LABEL	MEANING	LANGUAGE PORTRAIT
[+ obj + *to* infinitive]	verb with an object and an infinitive with *to*	Verbs
[+ obj + infinitive without *to*]	verb with an object and an infinitive without *to*	Verbs
[+ obj + v-*ed*]	verb with an object and a past participle	Get
[+ obj + v-*ing*]	verb with an object and the *-ing* form of another verb	-ing form of verbs
[+ obj + *wh-* word]	verb with an object and a question word	Clauses
past	past simple and past participle of a verb	Tenses
past part	past participle of a verb	Tenses
past simple	past simple of a verb	Tenses
pl	plural form of a noun	Plurals of nouns
pl n	plural noun, which has no singular form	
predeterminer	words like 'both' which come before other determiners	Determiners
prep	preposition	
pronoun	pronoun	
short form	short forms of words, such as 'I'm' (= I am)	Short forms
[+ sing/pl v]	noun which can be followed by either a singular or plural verb (in British and Australian English)	Varieties of English
[T]	transitive verb, which has an object	Verbs
[T; I + prep]	transitive verb which can be used as an intransitive verb when followed by a preposition. The particular preposition might be given, as in [T; I + *across*].	Verbs
[+ *that* clause]	word followed by a 'that' clause	Clauses
[+ *to* infinitive]	word followed by an infinitive with 'to'	
[+ two objects]	verb that has a direct object and an indirect object	Two objects
[U]	noun that does not have a plural form	
[usually in negatives and questions]	words that are not usually used in positive statements, such as 'any'	
[usually passive]	verb usually used in the passive form	
[usually pl]	noun usually used in the plural	
[usually sing]	noun usually used in the singular	
v	verb	
v aux	auxiliary verb such as 'do' or 'must'	Auxiliary Verbs
v adv	compound verb with adverb	Compound Verbs
v adv prep	compound verb with adverb and preposition	Compound Verbs
v adv, v prep	compound verb with adverb or preposition	Compound Verbs
v prep	compound verb with preposition	Compound Verbs
[+ v-*ed*]	verb followed immediately by a past participle	
[+ v-*ing*]	followed by the *-ing* form of a verb	-ing form of verbs
[+ *wh-* word]	followed by a clause introduced by a question word	Clauses

Usage labels in the dictionary

The following labels and abbreviations are explained in the Language Portraits on **Labels in the dictionary** at LABEL and **Varieties of English** at VARIETY.

Am	North American English	**law**	
approving		**literary**	
Aus	Australian English	**male**	
Br	British English	**medical**	
Canadian Eng	Canadian English	**not standard**	
dated		**old use**	
disapproving		**poetic**	
esp.	especially	**regional**	
female		**saying**	
fig.	figurative	**Scot Eng**	Scottish English
fml	formal	**slang**	
humorous		**specialized**	
infml	informal	**taboo**	
Irish Eng	Irish English	**trademark**	

CAMBRIDGE
INTERNATIONAL DICTIONARY of ENGLISH

CAMBRIDGE
UNIVERSITY PRESS

PUBLISHED BY THE PRESS SYNDICATE OF THE UNIVERSITY OF CAMBRIDGE
The Pitt Building, Trumpington Street, Cambridge CB2 1RP, United Kingdom

CAMBRIDGE UNIVERSITY PRESS
The Edinburgh Building, Cambridge CB2 2RU, United Kingdom
40 West 20th Street, New York, NY 10011–4211, USA
10 Stamford Road, Oakleigh, Melbourne 3166, Australia
Ruiz de Alarcón 13, 28014 Madrid, Spain
Dock House, The Waterfront, Cape Town 8001, South Africa

Visit our website at http://www.cambridge.org/elt/reference
Email comments about this book to cide@cambridge.org

First published 1995
Reprinted 1995, 1996, 1999, 2000

Defined words that we have a reason to believe constitute trademarks
have been labelled as such. However, neither the presence nor absence
of such labels should be regarded as affecting the legal status of any trademark.

Typeset by Computaprint, London

Printed in the United Kingdom by Clays Ltd, St Ives plc

Library of Congress Cataloguing in Publication data:
Cambridge international dictionary of English.
p. cm.
ISBN 0-521-48236-4. – ISBN 0-521-48421-9 (pbk.)
1. English language – Dictionaries. 2. English language – Textbooks
for foreign speakers.
PE1628.C23 1995
423 – dc21 95-155383
CIP

A catalogue record of this book is available from the British Library

ISBN 0 521 48236 4 hardback
ISBN 0 521 48421 9 paperback
ISBN 0 521 48469 3 flexicover
ISBN 0 521 48468 5 economy edition
ISBN 3 12 517918 1 Klett paperback
ISBN 3 12 517919 X Klett hardback

Editorial Team and Consultants

Editor-in-chief
Paul Procter

Editorial Consultants
John Ayto
Adrian Stenton
Penny Stock

Editors
Susan Allen-Mills
Ann Fiddes
Guy Jackson
Susan Jellis
Ann Kennedy
Daryl Tayar
Martin Tolley
Sally Webber
Susannah Wintersgill
Kate Woodford

American Editor
Paul Heacock

American Pronunciation
James Hartman – Editor

Australian Editor
Pam Peters

British Pronunciation
Peter Roach – Editor
Jane Setter
Helen Pandeli
Kimberley Parsons
Jonathan Rodgers

Citations
Annie Coulthard
Helen Kemp
Tom Leinster
Vivienne Painting
Jean Thomas

Clerical
Marie Allan

Cover Design
John Dunne
John Scully

Design
Peter Ducker
John Miles
Nick Newton

False Friends Editor
Diane Nicholls

False Friends
M F Allen
Maria Tereza Biderman
Daniel Blackman
Victoria Blanco Alonso
Somseen Chanawangsa
Christina Hottner
David Judah
Marie Kallkvist
Berit Larsson
Gillian Kay
Kirsten Malmkjær
Odile Martin
Madeleine Oliphant
Eleftheria Papanikolaou
Irina Pavlovskaya
Eva Přibilová
Pearl Spear
Hildegard Schaeffler
Jae-Mog Song
Olga Stankova
Emanuela Tasso
Halina Urbanska-Blackman

Illustrations Editor
Emma Malfroy

Illustrations
Corinne Burrows
Ray Burrows

Language Portrait Editor
Simon Baugh

Language Portraits
Elizabeth Austin
Kristine Brown
Ronald Carter
Annie Cornford
Fiona Currie
Coleen Degnan-Veness
Ben Duncan
Dominic Fisher
Diann Gruber
Roland Hindmarsh
Gillian Lazar
Christine Lindop
Andrew Littlejohn
Keith Mitchell
Jean Naterop
Felicity O'Dell
Paul Roberts
Roger Scott

Language Research
Pete Adams
Beth Boda
Julia Blackbeard
Charlotte Boynton
Carol June Cassidy
Helen Clark
Anna Cowper
Dewayne Crawford
Steve Davies
Adrienne Gavin
Ellen Head
Christina Hottner
Gillian Kay
Clea McEnery
Paula Parish
Sophia Pett
Jeremy Pettitt
Daniel Ponsford
Gavin Procter
Michael Procter
Damian Shaw
Hannah Stone

Learner Corpus
Philip Armit
Katie Martin
Polly Richards

Phrase Index
Jean Lloyd
Jean Thomas

Quotations
Julia Cresswell

Software Coordinator
Andrew Harley

Software and Corpus
Andy Cook
Robert Fairchild
Philip Makower

Usage Notes
Robert Hill

English Language Teaching Consultants

Ana Aguilar
Maggie Aldhamland
Cem Alptekin
Kenneth Anderson
Elizabeth Austin
Maria Tereza Biderman
Daniel Blackman
Vanessa Boutefeu
Kristine Brown
Alicia Peña Calvo
Paul Carne
Ron Carter
Annie Cornford
Ben Duncan
Marion Edwards
Chris Evenden
Frederick Featham
Dominic Fisher
Margaret Fowler
Richard Francis
Fernando Garcia Clemente
Malcolm Garfield
Claire Gipson
Claude-Françoise Grellet
Diann Gruber
Käthe Henke-Brown
Martin Hewings
Diana Hicks Lander
Roland Hindmarsh
Tom Hinton
Henri Holec
Rodney Huddleston
Ruth Jimack
Gillian Kay
Geneviève Krebs
Gillian Lazar
Christine Lindop
Andrew Littlejohn
Gillian Mansfield
Laura Matthews
Keith Mitchell
Ray Murphy
Felicity O'Dell
Paola Pace
Michel Perrin
Antonia Prodromou
Manfred Pulm
Jack Richards
Paul Roberts
Josef Schmid
Veronika Schnorr
Roger Scott
Mary Spratt
Klaus Stenzel
Simon Sweeney
Barbara Thomas
Desmond Thomas
Wolfgang Uhden
Clare West
Ian Winter
Katsuei Yamagishi
Asaji Yoneyama

Academic consultants

Juan Acordagoicoechea, Bibliograf (Bibl), Spain
Ted Briscoe, Cambridge Computer Laboratory (CCL), UK
Nicoletta Calzolari, Instituto di Linguistica Computazionale, CNR (Pisa), Italy
John Carroll, Cambridge Computer Laboratory (CCL), UK
Ann Copestake, Cambridge Computer Laboratory (CCL), UK
David Elworthy, Sharp Laboratories of Europe Ltd, Oxford, UK
Ulrich Heid, University of Stuttgart, Germany
Kechil Kirkham, Teknika, Cambridge, UK
Ian Johnson, Sharp Laboratories of Europe Ltd, Oxford, UK
Michael Milanovic, University of Cambridge Local Examinations Syndicate, UK
Margreet Moerland, Van Dale Lexicografie (Dale), Netherlands
Antonia Marti, Universitat Politecnica de Catalunya (UPC), Spain
Willem Meijs, Faculteit Engels, Universiteit van Amsterdam, Netherlands
Horacio Rodriguez Hontoria, Universitat Politecnica de Catalunya (UPC), Spain
M. Felisa Verdejo, Universitat Politecnica de Catalunya (UPC), Spain
Piek Vossen, Faculteit Engels, Universiteit van Amsterdam, Netherlands
Antonio Zampolli, Università di Pisa, Italy

Subject Advisers

Aerospace
Michael Rycroft

Agriculture
David Bond

Archaeology
Paul Bahn

Architecture and Building
Desmond Shaw-Taylor

Art
David Mannings

Astronomy
Jacqueline Mitton

Biology
Steven Parker

Board Games
Darren Grivvell (J.W. Spears)

Broadcasting and Communications
Michael Tooley

Building and Construction
David Holloway

Business and Finance
Ann Rixs
Adam Jacobs

Chemistry
Adam Jacobs

Chess
Andrew Harley

Clothes
Madeleine Ginsburg

Computer Technology
Philip Makower
Andrew Harley

Crafts
Brenda Ross

Dance
Janet Lansdale

Dentistry
Laurence Dobson

Economics
Steve Davies

Education
Deirdre Pettitt (UK)
Jean Heacock (US)

Electronics
Andrew Everard

Emergency Services
Harry Stonebridge

Energy
James McCarthy

Engineering
Jacques Heyman

Fishing
Alan Taylor

Food
John Ayto

Forestry
Jack Stewart

Games and Sports
Clive Ellis

Geography
Alison Miles

Heraldry
Harry Bedingfield

History
John Morrill

Household
Pat Roberts

Journalism
Ronald Carter

Language and Linguistics
John Ayto

Law (British)
Michael Procter

Law (USA)
Steven Neil

Literature and Mythology
Ian Ousby

Manufacturing
James McCarthy

Mathematics
Geoffrey Howson

Medicine
Stephen Lock

Metallurgy
Robert Cahn

Military and Nautical
Ian Kemp

Movies
Ian Christie

Music
Damian Shaw

Nautical
Derek Howse

Occult
Lee Stephen Gawtry

Outdoor Pursuits
Bruce Dance

Philosophy
Gavin Procter

Photography
George Hughes

Physics
Valerie Neil

Politics
John Haslam

Printing and Publishing
Roger Coleman

Psychology
Catherine Taylor

Religion
Andrew Harley
Linda Woodhead

Scouting
Barry Sheehan

Social Sciences
Susan Allen-Mills

Sport
Clive Ellis

Stamps and Coins
Stephen Harper-Scott
Peter Lawrence

Stationery
David Filz (Rymans)

Theatre
Philip Bretherton

Transport
Simon Bennett
Hugh Madgin

Contents

Grammar labels *inside front cover*

Usage labels and abbreviations *inside front cover*

Foreword by the Editor viii

How to find words and meanings ix

How to use the dictionary x

Grammar: The Parts of Speech xiii

The Dictionary 1

Defining Vocabulary (list of words used in definitions) 1702

Phrase Index (where to find idioms and other phrases) 1708

Pictures, Language Portraits and lists of False Friends 1772

Phonetic symbols used for pronunciations 1774

Foreword

The *Cambridge International Dictionary of English (CIDE)* is one of the most recent developments from the oldest publisher in the world, Cambridge University Press. Strangely, Cambridge has never published mainstream monolingual dictionaries before, although it has in the last twenty years become a major contributor to the field of English Language Teaching. It is therefore appropriate that this first dictionary should be designed for the foreign learner of English in any part of the world. The fresh approach that we have taken should appeal to all those who appreciate good lexicography based on solid scholarly principles and using the latest computer techniques, many of them developed by our computer team. Our first concern in writing *CIDE* has been clarity and simplicity, that is the clearest presentation we could devise with the minimum of the fuss and clutter that are the usual feature of dictionaries. There are no cumbersome numbers, and a specific innovation of *CIDE* is that each entry is for one core meaning to which the reader is immediately directed by the [GUIDE WORD], as in **bear** [ANIMAL] and **bear** [CARRY], or **bank** [ORGANIZATION] and **bank** [RAISED GROUND].

Within each entry is a rich range of information: the definition is written in a controlled Defining Vocabulary; inflected forms are given, as are examples and usage, idioms, compounds, collocations, quotations, false friends and grammatical description. Grammar codes are kept deliberately simple, and every one is attached to an example sentence. This means that the learner always has a model of each pattern before its description, and helps to ensure that the learner *produces* the correct form.

Pronunciations carry the authority of the latest edition of Daniel Jones's classic *English Pronouncing Dictionary*.

Behind the scenes lies the enormous software resource that has been created through the international Cambridge Language Survey (CLS). This gives lexicographers immediate access to all instances of any word within one hundred million words (including plurals, verb parts, etc.). Words in the corpus are tagged with their part of speech, so that all instances of *bear* (noun) with its plural *bears* can be retrieved at the press of a button. The corpus covers major varieties of English (British and US English being equally represented) and covers all kinds of writing. A special component, built in association with the University of Cambridge Local Examinations Syndicate (UCLES), is a learner corpus in which learner errors are codified for retrieval and analysis. This allows the learning difficulties of specific language groups to be targeted. Our selected false friends, presented by language, is one outcome of our work on problems of language interference.

Another aspect of clarity is speed of access. A major innovation of *CIDE* is the phrase index. Lexicographers have never in the past solved the problem of where entries for phrases and idioms are to be found. Is *kick the bucket* under *kick* or under *bucket*? The *CIDE* phrase index lists every phrase under every word that might be looked up. It then gives a page and line number. This makes it possible to find a phrase quickly that is hidden in a long entry like *go* or *come*.

Another innovation is the treatment of collocation, a word or phrase which is frequently used with another word or phrase in a way that sounds natural to native speakers. It is only in the last few years that it has been possible to find collocations by computer from a corpus, using statistical techniques which compare the overall frequency of a particular word (or its inflections) with the frequency with which other words are found nearby. Lexicographic intuitions, however sharp and well-tuned, are just not able to spot these reliably, but once the computer has thrown them up, a skilled lexicographer can quickly assess their importance to the learner. Lack of this information is one of the last serious barriers against a learner achieving fluency. *Rain* is *heavy* rather than *strong*, *tea* is *strong* rather than *powerful*, *frosts* are *hard* rather than *fierce*. Equally important and presented with equal rigour are the small 'lexically empty' words – the prepositions, adverbial particles, etc. – whose choice has to be right for fluency or comprehension. These are words like *in*, *out* and *with* which follow or precede parts of speech such as adjectives, nouns or verbs when used in particular meanings. People visit their family *at* Christmas, and are chummy *with* their neighbours.

CIDE is full of useful extra material. Over one hundred Language Portraits contain material that can be used as classroom topics; some will provide enough material for a whole lesson. Gathered together in one Portrait will be found information on a wide range of topics – grammar, vocabulary, punctuation, style, etc.

The pictorial illustrations break new ground in covering hundreds of everyday objects which are more satisfactorily described by a picture than by a definition. Again, British and American variants, so common in fields such as tools, cars or aircraft, are treated in depth. In specialist fields such as law, economics, medicine and engineering, entries have been checked for factual accuracy by experts. This technique is common in large dictionaries for native speakers, but not (surprisingly) in learners' dictionaries.

One of our major concerns has been completeness. *CIDE* provides more entries and more examples than has been possible in other learners' dictionaries. It covers British, American, Australian and other usages, pronunciations, spellings and grammatical patterns. Huge numbers of new words and phrases, so essential for those keeping in touch with changes in ideas and technology, are included. The cultural content is as fully international as we could make it, reflecting the fact that English is often used today as the only common tongue between groups of speakers of other languages. We have tried to be sensitive and unbiased in our treatment of gender, race and religion.

We hope you enjoy this new dictionary, the first in a new line of English-language reference books from Cambridge University Press. *Paul Procter*

How to find words and meanings

A FINDING A SINGLE WORD

You find words with one meaning in alphabetical order.

➜ **ear·plug** /£'ɪə·plʌg, $'ɪr—/ *n* [C usually pl] a small piece of soft material such as wax, cotton or plastic which you put into your ear to keep out noise or water

➜ **ear·ring** /£'ɪə·rɪŋ/, /$'ɪr·ɪŋ/, *n* [C] a piece of jewellery, usually one of a pair, worn in a hole in the ear or fixed to the ear by a fastener that does not go through the ear • *a pair of dangly earrings* • *gold earrings* • *He was wearing an earring in his left ear.* • *a stud/clip-on earring*

Some words are not given in their alphabetical place because the different parts of speech of a word are grouped together when they share a similar form and meaning. For this reason they do not always have a separate definition.

base [NOT HONOURABLE] /beɪs/ *adj* **-r**, **-st** *literary* not honourable and lacking in morals • *I accused him of having base motives.*

➜ **base·ly** /'beɪ·sli/ *adv literary* • *I shall lie basely to help them.*

➜ **base·ness** /'beɪ·snəs/ *n* [U] *literary*

base·ball /£'beɪs·bɔːl/, /$—bɑːl/*n* (the ball used in) a game played esp. in N America by two teams of nine players, in which a player hits a ball with a BAT and tries to run around four BASES on a large field before the other team returns the ball • *Jake never played baseball like the other kids.*

A reference will tell you where to find a word if the place where it is explained is more than five dictionary entries away from where you expect to find it.

earth·en·ware /£'ɜː·θᵊn·weəʳ, —ðᵊn—, $'ɜːr·θᵊn·wer/ *n* [U], *adj* (dishes, bowls, etc.) made of quite rough clay, often shaped with the hands

➜ **earth·i·ness** See at EARTHY

earth·ling /£'ɜːθ·lɪŋ, $'ɜːr—/ *n* [C] (esp. in stories) a human being, esp. when talked to or talked about by a creature from another planet

When a single word has a meaning which differs slightly from the definition, this is shown or explained in an example.

dec·o·rate (*obj*) [MAKE ATTRACTIVE] /'dek·ə·reɪt/ *v* to add something to (an object or place), esp. in order to make it more attractive • *They decorated the wedding car with ribbons and flowers.* [T] • *The birthday cake was made and*
➜ *decorated* (= covered with ICING) *by her aunt.* [T] •
➜ To decorate is also to paint the inside or outside of a house and/or put paper on the inside walls: *We're going to decorate the kitchen next week.* [T] *I hate the smell of paint when I'm decorating.* [I]

When a single word has more than one meaning, [GUIDE WORDS] help you to find which meaning you want. More commonly used meanings are usually given first.

deck [FLOOR] /dek/ *n* [C] a flat area for walking on, esp. one built across the space between the sides of a boat or a bus; a type of floor • *The waves washed over the ship's deck in the stormy sea.* • *When we've eaten, let's go up* **on** *deck and get some air.*

deck [SET OF CARDS] /dek/ *n* [C] *esp. Am* a set of cards used for playing card games • *We played our game of bridge with a new deck* (**of** *cards).*

deck *obj* [DECORATE] /dek/ *v* [T usually passive] to decorate or add something to (something) to make an effect • *The room was decked* **with** *flowers.* • *The statement was decked* **out with** *grand visions of the future and good intentions.*

deck *obj* [HIT] /dek/ *v* [T] *slang* to hit, esp. to hit and knock down • *If you do that again I'll deck you.*

Notice that with some words the different meanings shown by the guide words are not as clearly separate as in this example, because the different meanings shown in the guide words might share some common characteristics.

B FINDING WORDS IN GROUPS: THE PHRASE INDEX

Some phrases and combinations of words have a special meaning which is not clear from the meanings of the separate words. They are usually explained in examples following the definition for the *first* word of the combination (for example 'dead end' is found at **dead**, and not at **end**). You can use the Phrase Index at the end of the dictionary to check where a combination is explained. For example, if you want to find the phrase 'over my dead body', look in the Phrase Index for *any of the most important words* in the phrase: 'over', 'dead' or 'body'. At each of these you will find the page and exact line number for this phrase.

Some words, such as 'time' or 'put' have many guide words or examples. In long sections like this, the Phrase Index helps you to find a particular phrase, for example a compound noun like 'time share' or a verb combination such as 'put back'. The index contains references for compound verbs (phrasal verbs) and also verb–adverb or verb–preposition combinations which might be confused with them. In this way you can quickly find the different possible meanings of a phrase like 'put back'.

Sometimes you might not know whether or not a sentence contains a combination of words which has a special meaning. You can use the Phrase Index to check this. If you look up any important word in the sentence, you will find all the phrases which contain it. You might, for example, read the sentence *He came out of prison hoping to start with a clean sheet.* If you look up either 'clean' or 'sheet' in the Phrase Index, it will tell you that there is a phrase 'clean sheet'.

How to use the dictionary

The definition uses words from a list of under 2,000 common words (see Defining Vocabulary at the end of the dictionary). Words not in this list are in SMALL CAPITALS.

When a word has more than one meaning, the GUIDE WORDS help you to find the right one quickly.

Example sentences in *italics* are based on natural written and spoken English and show how the word is most commonly used.

Meanings that are slightly different from the main definition are explained:

- by a word or phrase in round brackets (= ...) within an example sentence
- by a complete sentence, not in italics, among the example sentences

A *single* word in **bold** shows that it is often found with the word being looked up.

Sometimes the main word and one or more other words are shown in **bold** together. This means that this group of words has a special meaning which is not clear from the meanings of the separate words.
For further explanation, see the Language Portrait on **Words used together** at WORD.

Special symbols mark words which learners might confuse with similar words in their own language. The dictionary contains useful lists of these words: see Language Portrait on **False Friends** at FALSE for an explanation of how to use these symbols and lists.

Labels in *italics* give style and usage information. When they are placed before the definition they are true for all uses of the word. See the list at the front of the dictionary and the Language Portrait on **Labels**.

Well-known phrases from popular songs, television, films, books, plays, and sayings by famous people are sometimes included after the examples.

galleon /'gæl·iən/ *n* [C] a large sailing ship with three or four MASTS (= poles for supporting sails), used both in trade and war from the 15th to the 18th centuries

gear ENGINE PART /£gɪəʳ, $gɪr/ *n* a device, often consisting of connecting sets of wheels with teeth around the edge, that controls how much power from an engine goes to the moving parts of a machine • *Does your car have four or five gears?* [C] • *I couldn't find reverse gear.* [U] • *The car should be* **in** *gear* (= with its gears in position, allowing the vehicle to move). [U] • *When you start a car you need to be* **in** *(Br) first/(Am)* **low** *gear.* • To *(Br)* **change**/*(Am also)* **shift** gear is to change the position of the gears to make the car go faster or more slowly. • *(Br)* A **gear lever/stick** (*(Am)* **stick shift** or **gearshift**) is a metal rod that you use to change gear in a car or other vehicle.

gear EQUIPMENT /£gɪəʳ, $gɪr/ *n* [U], *combining form* the equipment, clothes etc. that you use to do a particular activity • *fishing/camping/walking gear* • *When riding a bicycle you should wear the proper headgear* (= protection for your head). • *Police in* **riot** *gear* (= protective clothing) *arrived to control the protestors.* • *(infml) She spends a lot on clothes and is always wearing the latest gear* (= clothes).

gem /dʒem/, **gemstone** /£'dʒem,stəun, $—,stoun/ *n* [C] a jewel, esp. when cut into a particular regular shape • *She inherited £20 000 in gold and gems.* • If you say that someone or something is a gem you mean that they are especially good, pleasing or useful: *You've been an* **absolute** *gem – I couldn't have managed without your help.* ○ *And then he came out with a gem* (= clever remark) *about the absurdity of the situation.*

generous /'dʒen·ər·əs/ *adj* (esp. of a person) willing to give money, help, kindness, etc., esp. more than is usual or expected, or (of an object) larger than usual or expected • **It** *was most generous* (**of** *you*) **to** *lend me £100.* [+ *to* infinitive] • *She's very generous* **with** *her time – always ready to answer questions.* • *There's a generous* (= kinder than deserved) *review of the book in today's newspaper.*

girl /£gɜːl, $gɜrl/ *n* [C] a young woman, esp. one still at school • *Two girls showed us round the classrooms.* • Girl sometimes means daughter: *We have two girls.* ○ *My little girl is five.* • Adult women consider it offensive to be called girls by other people, esp. men, although this was common in the past, but they might call themselves or their friends girls: *Mum says she's going out with* **the** *girls tonight.* ○ *The girls at work gave it to me.* • Women workers as a group are often called girls: *shop/office girls* • *(Br dated infml humorous) He's just* **a big/great girl's blouse** (= a weak and cowardly man). • A **girl Friday** is a type of SECRETARY or general helper in an office, usually someone willing to do several different types of work

genie /'dʒiː·ni/ *n* [C] *pl* **genies** /'dʒiː·niz/ or **genii** /'dʒiː·ni·aɪ/ a magical spirit, originally in Arab traditional stories, who will do or provide whatever the person who controls it asks it to do. • Ⓓ Ⓕ

geocentric /£,dʒiː·əʊ'sen·trɪk, $—oʊ—/ *adj specialized* having the earth as its centre • *In 1543 Copernicus suggested instead of a geocentric model of the solar system, one in which the sun was central.*

gossamer /£'gɒː·sə·məʳ, $'gɒs·ə·mɚ/ *n* [U] the very thin thread that SPIDERS produce to make WEBS • *In the early morning the lawn was covered with gossamer* (**threads**). • *(fig.) The bride wore a delicate gossamer veil* (= one made of very delicate, light cloth). • *"A trip to the moon on gossamer* (= very delicate and light) *wings,/Just one of those things"* (from the song *Just One of Those Things* written by Cole Porter, 1935)

Parts of speech (verb, noun, adjective etc.) are given in *italics*. See the notes on grammar on the following pages.

Some words are given more than one part of speech. In these cases, a single definition explains all the parts of speech mentioned.

obj after a verb shows that it always has an object (it is transitive).

(obj) after a verb shows that it sometimes has an object (it can be transitive or intransitive).

Grammar information is explained using example sentences. Grammar codes are given in square brackets [ ]. See the list at the front of the dictionary.

- When grammar information is given *before the definition*, the grammar pattern is true for all uses of the word.
- When grammar information is given *after an example*, that grammar pattern is true only for particular uses of the word.

Irregular verb forms, plurals, comparatives and superlatives are shown.

British (£) and American ($) pronunciations are given using the international phonetic alphabet. The symbols are explained in the Pronunciation Table at the end of the dictionary.

Labels in *italics* show differences between British, American and Australian English. Words and phrases, spellings and particular meanings are labelled. See the Language Portrait on **Varieties of English** at VARIETY.

LP tells you that there is a Language Portrait which gives interesting extra information about this word or words connected with it.

PIC tells you that there is an illustration containing the word.

gabardine, gaberdine /£'gæb·ə·diːn, $'—ə-—/ *n* a thick cloth which is esp. used for making coats, or a long coat made from this cloth • *It says on the label it's made of gabardine.* [U] • *I was wearing my father's beige gabardine* [C]

gam·ing /geɪm·ɪŋ/ *n* [U], *adj* [not gradable] (of) the risking of money in games of chance esp. at a CASINO • The **gaming tables** are places where you can go to GAMBLE, esp. the tables on which people play cards or ROULETTE.

generate *obj* /£'dʒen·ᵊr·eit, $'—ə-—/ *v* [T] *fml or specialized* to cause to exist, or to produce • *Her latest film has generated a lot of* **interest/excitement** • *I'm afraid I can't generate much* **enthusiasm** *for the idea.* • *There has been a lot of* **publicity/controversy** *generated* **by** *this event.* • *The new development will generate 1500 new jobs.* • *These measures will increase the club's ability to generate* **revenue/income**. • *The wind farm may be able to generate enough* **electricity/power** *for 2000 homes.* • *The equipment generates a* **signal**.

gov·ern *(obj)* RULE /£'gʌv·ᵊn, $—ə-n/ *v* to control and direct the public business of (a country, city, group of people, etc.); to rule • *Military leaders have overthrown the president and are now governing the country.* [T] • *They accused the government of being unfit to govern.* [I]

grouse BIRD /graʊs/ *n* [C] *pl* **grouse** a small fat bird with feathered legs and feet, shot for sport and food • *They went grouse shooting at the weekend.*

grouse COMPLAIN /graʊs/ *v* [I] *infml* to complain, esp. often • *She's always grousing* **about** *her daughter's cooking.*

grow *(obj)* INCREASE /£grəʊ, $groʊ/ *v past simple* **grew** *past part* **grown** to increase in size or amount, or to become more advanced or developed • *This plant grows best in the shade.* [I] • *She has grown two centimetres taller in the past couple of months.* [L only + adj] • *Football's popularity continues to grow.* [I] • *The labour force is expected to grow by 2% next year.* [I] • *The male deer grows large branching horns called antlers.* [T] • *One aim of psychotherapy is to enable people to grow in all their relationships* (= to develop stronger emotions within relationships). [I]

gan·gli·on /£'gæŋ·gli·ən, £—ɒn, $—ən/ *n* [C] *pl* **ganglions** or **ganglia** *medical* a painful swelling, often on the back of the hand, or a mass of nerve cells, esp. appearing outside the brain or SPINE (= row of bones down the centre of the back).

glos·sary /£'glɒs·ᵊr·i, $'glɑː·sᵊr·i/ *n* [C] an alphabetical list, with meanings, of the words or phrases in a text that are difficult to understand • *The book would have been more useful if a glossary* **of** *technical terms and abbreviations had been included.*

gag JOKE /gæg/ *n* [C] *infml* a joke or story that is intended to amuse, esp. one told by a COMEDIAN • *I did a few opening gags about the quality of the band that was on before me.* • *(Am and Aus)* A gag is also a trick played on someone or an action performed to amuse other people.

great·ly /'greɪt·li/ *adv* Greatly means very much and is used esp. to show how much you feel or experience something: *I greatly regret not having told the truth.* ○ *She greatly admires her grandmother.* ○ *Her piano-playing has greatly improved/has improved greatly since I last heard her.*
• LP **Very, completely**

grill *obj* COOK /grɪl/, *Am also* **broil** /brɔɪl/ *v* [T] to cook (something) by direct heat, esp. under a very hot surface in a cooker • *I decided to grill the sausages rather than fry them.*
• PIC **Cooking**

The Cambridge Language Survey

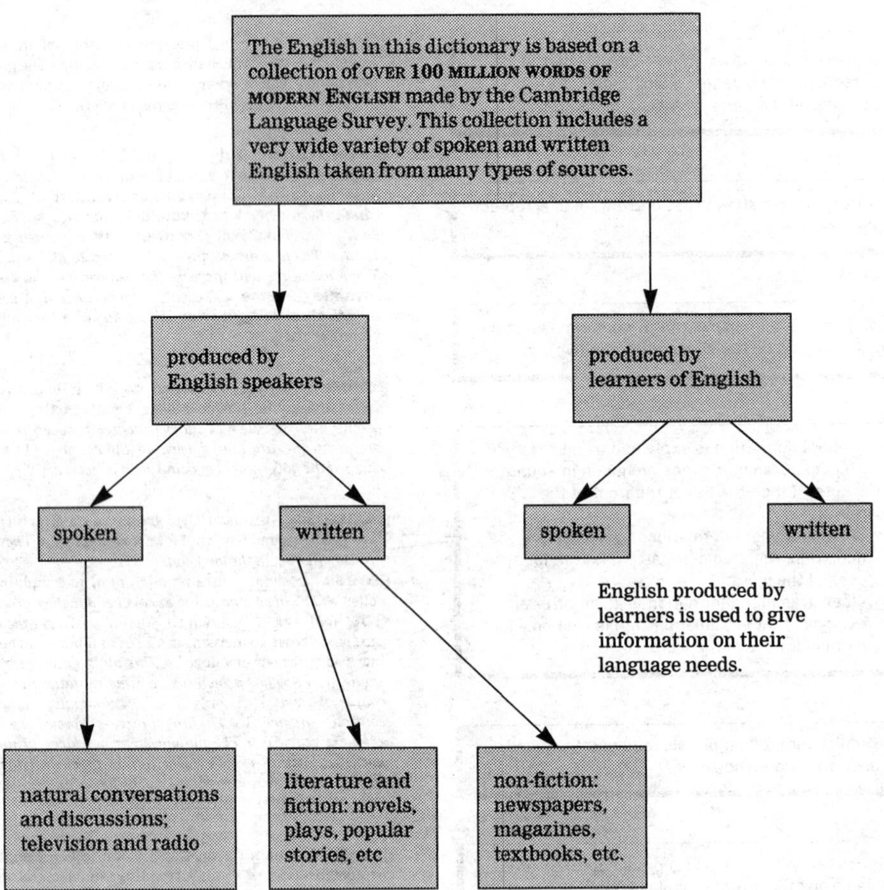
The English in this dictionary is based on a collection of OVER 100 MILLION WORDS OF MODERN ENGLISH made by the Cambridge Language Survey. This collection includes a very wide variety of spoken and written English taken from many types of sources.
produced by English speakers
produced by learners of English
spoken
written
spoken
written
English produced by learners is used to give information on their language needs.
natural conversations and discussions; television and radio
literature and fiction: novels, plays, popular stories, etc
non-fiction: newspapers, magazines, textbooks, etc.

Grammar: The Parts of Speech

The following table gives a simple explanation of each part of speech and says what important grammar information you can expect to find in the dictionary. It also refers to Language Portraits that give more information.

NOUNS

• **Main purpose:** Nouns name or refer to a person (*brother*), thing (*shoe*), substance (*oil*), quality (*completeness*) and so on. There are many compound nouns: *sportswear; fire-alarm; life jacket.*

• **Different forms:** Most nouns have a plural, usually formed with **-s/-es/-ies**: *boys; losses; parties.* Most compound nouns add **-s/-es/-ies** to the second part: *mountain tops; lunchboxes; cry-babies.* The dictionary gives all plurals which are formed in a different way.

Many nouns have a possessive form, usually formed by adding **'s** to the noun: **the dog's bowl; the old woman's kindness.**

A few nouns have different male and female forms: *waiter, waitress.* These are shown when they are important. See the Language Portrait **Using language that is not sexist** at SEXISM for information on the modern use of words like this.

• **Grammar:**

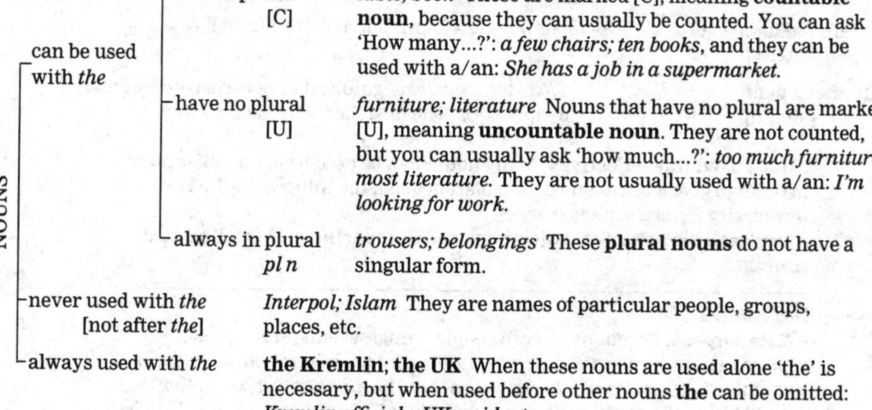

NOUNS
can be used with *the*
have a plural [C]
table; book These are marked [C], meaning **countable noun**, because they can usually be counted. You can ask 'How many...?': *a few chairs; ten books,* and they can be used with a/an: *She has a job in a supermarket.*
have no plural [U]
furniture; literature Nouns that have no plural are marked [U], meaning **uncountable noun**. They are not counted, but you can usually ask 'how much...?': *too much furniture; most literature.* They are not usually used with a/an: *I'm looking for work.*
always in plural *pl n*
trousers; belongings These **plural nouns** do not have a singular form.
never used with *the* [not after *the*]
Interpol; Islam They are names of particular people, groups, places, etc.
always used with *the*
the Kremlin; the UK When these nouns are used alone 'the' is necessary, but when used before other nouns **the** can be omitted: *Kremlin officials; UK residents.*

English has very many uncountable nouns, and often nouns that are countable in other languages are uncountable in English. Some nouns have both [C] and [U] uses, with a change of meaning: *The shop has sold five televisions today.* [C] / *Do you watch much television?* [U] • *These stretching exercises are good for your back.* [C] / *You really should take more exercise.* [U] Example sentences in the dictionary give important information about how a particular noun is used in singular and plural forms and with determiners such as *the, a/an,* and *some.*

• **Language Portraits:** Regular plural forms of nouns: see **Forms of words** at FORM. Rules for irregular plurals: see **Plurals of nouns** at PLURAL. Further information about [C] and [U] nouns: see **The definite and indefinite articles** at ARTICLE. See also **The possessive form** at POSSESS. Compound nouns: see **Words used together** at WORD.

ADJECTIVES

• **Main purpose:** Adjectives describe and give information about people, things, events, and so on.

Adjectives are applied to nouns, pronouns and clauses: *a* **kind** *friend* • *That was* **wonderful**. • *Finding the town was* **difficult**.

• **Different forms:** Adjectives do not have a plural, nor separate male and female forms. When they are used to compare things, some adjectives have **-er/-ier** and **-est/-iest** endings: *brave, braver, bravest* • *dry, drier, driest*.

• **Grammar:**

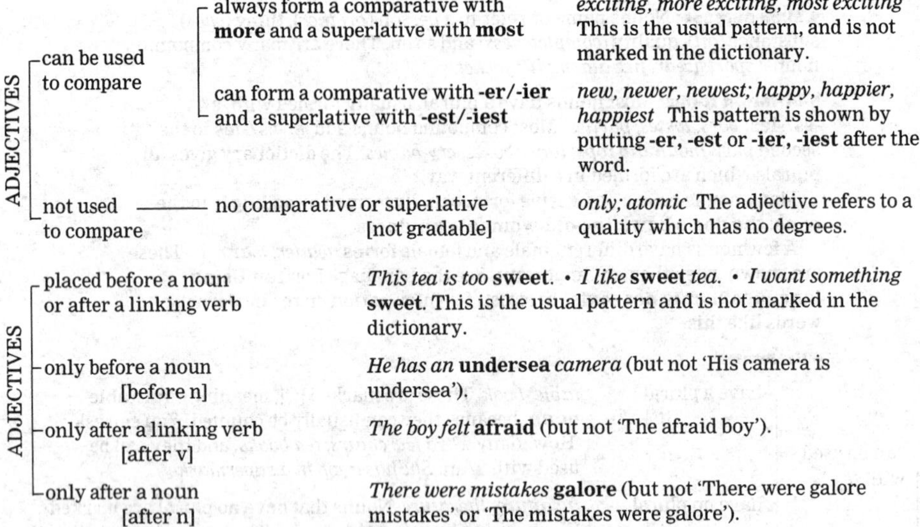

ADJECTIVES
can be used to compare
always form a comparative with **more** and a superlative with **most**
exciting, more exciting, most exciting This is the usual pattern, and is not marked in the dictionary.
can form a comparative with **-er/-ier** and a superlative with **-est/-iest**
new, newer, newest; happy, happier, happiest This pattern is shown by putting **-er, -est** or **-ier, -iest** after the word.
not used to compare
no comparative or superlative [not gradable]
only; atomic The adjective refers to a quality which has no degrees.
ADJECTIVES
placed before a noun or after a linking verb
This tea is too **sweet**. • *I like* **sweet** *tea.* • *I want something* **sweet**. This is the usual pattern and is not marked in the dictionary.
only before a noun [before n]
He has an **undersea** *camera* (but not 'His camera is undersea').
only after a linking verb [after v]
The boy felt **afraid** (but not 'The afraid boy').
only after a noun [after n]
There were mistakes **galore** (but not 'There were galore mistakes' or 'The mistakes were galore').

Nouns used like adjectives Many nouns can be used before another noun in order to give more detailed information about the thing: *a* **clothes** *brush, a* **university** *lecturer,* **space** *travel.*

• **Language Portraits:** See **Adjectives**, and **Comparing and grading** at COMPARE.

PRONOUNS

• **Main purpose:** Pronouns refer to people, things, events, etc. A pronoun replaces a noun or noun phrase when giving information about someone or something just mentioned: *Karen called, but* **she** *didn't stay long.* • *Tom bought* **himself** *a radio.* • *'Let's go out tonight.'* – **'That's** *a good idea.'* • *The eggs were cheap so we bought* **twelve**.

With some pronouns we might not know who or what is being referred to: **Who** *lives here?* • *Did* **anybody** *see you?* • **Something** *is burning.*

• **Different forms:** *This, that* and *I, he, she, it* have a plural form: **This** *is a new product.* / **These** *are new products.* • **It** *is a very rare animal.* / **They** *are very rare animals.*

I, he, she, we, they and *who* have a different form when they are the object of a verb or follow a preposition: *The police arrested* **him**. • *(fml) To* **whom** *am I speaking?* • *Except for you and* **me**, *nobody knows about this.* These pronouns (and also *it* and *you*) have a possessive form: *This bag is* **mine**. The personal pronouns also have a reflexive: *She couldn't see* **herself** *in the photograph.*

		plural				*plural*		
subject	I	we	he	she	it	they	you	who
object	me	us	him	her	it	them	you	who(m)
possessive	mine	ours	his	hers		theirs	yours	whose
reflexive	myself	ourselves	himself	herself	itself	themselves	yourself (sing.) yourselves (pl.)	

• **Grammar:** The form you should use depends on the noun which the pronoun replaces: **Mary** *has two children now – that little boy is* **hers**. Notice that *they* can be used to mean *he or she*: *Someone phoned you yesterday but* **they** *haven't called again.*

• **Language Portraits:** Modern non-sexist use of *he, she* and so on is explained in **Using language that is not sexist** at SEXIST. The pronouns *it* and *there* have special uses: see the Language Portraits at IT and THERE. See also **Reflexive verbs and pronouns** at REFLEXIVE.

DETERMINERS

• **Main purpose:** Determiners are used before nouns or noun phrases to make clear which particular person or thing is meant, or to give information about quantity: **the** *new government;* **a** *football;* **some** *bread;* **eleven** *boys; the* **other** *door;* **my** *shoes.*

A few determiners can be used immediately before other determiners: **both** *these apples;* **all** *that time;* **half** *the money;* **twice** *the cost.* These are marked *predeterminer*.

• **Different forms:** Determiners do not change their form, except for *a* (*an* before vowels), *this* (*these* before plural nouns), *that* (*those* before plurals), and the possessive determiners *my* (pl. *our*) and *his/her/its* (pl. *their*).

• **Grammar:**

- Some determiners showing quantity can only be used before one grammatical type of noun:

before singular [C] nouns	**every** *doctor,* **each** *day*
before plural [C] nouns	**both** *legs,* **many** *people,* **few** *problems,* **five** *languages*
before [U] nouns	*with* **much** *difficulty, we have* **little** *information*

  Examples and usage notes in the dictionary show which pattern(s) a particular determiner follows. See also the Language Portrait **Quantity words** at QUANTITY.

- When used before pronouns, determiners require 'of': **few of** *us,* **both of** *them,* **much of** *it,* **two of** *you.*

- Some words are used as both determiners and pronouns. They are called determiners when they come before a noun: **any** *news,* **few** *clouds,* **which** *bus.* They are pronouns when they are used alone, in order to replace a noun: *There isn't* **any**. • *He didn't tell me* **which**.

- Numbers are used as determiners, pronouns and sometimes as nouns:

as determiners, before a noun	*There were eight ships in the harbour.*
as pronouns, replacing a noun	*We counted the ships: there were eight of them/ there were eight.*
as nouns	*Two eights are sixteen.*

• **Language portraits:** The different types of determiners are explained in **Determiners**. Details on *the, a* and *an*: see **The definite and indefinite articles** at ARTICLE. The grammar of quantity determiners: see **Quantity words** at QUANTITY.

VERBS

• **Main purpose:** Verbs refer to an action, or to something happening, or to a state which exists: *She* **broke** *a cup.* • *The crops* **are growing**. • *You* **look** *hungry.* There are many compound verbs: *Tina and her boyfriend have* **fallen out** (= argued). • *I don't know how you* **put up with** (= bear) *the noise.*

• **Different forms:** In the present tense with *he/she/it* most verbs add **-s/-es/-ies**. The past simple and past participle usually end **-ed**. The present participle ends **-ing**. All other tenses and the passive are made using various forms of **be, do, have** or **will**. The dictionary gives all irregular forms and spellings.

• **Grammar of verbs:**

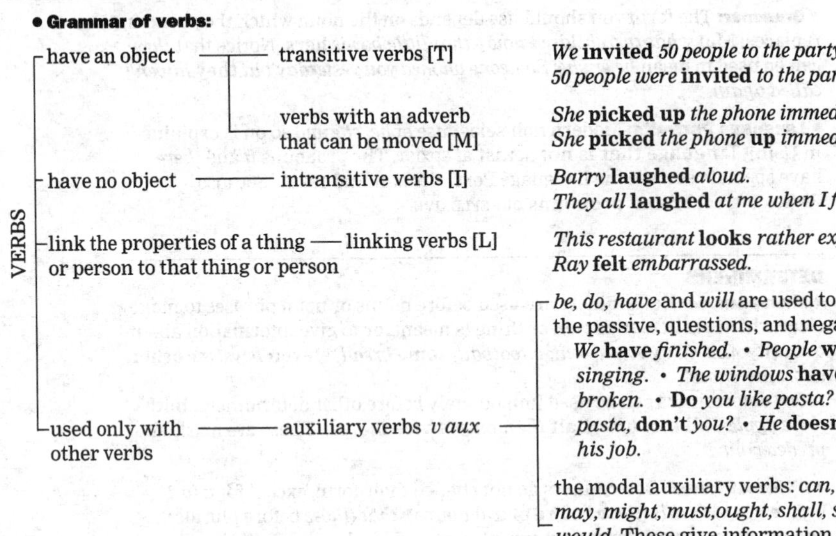

VERBS
have an object
transitive verbs [T]
We **invited** *50 people to the party.*
50 people were **invited** *to the party.*
verbs with an adverb that can be moved [M]
She **picked up** *the phone immediately./*
She **picked** *the phone* **up** *immediately.*
have no object
intransitive verbs [I]
Barry **laughed** *aloud.*
They all **laughed** *at me when I fell over.*
link the properties of a thing or person to that thing or person
linking verbs [L]
This restaurant **looks** *rather expensive.*
Ray **felt** *embarrassed.*
used only with other verbs
auxiliary verbs *v aux*
be, do, have and *will* are used to form tenses, the passive, questions, and negatives.
We **have** *finished.* • *People* **were** *singing.* • *The windows* **have been** *broken.* • **Do** *you like pasta?* • *You like pasta,* **don't** *you?* • *He* **doesn't** *enjoy his job.*
the modal auxiliary verbs: *can, could, may, might, must,ought, shall, should, will, would.* These give information about necessity and possibility, and are used to make suggestions, offers and requests.

- Many verbs can be used either with or without an object: *Some boys were kicking a can.* [T] • *Please stop kicking.* [I] These verbs are followed by *(obj)* in the dictionary, and example sentences are labelled [T] or [I].
- Verbs with an object can usually appear in passive sentences: *Someone stole my car last night* (active sentence). / *My car was stolen last night* (passive sentence). Notice that the object in the active sentence becomes the subject in the passive sentence.
- For [M] verbs both the possible positions of the adverb are shown, for example **knock down** *obj*, **knock** *obj* **down** *v adv* [M].
- Compound verbs might be [M], [T], [I] or both [T] and [I]. The labels *v adv* or *v prep* show if the compound verb contains an adverb or a preposition.
- If a verb is always used in a particular pattern, this is shown by a label before the definition. But if it is used in various patterns, these are shown in example sentences, with a label at the end.

• **Language Portraits:** The regular verb forms are explained in **Forms of words** at FORM, and in **Tenses**. For the main kinds of verbs see **Transitive and intransitive verbs** at VERB, **Linking verbs** at LINK, **Auxiliary verbs** at AUXILIARY, **Clauses,** and **Compound verbs** at COMPOUND. For information on particular grammar patterns, refer to the list of labels at the beginning of the dictionary.

ADVERBS

• **Main purpose:** Adverbs give information about how, when, where, etc. something happened or was done: *She stood up* **quickly**. • *I sent the order* **yesterday**. • *Mrs Brent lives* **next door**.

Some adverbs change the strength of adjectives, verbs or other adverbs: **fairly** *warm; I* **really** *admire him;* **too** *often.*

• **Different forms:** When they are used to compare things, most adverbs use *more* and *most*: *Please drive* **more carefully**. Some short adverbs have a comparative and superlative. These are formed in the same way as for adjectives, using **-er**/**-ier** and **-est**/**-iest**: *We arrived in Quebec* **sooner** *than I'd expected.* The dictionary shows these forms in the same way as for adjectives.

• Grammar:
The main difficulty with adverbs is using them in the right place, and example sentences show the usual position(s) an adverb takes. There are a few approximate rules:

- With intransitive verbs most adverbs usually come after the verb: *The wind blew* **hard**.
- With transitive verbs they usually come after the object: *He took the cat* **indoors**.
- Adverbs of frequency generally come after an auxiliary verb, but before a normal verb: *Betty should* **never** *lift anything heavy./Betty* **never** *lifts anything heavy.*

• Language Portraits: Adverbs, Comparing and grading at COMPARE, and **Very, completely** at VERY.

PREPOSITIONS

• Main purpose: Prepositions express relationships between people, things, actions, etc.: *I spoke* **to** *Mr Hall* **on** *Friday* **about** *the hole* **in** *our roof.* English uses prepositions more than many other languages, and one preposition often has several different meanings.

Prepositions are also used to introduce a phrase which completes the meaning of a verb, noun or adjective: *believe* **in**; *insist* **on**; *fear* **of**; *anxious* **about**. In these uses there is no rule for using one preposition rather than another. Examples in the dictionary show the preposition partners of a particular word.

• Grammar:

Prepositions can follow these types of words		These patterns can follow prepositions	
		the explosion	(noun)
(verb)	*I told him* **about**	*my trip to Poland*	(noun phrase)
(adjective)	*She was very interested* **in**	*them*	(pronoun)
(noun)	*He had no memory* **of**	*climb***ing** *the mountain*	(v-*ing* clause)
		wh*at had happened*	(clause with *wh-* word)

- Prepositions are not followed by an infinitive. Usually an *-ing* form is used instead: we say *I'm very keen* **on** *swimm***ing** and never 'I'm very keen on swim' or 'I'm very keen on to swim'. Notice that *to* is sometimes used as a preposition, when it can be followed by an *-ing* form: *We look forward* **to** *meet***ing** *you next week.*
- Prepositions are not followed by a *that* clause: we cannot say 'They waited for he arrived' or 'They waited for that he arrived', but use a different pattern such as *They waited for his arrival* or *They waited for him* **to** *arrive.*
- Some words are used both as prepositions and as adverbs. They are called prepositions when they come before a noun, pronoun, etc.: *My office was* **opposite** *Janet's.* They are adverbs when they are used alone: *Janet works* **opposite**.

• Language Portraits: Preposition partners: see **Words used together** at WORD. See also **Prepositions of movement** at PREPOSITION.

CONJUNCTIONS

• Main purpose: Conjunctions are used to connect together units of language. They can join:

WORDS: *He was tired* **but** *happy.* • *She loved to sing* **and** *dance.* • *You* **or** *Jim should do it.*
PHRASES: **Neither** *Mrs Malcolm* **nor** *any of her neighbours heard the noise.*
CLAUSES: **As** *it's my birthday, we're going for a meal.* • *Don't worry* **if** *you can't find it.*

• Grammar:

- Some conjunctions are used especially between clauses. They link the main clause of a sentence to a clause which is not of equal importance: *I used to swim every day* **because** *I lived by the sea.* • *We will sign the contract on Tuesday,* **unless** *Richards changes his mind.*

- When a conjunction introduces a phrase or clause one or two commas (,) are often used to separate the phrase or clause from the rest of the sentence: *Ms Harrison's company,* **unless** *I'm mistaken, has started exporting to Indonesia.* Notice that *and* does not generally require a comma.

• **Language Portraits: Comma.**

EXCLAMATIONS
• **Main purpose:** Exclamations are used especially in informal speech to show strong feelings such as surprise (*wow*), anger (*damn*), disgust (*ugh*) and pain (*ouch*). Some exclamations are used in particular situations, for example to greet someone (*hi*), make a request (*please*) or agree to something (*okay*). If the exclamation is said loudly or with strong feeling, an exclamation mark (!) is used, usually immediately after the exclamation: *Phew! It's hot this evening*.

• **Different forms:** Exclamations do not change their grammatical form.

• **Language Portraits: Exclamation mark** at EXCLAIM and **Phrases and customs** at PHRASE.

COMBINING FORMS
• **Main purpose:** Combining forms are words or parts of words which are added to the beginning or end of words to change or add meaning: **dis***interested, manage***ment**, *three***-legged**. They include the parts of words often called prefixes (for example *anti-*) and suffixes (for example *-ation*).

• **Different forms:** Combining forms added to the end of words follow the usual rules for the type of word that is made (verb, noun, adjective, etc.). For example the ending **-ify** is used to form a verb: *simpl***ify**, *simplifies, simplifying, simplified*.

• **Language Portrait: Combining forms** at COMBINE, **Opposite and negative meanings** at OPPOSITE.

A a

A LETTER (*pl* **A's**), **a** (*pl* **a's**) /eɪ/ *n* [C] the 1st letter of the English alphabet • **From A to B** means from one place to another: *You can now get computer software which helps drivers to work out the quickest route from A to B.* • **From A to Z** means including everything: *I want to know everything that's happened while I've been away, from A to Z.* • *(Am)* An **A-frame** is a simple house shaped like an A, with two of its four walls sloping inward and meeting at the top to act as a roof: *Our house is an A-frame.* ○ *They have an A-frame chalet somewhere in the mountains.* • An **A level** is a public examination in a particular subject taken in British schools by students aged 17 or 18, or the qualification obtained: *I failed my Maths A level.* [C] ○ *You usually need three A levels to get into university.* [C] ○ *She's taking Physics, Chemistry and Maths* **at** *A level* (= doing these examinations).

A MUSIC /eɪ/ *n pl* **A's** or **As** a note in Western music • *This concerto is in* **(the key of)** *A major.* [U] • *There are two As in this bar of music.* [C]

A MARK /eɪ/ *n pl* **A's** or **As** a mark in an exam or for a piece of work that shows that your work is thought of as excellent • *The teacher gave me an A for my essay.* [C] • *Sophie* **got** *A for English.* [U] • *She got* **straight** *As* (= All her marks were As) *in her end-of-year exams.* [C] • *(Am and Aus) Jim is a* **(straight)** *A student* (= All his marks were A). • An **A minus/A-** is a mark which is slightly lower than an A.

A ELECTRICITY /eɪ/ *n* [C] *abbreviation for* AMP

a NOT PARTICULAR /eɪ, ə/, **an** *determiner* used before nouns to refer to single things or people that have not been mentioned before, esp. when you are not referring to particular things or people, or you do not expect listeners or readers to know which particular things or people you are referring to • *Can I have a banana, please?* • *I wish I had enough money to buy a new car.* • *The only furniture in the room was a bed, a table and two chairs.* • *I've got a hole in my shoe.* • *There was a sudden loud noise.* • *What a shame that you couldn't go to the party.* • *We went to a really good restaurant last night.* • *A man stopped me and asked me how to get to the station.* • *I heard a child crying.* • *Is he a friend* **of** *yours* (= one of your friends)*?* • 'A' can be used to state what type of thing or person something or someone is: *She wants to be a doctor when she grows up.* ○ *Is this flower a primrose?* ○ *Their house is a 17th century cottage.* ○ *This is a very mild cheese.* ○ *Experts think that the recently discovered painting may be a Picasso* (= by Picasso). • 'A' can also be used to mean any or every thing or person of the type you are referring to: *A cheetah can run faster than a lion.* ○ *Vijay has just learnt to ride a bike.* ○ *A teacher needs to have a lot of patience.* • When used before particular nouns without any adjectives before them, 'a' can mean quite long or good: *We need to wait a while before making a final decision.* ○ *That's a thought* (= That's a good idea)*!* • 'A' can also be used before some uncountable nouns when you want to limit their meaning in some way, such as when describing them more completely or referring to one example of them: *I only have a limited knowledge of Spanish.* ○ *He has a great love of music.* ○ *There was a fierceness in her voice.* • 'A' is used before some nouns of action when referring to one example of the action: *Take a look at this, Jez.* ○ *I'm just going to have a wash.* ○ *There was a loud knocking at the door.* • 'A' can also mean a unit or a container of something, esp. something you eat or drink: *I'd love a coffee.* ○ *All I had for lunch was a yogurt.* • When two nouns are being referred to as one unit, you use 'a' before the first but not the second: *a cup and saucer* ○ *a knife and fork* • You use 'a' in front of a person's name when you are referring to someone whom you do not know: *There's a Ms Evans to see you.* ○ *Do you know a Julio Perez?* • 'A' can also be used in front of a famous person's name when you want to suggest that someone else has the same qualities as the famous person: *She may look good on the cinema screen but she'll never be a Greta Garbo.* • If you use 'a' in front of a person's family name, you mean that they are a member of that family: *I'd never have guessed he was a Wilson – he doesn't look anything like his brothers.* • 'A' is used before the names of days, months etc. to refer to one example of that day, month etc.: *My birthday is on a Friday this year.* ○ *Well, it's certainly been a June to remember!* • You can also use 'a' before some words expressing number or amount: *a few days* ○ *a bit of wool* ○ *a lot of money* • You use 'a' before consonants (a dog), or vowels which are pronounced as consonants (a university), and you use 'an' before vowels (an elephant). • LP> **Articles**

a ONE /eɪ, ə/, **an** *determiner* one • *a hundred* • *a thousand* • *a million* • *a dozen* • *Round the table were seated six men and a woman.* • 'A' can also be used after FRACTIONS: *half a mile* ○ *three-quarters of an hour* ○ *six-tenths of a second* • 'A' can also be used to mean each or every: *Take one tablet three times a day.* ○ *He earns $100 000 a* (= in one) *year.*

A4 /£ˌeɪ'fɔː, $-'fɔːr/ *n, adj* [not gradable] (paper) of a standard size used in Europe, measuring 21 centimetres x 29·7 centimetres • *The printer has run out of paper, could you get me some more A4?* [U] • *I must get this letter written – have you got a sheet of A4 I could use?* [U] • *A4 paper is twice as big as A5 and half the size of A3.* • *Is this paper A4 or something else?*

AA DEGREE /ˌeɪ'eɪ/ *n* [C] *abbreviation for* Associate in Arts (= a degree given by an American college to someone after they have completed a two-year course, or a person having this degree)

AA CARS /ˌeɪ'eɪ/ *n* [U + sing/pl v] **the AA** *abbreviation for* the Automobile Association (= an organization in Britain which gives help and information to drivers who are members of it) • *When my car broke down I called the AA and they arrived in just under an hour.* • *Anybody can buy AA products, but usually only AA members can use its services.*

AA ALCOHOL /ˌeɪ'eɪ/ *n* [U + sing/pl v; not after *the*] *abbreviation for* Alcoholics Anonymous (= an organization for people who drink too much alcohol and who want to cure themselves of this habit) • *AA help/helps thousands of people a year to stop drinking.* • *The doctor advised him to go to AA meetings where he could talk to other people who were also trying to stop drinking.*

AAA /ˌeɪ·eɪ'eɪ/ *n* [U + sing/pl v] *abbreviation for* American Automobile Association (= an organization in the US which gives help and information to drivers who are members of it)

AB /ˌeɪ'biː/ *n* [C] *Am for* BA (= a first college degree or someone having this degree) • LP> **Schools and colleges**

a·back /ə'bæk/ *adv* **take** *someone* **aback** to surprise or shock someone so much that they do not know how to behave for a short time • *I was taken aback* **by** *the strength of her feelings on the matter.* • *The news really took us aback.*

ab·a·cus /'æb·ə·kəs/ *n* [C] a square or rectangular frame holding an arrangement of small balls on metal rods or wires, which is used for counting, adding and subtracting • LP> **Mathematics**

a·ban·don *obj* /ə'bæn·dən/ *v* [T often passive] to leave (a place, thing or person) forever, or to stop doing (something) before you have finished it • *When the rebel troops arrived, the village had already been abandoned.* • *The party has now abandoned its policy of unilateral disarmament.* • *She abandoned her husband and children and went off with another man.* • *He abandoned everyone else* **to** *their* **fate** *and fled to safety.* • *We were sinking fast, and the captain gave the order to abandon* **ship**. • *The match was abandoned* (= stopped before it was finished) *at half-time because of the poor weather conditions.* • *They had to abandon* (= stop) *their attempt to climb the mountain.* • *"Abandon hope all ye who enter here" (Originally 'All hope abandon...')* (from Dante's *Inferno* III.4, 1265-1321)

a·ban·doned /ə'bæn·dənd/ *adj* • *An abandoned baby was found in a box on the hospital steps.* • *When her boyfriend left her, she felt very abandoned.*

a·ban·don·ment /ə'bæn·dən·mənt/ *n* [U] • *The abandonment of the land first began at the end of the last century.* • *Little can now be done to prevent the abandonment of the project.*

a·ban·don *obj* **to** *obj* /ə'bæn·dən/ *v prep* [T] to let (yourself) be controlled completely by (a feeling, way of living, etc.) • *He abandoned* **himself** *to his emotions.* • *She abandoned* **herself** *to a life of pleasure.*

a·ban·don /ə'bæn·dən/ *n* [U] • *We danced* **with (gay/ wild)** *abandon* (= lack of control and care).

a·ban·doned /əˈbæn·dᵊnd/ *adj* [before n] • *She threw off her cloak with an abandoned* (= uncontrolled and lacking in care) *gesture.*

a·base *obj* /əˈbeɪs/ *v* [T] *fml* to cause (yourself) to seem not to deserve respect or to be only of little importance, esp. in comparison with another person or God • *The president is not willing to abase him***self before** *the nation, and admit that he made a mistake.*

a·base·ment /əˈbeɪ·smənt/ *n* [U] • *The pilgrims knelt in* **self-***abasement.*

a·bashed /əˈbæʃt/ *adj* embarrassed and awkward in someone's presence, especially because of something you have done or said that they do not approve of • *She blushed, clearly abashed, and did not reply.* • *He looked rather abashed* **at** *her criticisms.* • *There was an abashed grin on Ted's face as he said, "Sorry, I guess I made a mistake."*

a·bate /əˈbeɪt/ *v* [I] to become less strong • *The storm/wind/rain has started to abate slightly.* • *The nurses' concern about cuts in funding for hospitals has not abated.* • *The fighting in the area shows no sign of abating.* • See also UNABATED. • ⓟ

a·bate·ment /əˈbeɪt·mənt/ *n* [U] • *a society for noise abatement*

ab·at·toir /£ˈæb·ə·twɑːʳ, $-twɑːr/, **slaugh·ter·house** *n* [C] a place where animals are killed for their meat

ab·bess /ˈæb·es/ *n* [C] a woman who is in charge of a CONVENT (= a place where religious women called NUNS live and work together)

ab·bey /ˈæb·i/ *n* [C] a building lived in by MONKS (= religious men) or NUNS (= religious women), in Britain esp. in the past. Some abbeys are now used as churches. • *Westminster Abbey*

ab·bot /ˈæb·ət/ *n* [C] a man who is in charge of a MONASTERY (= a place where religious men called MONKS live and work together)

ab·bre·vi·ate *obj* /əˈbriː·vi·eɪt/ *v* [T] to make (a word, sentence, book, etc.) shorter • *The name Susan is often abbreviated* **to** *Sue.* • *The European Monetary System is abbreviated* **as** *the EMS.* • *I've only seen an abbreviated* **version** *of the film.*

ab·bre·vi·a·tion /əˌbriː·viˈeɪ·ʃᵊn/ *n* [C] • *UN is the usual abbreviation* **for** *the United Nations.* • [LP] **Full stop**

ABC [ALPHABET] /ˌeɪ·biːˈsiː/ *n* [U], *Am usually* **ABCs** *pl n infml* the alphabet • *He's learning his ABC at school.* • *(fig.) What I need is a book containing the ABC* (= basic information about the facts and skills) **of** *carpentry.*

ABC [TELEVISION] /ˌeɪ·biːˈsiː/ *n* [U] **the ABC** *abbreviation for* the Australian Broadcasting Corporation (= a company that broadcasts on radio and television in Australia and is paid for by the government)

ab·di·cate *(obj)* /ˈæb·dɪ·keɪt/ *v* to give up (something, esp. a position of power, a responsibility or a right) formally • *King Edward VIII abdicated (the British throne) in 1936 so that he could marry Mrs Simpson, a divorced woman.* [I/T] • *She has abdicated all responsibility for the project.* [T] • *He abdicated his right to a share in the profits.* [T]

ab·di·ca·tion /ˌæb·dɪˈkeɪ·ʃᵊn/ *n* • *Do you know how many abdications* **from** *the British throne there have been?* [C] • *The council denied that their decision represented any abdication* **of** *responsibility.* [U]

ab·do·men /ˈæb·də·mən/ *n* [C] *specialized* the lower part of a person's or animal's body, which contains the stomach, bowels and other organs, or the end of an insect's body • *The patient is complaining of pain in the abdomen, doctor.* • [PIC] **Insects**

ab·dom·in·al /£æbˈdɒm·ɪ·nəl, $-ˈdɑː·mə-/ *adj* [not gradable] • *abdominal pains* • *an abdominal operation*

ab·duct *obj* /æbˈdʌkt/ *v* [T] to take (a person) away by using force • *The company director was abducted* **from** *his car by terrorists.*

ab·duc·tion /æbˈdʌk·ʃᵊn/ *n* • *There has been a series of abductions of young children* **from** *schools in the area.* [C] • *He was charged with abduction.* [U]

ab·duc·tor /£æbˈdʌk·təʳ, $-tɚ/ *n* [C] • *She was tortured by her abductors.*

a·bed /əˈbed/ *adj* [after v], *adv* [not gradable] *old use* in bed

ab·er·rant /əˈber·ᵊnt/ *adj fml* different from what is typical or usual, esp. in an unacceptable way • *aberrant behaviour/beliefs*

ab·er·ra·tion /ˌæb·əˈreɪ·ʃᵊn/ *n* a temporary change from the typical or usual way of behaving • **In a moment of** *aberration, she agreed to go with him.* [U] • *I'm sorry I'm late – I had a* **mental** *aberration and forgot we had a meeting today.* [C] • *He said that the decline in the company's sales*

last month was just a **temporary** *aberration.* [C] • *There is an aberration* (= a fault) *in the computer program.* [C]

a·bet *obj* /əˈbet/ *v* [T] **-tt-** to help or encourage (a person) to do something wrong or illegal • *They claimed that the riot had been abetted by the police.* • *His accountant* **aided and** *abetted him* **in** *the fraud/***in** *evading his taxes.*

a·bet·tor /£əˈbet·əʳ, $-ˈbeţ·ɚ/ *n* [C]

a·bey·ance /əˈbeɪ·ənts/ *n* [U] a state of not being used at present • *Hostilities between the two groups have been* **in** *abeyance since last June.* • *The project is being* **held in** *abeyance until agreement is reached on funding it.* • *The tradition has* **fallen into** *abeyance.*

ab·hor *obj* /£əˈbɔːʳ, $æbˈhɔːr/ *v* [T not *be abhorring*] **-rr-** to hate (something or someone) very strongly • *I have always abhorred insolence in children.* • *They abhor all forms of racism.*

ab·hor·rent /£əˈbɒr·ᵊnt, $æbˈhɔːr-/ *adj* • *I find his cynicism abhorrent.* • *His cynicism is abhorrent* **to** *me.* • *They have been accused of committing abhorrent acts of terrorism.*

ab·hor·rence /£əˈbɒr·ᵊnts, $æbˈhɔːr-/ *n* [U] • *She looked at him* **in/with** *abhorrence.* • *She has* **an** *abhorrence* **of** *change.*

a·bide *(obj)* [BEAR] /əˈbaɪd/ *v* [usually in negatives and questions] to accept (something or someone) willingly • *I* **can't** *abide her.* [T] • *He* **can't** *abide laziness.* [T] • *She* **never could** *abide seeing people enjoying themselves.* [+ v-ing]

a·bide [STAY] /əˈbaɪd/ *v* [I always + adv/prep] *old use* to live or stay somewhere • *He abided in the wilderness for forty days.* • *"Abide With Me"* (title of a hymn by Henry Francis Lyte, 1793-1847)

a·bid·ing /əˈbaɪ·dɪŋ/ *adj* [before n] • An abiding feeling, interest or belief is one which has lasted for a long time and will probably continue: *She has an abiding passion for ice skating.*

a·bide by *obj v prep* [T] to accept or obey (an agreement, decision, rule, etc.) • *Competitors must abide by the judges' decision.* • *I abide by my promise.*

a·bil·i·ty [POWER] /£əˈbɪl·ɪ·ti, $-ə·ţi/ *n* the physical or mental power or skill needed to do something • *Someone of her ability is bound to succeed.* [U] • *His failure was not due to lack of ability.* [U] • *She* **has** *the ability/a remarkable ability* **to** *summarize an argument in a few words.* [U + to infinitive] • *What I need is a camera which* **has** *the ability* **to** *focus automatically.* [U + *to* infinitive] • *She's a woman of considerable abilities.* [C] • *I have children in my class of very* **mixed** *abilities* (= different levels of skill or intelligence). [C] • *The children are taught in a* **mixed** *ability class.* • See also ABLE [CAN DO]; ABLE [SKILFUL].

-a·bil·i·ty [QUALITY] /£-əˈbɪl·ɪ·ti, $-ə·ţi/, **-i·bil·i·ty** *combining form* used to form nouns from adjectives ending in '-able' or '-ible', to mean the quality of being the stated adjective • *washability* • *likeability* • *stability* • *affordability* • *Student textbooks need to have readability* (= the quality of being well written and therefore easy and enjoyable to read). • *The latest computers are high on portability* (= the quality of being easily able to be carried from one place to another). • *Hollywood studios are not convinced of the bankability* (= power to earn money) *of their young female stars.*

ab·ject [EXTREME] /ˈæb·dʒekt/ *adj* (of the conditions in which someone lives) hopeless; of as low quality as possible • *They live in abject* **poverty/misery.** • *The conditions that these people live in are abject and shocking.*

ab·ject [WITHOUT SELF-RESPECT] /ˈæb·dʒekt/ *adj* (of a person or behaviour) not having any respect for yourself; not proud or brave • *an abject coward/beggar* • *an abject apology/request* • *This policy has turned out to be an abject failure.* • *She screamed in abject terror.* • *He is almost abject in his respect for his boss.*

ab·ject·ly /ˈæb·dʒekt·li/ *adv* • *He begged abjectly for forgiveness.*

ab·jure *obj* /£əbˈdʒʊəʳ, $-dʒʊr/ *v* [T] *fml* to say that you will no longer have or use; to give up • *He abjured his religion/his life of dissipation.*

a·blaze /əˈbleɪz/ *adj* [after v] burning very strongly or very brightly lit • *The house was ablaze, and the flames and smoke could be seen for miles around.* • *The ballroom was ablaze* (= brightly lit) **with** *lights.* • *(fig.) Her eyes were ablaze* (= bright) **with** *excitement.*

a·ble [CAN DO] /ˈeɪ·bl̩/ *adj* [after v; + *to* infinitive] (esp. used for tenses that do not use 'can' or 'could') having the physical or mental power, skill, time, money, opportunity, etc. needed • *Will she be able* **to** *cope with the work?* • *He's never been able* **to** *admit to his mistakes.* • *I'm sorry that I wasn't able* **to** *phone you yesterday.* • *He said that he was having financial difficulties and wasn't able* **to** *pay his bills.* • *I love the house – it's wonderful being able* **to** *see the sea from my window.* • *The answering machine is able* **to** *store messages that are up to two minutes in length.* • *Mary's* **more/better** *able* **to** *help you than I am.* • **The able-bodied** are healthy and strong people: *It's sometimes difficult for the able-bodied fully to appreciate the difficulties that disabled people encounter in their daily lives.* ○ *All the* **able-bodied** *young men were forced to join the army.* • See also ABILITY.

a·ble [SKILFUL] /'eɪ·bl̩/ *adj* **-r, -st** clever or good at what you do • *an able child/student/secretary/manager/teacher* • *I don't think he's able enough to do this type of work.* • *This problem is now being looked at by some of the ablest minds/ scientists in the country.* • *She's by far the ablest in the class.* • See also ABILITY.

a·bly /'eɪ·bli/ *adv* • *He performs his duties very ably.*

-a·ble [CAN BE] /-ə·bl̩/, **-i·ble** *combining form* added to verbs to form adjectives which mean able to receive the action of the stated verb • *breakable/washable/movable/ presentable* • *A countable noun is one that can be counted.* • [LP] **Combining forms**

-a·ble [WORTH BEING] /-ə·bl̩/, **-i·ble** *combining form* added to verbs to form adjectives which mean worth receiving the action of the stated verb • *an admirable person* • *an acceptable answer*

a·blu·tion /ə'bluː·ʃᵊn/ *n* [U] the act of washing yourself • *(fml) Ablution is carried out as part of some religious ceremonies.* • *(humorous) My girlfriend has loads of bottles of stuff that she seems to think are necessary for ablution!*

a·blu·tions /ə'bluː·ʃᵊnz/ *pl n* • *(humorous) I must just* **perform** *my ablutions* (= wash myself)*!*

ab·ne·gate *obj* /'æb·nɪ·geɪt/ *v* [T] *fml* not to allow yourself to have (something, esp. something which gives you pleasure) or to give it up • *He belongs to a small sect which abnegates pleasure.* • *They have abnegated* (= given up) *all their rights to the property.*

ab·ne·ga·tion /ˌæb·nɪ'geɪ·ʃᵊn/ *n* [U] *fml* • *He praised the army minister's 'enthusiasm, competence and abnegation'* (= not giving importance to himself or his desires or needs). • *Walking out on his family like that was* **a total** *abnegation* (= giving up) **of** *his responsibilities.*

ab·nor·mal /£æb'nɔː·məl, $-'nɔːr-/ *adj* different from what is usual or average, esp. in a way that is not desirable • *abnormal behaviour/weather/conditions* • *Tests have shown that he has an abnormal heart rhythm/some abnormal skin cells.* • *Like many pregnant women, she's worried that her baby might be born abnormal.*

ab·nor·mal·i·ty /£ˌæb·nɔː'mæl·ə·ti, $-nɔːr'mæl·ə·t̬i/ *n* • *genetic/congenital/neurological abnormalities* [C] • *An increasing number of tests are available for detecting* **foetal** *abnormalities.* [C] • *The X-rays showed some slight abnormality.* [U]

ab·nor·mal·ly /£æb'nɔː·mᵊl·i, $-'nɔːr-/ *adv* • *The success rate was abnormally high.*

Ab·o /£'æb·əʊ, $-oʊ/ *n* [C] *pl* **Abos** *Aus infml* an ABORIGINE. This word is generally considered offensive.

a·board /£ə'bɔːd, $-'bɔːrd/ *adv* [not gradable], *prep* on or onto (a ship, aircraft, bus or train) • *The flight attendant welcomed us aboard (the plane).* • *We spent two months aboard* **(ship)**. • *Hop/climb aboard!* • *The train's about to leave. All aboard!*

a·bode /£ə'bəʊd, $-'boʊd/ *n* [C usually sing] *fml or humorous* the place where someone lives • *The defendant* **is of no fixed** *abode.* • *Let me take you to my* **humble** *abode!*

a·bol·ish *obj* /£ə'bɒl·ɪʃ, $-'bɑː·lɪʃ/ *v* [T] to end (an activity, custom, etc.) officially • *I think bullfighting should be abolished.*

a·bo·li·tion /ˌæb·ə'lɪʃ·ᵊn/ *n* [U] • *William Wilberforce campaigned for the abolition of slavery in the late 18th and early 19th centuries.*

a·bo·li·tion·ist /ˌæb·ə'lɪʃ·ᵊn·ɪst/ *n* [C] • An abolitionist is a person who supports the abolition of something, such as the **death penalty** or SLAVERY.

a·bom·in·a·ble /£ə'bɒm·ɪ·nə·bl̩, $-'bɑː·mɪ-/ *adj* very bad or unpleasant • *The prisoners are forced to live in abominable conditions.* • *Your behaviour was abominable.* • *This tea tastes abominable.* • *(infml) The weather's been abominable this week.* • An **abominable snowman** is a YETI.

a·bom·in·a·bly /£ə'bɒm·ɪ·nə·bli, $-'bɑː·mɪ-/ *adv* • *He behaved abominably throughout the wedding reception.* • *The play was abominably acted.* • *How could you be so abominably cruel?*

a·bom·in·a·tion /£əˌbɒm·ɪ'neɪ·ʃᵊn, $-ˌbɑː·mɪ-/ *n dated* (something which causes) a strong feeling of hate or disgust • *I think that foxhunting is an abomination.* [C] • *Gerald's abomination of spending money should not be allowed to influence the committee's decision.* [U]

a·bom·in·ate *obj* /£ə'bɒm·ɪ·neɪt, $-'bɑː·mɪ-/ *v* [T not *be abominating*] *fml or dated* • *He abominates* (= hates very much) *cruelty of all kinds.*

ab·o·ri·gi·nal /ˌæb·ə'rɪdʒ·ɪ·nəl/ *adj* of or being a person or living thing which has existed in a country or continent since the earliest time known to people • *aboriginal forests* • *aboriginal inhabitants*

Ab·o·ri·gi·ne /æb·ə'rɪdʒ·ɪ·nəl/ *n* [C] a member of the race of dark-skinned people who were the first people to live in Australia • *Many Aborigines died when they came into contact with diseases introduced into Australia by Europeans.*

Ab·o·ri·gin·al /æb·ə'rɪdʒ·ɪ·nəl/ *adj, n* • *Aboriginal art* • *Aboriginal traditions* • An Aboriginal is an ABORIGINE. [C]

a·bort *obj* [STOP] /£ə'bɔːt, $-'bɔrt/ *v* [T] to cause (something) to stop or fail before it begins or before it is complete • *The plan/flight had to be aborted at the last minute.*

a·bor·tion /£ə'bɔː·ʃᵊn, $-'bɔːr-/ *n* [C] *slang* • *This project is a complete abortion* (= failure).

a·bort·ive /£ə'bɔː·tɪv, $-'bɔːr·t̬ɪv/ *adj* [not gradable] • An abortive attempt or plan is one that you have to give up because it has failed.

a·bort *(obj)* [END PREGNANCY] /£ə'bɔːt, $-'bɔːrt/ *v* to prevent (a baby that has not been born, or a pregnancy) from developing any further, usually by having a medical operation • *It is better to abort a pregnancy in its early stages rather than later on.* [T] • *Pregnant schoolgirls often choose to abort, so that they don't have to leave school to look after the baby.* [I] • *Do you think it's wrong to use aborted* **foetuses** *for medical research?* • *The doctor said that she did not want to see a return to the days when women aborted* **themselves** (= ended their pregnancies) *with knitting needles.* [T] • Abort can also mean **miscarry**. See at MISCARRIAGE. [I]

a·bor·tion /£ə'bɔː·ʃᵊn, $-'bɔːr-/ *n* • Abortion is the intentional ending of a pregnancy, usually by a medical operation: *She decided to* **have/get** *an abortion.* [C] ○ *Abortion is restricted in some American states.* [U] • Compare MISCARRIAGE; STILLBIRTH. • (DK) (E)

a·bor·tion·ist /£ə'bɔː·ʃᵊn·ɪst, $-'bɔːr-/ *n* [C] • An abortionist is a person who performs abortions to end unwanted pregnancies, esp. illegally and for money.

a·bound /ə'baʊnd/ *v* [I] to exist in large numbers • *Theories abound about how the earth began.* • *He said that he had experienced abounding* (= a lot of) *racism in his attempt to find a job.* • If something abounds **with/in** other things, it has a lot of them: *The coast here abounds in rare plants.*

a·bout [CONNECTED WITH] /ə'baʊt/ *prep* on the subject of; connected with • *"What's that book about?" "It's about the Spanish Civil War."* • *They were talking/laughing about his strange clothes.* • *He's always* **(going) on** *about what a great job he's got.* • *She was furious about our mistake.* • *I really don't know what all the fuss is about.* • *I wish you'd* **do something** *about* (= take action to solve the problem of) *your bedroom – it's a real mess.* • *(Br infml) Could you make me a coffee too* **while** *you're about* **it** (= while you're making one for yourself)*?* • *(esp. Br dated) Edward should be here by now. I don't know what on earth he could* **be about** (= could be doing). • *What exactly didn't you like about* (= in the character of) *the play?* • **There's something** *about* (= in the character of) *her attitude that worries me.* • **There's something** *(special/strange)* **about** *him* (= in his character). • **How/What about** (= I suggest) *a trip to the zoo/going to the zoo?* • *"Coffee, Sarah?" "No, thanks."* "**How/What about** *you* (= Would you like some), *Kate?"* • *"Let's go to Scotland this April." "Yes, but* **what about** (= have you considered the problem of) *the weather?"* • *"Is that your car?" "Yes,* **what** *about it* (= why are you asking me)*?"* This is sometimes said in an angry or threatening way.

a·bout [APPROXIMATELY] /ə'baʊt/ *adv* [not gradable] a little more or less than (a number, amount, etc.); approximately • *about six feet tall* • *about two months ago* • *(at) about four (o'clock)* • *The car was exactly what I was looking for, and* *the price was about right* (=approximately correct, or approximately what I wanted to pay), *so I bought it.* • *We're about* (=almost) *ready to leave.* • *I've had* **(just)** *about enough* (=I do not want any more) *of your complaining.* • *Well, I think* **that's** *about* **it** *for now* (=we have almost finished what we are doing for the present). *Shall we tidy up ready to start again tomorrow?* • LP› **Approximate numbers**

a·bout IN THIS PLACE /ə'baʊt/, *Am and Aus usually* **a·round** *adv* [not gradable], *prep, adj* [after v; not gradable] positioned or moving in or near a place, often without a clear direction, purpose or order • *She always leaves her clothes lying about (on the floor).* • *I was sitting about all morning waiting for the plumber.* • *They heard someone moving about outside.* • *I've been running about (the building) all morning trying to find you.* • *She must be about the place somewhere.* • *(Br fml) Do you have such a thing as a pen about* **you/your person** (=Have you got a pen)? • *Is John about* (=somewhere near)? • *There's a lot of flu about* (=many people have it) *at the moment.* • *You'll soon be* **up/out and about** (=healthy) *again.*

a·bout INTENDING /ə'baʊt/ *adj* [after v; + *to* infinitive; not gradable] having the intention of doing something immediately or almost starting to do something • *She was about* **to** *leave when Mark arrived so she stayed a little longer.* • *He looked as if he was about* **to** *burst into tears.* • *I'm not about* (=I am strongly determined not) **to** *say I'm sorry to him after the way he's behaved.*

a·bout–turn *Br and Aus* /£ə,baʊt'tɜːn, $-'tɜːrn/, *Am and Aus* **a·bout–face** /ə,baʊt'feɪs/ *n* [C] a change of direction or of someone's opinion or way of acting • *I'd only gone a little way down the street when I remembered I hadn't locked the door, so I* **made** *a quick about-turn and ran back to the house.* • *This is the Government's second about-turn* (=change of opinion) **on** *the issue.*

a·bove /ə'bʌv/ *adv* [not gradable], *prep* higher than or more than (something) • *The stars above (us) seemed cold and distant.* • *The helicopter was hovering above the building.* • *There's a mirror above the washbasin.* • *He waved the letter excitedly above his head.* • *Soft piano music floated down from above.* • *She's rented a room above a baker's shop.* • *Her name comes above mine on the list.* • *She was in the year above me at school.* • *In some countries, temperatures rarely rise above zero in winter.* • *Our rates of pay are above* **average.** • *The class is for children above* **the age of** *six.* • *The boots fasten above* (=just over) *the knee.* • *We could hardly hear each other speak above the music* (=because the music was so loud). • *In the end of term exams, Sophie came out above* (=was more successful than) *everyone else in the class.* • *A colonel is above* (=has a higher rank than) *a major in the British army.* • *He thinks he's above* (=better than or of a higher social class than) *everyone else.* • *She's been* **getting** *above* **herself** (=behaving as if she were more important than she really is) *recently.* • *(esp. Br humorous or dated) You're getting* **ideas** *above your* **station** (=you think that you are more important or of a higher social class than you really are)*!* • *He considers himself above travell***ing** (=too important to travel) *with us.* [+ v-*ing*] • *We've had orders* **from** *above* (=people in a more important position, or, less commonly, God). • Above can be used to mean more than: *She values her job above her family.* ○ *They value their freedom above* **(and beyond) all** *else.* ○ *Above* **all** (=Most importantly), *don't forget to write.* ○ *The officer was praised for showing courage above* **and beyond the call of duty** (=more than would usually be expected from someone in that job). • To be above something can be to be too good or honest for it: *She's above* **suspicion/criticism/reproach**. ○ *He's not above ly***ing** *to protect himself.* [+ v-*ing*] • When used in a piece of writing, above can mean higher on the page, or on a previous page: *Please send the articles to the address given above.* • If something is above you/your **head**, you do not understand it: *What he said was quite above me.* • *(fml)* The above-**mentioned** things or people are the things or people which were referred to earlier in a document or book. Compare UNDERMENTIONED. • *"This above all: to thine own self be true"* (Shakespeare, Hamlet 1.3)

a·bove /ə'bʌv/ *adj* [before n; not gradable] *fml* • *The way in which the blood is carried round the body is shown in the above diagram* (=one in a higher position on the same page).

a·bove /ə'bʌv/ *pl n* • **The above** are all of the people or things listed earlier: **All of** *the above are to be included.*

a·bove·board /£ə,bʌv'bɔːd, $-'bɔːrd/ *adj* [after v] *infml* (of a plan, business agreement, etc.) honest, not trying to deceive • *The deal was completely* **open and** *aboveboard.*

ab·ra·ca·dab·ra /,æb·rə·kə'dæb·rə/ *exclamation* said by someone who is performing a magic trick, in order to help them perform it successfully • *The magician waved his magic wand, cried 'Abracadabra', and pulled a white rabbit out of his hat.*

a·brade *obj* /ə'breɪd/ *v* [T] *specialized* to remove part of the surface of (something) by rubbing

a·bra·sive RUBBING /ə'breɪ·sɪv/ *adj, n* (of) a substance used for rubbing away the surface of something, esp. in order to clean it or make it shiny • *Is it OK to use an abrasive cleaner/powder/liquid/sponge to clean this bath, or will it scratch it?* • *You'll need a strong abrasive for cleaning this sink.* [C]

a·bra·sion /ə'breɪ·ʒᵊn/ *n* • *There seems to have been some abrasion of the surface.* [U] • An abrasion is a place where the surface of something, esp. skin, has been rubbed away: *She had a small abrasion on her knee.* [C]

a·bra·sive UNPLEASANT /ə'breɪ·sɪv/ *adj* (of people or their behaviour) upsetting and causing annoyance because of being unpleasant, rude and unkind • *I can't stand her abrasive manner.* • *If you criticize Pablo, he becomes very abrasive.*

a·bra·sive·ly /ə'breɪ·sɪv·li/ *adv*

a·bra·sive·ness /ə'breɪ·sɪv·nəs/ *n* [U]

a·breast /ə'brest/ *adv* (of two or more people or moving objects) next to each other and facing in the same direction • *We were running/cycling* **two** *abreast.* • *The motorcyclist came abreast* **of** *his car and shouted abuse at him.* • If you are abreast **of** a subject or situation, you stay informed about the most recent facts about it: *She's always abreast of the current political situation.* ○ *I try to* **keep** *abreast of what's happening in psychology.*

a·bridge *obj* /ə'brɪdʒ/ *v* [T] to make (a book, speech, article, etc.) shorter • *He's currently abridging his book so that it can be made into a film.* • *I've only read the abridged* **edition/version** *of her novel.*

a·bridg·ment, a·bridge·ment /ə'brɪdʒ·mənt/ *n* • *An abridgment* (=shortened form) **of** *the book has been published for younger readers.* [C] • *Because of space limitations, letters selected for publication in the newspaper are subject to abridgment* (=being made shorter). [U]

a·broad FOREIGN PLACE /ə'brɔːd/ *adj* [after v], *adv* [not gradable] in or to a foreign country or countries • *He's currently abroad on business.* • *The choir performs regularly both* **at home and** *abroad.* • *We always* **go** *abroad in the summer.*

a·broad OUT /ə'brɔːd/ *adj* [after v; not gradable] *literary or old use* outside; not at home • *Not a soul was abroad that morning.* • *(fig. fml) The rumour is abroad* (=is known and talked about by many people) *that she intends to leave the company.*

ab·ro·gate *obj* /£'æb·rəʊ·geɪt, $-rə-/ *v* [T] *fml* to end (a law, agreement, custom, etc.) formally • *The treaty was abrogated in 1929.*

ab·ro·ga·tion /£,æb·rəʊ'geɪ·ʃᵊn, $-rə-/ *n* [U] *fml* • *It seems that there has been* **an** *abrogation* **of** *the agreement.*

a·brupt SUDDEN /ə'brʌpt/ *adj* (of an event) sudden and not expected, often in an unpleasant way • *an abrupt change/movement* • *Our conversation came to an abrupt end when George burst into the room.* • *The road ended in an abrupt* (=sudden and very steep) *slope down to the sea.*

a·brupt·ly /ə'brʌpt·li/ *adv* • *The talks ended abruptly when one of the delegations walked out in protest.*

a·brupt·ness /ə'brʌpt·nəs/ *n* [U]

a·brupt NOT FRIENDLY /ə'brʌpt/ *adj* (of a person or the way they behave or speak) not friendly or polite and using few words; showing no interest in talking to other people • *an abrupt manner/reply* • *The headteacher is very abrupt* **with** *parents.*

a·brupt·ly /ə'brʌpt·li/ *adv* • *"I have nothing further to say," he said abruptly.*

a·brupt·ness /ə'brʌpt·nəs/ *n* [U]

ABS /,eɪ·biː'es/ *n* [U] *abbreviation for* anti-lock braking system (=a BRAKE fitted to some road vehicles that prevents uncontrolled sliding by reducing the effects of sudden braking)

ab·scess /'æb·ses/ *n* [C] a painful swollen area on or in the body which contains PUS (=a thick yellowish liquid) • *She had an abscess* **on** *her gum.*

ab·scond /£əb'skɒnd, $-'skɑːnd/ *v* [I] to go away suddenly and hide somewhere, esp. in order to escape from somewhere or because you have stolen something • *Two prisoners absconded last night.* • *She absconded* **from** *boarding school* **with** *her boyfriend.* • *They absconded* **with** (=stole) *£10 000 of the company's money.*

ab·scond·er /£æb'skɒn·dəʳ, $-'skɑːn·dɚ/ *n* [C] • *A 14 year-old absconder from a children's home in Bristol was found dead yesterday in London.*

ab·seil *esp. Br and Aus* /'æb·seɪl/, *Am usually* **rap·pel** *v* [I] to go down a very steep slope by holding on to a rope which is fastened to the top of the slope • *She abseiled* **down** *the rock face.*

ab·seil *esp. Br and Aus* /'æb·seɪl/, *Am usually* **rap·pel** *n* [C]

ab·sence /'æb·sᵊnts/ *n* the state or act of, or a period of, not being somewhere or of not existing • *A new manager was appointed* **during/in** *your absence* (=while you were away). [U] • *She has had repeated absences* (=acts of being away) **from** *work this year.* [C] • *He drew attention to the absence* (=lack) **of** *(any) concrete evidence against the defendant.* [U] • **In the** *absence* **of** *any more suitable candidates* (=because there were not any more suitable ones), *we decided to offer the job to Mr Conway.* [U] • *(saying)* 'Absence makes the heart grow fonder' means that we value people more when they are not with us.

ab·sent /'æb·sᵊnt/ *adj* [not gradable] • *John has been absent* (=away)**(from** *school/work/home) for three days now.* • *We drank a toast to absent* **friends**. • *Any sign of remorse was completely absent* (=lacking) **from** *her face.* • Someone can be described as being absent, or as having an absent **expression**, when they are not giving attention to what is happening near them, but are thinking of other things. • If you are **absent-minded**, you forget things, or do not give attention to what is happening near you because you are thinking of other things: *He's becoming very absent-minded.* ○ *She* **absent-mindedly** *left her shopping on the bus.* • LP› **Memory**

ab·sent·ly /'æb·sᵊnt·li/ *adv* • *She smiled at him absently* (=without thinking about what she was doing because she was thinking of other things).

ab·sent *obj* /æb'sent/ *v* [T] *fml* • *Saying "Would you please excuse me for a minute", he absented him***self** (=left) **(from** *the room).* • *You cannot choose to absent your***self** **(from** *work/school)* (=not go to work/school) *just because you want to.* • LP› **Reflexive pronouns and verbs**

ab·sent·ee /ˌæb·sᵊn'tiː/ *n* [C] • *There are several absentees in the school* (=people who are not present at school) *this week, because a lot of people have got flu.* • An *(Am)* **absentee ballot**/*(Aus)* **absentee vote** is a piece of paper which voters who are unable to be present at an election can vote on and send in by post: *Although we were in Sao Paolo at the time of the presidential election, we voted by absentee ballot.* • An **absentee landlord** is a person who rents out a house, apartment or farm to someone, but rarely or never visits it.

ab·sent·ee·i·sm /ˌæb·sᵊn'tiː·ɪ·zᵊm/ *n* [U] • *There has been a recent increase in absenteeism* (=people not going to work or school when they should be going).

ab·sinthe, **ab·sinth** /£'æb·sæ̃θ, £-sɪntθ, $-'-/ *n* [U] a strong green alcoholic drink with a bitter taste

ab·so·lute VERY GREAT /ˌæb·sə'luːt, '---/ *adj* [not gradable] very great or to the largest degree possible • *a man of absolute integrity/discretion/evil* • *I have absolute faith in her judgment.* • *There was no absolute proof of fraud.* • *He's an absolute* **certainty** *for the team.* • You can use absolute when you are expressing a strong opinion about someone or something: *He's an absolute idiot/moron!* ○ *You're an absolute angel/darling.* ○ *That's absolute* **rubbish/nonsense**. • An absolute **monarch/ruler** is one who rules completely, with unlimited power. • *"Absolute Beginners"* (title of a book by Colin MacInnes, 1959) • *"Power tends to corrupt and absolute power corrupts absolutely"* (from a letter written by Lord Acton, 1887)

ab·so·lute·ly /ˌæb·sə'luːt·li, '--ˌ--/ *adv* [not gradable] • *I believed/trusted him absolutely.* • *You must be absolutely silent or the birds won't appear.* • *We've achieved absolutely nothing today.* • Absolutely can be used to add force to a strong adjective which is not usually used with 'very', or to a verb expressing strong emotion: *It's absolutely impossible to work with all this noise!* ○ *The food was absolutely disgusting/delicious!* ○ *I absolutely loathe/adore jazz!* • Absolutely can also be used as a way of strongly saying yes. Absolutely **not** is a way of strongly saying no: *"It was an excellent film, though." "Absolutely!"* ○ *"Are you too tired to continue?" "Absolutely not!"* • LP› **Very, completely**

ab·so·lut·i·sm /£'æb·sə·luː·tɪ·zᵊm, $-t̬ɪ-/ *n* [U] • Absolutism is (the principle of) a political system in which a single ruler, group or political party has complete power over a country. • *"Every country has its own constitution: ours is absolutism moderated (sometimes 'tempered') by assassination"* (a Russian's description of his country reported by Count Munster, 1868)

ab·so·lute NOT CHANGING /ˌæb·sə'luːt, '---/ *adj* [before n] not dependent on anything else; true, right, or the same in all situations • *an absolute law/principle/doctrine* • *Do you think there's such a thing as absolute truth/beauty?* • *Her contribution was better than most, but* **in** *absolute* **terms** (=without comparing it with anything else) *it was still rather poor.* • Someone who wins an **absolute majority** in an election has the support of more than half of the voters. • **Absolute zero** is the lowest temperature possible, -273·15°C.

ab·solve *obj* /£əb'zɒlv, $-'zɑːlv/ *v* [T] *fml* (esp. in religion or law) to officially free (someone) from guilt or responsibility for doing, or seeming to have done, something wrong • *The priest absolved him* **(of** *all his sins).* • *The report absolved her* **from/of** *all blame for the accident.* • (CS)

ab·so·lu·tion /ˌæb·sə'luː·ʃᵊn/ *n* [U] • Absolution is the act of forgiving or being forgiven for a bad action or thought, esp. in Christian religions: *They came* **seeking** *absolution* **(for** *their guilt).* ○ *The priest* **gave** *the woman absolution* **(from/of** *her sins).* ○ *She was* **granted** *absolution.*

ab·sorb *obj* /£əb'zɔːb, $-'zɔːrb/ *v* [T] to take or suck (something) in, esp. gradually • *Plants absorb carbon dioxide.* • *In cold climates, houses need to have walls that will absorb heat.* • *Towels absorb moisture.* • *The drug is quickly absorbed* **into** *the bloodstream.* • *Our countryside is increasingly being absorbed* **by/into** *the large cities.* • To absorb facts, knowledge, ideas, information, etc. is to understand them completely and store them in your memory: *Have you absorbed all the details of the plan?* • To absorb a shock, force, change, etc. is to reduce its effect: *The barrier absorbed the main impact of the crash.* ○ *The effects of the job losses have been partially absorbed by the increase in training schemes.* • If someone's work, or a book, film, etc. absorbs them, or they are absorbed **in** it, their attention is given completely to it: *She was absorbed in her thoughts.* ○ *I was completely absorbed by your letter.* • See also SELF-ABSORBED.

ab·sorb·ent /£əb'zɔː·bᵊnt, $-'zɔːr-/ *adj* • *The new material is highly absorbent* (=can take in liquids). • *You'll need some absorbent paper/cloth to clean up that spilt milk.*

ab·sorb·en·cy /£əb'zɔː·bᵊnt·si, $-'zɔːr-/ *n* [U] • *The manufacturers claim that their tampons/sanitary towels have greater absorbency than competing brands.*

ab·sorb·ing /£əb'zɔː·bɪŋ, $-'zɔːr-/ *adj* • *The book I'm reading at the moment is very absorbing* (=It makes me give all my attention to it).

ab·sorp·tion /£əb'zɔːp·ʃᵊn, $-'zɔːrp-/ *n* [U] • *Some poisonous gases can enter the body by absorption through the skin.* • *He said that something should be done to halt the absorption* **of** *our village by the spreading town.* • *Her absorption* **in** *her work* (=giving of all her attention to it) *is so great that she thinks about nothing else.* • See also **self-absorption** at SELF-ABSORBED.

ab·stain /æb'steɪn/ *v* [I] to not do something, esp. something pleasurable that you think might be bad, or not to use your right to vote • *He took a vow to abstain* **from** *alcohol/smoking/sex.* • *She abstained* **(from** *voting) in the elections for chairperson.*

ab·stain·er /£æb'steɪ·nəʳ, $-nɚ/ *n* [C]

ab·sten·tion /æb'stentʃᵊn/ *n* • *Abstention* **from** *alcohol is essential while you are taking this medication.* [U] • *There were high levels of abstention* **(from** *voting) in the last elections.* [U] • *There were ten votes in favour, six against and three abstentions* (=votes which were neither for or against). [C]

ab·stin·ence /'æb·stɪ·nənts/ *n* [U] • *She said that the best way to avoid pregnancy was total abstinence* **from** *sex.*

ab·stin·ent /'æb·stɪ·nənt/ *adj* • *He's trying to give up drinking, and has managed to remain abstinent for two months now.* • (CS)

ab·stem·i·ous /æb'stiː·mi·əs/ *adj* not eating a lot of food or drinking a lot of alcohol, or not allowing yourself to do things which are enjoyable • *an abstemious meal/person* • *He has led a very abstemious life since he became a Christian.*

ab·stract [GENERAL] /ˈæb·strækt/ *adj* existing as an idea, feeling or quality, not as a material object, or (of an argument, discussion, etc.) general, not based on particular examples • *Truth and beauty are abstract concepts.* • *Her head's full of abstract ideas about justice and revolution.* • *This debate is becoming too abstract* (= general) – *let's have some hard facts!* • Abstract is also used to refer to a type of painting, drawing or SCULPTURE which tries to represent the real or imagined qualities of objects or people by using shapes, lines and colour, and does not show their outer appearance as would be seen in a photograph: *abstract art* ○ *an abstract painter* • An **abstract noun** is a noun which refers to a thing which does not exist as a material object: *'Joy', 'honesty' and 'liberty' are abstract nouns.* Compare **concrete noun** at CONCRETE [CERTAIN].

ab·stract /ˈæb·strækt/ *n* • **The abstract** refers to general ideas: *I have difficulty in dealing with the abstract – let's get down to some particulars.* ○ *We've only discussed the question* **in** *the abstract* (= without referring to any real examples) *so far.* • An abstract is a painting which represents the qualities of something, not its outer appearance. [C]

ab·strac·tion /æbˈstræk·ʃᵊn/ *n* [C] • *She's always talking in (empty) abstractions* (= in a general way, without real examples).

ab·stract [SHORT DOCUMENT] /ˈæb·strækt/ *n* [C] a shortened form of a speech, article, book, etc., giving only the most important facts or arguments • *This computer program puts the abstracts* **from** *hundreds of medical journals at doctors' fingertips.* • *There is a section at the end of the magazine which includes abstracts* **of** *recent articles/books.*

ab·stract /æbˈstrækt/ *v*

ab·stract·ed /£æbˈstræk·tɪd, $-t̬ɪd/ *adj* not giving attention to what is happening around you because you are thinking about something else • *He gave her an abstracted glance, then returned to his book.*

ab·stract·ed·ly /£æbˈstræk·tɪd·li, $-t̬ɪd-/ *adv* • *She gazed abstractedly out of the window.*

ab·struse /æbˈstruːs/ *adj* difficult to understand • *an abstruse philosophical essay* • *I found her argument very abstruse.*

ab·surd /£əbˈsɜːd, $-ˈsɜːrd/ *adj* ridiculous or unreasonable; foolish in an amusing way • **It** *was completely absurd* **(of** *him)* **to** *expect us to finish by Friday.* [+ *to* infinitive] • *What an absurd thing to say!* • *Don't be so absurd! Of course I want you to come.* • *It's an absurd situation – neither of them will talk to the other.* • *He looked absurd in those old-fashioned trousers.*

ab·surd·ly /£əbˈsɜːd·li, $-ˈsɜːrd-/ *adv* • *You're behaving absurdly* (= in a ridiculous way). • *The air fare was absurdly* (= unreasonably) *expensive.*

ab·surd·i·ty /£əbˈzɜː·dɪ·ti, £-ˈsɜː-, $-ˈzɜːr·də·t̬i/ *n* • *Standing there naked, I was suddenly struck by the absurdity* **of** *my position.* [U] • *There are all sorts of absurdities* (= things that are ridiculous) *in the proposal.* [C]

ABTA /ˈæb·tə/ *n* [U + sing/pl v; not after *the*] *abbreviation for* Association of British Travel Agents (= an organization in Britain which protects travellers and people on holiday if a company that arranges travel fails to do something or stops trading) • *The number of complaints by holidaymakers to ABTA has dropped by nearly a third so far this year.* • *Most reputable travel agents are ABTA members.*

a·bund·ant /əˈbʌn·dᵊnt/ *adj* more than enough • *We took an abundant* **supply** *of food with us when we went hiking in the mountains.* • *There is abundant* **evidence** *that cars have a harmful effect on the environment.* • *Cheap consumer goods are abundant* (= exist in large amounts) *in this part of the world.* • *The coastline is abundant* **in** (= has a lot of) *rare species of plants.*

a·bund·ance /əˈbʌn·dᵊnts/ *n* [U] • *There was* **an** *abundance* **of** *wine at the wedding.* • *We had wine* **in** *abundance.*

a·bund·ant·ly /əˈbʌn·dᵊnt·li/ *adv* • *The plant grows abundantly in woodland.* • *You've made your feelings abundantly* (= very) **clear**.

a·buse *obj* /əˈbjuːz/ *v* [T] to use or treat (someone or something) wrongly or badly, esp. in a way that is to your own advantage, or to use rude or cruel language to (someone) • *She is continually abusing her position/authority by getting other people to do things for her.* • *I never expected that he would abuse the* **trust** *I placed in him.* • *Several of the children had been* **sexually/physically/emotionally** *abused.* • *It's one of those cities where the people are really unfriendly and* **(verbally)** *abuse* (= use rude language to) *you all the time.*

a·buse /əˈbjuːs/ *n* • *an abuse* (= wrong use) *of privilege/power/someone's kindness* [C] • *sexual/physical/mental abuse* (= bad treatment) [U] • *She claimed to have been a victim of* **child** *abuse* (= the treatment of children in a bad, esp. sexual, way). [U] • **Drug** *and* **alcohol** *abuse* (= Using these substances in a bad way) *contributed to Brian's early death.* [U] • *They have for many years been involved in a campaign against the abuse* **of** (= refusal to allow) *human* **rights** *in their country.* [U] • *He* **hurled (a stream/torrent of)** *abuse at her* (= He shouted at her angrily and rudely) *when she turned up two hours late.* [U] • *'You idiot!' is a mild* **term of** *abuse* (= an insulting expression). [U] • *He said that he had experienced a lot of* **verbal** *abuse* (= the use of rude or cruel language) *from his co-workers.* [U]

a·bus·er /£əˈbjuː·zəʳ, $-zɚ/ *n* [C] • *a child abuser* • *a drug/substance/solvent abuser*

a·bus·ive /əˈbjuː·sɪv/ *adj* • Abusive means using rude and offensive words: *an abusive letter/telephone call* • *He always becomes abusive* **to** *everyone when he's drunk.*

a·bus·ive·ly /əˈbjuː·sɪv·li/ *adv*

a·but *(obj)* /əˈbʌt/ *v* [no passive] **-tt-** *fml* (of land or buildings) to be next to (something); to touch (something) on one side • *Mexico abuts* **(on)** *some of the richest parts of the United States.* [T; I + prep] • *Their house abutted* **(onto)** *the police station.* [T; I + prep]

a·buzz /əˈbʌz/ *adj* [after v] filled with noise and activity • *When we arrived, the party was in full swing and the room was abuzz.* • *The office was abuzz* **with** *the news that she was leaving.* • *The school was abuzz* **with** *excitement over the Queen's visit.* • *The air was abuzz* **with** *military helicopters, airlifting injured people and equipment.*

a·bys·mal /əˈbɪz·məl/ *adj* very bad • *abysmal poverty/working conditions* • *The film/meal was abysmal.* • *The standard of the students' work is abysmal.*

a·bys·mal·ly /əˈbɪz·məl·i/ *adv* • *an abysmally poor book*

a·byss /əˈbɪs/ *n* [C] a very deep hole which seems to have no bottom • *He was killed in a climbing accident when a rope broke and he fell into an abyss.* • *Space is like an abyss.* • *(fig.) The country is sinking/plunging into an abyss* (= bad state) **of** *violence and lawlessness.* • *(fig. literary) She found herself* **on the edge of** *an abyss* (= having to deal with a very difficult situation).

AC [ELECTRICITY] /ˌeɪˈsiː/ *n* [U] *specialized abbreviation for* alternating current (= electrical current which regularly changes the direction in which it flows) • Compare DC.

AC [AIR] /ˌeɪˈsiː/ *n Am abbreviation for* **air conditioner** or **air conditioning**, see at AIR [GAS] • *The car will cool down quickly once the AC kicks in.* [C] • *You can't live in Washington in the summer without AC.* [U]

a·ca·cia /əˈkeɪ·ʃə/ *n* [C/U] a tree from warm parts of the world which has small leaves and yellow or white flowers

ac·a·dem·ic [STUDYING] /ˌæk·əˈdem·ɪk/ *adj* relating to schools, colleges and universities, or connected with studying and thinking, not with practical skills • *academic subjects/qualifications/books* • *an academic institution* • *the academic year* (= the time, usually from September to June, during which students go to school or college) • *We must maintain/uphold academic standards.* • *They were in full academic dress, including gowns and hoods.* • A person who is academic is clever and enjoys studying: *I was never a particularly academic child.*

ac·a·deme /ˈæk·ə·diːm/ *n* [U] *fml* • Academe is the part of society, esp. universities, that is connected with study and thinking: *The 'town and gown' divide between academe and the rest of the population is growing wider.*

ac·a·dem·i·a /ˌæk·əˈdiː·mi·ə/ *n* [U] • Academia is either the part of society, esp. universities, that is connected with study and thinking, or it is the activity or job of studying: *We are seeking to strengthen the existing links between industry and academia.* ○ *A graduate of law and economics from Moscow State University, he had spent his career* **in** *academia.*

ac·a·dem·ic /ˌæk·əˈdem·ɪk/, *Am also* **a·cad·em·i·cian** *n* [C] • An academic is someone who teaches at a college, or who studies as part of their job: *The government has set up a committee of industrialists and academics to advise it.*

ac·a·dem·i·cally /ˌæk·əˈdem·ɪ·kli/ *adv* • *It may be that a child is bright, but not academically inclined.* • *They've compiled a league table of 100 of the most academically successful independent schools in England.* • *She's always done well academically.*

ac·a·dem·ic THEORETICAL /ˌæk·əˈdem·ɪk/ *adj* theoretical and not related to practical effects in real life • *a purely academic argument/question* • *Stop worrying about what to wear to her party – it's all academic anyway, because you haven't even been invited yet.*

a·cad·e·my /əˈkæd·ə·mi/ *n* [C] an organization intended to protect and develop an art, science, language, etc., or a school which teaches a particular subject or trains people for a particular job • *a military/police academy* • *the Royal Academy of Dramatic Art* • *She was the first woman to be elected to the French Academy.* • An **Academy Award** is a prize given in the US by the Motion Picture Academy to someone who has done good and successful work in films.

a·cad·em·ic·ian /əˌkæd·əˈmɪʃ·ᵊn/ *n* [C] • An academician is a member of an academy of art, science or literature: *In 1980 he became a Royal Academician.* ○ *In 1823 he became professor and academician at Munich.*

a cap·pel·la /£ˌæ·kəˈpel·ə, $ˌɑː-/ *adj, adv* [not gradable] *specialized* sung by a group of people without the help of any musical instruments • *The choir's poor ensemble is disastrously exposed in the a cappella passages.* • *Barbershop choirs sing a cappella.*

ac·cede AGREE /əkˈsiːd/ *v* [I] *fml* to agree to do what people have asked you to do • *He graciously acceded* **to** *our request.* • *It is doubtful whether the government will ever accede* **to** *the nationalists' demands for independence.*

ac·cede BECOME /əkˈsiːd/ *v* [I] *fml* to take an important position • *The diaries were written in 1837 when Queen Victoria acceded* **to the throne** (= became queen).

ac·cess·ion /əkˈseʃ·ᵊn/ *n* [U] *fml* • *1926 was the year of Emperor Hirohito's accession* **to the throne.** • *This latest scandal has raised new doubts over the accession of Sir Richard Binns* **to** *the role of chairman.*

ac·cel·er·ate *(obj)* /£əkˈsel·ə·reɪt, $ˈ-ɚ·eɪt/ *v* to move more quickly, or to make (something) happen faster or sooner • *He accelerated/The car accelerated to overtake the bus.* [I] • *Inflation is likely to accelerate this year, adding further upward pressure on interest rates.* [I] • *They use special chemical substances to accelerate the growth of crops.* [T] • *The director's mismanagement has accelerated the company's failure.* [T] • Compare DECELERATE. • LP **Driving**

ac·cel·er·a·tion /əkˌsel·əˈreɪ·ʃᵊn/ *n* [U] • *The acceleration* **in** *the decline of our industrial base is the fault of government cuts.* • *My car has very poor acceleration* (= it does not easily go faster).

ac·cel·er·a·tor /£əkˈsel·ə·reɪ·tər, $-ɚ·eɪ·t̬ɚ/ *n* [C] • *She put her foot down on the accelerator* (= the PEDAL in a car which makes it go faster). • In science, an accelerator is a machine which makes PARTICLES (= small pieces of matter) move very fast. • LP **Driving**

ac·cent PRONUNCIATION /ˈæk·sᵊnt/ *n* [C] the way in which people in a particular area, country, social class, etc. pronounce words • *He's got a strong French/Scottish/Birmingham/upper-class accent.* • *He speaks with a* **broad/pronounced/thick** (= strong) *Yorkshire accent.* • *Although French is her native language, she* **speaks with** *an impeccable English accent.* • *I tried to get rid of my Coventry accent when I went to university.* • *I thought I could detect a slight West Country accent.* • LP **Pronunciation, Varieties of English** Ⓙ

ac·cents /ˈæk·sᵊnts/ *pl n fig.* • *In the moralistic accents of today's leaders* (= the things the leaders say) *we hear echoes of a previous generation's hypocrisy.*

ac·cent·ed /£əkˈsen·tɪd, $-t̬ɪd/ *adj* • *He spoke in* **heavily** *accented English.*

ac·cent MARK /ˈæk·sᵊnt/ *n* [C] a mark written or printed over a letter to show you how to pronounce it • *an acute/grave/circumflex accent* • *Should there be an accent* **on** *'fete'?* • LP **Symbols** Ⓙ

ac·cent EMPHASIS /ˈæk·sᵊnt/ *n* [C] *specialized* a special emphasis given to a particular syllable in a word, word in a sentence, or note in a set of musical notes • *The accent comes/falls* **on** *the final syllable.* • *(fig.) This season the accent is definitely* **on** (= the most important or popular thing is) *long, flowing romantic clothes.* • LP **Stress in pronunciation** Ⓙ

ac·cent *obj* /əkˈsent/ *v* [T] *specialized* • *Accent the first note of every bar.* • *(fig.) In any advertising campaign, you must accent* (= emphasize) *the areas where your product is better than your competitors'.*

ac·cent·u·ate *obj* /əkˈsen·tju·eɪt/ *v* [T] to emphasize (a particular feature of something) or to make (something) more noticeable • *Her dress was tightly belted, accentuating the slimness of her waist.* • *I use eye-liner to accentuate my eyes.* • *The new policy only serves to accentuate the inadequacy of provision for the homeless.* • *"Accentuate the positive"* (song written by Jonny Mercer, 1944)

ac·cent·u·a·tion /əkˌsen·tjuˈeɪ·ʃᵊn/ *n* [U]

ac·cept *(obj)* /əkˈsept/ *v* to agree to take (something), or to take (something) as satisfactory, reasonable, true, etc. • *The former minister faces seven charges of accepting bribes.* [T] • *Do you accept credit cards?* [T] • *She was in London to accept an award for her latest novel.* [T] • *As a token of our gratitude for all the work you have done, we would like you to accept this small gift.* [T] • *I offered her an apology but she wouldn't accept it.* [T] • *The new telephones will accept* (= take) *coins of any denomination.* [T] • *I accept* (= take) *full responsibility for the failure of the plan.* [T] • *The manuscript was accepted* **for** *publication last week.* [T] • *She was accepted* **as** (= It was agreed that she could be) *a full member of the society.* [T] • *His fellow workers refused to accept him* (= to include him as one of their group). [T] • *He still hasn't accepted the situation* (= realized that he cannot change it). [T] • *The police refused to accept* (= believe) *her version of the story.* [T] • *I can't accept* (= make myself believe) **that** *there's nothing we can do.* [+ *that* clause] • *I don't accept* (= agree) **that** *government policy is at fault.* [+ *that* clause] • If you accept an offer or an invitation you say yes to it: *She's just accepted an invitation to the film star's fiftieth birthday party.* [T] ○ *I've offered her the job but I don't know whether she'll accept it.* [T] ○ *Union members agreed unanimously to accept management's offer of a 4·5% salary increase.* [T] ○ *"They've sent me an invitation." "Will you accept?"* [I] ○ *She's accepted* **to** *give the opening speech at our conference.* [+ *to* infinitive]

ac·cept·a·ble /əkˈsep·tə·bl̩/ *adj* • *Clearly we need to come to an arrangement that is acceptable* (= satisfactory) **to** *both parties.* • *So what is an acceptable level of radiation* (= one that people will agree is not too dangerous)? • *This kind of attitude is simply not acceptable* (= cannot be socially or morally approved of). • *(fml) Thank you so much for your gift. It was most acceptable* (= welcome). • *"Will a £50 donation be enough?" "Yes, that would be quite acceptable* (= enough)."

ac·cept·a·bly /əkˈsep·tə·bli/ *adv*

ac·cept·a·bil·i·ty /£əkˌsep·təˈbɪl·ɪ·ti, $-ə·t̬i/ *n* [U]

ac·cept·ance /əkˈsep·tᵊnts/ *n* • *I've had acceptances from three universities* (= Three universities have agreed to take me as a student). [C] • *The idea rapidly* **gained** *acceptance* (= became approved of) *in political circles.* [U]

ac·cept·ed /əkˈsep·tɪd/ *adj* • *'Speed bump' now seems to be the (generally) accepted term* (= most people use it) *for those ridges in the road that slow traffic down.*

ac·cess /ˈæk·ses/ *n* [U] the method or possibility of approaching a place or person, or the right to use or look at something • *The only access* **to** *the village is by boat.* • *The main access* **to** (= entrance to) *the building is at the side.* • *The tax inspector* **had/gained** *complete access* **to** *the company files.* • *The system has been designed to* **give** *the user quick and easy access* **to** *the required information.* • *The children's father was* **refused/granted** *access* **(to them)** *at any time* (= refused/given official permission to see them). • *(Br fml) Unfortunately, the theatre is* **difficult of** *access for wheel-chair users.* • *(Br)* An **access course** is a set of classes which people take so they can obtain a qualification which can be used to get into university or college: *She doesn't have A levels, but took an access course to get into university.* • An **access road/access route** is a road leading to a particular place, or *(Br)* to a MOTORWAY. • **Access time** is the time it takes a computer to find information.

ac·cess *obj* /ˈæk·ses/ *v* [T] • To access a computer file is to open it in order to look at or change information in it.

ac·cess·i·ble /əkˈses·ə·bl̩/ *adj* • *The resort is easily accessible* (= easy to reach) *by road, rail and air.* • *The problem with some of these drugs is that they are so very accessible* (= easy to obtain). • Accessible also means easy to understand: *Lea Anderson is a choreographer who believes in making dance accessible.* ○ *Covent Garden has made some attempt to make opera accessible* **to** *a wider public.*

ac·ces·si·bil·i·ty /£əkˌses·əˈbɪl·ɪ·ti, $-ə·t̬i/ *n* [U] • *Two new roads are being built to increase accessibility* **to** *the town centre.* • *The accessibility of her plays/poems means that she is able to reach a wide audience.*

ac·cess·ion /əkˈseʃ·ᵊn/ *n* [U] See at ACCEDE BECOME

ac·ces·so·ry EXTRA /£əkˈses·ᵊr·i, $ˈ-ɚ-/ *n* [C often pl] something added to a machine or to clothing which has a useful or decorative purpose • *She wore a green wool suit* *with* **matching** *accessories* (=shoes, hat, bag, etc.). • *Sunglasses are much more than a* **fashion** *accessory.* • *Accessories for the top-of-the-range car include leather upholstery, a compact disc player, electric windows and a sunroof.* • *(fig.) Our new laptop computer is the essential accessory for today's business executive.* • LP› **Shopping goods**

ac·cess·or·ize *obj, Br and Aus usually* **-ise** /£ək'ses·ər·aɪz, $-ə·aɪz/ *v* [T often passive] *esp. Am* • *She wears a little black dress, accessorized simply with a silver necklace.* • *The kitchen is basically finished now and it just needs to be accessorized.*

ac·cess·o·ry CRIMINAL /£ək'ses·ər·i, $'-ə-/ *n* [C] someone who helps another person to commit a crime but does not take part in it • *But if Karl Walker was not the murderer, nor an accessory* **to** *the murder, clearly he should not be in prison.* • *(law)* An **accessory before the fact** is someone who helps in the preparation of a crime. • *(law)* An **accessory after the fact** is someone who helps someone after they have committed a crime, by hiding them, etc.

ac·ci·dent /'æk·sɪ·dənt/ *n* [C] something which happens unexpectedly and unintentionally, esp. causing damage or injury • *John* **had** *an accident and spilled water all over his work.* • *Don't smack him – it was an accident.* • *She was injured in a car/road accident* (= when one car hit another). • *After my little accident* **with** *the chain saw, I've not been allowed to use it again.* • *I found her letter* **by** *accident, as I was looking through my files.* • *The play was a success* **more by accident than design** (= mainly by chance, not because it had been well organized). • *The baby* **had an accident** (= excreted unexpectedly). • An **accident-prone** person often has accidents, usually because they are very awkward or CLUMSY. • *(saying)* 'Accidents will happen' is what people say after an accident in order to make it seem less bad. • *(saying)* 'This was an accident waiting to happen' means that an accident was certain to happen at some time because something about the situation was already wrong or dangerous.

ac·ci·dent·al /£ˌæk·sɪ'den·təl, $-ṭəl/ *adj* • *Reports suggest that 11 soldiers were killed by accidental fire from their own side.* • *The site was located after the accidental discovery of bones in a field.* • **Accidental death** is a VERDICT (= opinion stated at the end of a trial) that is given when a death was the result of an accident and not of murder or SUICIDE.

ac·ci·dent·al·ly /£ˌæk·sɪ'den·təl·i, $-ṭəl-/ *adv* • *It got broken accidentally.* • If you do something **accidentally on purpose**, you do it intentionally but pretend it happened by chance: *I've never liked these glasses of Peter's. I might drop them one day – accidentally on purpose.*

ac·claim /ə'kleɪm/ *v, n* (to give) public approval and praise for someone's work, an action, a person, etc. • *She was universally/widely/publicly acclaimed* **for** *her contribution to the discovery.* [T] • *'Dinner Party', based on the* **critically** *acclaimed novel by Bill Davies, was made into a film last year.* [T] • *The new technique was acclaimed* **(as)** *a medical breakthrough.* [T + obj + *(as)* n] • *She is being acclaimed* (= publicly recognized) **as** *the greatest dancer of her generation.* [T] • *Despite the* **critical** *acclaim, the novel did not sell well.* [U] • *Hamlet was played by Romania's leading actor, Ion Caramitrou,* **to** *rapturous acclaim.* [U]

ac·clam·a·tion /ˌæk·lə'meɪ·ʃən/ *n* [U] *fml* • *His speech was greeted with (shouts of) acclamation* (= loud expressions of approval).

ac·cli·mat·ize *(obj), Br and Aus usually* **-ise** /£ə'klaɪ·mə·taɪz, $-ṭaɪz/, *Am also* **ac·cli·mate** /ə'klaɪ·meɪt, 'æk·lɪ-/ *v* to (cause to) change to suit different conditions of life, weather, etc. • *Even then, more time will be needed for the troops and equipment to become acclimatized* **to** *desert conditions.* [T] • *We found it impossible to acclimatize ourselves* **to** *the new working conditions.* [T] • *The defending champion is Grant Turner of England, who has acclimatized* **to** *the 90°F sunshine by spending the past month in Florida.* [I] • *"Why is it that it rains all the time in England?" "Don't worry – you'll soon acclimatize."* [I]

ac·cli·mat·iz·a·tion, *Br and Aus usually* **-i·sa·tion** /£əˌklaɪ·mə·taɪ'zeɪ·ʃən, $-ṭɪ-/ *n* [U]

ac·co·lade /'æk·ə·leɪd/ *n* [C usually sing] praise and approval • *This is his centennial year and he's been granted the* **ultimate** *accolade – his face on a set of three postage stamps.* • *In fact, the performance which won Irons his most important accolade yet was neither his most difficult nor his best.* • *Her approval was the* **highest** *accolade he could have received.*

ac·com·mo·date *obj* FIND A PLACE FOR /£ə'kɒm·ə·deɪt, $-'kɑː·mə-/ *v* [T] to provide with a place to live or to be stored in • *New students may be accommodated* **in** *halls of residence.* • *(fml) There wasn't enough space to accommodate the files.* • Ⓕ

ac·com·mo·da·tion /£əˌkɒm·ə'deɪ·ʃən, $-ˌkɑː·mə-/ *n* [U] *esp. Br and Aus* • *There's a shortage of cheap accommodation* (= places to live). • *We have first and third class accommodation* (= seats) *on this flight.* • *(Br)* An **accommodation address** *(Am* **mail drop***)* is an address where letters can be sent to a person which is different from the address where the person lives.

ac·com·mo·da·tions /£əˌkɒm·ə'deɪ·ʃənz, $-ˌkɑː·mə-/ *pl n Am* • *We have executive and standard accommodations* (= seats) *on this flight.*

ac·com·mo·date *obj* SUIT /£ə'kɒm·ə·deɪt, $-'kɑː·mə-/ *v* [T] to give what is needed to (someone), or to change (esp. yourself or your behaviour) to suit another person or new conditions • *The new policies fail to accommodate the disabled.* • *Some find it hard to accommodate them***selves to** *the new working conditions.* • *We always try to accommodate* (= help) *our clients* **with** *financial assistance if necessary.* • Ⓕ

ac·com·mo·dat·ing /£ə'kɒm·ə·deɪ·tɪŋ, $-'kɑː·mə·deɪ·ṭɪŋ/ *adj* • An accommodating person is eager or willing to help other people, for example by changing their plans, etc. to suit them: *I'm sure she'll help you – she's always very accommodating.*

ac·com·pa·ny *obj* /ə'kʌm·pə·ni/ *v* [T often passive] to go with (someone) or to be provided or exist at the same time as (something) • *Fenwick, accompanied* **by** *two bodyguards, refused to comment as he left the court.* • *Would you like me to accompany you* **to** *your room?* • *The course books are accompanied* **by** *four cassettes.* • *Depression is almost always accompanied* **by** *insomnia.* • *Bookings must be accompanied* **by** *payment for the full fare.* • *The salmon was accompanied* **by** (= served with) *a fresh green salad.* • *Miss Jessop accompanied Mr Bentley* **on** *the piano* (= played the piano while he sang or played another instrument).

ac·com·pa·ni·ment /ə'kʌm·pən·ɪ·mənt/ *n* • *A very dry champagne makes the ideal accompaniment* **for/to** *this dish.* [C] • *a song with piano accompaniment* [U] • *(humorous) We worked* **to the** *accompaniment* **of** (= while hearing the sound of) *Mr French's drill.* [U]

ac·com·pan·ist /ə'kʌm·pə·nɪst/ *n* [C] • *The singer's accompanist (on the piano) was Charles Harman.*

ac·com·plice /£ə'kʌm·plɪs, $-'kɑːm-/ *n* [C] a person who helps someone else to commit a crime or to do something morally wrong • *She was arrested, but her accomplice got away.*

ac·com·plish *obj* /£ə'kʌm·plɪʃ, $-'kɑːm-/ *v* [T] to finish (something) successfully or to achieve (something) • *The students accomplished the task in less than ten minutes.* • *She accomplished such a lot during her visit.* • *I feel as if I've accomplished nothing since I left my job.*

ac·com·plished /£ə'kʌm·plɪʃt, $-'kɑːm-/ *adj* • *She's a very accomplished* (= skilled) *pianist/painter/horsewoman.* • *He was accomplished* **in** *all the arts.*

ac·com·plish·ment /£ə'kʌm·plɪʃ·mənt, $-'kɑːm-/ *n* • *We celebrated the successful accomplishment* (= completion) *of our task.* [U] • *Cordon-bleu cookery is just one of her many accomplishments* (= skills). [C]

ac·cord AGREEMENT /£ə'kɔːd, $-'kɔːrd/ *n* (a formal) agreement • *An accord* **signed by** *the two sides in January brought a formal end to the war in Bougainville.* [C] • *On 31 May the two leaders signed a* **peace** *accord.* [C] • *Before 1987, the accord between the Labor government and the unions was a simple affair.* [C] • *The project is completely* **in** *accord* **with** *government policy.* [U] • *He left the meeting* **of his own accord** (= without being asked or told to leave). • *(Br)* **With one accord** *the delegates walked out of the conference* (= they did so together and in complete agreement). • Ⓒⓢ ⓇⓊⓈ

ac·cord with *obj* /£ə'kɔːd, $-'kɔːrd/ *v prep* [T] *fml* • *His version of events does not accord* (= agree) *with witnesses' statements.* • *Her speech did not accord with the latest party dogma.*

ac·cord·ance /£ə'kɔː·dənts, $-'kɔːr-/ *n* [U] • Something which is **in accordance with** a rule, law or belief follows or obeys it: *In accordance with her wishes, she was buried in France.*

ac·cord·ing·ly /£ə'kɔː·dɪŋ·li, $-'kɔːr-/ *adv* • *When we receive your instructions we shall* **act** *accordingly* (= we will obey the instructions). • *She's an expert in her field, and is*

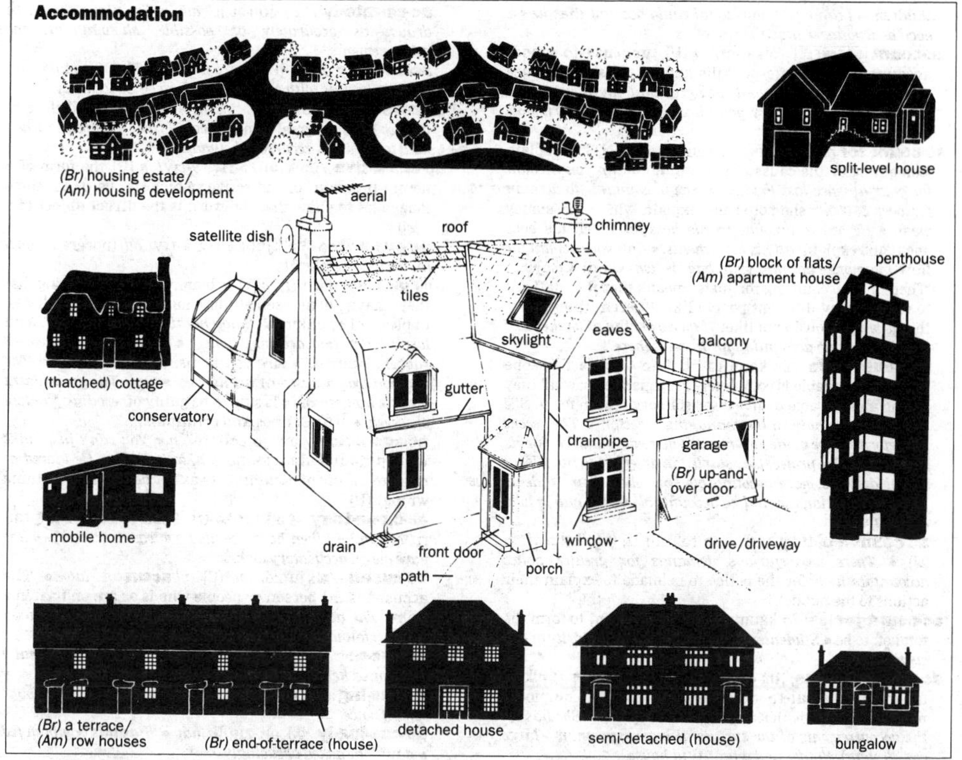

paid accordingly (= in a way suitable to her position). • *She was offended and accordingly* (= therefore) *refused to attend the meeting.*

ac·cord *obj* [GIVE] /£ə'kɔːd, $-'kɔːrd/ *v* [T] *fml* to give • *The massed crowds of supporters accorded him a hero's welcome.* [+ two objects] • *He had to put a brave face on the most hostile press coverage accorded any minister for many months.* [+ two objects] • *Certainly in our society teachers don't enjoy the respect that is accorded* **to** *doctors and lawyers.* • Ⓒ Ⓡ

ac·cord·ing to [AS STATED BY] /£ə'kɔː·dɪŋ, $-'kɔːr-/ *prep* as stated by • *According to Sarah they're not getting on very well at the moment.* • *According to our records you owe us $130.*

ac·cord·ing to [FOLLOWING] /£ə'kɔː·dɪŋ, $-'kɔːr-/ *prep* in a way that agrees with • *You're all put in different groups according to your ability.* • *Did it all go* **according to plan** (= Did it all happen as intended)? • *"From each according to his abilities, to each according to his needs"* (Karl Marx in *Criticism of the Gotha Programme*, 1875)

ac·cord·i·on /£ə'kɔː·di·ən, $-'kɔːr-/ *n* [C] a box-shaped musical instrument, held in the hands, consisting of a folded central part with a keyboard at each end, which is played by pushing the two ends towards each other • *When you hear accordion music in a film, you know they're trying to suggest a French atmosphere.* • **Accordion file** is *Am for* **concertina file**. See at CONCERTINA. • [PIC]**> File**

ac·cost *obj* /£ə'kɒst, $-'kɑːst/ *v* [T] *fml* to approach or stop and speak to (someone, esp. someone you do not know) in a threatening way • *I'm usually accosted by beggars and drunks as I walk to the station.* • *It's a bit unnerving to be accosted by a complete stranger as you walk along the street.*

ac·count [FINANCIAL SERVICE] /ə'kaʊnt/ *n* [C] an arrangement with a bank, shop, or other organization by which they take care of your money or allow you to buy things and pay for them later • *I've* **opened** *an account* **with** *a building society.* • *Have you got a* **bank** *account?* • *(Br and Aus) She* **paid the cheque into**/*(Am and Aus) She* **deposited the check in** *her account.* • *I need to* **draw** *some money* **out of** *my account.* • *Could you* **put** *it* **on**/**charge** *it* **to** *my account* (= can I pay for it later), *please?* • *Do you have an account* **at** *this store*/**with** *us, madam?* • *Could you please* **pay**/**settle** *your account in full* (= give us all the money you owe us). • A customer who does business with a company can be called an account: *If the advertising agency loses the United Beer account, it will make a big dent in their profits.* • [LP]**> Money**

ac·count·ant /£ə'kaʊn·tənt, $-ṭənt/ *n* [C] • An accountant is someone who keeps or examines the records of money received, paid and owed by a company or person: *Elaine's just got a job with a firm of accountants.*

ac·count·an·cy /£ə'kaʊn·tənt·si, $-ṭənt-/ *n* [U] • *He works in accountancy.* • *Irving is a consultant with accountancy firm Robson Rhodes.*

ac·counts /ə'kaʊnts/ *pl n* • Accounts are records of the money a person or company spends and receives: *I* **keep** *my own accounts.*

ac·count [REPORT] /ə'kaʊnt/ *n* [C] a written or spoken description of an event • *She* **gave** *a thrilling account* **of** *her life in the jungle.* • *He* **kept** *a detailed account* **of** *the suspect's movements.* • *Several eyewitnesses' accounts differed considerably from the official version of events.* • **By/From all accounts**, (= People say that) *San Francisco is a city it's easy to fall in love with.* • *She was* **brought/called to account for** (= made to explain) *her actions.* • **By** *his* **own account** (= He claims that) *he's quite wealthy.*

ac·count [REASON] /ə'kaʊnt/ *n* [U] **on account** because; for the reason • *She's angry on account* **of** *what you said over lunch about her husband.* • If something is said to be **on** someone's or something's **account**, it is because of that person or thing: *They were tired, but not any less enthusiastic on that account.* ○ *Please don't cook on my account* (= don't cook just for me) – *I'm perfectly happy with a sandwich.* • If something must **on no account/not on any account** be done, it must not be done at any time or for any reason: *Employees must on no account make personal telephone calls from the office.* ○ *Do not on any account be late for the meeting tomorrow.*

ac·count *obj* [JUDGE] /ə'kaʊnt/ *v* [T + obj + n/adj] *fml* to think of (someone or something) in the stated way; judge • *She was accounted a genius by all who knew her work.*

ac·count [IMPORTANCE] /ə'kaʊnt/ *n* [U] *fml* importance • *It's* **of** *no account to me whether he comes or not.* • *His opinion is* **of** *little account to me.*

ac·count [CONSIDER] /ə'kaʊnt/ *n* [U] **take into account/take account of** to consider or remember when judging a situation • *I hope my teacher will take into account the fact that I was ill just before the exams when she marks my paper.* • *A good architect takes into account the building's surroundings.* • *Britain's tax system takes no account of* *children.* • *I think you have to take into account* **that** *he's a good deal younger than the rest of us.*

ac·count USE WELL /ə'kaʊnt/ *n* [U] **turn/use to (good) account** *fml* to use (esp. skills and abilities) to produce good results • *I think we'd all agree that you turned your negotiating skills to very good account in this afternoon's meeting.*

ac·count for *obj* EXPLAIN /ə'kaʊnt/ *v prep* [T] to explain (something or the cause of something) • *Can you account for your absence last Friday?* • *She was unable to account for over $5000* (= she could not explain where the money was). • *He has to account* **to** *his boss for* (= tell his boss about and explain) *all his movements.* • *Can you account for* **how** *the money got into your bag?* [+ *wh-* word] • *(saying)* 'There's no accounting for taste' means that it is difficult to explain why different people like different things, esp. things which you do not like: *"I love working at weekends." "Well, there's no accounting for taste, is there!"*

ac·count·a·ble /£ə'kaʊn·tə·bl̩, $-t̬ə-/ *adj* • Someone who is accountable is completely responsible for what they do and must be able to give a satisfactory reason for it: *She is accountable only* **to** *the managing director.* ○ *The recent tax reforms have made government more accountable* **for** *its spending.* ○ *The project was started in an effort to* **hold** *local school districts more accountable* **for** *what their students learn.* ○ *Politicians should be accountable* **to** *the public who elected them.*

ac·count·a·bil·i·ty /£ə,kaʊn·tə'bɪl·ɪ·ti, $-t̬ə'bɪl·ə·t̬i/ *n* [U] • *There were furious demands for greater police accountability* (= for the police to be made to explain their actions to the public).

ac·count for BE /ə'kaʊnt/ *v prep* [L only + n] to form the total of; to be • *Students account for the vast majority of our customers.*

ac·cou·tre·ments, *Am also* **ac·cou·ter·ments** /£ə'kuː·trə·mənts, $ə'kuː·t̬ɚ·mənts/ *pl n fml* the equipment needed for a particular activity or way of life • *She has all the accoutrements of the successful businesswoman – large car, designer clothes and a beautiful house.*

ac·cred·it *obj* /ə'kred·ɪt/ *v* [T] to officially recognize, accept or approve of (someone or something) • *The agency was not accredited by the Philippine Consulate to offer contracts to Filipinos abroad.* • *Ambassadors must have the confidence of the governments* **to** *which they are accredited* (= that they officially represent).

ac·cred·it·ed /£ə'kred·ɪ·tɪd, $-t̬ɪd/ *adj* • *They're an accredited drama school.* • *Accredited war correspondents, photographers and artists will all be eligible for a medal.*

ac·cred·it·a·tion /£ə,kred·ɪ'teɪ·ʃən, $-'t̬eɪ-/ *n* [U] • *The college received/was given full accreditation in 1965.*

ac·cre·tion /ə'kriː·ʃən/ *n fml* gradual increase or growth by the addition of new layers or parts • *The fund was increased by the accretion of new shareholders.* [U] • *The room hadn't been cleaned for years and showed several accretions of dirt and dust.* [C]

ac·crue /ə'kruː/ *v* [I] *fml* to increase in number or amount over a period of time • *Interest will accrue* **on** *the account at a rate of 7%.* • *Little benefit will accrue* **to** *London* (= London will receive little benefit) *from the new road scheme.*

ac·cu·mu·late *(obj)* /ə'kjuː·mjʊ·leɪt/ *v* to collect a large number of (things) over a long period of time, or to gradually increase in number or amount • *As people accumulate more wealth, they tend to spend a greater proportion of their incomes.* [T] • *The company said the debt was accumulated during its acquisition of nine individual businesses.* [T] • *We've accumulated so much rubbish over the years.* [T] • *A thick layer of dust had accumulated in the room.* [I] • *If you don't sort out the papers on your desk on a regular basis they just keep on accumulating.* [I]

ac·cu·mu·la·tion /ə,kjuː·mjʊ'leɪ·ʃən/ *n* • *Despite this accumulation of evidence, the Government persisted in doing nothing.* [U] • *Accumulations of sand can be formed by the action of waves on coastal beaches.* [C]

ac·cu·mu·lat·or *Br and Aus* /£ə'kjuː·mjʊ·leɪ·tər, $-t̬ɚ/, *Am and Aus* **stor·age bat·ter·y** *n* [C] • An accumulator is a BATTERY that collects and stores electricity. • (PL) (RUS)

ac·cu·rate /'æk·jʊ·rət/ *adj* correct, exact and without any mistakes • *an accurate machine/clock* • *an accurate description/report* • *The figures they have used are just not accurate.* • *Her novel is an accurate reflection of life in post-war Spain.* • *She is always accurate* **in** *her use of language.* • *We hope to become more accurate* **in** *predicting earthquakes.*

ac·cu·rate·ly /'æk·jʊ·rət·li/ *adv* • *The plans should be drawn as accurately as possible, showing all the measurements.*

ac·cu·ra·cy /'æk·jʊ·rə·si/ *n* [U] • *The computer can predict changes with* **a surprising degree of** *accuracy.*

ac·cursed /£ə'kɜː·sɪd, £-'kɜːst, $-'kɜːrst/ *adj* [before n] *old use* causing great annoyance • *I can't get around like I used to – it's this accursed rheumatism!*

ac·cus·a·tive /£ə'kjuː·zə·tɪv, $-t̬ɪv/ *n* [U] the form of a noun, pronoun or adjective which is used in some languages to show that the word is the **direct object** of a verb

ac·cus·a·tive /£ə'kjuː·zə·tɪv, $-t̬ɪv/ *adj* [not gradable] • *the accusative plural*

ac·cuse *obj* /ə'kjuːz/ *v* [T] to blame (someone), saying that they have done something morally wrong, illegal, unpleasant or unkind • *"I had nothing to do with it." "Don't worry, I'm not accusing you."* • *He's been accused* **of** *robbery/murder.* • *Are you accusing me* **of** *lying?* • *The surgeon was accused* **of** *negligence.* • *(fml) The government* **stands** *accused* **of** (= is said to be guilty of) *eroding freedom of speech.* • LP **Crimes and criminals**

ac·cus·a·tion /,æk·jʊ'zeɪ·ʃən/ *n* • *You can't just make* **wild/unfounded** *accusations like that!* [C] • *He glared at me with an air of accusation* (= as if I had done something wrong). [U]

ac·cus·a·to·ry /£ə'kjuː·zə·tri, £,æk·jʊ'zeɪ·tər·i, $-tɔː·ri/ *adj fml* • *When he spoke his tone was accusatory.* • *She gave me an accusatory look.*

ac·cused /ə'kjuːzd/ *n* [C] *pl* **accused** *law* • **The accused** is the person or people who is or are on trial in a court: *The accused protested her innocence.* ○ *The accused were all found guilty.* • LP **Law**

ac·cus·er /£ə'kjuː·zər, $-zɚ/ *n* [C] • *She finally confronted her accuser.*

ac·cus·ing /ə'kjuː·zɪŋ/ *adj* • *an accusing glance/look/tone of voice*

ac·cus·ing·ly /ə'kjuː·zɪŋ·li/ *adv* • *"Has this dog been fed today?" she asked accusingly.*

ac·cus·tom *obj* **to** *obj* /£ə'kʌs·təm-, $-t̬əm-/ *v prep* [T] to make (someone, esp. yourself) familiar with (new conditions) • *It'll take time for me to accustom* **myself** *to the changes.*

ac·cus·tomed /£ə'kʌs·təmd, $-t̬əmd/ *adj* • *She performed the task with her accustomed* (= usual) *ease.* • *She quickly became accustomed* **to** *his messy ways.* • *I'm not accustomed* **to being** *treated like this* (= it is not a familiar experience for me). • *"I've grown accustomed to her face"* (title of a song by Alan Jay Lerner from the musical *My Fair Lady*, 1956)

ace PLAYING CARD /eɪs/ *n* [C] one of the four playing cards with a single mark or spot, which have the highest or lowest value in many card games • *the ace of hearts/clubs/spades/diamonds* • To **be/come within an ace of** losing/winning/death is to be very close to it: *She came within an ace of winning the match.* • If you have an **ace up** your **sleeve**/*(Am also)* **ace in the hole** you have some secret knowledge or skill which you have not yet used: *He knows something about the boss – that's his ace in the hole.* • Someone who **holds/has all the aces** has all the advantages: *In a situation like this, it's the big companies who hold all the aces.* • LP **Cards** PIC **Club, Diamond**

ace SKILLED PERSON /eɪs/ *n* [C] *infml* a person who is very skilled at something • *She's an ace* **at** *tennis.* • *He was a flying ace* (= was very skilled at flying aircraft) *in the First World War.*

ace /eɪs/ *adj* [not gradable] *dated slang* • *He's an ace footballer.* • *That's an ace* (= excellent) *bike you've got there.*

ace TENNIS /eɪs/ *n* [C] (in tennis) a SERVE (= a hit of the ball which starts play) which is so strong and fast that the other player cannot return the ball • *That's the third ace that Violente has* **served** *this match.*

a·cer·bic /£ə'sɜː·bɪk, $-'sɜːr-/ *adj fml* (esp. of someone's way of talking or manner) sharp, angry and hard • *The letters show the acerbic wit for which Parker was both admired and feared.* • *Buffett has been known to be acerbic in his criticism of Wall Street's executives.*

a·cer·bi·ty /£ə'sɜː·bə·ti, $-'sɜːr·bə·t̬i/ *n* [U] *fml* • *The acerbity of Osborne's two volumes of memoirs shocked a lot of people.*

a·ce·ta·mi·no·phen /£ə,siː·tə'mɪn·ə·fen, $-t̬ə-/ *n pl* **acetaminophens** or **acetaminophen** *Am* a medicine used to stop pain and reduce fever; PARACETAMOL • *Acetaminophen is recommended for people who shouldn't* *take aspirin.* [U] • *Take a couple of acetaminophen* (= pills containing this) *if you have a headache.* [C]

ac·e·tate /ˈæs·ɪ·teɪt/ *n* [U] a chemical substance made from ACETIC ACID, or a smooth artificial cloth made from this

a·ce·tic ac·id /£əˈsiː·tɪk, $-t̬ɪk-/ *n* [U] a colourless acid with a strong smell which is contained in vinegar

ac·e·tone /£ˈæs·ɪ·təʊn, $-t̬oʊn/ *n* [U] a strong-smelling colourless liquid which is used in the production of various chemicals and is sometimes added to paint to make it more liquid

a·ce·ty·lene /£əˈset·ə·liːn, $-ˈset̬-/ *n* [U] a colourless gas which burns with a very hot bright flame, used in cutting and joining metal

ache /eɪk/ *n* a continuous pain which is unpleasant but not strong • *As you get older, you have all sorts of aches* **and pains**. [C] • *I've got a* **dull** (= slight) *ache* **in** *my lower back.* [C] • Ache is often used in combinations: *earache/heartache/bellyache/headache/toothache/backache* ○ *I've had (a) stomach ache all morning.* [C/U] • LP› **Feelings and pains**

ache /eɪk/ *v* • *My head/tooth/back/stomach aches.* [I] • *I ache/I'm aching* **all over**. [I] • *I've got one or two aching muscles after yesterday's run.* [I] • *(fig.) Her heart ached* (= She felt very sad) *as she watched the children playing.* [I] • *(fig.) She ached* (= wanted very much) **to** *see him again.* [+ *to* infinitive] • *(fig.) He was lonely and aching* **for** *love.* [I]

ach·ing·ly /ˈeɪ·kɪŋ·li/ *adv literary* • Achingly is used to mean extremely: *Sung by the world's greatest tenor, this aria is achingly beautiful.* ○ *Nigel Bristow's revival of the play at the Alhambra theatre is fast, furious and achingly funny.*

ach·y /ˈeɪ·ki/ *adj* **-ier, -iest** *infml* • *I've been feeling tired and achy* (= full of pains) *all morning.*

a·chieve *obj* /əˈtʃiːv/ *v* [T] to succeed in finishing (something) or reaching (an aim), esp. after a lot of work or effort • *The government's training policy, he claimed, was achieving its* **objectives** *of increasing skills and providing for Britain's industrial future.* • *She finally achieved her* **ambition** *to visit South America.* • *I've been working all day, but I feel as if I've achieved nothing.* • *Though highly respected for her writing, she never achieved much commercial success.* • *He then started writing his own music, achieving international fame with the music and lyrics for 'Guys and Dolls' in 1950.* • *Democracy is very hard to achieve.* • See also UNDERACHIEVE.

a·chiev·a·ble /əˈtʃiː·və·bl̩/ *adj* • *Before you set your targets, make sure that they are achievable.*

a·chiev·er /£əˈtʃiː·vəʳ, $-vɚ/ *n* [C] • *Bond comes from a family of* **high** *achievers* (= successful people). • *Not enough attention is given to the* **low** *achievers in the class.* • An **over** achiever is someone who works very hard and achieves more than would be expected from a person of their mental abilities. • Someone who performs less well than would be expected is called an **under** achiever.

a·chieve·ment /əˈtʃiːv·mənt/ *n* • *Whichever way you look at it, an Olympic silver medal is a remarkable achievement for one so young.* [C] • *The Tale of Genji has been described as the greatest achievement of Japanese literature.* [C] • *It gives you a* **sense of** *achievement if you actually make it to the end of a very long book.* [U]

A·chil·les heel /əˈkɪl·iːz/ *n* [C usually sing] a small fault or weakness in a person or system that can result in its failure • *A misbehaving minister is regarded as a government's Achilles heel and is expected to resign.*

A·chil·les ten·don /əˌkɪl·iːz/ *n* [C] a small muscular cord just above the heel, connecting the heel bone to the muscles in the lower part of the leg • *An Achilles tendon injury has forced Elliot to withdraw from the World Championships.* • *My father tore his Achilles tendon while playing squash.*

ac·id LIQUID SUBSTANCE /ˈæs·ɪd/ *n* any of various usually liquid substances which can react chemically with and sometimes dissolve other materials • *acetic/hydrochloric/lactic/nitric/sulphuric acid* [U] • *The thieves had thrown acid in his face, which would have blinded him.* [U] • *Acids produce positively charged hydrogen atoms when dissolved in water.* [C] • *Vinegar is an acid.* [C] • *Because the pH of this liquid is less than 7·0 we can say it is an acid.* [C] • *It was thought that he disposed of the corpse in an acid bath.* • **Acid rain** is rain which contains unusually large amounts of harmful chemicals as a result of the burning of substances such as coal and oil. • An **acid test** is the true test of the value of something: *It looks good, but will people buy it? That's the acid test.*

ac·id /ˈæs·ɪd/ *adj* • *Lemon juice is quite acid.* • An acid **wit/remark/tone of voice** is sharp and shows the speaker's bad mood or criticism of something: *Unfortunately, the book has none of the acid wit of her earlier writings.* ○ *When she spoke her tone was acid.*

a·cid·ic /əˈsɪd·ɪk/ *adj* • *It's a rather acidic wine.* • *Many parts of Wales have naturally acidic soil.*

a·cid·i·fy *(obj)* /əˈsɪd·ɪ·faɪ/ *v* [I/T]

a·cid·i·ty /£əˈsɪd·ɪ·ti, $-ə·t̬i/ *n* [U] • *With its lemon flavour and refreshing acidity, this is the perfect summer wine.* • *High acidity levels in the water mean that the fish are not so large.*

ac·id·ly /ˈæs·ɪd·li/ *adv* • *"I suppose you expect me to thank you for coming," he said acidly* (= sharply and unpleasantly).

ac·id DRUG /ˈæs·ɪd/ *n* [U] *slang for* LSD (= an illegal drug which makes people see things that do not exist) • An **acid head** is a person who often takes the drug LSD.

ac·know·ledge *(obj)* /£əkˈnɒl·ɪdʒ, $-ˈnɑː·lɪdʒ/ *v* to accept, admit or recognize (something, or the truth or existence of something) • *She acknowledged having been at fault.* [+ v-*ing*] • *She acknowledged* **that** *she had been at fault.* [+ *that* clause] • *You must acknowledge the truth of her argument.* [T] • *Historians generally acknowledge her* **as** *a genius in her field.* [T] • *She is usually acknowledged* **to** *be one of our best artists.* [T + obj + *to* infinitive, usually passive] • *They refused to acknowledge* (= to recognize officially) *the new government.* [T] • *Please acknowledge* **receipt of** (= say that you have received) *this letter.* [T] • *The vicar gratefully acknowledged* (= showed or said he was grateful for) *their offers of help.* [T] • *He didn't even acknowledge my* **presence** (= show that he had seen me). [T] • *It is a truth universally acknowledged that airline food is awful.* [T] • *The government won't even acknowledge the existence of the problem.* [T]

ac·know·ledg·ment, **ac·know·ledge·ment** /£əkˈnɒl·ɪdʒ·mənt, $-ˈnɑː·lɪdʒ-/ *n* • *We sent her a copy of the book* **in** *acknowledgment of her part in its creation.* [U] • *I applied for four jobs, but I've only had one acknowledgment* (= letter saying that my letter has been received) *so far.* [C]

ac·know·ledg·ments, **ac·know·ledge·ments** /£əkˈnɒl·ɪdʒ·mənts, $-ˈnɑː·lɪdʒ-/ *pl n* • The acknowledgments at the beginning or end of a book are a short text where the writer names people or other works that have helped in writing the book.

ac·me /ˈæk·mi/ *n* [U] **the acme** *literary* the highest point of perfection or achievement • *To act on this world-famous stage is surely the acme* **of** *any actor's career.* • *"To subdue the enemy without fighting", he wrote, "is the acme* **of** *skill."*

ac·ne /ˈæk·ni/ *n* [U] a disease of the skin common in young people, in which small red spots appear, esp. on the face and neck • *He* **suffers from/gets/has** *really bad acne.* • *Acne is the curse of adolescence.*

ac·o·lyte /ˈæk·əl·aɪt/ *n* [C] a follower or helper, esp. someone who helps a priest in some Christian religious ceremonies

a·corn /£ˈeɪ·kɔːn, $-kɔːrn/ *n* [C] the fruit of the OAK tree, consisting of an oval nut growing inside a cup-like outer part • PIC› **Tree**

a·cous·tic /əˈkuː·stɪk/ *adj* relating to sound or hearing • *The microphone converts acoustic waves to electrical signals for transmission.* • *Animals use a whole range of acoustic, visual, and chemical signals in their systems of communication.* • An acoustic musical instrument is one that is not made louder by electrical equipment: *an acoustic guitar* • *(specialized)* An **acoustic coupler** is a device which allows computers to send and receive messages through a telephone.

a·cous·tic·ally /əˈkuː·stɪ·kli/ *adv* • *The new concert hall is acoustically far superior to* (= the sound can be heard better than at) *the old one.*

a·cous·tic /əˈkuː·stɪk/ *n* [C usually pl] • The acoustics of a building or room are the way in which its structural characteristics affect the qualities of musical or spoken sound that is heard in it: *The concert was recorded in a French church that is famous for its acoustics.* ○ *The acoustics in the lecture theatre aren't very good, so it's often difficult to hear what's being said.* • *(specialized) The song's rich harmonies suffered because of the* **dry** *acoustic of* (= short length of time that sounds lasted in) *the concert hall.*

a·cous·tics /əˈkuː·stɪks/ *n* [U] *specialized* • Acoustics is the scientific study of sound.

ac·quaint *obj* **with** *obj* /ə'kweɪnt/ *v prep* [T] *fml* to give (someone) information about (something) • *The Broadcasting Museum also offers Saturday workshops to acquaint children with the world of radio.* • *I'll be with you in a moment, if you'll just allow me a couple of minutes to acquaint myself with the rules of the game.* • *I haven't as yet been acquainted with the facts of the case.*

ac·quaint·ance /£ə'kweɪn·tᵊnts, $-ţᵊnts/ *n* [U always + *with*] *fml* • *Sadly, my acquaintance* **with** *Spanish literature is limited.* • *I'm afraid I have only a* **passing/slight/ nodding** *acquaintance* **with** *his works* (=I do not know them very well).

ac·quaint·ed /£ə'kweɪn·tɪd, $-ţɪd/ *adj* [after v; always + *with*] *fml* • *Police said the thieves were obviously well acquainted* **with** (=had knowledge of) *the alarm system at the department store.* • *Students who are already acquainted* **with** *one foreign language tend to find it easier to learn a new one.*

ac·quaint·ed /£ə'kweɪn·tɪd, $-ţɪd/ *adj* [after v] knowing or being familiar with a person • *"Do you know Daphne?" "No, I'm afraid we're not acquainted."* • *She returned to Paris, where she became acquainted* **with** (=got to know) *many well-known writers and artists.* • *I am not personally acquainted* **with** *the gentleman in question.*

ac·quaint·ance /£ə'kweɪn·tᵊnts, $-ţᵊnts/ *n* • An acquaintance is a person that you know but do not know very well and therefore do not consider truly a friend: *He has a lot of business acquaintances but very few real friends.* [C] • *(fml)* Acquaintance is used in a number of expressions about knowing or meeting people: *It was at the Mapstones' party that I first* **made** *his* **acquaintance** (=met him for the first time). [U] ○ *I wasn't sure about Darryl when I first met her, but* **on further acquaintance** (=knowing her a little more) *I rather like her.* [U] ○ *I was wondering which men* **of** *my acquaintance* (=that I know) *she might be interested in.* [U]

ac·quaint·ance·ship /£ə'kweɪn·tᵊnt·ʃɪp, $-ţᵊnt-/ *n* [U] • *Ours was a strictly professional acquaintanceship* (=relationship).

ac·qui·esce /ˌæk·wi'es/ *v* [I] *fml* to accept or agree to something, often unwillingly • *He reluctantly acquiesced* **to/in** *the plans.* • *She begged to be allowed to go and her parents finally acquiesced.*

ac·qui·es·cent /ˌæk·wi'es·ᵊnt/ *adj* • *She has a very acquiescent nature* (=agrees to everything without complaining).

ac·qui·es·cence /ˌæk·wi'es·ᵊnts/ *n* [U] • *I was surprised by her acquiescence* **to/in** *the scheme.*

ac·quire *obj* /£ə'kwaɪəʳ, $-'kwaɪɚ/ *v* [T] to obtain (something) • *He acquired the firm in 1978.* • *She acquired an original painting by Van Gogh.* • *I was wearing a* **newly/recently** *acquired jacket.* • *I* **seem to** *have acquired* (=obtained by unknown means) *two copies of this book.* • *I acquired* (=learnt) *a little Spanish while I was in Peru.* • *During this period he acquired* **a reputation** *for being a womanizer.* • *She's acquired some very unpleasant habits recently.* • *This wine is rather* **an acquired taste**. (=Many people dislike it at first, but they gradually start to like it after they have tried it a few times.)

ac·quir·er /£ə'kwaɪ·rəʳ, $-rɚ/ *n* [C] *esp. Am* • An acquirer is a business organization which buys other companies, usually to sell them again for profit: *A business of this size and with this much potential is sure to generate interest among potential acquirers.*

ac·qui·si·tion /ˌæk·wɪ'zɪʃ·ᵊn/ *n* • *The museum has been heavily criticized over its acquisition* **of** *the four-million-dollar sculpture.* [U] • *I like your earrings – are they a* **recent** *acquisition* (=did you get them recently)? [C]

ac·qui·si·tive /£ə'kwɪz·ɪ·tɪv, $-ə·ţɪv/ *adj slightly fml, esp. disapproving* • Acquisitive means eager to possess and collect things: *There's something in the actual act of shopping which makes one acquisitive.* ○ *We live in an acquisitive society which views success primarily in terms of material possessions.*

ac·quit *obj* DECIDE NOT GUILTY /ə'kwɪt/ *v* [T often passive] **-tt-** to decide officially in a court of law that (someone) is not guilty of a particular crime • *She was acquitted* **(of** *all the charges against her).* • *A Hong Kong court acquitted Graham Sykes and five associates* **of** *fraud charges.* • *Five months ago she was acquitted on a shoplifting charge.* • Compare CONVICT. • LP **Crimes and criminals**

ac·quit·tal /£ə'kwɪt·ᵊl, $-'kwɪţ-/ *n* • *The first trial ended in a hung jury, the second in acquittal.* [U] • *Of the three cases that went to trial, two ended in acquittals.* [C]

ac·quit *obj* PERFORM /ə'kwɪt/ *v* [T] **-tt-** *fml* to cause (yourself) to perform or behave in the stated way • *I thought that he acquitted* **himself** *admirably in today's meeting.* • LP **Reflexive pronouns and verbs**

a·cre /£'eɪ·kəʳ, $-kɚ/ *n* [C] a unit for measuring area, equal to 4047 square metres or 4840 square YARDS • *He's got 400 acres (of land) in Wales.* • LP **Units** DK NL

a·cre·age /£'eɪ·kᵊr·ɪdʒ, $-kɚ-/ *n* [U] • *What acreage is her estate* (=How big is it, measured in acres)?

ac·rid /'æk·rɪd/ *adj* (of a smell or taste) strong, bitter and unpleasant, causing a burning feeling in the throat • *Clouds of acrid* **smoke** *issued from the building.*

ac·ri·mo·ni·ous /£ˌæk·rɪ'məʊ·ni·əs, $-'moʊ-/ *adj fml* bitter and angry • *The whole issue provoked an acrimonious* **debate** *which lasted all afternoon.* • *It was an acrimonious* **dispute/row** *which made enemies of all the parties concerned.* • *It took 15 months of acrimonious* **negotiations** *to achieve the peace treaty.* • *My brief foray into marriage ended eight years ago in an acrimonious* **divorce**.

ac·ri·mo·ni·ous·ly /£ˌæk·rɪ'məʊ·ni·ə·sli, $-'moʊ-/ *adv fml* • *In 1967, he separated acrimoniously from his wife.* • *They argued acrimoniously about the case.*

ac·ri·mo·ny /'æk·rɪ·mə·ni/ *n* [U] *fml* • *We separated* **without** *acrimony.* • *The acrimony of the dispute has shocked a lot of people.*

ac·ro·bat /'æk·rə·bæt/ *n* [C] a person who entertains people by carrying out difficult and skilful physical actions, such as walking along a high wire • *I was always fascinated by the acrobats at the circus.*

ac·ro·bat·ic /£ˌæk·rə'bæt·ɪk, $-'bæţ-/ *adj* • *an acrobatic* (=skilled and graceful) *leap into the air* • *an acrobatic young dancer* • *He's very acrobatic.*

ac·ro·bat·ics /£ˌæk·rə'bæt·ɪks, $-'bæţ-/ *n* [U] • *He had spent the last ten years in a Peking Opera school, studying martial arts and acrobatics.*

ac·ro·nym /£'æk·rəʊ·nɪm, $-rə-/ *n* [C] an abbreviation consisting of the first letters of each word in the name of something, pronounced as a word • *AIDS is an acronym for Acquired Immune Deficiency Syndrome.*

a·cross /£ə'krɒs, $-'krɑːs/ *adv* [not gradable], *prep* from one side to the other of (something with clear limits, such as an area of land, a road, river, etc.), or on the opposite side of • *It's too deep to walk, but you can swim across.* • *She walked across the field/road.* • *They're building a new bridge across the river.* • *The library is just across the road.* • *(fig.) We tried to* **get** *our* **point** *across* (=make it understood), *but he just wouldn't listen.* • *(fig.) Voting took place peacefully across most of the country* (=in most parts of the country). • Travelling **across country** is travelling in a direction where roads or public transport do not go, or where main roads or railways do not go: *We'll have to cut across country until we can pick up a main road.* ○ *Getting a train across country from Cambridge to Chester can be difficult.* • Something which happens **across the board** happens or has an effect on people at every level and in every area: *The improvement has been across the board, with all divisions either increasing profits or reducing losses.* ○ *The initiative has* **across-the-board** *support.* • *(infml)* If you **put one across** someone, you succeed in deceiving them about something, esp. by telling them something which is not true but which they believe. • PIC **Prepositions of movement**

a·cros·tic /£ə'krɒs·tɪk, $-'krɑː·stɪk/ *n* [C] *specialized* a text, usually a poem, in which particular letters, such as the first letters of each line, spell a word or phrase

a·cry·lic /ə'krɪl·ɪk/ *adj* [not gradable], *n* (of or made from) a type of acid or a RESIN (=chemically produced sticky substance made from this acid and used in plastic, cloth or paint) • *an acrylic pullover/scarf/dress* • *acrylic socks* • *He used to paint in oils but he's started to use acrylics/paint in acrylic* [C/U] • *Use our acrylic paint for all your interior walls.*

act DO SOMETHING /ækt/ *v* [I] to do something for a particular purpose, or to behave in the stated way • *I'd recommend that you act immediately.* • *Make sure you act as soon as you receive my letter.* • *Engineers acted quickly* **to** *repair the damaged pipes.* [+ *to* infinitive] • *She acted without thinking.* • *He acted foolishly in leaving without us.* • *The anaesthetic acted* (=had an effect) *quickly.* • *Who is acting* **for/on behalf of** (=who is representing) *the defendant?* • *He acted* **as if** *he'd never met me before.* • *She acted* **as** (=performed the duty of) *guide for the group.* • *Some people say that capital punishment acts* **as** (=has the effect of being) *a deterrent.* • *The rose bushes acted* **as** (=had the effect of) *a screen around the front of the house.* • *Don't be so silly – you're acting* **like** *a child!* • *If he acts* **like** *an idiot he should expect to be treated like one!* • *He never acts* **on** *other people's advice* (= does what other people suggest). • *Acting* **on impulse** (= without thinking first) *can get you into a lot of trouble.* • If a person, esp. a child, **acts up**, they behave badly: *Sophie got bored and started acting up.* • *(infml)* If a machine or part of the body **acts up** it does not perform as well as it should: *My car always acts up in cold weather.* ○ *Her shoulder was acting up* (= hurting because of injury).

act /ækt/ *n* [C] • *an act* **of** *aggression/bravery/charity/love/madness/terrorism* • *a kind/thoughtless/brave/selfish act* • *The* **sexual** *act itself meant little to her.* • *The simple act of telling someone about a problem can help.* • *Primitive people regarded storms as an act* **of God**.

act·ing /£ˈæk·tɪŋ, $-t̬ɪŋ/ *adj* [before n; not gradable] • *She's the acting* (= temporary) *manager of the shop while her boss is away.* • See also **acting** at ACT [PERFORM].

act *(obj)* [PERFORM] /ækt/ *v* to play (a part); to perform in a film, play, etc. • *Ellis Pike was chosen to act the* **part** *of the lawyer in the film.* [T] • *Have you ever acted* **in** *a play before?* [I] • *Have you ever acted this role?* [T] • *I don't trust him – he always seems to be acting (a* **part***)* (= not being sincere). [I/T] • *(fig.) Why are you always acting* **the** (= behaving like a) *fool/martyr?* [T] • If you **act out** something/**act** something **out** you express your thoughts, emotions or ideas as actions or behaviour: *Children's negative feelings often get acted out in bad behaviour.* • *"Can't act, can't sing, can dance a little"* (said to be the report on the screen test of the dancer and actor Fred Astaire, 1899-1987)

act /ækt/ *n* [C] • An act is a person or group which performs a short piece in a show, or the piece that is performed itself: *a dance/comedy/juggling/trapeze act* ○ *Our next act is a very talented young musician.* ○ *They are a brilliant act.* ○ *They've got a very original act.* • *(fig.) Don't feel sorry for her – all this crying's just an act* (= is pretended and not sincere). • *(fig. disapproving) Rory, as usual,* **did** *his 'kind uncle' act with us* (= he copied the typical behaviour of a kind uncle). • *(fig.) Tim always* **does** *a* **disappearing/vanishing** *act* (= goes away) *whenever my mother comes to stay.* • An act is also a part of a play or opera: *Shakespeare's plays were written in five acts.* ○ *The hero does not enter until the second act/Act Two.* • To **get/muscle in on the act** means to take advantage of something that someone else started: *We did all the hard work of setting up the company, and now everyone wants to get in on the act.* • *(infml)* To **get** your **act together** is to organize yourself and your activities so that you do things in an effective way: *She's so disorganized – I wish she'd get her act together.* • *(infml)* Something or someone might be said to be **a hard/tough act to follow** if they are very good and will therefore be difficult for others to equal: *His presidency was very successful – it'll be a hard act to follow.* • *(infml)* If someone **puts on an act** they behave or speak in a false or artificial way: *He's just putting on an act for the boss's benefit.*

act·ing /£ˈæk·tɪŋ, $-t̬ɪŋ/ *n* [U] • *I want to get into acting* (= act as a job). • See also **acting** at ACT [DO SOMETHING].

act·or, *female also* **act·ress** /£ˈæk·təʳ, $-tɚ, -trəs/ *n* [C] • An actor or actress is someone who pretends to be someone else while performing in a film, theatrical performance, or television or radio programme: *"Who's your favourite actor?" "Robert de Niro."* ○ *She's the highest-paid actress in Hollywood.*

act [LAW] /ækt/ *n* [C] *law* a law or formal decision made by a parliament or other group of elected law-makers • *an act of parliament* • *the Betting and Gaming Act* • *Almost two hundred suspects were detained in Britain last year* **under** *the Prevention of Terrorism Act.* • *The state legislature* **passed** *an act banning the sale of automatic weapons.*

ac·tion [SOMETHING DONE] /ˈæk·ʃᵊn/ *n* (the process of) doing something, or something done, esp. for a particular purpose • *This problem calls for swift/prompt action from the government.* [U] • *Action* **to** *prevent the spread of the disease is high on the government's agenda.* [+ *to* infinitive] • *We must* **take** *action* (= do something) *to deal with the problem before it spreads to other areas.* [U] • *So what's the* **plan of** *action* (= What are we going to do)? [U] • *It's time to* **put** *our plan* **into** *action* (= to do it). [U] • *The complaints system swings* **into** *action* (= starts to work) *as soon as a claim is made.* [U] • *(humorous) The wheels of bureaucracy creaked* **into** *action* (= started to work very slowly). [U] • *Come on you lazy things, let's* **see** *some action* (= activity) *around here!* [U] • To **prod/spur** someone **into** action is to encourage them to do something: *The committee was spurred into action by the threat of government cuts.* [U] • *He's a* **man of** *action, not words* (= he is more effective doing things than thinking about and discussing them). [U] • *His films have a lot of action* (= many exciting things happen in them) *and not much dialogue.* [U] • *It was an* **action-packed** *film* (= full of exciting events). • *She was unable to justify her action* **in** *leaving the documents in her car.* (= She could not explain satisfactorily why she had done it.) [C] • *His actions since that morning have been eccentric and unpredictable.* [C] • *(infml)* If you want or ask for **a piece/slice of the action** you want to be included in an activity, esp. to get an advantage or profit. • *(Br and Aus)* An **action replay** (*Am and Aus* **(instant) replay**) is a showing again of part of a film, esp. of a sporting activity, often more slowly to show the action in detail: *They showed an action replay of the goal.* • An action is also a physical movement: *I'll say the words and you can mime the actions.* [C] ○ *The action of picking the baby up had made her back ache.* [C] ○ *It only needs a small wrist action* (= movement of the wrist) *to start the process.* [C] • *(saying)* 'Actions speak louder than words' means that what you do is more important and shows your intentions and feelings more clearly than what you say. • **The** action is also the main events in a book, play or film: *The main action of her latest novel* **takes place** *in medieval Spain.* [U] ○ *The action moves between bloody battle scenes and the domestic life of the families who are left behind.* [U] • Action is also fighting in a war: *We're* **going into** *action* (= going to fight) *tomorrow.* [U] ○ *Her younger son was* **killed in** *action.* [U] ○ *He was reported* **missing in** *action.* [U] ○ *He* **saw** *action* (= fought as a soldier) *in the trenches.* [U] • *An attack was expected, and the crew were at* **action stations** (= ready to fight). • To be **where the action is** is to be at the place where something important or interesting is happening: *A good journalist always manages to be where the action is.*

ac·tion [MOVEMENT] /ˈæk·ʃᵊn/ *n* [C] the way something moves or works, or the effect it has on something else • *We studied the action of the digestive system.* [U] • *The car has a very smooth braking action.* [C] • *The pumping action of the machine* (= the part of the machine which PUMPS) *needs repairing.* [C] • *They recorded the action of the drug* **on** *the nervous system.* [U]

ac·tion [LEGAL PROCESS] /ˈæk·ʃᵊn/ *n* a legal process that takes place and is decided in a court of law • *a libel action* [C] • *She* **brought** *an action* **(for** *negligence)* **against** *the hospital.* [C] • *A* **criminal** *action was* **brought against** *him.* [C] • *The book was halted in South Africa by a threat of* **legal** *action.* [U] • [LP] **Law**

ac·tion·a·ble /ˈæk·ʃᵊn·ə·bl̩/ *adj* [not gradable] *specialized* • If something is actionable, it gives someone a good reason for making an accusation in a law court: *She denies that her company has been involved in any actionable activity.*

ac·tiv·ate *obj* /£ˈæk·tɪ·veɪt, $-t̬ɪ-/ *v* [T] to cause (something) to start • *The alarm is activated by the lightest pressure.* • To activate a chemical reaction means to make it happen more quickly, especially by heating.

ac·tiv·a·tion /£ˌæk·tɪˈveɪ·ʃᵊn, $-t̬ɪ-/ *n* [U]

ac·tive /£ˈæk·tɪv, $-t̬ɪv/ *adj* busy in or ready to perform a particular activity • *physically/mentally active* • *She's 68 but she's still physically very active.* • *You've got to try to* **keep** *active* (= use your time and energy) *as you grow older.* • *Enemy forces remain active in the mountainous areas around the city.* • *She's very active* **in** (= involved in) *local politics.* • *Both of his parents were very* **politically** *active.* • *She emphasised that it was important to educate children before they became* **sexually** *active.* • *He tends to take a more active* **role** *in the team nowadays.* • *She's an active* **member** *of her trade union* (= not only belongs to it, but does work to help it). • *The movement has the active support of 2 000 people.* • *His regiment was sent* **on active service** (= to fight in a war). • An active VOLCANO is one that might ERUPT (= throw out hot liquid rock or other matter) at some time. • An active **verb** or **sentence** is one in which the subject is the person or thing which performs the stated action: *'Catrin told me' is an active sentence, and 'I was told by Catrin' is passive.*

ac·tive·ly /£ˈæk·tɪv·li, $-t̬ɪv-/ *adv* • *He's very actively* **involved** *in* (= does a lot of work for) *the local Labour Party.* • *It's nice having a man who actively* **encourages** *me to spend money.* • *I decided I wanted to change my job* *last year but I've only recently started actively looking for* (= trying hard to find) *one.*

ac·tiv·i·sm /£ˈæk·tɪ·vɪ·zᵊm, $-t̬ɪ-/ *n* [U] • Activism refers to the use of direct and noticeable action to achieve a result, usually a political or social one: *black/student activism* ○ *The levels of trade union and* **political** *activism in this country have greatly declined in the past fifteen years.*

ac·tiv·ist /£ˈæk·tɪ·vɪst, $-t̬ɪ-/ *n* [C] • An activist is someone who takes an active part in working for a political party or other organization: *He's been a trade union/party activist for many years.*

ac·tiv·i·ty /£ækˈtɪv·ɪ·ti, $-ə·t̬i/ *n* • *There was a lot of activity* (= people busy doing things) *in preparation for the Queen's visit.* [U] • *There's usually little political activity in August.* [U] • *There was a sudden* **flurry of** *activity when the director walked in.* [U] • *Ministers are concerned by the low level of* **economic** *activity.* [U] • *Garden plants are finally showing signs of activity after the long winter.* [U] • *The whole family was found guilty of terrorist activity* [U] • *His spare-time activities* (= things he enjoys doing) *include cooking, tennis and windsurfing.* [C usually pl] • *We offer our clients a wide range of outdoor/sporting/educational activities.* [C usually pl]

act·or, act·ress /£ˈæk·tər, $-tɚ, -trəs/ *n* [C] See at ACT [PERFORM]

ac·tual /ˈæk·tʃu·əl, -tju-, -tʃʊl/ *adj* [before n; not gradable] real; existing in fact • *She asked me to leave. Well, her actual words were "Get lost, you pig!"* • *We had estimated about 300 visitors, but the actual number was much higher.* • *I thought she was Portuguese, but* **in actual fact** *she's Brazilian.* • *The exams are in July, but the actual results* (= the results themselves) *don't appear until September.* • (CS) (D) (DK) (E) (F) (PL) (RUS)

ac·tu·al·i·ty /£ˌæk·tʃuˈæl·ə·ti, £-tju-, $-ə·t̬i/ *n fml* • *Where does one draw the line between fiction and actuality* (= fact)*?* [U] • *She cannot accept the tragic actuality* (= fact) *of his death.* [U] • *He's out of touch with the actualities of life in Africa.* [C usually pl] • **In actuality** (= really), *there were few job losses last year.*

ac·tu·al·ize *obj* /ˈæk·tʃu·ə·laɪz, -tju-/ *v* [T usually passive] *fml* • *We hope that this state of affairs will be actualized* (= will happen or take place) *as soon as possible.*

ac·tual·ly /ˈæk·tʃu·ə·li, -tju-, -tʃʊ·li/ *adv* [not gradable] • Actually means in fact, really: *I didn't actually see her – I just heard her voice.* ○ *I only intended to be there for a few days, but I actually ended up staying for a whole month.* • Actually is often used in sentences in which there is information that is in some way surprising or the opposite of what most people would expect: *I didn't like him at first, but in the end I actually got quite fond of him.* ○ *I'm one of the few people who doesn't actually like champagne.* ○ *Actually I rather like this music.* ○ *To think that I was actually in the same room as her!* ○ *(humorous) Don't tell me he actually agreed to pay for you! You are honoured!* • Actually is sometimes used as a way of making a sentence slightly more polite, for example when you are expressing an opposing opinion, correcting what someone else has said or refusing an offer: *"Alexander looks like he'd be good at sports." "Actually, he's not."* ○ *Actually, Gavin, it was Tuesday of last week, not Wednesday.* ○ *"Do you mind if I smoke?" "Well, actually, I'd rather you didn't."* ○ *Actually, I won't stay because I've got to go and collect the kids.* • (E) (F) (I) (PL)

ac·tu·a·ry /£ˈæk·tju·ə·ri, $-er·i/ *n* [C] a person who calculates the probability of accidents, such as fire, flood, loss of property, etc., and informs INSURANCE companies how much they should charge their customers

ac·tu·ate *obj* /ˈæk·tʃu·eɪt, -tju-/ *v* [T usually passive] to make (a machine) work or cause (a person) to act • *(specialized) A detonator is any device containing an explosive that is actuated by heat, percussion, friction, or electricity.* • *(fml) He has abandoned all ambition to become president and is now actuated wholly by altruism.*

a·cu·i·ty /£əˈkjuː·ə·ti, $-ə·t̬i/ *n* [U] *fml* accuracy and effectiveness (of EYESIGHT, hearing, or thought) • *Tiredness also affects visual acuity.* • *He was a man of great political acuity.*

ac·u·men /ˈæk·jʊ·mən/ *n* [U] skill in making correct decisions and judgments in a particular subject, such as business or politics • *She has considerable* **business/financial** *acumen.*

ac·u·punc·ture /£ˈæk·jʊ·pʌŋk·tʃər, $-tʃɚ/ *n* [U] a treatment for pain and illness in which thin needles are positioned just under the surface of the skin at special nerve centres around the body • *Acupuncture originated in China.*

a·cute [EXTREME] /əˈkjuːt/ *adj* (of something bad) extreme • *She was taken to hospital suffering from acute abdominal pains.* • *The company is said to be suffering from acute financial difficulties.* • *She felt acute embarrassment/anxiety/concern at his behaviour.* • *Because of the acute post-war* **shortage** *of construction materials, private building was severely restricted.* • *The problem of poverty is particularly acute in rural areas where one in three adults is unemployed.* • An acute illness is one that quickly becomes very severe: *acute gastritis/inflammation of the ear* ○ *an acute* **attack** *of appendicitis*

a·cute·ly /əˈkjuːt·li/ *adv* • *Management is acutely* (= fully) **aware/conscious** *of the resentment that their decision may cause.* • *Another scandal would be acutely* (= extremely) **embarrassing** *for the government.* • *It is often difficult to get acutely* (= extremely) *mentally ill patients into hospital.*

a·cute·ness /əˈkjuːt·nəs/ *n* [U] • *The government doesn't seem to be aware of the acuteness* **of** *the housing shortage.*

a·cute [ACCURATE/CLEVER] /əˈkjuːt/ *adj* (of the SENSES, intelligence, etc.) very good, accurate and able to notice very small differences • *acute eyesight/hearing* • *an acute sense of smell* • *a woman of acute intelligence/judgement* • *He gave an acute* (= clever, showing deep understanding) *analysis of the situation.* • *Her latest novel shows her usual acute observation of the English middle classes.*

a·cute·ly /əˈkjuːt·li/ *adv* • *The book is full of acutely perceptive observations.*

a·cute·ness /əˈkjuːt·nəs/ *n* [U]

a·cute [ANGLE] /əˈkjuːt/ *adj* (of an angle) less than 90 degrees • Compare OBTUSE [ANGLE].

a·cute (ac·cent) /əˈkjuːt/ *n* [C] a sign which is written above a letter in some languages, showing you how to pronounce the letter • *There's an acute accent on the e in blé which is the French word for corn.* • [LP]› **Symbols**

ad /æd/ *n* [C] *infml for* **advertisement**, see at ADVERTISE • *I often prefer the ads on TV to the actual programmes.* • *She works for an* **ad agency** (= advertising company).

AD /ˌeɪˈdiː/ *abbreviation for* Anno Domini (used in the Christian CALENDAR when referring to a year after Jesus Christ was born) • *in 1215 AD/AD 1215* • *during the seventh century AD* • Compare BC. • [LP]› **Dates**

ad·age /ˈæd·ɪdʒ/ *n* [C] a wise saying or PROVERB • *He remembered the* **old** *adage 'Look before you leap'.*

Ad·am /ˈæd·əm/ *n* [not after *the*] a Biblical character who was the first man made by God • The **Adam's apple** is the part of a man's throat that sticks out and tends to move up and down when he speaks or swallows: *Bernie has a big Adam's apple.*

ad·a·mant /ˈæd·ə·mənt/ *adj* impossible to persuade, or unwilling to change an opinion or decision • *I tried to persuade her to take the job but she was quite adamant* (**that** *she did not want it).* [+ *that* clause] • *He's absolutely adamant* **in/about** *not allowing smoking in his house.*

ad·a·mant·ly /ˈæd·ə·mənt·li/ *adv* • *The mayor is adamantly opposed to any tax increase.*

a·dapt *(obj)* /əˈdæpt/ *v* to change (something or yourself) to suit different conditions or uses • *Many software companies have adapted popular programs* **to** *the new operating system.* [T] • *The recipe here is a pork roast adapted* **from** *Caroline O'Neill's Louisiana Kitchen.* [T] • *We had to adapt our plans* **to** *fit Jack's timetable.* [T + obj + *to* infinitive] • *The play had been adapted* **for** (= changed to make it suitable for) *children.* [T] • *Davies is busy adapting Paul Brinkworth's latest novel* **for** *television.* [T] • *The good thing about children is that they adapt very easily* **to** *new environments.* [I] • *It took me a while to adapt* **to** *the new job.* [I] • (CS) (PL)

a·dapt·ed /əˈdæp·tɪd/ *adj* • *Both trees are* **well** *adapted* **to** *London's dry climate and dirty air.* • *He had a jacket with a* **specially** *adapted inside pocket to hold his pistol.*

a·dapt·a·ble /əˈdæp·tə·bl̩/ *adj* • Adaptable means able or willing to change in order to suit different conditions: *The survivors in this life seem to be those who are adaptable* **to** *change.* ○ *Human eyes are very adaptable optical sensors, able to respond to a wide range of light levels.*

a·dapt·a·bil·i·ty /£əˌdæp·təˈbɪl·ɪ·ti, $-ə·t̬i/ *n* [U] • *Adaptability is a necessary quality in an ever-changing work environment.*

ad·apt·a·tion /ˌæd·æpˈteɪ·ʃᵊn/ *n* • *Last year he starred in the film adaptation of Bill Cronshaw's best-selling novel.* [C]

• *Evolution occurs as a result of adaptation* **to** *new environments.* [U]

a·dapt·ive /ə'dæp·tɪv/ *adj* specialized • *Plant behaviour is often adaptive* (=shows the ability to change to suit different conditions) *– some turn their leaves towards the sun, others clamp down on insects, preventing their escape.*

a·dapt·or, a·dapt·er /£ə'dæp·təʳ, $-tɚ/ *n* [C] • An adaptor is a person who makes slight changes to a book, play or other piece of text so that it can be performed. • An adaptor is also a PLUG which can connect two or more pieces of equipment to the electrical supply. • PIC〉 **Plugs**

ADC /ˌeɪ·diː'siː/ *n* [C] *abbreviation for* **aide-de-camp**, see at AIDE

add *(obj)* /æd/ *v* to put (something) with something else to increase the number or amount or to improve the whole • *Beat the butter and sugar together and slowly add the eggs.* [T] • *She's added a Picasso* **to** *her collection.* [T] • *Her presence added a much needed sparkle* **to** *the occasion.* [T] • *Wasteful packaging can add several pence* **to** *the price of food.* [T] • *Her colleagues' laughter only added* **to** (=increased) *her embarrassment.* [I] • *She was sad, she said, but added* (=said also) **that** *she felt she had made the right decision.* [+ *that* clause] • *Have you anything to add* **to** *your earlier statement?* [I] • *"Oh, and thank you for all your help!" he added as he was leaving.* [+ clause] • *It's $45 – $50 if you add* **in** (=include) *the cost of postage.* [T] • *We added an extension* **on***/added* **on** *an extension at the back of the house.* [M] • *Don't forget to add* **on** *your travelling expenses/add your expenses* **on**. [M] • *If you add* (=calculate the total of) *three and four you get seven. (3 + 4 = 7)* [T] • *I'm not very good at adding* **up**! (=calculating the total of different numbers) [I] • *She added* **up** *the bill/added the bill* **up**. [M] • *The various building programmes add* **up to** (=give a total of, result in) *several thousand new homes.* [I] • *We thought we'd bought lots of food, but it didn't add up* **to much** (=did not seem to be a great amount) *when we'd spread it out on the table.* [I] • *Their proposals do not* **add up to** (=mean) *any real help for the poor.* • *It all* **added up to** (=resulted in) *a lot of hard work for all of us.* • *(infml) Why would she disappear the day before her holiday?* **It** *just* **doesn't add up.** (=There is no reasonable explanation for it.) • *They told me I was too old for the job, and then to* **add insult to injury** (=to make a bad situation worse) *they refused to pay my expenses!* • An **add-on** is a piece of equipment which can be connected to a computer to give it an extra use: *A modem is a useful add-on.* • LP〉 **Mathematics**

add·ed /'æd·ɪd/ *adj* [not gradable] • *He had the added disadvantage of being the only man present.* • *She lost her job last week, and now added* **to that** *she's pregnant again.*

ad·di·tion /ə'dɪʃ·ᵊn/ *n* • *Twice a week the children are tested in basic mathematical skills such as addition* (=calculating the total of different numbers put together) *and subtraction.* [U] • *Most working environments are improved by* **the** *addition* **of** (=adding) *a few plants and pictures.* [U] • *A secretary would be* **a welcome/useful** *addition* **to** *our staff.* [C] • **In** *addition* **to** *teaching, she also works in the holidays as a nurse.* [U] • **In** *addition* **to** *his flat in London, he has a villa in Italy and a castle in Scotland.* [U] • *(humorous) I hear you're expecting a small addition* **to** *the family* (=you are going to have a baby)*!* [C] • Ⓟ

ad·di·tion·al /ə'dɪʃ·ᵊn·ᵊl/ *adj* [not gradable] • *additional* (=extra) *costs/expenses/problems/difficulties* • *There will be an extra charge for any additional passengers.*

ad·di·tion·al·ly /ə'dɪʃ·ᵊn·ᵊl·i/ *adv* [not gradable] • *We were additionally* (=as well as everything else) *faced with trying to find somewhere to stay at two o'clock in the morning.* • *Additionally, we request a deposit of $200 in advance.*

ad·di·tive /£'æd·ɪ·tɪv, $-ə·t̬ɪv/ *n* [C] • An additive is a substance which is added to food in order to improve its taste or appearance or to preserve it: *food/chemical additives* ○ *This margarine is* **full of** *additives – just look at the label!* ○ *It says on the packet that these crisps contain no additives.*

ad·dend·um /ə'den·dəm/ *n* [C] *pl* **addenda** /ə'den·də/ *specialized* something that has been added or is to be added to a book, speech or document • *In a little-publicised addendum to the treaty the 12 EU leaders made a declaration on racism and xenophobia.*

ad·der /£'æd·əʳ, $-ɚ/ *n* [C] a poisonous snake

ad·dict /'æd·ɪkt/ *n* [C] a person who cannot stop doing or using something, esp. something harmful • *a drug/heroin/nicotine addict* • *a gambling addict* • *(humorous) I'm a chocolate/television/shopping addict.*

ad·dict·ed /ə'dɪk·tɪd/ *adj* • *She was addicted* **to** *heroin at the age of 14.* • *I'm addicted* **to** (=I very often eat/drink) *chocolate/vodka.* • *She's become addicted* **to** *love stories/horror films/football.* • *I know that if I start watching a soap opera I immediately become* **hopelessly** *addicted.*

ad·dic·tion /ə'dɪk·ʃᵊn/ *n* • *Her previous novel dealt with her recovery from* **drug** *addiction.* [U] • *For years she was dependent on drugs and drink and it was only in her fifties that she finally managed to* **overcome** *these addictions.* [C] • *Patrick is trying to cure himself of his addiction* **to** *alcohol.* [U]

ad·dict·ive /ə'dɪk·tɪv/ *adj* • An addictive drug is one which you cannot stop taking once you have started: *Narcotics such as morphine, heroin and cocaine are extremely addictive.* ○ *Tobacco is* **highly** *addictive and the tobacco industry knows this.* • Addictive is also used of any activity or food that you cannot stop doing or eating once you have started: *The problem with video games is that they're addictive.* ○ *These nuts are addictive – I can't stop eating them!* • Someone who is described as having an addictive **personality** very quickly becomes addicted to drugs, activities or food.

ad·dle *obj* /'æd·l̩/ *v* [T] *esp. humorous* to make (esp. a person's brain) confused and unable to think well • *I think my brain's been addled by the heat!*

ad·dled /'æd·l̩d/ *adj esp. humorous* • *I'm afraid my sun-addled* (=confused) *brain couldn't make any sense of the instructions.*

ad·dress HOME DETAILS /£ə'dres, $'æd·res/ *n* [C] the number of the house and name of the road and town where a person lives or works and where letters can be sent • *her business/home/temporary address* • *a change of address* • *He's changed his address again.* • *Could you give me your address, please?* • *I'll just look her phone number up in my address* **book**. • *(specialized)* In computing, an address tells you where in memory a piece of information can be found.

ad·dress *obj* /ə'dres/ *v* [T] • *She addressed* (=wrote the name and details of where the person lived on) *the letter and stuck a stamp on it.* • *The parcel was wrongly addressed.* • *So why did you open a letter that was addressed* **to** *me?*

ad·dress·ee /ˌæd·res'iː/ *n* [C] • *Postage will be paid by the addressee* (=the person whose name and address are written on the letter or parcel). • LP〉 **Letters**

ad·dress *obj* SPEAK TO /ə'dres/ *v* [T] *fml* to speak or write to (someone), or to direct information at (someone) • *She addressed the meeting with fire and passion.* • *He addressed a few introductory remarks* **to** *the audience.* • *He likes to be addressed* **as** *'Sir' or 'Mr Partridge'.* • *The essays on discipline are addressed primarily* **to** *young teachers.* • LP〉 **Titles and forms of address**

ad·dress /£ə'dres, $'æd·res/ *n* [C] • *She gave an address* (=a formal speech) **to** *the Royal Academy.*

ad·dress *obj* DEAL WITH /ə'dres/ *v* [T] to give attention to or deal with (a matter or problem) • *The problem of where we will raise the funds for the scheme has not yet been addressed.* • *People who want to ensure that global* **issues** *are addressed, he said, should be voting for the Greens.* • *It's a* **problem/question** *that hasn't as yet been addressed.*

ad·duce *obj* /£ə'djuːs, $-'duːs/ *v* [T] *fml* to give (proof, explanation, a reason, etc.) • *He claimed that Paul and I were having an affair, adducing* **as evidence** *the fact that we were once seen together in a bar.* • *She adduced several facts* **to support** *her thesis.*

ad·e·noids /'æd·ᵊn·ɔɪdz/ *pl n* (in the human body) the soft mass of flesh between the back of the nose and the throat, which sometimes makes breathing difficult • *She had her adenoids removed when she was a child.*

ad·e·noi·dal /ˌæd·ᵊn'ɔɪ·dᵊl/ *adj* [not gradable] • *He has an unpleasant adenoidal voice.* (=A lot of air comes through his nose when he speaks.)

a·dept /ə'dept/ *adj* skilled • *She's very adept* **at/in** *making people feel at their ease.* • *He was never very adept* **in** *the finer arts of conversation.* • *Tamsin Palmer gave an impressive and technically adept performance on the piano.*

a·dept·ly /ə'dept·li/ *adv* • *The president has adeptly avoided disclosing any estimates for the cost of the war.*

ad·e·quate /'æd·ə·kwət/ *adj* enough or satisfactory (for a particular purpose) • *We've got about twenty guests coming so if I put out a dozen chairs that should be adequate.* • *The reason I didn't do well in my exams is that I just didn't have adequate time to prepare.* • *It's not by any means a brilliant salary but it's adequate* **for** *our needs.* • *The council's provision for the elderly is* **barely** *adequate* (=is not enough). • *Will future oil supplies be adequate* **to** *meet world needs?* [+ *to* infinitive]

ad·e·quate·ly /ˈæd·ə·kwət·li/ *adv* • *Someone has to be there to make sure that the children are adequately fed and clothed.* • *While some patients can be adequately treated and cared for at home, others are best served by care in a hospital.*

ad·e·qua·cy /ˈæd·ə·kwə·si/ *n* [U] • *The adequacy of public health care has been brought into question.*

ad·here /£ədˈhɪəʳ, $-ˈhɪr/ *v* [I] *fml* to stick firmly • *These tiles are not properly adhered* **to** *the wall.*

ad·her·ent /£ədˈhɪə·rənt, $-ˈhɪr·ənt/ *adj fml* • *an adherent* (= sticky) *surface*

ad·he·sion /ədˈhiː·ʒən/ *n* [U] • Adhesion is the ability to stick: *At this stage a resin is used with a high level of adhesion.*

ad·he·sive /ədˈhiː·sɪv/ *adj, n* • *adhesive* (= sticky) *tape/paper* • *You'll need a/some strong adhesive* (= glue) *to mend that chair.* [C/U]

ad·here to *obj* /£ədˈhɪəʳ, $-ˈhɪr/ *v prep* [T] to continue to obey or maintain (esp. a rule, standard or belief) • *She adhered to her principles/ideals throughout her life.* • *They failed to adhere to the terms of the agreement/treaty.* • *He has always* **rigidly** *adhered to the precepts of the Church.* • *The translator has obviously adhered very* **strictly** *to the original text.*

ad·her·ence /£ədˈhɪə·rənts, $-ˈhɪr·ənts/ *n* [U] *fml* • *He was noted for his strict adherence* **to** *the rules.*

ad·her·ent /£ədˈhɪə·rənt, $-ˈhɪr·ənt/ *n* [C] *fml* • *She has long been an adherent* (= supporter) *of the Communist Party.*

ad hoc /£ˌædˈhɒk, $-ˈhɑːk/ *adv, adj* (made or happening) only for a particular purpose or need, not planned in advance • *an ad hoc committee/meeting* • *We deal with problems* **on an** *ad hoc* **basis** (= as they happen). • *The group met ad hoc, whenever the need arose.*

a·dieu /£əˈdjuː, £-ˈdjʊ, $-ˈduː/ *n, exclamation pl* **adieus** or **adieux** *literary or old use* goodbye • *Adieu then, my friend.* • *She* **bade** (= said to) *him adieu and left.*

ad in·fi·ni·tum /£ˌæd·ɪn·fɪˈnaɪ·təm, $-t̬əm/ *adv* [not gradable] forever, without ending • *"Why was she such a lousy boss?" "Oh, because she was unreasonable, disrespectful, rude, inconsiderate – I could go on ad infinitum."* • *Well, we all know about sitting through boring lunches where the guest speaker drones on and on ad infinitum.*

a·di·os /£ˌæd·iˈɒs, $-ˈoʊs/ *exclamation esp. Am infml* goodbye

ad·i·pose /£ˈæd·ɪ·pəʊs, £-pəʊz, $-ə·poʊs/ *adj* [before n] *specialized* of animal fat • *She's bought one of those massage machines that pummels at your adipose* **tissue** (= fat).

adj *abbreviation for* ADJECTIVE

ad·ja·cent /əˈdʒeɪ·sənt/ *adj fml* very near, next to, or touching • *She sat down on an adjacent sofa.* • *They work in adjacent buildings.* • *There was a cinema adjacent* **to** *where I lived/my house.*

ad·jec·tive /ˈædʒ·ek·tɪv/ *n* [C] a word that describes a noun or pronoun • *'Big', 'boring', 'purple', 'quick', 'obvious' and 'silvery' are all adjectives.* • LP **-ed and -ing adjectives, Comparing and grading, Stress in pronunciation**

ad·jec·tiv·al /ˌædʒ·ekˈtaɪ·vəl/ *adj* [not gradable] • *an adjectival phrase/group*

ad·jec·tiv·al·ly /ˌædʒ·ekˈtaɪ·vəl·i/ *adv* [not gradable] • *In 'kitchen table', the noun 'kitchen' is used adjectivally.*

ad·join *(obj)* /əˈdʒɔɪn/ *v* to be very near, next to, or touching • *The stables adjoin the west wing of the house.* [T] • *It's at this point that these three neighbourhoods adjoin.* [I]

ad·join·ing /əˈdʒɔɪ·nɪŋ/ *adj* [before n; not gradable] • *We asked for adjoining rooms* (= rooms next to each other).

ad·journ *(obj)* /£əˈdʒɜːn, $-ˈdʒɜːrn/ *v* to make a pause or rest in (esp. a meeting, trial, etc.) • *The meeting was adjourned* **until** *Tuesday/***for** *two days.* [T] • *Karpov adjourned (the chess game) a pawn ahead.* [T/I] • *Shall we adjourn* **for** *lunch?* [I] • *(fml or dated) Shall we adjourn* **to** (= go to) *the sitting room for coffee?* [I]

ad·journ·ment /£əˈdʒɜːn·mənt, $-ˈdʒɜːrn-/ *n* • *The defence attorney requested an adjournment.* [C] • *The court's adjournment means that a decision will not be reached until December at the earliest.* [U]

ad·judge *obj* /əˈdʒʌdʒ/ *v* [T] *fml* to announce or consider, esp. officially • *Half an hour into the game Paterson was adjudged* **to** *have fouled Peter Jackson and was sent off.* [+ obj + *to* infinitive] • *In October 1990, Mirchandani was adjudged bankrupt.* [+ obj + n/adj] • *Fairbanks was adjudged the winner, a decision which has outraged a good few members of the boxing fraternity.* [+ obj + n/adj]

ad·ju·di·cate *(obj)* /əˈdʒuː·dɪ·keɪt/ *v* to act as judge in (a competition or argument) • *He was asked to adjudicate* **on** *the dispute.* [I] • *They had to adjudicate* **upon** *the issue of whether the dismissal was fair or unfair.* [I] • *The (chess) game was adjudicated a win for Black.* [+ two objects]

ADJECTIVES

Most adjectives can go in three different places in a sentence:

- **Before nouns** as in *a beautiful day*. This is called the ATTRIBUTIVE position.
- **After verbs**, especially linking verbs like *be* and *seem*, as in *You are beautiful*. This is called the PREDICATIVE position.
- **After nouns, and pronouns ending in *-body, -one, -thing* and *-where*** as in *Someone beautiful*.

Some adjectives are found in only one of these positions:

ADJECTIVES USED ONLY BEFORE A NOUN [before n]

Adjectives that can only be used before a noun are labelled [before n]. They often:

- **are formed from nouns by adding the endings *-ar, -al* and *-ic***
  an **atomic** *bomb, the cold* **polar** *regions, the* **annual** *office party, a* **chronic** *illness, the* **presidential** *elections*
- **add emphasis** LP **Very, completely** at VERY.
  absolute *nonsense, a* **complete/utter** *fool, in* **extreme** *danger, an* **awful/damn** *mess, an* **in-depth** *report, she's a* **mere** *child*
- **limit the reference of the noun**
  my **only** *chance to go, on the* **same** *day, the* **entire/whole** *country, a* **single** *rose, your* **starting/initial** *salary*
- **refer to a relationship with the present**
  my **old** *friend, my* **present/previous/future** *wife, the* **late** *Mr Lucas* (= no longer living), *our* **new** *house, my* **former** *employer, her* **last/next/current** *book, the* **latest** *sports results*

ADJECTIVES USED ONLY AFTER VERBS [after v]

These adjectives often:

- **begin with *a-***
  She's **asleep/awake**. • *They're so* **alike**. *I'll be* **abroad** *until June.* • *I think he's still* **alive**. • *She's* **afraid/ashamed** *to tell you what she did.*
- **describe feelings or health**
  all right/fine • *unwell/poorly/sick* • *drunk* • *sorry* • *overjoyed* • *stressed/worked up/upset*

ADJECTIVES USED AFTER A NOUN [after n]

These adjectives often:

- **describe measurements or numbers**
  We're a couple of chairs **short** (= lacking). *Our group was about 20* **strong** (= in number).
- **are used in some fixed expressions, mainly after titles**
  He is the **heir apparent** • *The Prince* **Regent** *I work for TPC* **Incorporated**.

ad·ju·di·ca·tion /əˌdʒuː·dɪˈkeɪ·ʃᵊn/ *n* • *The legality of the transaction is still* **under** *adjudication in the courts.* [U] • *His adjudication was later found to be faulty.* [C]

ad·ju·di·cat·or /£əˈdʒuː·dɪ·keɪ·təʳ, $-t̬ɚ/ *n* [C] • *She acted as adjudicator in the dispute.*

ad·junct /ˈædʒ·ʌŋkt/ *n* [C] something added or connected to a larger or more important thing • *I hoped I would find the computer course a useful adjunct* **to** *my other studies.* • *In grammar, an adjunct is an adverb or adverbial phrase that gives extra information in a sentence.*

ad·jure *obj* /£əˈdʒʊəʳ, $-ˈdʒʊr/ *v* [T] *fml* to ask or order (someone) • *The judge adjured him* **to** *answer truthfully.* [+ obj + *to* infinitive]

ad·just *(obj)* /əˈdʒʌst/ *v* to change (something or yourself) slightly, esp. in order to make it more correct, effective, or suitable • *If the chair is too high you can adjust it to suit you.* [T] • *She adjusted her skirt, took a deep breath and walked into the room.* [T] • *I was amazed to see one of those old signs in the hotel lavatories saying 'Please adjust* (=make tidy) *your dress before leaving'.* [T] • *As a teacher you have to adjust your methods/approach to suit the needs of slower children.* [T] • *I can't adjust* **to** *living on my own.* [I] • *Her eyes slowly adjusted* **to** *the gloom.* [I] • *The lifestyle is so very different – it takes a while to adjust.* [I]

ad·just·a·ble /əˈdʒʌs·tə·bl̩/ *adj* • Adjustable means able to be changed to suit particular needs: *The height of the steering wheel is adjustable, and the seating is comfortable and supportive.* ○ *Is the strap on this helmet adjustable?* ○ *Guy, have you got an adjustable spanner?*

ad·just·er /£əˈdʒʌs·təʳ, $-tɚ/ *n* [C] *specialized* • *(Br)* A **loss** adjuster/*(Am)* **claims** adjuster is someone who works for an INSURANCE company (=organization which protects people financially against risks) and who decides how much money a claim against the company (for loss or injury) is worth.

ad·just·ment /əˈdʒʌst·mənt/ *n* • *She made a few* **minor** *adjustments* **to** *the focus of her camera.* [C] • *He has so far failed to make the adjustment* **from** *school* **to** *work.* [C] • *Children inevitably suffer problems of adjustment* **to** *their parents' divorce.* [U]

ad·ju·tant /ˈædʒ·ʊ·tᵊnt/ *n* [C] a military officer who does office work and is responsible for rules and punishment among the lower ranks

ad lib /ˌædˈlɪb/ *adj, adv* said without any preparation or thought in advance • *I'd forgotten the notes for my speech so I had to* **do** *it ad lib.* • *The spokeswoman made a few ad-lib comments for the press.*

ad–lib *(obj)* /ˌædˈlɪb/ *v* **-bb-** • *He not only couldn't ad-lib, he could barely put enough words together to form a sentence.* [I] • *She ad-libbed her way through the entire speech.* (=None of it was prepared before she made it.) [T]

ad·man /ˈæd·mæn/ *n* [C] *pl* **-men** a man who works in advertising • *The Republican Party imported a youthful English adman to help run its campaign.*

ad·mi·ni·ster *obj* MANAGE /£ədˈmɪn·ɪ·stəʳ, $-stɚ/ *v* [T] to control the operation or arrangement of something; to manage or govern • *The country was administered by the British until very recently.* • *The economy has been badly administered by the present government.*

ad·mi·ni·stra·tion /ədˌmɪn·ɪˈstreɪ·ʃᵊn/, *infml* **ad·min** *n* • *She has little experience in administration* (=in organizing a business, etc.). [U] • *Dr Whittle has complained that more of her time is taken up with petty administration than with treating the sick.* [U] • An administration in the United States is a period of government: *the Bush administration/the last Republican administration* [C]

ad·mi·ni·strat·ive /£ədˈmɪn·ɪ·strə·tɪv, $-t̬ɪv/ *adj* • *administrative work/duties* • *an administrative job/task/problem* • *Your responsibilities will be mainly administrative.*

ad·mi·ni·strat·ive·ly /£ədˈmɪn·ɪs·trə·tɪv·li, $-t̬ɪv-/ *adv* • *The changes were administratively complex.*

ad·mi·ni·strat·or /£ədˈmɪn·ɪ·streɪ·təʳ, $-t̬ɚ/ *n* [C] • *From 1969 to 1971, he was administrator of the Illinois state drug abuse program.* • *She works as a school administrator.*

ad·mi·ni·ster *obj* GIVE /£ədˈmɪn·ɪ·stəʳ, $-stɚ/ *v* [T] *fml* to cause someone to receive (something) • *to administer medicine/punishment/relief* • *A sedative had been administered* **to** *the patient.* • *Tests will be administered* **to** *schoolchildren at seven, twelve and sixteen years.* • *(fig.) The latest opinion polls have administered a severe blow* **to** *the party.* • To administer an **oath** (=official promise) **to** someone is to be present while they say the oath officially.

ad·mir·al /ˈæd·mɪ·rəl/ *n* [C] an officer of very high rank in the navy • *Admiral Nelson*

Ad·mir·al·ty /£ˈæd·mɪ·rəl·ti, $-t̬i/ *n* [U] **the Admiralty** in the past, in Britain, the government department in charge of the navy

ad·mire *obj* /£ədˈmaɪəʳ, $-ˈmaɪr/ *v* [T] to respect and approve of (someone or their behaviour), or to find (someone or something) attractive and pleasant to look at • *I've always admired her paintings.* • *I was just admiring your jacket, Delia – it's wonderful!* • *I admire your determination – I'd have given up long ago.* • *She admires (him* **for***) his originality.* • *I admire her* **for** *refusing to grow old.* • *He spends hours in the bathroom, admiring* **himself***/his profile in the mirror.* • Ⓟ

ad·mir·a·ble /ˈæd·mɪ·rə·bl̩/ *adj* • *I think you showed admirable* (=excellent) *tact/restraint/self-control in your answer.* • *The police did an admirable job in keeping the fans calm.*

ad·mir·a·bly /ˈæd·mɪ·rə·bli/ *adv* • *I think she coped admirably with a very difficult situation.*

ad·mi·ra·tion /ˌæd·mɪˈreɪ·ʃᵊn/ *n* [U] • *My admiration* **for** *that woman grows daily.* • *She gazed in admiration at his broad, muscular shoulders.*

ad·mir·er /£ədˈmaɪə·rəʳ, $-ˈmaɪr·rɚ/ *n* [C] • *She/He has many admirers* (=men/women who are attracted to her/him). • *She's got a* **secret** *admirer who keeps sending her gifts through the post.* • *The policy has few admirers* (=few people like it).

ad·mir·ing /£ədˈmaɪə·rɪŋ, $-ˈmaɪr·ɪŋ/ *adj* • *Annette was getting lots of admiring* **looks/glances** *in her new red dress.* • *She was surrounded by a group of admiring photographers.*

ad·mir·ing·ly /£ədˈmaɪə·rɪŋ·li, $-ˈmaɪr·ɪŋ-/ *adv* • *The women sitting opposite us were gazing admiringly at baby Joe.*

ad·mit *(obj)* ACCEPT /ədˈmɪt/ *v* **-tt-** to recognize or accept (something, often something bad) as true • *He admitted his guilt/mistake.* [T] • *She admitted* **(that)** *she had made a mistake.* [+ *(that)* clause] • *She admitted making a mistake.* [+ v-*ing*] • *At first he denied stealing the money but he later admitted* **(to)** *it.* [T; I + *to*] • *I wasn't entirely honest with him, I admit, but I didn't actually tell him any lies.* [I] • *The new law was generally admitted* **to** *be difficult to enforce.* [+ obj + *to* infinitive] • *In fact he's 43, but he only* **admits to** (=pretends to be) *36.* • To **admit defeat** means to accept that you have failed and give up: *After several attempts to untie the knot, I admitted defeat and cut through it with a knife.*

ad·mis·sion /ədˈmɪʃ·ᵊn/ *n* • *Her silence was taken as an admission* **of** *guilt/defeat.* [C] • *I felt he would see my giving up now as an admission* **that** *I was wrong.* [C + *that* clause] • **By/On** *his* **own** *admission* (=as he has said) *he has achieved little since he took over the company.* [U]

ad·mit·ted·ly /£ədˈmɪt·ɪd·li, $-ˈmɪt̬-/ *adv* [not gradable] • *Admittedly* (=I must accept even if I do not want to), *I could have tried harder – but I still don't think all this criticism is fair.* • *The policy is seen to have failed, although admittedly it was never treated fairly by the press.*

ad·mit *obj* ALLOW IN /ədˈmɪt/ *v* [T] **-tt-** to allow (someone or something) to come in • *Each ticket admits one member and one guest.* • *Men will not be admitted* **(to** *the restaurant) without a tie.* • *Spain was admitted* **to** *the European Community in 1986.* • *She was admitted* **to hospital** *suffering from shock.* • *The lecture theatre admits* (=has space for) *500 students.* • *(literary) A gap between the curtains admitted the faint glimmer of a street lamp.*

ad·mis·si·ble /ədˈmɪs·ɪ·bl̩/ *adj fml* • *The judge ruled that new* **evidence** *was admissible* (=could be allowed and considered in a legal court).

ad·mis·si·bil·i·ty /£ədˌmɪs·əˈbɪl·ɪ·ti, $-ə·t̬i/ *n* [U]

ad·mis·si·bly /ədˈmɪs·ɪ·bli/ *adv*

ad·mis·sion /ədˈmɪʃ·ᵊn/ *n* • *Admission* **to** *the exhibition will be by invitation only.* [U] • *The large London museums have all begun to* **charge** *admission.* [U] • *The admission* **charge/fee** *is £2.* [U] • *There's a notice outside the building which says 'No admission before 12 noon'.* [U] • *Half of all* **hospital** *admissions are emergencies, and these are treated straight away.* [C]

ad·mit·tance /£ədˈmɪt·ᵊnts, $-ˈmɪt̬-/ *n* [U] • *He was* **refused** *admittance* **to** (=not allowed in) *the club.* • *The enquiry centred on how the assassin had* **gained** *admittance* **to** (=succeeded in entering) *the building.* • *The sign read 'Private – no admittance'.*

ad·mit of *obj v prep* [T] *fml* to allow (something) or make it possible • *The present schedule does not admit of modification* (= it cannot be changed). • *The latest events admit of several interpretations.*

ad·mix·ture /£əd'mɪks·tʃəʳ, $-tʃɚ/ *n* [C usually sing] *specialized or fml* something added to something else • *Platinum combines with phosphorus and arsenic and is seldom found without an admixture* **of** *related metals.* • *Our party was composed principally of Japanese and Americans, with an admixture* **of** *Hungarians.*

ad·mon·ish *obj* /£əd'mɒn·ɪʃ, $-'mɑː·nɪʃ/ *v* [T] *fml* to express disapproval of (someone), esp. kindly, for their actions or behaviour, or to tell (someone) to do something • *His mother admonished him* **for** *eating too quickly.* • *Her teacher admonished her* **to** *work harder for her exams.* [+ obj + *to* infinitive]

ad·mon·i·tion /ˌæd·mə'nɪʃ·ᵊn/, **ad·mon·ish·ment** /£əd'mɒn·ɪʃ·mənt, $-'mɑː·nɪʃ-/ *n* [C] *fml* • *The most common parental admonition must surely be "Don't stay out late".* • *Despite the stern admonitions and entreaties of her parents and friends, she carried out her plan to join the army.*

ad·mon·i·to·ry /£əd'mɒn·ɪ·tᵊr·i, $-'mɑː·nə·tɔː·ri/ *adj fml* • *an admonitory remark*

ad nau·se·am /£ˌæd'nɔː·zi·æm, $-'nɑː-/ *adv* [not gradable] so many times or so much as to be very annoying or boring • *He talks ad nauseam about how clever his children are.*

a·do /ə'duː/ *n* [U usually in negatives] a lot of delay or unnecessary activity • *He agreed to the proposal* **without** *ado.* • *And so,* **without further** *ado, let me introduce tonight's speaker.* • *"I've had enough of this," she said, and,* **without more** *ado, walked out of the room.* • *He was buried* **with much** *ado* (= with a lot of activity) *in the graveyard of his local parish church.* • *"Much Ado About Nothing"* (title of a play by Shakespeare)

a·do·be /£ə'dəʊ·bi, $-'doʊ-/ *n* [U] a mixture of earth and STRAW (= dried grass) made into bricks and dried in the sun, used to build houses • *an adobe house*

ad·o·les·cent /ˌæd·ə'les·ᵊnt/ *adj, n* [C] (typical of) a young person between childhood and adulthood • *adolescent concerns/traumas/problems* • *The party was full of spotty adolescents.* • If adolescent is used of an adult or an adult's behaviour, it means silly and childish: *adolescent humour/behaviour* ○ *He's so adolescent sometimes!* • LP **Age**

ad·o·les·cence /ˌæd·ə'les·ᵊnts/ *n* • *He had a troubled adolescence.* [C] • *It's just another novel about the joys and sorrows of adolescence.* [U]

A·don·is /£ə'dəʊ·nɪs, $-'dɑː·nɪs/ *n* [C] a very beautiful or sexually attractive young man • *I saw Mira Shapur last night on the arm of some* **blond** *Adonis.*

a·dopt *(obj)* TAKE CHILD /£ə'dɒpt, $-'dɑːpt/ *v* to take (another person's child) into your own family, legally raising him or her as your own child • *They couldn't have children of their own so they adopted a couple of kids.* [T] • *A British couple yesterday lost their battle to adopt two Romanian orphans.* [T] • *She had the child adopted* (= She gave her baby to someone else to raise). [T] • *They have no children of their own, but they're hoping to adopt.* [I] • Compare FOSTER TAKE CARE OF. • LP **Relationships**

a·dopt·ed /£ə'dɒp·tɪd, $-'dɑːp-/ *adj* • *He's adopted, and he's never met his real parents.* • *They've got two adopted children and one of their own.*

a·dop·tion /£ə'dɒp·ʃᵊn, $-'dɑːp-/ *n* • *She was homeless and had to* **put** *her child* **up for** *adoption* (= asked for the child to be taken by another adult or family as their own). [U] • *The child was* **offered for** *adoption by a suitable family.* [U] • *The last ten years have seen a dramatic fall in the number of adoptions.* [C]

a·dopt·ive /£ə'dɒp·tɪv, $-'dɑːp-/ *adj* [not gradable] • *Her adoptive parents* (= the people who adopted her) *were very understanding about her desire to find her natural mother.*

a·dopt *obj* START /£ə'dɒpt, $-'dɑːpt/ *v* [T] to accept or start to use or put into action • *The party has adopted a more pragmatic approach towards arms reduction.* • *I think it's time to adopt a different strategy in my dealings with him.* • *The new tax would force companies to adopt energy-saving measures.* • *He's adopted a remarkably light-hearted attitude towards the situation.* • *The Labour party have tended to adopt more moderate policies in the last few years.* • *She adopted a stern tone while she spoke to him.* • *She was required to adopt a Polish accent for the film.* • *He adopted* (= stood or sat in) **a** *tragic* **pose** *by the window.*

a·dop·tion /£ə'dɒp·ʃᵊn, $-'dɑːp-/ *n* [U] • *Several suggestions have been offered for adoption by the panel.*

a·dopt *obj* CHOOSE /£ə'dɒpt, $-'dɑːpt/ *v* [T] to choose or claim as your own • *Dr Kennedy has been adopted* **as** *the party's candidate for South Cambridge.* • *Roz has adopted one or two funny mannerisms since she's been away.* • *She adopted Indian dress during her stay in the country.*

a·dopt·ed /£ə'dɒp·tɪd, $-'dɑːp-/ *adj* • *Spain is my adopted country* (= not the country where I was born, but the one where I have chosen to live).

a·dop·tion /£ə'dɒp·ʃᵊn, $-'dɑːp-/ *n* [U] • *England was Conrad's* **country of** *adoption.*

a·dore *(obj)* LOVE /£ə'dɔːʳ, $-'dɔːr/ *v* [not *be adoring*] to love (someone) very much, esp. in an admiring or respectful way, or to like something very much • *Both girls adored their father but seemed to think very little of their mother.* [T] • *She has one son and she adores him.* [T] • *Darling, I* **simply** *adore your blouse – where did you get it?* [T] • *I adore chocolate – I* **absolutely** *adore it.* [T] • *Don't you just adore lying in a hot bath?* [+ v-*ing*] • *"Pam, I adore you, Pam, you great big mountainous sports girl"* (John Betjeman in the poem *Pot Pourri from a Surrey Garden*, 1940)

a·dor·a·ble /£ə'dɔː·rə·bl̩, $-'dɔːr·ə-/ *adj* • A person or animal that is adorable makes you feel affectionate towards them because they have such qualities as charm, attractiveness or kindness: *I met your little nephew, Joe – isn't he just adorable!* ○ *Helen's just bought the most adorable puppy.* • Adorable is also used of things, often small things, to mean very attractive: *Oh, what an adorable little desk – I must have it!*

ad·or·a·tion /ˌæd·ə'reɪ·ʃᵊn/ *n* [U] • *What I find a bit strange is her complete adoration* (= complete love) *of her brother.*

a·dor·ing /ə'dɔː·rɪŋ/ *adj* • *I refuse to play the part of the adoring wife.*

a·dore *obj* WORSHIP /£ə'dɔːʳ, $-'dɔːr/ *v* [T] *fml* to worship as (sent from) god • *Let us adore God for all his works.*

ad·or·a·tion /£ˌæd·ə'reɪ·ʃᵊn, £-ɔː'-, $-ɚ'-/ *n* [U] • *The painting depicts the three wise men kneeling in adoration of the baby Jesus.*

a·dorn *obj* /£ə'dɔːn, $-'dɔːrn/ *v* [T usually passive] *literary* to make (something or someone) more beautiful by adding something decorative • *The altars were adorned* **with** *orange feathers, chrysanthemums and gold cloth.* • *The bride's hair was adorned* **with** *pearls and white flowers.*

a·dorn·ment /£ə'dɔːn·mənt, $-'dɔːrn-/ *n literary* • *On the living-room wall the only adornment, a painting of a female saint, stood out against the white surface.* [C] • *She never wore make-up, having a classically beautiful face that had little need of adornment.* [U] • *"What time he can spare from the adornment of his person he devotes to the neglect of his duties"* (W.H.Thompson referring to a professor at Cambridge University, 1810-86)

a·dren·a·lin /ə'dren·ᵊl·ɪn/ *n* [U] a HORMONE (= chemical substance) produced by the body when you are frightened, angry or excited, which makes the heart beat faster and prepares the body to react to danger • *I felt* **the** *adrenalin pumping through my body.* • *These arguments always* **get** *my adrenalin* **going** (= make me excited or angry). • *Adrenalin can also be made artificially for medical treatment.*

a·drift /ə'drɪft/ *adj* [after v], *adv* (of a boat) not tied up and therefore moving with the sea and wind, or *(fig.)* not controlled and without a clear purpose or direction • *He spent three days adrift on his yacht.* • *(fig.) Da Silva plays a bright, bookish, lonely student from New York, adrift in small-town Arizona.* • *Someone had* **cut** *the boat adrift* **from** *its moorings.* • To **cast/turn** someone adrift is to send them away without any support or help: *He made a very emotive speech all about homeless children cast adrift by society.* • *(infml)* To **come/go** adrift is to become loose: *The hem of my skirt's come adrift again.* • *(infml)* If plans **go** adrift they fail or do not produce the correct results: *Something seems to have gone adrift in our calculations.*

a·droit /ə'drɔɪt/ *adj* very skilful and quick in the way you think or move • *an adroit reaction/answer/movement of the hand* • *She became adroit* **at** *dealing with difficult questions.* • *Kimberley Smart is an adroit interviewer who knows when to keep her mouth shut.*

a·droit·ly /ə'drɔɪt·li/ *adv* • *She adroitly avoided the question.* • *He adroitly slipped the money into his pocket.*

a·droit·ness /ə'drɔɪt·nəs/ *n* [U]

ad·u·la·tion /ˌæd·jʊˈleɪ·ʃᵊn/ *n* [U] very great, often not deserved, admiration or praise for someone • *Durante is a born performer – she loves the excitement and she loves the adulation.*

ad·u·la·to·ry /£ˌæd·jʊˈleɪ·tᵊr·i, $ˈædʒ·ᵊl·ə·tɔː·ri/ *adj* • *I found myself irritated by the adulatory tone of her biography.*

ad·ult /ˈæd·ʌlt, əˈdʌlt/ *n* [C], *adj* (a person or animal that is) grown to full size and strength • *an adult male/elephant/sparrow* • *She spent most of her adult* **life** *in prison.* • *An adult under British law is someone over 18 years old.* • *Adults pay an admission charge but children get in free.* • *His behaviour/sense of humour is not very adult* (= it is childish, not suitable for his age). • *Let's try to be adult about this* (= we should behave or talk reasonably, like fully grown people). • Adult films, magazines and books are ones intended for sexual entertainment, and show naked people and describe sexual activity. • Adult **education** refers to classes, usually during the evening, for people who have finished their school education. • [LP] **Age**

ad·ult·hood /ˈæd·ʌlt·hʊd, əˈdʌlt-/ *n* [U] • *People in Britain legally* **reach** *adulthood at 18.* • *The disorder was once fatal in childhood but modern treatment permits many afflicted children to live into adulthood.* • *Responsibility, I suppose, is what defines adulthood.*

a·dul·ter·ate *obj* /£əˈdʌl·tə·reɪt, $-t̬ɚ·eɪt/ *v* [T] to make (something, esp. drink or food) weaker or of worse quality by adding something else • *There were complaints that the beer had been adulterated* **with** *water.*

a·dul·ter·at·ed /£əˈdʌl·tə·reɪ·tɪd, $-t̬ɚ·eɪ·t̬ɪd/ *adj* • *adulterated drugs* • *The Agency will also issue advice and warnings to the public and retailers about adulterated food.*

a·dul·ter·a·tion /əˌdʌl·təˈreɪ·ʃᵊn/ *n* [U]

a·dul·te·ry /£əˈdʌl·tᵊr·i, $-t̬ɚ·i/ *n* sex between a married man or woman and someone who is not their wife or husband • *Many people in public life have* **committed** *adultery.* [U] • *His second novel deals with the adulteries of middle-class New Englanders.* [C] • *"Thou shalt not commit adultery"* (Bible, Exodus 20.14)

a·dul·ter·er, *female* **a·dul·ter·ess** /£əˈdʌl·tə·rəʳ, $-t̬ɚ·ɚ, £-rəs, $-əs/ *n* [C] *old use* • *Her husband was a compulsive adulterer.*

a·dul·ter·ous /£əˈdʌl·tᵊr·əs, $-t̬ɚ-/ *adj* • *He had an adulterous relationship with his wife's best friend.*

ad·um·brate *obj* /ˈæd·əm·breɪt/ *v* [T] *fml* to give a general idea of (esp. something in the future), without details • *The play opens with a fierce storm which adumbrates the violence to follow.*

ad·um·bra·tion /ˌæd·əmˈbreɪ·ʃᵊn/ *n* [U] *fml*

adv *abbreviation for* ADVERB

ad·vance *(obj)* /£ədˈvɑːnts, $-ˈvænts/ *v* to go or move (something) forward, or to develop or improve (something) • *The fire advanced steadily through the forest.* [I] • *The troops advanced* **on** *the city* (= approached it, ready to attack). [I] • *We have advanced greatly in our knowledge of the universe.* [I] • *Her study has considerably advanced* (= helped) *the* **cause** *of equal rights.* [T] • *Could you advance me £50* (= pay it to me before the regular time) *until Tuesday?* [+ two objects] • *He's just trying to advance* (= improve) *his own* **career**. [T] • (P)

ad·vance /£ədˈvɑːnts, $-ˈvænts/ *n* • *Nothing could stop* **the** *advance* **of** *the flood waters.* [U] • *Recent advances* **in** *medical science mean that this illness can now be cured.* [C] • *She asked for a £300 advance* **on** *her salary* (= money paid before the regular time). [C] • *(fig.) She rejected his unwelcome advances* (= his attempts to make her sexually interested in him). [C] • *If you're going to come, please let me know* **in advance** (= before you come). • *She arrived* **in advance of** (= before) *everyone else.* • **Advance directive** is *Am for* **living will**, see at LIVE [HAVE LIFE].

ad·vance /£ədˈvɑːnts, $-ˈvænts/ *adj* [before n] • *advance payment/booking* (= done before the event) • *We got no advance* **warning** *of the changes.*

ad·vanced /£ədˈvɑːntst, $-ˈvæntst/ *adj* • *This is the most advanced* (= highly developed) *type of engine available.* • *(Am)* An **advanced class/course** is a school class which is doing work of a higher standard than is usual for students at that stage in their education.

ad·vance·ment /£ədˈvɑːnt·smənt, $-ˈvænt-/ *n* [U] • *All she was interested in was the advancement* (= improvement, development) *of her own career.*

ad·van·tage /£ədˈvɑːn·tɪdʒ, $-ˈvæn·t̬ɪdʒ/ *n* a condition giving a greater chance of success • *The advantage of booking tickets in advance is that you get better seats.* [C] • *Despite the* **twin** *advantages of wealth and beauty, she did not have a happy life.* [C] • **It** *would be* **to** *your advantage* (= It would improve the situation for you) **to** *agree to his demands.* [U + *to* infinitive] • *For a goalkeeper,* **it's** *a great advantage* **to** *have big hands.* [C + *to* infinitive] • *His height and reach* **give him** *a big advantage* **over** (= make him better than) *other boxers.* [C] • Advantage is the word used in tennis when a player has won the point after DEUCE: *Advantage Jackson!* [U] • *(Br fml) "Do you know how old I am?" "I'm afraid you* **have the** *advantage* **of** *me there* (= you know the answer but I do not)." [U] • To **take** advantage **of** a situation is to benefit intentionally from it: *Take advantage of this week's lower prices* (= Buy while prices are lower). [U] • *(disapproving)* To **take** advantage **of** a person or their qualities is to benefit selfishly from them without giving anything in return: *I think she takes advantage of his good nature.* [U]

ad·van·tag·eous /ˌæd·vænˈteɪ·dʒəs/ *adj* • *advantageous interest rates* • *I think you'd find it advantageous* **to** *pay by instalments.* • *The lower tax rate is particularly advantageous* **to** *poorer families.*

ad·van·tag·eous·ly /ˌæd·vænˈteɪ·dʒə·sli/ *adv*

ad·vent /ˈæd·vent, -vənt/ *n* [U] the (future) arrival (of an event, invention, person, etc.) • *Quills were the chief writing implement from the 6th century AD until* **the** *advent* **of** *steel pens in the mid 19th century.* • *Life in Britain was transformed by* **the** *advent* **of** *the steam engine.* • For Christians, Advent is the period of four weeks before Christmas. • An **Advent calendar** is a decorative piece of card, often hung on the wall, which has a small door-like opening for each of the days of the month before Christmas. People, esp. children, open one of these doors each day, finding a picture under it.

ad·ven·tist /ˈæd·ven·tɪst, -vən-/ *n* [C] • Adventists believe that Christ will return soon: *the Seventh Day Adventists*

ad·ven·ti·tious /ˌæd·vᵊnˈtɪʃ·əs, -ven-/ *adj fml* not expected or planned • *an adventitious event/situation*

ad·ven·ti·tious·ly /ˌæd·vᵊnˈtɪʃ·ə·sli, -ven-/ *adv fml* • *I came upon the painting quite adventitiously.*

ad·ven·ture /£ədˈven·tʃəʳ, $-tʃɚ/ *n* an unusual, exciting and possibly dangerous activity, journey, experience, etc., or the excitement produced by such activities • *She* **had** *some exciting adventures in Egypt.* [C] • *We got lost on the Metro – it was* **quite an** *adventure!* [C] • *Henry won't come – he's got no* **sense of** *adventure* (= he does not enjoy dangerous situations). [U] • *She's always looking for adventure.* [U] • An **adventure playground** is a public open space where children can play and climb on structures made of wood, metal, old tyres, etc. • *"To die will be an awfully big adventure"* (from the play and children's story *Peter Pan* by J.M.Barrie, 1904) • *"Hergé's Adventures of Tintin"* (book title, 1929) • (P)

ad·ven·tur·er /£ədˈven·tʃə·rəʳ, $-tʃɚ·ɚ/ *n* [C] • An adventurer is someone who enjoys and looks for dangerous and exciting experiences: *He was something of an adventurer, living most of his life abroad.* • *(disapproving)* An adventurer is also a person who takes risks, acts dishonestly or uses his or her sexual attractiveness to become rich or powerful: *He was portrayed in the press as a gold-digger and adventurer.*

ad·ven·tur·ous /£ədˈven·tʃᵊr·əs, $-tʃɚ·əs/ *adj* • *I think I'll try the snails for lunch – I'm feeling adventurous today.* • *She led an adventurous life.* • *He's not very adventurous sexually.*

ad·ven·tur·ous·ly /£ədˈven·tʃᵊr·ə·sli, $-tʃɚ·e-/ *adv* • *The availability of a greater variety of food has encouraged us as a nation to cook more adventurously.*

ad·verb /£ˈæd·vɜːb, $-vɜːrb/ *n* [C] a word which describes or gives more information about a verb, adjective, adverb or phrase • *In the following sentences, 'cheerfully', 'spotlessly', 'extremely', 'well', and 'right' are adverbs: She smiled cheerfully.* ○ *The house was spotlessly clean.* ○ *He's managing extremely well.* ○ *The shot was heard right outside the door.* • [LP] **Comparing and grading**

ad·verb·i·al /£ədˈvɜː·bi·əl, $-ˈvɜːr-/ *adj* [not gradable] • *an adverbial phrase*

ad·vers·a·ry /£ˈæd·və·sᵊr·i, $ˈæd·vɚ·ser-/ *n* [C] an enemy • *He saw her as his main adversary within the company.* • *You've come up* **against** *a* **powerful** *adversary.* • *"The Adversary of God and Man, Satan"* (Milton in *Paradise Lost*, 1667)

ad·vers·ar·i·al /£ˌæd·vəˈseə·ri·əl, $-vɚˈser·i-/ *adj* • Adversarial means involving opposition or disagreement:

ADVERBS

IMPORTANT TYPES OF ADVERBS

Different types of adverbs are used:

- **to describe how, where, when or how often something happens**

How?	*The dog barked* **loudly**.
	We enjoyed the film **a lot**.
Where?	*Come* **outside**.
	They built a factory **nearby**.
When?	*It's going to rain* **soon**.
	I haven't read the newspaper **yet**.
How often?	*You're* **always** *complaining*.
	I **usually** *cook dinner on Sunday*.

- **to change the strength of a verb, adjective or adverb**

verb:	*The car* **almost** *crashed*.
	The medicine helped him **enormously**.
adjective:	*It's* **rather** *cold. She was* **terribly** *excited by the news*.
adverb:	*We'll finish* **quite** *soon*.
	He talks **amazingly** *fast*.

LP **Very, completely** at VERY

- **to give information about the attitude of the speaker or writer**

Surprisingly, *all the children came on time.*
Unfortunately *I disagree with you.*
Perhaps *the team will win.*
It's **obviously** *too expensive.*

- **to join sentences or clauses**

Wilson's plan seemed good. His boss, **though**, *didn't like it.*
I don't know **why** *John went away.*
Tell me **when** *you have finished.*

- **before a preposition or adverb [before adv/prep]**

A few adverbs can be used immediately before another adverb or a prepositional phrase. They often mean 'exactly' or 'completely': *It broke* **right** *down the middle* (used with a prepositional phrase). • *Go* **right** *ahead* (used with an adverb). Other adverbs like this are: all, bang, full, smack.

POSITION OF ADVERBS

- Adverbs normally come after intransitive verbs: *Tara sings* **beautifully**.
- With transitive verbs the adverb should not be put between the verb and the object; it usually comes after the object: *They passed the test* **easily**.
- **Adverbs of frequency** normally come:
  after auxiliary verbs:
  Sue is **always** *borrowing other people's pens.*
  Simon may **sometimes** *be wrong.*
  before simple tenses of other verbs:
  The police **rarely** *go on strike.*
  My father **often** *slept in the afternoons.*
- Some adverbs can be placed at the beginning of a sentence to give them emphasis:
  Slowly *he raised the gun to his shoulder.*
  Possibly *your new plan will work.*

ORDER OF ADVERBS

When the sentence has more than one adverb, the normal order answers the questions how, where and when?

	HOW	WHERE	WHEN
The girls were playing	*quietly*	*outside.*	
We'll have to go		*back*	*soon.*

In the old days of two-party adversarial politics, voting was easy.

ad·verse /£'æd·vɜːs, £-'-, $æd'vɜːrs/ *adj* [before n] going against something, or harmful • *The match has been cancelled due to adverse* **weather conditions**. • *They received a lot of adverse* **publicity/criticism** *about the changes.* • *The advertising company responsible for the campaign say that they are surprised by the adverse public* **reaction** *to the poster.* • *A lot of local people are worried about the adverse* **impact** *that the road building scheme may have on the environment.* • *So far the drug is thought not to have any adverse* **effects**.

ad·verse·ly /£'æd·vɜː·sli, £-'--, $æd'vɜːr-/ *adv* • *A lot of companies have been adversely* (=in a harmful way) **affected** *by the recession.*

ad·vers·i·ty /£əd'vɜː·sə·ti, $-'vɜːr·sə·t̬i/ *n* a difficult or unlucky situation or event • *She was always cheerful* **in** *adversity.* [U] • *The road to happiness is paved with adversities.* [C]

ad·vert /£'æd·vɜːt, $-vɜːrt/ *n* [C] *Br infml for* **advertisement**, see at ADVERTISE • *There was an advert* **for** *the local radio station in last night's paper.* • *I always make a cup of tea during the adverts* (=the television advertisements). • *He looks like the man* **in** *the cigar adverts.*

ad·vert·ise *(obj)* /£'æd·və·taɪz, $-vɚ-/ *v* to make (something) known generally or in public, esp. in order to sell it • *We decided to advertise our car* (=to publish a description of it together with the price we wanted for it) *in the local newspaper.* [T] • *He advertises his services on the company noticeboard.* [T] • *I'm going to advertise* **for** (=put a notice in the newspaper, local shop, etc., asking for) *someone to clean my house.* [I] • *The extended news bulletin means that the remainder of this evening's programmes will be running twenty minutes later than advertised.* [T] • *He has always advertised* (=made generally known) *his willingness to talk to the press.* [T] • *There's no harm in applying for other jobs, but if I were you, I wouldn't advertise* **the fact** (=make it generally known) *at work.* [T] • Ⓕ

ad·vert·ise·ment /£əd'vɜː·tɪ·smənt, $'æd·vɜːr·taɪz·mənt/, *infml* **ad**, *Br infml* **advert** *n* [C] • *a television/newspaper/magazine advertisement* **for** *a new car* • *She scanned the job/property advertisements in the paper.* • *(fig.) I'm afraid I'm not a very good advertisement* **for** (=I do not show the good effects of) *the diet since I've actually put on weight!*

ad·vert·is·er /£'æd·və·taɪ·zəʳ, $-vɚ·taɪ·zɚ/ *n* [C] • *Whilst claiming to promote positive images of women, advertisers are in fact doing the very opposite.*

ad·vert·is·ing /£'æd·və·taɪ·zɪŋ, $-vɚ-/ *n* [U] • *Fiona works in advertising.* (=Her job is creating advertisements). • *I don't have much respect for the advertising industry.* • *They've set up a major advertising campaign.* • *"Half the money I spend on advertising is wasted, and the trouble is I don't know which half"* (Lord Leverhulme, 1851-1925)

ad·vert·or·i·al /£,æd·və'tɔː·ri·əl, $-'tɔːr·i-/ *n* [C] • An advertorial is an advertisement in a newspaper or magazine that is designed to look like an article by the writers of the magazine: *Some people don't like advertorials, because they think them deceptive.*

ad·vice /əd'vaɪs/ *n* [U] an opinion which someone offers you about what you should do or how you should act in a particular situation • *She* **gave** *me some* **good/bad/sound/unsolicited** *advice.* • *I think I'll* **take** *your advice, Huw, and get the green dress.* • *Let me* **give/offer** *you* **some/a piece of** *advice, Julia.* • *Look, if I want your advice, I'll ask for it* (=Stop telling me what I should do)! • *He asked (me) for my advice* **on** *the choice of a new car/***on** *what he should do.* • *My advice is* **to** *give yourself up to the police.* [+ *to* infinitive] • *He ignored my advice* **that** *he should sell his shares.* [+ *that* clause] • *Claire went to Paris* **on** *Sarah's advice.* • Advice is also, esp. in business, an official document that tells you that something has been done or will be done on a particular time: *We received advice* **of** *delivery next Tuesday/advice* **that** *the goods will be delivered next Tuesday.* [+ *that* clause] ○ *an advice note*

ad·vise *(obj)* /əd'vaɪz/ *v* • *I advised him* **to** *stay at home.* [T + obj + *to* infinitive] • *She was advised not* **to** *tell anyone.* [T + obj + *to* infinitive] • *His doctor advised (him)* **against** *smoking.* [always + prep] • *He advised* **that** *she (should) be patient.* [+ *that* clause] • *I advised Peter* **that** *he should get his hair cut.* [T + obj + *that* clause] • *He advised her* **to** *be patient.* [T + obj + *to* infinitive] • *I'd advise waiting until* *tomorrow.* [+ v-*ing*] • *She advised us* **when** *to come.* [+ obj + *wh-* word] • *She advises (the President)* (= gives information and suggests types of action) **on** *African policy.* [always + prep] • *Please advise us* **of** (= tell us) *the expected time of arrival.* [T] • *Our solicitors have advised* **that** *the costs could be enormous.* [+ *that* clause] • *You* **would be well-***advised* **to** (= It would be wise for you to) *have the appropriate vaccinations before you go abroad.* [+ *to* infinitive] • *Parents of small children* **would be ill-***advised* **to** (= It would be unwise for parents to) *take them into the area.* [+ *to* infinitive]

ad·vis·a·ble /əd'vaɪ·zə·bl̩/ *adj* • **It's** *advisable* **to** (= You should) *reserve a seat on this train.* [+ *to* infinitive] • *A certain amount of caution is advisable at this point.*

ad·vis·a·bil·i·ty /£əd,vaɪ·zə'bɪl·ɪ·ti, $-ə·t̬i/ *n* [U] • *They discussed the advisability of building so near to the airport.*

ad·vis·ed·ly /əd'vaɪ·zɪd·li/ *adv* • *This action is barbaric – and I use the word advisedly* (= on purpose and knowing what it means).

ad·vis·er /£əd'vaɪ·zəʳ, $-zɚ/, **ad·vis·or** *n* [C] • *She is the party's main economic adviser.*

ad·vis·o·ry /£əd'vaɪ·zᵊr·i, $-zɚ-/ *adj* • *She is employed by the president in an advisory capacity.*

ad·vo·cate *obj* /'æd·və·keɪt/ *v* [T] to speak in support of (an idea, course of action, etc.) • *She advocates tak***ing** *a more long-term view.* [+ v-*ing*] • *He advocates the return of capital punishment.* • (CS) (PL) (RUS)

ad·vo·cate /'æd·və·kət/ *n* [C] • *He's a strong advocate* **of** *state ownership of the railways.* • An advocate is also a lawyer who defends someone in a court of law.

ad·vo·ca·cy /'æd·və·kə·si/ *n* [U] • *She is renowned for her advocacy* **of** *human rights.*

adze /ædz/, *Am usually* **adz** *n* [C] a tool like an AXE with the blade at an angle of approximately 90° to the handle, which is used for cutting and shaping wood • [PIC] **Axe**

ae·gis /'iː·dʒɪs/ *n* [U] **under the aegis of** *someone or something*/**under** *someone's or something's* **aegis** with the protection or support of (someone or something, esp. an organization) • *The project was set up under the aegis of the university.* • *The conference was organized under the UN's aegis.*

ae·on /£'iː·ɒn, $-ɑːn/ *n* [C] *esp. Br for* EON • [LP] **Periods of time**

aer·ate *obj* /£eə'reɪt, $er'eɪt/ *v* [T] to add a gas to (a liquid, esp. a drink), or to let the air act on (something) • *Earthworms help to aerate the soil.* • *aerated water* • *aerated soil*

aer·a·tion /£eə'reɪ·ʃᵊn, $er'eɪ-/ *n* [U]

aer·i·al [RADIO] /£'eə·ri·əl, $'er·i-/, *Am and Aus also* **an·ten·na** *n* a structure made of metal rods or wires, often positioned on top of a building, vehicle, etc., which receives or sends out radio or television signals • [PIC] **Accommodation, Car**

aer·i·al [AIR] /£'eə·ri·əl, $'er·i-/ *adj* [not gradable] of, from, happening in or existing in the air • *Meanwhile, the massive aerial* **bombardment/bombing** *of military and strategic targets continued unabated.* • *The use of aerial* **photographs** *as a basis for mapping is increasing.* • *All aerial* **spraying** *of the fungicide has also been outlawed.* • *Aerial surveys have tried to track the dolphin population.*

aer·ie /£'ɪə·ri, $'ɪr·i/ *n* [C] *esp. Am for* EYRIE

aer·o– /£'eə·rəʊ, $'er·oʊ-/ *combining form* of the air or air travel • *aerodynamics/aeronautics*

aer·o·bat·ics /£,eə·rəʊ'bæt·ɪks, $,er·oʊ'bæt̬-/ *pl n* skilful movements in an aircraft, such as flying upside down or in a circle • *The crowd was entertained with a display of aerobatics.*

aer·o·bat·ics /£,eə·rəʊ'bæt·ɪks, $,er·oʊ'bæt̬-/ *n* [U] • *He enrolled in the air force, where he won a trophy for aerobatics.*

aer·o·bat·ic /£,eə·rəʊ'bæt·ɪk, $,er·oʊ'bæt̬-/ *adj* [not gradable] • *an aerobatic display*

aer·o·bics /£eə'rəʊ·bɪks, $er'oʊ-/ *n* [U] energetic physical exercises, often performed with a group of other people to music, which make the heart, lungs and muscles stronger and increase the amount of oxygen in the blood • *I really enjoy* **(doing)** *aerobics.* • *I go to aerobics* (= to a class where we are taught such exercises) *once a week.* • *I have a very good aerobics instructor/teacher called Nicky.*

aer·o·bic /£eə'rəʊ·bɪk, $er'oʊ-/ *adj* [not gradable] • *Adding aerobic* **exercise** *to your life will speed up weight loss, and tone up muscle to improve body shape.*

aer·o·drome /£'eə·rə·drəʊm, $'er·ə·droʊm/ *n* [C] *Br dated for* AIRFIELD

aer·o·dy·nam·ics /£,eə·rəʊ·daɪ'næm·ɪks, $,er·oʊ-/ *n* [U] the science which studies the movement of gases and the way solid bodies, such as aircraft, move through them

aer·o·dy·nam·ic /£,eə·rəʊ·daɪ'næm·ɪk, $,er·oʊ-/ *adj* • *aerodynamic principles* • *an aerodynamic design/car*

aer·o·dy·nam·ic·ally /£,eə·rəʊ·daɪ'næm·ɪ·kli, $,er·oʊ-/ *adv* • *aerodynamically designed/efficient*

aer·o·gramme, *Am and Aus also* **aer·o·gram** /£'eə·rəʊ·græm, $'er·ə-/ *n* [C] an AIRLETTER

aer·o·nau·tics /£,eə·rə'nɔː·tɪks, $,er·ə'nɑː·t̬ɪks/ *n* [U] the TECHNOLOGY and science of designing, building and operating aircraft

aer·o·nau·tic /£,eə·rə'nɔː·tɪk, $,er·ə'nɑː·t̬ɪk/ *adj* [not gradable] • *aeronautic design/engineering*

aer·o·nau·tic·al /£,eə·rə'nɔː·tɪ·kᵊl, $,er·ə'nɑː·t̬ɪ-/ *adj* [not gradable]

aer·o·plane *Br and Aus* /£'eə·rə·pleɪn, $'er-/, *Am* **air·plane** *n* [C] a vehicle designed for air travel, which has wings and one or more engines • *Concorde is a supersonic aeroplane.* • *He died in an aeroplane crash.* • *She has her own private aeroplane.*

aer·o·sol /£'eə·rəʊ·sɒl, $'er·ə·sɑːl/ *n* [C] a usually metal container in which liquids are kept under pressure and forced out in a SPRAY (= mass of small drops) • *an aerosol deodorant/paint/cologne/cream* • *The extremists sprayed aerosol insect repellent into the faces of police* • *CFC propellants, which are used to squirt many products through the nozzle of an aerosol, can damage the ozone layer.*

aer·o·space /£'eə·rəʊ·speɪs, $'er·oʊ-/ *adj* [before n; not gradable] producing or operating aircraft or spacecraft • *the aerospace industry* • *an aerospace company*

aes·thet·ic, *esp. Am* **es·the·tic** /£es'θet·ɪk, $-'θet̬-/ *adj* relating to (the enjoyment or study of) beauty, or (of an object or work of art) showing great beauty • *The new building has little aesthetic value/appeal.* • *This chair may be aesthetic but it's not very comfortable.*

aes·thet·ics, *esp. Am* **es·the·tics** /£es'θet·ɪks, $-'θet̬-/ *n* [U] • Aesthetics is the formal study of art, esp. with relation to the idea of beauty: *One of the central questions* **in** *aesthetics is whether beauty is in the eye of the beholder, or whether there is something within an object itself which makes it beautiful.* ○ *Eisenstein was the first to draw up and codify a formal aesthetics for the cinema.*

aes·thet·ic·al·ly, *esp. Am* **es·the·ti·cal·ly** /£es'θet·ɪ·kli, $-'θet̬-/ *adv* • *I like objects to be both functional and aesthetically* **pleasing**.

aes·thete, *Am also* **es·thete** /'iːs·θiːt/ *n* [C] • *Its ugliness would make an aesthete* (= person who understands and enjoys beauty) *like you shudder.* • *He does not accept, as the aesthetes proclaim, that good music must have violins in it.*

a·far /£ə'fɑːʳ, $-'fɑːr/ *adv* [not gradable] from or at a great distance • *People came* **from** *afar to see the show.* • *(humorous) I've never actually spoken to him – I've just admired him* **from** *afar.*

af·fa·ble /'æf·ə·bl̩/ *adj* friendly, kind, relaxed and easy to talk to • *He was relaxed and affable at Derrick's party.* • *He struck me as an affable sort of a man.* • *She was quite affable at the meeting.*

af·fa·bly /'æf·ə·bli/ *adv* • *He greeted us affably.* • *"It's good to see you," said Jackson, slapping me affably on the back.*

af·fa·bil·i·ty /£,æf·ə'bɪl·ɪ·ti, $-ə·t̬i/ *n* [U] *fml*

af·fair [MATTER] /£ə'feəʳ, $-'fer/ *n* [C] a situation or subject that is being dealt with or considered; a matter • *The meeting was addressed by an expert in South American affairs.* • *She organizes her* **financial** *affairs very efficiently.* • *He's always* **meddling in** (= trying to influence) *my/her/other people's affairs.* • *What I do in my spare time is my* **own** *affair* (= only involves me). • An affair is also a matter or situation which causes strong public feeling, usually of moral disapproval: *The arms-dealing affair has severely damaged the reputation of the government.* ○ *The President's* **handling** *of the affair has been criticised.* • **Affairs of state** are important government matters.

af·fair [RELATIONSHIP] /£ə'feəʳ, $-'fer/ *n* [C] a sexual relationship, esp. a secret one • *She's* **having** *an affair with a married man.* • *They had a torrid* **love** *affair in France.* • *The book doesn't make any mention of his* **extramarital** *affairs.*

af·fair [EVENT] /£ə'feəʳ, $-'fer/ *n* [C] an event • *The conference was a long and tedious affair.* • *The party was a very quiet affair and not at all what I'd been expecting.*

af·fair [THING] /£ə'feəʳ, $-'fer/ *n* [C] *infml* (used in descriptions) a thing • *She wore a long black velvet affair.* • *I can't remember what sort of car he has but it's a red sporty affair.*

af·fect *obj* [INFLUENCE] /ə'fekt/ *v* [T] to have an influence on • *The divorce affected every aspect of her life.* • *The team's performance was affected by the rain.* • *I think all the worry has affected my brain!* • *The disease only affects cattle.* • *I was deeply affected by the film* (= It caused strong feelings in me). • (CS) (RUS)

af·fect·ing /ə'fek·tɪŋ/ *adj fml* • *It was an affecting* (= producing strong feelings) *sight/moment.*

af·fect *obj* [PRETEND] /ə'fekt/ *v* [T] *fml esp. disapproving* to pretend to be or have • *Since going away to university he's affected a ridiculous upper class accent.* • *She affected a cough so that she could escape from the meeting.* • *He affects fancy outfits and often wears several rings and bracelets.* • (CS) (RUS)

af·fect·ed /ə'fek·tɪd/ *adj disapproving* • Affected means artificial and not sincere: *He has a very affected manner/style of writing* ○ *I hate that affected smile of hers.* ○ *I found her very affected.*

af·fect·ed·ly /ə'fek·tɪd·li/ *adv disapproving* • *She laughed affectedly.*

af·fect·a·tion /ˌæf·ek'teɪ·ʃᵊn/ *n disapproving* • *She has so many little affectations* (= ways of speaking and behaving that are not natural to her). [C] • *His manner reeks of falseness and affectation.* [U] • *"It doesn't concern me," he said with* **an** *affectation* **of** (= pretending) *nonchalance.*

af·fec·tion /ə'fek·ʃᵊn/ *n* a feeling of liking (someone or something) • *He* **had** *a* **deep** *affection for his aunt.* [C] • *She* **felt** *great/little/no affection* **for** *the child.* [U]

af·fec·tions /ə'fek·ʃᵊnz/ *pl n* • *He tried to* **win** *her affections* (= to persuade her to love him) *by bringing her flowers.* [C]

af·fec·tion·ate /ə'fek·ʃᵊn·ət/ *adj* • *She gave her daughter an affectionate kiss and put her to bed.* • *He's an affectionate little boy.*

af·fec·tion·ate·ly /ə'fek·ʃᵊn·ət·li/ *adv* • *She smiled affectionately at him.*

af·fi·da·vit /ˌæf·ə'deɪ·vɪt/ *n* [C] a written statement which someone makes after they have sworn officially to tell the truth, and which might be used as proof in a court of law

af·fil·i·ate *obj* /ə'fɪl·i·eɪt/ *v* [T often passive] to cause (a group) to become part of or form a close relationship with esp. a larger group or organization • *The school has affiliated it***self to***/is affiliated* **with** *a national association of driving schools.*

af·fil·i·ate /ə'fɪl·i·eɪt/ *n* [C] • *Our college is an affiliate* **of** *the university.*

af·fil·i·a·tion /əˌfɪl·i'eɪ·ʃᵊn/ *n* • *The group has affiliations* **with** *several organizations abroad.* [C] • *Their lack of affiliation* **to** *any particular bank allows them to give objective financial advice.* [U] • *(Br law)* Under an **affiliation order**, a man who is not married to the mother of his child is ordered by a law court to pay money to the mother to support his child.

af·fin·i·ty /£ə'fɪn·ɪ·ti, $-ə·ţi/ *n* a close similarity (between two things), or an attraction or sympathy (for someone or something), esp. because of shared characteristics • *The French have an affinity* **for** *cyclists unknown on the British side of the Channel.* [C] • *People really feel an affinity for dolphins and want to help them.* [C] • *There are several close affinities* **between** *the two paintings.* [C] • *She* **has/feels** *strong affinity* **for/with** *the homeless since her experiences in India.* [U]

af·firm *obj* /£ə'fɜːm, $-'fɜːrm/ *v* [T] to state (something) as true, or to state your support for (an idea, opinion, etc.) • *The suspect affirmed* **(that)** *he had been at home all evening.* [+ (*that*) clause] • *"The door was unlocked when I arrived," she affirmed.* [+ clause] • *She affirmed her intention to stand for the presidency.* • *The government affirmed its commitment to equal rights.* • *The delegates affirmed the right to freedom of speech.*

af·firm·a·tion /£ˌæf·ə'meɪ·ʃᵊn, $-ɚ'-/ *n* • *We welcome the government's affirmation of its intention to act.* [U] • *They ignored her, despite her repeated affirmations* **that** *she was telling the truth.* [C + *that* clause] • *The film is an affirmation* **of** *life.* [C] • An affirmation in a court of law is a promise to tell the truth, made without swearing on the Bible, for example by someone who is not a Christian.

af·firm·a·tive /£ə'fɜː·mə·tɪv, $-'fɜːr·mə·ţɪv/ *adj* • A statement which is affirmative shows agreement or says 'yes': *an affirmative answer/sentence/gesture/nod* • If a government or an organization takes **affirmative action**, it gives preference to women, black people, or other groups which are often treated unfairly, when it is choosing people for a job. • Compare NEGATIVE [NO].

af·firm·a·tive /£ə'fɜː·mə·tɪv, $-'fɜːr·mə·ţɪv/ *n* • *She asked the question expecting an affirmative.* [C] • *He replied* **in the** *affirmative* (= He said yes). [U] • *(esp. Am) "Were you in New York on March 3rd?" "Affirmative* (= Yes)*."*

af·firm·a·tive·ly /£ə'fɜː·mə·tɪv·li, $-'fɜːr·mə·ţɪv-/ *adv* • *She answered affirmatively.*

af·fix *obj* [FIX] /ə'fɪks/ *v* [T] *fml* to fix (one thing) to another, or to add • *She affixed a stamp* **to** *the envelope.* • *He affixed his signature* **to** *the contract.*

af·fix [WORD PART] /'æf·ɪks/ *n* [C] a letter or group of letters which are added to the beginning or end of a word to make a new word • *The affixes un- and -less are often used to make negative words, such as unhappy or careless.* • [LP] **Combining forms**

af·flict *obj* /ə'flɪkt/ *v* [T] to make (someone or something) suffer physically or mentally • *It is a disease which mainly afflicts individuals between 30 and 50 years of age.* • *He is afflicted* **with** *severe rheumatism.* • *These are a few of the problems which can afflict the elderly.*

af·flic·tion /ə'flɪk·ʃᵊn/ *n* [C] • *Malnutrition is one of the common afflictions of the poor.*

af·flu·ent /'æf·lu·ənt/ *adj* having a lot of money or possessions; rich • *an affluent person/nation/society* • *They have a relatively affluent way of life.* • *"The Affluent Society"* (title of a book by J.K.Galbraith, 1958)

af·flu·ence /'æf·lu·ənts/ *n* [U] • *Walking through the centre of the city I was struck by its air of affluence.* • *What we are seeing increasingly is a society of private affluence and public squalor.*

af·ford *obj* [BE ABLE] /£ə'fɔːd, $-'fɔːrd/ *v* [T] to have or do (something), esp. because you have enough money or time • *I don't know how he* **can** *afford a new car on his salary.* • *Few people are* **able to** *afford cars like that.* • **I can't** *afford* **to** *go out tonight.* [+ *to* infinitive] • *She* **couldn't** *afford the time off work to see him.* • *You* **can't** *afford* **to** *miss that film.* (= It is so good/important that you should see it.) [+ *to* infinitive] • *He* **can ill** *afford* **to** *fail any of his exams* (= It will cause him problems if he fails).

af·ford·a·ble /£ə'fɔː·də·bl̩, $-'fɔːr-/ *adj* • *That store sells nice clothes – and they're so/very/quite affordable* (= they are not expensive).

af·ford *obj* [GIVE] /£ə'fɔːd, $-'fɔːrd/ *v* [T] *fml* to allow someone to have (esp. something pleasant or necessary) • *The hut afforded little protection from the elements.* • *Her seat afforded her an uninterrupted view of the stage.* [+ two objects]

af·for·est *obj* /£ə'fɒr·ɪst, $-'fɔːr·əst/ *v* [T] to plant trees on (an area of land) in order to make a forest

af·for·est·a·tion /£æfˌɒr·ɪ'steɪ·ʃᵊn, $əˌfɔːr·ə-/ *n* [U]

af·fray /ə'freɪ/ *n* [C] *esp. law* a fight in a public place • *Wallace was* **charged with** *causing an affray at a Southampton nightclub.*

af·front /ə'frʌnt/ *n* [C] a remark or action intended to insult or offend someone • *She saw their rejection of her as an affront* **to** *her dignity.* • *The publication of this novel is an affront* **to** *our religion.*

af·front *obj* /ə'frʌnt/ *v* [T usually passive] • *an affronted look/glance* • *I was most affronted* **by** *his comments.* • *Maria, affronted* **at** *this implied criticism, left the room.*

af·ghan hound /'æf·gæn/ *n* [C] a tall thin dog with long silky hair and a pointed nose

a·fi·cion·a·do /£əˌfɪʃ·i·ə'nɑː·dəʊ, $-doʊ/ *n* [C] *pl* **aficionados** *fml* someone who is very interested in a particular subject; an enthusiast • *a club for model railway aficionados* • *He's an aficionado* **of** *French films/basketball.*

a·field /ə'fiːld/ *adv* **far afield** a long distance away • *We export our products to countries as far afield as Japan and Canada.* • *Our students come from Europe, Asia and even* **further** *afield.*

a·flame /ə'fleɪm/ *adj* [after v] *literary* burning, or red or golden as if burning • *The whole village was aflame.* • *It was autumn and the trees were aflame* **with** *colour.* • *Her cheeks were aflame* (= red) **with** *embarrassment/anger.* • *(fig.) Aflame* (= very excited) **with** *desire, he took her in his arms.*

a·float /£ə'fləʊt, $-'floʊt/ *adj* [after v] (partly) floating on water • *He mended the boat and it was soon afloat again.* • *She spent seven days afloat on a raft.* • *He managed to* **keep/**

stay *afloat by holding on to the side of the boat.* • *(fig.) Many small businesses are struggling to* **stay/keep** *afloat* (= to continue in business).

a•flut•ter /£ə'flʌt·əʳ, $-'flʌţ·ər/ *adj* [after v] *humorous* excited and nervous • *I'm* **all** *aflutter about meeting him after so long.* • *Paul had walked into the room and set my* **heart** *aflutter.*

a•foot /ə'fʊt/ *adj* [after v; not gradable] happening or being planned or prepared • **Something's** *afoot – the managers keep having secret meetings.* • *The children are very quiet – I think* **there's mischief/something** *afoot.*

a•fore /£ə'fɔːʳ, $-'fɔːr/ *adv* [not gradable], *prep, conjunction old use* BEFORE

a•fore•men•tioned /£ə'fɔː·men·tʃənd, $-'fɔːr-/ *adj* [not gradable], *n* **the aforementioned/the aforesaid** *fml* mentioned earlier • *The aforementioned/aforesaid Mr Highbrow then entered the cinema.* [before n] • *The aforementioned was/were seen waiting outside the building.* [C]

a•fraid FEARFUL /ə'freɪd/ *adj* [after v] feeling fear, or feeling anxiety about the possible results of a particular situation • *He was/felt suddenly afraid.* • *Knowing what he is capable of, you have every right to be afraid.* • *I've always been afraid* **of** *flying/heights/spiders.* • *She was afraid* **for** *her children* (= feared that they might be hurt). • *Don't be afraid* **to** *say what you think.* [+ *to* infinitive] • *They were afraid* **(that)** *their teacher would find out.* [+ *(that)* clause] • *She was afraid* **(that)** *he might be upset if she told him.* [+ *(that)* clause] • *The scientist was afraid* **of** *speaking out publicly for fear of losing his job.* • *"Who's afraid of the big bad wolf?"* (title of a song written by Frank E. Churchill, 1933)

a•fraid SORRY /ə'freɪd/ *adj* [after v; not gradable] (often used to introduce bad news or disagreement politely) sorry • *This is your room – it's rather small, I'm afraid.* • *I don't agree at all, I'm afraid.* • *I'm afraid you've completely misunderstood the question.* • *I'm afraid* **(that)** *we can't come this evening after all.* [+ *(that)* clause] • *"Did you write the report?" "I'm sorry, I'm afraid I didn't."* • *"Was she impressed with our work?" "I'm afraid not* (= No)*."* • *"Does this mean I've got to leave?" "I'm afraid so* (= Yes)*."*

a•fresh /ə'freʃ/ *adv* [not gradable] again, esp. starting from the beginning • *She tore up the letter and* **started** *afresh.* • *We agreed to* **look** *afresh at her original proposal.*

Af•ri•can /'æf·rɪ·kən/ *adj, n* [C] (a person) of or from Africa • An **african violet** is a small plant with purple, pink or white flowers which is grown in a container in a house. • LP **World regions**

Af•ri•kaans /£ˌæf·rɪ'kɑːns, $ˌɑː·frɪ'-/ *n* [U] a language which is related to Dutch and is spoken in South Africa • LP **Nations and nationalities**

Af•ri•kan•er /£ˌæf·rɪ'kɑː·nəʳ, $ˌɑː·frɪ'kɑː·nər/ *n* [C] • An Afrikaner is a South African person whose family were originally Dutch and whose first language is Afrikaans.

Af•ro HAIR /'æf·rəʊ, -roʊ/ *n* [C] *pl* **Afros** a way of arranging the hair so that it is very thick, curly and rounded, esp. like that of some black people • *I asked the hairdresser for an Afro.* • *an Afro comb/haircut/hairstyle*

Af•ro– CONTINENT /ˌæf·rəʊ-, ˌæf·roʊ-/ *combining form* of or connected with Africa • *Afro-Caribbean culture* • *Afro-American literature*

aft /£ɑːft, $æft/ *adj, adv* [not gradable] *specialized* in or towards the back part of a boat • *The large saloon opens on to the aft deck.* • *Graham sat aft, looking steadily out to the horizon.* • *Missiles were sited* **fore and** *aft* (= at the front and at the back) *on the ship.* • **Fore and** aft is sometimes used in non-boating situations to mean at both ends or sides: *Most of the work has gone into the auditorium, while only minor improvements have been possible fore and aft.* • *The paper was under his arm, sticking out fore and aft.*

af•ter /£'ɑːf·təʳ, $'æf·tər/ *prep, conjunction* following in time, place or order • *Shall we go for a walk after breakfast?* • *Some people believe in* **life** *after* **death**. • *Her name came after mine on the list.* • *There's a good film on the day after tomorrow.* • *She waited until* **well** *after midnight.* • *(Am) It's a quarter after (Br and Aus, Am also* **past***) four.* • *She just keeps on working,* **day** *after* **day**, **week** *after* **week** (= continuously), *without stopping.* • *We've had meeting after meeting* (= many meetings) *to discuss this point.* • *Jessie seemed very small after* (= in comparison with) *Michael's children.* • *After* (= Despite) *everything I've done for you, is this the way you treat me?* • *After* (= Because of) *what she did to me, I'll never trust her again.* • *The children have to learn to tidy up after them***selves** (= after they have made things untidy). • *She was asking/inquiring after* (= about) *you/your health.* • *She remembered as a child trailing after* (= behind) *her older brothers, wanting to join in their games.* • *She slammed the door after* (= behind) *her.* • *We ran after* (= followed) *him, but he escaped.* • *"And you needn't come back!" he shouted after her as she went away.* • *Could you lock up after you* (= when you leave)*, please?* • *She's named after* (= has the same name as) *her aunt.* • *(infml)* If you are after someone or something, you are looking for or trying to find them: *He's in hiding, but the police are after him.* ○ *I'm after a tie to go with this shirt.* ○ *He's after* (= wants for himself) *Jane's job.* ○ *I'm sure she's after my husband.* • After also means typical of or similar to the style of: *a painting after Titian* ○ *a concerto after Mozart* • *The rain has stopped, so the game will go ahead* **after all** (= despite problems or doubts). • *"Of course I admire her –* **after all** (= the fact is)*, she is a great politician."* • **After you** (= Please go in front of me or serve yourself with food before me), *Miss Taylor.* • **After you with** *the newspaper, Jack.* (= Please give it to me when you have finished with it.) • **After effects** are (usually bad) effects that follows an event, accident, etc., sometimes continuing for a long time or happening some time after it: **The** *after effects* **of** *the bomb are still being* **felt** *in Hiroshima.* ○ *Consumers are still* **feeling the** *after effects* **of** *the new sales tax.* ○ *He is not* **suffering from** *any bad after effects.* • LP **Time**

af•ter /£'ɑːf·təʳ, $'æf·tər/ *conjunction* • *The house was empty for three months after they moved out.* • **Soon/shortly** *after we joined the motorway, the car started to make a strange noise.* • *I went to the post office* **straight/immediately** *after I left you.*

af•ter /£'ɑːf·təʳ, $'æf·tər/ *adv* [not gradable] • *Hilary drove up and Nicholas arrived* **soon** *after.* • *I can't go next week – how about the week after* (= the following week)*?* • *(not standard) She got back at 4.30 and went to see Emilie after* (= afterwards).

af•ter /£'ɑːf·təʳ, $'æf·tər/ *adj* [not gradable] *literary* • *Miss Wilson became increasingly frail* **in** *after* **years** (= as she grew old).

af•ter– /£'ɑːf·tə-, $'æf·tər-/ *combining form* • *an after-dinner speech* • *an after-hours club* • *after-sales service*

af•ter•birth /£'ɑːf·tə·bɜːθ, $'æf·tər·bɜːrθ/ *n* [U] the material, including the PLACENTA, which is pushed out of a woman's or female animal's body soon after she has given birth

af•ter•care /£'ɑːf·tə·keəʳ, $'æf·tər·ker/ *n* [U] the care of people after they have left a hospital, prison, etc. • *A network of community services for aftercare and rehabilitation is being planned.* • *If she survives the operation, she will need expensive aftercare.* • *He was in hospital for a year before moving on to a psychiatric aftercare hostel.*

af•ter•glow /£'ɑːf·tə·gləʊ, $'æf·tər·gloʊ/ *n* [U] a pleasant feeling produced after an experience, event, feeling, etc. • *The team were* **basking in the** *afterglow* **of** *winning the cup.*

af•ter•life /£'ɑːf·tə·laɪf, $'æf·tər-/ *n* [U] the life, for example in heaven, which some people believe begins after death • *Humanists do not believe in an afterlife or immortality.* • *They'll be reunited in* **the** *afterlife.*

af•ter•math /£'ɑːf·tə·mæθ, £-mɑːθ, $'æf·tər-/ *n* [U] the period which follows an event, accident, etc., and the effects which it causes • *Many more people died* **in the** *aftermath* **of** *the explosion.* • *Large numbers of businesses went bankrupt* **in the** *aftermath* **of** *the recession.*

af•ter•noon /£ˌɑːf·tə'nuːn, £'---, $ˌæf·tər-/ *n* the period which starts at about twelve o'clock or after the meal in the middle of the day and ends at about six o'clock or when the sun goes down • *It was a sunny afternoon.* [C] • *She works three afternoons a week at the library.* [C] • *He works six days with just Saturday afternoons off.* [C] • *I can't see you today but we could make an appointment for one afternoon next week.* [C] • *My baby usually sleeps* **in the** *afternoons.* [C] • *Let's go to the park* **this** *afternoon.* [U] • *I spoke to her* **yesterday** *afternoon.* [U] • *I'll meet you* **tomorrow** *afternoon at about 3.30.* [U] • *Rachel's playing in a netball match* **on** *Wednesday afternoon.* [U] • *He's been in a bad mood* **all** *afternoon.* [U] • *I often go for a swim* **in the** *afternoon and then go back to the office and work late.* [U] • *She likes to have an afternoon nap.* • *We got an early-/mid-/late-afternoon flight.* • LP **Time**

afternoons *adv* [not gradable] *esp. Am* • *He plays tennis afternoons* (= every afternoon or on many afternoons).

af·ters /£'ɑːf·təz, $'æf·tɚz/ *n* [U] *Br infml* sweet food eaten at the end of a meal • *What's* **for** *afters, Dad?* • *Afters was trifle – it was scrummy.*

af·ter·shave /£'ɑːf·tə·ʃeɪv, $'æf·tɚ-/ *n* [U] a liquid with a pleasant smell which can be used on the face after SHAVING (= removing hair)

af·ter·shock /£'ɑːf·tə·ʃɒk, $'æf·tɚ·ʃɑːk/ *n* [C] a sudden movement of the Earth's surface which often follows an EARTHQUAKE and which is less violent than the first main movement • *The initial earthquake was followed by* **a series of** *aftershocks, which brought more destruction to an already devastated area.* • *(fig.) The aftershocks from the collapse of such a big company were still being* **felt** *weeks later on the New York stock exchange.*

af·ter·taste /£'ɑːf·tə·teɪst, $'æf·tɚ-/ *n* [C usually sing] the taste that a particular food or other substance leaves in your mouth when you have swallowed it • *The medicine left an unpleasant aftertaste.* • *(fig.) The trial, the judgment and the whole bitter aftertaste of the affair were more than she could stand.*

af·ter·thought /£'ɑːf·tə·θɔːt, $'æf·tɚ·θɑːt/ *n* [C usually sing] an idea, thought, plan, etc. which was not originally intended but is thought of at a later time • *She only asked me to her party* **as an** *afterthought.* • *Finally,* **almost** *as an afterthought, he made a plea for calm and restraint on the streets.* • *The pillars seem to have been* **added** *to the entrance* **as an** *afterthought.* • Ⓓ Ⓢ

af·ter·wards /£'ɑːf·tə·wədz, $'æf·tɚ·wɚdz/, *Am also* **af·ter·ward** /£'ɑːf·tə·wəd, $'æf·tɚ·wɚd/ *adv* [not gradable] after the time mentioned; later • *We had tea, and afterwards we sat in the garden for a while.* • *They separated, and* **soon/shortly** *afterwards Jane left the country.*

A·ga (cook·er) /'ɑː·gə/ *n* [C] *Br trademark* a large iron cooker which keeps its heat • *Agas used to burn coal but now they use oil, gas or electricity.* • *Our kitchen is much warmer since we had the Aga installed because it works all day and night.* • *Agas can also be used to heat water for use in the home.*

a·gain /ə'gen/ *adv* [not gradable] once more, or back to the original state or condition • *Could you spell your name again please?* • *If you do that again I'll smack you!* • *Deborah's late again.* • *We went to Edinburgh and* **back** *again all in one day.* • *You are reminded* **once** *again of the author's love of the sea.* • **"Never again!"** *I gasped as I got off the big dipper.* • *I think you'd better rub that out and* **start** *again.* • *I'm afraid it's been delayed* **yet** *again.* • *I've told you* **again and again** (= many times) *not to do that.* • *It's already taken me two hours – I don't want to have to do it* **(all) over again**. • You can say **then again** or **there again** when you have had a new thought that is different or opposite to what you have just said: *I'd like to travel more but, then again, staying at home does save money.*

a·gainst IN OPPOSITION /ə'gentst/ *prep* in opposition to • *She spoke against the decision to close the college.* • *Fifty people voted against the new proposal.* • *I'm very much against the idea that it is the woman's job to bring up the child.* • *The Lions are playing against Italy in the football cup finals tonight.* • *She's always rebelled against authority.* • *She sold the house even though it was against his wishes.* • *It's not that I'm prejudiced against older people, but I do think younger people should get better opportunities at work.* • *Miss Perrett argued that this policy discriminated against women.* • *They called a demonstration to protest against proposed job cuts.* • *Sanctions against the country should be lifted.* • *Stricter controls will help in the fight against inflation.* • *Criminal charges will be* **brought** *against the driver.* • *They decided not to take legal action against him.* • *They were* **up** *against a powerful pressure group.* • *We* **came** *up against a lot of problems in the course of building our extension.* • *The* **chances/odds** *against you winning such a competition are enormous.* • *It's against* **the law** (= illegal) *to leave children under a certain age alone in the house.* • *It's against my* **beliefs/principles** *to be nice to someone I dislike just because they're in a senior position.* • *Against* **all probability** (= although it was extremely unlikely) *we found ourselves in the same hotel as some people we used to know.* • *I wouldn't dare say anything against him* (= criticize him) *to his mother!* • To go against something means to go in the opposite direction to it: *The last part of the course was hard because I was running against the wind.* ○ *Commuting is not so bad when you are travelling against the traffic.* ○ *It was not an easy fight as they were going against the tide of public opinion.* • If you **have** something **against** someone you dislike them for some reason: *I've* **nothing** *against him – he's always been very pleasant to me – I just don't have much in common with him.* • If something is **against** your **better judgment** you think it would be wiser not to do it: *Persuaded by the others, but rather against his better judgment, he gave John the job.* • If you **come/find** yourself **up against a brick wall** you are unable to get any further with a plan, argument etc. because something is stopping you: *In its campaign to prevent the building, the department found itself up against a brick wall.* • *(infml)* If you are **up against it** you are having or are likely to have serious problems or difficulties: *With seven members of their own team missing, Hull are going to be up against it.* ○ *Many families are up against it, unable to afford even basic items.* • If something **counts/goes/works against** you it causes disadvantage to you: *Lack of experience will generally count against you in an interview.* • If you do something **against time/the clock** you do it as fast as possible and try to finish it before a certain time *We've been working against the clock to get the house decorated before the baby is born.* ○ *It was a real race against time to get all the costumes sewn for the play.* • LP **Opposites**

a·gainst /ə'gentst/ *adv* [not gradable] • *Are you* **for or** *against my proposal?* • *There was a majority of 173 with only 14 voting against.*

a·gainst TOUCHING /ə'gentst/ *prep* next to and touching or being supported by (something) • *It would save space if we put the bed against the wall.* • *I accidentally brushed against the wall which had just been painted.* • *He loved the feel of her soft hair against his skin.* • *The rain beat against her face as she struggled through the wind.* • *It sounded as if something was banging against the roof.* • *The police officer had him up against the wall, both arms behind his back.* • *She leant wearily against the door.*

a·gainst PROTECTION /ə'gentst/ *prep* as a protection or defence from the bad effects of • *We've insured the car against fire, theft and accident.* • *We were vaccinated against five different illnesses before we went to Egypt.* • *The police have to arm themselves against attack.*

a·gainst BACKGROUND /ə'gentst/ · *prep* with the background of or compared to • *Her pale skin looked ghostly white against the blackness of her hair.* • *Paintings look good against a simple white wall.* • *He earns $80000 a year* **as against** (= compared to) *my $40000.*

a·gape /ə'geɪp/ *adj* [after v], *adv* with the mouth open, esp. showing surprise • *The children watched, their eyes wide and their mouths agape, as the magician took a rabbit out of his hat.* • *The girls were agape* **with** *excitement.* • *The crowd stared agape as he climbed to the top of the building.*

ag·ate /'æg·ət/ *n* [C; U] a hard stone with strips of colour used in jewellery

age TIME SPENT ALIVE /eɪdʒ/ *n* the period of time someone has been alive or something has existed • *He never lets anyone know his real age.* [C] • *Do you know the age of that building?* [C] • *What age* (= how old) **is** *your brother?* [C] • *He's about your age.* [C] • *He's about the same age as you.* [C] • *She was 74* **years of** *age when she wrote her first novel.* [U] • *He left home* **at the** *age* **of** *16.* [C] • *I was married with four children* **at** *your age* **(when** *I* **was** *your age).* [C] • *You should know better* **at** *your age.* [C] • *Oh* **be/act** *your age* (= behave in a way suitable for someone as old as you)! [C] • *She's starting to* **show/look** *her age* (= to look as old as she is). [C] • *I'm really beginning to* **feel** *my age* (= feel old). [C] • *His girlfriend's twice his age* (= twice as old as he is). [C] • *Her skin was loose and wrinkled* **with** (= because of) *age.* [U] • *This cheese/wine improves* **with** *age* (= as it gets older). [U] • *Her temper doesn't improved with age!* [U] • *"What's the age* **limit**?" *"You have to be over 16."* • *He was prosecuted for having sex with a girl who was* **under** *age* (= younger than the age at which it is legal to have sex). [U] • *The clothes are being marketed for people in the over-50 age* **group** (= all the people who are over 50) • *The programmes are aimed at viewers in the 18-30 age* **range**. • *51% of enquiries were from those in the 25 to 40 age* **bracket**. • To **come/be of age** means to reach or be the age when you are legally recognized as an adult and become old enough to vote. • If something has **come of age**, it has reached its full successful development: *On the basis of this exhibition, her art can be said to have finally come of age.* • If something is **age-related**, it happens mostly to people of a certain age: *The disease is known to be strongly age-related.* • **Under-age drinkers** are people who are too young to drink alcohol in public places (younger than 18 in Britain and Australia)

DESCRIBING HUMAN AGE

Some words refer to periods in a human life, or to people at a particular age. It is often impossible to give exact limits for these words, for example to say at what age someone becomes 'middle aged'. The table below gives some *approximate* guidance.

		0	2	5	13	18	35	65	
	BIRTH	INFANCY	CHILDHOOD	YOUTH		ADULTHOOD	MIDDLE AGE	OLD AGE	DEATH
formal	(*Br*)foetus/ (*Am*)fetus	(newborn) infant	infant		young person young adult				the deceased the departed (*pl n*)
usual	unborn child unborn baby	(newborn) baby	toddler tot	child boy girl	youngster teenager adolescent young man/ woman	adult; man; woman		pensioner (*Br*)OAP (*Am*)retiree	corpse (= body) dead man/ woman
informal				kid lad (male)		guy; fella/fellow; (*Br*)bloke (these are all words for men)			
adjective forms		infant baby infantile*		juvenile* childish*	teenage adolescent*	adult	middle -aged	old; elderly retired (= not working)	dead (*fml*)deceased

*These words are often used in a disapproving way: *My father can be really* **childish** *if he doesn't get what he wants.* • *Don't be so* **adolescent**.

- A human being of any age can be called a person: *She was the first person to arrive.* The usual plural is 'people', and 'persons' is more formal: *20 000* **people** *came to the concert.* • *Many seriously ill* **persons** *require 24-hour care.*
- The word 'grown-up' is used esp. by children to refer to adults: *We were at the front and the* **grown-ups** *were at the back* • *Many* **grown-ups** *enjoy children's films.*
- Some people informally refer to women as 'ladies' and young women as 'girls', but this may be considered offensive.

For more expressions that describe someone's age, such as *in his 30s*, LP **Approximate numbers**

and do so illegally. • The **age of consent** is the age at which someone is considered by the law to be old enough to agree to have sex with someone. • *"Age cannot wither her, nor custom stale / Her infinite variety"* (Shakespeare, Antony and Cleopatra 2.2) • LP **Age, Measurements**

age *(obj)* /eɪdʒ/ *v* **ageing** or *Am and Aus usually* **aging** • *She's aged* (= She looks older) *since the last time we met.* [I] • *The brandy is aged* (= left to develop) *in oak for ten years.* [T usually passive]

ag·ed /ˈeɪ·dʒɪd/ *adj* • *an aged* (= old) *man* • *She has two rather aged aunts.* • *They've got one daughter, Isabel, aged 3* (= 3 years old). [before n]

ag·ed /ˈeɪ·dʒɪd/ *pl n* • *The hospital was built to meet the needs of* **the aged** (= old people).

age·ing, *Am and Aus usually* **ag·ing** /ˈeɪ·dʒɪŋ/ *adj* • *an ageing Hollywood actor* • *aging computers/machinery*

age·less /ˈeɪdʒ·ləs/ *adj* • Something which is ageless never seems to get or look older: *ageless youth/beauty* ○ *the ageless cathedral*

age PERIOD /eɪdʒ/ *n* [C] a particular period in time • *the Victorian age* • *the modern age* • *the nuclear age* • *It's an* **age-old** (= very old) *story of love and betrayal.* • LP **Periods of time**

-age ACTION /-ɪdʒ/ *combining form* used to form nouns which refer to the action or result of something • *blockage/shrinkage/wastage/wreckage* • *All breakages must be paid for.* • *The spillage from the oil tanker was a disaster for seabirds.* • LP **Combining forms, Stress in pronunciation**

-age STATE /-ɪdʒ/ *combining form* used to form nouns which refer to a state or condition • *bondage* • *a peerage* • *a shortage* • *They have a happy marriage.* • *It is not always possible to discover the true parentage* (= who the real parents are) *of an adopted child.*

-age PLACE /-ɪdʒ/ *combining form* used to form nouns which are names of places • *hermitage/orphanage/vicarage*

age·i·sm, *Am and Aus usually* **ag·i·sm** /ˈeɪ·dʒɪ·zᵊm/ *n* [U] treating people unfairly because of their age • *They didn't even consider her for the job because she was 46 – it was a typical case of ageism.*

age·ist, *Am and Aus usually* **ag·ist** /ˈeɪ·dʒɪst/ *adj* • *an ageist remark/job advertisement*

a·gen·da /əˈdʒen·də/ *n* [C] a list of matters to be discussed at a meeting • *There were several important items/points* **on** *the agenda.* • *The question of security* **high on** *the agenda for this afternoon's meeting.* • The agenda is also the matters which are waiting to be discussed or achieved: *Women's rights have been put back* **on** *the agenda* (= are being discussed publicly again). ○ *That's been* **on** *my agenda for three weeks and I still haven't done it.* ○ *The subject of safety must be placed* **high on/at the top of** *the agenda* (= must be discussed because it is very important). • *Education was placed firmly on the* **political** *agenda in the Prime Minister's week-end speech.* • *The opposition has* **set** *the election agenda* (= decided the subjects to be discussed). • *He stressed that the review was intended to identify staffing needs and there was no* **hidden** *agenda* (= secret plan) **to** *cut back on jobs.* [+ *to* infinitive] • (F) (GR) (NL)

a·gent REPRESENTATIVE /ˈeɪ·dʒᵊnt/ *n* [C] a person who acts for or represents another • *Please contact our agent in Spain for further information.* • *She's my agent* (= person representing an actor, artist, writer, etc.). • An agent is also someone who works secretly for the government or other organization: *an enemy/secret/undercover agent* • (T)

a·gen·cy /ˈeɪ·dʒᵊnt·si/ *n* [C] • An agency is a business which represents one group of people in dealing with another group: *an advertising/employment/estate/travel agency* • An agency is also a government organization: *an overseas-aid agency* • *the Central Intelligence Agency* • See also **agency** at AGENT CAUSE.

a·gent CAUSE /ˈeɪ·dʒᵊnt/ *n* [C] a person or thing that produces a particular effect or change • *a powerful cleaning agent* • *a raising agent for cakes* • *a clotting agent* • *(literary) He was the agent* **of their destruction.**

a·gen·cy /ˈeɪ·dʒᵊnt·si/ *n fml or literary* • *Sand dunes are formed* **by/through the** *agency* **of** *the wind* (=the wind formed them). • *She was freed from prison* **by/through the** *agency* **of** *her doctor* (=her doctor worked to free her). • See also **agency** at AGENT [REPRESENTATIVE].

a·gent prov·o·cat·eur /£ˌæʒ·ɑ̃ː·prəˌvɒk·əˈtɜːʳ, $ˌɑːʒ·ɑ̃ː·proʊˌvɑː·kəˈtɜːr/ *n* [C] *pl* **agents provocateurs** /£ˌæʒ·ɑ̃ː·prəˌvɒk·əˈtɜːʳ, $ˌɑːʒ·ɑ̃ː·proʊˌvɑː·kəˈtɜːr/ a person who is employed by the government, police, etc., to encourage people thought to be criminals or people who are working against the government to perform an illegal act so that they can be caught • *The leader of the riot was later discovered to have been an agent provocateur planted by the police.*

ag·glom·er·a·tion /£əˌglɒm·əˈreɪ·ʃᵊn, $-ˌglɑː·mə-/, **ag·glom·er·ate** /£əˈglɒm·ə·rət, $-ˈglɑː·mɚ·ət/ *n* [C] a large group of many (different) things gathered together • *a new agglomeration of five electronics companies* • *agglomerates of atoms* • *The country is an agglomeration of different ethnic and religious groupings.*

ag·grand·ize·ment, *Br and Aus usually* **–ise·ment** /əˈgræn·dɪz·mənt/ *n* [U] *esp. disapproving* increase in power, importance or wealth • *These foreign governments say they're concerned for human rights in our country, but territorial aggrandizement is their real aim.* • *He gives a lot of money to charity, but* **personal** *aggrandizement/* **self-***aggrandizement is his only motive.*

ag·gra·vate *obj* [MAKE WORSE] /ˈæg·rə·veɪt/ *v* [T] to make (esp. a bad situation or a disease) worse • *The situation will be aggravated if soldiers are brought into the city.* • *Attempts to restrict parking in the city centre have further aggravated the problem of traffic congestion.* • *In this case, the treatment only aggravated the injury/disease/ condition.* • *(Br law) He was found guilty of* **aggravated burglary** (=using a weapon while stealing). • *(law)* **Aggravated assault** is a serious type of violent attack on someone. There are different forms of aggravated assault.

ag·gra·vate *obj* [ANNOY] /ˈæg·rə·veɪt/ *v* [T] *infml* to annoy (someone) • *Men aggravate me when they go on about how impractical women are.* • *I was very aggravated by what she said.* • **It's** *extremely aggravating* **that** *I've got to work this weekend, so I can't go to the football match.* [+ *that* clause] • Some people do not consider this use of aggravate to be correct.

ag·gra·vat·ing /£ˈæg·rə·veɪ·tɪŋ, $-t̬ɪŋ/ *adj infml* • *We have extremely aggravating neighbours.* • **It** *was very aggravating* **to** *have to wait so long for the train.* [+ *to* infinitive]

ag·gra·va·tion /ˌæg·rəˈveɪ·ʃᵊn/ *n* [U] *infml* • *My sons are always in trouble and they're nothing but aggravation to me.* • Aggravation (also *Br and Aus slang* **aggro**) can also be used to mean trouble or difficulty: *I've been getting a lot of aggravation at work recently.* ○ *I was going to complain that my steak wasn't cooked properly, but I decided that it wasn't worth the aggravation.*

ag·gre·gate /ˈæg·rɪ·gət/ *n, adj* [not gradable] (something) formed by adding together several amounts or things; (a) total • *They purchased an aggregate* **of** *3000 shares in the company.* [C] • *Snowflakes are loose aggregates* **of** *ice crystals.* [C] • *Arsenal won only two of the three games, but got through to the final* **on** *aggregate* (=adding together all their goals). [U] • *The seven companies have an aggregate turnover of £5·2 million.* [before n]

ag·gre·gate *obj* /ˈæg·rɪ·geɪt/ *v* [T] • *I have aggregated* (=added together) *all the figures, and the grand total is 5 million.*

ag·gre·ga·tion /ˌæg·rɪˈgeɪ·ʃᵊn/ *n* [U] • *The aggregation* **of** *these twelve companies* **into** *a single multinational organization will mean big profits for some and unemployment for others.*

ag·gres·sion /əˈgreʃ·ᵊn/ *n* [U] spoken or physical behaviour which is threatening or involving harm to someone or something • *The hostages were rescued by special police trained in speed and aggression.* • *Some types of dog are bred for aggression.* • *The invading army has been accused of using* **naked** *aggression* **against** *a small and defenceless country.* • *We regard the presence of troops on our borders as an* **act of** *aggression.* • *She said that she had been a victim of male aggression* (=threatening behaviour). • *He seems to have a lot of aggression* (=the feeling of wanting to attack) **towards** *his parents.* • Aggression can also be used to refer to a type of playing in sports that is forceful and directed towards scoring points: *Their victory in the match was the result of a mixture of caution and aggression.*

ag·gres·sive /əˈgres·ɪv/ *adj* • *Some dogs are naturally aggressive.* • *If I criticize him he gets all aggressive and starts shouting.* • Aggressive can also mean being determined to win or succeed and using strong methods to achieve victory or success: *His victory was largely a result of his aggressive election campaign.* ○ *Thanks to our aggressive marketing tactics, our sales have risen sharply this year.* ○ *The two British players both won their first-round matches in aggressive style.*

ag·gres·sive·ly /əˈgres·ɪv·li/ *adv* • *The dog growled aggressively.* • *Small children often behave aggressively.* • *The company is aggressively* (=determinedly) *pursuing new business opportunities.* • *We have a good, skilful team, but we lost the match because we did not play aggressively* (=forcefully) *enough.*

ag·gres·sor /£əˈgres·əʳ, $-ɚ/ *n* [C] • An aggressor is a person, group or country who starts an argument, fight or war by attacking first: *In the conflict with Egypt in 1956, it was Britain who was seen as the aggressor by the international community.*

ag·grieved /əˈgriːvd/ *adj* unhappy, hurt and angry because of unfair treatment • *He felt aggrieved* **at** *not being chosen for the team.* • *She was understandably aggrieved* **that** *everyone else was given a pay increase and she wasn't.* [+ *that* clause] • *An aggrieved customer wrote to complain that he still hadn't received the book he had ordered several weeks ago.*

ag·gro /£ˈæg·rəʊ, $-roʊ/ *n* [U] *Br and Aus slang* violent or threatening behaviour, esp. between groups of young people • *There was some aggro between rival football fans at the station.* • Aggro (also **aggravation**) can also be used to mean trouble or difficulty: *She said that she was finding it hard to cope with the general aggro of life.* ○ *Why are you being so uncooperative? I don't need this aggro.*

a·ghast /£əˈgɑːst, $-ˈgæst/ *adj* [after v] suddenly filled with strong feelings of shock and anxiety or fear • *He looked at her aghast.* • *She was aghast* **at** *the extent of the damage to her car.* • *I was aghast* **to** *discover how much the repairs would cost.* [+ *to* infinitive]

ag·ile /£ˈædʒ·aɪl, $-ᵊl/ *adj* able to move about quickly and easily; NIMBLE • *My grandmother isn't as agile as she used to be.* • *Monkeys are very agile climbers.* • *You need to have agile fingers to do this kind of work.* • *The playing of the orchestra was neat and agile.* • *(fig.) For a man of 80, he has a remarkably agile mind* (=he thinks quickly and clearly). • *(fig.) She has shown herself to be a very agile politician* (=one who thinks and acts quickly and clearly).

a·gil·i·ty /£əˈdʒɪl·ɪ·ti, $-ə·t̬i/ *n* [U] • *He's got the agility of a mountain goat.* • *(fig.) This job requires considerable mental agility* (=the ability to think quickly and clearly).

a·gin /əˈgɪn/ *prep regional or infml* against • *Well, there's my suggestion! Are you for or agin it?*

ag·ing *esp. Am and Aus* /ˈeɪ·dʒɪŋ/ *present participle of* AGE [TIME SPENT ALIVE]

ag·i·sm /ˈeɪ·dʒɪ·zᵊm/ *n* [U] *esp. Am and Aus for* AGEISM

ag·i·tate [ARGUE] /ˈædʒ·ɪ·teɪt/ *v* [I] to argue energetically, esp. in public, in order to achieve a particular type of change • *The unions are agitating* **for** *higher pay.* • *As a young man, he had agitated* **against** *the Vietnam war.* • (KOR) (RUS)

ag·i·ta·tion /ˌædʒ·ɪˈteɪ·ʃᵊn/ *n* [U] • *The anti-war agitation is beginning to worry the government.* • *In 1920, women in America got the vote, after 72 years of agitation.*

ag·i·tat·or /£ˈædʒ·ɪ·teɪ·təʳ, $-t̬ɚ/ *n* [C] • *It is thought that the strike was the work of undercover political agitators.*

ag·i·tate *obj* [MAKE ANXIOUS] /ˈædʒ·ɪ·teɪt/ *v* [T] to make (someone) feel anxious and not calm • *The news will only agitate him – let's wait till tomorrow to tell him.* • (KOR) (RUS)

ag·i·tat·ed /£ˈædʒ·ɪ·teɪ·tɪd, $-t̬ɪd/ *adj* • *There's an agitated man on the phone insisting that a bomb is about to go off.* • *She became very agitated when her son failed to return home.*

ag·i·tat·ed·ly /£ˈædʒ·ɪ·teɪ·tɪd·li, $-t̬ɪd-/ *adv* • *"Come on! Come on! We'll be late," she said agitatedly.*

ag·i·ta·tion /ˌædʒ·ɪˈteɪ·ʃᵊn/ *n* [U] • *I paced up and down to conceal my agitation.* • *In her agitation as she was paying, she forgot to sign the cheque.* • *He arrived home in a* **state of** *agitation.*

ag·i·tate *obj* [SHAKE] /ˈædʒ·ɪ·teɪt/ *v* [T] to shake (a liquid) • *Pour the powder into the solution and agitate it until the powder has dissolved.* • (KOR) (RUS)

ag·it·prop /£'ædʒ·ɪt·prɒp, $-prɑːp/ *n* [U] (the spreading of) strongly political ideas or arguments expressed esp. through plays, art, books, etc. • *He stressed that his book was not intended as propaganda, but parts of it certainly seem like agitprop.* • *Agitprop plays are designed to persuade, not to entertain.*

a·glow /£ə'gləʊ, $-'gloʊ/ *adj* [after v] *literary* bright; shining with light and colour • *A fire was aglow in the hearth.* • *The city at night was aglow* **with** *lights.* • *His face was* **all** *aglow* **with** *health/excitement/triumph.*

AGM /ˌeɪ·dʒiː'em/ *n* [C] *abbreviation for* **annual general meeting**, see at ANNUAL

ag·no·sia /£ˌæg'nəʊ·zi·ə, $-'noʊ-/ *n* [U] an inability to recognize objects, caused by damage to the brain • *She has* **visual** *agnosia, but she can recognize objects if she touches them.*

ag·nos·tic /£æg'nɒs·tɪk, $-'nɑː·stɪk/ *n, adj* (someone) not knowing, or believing that it is impossible to know, whether a god exists • *Although he was born a Catholic, he was an agnostic for most of his adult life.* [C] • *Her agnostic parents completely failed to understand the depth of her religious beliefs.* • Agnostic can also mean not knowing whether something is true or right: *I'm agnostic* **about** *whether there really is a hell.* ○ *She said that she was agnostic* **about/on** *the government's education policy.* • Compare ATHEIST.

ag·nos·ti·ci·sm /£æg'nɒs·tɪ·sɪ·zᵊm, $-'nɑː·stə-/ *n* [U]

a·go /£ə'gəʊ, $-'goʊ/ *adv* [after n or adv; not gradable] back in the past; back in time from the present • *The dinosaurs died out 65 million years ago.* • *He left the house a year/an hour/just a minute ago.* • **Long** *ago*/**A long time** *ago, there lived a girl called Cinderella.*

a·gog /£ə'gɒg, $-'gɑːg/ *adj* [after v] excited; eager (to know or see more) • *We waited agog for news.* • *The audience was agog* **with** *expectation/excitement/curiosity.* • *She was* **all** *agog* **to** *hear what had happened.* [+ *to* infinitive]

ag·o·ny /'æg·ə·ni/ *n* (a state or feeling of) extreme physical or mental pain or suffering • *The people who had been injured in the bomb explosion lay screaming* **in** *agony.* [U] • *By not making a decision about what to do, we're just prolonging the agony.* [U] • *I was* **in** *an agony* **of** *doubt/indecision/suspense.* [C] • *We've both* **suffered** *agonies* **of** *guilt at what has happened.* [C] • An *(Br)* **agony aunt** (*Am* **advice columnist**) is a person, usually a woman, who publicly gives advice to people with personal problems, esp. in a regular magazine or newspaper article. A man who does this is sometimes called an **agony uncle**. • An *(Br)* **agony column** (*Am* **advice column**) is the part of a magazine or newspaper where letters from readers about their personal problems are printed, together with advice about how to deal with them. • *"The Agony and the Ecstasy"* (title of a novel by Irving Stone, 1961) • LP **Feelings and pains**

ag·o·nize, *Br and Aus usually* **–ise** /'æg·ə·naɪz/ *v* [I] • If you agonize **over/about** something, you spend time anxiously trying to make a decision about it: *She agonized for days about whether she should take the job.*

ag·o·nized, *Br and Aus usually* **–ised** /'æg·ə·naɪzd/ *adj* • *We heard an agonized* (= showing extreme physical pain) *cry.* • *She gave him an agonized* (= extremely anxious) *look.*

ag·o·niz·ing, *Br and Aus usually* **–is·ing** /'æg·ə·naɪ·zɪŋ/ *adj* • *The sudden pain above his heart was agonizing* (= extremely painful). • *They died an agonizing death.* • Agonizing can also mean causing extreme anxiety: *She went through an agonizing few weeks waiting for the results of the medical tests.* ○ *We are faced with an agonizing choice/decision/dilemma.*

ag·o·ra·pho·bi·a /£ˌæg·rə'fəʊ·bi·ə, $-'foʊ-/ *n* [U] *specialized* fear of open spaces, going outside, or distance from a place of safety • *My uncle* **suffers from** *agoraphobia, and when he goes out he finds it difficult to breathe.* • Compare CLAUSTROPHOBIA.

ag·o·ra·pho·bic /£ˌæg·rə'fəʊ·bɪk, $-'foʊ-/ *n* [C] • An agoraphobic is a person who suffers from agoraphobia.

ag·o·ra·pho·bic /£ˌæg·rə'fəʊ·bɪk, $-'foʊ-/ *adj* • *She said that the reason she doesn't go out much is because she's agoraphobic.*

a·grar·i·an /£ə'greə·ri·ən, $-'grer·i-/ *adj* related to the land, esp. farms, and its ownership, or (of a country) dependent on farming rather than industry • *This is prime agrarian land.* • *Agrarian production in the region has increased in recent years.* • *This part of the country is mainly agrarian* (= dependent on farming).

a·gree *(obj)* /ə'griː/ *v* to have the same opinion, or to accept (a suggestion or idea) • *I know what you think we should do, but I'm afraid I don't agree.* [I] • *Ann and I never seem to agree.* [I] • *I agree* **about** *Claire – she's not the right person for this job.* [I] • If you agree **with** an idea, action or organization, you approve of it: *I agree with letting children learn at their own pace.* [I] • *My father and I don't agree* **on** *very much.* [I] • *I agree whole-heartedly* **with** *Paul.* [I] • *All the members of the jury agree* **that** *Mr Thomas is guilty.* [+ *that* clause] • *Experts seem unable to agree* **whether** *the drug is safe or not.* [+ *wh*-word] • *"You're absolutely right," agreed George.* [+ clause] • *I suggested that we should meet, and they agreed* (= said yes). [I] • *The bank has agreed* (= is willing) **to** *lend me £5000 to buy a new car.* [+ *to* infinitive] • *(Br)* To agree something is to accept it: *We finally agreed a deal.* [T] • To agree **to** something is to agree it: *Both sides in the conflict have agreed to the terms of the peace treaty.* [I] • *We must stick to our agreed policy/price/story* (= the one that we have all accepted). [T] • *"So we'll meet at 5.30, shall we?" "Agreed* (= yes)*."* [T] • **It**'*s generally agreed* (= Most people think) **that** *eating too much fat is bad for you.* [T + obj + *that* clause] • If two or more people **are agreed**, they have the same opinion: *Are we all agreed* **(on** *that)?* ○ *The members are agreed* **that** *the proposal should be rejected.* [+ *that* clause] • If two or more statements, ideas, sets of numbers, etc. agree, they are the same or very similar: *We've got five accounts of what happened and none of them agree* **(with** *each other).* [I] • *(specialized)* If two words agree, or one word agrees **with** another word, they are grammatically related and one word changes its form between singular and plural, male and female, etc. when the other word's form changes. [I] • If you **agree to differ**, you stop trying to persuade someone else, who does not share your opinion, that your opinion is right, in order to avoid an argument. • If you say you **couldn't agree more/less**, you mean you completely agree/disagree.

a·gree·a·ble /ə'griː·ə·bl̩/ *adj* • If something or someone is agreeable (**to** someone or **to** different groups), they are acceptable to them: *The talks are aimed at finding a* **mutually** *agreeable solution.* ○ *The compromise is agreeable to both sides of the party.* ○ *Is it agreeable to you if we hold the meeting on Thursday?* • If someone is agreeable (**to** something), they are willing to do it: *Bring your wife too, if she's agreeable (to coming).* • See also AGREEABLE.

a·gree·ment /ə'griː·mənt/ *n* • *The whole family was* **in** *agreement* **(with** *Uncle Fred)* (= had the same opinion) **about/on** *what we should do.* [U] • *If the three parties cannot* **reach** *agreement* (= the same opinion) *now, there will be a civil war.* [U] • *I don't think you'll ever get Tony's agreement* **to** (= acceptance of) *these proposals.* [U] • *The two sides have* **reached** *an agreement* **to** *divide the money into two equal parts.* [C + *to* infinitive] • An agreement is also a decision or arrangement, often formal and written, between two or more groups or people: *The dispute was settled by an agreement that satisfied both sides.* [C] ○ *The government has* **entered into/signed** *an international arms-control agreement.* [C] ○ *If you* **make** *an agreement* **with** *someone, you should keep it.* ○ *They have* **broken (the terms of)** *the agreement* **on** *human rights.* [C] • *(specialized) In the sentence 'Kate was brushing her hair', 'Kate' and 'her' are* **in** *agreement* (= they are grammatically related). [U]

a·gree with *obj v prep* [T] to cause to feel healthy and happy • *You look well – the mountain air must agree with you.* • *Those onions I ate didn't agree with me* (= had a bad effect on my stomach and made me feel ill).

a·gree·a·ble /ə'griː·ə·bl̩/ *adj* pleasant; pleasing • *We spent an extremely agreeable evening with Mary and Edward yesterday.* • *The helpful flight attendants made our flight very agreeable.* • *He's a most agreeable* (= friendly and pleasant to be with) *person.* • *You might have been more successful in your job if you'd taken the trouble to* **make yourself** *more agreeable* (= pleasant) **to** *your boss.* • See also **agreeable** at AGREE.

a·gree·a·bly /ə'griː·ə·bli/ *adv* • Agreeably means with enjoyment or pleasure: *They were agreeably surprised to see that he had come after all.*

ag·ri·busi·ness /'æg·riˌbɪz·nɪs/ *n* [U] *specialized* the various businesses that are connected with producing, preparing and selling farm products • *Consumer protest at the way animals are treated is beginning to affect agribusiness.* • *In many countries, the agribusiness sector employs more labour and generates more income than any other sector of the economy.*

ag·ri·cul·ture /£ˈæg·rɪ·kʌl·tʃəʳ, $-tʃɚ/ *n* [U] farming • *Agriculture is still largely based on traditional methods in some countries.* • *The area depends on agriculture for most of its income.* • *70% of the country's population practises* **subsistence** *agriculture.* • Compare HORTICULTURE.

ag·ri·cul·tur·al /£ˌæg·rɪˈkʌl·tʃər·əl, $-tʃɚ·əl/ *adj* • *He said that the world's supply of agricultural land is shrinking fast, and every year produces less food.* • *She's studying agricultural science.* • *The country's economy is mainly agricultural* (=based on farming) *and depends on crops like coffee.*

a·ground /əˈgraʊnd/ *adj* [after v], *adv* [not gradable] (of a boat or ship) touching the ground or, where there is little water, touching the bottom of the sea, a lake, etc. and therefore unable to move • *The ship is currently aground off the Brittany coast.* • *The oil tanker* **ran/went** *aground* **on** *a mud bank in thick fog.* • *(fig.) The plans to send aid to the areas worst affected by the fighting have* **run** *aground* (=stopped because of difficulties).

ah /ɑː/, **aah** *exclamation* used to express understanding, pleasure, pain, surprise or the fact that you have noticed something • *Ah yes, now I see what's wrong – the wires have come loose.* • *Ah, it's wonderful to see you again.* • *Ah, that's terrible, you must have been in such pain.* • *Why has the train stopped? Ah, now we're off again.* • *Ah, Jessica, I'm glad you could make it.*

a·ha /ɑːˈhɑː/ *exclamation* used to express understanding of something being said or satisfaction at suddenly finding or understanding something • *"And this is the main computer?" "Aha."* • *Aha, now I've got you – you can't escape.*

ah·choo /əˈtʃuː/ *exclamation Am for* ATISHOO

a·head [IN FRONT] /əˈhed/ *adv* [not gradable] (directly) in front • *The road ahead looks rather busy – shall we turn off and go a different way?* • *Turn left at the traffic lights, and you'll see the hospital* **straight** *ahead.* • *We slowed down, to let the other cars get ahead* **of** *us.* • *I'm on the waiting list for a ticket, but there are ten people ahead* **of** *me.* • Ahead also means in a more advanced position: *The Prime Minister's speech* **put** *his party 5% ahead in the opinion polls.* • If someone or something is ahead **of** someone or something else, it is more advanced than them: *Sophie is* **way** (=far) *ahead of the other children in her class.* ○ *He claimed that his country was years ahead of the rest of the world in technological development.* • *"If you want to get ahead, get a hat"* (advertisement for hats, 1960s)

a·head [IN THE FUTURE] /əˈhed/ *adv* in or into the future; before • *He couldn't bear to think of the lonely year ahead.* • *You should* **think/plan/look** *ahead – what are you going to need on the trip?* • *We have a lot of hard work lying ahead* **of** *us.* • *The earthquake happened a year ahead* **of** *scientific predictions.* • *Is Italian time an hour ahead* **of** *or an hour behind English time?* • *Although I left home later than Jane, I arrived at the party ahead* **of** *her.* • *We sent our luggage* **on** *ahead, and it was there when we got to the hotel.* • *You* **go on** *ahead* **(of** *me), and I'll meet you at the cinema.* • *The project is* **moving** *ahead* (=developing) *quickly/slowly.* • *The government is* **pressing** *ahead* (=continuing) *with its plans to reorganize the health service.*

a·hem /əˈhem/ *exclamation esp. humorous* used to describe the little cough that someone gives to express slight embarrassment, amusement, doubt or disapproval, or to attract attention

a·his·tor·ic·al /£ˌeɪ·hɪsˈtɒr·ɪ·kəl, $-ˈtɑː·rɪ-/ *adj* not connected with history or with a historical understanding of past events • *The essay has a good style, but your argument is completely ahistorical.*

-a·holic, -o·hol·ic /£-əˈhɒl·ɪk, $-ˈhɑː·lɪk/ *combining form* unable to stop doing or taking • *a workaholic* • *a foodaholic* • *a chocoholic* • *an alcoholic*

a·hoy /əˈhɔɪ/ *exclamation* a shout used, esp. by people in boats, to attract attention • *Ahoy there!* • Ahoy can also be used, esp. on a boat or a ship, to mean that you can see something, usually something which is in the distance: *Land ahoy!* ○ *Ship ahoy!*

AI /ˌeɪˈaɪ/ *n* [U] *abbreviation for* **artificial intelligence** or **artificial insemination**, see at ARTIFICIAL

aid /eɪd/ *n* (something that provides) help or support • *He gets about* **with the** *aid* **of** *a walking stick.* [U] • *She* **went to the** *aid* **of** *a man trapped in his car.* [U] • *An anonymous millionaire has* **come to** *the company's aid by lending it the money it needs to keep it in business.* [U] • *The concert was* **in** *aid* **of** (=to collect money for) *famine relief.* [U] • *There is a huge market for slimming aids* (=things that make it easier to lose weight). [C] • *A thesaurus is a useful aid* **to** *writing* (=makes it easier to write) *well.* [C] • Aid is often used to refer to help in the form of food, money, medical supplies or weapons that is given by a richer country to a poorer country: *The Vatican has agreed to donate $80000 in* **humanitarian/emergency** *aid to countries affected by the war.* [U] ○ *The German Chancellor has pledged more* **financial/economic** *aid to the region.* [U] ○ *About a fifth of the country's income is in the form of* **foreign/overseas** *aid.* [U] ○ *America's aid budget for sending food, medicine and equipment to less developed countries is many times less than what Americans spend on dieting.* • **Aid to Families with Dependent Children** is *Am for* **child benefit**. See at CHILD. • *(Br infml)* **What's** *all this shouting* **in aid of?** (=What is the reason for this shouting?)

aid *obj* /eɪd/ *v* [T] • *Huge projects designed to aid* (=help) *poorer countries can sometimes do more harm than good.* • *His excuse for drinking brandy is that it's said to aid digestion.* • *The police announced that Mr Duggan was aiding them* **with** *their inquiries.* • *(law or humorous)* If you **aid and abet** someone, you help them do something illegal or wrong: *Three tax inspectors were accused of aiding and abetting the men charged with fraud.*

aide /eɪd/ *n* [C] a person whose job is to help someone important, such as a member of a government or a military officer of high rank • *a senior/close/top government aide* • *a military aide* • *an aide* **to** *the Prime Minister*

aide–de–camp /£ˌeɪd·dəˈkɑ̃ː, $-ˈkæmp/, **ADC** *n* [C] *pl* **aides-de-camp** /£ˌeɪd·dəˈkɑ̃ː, $-ˈkæmp/ • An **aide-de-camp** is a military or naval officer who helps an officer of higher rank: *He became Napoleon's aide-de-camp in 1804.* • **Aide-de-camp** is also another word for aide: *the Prime Minister's aide-de-camp*

AIDS, Aids /eɪdz/ *n* [U] *abbreviation for* Acquired Immune Deficiency Syndrome (=a serious disease caused by a virus which destroys the body's natural protection from infection, and which usually causes death) • *The symptoms of AIDS can take several years to develop.* • *In Britain, AIDS tests are now performed on all people who offer to become blood donors.* • *You can* **contract** *AIDS if your bodily fluids come into contact with the bodily fluids of someone else who is infected with HIV.* • *Don had* **full-blown** *AIDS for over a year before he died.* • Compare HIV.

ail *obj* [CAUSE DIFFICULTY] /eɪl/ *v* [T] to cause to be in difficulty, or to cause to be unhappy or upset • *The government seems to have no understanding of* **what** *ails the country.* • *I don't know* **what**'*s ailing her* (=making her unhappy or upset).

ail·ing /ˈeɪ·lɪŋ/ *adj* • Ailing means experiencing difficulty and problems: *The President's main task is to cure the country's ailing economy.* ○ *Measures have been taken to rescue the financially ailing company.* ○ *Ted asked me if I could help him fix his ailing car* (=his car that was not working).

ail *(obj)* [BE/MAKE ILL] /eɪl/ *v* to (cause to) be ill • *My grandmother had been ailing for years before she died.* [I] • *(slightly humorous) "So* **what**'*s ailing you, Mrs Brown?" "It's my leg, doctor."* [T]

ail·ing /ˈeɪ·lɪŋ/ *adj* [not gradable] • *He asked for some time off work so that he could visit his ailing father.*

ail·ment /ˈeɪl·mənt/ *n* [C] • *He died of a heart/respiratory/liver ailment* (=illness). • *She's always ill, always* **has** *some little ailment bothering her.*

ai·le·ron /£ˈeɪ·lə·rɒn, $-rɑːn/ *n* [C] *specialized* a movable part along the back edge of an aircraft's wing, used esp. to help the aircraft turn or to keep it level

aim *(obj)* [POINT] /eɪm/ *v* to point or direct (esp. a weapon) towards someone or something that you want to hit • *Aim (the arrow) a little above the target.* [I/T] • *He said that when he fired the gun, he had been aiming* **for** *his victim's shoulder, not her heart.* [I] • *Aim* **at** *the yellow circle.* [I] • *There are hundreds of nuclear missiles aimed* **at** *the main cities.* [T] • *She aimed* (=directed) *a kick* **at** *my shins.* [T] • To aim something that you do or say or write is to direct it towards someone whom you want to influence or towards achieving something: *These advertisements are specifically aimed* **at** *young people.* [T] ○ *The government's campaign is aimed* **at** *influencing public opinion.* [T] • *Let's aim* **for** (=go in the direction of) *Coventry first, and then we'll have a look at the map.* [I]

aim /eɪm/ *n* [U] • *He fired ten shots at the target, but his aim* (=act of pointing a weapon towards something) *was terrible, and he missed.* • *She raised her gun,* **took** *aim and fired, all in one smooth movement.*

aim [INTEND] /eɪm/ *v* [I] to intend; to plan or hope to achieve • *I aim* **to** *be a millionaire by the time I'm 35.* [+ *to* infinitive] • *We are aiming* **for** (= planning to achieve) *a 50% share of the German market.* • *The talks are aiming* **at** (= hoping to achieve) *a compromise.* • *She is aiming* **at** *winning a gold medal at the next Olympic games.*

aim /eɪm/ *n* [C] • An aim is a result that your plans or actions are intended to achieve: *My* **chief/main/ overriding** *aim* **in life** *is to be a good husband and father.* ○ *Our* **short-term** *aim is to deal with our current financial difficulties, but our* **long-term** *aim is to improve the company's profitability.* ○ *The leaflet has been produced* **with the** *aim* **of** *increasing public awareness of AIDS.* ○ *I don't know what his aims were* **in** *making such an accusation.*

aim·less /'eɪm·ləs/ *adj esp. disapproving* • *She said that her life seemed aimless* (= without any clear intentions, purpose or direction) *after her children left home.* • *I've always regarded bird-watching as a rather aimless activity, but I know that many people enjoy it.* • *Police said that the attack was an act of aimless violence.*

aim·less·ly /'eɪm·lə·sli/ *adv* • *While she waited, she walked aimlessly around the car park.*

aim·less·ness /'eɪm·lə·snəs/ *n* [U]

ain't /eɪnt/ *v not standard* am not, is not, are not, has not, have not • *"Is Terry here?" "No, he ain't coming into work today."* • *"Can I have a fag?" "No, I ain't got none left."* • *(saying)* 'If it ain't broke, don't fix it' means that if something is in a satisfactory state, there is no reason to try and change it.

air [GAS] /£eəʳ, $er/ *n* [U] the mixture of gases which surrounds the earth and which we breathe • *Air consists mainly of nitrogen and oxygen.* • *The air in the city is severely polluted.* • *I'm feeling a bit sick – I need some* **(fresh)** *air.* • *At the top of the mountain the air was* **thin** *and difficult to breathe.* • *Could you open a window – the air in this room is rather* **stale.** • *You should put some air in your tyres – they look flat to me.* • *We managed to see where the divers had gone under the water by watching the air* **bubbles** *that came to the surface.* • *Ever since she met Mark, she's been* **walking/floating on air** (= very happy). • **Air brakes** are brakes operated by air pressure which are used on large vehicles such as buses and trains to allow them to reduce speed or stop. • An **air conditioner** is a machine which keeps the air in a building cool. The system of keeping the air in a building or vehicle cool is called **air conditioning.** A building or room or vehicle in which the air is kept cool is **air-conditioned**: *It's really hot in here. Could you turn the air conditioner on?* ○ *I wish my car had air-conditioning.* ○ *I work in an air-conditioned office.* • An **air-cooled** engine is one that is kept cool by a flow of air. Compare **water-cooled** at WATER. • **Air-cushioned** *shoes* (= those which have spaces with air in them in the part of the shoe that you walk on) *are wonderfully comfortable.* • (An) **air freshener** is (a container which holds) a substance which makes a room or vehicle smell pleasant: *She put some air freshener in her bathroom.* • **Air mattress** is *Am for* AIRBED or LILO. • An **air pocket** is an area in the sky where the air is flowing differently from the way it is in the surrounding parts, which can sometimes cause aircraft to go up or down suddenly. • An **air-pistol** and an **air-rifle** are both types of gun that use air pressure to fire a PELLET (= small metal ball). See also AIRGUN. • See also AIRY [LIGHT]; AIRY [NOT SERIOUS]. • Ⓣ

air·less /£'eə·ləs, $'er-/ *adj disapproving* • In an airless place it is difficult to breathe or the air is not fresh: *an airless office* ○ *My hotel room was small, airless and uncomfortable.*

air [AREA] /£eəʳ, $er/ *n* [U] the space above, esp. high above, the ground • **The** *air was filled with millions of locusts/the scent of roses/terrified screams.* • *Throw your gun down and put your hands* **in the** *air.* • *The police fired* **into the** *air to clear the demonstrators from the streets.* • Air can also be used to refer to aircraft: *an air ambulance* ○ *an air crash/ disaster* ○ *an air fare* ○ *air travel* • *I hate travelling* **by** *air* (= in aircraft) *because I get horribly airsick.* • *We have supremacy* **in the** *air* (= Our aircraft are more powerful than those of our enemy). • *UN planes have made* **air drops** (= delivered supplies by dropping them from aircraft) *to 300 flood-hit villages.* • An **air force** is the part of a country's military forces which uses aircraft and fights in the air: *the United States Air Force* • *(Br and Aus dated)* An **air hostess** (also **flight attendant**) is a woman who serves passengers on an aircraft. • **Air power** is the force of a country's military aircraft and the ability of these aircraft to be used for attacking and defending the country: The decisive factor in their remarkable victory was their **superior** air power. • An **air raid** is an attack by enemy aircraft, usually dropping bombs: *an air raid* **shelter/siren** • **Air-sea rescue** is the act of using aircraft, including HELICOPTERS, and boats to try to save people in danger at sea: *An air-sea rescue* **operation** *was carried out to rescue passengers from the sinking ship.* • An **air terminal** is a building in an airport or in a place near an airport where aircraft passengers gather before their flight leaves or from which they leave after their flight has arrived. • **Air-to-air** means involving a weapon which is fired from an aircraft at another aircraft. **Air-to-ground/air-to-surface** means involving a weapon which is fired from an aircraft at a place on the ground: *an air-to-air missile* ○ *an air-to-ground attack* • **Air traffic control** is the activity of managing aircraft from the ground as they take off, fly and land, or it is the group of people who do this, who are also called **air traffic controllers.** • If something is **in the air**, you feel that it is happening or about to happen: *Love/ Change/Spring is in the air.* • If something such as a decision is **up in the air**, it is uncertain: *The whole future of the project is still up in the air.* • Ⓣ

air *(obj)* [BROADCAST] /£eəʳ, $er/ *v Am* to broadcast (something) on radio or television • *The interview with the President will air tomorrow morning.* [I] • *The game will be aired* **(live) on** *CBS at 7.00 tonight.* [T] • Ⓣ

air /£eəʳ, $er/ *n* [U] • If a programme or a person is **on/off** (the) air, they are/are not broadcasting on radio or television: *The radio station is on air from 6.00 a.m.* ○ *As soon as the war started, any broadcasts with a military theme were* **taken** *off the air.*

air [MANNER] /£eəʳ, $er/ *n* [C] manner or appearance • *She has* **an air of** *confidence about her.* • *Venice in winter has* **an** *air* **of** *mystery and sadness.* • *(disapproving)* If you **put on/give** yourself **airs (and graces)**, you behave as if you are more important than you really are. • *(disapproving) She's incredibly arrogant and full of* **airs and graces** (= a manner intended to make other people think she's important). • Ⓣ

air [TUNE] /£eəʳ, $er/ *n* [C] a simple tune • *Bach's Air on a G String* • Ⓣ

air *(obj)* [DRY] /£eəʳ, $er/ *v* to (cause to) become dry and/or fresh • *My mother always airs the sheets before she makes my bed.* [T] • *Leave the windows open to let the room air a bit.* [I] • Ⓣ

air·ing /£'eə·rɪŋ, $'er·ɪŋ/ *n* [U] • *The room was damp and smelly so we opened all the windows and gave it a good airing* (= made the air fresh and dry). • *(Br)* An **airing cupboard** is a heated cupboard where clothes, sheets, etc. that have been washed and are almost dry are put so that they can become completely dry. • [PIC] **Bathroom**

air *obj* [MAKE KNOWN] /£eəʳ, $er/ *v* [T] to make (your opinions, complaints, etc.) known to other people • *Putting a complaint in the suggestions box is one way of airing your* **grievances.** • *He'll air his* **views** *on the war whether people want to listen or not.* • Ⓣ

air·ing /£'eə·rɪŋ, $'er·ɪŋ/ *n* [C] • *The arguments for and against the proposals have* **had/been given** *a good airing* (= have been discussed in public).

air·bag /£'eə·bæg, $'er-/ *n* [C] a bag in a vehicle that automatically fills with air if the vehicle is involved in an accident, in order to protect the driver or a passenger from injury • *In the event of a collision, the airbag stops the driver of the car from hitting his or her chest on the steering wheel.*

air·base /£'eə·beɪs, $'er-/ *n* [C] a military airport, where military aircraft are kept and can land and take off

air·bed *Br and Aus* /£'eə·bed, $'er-/, *Am and Aus* **air mat·tress** *n* [C] a large rectangular rubber or plastic bag which you fill with air so that you can lie on it in water or use it as a bed • *He used a pump to inflate his airbed.* • *She floated lazily round the pool* **on** *an airbed.*

air·borne /£'eə·bɔːn, $'er·bɔːrn/ *adj* [not gradable] in the air, or carried by air or wind or by an aircraft; flying • *The airborne radioactive particles have covered a huge area of Russia.* • *Airborne troops were dropped by parachute behind enemy lines.* • *The old plane had great difficulty* **getting** *airborne* (= rising into the air). • *(fig.) We've got a lot to do before this project* **gets** *airborne* (= starts operating as intended).

air·brick /£'eə·brɪk, $'er-/ *n* [C] *Br and Aus* a special type of brick that has small holes in it which allow air to go through a wall • *When our new boiler was installed we had to have an airbrick fitted in the wall for ventilation.*

air·bridge /£'eə·brɪdʒ, $'er-/ *n* [C] *Br* a movable covered passage by which passengers can go from an airport building to an aircraft

air·brush /£'eə·brʌʃ, $'er-/ *n* [C] a machine that scatters paint using air pressure, which is used for painting or for delicate improvement work on photographs

air·brush *obj* /£'eə·brʌʃ, $'er-/ *v* [T] • *It's so obvious in the photo that her wrinkles have been airbrushed* **out** (= removed from the photograph by putting paint over them with an airbrush).

air·craft /£'eə·krɑːft, $'er·kræft/ *n* [C] *pl* **aircraft** any vehicle, with or without an engine, which can fly, such as an AEROPLANE, HELICOPTER or GLIDER • *a private/commercial/military aircraft* • *a jet aircraft* • *Five enemy aircraft have been shot down over the coast.* • An **aircraft carrier** is a large ship that carries military aircraft and has a long, flat surface where they can take off and land.

air·crew /£'eə·kruː, $'er-/ *n* [C + sing/pl v] all the people, including the PILOT, who work on an aircraft to fly it or to take care of the passengers

air·fare /£'eə·feə, $'er·fer/ *n* [C] the price of a journey by aircraft • *Transatlantic airfares are going up.*

air·field /£'eə·fiːld, $'er-/, *Br dated* **aer·o·drome** *n* [C] a level area where aircraft can take off and land, which has fewer buildings and services than an airport and is used by fewer passengers

air·gun /£'eə·gʌn, $'er-/ *n* [C] a gun which uses air pressure to fire a PELLET (= small metal ball)

air·head /£'eə·hed, $'er-/ *n* [C] *esp. Am slang* a person who cannot think clearly and does stupid things • *A couple of complete airheads walked right in front of me on my bike.*

air·let·ter /£'eə,let·əʳ, $'er,leṭ·ɚ/, **aer·o·gramme** *n* [C] a letter which is sent by aircraft, esp. one consisting of a single very thin sheet of paper which is folded and then stuck at the edges to form its own envelope

air·lift /£'eə·lɪft, $'er-/ *n* [C] an operation organized to move supplies or people, by aircraft, to or from a place that is difficult to reach because of war, flooding, etc.

air·lift *obj* /£'eə·lɪft, $'er-/ *v* [T] • *Israel secretly airlifted about 10 000 Jews* **out of** *war-torn Ethiopia.*

air·line /£'eə·laɪn, $'er-/ *n* [C] a business that operates regular services for carrying passengers and/or goods by aircraft • *What airline did you fly?*

air·lin·er /£'eə,laɪ·nəʳ, $'er,laɪ·nɚ/ *n* [C] a large passenger aircraft

air·lock [ROOM] /£'eə·lɒk, $'er·lɑːk/ *n* [C] a room between two other rooms that have different air pressure, which allows you to go from one to the other, without changing these pressures • *Airlocks are commonly found on submarines and manned spacecraft.*

air·lock [BUBBLE] /£'eə·lɒk, $'er·lɑːk/ *n* [C] a bubble in a pipe that prevents liquid from flowing along it

air·mail /£'eə·meɪl, $'er-/ *n* [U] a system of sending letters, parcels, etc. by aircraft • *If you send it* **(by)** *airmail, it'll be very expensive.* • *Airmail letters arrive much quicker than ones sent surface mail.*

air·man (*pl* **-men**), **air·wo·man** (*pl* **-women**) /£'eə·mən, $'er-, -,wʊ·mən/ *n* [C] a person who flies or helps to operate an aircraft, esp. a military one

air·plane /£'eə·pleɪn, $'er-/ *n* [C] *Am for* AEROPLANE

air·play /£'eə·pleɪ, $'er-/ *n* [U] (the amount of) broadcasting time that someone or something, such as a piece of recorded music, has on the radio • *Unless a song* **gets** *lots of airplay, it won't sell in the shops.* • Compare AIRTIME.

air·port /£'eə·pɔːt, $'er·pɔːrt/ *n* [C] a place where aircraft regularly take off and land, with buildings for passengers to wait in, equipment for controlling flights, etc. • *an international airport* • *a military airport* • *Gatwick Airport* • *an airport terminal/runway* • *airport delays/security/police* • *airport food*

air·ship /£'eə·ʃɪp, $'er-/ *n* [C] a large aircraft, used esp. in the past, without wings but filled with gas which is lighter than air and powered by engines. Passengers, letters, etc. were carried in an enclosed space below.

air·show /£'eə·ʃəʊ, $'er·ʃoʊ/ *n* [C] a public show of flying skills and special aircraft, often performed at an AIRBASE (= military airport) specially opened to visitors

air·sick /£'eə·sɪk, $'er-/ *adj* having the feeling that you will vomit because of the movement of an aircraft you are travelling in

air·sick·ness /£'eə·sɪk·nəs, $'er-/ *n* [U]

air·space /£'eə·speɪs, $'er-/ *n* [U] the air or sky above a country, which is considered to belong to that country • *The People's Republic has said it will shoot down any aircraft entering its airspace.*

air·speed /£'eə·spiːd, $'er-/ *n* [U] the speed of an aircraft, measured against the speed of the air through which it is moving • *Check your airspeed indicator.*

air·stream /£'eə·striːm, $'er-/ *n* [C] a current of air • *a strong south-westerly airstream* • *Migrating birds make use of airstreams to assist them on their long journey south.*

air·strike /£'eə·straɪk, $'er-/ *n* [C] an attack by military aircraft on a city, enemy soldiers, or their supplies, either by bombing or by firing guns

air·strip /£'eə·strɪp, $'er-/, **land·ing strip** *n* [C] a long flat piece of land from which trees, rocks, etc. have been removed so that aircraft can take off and land • *We landed at a tiny airstrip in the middle of the jungle.*

air·tight /£'eə·taɪt, $'er-/ *adj* (esp. of a container) completely closed so that no air can get in or out • *Biscuits will stay crisp if you keep them in an airtight tin.*

air·time /£'eə·taɪm, $'er-/ *n* [U] (the amount of) broadcasting time that someone or something has on television or radio • *The smaller political parties are campaigning to be allowed free airtime before general elections.* • Compare AIRPLAY.

air·waves /£'eə·weɪvz, $'er-/ *pl n* the radio waves used for broadcasting radio and television programmes, or more generally, radio or television broadcasting time • *The new series of Batman will be* **on the** *airwaves at 6 pm every Tuesday.* • *The airwaves are full of nothing but World Cup games and commentaries at the moment.*

air·way /£'eə·weɪ, $'er-/ *n* [C] the passage through the mouth and throat that carries air to the lungs • *When dealing with a road traffic accident casualty, lay them on their side and ensure the airway is clear and unobstructed.*

air·wor·thy /£'eə·wɜː·ði, $'er·wɜːr-/ *adj* (of an aircraft) in safe working condition; safe to fly

air·wor·thi·ness /£'eə·wɜː·ðɪ·nəs, $'er·wɜːr-/ *n* [U] • *a certificate of airworthiness* • *airworthiness trials*

air·y [SPACIOUS] /£'eə·ri, $'er·i/ *adj* **-ier, -iest** *approving* spacious and light • *The new offices are bright and airy, with high ceilings and lots of windows.*

air·i·ness /£'eə·rɪ·nəs, $'er·ɪ-/ *n* [U] *approving*

air·y [LIGHT] /£'eə·ri, $'er·i/ *adj* **-ier, -iest** light in appearance, manner, or movement • *She was wearing an airy outfit made of cream-coloured silk.* • *Fashion models stroll down the catwalk with an airy step.*

air·y [NOT SERIOUS] /£'eə·ri, $'er·i/ *adj* **-ier, -iest** *disapproving* not seriously considered • *These politicians make airy promises that they never keep.* • *(infml)* If something is **airy-fairy**, it is not practical or based on reality: *He spent his time dreaming up airy-fairy* **schemes** *that would never make the company any money.*

air·i·ly /'eə·rɪ·li, $'er-/ *adv disapproving* • *I get really annoyed when he airily* (= without seriously thinking about it) **dismisses** *anything I say as irrelevant.*

aisle /aɪl/ *n* [C] a long narrow space between rows of seats in an aircraft, cinema, church, etc., or between the rows of shelves in a large shop • *Would you like a seat by the aisle or would you prefer to be by the window?* • *He dreamed of the day he would* **take her down the aisle** (= marry her in a church). • *You'll find the shampoo and the soap in the fourth aisle along from the entrance.* • [PIC]> **Supermarket**

aitch /eɪtʃ/ *n* [C] (the name of) the letter *h* • *(Br disapproving)* If you say that someone **drops** their aitches, you mean that they do not pronounce the *h* at the beginning of words, so that they say, for example, 'ospital instead of hospital.

a·jar /£ə'dʒɑːʳ, $-dʒɑːr/ *adj* [after v] (of a door) almost closed; slightly open • *We left the door ajar so that we could hear what they were saying.*

aka /,eɪ·keɪ'eɪ/ *abbreviation for* also known as (= having as another name) • *James Brown, aka the 'Godfather of Soul', is one of my musical heroes.*

a·kim·bo /£ə'kɪm·bəʊ, $-boʊ/ *adj* [after n; not gradable] (of a person's arms) bent at the ELBOWS and with the hands on the hips • *The little boy stood* **(with) arms** *akimbo, and refused to move.*

a·kin /ə'kɪn/ *adj* [after v] similar; having some of the same qualities • *The way the police treated him was akin* **to** *the worst sort of torture.* • *They speak a language akin* **to** *French.*

-al /-əl/ *combining form* used to add the meaning 'connected with' to adjectives, or 'the action of' to nouns • *I have a*

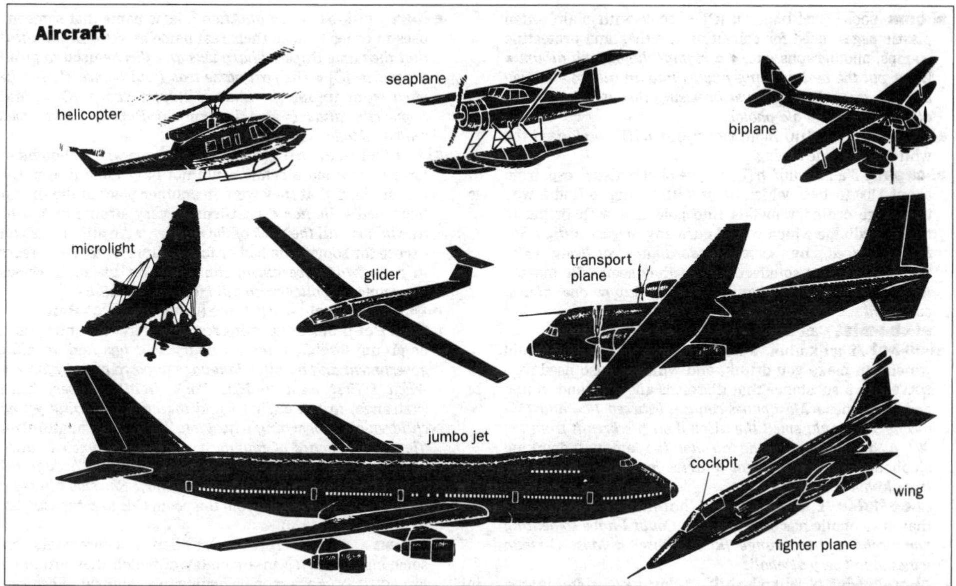

medical (=connected with medicine) *question for you.* • *If we get the bank's approval* (=act of approving) *the project can go ahead.* • LP> **Combining forms, Stress in pronunciation**

à la /ˈæl·æ/ *prep* in the style of • *She has her hair blonde and curly à la Marilyn Monroe.*

al·a·bas·ter /£ˌæl·əˈbæs·tər, $ˈæl·ə·bæs·tɚ/ *n* [U] an almost transparent white stone, used esp. for making decorative objects

à la carte /£ˌæl·əˈkɑːt, $-ˈkɑːrt/ *adj, adv* [not gradable] (of food in a restaurant) as separate dishes with different prices, rather than as a fixed complete meal at a total price • *You get more choice if you eat à la carte/from the à la carte* **menu**. • Compare TABLE D'HÔTE.

a·lack /əˈlæk/ *exclamation old use* **alas and alack**, see at ALAS

a·lac·ri·ty /£əˈlæk·rə·ti, $-t̬i/ *n* [U] *fml* speed and eagerness • *The United Nations has acted* **with** *alacrity and determination in this crisis.* • *She accepted the money* **with** *alacrity.*

A·lad·din's cave /əˈlæd·ɪnz/ *n* [U] *Br* a store of very many interesting or unusual objects • *The shop was* **a veritable** *Aladdin's cave* **of** *beautiful antiques.* • *He couldn't believe his eyes at the Aladdin's cave* **of** *treasure he found when the strongroom door swung open.*

à la mode MODERN /£æl·əˈməʊd, $-ˈmoʊd/ *adj, adv* in the most modern style or fashion • *Her clothes are very much à la mode.* • *She always dresses à la mode.*

à la mode FOOD /£æl·əˈməʊd, $-ˈmoʊd/ *adj* [after n] *Am* served with ice-cream • *apple pie à la mode*

a·larm ANXIETY /£əˈlɑːm, $-lɑːrm/ *n* [U] sudden anxiety and fear, esp. that something dangerous or unpleasant might happen • *I told her only half the story because I didn't want to* **cause** *her/***give** *her any* **cause for** *alarm.* • *The villagers have reacted with alarm to news of a proposed new airport.*

a·larm *obj* /£əˈlɑːm, $-lɑːrm/ *v* [T] • *The lack of books and the poor condition of the school buildings are alarming parents.* • *I was alarmed by reports of her disappearance.*

a·larmed /£əˈlɑːmd, $-lɑːrmd/ *adj* • *Please don't be alarmed, but your son has had a bit of an accident.* • *We are alarmed* **at** *this possibility.* • *I am alarmed* **to** *hear this news.* [+ *to* infinitive]

a·larm·ing /£əˈlɑː·mɪŋ, $-ˈlɑːr-/ *adj* • *an alarming noise* • *an alarming financial situation* • *There has been an alarming rise in the rate of inflation.*

a·larm·ing·ly /£əˈlɑː·mɪŋ·li, $-lɑːr-/ *adv* • *He shook her by the shoulders, but she took an alarmingly long time to open her eyes.* • *Alarmingly, the hole in the ozone layer has doubled in size this year.*

a·larm·ist /£əˈlɑː·mɪst, $-ˈlɑːr-/ *adj disapproving* • Something alarmist shows only the bad and dangerous things in a situation, and so worries people: *The government has dismissed newspaper reports of 200 dead as being alarmist.*

a·larm·ist /£əˈlɑː·mɪst, $-ˈlɑːr-/ *n* [C] *disapproving* • *Don't listen to the alarmists in the City – I am positive that we will double our profits this year.*

a·larm WARNING /£əˈlɑːm, $-lɑːrm/ *n* [C] (a loud noise, flashing light, etc., that gives) a warning of danger • *If there's any violence,* **raise/sound the** *alarm by pulling the emergency cord.* • *He screamed as loudly as he could to* **raise/give the** *alarm.* • *The first two bomb alerts were* **false** *alarms, but the third was the real thing.* • *(fig.) A local doctor was the first to* **raise the** *alarm* **about** (=make people understand the danger of) *this latest virus.* • *(fig.) The name* **rang** *alarm* **bells** *in her mind* (=made her think something about it was wrong). • An alarm is also a device which makes a loud noise to warn of danger to or from a particular thing: *a burglar/car/fire/smoke alarm* • If an electronic device such as a watch or computer has an alarm, it can be set to make a noise at a particular time. • An **alarm call** is a telephone call to wake you up at a particular time, for example in a hotel. • An **alarm (clock)** is a clock that you can set to wake you up at a particular time with a loud noise: *I've* **set the** *alarm* **for** *7.30.* ◦ *The alarm* **went off** *at 7.30.* • PIC> **Locks and home security**

a·larmed /£əˈlɑːmd, $-lɑːrmd/ *adj* [not gradable] • *This car is alarmed* (=has a device which makes a loud noise if anyone touches the car without permission).

a·las /əˈlæs/ *adv* [not gradable] *dated* used to express sadness or regret • *The building of the new school library will, alas, have to be postponed till next year.* • *I love football, but alas I have no talent as a player.* • *"Will you be able to come tomorrow?" "Alas, but no."*

a·las /əˈlæs/ *exclamation old use* • *Alas! My lover has forsaken me.* • **Alas and alack** is also an expression of sadness. • *"Alas, poor Yorick! I knew him, Horatio: a fellow of infinite jest"* (Shakespeare, Hamlet 5.1)

al·ba·tross /£ˈæl·bə·trɒs, $-trɑːs/ *n* [C] a large white bird with long strong wings, found esp. in the areas of the Pacific and S Atlantic oceans • If you say that something or someone is an albatross **(round your neck)**, you mean that you want to be free from them because they are causing you problems: *Her own supporters see her as an albatross who could lose them the election.*

al·be·it /£ɔːlˈbiː·ɪt, $ɑːl-/ *conjunction fml* (used to reduce the strength and effect of what has just been said) although • *The evening was very pleasant, albeit a little quiet.*

al·bi·no /£ælˈbiː·nəʊ, $-ˈbaɪ·noʊ/ *adj* [not gradable], *n* [C] *pl* **albinos** (a person or animal) with a condition that causes white skin and hair and pink eyes

al·bum RECORDING /ˈæl·bəm/ *n* [C] a recording of several pieces of music, usually on two sides, each lasting about 25 minutes • *Her new album has got two of her number-one hit singles on it.*

al·bum BOOK /ˈæl·bəm/ *n* [C] a book with plain, often plastic pages, used for collecting together and protecting stamps, photographs, etc. • *a stamp/photograph album* • *We've put the best wedding photos into an album – do you want to see?* • *We were just browsing through the* **family** *album, looking at old photos.*

al·bu·men /£ˈæl·bjʊ·mən, $ælˈbjuː-/ *n* [U] *specialized* the white part inside an egg

al·che·my /ˈæl·kə·mi/ *n* [U] a type of chemistry, esp. from about 1100 to 1500, which dealt with trying to find a way to change ordinary metals into gold and with trying to find a medicine which would cure any disease • *(fig.) She has managed,* **by** *some extraordinary alchemy* (=by methods that are so effective that they seem like magic), *to turn an unhappy family into a happy one almost overnight.*

al·che·mist /ˈæl·kə·mɪst/ *n* [C]

al·co·hol /£ˈæl·kə·hɒl, $-hɑːl/ *n* [U] a colourless liquid which can make you drunk, and which is also used as a SOLVENT (=a substance that dissolves another) and in fuel and medicines • *Most wines contain between 10% and 15% alcohol.* • *I could smell the alcohol on his breath from ten feet away!* • *I'm* **off** *the alcohol* (=I am not drinking alcoholic drinks) *– I've got to drive home later.* • *Do you like alcohol-***free** *lager?*

al·co·hol·ic /£ˌæl·kəˈhɒl·ɪk, $-ˈhɑː·lɪk/ *adj* • Something that is alcoholic has alcohol in it: *Could I have something non-alcoholic, like orange juice, please?* ○ *Most German wines aren't very alcoholic.*

al·co·hol·ic /£ˌæl·kəˈhɒl·ɪk, $-ˈhɑː·lɪk/, *slang* **al·ky, al·kie** *n* [C] • An alcoholic is a person who is unable to give up the habit of drinking alcohol very frequently and in large amounts.

al·co·hol·i·sm /£ˈæl·kə·hɒl·ɪ·zᵊm, $-hɑː·lɪ-/ *n* [U] • *Alcoholism* (=The uncontrollable habit of drinking alcohol) *cost me my job, my health and finally my family.*

al·cove /£ˈæl·kəʊv, $-koʊv/ *n* [C] a small space in a room, formed by one part of a wall being further back than the parts on each side • *Which shall we put in the alcove – a bed or bookshelves?* • (DK) (E)

al den·te /ælˈden·teɪ/ *adj* [not gradable] (of pasta or vegetables) cooked until still firm when bitten

al·der·man /£ˈɔːl·də·mən, $ˈɑːl·dɚ-/ *n* [C] *pl* **-men** (in Britain until 1974) a member of a local government chosen by the other members, or (in the US, Canada, Australia, etc.) an elected member of a city government

ale /eɪl/ *n* [C] any of various types of beer, esp. one that is darker, heavier and more bitter than other beer • *brown ale*

a·lert /£əˈlɜːt, $-ˈlɜːrt/ *adj* quick to see, understand and act in a particular situation • **Stay/Keep** *alert or you'll miss the planes when they fly by.* • *I'm not feeling very alert today – not enough sleep last night!* • *A couple of alert readers wrote in to the paper pointing out the mistake.* • *We're very alert* **to** (=we understand and give attention to) *the dangers of operating a nuclear power station.*

a·lert /£əˈlɜːt, $-ˈlɜːrt/ *n* • An alert is a warning to people to be/get ready to deal with something dangerous: *If there is an alert, don't panic, just make your way to the exit.* [C] • *The army was* **put on** *full alert as the peace talks began to fail.* [U] • *The police are* **on the** *alert* **for** (=watching carefully for) *any suspicious packages that might contain bombs.* [U] • *Security forces are on a high* **state of** *alert because of the President's visit.* [U]

a·lert *obj* /£əˈlɜːt, $-ˈlɜːrt/ *v* [T] • *An anonymous letter alerted police* **to** *the possibility of a terrorist attack at the airport.*

al·fal·fa /ˌælˈfæl·fə/ *n* [U] a plant grown as food for esp. farm animals, or used (before it is completely developed) in salads

al·fres·co /£ˌælˈfres·kəʊ, $-koʊ/ *adj, adv* [not gradable] (esp. of food and eating) outside • *They enjoyed an alfresco lunch on the patio.* • *Let's eat alfresco this evening – it's so hot inside.*

al·gae /ˈæl·giː/ *pl n* very simple, usually small plants, such as SEAWEED, that grow in or near water and do not have ordinary leaves or roots

al·ge·bra /ˈæl·dʒə·brə/ *n* [U] a part of mathematics in which signs and letters represent numbers

al·ge·bra·ic /ˌæl·dʒəˈbreɪ·ɪk/ *adj*

al·go·ri·thm /ˈæl·gə·rɪ·ðᵊm/ *n* [C] *specialized* a set of mathematical instructions that must be followed in a fixed order, and that, esp. if given to a computer, will help to calculate an answer to a mathematical problem

a·li·as /ˈeɪ·li·əs/ *n, conjunction* a false name that someone uses in order to keep their real name secret • *He admitted that the name Rupert Sharp was an alias he* **used** *to avoid the police.* [C] • *His real name was Paul Sopworth, but he often* **went under** *the alias of Rupert Sharp.* [C] • *Paul Sopworth, alias* (=also known as) *Rupert Sharp, was sentenced today to 3 years in jail.*

al·i·bi /ˈæl·ɪ·baɪ/ *n* [C] proof that someone who is thought to have committed a crime could not have done it, esp. the fact or claim that they were in another place at the time it happened • *He has a* **cast-iron** (=very strong) *alibi – he was in hospital the week of the murder.* • An alibi is also an excuse for something bad or for a failure: *After eight years in power, the government can no longer use the previous government's policy as an alibi* **for** *its own failure.*

A·lice band /ˈæl·ɪs/ *n* [C] *Br* a HAIRBAND • PIC› **Hair**

a·li·en /ˈeɪ·li·ən/ *adj* coming from a different country, race, or group; foreign • *It's a country that has had an alien government and an alien language imposed on it by force.* • *When I first went to New York, it all felt very alien* (=strange) *to me.* • *(fig.) I find the idea of sending young children off to boarding school totally alien* (=unnatural). • *(fig.) The practice of having a siesta after lunch is alien* (=strange or not familiar) **to** *the English.* • *"Through the sad heart of Ruth, when, sick for home,/ She stood in tears among the alien corn"* (from the poem *Ode to a Nightingale* by John Keats, 1820)

a·li·en /ˈeɪ·li·ən/ *n* [C] • An alien is a foreigner, esp. someone who lives in a country of which they are not a legal CITIZEN (=a person belonging to a country): *When war broke out the government rounded up thousands of aliens and put them in temporary camps.* • An alien is also a creature from a different world: *The radio play was so convincing that many people thought aliens were actually landing on the Earth.*

a·li·en·ate *obj* LOSE SUPPORT /ˈeɪ·li·ə·neɪt/ *v* [T] to cause (someone, or esp. a group of people) to stop supporting and agreeing with you or someone else • *All these changes to the newspaper have alienated its traditional readers.* • *If the nurses go on strike they may alienate public support for their pay claim.*

a·li·en·a·tion /ˌeɪ·li·əˈneɪ·ʃᵊn/ *n* [U] • *This short-sighted alienation of their own supporters may lose them the election.*

a·li·en·ate *obj* NOT WELCOME /ˈeɪ·li·ə·neɪt/ *v* [T] to cause (someone) to feel very distant from or not welcome to someone else • *Ten years in prison have alienated him* **from** *his family.*

a·li·en·a·tion /ˌeɪ·li·əˈneɪ·ʃᵊn/ *n* [U] • *She feels a terrible sense of alienation* **from** (=feeling of having no connection with) *everyone else around her.*

a·light BURNING /əˈlaɪt/ *adj* [after v] burning; on fire • *I had to use a bit of petrol to help me* **get** *the fire alight.* • *The rioters overturned several cars and* **set** *them alight.* • *His blankets apparently* **caught** *alight because he was smoking in bed.* • *The sky was alight* **with** (=brightly lit up by) *hundreds of fireworks.* • *(fig.) Her eyes were alight* (=bright) **with** *mischief.* • *(fig.) The flame of nationalism is spreading and* **setting** *new regions alight* (=creating high levels of interest and activity).

a·light GET OUT /əˈlaɪt/ *v* [I] *past* **alighted** or *dated* **alit** /əˈlɪt/ *fml* to get out of a vehicle, esp. a train or bus • *The suspect alighted* **from** *the train at Euston and proceeded to Heathrow.*

a·light TO LAND /əˈlaɪt/ *v* [I] *past* **alighted** or *dated* **alit** /əˈlɪt/ *fml* to land on something • *Two butterflies alighted gently* **on** *the flower.* • *(fig.) I spent the whole afternoon in various bookshops before alighting* **on** (=finding) *the perfect present for Peter.* • *(fig.) As she glanced round the room her eyes alighted* **upon** (=unexpectedly saw) *a painting of sunlit vineyards which reminded her of home.*

a·lign *obj* /əˈlaɪn/ *v* [T] to put (two or more things) into a straight line • *When you've aligned the notch on the gun* **with** *the target, fire!* • *Align the ruler* **and** *the middle of the paper and then cut it straight.* • *(fig.) The major unions are aligned* **with/behind** (=agree with and support) *the government on this issue.* • *(fig.) The party is under pressure to align itself more closely with industry* (=to support the aims of industry).

a·lign·ment /əˈlaɪn·mənt/ *n* • *The vibration in the steering wheel is happening because the wheels are* **out of** *alignment (***with** *each other).* [U] • *(fig.) The government is under pressure to bring safety standards on pollution* **into** *alignment* **with** *the rest of Europe.* [U] • *(fig.) New* *alignments* (= connections or agreements of support) *are being formed within the business community.* [C]

a·like /ə'laɪk/ *adj* [after v], *adv* similar; like each other • *You and your father don't* **look** *very much alike.* • *The boss* **treats** *us all alike* (= in the same way). • *Friends and family alike* (= both) *were devastated by the news of her suicide.*

al·i·ment·a·ry ca·nal /£æl·ɪ'men·tᵊr·i, $-t̬ɚ-/ *n* [C] the tube-like passage from the mouth, through the stomach to the ANUS, through which food travels during digestion • (RUS)

al·i·mo·ny /£'æl·ɪ·mə·ni, $-moʊ-/ *n* [U] *dated* a regular amount of money that a court of law orders a person, usually the man, to pay to their partner after a DIVORCE (= marriage that has legally ended)

a·live /ə'laɪv/ *adj* [after v; not gradable] living; having life; not dead • *I wonder if I'll be alive in 2050?* • *Doctors kept him alive on a life-support machine.* • *Since he became a grandparent, he is the proudest person alive* (= he is extremely proud). • *(fig.) She's a writer who really knows how to make her characters* **come** *alive* (= seem real and interesting). • *(fig.) Relatives of the missing sailors are struggling to keep hope alive* (= continue believing that the sailors will be found). • Alive is also used to mean active and energetic or exciting: *South American novels/Big cities/Young people are so alive.* ○ *If the soap opera had some younger characters, that would* **bring** *it alive* (= make it more interesting and exciting). ○ *The city centre really* **comes** *alive* (= becomes filled with activity) *on Friday and Saturday nights.* • If you are **alive to** something, you are thinking about it or aware of it: *I ski for the excitement, but I'm also always alive to the risks.* • If something is **alive with** something else, it is so covered with or full of them that it appears to be living and moving: *The grass was alive with ants.* ○ *The pond was alive with frogs.* • *Traditional jazz is still* **alive and well/kicking** (= active) *in New Orleans.* • *The book's* **alive and well** (= still exists, even though many people are no longer aware of it) **and** *making money for its author.*

al·ka·li /'æl·kᵊl·aɪ/ *n* [C] *pl* **alkalis** or **alkalies** *specialized* a substance which has the opposite effect or chemical behaviour to an acid

al·ka·line /'æl·kᵊl·aɪn/ *adj* • *Some plants will not grow in very alkaline soils.*

al·ky, al·kie /'æl·ki/ *n* [C] *slang* an **alcoholic**, see at ALCOHOL

all [EVERY ONE] /£ɔːl, $ɑːl/ *determiner, predeterminer, pronoun* every one (of), or the complete amount or number (of), or the whole (of) • *All animals have to eat in order to live.* • *All imported timber must be chemically treated against disease.* • *She's got four children, all under the age of five.* • *The cast all lined up on stage to take their bow.* • *Have you drunk all* **(of)** *the milk.* • *Have you drunk it all?* • *All the eggs got broken.* • *Now the money's all mine!* • *Not all my friends approved of what I did.* • *Where are you? I've been trying all day/week to contact you.* (D) • *She had £2000 under the bed and the thieves took it all.* • *I had to use all my powers of persuasion to get her to agree.* • *Do you remember all that trouble we had with the police last year?* • *Speed is all that matters* (= the most important thing) – *don't worry about any mistakes.* • *All* (= The only thing) *I need is a roof over my head and a decent meal.* • *The judge cleared the court of all* **but** (= everyone except) *herself and the witness.* • *Why do you get so angry with me all* **the time** (= very often)*?* • *It's very kind of you to come all* **the way** *to meet me.* • *"***All aboard***"* (= All passengers must get onto the ship), *shouted the Captain, "we sail in five minutes."* • *It's* **all (that)** *I* **can do to** (= I'm trying very hard to) *stay awake, this is so boring.* • **All in all** (= Considering everything), *I think you've done very well.* • *It's going to cost* **all of** (= at least) *a million dollars.* • *It's appalling – the book has sold* **all of** (= only) *200 copies.* • *Her parents died when she was a baby, so I was* **all the** (= the only) *family she ever had.* • *We're already two months behind schedule and now the computer people are going on strike –* **that/this is all** *we* **need** (= exactly what we don't want). • *The fairground strong man was offering to take on* **all-comers** (= anyone). • *(saying)* 'All good things must come to an end' means that nothing lasts forever. • *"All for one, and one for all"* (Alexandre Dumas in the novel *The Three Musketeers*, 1844) • *"I am made all things to all men"* (Bible, 1 Corinthians 9.22) • (LP) **Quantity words**

all– /£ɔːl-, $ɑːl-/ *combining form* • All- can be used in front of many nouns, adjectives and present participles: *an all-inclusive price* (= a price that includes all possible charges) ○ *an all-night bar* (= a bar that is open all night) ○ *an all-purpose tool/vehicle* (= one that can be used for many purposes) ○ *an all-weather hockey pitch* (= one that can be used in all weather conditions) *all-conquering armies* ○ *Profits are at an all-***time** *high/their all-***time** *best* (= are now the best ever reached). • **All-in wrestling** is a type of sport in which you fight without limits on your methods.

all [COMPLETELY] /£ɔːl, $ɑːl/ *adv* [before adv/prep; not gradable] completely • *This coat is all wool while the other one is a blend.* • *Is the milk all gone? I'll buy some more this afternoon.* • *The downstairs rooms were painted all in greens and blues.* • *The baby got food all* **over** *its bib.* • *Don't let those awful boys get you all upset.* • *She's been all over town/along the street looking for you.* • *Don't tell me any more – I've already heard all about it.* • *I used to have to work over-time, but, thankfully, that is all* **over** *now.* • *The Princess lived all* **alone/by herself** *in the middle of the forest.* • *I'm paying, so it's drinks all* **round** (= for everyone). • *It was a ghastly business all* **round** (= completely). • All is also used after a number to mean that both teams or players in a game have equal points: *The score at half-time was still four all.* • *Mum's* **not all that** (= not very) *keen on me having a disco for my party.* • *The game was* **all but** (= almost) *over by the time we arrived.* • *(Br and Aus) It was* **all go** (= extremely busy) *in town today.* • If you say that you are **all in**, you mean that you are very tired and unable to do anything more. • To **go all out** means to put all your energy/enthusiasm into what you are doing: *His parents went all out* **to** *make his birthday party special.* ○ *The team went all out* **for** *a win.* ○ *The publisher made an all-out effort to get the book out on time.* • *She's always talking – that's Claire,* **all over** (= that is typical of Claire). • If you say that things are **all over the place/***(Br also)* **all over the shop**, you mean that they are scattered in a lot of different places in an untidy way: *He'd gone out in a hurry and left his things all over the place.* ○ *They must have had a party – there were bottles and glasses and stuff all over the shop.* • *He'll be* **all smiles/apologies/charm** (= He will smile/APOLOGIZE a lot/be very charming) *when you meet him, but I wouldn't trust him an inch.* • *(infml disapproving) He's* **all mouth/talk** (= He never does any of the things that he says he will). • **All the** is used before comparative adjectives and adverbs to mean 'even' or 'much': *I've lost ten kilos in weight and I feel all the fitter for it.* ○ *Now that he's a star he'll be all the more difficult to work with.* ○ *She felt all the better* **for** *the drink.* • *(infml disapproving)* If you describe someone as **not all there**, you mean that they are slightly stupid or that they behave strangely: *My cousin is very nice, but she's not quite all there.* • *"All about Eve"* (film title, 1950) • See also ALL RIGHT.

all– /£ɔːl-, $ɑːl-/ *combining form* • *all-cotton socks* (= socks that are 100% cotton) • *When cooking the sauce, don't forget that all-***important** (= most or very important) *ingredient, fresh basil.* • *Baseball is such an all-***American** (= typically American) *sport.* • *Do you believe in an all-***powerful** *god* (= one with limitless power)*?* • An all-**star cast**/show/team/etc. is one that is full of excellent or famous actors or players. • *He gave/sounded/heard* **the all-clear** (= the signal that the danger was past). • *She's a fantastic* **all-round/***(Am also)* **all-around** *sportswoman* (= one with many different skills). • *(Br and Aus) He's an* **all-rounder** (= He is good at many different things).

Al·lah /'æl·ə/ *n* [not after *the*] the Islamic name for God

al·lay *obj* /ə'leɪ/ *v* [T] *fml* to make (a person's or group's fear, doubt, anger, etc.) less strong • *The government is desperately trying to allay public* **fears/suspicions/concern** *about the spread of the disease.*

al·lege *obj* /ə'ledʒ/ *v* [T] *fml esp. law* to state that (something bad) is a fact without giving proof • *The two men allege* **(that)** *the police forced them to make false confessions.* [+ (*that*) clause] • *Mr Smythe is alleged* **to** *have been at the centre of an international drugs ring.* [+ obj + *to* infinitive] • **It** *was alleged* **that** *Johnson had struck Mr Rahim on the head.* [+ *that* clause]

al·leged /ə'ledʒd/ *adj* [not gradable] *fml esp. law* • *It took 15 years for the alleged criminals* (= people thought to be criminals) *to prove their innocence.*

al·leg·ed·ly /ə'ledʒ·ɪd·li/ *adv* [not gradable] *fml esp. law* • *She's allegedly murdered three husbands, but she looks like a harmless old lady.*

al·le·ga·tion /ˌæl·ə'geɪ·ʃᵊn/ *n* [C] *fml esp. law* • An allegation is a statement made, without giving any proof, that someone has done something, esp. something wrong or illegal: *Several of her patients have made allegations* **of**

professional misconduct **about/against** *this doctor.* ○ *Allegations* **that** *Mr Dwight was receiving money from known criminals have caused a scandal.* [+ *that* clause]

al·le·giance /ə'liː·dʒᵊnts/ *n fml* loyalty and support for a ruler, country, group, belief, etc. • *Soldiers must* **swear** *allegiance* **to** *the Crown/the King.* [U] • *In many American schools, the students* **pledge** *allegiance* **(to the flag)** *at the beginning of the school day.* [U] • *As an Englishman who'd lived for a long time in France, he felt a certain conflict of allegiances when the two countries played soccer.* [C]

al·le·go·ry /£'æl·ə·gə·ri, $-gɔːr·i/ *n* (the style of) a story, play, poem, picture, etc. in which the characters and events represent particular qualities or ideas, related to some moral, religious or political meaning • *The play can be read as allegory.* [U] • *Saint Augustine's 'City of God' is an allegory* **of** *the triumph of Good over Evil.* [C]

al·le·gor·i·cal /£,æl·ə'gɒr·ɪ·kᵊl, $-'gɔːr-/ *adj*

al·le·gor·i·cal·ly /£,æl·ɪ'gɒr·ɪ·kli, $-'gɔːr-/ *adv*

al·le·lu·ia /,æl·ɪ'luː·jə/ *exclamation, n* [C] HALLELUJAH

Al·len key /'æl·ən/, **Al·len wrench** *n* [C] *trademark* an L-shaped metal tool with six sides that is used to turn a screw with a six-sided hole in the top

al·ler·gen /£'æl·ə·dʒən, $'-ɚ-/ *n* [C] *specialized* a substance which can cause an ALLERGY (= condition of the body reacting badly to something), but which is harmless to most people

al·ler·gy /£'æl·ə·dʒi, $'-ɚ-/ *n* [C] the condition of reacting badly to something, such as milk, the fur of particular animals or dust, causing someone who eats it, touches it or breathes it in to feel uncomfortable or become ill, although it is harmless to most people. • *Your skin problems are caused by an allergy* **to** *wheat.*

al·ler·gic /£ə'lɜː·dʒɪk, $-lɜːr-/ *adj* • *I'm allergic* **to** *cats./I have an allergic* **reaction** *to cats.* • *(fig. infml) My Dad's allergic* **to** (= he hates) *pop music.*

al·le·vi·ate *obj* /ə'liː·vi·eɪt/ *v* [T] *fml* to make (pain, problems, etc.) less severe • *The drugs did nothing to alleviate her pain/suffering.* • *This money should alleviate our financial problems.*

al·le·vi·a·tion /ə,liː·vi'eɪ·ʃᵊn/ *n* [U] • *the alleviation of poverty*

al·ley /'æl·i/, **al·ley·way** /'æl·i·weɪ/ *n* [C] a narrow road or path between buildings, or a path in a park or garden, esp. bordered by trees or bushes • *You'll find the dustbins in the alley.* • **Up/Down** your **alley** is *Am and Aus for* **up** your **street.** See at STREET. • *"Sally in our Alley"* (title of song written by Henry Carey, 1693-1743)

al·li·ance /ə'laɪ·ᵊnts/ *n* See at ALLY

al·lied /'æl·aɪd, ə'laɪd/ *adj* connected, esp. by a political or military agreement • *The allied nations managed to veto the suggestion.* • The **Allied forces** in World War Two were the armies of the countries that fought against Germany, Japan, Italy, etc. • *It takes a lot of enthusiasm, allied* **with/to** (= together with) *a love of children to make a good teacher.* • *(fml) Computer science and allied* (= similar) *subjects are not taught here.*

al·li·ga·tor /£'æl·ɪ·geɪ·tə^r, $-ţɚ/, *Am infml* **ga·tor** *n* [C] a large hard-skinned REPTILE (= type of animal) that lives in and near rivers and lakes in the hot wet parts of America and China. It has a long nose that is slightly wider and shorter than that of a CROCODILE • *(humorous)* People sometimes say 'See you later alligator,' 'In a while crocodile' when they are saying goodbye to each other.

all–in–one /£,ɔːl·ɪn'wʌn, $,ɑːl-/ *adj* [not gradable] doing the work of two or more usually separate parts • *(Br) an all-in-one baby suit/leotard* • *The new office machine is capable of acting as an all-in-one printer, document scanner, copier and fax machine.*

all–in–one /£,ɔːl·ɪn'wʌn, $,ɑːl-/ *n* [C] *Br* • An all-in-one is a piece of clothing that covers the whole body rather than being divided into a separate top and bottom part: *She wore a pink lycra all-in-one for her aerobics class.*

al·lit·er·a·tion /£ə,lɪt·ə'reɪ·ʃᵊn, $ə,lɪţ-/ *n* [U] the use, esp. in poetry, of the same sound or sounds, esp. consonants, at the beginning of several words that are close together • *'Round the rugged rocks the ragged rascal ran' uses alliteration.* • Compare ASSONANCE.

al·lo·cate *obj* /'æl·ə·keɪt/ *v* [T] to give (something) to someone as their share of a total amount, for them to use in a particular way • *The government is allocating £10 million* **for** *health education.* • *As project leader, you will have to allocate people jobs/allocate jobs* **to** *people.* [+ two objects] • *It is not the job of the investigating committee to allocate blame* **for** *the disaster/to allocate blame* **to** *individuals.*

al·lo·ca·tion /,æl·ə·keɪ·ʃᵊn/ *n* [U] • *the allocation of resources/funds/time*

al·lot *obj* /£ə'lɒt, $-'lɑːt/ *v* [T] **-tt-** to give (esp. a share of something available) for a particular purpose • *They allotted everyone a separate desk.* [+ two objects] • *They allotted a separate desk* **to** *everyone.* [+ two objects] • *The ministry of culture will be allotted about $6 million less this year.* [+ two objects] • *People rarely understand the difficulty of the job that has been allotted* **to** *us.* • *Three hours have been allotted* **to/for** *this task.* • *He's not satisfied with the* **role** *he's been allotted in the office.* [+ two objects] • *The museum is planning to increase the amount of* **space** *allotted to modern art.*

al·lot·ted /£ə'lɒt·ɪd, $-'lɑː·ţɪd/ *adj* [not gradable] • *The conference finished later than expected because the final speaker overran her allotted* **time** (= the time available for her to speak).

al·lot·ment /£ə'lɒt·mənt, $-'lɑːt-/ *n* • *The allotment of the company's shares to its employees is still to be decided.* [U] • *We have used up this year's allotment of funds.* [C]

al·lot·ment /£ə'lɒt·mənt, $-'lɑːt-/ *n* [C] *Br* a small piece of ground in or just outside a town that a person rents for growing vegetables, fruits or flowers

al·low *obj* PERMIT /ə'laʊ/ *v* [T] to let (someone) do something or let (something) happen; permit • *We must not allow these temporary problems* **to** *affect our long-term plans.* [+ obj + *to* infinitive] • *Do you think Dad will allow you to go to Pat's party?* [+ obj + *to* infinitive] • *He wouldn't allow them* **to** *leave until they'd paid the fine.* [+ obj + *to* infinitive] • *You're not allowed* **to** *talk during the exam.* [+ obj + *to* infinitive] • *She won't allow her novel* **to be** *made into a film.* [+ obj + *to* infinitive] • *Her proposals* **would** *allow* (= make it possible for) *more people* **to** *stay in full-time education.* [+ obj + *to* infinitive] • *Why has the project been allowed* **to** *continue if it's such a disaster?* [+ obj + *to* infinitive] • *The loophole has allowed hundreds of drink-drivers* **to** *avoid prosecution.* [+ obj + *to* infinitive] • *You won't be allowed* **to enter** *the country without a visa.* [+ obj + *to* infinitive] • *The government has* **refused to** *allow foreign journalists into the area for several weeks.* [+ obj + *to* infinitive] • *Prisoners have been moved to allow the demolition of part of the prison.* • *Pets aren't allowed in this hotel* (= You must not bring any animals with you when you stay here). • *Please allow me through* (= let me come/go through). • *Smoking is not allowed in this restaurant.* [+ v-*ing*] • *The manager does not allow smoking.* [+ v-*ing*] • *He didn't allow us enough time to finish the test.* [+ two objects] • *Red Cross officials were allowed* **access** *to the prison for the first time a few days ago.* [+ two objects] • *At the weekend I allow* **myself** (= I permit myself the special pleasure of having) *a box of chocolates.* [+ two objects] • *How much time do you allow your***self** (= make available to yourself) *to get ready in the morning?* [+ two objects] • *You are allowed one book each* (= That is all you are permitted to have). [+ two objects] • *(Br and Aus) The referee decided to allow* (= officially accept) *the goal.* • **Allow me** is a polite expression used when offering to do something: *Those bags are too heavy to carry by yourself – please, allow me* (**to** *help you*). • *(fml)* If a rule or situation **allows of** something, it permits it: *This rule allows of no exceptions.* ○ *The evidence allows of only one interpretation – he was murdered by his wife.* • LP **Two objects**

al·low·a·ble /ə'laʊ·ə·bḷ/ *adj* • *A certain level of error is allowable* (= permitted to happen). • *Taxpayers should claim as many allowable expenses* (= on which no taxes are paid) *as possible against their taxed income.*

al·low·ance /ə'laʊ·ᵊnts/ *n* [C] • *You'll have to pay a surcharge if you exceed your* **baggage/luggage** *allowance* (= the weight of luggage that a passenger is permitted to take on a flight). • *When I go abroad, I hardly ever use all my* **duty-free** *allowance* (= the amount of goods that can be bought without paying tax). • *The married couple's* **tax** *allowance* (= the amount of income that you can earn before you have to pay tax) *will rise in line with inflation.* • *The perks of the job include a company pension scheme and a generous* **travel** *allowance* (= money that an employee can spend while travelling on company business). • An allowance is *esp. Am for* **pocket money.** See at POCKET BAG. • An allowance is also money which parents give regularly to older children who are still at school or college to pay for some of their living expenses such as clothes and entertainment: *While he was at college, his parents gave him such a small allowance that he had to earn extra money working in a bar.*

al·low ADMIT /ə'laʊ/ *v* [+ (*that*) clause] *fml* to admit or agree (that something is true) • *She allowed* **that** *she might have been too suspicious.*

al·low for *obj v prep* [T] to take (something) into consideration; plan for (something) • *We allowed for living expenses of £20 a day.* • *You should allow for the plane* **being** *delayed.* [+ obj + v-*ing*] • *Have these prices been* **adjusted** *to allow for inflation?* • *We have to allow for the* **possibility** *that we might not finish on schedule.*

al·low·ance /ə'laʊ·ənts/ *n* • To **make allowance for** something is to prepare for the possibility of it: *We should make allowance for bad weather and have plenty of umbrellas available.* • To **make allowances for** someone or their characteristics is to take their characteristics into consideration and not judge them too severely: *You should make allowances for him – he's been quite ill recently.* ○ *"This is a poor piece of work." "Yes, but you should make allowances for the fact that she's only seven."*

al·loy METAL /'æl·ɔɪ/ *n* [C] a metal that is made by mixing two or more metals, or a metal and another substance, together • *Steel is an alloy* **of** *iron, carbon and other elements such as phosphorus and nickel.* • *Brass is an alloy of copper and zinc.* • *Standard features on the car include central locking, tinted glass, electric windows and alloy* **wheels.**

al·loy *obj* SPOIL /ə'lɔɪ/ *v* [T] *literary* to spoil or reduce in value • *My pleasure in receiving the letter was somewhat alloyed by its contents.*

all right SATISFACTORY /£ɔːl'raɪt, $ɑːl-/, **al·right** *adj* [after v], *adv* [not gradable] (in a way that is) satisfactory or reasonably good • *"What did you think of the film?" "It was all right. Nothing special."* • *Are you managing all right in your new job?* • *I wouldn't say she's rich, but she's* **doing** *all right* (= being reasonably successful). • *Is* **everything** *all right, madam?* • *(infml)* Sometimes **all right** means very good: *Gosh, this wine's all right, isn't it?* • *(Br infml)* **All right** can be used to greet someone at the same time as asking whether they are well: *"All right, John?" "Not bad thanks, and you?"* • *(slang)* **All right** can be used with the main emphasis on 'right' to express approval of what has been said or done: *"Did you hear I hit that creep who'd been pestering me?" "All* right*!"* • *(Br infml) Cor, he's* **a bit of all right** (= physically attractive). • *"I'm All Right, Jack"* (film title, 1959) • LP› **Meeting someone**

all right SAFE /£ɔːl'raɪt, $ɑːl-/, **al·right** *adj* [after v], *adv* safe, well or not harmed • *She was very ill for a while but she's all right now.* • *Are you sure you'll be all right on your own?* • *Did you get home all right* (= safely) *last night?* • *We got to London all right* (= without any problems), *but the car broke down on the way home.*

all right AGREED /£ɔːl'raɪt, $ɑːl-/, **al·right** *exclamation, adj* [after v; not gradable] used to show that something is agreed, understood or acceptable • *All right, I'll lend you the money.* • *All right, that's enough noise. Settle down and get on with your work.* • *Tell me as soon as you start to feel sick, all right?* • *"Are you sure you won't come for a drink with us?" "Well, all right then. If you insist."* • *All right, so I was wrong* (= I accept that I was wrong) *about him being the one who stole your wallet, but I still don't trust him.* • *I'd rather not go to Jane's party if that's all right* **with** *you.* • *Would it be all right* **if** *I didn't give you the money until tomorrow?* • *Chris wants to know* **if it'll** *be all right* **to** *come over to see us this evening.* [+ *to* infinitive] • *She seems to think that* **it's perfectly** *all right* **to** *break the law.* [+ *to* infinitive] • **It's/That's all right** is an answer to someone who has just thanked you for something or just said they are sorry for something they have done: *"Thanks a lot for the flowers." "It's all right* (= There's no need to thank me)*. I thought they might cheer you up."* ○ *"I'm sorry I broke the vase." "Oh, that's all right* (= it's not important)*. It wasn't very expensive."* ○ *"Oh, I'm terribly sorry!" "That's* **quite** (= completely) *all right."*

all right CERTAINLY /£ɔːl'raɪt, $ɑːl-/, **al·right** *adv* [not gradable] *infml* certainly or without any doubt • *"Are you sure he was the boy who hit you?" "Oh, it was him all right."*

all·spice /£'ɔːl·spaɪs, $'ɑːl-/ *n* [U] a powder made from a small fruit grown in hot countries, which is used as a spice in cooking

al·lude to *obj* /ə'luːd/ *v prep* [T] to refer to (someone or something) in a brief or indirect way • *She was far too polite to allude to the stain on his jacket.*

al·lu·sion /ə'luː·ʒən/ *n* [C] • *Don't* **make** *any allusions* **to** *her height* (= don't mention it, esp. when she is present). • *The film is full of allusions* **to** *Hitchcock* (= it intentionally makes you remember his films). • *Her novels are packed with* **literary** *allusions.*

al·lu·sive /ə'luː·sɪv/ *adj fml* • Something that is allusive contains a lot of allusions: *Her music is witty, ironic and allusive.* ○ *Literature tends to be very allusive, with Greek and Roman mythology, the Bible and Shakespeare being echoed over and over again.*

al·lu·sive·ness /ə'luː·sɪv·nəs/ *n* [U] *fml*

al·lure /£ə'ljʊər, £-'lʊər, $-'lʊr/ *n* [U] attraction, charm or excitement • *The allure of the moonlit swimming pool proved too much for them, and they all jumped in for a swim.* • *Most newspaper journalists find it hard to resist the allure of working in television.* • *Higher interest rates tend to increase a currency's allure to international investors.* • *He's an excellent actor, but he doesn't have the* **sexual** *allure that the role requires.* • *The town* **lost** *much of its allure when it became a seaside resort.* • Ⓓ Ⓝⓛ

al·lur·ing /£ə'ljʊə·rɪŋ, £-'lʊə-, $-'lʊr·ɪŋ/ *adj* • *I didn't find the prospect of a house with no electricity very alluring* (= attractive). • *She was wearing a most alluring dress at Sam's dinner party.*

al·lur·ing·ly /£ə'ljʊə·rɪŋ·li, £-'lʊə·rɪŋ·li, $-'lʊr·ɪŋ-/ *adv*

al·lu·vi·al /ə'luː·vi·əl/ *adj* [not gradable] *specialized* consisting of earth and sand that has been left by rivers, floods, etc. • *an alluvial plain* • *Some alluvial* **deposits** *are a rich source of diamonds.*

al·ly /'æl·aɪ/ *n* [C] a country that has agreed officially to give help and support to another one, esp. during a war, or a person who helps and supports someone else • *The President said that Britain would remain a vital ally of the United States.* • *North Korea is one of China's* **staunchest** *allies.* • *During World War One, Turkey and Germany were allies/Turkey was an ally of Germany.* • **The Allies** were the countries that fought against Germany, Italy and Japan in World War Two: *The Allies were led by the US, the UK, the USSR and France.* • *He is generally considered to be the Prime Minister's* **closest** (= greatest) *political ally.* • *She described him as a close friend and a* **dependable** *ally.*

al·ly *obj* /ə'laɪ/ *v* [T always + adv/prep] • *I refused to ally myself* **to/with** (= be friends with and support) *that mob.* • *After the last election, the socialists allied* **themselves** *with the communists to prevent the liberals taking power.*

al·li·ance /ə'laɪ·ənts/ *n* • An alliance is a group of countries, political parties or people who have agreed to work together because of shared interests or aims: *an Anglo-Japanese alliance* [C] ○ *An* **electoral** *alliance* **between** *the opposition parties would be the surest way of changing the government.* [C] ○ *Switzerland prides itself on being a neutral country which does not belong to any* **military** *alliance.* [C] ○ *Nato is sometimes called the Atlantic Alliance.* [C] • An alliance is also (the act of forming) such an agreement or connection: *The three smaller parties have* **forged/formed** *an alliance* **against** *the government.* [C] ○ *Some of us feel that the union is* **in** *alliance* **with** *the management against us.* [U]

al·lied /'æl·aɪd, ə'laɪd/ *adj* • *an allied offensive/attack/raid* ○ *allied bombers/commanders/forces/troops* • *The general admitted that civilian casualties were being caused by the allied* **bombing.** • Allied forces in World War Two were those of the countries that fought against Germany, Japan and Italy: *the Allied landings in Normandy* • *(fig.) It takes a lot of enthusiasm, allied* **with/to** (= combined with) *a love of children to make a good teacher.* • *(fig. fml) Computer science and allied* (= similar) *subjects are not taught here.*

al·ma mat·er /£,æl·mə'mɑː·tər, £-'meɪ·tər, $-'mɑː·t̬ɚ/ *n* [C usually sing] *fml or humorous* the school, college or university where you studied, or *(Am)* the official song of a school, college or university • *The vice-chancellor of the university is currently trying to persuade successful former students to support their poverty-stricken alma mater.* • *(Am) We ended our class reunion by singing the alma mater.*

al·ma·nac /'ɔːl·mə·næk, 'æl-/, **al·ma·nack** *n* [C] a book published every year that contains facts and information, either about a particular subject, or about important days, times of the sun rising and going down, changes in the moon, etc.

al·might·y GOD /£ɔːl'maɪ·ti, $-t̬i/ *adj* [not gradable] (of God) having the power to do everything • *I swear by Almighty* **God** *that the evidence which I shall give shall be the truth, the whole truth, and nothing but the truth.* • *(taboo)* **God almighty!** and **Christ almighty!** are expressions of anger or surprise.

Al·might·y /£ɔːl'maɪ·ti, $-t̬i/ *n* [U] • **The Almighty** is God: *We must pray to the Almighty for forgiveness.*

al·might·y BIG /£ɔːl'maɪ·ti, $-t̬i/ *adj* [before n] **-ier, -iest** *infml* very big, loud, serious, etc. • *All of a sudden we heard an almighty crash from the kitchen.* • *There was an almighty* **row** *when I asked them to leave.*

al·mond /£'ɑː·mənd, $'ɑːl-/ *n* [C] an edible oval nut with a hard shell, or the tree that it grows on • *Finish by sprinkling some* **chopped** *almonds over the cake.* • *(Br)* **Almond paste** is MARZIPAN. • PIC› **Nut**

al·most /£'ɔːl·məʊst, $'ɑːl·moʊst/ *adv* [not gradable] nearly but not quite • *She's almost thirty.* • *I almost wish I hadn't invited him.* • *She said yes almost before he'd finished speaking.* • *It'll cost almost as much to repair it as it would to buy a new one.* • *Almost* **all** *the passengers on the ferry were French.* • *They'll almost* **certainly** *forget to do it.* • *The number of bankruptcies almost* **doubled** *in the first six months of the year.* • *The town was almost* **entirely** *destroyed during the war.* • *We were bitten by mosquitoes almost* **every** *night.* • *You'll find beggars almost* **everywhere** *in the world.* • *Most forms of anti-social behaviour appear to be almost* **exclusively** *male.* • *Almost* **half** *of all the people who contract the disease make a complete recovery.* • *The new bridge is almost* **identical** *to the old one.* • *The boat sank almost* **immediately** *after it had struck the rock.* • *Most artists find it almost* **impossible** *to make a living from art alone.* • *This form of cancer is almost* **invariably** *fatal.* • *Until recently, the problem was almost* **universally** *ignored.*

alms /ɑːmz/ *pl n old use* clothing, food or money that is given to poor people • *In the past, people thought it was their religious duty to* **give** *alms to the poor.*

alms·house /'ɑːmz·haʊs/ *n* [C] *pl* **almshouses** /'ɑːmz ˌhaʊ·zɪz/ a private house built in the past where old or poor people could live without having to pay rent

al·oe /£'æl·əʊ, $-oʊ/ *n* [C] an evergreen plant with thick pointed leaves • **Aloe vera** is a type of aloe with a thick liquid in its leaves which is used to heal skin damaged by heat and in skin creams as a softener.

a·loft /£ə'lɒft, $-'lɑːft/ *adv* in the air or in a higher position • *She grabbed the string of sausages and* **held** *it aloft.* • *Bright scarves were* **held** *aloft by the two groups of football fans.* • *A huge balloon* **bore** (= carried) *the newly married couple aloft.*

a·lone WITHOUT PEOPLE /£ə'ləʊn, $-'loʊn/ *adj* [after v], *adv* without other people • *He likes being alone in the house.* • *She decided to climb the mountain alone.* • *We're alone together* (= there are just the two of us here) *at last, darling.* • *The Swedes are not alone* **in finding** *their language under pressure from the spread of English.* • *She's very disappointed about how things have developed, and she's* **not** *alone* **in that** (= other people are disappointed too). • *I don't like* **living** *alone.* • *Alone* **among** *his colleagues, he refused to ignore his boss's fraudulent business deals.* • *(infml)* To **go it alone** is to decide to do something by yourself and without help from other people: *I got fed up working in an office so I decided to go it alone and set up my own business at home.* • Compare LONELY.

a·lone ONLY /£ə'ləʊn, $-'loʊn/ *adj* [after n; not gradable] only or without any others • *She alone must decide what to do* (= no one else can do it for her). • *It's Jane, and Jane alone, who can help you out of this mess.* • *These facts alone* (= even if nothing else is considered) *show that he's not to be trusted.* • *You won't get the job through charm alone* (= you will need something else). • *The airfare alone would use up all my money* (= even if there was nothing else to pay for), *never mind the hotel bills.* • *Price alone is not a reliable indicator of quality.* • LP› **One**

a·long BESIDE /£ə'lɒŋ, $-'lɑːŋ/ *prep* in the same direction as, beside, or at a particular point on (something long and usually thin) • *We walked along the canal path.* • *Cars were parked* **all** *along the road.* • *My office is the third door along the corridor on the left.* • *I've been in this job for thirty years, and I've picked up a good deal of expertise* **along the way** (= during this time).

a·long FORWARD /£ə'lɒŋ, $-'lɑːŋ/ *adv* [not gradable] (esp. with verbs of movement) forward • *I was just strolling along the path when I heard a shout from behind the hedge.* • *You wait for ages for a bus, then three come along* (= arrive where you are) *at the same time.* • *Go along* (= Go) *to the careers office and have a chat with them.* • *The party was going along* (= developing) *successfully until Brian turned up with his drunken friends.* • *How far along are you in/with your essay* (= How much of it have you done)? • *Do you think he's been cheating us* **all along** (= from the beginning)?

a·long WITH YOU /£ə'lɒŋ, $-'lɑːŋ/ *adv* [not gradable] with you • *When they go to the beach they always* **bring** *their radio along.* • *Why don't you* **take** *him along* **with** *you when you go?* • *He was released from detention last week along* **with** *three other journalists.* • *I came* **along for the ride** (= just out of interest).

a·long·side /£əˌlɒŋ'saɪd, $ə'lɑːŋ·saɪd/ *prep, adv* [not gradable] beside, or together with • *A car pulled up alongside (ours).* • *The new pill will be used alongside existing medicines.* • *Most of the staff refused to* **work** *alongside the new team.* • *Britain* **fought** *alongside France, Turkey and Sardinia during the Crimean War.* • *Her latest novel does not* **rank** *alongside* (= is not as good as) *her earlier ones.* • *The stock market's burst of optimism* **sits uneasily** *alongside* (= does not suit) *the country's economic problems.*

a·loof /ə'luːf/ *adj* (of a person) unfriendly and refusing to take part in things • *Is she aloof and arrogant or just shy?* • *Whenever they started quarrelling, I would always* **remain** *aloof* (= not take part). • *Although many of his friends were politicians, he* **kept** *aloof* **from** (= avoided becoming involved in) *politics.*

a·loof·ness /ə'luːf·nəs/ *n* [U] • *I sensed a strange aloofness in her voice.* • *The church's aloofness from* (= lack of involvement in) *the current controversy will do little to resolve the matter.*

a·loud /ə'laʊd/ *adv* [after v; not gradable] in a voice loud enough to be heard; not silently or quietly • *He suddenly stopped whispering and spoke aloud.* • *He* **read** *her letter aloud to the rest of the family.* • *I couldn't help* **laughing** *aloud when she told me about her accident.* • *Some people are starting to* **wonder** *aloud* (= question publicly) *whether the economic reforms have gone too far.*

al·pac·a /æl'pæk·ə/ *n* [U] a type of wool used for making luxury clothes

al·pha, α /'æl·fə/ *n* [C] the first letter of the Greek alphabet, sometimes given as a mark for a student's work to show high quality • *I got an alpha plus for my last essay.* • *"I am the Alpha and Omega, the beginning and the ending"* (Bible, Revelations 1.8) • Compare BETA; GAMMA.

al·pha·bet /'æl·fə·bet/ *n* [C] a set of letters arranged in a fixed order which is used for writing a language • *The Urdu language has thirty-seven letters in its alphabet.* • *Russian and Bulgarian are written in the Cyrillic alphabet.* • *The pronunciations in this dictionary are given in the International Phonetic Alphabet.*

al·pha·bet·i·cal /£ˌæl·fə'bet·ɪ·kəl, $-'bet̬-/ *adj* • *an alphabetical list* • *The names are published* **in** *alphabetical* **order**.

al·pha·bet·i·cal·ly /£ˌæl·fə'bet·ɪ·kli, $-'bet̬-/ *adv* • *I've* **arranged** *the pictures of the animals alphabetically from aardvark to zebra.*

al·pine /'æl·paɪn/ *adj* relating to the Alps (= the highest mountains in Europe) or other mountainous areas • *alpine meadows/pastures* • *Our window looked out on a beautiful alpine scene.* • *Many Alpine ski resorts are suffering from a shortage of snow this winter.*

al·pine (plant) /'æl·paɪn/ *n* [C] • *Joe is an internationally renowned authority on alpines* (= plants that grow naturally in high mountain areas where trees are unable to grow).

al·ready /£ɔːl'red·i, $ɑːl-, '--/ *adv* [not gradable] earlier than the time expected, in a short time or before the present time • *Are you buying Christmas cards already? It's only September!* • *He inherited $10 000 yesterday and he's already decided what to do with it.* • *"Do you want to come to the Van Gogh exhibition with me?" "No, I've already* **seen** *it."* • *It's bad enough already* (= in its existing state) *– don't make it any worse.* • *We got caught up in the traffic and the concert had already* **begun** *by the time we arrived.* • *The company already* **owns** *three national newspapers.* • *She has only just completed her first television series, but her next project is already* **under way**. • *A test for the disease already* **exists**, *but the new test will be quicker and cheaper.* • *As I have already* **mentioned**, *I doubt that we will able to raise all the money we need.* • *"Would you mind giving the bath a quick clean?" "I've already* **done** *it."*

al·right /£ɔːl'raɪt, $ɑːl-/ *adj, adv* [not gradable], *exclamation* ALL RIGHT

Al·sa·tian /æl'seɪ·ʃən/, *esp. Am and Aus* **Ger·man shep·herd** *n* [C] a large, usually brown and black dog, often used for guarding buildings and in police work •

Alsatians look like wolves and have a reputation for being fierce. • PIC› **Dogs**

al·so /£'ɔːl·səʊ, $'ɑːl·soʊ/ *adv* [not gradable] additionally • *She's a photographer and also writes books.* • *I'm cold, and I'm also hungry and tired.* • An **also-ran** is someone in a competition who is unlikely to do well or who has failed. • Ⓓ

al·tar /£'ɔːl·tər, £'ɒl-, $-t̬ɚ/ *n* [C] a type of table used in ceremonies in a Christian church or in other religious buildings

al·ter *(obj)* CHANGE /£'ɒl·tər, $'ɑːl·t̬ɚ/ *v* (to cause a characteristic of something) to change, often slightly • *I took the coat back to the shop to have it altered.* [T] • *We've had to alter some of our plans.* [T] • *The waiter apologized and altered the figure on the bill.* [T] • *Although long-distance phone calls are going up, the charge for local calls will not alter.* [I] • *Giving up our car has* **radically** *altered our lifestyle.* [T]

al·ter·a·tion /£ˌɒl·tə'reɪ·ʃᵊn, $ˌɑːl·t̬ə-/ *n* • *Several police officers are being questioned about the alteration of the documents.* [U] • *The house needed extensive alterations when we moved in.* [C] • *Some alterations* **to** *our original plans might be necessary.* [C]

al·ter *obj* REMOVE ORGANS /£'ɒl·tər, $'ɑːl·t̬ɚ/ *v* [T] *esp. Am* to remove the sex organs from (an animal); used to avoid saying CASTRATE or SPAY • *We were planning to have Trixie altered, but she got pregnant before we had a chance to.*

al·ter·ca·tion /£ˌɒl·tə'keɪ·ʃᵊn, $ˌɑːl·t̬ɚ-/ *n* [C] *fml* a loud argument or disagreement • *According to witnesses, the altercation* **between** *the two men started inside the restaurant.* • *I'd like to avoid having another altercation* **with** *her if I possibly can.*

al·ter e·go /£ˌɒl·tə'riː·gəʊ, $ˌɑːl·t̬ɚ'iː·goʊ/ *n* [C] *pl* **alter egos** the side of someone's personality which is not usually seen by other people • *Clark Kent is Superman's alter ego.* • *Barbara Vine is the alter ego* (= the other less familiar name) *of the crime writer Ruth Rendell.*

al·ter·nate *(obj)* /£'ɒl·tə·neɪt, $'ɑːl·t̬ɚ-/ *v* [always + adv/prep] (to cause two things) to happen or exist one after the other repeatedly • *Her cheerfulness alternated* **with** *despair.* [I] • *The children alternated* **between** *being excited* **and** *tired.* [I] • *He alternated working in the office* **with** *long tours overseas.* [T]

al·ter·nate /£ɒl'tɜː·nət, $ɑːl'tɜːr-/ *adj* [before n; not gradable] • *The soldiers were in a state of alternate panic* **and** *bravado* (= they felt one thing, then the other). • *Private cars are banned from the city on alternate days* (= They can come in one day, then not on the next one, then on the next one, and so on). • *They ridiculed any alternate point of view* (= different from the one they have).

al·ter·nate·ly /£ɒl'tɜː·nət·li, $ɑːl'tɜːr-/ *adv* • *The film is alternately depressing and amusing.*

al·ter·nat·or /£'ɒl·tə·neɪ·tər, $'ɑːl·tɚ·neɪ·t̬ɚ/ *n* [C] • An alternator is an electrical device which produces a current that changes direction in a regular way.

al·ter·nat·ive /£ɒl'tɜː·nə·tɪv, $ɑːl'tɜːr·nə·t̬ɪv/, *esp. Am* **al·ter·nate** *n, adj* (something that is) different from something else, esp. from what is usual, and offering the possibility of choice • *There must be an alternative* **to** *people sleeping on the streets.* [C] • *We are not going to rule out every other alternative.* [C] • *I'm afraid I have* **no** *alternative* **but to** *ask you to leave* (= that is what I have to do). [C] • *The opposition parties have so far failed to set out an alternative strategy.* [before n] • *An alternative venue for the concert is being sought.* [before n] • *(esp. Am) They ridiculed any alternate point of view.* [before n] • Alternative **energy** means energy from moving water, wind, the sun and gas from animal waste: *The new policy is aimed at developing alternative energy* **sources** *and decreasing dependence on imported energy.* • Alternative **lifestyles/medicine/comedy** are things which are considered to be unusual and which tend to have a small but enthusiastic group of people who support them: *Alternative medicine includes treatments such as acupuncture, homeopathy, osteopathy and hypnotherapy.*

al·ter·nat·ive·ly /£ɒl'tɜː·nə·tɪv·li, $ɑːl'tɜːr·nə·t̬ɪv-/ *adv* • *We could go to the Indian restaurant,* **or** *alternatively* (= or instead of that), *we could try that new Italian place.*

al·though /£ɔːl'ðəʊ, $ɑːl'ðoʊ/ *conjunction* despite the fact that or but • *Although she's only three, her mother dresses her in grown-up clothes.* • *He decided to go, although I begged him not to.* • *She's very kind, although a bit bossy.* • *I'm rather shy, although I'm not as bad as I used to be.* • LP› **'-ough' pronunciation**

al·ti·me·ter /£'æl·tɪ·miː·tər, $æl'tɪm·ə·t̬ɚ/ *n* [C] a device used in an aircraft to measure how high it is from the ground

al·ti·tude /£'æl·tɪ·tjuːd, $-t̬ə·tuːd/ *n* [C] height above sea level • *We are currently flying* **at an altitude of** *15 000 metres.* • *Mountain climbers use oxygen when they reach* **higher** *altitudes.* • LP› **Measurements**

al·to /£'æl·təʊ, $-toʊ/ *n* [C] *pl* **altos** (a woman with) a low adult female singing voice or (a boy with) the lowest boys' singing voice • *She began by singing soprano, then changed to alto.* • An alto musical instrument has the same range of notes as the alto singing voice: *an alto saxophone*

al·to·ge·ther /£ˌɔːl·tə'geð·ər, $ˌɑːl·tə'geð·ɚ/ *adv* [not gradable] completely or in total • *That'll be £52·50 altogether, please.* • *He's bad-tempered, selfish and altogether* (= including everything) *an unpleasant man.* • *I'm not altogether sure I want that* (= I have doubts about it). • *It's all right working with him, but living with him would be a* **different** *matter altogether.* • *The government ought to* **abolish/scrap** *the tax altogether.* • *It is* **not** *altogether* **surprising** (= It is to be expected) *that he wants to go and live with his sister.* • *I think Graham will agree, but convincing Mary will be altogether* **more** (= much more) *difficult.* • *The new computer system won't* **eliminate** *paperwork altogether, but it'll reduce it dramatically.* • *She wrote less and less often, and eventually she* **stopped** *altogether.*

al·to·ge·ther /£ˌɔːl·tə'geð·ər, $ˌɑːl·tə'geð·ɚ/ *n* [U] *infml* • Someone who is **in the altogether** has no clothes on: *I wish you wouldn't keeping standing by the window in the altogether. Someone might see you.*

al·tru·i·sm /'æl·tru·ɪ·zᵊm/ *n* [U] willingness to do things which benefit other people, even if it results in disadvantage for yourself

al·tru·ist /'æl·tru·ɪst/ *n* [C] • *I'm not buying the factory because I'm an altruist. I expect it to be making me a lot of money in a few years' time.*

al·tru·ist·ic /ˌæl·tru'ɪs·tɪk/ *adj* • *I doubt whether her* **motives** *for donating the money are altruistic – she's probably looking for publicity.*

al·tru·is·ti·cal·ly /ˌæl·tru'ɪs·tɪ·kli/ *adv*

al·u·mi·ni·um *Br and Aus* /ˌæl·jʊ'mɪn·i·əm/, *Am* **a·lu·mi·num** /ə'luː·mɪ·nəm/ *n* [U] a light metallic element which is silver in colour and used esp. for making cooking equipment and aircraft parts • *an aluminium saucepan* • *Cover the fish with aluminium* **foil** *and cook over a low heat for 4 to 5 minutes.* • *We take all our aluminium* **cans** *for recycling.*

a·lum·nus *male* (*pl* **alumni**), *female* **a·lum·na** (*pl* **alumnae**) /ə'lʌm·nəs, -nə/ *n* [C] *esp. Am* someone who has left a school, college or university after completing their studies there • *the alumni of St MacNissi's College* • *Several* **famous** *alumni have agreed to help raise money for the school's restoration fund.*

al·ways /£'ɔːl·weɪz, $'ɑːl-/ *adv* [not gradable] every time, all the time or forever • *It's always cold in this room.* • *Will you always love me?* • *(usually disapproving) You're always complaining.* [+ v-*ing*] • *He* **almost** *always has breakfast in bed on a Saturday.* • *We've always* **wanted** *to buy our own house.* • *I always* **thought** *I'd have children eventually.* • *Lucy* **nearly** *always spells Susannah's name wrong.* • *He always* **seems** *to be complaining about something.* • *I've always* **felt** *I would go back there sometime.* • *She's always* **liked** *French food.* • Always is sometimes used with **can** or **could** to suggest another possibility: *If you miss this train you can always catch the next one.* • *"You always hurt the one you love"* (song written by Allan Roberts and Doris Fisher, 1944)

Alz·heim·er's (dis·ease) /£'ælts͵haɪ·məz, $-mɚz/ *n* [U] a disease of the nervous system that is common in old people and which results in the gradual loss of memory, speech, movement and the ability to think clearly • *an Alzheimer's patient* • *Alzheimer's disease affects an estimated one in five of the two million Britons over the age of 80.*

am BE /æm/ *I form of* BE • *I am sure she will be very successful in her new job.*

am MORNING, **a.m.** /ˌeɪ'em/ *adv* [not gradable] used when referring to a time between twelve o'clock at night and twelve o'clock in the middle of the day • *The most expensive time to use the phone in Britain is between 8am and 6pm on a weekday.* • *The first election results are expected around 1am.* • Compare PM TIME. • LP› **Time**

AM [RADIO] /ˌeɪˈem/ *n* [U] *abbreviation for* amplitude modulation (=type of radio broadcasting in which the strength of the signal changes, producing sound which is usually less clear than FM) • *You're listening to Radio Gold, broadcasting 24 hours a day on 909 AM.*

a·mal·gam·ate *(obj)* /əˈmæl·gə·meɪt/ *v* (to cause separate but related organizations or groups) to join or unite to form a larger organization or group • *The electricians' union is planning to amalgamate* **with** *the technicians' union.* [I] • *The different offices will be amalgamated* **as/into** *employment advice centres.* [T] • *How many members does the Amalgamated Engineering Union have?*

a·mal·gam /əˈmæl·gəm/ *n* [C] • *The Ecu is an amalgam* **of** (=a mixture of) *the currencies of the member states of the European Union.*

a·mal·gam·a·tion /əˌmæl·gəˈmeɪ·ʃən/ *n* • *The association was* **formed** *by the amalgamation of several regional environmental organizations.* [U] • *The company began as an amalgamation of small family firms.* [C]

a·man·u·en·sis /əˌmæn·juˈent·sɪs/ *n* [C] *pl* **amanuenses** /əˌmæn·juˈent·siːz/ *fml* a person whose job is to write down what another person says or to copy what another person has written • *Milton used an amanuensis to write some of his greatest poetry.*

a·mass *obj* /əˈmæs/ *v* [T] to get a large amount of (esp. money or information) by collecting it over a long period • *She has amassed a huge* **fortune** *from her novels.* • *Some of his colleagues envy the enormous* **wealth** *that he has amassed.* • *It was estimated that the state had amassed 100 to 200 atomic warheads.*

am·a·teur /£ˈæm·ə·təʳ, $-t̬ɚ/ *adj* taking part in an activity for pleasure, not as a job, or (of an activity) done for pleasure, not as a job • *an amateur astronomer/boxer/golfer/historian* • *amateur athletics* • *Lawton was an amateur singer until the age of 40, when he turned professional.* • *My sister's an* **enthusiastic** *amateur photographer.* • **Amateur dramatics** are theatrical performances in which the people involved are not paid but take part for their own enjoyment: *She trained as a teacher, but her love of amateur dramatics convinced her that acting was more than a hobby.* • Compare **professional** at PROFESSION.

am·a·teur /£ˈæm·ə·təʳ, $-t̬ɚ/ *n* [C] • *This tennis tournament is open to both amateurs and professionals.* • *(disapproving)* You can use the word amateur to describe someone who lacks skill in what they do: *The political leaders were accused of being bungling amateurs.* • Compare **professional** at PROFESSION.

am·a·teur·ish /£ˈæm·ə·tə·rɪʃ, $ˌæm·əˈtɜːr·ɪʃ/ *adj disapproving* • *A waiter who carried out an amateurish bank robbery with a toy gun has been given a five-year jail sentence.*

am·a·teur·ish·ly /£ˈæm·ə·tə·rɪʃ·li, $ˌæm·əˈtɜːr·ɪʃ-/ *adv disapproving* • *The house was redecorated recently, but it was very amateurishly done.*

a·ma·teur·ish·ness /£ˈæm·ə·tə·rɪʃ·nəs, $ˌæm·əˈtɜːr·ɪʃ-/ *n* [U] *disapproving* • *I wasn't impressed by the amateurishness of their performance.*

am·at·o·ry /£ˈæm·ə·tᵊr·i, $-tɔːr-/ *adj literary* relating to sexual love • *I'm not interested in hearing about your amatory experiences.*

a·maze *obj* /əˈmeɪz/ *v* [T] to cause (someone) to be extremely surprised; to ASTONISH • *I was amazed* **(by) how** *well he looked.* [+ obj + *wh-* word] • *You've done all your homework in an hour? You amaze me.* • **It** *amazes me* **that** *she's got the energy for all those parties.* [+ obj + *that* clause] • **It** *amazes me* **to** *think that Pat's now in charge of the company.* [+ obj + *to* infinitive] • **It** *amazes me* **how** *you can put up with living in such a dirty house.* [+ obj + *wh-* word] • **It never ceases to** *amaze me* **how** *he can talk for so long without ever saying anything interesting.* [+ obj + *wh-* word]

a·mazed /əˈmeɪzd/ *adj* • *She was amazed* **at** *how calm she felt after the accident.* • *I was* **absolutely** *amazed when I heard he'd been promoted.* • *Amazed, she stood and stared while the police arrested her husband.* • *Mr Graham was amazed* **to** *find 46 ancient gold coins inside the pot.* [+ *to* infinitive] • *I was amazed* **to hear** *that Chris had won first prize.* [+ *to* infinitive] • *We were amazed* **to discover** *that we'd been at school together.* [+ *to* infinitive]

a·maze·ment /əˈmeɪz·mənt/ *n* [U] • *She stared at the photograph* **in** *amazement* (=with great surprise). • *All his fellow students* **expressed** *amazement that he could have been part of such a violent organization.*

a·maz·ing /əˈmeɪ·zɪŋ/ *adj* • *This stain remover really works – it's amazing!* • *The new theatre is going to cost an amazing* (=very large) **amount** *of money.* • *(approving) This wine is really amazing* (=very good). • **It**'*s amazing* **to** *think that the managing director is only 23.* [+ *to* infinitive] • **It**'*s amazing* **that** *no one else has applied for the job.* [+ *that* clause] • *Her election victory was an amazing* **feat.** • *Cheryl found it* **truly** *amazing that her mother was better-looking than she was.* • *The amazing* **thing** *is that it was kept secret for so long.* • *I've just come back from Uganda, and it was a* **pretty** *amazing trip.* • *What an amazing* **coincidence**!

a·maz·ing·ly /əˈmeɪ·zɪŋ·li/ *adv* • *She plays the part amazingly well.* • *Her latest film is amazingly* **popular** *in Japan.* • *The food at that restaurant is amazingly* **good.** • *Amazingly* **enough** (=Very surprisingly), *no one else has applied for the job.*

am·a·zon /£ˈæm·ə·zᵊn, $-zɑːn/ *n* [C] *humorous* a tall strong or forceful woman • *The press portrayed me as some sort of amazon after I sailed around the world.*

am·a·zon·i·an /£ˌæm·əˈzəʊ·ni·ən, $-ˈzoʊ-/ *adj humorous* • *My sports mistress was a stern amazonian woman, with a piercing stare.*

A·ma·zon·i·an /£ˌæm·əˈzəʊ·ni·ən, $-ˈzoʊ-/ *adj* relating to the area around the Amazon river in South America • *He alleges that the company's oil-drilling operations are destroying the Amazonian* **rain forest** *where his tribe lives.*

am·bas·sa·dor /£æmˈbæs·ə·dəʳ, $-dɚ/ *n* [C] an important official who lives in a foreign country to represent his or her own country there, and who is officially accepted in this position by that country • *Britain's ambassador* **in** *Moscow has refused to comment.* • *She's a former ambassador* **to** *the United States.* • *When Iceland recognised Lithuania as an independent state, the Soviet Union* **recalled** *its ambassador in protest.* • *She was* **appointed** *ambassador to Spain three months ago.* • *Late last night, the French ambassador* **was summoned** *to the Foreign Office to discuss the crisis.* • *"An ambassador is an honest man sent to lie abroad for the good of the state"* (Remark by Sir Henry Wooton, 1604)

am·bas·sa·dor·i·al /£æmˌbæs·əˈdɔː·ri·əl, $-ˈdɔːr·i-/ *adj* • *He achieved ambassadorial rank* (=the rank of ambassador) *in 1958 when Eisenhower made him envoy to Romania.*

am·ber /£ˈæm·bəʳ, $-bɚ/ *n* a hard transparent yellowish-brown substance which was formed in ancient times from the liquid of trees and is used in jewellery • *He has a collection of prehistoric insects* **preserved in** *amber.* [U] • *Would you like an amber* **necklace** *for your birthday?* • *(Br)* Amber *(Am and Aus* **yellow**) is the yellowish-orange traffic light which shows between the green and the red to warn drivers that the lights are about to change: *The lights turned to amber.* [U] ○ *He almost had an accident when he drove through an amber that was just about to change to red.* [C] ○ *You should stop at an amber* **light**.

am·bi·dex·trous /ˌæm·bɪˈdek·strəs/ *adj* able to use both hands equally well • *My grandmother was ambidextrous, so she could write with both her left and her right hands.*

am·bi·ence /£ˈæm·bi·ᵊnts, $ˌɑːm·biˈɑːnts/ *n* [U] *literary* the character of a place or the quality it seems to have • *Despite being a busy city, Dublin has the ambience* **of** *a country town.*

am·bi·ent /ˈæm·bi·ᵊnt/ *adj* [before n] *specialized* (esp. of environmental conditions) existing in the surrounding area • *By being insulated from the outside world with extremely effective sound-proofing, the concert hall is virtually free of ambient* **noise.** • *A mammal or bird is able to keep its body temperature fairly constant, whatever fluctuations there may be in the ambient* **temperature.** • *A small change in ambient conditions, such as a slight drop in temperature, can cause a musical instrument to go out of tune.* • *Factors that affect the health of office workers include the design of desks and chairs, the ambient lighting and the angle of computer screens.*

am·big·u·ous /æmˈbɪg·ju·əs/ *adj* having or expressing more than one possible meaning, sometimes intentionally • *It was hoped that he would clarify the ambiguous remarks he made earlier.* • *The government has been ambiguous on this issue.* • *Her speech was* **deliberately** *ambiguous to avoid offending either side.* • *His reply to my question was* **somewhat** *ambiguous.* • *The* **wording** *of the agreement is ambiguous, so both interpretations are valid.* • *They've always had ambiguous* (=uncertain) **feelings** *about whether or not they should have children.*

am·bi·gu·ous·ly /æm'bɪg·ju·ə·sli/ *adv* • *Some questions were badly or ambiguously worded.*

am·bi·gu·i·ty /£ˌæm·bɪ'gjuː·ɪ·ti, $-ə·t̬i/ *n* • *We wish to remove any ambiguity* (=confusion) *concerning our demands.* [U] • *There are some ambiguities in the legislation.* [C]

am·bit /'æm·bɪt/ *n* [U] *fml* the range or limits of influence of something • *They believe that all the outstanding issues should* **fall within the** *ambit* **of** *the talks.*

am·bi·tion /æm'bɪʃ·ᵊn/ *n* a strong desire for success, achievement, power or wealth • *She's got a lot of ambition, so she's bound to be successful.* [U] • *His ambition is ultimately* **to** *run his own business.* [C + *to* infinitive] • *She denies that she has any* **political** *ambitions.* [C] • *She doubts whether she'll ever be able to* **fulfil** *her ambition.* [C] • *He died with only one* **unfulfilled** *ambition, which was to take photographs on a spaceflight.* [C] • *The important question is whether he is prepared to go to war to achieve his* **territorial** *ambitions.* [C] • *It was her* **life's** *ambition to publish a novel.* [C + *to* infinitive] • *My family are more important to me than politics and* **personal** *ambition.* [U] • *Her* **frustrated** *ambitions have made her extremely bitter and cynical.* [C] • *I've always had a* **burning** (=very great) *ambition to be a film director.* [C] • *The leaders of both parties have* **presidential** *ambitions.* [C] • *He attributes his failure to* **a lack of** *ambition.* [U] • *He has already* **achieved** *his main ambition in life – to become wealthy.* [C] • *After his heart attack, he abandoned his ambition* **to become** *Prime Minister.* [C + *to* infinitive]

am·bi·tious /æm'bɪʃ·əs/ *adj* • Someone who is ambitious has a great desire to be successful, powerful or wealthy: *She's extremely ambitious and intends to be running her own company by the time she's 30.* ○ *She's the sort of ambitious* **young** *professional that any company would be glad to have on its staff.* ○ *He's very ambitious* **for** *his children* (= He's anxious that they should be successful). • Something that is ambitious needs a great amount of skill and effort to be successful or be achieved: *She has some ambitious expansion* **plans** *for her business.* ○ *The tunnel was one of the most ambitious engineering* **projects** *ever undertaken* (=It needed more skill and effort than any other). ○ *The government has announced an ambitious* **programme** *to modernize the railway network.* ○ *The original completion date was* **over-ambitious**, *so we have had to delay the opening by six months.* ○ *The environment minister has set ambitious* **goals** *for the recycling of household waste.* ○ *There are bound to be problems with such an ambitious* **scheme**. • (RUS)

am·bi·tious·ly /æm'bɪʃ·ə·sli/ *adv* • *By the age of 11, she was ambitiously attempting to compose orchestral pieces.* • *Unemployment is ambitiously forecast to fall by 10% next year* (= It is unlikely that it will be possible to achieve this).

am·bi·va·lent /æm'bɪv·ə·lənt/ *adj* having two opposing feelings at the same time, or being uncertain about how you feel • *I must say I* **feel** *pretty ambivalent* **about** *whether or not we go to France this year.* • *He has understandably ambivalent* **feelings** *towards his father, who abused him throughout his childhood.* • *Professional soldiers have an ambivalent* **attitude** *to warfare – on the one hand, they enjoy their work, but on the other, they want to live.*

am·bi·va·lence /æm'bɪv·ə·lənts/ *n* [U] • *All the negotiators have expressed considerable ambivalence* **about** *the prospects for peace.* • *Her ambivalence* **towards** *marriage prevented her from making the commitment that he so desperately sought.*

am·bi·va·lent·ly /æm'bɪv·ə·lənt·li/ *adv*

am·ble /'æm·bl̩/ *v* [I always + adv/prep] to walk in a slow and relaxed way • *He ambled nonchalantly over to the phone.* • *She was just ambling* **along**, *going nowhere in particular.* • *She ambled* **down** *the street, stopping occasionally to look in the shop windows.* • *He blinked in the sunlight and ambled* **off** *towards the post office.*

am·ble /'æm·bl̩/ *n* [U] • *There's nothing I enjoy more than* **a** *leisurely amble across the moor.* • *The horse slowed to* **an** *amble* (= a slow walk, lifting both the legs on one side at the same time).

am·bro·si·a /£æm'brəʊ·zi·ə, £-ʒə, $-'broʊ·ʒə/ *n* [U] *literary* the food eaten by Greek and Roman gods, or a very pleasant food which could be compared with this • *The chocolate mousse she makes is sheer ambrosia* (=tastes extremely good).

am·bu·lance /'æm·bjʊ·lənts/ *n* [C] a special vehicle used to take ill or injured people to hospital • *Seventeen ambulances were needed to take the injured to hospital.* • *Quick,* **call** *an ambulance. I think he's had a heart attack.* • *We were woken regularly throughout the night by the wail of ambulance* **sirens**. • *I was an ambulance* **driver** *before I became a nurse.* • *An ambulance* **crew** *was called to his home, but he was dead by the time they arrived.* • *Many of the troubles of the ambulance* **service** *stem directly from management failures.* • *She was flown back to England by* **air** *ambulance for emergency surgery.* • *(infml)* An **ambulance chaser** is a lawyer or reporter who obtains work by taking advantage of someone else's misfortune without considering their feelings: *An ambulance chaser contacted her the day she was injured and persuaded her to sue the city council for negligence.* ○ **Ambulance-chasing** *journalists have been pestering her ever since her husband's affair was revealed.* • PIC› **Emergency services**

am·bu·lance·man (*pl* **-men**), **am·bu·lance·wo·man** (*pl* **-women**) /'æm·bjʊ·lənts·mən, -ˌwʊm·ən/ *n* [C] *Br and Aus* a person whose job is to drive an AMBULANCE and to help or give treatment to the people carried in it

am·bush *obj* /'æm·bʊʃ/ *v* [T] to attack (a person or a group of people) after hiding and waiting for them • *Five soldiers died after their bus was ambushed on a country road.* • *He was ambushed by* **gunmen** *on his way to work.*

am·bush /'æm·bʊʃ/ *n* • *Several passers-by were* **killed** *in the ambush.* [C] • *Fear of ambush prevents the police from going to high-risk areas.* [U] • If someone **lies in/ waits in** ambush they hide and wait for someone in order to attack them. [U]

a·me·ba /ə'miː·bə/ *n* [C] *pl* **amebas** or **amebae** /ə'miː·biː/ *esp. Am for* AMOEBA

a·me·bic /ə'miː·bɪk/ *adj* [not gradable] *esp. Am*

a·me·li·or·ate *obj* /ə'miː·ljə·reɪt/ *v* [T] *fml* to make (a situation) better or less bad • *Foreign aid is badly needed to ameliorate the effects of the drought.*

a·me·li·or·a·tion /əˌmiː·li·ə'reɪ·ʃᵊn/ *n* [U] *fml* • *We are hoping for* **an** *amelioration* **of** *the situation.*

a·men /ˌɑː'men, ˌeɪ-/ *exclamation fml* said or sung by Jews or Christians at the end of a prayer or sometimes a religious song to express agreement with what has been said • *May the grace of our Lord Jesus Christ be with you all. Amen.* • You can say **amen to that** to show that you agree strongly with something that someone has just said: *"Thank goodness we didn't go." "Amen to that!"*

a·men·a·ble /ə'miː·nə·bl̩/ *adj* willing to accept or be influenced by a suggestion • *She might be more amenable to the idea if you explained how much money it would save.* • *Do you think the new manager will* **prove** *more amenable* **to** *our proposals?* • *They are nice, amenable* (=well-behaved and easy to control) *dogs if they are trained in the right way.*

a·mend *obj* /ə'mend/ *v* [T] to change the words of (esp. a law or a legal document) • *MPs were urged to amend the law* **to** *prevent another oil tanker disaster.* [+ obj + *to* infinitive] • *In line 20, 'men' should be amended* (=changed) **to** *'people'.* • *Until the* **constitution** *is amended, the power to appoint ministers will remain with the president.* • *The country's constitution will have to be amended* **to allow** *its troops to take part in United Nations peacekeeping operations.*

a·mend·ment /ə'mend·mənt/ *n* • *He insisted that the book did not need amendment.* [U] • *I've made a few last-minute amendments* **to the** *article.* [C] • *Presidential power was reduced by a* **constitutional** *amendment in 1991.* [C] • An amendment is sometimes a change to a law that is not yet in operation and is still being discussed by a parliament: *An amendment to the* **bill** *was agreed without a vote.* [C] ○ *The amendments that she* **tabled** (=suggested for discussion) *were based on the most recent medical research.* [C] ○ *All amendments* **proposed** *by the opposition parties were defeated.* [C]

a·mends /ə'mendz/ *pl n* **make amends** to do something to show that you are sorry about something you have done • *Offenders should be allowed to make amends* **for** *their crimes.* • *She tried to make amends* **by** *inviting him out to dinner.*

a·me·ni·ty /£ə'miː·nɪ·ti, $ə'men·ə·t̬i/ *n* [C] something, such as a swimming pool or shopping centre, that is intended to make life more pleasant or comfortable for the people in a town, hotel or other place • *A sports centre, swimming pool and a multi-screen cinema are among the amenities that will be included in the redevelopment of the dockland area.* • *The 200-year-old jail is overcrowded, understaffed and* **lacking** *in basic amenities* (=things

SPELLING DIFFERENCES BETWEEN AMERICAN AND BRITISH ENGLISH

A number of words have a different spelling in British and American writing. The spelling in American English tends to be simpler, for example *behavior, center* and *jewelry* instead of *behaviour, centre* and *jewellery*. Important spelling differences are put into groups below. Spellings given in the middle column are acceptable in both types of English.

-our and -or

Br	*Br/Am*	*Am*
armour		armor
behaviour		behavior
colour		color
favour		favor
favourite		favorite
flavour		flavor
	glamour	glamor[a]
honour		honor
neighbour		neighbor
rumour		rumor

-re and -er

Br	*Br/Am*	*Am*
centre		center
	fibre	fiber[a]
	litre	liter[a]
	meagre	meager[a]
metre (length)		meter
	sombre	somber[a]
	theatre	theater[a]
	acre	

-ae- / -oe- and -e-

Br	*Br/Am*	*Am*
	archaeology	archeology
	aeon	eon
anaesthetic		anesthetic
	encyclopaedia*	
	encyclopedia[a]	
foetus		fetus
haemorrhage		hemorrhage
manoeuvre		maneuver
	aerial	

-ence and -ense

Br	*Br/Am*	*Am*
defence		defense
licence *(n)*		license *(n)*
	license *(v)*	
offence		offense
pretence		pretense

-ogue and -og

Br	*Br/Am*	*Am*
	analogue	analog
	catalogue	catalog[a]
	dialogue	dialog
	prologue[a]	prolog
	travelogue[a]	travelog
	rogue	

-amme and -am

Br	*Br/Am*	*Am*
	aerogramme	aerogram
	program (computer)	
programme		program
	telegram	
	kilogram	

-ll- and -l-

Br	*Br/Am*	*Am*
	councillor	councilor
	counsellor	counselor[a]
	(un)equalled	(un)equaled[a]
	install	instal
jewellery		jewelry
	marvellous	marvelous
	(un)rivalled	(un)rivaled[a]
	tranquillity	tranquility[a]
	travelled	traveled[a]
	traveller	traveler[a]
	woollen	woolen[a]
	controller	
	controlled	

-l and -ll

Br	*Br/Am*	*Am*
	appal	appall[a]
	distil	distill[a]
	enrol	enroll[a]
	enthral	enthrall[a]
	fulfil	fulfill[a]
instal	install*	
	instalment	installment[a]
	instil	instill[a]
skilful		skillful
	wilful	willful[a]

other common differences

Br	*Br/Am*	*Am*
analyse		analyze
paralyse		paralyze
	cosy	cozy
	ageing	aging
	eyeing	eying
	likeable	likable
	mileage[a]	milage
storey (building)		story
	embed[a]	imbed
	enclose[a]	inclose
	ensure	insure
	indefinable	undefinable
	axe	ax
cheque (money)		check
	dependence[a]	dependance
draught (wind etc.)		draft
	grey	gray
mould		mold
	plough	plow
	practise *(v)*	practice *(v)*
	practice *(n)*	practise *(n)*
	sceptical	skeptical
speciality		specialty
tyre (wheel)		tire

[a] the usual spelling in American English
* the usual spelling in British English

Verbs ending in '-ize' or 'ise'

The '-ize' spelling can be used in American, Australian and British English, and is the spelling used in the dictionary. The '-ise' spelling is found frequently in British and Australian English. The following words (which are not all verbs) should always be given the '-ise' ending in all varieties of English. Words are grouped by pronunciation.

aɪz	advertise	despise	otherwise	iːz	expertise (*n*)
	advise (*v*)	devise	revise		
	arise	disguise	supervise		
	clockwise	enterprise (*n*)	surprise	aɪs	concise (*adj*)
	compromise	exercise	wise		precise (*adj*)

needed to make it comfortable). • *The council has some spare cash which it proposes to spend on* **public** *amenities.*

A·mer·i·can /ə'mer·ɪ·kən/ *n, adj* (a person) of or from the continents of South or North America, esp. the US • *He said he was proud to be an American.* [C] • *They drive a big American car.* • If something is **as American as apple pie,** it is considered to be typical of America or Americans: *Leather jackets are as American as apple pie and Harley-Davidsons.* • The **American dream** is the belief that everyone in the US has the chance to be successful, rich and happy if they work hard. • *(Br and Aus)* **American football** (*Am* **football**) is a game for two teams of eleven players in which an oval ball is moved along the field by running with it or throwing it. Points are scored by moving the ball across the line at the end of the field or by kicking it between two posts. • An **American Indian** is a **Native American**. See at NATIVE. • LP **American spelling, Varieties of English**

A·mer·i·can·ize *obj, Br and Aus usually* **-ise** /ə'mer·ɪ·kᵊn·aɪz/ *v* [T] • *Linda Chan was born in Hong Kong but grew up in New York and quickly became Americanized.* • *(disapproving) Many European cities have been Americanized with burger bars and diners.*

A·mer·i·can·iz·a·tion /əˌmer·ɪ·kᵊn·aɪ'zeɪ·ʃᵊn/, *Br and Aus usually* **-i·sa·tion** *n* [U]

A·mer·i·can·i·sm /ə'mer·ɪ·kə·nɪ·zᵊm/ *n* [C] • An Americanism is a word or expression which originated in the United States but is used by people in other countries, esp. those where English is spoken: *'Have a nice day!' is an Americanism which many British people find extremely irritating.* ○ *Far from polluting the English language, I would say Americanisms such as 'show off' and 'beat up' have enriched it.*

a·mer·in·dian /ˌæm·ə'rɪn·di·ən/ *n* [C], *adj* [not gradable] of or from Central and South America, or a member of any of the original races of this area

am·e·thyst /'æm·ə·θɪst/ *n, adj* (the colour of) a transparent purple stone used for making jewellery • *Amethyst is a type of quartz.* [U] • *Her jewellery is encrusted with semi-precious stones such as garnets and amethysts.* [C] • *She was wearing a stunning amethyst dress at Paul's party.*

a·mi·a·ble /'eɪ·mi·ə·bl̩/ *adj* (of a person or their behaviour) pleasant and friendly • *For the last three days of the tour we had a more amiable guide.* • *So amiable was the mood of the meeting that a decision was soon reached.*

a·mi·a·bly /'eɪ·mi·ə·bli/ *adv* • *They were chatting quite amiably on the phone last night so I assumed they'd settled their differences.*

a·mi·a·bil·i·ty /£ˌeɪ·mi·ə'bɪl·ɪ·ti, $-ə·t̬i/ *n* [U] • *I hate all that false amiability that goes on at parties.*

am·ic·a·ble /'æm·ɪ·kə·bl̩/ *adj* (of a person or their behaviour) pleasant and friendly, esp. despite a difficult situation, or (of decisions, agreements, etc.) achieved without arguments or unpleasantness • *His manner was perfectly amicable but I felt uncomfortable.* • *Apparently it was an amicable* **parting**. • *Few people have amicable divorces.* • *We each argued for our own plans but eventually we reached an amicable* **agreement/solution/settlement**.

am·ic·a·bly /'æm·ɪ·kə·bli/ *adv* • *I hope we can settle this amicably.*

a·mid /ə'mɪd/, **a·midst** /ə'mɪdst/ *prep fml* in the middle of or surrounded by; among • *On the floor, amid mounds of books, were two small envelopes.* • *Placards amid the waving banners proclaimed the desire for independence.* • *Amidst the confusion the two men slipped away quietly without being noticed.* • *The new perfume was launched amid a fanfare of publicity.*

a·mid·ships /ə'mɪd·ʃɪps/ *adv* [not gradable] in the middle part of a ship

a·mi·no ac·id /£ə'miː·nəʊ, $-noʊ/ *n* [C] a chemical substance found in plants and animals • *In digestion, the protein foods we eat are broken down into the twenty-four amino acids of which they are made.* • *The ten essential amino acids which are necessary for growth cannot be made by the human body but must be supplied by food or drugs.*

a·miss /ə'mɪs/ *adj* [after v], *adv* wrong; not suitable or as expected • *I knew immediately that something was amiss.* • *Is there* **anything** *amiss?* • *The increased incidence of asthma was indicative of* **something** *amiss.* • *We searched thoroughly but could find* **nothing** *amiss.* • *A word of apology might* **not go/***(Br also)* **come amiss** (= would be suitable and might improve the situation). • *A sense of proportion would* **not go/***(Br also)* **come amiss** (= would be suitable and helpful) *in all of this.* • *He went on to say that he didn't* **take** *my comments* **amiss** (= was not unhappy or angry about them).

am·i·ty /£'æm·ɪ·ti, $-ə·t̬i/ *n* [U] *fml* friendship; a good relationship • *The two groups had lived* **in** *perfect amity for many years before the recent troubles.*

am·me·ter /£'æm·iː·tər, $-t̬ɚ/ *n* [C] a device for measuring the strength of an electric current in units called AMPS

am·mo·ni·a /£ə'məʊ·ni·ə, $-'moʊ-/ *n* [U] a gas with a strong unpleasant smell used in making explosives, FERTILIZERS and some cleaners

am·mo·ni·um /£ə'məʊ·ni·əm, $-'moʊ-/ *n* [U] *specialized* • *ammonium chloride* • *ammonium nitrate* • **Ammonium sulphate** is a white substance often used as a FERTILIZER (= a substance spread on the land to make plants grow well).

am·mu·ni·tion /ˌæm·jʊ'nɪʃ·ᵊn/, *infml* **am·mo** /£'æm·əʊ, $-oʊ/ *n* [U] objects that can be shot from a weapon, esp. bullets, bombs, etc. • *a good supply of ammunition* • *a shortage of ammunition* • *(fig.) His bad behaviour* **provided** *plenty of ammunition* **for** (= opportunities for criticism by) *his opponents.* • *"Praise the Lord and pass the ammunition"* (believed to have been said by Howell Forgy at Pearl Harbour, 1941)

am·ne·si·a /æm'niː·zi·ə, -ʒə/ *n* [U] loss of the ability to remember • *In his later life he suffered periods of amnesia.* • *Many of the survivors of the crash had amnesia, strongly suggesting they had head injuries.*

am·ne·sty /'æm·nɪ·sti/ *n* [C] a decision, esp. by a government, not to use the usual punishments for crime, or a period of time for which this lasts • *Most political prisoners were freed under the terms of the amnesty.* • *People who hand in illegal weapons will not be prosecuted during the amnesty.* • *The government refused to declare an amnesty* **for** *people who had not paid the disputed tax.* • **Amnesty International** is an international organization which works to persuade governments to release people who are in prison for their beliefs and to stop the use of TORTURE and punishment by death.

am·ni·o·cen·te·sis /£ˌæm·ni·əʊ·sen'tiː·sɪs, $-oʊ-/ *n pl* **amniocenteses** the removal with a needle of a small amount of the liquid that surrounds a baby in the mother's womb in order to examine the baby's condition • *Amniocentesis involves extracting a small amount of amniotic fluid* (= liquid surrounding the baby) *and analysing foetal cells within for evidence of abnormality.* [U] • *When I was pregnant with my third child I was offered an amniocentesis (test) because I was forty.* [C]

a·moe·ba, *esp. Am* **a·me·ba** /ə'miː·bə/ *n* [C] *pl* **amoebae** /ə'miː·biː/ or **amoebas** a very small simple organism consisting of only one cell

a·moe·bic, *esp. Am* **a·me·bic** /ə'miː·bɪk/ *adj* [not gradable] • **Amoebic dysentery** is an illness of the bowels caused by an amoeba.

a·mok /£ə'mɒk, $-'mʌk/ *adv* **run amok/amuck** to be out of control and act in a wild or dangerous manner • *The* *army ran amok after one of its senior officers was killed.* • *The two dogs ran amok in a school playground.* • *In the film a man clutching a chain saw runs spectacularly amok.*

a·mong /ə'mʌŋ/, **a·mongst** /ə'mʌŋst/ *prep* in the middle of or surrounded by (other things), or as part of a group of (people or things) • *I saw a few familiar faces among the crowd of young people who filled the hall.* • *There were several private yachts among the fishing boats in the harbour.* • *Talk about it among your***selves** (= talk to each other about it) *for a while.* • *He is among the best at chess in the world.* • *She has worked as an estate agent among* **other things** (= as well as other things).

a·mon·til·la·do /£ə,mɒn·tɪ'lɑː·dəʊ, $-,mɑːn·tə'lɑː·doʊ/ *n* [C] *pl* **amontillados** a brown Spanish SHERRY (= an alcoholic drink which is similar to strong wine) which is not very sweet

a·mor·al /£,eɪ'mɒr·əl, $,eɪ'mɔːr-/ *adj* [not gradable] without moral principles • *You could argue that humans are amoral and what guides them is not any sense of morality but an instinct for survival.* • *The society that he depicts is amoral and purposeless.* • Compare IMMORAL; MORAL.

a·mo·ral·i·ty /£,eɪ·mɒr'æl·ɪ·ti, $-mɔːr'æl·ə·t̬i/ *n* [U] • *The glorious thing about Almodovar's films is their unashamed amorality.*

a·mor·ous /£'æm·ə·rəs, $-ɚ·əs/ *adj* of or expressing sexual desire • *The film centres around the amorous* **adventures/exploits** *of its handsome hero, Mike Mather.* • *Charles was offended because Amanda had rejected his amorous advances.* • Ⓟ

a·morph·ous /£ə'mɔː·fəs, $-'mɔːr-, eɪ-/ *adj* having no fixed form or shape • *an amorphous* **mass** *of jelly* • *The party remains an amorphous organization held together by hatred of the former dictator rather than by any agreement about the future.*

a·mort·ize *obj, Br and Aus usually* **–ise** /£ə'mɔː·taɪz, $æm'ɔːr-/ *v* [T] *fml* to reduce a debt by paying small regular amounts • *There is a scheme to help people to amortize fuel debts.* • *The value of the machinery is amortized over its estimated useful life.*

a·mort·iz·a·ble, *Br and Aus usually* **–is·a·ble** /£ə'mɔː·taɪ·zə·bl̩, $-'mɔːr-/ *adj*

a·mort·iz·a·tion, *Br and Aus usually* **–i·sa·tion** /£ə,mɔː·tɪ'zeɪ·ʃən, $æm,ɔːr·t̬ə-/, **a·mort·ize·ment**, *Br and Aus usually* **–ise·ment** *n* [U]

a·mount /ə'maʊnt/ *n* [C] a collection or mass (esp. of something which cannot be counted) • *They didn't deliver the right amount* **of** *sand.* • *Small amounts* **of** *land were used for keeping animals.* • *He paid regular amounts* **of** *money to a charity.* • *I didn't expect the bill to come to this amount* (= of money). • *The new tax caused a huge amount* **of** *public anger.* • *I had* **a certain amount of** (= some) *difficulty finding the house.* • *You wouldn't believe* **the** *amount of trouble* (= what a lot of trouble) *I've had with this car.* • *We had* **any amount of** (= lots of) *people applying for the job.* • LP› **Measurements**

a·mount to *obj* /ə'maʊnt/ *v prep* [T not *be amounting*] to add up to, be in total, be equal to or be the same as • *The annual cost of income support to unmarried mothers amounted to £700 million in that year.* • *His behaviour amounted to serious professional misconduct.* • *He gave what amounted to an apology on behalf of his company.* • *Keeping silent in this case amounts to supporting the speaker.* [+ v-*ing*]

amp ELECTRICITY /æmp/, *fml* **amp·ere** /£'æm·peəʳ, $-pɪr/ *n* [C] the standard unit of measurement for the strength of an electrical current • *This piece of equipment needs a thirty-amp fuse.*

amp·er·age /£'æm·pə·rɪdʒ, $-prɪdʒ/ *n* [U] • The amperage of a piece of electrical equipment is the strength of electrical current needed to make it work.

amp SOUND /æmp/ *n* [C] *infml* an **amplifier**, see at AMPLIFY

amp·er·sand /£'æm·pə·sænd, $-pɚ-/ *n* [C] the sign (&) used for 'and' • LP› **Symbols**

am·phet·a·mine /£æm'fet·ə·miːn, £-mɪn, $-fet̬-/ *n* any of several types of drug used esp. as a STIMULANT (= a substance which makes the mind or body more active) • *Floyd was banned from racing after a drug test revealed traces of amphetamine in his urine.* [U] • *Most of the amphetamines seized came from the Netherlands.* [C]

am·phi·bi·an /æm'fɪb·i·ən/ *n* [C] an animal, such as the FROG, which lives both on land and in water, or a vehicle which can operate both on land or in water • *He hopes to explore the island, which he suspects has a wealth of treasures for those interested in amphibians and reptiles.* • *She is head of the amphibian house at the zoo.* • *Two amphibians ferry tourists out over the sands to the fort.*

am·phib·i·ous /æm'fɪb·i·əs/ *adj* [not gradable] • *amphibious animals* • *amphibious vehicles/aircraft* • *an amphibious landing/attack* (= from the sea onto the land)

am·phi·the·a·tre *esp. Br and Aus, Am usually* **am·phi·the·a·ter** /£'æmp·fɪ,θɪə·təʳ, $-fə,θiː·ə·t̬ɚ/ *n* [C] a circular or oval area of ground around which rows of seats are arranged on a steep slope, for watching plays, sports, etc. outside.

am·pho·ra /£'æm·fᵊr·ə, $-fɚ·ə/ *n* [C] *pl* **amphorae** or **amphoras** a long narrow clay container, wider at the top than at the base, which has two handles and was used in ancient times esp. for storing oil or wine • *Terracotta amphorae of local wine were taken to Rome for the emperor's feasts.*

am·ple /'æm·pl̩/ *adj* enough, esp. more than enough, or *(esp. humorous)* (esp. of body size) large • *You'll have ample* **opportunity** *to ask questions after the talk.* • *There's ample* **evidence** *to suggest that the lawyer in question knew exactly what she was doing.* • *We had ample warning of the factory closure.* • *There is ample capacity for freight on this railway line outside commuter peak times.* • *(humorous) She put her arms around me and drew me to her ample* (= large) **bosom**. • *(humorous) Judging by his ample* **girth** (= the large distance around his stomach), *I should imagine he enjoys his food.*

amp·ly /'æm·pli/ *adv* • *They face a hard task, as yesterday's discussions amply* (= clearly) *demonstrated.* • *Her complaint was amply justified.*

am·pli·fy *obj* /'æm·plɪ·faɪ/ *v* [T] to increase (something) in size, effect, detail, strength of sound, etc. • *The technology exists to complement and amplify the human mind.* • *A funeral can amplify the feelings of regret and loss for the relatives.* • *The amplified music was so loud I couldn't hear what she said.*

am·pli·fi·ca·tion /,æm·plɪ·fɪ'keɪ·ʃən/ *n* [U] • Amplification makes music or other sounds louder: *The band brought its own amplification.* ○ *The over-loud amplification spoilt the concert.* • Amplification can mean added detail: *The horror lies in the violence itself, which needs no amplification.*

am·pli·fi·er /£'æm·plɪ·faɪ·əʳ, $-ɚ/, *infml* **amp** *n* [C] • Amplifiers are electrical devices which make sounds louder. • PIC› **Musical instruments**

am·pli·tude LARGE AMOUNT /£'æm·plɪ·tjuːd, $-tuːd/ *n* [U] *fml* a large amount or wide range • *The sheer amplitude of the novel invites comparisons with Tolstoy and George Eliot.*

am·pli·tude CURVE /£'æm·plɪ·tjuːd, $-tuːd/ *n* [C usually sing] *specialized* the distance between the top and the base of a curve

am·poule, *Am also* **am·pule** /'æm·puːl/ *n* [C] a small, usually glass, container for a single measured amount of medicine, esp. for an INJECTION (= liquid medicine put into the body through a needle)

am·pu·tate *(obj)* /'æm·pjʊ·teɪt/ *v* to cut off (esp. part of the body) • *In the end they had to amputate his foot to free him from the wrecked car.* [T] • *In these cases there is no choice but to amputate.* [I] • *(fig.) He was faced with amputating* (= removing) *from the company the less profitable activities.* [T]

am·pu·ta·tion /,æm·pjʊ'teɪ·ʃən/ *n* • *Amputation of the limb is really a last resort.* [U] • *Most amputations in this region are the result of accidents with land mines.* [C]

am·put·ee /,æm·pjʊ'tiː/ *n* [C] • *At that time, it was quite common to see amputees* (= people who had had an arm or leg cut off) *begging on the streets.*

a·muck /ə'mʌk/ *adv* AMOK

am·u·let /£'æm·jʊ·lət, $-jə-/ *n* [C] an object worn because it is believed to protect against evil, disease, unhappiness, etc.

a·muse *(obj)* /ə'mjuːz/ *v* to entertain (someone), esp. by humorous speech or action or by making someone laugh or smile, or to keep (someone) happy, esp. for a short time • *I've brought with me an article from yesterday's paper that I thought might amuse you.* [T] • *At school she would always be devising games to amuse her classmates.* [T] • *I think* **it** *amuses him* **to** *see people make fools of themselves.* [T + obj + *to* infinitive] • *Toddlers don't need expensive toys and games to* **keep** *them amused.* [T] • *We amused* **ourselves** *by watching the passers-by.* [T] • *I bought a magazine to amuse* **myself** *while I was on the train.* [T] • *Apparently these* *stories are meant to amuse.* [I] • *I told Helena about what had happened and she was* **not amused** (=she was angry).

a·muse·ment /ə'mjuːz·mənt/ *n* • Amusement is the feeling of being entertained or made to laugh: *She looked at him* **with** *amusement.* [U] ○ *I looked on* **in** *amusement as they started to argue.* [U] ○ *The president's utterances, with their twisted syntax, missing nouns and pronouns, have long been a source of amusement.* [U] ○ *Carl came last in the race,* **(much) to** *my amusement*/**to** *my (great) amusement.* [U] ○ *I play the piano just* **for** *my* **own** *amusement* (=to entertain myself not other people). [U] • Amusements are activities that you can take part in for entertainment: *There was a range of* **fairground** *amusements, including rides, stalls and competitions.* [C] • An **amusement arcade** is a place in which you can pay to play games on machines. • *(Am and Aus)* An **amusement park** is a FUNFAIR or a **theme park**. See at THEME.

a·mus·ing /ə'mjuː·zɪŋ/ *adj* • *an amusing* (=entertaining) *story/person/situation* • *"Did you like the book?" "I* **found** *it mildly amusing."*

a·mus·ing·ly /ə'mjuː·zɪŋ·li/ *adv* • *On the subject of childbirth she is amusingly frank.*

an NOT PARTICULAR /æn/ *determiner* used instead of 'a' when the following word begins with a vowel sound • *an ugly face* • *an easy question* • *an interesting story* • *an orange* • *an appalling mistake* • *an honour*

-an BELONG TO /-ᵊn/, **-ean** /-iː·ən, -i·ən/, **-ian** /-i·ən/ *combining form* connected with or belonging to the stated place, group or type • *an American* • *a Canadian* • *a Christian* • *American apple pie* • *Italian opera* • LP **Combining forms, Stress in pronunciation**

an·a·bol·ic ste·roid /£'æn·ə·bɒl·ɪk, £-bɑː·lɪk/ *n* [C] a HORMONE (=substance that influences development and growth) that causes muscle and bone growth • *The International Olympic Committee has banned anabolic steroids because of their danger to athletes' health.* • *The weightlifter was disqualified from the competition after testing positive for anabolic steroids.*

a·na·chron·i·sm /ə'næk·rə·nɪ·zᵊm/ *n* [C] a person, thing or idea which exists out of its time in history, esp. one which happened or existed later than the period being shown, discussed, etc. • *For some people, marriage is an anachronism from the days when women needed to be protected.* • *The modern train was an obvious and distracting anachronism in the film about London in the 1950s.*

a·na·chron·is·tic /əˌnæk·rə'nɪs·tɪk/ *adj* • *He described the law as anachronistic* (=more suitable for an earlier time) *and ridiculous.*

a·na·chron·is·tic·ally /əˌnæk·rə'nɪs·tɪ·kli/ *adv*

an·a·con·da /£ˌæn·ə'kɒn·də, $-'kɑːn-/ *n* [C] a large South American snake which curls around a live animal and crushes it to kill it for food

a·nae·mi·a, *esp. Am* **a·ne·mi·a** /ə'niː·mi·ə/ *n* [U] a medical condition caused by having too few red blood cells, resulting in paleness and tiredness

a·nae·mic, *esp. Am* **a·ne·mic** /ə'niː·mɪk/ *adj* • *Lack of iron in your diet can make you anaemic.* • *(fig.) Both actors gave fairly anaemic* (=weak and not very exciting) *performances.*

an·aer·o·bic /£ˌæn·ə'rəʊ·bɪk, $-er'oʊ-/ *adj* [not gradable] not needing or without oxygen • *Some bacteria can only live in anaerobic* **conditions**.

an·aes·the·sia, *esp. Am* **an·es·the·sia** /ˌæn·əs'θiː·zi·ə, -ʒə/ *n* [U] a state in which someone does not feel pain, usually because of drugs they have been given, or *(specialized)* the inability to feel heat, cold, pain, touch, etc.

an·aes·thet·ic, *esp. Am* **an·es·thet·ic** /£ˌæn·əs'θet·ɪk, $-'θeţ-/ *n* • An anaesthetic is a substance that makes you unable to feel pain: *We'll take your tooth out* **under** *anaesthetic.* [U] • *Conditions are now so primitive in the town clinic that operations are frequently performed without anaesthetic.* [U] • A **general** anaesthetic is a drug which causes unconsciousness. [C] • A **local** anaesthetic causes loss of feeling just in one part of the body. [C] • *Sir Humphrey Davy discovered the anaesthetic effect of laughing gas.*

an·aes·thet·ist, *esp. Am* **an·es·thet·ist** /£ə'niːs·θə·tɪst, $-ţɪst/ *n* [C] • An anaesthetist is a doctor who gives anaesthetic to people in hospital.

an·aes·thet·ize *obj, Br and Aus usually* **-ise**, *esp. Am* **an·es·thet·ize** /£ə'niːs·θə·taɪz, $-ţaɪz/ *v* [T]

an·a·gram /'æn·ə·græm/ *n* [C] a word or phrase made by using the letters of another word or phrase in a different order • *'Neat' is an anagram* **of** *'a net'.*

a·nal /'eɪ·nəl/ *adj* [not gradable] See at ANUS

an·al·ges·ic /ˌæn·əl'dʒiː·zɪk/ *n, adj* (a type of drug) which stops you from feeling pain • *analgesic properties* • *an analgesic tablet* • *This cream contains a mild analgesic to soothe stings and bites.* [C]

an·a·logue, *Am also* **an·a·log** /£'æn·ə·lɒg, $-lɑːg/ *n* [C] something which is similar to or can be used instead of something else • *He has been studying the European analogues* **of** *the British Parliament.* • An analogue (*Am and Aus* analog) **recording** is made by changing the sound waves into electrical signals of the same FREQUENCY. • An analogue **clock/watch** is one that has HANDS (=narrow pointers) that show what time it is: *My grandmother can't stand those watches with digital read-outs, she always buys analogue models.* Compare DIGITAL.

a·nal·o·gy /ə'næl·ə·dʒi/ *n* (an example of) similarity in particular features • *He* **drew** *an analogy* **between** *the brain and a vast computer.* [C] • *Peters then offers an analogy* **between** *the balanced individual and a balanced society.* [C] • *It is sometimes easier to illustrate an abstract concept* **by** *analogy* **with** (=by comparing it with) *something concrete.* [U] • *A group was set up* **on the** *analogy* **of** (=based on a similar idea to) *a self-supporting community.* [C]

an·al·og·ous /ə'næl·ə·gəs/ *adj* • *The experience of mystic trance is in a sense analogous* **to** *sleep or drunkenness.*

an·a·lyse *obj Br and Aus, Am* **an·a·lyze** /'æn·ᵊl·aɪz/ *v* [T] to study or examine (something) in detail, in order to discover more about it • *The report analysed the effect of various child care subsidies.* • *The researchers analysed the purchases of 6300 households.* • *Firms must know what their waste is composed of or have it analysed to find out.* • *Water samples taken from streams were analysed* **for** *contamination by chemicals.*

a·nal·y·sis /ə'næl·ə·sɪs/ *n pl* **analyses** /ə'næl·ə·siːz/ • *Chemical analysis revealed a high content of copper.* [U] • *An analysis* **of** *seven years' work revealed errors and inconsistencies.* [C] • *I accepted her analysis* **of** (=examination of and judgment about) *the situation.* [C] • **In the last/final/ultimate analysis** means after everything has been considered: *What distinguishes all the species of plants and animals is, in the final analysis, differences in the way carbon atoms choose to bond.*

an·al·yst /'æn·ə·lɪst/ *n* [C] • *a financial/food/political/systems analyst*

an·a·lyt·ic·al /£ˌæn·ə'lɪt·ɪ·kᵊl, $-'lɪţ-/, **an·a·lyt·ic** /£ˌæn·ə'lɪt·ɪk, $-'lɪţ-/ *adj* • *He has a very analytical* **mind**. • *Some students have a more analytical approach to learning.*

an·ar·chi·sm /£'æn·ə·kɪ·zᵊm, $'-ɚ-/ *n* [U] the political belief that there should be little or no formal or official organization to society but that people should work freely together • *The group tends to be hostile to authority, with a fringe which borders on anarchism.*

an·ar·chist /£'æn·ə·kɪst, $'-ɚ-/ *n* [C] • *He was a poet, an anarchist and a vegan.* • *an anarchist group/slogan/bookshop* • *(disapproving)* An anarchist is also someone who wishes to destroy the existing government and laws: *anarchist tendencies/demonstrations*

an·ar·chist·ic /£ˌæn·ə'kɪs·tɪk, $-ɚ'-/ *adj*

an·ar·chy /£'æn·ə·ki, $'-ɚ-/ *n* [U] lack of organization and control, esp. in society because of an absence or failure of government • *What we are witnessing is the country's slow slide into anarchy.* • *The country has been in* **a state of** *anarchy since the inconclusive election.* • *If the pay deal isn't settled amicably there'll be anarchy in the factories.* • *Staff and volunteers in the office worked with an air of cheerful anarchy.*

an·ar·chic /£ə'nɑː·kɪk, $-'nɑːr-/ *adj* • *His parents had settled in the crowded ghettoes of the big city, surrounded by desperate poverty and anarchic violence.* • *Milligan's anarchic humour has always had the power to offend as well as entertain.*

a·nath·e·ma /ə'næθ·ə·mə/ *n* [U] something which is greatly disliked or disapproved of • *Credit controls are anathema* **to** *the government.* • *A university professor has declared the book anathema.* • *For older employees the new system is* **an** *anathema.*

a·nat·o·my /£ə'næt·ə·mi, $-'næţ-/ *n* [U] the scientific study of the inner structure of animals or plants • *An understanding of human anatomy is important to a dancer.*

[U] • *He studied medicine at five German universities, and in 1876 became professor of anatomy at Kiel.* [U] • *Today's lecture was on the anatomy* **of** *leaves/leaf anatomy.* [U] • *(esp. humorous)* Anatomy can be used to mean body: *On which part of her anatomy is she tattooed?* [C] • *(fig. literary) The whole play reads like an anatomy* (= examination) **of** *evil.* [C]

an·a·tom·ic·al /£ˌæn·əˈtɒm·ɪ·kəl, $-ˈtɑː·mɪ-/ *adj* [not gradable] • *anatomical drawings*

-ance /-ənts/ *combining form* See -ENCE

an·ces·tor /£ˈæn·ses·tər, $-tɚ/ *n* [C] a person, plant, animal or object that is related to one existing at a later point in time • *There were portraits of his ancestors on the walls of the room.* • *Studies suggest that life originated only once, from a single ancestor.* • *This wooden instrument is the ancestor of the modern metal flute.* • Compare **descendant** at DESCEND.

an·ces·tral /ænˈses·trəl/ *adj* [before n; not gradable] • *an ancestral home* • *ancestral rights* • *"And 'mid this tumult Kubla heard from far / Ancestral voices prophesying war!"* (Samuel Taylor Coleridge in the poem *Kubla Khan*, 1816)

an·ces·try /ˈæn·ses·tri/ *n* • *He was proud of his Native American ancestry.* [C] • *His wife was* **of** *royal ancestry.* [U] • *The family has* **traced** *its ancestry* **(back) to** *the Norman invaders.* [C] • *These buildings have an ancestry which can be* **traced back to** *Greece and Rome.* [C]

an·chor /£ˈæŋ·kər, $-kɚ/ *n* [C] a heavy metal object, usually shaped like a cross with curved arms, on a strong rope or chain, which is dropped from a boat into the water to prevent the boat from moving away • If you **drop** anchor, you lower the anchor into the water and stop: *We dropped anchor in the bay.* • When you **weigh** anchor, you pull up the anchor and sail away. • *The boat* **rode/lay/was at** *anchor* (= had stopped and was kept in the same place by its anchor). • *(fig.) This treaty has been called the anchor* (= strongest part) *of their foreign policy.* • *(fig.) She was my anchor when things were difficult for me* (= she helped me to keep things under control). • PIC **Ships and boats**

an·chor /£ˈæŋ·kər, $-kɚ/ *v* • *We anchor every evening and go ashore.* [I] • *Be careful where you anchor the boat.* [T] • *(fig.) The best plan is to anchor* (= fix) *everything in one proposal.* [T] • *(fig.) They are planting trees to try to anchor* **(down)** *the sand dunes.* [T/M]

an·chor·age /£ˈæŋ·kər·ɪdʒ, $-kɚ-/ *n* [C] • *The bay is well-known as a safe anchorage* (= place to anchor). • *The anchorage* **point** (= fixing point) *for the seat belt is not adjustable.*

an·chor·ite /£ˈæŋ·kər·aɪt, $-kɚ-/ *n* [C] someone who lives alone away from other people for religious reasons; a HERMIT

an·chor·man (*pl* **-men**), **an·chor·wo·man** (*pl* **-women**) /£ˈæŋ·kə·mæn, -mən, $-kɚ-, -ˌwʊm·ən/ *n* [C] a person whose job is to introduce a television or radio broadcast, esp. one containing many different items of news, discussions, etc. • *The late-night current affairs programme has a new anchorman.*

an·chor *obj* /£ˈæŋ·kər, $-kɚ/ *v* [T] *esp. Am* • *She will anchor* (= introduce) *the broadcast of Christmas greetings to the troops.*

an·cho·vy /£ˈæn·tʃə·vi, £ænˈtʃəʊ-, $ˈæn·tʃoʊ-/ *n pl* **anchovy** or **anchovies** a small fish with a strong salty taste • *Decorate the top of the pizza with anchovies/strips of anchovy* [C/U] • *anchovy paste*

an·cient /ˈeɪn·tʃənt/ *adj* of or from a long time ago, having lasted for a very long time, or *(infml)* very old • *ancient civilizations/rights/laws/rivalries* • *ancient monuments/ruins/woodlands* • *I've just finished reading a book on the ancient kingdoms of Mexico.* • *People have lived in this valley since ancient* **times**. • *History, ancient* **and modern**, *has taught these people an intense distrust of their neighbours.* • Ancient is sometimes used to refer to the period in European history from the earliest known societies to the end of the Roman empire: *the ancient Eyptians/Greeks/Romans* ○ *The ancient Britons inhabited these parts of England before the Roman invasion.* ○ *The museum has a large collection of sculptures dating from the ancient* **world**. • *(fig. infml) "Did you know Andy has a new job?" "Yeah, that's ancient* **history** (= that is so well known that it is not interesting)." • *(infml) You'd never think he was a wealthy man – he drives around in a really ancient car.*

an·cil·la·ry /£ænˈsɪl·ər·i, $ˈænt·sə·ler·i/ *adj* providing support or help; additional; extra • *ancillary staff/workers* • *ancillary equipment* • *an ancillary role* • *Campaigning to change government policy is ancillary* **to** *the charity's direct relief work.*

-an·cy, -en·cy /-ənt·si/ *combining form* See -ENCY

and ALSO /ænd/ *conjunction* used to join two words, phrases, parts of sentences or related statements together; also or in addition to • *Ann and Jim* • *boys and girls* • *knives and forks* • *We were wet and tired.* • *We kissed and hugged each other.* • *Tidy up your room. And don't forget to make your bed!* • *She bought the whole lot – house, farm, horses* **and all** (= and everything else). • *(slang)* **And all** means 'too', and can be used to make a meaning stronger: *I'd like some an' all.* ○ *"Were they the team that died in the plane crash?" "Yeah, and they were a great team and all."* • *She's an expert on English grammar* **and all that** (= and everything related to it). • **And/or** is used to mean that either one of two things or both of them is possible: *Many pupils have extra classes in the evenings and/or at weekends.* ○ *Cycling can be fun and/or exercise.* • **And so on/And so forth/And so on and so forth** means together with other similar things: *schools, colleges and so on* • LP **Comma**

and THEN /ænd/ *conjunction* used to join two parts of a sentence, one part happening after or because of the other part; then; after that; next; as a result; in order to • *I got dressed and (then)* (= next) *had my breakfast.* • *Stand over there and (then)* (= as a result) *you'll be able to see it better.* • *Bring the flowers into a warm room and (then)* (= as a result) *they'll soon open.* • *The car broke down and (so)* (= as a result) *we had to find a telephone.* • *I asked him to* **go** *and* **find** (= go in order to find) *my glasses.* • *Come and see* (= in order to see) *me tomorrow.* • *Don't go yet.* **Wait** *and* **see** (= wait in order to see) *what happens.* • *(infml)* **Try** *and get* (= Try to get) *some tickets for tonight's performance.*

and VERY /ænd/ *conjunction* (used to join two words, esp. two which are the same, to make their meaning stronger) • *She spends hours and hours* (= a very long time) *on the telephone.* • *The sound grew louder and louder* (= very loud). • *We laughed and laughed* (= laughed a lot). • *Make sure the water is* **nice/good** *and hot* (= very hot).

and BUT /ænd/ *conjunction* used to show a difference between two parts of a sentence; but • *You're a vegetarian and you eat fish?* • *This group are car drivers and that group never drive.* • **There are** *guide books and guide books* (= some are better than others).

an·dro·gyn·ous /£ænˈdrɒdʒ·ɪ·nəs, $-ˈdrɑː·dʒɪ-/ *adj* not clearly male or female, or *(specialized)* having both male and female features • *With her lean frame and cropped hair, Lennox has a fashionably androgynous look.*

an·dro·gyn·y /£ænˈdrɒdʒ·ə·ni, $-ˈdrɑː·dʒə-/ *n* [U] • *One or two of the earlier photos reveal an intriguing androgyny not normally associated with the actress.*

an·droid /ˈæn·drɔɪd/ *n* [C] a ROBOT (= computer-controlled machine) which is made to look like a human

an·ec·dote /£ˈæn·ɪk·dəʊt, $-doʊt/ *n* [C] a short often amusing story, esp. about something someone has done • *He told one or two amusing anecdotes about his years as a policeman.*

an·ec·dot·al /£ˌæn·ɪkˈdəʊ·təl, $-ˈdoʊ·t̬əl/ *adj* • **Anecdotal evidence** is information that is not based on facts or proper studies.

a·ne·mi·a /əˈniː·mi·ə/ *n* [U] *esp. Am for* ANAEMIA

a·nem·o·ne /əˈnem·ə·ni/ *n* [C] any of several types of small plant, wild or grown in gardens, with red, blue or white flowers

an·es·the·sia /ˌæn·əsˈθiː·zi·ə, -ʒə/ *n* [U] *esp. Am for* ANAESTHESIA

an·es·thet·ic /£ˌæn·əsˈθet·ɪk, $-θet̬-/ *n* [C] *esp. Am*

a·new /£əˈnjuː, $-ˈnuː/ *adv* [not gradable] *fml* again or one more time, esp. in a different way • *The film tells anew the story of his rise to fame and power.*

an·gel /ˈeɪn·dʒəl/ *n* [C] a good spiritual creature in stories or some religions, usually represented as a human with wings • *According to the Bible, an angel told Mary that she would have God's son Jesus.* • An angel is also someone who is very good, helpful or kind: **Be an** *angel and help me with this.* ○ *He's* **no angel** (= not good in every way) *but he can't be blamed for everything that has happened.* • In the theatre an angel is a person who provides money for a show to be planned. • Someone who is **on the side of the angels** is doing the right thing or is basically good: *He was, in this matter at least, firmly on the side of the angels.* • *What's the matter, angel?* [as form of address] • *(esp. Am)* **Angel food cake** is a light cake made without egg YOLKS or fat. • LP **Titles and forms of address**

an·gel·ic /æn'dʒel·ɪk/ *adj* • Angelic means very beautiful and very good: *an angelic voice/face/smile*
an·gel·ic·al·ly /æn'dʒel·ɪ·kli/ *adv*

an·gel·ic·a /æn'dʒel·ɪ·kə/ *n* [U] the green stem of a plant, preserved with sugar and used for decorating cakes and other sweet food, or the plant itself • *strips of angelica*

An·gel·us /'æn·dʒᵊl·əs/ *n* [U] **the Angelus** (a bell rung to show that it is time for) prayers said in the morning, in the middle of the day and in the evening in the Roman Catholic church

an·ger /£'æŋ·gəʳ, $-gɚ/ *n* [U] a strong feeling against someone or a situation which makes you want to hurt someone, be unpleasant, shout at someone, etc. • *I think he feels a lot of anger* **towards** *his father who treated him very badly as a child.* • *There is a danger that anger* **at** *the new law may turn into anti-government feeling.* • *The people showed no surprise or anger* **at** *their treatment.* • *He found it hard to contain/restrain/suppress* (= control) *his anger.* • *"Look Back in Anger"* (title of a play by John Osborne, 1956) • (N)
an·ger *obj* /£'æŋ·gəʳ, $-gɚ/ *v* [T] • *The remark angered him.* • *It always angers me to see so much waste.*
an·gry /'æŋ·gri/ *adj* **-ier, -iest** • *an angry look/voice* • *an angry crowd/person* • *(fig.) an angry* (= stormy) *sky* • Angry usually describes a temporary feeling and not a permanent characteristic: *I* **was/got** *really angry* **with** *her.* ○ *She made me really angry.* ○ *They were angry* **at/about** *the way they had been treated.* ○ *It makes me so angry when people are so thoughtless.* • *We are very angry* **that** *the government has done nothing to improve the situation.* [+ *that* clause] • *(fig.) On her leg was an angry* (= red and painful) *sore.*
an·gri·ly /'æŋ·grɪ·li/ *adv* • *"Don't do that!", she shouted angrily.* • *Demonstrators protested angrily following the jury's verdict.* • *The Prime Minister* **reacted** *angrily to claims that he had lied to the House of Commons.* • *Mike Walker angrily condemned/dismissed/rejected suggestions that he had moved football clubs for purely financial reasons.*

an·gi·na (pec·to·ris) /æn'dʒaɪ·nə/ *n* [U] a disease which repeatedly causes sudden strong pain in the chest because blood with oxygen is stopped from reaching the heart muscle by blocked ARTERIES • (CS) (PL) (RUS)

an·gi·o·pla·sty /£'æn·dʒi·əʊ,plæs·ti, $-oʊ-/ *n specialized* a medical operation to remove a blockage from an ARTERY (= a tube which allows blood to flow from the heart around the body) in a person who has ANGINA • *It was decided that (an) angioplasty wouldn't be necessary.* [C/U] • *He was back on his feet only two days after* **undergoing** *an angioplasty* **procedure**.

an·gle [SPACE] /'æŋ·gl̩/ *n* [C] the space between two lines or surfaces at the point at which they touch each other, measured in degrees • *The interior angles of a square are* **right** *angles or angles* **of** *90* **degrees**. • *The boat settled into the mud* **at** *a 35 degree angle/an angle of 35 degrees.* • *The plane's angle and speed of approach were too great.* • *The picture was hanging* **at an** *angle.* ○ *He wore his hat* **at** *a* **jaunty** *angle* (= not straight or vertical). • The angle of a building, table or anything with straight sides is its corner. • See also ANGULAR. • [PIC] Shapes
an·gle *obj* /'æŋ·gl̩/ *v* [T] • *The stage had been steeply angled* (= was sloping very noticeably).
an·gled /'æŋ·gl̩d/ *adj* • *His angled shot* (= from the side, not from straight in front) *beat the goalkeeper from 20 yards.*

an·gle [POSITION] /'æŋ·gl̩/ *n* [C] a position from which something is viewed, or a way of considering, judging or dealing with something • *The tower is visible* **from** *every angle/all angles.* • *I realised I was looking at it* **from** *the wrong angle.* • *Try looking at the problem* **from** *another angle/***from** *my angle.* • *We need to approach this* **from** *the angle* **of** *new participants.* • *What is the best news angle for this story?* • *The press was looking for* **a new/fresh angle on** *the story.*
an·gle *obj* /'æŋ·gl̩d/ *v* [T] • *The comic is angled* (= aimed) **at** *the 8-12 boys' market.*

an·gle for *obj* /'æŋ·gl̩/ *v prep* [T] *esp. disapproving* to try to get or achieve something • *He's clearly angling for a job.* • *She's been angling for an invitation for the last month.*

an·gler /£'æŋ·gləʳ, $-glɚ/ *n* [C] See at ANGLING

An·gli·can /'æŋ·glɪ·kən/ *n* [C], *adj* (a member) of the Church of England, or an international Church connected with it • *He's (an) Anglican.* • *His sister has just become an Anglican priest.* • *Desmond Tutu became the most famous Anglican archbishop in South Africa.* • *Outside England, the Anglican Church is often referred to as the Episcopal(ian) Church.*
An·gli·can·i·sm /'æŋ·glɪ·kə·nɪ·zᵊm/ *n* [U]

an·gli·ci·sm /'æŋ·glɪ·sɪ·zᵊm/ *n* [C] an English word or phrase that is used in another language • *'Le weekend' is an anglicism used by the French.*

an·gli·cize *obj, Br and Aus usually* **-ise** /'æŋ·glɪ·saɪz/ *v* [T] to make or become English in sound, appearance or character • *She married Norwegian immigrant Niels Larsen who later anglicized his name.*

an·gling /'æŋ·glɪŋ/ *n* [U] the sport of trying to catch fish with a rod, LINE (= plastic thread) and hook
an·gler /£'æŋ·gləʳ, $-glɚ/ *n* [C] • *Despite the rain, several anglers* (= people fishing) *were sitting on the river bank.*

An·glo– /£,æŋ·gləʊ-, $,æŋ·gloʊ-/ *combining form* of or connected with Britain or England • **Anglo-American** means British and American (usually US): *an Anglo-American agreement.* • **Anglo-Catholic** refers to the group in the Anglican church whose religious practice is similar to that of the Roman Catholic church. • An **Anglo-Indian** is a person with British and Indian parents or grandparents or *(dated)* an English person born or living in India. • **Anglo-Saxon** is used to describe the people who lived in England from about 600 AD and their language and customs, although it can also describe modern societies which are based on or influenced by English customs. See also WASP [PERSON]. • *"Anglo-Saxon attitudes"* (title of a novel by Angus Wilson, 1956)

an·glo·phile /£'æŋ·gləʊ·faɪl, $-glə-/ *n* [C], *adj* (a person who is not British) interested in, liking or supporting Britain and its people and customs

an·glo·phone /£'æŋ·gləʊ·fəʊn, $-glə·foʊn/ *n, adj specialized* (a person or country) speaking the English language, esp. as a usual method of official communication • *British people who live abroad often surround themselves with other anglophones in their social activities.* [C] • *The anglophone countries of Africa include Kenya and Zimbabwe.*

an·go·ra /£æŋ'gɔː·rə, $-'gɔːr·ə/ *n* [U] the wool, fibre or material made from the long soft hair of a type of rabbit or goat • *a jumper knitted* **in** *angora (wool)* • *an angora sweater*

an·go·stu·ra (bit·ters) /£,æŋ·gə'stjʊə·rə, $-gə'stʊr·ə/ *n* [U] a bitter liquid which can be used to flavour alcoholic drinks

an·gri·ly /'æŋ·grɪ·li/ *adv* See at ANGER

an·gry /'æŋ·gri/ *adj* See at ANGER

angst /£æŋkst, $ɑːŋkst/ *n* [U] strong anxiety and unhappiness, esp. about personal problems • *He is genuinely a man troubled by angst, by constant worries over the great spiritual questions.* • *All my children went through a period of late-adolescent angst.*

an·guish /'æŋ·gwɪʃ/ *n* [U] extreme unhappiness caused by physical or mental suffering • *His anguish* **at** *the outcome of the court case was very clear.* • *She spoke to him* **in** *great anguish.* • **In** *her anguish she forgot to leave a message.*
an·guished /'æŋ·gwɪʃt/ *adj* • *an anguished cry* • *an anguished letter to the newspapers* • *Politicians entered into two days of anguished* **debate** *following the release of this month's crime figures.*

an·gu·lar /£'æŋ·gjʊ·ləʳ, $-lɚ/ *adj* having a clear shape with sharp points • *Her features were too angular, her face a little too long for beauty.* • *He has a more angular figure than his father.*
an·gu·lar·i·ty /£,æŋ·gjʊ'lær·ɪ·ti, $-'ler·ə·t̬i/ *n* [U]

an·i·mal [CREATURE] /'æn·ɪ·məl/ *n* [C] a living creature, not a plant, which has any or all of the five SENSES of sight, hearing, smell, taste and touch, and which can move all or part of its body • *Humans, insects, reptiles, birds and mammals are all animals.* • *Animals are distinguished from plants by obtaining their nourishment from other living organisms or their remains.* • *People often forget that humans are animals, as are sponges and jellyfish.* • *I wouldn't really call myself an animal* **lover** *but I do quite like dogs.* • Animal often means an animal with four legs: *I like animals, but I hate slimy things like fish and snakes.* ○ *A lion is a* **wild** *animal, a dog is a* **domestic** *animal and a pig is a* **farm** *animal.* ○ *Surveys show that animal* **welfare** *has recently become a major concern for many schoolchildren.* ○ *A militant group of animal-***rights** *activists has claimed responsibility for a firebomb attack on the home of a prominent scientist.* • You can also say that a person who is very cruel or unpleasant or has no social manners is an animal: *He becomes an animal when he's had too much to* *drink.* • You can also say that someone or something is a particular type of animal to show what they are like: *She is a* **political** *animal at heart.* ○ *She is that* **rare animal** (= she has qualities or interests that are not usually found together), *a brilliant scientist who can communicate her ideas to ordinary people.* ○ *Feminism in France and England are rather* **different** *animals* (= are different). ○ *(humorous) A video-recorder that's easy to programme? There's* **no such** *animal* (= Such a thing does not exist)*!* • *(specialized)* **Animal husbandry** is the farming of animals to produce foods such as meat, eggs and milk. • **The animal kingdom** is the group of all living creatures that are animals. • *"It takes up to 40 dumb animals to make a fur coat. But only one to wear it."* (Lynx, a British animal-rights organization, 1980s) • *"My Family and Other Animals"* (title of a book by Gerald Durrell, 1956) • LP› **Plurals**

an·i·mal PHYSICAL /ˈæn·ɪ·məl/ *adj* [before n] relating to physical desires or needs, rather than spiritual or mental ones • *As an actor Olivier had a sort of animal* **magnetism**. • *Liz always knew that Dave wasn't the right man for her but she couldn't deny the animal* **attraction** *between them.* • If you are full of animal **spirits** you feel excited, happy and energetic.

an·i·mal·is·tic /£æn·ɪ·məˈlɪs·tɪk, $-t̬ɪk/ *adj fml disapproving* • *People he regarded as little more than a collection of animalistic* (= physical and not spiritual) *urges.*

an·i·mate ALIVE /ˈæn·ɪ·mət/ *adj* [not gradable] living; having life • *The world contains things which are animate, such as animals, and things which are inanimate, such as rocks.*

an·i·mate *obj* BRIGHT OR ACTIVE /ˈæn·ɪ·meɪt/ *v* [T] to make (someone) seem more bright, happy or active • *A sparkle in his eyes animated his face whenever he smiled.*

an·i·mat·ed /£ˈæn·ɪ·meɪ·tɪd, $-t̬ɪd/ *adj* • Animated means full of interest and energy: *There was an extremely animated discussion on the subject.* ○ *They must have been having an interesting conversation – they both looked very animated.* • In animated films, drawings, PUPPETS or models are photographed and shown in a way that makes them move and appear to be alive.

an·i·mat·ed·ly /£ˈæn·ɪ·meɪ·tɪd·li, $-t̬ɪd-/ *adv* • *The spectators were animatedly debating the likely result of the tennis final.*

an·i·ma·tion /ˌæn·ɪˈmeɪ·ʃən/ *n* • *During a fascinating lecture, the professor spoke with animation* (= enthusiasm and energy) *about her latest discoveries.* [U] • *Encyclopedias on compact disc include sound, illustrations and simple animations* (= moving pictures). [C] • *Thanks to* **computer** *animation* (= photographing drawings, etc. so that they appear to move), *it is now possible to make cartoon films much more quickly than in the past.* [U] • Ⓙ

an·i·mat·or /£ˈæn·ɪ·meɪ·təʳ, $-t̬ɚ/ *n* [C] • *Walt Disney is the most famous animator of feature-length films.*

an·i·mat·eur /£ˌæn·ɪ·məˈtɜː, $-tɜːr/ *n* [C] *Br* • An animateur is someone who uses energetic and interesting methods to teach performing arts such as dance and theatre.

an·i·mi·sm /ˈæn·ɪ·mɪ·zəm/ *n* [U] *specialized* the belief that all natural things, such as plants, animals, rocks, thunder and EARTHQUAKES, have spirits and can influence human events

an·i·mist /ˈæn·ɪ·mɪst/ *n* [C], *adj* [not gradable] *specialized*

an·i·mos·i·ty /£ˌæn·ɪˈmɒs·ɪ·ti, $-ˈmɑː·sə·t̬i/ *n* (an example of) strong, often active, dislike, opposition or anger • *The animosity* **between** *the rival candidates was obvious to the voters.* [U] • *Of course we're competitive but there's no* **personal** *animosity* **between us**. [U] • *In spite of his injuries, he* **bears no** *animosity* **towards** *his attackers.* [U] • *The European Community helped France and Germany forget the old animosities* **between** *them.* [C]

an·ise /ˈæn·ɪs, ænˈiːs/ *n* [U] a Mediterranean plant with small yellowish white flowers and seeds that taste of LIQUORICE

an·i·seed /ˈæn·ɪ·siːd/ *n* [U] the seeds of the anise plant, used to flavour sweets and LIQUEURS (= strong alcoholic drinks) and to make medicine for bowel problems • *aniseed balls*

an·kle /ˈæŋ·kl̩/ *n* [C] the joint which connects the foot to the leg, or the thin part of the leg just above the foot • *I fell over and* **sprained/twisted** *my ankle.* • *I want to get some* **ankle boots** (= short boots which cover only the foot and ankle) *for the winter.* • An **ankle sock** (*Am* **anklet**) is a short sock which covers only the foot and ankle. • PIC› **Body, Shoes**

an·klet JEWELLERY /ˈæŋ·klət/ *n* [C] a chain or ring worn as jewellery around the ANKLE (= part of the leg above the foot)

an·klet SOCK /ˈæŋ·klət/ *n* [C] *Am for* **ankle sock**, see at ANKLE

an·nals /ˈæn·əlz/ *pl n fml* yearly or historical records of the activities of a country or organization, or history in general • *The annals* **of** *the British Parliament are recorded in a publication called Hansard.* • *Quite whether he will* **go down in** *the annals* **of** *American history* (= be considered) *as a great leader remains to be seen.* • *The signing of the Treaty of Rome was the greatest event in the annals* **of** *European integration.*

an·neal *obj* /əˈniːl/ *v* [T] *specialized* to make (metal or glass) soft by heating and then cooling slowly

an·nex *obj* /ænˈeks/ *v* [T] to take possession of (something, esp. an area of land or a country) usually by force or without permission • *Britain annexed this small island west of Scotland in 1955.*

an·nex·a·tion /ˌæn·ekˈseɪ·ʃən/ *n* • *The annexations* **of** *Austria and the Sudetenland contributed to the outbreak of the Second World War.* [C] • *Territorial disputes are rarely resolved by the annexation of parts of other countries.* [U]

an·nexe *Br and Aus, Am* **an·nex** /ˈæn·ɪks/ *n* [C] an extra building added to a larger building • *Delicate and valuable books are kept in an air-conditioned annexe* **to** *the main library.* • *(fig.) Canadians get very upset when foreigners think of their country as simply an annexe* **to** *the US.*

an·ni·hi·late *obj* /əˈnaɪ·ɪ·leɪt/ *v* [T] to destroy completely so that nothing is left or *(infml)* to defeat completely • *By annihilating the smallpox virus, doctors have saved many lives.* • *The proposed road threatens to annihilate the last remaining meadow in our area.* • *(infml) In the Wimbledon tennis finals Jackson annihilated his opponent.* • *"The human race has today the means for annihilating itself"* (Max Born (nuclear physicist) in *Bulletin of Atomic Scientists*, 1957)

an·ni·hi·la·tion /əˌnaɪ·ɪˈleɪ·ʃən/ *n* [U] • *During the Cold War the threat of nuclear annihilation was always on people's minds.* • *(infml) The opposition party's candidate suffered annihilation* (= complete defeat) *at the polls.*

an·ni·ver·sa·ry /£ˌæn·ɪˈvɜː·sər·i, $-ˈvɜːr·sɚ-/ *n* [C] (the celebration of) the day on which an important event happened in a previous year • *We always celebrate our* **wedding** *anniversary with dinner in an expensive restaurant.* • *Tomorrow is the thirtieth anniversary* **of** *the revolution.* • LP› **Holidays**

an·not·ate *obj* /£ˈæn·əʊ·teɪt, $ˈ-ə-/ *v* [T] *fml* to add a brief explanation or opinion to (a text or drawing) • *The record company has annotated its new compilation of Beatles songs, giving details about how each recording was made.* • *Annotated editions of Shakespeare's plays help readers to understand old words.*

an·not·a·tion /£ˌæn·əʊˈteɪ·ʃən, $-əˈ-/ *n* • *The annotation of literary texts makes them more accessible.* [U] • *The revised edition of the book includes many useful annotations.* [C]

an·nounce *(obj)* /əˈnaʊnts/ *v* to state or make known, esp. publicly • *They announced the death of their mother in the local paper.* [T] • *She announced the winner of the competition* **to** *an excited audience.* [T] • *The Prime Minister has announced* **that** *public spending will be increased next year.* [+ *that* clause] • *(fig.) The first few leaves in the gutter announced* (= showed) *the beginning of autumn.* [T] • *(Am)* If you announce **for the presidency** or another political position, you make known publicly that you intend to be a CANDIDATE in an election. [I] • Ⓓ Ⓢ

an·nounce·ment /əˈnaʊnt·smənt/ *n* • *She* **made** *an important announcement* **to** *her parents* **about** *her engagement.* [C] • *The announcement* **of** *bad news is a daily task in hospitals.* [U]

an·nounc·er /£əˈnaʊnt·səʳ, $-sɚ/ *n* [C] • A radio/ television announcer introduces programmes or reads the news. • Ⓚⓞⓡ

an·noy *obj* /əˈnɔɪ/ *v* [T] to make (someone) slightly angry, esp. because of repeated actions • *Tim really annoyed me in the meeting this morning.* • *Sorry, am I annoying you?* • **It** *annoys me* **that** *she just assumes we'll all fit in with her plans.* [+ *that* clause] • **It** *really annoys me when people expect me to tip as well as pay a service charge in a restaurant.* • *What annoys me is the way he won't even listen to other people's suggestions.*

an·noy·ance /əˈnɔɪ·ənts/ *n* • *I can understand your annoyance – I'd be furious if she ever treated me like that.* [U] • **(Much)** *to our annoyance,* (= We were very annoyed that) *we couldn't see anything from the back row of the theatre.* [U] • *One of the greatest annoyances* (= things that caused us to be annoyed) *was being bitten by mosquitoes every night.* [C] • *"Few things are harder to put up with than the annoyance of a good example"* (Mark Twain *Pudd'nhead Wilson,* 1894)

an·noyed /əˈnɔɪd/ *adj* • *I was so annoyed* **with** *him for turning up late that I couldn't speak to him for half an hour.* • *He was annoyed* **at** *the way she tried to take over the whole meeting.* • *My parents were rather annoyed* **(that)** *I hadn't told them about the accident.* [+ (*that*) clause] • *She was annoyed* **to** *discover that her husband had taken her car keys.* [+ *to* infinitive]

an·noy·ing /əˈnɔɪ·ɪŋ/ *adj* • *It's really annoying when a train is late and there's no explanation.* • *He's got a number of annoying habits, like interrupting people when they're speaking.*

an·noy·ing·ly /əˈnɔɪ·ɪŋ·li/ *adv* • *Annoyingly enough, I'd just bought the hardback when the paperback edition came out.* • *They were annoyingly pleased with themselves whenever they got an answer right.*

an·nu·al /ˈæn·ju·əl, -jʊl/ *adj* [before n; not gradable] happening once every year, or relating to a period of one year • *an annual event/festival/convention/show/visit/holiday* • *annual income/salary/profit/interest/rainfall/subscription* • *Companies publish annual* **reports** *to inform the public about the previous year's activities.* • An *(Br and Aus)* **annual general meeting** *(abbreviation* **AGM**, *Am* **annual meeting**) is a meeting once every year in which a company or other organization discusses the past year's activities and elects new officers.

an·nu·al /ˈæn·ju·əl, -jʊl/ *n* [C] • An annual is a book or magazine published once a year, esp. for children, with the same title and style but different contents. • A plant which grows, produces seeds, and dies within one year is also called an annual. Compare BIENNIAL; PERENNIAL [PLANT].

an·nu·al·ly /ˈæn·ju·ə·li, -jʊ·li/ *adv* [not gradable] • *Your starting salary is £13 000 per annum and will be reviewed annually* (= once every year).

an·nu·al·ized, *Br and Aus usually* **-ised** /ˈæn·ju·ə·laɪzd, -jʊ·laɪzd/ *adj specialized* • *Exports fell at an annualized rate* (= the rate calculated over a year) *of 12·3%, while imports rose at a 7·5% pace.*

an·nu·i·ty /£əˈnjuː·ə·ti, $-t̬i/ *n* [C] a fixed amount of money paid to someone every year, usually until their death, or the INSURANCE agreement or investment which provides the money that is paid • *annuity policy/income* • *She receives a small annuity.*

an·nul *obj* /əˈnʌl/ *v* [T] **-ll-** *law* to officially announce (a law, agreement, marriage, etc.) as no longer existing and never to have existed legally • *Brian's second marriage was annulled because he never divorced his first wife.* • *Many laws made by the former regime have been annulled since the coup.*

an·nul·ment /əˈnʌl·mənt/ *n* • *Judges only* **grant** *marriage annulments in exceptional circumstances.* [C] • *The discovery of the election fraud has led to the annulment of 50 000 votes.* [U]

an·num /ˈæn·əm/ *n* See **per annum** at PER

an·nus mir·a·bil·is /ˌæn·əs·mɪˈrɑː·bɪ·lɪs/ *n* [C] *pl* **anni mirabiles** /ˌæn·iː·mɪˈrɑː·bɪ·liː/ *fml* a year of unusually good events • *This year has been Clare's annus mirabilis – she graduated from university, got a job at the BBC and had her thesis published.* • *1969 was the annus mirabilis in which man first landed on the moon.*

an·ode /£ˈæn·əʊd, $-oʊd/ *n* [C] *specialized* the positive part of an electrical CELL at which ELECTRONS leave a system • *A red wire is often attached to the anode which is also marked with the positive sign (+).* • Compare CATHODE.

an·od·ize *obj, Br and Aus usually* **-ise** /£ˈæn·əʊ·daɪz, $-oʊ-/ *v* [T] *specialized* to cover (a metal) with a layer of OXIDE (= a chemical combination of oxygen and one other element) by using an electric current • *The steel girders were anodized to protect them from corrosion.*

an·o·dyne /£ˈæn·əʊ·daɪn, $-oʊ-/ *adj fml esp. disapproving* intended to avoid causing offence or disagreement, esp. by not expressing strong feelings or opinions • *This is daytime television at its most anodyne.* • *The anodyne charm of soap operas is that they are so much easier to handle than life.* • *Somehow this avoids being just another silly pop song with anodyne lyrics about love and happiness.*

a·noint *obj* /əˈnɔɪnt/ *v* [T] (esp. in a religious ceremony) to make someone king or queen • *In 751 Pepin was anointed king* (= officially made king in a religious ceremony). [T + obj + n] • *(fig.) It remains to be seen whom the chairman will anoint* (= choose) **as** *his successor.*

anointed /£əˈnɔɪn·tɪd, $-t̬ɪd/ *adj* • *the anointed king* • *(fig.) Because she's worked so hard for the company, she's generally believed to be the anointed* **heir/successor** *to the presidency* (= the person who will become the company's president next).

a·noint·ment /əˈnɔɪnt·mənt/ *n* [U] • *The act of anointment raised the king above other laymen.*

a·nom·a·ly /£əˈnɒm·ə·li, $-ˈnɑː·mə-/ *n fml* a person or thing that is different from what is usual, or not in agreement with something else and therefore not satisfactory • *Statistical anomalies can make it difficult to compare economic data from one year to the next.* [C] • *The anomaly of the social security system is that you sometimes have more money without a job.* [U] • *Is it not something of an anomaly to have a president of one political persuasion and a prime minister of another?* [C]

a·nom·al·ous /£əˈnɒm·ə·ləs, $-ˈnɑː·mə-/ *adj fml* • *In a multicultural society is it not anomalous to have a blasphemy law which only protects one religious faith?*

a·nom·al·ous·ly /£əˈnɒm·ə·lə·sli, $-ˈnɑː·mə-/ *adv fml*

a·non [SOON] /£əˈnɒn, $-ˈnɑːn/ *adv* [not gradable] *old use or humorous* soon or in the near future • *See you anon.*

A·non [NAMELESS] /£əˈnɒn, $-ˈnɑːn/, **a·non** *n* (usually written at the end of a piece of writing) *abbreviation for* ANONYMOUS (= a writer whose name is not known) • *"Who wrote that poem?" "It says here it's by Anon."*

a·non·y·mous /£əˈnɒn·ɪ·məs, $-ˈnɑː·nə-/ *adj* (made or done by someone) with a name which is not known or not made public • *The money was donated by an anonymous* **benefactor**. • *Police said an anonymous* **caller** *warned just after midnight yesterday that a bomb was about to go off.* • *An attempt to implant an embryo using an egg from an anonymous woman* **donor** *was unsuccessful.* • *He received an anonymous* **letter** *threatening to disclose details of his affair if he didn't pay the money.* • *For reasons of personal safety, the informant wishes to* **remain** *anonymous.* • *(fig.) He has a rather anonymous face* (= His face is not unusual or different in any way).

a·non·y·mous·ly /£əˈnɒn·ɪ·mə·sli, $-ˈnɑː·nə-/ *adv* • *The donation was made anonymously.*

an·o·nym·i·ty /£ˌæn·ɒnˈɪm·ɪ·ti, $-əˈnɪm·ə·t̬i/ *n* [U] • *The police have reassured witnesses who may be afraid to come forward that they will be guaranteed anonymity* (= their names will not be requested or told to others). • *I love walking around a city where I'm not known – it's the anonymity* (= the state of not being known) *that I like.*

a·noph·e·les /£əˈnɒf·ɪ·liːz, $-ˈnɑː·fə-/ *n* [C] *pl* **anopheles** *specialized* a type of MOSQUITO (= a small flying insect), esp. one which spreads MALARIA to humans

an·o·rak *esp. Br* /ˈæn·ə·ræk/, *Am and Aus usually* **par·ka** *n* [C] a short, waterproof coat that protects the wearer against cold, wet and windy weather, usually with a part for covering the head • [PIC] **Coats and jackets**

an·o·rex·i·a (ner·vo·sa) /ˌæn·əˈrek·si·ə/ *n* [U] a serious illness often resulting in dangerous weight loss, in which a person, esp. a girl or woman, does not eat, or eats too little, because they fear fatness • *Reports of anorexia and other eating disorders are on the increase, with 6000 new cases in the UK every year.* • *She suggested that the main cause of anorexia nervosa is not the cultural desire for slimness, but the stresses of family life.* • Compare BULIMIA.

an·o·rex·ic /ˌæn·əˈrek·sɪk/, **an·o·rec·tic** /ˌæn·əˈrek·tɪk/ *adj* [not gradable], *n* [C] • *In her book she explores the complex and varied reasons which lead some of these women to become anorexic.* • *She looks anorexic to me.* • *Anorexics tend to be obsessional and perfectionist.*

an·oth·er [ADDITIONAL] /£əˈnʌð·əʳ, $-ɚ/ *determiner, pronoun* one more (person or thing) or an additional (amount) • *Would anyone like another piece of cake?* • *"Would you get me a bar of chocolate from the kitchen, darling." "Another (one), Patrick!"* • *We can fit another person in my car.* • *Danny's had* **yet** *another car accident – that's his fourth this year.* • **For** *another £30* (= For £30 more) *you can buy the model with remote control.* • *Just think,* **in** *another three months* (= three months from now) *it'll be summer again.* • *Many Americans feared the Gulf War would be another Vietnam.* • *A child prodigy who graduated from Oxford University when she was 13, she could well be another Isaac Newton* (= she could be as great a scientist as him). • *I'm not surprised he's feeling ill – he was eating* **one** *ice-cream* **after another**! • *(Br humorous)* **A.N. Other** at the end of a list of people refers to someone whose name is not yet known: *We've assigned as many tasks as we can to the staff we have, and rest are down to A.N. Other for now.* • *"Well, here's another fine mess (originally 'nice mess') you've gotten me into"* (Laurel and Hardy in their films, 1927-) • LP Determiners

an·oth·er DIFFERENT /£ə'nʌð·əʳ, $-ɚ/ *determiner, pronoun* a different (person or thing) • *She's ditched that dreadful boyfriend of hers and found herself another* **(one)**. • *Do you want to exchange this toaster for another* **(one)** *or do you want your money back?* • *We'll get out of this mess* **one way or another** (= in some way). • *Cars are useful, but whether they are good for the environment is* **another matter/thing altogether** (= a different situation which is likely to be judged differently). • *They gave* **one another** (= each other) *presents when they met at the airport.* • *Feeling guilty for the homeless is one thing, finding cheap secure accommodation for them is* **(quite) another (thing)** (= very different and likely to involve more problems or difficulties). • You can say something is **another story** when you do not want to discuss it now: *When we finally got home we found that we'd been burgled – but that's another story.* • *Oh, Dominic, you look as if you're* **in another world** (= you seem to be dreaming or thinking about something different to everyone else) • *"Tomorrow, I'll think of some way to get him back. After all, tomorrow is another day."* (Margaret Mitchell *Gone with the Wind*, 1936) • *"Another time, another place"* (title of novel and film by Jessie Kesson, 1983)

an·sa·phone, **an·sa·fone** /£'ɑːnt·sə·fəʊn, $'ænt·sə·foʊn/ *n* [C] *trademark* an ANSWERPHONE

an·swer REACTION /£'ɑːnt·səʳ, $'ænt·sɚ/ *n* [C] a reaction to a question, letter, telephone call, etc. • *The Minister promised to give a written answer* **to** *the MP's detailed question.* • *We've written to him asking him if he's free on that date but we haven't had an answer yet.* • *I've just rung him but there was no answer.* • *I didn't realise we had to write each answer on a new sheet of paper.* • *I got eight correct answers and two wrong ones in last week's exam.* • **In answer to** *your letter of May 30th, I am writing to accept your offer to publish my next novel.* • *(fig.) Channel 4 is independent television's answer* **to** (= is approximately the same as) *BBC2.* • *"The Answer to the Great Question of ....Life, the Universe and Everything....Is...Forty-two"* (Douglas Adams *Hitch Hiker's Guide to the Galaxy*, 1979) • *"But answer came there none"* (Sir Walter Scott in the poem *The Bridal of Triermain*, 1813) • *"Well, if I called the wrong number, why did you answer the phone?"* (from a cartoon by James Thurber, 1937)

an·swer *(obj)* /£'ɑːnt·səʳ, $'ænt·sɚ/ *v* • To answer is to say, write or do something as a reaction to a question, letter, telephone call etc.: *I can't answer (you) without more detailed information.* [I/T] ○ *I'd like to answer your* **question** *by posing another one.* [T] ○ *I wrote asking whether he'd be coming to the party but he hasn't answered yet.* [I] ○ *"I'd love to have dinner with you, but I won't be able to get there before nine o'clock," she answered.* [+ clause] ○ *She answered* **that** *she wouldn't be able to come before nine o'clock.* [+ *that* clause] ○ *Someone's at the door – would you answer it please?* [T] ○ *I phoned last night but nobody answered.* [I] • If someone who is believed to have committed a crime answers a **charge**, they are formally accused of it in a court of law, and asked to state whether they are guilty or not. [T] • *(fml) Does anyone here answer* **to the name of** *Wallis?* (= Is anyone here called Wallis?) [I] • *The company criticized in the documentary were given the opportunity to answer* **back** (= allowed to react publicly). [I] • *(Br)* If you **answer back** (*Am* **talk back**), you speak rudely when answering someone in authority: *The teacher told him off for answering back all the time.* • **Answering machine** is *esp. Am for* ANSWERPHONE. • An **answering service** is a company that receives and answers telephone calls for its customers.

an·swer SOLUTION /£'ɑːnt·səʳ, $'ænt·sɚ/ *n* [C] a solution to a problem • *There is no answer* **to the problem** *of environmental pollution.* • *There's no* **easy** *answer* **to the problem** *– we just have to work out the best way of dealing with it.*

an·swer *(obj)* MATCH /£'ɑːnt·səʳ, $'ænt·sɚ/ *v* [T; I always + *to*] to match (a description) • *A woman who answers* **(to)** *the suspect's description was seen in the area on the night of the crime.*

an·swer *obj* BE SUITABLE FOR /£'ɑːnt·səʳ, $'ænt·sɚ/ *v* [T] to be suitable for and satisfy (someone's needs) • *He showed me a computer that answered my requirements exactly.* • *I've got bit of furniture round the back that I think might answer your needs.*

an·swer for *obj v prep* [T] to take responsibility for (someone) • *I expect parents to answer for their children's behaviour.* • *"Why do you think there's so much violence nowadays?" "Well, violence on television has* **a lot to** *answer for* (= is the cause of much of it)*."* • *(Br) I can certainly answer for her* (= promise that she will show) *professionalism, and whole-heartedly recommend her to any employer.*

an·swer·a·ble /£'ɑːnt·sᵊr·ə·bl̩, $'ænt·sɚ-/ *adj* [after v] • *Soldiers who obey orders to commit atrocities should be answerable* **for** (= held responsible for) *their crimes.*

an·swer to *obj v prep* [T] to take orders from, obey and explain your actions to (someone) • *The great thing about working for yourself is that you don't have to answer to anyone.*

an·swer·a·ble /£'ɑːnt·sə·rə·bl̩, $'ænt-/ *adj* [after v] • *Any European central bank should be directly answerable* (= they should have to explain their actions) **to** *the European Parliament.* • *John works completely independently – he is answerable* **to** *nobody but himself* (= he takes responsibility for everything).

an·swer·phone *esp. Br* /£'ɑːnt·sə·fəʊn, $'ænt·sɚ·foʊn/, *esp. Am* **an·swer·ing ma·chine** *n* [C] a device connected to a telephone which answers calls automatically and records messages from callers • *She wasn't in so I* **left a message on** *her answerphone.* • *I rang several times last week, but I kept* **getting** *your wretched answerphone.* • LP Telephone

ant INSECT /ænt/ *n* [C] a very small insect which lives under the ground in large and highly organized social groups • *We've had another invasion of ants in the kitchen.* • *(dated humorous)* If you have **ants in** your **pants**, you cannot relax because you are excited or IMPATIENT about something. • See also ANTHILL. • PIC Insects

-ant PERFORM /-ənt/, **-ent** *combining form* (a person or thing) performing or causing the stated action • *assistant* • *participant* • *disinfectant* • *an expectant look* • *a defiant child*

ant·ac·id /ˌæn'tæs·ɪd/ *n* [C/U] a substance used to reduce or prevent acidity, particularly in the stomach

an·tag·on·i·sm /æn'tæg·ə·nɪ·zᵊm/ *n* (an example of) hate, extreme unfriendliness or active opposition, esp. between two (groups of) people • *The underlying antagonism* **between** *the two men doesn't exactly encourage party unity.* [U] • *There's a worrying degree of antagonism* **towards** *neighbouring states.* [U] • *The European Union has certainly helped to reduce the historic antagonisms* **between** *the countries of western Europe.* [C] • GR

an·tag·on·ist /æn'tæg·ə·nɪst/ *n* [C] • *The antagonists* (= opponents) *in this dispute are quite unwilling to compromise.* • Compare PROTAGANIST SUPPORTER.

an·tag·on·ist·ic /£ænˌtæg·ə'nɪs·tɪk, $-t̬ɪk/ *adj* • *We feel that the directors are adopting an unnecessarily antagonistic approach* **towards** (= are actively opposing) *these negotiations.* • *He's extremely antagonistic* (= shows unfriendliness and opposition) **towards** *all critics.*

an·tag·o·nize *obj, Br and Aus usually* **-ise** /æn'tæg·ə·naɪz/ *v* [T] • If you antagonize someone, you cause them to feel opposition or dislike towards you: *It's a very delicate situation and I've no wish to antagonize him.* ○ *With the publication of this controversial book, you risk antagonizing a large section of the population.*

An·tarc·tic /£æn'tɑːk·tɪk, $-'tɑːrk-/ *n* [U] **the Antarctic** the very cold area around the South Pole which includes Antarctica and the surrounding seas • *The protection of the Antarctic from commercial exploitation is an important goal of environmentalists.*

An·tarc·tic /£æn'tɑːk·tɪk, $-'tɑːrk-/ *adj* [not gradable] • *the Antarctic Ocean/Circle/Zone* • *an Antarctic explorer/expedition*

an·te RISK /£'æn·ti, $-t̬i/ *n* [C usually sing] the amount of money that must be paid, esp. in a game of POKER before a player can receive new cards; STAKE RISK • *a $30 ante* • *(fig.) The publisher* **upped the** *ante* (= raised the level of money to be paid) *for the biography by offering £200 000 more than her competitor.*

an·te- BEFORE /£ˌæn·ti-, $-t̬i-/ *combining form* before or in front of • *antedate* • *antenatal* • *anteroom* • Compare PRE- and POST-.

ant·eat·er /£'æntˌiː·təʳ, $-t̬ɚ/ *n* [C] a toothless mammal which eats ANTS or TERMITES and has a long nose and tongue

an·te·ced·ent /ˌæn·tiˈsiː·dᵊnt/ *n* [C] *fml* someone or something existing or happening before, esp. as the cause or origin of something existing or happening later • *Charles Babbage's mechanical calculating engines were the antecedents of the modern computer.* • *Many Christian festivals have pagan antecedents which stretch back into the distant past.* • *Some people see the pioneering novelist Dorothy Richardson as an antecedent of the Irish writer James Joyce.* • *Many people feel a great curiosity to find out about their antecedents.* • *(specialized)* An antecedent is also a word or phrase which a pronoun refers back to: *In the sentence 'Bill ran up to Roz and kissed her', 'Roz' is the antecedent of 'her'.*

an·te·ced·ent /ˌæn·tiˈsiː·dᵊnt/ *adj* [not gradable] *fml* • *When the college was established in 1546, it inherited a hall from each of three antecedent institutions.*

an·te·cham·ber /£ˈæn·tiˌtʃeɪm·bəʳ, $-t̬iˌtʃeɪm·bɚ/ *n* [C] an ANTEROOM

an·te·date *obj* /£ˌæn·tiˈdeɪt, $ˈæn·t̬i·deɪt/ *v* [T] *fml for* PREDATE

an·te·di·lu·vi·an /£ˌæn·ti·dɪˈluː·vi·ən, $-t̬i-/ *adj esp. humorous* extremely old-fashioned • *Their production techniques are positively antediluvian by modern standards.* • *My mother has some hopelessly antediluvian ideas about the role of women – she expects my girlfriend to iron my shirts for me!*

an·te·lope /£ˈæn·tɪ·ləʊp, $-t̬ᵊl·oʊp/ *n* [C] *pl* **antelope** /ˈæn·tɪ·ləʊp, $-t̬ᵊl·oʊp/ or **antelopes** a deer-like mammal with horns and long thin legs which allow it to run very fast • *Antelopes live in Africa and Asia and eat grass and leaves.* • *We saw a* **herd of** *antelope.*

an·te·nat·al /£ˌæn·tiˈneɪ·tᵊl, $-ˈneɪ·t̬ᵊl/, *esp. Am and Aus* **pre·na·tal** *adj* [before n; not gradable] happening or existing before birth • *antenatal care/screening/diagnosis* • *Over two-thirds of the women attending my antenatal* **class** *do so with their partners.* • *I've got an appointment at the antenatal* **clinic** *this afternoon.* • Compare POSTNATAL.

an·te·nat·al /£ˌæn·tiˈneɪ·tᵊl, $-ˈneɪ·t̬ᵊl/ *n* [C] *infml* • An antenatal is a specialist medical examination of a pregnant woman.

an·te·nat·al·ly /£ˌæn·tiˈneɪ·tᵊl·i, $-t̬ᵊl-/ *adv* [not gradable] • *Some foetal abnormalities can now be detected antenatally.*

an·ten·na [ORGAN] /ænˈten·ə/ *n* [C] *pl* **antennae** /ænˈten·iː/ either of a pair of long thin hair-like organs which are found on the heads of insects and CRUSTACEANS (= animals with hard outer shells) • *Sometimes a creature uses a pair of antennae to swim or attach itself to other animals or objects.* • *(fig.) Her finely-tuned political antennae helped her to sense problems that less-experienced politicians might not detect.* • *"Artists are the antennae of the race"* (Ezra Pound in *Literary Essays* 'Henry James', 1954) • [PIC〉] **Crustaceans**

an·ten·na [PART OF RADIO] /ænˈten·ə/ *n* [C] *pl* **antennas** *esp. Am and Aus* an AERIAL [RADIO] • *My neighbour has a tall radio antenna on his roof.* • [PIC〉] **Car**

an·te·pe·nul·ti·mate /£ˌæn·ti·pəˈnʌl·tɪ·mət, $-t̬i-/ *adj* [not gradable], *n* [C] *fml* (something which is) third from the last • *T is the antepenultimate letter of the name Martha.* • Compare PENULTIMATE.

an·te·ri·or /£ænˈtɪə·ri·əʳ, $-ˈtɪr·i·ɚ/ *adj* [before n; not gradable] *specialized* positioned at or towards the front • *Specimens for examination were taken from the anterior side of the left ventricle from each heart.* • Compare POSTERIOR.

an·te·room /£ˈæn·ti·rʊm, £-ruːm, $-t̬i-/, **an·te·cham·ber** *n* [C] *fml* a small room, esp. a waiting room, which leads into a larger, more important room • *The ministers waited for their meeting in the Cabinet anteroom.*

an·them /ˈænt·θəm/ *n* [C] a song which has special importance for a particular group of people, organization or country, often sung on a special occasion • *They usually play the* **national** *anthems of the teams at the beginning of a big international football match.* • *John Lennon's "Imagine" has become the anthem of peace-lovers all over the world.* • An anthem is also a short religious song sung by a CHOIR with ORGAN music.

an·them·ic /ænˈθem·ɪk/ *adj fml* • Music that is anthemic has qualities that are suitable for an anthem, such as a strong tune and seriousness.

an·ther /£ˈænt·θəʳ, $-θɚ/ *n* [C] the part of a flower that contains POLLEN (= the substance which causes other flower parts to produce seeds) • [PIC〉] **Flowers and plants**

ant·hill /ˈænt·hɪl/ *n* [C] a pile of earth, leaves, etc. created by ANTS when they are making their nests underground

an·thol·o·gy /£ænˈθɒl·ə·dʒi, $-ˈθɑː·lə-/ *n* [C] a collection of artistic works which have a similar form or subject, often those considered to be the best • *an anthology of modern quotations/American verse/humorous anecdotes* • *This Bob Dylan anthology includes some rare recordings of his best songs.* • *The exhibition is an anthology of anti-Stalinist works that had been hidden from the former regime.* • Compare OMNIBUS [BOOK OR PROGRAMME].

an·thol·o·gist /£ænˈθɒl·ə·dʒɪst, $-ˈθɑː·lə-/ *n* [C]

an·thol·o·gize *obj, Br and Aus usually* **-ise** /£ænˈθɒl·ə·dʒaɪz, $-ˈθɑː·lə-/ *v* [T] • *His poems are read in classrooms throughout the country and his short stories are frequently anthologized* (= included in anthologies).

an·thra·cite /ˈænt·θrə·saɪt/, **hard coal** *n* [U] a very hard type of coal which burns slowly and produces a lot of heat with very little smoke and a small flame

an·thrax /ˈæn·θræks/ *n* [U] a very infectious disease which causes fever, swelling and often death in animals, esp. sheep and cattle, and can be passed on to humans

an·thro·po- /£ˌænt·θrəʊ·pəʊ-, $-θrə·pə-/, **an·throp-** *combining form* relating to human beings • *anthropomorphism*

an·thro·po·cen·tric /£ˌænt·θrəʊ·pəʊˈsen·trɪk, $-θrə·pə-/ *adj fml* considering human beings and their existence as the most important and central fact in the universe

an·thro·po·cen·tri·sm /£ˌænt·θrəʊ·pəʊˈsen·trɪ·zᵊm, $-θrə·pə-/ *n* [U] *fml*

an·thro·poid /£ˈænt·θrəʊ·pɔɪd, $-θrə-/ *adj* [before n], *n* [C] (like) a human being or an APE (= large monkey) • *Gorillas, chimpanzees and gibbons are all anthropoid apes, having long arms, no tails and highly developed brains.* • *Monkeys, apes and humans are all anthropoids.*

an·thro·pol·o·gy /£ˌænt·θrəˈpɒl·ə·dʒi, $-ˈpɑː·lə-/ *n* [U] the study of the human race, its culture and society and its physical development

an·thro·po·log·ic·al /£ˌænt·θrə·pəˈlɒdʒ·ɪ·kᵊl, $-ˈlɑː·dʒɪ-/ *adj* • *anthropological research/fieldwork* • *the Anthropological Library/Department/Society*

an·thro·po·log·i·cal·ly /£ˌænt·θrə·pəˈlɒdʒ·ɪ·kli, $-ˈlɑː·dʒɪ-/ *adv*

an·thro·pol·o·gist /£ˌænt·θrəˈpɒl·ə·dʒɪst, $-ˈpɑː·lə-/ *n* [C] • Anthropologists are people who study scientifically human beings, their customs, beliefs and relationships.

an·thro·po·morph·i·sm /£ˌænt·θrə·pəʊˈmɔː·fɪ·zᵊm, $-pəˈmɔːr-/ *n* [U] the showing or treating of animals, gods and objects as if they are human in appearance, character or behaviour • *The books 'Alice in Wonderland', 'Peter Rabbit' and 'Winnie-the-Pooh' are classic examples of anthropomorphism.*

an·thro·po·morph·ic /£ˌænt·θrə·pəʊˈmɔː·fɪk, $-pəˈmɔːr-/ *adj*

an·ti- /£ˌæn·ti-, $-t̬i-, $-taɪ-/ *combining form* opposed to or against; opposite of or preventing • **Anti-ageing** substances are intended to prevent or limit the process of becoming old: *It's described on the bottle as 'an anti-ageing preparation to reduce fine lines and restore elasticity'.* • **Anti-aircraft** means intended to destroy or defend against enemy aircraft: *an anti-aircraft missile/gun/battery/weapon/position* • *anti-aircraft defences/fire* • People who are **anti-abortion** believe that ABORTION (= the intentional ending of a pregnancy by a medical operation) is morally wrong: *anti-abortion activists/groups* ○ *the anti-abortion movement* • *(disapproving)* **Anti-choice** means opposed to the idea that a pregnant woman should have the freedom to choose an ABORTION (= a medical operation to end a pregnancy) if she does not want to have a baby: *the anti-choice lobby* • **Anti-clerical** means opposed to organized religion having influence in politics and public life: *an anti-clerical law/constitution* ○ *In his novel 'The Power and the Glory', Graham Greene gives an account of an anti-clerical purge in Mexico.* ○ *I have ended up as a sort of open-minded agnostic but without any* **anti-clericalism**. • *(Br and Aus)* **Anti-clockwise** (*Am* **counterclockwise**) means in the opposite direction to the movement of the hand of a clock or watch: *"How do I get the top off this medicine bottle?" "Push it down and twist it anti-clockwise."* • **Anti-consumerist** means opposed to the idea that people should be able to buy an unlimited amount of goods, and to the effect that such freedom has on the physical and social conditions in which people live: *Graham doesn't have a car as a part of his anti-consumerist stance.* • An **anti-depressant** is a drug used to reduce feelings of sadness and hopelessness: *She's been* **on** *anti-depressants ever since her husband died.* ○ *anti-depressant drugs* • **Anti-federal(ist)**

means opposed to the establishment of a system of government in which power is divided between a single central government and several regional ones: *The Foreign Secretary assured anti-federalist MPs that he would not agree to anything which limited British sovereignty.* ○ *Many voters are staunch anti-federalists, opposed to the concept of regional government.* • An **anti-hero** is the central character in a play, book or film who does not possess traditionally HEROIC qualities, such as bravery, and is admired instead for what society generally considers to be weaknesses and faults: *He plays the classic anti-hero who drops out of society to join a world of impoverished artists and writers.* • An **anti-inflammatory** drug is used to reduce soreness and swelling: *Mira used to take anti-inflammatory drugs for her arthritis.* ○ *Aspirin is an* **anti-inflammatory.** • **Anti-lock** refers to a type of BRAKE which prevents the uncontrolled sliding of a vehicle by reducing the effects of sudden braking. • An **anti-missile** is a MISSILE (= flying weapon with its own engine) which is used for defence against attack from missiles. • **Anti-noise** is sound which is produced in such a way that it matches exactly and removes the effect of loud and possibly harmful noises, such as those produced by large engines in factories. • **Anti-nuclear** means opposed to the production and use of nuclear weapons, or to the production of electricity from nuclear power: *the anti-nuclear lobby/movement* ○ *Most environmentalists are vehemently anti-nuclear.* • An **anti-oxidant** is a substance which slows down the rate at which something decays because of OXIDIZATION (= combining with oxygen): *Anti-oxidants are used as preservatives to make food last a long time.* • **Anti-personnel** weapons are intended to kill or injure people rather than damage weapons or buildings, etc.: *anti-personnel mines* • An **anti-perspirant** is a substance which is put on the skin, esp. under the arms, in order to prevent or reduce PERSPIRATION (= the excretion of liquid through the skin). • **Anti-racist** means opposed to the unfair treatment of people who belong to other racial groups: *Tougher anti-racist legislation is essential for the protection of ethnic minorities.* ○ *A group of anti-racists were protesting in the town centre.* • **Anti-Semitism** is the strong dislike or cruel and unfair treatment of Jewish people: *Anti-semitism invariably reflects or foreshadows a diseased condition in European politics.* ○ *He was accused of being* **anti-Semitic**. ○ *In later life the American poet became a virulent* **anti-Semite**. • **Anti-social** means opposed or harmful to society, or tending to avoid spending time with other people: *Smoking is such an anti-social* **behaviour** *when you're in a room full of non-smokers.* ○ *Some people seem anti-social when in fact they are simply very shy.* ○ *It's hardly surprising that Richard doesn't have any friends when he behaves so* **anti-socially.** • **Anti-tank** weapons are those which destroy or damage enemy TANKS (= large military fighting vehicles): *anti-tank missiles/helicopters/rockets* • **Anti-viral** means intended to treat an infection or disease caused by a virus: *an anti-viral agent/drug* ○ **Anti-virals** *are used to destroy the enzyme which the AIDS virus needs to reproduce itself.* • Compare PRO- [SUPPORT]. • [LP> **Opposites** [PIC> **Clocks and watches**

an·ti /£'æn·ti, $-ţi/ *adj, prep, n* [C] *pl* **antis** *infml* • *We've received a lot of anti letters about* (= letters opposing) *that newspaper article.* • *Just because I won't join you, it doesn't mean that I'm anti* (= against) *you.* • *So what do you think about smoking in public places – are you (a) pro or (an) anti?* (= do you support or oppose it)*?*

an·ti·bac·te·ri·al /£ˌæn·ti·bæk'tɪə·ri·əl, $-ţi·bæk'tɪr·i-/ *adj* [not gradable] intended to kill or reduce the harmful effects of bacteria especially when used on the skin • *Her doctor recommended that she use an antibacterial facial wash for her spots.*

an·ti·bi·ot·ic /£ˌæn·ti·baɪ'ɒt·ɪk, $-ţi·baɪ'ɑː·ţɪk/ *n* a medicine or chemical that can destroy harmful bacteria in the body or limit their growth • *I'm* **taking** *antibiotics for a throat infection.* [C] • *The doctor has recommended a one-month* **course of** *antibiotics to clear up her acne.* [C] • *Some types of antibiotic are used to promote growth in farm animals.* [U] • *Beehive glue contains a substance which has an antibiotic effect and could be used in medicines.*

an·ti·bo·dy /£'æn·tiˌbɒd·i, $-ţiˌbɑː·di/ *n* [C] a PROTEIN produced in the blood which fights diseases by attacking and killing harmful bacteria • *Antibodies found in breast milk protect babies against infection.* • See also ANTIGEN.

An·ti·christ /£'æn·ti·kraɪst, $-ţi-/ *n* [C] originally the main enemy of Jesus Christ who was expected to rule the world until Jesus Christ's Second Coming, now any enemy of Jesus Christ or Christianity • *In the eyes of some extreme Protestants, the Pope is the Antichrist.* • *When rock 'n' roll first appeared, many people described it as the music of the Antichrist.*

an·ti·ci·pate *(obj)* /æn'tɪs·ɪ·peɪt/ *v* to imagine or expect that (something) will happen, sometimes taking action in preparation for it happening • *The police are anticipating trouble at tomorrow's football match.* [T] • *We had one or two difficulties along the way that we couldn't have anticipated.* [T] • *Are you anticipating a lot of people at the party tonight?* [T] • *They anticipate* **having** *several applicants for the job.* [+ v-ing] • *They anticipate* **that** *they will have several applicants for the job* [+ *that* clause] • *It's always better to anticipate a problem before it arises than to search for a solution afterwards.* [T] • *He should have anticipated* **that** *this would happen and tried to prevent it.* [+ *that* clause] • *At this stage we can't really anticipate* **what** *will happen.* [+ *wh-* word] • *The anticipated inflation figure is lower than last month's.* • *The army anticipated* (= took action in preparation for) *the explosion by evacuating the town.* [T] • *(fml) You shouldn't anticipate* (= spend before you receive) *your inheritance because it could be years before your parents die.* [T] • Ⓔ Ⓟ

an·ti·ci·pa·tion /ænˌtɪs·ɪ'peɪ·ʃən/ *n* [U] • *London share prices slipped back* **in** *anticipation* **of** *an* (= because of an expected) *overnight fall on Wall Street.* • *Hurricane-force winds have been predicted.* **In** *anticipation* **(of** *these)* (= In preparation for these), *the radio and television are broadcasting warnings to the public.* • Anticipation is a feeling of excitement about something that is going to happen in the near future: *The postponement of the film's sequel has held cinema-goers* **in eager** *anticipation for several months.* ○ *As with most pleasures, it's not so much the experience itself as the anticipation that is enjoyable.*

an·ti·cli·max /£ˌæn·ti'klaɪ·mæks, $-ţi-/ *n* an event or experience which causes disappointment because it is less exciting than was expected or because it happens immediately after a much more interesting or exciting event • *When you really look forward to something it's often an anticlimax when it actually happens.* [C] • *Coming home after a trip somewhere is always* **a bit of an** *anticlimax.* [C] • *The concert was* **something of an** *anticlimax because the star soloist never turned up.* [C] • *Even when you win a match there's often a sense of anticlimax – you always feel you could have played better or got a higher score.* [U]

an·ti·cli·mac·tic /£ˌæn·ti·klaɪ'mæk·tɪk, $-ţɪk/ *adj* • *There was so much publicity and hype beforehand, that the performance itself was a touch anticlimactic.*

an·ti·co·ag·ul·ant /£ˌæn·ti·kəʊ'æg·jʊ·lənt, $-ţi·koʊ-/ *n* [C], *adj* [not gradable] (a drug) which prevents or slows down the process of blood forming a CLOT (= a partly solid lump) • *Mosquitoes secrete an anticoagulant to keep blood from clotting as they suck it from their victims.*

an·tics /£'æn·tɪks, $-ţɪks/ *pl n* amusing, silly or strange behaviour • *But the rock-star whose stage antics used to include smashing guitars is older and wiser now.* • *The crowds were once again entertained by the number one tennis player's antics on and off the court.* • *(fig.) Prices were unsettled by the Deutschmark's antics on the foreign exchanges.*

an·ti·cy·clone /£ˌæn·ti'saɪ·kləʊn, $-ţi'saɪ·kloʊn/ *n* [C] an area of high ATMOSPHERIC pressure which causes calm weather • *Anticyclones cause cloudless blue skies and high temperatures in summer.* • *Anticyclones are common over the Pyrenees in winter, which is good for sun-lovers but bad for skiers.*

an·ti·dote /£'æn·ti·dəʊt, $-ţi·doʊt/ *n* [C] a chemical, esp. a drug, which limits the effects of a poison, or *(fig.)* a way of preventing or acting against something bad • *Sales of nerve gas antidotes increased dramatically before the war.* • *Anemone was at the time believed to be an antidote for scorpion poison.* • *(fig.) Regular exercise is the best antidote* **to** *tiredness and depression.* • *(fig.) High interest rates are the only known antidote* **to** *a persistent consumer boom.*

an·ti·freeze /£'æn·ti·friːz, $-ţi-/ *n* [U] a liquid which is added to water in order to lower the temperature at which it freezes, used esp. in car RADIATORS (= cooling systems) in very cold weather

an·ti·gen /£'æn·tɪ·dʒən, £-dʒen, $-ţi-/ *n* [C] *specialized* a substance that causes the production of ANTIBODIES in the body • *The faeces of dust mites contains antigens which trigger allergic reactions such as wheezing and coughing.*

an·ti·hi·sta·mine /£ˌæn·tiˈhɪs·tə·mɪn, £-miːn, $-t̬iˈ-/ *n* a type of drug which is used to treat illnesses caused by an extreme reaction to particular substances • *Antihistamine is often used to treat hay fever and insect bites.* [U] • *Mixing antihistamines with alcohol makes people drowsy.* [C]

an·ti·knock /£ˌæn·tiˈnɒk, $ˈæn·t̬iˈnɑːk/ *n* [U] a chemical which is added to the fuel of a car engine in order to make the fuel burn more effectively

an·ti·knock·ing /£ˌæn·tiˈnɒk·ɪŋ, $-ˈnɑː·kɪŋ/ *adj* [before n; not gradable] • *Increased use of unleaded petrol has reduced demand for antiknocking compounds.*

an·ti·log·a·rithm /£ˌæn·tiˈlɒg·ə·rɪ·ðəm, $-ˈlɑː·gɚ·ɪ-/, *infml* **an·ti·log** *n* [C] the number to which a LOGARITHM belongs • *The antilogarithm of 3 is 1000 because 10 cubed equals 1000.* • *100 and 10 are the antilogarithms of 2 and 1.*

an·ti·ma·cas·sar /£ˌæn·ti·məˈkæs·əʳ, $-t̬i·məˈkæs·ɚ/ *n* [C] a cloth, used mainly in the past, for putting over the back of a chair in order to keep it clean or to decorate it

an·ti·mo·ny /£ˈæn·tɪ·mə·ni, £ænˈtɪm·ə-, $ˈæn·t̬ə·moʊ-/ *n* [U] a metallic and poisonous element which is hard but easily broken and has a silvery white appearance. It is used to strengthen and harden other metals and to make SEMICONDUCTORS for computers.

an·ti·pa·sto /£ˌæn·tiˈpæs·təʊ, $-t̬iˈpɑː·stoʊ/ *n* [C] *pl* **antipastos** or **antipasti** /£ˌæn·tiˈpæs·ti, $-t̬iˈpɑː·sti/ something eaten at the beginning of an Italian meal, typically a small plate of HAM, sliced SAUSAGE or vegetables

an·ti·pa·thy /ænˈtɪp·ə·θi/ *n* (an example of) strong, often active, dislike, opposition or anger • *Despite the deep antipathies* **between** *them, the two sides have managed to negotiate an agreement.* [C] • *Declarations of racial antipathy* **against** *ethnic minorities will not be tolerated.* [U] • *He has no ideas of his own – his success depended purely on the electorate's antipathy* **to/towards** *his rival.* [U] • *Antipathy* **for** *the terrorist group usually increases after a bomb attack.* [U]

an·ti·pa·thet·ic /£ˌæn·ti·pəˈθet·ɪk, $-t̬i·pəˈθet̬-/ *adj fml* • *He said that antipathetic attitudes towards smokers were turning them into a persecuted minority.*

An·ti·pod·es /ænˈtɪp·ə·diːz/ *pl n* **the Antipodes** *esp. humorous* a way of referring to Australia and New Zealand by people living in the northern HEMISPHERE (= half of the earth) • *I'm not sure where we're going next summer but I rather fancy the Antipodes.*

An·ti·po·de·an /ænˌtɪp·əˈdiː·ən/ *n* [C], *adj esp. humorous* • *I knew his accent was Antipodean but I couldn't work out whether he was an Australian or a New Zealander.* • *Of course for Antipodeans it's now winter.*

an·ti·qua·ri·an /£ˌæn·tɪˈkweə·ri·ən, $-t̬ɪˈkwer·i-/ *adj, n* [C] (a person) connected with the trade, collection or study of old and valuable or rare objects, or with the study of (objects, artistic works and buildings from) the distant past • *an antiquarian bookshop/bookseller*

an·ti·qua·ri·an·i·sm /£ˌæn·tɪˈkweə·ri·ə·nɪ·zəm, $-t̬ɪˈkwer·i-/ *n* [U]

an·ti·qua·ry /£ˈæn·tɪ·kwə·ri, $-t̬ə·kwer·i/ *n* [C] *old use for* ANTIQUARIAN

an·ti·quat·ed /£ˈæn·tɪ·kweɪ·tɪd, $-t̬ə·kweɪ·t̬ɪd/ *adj* old-fashioned or unsuitable for modern society • *antiquated ideas/attitudes/values/laws/machinery/technology* • *Foreigners often find Britain's antiquated class system difficult to understand.* • *It will take many years to modernise these antiquated industries.* • *Compared with modern satellite dishes, ordinary TV aerials look positively antiquated.* • *(infml humorous) Now I'm thirty I feel positively antiquated* (= very old)*!*

an·tique /ænˈtiːk/ *n* [C], *adj* (something) made in an earlier period and collected and valued because it is beautiful, rare, old or of high quality, or related to the buying and selling of such items • *antique silver/jewellery/lace/furniture/china/coins/clocks/manuscripts* • *You can't give away Granny's old bookcase – it's a valuable antique.* • *My mother* **collects** *antiques.* • *She's married to an antique* **dealer**. • *Antique shops/stalls/markets/fairs/auctions are all places where you can buy antiques.*

an·ti·qui·ty /£ænˈtɪk·wɪ·ti, $-wə·t̬i/ *n* the distant past, esp. before the sixth century, or (something of) great age • *Cannabis has been used for medicinal purposes since antiquity.* [U] • *Before creating this sculpture, she studied all the masterpieces of* **classical** *antiquity.* [U] • *We took a special trip to see Stonehenge, a prehistoric monument of great antiquity.* [U] • *Under Greek law, all antiquities* (= objects of great age) *that are discovered in Greece belong to the government.* [C]

an·tir·rhi·num /£ˌæn·tɪˈraɪ·nəm, $-t̬ɪ-/ *n* [C] *fml for* SNAPDRAGON

an·ti·sep·tic /£ˌæn·tɪˈsep·tɪk, $-t̬ɪ-/ *n* a chemical used for preventing infection in an injury, esp. by killing bacteria • *Antiseptic is used to sterilize the skin before giving an injection.* [U] • *Many of the ingredients for antiseptics come from the rainforests.* [C]

an·ti·sep·tic /£ˌæn·tɪˈsep·tɪk, $-t̬ɪk/ *adj* • Antiseptic means completely free from infection: *In the 1870s and 1880s, doctors began to follow the principles of antiseptic surgery.* • *(fig. disapproving) There's an air of antiseptic cleanliness about the new town centre, with its covered shopping mall and luxuriant flower displays.* • *(fig. disapproving) I find a lot of modern buildings cold and antiseptic* (= lacking in imagination and character).

an·ti·sta·tic /£ˌæn·tiˈstæt·ɪk, $-t̬iˈstæt̬-/ *adj* providing a path for electricity and so preventing the problems which are caused when electricity collects on the surface of objects instead of flowing in a current • *Antistatic cloths improve the sound quality of records by making them attract less dust and fluff.*

an·ti·the·sis /ænˈtɪθ·ə·sɪs/ *n pl* **antitheses** /ænˈtɪθ·ə·siːz/ the exact opposite • *The antithesis* **of/to** *warmongering is pacifism.* [C] • *Their solution to the problem was* **in** *complete antithesis* **to** *mine.* [U] • *Thanks to the collapse of communism the political antithesis* **between** *Left and Right is less important.* [C] • *He is the very antithesis* **of** *his predecessor – young, male, indecisive and under-educated.* [U]

an·ti·thet·ic·al /£ˌæn·tɪˈθet·ɪ·kəl, $-t̬ɪˈθet̬-/, **an·ti·thet·ic** /£ˌæn·tɪˈθet·ɪk, $-t̬ɪˈθet̬-/ *adj* [not gradable] *fml* • *I've never understood how a couple can get on when their opinions on everything are absolutely antithetical* **(to** *each other).*

ant·ler /£ˈænt·ləʳ, $-lɚ/ *n* [C] a horn with branch-like parts which grows on the head of a usually male deer • *a pair of antlers* • *Deer shed their antlers each year and grow more branches as they get older.*

an·to·nym /£ˈæn·tə·nɪm, $-t̬ən·ɪm/ *n* [C] *specialized* a word which means the opposite of another word • *Two antonyms of 'light' are 'dark' and 'heavy'.* • Compare SYNONYM. • [LP] **Opposites**

an·to·nym·ous /£ænˈtɒn·ɪ·məs, $-ˈtɑː·nɪ-/ *adj specialized* • *'Long' and 'short' are antonymous (words).*

a·nus /ˈeɪ·nəs/ *n* [C] the opening at the end of the ALIMENTARY CANAL through which solid excrement leaves the body

a·nal /ˈeɪ·nəl/ *adj* [not gradable] • *the anal passage/sphincter* • Anal **sex/intercourse** is sex between two people in which a man's penis enters the other person's anus.

a·nal·ly /ˈeɪ·nə·li/ *adv* [not gradable] • *(esp. humorous)* Someone who is **anally retentive** (also **anal**, *Am usually* **anal retentive**) is too worried about being organized and tidy: *Don't you think Adrian's a bit anally retentive? Look how obsessively orderly everything is in his garage.*

an·vil [EQUIPMENT] /ˈæn·vɪl/ *n* [C] a heavy block of iron on which heated pieces of metal are shaped by hammering them into objects such as shoes for horses' HOOVES

an·vil [BONE] /ˈæn·vɪl/ *n* [C] *specialized* one of the small bones of the ear

anx·i·e·ty /£æŋˈzaɪ·ə·ti, $-t̬i/ *n, adj* [not gradable] (a cause of) an uncomfortable feeling of nervousness or worry about something that is happening or might happen in the future • *Children normally feel a lot of anxiety* **about** *their first day at school.* [U] • *Her son is a source of considerable anxiety.* [U] • *The British fail to comprehend the deep European anxiety* **for** *progress towards unification because Britain hasn't been invaded since 1066.* [U] • *Traffic jams, bad housing, too much concrete and too little grass are the main anxieties of people who live in urban areas.* [C] • *Peter's leaving at the end of this week – hence his anxiety* **to** *get his work finished.* [+ to infinitive] • *She treats phobias and generalized anxiety* **disorders** *at the clinic.* [before n]

anx·ious /ˈæŋk·ʃəs/ *adj* • *My mother always gets a bit anxious if we don't arrive when we say we will.* • *I saw my sister's anxious face at the window.* • *The drought has made farmers anxious* **about** *the harvest.* • *People are always anxious* **to** (= they want to) *know who is to blame for something awful.* [+ to infinitive] • *Banks, anxious* **to** (= wanting very much to) *reduce lending risks, have tightened up lending criteria.* [+ to infinitive] • *Developing countries which are anxious* **for** (= want very much) *hard currency can rarely afford to protect the environment.* • *I'm* *anxious* **that** *we* (=I want us to) *get there on time because I don't think there'll be many seats left.* [+ *that* clause]

anx·ious·ly /'æŋk·ʃə·sli/ *adv* • *We* **waited** *anxiously by the phone.* • *Tomorrow the government will release its anxiously* **awaited** *statistics on employment in August.*

an·y SOME /'en·i/ *determiner* [usually in negatives and questions], *pronoun* some, or even the smallest amount or number of • *Is there any of that lemon cake left?* • *"Do you have any basil?" "I'm sorry, there isn't any left."* • *I don't think there'll be any snow this Christmas.* • *There was hardly any food left by the time we got there.* • *"Is there some butter I could use?" "No, there's some margarine but there isn't any butter."* • *"Is there any more soup?" "No, I'm afraid there isn't any left."* • *I haven't seen any of his films.* • *I don't expect we'll have any* **more** *trouble from him.* • *I go to church for weddings but not for any* **other** *reason.* • *Are you sure there isn't any way of solving this problem?* • *Very* **few** *people,* **if** *any* (=probably none, in fact), *still believe that the Earth is flat.* • LP **Quantity words**

an·y NOT IMPORTANT WHICH /'en·i/ *determiner, pronoun* one of or each of (something) or a particular amount of (something), but it is not important which • *Absolutely any food would be better than nothing at all.* • *"Which of these cakes may I eat?" "Any."* • *The offer was that you could have any three items of clothing you liked for £30.* • *(infml) On Sundays I just wear any* **old** *thing* (=anything) *that I happen to find lying around.* • *Any of you* (=Each one of you but it is not important which) *should be able to answer this question.* • *Any idiot* (=Every person) *with a basic knowledge of French should be able to book a hotel room in Paris.* • *Any advice* (=Whatever advice) *that you can give me would be greatly appreciated.* • *Any* **minute/day/moment/time now** (=Very soon) *there's going to be a massive quarrel between those two.* • *There were a lot of computers at the exhibition, any (one) of which would have suited me perfectly.* • *You should be able to catch a bus at midnight, but* **in** *any* **case** (=whatever happens) *you can always take a taxi home.* • *I don't want to go out tonight – there's nothing on at the cinema and* **in** *any* **case** (=also and more importantly) *it's far too cold.*

an·y AT ALL /'en·i/ *adv* [usually in negatives and questions; not gradable] at all or in the least • *Can't you run any faster?* • *This television doesn't look any different from the other one you showed me.* • *None of us is getting any younger.* • *Are you feeling any better after your illness?* • *Houses in this area used to be a real bargain, but they're not cheap any* **more** (=now). • *This radio isn't any good* (=it's useless) *– I'll have to buy another.* • *I used to commute to work every day, but not any longer* (=but I've stopped doing that) *– now I have an office at home.* • *(Am infml) I tried talking him out of it, but that didn't help any – he still left home.*

an·y·bod·y /£'en·iˌbɒd·i, $-ˌbʌː·di/ *pronoun* ANYONE

an·y·how ANYWAY /'en·i·haʊ/ *adv* [not gradable] ANYWAY

an·y·how WITHOUT CARE /'en·i·haʊ/, *infml* **any old how** *adv* [not gradable] without care or interest; in an untidy way • *He looked a complete mess – hair sticking up on end and clothes dragged on just anyhow.*

an·y·more /£ˌen·i'mɔːʳ, $-'mɔːr/ *adv* [not gradable] *Am for* any more, see at MORE

an·y·one /'en·i·wʌn/, **an·y·bod·y** *pronoun* any person whatever, or (esp. in questions or negatives) some person • *I was so pleased when you rang – I hadn't spoken to anyone all day.* • *Anyone could dress well with as much money as he's got.* • *Anyone with an ounce of common sense would have checked their tyres before driving all that way.* • *Has anyone seen my glasses anywhere?* • *I've never met anyone so totally lacking in a sense of humour.* • *Was there anyone you knew at the meeting?* • *If anyone could persuade him to come to the party you could.* • *(usually humorous)* **Anyone who** is **anyone** means anyone who is well known or powerful: *In those days anyone who was anyone dined in this exclusive little restaurant.* • LP **Quantity words**

an·y·place /'en·i·pleɪs/ *adv* [not gradable] *Am for* ANYWHERE • *Oh just put it anyplace – it doesn't matter where.*

an·y·road /£'en·i·rəʊd, $-roʊd/ *adv* [not gradable] *Br not standard for* ANYWAY

an·y·thing /'en·i·θɪŋ/ *pronoun* any event, act or object whatever, or (esp. in questions or negatives) something • *If he eats anything with wheat in it he's very sick.* • *Let me know if anything happens won't you.* • *Is there anything I can do to help?* • *I didn't know anything about computers till I started this job.* • *Did you notice anything strange about him?* • *I was looking for a birthday present for my mother but I didn't find anything suitable.* • *Spending Christmas with him and his brother – I can't imagine anything worse!* • *Was there anything else you wanted to say or is that it?* • *Have you got anything less expensive? – I don't really want to spend that much on a bed.* • *She could be anything* (=any age) **between** *30* **and** *40.* • *She could be anything* (=any age) **from** *30* **to** *40.* • *"What did you do at the weekend?" "I don't think we did anything much."* • If you say that someone or something is **anything but** a particular quality, you mean that the person or thing is the opposite of that particular quality: *She's meant to be a very nice person but she was anything but nice the only time I've ever met her.* • *Does it look* **anything like** (=Is it similar to) *an eagle?* • *You don't eat* **anything like** (=You eat much less than) *the amount that you used to.* • *(infml) He's* **as** *fat* **as anything** (=very fat) • *(infml)* If you say that you would not do a particular thing **for anything (in the world)** it means that you certainly would not do it: *It was a fantastic party – I wouldn't have missed it for anything.* • *"Anything goes"* (title of a song written by Cole Porter, 1934) • *"Anything you can do, I can do better"* (from the song *Anything You Can Do* written by Irving Berlin, 1946) • *"Anything can happen in the next half hour"* (from the children's television show *Stingray*, 1965-) • LP **Quantity words**

an·y·time /'en·i·taɪm/ *adv* [not gradable] at a time which is not or does not need to be decided or agreed • *Call round to see me anytime.* • *(Am) We expect/don't expect the economic situation to change anytime* **soon**.

an·y·way /'en·i·weɪ/, **an·y·how**, *Am infml* **an·y·ways** *adv* [not gradable] whatever else is happening; not considering other things • *Of course I don't mind taking you home – I'm going that way anyway.* • *"I thought you said everyone had left." "Well, some of them have anyway."* • Anyway is often used in conversation without adding much meaning to what is being said: *Why don't we get rid of the car since we don't use it anyway?* ○ *What was he doing with so much of the company's money in his personal account anyway?* • In conversation anyway is used to change the subject, return to an earlier subject or get to the most interesting point: *(Well) anyway, if we could focus on the subject we came here to discuss and perhaps think about that problem some other time.* ○ *Anyway, in the end I didn't wear your jacket.*

an·y·where /£'en·i·weəʳ, $-wer/, *Am also* **an·y·place** *adv* [not gradable] in, to or at any place whatever or (esp. in questions or negatives) some place • *I think I've lost that green scarf of mine – I can't find it anywhere.* • *You won't find a prettier village anywhere in England.* • *Did you go anywhere interesting this summer?* • *Go anywhere in the world and you'll find some sort of hamburger restaurant.* • *Is there anywhere in particular you wanted to go to eat tonight?* • *I was wondering if there was anywhere I could go to to get this mended.* • *There are quite a few words that they use in that part of the country that you don't hear anywhere* **else**. • *As a teacher you could expect to be paid anywhere* (=any amount) **between** *£7* **and** *£15* • *(infml)He isn't* **anywhere near as** *popular as* (=He is much less popular than) *he used to be.* • *(infml) Are we* **anywhere near** (=close to) *finishing yet or is there still some way to go?* • *(infml) They live in some tiny little village* **miles from** *anywhere* (=a very long way from any main towns or villages). • If you say you are **not getting/going anywhere**, you mean that you are not improving or advancing a particular situation: *I've been sorting out my study all day but it's such a mess I don't feel I'm getting anywhere.*

AOB /£ˌei·əʊ'biː, $-oʊ'-/ *n* [U] *Br abbreviation for* any other business (=used at the end of the list of subjects to be discussed at a meeting)

A–OK /£ˌeɪ·əʊ'keɪ, $-oʊ'-/ *adv, adj* [not gradable] *Am* completely right or acceptable • *The doctor says I'm A-OK now, that there's absolutely nothing wrong with me.*

a·or·ta /£eɪ'ɔː·tə, $-'ɔːr·t̬ə/ *n* [C] the main ARTERY (=tube for carrying blood from the heart) which takes blood to the other parts of the body

a·pace /ə'peɪs/ *adv literary or old use* quickly • *The project is coming on apace* (=advancing quickly).

a·part SEPARATE /£ə'pɑːt, $-'pɑːrt/ *adv* separated by a distance or, less commonly, by time • *Stand with your feet wide apart and lower the top half of your body to the floor.* • *How far apart do you think I should put my stereo speakers?* • *We were asked to stand in two lines 3 metres apart.* • *The two lines of children moved slowly apart.* • *The garage, large enough for two cars, is set apart* **from** (=not joined to) *the house.* • *What's the age difference between you and your brother – are you two or three years apart?* • People might say that they are apart either when they are living or staying in separate places or when their relationship has ended and they no longer spend time together: *When you're apart you rely so heavily on the phone to keep in touch.* • Apart can also mean into smaller pieces: *These toys aren't well made – they* **come/fall** *apart far too easily.* ○ *My lamp isn't working but I don't want to* **take** *it apart* (= separate it into the pieces that make it up) *in case I can't put it together again.* • (J) (KOR)

a·part EXCEPT /£əˈpɑːt, $-ˈpɑːrt/ *adv* except for or not considering • *He works until nine o'clock every evening, and that's* **quite** *apart* **from** *the work he does over the weekend.* • *Apart* **from** *the salary/Salary apart, it's not a bad job.* • *Apart* **from** *you and me/You and me apart, I don't think there was anyone there under thirty.* • (J) (KOR)

a·part·heid /£əˈpɑː·taɪt, -teɪt, $-ˈpɑːr·t̬aɪt/ *n* [U] (in the past in South Africa) a political system in which people of different races are separated • *the long-awaited dismantling* (= end) *of apartheid*

a·part·ment *esp. Am* /£əˈpɑːt·mənt, $-ˈpɑːrt-/, *Br and Aus usually* **flat** *n* [C] a set of rooms for living in, esp. on one floor of a building • *I'll give you the keys to my apartment.* • *They have six holiday/luxury apartments for sale.* • Apartments is also used to refer to a set of large luxuriously decorated rooms in, for example, a public building or castle: *The Royal Apartments are open to the public.* • An **apartment house** or **apartment building** is *Am for* **block of flats**. See at BLOCK AREA. • PIC Accommodation (CS) (P) (PL) (RUS) (T)

ap·a·thet·ic /£ˌæp·əˈθet·ɪk, $-ˈθet̬-/ *adj* lacking interest or energy; unwilling to take action esp. over a matter of importance • *You're so apathetic* **about** *everything.* • *Don't be so apathetic – how are you going to get a job if you don't even write a letter?*

ap·a·thy /ˈæp·ə·θi/ *n* [U] • *The group fights widespread public apathy* **towards** *earthquake safety measures.* • *Sadly these kids attend schools where apathy exists among both the students and teachers.* • (GR)

ape ANIMAL /eɪp/ *n* [C] a type of monkey which has no tail and uses its arms to swing through trees • *Chimpanzees and gorillas are both apes.* • *(fig. slang) You're on my foot, you big ape* (= awkward, stupid person)*!* [as form of address] • *(Am slang) Your parents'll* **go ape/ape-shit** (= become extremely angry) *when they find out you've taken the car without asking.*

ape *obj* COPY /eɪp/ *v* [T] to copy (something or someone) badly and unsuccessfully • *He called the new building unoriginal and said that it merely aped the classical traditions.*

a·pe·ri·tif /əˌper·ɪˈtiːf/ *n* [C] an alcoholic drink, esp. one which is drunk before a meal • *Would you like an aperitif before dinner?* • *Martini is often drunk as an aperitif.*

ap·er·ture /£ˈæp·ə·tʃəʳ, $-ɚ·tʃɚ/ *n* [C] a small and often narrow opening, esp. one that allows light into a camera

a·pex TOP /ˈeɪ·peks/ *n* [C] *pl* **apexes** or **apices** /ˈeɪ·pɪ·siːz/ *specialized or fml* the highest point or top of something • *the apex of a triangle/house* • *He reached* **the** *apex* **of** *his career during that period.* • *The chairman could be said to be* **at** *the apex of the organization.*

ap·i·cal /ˈeɪ·pɪ·kəl/ *adj* [not gradable] *specialized or fml*

A·PEX TRAVEL /ˈeɪ·peks/ *n* [U], *adj* [before n] *abbreviation for* Advance Purchase Excursion (= a system of cheap travel tickets which must be bought a particular number of days before travelling) • *an APEX* **fare** • *If you make a booking at least fourteen days in advance you can buy an Apex ticket which will be half the standard price.*

a·phas·ia /əˈfeɪ·ʒə/ *n* [U] *medical* a medical condition in which a person is not able to speak or write or understand speech or writing because of damage to the brain

a·phas·ic /əˈfeɪ·zɪk/ *adj* [not gradable] *medical* • *The girl was aphasic because of brain damage suffered during a difficult birth.*

a·phid /ˈeɪ·fɪd/ *n* [C] any of various small insects, such as the GREENFLY, which suck the juices of plants for food

aph·o·ri·sm /£ˈæf·ə·rɪ·zəm, $-ɚ·ɪ-/ *n* [C] a short, cleverly phrased saying which is intended to express a general truth; a MAXIM • *Oscar Wilde was famous for such aphorisms as 'Experience is the name everyone gives to their mistakes'.*

aph·ro·dis·i·ac /£ˌæf·rəˈdɪz·i·æk, $-ˈdiː·ʒæk/ *n* [C] something, usually a drug or food, which is believed to cause sexual desire in people • *Are oysters really an aphrodisiac?* • *They say that power is an aphrodisiac.*

aph·ro·dis·i·ac /£ˌæf·rəˈdɪz·i·æk, $-ˈdiː·ʒæk/ *adj* • *She claims that champagne possesses aphrodisiac properties.*

a·pi·ar·y /£ˈeɪ·pi·ə·ri, $-er·i/ *n* [C] a place where people keep bees, esp. a collection of HIVES (= containers in which bees live) kept to provide HONEY (= the sweet substance made by bees)

ap·i·cal /ˈeɪ·pɪ·kəl/ *adj* [not gradable] See at APEX TOP

ap·i·ces /ˈeɪ·pɪ·siːz/ *pl of* APEX TOP

a·piece /əˈpiːs/ *adv* [after n; not gradable] each • *In good condition, dolls from this period sell for £500 apiece.*

a·plen·ty /£əˈplen·ti, $-t̬i/ *adj* [after n; not gradable] *old use* available in large amounts • *If that's not enough, there are shows, films and amusements aplenty.* • *Skilled workers aplenty are available to cope with earthquake damage.*

a·plomb /£əˈplɒm, $-ˈplɑːm/ *n* [U] confidence and style • *Rosalind conducted the meeting* **with** *characteristic aplomb/* **with** *her usual aplomb/***with all the** *aplomb* **of** *an experienced speaker.*

a·poc·a·lypse /£əˈpɒk·ə·lɪps, $-ˈpɑː·kə-/ *n* [U] a very serious event resulting in great destruction and change • *The book offers a vision of the future in which there is a great nuclear apocalypse.* • *If the factory closes it will make the town an industrial wasteland – to avoid an apocalypse of this kind we must attract new industry.* • **The** Apocalypse is a religious idea of the total destruction of the world: *The* **Four Horsemen of** *the Apocalypse were imaginary people thought to spread war, conquest, rough justice and death in the world.* • *"Apocalypse now"* (film title, 1979)

a·poc·a·lyp·tic /£əˌpɒk·əˈlɪp·tɪk, $-ˌpɑː·kə-/ *adj* • *The poem includes apocalyptic visions of a nuclear confrontation.* • *The group regularly gives apocalyptic warnings about our destruction of the environment.* • *(fig.) The minister's speech was apocalyptic, warning of the consequences of a further rise in inflation.*

a·poc·ryph·al /£əˈpɒk·rɪ·fəl, $-ˈpɑː·krɪ-/ *adj fml* (of a story) probably not true although often told and believed by some people to have happened • *He told one of those apocryphal* **stories** *about meeting a girl at the station who later turned out to have been dead for five years.* • *It's a good story but I dare say it's apocryphal.*

ap·o·gee /ˈæp·ə·dʒiː/ *n* [U] *fml* the most successful, popular or powerful point • *At their apogee, the novels of Spillane claimed worldwide sales of over 180 million.*

a·po·li·tic·al /£ˌeɪ·pəˈlɪt·ɪ·kəl, $-ˈlɪt̬-/ *adj* not interested in or connected with politics, or not connected to any political party • *The organization insists that it is apolitical and does not identify with any one particular party.*

a·pol·o·gist /£əˈpɒl·ə·dʒɪst, $-ˈpɑː·lə-/ *n* [C] *fml* a person who supports a particular belief or political system, esp. an unpopular one, and speaks or writes in defence of it • *communism and its apologists* • *There are few apologists* **for** *the old system.*

a·pol·o·gy *fml* /£əˈpɒl·ə·dʒi, $-ˈpɑː·lə-/, *fml or literary* **ap·o·lo·gia** /£ˌæp·əˈləʊ·dʒi·ə, $-ˈloʊ-/ *n* [C] • An apology is a formal explanation or defence of a belief or system, esp. one that is unpopular. • See also **apology** at APOLOGIZE. • (GR)

a·pol·o·gize, *Br and Aus usually* **-ise** /£əˈpɒl·ə·dʒaɪz, $-ˈpɑː·lə-/ *v* to tell someone that you are sorry for having done something that has caused them inconvenience or unhappiness • *He apologized* **publicly to** *me* **for** *his mistake.* [I] • *Trains may be subject to delay on the northern line – we apologize* **for** *any inconvenience caused.* [I] • *She apologized* **profusely for** *having to leave at 3.30 p.m.* [I] • *He apologized* **that** *the statistics had been inaccurate.* [+ *that* clause] • *(slightly fml) I* **do** *apologize* **if** *my voice is a little low – I've got rather a bad cold.* [I] • (LP) **Phrases and customs**

a·pol·o·get·ic /£əˌpɒl·əˈdʒet·ɪk, $-ˌpɑː·ləˈdʒet̬·ɪk/ *adj* • *She was so apologetic* (= sorry) **about** *forgetting my birthday it was almost embarrassing.* • *I hope he was suitably apologetic* (= sorry) **for** *breaking your glasses.*

a·pol·o·get·ic·ally /£əˌpɒl·əˈdʒet·ɪ·kli, $-ˌpɑː·ləˈdʒet̬-/ *adv* • *She offered us her burnt cakes and smiled apologetically.*

a·pol·o·gy /£əˈpɒl·ə·dʒi, $-ˈpɑː·lə-/ *n* [C] • An apology is an act of saying sorry: *He's demanding a* **full** *apology* **from** *the newspaper for making untrue allegations about his personal life.* ○ *"Was he at all sorry for what he'd done?" "Oh he was* **full of** *apologies* (= extremely sorry)." ○ *She complained to the company about its awful service and they sent her a* **written** *apology.* • *I have an apology to* **make** *to you – I'm afraid I opened your letter by mistake.* ○ *She* **owes** *him an apology for treating him so badly.* • *(infml esp. humorous) You're not coming out because you're tired? – That's* **an apology for a***n* (= an extremely bad) *excuse!* • See also **apology** at APOLOGIST.

a·pol·o·gies /£əˈpɒl·ə·dʒiz, $-ˈpɑː·lə-/ *pl n fml* • *I make no apologies* (= apology) *for what I said.* • If you cannot go to a meeting you send your apologies **(for absence)**: *The vice-chair has sent his apologies – he's abroad at present.*

ap·o·plec·tic /ˌæp·əˈplek·tɪk/ *adj usually humorous* extremely and noticeably angry, or in a state of violent excitement, usually caused by great anger • *He was apoplectic* **with** *rage/fury – I thought he was going to have a heart attack.*

ap·o·ple·xy /ˈæp·ə·plek·si/ *n* [U] • *In a* **fit of** *apoplexy* (= great anger), *he thumped the table with both hands.*

a·pos·ta·sy /£əˈpɒs·tə·si, $-ˈpɑː·stə-/ *n* [U] *fml* the act of giving up your religious or political beliefs and leaving a religion or a political party • *In those days apostasy was punishable by death.*

a·pos·tate /£əˈpɒs·teɪt, $-ˈpɑː·steɪt/ *n* [C] *fml* • An apostate is a person who has given up their religion or left a political party.

a·pos·tle /£əˈpɒs·l̩, $-ˈpɑː·sl̩/ *n* [C] any of the twelve followers of Jesus Christ whom he chose to teach other people about Christianity, or someone who strongly supports a particular belief or political movement • *the Apostle Paul* • *an apostle* **of** *world peace/liberty*

ap·os·tol·ic /£ˌæp·əˈstɒl·ɪk, $-ˈstɑː·lɪk/ *adj*

a·pos·tro·phe /£əˈpɒs·trə·fi, $-ˈpɑː·strə-/ *n* [C] the sign (') used in writing to show that a letter or a number has been omitted, or before or after s to show possession • *I'm* (= I am) • *they're* (= they are) • *'65* (= 1965) • *Helen's laugh* • *Charles' cooking* • *a baby's hand* • *babies' hands* • An apostrophe is also sometimes used before s to show the plural of a number or a letter: *the 1920's* ○ *I always forget there are four s's in possession.* • (LP) **Apostrophe**

a·poth·e·cary /£əˈpɒθ·ə·kri, $-ˈpɑː·θə-/ *n* [C] a person who in the past made and sold medicines

a·poth·e·o·sis /£əˌpɒθ·iˈəʊ·sɪs, $-ˌpɑː·θiˈoʊ-/ *n* [C] *pl* **apotheoses** /£əˌpɒθ·iˈəʊ·siːz, $-ˌpɑː·θiˈoʊ-/ *fml or literary* the best or most extreme example of something • *Her acting career* **achieved** *its apotheosis in that film.* • *Bad taste in clothes* **reached** *its apotheosis in the 1970s.* • *The new house is the apotheosis* **of** *a dream* (= a dream which has become fact) *for him.* • **The** apotheosis **of** someone is the act of making them into a god: *One of the large paintings showed the Apotheosis of the Emperor Trajan.*

ap·pal *obj* **(-ll-)**, *Am usually* **ap·pall** /£əˈpɔːl, $-ˈpɑːl/ *v* [T] to cause (someone) to have strong feelings of shock or of disapproval • *I was appalled* **at/by** *the lack of staff in the hospital.* • *The thought of someone else driving my car appals me.*

ap·pal·ling /£əˈpɔː·lɪŋ, $-ˈpɑː-/ *adj* • *He was upset by that appalling child murder case that was on the news last night.* • *Prisoners were kept in the most appalling conditions.* • Appalling can also be used to mean very bad: *I had an appalling headache.* ○ *The journey home was appalling.*

ap·pal·ling·ly /£əˈpɔː·lɪŋ·li, $-ˈpɑː-/ *adv* • *The number of casualties was appallingly high in both wars.* • *The whole play was appallingly* (= very badly) *acted.*

ap·pa·ra·tus EQUIPMENT /£ˌæp·əˈreɪ·təs, $-ˈræt̬·əs/ *n* a set of equipment or tools or sometimes a machine which is used for a particular purpose • *The new piece of apparatus was used in the experiment.* [C] • *The divers checked their breathing apparatus.* [U] • *I used to hate going on the climbing apparatus in the school gym.* [C] • (PIC) **Emergency services**

ap·pa·ra·tus ORGANIZATION /£ˌæp·əˈreɪ·təs, $-ˈræt̬·əs/ *n* [C] an organization or system, esp. a political one • *The whole apparatus of communism was already falling apart.* • *The book documents the government's apparatus of control and repression.*

ap·par·el /əˈpær·əl/ *n* [U] *fml or literary* clothes, esp. of a special type • *sports apparel* • If something **takes on** the apparel of something else it becomes like it: *The film has taken on the apparel of a musical.* • If you **wrap** something **in the** apparel **of** something else, you are trying to hide it: *They have cleverly wrapped their power in the noble apparel of the law.*

ap·par·ent /£əˈpær·ənt, $-ˈper-/ *adj* able to be seen or understood • *Her unhappiness was apparent* **to** *everyone.* • **It** *was becoming increasingly apparent* **that** *he could no longer look after himself.* [+ *that* clause] • *I was on the metro*

APOSTROPHE [']

An apostrophe is used:

- **to show that letters or numbers are missing**

  in short forms of verbs
  They're (= they are) *waiting outside.*
  We've (= we have) *just arrived.*
  Please don't (= do not) *bother.*
  (LP) **Short forms** at SHORT.

  in shortened words
  Rock 'n' Roll (= Rock and Roll) *music.*
  Grandparents, who needs 'em (= them) *?*
  I like him 'cos (= because) *he's so honest.*

  in dates
  I graduated in '88 (= 1988)

- **to show possession** ((LP) **Possessive form** at POSSESS)

  nouns not ending in s
  the girl's toy • *the children's bedroom*

  plural nouns ending in s
  a girls' school • *the Smiths' house*

  singular nouns ending in s
  Mr Jones's car or *Mr Jones' car*

  compound nouns
  my sister-in-law's baby

  indefinite pronouns
  someone's watch • *anybody's answer*

- **sometimes to form plurals or verb forms from letters or abbreviations**

  Her u's and n's look the same to me.
  I got two B's in my exams.
  He was KO'd (= knocked out) *in the third round.*

this morning when **for no** *apparent* **reason** *the man opposite suddenly screamed.* ● Apparent also means appearing or being understood in one way when the real situation is different: *There are one or two apparent discrepancies between the two reports.* ○ *She has this apparent innocence which, I suspect, she uses to her advantage.* ○ *They claimed the apparent deterioration in the economy was just a temporary change.*

ap·par·ent·ly /£ə'pær·ᵊnt·li, $-'per-/ *adv* ● Apparently means 'it appears', esp. when you are not certain of the truth of the information you are going to give, or want to distance yourself from it: *Well, apparently she's had enough of this country and she's heading off to Africa.* ○ *Apparently, we have to change all the labels on the books during the next week.* ○ *An eighty-year-old woman was badly hurt in what the police describe as an apparently motiveless attack* (= it appeared to have no purpose, such as stealing). ● People also use apparently to mean 'in fact' when the real situation is different from what they thought it was: *You know I told you Alice's party was on the 13th, well I saw her last night and apparently it's on the 14th.* ○ *She looks about 12 but apparently she's 14.* ○ *I thought they were married but apparently not* (= they are not married).

ap·pa·ri·tion /ˌæp·ə'rɪʃ·ᵊn/ *n* [C] the spirit of a dead person appearing in a form which can be seen ● *He claimed to have seen strange apparitions at night.*

ap·peal ATTRACT /ə'piːl/ *v* [I not *be appealing*] to interest or attract someone ● *I've never been skiing – it doesn't really appeal* (**to** *me*). ● *It's a programme designed to appeal mainly* **to** *16 to 25 year olds.* ● *I think what appeals* **to** *me about his painting is the colours he uses.* ● *I like boxing – it appeals* **to** *the savage in me.*

ap·peal /ə'piːl/ *n* [U] ● *Men worry about going bald because they think they will* **lose** *their* **sex** *appeal.* ● *Spielberg films have a* **wide** *appeal.* ● *Parties on river-boats have* **lost** *their appeal since one sank and several people died.*

ap·peal·ing /ə'piː·lɪŋ/ *adj* ● *The idea of not having to get up early every morning is rather appealing* (**to** *me*). ● Someone's expression might be described as appealing if it makes you want to help or protect them: *a little dog with appealing big brown eyes.*

ap·peal ARGUE /ə'piːl/ *v* [I] to formally request that esp. a legal or official decision is changed ● *The parents appealed* **against** *the school's decision not to admit the child.* ● *The footballer appealed* **to** *the referee* **for** *a free kick.* ● *(law)* To appeal is also to request a higher law court to consider again a decision made by a lower court, esp. in order to reduce or prevent a punishment: *The teenager has been* **given/granted leave** (= allowed) *by the High Court to appeal* **against** *her two-year sentence.* ○ *They're appealing* **to** *the High Court to reduce the sentence to a fine.*

ap·peal /ə'piːl/ *n* ● *The case went to the* **court of** *appeal/ the appeal court.* [U] ● *He won his appeal and the sentence was halved.* [C] ● *She has* **lodged** (= made) *an appeal* **against** *the severity of the fine.* [C] ● *The umpire has* **rejected** *the player's appeal against the linesman's decision.* [C]

ap·peal REQUEST /ə'piːl/ *v* to make a serious or formal request, esp. to the public, for money or help ● *They're appealing* **for** *clothes and blankets to send off to the earthquake victims.* [I] ● *The police are appealing* **to** *the public* **for** *any information about the missing girl.* [I] ● *The boss tried to appeal* **to** (= ask for support based on) *his employees' sense of loyalty by asking them to stay with the company in these difficult times.* [I] ● *Her students appealed* **to** *her* **for** *advice on completing the application forms.* [I] ● *Church leaders have appealed* **to** *the government* **to** *halt the war.* [+ *to* infinitive]

ap·peal /ə'piːl/ *n* ● *They're* **launching** (= starting) *an appeal to raise money for famine victims.* [C] ● *I could hear the note of appeal in her voice as she asked me to come and talk things over.* [U] ● *The police have issued an appeal* **to** *the public* **to** *stay away from the centre of town at the weekend.* [C + *to* infinitive]

ap·pear BE PRESENT /£ə'pɪəʳ, $-'pɪr/ *v* [I] to become noticeable or to be present ● *I was standing in my kitchen last night when this face suddenly appeared at the window.* ● *We'd been living in the house a month when dark stains started appearing on the wall.* ● *His name appears in the film credits for lighting.* ● *If she hasn't appeared* (= arrived) *by ten o'clock I'm going without her.* ● *The film, currently in the States, will be appearing on our screens* (= we will be able to see it) *later this year.* ● *I've noticed that smaller cars are starting to appear* (= be produced or sold) *again.* ● When the person being tried in a court case, the person accusing them and the lawyers for each appear in court they are there officially for the case to be heard. ○ *Both women will be appearing* **before** *magistrates later this week.* ○ *We have to appear* **in** *court next week.* ● If a lawyer appears **for** someone, he or she acts for the person: *Ms Hawley was appearing for the defence.*

ap·pear·ance /£ə'pɪə·rᵊnts, $-'pɪr·ᵊnts/ *n* [C] ● *It was his first appearance on television/television appearance* **as** *president.* ● *She was making a* **public** *appearance signing copies of her latest novel.* ● *This was the defendant's third* **court** *appearance for the same offence.* ● An appearance is an act of being present: *I didn't really want to go to the party but I thought I'd better* **put in an** *appearance* (= be present for a short time).

ap·pear SEEM /£ə'pɪəʳ, $-'pɪr/ *v* [not *be appearing*] to seem ● *You've got to appear* (**to be**) *calm in an interview even if you're terrified underneath.* [L (+ *to be*)] ● *I think to people who don't know him he probably appears* (**to be**) *rather unfriendly.* [L (+ *to be*)] ● *Things aren't always* **what** *they appear* (**to be**). [L (+ *to be*)] ● *She appears* **to** *be the girl's sister.* [+ *to* infinitive] ● *She appears* **to** *actually like the man, which I find incredible.* [+ *to* infinitive] ● *They appear* **to** *be keeping the details of the case a secret for the time being.* [+ *to* infinitive] ● **It** *appears* (**that**) *she was with someone when she left but nobody at the party knew who it was.* [+ (*that*) clause] ● **It** *appears* **to me** (*that*) (= I think that) *we need to make some changes.* [+ (*that*) clause] ● *(fml)* **It would** *appear* (**that**) (= It seems that) *nobody on board the aircraft actually had a licence to fly it.* [+ (*that*) clause] ● **There** *appears* **to** *be some mistake.* [+ *to* infinitive] ● **It** *appears* **as if/as though** *I was wrong.* [I always + adv/prep] ● *Everything was not* **as** *it appeared – secret deals had been done.* [I always + adv/prep] ● *I know* **how** *it must appear, but it's not really as bad as it looks.* [I always + adv/prep] ● *"Has he left?" "It appears* **not**/**so.**" [+ *not/so*] ● *"I think we're late." "***So** *it appears."* [after *so*] ● LP **It, There**

ap·pear·ance /£ə'pɪə·rᵊnts, $-'pɪr·ᵊnts/ *n* [U] ● The appearance of a person or a thing is the way that they look to other people: *a middle-aged man* **of** *smart appearance* ○ *You can* **alter/change** *the whole appearance* **of** *a room just by lighting it in a certain way.* ○ *There was nothing unusual about/in her physical appearance.* ● *Grey squirrels are rather rat-like* **in** *appearance* (= they look like rats). ● *The large car outside the house gave an immediate appearance* **of** *wealth* (= suggested wealthy people lived there).

ap·pear·ances /£ə'pɪə·rənt·sɪz, $-'pɪr·ᵊnt-/ *pl n* ● Appearances are what things look like rather than what they are made of, how they work, etc.: *You're so worried about appearances!* ● **To all appearances**/*(Am also)* **From all appearances** (= Judging from what can be seen) *I would say their marriage is fine but I think she gives him a bad time in private.* ● To **keep up appearances** is to continue living as if everything is the same as before so that people do not know you have personal problems, esp. money problems. ● *(saying)* 'Appearances can be deceptive' means things might not be what they seem: *What does it matter what someone wears or how long their hair is? – Appearances can be deceptive.* ● *(saying)* 'Appearances matter' means what you look like is important: *Put a smart suit on for your interview – appearances matter!*

ap·pear PERFORM /£ə'pɪəʳ, $-'pɪr/ *v* [I always + adv/prep] to perform publicly in a play, film, dance, etc. ● *Dave Gilmore is currently appearing* **as** *Widow Twanky in the Arts Theatre's production of "Puss in Boots".* ● *She appears briefly in the new Bond film.*

ap·pear·ance /£ə'pɪə·rənts, $-'pɪr·ᵊnts/ *n* [C] ● *He made his first* **stage/TV** *appearance at the age of six.*

ap·pease *obj* /ə'piːz/ *v* [T] *fml disapproving* (in arguments or war) to prevent further disagreement by giving to (the other side) an advantage that they have demanded ● *She claimed that the government had only changed the law in order to appease their critics.*

ap·pease·ment /ə'piːz·mənt/ *n* [U] ● *Appeasement of dictators, said the president, led to wide scale bloodshed.*

ap·pel·la·tion /ˌæp·ə'leɪ·ʃᵊn/ *n* [C] *fml* a name or title ● *Mussolini was known by the more familiar appellation 'Il Duce'.*

ap·pend *obj* /ə'pend/ *v* [T] *fml* to add (esp. something written to the end of the main piece of writing) ● *The author appends a short footnote* **to** *the text explaining the point.*

ap·pend·age /ə'pen·dɪdʒ/ *n* [C] *fml* something which exists as a smaller and less important part of something larger • *The committee is a* **mere** *appendage* **of** *the council and has no power of its own.* • *The organism has small leaf-like appendages.* • *(humorous) the* **male** *appendage* (= the penis) • *He hates being made to* **feel like** *an appendage* (= to feel unimportant).

ap·pen·dix [BODY PART] /ə'pen·dɪks/ *n* [C] *pl* **appendixes** /ə'pen·dɪk·sɪz/ a small tube-shaped part which is joined to the INTESTINES on the right side of the body and has no use in humans • *She* **had** *her appendix* **out** (= medically removed) *last summer.*

ap·pen·dec·to·my /ˌæp·en'dek·tə·mi, -ən-/ *n* [C] *specialized* • An appendectomy is a medical operation to remove the appendix.

ap·pen·di·ci·tis /£əˌpen·dɪ'saɪ·tɪs, $-t̬ɪs/ *n* [U] • Appendicitis is an illness in which the appendix is infected and painful and usually needs to be removed by an operation.

ap·pen·dix [BOOK PART] /ə'pen·dɪks/ *n* [C] *pl* **appendices** /ə'pen·dɪ·siːz/ or **appendixes** /ə'pen·dɪk·sɪz/ a separate part at the end of a book or magazine which gives additional information • *There's an appendix at the end of the book with a list of dates.*

ap·per·tain to *obj* /£ˌæp·ə'teɪn, $-ɚ'-/ *v prep* [T no passive] *fml* to be connected to or belong to, esp. in an official way • *She enjoyed the privileges appertaining to the office of chairman.*

ap·pe·tite /'æp·ɪ·taɪt/ *n* [C] a desire or need for something, esp. food • *She hasn't* **got much of** *an appetite* (= she does not eat much). • *All that walking has* **given** *me an appetite.* • *The children have* **got healthy/good** *appetites* (= they eat a lot). • *Fame and wealth has done nothing to* **curb** (= reduce) *her appetite* **for** *success.* • *He had a notorious sexual appetite.*

ap·pe·tiz·ing, *Br and Aus usually* **-is·ing** /'æp·ɪ·taɪ·zɪŋ/ *adj* • If something is or **looks** appetizing you think you will enjoy it: *Those cakes look a lot more appetizing than the healthier alternatives.* ○ *(fig.) I don't find the thought of spending six weeks at home a particularly appetizing* **prospect**.

ap·pe·tiz·er /£'æp·ɪ·taɪ·zəʳ, $-zɚ/, *Br and Aus usually* **-iser** *n* [C] a small amount of food eaten before a meal • *At 6:30, everyone gathered for drinks and appetizers in the lounge.* • *She passed round a large plate of appetizers and I took a cheese biscuit and a few nuts.* • *(esp. Am)* An appetizer is also the first part of a meal: *The average cost of a full three-course meal – appetizer, main course and dessert – including tip and a modest wine is about $25.*

ap·plaud *(obj)* [CLAP] /£ə'plɔːd, $-'plɑːd/ *v* to show enjoyment and/or approval of (esp. a performance, speech, etc.) by clapping the hands repeatedly to make a noise • *You should have heard the audience applaud – the noise was fantastic.* [I] • *She was applauded for a full five minutes after her speech.* [T]

ap·plause /£ə'plɔːz, $-'plɑːz/ *n* [U] • *His speech* **met with** (= received) *loud applause.* • *So let's have a* **round of** *applause, please,* **for** (= please applaud) *a very lovely and talented young lady who is going to sing for us.*

ap·plaud *obj* [PRAISE] /£ə'plɔːd, $-'plɑːd/ *v* [T] *fml* to say that you admire and agree with (a person's action or decision) • *We applaud the family's decision to remain silent over the issue.*

ap·ple /'æp·l̩/ *n* a round fruit with a firm white inside and a green, red or yellow skin, or the tree on which it grows • *I think I'll peel this apple – the skin is a bit tough.* [C] • *apple* **pie/sauce** • *an apple* **tree** • *Has the fruit salad got any apple in it?* [U] • *(dated) Their house is always in* **apple pie order** (= perfectly arranged and tidy). • *(dated)* If someone refers to a person as **the apple of** their **eye** it means that they like or love them and are proud of them: *His daughter was the apple of his eye.* • *(saying)* 'An apple a day keeps the doctor away' means that eating an apple each day will keep you healthy.

ap·ple·jack /'æp·l̩.dʒæk/ *n* [U] *esp. Am* a type of BRANDY (= a strong alcoholic drink) made from apples

ap·pli·ance /ə'plaɪ·ənts/ *n* [C] a device, machine or piece of equipment, esp. an electrical one that is used in the house such as a cooker, fire, washing machine, etc. • *electric/domestic/home/household appliances* • *The shop sells a large range of* **surgical** *appliances* (= pieces of medical equipment which are worn to correct a particular condition). • [LP] **Shopping goods, Switching on and off**

ap·pli·ca·ble /ə'plɪk·ə·bl̩/ *adj* See at APPLY [RELATE TO]

ap·pli·qué /'æp·lɪ·keɪ/ *n* [U] decorative work in which one piece of cloth is sewn or fixed onto another, or the activity of decorating cloth in this way

ap·pli·qué *obj* /'æp·lɪ·keɪ/ *v* [T usually passive] • *The animal shapes were appliquéd* **onto** *the cot quilt.* • *The dress was appliquéd* **with** *bold geometric designs.*

ap·ply [REQUEST] /ə'plaɪ/ *v* to request something, usually officially, esp. by writing or sending in a form • *By the time I saw the job advertised it was already too late to apply.* [I] • *Please apply in writing* **to** *the address below.* [I] • *We've applied* **to** *a charitable organization* **for** *a grant for the project.* [I] • *Tim's applied* **to** *join the police.* [+ *to* infinitive]

ap·pli·ca·tion /ˌæp·lɪ'keɪ·ʃən/ *n* • *a* **letter of** *application* [U] • *Free information will be sent out* **on** *application* **to** (= if you ask) *the central office.* [U] • *I've sent off applications* **for** *four different jobs.* [C] • *Have you filled in the application* **form** *for your passport yet?* • *South Africa has submitted an application* **to** *host the World Cup.* [C + *to* infinitive]

ap·pli·cant /'æp·lɪ·kənt/ *n* [C] • An applicant is a person who formally requests something, esp. a job or a place at college or university: *How many applicants did you have* **for** *the job?*

ap·ply [RELATE TO] /ə'plaɪ/ *v* [I] (esp. of rules or laws) to have a connection or be important • *That bit of the form is for UK citizens – it doesn't apply* **to** *you.* • *Those were old regulations – they don't apply any more.*

ap·pli·ca·ble /ə'plɪk·ə·bl̩/ *adj* • *This part of the law is only applicable* **to** *companies employing more than five people.* • *The new qualifications are applicable* **to** *all European countries.*

ap·pli·ca·tion /ˌæp·lɪ'keɪ·ʃən/ *n* [U] • *The new laws have (a) particular application* **to** *the self-employed.*

ap·ply *obj* [PUT ON] /ə'plaɪ/ *v* [T] to spread or rub (cream, paint, etc.) on a surface • *Apply the suntan cream liberally (to exposed areas) every three hours and after swimming.* • *The paint should be applied thinly and evenly.*

ap·pli·ca·tion /ˌæp·lɪ'keɪ·ʃən/ *n* • *Leave the paint to dry between applications.* [C] • *Regular application of the cream should reduce swelling within 24 hours.* [U]

ap·pli·ca·tor /£'æp·lɪ·keɪ·təʳ, $-t̬ɚ/ *n* [C] • An applicator is a device used to put something on or into a particular place: *Please use the sponge applicator provided.*

ap·ply *obj* [USE] /ə'plaɪ/ *v* [T] to make use of (something) or use it for a practical purpose • *He wants a job in which he can apply his foreign languages.* • *The court heard how the driver had failed to apply his brakes in time.* • *If you apply pressure to a cut it's meant to stop the bleeding.* • If you apply your**self** or your **mind to** something, you work hard at it, directing your abilities and efforts in a determined way so that you succeed: *You can solve any problem if you apply yourself.*

ap·plied /ə'plaɪd/ *adj* [before n] • An applied subject of study, esp. a science, is one which has a practical use: **pure and** *applied mathematics/science* ○ *The new statistics course is much more applied – certainly not as theoretical as the one I did.*

ap·pli·ca·tion /ˌæp·lɪ'keɪ·ʃən/ *n* • *The design has many applications* (= particular uses). [C] • Application is also the determination to work hard over a period of time in order to succeed at something: *Peter clearly has ability in this subject but lacks application.* [U] • An application is a computer program that is designed for a particular purpose: *In my business I use word processing and spreadsheet applications.* [C]

ap·point *obj* /ə'pɔɪnt/ *v* [T] to choose (someone) officially for a job or responsibility • *We've appointed three new teachers this year.* • *He's just been appointed* **(as)** *director of the publishing division.* • *A commission has just been appointed* **to** *investigate fraud claims.* [+ obj + *to* infinitive]

ap·point·ed /£ə'pɔɪn·tɪd, $-t̬ɪd/ *adj* [not gradable] • *I'd like to introduce our newly appointed members of staff.* • See also APPOINTED; SELF-APPOINTED.

ap·point·ee /əˌpɔɪn'tiː/ *n* [C] • An appointee is someone who has been chosen officially for a job or responsibility: *a government appointee* ○ *The new appointee will be working closely with both departments.*

ap·point·ment /ə'pɔɪnt·mənt/ *n* • *He was very pleased with his appointment* **as** *senior lecturer.* [U] • *We would like to announce* **the** *appointment* **of** *Julia Lewis* **as** *head of sales.* [U] • *Our department expects to* **make** *five new appointments* (= appoint five new people) *this year alone.* [C] • *Carter's Ltd, confectioners* **by** *appointment* **to** (= officially chosen by) *the Queen* [U] • See also APPOINTMENT.

ap·point·ed /£ə'pɔɪn·tɪd, $-t̬ɪd/ *adj fml* (of buildings or rooms) having furniture and equipment of a stated standard • *It says in the ad that the bathroom is spacious and well-appointed.* • *The room was poorly appointed and badly decorated.* • See also **appointed** at APPOINT; WELL-APPOINTED.

ap·point·ment /ə'pɔɪnt·mənt/ *n* a formal arrangement to meet or visit someone at a particular time and place • *I'd like to* **make** *an appointment* **with** *Doctor Evans this morning, please.* [C] • *She had to* **cancel** *her* **dental** *appointment.* [C] • *I've got an appointment* **to** *see Ms Edwards at two o'clock/a two o'clock appointment* **with** *Ms Edwards.* [C + *to* infinitive] • *If he didn't have a secretary to remind him, he wouldn't* **keep** (= remember to be present at) *any of his appointments.* [C] • *That's the second appointment he's* **missed** (= not been present at). [C] • *House for sale, two bedrooms. Viewing* **by** *appointment only.* [U] • See also **appointment** at APPOINT.

ap·point *obj* /ə'pɔɪnt/ *v* [T] • *(fml) A date has been appointed for the election.* • The appointed **time** is the time at which it has been agreed something will happen: *Ten minutes before the appointed time, he sat nervously outside her office.*

ap·por·tion *obj* /£ə'pɔː·ʃən, $-'pɔːr-/ *v* [T] *fml* to give or share out (esp. blame or money) among several people or things • *When we know how much is profit, then we can apportion the money* **(among/between** *us).* • *The investigation into the air crash would inevitably apportion* **blame** *(***to** *certain members of the crew).*

ap·po·site /'æp·ə·zɪt, -zaɪt/ *adj fml* suitable and right for the occasion • *an apposite comparison/phrase/quotation/remark/title* • *The film starts in a graveyard, an apposite image for the decaying society which is the theme of the film.*

appraise *obj* /ə'preɪz/ *v* [T] to examine (someone or something) in order to judge their qualities, success or needs • *At the end of each teaching practice, trainee teachers are asked to appraise their own* **performance**. • *All lecturers in this department are appraised at the end of each lecture course by the students who fill in a questionnaire.* • *Each of these approaches may be valuable in teaching the physician to appraise clinical evidence more systematically.* • *In co-operation with other professionals, social workers will appraise the individual's needs.* • *He coolly appraised the situation, deciding which person would be most likely to succeed.*

ap·prais·al /ə'preɪ·zəl/ *n* • *The newspaper gave an editorial appraisal* **of** *the government's achievements of the past year.* [C] • *We undertake regular job appraisals/job appraisal reviews.* [C] • *The article simply records the political changes of the last year – it doesn't give much actual appraisal.* [U]

ap·prais·ee /ə·preɪ'ziː/ *n* [C] • An appraisee is a person who is being appraised.

ap·prais·er /£ə'preɪ·zər, $-zɚ/ *n* [C] • An appraiser is a person who appraises someone or something: *You will discuss how well you have achieved your targets with your appraiser at the end of the year.* ○ *You should have this piece of furniture checked over by an* **antiques** *appraiser.* ○ *(esp. Am) He works as a* **real-estate** *appraiser.*

ap·pre·ci·a·ble /ə'priː·ʃə·bl/ *adj* (esp. of amounts or changes) large or noticeable enough to have an important effect • *There has been an appreciable drop in the number of unemployed since the new government came to power.*

ap·pre·ci·a·bly /ə'priː·ʃə·bli/ *adv* • *Her health has improved appreciably ever since she changed her treatment.*

ap·pre·ci·ate *(obj)* VALUE /ə'priː·ʃi·eɪt/ *v* to recognize or understand that (something) is valuable, important or as described • *He really appreciates fine furniture.* [T] • *We appreciate the need for immediate action.* [T] • *I appreciate* **that** *it's a difficult decision for you to make.* [+ *that* clause] • *I don't think you appreciate* **how** *much time I spent preparing this meal for you.* [+ *wh-* word] • You can use appreciate when you are thanking someone or showing that you are grateful: *We really appreciate all the help you gave us last weekend.* [T] ○ *I appreciate your making the effort to come.* [+ v-*ing*] • If you say you **would** appreciate something, you mean you would like it to happen: *I'd appreciate* **it** *if you could let me know* (= Please let me know) *in advance whether or not you will be coming.* [T] • Ⓕ Ⓟ

ap·pre·ci·a·tion /ə,priː·ʃi'eɪ·ʃən/ *n* [U] • *Max has no appreciation* **of** *the finer things in life.* • *The crowd cheered* **in** *appreciation when the fielder caught the ball.* • *Children rarely show any appreciation* **of/for** *what their parents do for them.* • *These flowers are a token of my appreciation* **of/for** *all your help.*

ap·pre·ci·at·ive /£ə'priː·ʃə·tɪv, $-t̬ɪv/ *adj* • *It's nice to have an appreciative audience.* • *I'm very appreciative* **of** *all the support you've given me.*

ap·pre·ci·at·ive·ly /£ə'priː·ʃə·tɪv·li, $-t̬ɪv-/ *adv* • *She smiled appreciatively at him.*

ap·pre·ci·ate INCREASE /ə'priː·ʃi·eɪt/ *v* [I] to increase (in value) • *The value of our house has appreciated* (= increased) **by** *50% in the last two years.* • *Our house has appreciated* **(in value) by** *50% in the last two years.* • Compare DEPRECIATE. • Ⓕ Ⓟ

ap·pre·ci·a·tion /ə,priː·ʃi'eɪ·ʃən/ *n* [U] • *There has been little appreciation* (= increase) **in** *the value of our house recently.*

ap·pre·hend *obj* CATCH /,æp·rɪ'hend/ *v* [T] *fml* to catch and take into police control (someone who has not obeyed the law); to ARREST • *The police have finally apprehended the killer.*

ap·pre·hen·sion /,æp·rɪ'hen·ʃən/ *n* [U] • *The apprehension of the drug dealers means that the streets of New York will be a little safer now.*

ap·pre·hend *(obj)* UNDERSTAND /,æp·rɪ'hend/ *v fml* to understand completely • *Are you sure you entirely apprehend the importance of completing these forms as accurately as possible?* [T] • *I completely fail to apprehend* **why** *you're behaving like this.* [+ *wh-* word]

ap·pre·hen·sion /,æp·rɪ'hen·ʃən/ *n* [U] *fml* • *Carl has no apprehension* (= understanding) **of** *what the world's really like.*

ap·pre·hen·sion /,æp·rɪ'hen·ʃən/ *n* [U] anxiety about the future; fear that something unpleasant is going to happen • *There is some apprehension in the office* **about** *who the new director will be.* • *Margot voiced the general apprehension when she asked "What will the changes mean for us?".* • *Diane waited* **with (a feeling of)** *apprehension for her examination results.* • *I arrived at the hospital* **in a state of** *apprehension about what the doctor would say.*

ap·pre·hen·sive /,æp·rɪ'hent·sɪv/ *adj* • *I'm very apprehensive* (= anxious) **about** *tomorrow's meeting.* • *She was apprehensive* **about/for** *her son's safety every time he went out on his motorcycle.* • *I've invited a lot of people to the party, but I'm a bit apprehensive* **that** *no one will come.* [+ *that* clause] • *He always has such an apprehensive expression on his face.*

ap·pre·hen·sive·ly /,æp·rɪ'hent·sɪv·li/ *adv* • *They looked at each other apprehensively.*

ap·pren·tice /£ə'pren·tɪs, $-t̬ɪs/ *n* [C] (esp. in the past) someone who has agreed to work for a skilled person for a particular period of time and often for low payment, in order to learn that person's skills • *Most of the work was done by apprentices.* • *My brother has just become an apprentice carpenter.*

ap·pren·tice *obj* /£ə'pren·tɪs, $-t̬ɪs/ *v* [T] • *The boy's parents apprenticed him* **to** *a blacksmith.* • *Michelangelo was apprenticed* **to** *Ghirlandaio in Florence for three years.*

ap·pren·tice·ship /£ə'pren·tɪs·ʃɪp, $-t̬ɪs-/ *n* • *a five-year apprenticeship* (= job as an apprentice) [C] • *He had two more years of apprenticeship* (= period of time working as an apprentice) *left.* [U]

ap·prise *obj* /ə'praɪz/ *v* [T] *fml* to tell; to inform • *The President has been apprised* **of** *the situation.*

ap·proach *(obj)* COME NEAR /£ə'prəʊtʃ, $-'proʊtʃ/ *v* to come near or nearer to (something or someone) in space, time, quality or amount • *We could just see the train approaching in the distance.* [I] • *If you look out of the window on the left of the bus, you'll see that we're now approaching the Tower of London.* [T] • *I see it's approaching lunchtime, so let's take a break now.* [T] • *In my opinion, no other composers even begin to approach* (= come near in quality to) *Mozart.* [T] • *The total amount raised so far is approaching* (= almost) *$1000.* [T] • *My grandfather is very active for a man approaching 80* (= who is almost 80 years old). [T] • If you approach someone you speak, write or visit them in order to make a request, business agreement, etc.: *We've just approached the bank* (= asked them for the first time) **for/about** *a loan.* [T] ○ *My boss isn't a very easy person to approach* (= it is difficult to talk to him or her). [T] ○ *I'm going to approach my uncle* **to** *see if he will give me a job.* [T]

ap·proach /£ə'prəʊtʃ, $-'proʊtʃ/ *n* • *The siren signalled the approach* **of** *an ambulance* (= that it was getting nearer). [U] • *Some shops have doors which open by themselves* **at** *the approach of a customer.* [U] • *Many kinds of birds fly south* at *the approach of winter* (= as winter gets nearer). [U] • *Please fasten your seat belts, the plane is now making its final approach* **(in)to** (= is coming near to and preparing to land at) *Heathrow.* [C] • *We got stuck in a traffic jam on the approach* **road**. • An approach is also an act of communicating with another person or group: *The hospital is* **making** *approaches* **to** *local businesses* (= asking them to help) *in their bid to raise money.* [C] ○ *I hear that Everton have* **made** *an approach* **to** (= an attempt to make a business arrangement with) *Arsenal to buy one of their players.* [C] ○ *She rejected the family's approaches* (= attempts to communicate with her). [C] • **The closest approach to** means the nearest (thing) to: *That was the closest approach to an apology that you'll ever get!* ○ *This is the closest approach* **to** *warm that* (= This is as warm as) *this house ever gets!* [C]

ap·proach·a·ble /£ə'prəʊ·tʃə·bl̩, $-'proʊ-/ *adj* • *The castle tower is approachable* (= It is possible to reach it) *only by going up some very steep steps.* • An approachable person is someone who is friendly and very easy to talk to: *Graham's always very approachable – why don't you talk the problem over with him?*

ap·proach *obj* DEAL WITH /£ə'prəʊtʃ, $-'proʊtʃ/ *v* [T] to deal with (something) • *We need to find the best way of approaching this problem.* • *I must tell him that I can't go to his graduation ceremony, but I don't quite know how to approach the subject.*

ap·proach /£ə'prəʊtʃ, $-'proʊtʃ/ *n* [C] • *Since our research so far has not produced any answers to this problem, we need to* **adopt** *a different approach* **to** *it.* • *I've just read an interesting book which has a new approach* **to** (= a new way of considering) *Shakespeare.* • *Michael is always very logical* **in** *his approach* (= the way he deals with things).

ap·pro·ba·tion /ˌæp·rəʊ'beɪ·ʃᵊn/ *n* [U] *fml* approval or agreement, often given by an official group; praise • *He had worked long and hard on the project and, when his efforts succeeded, the committee never gave him so much as a word of approbation.* • *The council has finally indicated its approbation of the plans.* • CS

ap·pro·pri·ate SUITABLE /£ə'prəʊ·pri·ət, $-'proʊ-/ *adj* suitable or right for a particular situation or occasion • *I didn't think his comments were very appropriate at the time.* • *I've been invited to her wedding but I haven't got anything appropriate to wear.* • *Her thin shoes weren't appropriate* **for** *such muddy paths.* • *Her remarks were considerate and very appropriate* **to** *the situation.* • *This isn't an appropriate occasion* **to** *discuss finance.* [+ *to* infinitive] • **It** *wouldn't be appropriate* **for** *me* **to** *comment.* [+ *to* infinitive] • *Please complete the appropriate parts of this form* (= the parts that are right or necessary for your particular situation) *and return it as soon as possible.*

ap·pro·pri·ate·ly /£ə'prəʊ·pri·ət·li, $-'proʊ-/ *adv* • *Those children aren't appropriately dressed for this cold weather.*

ap·pro·pri·ate·ness /£ə'prəʊ·pri·ət·nəs, $-'proʊ-/ *n* [U] • *He misjudged the appropriateness of the occasion for announcing that he was leaving.*

ap·pro·pri·ate *obj* TAKE /£ə'prəʊ·pri·eɪt, $-'proʊ-/ *v* [T] *fml* to take (something) for your own use, usually without permission, or to keep (a sum of money) to use for a particular purpose • *He lost his job when he was found to have appropriated some of the company's money.* • *My daughter is always appropriating my clothes!* • *There has been a lot of opposition to the government's plans to appropriate millions of pounds* (= keep them to use for) *for a new submarine.*

ap·pro·pri·a·tion /£əˌprəʊ·pri'eɪ·ʃᵊn, $-ˌproʊ-/ *n* • *His appropriation* **of** *company money lost him his job.* [U] • *(specialized)* An appropriation is a sum of money to be used for a particular purpose: *The committee approved an appropriation of £10 000.* [C]

ap·pro·pri·a·tions /£əˌprəʊ·pri'eɪ·ʃᵊnz, $-ˌproʊ-/ *pl n specialized* • *The foundation was promised a 7% increase to bring its appropriations* (= appropriation) *to $2·07 billion.*

ap·prove GOOD OPINION /ə'pruːv/ *v* [I] to have a positive opinion (of) • *She wanted to be a fashion model, but her parents didn't approve.* • *My mother doesn't approve* **of** *my brother's friends.* • *I don't approve* **of** *smoking in public places.* • *I thoroughly approve* **of** *what the government is doing.*

ap·prov·al /ə'pruː·vᵊl/ *n* [U] • *He showed his approval by smiling broadly.* • *Alan is someone who always needs the approval of other people/other people's approval.* • *She looked at her son* **with approval**. • *The council's plans have* **met with the** *approval* **of** *local residents.* • *Sam always tried hard to* **win** *his father's approval.*

ap·prov·ing /ə'pruː·vɪŋ/ *adj* • *She gave him an approving smile.*

ap·prov·ing·ly /ə'pruː·vɪŋ·li/ *adv* • *She smiled at him approvingly.*

ap·prove *obj* PERMIT /ə'pruːv/ *v* [T] to accept, permit or officially agree to (something) • *We had to wait months for the council to approve our plans to extend our house.* • *The court approved the sale of the property.* • *The minutes of the last meeting were approved.* • *Please will you approve my expenses.*

ap·prov·al /ə'pruː·vᵊl/ *n* [U] • *The teacher gave the student a* **nod of** *approval.* • *We'll buy the new computer system as soon as we have the approval* **of** *the directors.* • *I've bought these chairs* **on approval** (= I can return them without payment if they are not satisfactory).

ap·proved /ə'pruːvd/ *adj* • *What's the approved way* (= the way which is generally accepted as correct) *of dealing with this?* • *This school only offers approved language courses* (= those which have been accepted by an official organization). • *(Br dated)* **Approved school** is an old expression for **Young Offenders' Institution** (= type of prison for young people).

ap·prox /£ə'prɒks, $-'prɑːks/ *adv abbreviation for* APPROXIMATELY

ap·prox·i·mate /£ə'prɒk·sɪ·mət, $-'prɑːk/ *adj* almost, but not completely, correct or exact • *The train's approximate time of arrival is 10.30.* • *The approximate cost will be about $600.* • *Can you give me an approximate idea of what happened?*

APPROXIMATE NUMBERS

- **The most common ways of giving an approximate number are as follows:**

It costs **approximately** *$500.*
She weighs **about** *60 kilos.*
There are **around** *thirty flights a day.*
Some *65 scientists attended the conference.*
*(infml) She's got twenty-***odd** *cats.*
(written) Salary **c** *£12 000*
It's **roughly** *2 metres across.*
I'll be visiting ten **or so** *countries on my trip.*
A good *(= At least) 5 000 demonstrators turned up.*

Units like 'hundred' or 'thousand' can be put in the plural in order to give an approximate number: *hundreds of hours* • *dozens of friends* • *Sales have reached the millions.*

- **The following expressions are used with particular quantites:**

Temperatures will be **in the 30s** tomorrow.
She's sixtyish but she only looks **in her forties**.

- **The following ways of giving an approximate number are used for small numbers (usually more than two but less than ten):**

I have **a few** *questions.*
Several *paintings were stolen.*
They have won only **a handful of** *games.*

The expression 'a number of' can also be used when referring to small numbers greater than this: *Police have received* **a number of** *complaints.*

ap·prox·i·mate /£ə'prɒk·sɪ·meɪt, $-'prɑːk-/ *v fml* • *Student numbers this year are expected to approximate 5000* (= to be about 5000). [L only + n] • *The newspaper reports of the discussion only* **roughly** *approximated* **to** (= were not exactly the same as) *what was actually said.* [I always + adv/prep]

ap·prox·i·mate·ly /£ə'prɒk·sɪ·mət·li, $-'prɑːk-/ *adv* • *The job will take approximately three weeks, and cost approximately £1000.*

ap·prox·i·ma·tion /£əˌprɒk·sɪ'meɪ·ʃᵊn, $-ˌprɑːk-/ *n* [C] *fml* • *Could you give me a* **rough** *approximation* **of** *how* *many people will be coming* (= an amount that is close to the correct number but is not exact). • *What he said bore no approximation whatsoever* **to** *the truth* (= was not at all like the truth).

ap·pur·ten·ance /£əˈpɜː·tɪ·nənts, $-ˈpɜːr·t̬ɪ-/ *n* [C usually pl] *fml or humorous* a possession or piece of property; an additional feature • *Books and CDs are among the appurtenances* **of** *student life.*

APR /£ˌeɪ·piˈɑːr, $-ˈɑːr/ *n abbreviation for* Annual Percentage Rate (= the rate at which a borrower of money is charged, calculated over a period of twelve months) • *I'm paying an APR of 21% on the loan that I took out to buy a car.* [C] • *The interest rate on my credit card is currently 25.5% APR.* [U]

a·près–ski /ˌæp·reɪˈskiː/ *n* [U] social activities which take place in the evening at hotels and restaurants in places where people go to SKI • *I think I enjoy the après-ski more than the actual skiing!* • *The resort has a good range of après-ski entertainment.*

a·pri·cot FRUIT /£ˈeɪ·prɪ·kɒt, $-kɑːt/ *n* [C] a small round pale orange soft fruit with a furry skin • PIC› **Fruit**

a·pri·cot COLOUR /£ˈeɪ·prɪ·kɒt, $-kɑːt/ *n* [U] pale orange • *an apricot sweater*

A·pril /ˈeɪ·prəl/ (*abbreviation* **Apr**) *n* the fourth month of the year, after March and before May • *20(th) April/April 20(th)* [U] • *The meeting is* **on** *the fourth of April/April the fourth/ (esp. Am) April fourth* [U] • *I did an English course in Cambridge* **last** *April/I'm doing an English course in Cambridge next April.* [U] • *I met him* **in/during** *April.* [U] • *This has been one of the driest Aprils for many years.* [C] • An **April fool** is a trick played on someone, or the person who is tricked, on April 1st, which is **April Fools' Day**. • *"Oh, to be in England, / Now that April's there"* (Robert Browning in the poem *Home-Thoughts from Abroad*, 1845) • LP› **Dates, Holidays**

a pri·o·ri /£ˌeɪ·praɪˈɔː·raɪ, £-priːˈɔː·ri, $-ˈɔːr·aɪ/ *adj, adv fml* (of an argument) suggesting the probable effects of a known cause, or using general principles to suggest likely effects • *"It's freezing outside, you must be cold" is an example of a priori reasoning.*

a·pron CLOTHING /ˈeɪ·prən/ *n* [C] a piece of clothing which is worn over the front of other clothes to keep them clean while you are doing something dirty, esp. cooking or cleaning in the house • *Many people like to wear aprons while they are cooking or doing the washing up.* • **Apron strings** are the strips of material used to tie an apron round the body, or *(disapproving)* is a phrase used in referring to the way one person or group depends on another: *(disapproving) Free from the apron strings of home and family, she changed completely.* ○ *(disapproving) The subsidiary company has been reluctant to tug at, let alone cut, the apron strings.*

a·pron AIRPORT /ˈeɪ·prən/ *n* [C] the part of an airport in which aircraft are turned around, loaded, etc. • *There were three jumbos* **on** *the concrete apron.* • *Both passenger lounges have a good view of the runway and apron area.*

a·pron THEATRE /ˈeɪ·prən/, **a·pron stage** *n* [C] part of a stage in a theatre that is in front of the curtain and beside the area in which people who are watching the performance sit

ap·ro·pos RELATED, **a pro·pos** /£ˌæp·rəˈpəʊ, $-ˈpoʊ/ *adv* [not gradable], *prep fml* used to introduce something which is related to or connected with something that has just been said • *I had a long letter from my sister yesterday – apropos* **(of)** *which, have you heard from yours recently?* • *Apropos what you said yesterday, I think you were right.*

ap·ro·pos SUITABLE /£ˌæp·rəˈpəʊ, $-ˈpoʊ/ *adj fml* suitable in a particular situation or at a particular time • *I thought his remarks about her father were hardly apropos.*

apse /æps/ *n* [C] *specialized* the rounded or many-sided end of esp. the east end of a church

apt SUITABLE /æpt/ *adj* **-er, -est** suitable or right for a particular situation • *Chris produced an apt* **comment** *which summed up how we all felt.*

apt·ly /ˈæpt·li/ *adv* • *Decades earlier his Chicago team had aptly called him 'Joe Batters', a reference to his use of a baseball bat.*

apt·ness /ˈæpt·nəs/ *n* [U] *fml* • *The reviewer admired the aptness of the author's imagery.*

apt ABILITY /æpt/ *adj* having a natural ability or skill; clever • *We have some particularly apt students in the class this year.*

ap·ti·tude /£ˈæp·tɪ·tjuːd, $-tuːd/ *n* • Aptitude is natural ability or skill: *My son has no/little aptitude* **for** *sport.* [U] ○ *My daughter is* **showing** *an aptitude* **for/at** *maths.* [C] ○ *We will take your personal aptitudes and abilities into account.* [C] ○ *I had to take an* **aptitude test** (= a test to find out whether I had the natural ability to be suitable for that particular type of work) *before I began training as a nurse.*

apt·ness /ˈæpt·nəs/ *n* [U] *fml dated* • *an aptness* **for/at** *drawing*

apt LIKELY /æpt/ *adj* [after v; + *to* infinitive] likely • *The kitchen roof is apt to leak when it rains.*

A·qua Lung /ˈæk·wə·lʌŋ/ *n* [C] *trademark* a container of air which someone carries on their back while swimming under the water, which has a tube taking air to their mouth or nose to allow them to breathe • *Jacques Cousteau was the inventor of the Aqua-Lung.* • PIC› **Water sports**

aq·ua·ma·rine STONE /ˌæk·wə·məˈriːn/ *n* [U] a bluish green stone used in jewellery • *a ring set with aquamarines and pearls* [C] • *a brooch made of aquamarine* [U]

aq·ua·ma·rine COLOUR /ˌæk·wə·məˈriːn/ *n* [U] bluish green • *Rio de Janeiro is probably the most spectacular city on earth, with emerald mountains and an aquamarine sea.*

aq·ua·plane *Br* /ˈæk·wə·pleɪn/, *Am* **hy·dro·plane**, *Aus* **plane** *v* [I] (of a motor vehicle) to slide out of control on a wet road without touching the road's surface

a·qua·ri·um /£əˈkweə·ri·əm, $-ˈkwer·i-/ *n* [C] *pl* **aquariums** or **aquaria** /£əˈkweə·ri·ə, $-ˈkwer·i-/ a glass container in which fish and other water animals can be kept, or a building, usually open to the public, which holds many of these containers

A·qua·ri·us /£əˈkweə·ri·əs, $-ˈkwer·i-/ *n* [not after *the*] the eleventh sign of the ZODIAC, relating to the period 21 January to 19 February, represented by a person carrying water, or a person born during this period • *He was born* **under** *Aquarius* (= during this period). [U] • *I'm an Aquarius.* [C]

A·qua·ri·an /£əˈkweə·ri·ən, $-ˈkwer·i-/ *n* [C] • *She's an Aquarian* (= she was born during this period), *but she doesn't have a typical Aquarian personality.*

a·quat·ic /£əˈkwæt·ɪk, $-ˈkwæt̬-/ *adj* [not gradable] living or growing in, happening in, or connected with water • *Water lilies are aquatic plants.* • *I don't enjoy aquatic sports.*

a·quat·ic·ally /£əˈkwæt·ɪ·kli, $-ˈkwæt̬-/ *adv* [not gradable]

aq·ua·tint /ˈæk·wə·tɪnt/ *n* [C] a picture produced by cutting it into a COPPER sheet with acid and then printing it • *an aquatint by Picasso*

aq·ue·duct /ˈæk·wɪ·dʌkt/ *n* [C] a structure for carrying water across land, esp. one that looks like a high bridge with many arches, which carries pipes or a CANAL (= an artificial channel for river boats) across a valley

a·que·ous /ˈeɪ·kwi·əs/ *adj fml or specialized* of or like water; containing water; produced by water • *an aqueous solution*

aq·ui·line /ˈæk·wɪ·laɪn/ *adj esp. literary* of or like an EAGLE (= a large bird with a hooked beak which eats small animals) • *an aquiline nose* (= a nose curved like an EAGLE'S beak) • *aquiline features* (= a face with this type of nose)

Ar·ab /£ˈær·əb, $ˈer-/ *n* [C] a person from the Middle East or N Africa who speaks Arabic as a first language

Ar·ab /£ˈær·əb, $ˈer-/ *adj* [not gradable] • *The Arab countries include Iraq, Saudi Arabia, Syria and Egypt.*

A·ra·bi·an /əˈreɪ·bi·ən/ *adj* [not gradable] • *The Arabian peninsula is the area between the Red Sea and the Gulf, mostly occupied by Saudi Arabia.*

Ar·a·bic /£ˈær·ə·bɪk, $ˈer-/ *n* [U] • Arabic is the language of the people of the Middle East and N Africa: *There are many regional types of Arabic.*

Ar·a·bic /£ˈær·ə·bɪk, $ˈer-/ *adj* [not gradable] • *Arabic books are often beautifully illustrated.* • **Arabic numerals** are the signs (such as 1, 2, 3) used for writing numbers in many parts of the world. Compare **Roman numerals** at ROMAN CITY.

ar·a·besque POSITION /£ˌær·əˈbesk, $ˌer-/ *n* [C] a position in BALLET dancing in which the dancer stands on one leg with the other leg held out straight behind

ar·a·besque ART /£ˌær·əˈbesk, $ˌer-/ *n* a type of decoration, based on curving leaves, branches etc., found esp. in Islamic art

ar·a·ble /£ˈær·ə·bl̩, $ˈer-/ *adj* [U] (of farming and farm land) used for, or suitable for, growing crops • *arable farming/farmers/farms/land* • *a large arable area*

a·rach·nid /əˈræk·nɪd/ *n* [C] any of a group of small animals, similar to insects but with four pairs of legs, which include SPIDERS, SCORPIONS, TICKS and MITES

a·rach·no·pho·bi·a /£ə'ræk·nəˌfəʊ·bi·ə, $-ˌfoʊ-/ *n* [U] *specialized* a very deep fear of SPIDERS (=insect-like creature with eight legs)

ar·bi·ter /£'ɑː·bɪ·tər, $'ɑːr·bɪ·t̬ɚ/ *n* [C] someone who makes a judgment or solves an argument or decides what will be done • *Magazines are often the arbiters* **of** *taste.* • *He took on himself the role of moral arbiter of the nation.* • *The government will be the* **final** *arbiter in the dispute over the new road.* • An arbiter is also an **arbitrator**. See at ARBITRATE. • Ⓟⓛ

ar·bi·trage /£ˌɑː·bɪ'trɑːʒ, $'ɑːr·bɪ·trɑːʒ/ *n* [U] the method on the **stock market** of buying something in one place and selling it in another place at the same time, in order to make a profit from the difference in price in the two places

ar·bi·trag·eur /£ˌɑː·bɪ·trɑː'ʒɜːr, $'ɑːr·bɪ·trɑː·ʒɚ/ *n* [C] • An arbitrageur is a person who makes money from arbitrage.

ar·bi·trar·y /£'ɑː·bɪ·trə·ri, $'ɑːr·bə·trer-/ *adj* based on chance rather than being planned or based on reason, or *(disapproving)* based on personal power without considering people's wishes • *She made an arbitrary choice of the black shoes instead of the brown ones.* • *Our decision to go to Italy this summer rather than Spain was quite arbitrary.* • *(disapproving) an arbitrary ruler* (=ruling by uncontrolled personal power, not because others wish him or her to do so.) • *(disapproving) The company has been the subject of an arbitrary take-over* (=control has been taken of it without considering its wishes).

ar·bi·trar·i·ly /£ˌɑː·bɪ'treə·rɪ·li, $ˌɑːr·bɪ'trer·ɪ-/ *adv* • *We made the decision to go to Italy quite arbitrarily.* • *(disapproving) He gives his support to projects quite arbitrarily and never consults anyone else.*

ar·bi·trar·i·ness /£'ɑː·bɪ·trə·rɪ·nəs, $'ɑːr·bɪ·trer·ɪ-/ *n* [U] *disapproving* • *The arbitrariness of his action/choice/decision infuriated me.*

ar·bi·trate *(obj)* /£'ɑː·bɪ·treɪt, $'ɑːr-/ *v* to make a judgment in (an argument), usually because asked to do so by those involved • *The children were arguing about whose turn it was to ride on the bicycle, so their mother had to arbitrate.* [I] • *I've been asked to arbitrate* **between** *the opposing sides.* [I] • *An outside adviser has been brought in to arbitrate the dispute between the management and the union.* [T]

ar·bi·tra·tion /£ˌɑː·bɪ'treɪ·ʃən, $ˌɑːr-/ *n* [U] • *Both sides in the dispute have agreed to* **go to** *arbitration* (=to have the disagreement solved by an outside person who has been chosen by both sides).

ar·bi·trat·or /£'ɑː·bɪ·treɪ·tər, $'ɑːr·bɪ·treɪ·t̬ɚ/ *n* [C] • An arbitrator is a person whose official role is to make a decision between two people or groups who do not agree: *Both parties to the dispute agreed to* **appoint** *an* **expert/independent** *arbitrator.* • *In cases of divorce, the court often acts as the arbitrator in deciding which parent the children will live with.*

ar·bor·e·al /£ɑː'bɔː·ri·əl, $ɑːr'bɔːr·i-/ *adj specialized* of or living in trees • *Monkeys are arboreal animals.*

ar·bour *Br and Aus, Am and Aus* **ar·bor** /£'ɑː·bər, $'ɑːr·bɚ/ *n* [C] a sheltered place in a garden formed by trees and bushes which are grown to partly enclose it • *a rose arbour* • *"I will hide me in the arbour"* (Shakespeare, Much Ado About Nothing 2.3)

arc CURVE /£ɑːk, $ɑːrk/ *n* [C] (the shape of) part of a circle, or other curved line • *The crowd watched as the ball rose* **in** *a high arc and fell behind the boundary line.* • *They dug out the soil in an arc stretching about 4 metres from the wall.* • *The agricultural land spreading out in a 100-mile arc from the city is extremely fertile.*

arc /£ɑːk, $ɑːrk/ *v* [I] **arcs, arcing**, *past* **arced** • *The rocket arced gracefully* (=moved in the shape of an arc) *into the sky.*

arc ELECTRICAL FLOW /£ɑːk, $ɑːrk/ *n* [C] a powerful flow of electricity which goes across a space between two points • An **arc lamp** or **arc light** is a device which gives light produced by an electric arc. • **Arc welding** is the joining together of pieces of metal using an electric arc.

arc /£ɑːk, $ɑːrk/ *v* [I always + adv/prep] **arcs, arcing**, *past* **arced** • To arc is to make an electric arc: *A spark arced* **across** *when he attached the wire to the battery.*

ar·cade /£ɑː'keɪd, $ɑːr-/ *n* [C] a covered area or passage in which there are shops, or a covered passage joined to a building on one side and with columns and arches along the other side • *a shopping arcade*

Ar·ca·di·a /£ɑː'keɪ·di·ə, $ɑːr-/ *n* [U] *esp. literary* (a representation of) life in the countryside believed to be perfect

Ar·ca·di·an /£ɑː'keɪ·di·ən, $ɑːr-/ *adj*

ar·cane /£ɑː'keɪn, $ɑːr-/ *adj fml* known only by a few people; mysterious; secret • *The law profession has a long tradition of defending its more arcane* **procedures/rituals**. • *He was the only person who understood all the arcane* **details** *of the agreement.* • *This argument may* **seem** *arcane to those not closely involved in the world of finance.*

arch CURVED STRUCTURE /£ɑːtʃ, $ɑːrtʃ/ *n* [C] (something which has the shape of) a structure consisting of a curved top on two supports, which holds the weight of something above it, or is for decoration • *In many churches the side aisles are separated from the central aisle by a row of arches.* • *Where it crosses the valley, the railway line is supported by arches.* • *Passing through the arch, you enter an open courtyard.* • *Marble Arch is at the corner of Hyde Park in London.* • The arch of your foot is the raised curve on the bottom of it: *My father suffers from* **fallen arches**. • See also ARCHWAY. • Ⓒⓢ

arch *(obj)* /£ɑːtʃ, $ɑːrtʃ/ *v* • *At this point on the river, the trees arch* (=make the shape of an arch) *right* **over** *it.* [I] • *Her eyebrows arched in contempt.* [I] • *Cats often arch their* **backs** *when they're angry.* [T]

arched /£ɑːtʃt, $ɑːrtʃt/ *adj* • *The entrance to the cathedral is through an arched door* (=a door with a curved structure surrounding it).

arch NOT SERIOUS /£ɑːtʃ, $ɑːrtʃ/ *adj* **-er, -est** (of a person) amusing or not serious in a way that suggests you are behaving this way intentionally for the effect that it will have • *an arch smile/expression/tone* • *She was rather arch in her behaviour.* • Ⓒⓢ

arch·ly /£ɑːtʃ·li, $ɑːrtʃ-/ *adv* • *She smiled archly at him.* • *"I fail to understand what you are suggesting," said Clare archly.*

arch– MAIN /£ɑːtʃ-, $ɑːrtʃ-/ *combining form* most important; CHIEF • *an archbishop/archduke*

arch– EXTREME /£ɑːtʃ-, $ɑːrtʃ-/ *combining form* greater or esp. worse than others of the same type; extreme • *an arch-criminal/arch-enemy/arch-villain* • *He's always been an arch-opponent of the scheme.*

ar·chae·ol·o·gy, *esp. Am* **ar·che·ol·o·gy** /£ˌɑː·ki'ɒl·ə·dʒi, $ˌɑːr·ki'ɑː·lə-/ *n* [U] the study of the buildings, containers and other, usually buried, objects which belonged to people who lived in the past • *She teaches archaeology at the university.*

ar·chae·o·log·i·cal, *esp. Am* **ar·che·o·log·i·cal** /£ˌɑː·ki·ə'lɒdʒ·ɪ·kəl, $ˌɑːr·ki·ə'lɑː·dʒɪ-/ *adj* • *an archaeological dig/excavation* • *an area/site of archaeological interest*

ar·chae·o·log·i·cal·ly, *esp. Am* **ar·che·o·log·i·cal·ly** /£ˌɑː·ki·ə'lɒdʒ·ɪ·kli, $ˌɑːr·ki·ə'lɑː·dʒɪ-/ *adv* • *Crete is an archaeologically interesting island.*

ar·chae·ol·o·gist, *esp. Am* **ar·che·ol·o·gist** /£ˌɑː·ki'ɒl·ə·dʒɪst, $ˌɑːr·ki'ɑː·lə-/ *n* • An archaeologist is someone who studies the buildings, tools, etc. of people who lived in the past.

ar·cha·ic /£ɑː'keɪ·ɪk, $ɑːr-/ *adj* of or belonging to the distant past; from an ancient period in history • *The meaning of some archaic forms of writing is not always well understood today.* • *(infml humorous) My mum's clothes are absolutely archaic* (=very old-fashioned)*!*

ar·cha·ic·al·ly /£ɑː'keɪ·ɪ·kli, $ɑːr-/ *adv*

ar·cha·i·sm /£ɑː'keɪ·ɪ·zəm, $ɑːr-/ *n* [C] • An archaism is a word or expression that is not generally used any more.

arch·an·gel /£ɑː'keɪn·dʒəl, $ɑːr-, 'ˌ--/ *n* [C] an ANGEL (=a heavenly being) of the highest rank • *In the New Testament, the birth of Christ is announced to Mary by the Archangel Gabriel.*

arch·bi·shop /£ˌɑːtʃ'bɪʃ·əp, $ˌɑːrtʃ-, 'ˌ--/ *n* [C] a BISHOP (=an important priest) of the highest rank, esp. in particular groups of the Christian Church, in charge of churches and other bishops in a particular large area • *The Archbishop* **of Canterbury** *holds the highest position in the Church of England.*

arch·bish·op·ric /£ˌɑːtʃ'bɪʃ·ə·prɪk, $ˌɑːrtʃ-/ *n* [C] • An archbishopric is the period of time during which a person serves as an archbishop. • An archbishopric is also the area of which an archbishop is in charge.

arch·deacon /£ˌɑːtʃ'diː·kən, $ˌɑːrtʃ-, 'ˌ--/ *n* [C] (in the Anglican Church) a priest next in rank below a BISHOP

arch·di·o·cese /£ˌɑːtʃ'daɪə·sɪs, $ˌɑːrtʃ-/ *n* [C] the area of which an ARCHBISHOP in some Christian churches is in charge

arch·duke *male, female* **arch·duch·ess** /£ˌɑːtʃ'djuːk, $ˌɑːrtʃ'duːk, -'dʌtʃ·ɪs/ *n* [C] a person of the highest rank, esp. in the past in the Austrian royal family • *The assassination of (the) Archduke Ferdinand started off the first World War.*

arch·en·e·my /£ˌɑːtʃ'en·ɪ·mi, $ˌɑːrtʃ-/ *n* [C] an especially bad enemy • *George and Harry are archenemies.* • *(old use or literary)* **The Archenemy** *is the devil.*

ar·che·ol·o·gy /£ˌɑː·ki'ɒl·ə·dʒi, $ˌɑːr·ki'ɑː·lə-/ *n* [U] *esp. Am for* ARCHAEOLOGY

arch·er /£'ɑː·tʃəʳ, $'ɑːr·tʃɚ/ *n* [C] a person who shoots arrows from a BOW (=curved piece of wood with a tight string between each end) for sport or (in the past) as a weapon

arch·er·y /£'ɑː·tʃə·ri, $'ɑːr·tʃɚ·i/ *n* [U] • Archery is the art or sport of shooting arrows.

ar·che·type /£'ɑː·kɪ·taɪp, $'ɑːr-/ *n* [C] a typical example of something; the original model of something from which others are copied • *The United States is* **the** *archetype* **of** *a federal society.* • According to Jung, archetypes are common mental pictures which all people have from birth, and which appear frequently in art and literature. • *"The House of Commons, the archetype of all the representative assemblies which now meet"* (Thomas Macaulay in *History of England*, 1849)

ar·che·typ·al /£ˌɑː·kɪ'taɪ·pᵊl, $ˌɑːr-, '----/, **ar·che·typ·i·cal** *adj* • *an archetypal English gentleman*

ar·che·typ·i·cal·ly /£ˌɑː·kɪ'tɪp·ɪ·kli, $ˌɑːr-/ *adv*

ar·chi·pel·a·go /£ˌɑː·kɪ'pel·ə·gəʊ, $ˌɑːr·kɪ'pel·ə·goʊ/ *n* [C] *pl* **archipelagos** or **archipelagoes** a group of small islands or an area of sea in which there are many small islands • *the Hawaiian archipelago*

ar·chi·tect /£'ɑː·kɪ·tekt, $'ɑːr-/ *n* [C] a (qualified) person who designs new buildings and who makes certain that they are built correctly • *Bramante was the architect* **of** *St Peter's Cathedral in Rome.* • *Who are the architects* **for** *the new school?* • *(fig.) Bevan was the architect of* (= the person who planned) *the British National Health Service.*

ar·chi·tecture /£'ɑː·kɪ·tek·tʃəʳ, $'ɑːr·kɪ·tek·tʃɚ/ *n* [U] • *Jill is studying architecture* (= the art and science of designing and making buildings). • *We went to an interesting talk on Roman architecture* (= the style in which buildings were made by the Romans).

ar·chi·tec·tur·al /£ˌɑː·kɪ'tek·tʃᵊr·ᵊl, $ˌɑːr·kɪ'tek·tʃɚ-/ *adj* • *architectural drawings/plans* • *a building of architectural interest*

ar·chi·tec·tur·al·ly /£ˌɑː·kɪ'tek·tʃᵊr·ᵊl·i, $ˌɑːr·kɪ'tek·tʃɚ-/ *adv* • *Oak Park is architecturally interesting because it has several houses designed by the famous architect Frank Lloyd Wright.*

ar·chive /£'ɑː·kaɪv, $'ɑːr-/ *n* [C] (a place for keeping) the historical records of a place, organization, family, etc. • *I've been studying village records in the local archive.* • *His book is based entirely on archive material.*

ar·chiv·al /£ɑː'kaɪ·vᵊl, $ɑːr-/ *adj* [not gradable] • *I've been doing some archival research on my family history.*

ar·chives /£'ɑː·kaɪvz, $'ɑːr-/ *pl n* • *These old photographs should go into the family archives* (= archive).

ar·chiv·ist /£'ɑː·kɪ·vɪst, $'ɑːr-/ *n* [C] • An archivist is a person whose job is to take care of archives.

arch·ly /£ɑːtʃ·li, $ɑːrtʃ-/ *adv* See at ARCH NOT SERIOUS

arch·way /£'ɑːtʃ·weɪ, $'ɑːrtʃ-/ *n* [C] an entrance or passage formed by an arch

Arc·tic /£'ɑːk·tɪk, $'ɑːrk-/ *n* [U] **the Arctic** the most northern part of the world, which is very cold • *Polar bears live in the Arctic.* • **The Arctic Circle** is an imaginary line drawn round the world at approximately 70 degrees North.

Arc·tic /£'ɑːk·tɪk, $'ɑːrk-/ *adj* • *No trees grow in the Arctic regions* (= those of the most northern part of the world). • Arctic also means extremely cold: *The weather's really arctic today.*

ar·dent /£'ɑː·dᵊnt, $'ɑːr-/ *adj* showing strong feelings; eager • *He's an ardent supporter of the local football team.* • *I've never met such an ardent pacifist as Terry.* • *Paul is a very ardent lover.*

ar·dent·ly /£'ɑː·dᵊnt·li, $'ɑːr-/ *adv* • *She listened ardently to his every word.*

ar·dour *Br and Aus, Am and Aus* **ar·dor** /£'ɑː·dəʳ, $'ɑːr·dɚ/ *n* [U] a strong positive and enthusiastic feeling • *They showed great ardour* **for** *the cause of helping deprived children.* • *His ardour* **(for** *her)* *cooled after only a few weeks.*

ar·du·ous /£'ɑː·dju·əs, $'ɑːr·dʒu-/ *adj* difficult, tiring and needing a lot of effort • *an arduous climb/task/journey*

ar·du·ous·ly /£'ɑː·dju·ə·sli, $'ɑːr·dʒu-/ *adv*

ar·du·ous·ness /£'ɑː·dju·ə·snəs, $'ɑːr·dʒu-/ *n* [U]

are /£ɑːʳ, $ɑːr/ *we/you/they form of* BE • *Are you hungry?* • *They are very late.*

a·re·a PLACE /£'eə·ri·ə, $'er·i·/ *n* [C] a particular part of a place, piece of land, country, etc. • *All areas* (= all parts of the country) *will have some rain tonight.* • *The area* **of** *New York to the south of Houston Street is known as Soho.* • *Houses* **in the** *London* **area** (= in and around London) *are very expensive.* • *I'm an area manager* (= I am responsible for business in a particular part of the country or world) *for a computer company.* • *This is a very poor area* (= part of the town, country or world). • *We'll have to keep the birds off the area* (= part of the ground) *where we've planted the seeds.* • *Dogs are not allowed in the children's play area.* • *Please do not leave any litter in the picnic area.* • An area is also (part of) a subject or activity: *I'm particularly interested in the area* **of** *Greek art.* ○ *He asked me for my views on a recent book on Italian opera, but that's not really my area* (= a subject of which I have special knowledge). ○ *I'd like to work in the area* **of** *local government* (= I would like to do a job connected with local government). ○ *Starting school has opened up a lot of new areas for Sophie* (= has given her new experiences). • *The repairs to my car are going to cost* **in the area of** (= about) *£200.* • **Area code** is *Am and Aus for* **dialling code**. See at DIAL TELEPHONE. • LP› **Measurements, Units**

a·re·a MEASURE /£'eə·ri·ə, $'er·i·ə/ *n* the measure of a flat space • *The area* **of** *a rectangle is obtained by multiplying its length by its width.* [C] • *Meadow Farm is 50 square kilometres* **in area**. [U]

a·re·na /ə'riː·nə/ *n* [C] a large flat enclosed area used for sports or entertainment • *a circus/dance/sports arena* • *(fig.) We were surprised to see a new candidate* **enter** *the arena* (= become involved in an activity, esp. one involving argument and fighting) *just before the election.* • *(fig.) After 30 years in the political arena* (= of being involved in political activity) *our local member of parliament is retiring next year.*

aren't /£ɑːnt, $ɑːrnt/ *short form of* are not *or* (in questions) am not • *They aren't at work today.* • *We aren't going to the party.* • *I'm late again, aren't I?*

ar·gon /£'ɑː·gɒn, $'ɑːr·gɑːn/ *n* [U] a gas which is found in the air and is sometimes used to make electric lights

ar·got /£'ɑː·gəʊ, $'ɑːr·goʊ/ *n* words and expressions which are used by small groups of people and which are not easily understood by other people • *thieves' argot* [U] • *They spoke in a strange argot of their own, which no one else could understand.* [C]

ar·gue DISAGREE /£'ɑːg·juː, $'ɑːrg-/ *v* [I] to show disagreement, esp. strong disagreement, in talking or discussing • *The children are always arguing.* • *I wish you wouldn't argue* **with** *me all the time.* • *Liz and Brian spent a long time arguing* **over/about** *which film to go and see.* • *(infml) You can* **argue the toss** (= disagree) *all you like, but the decision has been made.*

ar·gu·a·ble /£'ɑːg·ju·ə·bḷ, $'ɑːrg-/ *adj* • *The book makes some arguable points* (= points about which there could be some disagreement). • *It is arguable which way is quicker.*

ar·gu·ment /£'ɑːg·jʊ·mənt, $'ɑːrg-/ *n* [C] • *The children* **had** *an argument* **about/over** *what game to play.* • **He got into an** *argument* **with** *Jeff in the pub last night.*

ar·gu·ment·a·tive /£ˌɑːg·jʊ'men·tə·tɪv, $ˌɑːrg·jʊ'men·ṭə·ṭɪv/ *adj disapproving* • *Don't be so argumentative.*

ar·gu·ment·a·tive·ly /£ˌɑːg·jʊ'men·tə·tɪv·li, $ˌɑːrg·jʊ'men·ṭə·ṭɪv-/ *adv*

ar·gue *(obj)* REASON /£'ɑːg·juː, $'ɑːrg-/ *v* to give the reasons for your opinion, idea, belief, etc. • *Henry is such a good lawyer because he argues so clearly* (= gives reasons for and against something in a clear way). [I] • *The minister argued* **for/in favour of/against** *making cuts in military spending.* [I] • *The minister argued* **that** *cuts in military spending were needed.* [+ *that* clause] • *You can argue the* **case** *either way.* [T] • *There was a* **well-argued** *article in the paper yesterday about the proposed changes in the health service.* • *Alan's parents are trying to argue him* **out of** *joining the army.* [I] • *The cost of this proposal argues* (= shows that we should decide) **for/against** *it.* [I] • *The cost of this proposal argues* (= shows) **that** *we should reject it.* [+ *that* clause] • See also WELL-ARGUED.

ar·gu·a·ble /£'ɑːg·ju·ə·bḷ, $'ɑːrg-/ *adj* • *Scientists have produced an arguable theory* (= one that can be supported with reasons) *about the cause of the disease.* • *It is arguable* **that** *Shakespeare was England's greatest playwright.*

ar·gu·a·bly /£'ɑːg·ju·ə·bli, $'ɑːrg-/ *adv* • *He is arguably one of the world's finest football players.* • *Arguably, the drug should not have been made available before it had been thoroughly tested.*

ar·gu·ment /£'ɑːg·ju·mənt, $'ɑːrg-/ *n* • *Now that we've heard all the arguments* (= reasons given) **for** *and* **against** *the proposal, shall we vote on it?* [C] • *Her husband was not convinced by her argument* **that** *they needed a bigger house.* [C + *that* clause] • *I don't think that's a very* **strong/convincing/powerful** *argument.* [C] • *They were engaged in argument for hours.* [U] • *The central argument* (= main point) **of** *the book is that some of the plays supposedly written by Shakespeare were actually written by someone else.* [C] • Ⓒⓢ Ⓔ Ⓟ ⓅⓁ ⓇⓊⓈ

ar·gy-barg·y /£,ɑː·dʒi'bɑː·dʒi, $,ɑːr·dʒi'bɑːr-/ *n* [U] *Br infml* loud argument or disagreement which is not usually very serious • *Did you hear all that argy-bargy last night?* • *There has been a lot of academic argy-bargy over the paper's findings.*

a·ri·a /£'ɑː·ri·ə, $'ɑːr·i-/ *n* [C] a song sung by one person in an opera

-a·ri·an /£-'eə·ri·ən, $-'er·i-/ *combining form* (a person who has) a connection with or belief in the stated subject • *a librarian* (= person who works in a LIBRARY) • *a vegetarian* (= a person who does not eat meat) • *humanitarian aid* (= help for injured, ill or hungry people)

ar·id /£'ær·ɪd, $'er-/ *adj* (of land or weather) having little rain; very dry • *The desert is so arid that nothing can grow there.* • *(fig.) I found his book extremely arid* (= uninteresting or dull). • *(fig.) After several arid years* (= years in which little was achieved), *the company has suddenly become very successful.*

A·ries /£'eə·riːz, $'er·iːz/ *n* [not after *the*] the first sign of the ZODIAC, relating to the period 21 March to 20 April, represented by a RAM, or a person born during this period • *I was born* **under** *Aries* (= during this period). [U] • *I'm an Aries.* [C]

a·right /ə'raɪt/ *adv old use or literary* correctly • *Did I* **hear/understand** *you aright?*

a·rise HAPPEN /ə'raɪz/ *v* [I] *past simple* **arose** /£ə'rəʊz, $-'roʊz/, *past part* **arisen** /ə'rɪz·ən/ to happen; to come into existence • *Should the* **opportunity** *arise, I'd love to go to China.* • *Could you work on Saturday, should the* **need** *arise* (= if it were to be necessary)? • *Are there any* **matters** *arising* **from** (= caused by) *the last meeting?* • *A strange smell arose* (= came) **from** *the bottom of the garden.*

a·rise GET UP /ə'raɪz/ *v* [I] *past simple* **arose** /£ə'rəʊz, $-'roʊz/, *past part* **arisen** /ə'rɪz·ən/ to get up • *(fml) We arose* (= got out of bed) *at seven.* • *(fml or literary) Arise* (= get up from a kneeling, sitting or lying position), *Sir Lancelot!* • *"I will arise and go now, and go to Innisfree"* (W.B.Yeats in the poem *The Lake Isle of Innisfree*, 1892)

ar·is·toc·ra·cy /£,ær·ɪ'stɒk·rə·si, $,er·ɪ'stɑː·krə-/ *n* [C] a class of people who hold high social rank • **The** *aristocracy has/have sent its/their children to this school for centuries.* [+ sing/pl v] • *(fig.) Judges are generally considered to be the aristocracy* (= the most powerful or highest members) **of** *the legal profession.*

ar·is·to·crat /£'ær·ɪ·stə·kræt, $'er-/ *n* [C] • *Many aristocrats* (= members of the aristocracy) *were killed in the French Revolution.* • *(fig.) In my view, peaches are* **the** *aristocrats* (= the best type) **of** *fruit.*

ar·is·to·crat·ic /£,ær·ɪ·stə'kræt·ɪk, $,er·ɪ·stə'kræt̬-/ *adj* • *She married a man from an aristocratic family* (= a family belonging to the aristocracy). • *He was admired for his aristocratic features* (= having a face which looked like that of an aristocrat).

a·rith·me·tic /£ə'rɪθ·mə·tɪk, $-t̬ɪk/ *n* [U] the process of making calculations such as adding, multiplying, etc. using numbers • *I'm not very good at arithmetic.* • *We've got an arithmetic test at school tomorrow.* • *The teacher always has to correct Nick's arithmetic.* • *I can't work out which of these packets of washing powder is cheaper – could you do* **the** *arithmetic for me?* • **Mental** arithmetic is calculations done in the mind: *He did some quick mental arithmetic and then checked his answer on the calculator.*

a·rith·met·i·cal /£,ær·ɪθ'met·ɪ·kəl, $,er·ɪθ'met̬-/, **a·rith·me·tic** /£,ær·ɪθ'met·ɪk, $,er·ɪθ'met̬-/ *adj* • *My son is very good at solving arithmetical problems.* • An **arithmetical/arithmetic progression** is a SEQUENCE (= ordered series) of numbers which increase or decrease by the same amount, such as 3, 6, 9..., or 9, 6, 3.

a·rith·met·i·cal·ly /£,ær·ɪθ'met·ɪ·kli, $,er·ɪθ'met̬-/ *adv*

ark SHIP /£ɑːk, $ɑːrk/, **No·ah's ark** *n* [U] (in the Bible) a large wooden ship built by Noah in order to save his family and a male and female of every type of animal when the world was covered by a flood • *(infml) My aunt's hat looked as if it came* **out of the ark** (= was very old-fashioned).

ark BOX /£ɑːk, $ɑːrk/ *n* [U] **the Ark of the Covenant** (in the Bible) a wooden box which contained the writings of Jewish law, and which represented to the people of Israel the presence of God leading them

arm BODY PART /£ɑːm, $ɑːrm/ *n* [C] either of the two long parts of the upper body which are fixed to the shoulders and have the hands at the end • *My arms ache from carrying this heavy bag.* • *Bill arrived at the party with his new girlfriend* **on** *his arm* (= her hand resting on his arm). • *She* **put/threw** *her arms* **round** *me, and gave me a hug.* • *He* **took/held** *her* **in** *his arms* (= held her closely). • The arm **of** a piece of clothing or furniture is a part of it that you put your arm in or on: *the arm of a jacket* ○ *the arm of a chair* • An arm **of** land or water is a long, thin part of it that is joined to a larger area. • An arm **of** an organization is a part of it that is responsible for a particular activity or place: *The British company is one arm of a large multinational.* ○ *The Royal Marines is one of the arms of the services.* • If you hold something **at arm's length**, you hold it as far away from your body as possible: *He carried the rubbish out at arm's length.* ○ *(fig.) She prefers to* **keep** *her relations at arm's length* (= avoid being friendly with them). • *(infml)* **An arm and a leg** means a lot of money: *These shoes* **cost** *me an arm and a leg.* • **Arm in arm** means with your arm resting on another person's: *We walked arm in arm along the river bank.* • **Arm-twisting** is the use of persuasion or threats which make it very difficult for someone to refuse to do something: *The vote was won only as the result of much arm-twisting by the government.* • **Arm wrestling** is a game played by two people who place the ELBOWS of their right arms on a table, hold hands and then try to push the other person's hand down onto the table. • PIC> **Arm**

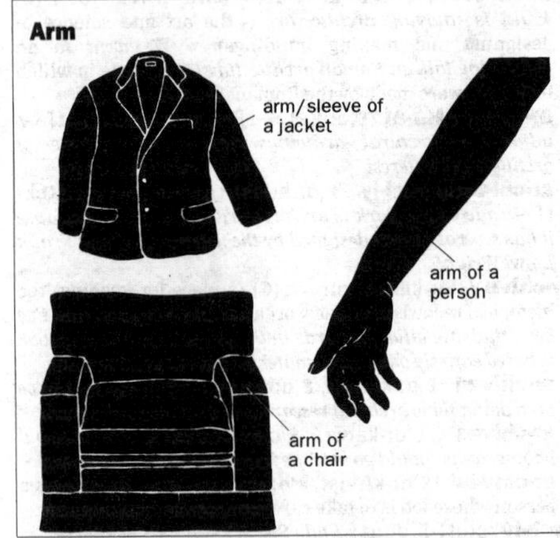

-armed /£-ɑːmd, $-ɑːrmd/ *combining form* • -armed means having the stated type of arm: *a one-armed person* • *a hairy-armed man*

arm·ful /£'ɑːm·fʊl, $'ɑːrm-/ *n* [C] • An armful is the amount that a person can carry in one or both arms: *She struggled along with an armful* **of** *clothes.*

arm *(obj)* PROVIDE WEAPONS /£ɑːm, $ɑːrm/ *v* to provide (yourself or others) with a weapon or weapons • *The tiny state is arming (itself) and preparing for war.* [I/T] • *Nobody knows who is arming the terrorists.* [T] • *I armed* **myself with** *a baseball bat and went to investigate the noise.* [T] • *(fig.) She armed* (= prepared) **herself for** *the interview by finding out all she could about the company in advance.* [T]

armed /£ɑːmd, $ɑːrmd/ *adj* [not gradable] • Armed means using or carrying weapons: *an armed robbery* ○ *armed conflict* ○ *These men are armed* **and dangerous**, *and should not be approached.* • *(fig.) Armed* **with** (= Prepared by having) *the knowledge that it was his birthday, I took some chocolates when I went to see him.* • The **armed forces** are a country's military forces, usually an army, navy and air force.

arms /£ɑːmz, $ɑːrmz/ *pl n* • *They have been charged with supplying arms* (= weapons and equipment used to kill and injure people) to the guerillas. • *An arms* **cache** *was discovered in South Wales.* • *The minister has called on the terrorists to* **lay down** *their arms* (=stop fighting). • *They are willing to* **take up** *arms* (=prepare to fight) ***(against** the government) if they have to.* • *The rebels now have thousands of people* **under arms** (=having weapons and being willing to fight). • *(infml) They're* **up in arms** (=very angry) **about/over** *the new management scheme.* • *There's an* **arms-control** *agreement between the superpowers limiting the number of weapons that each is allowed to possess.* • The **arms race** is the situation in which two or more countries try to have more and stronger weapons than each other. • *"To take arms against a sea of troubles, / And by opposing end them"* (Shakespeare, Hamlet 3.2)

ar·ma·da /£ɑː'mɑː·də, $ɑːr-/ *n* [C] a large group of ships (of war) • *The Spanish Armada was sent by the king of Spain to invade England in 1588.* • (CS)

ar·ma·dil·lo /£ˌɑː·mə'dɪl·əʊ, $ˌɑːr·mə'dɪl·oʊ/ *n* [C] *pl* **armadillos** a small animal found in S America, central America and the southern part of the US which has a body covered in hard bony strips that allow it to curl into a ball when attacked

Ar·ma·ged·don /£ˌɑː·mə'ged·ən, $ˌɑːr-/ *n* [U] a final war between good and evil at the end of the world, as described in the Bible, or, more generally, any event of great destruction • *These people expect the coming of Armageddon soon.* • *He said that unless people in western societies change the way in which they live, the world is heading for* **an** *environmental Armageddon.*

ar·ma·ments /£'ɑː·mə·mənts, $'ɑːr-/ *pl n*, **ar·ma·ment** *n* [U] (a country's) weapons or military equipment • *During the war, a lot of factories which normally produced other things had to be used for making armaments.* • *The country's armaments programme included developing their own nuclear weapons.* • *The new frigates had much heavier armament than their predecessors.* • Armament is also the process of a country increasing the number and strength of its weapons: *As the country prepares for war, more and more money is being spent on armament.*

arm·band /£'ɑːm·bænd, $'ɑːrm-/ *n* [C] a piece of material that a person wears around the arm as a sign of something, for example an official position • *All the stewards at the racetrack were wearing armbands.* • *People sometimes wear black armbands to show to show that a friend or relative has died.* • An armband is also a hollow ring-shaped piece of plastic, into which you blow air, which children who cannot swim wear on their arms in water, in order to help them float.

arm·chair /£'ɑːm·tʃeəʳ, $'ɑːrm·tʃer/ *n* [C] a comfortable chair with two resting places for the arms • *She sat in an armchair by the fire, reading a newspaper.* • Armchair can be used to refer to a person who knows, or claims to know, a lot about a subject without having direct experience of it: *an armchair gardener/traveller/cricketer* • PIC **Chair**

arm·hole /£'ɑːm·həʊl, $'ɑːrm·hoʊl/ *n* [C] an opening in a shirt, coat, etc. through which you put your arm

arm·i·stice /£'ɑː·mɪ·stɪs, $'ɑːr-/ *n* [C] an agreement between two countries or groups at war to stop fighting for a particular time, esp. to talk about possible peace • *A two-week armistice has been* **declared** *between the rival factions.*

arm·our *Br and Aus, Am and Aus* **arm·or** /£'ɑː·məʳ, $'ɑːr·mɚ/ *n* [U] strong protective covering, esp. for the body • *Police put on* **body** *armour before confronting the rioters.* • *In the past, knights used to wear* **(suits of)** *armour* (=protective covering made of metal) *in battle.* • *These grenades are able to* **pierce/penetrate** *the armour* **of** *tanks.* • Armour is also military vehicles that are covered in strong metal to protect them from attack: *The troops were backed by tanks, artillery and other heavy armour.* • Armour can also be a way of acting that a person has in order to protect themselves emotionally: *She's very hard to get to know, and few people have been able to* **penetrate** *her armour.* ○ *She saw his face soften, losing its armour.* • An **armour-plated** vehicle is one that has been covered with special protective metal.

arm·oured *Br, Am* **arm·ored** /£'ɑː·məd, $'ɑːr·mɚd/ *adj* • Armoured means protected by a strong covering, or using military vehicles protected by strong covering: *an armoured tank* ○ *armoured troops* ○ *an armoured division* (=military group) • An **armoured personnel carrier** is a special vehicle covered with strong metal which is used for carrying soldiers.

arm·our·er *Br, Am* **arm·or·er** /£'ɑː·mə·rəʳ, $'ɑːr·mɚ·ɚ/ *n* [C] • An armourer is a person who makes, repairs and supplies weapons.

arm·our·y *Br, Am* **arm·or·y** /£'ɑː·mə·ri, $'ɑːr·mɚ·i/ *n* [C] • A country's or a group's armoury is all the weapons and military equipment it possesses: *The two countries signed an agreement to reduce their nuclear armouries.* [C] • An armoury is also a place where weapons and other military equipment are stored: *Fighter planes have successfully bombed the enemy's main armoury.* [C] • *(fig.) The only weapon left in his armoury* (=The only way he had of behaving in order to protect himself emotionally) *was indifference.* [C]

arm·pit /£'ɑːm·pɪt, $'ɑːrm-/ *n* [C] the hollow place under your arm where your arm joins your body • *Whenever I do any kind of sport, I always get sweaty armpits.* • If somewhere is the **armpit of the Universe**, it is a place which is dirty and unpleasant and which smells bad.

arms /£ɑːmz, $ɑːrmz/ *pl n* See at ARM [PROVIDE WEAPONS]

ar·my /£'ɑː·mi, $'ɑːr-/ *n* [C] a military force, usually belonging to a country, that has the training and equipment to fight on land • *Both the armies suffered heavy losses in the battle.* • *When did you join* **the** (=a particular country's) *army?* • *He has decided on a career* **in the** *British Army.* • **The** *army was/were* (=Soldiers were) *called out to enforce the curfew.* [+ sing/pl v] • *The minister is believed to have been killed by the rebel army* (=group of fighters). • *(fig.) She brought an army* (=large group) **of** *supporters with her.* • **Army surplus** is clothes and equipment that are not needed by the army, and are made available for sale to the public: *He always dresses in army surplus/wears army surplus clothes.* ○ *We bought a lot of camping equipment at an army surplus store/(Am usually)* **army-navy store***/(Aus)* **army disposals store**. • *"An army marches on its stomach"* (believed to have been said by Napoleon, 1769-1821)

a·ro·ma /£ə'rəʊ·mə, $-'roʊ-/ *n* [C] a strong, usually pleasant smell • *The room was filled with the aroma* **of** *coffee.* • *This wine* **has** *a light fruity aroma.* • *These candles* **give off** *a fragrant aroma.* • *(fig.) There is an aroma* (=feeling) **of** *nostalgia about the film.* • LP **Smells**

ar·o·mat·ic /£ˌær·əʊ'mæt·ɪk, $ˌer·ə'mæt̬-/ *adj* • *Properly fried chicken should be golden, aromatic* (=with a pleasant smell) *and tasty.* • *He uses a lot of aromatic herbs in his cooking.*

a·ro·ma·ther·a·py /£əˌrəʊ·mə'θer·ə·pi, $-ˌroʊ-/ *n* [U] a form of treatment in which pleasant-smelling oils are rubbed into the skin, or the gas which they produce is breathed in • *Aromatherapy* **massage** *may help to relieve headaches, stress and pains.* • *Burning aromatherapy* **oils** *produces a pleasant fragrance which can help you relax.*

a·rose /£ə'rəʊz, $-'roʊz/ *past simple of* ARISE

a·round [IN THIS DIRECTION] /ə'raʊnd/, *esp. Br* **round** *prep, adv* [not gradable] in a position or direction surrounding, or in a direction going along the edge of or from one part to another (of) • *The family sat around the dinner table, sharing the day's news.* • *He put his arm around her.* • *A crowd had gathered around the scene of the accident.* • *She had a woollen scarf around her neck.* • *What do you measure around your waist?* • *The moon goes around the Earth.* • *One path goes around the forest and another one goes through it.* • *Go around the side of the building and the car park is at the back.* • *As the bus left, she turned around* (=so that she was facing in the opposite direction) *and waved goodbye to us.* • *He put the wheel on the* **right/wrong way** *around* (=facing the right/wrong way). • *The children were dancing around* (=from one part to another of) *the room.* • *I spent a year travelling around* (=from one part to another of) *Africa and the Middle East.* • *The museum's collection includes works of art from all around* (=all the different parts of) *the world.* • *When I went to look at a house I was thinking of buying, the estate agent showed me around* (=showed me the different rooms). • *She passed a plate of biscuits around* (=from one person to another). • *This virus has been going around (the school)* (=from one person to another (in the school)). • *You must* **come** *around (to my house)* (=visit me) *sometime soon.* • *That tune has been going around* **and around** (=I am continually hearing it) *in my head.* • *There's a great restaurant just* **around the corner** (=near to here). • *"Around the World in Eighty Days"* (title of a novel by Jules Verne, 1873) • PIC **Prepositions of movement**

a·round [APPROXIMATELY] /ə'raʊnd/ *adv* about; approximately • *around six feet tall* • *around two months* *ago* • *around four o'clock* • *She earns around forty thousand a year.* • *Around a hundred people wrote to the BBC to protest about the broadcast.* • [LP>] **Approximate numbers**

a·round [IN THIS PLACE] /ə'raʊnd/ *adv* [not gradable], *prep, adj* [after v] positioned or moving in or near a place, often without a clear direction, purpose or order • *He always leaves his clothes lying around (on the floor).* • *She went into town and spent two hours just walking around.* • *Let's take the children to the park so they can run around for a bit.* • *I used to live around* (= near) *here.* • *When you need her, she's never around* (= here or somewhere near). • *Will you be around* (= here or somewhere near) *next week?* • *There's a lot of flu around* (= a lot of people have it) *at the moment.* • *Mobile phones* **have been** *around* (= existed) *for quite a while.* • *(infml) You could say he***'s been** *around* (= has had a lot of experience of life). • You can say 'See you around' to someone when you leave them, as a very informal way of saying goodbye when you are not making a certain arrangement to meet again.

a·rouse *obj* /ə'raʊz/ *v* [T] to cause someone to have (a particular feeling) • *Her latest book has so far aroused little interest.* • *The new law has aroused much public concern.* • *They are trying to arouse sympathy for their cause.* • *Our* **suspicions** *were first aroused when we heard a muffled scream.* • See also ROUSE.

a·roused /ə'raʊzd/ *adj* • A person who is **(sexually)** aroused (by something) feels sexual excitement.

a·rous·al /ə'raʊ·zəl/ *n* [U] • *a state of* **(sexual)** *arousal* (= being sexually excited)

ar·peg·gi·o /£ɑː'pedʒ·i·əʊ, $ɑːr'pedʒ·i·oʊ/ *n* [C] *pl* **arpeggios** the notes of a musical CHORD played quickly one after the other instead of together

arr [ARRIVE] *v, n abbreviation for* **arrives** or **arrival** (used in TIMETABLES to show the time at which a bus, train or aircraft reaches a place) • *Flight 226: dep. 10.25, arr. 13.45.*

arr [ARRANGE] *adj* (of a piece of music) *abbreviation for* arranged (= changed so that it can be played in a different way)

ar·raign *obj* /ə'reɪn/ *v* [T] *law* (in a court of law) to formally accuse (someone) of a particular crime and ask them to state whether they are guilty or not • *He was arraigned* **on** *charges of aiding and abetting terrorists.*

ar·raign·ment /ə'reɪn·mənt/ *n* [C/U] *law* • (An) arraignment is the act of formally accusing someone of a crime in a court of law, and asking them to state whether they are guilty or not.

ar·range *(obj)* [PLAN] /ə'reɪndʒ/ *v* to plan or make preparations (for); to organize • *I'm trying to arrange my work so that I can have a couple of days off next week.* [T] • *The meeting has been arranged* **for** *Wednesday.* [T] • *They arranged* **to** *have dinner the following month.* [+ *to* infinitive] • *I've already arranged* **with** *him to meet at the cinema.* [+ *to* infinitive] • *She's arranged* **for** *her son* **to** *have swimming lessons.* [+ *to* infinitive] • *I'd deliberately arranged* **that** *they should arrive at the same time.* [+ *that* clause] • *We haven't yet arranged* **when** *to meet.* [+ *wh-* word] • An **arranged marriage** is one in which the parents chose whom their son or daughter will marry.

ar·range·ment /ə'reɪndʒ·mənt/ *n* • *You can only withdraw money from this account by* **(prior)** *arrangement* (= making plans to do so) **with** *the bank.* [U] • *They'd* **made** *all the arrangements* (= preparations) **for** *a huge party.* [C] • *Arrangements were made* **to** *move the prisoners to another jail.* [C + *to* infinitive] • *What are your current working arrangements* (= How do you organize your work)*?* [C] • *We* **had** *an arrangement* (= agreement) **that** *he would clean the house and I would cook.* [C + *that* clause] • *I'm sure we can* **come to** *an arrangement* (= reach an agreement). [C]

ar·range *obj* [PUT IN POSITION] /ə'reɪndʒ/ *v* [T] to put (something) in a particular order • *She arranged her birthday cards along the shelf.* • *Who arranged these flowers – they look beautiful?* • *His books are* **neatly** *arranged in alphabetical order.* • To arrange a piece of music is to change it so that it can be played in a different way, for example by a particular instrument: *Beethoven's fifth symphony has been arranged* **for** *the piano.*

ar·range·ment /ə'reɪndʒ·mənt/ *n* [C] • *There was a striking arrangement of dried flowers* (= a group of them which had been put in a particular order) *on the table.* • *This new arrangement* (= changed form) *of the piece is for saxophone and piano.*

ar·rang·er /£ə'reɪn·dʒəʳ, $-dʒɚ/ *n* [C] • *a flower arranger* • *The famous jazz musician, Duke Ellington, was a composer, arranger and pianist.*

ar·rant /£'ær·ənt, $'er-/ *adj* [before n] total; complete • *He dismissed the rumours as 'arrant nonsense'.*

ar·ray [LARGE GROUP] /ə'reɪ/ *n* a large group of things or people, esp. one which is attractive or causes admiration and often one which has been positioned in a particular way • *There was a glittering array* **of** *film stars at the festival.* [C] • *There was a splendid array* **of** *food on the table.* [C] • *They sat before an array* **of** *microphones and cameras.* [C] • *Soldiers in* **battle** *array* (= positioned in a particular way for fighting) *have been placed in position, ready to fight.* [U]

ar·ray *obj* /ə'reɪ/ *v* [T] • *A large number of magazines were arrayed* (= put where they could be seen) *on the shelf in the shop.* • *Arrayed* (= Standing in a group) *before him were 40 schoolchildren in purple and green.* • *Is this small country capable of fighting the forces arrayed* **against** (= opposing) *it?*

ar·ray [CLOTHES] /ə'reɪ/ *v, n fml* (to dress in) esp. splendid clothes • *The mayor was dressed in full ceremonial array.* [U] • *She was arrayed* **in** *a dress covered with sequins.* [T] • *They arrayed them***selves in** *robes in preparation for the ceremony.* [T] • *Brightly-arrayed couples waltzed across the floor.*

ar·rears /ə'rɪəz/ *pl n* money that is owed and that should have been paid in the past • *We must find some way of paying off our rent arrears.* • **In arrears** means owing money: *My account is* **badly** *in arrears.* ○ *They are in arrears* **on/with** *their mortgage payments.* • If someone is paid **in arrears**, they are paid at the end of the period of time during which the money was earned: *The workers in the factory are all paid a week in arrears.*

ar·rest *obj* [CATCH] /ə'rest/ *v* [T] (of the police) to use lawful authority to catch (someone) and take them to a place where they might be accused of a crime • *He was arrested when customs officers found drugs in his bag.* • *The police arrested her* **for** *drinking and driving.* • (NL)

ar·rest /ə'rest/ *n* • *Two arrests were made, but the men were later released without charge.* [C] • *She was stopped outside the shop and placed/put* **under** *arrest.* [U]

ar·rest *obj* [STOP] /ə'rest/ *v* [T] *fml* to stop or interrupt (the development of) • *The treatment has so far done little to arrest the spread of the cancer.* • (NL)

ar·rest *obj* [ATTRACT NOTICE] /ə'rest/ *v* [T] to attract or catch (someone's attention) • *One photo, of a small boy, arrested my* **attention.** • (NL)

ar·rest·ing /ə'res·tɪŋ/ *adj* • *She gave an arresting account of how she was rescued from a burning building.* • *His performance was arresting.* • *Naomi is an arresting-looking woman.*

ar·rive /ə'raɪv/ *v* [I] to reach a place, esp. at the end of a journey • *What time will your train arrive?* • *The rest of the family arrived the next day.* • *It was dark by the time we arrived* **at** *the station.* • *Early humans first arrived* **in** *this area over 25 000 years ago.* • *I arrived back* **to** *find* (= and found) *that my room had been burgled.* • *What time does the mail usually arrive* (= is it delivered)*?* • *I ordered some CDs over a month ago, but they still haven't arrived* (= I have not received them). • *The leaves starting to turn brown is a sign that autumn has arrived* (= begun). • *Sometimes it seems as if my birthday will never arrive* (= happen). • *Their baby Olivia arrived* (= was born) *on the date she was expected.* • *(fig. infml) He felt he had truly arrived* (= become successful) *when he got his first part in a Broadway play.* • *(fig.) We all argued about it for hours and eventually arrived* **at** (= reached) *a decision.*

ar·riv·al /ə'raɪ·vəl/ *n* • *Hundreds gathered to await the boxer's arrival* **at** *the airport.* [U] • **On** *arrival* **at** *the police station, they were taken to an interview room.* [U] • *We regret the late arrival* **of** *Flight 237.* [U] • *Sue and Michael are delighted to announce the arrival* (= birth) **of** *Emily, born on August 21.* [U] • *The arrival* (= introduction) *of satellite television changed the face of broadcasting.* [U] • *New arrivals* (= people who have just come to a place) *were being housed in refugee camps.* [C] • *(infml)* An arrival can also be a baby which has recently been born: *Their* **new** *arrival was keeping them busy.* [C] ○ *How's your latest arrival?* [C]

ar·ro·gant /£'ær·ə·gənt, $'er-/ *adj* unpleasantly proud and behaving as if you are more important than, or know more than, other people • *He's one of those arrogant people who think that they're always right about everything.* • *She's very arrogant in the way she behaves.*

ar·ro·gant·ly /£'ær·ə·gənt·li, $'er-/ *adv* • *The authorities had behaved arrogantly, she said.*

ar·ro·gance /£ˈær·ə·gᵊnts, $ˈer-/ *n* [U] • *He has a self-confidence that is sometimes seen as arrogance.*

ar·ro·gate *obj* /£ˈær·əʊ·geɪt, $ˈer·ə-/ *v* [T] *fml* to take (something) without having the right to do so • *He accused the group of arrogating* **to** *itself the power to punish people.*

ar·row /£ˈær·əʊ, $ˈer·oʊ/ *n* [C] a weapon that is like a long thin stick with a sharp point at one end and often feathers at the other, shot from a BOW • *Robin Hood asked to be buried where his arrow landed.* • An arrow is also a sign consisting of a straight line with an upside down V shape at one end of it, which points in a particular direction, and is used to show where something is: *I followed the arrows to the car park.* • Compare DART [WEAPON]. • [PIC]> **Bow**

ar·row·head /£ˈær·əʊ·hed, $ˈer·oʊ-/ *n* [C] the sharp point at the end of an arrow

ar·row·root /£ˈær·əʊ·ruːt, $ˈer·oʊ-/ *n* [U] a STARCH (= sticky tasteless food substance) in the form of powder, which is made from a W Indian plant and is used in cooking, esp. to thicken sauces

arse *Br and Aus* /£ɑːs, $ɑːrs/, *Am* **ass** *n* [C] *slightly taboo slang* the part of your body that you sit on; your bottom • *I got a sore arse from sitting on that hard chair.* • If you **do not know/cannot tell** your **arse from** your **elbow**, you are lacking in knowledge. • If someone tells you to **move/shift** your **arse**, they are rudely telling you to hurry up, or to get out of their way. • If someone tells you to **get off** your **arse**, or to **get** your **arse in gear**, they are rudely telling you to do some work or to hurry. • *(Br)* If you go **arse over tit/tip** or **arse about face** (*Am* **ass over teakettle**), you are upside down with your feet above your head, usually because you have fallen: *I fell off my bike and went arse over tit.* • *(Br)* An **arse-licker** (*Am* **ass-licker**) or **arse-kisser** (*Am* **ass-kisser**) is a person who tries to get other people to do things for them by being extremely pleasant to them in a way which is not sincere.

arse a·bout/a·round *Br and Aus* /£ɑːs, $ɑːrs/, *Am* **ass a·bout/a·round** *v adv* [I] *slightly taboo slang* to act in a silly way or waste time • *Stop arsing about, we've got work to do!*

arse·hole [UNPLEASANT PERSON] *Br* /£ˈɑːs·həʊl, $ˈɑːrs·hoʊl/, *esp. Am* **ass·hole** *n* [C] *taboo slang* an unpleasant, stupid person • *You've ruined my dress, you arsehole!*

arse·hole [BODY PART] *Br* /£ˈɑːs·həʊl, $ˈɑːrs·hoʊl/, *Am* **ass·hole** *n* [C] *taboo* the ANUS

arse·nal /£ˈɑː·sᵊn·ᵊl, $ˈɑːr-/ *n* [C] a building where weapons and military equipment are stored, or a collection of weapons • *The army planned to attack enemy arsenals.* • *The country has agreed to reduce its nuclear arsenal* (= collection of weapons). • *The arsenal* (= collection of weapons) *recovered from the jail included knives, axes and sticks.*

arsenic /£ˈɑː·sᵊn·ɪk, $ˈɑːr-/ *n* [U] a very poisonous element, often used to kill RATS and able to kill people

ar·son /£ˈɑː·sᵊn, $ˈɑːr-/ *n* [U] the crime of intentionally starting a fire in order to damage or destroy something, esp. a building • *A cinema was burnt out in north London last night. Police suspect arson.*

ar·son·ist /£ˈɑː·sᵊn·ɪst, $ˈɑːr-/ *n* [C] • *Police are blaming arsonists for the spate of fires in the Greenfields housing estate.*

art /£ɑːt, $ɑːrt/ *n* the making of what is expressive or beautiful, or things that are considered to be expressive or beautiful • *He said that, in his opinion, most people in our society do not really regard art as important.* [U] • *Can television and pop music really be considered art?* [U] • *I enjoyed the ballet, but it wasn't really* **great** *art.* [U] • Art is sometimes used to refer particularly to painting, drawing and SCULPTURE: *She is very good at music and art.* [U] ○ *He wants to be an art teacher when he's left college.* • Art can also be used to refer to paintings, drawings and SCULPTURES: *The gallery has an excellent collection of modern art.* [U] ○ *I went to an exhibition of Native American art.* [U] ○ *Peggy Guggenheim was one of the twentieth century's great art collectors.* ○ *The Frick is an art* **gallery** *in New York.* • An art is an activity through which people express particular ideas: *Drama is an art that is traditionally performed in a theatre.* [C] ○ *Do you regard film as entertainment or as an art?* [C] ○ *She is doing a course in the performing arts.* [C] • An art is also a skill or special ability: *Getting him to go out is* **quite** *an art* (= needs special skill). [C] ○ *There is a special art* **in/to** *knowing when to give up.* [C] • **Arts and crafts** are the skills of making objects, such as decorations, furniture and POTTERY (= objects made from clay), by hand. • **Art deco** is a style of decoration that was especially popular in the 1930s and uses simple shapes and lines and strong colours. • **Art nouveau** is a style of art and decoration that uses curling lines and plant and flower shapes. • Ⓢ

art·ist /£ˈɑː·tɪst, $ˈɑːr·t̬ɪst/ *n* [C] • An artist is someone who paints, draws or makes SCULPTURES: *Monet is one of my favourite artists.* • An artist is also someone who is very good at what they do, esp. when that is an activity such as singing or acting or dancing: *All the dancers in the company are real artists.* ○ *He described her as one of the greatest film artists of the 20th century.* ○ *I'm not just a window cleaner, I'm an artist.* ○ *Don't believe a word he says – he's just a* **con** *artist* (= a person skilled in trickery). • Compare ARTISTE. • Ⓡ

art·ist·ic /£ɑːˈtɪs·tɪk, $ɑːr-/ *adj* • *Artistic* (= Artists') *independence was increased when annual exhibitions of art began.* • If you are artistic, you are able to create or enjoy art: *His friends are all artistic – they're painters, musicians and writers.* ○ *There are some very artistic people in my drawing class.* • Artistic can also mean skilfully and attractively made: *That's a very artistic flower arrangement you have there.*

art·ist·ic·ally /£ɑːˈtɪs·tɪ·kli, $ɑːr-/ *adv* • *They set up a school for artistically gifted children.*

art·ist·ry /£ˈɑː·tɪ·stri, $ˈɑːr·t̬ɪ-/ *n* [U] • *You have to admire the artistry* (= skill) *of her novels.*

arts /£ɑːts, $ɑːrts/ *pl n* • **The arts** are the making or showing or performance of painting, acting, dancing, music, etc.: *More government money is needed for the arts.* • See also ARTS.

art·y /£ˈɑː·ti, $ˈɑːr·t̬i/ *adj* **-ier, -iest** *infml usually disapproving* • Arty means being or wishing to seem very interested in everything connected with art and artists: *The students at the college are all very arty types.* ○ *He has a pony tail, dresses in black, and wears sunglasses all the time – all very arty.* • Arty can also mean being or wishing to seem artistically skilful: *She's always dragging me along to these arty films that I can never understand.* ○ *The play had very arty lighting.* • *(Br infml)* If you are **arty-crafty** (*Am* **artsy-craftsy**), you make or enjoy decorative objects: *They run a little pottery shop and café and are very arty-crafty.* • *(disapproving)* If you are **arty-farty** (also **artsy-fartsy**), you wish to appear more educated or knowledgeable about art than you really are: *He is one of those arty-farty types who talk of nothing but the latest novel/play/exhibition.* • Ⓢ

art·e·fact *esp. Br* /£ˈɑː·tɪ·fækt, $ˈɑr·t̬ɪ-/, **ar·ti·fact** *n* [C] an object that is made by a person, such as a tool or a decoration, esp. one that is of historical interest • *Bowls and other artefacts were discovered during the excavations.* • *The museum's collection includes artefacts dating back to prehistoric times.*

ar·te·ry [TUBE] /£ˈɑː·tᵊr·i, $ˈɑːr·t̬ɚ-/ *n* [C] one of the thick tubes that carry blood from the heart to other parts of the body • *Hardening of the coronary arteries can lead to a heart attack.*

ar·te·ri·al /£ɑːˈtɪə·ri·ᵊl, $ɑːrˈtɪr·i-/ *adj* [not gradable] • *Smoking is very damaging to the arterial walls* (= the sides of the arteries).

ar·te·ry [ROAD/RAILWAY] /£ˈɑː·tᵊr·i, $ˈɑːr·t̬ɚ-/ *n* [C] an important road or railway • *I heard on the radio that all the main arteries leading into London are blocked with traffic.* • *This line is one of the major arteries of the country's rail network.*

ar·te·ri·al /£ɑː·tɪə·ri,ᵊl, $ɑːr·tɪr·i-/ *adj* • *Improvements have been made to arterial roads to cope with increased traffic.*

art·es·i·an well /£ɑːˈtiː·zi·ᵊn, $ɑːr·ti·ʒᵊn/ *n* [C] a WELL in which the water is forced to the surface by natural pressure

art·ful /£ˈɑːt·fᵊl, $ˈɑːrt-/ *adj* clever and skilful, esp. in getting what you want • *He has shown himself to be an artful politician.* • *She is an artful tennis player, which makes up for her relative lack of strength.* • *The prime minister dealt with the interviewer's questions in a very artful way.* • *"The Artful Dodger"* (name of a young thief in Charles Dickens' *Oliver Twist*, 1839)

art·ful·ly /£ˈɑːt·fᵊl·i, $ˈɑːrt-/ *adv* • *His clothes were artfully arranged to look stylishly casual.*

art·ful·ness /£ˈɑːt·fᵊl·nəs, $ˈɑːrt-/ *n* [U]

arth·ri·tis /£ɑːˈθraɪ·tɪs, $ɑːrˈθraɪ·t̬ɪs/ *n* [U] a serious condition in which a person's joints become painful, swollen and stiff • *She described herself as* **crippled with** *arthritis.*

arth·ri·tic /£ɑːˈθrɪt·ɪk, $ɑːrˈθrɪṭ-/ *adj, n* • *My mother is arthritic and her joints are swollen.* • *Her hands were swollen and arthritic.* • *Many arthritics* (= people suffering from arthritis) *find it difficult to climb stairs.* [C]

ar·tic *n* [C] *Br infml* an ARTICULATED truck

ar·ti·choke /£ˈɑː·tɪ·tʃəʊk, $ˈɑːr·ṭɪ·tʃoʊk/ *n* [C] a **globe artichoke**, see at GLOBE [ROUND OBJECT], or a JERUSALEM ARTICHOKE • [PIC]> **Vegetables**

ar·ti·cle [NEWSPAPER] /£ˈɑː·tɪ·kl̩, $ˈɑːr·ṭɪ-/ *n* [C] a piece of writing on a particular subject in a newspaper or magazine • *There was an interesting article* **on** *vegetarianism in the paper yesterday.*

ar·ti·cle [OBJECT] /£ˈɑː·tɪ·kl̩, $ˈɑːr·ṭɪ-/ *n* [C] a particular thing, esp. one which is one of several things of a similar type or in the same place • *In the gardening catalogue I saw several articles that I wanted to buy.* • *When our house was burgled, the police asked us to make a list of the missing articles.* • *Guests are advised not to leave any articles of value in their hotel rooms.* • *An article* **of clothing** *was found near the river.*

ar·ti·cle [GRAMMAR] /£ˈɑː·tɪ·kl̩, $ˈɑːr·ṭɪ-/ *n* [C] any of the English words 'a', 'an' and 'the' or words in other languages that do the same job as these • See **definite article** at DEFINITE; **indefinite article** at INDEFINITE. • [LP]> **Articles**

ar·ti·cle [LAW] /£ˈɑː·tɪ·kl̩, $ˈɑːr·ṭɪ-/ *n* [C] a separate part in a written document such as a legal agreement • *East and West Germany united under article 23 of the Bonn constitution.* • An **article of faith** is something that you believe in very strongly: *Socialism was an article of faith in his parents' home.* • *(Br and Aus)* A person who is **doing/in articles** is working in a law office while they are training to be a lawyer.

ar·ti·cled /£ˈɑː·tɪ·kl̩d, $ˈɑːr·ṭɪ-/ *adj* [not gradable] • *She is articled* **to** *a big law firm* (= she is working there as part of her training) *in the City of London.* • *Theo is an articled* **clerk**.

ar·ti·cu·late [CLEAR] /£ɑːˈtɪk·jʊ·lət, $ɑːr-/ *adj* able to express, or expressing, thoughts and feelings easily and clearly • *At the age of 93, he was still sharp-witted and articulate.* • *Our local vicar is an inspiring and articulate preacher.* • *She gave a witty, entertaining and articulate speech.*

ar·ti·cu·late·ly /£ɑːˈtɪk·jʊ·lət·li, $ɑːr-/ *adv* • *He was a journalist who wrote elegantly and articulately* (= in a clear style).

ar·ti·cu·late·ness /£ɑːˈtɪk·jʊ·lət·nəs, $ɑːr-/,
ar·ti·cu·lacy /£ɑːˈtɪk·jʊ·lə·si, $ɑːr-/ *n* [U]

ar·ti·cu·late *obj* [SAY] /£ɑːˈtɪk·jʊ·leɪt, $ɑːr-/ *v* [T] *fml* to express in words • *Do you think that women are more able than men to articulate their feelings?* • *Many people are opposed to the new law, but have had no opportunity to articulate their opposition.* • Articulate can also mean pronounce: *When children first learn to talk, there are some sounds that they find it difficult to articulate.*

ar·ti·cu·la·tion /£ɑːˌtɪk·jʊˈleɪ·ʃən, $ɑːr-/ *n* [U] • *A clearer articulation* (= expression) *of the government's aims would be helpful.* • *A good singer needs to have good articulation* (= a clear way of pronouncing words).

ar·ti·cu·lat·ed /£ɑːˈtɪk·jʊ·leɪ·tɪd, $ɑːrˈtɪk·jʊ·leɪ·ṭɪd/ *adj* (of a vehicle) consisting of two or more parts which bend where they are joined in order to help the vehicle turn corners • *an articulated vehicle* • *(Br) The road is closed because an articulated* **lorry** *(infml* **artic**, *Am and Aus infml* **semi**) *has overturned, shedding its load.*

ar·ti·fact /£ˈɑː·tɪ·fækt, $ˈɑːr·ṭɪ-/ *n* [C] an ARTEFACT

ar·ti·fice /£ˈɑː·tɪ·fɪs, $ˈɑːr·ṭɪ-/ *n fml* (the use of) a clever trick or something intended to deceive • *She seems to write with as little artifice as a bird when it sings.* [U] • *His remorse is just an artifice to gain sympathy.* [C]

ar·ti·fi·cial /£ˌɑː·tɪˈfɪʃ·əl, $ˌɑːr·ṭɪ-/ *adj* made by people, often as a copy of something natural, or *(disapproving)* not sincere • *I don't like wearing clothes made of artificial fibres.* • *He was born with only one ear, but surgeons have fitted him with an artificial one made of silicon.* • *A lot of people use artificial sweeteners in their tea or coffee.* • *Many citizens feel that the division of their country is artificial.* • *(disapproving) Their cheerfulness seemed rather strained and artificial.* • **Artificial insemination** (*abbreviation* **AI**) is the process of putting sperm into a female using methods which do not involve sexual activity between a male and female. In animals this method is used to improve the quality of the breed. • **Artificial intelligence** (*abbreviation* **AI**) is the study of how to produce machines that have some of the qualities that the human mind has, such as the ability to understand language, recognize pictures, solve problems and learn. • **Artificial respiration** is the act of forcing air in and out of the lungs of a person who has stopped breathing, esp. by blowing into their mouth and pressing their chest until they start breathing again: *Rescuers pulled the child from the river, and she was* **given** *artificial respiration.*

ar·ti·fi·cial·ly /£ˌɑː·tɪˈfɪʃ·əl·i, $ˌɑːr·ṭɪ-/ *adv* • *Most mushrooms sold in supermarkets have been grown artificially* (= not in natural conditions) *in manure.*

ar·ti·fi·ci·al·i·ty /£ˌɑː·tɪˌfɪʃ·iˈæl·ɪ·ti, $ˌɑːr·ṭɪˌfɪʃ·iˈæl·ə·ṭi/ *n* [U]

ar·til·lery /£ɑːˈtɪl·ər·i, $ɑːrˈtɪl·ɚ-/ *n* [U] (the part of the army which uses) very large guns that are moved on wheels or metal tracks • *Naval gunfire and ground-based artillery are generally less accurate than many aircraft-borne weapons.*

ar·ti·san /£ˈɑː·tɪ·zæn, $ˈɑːr·ṭɪ-/ *n* [C] a person who does skilled work with his or her hands • *In pre-1750 Europe, most artisans were involved in producing basic goods – cloth, shoes, bread, flour, building materials, and so on – although some did make luxury items.*

art·ist /£ˈɑː·tɪst, $ˈɑːr·ṭɪst/ *n* [C] See at ART

art·ist·ic /£ɑːˈtɪs·tɪk, $ɑːr-/ *adj*

art·ist·ic·ally /£ɑːˈtɪs·tɪ·kli, $ɑːr-/ *adv*

art·ist·ry /£ˈɑː·tɪ·stri, $ˈɑːr·ṭɪ-/ *n* [U]

art·iste /£ɑːˈtiːst, $ɑːr-/ *n* [C] a skilled entertainer esp. a dancer, singer or actor • *She was a popular French music-hall artiste in the late 19th century.* • *All the members of the family worked as circus artistes.*

art·less /£ˈɑːt·ləs, $ˈɑːrt-/ *adj* simple and honest; not wanting to deceive • *She's an artless young woman who would never dream of trying to mislead anyone.* • *"Why did you take the money?" the police officer asked the child. "Because I wanted it," came the simple and artless reply.*

art·less·ly /£ˈɑːt·lə·sli, $ˈɑːrt-/ *adv*

art·less·ness /£ˈɑːt·lə·snəs, $ˈɑːrt-/ *n* [U]

arts /£ɑːts, $ɑːrts/ *pl n* subjects, such as history, languages and PHILOSOPHY, that are not sciences • *At school I was quite good at arts, but hopeless at science.* • *Children should be given a well-balanced education in both the arts and the sciences.* • *Do you think it's more difficult for arts graduates/people who have done arts degrees to get a job?* • See also **arts** at ART. • [LP]> **Schools and colleges**

art·work /£ˈɑːt·wɜːk, $ˈɑːrt·wɜːrk/ *n* [U] the pieces of art, such as drawings and photographs, that are used in books, newspapers and magazines • *All the artwork in the book has been done by the author.*

art·y /£ˈɑː·ti, $ˈɑːr·ṭi/ *adj* **-ier, -iest** See at ART

as [COMPARISON] /æz/ *adv* [not gradable], *prep, conjunction* used to express the way in which something or someone is like something or someone else • *She'll soon be* **as** *tall* **as** *her mother.* • *I can't run* **as** *fast* **as** *you.* • *Her skin is* **(as)** *soft* **as** *a baby's.* • *I like this jacket better than that one, but it costs twice as much.* • *Paolo earns three times* **as** *much* **as** *I do.* • *With modern technology, even babies weighing* **as** *little* **as** *1 kilogram at birth can survive.* • *They live in the* **same** *town* **as** *my parents.* • *It's not* **as** *good* **as** *it used to be.* • *I'd never seen him looking* **so** *miserable* **as** *he did that day.*

as [BEING] /æz/ *prep* appearing to be, or being • *He went to the fancy-dress party dressed as a banana.* • *She was praised as an actress, but less so as a director.* • *As a child, Mary had lived in India.* • *Use your coat as* (= in the same way as) *a blanket.* • *The news came as no surprise.* • *What I said was meant as a joke.* • *The necklace was reported to the police as having been stolen.* [+ v-*ing*]

as [BECAUSE] /æz/ *conjunction* because • *As it was getting late, I decided to book into a hotel.* • *You can go first as you're the oldest.*

as [WHEN] /æz/ *conjunction* while; during the time that • *As I was getting into the car, I noticed a piece of paper on the floor.* • *He gets more attractive as he gets older.* • **As of/As from** (= Starting) *next month, all the airline's fares will be going up.*

as [ALTHOUGH] /æz/ *conjunction* although • *Angry as he was, he couldn't help smiling.*

as [SIMILAR] /æz/ *conjunction* in the way that; like • *Do as I say!* • *When I arrived at the party, someone else was dressed exactly as I was.* • *He got divorced,* **(just)** *as his parents had done years before.* • *As with his earlier movies, the special effects in his latest film are brilliant.* • *As is often the case with children, Amy was completely better by the time the doctor arrived.* • *As I thought, Danny was to blame.* • *As you* *know, I have a house in the country.* • *As I was just saying, I think the proposal needs further consideration.* • *Gather ye rosebuds, as Robert Herrick put it.* • *Knowing him as I do, I can't believe he would do such a thing.* • *As a matter of principle, I don't drink and drive.* • *He was thrilled.* **As for** (= Changing the subject to) *me, I got used to the idea.* • **As if/though** means in a way that suggests that something is the situation: *She looked as if she'd had some bad news.* ○ *My mouth felt as if I'd been eating the blanket.* ○ *They stared at me as if I was crazy.* ○ *Why is she so surprised? It isn't as if she wasn't warned* (= this certainly was not the situation). • **As if** can also be used for emphasis: *As if I didn't have enough problems already* (= I have a lot of problems and do not need any more)! ○ *He said that he didn't like the dress I was wearing. As if I cared* (= I do not care)! • *(esp. Am infml)* If you buy something **as is**, you accept it in its present condition: *All merchandise is sold as is – no refunds, no exchanges.* • If you say **as it is/stands/turns out/happens** or **as it was/stood/turned out/happened** or **as things are/stand** or **as things were/stood/turned out/happened**, you are referring to the real situation, rather than what might or should have happened: *We expected to arrive at 6.30, but as it was we didn't get there until after midnight.* ○ *As things stand, I don't think we can ask Elaine to take on any further work.* • **As it is** can also mean already: *No, I'm not buying you children anything else today – I've spent far too much money as it is.* • *(fml)* You can say **as you wish/like/prefer**, when you are agreeing to a request. This is sometimes used to show that you do not agree with or approve of the request: *"I want you to do this work again." "As you wish."* • **As to/As for** means to change the subject to: *As to where we'll get the money from, we'll talk about that later.* • **As to** means about: *I can't answer questions as to how long this will last.* ○ *He was uncertain as to which road to take.* • *(Br)* **As and when** (*Am and Aus* **If and when**) means at the time or in the way that: *We don't own a car, but we rent one as and when we need it.* • You use **as it were** to make what you say sound less certain or humorous: *He's a little on the large side, as it were* (= He is fat).

AS /ˌeɪˈes/ *n* [C] *Am abbreviation for* Associate in Science (= US degree)

asap /ˌeɪ·es·eɪˈpiː/ *abbreviation for* as soon as possible • LP› Letters

as·bes·tos /£æsˈbes·tɒs, $-tɑːs/ *n* [U] a soft greyish-white material that does not burn, and which is used in buildings, clothing, etc. as a protection against fire, and as a form of INSULATION (= way of stopping heat from escaping) • *blue/white/brown asbestos* • *Many countries have limited or banned the use of asbestos because of fears that its fibres cause diseases such as lung cancer if inhaled.*

as·bes·to·sis /£ˌæs·besˈtəʊ·sɪs, $-ˈtoʊ-/ *n* [U] • Asbestosis is a serious medical condition caused by breathing asbestos fibres into the lungs: *People who work with asbestos may develop lung cancer, asbestosis and other respiratory diseases years afterwards.*

as·cend *(obj)* /əˈsend/ *v literary or fml* to move up or climb (something) • *They slowly ascended the steep path up the mountain.* [T] • *The divers have begun to ascend* **to** *the surface of the water.* [I] • *There's a long flight of steps ascending* (= leading up) **to** *the cathedral doors.* [I] • *(fig.) He eventually ascended* (= advanced) **to** *the position of chief executive of America's fourth largest banking company.* [I] • *(fig.) I shall list my objections to the plan in ascending* (= increasing) **order** *of importance.* • To **ascend the throne** is to become queen or king.

as·cent /əˈsent/ *n* • *She made her first successful ascent* (= climb) *of Everest last year.* [C] • *We struggled up the slippery ascent* (= slope). [C] • *(fig.) The leader's ascent* (= advance) **to** *power was rapid and unexpected.* [U] • *"The Ascent of Man"* (title of a book by Jacob Bronowski, 1973)

as·cend·ant /əˈsen·dᵊnt/ *n* [U] *literary or fml* • *As a director, he is currently* **in the ascendant** (= has an important or increasing influence) *in Hollywood.*

as·cend·an·cy /əˈsen·dᵊnt·si/ *n* [U] • *They are in danger of losing their political ascendancy* (= controlling power). • *Supporters of the proposal are currently* **in the** *ascendancy* **(over** *its opponents)* (= are more powerful than them).

as·cer·tain *(obj)* /£ˌæs·əˈteɪn, $-ɚˈ-/ *v fml* to discover; to make certain • *The police have so far been unable to ascertain the cause of the explosion.* [T] • *I ascertained* **that** *no one could overhear us before I told Otto the news.* [+ *that* clause] • *Have you ascertained* **wh**ether *she's coming or not?* [+ *wh-* word]

a·scet·ic /£əˈset·ɪk, $-ˈset̬-/ *adj, n* avoiding physical pleasures and living a simple life, often for religious reasons, or a person who does this • *Her sister is extrovert and fun-loving, while she is ascetic and strict.* • *They live a very ascetic life.* • *There's something of the ascetic about Mr Martin.* • *He has spent most of his adult life living as an ascetic.* [C]

a·scet·ic·ally /£əˈset·ɪ·kli, $-ˈset̬-/ *adv*

a·scet·i·ci·sm /£əˈset·ɪ·sɪ·zᵊm, $-ˈset̬-/ *n* [U]

ASCII /ˈæs·ki/ *n* [U] *abbreviation for* American Standard Code for Information Interchange (= a way of storing numbers, letters or symbols for exchanging information between computer systems) • *Can you give me the document in ASCII format?*

a·scor·bic ac·id /£əˈskɔː·bɪk, $-ˈskɔːr-/ *n* [U] *specialized* a VITAMIN (= substance necessary in small amounts for bodily growth and good health) found esp. in fruit and vegetables • *Ascorbic acid is also known as Vitamin C.*

as·cot /£ˈæs·kət, $-kɑːt/ *n* [C] *Am* a SCARF with wide square ends which is made of silk or wool. It is worn around the neck and is often held in place with a decorative fastener; a CRAVAT

a·scribe *obj* **to** *obj* /əˈskraɪb/ *v prep* [T] to consider (something) to be caused, created or possessed by (someone or something); to ATTRIBUTE TO • *To what do you ascribe the phenomenal success of your new album, Lloyd?* • *After years of research, scholars have finally ascribed this anonymous play to Christopher Marlowe.* • *People like to ascribe human feelings to animals* (= believe animals have human feelings).

a·sep·tic /ˌeɪˈsep·tɪk/ *adj* medically clean or without infection • *an aseptic wound/dressing/bandage*

a·sex·u·al /ˌeɪˈsek·sju·ᵊl/ *adj* without sex, sexual organs or sexuality, or not interested in sexual relationships • *asexual reproduction/behaviour* • *Our relationship is completely asexual – we're like sister and brother.*

a·sex·u·al·ly /ˌeɪˈsek·sju·ᵊl·i/ *adv*

a·sex·u·al·i·ty /£ˌeɪ·sek·sjuˈæl·ɪ·ti, $-ə·t̬i/ *n* [U]

ash POWDER /æʃ/ *n* [U] the soft grey or black powder that is left after a substance, esp. tobacco, coal or wood, has burnt • *cigar/cigarette ash* • *When volcanoes erupt, they throw out a lot of ash which consists of fine particles of lava.* • **Ash blond/blonde** describes the colour of hair which is very pale yellow, almost white, and also refers to a person with such hair: *She's an ash-blonde.* ○ *He has ash-blond hair.* • **Ash Wednesday**, the first day of Lent, is named after the Christian tradition of drawing a cross on the front of the head with holy ashes.

ash·es /ˈæʃ·ɪz/ *pl n* • Ashes are what is left of something after it has been destroyed by fire, esp. what is left of a human body after it has been CREMATED (= burned in a formal ceremony): *My grandmother's ashes were scattered over the Yorkshire Moors where she had spent the last few years of her life.* ○ *Allied bombing left Dresden in ashes in 1945.* ○ *(fig.) In 1991, independent democratic states* **rose from** *the ashes of the former Soviet Union.*

ash·y /ˈæʃ·i/ *adj* • Something that is ashy consists of, or is covered with, or looks like ash.

ash TREE /æʃ/ *n* (the hard wood of) a forest tree which has a smooth grey BARK (= strong outer covering), small greenish flowers and seeds shaped like wings • *The cuckoo was perched amongst the upper branches of a tall ash.* [C] • *Ash is often used for making tool handles.* [U]

a·shamed /əˈʃeɪmd/ *adj* [after v] feeling guilty, anxious or awkward about something, or not approving of someone • *She ought to be thoroughly ashamed* **of** *herself* **for** *talking to her mother like that.* • *Oliver Twist was not ashamed* **of** *asking for more food.* • *He was not ashamed* **to** *ask for more.* [+ *(to)* infinitive] • *He was not ashamed* **that** *he had shouted at her.* [+ *(that)* clause] • *Owning an old car is nothing to be ashamed* **of**. • *He was too ashamed* **to** *admit (that) he had forgotten her name.* [+ *(to)* infinitive] • *I'm ashamed* **to** *be seen with you when you're behaving like that.* [+ *(to)* infinitive] • *How on earth could you do such a thing? I'm so ashamed* **of** *you!* • *I* **felt** *so ashamed when I heard what had happened.*

ash·can /ˈæʃ·kæn/ *n* [C] *dated Am for* DUSTBIN

ash·en /ˈæʃ·ᵊn/ *adj* lacking colour or looking like the pale grey colour of ASH POWDER • *Although she remained calm when she heard of her boyfriend's death, the shock showed in her ashen face.* • *The refugee's skin was ashen, indicating severe malnutrition.*

a·shore /£əˈʃɔːʳ, $-ˈʃɔːr/ *adj* [after v], *adv* [not gradable] towards or onto land from an area of water, or on land after

THE DEFINITE AND INDEFINITE ARTICLES, 'THE', 'AN' AND 'A'

How articles are used before nouns and noun phrases

The articles are most often used before nouns in order to refer to people, things, ideas and so on. Generally, no article is used before the names of particular people or places (see the table below for more details): *Oxford Street* • *President Saddam* • *(Mount) Everest* • *Lake Ontario* • *University College*. In the dictionary nouns like this are marked [not after *the*].

- **referring to a particular item that is not yet known: A / AN**
  The indefinite article is used to introduce a single item for the first time: *Is that noise* **an** *ambulance or* **a** *police car?* • *"Have you got* **a** *pen I could use?" "I've got* **a** *pencil. Will that do?"*

- **referring to one or more particular items that are known: THE**
  'The' is used when something introduced earlier is referred to again: *On my plate was a slice of meat, some potatoes and some cabbage.* **The** *meat was revolting, but I managed to eat* **the** *potatoes and cabbage.*
  'The' is also used when it is very clear what is being referred to, even if it has not been mentioned before: **The** *moon looks great tonight.* • **The** *telephone's ringing.* • *What's* **the** *date?* • *Can I use* **the** *bathroom?*

- **stating what type of thing something is: A / AN**
  'A' and 'an' can be used to say what class a particular person or thing belongs to: *He's* **an** *agricultural economist.* • *This is* **a** *wonderful surprise!* • *That bird looks* **like a** *white eagle.* • *She's employed* **as a** *personal assistant.*

- **general statements : usually NO ARTICLE**
  A noun that has no plural is labelled [U]. In general statements using [U] nouns, no article is used: *History was my favourite subject at school.* • *Light travels at 300,000 km per second.* • *Swimming benefits every muscle you've got.* • *Classical music will never be as popular as pop music.*
  Usually with [C] nouns the plural is used with no article: *Elephants cannot jump; kangaroos cannot help it.* • *Ladies first!*
  It is also possible to make general statements using a definite or indefinite article before a [C] noun: **An** *injured lion* (=any injured lion) *is* **an** *extremely dangerous animal.* • *Does* **the** *computer* (=Do computers in general) *really save time and money?* • **The** *Italians and* **the** *Scots are very different.*

- **making general or indefinite phrases refer to particular items: THE**
  In the left-hand sentences the nouns refer generally to a group of items, or to particular items that are not known. In the sentences on the right the noun phrases refer to particular things. The definite article is then required.

Normally I like music.	*Normally I like* **the** *music you like.*
Do you know any Nigerians?	*Do you know* **the** *Nigerians next door?*
Managers often complain.	**The** *managers in our office often complain.*
A man telephoned.	**The** *man who you visited yesterday telephoned.*

- **meaning 'one' or 'each': A / AN**
  The indefinite article is preferred to 'one' when talking about a single thing or person: *The thieves took* **a** *painting and four silver candlesticks.* • *He only stayed* **a** *day or two.* Notice also *a dozen, a hundred, a thousand, a million.*
  'One' is used for emphasis, or in order to contrast with other numbers: *Give me* **one** *good reason why I should!* • *Last year we had three thousand visitors, but only* **one** *thousand this year.*
  'A(n)' is used with units and some other words to mean 'each': *It costs £12.95* **a** *metre* (=each metre). • *He reads three books* **a** *week.* • *Only 800 calories* **a** *portion.*

How the articles are used with [C] and [U] nouns

Many [U] nouns in English are [C] in other languages, for example *advice, clothing, information, music.* [C] and [U] nouns are used differently with articles:

- 'The' can be used with [C] nouns, both singular and plural, and with [U] nouns. It is used when the particular reference of the noun phrase is known. Compare the sentences below:

Is there a message for me?	*She phoned four times but no-one gave me* **the** *message.*
Roses are less popular these days.	*I really must prune* **the** *roses this week.*
Industry needs up-to-date information.	**The** *newspaper industry paid $2 million for* **the** *information.*
Tony always ignores advice.	*Tony always ignores* **the** *advice that I give him.*

- 'A' and 'an' can be used only with nouns that are singular. Usually these are [C]: *Why don't you get* **a** *dog?* • **an** *early example of block printing.*
  A few [U] nouns can also take 'a(n)', especially when used after an adjective. The noun often refers to a particular actual example of a quality, idea or feeling: *Rachel has* **a** *good knowledge of Arabic.* • *There was* **an** *indefinable sadness in his voice.* • *I noticed* **a** *slight stiffness in his movement: he was hurt.*
  Sometimes 'a(n)' is used with the meaning 'a type of' before [U] nouns for substances: *Belvoir Spring is* **a** *sparkling mineral water.* • *Do you think we should use* **an** *acrylic paint?* It can also mean a unit or container of the substance mentioned: *I'd love* **a** *coffee.* • *I always have* **a** *yogurt for breakfast.*

- **Countable nouns used with no article**
  Some [C] nouns are used without an article in common expressions with 'at', 'by', 'in', 'on', 'out of': *Terry spent 10 years* **in** *jail/prison* (=he was a prisoner). • *(Br) The injured were taken* **to** *hospital.* • *He refused to get* **out of** *bed.* • *Does Lisa go* **to** (=attend) *school yet?* • *Shall we fly or go* **by** *train?* • *This was painted* **by** *hand.*
  All these nouns are also used in the usual way with articles: *There are 244 men in* **the** *prison* (=in this particular prison). • *Mary's gone to* **the** *hospital to visit Mrs Friedman.*

Example sentences in the dictionary show how particular nouns are used with 'a(n)', 'the' or with no article. The following table gives approximate rules for some common types of nouns:

a(n)	the	no article		
		•	countries (if singular)*	*Zimbabwe* • *South Korea* • (also *Africa, Asia* etc.)
•		•	days, months, holidays	*Come on Monday.* • *I was born on* **a** *Friday.* • *I'm going home for Christmas.*
		•	languages	*I'm trying to learn Dutch.*
		•	meals	*I don't usually have breakfast.* • *Dinner is at eight.*
•	•	•	musical instruments	*I play drums.* • *She's learning* **the** *piano.* • *He was playing* **a** *violin.*
		•	names (if singular)	*Patricia* • *Charles King* • *Smith, Harris and McIntyre*
	•	•	nationalities (ending -s)	**(the)** *Romanians* • **(the)** *Swedes*
	•		nationalities (other endings)	**the** *Chinese* • **the** *Dutch* • **the** *Swiss*
•			job names	*She was* **a** *dancer at one time.* • *He's* **an** *economist.*
		•	professions	*James is in business/teaching.* • *Medicine is a rewarding career.*
		•	shops (proper names)	*I'll get it from Boots.* • *Marks & Spencers* • *Macey's*
•	•		shops	*Buy some fruit from* **a/the** *greengrocer's* • **a/the** *newsagent's*
		•	sports and games	*Do you play chess?* • *She loves watching tennis.*
	•		titles used alone	**the** *Queen (of England)* • **the** *President* • **the** *Pope*
		•	titles before names	*Mr Gordon* • *Queen Elizabeth* • *Lord Chalmers*
	•	•	towns, streets	*Do you like Boston?* • *Where's Princess Road?* • **the** *High Street*
		•	years	*1985 was a very peculiar year.*
	•		years in groups	*He grew up during* **the** *1930s.* • **the** *eighties*

* Plural names of countries and some names of geographical areas take 'the': *We flew from the United States to the Caribbean.* LP **Nations and nationalities** at NATION and **World regions** at WORLD.

How the articles are used with other parts of speech

• **used before adjectives**

'The' is used before adjectives when they are used alone to refer to a group. Notice that a plural verb is required: **The** *young are so optimistic, aren't they?* • **the** *French* • **the** *unemployed*

Some adjectives refer to only one person or thing, and always require 'the': *She was* **the** *first/last to finish.* • *He sang* **the** *only song he knew.* • *They had exactly* **the** *same hairstyle.*

Superlatives require 'the': *It's* **the** *fastest growing economy in Asia.* • *She's* **the** *most intelligent and kindest woman I know.* (Notice that superlatives of adverbs also require 'the': *Which mistake do you make* **the** *most often?*)

• **used after predeterminers**

The articles are determiners, like 'my', 'your', 'this', 'that', 'those' etc., and so they cannot be used *before* another determiner. Phrases like 'the my brother' or 'a this friend' are impossible.
'A' and 'an' can be used *after* the predeterminers 'half', 'quite', 'rather', 'such' and 'what': *half* **an** *hour* • *quite/rather* **a** *long time* • *Such* **an** *interesting couple!* • *What* **a** *difference!*
'The' can be used after the predeterminers 'all', 'both', 'double', 'half' and 'twice': *all* **the** *information* • *both* **the** *boys* • *twice* **the** *weight.*

coming from an area of water • *to come/swim/wade/stagger/struggle ashore* • *to carry/bring something ashore* • *We gathered some pieces of wood which had washed ashore to make the fire.* • *Strong winds blew the ship ashore.* • *After twenty years at sea, it was hard for her to adjust to life ashore.* • *They stocked up on supplies while they were ashore.*

ash·tray /ˈæʃ·treɪ/ *n* [C] a small dish or container, sometimes decorative, in which smokers leave ash and cigarette ends • *"I really must give up smoking," said Ian, stubbing out another cigarette in the ashtray.*

ash·y /ˈæʃ·i/ *adj* See at ASH [POWDER]

A·sian /ˈeɪ·ʒᵊn/ *n* [C] someone who lives in or comes from the continent of Asia, or a member of a race originally from Asia • In the US, Canada, Australia and New Zealand, an Asian is usually someone from China, Japan or countries near them. • In the UK, an Asian is usually someone from India, Pakistan or countries near them.

A·sian /ˈeɪ·ʒᵊn/ *adj* • *The food production of a billion people depends on the Asian monsoons* (= where and when the rain falls in Asia). • *Asian-Americans are campaigning for greater recognition of the racial discrimination against them.* • *The police force is trying to increase the proportion of recruits from the Asian community.*

A·si·at·ic /£ˌeɪ·ziˈæt·ɪk, $-ˈæṭ-/ *adj specialized* relating to Asia, esp. when considering its physical position, or its plants and animals, rather than social or cultural matters • *Anatolia is the Asiatic region of Turkey* (= the part of Turkey which is in Asia rather than Europe). • LP **World regions**

a·side [TO ONE SIDE] /əˈsaɪd/ *adv* [not gradable] on or to one side • **Stand** *aside, please, and make way for the ambulance.* • *The doctor* **pulled** *aside the curtain and examined the patient.* • *She threw the newspaper aside in disgust.* • *She* **took** *me aside* (= out of hearing distance) *so that no-one would overhear her proposal.* • *(fig.)* **Leave** *the difficult questions aside for now and try to answer the easier ones.* • *(fig.) We'll have to* **put** *aside* (= out of our thoughts) *any demand for a pay increase until the company can afford one.* • *(fig.) Every week I* **put** *aside* (= saved) *a bit of money for a rainy day.* • *I've forgotten my cheque book, so could you* **put** *this book aside* (= keep this book) *for me and I'll come back later on.* • *(esp. Am) I hardly watch any television, aside* **from** (= except for/apart from) *news and current affairs.*

a·side [REMARK] /əˈsaɪd/ *n* [C] a remark made in a low voice which the speaker does not intend everyone to hear, or a remark or story in a speech or text which is not part of the main subject • *a quiet/conspiratorial/whispered aside* • *Responsible journalists know they should not quote the informal asides that politicians give in interviews.* • *The informative asides about rural life make this wine guide rather special.*

as·i·nine /ˈæs·ɪ·naɪn/ *adj* extremely stupid • *an asinine comment*

ask *(obj)* [QUESTION] /£ɑːsk, $æsk/ *v* to put (a question) to (someone), or to request (esp. an answer) from (someone) •

She asked me a question./(fml) She asked a question **of** *me.* [+ two objects] • *May I ask you a favour?/(fml) May I ask a favour* **of** *you?* [+ two objects] • *She asked a question* **about** *Welsh history.* [T] • *She asked me* **about** *Welsh history.* [T] • *She asked* **about** *Welsh history.* [I] • *She asked me* **whether** *I thought Welsh history should be studied more.* [T + obj + *wh-* word] • *I've no idea when the train departs. Ask the guard* **whether** *she knows.* [T + obj + *wh-* word] • *I asked the guard the time of the train's departure.* [+ two objects] • *I asked* **when** *the train would depart.* [+ *wh-* word] • *"What time does the train depart?" I asked.* [+ clause] • *"What are you doing?" he asked me.* [+ obj + clause] • *Should you require any assistance, Dr Howlett, please don't hesitate to ask.* [I] • **Don't ask me** (= I have no idea) *where you've left your spectacles.* • **If you ask me** (= In my opinion), *people should go on a training course before they become parents.* • *How could Jonathan afford to buy a new suit?* **You may well ask**/*(humorous)* **Well may you ask** (= It would be very interesting to know) – *I thought he was broke.* • *You should ask (your accountant)* **for** *some financial advice.* [I/T] • *You should ask your accountant* **to** *give you some financial advice.* [T + obj + *to* infinitive] • *I asked* **to** *see my accountant.* [+ *to* infinitive] • *I'd like to ask your* **advice/opinion** *on an awkward financial problem.* [T] • *Polite children always ask* **permission** *before they leave the dinner table.* [T] • *(fml) The solicitor asked* **that** *her client (should) be allowed to make a telephone call.* [+ *that* clause] • *(fml) We ask* **that** *any faulty goods (should) be returned in their original packaging.* [+ (*that*) clause] • *Our baby-sitter's just moved away, so we're asking* **around** *for* (= asking a lot of people to suggest) *a replacement.* [I] • If you ask **after**/*(Scot Eng)* **for** someone, you ask about how they are, their health, happiness, etc.: *She appreciates it when you ask* **after** *her elderly father.* [I] • If you are **asking for** something, you behave in a manner that is considered likely to cause problems for you: *Drinking alcohol before driving is really asking for* **trouble.** ○ *He's really asking for* **it** (= likely to fail), *if he thinks he can pass his exams without studying.* ○ *I'm not surprised she lost her job – she was asking for* **it.** ○ *It is totally wrong to say that women who dress attractively are asking* **to** *be* (= deserve to be) *assaulted or raped.* [+ *to* infinitive] • Something which is yours **for the asking** can be obtained simply by asking for it: *With three years' experience behind her, the promotion was Kate's for the asking.* • The **asking price** is the amount of money someone wants when they sell something, esp. a building or a piece of land: *The asking price for the flat was £44 500, so Sally made an initial offer of £40 000 for it.* • *"And so, my fellow Americans: ask not what your country can do for you – ask what you can do for your country."* (John F Kennedy, 1961) • LP **Say**

ask *obj* EXPECT /£ɑːsk, $æsk/ *v* [T] to expect or demand (something) • *Jamie's asking* (= expecting to be paid) *£50 000* **for** *his house.* • *Mike really asks too much* **of** *Caroline – he expects her to cook him dinner when she arrives home from work.* • **It's** *asking* **a lot** *when your boss wants you to work weekends as well as evenings.* • *It's the nicest present I've ever had – I* **couldn't** *ask* **for** (= hope to receive) *a better one.* • *You're* **as** *good a friend* **as** *anyone* **could** *ask* **for.** (= You are the best friend anyone could possibly hope to have.) • *"I got rhythm,/I got music,/I got my man/Who could ask for anything more?"* (Ira Gershwin, 1930)

ask *obj* INVITE /£ɑːsk, $æsk/ *v* [T] to request or invite (someone) to go somewhere with you or to come to your home • *Muriel's asked David* **to** *her party so she must like him.* • *"Are you going to Muriel's party, Jo?" "No, I haven't been asked."* • *Ian's asked us* **(over/round) for/to** *dinner next Friday.* • *In fact they've asked us* **to** *stay for the whole weekend.* [+ obj + *to* infinitive] • *Annie's asked Steve* **out** *to the cinema this evening.* • *I'd really like to ask Hamilton* **out** (= invite him on a DATE), *but I'm worried he'd say no.* • *I'd ask you* **in** (= invite you into my home) *for a coffee but I have to get up early for work in the morning.*

a·skance /£əˈskɑːnts, $-ˈskænts/ *adv* **look askance** to consider or think about someone or something with doubt, disapproval or a lack of trust • *Now that the city is a potential war zone, most people will be looking askance* **at** *the idea of a holiday there this year.*

a·skew /əˈskjuː/ *adj* [after v], *adv* not straight or level, or out of balance • *The table stood askew on its uneven legs.* • *The portrait was hanging askew on the wall.* • *I knocked her spectacles askew with my newspaper.* • *She put her lipstick on askew as she rushed to meet her friend.* • *With his shirt crumpled and school tie askew, it was obvious he'd been in a* fight. • *(fig.) Now that we have all the evidence, the jury's original verdict seems utterly askew.* • *(fig.) The balance between the vocal and instrumental parts was slightly askew, otherwise the concert was excellent.*

a·sleep /əˈsliːp/ *adj* [after v] sleeping or not awake • *I'm surprised to see you awake – ten minutes ago you were* **fast/sound** (= completely) *asleep.* • *I was so tired I* **fell** *asleep* (= I went to sleep) *during the lecture.* • Someone who is **(half)** asleep is not paying attention because they are tired or thinking about other things. • If your arm or leg is asleep, it cannot feel anything because it has been in the same position for so long that the blood supply has been cut off.

A/S lev·el /ˌeiˈes/ *n* [C] a British examination of a standard between GCSE and **A level** which allows more subjects to be studied than is possible at A level because less information needs to be learnt for it • *I'm doing* (= studying) *5 A/S levels instead of 3 A levels.* • *Are you doing A/S-level French?* • *I've got 3 A/S levels.*

asp /æsp, ɑːsp/ *n* [C] a small poisonous snake found esp. in N Africa which was a symbol of royalty in ancient Egypt • *When Queen Cleopatra committed suicide she forced an asp to bite her.* • DK

a·spar·a·gus /£əˈspær·ə·gəs, $-ˈsper-/ *n* [U] (a plant with) pale green juicy stems that are cooked and eaten as a vegetable • *asparagus* **spears** • *I thought we'd have asparagus tonight as a special treat.* • PIC **Vegetables**

as·par·ta·me /£ˈæs·pə·teɪm, $-pɚ-/, *trademark* **Nu·tra·Sweet** *n* [U] a very sweet substance which contains very little energy and is used instead of sugar to sweeten drinks and foods for people wanting to stay or become thin

as·pect FEATURE /ˈæs·pekt/ *n* [C] a particular feature of, or way of thinking about, a complicated problem, situation, idea, plan, or activity; a FACET • *You should consider all aspects* **of** *your decision, negative as well as positive.* • *Have you thought about the problem from every aspect?* • *What do you find is the most worrying aspect* **of** *this election result?* • *The most significant aspect* **of** *the election was not the victory of the opposition but the defeat of the ruling Communist party.* • *Lighting is a vitally important aspect* **of** *film-making.*

as·pect DIRECTION /ˈæs·pekt/ *n* [C] the direction in which a building, window, room or sloping field faces, or the view which can be seen because of this direction • *The dining room has a southern aspect which allows us to make the most of the sun.*

as·pect APPEARANCE /ˈæs·pekt/ *n fml* the appearance or VISUAL effect of a place, or the expression on a person's face • *The impressive aspect of this mountain has inspired many artists.* [C] • *With her precise use of language and intimidating aspect, she was a typical traditional schoolmistress.* [U] • *Although she was intimidating* **in** *aspect, she was warm and affectionate beneath the surface.* [U]

as·pect GRAMMAR /ˈæs·pekt/ *n* [U] *specialized* the form of a verb which shows how the meaning of a verb is considered in relation to time, typically expressing whether an action is complete, habitual or continuous

a·sper·i·ty /£əˈsper·ɪ·ti, $-ə·ṭi/ *n fml* (an example of) severity and force, esp. in speech, behaviour or weather • *She will be remembered for her asperity of speech which was both amusing and provocative.* [U] • *"How do you think that ridiculous idea is going to help us?" he demanded with asperity.* [U] • *We must send food aid to help Russia through the asperities of winter.* [C]

as·per·sions /£əˈspɜː·ʒənz, $-ˈspɜːr-, -ʃənz/ *pl n* **cast aspersions on** *fml* see at CAST PUT

as·phalt /£ˈæs·fɔːlt, $-fɑːlt/ *n* [U], *v* [T] (to cover esp. a roof or road with) a black sticky substance mixed with small stones or sand which forms a strong surface when it hardens • *an asphalted road/pitch/court* • KOR

as·phyx·i·ate *(obj)* /əsˈfɪk·si·eɪt/ *v fml* to (cause someone to) be unable to breathe, usually resulting in death; to SUFFOCATE • *The murder inquiry found that the children had been asphyxiated.* [T] • *The baby asphyxiated herself with a plastic bag.* [T] • *He asphyxiated* **on** *his own vomit after taking an overdose of sleeping pills.* [I]

as·phyx·i·a·tion /əsˌfɪk·siˈeɪ·ʃən/ *n* [U] • *Asphyxiation at birth caused irreparable brain damage.* • *Nerve gas causes death* **through** *asphyxiation by preventing messages reaching the muscles which control breathing.*

as·pic /ˈæs·pɪk/ *n* [U] a transparent JELLY made from animal bones which is used in cold savoury foods

as·pi·di·stra /ˌæs·pɪˈdɪs·trə/ *n* [C] a large evergreen plant, usually grown inside, which has purple flowers shaped like bells and long strong leaves • *The aspidistra is often regarded as a symbol of social respectability.* • *"Keep the Aspidistra Flying"* (George Orwell, 1936)

as·pi·rate /£ˈæs·pɪ·rət· $-pə·ət/ *n* [C] the sound represented in English by the letter 'h', in words such as 'house'

as·pi·rate *obj* /ˈæs·pɪ·reɪt/ *v* [T] • *The 'wh' sound in 'where' would usually be aspirated* (=pronounced as an aspirate) *by Scottish speakers.*

as·pi·ra·tion /ˌæs·pɪˈreɪ·ʃᵊn/ *n* [U]

as·pire /£əˈspaɪəʳ, $-ˈspaɪr/ *v* [I always + adv/prep] to have a strong desire or hope to do or have something • *Few people who aspire* **to/after** *fame ever achieve it.*

as·pir·ant /£ˈæs·pɪ·rᵊnt, £əˈspaɪ-, $ˈæs·pə·ᵊnt/ *n* [C] *fml* • *Aspirants to positions of power are prepared to do almost anything to fulfil their ambitions.* • (RUS)

as·pir·a·tion /£ˌæs·pɪˈreɪ·ʃᵊn, $-pəˈeɪ-/ *n* • *His early death caused many of his political aspirations to remain unfulfilled.* [C] • *Jane's aspirations* **to** *help others come from her own misfortune as a child.* [C + *to* infinitive] • *A dynamic economy is founded on the aspiration of entrepreneurs, which is rewarded by profit.* [U] • *"The young have aspirations that never come to pass, the old have reminiscences of what never happened."* (Saki in *Reginald*, 1904)

aspir·ing /£əˈspaɪə·rɪŋ, $-ˈspaɪr·ɪŋ/ *adj* • *Aspiring ballet dancers need to be strong as well as agile.*

as·pi·rin /ˈæs·pɪ·rɪn/ *n pl* **aspirin** or **aspirins** (a pill of) a common drug which reduces pain, esp. HEADACHES, fever and INFLAMMATION (=swelling and soreness) • *an aspirin overdose* • *As aspirin prevents the formation of blood clots, it is also used to treat heart attack and stroke victims.* [U] • *Aspirin should not be* **given** *to young children.* [U] • *I need some aspirin for my headache.* [C/U] • *I always* **take** *a couple of aspirin(s) when I feel a cold starting.* [C]

ass ANIMAL /æs/ *n* [C] a small strong horse, esp. a DONKEY, which is pale grey or brown and has long ears • *The donkey is a domesticated form of the African wild ass which has been used for thousands of years for carrying heavy loads.* • *(Irish Eng infml) Jane's* **not within an ass's roar of** *getting the promotion* (= She's very unlikely to achieve it).

ass PERSON /æs/ *n* [C] a person who does or says stupid things • *a pompous ass* • *Don't be such an ass! Of course you'll pass your English exam.* • *Simon always* **makes a** *complete* **ass of** *himself* (=behaves stupidly and looks ridiculous) *when he's had too much to drink.* • *(saying)* If you say 'the law is an ass', you mean that a law is so stupid that it should be changed or REPEALED (=removed from use).

ass BOTTOM /æs/ *n* [C] *esp. Am slightly taboo slang* ARSE • If someone tells you to **get** your ass somewhere, they want you to go there quickly: *Get your ass in my office immediately!* • If you **get** someone's ass, you find and punish them for something they have done: *Don't worry, the cops'll get that maniac's ass.* • If you **bore the ass off** someone/**bore** someone's **ass off** you bore them a lot: *That guy at the party bored the ass off me!* • If you **work the ass off** someone/**work** someone's **ass off**, you make them work very hard. • If you **work** your **ass off**, you work very hard: *I worked my ass off for that promotion and I still didn't get it.* • If you **talk** your **ass off**, you talk a lot or too much: • If you **talk** someone's **ass off**, you talk to them too much. • If you tell someone to **shove/stick/ram** something **up** their **ass**, you mean they should stop troubling you with it: *She wanted me to work over the weekend, but I told her to shove it up her ass.* • *(fig.) The journey was terrible – there was a sports car* **up** *my* **ass** (= driving too close to me) *all the way from Cambridge.* • *(Br)* If you are **up** someone's **ass** (*Am* **on** someone's **ass**), you are annoying them by refusing to leave them alone: *The police have been up my ass ever since I was done for speeding.* • *(Am taboo)* Ass is sometimes used by men to refer to sexual activity, or to women considered only as sex objects. Some people find this use offensive, whether or not the speaker intends it to be: *I really need some ass – I haven't had any for weeks.* ○ *I've never seen so much gorgeous ass.*

ass a·bout/a·round /æs/ *v adv* [I] *Am for* ARSE ABOUT/AROUND

as·sail *obj* /əˈseɪl/ *v* [T usually passive] *fml* to attack (someone) violently or criticize (someone) strongly • *The victim had been assailed* **with** *repeated blows to the head and body.* • *Although he had been cleared of the murder, he was assailed* **with** *insults and abuse as he left the court.* • To assail also means to cause someone to experience a lot of things that are difficult to deal with: *to be assailed* **by** *doubts/fears/problems/letters/reports* • *After her disappointing exam results, Chris was assailed* **by** *worries about her career.* • *The MP was assailed* **with** *awkward questions* **by** *the interviewer.*

as·sail·ant /əˈseɪ·lənt/ *n* [C] • *The majority of rape and murder victims already know their assailant* (=the person who physically attacked them) *before the crime is committed.* • *Politicians have few friends – their assailants come from every section of society.*

as·sas·sin /əˈsæs·ɪn/ *n* [C] a murderer, esp. one who kills a famous or important person for political reasons or in exchange for money • *John Lennon's assassin was Mark Chapman.* • *She* **hired** *an assassin to eliminate her rival.* • *(fig.) Following Margaret Thatcher's resignation, several of her former colleagues were accused of being her political assassins.* • LP **Crimes and criminals**

as·sas·sin·ate *obj* /əˈsæs·ɪ·neɪt/ *v* [T] • *Scotland Yard's anti-terrorist branch has uncovered a* **plot to** *assassinate the Queen.*

as·sas·sin·a·tion /əˌsæs·ɪˈneɪ·ʃᵊn/ *n* • *an assassination attempt* • *The risk of assassination has been reduced by modern security systems.* [U] • *Following the military coup it was feared that there would be a wave of assassinations of opposition leaders.* [C] • *(fig.)* **Character** *assassinations of rival candidates have become a regular feature of election campaigns.* [C] • *"Assassination is the extreme form of censorship."* (George Bernard Shaw, 1916)

as·sault /£əˈsɒlt, $-ˈsɑːlt/ *n, v* (to make) a sudden violent attack on (someone), esp. a sexual one • *Following a police arrest yesterday, a man has been charged with* **sexual** *assault.* [U] • *The number of* **indecent** *assaults has increased alarmingly over the past year.* [C] • *The Serbs* **launched** *a major* **military** *assault* **on** *a Croatian stronghold yesterday.* [C] • *(fig.) She died heroically during an assault* **on** (=an attempt to climb) *the world's second-highest mountain.* [C] • *(fig.) I'm really going to have to* **make** *an assault* **on** (=make a great effort to deal with) *all this paperwork before my holiday.* [C] • *(fig.) Women's groups have demanded a nationwide assault* **on** *sexism in the workplace.* [C] • *A woman and a man have been convicted of assaulting a police officer following last month's demonstration.* [T] • *The robber also attempted to* **sexually** *assault the woman but was scared off when she shouted for help.* [T] • *(Br)* An **assault course** (*Am* **obstacle course**) is an area of land on which soldiers have to run between and climb over or cross various objects which are designed to test their fitness and strength: *(fig.) Meetings with tax inspectors are often bureaucratic* **assault courses**. • *(law)* Assault is any act which causes someone to think they are in immediate danger of being physically harmed, whether or not injury follows. • *(law)* **Assault and battery** is *(Br)* a threat to attack someone followed either by a violent physical act or by touching which is not violent but is not intended to be friendly, or *(Am)* a violent physical attack on someone. • LP **Crimes and criminals**

as·say *obj* /əˈseɪ, æsˈeɪ/ *v* [T] *specialized* to perform an examination on (a chemical) in order to test its purity

as·sem·blage /əˈsem·blɪdʒ/ *n* a collection of things or a group of people or animals, or the process of joining or putting things together; an ASSEMBLY • *The party-goers were a diverse assemblage of students, artists and aspiring philosophers.* [C] • *A varied assemblage of birds was probing the mud for food.* [C] • *Assemblage of parts from other countries is an important aspect of manufacturing in the United Kingdom.* [U] • *Assemblage artists create three-dimensional works of art by sticking together ordinary objects in unusual ways.* Compare COLLAGE.

as·sem·ble *(obj)* /əˈsem·bl/ *v* to join or bring (parts) together in a single group or place, or (of parts) to come together like this • *When the fire alarm rang we assembled outside the emergency exit.* [I] • *Martha has assembled* (=brought together) *a fascinating collection of doll's houses.* [T] • *Martha assembled* (=joined the separate parts to make) *her latest doll's house very quickly.* [T] • *At the staff meeting, the manager told* **the assembled company** (=everyone there) *that no one would lose their job.*

as·sem·bler /£əˈsem·bləʳ, $-blə/ *n* [C] *specialized* a type of computer program which changes a program written in ASSEMBLY LANGUAGE into a machine language

as·sem·bly GATHERING /əˈsem·bli/ *n* a group of people, esp. one gathered together regularly for a particular purpose, such as government, or more generally, the process of gathering together, or the state of being together • *the United Nations General Assembly* • *British constitutional reform might involve national assemblies* (= parliaments) *for Wales and Scotland and regional assemblies for England.* [C] • *(Am)* An Assembly is one of the two parts of the government that makes laws in many US States: *the New York Assembly* ○ *The Senate and the Assembly put aside political differences to pass the aid package.* • An assembly in a school is a gathering of several classes for a group activity such as singing, a theatrical performance or a film: *All pupils are expected to attend school assembly.* [U] ○ *There's a religious assembly every morning.* [C] • *The* **right of** *free assembly* (= The freedom of people to gather in groups) *is essential in any country claiming to be democratic.* [U] • *If there was a fire, would you know which assembly* **point** *to go to?*

as·sem·bly·man (*pl* **-men**), **as·sem·bly·wo·man** (*pl* **-women**) /ə'sem·bli·mæn, -mən, -ˌwʊm·ən/ *n* [C] *Am* • An assemblywoman or man is someone who belongs to a part of the official law-making body in many US states.

as·sem·bly [JOINING] /ə'sem·bli/ *n* the process of putting together the parts of a machine or structure, or *(specialized)* the structure produced by this process • *Assembly is the factory's most automated stage of production.* [U] • *(specialized) The frame needs to be strong enough to support the engine assembly* (= structure). [C] • An **assembly line** is an arrangement of machines and workers in a factory, in which each has a particular job which has to be completed before the next stage of production is started by another worker: *(fig.) An education system should be more than a mere* **assembly line** *which adds qualifications at various stages.* ○ **Assembly-line** *workers need regular breaks to relieve boredom and keep them alert.*

as·sem·bly lan·guage *n* [U] *specialized* a computer language that is used for writing programs in such a way that they can be changed into a machine language

as·sent /ə'sent/ *n, v fml* (to give) agreement to an idea, plan or request, esp. after thinking about it in detail • *Will you* **give** *your assent* **to** *my proposal?* [U] • *Jane nodded her assent* **to** *my proposal.* [U] • *She assented* **to** *my proposal.* [I] • *Her latest film,* **by general** *assent* (= everyone agrees), *is her best yet.* [U] • *(Br) Before an Act of Parliament can become law, it needs to receive* **Royal** *Assent* (= an official signature) *from the monarch.* [U] • Compare DISSENT.

as·sert *obj* /£ə'sɜːt, $-'sɜːrt/ *v* [T] to state (an opinion), claim (a right) or establish (authority) forcefully • *It is nonsense to assert* **that** *smoking does not damage people's health.* [+ *that* clause] • *Throughout the Cold War, the Allies asserted their* **right** *to move freely between the two Berlins.* • *Teachers should assert greater* **control** *over their pupils.* • If you assert your**self**, you behave in a way which expresses your confidence, importance or power and earns you respect from others: *Women assert themselves more nowadays and do not tolerate unfair treatment from men like they once did.*

as·ser·tion /£ə'sɜː·ʃən, $-'sɜːr-/ *n* [C] • *Despite her assertion* **that** *she was innocent, she was found guilty.* [+ *that* clause] • *These repeated assertions* **that** *AIDS cannot be transmitted heterosexually are false.* [+ *that* clause]

as·sert·ive /£ə'sɜː·tɪv, $-sɜːr·t̬ɪv/ *adj* • Someone who is assertive behaves confidently and is not afraid to say what they want or believe: *If you really want the promotion, you'll have to be more assertive.*

as·sert·ive·ly /£ə'sɜː·tɪv·li, $-'sɜːr·t̬ɪv-/ *adv* • *The pianist played assertively* (= confidently) *throughout the concert.* • *Prince Charles condemned the assertively modernist style of architecture.*

as·sert·ive·ness /£ə'sɜː·tɪv·nəs, $-'sɜːr·t̬ɪv-/ *n* [U] • **Assertiveness training** teaches people how to communicate confidently and obtain what they want without annoying others.

as·sess *(obj)* /ə'ses/ *v* to judge or decide the amount, value, quality or importance of; to EVALUATE • *The insurers will need to assess the flood damage.* [T] • *They assessed the cost of the flood damage* **at** *£1500.* [T] • *Examinations are not the only means of assessing someone's ability.* [T] • *It's too early to assess the long-term consequences of the collapse of the Soviet Union.* [T] • *It's difficult to assess* **how** *they'll react to our suggestions.* [+ *wh-* word]

as·sess·a·ble /ə'ses·ə·bl̩/ *adj* • *(Br)* **Assessable income** is the amount of money which is considered when calculating tax payments.

as·sess·ment /ə'ses·mənt/ *n* • *Both their assessments of production costs were hopelessly inaccurate.* [C] • *Assessment of your symptoms will take a while, I'm afraid.* [U]

as·ses·sor /£ə'ses·əʳ, $-ɚ/ *n* [C] • *The assessor stated that the fire damage was not as severe as the hotel's owner had claimed.* • *(Br)* A **legal** assessor (*Am* **expert witness**) is someone with specialist knowledge who gives advice on a technical subject to a law court.

as·set /'æs·et, -ɪt/ *n* [C] a useful or valuable quality, skill or person, or a part of the usually valuable property of a person or organization which can be used for the payment of debts • *His eyes are his best asset* (= most attractive feature). • *I am confident that I will be a tremendous asset* **to** *your company.* • *A company's assets can consist of cash, investments, buildings, machinery, specialist knowledge or copyright material such as music or computer software.* • **Liquid** assets are money, or things which can easily be changed into money. • *(disapproving)* **Asset-stripping** involves buying an unsuccessful company cheaply, selling its assets separately at a profit, and then sometimes closing it down: *These so-called investors are just* **asset-strippers** *who believe the company is worth more dead than alive.* • Compare **liabilities** at LIABLE.

ass·hole /£'æs·həʊl, $-hoʊl/ *n* [C] *esp. Am slang for* ARSEHOLE

as·si·du·ous /ə'sɪd·ju·əs/ *adj* showing hard work, care, serious interest or attention to detail; DILIGENT • *assiduous investigation/research/efforts* • *an assiduous student/detective* • *The Government has been assiduous* **in** *the fight against inflation.* • *In spite of the rain, the assiduous spectators waited patiently for the delayed start of the game.*

as·si·du·ous·ly /ə'sɪd·ju·ə·sli/ *adv* • *Before apartheid ended, I assiduously avoided buying South African products.* • *She assiduously cultivated an intellectual image to attract intelligent men.*

as·si·du·ous·ness /ə'sɪd·ju·ə·snəs/ *n* [U]

as·sign *obj* [CHOOSE] /ə'saɪn/ *v* [T] to choose or decide on (the person who should do a job), or to give (a particular job or responsibility to someone) • *We've assigned Chris* **to** *the advertising campaign./We've assigned the advertising campaign* **to** *Chris./We've assigned Chris the advertising campaign.* [+ two objects] • *I've been assigned* **to** *interview the candidates.* [+ *(to)* infinitive] • *We'll have to assign a role* **to** *our new trainee.* • If someone is assigned to a place they are sent there to do a job: *Jane has been assigned* **to** *her newspaper's Berlin office.* • If you assign a time for a job or activity, you decide it will be done during that time: *Have you assigned a day* **for** *the interviews yet?* • If you assign a characteristic to something, you state that it possesses it: *The report assigned the* **blame** *for the accident* **to** *inadequate safety regulations.* ○ *We assign tremendous* **importance** *to training in our department.* ○ *Detectives have been unable to assign a motive* **for** *the murder.*

as·sign·ment /ə'saɪn·mənt, -'saɪm-/ *n* • *a foreign/diplomatic/freelance/photo assignment* (= job to be done) [C] • *a tough/taxing/formidable/dangerous assignment* [C] • *The journalist was killed by terrorists whilst* **on assignment** (= doing a job) *in Colombia.* • *Her assignment was* **to** *collect forensic evidence for the investigation.* [C + *to* infinitive] • *I have a lot of reading assignments to complete before the end of term.* [C] • *The assignment* **of** (= decision on who to) *blame for the disaster is impossible without more information.* [U]

as·sign *obj* [COMPUTING] /ə'saɪn/ *v* [T] *specialized* to put (a value) in a particular position in the memory of a computer

as·sign *obj* [GIVE LEGALLY] /ə'saɪn/ *v* [T] to give (property, money or rights) using a legal process • *Jane assigned her business* **to** *her grandchildren.*

as·sig·na·tion /ˌæs·ɪg'neɪ·ʃən/ *n* [C] *humorous or fml* a meeting, esp. a secret or forbidden one between lovers

as·si·mi·late *(obj)* /ə'sɪm·ɪ·leɪt/ *v* to take in, fit into, or become similar (to) • *The European Union should remain flexible enough to assimilate more countries quickly.* [T] • *You shouldn't expect immigrants to assimilate* **into** *an alien culture immediately.* [I] • *You'll need to assimilate* (= learn and understand) *all Einstein's work before doing this research.* [T] • *Contraceptive advice should be given in a way that can be easily assimilated by the public.* [T] • *By assimilating the styles of Van Gogh and Dufy she has produced some highly original paintings.* [T]

as·si·mi·la·tion /ə,sɪm·ɪ'leɪ·ʃᵊn/ *n* [U] • *The assimilation of ethnic Germans in the US was accelerated by the two world wars.*

as·si·mil·a·ble /ə'sɪm·ɪ·lə·bl/ *adj* • *A textbook needs to be assimilable* (= understandable) *to sell a lot of copies.*

as·sist *(obj)* /ə'sɪst/ *v fml* to help • *We assisted the firefighters* **in** *extinguishing the blaze.* [T] • *You will be expected to assist (the editor)* **with** *the selection of illustrations for the dictionary.* [I] • *(Br)* If someone is **assisting the police with/in their inquiries** it usually means they have been taken to the police station for official questioning about a crime. • Ⓔ Ⓟ

as·sist·ance /ə'sɪs·tᵊnts/ *n* [U] • *The company needs more* **financial** *assistance from the Government.* • *A £1 billion investment would be* **of** *considerable assistance to the railways.* • *"Can I be of any assistance, madam?" "Yes, do you sell these shoes in brown?"* • *Teachers can't* **give** *pupils any assistance in exams.* • If someone **comes to** your **assistance**, they help you. • Ⓔ

as·sist·ant /ə'sɪs·tᵊnt/ *n* [C] • An assistant helps someone else to do a job: *an assistant editor/manager/camera operator/gardener* • *(Br)* An assistant in a shop sells goods to customers and gives advice about the goods sold in the shop: *I'll just ask that* **sales** *assistant where the kitchenware department is.* • Ⓔ Ⓟ

as·siz·es /ə'saɪ·zɪz/ *pl n* (in Wales and England until 1971) one or more of the meetings of the most important court in each COUNTY (= region) which were usually held four times a year by a travelling judge

assn *n* [C] *abbreviation for* **association**, see at ASSOCIATE

as·soc *abbreviation for* ASSOCIATED, association or associate

as·so·ci·ate *(obj)* /£ə'səʊ·si·eɪt, $-'soʊ-/ *v* to join or connect (people, things or ideas) together, or to be connected (with a person, organization or idea) • *I don't want my children associating* **with** *drug-addicts and alcoholics.* [I] • *The terrorists' victim was not associated* **with** *any paramilitary group.* [T] • *Why do men associate enjoying themselves* **with** *getting drunk?* [+ v-*ing*] • *Why do men associate enjoyment* **with** *drunkenness?* [T] • *I'd rather not associate my***self with** *extremist political statements.* [T]

as·so·ci·ate /£ə'səʊ·si·ət, $-'soʊ-/ *n, adj* [not gradable] • An associate is someone who is closely connected to another person as a companion, friend or business partner: *A close associate of the author denied reports that she had cancer.* [C] • *Tina's party was very boring – it was full of her business associates.* [C] • Associate members of an organization are not full members of it. • In film or theatre, an associate director has a rank slightly lower than a DIRECTOR. • *(Am)* An **associate professor** is a high-ranking teacher in a college or university who has a lower rank than a PROFESSOR. • *(Am)* An **associate's degree** is the qualification given to a student by a **junior college** on successful completion of two years of study. • *(Am)* An Associate is someone who holds an associate's degree: *an associate of arts.* [C]

as·so·ci·a·tion /£ə,səʊ·si'eɪ·ʃᵊn, $-,soʊ/ *n* • An association is a group of people who are united in a single organization for a particular purpose: *the Association for the Advancement of Science* [C] • *The British Medical Association is/are campaigning for a complete ban on tobacco advertising.* [C + sing/pl v] • *If you continue your association* (= romantic involvement) **with** *that man, I'll stop paying your college fees.* [U] • *Our association* **with** (= involvement in) *the feminist movement began at university.* [U] • *Many cinema films are made* **in** *association* **with** *television companies nowadays.* [U] • *French bread has had positive associations for me* (= has made me think of pleasant things) *ever since I went on holiday to France.* [C] • *The association of ideas in original ways is the key to creativity.* [U] • *(Br fml)* **Association football** is another name for SOCCER.

as·so·nance /'æs·ᵊn·ᵊnts/ *n* [U] the repeated use, esp. in poetry, of a vowel in several words or parts of a word • *Examples of assonance include "back" and "cat", and "hit" and "heart".* • Compare ALLITERATION.

as·sort·ed [MIXED] /£ə'sɔː·tɪd, $-'sɔːr·ţɪd/ *adj* consisting of various types mixed together • *a case of assorted wines*

as·sort·ment /£ə'sɔːt·mənt, $-'sɔːrt-/ *n* [C usually sing] • *The police discovered a rich assortment* **of** *guns and explosives at the terrorist's house.* • *An unlikely/motley assortment* **of** *rock stars and politicians attended the charity concert.*

as·sort·ed [MATCHED] /£ə'sɔː·tɪd, $-'sɔːr·ţɪd/ *adj* matched or suited in personality • *The party guests were so* **ill-assorted** *that it was hardly surprising nobody would talk to each other.*

asst *adj abbreviation for* **assistant**, see at ASSIST

as·suage *obj* /ə'sweɪdʒ/ *v* [T] *fml* to reduce the strength of (a worry or an unpleasant emotion), or to satisfy (a desire, thirst or hunger) • *to assuage fears/grievances/concerns/guilt/anger* • *His grief at the premature death of his wife was assuaged by his strong religious beliefs.* • *Not even his promotion to managing director assuaged his desire for power.*

as·sume *obj* [ACCEPT] /£ə'sjuːm, $-'suːm/ *v* [T] to accept (something) to be true without question or proof • *We can't assume the suspects* **to** *be guilty simply because they've decided to remain silent.* [+ obj + *to* infinitive] • *We mustn't assume the suspects' guilt.* • *I assumed* **(that)** *you knew each other because you went to the same school.* [+ *(that)* clause] • **Let's** *assume* **(that)** *there's an election this month. What is the result likely to be, given the latest opinion polls?* [+ *(that)* clause]

as·sum·ing (that) /£ə'sjuː·mɪŋ, $-'suː-/ *conjunction* • *Even assuming (that) smokers do see the health warnings, I doubt they'll take any notice.*

as·sump·tion /ə'sʌmp·ʃᵊn/ *n* • *I find your assumptions* **about** *never-ending violence and terrorism depressing.* [C] • **On** *the assumption* **that** *the increased production targets can be reached, I've ordered extra raw materials.* [C + *that* clause] • *This so-called proof is mere assumption based on circumstantial evidence.* [U]

as·sume *obj* [PRETEND] /£ə'sjuːm, $-'suːm/ *v* [T] to pretend to have (a different name) or be someone you are not, or to express (a feeling) falsely • *Smith used the assumed name* (= false name) *of Jones when making his fraudulent social security claims.* • *To help her fit in with the islanders, Joan assumed a local Greek name.* • *During the investigation, two detectives assumed the identities of antiques dealers.* • *James assumed a look of indifference when he heard Anna was getting married, but we all knew he was upset.*

as·sume *obj* [TAKE CONTROL] /£ə'sjuːm, $-'suːm/ *v* [T] to take or claim (responsibility or control), sometimes without the right to do so, or to begin to possess (a characteristic) • *The new President assumes office at midnight tonight.* • *The terrorists assumed control of the plane and forced it to land in the desert.* • *The issue of starvation could assume frightening political proportions* (= could become a very big political problem).

as·sump·tion /ə'sʌmp·ʃᵊn/ *n* [U] • *The revolutionaries' assumption of power took the army by surprise.*

as·sure *obj* [SAY WITH CERTAINTY] /£ə'ʃɔːʳ, $-'ʃɜːr/ *v* [T] to tell something to (someone) confidently or firmly, or to cause (someone) to feel certain by removing doubt • *The unions assured the new owners* **of** *the workers' loyalty to the company.* • *"Don't worry, your car will be ready tomorrow," the mechanic assured him.* [+ obj + clause] • *She assured him* **(that)** *the car would be ready the next day.* [+ obj + *(that)* clause] • *The public can* **rest** *assured* (= feel confident) *that detectives are doing everything possible to find the murderer.*

as·sur·ance /£ə'ʃɔː·rənts, $-'ʃɜːr·ᵊnts/ *n* [U] • Assurance is a feeling of confidence and certainty in your abilities: *She sang* **with** *assurance* (= confidently) *throughout the performance.* ○ *Dr Green didn't have the assurance* **to** *lecture interestingly to so many students.* [+ *to* infinitive]

as·sured /£ə'ʃɔːd, $-'ʃɜːrd/, **self–as·sured** *adj* • Someone who is (self-)assured is very confident about their ability to do something: *She's impressive on TV because her style of presentation is very assured.*

as·sur·ed·ly /£ə'ʃɔː·rɪd·li, $-'ʃɜːr·ɪd-/ *adv* • *After a disappointing first set, Becker played assuredly* (= confidently) *and went on to win the match.*

as·sure *obj* [PROMISE] /£ə'ʃɔːʳ, $-'ʃɜːr/ *v* [T] to promise something to (someone), or to state publicly that something will certainly be done • *We would like to assure our customers* **of** *the best possible service.* • *The Prime Minister assured the electorate* **(that)** *taxes would not be increased after the election.* [+ obj + *(that)* clause]

as·sur·ance /£ə'ʃɔː·rənts, $-'ʃɜːr·ᵊnts/ *n* [C] • *Although he gave many assurances* **of** *his interest in our company, we never heard from him again.* • *Despite the Government's repeated assurances* **to** *the contrary, taxation has risen over the past decade.* • *She gave me her assurance* **that** *she would post the cheque immediately.* [+ *(that)* clause]

as·sure *obj* [MAKE CERTAIN] /£ə'ʃɔːʳ, $-'ʃɜːr/ *v* [T] to cause (something) to be certain • *The play's popularity has been* *assured by the critics' rave reviews.* • *You should reserve early to assure yourselves* **of** (= to be certain of obtaining) *the best tickets.*

as·sured /£ə'ʃɔːd, $-'ʃɜːrd/ *adj* • *Now that the finance has been secured, the production of the film is assured.*

as·sur·ed·ly /£ə'ʃɔː·rɪd·li, $-'ʃɜːr·ɪd-/ *adv* • *These problems might not be solved by money alone, but they will assuredly* (= certainly) *not be solved without it.*

as·sure *obj* PROTECT /£ə'ʃɔːʳ, $-'ʃɜːr/ *v* [T] *Br* (of an organization) to promise to pay a sum of money to a person (or their family) when a particular event happens, esp. their death, in return for small regular payments • *(fml) A person who either holds or gains from a life assurance policy is called* **the assured**.

as·sur·ance /£ə'ʃɔː·rᵊnts, $-'ʃɜːr·ᵊnts/ *n* [U] *Br* • Assurance is a type of INSURANCE against events, such as death, which will certainly happen, not ones such as illness, THEFT or fire, which might happen.

as·ter·isk /£'æs·tᵊr·ɪsk, $-tɚ-/ *n, v* (to mark with) a symbol shaped like a star which is used to refer readers to a note at the bottom of a page of text, or to show that a letter is missing from a word • *Sometimes taboo words are written with asterisks to avoid causing offence, such as sh*t, b*ll*cks.* [C] • *I have asterisked the books that are essential reading for the course.* [T]

ASTERISK [*]

One or more asterisks or stars can be used:

- **to refer to extra information given in a note, often at the bottom of the page**

> Check that the machine is set to the correct voltage* (110/240 volts.) If necessary, change the voltage setting by turning the control until the
>
> * Voltage setting is given on the red label on the back of the machine.

- **in forms, to give instructions**

> I wish to pay by cash / cheque / Visa / other *
>
> * Delete as appropriate (= cross out what you do not want)

- **to mark certain items, for example in lists and timetables**

> **Colour televisions: models SA1000*, SA1050, SA1200, SX750***
>
> *(Items marked * are available only in the UK)*

- **to avoid writing taboo words (a dash can be used instead)**

  **** *off!*

a·stern /£ə'stɜːn, $-'stɜːrn/ *adv, adj* [not gradable] behind a ship, or going backwards when in a ship • *The skipper went astern to gaze at the island she had just left.* • *Halfway through the race, his boat was 30km astern* (**of** *the leader).* • *Full steam astern!* (= Make the engine go backwards as fast as possible!)

as·ter·oid /£'æs·tᵊr·ɔɪd, $-tə·rɔɪd/, **plan·et·oid** /£'plæn·ə·tɔɪd, $-t̬ɔɪd/, *old use* **mi·nor plan·et** *n* [C] one of many rocky objects, varying in width from over 900 kilometres to less than one kilometre, which circle the sun. Most are situated between the ORBITS (= paths around the sun) of the planets Mars and Jupiter • *Asteroids are also known as 'minor planets'.*

asth·ma /'æs·mə/ *n* [U] a chest disease that lasts a long time, often caused by an ALLERGIC reaction, which makes breathing difficult by causing the air passages to become narrow or blocked • *an asthma sufferer* • *I think he's having an asthma* **attack**.

asth·ma·tic /£æs'mæt·ɪk, $-'mæt̬-/ *adj, n* • *an asthmatic attack/wheeze* • *She's been (an) asthmatic since her childhood.*

asth·ma·ti·cally /£æs'mæt·ɪ·kli, $-'mæt̬-/ *adv* • *(fig.) The rusty old car wheezed asthmatically into life.*

a·stig·ma·ti·sm /£ə'stɪg·mə·tɪ·zᵊm, $-t̬ɪ-/ *n* [U] a fault in the LENS of the eye which reduces the quality of sight, esp. a fault which stops the eye from FOCUSSING

as·tig·mat·ic /£ˌæs·tɪg'mæt·ɪk, $-'mæt̬-/ *adj* [not gradable], *n* [C]

a·stir /£ə'stɜːʳ, $-'stɜːr/ *adj* [after v] *literary or dated* out of bed and moving around, or in an excited state • *She was rarely astir later than 7 o'clock.* • *After the explosion, the hospital was astir* **with** *over-worked nurses and doctors.*

a·ston·ish *obj* /£ə'stɒn·ɪʃ, $-'stɑː·nɪʃ/ *v* [T] to surprise very much, sometimes causing lack of belief; to AMAZE • *I was astonished* **by** *the news of the divorce – they'd seemed so happy together.* • *It astonishes me* **that** *they're getting divorced.* [T + obj + *that* clause]

a·ston·ished /£ə'stɒn·ɪʃt, $-'stɑː·nɪʃt/ *adj* • *We were astonished* **to** *hear you'd failed all your exams.* [+ *to* infinitive] • *They looked astonished when I announced I was already pregnant again.* • *The doctors were astonished* **at** *the speed of her recovery.*

a·ston·ish·ing /£ə'stɒn·ɪ·ʃɪŋ, $-'stɑː·nɪ-/ *adj* • *Her first novel enjoyed an astonishing success.* • *It's astonishing* **to** *think that only a few years ago Communism dominated eastern Europe.* [+ *to* infinitive]

a·ston·ish·ing·ly /£ə'stɒn·ɪ·ʃɪŋ·li, $-'stɑː·nɪ-/ *adv* • *Astonishingly (enough), I've never visited King's College Chapel, even though I've always lived in Cambridge.* • *She solved the puzzle astonishingly quickly.* • *Prices rose astonishingly in Germany during the early 1920s.*

a·ston·ish·ment /£ə'stɒn·ɪʃ·mənt, $-'stɑː·nɪʃ-/ *n* [U] • *Her decision to resign was greeted* **with** *(gasps of) astonishment.* • **To the** *astonishment* **of** *her colleagues, she resigned.* • **To** *their astonishment, she resigned.* • *I laughed* **in** *astonishment when I heard the news.* • *Everyone* **expressed** *astonishment* **at** *his sudden death.*

a·stound *(obj)* /ə'staʊnd/ *v* to surprise (someone) so much that it shocks them, esp. with (news of) something completely unexpected • **It** *astounds me* **that** *anyone could ever consider declaring war.* [T + obj + *that* clause] • *The enormous changes in share prices continue to astound (the experts).* [I/T]

a·stound·ed /ə'staʊn·dɪd/ *adj* • *Psychologists were astounded* **to** *discover that volunteers in the experiment were often willing to inflict pain on others if they were told to.* [+ *to* infinitive]

a·stound·ing /ə'staʊn·dɪŋ/ *adj* • *an astounding fact/decision/revelation* • *an astounding* (= very great) *victory/achievement/success* • *I find it astounding* **that** *you could ever think of doing anything so terrible.* [+ *that* clause]

a·stound·ing·ly /ə'staʊn·dɪŋ·li/ *adv* • *Astoundingly, nobody noticed that the gold had been stolen until a year after the robbery.* • *They are an astoundingly* (= extremely) *attractive and successful couple.*

as·tra·khan /'æs·trə·kæn/ *n* [U] (a type of cloth which looks like) the skin of very young sheep from Astrakhan in S Russia which is covered in usually grey or black wool that is tightly curled and looks like fur • *Imitation astrakhan cloth is made from ordinary wool and mohair.* • *This hat is made of astrakhan.*

as·tral /'æs·trəl/ *adj* [before n; not gradable] relating to unknown forces and spirits; SUPERNATURAL • The **astral plane** is thought by some people to be where a person's spirit goes between dying and entering the spirit world. • An **astral projection** is an experience in which a person has the feeling that their **astral body** (= spiritual being) is temporarily separated from their physical body.

a·stray /ə'streɪ/ *adv* away from the correct path or way of doing something • *I'm sorry you haven't received my letter – it must have* **gone** *astray in the post.* • *After some brilliant exam results, he* **went** *astray, and now he's working as a cleaner.* • *I was* **led** *astray by an out-of-date map.* • *Parents always worry about their children being* **led** *astray by unsuitable friends.*

a·stride /ə'straɪd/ *adv, prep* (with one leg or part) on either side (of), or with legs wide apart • *She sat proudly astride her new motorbike.* • *(fig.) She sat astride a worldwide business empire.* • *East and West Berliners celebrated astride* (= on both sides of) *the newly redundant Wall.* • *Brandenburg lies astride the River Havel.* • *Michael Jackson posed provocatively with his legs astride.* • *"They give birth astride of a grave, the light gleams an instant, then it's night once more."* (Samuel Beckett, 1955)

a·strin·gent SEVERE /ə'strɪn·dʒᵊnt/ *adj* severe or bitter; HARSH • *astringent conversation/criticism/attacks/wit*

a·strin·gent·ly /ə'strɪn·dʒᵊnt·li/ *adv*

a·strin·gen·cy /ə'strɪn·dʒᵊnt·si/ *n* [U]

a·strin·gent MEDICINE /ə'strɪn·dʒᵊnt/ *adj, n* (a drug or cream) causing the skin or other tissue to tighten so that the flow of blood or other liquids stops • *You can use (an) astringent to make your skin less oily.* [C/U]

as·tro– /£'æs·trəʊ-, $-troʊ-/ *combining form* relating to space, the planets, stars or other objects in space, or to a structure in the shape of a star • *Astrobiology is concerned with finding and studying life on other planets.* • *Astrocytes are star-shaped cells in the tissue which surrounds nerve cells.*

a·strol·o·gy /£ə'strɒl·ə·dʒi, $-'strɑː·lə-/ *n* [U] the study of the movements and relative positions of the sun, moon, planets and stars, and the skill of describing the expected effect that these are believed to have on the character and behaviour of humans

a·strol·og·er /£ə'strɒl·ə·dʒəʳ, $-'strɑː·lə·dʒɚ/ *n* [C]

as·tro·log·ic·al /£ˌæs·trə'lɒdʒ·ɪ·kəl, $-'lɑː·dʒɪ-/ *adj* [not gradable] • *an astrological chart/forecast*

as·tro·naut /£'æs·trə·nɔːt, $-nɑːt/ *n* [C] a person who has been trained for travelling in spacecraft • See also COSMONAUT.

as·tro·naut·ics /£ˌæs·trəʊ'nɔː·tɪks, $-trə'nɑː·t̬ɪks/ *n* [U] • Astronautics is the TECHNOLOGY and science of travelling in space.

as·tro·nom·ic·al LARGE /£ˌæs·trə'nɒm·ɪ·kəl, $-'nɑː·mɪ-/, **as·tro·nom·ic** *adj* extremely large; IMMENSE • *an astronomical rent/bill/price/charge* • *The damage caused by the hurricane is astronomical.* • *AIDS is an astronomical problem which is immensely difficult to solve.*

as·tro·nom·i·cally /£ˌæs·trə'nɒm·ɪ·kli, $-'nɑː·mɪ-/ *adv* • *Oil prices have risen astronomically since the early 70s.* • *Income levels in Japan and India are astronomically different.*

as·tro·nom·ic·al SCIENTIFIC /£ˌæs·trə'nɒm·ɪ·kəl, $-'nɑː·mɪ-/ *adj* [before n; not gradable] connected with ASTRONOMY • *the British Astronomical Association* • *the Royal Astronomical Society* • *astronomical observations/instruments/projects*

a·stron·o·my /£ə'strɒn·ə·mi, $-'strɑː·nə-/ *n* [U] the scientific study of the universe as a whole and of objects which exist naturally in space, such as the moon, the sun, planets and stars

a·stron·om·er /£ə'strɒn·ə·məʳ, $-'strɑː·nə·mɚ/ *n* [C]

as·tro·phy·sics /£ˌæs·trəʊ'fɪz·ɪks, $-troʊ-/ *n* [U] the type of ASTRONOMY which uses physical laws and ideas to explain the behaviour of the stars and other objects in space

as·tro·phy·si·cal /£ˌæs·trəʊ'fɪz·ɪ·kəl, $-troʊ-/ *adj* [not gradable]

as·tro·phy·si·cist /£ˌæs·trəʊ'fɪz·ɪ·sɪst, $-troʊ-/ *n* [C] • *One of the greatest successes of astrophysicists has been their explanation of how energy is produced inside stars.*

A·stro·turf /£'æs·trəʊ·tɜːf, $-troʊ·tɜːrf/ *n* [U] *trademark* a type of artificial grass surface, used esp. for sports grounds

a·stute /£ə'stjuːt, $-'stuːt/ *adj* clever and quick to see how to take advantage of a situation; SHREWD • *an astute investor/businesswoman* • *Chris is an astute judge of ability.* • *His astute handling of this difficult situation saved her from disaster.* • *Her astute political sense stopped her from exploiting her opponent's misfortune.* • *Had he been more astute he might have stayed in power longer.*

a·stute·ly /£ə'stjuːt·li, $-'stuːt-/ *adv*

a·stute·ness /£ə'stjuːt·nəs, $-'stuːt-/ *n* [U]

a·sun·der /£ə'sʌn·dəʳ, $-dɚ/ *adv fml or literary* into forcefully separated pieces; apart • *to tear/rip/rend/split/put/blow asunder* • *The huts were blown asunder by the hurricane.* • *Their lives were torn asunder by the untimely deaths of their children.* • *"Those whom God hath joined together let no man put asunder."* (Book of Common Prayer, 1662)

a·sy·lum PROTECTION /ə'saɪ·ləm/ *n* [U] protection or safety, esp. that given by a government to foreigners who have been forced to leave their own countries for political reasons • *an asylum* **seeker** • *to* **seek/apply for/grant political** *asylum* • *Having sought asylum in the West for many years, the refugees were eventually granted it.* • Ⓔ

a·sy·lum HOSPITAL /ə'saɪ·ləm/ *n* [C] *dated* a mental hospital, or any other INSTITUTION giving shelter and other help to poor or suffering people • *Victorian asylums are closing because they cannot provide adequate standards of care.* • *Vincent Van Gogh painted 'Starry Night' during his year in a* **lunatic** *asylum.* • *"The world is becoming like a lunatic asylum run by lunatics."* (David Lloyd George in *The Observer* newspaper, 8 Jan 1933) • Ⓔ

a·sym·met·ric /ˌeɪ·sɪ'met·rɪk/, **a·sym·met·ric·al** /ˌeɪ·sɪ'met·rɪ·kəl/ *adj* with two halves, sides or parts which are not exactly the same in shape and size; without SYMMETRY • *Sugars and amino-acids have asymmetric molecules.* • *(fig.) Britain's trade with Japan is asymmetric* (=not equal) *because Britain imports far more than it exports.*

a·sym·met·ric·ally /ˌeɪ·sɪ'met·rɪ·kli/ *adv*

a·sym·me·try /eɪ'sɪm·ə·tri/ *n* • *Asymmetry in language learning means that learners tend to understand more than they can say.* [U] • *Although humans appear to be symmetric, there are a surprising number of asymmetries in their bodies.* [C]

at PLACE /æt/ *prep* used to show an exact position or particular place • *The next checkpoint is at map reference point 619 403.* • *We'll meet you at the entrance/the ticket office/the cinema.* • *I thought that bit at the beginning/end of the film was brilliant.* • *She's the one in pink standing at the bar/sitting at the table in the corner.* • *Have you seen the old man who lives at number 12?* • *She was standing at the top of the stairs when she fell.* • *She can hit the target every time at (a distance of) 50 metres* (=from 50 metres away). • *The dog came and lay down at* (=next to) *my feet.* • *There's someone at the door* (=someone is outside the door and wants to come in). • *We spent the afternoon at the museum/the beach/a football match* (= in that particular place). • *My number at work/home/the office/the bank* (=in that particular place) *is 215 4949.* • *I enjoyed my three years at university* (=in that particular place) *so much.* • *I'd love to stay at* **home** (=in that particular place) *and look after the kids, but I have to go out to work because we need the money.* • *Ali's at* (=eating) *lunch at the moment, can I take a message?*

at TIME /æt/ *prep* used to show an exact or a particular time • *The meeting is at 2.30 this afternoon.* • *What are you doing at Christmas this year?* • *I'm free at lunchtime – shall we meet then?* • *In theory, women can still have children at (the age of) 50.* • *I'm afraid the bells ring at regular intervals through the day.* • *At no* **time/point/stage** *did the company do anything illegal.* • *I'm busy at* **the moment**/*at* **present** (=now) – *can you call back later?* • *It's a shame I wasn't here to meet you – I was in London at* **the time** (=then). • *I'm sorry but I'm too busy to help you now – I can only do one thing* **at a time** (=during any one time or moment).

at DIRECTION /æt/ *prep* towards; in the direction of • *They smiled/waved/pointed/stared at us as we drove by.* • *As he lifted the gun, the policemen rushed/ran at him.* • *She aimed at the target, but missed.* • *I wish the baby would stop pulling at my hair.* • *"Look at me! Look at me!" called the little girl.* • *He can't be a good teacher if he's always shouting at the children.* • *What are you hinting at* (=about)*? Just tell me.* • *At* (=Making) *a rough guess, I'd say the job will take three or four weeks.*

at CAUSE /æt/ *prep* used to show the cause of something, esp. a feeling • *I was so happy/excited/surprised/depressed at the news.* • *Many people in the audience were crying at the film.* • *Why does nobody ever laugh at my jokes?* • *(infml) Don't be angry at her – she can't help being slow.* • *I'm here at your request.* • *It was the third time he'd got angry with her over nothing, and at* **that** *she just walked out.*

at CONDITION /æt/ *prep* used to show a state, condition or continuous activity • *The President announced that the country was at war.* • *I love watching the animals at play.* • *The strike means that no work is being done – everything is at a standstill* (=has stopped).

at AMOUNT /æt/ *prep* used to show a price, temperature, rate, speed, etc. • *I'm not going to buy those shoes at $150!* • *They're selling cornflakes at 50p off in the supermarket this week.* • *Inflation is running at 5%.* • *He denied driving at 120 mph/dangerous speeds.* • This meaning of 'at' can be shown using the sign @.

at JUDGMENT /æt/ *prep* used to show the activity in which someone's ability is being judged • *He's very good at getting on with people.* • *I'm terrible at all sports/at games.* • *It's too expensive, and probably out-of-date* **at that** (=as well).

at THE MOST /æt/ *prep* used before a superlative • *I'm afraid we can only pay you £5 an hour at (the) most.* • *At worst, we will only lose two days because of the strike.* • *My car was damaged in an accident yesterday, but at least no one was hurt.* • *Even playing at his best, he couldn't beat his Spanish opponent.*

at all *adv* (used to make negatives and questions stronger) in any way or of any type • *I'm* **not** *at all in a hurry – please don't rush.* • *I haven***'t** *been at all well recently.* • *He's had no food at all.* • *I'm afraid I've got* **nothing** *at all to say/* **nothing** *to say at all.* • *There was* **nobody** *at home at all when I called.* • *Is there any question/doubt/uncertainty at all about the way she died?* • *Why bother getting up at all when you don't have a job to go to?*

at·a·vi·stic /£ˌæt·ə'vɪs·tɪk, $ˌæṱ-/ *adj fml or specialized* (of behaviour) happening because of a very old natural and basic habit from the distant past, not because of a conscious decision or present need or usefulness • *an atavistic fear of the dark*

at·a·vi·sm /£'æt·ə·vɪ·zᵊm, $'æṱ-/ *n* [U]

ate /et, eɪt/ *past simple of* EAT

a·the·ist /'eɪ·θi·ɪst/ *n* [C] someone who believes that God or gods do not exist • *She has been a confirmed/proclaimed atheist for many years.* • Compare AGNOSTIC.

a·the·ist /'eɪ·θi·ɪst/, **a·the·ist·ic** /ˌeɪ·θi'ɪs·tɪk/ *adj* • *In 1967 Albania proclaimed itself the world's first atheist state.*

a·the·i·sm /'eɪ·θi·ɪ·zᵊm/ *n* [U]

ath·lete /'æθ·liːt/ *n* [C] a person who is very good at sports, esp. one who enters sports competitions, and who is healthy and strong • *He became a professional athlete at the age of 16.* • *She has the build of an athlete.* • *(fig. humorous) She has the reputation of being a real* **sexual** *athlete* (= someone who has sex in an energetic way or with many different people). • **Athlete's foot** is a disease in which the skin between the toes cracks and feels uncomfortable.

ath·let·ic /£æθ'let·ɪk, $-'leṱ-/ *adj* • *This college has a long tradition of athletic* (= connected with the sports of running, jumping, throwing, etc.) *excellence.* • *Are you feeling athletic* (= strong) *– could you carry this table?* • *She has a wonderfully athletic* (= strong and in good physical condition) *body.* • **Athletic support** is *fml for* JOCKSTRAP.

ath·let·ic·i·sm /£æθ'let·ɪ·sɪ·zᵊm, $-'leṱ-/ *n* [U] • *The team's superb athleticism* (= skill in running, jumping, throwing, etc.) *compensated for their lack of international experience.*

ath·let·ics /£æθ'let·ɪks, $-'leṱ-/ *n* [U] • Athletics (*Am* **track and field**) is the general name for a particular group of competitive sports, including running, jumping and throwing: *an athletics team/club/meeting* ○ *When I was at school I was always hopeless at athletics.* • LP **Sports**

–a·tion /-'eɪ·ʃᵊn/ *combining form* -ION ACTION • LP **Combining forms**

a·ti·shoo *Br* /ə'tɪʃ·uː/, **atch·oo**, *Am* **ah·choo** *exclamation* used, esp. in writing, to represent the sound of a sneeze

–a·tive /£-ə·tɪv, $-ə·ṱɪv/ *combining form* -IVE

at·las /'æt·ləs/ *n* [C] a book containing maps • *a road atlas* • *an atlas of the world* • An atlas can also be a book containing maps and diagrams showing where particular things are found: *a wine atlas* ○ *an atlas of British plants*

ATM /ˌeɪ·tiː'em/ *n* [C] *Am abbreviation for* automated teller machine, see at CASH

at·mos·phere AIR /£'æt·mə·sfɪəʳ, $-sfɪr/ *n* the mixture of gases that surrounds some planets, such as the Earth; the air • *The atmospheres of Mars and the Earth are very different.* [C] • If you say **the** atmosphere, you are usually referring to that of the Earth: *These factories are releasing toxic gases into the atmosphere.* [U] • The atmosphere in a place is the air that you breathe in it: *The atmosphere in the room was so stuffy I could hardly breathe.* [U]

at·mos·pher·ic /ˌæt·məs'fer·ɪk/ *adj* [not gradable] • *Plants are the main source of atmospheric oxygen.* • *If atmospheric* **conditions** *are right, it may be possible to see this group of stars tonight.* • *When divers have been deep underwater, they should be careful not to return to normal atmospheric* **pressure** *too quickly.*

at·mos·pher·ics /ˌæt·məs'fer·ɪks/ *pl n specialized* • Atmospherics are unusual conditions in the atmosphere, such as those caused by lightning, or the continuous crackling noise produced by a radio during these conditions.

at·mos·phere CHARACTER /£'æt·məs·fɪəʳ, $-fɪr/ *n* [U] the character or feeling or mood of a place or situation • *The atmosphere at home has been really tense since my brother had that big row with Dad.* • *There's a very friendly atmosphere in our office.* • *There has been* **an** *atmosphere* **of** *gloom in the factory since it was announced that it would be closing.* • *(approving)* If a place has atmosphere, it has a feeling of being pleasant and interesting or exciting: *The restaurant we went to last night had a lot of atmosphere, but the food wasn't very good.* ○ *He put on some soft music and turned the lights down in order to give the room a bit more atmosphere.*

at·mos·pher·ic /ˌæt·məs'fer·ɪk/ *adj approving* • If you describe something as atmospheric, you mean that it has a pleasant and often mysterious character: *an atmospheric poem/song* ○ *The stage lighting was highly atmospheric.*

at·oll /£'æt·ɒl, $-ɑːl/ *n* [C] a ring-shaped island formed of CORAL (= rock-like natural substance) which surrounds a LAGOON (= area of sea water) • *the Bikini atoll*

at·om /£'æt·əm, $'æṱ-/ *n* [C] the smallest unit of any chemical element, consisting of a positive NUCLEUS surrounded by negative ELECTRONS. Atoms can combine to form a MOLECULE. • *A molecule of carbon dioxide (CO_2) has one carbon atom and two oxygen atoms.* • *(fig.) He hasn't an atom* (= not even the smallest bit) **of** *sense, that boy.* • *(slightly dated)* An **atom bomb** (also **atomic bomb**) is a bomb that uses the explosive power that results from breaking the atom: *Over 200 000 Japanese people were killed or wounded when two atom bombs were dropped on Hiroshima and Nagasaki in 1945.* • *"The next war will be fought with atom bombs and the one after that with spears"* (Harold Urey, 'Sayings of the Week' in *The Observer* newspaper, 1946)

a·tom·ic /£ə'tɒm·ɪk, $-'tɑː·mɪk/ *adj* [not gradable] • *atomic energy/scientists* • *atomic structure/nuclei* • An **atomic bomb** is an **atom bomb**. • See also NUCLEAR. • GR

a·tom·ic·al·ly /£ə'tɒm·ɪ·kli, $-'tɑː·mɪ-/ *adv* [not gradable]

at·om·iz·er, *Br and Aus usually* **–iser** /£'æt·ə·maɪ·zəʳ, $'æṱ·ə·maɪ·zɚ/ *n* [C] a device that changes a liquid into small drops by forcing it out through a very small hole. • *Atomizers are used for putting on perfume.*

a·tone /£ə'təʊn, $-'toʊn/ *v* [I] *fml* to do something that shows that you are sorry for something bad that you did or for something that you failed to do • *The country's present leader has expressed a wish to atone* **for** *its actions in the past.* • *If he wins this race, it will atone* **for** *his recent string of defeats.*

a·tone·ment /£ə'təʊn·mənt, $-'toʊn-/ *n* [U] *fml* • *He said that young hooligans should do community service as atonement* **for** *their crimes.*

a·top /£ə'tɒp, $-'tɑːp/ *prep literary* on or at the top of • *The statue atop the tower seems to be guarding the town from attack.* • *She sat atop a two-metre high wall.*

a·tri·um /'eɪ·tri·əm/ *n* [C] *pl* **atriums** a very large room, often with glass walls or roof, esp. in the middle of a large shop or office building

a·tro·cious /£ə'trəʊ·ʃəs, $-'troʊ-/ *adj* of very bad quality, or (of an action) cruel and shocking • *I thought that was an atrocious film/piece of acting.* • *The weather has been atrocious all week.* • *Conditions in the prison were atrocious.* • *Terrorists are believed to have been responsible for this atrocious* (= cruel and shocking) *crime.*

a·tro·cious·ly /£ə'trəʊ·ʃə·sli, $-'troʊ-/ *adv* • *She's been learning the trumpet for years but she still plays atrociously* (= very badly). • *The children have been behaving atrociously.*

a·troc·i·ty /£ə'trɒs·ɪ·ti, $-'trɑː·sɪ·ṱi/ *n* • *They're on trial for* **committing** *hundreds of war-time atrocities* (= cruel and shocking acts) **against** *the civilian population.* [C] • *These people are guilty of acts of great atrocity* (= cruelty). [U]

at·ro·phy /'æt·rə·fi/ *v* [I] (of a part of the body) to be reduced in size and therefore strength, or, more generally, to become weaker • *After several months in a hospital bed, my leg muscles had atrophied.* • *In the 1980s, their political power gradually atrophied* (= became weaker).

at·ro·phy /'æt·rə·fi/ *n* [U]

at·tach *obj* CONNECT /ə'tætʃ/ *v* [T] to fasten, join or connect; to place or fix in position • *Use this lead to attach the printer* **to** *the computer.* • *I attached a photo* **to** *my application form.* • *A buckle has come off my shoe and I don't know how to attach it back on again.* • *In Britain, packets of cigarettes come with a government health warning attached (to them)* (= on them). • *(slightly fml) I attach* (= am sending, usually with a letter) *a copy of our latest report.* • If you attach your**self to** a person or group, or if you are attached **to** a group or organization, you join them, usually for a limited period of time: *Being on his own, he attached himself to a noisy group at the bar.* ○ *As an economics expert, she was attached to* (= worked for) *the Nigerian government as an adviser for six months.* • *(slightly fml)* To attach a particular quality **to** something is to consider it to have that quality: *I don't attach any importance/significance to these rumours.*

○ *She attaches great value to being financially independent.* • *(fml)* If you say that a particular quality attaches **to** someone or something, you mean that they have that quality: *Don't worry – it was an accident and no blame attaches to either of you.* ○ *Great honour attaches to winning this award.* [+ v-*ing*] • Compare DETACH.

at·tached /ə'tætʃt/ *adj* [before n; always + *to*] • *The children are very attached* **to** (= love) *their grandparents.* • *My son feels very attached* **to** *his old guitar, and he'd never sell it.*

at·tach·ment /ə'tætʃ·mənt/ *n* • *When I was doing an English course in Brighton, I* **formed** *a strong attachment* **to** (= feeling of affection for) *the other students in my class.* [C] • *She is unlikely to give up her lifelong attachment* **to** (= support of) *feminist ideas.* [U] • *He spent a year* **on** *attachment* **to** (= working with) *the War Office.* [U] • An attachment is an extra piece of equipment that can be added to a machine: *This food processor has a special attachment for grinding coffee.* [C]

at·tach *obj* [TAKE GOODS] /ə'tætʃ/ *v* [T] *law* to take (money or possessions) officially from someone, or to ARREST them, usually because they have failed to pay money that they owe

at·tach·ment /ə'tætʃ·mənt/ *n law* • (An) attachment is the act of ARRESTING a person for failing to obey the order of a court, or of officially taking their property because they have failed to pay money that they owe. [C/U]

at·tach·é /ə'tæʃ·eɪ/ *n* [C] a person who works in an EMBASSY and has a particular area of responsibility in which they have specialist knowledge • *a naval/military/press/cultural attaché*

at·tach·é case *n* [C] a hard-sided rectangular case, used esp. for carrying business papers; a type of BRIEFCASE

at·tack /ə'tæk/ *v* to try to hurt or defeat using violence • *Most wild animals won't attack humans unless they are provoked.* [T] • *I was/got attacked last night by a couple of guys with knives.* [T] • *Army forces have been attacking (the town) since dawn with mortar and shell fire.* [I/T] • *Napoleon attacked Russia in 1812 and was defeated and forced to retreat.* [T] • If you attack someone or something, such as an organization or idea, you criticize them strongly: *She wrote an article attacking the judges and their conduct of the trial.* [T] ○ *The report attacks the idea of exams for 7 and 8 year olds.* [T] • If something, such as a disease or a chemical, attacks something, it damages it: *These rose bushes are being attacked by greenfly.* [T] ○ *AIDS attacks the body's immune system.* [T] ○ *The acid will attack plastic surfaces.* [T] • In sports, to attack is to play in a determined way and to try to score points: *The players must attack more, or the team is going to lose this match.* [I] ○ *The players must keep attacking the ball/the goal* (= determinedly try to score points by kicking or hitting the ball (towards the goal)), *or the team is going to lose this match.* [T] • *(fig.) We have to attack* (= begin to deal with) *these problems now and find some solutions.* [T] • *(fig.) The children rushed in and eagerly attacked the food* (= quickly started to eat it). [T] • *"Attack of the Killer Tomatoes"* (film title, one of many horror films with titles beginning 'Attack of the...', 1978) • Compare DEFEND. • Ⓘ Ⓙ

at·tack /ə'tæk/ *n* • *The soldiers fell victim to an* **all-out/surprise** *attack by enemy forces.* [C] • *Enemy forces have* **made** *an attack* **on/against** *the city.* [C] • *These bomb blasts suggest that the terrorists are* **(going) on the** *attack* (= trying to defeat or hurt other people) *again.* [U] • *The town is* **under** *attack* **from** (= is being attacked by) *warships in the bay.* [U] • *The government has* **come under** *attack* **from all sides** (= is being widely and severely criticized) *for cutting education spending.* [U] • *The Department of Health have* **launched** *a major attack* **on** (= attempt to deal with) *smoking.* [C] • An attack is also a sudden and short period of illness: *an attack of asthma/flu/malaria* [C] • If you **have** or are **overcome by** an attack **of hiccups/the giggles/nerves/shyness etc.**, you experience this and cannot control it. [C] • In some sports, the attack is the part of a team which tries to score points: *The team has a strong attack, but its defence is weak.* [C] ○ *The team is strong (Br)* **in**/*(Am)* **on** *attack but useless in defence.* [U] • In sports, attack is also the activity of playing in a determined way and trying to score points: *The team needs to put some more attack into its game.* [U]

at·tack·er /£ə'tæk·əʳ, $-ɚ/ *n* [C] • *The old lady never even saw her attackers.* • *He has been one of the strongest attackers* **of** (= people who have criticized) *the government's policies.*

at·tain *obj* /ə'teɪn/ *v* [T] *fml* to reach or succeed in getting (something); to achieve • *He has attained the highest grade in his music exams.* • *We need to identify the best ways of attaining our* **objectives/goals.** • *India attained independence in 1947, after decades of struggle.* • *These trains are capable of attaining very high speeds.*

at·tain·a·ble /ə'teɪ·nə·bl̩/ *adj fml* • *We must ensure that we do not set ourselves goals that are not attainable.*

at·tain·ment /ə'teɪn·mənt/ *n fml* • *Student levels/standards of punctuality, behaviour and attainment* (= achievement) *are very low.* [U] • *The department has been set some very high attainment* **targets.** • A person's attainments are the things they have done and the skills they have learned. [C]

at·tempt *(obj)* /ə'tempt/ *v* to try or make an effort (to make or do (something, esp. something difficult)) • *He attempted a joke, but it was received in silence.* [T] • *There's no point in even attempting an explanation – he'll never listen.* [T] • *They are attempting a very difficult climb.* [T] • *She's attempting* **to** *swim across the Channel next month.* [+ *to* infinitive] • *(law) A man is being questioned in relation to the attempted* **murder/robbery** *last night.*

at·tempt /ə'tempt/ *n* [C] • *It was a brave attempt that was always doomed to failure.* • *She* **made** *a few half-hearted attempts* **to** *join in their conversation.* [+ *to* infinitive] • *None of our attempts* **to** *contact Dr James were successful.* [+ *to* infinitive] • *None of our attempts* **at** *contacting Dr James were successful.* • *I've been learning to paint animals – this is one of my early attempts* (= examples of my work). • An attempt **on** someone's **life** is an act of trying to kill them: *This bomb is the third attempt on the President's life this year.*

at·tend *(obj)* [BE PRESENT] /ə'tend/ *v slightly fml* to be at or go to (an event, place, etc.) • *A large number of people attended the funeral/the meeting/the court.* [T] • *The trial will be on the 15th, but you don't have to attend if you would prefer not to.* [I] • To attend is also to go officially and usually regularly to a place: • *Which school do your children attend?* [T] ○ *I attended the classes/seminars/lectures for a month or two.* [T] ○ *The doctor asked me which ante-natal clinic I was attending.* [T] • See also **attend** at ATTENTION [NOTICE]; WELL-ATTENDED. • Ⓘ

at·tend·ance /ə'ten·dᵊnts/ *n* • *Attendance* **at** *lectures is compulsory.* [U] • *Attendances* **at** *church are falling* (= Fewer people are regularly going there). [C]

at·tend *(obj)* [PROVIDE HELP] /ə'tend/ *v* to provide a service to (someone), esp. as part of your job; to care for or deal with (someone or something) • *The Princess was attended by her ladies-in-waiting.* [T] • *The prime minister always has her own doctor attending* **(on)** *her.* [T; I + prep] • *The doctors try to attend* **(to)** *the worst injured soldiers first.* [T; I + prep] • *Tom, could you attend* **to** *the customers, please?* [always + prep] • *I always have so many things to attend* **to**, *when I come into the office after a trip abroad.* [always + prep] • See also **attend** at ATTENTION [NOTICE]. • Ⓘ

at·tend·ance /ə'ten·dᵊnts/ *n* [U] • *The singer never goes out without his security men* **in** *attendance* (= with him and taking care of him). • *Now that she's the boss, she has a couple of secretaries* **in** *attendance* **(on** *her)* (= helping her).

at·tend·ant /ə'ten·dᵊnt/ *n* [C] • *The Prince was followed by five or six attendants* (= people providing him with service). • An attendant is also someone whose job is to be in a place and help visitors or customers: *a cloakroom/museum attendant*

at·ten·tion /ə'ten·tʃᵊn/ *n* [U] • *It's a pretty house, but those door and window frames are rotten and will* **need** *a lot of attention* (= care given to them). • *If think you should seek* **medical** *attention* (= visit a doctor) *for that cut.* • *(fml) The letter is marked* **'For the** *attention* **of** (= to be dealt with by) *Ms Kramer'.* • See also ATTENTION [NOTICE]; ATTENTION [WAY OF STANDING].

at·ten·tive /£ə'ten·tɪv, $-t̬ɪv/ *adj* • If someone is attentive, they are very helpful and take care of you: *I had very attentive and loving parents.* ○ *He was very attentive* **to** *her when she was ill in bed.* ○ *A good teacher is always attentive* **to** *his or her students'* **needs.**

at·ten·tive·ly /£ə'ten·tɪv·li, $-t̬ɪv-/ *adv*

at·ten·tive·ness /£ə'ten·tɪv·nəs, $-t̬ɪv-/ *n* [U]

at·tend *obj* [RESULT IN] /ə'tend/ *v* [T] *fml* to happen as a result of, and at the same time as • *Are you sure you'd like the publicity which would attend a career in television.* • *This job is attended by a certain amount of danger.* • *Do you fully appreciate the consequences that attend this decision?* • See also **attend** at ATTENTION [NOTICE]. • Ⓘ

at·tend·ant /ə'ten·dənt/ *adj* [not gradable] *fml* • *There are too many risks attendant* **on** (= resulting from) *such a large investment of money.*

at·ten·tion NOTICE /ə'ten·tʃən/ *n* [U] notice, thought or consideration • *Could I have your attention, please?* • *They're organizing a campaign to* **draw/call** *people's attention* **to** *the environmentally harmful effects of using their cars.* • *He likes being* **the centre of** *attention* (= having a lot of people notice him) • *I knocked on the window to* **get/attract/catch** *her attention* (= make her notice me). • *After an hour, my attention started to* **wander** (= I stopped taking notice). • *Don't* **pay** *any attention* **to** (= take any notice of) *Nina – she doesn't know what she's talking about.* • *If you don't* **pay** *attention* (= listen carefully) *now, you'll get it all wrong later.* • *From the ship's loudspeakers came a sudden command, "Attention all personnel* (= Listen carefully everyone)*!"* • *I'll* **give** *your proposal my* **full/undivided** *attention* (= I'll consider it carefully). • *Many countries are starting to* **turn** *their attention* **to** (= to consider) *new forms of energy.* • *Members of the terrorist group have spent the last two years in hiding, trying to escape the* **unwelcome** *attention of the secret police* (= trying to avoid their notice because they want to hurt them). • Your **attention span** is the length of time you can keep your thoughts and interest fixed on something: *Young children have quite short attention spans.* • See also **attention** at ATTEND PROVIDE HELP.

at·ten·tions /ə'tent·ʃənz/ *pl n* • *Many countries are starting to* **turn** *their attentions* (= attention) **to** *new forms of energy.*

at·tend /ə'tend/ *v* [I] *fml* • *There's no point in your coming to my classes if you're not going to attend* (= listen carefully) *(to what I say).* • See also ATTEND.

at·ten·tive /£ə'ten·tɪv, $-t̬ɪv/ *adj* • *It's always a pleasure to lecture to an attentive audience* (= one that listens carefully).

at·ten·tive·ly /£ə'ten·tɪv·li, $-t̬ɪv-/ *adv* • *The children sat* **listening** *attentively to the story.*

at·ten·tion WAY OF STANDING /ə'ten·tʃən/ *n* [U] (esp. in the armed forces) a way of standing, with the feet together, arms by your sides, head and shoulders back and not moving • *The soldiers were standing* **at** *attention* (= in this way). • *The soldiers stood* **to** *attention* (= got into this way of standing). • Attention is also said to soldiers as an order to them to stand in this way: *"Attention!" yelled the sergeant.*

at·ten·u·ate *obj* /ə'ten·ju·eɪt/ *v* [T] *fml or specialized* to make (something) smaller, thinner or weaker • *Radiation from the sun is attenuated by the Earth's atmosphere.*

at·ten·u·at·ed /£ə'ten·ju·eɪ·tɪd, $-t̬ɪd/ *adj fml or specialized* • *The television signal is attenuated because of the high hills around the receiver.* • *They were shocked by the attenuated bodies of the children in the refugee camps.*

at·ten·u·a·tion /əˌten·ju'eɪ·ʃən/ *n* [U] *fml or specialized*

at·test *(obj)* /ə'test/ *v* to show (something) or to say or prove that something is true • *Thousands of people came out onto the streets to attest their support for the democratic opposition party.* [T] • *The number of old German cars still on the road attests* **(to)** *the excellence of their manufacture.* [T; I + *to*] • *As his career attests, he is a cricketer of world-class standard.* [I] • *(specialized) The will needs to be attested* (= signed to show that the signature of the person who made the WILL is correct) *by three witnesses.* [T]

at·test·a·tion /£ˌæt·es'teɪ·ʃən, $ˌæt̬-/ *n* [C] *specialized* • An attestation is a formal statement which you make and declare to be true.

at·tic /£'æt·ɪk, $'æt̬-/, **loft** *n* [C] the space or room at the top of a building, under the roof, often used for storing things • *I've got boxes of old clothes in the attic, which I really should throw away.* • *Susie has a tiny attic (bed)room at the top of the house.*

at·tire /£ə'taɪər, $-'taɪr/ *n* [U] *fml* clothes, esp. of a particular or formal type • *I hardly think jeans are appropriate attire for a wedding.*

at·tired /£ə'taɪəd, $-'taɪrd/ *adj* [after v; not gradable] • *She was completely attired in black, from head to foot.*

at·ti·tude OPINION /£'æt·ɪ·tjuːd, $'æt̬·ɪ·tuːd/ *n* (a) feeling or opinion about something or someone, or a way of behaving that follows from this • *It's often very difficult to change people's attitudes.* [C] • *She takes the attitude* **that** *children should be allowed to learn at their own pace.* [U + *that* clause] • *The government's attitude* **to(wards)** *the refugees is not sympathetic.* [U] • *He seems to have undergone a change* **in/of** *attitude recently, and has become much more co-operative.* [U] • *I don't like your attitude* (= the way you are behaving). [U] • *That boy has a real attitude* **problem** (= behaves in a way that makes it difficult for other people to have a relationship with him or work with him). • If you say that someone **has** attitude, you mean that they are confident and independent, sometimes in a rude or unpleasant way. [U]

at·ti·tude POSITION /£'æt·ɪ·tjuːd, $'æt̬·ɪ·tuːd/ *n* [C] a position of the body; POSTURE • *She lay sprawled across the sofa, in an attitude* **of** *complete abandon.* • If you **strike** an attitude, you hold your body in a way which suggests a particular quality or feeling: *He struck an attitude* **of** *offended dignity and marched out of the room.*

at·torn·ey /£ə'tɜː·ni, $-'tɜːr-/ *n* [C] *Am* a LAWYER • *a defense attorney* • *an attorney for the plaintiff* • *a civil/criminal attorney* • LP> **Law**

At·torn·ey Gen·er·al *n* [C] *pl* **Attorneys General** or **Attorney Generals** • An **Attorney General** is the top legal officer in some countries, who advises the king or queen or government.

at·tract *obj* /ə'trækt/ *v* [T] (of people, things, places, etc.) to pull or draw someone or something towards them, by the qualities, esp. positive and admirable ones, which they have • *These flowers are brightly coloured in order to attract butterflies.* • *The circus is attracting huge* **crowds/audiences.** • *Magnets attract iron filings.* • *The government is trying to attract industry* **to** *the area* (= to persuade people to place their industry there). • *Her ideas have attracted a lot of* **attention/support/criticism** *in the scientific community.* • If someone is attracted **to** someone else or is attracted **by** their qualities, they like, admire or want them: *She doesn't attract me physically/sexually.* ○ *I'm not physically/sexually attracted* **to/by** *him.* ○ *I'm attracted* **to/by** *the idea of marriage, but I don't want to have children.*

at·trac·tion /ə'træk·ʃən/ *n* • *The magnets are only small, so the attraction* (= pulling force) *is weak.* [C] • *Skiing* **holds** *no attraction* **for** *me* (= I do not want to do it). [U] • *I don't understand the attraction* **of** (= what is interesting or pleasurable about) *getting your ears pierced.* [U] • *She felt an immediate (physical) attraction* **to** (= interest in) *him.* [U] • An attraction is something which makes people want to go to a place: *Life in London has so many attractions – nightclubs, good restaurants and so on.* [C] ○ *The lions are the circus'* **main** *attraction.* [C] ○ *Paris has such famous* **tourist** *attractions such as the Louvre and the Eiffel Tower.* [C]

at·trac·tive /£ə'træk·tɪv, $-t̬ɪv/ *adj* very pleasing in appearance or sound, or causing interest or pleasure • *He's so attractive, I wish he'd ask me out.* • *She's so attractive, but I'd never dare ask her out.* • *They have very attractive children.* • *The house was set in attractive countryside near Oxford.* • *He sounds very attractive on the phone.* • *She's not beautiful, but I find her incredibly attractive* (= interesting and pleasant) *because she seems so full of life and fun.* • *Spending 18 hours on a plane isn't a very attractive* (= pleasant) *prospect.* • *The salary they're offering is very attractive* (= interesting because of being to my advantage), *but I still don't want the job.*

at·trac·tive·ly /£ə'træk·tɪv·li, $-t̬ɪv-/ *adv* • *She always dresses very attractively.* • *Their house is very attractively decorated.*

at·trac·tive·ness /£ə'træk·tɪv·nəs, $-t̬ɪv-/ *n* [U] • *She doesn't have to worry about her attractiveness – everyone thinks she's beautiful.* • *High mortgage rates have decreased the attractiveness of owning your own house.*

at·tri·bute /'æt·rɪ·bjuːt/ *n* [C] a quality or feature of something, esp. one that is a central part of its nature • *Organizing ability is an essential attribute for a good manager.* • *One of the main attributes* **of** *this plastic is its ability to bend without breaking.*

at·tri·bute *obj* **to** *(obj)* /ə'trɪb·jʊt, -juːt/ *v prep* to say or think that (something) is the result or work of (something or someone else); to ASCRIBE TO • *The doctors have attributed the cause of the illness to an unknown virus.* [T] • *To what do you attribute this delay?* [T] • *We attribute our success to* **being** *in the right place at the right time.* [+ v-ing] • *Most experts have attributed the drawing to Michelangelo.* [T] • If you attribute a particular quality or feature to someone or something, you meant that you think that they have it: *I wouldn't dream of attributing such a lack of judgment to you.* [T]

at·tri·but·a·ble /£ə'trɪb·ju·tə·bl̩, $-t̬ə-/ *adj* • *Do you think that these higher-than-average temperatures are attributable* **to** *global warming?*

at·tri·bu·tion /ˌæt·rɪˈbjuː·ʃᵊn/ *n* [U] • *The usual attribution* **of** *the work* **to** *Leonardo is now disputed by several experts.*

at·tri·bu·tive /£əˈtrɪb·jʊ·tɪv, $-t̬ɪv/ *adj* [not gradable] *specialized* (of the position or use of an adjective, noun or phrase) before a noun • *In 'a sudden movement', 'sudden' is an adjective in the attributive position.* • *In 'the television aerial', 'television' is a noun used in an attributive way.* • LP› **Adjectives**

at·tri·bu·tive·ly /£əˈtrɪb·jʊ·tɪv·li, $-t̬ɪv-/ *adv* [not gradable]

at·tri·tion /əˈtrɪʃ·ᵊn/ *n* [U] *slightly fml* the gradual weakening and destroying of (something, esp. the strength or confidence of an enemy) by repeatedly attacking it • *Feminists are struggling to stop the attrition* **of** *women's rights in the country.* • *Repeated criticisms from his colleagues led to the gradual attrition* **of** *his argument.* • *Terrorist groups and the government have been engaged in a costly* **war of** *attrition since 1968.* • Attrition is also *Am and Aus for* **natural wastage**. See at NATURE LIFE.

at·tuned to /£əˈtjuːnd, $-ˈtuːnd/ *adj* able to understand or being very familiar with • *A good nurse has to be attuned to the needs of his or her patients.* • *These workers are so attuned to their jobs that they can do them almost without thinking.* • *He's very attuned to the latest developments in modern music.* • If your **ears** are attuned to a particular sound, they are able to recognize it very easily: *Her ears are attuned to even the slightest variation in her baby's breathing.*

a·typ·i·cal /ˌeɪˈtɪp·ɪ·kᵊl/ *adj* not typical; different from all the others of its type • *The play is a comedy and therefore an atypical example of his writing.* • *They are atypical* **of** *the way most Americans live.*

au·ber·gine *Br* /£ˈəʊ·bə·ʒiːn, $ˈoʊ·bɚ-/, *Am and Aus* **egg·plant** *n* [C] an oval-shaped vegetable with a shiny dark purple skin, which is usually eaten cooked • PIC› **Vegetables**

au·burn /£ˈɔː·bən, $ˈɑː·bɚn/ *adj* (of hair) reddish brown in colour • *My sister is auburn-haired.*

auc·tion /£ˈɔːk·ʃᵊn, $ˈɑːk-/ *n* a usually public sale of goods or property, where people make higher and higher BIDS (= offers of money) for each item, until it is sold to the person who will pay the highest price • *Do you want to come to the furniture auction with me?* [C] • *They're* **holding** *an auction* **of** *jewellery on Thursday.* [C] • *The painting will be sold* **at**/*(Br also)* **by** *auction next week.* [U] • *The house and its contents are being* **put up for** *auction.* [U]

auc·tion *obj* /£ˈɔːk·ʃᵊn, $ˈɑːk-/ *v* [T] • *The stamps will be auctioned* (= sold by public auction) *tomorrow.* • *The family is auctioning* **(off)** *its art collection.* [T/M]

auc·tion·eer /£ˌɔːk·ʃəˈnɪəʳ, $ˌɑːk·ʃəˈnɪr/ *n* [C] • An auctioneer is a person in charge of an auction who calls out the prices that people offer.

au·da·cious /£ɔːˈdeɪ·ʃəs, $ɑː-/ *adj* brave and fearless; having or showing a willingness to take risks • *The prisoners had an audacious escape plan involving two helicopters.* • *What an audacious idea/suggestion!* • *He described the plan as ambitious and audacious.* • If a person is audacious, they are willing to risk being rude and to not show respect.

au·da·cious·ly /£ɔːˈdeɪ·ʃə·sli, $ɑː-/ *adv*

au·da·cious·ness /£ɔːˈdeɪ·ʃə·snəs, $ɑː-/ *n* [U]

au·da·ci·ty /£ɔːˈdæs·ɪ·ti, $ɑːˈdæs·ɪ·t̬i/ *n* [U] • *It took a lot of audacity* (= bravery) **to** *stand up and criticize the chairman.* [+ *to* infinitive] • *(disapproving) He* **had the** *audacity* (= rudeness) **to** *blame me for his mistake.* [+ *to* infinitive]

au·di·ble /£ˈɔː·dɪ·bl̩, $ˈɑː-/ *adj* loud enough to be heard • *The lecturer spoke so quietly that he was barely/scarcely audible at the back of the hall.* • *She gave an audible sigh of relief.*

au·di·bly /£ˈɔː·dɪ·bli, $ˈɑː-/ *adv* • *Our teacher was audibly suffering from a cold.*

au·di·ence /£ˈɔː·di·ənts, $ˈɑː-/ *n* [C + sing/pl v] the group of people gathered in one place to watch or listen to a play, film, speaker, etc., or the (number of) people watching or listening to a particular television or radio programme, or reading a particular book • *She lectures to audiences all over the world.* • *He's a very good public speaker because he knows how to get an audience on his side.* • *The audience was/were clearly delighted with the performance.* • *The magic show had a lot of audience* **participation**, *with people shouting things to the performers and going up on stage.* • *The television company has* **lost** *a large part of its audience* (= the group of people who watch its programmes) *since it changed its programming.* • *Her latest book should appeal to a large audience* (= should be read by a large number of people). • An audience is also a formal meeting that you have with an important person: *She had a private audience* **with** *the king.* • Ⓔ Ⓘ

au·di·o /£ˈɔː·di·əʊ, $ˈɑː·di·oʊ/ *adj* [not gradable] connected with sound and the recording and broadcasting of sound • *an audio cassette* • *audio tape* • *an audio signal* • *The hardware store is having a sale of* **audio-visual** *equipment/aids/software.*

au·dit *obj* FINANCE /£ˈɔː·dɪt, $ˈɑː-/ *v* [T] *specialized* to make an official examination of (the ACCOUNTS of a business)

au·dit /£ˈɔː·dɪt, $ˈɑː-/ *n* [C] • *The company has an audit at the end of each financial year.*

au·di·tor /£ˈɔː·dɪt·əʳ, $ˈɑː·dɪ·t̬ɚ/ *n* [C] • *The external auditors come in once a year.*

au·dit *obj* EDUCATION /£ˈɔː·dɪt, $ˈɑː-/ *v* [T] *Am and Aus* to go to (a class or educational course) for pleasure or interest, without being tested or receiving a qualification at the end • *As a senior citizen, Bill is allowed to audit university classes.*

au·di·tion /£ɔːˈdɪʃ·ᵊn, $ɑː-/ *n* [C] a short performance that an actor, musician, dancer, etc. gives in order to show their ability and suitability for a particular play, film, show, etc. • *His audition went well and he's fairly hopeful about getting the part.* • *The director is* **holding** *auditions next week* **for** *the major parts.* • Ⓟ

au·di·tion *(obj)* /£ɔːˈdɪʃ·ᵊn, $ɑː-/ *v* • *I'm auditioning* **for** (= trying to get) *the part of Lady Macbeth.* [I] • *We're auditioning* (= testing) *local rock bands* **for** *the music festival.* [T]

au·di·tor·i·um /£ˌɔː·dɪˈtɔː·ri·əm, $ˌɑː·dɪ·tɔːr·i-/ *n* [C] *pl* **auditoriums** or **auditoria** /£ˌɔː·dɪˈtɔː·ri·ə, $ˌɑː·dɪ·tɔːr·i-/ the part of a theatre, or similar building, where the people who are watching and listening sit, or *(esp. Am)* a large public building such as a theatre • *No smoking in the auditorium.*

au·di·tory /£ˈɔː·dɪ·tri, $ˈɑː-/ *adj* [not gradable] *specialized* of or about hearing; AURAL • *It's an artificial device which stimulates the auditory areas of the brain.*

au fait /£ˌəʊˈfeɪ, $ˌoʊ-/ *adj* familiar with or informed about (something) • *Bill is very au fait* **with** *the latest developments in computers.*

au·ger /£ˈɔː·gəʳ, $ˈɑː·gɚ/ *n* [C] a tool consisting of a twisted rod of metal fixed to a handle, used for making large holes in wood or in the ground

aught /£ɔːt, $ɑːt/ *pronoun old use or regional* anything • *Is there aught for supper?* • *I haven't seen her and she could be in Australia* **for aught** *I* **know/care** (= it is something I do not care about).

aug·ment *obj* /£ɔːgˈment, $ɑːg-/ *v* [T] *fml* to make (something) bigger or more complete by adding something to it • *With the birth of his third son, he found it necessary to do something to augment his income.* • *New York City draws water from the Hudson River to augment reservoirs when they are low.* • *The report recommends the use of private resources to augment government services in some areas.*

aug·ment·a·tion /£ˌɔːg·menˈteɪ·ʃᵊn, $ˌɑːg-/ *n* [C/U]

au gra·tin /£ˌəʊˈgræt·æ̃, $ˌoʊˈgrɑː·t̬ᵊn/ *adj* [after n; not gradable] cooked with a covering of cheese or small pieces of bread mixed with butter • *potatoes au gratin*

au·gur *(obj)* /£ˈɔː·gəʳ, $ˈɑː·gɚ/ *v fml* to be a sign of (esp. good or bad things) in the future • *The company's sales figures for the first six month augur* **well** *for the rest of the year.* [I always + adv/prep] • *Their recent string of defeats augur* **ill/badly for** *the team.* [I always + adv/prep] • *Do you think that this recent ministerial announcement augurs* (= is a sign of) *a shift in government policy?* [T]

au·gu·ry /£ˈɔːg·jʊ·ri, $ˈɑːg·jɚ·i/ *n fml* • An augury is a sign of what might happen in the future: *These sales figures are a good augury* **for** *another profitable year.* [C] • Augury is also the skill of knowing what will happen in the future: *His remarkable recovery defied all medical augury.* [U]

au·gust IMPORTANT /£ɔːˈgʌst, $ɑː-/ *adj literary* having great importance and esp. of the highest social class • *The society's august patron, the Duke of Norfolk, gave a speech at the annual dinner.*

Au·gust MONTH /£ˈɔː·gəst, $ˈɑː-/ (*abbreviation* **Aug**) *n* the eighth month of the year, after July and before September • *13(th) August/August 13(th)/13(th) Aug/Aug 13(th)* [U] • *We're going to Australia* **on** *the first of August/August the first/(esp. Am) August first.* [U] • *We've got* *friends coming at the end of August.* [U] • *They got married* **last** *August/are getting married* **next** *August.* [U] • *Cairo* **during/in** *August is unbearably hot and crowded.* [U] • *It was one of the hottest Augusts on record.* [C] • LP› **Dates**

aunt /£ɑːnt, $ænt/, *infml* **aunt·ie** /£'ɑːn·ti, $'æn·ţi/, **aunt·y** *n* [C] the sister of someone's father or mother, or the wife of someone's uncle • *It makes me feel awfully old when my brother's children call me aunt.* • *She's just an old family friend, not an actual relation, but I've always called her Auntie Sheila.* • *Hello, aunt/Hello, Aunt Margaret.* [as form of address] • PIC› **Family tree**

au pair /£ˌəʊ'peəʳ, $ˌoʊ'per/ *n* [C] a foreign person, usually a young woman, who lives with a family in order to learn their language and who looks after the children or cleans the house in return for meals, a room and a small payment • *We've got a Swiss au pair living with us for a year.*

au·ra /£'ɔː·rə, $'ɔːr·ə/ *n* [C] a feeling or character that a person or place seems to have • *She seems to* **have** *a strange aura.* • *The woods* **have** *an aura* **of** *mystery.* • *There's an aura* **of** *sadness* **about** *him.* • Aura is sometimes used to refer to a type of light that some people say they can see around people and animals.

au·ral /£'ɔː·rəl, $'ɔːr·əl/ *adj* [not gradable] relating to hearing • *The opera was an aural as well as a visual delight.* • *Language teachers often use aural material, such as tapes, to help their students learn to understand the language when it is spoken.*

au·re·ole /£'ɔː·ri·əʊl, $'ɔːr·i·oʊl/ *n* [C] *literary* a bright circle of light, esp. around the head; a HALO

au·ro·ra au·stra·lis /£əˌrɔː·rə·ɒs'trɑː·lɪs, $-ˌrɔːr·ə·ə'strɑː-/ *n* [U] **the aurora australis** *(also* **the Southern Lights***)* a pattern of differently coloured lights that are sometimes seen in the night sky in the most southern parts of the world • Compare AURORA BOREALIS.

au·ro·ra bo·re·al·is /£əˌrɔː·rə·bɒr·i'ɑː·lɪs, $-ˌrɔːr·ə·bɔːr·i'æl·ɪs/ *n* [U] **the aurora borealis** *(also* **the Northern Lights***)* a pattern of differently coloured lights that are sometimes seen in the night sky in the most northern parts of the world • Compare AURORA AUSTRALIS.

aus·pi·ces /£'ɔː·spɪ·sɪz, $'ɑː-/ *pl n* the control, encouragement, approval and support (of) • *Financial aid is being provided to the country* **under the** *auspices* **of** *the International Monetary Fund.* • *The withdrawal of troops will be carried out* **under** *United Nations' auspices.* • *The prisoners are being freed* **under** *international auspices.*

aus·pi·cious /£ɔː'spɪʃ·əs, $ɑː-/ *adj fml* suggesting a positive and successful future • *They won their first match of the season 5-1 which was an auspicious* **start/beginning.** • *Our first meeting was not auspicious – we had a huge argument.*

aus·pi·cious·ly /£ɔː'spɪʃ·ə·sli, $ɑː-/ *adv fml*

Aus·sie /£'ɒz·i, $'ɑː·zi/ *adj* [not gradable], *n* [C] *slang* Australian, or an Australian person

au·stere /£ɔː'stɪəʳ, $ɑː'stɪr/ *adj* without comfort; plain and without decoration; severe • *I had an austere childhood because it was during the war and there were no luxuries then.* • *The courtroom was a large dark chamber, an austere place.* • *The room with its white walls was bare, austere and beautiful.* • *She has an austere elegance in her plain grey and black clothes.* • *He was a tall, austere, forbidding figure.*

au·stere·ly /£ɔː'stɪə·li, $ɑː'stɪr-/ *adv* • *Her simple dress was austerely elegant.*

au·ster·i·ty /£ɔː'ster·ɪ·ti, $'ɑː·ster·ɪ·ţi/ *n* • *The wartime austerity* (= lack of luxuries and comfort) *of my early years prepared me for later hardships.* [U] • *The austerities of life in a small rural community were not what I was used to.* [C] • *The government believes that its austerity programme will reduce inflation but people are angry at the loss of jobs and services.*

Au·stral·a·sian /£ˌɒs·trə'leɪ·ʒən, $ˌɑː·strə-/ *n* [C], *adj* (a person or thing) of or from Australasia (= the area of the world consisting of Australia and New Zealand and the islands near them) • LP› **World regions**

au·then·tic /£ɔː'θen·tɪk, $ɑː'θen·ţɪk/ *adj* real or true; being in fact what it is claimed to be; GENUINE • *an authentic 1920s dress* • *an authentic Goya drawing* • *He was there and saw what happened, so his is the only authentic account.* • *She speaks with the authentic voice of the British working class.*

au·then·ti·cate *obj* /£ɔː'θen·tɪ·keɪt, $ɑː'θen·ţɪ-/ *v* [T] • *They used carbon dating tests to authenticate the claim that the skeleton was 2 million years old.*

au·then·ti·ca·tion /£ɔːˌθen·tɪ'keɪ·ʃən, $ɑːˌθen·ţɪ-/ *n* [U]

au·then·tic·i·ty /£ˌɔː·θen'tɪs·ɪ·ti, $ˌɑː·θen'tɪs·ə·ţi/ *n* [U] • *The poems are supposed to be by Sappho, but they are actually of doubtful authenticity.* • *The authenticity of her story is beyond doubt.*

au·thor /£'ɔː·θəʳ, $'ɑː·θɚ/ *n* [C] the writer of a book, article, play, etc. • *The copy of the novel I bought was signed by the author.* • *Barry Black is the author* **of** *two books on French history.* • *(fml)* Author can also be used to refer to a person who begins or creates something: *She's the author* **of** *the company's recent success/***of** *all our troubles.*

au·thor *obj* /£'ɔː·θəʳ, $'ɑː·θɚ/ *v* [T] • *He has authored* (= written) *more than 30 books.* • *(fig. esp. Am) The deal is being authored* (= arranged) *by a Greek diplomat.*

au·thor·i·al /£ɔː'θɔː·ri·əl, $ɑː'θɔːr·i-/ *adj* [not gradable] • *Can we learn anything about authorial* **intention** (= what the author intended to communicate) *by looking at what the characters say in the book?* • *It is the lack of an authorial* **voice** (= the real personality of the author) *in her novels that makes them so difficult.*

au·thor·ship /£'ɔː·θə·ʃɪp, $'ɑː·θɚ-/ *n* [U] • *The article is of unknown authorship* (= It is not known who wrote it). • *She is being attacked for her authorship* **of** (= being the person who wrote) *the policy document.*

au·thor·i·ta·ri·an /£ˌɔː·θɒr·ɪ'teə·ri·ən, $əˌθɔːr·ɪ'ter·i-/ *adj disapproving* demanding total obedience and refusing to allow people freedom to act as they wish • *an authoritarian regime/government/ruler* • *His manner is extremely authoritarian.*

au·thor·i·ta·ri·an /£ˌɔː·θɒr·ɪ'teə·ri·ən, $əˌθɔːr·ɪ'ter·i-/ *n* [C] • *My father was a real authoritarian, and we used to fight a lot when I was a teenager.*

au·thor·i·ta·ri·an·i·sm /£ɔːˌθɒr·ɪ'teə·ri·ə·nɪ·zəm, $əˌθɔːr·ɪ'ter-/ *n* [U]

au·thor·i·ty /£ɔː'θɒr·ɪ·ti, $ə'θɔːr·ɪ·ţi/ *n* (a person or people who have) the moral or legal right or ability to control • *The United Nations has* **used/exerted/exercised** *its authority* **to** *restore peace in the area.* [U] • *We need to get the support of someone* **in** *authority* (= an important or high ranking person). [U] • *They've been acting illegally and without authority* (= permission) *from the council.* [U] • *I'll give my lawyers authority* (= permission) **to** *act on my behalf.* [U + *to* infinitive] • *He's got no authority* **over** (= ability to control) *his students.* [U] • *She seemed to speak* **with** *authority* (= as if she was in control or had special knowledge). [U] • An authority is a group of people with official responsibility for a particular area of activity: *the port/police/health/education authority* [C] ○ *the Atomic Energy Authority* [C] ○ *We shall abolish the local councils and create a single, central authority.* [C] • An authority **on** a subject is an expert on it: *She's a world authority on 19th-century Irish history.* [C] • To **have it on** someone's **authority** is to have been told it by them: *I have it on Jim's authority* **that** *the meeting has been cancelled.* ○ *We have it on* **good** *authority* (= Someone who knows has told us) **that** *you're getting married soon.*

au·thor·i·ta·tive /£ɔː'θɒr·ɪ·tə·tɪv, $ə'θɔːr·ɪ·ţə·ţɪv/ *adj* • *She has an authoritative* (= seeming to have an ability to control) *manner that at times is almost arrogant.* • *The book is an authoritative* (= containing complete information) *account of the Easter Rising.*

au·thor·i·ta·tive·ly /£ɔː'θɒr·ɪ·tə·tɪv·li, $ə'θɔːr·ɪ·ţə·ţɪv-/ *adv*

au·tho·ri·ties /£ɔː'θɒr·ɪ·tiz, $ə'θɔːr·ɪ·ţiz/ *pl n* • **The authorities** are the group of people with official responsibilities for a particular area: *I'm going to report all these holes in the road to the authorities.*

au·thor·ize *obj, Br and Aus usually* **-ise** /£'ɔː·θər·aɪz, $'ɑː·θɚ-/ *v* [T] to give official permission for (something) to happen, or to give (someone) official permission (to do something) • *Who authorized this expenditure?* • *The invasion was authorized by the president.* • *I authorized my bank* **to** *pay her £3000.* [+ obj + *to* infinitive]

au·thor·i·za·tion, *Br and Aus usually* **-i·sa·tion** /£ˌɔː·θər·aɪ'zeɪ·ʃən, $ˌɑː·θɚ-/ *n* • *This information cannot be disclosed without authorization* **from** *a minister.* [U] • *The authorization* **to** *sell the shares arrived too late.* [C + *to* infinitive]

au·ti·sm /£'ɔː·tɪ·zəm, $'ɑː·ţɪ-/, *Am also* **in·fan·tile au·ti·sm** *n* [U] a failure to develop social abilities, language and other communication skills to the usual level, together with a severe limitation on the number of a

AUSTRALIAN ENGLISH

Australians use words from both British and American English and have created many words of their own. In the following lists, the usual British words are on the left, usual American words on the right. **The most common word in Australian English is given in bold type.** Sometimes Australians use both words (e.g. biscuit and cookie), though the American word has usually arrived more recently. For more information on the relationship between Australian, British and American English LP **Varieties of English** at VARIETY.

CLOTHING

BRITISH	AMERICAN
bowler (hat)	**bowler** (hat)/derby
bumbag	fanny pack
dinner jacket	tuxedo
plimsolls	**sneakers**
rucksack	**backpack**
trainers	**running shoes**
trousers	pants
pants/**underpants**	**underpants**
vest/**singlet**	undershirt
waistcoat	**vest**

TELEPHONE AND POSTAL SERVICE

BRITISH	AMERICAN
dialling code	**area code**
engaged	busy
ex-directory number	**unlisted number**
mailshot	**mass mailing**
post (n, v)	**mail** (n, v)
post box	**mailbox**
reverse charge call	collect call

CARS, TRAINS AND ROADS

BRITISH	AMERICAN
(railway) **points**	switches
bonnet	hood
boot	trunk
central reservation	**median strip**
demist (v)	defog (v)
dual carriageway	**divided highway**
flyover	**overpass**
funnel	**funnel**/smokestack
high street	main street
junction	**intersection**
kerb	curb
lorry	**truck**
luggage van	baggage car
number plate	licence plate
petrol	gas
pink (v)	**ping** (v)
puncture (n)	**flat** (n)
railway	railroad
ringroad	beltway
roundabout	*also* traffic circle
saloon	**sedan**
silencer	**muffler**
to change gear	to shift gear

TOOLS AND ELECTRICAL

BRITISH	AMERICAN
blowlamp	**blowtorch**
earth	ground
ironmongery	**hardware**
paraffin	**kerosene**
pneumatic drill	**jackhammer**
power point	electric outlet

GAMES AND SPORTS

BRITISH	AMERICAN
hockey	field hockey
ice hockey	hockey
noughts and crosses	tic-tac-toe
pack (of cards)	deck
patience	solitaire
press-up	**push-up**

WORK AND MONEY

BRITISH	AMERICAN
curriculum vitae	**resumé**
holiday	vacation
let	rent
pay packet	pay envelope
rise (in pay)	**raise** (in pay)
rota	**roster**

KITCHEN

BRITISH	AMERICAN
clingfilm	**plastic wrap**
clothes peg	clothes pin
cooker	**stove**/**range**
cornflour	cornstarch
frying pan	**frying pan**/skillet
grill (v)	**grill**/broil
hob	**stovetop**
jug	pitcher
laundrette	*(trademark)* **laundromat**
plain flour	all-purpose flour
tap	faucet

FOOD, FRUIT AND VEGETABLES

BRITISH	AMERICAN
lager (=a light beer)	**beer**
bilberry	**blueberry**
biscuit	**cookie**
crisps (=a cold snack)	**potato chips**
chips (=part of a meal)	**french fries**
cos lettuce	**romaine lettuce**
courgette	**zucchini**
jam	jelly
jelly	jello/*(trademark)* Jell-O
maize	**corn**
mangetout	**snow peas**
mince	ground meat
pudding	**dessert**/sweet

BABIES

BRITISH	AMERICAN
cot	crib
cotton wool	cotton
dummy	pacifier
nappy	diaper
pram	baby carriage
pushchair	**stroller**
quin	quint

person's activities and interests • *Autism is four times more common in boys than in girls.*

au·tis·tic /£ɔː'tɪs·tɪk, $ɑː-/ *adj* • *One child in 5000 is autistic.*

au·to CARS /£'ɔː·təʊ, $'ɑː·t̬oʊ/ *adj* [before n; not gradable] relating to cars • *auto parts/components/repairs/insurance/dealers/mechanics/engineers* • *the auto industry/market/business* • LP **Driving**

au·to /£'ɔː·təʊ, $'ɑː·t̬oʊ/ *n* [C] *pl* **autos** *Am dated* • An auto is a car: *She jumped out of her auto and ran to the phone booth.*

au·to– AUTOMATIC /£'ɔː·təʊ, $'ɑː·t̬oʊ/ *combining form* of or by yourself, or operating independently or automatically • *an autofocus camera* (= one with a device to make the picture clear automatically)

au·to·bahn /£'ɔː·təʊ·bɑːn, £'aʊ-, $'ɑː·t̬oʊ-/ *n* [C] a MOTORWAY in Germany

au·to·bi·og·raph·y /£,ɔː·təʊ·baɪ'ɒg·rə·fi, $,ɑː·t̬ə·baɪ'ɑː·grə-/ *n* (a book containing) the story of a person's life, written by that person, or the area of literature relating to such books • *The TV series 'An Angel at my Table' was based on the autobiographies of the New Zealand author Janet Frame.* [C] • *She specialized in nineteenth century autobiography.* [U] • *His life story is recounted in two fascinating volumes of autobiography.* [U] • Compare BIOGRAPHY.

au·to·bi·og·ra·pher /£ˌɔː·təʊ·baɪˈɒg·rə·fəʳ, $ˌɑː·t̬ə·baɪˈɑː·grə·fɚ/ *n* [C] • *Biographers tend to be more accurate and objective than autobiographers.*

au·to·bi·o·graph·ic·al /£ˌɔː·təʊˌbaɪ·əʊˈgræf·ɪ·kᵊl, $ˌɑː·t̬əˌbaɪ·ə-/ *adj* • *an autobiographical essay/story/novel/poem/song* • A character who is autobiographical is based on the author. • *Nearly all François Truffaut's films were autobiographical.*

au·toc·ra·cy /£ɔːˈtɒk·rə·si, $ɑːˈtɑː·krə-/ *n* government by a single person or small group that has unlimited power or authority, or the power or authority of such a person or group • *The victory against autocracy was won after years of struggle.* [U] • *Her autocracy had become so absolute that none of her colleagues dared question her policies.* [U] • An autocracy is also a country or society which has this form of government: *The novel is about an east European military autocracy threatened by a popular uprising.* [C]

au·to·crat /£ˈɔː·tə·kræt, $ˈɑː·t̬ə-/ *n* [C] • *He was condemned for being a right-wing autocrat who ruled his country by brute force.* • *Business colleagues described her as an ambitious autocrat who did what she wanted without any regard for other people.*

au·to·crat·ic /£ˌɔː·təˈkræt·ɪk, $ˌɑː·t̬əˈkræt̬-/ *adj* • *an autocratic ruler/regime/policy/measure* • *an autocratic style of government/leadership/management* • *The President resigned after 30 years of autocratic rule.* • *Her autocratic manner lost her many potential allies.*

au·to·crat·ic·al·ly /£ˌɔː·təˈkræt·ɪ·kli, $ˌɑː·t̬əˈkræt̬-/ *adv*

au·to·cross /£ˈɔː·təʊ·krɒs, $ˈɑː·t̬oʊ·krɑːs/ *n* [U] the sport of racing cars around a rough grass track

Au·to·cue *Br trademark* /£ˈɔː·təʊ·kjuː, $ˈɑː·t̬oʊ/, *Am and Aus trademark* **Tel·e·Promp·Ter** *n* an electronic device which makes it possible for broadcasters to read text while looking directly at the television camera • *The studio was thrown into chaos when the autocue broke down.* [C] • *Newsflashes often have to be read without autocue.* [U]

au·to·e·rot·ic·i·sm /£ˌɔː·təʊ·ɪˈrɒt·ɪ·sɪ·zᵊm, $ˌɑː·t̬oʊ·ɪˈrɑː·t̬ɪ-/ *n* [U] the use of your own body and imagination to obtain sexual pleasure

au·to·e·rot·ic /£ˌɔː·təʊ·ɪˈrɒt·ɪk, $ˌɑː·t̬oʊ·ɪˈrɑː·t̬ɪk/ *adj*

au·to·graph /£ˈɔː·tə·grɑːf, $ˈɑː·t̬ə·græf/ *n* [C] a signature, esp. of a famous person • *He mistook me for Madonna and asked for my autograph.*

au·to·graph *obj* /£ˈɔː·tə·grɑːf, $ˈɑː·t̬ə·græf/ *v* [T] • If you autograph something, you write your signature on it, often for someone else to keep: *I got Paul McCartney to autograph my T-shirt.* ○ *Would you autograph this book/drawing/album/football for me?* ○ *She gave me an autographed photograph of herself.*

au·to–im·mune /£ˌɔː·təʊ·ɪˈmjuːn, $ˌɑː·t̬oʊ-/ *adj* [before n; not gradable] *specialized* caused by ANTIBODIES attacking substances that are naturally found in the body • *One type of diabetes is an auto-immune disorder that may be triggered by a virus.*

Aut·o·mat /£ˈɔː·təʊ·mæt, $ˈɑː·t̬ə-/ *n* [C] *Am trademark* a restaurant where food is obtained from enclosed boxes whose doors open when money is put in

au·to·mate *obj* /£ˈɔː·tə·meɪt, $ˈɑː·t̬ə-/ *v* [T] to make (esp. a process in a factory or office) operate by machines or computers, so reducing the amount of work done by humans and the time taken to do the work • *Massive investment is needed to automate the production process.*

au·to·mat·ed /£ˈɔː·tə·meɪ·tɪd, $ˈɑː·t̬ə·meɪ·t̬ɪd/ *adj* • *an automated factory/plant/system/service* • *(fully) automated production/machinery/equipment/scanning/monitoring* • *Flying has become so automated that pilots risk falling asleep through boredom.* • **Automated teller machine** (*Am abbreviation* **ATM**) is *fml for* **cash dispenser**. See at CASH.

au·to·ma·tion /£ˌɔː·təˈmeɪ·ʃᵊn, $ˌɑː·t̬ə-/ *n* [U] • *office/factory automation*

au·to·mat·ic [INDEPENDENT] /£ˌɔː·təˈmæt·ɪk, $ˌɑː·t̬əˈmæt̬-/ *adj* able to operate independently of human control • *an automatic (control) system/mechanism* • *An automatic pistol or rifle can fire repeatedly without the need to pull the trigger more than once.* • *An automatic washing machine is one which, when it has been switched on, completes a wash without any more human control.* • **Automatic transmission** enables a vehicle to change GEAR without being controlled by the driver. A car with this device is called an automatic. Compare **manual transmission** at MANUAL [BY HAND]. • (NL)

au·to·mat·ic /£ɔː·təˈmæt·ɪk, $ɑː·t̬əˈmæt̬-/ *n* [C] • An automatic is a machine with some features which operate independently of human control: *Our washing machine is an automatic* (= when it has been filled and switched on, it completes a wash without any more human involvement). ○ *I prefer driving an automatic* (= a car whose GEARS change automatically). • [LP]> **Driving**

au·to·mat·ic·al·ly /£ˌɔː·təˈmæt·ɪ·kli, $ˌɑː·t̬əˈmæt̬-/ *adv* • *The camera adjusts the lens aperture and shutter speed automatically.*

au·to·mat·ic [NOT CONSCIOUS] /£ˌɔː·təˈmæt·ɪk, $ˌɑː·t̬əˈmæt̬-/ *adj* done without thinking about it • *Life would be impossible if digestion wasn't an automatic process.* • *When driving becomes automatic, the risk of an accident increases.* • (NL)

au·to·mat·ic [CERTAIN] /£ˌɔː·təˈmæt·ɪk, $ˌɑː·t̬əˈmæt̬-/ *adj* certain to happen; INEVITABLE • *an automatic right* • *Citizenship is automatic for children born in this country.* • *Should a life sentence be automatic for men convicted of rape?* • (NL)

au·to·mat·ic·al·ly /£ˌɔː·təˈmæt·ɪ·kli, $ˌɑː·t̬əˈmæt̬-/ *adv* • *Employees who steal from the warehouse will be dismissed automatically.* • *Nurses' salaries should increase automatically every year.*

au·to·ma·ton /£ɔːˈtɒm·ə·tᵊn, $ɑːˈtɑː·mə·t̬ᵊn/ *n* [C] *pl* **automatons** or **automata** /£ɔːˈtɒm·ə·tə, $ɑːˈtɑː·mə·t̬ə/ a machine which operates on its own without the need for human control, or a person who acts like a machine without considering what they are doing, esp. because they are bored or tired • *Halfway through the exam, I turned into an automaton and was writing without thinking.*

au·to·mo·bile /£ˈɔː·tə·məʊ·biːl, $ˈɑː·t̬ə·moʊ-/ *n* [C] *esp. Am fml* a car • *the automobile industry* • *The Automobile Association (AA) and the Royal Automobile Club (RAC) in Britain and the American Automobile Association in the US are organizations which offer advice and repair services to motorists, and publish road maps and guide books.* • [LP]> **Driving**

au·to·mo·tive /£ˌɔː·təˈməʊ·tɪv, $ˌɑː·t̬əˈmoʊ·t̬ɪv/ *adj* [before n; not gradable] relating to road vehicles • *the automotive industry/business/trade/market* • *automotive research/manufacturing/engineers/components/parts*

au·ton·o·my /£ɔːˈtɒn·ə·mi, $ɑːˈtɑː·nə-/ *n* [U] the right of a group of people to govern itself, or to organize its own activities • *Demonstrators demanded immediate autonomy* **for** *their region.* • *The universities are anxious to preserve their autonomy* **from** *central government.*

au·ton·o·mous /£ɔːˈtɒn·ə·məs, $ɑːˈtɑː·nə-/ *adj* • *an autonomous region/province/republic/homeland/assembly/council* • *The majority of Scots favour an autonomous Scotland involving devolution or complete independence.* • *The local groups are autonomous* **of** *the national organization.*

au·to–pi·lot, **au·to·pi·lot** /£ˈɔː·təʊˌpaɪ·lət, $ˈɑː·t̬oʊ-/, **au·to·mat·ic pi·lot** *n* a device which keeps aircraft, spacecraft and ships moving in a particular direction without human involvement • *The captain switched off the autopilot and took back control of the airliner.* [C] • *The plane was* **on** *autopilot when it crashed.* [U] • A person **on autopilot** is doing something without consciously thinking about it or without making an effort: *The pianist coasted along on autopilot throughout her mediocre performance.*

au·top·sy /£ˈɔː·tɒp·si, $ˈɑː·tɑːp-/ *n* the cutting open and examination of a dead body in order to discover the cause of death; POSTMORTEM • *We are going to have to* **carry out/perform** *an autopsy.* [C] • *The autopsy* **on** *the prisoner showed that she had been taking drugs.* [C] • *The body arrived for autopsy at the Dallas hospital.* [U] • *Small pieces of tissue are taken from the body at autopsy and sent to the lab for testing.* [U]

au·top·sy *obj* /£ˈɔː·tɒp·si, $ˈɑː·tɑːp-/ *v* [T] • *The body of the 45-year-old squash player has been autopsied by experts looking for evidence of heart disease.*

au·to·sug·ges·tion /£ˌɔː·təʊ·səˈdʒes·tʃᵊn, $ˌɑː·t̬oʊ-/ *n* [U] the influencing of your physical or mental state by thoughts and ideas which come from yourself rather than from other people • *Autosuggestion is the power of mind over matter – if you convince yourself that you are cured, you will be.*

au·to·sug·ges·tive /£ˌɔː·təʊ·səˈdʒes·tɪv, $ˌɑː·t̬oʊ-/ *adj* • *Autosuggestive techniques can help in the treatment of diseases which cannot be cured by conventional medicine.*

au•tumn /£ˈɔː·təm, $ˈɑː·t̬ᵊm/, *Am also* **fall** *n* the season of the year between summer and winter, lasting from September to November north of the equator and from March to May south of the equator, when fruits and crops become ripe and are gathered, and leaves fall • *We like to travel* **in the** *autumn when there are fewer tourists.* [U] • *We always clear out the garage* **in** *early/late autumn.* [U] • *Last autumn we went to Germany – this/next autumn we're going to Austria.* [C] • *Martha used to spend her autumns with friends in southern France.* [C] • *We enjoyed a very warm autumn last year.* [C] • *Autumn* **colours** *are the browns, oranges and yellows of autumn leaves.* • Someone's **autumn years** are the later years of their life, esp. after they have stopped working.

au•tum•nal /£ɔːˈtʌm·nəl, $ɑː-/ *adj* • *autumnal colours/hues/tints/gales/rain/sunlight* • *an autumnal landscape/atmosphere/feeling*

aux•il•i•a•ry /£ɔːgˈzɪl·i·ᵊr·i, $ɑːgˈzɪl·i·er-/ *adj, n* (someone or something) giving help or support, esp. to a more important person or thing • *auxiliary staff* • *an auxiliary vessel/engine/power unit/system* • *The assistants will receive auxiliary rates of pay.* • *(Br)* **Auxiliary nurses/Nursing auxiliaries** (*Am* **Nurses' aides**) (*Aus* **Nursing aids**) help nurses to take care of people. [C] • Auxiliaries are soldiers of one country who fight for another country. [C usually pl] • An **auxiliary (verb)** gives grammatical information, for example about tense, which is not given by the main verb of a sentence: *The first verb in each of the following sentences is an auxiliary – 'When did you arrive?', 'I would love a drink', 'She has finished her book'.* [C] • LP **Auxiliary verbs**

AV /ˌeɪˈviː/ *adj Am abbreviation for* **audio-visual**, see at AUDIO • *Our teacher sent us to the AV room for an overhead projector.*

a•vail /əˈveɪl/ *n* [U usually in negatives] use, purpose, advantage, or profit • *I tried to persuade her not to resign, but* **to no** *avail.* • *We've economised as much as possible, but* **to little/to no great** *avail, since we still owe a lot of money.* • *The doctors' efforts to save the child were* **to/of no** *avail.*

a•vail *obj* /əˈveɪl/ *v* [+ two objects] *dated* • **It avails** *you* **nothing** (= It is hopeless for you) **to** *complain about all your predicaments.* [+ *to* infinitive]

a•vail *obj* **of** *obj v prep* [T] • If you avail yourself of something, you use it to your advantage or benefit: *Employees should avail themselves of the opportunity* **to** *buy cheap shares in the company.* [+ *to* infinitive] • LP **Reflexive pronouns and verbs**

a•vail•a•ble /əˈveɪ·lə·bl̩/ *adj* able to be obtained, used, or reached • *Is this dress available in a larger size?* • *Our autumn catalogue is now available* **from** *our usual stockists.* • *There's no money available* **for** *tax cuts this year.* • *It is vital that food is made available* **to** *the famine areas.* • *I'm afraid I'm not available* **to** *do the show on the 19th.* [+ *to* infinitive] • *Every available officer will be assigned to the investigation.* • *Paul's not available at present. Should I ask him to call you back?* • *Did you know John's available again? He's just finished his relationship with Chris.* • *Do you have an afternoon available this week to meet the President?*

a•vail•a•bil•i•ty /£əˌveɪ·ləˈbɪl·ɪ·ti, $-ə·t̬i/ *n* [U] • *The ready availability of guns has contributed to the escalating violence.* • *Abortion rates are high because the availability of contraceptives is limited.*

av•a•lanche /£ˈæv·ᵊl·ɑːntʃ, $-æntʃ/ *n* [C] a large amount of ice, snow and rock falling quickly down the side of a mountain, or *(fig.)* the sudden arrival of (too) many things • *Skiers should avoid the area because of the high risk of avalanches.* • *(fig.) We were swamped by an avalanche* **of** *letters/phone calls/claims/complaints/publicity* • *(fig.) Chinese leaders feared that the avalanche* **of** *change in eastern Europe might descend upon their own country.*

av•ant•garde /£ˌæv·ɑ̃ːˈgɑːd, $-ˈgɑːrd/ *n* [C + sing/pl v] **the avantgarde** (the work of) the painters, writers, musicians and other artists whose ideas, styles and methods are highly original or modern in comparison to the period in which they live • *the Western avantgarde* • *New York is the international capital of the musical avantgarde.*

av•ant–garde /£ˌæv·ɑ̃ːˈgɑːd, $-ˈgɑːrd/ *adj* • *avant-garde art/cinema/painting/fashion* • *an avant-garde architect/dancer/composer/sculpture/production/movement* • *It was one of the first avant-garde works to appeal to a wide audience.*

av•a•rice /£ˈæv·ᵊr·ɪs, $ˈ-ə-/ *n* [U] *fml* an extremely strong desire to obtain or keep wealth; GREED • *She earned wealth* **beyond the dreams of** *avarice* (= an extremely large amount of money) *from her business empire.* • *No one believes that football clubs are not motivated by avarice.* • *"I am rich beyond the dreams of avarice"* (Edward Moore in the play *The Gamester*, 1753)

av•a•ri•cious /ˌæv·əˈrɪʃ·əs/ *adj fml* • *The employees of the avaricious tycoon were over-worked and under-paid.*

av•a•ri•cious•ly /ˌæv·əˈrɪʃ·ə·sli/ *adv fml*

Ave /æv/ *n* [U] *abbreviation for* AVENUE, usually used in writing after the name of a road • *13 Victoria Ave*

a•venge *obj* /əˈvendʒ/ *v* [T] to do harm to or punish the person responsible for (something bad done to you or your family or friends) in order to achieve a fair situation • *She killed her father to avenge her mother/her mother's suffering.* • *Scotland's stunning victory avenged last year's humiliating defeat by Wales.* • *The cyclist avenged her***self on** *the dangerous driver by reporting him to the police.* • *At the end of the film, the murderer is killed by his victim's avenging girlfriend.*

a•veng•er /£əˈven·dʒəʳ, $-dʒɚ/ *n* [C] • *John Wayne stars as a grief-stricken avenger on the trail of his brother's killer.*

av•e•nue ROAD /£ˈæv·ə·njuː, $-nuː/ *n* [C] a wide road, with trees or tall buildings on both sides, or a wide countryside path or road with trees on both sides, esp. *(Br)* one which leads to a large house • *Madison Avenue* • *One of the world's most beautiful avenues is the Champs Elysées in Paris.* • *(Br) A broad avenue of lime trees led up to a grand entrance with huge oak doors.*

av•e•nue POSSIBILITY /£ˈæv·ə·njuː, $-nuː/ *n* [C] a method or way (of doing something); a possibility • *We should* **explore/pursue** *every avenue in the search for an answer to this problem.* • *Only two avenues are* **open** *to us – either we accept his offer or we give up the fight completely.*

a•ver *obj* /£əˈvɜːʳ, $-ˈvɜːr/ *v* [T] **-rr-** *fml* to state the truth of (something) strongly; ASSERT • *The lawyer averred her client's innocence.* • *"He's guilty, I tell you," she averred.* [+ clause] • *She averred* **that** *he was guilty.* [+ *that* clause]

av•er•age AMOUNT /£ˈæv·ᵊr·ɪdʒ, $ˈ-ɚ-/ *n* the result obtained by adding two or more amounts together and dividing the total by the number of amounts • *The average of the three numbers 7, 12 and 20 is 13, because the total of 7, 12 and 20 is 39, and 39 divided by 3 is 13.* [C] • *Prices have risen by an average* **of** *4% over the past year.* [C] • *She walked 8 km in two hours, so her average was 4 km per hour.* [C] • *My income's rather variable, but I earn £53 a day* **on** *average.* [U]

av•er•age /£ˈæv·ᵊr·ɪdʒ, $ˈ-ɚ-/ *adj* [before n; not gradable] • *average earnings/income/rainfall* • *The average age of the US soldiers who fought in the Vietnam War was 19.*

av•er•age *(obj)* /£ˈæv·ᵊr·ɪdʒ, $ˈ-ɚ-/ *v* • *Enquiries to our office average 1000 calls a month.* [L only + n] • *Many doctors average* (= work an average of) *70 hours a week.* [T] • *Trainee accountants average* (= earn an average of) *£12 000 per year.* [T] • *I'd like you to average* **(out)** (= calculate the average of) *the column of figures on page 34.* [T] • *My annual holiday varies, but it averages* **out at** (= has as its average) *five weeks a year.* [I]

av•er•age USUAL STANDARD /£ˈæv·ᵊr·ɪdʒ, $ˈ-ɚ-/ *n* a standard or level which is considered to be typical or usual • *The audience figures were lower than average for this sort of film.* [U] • *In western Europe, a 7- to 8-hour working day is about* **the** *average* (= typical). [U] • **On** *average, people who don't smoke are healthier than people who do.* [U] • *The quality of candidates was* **(well) below/above** *average.* [U] • *I expect to spend* **an** *average* **of** *$15 to $20 on a meal in a restaurant.* [C]

av•er•age /£ˈæv·ᵊr·ɪdʒ, $ˈ-ɚ-/ *adj* [not gradable] • *The average person (in the street) is a lot better off than they were forty years ago.* • *His first novel was not particularly good or bad, just average.* • *The teachers were pleased with the above-average results.* • *We don't want Einstein, just someone of average ability.*

av•er•age•ly /£ˈæv·ᵊr·ɪdʒ·li, $ˈ-ɚ-/ *adv* • *Jim's an averagely attractive man.*

av•er•age out *v adv* [I] • *The highs and lows of life tend to average out* (= be equal in amount) *in the end.*

a•verse /£əˈvɜːs, $-ˈvɜːrs/ *adj* [after v; always + *to*] strongly disliking or opposed to • *Few MPs are averse* **to** *the attention of the media.* • *I wouldn't be averse* **to** *inheriting* (= I would very much like to inherit) *a million pounds!* • *She's not averse* **to** *good champagne – in fact she's very keen on it!*

a•ver•sion /£əˈvɜː·ʃᵊn, £-ʒᵊn, $-ˈvɜːr·ʒᵊn/ *n* [C usually sing] • An aversion is (a person or thing which causes) a

AUXILIARY VERBS

Auxiliary verbs are marked *v aux* in the dictionary. **Be, do, have** and **will** are the auxiliary verbs which give information about the tense of the main verb. **Be** is also used to form the passive.

Can, could; may, might; shall, should; will, would; must and **ought** are the important *modal auxiliary verbs*; they give other information about the main verb, for example about necessity or possibility.

Need, used to and **dare** can follow some of the grammar patterns of modal auxiliaries, but are also used like ordinary verbs. They are not marked *v aux* in the dictionary.

IMPORTANT USES OF AUXILIARY VERBS

- **to ask questions:**
  Did *you go to the concert?*
  Can *your friend speak Spanish?*
- **to make negatives:**
  Sally **didn't** *go to the concert.*
  He **shouldn't** *work so hard.*
- **to avoid repeating the main verb** especially in questions and short answers:
  Jamie had forgotten all about it and I **had** *too.*
  "It's a nice day today, **isn't** *it?" "Yes, it* **is**.*"*
  *"***Will** *you phone me tomorrow?" "Yes, I* **will**.*"*
  "You'll forget to buy the milk." "Oh no I **won't**.*"*
- **to emphasize something** (in speaking, the auxiliary verb is given heavy stress)
  I **do** *believe you.*
  I disagree. I think we **should** *invite him.*

IMPORTANT GRAMMAR OF AUXILIARY VERBS

Auxiliary verbs do not use *'do'* or *'did'* when forming negatives or questions:

- **negatives**

auxiliary verb	*She has visited Canada.*	*She has***n't** *visited Canada.*
modal auxiliary	*We should go now.*	*We should***n't** *go now.*
(ordinary verb	*You enjoy football.*	*You* **don't** *enjoy football.*)

- **questions**
  - ordinary question form

auxiliary verb	*She has visited Canada.*	**Has she** *visited Canada?*
modal auxiliary	*We should go now.*	**Should we** *go now?*
(ordinary verb	*You enjoy football.*	**Do you** *enjoy football?)*

  - question using a short form in the negative

auxiliary verb	*She has visited Canada.*	*She has visited Canada,* **hasn't she***?*
modal auxiliary	*We should go now.*	*We should go now,* **shouldn't we***?*
(ordinary verb	*You enjoy football.*	*You enjoy football,* **don't you***?*)

  - question showing the speaker doubts or is surprised at the statement

auxiliary verb	*She has visited Canada.*	*She has visited Canada,* **has she***?*
modal auxiliary	*We should go now.*	*We should go now,* **should we?**
(ordinary verb	*You enjoy football.*	*You enjoy football,* **do you***?*)

- **short forms are often used**, especially in informal situations:
  - statements: *I'm, he's, she'd, we'll*
  - negatives and questions: *they can't, he isn't, he's not, aren't I?*

  LP **Short forms**

SPECIAL GRAMMAR OF MODAL AUXILIARY VERBS

- **they are usually followed by an infinitive without** *to*
  You should thank him. • *He would always smile at us.*
  But notice that **ought** and **used** take a *to* infinitive: • *You ought* **to** *thank him.* • *He always used* **to** *smile at us.*
- **they have very few different forms**
  - the third person singular does not take -s *I can, he can*
  - there is no past participle or *-ing* form
  - there is no infinitive
- **they cannot follow another verb**
  Because modal auxiliaries do not have infinitive or *-ing* forms, they cannot follow another verb. For example, you cannot say *'Will I must show my passport?'* You need to replace the auxiliary with a different expression: *Will I* **have to** *show my passport?* Other examples:
  I want to **be able to** *sleep tonight.* (replacing *can*)
  She may **be ready/willing to** *help us.* (replacing *will*)
  I hate **having to** *take my medicine.* (replacing *must* or *ought*)

- **they are used in very few tenses**
  - Modal auxiliaries are not used in the future, perfect or continuous.
  - **Could**, **might**, **should** and **would** look like past forms, but are more often used with particular meanings of their own which are explained separately in the dictionary.
  - Modal auxiliaries *are* sometimes used to express past time:
    - **Could** is used as the past simple of **can** in all its meanings. **Would** is used as the past simple of **will** (CAN) meaning to be able to do something.
      I **couldn't** *understand what she said.*
      We **couldn't** *smoke anywhere in the building.*
      The car **would** *barely start this morning.*
    - in indirect speech **could, might, should** and **would** are used as past forms:
      "It **may** *be dangerous," he said. / He said it* **might** *be dangerous.*
      must, **need** and **ought** are also sometimes used in this way:
      "You **must** *take more exercise." / She said I* **must** *take more exercise.*
    - using **have** + *past participle*:
      You **should have** *asked him.* • *You* **may have** *won a $10 000 prize.*
      Ursula **ought to have** *apologized.* • *Her car* **might have** *broken down.*
      The explosion **must have** *occurred at 2.30 in the morning.*
      (Notice that **dare** and **used to** do not follow this pattern.)

feeling of strong dislike or a lack of willingness to do something: *I felt an instant aversion* **to** *his parents.* ○ *She has a deep aversion* **to getting** *up in the morning.* ○ *Greed is my* **pet** *aversion* (=the thing I dislike most of all). • **Aversion therapy** is a method of treating habits or types of behaviour that are not desirable by causing the patient to connect them with unpleasant feelings: *Despite what many people think, aversion therapy is no longer used by professional psychologists in this country.*

a·vert *obj* [PREVENT] /£əˈvɜːt, $-ˈvɜːrt/ *v* [T] to prevent (something bad) from happening; avoid • *to avert a crisis/war/conflict/confrontation/strike/famine* • *to avert (an) economic collapse* • *Starvation can only be averted with massive food aid from the West.*

a·vert *obj* [TURN] /£əˈvɜːt, $-ˈvɜːrt/ *v* [T] to turn away (your eyes or thoughts) • *The police officer averted his gaze/eyes* **from** *the mutilated corpse.* • *We tried to avert our thoughts* **from** *our massive financial problems.*

a·viar·y /£ˈeɪ·vi·ə·ri, $-er·i/ *n* [C] a large cage or enclosure in which birds are kept as pets

a·vi·a·tion /ˌeɪ·viˈeɪ·ʃən/ *n* [U] the activity of flying aircraft, or of designing, producing and maintaining them • *aviation fuel* • *the British Civil Aviation Authority* • *the US Federal Aviation Administration*

a·vi·a·tor /£ˈeɪ·vi·eɪ·tər, $-t̬ɚ/ *n* [C] *dated* • *Amy Johnson was a pioneering aviator who made record-breaking flights to Australia and South Africa in the 1930s.*

av·id /ˈæv·ɪd/ *adj* extremely eager or interested • *an avid collector/reader/consumer/supporter/viewer/fan/audience* • *She was an avid proponent of equal rights for immigrants.* • *She was avid* **for** *equal rights for immigrants.* • *Jane has always had an avid desire to become an engineer.*

av·id·ly /ˈæv·ɪd·li/ *adv* • *She remained avidly anti-Communist throughout the years of dictatorship.* • *The winners avidly awaited their prizes.* • *We watched the film avidly from beginning to end.*

a·vid·i·ty /£əˈvɪd·ɪ·ti, $-ə·t̬i/ *n* [U]

a·vi·on·ics /£ˌeɪ·viˈɒn·ɪks, $-ˈɑː·nɪks/ *n* [U] the science and TECHNOLOGY of the electronic devices used in AERONAUTICS and ASTRONAUTICS • *Avionics forms an important part of the defence industry.*

a·vi·on·ics /£ˌeɪ·viˈɒn·ɪks, $-ˈɑː·nɪks/ *pl n* • The avionics of an aircraft or spacecraft are its electronic devices: *The sophisticated avionics enable the helicopter to operate at night.*

a·vi·on·ic /£ˌeɪ·viˈɒn·ɪk, $-ˈɑː·nɪk/ *adj* [not gradable] • *Aircraft today use complex avionic systems.*

av·o·ca·do (pear) /£ˌæv·əˈkɑː·dəʊ, $-doʊ/ *n* [C/U] *pl* **avocados** or **avocadoes** a tropical fruit with thick green or purple skin and oily green or yellow edible flesh which has a very large round seed at the centre and which grows on trees • PIC **Fruit**

a·void *obj* /əˈvɔɪd/ *v* [T] to stay away from (someone or something), or prevent (something) from happening or not allow yourself to do (something) • *You really should avoid him – he'll only try to borrow money from you.* • *Do you think Tim's avoiding me? I haven't seen him for a month.* • *I try to avoid supermarkets on Saturdays – they're always so busy.* • *I try to avoid* **going** *shopping on Saturdays.* [+ v-*ing*] • *The report* **studiously** *avoided any mention of the controversial plan.* • *The plane* **narrowly** *avoided disaster when one of the engines cut out on take-off.* • *I left the pub to avoid a fight* (=prevent a fight from happening). • *Unnecessary paperwork should be avoided* (=prevented) **at all costs**. • *The politicians were* **anxious to** *avoid* (=prevent) *the embarrassment of an environmental disaster.* • To **avoid** someone or something **like the plague** is to be determined to avoid it completely: *She avoids him like the plague now she knows what he did.* ○ *Since the scare about mad cow disease, I've avoided beef like the plague.*

a·void·a·ble /əˈvɔɪ·də·bl̩/ *adj* • *an avoidable mistake/accident/disaster* • *Car theft is the commonest type of avoidable crime.* • *In spite of these latest threats, war may still be avoidable.*

a·void·ance /əˈvɔɪ·dənts/ *n* [U] • *The avoidance of injury should take priority in sports like rugby.* • **Tax** avoidance is the reduction, by legal methods, of the amount of tax that a person or company pays.

a·vow *obj* /əˈvaʊ/ *v* [T] *fml* to state or admit (something) • *The terrorists avowed* **that** *they regretted what they had done.* [+ *that* clause] • *It is a society in which homosexuality is rarely avowed.*

a·vowed /əˈvaʊd/ *adj* [before n] • *The Government's avowed commitment/intent/purpose/aim/goal/desire is to reduce tax.* • *He is an avowed traditionalist and against reform of any kind.*

a·vow·ed·ly /əˈvaʊ·ɪd·li/ *adv* • *an avowedly feminist author*

a·vow·al /əˈvaʊ·əl/ *n* • *They were imprisoned for their avowal* **of** *anti-government beliefs.* [U] • *Her public avowals* **to** *reduce crime have yet to be put into effect.* [C + *to* infinitive]

a·vun·cu·lar /£əˈvʌŋ·kjʊ·lər, $-lɚ/ *adj* friendly, caring or helpful, like the expected behaviour of an uncle • *David's an avuncular, quietly-spoken man.* • *His avuncular image belies his steely determination.*

a·vun·cu·lar·ly /£əˈvʌŋ·kjʊ·lə·li, $-lɚ-/ *adv*

a·wait *obj* /əˈweɪt/ *v* [T] *fml* to wait for, or be waiting for (something) • *He is anxiously awaiting the result of the medical tests.* • *A marvellous reception awaited me on my first day at work.* • *A lot of hard work awaits you at university.* • *The* **long/eagerly** *awaited sequel is now available on video.*

a·wake /əˈweɪk/ *adj* [after v] not sleeping • *"Is Mark awake yet, Caroline?" "Yes, he's* **wide** (=completely) *awake and running around his bedroom."* • *I find it so difficult to* **stay** *awake during history lessons.* • *I drink a lot of coffee to* **keep** *me awake.* • *She used to* **lie** *awake at night worrying about how to pay the bills.* • *(fig.) Businesses need to be awake* **to** (=aware of) *the advantages of European integration.*

a·wake *(obj)* /əˈweɪk/ *v past simple* **awoke** /£əˈwəʊk, $-ˈwoʊk/ or *Am also* **awaked**, *past part* **awoken** /£əˈwəʊ·kən, $-ˈwoʊ-/ *literary* • *I awoke* (=woke up) *at seven o'clock.* [I] • *She awoke me* (=woke me up) *at seven.* [T] • *(fig.) The chance meeting awoke* (=started again) *the old passion between them.* [T] • *(fig.) Young people need to awake* **to** (=become aware of) *the risks involved in casual sex.* [I]

a·wak·en *(obj)* /əˈweɪ·kən/ *v literary* to stop sleeping • *They were awakened by the sound of rebel gunfire.* [T] • If a desire, interest or emotion awakens or is awakened **in** you, you become aware of it for the first time: *A passion for French food awakened in me after my holiday in Paris.* [I] ○

My holiday in Paris awakened a passion for French food in me. [T] ○ *I wish I could awaken some interest in English grammar in my students.* [T] • If you awaken someone **to** something, you make them aware of it or make them remember it: *I awakened him to his responsibilities for his children.* [T]

a·wak·en·ing /ə'weɪ·kᵊn·ɪŋ/ *n* [C usually sing] • *His religious awakening came after the tragic death of his parents.* • *Environmentalists were pleased by the awakening of public concern about the ozone layer.* • *If you think they're going to reduce taxes, you're in for a* **rude** *awakening* (= you will be unpleasantly surprised).

a·ward *obj* /£ə'wɔːd, $-'wɔːrd/ *v* [T] to give (money or a prize) following an official decision • *The jury awarded libel damages of £100 000.* • *The university has awarded Jane a $500 travel grant./The university has awarded a $500 travel grant* **to** *Jane.* [+ two objects] • LP> **Schools and colleges**

a·ward /£ə'wɔːd, $-'wɔːrd/ *n* [C] • *They have authorized awards of £900* **to** *each of the victims.* • *Who do you think should win the Academy Award for Best Director this year?*

a·ware /£ə'weəʳ, $-'wer/ *adj* [after v] knowing that something exists, or having knowledge or experience of a particular thing • *Are you aware* **that** *your car is parked on a double yellow line?* [+ *that* clause] • *Are you aware* **how much** *the fine for this offence is?* [+ *wh-* word] • *Is he aware* **of** *the price of shoes like those?* (= Does he realize that they are very expensive?) • *I am* **well/acutely** (= very) *aware* **of** *the problems caused by this new road – it runs right past my office.* • *I've been aware* **of** (= I have felt) *a strange presence in the flat ever since he died.* • *"Has Claude paid the phone bill?" "Not as far as I'm aware."* (= I don't think so) • Aware also means having special interest in or experience of something and so being well informed of what is happening in that subject at the present time: *ecologically aware* ○ *sexually aware* ○ *She's so politically aware because she's always reading newspapers.*

a·ware·ness /£ə'weə·nəs, $-'wer-/ *n* [U] • *Public awareness* **of** *the problem will make politicians take it seriously.* • *Environmental awareness has increased dramatically over the past decade.*

a·wash /£ə'wɒʃ, $-'wɑːʃ/ *adj* [after v] covered with a liquid, esp. water, or *(fig.)* having an amount of something which is very large or larger than necessary or desirable • *The floor was awash after the bath overflowed.* • *(fig.) Parliament is awash* **with** *rumours/reports that the Chancellor is about to resign.* • *(fig.) The office is already awash* **with** *computers, so why do we need another one?* • *(fig.) The city is awash* **with** *drugs and the police are powerless to do anything about it.*

a·way SOMEWHERE ELSE /ə'weɪ/ *adj, adv* [not gradable] somewhere else, or to or in a different place, position or situation • *Ms Watson is away on holiday until the end of the week.* • *Keep/Stay away* **from** *strange men* (= Do not go near them or talk to them). • *Just go away and leave me alone, will you?* • *The sight was so horrible that I had to look/turn away.* • *Air pollution has become so awful in the city that I've decided to move away.* • *(fig.) I'd like to move (our discussion) away* **from** (= I'd like to talk about something other than) *the election campaign.* • *The recent flood has swept away the footbridge.* • *I've given away all my old clothes to charity.* • *Would you like your burger to eat in or take away?* • An away match/game/fixture is played at an opposing team's sports ground: *We lost the away game but won both the home games.* • LP> **Sports** PIC> **Prepositions of movement**

a·way DISTANT /ə'weɪ/ *adv* [not gradable] at a distance (of or from here) • *How far away is the station?* • *The office is a half-hour drive away.* • *We live 5 km away* **from** *each other.* • *Life's so much quieter away* **from** *the city.* • *I want to get as far away as possible from that dreadful man.* • *(infml) Oh, it's* **miles** *away* (= a long distance from here). • *(fig.) I called her several times but she didn't hear – she was miles away* (= not giving any attention).

a·way IN THE FUTURE /ə'weɪ/ *adv* [not gradable] in the future; from now • *My English exam's only a week away and I haven't even started to prepare.* • *My exam's still three weeks away, so I've got plenty of time.*

a·way INTO PLACE /ə'weɪ/ *adv* [not gradable] in or into the usual or a suitable (esp. enclosed) place • *Would you put the ice-cream away in the freezer.* • *My grandparents had £800 hidden away in an old shoe box.*

a·way GRADUALLY /ə'weɪ/ *adv* [not gradable] gradually until mostly or completely gone • *to wear/rust away* • *All the water's boiled away and the saucepan's ruined.* • *The music faded/died away as the procession moved slowly up the street.* • *All the snow had melted away.* • *You should go to see the dentist before your teeth rot away completely.* • *We used to while away* (= spend time at) *the weekends at my aunt's cottage in the country.* • *We danced the night away* (= until the night was over).

a·way CONTINUOUSLY /ə'weɪ/ *adv* [not gradable] continuously or repeatedly, or busily • *I forgot all about the kettle and left it boiling away for half an hour.* • *I was still writing away when the exam finished.* • *Chris has been working/hammering away in the garden all day.* • *You two never pay attention, you're always chattering/laughing away.* • *Poor Diane hasn't slept a wink – she was coughing away all night.*

awe /£ɔː, $ɑː/ *n* [U] a feeling of great respect usually mixed with fear or surprise • *The sight of Father Christmas* **filled** *the children with awe.* • *I've always* **held** *pianists in awe, because I'd like to have become one myself.* • *I am quite* **in** *awe* **of** *brain surgeons.* • *You can't help but* **stand in** *awe* **of** (= respect greatly and fear slightly) *such powerful people.* • If something is awe-**inspiring**, it causes you to admire or respect it greatly: *Niagara Falls is a really awe-inspiring sight.* ○ *Her knowledge of computers is quite awe-inspiring.*

awe *obj* /£ɔː, $ɑː/ *v* [T] *Br* **aweing** or *Am* **awing** • *I was awed but not frightened by the huge gorilla.* • *Her paintings have awed and amazed the public for half a century.* • *The audience was awed* **into** *silence by her stunning performance.*

awed /£ɔːd, $ɑːd/ *adj* • *awed humility/reverence/respect/admiration* • *"How does she manage to run so fast at her age?" he asked in awed tones.*

awe·some /£'ɔː·səm, $'ɑː-/ *adj* causing feelings of great admiration, respect or fear • *an awesome performance/spectacle/achievement/event/experience* • *We would then face the awesome* **prospect** *of nuclear war.* • *Berliners now had the awesome* **task** *of dismantling the Wall.* • *(Am slang) He looks* **totally** *awesome* (= extremely good) *in his new suit.*

awe·struck /£'ɔː·strʌk, $'ɑː-/, **awe·strick·en** *adj* filled with feelings of admiration or respect • *an awestruck admirer/fan/visitor/tourist* • *I could tell she was impressed from the awestruck expression on her face.*

aw·ful BAD /£'ɔː·fᵊl, $'ɑː-/ *adj* (very) bad, unpleasant, or of low quality • *The bomb victims suffered some awful injuries.* • *We've had an awful journey – there was heavy traffic all the way.* • *Isn't all this wind and rain awful?* • *That awful man is always harassing the women in the office.* • *What an awful thing to say.* • *Would life be so awful without a car?* • *That food* **smells** *awful – is it safe to eat?* • *You* **look** *awful. Have you seen a doctor?* • *My head* **feels** *awful – I think I must have flu.* • *"Great God! this is an awful place"* (Captain R.F. Scott writing about the South Pole, 1912)

aw·ful·ly /£'ɔː·fᵊl·i, $'ɑː-/ *adv* • *England played awfully throughout the game.*

aw·ful·ness /£'ɔː·fᵊl·nəs, $'ɑː-/ *n* [U] • *You can't appreciate the true/sheer awfulness of war until you've actually experienced it.*

aw·ful VERY GREAT /£'ɔː·fᵊl, $'ɑː-/ *adj* [before n] very great • *It was an awful risk to take on that job, but it proved worthwhile in the end.* • *The president is heading for an awful beating in the next election.* • *I don't know an awful lot* (= very much) *about art, but I'm learning.* • *Fortunately it won't make an awful lot of difference if I don't pass the test.*

aw·ful·ly /£'ɔː·fᵊl·i, $'ɑː-/, *Am infml also* **aw·ful** *adv* • If you use 'awfully' before an adjective or adverb, it means 'very' or 'extremely': *I'm not awfully good at skiing – in fact I'm rather bad.* ○ *I can't ski awfully well.* ○ *It's an awfully long time since we last saw each other.* ○ *It's an awfully long way to the shops.* ○ *I'm awfully sorry, but we've forgotten to reserve you a table.* • *(fml dated) Would you mind awfully* (= very much) *if I didn't accompany you to the dance?* • LP> **Very, completely**

a·while /ə'waɪl/ *adv* [not gradable] for a short time • *Stay awhile and rest.* • *I'd like to rest awhile before we continue hiking.*

awk·ward DIFFICULT /£'ɔː·kwəd, $'ɑː·kwɚd/ *adj* difficult to use, do, or deal with • *Some of the questions were rather awkward, but I still enjoyed the exam.* • *It was an awkward ascent, but we reached the top eventually.* • *It was an awkward corner to get round, so take it slowly.* • *That journalist's an awkward* **customer** (= a difficult person to deal with) *– she's always asking politicians the questions that they'd prefer not to answer.* • *My car's awkward* **to**

drive./ My car's an awkward car **to** *drive.* [+ *(to)* infinitive] • *He responded well to a very awkward situation.* • *"We could make things very awkward* **for** *you if you refuse to cooperate," the detective threatened.*

awk·ward·ly /£'ɔː·kwəd·li, $'ɑː·kwɚd-/ *adv* • *The car was parked awkwardly across the pavement.* • *Owners should not abandon their dogs when they become awkwardly large.*

awk·ward [ANXIOUS] /£'ɔː·kwəd, $'ɑː·kwɚd/ *adj* causing inconvenience, anxiety or embarrassment • *an awkward position/situation* • *Her controversial comment was followed by an awkward silence.* • *They'd chosen an awkward time to call as I'd just got into the bath.* • *The police asked some awkward questions about where the money had come from.* • If someone **feels** awkward they feel embarrassed or nervous: *I always feel awkward when I'm with Chris – he's so difficult to talk to.* ○ *I hate being the first to arrive at a party – it makes me feel so awkward.*

awk·ward·ly /£'ɔː·kwəd·li, $'ɑː·kwɚd-/ *adv* • *The publication of the economic statistics was awkwardly timed for the Government.* • *He sat awkwardly at the back of the classroom while the teacher criticised his essay.*

awk·ward·ness /£'ɔː·kwəd·nəs, $'ɑː·kwɚd-/ *n* [U] • *In spite of the divorce there was no awkwardness between them – in fact they seemed very much at ease.*

awk·ward [NOT HELPFUL] /£'ɔː·kwəd, $'ɑː·kwɚd/ *adj esp. Br* (intentionally) not helpful; UNCOOPERATIVE • *Just stop being so awkward and help me push the car, will you!* • *It's rather awkward* **of** *you to refuse to do this job.*

awk·ward·ly /£'ɔː·kwəd·li, $'ɑː·kwɚd-/ *adv*

awk·ward [GRACELESS] /£'ɔː·kwəd, $'ɑː·kwɚd/ *adj* lacking grace or skill when moving; INELEGANT • *an awkward posture*

awk·ward·ly /£'ɔː·kwəd·li, $'ɑː·kwɚd-/ *adv* • *an awkwardly arranged vase of flowers* • *She fell awkwardly when she was skiing and twisted her ankle.* • *Her uncomfortable shoes made her walk awkwardly.* • *He contorted himself awkwardly to fit inside the tiny car.*

awn·ing /£'ɔː·nɪŋ, $'ɑː-/, *Am* **sun·shade**, *Aus* **sun·blind** *n* [C] a piece of material such as CANVAS or plastic supported by a frame and used to protect from the sun or rain • *The gaily striped awnings of the little shops and market stalls made an attractive scene.* • *Annie's fall from the hotel window was broken by a restaurant awning.* • *The sun beat down through the yellow awnings on passengers dozing on the deck.* • *We parked the caravan and then set about putting the awning up.*

a·woke /£ə'wəʊk, $-'woʊk/ *past simple of* AWAKE

a·wo·ken /£ə'wəʊ·kən, $-'woʊ-/ *past participle of* AWAKE

AWOL /£'eɪ·wɒl, $-wɑːl/ *adj* [after v; not gradable] *abbreviation for* (esp. of soldiers) Absent Without LEAVE (= permission) • *The pilot is serving 22 days detention for* **going** *AWOL.* • *(fig.) Two computers have* **gone** *AWOL* (= been borrowed without permission or stolen) *from the office.* • *Half the squad is still AWOL.*

awry /ə'raɪ/ *adj* [after v], *adv* not in the intended manner, or out of position • *Everything that* **goes** *awry* (= wrong) *in the town is blamed on the nuclear power station.* • *The strike has sent the plans for investment seriously awry.* • *We couldn't hear the cello very well because the balance with the piano was awry.* • *He was a scruffy man whose clothes were always hopelessly awry* (= untidy).

aw–shucks /ɔː'ʃʌks/ *adj Am* showing a shy or a modest character or way of behaving • *After the rescue he just shrugged and gave an aw-shucks smile that suggested anyone could have done it.* • See also SHUCKS.

axe [TOOL], *Am also* **ax** /æks/ *n* [C] a tool used for cutting wood and which consists of a heavy iron or steel blade at the end of a long wooden handle • *Julian used an axe to chop the old apple tree down.* • If you **have an axe to grind** you have a personal, sometimes secret, reason for wanting something to happen, or a particular idea or belief that you are always trying to persuade other people to agree with, or a good reason for complaining about something: *Environmentalists have no political axe to grind – they just want to save the planet.* ○ *He's always grinding his axe about avoiding sexism and racism.* ○ *Tim certainly has an axe to grind now that his salary has been reduced.* • See also BATTLEAXE. • [PIC] **Axe**

axe *obj* [REDUCE], *Am also* **ax** /æks/ *v* [T] to reduce (services, jobs, payments) greatly or completely without warning or in a single action • *Rural railway lines risk being axed because they are unprofitable.* • *The city council is axing recycling facilities in order to save money.* • *Because of the recession the company is to axe 350 jobs/20% of the workforce.* • *The TV series/magazine will be axed owing to a decline in popularity.* • *The committee is likely to recommend the axing of the nuclear project.*

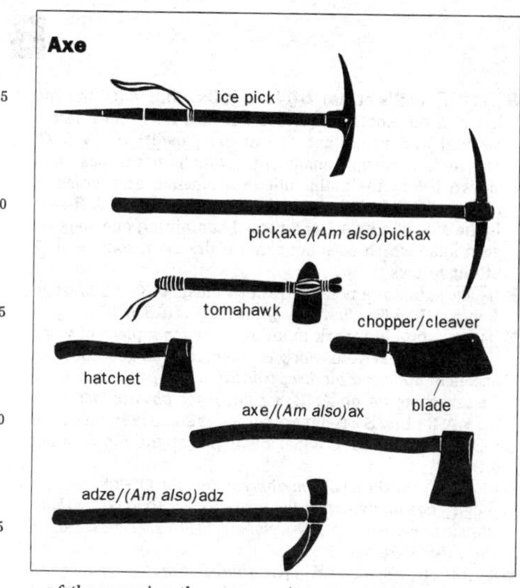

axe, *Am also* **ax** /æks/ *n* • If a person **gets the axe** they lose their job: *They got the axe after they were discovered stealing computers from the office.* • If a service, plan, etc. **gets the axe** it is stopped or prevented from happening: *Religious programmes will be the first to* **get** *the axe* (= be removed) *if she's put in charge of the station.*

ax·i·om /'æk·si·əm/ *n* [C] a statement or principle which is generally accepted to be true, but is not necessarily so • *It is a widely held axiom that governments should not negotiate with terrorists.* • *The victorious team had skilfully demonstrated the old axiom about attack being the best form of defence.* • *(specialized)* In mathematics, science, etc., an axiom is a formal statement or principle from which other statements can be obtained: *Euclid's axioms form the foundation of his system of geometry.*

ax·i·o·mat·ic /£ˌæk·si·ə'mæt·ɪk, $-'mæţ-/ *adj* • *It is an axiomatic* (= obvious and not needing to be proved) *fact that governments rise and fall on the state of the economy.* • *It seems axiomatic that everyone would benefit from a better scientific education.*

ax·i·o·mat·ic·al·ly /£ˌæk·si·ə'mæt·ɪ·kli, $-'mæţ-/ *adv*

ax·is /'æk·sɪs/ *n* [C] *pl* **axes** /'æk·siːz/ a real or imaginary straight line which goes through the centre of a spinning object, or a line which divides a SYMMETRICAL shape into two equal halves, or a line on a GRAPH used to show the position of a point • *The Earth revolves about the axis which joins the North and South Poles.* • *It has been predicted that the Earth will tilt on its axis, causing catastrophic famine and disease.* • *The diameter of a circle is also an axis.* • *Plot distance on the vertical Y-axis against time on the horizontal X-axis.* • An axis between esp. governments or politicians is an agreement to work together to achieve a particular aim: *the Franco-German axis* • The **Axis Powers** in World War Two were Germany, Italy and Japan.

ax·le /'æk·sl̩/ *n* [C] a bar connected to the centre of a circular object such as a wheel which allows or causes it to turn, esp. one connecting two wheels of a vehicle • (J)

a·ya·tol·lah /£ˌaɪ·ə'tɒl·ə, $-'toʊ·lə/ *n* [C] a religious leader of Shiite Muslims in Iran

aye /aɪ/ *adv* [C; not gradable], *n* another word for yes, or a vote or voter in support of a suggestion, idea, law, etc. • *"Would you prefer not to work?" "Oh aye, I'd stop tomorrow if I could."* • *"Aye, aye, Captain," said the sailor, nodding her head.* • *All those who support this proposal say "Aye".* • *In the British parliament, MPs are divided into the Ayes and the Noes when they vote.*

AZT /£ˌeɪ·zed'tiː, $-ziː'-/ *n* [U] a drug used in the treatment of AIDS • *Among the drugs he took was AZT, which may control symptoms in some AIDS cases.*

a·zure /£'æʒ·ər, £'æz·jʊər, $-ɚ/ *adj* [U], *n* (having) the bright blue colour of the sky on a sunny day • *The once azure skies of Athens have been ruined by atmospheric pollution.*

B b

B [LETTER] (*pl* **B's** or **Bs**), **b** (*pl* **b's** or **bs**) /biː/ *n* [C] the 2nd letter of the English alphabet • **B and B** is *abbreviation for* **bed and breakfast**. See at BED [FURNITURE]. • A **B-movie** is a cheaply made film, which in the past was shown before the main film in a cinema, and which is often not well written and contains bad acting. • A **B-side** is the side of a SINGLE (=a record containing one song on each side) which does not contain the main song. • [LP] **Silent letters**

B [MUSIC] /biː/ *n* a note in Western music • *Bach's Mass in B minor* [U] • *The first note of the song is a B.* [C]

B [MARK] /biː/ *n* a mark in an exam or for a piece of work that shows that your work is thought of as good but not excellent • *I was a bit disappointed just to be given a B, as I was hoping for an A.* [C] • *I* **got** *B for physics last term.* [U] • A **B plus/B+** is a mark which is slightly higher than a B. A **B minus/B-** is a mark which is slightly lower than a B.

b [NUMBER], *Br* **bn** *n* [C] *Am abbreviation for* BILLION

b [BORN] *adj abbreviation for* BORN [BEGAN TO EXIST] • *John Winston Lennon (b. 9 October 1940, Liverpool, d. 8 December 1980, New York).*

BA /ˌbiːˈeɪ/, *Am also* **AB** *n* [C] *abbreviation for* Bachelor of Arts (=a first college degree in the **arts** or **social sciences**, or someone having this degree) • *Farida* **has** *a BA* **in** *history* **from** *the University of Sussex.* • *Jake is* **doing** *a BA at Edinburgh University.* • *Both their children are now BAs.* • [LP] **Schools and colleges**

baa /£bɑː, $bæ/ *v, n* **baas, baaing**, *past* **baaed** (to make) the sound that a sheep or LAMB makes • *From the fields we could hear sheep baaing.* [I] • *We heard the neigh of a horse, and the baa of a sheep.* [C] • *"Baa, baa, black sheep, have you any wool?"* (traditional children's song)

bab·ble *(obj)* [TALK] /ˈbæb·l̩/ *v* to talk or say (something) in a quick, confused, excited or foolish way • *Don't babble – I can't understand what you're saying.* [I] • *The children babbled excitedly among themselves.* [I] • *You were babbling* **incoherently** *in your sleep last night.* [I] • *She was babbling something* **about** *her ring being stolen.* [T] • *"It wasn't me – I don't know anything about it," babbled Jason.* [+ clause]

bab·ble /ˈbæb·l̩/ *n* [U] • *We listened to Isabel's childish babble* (=quick, confused or foolish talk) *as she played.* • *I could hear the babble* (=low continuous sound) **of** *voices in the next room.*

-bab·ble /-ˌbæb·l̩/ *combining form* • -babble is confusing talk about the stated subject: *computer-babble* ○ *psycho-babble* (=confusing talk about the way in which the human mind works) ○ *Euro-babble* (=confusing talk about Europe)

bab·ble [WATER NOISE] /ˈbæb·l̩/ *v* [I] *literary* (of a stream) to make the low, continuous noise of water flowing over stones • *A small stream babbles through the valley.* • *They rested a while by a babbling* **brook**.

babe /beɪb/ *n* [C] *literary* a small baby or *(infml)* an affectionate way of addressing a wife, husband, lover, etc. • *a newborn babe* • *(infml) It's up to you, babe. I'll do whatever you say.* • A babe is also an attractive young person, often someone who is an actor or a singer of popular music: *a Hollywood babe* ○ *He said that he enjoyed watching the babes on the beach.* • **Babes in arms** (=very small babies) *are not allowed in the cinema.* • *"Out of the mouths of babes and sucklings hast thou perfected praise"* (Bible, Matthew 21.16) • [LP] **Titles and forms of address**

ba·bel /ˈbeɪ·bəl/ *n* [C usually sing] a state of confusion caused by many people talking at the same time or using different languages • *Communication between different computers has been made difficult by the babel* **of** *computer languages used by different machines.*

ba·boon /bəˈbuːn/ *n* [C] a type of large monkey found in Africa and S. Asia, which has a long pointed hairless face and large teeth • [PIC] **Apes and monkeys**

ba·by /ˈbeɪ·bi/ *n* [C] a very young child, esp. one that has not yet begun to walk or talk • *a newborn baby* • *a six-week-old baby* • *a baby boy* • *baby clothes* • *baby food* • *Sandra* **had** *a baby* (=gave birth to it) *on May 29th.* • *Lucy and Eric are* **expecting** *a baby* (=it is expected to be born) *in the autumn.* • *Owen is the baby* (=the youngest person) *of the family.* • Baby animals are young animals: *a baby elephant* ○ *a baby chick* • Baby vegetables are types of vegetable that are specially grown to stay small: *a baby cauliflower* ○ *baby carrots* • *(disapproving)* Baby can be used to refer to an adult or esp. an older child who is crying or behaving childishly: *Don't be a such a baby – this won't hurt a bit!* • *(esp. Am)* 'Baby' is an affectionate way of addressing a wife, husband or lover: *I love you, baby.* [as form of address] • *(infml)* Your baby is something that you have a special interest in and responsibility for: *I don't know much about the project – it's Philip's baby.* • A **baby boom** is a large increase in the number of babies born among a particular group of people during a particular time: *There was a baby boom in Britain and the US after World War II.* ○ *They are part of the baby-boom* **generation**. • A **baby boomer** is a person who was born during a baby boom, esp. the one that happened in Britain and the US between approximately 1945 and 1965. • **Baby carriage/Baby buggy** is *Am for* PRAM. • *(Br)* A **baby-minder** is a CHILDMINDER. • **Baby milk** is artificial milk which can be given to babies instead of milk from their mother. • **Baby talk** means the words that a very young child uses, or the words used by some adults when they talk to babies. • A **baby tooth** (also **milk tooth**) is any of the set of teeth that young children or some other young mammals have, until they fall out and are replaced by a new permanent set. • *"I'll be your baby tonight"* (title of a song by Bob Dylan, 1968) • [LP] **Age, Titles and forms of address** Ⓟ

ba·by *obj* /ˈbeɪ·bi/ *v* [T] *infml* • *The boys were now ten and twelve and didn't want their mother to baby them* (=to treat them as if they were still very young children).

ba·by·ish /ˈbeɪ·bi·ɪʃ/ *adj disapproving* • *The older children found the toys too babyish.*

ba·by·hood /ˈbeɪ·bi·hʊd/ *n* [U] • Babyhood is the period of time when you are a baby: *A series of photographs on their mantelpiece show their daughter's progression from babyhood to adolescence.*

ba·by·sit *(obj)* /ˈbeɪ·bi·sɪt/, **sit** *v* **-tt-** to take care of (someone's baby or child) while that person is out, usually by going to their home • *I'm babysitting* **for** *Jane on Tuesday evening while she goes to her yoga class.* [I] • *Seth earns extra pocket money by babysitting.* [I] • *I'm going to babysit my brother's kids for the weekend.* [T]

bab·y·sit·ter /£ˈbeɪ·biˌsɪt·əʳ, $-ˌsɪt̬·ɚ/, **sit·ter** *n* [C] • *I promised the babysitter that we'd be home by midnight.*

bac·cha·na·li·an /ˌbæk·əˈneɪ·li·ən/ *adj literary* (esp. of a party) involving a lot of drinking of alcohol, uncontrolled behaviour and possibly sexual activity • *a Bacchanalian orgy*

bac·cy /ˈbæk·i/ *n* [U] *slang for* TOBACCO

bach·e·lor /£ˈbætʃ·əl·əʳ, $-ɚ/ *n* [C] a man who has never married • *He remained a bachelor until he was well into his 40s.* • *Simon is a* **confirmed** *bachelor* (=He is unlikely ever to want to get married). • *She could have had her pick of* **eligible** (=desirable because of being rich and attractive) *bachelors, but she married a boy she'd known all her life.* • *He says that he's enjoying his bachelor life and has no plans to marry yet.* • *André lives in a bachelor apartment in Paris.* • A **Bachelor's degree** is a first degree at college or university.

ba·cil·lus /bəˈsɪl·əs/ *n* [C] *pl* **bacilli** /bəˈsɪl·aɪ/ a bacterium which is shaped like a rod. There are various types of bacillus, some of which can cause disease • *Some bacilli can cause fatal illnesses.*

back [RETURN] /bæk/ *adv* [not gradable] in, into or towards a previous place or condition, or an earlier time • *When you take the scissors, remember to put them back.* • *She went to America for two years, but now she's come back.* • *He left a note saying 'Gone out. Back soon'.* • *Do you think we can get to Madrid* **and** *back from here in a day?* • *He looked back* (=looked behind him) *and saw they were following him.* • *(fig.) Don't look back* (=think of the past), *concentrate on the present!* • *Looking at her old photographs* **brought** *back* (=made her remember) *a lot of memories.* • *His girlfriend left him last month and he badly* **wants** *her back* (=to return to him). • *I was woken by a thunderstorm, and I couldn't* **get** *back* (=could not return) **to** *sleep.* • *I would never have thought that flared trousers would* **come** *back* (=would return) **into fashion**, *but they did.* • *The last time we saw Lowell was back* (=at an earlier time) *in January.* • *The school was built* **way** *back* (=at an earlier time) *in the 19th* *century.* • *This tradition dates back to* (= to the earlier time of) *the 16th century.* • *Mrs Mackay has lived in that house* **as** *far back* (= for as long a period of time) **as** *I can remember.* • Back can also mean in return: *If he hits me, I'll* **hit** *him back.* ○ *You're not just going to let her say those things about you without* **fighting** *back, are you?* ○ *I'll* **get** *her back/***get** *back* **at** *her/***pay** *her back* (= I will do something unpleasant to her in return) **for** *what she did.* • Back can also mean in reply: *I'm busy at the moment – can I call you back?* ○ *I wrote to Donna several months ago, but she hasn't written back yet.* • **Back to the drawing board/Back to square one** means that something you have done has been unsuccessful and you must start again. • *"I'll be back"* (expression used by Arnold Schwarzenegger in the *Terminator* films, 1984-) • PIC› **Prepositions of movement** KOR

back /bæk/ *adj* [not gradable] • *She went to America for two years, but now she's back* (= has returned). • *1940s fashions seem to be back* (= fashionable again) *this year.* • A **back copy, back issue** or **back number** of a newspaper or magazine is one of an earlier date than the one now on sale. KOR • **Back talk** is *Am for* BACKCHAT.

back FARTHER AWAY /bæk/ *adv* [not gradable] farther away in distance • *If we push the table back against the wall, we'll have more room.* • *This machine is dangerous –* **stand (well)** *back.* • *"***Keep** *back!" he shouted, "Don't come any closer!"* • *The dentist told her patient to* **lie** *back in the chair.* • *He* **sat** *back on the sofa.* • *She* **threw** *back her head and laughed uproariously.* • *The house is set back* **from** *the road.* • *Marsha always wears her hair* **tied** *back* **from** *her face.* • *Don't let anything* **hold** *you back* (= stop you from doing what you want to do). • *She swayed gently* **back and forth** (= moving first in one direction and then in the opposite one) *to the music.* • KOR

back *(obj)* /bæk/ *v* • *Ann gave up driving when she backed the car* (= drove it backwards) **into** *the garage door.* [T] • *I failed my driving test because I was no good at backing* (= driving backwards) *round corners.* [I always + adv/prep] • *Please could you back your car* **up** (= drive it backwards) *so that I can get mine out of the drive.* [M] • *I backed* **away** (= walked backwards) *nervously.* [I always + adv/prep] • *The gunman shouted to the police officer, "Back* **off** (= move away), *and no one will get hurt."* [I always + adv/prep] • *(fig.) She started to criticize me, then suddenly backed* **off** (= stopped). [I always + adv/prep] • If you **back down,** you admit that you were wrong or that you have been defeated: *Eventually, Roberto backed down and apologized.* ○ *Local residents have forced the local council to back down* **from/on** *its plans to build a nightclub in their street.* • To **back out** is to decide not to do something that you had said you would do: *You agreed to come. You can't back out now!* ○ *They backed out* **of** *the deal the day before they were due to sign the contract.* • PIC› **Driving**

back FARTHEST PART /bæk/ *n* [U] the inside or outside part of an object, vehicle, building, etc. that is farthest from the front • *He jotted her name down on the back* **of** *an envelope.* • *There are notes at the back* **of** *the book.* • *I found my tennis racket at the back* **of** *the cupboard.* • *We sat at the back* **of** *the bus.* • *Two small children were asleep in the back* **of** *the car.* • *Our seats were right at the back* **of** *the theatre.* • *The bathroom is at the back* **of** *the house.* • *There is a beautiful garden* **at** *the back* **of***/(Am also)* **in** *back* **of** (= behind) *the house.* • *He put his jacket on the back* **of** *his chair* (= the part of the chair which you put your back against when you sit on it). • *(Br and Aus) You've put your jumper on* **back to front** *(esp. Am* **backwards***)* (= with the back part at the front). • *She knows her part in the play* **back to front** (= very well). • *"Where's Ted?" "He's (Br and Aus)* **out/round the back***/(Am)* **out back** (= in the area behind the house)." • *If there's no reply at the front door, come* **round the back** (= to the part of the house that is furthest from the front). • **The** back **of** your **hand** is the side that has hair growing on it. • *I know this area* **like the back of** *my* **hand** (= I know it very well). • *They live in some village in* **the back of beyond** (= far away from any big town). • If something is **at/in the back of** your **mind,** you intend to do it, but are not actively thinking about it: *It's been at the back of my mind to call José for several days now, but I haven't got round to it yet.* • **Back saw** is *Am for* **tenon saw.** See at TENON. • KOR

back /bæk/ *adj* [before n; not gradable] • *She left the house by the back* **door.** • *(fig.) The president is trying to introduce price rises through the back door* (= indirectly). • *The back* **seat** *(of the car) folds down.* • If someone **takes a/the back seat,** they choose not to be in a position of responsibility in an organization or activity. • A **back-seat driver** is a passenger in a car who keeps giving advice to the driver that the driver has not asked for: *(fig.) It is expected that the former prime minister will be a back-seat driver* (= have a controlling influence on what happens) *in the new government.* • *Our cat has broken one of her back* **legs** (= legs farthest from her head). • If something is **on the back burner,** it is temporarily not being dealt with or considered, esp. because it is not urgent or important: *We've had to* **put** *our plans to buy a new car on the back burner for a while.* • *(Br)* **Back passage** is used to avoid saying RECTUM. • A **back road** is a small road which does not have much traffic on it. • The **back streets** of a city or town are the older and poorer areas. • *(Br and Aus)* A **back-street abortion***/(Am)* **back-alley abortion** is an illegal and dangerous operation to end a pregnancy done by someone who is not medically qualified.

back *(obj)* /bæk/ *v* • *The material is backed* **with** *a heavy lining* (= has another material put onto the back of it to make it stronger or protect it). [T] • *The house* **backs onto** *a narrow alley* (= has a narrow passage behind it).

back·ing /ˈbæk·ɪŋ/ *n* [C/U] • *It's strong cloth – it might be useful as (a) backing* (= something put on the back of something else in order to make it stronger or protect it).

back *obj* SUPPORT /bæk/ *v* [T] to give support to (someone or something) with money or words • *The management has refused to back our proposals for change.* • *The horse I backed* (= risked money on so that I could win more money if it won a race) *came in last.* • *(fig.) In all his years as a book publisher, he rarely backed the wrong horse* (= supported someone or something or an action that was unsuccessful). • *He backed* **(up)** (= supported) *his claim with a sheaf of documents.* [T/M] • *Will you back me* **up** (= say that I am telling the truth) *if I say that I never saw him?* [M] • *(specialized)* To **back up** computer information, or to **back** computer information **up** is to make an extra copy of it which you keep separately from your computer. See also BACKUP. • KOR

back·ing /ˈbæk·ɪŋ/ *n* [U] • *If I go ahead with the plan, can I count on your backing* (= support, esp. with money)? • Backing is also music or singing which is played or performed to support a song or tune, esp. a popular one: *a backing track* ○ *She sang as part of an all-women backing (Am and Aus usually* **backup***)* **group.**

back·er /£ˈbæk·əʳ, $-ɚ/ *n* [C] • *We need financial backers* **for** *the project.*

-backed /-bækt/ *combining form* • *government-backed contracts* • *bank-backed loans* • *US-backed intervention*

back BODY PART /bæk/ *n* [C] the part of your body that is opposite to the front, from your neck to the top of your legs • *Sleeping on a bed that is too soft can be bad for your back.* • *He lay* **on** *his back, staring at the ceiling.* • *Harry spent six weeks* **on** *his back* (= lying in bed because of illness or injury) *after his car accident.* • *I'm going to get dressed now – please* **turn** *your back* (= turn round so that you cannot see me). • *(fig.) Don't* **turn** *your back* **on** *us now* (= refuse to help or to have anything to do with us). • *If you lift that suitcase you might* **put** *your back* **out** (= cause a serious injury to your back). • *What do they say about me* **behind** *my* **back** (= when I am not there)? • *They have carried on their business operations (by* **riding)** **on the back of** (= by using) *established firms.* • If you achieve something **on the back of** an earlier success, you achieve it soon after that success, and as a result of it: *The advertising agency secured the contract on the back of their previous successful campaigns.* • *He owes money to everyone – he's really* **got** *his* **back to the wall***/his* **back is** *really* **to the wall** *now* (= he has serious problems). • *(infml) Why don't you* **get off** *my* **back** (= stop criticizing me)? • *Come on!* **Put** *your* **back into it** (= make more of a physical effort)! • *(infml) He's only trying to* **put/get** *your* **back up** (= annoy you). • A **back-stabber** is someone who says harmful things about you when you are not there to defend yourself or your reputation. See also **stab** someone **in the back** at STAB. • *"With our backs to the wall, and believing in the justice of our cause, each one of us must fight on to the end"* (Earl Haig's order to British troops, 1918) • KOR

back SPORT /bæk/ *n* [C] (in some sports, such as football or HOCKEY) one of the players in a team who try to stop players from the other team from scoring goals, rather than trying to score goals themselves • Compare FORWARD SPORT. • KOR

back up *v adv* [I] (esp. of traffic or water) to collect in a place because something is preventing it from moving • *The traffic is starting to back up on the M25.* • *Our sink is backing up* (= water is not flowing out of it) *– we'd better call a plumber.*

backed up /bækt/ *adj* • *The traffic is backed up* (= has formed a line which is not moving) *for six miles on the road to the coast.* • *Our sink is backed up* (= water is not flowing out of it).

back·ache /ˈbæk·eɪk/ *n* a pain in your back • *Many people who work in offices get backache because they do not sit at their desks properly.* [U] • *Doing all that gardening has given me a dreadful backache.* [C] • [LP]› **Feelings and pains**

back·bench /bækˈbentʃ/ *n* [C] (the seats in the British parliament used by) members who do not have official positions in the government or in an opposition political party • *Following his resignation, the former Chancellor of the Exchequer has returned to the backbenches.* • *The Prime Minister expects strong support from the Labour backbenches.* • *Unless there is a surprise backbench revolt, the proposal is likely to be accepted.* • Compare FRONTBENCH.

back·bench·er /£bækˈben·tʃəʳ, $-tʃ ɚ/ *n* [C] • *The advantage of being a backbencher is that you can speak your mind.* • Compare **frontbencher** at FRONTBENCH.

back·bit·ing /£ˈbæk·baɪ·tɪŋ, $-t̬ɪŋ/ *n* [U] unpleasant and unkind words that are said about someone who is not there • *A lot of backbiting goes on in our office.*

back·bone [BONES] /£ˈbæk·bəʊn, $-boʊn/ *n* [C] the SPINE [BONE] • *She stood with her backbone rigid.* [C] • *(fig.) The Pennines are the backbone* (= central row of mountains) **of** *England.* [C] • **The** backbone **of** something is the most important part of it and gives it support and strength: *Farming and cattle-raising are the backbone of the country's economy.* [U] ○ *They have been the backbone of the local golf club for years.* [U]

back·bone [STRENGTH] /£ˈbæk·bəʊn, $-boʊn/ *n* [U] strength, bravery or strength of character • *The manager has taken on four new players in an attempt to* **put** *some backbone* **into** *the team.* • *I don't think Robin* **has** *the backbone for this kind of job.* • *Will he* **have** *the backbone* **to** *tell them what he thinks?* [+ *to* infinitive] • *The new prime minister isn't* **showing** *much backbone so far.* • (OK) (N)

back·break·ing /ˈbæk·breɪ·kɪŋ/ *adj* needing a lot of hard physical effort and very tiring • *Digging the garden was backbreaking* **work**.

back·chat /ˈbæk·tʃæt/, *Am usually* **back talk** *n* [U] rude remarks made when answering someone in authority • *That's enough of that backchat! You'll do as you're told.*

back·comb *obj Br* /£ˈbæk·kəʊm, $-koʊm/, *Am and Aus* **tease** *v* [T] to hold (your hair) away from your head and COMB it towards your head, in order to make it look thicker

back·date *obj* /ˌbækˈdeɪt, ˈ--/ *v* [T] to make (something) effective from an earlier time • *They got a pay rise in March which was backdated* **to** *January.* • *We were late paying our electricity bill, so we backdated* (= wrote an earlier date on) *the* **cheque** *when we sent it.* • Compare PREDATE; POSTDATE.

back·drop /£ˈbæk·drɒp, $-drɑːp/, *esp. Br* **back·cloth** *n* [C] a large piece of cloth with buildings, countryside, etc. painted on it that is hung at the back of a stage during a performance • *A moonlit sky was painted on the backdrop for the second act of the ballet.* • *(fig.) The mountains form a dramatic backdrop* **to** (= can be seen behind) *the little village.* • *(fig.) Their love affair began* **against** *a backdrop* **of** *war* (= while war was happening).

back·fire [HAVE RESULT] /£ˌbækˈfaɪəʳ, $-ˈfaɪr/ *v* [I] (of a plan) to have the opposite result from the one you intended • *Her* **plans** *to make him jealous backfired* **on** *her when he went off with her best friend.* • *The company's* **tactics/strategy** *to expand their market backfired.*

back·fire [MAKE NOISE] /£ˈbæk·faɪəʳ, $-faɪr/ *v* [I] (of an engine) to make a loud noise as a result of fuel burning too early • *I was woken by the sound of a truck backfiring.*

back·gam·mon /ˈbæk·gæm·ən/ *n* [U] a game for two people in which you throw DICE and move circular pieces around a special board with narrow triangular shaped patterns on it • [PIC]› **Games**

back·ground [THINGS BEHIND] /ˈbæk·graʊnd/ *n* the things that can be seen or heard behind other things that are closer or louder • *The little figure that you can just see* **in the** *background* **of** *the photograph is me.* [U] Compare FOREGROUND. • *If you listen carefully to this piece of music, you can hear a flute* **in the** *background.* [U] • *We couldn't hear what they were saying on the tape – there was too much background* **noise**. • *He has written the background* **music** *for a number of films.* • *(fig.) He keeps himself to himself – likes to stay* **in the** *background* (= not to be noticed). [U] • *(fig.) Her worries about her job have* **faded into** *the background* (= become less important or noticeable) *since she learnt about her father's illness.* [U] • A background is what can be seen behind the main things or people in a picture: *The artist himself did not paint the backgrounds* **to** *his pictures – they were done by his pupils.* [C] ○ *He has photographed her* **against** *lots of different backgrounds.* [C] ○ *They were filmed* **against** *a background* **of** *dark fir trees.* [C] ○ *The book's cover has white lettering* **on** *a blue background.* [C] • Background can also mean the conditions that existed before a particular event happened, and which help to explain why it happened: *To understand the present conflict, we need to consider the historical and political background* **to** *it.* [U] ○ *These decisions have had to be taken* **against a** *background of high unemployment.* [U] ○ *Can you give me some background* **on** (= information about the conditions that existed before) *the situation?* [U] • Background can also be used to refer to something that is done before, and in preparation for, something else: *Students are expected to do some background reading before the course starts.* ○ *The training programme is designed to provide background knowledge of the business world.* ○ *The book provides background* **information** *on the history of the region.*

back·ground [EXPERIENCE] /ˈbæk·graʊnd/ *n* your family and your experience of education, living conditions, wealth, etc. • *Their marriage will never work – their backgrounds are too different.* [C] • *The school has pupils* **from** *many different* **ethnic/cultural/religious** *backgrounds.* [C] • *She works with children from* **deprived/disadvantaged** *backgrounds.* [C] • *They* **come from** *a* **privileged/wealthy** *background.* [C] • *Do you have any background* **in** (= experience of) *publishing?* [U] • *He has a background* **in** (= experience of) *classical music.* [C]

back·hand /ˈbæk·hænd/ *n* [C] a way of hitting the ball in games such as tennis where the arm is brought across the body with the back of the hand facing the direction of movement of the ball • *He's got a great backhand.* • *What a wonderful backhand return!* • *She kept serving to my backhand, which she knew was my weaker stroke.* • Compare FOREHAND.

back·hand·ed /ˌbækˈhæn·dɪd/ *adj* (of something said) seeming pleasant but possibly critical or unkind in reality • *a backhanded* **compliment**

back·hand·er /£ˌbækˈhæn·dəʳ, $-dɚ/ *n* [C] *infml for* BRIBE

back·lash /ˈbæk·læʃ/ *n* [C] a strong feeling among a group of people in reaction to a tendency or recent events in society or politics • *The new President encouraged the backlash* **against** *'moral laxity'.* • *The accident has* **provoked/produced** *a backlash among local people who claim that the road is dangerous.*

back·less /ˈbæk·ləs/ *adj* [not gradable] (of a dress) not covering most of your back

back·list /ˈbæk·lɪst/ *n* [C] (a list of) all the books a particular publisher has produced in the past which are still available • *a publisher's backlist* • *Not many of today's new titles will be* **on** *the backlists in ten years' time.*

back·lit /ˈbæk·lɪt/ *adj* [not gradable] lit up from behind, esp. in order to create a special effect • *a backlit stage* • *His trophies were proudly displayed in a backlit cabinet.* • *Someone was standing in the doorway, backlit from the other room.*

back·log /£ˈbæk·lɒg, $-lɑːg/ *n* [C usually sing] a large amount of things that you should have done before and must do now • *I've got a huge backlog* **of** *work to do.* • *Employees are being asked to work extra hours in order to* **clear** *the company's backlog* **of** *orders.*

back·pack /ˈbæk·pæk/ *n* [C] *Am for* RUCKSACK • [PIC]› **Luggage**

back·pack /ˈbæk·pæk/ *v* [I] • *We backpacked/went backpacking* (= travelled with our possessions in backpacks) *around Thailand.*

back·pack·er /£ˈbækˌpæk·əʳ, $-ɚ/ *n* [C] • A backpacker is a person who travels with their possessions in a backpack.

back·ped·al /ˈbæk·ped·əl, -ˈ--/ *v* [I] **-ll-** or *Am usually* **-l-** to PEDAL backwards on a bicycle, or *(fig.)* to change an opinion that you had expressed before, or do something different from what you had said you would do • *Some types of bike have brakes which you operate by backpedalling.* • *(fig.) As soon as I said I thought she was wrong, she started* *backpedalling.* • *(fig.) He said he'd help, but now he's starting to backpedal (***on** *his promise).*

back·room /bæk'ruːm, '--, -rʊm/ *n* [C] a room in which work or other activities are done out of public view or secretly • *a backroom worker* • *backroom staff* • *backroom negotiations* • *The leaflets had been produced in a backroom in Amsterdam.* • *He runs a small printing business in a backroom of his house.* • **Backroom boys** are people in an organization whose work is not seen by the public: *the newspaper's backroom boys*

back·side /bæk'saɪd, '--/ *n* [C] *infml* the part of the body that you sit on; your bottom • *After cycling for the whole day, my backside was very sore.* • *She's so lazy – she needs* **a boot/kick up the backside** (= someone should tell her to do something). • **Get off** *your* **backside** (= Do not be so lazy) *and do some work!* • *I do all the work, while all you do is* **sit (around) on** *your* **backside** (= do nothing) *all day.*

back·slap·ping /'bæk,slæp·ɪŋ/ *n* [U] a noisy expression of happiness and positive feelings, usually showing admiration for a shared success • *There was a party after the ceremony where much drinking and backslapping went on.* • *The opening of the new theatre a month ahead of schedule brought backslapping all round.* • *The meeting was one of those backslapping occasions when everyone congratulates each other.*

back·slide /'bæk·slaɪd/ *v* [I] *past* **backslid** /'bæk·slɪd/ to go back to doing something bad when you have been doing something good, esp. to stop working hard or to fail to do something that you had agreed to do • *We were making good progress on this project for a while, but now things have begun to backslide and we're behind schedule.* • *I've been trying to lose weight by going on a diet, but I've been backsliding a bit recently.* • *The government seems to be backsliding* **over/on/from** (= failing to keep) *its promise not to raise taxes.*

back·stage /'bæk·steɪdʒ, -'-/ *adj, adv* in the area behind the stage in a theatre, esp. the rooms in which actors change their clothes or where equipment is kept • *We went backstage after the show to meet the actors.* • *For backstage workers, the week before the Festival is the busiest of all.* • *(fig.) The organizers say it's a fair contest but who knows what goes on backstage* (= where the public cannot see)*?* • *(fig.) The unions were involved in backstage* (= secret) *negotiations with the management.*

back·stop [PLAYER] /£'bæk·stɒp, $-stɑːp/ *n* [C] (in ROUNDERS) a player who stands directly behind the player from the opposing team who is trying to hit the ball, and attempts to catch the ball after it has been thrown if the person does not hit it • *The team needs a more reliable backstop.* • *(Am)* Backstop is also *infml for* **catcher**. See at CATCH [TAKE HOLD]. • *(fig.) These measures are intended to be a backstop* (= a protection) *against higher inflation.*

back·stop [FENCE] /£'bæk·stɒp, $-stɑːp/ *n* [C] (in baseball) a high fence behind the player hitting the ball, which prevents balls from leaving the playing area if they are not hit or caught

back·stroke /£'bæk·strəʊk, $-stroʊk/ *n* [U] a way of swimming in which you lie on your back and move one arm and then the other straight behind you so that they pass the sides of your head, while kicking with your legs • *Can you do* **(the)** *backstroke?*

back·track /'bæk·træk/ *v* to go back along a path you have just followed, or *(fig.)* to say that you did not mean something you said earlier or that you have changed your opinion • *We went the wrong way and had to backtrack till we got to the right turning.* [I] • *(fig.) "All right," he backtracked, "It's possible that I was mistaken."* [+ clause] • *(fig.) The officers were forced to backtrack* **on** *their statements.* [I] • *(fig.) She refused to backtrack* **from** *her criticisms of the proposal.* [I]

back·up /'bæk·ʌp/ *n* (someone or something that provides) support or help, or something that you have arranged in case your main plans, equipment, etc. go wrong • *We're going to need some professional backup for this project.* [U] • *The hospital has a backup generator in case there is a power failure.* • *The party is going to be outdoors, so we'll need to organize somewhere as* **a** *backup in case it rains.* [U] • *Remember, your colleagues are your backup* **system** *when things go wrong.* • *(Am) He's a backup* (= plays if the person who usually plays is not available) *for the Dallas Cowboys.* [C] • *(Am) She used to be a backup singer for* (= sing with) *Whitney Houston.* • A backup is also a copy of information that is held on computer, which is stored separately from the computer: *Before we leave work each day, we* **make** *a backup* **of** *all the records we have entered into the computer that day.* [C] ○ *The department's backup* **disks** *are all stored in a different building.*

back·ward /£'bæk·wəd, $-wɚd/ *adj* not advanced • *When he was a child, his teachers thought he was backward* (= unable to learn as much as most children). • *People still think of it as a backward country/region/area* (= one without industry or modern machines). • If someone is **backward in coming forward**, they are shy and do not willingly express their opinions or wishes: *I'm sure Matt will tell you what he thinks of the idea – he's not usually backward in coming forward.* • See also **backward** at BACKWARDS.

back·ward·ness /£'bæk·wəd·nəs, $-wɚd-/ *n* [U] • *They were accused of backwardness* (= very old-fashioned ways) *because they had no washing machine.*

back·wards /£'bæk·wədz, $-wɚdz/, *Am and Aus also* **back·ward** *adv* [not gradable] towards the direction which is opposite to the one in which you are facing or opposite to the usual direction • *I walked backwards towards the door.* • *He took* **a step** *backwards to allow her to pass.* • *(fig.) This will be seen as* **a step** *backwards* (= as a return to older and less effective ways). • *He began counting backwards: "Ten, nine, eight ..."* • *Paul paced anxiously* **backwards and forwards** (= first in one direction and then in the opposite one). • To **bend/lean over backwards** is to try very hard to do something: *I've been bending over backwards trying to help you and this is all the thanks I get.* • Compare FORWARDS.

back·ward /£'bæk·wəd, $-wɚd/ *adj* • *She left without a backward* (= directed behind her) **glance**. • *He did a brilliant backward* (= directed towards his back) **somersault**. • *(fig. disapproving) The business is rapidly losing money because of their* **backward-looking** (= old-fashioned) *ideas.*

back·wash /£'bæk·wɒʃ, $-wɑːʃ/ *n* [U] the backward movement of waves, or the backward movement of water caused by something, such as a boat, passing through it, or *(fig.)* an indirect effect • *The water-skier was caught in the backwash from a passing motorboat, and fell off his skies.* • *(fig.) The economic and political backwash* **of** *the war is still being felt.* • *(fig.) The backwash* **of** *the President's resignation is still swirling round the capital.*

back·wa·ter /£'bæk·wɔː·tər, $-wɑː·t̬ɚ/ *n* [C] a part of a river where the water does not flow, or *(fig. disapproving)* a place which is not influenced by new ideas or events that happen in other places, and which does not change • *We tied the boat up in a quiet backwater overnight.* • *(fig.) He grew up in a rural backwater.* • *(fig.) She decided that life in the backwaters* **of** *Yorkshire was too dull, so she moved to London.* • *(fig.) This town is a real* **cultural** *backwater – it doesn't even have a cinema.* • Compare JERKWATER.

back·woods /'bæk·wʊdz/ *pl n* **the backwoods** a place in the countryside which is a long way from any town and in which not many people live • *They spent their childhood* **in** *the backwoods.* • *Not many people live in this small backwoods town.*

back·yard /£bæk'jɑːd, $-'jɑːrd/ *n* [C] *Br* a small enclosed space at the back of a house, usually with a hard surface • *The house has a small backyard, surrounded by a high brick wall.* • *(Am and Aus)* A backyard is a space at the back of a house, usually enclosed by a fence, and covered with grass. • *(fig.) These people don't want a nuclear power station to be built* **in** *their backyard* (= near to where they live). • *(fig.) The country should take a look at what is happening* **in** *its* **own** *backyard* (= in itself) *before criticizing what is taking place in other countries.*

ba·con /'beɪ·kən/ *n* [U] (thin slices of) meat from the back or sides of a pig that has been salted, and sometimes also smoked, which is often eaten fried • *I had a mug of tea and a bacon sandwich.* • *Eddie ate six* **rashers** *of bacon for breakfast.* • *He cooked us all a big breakfast of* **bacon and eggs** (= fried bacon and eggs). • *Since their father died, there's been no-one to* **bring home the bacon** (= earn money for the family to live on). • *Everyone is relying on them to* **bring home the bacon** (= succeed) *for Britain at the next Olympic games.*

bac·te·ri·a /£bæk'tɪə·ri·ə, $-'tɪr·i-/ *pl n* very small organisms that live in air, earth, water, plants and animals, and are the cause of some diseases • *Bacteria in drinking water have spread the illness.* • *Illnesses caused by bacteria can often be treated with antibiotics.*

bac·te·ri·al /£bæk'tɪə·ri·əl, $-'tɪr·i-/ *adj* [not gradable] • A bacterial **infection** is one caused by bacteria.

bac·te·ri·ol·o·gy /£bæk,tɪə·ri'ɒl·ə·dʒi, $-,tɪr·i'ɑː·lə-/ *n* [U] the scientific study of bacteria and other very small living things, esp. those which cause disease

bac·te·ri·o·log·i·cal /£bæk,tɪə·ri·ə'lɒdʒ·ɪ·kəl, $-,tɪr·i·ə'lɑː·dʒɪ-/ *adj* [not gradable] • *Bacteriological* **warfare** *uses bacteria to cause death and disease in humans.*

bac·te·ri·ol·o·gist /£bæk,tɪə·ri'ɒl·ə·dʒɪst, $-,tɪr·i'ɑː·lə-/ *n* [C]

bad UNPLEASANT /bæd/ *adj* **worse** /£wɜːs, $wɜːrs/, **worst** /£wɜːst, $wɜːrst/ unpleasant; causing difficulties or harm • *Our holiday was spoiled by bad* **weather**. • *We've just had some very bad* **news**. • *She woke from a bad* **dream**. • *I had a very bad* **night** (= did not sleep well) *last night.* • *Watch out – he's* **in a** *bad* **mood/temper** (= being unpleasant to everyone). • *Don't be so* **bad-tempered** (= unpleasant to everyone)*!* • *She's just a bad* **loser** (= She is unpleasant when she loses). • *The company has been getting a lot of bad* **publicity**/*getting a bad* **press** (= harmful things have been written or said about it) *recently.* • *The queues were so bad* (= unpleasantly long) *that I didn't bother waiting.* • *The company's financial situation is* **looking** *rather bad* (= likely to be difficult) *at the moment.* • *The damage caused by the storm was* **nothing like as/nowhere near as** *bad* (= not as serious) **as** *we'd feared it might be.* • *Breathing in other people's cigarette smoke is bad* **for** *you* (= has a harmful effect on your health). • *This is rather a bad* (= not convenient or suitable) *time for me to talk. Can I call you back later?* • *"How are things?" "***Not too bad** (= Quite good).*"* • *Five million dollars! That's* **not bad** (= very good)*!* • You can say that something is **too bad** if you want to express sympathy: **It's** *too bad* **that** *she lost all her things in the fire.* • You can also say that something is **too bad** if you want to express a lack of sympathy: *"But I've been sick!" "***(That's)** *too bad – you still have to get this piece of work done by Friday."* • If you **give** something **up as a bad job**, you stop trying to do it because you have been unable to do it successfully: *I can't mend this iron – I'm going to give it up as a bad job.* • If a situation **goes from bad to worse**, it was difficult and unpleasant, and is becoming even more so: **Things** *have gone from bad to worse recently.* • If someone has **got it bad**, they have become deeply in love: *You can tell he's got it bad because he can't concentrate on his work and he talks about her all the time.* • *There has been* **bad blood/bad feeling** (= feelings of hate and lack of trust) **between** *the two families for years.* • *He had few friends because of his* **bad breath** (= breath that smelled unpleasant). • A **bad debt** is one that is not likely to be paid: *The bank expects to lose £703 million of last year's profits as a result of bad debts.* • *(saying)* 'Bad news travels fast' means that you hear about bad things more quickly than you hear about good ones: *"Mary told me you lost your job." "Bad news travels fast, doesn't it?"*

bad /bæd/ *n* [U] • *You have to* **take the bad with the good** (= accept the unpleasant things in life, as well as the pleasant ones).

bad /bæd/ *adv* • Bad is *Am infml for* **badly** (= very much): *He needs the money real bad.* ○ *My arm hurts so bad.*

bad·ly /'bæd·li/ *adv* **worse** /£wɜːs, $wɜːrs/, **worst** /£wɜːst, $wɜːrst/ • *She was badly affected by the events in her childhood* (= They had a powerful or harmful effect on her). • *They* **came out** *of the affair rather badly* (= They were damaged by it). • *None of the passengers had been badly* (= seriously) **hurt/injured/wounded** *in the accident.* • *You don't deserve to have been* **treated** *so badly* (= in a harmful way). • *They were rather* **badly-off** (= had little money) *in the first years of their marriage.* • Badly can also mean very much: *He needs the money really badly.* ○ *My arm hurts very badly.* ○ *They are badly* **in need of** *help.* ○ *The hospital was badly-***off for** *funds* (= needed them very much).

bad LOW QUALITY /bæd/ *adj* **worse** /£wɜːs, $wɜːrs/, **worst** /£wɜːst, $wɜːrst/ of unacceptably low quality; not acceptable • *I thought the film was really bad.* • *Bad teachers can make children hate a subject.* • *The plumber made rather a bad job of mending our pipes.* • *The match has been postponed because of bad light.* • *Are the company's current difficulties a result of bad* (= harmful) **luck** *or bad* (= of low quality) **judgment***?* • *He has some very bad* **habits**. • *In some parts of the world, it is considered bad* **manners** *to pick up food or cutlery with the left hand.* • *Bobby was sent home from school for bad* **behaviour**. • *That remark was* **in (rather)** *bad* **taste**, *wasn't it?* • *(Br dated) It's bad* **form** *to be late on your first day.* • *I'm very bad* **at** *cooking* (= cannot do it very well). • To **feel** bad is to feel ashamed and sorry: *Knowing that I hurt her makes me feel really bad.* ○ *I feel bad* **about** *letting them down.* • **Bad faith** is dishonest or unacceptable behaviour: *He was accused of bad faith in breaking his promise.* ○ *They* **acted in** *bad faith by selling her a car that they knew to be faulty.* • **Bad language** is words that are considered offensive or taboo by most people: *I think there's too much bad language on television.*

bad·ly /'bæd·li/ *adv* • *He drives badly.* • *These shoes are really badly made.* • *The event was very badly organized.* • *You behaved very badly.* • *Their children are extremely badly-***behaved**. • *Don't* **think** *badly* **of** *me* (= Do not think that I have behaved in an unacceptable way, will you)*?* • *I* **feel** *badly* (= ashamed) **about** *putting you to so much trouble.*

bad EVIL /bæd/ *adj* **worse** /£wɜːs, $wɜːrs/, **worst** /£wɜːst, $wɜːrst/ (of people or actions) evil or morally unacceptable • *There are a lot of bad people in the world.* • *Lying is a really bad thing to do.* • *It was one of those films where it wasn't easy to tell the good guys from the bad* **guys**. • *He's not a* **bad lot** (= an evil person) *– just a bit wild.*

bad·dy /'bæd·i/, **bad·die** *n* [C] *infml* • *In the old cowboy films, the baddies* (= evil people) *always get beaten in the end.*

bad·ness /'bæd·nəs/ *n* [U] • *There is goodness and badness in everyone.*

bad PAINFUL /bæd/ *adj* **worse** /£wɜːs, $wɜːrs/, **worst** /£wɜːst, $wɜːrst/ causing or experiencing pain • *She can't walk up all those steps, not with her bad leg!* • *That's a bad cough you've got.* • *I felt really bad when I woke up after my operation.*

bad DECAYED /bæd/ *adj* [not gradable] harmful to eat because of being decayed • *Don't eat that apple – it's bad.* • *We'd better eat this chicken before it* **goes** *bad.*

bade /bæd/ *past simple of* BID TELL

badge /bædʒ/ *n* [C] a small piece of metal, plastic, cloth, etc., with words or a picture on it, that is pinned or sewn to your clothing, often to show your support for a political organization or belief, or your rank, or membership of a group, etc. • *She wore a T-shirt covered in badges.* • *At the meeting, we all had to wear badges with our names on.* • *He was wearing a badge that said 'You can't hug a child with nuclear arms'.* • *For Tony, owning a Mercedes was* **a badge of** *success* (= showed that he was successful).

bad·ger ANIMAL /£'bædʒ·əʳ, $-ɚ/ *n* [C] an animal with greyish brown fur, a black and white head and a pointed face, which lives underground and comes out to feed at night • PIC **Wild animals in Britain**

bad·ger *obj* ASK /£'bædʒ·əʳ, $-ɚ/ *v* [T] to persuade (someone) by telling them repeatedly to do something, or to question (someone) repeatedly • *Stop badgering me – I'll do it when I'm ready.* • *She badgered her boyfriend* **into** *taking up regular exercise.* • *Every time they go to the shop, the children always badger their father* **to** *buy them sweets.* [+ obj + *to* infinitive] • *As soon as I got back, they all badgered me* **with** *questions.*

bad·i·nage /'bæd·ɪ·nɑːʒ/ *n* [U] *literary or humorous* remarks or conversation that are joking and not serious; BANTER • *The two team-mates exchanged handshakes and badinage for a group of photographers.* • *But enough of this badinage! What are you really here for?*

bad·lands /'bæd·lændz/ *pl n* a dry area without plants and with large rocks that the weather has worn into strange shapes, esp. the area like this in Dakota and Nebraska in the US

bad·min·ton /'bæb·mɪn·tən/ *n* [U] a sport in which two or four people hit a SHUTTLECOCK (= a small feathered object) over a high net

bad·mouth *obj* /'bæd·maʊθ, -maʊð/ *v* [T] *Am and Aus* to criticize (someone or something) in a very unpleasant manner • *Stop badmouthing me.* • *I don't think you should badmouth Sarah/the medical profession/the tax system like that.*

baf·fle *obj* /'bæf·l̩/ *v* [T often passive] to cause (someone) to be completely unable to understand or explain something • *She was* **completely** *baffled* **by** *his strange behaviour.* • *Her strange note baffled me.*

baf·fle·ment /'bæf·l̩.mənt/ *n* [U] • *"But how did you get in?" he asked* **in** *complete bafflement.*

baf·fling /'bæf·lɪŋ/ *adj* • *I found what he was saying* **completely** *baffling.* • **It's** *baffling* **that** *she left without saying goodbye.* [+ *that* clause]

bag CONTAINER /bæg/ *n* [C] a container made out of paper or thin plastic in which you put things you have bought, or

a stronger container made of leather, plastic or other material, usually with a handle, in which you carry personal things or clothes and other items that you need for travelling • *a paper/plastic bag* (= a bag made of paper/plastic) • *a shopping bag* (= a bag in which shopping is carried) • *Stella was carrying a little velvet bag with a gold chain on it.* • *I'd like two pints of beer and two bags* (= plastic containers) **of** *(Br) crisps/(Am and Aus) potato chips, please.* • *Don't eat that whole bag* **of** (= the amount the bag contains) *sweets at once.* • *"I've* **packed** *my bags* (= I've put my possessions in cases/bags) *and I'm off!" Charlie shouted from the door.* • *The child was just* **a bag of bones** (= extremely thin) *when we found her.* • **Bag of tricks** means everything: *At the end of term I have to take all my things home from college, then I have to take* **the whole** *bag of tricks back again at the beginning of the next term.* • Someone who has **bags under** their **eyes** has dark loose or swollen skin there because of extreme tiredness or old age. • *Don't worry about the tickets – they're* **in the bag** (= certain to be obtained). • *(dated slang) Tennis* **isn't (really) my bag** (= I am not interested in it)*, I'm afraid.* • A **bag lady** is a woman who has no home and who carries all her possessions around with her in plastic bags. • See also BAGS [LOTS]. • [PIC]› **Bags, Containers**

bag *obj* /bæg/ *v* [T] **-gg-** • *Shall I bag* **(up)** *those tomatoes* (= put them in a bag) *for you?* [T/M]

bag·ful /ˈbæg·fʊl/ *n* [C] • *a bagful* (= the amount that a bag contains) *of shoes/socks/shirts* • A bagful is also a large amount: *a bagful of tunes/memories/dreams* ○ *Clinton picked up a bagful of votes from the youth of America.*

bag *obj* [OBTAIN] /bæg/ *v* [T] **-gg-** *infml* to get (something) before other people have a chance to take it • *Bag us some decent seats/Bag some decent seats* **for us** *if you get there first, won't you.* [+ two objects] • See also BAGS [CLAIM FIRST].

bag *obj* [KILL] /bæg/ *v* [T] **-gg-** to hunt and kill (an animal or bird)

bag [WOMAN] /bæg/ *n* [C] *slang* a rude and insulting name for a woman • *You old bag!* [as form of address]

bag *obj* [CRITICIZE] /bæg/ *v* [T] **-gg-** *Aus infml* to criticize or laugh at (someone or something) in an unkind way • *Stop bagging her* **(out)** *– she's doing her best.* [T/M]

bag·a·telle [SMALL AMOUNT] /ˌbæg·əˈtel/ *n* [C usually sing] *literary or fml* something, esp. a sum of money, that is small and unimportant • *A thousand pounds is* **a mere** *bagatelle* **to** *him.*

bag·a·telle [GAME] /ˌbæg·əˈtel/ *n* [C] a game in which small balls are hit, usually by a small rod on a spring which the player pulls, towards numbered holes on a board with a rounded end

ba·gel, bei·gel /ˈbeɪ·gəl/ *n* [C] a small soft chewy loaf of bread in the shape of a ring • *For Sunday brunch, we like to have bagels with cream cheese and smoked salmon.* • [PIC]› **Bread and cakes**

bag·gage [BAGS] /ˈbæg·ɪdʒ/ *n* [U] *esp. Am* all the cases and bags that you take with you when you travel; LUGGAGE • *I take as little baggage as possible with me when I travel.* • *We had to wait a long time in the baggage reclaim area for our bags to be removed from the plane.* • *How many* **pieces of** *baggage do you have?* • *We had to pay extra for our* **excess** *baggage* (= our bags and cases which weighed more than was allowed). • Your **baggage allowance** is the weight or number of cases and bags that you are allowed to take onto an aircraft without paying extra. • A **baggage handler** is a person who takes passengers' bags and cases, and puts them onto an aircraft or removes them from an aircraft. • **Baggage car** is *Aus and Am for* **luggage van**. See at LUGGAGE. • **Baggage room** is *Aus and Am for* **left-luggage office**. See at LEAVE [NOT TAKE].

bag·gage [FEELINGS] /ˈbæg·ɪdʒ/ *n* [U] the beliefs and feelings that you have which influence how you think and behave • *The new prime minister has shown that he is quite prepared to set aside some of the ideological baggage of the past.* • *We all* **carry** *a lot of* **emotional** *baggage around with us.*

bag·gy /ˈbæg·i/ *adj* **-ier, -iest** (of clothes) hanging loosely because of being too big or having been stretched • *baggy trousers* • *a baggy sweater* • *My T shirt went all baggy in the wash.*

bag /bæg/ *v* [I] **-gg-** • *I hate these trousers – they bag* **(out)** (= hang loosely) *at the back.*

bags /bægz/ *pl n Br dated* • Bags are trousers with a wide and loose style: *Oxford bags* • See also BAG.

bag·pipes /ˈbæg·paɪps/ *pl n* a type of musical instrument, played esp. in Scotland and Ireland, from which you produce sound by blowing air into a leather bag and forcing it out through pipes • *A man wearing a* *kilt was* **playing the** *bagpipes.* • *Bagpipes are often* **played** *at Scottish Hogmanay celebrations.*

bag·pipe /ˈbæg·paɪp/ [before n] • *Do you like bagpipe music?*

bags LOTS /bægz/ *pl n esp. Br and Aus infml* a lot of (something) • *Help yourself to some more cake – there's bags left.* • *Come and stay with us – we've got bags* **of** *room.* • *She's rich, beautiful and has bags* **of** *style.* • See also BAG CONTAINER.

bags *obj* CLAIM FIRST /bægz/, **bag·sy** /ˈbæg·zi/ *v* [T] *Br and Aus infml* (used esp. by children) to have the right to have or do (something) because you say you want it first • *I bagsed it first!* (= I said I wanted it first so I should have it, not you.) • *"Who wants to go first?" "Bags me!* (= I want to.)" • *Bags I sit in the front seat!* (= I said I wanted to do it first, so I should do it, not you.) • See also BAG OBTAIN.

ba·guette /bægˈet/, **French stick**, **French loaf** *n* [C] a long thin white loaf of bread, of a type which originally came from France • *He cut the baguette in half and filled it with ham, lettuce and tomato.*

bah /bɑː/ *exclamation dated* an expression of annoyance or disapproval • *Scrooge, a character in Charles Dickens' book 'A Christmas Carol', was always saying "Bah! Humbug!".*

bail MONEY /beɪl/ *n* [U] a sum of money which a person who has been accused of a crime pays to a law court so that they can be released until their trial. The payment is a way of making certain that the person will return to court for trial, at which point the money is returned. • *Bail was set at £50 000.* • *He was* **released/remanded on** *bail* **(of** *$100 000).* • *Because of a previous conviction, the judge refused to* **grant** *bail* (= allow the accused person to be released). • *Her parents have agreed to* **put up/stand/(Am) post** (= pay) *bail* **for** *her.* • *They* **jumped** *bail* (= did not come back for trial after being released on bail) *and fled to Spain.* • *Somerset police report that a third of all crimes are committed by people* **out on** *bail* (= who have been released before going on trial).

bail *obj* /beɪl/ *v* [T] • *The head of the police traffic department was yesterday bailed* (= released having paid a sum of money) *for three weeks on drink-driving offences.* • *His wife refused to bail him* **out** (= to pay the money needed in order for him to be released). [M] • *(fig.) She keeps running up huge debts and asking friends to bail her* **out** (= help her, esp. with money). [M] • *He was bailed* **to** *appear at the Magistrates' Court next month.* [+ obj + *to* infinitive]

bail *(obj)* REMOVE WATER, *Br and Aus also* **bale** /beɪl/ *v* to remove (water) from a boat using a container • *The boat's sinking! Start bailing quickly!* [I] • *He started frantically bailing water* **(out)**. [T/M]

bail out, *Br and Aus also* **bale out** /beɪl/ *v adv* [I] to jump out of an aircraft with a PARACHUTE because the aircraft is about to have an accident • *The plane's engine failed and the pilot was forced to bail out.* • To bail out is also to stop doing or being involved with something: *The book I was reading was so boring that I bailed out after the first couple of chapters.* ○ *The company she was working for was failing, so she bailed out and set up her own business with a friend.* ○ *The actor has bailed out* **of** *the film after only three weeks' shooting.*

bai·liff BRITISH OFFICIAL /ˈbeɪ·lɪf/ *n* [C] (in Britain) an official who takes away someone's possessions when they owe money • *They didn't pay their rent, so the landlord* **called/sent in** *the bailiffs.*

bai·liff AMERICAN OFFICIAL /ˈbeɪ·lɪf/ *n* [C] *Am* (in some parts of the US) an official who is responsible for prisoners who are appearing in court

bai·liff LAND /ˈbeɪ·lɪf/ *n* [C] *Br* a person whose job is to take care of someone else's land or property

bails /beɪlz/ *pl n* the two small pieces of wood on top of the STUMPS in a game of cricket • PIC **Sports**

bairn /£ beən, $ bern/ *n* [C] *Scot Eng or regional* a child

bait FOOD /beɪt/ *v, n* (to use) a small amount of food put on a hook or in a special device to attract and catch a fish or animal • *They were digging up worms to use for bait.* [U] • *The fish nibbled at the bait on the hook.* [U] • *We put down some* **poisoned** *bait to kill the rats.* [U] • *Have you got any stale cheese that I can bait the mousetrap* **with**? [T] • *(fig.) Free holidays were* **offered as (a)** *bait* **to** (= a way of attracting) *customers.* [C/U] • *(fig.) I told my sister I'd lend her my new shirt if she let me borrow her jacket, but she didn't* **rise to/take/swallow** *the bait* (= I wasn't able to trick her into doing it). [U]

bait *obj* MAKE ANGRY /beɪt/ *v* [T] to intentionally make (a person) angry by saying or doing things to annoy them, or to make dogs attack (an animal) for cruel entertainment • *She enjoys baiting her brother by teasing him about his strange hobbies.* • *In the past,* **bear-baiting** *was a common form of entertainment in Britain.*

baize /beɪz/ *n* [U] thick, usually green, woollen material used to cover the special tables on which SNOOKER, BILLIARDS and card games are played

bake *(obj)* /beɪk/ *v* to cook inside a cooker, without using added liquid or fat • *She spent the afternoon baking some bread/a cake/biscuits/cookies.* [T] • *I made the icing while the cake was baking.* [I] • *Would you prefer a baked potato or French fries?* [T] • *I love the smell of freshly baked bread* [T] • *Bake* **at** *180°C for about 20 minutes.* [I] • *Bake* **for** *5-7 minutes in a preheated oven.* [I] • Earth, clay, etc. can be baked at a high temperature, until they become hard in order to make bricks. [T] • *(infml)* If someone or something is baking, they are very hot: *I'm baking in this heavy coat!* [I] ○ *It's baking outside.* [I] • **Baked Alaska** is a dish consisting of a cake base with ice cream on top covered with MERINGUE (= a mixture made of sugar and the white part of eggs) which is cooked for a very short time at a high temperature. • **Baked beans** are HARICOT beans cooked in TOMATO sauce, sugar and spices, and usually put into metal containers. • **Baking powder** is a special mixture of powders used to make cakes rise and become light when they are baked. • **Baking soda** is BICARBONATE OF SODA. • *Put alternate layers of vegetables and cheese into a* **baking dish** (= an open container, usually made from clay, used in cooking). • *Lightly grease a* **baking sheet** (= flat metal dish used in cooking) *with vegetable oil.* • *Pour the mixture into an eight-inch* **baking tin** (= open metal container used in cooking). • *Put the chocolate mixture into a* **baking tray** (= a flat metal dish with low sides used in cooking). • PIC **Cooking, Peas and beans**

ba·ker /£ ˈbeɪ·kəʳ, $ -kɚ/ *n* [C] • A baker is a person whose job is to make bread and cakes for sale, or to sell bread and cakes.

ba·ker's /£ ˈbeɪ·kəz, $ -kɚz/ *n* [C] *pl* **bakers** or **bakers'** *esp. Br* • A baker's is a shop where bread and cakes are sold and sometimes made: *Go down to the baker's and buy me some cream buns, would you?* • *(dated)* A **baker's dozen** is 13.

ba·ker·y /£ ˈbeɪ·kᵊr·i, $ -kɚ·i/ *n* [C] • *She used to work in the local bakery* (= a place where bread and cakes are made and sometimes sold).

Bake·lite /ˈbeɪ·kə·laɪt/ *n* [U] *trademark* a type of hard plastic used esp. in the past • *a 1940s Bakelite radio* • *a Bakelite telephone*

bal·a·cla·va /ˌbæl·əˈklɑː·və/ *n* [C] a closely fitting woollen covering for the head with only the face left not covered • PIC **Hats**

bal·a·lai·ka /ˌbæl·əˈlaɪ·kə/ *n* [C] a type of musical instrument with a three-sided body and three strings, played esp. in Russia

bal·ance EQUALITY /ˈbæl·ᵊnts/ *n* [U] a state where things are of equal weight or force; EQUILIBRIUM • *The toddler wobbled and* **lost** *his balance* (= started to fall sideways) *and fell off the low wall.* • *She had to hold onto the railings to* **keep** *her balance* (= to stop herself from falling). • *New tax measures are designed to* **redress** *the balance* (= make the situation more equal) *between rich and poor.* • *We must* **strike a** *balance* **between** *reckless spending* **and** *penny-pinching* (= try to have something between these two things). • *This development may* **upset the delicate** *balance* **between** *the two countries.* • *The eradication of one tiny species can seriously affect* **the natural** *balance* (= the state where everything works together). • *I think,* **on balance** (= having considered all the facts), *I did treat you unfairly.* • *Her sudden friendliness* **threw** *him* **off balance** (= made him surprised and confused). • *Both countries have a vested interest in maintaining* **the balance of power** (= a position where both sides have equal power). • *When the election is over, this will be the party* **holding the balance of power** (= able to give its support to one or other side, and so deciding who will win). • The balance on a piece of electronic equipment for playing music is the particular mixture of different sounds or the device which controls this: *The drums were too strong, so we adjusted the balance.* • A country's **balance of payments** or **balance of trade** is the difference between the money from EXPORTS (= goods and services sold to other countries) and the cost of IMPORTS (= goods and services bought from other countries): *The balance of payments crisis led to the president's downfall.*

bal·ance *(obj)* /ˈbæl·ᵊnts/ *v* • *The flamingoes balanced gracefully* (=stood without falling) **on** *one leg.* [I] • *She walked along, a huge pot balanced effortlessly* **on** *her head.* [T] • *I had to balance the children's needs* **against** *my own* (= decide which were more important). [T] • *It seems a lot to spend this month, but we won't be spending much in July and August so it'll balance* **out** *over the year* (= the amounts will be equal over a period of time). [I] • *If the business loses any more money, we won't be able to* **balance the books** *this year* (= make certain that the amount of money spent is not more than the amount received). • *Stringent measures were introduced so that the government could* **balance** *its* **budget/balance the economy** (= make certain that the amount of money spent is not greater than the amount received). • *I found myself having to do a* **balancing act between** *work* **and** *family* (= trying to give care and attention to both things).

bal·anced /ˈbæl·ᵊntst/ *adj* • *The news programme prided itself on its balanced reporting* (= one that considered all sides). • *The committee is* **evenly** *balanced, with six members from each party.* • *She's in love with him so she's hardly capable of a balanced* **judgment** (= one that fairly considers all the facts) *about him.* • A **balanced diet** is a combination of the correct types and amounts of food: *If you have a balanced diet, you are getting all the vitamins you need.* • See also WELL-BALANCED.

bal·ance WEIGHING DEVICE /ˈbæl·ᵊnts/ *n* [C] a device used for weighing things. It consists of two dishes hanging on a bar which shows when the contents of both dishes weigh the same. • If a situation is **in the balance** it has reached a stage where it will soon be decided one way or another: *Her job was in the balance for some months, but now the company has decided to expand, so her future is assured.* ○ *The game* **hung** *in the balance until the last seconds when an exciting point decided it.* • PIC› **Laboratory**

bal·ance AMOUNT /ˈbæl·ᵊnts/ *n* [C usually sing] the amount of money you have in a bank account, or the amount of something that you have left after you have spent or used up the rest • *I've no idea what the balance in my account is.* • *Once we know how much money we'll need, let's spend* **the** *balance* (= the amount left). • *The company's success is reflected in its healthy* **bank** *balance.* • A **balance sheet** is a statement that shows the value of a company's ASSETS (= items of positive value) and its debts. • LP› **Money**

bal·co·ny /ˈbæl·kə·ni/ *n* [C] an area with a wall or bars around it that is joined to the outside wall of a building on an upper level, or an area of seats at an upper level in a theatre • *We had drinks on the hotel balcony.*

bald HAIRLESS /£bɔːld, $bɑːld/ *adj* **-er, -est** without any hair on the head • *At twenty he was already* **going bald**. • *(humorous) He was* **as bald as a coot** (= completely bald). • A **bald eagle** is a large North-American EAGLE with a white head. • A *(Br and Aus)* **bald patch**/*(Am)* **bald spot** is an area of head without hair. • A **bald tyre** is one that has worn away to become very smooth and therefore dangerous. • ⓘ

bald·ing /£ˈbɔːl·dɪŋ, $ˈbɑːl-/ *adj* • *Eammon was plump and balding* (= becoming bald) *but very attractive to women.*

bald·y, bald·ie /£ˈbɔːl·di, $ˈbɑːl-/ *n* [C] *humorous* • Baldy is the name used unkindly to refer to someone who has lost or is losing the hair on their head: *"Hey, baldy!"* [as form of address]

bald·ness /£ˈbɔːld·nəs, $ˈbɑːld-/ *n* [U] • *Men often see baldness as a sort of personal tragedy.*

bald PLAIN /£bɔːld, $bɑːld/ *adj* **-er, -est** basic and with no unnecessary words; not detailed • *There was just this bald statement of resignation – no explanation or anything.* • ⓘ

bald·ly /£ˈbɔːld·li, $ˈbɑːld-/ *adv* • *To put it baldly, I can't afford to take the risk.*

bald·ness /£ˈbɔːld·nəs, $ˈbɑːld-/ *n* [U] • *The baldness* (= directness) *of her question shocked him.*

bal·der·dash /£ˈbɔːl·də·dæʃ, $ˈbɑːl·dɚ-/ *n* [U], *exclamation dated* nonsense; something that is stupid or not true • *That's absolute balderdash, old chap!* • *"Balderdash!" he spluttered indignantly.*

bale LARGE AMOUNT /beɪl/ *n* [C] a large amount of something such as HAY (= dry grass), paper, wool or cloth that has been tied tightly together

bale *(obj)* /beɪl/ *v* • *We were baling* **(up)** (= tying up) *the hay all day.* [T] • *They bought a special machine for baling.* [I]

bale *(obj)* REMOVE WATER /beɪl/ *v esp. Br and Aus* to BAIL REMOVE WATER

bale out *v adv* [I] *Br and Aus also* to BAIL OUT.

bale·ful /ˈbeɪl·fᵊl/ *adj* full of evil intentions, or expressing blame and sadness • *He gave me a baleful* (= threatening) *look.* *'You'd better give me that money'* • *The dog gave me a baleful, you've-forgotten-to-take-me-for-a-walk look.*

bale·ful·ly /ˈbeɪl·fᵊl·i/ *adv* • *She glared balefully at me.*

balk BE UNWILLING, **baulk** /£bɔːk, $bɑːlk/ *v* [I] to be unwilling to do something or let something happen • *I balked* **at** *the prospect of spending four hours on a train with him.*

balk WOOD /£bɔːk, $bɑːlk/, **baulk** *n* [C] a rough thick piece of wood

ball ROUND OBJECT /£bɔːl, $bɑːl/ *n* [C] any spherical object, esp. one used as a toy by children or in various sports such as tennis and football • *a golf/rugby/tennis ball* • *a beach ball* • *Just try to concentrate on* **hitting** *the ball.* • *She* **bounced** *the ball past her opponent.* • *He bowled him a fast ball* (= a ball thrown at a fast speed). • *The kitten* **curled** *itself* **into a** *ball.* • A ball of string or wool is an amount of it in a round shape. • The ball of your foot or thumb is the rounded part where the toes join the foot and the thumb joins the hand. • *She knows everything – she's really* **on the ball** (= very aware of everything and quick to act). • To **start/set/get the ball rolling** is to do something first that you want lots of other people to do: *I decided to set the ball rolling and got up to dance.* • *It's up to you what to do –* **the ball is in** *your* **court** *now* (= you are responsible for making the next decision or doing the next thing). • A **ball bearing** is a small metal ball or several of these arranged in a ring to make particular parts of a machine move more easily. • In esp. tennis, a **ball boy/girl** is someone who picks up balls which have been used and gives them back to the players: *Children from the local schools act as ball girls and ball boys at Wimbledon.* • *(Am)* A **ball game** is a baseball match. • If something is **a whole new/completely different ball game** it is a new experience or something very different from what has existed before: *Sharing a flat with someone is a whole new ball game for me.* • *The hip joint is a* **ball-and-socket** *joint.* • *"Great Balls of Fire"* (title of a song by Jerry Lee Lewis, 1957)

ball DANCE /£bɔːl, $bɑːl/ *n* [C] a large formal occasion where people dance • *Did you go to the Summer Ball last year?* • *I* **had a ball** (= really enjoyed myself)*!*

bal·lad /ˈbæl·əd/ *n* [C] a song or poem that tells a story, or (in popular music) a slow love song

bal·last /ˈbæl·əst/ *n* [U] heavy matter such as sand or stone that is used at the bottom of a ship or a BALLOON to make it heavier, or the small stones on which railways and roads are made

ball·cock /£ˈbɔːl·kɒk, $ˈbɑːl·kɑːk/ *n* [C] a device in a water TANK that consists of a floating ball fixed to a rod which controls the level of water • PIC› **Bathroom**

bal·le·ri·na /ˌbæl·əˈriː·nə/ *n* [C] a female BALLET dancer

bal·let /£ˈbæl·eɪ, $-ˈ-/ *n* (a theatrical work with) a type of dancing where carefully organized movements tell a story or express an idea • *Henry had never been to a ballet before.* [C] • *Do you prefer* **modern** *ballet to* **classical** *ballet?* [U] • *Ballet* **dancers** *have to be strong and very supple.* • *Margot Fonteyn was a prima ballerina in the Royal Ballet* (= a particular group of ballet dancers in Britain). • *By the age of fifteen he had already composed his first ballet* (= the music for a ballet). [C] • **Ballet shoes** are a type of flat soft shoe worn by ballet dancers. • LP› **'-et' words** PIC› **Shoes**

bal·let·ic /£bəˈlet·ɪk, $-ˈlet̬-/ *adj* • *balletic movements* • *The most skilful footballers have a control of their bodies which is almost balletic.*

ball·gown /£ˈbɔːl·gaʊn, $ˈbɑːl-/ *n* [C] a formal dress that is often made from an expensive material and usually has a long skirt • *a taffeta/silk ballgown*

bal·li·stics /bəˈlɪs·tɪks/ *n* [U] the study of objects that are shot or thrown through the air, such as a bullet from a gun

bal·li·stic /bəˈlɪs·tɪk/ *adj* • A **ballistic missile** is one that is powered as it rises but then falls freely.

bal·loon /bəˈluːn/ *n* [C] a small, very thin rubber bag that you blow air into or fill with a light gas until it is round in shape, used for decoration at parties or as a children's toy, or a very large strong bag that is filled with hot air or gas that can carry people in a container fixed to it • *We tied balloons and streamers to the ceiling ready for the party.* • *People first flew in a balloon in 1783.* • A balloon is also a **speech bubble**. See at SPEECH SAY WORDS. • *That was the* *year when* **the balloon went up** (=when an unpleasant situation began).

bal·loon·ist /bəˈluː·nɪst/ *n* [C] • A balloonist is a person who takes part in the sport of travelling by balloon: *He's a keen balloonist.*

bal·loon /bəˈluːn/ *v* [I] • *The tent ballooned* **(out)** (= became rounded in shape) *in the wind.* • *(fig.) The rumours soon ballooned* **into** (=quickly became) *a full-grown scandal.*

bal·lot /ˈbæl·ət/ *n* [C] a system or occasion of secret voting • *Representatives were elected* **by** *ballot.* • *They decided to* **hold a** *ballot* (=organize a ballot). • *Let's* **put** *it* **to the ballot** (=vote secretly on it). • A **ballot (paper)** is a piece of paper on which you write your vote. • **Ballot-rigging** is getting the election result you want by an illegal method: *Rumours of ballot-rigging discouraged many from voting.*

bal·lot *obj* /ˈbæl·ət/ *v* [T] • *The union decided to ballot its members on the issue* (=find out their views by organizing a secret vote).

ball·park /£ˈbɔːl·pɑːk, $ˈbɑːl·pɑːrk/ *n* [C] *Am* a large structure enclosing a field on which ball games, esp. baseball games, are played

ball·park fig·ure *n* [C] *esp. Am* a number which is a guess, but which you believe is near the correct number • *We'll have to go away and cost this carefully, but as a ballpark figure I'd say that it'll be about two million dollars.*

ball·point, *fml* **ball·point pen** /£ˈbɔːl·pɔɪnt, $ˈbɑːl-/, *esp. Br, Aus also (trademark)* **Bi·ro** *n* [C] a pen with a small metal ball at the end that puts ink on the paper • *We aren't allowed to write* **in** *ballpoint at school.* • PIC> **Stationery, Writing instruments**

ball·room /£ˈbɔːl·rʊm, -ruːm, $ˈbɑːl-/ *n* [C] a large room that is used for dancing • **Ballroom dancing** is a type of dancing where a man and a woman dance together using steps and movements to special music, such as the WALTZ or TANGO.

balls /£bɔːlz, $bɑːlz/ *pl n, exclamation slang for* TESTICLES • *She fought off her attacker by kicking him in the balls.* • If you **have** someone **by the the balls**, you have them in a position where you have power over them. • Balls can also mean complete nonsense or stupidity: *What he said was* **(a load of)** *balls.* ○ *"All men are pigs." "Balls* (=I completely disagree)*!"* • Balls can also mean bravery: *It* **takes (a lot of)** *balls to go off alone like that.* ○ *You have to admit it – the woman's* **got** *balls!*

balls·y /£ˈbɔːl·zi, $ˈbɑːl-/ *adj Am* • *She's one ballsy* (= strong-minded) *lady!*

balls up *(obj) Br and Aus,* **balls** *(obj)* **up** /£bɔːlz, $bɑːlz/, *Am* **ball up** *v adv slang* to spoil (something) by making a mistake or doing something stupid • *Trust me to balls up the interview.* [M] • *Oh no – have I ballsed up again?* [I]

balls–up /£ˈbɔːlz·ʌp, $ˈbɑːlz-/ *n* [C] *slang* • *The whole trip was a complete balls-up* (=failure).

bal·ly /ˈbæl·i/ *adj* [before n; not gradable] *dated slang* used to express anger or annoyance with something or someone • *I'll have to do the whole bally thing again!*

bal·ly·hoo /£ˌbæl·ɪˈhuː, $ˈ---/ *n* [U] *dated slang* a lot of noise and activity, often with no real purpose • *I can't see what all this ballyhoo is about.*

balm /bɑːm/ *n* an oil that is obtained from particular tropical trees and used esp. to treat injuries or reduce pain, or *(fig.)* something that gives comfort • *The firm is selling a new skin balm.* [C] • *(fig.) Friendship is certainly the finest balm for the pangs of disappointed love.* [C] • *(fig.) Her words were balm* **to** *me.* [U]

balm·y /ˈbɑː·mi/ *adj* **-ier, -iest** (of weather) pleasantly warm • *It was a balmy* **night** *and we sat on the grass talking until after midnight.*

ba·lo·ney /£bəˈləʊ·ni, $-ˈloʊ-/ *n* [U] *infml* nonsense • *Baloney! Tell the truth!* • *That's* **a load of** *baloney if you ask me.* • *"No matter how thin you slice it, it's still baloney"* (A.E.Smith in a speech, 1936)

bal·sa (wood) /£ˈbɒl·sə, $ˈbɑːl-/ *n* [U] very light wood which is soft and easily cut, sometimes used in making model aircraft

bal·sam /£ˈbɒl·sᵊm, $ˈbɑːl-/ *n* [U] a pleasant-smelling substance used as the base for medical or beauty treatments, or *(fig.)* anything believed to heal the body or mind • *a balsam shampoo* • *(fig.) Great literature is a balsam to the soul.*

bal·u·strade /ˌbæl·əˈstreɪd, ˈ---/ *n* [C] a RAILING or wall to prevent people from falling over the edge of stairs, a BALCONY, etc.

bam·boo /bæmˈbuː/ *n* [U] a tall tropical grass with hard hollow stems, or the stems of this plant • *I looked at the photograph in the bamboo frame.* • *I use bamboo* **canes** *to support tall plants in the garden.*

bam·boo·zle *obj* /bæmˈbuː·zl̩/ *v* [T] *infml* to trick or deceive someone, often by confusing them • *She was bamboozled* **into** *telling them her credit card number.*

ban *obj* /bæn/ *v* [T] **-nn-** to forbid, esp. officially • *The film was banned* (=the government prevented it from being shown) *for thirteen years.* • *Smoking is banned in this restaurant.* [+ v-ing] • *They'd been banned from the pub* **for** *rowdiness* (=they were not allowed to go into it). • *She was banned* **from** *driving for two years.* • *"Ban the bomb"* (phrase used by people opposed to nuclear weapons, 1953-)

ban /bæn/ *n* [C] • *There should be a ban* **on** *talking and eating loudly in cinemas* (=an order preventing this).

ba·nal /bəˈnɑːl/ *adj* boring, ordinary and not original • *He just sat there making banal remarks all evening.*

ba·nal·i·ty /£bəˈnæl·ə·ti, $-t̬i/ *n* • *The banality of the final line spoiled the whole poem.* [U] • *The film is predictable, full of banalities and tediously dull.* [C]

ba·na·na /£bəˈnɑː·nə, $-ˈnæn·ə/ *n* a long curved fruit with a usually yellow skin and soft, sweet flesh inside • *Have a banana, Roger.* [C] • *Decorate the dessert with sliced banana.* [U] • *A banana tree has long green leaves which grow from the top of a central stem.* • *(disapproving)* A **banana republic** is a small country, esp. in S and Central America, that is poor and often badly and immorally ruled. • *(Br infml)* A **banana skin** is a sudden unexpected situation that makes a person appear foolish or causes them difficulty: *Trying to keep the story out of the newspapers turned out to be another banana skin for the prime minister.* • A **banana split** is a sweet dish made of a banana cut in half with ice cream and cream on top. • *"Yes, we have no bananas"* (title of a song written by Frank Silver and Irving Cohn, 1923) • PIC> **Fruit, Tree**

ba·na·nas /£bəˈnɑː·nəz, $-ˈnæn·əz/ *adj* [after v] *infml* silly • *He must be bananas to do a crazy thing like that.* • *She'll* **go** *bananas when you tell her the news* (=she will be extremely angry or very excited and pleased).

band MUSICIANS /bænd/ *n* [C] a group of musicians who play modern music together • *a rock band* • *a brass band* • *a dance band* • *Are you going to see the band at the Corn Exchange tonight?* • *The Beatles are probably the most famous band in the world.* • *I could hear a jazz band playing.* • *"The Band Played On"* (title of a song written by John F. Palmer, 1895) • *"Band on the Run"* (title of a song by Paul McCartney and Wings, 1974)

band STRIP /bænd/ *n* [C] a thin flat piece of cloth, elastic, metal or other material put around something to fasten or strengthen it, or a long narrow piece of colour, light, etc. that is different from what surrounds it • *It was a treasure chest with thin bands of black metal round it.* • *A narrow band of grass separated the greenhouse from the vegetable garden.* • *The parrot was green with red and grey bands on its wings.*

band RANGE /bænd/ *n* [C] a particular range of values, numbers, etc. • *The scheme is devised for young people in the 15 – 20* **age** *band.* • *Radio signals are transmitted in different bands.*

band GROUP /bænd/ *n* [C] a group of people who share the same interests or beliefs, or who have joined together for a special purpose • *a guerilla band* • *The former president still has a small band of supporters.*

band to·geth·er /bænd/ *v adv* [I] • *We decided to band together* (=join together as a group) *and organize a protest.*

ban·dage /ˈbæn·dɪdʒ/, *Am also* **gauze** *n* [C] a long narrow piece of cloth which is tied around an injury or a part of someone's body that has been hurt • *She offered to put a bandage on his arm.* • PIC> **Medical equipment**

ban·dage *obj* /ˈbæn·dɪdʒ/ *v* [T] • *You ought to bandage* **(up)** *that cut.* [M] • *Jess the dog gazed sorrowfully at her bandaged paw.*

Band–Aid /ˈbænd·eɪd/ *n* [C] *trademark* a type of **sticking plaster** that you use to cover small cuts on your body • *(esp. Am and Aus)* A **band-aid solution** is one which does not deal with a problem in detail or permanently.

ban·dan·na /bænˈdæn·ə/ *n* [C] a large brightly coloured HANDKERCHIEF that is worn around your neck or head • PIC> **Clothes**

ban·di·coot /ˈbæn·dɪ·kuːt/ *n* [C] a type of MARSUPIAL (= small animal which lives in a bag on its mother's body after birth) which lives in Australia

ban·dit /ˈbæn·dɪt/ *n* [C] an armed thief, esp. one belonging to a group that attack people travelling through the countryside • (PL)

band·lead·er *dated* /£ˈbænd,liː·dəʳ, $-dɚ/ *n* [C] a person who leads a large group of esp. jazz musicians while they play, and who often plays an instrument at the same time • *Glenn Miller was one of the most famous bandleaders of the 1930s.*

band·mas·ter /£ˈbænd,mɑː·stəʳ, $-,mæs·tɚ/ *n* [C] a person who leads the music of a military BAND or a **brass band**

bands·man /ˈbændz·mən/ *n* [C] *pl* **-men** a person who plays a musical instrument in a military BAND or a **brass band**

band·stand /ˈbænd·stænd/ *n* [C] a covered place where musical groups can play outside

band·wag·on /ˈbænd,wæg·ᵊn/ *n* [C usually sing] an activity, group, movement, etc. that has become successful or fashionable and so attracts many new people • *a bandwagon effect* • *The success of the product led many firms to try to* **jump/climb/get on the bandwagon** (= copy it in order to have the same success).

band·y [CURVED] /ˈbæn·di/ *adj* **-ier**, **-iest** (of legs) curving out at the knees • *I couldn't help laughing at his bandy legs.* • *He was short and bandy-legged.*

band·y *obj* [SPEAK] /ˈbæn·di/ *v* [T] to speak of (something) without careful consideration or attention • *I don't like these rumours about me being bandied* **about**. • *Large figures were bandied* **about** (= mentioned frequently), *but no money was ever paid.* • *(dated) I haven't come here to* **bandy words** (= argue) *with you.*

bane /beɪn/ *n* [U] **the bane** a cause of continual trouble or unhappiness • *Keeping noise levels low is the bane* **of** *airport administration.* • *That cat is* **the bane of** *my* **life** (= always causing me trouble)*!* • (N)

bang *(obj)* [NOISE] /bæŋ/ *v* to (cause something to) make a sudden very loud noise or noises • *She banged her fist angrily on the table.* [T] • *Outside a door was banging in the wind.* [I] • *He could hear someone banging* **at** *the door with their fists.* [I] • *I could hear her in the kitchen banging* **about** (= doing things noisily). [I] • *At the weekend he's always banging* **away** *in the garage* (= making repeated noises as if with a hammer). [I] • *(infml disapproving) My parents are always* **banging on about** (= talking repeatedly about) *how much better life was 20 years ago.* • To **bang the drum** is to tell as many people as possible about something, esp. a belief or idea, so that they will support it: *Labour are banging the drum for a united Europe.*

bang /bæŋ/ *n* [C] • *They heard a bang, followed by a scream, from the next room.* • *The window slammed shut with a loud bang.* • *(infml)* If a party or event is said to **go with a bang** (*Am* **go over with a bang**), it is very successful. • *"This is the way the world ends / Not with a bang but a whimper"* (from T.S.Eliot's poem *The Hollow Men*, 1925)

bang /bæŋ/ *exclamation* • *"Bang! Bang! You're dead" said the child, pointing a plastic gun at me.* • *The balloon* **went** *bang* (= made a sudden loud noise) *when it landed on the prickly bush.* • *(infml) Oh well,* **bang goes** *my chance* (= my chance has gone completely) *of becoming a millionaire overnight.*

bang *obj* [HIT] /bæŋ/ *v* [T] to hit (a part of the body) accidentally against something • *He tried to stand up, but banged his head* **against/on** *the table and fell down again.*

bang /bæŋ/ *n* [C] • *I think she must have got a bang* (= hit) **on** *the head.*

bang [SEX] /bæŋ/ *v* [I] *taboo slang* to have sex • *They could be heard banging* **away** *every night.*

bang [EXACTLY] /bæŋ/ *adv* [before adv/prep; not gradable] *infml* exactly or directly • *The car came to a halt bang* **in the middle of** *the road.* • *I live bang* **opposite** *the cinema.* • *I turned the corner and walked* **slap bang into** *him.* • *The company's new software is bang* **up-to-date**. • *What was your answer? 76? That's absolutely* **bang on** (= exactly right)*!*

bang up *obj*, **bang** *obj* **up** *v adv* [M] *slang* to lock (someone) up, esp. in a police STATION (= office) or prison • *She's terrified of him and won't make a statement until we've got him banged up in the cells.*

bang·er [CAR] /£ˈbæŋ·əʳ, $-ɚ/ *n* [C] *Br* a very old car in bad condition

bang·er [EXPLOSIVE] /£ˈbæŋ·əʳ, $-ɚ/ *n* [C] *Br and Aus* a small noisy FIREWORK (= explosive device)

bang·er [FOOD] /£ˈbæŋ·əʳ, $-ɚ/ *n* [C] *Br infml for* SAUSAGE • *It's bangers* **and mash** (= potatoes) *for tea!*

ban·gle /ˈbæŋ·gl̩/ *n* [C] a ring of stiff plastic, metal, etc. worn around the wrist or arm as jewellery • PIC> **Jewellery**

bangs /bæŋz/ *pl n Am for* a FRINGE [HAIR] • *We wore ponytails with bangs when we were in school.* • PIC> **Hair**

ban·ish *obj* /ˈbæn·ɪʃ/ *v* [T] to send (someone) away from their country and forbid them to come back • *They were banished* **from** *their country for criticizing the government.* • *They were banished* (= sent out) **from** *the library for making a noise.* • *He was banished* **to** *an uninhabited island for a year.* • *(fig.) In an ideal world, preventive medicine would banish* (= get rid of) *premature death.* • *(fig.) You must try to banish* (= get rid of) *all thoughts of revenge* **from** *your mind.*

ban·ish·ment /ˈbæn·ɪʃ·mənt/ *n* [U]

ban·i·ster /£ˈbæn·ɪ·stəʳ, $-stɚ/ *n* [C], **ban·i·sters** *pl n* the row of poles at the side of stairs and the wooden or metal bar on top of them • *Aunt Agatha could never resist the urge to slide down the banisters.*

ban·jo /£ˈbæn·dʒəʊ, $-dʒoʊ/ *n* [C] *pl* **banjos** or **banjoes** a stringed musical instrument with a long neck and a hollow circular body

bank [ORGANIZATION] /bæŋk/ *n* [C] an organization where people and businesses can invest or borrow money, change it to foreign money, etc., or a building where these services are offered • *The banks have been accused of exploiting small firms.* • *The bank that Shaun works in is in the town centre.* • *You should keep your savings* **in** *a bank.* • *This bank has branches* (= buildings and offices that form part of it) *all over the country.* • *I had to take out a bank* **loan** *to start my own business.* • *I got an angry letter from my* **bank manager** (= the person in charge of a bank) *the other day.* • A bank of something, such as blood or human organs for medical use, is a place which stores these things for later use: *a blood bank* ○ *a sperm bank* • In GAMBLING, the bank is money that belongs to the owner and can be won by the players. • A **bank account** is an arrangement with a bank where the customer puts in and removes money and the bank keeps a record of it. • Your **bank balance** is the amount of money that you have in the bank. • **Bank charges** are sums of money paid by the customer for the bank to perform various services: *When my statement came I noticed some unexpected bank charges.* • *(Br)* A **bank holiday** is an official holiday when banks and most businesses are closed for a day. • The **bank rate** is the amount of INTEREST that a bank charges, esp. the lowest amount that it is allowed to charge, when it lends money. • A **bank statement** is a printed record of the money put into and removed from a bank account. • LP> **Money** (I) (T)

bank *(obj)* /bæŋk/ *v* • *I used to bank* **with** *Lloyd's* (= keep my money there). [I] • *You ought to bank that money* (= put it in a bank) *as soon as possible.* [T]

bank·a·ble /ˈbæŋ·kə·bl̩/ *adj* • *She is currently Hollywood's most bankable actress* (= Her films make large profits).

bank·a·bil·i·ty /£bæŋ·kəˈbɪl·ɪ·ti, $-ə·t̬i/ *n* [C] • *His bankability* (= ability to make money) *as a pop star decreased as he got older.*

bank·er /£ˈbæŋ·kəʳ, $-kɚ/ *n* [C] • *She was a successful banker* (= someone with an important position in a bank) *by the time she was forty.* • The banker in GAMBLING games is the person responsible for looking after the money. • **Banker's card** is another name for a **cheque card**. See at CHEQUE. • **Banker's order** is another name for a **standing order**. See at STANDING [PERMANENT].

bank·ing /ˈbæŋ·kɪŋ/ *n* [U] • *The intricacies of international banking* (= the business of operating a bank) *remained a mystery to him.*

bank [RAISED GROUND] /bæŋk/ *n* [C] sloping raised land, esp. along the sides of a river, or a pile or mass of earth, clouds, etc. • *By the time we reached the opposite bank, the boat was sinking fast.* • *These flowers generally grow on sloping* **river banks** *and near streams.* • *A dark bank* **of** *cloud loomed on the horizon.* • A bank of buttons or switches on a machine is a large number of them, usually arranged in rows. • (I) (T)

bank *(obj)* /bæŋk/ *v* • *The snow had banked* **up** (= formed into a mass) *in the corner of the garden.* [I] • *We banked* **up** *the fire* (= put more coal on it) *to keep it burning all night.* [M]

bank [TURN] /bæŋk/ *v* [I] (of an aircraft) to fly with one wing higher than the other when turning • *We felt the plane bank steeply as it changed direction.* • (I) (T)

bank on *(obj) v prep* to expect (something) or depend on (something) happening • *Can I bank on your support?* [T] • *I wouldn't bank on him* **being** *there.* [T + obj + v-*ing*] • *"Do you think she'll come?" "I wouldn't* **bank on it***".* [T] • *I'd banked on getting a pay rise this year.* [+ v-*ing*]

bank·note /£'bæŋk·nəʊt, $-noʊt/ *n* [C] a piece of printed paper that has a particular value as money • *a £20 banknote* • *Hidden in the suitcase were* **wads of** *banknotes.*

bank·roll *obj* /£'bæŋk·rəʊl, $-roʊl/ *v* [T] *infml* to support (a person or activity) financially • *Why is Hollywood prepared to go on bankrolling this director when he's obviously incompetent?*

bank·rupt /'bæŋ·krʌpt/ *adj law* unable to pay what you owe, and having control of your financial matters given, by a court of law, to a person who sells your property to pay your debts • *He* **went** *bankrupt after only a year in business.* • *The recession has led to many small businesses* **going** *bankrupt.* • *(infml)* Bankrupt is also used to mean having no money: *(humorous) I shall go bankrupt if you children keep on asking for more pocket money!* • *(fig.) He believes that modern society is morally bankrupt* (= is completely lacking in morals).

bank·rupt *obj* /'bæŋ·krʌpt/ *v* [T] *law* • *They feared that the loss would bankrupt them* (= cause them to become bankrupt).

bank·rupt /'bæŋ·krʌpt/ *n* [C] *law* • *He was* **declared** *a bankrupt* (= stopped by a court of law from managing his own financial matters) *in 1991.*

bank·rupt·cy /'bæŋ·krəpt·si/ *n law* • *The company was forced into bankruptcy.* [U] • *The toll of bankruptcies was rising daily.* [C]

ban·ner /£'bæn·əʳ, $-ɚ/ *n* [C] a long piece of cloth, often stretched between two poles, with a sign written on it, usually carried by people taking part in a march • *The demonstrators walked along the street, waving banners and shouting angrily.* • *(fig.) He continues to* **carry** *the banner of* (= support strongly) *liberal politics.* • *(fig.) They won the election* **under** *the banner of* (= by stating that they supported) *lower taxes.* • A **banner headline** is a large title of a story in a newspaper that stretches across the top of the front page.

ban·nock /'bæn·ək/ *n* [C] *esp. Scot Eng* a flat cake made of OATMEAL

banns /bænz/ *pl n* a public announcement, made in a church, that two people are going to get married • *The banns were* **published** *in their local parish church.*

ban·quet /'bæŋ·kwɪt/ *n* [C] a large formal meal for many people, often followed by speeches in honour of someone • *Medieval banquets are held in the castle once a month.* • *The Lord Mayor's banquet is held in London.*

ban·quet·ing /£'bæŋ·kwɪ·tɪŋ, $-t̬ɪŋ/ *n* [U] • *The hotel has one large room which is used for banqueting.* • *The dinner is to be held in the banqueting hall/suite.*

ban·shee /'bæn·ʃiː/ *n* [C] a female spirit in traditional Irish stories whose crying sound tells you that someone in your family is going to die

ban·tam /£'bæn·təm, $-t̬əm/ *n* [C] a small breed of chicken

ban·tam·weight /£'bæn·təm·weɪt, $-t̬əm-/ *n* [C] a boxer weighing between 51 and 53·5 kilograms

ban·ter /£'bæn·təʳ, $-t̬ɚ/ *n* [U] conversation which is amusing and not serious; BADINAGE • *He considered himself a master of witty banter.*

ban·ter /£'bæn·təʳ, $-t̬ɚ/ *v* [I] • *We stood around bantering while we waited.*

ban·ter·ing /£'bæn·tᵊr·ɪŋ, $-t̬ɚ-/ *adj* • *I grew weary of his bantering style of conversation.*

ban·yan /'bæn·jæn/ *n* [C] an Indian fruit tree with branches that grow down into the ground to form additional trunks

bap /bæp/ *n* [C] *Br* a round soft form of bread which is usually smaller than a loaf • *a granary/breakfast bap* • *Please buy me a dozen white baps from the baker's.*

bap·ti·sm /£'bæp·tɪ·zᵊm, $-t̬ɪ-/ *n* a Christian ceremony in which a person has water poured on their head, or are covered briefly in water, to show that they have become a member of the Christian Church • *All the family attended the baptism of the first grandchild.* [C] • *Some clergymen wanted to limit baptism to the children of church-goers.* [U] • A **baptism of fire** is a difficult first experience of something: *My first job involved working with children – it was a real baptism of fire!*

bap·tize *obj, Br and Aus usually* **-ise** /bæp'taɪz/ *v* [T usually passive] • *Were you baptized a Catholic?* [+ obj + n] • *I was baptized Elizabeth* (= given the name Elizabeth when I was baptized), *but my friends call me Beth.* [+ obj + n] • See also CHRISTEN.

Bap·tist /£'bæp·tɪst, $-t̬ɪz/ *n* [C] a member of a Christian group that believes that baptism should not happen until a person is old enough to understand its meaning

bar POLE /£bɑːʳ, $bɑːr/ *n* [C] a straight stick esp. one made of metal, or something that has been made into a rectangular shape • *She picked up a metal bar and waved it threateningly.* • *The gorilla rattled the bars of its cage.* • *(infml) He's spent most of his life* **behind bars** (= in prison). • *a bar of chocolate/soap* • The bar of an electric heater is a long thin wire in the shape of a spring which is wrapped tightly around a tube. When electricity passes through it, it produces heat and red light: *It's very warm in here. Do you really need both bars on?* • Bar is also *Am for* STRIPE MATERIAL. • A **bar chart/graph** (also **histogram**) is a mathematical picture in which different amounts are represented by thin vertical or horizontal rectangles which have the same width but vary in height or length. • A **bar code** is a small rectangle of thick and thin black lines which is printed on food wrappers, book covers, etc. and allows a computer to read information about the item, such as the price. • PIC› **Bar**, **Supermarket**

bar *obj* /£bɑːʳ, $bɑːr/ *v* [T] **-rr-** • *We barred* (= put bars across) *the door to stop anyone getting into the room.*

barred /£bɑːd, $bɑːrd/ *adj* [not gradable] • *They arrived at the house to find the door locked and barred* (= with a bar of wood or metal across the front of it). • *The burglary rate is so high that most of the houses in the area have barred windows.*

bar DRINKING PLACE /£bɑːʳ, $bɑːr/ *n* [C] a place where esp. alcoholic drinks are sold and drunk, or the area in such a place where the person serving the drinks stands • *They* *noticed him going into the hotel bar.* • *There weren't any free tables, so I sat on a stool at the bar.* • *Ask the guy* **behind** *the bar* (= serving drinks there) *for some change for the phone.* • *(esp. Am) Let's go for a drink – where's the nearest bar?*

bar MUSIC /£bɑːʳ, $bɑːr/, *Am also* **meas·ure** *n* [C] one of the small equal parts into which a piece of music is divided, containing a fixed number of beats • *The band played the first few bars, and then everyone joined in with the singing.* • *Waltzes have three beats* **in/to the** *bar* (= in each bar). • A *(Br and Aus)* **bar line**/*(Am)* **bar** is the vertical line that divides one bar from another in a written piece of music. • PIC〉 **Bar**

bar *obj* PREVENT /£bɑːʳ, $bɑːr/ *v* [T] **-rr-** to prevent (something or someone) from doing something or going somewhere, or to forbid (something) • *The centre of the town was barred* **to**/*(Am usually) barred* **off to** *football supporters.* • *The incident led to him being barred* **from** *the country/barred* **from** *playing for England.* • *The government has acted to bar this kind of tobacco* (= make using, selling or producing it illegal). • *I tried to push past her but she barred my* **way/path** (= stood in front of me and prevented me from getting past).

bar /£bɑːʳ, $bɑːr/ *n* [C] • *A lack of formal education is no bar* **to** *becoming rich* (= does not make it impossible to become rich).

bar EXCEPT /£bɑːʳ, $bɑːr/ *prep slightly fml* except • *Everyone is leaving the village, bar the very old and ill.* • *They're the best songwriters of this century, bar* **none** (= no one else is better). • *(Br)* If an activity is **all over bar the shouting**, the result of it is known, but it has not been officially completed or stated, so people can still claim that a different result is possible: *With practically all the results declared, the Nationalist Party has 68% of the vote, so it's all over bar the shouting.*

bar·ring /£'bɑː·rɪŋ, $'bɑːr·ɪŋ/ *prep* • *I can't understand why anybody, barring* (= except for) *a masochist, would want to play such a violent game.* • *We should arrive at ten o'clock, barring any* (= if there are no) *unexpected delays.*

Bar LAWYERS /£bɑːʳ, $bɑːr/ *n* [U + sing/pl v] **the Bar** *Br and Aus* lawyers who are allowed to argue a case in a higher court, or *(Am)* all lawyers thought of as a group • *(Br and Aus)* To be **called to** the Bar is to qualify as a lawyer who can argue a case in a higher court. • *(Am)* To be **admitted to** the Bar is to qualify as a lawyer.

barb /£bɑːb, $bɑːrb/ *n* [C] the sharp part which points backwards from a fish hook or arrow, making it hard to remove it from something, or *(fig.)* a remark that is clever but cruel and hurtful • *(fig.) I tried to ignore their barbs about my new jacket.* • *(fig.) Nobody was left in any doubt that the barb was* **aimed at** *the president.*

barbed /£bɑːbd, $bɑːrbd/ *adj* • *(fig.) She made some rather barbed* (= critical and unkind) *comments about my lifestyle.* • **Barbed wire** is a type of strong wire with sharp points on it, used to prevent people or animals from entering or leaving a place, esp. a field: *a barbed wire fence* • PIC〉 **Farming**

bar·bar·i·an /£bɑː'beə·ri·ən, $bɑːr'ber·i·/ *n* [C] a member of a group of people from a very different country or culture that is considered to be less socially advanced and more violent than your own • *The walled city was attacked by barbarian hordes.* • *(disapproving)* A barbarian is also a person with little education who has no interest in art and culture: *How can you call those barbarians your friends?* ○ *Those barbarians at the council want to knock down the church and build a car park instead.*

bar·bar·ic /£bɑː'bær·ɪk, $bɑːr-/ *adj* extremely cruel and unpleasant • *She found the idea of killing animals for pleasure barbaric.* • *This barbaric practice should be banned immediately.* • *He was rough and barbaric, but she found him very attractive.* • *My wife thinks it is barbaric* (= extremely rude and unacceptable) *to read a newspaper at the breakfast table.*

bar·bar·i·sm /£'bɑː·bə·rɪ·zᵊm, $'bɑːr·bɚ·ɪ-/ *n* [U] • Barbarism is extremely cruel and unpleasant behaviour: *He witnessed some appalling acts of barbarism during the war.*

bar·bar·i·ty /£bɑː'bær·ə·ti, $bɑːr'bær·ə·t̬i/ *n* • *This barbarity* (= extreme cruelty) *must cease!* [U] • *The dictatorship has been responsible for countless barbarities* (= extremely cruel acts). [C]

bar·bar·ous /£'bɑː·bᵊr·əs, $'bɑːr·bɚ-/ *adj fml or literary* • Behaviour that is barbarous is extremely cruel or unpleasant, or fails to reach acceptable social standards: *She condemned the murder as an outrageous and barbarous act* ○ *The barbarous treatment of the refugees is something that a civilized society should be ashamed of.* ○ *How can they forgive such barbarous* **behaviour**?

bar·be·cue, *infml* **Bar–B–Q** /£'bɑː·bɪ·kjuː, $'bɑːr-/, *infml* **bar·bie** /£'bɑː·bi, $'bɑːr-/ *n* [C] a metal frame on which meat, fish or vegetables are cooked outside over a fire, or a meal prepared using such a frame which is eaten outside, often during a party • *They had a barbecue on their patio on Sunday.* • **Barbecue sauce** is a very spicy sauce which is used to flavour food cooked on a barbecue.

bar·be·cue *obj* /£'bɑː·bɪ·kjuː, $'bɑːr-/ *v* [T] • *Their traditional sausages are delicious grilled or barbecued.*

barb·er /£'bɑː·bəʳ, $'bɑːr·bɚ/ *n* [C] a man whose job is cutting men's hair • *As well as a haircut, a man can have a shave or get his beard trimmed when he goes to a barber.* • A **barber's pole** is a pole with red and white strips that traditionally is put on the front of a barber's shop.

barb·er's /£'bɑː·bəz, $'bɑːr·bɚʒ/ *n* [C], *Am also* **barb·er·shop** *n* [C] *pl* **barbers** or **barbers'** • A barber's is a shop where a barber works: *He always has his hair cut at an old-fashioned barber's.*

barb·er·shop /£'bɑː·bə·ʃɒp, $'bɑːr·bɚ·ʃɑːp/ *n* [U] a type of singing in which four, usually male, voices in close combination perform popular romantic songs, esp. from the 1920s and 1930s • *They're planning to have a barbershop* **quartet** *at their wedding reception.*

bar·bi·tu·rate /£bɑː'bɪt·jʊ·rət, $bɑːr-/ *n* [C] a strong drug that makes people calm or helps them to sleep • *He died from an overdose of alcohol and barbiturates.*

bard /£bɑːd, $bɑːrd/ *n* [C] *literary* a poet • Shakespeare is sometimes referred to as **the Bard**.

bare /£beəʳ, $ber/ *adj* **-r, -st** without any clothes or not covered by anything • *Her arms were bare and covered in freckles.* • *Don't walk around outside* **in** *your* **bare feet**. See also BAREFOOT. • *Their flat has a bare wooden floor* (= one not covered by anything). • *The landscape was windswept and bare* (= it had no trees or plants on it). • *The cupboard/room was completely bare* **(of** *food/furniture)* (= there was nothing in it). • *I just packed the bare* **essentials** (= the most basic things). • *There isn't much time, so I'll just give you the bare* **facts/details** (= I'll only give you the most important information). • *She eats only the bare* **minimum** (= the least possible) *to stay alive.* • *She* **lays bare** (= talks very honestly about) *her three unhappy marriages in her autobiography.* • *He wrestled the lion to the ground* **with** *his* **bare hands** (= without using any weapons). • The **bare bones** of something are the most important facts that relate to it, providing a structure to which more detail might be added later: *She only told me* **the** *bare bones* **of** *the story, so I don't know precisely what happened.* ○ *The negotiators believe they will soon have* **the** *bare bones* **of** *a peace agreement.* • *(specialized)* In grammar, the **bare infinitive** is the infinitive form of a verb without the word 'to': *In the sentence 'Let her go, she's done nothing wrong!', the bare infinitive is the word 'go'.*

bare *obj* /£beəʳ, $ber/ *v* [T] • *The men bared their* **heads** (= took their hats off as a sign of respect) *as they entered the church.* • *He became nervous when the dog growled and bared its* **teeth** *at him* (= showed its teeth to him). • *I* **bared** *my* **heart/soul** *to him* (= told him my most secret thoughts and feelings), *and then he went and told everyone in the office what I'd said.*

bare·back /£'beə·bæk, $'ber-/ *adj, adv* [not gradable] without a SADDLE (= leather seat) on the back of a horse that is being ridden • *a bareback rider* • *Is it difficult* **riding** *bareback?*

bare·faced /£'beə·feɪst, $ber-/ *adj disapproving* not trying to hide your bad behaviour • *That's a barefaced* **lie**!

bare·foot /£beə'fʊt, $'ber-/ *adj, adv* [not gradable] not wearing any shoes or socks • *We took off our shoes and socks and* **walked** *barefoot along the beach.* • *Most of the children in the village were barefoot.* • *"Barefoot in the Park"* (film title, 1967)

bare·head·ed /£beə'hed·ɪd, $ber-/ *adj, adv* [not gradable] without any covering on your head

bare·ly /£'beə·li, $'ber-/ *adv* [not gradable] by the smallest amount; almost not • *They have barely enough* (= no more than what is needed) *to pay the rent this month.* • *She was barely* (= only just) *fifteen when she won her first championship.* • *He had barely* (= only very recently) *left the office when a huge explosion ripped through the building.*

barf /£bɑːf, $bɑːrf/ *v* [I] *esp. Am slang* to vomit • *He drank far too much at the party and barfed all over the carpet.* •

(fig.) Just the thought of going to the hospital makes me barf (= feel ill).

barf /£bɑːf, $bɑːrf/ *n* [C/U] *esp. Am slang* • A **barf bag** is a waterproof paper bag provided for each passenger on an aircraft in case they need to vomit.

bar·gain AGREEMENT /£'bɑː·gɪn, $'bɑːr-/ *n* [C] an agreement between two people or groups in which each promises to do something in exchange for something else • *"I'll tidy the kitchen if you clean the car." "OK, it's a bargain."* • *The management and employees eventually* **struck/made** *a bargain* (= reached an agreement). • *(fig.) He's intelligent, witty, a loving husband and an excellent cook* **into the bargain**/*(Am also)* **in the bargain** (= in addition to all these things).

bar·gain *(obj)* /£'bɑː·gɪn, $'bɑːr-/ *v* • *The unions bargain* **with** *the employers for better rates of pay each year.* [I] • *I realized that by trying to gain security I had bargained* **away** *my freedom* (= exchanged it for something of less value). [M] • *(fig.) He hadn't bargained* **on** *her extreme anger/be***ing** *so angry* (= he had not expected this). [I] • *(fig.) This was the one thing we hadn't bargained* **for** (= we were not expecting). [I] • *(fig.) She got more than she'd bargained* **for** (= than she was expecting) *when she rescued the cat, as it gave birth soon afterwards.* [I] • *(fig. Am) I'll bargain* (= I expect) **that** *he will compete at the next Olympic games.* [+ *that* clause] • A **bargaining chip**/*(Br)* **counter** is something which someone else wants that you are willing to lose in order to reach an agreement: *The missiles were used as a bargaining chip in the negotiations for economic aid.* • *Rising unemployment has diminished the* **bargaining power** *of people with jobs* (= their ability to get what they want).

bar·gain LOW PRICE /£'bɑː·gɪn, $'bɑːr-/ *n* [C] something on sale at a lower price than its true value • *This coat was half-price, a real bargain.* • *The airline regularly offers last-minute bookings at bargain* **prices.** • A **bargain basement** is an underground room in a shop where items are sold at reduced prices: *Jonathan manages to buy all his clothes at bargain-basement prices* (= very cheaply). • *The sales had started and the* **bargain hunters** (= people looking for things at a low price) *were out in force.* • LP› **Expensive**

barge *(obj)* HURRY /£bɑːdʒ, $bɑːrdʒ/ *v* [always + adv/prep] to hurry somewhere or through a place in a rude and forceful way • *They barged* **through** *the crowd.* [I] • *When the doors opened she barged her way* **to** *the front of the queue.* [T] • *The man barged* (= pushed) **into** *her and ran on without stopping.* [I] • *I wish he'd knock instead of just barging* **in** (= hurrying in rudely). [I] • *(fig.) Sorry to barge* **in** (= interrupt), *but I couldn't help overhearing what you were saying.* [I]

barge BOAT /£bɑːdʒ, $bɑːrdʒ/ *n* [C] a long boat with a flat bottom, used for carrying heavy loads on rivers or CANALS (= artificial rivers) • PIC› **Canal**

bar·i·tone /£'bær·ɪ·təʊn, $-toʊn/ *n* [C] a man with a singing voice that is lower than a TENOR but not as low as a BASS, or a musical instrument with this range • *He was one of the last baritones to accompany her.* • *a baritone saxophone* • *Leo began to sing in a fine baritone voice.*

ba·ri·um meal *Br and Aus* /£'beə·ri·əm, $'ber·i-/ *n* [C], *Am* **ba·ri·um sul·phate** *n* [U] a chemical that is swallowed by a person just before an X-RAY is taken of their stomach and bowels, so that these organs can be seen clearly

bark DOG /£bɑːk, $bɑːrk/ *v, n* (to make) the loud, rough noise that a dog and some other animals make • *They heard a dog barking outside.* [I] • *Our dog gave a loud bark and rushed to the door, wagging her tail.* [C] • *(fig.) The sergeant barked* **(out)** (= shouted quickly in a rough voice) *a succession of orders to the new recruits.* [T/M] • *(infml) Don't let her frighten you, her* **bark is worse than** *her* **bite** (= she is not as unpleasant as she seems). • *(infml)* If you are **barking up the wrong tree**, you are wrong about something, or you will not be successful in what you are trying to achieve: *Chris suspects Mark of stealing her watch, but I reckon she's barking up the wrong tree.* ○ *I think the researchers are barking up the wrong tree.*

bark·ing /£'bɑː·kɪŋ, $'bɑːr-/ *adj* [after v], *adv Br dated infml* • If someone is barking **(mad)** they do things which are extremely foolish, or their behaviour is very unusual and socially unacceptable: *She must have been barking mad to lend him so much money.* ○ *Her brother's absolutely barking – he wanders around town all day swearing at everyone.*

bark TREE /£bɑːk, $bɑːrk/ *n* [U] the hard outer covering of a tree • *He took a knife from his bag and cut their initials into the bark.*

bar·keep·er /£'bɑːˌkiː·pəʳ, $'bɑːrˌkiː·pɚ/ *n* [C] *Am* a person who serves drinks in a bar, or the owner or manager of a bar • *She spent the summer working as a barkeeper at the resort.*

bar·ley /£'bɑː·li, $'bɑːr-/ *n* [U] a tall grass-like plant with long straight hairs growing from the head of each stem, or the grain obtained from this plant which is used for food and for making beer and WHISKY. • *They looked out across the fields of waving barley.* • A **barley sugar** is a hard sweet made from boiled sugar. • *(Br)* **Barley water** is a drink made from barley and fruit juice, or *(Am and Aus)* a drink made from barley and water boiled together for the purpose of making an ill person feel better.

bar·maid /£'bɑː·meɪd, $'bɑːr-/ *n* [C] a female BARTENDER

bar·man /£'bɑː·mən, $'bɑːr-/ *n* [C] *pl* **-men** *esp. Br* a male BARTENDER

bar mitz·vah /£bɑː'mɪts·və, $bɑːr-/ *n* [C] (in the Jewish religion) a ceremony held to celebrate a boy reaching the age of 13, in which he is given the responsibilities and duties of an adult man

barm·y /£'bɑː·mi, $'bɑːr-/ *adj* **-ier, -iest** *esp. Br infml* behaving strangely, or very silly • *Love had made him a little barmy.* • *It was another one of her barmy ideas.*

barn /£bɑːn, $bɑːrn/ *n* [C] a large building on a farm in which HAY (= dried grass) and grain are kept • A **barn dance** is an informal dance in which people do traditional dancing in rows and circles, changing partners regularly. • PIC› **Farming**

bar·na·cle /£'bɑː·nə·kl̩, $'bɑːr-/ *n* [C] a small sea creature with a shell that sticks very tightly and in large numbers to rocks and the bottom of boats

barn·ey /£'bɑː·ni, $'bɑːr-/ *n* [C] *esp. Br infml* a loud argument • *The neighbours were having a bit of a barney last night.*

barn·storm *(obj)* /£'bɑːn·stɔːm, $'bɑːrn·stɔːrm/ *v esp. Am* to travel to a lot of small towns and make political speeches to try to obtain people's votes or support • *During the election campaign Roberta Smith barnstormed the country, thrilling audiences with her speeches.* [T] • *He plans to barnstorm across the state to generate public support for his legislation.* [I] • *During his barnstorming campaign for the presidential election, he travelled 18 000 miles, making 600 speeches to five million people.* • In the past, to barnstorm was to travel to a lot of small towns and perform flying tricks in aircraft. [I/T]

barn·yard /£'bɑːn·jɑːd, $'bɑːrn·jɑːrd/ *n* [C] *esp. Am for* FARMYARD

ba·ro·me·ter /£bə'rɒm·ɪ·təʳ, $-'rɑː·mɪ·t̬ɚ/ *n* [C] a device that measures air pressure and shows when the weather is likely to change • *The arrow on the barometer was pointing to 'Stormy'.* • *(fig.) This survey is considered to be a reliable barometer* **of** *public opinion* (= a good way of showing what people think). • PIC› **Meters and gauges**

bar·on /'bær·ᵊn/ *n* [C] (the title of) a British man who has the lowest rank in the highest social class • *Are you a friend of Baron Wendleton's?* • A baron is also an extremely powerful person in a particular area of business: *a media/press baron* • *a cocaine/drug baron*

bar·on·ess /'bær·ᵊn·es, ˌ--'-/ *n* [C] • A baroness is a British woman who has the lowest rank in the highest social class, or who is the wife of a baron.

ba·ron·i·al /£bə'rəʊ·ni·əl, $-'roʊ-/ *adj* • *They lived in baronial* (= great) *splendour in a mansion surrounded by vast gardens.*

bar·on·y /'bær·ᵊn·i/ *n* [C] • A barony is the rank of a baron, or the land owned by a baron.

bar·on·et /'bær·ᵊn·et, ˌ--'-/ *n* [C] a man who has the lowest title of honour that can be given in Britain, below a BARON but above a KNIGHT, and which is given from father to son • *Mr Thatcher was created a baronet in 1990 and is now called Sir Denis Thatcher.*

bar·on·et·cy /'bær·ᵊn·et·si/ *n* [C] • *Robert's grandfather was given the baronetcy* (= rank of baronet) *after the war.*

ba·roque /£bə'rɒk, $-'rɑːk/ *adj* relating to the heavily decorated style in buildings, art and music that was popular in Europe in the 17th century and the early part of the 18th century • *baroque architecture* • *Rubens and Caravaggio were two of the greatest Baroque painters.*

bar·rack *(obj)* /'bær·ək/ *v Br* to shout loudly in order to interrupt (someone that you disagree with) • *Every time the minister got up to speak he was barracked mercilessly.* [T] •

(Aus) To barrack **for** a football team is to shout encouragement to the players. [I] • (DK)

bar·rack·ing /ˈbær·ə·kɪŋ/ *n* [U] *Br* • *She could not make herself heard above the constant barracking* (= shouting).

bar·racks /ˈbær·əks/ *n* [C + sing/pl v] *pl* **barracks** a building or group of buildings where soldiers live • *The barracks was/were surrounded by a high wall.* • (CS)

bar·ra·cout·a /£ˌbær·əˈkuː·tə, $-t̬ə/ *n* [C] a fish of the south Pacific, used for sport and food

bar·ra·cu·da /ˌbær·əˈkuː·də/ *n* [C] a large tropical sea fish with sharp teeth, that eats other fish and can attack people • *(fig. Am) In the world of high finance, you have to keep an eye on the barracudas* (= selfish people who do business in bad ways). • PIC〉 **Fish**

bar·rage [ATTACK] /£ˈbær·ɑːʒ, $bəˈrɑːʒ/ *n* [C usually sing] continuous firing of large guns to protect soldiers advancing on an enemy, or *(fig.)* a great number of complaints, criticisms or questions suddenly directed at someone • *an artillery barrage* • *(fig.) a barrage of criticism/questions* • *(fig.) The TV station has received a barrage* **of** *complaints about the amount of violence in the series.* • A **barrage balloon** is a large BALLOON, esp. one of a group that are tied to the ground with steel ropes in order to stop enemy aircraft which are flying low.

bar·rage [STRUCTURE] /£ˈbær·ɑːʒ, $bəˈrɑːʒ/ *n* [C] a structure that is built across a river to make the water deeper so that boats can travel more easily or to provide water for farming • *The proposed* **tidal** *barrage would generate enough electricity to supply between 60 000 and 80 000 homes.*

barre /£bɑːʳ, $bɑːr/ *n* [C] a horizontal bar fixed at a convenient height for dancers to hold on to and help them balance while exercising • PIC〉 **Bar**

bar·rel [CONTAINER] /ˈbær·ᵊl/ *n* [C] a large container, made of wood, metal or plastic, with a flat top and bottom and curved sides that make it fatter in the middle • *The apples were stored in barrels in the barn.* • *They drank a barrel of beer* (= the contents of a barrel) *at the party.* • In the oil industry, a barrel of oil is equal to 159 litres. • *(infml) I wouldn't say he's* **a barrel of laughs/fun** (= an amusing person). • *(infml)* If someone has you **over a barrel** they have put you in a very difficult situation in which you have no choice about what you do: *She knows I need the work so she's got me over a barrel in terms of what she pays me.* • A **barrel organ** is a large musical instrument that plays music when you turn a handle on the side. In the past, barrel organs were played outside to entertain people, often with a monkey sitting on top. • A **barrel roll** is a movement of an aircraft in which it turns over and then back up again. • PIC〉 **Containers**

bar·rel [GUN PART] /ˈbær·ᵊl/ *n* [C] the long part of a gun that is shaped like a tube

bar·ren /ˈbær·ᵊn/ *adj* unable to produce plants or fruit, or *(literary or specialized)* unable to have babies • *We drove through a barren, rocky* **landscape**. • *(literary) They longed for a child but she was barren.* • *(fig.) She became very depressed during the barren* (= not productive) *years when she was unable to paint.* • Compare FERTILE [LAND].

bar·rette /bəˈret/ *n* [C] *Am for* **hair slide**, see at HAIR • PIC〉 **Hair**

bar·ri·cade /ˈbær·ɪ·keɪd, --ˈ-/ *n* [C] a line or pile of objects put together, esp. quickly, to stop people from going where they want to go • *During the disturbance, the inmates damaged furniture and other property before* **erecting** *a barricade between themselves and prison officers.* • *There are unconfirmed reports of several deaths among demonstrators who were* **manning** *barricades to stop the tanks.*

bar·ri·cade *obj* /ˈbær·ɪ·keɪd, --ˈ-/ *v* [T] • *Inside the jail, prisoners had barricaded themselves* **into** *their cells* (= put something heavy against the door to stop anyone from getting in). • *Terrified villagers have barricaded themselves* **into** *their houses.*

bar·ri·er /£ˈbær·i·əʳ, $-ɚ/ *n* [C] a long pole, fence, wall or natural feature, such as a mountain or sea, that stops people from going somewhere, or *(fig.)* anything that prevents people from being together or understanding each other • *Barriers have been erected all along the route that the Pope will take.* • *Passengers are requested to show their tickets at the barrier* (= the gate in some railway stations through which you must go to get a train). • *The mountains acted as a natural barrier* **to** *the spread of the disease.* • *(fig.) Despite the* **language** *barrier* (= not speaking the same language), *they soon became good friends.* • *(fig.) Shyness is one of the biggest barriers* **to** *making friends* (= something that makes this difficult). • *(Br)* **Barrier cream** is a cream that stops dirt or chemicals from getting through to the skin.

bar·ring /£ˈbɑː·rɪŋ, $ˈbɑːr·ɪŋ/ *prep* See at BAR [EXCEPT]

bar·rist·er /£ˈbær·ɪ·stəʳ, $-stɚ/ *n* [C] a lawyer in Britain, Australia, etc. who is qualified to argue a case in higher and lower law courts • LP〉 **Law**

bar·row /£ˈbær·əʊ, $-oʊ/ *n* [C] a WHEELBARROW, or *(Br)* a vehicle moved by a person from which esp. fruit and vegetables are sold at the side of a road • *(Br)* A **barrow boy** is a man or boy who sells esp. fruit and vegetables from a barrow.

bar·ten·der *esp. Am* /£ˈbɑːˌten·dəʳ, $ˈbɑːrˌten·dɚ/, *Am* **bar·keep·er**, *esp. Br* **bar·man (-men)**, *female* **bar·maid** *n* [C] someone who serves drinks in a bar • *Most of the bartenders who work here are students.* • (T)

bar·ter *(obj)* /£ˈbɑː·təʳ, $ˈbɑːr·t̬ɚ/ *v* to exchange (goods) for other things rather than for money • *He bartered his stamp collection* **for** *her comics.* [T] • *At the market, you can barter* **for** *souvenirs with Western consumer goods such as jeans and lipstick.* [I]

bar·ter /£ˈbɑː·təʳ, $ˈbɑːr·t̬ɚ/ *n* [U] • *The currency has lost so much of its value that barter has become the preferred way of doing business.*

bas·alt /£ˈbæs·ɒlt, $-ɑːlt/ *n* [U] a type of black rock that comes from a VOLCANO

base [BOTTOM] /beɪs/ *n* [C] the bottom part of an object, on which it rests, or the lowest part of something • *This drinking glass is made of crystal and has a heavy base.* • *'Wedgwood' was written on the base of the cup.* • *At the base of the cliff was a rocky beach.* • *This cream provides an excellent base for your make-up* (= a good bottom layer on which other layers can be put). • *(fig.) A strong economy depends on a healthy* **manufacturing** *base.* • *(Br specialized)* The **base rate** is the percentage rate decided by the government or the Bank of England which banks use when deciding how much to charge for lending money: *The interest rate on Caroline's mortgage is fixed at two percent above the base rate for five years.* • (P)

base [MAIN PLACE] /beɪs/ *n* [C] the main place where a person lives and works, or a place that a company does business from, or a place where there are military buildings and weapons and where members of the armed forces live • *I spend a lot of time in Brussels, but London is still my base.* • *Nice is an excellent base for* (= place to stay when) *exploring the French Riviera.* • *With the ending of the Cold War, a lot of American bases in the UK have been closed.* • In the game of baseball, a base is one of the four positions on a square that a player must reach to score a point. • A **base camp** is a place where food and general supplies are kept, esp. for people climbing a mountain. • (P)

base *obj* /beɪs/ *v* [T usually passive; always + adv/prep] • *Where is your firm based?* • *He was based in* (= He lived in or was at a military establishment in) *Birmingham during the war.*

-based /-beɪst/ *combining form* • *a Manchester-based company* • *community-based programs* • *land-based missiles* (= ones which are fired from the ground)

base [MAIN PART] /beɪs/ *n* [C usually sing] the main part of something • *A Manhattan is a cocktail with a whisky base.* • *(specialized)* In grammar, the **base form** of a verb is the simplest form, without a special ending: *The base form of 'calling' is 'call'.* • (P)

base *obj* /beɪs/ *v* [T usually passive] • *The film is based* **on** *a short story by Thomas Mann* (= the film was developed from the story). • *I feel he's doing something wrong, but I've got nothing to base it* **on** (= I have no proof).

-based /-beɪst/ *combining form* • *This is a cream-based sauce* (= Cream is the main thing in it).

base·less /ˈbeɪ·sləs/ *adj* • A baseless claim or belief is not based on facts: *baseless accusations/allegations/rumours* ○ *The reports that he has been involved in corruption are completely baseless.*

base [NOT HONOURABLE] /beɪs/ *adj* **-r, -st** *literary* not honourable and lacking in morals • *I accused him of having base motives.* • *(specialized)* A **base metal** is a common metal such as LEAD, TIN or COPPER which is not a precious metal and which reacts easily with other chemicals. • (P)

base·ly /ˈbeɪ·sli/ *adv literary* • *I shall lie basely to help them.*

base·ness /ˈbeɪ·snəs/ *n* [U] *literary*

base [MATHEMATICS] /beɪs/ *n* [C usually sing] *specialized* the number on which a counting system is built • *The normal counting system uses base 10, but computers use base 2.* • *A binary number is a number written* **in** *base 2, using the two numbers 0 and 1.* • *5 in base 10 is 101 in base 2, and 3 in base 10 is 11 in base 2.* • The base is also the number which must be multiplied by itself a particular number of times to produce another number, when you represent the other number using a LOGARITHM: *The logarithm of 1 000 000 is six, if the base is ten.* • Ⓟ

base [CHEMISTRY] /beɪs/ *n* [C] *specialized* a base is a chemical that dissolves in water and combines with an acid to create a SALT • *Caustic soda is a base which reacts with hydrochloric acid to give water and sodium chloride.* • Ⓟ

base·ball /£ˈbeɪs·bɔːl, $-bɑːl/ *n* (the ball used in) a game played esp. in N America by two teams of nine players, in which a player hits a ball with a BAT and tries to run around four BASES on a large field before the other team returns the ball • *Jake never* **played** *baseball like the other kids.* [U] • *He had a baseball and a couple of bats in his sports bag.* [C] • A **baseball cap** is a tightly fitting hat, originally worn by baseball players, with a long flat piece at the front to protect the eyes from the sun: *He thinks it's cool to wear his baseball cap back-to-front.* • A **baseball jacket** is a jacket made of a shiny material which fits tightly round the waist and fastens with a ZIP: *Baseball jackets are worn by baseball players to keep them warm when they are not on the field, and by other people in informal situations.* • [LP› **Sports** [PIC› **Coats and jackets, Hats**

base·board /£ˈbeɪs·bɔːd, $-bɔːrd/ *n* [C/U] *Am for* SKIRTING BOARD • [PIC› **Room**

base·line /ˈbeɪs·laɪn/ *n* [C usually sing] a line on a sports field such as the one in tennis marking the end of the playing area or the one in baseball marking the path along which players run • *She delivered a final serve from* **the** *baseline to win the match.* • A baseline is also an imaginary line used as a starting point for making comparisons: *He* **used** *his friend Jack's salary* **as a** *baseline to measure how much he should be earning himself.*

base·ment /ˈbeɪ·smənt/ *n* [C] a part of a building consisting of rooms that are partly or completely below the level of the ground • *Our kitchenware department is in the basement.* • *a basement flat/apartment*

bas·es /ˈbeɪ·siːz/ *pl of* BASE or BASIS

bash *(obj)* [HIT] /bæʃ/ *v infml* to hit hard, or *(fig.)* to attack with words • *He bashed his arm* **against** *a shelf.* [T] • *I got this bruise when I bashed my knee.* [T] • *I could hear her bashing* **away on** *a typewriter* (= hitting the keys loudly). [I] • *(fig.) It's not fair to keep bashing the secretaries* (= criticizing them severely). [T]

bash /bæʃ/ *n* [C usually sing] • *I jumped up too quickly and got a bash* **on** *the head.*

-bash·er /£-ˈbæʃ·əʳ, $-ɚ/ *combining form disapproving* • A **gay/queer**-basher is someone who hates homosexuals and attacks them violently. • A **union**-basher is someone who strongly criticizes **trade unions**. • A **Bible**-basher (*Am usually* **Bible-thumper**) is someone who forcefully or enthusiastically tries to make other people believe in Christianity.

-bash·ing /-ˈbæʃ·ɪŋ/ *combining form disapproving* • **Gay/Queer**-bashing is violence directed at homosexuals. • **Union**-bashing is strong criticism of **trade unions**. • A **Bible**-bashing (*Am usually* **Bible-thumping**) Christian is one who forcefully or enthusiastically tries to make other people believe in Christianity.

bash [PARTY] /bæʃ/ *n* [C] *infml* a party • *He had a big bash for his 18th birthday.*

bash [ATTEMPT] /bæʃ/ *n* [U] **have a bash** *Br infml* to try to do (something you have not done before) • *Learning Russian is really interesting. Why don't you have a bash* (**at** *it)?*

bash on *v adv* [I] *Br infml* to continue doing something that is difficult, boring or takes a long time • *Oh well, that's enough chatting. I suppose I'd better bash on with this essay.* • See also CARRY ON [CONTINUE].

bash·ful /ˈbæʃ·fəl/ *adj* tending to feel uncomfortable with other people and be embarrassed easily; shy • *He felt rather bashful* **about** *taking his clothes off in front of the doctor.* • *She gave a bashful* (= embarrassed) **smile** *as he complimented her on her work.*

bash·ful·ly /ˈbæʃ·fəl·i/ *adv*

bash·ful·ness /ˈbæʃ·fəl·nəs/ *n* [U]

ba·sic /ˈbeɪ·sɪk/ *adj* providing the base or starting point from which something can develop; simple or without complication • *I really need to get some basic financial advice.* • *He only has a basic command of English* (= He only knows the most important and simple words and expressions). • *The basic* (= most important) *problem is that they don't talk to each other enough.* • *Being loved was basic* **to** *her happiness* (= necessary for her to be happy). • *The car she bought was pretty basic* (= had only simple features) – *she didn't want one with a lot of gadgets.* • *The rise in prices of basic* **foodstuffs***, such as meat, cheese and sugar, has led to strikes and demonstrations.* • A **basic salary** is what a person earns before other sums of money, such as payments for working extra hours, are added.

ba·sics /ˈbeɪ·sɪks/ *pl n* • The basics are the simplest and most important facts, ideas or things connected with something: *Pat has promised to teach me* **the** *basics* **of** *sailing, but I haven't got time at the moment.* • *The country's biggest supermarket chain is to cut its prices on 500 items, ranging from basics, such as coffee and eggs, to luxury goods.* • If you get **back to basics**, you start to give your attention to the simplest and most important matters after ignoring them for a while: *Electric guitars dominated her last album, but for her latest one she has got back to basics and used only acoustic instruments.* ○ *Teaching the correct use of the apostrophe is part of a new back-to-basics campaign to raise standards in grammar, punctuation and spelling.*

ba·sic·al·ly /ˈbeɪ·sɪ·kli/ *adv* [not gradable] • Basically is used when referring to the main or most important characteristic or feature of something: *My job is basically to make sure that the computer system keeps working properly.* ○ *Basically,* (= The most important thing is that) *they want a lot more information about the project before they will put any money into it.* ○ *His lawyer described him as a basically* **decent** *man whose desperate circumstances had driven him to shoplifting.* ○ *"So what's the difference between these two TVs?" "Well, they're basically* **the same***, but the more expensive one comes with a remote control."* ○ *The car's basically* **sound** (= in good condition), *but the paintwork needs a bit of attention.* ○ *The village has remained basically* **unchanged** *for over 300 years.*

BASIC /ˈbeɪ·sɪk/ *n* [U] a common language for programming computers which uses instructions that are similar to English • *BASIC is comparatively slow in executing its instructions, but it is simple enough for anyone who is interested to have a go at programming.*

bas·il /£ˈbæz·əl, $ˈbeɪ·zəl/ *n* [U] a herb with a sweet smell which is added to add flavour in cookery • *Basil goes well with tomatoes and is used to make pesto sauce.* • [PIC› **Herbs and spices**

ba·sil·i·ca /bəˈsɪl·ɪ·kə, -ˈzɪl-/ *n* [C] a public building in ancient Rome which was round at one end and had two rows of columns supporting the roof, or an often very old church with a similar design

ba·sin /ˈbeɪ·sən/ *n* [C] *esp. Br* an open round container shaped like a bowl with sloping sides, used for holding food or liquid • *Put the ingredients into a large basin and mix well.* • A basin is also the amount of something that a basin can hold: *After he'd finished cleaning his boots, he poured the basin* **of** *water over the lawn.* • *(esp. Am)* Basin is also another name for WASHBASIN: *I've cleaned the basin and scrubbed the bath.* • The basin of a river, lake or sea is the area of land from which streams run into it. • A basin is also a sheltered area of deep water where boats are kept. • (CS) (RUS)

ba·sis /ˈbeɪ·sɪs/ *n* [C] *pl* **bases** /ˈbeɪ·siːz/ the most important facts, ideas, etc. from which something is developed • *This design was the basis* **for** *the large painting he did later.* • *Their proposals have no proven scientific basis.* • *Decisions were often made* **on the** *basis* **of** (= using) *incorrect information.* • A basis is also a way or method of doing something: *Most of our staff work for us* **on a voluntary** *basis* (= They work without being paid).

bask /£bɑːsk, $bæsk/ *v* [I always + adv/prep] to lie or sit enjoying the warmth esp. of the sun • *We sat out on the balcony, basking* **in** *the sun.* • *(fig.) He had done the right thing, and for a while he basked* **in** (= enjoyed) *his mother's approval.* • (DK)

bas·ket /£ˈbɑː·skɪt, $ˈbæs·kɪt/ *n* [C] a light container, often with a handle, which is made of thin bendable strips of wood or plastic woven together and is used for carrying or storing things • *a shopping basket* • *a wicker basket* • *a laundry/clothes basket* • *Susannah's very pleased with her*

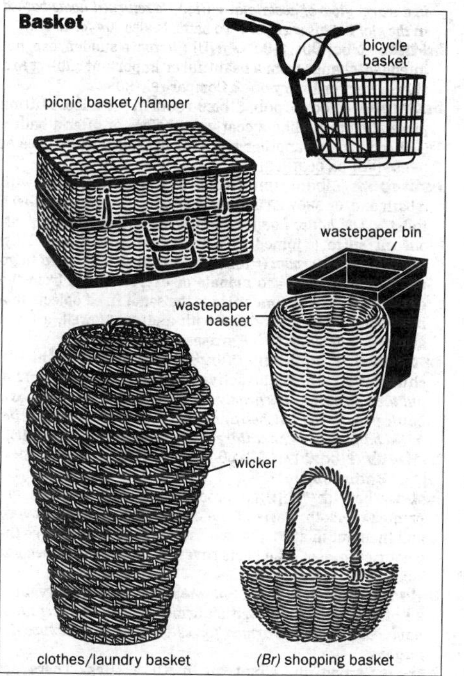

new **picnic** *basket.* • *We picked lots of strawberries, but we'd eaten half the basket* (= the contents of the basket) *by the time we got home.* • In the game of BASKETBALL, a basket is an open net hanging from a metal ring through which the players try to throw the ball to score points for their team, or the successful throwing of the ball through the ring. • A basket of something is a group of related things: *The value of the pound against a basket* **of** *world* **currencies** *has fallen to 81% of its 1985 value.* • A **basket case** is an unkind name for someone who is not able to handle the demands and pressures of life. • A **basket case** is also a country or company that is very unsuccessful financially: *Twenty years ago the country was an* **economic** *basket case.* ○ *He has a lot of experience of turning basket cases into profitable companies.* • See also WASTEPAPER BASKET. • [PIC]> **Basket, Bicycles, Sports**

bas·ket·ful /£'bɑː·skɪt·fʊl, $'bæs·kɪt-/ *n* [C] • A basketful of something is the amount of it that a basket can hold: *a basketful of apples*

bas·ket·work /£'bɑː·skɪt·wɜːk, $'bæs·kɪt·wɜːrk/, **bas·ket·ry** /£'bɑː·skɪ·tri, $'bæs·kɪ-/ *n* [U] • Basketwork is the making of baskets and other objects by weaving together thin bendable strips of wood.

bas·ket·ball /£'bɑː·skɪt·bɔːl, $'bæs·kɪt·bɑːl/ *n* [C/U] (a ball used in) a game played by two teams of five men or six women who score points by throwing a large ball through an open net hanging from a metal ring • [LP]> **Sports**

basque [CLOTHING] /bæsk, bɑːsk/ *n* [C] a type of tight-fitting underwear for women which covers the top part of the body and provides support for the breasts • *Basques became very popular after Madonna wore one which had been designed by Jean-Paul Gaultier.*

Basque [RACE] /bæsk, £bɑːsk/ *n, adj* (connected with) a member of a race living in the area around the W Pyrenees in Spain and France, or the language of this race • *There are about 805 000 Basques in Spain and 130 000 in France.* [C] • *Approximately half a million people speak Basque, which is unrelated to any other language.* [U] • *The city of Bilbao is a centre of Basque* **nationalism**.

bas–re·lief /ˌbæs·rɪ'liːf/ *n* a type of art in which shapes are cut from the surrounding stone so that they stand out slightly against a flat background, or a work of art done in this way • *The exhibition has three-dimensional sculpture, large amounts of bas-relief and architectural carving.* [U] • *One of the advantages of profiling* **in** *bas-relief is that it allows the background to be carved before the figures are finished.* [U] • *The stone gateway bears bas-relief depictions of Egyptian archers and their chariots.* • *Gravestone decorations included bas-reliefs* (= works of art) *showing the dead man and his dog.* [C]

bass [MUSICAL RANGE] /beɪs/ *n* the lowest range of musical notes, or a man with a singing voice in this range • *He* **sings** *bass.* [U] • *Italy's leading bass was to give a concert in the park.* [C] • A bass is also a **double bass**. [C] See at DOUBLE [TWICE]. • On a radio, music system, etc. the bass is the set of low musical sounds or the button that controls them: *There's too much bass.* [U] ○ *Turn down the bass.* [U] • A **bass drum, bass (guitar)**, **bass saxophone** or other bass musical instrument is one that produces the lowest musical sound of the group of instruments of the same type: *He plays (the) bass (guitar).* • [PIC]> **Musical instruments**

bass·ist /'beɪ·sɪst/ *n* [C] • A bassist plays either the **bass guitar** or the **double bass**.

bass [FISH] /bæs/ *n* [C] *pl* **bass** a type of fish found in rivers or the sea

bas·set (hound) /'bæs·ɪt/ *n* [C] a type of dog with smooth hair, a long body, short legs and long ears

bas·soon /bə'suːn/ *n* [C] a musical instrument of the WOODWIND group, consisting of a long wooden pipe, metal keys and two REEDS, which plays low notes • [PIC]> **Musical instruments** (DK) (S)

bas·tard [UNPLEASANT] /£'bɑː·stəd, $'bæs·tɚd/ *n* [C] *taboo* an extremely unpleasant person, esp. a man, or an unpleasant or difficult activity • *I've never met a such a bastard.* • *He was a* **real/right** *bastard* **to** *his wife.* • *You lied to me,* **you** *bastard!* [as form of address] • *(humorous) Trust him to win again – he's a* **jammy/lucky** *bastard* (= I don't think he deserves it)*!* • *This crossword's a bastard* (= difficult to do). • (DK) (NL)

bas·tard [CHILD] /£'bɑː·stəd, $'bæs·tɚd/ *n* [C] *old use* a person born to parents who are not married to each other; an ILLEGITIMATE child • *She was never concerned about being born a bastard.* • *He was born in 1798, the bastard son of a country squire and his mistress.* • *"Now, gods, stand up for bastards"* (Shakespeare, King Lear 1.2) • (DK) (NL)

bas·tard·ize *obj, Br and Aus usually* **–ise** /£'bɑː·stə·daɪz, $'bæs·tɚ-/ *v* [T] to change (something) in a way which makes it fail to represent the values and qualities that it is intended to represent • *The plot of the classic novel was bastardised with an obligatory Hollywood happy ending.* • *He criticizes those who bastardize Shakespeare, slice up Beethoven symphonies and re-orchestrate great operas.*

bas·tard·ized, *Br and Aus usually* **–ised** /£'bɑː·stə·daɪzd, $'bæs·tɚ-/ *adj* • *a bastardized* **form** *of the word/language* • *a bastardized* **version** *of the song*

baste *obj* [POUR] /beɪst/ *v* [T] to pour hot fat and liquid over (esp. meat while it is cooking) • *Baste the turkey at regular intervals during cooking.*

baste *obj* [SEW] /beɪst/ *v* [T] *esp. Am and Aus for* TACK [SEW] • *Baste the seams.*

bas·ti·on /'bæs·ti·ən/ *n* [C] something which maintains or defends esp. a belief or a way of life that is disappearing or threatened • *British public schools were described as 'a bastion* **of** *upper-class privilege'.* • *The club regarded itself as one of the* **last** *bastions* **of** *male supremacy.* • A bastion is also a part of the wall of a castle that sticks out from it in order to protect it.

bat [STICK] /bæt/ *n* [C] a specially shaped piece of wood used for hitting the ball in many games • *a baseball/cricket/rounders/table tennis bat* • *(Br and Aus infml) I didn't ask her to buy them a present – she did it* **off** *her* **own bat** (= without anyone telling or asking her to). • *(Am)* If something is done **off the bat** it is done immediately: *You can't expect to be accepted in a new town* **right/straight** *off the bat.* • See also BATSMAN. • [PIC]> **Sports**

bat *(obj)* /bæt/ *v* **-tt-** • *He batted the ball high into the air.* [T] • *Jones will be the first to bat.* [I]

bat·ter /£'bæt·əʳ, $'bæţ·ɚ/, **hit·ter** *n* [C] • In baseball, the batter is the person whose turn it is to hit the ball or a person who is good at this activity. • The **batter's box** is the place where the batter stands when he is trying to hit the ball. • [PIC]> **Box**

bat [ANIMAL] /bæt/ *n* [C] a small flying animal with big ears and leathery wings which is active at night • *As twilight fell they could just see the bats swooping in and out from under the roof.* • *(infml dated disapproving)* A person who **has bats in the belfry** is silly and foolish with confused behaviour. See also BATS; batty. • *"Bat out of Hell"* (title of a record by Meat Loaf, 1979)

bat *obj* [EYE] /bæt/ *v* [T] **-tt-** (esp. of women) to open and close (your eyes) quickly several times, esp. to attract attention or admiration • *She smiled and batted her* **eyelashes** *at him.* • If you do **not bat an eyelid** you show no sign of surprise or worry when something unexpected happens: *Gail didn't bat an eyelid when Mark told her that he had crashed the car.*

batch /bætʃ/ *n* [C] a group of things or people dealt with at the same time or considered similar in type • *The travel agent gave us a batch* **of** *holiday leaflets and brochures.* • *The cook brought in a fresh batch* **of** *homemade cakes.* • *We looked at the job applications* **in** *two batches.* • *The* **latest** *batch* **of** *economic statistics underlines fears that domestic demand is too strong.* • If you **batch-bake** you make a large number of cakes at the same time, esp. to freeze some for future use. • **Batch processing** is when a computer does several jobs, one after the other.

bat·ed /£ˈbeɪ·tɪd, $-t̬ɪd/ *adj* [not gradable] **with bated breath** anxiously or excitedly • *I waited for the results with bated breath.*

bath *Br and Aus* /£bɑːθ, $bæθ/ *n* [C] a long plastic, metal or CERAMIC container which can be filled with water so that a person can sit or lie in it to wash their whole body (*Am usually* **bathtub** or **tub**), or the act of washing in this way • *The bath was cracked and would need replacing.* • *There was a shelf over the end of the bath with glass ornaments on it.* • A bath is also a period of sitting in a bath in order to wash: *I haven't time for a bath, so I'll just have a shower.* ○ *He* **had/***(esp. Am)* **took** *a* **(cold/hot/tepid/warm)** *bath.* • *It was his turn to* **give** *the baby/the dog a bath* (= wash it in a bath). • If you **run** (someone) a bath you fill a bath with water for washing: *The phone rang while I was running (myself) a bath.* ○ *I'll run you a bath while you take off those wet clothes.* • A bath can also be a health treatment: *mud baths* • *thermal baths* • A bath is also any container holding liquid: *The material is immersed in a bath* **of** *pink dye for two hours.* ○ *The garden has a beautiful stone* **bird** *bath in which you will often see small birds splashing.* • Bath is used with other words to refer to things used in or near a bath: *bath oil* ○ *a bath pillow* • **Bath cubes/salts** are small hard pieces that you put in the bath water to make it smell pleasant and/or to make the water dissolve soap more easily. • A **bath mat** is either a cover that you stand on after getting out of a bath or SHOWER to stop the floor from getting wet or a piece of rubber which is put inside the bath or SHOWER to prevent you sliding and falling. • A **bath rack** is a set of metal bars or an open plastic container which is put across a bath and used to hold washing equipment such as soap. • A **bath towel** is a large TOWEL (= piece of cloth) with which you dry yourself after a bath or SHOWER. • [PIC] **Bathroom, Rack**

baths /£bɑːðz, $bæðz/ *n* [C + sing/pl v] *pl* **baths** • *(dated Br and Aus)* A baths is a **swimming baths**. See at SWIM [MOVE IN WATER]. • A baths is a place where people can go to have esp. a hot bath: *the public baths* ○ *the Turkish baths* ○ *An old Roman baths was discovered during the building work.*

bath *(obj) Br and Aus* /£bɑːθ, $bæθ/, *Am* **bathe** *v* • To bath is to wash in a bath: *She baths every morning.* [I] ○ *It's time to bath the baby.* [T] • [LP] **Reflexive pronouns and verbs**

bathe [SWIM] /beɪð/ *v* [I] to swim, esp. in the sea, a river or a lake • *Children who had bathed* **in** *sewage-contaminated sea water suffered from vomiting, diarrhoea and fever.* • *Watching the elephants come down to the river each evening to drink and bathe was one of the highlights of our holiday.*

bathe *Br* /beɪð/ *n* [U] • *The children had gone to the beach for a bathe.*

bath·er /£ˈbeɪ·ðəʳ, $-ðɚ/ *n* [C] • *At Wittering, Sussex, a woman bather was dragged unconscious from the sea.* • *There is a campaign along the Riviera to force bathers to cover up before leaving the beaches.*

bath·ing /ˈbeɪ·ðɪŋ/ *n* [U] • *At midnight they all decided to* **go** *bathing.* • *The resort has two wonderful sandy bathing beaches.* • *The report was critical of bathing-water quality.* • *(esp. Br and Aus)* A **bathing costume/bathing suit** is a **swimming costume**. See at SWIM [MOVE IN WATER]. • **Bathing trunks** are **swimming trunks**. See at SWIM [MOVE IN WATER].

bathe *obj* [COVER] /beɪð/ *v* [T] to cover with a liquid, esp. in order to make part of the body feel better, or *(fig.)* to cover with something that causes a pleasant feeling or appearance • *I bathed my sore eyes* **with** *water.* • *I bathed my feet* **in** *warm water.* • *He was shaking and his face was bathed* **in sweat.** • *(fig.) In the afternoon the sun bathes the city* **in** *shades of pink and gold.* • *(fig.) Their past is bathed in a warm glow of nostalgia.* • *(fig.) He returned home bathed* **in** *the glory of his success.* • To bathe is also *Am for* to BATH.

ba·thos /£ˈbeɪ·θɒs, $-θɑːs/ *n* [U] *literary* a sudden, esp. not intended, change from a beautiful or important subject to a silly or very ordinary one • Compare PATHOS.

bath·robe /£ˈbɑːθ·rəʊb, $ˈbæθ·roʊb/ *n* [C] a loose-fitting piece of clothing like a coat worn before or after a bath • Bathrobe is also another word for **dressing gown**. See at DRESS [PUT ON CLOTHES].

bath·room /£ˈbɑːθ·rʊm, £-ruːm, $ˈbæθ-/ *n* [C] a room with a bath and/or SHOWER and often a toilet, or *(Am and Aus)* a toilet • *The house has four bedrooms and two bathrooms, one* **en suite** (= joined to a bedroom). • *(Am and Aus) Where's the bathroom* (= toilet)*?* • *(Am and Aus) I need* **to go to the bathroom** (= to urinate or excrete waste from the bowels). • A **bathroom suite** is the set of fixed objects in a bathroom which includes a bath and/or SHOWER, a toilet and a WASHBASIN. • [LP] **Phrases and customs**

bath·time /£ˈbɑːθ·taɪm, $ˈbæθ-/ *n* the time at which a child has a bath, or the activity of bathing • *Let's start to put the toys away – it's nearly bathtime.* [U] • *Bathtime was a battleground for Rachel and her mother, because Rachel hated baths.* [U] • *The children have different bathtimes.* [C]

bath·tub /£ˈbɑːθ·tʌb, $ˈbæθ-/, **tub** *n* [C] *Am for* BATH • [PIC] **Bathroom**

bat·ik /bætˈiːk/ *n* [U] a process in which patterns are printed on cloth. Parts of the cloth are covered with wax, and then put in a DYE (= a special liquid used to change the colour of things). The parts covered in wax do not become coloured.

bat·man /ˈbæt·mən/ *n* [C] *pl* **-men** the personal servant of an officer esp. in the British armed forces • *Officers also have batmen in the armed forces of other Commonwealth nations.*

bat·on /£ˈbæt·ɒn, $ˈbæt̬·ᵊn/ *n* [C] a stick. There are different types with several different uses. • A baton is used by a CONDUCTOR (= person who controls the performance of a group of musicians) to show the speed of the music. • In some races a baton is given from one runner to another as they run. • A baton is used by a MAJORETTE (= a young woman or girl) who marches in front of a musical group wearing a uniform and spins the baton and throws it into the air. • A baton (*Br and Aus usually* **truncheon**, *Am usually* **nightstick**) is a thick, heavy stick used as a weapon by the police. • *(Br)* A **baton charge** is when a large group of police run forward in an attacking movement carrying their batons. • (PL) (RUS)

bats /bæts/ *adj* [after v] *infml dated disapproving for* silly and foolish with confused behaviour • *She's bats.*

bats·man (*pl* **-men**), **bats·wo·man** (*pl* **-women**) /ˈbæt·smən, -ˌswʊm·ən/ *n* [C] in cricket, a person whose turn it is to hit the ball or a person who is regularly does this activity • *There was applause as the batsman walked out to the wicket.* • *He was a former England batsman/the team's best batsman.* • [PIC] **Sports**

bat·tal·i·on /bəˈtæl·i·ən/ *n* [C] a military unit consisting of three or more COMPANIES

bat·ten /£ˈbæt·ᵊn, $ˈbæt̬-/ *n* [C] a long piece of wood, often fixed to something to strengthen it

bat·ten *obj* /£ˈbæt·ᵊn, $ˈbæt̬-/ *v* [T] • *The boxes were securely battened* (= fastened with pieces of wood) *before the journey.* • To **batten down the hatches** is to fasten the entrances to the lower part of a ship using wooden boards or *(fig. infml)* to prepare for a difficult situation: *(fig. infml) My sister's children were coming to stay so we had to batten down the hatches.* • To **batten on** someone is to live well by using that person's money or position.

bat·ter *(obj)* [HIT] /£ˈbæt·əʳ, $ˈbæt̬·ɚ/ *v* to hit and behave violently towards (a person, esp. a woman or child) repeatedly over a long period of time or to hit (something) with force many times • *No-one seemed to realize that the child's stepfather had been battering her for years.* [T] • *The paramilitaries battered him to death with a rifle-butt.* [T] • *He was battering* **(at/on)** *the door with his fists and howling.* [T; I + prep] • *The waves battered* **(against)** *the rocks at the bottom of the cliff.* [T; I + prep] • *The burglars had battered* **down** *the door of the house* (= hit it so hard that it broke and fell down). [M] • [LP] **Crimes and criminals** (E) (P)

bat·tered /£ˈbæt·əd, $ˈbæt̬·ɚd/ *adj* • *The group set up a sanctuary for battered* **wives.** • Something which is battered is damaged, esp. by being used a lot: *a battered car/hat* ○ *battered furniture/toys* ○ *a battered economy/image*

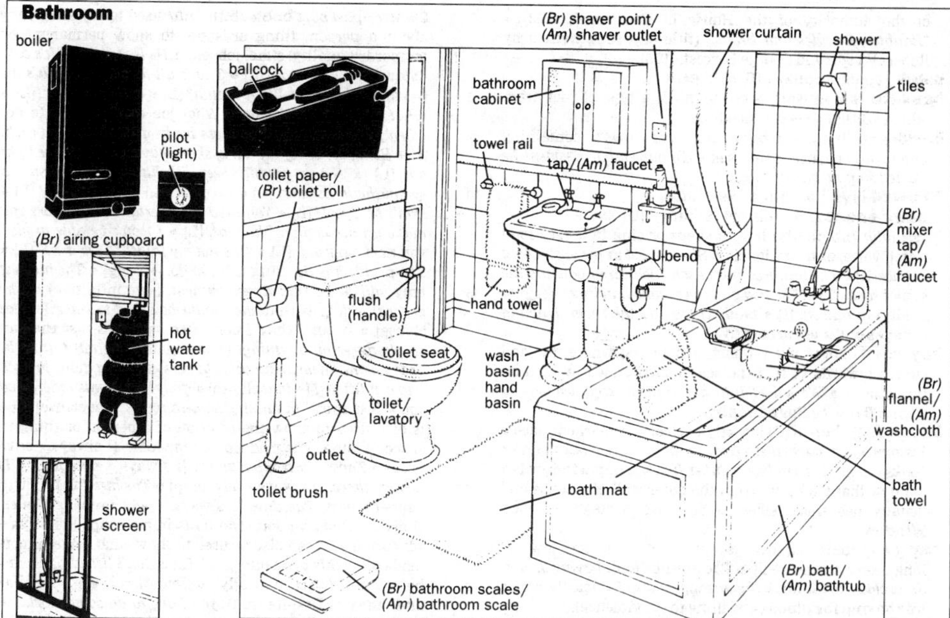

bat·ter·ing /£'bæt·ᵊr·ɪŋ, $'bæţ·ɚ·ɪŋ/ *n* • *People were shocked to hear about* **baby** *battering by a such a respectable couple.* [U] • *(infml) Once again, our team had* **taken** *a battering* (= had been defeated heavily). [C] • A **battering ram** is a long heavy pole which was used by armies in the past to break down esp. castle doors, and which is now used by police and fire officers to break down house doors.

bat·ter·y /£'bæt·ᵊr·i, $'bæţ·ɚ·i/ *n* [U] **assault and battery** • See at ASSAULT.

bat·ter FOOD /£'bæt·əʳ, $'bæţ·ɚ/ *n* [U] a mixture of flour, eggs and milk, used to make PANCAKES or to cover food before frying it • *Do you prefer fish* **in** *batter or in breadcrumbs?* • Ⓔ Ⓟ

bat·tered /£'bæt·əd, $'bæţ·ɚd/ *adj* • *battered cod* • *The courgettes, lightly battered, were fried and served with fresh lemon sauce.*

bat·ter·y ELECTRICAL DEVICE /£'bæt·ᵊr·i, $'bæţ·ɚ·i/ *n* [C] a device that produces electricity to provide power for radios, cars, etc. • *an alkaline battery* • *a rechargeable/ solar battery* • *a battery-operated hair dryer* • *a battery-powered car* • *This alarm clock takes two medium-sized batteries.* • *The toy costs £50 – batteries not included* (= not provided with it and must be bought separately). • *I think the battery is* **dead/gone/(Br esp. of a car battery)** *flat* (= has lost its power).

bat·ter·y LARGE NUMBER /£'bæt·ᵊr·i, $'bæţ·ɚ·i/ *n* [C] a number of things of a similar type • *In the kitchen an impressive battery* **of** *stainless steel utensils hangs on the wall.* • *A battery* **of** *experts failed to discover the cause of the accident.* • *A* **whole** *battery* **of** *measures was tried in an attempt to get them to give up cigarettes.* • A battery is also a number of large guns and similar weapons operating together in the same place: *The shore battery opened fire.* • *(Br and Aus)* A battery is also a system of producing a large number of eggs cheaply by keeping a lot of chickens in rows of small cages: *battery* **farming** ○ *They refused to eat eggs laid by battery* **hens**.

bat·tle /£'bæt·l̩, $'bæţ·/ *n* [C] a fight between armed forces, or *(fig.)* an argument between two groups or against a situation that a group wishes to change • *The Battle of the Somme in 1916 was the bloodiest battle ever fought, with over a million deaths.* • *Her only brother was killed* **in** *battle* (= while fighting). • *(fig.) The aid agency continues the battle* **against** *ignorance and superstition.* • *(fig.) The two companies fought a fierce battle* **for** *control of the market.* • *(fig.) The battle* **for** *women's rights still goes on.* • *No agreement was reached and both sides prepared to* **do battle** (= fight or argue with each other). • A **battle of wits** is when two people or two groups use their intelligence and ability to think quickly to try to defeat each other. • A **battle cry** is a shout given by soldiers as they run towards the enemy or *(fig.)* a phrase used by people supporting a particular cause: *A famous battle cry is 'God for Harry! England and St George!' from Shakespeare's play Henry V.* • *(fig.) 'Reclaim the night' was the battle cry of women fighting for the right to walk safely at night.* • *"The battle of Waterloo was won on the playing fields of Eton"* (believed to have been said by The Duke of Wellington, 1769-1852)

bat·tle /£'bæt·l̩, $'bæţ·/ *v* [I] • *Twenty years ago this summer, police battled with residents in this inner city area for three days.* • *The governments agreed to resume diplomatic and economic relations, seven years after the two nations battled over territory.* • *(fig.)* To battle is also to try hard to achieve something in a difficult situation: *He had to battle* **against** *prejudice to get a job.* ○ *The parents battled* **for** *the right to be involved in the decision-making.* ○ *We battled* **with** *the elements* **to** *get the roof fixed.*

bat·tler /£'bæt·ləʳ, $'bæţ·lɚ/ *n* [C] • A battler is a person who has continually worked under great difficulties to achieve things.

bat·tle·axe WEAPON *Br and Aus, Am* **bat·tle–ax** /£'bæt·l̩.æks, $'bæţ-/ *n* [C] a large AXE used as a weapon in the past

bat·tle·axe WOMAN *Br and Aus, Am* **bat·tle–ax** /£'bæt·l̩.æks, $'bæţ-/ *n* [C] a fierce and unpleasant older woman with strong opinions • *Their headmistress was regarded as an* **old** *battleaxe.*

bat·tle·dress /£'bæt·l̩.dres, $'bæţ-/ *n* [U] uniform worn by soldiers and other military groups esp. when they go to fight

bat·tle·field /£'bæt·l̩.fiːld, $'bæţ-/ *n* [C] a place where a BATTLE is being fought or has been fought in the past • *They carried the wounded from the battlefield.* • *First aid is now a battlefield priority.* • *a Civil War battlefield* • *(fig.) The companies' battlefield is the world's biggest and most sophisticated market for cars.* • *(fig.) Thirty people were injured in the ensuing fracas that turned the restaurant into a battlefield* **of** *broken glass and overturned tables.*

bat·tle·ground /£'bæt·l̩.graʊnd, $'bæţ-/ *n* [C] a BATTLEFIELD or *(fig.)* a subject on which people strongly disagree • *(fig.) Bathtime was a battleground for the five year old and her mother.*

bat·tle·ments /£'bæt·l̩.mənts, $'bæţ-/ *pl n* a wall around the top of a castle with regular spaces in it through which the people inside the castle can shoot

bat·tle·ship /£'bæt·l̩.ʃɪp, $'bæţ-/ *n* [C] a very large military ship with big guns

bat·ty /£'bæt·i, $'bæţ-/ *adj* **-ier, -iest** *infml disapproving* silly and foolish with confused behaviour • *His batty old aunt kept knitting him ugly jumpers.*

bau·ble /£'bɔː·bl̩, $'bɑː-/ *n* [C] a shiny decoration, or a piece of bright but cheap jewellery • *"What shall we do with the bauble? Take it away! (often quoted as 'take away that bauble')"* (Oliver Cromwell referring to the mace (= symbol of the authority of the House of Commons), 1653) • *"Baubles, Bangles and Beads"* (title of a song written by Robert Wright and George Forrest, 1955)

baulk /£bɔːk, $bɑːlk/ *v* [I], *n* [C] BALK

baux·ite /£ˈbɔːk·saɪt, $ˈbɑːk-/ *n* [U] a type of rock from which ALUMINIUM is produced

bawd·y /£ˈbɔː·di, $ˈbɑː-/ *adj* **-ier, -iest** containing humorous remarks about sex • *To our embarrassment he started singing bawdy songs.*

bawd·i·ly /£ˈbɔː·dɪ·li, $ˈbɑː-/ *adv*

bawd·i·ness /£ˈbɔː·dɪ·nəs, $ˈbɑː-/ *n* [U]

bawl *(obj)* /£bɔːl, $bɑːl/ *v* to shout or sing in a very loud rough voice, or to cry loudly • *She bawled* **at** *me to sit down at once.* [I] • *The hall was full of schoolchildren bawling the school song.* [T] • *The two girls were now bawling* (= crying loudly) *in unison.* [I] • *Lindy came into the room, bawling her* **eyes out** (= crying loudly). [T]

bay COAST /beɪ/ *n* [C] a part of the coast where the land curves inwards so that the sea is surrounded by land on three sides • *We sailed into a beautiful, secluded bay.* • *Dublin Bay* • *the Bay* **of** *Naples*

bay SPACE /beɪ/ *n* [C] a partly enclosed or marked space • *Visitors must park their cars in the marked bays.* • *The books you need are in bay number five.* • A **bay window** is a window that sticks out from the outer wall of a house and usually has three sides. • See also SICKBAY. • PIC **Window**

bay CALL /beɪ/ *v* [I] (of dogs and WOLVES) to make a low and long deep cry repeatedly • *The* **hounds** *were baying as they drew closer to the fox.* • *(fig. disapproving) By now the crowd was* **baying for blood** (= wishing to see violence).

bay TREE /beɪ/ *n* [C] a small evergreen tree, the leaves of which are dried and used in cooking to add flavour • PIC **Herbs and spices**

bay HORSE /beɪ/ *n* [C] a reddish brown horse

bay PREVENT HARM /beɪ/ *n* [U] **hold/keep at bay** to prevent (someone or something unpleasant) from harming you • *She left the light on at night to keep her fears at bay.* • *Exercise can help keep fat at bay.*

bay CAUGHT /beɪ/ *n* [U] **at bay** (of an animal) about to be caught or attacked • *A frightened animal at bay can turn violent.*

bay·o·net /ˈbeɪ·ə·nət/ *n* [C] a long sharp blade fixed on to a RIFLE (= gun) • *Fix bayonets!* • *The soldiers were ordered to do bayonet practice.* • PIC **Knife**

bay·o·net *obj* /ˈbeɪ·ə·nət/ *v* [T] **-t-** or **-tt-** • *He viciously bayoneted the straw dummy.*

bay·ou /ˈbaɪ·uː/ *n* [C] (in the southern US) an area of slowly moving water away from the main river

bazaar /£bəˈzɑːʳ, $-ˈzɑːr/ *n* [C] an area of small shops and people selling things esp. in the Middle East and India, or any group of small shops or people selling goods of the same type • *The tourists were bargaining/haggling for cheap consumer goods in the covered bazaar.* • *The wide pavement on one side of the street has become an open-air bazaar with stalls and street traders.* • *These weapons are available in international arms bazaars.* • *We spent the morning happily exploring an antiques bazaar.* • A bazaar is also an event where people sell things to raise money esp. for an organization which helps other people: *a Christmas bazaar* ◦ *A group of friends organized bazaars and jumble sales to raise money for medical treatment for the children injured in the war.*

ba·zoo·ka /bəˈzuː·kə/ *n* [C] a long tube-shaped gun, fired from the shoulder, which is used to fire ROCKETS at esp. military vehicles

BBC /ˌbiː·biːˈsiː/, *Br infml* **Beeb** *n* [U] *abbreviation for* British Broadcasting Corporation (= a British organization that broadcasts on television and radio in Britain and is paid for by a charge on everyone who has a television) • **The** *BBC faces increasing competition from the commercial channels, cable and satellite TV.* • *The new series is on BBC 1/BBC 2 every Tuesday night.* • **BBC Pronunciation** is the standard way in which middle class speakers of southern British English pronounce words. • Compare ITV. • LP **Pronunciation**

BC /ˌbiːˈsiː/ *abbreviation for* Before Christ (used in the Christian CALENDAR when referring to a year before Jesus Christ was born) • *Dinosaurs became extinct 62 million years BC.* • *The Battle of Actium took place in 31 BC.* • Compare AD. • LP **Dates**

be QUALITY /biː/ *v* I **am** /æm/ you/we/they **are** /£ɑːʳ, $ɑːr/ he/she/it **is** /ɪz/, **being** /ˈbiː·ɪŋ/, *past simple* I/he/she/it **was** /£wɒz, $wɑːz/ you/we/they **were** /£wɜːʳ, $wɜːr/, *past part* **been** /biːn, bɪn/ used to say something about a person, thing or state, to show permanent or temporary quality, state, job, etc. • *He is rich.* [L] • *It's cold today.* [L] • *I'm Andy.* [L] • *That's all for now.* [L] • *It's me* (= I am here). [L] • *What is that?* [L] • *She's a doctor.* [L] • *What do you want to be* (= What job do you want to do) *when you grow up?* [L] • *These books are* (= cost) *50p each.* [L] • *Being afraid of the dark, she always slept with the light on.* [L] • *Never having been ill himself, he wasn't a sympathetic listener.* [L] • *Be quiet!* [L] • *Do be quiet!* [L] • *Don't be a fool!* [L] • *You need to be certain/sure before you make an accusation like that.* [L] • *I won't be able to visit you next weekend.* [L] • *"It's not my fault!" "Yes it is!"* [L] • *The problem is deciding what to do.* [+ v-ing] • *The hardest part will be* **to** *find a replacement.* [+ to infinitive] • *The general feeling is* **that** *she should be asked to leave.* [+ *that* clause] • **It**'*s not* **that** *I don't like her* – **it**'*s just* **that** *we rarely agree on anything!* [+ *that* clause] • *(fml) Can* **it** *be* **that** *no-one knew about this old person, living alone in such bad conditions?* [+ *that* clause] • *(fml) Have I misunderstood you* – *is* **it that** *I'm missing something?* [+ *that* clause] • Be is also used to show the position of a person or thing in space or time: *The food was on the table.* [I always + adv/prep] ◦ *Tony's in trouble again.* [I always + adv/prep] ◦ *Is anyone there?* [I always + adv/prep] ◦ *The meeting is* (= will happen) *next Tuesday.* [I always + adv/prep] ◦ *Waiter,* **there**'*s a fly in my soup* (= a fly is in my soup). [I always + adv/prep] • Be can also be used to show what something is made of: *Is this plate pure gold?* [L] • *Don't listen to others* – **be** *your***self** (= act naturally). • *(fml) "I'm tired."* "**Be that as it may** (= Despite that), *you have to do some work."* • The **be-all and end-all** is the most important thing: *Not everybody agreed that winning was the be-all and end-all.* ◦ *She added, " We don't want investment banking to be the be-all and end-all* **of** *a Harvard MBA".* ◦ *It was the period when everyone saw men in space as the be-all and end-all* **of** *space exploration.* ◦ *Don't worry if you can't find that photo for me – it's not the be-all and end-all* (= it's not very important).

be CONTINUE /biː/ *v aux* [+ v-*ing*] I **am** /æm/ you/we/they **are** /£ɑːʳ, $ɑːr/ he/she/it **is** /ɪz/, **being** /ˈbiː·ɪŋ/, *past simple* I/he/she/it **was** /£wɒz, $wɑːz/ you/we/they **were** /£wɜːʳ, $wɜːr/, *past part* **been** /biːn, bɪn/ used with the present participle of other verbs to describe actions that are or were still continuing • *Don't talk about that while I'm eating.* • *You're being very selfish.* • *She's studying to be a lawyer.* • *It's raining.* • *The audience clearly wasn't enjoying the show.* • *You're always complaining.* • *I'll be coming back* (= I plan to come back) *on Tuesday.* • LP **Auxiliary verbs, Tenses**

be PASSIVE /biː/ *v aux* [+ v-ed] I **am** /æm/ you/we/they **are** /£ɑːʳ, $ɑːr/ he/she/it **is** /ɪz/, **being** /ˈbiː·ɪŋ/, *past simple* I/he/she/it **was** /£wɒz, $wɑːz/ you/we/they **were** /£wɜːʳ, $wɜːr/, *past part* **been** /biːn, bɪn/ used with the past participle of other verbs to form the passive • *She didn't jump she was pushed.* • *I'd like to go but I haven't been asked.* • *Troublemakers are encouraged to leave.* • *A body has been discovered by the police.* • *The problems have been gone into very thoroughly.*

be ALLOW /biː/ *v* [+ *to* infinitive] I **am** /æm/ you/we/they **are** /£ɑːʳ, $ɑːr/ he/she/it **is** /ɪz/, **being** /ˈbiː·ɪŋ/, *past simple* I/he/she/it **was** /£wɒz, $wɑːz/ you/we/they **were** /£wɜːʳ, $wɜːr/, *past part* **been** /biːn, bɪn/ used to say that someone must or should do (something) • *You're* **to** *sit in the corner and keep quiet.* • *Their mother said they were* **not to** (= not allowed to) *play near the river.* • *There's no money left – what are we* **to** *do?*

be FUTURE /biː/ *v* [+ *to* infinitive] I **am** /æm/ you/we/they **are** /£ɑːʳ, $ɑːr/ he/she/it **is** /ɪz/, **being** /ˈbiː·ɪŋ/, *past simple* I/he/she/it **was** /£wɒz, $wɑːz/ you/we/they **were** /£wɜːʳ, $wɜːr/, *past subjunctive* **were**, *past part* **been** used to show that something will happen in the future • *We are* **to** (= We are going to) *visit Australia in the spring.* • *She was* **never to** *see* (= She never saw) *her brother again.* • Be is also used in CONDITIONAL sentences to say what might happen: *If I were* **to** *refuse they'd be very annoyed.* ◦ *(fml) Were I* **to** *refuse they'd be very annoyed.* • LP **Conditionals, Tenses**

be CAN /biː/ *v* [+ *to* infinitive] I **am** /æm/ you/we/they **are** /£ɑːʳ, $ɑːr/ he/she/it **is** /ɪz/, **being** /ˈbiː·ɪŋ/, *past simple* I/he/she/it **was** /£wɒz, $wɑːz/ you/we/they **were** /£wɜːʳ, $wɜːr/, *past part* **been** /biːn, bɪn/ used to say what can happen • *The exhibition of modern prints is currently* **to** *be seen at the City Gallery.*

be EXIST /biː/ *v* [I] I **am** /æm/ you/we/they **are** /£ɑːʳ, $ɑːr/ he/she/it **is** /ɪz/, **being** /ˈbiː·ɪŋ/, *past simple* I/he/she/it **was** /£wɒz, $wɑːz/ you/we/they **were** /£wɜːʳ, $wɜːr/, *past part* **been** /biːn, bɪn/ to exist or live • *(fml) Such terrible suffering should never be.* • *(old use or literary) By the time the letter reached them their sister had ceased to be.* • **There**'*s no room* (=no space exists) *in here.* • **There** *was no sound.* • *"To be, or not to be: that is the question"* (Shakespeare, Hamlet 3.1) • *"And God said, Let there be light: there was light"* (Bible, Genesis 1.3) • *"Whatever is, is right"* (Alexander Pope in the poem *Essay on Man*, 1733) • LP> **There**

beach /biːtʃ/ *n* [C] an area of sand or small stones beside the sea or other area of water such as a lake • *We would go to the beach in the morning and stay there all day.* • *We spent the day* **on** *the beach.* • *There are* **pebble/sandy/shingle/stony** *beaches on the north coast.* • Beach is used with other words to refer to things usually used or found on or near a beach: *a beach café* ○ *a children's beach club* ○ *a beach hotel/house/hut* ○ *a beach towel* ○ *beach shoes* ○ *a beach umbrella* • A **beach ball** is a large, light brightly coloured ball filled with air that people play with esp. on the beach. • A **beach buggy** is a small car with large wheels and open sides that you can drive on sandy beaches. • A **beach bum** is someone, esp. a man, who spends most of his time enjoying himself on the beach. • A **beach resort** is a place where people can go for holidays which has a beach and beach activities as its main attraction.

beach *obj* /biːtʃ/ *v* [T] • *The boat had been beached* (= pulled or forced out of the water) *near the rocks.* • A beached **whale/dolphin** is one that has come on to the beach and cannot return to the water.

beach·comb·er /£ˈbiːtʃˌkəʊ·məʳ, $-ˌkoʊ·mɚ/ *n* [C] a person who walks along beaches looking for objects of value or interest

beach·front /ˈbiːtʃ·frʌnt/ *n* [C] *Am* a strip of land along a beach • *a house on the beachfront* • *a beachfront property*

beach·head /ˈbiːtʃ·hed/ *n* [C] an area of land beside the sea or a river that an attacking army has taken control of and from where it can advance into enemy country • *The troops quickly* **established** *a beachhead and were preparing to advance.* • Compare BRIDGEHEAD.

beach·wear /£ˈbiːtʃ·weəʳ, $-wer/ *n* [U] clothes that are meant to be worn on a beach • LP> **Shopping goods**

bea·con /ˈbiː·kᵊn/ *n* [C] a light or fire on the top of a hill that acts as a warning or signal • *As part of the centenary celebrations* **a chain of** *beacons was* **lit** *across the region.* • *Honesty shone from him* **like a** *beacon.* • *(fig.) She* **lit** *a beacon* **of** *hope for the whole world.*

bead /biːd/ *n* [C] a small coloured often round piece of plastic, wood, glass, etc. with a hole through it. It is usually put on a string with a lot of others to make jewellery. • *She wore a necklace of brightly coloured wooden beads.* • *(fig.) Beads* (=Drops) **of** *sweat stood out on his forehead.* • PIC> **Jewellery**

bead·ed /ˈbiː·dɪd/ *adj* • *She wore an elaborately beaded twenties-style dress.* • *After an hour of aerobics your face will be beaded* **with** *sweat.*

bead·ing /ˈbiː·dɪŋ/ *n* [C/U] a long thin piece of wood stuck to the edge of, or used to decorate, wood used in furniture, picture frames, etc.

bead·y /ˈbiː·di/ *adj* **-ier, -iest** *disapproving* (of eyes) small and bright, esp. like a bird's eyes • *His beady little eyes were fixed on the money I held out.* • *She's always got her beady eyes on what I'm doing* (= She watches me closely).

bea·gle /ˈbiː·gḷ/ *n* [C] a dog with short hair, a black, brown and white coat, short legs and long ears • *Snoopy is the world's most famous beagle.*

beak BIRD'S MOUTH /biːk/ *n* [C] the hard pointed part of a bird's mouth • *Birds use their beaks to pick up food.* • *(infml) He'd be quite handsome if it wasn't for that great beak* (= large nose) *of his.* • PIC> **Birds**

beak JUDGE /biːk/ *n* [C] *Br dated slang* a judge • *He was up before the beak last month.*

beak·er /£ˈbiː·kəʳ, $-kɚ/ *n* [C] a cup, usually with no handles, used for drinking, or a glass or plastic container used in chemistry • *She gave the children beakers* **of** *juice.* • PIC> **Laboratory**

beam LIGHT /biːm/ *n* [C] a line of light that shines from an object that gives out light, or a line of RADIATION or PARTICLES • *We could just pick out the path in the weak beam of the (Br and Aus usually) torch/(Am)* **flashlight**. • *The rabbit stopped, mesmerized by the beam* **of** *the car's headlights.* • *The missiles home in on the* **laser** *beam.* • *The company has developed a new way of sterilizing syringes using an* **electron** *beam.* • See also MOONBEAM; SUNBEAM.

beam *(obj)* /biːm/ *v* • *The midday sun beamed* (=shone brightly) **down on** *the boat as it drifted along.* [I] • *The concert was beamed* (=broadcast) *by satellite all over the world.* [T] • *(fig.) This mailing technique is used to beam* (= direct) *goods and services to likely consumers.* [T] • *"Beam me up, Scottie"* (popular phrase based on the *Star Trek* television series, 1966-)

beam WOOD /biːm/ *n* [C] a long thick piece of wood, metal or concrete, esp. used to support weight in a building or other structure • *The sitting room had* **exposed wooden** *beams and a large fireplace.* • In the sport of women's GYMNASTICS, **the** beam is a wooden bar on which the competitors balance and perform movements. • *(Br infml dated)* If you are **on** your **beam-ends** you have little or no money left. • PIC> **Sports**

beam SMILE /biːm/ *v* to smile with obvious pleasure • *She beamed* **with** *delight/pleasure at his remarks.* [I] • *The child beamed* **at** *his teacher as he received the award.* [I] • *"I'm so pleased to see you," he beamed* (=said as he smiled). [+ clause]

beam·ing /ˈbiː·mɪŋ/ *adj* • *She gave a beaming* (=wide and happy) **smile**.

bean /biːn/ *n* [C] a seed, or the POD (=case) containing seeds, of various climbing plants, eaten as a vegetable • *green beans* • *runner beans* • *French beans* • *baked beans* • *Coffee beans are the bean-like seeds of the coffee tree.* • *(infml) I'd like to help but I haven't (got)* **a bean** (=I haven't any money) , *I'm afraid.* • **Bean curd** is TOFU. • *(Am and Aus infml disapproving)* A **bean counter** is an ACCOUNTANT (=person who works in finance), esp. one who works for a large company and does not like to allow employees to spend money: *It looked like the project was sure to be approved, but the bean counters said it wasn't cost-effective.* ○ *It's clear that the bean counters and the number crunchers don't have a clue about what's going on in the real world.* • *(Br and Aus infml)* A **bean feast** is a party or social occasion. • PIC> **Peas and beans**

bean·bag /ˈbiːm·bæg/ *n* [C] a large cloth bag filled with dried beans or some other filling and sewn up, which is for sitting on, or a much smaller bag of the same type used as a children's toy • *The beanbag/(Am also)* **beanbag chair** *(Br also* **sag bag***) split when he sat down heavily on it and the stuffing/filling poured out onto the floor.* • *The children were trying to juggle with small beanbags.*

bean·o /£ˈbiː·nəʊ, $-noʊ/ *n* [C] *pl* **beanos** *dated infml* a party

bean·pole /£ˈbiːm·pəʊl, $-poʊl/ *n* [C] *infml humorous* a very tall thin person

bean·sprout /ˈbiːn·spraʊt/ *n* [C] a bean with a small SHOOT, esp. used lightly cooked or raw in Chinese food

bear ANIMAL /£beəʳ, $ber/ *n* [C] a large, strong wild mammal with a thick furry coat that lives esp. in colder parts of Europe, Asia and N America • *a brown/black bear* • *a bear cub* (=young bear) • *(infml) You're* **like a bear with a sore head/(Am also) a (real) bear** (=very bad-tempered) *today.* • A **bear hug** is the action of putting your arms around someone very tightly and quite roughly. • *"I am a Bear of Very Little Brain, and long words Bother me"* (A.A.Milne in the children's book *Winnie-the-Pooh*, 1926) • See also GRIZZLY; KOALA; TEDDY.

bear·ish /£ˈbeə·rɪʃ, $ˈber·ɪʃ/ *adj* • *The actor's bearish bulk makes him ideal for certain types of strong silent heroes.* • See also **bearish** at BEAR FINANCE.

bear *obj* CARRY /£beəʳ, $ber/ *v* [T] *past simple* **bore** /£bɔːʳ, $bɔːr/, *past part* **borne** /£bɔːn, $bɔːrn/ or *Am also* **born** *slightly fml* to carry and move (something) to a place • *At Christmas the relatives descend on the house bearing* **gifts**. • *The sound of the ice-cream van was borne into the office on the wind.* • *The waiters bore trays of cucumber sandwiches, cakes and vol au vents into the room and offered them to the guests.* • *There's a brief paragraph which recalls how, 100 years ago, ships sailed from Hull bearing immigrants to the New World.* • *(fml) He bore* **himself** (=moved and behaved) *with dignity, head held high.*

bear·er /£ˈbeə·rəʳ, $ˈber·ɚ/ *n* [C] • *Why are you always the bearer* **of** (=the person who brings) **bad news**? • *He was a* **(coffin/pall)** *bearer* (=one of the people who carried it) *at his father's funeral.* • *(specialized)* The bearer **of** an official document or bank note, is the person who owns it. The phrase 'I promise to pay the bearer on demand' appears on British bank notes and means that the note is worth the amount written on it.

bear·ing /£'beə·rɪŋ, $'ber·ɪŋ/ *n* [U] *slightly fml* • *She had a proud, distinguished bearing* (=way of moving and behaving). • See also BEARING; **bearing** at BEAR [CHANGE DIRECTION], BEAR ON.

bear *obj* [SUPPORT] /£beəʳ, $ber/ *v* [T] *past simple* **bore** /£bɔːʳ, $bɔːr/, *past part* **borne** /£bɔːn, $bɔːrn/ or *Am also* **born** to hold or support (something) • *The chair, too fragile to bear her* **weight**, *collapsed.*

-bear·ing /£-ˌbeə·rɪŋ, $-ˌber·ɪŋ/ *combining form* • *a load-bearing wall*

bear *(obj)* [ACCEPT] /£beəʳ, $ber/ *v past simple* **bore** /£bɔːʳ, $bɔːr/, *past part* **borne** /£bɔːn, $bɔːrn/ or *Am also* **born** to accept, TOLERATE or ENDURE esp. something unpleasant • *The strain must have been enormous but she bore it well.* [T] • *Tell me now! I can't bear* **the suspense**! [T] • *It's your decision – you must bear* **the responsibility** *if things go wrong.* [T] • *He had borne* **the burden of** *guilt for many years.* [T] • *He couldn't bear* **to** *see the dog in pain.* [+ to infinitive] • *Being bored is something she can't bear.* [+ v-ing] • *What might have happened* **doesn't bear thinking about** (=is too frightening to imagine).

bear·a·ble /£'beə·rə·bl̩, $'ber·ə-/ *adj* • *As far as she was concerned, only the weekends made life bearable* (=able to be lived through).

bear *obj* [KEEP] /£beəʳ, $ber/ *v* [T] *past simple* **bore** /£bɔːʳ, $bɔːr/, *past part* **borne** /£bɔːn, $bɔːrn/ or *Am also* **born** to have or continue to have (something) • *Their baby bears* **a** *strong* **resemblance/an uncanny likeness to** *its grandfather.* • *He still bears a scar on his head from when he tripped on the front step.* • *(fig.) She's had a terribly unhappy year last year and still bears* **the scars** (=still suffers emotional pain). • *The stone plaque bearing his name was smashed to pieces.* • *On display were boxing gloves which bore Rocky Marciano's signature.* • *I don't bear them a* **grudge/any ill feeling/***I don't bear a* **grudge/any ill feeling against/towards** *them* (=I do not continue to have a dislike for them). [+ two objects] • *Thank you for your advice, I'll bear it* **in mind** (=will remember and consider it).

bear *obj* [PRODUCE] /£beəʳ, $ber/ *v* [T] *past simple* **bore** /£bɔːʳ, $bɔːr/, *past part* **borne** /£bɔːn, $bɔːrn/ or *Am also* **born** to give birth to (young) or (of a tree or plant) to give or produce (esp. fruit or flowers) • *She had borne six children by the time she was thirty.* • *When his wife bore him* **a child** *he could not hide his delight.* [+ two objects] • *Most animals bear their young in the spring.* • *The pear tree they planted has never borne* **fruit**. • *(fig.) Eventually her efforts bore* **fruit** (=were successful) *and she got the job she wanted.* • If you **bear testimony/witness** to something you say you know something happened or is true, from your own experience: *She bore witness* **to** *his gentle treatment of distressed patients.* ○ *(fig.) The iron bridge bears witness* **to** *the skills developed in that era.* • *(old use)* If you **bear false witness** you lie.

-bear·ing /£-ˌbeə·rɪŋ, $-ˌber·ɪŋ/ *combining form* • *ore-bearing rocks* • *an interest-bearing account*

bear [CHANGE DIRECTION] /£beəʳ, $ber/ *v* [I always + adv/prep] *past simple* **bore** /£bɔːʳ, $bɔːr/, *past part* **borne** /£bɔːn, $bɔːrn/ or *Am also* **born** to change direction slightly so that you are going (in a particular direction) • *The path followed the coastline for several miles, then bore inland.* • *To get to Portsmouth from here, you need to bear south.* • *After you go past the church keep bearing* **left/right**.

bear·ing /£'beə·rɪŋ, $'ber·ɪŋ/ *n* [C] *specialized* • A bearing is an exact position, measured CLOCKWISE (=to the right) from north. Bearings are given as three numbers: *Nottingham is 70 km from Birmingham* **on a** *bearing* **of** *045 degrees.* ○ *What is the bearing of Birmingham* **from** *Nottingham?* • *The yachtsman* **took** *a bearing* **on** (=found his position by using) *the lighthouse.* ○ *We took a* **set of** *bearings,* ○ *They* **plotted** *their bearing on the chart.* • See also BEARING; **bearing** at BEAR [CARRY], BEAR ON.

bear·ings /£'beə·rɪŋz, $'ber·ɪŋz/ *pl n* • *The road system was so complicated that we had to stop to get/find/take our bearings* (=discover our exact position) *several times.* • *They* **lost** *their bearings* (=did not know where they were) *in the dark.* • *(fig.) It took me a while to get/find my bearings in the new job* (=become familiar with the new situation).

bear [FINANCE] /£beəʳ, $ber/ *n* [C] *specialized* a person who sells shares when prices are expected to fall in order to make a profit by buying them back again at a lower price • A **bear market** is a time when the price of shares is falling and a lot of people are selling them. • Compare BULL [BUYER].

bear·ish /£'beə·rɪʃ, $'ber·ɪʃ/ *adj specialized* • Bearish means expecting a fall in prices: *The overall oil price outlook is expected to remain bearish.* • *Wall Street would be sensible to be bearish on airline shares.* • See also **bearish** at BEAR [ANIMAL].

bear down on *obj v adv prep* [T] to move threateningly towards (someone or something) • *The teacher bore down on the class looking furious.* • *I looked up to see the car bearing down on me, out of control.*

bear on *obj v prep* [T] *slightly fml* to be connected or related to; to influence • *I don't see how that information bears on this case.*

bear·ing /£'beə·rɪŋ, $'ber·ɪŋ/ *n* [U] • *That had a/no/some bearing* **on** (=had a/no/some influence) *our decision to move to another area of town.* • *Your remark* **didn't** *have* **any** *bearing* **on** *what happened.* • See also BEARING; **bearing** at BEAR [CARRY], BEAR [CHANGE DIRECTION].

bear out *obj*, **bear** *obj* **out** *v adv* [M] to support the truth of (something) • *His version of events just isn't borne out by the facts.* • *If you tell them what happened I will bear you out* (**on** *it*).

bear up *v adv* [I] (of people) to show bravery despite difficulties, or (of things) to be strong enough to support close examination or pressure • *Bear up! This will soon be over.* • *"How is she since the funeral?" "Oh, she's bearing up."* • *Her claims just don't bear up under questioning.*

bear with *obj v prep* [T] to be patient with (someone) • *If you'll just bear with me* **for a moment**, *I'll find you a copy of the drawings.*

beard [HAIR] /£bɪəd, $bɪrd/ *n* [C] the hair that some men allow to grow on the lower part of their face • *The old man had a flowing white beard.* • *He had tried to* **grow** *a beard without success.* • *He* **shaved off** *his beard but kept his moustache.* • A goat's beard is the long hair that grows under its mouth. • [PIC] **Hair**

beard·ed /£'bɪə·dɪd, $'bɪr·dɪd/ *adj* [not gradable] • *A thin, bearded* (=with a beard) *man sat opposite me on the train.*

beard *obj* [VISIT] /£bɪəd, $bɪrd/ *v* [T] *literary or dated* to visit someone important or powerful in the place where they work or live, in order to speak to them about a difficult situation • *I managed to beard the boss* **in** *her office this morning, and tell her my concerns about the project.* • *A group of journalists bearded the president* **in his den/lair** (=the place where he works) *to ask him how he proposed to deal with the crisis.* • *Someone is going to have to* **beard the lion in** *his/her* **den** (=visit an important person) *and report what's gone wrong.*

bear·ing /£'beə·rɪŋ, $'ber·ɪŋ/ *n* [C] a part of a machine which supports another part that turns round • *a wheel bearing* • *a roller bearing* • See also **bearing** at BEAR [CARRY], BEAR [CHANGE DIRECTION], BEAR ON.

bear·skin [BEAR] /£'beə·skɪn, $'ber-/ *n* [C] the fur-covered skin of a bear, esp. when it has been removed from its body • *The people who live in this region wear bearskins to keep themselves warm.* • *An old bearskin* **rug** *lay on the floor.*

bear·skin [HAT] /£'beə·skɪn, $'ber-/ *n* [C] a tall black fur hat which is worn by particular soldiers, esp. on ceremonial occasions • *They stood watching the Guards in their bearskins outside Buckingham Palace.*

beast /biːst/ *n* [C] a wild animal, or *(infml)* an unpleasant, annoying or cruel person • *Lying in their tent, they could hear the noises of wild beasts moving about in the darkness outside.* • *The room wasn't fit for man or beast.* • *(infml) Her children are horrible little beasts.* • *(infml) He used to beat her and threaten her – he was a real beast* **to** *her.* • *(infml) Don't do that, you beast!* [as form of address] • *(infml) Money* **brings out the** *beast* **in** *her* (=shows the unpleasant side of her). • *(literary)* A **beast of burden** is an animal such as a DONKEY or an OX which is used to carry or pull things.

beast·ly /'biːst·li/ *adj* **-ier, -iest** *infml* • *We've had beastly* (=very bad) *weather all summer.* • *Why are you being so beastly* (=unkind) **to** *me?*

beast·ie [ANIMAL] /'biː·sti/ *n* [C] *Scot Eng or humorous* an animal • *A lot of beasties live in the forest.* • *(humorous) These otters are particularly vicious beasties, with very sharp teeth.*

beast·ie [INSECT] /'biː·sti/ *n* [C] *infml* an insect • *Keep still, you've got a beastie in your hair.*

beat *(obj)* [HIT] /biːt/ *v past simple* **beat**, *past part* **beaten** /£'biː·tᵊn, $-t̬ᵊn/ or **beat** to hit repeatedly (with a hand, stick, or other object) • *They saw him beating his dog with a stick.* [T] • *The child had been* **brutally/savagely** *beaten.* [T] • *The muggers beat her* **to death.** [T] • *He was beaten* **senseless.** [T + obj + adj] • *Her husband had beaten her* **black and blue.** [T + obj + adj] • *She beat the* **drum** *slowly.* [T] • *The rain was beating* **(down)** *incessantly* **on** *the tin roof.* [I always + adv/prep] • *The tropical sun* **beat down** *mercilessly* (= shone with great heat). • To **beat** someone **down** is to persuade them to charge you a lower amount of money for something: *He wanted £50 for the bike, but I managed to beat him down* **(to** *£35).* • *The firemen beat* **back** *the blaze* (= stopped it from spreading). [M] • *She beat* **off** *her attacker* (= made him go away) *by hitting him with her handbag.* [M] • *They beat* **out** *the fire* (= stopped it from burning) *by striking it with a blanket.* [M] • *Two men beat a woman* **up** (= hit her repeatedly and with great force) *while she was on her way home last night.* [M] • *The men claimed that the police had beaten the confession* **out of** *them* (= hit them until they admitted that they had committed a crime). [T] • *To make an omelette you must first beat* (= mix repeatedly using a utensil) *the eggs.* [T] • If you beat a **path** through an area where long grass or bushes grow closely together, you form a path by hitting the plants with your hands or an object, or by stepping on them: *We beat a path* **through** *the undergrowth.* [T] • To **beat a path to** someone's **door** is to be eager to buy or obtain something from them: *I tried to sell my old bike by advertising it in the local paper, but I didn't have a lot of people beating a path to my door.* • To **beat about the bush**/*(Am also)* **beat around the bush** is to avoid talking about what is important: *"Don't beat about the bush – get to the point!" she said impatiently.* ○ *Well, not to beat about the bush, I ended up offering him the money.* • If you **beat** someone's **brains out**, you hit them with great force: *Do that again, and I'll beat your brains out.* • To **beat** your **brains out** is to spend a lot of time worrying about or thinking about how to deal with a problem: *I've been beating my brains out for hours trying to decide what to do next.* • To **beat** your **breast/chest** is to show great sadness or guilt in an obvious or public way: *There's no point in beating your breast about losing the money – you won't get it back.* • *(slang)* **Beat it!** (= Go away!) • *She burst into tears, so I* **beat a (hasty) retreat** (= ran away from something unpleasant) . • *"Speak roughly to your little boy and beat him when he sneezes"* (from the book *Alice in Wonderland* by Lewis Carroll, 1865) • PIC› **Food preparation**

beat·en /£'biː·tᵊn, $-t̬ᵊn/ *adj* • *She was wearing a necklace of beaten gold* (= gold made flat by having been hit repeatedly with a hard object). • *The farmhouse we stayed in was completely* **off the beaten track**/*(Am also)* **off the beaten path** (= in a place where not many people go).

beat·er /£'biː·tər, $-t̬ɚ/ *n* [C] • A beater is a device which is used for repeatedly hitting something, esp. in order to clean it, or for mixing esp. foods. Beater is often used as a combining form: *an electric beater* ○ *a carpet-beater* ○ *an egg-beater* • Beater is often also used as a combining form to mean a person who repeatedly hits people, esp. members of their family: *a child-beater* ○ *a wife-beater* • A beater is also a person paid by hunters to force birds and animals into a place where they can be seen and therefore shot.

beat·ing /£'biː·tɪŋ, $-t̬ɪŋ/ *n* [C] • *She* **gave** *her son a severe beating.*

beat *obj* DEFEAT /biːt/ *v* [T] *past simple* **beat**, *past part* **beaten** /£'biː·tᵊn, $-t̬ᵊn/ or **beat** to defeat or do better than • *She thought her exam had gone badly but she managed to beat everyone else in the class.* • *Simon always beats me* **at** *tennis.* • *Holland beat Belgium* **(by)** *3-1.* • *Our team was* **comfortably/easily/soundly** *beaten in the first round of the competition.* • *The nationalists were* **narrowly** *beaten in the local election.* • *He beat me* **fair and square** (= without cheating). • *They were beaten* **hands down** (= completely) *by their opponents.* • *She has beaten her own* **record** *of three minutes ten seconds.* • *(Am)* He beat **out** *all the top competitors in his sport.* [M] • *(infml) Taking the bus sure beats* (= is better than) *walking there.* [+ v-*ing*] • *(slang) Taking the bus beats* **the hell out of** (= is much better than) *walking all the way there.* • *In my opinion, you can't beat* (= there is nothing better than) *a cold beer on a hot afternoon.* • *You can't beat our local Italian restaurant* **for** (= it is the best restaurant for providing) *a good pizza.* • To beat something that is going to happen is to take action before the thing happens: *Let's try to beat the traffic problems by leaving early in the morning.* ○ *I always do my shopping early to beat* **the rush.** • To **beat** someone **at** their **own game** is to use to your own advantage the methods by which they tried to defeat you. • To **beat** someone **to it** is do something before someone else does it: *I was just going to tidy up the kitchen, but you've beaten me to it.* • To **beat the pants off** someone/*(Br)* **beat** someone **hollow** is to defeat them easily and by a great amount. • *(Am)* To **beat the rap** is to escape or avoid blame or punishment. • *(slang)* **That beats everything**/*(Am also)* **That beats all** are expressions showing surprise and disbelief: *You mean she just left her job without telling anyone she was going? Well, that beats everything!* • *(slang)* **It beats me/What beats me is** (= I cannot understand) *how that idiot got the job.* • *(saying)* 'If you can't beat 'em, join 'em' means if you cannot do things in the way you want to do them because of what other people are doing, you should change so that you do what the other people are doing. • LP› **Sports**

beat·ing /£'biː·tɪŋ, $-t̬ɪŋ/ *n* [C] • *Our team* **took** *a beating* (= was defeated) *in our last match.* • If something will **take some beating**, it is so good that it is hard to improve on it: *Lewis's new world record will take some beating.*

beat *(obj)* MOVEMENT /biːt/ *v past simple* **beat**, *past part* **beaten** /£'biː·tᵊn, $-t̬ᵊn/ or **beat** to (cause to) make a regular movement or sound • *Although he was badly injured, his heart was still beating.* [I] • *The doctor could feel no pulse beating.* [I] • *The hummingbird beats its wings at great speed.* [T] • *The drums beat* **(out)** *in the still night.* [I] • To beat **out** a rhythm is to make a regular sound or movement to music: *She beat the rhythm out with her hands.* [M] • To beat **time** is to make a regular sound or movement to music. [T]

beat /biːt/ *n* • *My heart missed a beat when she said, "Yes, I'll marry you".* [C] • *He tapped his foot to the beat* (= rhythm) *of the music.* [U] • In music, a beat is a regular emphasis, or a place in the music where such an emphasis is expected: *The guitar comes in* **on** *the third beat.* [C] ○ *Make sure you play* **on the beat** (= on the beats). [U] • *"The beat goes on"* (title of song by Sonny and Cher, 1967)

beat AREA /biːt/ *n* [C usually sing] an area for which someone, such as a police officer, has responsibility as part of their job • *Bob has worked as an officer* **on** *this particular beat for 20 years.* • A police officer who is **on the** beat/ **walking the** beat is on duty, walking around rather than driving in a police car.

beat TIRED /biːt/ *adj* [after v] *infml* extremely tired • *I'm beat – I'm going to bed.* • *(Br) You've been working too hard, you look* **dead** *beat.* • See also DEADBEAT PERSON, DEADBEAT IN DEBT.

beat gen·er·a·tion *n* [U] (esp. in the US in the 1950s) young people who did not follow accepted principles and customs but who valued personal experience instead

be·a·ti·fic /ˌbiː·ə'tɪf·ɪk/ *adj literary* expressing happiness and calmness, esp. in a holy way • *The angels in the painting have beatific* **smiles.**

be·a·tif·i·cally /bɪə'tɪ·fɪ·kli/ *adv*

be·at·i·fy *obj* /£bi'æt·ɪ·faɪ, $-'æt̬-/ *v* [T] (of the Pope) to announce formally that someone who is dead has lived a holy life, usually as the first stage in making that person a SAINT

be·at·i·fi·ca·tion /£biˌæt·ɪ·fɪ'keɪ·ʃᵊn, $-ˌæt̬-/ *n* [C/U]

Be·at·i·tudes /£bi'æt·ɪ·tjuːdz, $-'æt̬·ɪ·tuːdz/ *pl n* (in the Bible) a group of statements made by Jesus Christ • *"Blessed are the meek, for they shall inherit the earth" is one of* **the** *Beatitudes.*

beat·nik /'biːt·nɪk/ *n* [C] (esp. in the 1950s and 1960s) a young person who did not accept society's customs and principles, and who had long hair and wore untidy clothes

beat-up /£'biːt·ʌp, $'biːt̬-/, **beat·en-up** /£ˌbiː·tᵊn'ʌp, $-t̬ᵊn-/ *adj infml* (of things) in bad condition • *He's got loads of money but he's still driving around in that beat-up old car.*

beau /£bəʊ, $boʊ/ *n* [C] *pl* **beaus** or **beaux** *dated* a male admirer or BOYFRIEND

beau monde /£ˌbəʊ'mɔ̃d, $ˌboʊ'mɑːnd/ *n* [C] **the beau monde** *dated* the group of rich and fashionable people

beaut /bjuːt/ *n* [C] *infml dated* something which, or someone who, is very good or noticeable • *Let me have a look at that bruise. Oh, that's a beaut!* • *His new car is a beaut.*

beaut /bjuːt/ *adj Aus infml* • *That was a beaut dinner, Mike!*

beau·te·ous /£'bjuː·ti·əs, $-t̬i-/ *adj poetic* very attractive to look at; beautiful • *"How beauteous mankind is! O brave new world that has such people in't"* (Shakespeare, Tempest 5.1)

beau·ti·cian /bjuːˈtɪʃ·ᵊn/ *n* [C] a trained person whose job it is to improve the appearance of a customer's face, body and hair, using creams and other types of treatment, often in a **beauty salon**

beau·ty /£ˈbjuː·ti, $-t̬i/ *n* the quality of being pleasing, esp. to look at, or someone or something that gives great pleasure, esp. by being looked at • *In ancient Greek stories, Helen of Troy was a woman of great beauty.* [U] • *We were speechless at the beauty of the view from the top of the mountain.* [U] • *This is an area of outstanding* **natural/scenic** *beauty.* [U] • *The piece of music he played had* **a** *haunting beauty.* [U] • *Some women spend a lot of money on beauty* **products/treatments**. • *She was a great beauty* (= a beautiful woman) *when she was young.* [C] • *(infml)* A beauty is also something that is an excellent example of its type: *Your roses are beauties this year.* [C] ○ *"That's a* **real** *beauty!" he said admiringly of her new car.* [C] • *(infml) The beauty* **of** *this plan* (= what makes it good) *is that it won't cost too much.* [U] • A **beauty contest/pageant** is a competition in which women are judged for their physical attractiveness. • A **beauty queen** is a woman who wins a beauty contest. • A **beauty salon/beauty parlour**/*(Am also)* **beauty shop** is a place where (usually) women go to have their hair, face and body given special treatments to improve their appearance. • *(humorous)* **Beauty sleep** is the sleep that you need in order to feel and look healthy and attractive: *I always feel terrible if I don't get my beauty sleep.* • A **beauty spot** is a place in the countryside which is particularly attractive. • A **beauty spot** is also a small dark mark (which in the past was often artificial) on a woman's face. • *(saying)* 'Beauty is in the eye of the beholder' means that not all people have the same opinions about what is attractive. • *(saying)* 'Beauty is only skin deep' means that a person's character is more important than how they look. • *"Beauty is truth, truth beauty, – that is all / Ye know on earth, and all ye need to know"* (John Keats in *Ode on a Grecian Urn*, 1820)

beau·ti·ful /£ˈbjuː·tɪ·fᵊl, $-t̬ɪ-/ *adj* • Beautiful means very pleasing to look at: *You see lots of nice houses, but rarely a beautiful one.* ○ *There were some* **breathtakingly/exquisitely/stunningly** *beautiful paintings in the exhibition.* ○ *Come on, beautiful.* [as form of address] • Beautiful also means very pleasing to experience: *The radio station claims that it plays 'the world's most beautiful music'.* ○ *Ann makes beautiful cakes.* ○ *What beautiful weather we're having.* • Beautiful can also mean very kind: *Terry is a beautiful person.* ○ *You did a beautiful thing in helping those poor children.* • **The beautiful people** are people who are very fashionable and have a lot of money: *This café is a favourite haunt of the beautiful people.* • **The beautiful people** are also people, esp. in the 1960s and 1970s, who believed in peace and love, were opposed to many of the accepted ideas about how people should live, and often lived in groups. • *"Have nothing in your houses that you do not know to be useful, or believe to be beautiful"* (William Morris in *Hopes and Fears for Art*, 1882) • *"Oh, what a beautiful morning, / Oh, what a beautiful day! / I got a beautiful feeling / Everything's going my way"* (from the song *Oh what a Beautiful Morning* written by Oscar Hammerstein II, 1943)

beau·ti·ful·ly /£ˈbjuː·tɪ·fᵊl·i, $-t̬ɪ-/ *adv* • *She dresses beautifully.* • *He plays the piano beautifully.* • *The children behaved beautifully* (= very well). • *Their house is beautifully decorated.*

beau·ti·fy *obj* /£ˈbjuː·tɪ·faɪ, $-t̬ɪ-/ *v* [T] *esp. humorous* • To beautify someone or something is to improve their appearance: *I'm just going to beautify myself – it should only take a few hours.*

beau·ti·fi·ca·tion /£ˌbjuː·tɪ·fɪˈkeɪ·ʃᵊn, $-t̬ɪ-/ *n* [U]

beaux /£bəʊz, $boʊz/ *pl of* BEAU

bea·ver ANIMAL /£ˈbiː·vəʳ, $-vɚ/ *n* [C] *pl* **beavers** or **beaver** a small animal with smooth fur, sharp teeth and a large flat tail, which lives in a DAM (= a wall of sticks and earth) that it builds across a river • *Beavers are traditionally thought of as being hard-working, but recent research has shown that in fact they are not.* • *(infml)* Beaver can also be used to mean a person who works very hard.

bea·ver CHILD /£ˈbiː·vəʳ, $-vɚ/, **Beav·er Scout** *n* [C] a child aged between 6 and 8 years old who is a member of the international youth organization called the Scouts • *Jack and his sister belong to a Beaver* **colony** (= group).

bea·ver a·way /£ˈbiː·vəʳ, $-vɚ/ *v adv* [I] *infml* to work hard, esp. for a long time • *She has been beavering away* **at** *that essay for hours.*

be·bop, bop /£ˈbiː·bɒp, $-bɑːp/ *n* [U] a type of jazz music first played by small groups of esp. black American musicians in the 1940s

be·calmed /bɪˈkɑːmd/ *adj* (of boats with sails) not moving because of lack of wind • *In earlier times, sailors sometimes died if their ship was becalmed for a long time.* • *(fig.) Steps are being taken to retrieve the negotiations from their present becalmed* (= not advancing) *state.*

be·cause /£bɪˈkɒz, $-ˈkɑːz/ *conjunction* for the reason that • *"Why did you do it?" "Because Carlos told me to".* • *"Why can't I have an ice-cream?" "Because I say so, that's why!"* • *We can't go to Julia's party because we're going away that weekend.* • *The reason she's so irritable is because she's tired.* • *Because he was so late, he was driving too fast, and he had an accident.* • **Just** *because I'm lending you my dress for tonight, that doesn't mean you can borrow it whenever you want to.* • *(infml) Have you been away, because* (= the reason I am asking is that) *we haven't seen you recently?*

be·cause of *prep* • *The train was delayed because of* (= as a result of) *bad weather.* • *He has been off school for several days because of illness.* • *Because of an emergency, the doctor will not be available for several hours.* • *We didn't get home till after midnight because of miss***ing** *the bus.* [+ v-*ing*]

beck STREAM /bek/ *n* [C] *regional* a small stream

beck WILLING /bek/ *n* [U] **at** *someone's* **beck and call** always willing and able to do whatever someone asks • *Go and get it yourself! I'm not at your beck and call, you know.*

beck·on *(obj)* /ˈbek·ᵊn/ *v* to move your hand or head in a way that tells someone to come nearer • *The customs official beckoned the woman with the large suitcase* **to** *his counter.* [T] • *"Hey you!", she called, beckoning me* **over** *with her finger.* [T] • *He beckoned* **to** *me, as if he wanted to speak to me.* [I] • *They beckoned us* **to** *join them.* [T + obj + *to* infinitive] • *(fig.)* **For** *many young people, the bright lights of London beckon* (= are interesting and attract people to them), *though a lot of them end up sleeping on the streets.* [I] • *(fig.) She's an excellent student,* **for** *whom a wonderful future beckons* (= looks likely to happen). [I]

be·come BE /bɪˈkʌm/ *v* [L] *past simple* **became** /bɪˈkeɪm/, *past part* **become** to start to be • *I was becoming increasingly suspicious of his motives.* • *It was becoming cold, so we lit the fire.* • *After giving up smoking, he became fat and irritable.* • *Margaret Thatcher became Britain's first woman prime minister in 1979.* • *He has just become a father.* • Ⓓ

be·come *obj* SUIT /bɪˈkʌm/ *v* [T] *past simple* **became** /bɪˈkeɪm/, *past part* **become** *dated* to cause to look attractive or to be suitable for • *That colour really becomes you.* • *This sort of vulgar language hardly becomes* (= is suitable for) *a man in your position, vicar.* • *"Nothing in his life/ Became him like the leaving it"* (Shakespeare, Macbeth 1.3) • Ⓓ

be·com·ing /bɪˈkʌm·ɪŋ/ *adj dated* • *That's a most becoming* (= attractive) *dress, my dear.* • *That kind of behaviour is not very becoming* (= suitable) **for** *a teacher.*

be·come of *obj v prep* [T] to happen to someone or something • *Whatever became of old Watson* (= Where is he now and what is he doing)?

bec·que·rel /ˌbek·əˈrel/ *n* [C] *specialized* a unit of measurement for RADIOACTIVITY

BEd /biːˈed/ *n* [C] *abbreviation for* Bachelor of Education (= a degree taken by some teachers, or a person having this degree) • LP〉 **Schools and colleges**

bed FURNITURE /bed/ *n* [C] a large rectangular piece of furniture, often with four legs, which is used for sleeping on • *He lived in a room with only two chairs, a bed and a table.* • *He likes to have breakfast* **in** *bed on a Saturday morning.* • *She didn't get* **out of** *bed till lunchtime today.* • *I'm exhausted – I'm going* **to** *bed* (= going to get into a bed in order to sleep). • *I always* **put** *the children* **to** *bed* (= make certain that they get into a bed and are comfortable there ready for going to sleep) *at 7.30 p.m.* • To **put** something that is printed **to bed** is to begin printing it. • *The hospital staff was concerned that there would not be enough beds for incoming patients* • *We couldn't get a bed* (= a place to stay for the night) *at a hotel anywhere in the city.* • **In bed** means connected with sex: *They went to see their doctor because they were having problems in bed.* ○ *He may be good-looking, but is he good in bed* (= a skilful lover)? ○ *She found her boyfriend in bed with another woman.* • If a person is **in bed with** someone or an organization, they are involved with them and have to do things for them. This often means that the person cannot be completely trusted: *The newspaper*

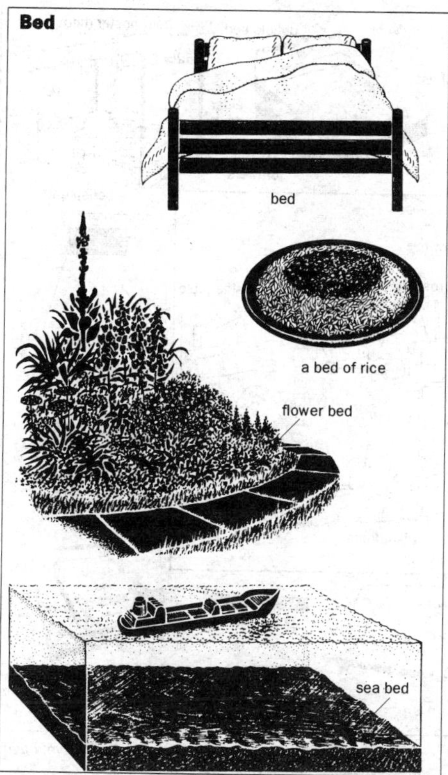

editor is obviously in bed with the President. • If you **go to bed with** someone, you have sex with them. • If a person has **got out of bed (on) the wrong side**/*(Am also)* **got up on the wrong side of the bed** they are in a bad mood and are easily annoyed all day. • When someone **makes the bed**, they put sheets and covers, or a DUVET on the bed, and/or make these smooth so that the bed is comfortable to sleep in. • **A bed of nails** is a difficult situation or way of life. • **Bed and board** is *esp. Br for* **board and lodging**. See at BOARD [STAY]. • **Bed and breakfast** (*abbreviation* **B and B**) means (a small hotel or private house offering) a room in which you can stay for the night and a morning meal: *We're staying at a farm that* **does** *bed and breakfast.* ○ *There are several bed and breakfast* **places** *near the station.* ○ *Can you recommend a good bed and breakfast near Brighton?* • A **bed-bath** is a careful and complete wash that you give to someone who is ill in bed. • **Bed linen** is the sheets, PILLOWCASES and covers for DUVETS that you put on a bed. • *(Br)* **Bed-sitting room** is *fml for* BEDSIT. • **Bed-wetting** is the act or habit, which is often found among young children, of urinating while sleeping. • *(saying)* 'You have made your bed and now you must lie in it' means that you must accept the unpleasant results of something you have done. • *"And so to bed"* (Samuel Pepys ending the day's entry in his *Diary*, 1660-) • [PIC〉] **Bed**

bed *(obj)* /bed/ *v* **-dd-** • *(dated) The French writer, Georges Simenon, claimed that he had bedded* (= had sex with) *over 10 000 women.* [T] • *I* **bedded down** (= slept) *on the couch for the night.* • *It did not take the procedure long to* **bed down** (= become established.)

bed [BOTTOM] /bed/ *n* [C] the bottom or something that serves as a base • *Many strange plants and fish live on the sea bed.* • *The railway was built on a bed* **of** *solid rock.* • A bed **of** a particular food is a pile of that food on top of which other food is placed as a meal: *a bed of rice* ○ *a bed of lettuce* • [PIC〉] **Bed**

bed [AREA OF GROUND] /bed/ *n* [C] a piece of ground used for planting flowers • *They've got some beautiful* **flower** *beds in their garden.* • **A bed of roses** is an easy and happy existence. • [PIC〉] **Bed**

bed out *obj*, **bed** *obj* **out** *v adv* [M] • *May is the time to bed out the geraniums* (= move them from inside and plant them outside.)

bed·ding /ˈbed·ɪŋ/ *adj* [not gradable] • A **bedding plant** is a type of plant which is planted outside in a bed when it is beginning to flower, and dug up when it has finished flowering.

be·daub *obj* /£bɪˈdɔːb, $-ˈdɑːb/ *v* [T usually passive] to cover very roughly with something sticky or dirty • *The child's face was bedaubed* **with** *chocolate.*

bed·bug /ˈbed·bʌg/ *n* [C] a very small insect which lives mainly in beds and feeds by sucking people's blood

bed·clothes /£ˈbed·kləʊðz, $-kloʊðz/ *pl n* the sheets and covers which you put on a bed

bed·ding /ˈbed·ɪŋ/ *n* [U] the covers on a bed, or the dry grass, etc., that an animal sleeps on

be·deck *obj* /bɪˈdek/ *v* [T often passive] to decorate or cover • *The hall was bedecked* **with** *flowers.*

be·dev·il *obj* /bɪˈdev·əl/ *v* [T often passive] **-ll-** or *Am usually* **-l-** to confuse, annoy or cause problems or difficulties for someone or something • *Ever since I started playing tennis, I've been bedevilled* **by** *back pains.* • *Serious economic problems are bedevilling the country.*

bed·fel·low /£ˈbedˌfel·əʊ, $-oʊ/ *n* [C] a person connected with another in a particular activity • *The priest and the politician made* **strange/odd/unlikely** *bedfellows in their campaign for peace.*

bed·lam /ˈbed·ləm/ *n* [U] a noisy lack of order • *When the teacher left the room, complete bedlam broke out.* • *It was bedlam at the football ground.*

Bed·ou·in, **Bed·u·in** /ˈbed·u·ɪn/ *adj* [not gradable], *n pl* **Bedouin** or **Bedouins** (of or connected with) an Arab person living in or near the desert • *They are members of a Bedouin tribe.* • *Bedouins often lead a nomadic life.* [C]

bed·pan /ˈbed·pæn/ *n* [C] a flat dish used as a toilet by people who are too ill to get out of bed

bed·post /£ˈbed·pəʊst, $-poʊst/ *n* [C] one of the four corner poles that support a bed, and to which the vertical boards at each end of the bed are fixed • *In some countries, children traditionally hang stockings on the bedpost at Christmas, hoping that they will be filled with presents.* • **Between you, me and the bedpost** (= I'm telling you a secret), *I think he's lying.*

be·drag·gled /bɪˈdræg·ḷd/ *adj* (of a person, esp. their clothes and hair) wet, and often also dirty and untidy • *A few bedraggled passengers stood in the rain, waiting for the train.* • *The children ran into the house, dirty and bedraggled from playing in the garden.*

bed·rid·den /ˈbed·rɪ·dən/ *adj* having to stay in bed because of illness or injury • *His aunt was 93 and bedridden.* • *After hurting my leg, I was bedridden for a whole month.* • *Bedridden patients are often given exercises to help prevent their muscles from becoming stiff.*

bed·rock /£ˈbed·rɒk, $-rɑːk/ *n* [U] the hard area of rock in the ground which holds up the loose earth above • *(fig.) Some people believe that the family is* **the** *bedrock* **of** (= the strong base of) *society.*

bed·room /ˈbed·rʊm, -ruːm/ *n* [C] a room used for sleeping in • *Our ideal home would have four bedrooms.* • *The house has a large* **master** *bedroom with its own bathroom.* • *You can stay in our* **guest/spare** *bedroom if you like.* • Bedroom can also mean connected with sex: *The play contained several bedroom* **scenes**. ○ *He has bedroom* **eyes** (= looks as if he is interested in sex). • *(Am)* A **bedroom community** is a **dormitory suburb**. See at DORMITORY.

-bed·roomed /-ˈbed·rʊmd, -ruːmd/ *combining form* • *a two-bedroomed house* (= a house having two bedrooms)

bed·side /ˈbed·saɪd/ *n* [U] the area beside a bed • *I find it useful to have a telephone* **at** *my bedside.* • *She sat* **by** *her son's bedside all night, watching for signs of his recovery.* • *I keep a bedside lamp on all night.* • A **bedside manner** is the way in which a doctor treats people who are ill, esp. in relation to kind, friendly and understanding behaviour: *He has a lovely bedside manner.* • A **bedside table** (*Am* **night stand/table**) is a small table which is kept beside a bed. • [PIC〉] **Beds and bedroom, Table**

bed·sit /ˈbed·sɪt/, **bed·sit·ter** /£ˈbedˌsɪt·əʳ, $-ɚ/, *fml* **bed-sit·ting room** /£ˌbedˈsɪt·ɪŋ-, $-ˈsɪṭ-/ *n* [C] *esp. Br* a rented room which has a bed, table, chairs and somewhere to cook in it • *He lives in a tiny student bedsit.*

bed·sore /£ˈbed·sɔːʳ, $-sɔːr/ *n* [C] a painful mark on the body caused by having to lie in bed for a long time

bed·spread /ˈbed·spred/, **coun·ter·pane**, **cov·er·let** *n* [C] a decorative cover put on a bed, on top of sheets and BLANKETS • [PIC〉] **Beds and bedroom**

bed·stead /ˈbed·sted/ *n* [C] the wooden or metal frame of an old-fashioned bed

Beds and bedroom

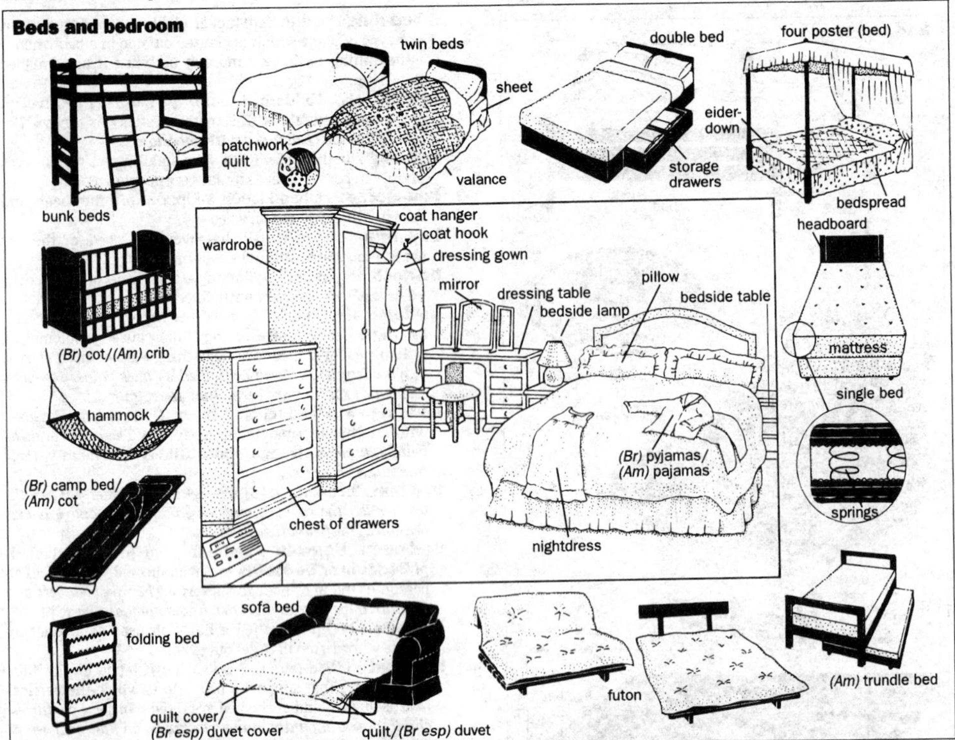

bed·time /ˈbed·taɪm/ *n* [U] the time at which you usually get into your bed in order to sleep • *Put your toys away now, it's bedtime.* • *Eleven o'clock is past my bedtime.* • *I like to have a hot drink* **at** *bedtime.* • *He always reads his children a bedtime* **story** *every night.*

Bed·u·in /ˈbed·u·ɪn/ *adj* [not gradable], *n* BEDOUIN

bee [INSECT] /biː/ *n* [C] a flying insect which has a yellow and black body and four transparent wings. There are various types of bee. • *As we sat in the garden, we could hear the bees buzzing from one flower to the next collecting nectar.* • *A* **swarm of** *bees flew into the garden.* • *My arm swelled up where I was* **stung** *by a bee.* • **Worker** *bees provide food for the* **queen** *bee which produces young.* • *(humorous)* To be **as busy as a bee**/**a busy bee** is to move quickly about doing many things. • To **have a bee in** your **bonnet** is to have a continual and fixed interest in something: *She never stops talking about dieting – she's got a real bee in her bonnet about it.* • *(Br infml)* Someone or something that is **the bee's knees** is excellent or of extremely high standard: *Eleanor thinks Richard is the bees' knees, though I can't imagine why.* • A **bee-keeper** is someone who looks after bees for pleasure or as a business, to eat or sell their HONEY. The activity of looking after bees is called **bee-keeping**: *Bee-keeping isn't as dangerous as it looks, as the bees are quite friendly once they get to know you.* • See also BUMBLEBEE.

bee [GROUP] /biː/ *n* [C] *Am and Aus* a group of people who come together in order to take part in a particular activity • *a sewing bee* • *a working bee*

Beeb /biːb/ *n* [U] **the Beeb** *Br infml for* the BBC

beech /biːtʃ/ *n* (the wood of) a tree with a smooth grey trunk and leaves which fall in winter or early spring • *a row of beeches* [C] • *a chair made of beech* [U] • *a beech floor/hedge*

beef [MEAT] /biːf/ *n* [U] the flesh of cattle which is eaten • *The spaghetti sauce is made from* **minced** *beef.* • *People in England often have* **roast** *beef* **and Yorkshire pudding** *for lunch on Sundays.* • *He is a beef* **cattle** *farmer.* • Beef is sometimes used of fruit or vegetables, to mean large: *a beef tomato* • *(infml)* Beef can also mean strength, power or force: *He said that the newly published government report didn't have much beef in it.* ○ *Push harder! Put some beef into it!* • Ⓢ

beef·y /ˈbiː·fi/ *adj* **-ier, -iest** *infml* • A beefy person is someone who looks strong, heavy and powerful: *a beefy footballer* • Beefy also means powerful and effective: *I want to buy myself a beefier computer.*

beef up *obj*, **beef** *obj* **up** /biːf/ *v adv* [M] *slang* • To beef up something is to make it stronger or more important: *We need to find some new players to beef up the team.* ○ *The company has plans to beef up its production.* ○ *Your report on the new car park is fine, but why don't you beef it up a bit* **with** *some facts?*

beef [COMPLAIN] /biːf/ *v* [I], *n* [C] *infml* (to make) a complaint • *He was beefing* **about** *having to do the shopping.* • *My main beef* **about** *the job is that I have to work on Saturdays.* • Ⓢ

beef·bur·ger /£ˈbiːfˌbɜː·gəʳ, $-ˌbɜːr·gɚ/ *n* [C] a HAMBURGER

beef·cake /ˈbiːf·keɪk/ *n slang* a man with a muscular body to which he likes to attract esp. women's attention, or men with such bodies as shown in pictures or in shows • *A couple of young beefcakes were trying to chat up two girls in the bar.* [C] • *Her friends gave her a calendar that was all pictures of beefcake.* [U] • *He was standing by the side of the pool in a beefcake pose.* [U] • Compare CHEESECAKE [WOMEN].

Beef·eat·er /£ˈbiːˌfiː·təʳ, $-t̬ɚ/ *n* [C] a guard at the Tower of London who wears a 16th century uniform

bee·hive [CONTAINER] /ˈbiː·haɪv/ *n* [C] a box-like container in which bees are kept so that their HONEY (= the sweet substance they produce) can be collected

bee·hive [HAIR] /ˈbiː·haɪv/ *n* [C] (originally in the 1960s) a woman's hairstyle in which the hair is worn piled high on the head

bee·line /ˈbiː·laɪn/ *n* [U] **make a beeline for** to go directly and quickly towards • *At parties he always makes a beeline for the prettiest woman in the room.*

been /biːn/ *past participle of* BE • Been is also used to mean visited, travelled or arrived: *I've never been to Kenya, but I hope to visit it next year.* ○ *The postman hasn't been here yet.* ○ *The doctor's just been* (= has arrived and left). • Been is used as the past participle of 'go' when the action referred to is finished: *She's been to the hairdresser's* (= and now she has returned).

beep *(obj)* /biːp/ *v* to (cause to) make a short loud sound • *The taxi-driver beeped (his horn) impatiently* **at** *the cyclist.* [I/T] • *I don't like those watches that keep beeping every hour.* [I]

beep /biːp/ *n* [C] • *The microwave will give three beeps when the food is cooked.* • *The voice on the answerphone said "Please leave any message after the beep".*

beep·er /£ˈbiː·pəʳ, $-pɚ/ *n* [C] • Beeper is *esp. Am for* **pager**, see at PAGE [CALL].

beer /£bɪəʳ, $bɪr/ *n* an alcoholic drink made from grain • *He asked for a pint of beer.* [U] • *I prefer* **draught** *beer to* **keg** *beer.* [U] • *This beer is* **brewed** *in Mexico.* [U] • *After a hard day's work I enjoy a beer* (= a glass or container of beer) *or two.* [C] • *(infml)* A **beer belly/gut** is the fat stomach that a man develops when he has drunk a lot of beer for many years. • A **beer garden** is an area of land belonging to a PUB where people can sit outside and have a drink. • A **beer mat** is a small piece of cardboard which you put under a glass to protect a table surface. • (J)

beer·y /£ˈbɪə·ri, $ˈbɪr·i/ *adj* • Beery means smelling of beer: *beery breath* ○ *a beery kiss*

bees·wax /ˈbiːz·wæks/ *n* [U] the fatty substance which bees produce to make the structures in which they store their HONEY, and which is used for making candles and POLISH for wood

beet /biːt/ *n* [C/U] the large round white root of a plant. There are various types of beet, some of which are given as food to animals and some of which are used for making sugar. • Beet is also *esp. Am for* BEETROOT.

bee·tle [INSECT] /£ˈbiː·tl̩, $-t̬l̩/ *n* [C] an insect with a hard shell-like back. There are various different types of beetle. • *a black beetle* • *a death watch beetle* • *a dung beetle*

bee·tle [HURRY] /£ˈbiː·tl̩, $-t̬l̩/ *v* [I] *esp. Br infml* to go somewhere or do something quickly • *Hoping to miss the traffic jams, she beetled* **(off)** *home at four o'clock.* • *He's been beetling* **away** *at his work all morning.*

bee·tle–browed /£ˈbiː·tl̩·braʊd, $-t̬l̩-, --ˈ-/ *adj* having EYEBROWS (= lines of hair above the eyes) which are dark and untidy or long

beet·root /ˈbiː·truːt/, *Am usually* **beet** *n* the small round dark red root of a plant, which is eaten cooked as a vegetable, esp. cold in salads • *She made a delicious beetroot and apple salad.* [U] • *You have to cook the beetroots before you can eat them.* [C] • *(Br)* To **go/turn beetroot (red)** or **go/turn as red as a beetroot** or *(Am)* **go/turn as red as a beet** is to have a red face because you are embarrassed: *Whenever I talked about his past life, he would go beetroot.* • [PIC]› **Vegetables**

be·fall *(obj)* /£bɪˈfɔːl, $-ˈfɑːl/ *v past simple* **befell** /bɪˈfel/, *past part* **befallen** /£bɪˈfɔː·lən, $-ˈfɑː-/ *old use* (esp. of something bad) to happen (to) • *Should any harm befall me on my journey, you may open this letter.* [T] • *We will carry on, whatever befalls.* [I] • (S)

be·fit *obj* /bɪˈfɪt/ *v* [T] **-tt-** *fml* to be suitable or right for • *She was buried in the cathedral, as befits someone of her position.*

be·fore [EARLIER] /£bɪˈfɔːʳ, $-ˈfɔːr/ *prep, adv* [not gradable], *conjunction* at or during a time earlier than (the thing mentioned) • *You should always wash your hands before meals.* • *Before leav***ing** *he said good-bye to each of them.* [+ v-ing] • *She has had a hard life, and has grown old before her* **time**. • *He said he had never seen her before.* • *His friends, with whom he had been at a party only the night before, were shocked at his sudden death.* • *Although I left after Martin, I arrived before he did.* • *Before he could reach the door, she quickly locked it, and turned to him with a smile.* • *Before we finally make a decision on this, does anyone want to say anything else?* • *Before you criticize me, I think you should let me explain why I acted in the way I did.* • *It was an hour before* (= until) *the police arrived.* • *She had to give the doorman a tip before* (= in order that) *he would help her with her suitcases.*

be·fore [IN FRONT] /£bɪˈfɔːʳ, $-ˈfɔːr/ *prep* in front of • *The letter K comes before L in the Roman alphabet.* • *Many mothers put their children's needs before their own.* • *We have the whole weekend before us – what shall we do?* • *He stood up before a whole roomful of people, and asked her to marry him.* • *(fml) I stand before you to ask your forgiveness.* • *The task before him* (= that he had to deal with) *seemed impossible, but he was determined to succeed.* • To be before someone or a group of people, is to be formally considered or examined by that person or group: *The proposal before the committee is that we try and reduce our spending by 10%.* ○ *Our case is* **coming** *before the court week.* ○ *The men* **appeared** *before the judge yesterday.* • If a place is before another place, you will arrive at it first when you are travelling towards the second place: *The bus stop is just before the school.* ○ *When you're travelling north in England, York is before Newcastle.*

be·fore·hand /£bɪˈfɔː·hænd, $-ˈfɔːr-/ *adv* [not gradable] earlier (than a particular time); in advance • *I knew she was coming that afternoon because she had phoned beforehand to say so.*

be·friend *obj* /bɪˈfrend/ *v* [T] to be friendly towards (esp. someone who needs help) • *Alone in the big city, he was befriended by an old lady.* • *Clare has befriended a new child in her class at school.*

be·fud·dled /bɪˈfʌd·l̩d/ *adj* confused • *Befuddled by drink, he could not remember where he had left his bike.* • *I'm so tired, my poor befuddled brain can't absorb any more.*

beg *(obj)* /beg/ *v* **-gg-** (of someone poor) to ask for food or money, or (of anyone) to request strongly and without pride • *There are more and more homeless young people begging* **on the streets** *these days.* [I] • *She had to beg* **for** *money and food for her children.* [I] • *They begged* **for** *mercy.* [I] • *(fml) Stop it, I beg you!* [T + obj + clause] • *"Please, please forgive me!" she begged (him).* [T + (obj) + clause] • *I'm dying for a cigarette. Could I beg one* **off/from** *you?* [T] • *He begged her* **to** *stay, but she simply laughed and put her bags in the car.* [T + obj + *to* infinitive] • *She begged* **that** *her name not be printed in the newspaper.* [+ *that* clause] • If a dog begs, it sits with its front legs in the air as if to ask for something: *They have trained their dog to* **sit up and** *beg.* [I] • To **beg the question** is to avoid dealing with a particular matter, or to accept that something that is being considered is true, without question or proof: *Spending the summer travelling round India is a great idea, but it begs the question* **of** *how we can afford it.* ○ *To discuss the company's future begs the question whether it has a future.* • To **beg off** is to ask to be allowed not to do something that you are expected to be doing: *She begged off early* **from** *the party because she was so tired.* • *(infml)* If something is **going begging**, it is available to be taken because no one else wants it: *If that bottle of wine is going begging, I'll have it.* • **I beg to differ/disagree** is a polite way of saying "I do not agree". • *(saying)* 'Beg, borrow or steal' means that you will do whatever is necessary to obtain something: *I must get a dress for the ball, whether I have to beg, borrow or steal one.* • **I beg your pardon** is a polite way of saying "I am sorry" or "Could you repeat what you just said?". • [LP]› **Phrases and customs**

be·get *obj* /bɪˈget/ *v* [T] **begetting**, *past simple* **begot** /£bɪˈgɒt, $-ˈgɑːt/ or *esp. old use* **begat** /bɪˈgæt/, *past part* **begotten** /£bɪˈgɒt·ən, $-ˈgɑː·t̬ən/ or **begot** /£bɪˈgɒt, $-ˈgɑːt/ *literary or old use* to be the father of • *It was said that Sir William had begotten several illegitimate children.* • *In the Bible it says that Adam begat Cain and Abel.* • *(fig.) Poverty begets* (= causes) *hunger, and hunger begets crime.*

beg·gar /£ˈbeg·əʳ, $-ɚ/ *n* [C] a poor person who lives by asking others for money or food • *Crippled beggars lined the road which led to the temple.* • *(infml)* Beggar can also be used to refer to a person, esp. when you are expressing an opinion about something that they have done, or has happened to them: *You've won again, you lucky beggar.* ○ *Those children have been running about in my rose garden again, the little beggars* (= annoying people)*!* • **Beggar-my-neighbour** is a type of card game played by two people in which the winner is the player who wins all the cards. • *(saying)* 'Beggars can't be choosers' means that if you cannot have what you want, then you should accept whatever you are given without complaining: *I've just won a holiday in Brighton! I wish it was in the Caribbean, but beggars can't be choosers I suppose.*

beg·gar *obj* /£ˈbeg·əʳ, $-ɚ/ *v* [T] • *His cruelty* **beggared belief/description** (= was impossible to believe/describe). • *"For her person it beggar'd all description"* (Shakespeare, Anthony and Cleopatra 2.2)

beg·gar·ly /£ˈbeg·ə·li, $ˈ-ɚ-/ *adj dated* • *The council voted to give the new project a beggarly* (= small and not generous) *amount of money.*

be·gin *(obj)* /bɪˈgɪn/ *v* **beginning**, *past simple* **began** /bɪˈgæn/, *past part* **begun** /bɪˈgʌn/ to start (to be, do, etc.) • *I began the book six months ago, but I can't seem to finish it.* [T] • *Now the owner of a huge chain of restaurants, she began (her career) as a humble waitress.* [I/T] • *I have so much to tell you, I don't know where to begin.* [I] • *What time does the concert begin?* [I] • *The bridge was begun five years ago and the estimated cost has already doubled.* [T] • *The film they want to watch begins* **at** *seven.* [I] • *If you want to learn to play a musical instrument, it might be a good idea to begin* **on** *something simple.* [I] • *The play begins* **with** *the sisters in the kitchen together.* [I] • *The word 'cat' begins* **with** *the letter 'c'.* [I] • *The meeting began* **promisingly**, *but then things started to go wrong.* [I] • *Jane has just begun* *learning to drive.* [+ v-*ing*] • *After waiting for half an hour she was beginning* **to** *get angry.* [+ *to* infinitive] • *"Well," he began* (= started by saying). *"I don't quite know how to tell you this."* [+ clause] • If you **can't (even) begin to** do something, it is very difficult for you to do it: *I can't begin to explain how I ended up on the roof.* ○ *As a top businessman, he couldn't even begin to imagine/understand real poverty.* • *There were six of us* **to begin with** (= at first), *then two people left.* • *The hotel was awful!* **To begin with** (= first), *our room was far too small. Then we found that the shower didn't work.*

be·gin·ner /£bɪˈgɪn·əʳ, $-ɚ/ *n* [C] • *This class is for beginners* (= people who are just starting to do the activity) *only.* • *After my first tennis lesson, the teacher said that I was* **not bad for a** *beginner.* • *When I won the first contest I entered, he put it down to* **beginner's luck** (= unexpected and probably brief early success). • *(Am and Aus)* **Beginners' slopes** are **nursery slopes**. See at NURSERY [FOR CHILDREN].

be·gin·ning /bɪˈgɪn·ɪŋ/ *n* • *On the first day in her new job, she was an hour late – it was not an* **auspicious/promising** *beginning* (= start). [C] • *The students are all returning to college ready for the beginning* **of** *term.* [U] • *Notes on how to use this dictionary can be found* **at the beginning of** *the book.* [U] • *She sat down and read the book straight through* **from** *beginning* **to end**. [U] • *I enjoyed my job* **at/in** *the beginning* (= when I started it), *but I'm bored with it now.* [U] • *The city had its beginnings* (= origins) *in Roman times.* • *It was the* **beginning of the end** (= the point where things start to get gradually worse) *for their marriage when he started seeing another woman.* • *"I think this is (sometimes 'could be') the beginning of a beautiful friendship"* (Rick (Humphrey Bogart) to Louis (Paul Henreid) at the end of the film *Casablanca*, 1942) • *"In the beginning was the Word"* (Bible, St John 1.1) • *"I like a film to have a beginning, a middle and an end, but not necessarily in that order"* (believed to have been said by Jean-Luc Godard, 1930-1995) • *"In my beginning is my end"* (T.S.Eliot in the poem *East Coker*, 1940)

be·gone /£bɪˈgɒn, $-ˈgɑːn/ *exclamation old use or literary* go away • *"Begone!" he shouted. "And never let me see your face again!"*

be·go·ni·a /£bɪˈgəʊ·ni·ə, $-ˈgoʊ-/ *n* [C] a type of garden plant with brightly coloured waxy flowers and decorative leaves

be·grudge *obj* /bɪˈgrʌdʒ/ *v* [T] to allow or give unwillingly • *I don't begrudge him his freedom./I don't begrudge his freedom* **to** *him.* [+ two objects] • *They begrudged every day they had to stay with their sick father.* • *She begrudged paying so much for an ice-cream cone.* [+ v-*ing*]

be·guile *obj* /bɪˈgaɪl/ *v* [T] *literary* to charm, attract or interest, sometimes in order to deceive • *He was completely beguiled by her beauty.* • *Florence beguiled her grandchildren with tales of what life had been like when she was young.* • *The salesman beguiled him* **into** *buying a car he didn't want.*

be·guil·ing /bɪˈgaɪ·lɪŋ/ *adj* • *Two weeks in the Caribbean is a beguiling* (= attractive) *prospect.* • *That's a beguiling* (= interesting) *argument, but I'm not convinced by it.*

be·guil·ing·ly /bɪˈgaɪ·lɪŋ·li/ *adv* • *She smiled beguilingly at him.*

be·gun /bɪˈgʌn/ *past participle of* BEGIN

be·half /£bɪˈhɑːf, $-ˈhæf/ *n* [U] **on behalf of** *someone*/**on** *someone's* **behalf** representing; instead of • *On behalf of the company as a whole, I would like to thank you for all your work.* • *Unfortunately, George cannot be with us today so I am pleased to accept this award on his behalf.* • *Please don't leave on my behalf* (= because of me).

be·have *(obj)* /bɪˈheɪv/ *v* to act in a particular way, or to be good by acting in a way which has society's approval • *She always behaves* **well/badly** *when her aunts come to visit.* [I] • *Our job is to show people the need to behave responsibly in or close to the sea.* [I] • *Whenever there was a full moon he would start behaving strangely.* [I] • *What a well-behaved little boy!* • *You must behave (your***self***) at the party!* [I/T] • *He's thirty now, it's time that he started behaving (him***self***).* [I/T] • See also WELL-BEHAVED. • [LP] **Reflexive pronouns and verbs**

be·hav·iour *Br and Aus, Am and Aus* **be·hav·ior** /£bɪˈheɪ·vjəʳ, $-vjɚ/ *n* [U] • Behaviour is a way of acting: *Her behaviour is often appalling.* ○ *He was well-known for his violent and threatening behaviour.* • If someone is **on** their **best behaviour** they act with great politeness, esp. for a particular reason: *After she threatened to leave him, he was on his best behaviour for a few months.* • *(specialized)* In PSYCHOLOGY, **behaviour therapy** is the general name for a form of treatment which tries to change someone's particular unwanted behaviour rather than treating the causes.

be·ha·viour·al *Br and Aus, Am and Aus* **be·hav·io·ral** /£bɪˈheɪ·vjə·rəl, $-vjɚ·əl/ *adj* [not gradable] • *She studied behavioural* **psychology** *at college.*

be·hav·iour·i·sm *Br and Aus, Am and Aus* **be·hav·io·ri·sm** /£bɪˈheɪ·vjə·rɪ·zᵊm, $-vjɚ·ɪ-/ *n* [C] *specialized* • Behaviourism is a theory which emphasizes watching human actions and behaviour to discover facts esp. about the human brain, rather than looking at private conscious experience or mental events.

be·ha·vi·our·ist *Br and Aus, Am and Aus* **be·hav·io·rist** /£bɪˈheɪ·vjə·rɪst, $-vjɚ·ɪst/ *adj, n* • *He's written a behaviourist* **account** *of the emotions.* • A behaviourist is someone who supports the theory of behaviourism, and may use it in their work or studies: *She's a strict behaviourist.* [C]

be·head *obj* /bɪˈhed/ *v* [T] to cut off the head of (a person or animal)

be·hest /bɪˈhest/ *n* [U] *fml* an order or request • *The budget proposal was adopted* **at** *the president's behest/***at the** *behest* **of** *the president.* • *(humorous) He took the dog for a walk at my behest.*

be·hind [BACK] /bɪˈhaɪnd/ *prep, adv* [not gradable] at the back (of) • *Look behind you!* • *I've put the letter behind the fruit bowl.* • *The path was too narrow for two people so the boy walked behind.* • *(fig.) I knew that behind* (= hidden by) *her smile was sadness.* • *(fig.) Marie Curie was the woman behind* (= responsible for) *enormous changes in the science of chemistry.* • *(fig.) He wondered what was behind* (= the true reason for) *his neighbour's sudden friendliness.* • *As hard as she tried, she always* **fell** *behind the other swimmers in the races.* • *After visiting a friend I was annoyed to discover when I got home that I'd* **left** *my bag behind* (= in the place I had left). • *After the party a few people* **stayed** *behind* (= stayed when others had gone) *to help clear up.* • *He was behind* **with** (= delayed in) *his work for the German course.* • *The old woman was behind* **with** (= late paying) *the rent.* • *Since he got his license he has spent all his free time* **behind the wheel** *of* (= driving) *his parents' car.* • If you are **behind** someone **(all the way)** you support them (completely) in what they intend to do: *My friends said they would be behind me (all the way) if I applied for the course.* • *(saying)* 'Behind every great/successful man there stands a woman' means while men enjoy the fame it is often their wives who give them the confidence or do a lot of the work. • *"Get thee behind me, Satan"* (Bible, Matthew 15.23) • *"The Girl I Left Behind Me"* (title of a traditional song)

be·hind [BODY PART] /bɪˈhaɪnd/ *n* [C] *infml* the part of the body on which a person sits; BOTTOM • *He tripped and fell on his behind.* • *Why don't you* **get off** *your behind* (= stand up) *and do something!*

be·hind·hand /bɪˈhaɪnd·hænd/ *adv slightly fml* delayed in doing something or slower doing something then expected • *I worked late last night because I was behindhand* **with** *my accounts.*

be·hold *obj* /£bɪˈhəʊld, $-ˈhoʊld/ *v* [T] *past* **beheld** /bɪˈheld/ *esp. old use* to see or look at • *The new bridge is an incredible sight to behold.* • *Behold, he's not so confident now!* • The expression **lo and behold** is used to attract attention to something surprising: *We were just talking about Mike, and lo and behold, he appeared.* • *"Behold her, single in the field,/ Yon solitary Highland lass"* (in the poem *The Solitary Reaper* by William Wordsworth, 1807) • (N)

be·hold·er /£bɪˈhəʊl·dəʳ, $-ˈhoʊl·dɚ/ *n* [C] *esp. old use* • (N) (NL)

be·hold·en /£bɪˈhəʊl·dᵊn, $-ˈhoʊl-/ *adj* [after v] *fml* feeling you have a duty to someone because they have done something for you • *She wanted to be independent and beholden* **to** *no-one.* • *Thank you for driving me all that way, I'm beholden* **to** *you.*

be·hove *obj Br and Aus* /£bɪˈhəʊv, $-ˈhoʊv/ *v* [T + obj + *to* infinitive] **it behoves** *someone* **to** *(Am* **it behooves** *someone* **to***) fml dated* it is right for (someone) to do something • *When you are speaking to a policeman it behoves you to be polite.* • *It* **ill** *behoves you to* (= you should not) *speak so rudely of your parents.*

beige /beɪʒ/ *adj, n* [U] (of) a pale creamy brown colour

bei·gel /ˈbeɪ·gᵊl/ *n* [C] a BAGEL

being [PERSON] /ˈbiː·ɪŋ/ *n* a person or thing that exists or the state of existing • *A nuclear war would kill millions of living beings.* [C] • *Strange beings from another planet/*

outer space are still a popular subject for many sci-fi films. [C] • *He was a very gentle being who was much loved by all those who knew him.* [C] • *The new laws* **come into** *being* (= start to take effect) *in September.* [U] • *We do not know exactly how life first* **came into** *being* (= began to exist.) [U]

being BE /ˈbiː·ɪŋ/ *present participle of* BE

be·jewelled /bɪˈdʒuː·əld/, *Am usually* **be·jeweled** *adj* wearing a lot of jewellery or decorated with jewels • *Bejewelled women decorate the fashionable charity balls.*

be·la·bour *obj Br and Aus, Am and Aus* **be·la·bor** /£bɪˈleɪ·bəʳ, $-bɚ/ *v* [T] to explain (something) more than necessary, or *(dated)* to hit (someone or something) hard and repeatedly • *There's no need to belabour the* **point** *– you're angry I'm late and you don't need to keep reminding me.* • *(dated) She belaboured him* **with** *her walking stick.* • *(fig.) The protester belaboured the speaker* **with** *insults.*

be·lat·ed /£bɪˈleɪ·tɪd, $-t̬ɪd/ *adj* coming later than expected • *Two days after he had crashed my car he made a belated apology.* • *They did make a belated* **attempt** *to reduce the noise.* • *Belated birthday greetings!*

be·lat·ed·ly /£bɪˈleɪ·tɪd·li, $-t̬ɪd-/ *adv*

belch *(obj)* /beltʃ/ *v* to allow air from the stomach to come out noisily through the mouth • *Making his way unsteadily towards the seat, he belched and hiccupped noisily.* [I] • *(fig.) The exhaust pipe belched* **(out)** (= produced) *dense petrol fumes.* [T]

belch /beltʃ/ *n* [C] • *The baby let out a loud, satisfied belch.*

be·lea·guered /£bɪˈliː·gəd, $-gɚd/ *adj* surrounded by an army or *(fig.)* troubled by someone or a situation • *The occupants of the beleaguered city had no means of escape.* • *(fig.) The arrival of the fresh medical supplies was a welcome sight for the beleaguered* (= extremely busy) *doctors working in the refugee camps.*

bel·fry /ˈbel·fri/ *n* [C] the tower of a church where the bells are hung

be·lie *obj* /bɪˈlaɪ/ *v* [T] **belying**, *past* **belied** to show (something) to be false, or to hide (something such as an emotion) • *Television pictures of starving children belie official reports that normal life is continuing.* • *Her calm face belied the terror she was feeling.*

be·lief /bɪˈliːf/ *n* the feeling of certainty that something exists or is true • *She holds strong beliefs and expresses them frequently.* [C] • *His belief* **in** *God gave him hope during difficult times.* [U] • *All non-violent religious and political beliefs should be respected equally.* [C] • *It is my (firm) belief* **that** *nuclear weapons are immoral.* [C + *that* clause] • *Recent revelations about corruption have* **shaken** *many people's belief* **in** (= caused people to have doubts about) *the police.* [U] • *The brutality of the murders was* **beyond** *belief* (= too difficult to be imagined). [U] • *He called at her house* **in the** *belief* **that** (= confident that) *she would lend him the money.* [U] • **To the best of** *my* **knowledge/***(Br also)* **belief** (= From what I know and understand from the information that I have) *the chemicals which were found are not dangerous.*

be·lieve *(obj)* /bɪˈliːv/ *v* to think that something is true, correct or real • *Strangely, no one believed us when we told them we'd been visited by a creature from Mars.* [T] • *He believes* **that** *all children are born with equal intelligence.* [+ *that* clause] • *She's arriving tomorrow, I believe.* [+ clause] • *"Is she coming alone?" "We believe* **not/so** (= We think she is not/is)*."* [+ *not/so*] • *You wouldn't believe* **who** *Ed's going to marry.* [+ *wh-* word] • *I believe her* **to** *be the finest violinist in the world.* [T + obj + *to* infinitive] • *The robbers are believed* **to** *have escaped via Heathrow Airport.* [T + obj + *to* infinitive] • *All the crew are missing, believed dead.* [T + obj + adj] • To believe **in** something is to be certain that it exists: *Do you believe in reincarnation?* [I always + prep] • To believe **in** someone/something is to have confidence in that person or thing: *I believe in the fundamental goodness of human nature.* [I always + prep] • *So he told you she was just a friend, did he? I don't* **believe a word** (= any) *of it!* • *He's upstairs doing his homework,* **believe it or not/would you believe it?** (= it is true, although it seems unlikely). • *She* **could hardly/couldn't believe** *her* **eyes/ears** *when she saw/heard* (= was so surprised that she thought she imagined) *what happened on the bus.* • *I* **couldn't believe** *my* **luck** (= was very surprised and very pleased) *when I heard that I'd inherited my uncle's fortune.* • To **make believe** something is to pretend it: *Let's make believe we are pirates and search for treasures.* See also MAKE-BELIEVE. • If you say you **will believe** something **when** you **see it** you mean it seems so unlikely that you will not think it is true until you see proof of it: I'll believe someone on a motorcycle can jump over seventeen cars when I see it. • *"When my love swears that she is made of truth,/ I do believe her, though I know she lies"* (William Shakespeare, Sonnett 138) • *"Believe it or not"* (title of a newspaper column by R.L.Ripley, 1893-1949)

be·liev·a·ble /bɪˈliː·və·bl̩/ *adj* • *I didn't enjoy the film because I didn't think the characters were believable* (= like real life).

be·liev·er /£bɪˈliː·vəʳ, $-vɚ/ *n* [C] • A believer is a person who has a religious belief or who has confidence in the good of something: *She's became a believer after she survived a terrible accident.* ○ *Harvey's a* **(great)** *believer* **in** *health food.* ○ *I'm a* **(great)** *believer* **in** *allowing people to make their own mistakes.* • *"Then I saw her face, now I'm a believer"* (song written by Neil Diamond and sung by The Monkees, 1967)

Be·li·sha bea·con /bəˈliː·ʃə/ *n* [C] (in Britain) a post with a flashing orange light on top which shows someone who is walking where they can cross a road • PIC› **Road**

be·lit·tle *obj* /£bɪˈlɪt·l̩, $-ˈlɪt̬-/ *v* [T] to make (an action or a person) seem unimportant • *Though she had spent hours fixing the computer he belittled her efforts, dismissing it as 'basic mechanics'.* • *Stop belittling yourself – your work is highly valued.*

bell /bel/ *n* [C] a hollow metal object shaped like a cup which makes a ringing sound when hit by something hard, esp. a CLAPPER • *The church bells* **rang (out)** *to welcome in the New Year.* • *The sound of a bicycle bell caused me to jump out of the way.* • *I stood at the front door and* **rang** *the bell (also* **doorbell***) several times, but the house seemed empty.* • *"There's the bell* (= the sound of the bell) *for lunch." "Good, I'm starving."* • If something is as **clear/sound as a bell** it is in perfect condition: *Her memory is as clear as a bell.* • *(Br infml)* **Give me a bell** (= telephone me) *sometime next week, won't you?* • *When Frank suggested coming to stay for a couple of days,* **warning/alarm bells rang (in** *my* **head)** (= I thought something was wrong). • *(Am and Aus infml)* To do something or go somewhere **with bells on** is to do it or go there eagerly: *I'll be at the party with bells on.* • **Bell-bottoms** are trousers that are very wide below the knee. • A **bell jar** is a large glass cover shaped like a bell used to cover chemical equipment, esp. to prevent any gas produced from escaping. • A **bell-pull** is a cord or handle that is pulled to ring a bell. • A **bell-push** is a button, usually by the front door of a house, which makes a bell ring inside. • A **bell-ringer** is a **campanologist**. See at CAMPANOLOGY. • *"... never send to know for whom the bell tolls; it tolls for thee"* (*Meditation XVII* by John Donne, 1624) • PIC› **Bicycles, Laboratory**

bel·la·don·na /£ˌbel·əˈdɒn·ə, $-ˈdɑː·nə/ *n* [U] **deadly nightshade**, see at DEAD NOT LIVING

bell·boy /ˈbel·bɔɪ/, *Am also* **bell·hop** /£ˈbel·hɒp, $-hɑːp/ *n* [C] a man in a hotel employed to carry cases, open doors, etc.

belle /bel/ *n* [C] *dated* a beautiful and charming woman or one who is beautifully dressed • *She wore a dress of crimson silk to the dinner and was* **the belle of the ball** (= the most attractive woman there).

bel·li·cose /£ˈbel·ɪ·kəʊs, $-koʊs/ *adj fml* wishing to fight or start a war • *The general made some bellicose statements about his country's military strength.*

bel·li·ger·ent /£bəˈlɪdʒ·ər·ənt, $ˈ-ɚ-/ *adj disapproving* wishing to fight or argue, or *(specialized)* fighting a war • *I don't know why she always seems so belligerent* **towards** *me.* • *Giving the ticket collector a belligerent look, he said he wouldn't pay his fare.* • *(specialized) The belligerent countries are having difficulties funding the war.*

bel·li·ger·ence /£bəˈlɪdʒ·ər·ənts, $ˈ-ɚ-/, **bel·li·ger·en·cy** /£bəˈlɪdʒ·ər·ənt·si, $ˈ-ɚ-/ *n* [U] *disapproving* • *I can't stand his belligerence* (= his wish to argue with people all the time).

bel·li·ger·ent·ly /£bəˈlɪdʒ·ər·ənt·li, $ˈ-ɚ-/ *adv disapproving* • *"Are you saying I'm fat?" she said belligerently.*

bel·low *(obj)* /£ˈbel·əʊ, $-oʊ/ *v* to shout in a loud voice, or (of a cow or large animal) to make a loud, deep sound • *"Keep quiet!" the headmaster bellowed across the room.* [+ clause] • *We could hear the sergeant bellowing commands to his troops.* [T] • *After a while the bull began to bellow* **in** *pain.* [I]

bel·low /£ˈbel·əʊ, $-oʊ/ *n* [C] • *He gave a bellow* **of** *rage.*

bel·lows /£'bel·əʊz, $-oʊz/ *pl n* a tool used to blow air, especially into a fire to make it burn better • *a* **pair of** *bellows* • PIC> **Fires and space heaters**

bel·ly BODY PART /'bel·i/ *n* [C] *infml* the stomach • *For the first time in weeks he fell asleep with a full belly and a happy heart.* • *Now six months pregnant, Gina's belly had begun to swell.* • *The tiny children, their bellies swollen from hunger, stared dumbly at the cameras.* • *(fig.) The belly* (= bottom part) *of the aircraft was painted red.* • *(infml)* (used esp. by or to children) A **belly button** is a NAVEL. • A **belly dance** is a dance of Eastern origin in which a woman (a **belly-dancer**) moves the lower parts of her body to music. • A **belly flop** is when someone jumps awkwardly into water and their body falls flatly and painfully on the water. • A **belly laugh** is a loud, uncontrolled laugh: *She let out a real belly laugh when she heard what had happened.* • *(Am infml)* To **go/turn belly up** is to come to an end usually because of failure or death: *The business went belly up after only six months in operation.*

-bel·lied /-'bel·ɪd, -id/ *combining form* • *pot-bellied* • *big-bellied*

bel·ly·ful /'bel·i·fʊl/ *n* [U] *infml* • *What a feast – I feel like I've got a real bellyful!* • A bellyful is also more than enough of something: *I've* **had a** *bellyful* **of** *their lies, so I'm leaving today.*

bel·ly BECOME ROUND /'bel·i/ *v* [I] (esp. of sails) to become rounded • *The yacht picked up speed as the sails bellied* **out** *in the wind.*

bel·ly·ache /'bel·i·eɪk/ *n* [C] *infml* a pain in the stomach • *I've got this awful bellyache, I think I'm going to be sick!*

bel·ly·ache /'bel·i·eɪk/ *v* [I] *infml* • To bellyache is to complain: *I wish you'd stop your bellyaching and just get on with the job.*

be·long /£bɪ'lɒŋ, $-'lɑːŋ/ *v* [I] to be in the right place or (of a person) to feel this way • *The table belongs* **in** *the sitting-room, so please put it back there straight away.* • *Where do these spoons belong?* • *Your shoes belong under the bed or in your cupboard, not beside the door.* • *She told me she felt as if she didn't belong* **in** *her job anymore.* • *That sort of person belongs* **in** (= should be in) *jail.* • *All his life he's never felt as if he belonged* (= he has never felt wanted) *anywhere.*

be·long to *obj v prep* [T] to be the property of (someone) or to be a member of (a group) • *This book belongs to Sarah – I must give it back to her.* • *You shouldn't take what doesn't belong to you.* • *She belongs to an elite club which is very hard to get into.* • *This strange vegetable belongs to the potato family.*

be·long·ings /£bɪ'lɒŋ·ɪŋz, $-'lɑːŋ-/ *pl n* • A person's belongings are the things that they own, esp. those which can be carried: *I put a few* **personal** *belongings in a bag and left the house for the last time.*

be·lov·ed /bɪ'lʌv·ɪd, -'lʌvd/ *n, adj slightly fml* (someone or something that is) loved very much • *Her beloved husband died last year.* • *She was forced to leave her beloved Paris and return to Lyon.* • *Eric was a gifted teacher beloved* **by** *all those he taught over the years.* • *I gave a dozen roses to my beloved* (= the person who is loved by me). [U]

be·low /£bɪ'ləʊ, $-'loʊ/ *adv* [not gradable], *prep* in a lower position (than), under • *From the top of the skyscraper the cars below us looked like insects.* • *The sun shone on the hilltop, while below in the valley it was foggy and cold.* • *Do you usually wear your skirts above or below the knee?* • *The author's name was printed below the title.* • *The sun sank below the horizon.* • *They have three children below* **the age of** (= younger than) *four.* • *A corporal in the army is below a sergeant in rank.* • *The temperature has fallen below zero/freezing* (= cooled to less than zero) *recently.* • *Last night it was eight degrees below* (= eight degrees less than zero). • *His marks in English have been* **(way)** *below* (= (much) less than) **average** *for some time now.* • *She has three people* **working** *below her* (= people to whom she gives orders). • *(fml) For further information on this subject,* **see** *below* (= later in this book). • *The ship's captain went* **(down)** *below* (= to the lower, covered part of the ship). • *(infml)* If a remark is **below the belt** it is particularly hurtful and unfair.

belt CLOTHING /belt/ *n* [C] a strip of leather or material worn around the waist to support clothes or for decoration • *She* **fastened** *her belt tightly around her waist.* • *He had eaten so much that he had to* **undo** *his belt a couple of notches.* • A belt is also a continuous strip of material that moves round: *When you get into the arrivals hall, wait by the belt till your luggage comes through.* • A belt is also an area, usually just outside a city, where a particular group of people live, such as the **commuter belt** and **stockbroker belt**, or an area that is known for a particular characteristic, such as the **cotton belt.** • *(Br infml)* **Belt and braces** is when two or more actions are done to be extra careful about something when only one is really necessary: *I wrote to them and telephoned as well – belt and braces, I admit.* • To have something **under** your **belt** is to have learned or succeeded in something which might be a benefit in the future: *That typing course is a good thing to have under your belt.* • LP> **Dressing and undressing**

belt *obj* /belt/ *v* [T] • *I belted my coat* (= tied it with a belt) *tightly.* • *(infml)* **Belt up** means put on your **seat belt**, see at SEAT FURNITURE: *Don't forget, belt up before you drive off.*

belt MOVE FAST /belt/ *v* [I] *slang* (esp. of a vehicle) to travel with great speed • *The car was belting* **along/down** *the road, we were sure it was going to crash.*

belt *obj* HIT /belt/ *v* [T] *infml* to hit hard, esp. with violence • *He belted him* **on** *the jaw.* • *Furious, he belted the ball down the fairway and stormed after it.* • *(fig.) The choir belted* **out** (= sang very loudly) *the big tune.* [M]

belt /belt/ *n* [C] *infml* • *a belt* **on** *the jaw*

belt up *v adv* [I] *Br and Aus slang* to stop talking and keep quiet • *If you kids don't belt up I won't take you to the match.*

belt·way /'belt·weɪ/ *n* [C] *Am for* **ring road**, see at RING CIRCLE • PIC> **Ring**

be·ly·ing /bɪ'laɪ·ɪŋ/ *pres part of* BELIE

be·moan *obj* /£bɪ'məʊn, $-'moʊn/ *v* [T] *fml* to complain about or express sadness because of • *Researchers at universities are always bemoaning their lack of funds.* • *What an opera – the heroine bemoaned her* **fate** *throughout the entire third act!*

be·mused /bɪ'mjuːzd/ *adj* slightly confused or lost in thought • *I must admit that I was rather bemused* **by** *his sudden anger.* • *She gave me a bemused* **look** *when he told her he was studying the common flea.*

bench /bentʃ/ *n* [C] a long, usually hard, seat for two or more people, often found in public places, or a long table for working at • *a park bench* (= a seat for people to rest on in a public garden) • *a work bench* (= a table for working at) • In sport, **the** bench is a seat or area of seats where players sit during a game when they are not playing: *He was dropped from the team, and spent the last few weeks of the season on the bench.* • **The bench** is used in a court of law to describe a judge (or judges) as well as the place on which they sit: *Kindly address your remarks to the bench, Mr Smith.* • To **serve/sit on the** bench is to work as a judge or MAGISTRATE. • *(Am)* To **take the** bench is to become a judge or MAGISTRATE. • *(Am)* If a judge **takes the** bench they begin a formal meeting of a law court. • In the British parliament, a bench is one of the seats used by the members: *There was jeering from both the Labour and Conservative benches.* • *(Aus)* A **bench (top)** is a WORKTOP. • PIC> **Chair**

bench·mark /£'bentʃ·mɑːk, $-mɑːrk/ *n* [C usually sing] a mark made on something such as a post used as a point for measuring things by • *(fig.) Despite her behaviour off-stage her performances set a new benchmark* (= standard) *for singers throughout the world.*

bench·mark /£'bentʃ·mɑːk, $-mɑːrk/ *adj* [not gradable] • *This is a benchmark case for legal history.*

bend *(obj)* /bend/ *v past* **bent** /bent/ to (cause to) curve • *I bent* **down** *and picked up the gold necklace lying on the road.* [I] • *Now, bend* **forward/over** *and touch your toes!* [I] • *Make sure you bend your knees and keep your back straight when you're picking up heavy objects.* [T] • *The trees were bending in the wind.* [I] • *The road bends to the left after the first set of traffic lights.* [I] • *After her fall she complained that she couldn't bend her leg properly.* [T] • *I dropped the fork and bent it.* [T] • *(fig.) The local council was forced to bend* **to** *public pressure* (= it had to change a course of action because of general opinion). [I] • *(infml)* To **bend** someone's **ear** is to talk too much, esp. about problems: *He's a real nuisance, he's always trying to bend my ear about the difficulties he has at work.* • To **bend the law/rules** is to break the rules in way that is considered to be unimportant or not harmful: *Can't you bend the rules a little – I was only a few minutes late?* • *He was* **bent double** (= bending forward) *because he was laughing so much.* • See also BENT.

bend /bend/ *n* [C] • *There's a bend in the pipe so you can't see from one end to the other.* • *The car came* **round the** *bend on the wrong side of the road.* • To be/go **round the bend** is to be/become mentally confused or unable to act in a reasonable way: *I think the old man's round the bend.* ◦ *If I'd had to stay there any longer I'd have* **gone** *round the bend.* •

(infml) To **drive/send** someone **round the bend** means to make someone bored and/or angry: *Staying at home all day was driving her round the bend.* ○ *People who tell you to 'smarten up or you'll never get a job' drive me round the bend.*

bend·a·ble /ˈben·də·bl̩/ *adj* ● Something which is bendable can be bent: *bendable copper pipe*

bend·ed /ˈben·did/ *adj* ● *(fml)* **On bended knee** in a position where the knee of one of their legs is touching the floor: *He* **went down** *on bended knee to ask her to marry him.*

bend·y /ˈben·di/ *adj* **-ier**, **-iest** ● Something which is bendy has many bends in it or can be easily bent: *a bendy road* ○ *a bendy toy*

bend·er /£ˈben·dər, $-dɚ/ *n* [C] *infml* a period during which a large amount of alcoholic liquid is drunk ● *They went* **on** *a bender for two days after they won the championship.*

bends /bendz/ *pl n* **the bends** See **decompression sickness** at DECOMPRESS

be·neath /bɪˈniːθ/ *prep* in or to a lower position than, under ● *Jeremy hid the letter beneath a pile of papers.* ● *We huddled together for warmth beneath the blankets.* ● *I had arranged to meet him beneath the statue in the park.* ● *After weeks at sea, it was wonderful to feel firm ground beneath our feet once more.* ● *You'd never guess it, but beneath* (= hidden by) *his cool exterior there beats a heart of pure passion.* ● *Emma was so tired and hungry that her legs were beginning to* **give way** *beneath her* (= she was about to fall over). ● *She always thought that she had* **married** *beneath her* (= that she had married someone of a lower social position). ● *I would have thought that making a nasty comment like that was beneath him* (= he would not be expected to say it).

ben·e·dict·ine /ˌben·ɪˈdɪk·tiːn/ *n* [U] a type of LIQUEUR (= a strong alcoholic drink)

ben·e·dic·tion /ˌben·ɪˈdɪk·ʃᵊn/ *n* [C] a prayer asking God for help and protection

ben·e·fac·tor, *female also* **ben·e·fac·tress** /£ˈben·ɪ·fæk·tər, $-t̬ɚ, -trəs/ *n* [C] someone who gives money to help an organization, society or person

ben·e·fi·cia·ry /£ˌben·ɪˈfɪʃ·ᵊr·i, $-i·er·i/ *n* [C] a person or group who receives money, advantages, etc. as a result of something else ● *Her husband was the chief beneficiary* **of** *her will.* ● *The main beneficiaries of the new law will be those living on or below the poverty line.*

be·ne·fi·cent /bɪˈnef·ɪ·sᵊnt/ *adj fml* helping people and doing good acts ● *a beneficent aunt*

ben·e·fit *(obj)* /ˈben·ɪ·fɪt/ *v, n* **-t-** or *Br also* **-tt-** (to receive or give) a helpful or good effect, or something intended to help ● *The discovery of oil brought many benefits to the town.* [C] ● *One of the many benefits* **of** *foreign travel is learning how to cope with the unexpected.* [C] ● *He's had* **the** *benefit* **of** *an expensive education and yet he continues to work as a waiter.* [U] ● *I didn't* **get/derive (much)** *benefit* **from** *school.* [U] ● **For the** *benefit* **of** (= Especially for) *those who weren't listening the first time, I will repeat the question.* [U] ● *With the benefit* **of hindsight** (= Helped by the knowledge since learned) *it is easy for us to see where we went wrong in the past.* [U] ● *(slightly fml) She drinks a lot less now,* **to the** *benefit* **of** (= resulting in an improvement in) *her health as a whole.* [U] ● *I feel that I have benefited greatly* **from** *her wisdom.* [I] ● *How can we benefit those who most need our help?* [T] ● *I didn't know whether his story was true or not, but I decided to* **give him the benefit of the doubt** (= to accept something as true although it is not certain). ● Benefit is also the money given by the government to people who need financial help, for example because they cannot find a job: *unemployment benefit* [U] ○ *I'm* **on** *benefit at the moment.* [U] ● A **benefit concert** is a musical performance held to raise money for people in need, where the performers usually play for free.

ben·e·fi·cial /ˌben·ɪˈfɪʃ·ᵊl/ *adj* ● *The improvement in sales figures had a beneficial* (= helpful or good) **effect/ influence** *on the company as a whole.* ● *A stay in the country will be beneficial* **to** *his health.*

be·nev·o·lent /bɪˈnev·ᵊl·ᵊnt/ *adj* kind and helpful ● *He was a benevolent old man, he wouldn't hurt a fly.* ● A **benevolent fund** is an amount of money (given by others) used to help particular people in need. ● A **benevolent society** is an organization which gives money to and helps a particular group of people in need: *a benevolent society for sailors' widows*

be·nev·o·lence /bɪˈnev·ᵊl·ᵊnts/ *n* [U]

be·nev·o·lent·ly /bɪˈnev·ᵊl·ᵊnt·li/ *adv* ● *She smiled benevolently at me when I offered to help carry the shopping.*

be·night·ed /£bɪˈnaɪ·tɪd, $-t̬ɪd/ *adj literary* without knowledge or morals ● *Some of the early explorers thought of the local people as benighted savages who could be exploited.*

be·nign /bɪˈnaɪn/ *adj* pleasant and kind ● *Martha is a benign old lady who wouldn't hurt a fly.* ● If a CANCER (= a growth in or on a body) is benign it is not likely to cause death: *She wept in relief when the tumour turned out to be benign.* Compare MALIGNANT.

be·nign·ly /bɪˈnaɪn·li/ *adv* ● *The policeman smiled benignly at the motorist.*

bent [BEND] /bent/ *past simple and past participle of* BEND

bent [SKILL] /bent/ *n* [U] a natural skill ● *She has* **a** *scientific bent/***a** *bent* **for** *science.* ● *"They fool me to the top of my bent* (= to my limit)" (Shakespeare, Hamlet 3.2)

bent [DISHONEST] /bent/ *adj esp. Br slang* (esp. of a person in a position of authority) dishonest ● *a bent copper*

bent [HOMOSEXUAL] /bent/ *adj dated disapproving* (esp. of men) homosexual

bent on /bent/ *adj* [after v] determined to (do or have something) ● *He was bent on getting married as soon as possible.* ● *She became bent on destruction/revenge after the gunman was found innocent in court.*

be·numb·ed /bɪˈnʌmd/ *adj fml* unable to feel because of cold, shock, etc. ● *a face benumbed with cold*

ben·zene /ˈben·ziːn/ *n* [U] a colourless liquid from which many other chemicals can be made ● *A benzene molecule is made of six carbon atoms joined in a ring, each one with a hydrogen atom attached.* ● (CS) (D) (NL) (PL) (S)

be·queath *obj* /bɪˈkwiːð/ *v* [T + two objects] *fml* to arrange to give (esp. money or property) to others after your death ● *Her father bequeathed her the family fortune/bequeathed the family fortune* **to** *her in his will.* ● *Picasso bequeathed Spain and France most of his paintings and sculptures/bequeathed most of his paintings and sculptures* **to** *Spain and France.*

be·quest /bɪˈkwest/ *n* [C] the money or property belonging to someone which they say that, after their death, they wish to be given to other people ● *Her will included small bequests* **to** *her family, while most of her fortune went to a home for retired donkeys.*

be·rate *obj* /bɪˈreɪt/ *v* [T] *fml* to speak in an angry manner to (someone) ● *His mother berated him* **for** *making a mess.*

be·reaved /bɪˈriːvd/ *adj* [not gradable] having a close relative or friend who has died ● *Our neighbour has recently been bereaved.* ● *The bereaved parents wept silently beside the grave.* ● *(fml) Last year he was tragically bereaved* **of** *his brother.*

be·reaved /bɪˈriːvd/ *pl n* ● *It is generally accepted that* **the** *bereaved* (= people whose relatives or friends have died) *should receive proper counselling after a tragedy.*

be·reave·ment /bɪˈriːv·mənt/ *n* ● Bereavement is the experience of having a close relative or friend who has died: *She has recently* **suffered** *a bereavement.* [C] ○ *Parents who have lost a child often never get over their bereavement.* [U]

be·reft /bɪˈreft/ *adj* [after v] *fml* lacking something or feeling great loss ● *Alone now and almost penniless, he was bereft* **of** *hope.* ● *After the last of their children had left home the couple* **felt** *utterly bereft.*

ber·et /£ˈber·eɪ, $bəˈreɪ/ *n* [C] a round flat hat made of soft material ● [LP]> **'-et' words** [PIC]> **Hats**

berk, **burk** /£bɜːk, $bɜːrk/ *n* [C] *Br and Aus slang* a stupid person; a person for whom you feel dislike and lack of respect ● *I felt a* **right** *berk when I couldn't remember where I'd parked the car.* ● *Get out of the way, you berk!*

ber·ry /ˈber·i/ *n* [C] a small round fruit on particular plants and trees ● *The berries of this plant look delicious but in fact contain a deadly poison.*

ber·serk /£bəˈzɜːk, $-ˈzɜːrk/ *adj* out of control and violent ● *Maddened by pain the horse* **went** *berserk kicking at the walls of his stable.* ● *(fig. infml) My mother will* **go** *berserk* (= be extremely angry) *when she finds out that I've ruined her best dress.*

berth /£bɜːθ, $bɜːrθ/ *n* [C] a bed in a boat, train, etc., or a place for a ship or boat to stay in a port ● *She booked a berth on the train from London to Aberdeen.*

berth /£bɜːθ, $bɜːrθ/ *v* ● *We've heard that the pilot hopes to berth* (= bring into port) *the tanker as soon as the engines are running again.* [T] ● *The ship berthed* (= was tied up at the port) **at** *Sydney and so we spent a day touring the city.* [I]

be·seech *obj* /bɪˈsiːtʃ/ *v* [T] *past* **beseeched** or **besought** /£bɪˈsɔːt, $-ˈsɑːt/ *fml* to ask for something in a

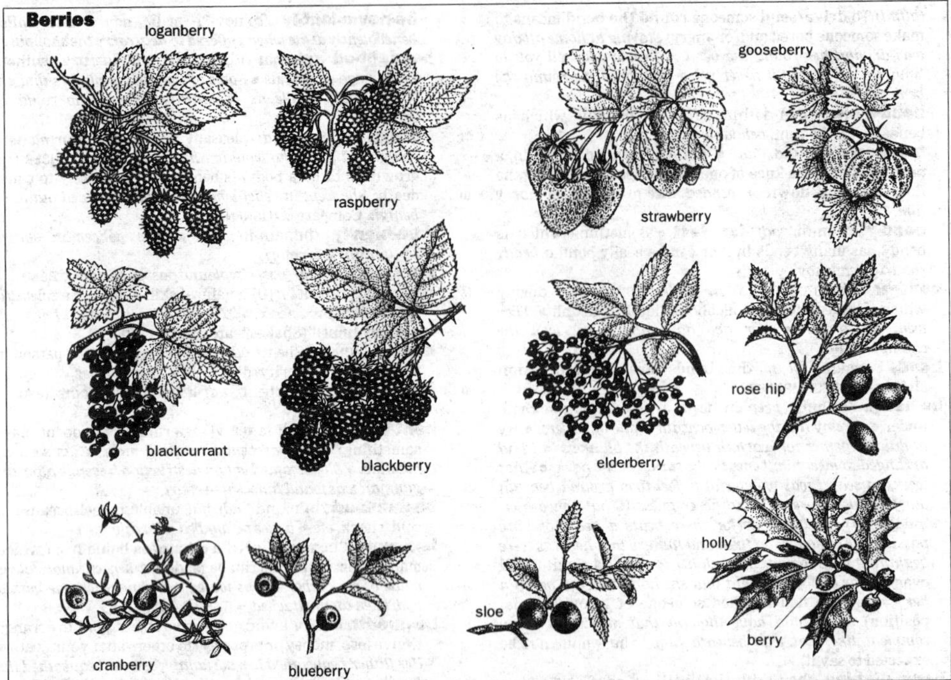

needy and anxious way; BEG • *They beseeched her not* **to** *climb the mountain that day, but she wouldn't listen.* [+ obj + *to* infinitive] • *Stay a little longer, I beseech you!*

be·set /bɪˈset/ *adj* [after v; always + adv/prep] troubled (by); surrounded (by); full (of) • *Her path to becoming an artist in her own right was beset* **by/with** *difficulties.* • *With the amount of traffic nowadays, even a trip across town is beset* **by/with** *dangers.*

be·side /bɪˈsaɪd/ *prep* at the side of, next to • *Come and sit here beside me.* • *The baby elephant stood beside its mother at the waterhole.* • *Our school was built right beside a river.* • *(fig.) Those books seem rather dull beside* (= compared to) *this one.* • *The exact cost is* **beside the point** (= not really connected with what is being talked about), *I wish you'd stick to discussing whether the road should be built at all.* • If you are **beside yourself with** a particular feeling or emotion it is so strong that it makes you almost out of control: *He was beside himself with grief when his dog died.* ○ *When she passed the exam at last she was beside herself with joy.*

be·sides /bɪˈsaɪdz/ *adv* [not gradable], *prep* in addition to; also • *Do you play any other sports besides ice-skating and darts?* • *She told me that she has two other cars besides the one she drives to work.* • *I've had job offers from two firms of international lawyers and plenty more besides.* • *She won't mind your being late – besides, it's hardly your fault.*

be·siege *obj* /bɪˈsiːdʒ/ *v* [T] to surround (something such as a town), esp. with an army, to prevent people or supplies getting in or out • *The town had been besieged for two months but still resisted the aggressors.* • *(fig.) When the pop star tried to leave her hotel she was besieged* **by** (= surrounded by) *waiting journalists and fans.* • *(fig.) After showing the controversial film the television company was besieged* **with** (= received many) *phone calls and letters.*

be·smeared /£bɪˈsmɪəd, $-ˈsmɪrd/ *adj* [after v] *fml* marked with dirt, oil, etc. • *His face was besmeared* **with** *chocolate and dirt.* • *(fig.) The teacher's reputation was besmeared* (= damaged) *by students' accusations of unfair grading.*

be·smirch *obj* /£bɪˈsmɜːtʃ, $-ˈsmɜːrtʃ/ *v* [T] *literary* to doubt the honour of (a person or esp. their reputation) • *His jealous brother besmirched him in front of a large group of his colleagues.*

be·sot·ted /£bɪˈsɒt·ɪd, $-ˈsɑː·t̬ɪd/ *adj* completely in love and therefore likely to behave in an unusual way or be foolish • *He was so completely besotted* **with** *her that he couldn't see how badly she treated him.*

be·sought /£bɪˈsɔːt, $-sɑːt/ *past simple and past participle of* BESEECH

be·spat·tered /£bɪˈspæt·əd, $-ˈspæt̬·əd/ *adj* [after v] covered with spots of liquid • *The backs of my legs were bespattered* **with** *mud after walking home in the rain.*

be·speak *obj* /bɪˈspiːk/ *v* [T] *past simple* **bespoke** /£bɪˈspəʊk, $-ˈspoʊk/, *past part* **bespoken** /£bɪˈspəʊ·kᵊn, $-ˈspoʊ-/ *fml* to suggest or show • *His letter bespeaks his willingness to mend his ways.*

be·spec·ta·cled /bɪˈspek·tɪ·kḷd/ *adj* [not gradable] *fml* wearing SPECTACLES (= glasses) • *If he has grown older, it scarcely shows on his eager, bespectacled face.*

be·spoke /£bɪˈspəʊk, $-ˈspoʊk/ *adj* [not gradable] *esp. Br fml* (of clothing) specially made to fit a particular person • *They have set up a business in London producing bespoke* **tailoring** (= jackets, trousers and skirts) *for men and women.* • A bespoke **tailor** is a person who makes or sells clothing that is specially made for the customer.

best SUPERLATIVE OF GOOD /best/ *adj* [not gradable] of the highest quality, or being the most suitable, pleasing or effective type of thing or person • *This is the best meal I've ever had.* • *He's one of our best students.* • *Are you sure this is the best way of doing it?* • *What's the best* (= shortest or quickest) *way to get to the station?* • *Your parents only want what is best* **for** *you.* • *She was my best* **friend** (= She was the friend for whom I had the most affection) *at school.* • **It's** *best* (= It is wise) **to** *try and get to the supermarket before the rush starts.* [+ *to* infinitive] • To **be on** your **best behaviour** is to behave extremely well and be very polite on a particular occasion: *I want you to be on your best behaviour while Aunt Ethel is here.* • If you say **may the best man/person win** before a race or competitive activity, you mean you want the person who is the fastest, strongest or most skilled to win or succeed. • To **put** your **best foot forward** is to try as hard as you can. • *(infml)* If you describe someone or something as **the best thing since sliced bread**, you think they are an excellent person or thing: *She thinks her new boyfriend is the best thing since sliced bread.* • *Adults are fond of telling children that the time they spent at school is* **the best days of** *their* **life** (= the most pleasant time they will ever have). • **With the best will in the world** (= Although I want to if I possibly can) *I can't employ him in the shop unless I can trust him.* • The **best before date** on food or drink is the day or month before which it should be eaten or drunk. • *(infml)* Your **best bet** is the action which is most likely to be successful: *If you want to get to the station before 10 o'clock, your best bet would be to take a taxi.* • *(specialized)* The **best boy** is the person who helps the GAFFER (= the most important electrician) when a film or television programme is being made. • The **best man** at a marriage ceremony is the male friend or relative of the BRIDEGROOM who stands with him and gives him emotional support during the ceremony. • **Best wishes** is a polite way of finishing a letter to a person whom you know quite well. • *(saying)* 'The best things come in small packages/parcels.' • *"The Best Things in Life are Free"* (song written by Buddy de Sylva, 1927)

best [SUPERLATIVE OF WELL] /best/ *adv* [not gradable] in the most suitable, pleasing or satisfactory way, or to the greatest degree • *Which evening would suit you best for the party?* • *Ayers Rock is best seen at sunset when it seems to change colour.* • *He couldn't decide which one he* **liked** *best* (= preferred). • *It is a difficult passage, but just translate it* **as best** *you* **can** (= as well as you can). • *"Do you think I should take this job or try for another?" "You should* **do as** *you* **think best** (= you should use your judgment to decide which choice to make)." • **Had best** can be used to show that an action is advisable, desirable or necessary: *You had best tell her* (= It would be wise if you told her) *that you won't be able to come to her party.* ○ *We'd best be going now* (= We should go now). • Best can also mean to the greatest degree when it is used as the superlative of adjectives beginning with 'good' or 'well': *They were the best-dressed couple at the party.* ○ *He was voted the best-looking* (= most attractive) *actor in Hollywood.*

best [EXCELLENT] /best/ *n* [U] the most excellent in a group of things or people • *My tastes are simple – I only like* **the** *best.* • *He wanted* **the** *best for his children – good schools, a nice house and trips abroad.* • *I like all of Hitchcock's films, but I think 'Notorious' is* **the** *best.* • *All the singers were good, but Maria was easily* **the** *best.* • *Chris and I are* **the** *best* **of** *friends* (= We are very close friends). • *I'm sorry that this isn't a very nice room, but it's* **the** *best* (= the most pleasant) *I could get.* • *My essay isn't great, but it's* **the** *best I could do in the time available.* • *(infml)* If you are saying goodbye to someone whom you will not see for a long time, you can say **all the best!** to wish them a happy and successful future. • *The food was bland* **at best** (= even considering it as kindly as possible), *and at worst completely inedible.* • *The documentary was an example of investigative journalism* **at** *its* **best** (= at the highest standard achievable). • *I'm not* **at** *my* **best** (= I am not very active or intelligent) *in the morning.* • *Our car doesn't go fast even* **at the best of times** (= even when everything is going well), *but today it's incredibly slow.* • *There was wonderful food, good company, and* **best of all** (= the most pleasing thing was) *a jazz band.* • **Best of luck** is an expression used to wish someone success before an exam or an activity which might be difficult or cause problems: *Best of luck* **with** *your exams!* ○ *We would like to wish you* **the** *(very) best of luck* **with** *your move to the States.* • *If you like skiing and swimming, the island allows you to enjoy* **the best of both worlds** (= the advantages of two very different things). • In a sport such as tennis, if you play **the best of** a particular number of games, you play that number of games and the winner is the player who wins the greatest number of those games: *Shall we play the best of five?* • To **do/try** your **(level/very) best** is to make the greatest effort possible: *It doesn't matter if you fail, just do your best.* • If you **have had the best of** something, you have enjoyed the most pleasant part of it, and everything that remains is worse: *I think we've already had the best of the hot weather this summer.* • If you **make the best of** something/*(Br)* **make the best of a bad job**/*(Am)* **make the best of a bad situation**, you make an unsatisfactory situation as pleasant as possible: *We'll have to spend the night in this awful place, so we might as well make the best of it.* • If an action is **for the best**, it is done to improve a situation or produce a good result, although it might seem unpleasant at the time: *I know it's hard for you to leave Michael, but it's for the best.* • If something **turns out/is all for the best**, it has a good result despite seeming bad at the time: *Failing my exams was awful, but it all turned out for the best because I managed to get a job almost immediately.* • *Just do the work* **to the best of** *your* **ability** (= as well as you can). • *He's arriving tomorrow,* **to the best of my knowledge** (= I believe that this is true from the information available). • *He can dance* **with the best of them** (= as well as anyone). • *"Grow old along with me! / The best is yet to be"* (Robert Browning in the poem *Rabbi Ben Ezra*, 1864) • *"All is for the best in the best of all possible worlds"* (from Voltaire's novel *Candide*, 1759)

best *obj* [DEFEAT] /best/ *v* [T] *fml* to defeat (someone) in a fight or competition • *He bested his opponent in just two rounds.*

best /best/ *n* [U] • *His illness* **got the best of** (= defeated) *him over time.* • *Lisa* **got the best of** (= obtained an advantage over) *her opponent in the last half of the game.*

bes·ti·al /ˈbes·ti·əl/ *adj disapproving* cruel or animal-like • *The soldiers were accused of carrying out atrocities in the most bestial fashion against unarmed civilians.*

bes·ti·al·i·ty /£ˌbes·tiˈæl·ə·ti, $-t̬i/ *n* [U] *disapproving* • *The unspeakable bestiality* (= cruelty) *of Auschwitz and the other death camps led many people to reject their faith in the fundamental goodness of humanity.* • See also BESTIALITY.

bes·ti·al·i·ty /£ˌbes·tiˈæl·ə·ti, $-t̬i/ *n* [U] sex between a person and an animal • See also **bestiality** at BESTIAL.

bes·ti·ar·y /£ˈbes·ti·ə·ri, $-er·i/ *n* [C] (in the Middle Ages) a book containing descriptions of real and imaginary animals which was intended to teach morals and to entertain

be·stir *obj* /£bɪˈstɜːʳ, $-ˈstɜːr/ *v* [T] **-rr-** *fml* to make active after a period of rest • *After several months of indifference, the residents finally started to bestir them***selves to** *stop the motorway from being built near their homes.* [+ obj + *to* infinitive] • *(humorous) Bestir your***self** *from that chair and make me a cup of tea, would you?* • *(fig.) Share prices rose sharply yesterday, bestirred by the news of a cut in interest rates.*

be·stow *obj* /£bɪˈstəʊ, $-ˈstoʊ/ *v* [T] *fml* to give (something) as an honour or present • *The Chancellorship of the University was bestowed* **upon** *her in 1992.* • *The George Cross is a decoration that is bestowed* **on** *British civilians for acts of great bravery.* • *He saw writers and artists as being important to the state for they could bestow credibility* **on** *the regime.*

be·stow·al /£bɪˈstəʊ·əl, $-ˈstoʊ-/ *n* [U] *fml* • *She knelt to receive her father's blessing which represented a bestowal of consent* **upon** *her forthcoming marriage.*

be·strew *obj* /bɪˈstruː/ *v* [T] *past simple* **bestrewed**, *past part* **bestrewn** /bɪˈstruːn/ or **bestrewed** *literary* to lie covering (a surface), or to cover (a surface) with things that are far apart and in no particular arrangement • *Autumn leaves bestrewed the lawn.* • *During the festival, the city streets are bestrewn* **with** *flowers.*

be·stride *obj* /bɪˈstraɪd/ *v* [T] *past simple* **bestrode** /£bɪˈstrəʊd, $-ˈstroʊd/, *past part* **bestridden** /bɪˈstrɪd·ən/ *fml* to sit or stand with a leg on either side of (an object or animal) • *He bestrode the chair as though it were a horse.* • *"Why man, he doth bestride the narrow world / like a Colossus* (= a very big statue)*"* (Shakespeare, Julius Caesar 1.1)

best·sel·ler /£ˈbestˌsel·əʳ, $-ɚ, ˌ-ˈ--/ *n* [C] a book which is extremely popular and has sold in very large numbers • *Jeffrey Archer's novels are all bestsellers.* • *Her latest novel has gone to number two in the bestseller list* (= the list that shows which books are the most popular at that time).

best·sell·ing /ˈbestˌsel·ɪŋ/ *adj* [not gradable] • *He has received royalties of several million from his bestselling autobiography.* • *She's a* **bestselling** *author* (= Her books are extremely popular).

bet *(obj)* /bet/ *v* **betting**, *past* **bet** or **betted** to risk (a sum of money) on the unknown result of an event, such as a horse race, in the hope of winning more money • *He regularly goes to the races and bets heavily.* [I] • *I never bet* **on** *certainties.* [I] • *She bet £500 000* **on** *the horse which came in second.* [T] • *I bet you $25* **that** *I'll get there before you.* [T + two objects + *that* clause] • *(infml)* If you bet (someone) that something is true or will happen, you are certain that it is true or will happen: *I bet you* **(that)** *she's missed the bus.* [T + obj + (*that*) clause] ○ *I bet* **(that)** *he won't come* [+ (*that*) clause] • *(infml)* If you say **I/I'll bet** in answer to something that someone has said, you mean that you agree with them: *"I was so relieved that I didn't have to clean up after the party." "I bet* (= I am not surprised) *you were."* • *(infml)* **You bet** can be used to emphasize a statement or to mean 'certainly': *"Are you coming to the party?" "You bet* (= certainly)*!"* • *(infml)* If you say **(how much) do you want to bet?** in answer to something that someone has said, you mean that you are certain that they are wrong: *"I'm sure she won't come and visit us." "How much do you want to bet?"* • *(infml)* If you say **don't bet on it/I wouldn't bet on it**, you mean that you think what someone has just said is unlikely to be true or to happen: *"Do you think they'll give me back the money they owe me?" "I wouldn't bet on it."* • *(infml) You can* **bet your boots/bottom dollar/shirt/***(Am slang)* **ass** (= be certain) *she'll be there to meet me.* • [LP] **Two objects**

bet /bet/ *n* [C] • A bet is an amount of money which you risk on the unknown result of an event, such as a horse race: *He* **placed/put** *a bet* **on** *the horse which was the favourite to win.* • *(infml)* A bet is also a guess or opinion: *My bet is their baby will be a girl.* [+ *(that)* clause] • If you **make a bet with** someone about something, you both have different opinions about whether it is true or will happen: *She made a bet with her brother* **about** *whether their mother would notice the broken vase.* • If you do something **for**/*(Am usually)* **on** a bet, you do it because someone says that you cannot or will not do it: *She jumped in the fountain for a bet.* • *Putting your savings in a high-interest account is* **a good** *bet*/*your* **best** *bet* (= the wisest thing to do). • *It is a* **fair** *bet* (= It is quite likely) **that** *the government will not act on any of the recommendations in the report.* [+ *(that)* clause] • *It's a* **safe** *bet* (= It is very likely) **that** *he won't remember my birthday tomorrow.* [+ *(that)* clause]

bet·ting /£ˈbet·ɪŋ, $ˈbeṭ-/ *n* [U] • Betting is the habit of putting bets on horse races or other competitions: *Betting can be as addictive as drinking or smoking.* • *(Br)* A **betting shop** is a place where people go to bet on horse races or other competitions.

be·ta, β /£ˈbiː·tə, $ˈbeɪ·ṭə/ *n* [C] the second letter of the Greek alphabet, sometimes given as a mark for a student's work to show good quality • *I got a beta minus for my long essay.* • Compare ALPHA; GAMMA.

be·tel /£ˈbiː·tᵊl, $-ṭᵊl/ *n* [U] a plant that grows in south east Asia which has leaves and red nuts that act as a drug when chewed

bête noire /£betˈnwɑːʳ, $-ˈnwɑːr/ *n* [C] *pl* **bêtes noires** *disapproving* a person or thing that you particularly dislike or that annoys you • *My particular bête noire is cigarette ends being left in half-empty glasses.*

be·tide *(obj)* /bɪˈtaɪd/ *v literary* to happen (to) • *We will remain true to one another, whatever betides (us) in years to come.* [I/T]

be·to·ken *obj* /£bɪˈtəʊ·kᵊn, $-ˈtoʊ-/ *v* [T] *old use* to be a sign of (something) • *He gave her a gift to betoken his gratitude.*

be·tray *obj* [NOT LOYAL] /bɪˈtreɪ/ *v* [T] to not be loyal to your country or a person who thinks you love or support them, often by doing something harmful such as helping their enemies • *He was accused of betraying his country during the war.* • *She felt betrayed by her mother because she couldn't talk to her about her problems.* • *For years they betrayed Britain's secrets* **to** *Russia.* • *(fml) He promised never to betray her* (= never to leave her for another person). • *(fml)* If someone betrays something such as a promise, they do not do what they said they would: *The government has been accused of betraying its election promises.* ○ *He claims that by signing the treaty, the group has betrayed* (= not followed) *its ideals.* • If someone **betrays** your **trust**, they make you question your confidence in them: *By staying out so late, they have betrayed my trust.* • *"If I had to choose between betraying my country and betraying my friend, I hope I should have the guts to betray my country"* (from E.M.Forster's *Two Cheers for Democracy*, 1951)

be·tray·al /bɪˈtreɪ·əl/ *n* • *I felt a sense of betrayal when my friends refused to support me.* [U] • *It was an act of betrayal which, according to the law, was punishable by death.* [U] • *This was the first in a series of betrayals.* [C]

be·tray *obj* [SHOW] /bɪˈtreɪ/ *v* [T] to show (feelings, thoughts or a particular characteristic) without intending to • *If he is nervous on stage, he does not betray it.* • *Although she often seems quite cold and harsh, her smiling eyes betray her true nature.* • *He wanted to write an emotive novel, but the book betrays too much anger to be effective.* • *The simple, linear style in which she paints betrays a mixture of influences.*

be·troth *obj* /£bɪˈtrəʊð, $-ˈtroʊð/ *v* [T usually passive] *fml or old use* to cause (someone) to promise formally to marry someone • *She was betrothed* **to** *her cousin at an early age.*

be·troth·al /£bɪˈtrəʊ·ðᵊl, $-ˈtroʊ-/ *n* [C] *fml or old use* • *The play revolves round the betrothal of a duke* **to** *a doctor's daughter.*

be·trothed /£bɪˈtrəʊðd, $-ˈtroʊðd/ *n* [C] *pl* **betrothed** *fml or old use* • *He sent a dozen roses to his betrothed* (= the woman whom he had promised to marry). • *She gave a large party in honour of the betrothed* (= the two people who had promised to marry one another).

bet·ter [COMPARATIVE OF GOOD] /£ˈbet·əʳ, $ˈbeṭ·ɚ/ *adj* [not gradable] of a higher standard, or more suitable, pleasing or effective than other things or people • *He stood near the front to get a better view of the procession.* • *Relations between the two countries have never been better.* • *The phone call could not have come at a better time.* • *It's much better to have a small cosy room than a big cold one.* • *The film was better* **than** *I expected.* • *This is a better restaurant* **than** *the last one we went to.* • *She thinks they will have a better life in the US* **than** *in their own country.* • *She is much better* **at** *tennis than I am.* • *It is* **far** (= much) *better to save some of your money than to spend it all at once.* • *Fresh vegetables are better* **for** *you* (= They are more beneficial to you) *than canned ones.* • *The longer you keep this wine,* **the** *better it tastes* (= It has a better flavour if you keep it for a long time). • *The only hotel in town was filthy, but it was* **better than nothing**. • If you are or get better after an illness or injury, you are healthy and no longer ill: *I was rather ill last week, but I'm much better now.* ○ *Are you feeling any better today?* ○ *I hope you get better soon.* ○ *I felt (all the) better* **for** (= I felt I had obtained both physical and mental benefits from) *a quick walk.* • If you say **better luck next time** to someone, you mean that you hope they will succeed when they try again: *I'm sorry to hear that you failed your driving test, but better luck next time.* • If a situation **gets better**, it improves: *Even after the cease-fire, the situation in the capital got no better and the violence continued.* • If a person **gets better** at an activity, they improve their skills in it: *She practises the piano every day after school and she's getting much better at it.* • If you **go one better** than someone else, you do something which is more advanced or more generous than them: *I gave her a card, but my brother had to go one better and bought her an expensive present.* • If you say that someone is **no better than** a person who is unpleasant or unkind, you mean that they have behaved in a similar way to this type of person: *"People who don't pay their bus fares are no better than common criminals," she told him.* • *(dated)* A person's **better half** is their husband, wife or usual sexual partner. • A person's **better nature** is the more honourable or moral side of their character. • *(saying)* 'Better late than never' is used when someone or something is late, and it means that it is better for them to be late than for them never to arrive or happen. • *(saying)* 'Better safe than sorry' means it is wise to be extremely careful and protect yourself against all types of risk rather than be careless and harm yourself. • *(saying)* 'Better the devil you know (than the devil you don't)' means it is wiser to choose something which is familiar when you have to make a choice in which none of the possibilities seem very good. • *"'Tis better to have loved and lost / Than never to have loved at all"* (from Alfred Tennyson's poem *In Memoriam*, 1850) • *"You're a better man than I am, Gunga Din!"* (Rudyard Kipling in the poem *Gunga Din*, 1892)

bet·ter [COMPARATIVE OF WELL] /£ˈbet·əʳ, $ˈbeṭ·ɚ/ *adv* in a more suitable, pleasing or satisfactory way, or to a greater degree • *The next time he did the test, he was better prepared.* • *She did much better* (= She was more successful) *in the second part of the exam.* • *Nothing demonstrates the need for immediate international aid better* (= more) *than this crisis.* • *There is nothing I* **like** *better than* (= I very much like) *lying in bed on Sunday morning, listening to the radio.* • *I* **like** *this jacket much better than* (= I prefer it to) *the one I saw in the other shop.* • *She knows her way around the college better* **than** *I do.* • *Some questions are better left unanswered* (= It is wise not to answer them). • Better can also mean 'to a greater degree' when it is used as the comparative of adjectives beginning with 'good' or 'well': *She is better-looking* (= more attractive) *than her brother.* ○ *He is much better-known for his poetry than his song-writing.* • *Why don't you give her a call, or* **better still/even better** (= it would be more satisfactory to) *go and see her in person?* • If someone is **better-off**, they have more money than they used to have or more money than most other people: *She was much better-off when she got promoted, and even had enough money to buy a new car.* ○ *When his parents died, he found himself $100 000 better-off* (= he had $100 000 more than he used to). ○ *Better-off people usually live in bigger, more luxurious homes.* ○ *The tax on domestic fuel will not have a very serious impact on* **the** *better-off* (= people who are richer than most others). • If someone is **better-off** after something has happened, they are in a more satisfactory or acceptable situation: *This house is much too small for all of you – you'll be much better-off when you move into a larger place.* • *You would* **do better** (= It would be wiser) **to** *bring the plants inside when the weather gets colder.* [+ *to* infinitive] • **Had better** is sometimes used to give advice or to make a threat: *You'd* *better* (= You should) *go home now before the rain starts.* [+ infinitive without *to*]

bet·ter IMPROVEMENT /£ˈbet·əʳ, $ˈbet̬·ɚ/ *n* [U] something that is of a higher standard than others • *He ran the 100 metres in 9·91 seconds, and I have not seen better* (= a faster result) *this year.* • *I didn't think he would go out without telling me – I expected better* **of** *him* (= I thought he would have behaved in a more responsible way). • *If you can go there this afternoon,* **so much/all the better** (= it will be more advantageous). • If you do something **for better or (for) worse**, you accept the bad results of the action as well as the good ones: *I decided to follow her advice, for better or for worse.* • If something changes **for the better**, it improves: *He does not think that things have changed for the better since the new government came to power.* ○ *She has helped to transform for the better the country's international position and economic prospects.* • *He fought fiercely but his opponent was strong and easily* **got the better of** (= defeated) *him.* • If a feeling **gets the better of** you, you cannot stop yourself from letting that feeling make you do something, despite knowing that what you are doing is forbidden or wrong: *Her curiosity got the better of her and she opened the door and peeped inside.* ○ *I tried to resist another piece of cake, but my greed got the better of me and I took one.*

bet·ters /£ˈbet·əz, $ˈbet̬·ɚz/ *pl n* • Your betters are people of a higher rank or social position than you: *As children, we were taught not to argue with our* **elders and** *betters.*

bet·ter *obj* IMPROVE /£ˈbet·əʳ, $ˈbet̬·ɚ/ *v* [T] to improve (a situation, condition or person) • *The organization was established to better conditions for the handicapped.* • *He tried to better him***self** (= increase his chances of future success) *by taking evening classes.*

bet·ter·ment /£ˈbet·ə·mənt, $ˈbet̬·ɚ-/ *n* [U] • *Several changes have been made to the rules of rugby for the betterment* (= improvement) *of the sport.* • *Education is one of the surest ways to achieve* **self-***betterment* (= to increase your chances of future success).

be·tween SPACE /bɪˈtwiːn/ *prep, adv* [not gradable] in or into the space which separates two places, people or objects • *The town lies half-way between Rome and Florence.* • *Standing between the two adults was a small child.* • *She squeezed between the parked cars and ran out into the road.* • *A narrow path ran* **in** *between the two houses.* • If something is between two amounts, it is greater than the first amount but smaller than the second: *She weighs between 55 and 60 kilograms.* ○ *The temperature in the north east will be between 20 and 25 degrees today.* ○ *Estimates for the cost of the job vary between £3 000 and £5 500.* ○ *The room was either extremely cold or hot, never anything* **in** *between* (= in the middle). • PIC **Prepositions of movement**

be·tween TIME /bɪˈtwiːn/, **in be·tween** *prep, adv* in the period of time which separates two different times or events • *You shouldn't eat between meals.* • *There is a break of ten minutes between classes.* • *The shop is closed for lunch between 12.30 and 1.30.* • *Come along to our house between eight and eight-thirty this evening.* • *The competition is open to children between six and twelve years of age.* • *She left school at three, but didn't arrive home until six, so where was she in between* (= during that time)? • *In between sobs, he managed to tell them what had happened.* • *If you only go to the supermarket once a month, what do you do* **between times** (= in the period between visits)?

be·tween AMONG /bɪˈtwiːn/ *prep* shared among two or more people or things • *The money was divided equally between several worthy causes.* • *We drank two bottles of wine between four of us.* • *All we had was half a loaf of bread and a bottle of water between us.* • *Trade between the two countries* (= Their trade with each other) *has increased sharply in the past year.* • *A close friendship had existed between them* (= They had been very good friends) *for several years.* • *There is a great deal of similarity between Caroline and her mother* (= They are very similar). • *There has always been a good relationship between locals and tourists in the resort.* • *The students did a 20-mile run, and between them* (= by their shared efforts) *they managed to raise over £500 for charity.* • *Between them* (= By their shared efforts), *they scored five goals during the match.* • *You'll have to* **choose** *between a holiday or a new washing machine* (= You will have to choose either one thing or the other) – *we can't afford them both.* • *She was* **torn** *between loyalty to her father and love for her husband* (= She could not decide which one to support). • A discussion, argument or game between two or more people or groups of people involves both people or groups: *The negotiations between the union and management have broken down.* ○ *There has always been a fierce rivalry between the two clubs.* ○ *Tonight's match is between the New Orleans Saints and the Los Angeles Rams.* • **Between ourselves/Between you and me/***(humorous)* **Between you, me and the bedpost/gatepost** is an expression used to tell someone that what you are about to say should be kept secret: *Between you and me, I think she's been telling lies.* ○ *Don't tell this to anyone else – it's just between ourselves.*

be·tween CONNECTING /bɪˈtwiːn/ *prep* connecting two or more places, things or people • *There is a regular train service between Glasgow and Edinburgh.* • *There is one scheduled flight each week between London and Beijing.* • *A high-speed rail link operates between Paris and the Channel Tunnel.* • *The survey shows a link between asthma and air pollution.* • Between also means from one place to another: *He commutes daily between Leeds and Manchester.*

be·tween SEPARATING /bɪˈtwiːn/ *prep* separating two places or things • *The wall between East and West Berlin came down in 1989.* • *The report states that the gap between the rich and the poor has increased dramatically over the past decade.* • *These washing powders look the same, so what's the* **difference** *between them* (= in what way are they different)? • If something **comes between** two people, it harms their relationship: *"Don't let one little mistake come between us!" he begged.*

be·twixt /bɪˈtwɪkst/ *adv* [not gradable], *prep* **betwixt and between** between two positions, choices or ideas and unable or unwilling to decide between them • *She's neither for nor against us, but seems to want to remain on a path betwixt and between.* • *He found it difficult to choose betwixt and between* (= between) *two great opportunities.* • *(saying)* 'There's many a slip betwixt cup and lip' means that many bad things might happen before something is completed.

bev·el *obj* /ˈbev·əl/ *v* [T] *Br and Aus* **-ll-** or *esp. Am* **-l-** to give (a piece of wood or metal) a sloping edge • *He bevelled the edges of the bookcase.*

bev·el /ˈbev·əl/ *n* [C] • *She put a bevel* (= a sloping edge) *on the end of the table top.*

bev·elled *Br and Aus, esp. Am* **bev·eled** /ˈbev·əld/ *adj* • *A picture frame often has bevelled* **edges**.

bev·er·age /£ˈbev·ər·ɪdʒ, $ˈ-ɚ-/ *n* [C] *fml or specialized* a drink of any type • **Hot** *beverages include tea, coffee and hot chocolate.* • *We do not sell any* **alcoholic** *beverages.*

bev·vy /ˈbev·i/ *n* [C] *Br slang* an alcoholic drink • *Are you coming down the pub for a bevvy?*

bev·y /ˈbev·i/ *n* [C] a large group of people, esp. women or girls, or a large group of similar things • *Victorian postcards often featured bevies* **of** *bathing beauties.* • *A bevy* **of** *tariffs and taxes means that a foreign car costs twice as much as a similar domestically produced vehicle.* • A bevy is also a large group of a particular type of bird: *a bevy of quail/larks*

be·wail *obj* /bɪˈweɪl/ *v* [T] *fml or literary* to express great sadness about (something) • *He bewailed his sudden misfortune and the loss of his most treasured possessions.* • *She spent the evening bewailing the fact that no one ever listened to what she had to say.*

be·ware *(obj)* /£bɪˈweəʳ, $-ˈwer/ *v* (used in warnings) to be very careful about (something or someone) • *The mountains are a paradise for climbers and skiers – though beware, wolves still roam there.* [I] • *Beware salespeople who promise offers that seem too good to be true.* [T] • *You should beware* **of** *undercooked food when staying in hot countries.* [I] • *Beware* **of** *falling asleep while sunbathing.* [I] • Beware is often used on signs: *Beware* **of** *the dog.* [I] ○ *Beware – poisonous chemicals.* [I] • *"Beware the Ides* (= 15th) *of March"* (Shakespeare, Julius Caesar 1.1) • *"Beware the Fury of a Patient Man"* (from the poem *Absalom and Achitophel* by John Dryden, 1681) • Beware is only used in commands and warnings.

be·whis·kered /£bɪˈwɪs·kəd, $-kɚd/ *adj literary* (of a man) with facial hair on the lower part or sides of the face • *He was a bewhiskered, distinguished-looking gentleman.*

be·wigged /bɪˈwɪgd/ *adj* [not gradable] *literary* wearing a covering of artificial hair on the head • *The bewigged and robed judge stared sternly at the accused before passing sentence.*

be·wil·der *obj* /£bɪˈwɪl·dəʳ, $-dɚ/ *v* [T] to confuse (someone) by being difficult to understand or by not being familiar • *The instructions that came with the microwave completely bewildered me.* • *A new environment can* *bewilder and frighten a child.* • *She was completely bewildered by his critical remarks* (=She did not understand why he had criticized her).

be·wil·dered /£bɪˈwɪl·dəd, $-dərd/ *adj* • *Arriving in a strange city at night, I felt alone and bewildered.*

be·wil·der·ing /£bɪˈwɪl·dər·ɪŋ, $-dər·ɪŋ/ *adj* • *He gave me directions to his house, but I found them so utterly bewildering that I had to ask several people how to get there.* • If a range or choice of things is bewildering, it is so big that you find it hard to decide what you want: *The college offers a bewildering range of subjects that can be studied to degree level.* ○ *He opened the cupboard to find a bewildering* **array** *of lotions, creams and tablets.*

be·wil·der·ment /£bɪˈwɪl·də·mənt, $-dər-/ *n* [U] • *He was in a complete state of bewilderment and did not know what to do next.* • *As he walked through the door, she stared at him* **in** *utter bewilderment.*

be·witch *obj* /bɪˈwɪtʃ/ *v* [T] to put a magic SPELL (=effect) on (someone or something) in order to control them, or *(fig.)* to charm (someone) greatly so that you have the power to influence them • *The magician bewitched the broom and made it come to life.* • *19 people accused of bewitching a group of children were hanged in Salem in 1692.* • *(fig.) He was bewitched by her radiant beauty.* • *(fig.) His idealistic message about the need for peace seemed to bewitch an entire generation.* • *"Bewitched, Bothered and Bewildered"* (title of a song written by Lorenz Hart, 1941)

be·witch·ing /bɪˈwɪtʃ·ɪŋ/ *adj* • *(fig.) He was mesmerized by her bewitching green eyes.*

be·yond [FURTHER AWAY] /£bɪˈɒnd, $-ˈɑːnd/ *prep, adv* [not gradable] further away in the distance (than something) • *In the distance, beyond the river, was a small town.* • *From the top of the hill we could see our house and the woods beyond.* • *(disapproving)* If someone **cannot see beyond** something, their attention is fixed on that thing and they are unable to see other qualities it might have or understand what the result of their actions will be: *She claims that by selling off council housing, the government cannot see beyond immediate profits.*

be·yond [OUTSIDE A LIMIT] /£bɪˈɒnd, $-ˈɑːnd/ *prep, adv* [not gradable] outside or after (a stated limit) • *Few people live beyond the age of a hundred.* • *The builder will have to pay us compensation if the work continues beyond the agreed completion date.* • *This work could take us into the year 2000 and beyond.* • *Beyond a certain level of tiredness, it is impossible to work productively.* • *At present, there are no women in the police force holding posts beyond the rank of* (=of a higher rank than) *chief superintendent.* • *I've got nothing to tell you beyond* (=in addition to) *what I told you earlier.* • *The repercussions of this cut in spending will be felt throughout the education system and beyond* (=in other areas). • *My job* **goes** *beyond* (=is more than) *just teaching – my aim is to encourage the children to think for themselves.* • *The effect of information technology* **goes far** *beyond* (=It has a great effect on more areas than just) *those firms that make electronic products.* • *His thoughtlessness is beyond* **belief** (=It is so great that it is almost too impossible to believe). • *His story is beyond the* **bounds** *of credibility* (=It cannot be true). • *(literary) Her beauty is beyond* **compare** (=It is so great that nothing can be compared to it). • *Tonight's performance has been cancelled due to circumstances beyond our* **control** (=events which we are unable to deal with). • *(esp. humorous) Sam? Oh, he's beyond* **help** (=too stupid/ill/etc. to be worth trying to help). • *She has always lived beyond her* **means** (=She has always spent more than she has earned). • *His honesty is beyond* **question** (=It cannot be doubted). • *Sports cars such as Ferraris and Porsches are priced beyond the* **reach** *of most people* (=They are too expensive for most people to buy). • *Since becoming a mother, she has changed beyond* **recognition** (=her character has completely changed). • *He survived the accident, but his car was damaged beyond* **repair** (=It could not be repaired). • *(infml)* If something is beyond you, you are unable to understand it: *I'm afraid computer studies is completely beyond me.* ○ *How he can live with a dog that barks constantly is beyond me.* • **From beyond the grave** means after a person has died: *The message came from a voice from beyond the grave.* • If something is **beyond a joke**, it has stopped being amusing and is now a serious matter: *I used to think he was funny, but his behaviour has now gone way beyond a joke.* • If someone's behaviour is **beyond the pale**, it is unacceptable: *Her recent conduct is beyond the pale.* • *(law)* If a legal case or a person's guilt is proved *(Br and Aus)* **beyond reasonable doubt**/*(Am)* **beyond a reasonable doubt**, there is enough proof for the person accused of a crime to be judged guilty: *Her guilt was established beyond reasonable doubt and she was sentenced to five years in prison.* • If you know or believe something **beyond a shadow of a doubt**, you are certain that it is true: *He is responsible beyond a shadow of a doubt.* ○ *They knew beyond a shadow of a doubt that they were going to win the match.* • *Suddenly she was rich* **beyond** *her* **wildest dreams** (=She was richer than she had ever thought possible).

BFPO /£ˌbiː·ef·piːˈəʊ, $-ˈoʊ/ *n* [U] *abbreviation for* British Forces Post Office • *BFPO is used as part of an address for letters sent to members of the British armed forces living in other countries.*

bi– [TWICE] /baɪ-/ *combining form* twice, or once every two • *We meet bi-monthly* (=twice every month or once every two months). • [LP] **Two**

bi– [TWO] /baɪ-/ *combining form* having two • *a biped* (=an animal which walks on two legs) • *a biplane* (=an old-fashioned aircraft with two wings)

bi·an·nu·al /baɪˈæn·ju·əl/ *adj* [before n; not gradable] happening twice a year • *He holds a biannual exhibition of his work in Milan.* • *The committee has just published its biannual report on major building projects.* • Compare ANNUAL; BIENNIAL.

bi·as [PREFERENCE] /ˈbaɪ·əs/ *n* a tendency to support or oppose a particular person or thing in an unfair way by allowing personal opinions to influence your judgment • *The government has accused the media of bias.* [U] • *Reporters must be impartial and not show political bias.* [U] • *A committee has been established to address the problem of racial and sexual bias within the industry.* [U] • *There was clear evidence of a strong bias* **against** *the workers in the news report.* [C usually sing] • *There has always been a slight bias* **in favour of/towards** *employing arts graduates in the company.* [C usually sing] • If someone has or shows a bias towards a particular subject or thing, they prefer it to other things: *She showed a scientific bias at an early age.* [C usually sing]

bi·as *obj* /ˈbaɪ·əs/ *v* [T] **-ss-** or *Am usually* **-s-** • *Both sides were given an equal opportunity to express their views in the programme, an approach which does not bias the reporting* (=does not let it show unfair support for one side). • *The judge ruled that the information should be withheld on the grounds that it would bias the jury* **against** (=influence them unfairly against) *the accused.*

bi·ased, *esp. Br* **bi·assed** /ˈbaɪ·əst/ *adj* • If someone is biased, they show an unreasonable preference or dislike for a person or group of people based on personal opinions: *The police should not be biased in any way.* ○ *The newspapers gave a very biased report of the meeting.* ○ *I think she's very intelligent, but then I am slightly biased since she's my sister.*

bi·as [CLOTHING] /ˈbaɪ·əs/ *n* [U] *specialized* a direction diagonally across the threads of woven material • *The dresses in his new winter collection are all cut* **on the bias** (=in a diagonal direction across the cloth). • *She uses bias-***cutting** *techniques to give the clothes grace and fluidity.* • *The jacket has bias-***cut** *sleeves.*

bi·ath·lon /£baɪˈæθ·lən, $-lɑːn/ *n* [C] a sporting event in which the competitors must SKI (=travel over snow) along a 20-kilometre area of land carrying a gun and shoot at four fixed objects • Compare DECATHLON; HEPTATHLON; PENTATHLON.

bib /bɪb/, **feed·er** *n* [C] a cover made of cloth or plastic which is worn by young children when eating to prevent their clothes from getting dirty • *He's just spilt apple juice all down his bib.* • *(dated)* Your **best bib and tucker** means your best clothes which you wear on special occasions.

Bi·ble /ˈbaɪ·bl̩/, **Ho·ly Bi·ble** *n* (a copy of) the holy book of the Christian religion consisting of the Old and New Testaments, or the holy book of the Jewish religion consisting of the Law, the Prophets and the Writings • *In* **the** *Bible it says that Adam and Eve were the first human beings.* [U] • *He studies* **the** *Bible every day.* [U] • *Her parents gave her a bible when she was a young child.* [C] • *He used to give out the bibles and hymn books in church.* [C] • *Bible-***reading** *classes are held in the church hall every Thursday evening.* • A bible is also a book which gives important advice and information about a particular subject: *Vogue magazine quickly became the bible of fashionable women.* [C] • *(infml disapproving)* A **Bible-basher**/*(esp. Am)* **Bible-thumper** is a person who tries in a forceful or enthusiastic way to persuade other people to believe in Christianity and to believe that what the Bible says is true: *He is an evangelical minister who has been described by the press as a Bible-basher.* ○ *I get really fed up with all her* **Bible-bashing**/*(esp. Am)* **Bible-thumping** (= forceful or enthusiastic attempts to persuade other people to believe in Christianity). • The **Bible Belt** is the southern and central regions of the United States where many people have traditional Christian beliefs and believe that what is written in the Bible is completely true.

bib·li·cal /ˈbɪb·lɪ·kᵊl/ *adj* [not gradable] • Biblical means in or relating to the Bible: *They named their son Isaac after the biblical character.* ○ *She has traced the history of the Christian religion from biblical* **times** (= the time in which Jesus was said to have lived) *to the present day.* • **In the biblical sense** refers to the original meaning of a word as it is used in the first English form of the Bible: *'To know' in the biblical sense means to have sex.* ○ *Simon and I are living together – but not in the biblical sense* (= we are not sexual partners).

bib·li·og·ra·phy /£ˌbɪb·liˈɒg·rə·fi, $-ˈɑː·grə-/ *n* [C] a list of the books and articles that have been used by someone when writing a particular book or article • *Other sources of information are found in the bibliography at the end of this article.*

bib·li·o·phile /ˈbɪb·li·ə·faɪl/ *n* [C] *fml* a person who loves or collects books

bi·cam·er·al /£ˌbaɪˈkæm·ᵊr·ᵊl, $-ɚ·əl/ *adj* [not gradable] *specialized* (of a government group) with two parts, such as the Senate and the House of Representatives in the United States • *The country is governed by a bicameral Federal Parliament.*

bi·car·bo·nate of so·da /£baɪˈkɑː·bᵊn·et-, $-ˈkɑːr-/, *infml* **bi·carb** /£ˈbaɪ·kɑːb, $-kɑːrb/, **so·di·um bi·car·bo·nate**, *Am and Aus also* **bak·ing so·da** *n* [U] a white powder used to make foods rise in baking, and sometimes to cure stomach pains or stop small fires burning • *Mix together 250g plain flour and a teaspoon of bicarbonate of soda and then add to the cake mixture.*

bi·cen·te·na·ry /£ˌbaɪ·senˈten·ᵊr·i, £-ˈtiː·nᵊr-, $ˈten·ɚ-/, *esp. Am* **bi·cen·ten·ni·al** /ˌbaɪ·senˈten·i·əl, -ˈtiː·ni-/ *n* [C] the day or year which is 200 years after a particular event, esp. an important one; the 200th ANNIVERSARY • *A statue was erected to mark the bicentenary* **of** *the composer's birth.* • *A fireworks display and open-air concert has been planned for the bicentenary celebrations.*

bi·ceps /ˈbaɪ·seps/ *n* [C] *pl* **biceps** the large muscle at the front of the upper arm • *He has bulging biceps from spending hours at the gym every day.* • Compare TRICEPS.

bick·er /£ˈbɪk·əʳ, $-ɚ/ *v* [I] *disapproving* to argue about unimportant matters • *Will you two stop bickering!* • *They're always bickering* **with** *each other* **about/over** *their personal problems.*

bick·er·ing /£ˈbɪk·ᵊr·ɪŋ, $ˈ-ɚ-/ *n* [U] *disapproving* • *The council finally elected a leader after several days of bickering.* • *He left the company because he couldn't stand the constant bickering* **between** *the staff and the managers.*

bick·ie *Br and Aus* /ˈbɪk·i/, *Aus also* **bik·kie** *n* [C] *infml for* BISCUIT [FLAT CAKE] • *I've bought a packet of choccy* (= chocolate) *bickies for tea.*

bi·cy·cle /ˈbaɪ·sɪ·kl̩/, *infml* **bike**, *fml* **cy·cle** *n* [C] a two-wheeled vehicle that is moved by using the feet to turn PEDALS (= the parts of the vehicle which supply power to the wheels) • *I go to work* **by** *bicycle.* • *He* **got on** *his bicycle and rode off.* • *You should never* **ride** *your bicycle without lights at night.* • *Do you want to come on a bicycle* **ride** *tomorrow?* • *She put her books in her bicycle* **basket**. • *My tyres are flat. Can I borrow your bicycle* **pump**? • A **women's/ladies'** bicycle has a low diagonal bar between the seat and the HANDLEBARS rather than a high horizontal one. • [PIC] **Basket, Bicycles**

bid *(obj)* [OFFER] /bɪd/ *v* **bidding**, *past* **bid** to offer (a particular amount of money) for something which is for sale and compete against other people to buy it, esp. at a public sale of goods or property • *She knew she could not afford the table which was being auctioned, so she did not bid.* [I] • *The communications group has shown an interest in bidding* **for** *the company.* [I] • *A foreign collector has bid £500 000* **for** *the portrait.* [T] • *What am I bid* **for** *this fine vase?* [+ two objects] • If two or more people bid for a job, they compete with each other to do the work by offering to do it for a particular amount of money: *The department is trying to ensure fairer competition among firms bidding* **for** *government contracts.* [I] • If someone bids to do something, they compete with other people to do it: *Paris is bidding* **to** *host the next Olympics.* [+ *to* infinitive] ○ *Scotland is bidding* **against** *England* **to** *host the world championships next year.* [+ *to* infinitive]

bid /bɪd/ *n* [C] • A bid is an offer of a particular amount of money for something which is for sale: *I made a bid of $150* **for** *the painting.* ○ *She* **made/put in** *a bid of £69 000 for the flat, which was accepted.* • A bid is also an offer to do something when you are competing with other people to do it: *Sydney* **made** *a successful bid* **to** *host the Olympic Games in the year 2000.* [+ *to* infinitive] ○ *I gave the job to the contractors who* **made/gave** *the lowest bid* (= who offered to do the work for the lowest amount of money). • A bid **for** something is an attempt to achieve or obtain it: *Her bid for re-election was unsuccessful.* ○ *He struggled with a prison guard and made a sudden bid for freedom.* ○ *She has given over $1 million to charity in a bid for respectability.* ○ *The company has managed to fight off a hostile* **takeover** *bid* (= to stop another company from obtaining control of it). • A bid **to** do something is an attempt to do it: *The government has reduced the cost of borrowing in a bid* **to** *get the economy moving again.* [+ *to* infinitive] ○ *The president has suspended parliament for a month in a* **desperate** *bid* **to** *prevent a serious challenge to his presidency.* [+ *to* infinitive]

bid·der /£ˈbɪd·əʳ, $-ɚ/ *n* [C] • *In an auction, goods or property is sold to the* **highest** *bidder* (= the person who offers the most money for it).

bid·ding /ˈbɪd·ɪŋ/ *n* [U] • *Most of the bidding at the auction was done by telephone.* • If someone **opens** the bidding at a public sale of goods, they make the first offer of money for an object on sale: *Who will open the bidding for this delightful 18th century bookcase?*

bid *obj* [TELL] /bɪd/ *v* [T] **bidding**, *past simple* **bid** or **bade** /bæd/, *past part* **bidden** /ˈbɪd·ᵊn/ or **bid** *fml or dated* to give (a greeting) to (someone), or to ask (someone) to do something • *They bade her good morning.* [+ two objects] • *I must now bid you* **farewell** (= say goodbye to you). [+ two objects] • *(literary) She bade her hopes* **farewell** (= She stopped being hopeful). [+ two objects] • *The king and queen had bidden* (= invited) *guests from all over the kingdom to their daughter's christening.* • *He bade* (= asked) *them* **(to)** *leave at once.* [+ obj + (*to*) infinitive]

bid·ding /ˈbɪd·ɪŋ/ *n* [U] *fml or dated* • **At** *my grandmother's bidding* (= request), *I wore my best dress.* • *You must* **do** (= obey) *your father's bidding* (= orders), *young man.*

bid·dy /ˈbɪd·i/ *n* [C] *infml disapproving* an old woman • *That stupid* **old** *biddy should mind her own business.*

bide *obj* /baɪd/ *v* [T] **bide** *your* **time** to wait patiently for a good opportunity to do something • *She was biding her time until she could get her revenge.*

bi·det /£ˈbiː·deɪ, $bɪˈdeɪ/ *n* [C] a small low bath in which a person washes their bottom and sex organs • [LP] **'-et' words**

bi·en·ni·al /baɪˈen·i·əl/ *adj* [not gradable] happening once every two years • Compare ANNUAL; BIANNUAL.

bi·en·ni·al /baɪˈen·i·əl/ *n* [C] • A biennial is a plant that lives for two years, producing seeds and flowers in its second year. • Compare ANNUAL; PERENNIAL [PLANT].

bier /£bɪəʳ, $bɪr/ *n* [C] a movable frame on which a dead body or a COFFIN (= a box for holding a dead body) is carried before a funeral

biff *obj* /bɪf/ *v* [T] *infml* to hit (someone), esp. with the FIST (= the hand with the fingers held tightly in) • *I biffed him hard in the stomach.*

biff /bɪf/ *n* [C] *infml* • *I'll give you a biff* (= a hit) *on the nose if you don't shut up.*

bi·fo·cals /£ˌbaɪˈfəʊ·kᵊlz, $-ˈfoʊ-/ *pl n* glasses with LENSES (= curved pieces of glass which improve your sight) that are divided into two parts. The upper half is for looking at things far away and the lower half is for reading or for looking at things that are near

bi·fo·cal /£ˌbaɪˈfəʊ·kᵊl, $-ˈfoʊ-/ *adj* [not gradable] • *bifocal lenses* • *If you are both short-sighted and long-sighted, you need bifocal spectacles or contact lenses.*

bi·fur·cate *(obj)* /£ˈbaɪ·fə·keɪt, $-fɚ-/ *v fml* (of roads, rivers, branches) to divide into two parts • *A sample of water was taken from the point where the river bifurcates.* [I] • *(fig.) The responsibility for policing the region was bifurcated* (= divided) *between the secretary of state and the secretary of the interior.* [T]

big [LARGE] /bɪg/ *adj* **bigger, biggest** large in size or amount • *He was a big, burly man.* • *My sister's much bigger than I am.* • *Could I try these shoes in a bigger size?* • *They live in a big house in the country.* • *He has blonde hair and*

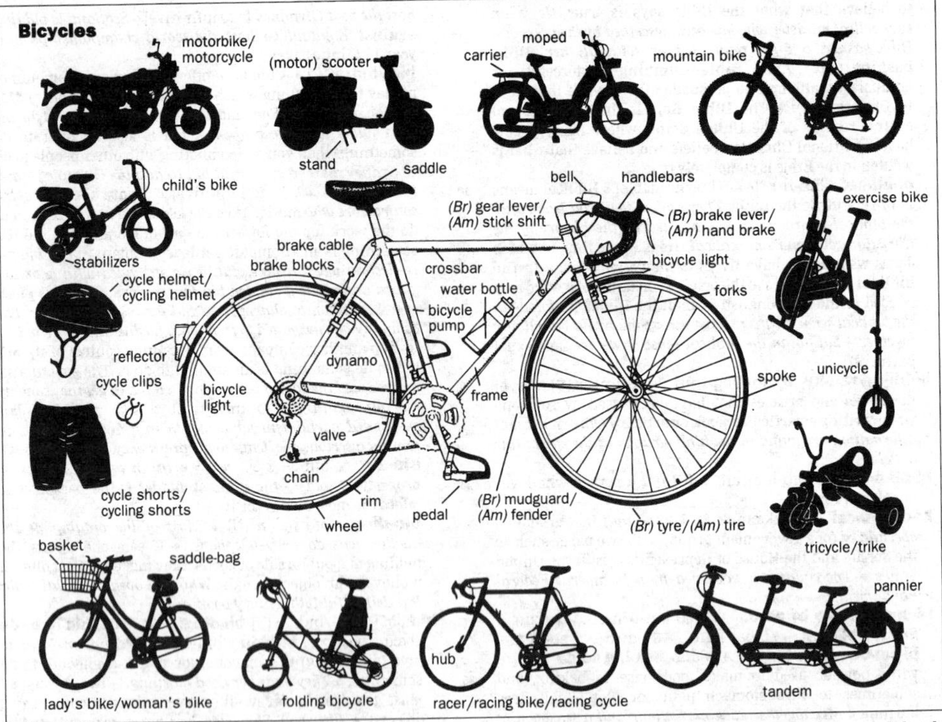

big blue eyes. • *She was offered a big increase in salary to stay with the company.* • *More and more people have been coming to the big cities looking for work.* • *I had a* **great** *big slice of chocolate cake for tea.* • *350 people took part in the region's biggest-***ever** *cycle race.* • *(infml) You write August with a big* (= capital) *'a'.* • *(infml) She's always been a big* **spender** (= She has always spent a lot of money). • *(infml) You're not a very big* **eater**, *are you?* (= You do not eat a lot). • *(infml)* Big can also mean older or more like an adult: *He wanted to play with the big* (= older) *boys.* See also **big boys** at BIG [IMPORTANT]. ○ *Her big* (= older) **sister/brother** *told her to go away.* ○ *(fig.) The magazine has now found its own style and direction after several months of emulating its big* **brother/sister** *in the States* (= copying the style of the magazine which was owned by the same company and begun before it). See also **Big Brother** at BIG [IMPORTANT]. ○ *Don't cry – you're a big girl now* (= You are too old to cry). ○ *I'm ashamed of you. You're big enough to know better* (= at an age where you should know that your behaviour is not acceptable). • *(infml)* Big can also be used to add emphasis: *You're a big* (= such a) *bully!* ○ *He fell for her* **in a** *big* **way** (= He was greatly attracted to her). • *(infml)* If someone is **big on** something, they like it very much: *I'm not very big on classical music.* • *(infml disapproving)* If you say that something that someone has done for a particular person was **really/very big of** them, you mean that you do not think it was very generous: *"I let him stay on my floor when he came to visit." "That was very big of you."* ○ *It was really big of him* **to** *buy me a cup of tea.* [+ *to* infinitive] • *He likes getting big presents –* **the bigger the better** *as far as he's concerned* (= he thinks that something that is bigger must be more valuable or desirable). • *(infml)* New York City is sometimes known as **the Big Apple**: *She found that Tokyo was more than twice as expensive to live in as the Big Apple.* ○ *He's planning to visit the States and* **take a bite of** *the Big Apple* (= become familiar with New York). • A **big band** is a group of musicians who play jazz and dance music: *He plays the saxophone in a big band.* ○ *Big band* **music** *was very popular during the 1930s and 40s.* • The **big bang theory** is the belief that the universe originated as the result of a large explosion of a single mass of matter. • *(Am infml)* The **Big Board** is the New York Stock Exchange (= the place where parts of the ownership of companies are bought and sold): *In Big Board composite trading yesterday, the company's shares closed at $44·50.* • *(Br and Aus)* A **big dipper** *(esp. Am* **roller coaster***)* is a type of small railway in an amusement park with carriages that travel very quickly along a narrow track that slopes and bends suddenly. • **Big Dipper** is also *Am for* **the Plough**. See at PLOUGH [STARS]. • *(Br and Aus specialized)* A **big end** in a car engine is the larger end of a rod that connects the PISTONS (= the tubes that send the power to the wheels) to the CRANKSHAFT (= the main rod in a car engine). • **Big game** means large wild animals when hunted and shot for sport: *Tour operators are encouraging people to go to the region's unspoilt forests to hunt big game.* • If someone is **big-hearted**, they are kind and generous: *The film has been very popular among children, with its evil villain, big-hearted hero and exciting plot.* • *(infml)* **Big money**/*(esp. Am)* **Big bucks**/*(Aus also)* **Big bickies** means a large amount of money: *It'd cost big money to fund a project like that.* ○ *Tournaments need to offer big bucks prize money to attract top players.* • *(infml disapproving)* If someone is or has a **big mouth**, they tend to say things which are meant to be kept secret: *You've got such a big mouth.* ○ *Just keep your big mouth* **shut** *and don't say anything to her!* ○ *He went and* **opened** *his big mouth and told them the whole story.* • *(infml)* The **Big Smoke** means a large city, esp. London: *I wouldn't like to live in the Big Smoke.* • Your **big toe** is the largest toe on your foot. • A **big top** is the main tent in a CIRCUS (= a show with acts of skill and danger). • *(Br)* A **big wheel** *(Am and Aus* **ferris wheel***)* in an amusement park is a large vertical wheel with seats, for people to sit on, which stay horizontal as the wheel turns round. • *(infml)* A **big word** is a long, difficult word, or a word which expresses a serious or important idea: *He tried to impress his teachers by using big words in all his essays.* ○ *When I told her we needed a new computer system, she said that 'need' was a big word and that although we might like a new system, we didn't need one.* • *"Oh Grandmama! What big eyes you've got." "All the better to see you with." "Oh Grandmama! What big teeth you've got." "All the better to eat you with."* (from the fairy story *Little Red Riding Hood*) • [LP] **Measurements**

big [IMPORTANT] /bɪɡ/ *adj* **bigger, biggest** important, because of being powerful, influential or having a serious effect • *He had a big decision to make about his future.* • *There's a big difference between starting up a business and just talking about it.* • *The big story in the news this week is the minister's resignation.* • *Tonight's big game is between Real Madrid and Nottingham Forest.* See also **big game** at BIG [LARGE]. • *The four big high street banks are all planning to cut their staffing levels.* • *It's taken us four years to complete this project, so today's a big day for us.* • *(infml)*

The **big day** is also the day when you get married: *When's the big day, then?* • *(infml)* To be big **in** a place or type of work is to be important or famous in that place or that type of work: *They're big in Japan, but no one's heard of them here.* ○ *She's big in marketing and owns three major companies.* • *(infml)* If a product or activity is big, it is extremely popular: *Grunge music was very big in the early 1990s.* • *(infml)* If you say **big deal** to someone, you mean that you do not think that what they have said or done is important or special: *So you've got a part-time job in the supermarket? Big deal!* ○ *"I ran five miles this morning." "Big deal! I ran ten."* • *(infml)* If you say that something is **no big deal**, you do not think it is important or special: *"I was really sorry to hear about your accident." "Oh, it was no big deal* (= it was not serious) *– I just had a few cuts and bruises."* • *(infml)* Someone who **has big ideas** about something has plans for their future which will require great effort, skill and luck to be achieved: *She's got big ideas* **about** *becoming a football manager.* • *(infml)* If you say to someone **what's the big idea**, you want to know why they have done something annoying: *Don't turn the TV off – I was watching it. What's the big idea?* • *(infml disapproving)* If someone is **too big for** their **boots**, they behave as if they are more important than they really are: *Since he got that promotion, he's been getting much too big for his boots.* • *(infml)* If someone **makes it big**, they become famous or successful. • *(infml)* The **big boys** are the most important people in an activity or organization, or the most powerful and influential businesses in a particular area: *He started off playing in junior competitions, but now he's up there with the big boys playing in international matches.* ○ *We're only a small business and don't have the capital to compete with the big boys.* • **Big Brother** is a government, ruler or person in authority that has complete power and that tries to control people's behaviour and thoughts and limit their freedom: *The introduction of police speed cameras on main roads has left many people with the impression that we are entering a Big Brother society.* • **Big business** is powerful and influential businesses and financial organizations when considered as a group: *The president believes in strengthening the ties between big business and the community.* ○ *The party receives most of its financial support from big business.* • If something is **big business**, it makes a lot of money: *Health clubs are big business these days.* ○ *Private publishing is big business – a rough estimate is that one book in ten is printed privately.* • *(infml)* A **big fish/gun/noise/shot** is a person who has an important or powerful position in a group or organization: *He's a big shot in the city* (= in the financial world). ○ *You might have been a big fish* **in a small pond** *at school, but you'll feel lost when you first go to university.* • *(disapproving)* If someone is/has a **big-head** or is **big-headed**, they think that they are cleverer or more important than they are: *He's always boasting. He's such a big-head!* Compare **swollen head** at SWOLLEN [LARGER]. ○ *She's so big-headed!* Compare **swollen-headed** at SWOLLEN [LARGER]. • *(infml)* The **big league** is the top level of a particular sport, business or activity in which there is the greatest competition and the greatest opportunity for success: *He is about to join the big league of Formula 1 in time for the start of the new season at the South African Grand Prix.* ○ *For the magazine to be successful, it will have to compete in the big league against leading weekly women's magazines.* ○ *We're not playing at local politics here – this is big league stuff.* • *(Am infml)* The **Big Mo** is the force which keeps an event developing after a start has been made: *The Democrats are determined to* **keep up** *the Big Mo in the election campaign.* • *(infml)* A **big name** is a famous or important person: *Are there any big names in the movie?* ○ *She's a big name* **in politics**. • *(infml)* **The big time** is the state of being famous or successful: *She wanted to* **hit** *the big time* (= become famous or successful). ○ *You've really* **made** *the big time now* (= become famous or successful). ○ *He's one of the big-time boys now* (= He is rich and successful). • *(saying)* 'The bigger they are, the harder they fall' means that the more important or powerful a person is, the more difficult it is for them when they lose that power or important position. • *"Big Brother is watching you"* (George Orwell in the novel *1984*, 1949)

big·gie /ˈbɪg·i/ *n* [C] *infml* • A biggie is something which is very important or successful: *The new Arnold Schwarzenegger movie will be the Hollywood biggie this summer.* ○ *Of all the company's products, this one's* **the** *biggie.*

bi·ga·my /ˈbɪg·ə·mi/ *n* [U] the crime of marrying a person while already legally married to someone else • *In court, he admitted that he had* **committed** *bigamy with a woman when he was living in Canada.* • Compare MONOGAMY; POLYGAMY.

bi·ga·mist /ˈbɪg·ə·mɪst/ *n* [C] • *He was accused of being a bigamist for having married his second wife before being legally divorced from his first wife.*

bi·ga·mous /ˈbɪg·ə·məs/ *adj* [not gradable] • *a bigamous marriage*

bi·ga·mous·ly /ˈbɪg·ə·mə·sli/ *adv* [not gradable] • *She has been married four times, once bigamously.*

Big·foot /ˈbɪg·fʊt/, **Sas·quatch** /ˈsæs·kwætʃ/ *n* [C] a large hairy human-like creature reported to exist in the NW United States and W Canada

bi·got /ˈbɪg·ət/ *n* [C] *disapproving* a person who has strong, unreasonable beliefs and who thinks that anyone who does not have the same beliefs is wrong • *a religious bigot* • *He was known to be a loud-mouthed, opinionated bigot.*

bi·got·ed /£ˈbɪg·ə·tɪd, $-t̬ɪd/ *adj disapproving* • *She's so bigoted that she refuses to accept anyone who doesn't think like her.*

big·ot·ry /ˈbɪg·ə·tri/ *n* [U] *disapproving* • *religious/racial bigotry* • *The organization is dedicated to fighting bigotry and racism in America.* • *Commentators believe there is no other reason for the latest killings than a renewed wave of bigotry and hatred.*

big·wig /ˈbɪg·wɪg/ *n* [C] *infml* a person who has an important or powerful position • *We were invited to a lunch with* **local** *bigwigs.* • *She has called a meeting of* **party** *bigwigs to discuss their strategy for the next election.*

bi·jou /ˈbiː·ʒuː/ *adj* [before n] (esp. of a building) small but attractive and fashionable • *The harbour front is lined with bijou cafés and bars.* • *The estate agent described the flat as a bijou* **residence**.

bike /baɪk/ *n* [C] *infml* a bicycle • *It would be better for the environment if more people used bikes rather than cars.* • *My youngest child is learning how to* **ride** *a bike.* • *I can't* **get on** *this bike because the seat is too high.* • *This must be a* **child's** *bike – it's far too small for me.* • A bike can also be a motorcycle: *He's got a brand new 750 cc bike.* • *(Br slang)* **On your bike**/*(not standard)* **On yer bike** means go away. • *(esp. Br)* A **bike shed** (also **cycle shed**) is a small building in which bicycles are stored: *Your bike will be more secure if you leave it in the bike sheds.* ○ *One of the teachers caught them smoking behind the bike sheds at school.* • *"I grew up in the Thirties with our unemployed father. He did not riot, he got on his bike and looked for work"* (Norman Tebbit, 1981) • [PIC] **Bicycles** (J)

bike /baɪk/ *v* [I] *infml* • *Should we bike to the park* (= go there by bicycle), *or walk?*

bik·er /£ˈbaɪ·kəʳ, $-kɚ/ *n* [C] *infml* • A biker is someone who rides a motorcycle or bicycle: *This path can be used by bikers or people on foot.* • See also BIKER.

bik·er *Br and Am* /£ˈbaɪ·kəʳ, $-kɚ/, *Aus* **bik·ie** /ˈbaɪ·ki/ *n* [C] *infml* a member of a GANG (= group) of motorcyclists • *We were overtaken by a crowd of bikers doing over 90 mph.* • See also **biker** at BIKE.

bi·ki·ni /bɪˈkiː·ni/ *n* [C] a two-piece **swimming costume** for women • *a bikini top* • *bikini bottoms/briefs* • *One-piece swimming costumes are more fashionable than bikinis this year.* • *The beach was full of bikini-***clad** *women* (= women dressed in bikinis) *trying to improve their tans.*

bik·kie /ˈbɪk·i/ *n* [C] *Aus infml for* BISCUIT [FLAT CAKE]

bi·la·bi·al /ˌbaɪˈleɪ·bi·əl/ *adj* [not gradable] *specialized* (of a sound) made using both lips • *'P' is a bilabial consonant.*

bi·lat·er·al /£ˌbaɪˈlæt·əʳ·əl, $-ˈlæt̬·ɚ-/ *adj* [not gradable] involving two groups or countries • *Canada and the United States have been negotiating a bilateral free-trade deal.* • *France and Germany have signed a bilateral* **agreement** *to help prevent drug smuggling.* • Compare MULTILATERAL; UNILATERAL.

bil·ber·ry /£ˈbɪl·bəʳr·i, $-ber-/ *n* [C] (the dark blue fruit of) a small bush which grows wild in Great Britain and N Europe, similar to a BLUEBERRY

bil·by /ˈbɪl·bi/ *n* [C] a type of RAT which lives in Australia and which has grey fur and long ears like a rabbit

bile /baɪl/ *n* [U] a bitter golden-yellow liquid produced by the LIVER (= a large organ in the body which cleans the blood) which helps to digest fats, or *(fig.)* bitterness or anger • *Meat-eaters must produce extensive bile* **acids** *in their intestines to properly digest the meat that they eat.* • *(fig.) His article was full of loathing and bile.* • *(fig.) She* *reserves her bile for her former political colleague, whose politics she now describes as "the vilest on earth".*

bi·li·ous /ˈbɪl·i·əs/ *adj* • Bilious means relating to an illness caused by too much bile, which can cause vomiting: *She suffered from bilious* **attacks.** • If someone is bilious, they are always in a bad mood: *He was a bilious old gentleman.* • Something which is bilious is extremely unpleasant: *His shirt was a bilious shade of green.*

bilge [TALK] /bɪldʒ/ *n* [U] *dated slang* worthless talk; nonsense • *Don't talk such bilge!*

bilge [SHIP] /bɪldʒ/ *n* [C usually pl] the bottom inside part of a ship where dirty water collects • *The bilges had been pumped and the ship was ready to set sail once again.* • **Bilge water** is the dirty water that collects in the bottom inside part of a ship.

bi·lin·gual /baɪˈlɪŋ·gwəl/ *adj* [not gradable] (of a person) able to use two languages for communication, or (of a thing) using or involving two languages • *She works as a bilingual secretary for an insurance company.* • *They have just published a major new edition of their French English bilingual dictionary.* • Compare MONOLINGUAL; MULTILINGUAL; TRILINGUAL.

bill [REQUEST FOR PAYMENT] /bɪl/ *n* [C] a request for payment of money owed, or the piece of paper on which it is written • *an electricity/gas/phone bill* • *They sent us a bill* **for** *the work they had done.* • *They asked the waitress for the bill.* • *Could we have the bill, please?* • *Her mother agreed to* **foot** (=pay) *the bill.* • *She* **ran up** (=caused herself to have) *a huge phone bill talking to her boyfriend for hours.* • [PIC> **Bill** Ⓣ

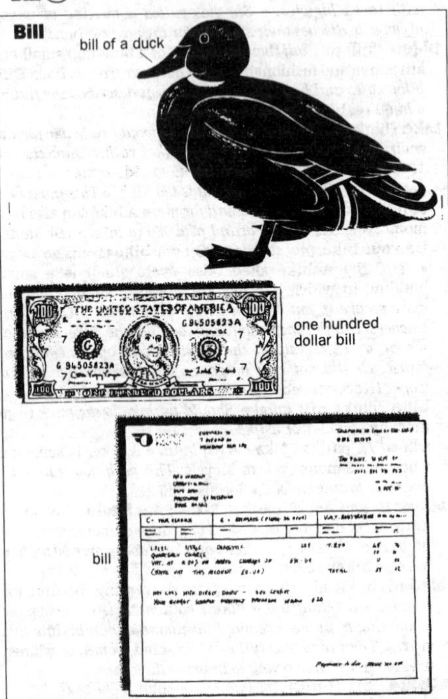

bill *obj* /bɪl/ *v* [T] • *Bill me* (=Give me a bill) *for any expenses you incur.*

bill·ing /ˈbɪl·ɪŋ/ *n* [U] • *itemized* (=detailed) *billing*

bill [MONEY] *esp. Am* /bɪl/, *Br and Aus usually* **note** *n* [C] a piece of paper money • *a* **dollar/one-dollar** *bill* • *a* **ten-dollar** *bill* • See also BILLFOLD. • [LP> **Money** [PIC> **Bill** Ⓣ

bill [LAW] /bɪl/ *n* [C] a formal statement of a planned new law that is discussed by a parliament before being voted on • *The bill was* **amended** (=changed). • *When a bill is* **passed** *in parliament it becomes law.* • *(infml) The bill was* **thrown out** *on first reading* (=it did not go past the first stage of discussion and will not become law). • **A bill of rights** is a statement of the basic laws which are meant to protect a country's citizens from injustice. • Ⓣ

bill [NOTICE] /bɪl/ *n* [C] a notice giving information about esp. an event or performance • *The sign 'Post no bills' means it is forbidden to stick notices on the wall.* • *There were lots of big names* **on the bill** (=famous people in the performance). • To **head/top the bill** is to be the most important actor in a show. • To **fill/fit the bill** is to be exactly what is needed in a certain situation: *That box will fill the bill nicely.* • *(dated)* In a restaurant a **bill of fare** is a MENU. • A **bill poster** or a **bill sticker** is someone who sticks notices onto walls. **Bill posting** is the activity of doing this. • Ⓣ

bill *obj* /bɪl/ *v* [T] • To bill someone is to describe them, esp. on a theatre poster: *They billed her* **as** *'the woman with rubber bones'.* ○ *The young author was billed* **as** *'the new Beckett'.*

bill·ing /ˈbɪl·ɪŋ/ *n* [U] • Billing is information, esp. about a performance: *The film didn't receive much advance billing.* ○ *Unfortunately, the show never* **lived up to** (=was not as good as) *its billing.* • A person who has **star/top** billing is the star of the show.

bill [BIRD] /bɪl/ *n* [C] *specialized or fml* the beak of a bird • [PIC> **Bill** Ⓣ

bill /bɪl/ *v* [I] • *(humorous)* When two people **bill and coo** they kiss each other and quietly speak words of love.

Bill [POLICE] /bɪl/ *n* [U] **the (Old) Bill** *Br slang* the police • *He's in trouble with the Old Bill again.*

bil·la·bong /£ˈbɪl·ə·bɒŋ, $-bɑːŋ/ *n* [C] *Aus* a low area of ground where a river used to be, which only fills up with water when the river floods

bill·board /£ˈbɪl·bɔːd, $-bɔːrd/ *n* [C] *Aus and Am for* HOARDING [ADVERTISEMENT]

bil·let /ˈbɪl·ɪt/ *n* [C] a place for esp. soldiers to stay in for a short time • *I found a billet in a flimsy shelter with five other men who were lying side by side.* • *Our billets were about a mile out of town, in a row of farm cottages.* • (NL)

bil·let–doux /ˌbiː·jeɪˈduː/ *n* [C] *pl* **billets-doux** /ˌbiː·jeɪˈduː/ *humorous or literary* a love letter

bill·fold /£ˈbɪl·fəʊld, $-foʊld/ *n* [C] *Am for* WALLET

bill·hook /ˈbɪl·hʊk/ *n* [C] a tool with a wide blade on top of a long pole used for cutting branches off trees

bil·liards /£ˈbɪl·i·ədz, $ˈbɪl·jərdz/ *n* [U] a game played by two people on a table covered in green cloth in which a CUE (=a long pole) is used to hit balls against each other and into pockets around the table

bil·liard /£ˈbɪl·i·əd, $ˈbɪl·jərd/ *adj* [before n; not gradable] • *a billiard table* • *a billiard ball*

bil·lion /ˈbɪl·jən/ *n* [C] 1 000 000 000, or *(Br dated)* 1 000 000 000 000 • *Cosmetics is a billion dollar industry – the profits are huge,* • [LP> **Hundred** (CS)

bil·lion·aire /£ˌbɪl·jəˈneər, $-ˈner/ *n* [C] • A billionaire is a person who has at least 1 000 000 000 *(Br also* 1 000 000 000 000) in any country's money, or who owns land buildings or possessions worth this amount.

bil·low /£ˈbɪl·əʊ, $-oʊ/ *v* [I] to spread over a large area, or (esp. of items made of cloth) to become filled with air and appear to be larger • **Smoke** *billowed* **(out)** *from the burning building.* • *The sheets/shirts hanging on the line billowed in the breeze.* • *We watched the boats with their billowing sails.* • *(fig.) Their small disagreement soon billowed* (=quickly grew larger) **into** *a more serious conflict.* • *(fig.) Billowing* (=Quickly increasing) *corruption was one of the factors which led to civil war.*

bil·low /£ˈbɪl·əʊ, $-oʊ/ *n* [C usually pl] • *Billows* **of smoke** *blown across the road by the wind made my eyes water.*

bil·ly /ˈbɪl·i/, **bil·ly·can** /ˈbɪl·i·kæn/ *n* [C] *Br and Aus* a metal container used for cooking outside over a fire

bil·ly (club) /ˈbɪl·i/ *n* [C] *Am for* TRUNCHEON

bil·ly (goat) /ˈbɪl·i/ *n* [C] a male goat

bil·ly–o /£ˈbɪl·i·əʊ, $-oʊ/ *n* [U] **like billy-o** *Br and Aus dated slang* a lot or very quickly, strongly, etc. • *Run like billy-o!* • *We worked like billy-o to get it finished.*

bim·bo /£ˈbɪm·bəʊ, $-boʊ/ *n* [C] *pl* **bimboes** or **bimbos** *disapproving slang* a young woman considered to be attractive but not intelligent • *He went out with a succession of* **blonde** *bimbos.*

bi·month·ly /ˌbaɪˈmʌntθ·li/ *adj, adv* [not gradable] happening or appearing every two months or twice a month • *a bimonthly publication/report* • *The magazine is published bimonthly, with six issues a year.* • *To keep a close check on progress we will have a bimonthly meeting* (=a meeting every two weeks) *for the next three months.*

bin [WASTE] *Br and Aus* /bɪn/, *Am usually* **can** *n* [C] a container for waste • *a litter bin* • *a pedal bin* • *a rubbish bin* • *a wastepaper bin* • *The supermarket has installed* **recycling** *bins for old newspapers, bottles and cans.* • *Do you want this or shall I* **throw** *it* **in** *the bin?* • *He immediately* **consigned** *the letter* **to** *the bin.* • *(fig.) The* *project was* **consigned to** *the bin* (= it was not considered to be good and was not continued). • *(Br)* A bin is also a DUSTBIN. • *(Br)* A **bin bag/liner** is a **dustbin bag/liner**. See at DUSTBIN. • **Bin man** is *Br infml for* DUSTMAN.

bin *obj* /bɪn/ *v* [T] **-nn-** *Br* • *Shall I bin these old shoes* (= throw them in the bin)? • *"Do you want to keep this newspaper?" "No, bin it."*

bin STORAGE /bɪn/ *n* [C] a large storage container • *a bread bin* • *a compost bin* • *a grain/corn bin* • *storage bins*

bi·na·ry /£ˈbaɪ·nᵊr·i, $-nə-/ *adj* [not gradable] consisting of two parts • *Computers operate using* **binary numbers** (= the values 0 and 1).

bind *(obj)* TIE /baɪnd/ *v past* **bound** /baʊnd/ to tie tightly or to fasten • *They bound an umbrella* **to** *a pole to get some shade.* [T] • *(fig.) Jonas is inextricably bound* **to** *his mother – as her health deteriorates, so does his sanity.* [T] • *Use strong string to bind the bundles of sticks* **together**. [T] • *(fig.) The things which bind them* **together** *are greater than their differences.* [T] • *The prisoner was bound* **hand and foot**. [T] • To bind **(up)** a part of the body, esp. a part which is damaged, is to tie something round it: *He had already bound (a strip of cloth round) the wound when I arrived.* [T] • To bind the edges of something such as a jacket is to sew or stick material along it to make it stronger or to decorate it. [T] • To bind also means to make separate pieces of paper into a book: *There are several different ways to bind a book, for example you can stitch or stick the pages together.* [T] ○ See also BOOKBINDING. • To bind someone **to** secrecy or to a promise is to force them to keep the promise or secret: *His sister had been bound to secrecy.* [T] • When an egg or water is used esp. in cooking to bind something it provides a way of making everything stick together in a solid mass: *Use an egg to bind the stuffing.* [T] ○ *The mixture wouldn't bind* **(together)**. [I]

bind·er /£ˈbaɪn·dəʳ, $-dɚ/ *n* [C] • A binder is a removable hard cover in which papers or magazines are stored: *a leather/plastic binder* • A binder is also a BOOKBINDER.

bind·ing /ˈbaɪn·dɪŋ/ *n* • The binding of a book is the type of cover it has: *embossed leather bindings* [C] ○ *What kind of binding does the book have – is it hardback or softback?* [U] • Binding is also a thin strip of material which can be sewn along the edges of clothes or other objects. [U]

bound /baʊnd/ *adj* • *We found the girl in the bedroom bound* (= tied) **and gagged**. • *All fifteen volumes of the book, bound* (= covered) *in green leather, stood behind him on her writing table.*

-bound /-baʊnd/ *combining form* • A book which is -bound is covered or held together in the stated way: *a leather-bound book* ○ *a spiral-bound notebook* • Clothes or other objects which are -bound have the edges covered in the stated way: *leather-bound cuffs*

bind UNPLEASANT SITUATION /baɪnd/ *n* [U] *infml* a difficult situation in which you are prevented from acting as you might like • *Having to visit her every week is* **a** *terrible* **bind**. • *Borrowing money may* **put** *you* **in a** *real* **bind**.

bind·ing /ˈbaɪn·dɪŋ/ *adj* (esp. of an agreement) which cannot be legally avoided or stopped • *a binding agreement* • *The contract wasn't legally binding.*

bind·weed /ˈbaɪnd·wiːd/ *n* [U] a wild plant with white and pink flowers that twists itself around other plants as it grows

binge /bɪndʒ/ *n* [C] *infml* an occasion when an activity is done in an extreme way, esp. eating, drinking or spending money • *a drinking/eating/spending binge* • *The annual office binge* (= party) *is in December.* • To **go on a** binge is to drink a lot of alcohol in a short time. • A **shopping** binge is an occasion when you buy a lot of clothes, jewellery, etc. • *Her illness involved periods of* **binge-eating** *and then making herself sick.*

binge /bɪndʒ/ *v* [I] **binging** or **bingeing** *infml* • A person who binges eats in an uncontrolled way, sometimes as part of an illness: *I tend to binge* **on** *chocolate when I'm watching TV!* ○ *She went through periods of bingeing (also* **binge-eating**).

bin·go GAME /£ˈbɪŋ·gəʊ, $-goʊ/ *n* [U] a game in which prizes can be won by marking all the numbers on a card that match others that are chosen by chance

bin·go SURPRISE /£ˈbɪŋ·gəʊ, $-goʊ/ *exclamation infml* an expression of surprise and, usually, pleasure • *I was just about to borrow some money when bingo! – the cheque arrived.*

bi·noc·u·lars /£bɪˈnɒk·jʊ·ləz, $-ˈnɑː·kjʊ·lɚz/ *pl n* a pair of jointed tubes with glass at either end that you look through to see things far away • *a pair of binoculars* • *I watched the birds* **through** *my binoculars.*

bi·o- /£ˈbaɪ·əʊ-, $-oʊ-/ *combining form* connected with life and living things • *bioethics* • *biodiversity*

bi·o·chem·i·cal /£ˌbaɪ·əʊˈkem·ɪ·kəl, $-oʊˈ-/ *adj* connected with the chemistry of living things

bi·o·chem·i·cal·ly /£baɪ·əʊˈkem·ɪ·kli, $-oʊˈ-/ *adv*

bi·o·chem·is·try /£ˌbaɪ·əʊˈkem·ɪ·stri, $-oʊˈ-/ *n* [U] the scientific study of the chemistry of living things such as animals, plants, and body organs

bi·o·chem·ist /£ˌbaɪ·əʊˈkem·ɪst, $-oʊˈ-/ *n* [C]

bi·o·de·grad·a·ble /£ˌbaɪ·əʊ·dɪˈgreɪ·dɪ·bl̩, $ˌ-oʊ-/ *adj* able to decay naturally and harmlessly • *Biodegradable packaging helps to limit the amount of harmful chemicals released into the atmosphere.*

bi·o·de·grade /£ˌbaɪ·əʊ·dɪˈgreɪd, $ˌ-oʊ-/ *v* [I] • *Some plastics are designed to rot or biodegrade when their useful life is over.*

bi·o·feed·back /£ˌbaɪ·əʊˈfiːd·bæk, $-oʊˈ-/ *n* [U] a method by which a person learns to control their heart rate or other physical or mental processes by using information from recordings of those processes • *Stress-management techniques such as biofeedback, massage therapy and self-hypnosis have been used with some success.* • *By using biofeedback, people can shift the balance of electrically measured brain activity back and forth between hemispheres at will.* • *The biofeedback technique can help to reduce stress.*

bi·og·ra·phy /£baɪˈɒg·rə·fi, $-ˈɑː·grə-/ *n* the life story of a person written by someone else • *Famous people often have several very different biographies written about them.* [C] • *He wrote a biography* **of** *Churchill.* [C] • *Do you prefer biography* (= literature about people's life stories) *or fiction?* [U] • Compare AUTOBIOGRAPHY; HAGIOGRAPHY.

bi·og·raph·er /£baɪˈɒg·rə·fəʳ, $-ˈɑː·grə·fɚ/ *n* [C] • *Boswell was Dr Johnson's biographer* (= wrote his life story).

bi·o·graph·i·cal /£ˌbaɪ·əʊˈgræf·ɪ·kᵊl, $-oʊˈ-/ *adj* • *There was a biographical note about the author on the back of the book.*

bi·ol·o·gy /£baɪˈɒl·ə·dʒi, $-ˈɑː·lə-/ *n* [U] the scientific study of the natural processes of living things • *human biology* • *marine biology* • *molecular biology* • *social biology* • *I studied biology at university.* • *The book deals with the reproductive biology* **of** *the buffalo.*

bi·o·log·ic·al /£ˌbaɪ·əˈlɒdʒ·ɪ·kᵊl, $-ˈlɑː·dʒɪ-/ *adj* • Biological means connected with the natural processes of living things: *the biological sciences* ○ *The biological* **cycle/rhythm** *of a plant is affected by light and heat.* ○ *Eating is a biological* **necessity**! • Your **biological clock** is your body's natural habit of sleeping, eating, growing, etc. at particular times: *Doctors believe that sufferers from this disease have no control over their biological clocks, which appear not to respond to light or dark.* • *(infml)* When a woman talks about her **biological clock** or says her biological clock **is ticking (away)** she means that she is worried that she is getting too old to be able to reproduce. • **Biological control** is the use of one plant or animal to control another, esp. to prevent disease or damage. • A **biological father/mother/parent** is the parent who caused a person to be born, although they may not be their legal parent or the parent who raised them. • **Biological warfare** and **biological weapons** involve the use of living matter such as bacteria to seriously harm and kill people and animals and damage crops. • **Biological washing liquid/powder** uses ENZYMES (= natural chemicals) to remove dirt. See also **non-bio** at NON.

bi·o·log·ic·al·ly /£ˌbaɪ·əˈlɒdʒ·ɪ·kli, $-ˈlɑː·dʒɪ-/ *adv* • *biologically active/stable chemicals* • *biologically based/determined handicaps*

bi·ol·og·ist /£baɪˈɒl·ə·dʒɪst, $-ˈɑː·lə-/ *n* [C] • A biologist is a scientist who studies biology.

bi·on·ic /£baɪˈɒn·ɪk, $-ˈɑː·nɪk/ *adj* using artificial materials and methods to produce esp. a human activity or movement • *These patients were among the first to have a new operation to replace hopelessly damaged discs in the spine with bionic bubbles.* • *(humorous)* Bionic is also used to refer to a person who has greater powers of strength, speed etc. than seem to be possible for a human: *a bionic man/woman*

bi·o·phy·sics /£ˌbaɪ·əʊˈfɪz·ɪks, $-oʊˈ-/ *n* [U] the science that uses the laws and methods of physics to explain biology

bi·op·ic /£baɪˈɒp·ɪk, $-ˈɑː·pɪk/ *n* [C] *infml* a film about the life of a real person

bi·op·sy /£ˈbaɪ·ɒp·si, $-ɑːp-/ *n* [C] the examination of cells taken from a living body to find out about any disease it might have

bi·o·rhy·thm /£ˈbaɪ·əʊ·rɪ·ðᵊm, $ˈ-oʊ-/ *n* [C] a regular pattern of changes in part of an organism over a period of time • *During a long period of captivity or confinement your biorhythms can re-adjust to a time clock which may not be a 24-hour cycle.*

bi·o·sphere /£ˈbaɪ·əʊ·sfɪəʳ, $-oʊ·sfɪr/ *n* [U] *specialized* the part of the Earth's environment where life exists

bi·o·tech·nol·o·gy /£ˌbaɪ·əʊ·tekˈnɒl·ə·dʒi, $-oʊ·tekˈnɑː·lə-/ *n* [U] the use of living things, esp. cells and bacteria, in industrial processes • *The companies are pouring trillions of yen into biotechnology research, especially for pharmaceuticals and new seeds.* • *The first biotechnology patent was awarded for a bug that could be persuaded to 'digest' crude oil.*

bi·par·tis·an /£ˌbaɪˈpɑː·tɪ·zæn, $ˈpɑːr·t̬ɪ-/ *adj* [not gradable] supported by or consisting of two political parties • *There was a bipartisan agreement on the need for discussions.*

bi·ped /ˈbaɪ·ped/ *n* [C] *specialized* an animal with two feet • Compare QUADRUPED.

bi·plane /ˈbaɪ·pleɪn/ *n* [C] an early type of aircraft with two sets of wings, one above the other • Compare MONOPLANE. • [PIC]〉 **Aircraft**

bi·pol·ar de·pres·sion /£baɪˌpəʊ·ləʳ, $-ˌpoʊ·lɚ/ *n* [U] *specialized for* **manic depression**, see at MANIC.

birch [TREE] /£bɜːtʃ, $bɜːrtʃ/ *n* [C] a tree with a smooth, often white BARK (=outer covering) and thin branches

birch [PUNISHMENT] /£bɜːtʃ, $bɜːrtʃ/ *n* [U] **the birch** an official punishment in the past, which involved hitting a person across the bottom with a stick, or the stick itself • *Some politicians are in favour of* **bringing back** *the birch* (=allowing this punishment to happen again).

birch *obj* /£bɜːtʃ, $bɜːrtʃ/ *v* [T] • *"These young hooligans ought to be birched* (=hit with the birch)*," growled the old man.*

bird [CREATURE] /£bɜːd, $bɜːrd/ *n* [C] a creature with feathers and wings, usually able to fly • *caged/wild birds* • *migrating/migratory birds* • *nesting birds* • *sea birds* • *wading birds* • *Birds build nests and lay eggs in them in the spring.* • *The birds were* **chirping** *and* **squawking** *at four o'clock this morning!* • *Penguins and ostriches are* **flightless** *birds* (=they cannot fly). • *We watched a* **flock** *of birds wheeling and turning over the field.* • *He was very good at imitating bird* **calls**. • *The car had been parked under a tree and was covered with bird* **droppings**. • *She works at a small bird* **sanctuary** *on the east coast.* • *(humorous)* **The birds and the bees** means the basic facts about sex: *She's only six, but she knows about the birds and the bees.* • *(Am and Aus infml)* If something is **(strictly) for the birds** it is worthless or ridiculous. • To be **(as) free as a bird** is to feel completely free. • *(infml)* If you describe someone as a **bird-brain** or **bird-brained** you think they are stupid. • To have **a bird's eye view** is to look at something from very high up so that you see a large area below you: *Climb to the top of the Eiffel Tower if you want a bird's eye view* **of** *Paris.* • **Bird dog** is *Am for* **gun dog**. See at GUN. • A **bird of paradise** is a bird found in New Guinea, of which the male has brightly coloured feathers. • A **bird of passage** is a bird which MIGRATES (=moves from one area to another when the season changes). See also at BIRD [PERSON]. • A **bird of prey** is a bird, such as a HAWK or an EAGLE, that kills and eats small birds and animals. • A **bird-scarer** is a device or a person involved in keeping birds away, esp. from crops or airports. • A **bird table** is a raised structure outside a building on which food for wild birds is placed: *Lots of different birds visit our bird table in the winter months.* • **Bird-watching** is the hobby of studying wild birds in their natural surroundings. A person who does this is a **bird-watcher**. • *(saying)* 'A bird in the hand (is worth two in the bush)' means that you should not risk losing something you already have by trying to get something you think might be better. • *"She was only a bird in a gilded cage"* (title of a song written by A.J.Lamb, 1900) • *"Like a bird on a wire"* (song by Leonard Cohen, 1968) • See also DICKYBIRD; HUMMINGBIRD; SONGBIRD.

bird·like /£ˈbɜːd·laɪk, $ˈbɜːrd-/ *adj* • *He was a little birdlike man with a pointed nose and darting eyes.*

bird [PERSON] /£bɜːd, $bɜːrd/ *n* [C] *(infml)* a person of the type stated, or *(Br and Aus slang)* a (young) woman • *(infml) He's an* **odd/rare bird**. • *(infml)* An **old** bird is an older woman: *(disapproving) This* **old** *bird was lecturing the shop assistant about the way she had been spoken to.* ○ *(approving) She's a* **game** *old bird* (=unexpectedly energetic and willing to do risky things). • *(Br and Aus slang) Let's go down to the pub and see if we can* **pick up/pull** *a couple of birds.* • A **bird of passage** is a person who does not stay long in one place, job, etc.: *At present the organization has to rely on young, inexperienced graduates who are usually birds of passage.* See also at BIRD [CREATURE]. • *(slightly disapproving)* **Birds of a feather** are two people who are similar in character: *He'll get on well with Anthony – they're birds of a feather.* • *(saying)* 'Birds of a feather flock together' means people join together in an activity because they have similar characters or interests, esp. ones of which you disapprove. • *(saying)* 'The bird has/birds have flown' means that the person(s) you were looking for has/have gone away or escaped.

bird [PRISON] /£bɜːd, $bɜːrd/ *n* [U] **do bird** *Br, Aus dated slang* to spend time in prison

bird·cage /£ˈbɜːd·keɪdʒ, $ˈbɜːrd-/ *n* [C] a container in which birds are kept so that people can look at them • *We keep our budgies in a birdcage in the kitchen.*

bird·house /£ˈbɜːd·haʊs, $ˈbɜːrd-/ *n* [C] *pl* **birdhouses** /£ˈbɜːdˌhaʊ·zɪz, $ˈbɜːrd-/ *Am for* **nesting box**, see at NEST

bird·ie [BIRD] /£ˈbɜː·di, $ˈbɜːr-/ *n* [C] (a word used by or to children) a small bird • A photographer sometimes says to a child "**Watch the birdie**" wanting them to look at the camera to see the little light that appears there.

bird·ie [GOLF] /£ˈbɜː·di, $ˈbɜːr-/ *n* [C] (in golf) getting the ball into the hole in one shot (=hit) less than PAR (=the expected number) for that hole

bird·ie [NET GAME] /£ˈbɜː·di, $ˈbɜːr-/ *n* [C] *Am for* SHUTTLECOCK

bird·like /£ˈbɜːd·laɪk, $ˈbɜːrd-/ *adj* See at BIRD [CREATURE]

bird·seed /£ˈbɜːd·siːd, $ˈbɜːrd-/ *n* [U] seeds for feeding birds

bird·song /£ˈbɜːd·sɒŋ, $ˈbɜːrd·sɑːŋ/ *n* [U] the sound or calls of a bird or birds • *I wake each morning to the sound of birdsong.*

Bi·ro *esp. Br* /£ˈbaɪ·rəʊ, $-roʊ/ *n* [C] *pl* **Biros** *trademark* a type of BALLPOINT • *Can I borrow your biro for a minute?* • [PIC]〉 **Stationery, Writing instruments**

birth /£bɜːθ, $bɜːrθ/ *n* the occasion when a baby comes out of its mother's body • *The birth* **of** *their first child was a joyous occasion.* [C] • *More men are present* **at the** *births of their children these days.* [C] • *The sheep died soon after the birth of her lambs.* [C] • *Their son weighed eight pounds* **at** *birth.* [U] • *The application form will ask for your* **country/place of** *birth* (=where you were born). [U] • *Oscar Wilde was Irish* **by birth** (=he was born in Ireland). • A birth is also a child which is born: *The percentage of* **live** *births* (=children who are born alive and continue to live) *continues to increase.* [C] ○ *Registration of births* **and deaths** *became compulsory in 1871.* [C] • Birth also refers to your family situation: *He had received all the advantages of birth* (=having been born into a family of a high social class) *and an expensive education.* [U] ○ *She was of* **low/noble** *birth* (=born into the lowest/highest social class). [U] ○ *The children suffered the stigma* **of** *illegitimate birth* (=being born to parents were not married). [U] • When a woman **gives birth** she causes one or more babies to come out of her body: *They were delighted when she gave birth* **to** *a healthy* **child**. ○ *She gave birth* **to** *twins.* ○ *(fig.) The extraordinary experience gave birth* **to** *his latest novel* (=caused it to happen). • A **birth certificate** is a document recording a baby's birth including such information as name, time, place, and parents. • **Birth control** means the various methods or types of equipment that allow people to have sex without having children as a result. • A **birth control pill** (*infml* **the pill**) is a pill taken by a woman that prevents her from becoming pregnant if she has sex. • A **birth defect** is a physical or chemical problem with some body part(s) or process which is present at birth. • A **birth mother/parent** is a **biological mother/parent**. See at BIOLOGY. • The **birth rate** is the number of births which happen during a period of time in a particular place: *There was concern at the* **falling/rising** *birth rate.* • [LP]〉 **Age**

birth·day /£ˈbɜːθ·deɪ, $ˈbɜːrθ-/ *n* [C] the day that is an exact year or number of years after a person was born • *Happy birthday (to you)!* • *Are you going to Ellen's birthday party next week?* • *It's her 21st birthday.* • *What did you get* **for** *your birthday* (=What present(s) did you receive)? • *(infml humorous)* If you are **wearing/in** your **birthday suit** you have no clothes on. • *"Happy Birthday to You"*

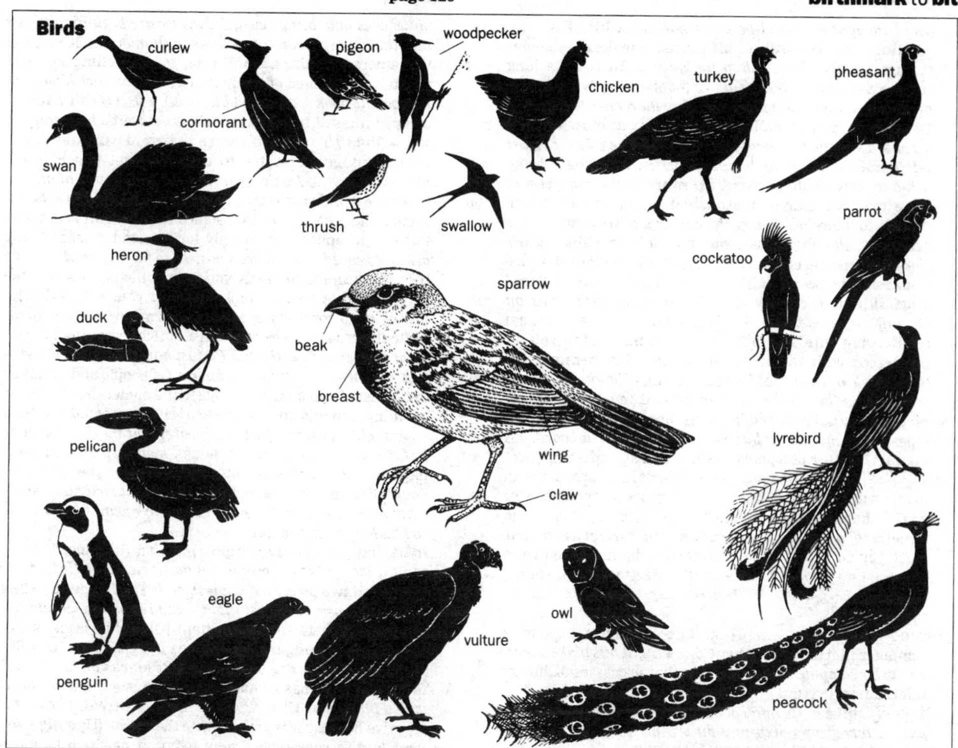

(song traditionally sung round the birthday cake, written by Pattie S.Hill, 1935)

birth·mark /£ˈbɜːθ·mɑːk, $ˈbɜːrθ·mɑːrk/ *n* [C] a brownish or reddish mark which is on a person's skin from when they are born

birth·place /£ˈbɜːθ·pleɪs, $ˈbɜːrθ-/ *n* [C usually sing] the house, town, etc. where a person was born • *Salzburg is famous as Mozart's birthplace.*

birth·right /£ˈbɜːθ·raɪt, $ˈbɜːrθ-/ *n* [C/U] something which is received or owned because of esp. your family or social situation, without having to be worked for or bought • *Let's face it, career women pose a real threat to men who see the better-paid, more powerful jobs as their birthright.* • *Many people were suddenly deprived of the power and influence they've come to enjoy almost as a birthright.* • *This culture takes food, wine and leisure as its birthright.* • *The documentary traced how a people who had no concept of territory as absolute possession were driven out of their birthright.* • *(fig.) He claimed the government were persuaded to* **sell** *their birthright and betray their friends, in order to cling to office* (= give up something valuable in order to get something which is wanted more).

bis·cuit FLAT CAKE *Br and Aus* /ˈbɪs·kɪt/, *Br and Aus infml* **bick·ie**, *Aus also* **bik·kie**, *Am, Aus also* **cook·ie** *n* [C] a flat small cake that is dry, hard and usually sweet • *chocolate/ginger biscuits* • *homemade biscuits* • *a packet of biscuits* • *Would you like some* **cheese and** *biscuits (Am* **crackers**)? • **Tea and** *biscuits was brought in to the meeting at 3.30 p.m.* • *What kind of biscuit do you like best?* • **Cheese** biscuits (*Am* **crackers**) are the different types of usually savoury biscuit that are eaten with cheese, or savoury biscuits which contain cheese. • *I usually mix* **dog** *biscuits with the other food I give my dog.* • *(infml)* If you say that something or someone **(really) takes the biscuit** you mean that someone has done something that you find particularly annoying or surprising. • PIC〉 **Bread and cakes, Containers**

bis·cuit RAISED BREAD /ˈbɪs·kɪt/ *n Am* a small soft raised bread • *baking-powder biscuits*

bi·sect *obj* /baɪˈsekt/ *v* [T] to divide into two, usually equal, parts • *The new road will bisect the town.*

bi·sex·ual /baɪˈsek·sju·əl/ *n* [C], *adj* [not gradable] (a person who is) attracted to both men and women • *He is (a) bisexual.* • Compare HETEROSEXUAL; HOMOSEXUAL.

bi·shop /ˈbɪʃ·əp/ *n* [C] a priest of high rank who is in charge of the priests of lower rank in a particular area • *the Bishop* **of** *Durham* • *Bishop Desmond Tutu* • In the game of CHESS, a bishop is a piece, sometimes in the shape of a bishop's hat, that can only move diagonally along squares of the same colour: *Each player has two bishops at the start of the game, one which moves on the black squares and the other which moves on the white.* • PIC〉 **Games**

bi·shop·ric /ˈbɪʃ·ə·prɪk/ *n* [C] • A bishopric is the period of time during which a person serves as a bishop. • A bishopric is also the area of which a bishop is in charge.

bi·son /ˈbaɪ·sᵊn/ *n* [C] *pl* **bisons** or **bison** a large wild animal, similar to a cow but having a larger head and hairy shoulders, found esp. in N America • *Large herds of bison used to live on the plains of N America.*

bisque /biːsk, bɪsk/ *n* [U] a thick creamy soup esp. made from SHELLFISH (= water animals with shells)

bi·stro /£ˈbiː·strəʊ, $-stroʊ/ *n* [C] *pl* **bistros** a small informal restaurant or bar, esp. in a French style

bit AMOUNT /bɪt/ *n* [C] *infml* a (small) piece or amount of something • *I can't eat all this chocolate – would you like a bit?* • *She broke the shells into* **little** *bits.* • *The boys just read/watched the* **funny/juicy/sad** *bits* (= parts of a story/film). • *There were bits* **of** *glass/paper all over the floor.* • **A bit (of)** means a small amount of something, or some: *She tries to do a bit of exercise every day.* ○ *I've just had a bit of* **luck** – *John says he can get me tickets for the show.* • *I'm just going out* **for a bit** (= for a short time). • *You go – I'll come along* **in a bit** (= after a short time). • **A bit (of)** means slightly or slight and is used to make esp. a critical or disapproving statement less strong: *The dress is a bit* **too** *big for me.* ○ *That was a bit silly, wasn't it?* ○ *I'm a bit nervous/worried.* ○ *By midnight I was a bit peckish.* ○ *This job's a bit fiddly/tricky.* ○ *It's a* **wee/teeny** *bit difficult to follow his explanations.* ○ *"Would you like a bit* **more** *(cake)?" "Yes please, just a bit."* ○ *The house is a (little) bit* **like** (= similar to) *a Swiss chalet.* ○ *Mary's put on a bit of weight, hasn't she?* ○ *He's a bit of a bore.* ○ *It's a bit of a nuisance.* • **A bit** can also be used to make a critical or disapproving statement stronger: *This soup's a bit cold* (= too cold), *isn't it?* ○ *This path is a bit steep* (= too steep). • **Not a bit** is used to make a negative statement stronger: *She wasn't a bit worried* (= not worried in any way) *about her exams.* ○ *My parents were not a bit happy* (= were very unhappy) *about my choice.* ○ *She was not* **the least/slightest** *bit sorry* (= not sorry in any way) *for hurting my feelings.* ○ *She's not a bit* **like** (= definitely not similar to) *me.* ○ *"Are you getting tired?" "Not a bit* (= definitely not). *"* •

(Br) I thought he would be sorry but **not a bit of it** (=he certainly wasn't). • **Quite a bit** is used to make a statement stronger: *You've been asleep for quite a bit* (=for a long time). ○ *She's got quite a bit of* (=a lot of) *money.* • **Bit by bit** means slowly or gradually: *I saved up the money bit by bit.* • **To bits** means into small pieces: *The car was* **blown** *to bits.* ○ *The sea smashed the boat to bits against the rocks.* ○ *It just* **fell/came** *to bits in my hands, honestly.* • *I thought being asked to miss my lunch was* **a bit much** (=the request was more than was fair or reasonable). • *The salesman who tried to convince me to buy the car was* **a bit much** (=his behaviour was more than was fair or reasonable). • *(Br slang)* If someone is described as **a bit of all right** they are considered to be attractive. • *(Br slang)* A **bit of fluff/stuff/skirt** is a sexually attractive woman: *She's a nice bit of stuff!* • *(humorous)* A **bit on the side** is a sexual relationship with someone who is not married to you, or the person with whom you have the relationship: *We've thought for a while that he was* **having** *a bit on the side.* ○ *She was his 'bit on the side' for several years.* • **Bits and pieces/** *(Br also)* **bits and bobs** are small things of different types: *I keep my sewing bits and pieces in that cupboard.* • A **bit part** in a film or a play is a small and unimportant part.

bit HORSE /bɪt/ *n* [C] a piece of metal put in a horse's mouth to allow the person riding it to control its movements • To **chafe/champ at the bit** is to be eager and impatient to do something. • If you **have/get/take the bit between** your **teeth** you do what you have decided to do in a forceful and energetic way: *She was reluctant to take the responsibility, but once she got the bit between her teeth there was no stopping her.*

bit COMPUTER /bɪt/ *n* [C] a unit of information in a computer that must be either 0 or 1 • *Eight bits make a byte.* • *a 32-bit computer* (=a computer that processes 32 bits of information at a time)

bit COIN /bɪt/ *n* [C] *infml* a small coin • *(in Britain in the past) a threepenny/sixpenny bit* • *(Am)* Two bits have the value of 25 CENTS. See also **two-bit** at TWO.

bit TOOL /bɪt/ *n* [C] the part of a tool used for cutting or DRILLING (=making holes)

bit BITE /bɪt/ *past simple of* BITE

bitch ANIMAL /bɪtʃ/ *n* [C] a female dog

bitch COMPLAIN /bɪtʃ/ *v* [I] to complain and make unkind remarks about someone or something • *They're always bitching* **about** *their friends.*

bitch /bɪtʃ/ *n* • *Most of us enjoy having* **a (good)** *bitch* (=talking and complaining about people not present) *from time to time.* [U] • A bitch is also a woman who is unkind or unpleasant to other people: *She can be a real bitch sometimes.* [C] ○ *The bitch told him what I'd said.* [C] ○ *You bitch – you knew I wanted to keep it secret!* [as form of address] • *"The Bitch is Back"* (title of a song by Elton John, 1974)

bitch·i·ness /ˈbɪtʃ·ɪ·nəs/ *n* [U] • *She was unpleasant to work with because of her bitchiness.*

bitch·y /ˈbɪtʃ·i/ *adj* **-ier, -iest** • *a bitchy remark* • *a bitchy person*

bite *(obj)* /baɪt/ *v past simple* **bit** /bɪt/, *past part* **bitten** /£ˈbɪt·ən, $ˈbɪt̬-/ to use your teeth to cut into something • *When her puppy bit me Joan told me that it was "only playing".* [T] • *The boys were kicking, biting and scratching as she dragged them into the room.* [I] • *He bit* **(into)** *the apple.* [T; I + *into*] • *She finished sewing and bit* **off** *the end of the thread.* [M] • *An insect bit me on the arm.* [T] • *(fig.) The racing bug bit him badly/He got badly bitten by the racing bug* (=he developed a strong interest in racing) *in his teens.* [T] • *One of those waiting for interview was looking very nervous, biting his* **lip(s)** (=holding esp. his lower lip between his teeth) *and moving on his chair.* [T] • *(fig.) We found his speech so funny we had to bite our lips* (=hide the emotion we felt) *– it was meant to be a serious occasion.* [T] • *She can't stop biting her* **nails.** [T] • When a fish bites it takes the food from the hook and is caught as a result: *The fish aren't biting today.* [I] ○ *(fig.) My house is for sale but nobody seems to be biting* (=no one is showing any interest). [I] • When car tyres bite the road, they take a firm hold of the surface and do not slide. [T] • If a new law, tax, activity, etc. bites, its unpleasant effects start to be felt: *When the recession* **began/started** *to bite, people spent less on eating out in restaurants.* [I] ○ *These changes always bite the elderly* **hard.** [T] • *The cold began to bite* **into** *their bones* (=be felt unpleasantly in their body). [I] • To **bite into** something is also to remove part of it: *Her job was demanding and began to bite* **(deep)** *into her free time.* ○ *Our parent company's patience is now being rewarded, as we are beginning to bite into the share of our competitors.* • *(humorous)* If you say that a person or thing **won't bite**, you are telling someone not to be frightened of them: *Just go and ask her if you can borrow the book – she won't bite (you).* • *(Br) He* **bit back** (=stopped himself from saying) *the cruel words he wanted to say.* • *(infml)* To **bite off (more than** you **can chew/cope with/manage)** is to try to do something which is too difficult for you: *Don't try and bite off too much at once.* ○ *When it expanded into toys, the company bit off more than it could chew.* • *(infml)* To **bite** someone's **head off** is to speak to them in anger and sharply for no good reason: *I only asked if I could help – there's no need to bite my head off!* • To **bite the hand that feeds** you is to act badly towards the person who is helping or has helped you. • To **bite the bullet** is to force yourself to perform an unpleasant or difficult action or to be brave in a difficult situation: *I don't want to go to the dentist but I'll just have to bite the bullet.* • *(esp. humorous)* To **bite the dust** is (of people and animals) to fall, esp. from a moving object, and sometimes to die, or (of things) to end in failure: *As they came round the bend several riders bit the dust.* ○ *His career bit the dust when he lost his job.* ○ *There wasn't enough money so another good idea bit the dust!* • If you **bite** your **tongue** you stop yourself from saying something: *I wanted to tell him exactly what had happened, but Margaret didn't want him to know so I had to bite my tongue.*

bite /baɪt/ *n* • *The puppy* **gave** *me* **a** *bite* (=bit me). [C] • *He* **took a** *bite* (=bit a piece) *out of the apple.* [C] • *He* **had** *two bites* (=bit two pieces) **of** *apple then threw it away.* [C] • *The mosquitoes were bad last night – you're covered in bites* (=sore places where you were bitten). [C] • A bite is also a fish caught by a fishing line: *Ah, at last I've got a bite.* [C] • *She got away from the dog but she had bite* **marks** *on her leg.* • If food has bite it has a sharp or strong taste: *I like mustard with a bit of bite.* [U] • *(fig.) This satire* **has (real)** *bite* (=it is effective because it is very close to the truth). [U] • *(fig.) You need to give your report more bite* (=it needs to be more powerful). [U] • *(infml) Let's* **have a bite to eat** (=Let's have some food) *before we go out.* • **A/Another/A double/A second bite of the cherry** is an/another opportunity to do something: *Job-sharing lets everyone get a bite of the cherry.* ○ *The team seized their chance of a second bite of the cherry.* • *They cut the cheese into* **bite-sized** *pieces* (=pieces small enough to put into your mouth whole). • See also SOUNDBITE.

bit·er /£ˈbaɪ·tər, $-t̬ɚ/ *n* • **The biter is bit** means that a person who has caused some harm is then hurt in some way: *He's always very been keen to expose other people's faults, so the newspaper article about his criminal connections was* **a** *clear* **case of** *the biter being bit.*

bit·ing /£ˈbaɪ·tɪŋ, $-t̬ɪŋ/ *adj disapproving* • Biting **cold** or a biting **wind** is very cold and severe and seems to cut through your body. • If someone makes biting **remarks** or has a biting **wit**, they say things that are critical, often in a clever way.

bit·ter TASTE /£ˈbɪt·ər, $ˈbɪt̬·ɚ/ *adj* **-er, -est** with an unpleasantly sharp taste • *a bitter flavour/taste* • *a bitter-tasting liquid* • *Marmalade is usually made with bitter, not sweet, oranges.* • *Bitter* **almonds** *contain a chemical which gives them a bitter taste.* • **Bitter chocolate** *(Am usually* **bittersweet chocolate**) is **plain chocolate**. See at PLAIN WITH NOTHING ADDED. • **Bitter lemon** is a fizzy drink with a slight taste of LEMON which is not alcoholic but which is sometimes mixed with alcoholic drinks. • **Bitter fruits** are unpleasant results: *The unemployed are* **tasting** *the bitter fruits* **of** *the market economy.* • **A bitter pill (to swallow)** or **bitter medicine** is something that is very unpleasant but must be accepted: *Failure to become a lawyer was a bitter pill for him.* ○ *She tried to* **sweeten** *the bitter medicine/pill by saying he would only have to stay one week.*

bit·ter /£ˈbɪt·ər, $ˈbɪt̬·ɚ/ *n* [U] *Br and Aus* • Bitter is a type of dark brown beer with a bitter taste: *a pint of bitter* • Compare MILD SLIGHT.

bit·ter·ness /£ˈbɪt·ə·nəs, $ˈbɪt̬·ɚ-/ *n* [U] • *the characteristic slight bitterness of chicory*

bit·ters /£ˈbɪt·əz, $ˈbɪt̬·ɚz/ *n* [U] • Bitters is a strong bitter alcoholic drink made from spices and plant products that is mixed with other alcoholic drinks.

bit·ter ANGRY /£ˈbɪt·ər, $ˈbɪt̬·ɚ/ *adj* **-er, -est** (of a person) angry and unhappy because unable to forget bad things which happened the past or (of an experience) causing deep pain or anger • *She was not bitter* **about** *what had happened to her.* • *He gave me a bitter look.* • *Failing the* *final exams was a bitter* **disappointment** *for me.* • *The brothers are bitter* **enemies** (=they hate each other). • *She learnt through bitter* **experience** *that he was not to be trusted.* • *The bitter* **irony** *is that the hospice treating AIDS patients is rich from the legacies of grateful dying patients.* • *Her childhood had left her with bitter* **memories** *of family life.* • *He felt that no-one had supported him and he became bitter* **and twisted** (=angry and unhappy). • Bitter is often used with words which mean argument: *a bitter dispute/feud* ○ *a bitter fight/row* ○ *bitter recriminations* ○ *a bitter struggle/wrangle* • The **bitter end** is death: *He stayed by her bedside until the bitter end* (=her death). • If something is done **to the bitter end** it is completed although the person doing it finds it extremely unpleasant: *I pursued my claim to the bitter end.*

bit·ter·ly /£'bɪt·ə·li, $'bɪṭ·ɚ-/ *adv* • *I wept bitterly* (=feeling great pain) *when I heard the news.* • *She was bitterly disappointed* (=felt great disappointment) *not to get the job.* • LP› **Very, completely**

bit·ter·ness /£'bɪt·ə·nəs, $'bɪṭ·ɚ-/ *n* [U]

bit·ter COLD /£'bɪt·əʳ, $'bɪṭ·ɚ/ *adj* unpleasantly and extremely cold • *a bitter wind/winter* • *bitter weather* • *It's bitter outside today.*

bit·ter·ly /£'bɪt·ə·li, $'bɪṭ·ɚ-/ *adv* • *Last Friday was a bitterly cold day.*

bit·tern /£'bɪt·ən, $'bɪṭ·ɚn/ *n* [C] a type of European water bird which has long legs and is related to the HERON

bit·ter·sweet EMOTION /£,bɪt·ə'swiːt, $,bɪṭ·ɚ-, '---/ *adj* containing a mixture of sadness and happiness • *The release of the first prisoner was bittersweet for the relatives of other hostages.*

bit·ter·sweet TASTE /£,bɪt·ə'swiːt, $,bɪṭ·ɚ-, '---/ *adj* both bitter and sweet • *I love the bittersweet taste of kumquats.* • **Bittersweet chocolate** is *Am for* **bitter chocolate**. See at BITTER TASTE.

bit·ty /£'bɪt·i, $'bɪṭ-/ *adj* **-ier, -iest** *Br and Aus infml* (seeming as if) made up of a lot of different things that do not fit together • *Several authors contributed a chapter each which made the book seem rather bitty.* • *I enjoyed the film but I found it quite bitty – it kept jumping from the story of one family to another.*

bi·tu·men /£'bɪtʃ·ʊ·mən, $bɪ'tuː-/ *n* [U] a black sticky substance (such as TAR or ASPHALT) used for making roads and roofing materials

bi·vou·ac /'bɪv·u·æk/ *n* [C] a temporary shelter to sleep outside in, which is not a tent • *The children made a bivouac at the bottom of the garden with some poles and an old blanket.* • *In worsening weather with darkness closing in, the climbers prepared a bivouac and settled down for the night.* • A bivouac **(tent)** is a small light tent just big enough for one or two people to lie in.

bi·vou·ac /'bɪv·u·æk/ *v* [I always + adv/prep] **bivouacking**, *past* **bivouacked** • *The soldiers bivouacked in the mountains for two nights.*

bi·week·ly /baɪ'wiː·kli/ *adj, adv* [not gradable] happening or appearing every two weeks or twice a week • *a biweekly hospital appointment*

bi·zarre /£bɪ'zɑːʳ, $-'zɑːr/ *adj* strange and unusual • *a bizarre episode/event/situation* • *Many of the homeless exhibit bizarre* **behaviour**, *which reinforces the myth that homelessness is really a psychiatric problem.* • *The incident adds a bizarre* **twist** *to last week's escalating cycle of violence in the province.* • Ⓟ

bi·zarre·ly /£bɪ'zɑː·li, $-'zɑːr-/ *adv*

bi·zarre·ness /£bɪ'zɑː·nəs, $-'zɑːr-/ *n* [U]

BL /,biː'el/, **LLB** /,el·el'biː/ *n* [C] *Am abbreviation for* Bachelor of Laws (=degree in law) • LP› **Schools and colleges**

blab *(obj)* /blæb/ *v* **-bb-** *infml* to talk carelessly or too much, often causing a secret to be known • *She blabbed the whole story* **to** *her mother.* [T] • *Someone blabbed* **to** *the press.* [I]

blab·ber /£'blæb·əʳ, $-ɚ/ *v* [I] *infml* to talk a lot, esp. in a way that is considered foolish • *He's always blabbering* **on about** *computers.*

blab·ber·mouth /£'blæb·ə·maʊθ, $'-ɚ-/ *n* [C] *infml* a person who talks carelessly, often telling other people your secrets

black DARK IN COLOUR /blæk/ *adj, n* **-er, -est** (of) the darkest colour there is, like night without light • *black shoes* • *a black car* • *When the storm started the sky was* **as** *black* **as night** (=very dark). • *She often dresses* **in** *black* (=in black clothes). [U] • *At last my bank account is* **in the black** (=has money in it). Compare **in the red** at RED COLOUR. • To be **black and blue** is to have dark marks on your skin, often as a result of being hit repeatedly: *His arm was black and blue.* • *This is a well-known children's joke: "What's black and white and red (=read) all over?" "A newspaper!"* • **Black and white** refers to photography that does not have any colours except black, white and grey: *black-and-white photos* ○ *The old newsreels were filmed* **in** *black and white.* • If you want something **(down) in black and white** you want it in a reasonably finished form in writing: *I'd like to* **see** *the proposal down in black and white before I comment on it.* • To **see things in black and white** is to have a simple view of what is right and wrong or good and bad: *He always sees things in black and white – he can never accept that there are grey areas to most of these questions.* • A **black-and white** situation is one where it is easy to decide what is right and wrong: *Disarmament isn't a black-and-white issue for me.* • A **black belt** is the symbol of, or is a name for, someone who has reached a very high standard in the sport of JUDO or KARATE: *He's got a black belt.* ○ *He's a black belt.* • A **black box** is a small machine that records information about an aircraft during its flight, and which is used to discover the cause of an accident. • **Black coffee** is coffee without milk or cream. • The **Black Country** is the industrial area in the West Midlands of England. • A **black eye** is the result of the eye being hit, when the skin around the eye becomes BRUISED (=dark in colour): *He'd been fighting at school and came home with a black eye.* • A **black-eyed bean**/*(Am also)* **black-eyed pea** is a type of small edible bean. • A **black hole** is *(specialized)* a region in space where GRAVITY is so strong that nothing, not even light, can escape, or *(fig.)* an imaginary place in which things are lost: *(fig.) The office, often criticized as a black hole for applications, has created a new record-keeping system.* • The expression **the Black Hole of Calcutta** is used to refer to an unpleasantly full and hot room: *One guest at the crowded reception was heard to mutter, "it's like the Black Hole of Calcutta in here".* • **Black ice** is a dangerous type of ice on roads which is so thin that it is the same colour as the road and cannot be seen by a driver. • *(dated)* A **Black Maria** is a police vehicle used to transport prisoners. • **Black pepper**, made from crushing whole black PEPPER seeds, adds a strong flavour to foods. • **Black pudding** is a type of SAUSAGE (=food in a tube-like case) made of pig's blood, fat and grain, which is very dark in colour. • **Black tie** means the clothes worn on formal occasions. For men this is a black **bow tie**, white shirt and black suit, and for women a long dress: *We're going to a black-tie event.* • PIC› **Peas and beans**

black *obj* /blæk/ *v* [T] • *The commandos blacked their faces* (=put a black substance on them to hide their paleness). • *He blacked his riding boots* (=cleaned them with a black substance). • *(dated) The attacker blacked the old man's eye and ran off* (=made his eye dark by hitting it). • PIC› **Eye**

black·en *obj* /'blæk·ᵊn/ *v* [T] • *The interior of the house is still blackened from the fire/***smoke-blackened**. • *The folds of the curtains were blackened* **with** *dirt.*

black·ness /'blæk·nəs/ *n* [U] • *The blackness of the forest at night frightened him.*

black BAD /blæk/ *adj* used in these words and phrases to mean bad, without hope or evil. Some people avoid using black to mean bad, as it might offend black people. • *When his business failed he experienced black* **despair**. • *The future looked black* (=without hope). • *His father looked* **as black as thunder** (=extremely angry). • If you **paint a (very) black picture** of a situation you describe it as extremely bad. • If a person is **not as black as** they are **painted** they are not as bad as people say they are. • A **black comedy** is a film, play, etc. that looks at the amusing side of things we usually take very seriously, like death and illness. • The **Black Death** was an illness (a form of BUBONIC PLAGUE) that killed millions of people in Europe and Asia in the 14th century. • The **black economy** of a country is the income of those people who avoid paying taxes. • **Black humour** is an amusing way of looking at or treating something that is serious or sad. • A **black look** is one that is full of anger and hate: *She gave me a black look.* • **Black magic** is a type of magic that is believed to use evil spirits to do harmful things. • A **black mark** is something you have done that makes people consider you as bad in some way: *If I'm late for work again it will be another black mark* **(against** *me).* • The **black market** is things bought and sold, money changed, etc. illegally: *During the war they bought food* **on** *the black market.* ○ *They bought electrical goods from a* **black marketeer** (=person selling goods illegally). • A **Black Mass** is a ceremony in which the Devil is worshipped instead of the Christian God. • A **black mood** is a very unhappy and hopeless feeling: *Since his wife died he has had black moods and feelings of despair.* ○ *She was* **in** *one of her black moods today.* • A **black sheep** is a person who has done something bad, esp. something which brings embarrassment and loss of respect to the family: *He's the black sheep* **of the family**. ○ *I never heard anyone mention my uncle – I think he was a bit of a black sheep.* • *(Br)* A **black spot** is a place on a road that is considered to be dangerous because several accidents have happened there, or a place where something is particularly bad: *This corner is an* **accident** *black spot.* ○ *This region has been a black spot* **for** *unemployment in recent years.* • A **black widow** is a very poisonous SPIDER (= an insect-like creature with eight legs) that lives in warm areas.

black *obj* /blæk/ *v* [T] • If a trade union blacks particular goods or people it refuses to handle or work with them.

black·en *obj* /ˈblæk·ᵊn/ *v* [T] • If you blacken an **image**/a **name**/etc. you make it less good: *The financial crash of a well-known bank blackened the image of investment for many small investors.* ○ *The island's name has been blackened by the travel writer in his latest book – he calls it scruffy and expensive.*

black PEOPLE /blæk/ *adj, n* **-er, -est** (a person) with black or dark brown skin, or of or for people with skin of this colour. Black is used esp. of people who live in Africa or whose family originally came from Africa • *They wouldn't employ me because I was black.* • *black culture* • *the black vote* • *the black part of town* • *He was the first black to join that firm of lawyers.* [C] • **Black Africa** is the part of Africa south of the Sahara Desert. • *"Say it loud – I'm black and I'm proud"* (title of a song by James Brown, 1968)

black·ball *obj* /£ˈblæk·bɔːl, $-bɑːl/ *v* [T] to vote against allowing (someone) to be a member of an organization or group • *His membership of the society was initially blackballed on account of an old dispute between himself and a couple of the committee members.*

black·ber·ry /£ˈblæk·bᵊr·i, $-ber-/ *n* [C] a small dark purple fruit that grows wild in Europe and is usually cooked before being eaten • *blackberry and apple pie* • PIC> **Berries**

black·ber·ry·ing /£ˈblæk·bᵊr·i·ɪŋ, $-ber-/ *n* [U] • *We* **went** *blackberrying* (= into the countryside to gather blackberries) *last Sunday.*

black·bird /£ˈblæk·bɜːd, $-bɜːrd/ *n* [C] a European bird, of which the male has black feathers and a bright yellow beak and the female has brown feathers

black·board /£ˈblæk·bɔːd, $-bɔːrd/ *n* [C] a dark surface on a wall or frame on which a teacher writes with CHALK • *Look at these words that I've written up on the blackboard – what is similar about them?* • The **blackboard jungle** is the way of life and activity connected with schools, esp. when it is seen as difficult, uncontrolled and confusing.

black·boy /ˈblæk·bɔɪ/ *n* [C] *Aus* a kind of Australian tree which has long thin leaves like grass

black·cur·rant /£blækˈkʌr·ᵊnt, $ˈblæk,kɜːr-/ *n* [C] a small round dark purple fruit that grows on a bush in gardens and is usually cooked before being eaten • *apple and blackcurrant pie* • *blackcurrant cheesecake* • *blackcurrant* **jam** • PIC> **Berries**

black·en *obj* /ˈblæk·ᵊn/ *v* [T] See at BLACK DARK IN COLOUR, BLACK BAD

black·fly /ˈblæk·flaɪ/ *n* a small insect with two wings that sucks the juices of plants for food; a type of APHID • *Blackflies lay their eggs in rivers or streams.* [C] • *Do your broad beans suffer from blackfly* (= are they attacked by blackflies)*?* [U]

black·guard /£ˈblæg·ɑːd, £-əd, $-ɑːrd/ *n* [C] *dated* a person, esp. a man, who is not honourable and has no moral principles

black·head /ˈblæk·hed/ *n* [C] a very small dark spot on the skin caused by a blocked PORE (= small hole in the skin's surface) • *Mark was in the bathroom squeezing the blackheads on his chin.*

black·jack CARD GAME /ˈblæk·dʒæk/, **pon·toon** *n* [U] a type of card game played for money

black·jack WEAPON /ˈblæk·dʒæk/ *n* [C] *Am* a short thick metal stick covered in rubber or leather used to hit people with; a COSH

black·leg /ˈblæk·leg/ *n* [C] *Br disapproving* a person who works while others that they work with are on STRIKE (= not working because of a disagreement with employers); a SCAB WORKER

black·list /ˈblæk·lɪst/ *v, n* (to put someone on) a list of people who are considered by a particular authority or group to have done wrong or who are not to be trusted • *In the 1950s she was put on a government blacklist because she had once visited the Soviet Union.* [C] • *They were blacklisted because of their extreme right-wing views.* [T]

black·mail /ˈblæk·meɪl/ *n* [U] the action of obtaining money from people or forcing them to do something by threatening to make known a secret of theirs or to harm them • *The journalist* **used** *blackmail to make the lawyer give him the documents.* • *In a position of authority a weakness for the opposite sex leaves you* **open** *to blackmail.* • LP> **Crimes and criminals**

black·mail *obj* /ˈblæk·meɪl/ *v* [T] • *They tried to blackmail me* (**into** *giving them the money).*

black·mail·er /£ˈblæk,meɪ·ləʳ, $-lɚ/ *n* [C] • *She had a call from a blackmailer who demanded $50 000 for the return of the photos.*

black·ness /ˈblæk·nəs/ *n* [U] See at BLACK DARK IN COLOUR

black·out HIDE /ˈblæk·aʊt/ *n* [C] a time when all lights must be hidden by law, or when there is no light or power because of an electricity failure • *The war-time blackouts were strictly enforced by special wardens.* • *The electricity failed during the storm and we had a blackout of several hours.* • *(fig.) There was a* **news** *blackout* (= no information was given publicly) *while the police operation was taking place.*

black out *obj*, **black** *obj* **out** *v adv* [M] • *The rules were that houses had to be completely blacked out after dark to prevent them being seen by enemy aircraft.* • *(fig.) The news of the kidnapping was blacked out* (= no information about it was given publicly) *until the police could find the child.*

black·out UNCONSCIOUSNESS /ˈblæk·aʊt/ *n* [C] a short period of unconsciousness • *He can't drive because he suffers from blackouts.* • *She must have* **had** *a blackout because she can't remember anything that happened to her.*

black out *v adv* [I] • *Someone hit him on the back of the head and he blacked out immediately* • *The shock was so great that she blacked out.*

black·smith /ˈblæk·smɪθ/ *n* [C] a person who makes and repairs iron tools and HORSESHOES

blad·der /£ˈblæd·əʳ, $-ɚ/ *n* [C] a bag-like organ inside the body of a person or animal where urine is stored before it leaves the body • *I must go and* **empty** *my bladder* (= urinate). • *Running on a* **full** *bladder is not a good idea.*

blade PART OF KNIFE /bleɪd/ *n* [C] the thin flat part, esp. of a tool or weapon, often having a cutting edge • *a knife blade* • *a razor blade* • *a skate blade* • *the blade of a propeller* • *the blade of an oar* • *This blade needs sharpening.* • Blade is also used in the names of other objects which are similar in shape to a blade, being flat, thin and sometimes long: *a shoulder blade* ○ *a blade of grass* • PIC> **Axe, Blade, Knife** Ⓢ

blade MAN /bleɪd/ *n* [C] *dated literary* an attractive and confident young man • *a dashing young blade* • Ⓢ

blah blah (blah) /ˌblɑː·blɑːˈblɑː/ *exclamation infml* a phrase used to represent boring speech • *He came out with all the usual stuff about there not being enough money to take on extra staff blah blah blah.*

blame *obj* /bleɪm/ *v* [T] to believe or state that (someone or something) is responsible for (something bad) happening • *Well don't blame me* (= It is not my fault) *if you miss the bus!* • *It's a disgrace that children should behave like that – I blame the parents.* • *Hugh blames his mother* **for** *his lack of confidence* (= He believes that it is her fault). • *Hugh blames his lack of confidence* **on** *his mother.* • *Careless campers were blamed* **for** *starting the forest fires.* • *"When this project is finally finished I'm going to take a good long holiday." "I* **don't blame you** (= I think that is the right thing to do)*."* • *You can't really blame Helen* **for** *not wanting to get involved* (= Her feelings are understandable). • *The hot weather is partly* **to blame for** (= the reason for) *the water shortage.* • *(saying)* People say 'a bad workman blames his tools' when someone has blamed other people or things for their own mistakes.

blame /bleɪm/ *n* [U] • *Health officials* **put** *the blame* **for** *the disease* **on** (= state that the reason for the disease is) *poor housing conditions.* • *If anything goes wrong, I'll* **take** *the blame* (= I will state that it is my fault). • *She* **laid/put** *the blame* **on** *him* **for** *the accident* (= she said it was his fault). • *They tried to* **pin** (= put) *the blame for the killing on an innocent army officer.* • *We want to find out what happened, not to* **apportion** *blame* (= to say someone or

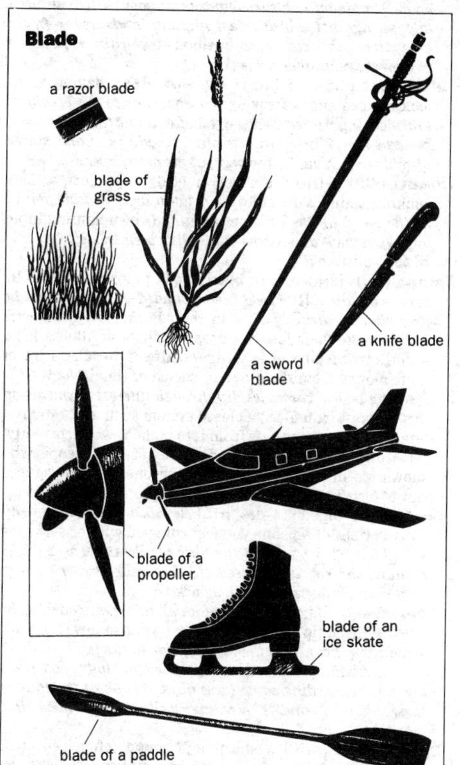

something was wrong). • *Chris placed the blame for rising crime* **squarely** *with the media.* • *It is clear that no blame* **attaches to** *the management of the operation* (= the management was not faulty).

blame·less /ˈbleɪm·ləs/ *adj* • *It was mainly my fault, but she wasn't entirely blameless* (= without fault).

blame·wor·thy /£ˈbleɪmˌwɜː·ði, $-ˌwɜːr-/ *adj fml* • *He does not feel that he is blameworthy* (= that he has done anything wrong).

blanch *(obj)* PALE /£blɑːntʃ, $blæntʃ/ *v* to turn or make pale • *While most people would blanch at the prospect of so much work, Daniels seems to positively enjoy it.* [I] • To blanch a plant is to make it white by covering it up as it is growing, so that the light does not reach it. [T]

blanch *obj* BOIL /£blɑːntʃ, $blæntʃ/ *v* [T] to put (esp. vegetables) into boiling water for a few minutes, to whiten, to remove skins, to get rid of strong flavours, or to prepare for freezing • *blanched almonds* • *Drop the tomatoes into the boiling water and blanch them for 20 to 30 seconds.*

blanc·mange /£bləˈmɒ̃nʒ, $-ˈmɑːndʒ/ *n* [U] a cold sweet food made from milk, sugar and CORNFLOUR (= a fine flour) • *jelly and blancmange*

bland /blænd/ *adj* **-er, -est** *usually disapproving* lacking a strong taste or character or lacking in interest or energy • *I find chicken a little bland unless it's cooked in a really spicy sauce.* • *Pop music these days is so bland.* • *From his holiday home by an Austrian lake, the chancellor issued a bland statement which calmed things only briefly.*

bland·ly /ˈblænd·li/ *adv* • *We've never been anything more than blandly polite to each other.*

bland·ness /ˈblænd·nəs/ *n* [U]

blan·dish·ments /ˈblæn·dɪʃ·mənts/ *pl n* pleasant words or actions meant to persuade • *The couple resisted the media's blandishments to reveal their wedding date.*

blank /blæŋk/ *adj* **-er, -est** carrying no information or mark; empty or clear • *a blank tape* • *a blank page/sheet* • *There's a blank space at the bottom of the form for you to sign your name in.* • *Sitting staring at a blank screen isn't going to do much good.* • *(fig.) My enquiries drew only blank* (= showing no understanding) **stares**. • *(fig.) I never know what Jayne's thinking – she has such a blank* (= showing no interest or feeling) *expression.* • A **blank cheque** is one that has been signed but does not yet have the amount of money written on it. • **Blank verse** is a type of poetry that does not RHYME (= words at the end of lines do not have the same sound), usually with ten syllables in each line: *Shakespeare's plays are mostly written in blank verse.* • Ⓓ Ⓝ ⓃⓁ

blank·ly /ˈblæŋ·kli/ *adv* • *(fig.) I asked him if he knew what had happened but he just* **stared** *blankly* (= showing no understanding) *at me.*

blank /blæŋk/ *n* [C] • A blank is a space left in a piece of writing, or on a form, for information to be added: *Fill in the blanks in this form.* • A blank is also something not yet marked or finished, such as a door key that is not yet cut. • A **blank (cartridge)** is a CARTRIDGE containing explosive but no bullet: *He* **fired** *a blank at the police officers.* • *(fig.) My mind was* **a (complete)** *blank* (= I could not remember or think of anything).

blank out *obj*, **blank** *obj* **out** *v adv* [M] • If you blank out something that is written, you intentionally cover it over so that it cannot be read: *Some of the names in the report have been blanked out.* • If you blank a memory out you forget it, often because it is unpleasant and you would prefer not to remember it: *I don't remember anything about that period in my life – I must have blanked it out.*

blan·ket COVER /ˈblæŋ·kɪt/ *n* [C] a cover, often of wool or similar material, for keeping in warmth (as on a bed) • *Do you prefer sheets and blankets or a duvet?* • *(fig.) The ground was covered by a thick blanket of snow.* • *(fig.) A blanket of gloom enveloped the losing team.* • Ⓒⓢ Ⓢ

blan·ket *obj* /ˈblæŋ·kɪt/ *v* [T] • To blanket something is to cover it completely with a thick layer: *A massive snowfall has in recent days blanketed south-eastern Turkey.* ○ *The helicopter started down, and immediately they were blanketed in fog.*

blan·ket UNLIMITED /ˈblæŋ·kɪt/ *adj* [before n] referring to everything, including all cases • *'Man' used to be an accepted blanket* **term** *for both men and women* (= a word which covered the whole group), *but is now often seen as sexist.* • **Blanket bombing** is when a lot of bombs are dropped over a large area such as a city, without aiming for any particular buildings.

blare *(obj)* /£bleəʳ, $bler/ *v*, *n* (to make) an unpleasantly loud noise • *The loudspeakers blared* **across** *the square.* [I] • *The radio was blaring* **out** *loud music.* [M] • *The music begins with a blare of trumpets.* [U]

blar·ney /£ˈblɑː·ni, $ˈblɑːr-/ *n* [U] words that are charming nonsense, intended to please or deceive • *He's got a good line in blarney, but don't believe a word of it.*

bla·sé /ˌblɑːˈzeɪ/ *adj* bored or not excited, or wishing to seem so • *He flies first class so often he's become blasé* **about** *it.*

blas·pheme /ˌblæsˈfiːm/ *v* [I] to use words which show a lack of respect for God or religion, or to swear • *I began to rage and blaspheme* **(against)** *God.*

blas·phem·ous /ˈblæs·fɪ·məs/ *adj* • A blasphemous remark or action is believed to be offensive to God or religion: *Some people say that it is blasphemous to say that God might be a woman.*

blas·phem·ous·ly /ˈblæs·fɪ·mə·sli/ *adv*

blas·phe·my /ˈblæs·fə·mi/ *n* • *Several of Epstein's symbolic sculptures resulted in accusations of indecency and blasphemy.* [U] • *(fig.) Elvis Presley fans think that any criticism of him is a blasphemy.* [C]

blast *(obj)* DESTROY /£blɑːst, $blæst/ *v* to destroy (something or someone) by using explosives or other great force • *The centre of the city has been blasted by repeated bombing.* [T] • *The gunmen blasted the bus* **with** *a hail of bullets.* [T] • *A tunnel was to be blasted through the mountains* (= made by removing rock with explosives). [T] • *The heavy winds blasted through the trees.* [I] • *They heard the guns blasting* **away** *all night* (= firing loudly and continuously). [I] • *(fig.) The opposition blasted* (= criticized very strongly) *the government for high inflation.* [T] • *(fig.) Their latest record blasted (its way) up the charts* (= moved very quickly because of its popularity). [I/T] • *The rocket is due to* **blast off** (= leave the ground) *at two o'clock.* • See also SANDBLAST.

blast /£blɑːst, $blæst/ *n* [C] • A blast is an explosion: *Three people were injured* **in** *the blast.* • A blast is also a sudden strong blow of air or a sudden loud noise: *A blast* **of** *cold air hit him as he opened the window.* ○ *I was woken up by a sudden blast* **of** *music from the next room.* ○ *The headteacher blew three blasts* **on** *a whistle to summon the pupils.* • *(humorous)I haven't heard that record for ages – that's a real* **blast from the past** (= something that happened a long time ago that I had almost forgotten about). • A **blast furnace** is a container that is use for producing iron by mixing iron ORE, COKE and LIMESTONE in it and blowing extremely hot air through the mixture. • **Blast-off** is the moment when a spacecraft leaves the ground: *Five seconds to blast-off!*

blast·ed /£ˈblɑː·stɪd, $ˈblæs·t̬ɪd/ *adj literary* • A blasted plant or piece of land has been damaged or destroyed by extreme cold, heat or wind: *a blasted heath*

blast [EVENT] /£blɑːst, $blæst/ *n* [C usually sing] *Am infml* an exciting or enjoyable experience or event, often a party • *You should have come with us last night, we had a real blast!*

blast (it) /£blɑːst, $blæst/ *exclamation dated slang* an expression of anger or annoyance • *Oh blast! I've left my keys at home!*

blast·ed /£ˈblɑː·stɪd, $ˈblæs·t̬ɪd/ *adj* [before n; not gradable] *slightly dated slang* • Blasted is used in phrases to express anger or annoyance: *I've forgotten my blasted keys!*

blast·ed /£ˈblɑː·stɪd, $ˈblæs·t̬ɪd/ *adj* [after v] *Am slang* drunk • *Patrick got blasted again last night.*

bla·tant /£ˈbleɪ·tᵊnt, $-t̬ᵊnt/ *adj* (esp. of something bad) obvious or intentional • *Aquino said he was angry after reading the article "because it was a blatant* **lie** *and showed a reckless disregard for the truth."* • *The whole episode was a blatant attempt to gain publicity.*

bla·tant·ly /£ˈbleɪ·tᵊnt·li, $-t̬ᵊnt-/ *adv* • *It was blatantly* **obvious** *that she was telling a lie.* • *Their continued imprisonment was condemned by civil liberties groups as 'blatantly unjust'.*

blath·er /£ˈblæð·əʳ, $-ɚ/, **bleth·er** *v* [I] to talk in a foolish way • *He blathered* **on** *for half an hour about his high-paying job.* • *What the devil was Michael blethering* **on** *about at this morning's meeting?*

blath·er /£ˈblæð·əʳ, $-ɚ/, **bleth·er** *n* [U] • *I'm tired of his blather.*

blaze [BURN] /bleɪz/ *v* [I] to burn brightly and strongly • *The fires in the oil wells blazed for days.* • *The sun was blazing* **down** *that afternoon.* • *There was a mood of excitement inside: the cameras were filming and powerful lights blazed.* • *(fig.) The fields around the house blazed* **with** (=were very bright with) *poppies.* • *(fig. literary) Isaac's eyes suddenly blazed* (=suddenly looked very bright) **with** *anger.*

blaze /bleɪz/ *n* • *Firefighters took two hours to control the blaze* (=the big fire). [C] • *(fig.) The garden is a blaze* **of** *colour* (=has a lot of bright colours in it) *at this time of year.* [U] • *(fig.) The 19th century went out in* **a** *blaze* **of glory** (=ended in an exciting way). [U] • *(fig.) The book was launched in* **a** *blaze* **of publicity** (=with a large amount of PUBLICITY). [U]

blaz·ing /ˈbleɪ·zɪŋ/ *adj* • *We quickly grew tired in the blazing* (=very hot) **sunshine**. • *I had to leave the blazing* **heat** *of the midday sun.* • *The deer was startled by the blazing* (=very bright) **headlights** *of the approaching car.* • *(fig.) They used to have some blazing* **rows** (=very fierce arguments) *over money.*

blaze [MARK] /bleɪz/ *n* [C] a white mark on the face of a horse or other animal

blaze *obj* [DO SOMETHING NEW] /bleɪz/ *v* [T] **blaze a trail** to do something that no-one has ever done before • *Elvis Presley blazed a trail in pop music.*

bla·zer /£ˈbleɪ·zəʳ, $-zɚ/ *n* [C] a type of jacket, usually with metal buttons, which is traditionally worn at sporting events • *The men in the yacht club wear navy blazers with gold buttons.* • *I've still got my old* **school** *blazer with the school badge sewn onto the pocket.* • *Martin was looking characteristically elegant in a blazer and beige trousers.*

bla·zes /ˈbleɪ·zɪz/ *pl n dated infml* used to give force to something you feel angry about • *What* **the** *blazes did he do that for?* • **Go to blazes!** (=Go away, leave me alone!)

bla·zon *obj* /ˈbleɪ·zᵊn/ *v* [T] EMBLAZON

bleach /bliːtʃ/ *n* [U] a liquid or powder used to clean or to remove colour • *My grandmother doesn't think a toilet has been properly cleaned unless it's had half a bottle of bleach poured down it.* • *Do you think Lucy puts bleach on her hair* (=uses bleach to make it lighter in colour)*?*

bleach *obj* /bliːtʃ/ *v* [T] • *Nicki's face was brown and the sun had bleached the ends of her hair.* • *Gary's had his hair bleached again.*

bleach·ers /£ˈbliː·tʃəz, $-tʃɚz/ *pl n Am* a sloping area of seats at a sports ground which are not covered and are therefore not expensive to sit in

bleak /bliːk/ *adj* **-er, -est** (esp. of a place or the weather) cold and not welcoming, or (of a situation) hopeless • *The house stands on a bleak, windswept moor.* • *It is a bleak tale, set against a bleak East Anglian landscape.* • *In the long term, the economic* **outlook** *is bleak.* • *Business* **prospects** *remain very bleak.*

blear·y /£ˈblɪə·ri, $ˈblɪr·i/ *adj* **-ier, -iest** having tired-looking, red and watery eyes • *She came to the breakfast table looking rather bleary-***eyed** *after a late night.*

blear·i·ly /£ˈblɪə·rɪ·li, $ˈblɪr·ɪ-/ *adv* • *Carl stared blearily* (=in a very tired way) *at the newspaper.*

bleat /bliːt/ *v* [I] (of a sheep or goat) to produce a high, shaking sound • *In the field a lamb was bleating for its mother.* • *(fig.) She's always bleating* (=complaining in an annoying way) *about how badly she's been treated.*

bleat /bliːt/ *n* [C]

bleed *(obj)* /bliːd/ *v past* **bled** /bled/ to lose blood • *Your arm is bleeding.* [I] • *He'd been wounded in the arm and he was bleeding heavily.* [I] • In the past, to bleed someone was to make them lose blood, as a cure for an illness. [T] • *(infml)* To **bleed** someone **dry/white** is to take a lot of their money from them over a period of time: *The West is bleeding poorer countries dry through interest payments on their debts.* • You bleed a closed system such as a RADIATOR or a BRAKE to remove air from it to make it work correctly. [T] • *(disapproving)* A **bleeding heart** is someone who shows too much sympathy for everyone: *He said he was sick of bleeding-heart liberal politicians.*

bleed·er /£ˈbliː·dəʳ, $-dɚ/ *n* [C] *Br taboo* a person, usually a man or child, esp. one you feel annoyed with or sorry for • *Children? I can't stand the little bleeders!* • *Three weeks holiday, eh? You lucky bleeder!* • *The poor bleeder's got to have another operation on his back.*

bleed·ing /ˈbliː·dɪŋ/ *adj* [before n], *adv* [not gradable] *Br taboo* • Bleeding is used to express your annoyance with something: *I can't get the bleeding car to start!* ○ *Well don't look so bleeding pleased with yourself!* ○ *Hollywood films are all the bleeding same these days.* ○ *Look at the state of these shoes – and I bleeding well cleaned them this morning!*

bleep /bliːp/ *n* [C] a short high sound (often repeated) made by a machine • *He wears a wristwatch with an irritating bleep.* • *You must have had loads of messages on your answering machine – there were a lot of bleeps.*

bleep *(obj)* /bliːp/ *v* • *I heard his alarm clock bleeping this morning.* [I] • To bleep someone is to call them by sending a signal to a BLEEPER (=small machine) which they carry: *Doctors are often bleeped in the night.* [T]

bleep·er /£ˈbliː·pəʳ, $-pɚ/ *n* [C] • A bleeper is a small machine which can be carried or worn and which produces a short high sound to attract someone's attention.

blem·ish /ˈblem·ɪʃ/ *n* a mark on something that spoils its appearance • *It says on the bottle that the make-up will conceal freckles, scars and other minor* **skin** *blemishes.* [C] • *If you buy organic fruit and vegetables you have to put up with a few blemishes.* [C] • *(fig.) She is perhaps the only member of the royal family who still enjoys a blemish-***free** (=without moral faults) *reputation.* • *(fig.) Is any politician's record without blemish on this issue?* [U]

blem·ish *obj* /ˈblem·ɪʃ/ *v* [T] • *(fig.) It seems that this latest revelation has seriously blemished* (=spoilt) *the governor's* **reputation**.

blench /blentʃ/ *v* [I] to feel great fear and disgust at the thought of doing something, or *(humorous)* to be very unwilling to do something • *She blenched* **at** *the thought of picking up the dead animal.* • *(humorous) My sister blenches* **at** *the very thought of changing a baby's dirty nappy.*

blend *(obj)* /blend/ *v* to mix or combine together • *Blend the ingredients* **(together)** *into a smooth paste.* [T] • *The music of the violin blended sweetly* **with** *her voice.* [I] • *The armchair blends well* **with** *the colour of the carpet.* [I] • *I tried to blend* **into** (=to look similar to) *the crowd, but I was obviously not dressed for the occasion.* [I] • *The chameleon survives by blending* **in with** (=looking similar to) *its background.* [I]

blend /blend/ *n* [C] • *Her approach to decor is an exciting blend* (=mixture) *of old and new.* • *This coffee is a rich blend* (=mixture of different types) *of the best beans, it says on the label.*

blend·ed /ˈblen·dɪd/ *adj* • A drink which is blended contains two or more different types of the same product: *blended whisky/coffee/tea*

blend·er /£ˈblen·dəʳ, $-dɚ/ *n* [C] • A blender is an electric machine used in the kitchen for breaking down foods or making smooth liquid substances from soft foods and liquids. • PIC› **Kitchen**

bless *obj* /bles/ *v* [T] *past* **blessed** /blest, 'bles·ɪd/ or *literary* **blest** /blest/ to ask for God's help and protection for (someone or something), or to call or make (someone or something) holy • *The priest blessed the people in church, saying "God be with you".* • *Fortunately we were* **blessed with** (= lucky in having) *fine weather.* • **Bless you!** is a phrase which is said to someone who has just sneezed. • *(dated)* **Bless my soul!, Bless me!, Well I'm blessed!** are expressions of surprise. • **Bless you** or *(dated)* **bless your heart!** is an expression which you use when you are grateful for something kind that someone has done for you: *"Here, let me help you with your shopping." "Bless you my dear."* • *(humorous saying)* 'Bless his/her (little) cotton socks' is sometimes said of someone, esp. an adult, when you are pretending that you feel affection for them. • *"'God bless us every one!' said Tiny Tim"* (Charles Dickens in *A Christmas Carol*, 1843) • LP› **Phrases and customs**

bless·ed /blest, 'bles·ɪd/ *adj* • Blessed means holy: *Blessed are the meek for they shall inherit the earth.* • **The Blessed Virgin** is a name for the mother of Christ. • Blessed also means bringing happiness and good luck: *At last the blessed rain fell on the dry fields.* • *(infml)* Blessed is also an expression of annoyance: *Take that blessed cat out!*

bless·ing /'bles·ɪŋ/ *n* [C] • *The mass always ends with a blessing* (= the priest asking God to look after the people). • *(fig.) Her father refused to* **give** *his blessing* **to** (= approval to) *their marriage.* • *(fig.) The government has* **given** *its blessing* **to** (= approved) *a plan to improve the rights of children.* • Something that is extremely lucky is sometimes described as a blessing: *It was a blessing that no one was killed in the accident.* • A **blessing in disguise** is something that seems bad or unlucky at first, but results in something good happening later: *The ending of that relationship was a blessing in disguise really, since it meant that I focused on my career.*

bleth·er /£'bleð·əʳ, $-ɚ/ *n, v* BLATHER

blew /bluː/ *past simple of* BLOW

blight /blaɪt/ *v, n* (to cause) disease and death in plants or severe damage to things • *A* **potato** *blight destroyed the main food supply of Irish peasants in the 1840s, and hundreds of thousands starved to death.* [C] • *His arrival* **cast a** *blight* **on** (= spoiled) *the wedding day.* [U] • *A broken leg blighted* (= spoiled) *her* **chances** *of winning the ballroom dancing championship.* [T]

blight·er /£'blaɪ·təʳ, $-t̬ɚ/ *n* [C] *Br infml dated* a man or child, esp. an annoying one • *The little blighters next door have trampled all over my flowers again.*

bli·mey /'blaɪ·mi/ *exclamation Br infml dated* an expression of surprise • *Blimey, what a lot of food!* • LP› **Phrases and customs**

blimp /blɪmp/ *n* [C] a small AIRSHIP (= an aircraft that floats in the air)

blimp·ish /'blɪm·pɪʃ/ *adj Br infml* (esp. of an old man) having old-fashioned military principles and too much pride in his country • *a blimpish old colonel* • See also **colonel blimp** at COLONEL.

blind SIGHT /blaɪnd/ *adj* **-er, -est** unable to see • *She's been blind since birth.* • *He started to* **go** (= become) *blind in his sixties.* • *My dog is very old and she's blind* **in** *one eye.* • *(fig.) She seems to be blind* **to** (= not aware of) *his faults.* • *(fig.) He was blind* **with** *fury* (= He was so angry that he was not able to behave reasonably). • Blind **anger/faith/panic/prejudice** are extreme feelings that are without thought or reason. • *(infml humorous)* If you are **as blind as a bat** you are unable to see very well: *I can't read the subtitles on films anymore – I'm as blind as a bat.* • *(Br infml)* If you say that someone is **not taking a blind bit of notice** you mean that they are not paying attention at all: *He didn't take a blind bit of notice of what I said.* • A **blind alley** is a situation or method that you have tried and discovered to be of no use: *This sort of thinking just seems to be* **leading** *us* **up/down** *a blind alley.* • A **blind date** is when two people who have never met each other go out for a romantic social meeting. It may also refer to either of these two people: *Elaine has arranged for me to go* **on** *a blind date this Saturday with a bloke that she knows through work.* • **Blind man's buff** is a children's game in which one person who has a cloth tied over their eyes tries to catch the others. • Your **blind side** is an area in your range of sight where you cannot see clearly. See also BLINDSIDE. • A **blind spot** is an area that you are not able to see, esp. as a driver, the part of a road which is behind and slightly to one side of a car: It can be very dangerous if there's a vehicle **in** your blind spot. ○ *(fig.) I am quite good at English, but I have a bit of a blind spot* (= a lack of ability or understanding) *where spelling is concerned.* • LP› **Eye and seeing** (NL)

blind *obj* /blaɪnd/ *v* [T] • *She was blinded* (= made permanently blind) *in an accident at an early age.* • *Turning the corner the sun blinded me* (= made me unable to see for a moment) *so I didn't see the other car.* • *(fig.) We mustn't let our prejudices blind us* **to** (= make us unable to notice or understand) *the facts of the situation.* • *(Br and Aus)* To **blind** someone **with science** is to confuse someone by using difficult or technical words to describe something.

blind /blaɪnd/ *pl n* • **The blind** are people who are unable to see: *She trains guide dogs for the blind.* • **(A case of) the blind leading the blind** is a situation where a person who knows nothing is getting advice and help from someone who knows almost nothing. • *(saying)* 'In the country of the blind, the one-eyed man is king.'

blind·ness /'blaɪnd·nəs/ *n* [U] • *Her blindness* (= The fact that she is blind) *doesn't stop her from having a full and active life.* • *(fig.) Clea has a complete blindness* **to** (= inability to recognize) *her friend's faults.*

blind·ing /'blaɪn·dɪŋ/ *adj* • A blinding light is an extremely bright one: *There was loud bang and a sudden blinding* **light**. ○ *At that moment a blinding* **flash** *ripped across the blue of the sky.* ○ *(fig.) The answer came to her in a blinding* (= sudden and surprising) *revelation.*

blind·ly /'blaɪnd·li/ *adv* • *The room was completely dark and I fumbled blindly for the door.* • *(fig.) The aim of education is to teach young people to think for themselves and not follow blindly* (= without knowledge or understanding) *other people's prejudices.*

blind WINDOW /blaɪnd/, *Am and Aus* **shade** *n* [C] a cover for a window made of a single piece or strips of cloth, paper or plastic that is pulled up or down by a string • *a roller blind* • *a Venetian blind* • *a vertical blind* • *I pulled the blind down to block out the light.* • PIC› **Window** (NL)

blind EXTREMELY /blaɪnd/ *adv* **blind drunk** *infml* extremely drunk • (NL)

blind·ers /£'blaɪn·dəz, $-dɚz/ *pl n Am for* BLINKERS

blind·fold /£'blaɪnd·fəʊld, $-foʊld/ *n, v* (to put on) a strip of cloth which covers someone's eyes to stop them from seeing • *I untied the blindfold and looked around.* [C] • *She was blindfolded and taken somewhere in the back of a van.* [T]

blind·fold /£'blaɪnd·fəʊld, $-foʊld/ *adv* [not gradable] • *I've been there so often I could probably drive there blindfold.*

blind·side *obj* /'blaɪnd·saɪd/ *v* [T usually passive] *Am* to surprise (someone), usually with harmful results • *The recession blindsided a lot of lawyers who had previously taken for granted their comfortable income.*

blink *(obj)* EYE MOVEMENT /blɪŋk/ *v* to close and then open (the eyes) quickly once or several times • *Actors in films have to teach themselves not to blink very often.* [I] • *You've got something in your eye – try blinking your eyes a few times.* [T] • *As he opened the letter he found it hard to blink* **back** *his tears.* [T] • *(fig.) "How did Harry react when you told him you were expecting twins?" "He didn't even blink* **at** (= express any surprise at) *the news."* [I] • *(fig.) The warning light blinked* (= flashed on and off) *insistently in the darkness.* [I] • (D) (NL)

blink /blɪŋk/ *n* [U] • **A blink of an eye** is a very short space of time: *In a blink of an eye he had disappeared.*

blink FAULTY /blɪŋk/ *n* [U] **on the blink** *infml* not working correctly • *The chocolate machine's on the blink again.* • (D) (NL)

blink·ered /£'blɪŋ·kəd, $-kɚd/ *adj Am and Aus* (of a person) unable or unwilling to understand other people's beliefs, or (of a belief) showing an inability or unwillingness to understand other people • *He's so blinkered in his outlook.* • *Sadly our politicians take a rather blinkered approach to problem solving.*

blink·ers *Br and Aus* /£'blɪŋ·kəz, $-kɚz/, *Am* **blind·ers** *pl n* two pieces of leather that are put at the side of a horse's eyes so that it can only see forward • *Both horses perform best when racing* **in** *blinkers.* • If a person is described as wearing blinkers, it means that they can only see things one way and are not willing or able to consider other possibilities.

blink·ing /'blɪŋ·kɪŋ/ *adj* [before n; not gradable] *Br infml dated* an expression of annoyance • *I wish they'd turn down that blinking music!*

blip /blɪp/ *n* [C] a small spot of light, sometimes with a short sharp sound, that appears on a RADAR screen, or a sudden sharp V-shaped bend in a line on a computer screen • *(fig.) Last month's rise in inflation was described by the chancellor as only a blip* (=temporary change), *and the figure should continue to fall in future.*

bliss /blɪs/ *n* [U] perfect happiness • *Two weeks lying on a beach is my idea of* **(pure/sheer)** *bliss.* • *The couple led a life of apparent* **domestic/wedded** *bliss.* • *It's bliss to be able to lie back and just forget all about your worries.*

bliss·ful /ˈblɪs·fᵊl/ *adj* • *We spent a blissful year together before things started to go wrong.* • *She was* **in** *blissful ignorance* (=did not know the unpleasant facts) *of the true situation.*

bliss·ful·ly /ˈblɪs·fᵊl·i/ *adv* • *They were blissfully* **happy** *together.* • *I look back on those two months and realise that I was blissfully* **unaware** *of the problems to come.*

bli·ster /£ˈblɪs·təʳ, $-tɚ/ *n* [C] a painful red swelling on the skin, usually caused by burning or by continuous rubbing • *New shoes always give me blisters.* • *The wall she had just painted was covered in blisters* (=rounded swellings).

bli·ster *(obj)* /£ˈblɪs·təʳ, $-tɚ/ *v* • *The sun had blistered his back/the paintwork.* [T] • *I burnt my shoulders over the weekend and they're starting to blister.* [I]

bli·stered /£ˈblɪs·təd, $-tɚd/ *adj* • *Their feet were blistered and bleeding after the long walk to the border.*

bli·ster·ing /£ˈblɪs·tᵊr·ɪŋ, $-tɚ-/ *adj* • *We went out in the blistering* (=extreme) **heat**. • *The runners set off at a blistering* (=very fast) *pace.* • Blistering **remarks/sarcasm** are words that express deep anger and are very unkind.

blithe /blaɪð/ *adj* **-r, -st** *dated* happy and without worry • *a blithe comment* • *"Hail to thee, blithe Spirit! / Bird thou never wert* (=were)*"* (Percy Bysshe Shelley in the poem *To a Skylark*, 1819)

blithe·ly /ˈblaɪð·li/ *adv* • *She blithely agreed to the contract without realising what its consequences would be.* • *He left the house blithely* **unaware** *that he was still wearing his pyjamas.* • *She blithely* **ignored** *all the advice her mother gave her.*

bli·ther·ing /£ˈblɪð·ᵊr·ɪŋ, $ˈ-ɚ-/ *adj* [not gradable] **blithering idiot** an extremely stupid person, often one who talks nonsense • *You blithering idiot! You could have killed me with that knife.*

blitz /blɪts/ *v, n* (to make) a fast, violent attack on a town, city, etc. usually with bombs dropped from aircraft • *Coventry was blitzed mercilessly during the Second World War.* [T] • *They carried out a blitz* **on** *the industrial parts of the town.* [C] • *(fig.) The launch of the new car was accompanied by a* **media** *blitz* (=a lot of activities to attract the attention of the public) *involving newspapers, magazines, television and radio.* [C] • *(infml)* To have a blitz on something is to make a great effort to do something that needs to be done: *We* **had a** *blitz* **on** *the house at the weekend and cleaned it completely.* [U] ○ *The President is to launch* **a** *blitz* **on** *teenage crime accompanied by drastic reform of the police and prison services.* [U] • *(specialized)* In the game of CHESS, a blitz sometimes happens at the end of a timed game, when both players have to make a lot of moves in a very short period before the time allowed is past. [C] • **The Blitz** refers to the big attacks on British towns made by German aircraft in 1940-1: *She was killed* **in/during** *the Blitz.*

blitz·krieg /ˈblɪts·kriːg/ *n* [C] a sudden attack involving aircraft and forces on the ground that is intended to surprise the enemy and defeat it quickly • *In a blitzkrieg, the attack is concentrated on the enemy's rear, rather than its front where there is more resistance.*

bliz·zard /£ˈblɪz·əd, $-ɚd/ *n* [C] a severe snow storm with strong winds • *We once got* **stuck in** *a blizzard for six hours on the road across the moors.* • *Most of Devon and Cornwall was cut off* **during** *the 1978 blizzards.* • *In Sussex, blizzard* **conditions** *made the main roads almost impassable.* • A blizzard of things is a large amount of them arriving or being produced together, esp. in a confusing or badly organized way: *It's easy to be overwhelmed by the blizzard* **of** *statistics that the computer prints out.* ○ **A** *blizzard* **of** *leaflets will be falling through the country's letterboxes during the election campaign.*

bloat·ed /£ˈbləʊ·tɪd, $ˈbloʊ·t̬ɪd/ *adj* swollen and rounded because of containing too much air, liquid or food • *Drowned bodies are often horribly bloated.* • *I hate that bloated* (=uncomfortably full) **feeling** *you get when you've had too much to eat.* • *(fig.) The organization has become a bloated* (=unnecessarily large) **bureaucracy** *which is overstaffed and wasteful.*

bloat·er /£ˈbləʊ·təʳ, $ˈbloʊ·t̬ɚ/ *n* [C] a HERRING or MACKEREL (=type of fish) that has been preserved with salt and lightly smoked

blob /£blɒb, $blɑːb/ *n* [C] a fat round drop, usually of something sticky or thick, or *(infml)* a fat person • *a blob* **of** *glue/paint* • *(infml) You fat blob!* [as form of address]

bloc /£blɒk, $blɑːk/ *n* [C] a group of countries or people that have similar political interests • *The European Union is a powerful* **trading/trade** *bloc.* • *The economies of the* **former Eastern/Communist** *bloc countries have made rapid progress towards free-market capitalism.*

block LUMP /£blɒk, $blɑːk/ *n* [C] a solid straight-sided lump of hard material • *a block of wood* • *a large block of ice* • *(Am)* If something is **on the block**, it is being sold at an AUCTION (=a public sale where people compete to buy things by offering more money than other people). • In the past, **the** block was a large piece of wood on which criminals had their head cut off: *(fig.) I'm not going to* **put** *my* **head on** *the block* (=take the risk of great harm to myself) *for you.* • **Block capitals** or **block letters** is a style of writing in which each letter of a word is written separately and clearly using the capital letters of the alphabet: *Please print your name and address in block letters.* • A **block and tackle** is a device used for raising objects off the ground which consists of one or more small wheels connected to a high part of a building with a rope or chain moving over them. • PIC **Writing**

block GROUP /£blɒk, $blɑːk/ *n* [C] a group of things considered together • *a block of tickets/seats/shares* • *Corporate-hospitality firms make block* **bookings** (=buy large numbers of seats) *at big sporting events.* • A **block vote** is a large number of votes that are made in the same way by one person who represents a large group of people: *The days of the British trade union block vote seem to be coming to an end.*

block BUILDING /£blɒk, $blɑːk/ *n* [C] a large, usually tall building divided into separate parts for use as offices or homes by several different organizations or people • *an office block* • *(Br and Aus) a tower block* • *(Br and Aus) They lived in the same block of flats (Am* **apartment building** *or* **apartment house***).* • PIC **Accommodation, Office**

block AREA /£blɒk, $blɑːk/ *n* [C] the area between roads, esp. in towns and cities, or the length of this area • *(Am and Aus) The museum is just six blocks away.* • *(Am) My friend and I live* **on the** *same block* (=the same road between two other roads which cross it.) • *He only lives* **around the** *block* (=around the corner of the road).

block *obj* PREVENT /£blɒk, $blɑːk/ *v* [T] to prevent movement through (something) or to prevent (something) from happening or succeeding • *A fallen tree is blocking the road.* • *All the roads out of the town were blocked* **off** (=cars were prevented from using them) *by the police.* [M] • *My view was blocked by a tall man in a hat standing in front of me.* • *Another car had parked behind me and blocked me* **in**. [M] • *Unfortunately, a tree near the window blocks* **(out)** *the sun* (=stops the light from coming in). [T/M] • *(fig.) He's trying to block* **out** (=stop himself thinking about) *the accident.* [M] • *Every autumn dead leaves block* **(up)** *the drains.* [T/M] • *Her parents were blocking her* **progress** (=stopping her from succeeding). • *A group of politicians blocked the* **proposal** (=stopped it from being completed.)

block /£blɒk, $blɑːk/ *n* [C usually sing] • *A block* **in** (=An object blocking) *the pipe was preventing the water from coming through.*

block·age /£ˈblɒk·ɪdʒ, $ˈblɑː·kɪdʒ/ *n* • *There are thousands of collapses and blockages in British sewers every year.* [C] • *Angina is usually caused by the narrowing or blockage of one or more of the arteries which supply the heart muscle with blood.* [U]

blocked /£blɒkt, $blɑːkt/ *adj* • *The roads are blocked* **(up)**. • *I've got a sore throat and a blocked* **(up) nose**.

block·ade /£blɒkˈeɪd, $blɑːˈkeɪd/ *n* [C] the surrounding of a country or place by soldiers or ships to stop people or goods from going in or out • *to impose a blockade* • *The Soviet blockade* **of** *Berlin was* **lifted** *in May 1949.* • *Combined with the* **naval** *blockade, a well-directed air assault could force a surrender within days.* • *There is still some hope that the* **economic** *blockade will work and make military intervention unnecessary.*

block·ade *obj* /£blɒkˈeɪd, $blɑːˈkeɪd/ *v* [T] • *The Estonian port of Tallinn was blockaded for a time by Soviet* *warships.* • *In three days of angry protests, thousands of peasants blockaded traffic and held police officers hostage.*

block·bust·er /£ˈblɒkˌbʌs·təʳ, $ˈblɑːkˌbʌs·tɚ/ *n* [C] *infml* a book or film that is very successful, esp. because of its exciting contents • *Her latest blockbuster is the best-selling book so far this year.* • *a blockbuster movie/novel*

block·head /£ˈblɒk·hed, $ˈblɑːk-/ *n* [C] *dated infml* a stupid person • *Those blockheads have screwed up the whole project.*

bloke /£bləʊk, $bloʊk/ *n* [C] *Br and Aus infml* a man, often one who is considered to be ordinary • *Paul's a really* **good** *bloke* (=I like him a lot). • *I'm no hero – I'm just an* **ordinary** *bloke doing my job.* • *Her new boyfriend's a* **funny (sort of)** *bloke* (=slightly strange). • LP **Age**

bloke·ish, blok·ish /£ˈbləʊ·kɪʃ, $ˈbloʊ-/ *adj Br infml* • A man who is blokeish behaves in a way that is traditionally considered to be typical of an ordinary man: *Her new boyfriend's a bit too blokeish for my liking – he's always talking about football and cars.*

blonde *esp. female* **(-r, -st)**, *esp. male* **blond (-er, -est)** /£blɒnd, $blɑːnd/ *n, adj* (a person) with pale yellow or golden hair • *beautiful blonde hair* • *blonde highlights* • *a tall blonde woman* • *People think I'm a* **natural** *blonde, but actually my hair's dyed.* [C] • *(saying)* 'Blondes have more fun' means that a woman with lightly coloured hair is often considered more attractive than other women and so has the admiring attention of more men. • *"Blonde Bombshell"* (used to describe the film actress Jean Harlow, (1911-37)) • *"Gentlemen Prefer Blondes"* (title of a book by Anita Loos, 1925)

blood LIQUID /blʌd/ *n* [U] the red liquid that is sent around the body by the heart and carries oxygen and important substances to organs and tissue and removes waste products • *He lost a lot of blood in the accident.* • **fig.** *Our team scored the opening goal, so it was* **first** *blood* (=first success in competition with someone else) **to** *us.* • *(fig.) The company has brought in some* **fresh** *blood* (=young, energetic and enthusiastic people) *in an effort to revive its fortunes.* • To **give** or **donate** blood is to allow a trained person to take some blood from your body so that it can be stored and is ready to be given to people who have a lost a lot of blood during an accident or operation. • If something **makes** your **blood boil** it makes you extremely angry: *The way they have treated those people makes my blood boil.* • If you are **after** someone's **blood**, you are very angry with them and are threatening to harm them: *You'd better stay out of her way – she's after your blood.* • If something makes your **blood run cold**, it frightens you very much: *My blood ran cold when I heard the tapping on the window.* • *(infml)* **Blood and guts** is a way of describing violence that seems very real: *There was a bit too much blood and guts in the film for my liking.* • If your **blood is up**, you are feeling very angry. • *Persuading Chris to buy a round of drinks is like* **getting blood out of a stone** (=extremely difficult because he is unwilling to spend money). • A **blood bank** is a cool place where blood is stored before it is used in hospitals. • A **blood count** is (a medical test of) the number of red and white blood cells in a person's blood. • A **blood donor** is a person who allows some of their blood to be taken to help others who need it. • A person's **blood group** or **blood type** is the type of blood which they have in their body and which cannot be mixed safely with other types: *She belongs to a rare blood group.* • **Blood lust** is the wish to be excited by being violent or watching other people being violent. • *(disapproving)* **Blood money** is money paid to the family of a murdered person or money paid to have someone murdered. • **Blood money** is also money that is paid to a person either for supplying information or for helping in some indirect way to cause the death of someone else. • **Blood poisoning** (also *specialized* **septicaemia)** is a serious illness in which an infection spreads through the blood, or (also *specialized* **toxaemia)** the condition of having a poisonous substance or substances in your blood. • **Blood pressure** is a measure of the pressure at which the blood flows through the body: *The nurse will* **take** *your blood pressure in a moment.* ○ *Both very* **high** *blood pressure and very* **low** *blood pressure can be dangerous to health.* • Something that is **blood-red** is the bright red colour of fresh blood. • A **blood sport** is any sport that involves animals being killed or hurt to excite the people watching or taking part: *Blood sports include foxhunting and cock-fighting.* • A **blood test** is a scientific examination of a person's blood to find out whether they have any diseases or lack any important substances. • A **blood transfusion** is a process in which blood that has been taken from one person is put into another person's body, esp. after an accident or during an operation. • A **blood vessel** is any of the tubes through which blood flows in the body: *Veins and arteries are blood vessels.* ○ *(humorous) I almost* **burst a blood vessel** (=It was a great physical effort) *trying to carry her suitcase.* ○ *(humorous) Don't* **burst a blood vessel** (=Don't be so angry)*!*

blood·y /ˈblʌd·i/ *adj* **-ier, -iest** • *He had a bloody* **nose** (=nose covered with blood) *and a twisted ankle.* • *A bloody* (=extremely violent) *war had raged for years.* • *It was a* **long and** *bloody battle and many men were killed.* • A **Bloody Mary** is an alcoholic drink made of VODKA and TOMATO juice. • *"My head is bloody, but unbowed"* (from the poem *Invictus* by W.E.Henley, 1888)

blood·i·ly /ˈblʌd·ɪ·li/ *adv* • *All the demonstrations were bloodily suppressed by government forces.*

-blood·ed /-ˈblʌd·ɪd/ *combining form* • *Mammals are* **warm-***blooded and reptiles are* **cold-***blooded.*

blood·ied /ˈblʌd·id/ *adj literary* • Something that is bloodied is covered in blood: *His bloodied body was discovered in a ditch half a mile from his home.*

blood·less /ˈblʌd·ləs/ *adj* • A bloodless military operation is one which results in no deaths: *The rebel soldiers seized power in a bloodless* **coup.** • When a person's face or skin is bloodless, it is very pale: *His face was thin and bloodless.*

blood *obj* FIRST EXPERIENCE /blʌd/ *v* [T] to give (someone) their first experience of something • *They decided to blood him in the full international team at the age of only 18.*

blood FAMILY /blʌd/ *n* [U] family relationship by birth rather than marriage • *They are related* **by** *blood.* • *She has Russian blood in her* (=a parent, grandparent, etc. of hers was Russian). • *Painting must* **be/(Br also) run in** *his blood* (=come from his parents, grandparents, etc.), *as his father and grandmother were artists too.* • *(saying)* 'Blood is thicker than water' means family connections are always more important than friendships. • A **blood brother** is a man who has promised to treat another man as his brother in a ceremony in which they cut themselves and mix their blood together. • A **blood relation** is a person who is related to you by birth rather than through marriage. • **Blood ties** are the relationships that exist by birth rather than through marriage. • LP **Relationships**

blood·bath /£ˈblʌd·bɑːθ, $-bæθ/ *n* [C] an extremely violent event in which a great number of people are killed • *Is there nothing that the outside world can do to* **prevent** *a bloodbath?*

blood·curd·ling /£ˈblʌd·kɜː·dl·ɪŋ, $-kɜːr-/ *adj* causing a feeling of extreme fear • *a bloodcurdling story about a vicious murder*

blood·hound /ˈblʌd·haʊnd/ *n* [C] a large dog that has a very good ability to smell things and is used for hunting animals or finding people who are lost

blood·let·ting /£ˈblʌdˌlet·ɪŋ, $-ˌleṭ-/ *n* [U] killing and violence, esp. between enemy groups involved in an argument that has existed for a long time

blood·line /ˈblʌd·laɪn/ *n* [C] all the members of a family group of people or animals over a period of time, esp. when thought of in connection with the shared family characteristics that they have • *Ismaili Muslims believe that a bloodline joins the Aga Khan to Muhammed.* • *This is a pedigree poodle – her bloodline is pure.*

blood·shed /ˈblʌd·ʃed/ *n* [U] a great amount of killing and violence • *The army was brought in to try to prevent further bloodshed.*

blood·shot /£ˈblʌd·ʃɒt, $-ʃɑːt/ *adj* (of the eyes) with the white part red or pink because of swelling and soreness • *Hayfever gives me a runny nose and bloodshot* **eyes.**

blood·stain /ˈblʌd·steɪn/ *n* [C] a mark made by blood, often as a result of a violent event • *His car was found abandoned with bloodstains on the driver's seat.*

blood·stained /ˈblʌd·steɪnd/ *adj* • *Bloodstained clothing* (=Clothing marked with blood) *was found near the scene of the attack.*

blood·stock /£ˈblʌd·stɒk, $-stɑːk/ *n* [U] horses that have been specially bred for racing

blood·stream /ˈblʌd·striːm/ *n* [C usually sing] the flow of blood around the body • *The drug can be taken orally, but it works more quickly if it is injected directly into* **the** *bloodstream.*

blood·suck·er /£ˈblʌd·sʌk·əʳ, $-ɚ/ *n* [C] an animal or insect that sucks blood from other animals • *Leeches and mosquitoes are bloodsuckers.*

blood·thirst·y /£'blʌd,θɜː·sti, $-,θɜːr-/ *adj* eager to see or take part in violence and killing • *The Vikings were cruel and bloodthirsty warriors.*

blood·y ANGER /'blʌd·i/ *adj* [before n], *adv esp. Br and Aus slang* used to express anger and annoyance emphatically • *I've had a bloody* **awful** *week.* • *"How did you do in your exams?" "Bloody* **badly**.*"* • *It's a bloody* **disgrace** *that some war widows don't get a decent pension.* • *Which bloody* **idiot** *left this knife lying on the floor?* • *(humorous) "Jane's train has been delayed so she'll be late for the meeting." "Oh that's bloody* **marvellous** (= extremely annoying), *that is!"* • *This computer's bloody* **useless***! It's always going wrong.* • *I wish you'd stop complaining and bloody* **well** *get on with your job.* • *Don't you tell me what to do! I'll do what I bloody* **well** *like in my own house.* • **Bloody hell** is an expression of great annoyance which some people find offensive: *Bloody hell! I've lost my wallet.* ○ *What the bloody hell did you do that for?* ○ *What the bloody hell do you think you're doing in my office?* • Someone who is **bloody-minded** is an awkward person who makes things difficult for others and opposes their views for no good reason: *I don't know why they're refusing to cooperate with us. I suppose they're just being bloody-minded.* ○ *I reckon it was sheer* **bloody-mindedness** *that made him reject your proposal.*

blood·y EMPHASIS /'blʌd·i/ *adj* [before n], *adv esp. Br and Aus slang* used to emphasize an adjective, adverb or noun • *Nothing's perfect in life and it would be bloody* **boring** *if it was.* • *You must think I'm a bloody* (= a very great) **fool**. • *Tina's working for an insurance company in Paris and earning bloody* **good** (= a very large amount of) *money.* • *I had a bloody* **good laugh** (= a very enjoyable time) *at Mary's wedding.* • *"He's decided not to bring his kids to the party." "And a bloody* **good thing** *too. They always cause trouble."* • *I had a bloody* **marvellous** *time in Berlin.* • *He looked bloody* **stupid** *in that ridiculous hat.* • *I'm afraid there's* **not a** *bloody* **thing** (= nothing at all) *you can do about it.* • *"I can't see a bloody* **thing** (= I can't see anything at all)*," she said, peering through the keyhole.* • *She's done bloody* **well** *to reach the semi-final.*

bloom /bluːm/ *v* [I] (of a plant or tree) to produce flowers, or (of a flower) to open or be open • *These flowers will bloom all through the summer.* • *(fig.) Rimbaud's poetic genius bloomed* (= produced its best) *early and then died away.*

bloom /bluːm/ *n* [C] • A bloom is a flower on a plant: *Their garden was full of wonderful blooms.* • *(literary) The house had been filled with sweet-smelling blooms* (= cut flowers). • *The roses* **come into bloom** (= start to produce flowers) *at this time of year.* • *The apple trees are* **in (full) bloom** (= producing all their flowers) *at the moment.* • *(fig. literary) He was only nineteen but* **the bloom of youth** (= the young freshness) *had already disappeared from his face.*

bloom·ing /'bluː·mɪŋ/ *adj* [not gradable] • A person who is blooming has a healthy, energetic and attractive appearance: *She's been blooming since she came out of hospital.*

bloom·er MISTAKE /£'bluː·mər, $-mɚ/ *n* [C] *Br dated slang* a silly or embarrassing mistake which does not have serious results • *I made* **an awful** *bloomer when I introduced Mary's new boyfriend using her ex-husband's name.*

bloom·er BREAD /£'bluː·mər, $-mɚ/ *n* [C] *Br* a type of large loaf which has diagonal cuts on the top

bloom·ers /£'bluː·məz, $-mɚz/ *pl n* long loose trousers that were tight around the bottom of the legs and were worn under a short skirt by women in the middle of the 19th century, or *(esp. humorous)* long loose underwear worn below the waist by women

bloom·ing /'bluː·mɪŋ/, **bloom·in'** /'blu·mɪn/ *adj* [before n], *adv esp. Br infml* extreme(ly) or great(ly) • *It's* **a** *blooming disgrace!* • *I'm not going to bloomin' well apologise to him!* • *She did blooming well to reach the final.* • See also **blooming** at BLOOM.

bloop·er /£'bluː·pər, $-pɚ/ *n* [C] *esp. Am humorous* an amusing mistake made by an actor or television personality during the making of a film or television programme, which is cut out of the end product • *Some TV shows are made up entirely of bloopers from movies and other shows.*

blos·som /£'blɒs·ᵊm, $'blɑː·sᵊm/ *v* [I] (of a tree or plant) to produce flowers before producing edible fruit, or *(fig.)* (of a person) to become more attractive, successful or complete • *The cherry tree is beginning to blossom.* • *(fig.) Since their first meeting their friendship has blossomed* (= they have become good friends). • *(fig.) He has really blossomed* **(out)** *recently* (= He has become an attractive and interesting person). • *(fig.) She is suddenly blossoming* **into** (= becoming) *a very attractive woman.* • *(fig.) Sean and Sarah's friendship blossomed* **into** *love.* • *(fig.) War put an end to their blossoming* (= developing) *love affair.*

blos·som /£'blɒs·ᵊm, $'blɑː·sᵊm/ *n* • *The grass was covered with white blossoms.* [C] • *The scent of apple blossom filled the air.* [U] • *All along the road the trees are* **in (full) blossom** (= flowering). • PIC> **Tree**

blot SPOIL /£blɒt, $blɑːt/ *v, n* **-tt-** (to make) a dirty mark with ink • *His homework was badly written and covered in* **ink** *blots.* [C] • *(fig.) Being caught stealing was* **a** *blot* **on** (= a bad mark against) *her character.* [C] • *(Br and Aus)* To **blot** your **copybook** is to do something that makes you seem less deserving of trust or respect: *I've blotted my copybook* **by** *forgetting an important meeting at work.* • A **blot on the landscape** is something such as an ugly building that spoils a pleasant view: *The proposed power station will be a horrendous blot on the landscape.* • If something blots **out** the sun it stops any light from coming through: *A dark cloud suddenly blotted out the sun.* • To blot **out** a memory or thought is to avoid thinking about it.

blot *obj* DRY /£blɒt, $blɑːt/ *v* [T] **-tt-** to dry a wet surface by pressing something soft and absorbent against it • *After signing my name I blotted the paper.* • *She put on her lipstick and then carefully blotted her lips* **with** *a tissue.* • *Fry the fillets for three minutes on each side and blot* **up** *any excess oil before serving.* • **Blotting paper** is thick soft paper which you press onto a piece of paper on which you have just written in ink, in order to dry the ink.

blot·ter /£'blɒt·ər, $'blɑː·t̬ɚ/ *n* [C] • A blotter is a large piece of blotting paper with a stiff back which is used to absorb ink and is often put on the top of a DESK to protect it when writing: *Gerald has a big old-fashioned desk, with a large blotter on it.*

blotch /£blɒtʃ, $blɑːtʃ/ *n* [C usually pl] a mark of an irregular shape, such as on a person's skin • *Her face was covered in purple blotches.*

blotch·y /£'blɒtʃ·i, $'blɑː·tʃi/ *adj* **-ier, -iest** • *He'd been crying and his face was all swollen and blotchy.*

blot·to /£'blɒt·əʊ, $'blɑː·t̬oʊ/ *adj dated slang* extremely drunk • *I got completely blotto at Jeremy's wedding.*

blouse /£blaʊz, $blaʊs/ *n* [C] a shirt for a woman or girl • *She was wearing a white silk blouse.* • PIC> **Clothes** (F) (GR)

blou·son /£'bluː·zɒn, $-sɑːn/ *n* [C] a piece of clothing, such as a loose short jacket, which is worn on the upper body and fits tightly around the waist • *She was wearing a silk blouson* **(jacket)**.

blow *(obj)* SEND OUT AIR /£bləʊ, $bloʊ/ *v past simple* **blew** /bluː/, *past part* **blown** /£bləʊn, $bloʊn/ to send out a stream of air, or to move (something) or be moved with a stream of air • *The wind was blowing* **harder** *every minute.* [I] • *On the beach the letter blew* **away** *and I had to run after it.* [I] • *The gale-force wind had blown the fence* **down**. [T] • *She blew* **on** *the fire to help it to light.* [I] • *I blew the dust* **off** *the old book.* [T] • *(Am) (fig.) Just blow* **off** *his comments* (= do not take them seriously), *he's only joking.* [I] • *I wish you wouldn't blow smoke* **in** *my face.* [T] • *He scored the winning goal just before the whistle blew* (= had a stream of air sent through so that it made a sound). [I] • To blow a musical instrument is to make it produce a sound by sending air through it from your mouth. [T] • *(Am) (infml) They* **blew** *the other team* **away** (= severely defeated them) *in the second half of the game.* • *(infml) Winning the Olympic gold medal really* **blew** *her* **away** (= caused strong emotions in her). • To blow your **nose** is to force air from your lungs through it to clear it. [T] • To blow someone **a kiss** or blow **a kiss at** someone is to kiss your hand and blow on it in the direction of someone. [T] • *(Br)* To **blow the cobwebs away** is to get rid of feelings of tiredness, usually with fresh air or exercise: *A five mile jog in the rain certainly blew the cobwebs away.* • *(dated)* If you **blow the gaff** you let something that is secret be known: *Don't blow the gaff* **on** *us about putting the rat in his desk.* • If a person **blows hot and cold** about something, they are very interested in it at one time, but soon after do not seem interested in it : *He's been blowing hot and cold* **about** *the trip to Holland ever since I first suggested it.* • *These pictures will* **blow the lid off** (= make known to the public) *his illegal activities.* • *He lifts weights after work to* **blow off steam** (= to become free from worry or anger). • If you **blow** your **own trumpet/horn**, you tell everyone proudly about your successes or achievements. • *(infml)* To **blow the whistle** on someone or something is to cause something bad to stop, esp. by bringing it to the attention of other people. • *After the dinner party had ended she blew* **out** *the candles* (=stopped the flames from burning by blowing on them). [M] • *The sudden breeze made the candles blow* **out**. [I] • *The storm raged all night but by morning it had blown* **over**/*blown itself* **out** (=stopped). [T] • *I thought that after a few months the argument would* **blow over** (=be forgotten about). • When a storm blows **up** it begins. [I] • To blow **up** tyres etc. is to fill them with air: *Would you help me blow up these balloons?* [M] • A photograph or picture that is blown **up** is printed in a larger size. [M] • To **blow-dry** your hair is to make it dry by using an electric **hair dryer** (=a small machine that blows warm air). • *(taboo slang)* A **blow job** is a sexual activity in which a man's penis is excited by the touch of someone's mouth. • *"Blow, blow thou winter wind, / Thou art not so unkind / As man's ingratitude"* (Shakespeare, As You Like It 2.7) • *"The answer, my friend, is blowin' in the wind"* (from the song *Blowin' in the Wind* by Bob Dylan, 1962)

blow /£bləʊ, $bloʊ/ *n* [C usually sing] • *She gave the boy a tissue and told him to have a good blow* (=to blow his nose well). • *(Br dated) Shall we go out for a blow* (=a walk in the fresh air)*?*

blow·y /£'bləʊ·i, $'bloʊ-/ *adj* **-ier**, **-iest** *infml* • *It was a very blowy* (=windy) *day.*

blow *(obj)* DESTROY /£bləʊ, $bloʊ/ *v past simple* **blew** /bluː/, *past part* **blown** /£bləʊn, $bloʊn/ to (cause to) become destroyed by a bomb, technical failure, etc. • *His car had been blown* **to** *pieces.* [T] • *The strength of the explosion blew her leg* **off**. [M] • *The terrorists blew* **up** (= destroyed by bombing) *the parliament buildings.* [M] • If an electrical FUSE (=short thin piece of wire) blows or if you blow **a** fuse something electrical stops working because it is receiving too much electricity. [I/T] • If a tyre blows it suddenly gets a hole in it and goes flat. [I] • *When someone surprises him it sure* **blows** *his* **cool** (= makes him upset). • *I was pretending to be her sister until she* **blew** *my* **cover** (=let people know who I really was). • *(infml dated)* If someone **blows a gasket** they suddenly become very angry: *When he told her how much it cost, she blew a gasket.* • *(infml)* To **blow** your **lid/top/stack** is to become extremely angry: *My father will blow his top when he sees what happened to the car.* • *(infml)* If a person **blows** someone's **brains out** they kill that person by shooting them in the head: *After two earlier suicide attempts, she finally succeeded in blowing her brains out.* • *(infml)* To blow a large amount of money is to spend it, esp. on things that are not really necessary: *When I first got paid I blew it all on a night out.* [T] • *(infml)* If you **blow it** or **blow** your **chance** you fail to take advantage of an opportunity by doing or saying something wrong: *I guess I blew it when I turned down that job offer, didn't I?* • *(infml)* If something **blows** your **mind** you find it very exciting and unusual. See also **mind-blowing** at MIND THOUGHTS. • *When he says he has been all over the world he's just* **blowing smoke** (=not telling the exact truth, often to make himself seem better than he really is). • *(infml)* **Blow the expense** (=I don't care about how much it costs)*! We need a new car.* • *(infml dated)* **Blow it!** is used to express annoyance: *Oh, blow it! I've forgotten to invite Paul to the party.* • *(infml dated)* **Well, I'll be blowed!** and **Blow me!** are used to express great surprise: *"Kate's decided to get married." "Well, I'll be blowed!"* • *(infml dated)* **I'm blowed if I'm going to** *pay for his taxi home* (=I am determined not to pay for it).

blow HIT /£bləʊ, $bloʊ/ *n* [C] a hard hit with a hand or a weapon • *A sharp blow to the stomach sent him spinning to the floor.* • *They almost* **came to blows** (=had a physical fight) **over** *the last sausage.* • *(fig.) Her death at twenty* **came as a (terrible)** *blow* (=was a sudden shock with very damaging effects) **to** *her parents.* • *(fig.) Losing his job was a severe blow* **to** (=had a very damaging effect on) *his confidence.* • A **blow-by-blow** account/description is one in which every detail and action of an event is described: *I almost fell asleep as he gave me a blow-by-blow account of his day at the bank.*

blow a·way *obj*, **blow** *obj* **a·way** *v adv* [M] to kill (a person) by shooting them • *I'm gonna blow him away when I catch up with him.*

blow·er /£'bləʊ·əʳ, $'bloʊ·ɚ/ *n* [U] **the blower** *Br and Aus infml* the telephone • *Get* **on** *the blower and invite him round.*

blow·fly /£'bləʊ·flaɪ, $'bloʊ-/ *n* [C] a fly which puts its eggs in decaying meat, excrement and injuries in which the skin is broken

blow·hard /£'bləʊ·hɑːd, $'bloʊ·hɑːrd/ *n* [C] *Am infml* a person who likes to talk about how important they are • *Stop being such a blowhard! Do you have to talk about yourself the whole time?*

blow·hole /£'bləʊ·həʊl, $'bloʊ·hoʊl/ *n* [C] an opening in the top of the head of a WHALE (=large sea mammal) through which it breathes

blow·out EXPLOSION /£'bləʊ·aʊt, $'bloʊ-/ *n* [C] *esp. Am* a sudden bursting of a tyre on a road vehicle while it is moving quickly • *The car skidded all over the road after a* **high speed** *blowout.*

blow·out MEAL /£'bləʊ·aʊt, $'bloʊ-/ *n* [C] *Br infml* a very large meal, or *(Am infml)* a party or social occasion • *We went out on Saturday night and had a* **real** (=large) *blowout.*

blow·pipe *Br and Aus* /£'bləʊ·paɪp, $'bloʊ-/, *Am* **blow·gun** /£'bləʊ·gʌn, $'bloʊ-/ *n* [C] a weapon in the shape of a tube with which arrows are fired by blowing through it

blows·y (**-ier**, **-iest**), **blow·zy** (**-ier**, **-iest**) /£'blaʊ·zi, $-si/ *adj* (of a woman) untidy looking, quite fat and wearing clothes that are brightly coloured or too tight

blow·torch /£'bləʊ·tɔːtʃ, $'bloʊ·tɔːrtʃ/, *Br also* **blow·lamp** /£'bləʊ·læmp, $'bloʊ-/ *n* [C] a tool used to heat metal or remove paint from a surface by producing an extremely hot flame

blow·y /£'bləʊ·i, $'bloʊ-/ *adj* See at BLOW SEND OUT AIR

blub·ber CRY /£'blʌb·əʳ, $-ɚ/, *Br infml* **blub** /blʌb/ *v* [I] **-bb-** *disapproving* to cry in a noisy and childish way • *He just stood there blubbering when I told him I was leaving him.* • *(Br infml) Oh stop blubbing! Your knee can't hurt that much.*

blub·ber FAT /£'blʌb·əʳ, $-ɚ/ *n* [U] the thick layer of fat under the skin of sea mammals such as WHALES which keeps them warm, or *(infml)* human fat • *The hunting of whales for oil, meat, and blubber has resulted in a serious decline in whale populations and the near-extinction of several species.* • *(infml) He's gone on a diet to try to lose some of his blubber before his wedding.*

blud·geon *obj* /'blʌdʒ·ᵊn/ *v* [T] to hit (someone) hard and repeatedly with a heavy weapon • *The two boys had been mercilessly bludgeoned* **to death**. • *(fig.) The children bludgeoned their parents* **into** *taking* (=forced them to take) *them to the zoo.*

blud·geon /'blʌdʒ·ᵊn/ *n* [C] • A bludgeon is a heavy stick which is thick at one end and is used as a weapon.

blue COLOUR /bluː/ *adj, n* **-r**, **-st** (having) the colour of the sky without clouds on a bright day, or a darker or lighter variety of this • *He wore a faded blue shirt that matched his pale blue eyes.* • *It was a sky of* **deepest blue**. • *It was freezing outside and her hands were blue* **with cold** (= slightly blue because of the cold) *when she came in.* • If you say or shout something **until** you are **blue in the face**, you are wasting your efforts because you will get no results: *You can tell her to tidy her room until you are blue in the face, but she won't listen to you.* • If something happens **out of the blue**, it is completely unexpected: *One day, out of the blue, a girl rang up and said she was my sister.* • *He has a bath* **once in a blue moon** (=very rarely). • *She* **screamed/shouted blue murder** (=made a lot of noise and complained loudly) *when she had to go to the dentist's.* • *(Br and Aus dated)* If you are **in a blue funk** (*Am* **in a funk**) about something, you are in a state of anxiety, fear and sometimes confusion: *He's in a blue funk about his job interview.* • A **blue baby** is a baby born with slightly blue skin, usually because it has something wrong with its heart. • **Blue-black** is very dark blue that sometimes looks blue and sometimes black. • A **blue-blooded** person is someone who is born into a family which belongs to the highest social class. • **Blue cheese** is a cheese with a strong flavour that has thin blue lines of bacteria going through it: *Stilton and Roquefort are popular types of blue cheese.* • A **blue chip** company or investment is one that is considered to be safe and certain to make a profit: *Much of her personal fortune has been made from investments in blue chip companies.* • **Blue collar** workers are people who do physical or unskilled work in a factory rather than office work. • *(Br and Aus infml disapproving)* A **blue-eyed boy** (*Am* **fair-haired boy**) is a boy or man who is particularly liked and is treated well by someone, usually in authority. • *(infml)* **Blue-eyed soul** is a name for **soul music** played by white people. • **Blue-green algae** is a poisonous type of plant that grows on the surface of lakes in warm weather. • **Blue jeans** are trousers made of blue DENIM (=a strong cotton cloth). • *(Am infml)* A **blue law** is a law that limits activities, such as shopping or working on Sundays, which are considered to be immoral for religious reasons: *The town's blue laws were recently repealed and now you can buy liquor on a Sunday.* • If a person goes over a piece of writing with a **blue pencil**, they remove or change some of the words to improve it or make it acceptable. • A **blue riband**/*(esp. Am)* **blue ribbon** is a prize in a competition in the form of a blue RIBBON (=a woven strip of material): *Redland Middle School in Rockville has received a Blue Ribbon of excellence for the third time in eight years.* ○ *(fig. Am) The professor is a member of several* **blue-ribbon** (= expert) *scientific committees.* • A **blue tit** is a small European bird with a blue head and wings and a yellow front. • *"But don't you step on my blue suede shoes"* (from the song *Blue Suede Shoes* sung by Elvis Presley and by Carl Perkins, 1956)

blu·ish, blue·ish /ˈbluː·ɪʃ/ *adj* • Something that is bluish is slightly blue: *I want to buy a bluish-grey suit for an important job interview.*

blue·ness /ˈbluː·nəs/ *n* [U]

blue SEXUAL /bluː/ *adj* **-r, -st** showing or mentioning sexual activity in a way that offends many people • *a blue joke* • *a blue movie/film* • *His type of humour is a bit too blue for my tastes.*

blue SAD /bluː/ *adj* [after v] **-r, -st** *infml* feeling or showing sadness • *He's been feeling really blue since he failed his exams.* • *"When I'm feelin blue, all I have to do is take a look at you, then I'm not so blue"* (from the song *A Groovy Kind of Love* by The Mindbenders, 1965)

blues /bluːz/ *n* [U + sing/pl v] • **The blues** is a type of slow sad music, originally from the southern US, in which the singer often sings about his or her difficult life and bad luck in love: *Can you name any famous blues* **singers**? ○ *Billie Holiday was famous for* **singing** *the blues.* ○ *I'm gonna sing you a classic blues* **number** (=song) *now.* • *(infml)* If you **have the blues**, you feel sad: *He's had the blues real bad since his wife left him.* • *"The Blues Brothers"* (title of a film, 1980)

blue SPORTSPERSON /bluː/ *n* [C] a person who has played a sport for Oxford or Cambridge University against the other university • *The England captain is a former Cambridge blue.*

blue·bell /ˈbluː·bel/ *n* [C] a small European plant that usually grows in woods and has blue flowers shaped like bells • Bluebell is also *Scot Eng for* HAREBELL.

blue·ber·ry /ˈbluː·bᵊr·i, -ˌber-/ *n* [C] (the dark blue fruit of) a bush that is grown in N America, similar to a BILBERRY • *"I found my thrill on Blueberry hill"* (song by Fats Domino and others, 1941) • PIC› **Berries**

blue·bird /£ˈbluː·bɜːd, $-bɜːrd/ *n* [C] a small blue singing bird found in N America

blue·bot·tle /£ˈbluː·ˌbɒt·l̩, $-ˌbɑː·t̬l̩/ *n* [C] a big FLY (=type of insect) with a dark blue shiny body

blue·grass /£ˈbluː·grɑːs, $-græs/ *n* [U] a type of COUNTRY music from the southern US played on stringed instruments such as guitars, BANJOS and VIOLINS

blue·jay /ˈbluː·dʒeɪ/ *n* [C] a small N American bird with a bright blue back, a grey front and feathers that stand up on the top of its head

blue·print /ˈbluː·prɪnt/ *n* [C] a photographic copy of an early plan for a building or machine, with white lines on a blue background • *She was charged with spying after she was caught trying to steal the blueprint of a top-secret missile system.* • A blueprint is also an early plan or design which explains how something might be achieved: *It is unlikely that their blueprint* **for** *economic reform will be put into action.*

blue·stock·ing /£ˈbluː·ˌstɒk·ɪŋ, $-ˌstɑː·kɪŋ/ *n* [C] *dated* an intelligent and highly educated woman who spends most of her time studying and is therefore not approved of by some men

bluff PRETEND /blʌf/ *v* to deceive (someone) by making them think either that you are going to do something when you really have no intention of doing it, or that you have knowledge that you do not really have, or that you are someone else • *Is he going to jump or is he only bluffing?* [I] • *Tony seems to know a lot about music, but sometimes I think he's only bluffing.* [I] • *She bluffed the doorman* **into** *thinking that she was a reporter.* [T] • If you **bluff** your **way** into or out of a situation, you get yourself into or out of it by deceiving people: *However did Mina manage to bluff her way* **into** *that job?* [T] ○ *He's one of those people who is very good at bluffing their way* **out of** *trouble.* [T]

bluff /blʌf/ *n* [C] • *When she said she was going to leave him, he thought it was* **only** *a bluff.*

bluff CLIFF /blʌf/ *n* [C] a cliff or very steep bank

bluff TOO HONEST /blʌf/ *adj* **-er, -est** direct or too honest, esp. in a way that some people find rude • *Despite her bluff* **manner**, *she's actually a very kind woman.*

blu·ish /ˈbluː·ɪʃ/ *adj* See at BLUE COLOUR

blun·der MISTAKE /£ˈblʌn·dəʳ, $-dɚ/ *v, n* (to make) a big mistake, especially as a result of lack of care or thought • *A woman died of a rare disease yesterday after she was infected as a result of a hospital blunder.* [C] • *I* **committed** *a bit of a blunder by calling his new wife by his ex-wife's name.* [C] • *He said that the tax was the biggest political blunder that the government had ever* **made**. [C] • *I blundered badly in the boss's eyes by losing the firm an important client.* [I] • *That was a really stupid thing to do, you blundering idiot!*

blun·der MOVE /£ˈblʌn·dəʳ, $-dɚ/ *v* [I always + adv/prep] to move in a awkward way • *I could hear him blundering* **around** *in the darkness.* • *The two countries seem to be blundering* **into/towards** *war.*

blun·der·er /£ˈblʌn·dᵊr·əʳ, $-dɚ·ɚ/, *Am also* **blun·der·buss** *n* [C] • *I'm sorry I knocked your coffee over – I'm such a blunderer* (=awkward person).

blun·der·buss GUN /£ˈblʌn·də·bʌs, $-dɚ-/ *n* [C] an old-fashioned gun with a wide mouth that shoots a lot of small metal balls

blun·der·buss PERSON /£ˈblʌn·də·bʌs, $-dɚ-/ *n* [C] *Am for* **blunderer**, see at BLUNDER MOVE

blunt NOT SHARP /blʌnt/ *adj* **-er, -est** (of a pencil, knife, etc.) not able to cut; not sharp • *This knife's too blunt to cut vegetables, please could you sharpen it?* • *The police think that he was murdered with some kind of blunt instrument.*

blunt *obj* /blʌnt/ *v* [T] • *I blunted the scissors* (=made them less sharp) *by using them to cut paper.* • *(fig.) My recent bad experience has rather blunted* (=made less strong) *my* **enthusiasm** *for travel.*

blunt RUDE /blʌnt/ *adj* **-er, -est** saying what you think without trying to be polite or caring about other people's feelings • *I'll be blunt – that last piece of work you did was terrible.* • *I've had a rather blunt letter from my bank manager about the state of my account.*

blunt·ly /ˈblʌnt·li/ *adv* • *She bluntly told me the bad news.* • *To put it bluntly, I can't afford it.*

blunt·ness /ˈblʌnt·nəs/ *n* [U] • *A lot of people are offended by his bluntness.*

blur /£blɜːʳ, $blɜːr/ *n* [U] something whose shape is not clear • *If I don't wear my glasses, everything is* **a** *blur.* • *The landscape was* **just a** *blur as we sped along on our motorbikes.* • A blur is also something that you cannot remember clearly: *It all happened so long ago that it's* **just a** *blur to me now.* ○ *The last few days seem to have gone by* **in a** *blur.*

blur *(obj)* /£blɜːʳ, $blɜːr/ *v* **-rr-** • *As she drifted into sleep, the doctor's face began to blur and fade.* [I] • *It was one of those films that blur* (=make less clear) *the* **line/distinction/boundary** *between reality and fantasy.* [T]

blurred /£blɜːd, $blɜːrd/ *adj* • *The photograph was blurred* (=not clear) *and it was hard to recognize him at first.* • *My eyes were blurred* **with** (=I could not see clearly because of) *tears.* • *Do you agree that male and female roles are becoming blurred* (=less clearly separated)?

blur·ry /£ˈblɜː·ri, $ˈblɜːr·i/ *adj* • *The picture on our television has become rather blurry.*

blurb /£blɜːb, $blɜːrb/ *n* [C] a description of the contents of a book, film, etc. that is written by the people who have produced the book, film, etc., and is intended to make people want to buy the book or see the film or show • *The blurb on the back of the book says that it 'will touch your heart'.* • *According to the blurb, the film is 'entertainment for all the family'.*

blurt out *(obj)* /£blɜːt, $blɜːrt/ *v adv* to say (something) suddenly and without thinking of the results • *To his friends' surprise, he blurted his secret out one night.* [M] • *She suddenly blurted out, "I can't do it".* [+ clause] • *Anna was amazed when late one evening, Gianni blurted out* **that** *he loved her.* [+ *that* clause]

blush /blʌʃ/ *v* [I] to become pink in the face, usually from embarrassment • *She blushes furiously whenever she sees him.* • *I always blush when I speak in public.* • *I blush* **to think of** *what a fool I made of myself last night.* • *He blushed* **at the thought of** *what he'd done.* • *"Man is the* *only animal that blushes. Or needs to."* (Mark Twain in the book *Following the Equator*, 1897)

blush /blʌʃ/ *n* [C] • *A blush of shame crept up his face.*

blush·er /£ˈblʌʃ·əʳ, $-ɚ/, *Am also* **blush** *n* (a) powder or cream that is put on the CHEEKS (= the sides of the face) to make them look pink • *She finished her make-up by putting on some blusher.* [U] • *I bought myself a pale pink blusher.* [C] • PIC› **Cosmetics**

blus·ter SPEAK /£ˈblʌs·təʳ, $-tɚ/ *v* to speak in a loud angry or offended way, usually with little effect • *"You had no right to do it, no right at all," he blustered.* [+ clause] • *He blustered and shouted at everyone.* [I]

blus·ter /£ˈblʌs·təʳ, $-tɚ/ *n* [U] • *I knew that it was all bluster and he wasn't really angry with me.*

blus·ter BLOW /£ˈblʌs·təʳ, $-tɚ/ *v* [I] (of the wind) to blow fiercely • *A gale was blustering round the house.*

blus·ter·y /£ˈblʌs·tᵊr·i, $-t̬ɚ-/ *adj* **-ier, -iest**

Blu–Tack /ˈbluː·tæk/ *n* [U] *trademark* a soft sticky substance used for temporarily fixing something to a surface, esp. something light to a wall. It can be used more than once • *Helga used Blu-Tack to put some posters up on her bedroom wall.* • PIC› **Stationery**

BM *Am* /ˌbiːˈem/, *Br and Aus* **MB** *n* [C] *abbreviation for* Bachelor of Medicine (= a degree in medicine or a person having this) • LP› **Schools and colleges**

bm /ˌbiːˈem/ *n* [C] *Am abbreviation for* **bowel movement**, see at BOWEL

bn *Br, Am* **b** *n* [C] *abbreviation for* BILLION

BO /£ˌbiːˈəʊ, $-ˈoʊ/ *n* [U] *abbreviation for* **body odour**, see at BODY PHYSICAL STRUCTURE

bo·a /£ˈbəʊ·ə, $ˈboʊ-/ *n* [C] a long thin piece of clothing made of feathers and worn around the neck, esp. by women • *Young women in the 1920s often wore* **feather** *boas.*

bo·a (con·strict·or) /£ˈbəʊ·ə, $ˈboʊ-/ *n* [C] a large, strong snake, found in South and Central America, that kills animals and birds by wrapping itself around them and crushing them to death

boar /£bɔːʳ, $bɔːr/ *n* [C] a male pig kept for breeding on a farm, or a type of wild pig • Compare HOG ANIMAL; SOW ANIMAL.

board WOOD /£bɔːd, $bɔːrd/ *n* [C] a thin flat piece of cut wood or other hard material • *The hurricane was coming and people were nailing boards across their windows.* • *He put the washed vegetables on a (Br and Aus)* **chopping**/ *(Am)* **cutting** *board and began to cut them up.* • *There was a board* (= a flat piece of wood or other hard material with a message written on it) *outside the house saying 'For Sale'.* • A board is also a flat piece of wood or other hard material with a special pattern on it, used for playing games: *Chess is played on a similar board to draughts.* • A **board game** is any game, such as CHESS, DRAUGHTS and many others, in which small pieces are moved around on a board with a pattern on it. • A board can be a BLACKBOARD: *The teacher asked you to write your name up on* **the board.** • A board can also be a **notice board**. See at NOTICE INFORMATION: *I stuck the notice on* **the** *board.* • A board can also be a **diving board**: *I dived off the top board today, Dad.* ○ See at DIVE MOVE DOWN. • To **go by the board** is to be forgotten or omitted: *It's a shame they let the scheme for the new swimming pool go by the board.* • **Board shorts** are *Aus for* **bathing trunks**. See at BATHE SWIM. • See also ABOVEBOARD; BREADBOARD; SOUNDBOARD. • PIC› **Games, Kitchen, Office**

board *obj* /£bɔːd, $bɔːrd/ *v* [T] • *Rumours of a riot had led several shopkeepers to board* **(up/over)** *their windows* (= to cover them with boards). [T/M]

boards /£bɔːdz, $bɔːrdz/ *pl n* • *(dated)* **The boards** are the stage in a theatre: *He's been* **on/treading** *the boards* (= has been an actor) *for nearly 50 years now.* • In **ice hockey** (= a team game played on ice), **the boards** are the wooden fence surrounding the ice surface: *Two players crashed into the boards.*

board PEOPLE /£bɔːd, $bɔːrd/ *n* [C + sing/pl v] the group of people who are responsible for controlling and organizing a company or organization • *Every decision has to be passed by* **the board (of directors)**. • *She started in the firm by making the tea and now she's* **on the board**. • *The board* **of governors** *meet/meets once a month to discuss school policy.* • *(Am)* A **board of education** is a group of people who have been elected to organize the management of the local school system of a particular area: *The county Board of Education has decided to cancel high school gymnastics and golf programs.*

boards /£bɔːdz, $bɔːrdz/ *pl n Am* • Boards are an examination given by an organization: *This is my last chance to pass the medical boards.*

board *(obj)* STAY /£bɔːd, $bɔːrd/ *v* to pay to sleep and eat meals in someone's house, or in a building that they own, or at a school, or to provide these services for (someone) • *During his stay in England he boarded* **with** *a family in Bath.* [I] • *When you went to school were you a day-student or did you board* (= sleep and eat there during school time)*?* [I] • *She boarded* (= provided meals and somewhere to sleep for) *a lodger at her house.* [T] • If you board a pet animal, you arrange for it to be temporarily taken care of at a place other than its home: *They used to board the dog* **out** *when they went on business trips.* [T]

board /£bɔːd, $bɔːrd/ *n* [U] • Board means meals provided when you are staying somewhere: *How much does it cost per week for board* **and lodging**/*(esp. Br)* **bed and** *board*/*(Am usually)* **room and** *board* (= all meals and a room to sleep in)*?*

board·er /£ˈbɔː·dəʳ, $ˈbɔːr·dɚ/ *n* [C] • A boarder is a student who lives at her or his school during school time, returning home only during the holidays. • Compare **day pupil** at DAY.

board·ing /£ˈbɔː·dɪŋ, $ˈbɔːr-/ *adj* [before n; not gradable] • Boarding is used to refer to the arrangement by which students sleep and eat meals at their school during school time: *Both their children go to boarding* **school**. ○ *Boarding* **fees** *at most private schools are extremely expensive.* • Boarding is also used to refer to the arrangement by which pet animals are temporarily kept and cared for in a place which is not their home: *We'll have to put the dogs in boarding* **kennels** *while we're away.* • A **boarding house** is a private house that a person pays to stay in and receive meals. • LP› **Schools and colleges**

board *(obj)* GET ON /£bɔːd, $bɔːrd/ *v* to get onto or allow people to get onto (a boat, train or aircraft) • *At London airport she boarded a plane to Australia.* [T] • *Will passengers waiting to board please go to the ticket counter.* [I] • *"Attention, we are boarding Flight 701 immediately," the airline attendant announced.* [T]

board /£bɔːd, $bɔːrd/ *n* [U] • *Waving goodbye to everyone, she got* **on board** (= got onto) *the train.* • *As soon as I was* **on board** (= on the boat, train or aircraft), *I began to have second thoughts about leaving.* • To **take/bring someone on board** is to arrange for them to join a group or team, esp. for a special purpose: *Let's* **bring** *Jane* **on board** *for the Saudi deal – she's the expert.* • To **take on board** a job or responsibility, or to **take** a job or a responsibility **on board**, is to agree to do it. • To **take on board** information or an idea, or to **take** information or an idea **on board** is to understand and accept it.

board·ing /£ˈbɔː·dɪŋ, $ˈbɔːr-/ *adj* [not gradable] • *(Br)* A **boarding card**/*(Am and Aus)* **boarding pass** is a card that a passenger must have to be allowed to enter an aircraft or a ship.

board·er /£ˈbɔː·dəʳ, $ˈbɔːr·dɚ/ *n* [C] • A boarder is someone who gets on a boat, train or aircraft.

board·ing /£ˈbɔː·dɪŋ, $ˈbɔːr-/ *n* [U] a collection of boards that have been fastened side by side to each other

board·room /£ˈbɔːd·rʊm, £-ruːm, $ˈbɔːrd-/ *n* [C] a room where the people who control a company or organization meet

board·walk *Am* /£ˈbɔːd·wɔːk, $ˈbɔːrd·wɑːk/ *n* [C] a path made of wooden boards built along a beach • *"Under the Boardwalk"* (song by The Drifters, 1964)

boast *(obj)* SPEAK PROUDLY /£bəʊst, $boʊst/ *v disapproving* to speak too proudly or happily about what you have done or what you own; to BRAG • *He didn't talk about his top exam results in case people thought he was boasting.* [I] • *She boasted* **of/about** *how she had written a novel when she was only 15.* [I] • *Parents enjoy boasting* **about** *their children's achievements.* [I] • *They boasted* **that** *they had never had an accident yet.* [+ *that* clause] • *"I won," boasted Tim.* [+ clause]

boast /£bəʊst, $boʊst/ *n* [C] *disapproving* • **It is** *her proud boast* **that** *she has never missed a single episode of the soap opera.* [+ *that* clause] • *His claim to be a great director was only an* **empty** *boast* (= He said it to make himself seem more important).

boast·ful /£ˈbəʊst·fᵊl, $ˈboʊst-/ *adj disapproving* • If you are boastful, you have a tendency to praise yourself and what you have done.

boast·ful·ly /£ˈbəʊst·fᵊl·i, $ˈboʊst-/ *adv disapproving*

boast·ful·ness /£'bəʊst·fəl·nəs, $'boʊst-/ *n* [U] *disapproving*

boast *obj* [POSSESS] /£bəʊst, $boʊst/ *v* [T not *be boasting*] to have or possess (something to be proud of) • *Ireland boasts beautiful beaches, great restaurants and friendly locals.*

boat /£bəʊt, $boʊt/ *n* [C] a small vehicle for travelling on water, or *(infml)* a ship • *a rowing/sailing boat* • *a fishing boat* • *We took turns in rowing the boat up the river.* • *The little boats sailed slowly out of the harbour.* • *(infml) Are you travelling* **by** *boat or by air?* • *(infml) I'm* **taking the** *boat from Dover to Calais.* • A **boat hook** is a long pole with an iron hook on the end, used by a person on land to pull a boat towards them or away from other boats. • **Boat people** are people who have left their country by boat, usually in the hope of finding safety in another place. • A **boat train** is a train that travels to or from a port at times that connect with a particular ship's leaving or arriving.

boat·ing /£'bəʊ·tɪŋ, $'boʊ·t̬ɪŋ/ *n* [U] • *They decided to* **go** *boating on the lake last Sunday.* • *There have been several boating accidents on the river this month.*

boat·load /£'bəʊt·ləʊd, $'boʊt·loʊd/ *n* [C] • *boatloads of refugees/tourists* (= the amount of these people that can be transported by a boat) • *A whole boatload* **of** *oil* (= The amount of this substance that can be transported by a boat) *was discharged into the ocean, destroying the marine life of that entire area.* • *Following the military coup, people are leaving the island in boatloads/by the boatload* (= in large numbers, travelling by boat). • *(fig. infml) The movie company made boatloads* (= a large amount) *of money on that project.*

boat·er /£'bəʊ·tər, $'boʊ·t̬ɚ/ *n* [C] a stiff hat made of STRAW (= dried wheat stems) with a flat top

boat·house /£'bəʊt·haʊs, $'boʊt-/ *n* [C] *pl* **boathouses** /£'bəʊt,haʊ·zɪz, $'boʊt-/ a small building beside a river or lake, and in which boats are kept

boat·swain /£'bəʊ·sən, $'boʊ-/, **bo·sun**, **bo'sun**, **bo's'n** *n* [C] the officer on a ship who is responsible for looking after the ship's equipment

boat·yard /£'bəʊt·jɑːd, $'boʊt·jɑːrd/ *n* [C] a place where boats are made, kept or repaired

bob *(obj)* [MOVE] /£bɒb, $bɑːb/ *v* **-bb-** to move (something) up and down quickly and gently • *In the harbour, the boats bobbed gently on the water.* [I] • *I dropped the bottle into the sea and watched it bob* **(up)** (= come back up) *to the surface a moment later.* [I] • *Suddenly a head bobbed* **up** (= appeared suddenly) *from behind the hedge.* [I] • *He bobbed his head* (= moved it down and then up) *briefly to say hello.* [T] • *She bobbed* **(a curtsy)** (= made a movement consisting of bending at the knees as a sign of respect) **to** *the Queen.* [I/T]

bob /£bɒb, $bɑːb/ *n* [C] • *With a quick bob* **of** *her* **head** *she indicated that I should come in.*

bob [HAIRSTYLE] /£bɒb, $bɑːb/ *n* [C] a hairstyle that is short at the front while the other hair is cut to neck length all around the head • *I've had my hair* **in a** *bob for quite a long time now.* • [PIC] **Hair**

bobbed /£bɒbd, $bɑːbd/ *adj* [not gradable] • *She had short, bobbed hair and a toothy grin.*

bob [MONEY] /£bɒb, $bɑːb/ *n* [C] *pl* **bob** *Br dated infml* a SHILLING (= a British coin used in the past that was worth 5p) • *That coat cost me forty bob in 1956.* • [LP] **Money**

Bob [DESIRED RESULT] /£bɒb, $bɑːb/ *n* [U] **Bob's your uncle** *Br infml* used to mean that the result of an action that is being described will be quick and simple • *Just tell them you're a friend of mine and, Bob's your uncle, you'll get the job.*

bob·bin /£'bɒb·ɪn, $'bɑː·bɪn/ *n* [C] a small round or tube-shaped object around which thread is put, often before putting it in a sewing machine • [PIC] **Handicraft**

bob·ble *esp. Br* /£'bɒb·l̩, $'bɑː·bl̩/, *Am and Aus* **pom–pom** *n* [C] a small round ball of soft material used as decoration • A *(Br)* **bobble hat** (*Am* **stocking cap**, *Aus* **beanie**, *Canadian Eng* **tuque**) is a woollen hat with a small round ball, made from short pieces of wool stitched together, on top. • [PIC] **Hats**

bob·by /£'bɒb·i, $'bɑː·bi/ *n* [C] *Br infml slightly dated* a police officer • *Have the days of the friendly* **local** *bobby on the beat gone forever?* • *Bobbies* **on the beat** *in Cambridgeshire have called on police chiefs to arm them with pepper gas.*

bob·by pin /£'bɒb·i, $'bɑː·bi/ *n* [C] *Am and Aus for* HAIRGRIP

bobs /£bɒbz, $bɑːbz/ *pl n* **bits and bobs**, see at BIT [AMOUNT]

bob·sleigh *Br and Aus* /£'bɒb·sleɪ, $'bɑːb-/, *Am* **bob·sled** /£'bɒb·sled, $'bɑːb-/ *n* [C] a small vehicle that has long metal blades fixed to its bottom and is built for racing down ice-covered tracks • [PIC] **Winter sports**

bod [PERSON] /£bɒd, $bɑːd/ *n* [C] *Br and Aus infml* a person • *Some bod came in and told us not to make so much noise.* • *She's a bit of an* **odd bod**.

bod [BODY] /£bɒd, $bɑːd/ *n* [C] *Am infml for* BODY • *That guy has a great bod!* • *You really should work out more and get that bod of yours in shape.*

bo·da·cious /£bəʊ'deɪ·ʃəs, $boʊ-/ *adj esp. Am slang* very large or important, or very enjoyable or admirable • *That was the most bodacious party, dude!* • *The Taj Mahal – bodacious!*

bode *(obj)* /£bəʊd, $boʊd/ *v* to be a sign of (esp. good or bad things) in the future • *As far as the company's future is concerned, these recently published figures bode* **ill**/*do not bode* **well**. [I] • *There are fears that the hurricane bodes disaster* **for** *those areas in its path.* [T] • *It is not yet clear what these changes will bode* **for** *the local community.* [T]

bo·de·ga /£bə'deɪ·gə, $boʊ-/ *n* [C] *Am* a small shop that sells food and other items, mostly to Spanish-speaking customers • *If you're out of beans, I can always run down to the bodega to pick some up.*

bodge /£bɒdʒ, $bɑːdʒ/ *n* [C], *v* [T] *Br for* BOTCH

bod·ice /£'bɒd·ɪs, $'bɑː·dɪs/ *n* [C] the upper part of a woman's dress, or *(old use)* a piece of women's underwear that fits tightly to the body above the waist • *She was wearing a ballgown with a* **fitted** *bodice* (= with the upper part cut to fit closely to the body). • *(Am)* A **bodice-ripper** is a romantic story in which the main female character is sexually attacked.

bod·kin /£'bɒd·kɪn, $'bɑːd-/ *n* [C] a large needle that does not have a sharp point, used esp. for pulling TAPE through cloth

bo·dy [PHYSICAL STRUCTURE] /£'bɒd·i, $'bɑː·di/ *n* [C] the whole physical structure that is a person, animal, etc., or the main part of it without the head or without the head, arms and legs • *They began to move their bodies in time to the music.* • *A good diet and plenty of exercise will help you to keep your body healthy.* • *She rubbed sun lotion over her entire body.* • *He had a fat body but rather thin legs and arms.* • *(dated) How is a body* (= a person) *supposed to live in these conditions?* • A body is also a dead person: *A body was washed up on the beach last week.* ○ *His family are sure that he was murdered, but his body has never been found.* [LP] **Age** • The body of a vehicle, such as a car or an aircraft, is the painted metal shell that covers it. See also BODYWORK. • *(esp. Br)* A body (*Am usually* **bodysuit**) is a piece of women's clothing which fits tightly over the chest, stomach, bottom, and sometimes also the arms, but not the legs, and which usually has a fastening between the legs. • To **keep body and soul together** is to be able to pay for food, clothing, a place to live, etc.: *His wages are barely enough to keep body and soul together.* • A **body bag** is a heavy plastic bag used to transport dead people, esp. soldiers who have been killed in a war. • A **body blow** is something that causes serious problems and disappointment for a person trying to do something: *Having all her files stolen came as a real body blow to her when she was trying to finish her research.* • **Body-building** means doing special exercises to make the muscles bigger. A **body builder** is someone who regularly does exercises to make their muscles bigger. • *(infml)* Your **body clock** is your body's natural tendency to sleep, eat, etc. at certain times. • **Body language** is the movements or positions by which you show other people your feelings without using words: *The study of body language can tell us whether two people like each other or not.* ○ *I could tell from her body language that she was very embarrassed.* • **Body odour** (*abbreviation* **BO**) is the unpleasant smell of a person's body that is caused by SWEAT. • A **body snatcher** is a person who, esp. in the past, stole the bodies of dead people and sold them to scientists who wanted to perform experiments on them. • A **body stocking** is an item of clothing made of thin material that tightly covers the whole body, except for the head, and which is often worn by dancers. • *"I know I have the body of a weak and feeble woman, but I have the heart and stomach* (= bravery) *of a king, and of a king of England too"* (speech by Queen Elizabeth I on the approach of the Spanish Armada, 1588) • [PIC] **Clothes**

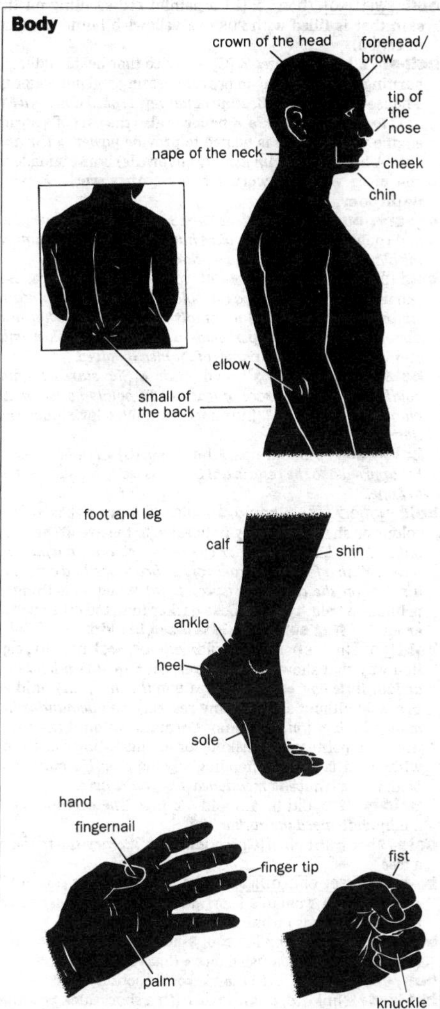

-bod·ied /£-ˈbɒd·id, $-ˈbɑː·did/ *combining form* • -bodied means having the stated type of body: *a long-bodied insect* ○ *a soft-bodied doll* ○ *a steel-bodied car*

bod·i·ly /£ˈbɒd·ɪ·li, $ˈbɑː·dɪ-/ *adv, adj* [not gradable] • *He carried her bodily* (= lifted her body and moved her) *up the stairs.* • *(fig.) The old house was moved bodily* (= The whole structure was moved) *to a new site when the bypass was built.* • *Some illnesses are caught by coming into contact with the bodily* **fluids** (= blood, SALIVA, etc.) *of people who are suffering from them.* • *Two men were following me in such a threatening way that I was afraid they were going to cause me bodily* **harm**. • Bodily **functions** and bodily **needs** are the things the body does or feels a need to do that are not under the control of the mind.

bo·dy GROUP OF PEOPLE /£ˈbɒd·i, $ˈbɑː·di/ *n* [C] a group of people who have joined together for a particular reason • *a governing body* • *an advisory body* • *The government is an* **elected** *body intended to represent the people.* • *The RSPCA is a respected body working for animal welfare.* • *There is a large body* (= group) **of** *people who are unaware of their basic rights.* • *The cleaning staff went* **in a** *body* (= as a group) *to the manager to complain.* • *(fml)* The **body politic** is all the people of a particular country under a certain government.

bo·dy AMOUNT /£ˈbɒd·i, $ˈbɑː·di/ *n* [C] an amount (of something) • *There is a growing body* **of** *evidence to support their claim.* • *She collected a huge body* **of** *information and data for her book.* • *A substantial body* **of opinion** (= A large group of people) *opposes change.* • *(fml)* A body **of** water is an area of water, such as a lake.

bo·dy MAIN PART /£ˈbɒd·i, $ˈbɑː·di/ *n* [U] **the body** the main part of a book, article, etc., or the main part of a large building • *I thought the most interesting details in the book were not in the body* **of** *the text, but in the notes at the end.* • *The body* **of** *the cathedral is always crowded with tourists.*

bo·dy OBJECT /£ˈbɒd·i, $ˈbɑː·di/ *n* [C] *specialized* a separate object • *The distance between the two bodies in space was measured daily.*

bo·dy FULLNESS /£ˈbɒd·i, $ˈbɑː·di/ *n* [U] a strong quality • *This Bordeaux* **has** *a flowery bouquet and plenty of body* (= strong flavour). • *Conditioner is used to give limp hair more body* (= thickness).

-bod·ied /£-ˈbɒd·id, $-ˈbɑː·did/ *combining form* • *a medium-bodied wine* • *a full-bodied whisky*

bo·dy·guard /£ˈbɒd·i·gɑːd, $ˈbɑː·di·gɑːrd/ *n* [C] a person paid to protect another person in case of attack • *The prince is always accompanied by his bodyguards.* • A bodyguard is also a group of people paid to protect another person in case of attack: *Her bodyguard was/were unable to protect her.* [+ sing/pl v]

bo·dy·surf /£ˈbɒd·i·sɜːf, $ˈbɑː·di·sɜːrf/ *v* [I] to SURF (= travel on a wave to the beach) without a floating board, lying face down in the water

bo·dy·warm·er *Br* /£ˈbɒd·iˌwɔː·məʳ, $ˈbɑː·diˌwɔːr·mɚ/, *Am* **down vest** *n* [C] a short jacket without sleeves which is made of thick cloth and fits closely to your body • PIC **Coats and jackets**

bo·dy·work /£ˈbɒd·i·wɜːk, $ˈbɑː·di·wɜːrk/ *n* [U] the painted metal shell that covers a car, aircraft, etc. • *My car's engine is in quite good condition, but the bodywork is in a terrible state.* • *(Am)* Bodywork is also the process of making or repairing the outer shell of a vehicle.

Boer /£bɜːʳ, $bɔːr/ *n* [C] a white person in South Africa related to the Dutch people who went to live there in the 17th century

boff *obj* /£bɒf, $bɑːf/ *v* [T] *Am slang* to have sex with (someone) • *She boffed him once before dinner, then again after the guests left.*

bof·fin /£ˈbɒf·ɪn, $ˈbɑː·fɪn/ *n* [C] *esp. Br and Aus infml* a scientist who is considered to know a lot about science but who is not thought to be interested in other things • *a technical boffin* • *a computer boffin*

bog WET AREA /£bɒg, $bɑːg/ *n* (an area of) soft, wet earth • *The path goes across an area of bog.* [U] • *She said that the gradual erosion of* **peat** *bogs in Britain and Ireland should be stopped.* [C] • *(Br and Aus disapproving slang)* If an Irish person is described as **bog Irish**, it means that they are thought of as being from the countryside and without much experience or understanding of life anywhere else.

bog·gy /£ˈbɒg·i, $ˈbɑː·gi/ *adj* **-ier**, **-iest** • *We walked across a stretch of boggy* (= soft and wet) *ground.*

bog TOILET /£bɒg, $bɑːg/ *n* [C] *Br and Aus slang* a toilet • *I'm just going to nip to the bog.* • *We've run out of bog paper/roll.*

bog down *(obj)*, **bog** *(obj)* **down** /£bɒg, $bɑːg/ *v adv* to (cause to) become unable to advance • *Delays in introducing their new product line have bogged the company down.* [M] • *The fact that neither side is willing to see the other's point of view is bogging down the* **negotiations/talks**. [M] • *(esp. Am) In recent months, the economy has bogged down.* [I]

bogged down /£ˌbɒgd-, $ˌbɑːgd-/ *adj* • *Our car* **got/became** *completely bogged down* (= unable to move) *in the mud.* • *I can't go out tonight, I'm really bogged down* (= have too much work to do). • *Don't let yourself* **get** *bogged down* **in** (= become too busy because of having to deal with) *too much paperwork.* • *The talks have* **become** *bogged down* **in** (= are unable to advance because of giving too much attention to) *detail.*

bog off /£bɒg, $bɑːg/ *v adv* [I] *slang* to go away; to leave • *"Where's Kevin?" "I don't know. I think he's bogged off home."* • *Bog off and leave me alone.*

bo·gey FEAR /£ˈbəʊ·gi, $ˈboʊ-/, **bo·gy**, *Am also* **bo·gie** *n* [C] a particular fear, esp. one not based on reason • *Committing himself in a relationship is his biggest bogey.* • A **bogey man** (also **bogy man**, *Am also* **boogeyman**) is an imaginary evil person whom adults pretend exists, as a way of frightening children: *Be good, or the bogey man will come and get you!*

bo·gey NOSE *Br and Aus* /£ˈbəʊ·gi, $ˈboʊ-/, *Am* **boo·ger** *n* [C] *slang* a piece of dried MUCUS from inside the nose

bog·gle *(obj)* /£ˈbɒg·l̩, $ˈbɑː·gl̩/ *v* to (cause to) have difficulty imagining or understanding something • *What she said made the imagination boggle.* [I] • *The* **mind**

boggles **at** *the amount of money they spend on food.* [I] • *It rather boggles the* **mind**, *doesn't it?* [T] • To boggle is also not to know how to deal with something: *He boggled* **at** *the suggestion.* [I] • See also **mind-boggling** at MIND THOUGHTS.

bog stand·ard *adj Br infml* completely ordinary; not having anything special added • *My new car is a completely bog standard model.* • *He's buying himself a computer, but he only wants something bog standard.*

bo·gus /£ˈbəʊ·gəs, $ˈboʊ-/ *adj* false, not real or not legal • *Hitler's diaries were eventually recognized as bogus.* • *The politicians dismissed their protest as a bogus argument intended to take attention away from the real issues.* • *She produced some bogus documents to support her claim.*

bo·hem·i·an /£bəʊˈhiː·mi·ən, $boʊ-/ *n* [C] a person who is interested in art, music and/or literature and lives in a very informal manner that does not follow usually accepted ways of behaving • *He thought of himself as a bohemian and liked to do as he pleased.*

bo·hem·i·an /£bəʊˈhiː·mi·ən, $boʊ-/ *adj* • *Paris is sometimes thought to be the classic place in which to lead a bohemian life.*

boil *(obj)* HEAT /bɔɪl/ *v* to (cause to) reach the temperature at which a liquid starts to turn into a gas • *Liquid nitrogen boils at a very low temperature.* [I] • *If you give water to a small baby to drink, you should boil it first.* [T] • When a container boils, esp. one used for cooking, or you boil a container, it is heated until the liquid in it starts to turn into a gas: *The saucepan's boiling.* [I] ○ *Could you boil a kettle for me?* [T] • If food boils, or you boil food, it is cooked by being put in water which is heated until it starts to turn into a gas: *The carrots are boiling.* [I] ○ *I boiled some potatoes for dinner.* [T] • If you boil clothes, you wash them in a container of very hot water. [T] • When a liquid boils **away**, it all turns into a gas so that none of it is left in liquid form. [I] • When you boil **down** a liquid or food, or it boils **down**, you heat it so that part of it is turned into gas, and its amount is reduced: *You make jam by boiling down fruit.* [M] ○ *Leave the sauce to boil down.* [I] • To **boil down** information, or to **boil** information **down**, is to reduce it, usually so that it contains only its most important parts: *The journalist boiled down his lengthy report to just a few paragraphs.* • To **boil down to** something is to be the reason for it: *The problem* **all** *boils down to a lack of money.* • If a container or food boils **dry**, all the liquid in the container in which the food was cooking has turned to gas. [I] • When a liquid boils **over**, it rises up as it starts to turn into a gas, and flows over the edge of its container: *Careful, the milk's boiling over!* [I] • If a container boils **over**, the liquid in it rises up as it starts to turn into a gas, and flows over the edge: *That saucepan is boiling over.* [I] • When a person or situation **boils over**, they suddenly become out of control or violent. • If you boil **up** a liquid (or food), you heat liquid in a container (and cook food in it): *Could you boil some water up for me?* [M] ○ *I'll just boil up the peas, then dinner will be ready.* [M] • If a difficult situation **boils up**, it becomes more difficult and dangerous: *Trouble has been boiling up in the prison for weeks.* • If a person says that they **can't boil an egg**, they mean that they are unable to cook even the simplest meal. • PIC› **Cooking**

boil /bɔɪl/ *n* [U] • *You'll need to give those towels* **a** *boil* (= wash them in very hot water) *in order to get them clean* • If you **bring** something **to** *(Br)* **the**/*(Am)* **a** boil, or **let** something **come to** *(Br)* **the**/*(Am)* **a** boil, you heat it until it boils: *Bring the water to the boil, then add the pasta.* • *(Br)* When a person goes **off the boil**, they lose interest: *We were almost ready to sign the contract with them when they seemed to go off the boil.*

boiled /bɔɪld/ *adj* [not gradable] • *boiled eggs* • *boiled bacon* • *a* **hard-/soft-***boiled egg* (= one boiled for a long/short time) • *(Br)* A **boiled sweet** (*Am* **hard candy**) is a hard, often brightly coloured, sweet.

boil·ing /ˈbɔɪ·lɪŋ/ *adj* [not gradable] *fig. infml* • *She scalded herself on some boiling water.* • Boiling can also mean very hot: *We don't usually have such boiling* **(hot)** *weather in England.* ○ *I wish I'd worn something cooler – I'm boiling.* • *(infml)* Boiling can also mean extremely angry: *He was boiling* **with** *rage.* • The **boiling point** of a liquid is the temperature at which it becomes a gas: *The boiling point of water is 100°C.* • *(fig.) The situation in the inner city was* **reaching boiling point** (= about to go out of control and become violent) *so the police were out in force.*

boil SWELLING /bɔɪl/ *n* [C] a painful red swelling on the skin that is filled with PUS (= a yellowish liquid from an infection)

boil·er /£ˈbɔɪ·ləʳ, $-lɚ/ *n* [C] a device that heats water by burning gas or oil, esp. to provide heating and hot water in a house • *Our central heating boiler has broken down – we'll need to call a plumber.* • A boiler is also the part of a steam engine where water is heated to provide power. • *(Br and Aus)* A **boiler suit** (*Am usually* **coveralls**) is a suit made in one piece which is worn for doing dirty work. • PIC› **Bathroom**

bois·ter·ous /£ˈbɔɪ·stᵊr·əs, $-stɚ-/ *adj* noisy, energetic and rough • *The children were having a boisterous game in the playground.* • *Calm down – don't be so boisterous!*

bold BRAVE /£bəʊld, $boʊld/ *adj* **-er, -est** brave; not fearing danger • *She was a bold and fearless mountain-climber.* • *Their refusal to comply was a bold but hopeless gesture.* • *The newspaper made a bold* **move**/*took a bold* **step** *by publishing the names of the men involved.*

bold·ly /£ˈbəʊld·li, $ˈboʊld-/ *adv* • *She stared at him boldly, showing no trace of fear.* • *"To boldly go where no man has gone before"* (introduction to the television series *Star Trek*, 1966-)

bold·ness /£ˈbəʊld·nəs, $ˈboʊld-/ *n* [U] • *The boldness of his approach to the restaurant business led to his sudden rise to fame.*

bold NOTICEABLE /£bəʊld, $boʊld/ *adj* **-er, -est** strong in colour or shape, and very noticeable to the eye • *They had painted the kitchen in bold colours – crimson, purple and blue.* • *With a few bold strokes of her brush she had captured his face on the canvas.* • *(specialized)* When something is printed **in** bold **(type)** it looks darker than the other words around it: **This sentence is printed in bold**.

bold NOT SHY /£bəʊld, $boʊld/ *adj* **-er, -est** not shy, esp. in a way that shows a lack of respect • *He was a bold and defiant little boy.* • *She marched into the shop,* **(as) bold as brass** (= without showing any respect), *and demanded her money back.* • *(fml)* **If I may be/make so bold (as to)** is used as a polite way of asking for or suggesting something without, it is hoped, offending anyone else: *If I may be so bold, you still haven't mentioned why you're here.*

bold·ly /£ˈbəʊld·li, $ˈboʊld-/ *adv* • *These people have boldly challenged the authorities.*

bole /£bəʊl, $boʊl/ *n* [C] *specialized or literary* the trunk of a tree

bo·le·ro PIECE OF CLOTHING /£bəˈleə·rəʊ, $-ˈler·oʊ/ *n* [C] *pl* **boleros** a woman's short jacket that stops just above the waist and has no buttons

bo·le·ro DANCE /£bəˈleə·rəʊ, $-ˈler·oʊ/ *n* [C] *pl* **boleros** (the music for) a Spanish dance • *Ravel's Bolero*

boll /£bəʊl, $boʊl/ *n* [C] the seed of the cotton plant

bol·lard /£ˈbɒl·ɑːd, $ˈbɑː·lɚd/ *n* [C] a short thick post that boats can be tied to, or *(esp. Br)* a post that is put in the middle or at the end of a road to prevent vehicles from going any further

bol·lock·ing /£ˈbɒl·ə·kɪŋ, $ˈbɑː·lə-/ *n* [C] *Br slightly taboo slang* angry words spoken to someone who has done something wrong • *She gave me a good bollocking for being late.*

bol·locks BODY PART /£ˈbɒl·əks, $ˈbɑː·ləks/ *pl n Br and Aus slightly taboo slang* TESTICLES • *Ouch! That caught/hit me right in the bollocks!*

bol·locks NONSENSE /£ˈbɒl·əks, $ˈbɑː·ləks/ *n* [U] *Br slightly taboo slang* nonsense • *What he said was* **a load of** *bollocks.* • *Bollocks* **to** *that* (= that's nonsense)*!*

bol·locks up *obj Br and Aus*, **bol·locks** *obj* **up**, *Am* **bol·lix up** *v adv* [M] • *They completely bollocksed up* (= spoilt by making mistakes) *the game.* • *Try not to bollocks it up* (= make mistakes) *this time!*

bo·lo·gna /£bəˈlɒn·jə, $-ˈloʊ·njə/, **ba·lo·ney** /£bəˈləʊ·ni, $-ˈloʊ-/ *n* [U] *Am and Aus* a cooked, smoked SAUSAGE (= mixed meat in a tube shape) which is sliced and eaten cold • *He made himself a bologna and cheese sandwich for lunch.*

bo·lo·ney /£bəˈləʊ·ni, $-ˈloʊ-/ *n* [U] BALONEY

Bol·she·vik /£ˈbɒl·ʃə·vɪk, $ˈboʊl-/ *adj* [C], *n* connected with the political system introduced by Lenin in Russia in 1917, or a supporter of that form of system

Bol·she·vi·sm /£ˈbɒl·ʃə·vɪ·zᵊm, $ˈboʊl-/ *n* [U]

bolsh·y **(-ier, -iest)**, **bolsh·ie** **(-r, -st)** /£ˈbɒl·ʃi, $ˈboʊl-/ *adj Br infml* (of a person) tending to argue and make difficulties • *He's a bit bolshy these days.*

bol·ster *obj* SUPPORT /£ˈbəʊl·stəʳ, $ˈboʊl·stɚ/ *v* [T] to support or make stronger • *They had to bolster the roof before searching for survivors in the rubble.* • *More money is* *needed to bolster the industry.* • *Everyone needs to be bolstered* **(up)** (= encouraged) *once in a while.* • *She tried to bolster my* **confidence/morale** (= encourage me, make me feel stronger) *by telling me that I had a special talent.* • *They need to do something to bolster* (= improve) *their* **image**. • *I need to find some way of bolstering* (= increasing) *my earnings.* • *Troop movements on the border have bolstered* (= increased) *fears that the country is planning to invade its neighbour.*

bol·ster [FOR SLEEPING] /£ˈbəʊl·stəʳ, $ˈboʊl·stɚ/ *n* [C] a long firm cylindrical PILLOW

bolt [LOCK] /£bəʊlt, $boʊlt/ *n* [C] a metal bar on a door or window that slides across to lock it closed • *I closed the window and* **drew the** *bolt.* • PIC› **Bolt, Locks and home security**

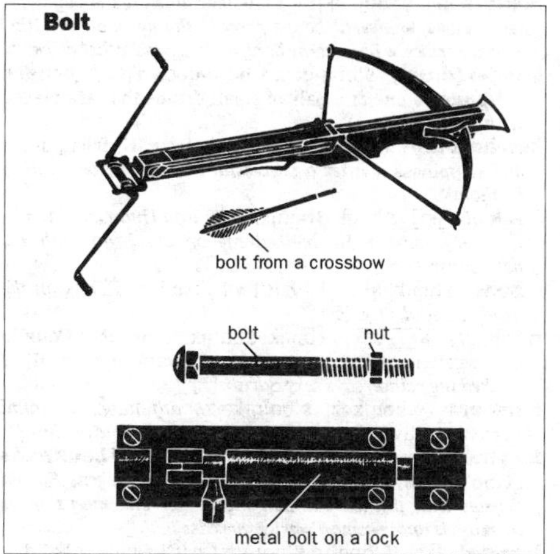

bolt *(obj)* /£bəʊlt, $boʊlt/ *v* • *Have you locked and bolted the door?* [T] • *The door bolts on the inside.* [I]

bolt [SCREW] /£bəʊlt, $boʊlt/ *n* [C] a screw-like metal object without a point which is used with a NUT (= a circular piece of metal) to fasten things together • *All the bolts needed to be tightened.* • PIC› **Bolt, Tools**

bolt *obj* /£bəʊlt, $boʊlt/ *v* [T always + adv/prep] • *I bolted* (= fastened with a bolt) *the rack back* **onto** *the bicycle.* • *On a ship the furniture is often bolted* **to** *the deck.*

bolt [LIGHTNING] /£bəʊlt, $boʊlt/ *n* [C] a flash of lightning that looks like a white line against the sky • *The house next to ours was struck by a bolt* **of lightning**. • *The news of their marriage was* **a bolt from/out of the blue** (= was completely unexpected). • See also THUNDERBOLT.

bolt *(obj)* [MOVE QUICKLY] /£bəʊlt, $boʊlt/ *v* to move very fast, esp. as a result of being frightened • *Frightened by the car horn, the horse bolted.* [I] • *She bolted* **to** *the phone to ring for an ambulance.* [I] • To bolt **(down)** your **food** is to eat it very fast. [T/M]

bolt /£bəʊlt, $boʊlt/ *n* [U] • *When he saw me arrive he tried to* **make a bolt for** (= quickly escape through) *the exit.* • *(esp. Br and Aus)* A **bolt-hole** is a place where you can hide, esp. to escape from other people.

bolt [ROLL] /£bəʊlt, $boʊlt/ *n* [C] a length or roll of cloth or WALLPAPER (= paper that covers walls)

bolt [STICK] /£bəʊlt, $boʊlt/ *n* [C] a type of short ARROW (= a thin stick-like weapon with a point at one end) shot from a CROSSBOW (= a type of weapon) • PIC› **Bolt**

bolt [STRAIGHT] /£bəʊlt, £bɒlt, $boʊlt/ *adv* [not gradable] **bolt upright** vertical and very straight • *Suddenly she* **sat** *bolt upright as if something had startled her.* • *Her back was bolt upright and her legs were stretched out straight in front of her.*

bomb [WEAPON] /£bɒm, $bɑːm/ *n* [C] a weapon that explodes and is used to kill or hurt people or to damage buildings • *A 100-pound bomb* **exploded/went off** *today, injuring three people.* • *The terrorists had* **planted** *a bomb near the police station.* • *During the Second World War, the British* **dropped** *a huge number of bombs on Dresden.* • **The bomb** is one or more **atom bombs**: *The US was the first country to have the bomb.* ○ See at ATOM. • *(Br infml)* **A bomb** is a lot of money: *That coat must have cost a bomb.* • When a vehicle **goes like a bomb**, it can go very fast. • *(Br infml)* An event that **goes like a bomb** or **goes a bomb** is very successful: *The party's really going a bomb, isn't it?* • A *(Br)* **bomb disposal unit**/*(Am)* **bomb squad** is a group of people whose job it is, once a bomb has been found, to prevent it from exploding or to remove it so no one is hurt. • A **bomb scare** is a warning that a bomb has been left in a building/area and people are told to leave. • *"Come, friendly bombs, and fall on Slough! / It isn't fit for humans now"* (John Betjeman in the poem *Slough*, 1937)

bomb *obj* /£bɒm, $bɑːm/ *v* [T] • *Planes bombed* (= dropped bombs on) *the city every night.* • *This pub was bombed* (= a bomb exploded in it) *a few years ago.* • *The building was completely bombed* **out** (= completely destroyed by a bomb).

bomb·ing /£ˈbɒm·ɪŋ, $ˈbɑː·mɪŋ/ *n* • *Heavy bombing has gutted the city.* [U] • *In the 1970s, there was a* **wave of** *bombings in London.* [C]

bomb·er /£ˈbɒm·əʳ, $ˈbɑː·mɚ/ *n* [C] • A bomber is a person who uses bombs or an aircraft that drops bombs: *Rajiv Gandhi is believed to have been killed by a suicide bomber* (= a person who carries a bomb on their body). ○ *The invasion on land was supported by bombers in the air.* • A **bomber jacket** is a short jacket that fits tightly at the waist, often made of leather. • PIC› **Coats and jackets**

bomb [FAILURE] /£bɒm, $bɑːm/ *n* [U] *Am and Aus infml* something which has failed • *The play was a real bomb.*

bomb /£bɒm, $bɑːm/ *v* [I] *Am and Aus infml* • *Her last book really bombed* (= failed).

bomb [GO FAST] /£bɒm, $bɑːm/ *v* [I always + adv/prep] *infml* to travel very fast in a vehicle • *They bombed around the racetrack at 150 miles an hour.*

bom·bard *obj* /£bɒmˈbɑːd, $bɑːmˈbɑːrd/ *v* [T] to attack with continuous shooting or bombs • *The troops bombarded the city, killing and injuring hundreds.* • *(fig.) After she had stopped speaking, the children bombarded her* **with** (= asked her a lot of) *questions.* • *(fig.) When we got married, we were bombarded* **with** (= received a lot of) *presents.*

bom·bard·ment /£ˌbɒmˈbɑːd·mənt, $ˌbɑːmˈbɑːrd-/ *n* • *The use of modern weapons has made it more difficult to protect civilians from* **aerial** *bombardment.* [U] • *Trapped militia were pounded by air, tank and mortar bombardments in the battle for the town.* [C] • *(fig.) Fortunately the new Governor was prepared for the bombardment of questions from* (= being asked many questions by) *the press.* [U]

bom·bard·ier /£ˌbɒm·bəˈdɪəʳ, $ˌbɑːm·bəˈdɪr/ *n* [C] a soldier with a low rank in the ARTILLERY of some armies, or a military person who aims bombs (and sometimes releases them) from an aircraft

bom·bast·ic /£bɒmˈbæs·tɪk, $bɑːm-/ *adj* using long and important-sounding words, usually to make people think you know more than you do • *a bombastic preacher* • *a bombastic statement*

bom·bast /£ˈbɒm·bæst, $ˈbɑːm-/ *n* [U]

bombed /£bɒmd, $bɑːmd/ *adj Am infml* experiencing the strong effect of alcohol or illegal drugs; STONED • *He said he'd been really bombed the night before.*

bomb·shell [NEWS] /£ˈbɒm·ʃel, $ˈbɑːm-/ *n* [C usually sing] a sudden and often unpleasant piece of news • *Her decision not to stand for election came as a bombshell to her supporters.* • *He* **dropped** *his bombshell last week when he said he was leaving.*

bomb·shell [WOMAN] /£ˈbɒm·ʃel, $ˈbɑːm-/ *n* [C] a very attractive woman • *a* **blonde** *bombshell*

bomb·site /£ˈbɒm·saɪt, $ˈbɑːm-/ *n* [C] an empty area in a town where all the buildings have been destroyed by a bomb

bo·na fi·de /£ˌbəʊ·nəˈfaɪ·di, $ˌboʊ-/ *adj* real; not false • *The new law meant that bona fide charities would suffer as well as the false ones.*

bo·na fi·des /£ˌbəʊ·nəˈfaɪ·diːz, $ˌboʊ-/ *pl n* • *(law)* Your bona fides are your good or sincere intentions.

bo·nan·za /bəˈnæn·zə/ *n* [C] something from which large profits are made • *The rise in house prices meant that those who were selling enjoyed a bonanza.* • *April was a bonanza month* (= a month when large profits were made) *for car sales.* • *(fig.) The magazine will hold another fashion bonanza* (= a big and exciting event) *in the spring.*

bond [CONNECTION] /£bɒnd, $bɑːnd/ *n* [C] a close connection joining two or more people • *the bond(s) of friendship/love* • *There has been a close bond* **between** *them ever since she saved him from drowning.* • *The moments after birth are vital for the bond* (= feeling of love) **between** *mother* **and** *child.* • *In societies with strong family bonds* (= relationships), *people tend to live longer.* • (J) (KOR) (NL)

bond *obj* /£bɒnd, $bɑːnd/ *v* [T] • *The training was devoted to bonding the group into a closely-knit team.*

bond·ing /£'bɒn·dɪŋ, $'bɑːn-/ *n* [U] • Bonding is the process by which a close emotional relationship is developed: *Much of the bonding between mother and child takes place in those early weeks.*

bond *(obj)* GLUE /£bɒnd, $bɑːnd/ *v* to stick materials together, esp. using glue • *This new adhesive can bond metal* **to** *glass.* [T] • *The two pieces will bond in less than a minute.* [I] • (J) (KOR) (NL)

bond /£bɒnd, $bɑːnd/ *n* [C] • *When the glue has set, the bond* (=joint) *formed is watertight.*

bond DOCUMENT /£bɒnd, $bɑːnd/ *n* [C] an official paper given by the government or a company to show that you have lent them money that they will pay back to you at an **interest rate** that does not change • *I invested some money in savings bonds.* • (J) (KOR) (NL)

bond PROMISE /£bɒnd, $bɑːnd/ *n* [C] a written agreement or promise • *They entered into a solemn bond which was signed in our presence.* • *(Am law)* A bond is a sum of money that is paid to formally promise that someone (who is then released from prison where they have been waiting to be put on trial for a crime they are accused of) will appear for trial: *The judge ordered that he* **post** *a $10 000 bond pending his appeal of the verdict.* • (J) (KOR) (NL)

bond·age SERVANT /£'bɒn·dɪdʒ, $'bɑːn-/ *n* [C] *literary* the state of being another person's SLAVE (=servant owned by someone and with no personal freedom) • *The slaves were kept* **in** *bondage until their death.* ○ *(fig.) They aim to deliver the people who are* **in** *bondage* **to** (=being controlled by) *superstitious beliefs.*

bond·age SEX /£'bɒn·dɪdʒ, $'bɑːn-/ *n* [U] the act of being tied up to get sexual pleasure • *The films featured scenes of men in bondage or subjected to beatings by women.* • *They were* **into** (=They liked) *bondage.*

bonds /£bɒndz, $bɑːndz/ *pl n literary* the ropes or chains that hold prisoners and prevent them moving around or escaping • *Loose his bonds and set him free.* • *(fig.) She longed to escape from the bonds of* (=being prevented from doing what she wanted by) *children and housework.*

bone /£bəʊn, $boʊn/ *n* any of the hard parts inside a human or animal that make up its frame • *The jagged bone of his broken arm was protruding through the skin.* [C] • *The child was so thin that you could see her bones.* [C] • *Some human bones were found by a Norfolk farmer last week, when he was ploughing one of his fields.* [C] • *Knives with handles made of bone should not be put in a dishwasher.* [U] • *All our cutlery has bone handles.* • Bone is also the bone in meat or fish: *There's still a lot of meat left on the bone – shall I slice some off for you?* [C] ○ *I don't like fish because I hate the bones.* [C] • A **bone of contention** is something that two or more people argue about fiercely over a long period of time. • *I waited for the bus for so long that I was frozen* **to the bone** (=all the way through) *when it arrived.* • *I've got* **a bone to pick with** *you* (=I want to talk to you about something you have done that has made me angry), *you've been using my shaver again.* • To **make no bones about** (doing) something is not to try to hide your feelings: *He made no bones about his dissatisfaction with the service.* • **Bone china** is a delicate and expensive type of CHINA made using animal bone powder. • Something that is **bone dry** is completely dry: *I hung my wet swimsuit on the balcony and twenty minutes later it was bone dry.* • *(Br) He never does any exercise – he's* **bone idle** (=very lazy). • **Bone marrow** is MARROW TISSUE. • **Bone meal** is a substance made from crushed dried bones that is used to improve the earth to make plants grow better.

-boned /£-bəʊnd, $-boʊnd/ *combining form* • *She is* large-boned (=has large bones) *so she seems big, but she's not fat.*

bon·y /£'bəʊ·ni, $'boʊ-/ *adj* **-ier, -iest** • *Her long bony* (=very thin) *hands clasped the book.*

bone *obj* /£bəʊn, $boʊn/ *v* [T] • *Ask the fishmonger to bone the fish* (=take its bones out) *for you.*

bone·less /£'bəʊn·ləs, $'boʊn-/, *Am also* **boned** /£bəʊnd, $boʊnd/ *adj* [not gradable] • *boneless breast of chicken*

bone up /£bəʊn, $boʊn/ *v adv* [I] *infml* to learn as much as you can about something for a special reason • *She boned up* **on** *economics before applying for the job.*

bone·head /£'bəʊn·hed, $'boʊn-/ *n* [C] *slang* a stupid person

bon·er MISTAKE /£'bəʊ·nəʳ, $'boʊ·nɚ/ *n* [C] *Am and Aus infml* a mistake which causes embarrassment to the person who makes it • *Oops! What a boner!* • *The president admitted that the US had committed a boner by sending in troops.*

bon·er PENIS /£'bəʊ·nəʳ, $'boʊ·nɚ/ *n* [C] *esp. Am taboo slang* a penis when it is hard

bone·shak·er /£'bəʊn,ʃeɪ·kəʳ, $'boʊn,ʃeɪ·kɚ/ *n* [C] *infml humorous* a very old, uncomfortable vehicle

bon·fire /£'bɒn·faɪəʳ, $'bɑːn·faɪr/ *n* [C] a large fire that is made outside to burn unwanted things or for pleasure • *We had been building a huge bonfire for weeks.* • *(Br)* **Bonfire night** is another name for GUY FAWKES NIGHT, the night of November 5 when many people in Britain light bonfires and have FIREWORKS. • *"The Bonfire of the Vanities"* (title of a novel by Tom Wolfe, 1987) • LP **Holidays** PIC **Fires and space heaters**

bong /£bɒŋ, $bɑːŋ/ *n* [C] a musical noise made esp. by a large clock • *Several bongs precede the news on the BBC World Service.* • *I heard the bong of the grandfather clock.*

bong·o (drum) /£'bɒŋ·gəʊ, $'bɑːŋ·goʊ/ *n* [C] *pl* **bongos** or **bongoes** one of a pair of small drums that are played with the hands

bon·hom·ie /£,bɒn·ə'mi, $,bɑː·nə'miː/ *n* [U] friendliness and happiness • *After a successful meeting he was full of bonhomie.*

bonk *obj* HIT /£bɒŋk, $bɑːŋk/ *v* [T] *infml humorous* to hit, not very hard • *He bonked me on the head with his newspaper.*

bonk /£bɒŋk, $bɑːŋk/ *n* [C] • *I gave him a bonk on the head and said, "Get lost!".*

bonk *(obj)* HAVE SEX /£bɒŋk, $bɑːŋk/ *v Br taboo slang* to have sex (with) • *They were bonking* **(away)** *for hours.* [I] • *I bonked the prince, says sexy Sarah.* [T]

bonk·ers /£'bɒŋ·kəz, $'bɑːŋ·kɚz/ *adj* [after v] *infml humorous* silly or stupid • *She must be bonkers to do that.*

bon mot /£,bɔ̃'məʊ, $,bɑːn'moʊ/ *n* [C] *pl* **bons mots** /£,bɔ̃'məʊ, $,bɑːn'moʊ/ a clever remark • *It was Harold Wilson who penned the bon mot that "one man's wage increase is another man's price increase".*

bon·net HAT /£'bɒn·ɪt, $'bɑː·nɪt/ *n* [C] a type of hat that covers the ears and is tied under the head, worn by babies or, esp. in the past, by women • PIC **Hats**

bon·net METAL COVER *Br and Aus* /£'bɒn·ɪt, $'bɑː·nɪt/, *Am* **hood** *n* [C] the metal cover over the part of a car where the engine is • *I looked under the bonnet and clouds of smoke poured out.* • PIC **Car**

bon·ny /£'bɒn·i, $'bɑː·ni/ *adj* **-ier, -iest** *esp. Scot Eng* beautiful and healthy • *a bonny baby* ○ *a bonny lass*

bon·sai /£'bɒn·saɪ, $,bɑːn'saɪ/ *n* [U] the method of growing very small trees by continually cutting the roots and branches and growing them in small containers • *a bonsai tree*

bo·nus /£'bəʊ·nəs, $'boʊ-/ *n* [C] an extra amount of money that is given to you as a present or reward in addition to the money you were expecting • *a productivity bonus* ○ *a Christmas bonus* • *He paid me and added a bonus for the new customers I had signed up.* • *The company used to give discretionary bonus payments.* • *(fig.) I love the job, and it's an* **added** *bonus* (=a pleasant additional thing) **that** *it's so close to home.*

bon vi·vant (*pl* **bons vivants**) /£,bɔ̃·viː'vɑ̃ː, $,bɑːn·viː'vɑːnt/, *Br also* **bon vi·veur** /£,bɔ̃·viː'vɜːʳ, $,bɑːn·viː'vɜːr/ *n* [C] a person who enjoys good food and wines and likes going to restaurants and parties

bon voy·age /£,bɔ̃·vɔɪ'ɑːʒ, $,bɑːn·vwaɪ-/ *exclamation* a phrase meaning 'enjoy your journey', that is said to people who are going away • LP **Phrases and customs**

bon·y /£'bəʊ·ni, $'boʊ-/ *adj* See at BONE

bon·zer /£'bɒn·zəʳ, $'bɑːn·zɚ/ *adj Aus dated infml* very good or pleasant

boo DISAPPROVAL /buː/ *v* he/she/it **boos**, **booing**, *past* **booed** to make an expression of strong disapproval or disagreement • *People at the back started booing loudly.* [I] • *Her singing was so bad that she was booed* **off** *the stage.* [T]

boo /buː/ *n* [C] *pl* **boos** • *He was greeted by boos and hisses.* • *(Am) You* **never said boo** (=did not say anything) *to me about going to your mother's this weekend.*

boo SURPRISE /buː/ *exclamation* an expression, usually shouted, used to surprise and frighten someone who does not know you are near them • *She would jump out of cupboards and shout 'Boo!' at people.*

boob MISTAKE /buːb/ *v, n Br infml* (to make) a silly mistake • *The leaflet boobed* **by** *calling her a county champion rather than a world champion.* [I] • *He boobed rather badly* **by** *not asking her first if he could borrow her* *stereo.* [I] • *Forgetting the President's name was a bit of a boob.* [C]

boob BREAST /buːb/ *n* [C] *slang* a woman's breast • *She had blonde hair, big boobs and wore tight clothes.*

boo–boo /ˈbuː·buː/ *n* [C] *pl* **boo-boos** *infml* a mistake • *Oops, I think I made a boo-boo there – I hope she's not too upset.* • *(Am infml)* A boo-boo can also be a slight injury: *Carol fell down and got a boo-boo on her hand.*

boob·y /ˈbuː·bi/, *Am also* **boob** *n* [C] a stupid person • A **booby prize** is a prize given as a joke to the person who finishes last in a competition. • A **booby trap** is something that is meant to give someone a, usually unpleasant, surprise. To **booby-trap** a place is to play this sort of joke there: *They put a bucket of water on top of his door as a booby trap.* ○ *She had booby-trapped the door with a bag of flour which fell on my head as I walked through.* • A **booby-trap** is a bomb, hidden in something that looks harmless, and which explodes when it is touched. To **booby-trap** a place is to put such a bomb in it: *Police in Northern Ireland have had to be constantly on the lookout for booby traps.* ○ *The booby-trap bomb was hidden in a bag of shopping.* ○ *The politician's car had been booby-trapped and exploded as he drove off.*

boo·ger /£ˈbuː·gəʳ, $-gɚ/ *n* [C] *Am for* BOGEY NOSE

boog·ey·man (*pl* **-men**) /ˈbuː·gi·mæn/ *n* [C] *Am for* **bogey man**, see at BOGEY FEAR

boog·ie /ˈbuː·gi/ *v* [I] **boogieing**, *past* **boogied** to dance to POP music • *We boogied away all night long.*

boog·ie /ˈbuː·gi/ *n* [U] • *I enjoy a good boogie from time to time.*

boo·hoo /ˌbuːˈhuː/ *exclamation* the sound of noisy, childish crying • *"Boohoo!" she wailed "I'm lost."*

book TEXT /bʊk/ *n* [C] a set of pages that have been fastened together inside a cover to be read or written in • *I took a book with me to read on the train.* • *Their walls were lined with books.* • *She wrote a book* **on** *car maintenance.* • *Look up the number in* **the book** (=a **telephone directory**). • In a very long book such as the Bible, a book is one of the parts into which it is divided: *The book of Job.* • A book **of** stamps, matches, tickets, etc. is a number of these items fastened together inside a cover. • *She likes good films and* **in my book** (=in my opinion) *that makes her all right.* • To **open/start/keep a** book **on** something is when a BOOKMAKER accepts and pays out sums of money which are risked on a particular result: *They've already opened a book on the result of the next World Cup.* • A **book club** is an organization in which members can buy books more cheaply than in the shops: *I joined a book club and got this big atlas for only £5.* • *(Br)* A **book token** is a card worth a particular amount of money that is given as a present, and which can only be used to buy a book: *Jamie got a £10 book token for his birthday from Auntie Marion.*

books /bʊks/ *pl n* • A company's books are its written records of money that has been spent or received: *At the end of the year the accountant goes over* **the books**. • **The** books is also the list of people who are employed by a company or who (pay to) belong to a club, society, sports team, etc.: *There are 256 people* **on** *the books at the cement works.* ○ *The nursery has 30 babies on the books and 13 on the waiting list.* ○ *The secretary of our tennis club says we've only got 22 members on our books at present.* ○ *Bob Matthewson had two seasons on Bolton's books before becoming a League referee.* ○ *Rachel had been signed up on the books of a model agency.* • If you are **in** someone's **good/bad books** they are pleased/annoyed with you: *Emily is in the teacher's good books lately.* ○ *I forgot to phone him so now I'm in his bad books.*

book *(obj)* ARRANGE /bʊk/ *v* to arrange to have (a seat, room, entertainer, etc.) at a particular time in the future • *I've booked us two tickets to see 'Carmen'/I've booked two tickets* **for** *us to see 'Carmen'.* [+ two objects] • *She'd booked a table for four at their favourite restaurant.* [T] • *Will booked a seat on the evening flight to Edinburgh.* [T] • *We were advised to book early if we wanted to get a room.* [I] • *They booked a jazz band for their wedding.* [T] • *We've booked* **to** *fly to Morocco on Friday.* [+ to infinitive] • *The hotel/restaurant/theatre is* **fully booked (up)** (=all the rooms/tables/tickets have been taken). [T] • *I'd like to go but I'm afraid I'm booked* **up** (=I have arranged to do other things) *until the weekend.* [T] • *I've booked you* **in** (=arranged a room for you) *at the Savoy.* [T] • *As soon as she arrived in Tokyo she booked* **in** (=reported her arrival and signed an official book) *at her hotel.* [I]

book·ing /ˈbʊk·ɪŋ/ *n* [C] • *Bookings are still available for that flight.* • *Bookings to Greece are 20% up on last year.* • *We* **made** *the booking three months ago.* • *Julian was ill so we had to* **cancel** *the booking.* • *The show had already taken £4 million in* **advance** *bookings.* • *I filled in the booking* **form** *and sent it off with a cheque for £30.* • *(Br and Aus)* A **booking clerk** is a person who sells tickets, esp. in a railway station or airport. • *(Br and Aus)* A **booking office** is a place, usually in a theatre, where tickets can be bought before a performance.

book *obj* MAKE A RECORD /bʊk/ *v* [T] (of a police officer, REFEREE, etc.) to write down the name of (someone who has done something wrong) in an official record • *A player in a football match who is booked twice in a game is sent off the field.* • *My grandmother was booked* **for** *speeding last week.*

book·a·ble /ˈbʊk·ə·bl̩/ *adj* [not gradable] that can be arranged before the time it happens

book·bind·ing /ˈbʊkˌbaɪn·dɪŋ/ *n* [U] the skill of fastening loose pages together inside a cover to make a book

book·bind·er /£ˈbʊkˌbaɪn·dəʳ, $-dɚ/ *n* [C]

book·bind·er's /£ˈbʊkˌbaɪn·dəz, $-dɚz/ *n* [C] *pl* **bookbinders** or **bookbinders'** • A bookbinder's is a place where bookbinders work: *I took the manuscript down to the bookbinder's to get it bound.*

book·case /ˈbʊk·keɪs/ *n* [C] a piece of furniture with shelves to put books on • PIC **Room**

book·end /ˈbʊk·end/ *n* [C] an object used, esp. in pairs, to keep a row of books standing vertically

book·ie /ˈbʊk·i/ *n* [C] *infml for* BOOKMAKER

book·ish /ˈbʊk·ɪʃ/ *adj esp. disapproving* enjoying reading books, esp. serious books • *People thought of her as bookish and rather prim.* • *He had a bookish and rather shy look about him.*

book·keep·ing /ˈbʊkˌkiː·pɪŋ/ *n* [U] the job or activity of keeping an exact record of the money that has been spent or received by a business or other organization • *She taught herself bookkeeping and started up her own company.* • *I always found* **double-entry** *bookkeeping difficult to understand.*

book·keep·er /£ˈbʊkˌkiː·pəʳ, $-pɚ/ *n* [C]

book·let /ˈbʊk·lət/ *n* [C] a very thin book with a small number of pages and a paper cover, often giving information about something • *We bought a booklet about the castle from the tourist office.*

book·mak·er /£ˈbʊkˌmeɪ·kəʳ, $-kɚ/, *infml* **book·ie** *n* [C] a person who accepts and pays out sums of money risked on a particular result, esp. of horse races • *The rain held off, punters were happy and the bookmakers did a decent trade.*

book·mak·er's /£ˈbʊkˌmeɪ·kəz, $-kɚz/ *n* [C] *pl* **bookmakers** or **bookmakers'** • A bookmaker's is a place where bookmakers work: *He went down to the bookmaker's in Chesterton Road to place a bet on the race.* ○ *Mr Smith won several hundred pounds at the bookmaker's by backing his party's chances.*

book·mark /£ˈbʊk·mɑːk, $-mɑːrk/, **book·mark·er** /£ˈbʊkˌmɑː·kəʳ, $-ˌmɑːr·kɚ/ *n* [C] a piece of card, leather or plastic that you put between the pages of a book so that you can find a page again quickly

book·mo·bile /£ˈbʊkˌmə·biːl, $-ˌmoʊ-/ *n* [C] *Am for* **mobile library**, see at MOBILE

book·plate /ˈbʊk·pleɪt/ *n* [C] a decorative piece of paper stuck inside the front cover of a book to show who owns it

book·sel·ler /£ˈbʊkˌsel·əʳ, $-ɚ/ *n* [C] a person or company that sells books

book·shelf /ˈbʊk·ʃelf/ *n* [C] *pl* **bookshelves** a shelf in a BOOKCASE

book·shop *esp. Br and Aus* /£ˈbʊk·ʃɒp, $-ʃɑːp/, *Am usually* **book·store** /£ˈbʊk·stɔːʳ, $-stɔːr/ *n* [C] a shop where books are sold

book·stall /£ˈbʊk·stɔːl, $-stɑːl/ *n* [C] *esp. Br and Aus* a table or a very small shop with an open front where books, magazines, etc. are sold • *I stopped at the station bookstall to get a magazine to read on the train.*

book·worm /£ˈbʊk·wɜːm, $-wɜːrm/ *n* [C] a person who reads a lot • *She's a real bookworm – she's always got her head in a book.*

boom PERIOD OF GROWTH /buːm/ *v, n* (to have) a period of sudden growth, esp. one that results in a lot of money being made • *Here, as elsewhere, the leisure industry is booming.* [I] • *This year has seen a boom* **in** *book sales.* [C] • *The insurance business has been characterised by a vicious cycle of boom and* **bust** *as companies go in and out of businesses and prices rise and fall.* [U] • *The consumer boom of the 1980s led to an explosion of shopping centre development.* [C] • *It* *was here that the property boom of the eighties really began.* [C] • *The Prime Minister is predicting a boom time for British business.* • *Aberdeen became a* **boom town** (= a town where lots of people have become rich) *when oil was discovered in the North Sea.*

boom SOUND /buːm/ *v, n* (to make) a very deep and loud hollow sound • *The cannons boomed* **(out)** *in the night.* [I] • *He boomed* **(out)** *an order to the soldiers.* [T] • *We heard a boom in the distance as the bomb went off.* [C] • *(Am)* A **boom box** is a large radio and TAPE player you can carry with you.

boom·ing /ˈbuː·mɪŋ/ *adj* • *a booming voice*

boom BOATING /buːm/ *n* [C] (on a boat) a long movable pole that has the main sail fastened to it • *The boom swung round and he was hit on the head.*

boom FILMING /buːm/ *n* [C] (in television or film-making) a long movable pole that has a MICROPHONE on one end and is held over the actors so that it cannot be seen by the viewers • *Sound recording is supervised by the floor mixer, while the boom operator positions the microphone during shooting.*

boom·er·ang /ˈbuː·mə·ræŋ/ *n* [C] a curved stick that, when thrown in a particular way, comes back to the person who threw it • *The Australian Aborigines originally used boomerangs as weapons.*

boom·er·ang /ˈbuː·mə·ræŋ/ *v* [I] • If something boomerangs **on** you it brings a harmful result instead of the intended good one: *Our plan to take over the business might boomerang on us.*

boon /buːn/ *n* [C usually sing] something that is very helpful and improves the quality of life • *The convenience of cashless shopping has proved a boon to millions.* • *Guide dogs are a great boon to the partially sighted.* • *(literary)* A boon **companion** is a very close friend.

boon·docks /£ˈbuːn·dɒks, $-dɑːks/ *pl n* **the boondocks** *Am and Aus disapproving* any area in the country that is quiet, has few people living there and is a long way away from a town or city

boor /£bʊəʳ, $bʊr/ *n* [C] a person who is rude and does not consider other people's feelings

boor·ish /£ˈbʊər·ɪʃ, $ˈbɔː·rɪʃ/ *adj* • *I found him rather boorish and aggressive.*

boost *obj* /buːst/ *v* [T] to improve or increase • *The theatre managed to boost its audiences by cutting the price of the tickets.* • *Share prices were boosted* **by** *reports of the President's recovery.* • *I tried to boost his* **ego** (= make him feel more confident) *by praising his cooking.* • *(infml) She appeared on various talk shows to boost* (= make more popular) *her new book.*

boost /buːst/ *n* [C usually sing] • *The lowering of interest rates will give a much-needed boost* (= improvement) **to** *the economy.* • *Passing my driving test gave a boost* **to** *my* **confidence**.

boost·er /£ˈbuː·stəʳ, $-stɚ/ *n* [C] • *Certainly, a successful end to the war will be a confidence booster.* • *Seeing the poor performance of their opponents the previous day was a great morale booster to the young team.* • *The two rocket boosters attached to the shuttle's belly drop back to sea and are reused.* • A **booster seat** is a removable extra seat put onto a car seat for a child to sit on in order to make the child high enough for the **seat belt** to fit safely.

boost·er /£ˈbuː·stəʳ, $-stɚ/ *n* [C] an additional small amount of a drug given to strengthen the effect of the same drug given some time before to protect a person from illness • *Julian had a typhoid vaccination last year but needed a booster this year before going to India.*

boot SHOE /buːt/ *n* [C] a type of shoe that covers the whole foot and the lower part of the leg • *ankle boots* ○ *wellington boots* ○ *walking boots* ○ *riding boots* • *I put on my coat and new leather boots.* • *She was wearing the sort of thick heavy boots that soldiers wear.* • If you say that **the boot is on the other foot**, you mean that a situation is now the opposite of what it was and esp. that someone who was weak now has power. • *"These Boots are Made for Walking"* (title of a song written by Lee Hazlewood, 1966) • PIC› **Shoes** (PL)

boot KICK /buːt/ *v, n infml* (to give) a hard kick with the foot • *He gave the ball a good boot and it landed at the far side of the field.* • If you **get/are given the boot** you are dismissed from your job: *She got the boot because she stole money from the till.* ○ *(fig.) My boyfriend was more interested in watching football than in going out so I gave him the boot* (= ended my relationship with him). • To **put the boot in** is to kick someone when they are already on the ground: *The thugs hit him, knocked him down and proceeded to put the boot in till he was unconscious.* ○ *(fig.) We've got enough problems on our hands – don't you come and put the boot in* (= make the situation worse). • (PL)

boot CAR *Br and Aus* /buːt/, *Am* **trunk** *n* [C] a covered space at the back of a car, for storing things in • *They found a body in the boot.* • *We loaded the boot and set off for our holiday.* • PIC› **Car** (PL)

boot *(obj)* MAKE READY /buːt/, **boot up** *v specialized* (of a computer) to (cause to) become ready for use by getting necessary information into the computer's memory • (PL)

boot ALSO /buːt/ *n* [U] **to boot** in addition, also • *He is kind, handsome and wealthy to boot.* • (PL)

boot·ee, *Am also* **boot·ie** /£ˈbuː·ti, $-t̬i/ *n* [C] a baby's soft boot that is often made of wool • PIC› **Shoes**

booth /£buːð, $buːθ/ *n* [C] a small enclosed box-like space that a person can go into • *a telephone booth* ○ *a polling booth* • A booth is also a partly enclosed area, a table or small tent at a FAIR (= public event with entertainment), EXHIBITION (= an event where a collection of things is shown), etc.: *There was a man standing outside one of the booths at the fair encouraging people to have a ride on the ghost train.* ○ *Our company's booth at the exhibition was right next to our main competitor.* • PIC› **Box**

boot·lace /ˈbuːt·leɪs/ *n* [C] a long thin cord or strip of leather used to fasten boots

boot·leg /ˈbuːt·leg/ *adj* [not gradable] illegally made or copied • *Some people had brought bootleg liquor to the party.* • *Police are cracking down on bootleg tapes being sold on the streets.*

boot·leg *(obj)* /ˈbuːt·leg/ *v* **-gg-** • *He was caught bootlegging videotapes.* [T] • *She bootlegged, sold drugs and shoplifted to make ends meet.* [I]

boot·leg·ger /£ˈbuːt·leg·əʳ, $-ɚ/ *n* [C]

boot·straps /ˈbuːt·stræps/ *pl n* **pull/haul** *yourself* **up by** *your* **bootstraps** to succeed by your own hard work and without any help from anyone else

boot·y /£ˈbuː·ti, $-t̬i/ *n* [U] any valuable items or money stolen by an army at war or by thieves • *Napoleon's booty comprised some of Europe's best paintings.* • *Caesar's army plundered the camp capturing many slaves and much booty.* • *After the earthquake looters stormed through the shops and made off with carloads of booty.*

booze /buːz/ *v, n infml* (to drink) alcohol • *They always go boozing after their football match.* [I] • *She's a bit too fond of the booze for her own good.* [U] • *The party's at Kate's on Friday night – bring some booze.* [U] • *(Br) Every Friday night Rick and Susie would go out* **on the booze** (= to drink a lot of alcohol). [U] • *(infml)* A **booze-up** is a party or similar occasion where people drink a lot of alcohol: *Peter's leaving tomorrow so we're going to have a booze-up in the evening.* • *(Aus)* A **booze bus** is a police vehicle from which officers test drivers' breath to see how much alcohol they have drunk.

booz·y /ˈbuː·zi/ *adj* **-ier, -iest** *infml* • *They enjoy a boozy* (= drinking a lot of alcohol) *night out once in a while.* • *In the musical she plays the coarse, boozy, widowed mum.* • *His boozy* (= smelling of alcohol) *breath could be smelt as soon as he came into the room.*

booz·er /£ˈbuː·zəʳ, $-zɚ/ *n* [C] *infml* • A boozer is a person who drinks a lot: *She's a big boozer.* • *(Br)* A boozer is a PUB (= building where alcoholic drinks can be bought and drunk): *He went down to his local boozer to see his friends.*

bop DANCE /£bɒp, $bɑːp/ *v* [I] **-pp-** *infml* to dance to POP music • *They all began to bop* **to** *the music.*

bop /£bɒp, $bɑːp/ *n* [U] • *There are a couple of decent clubs where you can go for a bop.*

bop·py /£ˈbɒp·i, $ˈbɑː·pi/ *adj* **-ier, -iest** *infml* • *I feel like dancing – have you got any boppy music* (= music that is good for dancing to)*?*

bop *obj* HIT /£bɒp, $bɑːp/ *v* [T] **-pp-** *infml* to hit • *He found he had bopped a policeman* **on the** *head by mistake.*

bop MUSIC /£bɒp, $bɑːp/, **be-bop** *n* [U] a type of jazz music first played by small groups in the 1940s

bo·rax /£ˈbɔː·ræks, $ˈbɔːr·æks/ *n* [U] a white powder used to make glass and cleaning products

Bor·deaux /£bɔːˈdəʊ, $bɔːrˈdoʊ/ *n pl* **Bordeaux** (a type of) white and esp. red wine from the Bordeaux area of France • *You can't go wrong choosing Bordeaux.* [U] • *They've got several nice Bordeaux in stock.* [C]

bor·del·lo /£bɔːˈdel·əʊ, $bɔːrˈdel·oʊ/ *n* [C] *pl* **bordellos** *literary* a BROTHEL

bor·der DIVISION /£ˈbɔː·dəʳ, $ˈbɔːr·dɚ/ *n* [C] the line that divides one country from another • *The towns near the* *border have suffered some of the worst bombing.* • *We got across the border without being searched.* • *The train crosses the border* **between** *France and Spain.* • *The two countries have been locked in border disputes for years.* • [PIC] **Edge**

bor·der *(obj)* /£ˈbɔː·dəʳ, $ˈbɔːr·dɚ/ *v* • *Swaziland borders* (= is next to) *South Africa and Mozambique.* [T] • *(fig.) Her behaviour showed eccentricity bordering* **on** (= almost the same as or coming close to) *insanity.* [I]

bor·der·ing /£ˈbɔː·dᵊr·ɪŋ, $ˈbɔːr·dɚ-/ *adj* [not gradable] • *Many people travel from bordering counties to work in the city.*

bor·der [EDGE] /£ˈbɔː·dəʳ, $ˈbɔːr·dɚ/ *n* [C] a strip that goes around or along the edge of something, often as decoration • *The dress was white with a delicate lace border.* • *That picture would look better with a border (around it).* • *Walkers are requested to keep to the borders of the field.* • *By May you should have planted your borders* (= the narrow strips of ground around a garden which are usually planted with flowers). • [PIC] **Edge, Garden**

bor·der *obj* /£ˈbɔː·dəʳ, $ˈbɔːr·dɚ/ *v* [T] • *Crumbling stone walls bordered the road as we drove along.* • *The colleges that border the river all have their own boats for the students.* • [PIC] **Edge**

bor·der·line /£ˈbɔː·də·laɪn, $ˈbɔːr·dɚ-/ *adj* between two very different conditions, with the possibility of belonging to either one of them • *Only in borderline* **cases** (= cases where students might succeed or fail) *will pupils have an oral exam.* • *She was very much a borderline candidate so I'm not surprised she has failed.*

bor·der·line /£ˈbɔː·də·laɪn, $ˈbɔːr·dɚ-/ *n* [C usually sing] • *The borderline* (= the line that separates two qualities) **between** *friendship and intimacy is often hard to define.*

bore *obj* [FAIL TO INTEREST] /£bɔːʳ, $bɔːr/ *v* [T] to talk or act in a way that makes (someone) lose interest and become tired • *"Am I boring you?" she asked anxiously.* • *The speaker was boring everybody – you could see it on their faces.*

bore /£bɔːʳ, $bɔːr/ *n* [C] • *All he talks about is his stamp collection – he's becoming an awful bore* (= an uninteresting person). • *"Come on into the water, Henry, don't be a bore!"* • *(infml)* A bore is also something that is annoying or unpleasant to do: *Ironing shirts is such a bore.* ○ *It's an awful bore cooking a meal every night.* [+ v-ing] ○ *It's such a bore* **to** *have to write this out all over again.* [+ *to* infinitive] ○ *It's raining again – what a bore!*

bored /£bɔːd, $bɔːrd/ *adj* • *(infml) I sat there pretending to listen but I was* **bored stiff/bored to tears/bored to death** (= completely uninterested). • *(infml) I was* **bored rigid** (= made very bored) *by the lecture.* • *He was getting bored* **with/of** *doing the same thing every day.*

bor·ing /£ˈbɔː·rɪŋ, $ˈbɔːr·ɪŋ/ *adj* • *She finds opera boring.* • *It was boring to sit on the plane with nothing to read.* • *It was a boring lecture so I amused myself by sketching the lecturer.* • *The new building was rather boring and conventional.* • *Jim said he found the subject incredibly boring.* • *The film was so boring I fell asleep.* • *We've had boring old carrots with every meal this week.*

bor·ing·ly /£ˈbɔː·rɪŋ·li, $ˈbɔːr·ɪŋ-/ *adv* • *The film has a boringly predictable ending.*

bore·dom /£ˈbɔː·dəm, $ˈbɔːr-/ *n* [U] • *They had started quarrelling* **out of** *sheer boredom.*

bore *(obj)* [MAKE A HOLE] /£bɔːʳ, $bɔːr/ *v* to make a hole (in something) using a tool • *He used a drill to bore a hole in the wall above the fireplace.* [T] • *The workmen bored* **through** *the rock.* [I always + adv/prep] • *A tunnel has been bored under the Channel to link England and France.* [T] • *(fig.) Her eyes bored* **into** *me* (= looked at me very hard) *and I had to look away.* [I always + adv/prep]

bore /£bɔːʳ, $bɔːr/, *Am usually* **gauge** *n* [U] *specialized* • The bore of a pipe or tube is the cylindrical hole along its length or the diameter (= measurement across the widest part) of this hole: *You need a pipe with a fairly narrow bore/ a bore of 16 millimetres.*

-bore *esp. Br* /£-bɔːʳ, $-bɔːr/, *Am usually* **gauge** *combining form* • -bore is used to express the width of a circular hole in a cylindrical object, esp. the inside of a gun BARREL: *a small-bore rifle* ○ *a twelve-bore shotgun*

bore [WAVE] /£bɔːʳ, $bɔːr/ *n* [C] a very large wave that runs from the sea up a narrow river at particular times of year • *the Severn Bore*

bore [BEAR] /£bɔːʳ, $bɔːr/ *past simple of* BEAR

bore·hole /£ˈbɔː·həʊl, $ˈbɔːr·hoʊl/ *n* [C] a deep hole made in the ground when looking for oil, gas or water • *We must sink boreholes, so that people will have water to drink and cook with.* • *They obtained information about the rock by drilling boreholes.*

born [BEGAN TO EXIST] /£bɔːn, $bɔːrn/ *adj* [not gradable] **be born** to come into existence by birth • *She was born in 1950.* • *I was born English but later became an American citizen.* • *We hoped to see a lamb being born when we visited the farm.* • *Diana was born* **into** *a wealthy and aristocratic family.* • *Stevie Wonder was born blind* (= was blind from birth). • *Ann was born* **and brought up** *in Ealing.* • *Born blind, she nevertheless became an international concert pianist.* • *The toll of babies born* **with** *AIDS is rising.* • *(fml) This was a child born* **to/of** *educated parents.* • *(fig.) His arrogance is born* **of** (= comes from) *a conviction that he is a superior being.* • *(fig.) It was in that year that the idea of independence was born* (= began to exist). • *She's a Dubliner* **born and bred** (= she has spent all her early life there). • To be **born with a silver spoon in** your **mouth** is to have a high social position and wealth from birth. • *"Don't try to fool me. I* **wasn't born yesterday** (= I am not as stupid as you seem to think), *you know."* • If someone says they **wish** they**'d never been born** they are expressing the deep unhappiness they feel: *"When I've finished with you you're going to wish you'd never been born," he threatened.* • A **born-again Christian** is one who has decided to accept a particular type of EVANGELICAL Christianity, esp. after a deep spiritual experience: *Cliff Richard is a born-again Christian.* ○ *(fig.) My mother is a born-again health freak* (= she has become extremely enthusiastic about health). • *"Born to Run"* (song by Bruce Springsteen, 1975) • *"Born in the USA"* (song by Bruce Springsteen, 1984) • *"Born to be Wild"* (song by Steppenwolf, 1969) • *"Born with the gift of laughter and a sense that the world was mad"* (Rafael Sabatini in the novel *Scaramouche*, 1921) • [LP] **Age**

-born /£-bɔːn, $-bɔːrn/ *combining form* • *newborn* • *stillborn* • *Ben Okri is a Nigerian-born poet and novelist.* • *In the past the first-born son inherited everything.*

born [NATURAL] /£bɔːn, $bɔːrn/ *adj* [not gradable] having a natural ability or tendency • *It was obvious from her childhood that Rachel was a born writer.* [before n] • *With those long legs Joel is a born athlete.* [before n] • *I felt born* **to** *look after animals.* [+ *to* infinitive]

borne [BEAR] /£bɔːn, $bɔːrn/ *past participle of* BEAR • *(Br fml)* If something **is borne in on/upon** someone they are made to understand it: *Suddenly it was borne in on him that he was becoming too old to start a new career.*

-borne [MOVED BY] /£-bɔːn, $-bɔːrn/ *combining form* carried or moved in this way • *airborne* • *waterborne*

bor·ough /£ˈbʌr·ə, $ˈbɜːr·oʊ/ *n* [C] a town, or a division of a large town • *London is made up of 32 boroughs while New York has 5.* • [LP] **'-ough' pronunciation**

bor·row *(obj)* [RECEIVE] /£ˈbɒr·əʊ, $ˈbɑːr·oʊ/ *v* to get or receive (something) from someone with the intention of giving it back after a period of time • *Could I borrow your bike* **from** *(not standard* **off***) you until next week?* [T] • *She used to borrow money and not bother to pay it back.* [T] • *Brazil has had to borrow heavily to survive.* [I] • *He borrowed* (= took away for a particular period) *a novel from the library.* [T] • *(fig.) English has borrowed* (= takes and uses as its own) *(many words)* **from** *French.* [I/T] • To **live/exist on borrowed time** is to continue living after a point at which you might easily have died: *Since his cancer was diagnosed he feels as if he's living on borrowed time.* ○ *(fig.) It is unlikely that serious decisions will be taken by a minority government living on borrowed time* (= still governing when most people would have expected them to have stopped). • Compare LEND. • [LP] **Borrow**

bor·row·er /£ˈbɒr·əʊ·əʳ, $ˈbɑːr·oʊ·ɚ/ *n* [C] • *Building societies are encouraging borrowers* (= people or organizations who borrow). • *"Neither a borrower nor a lender be"* (Shakespeare, Hamlet 1.3)

bor·row·ing /£ˈbɒr·əʊ·ɪŋ, $ˈbɑːr·oʊ-/ *n* • *Public borrowing has increased in recent years.* [U] • *A ministry exists in France to limit the French language's borrowings* (= the words it takes to use as its own) *from other languages.* [C]

bor·row *obj* [SUBTRACTION] /£ˈbɒr·əʊ, $ˈbɑː·roʊ/ *v* [T] to put a number into a different column when doing subtraction • *To take 26 away from 53, first borrow a 10 from from the 50 (leaving a 4 in the 10's column) to make the 3 into 13. Then you can take the 6 away.*

borscht, borsch /£bɔːʃt, $bɔːrʃt/ *n* [U] a type of soup made from BEETROOT (= a small dark red vegetable) •

BORROW, LEND, HIRE, RENT

NO PAYMENT IS NEEDED

• **Things or money are given for free.**

to borrow — *Can I borrow your bike? I'll return it in a few days.*
He borrowed £50 **from** *my sister and never gave a penny back.*

to lend — *I can lend you a jacket/lend a jacket* **to** *you if you need one.* [+ two objects]
About that money I lent you – when can you pay me back?

to loan *(esp. Am)* — *A TV company loaned him video-recording equipment for his trip.* [+ two objects]

PAYMENT IS NECESSARY

• **Money**

The money must be paid back, and the borrower usually has to pay **interest** (= extra money).

to borrow — *Many small businesses borrow heavily in order to buy equipment.*

to lend — *The organisation was set up to lend* **to** *farmers.*

a loan — *She got a small loan* **from** *the bank to buy her van.*

a debt — A debt is any money or property you owe: *They took out $1.5 million in loans and now can't repay their debts.* • *The corporation is deeply* **in debt**.

• **Things**

In *(Am)* it is usual to use 'rent' rather than 'hire'.

to hire/rent — *We want to hire a car for a week. How much will it cost?*
How much do you charge for hiring **out** *a fishing boat? Is this one* **for hire**?
You can rent a suit if you can't afford to buy one.

to lease — When you lease something you make a written legal agreement to pay money in order to use something for an agreed time: *We leased our photocopiers* **from** *Modern Office Supplies.* • *They have leased a printer* **to** *us for five years.*

• **Land or property**

'Let' is *(esp. Br)* and the usual *(Am)* word is 'rent'.

to let — *They went abroad and let their house* **to** *a Japanese family.*
The sign outside the building said (Br) 'Flats to let'/(Am) 'Apartments for rent'.

to rent — *I needed to be in London for a month, so I rented a room in a student house.*

(the) rent — *Don't forget the rent is due* (= should be paid) *tomorrow.*
Rents in Paris are extremely high.

to lease — *The landlord decided to lease the ground floor of the building* **to** *a shoe shop.*

• **Work or a service**

In *(Br)* someone is usually hired for work only temporarily; in *(Am)* to hire means to begin to employ.

to hire — *We need to hire another secretary for a couple of months until Jane comes back.*
Al's garage is doing fine – he's hired four more mechanics.

to hire out — *I've decided to hire myself out as a cook for company lunches.*

Borscht is often chilled in the refrigerator before being served.

bor·stal /£ˈbɔː·stᵊl, $ˈbɔːr-/ *n* [C] *Br* (in the past) a prison for boys who are too young to be sent to an ordinary prison • *He was sent to borstal for shoplifting.* • *Many boys in borstals are taught more serious crimes by older boys.*

bosh /£bɒʃ, $bɑːʃ/ *exclamation, n* [U] *dated* nonsense or foolishness • *Don't talk such bosh!*

bo's'n /£ˈbəʊ·sᵊn, $ˈboʊ-/ *n* [C] a BOATSWAIN

bo·som /ˈbʊz·ᵊm/ *n* [C usually sing] *fml or literary* a woman's breasts or the front of a person's chest, esp. when thought of as the centre of human feelings • *Her* **ample** *bosom wobbled as she laughed.* • *She* **held** *him tightly* **to** *her bosom.* • *A dark jealousy stirred* **in** *his bosom.* • *(fml or humorous) They intend to spend Christmas* **in the bosom of** (= close to, protected by and loved by) *their family.* • A **bosom friend/buddy/pal** is a friend that you like very much and are very close to.

bo·som·y /ˈbʊz·ᵊm·i/ *adj* • *She was tall and bosomy* (= had large breasts).

boss [MANAGER] /£bɒs, $bɑːs/ *n* [C] the person who is in charge of an organization and who tells others what to do • *She was the boss of a large international company.* • *The meeting was chaired by the former boss of a Hartlepool building firm.* • *The boss has just told me he's sacking me.* • *I started up my own business and now I'm my* **own** *boss* (= I work for myself and no one tells me what to do). • *(infml) Who's the boss* (= the person who makes all the important decisions) *in your house?* • Ⓙ

boss *obj* /£bɒs, $bɑːs/ *v* [T] *infml disapproving* • *She's bossed and nagged him ever since they got married.* • *I wish he's stop bossing me* **around/about** (= telling me what to do).

bos·sy /£ˈbɒs·i, $ˈbɑː·si/ *adj* **-ier, -iest** *disapproving* • *He thought she was bossy* (= was always telling him what to do), *and she thought he was a slob.* • **Bossy boots** is a name used by children for someone who is very bossy.

bos·si·ness /£ˈbɒs·ɪ·nəs, $ˈbɑː·sɪ-/ *n* [U] *disapproving*

boss [DECORATION] /£bɒs, $bɑːs/ *n* [C] a rounded, raised decoration such as on a SHIELD or a ceiling

boss [GOOD] /£bɒs, $bɑːs/ *adj Am infml* very good or excellent • *It was a boss party, with boss music and boss babes.*

boss–eyed /£ˈbɒs·aɪd, £,-ˈ-, $ˈbɑːs-/ *adj Br slang* with eyes that look inwards towards the nose; CROSS-EYED

bo·sun /£ˈbəʊ·sᵊn, $ˈboʊ-/ *n* [C] a BOATSWAIN

bot·a·ny /£ˈbɒt·ᵊn·i, $ˈbɑː·ṭᵊn-/ *n* [U] the scientific study of plants

bo·tan·ic·al /bəˈtæn·ɪ·kᵊl/ *adj* [not gradable] • *The tropical rain forests contain more than half of the earth's 250 000 botanical species.* • A **botanic(al) garden** is a garden, which is usually open to the public, where a wide range of plants are grown for scientific research and educational purposes: *I usually go for a stroll around the botanical garden during my lunch break.*

bot·an·ist /£ˈbɒt·ᵊn·ɪst, $ˈbɑː·ṭᵊn-/ *n* [C] • *Botanists are concerned that construction of the road would destroy the habitat of several rare plant species.*

botch *obj* /£bɒtʃ, $bɑːtʃ/, *Br also* **bodge** *v* [T] to spoil (something) by doing it badly • *The funding was withdrawn after they botched* **(up)** *the first stage of the research.* • *She tried to jump over the fence, but she botched* **it** (= jumped badly) *and twisted her ankle.* • *Our landlord redecorated the bedroom, but it was such a botched* **job** (= it was so badly done) *that we decided to redo it.* • *Thousands of women are infertile as a result of botched* **abortions**. • *He eventually sought psychiatric help after a botched* **suicide** *attempt.* • *The leaders of the botched* **coup** *will remain in prison until after the presidential election.*

botch /£bɒtʃ, $bɑːtʃ/, *Br and Aus also* **botch–up** /£ˈbɒtʃ·ʌp, $ˈbɑːtʃ-/, *Br also* **bodge** *n* [C] • *The company made a series of botches before it went bankrupt.* • *(Br) The concert was very badly organized. In fact, the whole thing was a real botch-up.*

both /£bəʊθ, $boʊθ/ *predeterminer, determiner, pronoun* (referring to) two people or things together • *Both my parents are journalists.* • *Her interest in the newspaper business came from her parents, both* **of whom** *were journalists.* • *She has written two novels, both* **of which** *have been made into television series.* • *Both Mike and Jim have red hair./Mike and Jim both have red hair.* • *How was I to choose between the two? I loved them both/I loved both* **of** *them.* • *The problem with both* **of these** *proposals is that they are hopelessly impractical.* • *Are both* **of us** *invited, or just you?* • *Would you like milk or sugar or both?* • *I felt both happy and sad* (=I had these two emotions) *at the same time.* • *Both men* **and** *women have written to complain that the advertisement was sexist.* • *Our products need to be competitive* **in terms of** *both quality and price.* • *It will be very difficult to find an agreement that will satisfy both* **parties.** • *In both* **cases,** *a coded warning was received from the bombers before the explosion.* • *I think it's important to listen to both* **sides** *of the argument.* • *The film was very popular on both sides of the Atlantic* (=in the US and the UK). • *Improved child-care facilities would benefit both* **sexes,** *not just women.* • *There is a growing awareness in both* **countries** *of their common history and culture.* • *Sunday's game will be the last match of the season for both* **teams.** • *Both* **groups** *have complained of discrimination.* • *Traffic was moving very slowly in both* **directions** *for about an hour after the accident.* • *She sharpened the stick carefully at both* **ends.** • *Scepticism about the official figures comes from both* **ends** *of the political spectrum.* • *I had been looking forward to a delicious meal with excellent service, but I was disappointed on both* **counts** (=neither the service nor the meal were as good as I had hoped). • *I failed my driving test because I didn't keep both* **hands** *on the steering wheel.* • *Both* **houses** *of Congress have begun their debate on granting the President authority to commit US troops to war.* • *She has expressed doubts about the validity of both* **sets of** *statistics.* • *There has been a build-up of troops on both* **sides of** *the border in recent weeks.* • LP› **Quantity words, Two**

both·er MAKE AN EFFORT /£ˈbɒð·əʳ, $ˈbɑː·ðɚ/ *v* [usually in negatives] to make the effort to do something, or to take the trouble to do something • *He hasn't even bothered* **to** *write.* [+ *to* infinitive] • *She should have phoned them, but she just didn't bother.* [I] • *Don't bother* **(about/with) doing** *the laundry.* [+ v-*ing*] • *You'd have found it if you'd bothered* **looking/to** *look.* [+ v-*ing*; + *to* infinitive] • *You won't get any credit for doing it,* **so why** *bother?* [I] • *"I've mended that cup for you." "Thanks, but you* **needn't have** *bothered. I bought a new one this morning."* [I] • *He went to all the trouble of organizing a leaving party for her, and she didn't even bother* **to** *turn up.* [+ *to* infinitive] • *Why did* **nobody** *bother* **to** *tell me something was wrong?* [+ *to* infinitive] • *He walked out of the office* **without** *bothering* **to** *say goodbye.* [+ *to* infinitive] • *About 25% of the electorate didn't bother* **to vote** *in the last election.* [+ *to* infinitive] • If you **cannot be bothered** to do something, you are unwilling to make the effort that is needed to achieve it: *I asked him to go to the post office for me, but he just couldn't be bothered.* ○ *I can't be bothered* **to** *cook this evening.*

both·er /£ˈbɒð·əʳ, $ˈbɑː·ðɚ/ *n* [U] • *Some people don't have church weddings because they don't want* **the** *bother* (= they don't want to make the effort that is necessary). • *"You really shouldn't have." "It was no bother."* • *He* **went to (all) the** *bother* **of** *making her a birthday cake* (= he made a lot of effort), *but she felt too ill to eat any of it.* • *It hardly seems* **worth** *the bother to go all that way for a dinner party.*

both·er *(obj)* ANNOY /£ˈbɒð·əʳ, $ˈbɑː·ðɚ/ *v* to annoy, worry or cause problems for (someone) • *Don't bother me now. Can't you see I'm trying to work?* [T] • *I'm sorry to bother you, but could you direct me to the station?* [T] • *The heat was beginning to bother him, so he went inside.* [T] • *She threatened to call the police if he didn't stop bothering her.* [T] • *It doesn't bother me if he doesn't turn up.* [T] • *"I hardly ever see my parents." "Doesn't that bother you at all?"* [T] • *The villagers don't seem to be bothered by all the tourists.* [T] • *Do they bother* **about** *punctuality in your job?* [I]

both·er /£ˈbɒð·əʳ, $ˈbɑː·ðɚ/ *n* [U], *exclamation* • *I don't want to be* **a** *bother, but would you mind typing this for me?* • *I had a bit of bother getting hold of his phone number.* • *(Br infml) I got into* **a spot of** *bother* (= a small amount of difficulty) *with my bank manager when I wasn't paid on time.* • *(Br infml) There was* **a spot of** *bother* (=fighting) *in town last night.* • *"Oh bother!" exclaimed Chris, as it started to rain. "I've left my umbrella at home."*

both·ered /£ˈbɒð·əd, $ˈbɑː·ðɚd/ *adj* • *"If the music's too loud for you, I'll turn it down." "I'm not bothered* (= It is not annoying me)." • *The bright sunshine made him feel* **hot and** *bothered* (= hot and uncomfortable).

both·er·a·tion /£ˌbɒð·əˈreɪ·ʃən, $ˌbɑː·ðə-/ *exclamation dated* an expression of annoyance • *Oh botheration! I can't find my keys anywhere.*

both·er·some /£ˈbɒð·ə·səm, $ˈbɑː·ðɚ-/ *adj dated* causing annoyance or trouble • *a bothersome little man* • *bothersome noise*

bot·tle CONTAINER /£ˈbɒt·l̩, $ˈbɑː·t̬l̩/ *n* [C] a container for liquids, usually made of glass or plastic, with a narrow neck • *a milk bottle* • *a wine bottle* • *a bottle* **of** *beer/whisky* • *She bought an expensive bottle* **of** *perfume/aftershave in London.* • *He uncorked another bottle* **of** *champagne and refilled our glasses.* • *His father used to drink a bottle* **of** *gin* (= the contents of a bottle) *a day.* • *Should I get a two-***litre** *bottle of lemonade, or will one litre be enough?* • **Fill** *the bottle with water and put the cap on firmly.* • *We take all our* **empty** *bottles and jars for recycling.* • **Plastic** *bottles are lighter than glass ones.* • A **baby's bottle** is a special container with a rubber top used for giving liquid, esp. milk, to a baby: *The baby had finished her bottle.* • *Most medical experts believe the breast to be better than* **the** *bottle* (= the method of feeding usually using artificial milk) *for your baby.* • To **bottle-feed** a baby is to feed it with a bottle rather than the breast: *I decided to bottle-feed Amy rather than breast-feed her.* ○ *She started* **bottle-feeding** *her baby when she went back to work.* • A **bottle bank** is a large container into which people put empty bottles so that the glass can be used again. • Something that is bottle **green** is very dark green in colour. • A **bottle top** is usually the circular piece of metal used to close a glass bottle of beer. It can also mean any top used to close a bottle. • PIC› **Bottles and flasks, Coverings, Top**

bot·tle *obj* /£ˈbɒt·l̩, $ˈbɑː·t̬l̩/ *v* [T] • *The wine was bottled* (= put into bottles) *near the vineyard.* • *To bottle fruit you put fresh fruit into special containers.* • *The apartment was centrally heated, and we had bottled* **gas** *to cook with.* • **Bottled water** (= Water that is sold in bottles) *is becoming increasingly popular because of the public's worries about the safety of tap water.* • When a person **bottles** things **up**, they refuse to talk about things that make them angry or worried: *Feelings that had been bottled up for years came flooding out.*

bot·tle ALCOHOL /£ˈbɒt·l̩, $ˈbɑː·t̬l̩/ *n* [U] **the bottle** *infml* the habit of regularly drinking a lot of alcohol • *With often disastrous consequences, some writers have considered the bottle as necessary as the pen.* • *(infml)* To be **on the bottle** is to drink a lot regularly: *He tried to give it up, but after a few months he was back on the bottle.* • *She started to* **hit** *the bottle* (= drink too much alcohol) *after she had her third child.* • *He was once a brilliant academic, but he* **took to the bottle** (= started to drink a lot regularly) *when his wife died.*

bot·tle BRAVERY /£ˈbɒt·l̩, $ˈbɑː·t̬l̩/ *n* [U] *Br slang* bravery or willingness to take risks • *It took* **a lot of** *bottle to do what she did.*

bot·tle out /£ˌbɒt·l̩, $ˌbɑː·t̬l̩/ *v adv* [I] *Br slang* • *I was going to enter a belly-dancing contest, but I bottled out* (= stopped being brave or confident enough to do it) *at the last minute.*

bot·tle·neck /£ˈbɒt·l̩.nek, $ˈbɑː·t̬l̩-/ *n* [C] a place where a road becomes narrow, or a place where there is often a lot of traffic, causing the traffic to slow down or stop • *Roadworks are causing bottlenecks in the city centre and long delays can be expected.* • *(fig.) Is there any way of getting round this bureaucratic bottleneck* (= problem which delays development)?

bot·tom LOWEST PART /£ˈbɒt·əm, $ˈbɑː·t̬əm/ *n* [C usually sing] the lowest part of something • *He stood at the bottom of the stairs and called up to me.* • *Extra information will be found at the bottom of the page.* • *The box had sunk to the bottom of the sea/the sea bottom.* • *The bottom of the mug* (= The base on which it stands) *had left a mark on the table.* • *The potatoes have burned and stuck to the bottom* (= the lowest inside surface) *of the pan.* • *They live at the bottom of our street* (= the other end of the street from us). • *The apple tree at the bottom* (= end) *of the garden is beginning to blossom.* • *At school, Einstein was (at the) bottom of* (= the least successful student in) *his class.* • *The manager of the hotel started* **at the** *bottom* (= in one of the least important jobs) *30 years ago, as a porter.* • *The rich usually get richer, while the people* **at the** *bottom* (= at the lowest position in society) *stay there.* • *The bottom has* **dropped out of** *the fur*

Bottles and flasks

coat market (=people have stopped buying these products). • A bottom is sometimes the lower part of an item of clothing that consists of two parts: *a bikini bottom* ○ *Have you seen my* **pyjama/tracksuit** *bottoms anywhere?* • *"I'm going to* **get to the bottom of** *this* (=to find out the truth of the situation)*," he snarled.* • *The desire for money is* **at the** *bottom* **of** (=the real reason for or the cause of) *much of the world's violence.* • *Jealousy is,* **at bottom** (=in fact), *lack of self-confidence.* • *When I said I loved you, I meant it* **from the bottom of** *my* **heart** (=very sincerely). • *(infml)* **Bottoms up!** is sometimes said by people just before they begin to drink an alcoholic drink to express friendliness towards each other. • *(Br) Kate's grandmother has given her a quilt for her* **bottom drawer** *(Am* **hope chest**, *Aus* **glory box***)* (=the collection of things that a young woman traditionally makes for use after she has married). • The **bottom line** in the accounts of a company or organization is the final line which states the total profit or loss that has been made: *How will the rise in interest rates affect our bottom line?* • The **bottom line** is also the final result or the most important consideration of a situation, activity or discussion: *The bottom line is that we need another ten thousand dollars to complete the project.* • **knock the bottom out of** at KNOCK [HIT]; **rock bottom** at ROCK [STONE]; **from top to bottom** at TOP [HIGHEST PART].

bot·tom [BODY PART] /£ˈbɒt·ᵊm, $ˈbɑː·t̬əm/ *n* [C] the part of your body at the top of your legs on which you sit • *I'll smack your bottom if you do that again!*

bot·tom out /£ˌbɒt·əm, $ˌbɑː·t̬əm/ *v adv* [I] to have reached the lowest point in a continuously changing situation and to be about to improve • *The government claims that the recession is bottoming out.*

bot·tom·less /£ˈbɒt·əm·ləs, $ˈbɑː·t̬əm-/ *adj* [not gradable] without a limit or end • *The generosity of the local people is bottomless.* • *(fig.) Each day we ventured on to larger rocks from which we flung ourselves into the bottomless* (=very deep) *sea.* • *The government's pockets are not bottomless* (=It does not have unlimited amounts of money), *so it has to find a way of reducing expenditure.* • *We'll be pouring money into a* **bottomless pit** (=spending an unlimited amount of money) *if we try to keep that factory open.*

bot·ul·i·sm /£ˈbɒt·jʊ·lɪ·zᵊm, $ˈbɑː·tʃə-/ *n* [U] a type of poisoning caused by bacteria that exist in badly preserved food • *Botulism affects the central nervous system, causing paralysis, hallucinations and vomiting, and is often fatal.*

bou·doir /£ˈbuːd·wɑːʳ, $-wɑːr/ *n* [C] a luxurious room used in the past by a woman for sleeping, dressing, relaxing and entertaining • *As he was going upstairs, the Duchess called him into her boudoir and showed him a letter she had just received.*

bouf·fant /£ˈbuː·fɒ̃ŋ, $-fɑːnt/ *n* [C] a type of hairstyle in which the hair is arranged in a high rounded shape

bou·gain·vil·le·a /ˌbuː·gᵊnˈvɪl·i·ə/ *n* [C; U] a climbing plant, common in hot countries, that has red and purple flowers

bough /baʊ/ *n* [C] *esp. literary* a large branch of a tree • [LP] **'-ough' pronunciation**

bought /£bɔːt, $bɑːt/ *past simple and past participle of* BUY • *Aren't you going to show me what you've bought?*

bouil·la·baisse /ˌbuː·jəˈbes/ *n* [U] a thick strongly-flavoured soup, made from fish, vegetables and spices, which originated in the south of France

bouil·lon /£ˈbuː·jɒ̃ŋ, $ˈbʊl·jɑːn/ *n* [U] a thin clear soup made by boiling meat and vegetables in water • **Bouillon cube** is *Am for* **stock cube**. See at STOCK [FLAVOUR].

boul·der /£ˈbəʊl·dəʳ, $ˈboʊl·dɚ/ *n* [C] a large rounded rock that has been smoothed by the action of the weather • *In 1952, severe floods carried 2000 tons of boulders down to the Devon town of Lynmouth, killing 38 people.*

boules /buːl/ *n* [U] a game played between two players or teams outside on rough ground, esp. in France, in which metal balls are thrown so that they land as close as possible to a smaller ball • *We spent the evening sitting outside a café, watching a couple of old men playing boules.*

bou·le·vard /£ˈbuː·lə·vɑːd, $ˈbʊl·ə·vɑːrd/ *n* [C] a wide road in a city, usually with trees on each side or along the centre • *In the 1850s Baron Haussmann replaced the narrow streets of Paris with wide boulevards.*

bounce *(obj)* [JUMP] /baʊnts/ *v* to (cause to) move up or away after hitting a surface • *The ball hit the ground and bounced high into the air.* [I] • *The basketball player bounced the ball along the ground.* [T] • *(fig.) Television pictures from all over the world are bounced* **off** (=are sent to and come down somewhere else from) *satellites.* [T] • *Her bag bounced* (=moved up and down) *against her side as she walked along.* [I] • *The children had broken the bed by bouncing* (=jumping up and down) *on it.* [I] • *(fig.) Tom bounced* **in** (=walked in with an up and down movement), *smiling broadly.* [I] • *He bounced the baby* (=lifted it up and down) *on his knee.* [T] • *(fig.) Although she was disappointed about not getting the job, Jane soon* **bounced back** (=soon returned to her usual activities and happiness after an unpleasant experience).

bounce /baʊnts/ *n* • *In tennis you must hit the ball before its second bounce.* [C] • *This shampoo will give dull, lifeless hair bounce* (=make it look thick and springy) *and shine.* [U] • *(fig.) She was always smiling and had loads of bounce* (=was happy and energetic). [U]

bounc·y /ˈbaʊnt·si/ *adj* **-ier, -iest** • *Hard ground makes balls more bouncy.* • *(fig.) He's always bouncy* (=happy and energetic) *in the morning.*

bounce *(obj)* [NOT PAY] /baʊnts/ *v infml* (to cause a CHEQUE) to not be paid or accepted by a bank because of a lack of money in the account • *He paid me by cheque but it bounced.* [I] • *To my horror the bank bounced the cheque.* [T]

bounc·er /£ˈbaʊnt·səʳ, $-sɚ/ *n* [C] *infml* a strong man paid to stand outside a bar, party, etc. and either stop people who cause trouble from coming in or force them to leave • *He was a* **nightclub** *bouncer before he became a boxer.*

bounc·ing /ˈbaʊnt·sɪŋ/ *adj* [before n] (esp. of a baby) healthy and energetic • *We've got two grandchildren – a three-year-old girl and a bouncing baby boy.*

bound BIND /baʊnd/ *past simple and past participle of* BIND TIE

bound CERTAIN /baʊnd/ *adj* [after v; not gradable] certain or extremely likely to happen • *These two young musicians are bound* **for** *international success* (= They are certain to be successful). • *You're bound* **to** *forget people's names occasionally.* [+ *to* infinitive] • *You're bound* **to feel** *nervous about your interview.* [+ *to* infinitive] • *He's bound* **to fail** *the exam if he doesn't do any revision.* [+ *to* infinitive] • *It was bound* **to happen** *sooner or later.* [+ *to* infinitive] • *(dated or humorous) He's in the pub,* **I'll be bound** (= I am certain). • *(fml)* **I'm** *bound* **to** *say that I've never liked their children.* [+ *to* infinitive] • *(Am) They are* **bound and determined** (= seriously intending) *to build their own house someday.*

bound FORCED /baʊnd/ *adj* [after v; + *to* infinitive] having a moral or legal duty to do something • *The company is bound by a special agreement* **to** *involve the union in important decisions.* • *She* **feels (duty)** *bound* **to** *tell him everything.* • *She is not* **legally** *bound* **to** *pay the debts, but she has agreed to do so as a gesture of goodwill.* • *Although he's my son, I felt* **morally** *bound* **to** *tell the police what he'd done.*

bound *obj* BORDER /baʊnd/ *v* [T] to mark or form the limits of • *The village is bounded on one side* **by** *a river.* • *The kingdom of Lesotho is completely bounded by South Africa.*

bound·less /ˈbaʊnd·ləs/ *adj* • *He is a man of apparently boundless* (= unlimited) *optimism.* • *She has boundless* **energy** *and* **enthusiasm**.

bounds /baʊndz/ *pl n* • *The school declared that the town was* **out of bounds** *to its pupils* (= that they were forbidden from going there). • *It's not* **beyond the** *bounds* **of** *possibility* (= It's not impossible) *that they'll win the match, but it doesn't seem very likely.* • *Surely it cannot be* **beyond the** *bounds* **of** *human ingenuity* (= it must be possible) *to find a more efficient way of collecting the tax.* • *The committee felt that newspaper coverage of the murder* **went beyond** *reasonable bounds.* • *What you did was* **outside the** *bounds* **of** *acceptable behaviour for an employee of this company.* • *All our trading activities are* **within the** *bounds* **of** *the law* (= are legal). • *His desire for political power apparently* **knows no** *bounds* (= seems to be unlimited).

bound DIRECTION /baʊnd/ *adj* [not gradable] going to • *She was on a plane bound* **for** *Moscow when she fell ill.* • *So where are you bound tomorrow?*

-bound /-baʊnd/ *combining form* • *Northbound traffic* (= Traffic which is travelling north) *is moving very slowly because of the accident.* • *(Am) The line did not close completely, but inbound and outbound trains* (= trains which were arriving and leaving) *had to share one of the two tracks near the station.*

-bound PREVENTING LEAVING /-baʊnd/ *combining form* (causing people to be) unable to leave a place because of an unwanted condition • *During his long illness he was completely housebound* (= he could not leave the house). • *She has been wheelchair-bound for several years.* • *The road is fogbound* (= covered by fog) *and driving conditions are extremely hazardous.* • *There have been no flights into or out of the snowbound/strikebound airport for 48 hours.* • See also **-bound** at BOUND DIRECTION.

bound JUMP /baʊnd/ *v* [I always + adv/prep] to move quickly with large jumping movements • *The kangaroo bounded across the road.*

bound /baʊnd/ *n* [C] • *With one bound* (= quick large jump) *the dog was over the fence.*

bound up /baʊnd/ *adj* [after v] closely connected or involved • *The reasons why the legislation was introduced are complex and bound up* **with** *the history of immigration into this country.* • *The survival of these creatures is* **intimately** *bound up with the health of the ocean.* • *Britain's fate is* **inextricably** *bound up with Europe's.*

bound·a·ry /£ˈbaʊn·dᵊr·i, -dri, $-dɚ-/ *n* [C] an often imaginary line that marks the edge or limit of something • *We crossed the state boundary at midnight.* • *The Ural mountains mark the boundary* **between** *Europe and Asia.* • *The company has ambitious plans to expand* **beyond** *national boundaries.* • *Residents are opposed to the village being placed* **within** *the city boundary.* • *Officials are insisting that there will be no* **redrawing** *of the boundary between their countries.* • *(fig.) The film is excessively violent and* **transgresses** *the boundaries* (= limits) *of good taste.* • *(fig.) Electronic publishing is* **blurring** *the boundaries between dictionaries and encyclopedias* (= making the differences between them less clear).

bound·en du·ty /ˈbaʊn·dᵊn/ *n* [U] *dated or humorous* something that you feel you must do • *She felt that it was her bounden duty to tell the police about the incident.*

bound·er /£ˈbaʊn·dəʳ, $-dɚ/ *n* [C] *dated* a man who behaves badly or immorally, esp. in his relationships with women • *You don't want to get involved with that brother of hers. He's a real bounder, you know.*

boun·ty REWARD /£ˈbaʊn·ti, $-t̬i/ *n* [C] a sum of money paid as a reward • *A bounty of $10 000 has been offered for the capture of his murderer.* • *The military government has placed a bounty on the heads of many of its opponents* (= It has offered a reward to people who kill them). • A **bounty hunter** is someone who searches for criminals or hunts animals in exchange for a reward.

boun·ty GENEROSITY /£ˈbaʊn·ti, $-t̬i/ *n* [U] *literary* generosity or a large amount • *The charity is totally dependent on the Church's bounty.* • *The pilots said the retreating enemy forces presented a bounty of targets.*

boun·ti·ful /£ˈbaʊn·tɪ·fᵊl, $-t̬ɪ-/ *adj literary* • *If the British were as bountiful* (= generous) *as the Americans, donations to charities would more than treble.* • *We found a bountiful* (= large) **supply of** *coconuts on the island.*

bou·quet FLOWERS /£bʊˈkeɪ, £bəʊ-, $boʊ-/ *n* [C] an often large group of flowers that have been fastened together and attractively arranged so that they can be given as a present or carried on formal occasions • *At the end of her performance she was presented with a big bouquet* **of** *roses.* • *Chris sent me a lovely bouquet* **(of flowers)** *when I was in hospital.* • *Her* **wedding** *bouquet consisted of roses and ivy.* • LP **'-et' words** Ⓕ

bou·quet SMELL /£bʊˈkeɪ, $boʊ-/ *n* [C] *specialized* the characteristic smell of a wine or LIQUEUR (= strong sweet alcoholic drink) • *This wine has a rich, oaky bouquet.* • Ⓕ

bour·bon /£ˈbɜː·bᵊn, $ˈbɜːr-/ *n* a type of American WHISKEY (= a strong alcoholic drink) • *Bourbon is made by distilling maize and rye.* [U] • *I'll have a bourbon on the rocks/and water/and soda.* [C]

bourge·ois /£ˈbɔːʒ·wɑː, $ˈbʊrʒ-/ *adj, n* [C] *disapproving* (a person) belonging to or typical of the **middle class** (= a social group between the rich and the poor), esp. in supporting established customs and values, and/or in having a strong interest in money and possessions • *She's become terribly bourgeois since she joined the golf club.* • *He would often escape his hectic life in 19th-century Paris, leaving behind the petty restrictions of the bourgeois society he so despised.*

bourge·ois·ie /£ˌbɔːʒ·wɑːˈziː, $ˌbʊrʒ-/ *n* [U + sing/pl v] • *The new bourgeoisie, which was created by the Industrial Revolution, had money to spend and wanted to travel.* • In Marxist theory, **the bourgeoisie** is the part of society, including bankers, employers and industrialists, which owns most of the wealth and takes advantage of ordinary workers: *The July Revolution in Paris in 1830 resulted in the establishment of a more liberal régime dominated by the wealthy bourgeoisie.*

bout BRIEF PERIOD /baʊt/ *n* [C] a brief period of illness or involvement in an activity • *She had a bout* **of** *flu over Christmas.* • *Towards the end of his life he* **suffered from** *periodic bouts of insanity.* • *He's* **prone to** *severe bouts of depression.* • *The printers were too ill to turn up for work after a* **drinking** *bout* (= brief period of drinking a lot of alcohol) *the previous night.*

bout SPORT /baʊt/ *n* [C] a boxing or WRESTLING match • *He's a former heavyweight champion and is expected to win the bout easily.*

bou·tique /buːˈtiːk/ *n* [C] a small shop that sells fashionable clothes, shoes, jewellery, etc. • *Some of Rome's best boutiques and restaurants occupy former churches.* • Ⓕ

bov·ine /£ˈbəʊ·vaɪn, $ˈboʊ-/ *adj (specialized)* connected with cows or *(fig.)* like a cow because slow or stupid • *(specialized) The bovine growth hormone can boost cows' milk production by up to 25%.* • *(fig.) He was a gentle, rather bovine man.* • See also BSE.

bov·ver /£ˈbɒv·əʳ, $ˈbɑː·vɚ/ *n* [U] *Br infml* violent or threatening behaviour • **Bovver boots** are heavy, thick boots traditionally used for kicking people in fights. • A **bovver boy** is a young man who likes fighting and trouble.

bow BEND /baʊ/ *v, n* (to make) a brief bending forward movement of the head or body, esp. as a way of showing someone respect or expressing thanks to people who have been watching you perform • *They bowed* **to** *the Queen before speaking.* [I] • *He* **gave** *a deep bow* **to** *the assembled crowd.* [C] • *The audience applauded enthusiastically, and* *she came back on stage to* **take** *another bow.* [C] • *She bowed her* **head** *in shame and sadness.* [T] • *We knelt down and bowed our* **heads** *in prayer.* [T] • *He bowed* **down** (= very low) *before* (= in front of) *the king and begged for mercy.* [I] • *(fig.) He expects me to bow* **down** *to* (= agree to obey) *him and do everything he tells me.* [I] • *(fig.) Eventually the government was forced to bow* **to** (= accept unwillingly) *public* **pressure** *and reform the tax.* [I] • *(fig.) She'll be bowing* **out** (= leaving her job) *at the end of the month, after presenting the programme for eight years.* [I] • *(disapproving)* If you **bow and scrape** you show too much politeness or attention to someone: *You don't need to bow and scrape every time you see the boss.* • Compare CURTSY.

bowed /baʊd/ *adj* • *He struggled along the path, bowed* (= bent over) **under** *the weight of the heavy bags he was carrying.*

bow FRONT PART /baʊ/ *n* [C], **bows** *pl n* the front part of a ship • *The bow/bows of the ship was/were badly damaged in the collision.* • *The ferry sank after leaving port with its bow doors open.* • *(fig.) The opposition party has fired a warning shot across the government's bows* (= has given them something to worry about). • Compare STERN SHIP PART. • PIC› **Bow, Ships and boats**

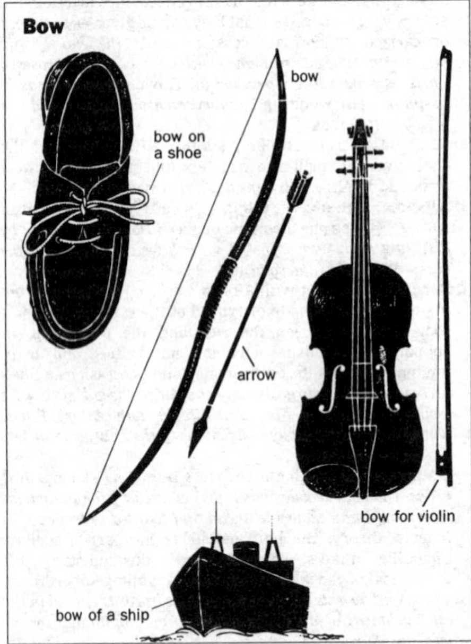

bow WEAPON /£bəʊ, $boʊ/ *n* [C] a weapon for shooting arrows, often used for sport, made of a long thin piece of wood bent into a curve by a tightly stretched string • *Robin Hood was armed with only his bow* **and arrows.** • A **bow-legged** person is someone with legs that curve out at the knees. • A **bow window** is a curved window that sticks out from the wall of a house. • *"Bring me my bow of burning gold"* (William Blake in the hymn *Jerusalem*, 1804-10) • See also CROSSBOW. • PIC› **Bow, Window**

bowed /£bəʊd, $boʊd/ *adj* • *The table had delicate bowed* (= curved) *legs.*

bow MUSIC /£bəʊ, $boʊ/ *n* [C] a long thin piece of wood with hair from the tail of a horse stretched along it which is used to play musical instruments that have strings • *Violins are played with bows.* • PIC› **Bow, Musical instruments**

bow KNOT /£bəʊ, $boʊ/ *n* [C] a knot with two curved parts and two loose ends which is used as a decoration or to tie shoes • *I tied the ribbon around the parcel in a pretty bow.* • A **bow tie** is a special type of TIE (= a strip of cloth put around a collar) in the shape of a bow, worn especially on formal occasions. • PIC› **Bow, Clothes**

bowd·ler·ize *obj, Br and Aus* **-ise** /ˈbaʊd·lə·raɪz/ *v* [T] *disapproving* to remove from (a book, play or film) language or parts that are considered to be unsuitable or offensive • *They decided to bowdlerize the film by cutting out all the nude scenes when it was shown on television.* • *The version of the play that I saw had been dreadfully bowdlerized.*

bowels /ˈbaʊ·əlz, baʊəlz/ *pl n, specialized* **bowel** *n* [C] a long tube through which food travels from the stomach and out of the body while it is being digested, esp. the larger part of this tube in humans, where excrement is formed; the INTESTINE • *Eating plenty of fresh fruit and vegetables can reduce the risk of bowel* **cancer/cancer** *of the bowel.* • *(medical)* If you **move** your bowels, you excrete the solid waste that they contain. • *(medical) Are your* **bowel movements** *normal?* (= Is your body regularly excreting solid waste?) • The bowels of something are the parts of it that are furthest away from the outside: *The paintings were stored in the bowels of the castle throughout the war.* ○ *People used to believe that monsters lived deep in the bowels of the* **earth.**

bower /£ˈbaʊ·əʳ, £baʊəʳ, $-ɚ/ *n* [C] *literary* a pleasant sheltered place in a wood or garden made by weaving together tree branches and plant stems • *They sat under the leafy bower at the end of the garden and watched the sun set.*

bowl DISH /£bəʊl, $boʊl/ *n* [C] a round container that is open at the top and is deep enough to hold fruit, sugar, etc., or the rounded inside part of something • *a soup/cereal/salad/sugar bowl* • *a bowl of soup/rice/porridge* • *She eats a bowl* (= the contents of a bowl) **of** *cereal every morning.* • *Government cutbacks have forced the university to go to large companies with a* **begging** *bowl* (= asking for money). • *Sift the flour and baking powder into a* **mixing** *bowl.* • *The* **toilet** *bowl was cracked and stained, and the walls were covered in mould.* • *(Br) Just put the dirty dishes in the* **washing-up** *bowl, and I'll do them later.* • **Life is just a bowl of cherries** is an expression which means that everything is excellent: *Life's just a bowl of cherries for her – she's so rich that she'll never need to worry about money.* • *(esp. Am)* A bowl is also a large bowl-shaped building which is used for important sporting events or musical performances. • PIC› **Cutlery, Pan**

bowl *(obj)* CRICKET /£bəʊl, $boʊl/ *v* to throw a ball towards a BATSMAN using a vertical circular movement of the arm while running • *Pringle was tired after bowling for an hour.* [I] • *He's injured his shoulder, so he'll have to bowl* **underarm** (= without raising his arm). [I] • To bowl someone **(out)** is to make them have to leave the cricket field by hitting the WICKET behind them with the ball: *I was bowled out for 34* (= after I had scored 34 RUNS). [T] • *(fig.) They bowled* **down/along** (= went fast along) *the street on their new bicycles.* [I]

bowl·er /£ˈbəʊ·ləʳ, $ˈboʊ·lɚ/ *n* [C] • *It isn't easy to score runs against* **fast/pace** *bowlers* (= cricketers who bowl fast). • A **spin** bowler makes the ball spin so that when it hits the ground it bounces in an unexpected way, making it difficult to hit. • PIC› **Sports**

bowl·ing /£ˈbəʊ·lɪŋ, $ˈboʊ-/ *n* [U] • *The England captain* **opened the** *bowling* (= bowled first).

bowl ROLL /£bəʊl, $boʊl/ *v* to roll (a ball) along a smooth grass or artificial surface during a game • *It's your turn to bowl.* [I] • *Stop messing about and bowl the ball!* [T] • A **bowling green** is an area of very short, smooth grass where you can play **bowls.**

bowl /£bəʊl, $boʊl/ *n* [C] • A bowl is a large ball used in the game of **bowls**, or a heavy ball with three holes for the fingers used in **bowling.**

bowl·ing /£ˈbəʊ·lɪŋ, $ˈboʊ-/, **ten·pin bowl·ing**, *Am* **ten·pins** *n* [U] • Bowling is a game played inside in which you roll a heavy ball down a track to try to knock down a group of wooden objects: *My brother has recently taken up (tenpin) bowling.* ○ *The aim in bowling is to knock down all the pins with one or two bowls.* • A **bowling alley** is either a building in which you can go bowling or a narrow track along which balls are rolled during a bowling game.

bowls /£bəʊlz, $boʊlz/ *n* [U] • Bowls is a game played either outside on smooth grass or inside on an artificial surface in which the players roll a large black or brown ball as close as possible to a smaller white ball: *Bowls is one of the most popular sports in Britain.*

bowl o·ver *obj*, **bowl** *obj* **o·ver** *v prep* [T usually passive] to knock (someone) to the ground by running into them, or *(fig.)* to surprise and please (someone) greatly • *She was almost bowled over by a huge dog as it ran around the corner.* • *(fig.) She was bowled over when she heard she'd won the competition.* • *(fig.) Most people are bowled over when they see this painting.* • *(fig.) I was bowled over* (= greatly charmed) *by his good looks and witty conversation.*

bowl·er (hat) /£ˈbəʊ·ləʳ, $ˈboʊ·lɚ/, *Am also* **der·by** *n* [C] a man's hat that is black and has a round hard top • *The train was crowded with businessmen in bowler hats and pinstripe* *suits.* • *The* **bowler-hatted** (= wearing a bowler hat) *British businessman is not as common a sight as he used to be.* • PIC〉 **Hats**

bow-wow /ˌbaʊˈwaʊ, ˈ--/ *exclamation* [C], *n infml* a child's word for a dog or the sound that a dog makes • *Why can't we have a bow-wow, Dad?* • *A cow goes 'moo' and a dog goes 'bow-wow'.*

box CONTAINER /£bɒks, $bɑːks/ *n* [C] an often square-shaped container with stiff sides and sometimes a lid • *a cardboard box* • *a cigar box* • *a matchbox* • A box can also be a box and its contents, or just the contents of a box: *a box of matches* ○ *He ate a whole box of chocolates while he was watching that film.* • A box is also any square or rectangular space on a form, sports field, road etc. which is separated from the main area by lines: *If you would like more information, mark this box.* • A box is sometimes a small enclosed space: *a jury/telephone box* • *(fig.) Their new house is just a box* (= a small uninteresting place to live). • In a theatre or at the side of a sports field, a box is a small seating area for important people which has been separated from other seating and has a good view: *Can you see Prince Charles in the* **royal** *box?* • *(Br and Aus)* In sport, a box (*Am* **cup**) is a curved piece of hard plastic worn by men to protect their outer sex organs. • *(infml) There's nothing worth watching on* **the box** (= television). • *(Br)* A **box junction** (*Am* **box**) is a place where two roads cross with a square of yellow lines painted in the centre which you can drive over only when the road in front is clear. • **Box lunch** (also **bag lunch**) is *Am for* **packed lunch**. See at PACK PUT INTO. • A **box number** is a number you can give instead of your address, esp. in newspaper advertisements: *Please reply to Box 307, The Times, London.* • A **box office** in a theatre or cinema is the place where tickets are sold: *Does the box office accept credit card bookings over the phone?* ○ *Her last film was a surprise box office hit* (= was surprisingly popular). ○ *In 1990, American films accounted for 58 per cent of box office* **receipts/takings** *in France.* • *(Br and Aus)* A **box spanner** (*Am* **box wrench**) is a cylindrical tool with a six-sided end that is used for screwing and unscrewing NUTS and BOLTS in places that are difficult to reach. • A **box spring** is a spring or set of springs attached to a frame and enclosed in a cloth covering for supporting a bed. • PIC〉 **Box, Containers, Tools** GR

box *obj* /£bɒks, $bɑːks/ *v* [T] • *Should I box these shoes* **(up)** (= put them in a box) *for you, or would you like to wear them straightaway?* • *Her forthcoming live album will be released as a three-CD boxed* **set**. • *When I came back I found my car had been boxed* **in** (= other cars were so close to it that I could not move it). • *(fig.) He feels boxed* **in** (= limited) *at work and wants greater freedom to develop his ideas.*

boxy /£ˈbɒk·si, $ˈbɑːk-/ *adj* • Something that is boxy is shaped like a box: *The car has a rather old-fashioned boxy shape, but it's very practical.* • *The trouble with many small houses is that they tend to be boxy.*

box TREE /£bɒks, $bɑːks/ *n* [U] a small evergreen tree with small shiny leaves • *Box is often planted close together to form a hedge around the edge of a garden.* • See also BOXWOOD. • GR

box·car /£ˈbɒks·kɑːʳ, $ˈbɑːks·kɑːr/ *n* [C] *Am* a railway carriage with a roof which is used for carrying goods

box·er /£ˈbɒk·səʳ, $ˈbɑːk·sɚ/ *n* [C] a dog of medium size with short light brown hair and a short flat nose • See also **boxer** at BOXING.

box·ing /£ˈbɒk·sɪŋ, $ˈbɑːk-/ *n* [U] a sport in which two competitors fight by hitting each other with their hands • *Boxing involves punching your opponent with your fists while wearing protective gloves.* • *Many doctors believe that boxing is too dangerous and should be banned.* • *He's a former world heavyweight boxing champion.* • *The first known boxing* **match** *in Britain took place in 1681 between the Duke of Albemarle's butler and butcher.* • **Boxing gloves** are a pair of large thick hand coverings that are worn for protection when boxing. • A **boxing ring** is a small enclosed area where boxers compete. • LP〉 **Sports** PIC〉 **Ring**

box *(obj)* /£bɒks, $bɑːks/ *v* • *He used to box every weekend.* [I] • *I've boxed* **(against)** *some of the best.* [T; I + adv/prep] • If you **box** someone's **ears** or **give** someone **a box on the ears**, you hit them on the ears, usually as a punishment: *I'll box your ears if you say that again.*

box·er /£ˈbɒk·səʳ, $ˈbɑːk·sɚ/ *n* [C] • *He was a* **heavyweight** *boxer before he became an actor.* • **Boxer shorts** (also **boxers**) are an item of loosely-fitting men's underwear similar to the short trousers ending above the knee which are worn by boxers.

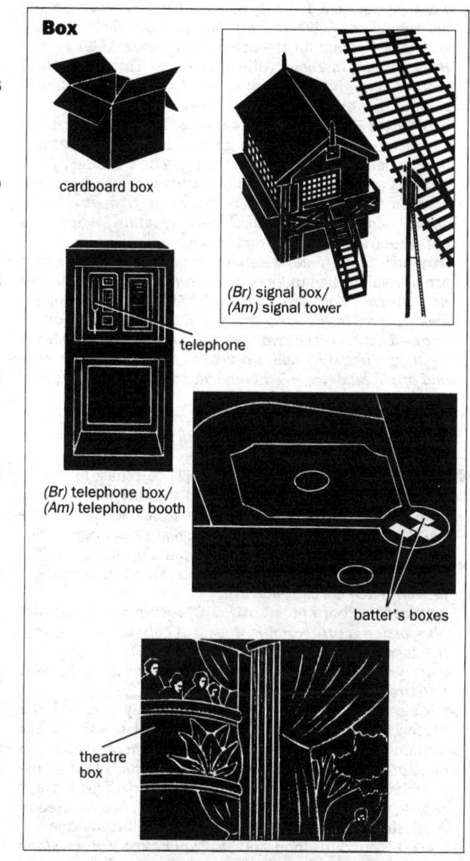

Box·ing Day /£ˈbɒk·sɪŋ, $ˈbɑːk-/ *n* [U; C] (in England, Wales and Canada) a public holiday which is the first day after Christmas Day that is not a Saturday or Sunday • *Have you got any plans for Boxing Day?*

box·room /£ˈbɒks·ruːm, -rʊm, $bɑːks-/ *n* [C] *Br* a small room in a house used for storing large objects such as cases and furniture

box·wood /£ˈbɒks·wʊd, $ˈbɑːks-/ *n* [U] a hard wood obtained from a BOX tree • *Boxwood is used for making small carved objects and tool handles.*

boy /bɔɪ/ *n* [C] a male child or, more generally, a male of any age • *a teenage/adolescent boy* • *Is it nature or nurture that makes* **girls and** *boys think so differently?* • *When my father was a* **young** *boy he used to walk three miles to school.* • *You've been a very* **naughty** *boy!* • *Their* **little** *boy* (= Their young son) *is very sick.* • *Johnny was a* **local boy made good** (= a man from the area who had achieved success). • *He used to like spending Friday nights with* **the boys** (= his male friends). • *Derek plays football, drinks a lot of beer and generally acts like* **one of the boys** (= a typical male). • *(saying)* 'Boys will be boys' means you should not be surprised when boys act in a rough, noisy or selfish way because this is considered to be part of the male character. • *(infml)* The **boys in blue** is an affectionate name for the police: **The** *boys in blue have a very difficult job and need all the support they can get.* • **The** boys or **our** boys is an approving way of speaking about your country's soldiers: *We must not forget our boys serving far from home.* • **(Oh) boy!** is an exclamation which is used to express excitement or to say something emphatically: *Boy, that was good!* • *(Br dated)* **My boy** is a friendly way of addressing a man: *Look here, my* **(dear)** *boy, this simply won't do.* • *(infml) It was the usual* **boy-meets-girl** *sort of film* (= involving a traditional love story). • **Boy Scout** is *dated for* a member of the SCOUTS. • *(Am)* A **boy toy** is a sexually attractive young man, esp. one who has relationships with older, powerful, or successful people. See also **toy boy** at TOY GAME. • A **boy wonder** is a young man who has achieved more than what is expected for his age. • *"The boy stood on the burning deck / Whence all but he had fled"* (Felicia Dorothea Hemans in the poem *Casabianca*, 1849) • *"The Boys are Back in Town"* (title of a song by Thin Lizzy, 1976) • *"Boys and girls come out to play"* (traditional nursery rhyme) • See also HOMEBOY. • LP› **Age** (KOR) (T)

boy·hood /ˈbɔɪ·hʊd/ *n* [U] • Boyhood is the period when a person is a boy, and not yet a man, or the state of being a boy: *I had* **a** *very happy boyhood.* ∘ *The transition from boyhood to manhood can be a confusing period.* ∘ *It was his boyhood* **ambition/dream** *to become a film director.* ∘ *James Bond was a boyhood* **hero** *of mine.* • See also **childhood** at CHILD; **girlhood** at GIRL.

boy·ish /ˈbɔɪ·ɪʃ/ *adj* • Behaviour or characteristics that are boyish are like those of a boy: *a boyish grin* ∘ *She had her hair cut in a boyish style.* ∘ *Her father is a shy, boyish-looking man in his early fifties.* ∘ *Even as an old man he retained his boyish* **charm**. ∘ *He's full of boyish* **enthusiasm** *for the project.* ∘ *He had a beardless boyish* **face**, *fair hair and bright blue eyes.* ∘ *She found his boyish* **good looks** *very attractive.*

boy·ish·ly /ˈbɔɪ·ɪʃ·li/ *adv* • *Mark grinned boyishly when I asked him where he'd been.* • *He is still boyishly handsome at the age of 45.*

boy·cott *obj* /£ˈbɔɪ·kɒt, $-kɑːt/ *v* [T] to refuse to buy (a product) or take part in (an activity) as a way of expressing strong disapproval • *People were urged to boycott the country's products to force it to change its policies.* • *The union called on its members to boycott the meeting.* • *The party has threatened to boycott the* **election** *because it believes it will not be democratic.*

boy·cott /£ˈbɔɪ·kɒt, $-kɑːt/ *n* [C] • *A boycott* **of/against** *all sporting events began in June.* • *A* **consumer** *boycott of the company's products eventually led to a change in its employment policy.* • *The* **economic** *boycott will not be lifted until free elections are announced.*

boy·friend /ˈbɔɪ·frend/ *n* [C] a man or boy with whom a person is having a romantic or sexual relationship • *She wouldn't stop talking about her new boyfriend.* • *Her parents don't approve of her living with her boyfriend.* • *Cathy's* **ex**-*boyfriend was a really nice guy.* • *She invited all her* **former** *boyfriends to the wedding.* • *I've never had a* **steady** *boyfriend.* • Compare GIRLFRIEND. • LP› **Relationships**

bo·zo /£ˈbəʊ·zəʊ, $ˈboʊ·zoʊ/ *n* [C] *pl* **bozos** *esp. Am slang* a stupid person • *Some bozo on a motorbike almost ran me over while I was out shopping.*

bra /brɑː/, **bras·si·ere** *n* [C] a piece of woman's underwear that supports the breasts

braai /braɪ/ *n* [C] (in South Africa) a BARBECUE • *Would you like to come to our braai this evening?*

braai *(obj)* /braɪ/ *v* • *We decided to braai (the meat) outside because it was sunny.* [I/T]

brace *obj* PREPARE /breɪs/ *v* [T] to prepare (yourself) physically or mentally for something unpleasant • *The passengers were told to brace* **themselves** (=to press their bodies hard against something or hold them very stiff) **for** *a crash landing.* • *She told me she had some bad news for me and I braced* **myself for** *a shock.* • (I)

brace SUPPORT /breɪs/ *n* [C] something that connects, fastens, strengthens or supports • *I had to wear a brace (Am and Aus usually* **braces**) *for my crooked teeth when I was a teenager.* • *He was recently fitted with a brace for his bad back.* • A **brace and bit** is a tool worked by hand for making holes in wood. • (I)

bra·ces /ˈbreɪ·sɪz/ *pl n* • *(Br and Aus)* Braces (*Am* **suspenders**) are pair of adjustable straps which stretch from the front of the trousers over your shoulders to the back to hold them up: *a pair of braces* • *(Am)* Braces are CALLIPERS LEG SUPPORT.

brace *obj* /breɪs/ *v* [T] • *The side wall of the old house was braced* **with** *a wooden support to prevent it from collapsing.*

brace PAIR /breɪs/ *n* [C] *pl* **brace** two things of the same type, esp. two wild birds that have been killed for sport or food • *a brace* **of** *pheasants* • (I)

brace·let /ˈbreɪ·slət/ *n* [C] a piece of jewellery which is worn around the wrist or arm • *a gold/silver/diamond bracelet* • *a chain bracelet*

brac·ing /ˈbreɪ·sɪŋ/ *adj* (esp. of air or an activity) healthy and fresh • *How do you fancy a bracing walk on the beach after lunch?*

brack·en /ˈbræk·ən/ *n* [U] a large FERN (=a type of plant) that grows thickly in open areas of countryside, esp. on hills, and in woods • *Bracken is poisonous and is not grazed by animals such as sheep and rabbits.*

brack·et SYMBOL /ˈbræk·ɪt/ *n* [C usually pl] either of two symbols put around a word, phrase or sentence in a piece of writing to show that what is between them should be considered as separate from the main part • *Biographical information is included* **in** *brackets.* • *(Br) You should include the date of publication in* **round** *brackets (also esp. Am and Aus* **parentheses**) *after the title.* • *Grammar patterns in this dictionary are shown in (Br)* **square** *brackets/(Am and Aus) brackets. For example, a countable noun is marked* [C]. • LP› **Brackets**

BRACKETS / PARENTHESES ( )

(Br) Round brackets/*(esp. Am)* parentheses are used:

- **to give extra information such as dates, numbers and amounts of money**

  Haydn (1732–1809) wrote over 100 symphonies.
  The figures given earlier (see p. 76) show a clear increase in sales.
  Telephone: Cambridge (01223) 73762
  The cost of his plan (£5 million) makes it quite unrealistic.

- **to add an explanation, extra information or an extra thought**

  Lucas was carrying 100g of Semtex (a high explosive) in his luggage.
  I'll see you on Tuesday (I can't come tomorrow, I'm just too busy).

- **to give another word or phrase which means the same as part of the sentence, or can replace it**

  Bake the cake at 200°C (Gas Mark 6) for 2 hours.

- **with numbers or letters, to separate items in lists or parts of a text**

  (1) Insert a cassette. (2) Press the PLAY and RECORD buttons.

(Br) Square brackets/*(esp.Am)* brackets are the [ ] symbols. They are used esp. in specialized writing, for example textbooks.

brack·et *obj* /ˈbræk·ɪt/ *v* [T] • *I've bracketed* (=put brackets around) *the bits of text that could be omitted.*

brack·et GROUP /ˈbræk·ɪt/ *n* [C] a set group with fixed upper and lower limits • *They were both surgeons in a high* **income** *bracket.* • *Most British university students are in the 18 – 22* **age** *bracket.* • *Her pay rise brought her into a new* **tax** *bracket.*

brack·et *obj* /ˈbræk·ɪt/ *v* [T] • If you bracket two or more things or people, you consider them to be similar or connected to each other: *Most English people bracket American and Canadian accents* **together**. ∘ *Her mother shouldn't bracket him* **with** *her previous boyfriends – this one's completely different.*

brack·et SUPPORT /ˈbræk·ɪt/ *n* [C] a piece of metal, wood or plastic, usually L-shaped, that is fastened to a wall and used to support something such as a shelf • PIC› **Tools**

brack·ish /ˈbræk·ɪʃ/ *adj* (of water) slightly salty • *All they had to drink was brackish* **water**.

brad·awl /£ˈbræd·ɔːl, $-ɑːl/ *n* [C] a small sharp tool used for making holes • PIC› **Tools**

brag /bræg/ *v* [I] **-gg-** *infml disapproving* to speak in a too proud or happy way about what you have done or what you own; to BOAST SPEAK PROUDLY • *She was always bragging* **about** *her cottage in Italy.* • *They bragged* **that** *they had never been beaten.* [+ *that* clause]

brag·gart /£ˈbræg·ət, $-ɚt/ *n* [C] *dated disapproving* • A braggart is someone who proudly talks a lot about themselves and their achievements or possessions.

brah·min, **brah·man** /ˈbrɑː·mɪn/ *n* [C] a member of the highest CASTE (=social group) of Hindus • *Brahmins traditionally become priests in the Hindu religion.*

braid CLOTH /breɪd/, **braid·ing** *n* [U] a thin strip of cloth or twisted threads which is fixed onto clothes, uniform or other items made of cloth as decoration • *The skirt had two rows of red braid round the hem.* • *The captain of the ship wore a peaked cap decorated with* **gold** *braid* (=twisted gold threads).

braid [HAIR] /breɪd/ *v* [T; I], *n* [C] *esp. Am for* PLAIT • [PIC] **Hair**

Braille /breɪl/ *n* [U] a system of printing for blind people in which each letter is represented as a raised pattern which can be read by touching with the fingers • *The book has been printed in six languages and in Braille.* • *a Braille book* • [PIC] **Writing**

brain /breɪn/ *n* [C] the organ inside the head that controls thought, memory, feelings and activity • *The surgeon used a laser to make a small incision into the brain/into the boy's brain.* • *Some foods are made from animal brains.* • *The* **left/right** *brain is the left/right* **hemisphere** (= half) *of the brain.* • *They examined changes in the brain cells/tissue of sufferers from the disease.* • *Professional boxers are at risk of suffering from brain* **damage**. • *His wife died from a brain* **tumour**. • *The relationship of brain size to intelligence is a matter of dispute.* • Brain is used to refer to intelligence: *Marie has an amazing brain* (= is very intelligent). ○ *That can't possibly be the right way to do it –* **use your brain!** • *Her brain was being* **addled** (= She was confused) *by the conflicting arguments.* • *The conspiracy of which they were falsely accused did not exist, save in the* **fevered** (= too excited by imagination) *brains of the secret police.* • *(infml)* A brain is also a very intelligent person, esp. one who has spent a lot of time studying: *We've got the best brains in the land working on this problem.* • *(infml disapproving) You've got cars* **on the brain** (= You never stop thinking and talking about them), *can't we change the subject?* • **Brain death** happens when a person's brain stops working and they become **brain dead** even though a machine might be causing their heart to beat: *She was declared to be brain dead and her family allowed the life-support machine to be switched off.* • A **brain drain** is when large numbers of educated and highly skilled people leave their own country to live and work in another one where pay and conditions are better: *Ireland has suffered a huge brain drain in recent years.* • *(infml)* **Brain power** is your intelligence or your ability to think: *Clea has plenty of brain power in the morning, but it wears off after lunch.* • A **brain teaser** is a problem for which it is hard to find the answer, esp. one which people enjoy trying to solve as a game: *I can't work out how she knew where I lived – it's a real brain teaser.* ○ *The paper publishes two brain teasers every Saturday.* • *(Am)* A **brain trust** is a group of people who advise a leader: *The candidate's brain trust is gathering this weekend to plan strategy for the primary election.* • A **brain wave** is any of several patterns of electrical activity in the brain. See also BRAINWAVE.

brain *obj* /breɪn/ *v* [T] *infml* • To brain someone is to hit them: *I'll brain you if you don't keep quiet.*

-brained /-breɪnd/ *combining form* • *These dinosaurs were large-brained and more intelligent than most.* • *(disapproving)* -brained is used in various phrases to describe someone as stupid or badly organized: *bird-brained* ○ *harebrained* ○ *scatterbrained*

brain·less /ˈbreɪn·ləs/ *adj* • *What sort of brainless* (= stupid) *idiot would do that?*

brains /breɪnz/ *pl n* • *The animal's brains* (= brain) *were visible through the damaged skull.* • *I hope the baby has his mother's brains* (= intelligence) *and his father's good looks.* • *Tom's* **got/has** *brains but is too lazy to use them* (= he's clever but doesn't use his advantage). • *I decided to* **pick** *his* **brains** (= ask for information from a person who knows a lot) *about computers.* • *This job needs* **more brains than brawn** (= more use of intelligence than use of strength).

brains /breɪnz/ *n* [U] • **The brains** is the cleverest person of a group, esp. the person who plans what the group will do: *My little brother's the brains* **of** *the family.* ○ *Smith was the brains* **behind** *the biggest art theft in recent times.*

brain·y /ˈbreɪ·ni/ *adj* **-ier**, **-iest** *infml* • *Sarah was beautiful and brainy* (= clever).

brain·child /ˈbreɪn·tʃaɪld/ *n* [U] *pl* **brainchildren** /ˈbreɪntʃɪl·drən, ˈbreɪntʃʊl-/ a clever and original idea, plan or invention • *The project was* **the** *brainchild* **of** *one of the students.*

brain·storm *(obj)* [SUGGEST] /£ˈbreɪn·stɔːm, $-stɔːrm/ *v* (of a group of people) to suggest a lot of ideas for (a future activity) very quickly before considering some of them more carefully • *The team got together to brainstorm (the project).* [I/T]

brain·storm·ing /£ˈbreɪnˌstɔː·mɪŋ, $-ˌstɔːr-/ *n* [U] • *We need to do some brainstorming before we get down to detailed planning.* • *We're having a brainstorming* **session** *on Friday.*

brain·storm [MENTAL STATE] /£ˈbreɪn·stɔːm, $-stɔːrm/ *n* [C] *Br infml* a sudden state of being unable to think clearly • *I must have* **had** *a brainstorm – I went shopping and forgot to take any money.* • Brainstorm is also *Am for* BRAINWAVE.

brain·teas·er /£ˈbreɪnˌtiː·zəʳ, $-zɚ/ *n* [C] a **teaser**, see at TEASE

brain·wash *obj* /£ˈbreɪn·wɒʃ, $-wɑːʃ/ *v* [T] *disapproving* to make (someone) believe only what you want them to believe by continually telling them that it is true and preventing any other information from reaching them • *The government is trying to brainwash the people* **into** *thinking that a war is necessary.* • *Many people thought the religious sect was guilty of brainwashing.*

brain·wave /ˈbreɪn·weɪv/, *Am also* **brain·storm** *n* [C] *infml* a sudden clever idea • *I couldn't see how I could get home from the station – then I* **had a** *brainwave, Eric could meet me.* • See also **brain wave** at BRAIN.

braise *obj* /breɪz/ *v* [T] to cook (meat, fish or vegetables) slowly in a covered dish in a little fat and liquid • *braised celery* • *braising steak*

brake /breɪk/ *n* [C] a device which makes a vehicle go slower or stop by pressing against the wheel, or a bar or handle which makes this device work • *She had no brakes on her bicycle.* • *The taxi driver suddenly* **applied** *his brakes.* • *(infml) I* **slammed on** (= quickly used) *the brake but it was too late.* • *I pressed my foot down hard on the brake* (= bar which makes the brakes work) *but to my horror the car did not slow down.* • *All our new models have* **anti-lock** *brakes.* • *The garage checked the brake fluid/brake linings/brake pads.* • *Suddenly we heard a* **screech/squeal of brakes** (= the noise of a car suddenly stopping) *and saw the car swerve to miss the cyclist.* • To **put a brake/the brakes on** is to slow down or stop an activity: *The government has put a brake on further spending.* • **Brake lights** are the red lights at the back of a motor vehicle that light up when the brakes are used. • **Brake blocks** are the rectangular pieces of rubber which press against the wheels of a bicycle to slow or stop them when the brakes are used. • **Brake cables** are the wires on a bicycle which connect the part of the brake you press with your hand to the part which stops the wheel. • The **brake pedal** is the bar which you push down with your foot to make a vehicle slow down or stop. • See also HANDBRAKE. • [PIC] **Bicycles, Car** (KOR)

brake /breɪk/ *v* [I] • *When it's icy brake* **gently**. [I] • *He would zoom up to junctions and brake* **fiercely/hard/sharply** *at the last minute.* [I]

bram·ble /ˈbræm·bl̩/ *n* a wild bush with THORNS (= sharp pointed growths on stem), which produces BLACKBERRIES, or *(esp. regional)* the fruits themselves • *We pushed our way with difficulty through low brambles.* [C] • *The garden was overgrown with bramble and honeysuckle.* [U] • *We picked basketfuls of brambles on that one bank alone.* [C] • *bramble jam* • *(esp. Am)* A bramble is also any wild bush with THORNS. [C]

bran /bræn/ *n* [U] the outer covering of grain that is separated when making white flour. Bran is added to other foods because it contains a lot of the FIBRE needed for a healthy body. • *wheat bran* • *Both these breakfast cereals have added bran.* • [PIC] **Cereals**

branch [TREE PART] /£brɑːntʃ, $bræntʃ/ *n* [C] one of the parts of a tree that grows out from the main trunk and has leaves, flowers or fruit on it • *bare/leafy/flowering branches* • *After the storm there were branches and twigs all over the ground.* • *The* **overhanging** *branches swayed in the breeze.* • *(fig. esp. Am) This branch of the river* (= single stream that joins or leaves the main flow) *eventually empties into the Atlantic.* • A **branch line** is a railway that goes from the main railway to small towns and countryside areas. • [PIC] **Tree**

branch /£brɑːntʃ, $bræntʃ/ *v* [I] • *The top of the tree had been cut off to encourage it to branch* **(out)** (= produce branches) *lower down.* • *(fig.) The road branches* (= divides into two) *at the bottom of the hill.* • *(fig.) We drove down a narrow track that branched* **off** *from the main road* (= started from it and went in a different direction).

branch [PART] /£brɑːntʃ, $bræntʃ/ *n* [C] a part of something larger • A branch is one of the offices or groups that form part of a large business organization: *I used to work in the* **local** *branch* **of** *a large bank.* ○ *The supermarket chain is planning to open a new branch in the town in the near future.* ○ *Four thousand jobs have been lost throughout the branch* **network**. ○ *She's a branch* **manager**. ○ *Take the forms into your local branch* **office**. • *Immunology is a* *branch* **of** *biological science* (= a subject that is part of a bigger subject). • *One branch* **of** *their family* (= One group of relatives) *went into business.*

branch out *v adv* [I] to start to do something different from what you usually do • *Bernadine told her she needed to get out of the house and branch out socially.* • *It is possible to branch out* **from** *IT to jobs in banking, accountancy, teaching and so on.* • *The clothes manufacturer recently branched out* **into** *children's wear.* • *After a couple of years working for a design company she branched out* **on** *her* **own** (= started her own business).

brand [PRODUCT] /brænd/ *n* [C] a type of product made by a particular company • *This isn't my usual brand* **of** *deodorant.* • *(fig.) Do you like his brand* (= particular type) **of** *humour?* • *Would you swap new 'Sparkle' for this well-known brand?* • *(Br) When I go to a supermarket I usually buy* **own** *(Am* **store**/*Aus* **generic**) *brands* (= the cheaper products with the shop's own name on them). • A **brand name** is the name by which a particular product is sold. • **Brand loyalty** is the tendency always to buy the same named product: *All manufacturers want to encourage brand loyalty to their own product.*

brand *obj* [JUDGE] /brænd/ *v* [T + obj + (*as*) n/adj; usually passive] to say that you think (someone) is (something bad) • *Because of one minor offence he was branded* **(as)** *a common criminal.* • *From then on they were branded* **(as)** *traitors.* • *The newspapers have branded the rebel MP disloyal.*

brand *obj* [MARK] /brænd/ *v* [T] to mark (esp. a cow) by burning its skin to show you own it • *The cattle were branded with an A in a circle.* • A **branding iron** is a long piece of metal with a special design at one end used to put an owner's mark on esp. cows.

brand /brænd/ *n* [C] • *Smith always uses a 'Bar T' brand on his cattle.*

brand [FLAME] /brænd/ *n* [C] *literary* a piece of burning wood used to give light

brand·ish *obj* /ˈbræn·dɪʃ/ *v* [T] to wave (something) in the air in a threatening or excited way • *He rushed into the room brandishing a letter.* • *She brandished a saucepan* **at** *me so I ran out of the kitchen.*

brand–new /£ˌbrændˈnjuː, $-ˈnuː/ *adj* [not gradable] completely new, esp. not yet used • *How can he afford to buy himself a brand-new car?* • *They brought their brand-new baby to show us.*

bran·dy /ˈbræn·di/ *n* a strong alcoholic drink, usually made from wine and sometimes flavoured with fruits • *French brandy* [U] • *cherry/peach brandy* [U] • *He always has a large brandy* (= glass of brandy) *and a cigar after dinner.* [C] • **Brandy butter** is made of sugar, butter and brandy and served esp. at Christmas in Britain on **Christmas pudding** and MINCE PIES. • A **brandy snap** is a thin hard biscuit which is rolled into a tube.

brash /bræʃ/ *adj* **-er, -est** *disapproving* (of people) showing too much confidence and too little respect, or (of clothes) too bright and colourful • *He was a rather brash young city type with more money than manners.* • *Don't you think that suit's a bit brash for a funeral?*

brash·ness /ˈbræʃ·nəs/ *n* [U]

brass [METAL] /£brɑːs, $bræs/ *n* a bright yellow metal made from COPPER and ZINC • *The door handles were made of brass and needed cleaning and polishing regularly.* [U] • *The mantlepiece was lined with brightly polished brass ornaments.* • In a church, a brass is a thin piece of brass on the floor or wall with a picture or writing cut into it: *The church has several beautiful medieval brasses.* [C] • *(Br slang) It's* **brass monkey weather** (= extremely cold weather) *today.* • *Let's* **get down to brass tacks** (= consider the most important and basic facts of a situation) – *who is going to pay for it all?* • *(Am slang)* A **brass hat** is a military officer of very high rank. • **Brass knuckles** is another name for a **knuckle-duster**. See at KNUCKLE. • **Brass-rubbing** involves putting a sheet of paper on top of a brass in a church and rubbing it with a special pencil to make a picture.

brass·y /£ˈbrɑː·si, $ˈbræs·i/ *adj* • *a brassy yellow*

brass [MUSICAL INSTRUMENTS] /£brɑːs, $bræs/ *adj* [before n] (of a musical instrument) made of metal and played by blowing • *The trumpet and trombone are brass instruments.* • *He plays in the brass section of the orchestra.* • A **brass band** is one that consists mostly of brass musical instruments. • Compare PERCUSSION; WOODWIND. • [PIC]› **Musical instruments**

brass /£brɑːs, $bræs/ *n* [U + sing/pl v] • **The brass** is/are the group of brass instruments or players in a BAND or ORCHESTRA: *I think the brass is too loud in this recording.*

brass·y /£ˈbrɑː·si, $ˈbræs·i/ *adj* **-ier, -iest** • *I love the big brassy sound* (= having lots of brass instruments) *of the 1930s bands.* • *(disapproving) He had a brassy* (= unpleasantly loud) *voice.*

brass [CONFIDENCE] /£brɑːs, $bræs/ *n* [U] *infml* complete self-confidence and lack of fear • *(approving) I'll say this for her – she's got plenty of brass!* • *(disapproving) How did they* **have the brass to** *do it?* • *(disapproving) She must have a (Br)* **brass neck**/*(Am slang)* **brass balls** (= great self-confidence) *to ask for a day off when we're so busy.*

brass·y /£ˈbrɑː·si, $ˈbræs·i/ *adj* **-ier, -iest** *disapproving* • *To succeed as a journalist a woman might have to appear somewhat brassy* (= loud and self-confident) *and fearless.*

brass [MONEY] /£brɑːs, $bræs/ *n* [U] *Br dated infml* money • *He made plenty of brass out of his scrap business.*

brassed off /£brɑːst, $bræst/ *adj* [after v] *infml* annoyed and bored • *After waiting thirty minutes for a bus he was really brassed off.* • *I'm really brassed off* **with** *the stupid comments he keeps making.*

bras·se·rie /£ˈbræs·ə·ri, $ˌbræs·əˈriː/ *n* [C] a French-style restaurant that serves cheap and quite simple food

bras·si·ere /£ˈbræz·i·eəʳ, $-er/ *n* [C] *fml for* BRA • Ⓕ

brat /bræt/ *n* [C] *infml disapproving* a child, esp. one who behaves badly • *How many brats do they have now?* • *She's a* **spoilt** *brat, never happy with what she has.*

bra·va·do /£brəˈvɑː·dəʊ, $-doʊ/ *n* [U] a show of bravery, esp. when unnecessary and dangerous, to make people admire you • *Their behaviour was just* **sheer** *bravado.* • *It was an* **act of** *bravado that made him ask his boss to resign.*

brave [FEARLESS] /breɪv/ *adj* **-r, -st** showing no fear of dangerous or difficult things • *They were brave children and did not cry or make a fuss.* • *The cousins, a brave and resourceful pair, are constantly facing adventures in this amusing film.* • *She was very brave* **to** *climb the cliff as a fund-raising stunt.* [+ to infinitive] • *Of the three organizations criticized, only one was brave* **enough to** *face the press.* [+ to infinitive] • *Richards has made a brave* **attempt** *to expose farming objectives to public debate.* • *Laura* **made a** *brave* **stab at** (= tried hard to give) *a smile.* • *Some brave* **souls** *still cling to their hopes.* • **It's a** *brave person* **who** *tries to argue with him* (= he is a difficult person to disagree with). • **It takes a** *brave man/woman* **to** *predict* (= There is a risk involved in guessing) *how interest rates will go at the moment.* • *This action will cause problems, despite the bank's brave* **talk/words** *about carrying on as if nothing had happened.* • To **put on a brave face** or **put a brave face on** a situation, is to behave as if a problem is not important: *He was obviously worried when the child was late but he put on a brave face and said he thought she'd soon be home.* ○ *Her name wasn't on the list of winners but she put a brave face on* **it**. • **Brave new** is used to refer to something new, esp. to suggest that there is some doubt that it can be good or successful: *The government revealed its brave new approach to homelessness at the press conference.* ○ *They introduced customers to the brave new world of telephone banking.* • *"None but the brave deserve the fair"* (John Dryden in the poem *Alexander's Feast*, 1697) • *"Brave New World"* (title of book by Aldous Huxley, 1932) • *"Scotland the Brave"* (title of a traditional Scottish tune) • Ⓓ Ⓘ Ⓟ

brave *obj* /breɪv/ *v* [T] • *Shall we brave the snow and go for a walk* (= go for a walk even though it is snowing)? • *I was quite frightened by the way the boys approached me, but decided to brave it* **out** (= show no fear). [M] • *(literary) She braved the* **wrath** *of her parents by refusing to marry the man they had chosen.*

brave·ly /ˈbreɪv·li/ *adv* • *"The pain is getting less," she said bravely.*

brav·er·y /£ˈbreɪ·vᵊr·i, $-vɚ-/ *n* [U] • *They were awarded medals for their remarkable bravery.*

brave [FIGHTER] /breɪv/ *n* [C] *dated* a young male Native American Indian WARRIOR (= fighting man). This is considered offensive. • Ⓓ Ⓘ Ⓟ

brav·o /£ˌbrɑːˈvəʊ, £ˈ–, $ˈbrɑː·voʊ/ *exclamation dated or humorous* an expression used to show your pleasure when someone has done something well

brav·u·ra /£brəˈvjʊə·rə, $-ˈvjʊr·ə/ *n* [U] unnecessary actions to make what is being done look more exciting or clever than it is • *The show was mostly bravura with no real substance.* • *He gave a bravura* **performance**.

brawl /£brɔːl, $brɑːl/ *v, n* (to take part in) a noisy, rough, uncontrolled fight • *The young men had nothing better to do than brawl in the streets.* [I] • *A* **drunken** *brawl had broken out in the bar.* [C]

brawn STRENGTH /£brɔːn, $brɑːn/ *n* [U] physical strength and big muscles • *She said she preferred brawn to brains* (= a man who is physically attractive rather than a clever one).

brawn·y /£ˈbrɔː·ni, $ˈbrɑː-/ *adj* **-ier, -iest** • *He was a big brawny man with huge hands.*

brawn FOOD /£brɔːn, $brɑːn/ *n* [U] *Br and Aus* meat from the head of a pig cooked and pressed into a block

bray /breɪ/ *v* [I] to make a loud, unpleasant noise like a DONKEY (= an animal like a small horse) • *The mules suddenly started braying.* • *She had a loud, braying laugh.*

bra·zen /ˈbreɪ·zᵊn/ *adj* clear and obvious, without any attempt to be hidden • *There were instances of brazen cheating in the exams.* • *They showed a brazen disregard for private property.* • *He told me a brazen* **lie.** • *(humorous) She'd like to ask him out but is afraid he'll think her a* **brazen hussy** (= a woman who wants to attract sexual attention).

bra·zen·ly /ˈbreɪ·zᵊn·li/ *adv*

bra·zen out *obj* /ˈbreɪ·zᵊn/ *v adv* [M] • To brazen (something) out is to act confidently and not admit that a problem exists: *Much of the present difficulty might have been avoided if the management had not chosen simply to brazen out its position.* ○ *I decided to brazen* **it** *out and hoped they wouldn't notice the scratch on the car.*

braz·i·er /£ˈbreɪ·ʒəʳ, $-ʒɚ/ *n* [C] a metal container for burning coal, used to give warmth to people who have to be outside in cold weather or to cook on • *A group of workmen were standing drinking tea round a brazier.* • *Chestnuts were roasting on a brazier in the street.*

Bra·zil nut /brəˈzɪl/ *n* [C] (a tree in S America which grows) an edible nut • PIC› **Nut**

breach BREAK /briːtʃ/ *n* [C] an act of breaking a law, promise, agreement or relationship • *Will discussions with other companies constitute a breach* **of/in** *our agreement?* • *The incident led to a serious breach* **in** *their friendship.* • *His refusal to work on a Sunday was a breach* **of contract.** • *They said I wouldn't have to do any housework as an au pair so making me clean the bedrooms was a breach* **of promise.** • *There have been serious* **security** *breaches* (= Secrets have been discovered by members of the public). • *The cinema was* **in breach of** (= was breaking) *the Health and Safety Act for having no fire doors.* • *(law)* A **breach of the peace** is illegal noisy or violent behaviour in a public place.

breach *obj* /briːtʃ/ *v* [T] *fml* • *They breached the agreement they had made with their employer.*

breach OPENING /briːtʃ/ *v, n* (to make) an opening in a wall or fence, esp. in order to attack someone or something behind it • *Their defences were easily breached.* [T] • *A cannon ball had made a breach in their castle walls.* [C] • *"Once more unto the breach, dear friends, once more; / Or close the wall up with our English dead."* (Shakespeare, Henry V 3.1)

bread /bred/ *n* [U] a food made from flour, water and usually YEAST mixed together and baked • *a slice of bread* • *a loaf of bread* • *white/brown bread* • *granary/wholemeal bread* • *rye bread* • *sliced bread* • *unleavened bread* (= made without YEAST) • *bread rolls* • *There was nothing in the cupboard but a few* **crusts of** *bread.* • *This bread is* **fresh/stale.** • *Do you* **bake** *your own bread?* • *We often have bread* **and cheese** *for lunch.* • In some cases, bread can be used in its plural form, breads, to mean types of bread: *Supermarkets sell many different breads, from French sticks to pitta bread.* • *(fml) He* **earned** *his* **(daily) bread** (= earned money to live on) *as a top banker in the city.* • *(dated slang) I needed some bread* (= money) *so I worked as a waiter.* • *Gardening is my* **bread and butter** (= how I earn enough money to live) *at the moment.* • **Bread and butter** ideas or problems are the basic things that directly relate to most people: *Health and education are the sort of bread-and-butter* **issues** *that people vote on.* • **Bread and circuses** is used to refer to activities which are designed for keeping people happy so that they do not ask difficult questions: *The whole news story smacks of bread and circuses – a conspiracy to keep the voters' minds off the major issues of the day!* • A **bread basket** is an open container in which bread is put on a table during a meal. • A **bread basket** is also a large farming area of a country or region which produces much more food than it needs locally, allowing it to support other areas: *The Eastern Province is the country's bread basket.* • A *(Br and Aus)* **bread bin**/*(Am)* **bread box** is a container in which bread is stored. • A **bread knife** is a long sharp knife that has a row of sharp points along one edge and is used to cut bread. • *(saying)* 'Man cannot live by bread alone' means that people need not just food, but also poetry, art, music, etc. to live happily. • *"Man shall not live by bread alone, but by every word that proceedeth out of the mouth of God"* (Bible, Matthew 4.4) • PIC› **Cutlery, Kitchen, Knife**

bread·board /£ˈbred·bɔːd, $-bɔːrd/ *n* [C] a wooden board that is used to cut bread on

bread·crumb /ˈbred·krʌm/ *n* [C] a very small piece of dried bread, esp. used in cooking • *Before baking, cover the mixture with a layer of breadcrumbs for a crunchy topping.*

bread·ed /ˈbred·ɪd/ *adj* [not gradable] covered in BREADCRUMBS before being cooked • *breaded chicken breasts*

bread·fruit /ˈbred·fruːt/ *n* [C] *pl* **breadfruit** or **breadfruits** a type of large round tropical fruit which when baked looks and feels like bread

bread·line INCOME /ˈbred·laɪn/ *n* [U] **the breadline** *Br* the level of income someone has when they are extremely poor • *If as a student you are* **on/close to/just above/below** *the breadline, you should make the most of all available benefits and grants.* • *Many families of the unemployed are/are* **living** *on or below the breadline* (= on very little money).

bread·line GROUP /ˈbred·laɪn/ *n* [C] *Am* a group of people waiting outside a particular building to be given food • *You'll see breadlines outside many New York churches at lunchtime.*

breadth /bredθ, bretθ/ *n* [U] the distance from one side to another, or *(fig.)* the quality of consisting of or including many different things • *The length of this box is twice its breadth.* • *(fig.) The breadth of her political vision has long been recognized.* • *(fig.) He showed an astonishing breadth of learning* (= he knew about many different subjects) *for one so young.* • *(fig.) He was not known for his* **breadth of mind** (= willingness to consider all opinions). • See also BROAD WIDE.

bread·win·ner /£ˈbred,wɪn·əʳ, $-ɚ/ *n* [C] the person in a family who works to provide the money that the family needs to live on • *Men are often expected to be the breadwinner in a family.*

break *(obj)* DAMAGE /breɪk/ *v past simple* **broke** /£brəʊk, $broʊk/, *past part* **broken** /£ˈbrəʊ·kᵊn, $ˈbroʊ-/ to (cause to) separate suddenly or violently into two or more pieces, or to (cause to) stop working by being damaged • *The dish fell to the floor and broke.* [I] • *Charles is always breaking glasses.* [T] • *She broke a tooth on a cherry stone.* [T] • *They broke a window to get into the house.* [T] • *I dropped the vase and it broke* **into pieces.** [I] • *I think I've broken your cassette player.* [T] • *Kate sat on the chair and it broke.* [I] • *We heard the sound of breaking glass.* • *She fell awkwardly and broke her arm/hip/etc.* (= broke the bone(s) in her arm/hip/etc.). [T] • *(fig. infml) He was breaking his* **back/***(Am slang)* **ass** (= working extremely hard) *trying to finish the work on time.* [T] • *These new taxes will* **break the back of** (= make life difficult or impossible for) *the working poor.* • *(Br and Aus) We can* **break the back of** *this work* (= get most of it done) *today if we really try.* • *(fig.) She really broke her mother's* **heart** (= hurt her feelings very much) *when she left home.* [T] • *(fig.) He's broken a lot of girls'* **hearts** (= caused them to love him without sharing their feelings). [T] • *(humorous) It only costs £2. That's not going to* **break the bank** (= it is not very much money). • *The car* **broke down** (= stopped working) *at the traffic lights.* • *When we gave her the bad news she* **broke down** (= became very upset) *and cried.* • A **make-or-break situation** is one that will bring great success or complete failure. • **Breaking point** is the stage at which your control over yourself or a situation is lost: *The situation reached breaking point when his son crashed the family car.* ○ *Her nerves were* **at** *breaking point.*

break /breɪk/ *n* [C] • *There's a break in the pipe.*

break·a·ble /ˈbreɪ·kə·bl̩/ *adj* • *Have you got anything breakable in your bag?* • *Liquids are permitted only in cans – not in breakable bottles.* • *These old crystal glasses are very breakable, so pack them carefully.*

break·age /ˈbreɪ·kɪdʒ/ *n* [C] • A breakage is something that has been broken: *The customer must* **pay for** *any breakages.*

-break·er /£-ˈbreɪ·kəʳ, $-kɚ/ *combining form*

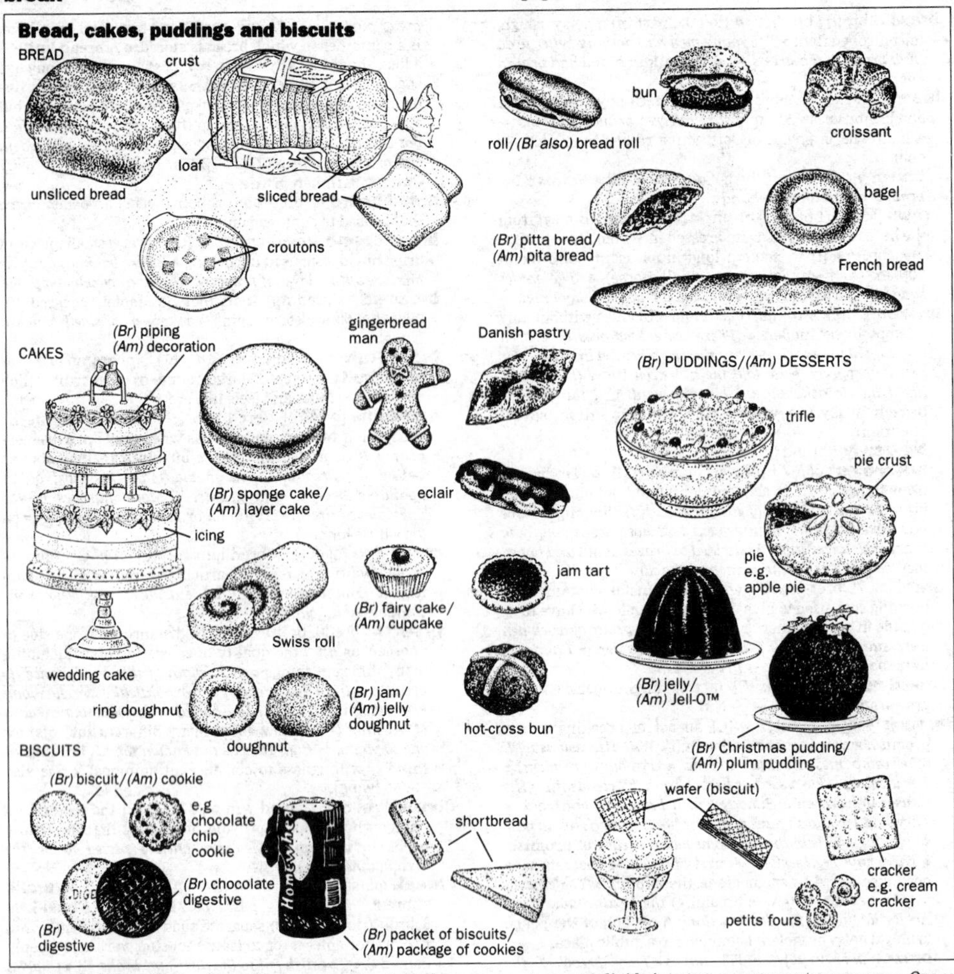

break *(obj)* USE FORCE /breɪk/ *v past simple* **broke** /£brəʊk, $broʊk/, *past part* **broken** /£ˈbrəʊ·kən, $ˈbroʊ-/ to go somewhere or do (something) by force • *She clung to him but he managed to break* **away (from** *her)* (= free himself forcefully). [I always + adv/prep] • *"Let me in or I'll break the door* **down** (= enter using force)," *he roared.* [M] • *(fig.) The talks were meant to break down* **barriers** (= improve people's views of each other) *between the two groups.* [M] • *The horse tried to break* **free** *from its stable.* [I always + adv/prep] • *She broke* (= forcefully removed herself from) *her brother's* **hold** *and ran away.* [T] • *I came back to the house to discover that thieves had broken* **in** (= forced their way into the house) *and stolen everything.* [I always + adv/prep] • *Car alarms are intended to stop people from breaking* **into** (= forcing their way into) *cars.* [I always + adv/prep] • *In the storm the boat broke* **loose** *from its moorings.* [I always + adv/prep] • *The thieves broke the safe* **open** *and stole the diamonds.* [M] • *He decided that he was going to break* **out (of** *jail)* (= escape from prison) *that summer.* [I always + adv/prep] • *I tried to break* **through** (= force a way through) *(the crowd) but it was impossible.* [I always + adv/prep] • *The police broke* **up** *the fight* (= ended it forcefully). [M] • **Breaking and entering** is illegally forcing your way into a house, esp. to steal. • A **break-in** is an occasion when a building is entered illegally by a criminal or criminals, usually by damaging a window or door, esp. in order to steal.

break /breɪk/ *n* [C] • *A group of prisoners* **made a** *break* (= escaped) *from the jail some years back.* See also BREAKOUT.

-break·er /£-ˈbreɪ·kər, $-kɚ/ *combining form* • A -breaker is someone who uses force to go into or open the stated thing: *a house-breaker* ○ *a safebreaker*

break *(obj)* DIVIDE /breɪk/ *v past simple* **broke** /£brəʊk, $broʊk/, *past part* **broken** /£ˈbrəʊ·kən, $ˈbroʊ-/ to (cause to) divide into two or more parts or groups • *One or two of the tourists broke* **away (from** *the tour group)* (= left it) *and wandered on their own.* [I] • *These enzymes break* **down** *food in the stomach* (= cause food to separate into smaller pieces). [M] • *I asked for my exam result to be broken* **down** (= divided into smaller parts) **into** *the marks for each paper.* [M] • *Break* **off** (= Remove by breaking) *a piece of chocolate for me, would you?* [M] • *The emigration of young people often breaks* **up** *families* (= causes them to separate). [M] • *(infml esp. Am) That show really* **broke** *me* **up** (= made me laugh a lot). • To break **(up)** the **ground/soil** is to dig an area that has not been dug: *We could use a machine to break (up) the ground first.* [T/M] • *The builders expect to* **break ground** (= start digging the base for a new building) *next week.* • To **break fresh/new ground** is to do or discover something new: *This recovery technique breaks new ground.* • *(fml old use)* To **break bread** is to eat a meal. • To **break bread** is also to take **holy communion**. • *(infml) Someone suggested that we play a party game to* **break the ice** (= remove feelings of embarrassment among people who have not met before). See also **ice-breaker** at ICE. • If something **breaks the mould**, it is new and different: *Their approach to sports teaching broke the mould.* • *His medical colleagues advised him not to* **break ranks** (= be disloyal to the group to which he belonged) *by talking about the hospital's problems to the newspapers.*

break·er /£ˈbreɪ·kər, $-kɚ/ *n* [C] • A **breaker's yard** is a place where old cars are taken to pieces and sold as parts for repairing other cars.

break *(obj)* INTERRUPT /breɪk/ *v past simple* **broke** /£brəʊk, $broʊk/, *past part* **broken** /£ˈbrəʊ·kən, $ˈbroʊ-/ to interrupt or to stop (something) for a brief period • *Shall we break* **(off) for** *lunch?* [I always + adv/prep] • *They decided to break their* **journey** *at Singapore.* [T] • *He broke* **(off)** *his holiday to attend a business meeting.*

[T/M] • *I needed something to break* **the monotony** *of my typing job.* [T] • *He swerved around the dog without breaking his* **step/stride** (=interrupting his walking speed). [T] • *The doorbell rang, breaking my* **train of thought** (=interrupting my thoughts). [T] • *Amazingly, he was saved by some trees which broke his* **fall** (=made its effect much weaker). [T] • *As she was talking, he suddenly* **broke in** (=interrupted her), *saying, "That's a lie".* • *We* **broke up** (=classes in school or college stopped) **for** *the holidays in June.*

break /breɪk/ *n* • A break is an interruption: *There was a temporary break* **in** *the cold weather one day and we went swimming.* [C] • A break is also the short period of advertisements between esp. television programmes: *I'll make a cup of coffee during the next* **(commercial)** *break.* [C] ○ *The presenter said, "After the break we will be discussing the relationships between parents and teenagers".* [C] • A break is also a short period of rest, when food or drink is sometimes eaten: *Shall we have a break now?* [C] ○ *We'll* **take** *another break at 10.30.* [C] ○ *They worked through the night without a break.* [C] ○ *We used to go to the school library during the* **lunch** *break.* [C] ○ *Is it time for our* **tea/coffee** *break?* [C] ○ *Do you usually* **take** *a* **morning/afternoon** *break* (=stop for a rest, esp. to have a drink and sometimes a small amount of food)? [C] • *(esp. Br)* Break is the regular time in the middle of the morning or afternoon for school students to talk or play and have some food or drink if they wish: *During break everyone was talking about the rock star's death.* [U] • A break is also a time away from work or your regular activity, or a holiday: *Take a couple of weeks off – you need a break.* [C] ○ *How long is the Christmas break this year?* [C] ○ *We decided to have a* **short/spring/winter/weekend** *break in Paris.* [C] ○ *I'll read your report* **over** (=during) *the Easter break.* [C] ○ *I need a break* **from typing**. [C] • **Give me a break** (=Stop annoying me)!

break *(obj)* END /breɪk/ *v past simple* **broke** /£brəʊk, $broʊk/, *past part* **broken** /£ˈbrəʊ·kᵊn, $ˈbroʊ-/ to destroy or end (something), or to come to an end • *Someone switched a radio on, breaking the romantic mood.* [T] • *She laughed and that broke the tension in the room.* [T] • *Eventually someone spoke, breaking the silence.* [T] • *I used to smoke but I managed to break the* **habit**. [T] • *We tried to break him* **of the habit** *of telling lies.* [T] • *The warm weather broke at the end of August.* [I] • *The enemy were unable to break the* **code** (=understand it and so make it useless). [T] • *The government tried to break the* **deadlock** (=end the disagreement) *between management and the trade union.* [T] • *She broke* (=did better than) *the* **record** *for the 5000 metres.* [T] • *Outside workers were brought in in an attempt to break* (=end) *the* **strike**. [T] • *They tried to break his* **will** (=make him lose his control) *but he resisted.* [T] • *He thought she would break* (=lose her self-control) *under the strain.* [I] • To break **(off)** a relationship is to end it: *He was so angry that he broke off his friendship with her.* [M] ○ *They've broken* **(off)** *their engagement.* [T/M] ○ *The governments have broken off diplomatic relations.* [M] • To break **(up)** is to end a relationship: *The quarrel caused him to break* **with** *his brother.* [I] ○ *Their marriage is breaking up.* [I] ○ *Jenny and George have broken up.* [I] • To **break up** is to (cause to) end: *The meeting broke up at ten to three.* ○ *I don't want to break up* **the party** (=cause all the people present to think that they should leave) *but I really have to go now.* ○ *(infml)* **Break it up** (=Stop fighting), *you two!* • To **break camp** is to put away your tent and leave the place where you have been staying: *They broke camp at dawn and began the ascent of Mount Ararat.* • To **break even** is to have no profit or loss at the end of esp. a business activity: *After paying for our travel costs, we* **barely** (=only just) *broke even.* • *We decided to* **break with** (=intentionally not continue) *tradition and not spend Christmas with our family.* • *"I wish that we were making up again/ Instead of breaking up again/ 'Cos breaking up is hard to do"* (from the song *Breaking Up is Hard To Do* by Neil Sedaka, 1972)

break /breɪk/ *n* [C] • *Their decision to not call their daughter Jane was a break with* (=was intentionally different from) *family tradition.* • If you **make a/the break**, you stop having a close relationship with someone, esp. living with them, or you change a course of action that you have had for a long time: *At 20, she felt she had to make the break from her family and go and live alone.* ○ *You've been in that job for years – it's time you made the break.* ○ *When a relationship ends, it's often best to make a* **clean/complete** *break* (=suddenly and completely stop having any connections with each other).

-break·er /£-ˈbreɪ·kəʳ, $-kɚ/ *combining form* • A -breaker is a someone or something that ends something or causes it to end in some way: *a record-breaker* ○ *a code-breaker*

break *obj* DISOBEY /breɪk/ *v* [T] *past simple* **broke** /£brəʊk, $broʊk/, *past part* **broken** /£ˈbrəʊ·kᵊn, $ˈbroʊ-/ to fail to keep (a law, rule or promise) • *He didn't know he was breaking* **the law** (=doing something illegal). • *She broke her* **promise/word** *to me* (=did not do what she promised she would). • *His actions broke* **all the rules** *(and* **regulations***)* (=it was not the legal or expected way to behave).

-break·er /£-ˈbreɪ·kəʳ, $-kɚ/ *combining form* • *a lawbreaker* (=a person who breaks the law)

break *(obj)* NOTICE /breɪk/ *v past simple* **broke** /£brəʊk, $broʊk/, *past part* **broken** /£ˈbrəʊ·kᵊn, $ˈbroʊ-/ to come or bring to notice; to (cause to) be known • *When the* **scandal** *broke* (=came to public notice) *the company director committed suicide.* [I] • *It was the Observer newspaper which first broke the* **story** (=told the public) *about the smuggling ring.* [T] • *I don't want to be the one to break* **the news to** *him* (=tell him the bad news). [T] • *(fig.) Dawn broke* (=happened) **over** *the city.* [I] • When an animal or person **breaks cover**, they run out of their hiding place. • *(sometimes humorous)* **Break it to** *me gently* (=Tell me the bad news in a kind way). • To **break wind** is to let out digestive gas from the bowels through the bottom.

break /breɪk/ *n* [U] *literary* • *We set out at* **the** *break* **of day** (=as the sun was rising). • See also DAYBREAK.

break OPPORTUNITY /breɪk/ *n* [C] an opportunity for improving a situation, esp. one which happens unexpectedly • *She* **got** *her main break as an actress in a Spielberg film.* • *It was a* **lucky** *break finding the address of his mother – she was able to tell us where he had moved to.*

break MOVE /breɪk/ *v* [I] (of waves) to reach and move over the beach, hit a cliff or wall, etc. • *A huge wave broke on the shore/over the boat.* • *(fig.) A wave of nationalism seemed poised to break over* (=about to begin in) *the socialist strongholds of the industrial valleys.*

break·er /£ˈbreɪ·kəʳ, $-kɚ/ *n* [C] • A breaker is a large sea wave, esp. one that hits the coast.

break CHANGE /breɪk/ *v* [I] *past simple* **broke** /£brəʊk, $broʊk/, *past part* **broken** /£ˈbrəʊ·kᵊn, $ˈbroʊ-/ (of voices) to change from one state to another • *When a boy's voice breaks it begins to sound like a man's.* • *Her voice was breaking* (=changing in level) **with** *emotion as she pleaded for her child's return.*

break *obj* SPORT /breɪk/ *v* [T] **broke** or **broken break serve** (in tennis) to win a game in which another player is SERVING (=hitting the ball first) • *Sampras broke Ivanisevic's serve in the second set.*

break /breɪk/ *n* [C] • *Becker must get another break* **(of serve)** *to win tennis's most prestigious prize.* • In tennis if you win a **break point**, you have broken (=won a game against) the opposing player's SERVE. • In SNOOKER and BILLIARDS, a break is the number of points that a player gets during one turn at hitting the balls.

break in *obj* MAKE COMFORTABLE, **break** *obj* **in** *v adv* [M] to wear (new shoes) or use (new equipment) for short periods to make them more comfortable • *I got blisters because I hadn't broken in my walking boots properly.* • *You'll have to break your new baseball mitt in before you can use it in a game.* • Break in is also *Am for* RUN IN USE CAREFULLY.

break in *obj* PREPARE, **break** *obj* **in** *v adv* [M] to prepare or train (esp. a horse) to take a rider and be obedient to control • *They were wild ponies which had never been broken in.* • *(fig.) The boss did not believe in breaking his staff in* **gently** *– he expected them to work efficiently from the first day.*

break into *obj v adv* [T] to begin suddenly to do (something) • *He felt so happy that he broke into song* (=suddenly began to sing). • *She walked quickly, occasionally breaking into a run* (=starting to run).

break out *v adv* to begin suddenly (doing something) • *An argument broke out* **in** *the classroom between the children.* [I] • *A storm broke out during the night.* [I] • *War broke out* **in** *1914.* [I] • *"Can we go soon?" he broke out* (=said suddenly). [+ clause] • *They broke out laughing/singing.* [+ v-ing]

break out in *obj v adv prep* [T] suddenly to begin to show or become covered in (something) • *After eating chocolate* *she would break out in* **spots/a rash.** • *It didn't take much exercise to make him break out in (a) sweat* (= make him sweat). • *When I heard the noise I broke out in* **a cold sweat** (= felt great fear).

break·a·way /ˈbreɪ·kə·weɪ/ *n* [C] an act of separation from a group, esp. because of disagreement • *The sports association accepted the inevitability of a breakaway by the elite clubs.* • *The breakaway group formed a new political party.* • See **break away** at BREAK [DIVIDE].

break–danc·ing /£ˈbreɪk,dɑːnt·sɪŋ, $-ˌdænt-/ *n* [U] a highly energetic form of dance often performed outside in the middle of cities, esp. by groups of young men • *Break-dancing was developed by the black urban youth of America.*

break·down [FAILURE] /ˈbreɪk·daʊn/ *n* [C] a failure to work or be successful • *I had a breakdown* (= my car stopped working) *in the middle of the trip.* • *Both sides blamed each other for the breakdown* **of** *talks.* • *Parents and teenagers often suffer from a breakdown* **in communications.** • *(Br)* A **breakdown truck** (*Am and Aus* **tow truck** or **wrecker**) is a truck which has special equipment for removing vehicles which cannot be driven, and taking them to a place where they can be repaired or separated into pieces. • See also **break down** at BREAK [DAMAGE]. • [PIC] **Vehicles**

break·down [DIVISION] /ˈbreɪk·daʊn/ *n* a division of something into smaller parts • *We asked for a breakdown* **of** *the accident figures* **into** *day time and night time.* [C] • *The rate of breakdown of muscle protein was assessed.* [U] • See also **break down** at BREAK [DIVIDE].

break·down [ILLNESS] /ˈbreɪk·daʊn/ *n* [C] a **nervous breakdown**, see at NERVES

break·fast /ˈbrek·fəst/ *n* a meal eaten in the morning as the first meal of the day • *She likes a big/light breakfast.* [C] • *What do you* **have for** *breakfast?* [U] • *Make sure you have some breakfast before you go out.* [U] • *No quarrelling* **at the** *breakfast* **table** (= while eating breakfast)*!* • **Breakfast television** is the television shows that are on early in the morning.

break·fast /ˈbrek·fəst/ *v* [I] *fml* • *They breakfasted hurriedly* **on** *tea and toast.*

break·neck /ˈbreɪk·nek/ *adj* [before n] carelessly fast and dangerous • *They were cycling along* **at** *breakneck* **speed/ at a** *breakneck* **pace.**

break·out /ˈbreɪk·aʊt/ *n* [C] a violent escape, esp. by a group, from prison • *There has been a mass breakout* **from** *one of Germany's top security jails.* • See also **break out** at BREAK [USE FORCE].

break·through /ˈbreɪk·θruː/ *n* [C] an important discovery that helps to provide an answer to a problem • *Scientists are hoping for a breakthrough* **in** *the search for a cure for the disease.* • *An important breakthrough* **in** *negotiations has been achieved.*

break·up [DIVISION] /ˈbreɪk·ʌp/ *n* [U] a gradual division into smaller pieces • *It was feared that the breakup* **of** *the oil tanker would result in further pollution.*

break·up [END] /ˈbreɪk·ʌp/ *n* [C] the coming to an end of a business or personal relationship caused by the separation of those involved • *Long separations had contributed to their* **marriage** *breakup.* • *The breakup* **of** *the pop group came as no surprise.* • *The financial collapse led to the breakup* **of** *his business empire.*

break·wa·ter /£ˈbreɪk,wɔː·təʳ, $-ˌwɑː·t̬ɚ/ *n* [C] a very large wall that is built from the coast out into the sea to protect a beach or HARBOUR (= a walled shelter for boats) from big waves

bream /briːm/ *n pl* **bream** or **breams** a type of edible fish found esp. in lakes and rivers • *A lot of bream are found in quiet lowland lakes and rivers in Northern Europe.* [C] • *They don't have bream on the menu.* [U] • **Sea** bream is a sea fish like a bream. [C/U]

breast [OF A WOMAN] /brest/ *n* [C] either of the two soft, rounded parts of a woman's chest that can produce milk after she has a baby • *When a woman becomes pregnant her breasts tend to grow larger.* • *He stroked/caressed/fondled her breasts.* • *She had breast* **cancer** *when she was younger but recovered and lived to a ripe old age.* • *Do you think she's had breast* **implants** *or are they naturally that size?* • To **breast-feed** a baby is for a mother to feed it with milk directly from her breast rather than with artificial or cow's milk from a bottle. • *I'm a great believer in* **breast-feeding.** • *(saying)* 'Breast is best' means that feeding babies with mothers' breast milk is healthier than feeding them with artificial or cow's milk.

–breast·ed /£-ˈbres·tɪd, $-t̬ɪd/ *combining form* • *a big/ small-breasted woman*

breast [CHEST] /brest/ *n* the front part of a bird's body, or *(esp. literary)* a chest • *The robin is famous for its red breast.* [C] • *Do you prefer breast or leg of chicken?* [U] • *I had a cold* **chicken** *breast and salad for lunch.* [C] • *(literary) The dagger entered his breast.* [C] • *He put a silk hanky in his breast* **pocket** (= a pocket on the top front part of a shirt or coat). • *(literary)* A person's breast is considered as the centre of their feelings: *A feeling of love surged* **in** *his breast.* [C] • [PIC] **Birds**

–breast·ed /£-ˈbres·tɪd, $-t̬ɪd/ *combining form* • A **double**-breasted jacket or coat has two sets of buttons and two wide parts at the front, one of which covers the other when the buttons are fastened. • A **single**-breasted jacket or coat fastens in the centre with one row of buttons.

breast·bone /£ˈbres*t*·bəʊn, $-boʊn/, *medical* **ster·num** *n* [C] the long vertical bone that is in the centre of the chest

breast·plate /ˈbres*t*·pleɪt/ *n* [C] a piece of ARMOUR (= metallic military clothing worn in the past) that protects the chest

breast·stroke /£ˈbres*t*·strəʊk, $-stroʊk/ *n* [U] a way of swimming in which the arms make a circular movement in front of the body while the knees are brought up towards the body and then kicked out and back • *Can you* **do** *breaststroke, Rosie?*

breath /breθ/ *n* the air that you take into and let out of your lungs • *After running I didn't have any breath left to shout for help.* [U] • *Without pausing to* **draw** *breath* (= breathe) *she told me everything.* [U] • *I had to stop running for a few minutes to* **catch** *my breath/***get** *my breath* **back** (= be able to breathe comfortably again). [U] • *I'd just been for a run and I was rather* **short of** *breath* (= unable to breathe deeply). [U] • *He burst into the room, red-faced and* **out of** *breath* (= unable to breathe comfortably because of tiredness or excitement). [U] • *How long can you* **hold** *your breath* (= stop breathing) *for?* [U] • *(fig.) The whole country* **held** *its breath* (= waited anxiously) *as it waited for news.* [U] • *He was gasping for breath when they pulled him from the water.* [U] • *The doctor told me to* **take a deep** *breath* (= breathe in a lot of air). [C] • *There wasn't a* **breath of air** (= the smallest amount of wind) *in the desert.* • *Shall we go out for* **a breath of (fresh) air** (= go outside for a short time)*?* • *She's so cheerful and lively – it's like* **a breath of fresh air** (= everything seems better) *when she visits.* • *The beauty of the Taj Mahal* **took** *my* **breath away** (= was so surprising that I felt as though I could not breathe easily). • *He said he didn't love her any more but* **in the same/next breath** (= the next moment) *said how wonderful she was.* • *"Let's go," she muttered* **under** *her* **breath** (= very quietly so that other people could not hear). • *She asked him* **with** *her* **last/dying breath** (= just before she died) *to look after her child.* • A **breath freshener** is something you eat to make your breath smell pleasant: *People often suck a peppermint as a breath freshener.* • A **breath test** is a test in which the police ask a driver to blow into a BREATHALYSER (= a bag-like device) to show whether they have drunk too much alcohol to be allowed to drive.

breathe *(obj)* /briːð/ *v* • To breathe is to take air into the lungs and let it out again: ○ *It's so airless in here – I can hardly breathe.* [I] ○ *The instructor told us to breathe* **in** *deeply and then breathe* **out** *slowly.* [I] ○ *(fig.) She'd passed the test and she could breathe* **again/more easily** (= feel calm because a difficult or dangerous situation has ended). [I] • *I'm sorry if I'm breathing* (= letting out air containing) *garlic fumes all* **over** *you!* [T] • *"Here they come," he breathed* (= said very quietly). [+ clause] • *We need some new people to* **breathe life into** (= bring new ideas and energy to) *this project.* • *(literary) Her eyes fluttered open for a moment and then she* **breathed** *her* **last** (= died). • *(disapproving)* If someone **breathes down** your **neck**, they stay close to you, watching everything that you do: *It's awful having a boss who breathes down your neck all the time.* • *(specialized)* If you let **wine** breathe, you open the bottle for a short time before you intend to drink from it in order to improve the wine's flavour. [I]

breath·ing /ˈbriː·ðɪŋ/ *n* [U] • *She lay awake listening to her sister's steady breathing.* • *I could hear the sound of* **heavy** *breathing as he slowly climbed the stairs.* • *He felt he needed a* **breathing space** (= a period of rest or a change) *between school and university and took a year out.*

breath·er /£ˈbriː·ðəʳ, $-ðɚ/ *n* [C] • A breather is a brief rest: *He'd been working hard and felt he needed (to* **have/**

take *a breather*. • Breather is *Am for* **heavy breather**. See at HEAVY [TO A GREAT DEGREE].

breath·less /ˈbreθ·ləs/ *adj* • *I was breathless* (= unable to breathe easily) *after swimming three miles.* • *That one kiss had left her breathless with excitement.*

breath·y /ˈbreθ·i/ *adj* **-ier, -iest** • *Marilyn Monroe was famous for her breathy* (= sexy because the breath can be heard) *voice.*

breath·a·lyse *obj* /ˈbreθ·ᵊl·aɪz/ *v* [T] *Br and Aus* to test (a driver's) breath to see how much alcohol they have drunk • *The officer noticed his breath smelled of alcohol and breathalysed him.*

breath·a·lys·er *Br and Aus, Am* **breath·al·yz·er** /£ˈbreθ·ᵊl·aɪz·əʳ, $-ɚ/ *n* [C] *trademark* • A breathalyser is a device like a small bag with a tube at one end, which the police can ask a driver to blow into to see how much alcohol the driver has drunk.

breath·tak·ing /ˈbreθˌteɪ·kɪŋ/ *adj* extremely exciting, beautiful or surprising • *It's a long climb up the hill but once you're up there the view is breathtaking.* • *His performance is described in the paper as 'a breathtaking display of physical agility'.* • *With breathtaking audacity he dared to suggest that I clean up after him.*

breath·tak·ing·ly /ˈbreθˌteɪ·kɪŋ·li/ *adv* • *The scenery really was breathtakingly* **beautiful**.

breech·es /ˈbrɪtʃ·ɪz, ˈbriː·tʃɪz/, *Am* **britch·es** *pl n* tight trousers that do not cover the whole of the leg • *riding breeches*

breed *(obj)* /briːd/ *v past* **bred** /bred/ to keep (animals or plants) for the purpose of producing young animals or plants with chosen qualities, or (of animals) to have sex and reproduce • *My father breeds alpine plants.* [T] • *American pit bull terriers are bred* **for** *their fighting instincts.* [T] • *The blackbird, like most birds, breeds in the spring.* [I] • *(fig.) Favouritism breeds* (= produces) **resentment**. [T] • See also INBRED [ESTABLISHED]; INBRED [RELATED]; PUREBRED; THOROUGHBRED; WELL-BRED.

breed /briːd/ *n* [C] • A breed is a particular type of animal or plant: *The Manx breed* **of** *cat has no tail.* ○ *This is a particularly hardy breed of sheep.* ○ *There was a tent at the show where they had lots of* **rare** *breeds of animals.* • *(infml)* A breed is also a type of person: *Arletty was that* **rare** *breed* **of** *actress – beautiful, sexy and funny at the same time.* ○ *A* **new** *breed* **of** *film-maker has taken over Hollywood.* ○ *Authentic blues singers tend to be a* **dying** *breed these days.*

breed·er /£ˈbriː·dəʳ, $-dɚ/ *n* [C] • *She was one of the country's top sheep breeders.*

breed·ing /ˈbriː·dɪŋ/ *n* [U] • *The family's business was horse-breeding.* • *We used to keep pigs for breeding purposes.* • *The penguins' breeding* **season** *has begun.* • *These animals always return to the same breeding* **ground** (= the place where they produce their young). • *Dirty water and poor sanitary conditions are rich breeding* **grounds** *for* (= they produce a lot of) *disease.* • *Poor housing conditions are a breeding* **ground** *for* (= they produce a lot of) *teenage crime.* • *(dated)* A person who has **(good)** breeding has been trained in their childhood to be polite and behave correctly: *That boy lacks breeding.*

breeze [WIND] /briːz/ *n* [C] a light and pleasant wind • *There's a nice breeze today.* • *She stood still for a moment and let the gentle breeze cool her face.* • *It doesn't feel so hot on the beach because you get the* **sea** *breeze.* • *A breeze came up and filled the sails.*

breez·y /ˈbriː·zi/ *adj* **-ier, -iest** • *It was a sunny, breezy day* (= one with quite strong but pleasant winds), *just right for sailing.*

breeze [WALK] /briːz/ *v* [I always + adv/prep] to walk somewhere quickly and confidently, without anxiety or embarrassment • *She just breezed* **in** *as if she'd only been away a day instead of a year.* • *The nurse rapped on my door and, without waiting for an answer, breezed* **into** *the room.*

breez·y /ˈbriː·zi/ *adj* • *He had the breezy* (= happy and confident) *manner of a salesman.* • *You seem very* **bright** **and** *breezy* (= happy) *today.*

breeze [SOMETHING EASY] /briːz/ *n* [C usually sing] *infml* something which is easy to achieve, often unexpectedly • *You won't have any problems with the entrance test – it's an absolute breeze.*

breeze /briːz/ *v* [I always + adv/prep] *infml* • *She breezed* **through** (= easily completed) *the song as though she'd been singing it for years.* • *(esp. Am) He was re-elected with both Republican and Democratic backing, and in 1985 he breezed* **to** *victory* (= won easily) *with 78% of the vote.*

breth·ren /ˈbreð·rən/ *pl n dated* (used as a form of address to members of an organization or religious group) brothers

brev·i·ty /£ˈbrev·ɪ·ti, $-ə·t̬i/ *n* [U] lasting only a short time or using only a few words; shortness • *The first of these two poems is an anguished reflection on the brevity of life.* • *The later essays were written with admirable clarity and brevity.* • *Brevity is, in almost everything, a virtue.* • *"Brevity is the soul of wit"* (Shakespeare, Hamlet 2.2)

brew *(obj)* /bruː/ *v* (of tea or coffee) to become stronger in taste in the container in which it is made, or to make (a hot drink or beer) • *I'll just let the* **tea** *brew for a minute before I pour it.* [I] • *He brewed us some coffee./He brewed some coffee* **for** *us.* [+ two objects] • *This* **beer** *has been brewed using traditional methods.* [T] • *(fig.) A storm was brewing* (= about to start) *outside.* [I] • *(fig.) It was too quiet – I felt that trouble was brewing* (= about to start). [I]

brew·er /£ˈbruː·əʳ, $-ɚ/ *n* [C] • *A survey suggested that 60% of pub tenants felt no pressure from their brewer* (= a person or company that makes beer) *over this issue.* • *The inquiry said pubs under the* **big** *brewers' control should be allowed to sell one ale from an independent supplier.*

brew /bruː/ *n* [C] • *This brew* (= type of beer) *is only sold in the north of England.* • *They gave her a strange brew* (= a drink made of various mixtures) *to drink.* • *(fig.) War, with its fear, its deprivation, its excitement and violence makes for a very* **heady** *brew* (= powerful combination).

brew·er·y /£ˈbrʊə·ri, $ˈbrʊr·i/ *n* [C] a company that makes beer or a place where beer is made • *Most pubs in England are owned by one of only a few large breweries.*

briar, brier /£ˈbraɪəʳ, $braɪr/ *n* [C] a wild rose bush with long stems and sharp THORNS

bribe *obj* /braɪb/ *v* [T] to try to make (someone) do something for you by giving them money, presents or something else that they want • *He escaped and fled to England after his family bribed officials.* • *Then came revelations that the police had concealed evidence and bribed witnesses.* • *They bribed the waiter* **(with** *a ten-pound note)* **to** *find them a table* [+ obj + *to* infinitive] • *I tried to bribe my brother* **into** *disappearing for the afternoon by offering him the use of my car.* • [LP] **Crimes and criminals**

bribe /braɪb/, *infml* **back·hand·er** *n* [C] • *He was accused of* **accepting/taking** *bribes* (= money or presents given in exchange for doing something special) *from wealthy businessmen.*

brib·er·y /£ˈbraɪ·bᵊr·i, $-bɚ-/ *n* [U] • *The organization was rife with bribery and corruption.*

bric–a–brac /ˈbrɪk·ə·bræk/ *n* [U] small decorative objects of various types and of no great value • *It's one of those shops that sells antiques and bric-a-brac.*

brick [BUILDING BLOCK] /brɪk/ *n* [C] a rectangular block of hard material used for building walls and houses • *Someone had thrown a brick through the shop window.* • *We lived in a Victorian terrace of* **red**-*brick houses.* • *He was so embarrassed – his face went brick*-**red** (= a dark red). • *(fig.) I was nearly forty when I finally invested in* **bricks and mortar** (= bought a home). • *(saying)* 'You can't make bricks without straw' means that you cannot make something without the necessary materials. • *"Another Brick in the Wall"* (song by Pink Floyd, 1979) • See also AIRBRICK; FIREBRICK; REDBRICK. • [PIC] **Building and construction**

brick *obj* /brɪk/ *v* [T always + adv/prep] • To brick **in/up** something is to build a wall of bricks around something or to fill something with bricks: *The doors and windows had been bricked up to prevent squatters from getting in.* • *In an attempt to stop the fighting, one side of the city was bricked* **off** (= a brick wall was built to separate it) *from the other.*

brick [GOOD PERSON] /brɪk/ *n* [C usually sing] *dated or humorous* a very helpful and kind person who can be trusted • *Thanks for bringing all that food along to the party, Tony,* **you're a** *brick!* • Brick is often used humorously to mean the opposite: *Thanks for leaving me on my own with eleven children to entertain, Richard,* **you're a** *real brick!*

brick·bat /ˈbrɪk·bæt/ *n* [C] a spoken attack; an insult • *The members of parliament hurled brickbats at the minister.*

brick·lay·er /£ˈbrɪkˌleɪ·əʳ, $-ɚ/, *Br and Aus infml* **brick·ie** /ˈbrɪk·i/ *n* [C] a person who builds walls or buildings using bricks, esp. as a job

brick·lay·ing /ˈbrɪkˌleɪ·ɪŋ/ *n* [U] • *Bricklaying is a skilled job.*

brick·work /£ˈbrɪk·wɜːk, $-wɜːrk/ *n* [U] the bricks in a wall or walled building

bride /braɪd/ *n* [C] a woman who is about to get married or has just got married • *He returned to New York in 1946 with his lovely* **young** *bride.* • *A car turned up to take the bride* **and groom** *to the reception.* • *As the* **mother of the** *bride, I feel obliged to wear something really spectacular.* • *(humorous) May I kiss the* **blushing** *bride?* • *I was 38 when I married, hardly a* **child** *bride* (= a very young woman getting married). • A **bride-to-be** is a woman who is going to be married soon.

brid·al /ˈbraɪ·dəl/ *adj* [not gradable] • Bridal means of a woman about to be married, or of a marriage ceremony: *The magazine had a section on bridal wear* (= the clothes that a woman wears at her marriage). ○ *We stayed in the hotel's bridal* **suite** (= the rooms for recently married people).

bride·groom /ˈbraɪd·grʊm, -gruːm/, **groom** *n* [C] a man who is about to get married or has just got married • *The bridegroom himself was late for the ceremony.*

brides·maid /ˈbraɪdz·meɪd/ *n* [C] a girl or woman who during the marriage ceremony helps the woman who is getting married • *The bridesmaids were in peach-coloured satin.* • *She wondered if she was destined to be* **always a/the bridesmaid, never the bride** (= She asked herself if she would ever get married).

bridge [LARGE STRUCTURE] /brɪdʒ/ *n* [C] a structure that is built over a river, road or railway to allow people and vehicles to cross from one side to the other • *We drove* **across/over** *the bridge.* • *The Brooklyn Bridge spans the East River from Brooklyn to Manhattan.* • *When the Golden Gate bridge was built, it was the world's longest* **suspension** *bridge.* • *(fig.) Voluntary work can provide a bridge* (= something that allows you gradually to make the change) **between** *staying at home* **and** *working full-time.* • *"Bridge over Troubled Water"* (title of a song by Simon and Garfunkel, 1970) • [PIC] **Bridge**

bridge *obj* /brɪdʒ/ *v* [T] • *In the Middle Ages the river had been bridged* (= a bridge had been built over it) *with slabs of rock.* • *(fig.) The group exists to try to bridge* **the gap** *between* (= bring together) *the unemployed and employers who need workers.* • *(fig.) This play successfully bridges* **the gap** *between high and low culture* (= makes it seem as if these things are not so different). • *(Br and Aus)* A **bridging loan**/*(Am)* **bridge loan** is an arrangement by which a bank lends a person some money for a short time until that person can get the money from somewhere else, often so that they can buy another house before they sell their own.

bridge [TEETH] /brɪdʒ/ *n* [C], *esp. Am* **bridge·work** /£ˈbrɪdʒ·wɜːk, $-wɜːrk/ *n* [U] (a piece of) material that contains one or more artificial teeth and is kept in place by being fastened to the natural teeth • *My dentist says I'm going to have to have a bridge.* • *She had some bridgework put in when she became a TV presenter.*

bridge [NOSE] /brɪdʒ/ *n* [C usually sing] the top part of the nose, between the eyes, or (on a pair of glasses) the piece that is supported by the top part of the nose • *The blow caught him right on the bridge of his nose.*

bridge [MUSICAL INSTRUMENT] /brɪdʒ/ *n* [C] on a musical instrument such as a guitar or VIOLIN, the small piece of wood over which the strings are stretched

bridge [PART OF A SHIP] /brɪdʒ/ *n* [C] the raised part of a ship on which the CAPTAIN and other officers stand and from where they control the movement of the ship • *The captain stood on the bridge and surveyed the empty sea.*

bridge [GAME] /brɪdʒ/ *n* [U] a card game, similar to WHIST, for four players who form two partnerships and try to win the cards they say they will win

bridge·head /ˈbrɪdʒ·hed/ *n* [C] a good position that an army has taken in enemy land from which it can attack the enemy more effectively • *The advance troops* **established a** *bridgehead early in the fighting.* • *(fig.) A lot of these companies are looking to European markets, and Britain is a natural bridgehead.* • Compare BEACHHEAD.

bri·dle [CONTROL] /ˈbraɪ·dl̩/ *n* [C] a set of leather strips that are put around a horse's head to allow its rider to control it • A **bridle path** is a small track in a park in the countryside, originally intended to be used only by people riding or walking horses, but often also used by people going on walks.

bri·dle *obj* /ˈbraɪ·dl̩/ *v* [T] • *Polly saddled and bridled* (= put a bridle on) *her favourite horse.*

bri·dle [SHOW ANGER] /ˈbraɪ·dl̩/ *v* [I] to show sudden annoyance • *She bridled* **at** *the suggestion that she had been dishonest.*

bri·dle·way /ˈbraɪ·dl̩·weɪ/ *n* [C] a **bridle path**, see at BRIDLE [CONTROL].

Brie /briː/ *n* [U] a soft French cheese with a white outside and a yellowish creamy inside • *I prefer Brie to Camembert.*

brief [SHORT IN TIME] /briːf/ *adj* **-er, -est** lasting only a short time or containing few words • *His speech was witty and mercifully brief.* • *I had a brief look at the newspaper over breakfast.* • *"I'll be brief," she said. "The theatre needs more money to survive."* • *It'll only be a brief visit because we really haven't much time.* • *Rory had a brief* **flirtation** *with acting when he was in his twenties.* • *After a brief* **spell/stint** *in the army, he started working as a teacher.* • *The company issued a brief* **statement** *this morning disclaiming all responsibility for the accident.* • *I get a brief* **respite** *at Christmas and then two days later I'm back at work.* • Brief can also be used to express how quickly time goes past: *For a few brief weeks we were very happy.* • *"Brief Encounter"* (Film title, 1945) • (NL)

brief /briːf/ *n* [U] • If something is said **in** brief, it is said in a very short form, with very few details: *In brief, then, has the government lost its nerve?* ○ *"So you didn't enjoy the party then." "In brief, no."*

brief·ly /ˈbriː·fli/ *adv* • *We chatted briefly* (= for a short time) *about the weather.* • *Briefly* (= Using few words), *the company needs to cut its expenditure.*

brief [SHORT IN LENGTH] /briːf/ *adj* (of clothes) very short • *She was wearing a rather brief skirt, as I recall.* • (NL)

brief *obj* [GIVE INSTRUCTIONS] /briːf/ *v* [T] *fml* to give (someone) instructions or information about what they should do or say • *We had already been briefed* **about/on** *what the job would entail.* • *(law)* A SOLICITOR briefs a BARRISTER by giving him or her all the details about the case that he or she is to argue in a court of law. • Compare DEBRIEF. • (NL)

brief /briːf/ *n* [C] *Br and Aus* • *It was my brief* (= I was instructed) **to** *make sure that the facts were set down accurately.* [+ *to* infinitive] • *(law)* A brief is a document or set of documents containing the details about a court case which is prepared by a SOLICITOR and given to the BARRISTER who is to argue the case in court.

brief·ing /ˈbriː·fɪŋ/ *n* • *They received (a) thorough briefing* (= the information that is given to someone just before they do something) *before they left the country.* [C/U] • *We had to attend a briefing* (= a meeting where information is given) *once a month.* [C]

brief·case /ˈbriːf·keɪs/ *n* [C] a usually flat rectangular case, used esp. for carrying business papers • [PIC] **Luggage**

briefs /briːfs/ *pl n* a piece of underwear worn by men and women, covering the area between the waist and the tops of the legs • *cotton briefs*

brier /£ˈbraɪər, $braɪr/ *n* [C] a BRIAR

brig /brɪg/ *n* [C] *Am* a prison, esp. one on a US navy ship or at a US military station

bri·gade /brɪˈgeɪd/ *n* [C] one of the groups into which an army is divided, consisting of two or more BATTALIONS • *Jones and Rigby fought in the same brigade during the war.* • *(fig. humorous) Since she gave up smoking she's joined the anti-smoking brigade* (= the people who are very opposed to smoking and frequently express this opinion). • (CS)

bri·gad·ier /£ˌbrɪg·əˈdɪər, £ˈ---, $-ˈdɪr/, **bri·gad·ier–gen·er·al** *n* [C] an officer in a British or Commonwealth army of the rank above a COLONEL and below a **major-general**, and who is in charge of a BRIGADE • *(Am)* A **brigadier-general** is an officer of the US Army of the same rank as a brigadier.

bri·gand /ˈbrɪg·ənd/ *n* [C] *literary* an armed thief, esp. one of a group living in mountains or forests and stealing from people travelling through the area

bright [LIGHT] /braɪt/ *adj* **-er, -est** full of light, shining • *It was a warm, bright day with no wind.* • *It's a south-facing room so it's bright and airy.* • *The lights are too bright in here – they're hurting my eyes.* • *A bright star was shining in the East.* • *In 1983 I moved to London, attracted by the bright* **lights** *of the city.* • *When she looked up her eyes were bright* **with** *tears.* • *"All things bright and beautiful/ All creatures great and small,/ All things wise and wonderful – / The Lord God made them all"* (From the hymn *All Things Bright and Beautiful* by Mrs C.F. Alexander, 1848) • (D)

bright·en *(obj)* /£ˈbraɪ·tən, $-t̬ən/ *v* • *It was rainy and overcast in the morning, but* **it** *brightened* **up** (= the sky

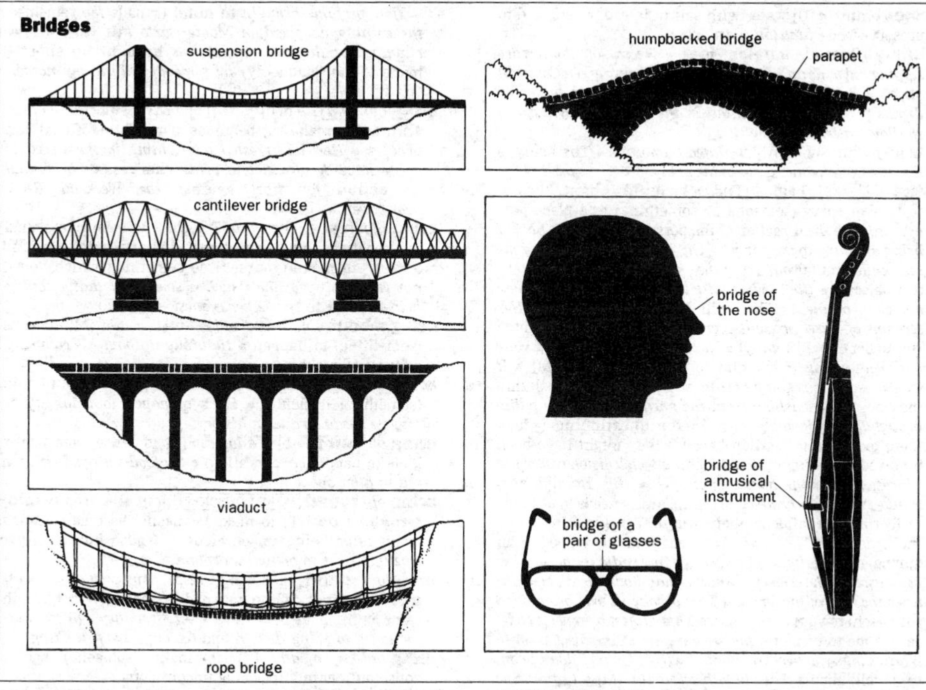

became lighter and the sun shone) in the afternoon. [I] • *It was a small dark room, without so much as a chink of light to brighten the gloom.* [T] • *The sponged yellow walls are Angie's own handiwork, to brighten* **up the place** *a bit* (= make it brighter and therefore more pleasant). [M]

brights /braɪts/ *pl n Am* • A car's brights are its HEADLIGHTS (= the powerful lights at the front) on full power.

bright·ly /ˈbraɪt·li/ *adv* • *She walked into a brightly lit room.* • *He polished his shoes until they* **shone brightly**.

bright·ness /ˈbraɪt·nəs/ *n* [U] • *He walked outside and the brightness of the sun made him blink.*

bright COLOUR /braɪt/ *adj* **-er, -est** strong in colour • *He was wearing a bright green suit and an orange tie.* • *He said hello and I felt my face turn bright red.* • *She wears bright pink lipstick.* • Ⓓ

bright·ly /ˈbraɪt·li/ *adv* • *The book had pictures of brightly coloured animals.*

bright INTELLIGENT /braɪt/ *adj* **-er, -est** (of a person) clever and quick to learn • *They were bright children, always asking questions.* • *He was nice enough but he didn't seem very bright.* • *She was enthusiastic and full of bright* **ideas** (= clever ideas) *and suggestions.* • *(humorous) Whose bright* **idea** (= stupid idea) *was it to send the documents out before they were complete?* • *(Br) Some* **bright spark** (= stupid person) *has broken the computer!* • Ⓓ

bright HAPPY /braɪt/ *adj* full of hope or happiness • *You're very bright* **and cheerful** *this morning.* • *At last things are starting to look brighter* **for** *British businesses.* • *The* **future** *seemed bright* (= likely to be good) *for these children.* • *She seemed very bright* **and breezy** (= happy and confident) *today.* • *We'll set off for the coast bright* **and early (in the morning)** (= early in the morning) *so we can have most of the day there.* • *He always leaps out of bed* **bright-eyed and bushy-tailed** (= in a good mood and energetic). • Ⓓ

bright·en *(obj)* /£ˈbraɪ·tᵊn, $-t̬ᵊn/ *v* • *Her eyes brightened* (= looked happier and more hopeful) *when she saw the letter on the floor.* [I] • *Market prospects, he reassured his audience, had brightened* (= started to give more cause for hope) *in the last twelve months.* [I] • *There are, however, one or two items of good news to brighten* (= cause to look more hopeful) *the economic picture a bit.* [T]

bright·ly /ˈbraɪt·li/ *adv* • *She walked into the room smiling brightly* (= happily and full of hope). • *"Only three more days of work and then I'm off," she said brightly.*

brill /brɪl/ *adj, exclamation Br and Aus short for* BRILLIANT • *I like your hat – it's brill!* • *"I got the tickets." "Oh, brill, that's really good news."*

bril·li·ant CLEVER /ˈbrɪl·i·ənt/ *adj* extremely clever or highly skilled • *Her mother was a brilliant scientist.* • *It was in many ways a brilliant plan.* • *She seemed to have a brilliant career ahead of her* (= was likely to be extremely successful).

bril·li·ant·ly /ˈbrɪl·i·ənt·li/ *adv* • *He seems to do everything brilliantly – piano playing, skiing, tap-dancing.* • LP› **Very, completely**

bril·li·ance /ˈbrɪl·i·ənts/ *n* [U] • *Her first novel showed signs of brilliance.*

bril·li·ant SHINING /ˈbrɪl·i·ənt/ *adj* full of light, shining or bright in colour • *The sky was a brilliant, cloudless blue.* • *I dived into the brilliant water.* • *The rooms were all painted brilliant white.* • *(fig.) He flashed me a brilliant smile.*

bril·li·ant·ly /ˈbrɪl·i·ənt·li/ *adv*

bril·li·ance /ˈbrɪl·i·ənts/ *n* [U] • *I had never seen diamonds shine with such brilliance before.*

bril·li·ant VERY GOOD /ˈbrɪl·i·ənt/ *adj Br infml* very good • *"Did you like the film?" "I thought it was brilliant."* • *She's got a brilliant sense of humour.* • *Oh, brilliant! My parcel's arrived.*

bril·li·ant·ine /ˈbrɪl·i·ən·tiːn/ *n* [U] a type of oil used to make esp. men's hair smooth and shiny

bril·li·ant·ine *obj* /ˈbrɪl·i·ən·tiːn/ *v* [T] • *The fifties were the days of brilliantined hair for boys and pony-tails for girls.*

brim PART OF HAT /brɪm/ *n* [C usually sing] the bottom part of a hat that sticks out all round • *He wore a battered felt hat with the brim pulled down over his eyes.* • Compare CROWN TOP PART. • PIC› **Hats**

-brimmed /-brɪmd/ *combining form* • *She wore a* **wide-***brimmed hat.*

brim TOP /brɪm/ *n* [C] the very top edge of a container • *She poured the cream until it reached the brim.* • *He went round the table filling each fluted glass until the froth reached the brim.* • *He* **filled** *the jug* **to the** *brim.* • *She passed him the plastic mug,* **filled/full to the** *brim* **with** *hot black coffee.*

brim /brɪm/ *v* [I] **-mm-** • *Her eyes brimmed* **with tears** (= filled up with tears). • *(fig.) His recent triumphs have left the tennis ace brimming* **(over) with** (= full of) *confidence and energy.* • *(fig.) Her eyes are her most arresting feature, dark and shrewd but brimming* **(over) with** (= full of) *humour.*

brim·ful /brɪmˈfʊl/ *adj* [after v; not gradable] • Something which is brimful **of** something is full of it: *Nobody could call this year's Cannes film festival brimful of wonderful surprises.*

brim·stone /£ˈbrɪm·stəʊn, $-stoʊn/ *n* [U] *old use* the chemical SULPHUR

brine /braɪn/ *n* [U] water with salt in it, esp. when used to preserve food • *tuna/olives* **in** *brine*

brin·y /ˈbraɪ·ni/ *adj* **-ier, -iest** • *We sat on the terrace sipping red wine and eating bread with briny green Corsican olives.* • *For most of the year the whales hide in the briny depths* (= in the deep sea) *but in the summer they bask in shallow water.*

brin·y /ˈbraɪ·ni/ *n* [U] *Br dated humorous* • **The** briny is the sea: *Do you fancy a dip in the briny?*

bring *obj* [TAKE] /brɪŋ/ *v* [T] *past* **brought** /£brɔːt, $brɑːt/ to take or carry (someone or something) to a place or a person, or in the direction of the person speaking • *"Shall I bring anything to the party?" "Oh, just a bottle."* • *Bring me that knife, would you/Bring that knife* **to** *me, would you?* [+ two objects] • *(fig.) What will the future bring for these homeless people* (= What will happen to them?) • *Her screams of 'Fire' brought everyone running* (= made them run to her). [+ obj + v-*ing*] • *Next time you come, bring your boyfriend* **along** (= ask him to come with you). [M] • *It looked as if it was going to rain, so I brought* **in** (= took into the house) *the washing from the garden.* [M] • *The police brought several young men* **in for questioning** (= took them to the police station because they might have been involved in a crime). [M] • *Teaching by television can bring education* **into** *the homes of people.* • *(fig. Br and Aus) Paulo's very shy – he needs bringing* **out** (= needs to be made to feel more confident about himself). • *(fig.) His wife's encouragement brought him* **through** (= helped him during) *the bad times.* • *I've brought my radio* **to** *the office so I can listen to the cricket.* • *Another half hour's walk brought us* **to** *the edge of the forest.* • *This broadcast was brought* **to** *you* (= sent to you) *by satellite.* • *This subject brings me* **to** (= causes me to come to) *the second part of the discussion.* • *What brings you here* **to** *London?* • *(fig.) Oh no – don't bring* **up** (= talk about) *that old subject again.* [M] • *(infml) She was crying so much I thought she'd* **bring up** (= vomit) *her breakfast.* See also BRING UP. • *You two go ahead and I'll* **bring up the rear** (= be last). • *When they visit us they always bring their dog* **with** *them.* • To **bring** someone **to book** is to punish them and make them explain their behaviour. • *(Br and Aus)* A **bring and buy sale** is a sale, usually to collect money for a CHARITY, where people bring things to be sold and buy things brought by other people. • (D) (DK)

bring *obj* [CAUSE] /brɪŋ/ *v* [T] *past* **brought** /£brɔːt, $brɑːt/ to cause, result in or produce (a state) • *Her presence has brought us so much happiness./Her presence has brought so much happiness* **to** *us.* [+ two objects] • *The explosion brought the whole building crashing to the ground.* [+ obj + v-*ing*] • *Few politicians are in favour of bringing* **back** *hanging* (= causing it to come into use again). [M] • *That music always brings* **back** *happy* **memories** (= causes them to be thought of). [M] • *Several trees were brought* **down** (= made to fall) *by the storms.* [M] • *The people succeeded in bringing* **down** *the dictator* (= causing him or her to lose power). [M] • *When is the government going to bring* **down** *inflation* (= cause it to become less)*?* [M] • *(Br) The elections were brought* **forward** (= caused to happen earlier) *by three months.* [M] • *The documentary brought* **home to** *him* (= made him aware of) *the seriousness of the situation.* • *(Br) The government is bringing* **in** *a law* (= making a new law) *to reduce junior doctors' working hours.* [M] • *The restaurant chain brings* **in** (= produces) *a profit of millions of pounds a year.* [M] • *(law) The jury brought* **in** (= produced) *a verdict of not guilty.* [M] • *A new type of electronic encyclopedia has been brought* **into being** (= made to exist). [M] • *The loud music brought* **on** (= caused) *another one of his headaches.* [M] • *You'll only bring trouble* **on** *yourself* (= cause trouble for yourself) *if you disobey.* • *I see they've brought* **out** (= produced for general sale) *a new lap-top word processor.* [M] • *A crisis can bring* **out** (= produce) *the best and the worst in people.* [M] • *The closure of the factory brought poverty* **to** *the town* (= resulted in it becoming poor). • *Her remarkable achievements have brought fame* **to** *her small home town* (= resulted in it becoming famous). • *What could have brought him* **to** (= caused him to feel) *this state of despair?* • *His parents brought a lot of pressure* **to bear** *on him* (= strongly tried to influence him) *to improve his grades.* • *Bring the water (Br and Aus)* **to the boil***/(Am)* **to a boil** (= make it start boiling). • *The actor suddenly brought the interview* **to an end** (= caused it to end). • *The sharp pain brought* **tears to** *my* **eyes** (= made me cry). • *Another investigation may bring* **to light** (= cause to be known) *other corrupt practices.* • *Your perfume brought* **to mind** (= made me remember) *the evening we spent in Monte Carlo this year.* • *I was running for the bus when I was* **brought up short** (= made to stop suddenly) *by someone calling my name.* • (D) (DK)

bring *obj* [LAW] /brɪŋ/ *v* [T] *past* **brought** /£brɔːt, $brɑːt/ to make or begin as part of an official legal process • *He was arrested for fighting in the street, but police have decided not to bring* **charges**. • *She brought an* **action** *for libel* **against** *the Weekend Record newspaper.* • (D) (DK)

bring *obj* [FORCE] /brɪŋ/ *v* [T + obj + *to* infinitive; usually in negatives and questions] *past* **brought** /£brɔːt, $brɑːt/ to make (yourself) do something which you do not want to do • *She's such a sweet girl that I couldn't bring my***self to** *refuse her request.* • (D) (DK)

bring a·bout *obj*, **bring** *obj* **a·bout** *v adv* [M] to cause (something) to happen • *He brought about his company's collapse by reckless speculation.*

bring off *obj*, **bring** *obj* **off** *v adv* [M] to succeed in doing (something difficult) • *She's managed to bring off the biggest cheque fraud in history.*

bring *obj* **out in** *obj v adv prep* [T] to cause (someone) to have (a particular condition) • *Seafood always brings me out in huge spots.*

bring *obj* **round** [MAKE CONSCIOUS], *esp. Am usually* **bring a·round** *v adv* [T] to make (someone) become conscious again after being unconscious • *I gave him a sniff of smelling salts to bring him round.*

bring *obj* **round** [PERSUADE], *esp. Am usually* **bring a·round** *v adv* [T] to persuade (someone) to have the same opinion as you have • *At first they refused but I managed to bring them round (***to** *my way of thinking).*

bring *obj* **to** *v adv* [T] to make (someone) become conscious again after being unconscious

bring up *obj*, **bring** *obj* **up** *v adv* [M] to care for (a child) until it is an adult, often giving it particular beliefs • *When their parents died an aunt brought them up.* • *They brought her up* **(as/to be)** *a Catholic.* [+ obj + (*as/to be/as*) n/adj] • *David was brought up* **to** *respect authority.* [+ obj + *to* infinitive] • *She seemed to be a* **well/badly** *brought-up young girl* (= was taught to behave well/badly as a child). • See also **bring up** at BRING [TAKE].

brink /brɪŋk/ *n* [U] the point where something is about to begin, or *(literary)* the edge of a cliff or other high area • *Extreme stress had driven him to* **the** *brink* **of** *a nervous breakdown.* • *Scientists are* **on the** *brink* **of** (= extremely close to) *a major new discovery.* • *His company are reported to be* **teetering on the** *brink* **of** *bankruptcy/collapse/ruin.* • *(literary) She stood swaying* **on the** *brink* **of** *the gorge.*

brink·man·ship /ˈbrɪŋk·mən·ʃɪp/ *n* [U] the activity, esp. in politics, of trying to get what you want by pretending that if you do not get it, you will do something dangerous • *"If it turns out otherwise, I will simply go, and someone else can assume the responsibility," said the leader, resorting to brinkmanship.*

bri·oche /£ˈbri·ɒʃ, $-ɑːʃ/ *n* [C/U] a loaf of soft, slightly sweet bread made with eggs and butter

bri·quette, bri·quet /brɪˈket/ *n* [C] a small block made from coal dust or PEAT, used as fuel in a fire

brisk /brɪsk/ *adj* **-er, -est** quick, energetic and active • *My mother goes for a brisk walk every day.* • *If we walk at a brisk* **pace** *we should get there on time.* • *Her tone on the telephone was brisk* (= she spoke quickly, wasting no time and using few words) **and businesslike**. • *A brisk* (= cold but pleasant) *wind blew over the moors.* • *The heat wave means that shops are doing a brisk* **trade in** *electric fans* (= selling a lot quickly).

brisk·ly /ˈbrɪsk·li/ *adv* • *She walked briskly into town.* • *The new shopping centre traded briskly in basic goods, many shops offering sales and reductions.* • *"Let's get it over with," he said briskly.*

brisk·ness /ˈbrɪsk·nəs/ *n* [U]

bri·sket /ˈbrɪs·kɪt/ *n* [U] meat from the chest of a cow

brist·le /ˈbrɪs·l̩/ *n* a short stiff hair, usually one of many • *The only paintbrushes we could find were old and had lost most of their bristles.* [C] • *The best quality men's shaving brushes are made from badger bristle* (= hairs). [U] • [PIC] **Brush**

brist·le /ˈbrɪs·l̩/ *v* [I] • *The cat's fur bristled* (= the hairs stood up stiffly) *and it arched its back.* • *(fig.) She bristled* (= showed anger) **at** *the suggestion that she had in any way neglected the child.* • *(fig.) It was a Saturday* *afternoon and the town was bristling* **with** (= full of) *people.*

brist·ly /ˈbrɪs·li/ *adj* **-ier, -iest** • *He had furry straight eyebrows and bristly* (= short, sticking up) *hair cropped short.* • *Your bristly chin tickles me when we kiss!*

Brit /brɪt/ *n* [C] *infml* a British person • *A gang of tourists walked into the bar and you could just tell by their clothes they were Brits.*

britch·es /ˈbrɪtʃ·ɪz/ *pl n Am for* BREECHES

Brit·ish /£ˈbrɪt·ɪʃ, $ˈbrɪt̬-/ *adj* of the United Kingdom of Great Britain and Northern Ireland • *He's got a British passport.* • *The British weather is somewhat unpredictable.* • **British Summer Time** (*abbreviation* **BST**) is the time used in Britain from late March to late October that is one hour later than Greenwich Mean Time. • *"The British are coming"* (Colin Welland on the British film industry, using a cry from the American War of Independence, 1982)

AREAS OF BRITAIN

Different names for Britain and its parts:

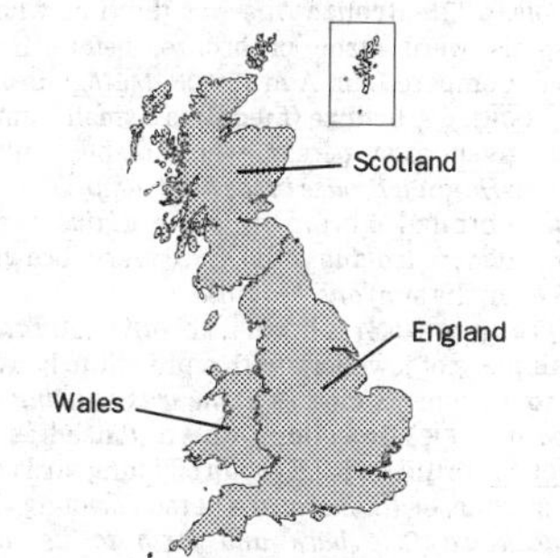

Britain/Great Britain

The UK/the United Kingdom

- **The British Isles** is not a nation but a name for all the islands of Britain and Ireland considered as a group.
- The UK is divided into political areas called **counties**. The **home counties** surround London.

Brit·ish /£ˈbrɪt·ɪʃ, $ˈbrɪt̬-/ *pl n* • **The British** are people from Britain.

Brit·ish·er /£ˈbrɪt·ɪ·ʃəʳ, $ˈbrɪt̬·ɪ·ʃɚ/ *n* [C] *Am* • A Britisher is a British person.

Brit·on /£ˈbrɪt·ᵊn, $ˈbrɪt̬-/ *n* [C] a British person • *Six Britons are believed to have been involved in the accident.* • *The* **Ancient** *Britons inhabited these islands before the Anglo-Saxon invasions.*

brit·tle /£ˈbrɪt·l̩, $ˈbrɪt̬-/ *adj* delicate and easily broken • *As you get older your bones become increasingly brittle.* • *The pond was covered in a brittle layer of ice.* • *(fig.) She gave a brittle* (= unkind) *laugh and turned away.*

bro /£brəʊ, $broʊ/ *n* [C] *pl* **bros** *esp. Am infml for* BROTHER • *I used to call my little bro 'Pipsqueak'.* • *Hey, bro, what's happening?* [as form of address]

broach *obj* [BEGIN] /£brəʊtʃ, $broʊtʃ/ *v* [T] to begin a discussion of (something difficult) • *At some point we've got to discuss money but I don't know quite how to broach the subject with him.* • *So how are you going to broach the issue?*

broach *obj* [OPEN] /£brəʊtʃ, $broʊtʃ/ *v* [T] *fml or humorous* to open (a bottle or BARREL) in order to drink its contents • *Shall we broach another cask of wine?*

broach [JEWELLERY] /£brəʊtʃ, $broʊtʃ/ *n* [C] *Am for* BROOCH

broad [WIDE] /£brɔːd, $brɑːd/ *adj* **-er, -est** very wide • *We walked down a broad street lined with trees.* • *He flashed a broad* **grin** *at us.* • *My brother is very broad-***shouldered**. • If something is a particular distance broad, it measures this distance from side to side: *This river is over 100 metres broad at its widest point.* • *O'Connell Bridge in Dublin is famous for being broader than it is long.* • *She dropped a broad* **hint** (= one that is very easy to understand) *that her guests should leave.* • *Thieves had broken into the car* **in broad daylight** (= during the day rather than at night) *and stolen the stereo.* • *(dated humorous) Her mother was fairly* **broad in the beam** (= had wide hips and a large bottom). • A **broad bean** is a large edible pale green bean. • **Broad jump** is *Am for* **long jump**. See at LONG [DISTANCE]. • Compare NARROW.

broad·en *(obj)* /£ˈbrɔː·dᵊn, $ˈbrɑː-/ *v* • *The track broadens* (= becomes wider) *and becomes a path at this point.* [I] • *They are broadening the road* (= making it wider) *to speed up the flow of traffic.* [T]

broad·ness /£ˈbrɔːd·nəs, $ˈbrɑːd-/ *n* [U] • *She was struck by the broadness of his back.*

broad [GENERAL] /£brɔːd, $brɑːd/ *adj* including a wide range of things; general • *The politician gave a broad* **outline** *of his proposals.* • *The magazine covers a broad* **range** *of subjects, from sewing to psychology.* • *We are in broad* **agreement** (= We agree about most things). • *Romantic comedies usually have a broad* **appeal** (= are liked by many people). • *The law is intended to help a broad* **cross-section** (= a great number of different people) *of the population.*

broad·en *obj* /£ˈbrɔː·dᵊn, $ˈbrɑː-/ *v* [T] • To broaden something is to increase the range of it: *They've introduced all sorts of new elements to that programme in order to broaden its* **appeal**. ○ *Living in India for eight months certainly broadened my outlook on life.* ○ *I hoped that going to university might broaden my* **horizons** (= increase the range of my knowledge and experience). ○ *He decided to broaden* **(out)** *the discussion to include health issues.* [T/M]

broad·ly /£ˈbrɔːd·li, $ˈbrɑːd-/ *adv* • *I broadly agree with you.* • *Broadly* **speaking**, *don't you think women make better drivers than men?*

broad [STRONG] /£brɔːd, $brɑːd/ *adj* **-er, -est** (of an ACCENT (= way of speaking)) strong and noticeable, showing where the speaker comes from • *His mother has a broad Yorkshire* **accent** *and yet he speaks with almost no accent.* • *A man addressed me in a broad Australian accent.*

broad [WOMAN] /£brɔːd, $brɑːd/ *n* [C] *esp. Am slang* a woman • *So this broad walks into the bar and I think I know her face from somewhere.*

broad·cast /£ˈbrɔːd·kɑːst, $ˈbrɑːd·kæst/ *v*, *n past* **broadcast** or *Am also* **broadcasted** (to send out) sound or pictures which are carried over distances using radio waves • *a radio/television broadcast* [C] • *We watched a* **live** *broadcast of the concert.* [C] • *Radio Caroline used to broadcast* **from** *a boat in the North Sea.* [I] • *The tennis championship is broadcast* **live** *to several different countries.* [T] • *(infml) I told Patrick that I was having an operation but asked him not to broadcast* (= tell everyone) **the fact**. [T]

broad·cast·er /£ˈbrɔːdˌkɑː·stəʳ, $ˈbrɑːdˌkæs·tɚ/ *n* [C] • *He was a famous broadcaster* (= a person who presents discussions or information on radio or television) *in the 1930s.*

broad·cast·ing /£ˈbrɔːdˌkɑː·stɪŋ, $ˈbrɑːdˌkæs·tɪŋ/ *n* [U] • *Huge amounts of money are spent on sports broadcasting.*

broad·mind·ed /£ˌbrɔːdˈmaɪn·dɪd, $ˌbrɑːd-/ *adj approving* willing to accept other people's behaviour and beliefs, esp. sexual behaviour • *At seventy she was surprisingly broadminded.* • Compare **narrow-minded** at NARROW.

broad·mind·ed·ness /£ˌbrɔːdˈmaɪn·dɪd·nəs, $ˌbrɑːd-/ *n* [U] *approving* • *My parents always prided themselves on their broadmindedness.*

broad·sheet /£ˈbrɔːd·ʃiːt, $ˈbrɑːd-/ *n* [C] *Br and Aus* a newspaper that is printed on large paper or an advertisement printed on a large sheet of paper • *In*

Britain, the broadsheets are generally believed to be more serious than the tabloids.

broad·side /£ˈbrɔːd·saɪd, $ˈbrɑːd-/ *n* [C] a strong written or spoken attack (on someone), or *(specialized)* the firing of all the guns on one side of a military ship at the same time • *The opposition* **fired/launched** *yet another broadside* **at** *the prime minister.*

bro·cade /brəˈkeɪd/ *n* [U] heavy decorative cloth with a raised design often of gold or silver threads • *She wore a heavy brocade gown.*

broc·coli /£ˈbrɒk·əl·i, $ˈbrɑː·kəl-/ *n* [U] a vegetable with a thick green stem and a tight green or purple tree-like top • PIC› **Vegetables**

bro·chure /£ˈbrəʊ·ʃəʳ, $broʊˈʃʊr/ *n* [C] a type of small magazine that contains pictures and information on a product or a company • *They brought home heaps of* **travel** *brochures.*

brogue /£brəʊg, $broʊg/ *n* [C usually sing] an Irish or sometimes Scottish way of speaking English • *She spoke in her soft lilting brogue.*

brogues /£brəʊgz, $broʊgz/ *pl n* strong leather shoes, usually worn by men, often with a pattern in the leather • PIC› **Shoes**

broil *obj* /brɔɪl/ *v* [T] *Am for* GRILL COOK • PIC› **Cooking**

broil·ing /ˈbrɔɪ·lɪŋ/ *adj* [not gradable] *Am infml* • *It was already broiling* (= very hot weather) *by breakfast time.*

broil·er /£ˈbrɔɪ·ləʳ, $-lɚ/ *n* [C] a young chicken suitable for ROASTING or GRILLING • **Broiler pan** is *Am for* **grill pan**. See at GRILL COOK. • PIC› **Kitchen, Pan**

broke BREAK /£brəʊk, $broʊk/ *past simple of* BREAK

broke POOR /£brəʊk, $broʊk/ *adj* [after v] *infml* without money • *I can't afford to go on holiday this year – I'm* **(flat)** *broke.* • *(infml) Many small businesses* **went** *broke* (= lost all their money) *during the recession.* • *(infml)* To **go for broke** is to risk everything in the hope of having great success.

brok·en BREAK /£ˈbrəʊ·kən, $ˈbroʊ-/ *past participle of* BREAK

brok·en DAMAGED /£ˈbrəʊ·kən, $ˈbroʊ-/ *adj* [not gradable] damaged, no longer able to work • *He attacked the man with a broken bottle.* • *My watch is broken.* • *Careful – there's broken* **glass** *on the floor.* • *(fig.) He was* **a broken man** (= very sad and completely changed) *after his wife died.* • *They lived for months in a* **broken-down** *van* (= one that did not work any more). • *She was* **broken-hearted** (= extremely unhappy) *when her boyfriend left her.*

brok·en INTERRUPTED /£ˈbrəʊ·kən, $ˈbroʊ-/ *adj* interrupted or not continuous • *Nicki and Steve have had a lot of broken* **nights** (= nights with only short periods of sleep) *since their baby was born.* • *He tried to explain what had happened in broken* (= not spoken easily and stopping a lot) *English.*

brok·en ENDED /£ˈbrəʊ·kən, $ˈbroʊ-/ *adj* [not gradable] destroyed or ended • *a broken engagement* • *She comes from a broken* **home** (= one where the parents have separated). • *Broken* **marriages** *are becoming more common.*

brok·en NOT KEPT /£ˈbrəʊ·kən, $ˈbroʊ-/ *adj* [not gradable] (of a law, rule or promise) disobeyed or not kept • *a broken promise/vow*

bro·ker /£ˈbrəʊ·kəʳ, $ˈbroʊ·kɚ/ *n* [C] a person who buys and sells foreign money, shares in companies, etc., for other people, or a person who talks to opposing sides, esp. governments, making arrangements for them or bringing to an end disagreements • *a commodity/insurance/mortgage broker.* • *I resisted the urge to call my broker and instruct him to sell all my stocks.* • *He works for a firm of broker-dealers.* • *During the war Wallas became a power-broker in English governmental circles.* • *He was a man of God, a peace broker, prepared to listen and talk to anyone if it helped to free hostages.*

brok·er *obj* /£ˈbrəʊ·kəʳ, $ˈbroʊ·kɚ/ *v* [T] • *It was Ovitz who brokered the multi-billion dollar deal between the two companies.* • *So far the foreign ministers have failed in their attempts to broker a ceasefire.* • *The accord was one of the broadest the United Nations has brokered in 14 months of warfare.*

brol·ly /£ˈbrɒl·i, $ˈbrɑː·li/ *n* [C] *esp. Br and Aus infml for* UMBRELLA

brom·ide /£ˈbrəʊ·maɪd, $ˈbroʊ-/ *n* [C/U] a drug used to calm down people who are very unhappy or worried • *He took a/some bromide to calm his nerves.* • A bromide is also a remark or statement about something that, although it might be true, is boring and meaningless because it has been said so many times before.

bronch·i·al /£ˈbrɒŋ·ki·əl, $ˈbrɑːŋ-/ *adj* [not gradable] of or being the pipes that carry air from the WINDPIPE (= tube in the throat) to the lungs • *bronchial tubes* • *He had bronchial* **pneumonia** *as a child.*

bronch·i·tis /£brɒŋˈkaɪ·tɪs, $brɑːŋˈkaɪ·t̬ɪs/ *n* [U] an illness in which the BRONCHIAL tubes become infected and swollen, resulting in coughing and difficulty in breathing

bron·co /£ˈbrɒŋ·kəʊ, $ˈbrɑːŋ·koʊ/ *n* [C] *pl* **broncos** a wild horse of the western US

bron·to·saur·us /£ˌbrɒn·təˈsɔː·rəs, $ˌbrɑːn·t̬əˈsɔːr·əs/ *n* [C] *pl* **brontosauruses** or **brontosauri** /£ˌbrɒn·təˈsɔː·raɪ, $ˌbrɑːn·t̬əˈsɔːr·aɪ/ a large DINOSAUR that ate plants and had four legs, a long neck and tail and a small head

Bronx cheer /£brɒŋks, $brɑːŋks/ *n* [C] *Am slang for* RASPBERRY SOUND

bronze /£brɒnz, $brɑːnz/ *adj* [not gradable], *n* (of) a hard metal made of COPPER and TIN • *The church bell is made of bronze.* [U] • *Rodin is famous for his bronze* (= statue made of bronze) *'The Thinker'.* [C] • *The bronze river* (= yellowish brown, the colour of bronze) *wound its way through the valley below.* • The **Bronze Age** was the time when tools and weapons were made of bronze, before iron was discovered. Compare **Iron Age** at IRON METAL; **Stone Age** at STONE ROCK. • A **bronze (medal)** is a small round piece of bronze given to a person who finishes third in a competition: *He* **got** *a bronze in the high jump.*

bronzed /£brɒnzd, $brɑːnzd/ *adj* • *Elaine came back from her holiday looking bronzed* (= very brown from having been in the sun) *and beautiful.*

brooch, *Am also* **broach** /£brəʊtʃ, $broʊtʃ/, *Am also* **pin** *n* [C] a small piece of jewellery with a pin at the back that is fastened to a woman's clothes • *She was wearing a small silver brooch.* • PIC› **Jewellery, Pins and needles**

brood GROUP /bruːd/ *n* [C] a group of young birds all born at the same time, or *(humorous)* a person's young children • *The blackbird flew back and forth to its brood.* • *(humorous) Ann was at the party with her brood.* • A **brood mare** is a female horse kept especially for breeding.

brood·y /ˈbruː·di/ *adj* **-ier, -iest** • *The hen was now broody* (= ready to sit on her eggs). • *(infml)* A person, esp. a woman or girl, who is broody feels as if she would like to have a baby: *Much to her surprise, Ruth started feeling broody in her late twenties.*

brood·i·ness /ˈbruː·di·nəs/ *n* [U] • *It always brings on an attack of broodiness when I go and see my sister and her children.*

brood THINK /bruːd/ *v* [I] to think silently for a long time about things that make you sad, worried or angry • *I wish she wouldn't sit brooding in her room all day.* • *He sat at his desk, brooding* **darkly on/over** *why she had left him.*

brood·ing /ˈbruː·dɪŋ/ *adj* • *He stood there in the corner of the room, a dark, brooding* (= worrying) **presence**.

brood·y /ˈbruː·di/ *adj* **-ier, -iest** • *Mike Welbrock plays the broody* (= always thinking unhappy thoughts), *self-centred teenager.*

brook STREAM /brʊk/ *n* [C] a small stream • *I could hear the sound of a* **babbling** *brook.*

brook *obj* ALLOW /brʊk/ *v* [T] *fml* to allow or accept (esp. difference of opinion or intention) • *At this point the waiter suggested it was time to go and would brook no disagreement.* • *The prime minister's unwillingness to brook dissent has been particularly noticeable of late.* • *She won't brook any criticism of her work.*

broom BRUSH /bruːm, brʊm/ *n* [C] a brush with a long handle, used for cleaning the floor • *Take this broom and get busy, I want the whole shop swept out.* • *The broom* **handle** *has broken.* • See also BROOMSTICK. • PIC› **Brush**

broom PLANT /bruːm/ *n* [U] a wild and garden bush with small yellow flowers

broom·stick /ˈbruːm·stɪk, ˈbrʊm-/ *n* [C] a long brush made of sticks, esp. of the type traditionally used by WITCHES for flying around on in children's stories • *Every Hallowe'en, Warty the witch would fly around on her broomstick with her long pointed black hat and her long pointed black cat.* • *"Bedknobs and Broomsticks"* (title of a film about friendly witches, 1971) • PIC› **Brush**

Bros. /£brɒs, $brɑːs/ *pl n abbreviation for* brothers (when used in a company's name) • *He hired a suit from Moss Bros.*

broth /£brɒθ, $brɑːθ/ *n* [U] a thin soup, usually with vegetables or rice in it, traditionally made with the liquid in which meat bones have been boiled • *turkey broth*

broth·el /£ˈbrɒθ·əl, $ˈbrɑː·θəl/ *n* [C] a place where men go and pay to have sex with PROSTITUTES

bro·ther /£ˈbrʌð·əʳ, $-ɚ/ *n* [C] a man or boy with the same parents as another person • *Do you have any brothers and sisters?* • *I have three brothers and a sister.* • *Johnny is my younger/older/big/baby/little brother.* • *It's your brother on the phone.* • 'Brothers' is a way of speaking to or of people who are members of the same group or who share a similar way of thinking: *Let us unite, brothers!* [as form of address] • Brother is the title of a man, such as a MONK, who belongs to a religious organization: *Brother Michael and Brother John were deep in conversation.* • 'I am not my brother's keeper' means that you are not responsible for what someone else does or for what happens to them. • LP **Relationships** PIC **Family tree**

bro·ther–in–law /£ˈbrʌð·ə·rɪn·lɔː, $-ɚ·ɪn·lɑː/ *n* [C] *pl* **brothers-in-law** or *Br also* **brother-in-laws** • A person's **brother-in-law** is the brother of their husband or wife, or the man who is married to their sister, or the man who is married to the sister of their wife or husband.

bro·ther·ly /£ˈbrʌð·əl·i, $-ɚ·li/ *adj* • *Can I give you some brotherly* (=affectionate and interested, as from a brother) *advice?* • *It was an act of brotherly* **love** (= kindness to other humans).

bro·ther·hood /£ˈbrʌð·ə·hʊd, $ˈ-ɚ-/ *n* [C + sing/pl v] (the members of) a particular organization or (more generally) friendship and loyalty • *The various groups eventually fused into a single brotherhood.* • *The ideal of the brotherhood* **of man** (= where everyone loves each other) *is still far from reality.*

brougham /bruːm/ *n* [C] a light carriage pulled by a single horse and ridden in by two to four people, used in Europe and N. America in the 19th century

brought /£brɔːt, $brɑːt/ *past simple and past participle of* BRING

brou·ha·ha /ˈbruː·hɑː·hɑː/ *n* [U] *infml* a lot of noise or angry complaining (about something) • *There was a brouhaha* **over** *the new production of 'The Magic Flute'.*

brow /braʊ/ *n* [C usually sing] *slightly literary* the FOREHEAD (=the flat part of the face above the eyes and below the hair) • *He paused at the top of the hill and* **mopped** *his brow* (=rubbed the wetness away). • *She* **wrinkled** *her brow as she thought.* • *(fig.) As the car came* **over the** *brow* (= the top part) *of the hill it swerved wildly.* • PIC **Body**

brow·beat *obj* /ˈbraʊ·biːt/ *v* [T] *past simple* **browbeat**, *past part* **browbeaten** /£ˈbraʊˌbiː·tən, $-t̬ən/ to try to force (someone) to do something by threatening them or using strong and unfair persuasion • *Don't be browbeaten* **into** *working more hours than you want.* [+ obj + v-*ing*]

brown /braʊn/ *adj, n* **-er, -est** (of) the colour of chocolate or earth • *Both my parents have* **dark** *brown hair.* • *The autumn leaves formed a thick brown carpet underfoot.* • *Her skin is quite pale in the winter but she* **goes** *very brown in the sun.* • *His eyes were of a deep dark brown.* • *(Am)* To **brown-bag** is to have a meal in the middle of the day esp. with other people, to which you take your own food, usually in a brown paper bag: *If the weather's fine I thought we might brown-bag it outside somewhere.* ○ *We're having a* **brown-bag lunch** *in the park tomorrow – do you want to join us?* • **Brown bread** is bread which is light brown in colour, often still containing all the natural features of the grain in it. • **Brown rice** is rice which still has its outer covering. • **Brown paper** is a strong type of brown paper which is often used for wrapping items in when they are to be sent through the post. • **Brown sugar** is sugar that has only been partly REFINED.

brown *(obj)* /braʊn/ *v* • *I browned* (=made brown by cooking) *the meat quickly in a frying pan before putting it into the oven to cook.* [T] • **Lightly** *brown the onion before adding the liquid.* [T] • *Allow the onion rings to brown before adding the spices.* [I] • *(Br and Aus infml dated)* To be **browned off** is to be tired and annoyed with something: *I think she gets a bit browned off with him borrowing the car all the time.*

brown·ish /ˈbraʊ·nɪʃ/ *adj* • Brownish means slightly brown: *She's got strange brownish-green eyes.*

Brown·ie GIRL /ˈbraʊ·ni/, *Br* **Brownie Guide** *n* [C] a girl aged between 7 and 10 years old who is a member of the international organization for young women called the Guides, or the Girl Scouts in the US • *New Brownies make a promise to be kind and helpful.* • *The girls wanted to join a Brownie* **pack** (= group). • *(humorous)* If you **get/score brownie points**, you get approval for your actions, esp. by doing something helpful: *I thought I could score some brownie points with my mother-in-law by offering to cook dinner.*

brown·ie CAKE /ˈbraʊ·ni/ *n* [C] *esp. Am* a small square chocolate cake often with nuts in it

brown·stone /£ˈbraʊn·stəʊn, $-stoʊn/ *n* [C] *esp. Am* a house with its front built of a reddish brown stone, esp. common in New York City

browse LOOK /braʊz/ *v* [I] to look through a book or magazine in a relaxed, enjoyable way, looking briefly at several pages, or to walk around a shop looking at several items without intending to buy any of them • *Roz would spend entire days browsing in the bookshops on Charing Cross Road.* • *I was browsing* **through** *a magazine one day when a photograph caught my eye.* • *"Are you looking for anything in particular, madam?" "No, I'm just browsing."*

browse /braʊz/ *n* [U] • *We went for a browse around an antique shop.* • *I* **had** *a browse* **through** *the books on his desk.*

browse FEED /braʊz/ *v* [I] (of animals) to feed on grass, leaves, etc. in a relaxed way • *The young deer were browsing (***on** *grass) under the trees.*

bruise /bruːz/ *n* [C] an injury or mark where the skin has not been broken but is darker in colour, often as a result of being hit by something • *His arms and back were* **covered in** *bruises.* • *Your legs are covered in* **bumps and** *bruises – what have you been doing?* • *She had a few* **cuts and** *bruises but nothing serious.* • *I noticed a dark purple bruise on her throat.* • *One or two of the peaches had bruises on them which I had to cut out.*

bruise *(obj)* /bruːz/ *v* • *So how did you bruise your arm?* [T] • *The problem with ripe fruit is that it bruises easily.* [I] • *(fig.) I don't think it broke Jamie's heart when Cherise left him, but it certainly bruised his* **ego** (= hurt him because he felt less important and valuable). [T]

bruised /bruːzd/ *adj* • *She was* **badly** *bruised but otherwise unhurt.* • *She was all* **battered and** *bruised having fallen off her bike the day before.* • *(fig.) The break-up of a love affair generally leaves both partners feeling rather bruised* (= hurt emotionally).

bruis·ing /ˈbruː·zɪŋ/ *n* [U], *adj* • *The bruising* (= These bruises) *should soon become less painful.* • *(fig.) I had a bruising* **encounter** (= an unpleasant meeting) *with my ex-husband last week.*

bruis·er /£ˈbruː·zəʳ, $-zɚ/ *n* [C] *infml humorous* a big strong man, or a large fat, esp. boy baby • *Helen's boyfriend looked like a bit of a bruiser – I wouldn't like to meet him down a dark alley!* • *She's such a petite woman and yet she's got a real bruiser of a baby.*

bruit *obj* /bruːt/ *v* [T usually passive] *fml or humorous* to tell everyone (a piece of news) • *It's been bruited* **abroad/around** *that he's going to leave the company.*

brum·by /ˈbrʌm·bi/ *n* [C] *Aus* a wild horse, esp. one that has escaped from a farm

brunch /brʌntʃ/ *n* [C] a meal eaten in the late morning; a combination of BREAKFAST and LUNCH • *We had a Sunday brunch of champagne and bagels.*

brun·ette /bruˈnet/ *n* [C] a white woman or girl with dark hair • *Me, I prefer brunettes to blondes.*

brunt /brʌnt/ *n* [U] **the brunt of** the main force of (esp. something unpleasant) • *The people of this area have* **taken/borne** *the brunt of the missile attacks.* • *Small companies are* **feeling** *the* **full** *brunt of the recession.* • *He seemed to have* **escaped** *the* **full** *brunt of his critics' censure.* • *For the first time in many years, the brunt of the snow hit the south-east.*

brush TOOL /brʌʃ/ *n* [C] an object with short pieces of stiff hair, plastic or wire fixed into a usually wooden or plastic base or handle, which is used for cleaning, tidying the hair or painting • *If my hair looks a mess, it's because I can't find my brush.* • *The bristles on this brush are worn out.* • *You'll need a brush to get those crumbs up.* • *He paints with a very fine brush.* • Brush is often used as a combining form: *a hairbrush* ○ *a toothbrush* ○ *a paintbrush* ○ *a clothes/lavatory/nail/scrubbing/shaving/shoe brush* • **A** brush is also an act of cleaning with a brush: *These shoes need a good brush.* ○ *Don't forget to* **give** *your hair a brush before you go out.* ○ *Have you* **given** *your teeth a brush, Rosie?* • PIC **Brush, Drawing and painting**

brush *(obj)* /brʌʃ/ *v* • *When did he last brush his* **teeth**, *she wondered.* [T] • *She brushed her* **hair** *with long, regular strokes.* [T] • *My trousers got covered in mud, but luckily I was able to brush them clean.* [T + obj + adj] • *Would you brush the hairs* **off** *the back of my coat for me* (=remove

always + adv/prep] • If you brush yourself or your clothes **off** or *(Br also)* **down**, you remove dust, dirt, hair, etc. from your clothes using your hands or a brush: *When she fell off her bike, she just got up, brushed herself down and rode off again.* [T] • *Jackie brushed her hair out of/from her eyes* (= pushed it away from her eyes with her hands). [T] • *He brushed his tears/a fly* **away** (= removed them with a movement of his hand). [M] • *(fig.) She brushed their objections* **aside** (= refused to consider them seriously), *saying "Leave it to me."* [M] • *(fig.) He just brushed* **off** (= ignored) *all their criticisms.* [M] • If you **brush** someone **off** or **give** someone **the brush-off**, you refuse to talk or be pleasant to them: *I tried to be friendly but he brushed me off.* ○ *So she's given you the brush-off, has she?*

brushed /brʌʃt/ *adj* [not gradable] • *Her nightdress was made of brushed* **nylon/cotton** (= cloth treated to make it soft and furry).

brush *(obj)* TOUCH /brʌʃ/ *v* to touch (something) quickly and lightly or carelessly • *His lips gently brushed her cheek and he was gone.* [T] • *Charlotte brushed* **against** *him* (= touched him quickly and lightly with her arm or body) *as she left the room.* [I always + adv/prep] • To brush **past/by** (someone) is to walk quickly past them, usually because you do not want to speak to them: *Ignoring their protests, Newman brushed past waiting journalists.* [I always + adv/prep] ○ *She brushed straight by, without even looking at me.* [I always + adv/prep]

brush /brʌʃ/ *n* [C usually sing] • *He felt the brush* **of** *her hand on his* (= her hand touched his lightly and quickly). • A brush **with** something or someone is an experience of dealing with or facing it or them, which is usually unpleasant: *Jim* **had** *a brush with death* (= was nearly killed) *on the motorway.* ○ *I* **had** *a brush with* (= an unpleasant meeting or disagreement with) *my boss this morning.* ○ *Being stopped for speeding was Jo's first brush* **with the law** (= experience of being in trouble with the police).

brush BUSHES /brʌʃ/ *n* [U] *Am* small low bushes or the rough land they grow on, or BRUSHWOOD • *The land was covered in low brush and rocky outcrops.* • *The dry weather has increased the risk of brush* **fires**.

brush TAIL /brʌʃ/ *n* [C] the tail of a FOX

brush up on *obj v adv prep* [T] to improve your knowledge of (something already learned but partly forgotten) • *I thought I'd brush up on my French before going to Paris.*

brush·stroke /£ˈbrʌʃ·strəʊk, $-stroʊk/ *n* [C usually pl] the way in which esp. paint is put on to a surface with a brush, or *(fig.)* the way in which a plan or idea is explained • *The artist painted this picture using tiny/vigorous/swirling brushstrokes* (= movements of the brush). • *(fig.) She sketched out her idea of the perfect lover using only the broadest brushstrokes* (= without giving us any details).

brush·wood /ˈbrʌʃ·wʊd/, **brush** *n* [U] small branches that have broken off from trees and bushes • *We gathered some brushwood to make a fire.*

brush·work /£ˈbrʌʃ·wɜːk, $-wɜːrk/ *n* [U] the particular style that an artist has of putting paint with a brush onto the painting • *Van Gogh then studied in Paris where he developed his individual style of brushwork and a more colourful palette.*

brusque /£bruːsk, $brʌsk/ *adj* quick and rude in manner or speech • *I got his secretary who was rather brusque* **with** *me and told me to call back later.*

brusque·ly /£ˈbruː·skli, $ˈbrʌs·kli/ *adv* • *"I simply haven't got time to deal with the problem today," she said brusquely.*

brusque·ness /£ˈbruːsk·nəs, $ˈbrʌsk-/ *n* [U]

brus·sels sprout /ˌbrʌs·əlzˈspraʊt/, *Br also* **brus·sel sprout**, **sprout** *n* [C] a green vegetable like a very small CABBAGE that is boiled and eaten • *Most children don't like brussels sprouts.* • PIC **Vegetables**

brut·al /£ˈbruː·təl, $-t̬əl/ *adj* cruel, violent and completely without human feelings • *He had been a brutal dictator and had many enemies.* • *He had presided over a brutal regime in which thousands of people had 'disappeared' in mysterious circumstances.* • *She was taken to a small cell where she was subjected to a brutal beating.* • *He was imprisoned in 1945 for the brutal* **murder** *of a 12-year old school girl.* • Brutal can also mean unpleasantly truthful: *She spoke with brutal* **honesty** *– I was too old for the job.* ○ *How could I tell him the brutal truth – that I had stopped loving him and that's why I had left him.* • (NL)

brut·al·ly /£ˈbruː·təl·i, $-t̬əl-/ *adv* • *The old man had been brutally attacked/murdered.* • *It is the mind-set of brutally repressive regimes everywhere – if you oppose the system, you will be destroyed.* • *Be brutally* **honest/frank** *with me* (= Tell me the unpleasant truth). *Do I look fat in this dress?*

brut·al·i·ty /£bruːˈtæl·ə·ti, $-t̬i/ *n* • *Seeing so much brutality* (= cruelty) **towards** *prisoners had not hardened them to it.* [U] • *The brutalities of war are glossed over in news reports.* [C] • (NL)

brut·al·ize *obj, Br and Aus usually* **-ise** /£ˈbruː·təl·aɪz, $-t̬əl-/ *v* [T] • To brutalize someone is to treat them in a cruel and violent way: *It is claimed that the police routinely* *brutalize prisoners.* • To brutalize someone is also to make them cruel and remove from them all human feelings by continually treating them in a cruel and violent way: *So many children who commit violent crimes have themselves been brutalized by years of abuse and neglect.*

brute /bruːt/ *n* [C] a rough and sometimes violent man • *Take your hands off me, you brute!* [as form of address] • *He won't let her see her friends, the selfish brute.* • A brute can also be an animal, esp. a large one: *Your dog's an ugly brute, isn't it?* ○ *The oldest elephant was lame, poor brute.*

brute /bruːt/ *adj* [before n; not gradable] • *In the end she used brute* **force** (=simple physical strength) *to push him out.*

brut·ish /£ˈbruː·tɪʃ, $-ṭɪʃ/ *adj* • *Nicola Colman plays the part of the long suffering wife, Peter Davison her brutish* (=cruel and without human feeling) *husband.*

bruv /brʌv/ *n* [C usually sing] *Br infml humorous for* BROTHER • *I know he's a bit of an idiot but he's still my bruv, ain't he.* • *All right, bruv, how're you doing, mate?* [as form of address]

BS /ˌbiːˈes/ *n, v, exclamation Am abbreviation for* BULLSHIT

BSc /ˌbiː·esˈsiː/, *Am also* **BS** /ˌbiːˈes/ *n* [C] *abbreviation for* Bachelor of Science (=a first level college degree in science, or someone having this degree) • *C.G. Smith, BSc* • LP› **Schools and colleges**

BSE /ˌbiː·esˈiː/ *n* [U] *Br* bovine spongiform encephalopathy (=a disease in cattle which damages the brain and causes the death of the animal)

BST /ˌbiː·esˈtiː/ *n* [U] *abbreviation for* **British Summer Time**, see at BRITISH

bub /bʌb/ *n* [C] *Am infml dated* a way of addressing a man, sometimes in a slightly angry way • *That may be what you do at home, but listen bub, you don't do it here!* • LP› **Titles and forms of address**

bub·ble /ˈbʌb·l̩/ *n* [C] a ball of air in a liquid or a delicate hollow sphere floating on top of a liquid or in the air • *As water begins to boil, bubbles rise ever faster to the surface.* • *I plunged my arms into the thick bubbles and furiously began scrubbing the pots.* • *I love champagne – I think it's the bubbles that make it so nice.* • *Rosie was out in the garden* **blowing** *bubbles.* • *(fig.) She was blissfully happy until one day, suddenly, the bubble* **burst** (=that happy state suddenly ended). • *(esp. Br)* **Bubble and squeak** is a food made by mixing together and heating cooked potato and CABBAGE. • **Bubble bath** is a special liquid soap with a pleasant smell that you put in a bath to make lots of bubbles: *She was looking forward to a relaxing bubble bath* (=a bath with this soap in it) *when she got home.* • **Bubble gum** is **chewing gum** that you can blow into the shape of a bubble. • *(specialized)* **Bubble-jet** printing is a very fast and quiet method of printing in which the ink is directed electronically onto the paper. • *(trademark)* **Bubble wrap** is a sheet of plastic bubbles that is used for wrapping items in order to protect them, for example, when they are being posted or delivered somewhere. • *"I'm Forever Blowing Bubbles"* (title of a song written by Joan Kenbrovin and J.W. Kellette, 1919)

bub·ble /ˈbʌb·l̩/ *v* [I] • *Is the stew bubbling yet?* • *We could hear the porridge beginning to bubble* (=make the sound of bubbles rising to the top). • *(fig.) Feelings of anger and shame were bubbling* (=very active) *inside me.* • *(fig.) She was bubbling* **(over)** *with excitement/enthusiasm* (=full of it and expressing it to everyone).

bub·bly /ˈbʌb·li/ *n* [U] *infml* • Bubbly is CHAMPAGNE (=expensive fizzy white or pink alcoholic drink): *Let's* **crack open** *a bottle of bubbly to celebrate.* • See also BUBBLY.

bub·bly /ˈbʌb·li/ *adj infml* (esp. of a woman or girl) attractively full of energy and enthusiasm • *She's got a lovely bubbly personality.* • See also **bubbly** at BUBBLE.

bu·bon·ic plague /£bjuːˈbɒn·ɪk, $-ˈbɑː·nɪk/ *n* [U] a very infectious disease spread by RATS (=animals like large mice) causing swellings, fever and usually death. In the 14th century it killed half the people living in Europe.

buc·can·eer /£ˌbʌk·əˈnɪəʳ, $-ˈnɪr/ *n* [C] a person who attacked and stole from ships at sea, esp. in the 17th and 18th centuries; a PIRATE CRIMINAL

buck MONEY /bʌk/ *n* [C] *infml* a DOLLAR • *(esp. Am and Aus) She left home with a couple of bucks in her pocket and the shirt on her back.* • Buck is used in a number of expressions about money, usually expressions referring to a lot of money: *He earns* **mega-bucks** (=a lot of money) *working for an American bank.* ○ *Writing a best-selling novel is a good way to* **make a fast/quick/an easy** *buck* (=earn money easily and not always honestly). • LP› **Money**

buck ANIMAL /bʌk/ *n* [C] *pl* **buck** *or* **bucks** the male of some animals, such as deer and rabbits, or a male or female ANTELOPE in South Africa • *There was a big buck rabbit sitting calmly among the lettuces.* • **Bucks party** is *Aus for* **stag party**. See at STAG ANIMAL. • Compare DOE.

buck RESPONSIBILITY /bʌk/ *n* [U] *infml* responsibility for getting something done • **Buck-passing** is when you give a difficult problem to someone else for them to deal with although it should really be your responsibility: *"The time for buck-passing has passed," said the politician.* • *(saying)* 'The buck stops here' means that the person speaking is responsible for making decisions and will take the blame if things go wrong.

buck *(obj)* JUMP /bʌk/ *v* (of a horse) to jump into the air with all four feet off the ground and the back arched • *When he tried to put a saddle on it, the horse bucked wildly.* [I] • See also BUCK UP.

buck *obj* BE DIFFERENT /bʌk/ *v* [T] **buck the trend** to be noticeably different from the way that a situation is developing generally, esp. in connection with financial matters • *January's newspaper circulation figures show that the 'quality' daily newspapers have bucked the trend of a market sector that continues to decline.* • *In late trading Friday, Jaguar shares bucked the downward tide in London's stock market and rose five pence to 725 pence ($11·44).*

buck MAN /bʌk/ *n* [C] *literary* a stylish young man in the 18th and 19th centuries • *A Regency buck*

buck up *(obj)*, **buck** *(obj)* **up** *v adv infml* to become or make happier or more positive • *(dated) Oh, buck up for heaven's sake, Anthony! I'm sick of looking at your miserable face.* [I] • *She was told that if she didn't buck her* **ideas** *up* (=start working in a more positive way), *she'd be out of a job.* [M]

buck·et /ˈbʌk·ɪt/ *n* [C] a container with an open top and a handle, often used for carrying liquids • *Armed with a bucket and a mop, I started washing the floor.* • *I took my two-year old nephew down to the beach with his bucket* **and spade**. • *The waiter brought a bottle of champagne in a silver* **ice** *bucket to our table.* • *She mistook the fire bucket for modern art.* • *I threw a bucket* (=the amount a bucket contains) *of cold water over him to sober him up.* • *(infml) The rain came down* **in buckets** (=in great amounts). • *(infml) That was such a sad film – I* **wept buckets** (=cried a lot) *at the end of it.* • *(infml) He earns* **bucket-loads** (=a lot) *of money.* • A **bucket seat** is a rounded seat with high sides for one person, esp. in an old-fashioned car. • PIC› **Cleaning, Cutlery** Ⓢ

buck·et /ˈbʌk·ɪt/ *v* [I] *Br and Aus infml* • **It/The rain** *bucketed* **down** (=it rained heavily) *all weekend.*

buck·et shop *n* [C] *Br infml* a travel company that sells aircraft tickets at a low price

buck·le FASTENER /ˈbʌk·l̩/ *n* [C] a piece of metal at one end of a belt or strap, used to fasten the two ends together and often also as a decoration • *Andy's favourite belt has a buckle with his name engraved on it.* • *She gazed proudly at the shiny buckles on her shoes.* • *Deep in thought, Marsha* **fastened/did up** *the buckle on her briefcase.* • LP› **Dressing and undressing** PIC› **Shoes**

buck·le *obj* /ˈbʌk·l̩/ *v* [T] • *She bent over to buckle her* **shoes**. • *Grant buckled his seat* **belt**. • *He buckled his raincoat* (=fastened the belt) *tightly and set off on foot.* • *The plane was about to take off so I buckled* **myself into** *my seat* (=fastened the safety belt around me).

buck·led /ˈbʌk·l̩d/ *adj* • *She was wearing a tightly buckled belt to show off her thin waist.* • *On his feet he wore buckled patent leather slippers.* • *All 50 states now require infants and children to travel buckled* **into** *a car seat or safety belt.*

buck·le *(obj)* BEND /ˈbʌk·l̩/ *v* to bend or become bent, often as a result of force, heat or weakness • *The intense heat from the fire had caused the factory roof to buckle.* [I] • *Both* **wheels** *on the bicycle had been badly buckled.* [T] • *I felt faint and my* **knees** *began to buckle.* [I] • *(fig.) But these were difficult times and a lesser man would have buckled* **under the strain** (=been unable to deal with the situation). [I]

buck·le down *v adv* [I] to start working hard • *He'll have to buckle down* **(to** *his work) soon if he wants to pass these exams.*

buck na·ked *adj Am infml* completely naked • *I ran down the stairs, buck naked, to answer the phone.*

buck·shot /£ˈbʌk·ʃɒt, $-ʃɑːt/ *n* [U] large pieces of metal which are often in the shape of balls fired from a SHOTGUN when hunting animals

buck·skin /ˈbʌk·skɪn/ *n* [U] soft, strong leather made from the skin of a deer or a sheep

buck tooth /bʌk/ *n* [C] *pl* **buck teeth** *infml* an upper front tooth that sticks out

buck·wheat /ˈbʌk·wiːt/ *n* [U] small dark grain used for feeding animals and for making flour

bu·col·ic /£bjuˈkɒl·ɪk, $-ˈkɑː·lɪk/ *adj literary* related to the countryside • *The painting shows a typically bucolic scene with peasants harvesting crops in a field.*

bud PLANT PART /bʌd/ *n* [C] a small part of a plant which sticks out from a branch or stem and will develop into a flower or leaf • *The trees all around were covered in buds.* • *In the garden most of the plants are* **in bud** (= covered with buds). • *"Rough winds do shake the darling buds of May"* (Shakespeare, Sonnet 18) • PIC› **Flowers and plants**

bud /bʌd/ *v* [I] **-dd-** • *The unusually cold winter has caused many plants to bud* (= produce buds) *late this year.*

bud·ding /ˈbʌd·ɪŋ/ *adj* [not gradable] • *(fig.) The budding* (= beginning) *journalist was printing his own newspaper at an early age.* • *(fig.) While still at school she was clearly a budding* **genius** (= showing how clever she would become).

bud MAN /bʌd/, **bud·dy** *n* [C] *Am infml* a way of addressing a man, sometimes used to show anger • *Look, bud, it wasn't broken when I left it with you!* [as form of address] • LP› **Titles and forms of address**

Bud·dhi·sm /ˈbʊd·ɪ·zᵊm/ *n* [U] a religion that originally comes from India and teaches that personal spiritual improvement will lead to a person escaping from human suffering

bud·dhist /ˈbʊd·ɪst/ *n* [C]

bud·dy /ˈbʌd·i/ *n* [C] *infml* a close friend • *Bob and I have been great buddies for years.* • *(Am)* Buddy is sometimes used when speaking to another man, esp. if annoyed: *Drink up and go home, buddy.* • LP› **Titles and forms of address**

budge *(obj)* /bʌdʒ/ *v* [usually in negatives] to move or change (something) a little • *I've tried moving the desk but it won't budge/I can't budge it.* [I/T] • *Despite the risk of losing their jobs, they won't budge* **from/on** *their position.* [I] • *(Br infml)* You can say **budge up** to someone to ask them to move along a seat to let someone else sit beside you: *Hey, budge up, there's room for another one on the bench and the game is about to start.*

bud·get FINANCIAL PLAN /ˈbʌdʒ·ɪt/ *n* a plan to show how much money a person or organization will earn and how much they will need or be able to spend • *The firm has* **drawn up** *a budget for the coming financial year.* [C] • *Libraries are finding it increasingly difficult to remain* **within** *(their) budget.* [C/U] • *The government's Budget will mix new taxes and spending cuts.* [C] • *It's still too early to say if the building will be completed* **on** *budget* (= in agreement with the financial plan). [U]

bud·get *(obj)* /ˈbʌdʒ·ɪt/ *v* • *I must budget* (= plan how to spend) *my wages carefully between rent, food and clothing.* [T] • *(fig.) He has so many friends that he has to budget his time* (= plan how he will use his time) *to be able to see them all.* [T] • To budget also means to save money in a planned way: *She budgets* **for** *one holiday abroad every year.* [I] • *The department budgeted* **to** *spend £4m this year.* [+ to infinitive]

bud·get·a·ry /£ˈbʌdʒ·ɪ·tri, $-ter·i/ *adj* [not gradable] • *budgetary constraints* • *The President was criticized for his stringent budgetary* **policy**.

bud·get CHEAP /ˈbʌdʒ·ɪt/ *adj* [before n] low in price; cheap • *budget holidays* • *budget prices* • LP› **Expensive**

bud·gie /ˈbʌdʒ·i/, *slightly fml* **bud·ge·ri·gar** /£ˈbʌdʒ·ə·rɪ·gɑːʳ, $-ɚ·ɪ·gɑːr/ *n* [C] a small, brightly coloured bird often kept as a pet in Britain

buff COLOUR /bʌf/ *n, adj* (of) a pale yellowish brown colour • *The letter arrived in a buff envelope.*

buff *obj* MAKE SHINE /bʌf/ *v* [T] to rub (an object made of metal, wood or leather) in order to make it shine, esp. using a soft cloth • *Let the wax dry on the wood then buff* **(up)** *the table with a cloth.* [T/M]

buff PERSON /bʌf/ *n* [C] *infml* a person who knows a lot about and is very interested in a particular subject • *a computer/opera/railway buff* • *She was a* **film/movie** *buff who went to the cinema at least three times a week.*

buff NAKED /bʌf/ *n* [U] **in the buff** with no clothes on • *We were a little surprised that she answered the door in the buff.*

buf·fa·lo /£ˈbʌf·ə·ləʊ, $-loʊ/ *n* [C] *pl* **buffaloes** or **buffalo** a large animal of the cattle family with long curved horns found in Africa, Asia and the US • *Great herds of buffalo migrated across the plains.*

buf·fer PROTECTOR /£ˈbʌf·əʳ, $-ɚ/ *n* something or someone that helps protect from harm • *Friends are excellent buffers in times of crisis.* [C] • *I bought a house as a buffer* **against** *inflation.* [C] • On a railway a buffer is either of the two protective metal parts at the front and back of a train that reduce damage if it hits something. There are also usually two buffers at the end of a track. [C] • A buffer is also a chemical that keeps a liquid from becoming more or less acidic. [C/U] • A **buffer state** is a peaceful country between two larger countries that reduces the chances of war between them.

buf·fer *obj* /£ˈbʌf·əʳ, $-ɚ/ *v* [T] • *It is foolish to believe that romantic love will buffer you against life's hardships.*

buf·fer FOOLISH MAN /£ˈbʌf·əʳ, $-ɚ/, **old buf·fer** *n* [C] *Br infml* a foolish, esp. old man • *Some* **old** *buffer was saying that nothing needed to be changed.*

buf·fet MEAL /£ˈbʊf·eɪ, $bəˈfeɪ/ *n* [C] a meal where people serve themselves from a variety of types of usually cold food and often eat standing up • *Are you having a sit-down meal or a buffet at the wedding?* • *(Br)* A buffet is also a restaurant at a station, where food and drinks can be bought and eaten. • *(esp. Br)* A **buffet car** on a train is a carriage where food and drinks can be bought. • LP› **'-et' words**

buf·fet *obj* HIT /ˈbʌf·ɪt/ *v* [T often passive] (of wind, rain, etc.) to hit (something) repeatedly and with great force • *The little boat was buffeted mercilessly by the waves.*

buf·foon /bəˈfuːn/ *n* [C] a person who does silly things, usually to make other people laugh • *Doesn't he get tired of* **playing the** *buffoon in class?*

buf·foon·e·ry /£bəˈfuː·nᵊr·i, $-nɚ-/ *n* [U] • *Enough of this buffoonery – everyone back to work!*

bug INSECT /bʌg/ *n* [C] *infml* a very small insect such as a BEDBUG • *She's allergic to the bugs that live in cats' fur.* • To be **bug-eyed** or to have **bug eyes** is to have eyes that stick out: *He stared at her in bug-eyed surprise.*

bug·gy /ˈbʌg·i/ *adj Am* • *The garden is too buggy* (= full of bugs) *to eat in.*

bug ILLNESS /bʌg/ *n* [C] *infml* a bacteria or a virus causing an illness that is usually not serious • *I* **had** *a* **tummy** *bug last week.* • *There's a bug* **going around** (= an illness that many people are getting).

bug FAULT /bʌg/ *n* [C] an unexpected mistake or problem in the way something, esp. a computer program, works • *This new database software is full of bugs.* • *A bug caused the company's computer system to crash.* • *There were a few bugs in the reorganization plan.*

bug DEVICE /bʌg/ *n* [C] a very small device fixed on to a telephone or hidden in a room that allows you to listen to what people are saying without them knowing • *We've discovered that someone, presumably from a rival company, has* **planted** *a bug in the conference room.*

bug *obj* /bʌg/ *v* [T] **-gg-** • *She suspected that her phone had been bugged* (= that a listening device had been hidden inside it).

bug *obj* ANNOY /bʌg/ *v* [T] **-gg-** *infml* to annoy, worry or upset • *His persistent moaning about his personal problems has been really bugging me lately.* • *Why must they keep bugging me about the rent?*

bug ENTHUSIASM /bʌg/ *n* [U] *slightly infml* a very strong enthusiasm for something • *I don't think I could ever* **catch/get** *the train-spotting bug.* • *He's been* **bitten by** *the sailing bug.*

bug·bear /£ˈbʌg·beəʳ, $-ber/ *n* [C] a particular thing that annoys or upsets you • *Smoking is a particular bugbear* **of** *his.*

bug·ger ANNOYANCE /£ˈbʌg·əʳ, $-ɚ/ *n* [C] *slightly taboo slang* a person who is annoying, silly or who you feel sympathy for, or a thing that is annoying or difficult to do • *He's such a bugger, always letting people down.* • *You* **stupid/silly** *bugger – you've ruined my dress!* • *The* **poor** *bugger has nowhere else to sleep.* • *This instruction book is a bugger* (= very difficult) *to understand.* • *(Br and Aus slang)* The phrase **bugger all** means very little or nothing: *You've done bugger all to help.*

bug·ger /£ˈbʌg·əʳ, $-ɚ/ *exclamation esp. Br and Aus slightly taboo slang* • Bugger is a swear word often used to express annoyance: *Oh bugger, it's raining again!* ○ *Bugger, I've forgotten the keys.* • Also, **bugger it** and **bugger me** can be used to show annoyance or surprise: *If* *they're not prepared to wait then bugger it – they'll have to go without dinner.* o *Bugger me – did you see that?*

bug·ger *obj* /£ˈbʌg·əʳ, $-ɚ/ *v Br and Aus slightly taboo slang* • *Stop buggering* **about** (= doing silly things), *you might hurt yourself!* [I] • *Stop buggering me* **about** (= stop treating me badly) *and tell me the truth!* [T] • *He's buggered* **(up)** (= broken) *the computer.* [T/M] • *I've buggered* **(up)** (= spoiled) *my chances of success.* [T/M] • *"***Bugger off!***"* (= go away) *he shouted at the cat in his garden.* [I] • *No one else was still at work so I decided to* **bugger off** (= leave) *early too.* [I] • *"Bugger Bognor"* (the last words of George V, 1936)

bug·gered /£ˈbʌg·əd, $-ɚd/ *adj Br and Aus slightly taboo slang* • *The television's buggered* (= broken). • *After a weekend's partying they were buggered* (= very tired). • If someone says they are **buggered if** they will do something they refuse to do it: *I'm buggered if I'll say sorry to her.*

bug·ger *obj* HAVE SEX /£ˈbʌg·əʳ, $-ɚ/ *v* [T] *taboo or law* to have sex in which a man's penis enters the other person's ANUS (= the opening through which solid excrement leaves the body)

bug·ger·y /£ˈbʌg·ᵊr·i, $ˈ-ɚ-/ *n* [U] *taboo or law*

bug·gy BABY CHAIR *Br* /ˈbʌg·i/, *Am and Aus* **stroll·er** *n* [C] a PUSHCHAIR • Buggy is *Am for* PRAM. • PIC› **Chair**

bug·gy CAR /ˈbʌg·i/ *n* [C] a small car usually with no roof which is designed for driving on rough ground • *a golf/dune buggy* • PIC› **Vehicles**

bug·gy CARRIAGE /ˈbʌg·i/ *n* [C] (esp. in the past) a light carriage pulled by one horse • *a horse-drawn buggy*

bu·gle /ˈbjuː·gl̩/ *n* [C] a musical instrument made of BRASS (= a type of metal) like a small TRUMPET used esp. in the army

build *(obj)* /bɪld/ *v past* **built** /bɪlt/ to make (something) by putting bricks or materials together • *They're building new houses by the river.* [T] • *The birds built their nest in the small fir tree.* [T] • *These old houses are built* (= made) **of** *stone.* [T] • *Contractors have started building on waste land near the town.* [I] • *She built me a bookcase./She built a bookcase* **for** *me.* [+ two objects] • *They built picture frames* **from/out of** *driftwood they found on the beach.* [T] • *The hotel had been built* **into** *the side of the rock* (= part of the hotel was inside the rock). [T] • *The conservatory was built* **on/onto** (= added to) *the house a few years ago.* [T] • *Of course, in those days houses were built* **to last** (= were built with the intention of making them last). [T] • *(fig.) We want to build* (= gradually make) *a better future for our children.* [T] • *(fig.) The film was built* **around** (= based on) *an improbable storyline.* [T] • *(fig.) Inequalities are often built* **into** (= cannot be separated from) *society.* [T] • *(fig.) When drawing up a contract it is vital to build* **in** (= include) *safety procedures.* [M] • *(fig.) A good relationship is built* (= based) **on** *trust.* [T] • *(fig.) We must build* **on** (= use as a base) *our reputation to expand the business.* [I] • *(saying)* 'Rome wasn't built in a day' means you can't expect to do important things very quickly.

build /bɪld/ *n* [C] • *She was small and of slight/slim build* (= had this type of body shape). • *He* **has the** *build* **of** (= a body like that of) *a top athlete.*

build·er /£ˈbɪl·dəʳ, $-dɚ/ *n* [C] • *There are a lot of Irishmen working as builders* (= people who make buildings) *in London.*

built /bɪlt/ *adj* [not gradable] • If you say that someone is built in a particular way you mean that their body is of the stated type: *He was tall and* **heavily/well** *built.* o *She is* **slightly** *built but her illness has made her look much thinner.* • If a room or place has **built-in** objects, esp. furniture they are attached and cannot be easily removed: *All the rooms have built-in* **cupboards/wardrobes**. o *(fig.) Some reference books have built-in* **obsolescence** (= they are made so that they will become dated before long). • A place that is **built-up** is one where there are a lot of buildings: *After several hours we drove into a built-up* **area**.

build up *(obj)*, **build** *(obj)* **up** *v adv* to (cause to) increase or become larger or stronger • *Traffic on the new bypass is building up.* [I] • *Tension is building up* **between** *the two communities.* [I] • *They gave him soup to build up his* **strength** [M] • *They gave him soup to build him up* (= make him stronger). [T] • *It took her ten years to build up her publishing business* (= make it strong and successful). [M] • To **build up** something/**build** something **up** also means to praise it, esp. in a way which will influence peoples' opinions: *For weeks the media has been building up the national basketball team.*

build–up /ˈbɪld·ʌp/ *n* [C] • *The build-up* (= increase) *of troops in the region makes war seem more likely.* • *The group got a big build-up* (= a lot of praise) *before their tour, being touted by many as the next Beatles.*

build·ing /ˈbɪl·dɪŋ/ *n* a structure with walls and a roof such as a house or factory, or the business of making buildings • *The once-empty site was now covered with buildings.* [C] • *It's not a very beautiful building but it's comfortable to be in.* [C] • *He started off in the building* **trade** *before opening his own restaurant.* [U] • *(fig.) Science and the arts are the building* **blocks** *of* (= the basic things that make) *a good education.* [U] • A **building site** is a piece of land on which a house or other building is being built. • *(Br and Aus)* A **building society**/*(Am and Aus)* **savings and loan association** is a business that lends you money if you want to buy a house or pays you INTEREST on money you invest there.

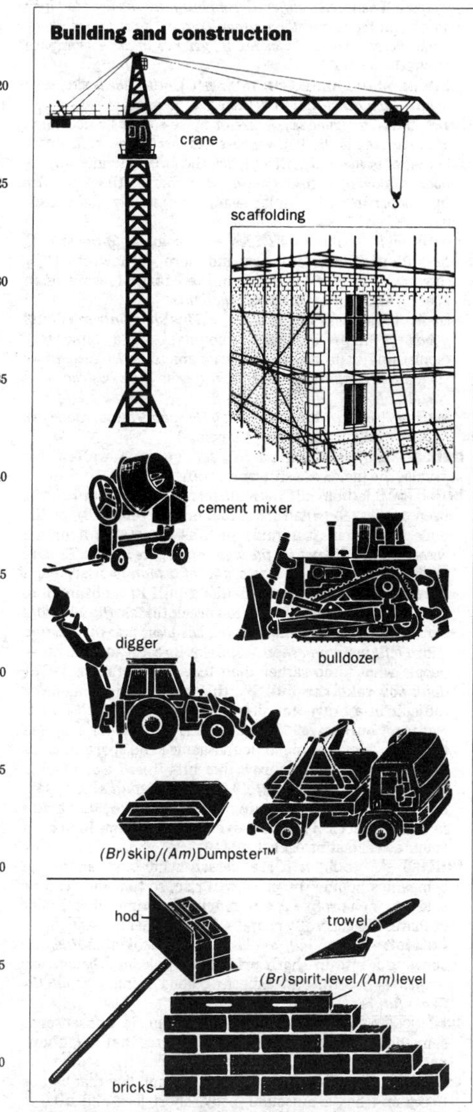

bulb PLANT /bʌlb/ *n* [C] a round root of some plants from which the plant grows • *Tulips, onions and lilies all grow from bulbs.* • *Plant the bulbs in soil 15 centimetres apart and three to five centimetres deep.* • PIC› **Flowers and plants**

bulb·ous /ˈbʌl·bəs/ *adj* • *(fig.) He had tiny eyes and a huge bulbous* (= fat and round) *nose.*

bulb LIGHT /bʌlb/ *n* [C] a **light bulb**, see at LIGHT BRIGHTNESS • PIC› **Lights**

bulge /bʌldʒ/ *v* [I] to stick out or be swollen • *He chewed the toffee, his cheeks bulging.* • *Her eyes bulged in surprise when she saw the house.* • *Flesh bulged* **out** *where the elasticated clothing was too tight.* • *His stomach was bulging* **over** *the* *top of his waistband.* • *(infml) Once all the guests had arrived the room was* **bulging at the seams** (= very full).

bulge /bʌldʒ/ *n* [C] • *I wondered what the bulge* (= swelling) *in her coat pocket was.* • *There was a bulge* (= sudden increase that soon returned to the usual level) **in** *spending in the early part of the year.*

bulg·ing /ˈbʌl·dʒɪŋ/ *adj* • *She dragged her bulging suitcase up the stairs.*

bu·lim·i·a (ner·vo·sa) /£bʊˌlɪm·i·ə·nɜːˈvəʊ·sə, £-ˈliː·mi-, $-nɜːrˈvoʊ-/ *n* [U] *medical* a mental illness in which someone, esp. a woman, stops eating, or eats without stopping for long periods, then eats uncontrollably and in large amounts, before taking action, often vomiting, to remove the food from their body • *Bulimia is partly motivated and maintained by a person's concern over their weight and shape.* • *When Helen suffered from bulimia, she used to binge on certain foods and then either exercise, take laxatives, or make herself vomit in order to get rid of it.* • Compare ANOREXIA.

bu·lim·ic /bʊˈlɪm·ɪk, -ˈliː·mɪk/ *n* [C], *adj* • *She is supposed to have been (a) bulimic when she was younger.*

bulk /bʌlk/ *n* largeness of size or mass • *It was a document of surprising bulk.* [U] • *She eased her large bulk* (= big body) *out of the chair.* [C] • *In fact,* **the bulk of** (= most of) *the book is taken up with criticizing other works.* [U] • *The office buys paper* **in bulk** (= in large amounts) *to keep down costs.* [U]

bulk *(obj)* /bʌlk/ *v* • *I added some potatoes to the stew to bulk it* **out** (= make it larger and more satisfactory). [T] • *(literary) Fears of his death* **bulked large** (= were often present and important) *in her thoughts.*

bulk /bʌlk/ *adj* [not gradable] • *This shop only sells bulk goods* (= things in large amounts). • To bulk **buy** (something) is to buy (it) in large amounts: *Because we're such a large family we find it cheaper to bulk buy foods we eat a lot of.*

bulk·y /ˈbʌl·ki/ *adj* **-ier, -iest** • *Her padded coat made her look very bulky* (= large and shapeless).

bulk·head /ˈbʌlk·hed/ *n* [C] *specialized* a wall which divides the inside of a ship or aircraft

bull [ANIMAL] /bʊl/ *n* [C] a male form of cattle that has not been CASTRATED (= had its sexual organs removed), or the male of particular animals such as the ELEPHANT or the WHALE • *They did not see the sign by the gate saying 'Beware of the bull'.* • *(fig.) He was a bull of a man* (= a large and strong man). • If someone is like **a bull in a china shop** they are very careless and often break things: *(fig.) We told her it was a delicate situation but she went into the meeting* **like** *a bull in a china shop* (= she was forceful and told other people what to do rather than listening to them). • *Why don't you* **take the bull by the horns** (= do something difficult in a brave and determined way) *and tell him to leave?* • A **bull's-eye**/*(Br also)* **bull** is the circular centre of the object aimed at in particular games and sports such as DARTS, or the shot or throw that hits this: *I was amazed when I got a bull's-eye.* ○ *(fig.) You* **hit** *the bull's-eye* (= said or did exactly the right thing) *when you asked him where he'd been at noon.* • A **bull's-eye** is also the name for a hard round sweet tasting of PEPPERMINT.

bull [BUYER] /bʊl/ *n* [C] a person who buys shares in companies hoping the price will rise, so that they can be sold later at a profit • A bull **market** is a time when prices of shares are generally rising. • Compare BEAR [FINANCE].

bull·ish /ˈbʊl·ɪʃ/ *adj* • *The market is looking bullish* (= showing a rise in share prices). • *(fig.) She's being very bullish* (= hopeful and expecting good things) *about the firm's future.*

bull [NONSENSE] /bʊl/ *n* [U] *infml* complete nonsense or something that is not true • *Don't* **give** *me* **that** *bull* **about** *not knowing the time.*

bull·dog /£ˈbʊl·dɒg, $-dɑːg/ *n* [C] a small dog that can be fierce and has a muscular body, short legs and a large square-shaped face • *(Br and Aus)* A **bulldog clip**/*(Am* **clip**) is a simple, usually metal, device used for holding pieces of paper together. • [PIC] **Dogs, Stationery**

bull·doz·er /£ˈbʊlˌdəʊ·zəʳ, $-ˌdoʊ·zɚ/ *n* [C] a heavy vehicle with a large blade in front used for pushing earth and stones along and for flattening areas of ground at the same time • [PIC] **Building and construction**

bull·doze *obj* /£ˈbʊl·dəʊz, $-doʊz/ *v* [T] • *The township was bulldozed* **(flat)** *in the 1950s.* • If you bulldoze someone to do something you force them to do it although they may not want to: *She bulldozed her daughter* **into** *buying a new dress.* ○ *He bulldozed his plans* **through** *the committee.*

bul·let /ˈbʊl·ɪt/ *n* [C] a small object, usually made of metal and often with a pointed end, that is fired from a gun, or this and its cylindrical holder containing explosive that is put into a gun • *A bullet had lodged in the boy's leg.* • *Soldiers started* **firing** *bullets above the crowd.* • A bullet is also a symbol, often a small black circle, used in printing and sometimes in writing either to show the beginning of or to separate items in a list. • Something which is **bullet-proof** prevents bullets from going through it: *bullet-proof glass* ○ *a bullet-proof vest* • A **bullet-headed** person has a small head, usually with very short hair. • [LP] **Symbols**

bul·let·in /£ˈbʊl·ə·tɪn, $-t̬ɪn/ *n* [C] a short news programme on television or radio often about something that has just happened, or a short newspaper printed by an organization • *an hourly news bulletin* • *They listened to the daily bulletin on their crackling radio.* • *I had just heard a bulletin* **that** *John Lennon had been shot.* [+ *that* clause] • *The company publishes a fortnightly bulletin for its staff.* • **Bulletin board** is *Am for* **notice board**. See at NOTICE [INFORMATION]. • A **bulletin board** is also a system for sending messages between computers. • [PIC] **Office**

bull·fight /ˈbʊl·faɪt/ *n* [C] a traditional public entertainment in Spain, Portugal, Latin America and the South of France where a person shows their bravery by fighting a BULL using pointed sticks, and sometimes killing it • *Have you ever been to a bullfight?*

bull·fight·er /£ˈbʊlˌfaɪ·təʳ, $-t̬ɚ/ *n* [C] • *Paquirri, the famous bullfighter, was gored to death.*

bull·fight·ing /£ˈbʊlˌfaɪ·tɪŋ, $-t̬ɪŋ/ *n* [U]

bull·finch /ˈbʊl·fɪntʃ/ *n* [C] a small European bird that has a black head and a pink chest and is found in woods and gardens

bull·frog /£ˈbʊl·frɒg, $-frɑːg/ *n* [C] a large N American FROG (= type of animal) that makes a loud deep rough noise

bull·head·ed /ˈbʊlˌhed·ɪd, -ˈ--/ *adj disapproving* very determined to do what you want to do, esp. without considering other people's feelings

bull·horn /£ˈbʊl·hɔːn, $-hɔːrn/ *n* [C] *Am for* MEGAPHONE

bul·li·on /ˈbʊl·i·ən/ *n* [U] gold or silver in the form of bars • *gold bullion*

bull·ish /ˈbʊl·ɪʃ/ *adj* See at BULL [BUYER]

bul·lock /ˈbʊl·ək/ *n* [C] a male form of cattle that has been CASTRATED (= had its sexual organs removed)

bull·ring /ˈbʊl·rɪŋ/ *n* [C] a circular area surrounded by seats used for BULLFIGHTS

bull·shit /ˈbʊl·ʃɪt/ (*Am abbreviation* **BS**) *exclamation, n* [U], *adj slightly taboo slang* complete nonsense or something that is not true • *Bullshit! I don't believe a word of what you've said.* • *His excuse is* **a load of** *bullshit.* • *She gave some bullshit excuse for not showing up.*

bull·shit *(obj)* /ˈbʊl·ʃɪt/ *v* **-tt-** *slightly taboo slang* • *He tried to bullshit me* (= persuade me by saying things that are not true) *into buying his old car.* [T] • *Quit bullshitting, will you!* [I]

bull·shit·ter /£ˈbʊlˌʃɪt·əʳ, $-ɚ/ *n* [C] *slightly taboo slang* • *He was one of the biggest bullshitters I've ever heard.*

bull ter·ri·er *n* [C] a strong-looking type of dog with short hair

bul·ly *obj* [FRIGHTEN] /ˈbʊl·i/ *v* [T] to hurt or frighten other people, often forcing them to do something they do not want to do • *Our survey indicates that one in four children is bullied at school.* • *Don't let anyone bully you* **into** *doing something you don't want to do.*

bul·ly /ˈbʊl·i/ *n* [C] • *You're just a* **big** *bully!* • *Teachers usually know who the bullies are in a class.* • *(infml dated)* A **bully boy** is a rough and threatening man, esp. one paid by someone to hurt or frighten other people. *bully-boy tactics*

bul·ly [EXPRESSION] /ˈbʊl·i/ *adj* [not gradable] **bully for** *humorous* an expression used to show that you do not think what someone has done or said is very exciting or interesting • *"He's started ironing his own shirts." "Well, bully for him!"*

bul·rush /ˈbʊl·rʌʃ/ *n* [C] a plant with tall stems that grows near rivers and lakes

bul·wark /£ˈbʊl·wək, $-wɚk/ *n* [C] something that protects you from dangerous or unpleasant situations • *My savings were to be a bulwark* **against** *unemployment.*

bum [BODY PART] /bʌm/ *n* [C] *esp. Br and Aus infml* the part of the body that you sit on; bottom

bum [PERSON] /bʌm/ *n* [C] *infml* a useless person or one who is not responsible, or *(Am)* a TRAMP (= a person who has no home or job and lives by asking other people for money) • *He left his wife just before she gave birth? What a* *bum!* • *(Am) The wealthy people of Manhattan wanted to drive the bums out of their area.*

bum *obj* /bʌm/ *v* [T] **-mm-** • *Could I bum* (= get for free) *a coffee* **off** *you?* • *I wish you'd stop* **bumming around/about** (= lazily doing nothing) *and look for a job.* • *After college she spent a year* **bumming around** (= travelling around with very little money) *the States.*

bum [BAD] /bʌm/ *adj* [before n] *slang* bad in quality or worthless • *He gave us bum directions, but we eventually found the place.* • *(Am and Aus) Her suggestion that we ate at that restaurant was a* **bum steer** (= a bad suggestion).

bum·bag *Br and Aus* /ˈbʌm·bæg/, *Am* **fan·ny pack, waist pack** *n* [C] a small bag fixed to a long strap which you fasten around your waist, and which is used for carrying money, keys and other personal possessions • [PIC]› **Bags**

bum·ble /ˈbʌm·bl̩/ *v* [I] to speak or move in a confused way • *George seems to bumble* **along** *through life happily enough.*

bumb·ling /ˈbʌm·blɪŋ/ *adj* • *He was a bumbling but well-meaning old gentleman.* • *I've never seen such bumbling incompetence!*

bum·ble·bee /ˈbʌm·bl̩·biː/ *n* [C] a large hairy bee • [PIC]› **Wasps and bees**

bumf, bumph /bʌmpf/ *n* [U] *esp. Br and Aus infml* printed information such as advertisements that is usually unwanted and not interesting • *I got a load of bumf from my bank today.* • Bumf is also documents, forms, etc. that are very boring but have to be dealt with: *You wouldn't believe the amount of bumf we received from the local council when we applied for a grant!*

bum·mer *Am* /£ˈbʌm·əʳ, $-ɚ/ *exclamation, n* [C] something that is unpleasant or difficult to do or experience • *That exam was a real bummer.* • *(Am) Oh, bummer! I locked my keys in the car.*

bump [SWELLING] /bʌmp/ *n* [C] (on something alive) a raised swelling or (on something which is generally flat and usually hard) a raised, uneven part • *Tim had a nasty bump on his head from when he'd fallen over.* • *Her bicycle hit a bump in the road and threw her off.* • *(Br humorous) Heavily pregnant by now, Alice and her bump* (= the shape made by the baby growing inside her) *went shopping.*

bump·y /ˈbʌm·pi/ *adj* **-ier, -iest** • *We drove along a narrow, bumpy* (= uneven and rough) *road.* • *The track was full of holes and we had a bumpy* **ride** (= an uncomfortable and rough ride) *in the truck.* • *(fig.) She's had a bumpy* **ride** (= a difficult time) *at work over the last few months.* • *It might be a bumpy* **flight** (= an uncomfortable and rough flight) *because there's a lot of air turbulence ahead.* • *"Fasten your seat-belts, it's going to be a bumpy night"* (Bette Davis in the film *All About Eve*, 1950)

bump /bʌmp/ *v* [I always + adv/prep] • To bump means to travel, usually in a vehicle, in an uncomfortable way because the surface you are moving over is rough: *We bumped* **along** *the track in our car holding on to our seats.*

bump *(obj)* [HIT] /bʌmp/ *v* to hit (something) with force, esp. accidentally • *When he was parking his car he bumped the car in front of him.* [T] • *She bumped* **into** *his tray, knocking the food onto his lap.* [I] • *(fig.) We bumped* **into** (= accidentally met) *Kate when we were in London last week.* [I]

bump /bʌmp/ *n* [C] • *(infml) She got a bump* **on the** (= She hit her) *head when she fell off her bicycle, but luckily she wasn't hurt.* • *We heard a bump* (= the sound of something falling to the ground) *from the next room.* • A bump is also an accident involving a car, esp. one which is not serious: *A van drove into their car but luckily it was just a bump.* • **Bump start** means **push start.** See at PUSH [USE PRESSURE]. • *"From ghoulies and ghosties* (= evil spirits and ghosts) *and long-leggety beasties* (= long-legged beasts)*/ And things that go bump in the night, / Good Lord, deliver us!"* (Traditional countryside prayer)

bump off *obj*, **bump** *obj* **off** *v adv* [M] *slang* to kill (a person) • *They tried to have him bumped off by their thugs.*

bump up *obj*, **bump** *obj* **up** *v adv* [M] *infml* to increase (the amount or size of something, esp. a price) • *The distributors will probably bump up the price of the software when the next version is released.*

bump·er [CAR PART] /£ˈbʌm·pəʳ, $-pɚ/ *n* [C] a horizontal strip along the lower front and lower back part of a motor vehicle to help protect it from accidents • *By eight o'clock the traffic was* **bumper to bumper** (= there were so many cars and they were so close that they almost touched). • A **bumper car**/*(Br and Aus also)* DODGEM is a small electric car driven for entertainment in a special enclosed space where the aim is to try to hit or avoid other similar cars. • *"Pull up to the bumper, baby"* (song by Grace Jones, 1981) • [PIC]› **Car, Nose**

bump·er [BIG] /£ˈbʌm·pəʳ, $-pɚ/ *adj* [before n] unusually large in amount • *Farmers have reported a bumper* **crop** *this year.*

bumph /bʌmpf/ *n* [U] BUMF

bump·kin /ˈbʌmp·kɪn/, **coun·try bump·kin** *n* [C] *infml* a person from the countryside who is (considered to be) awkward and stupid

bump·tious /ˈbʌmp·ʃəs/ *adj* unpleasantly confident • *There are some jobs in which a bumptious young man like that should be very successful.*

bump·tious·ness /ˈbʌmp·ʃə·snəs/ *n* [U]

bun [FOOD] /bʌn/ *n* [C] a small sweet usually round cake • *I had a cup of tea and a bun at four o'clock.* • *(esp. Am)* A bun can also be a small round loaf of bread, esp. one which is cut horizontally and holds a piece of cooked meat: *a (ham)burger bun* • *(dated humorous)* To have **a bun in the oven** is to be pregnant. • [PIC]› **Bread and cakes**

bun [HAIRSTYLE] /bʌn/ *n* [C] a woman's hairstyle where the hair is gathered into a round shape at the back of the head • *She wore her hair* **in a** *bun.*

bun [BOTTOM] /bʌn/ *n* [C usually pl] *esp. Am and Aus slang* a BUTTOCK (= one side of a person's bottom) • *I get sore buns from riding a bicycle.*

bunch /bʌntʃ/ *n* [C] a number of things of the same type fastened or closely grouped together, or a group of people • *a bunch of grapes/bananas/keys* • *His friends are just a bunch* **of** *hooligans.* • *I bought a bunch* **of flowers** *in the market.* • *Let me straighten out your shirt – it's all* **in a** *bunch at the back.* • *(infml) They're a nice bunch* (= group of people). • *(esp. Am infml) The reorganization will give us a whole bunch* (= a lot) *of problems.* • *I like all her family but Gerard is* **the best/pick of the bunch** (= the most pleasant person among them). • A person or thing that is **the best of a bad bunch** is the one you think is not as bad as the others, although you do not really like any of them. • *(dated humorous slang)* If you **give** someone **a bunch of fives** you hit them hard with your hand closed: *If he keeps on boasting like that someone will give him a bunch of fives.*

bunch·es /ˈbʌnt·ʃɪz/ *pl n Br* • If a girl has her hair in bunches it is tied together in two parts with one at each side of her head: *As a little girl she wore her hair* **in** *bunches.* • [PIC]› **Hair**

bunch *(obj)* /bʌntʃ/ *v* [always + adv/prep] • *The monkeys bunched* **together/up** (= were in a tight group) *in their cage.* [I] • *Make sure the wet sheets aren't bunched* **up** (= gathered together in places) *otherwise they won't dry properly.* [T]

bun·dle /ˈbʌn·dl̩/ *n* [C] a number of things that have been fastened or are held together, often so that they can be carried • *a bundle of clothes/newspapers/books* • *He came in carrying a bundle* **of** *sticks for the fire.* • *All her clothes and belongings were wrapped in a bundle* (= contained in a cloth which was tied closed). • *(infml)* Some people affectionately refer to a baby as a bundle: *Three days after the birth, Paul and Sandra took their* **(precious)** *bundle* **(of joy)** *home.* • *He's not exactly* **a bundle of laughs/joy** (= an amusing person), *is he?* • *Sorry for shouting – I'm* **a bundle of nerves** (= extremely nervous) *these days.* • *(Br infml) I don't* **go a bundle on** (= I don't much like) *his taste in clothes.* • *(infml) When they sold their business they* **made a bundle** (= got a lot of money).

bun·dle *(obj)* /ˈbʌn·dl̩/ *v* [always + adv/prep] • *He bundled his clothes* **into** *the washing machine* (= pushed them into it in an untidy bundle). [T] • *She was bundled* (= pushed quickly and roughly) **into** *the back of the car.* [T] • *We all bundled* (= quickly moved together in a way which was not orderly) **into** *the back of the jeep.* [I] • *The children were bundled* (= sent quickly) **off** *to school every morning.* [T] • To **bundle up** means to wear warm clothes, esp. lots of them: *I'd advise you to bundle (yourself) up well – it's going to be very cold today.*

bung [CLOSING DEVICE] *esp. Br* /bʌŋ/, *Am usually and Aus also* **stop·per** *n* [C] a round piece of rubber or wood that is used to close the hole in a container • [PIC]› **Laboratory**

bung *obj* /bʌŋ/ *v* [T] • *We managed to bung* **(up)** (= close) *the hole in the ceiling with some paper.* [T/M] • *I've got a bad cold and my* **nose** *is/I'm all bunged* **up** (= my nose is blocked).

bung *obj* [PUT] /bʌŋ/ *v* [T always + adv/prep] *esp. Br and Aus infml* to put or send (something) somewhere in a careless way • *"Where shall I put your coat?" "Oh, bung it* *anywhere.* • *Will you bung another coin* **in/into** *the machine.*

bun·ga·low /£ˈbʌŋ·gᵊl·əʊ, $-oʊ/ *n* [C] a house that has only one STOREY (= floor) • *It was a seaside town filled with small white bungalows.* • PIC〉 **Accommodation**

bun·gee (cord) /ˈbʌn·dʒi/ *n* [C] *esp. Am* a stretchable cord with a hook at each end which is used to hold things in place, esp. on a bicycle or car • *We carried our groceries by strapping them to the back of our bikes with bungee cords/ with bungees.* • **Bungee jumping** or **bungy jumping** is the sport of jumping off a very high bridge or similar structure with a long elastic rope tied to your legs. The rope pulls you back before you hit the ground.

bun·gle *(obj)* /ˈbʌŋ·gl̩/ *v* to do (something) badly or unsuccessfully • *The attempted robbery was badly bungled and a guard was shot.* [T] • *Our tour operators really bungled – they booked us on the wrong flight!* [I]

bun·gler /£ˈbʌŋ·glər, $-glɚ/ *n* [C] • *He's very good at intellectual tasks but if he tries to fix anything mechanical he's a hopeless bungler.*

bun·gling /ˈbʌŋ·glɪŋ/ *adj* • *What bungling idiot wired up the plug like this!*

bun·ion /ˈbʌn·jən/ *n* [C] a painful swelling on the first joint of the big toe

bunk BED /bʌŋk/ *n* [C] a narrow bed that is fixed to a wall, esp. in a boat or a train • A **bunk bed** is a piece of furniture consisting of two beds fixed together by a frame with one above the other, or one of these beds: *The twins sleep in a bunk bed.* • PIC〉 **Beds and bedroom**

bunk SLEEP /bʌŋk/ *v* [I] *infml* to sleep • *We were able to bunk* **(down)** *in a spare room for the night.*

bunk NONSENSE /bʌŋk/, **bunk·um** /ˈbʌŋ·kᵊm/ *n* [U] *dated infml* complete nonsense or something that is not true • *Most economists think his theories are sheer bunk.* • *"History is bunk (Originally 'History is more or less bunk')"* (remark by Henry Ford, 1916)

bunk GO AWAY /bʌŋk/ *n* [U] **do a bunk** *Br and Aus slang* to leave suddenly and unexpectedly • *They'd done a bunk without paying the rent.*

bunk off *(obj) v adv, v prep Br slang* to avoid (a responsibility or duty) • *A lot of people bunk off* (= leave) *early on Friday.* [I] • *It was a sunny day so they decided to bunk off* (= not go to) *school.* [T]

bun·ker SHELTER /£ˈbʌŋ·kər, $-kɚ/ *n* [C] a shelter, usually underground, that has strong walls to protect the people inside it from bullets and bombs • *The bunker could only be damaged by a direct hit from a very large bomb.*

bun·ker HOLLOW AREA /£ˈbʌŋ·kər, $-kɚ/, *Am also* **sand trap** *n* [C] (in the game of golf) a hollow area of ground filled with sand that is difficult to hit a ball out of

bun·ny (rab·bit) /ˈbʌn·i/ *n* [C] (esp. used by or to children) a rabbit

bun·sen burn·er /ˌbʌn·sᵊn/ *n* [C] a small device that burns gas to produce a smokeless flame which is used to heat things in scientific work and experiments • PIC〉 **Laboratory**

bunt·ing /£ˈbʌn·tɪŋ, $-t̬ɪŋ/ *n* [U] rows of brightly-coloured little flags that are hung across roads or above a stage as decoration for special occasions

buoy /£bɔɪ, $ˈbuː·i/ *n* [C] a floating object on the top of the sea which is used for directing ships and warning them of possible danger • PIC〉 **Emergency services**

buoy *obj* /£bɔɪ, $ˈbuː·i/ *v* [T] • *The very salty water buoyed her* **(up)** (= prevented her from sinking) *as she swam.* • *(fig.) House prices have been buoyed* (= kept high) *in the area by the possibility of a new factory opening.* • *(fig.) She was buoyed* **(up)** (= made happier) *by the warm reception her audience gave her.*

buoy·an·cy /ˈbɔɪ·ᵊnt·si/ *n* [U] • *We tested the boat for its buoyancy* (= ability to float). • *(fig.) He was a man of remarkable buoyancy* (= ability to stay happy despite difficulties).

buoy·ant /ˈbɔɪ·ᵊnt/ *adj* • *Most woods are buoyant* (= float). • *(fig.) After reading the letter he was in a buoyant* (= happy) **mood**.

buoy·ant·ly /ˈbɔɪ·ᵊnt·li/ *adv*

bur /£bɜːr, $bɜːr/ *n* [C] a BURR SEED

Bur·ber·ry /£ˈbɜː·bᵊr·i, $ˈbɜːr·ber-/ *n* [C] *trademark* a light high-quality waterproof coat

bur·ble MAKE SOUND /£ˈbɜː·bl̩, $ˈbɜːr-/ *v* [I] to make a low continuous bubbling sound, like water moving over stones • *The stream burbled over small rocks and boulders on its way through the valley.*

bur·ble *(obj)* TALK /£ˈbɜː·bl̩, $ˈbɜːr-/ *v* to talk (about something) in a confused way • *She was burbling* **(on) about** *what she'd do if she won the money.* [I] • *The driver burbled something about being hit on the head and then passed out.* [T] • *He was just burbling* **away**, *not making sense to anyone.* [I]

bur·den /£ˈbɜː·dᵊn, $ˈbɜːr-/ *n* [C] a heavy load that you carry or *(fig.)* a difficult duty or responsibility you have to bear • *The little donkey struggled under its* **heavy burden**. • *(fig.) Buying a house often places a big financial burden* **on** *young couples.* • *(fig.) There were crushing tax burdens* **on** *the poor.* • *(fig.) "I don't want to be* **a** *burden* **to** *you," her elderly father said.* • *(fig.) These feelings of remorse are a* **heavy** *burden* **to bear**. • In law, the **burden of proof** is the responsibility for proving something: *The burden of proof lies with the authority or person that accuses.* • *"The White Man's Burden"* (title of a poem by Rudyard Kipling, 1899)

bur·den *obj* /£ˈbɜː·dᵊn, $ˈbɜːr-/ *v* [T] • *I don't want to burden* (= trouble) *you* **with** *my problems.*

bur·den·some /£ˈbɜː·dᵊn·səm, $ˈbɜːr-/ *adj fml* • *Will the extra tasks be too burdensome* (= troublesome) *for you?*

bu·reau ORGANIZATION /£ˈbjʊə·rəʊ, $ˈbjʊr·oʊ/ *n* [C] *pl* **bureaux** /£ˈbjʊə·rəʊ, £-əʊz, $ˈbjʊr·oʊ, $-oʊz/ or *Am and Aus usually* **bureaus** an organization, often formed by a government, or a business that collects or provides information, or *(esp. Am)* a division of a large organization • *Her disappearance was reported to the police department's Missing Persons Bureau.* • *(esp. Am) I work in the New York bureau of a large news agency.*

bu·reau FURNITURE /£ˈbjʊə·rəʊ, $ˈbjʊr·oʊ/ *n* [C] *pl* **bureaux** /£ˈbjʊə·rəʊ, £-əʊz, $ˈbjʊr·oʊ, $-oʊz/ or **bureaus** *(Br)* a piece of furniture with a lid that opens to form a writing surface, or *(Am)* a piece of furniture having drawers used for keeping items in such as clothes

bu·reau·cra·cy /£bjʊəˈrɒk·rə·si, $bjʊˈrɑː·krə-/ *n esp. disapproving* a system for controlling or managing a country, company or organization that is operated by a large number of officials who are employed to follow rules carefully, or the officials, or the system of rules • *It's difficult for outsiders to understand the bureaucracy of India.* [C] • *I had to deal with the university's bureaucracy before I could change from one course to another.* [C] • *The bureaucracy surrounding getting a visa can be horrendous.* [U]

bu·reau·crat /£ˈbjʊə·rə·kræt, $ˈbjʊr·ə-/ *n* [C] • *It turned out she was one of those* **faceless** *bureaucrats who control our lives.*

bu·reau·crat·ic /£ˌbjʊə·rəˈkræt·ɪk, $ˌbjʊr·əˈkræt̬-/ *adj* • *I had a lot of bureaucratic hassle* (= long and difficult dealings with officials) *trying to get the information I needed.* • *The company was inefficient because it was highly bureaucratic.*

bu·reau de change /dəˈʃɑːʒ/ *n* [C] an office where you can change money of one country for that of another

bur·geon /£ˈbɜː·dʒᵊn, $ˈbɜːr-/ *v* [I] *literary* to develop or grow quickly • *In those happy, carefree days love burgeoned between them.*

bur·geon·ing /£ˈbɜː·dʒᵊn·ɪŋ, $ˈbɜːr-/ *adj* • *The company hoped to profit from the burgeoning* (= quickly developing) *communications industry.*

bur·ger /£ˈbɜː·gər, $ˈbɜːr·gɚ/ *n* [C] *infml for* HAMBURGER • *I just had a burger and chips for lunch.* • Burger is often used as a combining form to refer to HAMBURGERS cooked in a particular way, or other foods cut into very small pieces and pressed into a round flat shape: *a cheeseburger* ○ *a veggieburger*

burgh·er /£ˈbɜː·gər, $ˈbɜːr·gɚ/ *n* [C] *humorous* a person of the middle social classes who lives in a city • *The respectable burghers of Edinburgh did not conceal their dismay.*

bur·glar /£ˈbɜː·glər, $ˈbɜːr·glɚ/ *n* [C] a person who illegally enters buildings and steals things • A **burglar alarm** is a device on a building that gives a warning, such as making a loud noise or flashing a light, or informs the police if someone tries to illegally enter the building. • LP〉 **Crimes and criminals**

bur·glar·y /£ˈbɜː·glᵊr·i, $ˈbɜːr·glɚ-/ *n* [C] • *Last year the number of burglaries* (= crimes of illegally entering a place and stealing things) *reported in the city increased by 7%.*

bur·gle *obj* /£ˈbɜː·gl̩, $ˈbɜːr-/, *Am usually* **bur·glar·ize** /£ˈbɜː·glə·raɪz, $ˈbɜːr-/ *v* [T] • *When they returned they found that their home had been burgled* (= someone had entered it illegally and stolen things from it).

bur·i·al /ˈber·i·əl/ *n* the act of putting a dead body into the ground, or the ceremony connected with this • *We went back to Ireland for my uncle's burial.* [C] • *Nowadays many* *people prefer cremation to burial.* [U] • A burial **at sea** is a ceremony in which the body of a person who has died on a ship is put into the sea. [C] • A **burial ground** is an area of land where dead bodies are buried: *The house was built on an ancient burial ground.* • See also BURY.

burk /£bɜːk, $bɜːrk/ *n* [C] a BERK

bur·lap /£ˈbɜː·læp, $ˈbɜːr-/ *n* [U] *Am usually for* HESSIAN

burlesque [WRITING] /£bɜːˈlesk, $bɜːr-/ *n* a type of writing or acting that intends to make a serious piece of work look foolish • *The novel is a burlesque of a Dickens work.* [C] • *Her latest play features satire and burlesque.* [U]

burlesque [SHOW] /£bɜːˈlesk, $bɜːr-/ *n* [U] a theatrical entertainment in the US in the late 19th and early 20th centuries that had amusing acts and a STRIPTEASE (= a performance in which someone removes their clothes)

burl·y /£ˈbɜː·li, $ˈbɜːr-/ *adj* **-ier, -iest** (of a person) large and strong • *He looked up and saw a burly policeman approaching him.*

burn *(obj)* [BE ON FIRE] /£bɜːn, $bɜːrn/ *v past* **burnt** /£bɜːnt, $bɜːrnt/ or **burned** to be on fire or produce flames • *A fire was burning brightly in the fireplace.* [I] • *Helplessly we watched our house burning.* [I] • *The wood was wet and would not burn.* [I] • *This heater will burn both gas and oil* (= use them as fuel). [T] • *(infml) My old car really burns* **(up)** *fuel* (= uses a lot of it). [T/M] • *(fig.) I saw a light burning in her window* (= there was a light there). [I] • *(fig.) Running is an excellent way to burn* **off** (= get rid of) *excess energy.* [M] • *(fig.) Mary was burning* **to** (= wanting very much to) *tell us her news.* [+ *to* infinitive] • *(fig.) "You're burning* **(up)** (= You have a high fever)*!" she said, touching his forehead.* [I] • *Meteorites often burn* **up** (= are destroyed by fire) *in the atmosphere before they reach the earth.* [I] • *(fig.) He was burnt* **up with** (= feeling continuous and painful) *jealousy and suspicion.* [I] • *(fig.) His face burned* **with** (= felt very hot because of) *embarrassment/shame/anger.* [I] • *(fig.) They were both burning* **with** (= feeling very strong) *desire/passion.* [I] • To **burn the candle at both ends** is to work from early in the morning until late at night and so get very little rest: *Fine, so you've got a lot of work to do, but if you keep burning the candle at both ends you'll make yourself ill.* • When you **burn the midnight oil** you work late into the night: *He's been burning the midnight oil over the last few weeks because he's been trying to finish writing up his project work.* • *"To burn always with this hard, gemlike flame, to maintain this ecstasy, is success in life"* (Walter Pater in *Studies in the History of the Renaissance*, 1893)

burn·er /£ˈbɜː·nəʳ, $ˈbɜːr·nɚ/ *n* [C] • A burner is the part of a cooker, light, etc. that produces flame or heat.

burn·ing /£ˈbɜː·nɪŋ, $ˈbɜːr-/ *adj* • *a burning forest* • A burning interest, desire or wish is one that is very strong: *He has a burning interest in the preservation of the rainforests.* • A burning **question** or **issue** is one a lot of people have very strong opinions about: *The plan to build a new road through the area is a burning issue in the community at the moment.*

burn *(obj)* [DAMAGE] /£bɜːn, $bɜːrn/ *v past* **burnt** /£bɜːnt, $bɜːrnt/ or **burned** to (cause to) be hurt, damaged or destroyed by fire or extreme heat • *He was badly burnt in the blaze.* [T] • *She burnt his old love letters.* [T] • *The scalding hot tea burnt my tongue.* [T] • *Oh no! I've burnt the dinner again!* [T] • *The brandy they made me drink burned my throat* (= felt painfully hot). [T] • *On her first day in the Caribbean Josie was badly burned* (= her skin became red and painful from too much sun). [T] • *Fair-skinned people burn easily.* [I] • *Unable to escape, six people were burnt* **alive**/*burnt* **to death** (= died by burning) *in the building.* [T] • *I left the fire to burn* **(itself) out** (= stop burning because there was nothing left to burn). [T] • *The vegetables were burnt* **to a crisp** (= badly burnt). [T] • *(fig.) He'd been burnt* (= very hurt) *by his last love affair.* [T] • If something **burns a hole in** your **pocket**, you are very eager to do something with it: *She went to the shops with her* **money** *burning a hole in her pocket* (= she was eager to spend it). • *In the 14th century women thought to be witches were* **burnt at the stake** (= killed by being kept in a fire). • If you are in a situation and you **burn** your **boats/bridges** you destroy all possible ways of going back to that situation: *If you walk out on your job now you'll be burning your boats with them because they won't employ you again.* • *They came back to find that their house had* **burnt down** (= had been destroyed by fire). • *The building was* **burned to the ground** (= completely destroyed by fire) *ten years ago.* • If something **burns out** it stops working because of damage from heat: *It looks like the starter motor on the car has burnt out.* ○ *(fig.) Stop working so hard – you'll burn yourself out* (= become ill because of tiredness). See also BURNOUT. • *After the fire the factory was completely* **burnt-out**/*just a* **burnt-out** *shell* (= the inside had been destroyed by fire). • *(infml)* If someone **gets/has** their **fingers burnt** or **burns** their **fingers** they suffer from a bad decision or a foolish action: *She'd tried to make money by investing in stocks but she got her fingers badly burnt/burnt her fingers badly because the market collapsed.*

burn /£bɜːn, $bɜːrn/ *n* [C] • *One rescue worker caught in the explosion sustained severe burns on many parts of his body.* • *I noticed a cigarette burn in the carpet.* • See also HEARTBURN; SUNBURN.

burn·ing /£ˈbɜː·nɪŋ, $ˈbɜːr-/ *adj* • *Suddenly she felt a burning* **(sensation)** (= feeling of heat) *in her throat.*

burnt /£bɜːnt, $bɜːrnt/ *adj* • A **burnt offering** is something, such as an animal, that has been burned in honour of a god, or *(Br humorous)* a meal that has been spoiled by burning.

burn [STREAM] /£bɜːn, $bɜːrn/ *n* [C] *Scot Eng* a small stream

burn·ish *obj* /£ˈbɜː·nɪʃ, $ˈbɜːr-/ *v* [T] *esp. literary* to rub (metal) until it is smooth and shiny

burn·ished /£ˈbɜː·nɪʃt, $ˈbɜːr-/ *adj esp. literary* • *(fig.) I envied her slim figure and burnished* (= smooth brown) *skin.*

burn·out /£ˈbɜːn·aʊt, $ˈbɜːrn-/ *n* [U] extreme tiredness usually caused by working too much • *She* **suffered** *burnout after doing her last exam.* • See also **burn out** at BURN [DAMAGE].

burp /£bɜːp, $bɜːrp/ *v, n* (to make) the noise of gas coming up from the stomach and out through the mouth • *Someone burped loudly at the back of the hall.* [I] • *The baby gave a contented burp and dribbled milk onto his shoulder.* [C] • If you burp a baby you rub its back gently to help air to come out of its stomach. [T]

burr [SOUND] /£bɜːʳ, $bɜːr/ *n* [C] a way of speaking English with noticeable 'r' sounds, or (esp. of machines) a low continuous sound • *He spoke in a soft West Country burr.* • *They could hear the burr of a printing machine.*

burr [SEED], **bur** /£bɜːʳ, $bɜːr/ *n* [C] a very small round seed container that sticks to clothes and to animals' fur because it is covered in little hooks • *After she walked through the long grass her socks were covered with burrs.*

bur·ri·to /£bəˈriː·təʊ, $-ˈriː·t̬oʊ/ *n* [C] *pl* **burritos** a type of Mexican food made by folding a thin round piece of bread and putting meat, beans and cheese inside it

bur·row /£ˈbʌr·əʊ, $ˈbɜːr·oʊ/ *n* [C] a hole in the ground dug by an animal such as a rabbit, esp. to live in • *The dog had chased a rabbit into its burrow but then got stuck.*

bur·row *(obj)* /£ˈbʌr·əʊ, $ˈbɜːr·oʊ/ *v* [always + adv/prep] • *Rats had burrowed* **into** *the bank of the river.* [I] • *The worm burrowed its way* **under** *the earth.* [T] • *(fig.) I burrowed* **through** *the clothes in the drawer* (= made digging movements) *looking for a clean pair of socks.* [I] • *(fig.) Suddenly shy, our young daughter burrowed her head* **into** *my shoulder* (= tried to hide there). [T]

bur·sar /£ˈbɜː·səʳ, $ˈbɜːr·sɚ/ *n* [C] the person in a college, school or university responsible for controlling its finances

bur·sa·ry /£ˈbɜː·sᵊr·i, $ˈbɜːr·sɚ-/ *n* [C] *Br* a sum of money given to a person by an organization, such as a university, to pay for them to study

burst *(obj)* /£bɜːst, $bɜːrst/ *v past* **burst** or *Am also* **bursted** to (cause to) break open or apart suddenly • *Balloons make me nervous – I hate it when they burst.* [I] • *The river was threatening to burst its* **banks**. [T] • *Driving down the road a tyre burst and she had to stop the car.* [I] • *During the winter one of the water pipes burst and we had a flood in the house.* [I] • *Not stopping to knock, the children burst* **into** *the room/burst* **in** (= hurried into the room). [I] • *Suddenly the door burst* **open** (= opened suddenly and forcefully) *and police officers carrying guns rushed in.* [I] • *(fig. humorous) If I eat any more cake I'll burst* (= I cannot eat anything else)*!* [I] • *(fig.) Tom was bursting* (= very eager) **to** *tell everyone the news.* [+ *to* infinitive] • *(fig.) I'm bursting* (= I urgently need) **to** *go to the loo!* [+ *to* infinitive] • *(fig.) I knew they were bursting* **with** (= full of) *curiosity but I said nothing.* [I] • *(infml) When all the family come home the house is* **bursting at the seams** (= extremely full). • *Katya* **burst in on** *him* (= suddenly entered the room he was in) *without warning.* • If you **burst into song/tears/laughter** you suddenly begin to sing/cry/laugh: *Much to* *my surprise Ben suddenly burst into song.* • If something **bursts into flames** it suddenly burns fiercely and produces a lot of flames: *Smoke started pouring out from underneath, then the truck burst into flames.* • *Without warning she* **burst out laughing/crying** (= suddenly started to laugh/cry). • *"Don't go!" he* **burst out** (= said suddenly and loudly). • Ⓢ

burst /£bɜːst, $bɜːrst/ *n* [C] • *Get a plumber quickly – there's been a burst* (= a break in a pipe) *in the kitchen and there's water all over the floor!* • A burst can also mean a sudden increase in something, esp. for a short period: *If we put on a burst* **of speed** *we can lose them.* • A burst can also be a short period of something, esp. one that starts suddenly: *There was a burst of applause/laughter/activity.*

bur·ton /£ˈbɜː·tᵊn, $ˈbɜːr·t̬ᵊn/ *n* [U] **go for a burton** *Br infml dated* to be spoiled or lost • *That's our quiet evening in* **gone for a burton.**

bu·ry *obj* /ˈber·i/ *v* [T] to put (a dead body) into the ground, or to put (something) into a hole in the ground and cover it • *His father is buried* **in** *a plot on the hill.* • *The dog trotted off to bury its bone.* • *If an avalanche strikes, skiers can be buried* **alive** *by snow.* • *There might even be buried* **treasure** *on the island.* • *(fig.) He'd had to bury* (= hide) *his pain over the years.* • *(fig.) She buried* (= hid) *her face* **in** *her hands and began to sob.* • *(fig.) Wanting to write without being interrupted, she buried* (= hid) *herself* **in** *a remote farmhouse.* • *(fig.) I found the article buried* **(away)** (= in a place that was difficult to find) *in the business section of the newspaper.* • If you say you have buried a relative you mean that they have died and you went to the ceremony at which their body was put in the ground: *Our neighbour buried both her grandparents last year.* • If two people **bury the hatchet** they stop disagreeing with each other: *Can't you two bury the hatchet and get back to a normal working relationship!* • *"I come to bury Caesar, not to praise him"* (Shakespeare, Julius Caesar 3.2) • *"Bury my heart at Wounded Knee"* (line from the poem *American Names* by Stephen Benét used as the title of book by Dee Brown, 1927) • See also BURIAL.

bus /bʌs/ *n* [C] *pl* **buses** or *Am also* **busses** a large motor vehicle in which people are driven from one place to another • *I got on the bus outside our house and got off at the shopping centre.* • *You should* **take the** *bus/***go by** *bus* (= travel by bus) *if you want to see the sights.* • *If you want to be bus* **driver** *you have to take a special driving test.* • *(Am)* A **bus boy** is a person who helps someone serve in a restaurant, esp. by removing dirty dishes and bringing clean ones. • A **bus conductor** is a person on some buses who takes your money and gives you a ticket. • A **bus lane** is a specially marked wide strip on a road, usually along one or both sides, on which only buses are allowed to travel. • A **bus-shelter** is a place to wait for buses that has a roof and usually sides to prevent you from getting wet if it rains. • A **bus station** is a place where buses start and end their journeys. • A **bus stop** is a place, usually marked by a pole with a sign, where a bus stops to let passengers get on and off. • See also MINIBUS; OMNIBUS [TRANSPORT]; TROLLEYBUS. • [PIC]> **Road**

bus *(obj)* /bʌs/ *v* **-ss-** or *Am usually* **-s-** • *Shall we walk to the cinema or bus* (= travel by bus)*?* [I] • *Demonstrators were bussed in from all parts of the country to attend the protest rally.* [T] • In the US children who are bussed to school are taken by bus to school in another area every day: *Anna will have to be bussed to junior high, since the building's on the other side of town.* [T]

bus·by /ˈbʌz·bi/ *n* [C] a fur hat worn by some British soldiers on ceremonial occasions

bush [PLANT] /bʊʃ/ *n* [C] a plant with many small branches growing either directly from the ground or from a hard woody stem, giving the plant a rounded shape • *The hill was covered in flowering bushes.* • *Our dog ran off into some bushes when we were walking in the forest.* • *Suddenly, we heard a noise in the bushes beside us.* • *(fig.) The baby was born with a surprising bush* **of** *black hair* (= a large amount of hair). • Bush can be used as a combining form to mean a plant of a particular type: *a currant bush* ○ *a rose bush* • [PIC]> **Garden**

bush [AREA OF LAND] /bʊʃ/ *n* [U] (esp. in Australia and Africa) an area of land covered with natural bushes and trees which has never been farmed and where there are very few people • *He decided to live out in* **the** *bush for six months.* • A **bush fire** is a fire burning in the bush that is difficult to control and sometimes spreads quickly: *A series of bush fires came very close to destroying several suburbs of Sydney this year.* • *(humorous dated) The rumour of closure quickly spread through the factory by* **bush telegraph** (= by people talking, esp. in an informal way). • See also BUSHMAN; BUSHRANGER; BUSHWALKING.

bushed /bʊʃt/ *adj* [after v] *infml* very tired • *I spent the whole morning mowing grass and now I'm bushed.* • *(Aus)* Bushed also means lost and/or confused.

bush·el /ˈbʊʃ·ᵊl/ *n* [C] a unit of volume equal to approximately 36·4 litres in Britain or 35·2 litres in the US • *a bushel of wheat* • *In the old way of measuring, a British bushel is equal to eight gallons.*

bush·man *(pl* **-men)** /ˈbʊʃ·mən/ *n* [C] *esp. Aus* a person who lives or knows by experience how to live in the BUSH (= a wild area of land)

bush·rang·er /£ˈbʊʃˌreɪn·dʒəʳ, $-dʒɚ/ *n* [C] *Aus* (in the past) a criminal or thief who lived in the BUSH (= wild area of land)

bush·walk·ing /£ˈbʊʃˌwɔː·kɪŋ, $-ˌwɑː-/ *n* [U] *Aus* the sport of walking through the BUSH (= wild area of land)

bush·y /ˈbʊʃ·i/ *adj* **-ier, -iest** (of hair or fur) growing very thickly • *We could see a squirrel's bushy* **tail** *sticking out from behind the tree's trunk.* • *He glared at me from under his bushy* **eyebrows.**

bus·i·ly /ˈbɪz·ɪ·li/ *adv* See at BUSY

bu·si·ness [SELLING] /ˈbɪz·nɪs/ *n* the activity of buying and selling goods and services, or a particular company that does this, or work in general rather than pleasure • *She's finished college and now she works* **in** *business.* [U] • *He's* **in the** *frozen food* **business.** [C] • *The two brothers started up/built up/established a clothes retailing business.* [C] • *Peter ended up in charge of the business.* [C] • *Our firm* **does** *a lot of business* **with** *overseas customers.* [U] • *Eventually they found a consultant they felt they could* **do** *business* **with** (= with whom they could work well). [U] • *Currently, there are fewer firms* **in** *business* (= operating) *in the area than ever before.* [U] • *(infml) Once we get the computer installed we'll* **be in business** (= we will be able to start doing what we planned). • *This new tax will put a lot of small firms* **out of** *business* (= they will stop operating). [U] • *She* **set up in** *business* (= started her own company) *as a management consultant.* [U] • *How is business* (= Are you selling much) *at the moment?* [U] • *Business is good/brisk/booming/flourishing* (= I'm selling a lot). [U] • *Business is bad/slack/quiet* (= I'm not selling much). [U] • *Is your visit to this country for business or pleasure?* [U] • *I'm in Baltimore* **on** *business.* [U] • *My sister had a business appointment she couldn't cancel.* • *If the introductions are over I'd like to* **get down to business** (= start talking about the matter to be discussed). • If a person or organization is **in the business of** doing something then it is what they do: *The intelligence service is* **not** *in the business of routinely monitoring the activities of law-abiding citizens.* • If you travel **business class** on an aircraft you have better conditions, such as wider seats and free drinks, than if you travel cheaper. • *(infml)* The **business end** of something, such as a knife or a gun, is the end which does the work or damage rather than the handle. • A **business park** is an area that is specially designed to have business offices, small factories, etc. • **Business people** are the men and/or women who work in business, esp. those who have important positions in it: *Many business people will be concerned by the proposed increase in interest rates.* • *(saying)* 'Business as usual' means that things are continuing as they always do, despite a difficult situation. • *(saying)* 'Business before pleasure' means that business is more important than entertainment and enjoyment. • *"There's No Business like Show Business"* (title of song written by Irving Berlin, 1946) • *"The business of America is business"* (Speech by Calvin Coolidge, 1925) • *"We can do business together (often quoted in the form 'Someone you can do business with')"* (Margaret Thatcher of Mr Gorbachev, 1984) • [LP]> **Letters, Work**

bu·si·ness [IMPORTANT MATTERS] /ˈbɪz·nɪs/ *n* [U] important and serious matters • *Arranging a trip abroad is* **a** *time-consuming business.* • *These killings are* **a** *dreadful business.* • *I* **make it** *my business* (= I feel it is my particular duty) *to check the monthly accounts.* • *Watch out – she* **means** *business* (= is determined to get things done) *this time.* • *We've got some* **unfinished** *business to discuss* (= We still have something important to discuss). • *It took ages to sort out the documentation needed to get into the country –* **what a business** (= what an annoying and difficult matter it was)*!* • *(Br slang) The new player in the team is* **the business** (= extremely good). • *(Br slang)* To **do the business** is to have sex.

bu·si·ness THINGS YOU DO /ˈbɪz·nɪs/ *n* [U] the things that you do or the matters which relate only to you • *I got on with* **the** *business* **of** *filling in the form.* • *What she does with her life is her business – only she can decide what she should do.* • *You* **had no business** (= should not have been) *reading my private letters.* • *(dated) He was scribbling away* **like nobody's business** (= very quickly). • *(infml) When I asked him what he was doing he told me to* **mind** *my* **own business**/*it was* **none of** *my* **business** (= it did not involve me). • *"It is the business of the wealthy man / To give employment to the artisan"* (from the poem 'Lord Finchley' in Hilaire Belloc's *More Peers*, 1911)

bu·si·ness·like /ˈbɪz·nɪs·laɪk/ *adj* getting things done in a quick and practical way • *"Sign here," she said, suddenly businesslike.* • *The meeting was brief and businesslike with a lot of decisions being made.*

bu·si·ness·man (*pl* **-men**), **bu·si·ness·wo·man** (*pl* **-women**) /ˈbɪz·nɪs·mən, -ˌwʊm·ən/ *n* [C] a person who works in business, esp. if they have a high position in a company • *He was a successful businessman before becoming a writer.* • *She's a good/shrewd businesswoman who's popular with her staff.*

busk /bʌsk/ *v* [I] *Br and Aus* to play music or sing in a public place so that the people who are there will give money • *A lot of music students busk in their vacation to earn some extra money.*

busk·er /£ˈbʌs·kəʳ, $ˈbʌs·kɚ/ *n* [C] • *I refuse to give money to any busker playing Simon and Garfunkel.*

bus·man's hol·i·day /ˈbʌs·mənz/ *n* [C] a holiday where you do something similar to your usual work instead of having a rest from it

bus·ses *Am also* /ˈbʌs·ɪz/ *pl of* BUS

bust *obj* BREAK /bʌst/ *v* [T] *past* **bust** or *Am usually* **busted** *infml* to break (something) • *Oh no! I've bust his CD player.* • *Harry and his girlfriend bust* **up** (= separated) *last week.* • *(slang)* When the police bust a person they ARREST him or her, or when they bust a building or a place they ARREST people in it who they believe are breaking the law: *The police busted him because they think he's involved with a terrorist group.* • Ⓘ Ⓙ

bust /bʌst/ *n* [C] • *(slang)* A bust is an occasion when police ARREST people who are thought to have broken the law: *In their latest* **drugs** *bust police entered a warehouse where cocaine dealers were meeting.* • *(Br and Aus infml)* A **bust-up** is a serious argument, esp. one which ends a relationship: *She* **had** *a big bust-up* **with** *her brother-in-law.*

bust /bʌst/, *Am also* **bust·ed** *adj* [after v; not gradable] *infml* • *I think my watch is bust.* • When a company **goes bust** it is forced to close because it is financially unsuccessful: *More than twenty companies in the district went bust during the last three months.*

bust HEAD /bʌst/ *n* [C] a statue of the head and shoulders of a person • *There was a bust* **of** *Mahler on his desk.* • PIC **Sculpture** Ⓘ Ⓙ

bust BREASTS /bʌst/ *n* [C] a woman's breasts, or the measurement around a woman's body at the level of her breasts • *She had a small bust and long legs.* • *I couldn't find anything in the shop in my bust size.* • Ⓘ Ⓙ

bust·y /ˈbʌs·ti/ *adj* **-ier, -iest** *infml* • *Charlene was a busty* (= having large breasts) *blonde with a laugh like a chain saw.*

bust·er DISLIKED PERSON /£ˈbʌs·təʳ, $-tɚ/ *n* [U] *infml* used to address a man or a boy you do not like • *Cut it out, buster!* • LP **Titles and forms of address**

-bust·er DESTROYER /£-ˌbʌs·təʳ, $-tɚ/ *combining form* a person or things intended to destroy the stated thing • *a ghostbuster* • *a tankbuster*

bus·tle BE BUSY /ˈbʌs·l̩/ *v* [I] to do things in a hurried and busy way • *Thora bustled* **about** *the flat, getting everything ready.* • *My aunt bustled* **in** *with the shopping in one arm and the baby in the other.*

bus·tle /ˈbʌs·l̩/ *n* [U] • *I sat in a café, watching the* **(hustle and)** *bustle* (= busy activity) *of the street outside.*

bust·ling /ˈbʌs·lɪŋ/ *adj* • *This used to be a bustling* (= full of busy activity) *town but a lot of people have moved away over recent years.* • *The house, usually bustling* **with** *activity, was strangely silent.* • If a person is bustling they seem always to be busy and they make lots of quick movements: *A bustling little man led them into the funeral parlour.*

bus·tle DRESS /ˈbʌs·l̩/ *n* [C] a type of frame or mass of cloth worn at the back of a dress below the waist by women in the late 19th century to make the dress stick out

bu·sy /ˈbɪz·i/ *adj* **-ier, -iest** (of a person) actively involved in doing something or having a lot of things to do, or (of a time or place) where a lot of things are happening • *Don't talk to me now – can't you see I'm busy?* • *The kids are busy* **with** *their homework.* • *She's busy writing out the wedding invitations.* • *I'm afraid I'm very busy this week so I can't see you.* • *Their house is near a very busy road.* • *Have a rest – you've had a busy day.* • *(disapproving) Her dress is a bit busy* (= has too much decoration or too many colours), *isn't it?* • *(esp. Am) I tried to call you on the phone earlier but the line was busy* (= being used). • LP **Telephone**

bu·sy *obj* /ˈbɪz·i/ *v* [T] • *To pass the time he busied himself* **with/by** (= made himself busy by) *tidying up the room.*

bus·i·ly /ˈbɪz·ɪ·li/ *adv* • *Grandma busily set to work cleaning the dolls' house.* • *She's busily reorganizing the company to increase profits.*

bu·sy·bod·y /£ˈbɪz·iˌbɒd·i, $-ˌbɑː·di/ *n* [C] *infml* a person who is too interested in things that do not involve them • *Some interfering busybody had rung the police.*

but DIFFERENCE /bʌt/ *conjunction* used to express a difference or introduce an added statement • *She's very hard-working but not very imaginative.* • *I love tennis but I like walking too.* • *This is not caused by evil, but by simple ignorance.* • *The play's good, but not that good – I've seen better.* • *The phone rang, but only for a few seconds.* • *I'm sorry, but I think you're wrong when you say she did it deliberately.* • *Call me old-fashioned, but I like handwritten letters.* • *I can understand his unhappiness. But to attempt suicide!* • *"She said she's leaving." "But why?"* • *You can invite Keith to the party, but please don't ask that friend of his.* • *We must not complain about the problem, but* (= instead we must) *help to put it right.* • *She's not a painter but a writer* (= She is a writer, not a painter). • *She's* **not only** *a painter but* **also** *a writer* (= She is both). • *He said he hadn't been there, but* **then** (= it is not surprising that) *he would say that.* • *I think it's true, but* **then** (= it should be understood that), *I'm no expert.*

but /bʌt/ *n* [C] • If you say about something that (there are/there can be) **no/not any buts (about it)**, you mean that it is certain, and either it will happen or you will not hear any arguments against it: *We're going to visit your aunt tomorrow and there'll be no buts about it.* ○ *Jim is going to be in charge for the rest of the week and I don't want to hear any buts.* • *"But me no buts"* (saying, meaning don't make excuses, popularized by Sir Walter Scott in his novel *The Antiquary*, 1816)

but EXCEPT /bʌt/ *prep, conjunction* except • *Eventually,* **all** *but* **one** *of them promised to come to his leaving party.* • *He's* **anything** *but violent* (= not violent in any way). • *I'd have crashed the car but* **for** *your warning.* • *This is the* **last** *episode but* **one** (= one before the last) *of this drama serial.* • *She's one of those guests who does* **nothing** *but complain.* • *This car has been* **nothing** *but trouble – it's always breaking down!*

but ONLY /bʌt/ *adv* [not gradable] *fml* only; just • *She's but a young girl!* • But can also be used to give force to a statement: *Everyone, but everyone, will be there.*

bu·tane /ˈbjuː·teɪn/ *n* [U] a chemical containing carbon that is used as a fuel

butch /bʊtʃ/ *adj* **-er, -est** (of a woman) copying particular features of men's appearance and behaviour, or (of a man) being muscular and behaving in a manly way • *She didn't look butch enough to get into the nightclub.* • *My current girlfriend isn't as butch as the last one.* • *I immediately noticed the big, butch man in the corner.*

butch·er /£ˈbʊtʃ·əʳ, $-ɚ/ *n* [C] a person who sells meat in a shop • *Our local butcher is very good, he's always happy to prepare joints of meat specially.* • Someone who murders a lot of people can be called a butcher: *Klaus Barbie was called the Butcher of Lyons.*

butch·er *obj* /£ˈbʊtʃ·əʳ, $-ɚ/ *v* [T] • *The sheep were taken abroad where they were butchered* (= killed and then prepared) *for meat.* • *Need so many young men be senselessly butchered* (= murdered) *in war?*

butch·er's /£ˈbʊtʃ·əz, $-ɚz/ *n* [C] *pl* **butchers** or **butchers'** • A butcher's is a shop where butchers work: *There's a butcher's on the main road into the city.*

butch·er·y /£ˈbʊtʃ·ᵊr·i, $ˈ-ɚ-/ *n* [U] • *His father taught him all about butchery* (= preparing meat for sale). • *The butchery* (= cruel murder) *of innocent people by this dictator must be stopped.*

butch·er's /£ˈbʊtʃ·əz, $-ɚz/ *n* [U] *Br and Aus slang* a look at something • *Let's* **have a/Give us a** *butcher's* **at** *your present, then.*

but·ler /£ˈbʌt·ləʳ, $-lɚ/ *n* [C] the most important male servant in a house, usually responsible for organizing the other servants

butt THICK END /bʌt/ *n* [C] the thick end of something, esp. a RIFLE (=type of gun) • *They struck him with their rifle butts.*

butt CIGARETTE /bʌt/ *n* [C] the part of a finished cigarette that has not been smoked • *The ashtray was overflowing with cigarette butts.*

butt BOTTOM /bʌt/ *n* [C] *Am slang* a person's bottom • *She told him to* **get off** *his butt and do something useful.* • **Butt naked** means completely naked.

butt *(obj)* HIT /bʌt/ *v* to hit (something) hard with the head or the horns • *The thug butted him* **on the head.** [T] • *Be careful of that ram – it butts!* [I]

butt /bʌt/ *n* [C] • *He* **gave** *his attacker a butt and then ran as fast as he could.*

butt in /bʌt/ *v adv* [I] *infml* • *Sorry to butt in* **(on** *you)* (= interrupt you) *like this.*

butt PERSON /bʌt/ *n* [C usually sing] a person who is joked about or laughed at • *He was fed up with being* **the butt of** *their jokes.*

butt CONTAINER /bʌt/ *n* [C] a large container used to store liquids • *The* **(rain) water** *butt was almost empty.*

but·ter /£ˈbʌt·əʳ, $ˈbʌt̬·ɚ/ *n* [U] a pale yellow fatty solid made from cream that is spread on bread or used in cooking • *a butter dish* • *We were served scones with butter and jam.* • *Have some* **bread/toast and** (= spread with) *butter.* • *Tommy looked as if* **butter wouldn't melt in** *his* **mouth** (= he looked as if he would never do anything wrong, although you feel certain he would). • PIC› **Cutlery**

but·ter *obj* /£ˈbʌt·əʳ, $ˈbʌt̬·ɚ/ *v* [T] • *She buttered a piece of bread for herself.* • *(infml) You'll have to* **butter** *them* **up** (= praise or try to please them) *a bit before they'll agree.*

but·tered /£ˈbʌt·əd, $ˈbʌt̬·ɚd/ *adj* • *For breakfast I'd like coffee, juice, eggs and buttered toast, please.* • *"I never had a piece of toast / Particularly long and wide, / But fell upon the sanded floor, / And always on the buttered side"* (verse by James Payn, 1884)

but·ter·y /£ˈbʌt·ᵊr·i, $ˈbʌt̬·ɚ-/ *adj* **-ier, -iest** • *With tea she served some lovely buttery* (= containing a lot of butter) *biscuits.* • See also BUTTERY.

but·ter bean *n* [C] a LIMA BEAN • PIC› **Peas and beans**

but·ter·cup /£ˈbʌt·ə·kʌp, $ˈbʌt̬·ɚ-/ *n* [C] a small bright yellow wild flower • PIC› **Flowers and plants**

but·ter·fin·gers /£ˈbʌt·əˌfɪŋ·gəz, $ˈbʌt̬·ɚˌfɪŋ·gɚz/ *n* [C] *pl* **butterfingers** *humorous* a person who drops things they are carrying or trying to catch • *"Butterfingers!" she called as I dropped the hot plates.* [as form of address]

but·ter·fly /£ˈbʌt·ə·flaɪ, $ˈbʌt̬·ɚ-/ *n* [C] a type of insect with large often brightly coloured wings • *The zoo has a large collection of butterflies.* • *(fig.) Melanie is a social butterfly* (= a person only interested in pleasure). • *(infml)* If you say you have **butterflies (in** your **stomach)** you mean you are feeling very nervous, usually about something you are about to do. • A butterfly is also the small metal part put on the back of a STUD (= piece of jewellery worn in the ear) that keeps it in place. • **The butterfly** or **butterfly stroke** is a way of swimming on your front by kicking with your legs while raising your arms together out of the water and then bringing them down in front of you. • *"Float like a butterfly, sting like a bee"* (Muhammad Ali, previously known as Cassius Clay, describing his boxing style, 1964) • PIC› **Insects, Jewellery**

but·ter·milk /£ˈbʌt·ə·mɪlk, $ˈbʌt̬·ɚ-/ *n* [U] the liquid that is left after taking the fat from cream to make butter, used in cooking

but·ter·scotch /£ˈbʌt·ə·skɒtʃ, $ˈbʌt̬·ɚ·skɑːtʃ/ *n* a hard light-brown coloured sweet food made by boiling butter and water together • *Would you like a/some butterscotch?* [C/U]

but·ter·y /£ˈbʌt·ᵊr·i, $ˈbʌt̬·ɚ-/ *n* [C] *esp. Br* a room where you can buy meals and drinks, esp. in a college or university • See also **buttery** at BUTTER.

but·tock /£ˈbʌt·ək, $ˈbʌt̬-/ *n* [C usually pl] either side of a person's bottom

but·ton /£ˈbʌt·ᵊn, $ˈbʌt̬-/ *n* [C] a small usually circular object used to fasten a shirt, coat, etc., or a small sometimes circular object that you press to operate a device or a machine • *I* **did up/undid** (= fastened/unfastened) *the buttons on my blouse.* • *He pressed the button and the doorbell rang.* • *You can't expect to get everything you need* **at the push of a button** (= very easily). • *(esp. Am) She was* **right on the button** (= exactly correct) *when she said I'd regret moving out.* • **Button-fly** trousers are trousers which fasten at the front with buttons. • LP› **Dressing and undressing, Switching on and off**

but·ton *obj* /£ˈbʌt·ᵊn, $ˈbʌt̬-/ *v* [T] • *Button* **(up)** *your coat, it's cold out.* • *(esp. Am infml)* The expression **button it** is a forceful way of telling someone to stop talking: *Button it, OK! I'm trying to think.* • A **button-down collar** on a shirt is a collar that has the pointed ends fastened to the shirt by buttons. • PIC› **Clothes**

but·ton·hole HOLE /£ˈbʌt·ᵊn·həʊl, $ˈbʌt̬·ᵊn·hoʊl/ *n* [C] a hole that a button is pushed through to fasten a shirt, coat, etc. • *(esp. Br)* A buttonhole is also a flower that a man wears in the buttonhole of, or pinned to, his jacket on a special occasion such as a marriage ceremony.

but·ton·hole *obj* MAKE LISTEN /£ˈbʌt·ᵊn·həʊl, $ˈbʌt̬·ᵊn·hoʊl/ *v* [T] to stop (someone) and make them listen to you • *Greg buttonholed me about sales figures when I came out of the meeting.*

but·tress /ˈbʌt·rəs/ *n* [C] a structure made of stone or brick which sticks out from and supports a wall of a building • *Soon after the church was built buttresses had to be built along the south wall because it was beginning to collapse.*

but·tress *obj* /ˈbʌt·rəs/ *v* [T] • *It was decided to buttress* (= build buttresses to support) *the crumbling walls.* • *(fig.) The arguments for change are buttressed* (= given force and strength) *by events elsewhere.*

but·ty /£ˈbʌt·i, $ˈbʌt̬-/ *n* [C] *Br regional* a SANDWICH

bux·om /ˈbʌk·sᵊm/ *adj* (of a woman) healthy-looking and slightly fat, with large breasts • *He fell in love with a buxom hairdresser.*

buy *obj* PAY FOR /baɪ/ *v* [T] *past* **bought** /£bɔːt, $bɑːt/ to obtain (something) by paying money for it • *Eventually she had saved enough money to buy a small car.* • *He bought his mother some flowers/He bought some flowers* **for** *his mother.* [+ two objects] • *The company was set up to buy and sell shares on behalf of investors.* • *I bought my camera* **from/** *(infml)* **off** *a friend of mine.* • *(Br) We bought* **in** (= bought for future use) *lots of tinned food in case of heavy snow.* • *McDowell was trying to buy* **into** *the newspaper business* (= buy a part of it to have some control over it). • If you buy someone **(off)** you get their help, esp. in a matter that may not be legal, by giving them money: *They tried to buy the guard at the bank off but he told the police and the gang were arrested.* [T/M] • In business, to buy someone **out** is to give them money so that you own the part of the business that previously belonged to them. *Allied Chemicals have been trying to buy out their competitor's share in the target company.* [M] • *(Br)* In the armed forces, if you **buy yourself out** you pay a sum of money so that you can leave earlier than you had previously agreed to. • To buy **up** something is to buy large amounts of it, or all that is available: *He bought up all the land in the surrounding area.* • *(fig.) What will we have to do to buy her* **silence** (= to make her not tell anyone what she knows)? • *(Am infml)* If you **buy the farm** you die: *I'm afraid Pat's bought the farm this time.* • *He tried to* **buy time** (= be allowed more time) *by saying he hadn't been well.* • *The government warned people against* **panic buying** (= buying food and supplies because of the fear that they might soon all be sold.) • *"Can't Buy me Love"* (title of song by The Beatles, 1964)

buy /baɪ/ *n* [C] • *This jacket was a really* **good/bad** *buy* (= it was/was not worth the money I paid for it).

buy·er /£ˈbaɪ·əʳ, $-ɚ/ *n* [C] • *He's still looking* **for** *a buyer* **for** (= someone to buy) *his house.* • *She's the buyer* (= the person who decides what will be bought) *for a stylish boutique in Dublin.* • A **buyer's market** is a time when there are more goods for sale than there are people to buy them, so prices tend to be low.

buy *obj* BELIEVE /baɪ/ *v* [T] *past* **bought** /£bɔːt, $bɑːt/ *slang* to believe that something is true • *She'll never buy that story about you getting lost!* • *I like the idea of getting married but I don't buy* **into** (= accept as true) *the traditional view of what marriage should be all about.*

buy it *v adv Am slang* to be killed • *He was going to buy it sooner or later.* • *Marvin's bought it!*

buy·out /ˈbaɪ·aʊt/ *n* [C] (in business) a situation where a person or group buys all the shares belonging to a company and so gets control of it • *a management buyout* ○ *a leveraged buyout* • See also **buy out** at BUY PAY FOR.

buzz *(obj)* /bʌz/ *v* to make a continuous low sound such as the one a bee makes • *The bee buzzed* **from** *flower* **to** *flower.*

[I] • *A fly had got into the car and was buzzing* **around** *furiously.* [I] • *(fig.) Reporters were buzzing* **around** (= moving around busily), *trying to get the full story.* [I] • *(fig.) Thoughts buzzed* **around** *my head/My head was buzzing* **with** *thoughts* (=I was thinking about a lot of different things). [I] • *He complained that his ears were buzzing* (= that there was a unpleasant buzzing sound in his ears). [I] • *(fig.) The place was buzzing* **with** *excitement* (= was full of excited talk and activity). [I] • *(infml) Frances buzzed* **(for)** *her colleague* (= called that person by using a telephone that buzzes). [I/T] • If an aircraft buzzes a place it flies over it very low and fast: *Everyone scattered, screaming, as the plane buzzed them repeatedly.* [T]

buzz /bʌz/ *n* • *I heard a buzz* (= a continuous low sound) *and then saw the plane in the distance.* [C] • *(fig.) From the next room I could hear* **the** *buzz* **of** (= the sound of) *conversation.* [U] • *(infml) I* **get a** *real* **buzz from** (=I experience excitement by) *cycling fast.* • *(infml)* If you **give** someone **a buzz** you telephone them: *I'll give you a buzz next week to arrange a time for the meeting.*

buzz·er /£ ˈbʌz·əʳ, $-ɚ/ *n* [C] • *I pressed the buzzer* (= an electronic device that makes a buzzing sound) *and after a while someone came to the door.*

buzz off *v adv* [I] *infml* to go away • *"Buzz off!" growled Celia.*

buz·zard /£ ˈbʌz·əd, $-ɚd/ *n* [C] a large European bird that is a type of HAWK with brown, grey or white feathers that kills small animals on the ground for food, or a type of North American VULTURE that feeds on the flesh of animals that are already dead

buzz word *n* [C] a word or expression that originally had a technical use but has become fashionable by being used a lot, esp. on television and in the newspapers • *'Meltdown' is a buzz word which is still quite common.*

by [CAUSE] /baɪ/ *prep* used to show the person or thing that does something • *The motorcycle was driven by a tiny bald man.* • *We were amazed by what she told us.* • *I'm reading some short stories (written) by Chekhov.* • *The book was translated by a well-known author.* • *I felt frightened by the anger in his voice.* • *By all accounts she was good with children.* • *(specialized)* A **by-line** is a line at the top of a newspaper or magazine article giving the writer's name. See also BYLINE. Compare DATELINE and HEADLINE.

by [METHOD] /baɪ/ *prep* used to show how something is done • *They travelled across Europe by train/car.* • *She did the decorating* **(all)** *by herself* (= alone, without help from anyone). • *We went in by* (= through) *the front door.* • *Do you wish to be paid in cash or by* **cheque**? • *He learned English by* **listening** *to the radio.* [+ v-ing] • *Suddenly, she grabbed him by the arm* (= took hold of this part of his body). • *I refuse to live by* (= following) *their rules.* • *He's a plumber by trade/profession* (= that is his job). • *It's all right by me* (= to me) *if we leave early.*

by [NOT LATER THAN] /baɪ/ *prep* not later than; at or before • *She had promised to be back by five o'clock.* • *The application must be in by the 31st to be accepted.* • *By the time I got to the station the train had already gone.*

by [MEASUREMENT] /baɪ/ *prep* used to show measurements or amounts • *Our office floor space measured twelve metres by ten* (= was twelve metres in one direction and ten in the other). • *Their wages were increased by 12%.* • *Freelance workers are paid by the hour* (= for every hour they work). • *These telephones have sold by the thousand.*

by [DURING] /baɪ/ *prep* during • *We travelled by night and rested by day.* • *(dated) You will find happiness* **by and by** (= gradually).

by [NEAR] /baɪ/ *prep, adv* [not gradable] near, beside or (in distance or time) past • *A small child stood sullenly by her side.* • *He wanted to keep her close by him always.* • *The policewoman walked by* (= past) *(them) without saying a word.* • *"The fundamental things apply/As time goes by"* (song in the film *Casablanca*, Herman Hupfield, 1931)

bye(–bye) /ˈbaɪ·baɪ/ *exclamation infml* goodbye • *Are you going? Bye then.* • *Bye-bye, see you tomorrow.* • *(Am infml)* The expression to **go bye-bye** means to leave and it is often used to children: *It's time to go bye-bye.* • *(esp. Br infml)* The expression **go to bye-byes** is used by or to young children to mean go to sleep or to bed: *It's getting late – it's time for you to go to bye-byes.* • [LP] **Meeting someone**

by–e·lec·tion /ˈbaɪ·ɪˌlek·ʃᵊn/ *n* [C] a special election which happens at a different time from a main election to choose a member of parliament or representative to replace one who has died or left their job

by·gone /£ ˈbaɪ·ɡɒn, $-ɡɑːn/ *adj* [before n; not gradable] belonging to or happening in a past time • *a bygone era* • *The empty factories are relics of a bygone age, no longer required by the modern world.*

by·gones /£ ˈbaɪ·ɡɒnz, $-ɡɑːnz/ *pl n* • If you say **let bygones be bygones** you are telling someone they should forget about unpleasant or hurtful things that have happened in the past: *Forget about the argument you two had, just let bygones be bygones and be friends again.*

by·law, bye–law /£ ˈbaɪ·lɔː, $-lɑː/ *n* [C] a law that is made by an official local organization that only relates to its particular region • A bylaw is also a rule which governs the members of an organization.

by·line /ˈbaɪ·laɪn/ *n* [C] (in football) the line which marks the two shorter ends of the playing field, and which the ball must not pass over if play is to continue • See also **by-line** at BY [CAUSE]. Compare **goal line** at GOAL [GAME].

BYOB /£ ˌbiː·waɪ·əʊˈbiː, $-oʊ-/ *abbreviation for* bring your own bottle (= a request, esp. to people coming to a party, that they bring wine, beer, etc.)

by·pass *obj* /£ ˈbaɪ·pɑːs, $-pæs/ *v* [T] to avoid (something) by going around it • *We were in a hurry so we decided to bypass Canterbury because we knew there'd be a lot of traffic.* • *(fig.) I decided to bypass the boss* (= to act without his or her permission) *and make the decision myself.* • *(fig.) We must not bypass* (= avoid talking about) *such an important issue.*

by·pass /£ ˈbaɪ·pɑːs, $-pæs/ *n* [C] • A bypass is a road built around a city to take traffic around the edge of it rather than through it. • A **bypass (operation)** is a medical operation in which the flow of a person's blood is changed to avoid a diseased part of their heart: *a triple bypass operation* ○ *Her grandfather has recently had coronary bypass surgery.*

by·play /ˈbaɪ·pleɪ/ *n* [U] things that happen, esp. in a play, at the same time as the main action but that are less important than it

by–prod·uct /£ ˈbaɪˌprɒd·ʌkt, $-ˌprɑː·dəkt/ *n* [C] something that is produced as a result of making something else, or something unexpected that happens as a result of something • *Buttermilk is a by-product* **of** *making butter.* • *An increased rate of illness is sometimes said to be one of the by-products* **of** *overcrowded housing.*

byre /£ baɪəʳ, $ baɪr/ *n* [C] *Br dated or literary* a building in which cattle are kept; a COWSHED

by·stand·er /£ ˈbaɪˌstæn·dəʳ, $-dɚ/ *n* [C] a person who is standing near and watching something that is happening but is not taking part in it • *Bystanders were questioned by the police about the violent attack.* • *Many* **innocent** *bystanders were injured by the explosion.* • See also **stand by** at STAND [VERTICAL].

byte /baɪt/ *n* [C] *specialized* a unit of computer information, consisting of a group of (usually eight) BITS • See also GIGABYTE; KILOBYTE; MEGABYTE.

by·way /ˈbaɪ·weɪ/ *n* [C] a small road that not many cars or people travel on • *When we're on holiday we prefer to travel on byways rather than main roads.*

by·word /£ ˈbaɪ·wɜːd, $-wɜːrd/ *n* [C] a person or thing that is very closely connected with a particular quality • *Their shops are a byword* **for** *good value.* • *'Choice' has become a byword* (= a common phrase) *among educationalists.*

by·zant·ine /bɪˈzæn·taɪn, ˈbɪz·ᵊn·tiːn/ *adj fml disapproving* difficult to understand and complicated • *The procedures surrounding legal redress are byzantine.*

C c

C LETTER (*pl* **C's** or **Cs**), **c** (*pl* **c's** or **cs**) /siː/ *n* [C] the 3rd letter of the English alphabet • *Does she spell her name with a C or with a K?* • *(Am)* A **C-note** is a note with the value of 100 DOLLARS. • LP› **Silent letters**

C MUSIC /siː/ *n* [C] a note in Western music • *This song is in* **(the key of)** *C.* [U] • *Play a C, then an E, then a G.* [C]

C MARK /siː/ *n* a mark in an exam or for a piece of work which shows that your work is average or acceptable and not particularly good or bad • *Rachel got a C for her French exam.* [C] • *I got C for Biology last year – I hope I'll get B this year.* [U] • A **C plus/C+** is a mark which is slightly higher than a C. A **C minus/C -** is a mark which is slightly lower than a C.

C NUMBER, **c** /siː/ *n* [C] the sign used in the Roman system for the number 100

C TEMPERATURE /siː/ *n* [after n] *abbreviation for* CELSIUS • *The temperature today reached 25°C.* • LP› **Units**

c ABOUT, **ca** *prep abbreviation for* CIRCA • LP› **Approximate numbers**

cab PART OF VEHICLE /kæb/ *n* [C] the separate part at the front of a vehicle in which the driver sits • *A coat and some maps were stolen from the cab of his truck.*

cab VEHICLE /kæb/ *n* [C] *esp. Am and Aus for* TAXI (= a car with a driver that you pay to use) • *The cabs were lined up outside the station.* • *It will save time if we go* **by cab.** • In the past a cab was a vehicle pulled by a horse, with a driver, which you pay to use. • **Cab stand** is *Am for* **taxi rank.** See at TAXI VEHICLE. • See also MINICAB.

ca·bal /£kəˈbæl, -ˈbɑːl/ *n* [C] *disapproving* a small group of people who plan secretly to take (esp. political) action • *He was assassinated by a cabal* **of** *aides within his own regime.*

cab·a·ret /£ˈkæb·ə·reɪ, $-ɚ-eɪ/ *n* a performance of popular music, singing or dancing, esp. in a restaurant or bar • *The club has a good reputation for its cabaret.* [C] • *She is appearing* **in** *cabaret for the next three weeks.* [U] • *They used to have a famous cabaret* **act.** • LP› **'-et' words** Ⓔ Ⓟ

cab·bage /ˈkæb·ɪdʒ/ *n* a large round vegetable that is often green and which can be eaten cooked or raw • *a savoy cabbage* [C] • *red/white cabbage* [U] • *My cabbages* (= cabbage plants) *didn't grow well this year.* [C] • *Children never seem to like eating cabbage.* [U] • *(Br taboo)* A cabbage is someone who has lost all their powers of thought or speech usually as the result of a serious accident or illness. [C]

cab·bie *infml,* **cab·by** /ˈkæb·i/, *esp. Am* **cab·driv·er** /£ˈkæbˌdraɪ·vəʳ, $-vɚ/ *n* [C] a driver of a car that you pay to use • *Cabbie, how far is it to Johnson Street?* [as form of address]

ca·ber /£ˈkeɪ·bəʳ, $-bɚ/ *n* [C] a long heavy wooden pole which is thrown in competitions in Scotland • *At the Highland Games he proved to be a champion at* **tossing** (= throwing) *the caber.*

cab·in ROOM /ˈkæb·ɪn/ *n* [C] a space in a vehicle (esp. an aircraft or a boat), like a small room, for passengers or the people operating the vehicle • *The best passenger cabins on ocean liners are rather like small hotel rooms.* • In the past a **cabin boy** was a boy who was a servant on a ship. • In an aircraft, the **cabin crew/staff** take care of the passengers. • A **cabin cruiser** is a boat powered by a motor with one or more small cabins for sleeping in. • PIC› **Ships and boats** Ⓓ Ⓔ

cab·in HOUSE /ˈkæb·ɪn/ *n* [C] a small simple house • *We stayed in a cabin in the mountains for two weeks.* • Ⓓ Ⓔ

cab·i·net FURNITURE /ˈkæb·ɪ·nət/ *n* [C] a piece of furniture with shelves, cupboards, or drawers which is used for storing or showing decorative things • *Valued pieces of china may be displayed in a glass-fronted cabinet.* • A **bathroom** cabinet is a small cupboard for storing all the things used in a bathroom. • A **filing** cabinet is a set of large drawers for storing documents, letters, etc. • A **cabinet maker** is a person who makes or repairs good furniture. • PIC› **Bathroom, File** Ⓔ Ⓕ Ⓟ (RUS)

cab·i·net GOVERNMENT /ˈkæb·ɪ·nət/ *n* [C + sing/pl v] a small group, esp. of those elected to government, who make the main decisions about what should happen • *The Cabinet meet/meets every Thursday.* • *All these issues are regularly discussed* **in** (= in a meeting of the) *cabinet.* • *She has become a cabinet* **minister.** • *(Br)* A cabinet **reshuffle** is a change in the members of the cabinet.

ca·ble WIRE /ˈkeɪ·bl̩/ *n* (a length of) wire, esp. twisted into thick strong rope or used to carry electricity • *The cable snapped and the boat floated away from the bank.* [C] • *He tripped over a coil of cable.* [U] • *There were cables for telephones, lights and computers all over the floor.* [C] • *The road has been dug up in order to* **lay** *cables.* [C] • A **cable car** is a vehicle which hangs from a cable fixed to tall poles and transports people up steep slopes or *(Am)* a vehicle on a **cable railway.** • A **cable railway** uses cables under the road to pull passenger vehicles up steep slopes. • **Cable stitch** is a pattern of wool used in KNITTING which looks like twisted cables. • **Cable (television/TV)** is a system of sending television pictures and sound along cables: *Have you got cable (television) yet?* ○ *We* **subscribe** *to several cable* **channels.** • Cable is also a type of telephone system which sends messages and sound along cables: *The office has gone over to cable/to a cable number.*

ca·ble MESSAGE /ˈkeɪ·bl̩/ *n* [C] (in the past) a message sent by electric signal

ca·ble *(obj)* /ˈkeɪ·bl̩/ *v*

ca·boose /kəˈbuːs/ *n* [C] *Am for* **guard's van,** see at GUARD

ca·ca·o /£kəˈkɑː·əʊ, -ˈkeɪ-, $-oʊ/ *n* [U] the seeds of a tropical tree from which chocolate and COCOA are made • *cacao beans*

cache /kæʃ/ *n* [C] a secret or hidden store of things, or the place where they are kept • *an arms cache* • *a cache* **of** *explosives/weapons/drugs*

cach·et /£ˈkæʃ·eɪ, $-ˈ-/ *n* [U] a quality which marks someone or something as special and worth respect and admiration • *They have* **the** *international cachet that comes from wealth.* • *This type of jacket used to have* **a certain** *cachet.* • LP› **'-et' words**

cack–hand·ed /ˌkækˈhæn·dɪd/ *adj Br and Aus slang* awkward, without skill; CLUMSY • *That's a cack-handed way of going about it!*

cack·le /ˈkæk·l̩/ *v* [I] to make the loud, unpleasant sound of a chicken, or *(fig.)* to laugh or talk in a loud, high voice • *The hens cackled in alarm.* • *(fig.) A group of ladies were cackling in a corner.*

cack·le /ˈkæk·l̩/ *n* [C] • *The chicken gave a cackle as it laid an egg.* • *(fig.) Their cackles of amusement could be heard in the next room.*

ca·coph·o·ny /£kəˈkɒf·ə·ni, $-ˈkɑː·fə-/ *n* [U] an unpleasant mixture of loud sounds • *What a cacophony!* • *As we entered the farmyard we were met with a cacophony* **of** *animal sounds.*

ca·coph·on·ous /£kəˈkɒf·ə·nəs, $-ˈkɑː·fə-/ *adj*

cac·tus /ˈkæk·təs/ *n* [C] *pl* **cactuses** or **cacti** /ˈkæk·taɪ/ any of many types of desert plant with thick stems for storing water and usually SPINES (= sharp points)

cad /kæd/ *n* [C] *dated disapproving* a man who behaves badly to women • *He's a cad and a bounder – I'm not in the least surprised he let you down.*

ca·dav·er /£kəˈdæv·əʳ, $-ɚ/ *n* [C] *medical* a dead human body, esp. one used by students for study

ca·dav·er·ous /£kəˈdæv·ᵊr·əs, $ˈ-ɚ-/ *adj* • *cadaverous features* (= looking pale and thin like a person who is about to die)

cad·die, cad·dy /ˈkæd·i/ *n* [C] a person who carries the equipment for someone who is playing golf

cad·die, cad·dy /ˈkæd·i/ *v* [I] **caddying,** *past* **caddied** • *Can you caddie* **for** *me on Saturday?*

cad·dy /ˈkæd·i/, **tea cad·dy** *n* [C] a small container, esp. one for storing tea leaves

ca·dence VOICE /ˈkeɪ·dᵊnts/ *n* [C] a regular rise and fall of sound, esp. of the human voice

ca·dence MUSIC /ˈkeɪ·dᵊnts/ *n* [C] *specialized* a set of CHORDS (= different notes played together) at the end of a piece of music

ca·det /kəˈdet/ *n* [C] a student in the armed forces or the police, or a member of particular uniformed organizations for young people

cadge *(obj)* /kædʒ/ *v infml often disapproving* to (try to) get (something) from someone else without paying for it or doing anything in exchange • *Can I cadge a lift home?* [T] • *He's always cadging free meals and free trips* **from/off** *his clients.* [T] • *I think she was cadging* **for** *a bed for the night but I ignored it.* [I]

cadg·er /£ˈkædʒ·əʳ, $-ɚ/ *n* [C] • *They were cadgers who made a living by writing begging letters to old ladies.*

cad·re /£ˈkɑː·dəʳ, $-dɚ/ *n* [C] (a member of) a small group of trained people who form the basic unit of a military, political or business organization

cae·sar·e·an (sec·tion), **cae·sar·i·an**, *Am usually* **ce·sar·e·an** /£sɪˈzeə·ri·ən, $-ˈzer·i-/, *medical* **section** *n* [C] an operation in which a woman's stomach and womb are cut to allow a baby to be born • *I had to have a caesarean.* • *The doctor suggested I might consider a caesarean section.* • *The baby was born* **by** *caesarean.* • *It was a caesarean* **birth/delivery** *and mother and baby are doing well.*

caf·é, **caf·e** /ˈkæf·eɪ/, *Br infml* **caff** /kæf/ *n* [C] a restaurant where only small meals and drinks that usually do not contain alcohol are served • *There's a little cafe on the corner that serves very good coffee – let's stop there.* • Ⓔ Ⓟ

caf·e·te·ri·a /£ˌkæf·əˈtɪə·ri·ə, $-ˈtɪr·i-/ *n* [C] a restaurant (often in a big shop, a college or an office building) where people collect food and drink from a serving area and take it to a table themselves after paying for it

caf·e·ti·ere /£ˌkæf·əˈtjeəʳ, $-ˈtjer/ *n* [C] a glass container for making coffee in which hot water is poured onto crushed coffee beans and then a metal or plastic FILTER (= net) is pushed down into the container to keep the solids at the bottom • *a six-cup cafetiere*

caf·feine /ˈkæf·iːn/ *n* [U] a chemical, found for example in tea and coffee, which is a STIMULANT (= something which makes people more active)

caf·tan, **kaf·tan** /£ˈkæf·tæn, $-tæn/ *n* [C] a loose piece of clothing, long or short with wide sleeves, of the type worn in the East • *Kaftans were popular in the West during the 1960's and 70's.*

cage /keɪdʒ/ *n* [C] a space surrounded on all sides by bars or wire in which animals or birds are kept, or something which is similar to this in form or purpose • *Zoos are moving away from keeping animals in small cages.* • *Richard's rabbit cage was kept in the yard.* • *(fig.) When I was ill my room was my cage* (= felt like a prison). • *"A Robin Redbreast in a Cage/ Puts all Heaven in a Rage"* (William Blake in the poem *Auguries of Innocence*, 1803)

cage *obj* /keɪdʒ/ *v* [T] • *caged birds/animals* • *Sam's been prowling about* **like a** *caged* **animal** *all morning – I wish he'd sit down.* • *"I know why the caged bird sings"* (title of a book by Maya Angelou, 1969)

cage·y /ˈkeɪ·dʒi/ *adj* **cagier**, **cagiest** *infml* unwilling to give information • *He was very cagey* **about** *what happened at the meeting.*

cag·i·ly /ˈkeɪ·dʒɪ·li/ *adv infml* • *"I'll have to think about it," she replied cagily.*

cag·i·ness /ˈkeɪ·dʒɪ·nəs/ *n* [U] *infml* • *I thought there was a certain amount of caginess in his manner.*

ca·goule, **ka·goul**, **ka·goule** /kəˈguːl/ *n* [C] *Br* a light waterproof jacket which protects the wearer against wet and windy weather and which has a HOOD (= a part that can cover the head) • *Bad weather is likely so please wear walking boots and a kagoul.* • PIC› **Coats and jackets**

ca·hoots /kəˈhuːts/ *pl n* **in cahoots (with)** *infml* acting together with others for an illegal or dishonest purpose • *A banker and a government minister were in cahoots over a property deal.* • *The robber was in cahoots with a bank employee.*

cairn /£keən, $kern/ *n* [C] a small pile of stones made, esp. on mountains, to mark a place or as a MEMORIAL (= to make people remember someone or something) • *We followed the line of cairns across the open hillside.* • *Finally we reached the summit and stood by the cairn to admire the view.*

ca·jole *(obj)* /£kəˈdʒəʊl, $-ˈdʒoʊl/ *v* to persuade (someone) to do (something they might not want to do) by pleasant talk and (sometimes false) promises • *He really knows how to cajole people* **into** *doing what he wants.* [T] • *I managed to cajole her* **out of** *leaving too early.* [T] • *The most effective technique is to cajole rather than to threaten.* [I]

Ca·jun /ˈkeɪ·dʒᵊn/ *n* [C] a member of a group of people living in southern Louisiana in the US • *Cajuns are an ethnic group of people who are descended from the French-speaking peoples of the Maritime Provinces of Canada.*

Ca·jun /ˈkeɪ·dʒᵊn/ *adj* [not gradable] • *Cajun cooking/food* • *New Orleans is the home of Cajun music/dance.*

cake FOOD /keɪk/ *n* a sweet type of food made with a mixture of flour, eggs, fat and sugar • *chocolate/fruit/sponge cake* [U] • *a birthday/Christmas cake* [C] • *cream/small iced cakes* [C] • *He* **made/baked** *a delicious cake.* [C] • *Would you like a piece of/a slice of/some cake.* [U] • *(infml dated) To her, translating from French to Dutch is* **a piece of cake** (= very easy). • **The cake** means the amount of money, goods, etc., available: Everyone should have a fair slice of the cake. ○ *MTV currently has the largest share of the TV music cake* (= market). ○ *The national cake is being cut to suit the rich and powerful.* • *To want more local services but also to pay less tax is to want to* **have** *your* **cake and eat it** (= have/do two things that it is impossible to have/do together). • *"Let them eat cake"* (believed to have been said by Marie Antoinette, but recorded earlier) • *"Dost thou* (= do you) *think, because thou art virtuous, there shall be no more cakes and ale?"* (Shakespeare, Twelfth Night 2.3) • See also OATCAKE, PANCAKE. • Ⓢ

cake SHAPE /keɪk/ *n* [C] a small flat object made by pressing together a soft substance • *a fish/potato cake* ○ *a cake* **of** *soap* ○ *cattle cake* (= dried food for cattle) • Ⓢ

cake *(obj)* TO COVER /keɪk/ *v* to thickly cover and dry out • *boots caked* **with** *mud* [T] ○ *hair caked* **with** *blood* [T] • *The men were caked* **in** *layers of filth and grime.* [T] • *Her make-up had caked and she looked tired.* [I] • Ⓢ

cake·walk /£ˈkeik·wɔːk, $-wɑːk/ *n* [U] *Am infml* something which is very easy to achieve, or a one-sided competitive event where the opposition gives up without a fight • *Doing my exams was a cakewalk this semester.* • *The first round of the 200 meters was a cakewalk* **for** *Carl Lewis.* • *The Superbowl was a cakewalk* **for** *the Forty-Niners.*

cal·a·bash /ˈkæl·ə·bæʃ/ *n* [C] (a tropical plant which produces) a large fruit, the outside of which becomes hard when dried and can be used as a container

cal·a·mine (lo·tion) /ˈkæl·ə·maɪn/ *n* [U] a pink liquid used to reduce pain on sore skin • *Your shoulders look terribly sunburnt – put some calamine on them.*

ca·lam·i·ty /£kəˈlæm·ɪ·ti, $-ə·t̬i/ *n* [C] a serious misfortune causing loss and suffering • *A series of calamities ruined them – floods, a failed harvest and the death of a son.* • Ⓘ

ca·lam·i·tous /£kəˈlæm·ɪ·təs, $-t̬əs/ *adj* • *They feared the calamitous consequences of yet another war.*

ca·lam·i·tous·ly /£kəˈlæm·ɪ·tə·sli, $-t̬ə-/ *adv* • *Despite a change of name the party's vote has fallen calamitously.*

cal·ci·fy *(obj)* /ˈkæl·sɪ·faɪ/ *v* [I/T] to become or make hard, esp. by the addition of substances containing CALCIUM

cal·ci·um /ˈkæl·si·ᵊm/ *n* [U] a chemical element which is present in teeth, bones and CHALK

cal·cu·late *(obj)* /ˈkæl·kjʊ·leɪt/ *v* to judge (the number or amount of something) by using the information that you already have, and adding, multiplying, subtracting or dividing numbers • *The cost of the damage caused by the recent storms has been calculated* **as/at** *over £5 million.* [T] • *The new tax system would be calculated* **on** *the value of property owned by an individual.* [T] • *At some stage we need to calculate* **when** *the project will be finished.* [+ *wh-* word] • *He's calculated* **that** *it would take him two years to save up enough for a car.* [+ *that* clause]

cal·cu·la·tion /ˌkæl·kjʊˈleɪ·ʃᵊn/ *n* • *The calculations that you* **did/made** *contained a few inaccuracies.* [C] • *It took some calculation, but I've worked out how much money we'll need for the project.* [U]

cal·cu·lat·or /£ˈkæl·kjʊ·leɪ·təʳ, $-t̬ɚ/ *n* [C] • A calculator is a small electronic device which is used for doing calculations: *a* **pocket** *calculator* ○ *You won't be allowed to take a programmable calculator into the exam.* • LP› **Mathematics**

cal·cu·late on *obj v prep* [T] to expect or depend on (esp. a particular amount or time); COUNT ON • *We're calculating on about 30 guests for the reception and 60 for the party afterwards.* • *I would have arrived earlier, but I hadn't calculated on the train* **being** *so late.* [+ obj + *v-ing*]

cal·cu·lat·ed /£ˈkæl·kjʊ·leɪ·tɪd, $-t̬ɪd/ *adj* planned or arranged in order to produce a particular effect • *It's one of those awful film endings which is calculated* **to** *make you cry.* [+ *to* infinitive] • *It's a policy that was hardly calculated* **to** (= will not) *win votes.* [+ *to* infinitive] • A **calculated risk** is a risk which you consider worth taking because the result, if it is successful, will be so good: *The director took a calculated risk in giving the film's main role to an unknown actor.*

cal·cu·lat·ing /£ˈkæl·kjʊ·leɪ·tɪŋ, $-t̬ɪŋ/ *adj* tending to control situations for your own advantage in a way that is slightly unpleasant and causes people not to trust you • *In the film she's depicted as a very* **cold and** *calculating character.*

cal·cu·la·tion /ˌkæl·kjʊˈleɪ·ʃᵊn/ *n* [U] • *There's an element of calculation in his behaviour that makes me distrust him.*

cal·cu·lus /'kæl·kjʊ·ləs/ *n* [U] *specialized* an area of advanced mathematics in which continually changing values are studied • *I'm specializing in differential and integral calculus.*

cal·dron /£'kɔːl·drən, $'kɑːl-/ *n* [C] *Am for* CAULDRON

cal·en·dar /£'kæl·ɪn·dəʳ, $-dɚ/ *n* [C] a printed table showing the arrangement of the days, weeks and months of the year, or a system for deciding the beginning and end of years, their total length and the parts into which they are divided • *He's got a calendar on his office wall with different photographs of Paris for each month.* • *You should turn over your calendar – it's the 1st of March today.* • *There's a calendar in the back of your diary.* • *the Jewish/Muslim calendar* • A **calendar month** is one of the twelve named months that the year is divided into: *Your salary will be paid on the third week of each calendar month.* • A **calendar year** is a period of 365 or 366 days, starting on January 1st and ending on December 31st. • A calendar is also a list of events and dates within a particular year that are important for an organization or for the people involved in a particular activity: *The athletics meeting at Crystal Palace promises to be a major event in this year's sporting calendar.* • LP **Calendar** CS PL

calf ANIMAL /£kɑːf, $kæf/ *n* [C] *pl* **calves** /kɑːvz/ a young cow, or the young of various other large mammals, including ELEPHANTS, GIRAFFES and WHALES • If a cow is **in calf**, it is pregnant. • See also CALVE.

calve /£kɑːv, $kæv/ *v* [I] • When a cow calves it gives birth to a calf: *Four cows calved overnight.* ○ *The calving was difficult and we had to call a vet.*

calf LEG /£kɑːf, $kæf/ *n* [C] *pl* **calves** /£kɑːvz, $kævz/ the curved fleshy part at the back of the human leg between the knee and the foot • *She's been unable to play since January because of a torn calf* **muscle**. • *The captain expects to have recovered from his calf* **injury** *in time for Saturday's game against Ireland.* • *I think I'll wear a* **calf-length** *skirt* (= one which ends at the middle point between the knee and the foot) *for the interview.* • PIC **Body**

calf·skin /£'kɑːf·skɪn, $'kæf-/, **calf** *n* [U] leather made from the skin of a young cow • *calfskin boots* • *a calfskin bag*

cal·i·brat·ed /£'kæl·ɪ·breɪ·tɪd, $-t̬ɪd/ *adj specialized* (of tools or other devices) adjusted or marked for making accurate measurements • *a calibrated stick for measuring the amount of oil in an engine*

cal·i·brate *obj* /'kæl·ɪ·breɪt/ *v* [T] *specialized* • *The meter needs to be carefully calibrated before any measurements are made.*

cal·i·bra·tion /ˌkæl·ɪ'breɪ·ʃən/ *n* [C; U] *specialized*

cal·i·bre QUALITY, *Am usually* **cal·i·ber** /£'kæl·ɪ·bəʳ, $-bɚ/ *n* [U] the degree of quality or excellence of someone or something • *If teaching paid more it might attract people* **of** *(a) higher calibre.* • *The competition entries were* **of** *such (a)* **high** *calibre that judging them was very difficult.*

cal·i·bre MEASUREMENT, *Am usually* **cal·i·ber** /£'kæl·ɪ·bəʳ, $-bɚ/ *n* [C; U] the width of the inside of a pipe, esp. of the long cylindrical part of a gun, or the width of a bullet

cal·i·co /£'kæl·ɪ·kəʊ, $-koʊ/ *n* [U] a heavy plain cloth made from cotton

cal·i·pers /£'kæl·ɪ·pəz, $-pɚz/ *pl n Am for* CALLIPERS TOOL

ca·liph /'keɪ·lɪf/, **ca·lif**, **kha·lif** *n* [C] (in the past) a Muslim ruler • *Fatima was the youngest daughter of the Prophet Mohammed and was also the wife of the fourth Muslim caliph, Ali.*

cal·is·then·ics /ˌkæl·ɪs'θen·ɪks/ *n* [U + sing/pl v] CALLISTHENICS

call *obj* NAME /£kɔːl, $kɑːl/ *v* [T + obj + n] to give (someone or something) a name, or to know or address (someone) by a particular name • *They've called the twins Katherine and Thomas.* • *What's that actor called that we saw in the film last night?* • *His real name is Jonathan, but they've always called him 'Johnny'.* • *What's her new novel called?* • *I wish he wouldn't keep calling me 'dear' – it's so patronising!* • *Martha refuses to eat spaghetti – she calls it 'worms'.* • If a person, esp. a child, calls someone **names**, he or she addresses that person with a name which is intended to be offensive: *Tom's worried that if he wears glasses at school the other children will call him names.*

call *(obj)* TELEPHONE /£kɔːl, $kɑːl/ *v* to telephone (someone) • *He called (you) last night when you were out.* [T] • *She called (me) this morning at the office and we had a brief chat.* [T] • *I've been calling all morning but I can't get any answer.* [I] • *I'm a bit busy – can I call you* **back** *later?* [T] • *If you're ever followed by a stranger again you should call the police.* [T] • *I just called* **to** *say I love you.* [I] • (esp. Am) *Can I call you* **up** *at your apartment?* [T] • (Am) If you **call collect** (*Am also, Br and Aus* **reverse (the) charges**), you make a call which is paid for by the person who receives it. • LP **Telephone**

call /£kɔːl, $kɑːl/ *n* [C] • *I got a call* **from** *an old college friend last night.* • *If there are any calls* **for** *me could you write them down next to the telephone?* • *I've just got a couple of calls to* **make**. • *That decorator you rang about painting the house – did he ever* **return** *your call?* • *The radio station* **received** *a lot of calls complaining about the show's bad language.* • *Telephone calls during peak hours are charged at a higher rate.* • (Br) A **call box** (also **public (tele)phone, (tele)phone booth**, *Br and Aus* **(tele)phone box**), is an enclosed or partly enclosed area in a public place where people can use a telephone. • A **call girl** is a female PROSTITUTE (= person who is paid for sexual services) who arranges her meetings with customers over the telephone. • **Call-in** is *Am for* **phone-in**. See at PHONE.

call·er /£'kɔː·ləʳ, $'kɑː·lɚ/ *n* [C] • A caller is someone who makes a telephone call, often a member of the public who is telephoning a radio or television programme while it is being broadcast: *Hold the line please, caller. I'm trying to connect you.* [as form of address] ○ *I'd just like to comment on what your previous caller was saying.*

call VISIT /£kɔːl, $kɑːl/ *v* [I] to visit someone, esp. for a short time • *Shall we call* **in on** *Martin/(Br also)* **round at** *Martin's this evening?* • *Could you call* **in at**/*(Br also)* **round at** *the shops on your way home and get some milk?* • *The electrician must have called this morning when we were out – there's a note on the door mat.* • *If she's not in I'll call* **back** *later.* • If you call **by**, you visit somewhere for a short while on your way to somewhere else: *I just thought I'd call by on my way into town.* • If you call **for** someone or something, you visit a place with the intention of collecting someone or something: *She's going to call for you at eight o'clock and she wants you to be ready to leave straightaway.* ○ *I was wondering when I could call for the gloves that I left at your house last night.*

call /£kɔːl, $kɑːl/ *n* [C] • A call can be a short official visit, usually made by someone whose job is connected with health: *Doctor Seward is out* **on a** *call this morning.* ○ *The nurse has got a few calls to* **make** *this afternoon.* • Some types of workers, esp. doctors, are described as being **on call** if they are available to make official visits at any time when they are needed, whether they are at home or at work: *She's a doctor so she's often on call at the weekend, even when she's at home.* • (slightly dated) *I thought I'd* **pay** *a call* **on** (= visit) *an old friend of mine this weekend.*

call·er /£'kɔː·ləʳ, $'kɑː·lɚ/ *n* [C] • (dated) *The nearest village is ten miles away, so we don't get many callers* (= visitors) *here.*

call *(obj)* SHOUT/CRY /£kɔːl, $kɑːl/ *v* to say something in a loud voice, esp. in order to attract someone's attention, or (of animals) to make a loud, high sound, esp. to another animal • *Someone in the crowd called* **out** *his name but he couldn't see who.* [T] • *Did you call?* [I] • *"Hey, you! Come over here!" she called.* [+ clause] • *The blackbird called* **to** *its mate.* [I]

call /£kɔːl, $kɑːl/ *n* [C] • *The whale has a very distinctive call.* • *She could hear calls* **for help** *from inside the burning building.* • *I'll be in the next room, so* **give** *me a call if you need any help.* • If someone **stays within** call of you, they stay near enough for you to be able to attract their attention by shouting to them: *When we were children we were allowed to wander away from our parents so long as we stayed within call.*

call *(obj)* ASK TO COME /£kɔːl, $kɑːl/ *v* to ask (someone) to come to you • *She called me* **over** *to where she was sitting.* [T] • *I keep the bedroom door open in case the children call* **(for)** *me in the night.* [I/T] • *I was called* **to** *an emergency meeting this morning.* [T] • *Could you call* **in** *the next interviewee, please?* [M] • *At school she was always being called* **into** *the headteacher's office.* [T] • *His bank has called him* **in** *again to discuss the money that he owes them.* [T] • If a bank calls **in a loan** they demand that the money is paid back to them. [M] • *Leading supermarkets have called* **back** (= asked to be returned) *the mineral water after traces of poison were found in two bottles.* [M] • To **call** something **to mind** is to remember it: *Her name is familiar, but I can't quite call to mind where I've heard it.* • (fml) *The fact that a party can be voted into power by a minority of the electorate* **calls into question** (= causes doubts about) *the country's*

CALENDAR: REFERRING TO POINTS IN TIME

In the calendar below, **TODAY** is Wednesday 16th July. From this point in time, other days can be referred to by the phrases given in their boxes. For example, Friday 18th is *the day after tomorrow*.

SUN	MON	TUES	WED	THURS	FRI	SAT
		1	**2** (*esp. Br*) a fortnight ago	**3**	**4**	**5**
6 the Sunday before last	**7** last Monday	**8** last Tuesday	**9** last Wednesday	**10** last Thursday	**11** last Friday	**12** last Saturday
13 last Sunday	**14** the day before yesterday	**15** yesterday	**16** **TODAY**	**17** tomorrow	**18** the day after tomorrow	**19** next Saturday
20 next Sunday	**21** next Monday	**22** next Tuesday	**23** next Wednesday, a week today, today week	**24** next Thursday, a week (from) tomorrow, tomorrow week	**25** next Friday	**26** Saturday week, a week on Saturday
27	**28**	**29**	**30** (*esp. Br*) a fortnight today	**31**		

You can refer to weeks or months using 'last' and 'next' in the same way. In America a week is from Sunday to Saturday, so *this week* is July 13–19, next week is July 20–26, and so on. Often in Britain a week is from Monday to Sunday.

The expressions 'this Saturday', 'this Sunday' and 'this weekend' can mean either *next* or *last Saturday* and so on, depending on the situation. This can sometimes cause confusion.

LP **Common ways of giving the date** at DATE, and **Periods of time** at PERIOD.

electoral system. • *"For many are called, but few are chosen"* (Bible, Matthew 22.14)

call *obj* CONSIDER /£kɔːl, $kɑːl/ *v* [T + obj + n] to consider to be • *He knows a lot of people, but only one or two that he'd call close friends.* • *One sandwich and a lettuce leaf – I don't call that a meal!* • *I'm not calling you a liar – I'm just suggesting that you misunderstood the facts of the situation.* • *A woman gets six months in prison for stealing food and a rapist only gets a fine and they call that justice!* • *"Actually Andrew, people usually say excuse me when they push past someone else – it's called manners!"* • *I don't know exactly how much you owe me, but let's call it £10.* • *I paid for last week's shopping and you paid for this week's, so let's* **call it quits** (= agree not to owe each other anything). • *(infml) I'm getting a bit tired now – shall we* **call it a day** (= stop the work we are doing)? • *(infml usually humorous)* If someone **calls a spade a spade** they are not frightened to say the truth about something, even if it is not polite or pleasant. • If you can **call** something your **own**, you can reasonably consider it to belong to you: *I don't want to live in a particularly big house. I just want a place I can call my own.* ○ *The President has had very few ideas that he can genuinely call his own.*

call *obj* WAKE UP /£kɔːl, $kɑːl/ *v* [T] to wake (someone) up • *If I'm not up by eight o'clock could you call me, please?*

call /£kɔːl, $kɑːl/ *n* [C] • *What time do you want me to* **give** *you a call tomorrow morning?*

call *(obj)* DEMAND /£kɔːl, $kɑːl/ *v* to demand or to deserve • *The opposition parties are calling* **for** *the minister's resignation over the scandal.* [I] • *You've been promoted? This calls* **for a celebration***!* [I] • *It's the sort of work that calls* **for** *a high level of concentration.* [I] • *They're calling* **on** *all men and boys over the age of 14 to join the army.* [I] • *(fml) I now call* **on** *everyone to raise a glass to the happy couple.* [I] • *(fig. fml) She would have to* **call on** (= use) *all her strength if she was to survive the next few months.* • *The chairwoman called* **(for) order***/called the meeting* **to order** (= demanded that everyone stop talking so that the meeting could start or continue). [T] • *He told you that you were an idiot? Well, I don't think that was* **called for** (= I think it was rude and not deserved)*!* • If someone is falsely claiming to know something, or threatening to do something that they are not able to, you might **call** their **bluff** by making them prove their knowledge or by telling them to perform the action that they were threatening you with. • *(Am)* You **call** your **shot** by stating clearly your intentions. •

Someone who **calls the tune/shots** is in the position of being able to make the decisions which will influence a situation.

call /£kɔːl, $kɑːl/ *n* • *There's* **not much** *call* **for** (= There's little public demand for) *fur coats these days.* [U] • *Management have so far ignored the union's calls* **for** *stricter safety regulations.* [C] • *(fml or humorous) I certainly don't think there's any call* **for** *that sort of language, young lady!* [U] • *(usually humorous)* **A/The call of nature** refers to the need to urinate or excrete the contents of the bowels: *Would you excuse me for a moment? I just need to* **answer** *a call of nature.* • *"The Call of the Wild"* (title of a book by Jack London, 1903)

call *obj* [DECIDE ON] /£kɔːl, $kɑːl/ *v* [T] to decide officially to have (a particular event) or take (particular action) • *The managing director has called* **a meeting** *to discuss pay levels.* • *The papers are predicting that the Prime Minister will call* **an election** *in the spring.* • *It's reckoned that the unions will call* **a strike** *if management will not agree to their demands.* • *They had to call* **a halt to** (= end) *the match because of the heavy rain.*

call forth *obj*, **call** *obj* **forth** *v adv* [M] *fml* to cause (something) to exist • *The proposed shopping centre has called forth an angry response from local residents.*

call off *obj* [STOP ACTIVITY], **call** *obj* **off** *v adv* [M] to decide that (a planned event, esp. a sporting one) will not happen, or to end (an activity) because it is no longer useful or possible • *Tomorrow's match has been called off because of the icy weather.* • *The police have called off the search for the missing child until dawn tomorrow.*

call off *obj* [STOP ATTACK], **call** *obj* **off** *v adv* [M] *slightly fml* to order (esp. a dog) to stop attacking someone or something • *I shouted to him to call his dog off, but he just laughed at me.*

call up *obj* [MILITARY], **call** *obj* **up**, *Am usually* **draft** *v adv* [M] to order (someone) to join the armed forces • *He was called up when the war began.*

call–up /£ˈkɔːl·ʌp, $ˈkɑːl-/, *Am also* **draft** *n* [C] • *She was very upset when her boyfriend received his call-up papers* (= was officially ordered to join the armed forces).

call up *obj* [COMPUTING], **call** *obj* **up** *v adv* [M] to find and show (information) on a computer screen • *You can use the search facility to call up all the occurrences of a particular word in a document.* • *Could you call last year's sales figures up for me?*

cal·lan·et·ics /£kæl·əˈnet·ɪks, $-ˈneţ-/ *n* [U] *Br trademark* a system of physical exercise which involves frequently repeated small movements of the muscles and is intended to make the body firmer and more attractively shaped

cal·li·graph·y /kəˈlɪg·rə·fi/ *n* [U] (the art of producing) beautiful writing, often created with a special pen or brush • *There's some wonderful calligraphy in these old manuscripts.* • *Susannah won the calligraphy prize when she was at school.* • [PIC] **Writing**

call·ing /£ˈkɔː·lɪŋ, $ˈkɑː-/ *n* [C] *fml* a job, esp. a religious one or one such as medicine, in which you help others • *I'm glad she's going into medicine. It's a very worthy calling.*

cal·li·pers [TOOL] *Br and Aus, Am* **cal·i·pers** /£ˈkæl·ɪ·pəz, $-pɚz/ *pl n* a device for measuring widths or distances, consisting of two long thin movable pieces of metal fixed together at one end

cal·li·pers [LEG SUPPORT] *Br and Aus* /£ˈkæl·ɪ·pəz, $-pɚz/, *Am* **bra·ces** *pl n* metal supports which are fastened to the legs of people who have difficulties with walking

cal·lis·then·ics, cal·is·then·ics /ˌkæl·ɪsˈθen·ɪks/ *n* [U + sing/pl v] (a system of) simple physical exercises that are done to make the body firm, able to stretch easily and more attractive

cal·lous /ˈkæl·əs/ *adj* unkind or cruel; without sympathy or feeling for other people • *It might sound callous, but I don't care if he's homeless. He's not living with me!*

cal·lous·ly /ˈkæl·ə·sli/ *adv*

cal·lous·ness /ˈkæl·ə·snəs/ *n* [U]

cal·low /£ˈkæl·əʊ, $-oʊ/ *adj* **-er, -est** *disapproving* (esp. of young people) behaving in a way that shows a lack of experience, confidence or wisdom • *Mark was just a callow* **youth** *of sixteen when he arrived in Paris.*

cal·lus /ˈkæl·əs/ *n* [C] an area of hard thickened skin, esp. on the feet or hands • *He had workman's hands which were rough and covered with calluses.*

calm /kɑːm/ *adj* **-er, -est** peaceful and quiet; without hurried movement, anxiety or noise • *After a night of fighting, the streets are now calm.* • *He has a very calm manner, which is useful in this hectic office.* • *She's not very good at* **keeping/staying** *calm in difficult situations.* • Calm can also be used to describe weather which is not windy or the sea or a lake when it is still and has no waves. • (P)

calm *(obj)* /kɑːm/ *v* • *He was trying to calm a screaming baby by rocking it back and forth.* [T] • *She sat down and took a few deep breaths to calm herself* **(down)**. [T] • *Nick was furious when I told him we couldn't afford to go to Mexico, but he soon calmed* **down**. [I] • *Calm* **down**, *for goodness sake. It's nothing to get excited about!* [I] • *She had a very calming* **influence** *on her husband.* • *He placed a calming hand on the child's shaking shoulder.* • Something or someone which calms your **fears** makes you feel less anxious about something. [T]

calm·ly /ˈkɑː·m·li/ *adv* • *She reacted surprisingly calmly to the news of his death.*

calm·ness /ˈkɑːm·nəs/, *esp. literary* **calm** *n* [U] • *She had never felt such calmness before. It was as if all her worries had disappeared.* • *It was the calm of the countryside that he loved so much.* • **The calm before/after the storm** is a quiet or peaceful period before/after a period during which there is great activity, argument or unpleasantness: *He decided to take advantage of the calm before the storm and relax for a few minutes before the guests arrived.* ○ *After all her suffering, she felt she was entering a peaceful stage in her life, the calm after the storm.*

Cal·or gas /£ˈkæ·lə, $-lɚ-/ *n* [U] *Br trademark* a type of gas which is sold in metal containers and can be taken to places where there is no gas supply and used for heating and cooking • *We took a calor gas* **stove** *for cooking on when we went camping.*

cal·or·ie [FOOD] /£ˈkæl·ᵊr·i, $ˈ-ɚ-/ *n* [C] a unit of energy which is used as a measurement for the amount of energy which food provides • *There are about fifty calories in an apple.* • *An athlete in training needs a lot of calories.* • *This drink can only help you to lose weight as a part of a calorie-***controlled diet**. • *He found calorie-***counting** *the best way of losing weight.*

cal·or·if·ic /ˌkæl·əˈrɪf·ɪk/ *adj* • *Although it's only a quick snack, a hamburger is very calorific* (= it contains a lot of calories.) • *Fatty foods have a high calorific* **value**.

cal·or·ie [HEAT] /£ˈkæl·ᵊr·i, $ˈ-ɚ-/ *n* [C] *specialized* a unit of heat energy equal to either 4·19 or 4190 JOULES • *A calorie is the amount of heat required to increase the temperature of one gram of water by one degree Celsius.*

cal·um·ny /ˈkæl·əm·ni/ *n fml* (the act of making) a statement about someone which is not true and is intended to damage the reputation of that person • *He was subjected to the most vicious calumny, but he never complained and never sued.* [U] • *She has been the victim of a series of completely unjustified calumnies.* [C]

cal·va·dos /£ˈkæl·və·dɒs, $-doʊs/ *n* [U] a strong alcoholic drink made from apples; a type of BRANDY • *Calvados is made in Normandy in northern France.*

calve /kɑːv/ *v* See at CALF [ANIMAL]

calves /kɑːvz/ *pl of* CALF

cal·vin·ist /ˈkæl·vɪ·nɪst/, **cal·vin·ist·ic** /ˌkæl·vɪˈnɪs·tɪk/ *adj* relating to the Christian teachings of John Calvin, esp. the belief that God is responsible for saving people from evil • *Calvinist doctrine* • *(fig.) Her parents have very calvinist attitudes* (= They have severe moral standards and consider pleasure to be wrong or unnecessary).

Cal·vin·ist /ˈkæl·vɪ·nɪst/ *n* [C] • *The Dutch are a pretty fun-loving people, especially when you consider that they are Calvinists.*

ca·lyp·so /£kəˈlɪp·səʊ, $-soʊ/ *n* [C] *pl* **calypsos** or **calypsoes** a type of popular West Indian song whose words, often invented as the song is sung, usually deal with a subject of interest at the present time

cam·a·rad·e·rie /£ˌkæm·əˈrɑː·dᵊr·i, $-dɚ-/ *n* [U] *slightly fml* a feeling of friendliness towards people with whom you work or share an experience • *When you've been climbing alone for hours there's a tremendous sense of camaraderie when you meet another climber.*

cam·ber /£ˈkæm·bəʳ, $-bɚ/ *n* [C] a gradual slope down from the middle of a road to each edge which helps water to flow off it

cam·cord·er /£ˈkæmˌkɔː·dəʳ, $-ˌkɔːr·dɚ/ *n* [C] a combination of a small VIDEO camera and recording device in a single unit which can be held easily in one hand • *Colour LCD screens are ideal for portable battery-operated equipment such as laptop computers and camcorders.*

came /keɪm/ *past simple of* COME

cam·el ANIMAL /ˈkæm·ᵊl/ *n* [C] a large animal with a long neck that lives in desert areas and has either one or two HUMPS (= large lumps) on its back • *"It is easier for a camel to go through the eye of a needle, than for a rich man to enter into the kingdom of God"* (Bible, Matthew 19.24)

cam·el CLOTH /ˈkæm·ᵊl/, **cam·el hair** *n* [U] a soft brown woollen cloth used to make coats

ca·mel·li·a /kəˈmiː·li·ə/ *n* [C] a bush with dark shiny leaves and large, esp. white, pink or red flowers which are similar to roses

Cam·em·bert /£ˈkæm·ᵊm·beə, $-ber/ *n* [C/U] a soft French cheese with a white outside and a yellowish creamy inside

cam·e·o PERFORMANCE /£ˈkæm·i·əu, $-ou/ *n* [C] *pl* **cameos** a small but noticeable part, esp. in a film or play, usually performed by a famous actor • *Olivier appears briefly towards the end of the film in a comic cameo* **role/part**.

cam·e·o JEWELLERY /£ˈkæm·i·əu, $-ou/ *n* [C] *pl* **cameos** a piece of usually oval jewellery on which there is a head or other shape of one colour on a background of a noticeably different colour • *a cameo* **brooch** • PIC› **Jewellery**

cam·era /ˈkæm·rə/ *n* [C] a device for taking photographs or making films or television programmes • *I forgot to take my camera with me to Portugal, so I couldn't take any photos.* [C] • *Television camera* **crews** *broadcast the event all round the world.* • *They must be filming in the street because there are cameras down there.* [C] • *Smile, you're* **on camera** (= being filmed)*!* • *It was said of Marilyn Monroe that the camera loved her* (= that she looked very attractive on film and in photographs). [C] • If someone is **camera-shy**, they dislike or feel nervous about having their photograph taken: *"Where's Nicki in this photo?" "Oh, hiding in the background – she's really camera-shy."* • *The* **camera work** *in* (= skill involved in filming) *some of these animal documentaries is fantastic.* • See also IN CAMERA. • (RUS)

cam·era·man (*pl* **-men**), **cam·era·wo·man** (*pl* **-women**), **cam·era op·e·rat·or** /ˈkæm·rə·mæn, -mən, -ˌwʊm·ən/ *n* [C] a person who operates a camera when films or television programmes are being made

cam·i·knick·ers /£ˈkæm·iˌnɪk·əz, $-ɚz/ *pl n Br* a piece of women's underwear consisting of a light part to cover the top half of the body connected to a pair of KNICKERS

cam·i·sole /£ˈkæm·ɪ·səul, $-soul/ *n* [C] a light piece of women's underwear for the top half of the body with thin straps that go over the shoulders

cam·o·mile /ˈkæm·ə·maɪl/ *n* [C; U] a pleasant smelling plant whose white and yellow flowers have uses in medicine and are also used to make tea • *camomile* **tea**

cam·ou·flage /ˈkæm·ə·flɑːʒ/ *n* [U] (the military use of) leaves, branches and paints for hiding people or equipment • *Using smoke as* **(a)** *camouflage, the army advanced up the hill.* • Camouflage is also the way that the colour or shape of an animal or plant appears to mix with its surroundings to prevent it from being seen by attackers: *The lizard's light brown skin acts as* **(a)** *camouflage in the desert sand.* • Camouflage can refer to anything which is intended to hide something because, for example, it is unattractive: *This cream is an excellent camouflage for spots, blemishes and scars.*

cam·ou·flage *obj* /ˈkæm·ə·flɑːʒ/ *v* [T] • *The troops had camouflaged themselves so effectively that the enemy didn't notice them approaching.* • *Camouflaged by its green skin, the frog rested safely in the undergrowth by the water.* • *(fig.) He always wore a hat as a way of camouflaging* (= hiding) *his baldness.*

camp TENTS/BUILDINGS /kæmp/ *n* a place where people stay in tents or other temporary structures • *We* **pitched** *camp* (= set up our tents) *by the lakeside.* [U] • *(Br) As a boy, Chris spent a lot of his holidays* **on camp**. [U] • *The military base was once the site of a* **peace** *camp of women opposed to nuclear weapons.* [C] • A camp can also be a group of buildings or tents where an army stays while training or fighting: *a* **military/army** *camp* [C] • A camp can also be a group of buildings that have been built as a temporary way of dealing with a problem: *Thousands are living in appalling conditions in the* **refugee** *camps.* [C] ○ *During the war he was held in a* **prison** *camp.* [C] • *(Br and Aus)* A **camp bed** (*Am* **cot**) is a light bed, usually made of a strong fabric stretched over a metal frame, which can be folded so that it uses little space when it is being stored. • PIC› **Beds and bedroom** (I) (NL)

camp /kæmp/ *v* [I] • *We camped on one of the lower slopes of the mountain.* • *We used to* **go camping** *in Spain when I was a child.* • If you camp **out**, you sleep outside in a tent.

camp·er /£ˈkæm·pəʳ, $-pɚ/ *n* [C] • A camper is a person who is staying in a tent. • A camper *(Br also, and Aus)* **camper van**, *(Am also)* **RV** is a large motor vehicle in which you can sleep, store a lot of equipment and often cook. See also DORMOBILE. • PIC› **Vehicles**

camp·ing /ˈkæm·pɪŋ/ *n* [U] • *I love the freedom of camping.* • *Is there a shop round here that sells camping* **equipment***?* • **Camping ground** is *Aus for* CAMPSITE. • (GR)

camp STYLE /kæmp/ *adj* **-er, -est** *infml* (of a man) behaving and dressing in a way that is similar to a woman and often intended to be noticed by others or, (of people or styles in general) intentionally artificial, usually in a way that is amusing • *What's the name of that amazingly camp actor with the high voice and a funny walk?* • *Their shows are always incredibly camp and flamboyant.* • (I) (NL)

camp /kæmp/ *n* [U] *infml* • *The latest production of the opera is very* **high** *camp – all the men are dressed up as women.* • *He was a master of innuendo and* **high**-*camp comedy.*

camp /kæmp/ *v* [I] *infml* • If an actor **camps it up**, he or she gives an artificial and often amusing performance in which emotions are expressed too strongly and the movements of the hands and body are more noticeable than they would usually be.

camp OPINION /kæmp/ *n* [C + sing/pl v] a group of people who share an opinion, esp. a political one • *The pro-abortion camp are fighting to decriminalize abortion.* • *The party is divided into two distinct camps over the legislation.* • A **camp follower** is a person who is interested in and supports a particular political party or other organization but is not a member of it. • (I) (NL)

cam·paign /kæmˈpeɪn/ *n* [C] a planned group of esp. political, business or military activities which are intended to achieve a particular aim • *The protests were part of their campaign* **against** *building development in the area.* • *This is the latest act of terrorism in a long-standing and bloody campaign* **of violence**. • *The endless public appearances and shaking of hands are an inevitable part of an* **election** *campaign.* • *She's the campaign* **organizer** *for the Labour Party.* • *She went on the* **campaign trail** (= to the places where someone who wants to be elected goes to make speeches) *around the Southern states with Clinton before the 1992 election.* • Campaigns often involve the spreading of information: *The government have just* **launched** (= begun) *their annual Christmas campaign* **to** *stop drunken driving.* [+ *to* infinitive] • **Advertising** campaigns are intended to bring a particular product to the public's attention: *The jeans company's latest advertising campaign involves photographs of animals dressed up as people.* • A **military** campaign is a group of connected actions or movements that forms part of a war. • (T)

cam·paign /kæmˈpeɪn/ *v* [I] • *They've been campaigning for years* **to** *get him out of prison.* [+ *to* infinitive] • *He's spending a lot of his time at the moment campaigning* **for/on behalf of** *the Animal Liberation Front.* • *They're busy campaigning* **against** *the building of a new motorway near here.*

cam·paign·er /£ˌkæmˈpeɪ·nəʳ, $-nɚ/ *n* [C] • A campaigner is a person who takes part in organized activities which are intended to change something in society: *an anti-alcohol campaigner* ○ *She's a campaigner* **for** *Friends of the Earth.*

cam·pan·ol·o·gy /£ˌkæm·pəˈnɒl·ə·dʒi, $-ˈnɑː·lə-/ *n* [U] *specialized* the art or skill of ringing bells to make music

cam·pan·o·log·ist /£kæm·pəˈnɒl·ə·dʒɪst, $-nɑː·lə-/ *n* [C] *specialized*

camp·fire /£ˈkæmp·faɪəʳ, $-faɪr/ *n* [C] a fire outside which is made and used esp. by people who are staying in tents

cam·phor /£ˈkæm·fəʳ, $-fɚ/ *n* [U] a white or colourless substance with a strong smell which is sometimes used in medicine to reduce pain or ITCHING

camp·site /ˈkæmp·saɪt/, **camp·ing site**, *Aus* **camp·ing ground**, *Am usually* **camp·ground** *n* [C] a piece of land where people on holiday can stay in tents, usually with toilets and places for washing • *The campsite is in a beautiful location next to the beach.* • *(Am)* A campsite is also a place for one tent at a place where people stay in tents: *Our tent was so large that they charged us for two campsites.*

cam·pus /ˈkæm·pəs/ *n* the buildings of a large school, college or university and the land that surrounds them •

There's accommodation for about five hundred students **on** *campus.* [U] • *The campus at Warwick University has a really impressive arts centre.* [C]

cam·shaft /£'kæm·ʃɑːft, $-ʃæft/ *n* [C] a device which causes the VALVES of an engine to open or close at the correct time

can CONTAINER /kæn/ *n* [C] a closed metal container, esp. a cylindrical one in which some types of drink and food are sold • *We recycle all our empty food and drink cans.* • *After the party, the floor was littered with empty beer/lager cans.* • A can is also the amount of food or drink that is contained in a can: *I've drunk two cans of lemonade, and I'm still thirsty!* ○ *You'll need a can (Br and Aus also* **tin**) *of beans/tuna/pineapple for that recipe.* • A can might also be a larger metal container, esp. one with a lid, handle and shaped opening for pouring: *a* **petrol/oil** *can* • *(Am infml)* **The can** is sometimes used to mean prison: *He spent ten years in the can for armed robbery.* • *(Am infml)* **The can** is sometimes also used to mean toilet: *I'm just going to the can. I'll be back in a moment.* • *(infml)* If a film is **in the can**, filming has been completed and it is ready to be prepared for showing to the public. • *(infml)* People sometimes refer to a difficult problem as a **can of worms**, esp. when it is a situation which they really do not want to deal with: *Corruption is a serious problem, but nobody has yet been willing to* **open** *up that can of worms.* • A **can opener** *(Br and Aus also* **tin opener**) is a tool for opening cans of food. • PIC **Containers, Kitchen** NL

can *obj* /kæn/ *v* [T] **-nn-** • Food and drink is canned when it is put into a closed metal container without air: *He works in a factory where they can fruit.* • *(esp. Am infml)* If you can something you stop doing it: *I wish the people next door would can that noise.* ○ *Hey, can* **it**, *would you? I'm trying to sleep.*

canned /kænd/ *adj* [not gradable] • Something which is canned is preserved and sold in a can: *canned (also Br and Aus* **tinned**) *food/fruit/tomatoes* ○ *Do you prefer canned or bottled beer?* • *(disapproving)* **Canned laughter** is recordings of laughter that have been added to a humorous radio or television programme when something amusing has been said or done: *The show was full of canned laughter, but it didn't make the jokes any funnier.* • *(disapproving)* **Canned music** is recorded music of low quality which is played quietly and continuously in public places to make people feel relaxed: *As soon as the aircraft lands they switch on the canned music.* See also MUZAK; **piped music** at PIPE TUBE.

can·ne·ry /£'kæn·ᵊr·i, $'-ɚ-/ *n* [C] • A cannery is a factory where food is put into cans.

can ABILITY /kæn/ *v aux* [+ infinitive without *to*; not *be canning*] he/she/it **can**, *past simple* **could** /kʊd/ to be able to • *Can you drive?* • *She can speak four languages.* • *I can't eat anything with mushrooms in – they make me ill.* • *We can have the coat ready for you by tomorrow, madam.* • *Can you read that sign from this distance?* • *The doctors are doing all that they can, but she's still not breathing properly.* • *Do the best you can – I realize the circumstances are not ideal.* • *If the party is awful we can* **always** *leave* (= that would be one possible solution to our problem). • *"She's really furious about it." "Can you blame her?* (= I'm not surprised)*"* • *(Am) "Will you mail this letter for me, please?"* "**Can do** (= Yes, I can and I will)"/"**No can do** (= No I can't)." • *(Am)* If someone has a **can-do** character or a can-do approach to a problem, they are very positive about their ability to achieve success: *Her can-do* **attitude** *is what made her our choice for the job.* • LP **Auxiliary verbs** NL

can PERMISSION /kæn/ *v aux* [+ infinitive without *to*; not *be canning*] he/she/it **can**, *past simple* **could** /kʊd/ *infml* to be allowed to, either by general or personal permission • *You can park over there – there's a sign telling you to.* • *Can I have one of your tissues, please?* • *You can have a piece of cake if you eat your vegetables!* • *Can* is the word usually used in standard spoken English when asking for permission. It is acceptable in most forms of written English, although in very formal writing, such as official instructions, *may* is usually used instead: *Persons under 14 unaccompanied by an adult may not enter.* • NL

can REQUEST /kæn/ *v aux* [+ infinitive without *to*; not *be canning*] he/she/it **can**, *past simple* **could** /kʊd/ *infml* used informally to request something • *If you see Adrian can you tell him* (= please tell him) *I'm in London next weekend.* • *"Can't you move your chair in a bit, please?" "I'm sorry, but there isn't any more room."* • *Can you make a little less noise, please. I'm trying to work.* • Less commonly, can might be used in orders or threats, usually ones which are given angrily: If you carry on being horrible to your sister, Sophie, you can just go to bed! • NL

can POSSIBILITY /kæn/ *v aux* [+ infinitive without *to*; not *be canning*] *past simple* **could** /kʊd/ used to express possibility in the present, although not in the future • *You can get stamps from the local newsagents.* • *You can get very nasty skin diseases from bathing in dirty water.* • *Smoking can cause cancer.* • *Noise can be quite a problem when you're living in a flat.* • *He can be really annoying at times* (= He is sometimes very annoying). • *He can't* **have**/*I don't think he can* **have** *seen it coming.* • Can't might be used to express lack of belief: *You can't be hungry already – you only had lunch two hours ago!* ○ *You can't be serious! Are you really going to wear that hat?* • NL

can OFFER /kæn/ *v aux* [+ infinitive without *to*; not *be canning*] *past simple* **could** /kʊd/ used in polite offers of help • *Can I help you with those bags?* • *I'm afraid Ms Ferguson has already left the office. Can I be of any help?* • NL

ca·nal /kə'næl/ *n* [C] a long channel of water which is artificially made either for boats to travel along or for taking water from one area to another • *Canals were the main method of transporting goods until the mid-19th century.* • *In Britain nowadays, canals are used mainly for pleasure, by people travelling in long, narrow boats called barges or narrow boats.* • *The Panama Canal provides a crucial shipping link between the Atlantic and Pacific oceans.* • A **canal boat** (also **narrow boat**) is a long narrow boat which is used on a canal. • See also ALIMENTARY CANAL.

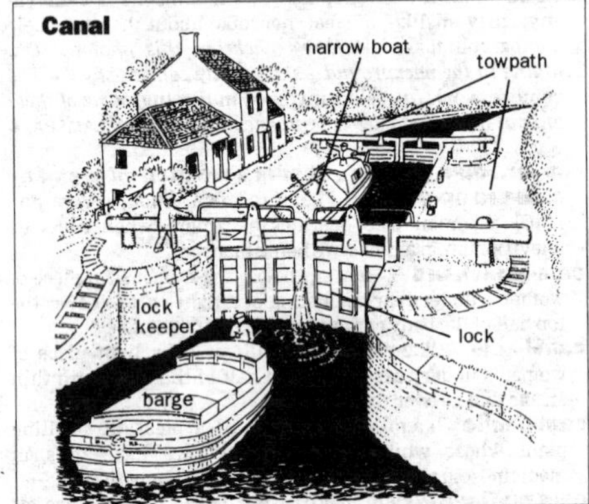

can·a·pé /'kæn·ə·peɪ/ *n* [C] a small thin piece of bread or biscuit with a piece of savoury food, such as cheese, fish or meat, on the top, which is served with drinks, esp. at a party • *They used to have glamorous drinks parties where a butler in white gloves served fine wines and elegant canapés from silver trays.*

ca·nard /£'kæn·ɑːd, $kə'nɑːrd/ *n* [C] *literary* a false report or piece of information which is intended to deceive people • *The newspaper's editor denies she tried to increase sales by printing the canard* **that** *the famous couple were about to get divorced.*

ca·na·ry /£kə'neə·ri, $-'ner·i/ *n* [C] a small yellow bird which is well known for its singing and is sometimes kept as a pet in a cage

ca·nas·ta /kə'næs·tə/ *n* [U] a card game for two to six people which is played with two sets of cards

can·can /'kæŋ·kæn/ *n* [C] a fast dance, originally performed in France in the 19th century, in which a row of women on a stage kick their legs high and lift their skirts

can·cel *(obj)* /'kænt·sᵊl/ *v* **-ll-** or *Am usually* **-l-** to decide that (something which has been arranged in advance) will not happen, or to state that you no longer wish to use or pay for (something which you have already ordered) • *They've had to cancel tomorrow's football match because of the bad weather.* [T] • *The 7.10 train to London has been cancelled.* [T] • *We were planning to go camping, but we had to cancel at the last minute because two of our party were ill.* [I] • *I think I'll cancel the theatre tickets and get my money back.* [T] • If you cancel a **cheque** you stop the money which you ordered to be paid from being paid. [T] • If a postage stamp is cancelled, it is marked to show it has been used and cannot be used again. [T]

can·cel·la·tion /ˌkænt·sᵊlˈeɪ·ʃᵊn/ *n* • *The theatre tickets were sold out, so we waited to see if there were any cancellations* (= if any tickets were returned by the people who bought had them). [C] • *Many trains are subject to cancellation because of the flooding.* [U]

can·cel out *obj*, **can·cel** *obj* **out** *v adv* [M] to remove the effect of (one thing) by doing another thing which has the opposite effect • *This month's pay cheque will cancel out his debt, but it won't give him any extra money.*

can·cer DISEASE /£ˈkænt·səʳ, $-sɚ/ *n* (a serious medical condition often resulting in death, caused by) a diseased and uncontrolled growth in the body; a CARCINOMA • *a benign/malignant/dangerous cancer* [C] • *cancer* **of** *the stomach* [U] • *(fig.) Drug abuse is a cancer* (= spreading evil) *which is destroying our society.* [C] • See also CARCINOGEN.

can·cer·ous /£ˈkænt·sᵊr·əs, $-sɚ-/ *adj* • *a cancerous growth/tumour*

Can·cer SIGN /£ˈkænt·səʳ, $-sɚ/ *n* [not after *the*] the fourth sign of the ZODIAC, relating to the period from 22 June to 22 July, represented by a CRAB (= sea animal with a hard shell), or a person born during this period • *Jeremy was born* **under** *Cancer* (= during this period). [U] • *Tyler is a Cancer.* [C]

Can·ce·ri·an /£kænˈsɪə·ri·ən, $-ˈsɪr·i-/, **Can·ce·re·an** *n* [C] • *Cancerians are supposed to be romantic and home-loving people.*

can·del·a·bra /ˌkæn·dɪˈlɑː·brə/ *n* [C] *pl* **candelabra** or **candelabras** a decorative holder for several candles or lights • PIC› **Lights**

can·did /ˈkæn·dɪd/ *adj approving* truthful and honest, esp. about something difficult or painful • *The two presidents have had candid talks about the current crisis.* • **To be** *candid* **with** *you, I think you're making a dreadful mistake.* • *"Candid Camera"* (title of a television show, 1949-) • See also CANDOUR. • Ⓔ Ⓟ

can·did·ly /ˈkæn·dɪd·li/ *adv* • *Candidly, Paul, I was hoping you would pay at least half the bill.* • *It's almost impossible to get politicians to talk candidly about their ambitions.*

can·di·da /ˈkæn·dɪ·də/ *n* [U] *specialized* a type of FUNGUS which can cause a vaginal infection in adult women and an infection of the mouth and throat esp. in young children • *Candida is the yeast-like fungus which can lead to thrush.*

can·di·date /ˈkæn·dɪ·dət, -deɪt/ *n* [C] a person who is competing to get a job or elected position, or *(Br and Aus also)* someone who is taking an exam • *There are three candidates standing in the election.* • *(Br and Aus) Candidates must write their names on the top page of the exam paper.* • *(fig.) The English Department is a likely candidate* **for** (= likely to be chosen for) *staff cuts.* • Ⓝⓛ Ⓡⓤⓢ

can·di·da·cy /ˈkæn·dɪ·də·si/, *Br also* **can·di·dat·ure** /£ˈkæn·dɪ·də·tʃəʳ, $-tʃɚ/ *n* [U] • *She is expected to* **announce** *officially her candidacy* (= the fact that she is a candidate) *for president early next week.*

can·dle /ˈkæn·dḷ/ *n* [C] a usually cylindrical piece of wax with a WICK (= piece of string) in the middle of it which produces light as it slowly burns • *There was a power cut last night, and we had to light lots of candles.* • If you say that someone or something **can't hold a candle** to someone or something else, you mean that they are not as good: *The pop music of today can't hold a candle to the great songs of the 60s and 70s.* • *"She would rather light a candle than curse the darkness"* (Adlai Stevenson about Eleanor Roosevelt, 1962) • *"Candle in the Wind"* (title of a song by Elton John, 1974) • PIC› **Lights**

can·dle·light /ˈkæn·dḷ·laɪt/ *n* [U] the light that a candle produces when it is burning • *She loves the romance of dining by candlelight.*

can·dle·lit /ˈkæn·dḷ·lɪt/ *adj* [before n; not gradable] • *The restaurant is a wonderful setting for a candlelit* **dinner**.

can·dle·stick /ˈkæn·dḷ·stɪk/ *n* [C] a usually decorative holder for a candle • PIC› **Lights**

can·dour *Br and Aus, Am and Aus* **can·dor** /£ˈkæn·dəʳ, $-dɚ/ *n* [U] the quality of being truthful and honest, esp. about a difficult or embarrassing subject • *"We really don't know what to do about it," she said with surprising candour.* • See also CANDID.

can·dy /ˈkæn·di/ *n esp. Am* a sweet, sweets or (a piece of) chocolate • *Hey, Mom, can I have some candy/candies?* [U; C] • *Why don't you take Martha to the candy* **store** *and buy some candy* **bars**? • *(Am slang)* A **candy-ass** is a cowardly person: *You've got to learn to stand up for yourself and stop being such a candy-ass* **wimp**. • Something that is **candy-striped** has narrow strips of white and a bright colour such as pink: *He was wearing a candy-striped shirt which looked dreadful with his brown trousers.*

can·died /ˈkæn·did/ *adj* [not gradable] • Something that has been candied has been preserved with sugar: *candied fruit* • **Candied peel** is the skin of lemons and oranges which is preserved with sugar and used for making cakes: *Granny puts candied peel in her Christmas cakes.*

can·dy·floss *Br, Am* **cot·ton can·dy**, *Aus* **fair·y floss** /£ˈkæn·di·flɒs, $-flɑːs/ *n* [U] a large soft ball of white or pink sugar in the form of thin threads which is usually sold on a stick and eaten at FAIRS and amusement parks

cane /keɪn/ *n* the long hollow stems of particular plants such as BAMBOO • *Long pieces of cane are used to make furniture and to weave baskets.* [U] • *a cane chair* • Sometimes a cane is a tall bamboo stick which is used to hold weak plants in a vertical position. [C] • A cane is also a long stick used esp. by old, ill or blind people to help them walk. [C] • A cane can also be a thin stick used for hitting people, esp. in the past as a school punishment: *He* **got** (= was hit with) *the cane for cheating.* [U]

cane *obj* /keɪn/ *v* [T] • *Don't you think caning young children* (= punishing them by hitting them with canes) *is barbaric?*

ca·nine /ˈkeɪ·naɪn/ *adj* relating to or similar to a dog • *She's a specialist in canine psychology and behaviour.* • *The city's canine population* (= The number of dogs in the city) *has grown dramatically over recent years.*

ca·nine (tooth) /ˈkeɪ·naɪn/ *n* [C] • A canine (tooth) is one of four pointed teeth in the mouths of humans and some other animals. • Compare INCISOR; MOLAR.

can·is·ter /£ˈkæn·ɪ·stəʳ, $-stɚ/ *n* [C] a hard usually cylindrical container used for storing objects or substances • *a plastic/metal/waterproof canister* • *The police fired* **tear gas** *canisters into the crowd.* • **Canister vacuum cleaner** is *Am for* **cylinder vacuum cleaner**. See at VACUUM. • PIC› **Cleaning**

can·ker /£ˈkæŋ·kəʳ, $-kɚ/ *n* [C] *specialized or fml* a disease which attacks the wood of trees, or the mouths and ears of animals and people • A canker is also something evil that spreads through a person's mind, an organization or a society: *Poverty is a canker eating away at the heart of society.*

can·na·bis /ˈkæn·ə·bɪs/ *n* [U] a usually illegal drug which is made from the dried leaves and flowers of a variety of the HEMP plant and produces a feeling of pleasant relaxation when smoked or eaten • *Are you in favour of the legalization of cannabis?*

can·nel·lo·ni, **can·ne·lo·ni** /£ˌkæn·ᵊlˈəʊ·ni, $-ˈoʊ-/ *n* [U] tubular pasta filled usually with cheese or meat

can·ni·bal /ˈkæn·ɪ·bᵊl/ *n* [C] a person who eats human flesh, or an animal which eats the flesh of animals of its own type

can·ni·bal·i·sm /ˈkæn·ɪ·bᵊl·ɪ·zᵊm/ *n* [U]

can·ni·bal·i·stic /ˌkæn·ɪ·bᵊlˈɪs·tɪk/ *adj*

can·ni·bal·ize *obj, Br and Aus usually* **-ise** /ˈkæn·ɪ·bᵊl·aɪz/ *v* [T] to take parts from (a machine or vehicle) in order to make or repair another machine or vehicle • *He bought an old engine and cannibalized it for spare parts.*

can·non GUN /ˈkæn·ən/ *n* [C] *pl* **cannon** or **cannons** a large powerful gun fixed to an aircraft, ship or land vehicle • In the past, a cannon was a large gun which was usually fixed on a carriage and was used on land or at sea to fire heavy metal or stone balls. • A **cannon ball** is a heavy metal or stone ball that was fired from a cannon. • If you describe soldiers as **cannon fodder**, you mean that they are not considered important by their officers and are sent into war without their leaders caring if they die.

can·non KNOCK /ˈkæn·ən/ *v* [I always + adv/prep] *Br and Aus* to knock or hit against (someone or something) suddenly, forcefully and usually unintentionally • *I was rushing along with my head down when I cannoned into an old lady walking the other way.*

can·non·ade /ˌkæn·əˈneɪd/ *n* [C] a period of continuous heavy firing of large guns, esp. as part of an attack

can·not /£ˈkæn·ɒt, $-ɑːt/ *v aux fml or Am* can not; to be unable or not allowed to • *I cannot predict what will happen next year.* • *If we persevere, we* **cannot but** (= will certainly) *succeed.*

can·ny CLEVER /ˈkæn·i/ *adj* **-ier**, **-iest** thinking quickly and cleverly, esp. in business or financial matters • *These salesmen are a canny lot.* • *She struck a canny bargain with her ex-employer.* • *Canny investors are starting to worry that the stockmarket might be due for a sharp fall.*

can·ni·ly /ˈkæn·ɪ·li/ *adv*

can·ny PLEASANT /ˈkæn·i/ *adj Br regional approving* good or pleasant • *That new boyfriend of yours is a canny lad.* • *We had a canny time at the seaside last weekend.*

ca·noe /kəˈnuː/ *n* [C] a small light narrow boat, pointed at both ends and moved using a PADDLE (=a short pole with a flat blade) • Canoe is also *Br for* KAYAK. • PIC› **Ships and boats, Water sports**

ca·noe /kəˈnuː/ *v* [I always + adv/prep] **canoeing**, *past* **canoed** • *They canoed across the lake.*

ca·noe·ing /kəˈnuː·ɪŋ/ *n* [U] • *She's involved in a lot of outdoor activities like hiking and canoeing.* • *They died in a canoeing accident.*

ca·noe·ist /kəˈnuː·ɪst/ *n* [C] • *She's a very experienced canoeist.*

can·on STANDARD /ˈkæn·ən/ *n* [C usually pl] *fml or specialized* a rule, principle or law, esp. in the Christian Church, relating only to the Church and its members

ca·non·ic·al /£kəˈnɒn·ɪ·kəl, $-ˈnɑː·nɪ-/ *adj* [not gradable]

can·on WRITINGS /ˈkæn·ən/ *n* [C usually sing] *specialized* all the writings or other works known to be by a particular person • *Some scholars would not strictly include these plays in the Shakespearean canon.*

can·on PRIEST /ˈkæn·ən/ *n* [C] a Christian priest, often one who works in a CATHEDRAL, or a title given as an honour to some priests

can·on·ize *obj, Br and Aus usually* **-ise** /ˈkæn·ə·naɪz/ *v* [T] (esp. in the Roman Catholic Church) to announce officially (a dead person) to be a SAINT (=holy person who deserves honour)

ca·noo·dle /kəˈnuː·dl̩/ *v* [I] *dated infml humorous* (of two people) to kiss and hold each other in a sexual way • *It was very embarrassing when I discovered them canoodling* (**with** *each other*) *in the living room.*

can·o·py /ˈkæn·ə·pi/ *n* [C] a cover or type of roof for shelter or decoration, or the branches and leaves that spread out at the top of a group of trees forming a type of roof • *The canopy of a tropical rain forest is home to many thousands of species of animals.* • A canopy over a bed or outside a shop or restaurant is a piece of cloth, plastic or other material which is supported above or in front of it for decoration or shelter: *The Queen's four poster bed had a golden canopy.* ○ *We sat drinking our coffee under the canopy, grateful for the shade.* • In a military aircraft, the canopy is a transparent part which covers the place where the people flying the aircraft sit. • A canopy is also the large circular piece of cloth that is the main part of a PARACHUTE. • *(fig. literary) The sun was like a lamp hanging from the canopy of the sky.*

cant /kænt/ *n* [U] statements on esp. religious or moral subjects which are not sincerely believed by the person making them • *Shelley's friendship with Byron was rooted in their shared contempt for cant and hypocrisy.* • Cant is also special words used by a particular group of people such as thieves, lawyers or priests: *Sometimes words that were originally cant come to be used in the general language.*

can't /£kɑːnt, $kænt/ *short form of* cannot • *Speak up! I can't hear you.* • *This can't be* (=is very unlikely to be) *right.* • *(infml) I wasn't anywhere near the house when the window was broken so you* **can't hang/pin that on** *me* (=cannot say that I am responsible)*!* • Can't might be used when you are suggesting that someone do something, esp. when it seems the obvious thing to do: *Can't you just take the dress back to the shop if it doesn't fit?* • *"Can't pay, won't pay"* (title of a play by Dario Fo, 1975)

can·ta·loupe, **can·ta·loup** /£ˈkæn·tə·luːp, $-t̬ə-/, *Aus also* **rock·mel·on** *n* [C] a type of small round MELON with yellow or green skin and orange flesh

can·tan·ker·ous /£ˌkænˈtæŋ·kər·əs, $-kɚ-/ *adj* (of a person) bad-tempered; tending to argue and complain a lot • *Grandad never stops complaining, the cantankerous old bugger.*

can·ta·ta /£kænˈtɑː·tə, $kənˈtɑː·t̬ə/ *n* [C] a short musical work, with words usually based on a religious subject • Compare ORATORIO.

can·teen RESTAURANT /kænˈtiːn/ *n* [C] a small place in a factory, office, etc. where food and meals are sold, often at a lower than usual price • GR

can·teen KITCHEN EQUIPMENT /kænˈtiːn/ *n* [C] *Br and Aus* (a small flat case containing) a complete set of knives, forks and spoons • *We're giving them a canteen* **of cutlery** *as a wedding present.* • GR

can·teen CONTAINER /kænˈtiːn/ *n* [C] a small container for carrying esp. water or other drink, used esp. by soldiers or travellers • PIC› **Jug** GR

can·ter /£ˈkæn·tər, $-t̬ɚ/ *v* [I] (of a horse) to move at a fast but easy and comfortable speed which is faster than a TROT and slower than a GALLOP • *The horsemen cantered round the field a few times.*

can·ter /£ˈkæn·tər, $-t̬ɚ/ *n* [C usually sing] • *The horses set off* **at a canter**. • *I went for a canter* (=ride at medium speed on a horse) *across the fields.*

can·ti·le·ver /£ˈkæn·tɪ·liː·vər, $-t̬ɪ·liː·vɚ/ *n* [C] *specialized* a long bar or beam which is fixed at only one end to a vertical support and is used to hold a structure such as an arch, bridge or shelf in position • A **cantilever bridge** is made from two cantilevers which are joined in the middle. • PIC› **Bridge**

can·ton /£ˈkæn·tɒn, $-tɑːn/ *n* [C] a political region or local government area in some countries, esp. one of the 23 political regions into which Switzerland is divided • *She's a Swiss from the Italian-speaking canton of Ticino.*

can·vas /ˈkæn·vəs/ *n* strong rough cloth made from cotton, HEMP or JUTE, used for making tents, sails, bags or strong clothes • *Her shoes were made of canvas.* [U] • *Most of the soldiers carried canvas bags.* • *I love sleeping* **under canvas** (=in a tent). • A canvas is a piece of this cloth used by artists for painting on, usually with oil paints, or the painting itself: *These two canvases by Hockney would sell for £500 000.* [C] • PIC› **Drawing and painting**

can·vass *(obj)* OBTAIN SUPPORT /ˈkæn·vəs/ *v* to try to obtain (political support or votes), esp. by visiting all the houses in an area • *I've been out canvassing (support/votes* **for** *the Labour Party) every evening this week.* [I/T]

can·vass /ˈkæn·vəs/ *n* [C] • *a door-to-door/house-to-house canvass*

can·vas·ser /£ˈkæn·və·sər, $-sɚ/ *n* [C] • *We find that people in rural areas often respond better to personal calls from party canvassers than to a sustained media campaign.*

can·vass *obj* ASK /ˈkæn·vəs/ *v* [T] to try to discover (information or opinions) by asking (people) • *The council has been canvassing local* **opinion**/*local people to get their thoughts on the proposed housing development.*

can·vass *obj* SUGGEST /ˈkæn·vəs/ *v* [T] *Br and Aus fml* to suggest (an idea or plan) for consideration • *Wind and wave power are now being seriously canvassed as the solution to our energy problems.*

can·yon /ˈkæn·jən/ *n* [C] a large valley with very steep sides and usually a river flowing along the bottom • *The Grand Canyon in the USA is 1900 metres deep and 25 kilometres wide at its maximum.*

cap HAT /kæp/ *n* [C] a soft light hat which either fits closely to the head or is flat with a curved part sticking out at the front, and which is worn esp. as part of a uniform • *a workman's/soldier's/schoolboy's cap* • *When she goes walking in the countryside, my sister likes to wear a* **flat/cloth** *cap.* • *In some countries, police officers wear* **peaked** *caps.* • *I always wear a plastic* **shower** *cap to keep my hair dry in the shower.* • *Professional swimmers usually wear rubber* **swimming** *(Am usually* **bathing**) *caps.* • *(esp. Br)* When a sportsperson plays for their national team they receive a special cap as a symbol of this achievement: *Davis has 17 Scottish caps* (=has played for Scotland 17 times). ○ *He is one of four Turin players to* **win** *caps this season.* • If you go to someone **cap in hand**, you ask them very respectfully for something, esp. money or forgiveness. • PIC› **Hats**

cap *obj* /kæp/ *v* [T] **-pp-** • *She's been capped for* (=has played for) *Scotland 17 times.*

-capped /-kæpt/ *combining form* • *a cloth-capped old man*

cap *obj* LIMIT /kæp/ *v* [T] **-pp-** to put a limit on (the amount of money that can be charged or spent in connection with a particular activity) • *High spending councils have all been rate/charge capped.* • *We're trying to cap costs by keeping salary increases low.* • *Our mortgage is capped at 8·75% for five years.*

cap /kæp/ *n* [C] • *Central government has imposed a cap* (=limit) **on** *local tax increases.* • *(Am) The team will have to cut a player or two if it plans to stay under the league's* **salary** *cap.*

cap COVER /kæp/ *n* [C] a small usually protective lid or cover • *The label on the bottle says 'Twist cap to open', but I can't get it off.* • *The camera has a* **lens** *cap to protect the lens surface.* • A cap is also an artificial protective covering on a tooth. • *(fig.) The damaged nuclear reactor was covered with a cap* (=protective layer) **of** *concrete 20 feet thick.* • PIC› **Coverings**

cap *obj* /kæp/ *v* [T] **-pp-** • *The mountain was capped* **with** (=The top of it was covered by) *snow.* • *My teeth were in a* *terrible state, so I had most of them capped* (= protected with an artificial covering). • *(fig.) I capped their stories* (= told a better one) **with** *a joke which had them all laughing.* • *(fig.) It's been a terrible week and now,* **to cap it all** (= in addition to all the other (bad) things that have happened) *I've got a cold.*

-capped /-kæpt/ *combining form* • *a snow-capped mountain*

cap BIRTH CONTROL *Br* /kæp/, **di·aph·ragm**, *Br* **Dutch cap** *n* [C] a circular rubber CONTRACEPTIVE device which a woman fills with a cream that kills sperm and puts inside her vagina before having sex to prevent herself from becoming pregnant

cap EXPLOSIVE /kæp/ *n* [C] a very small amount of explosive powder in a paper container, used esp. in toy guns to produce a loud noise

ca·pa·ble /ˈkeɪ·pə·bl̩/ *adj* able; (of people) skilful and effective, or (of people or things) having enough ability or power to do something • *She's a very capable woman/worker/judge.* • *We need to get an assistant who's capable and efficient.* • *(humorous) I'm going away next week, so I'll be leaving everything in your* **capable hands** (= for you to deal with). • *Only the Democratic Party is capable* **of** *running the country.* • *A force 10 wind is capable* **of** *blowing* (= able and likely to blow) *the roofs off houses.* • *When she's drunk she's capable* **of** *saying* (= able and likely to say) *awful, rude things.* • *I think your plan is capable* **of** *being* (= could be) *improved.*

-ca·pa·ble /-ˈkeɪ·pə·bl̩/ *combining form* • *These are nuclear-capable aircraft* (= They can carry nuclear weapons).

ca·pa·bil·i·ty /£ˌkeɪ·pəˈbɪl·ɪ·ti, $-ə·t̬i/ *n* • *With the new machines we finally have the capability* (= power) **to** *do the job properly.* [U + *to* infinitive] • *These tests are beyond the capability* (= ability) *of an average 12-year- old.* [U] • *The old computer's capabilities* (= effectiveness) *were limited.* [C] • *Several countries are trying to develop a* **nuclear** *capability* (= weapons needed to fight a nuclear war). [C]

ca·pa·bly /ˈkeɪ·pə·bli/ *adv* • *She drove very capably.*

ca·pa·cious /kəˈpeɪ·ʃəs/ *adj fml* able to contain a lot; having lots of space • *a capacious pocket/handbag/auditorium* • *a capacious mind* • *There was a rather fat man wearing a capacious stripy suit.*

ca·pac·it·or /£kəˈpæs·ɪ·tər, $-t̬ɚ/ *n* [C] *specialized* a device which collects and stores electricity, and is an important part of electronic equipment such as televisions and radios

ca·pac·i·ty AMOUNT /£kəˈpæs·ə·ti, $-t̬i/ *n* the total amount that can be contained or produced, or (esp. of a person or organization) the ability to do a particular thing • *The stadium has a* **seating** *capacity of 50 000.* [C] • *The game was watched by a capacity* **crowd/audience** *of 50 000* (= the place was completely full). • *(fml or humorous) No, you can't come with us, the car's already* **full to** *capacity* (= completely full). [U] • *She's got an amazing capacity* **for** *alcohol* (= She can drink a lot without getting drunk). [C] • *She has a great capacity* **for** *hard work.* [C] • *The purchase of 500 tanks is part of a strategy to increase military capacity by 25% over the next five years.* [U] • *It seems to be* **beyond** *his capacity* **to** (= He seems to be unable to) *follow simple instructions.* [C + *to* infinitive] • *Do you think it's* **within** *his capacity* **to** (= Do you think he'll be able to) *do the job without making a mess of it?* [C + *to* infinitive] • *The generators each have a capacity* **of** (= can produce) *1000 kilowatts.* [C] • *The larger cars have bigger capacity engines* (= the engines are bigger and more powerful). • *All our factories are working* **at (full)** *capacity* (= are producing goods as fast as possible). [U] • *We are running* **below** *capacity* (= not producing as many goods as we are able to) *because of cancelled orders.* [U] • *He suffered a stroke in 1988, which left him unable to speak, but his* **mental** *capacity* (= his ability to think and remember) *wasn't affected.* [C] • See also CAPACIOUS. • LP **Measurements**

ca·pac·i·ty POSITION /£kəˈpæs·ə·ti, $-t̬i/ *n* [C] *fml* a particular position or job; a ROLE • *In his capacity* **as** *secretary of the residents association, he regularly attends meetings of the community policing committee.* • *She was speaking in her capacity* **as** *a novelist, rather than as a television presenter.*

cape LAND /keɪp/ *n* [C] a very large piece of land sticking out into the sea • *the Cape of Good Hope* • (J)

cape COAT /keɪp/ *n* [C] a type of loose sleeveless coat which is fastened at the neck and hangs from the shoulders • *A cape is similar to a cloak, but it is usually shorter.* • (J)

caped /keɪpt/ *adj* [not gradable] • *Batman, the comic-book hero, was also called 'The Caped Crusader'.*

ca·per JUMP /£ˈkeɪ·pər, $-pɚ/ *v* [I] *slightly literary* to jump about in an energetic, happy way • *The dancers capered* **through** *their routines to great applause.*

ca·per ACTIVITY /£ˈkeɪ·pər, $-pɚ/ *n* [C] *dated* an illegal, unusual or amusing activity • *He took part in a caper last year which involved smuggling guns into Germany.* • *They hope that their bizarre capers will raise £2000 for charity.*

ca·per FOOD /£ˈkeɪ·pər, $-pɚ/ *n* [C usually pl] a small dark green flower BUD which is used in sauces to give a slightly sour taste to food

ca·pil·la·ry /£kəˈpɪl·ər·i, $ˈ-ɚ-/ *n* [C] *specialized* a very thin tube, esp. one of the smaller tubes that carry blood around the body

cap·i·tal (let·ter) /£ˈkæp·ɪ·tᵊl, $-t̬ᵊl/ *n* [C] a letter of the alphabet in the form and larger size that is used at the beginning of sentences and names • *THIS SENTENCE IS PRINTED* **IN** *CAPITALS/CAPITAL LETTERS.* • LP **Capital letters**

cap·i·tal /£ˈkæp·ɪ·tᵊl, $-t̬ᵊl/ *adj* [not gradable] • *Do you write 'calvinist' with a capital 'C'?* • *Why have you made half the letters capital?* • *I'm hungry* **with a capital** *H* (= I'm very hungry).

cap·i·tal·ize *obj, Br and Aus usually* **-ise** /£ˈkæp·ɪ·tᵊl·aɪz, $-t̬ᵊl-/ *v* [T] • *The names of political parties are always capitalized, e.g. the Green Party.*

cap·i·tal·i·za·tion, *Br and Aus usually* **-i·sa·tion** /£ˌkæp·ɪ·tᵊl·aɪˈzeɪ·ʃᵊn, $-t̬ᵊl-/ *n* [U] • *The capitalization of all nouns in German can be very confusing when you are just starting to learn the language.*

cap·i·tal CITY /£ˈkæp·ɪ·tᵊl, $-t̬ᵊl/ *n* [C] a city which is the centre of government of a country or smaller political area • *Los Angeles is the capital of Los Angeles County.* • *Australia's capital city is Canberra.* • *(fig.) London used to be the financial capital of the world.* • (RUS)

cap·i·tal MONEY /£ˈkæp·ɪ·tᵊl, $-t̬ᵊl/ *n* [U] wealth, esp. a large amount of money used for producing more wealth or for starting a new business • *She leaves her capital untouched in the bank and lives off the interest.* • *We've* **put** *£20 000 capital* **into** *the business, but we're unlikely to see any return for a few years.* • **Capital assets** are the buildings and machines owned by an organization such as a business. • **Capital gains** are profits made by selling something, esp. buildings or machines. • An industry, business or process that is **capital intensive** needs a lot of money to buy buildings and equipment in order to start operating: *As agriculture became more capital intensive, many farm labourers moved to the towns and cities to look for work.* • **Capital investment** or **capital expenditure** is money which is spent on buildings and equipment to increase the effectiveness of a business. • If you **make capital (out) of/from** a situation, you use it to obtain an advantage for yourself: *The Opposition is making a lot of* **political** *capital out of the Goverment's failure to invest in education.* • (RUS)

cap·i·tal·ize *obj, Br and Aus usually* **-ise** /£ˈkæp·ɪ·tᵊl·aɪz, $-t̬ᵊl-/ *v* [T] • *We capitalized* (= sold) *our* **assets** *to avoid bankruptcy.* • *The business* **is under capitalized** (= has too little money to be able to develop).

cap·i·tal·i·za·tion, *Br and Aus usually* **-i·sa·tion** /£ˌkæp·ɪ·tᵊl·aɪˈzeɪ·ʃᵊn, $-t̬ᵊl-/ *n* [U]

cap·i·tal EXCELLENT /£ˈkæp·ɪ·tᵊl, $-t̬ᵊl/ *adj Br dated approving* very good or excellent • *That's a capital idea!* • (RUS)

cap·i·tal DEATH /£ˈkæp·ɪ·tᵊl, $-t̬ᵊl/ *adj* [before n; not gradable] (of a crime) punishable by death • *In certain countries, importing drugs is a capital* **offence.** • **Capital punishment** (also **the death penalty**) is punishment by death, as ordered by a legal system. • (RUS)

cap·i·tal BUILDING /£ˈkæp·ɪ·tᵊl, $-t̬ᵊl/ *n* [C] *specialized* the top part of a column • (RUS)

cap·i·tal·ism /£ˈkæp·ɪ·tᵊl·ɪ·zᵊm, $-t̬ᵊl-/ *n* [U] an economic, political and social system based on private ownership of property, business and industry, and directed towards making the greatest possible profits for successful organizations and people • *Capitalism is also based upon the free exchange of goods and services in the world market.* • Compare COMMUNISM; SOCIALISM.

cap·i·tal·ist /£ˈkæp·ɪ·tᵊl·ɪst, $-t̬ᵊl-/, **cap·i·tal·ist·ic** /£ˌkæp·ɪ·tᵊlˈɪs·tɪk, $-t̬ᵊl-/ *adj* • *a capitalist economy/country/system* • *(disapproving) We must protect ourselves against these ruthless capitalistic nations.*

CAPITAL LETTERS

Capital letters are generally used with words that are being used as names, or that have a special importance. A capital letter is used at the beginning of:

- **a sentence, and any complete sentence put in quotation marks [' ' or " "]**
  The shops are closed today.
  She whispered "Can you hear me?"
  "As soon as the bus arrives," he said, "take your bags to the back".
- **proper nouns, that is, the names of particular people, places and things.** These include place names, towns, countries, nationalities and geographical areas; businesses and organisations; days and months, and times in history.
  John R. Tennant • 133 High Street • San Francisco
  the United States of America • Europe • two Germans and an Italian
  I'm trying to learn Japanese.
  a job working for Central Bank • Cooper and Sons Ltd
  members of the National Union of Teachers
  She's leaving on 10th June – that's next Tuesday. • during the Middle Ages
- **adjectives taken from names or proper nouns.** (But when these words have an independent meaning, they usually have no capital letter.)
  Shakespearean drama • a Marxist government • the British economy • an old Victorian house
  BUT: *a china plate • a hamburger and french fries • a glass of scotch*
- **the following words only when they are used as (part of) a name:** words for directions (*north, south* etc.); words like *river, lake, sea*; and words like *road* and *street* used in addresses.
  South Africa BUT *the countries of southern Africa*
  the political leaders of the West BUT *He drove east for three hours.*
  a walking holiday in the North-East
  the Yellow River BUT *a sample of river water*
  Lake Erie • the Red Sea • Mount Everest
  134 Dewey Road BUT *she crossed the road*
  Central Park BUT *a walk in the park*
  staying at the Station Hotel BUT *a cheap hotel*
- **people's titles when they come before the name or** (*esp. in Br use*) when a title is used alone instead of the name
  Ms Eliot • Mr Salmon • Sir Edward BUT *Can I help you, sir?*
  Dr Grey • Good morning, Doctor. BUT *She's a doctor.*
  Queen Elizabeth • (Br) a visit by the Queen BUT *the early kings of England*
  President Kennedy BUT *(Am) re-elect the president • America's first president*
- **words for members of a family when they are used as a title before a name, or used alone instead of the name.** Family words do *not* have capitals after my, your etc.
  Uncle Ben and Aunt Freda BUT *visit your uncle and aunt*
  Yes, Dad BUT *he hasn't got a dad*
  a letter to Mother BUT *I wrote to my mother*
- **religions (and their adjectives) and the highest God**
  the history of Hinduism • he is a Christian • according to Islamic law
  I know God listens to our prayers. BUT *'Polytheism' is the belief in many gods.*
- **important words in titles of books, etc and in headlines in newspapers, etc.** This means at least the first word and all nouns and adjectives (some writers put other words in capitals too)
  A Modern Guide to the Ancient World • How to start a Small Business

Notice that words like 'south', 'father', 'king' that have a capital letter only in certain uses are spelled with small letters in the dictionary. Common uses with capitals can be found in the examples.

cap·i·tal·ist /£ˈkæp·ɪ·tᵊl·ɪst, $-t̬ᵊl-/ *n* [C] • A capitalist is someone who has great wealth invested in a business or who supports capitalism: *During this period there was a redistribution of income away from labourers towards landowners and capitalists.* ○ *He's always trying to persuade his socialist friends to become capitalists.* ○ *(disapproving) She said I was a filthy capitalist for charging her interest on the money I lent her.*

cap·i·tal·ize on *obj, Br and Aus usually* **-ise** /£ˈkæp·ɪ·tᵊl·aɪz, $-t̬ᵊl-/ *v prep* [T] to use (esp. a situation) to your own advantage • *The Labour Party is capitalizing on local discontent over low living standards.* • *She capitalized on her knowledge and experience to get a new and better paid job.*

cap·i·ta·tion /ˌkæp·ɪˈteɪ·ʃᵊn/ *n* [C] *specialized* a tax, charge or amount which is fixed at the same level for everyone • *Doctors receive capitation of £13·85 per patient and therefore lose money when someone transfers to another doctor.*

ca·pi·tu·late /kəˈpɪt·ju·leɪt/ *v* [I] to accept military defeat, or *(fig.)* to accept something or agree to do something unwillingly • *Their forces capitulated five hours after the Allied bombardment of the city began.* • *(fig.) The sports minister today capitulated* **to** *calls for his resignation.*

ca·pi·tu·la·tion /kəˌpɪt·juˈleɪ·ʃᵊn/ *n* • *During the war, we never contemplated capitulation* **(to** *the enemy).* [U] • *Repeated management capitulations* **on** *wage increases have made the company's financial situation worse.* [C]

cap·puc·ci·no /£ˌkæp·uˈtʃiː·nəʊ, $-noʊ/ *n pl* **cappuccinos** (a cup of) coffee made with heated milk which is served with a thick mass of bubbles and often powdered chocolate on the top • *Do you prefer espresso or cappuccino?* [U] • *Two cappuccinos and a pot of Earl Grey, please.* [C]

ca·price /kəˈpriːs/ *n literary* (the tendency to have) a sudden and usually foolish desire to have or do something, or a sudden and foolish change of mind or behaviour; a WHIM • *The $300 million palace was built to satisfy the caprice of one man.* [U] • *(fig.) The dam protects the region from Nature's caprices.* [C]

ca·pri·cious /kəˈprɪʃ·əs/ *adj literary* • *capricious children* • *He was a cruel and capricious tyrant.* • *She writes* *songs about capricious love and wounded hearts.* • See also FICKLE.

ca·pri·cious·ly /kəˈprɪʃ·ə·sli/ *adv*

ca·pri·cious·ness /kəˈprɪʃ·ə·snəs/ *n* [U]

Cap·ri·corn /£ˈkæp·rɪ·kɔːn, $-kɔːrn/ *n* [not after *the*] the tenth sign of the ZODIAC, relating to the period from 23 December to 20 January and represented by a goat, or a person born during this period • *She was born* **under** *Capricorn* (=during this period). [U] • *Capricorns are supposed to be serious and hard working.* [C]

cap·si·cum /ˈkæp·sɪ·kəm/ *n* [C/U] *specialized* a PEPPER [VEGETABLE]

cap·size *(obj)* /kæpˈsaɪz/ *v* to (cause a boat or ship to) turn upside down accidentally while on water • *A huge wave capsized the yacht.* [T] • *When the boat capsized we were trapped underneath it.* [I] • *(fig.) Bringing in a Hollywood actor with a big ego might capsize* (=destroy) *the production.* [T]

cap·stan /ˈkæp·stən/ *n* [C] a machine with a spinning vertical cylinder which is used, esp. on ships, for pulling heavy objects with a rope • A capstan is also a thin spinning cylinder in a **tape recorder** which pulls the TAPE through the machine when it is pushing against a rubber wheel.

cap·sule [SPACECRAFT] /£ˈkæp·sjuːl, $-səl/ *n* [C] the part of a spacecraft in which the people on it live and in which they return to Earth

cap·sule [MEDICINE] /£ˈkæp·sjuːl, $-səl/ *n* [C] a measured amount of medicine in a very small rounded container which you swallow

cap·tain /£ˈkæp·tɪn, $-tən/ *n* [C] a person in charge, esp. of a ship or an aircraft, or a leader of a sports team • *This is your captain speaking. We expect to be landing at London Heathrow in an hour's time.* • *It's unusual to have a goalkeeper as (the) captain of a football team.* • In the army, navy or US air force, and in US police and fire departments, Captain is an officer's rank: *Captain Sam Hill R.N.* ○ *Mike Ransom was promoted to captain and then became a battalion chief.* • A **captain of industry** is a person who has an important job in industry and who can influence company and national planning: *In a speech to captains of industry, she predicted economic growth of 3·5% next year.* • [LP]› **Sports**

cap·tain *obj* /£ˈkæp·tɪn, $-tən/ *v* [T] • *She captained the Welsh netball team for 5 years.*

cap·tain·cy /£ˈkæp·tɪn·si, $-tən-/ *n* • *Her captaincy of the Welsh team was very successful.* [C] • *Having the captaincy of the team is a great responsibility.* [U]

cap·tion /ˈkæp·ʃən/ *n* [C] brief text under a picture in a book, magazine or newspaper which describes the picture or explains what the people in it are doing or saying

cap·tious /ˈkæp·ʃəs/ *adj fml* tending to express criticisms about unimportant matters

cap·tiv·ate *obj* /ˈkæp·tɪ·veɪt/ *v* [T] to hold the attention of (someone) by being extremely interesting, exciting, charming or attractive • *With her beauty and charm she captivated film audiences everywhere.* • *Her speeches are full of captivating wit and warmth.*

cap·tive /ˈkæp·tɪv/ *n* [C] a person or animal whose ability to move or act freely are limited by being in an enclosed space; a prisoner, esp. a person held by the enemy during a war • *When the town was recaptured we found soldiers who had been captives for several years.*

cap·tive /ˈkæp·tɪv/ *adj, adv* • *The terrorists* **took/held** *several British diplomats captive as hostages.* • *Animal rights groups want the release of all captive animals used for cosmetics testing.* • *The gypsy musician on the train had a captive* **audience** (=group of people who have to watch and listen because they cannot leave).

cap·tiv·i·ty /£kæpˈtɪv·ɪ·ti, $-ə·t̬i/ *n* [U] • *All the hostages, when* **released from** *captivity, looked remarkably fit and well.* • *Animals bred* **in** *captivity would probably not survive if they were released into the wild.*

cap·tor /£ˈkæp·təʳ, $-tɚ/ *n* [C] a person who has CAPTURED (=caught) a person or animal and is refusing to release them

cap·ture *obj* /£ˈkæp·tʃəʳ, $-tʃɚ/ *v* [T] to take (someone) as a prisoner, or to take (something) into your possession, esp. by force • *Two of the soldiers were killed and the rest were captured.* • *Rebel forces captured the city after a week-long battle.* • *(fig.) The Democratic Party captured 70% of the vote/captured control of the legislature.* • *(fig.) The American drive to land a man on the Moon captured the imagination/attention of the whole world.* • *(fig.) A passer-by captured the whole incident* **on film** (=recorded it with a camera). • *(fig.) It would be impossible to capture* (=represent) *her beauty in a painting.* • *(specialized)* If a machine such as a computer captures information, it takes it in and stores it.

cap·ture /£ˈkæp·tʃəʳ, $-tʃɚ/ *n* [U] • *They lived in terror of capture by enemy soldiers.*

car /£kɑːʳ, $kɑːr/, *esp. Br dated or fml* **mo·tor car**, *esp. Am fml* **au·to·mo·bile** *n* [C] a road vehicle with an engine, usually four wheels and seating for between one and four people • *a car chase* • *a car accident* • *a car factory* • *She goes/drives to work* **by car**. • *A car whizzed round the corner and knocked the old lady over.* • A car is also the part of a larger vehicle in which the passengers or goods travel: *The passengers in an airship travel in the car which hangs underneath.* ○ *The train has both a* **restaurant** *car* (=carriage with a restaurant) *and a* **sleeping** *car* (=carriage with beds). • A **car bomb** is a bomb put inside a car and left to explode in a public place. • *(Br)* A **car-boot sale** (*Am* **swap meet**, *Aus* **garage sale**) is an event where people sell their unwanted possessions from the backs of their cars. • A **car ferry** is a ship designed for carrying vehicles and passengers. • *(Br and Aus)* A **car park** is an area of ground (*Am and Aus* **parking lot**) or a building (*Am* **parking garage**) where there is space for vehicles to be parked. • A **car phone** is a telephone which is kept and used in a car and is connected to the telephone system by radio. • *(Am and Aus)* A **car pool** is a group of cars owned by a company or other organization which can be used by any of its employees. • *(Am and Aus)* A **car pool** is also a group of people who travel together, esp. to work or school, usually in a different member's car each day: **Car-pooling** *is cheaper and more environmentally friendly than commuting alone in your car every day.* • A **car wash** is a machine which you can drive through to have your car cleaned automatically. • [LP]› **Driving** Ⓕ

ca·rafe /ˈkær·əf, kəˈræf/ *n* [C] (the amount contained in) an open glass container for serving wine or water esp. in a restaurant • *Shall we order another carafe of red wine?* • [PIC]› **Bottles and flasks**

car·a·mel /£ˈkær·ə·məl, $ˈkɑːr·məl, $ˈker·ə-/ *n* burnt sugar used to give flavour and a brown colour to food • *Use caramel to darken the custard.* [U] • Caramel is also a sticky brown sweet made from sugar which has been heated with milk, butter or cream in hot water: *Caramels are softer than toffees.* [C] ○ *I love chocolates with caramel centres.*

ca·ra·mel·ize *(obj), Br and Aus usually* **-ise** /£ˈkær·ə·məl·aɪzd, $ˈkɑːr·məl-, $ˈker·ə-/ *v* • *Wait until the sugar has caramelized* (=turned into caramel) *before adding the banana.* [I] • Food that has been caramelized has been covered in caramel. [T]

car·a·pace /£ˈkær·ə·peɪs, $ˈker-/ *n* [C] *specialized* a hard shell that covers and protects animals such as CRABS and TORTOISES • *(fig.) No sense of guilt ever penetrated his moral carapace.*

car·at /£ˈkær·ət, $ˈker-/ *n* [C] *pl* **carats**, before n **carat** a unit for measuring the weight of jewels or (*Am usually* **karat**) the purity of gold • *A one-carat diamond weighs 0·2 grams.* • *24-carat gold is the purest.*

car·a·van [VEHICLE] *Br* /£ˈkær·ə·væn, $ˈker-/, *Am* **trail·er** *n* [C] a wheeled vehicle for living or travelling in, esp. for holidays, which contains beds and cooking equipment and can be pulled by a car • *(Br)* A **caravan site** (*Am* **trailer park**, *Aus* **caravan park**) is an area of ground where caravans can be parked, esp. by people spending their holidays in them. • *Old-fashioned gypsy caravans are painted wooden vehicles that are pulled by horses.* • [PIC]› **Vehicles**

car·a·van·ning *Br* /£ˈkær·ə·væn·ɪŋ, $ˈker-/, *Am* **trail·er camp·ing** *n* [U] • *We take the children camping or caravanning every summer.*

car·a·van [GROUP] /£ˈkær·ə·væn, $ˈker-/ *n* [C] a group of people with vehicles or animals who travel together for safety through a dangerous area, esp. across a desert on CAMELS

car·a·way /£ˈkær·ə·weɪ, $ˈker-/ *n* [C/U] a short plant whose small fruits, which look like seeds and have a flavour similar to but weaker than ANISEED, are used in food, esp. for making bread or cake • *Seed cake sometimes contains caraway* **seeds**.

car·bine /£ˈkɑː·baɪn, $ˈkɑːr-/ *n* [C] *specialized* a short light gun, originally used by soldiers on horses, which is fired from the shoulder

Car (exterior)

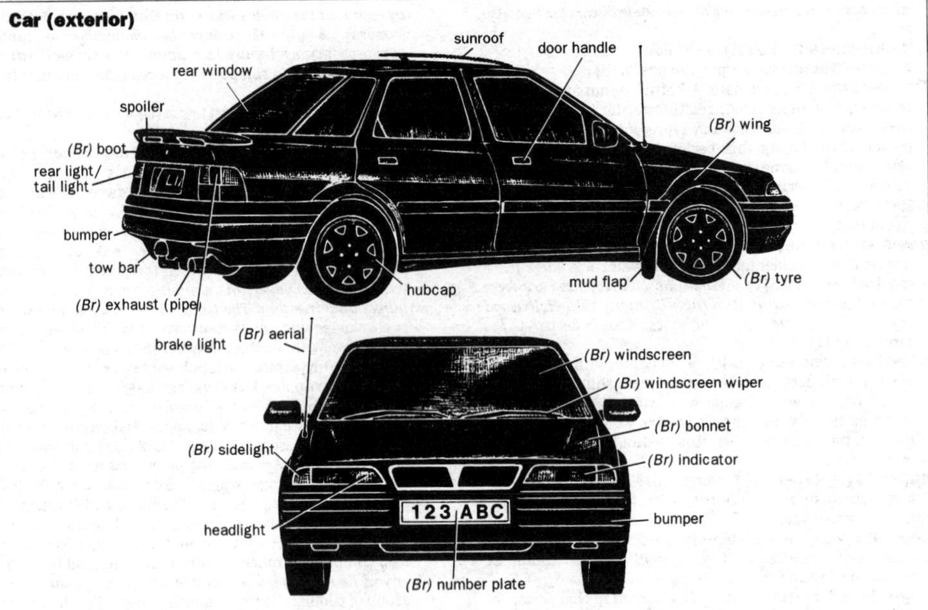

car parts in American English

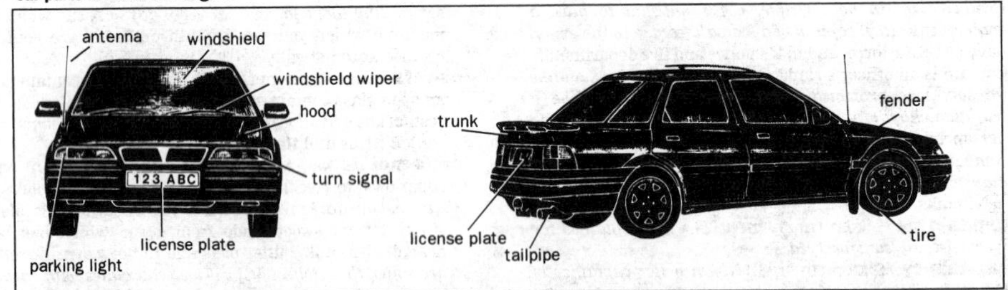

car·bo·hy·drate /£ˌkɑː·bəʊ'haɪ·dreɪt, $ˌkɑːr-/ *n* (food containing) any of several substances such as sugar or STARCH which provide the body with energy • *Bread, potatoes, pasta and rice are all high in carbohydrate(s).* [U; C] • *Athletes usually eat a high carbohydrate diet.*

car·bol·ic /£kɑː'bɒl·ɪk, $kɑːr'bɑː·lɪk/ *adj* [not gradable] coming from **coal tar** (= a substance produced when coal is heated until it changes to a gas and then made liquid by cooling) • *carbolic soap* • **Carbolic acid** is a liquid which destroys bacteria and is used for cleaning injuries or surfaces to prevent disease.

car·bon /£'kɑː·bᵊn, $'kɑːr-/ *n* [U] a simple chemical substance, which exists in its pure form as DIAMOND or GRAPHITE, and is an important part of other substances such as coal and oil, as well as being contained in all plants and animals • *Carbon compounds are the basis of all living matter.* • **Carbon (paper)** is thin paper with a covering of carbon or other dark-coloured substance on one side which is used between sheets of writing to make copies: *This copy's very faint – I need a new sheet of carbon.* • A **carbon (copy)** is a copy made with carbon paper: *I'd better make a carbon* **of** *this memo.* ○ *(fig.) She's a* **carbon copy of** (= is exactly like) *her mother.* • **Carbon dioxide** is the gas formed when carbon is burned, or when animals breathe out: *carbon dioxide emissions* • **Carbon monoxide** is the poisonous gas formed by the burning of carbon, esp. in the form of car fuel: *Levels of carbon monoxide in the air are worryingly high.* ○ *A postmortem revealed that he had died from carbon monoxide poisoning.* • **Carbon dating** is a method of calculating the age of extremely old objects by measuring the amount of a particular type of carbon in them: *Carbon dating has put the date of the skeleton at about 4000 BC.* • PIC〉 **Stationery**

car·bon·if·er·ous /£ˌkɑː·bə'nɪf·ᵊr·əs, $ˌkɑːr·bə'nɪf·ɚ-/ *adj specialized* • Carboniferous **rocks** are rocks containing coal. • **The Carboniferous (period)** is the period of the world's history during which coal was formed.

car·bon·ize *(obj), Br and Aus usually* **-ise** /£'kɑː·bᵊn·aɪz, $'kɑːr-/ *v specialized* • To carbonize something is to change it to carbon by burning it. [T] • If something carbonizes, it changes to carbon by burning. [I]

car·bon·at·ed /£'kɑː·bᵊn·eɪ·tɪd, $'kɑːr·bᵊn·eɪ·t̬ɪd/ *adj* (of a drink) fizzy because it contains **carbon dioxide** • *carbonated drinks/water*

car·bun·cle SWELLING /£'kɑː·bʌŋ·kl̩, $'kɑːr-/ *n* [C] *specialized* a large painful swelling under the skin • *Victims of the plague developed carbuncles and swellings in the groin and armpits.* • *"Like a monstrous carbuncle on the face of a much-loved and elegant friend"* (Prince Charles describing a new building in a speech to the Institute of British Architects, 1984)

car·bun·cle JEWEL /£'kɑː·bʌŋ·kl̩, $'kɑːr-/ *n* a dark red jewel • *a ring set with pearls and a carbuncle* [C] • *a brooch made of carbuncle* [U]

car·bu·ret·tor *Br, Am* **car·bu·ret·or** /£ˌkɑː·bjə'ret·əʳ, $ˌkɑːr·bjə'ret̬·ɚ/ *n* [C] the part of an engine which mixes fuel and air, producing the gas which is burnt to provide the power needed to operate the vehicle or machine

car·cass, *Br also* **car·case** /£'kɑː·kəs, $'kɑːr-/ *n* [C] the parts left of a dead animal, or the frame of an object, such as a car or ship • *Vultures flew around in the sky waiting to pick at the carcass* **of** *the deer.* • *I saw children swimming in an old irrigation ditch alongside the* **rotting** *carcass of an ox.* • *Carcasses of burnt-out vehicles lined the roads near the scene of the worst fighting.* • *You can make soup by boiling chicken carcasses.* • *(slang) Move your great carcass* (= your body) *out of that chair!*

car·cin·o·gen /£kɑː'sɪn·ə·dʒᵊn, $kɑːr-/ *n* [C] a substance which causes CANCER (= a serious illness involving diseased growths in the body) • *The American government classifies both asbestos and environmental tobacco smoke as class one carcinogens.*

car·cin·o·gen·ic /£ˌkɑː·sᵊn·əʊ'dʒen·ɪk, $ˌkɑːr·sᵊn·oʊ-/ *adj* • A carcinogenic substance is one which causes

CANCER: *He estimated that the average American consumes about 45 micrograms of possibly carcinogenic man-made pesticide residues in a day.*

car·cin·o·ma /£kɑː·sɪˈnəʊ·mə, $kɑːr·sɪˈnoʊ-/ *n* [C] *specialized* a diseased growth which forms on or inside the body; a TUMOUR

card STIFF PAPER /£kɑːd, $kɑːrd/ *n* (a piece of) thick stiff paper • *The children are making party hats out of coloured card.* [U] • *I have all my friends' addresses written on cards* (=small plain rectangular pieces of stiff paper). [C] • A **card index** is a box for storing cards in a particular order. • *(Br)* A **card vote** is a **block vote** in which the number of members of the organization which the voter represents is recorded on a card that the voter gives in. • See also PHONECARD; RAILCARD; SCORECARD. • PIC› **Stationery** Ⓓ

card GAME /£kɑːd, $kɑːrd/, **play·ing card** *n* [C] one of a set of 52 small rectangular pieces of stiff paper each with a number and one of four signs printed on it, used in games • *After dinner, Ted got out a* **pack**/*(Am also)* **deck** *of cards* • *John* **shuffled** (=mixed up) *the cards before he* **dealt** *them* **(out)** (=gave them to the players). • *Whist is my favourite card* **game**. • *a card table* • If you have a few **cards up** your **sleeve**, you have a secret plan to improve your situation which you will put into action at the most advantageous moment: *Well, Alan, England have definitely been the weaker side in the first half, but I think they've still got one or two cards up their sleeve.* • If you **keep/hold** your **cards** (very) **close to** your **chest** you are very secretive about your intended actions: *You never quite know what Barry's going to do next – he keeps his cards very close to his chest.* • Your **best/strongest/trump card** is your main advantage over others: *William finally* **played** *his trump card when he took Camilla to his parents' house – an enormous manor in deepest Sussex.* • If you **put/lay** your **cards on the table** you are honest about your feelings and intentions: *I thought it was time to lay my cards on the table, so I told him that I had no intention of marrying him.* • If someone **has/holds all the cards** they are able to control the situation. • An event that is **on the cards**/*(Am also)* **in the cards** is likely: *"So you think there'll be an election next year." "I think it's on the cards."* • See also CARDSHARP. • LP› **Cards** Ⓓ Ⓘ

cards /£kɑːdz, $kɑːrdz/ *n* [U + sing/pl v] • Cards is any of a range of games played with cards, such as POKER, WHIST and BRIDGE: *I've never been much good at cards.* ○ *Shall we* **have a game of/play** *cards?*

card PERMISSION /£kɑːd, $kɑːrd/ *n* [C] a small rectangular piece of card or plastic, often with your SIGNATURE, photograph or other information proving who you are, which allows you to do something, such as make payment, obtain money from a bank or enter a particular place • *I don't have any cash – can I* **put** *this* **on** (=pay using) *my* **(credit/charge)** *card?* • *Jim, why don't you use your card to pay for the hotel?* • *A lot of shops won't accept cheques unless you have a* **(cheque/***Br also* **banker's)** *card with you.* • *The bank's closed now, but I can get some money out with my* **(cash)** *card.* • *I don't have any change for the phone but I do have a* **(phone)** *card, if that's of any use.* • *"Are you coming to aerobics tonight?" "Yes but I've left my* **(membership)** *card at home so I hope they let me in."* • *You usually have to show your (membership) card at the door.* • A **card-carrying member** of an organization is an active and involved member: *My brother's a card-carrying member of the Green Party.* • See also CARDHOLDER. • LP› **Money** Ⓓ Ⓘ

card *obj* /£kɑːd, $kɑːrd/ *v* [T] *Am* • To card someone is to ask them to show you a document, esp. an **identity card**, in order to prove how old they are: *She looks really young – she's always being carded when she goes into bars.*

card GREETINGS /£kɑːd, $kɑːrd/ *n* [C] a rectangular piece of stiffened paper, folded in half, with a picture on the front and often a message printed inside, sent on a special occasion • *anniversary/birthday/Christmas/get-well/greetings/valentine cards* • *It's Steve's birthday on Thursday – I must* **send** *him a card.* • *We received lots of cards when our baby was born.* • A card can also be a POSTCARD (= a card, often with a photograph or picture on one side, which can be addressed and sent without an envelope): *Terry sent us a card* **of** *the Empire State Building from New York.* • Ⓓ Ⓘ

card INFORMATION /£kɑːd, $kɑːrd/ *n* [C] a small rectangular piece of stiff paper with information printed on it, esp. a person's job title, business address and telephone number • *Here, let me give you my* **(business)** *card.* • Ⓓ Ⓘ

card PERSON /£kɑːd, $kɑːrd/ *n* [C] *dated infml* an amusing or strange person • *You're such a card, Patrick!* • Ⓓ Ⓘ

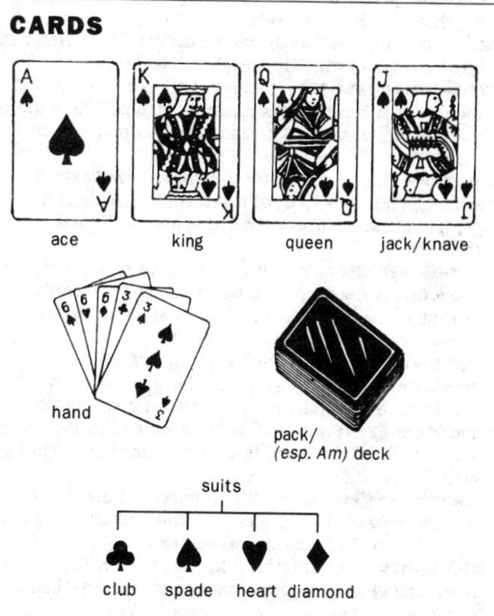

You refer to particular playing cards by using 'of' followed by the name of the suit: *the ace of spades; the queen of hearts; the two of clubs.*

A **pack**/*(esp. Am)* **deck** of cards is a set of playing cards.

The **dealer** is the person who **shuffles** (= mixes up) the pack before playing a game, and then **deals** (= gives out) cards to the other players.

The set of cards which a player has is his or her **hand**. A hand is also a (single part of a) game of cards.

car·da·mom, *Br also* **car·da·mum**, *Am also* **card·a·mon** /£ˈkɑː·də·məm, $ˈkɑːr-/ *n* an E. Indian plant, the seeds of which are used as a spice, esp. in Asian food • *cardamom seeds* • *Cardamoms have blue flowers.* [C] • *Add two teaspoonsful of ground cardamom.* [U]

card·board /£ˈkɑːd·bɔːd, $ˈkɑːrd·bɔːrd/ *n* [U] material like very thick stiff paper, usually pale brown in colour, which is used esp. for making boxes • *The children were playing with a toy farm made out of cardboard.* • *She brought the shopping home in a cardboard* **box**. • *We were standing next to a cardboard* **cutout** *of the actor in the cinema foyer.* • *(fig. disapproving) I've never enjoyed his plays – somehow all his characters are all cardboard* (=artificial). • PIC› **Box**

card·hold·er /£ˈkɑːdˌhəʊl·dəʳ, $ˈkɑːrdˌhoʊl·dɚ/ *n* [C] *Am* someone who has been given permission to use a card which allows them to do something, esp. a **cheque card** or a **credit card** (=small plastic card which can be used as a method of payment) • *Visa operates through a network of member banks and has 55 million cardholders in Europe.*

car·di– /£ˈkɑː·di-, $ˈkɑːr-/, **car·di·o–** *combining form specialized* of the heart • *the cardiovascular* (=heart and blood) *system* • *The machine measures cardiopulmonary* (=heart and lung) *functions.*

car·di·ac /£ˈkɑː·di·æk, $ˈkɑːr-/ *adj* [not gradable] of the heart or heart disease • Cardiac **arrest** is a condition in which the heart stops beating.

car·di·gan /£ˈkɑː·dɪ·gən, $ˈkɑːr-/, *Br infml* **car·dy** /£ˈkɑː·di, $ˈkɑːr-/, **car·die** *n* [C] a woollen piece of clothing which covers the upper part of the body and the arms, fastening at the front with buttons, and usually worn over other clothes • *I'm knitting a cardigan for the neighbour's new baby.* • PIC› **Clothes**

car·di·nal PRIEST /£'kɑː·dɪ·nəl, $'kɑːr-/ *n* [C] any of a number of priests of high rank in the Roman Catholic Church who elect the Pope • *Cardinal Hume*

car·di·nal IMPORTANT /£'kɑː·dɪ·nəl, $'kɑːr-/ *adj* [before n] of great importance; main • *a cardinal rule/error/sin* • **Cardinal points** are the four main points of the compass – North, South, East and West.

car·di·nal BIRD /£'kɑː·dɪ·nəl, $'kɑːr-/ *n* [C] a N American bird, the male of which has bright red feathers

car·di·nal (num·ber) /£'kɑː·dɪ·nəl, $'kɑːr-/ *n* [C] a number which represents amount, such as 1, 2, 3, rather than order, such as 1st, 2nd, 3rd • Compare ORDINAL (NUMBER).

car·di·o– /£kɑː·di·əʊ, $-oʊ-/ *combining form* CARDI-

car·di·og·ra·phy /£,kɑː·di'ɒg·rə·fi, $,kɑːr·di'ɑː·grə-/ *n* [U] *specialized* the use of a machine to record the beating of the heart

car·di·o·graph /£'kɑː·di·ə·græf, $'kɑːr-, £-grɑːf/ *n* [C] *specialized* • *The cardiograph* (=machine for recording the beating of the heart) *is one of the most useful tools doctors have in the fight against heart disease.*

car·di·o·gram /£'kɑː·di·ə·græm, $'kɑːr-/ *n* [C] *specialized* • A cardiogram is the picture drawn by a cardiograph which shows a record of the heart's activity.

car·di·ol·o·gy /£,kɑː·di'ɒl·ə·gi, $,kɑːr·di'ɑː·lə-/ *n* [U] *specialized* the study and treatment of medical conditions of the heart

car·di·ol·o·gist /£,kɑː·di'ɒl·ə·dʒɪst, $,kɑːr·di'ɑː·lə-/ *n* [C] *specialized* • *I've got an appointment with the cardiologist* (=heart specialist) *next month.*

card·phone /£'kɑːd·fəʊn, $'kɑːrd·foʊn/ *n* [C] a public telephone which you operate using a special card instead of coins

card·punch *Br* /£'kɑːd·pʌntʃ, £'kɑːb-, $'kɑːrd-/, *Am and Aus* **key·punch** *n* [C] (esp. in the past) a machine for putting information onto cards so that it can be read by a computer

card·sharp /£'kɑːd·ʃɑːp, $'kɑːrd·ʃɑːrp/ *n* [C] a person who earns money by playing cards dishonestly

car·dy /£'kɑː·di, $'kɑːr-/ *n* [C] *Br infml for* CARDIGAN

care PROTECTION /£keəʳ, $ker/ *n* [U] the process of or responsibility for protecting and giving special attention to someone or something • *The standard of care at our local hospital is excellent.* • *Mira's going to be very weak for a long time after the operation, so she'll need a lot of care.* • *Nurseries are responsible for the children* **in** *their* **care**. • Care is often used as a combining form: *I need some advice on skin care/healthcare/babycare/childcare/daycare.* • To **take care of** someone or something is to be responsible for, give attention to or protect them or it: *My parents are going to take care of the house while we're away.* ○ *Take* **good** *care of that girl of yours, Patrick – she's very special.* ○ *Don't worry about me, I can take care of* **myself** (=I do not need anyone else to protect me.) • To **take care of** something also means to deal with it: *If you can sort out the drink for the party, I'll take care of the food.* ○ *All the travel arrangements have been taken care of.* ○ *No, you paid for dinner last time, let me take care of* (=pay for) *it.* • *(infml)* People sometimes say **Take care**, or less commonly, **Take care of yourself** when they are saying goodbye to someone: *"Bye, Melissa." "Goodbye Rozzie, take care."* • *(Br)* Children who are **in care** or who have been **taken/put into care** are not living with their natural parents but instead with a national or local government organization or another family: *Both children were taken into care when their parents died.* • If someone is **care of** (*abbreviation* **c/o**) someone else, it means that letters can be sent to them at the address of that person: *Paul Brinkworth, c/o Anthony Edwards, 23 Mill Road.*

care for *obj v prep* [T] • To care for a person or animal is to provide them with what they need and to protect them, esp. because they are young or ill: *Who'll care for the children when Sandra's in hospital?* ○ *She can't go out to work because she has to stay at home to care for her elderly mother.* ○ *It's good to know that the dogs will be well cared for while we're away.*

car·er /£'keə·rəʳ, $'ker·ɚ/, *specialist or Am also* **care·giver**, *Am also* **care·tak·er** *n* [C] • *Now that Jane has gone back to work, Ken is the children's main carer* (=the main person who cares for them).

car·ing /£'keə·rɪŋ, $'ker·ɪŋ/ *adj* • Someone who is caring is kind and gives emotional support to others: *I've always thought of Jo as a very caring person.* • *(Br)* The **caring professions** are jobs such as nursing which involve caring for people: *Fewer graduates are taking jobs in industry, choosing instead careers in the civil service, the universities and the 'caring' professions.*

care ATTENTION /£keəʳ, $ker/ *n* [U] serious attention, esp. to the details of a situation or something • *She painted the window frames* **with** *great care so that no paint got onto the glass.* • *You need to* **take** *a bit more care* **with** *your spelling.* • *The roads are icy, so drive* **with** *care* (=drive with attention so that you do not have an accident). • **Take** *care on these busy roads* (=Drive with attention so that you do not have an accident). • **Take** *care* **not to** (=Make certain that you do not) *spill your coffee.* [+ *to* infinitive] • **Take** *care* (=Make certain) **that** *you don't fall.* [+ *that* clause] • *The parcel had a label on it saying* **'Handle with care'**. • *(Br dated)* **Have a care** means 'be more careful'.

care·ful /£'keə·fəl, $'ker-/ *adj* • *Norwich welcomes careful drivers* (=people who drive with care in order to avoid accidents)*!* • **Be** *careful* **with** *the glasses* (=take care so that you don't break them). • **Be** *careful* **of/about** *the ice on the road.* • *He's in a really foul temper so be careful* **(about/of)** *what you say to him.* • **Be** *careful* **where** *you put that hot pan.* [+ *wh-* word] • **Be** *careful* **to** *look both ways when you cross the road.* [+ *to* infinitive] • **Be** *careful* **carrying** *those heavy bags.* [+ *v-ing*] • *(Be) careful* **(that)** *you don't fall.* [+ (*that*) clause] • *Michael is a very careful worker* (=gives attention to detail). • *After careful* (=detailed) *consideration of your proposal, I regret to say that we are unable to accept it.* • *(Br dated)* People sometimes say **Careful how you go** when they say goodbye to someone.

care·ful·ly /£'keə·fəl·i, $'ker-/ *adv* • Carefully means with great attention: *The doctor examined her patient carefully.* ○ *She carefully folded the letter and put it in her pocket.* ○ *Drive carefully* (=with care, so that you avoid any danger) *on those icy roads.*

care·less /£'keə·ləs, $'ker-/ *adj* • Careless means not taking or showing enough care and attention: *Careless drivers cause accidents.* ○ *She broke two glasses? That was a bit careless* **of** *her.* ○ *Sian has always been careless* **with money** (=does not take enough care of it and is likely to spend too much of it or to lose it). ○ *My son's teacher says that his work is often rather careless.* ○ *He made a careless* (=without thinking) *remark about her appearance that really upset her.* • *"Careless talk costs lives"* (warning used on posters during the Second World War, 1939-45)

care·less·ly /£'keə·lə·sli, $'ker-/ *adv* • *I found your glove which you'd carelessly dropped outside.* • *He told me off for driving carelessly.*

care·less·ness /£'keə·lə·snəs, $'ker-/ *n* [U]

care WORRY /£keəʳ, $ker/ *n* a feeling of worry or anxiety • *Isn't it good to see all those children playing, completely* **free from** *care* (=without any worries). [U] • *She seemed weighed down by all her cares.* [C] • *You look as if you have* **all the cares of the world on** *your* **shoulders** (=You look very worried). • *Look at her,* **not/without a care in the world** (=not having any worries).

care /£keəʳ, $ker/ *v* • *He claims he doesn't mind that she won't go out with him, but actually I think he cares quite a lot* (=he's quite upset). [I] • *"Was Lorna happy about the arrangements?" "I* **don't know and** *I don't care."* [I] • *I really don't care* (=It's not important to me) **whether** *we go out or not.* [+ *wh-* word] • *I don't care* **how** *much it costs, just buy it.* [+ *wh-* word] • *She's never cared very much* **about** *her appearance* (=Her appearance has never been important to her). [I] • *(infml) I* **couldn't care less** (=It isn't important to me) *about what we have for supper.* • *(infml) "Mike's really fed up about it." "I* **couldn't care less** (=That does not worry or upset me at all)*."* • *(infml) You can do what you like* **for all** *I* **care** (=It isn't important to me what you do). • *(infml) He said he didn't approve of what I'd done,* **as if** *I* **cared** (=it wasn't important to me). • *(infml) "It looks as if Scotland are going to win."* **"Who cares?"** (=It isn't important to me).

care·less /£'keə·ləs, $'ker-/ *adj* • Careless means relaxed, natural and free from anxiety: *She has a certain careless simplicity about her which I rather envy.* • See also CAREFREE.

care·less·ly /£'keə·lə·sli, $'ker-/ *adv* • *She wandered carelessly through the park.*

care·less·ness /£'keə·lə·snəs, $'ker-/ *n* [U]

care WANT /£keəʳ, $ker/ *v fml* (used in polite offers and suggestions) to want something • **Would** *you care* **for** *a drink?* [I + *for*] • **Would** *you care* **to** *join us for dinner?* [+ *to* infinitive]

care for *obj* /£keəʳ, $ker/ *v prep* [T] to like (something or someone) • *(slightly fml) I have to say I don't much care for modern music.* • *(slightly fml) Your father thought she was nice but Camille and I didn't care for her.* • To care for someone is also to feel affectionate and often romantic towards them: *You know I care for you, Peter.* ○ *(humorous) I didn't know you cared* (= I didn't know that you felt romantic towards me)*!*

ca·reen /kəˈriːn/ *v* [I] to go forward quickly while moving from side to side • *The driver lost control of his car when the brakes failed, and it went careening* **down** *the hill.*

ca·reer JOB /£kəˈrɪəʳ, $-ˈrɪr/ *n* [C] a job for which you are trained and in which it is possible to advance during your working life, so that you get greater responsibility and earn more money • *He's hoping for a career* **in** *the police force/***as** *a police officer.* • *When he retires he will be able to look back over a* **brilliant** *career* (= a working life which has been very successful). • *It helps if you can move a few rungs up the career* **ladder** *before taking time off to have a baby.* • *I took this new job because I felt that the career* **prospects** *were much better.* • *It looks as though Francis is going to be a career politician* (= will spend his life working as a politician). • *Elaine has become a real career* **woman/girl** (= is interested in and spends most of her time on her job). • *Judith is very career-***minded/-oriented** (= gives a lot of attention to her job). • Ⓔ

ca·reer·ist /£kəˈrɪə·rɪst, $-ˈrɪr·ɪst/ *n* [C] • A careerist is someone who thinks that their career is more important than anything else, and who will do anything, even something unfair, to be successful in it: *Return to work before your baby has started to walk and you risk being seen as a ruthless careerist.* ○ *It was difficult not to feel intimidated by his high-earning, careerist sisters.*

ca·reers /£kəˈrɪəz, $-ˈrɪrz/ *adj* [before n; not gradable] • *(Br)* A careers **adviser/teacher/officer** (*Am* **guidance counselor**) is someone who gives people information about jobs.

ca·reer MOVE /£kəˈrɪəʳ, $-ˈrɪr/ *v* [I always + adv/prep] (esp. of a vehicle) to move fast and uncontrollably • *The coach careered* **down** *a slope and collided with a bank.* • *The wreckage was all that was left of a sports car which careered out of control, killing two people.* • Ⓔ

care·free /£ˈkeə·friː, $ˈker-/ *adj* having no worries, problems, or anxieties; happy • *I remember my carefree student days.* • *People always tend to look back on their childhood as a carefree time.*

care·ful /£ˈkeə·fᵊl·nəs, $ˈker-/ *adj* See at CARE ATTENTION

care·giver /£ˈkeəˌgɪv·əʳ, $ˈkerˌgɪv·ɚ/ *n* [C] *esp. Am or specialized for* **carer**, see at CARE PROTECTION • *a professional caregiver* • *The role of caregiver in this society is often taken on by women.*

care·less /£ˈkeə·ləs, $ˈker-/ *adj* See at CARE ATTENTION, CARE WORRY

car·er /£ˈkeə·rəʳ, $ˈker·ɚ/ *n* See at CARE PROTECTION

ca·ress /kəˈres/ *n, v* (to give) a gentle loving touch or kiss • *Gently he caressed the back of her neck.* [T] • *They murmured to each other as they caressed.* [I] • *(fig.) The warm ocean breeze caressed* (= blew gently over) *her skin.* [T] • *She melted under the warmth of his caresses.* [C]

care·tak·er BUILDING WORKER *Br* /£ˈkeəˌteɪ·kəʳ, $ˈkerˌteɪ·kɚ/, *Am and Scot Eng* **janitor**, *Am also* **cus·to·di·an** *n* [C] a person employed to take care of a large building, such as a school, and who deals with the cleaning, repairs, etc. • *At the end of the day, the children put their chairs on their desks so that the caretaker could sweep the floor of the classroom.* • *(fig.)* A caretaker **government**, official organization or position is one which holds power for a short period of time until a new one is chosen.

care·tak·er PROTECTOR /£ˈkeəˌteɪ·kəʳ, $ˈkerˌteɪ·kɚ/ *n* [C] *Am for* **carer**, see at CARE PROTECTION

care·worn /£ˈkeə·wɔːn, $ˈker·wɔːrn/ *adj* appearing tired, worried and unhappy • *Her mother, who couldn't have been much more than thirty, looked old and careworn.*

car·fare /£ˈkɑː·feəʳ, $ˈkɑːr·fer/ *n* [U] *Am* the money paid by a passenger for travelling in a bus, TAXI, etc. • *You'll need a couple of dollars for carfare.*

car·go /£ˈkɑː·gəʊ, $ˈkɑːr·goʊ/ *n pl* **cargoes** or **cargos** (a load of) the goods carried by a ship, aircraft or other large vehicle • *a cargo ship/plane/vessel* • *The ship was carrying a cargo* **of** *wool from England to France.* [C] • *This aircraft is for passengers only, it doesn't take any cargo.* [U] • Ⓕ Ⓟ

car·hop /£ˈkɑː·hɒp, $ˈkɑːr·hɑːp/ *n* [C] *Am infml* a person who serves food at a **drive-in** restaurant (= a restaurant in which people eat their meals in their cars)

Car·ib·be·an /£ˌkær·ɪˈbiː·ᵊn, £kəˈrɪb·i-, $ˌker·ɪˈbiː·ᵊn/ *n* [U] **the Caribbean** the sea which is east of Central America and north of S America, the islands found there or the countries which border this sea • *They're holidaying somewhere in the Caribbean.* • LP **World regions**

Car·ib·be·an /£ˌkær·ɪˈbiː·ᵊn, £kəˈrɪb·i-, $ˌker·ɪˈbiː-/ *adj* • *Caribbean food* • *a Caribbean restaurant* • *Derek Wallcott is one of the most famous Caribbean poets.*

car·i·bou /£ˈkær·ɪ·buː, $ˈker-/ *n* [C] *pl* **caribous** or **caribou** a N. American REINDEER (= a large deer with long branch-like horns)

car·i·ca·ture /£ˈkær·ɪ·kə·tʃʊəʳ, $ˈker·ɪ·kə·tʃʊr/ *n* (the art of making) a drawing or written or spoken description of someone which makes part of their appearance or character more noticeable than it really is, and which can make them look ridiculous • *There was a wonderful caricature* **of** *the prime minister in the newspaper yesterday.* [C] • *There are caricatures that indulge their subjects and caricatures that criticise them.* [C] • *The characters in his early novels are a lot subtler than the overblown caricatures in his more recent work.* [C] • *(fig.) Over the years he's become a grotesque caricature* **of** *himself.* [C] • *Of course Tanner's paintings have always been more caricature than strict portraiture.* [U]

car·i·ca·ture *obj* /£ˌkær·ɪ·kəˈtʃʊəʳ, $ˌker·ɪ·kəˈtʃʊr/ *v* [T] • *Charles Dickens caricatured lawyers* (= represented them in a way which made them look ridiculous) *in several of his novels.*

car·i·ca·tur·ist /£ˌkær·ɪ·kəˈtʃʊə·rɪst, $ˌker·ɪ·kəˈtʃʊr·ɪst/ *n* [C] • A caricaturist is a person who makes caricatures.

ca·ries /£ˈkeə·riːz, $ˈker·iːz/ *n* [U] *fml or medical* decay in the teeth or bones • *Children who eat a lot of sweets are more likely to suffer from* **dental** *caries.*

ca·ril·lon /kəˈrɪl·jən/ *n* [C] (a tune played on) a set of bells, usually hung in a tower

car·ing /£ˈkeə·rɪŋ, $ˈker·ɪŋ/ *adj* See at CARE PROTECTION

car·jack·ing /£ˈkɑːˌdʒæk·ɪŋ, $ˈkɑːrˌdʒek-/ *n* [C/U] *esp. Am* (an act of) stealing someone's car while they are in it by using physical force or threats • *The two police officers arrived at the scene of the carjacking within five minutes.*

car·mine /£ˈkɑː·maɪn, $ˈkɑːr-/ *adj, n* [U] (of a) deep bright red colour • *I found myself in a room full of carmine-nailed women dripping with furs and diamonds.*

car·nage /£ˈkɑː·nɪdʒ, $ˈkɑːr-/ *n* [U] the violent killing of large numbers of people, esp. in war • *The Battle of the Somme was a scene of dreadful carnage.* • *The country's breakup would undoubtedly lead to chaos and carnage.* • *Something must be done to reduce the carnage* (= death and injury of people in car accidents) *on our roads each year.*

car·nal /£ˈkɑː·nəl, $ˈkɑːr-/ *adj fml* relating to the physical feelings and desires of the body; sexual • *carnal desires* • *carnal pleasures* • *(fml or law)* **Carnal knowledge** is sex.

car·nal·i·ty /£kɑːˈnæl·ɪ·ti, $kɑːrˈnæl·ə·t̬i/ *n* [U] *fml* • *In the last scene of the ballet the young princess throws herself upon her lover in a moment of pure carnality.*

car·na·tion /£kɑːˈneɪ·ʃᵊn, $kɑːr-/ *n* [C] (a plant with) a small flower with a sweet smell, which is usually white, pink, or red • *He presented her with a bouquet of red carnations.* • *They were wearing carnations in their buttonholes so I assumed they'd all been to a wedding.* • PIC **Flowers and plants**

car·ni·val /£ˈkɑː·nɪ·vᵊl, $ˈkɑːr-/ *n* [C] (a special occasion or period of) public enjoyment and entertainment involving wearing unusual clothes, dancing, and eating and drinking, usually held in the roads of a city • *Mardi Gras is a carnival held just before the beginning of Lent in New Orleans and Rio de Janeiro.* [C] • *There's a real carnival atmosphere in the streets.* • Carnival is also *Am for* FUNFAIR and FETE.

car·ni·vore /£ˈkɑː·nɪ·vɔːʳ, $ˈkɑːr·nɪ·vɔːr/ *n* [C] an animal that eats meat • *Lions and tigers are carnivores, while sheep and goats mainly eat grass.* • *(humorous) I did mostly vegetarian food but put a couple of meat dishes out for the carnivores* (= people who eat meat). • Compare HERBIVORE.

car·ni·vo·rous /£kɑːˈnɪv·ᵊr·əs, $kɑːrˈnɪv·ɚ-/ *adj* • *Lions and tigers are carnivorous* (= eat meat).

car·ob /£ˈkær·əb, $ˈker-/ *n* (the dark brown bean-like fruit of) a Mediterranean tree • *Carob is sometimes used in sweet foods as a healthier alternative to chocolate.* [U] • *The carob is also known as the locust tree.* [C]

car·ol /£'kær·əl, $'ker-/ *n* [C] a happy and/or religious song, esp. sung at Christmas • *a carol concert* • *a carol service* (= a Church ceremony at which carols are sung) • *carol music* • *'Silent Night' is my favourite* **(Christmas)** *carol.* • **Carol singers** (*Am usually* **carolers**) are people who go from house to house singing carols at Christmas. In Britain this is done in order to collect money, usually to help people in need: *We had some carol singers round last night.* ○ *We go* **carol-singing** *for charity every Christmas.* • LP> **Holidays**

car·ol /£'kær·əl, $'ker-/ *v* [I] **-ll-** or *Am usually* **-l-** • *As we stood outside the church, we could hear the choir carolling* **(away)** (= singing happily) *inside.* • *Last Christmas we went carolling* (= went from house to house singing carols) *to raise money for the homeless.* • *(fig.) At dawn, the silence of the night was broken by the sound of the birds carolling in the trees.*

car·ot·ene /£'kær·ə·tiːn, $'ker-/ *n* [U] an orange-yellow or red PIGMENT (= substance which gives colour) contained in some foods • *Carrots contain a lot of carotene, which is a good source of Vitamin A.* • *Flamingoes are pink because their diet is rich in carotene.*

ca·rouse /kə'raʊz/ *v* [I] to enjoy yourself by drinking alcohol and speaking and laughing loudly in a group of people • *They'd been up carousing till dawn the night before and looked exhausted.*

ca·rous·el AMUSEMENT /£,kær·ʊ'sel, $,ker·ə-/ *n* [C] *esp. Am for* **merry-go-round**, see at MERRY HAPPY

ca·rous·el MOVING STRIP /£,kær·ʊ'sel, $,ker·ə-/ *n* [C] a continuous moving strip on which airport passengers' bags are put for collection • *As always our luggage was the last to appear on the carousel.*

Ca·rou·sel CONTAINER /£,kær·ʊ'sel, $,ker·ə-/ *n* [C] *trademark* a circular device in which SLIDES (= small pieces of photographic film) for a PROJECTOR are held

carp COMPLAIN /£kɑːp, $kɑːrp/ *v* [I] to complain continually about unimportant matters • *He's convinced that however much people carp about junk mail, most couldn't live without it.* • *I can't stand the way he's always carping.* • *She never stops carping* **at** *him.* • *After years of having to listen to her carping* **criticism**, *he finally left her.*

carp FISH /£kɑːp, $kɑːrp/ *n* [C] *pl* **carp** or **carps** a large edible fish which lives in lakes and rivers

car·pen·ter /£'kɑː·pɪn·təʳ, $'kɑːr·pɪn·t̬ɚ/ *n* [C] a person whose job is making and repairing wooden objects and structures • *We've found a good carpenter to build some bookshelves for us.*

car·pen·try /£'kɑː·pɪn·tri, $'kɑːr-/ *n* [U] • *Martin is learning carpentry* (= the skill of making and repairing wooden objects). • *That staircase of theirs is the most beautiful piece of carpentry* (= work done by a carpenter).

car·pet /£'kɑː·pɪt, $'kɑːr-/ *n* (a shaped piece of) thick woven material, either woollen or woollen-like, for covering floors • *We've just had a new carpet* **fitted/laid** *in our bedroom.* [C] • A *(Br)* **fitted**/*(Am)* **wall-to-wall** carpet is one which covers the whole floor of a room from wall to wall. [C] • *She cut up some bits of old carpet for the children's playhouse.* [U] • *(fig.) Our lawn is* **a carpet of** (= is covered with) *daisies.* [U] • *(fig.) There's* **a carpet** (= a thick layer) **of snow** *outside.* [U] • *(infml dated) Patrick was* **on the carpet** (= in trouble with someone in authority) *for crashing a company car that he hadn't even asked permission to use.* • *When Mark gets home from work, he likes to put on his* **carpet slippers** (= soft shoes worn inside) *and sit down to read the newspaper.* • **Carpet bombing** is the act of dropping a lot of bombs all over a particular area so that it will be destroyed. • A **carpet sweeper** is a machine with a brush fixed to the bottom of it for cleaning carpets. • (KOR)

car·pet *obj* /£'kɑː·pɪt, $'kɑːr-/ *v* [T] • *We need to carpet the stairs* (= cover them with carpet). • *(fig. infml) He was carpeted* (= severely criticized) *by his boss* **for failing** *to turn up to work last week.*

car·pet·ed /£'kɑː·pə·tɪd, $'kɑːr·pə·t̬ɪd/ *adj* • *I don't understand why people have carpeted bathrooms.* • *(fig.) In spring this area is carpeted* (= covered) *with bluebells.*

car·pet·ing /£'kɑː·pɪ·tɪŋ, $'kɑː·pɪ·t̬ɪŋ/ *n* [U] • *The floors and walls were marble, the carpeting* (= carpets) *plush and the furniture richly upholstered.*

car·pet·bag·ger /£'kɑː·pɪt,bæg·əʳ, $'kɑːr·pɪt,bæg·ɚ/ *n* [C] *esp. Am disapproving* a person who tries to become a politician in an area away from their home because they think there is a greater chance of succeeding there

car·port /£'kɑː·pɔːt, $'kɑːr·pɔːrt/ *n* [C] a shelter for cars which has a roof and one or more open sides, and which can be built against the side of a house

car·riage VEHICLE /£'kær·ɪdʒ, $'ker-/ *n* [C] either a vehicle with four wheels which is usually pulled by horses and was used esp. in the past, or *(Br)* any of the separate wheeled parts of a train in which the passengers sit • *Kate was driven to the church for her wedding in a beautiful* **horse-drawn** *carriage.* • *(Br) The middle three carriages of the train are for first-class passengers only.* • *(Br) Ten minutes into the journey I noticed an attractive dark-haired man sitting in the same* **railway** *carriage.* • *"Love and marriage, love and marriage, go together like a horse and carriage"* (from a song written by Sammy Cahn, 1955)

car·riage TRANSPORTING /£'kær·ɪdʒ, $'ker-/ *n* [U] *Br* (the cost of) transporting goods • *That will be £150, carriage included.* • If goods are sent **carriage forward** it means that the person receiving them will pay for the cost of sending them. • If goods are sent **carriage free/paid**, it means that the cost of sending them has been paid by the sender. • A **carriage clock** is a rectangular clock with a handle which can be easily carried from one place to another. • PIC> **Clocks and watches**

car·riage BODY MOVEMENT /£'kær·ɪdʒ, $'ker-/ *n* [U] *fml* the way in which a person moves or keeps their body when they are standing, sitting or walking • *I noted his upright carriage and immediately assumed that he had a military background.*

car·riage·way /£'kær·ɪdʒ·weɪ, $'ker-/ *n* [C] *Br* one of the two halves of a MOTORWAY or other wide road which has two or more parallel divisions for keeping apart faster and slower cars travelling in the same direction • *The accident blocked the southbound carriageway for several hours.*

car·ri·on /£'kær·i·ən, $'ker-/ *n* [U] dead or decaying flesh • *On the road ahead a crow tugs on some carrion and flies up slowly as we approach.* • A **Carrion crow** is a European bird which feeds on carrion.

car·rot VEGETABLE /£'kær·ət, $'ker-/ *n* a long pointed orange root eaten as a vegetable • *carrot cake/juice/salad/soup* • *Eat up your carrots, they're good for you.* [C] • *Did you put any carrot in this soup?* [U] • *(infml)* A **carrot-top** is a person with orange-coloured hair: *Joe's blond and Rosie's a carrot-top.* • PIC> **Vegetables**

car·rot·y /£'kær·ə·ti, $'ker·ə·t̬i/ *adj* • *Leo has bright carroty* (= orange) **hair**.

car·rot REWARD /£'kær·ət, $'ker-/ *n* [C] *infml* something that is offered to someone in order to encourage them to do something • *"Have you tried offering your son some sort of reward if he works harder?" "Yes, I've tried* **dangling/holding out/offering** *all sorts of carrots but nothing works."* • **The carrot and the stick** refers to a system in which you are rewarded for some actions and threatened with punishment for others: *The teacher's method of handling the children is to use the carrot and the stick.* ○ *Sometimes I just have to resort to the* **carrot-and-stick** *approach with my children.*

car·ry *obj* TRANSPORT /£'kær·i, $'ker-/ *v* [T] to transport or take from one place to another • *Would you like me to carry your bag for you?* • *She carried her tired child upstairs* **to** *bed.* • *These books are too heavy for me to carry.* • *I'm so tired, my* **legs** *won't carry me* (= I can't walk) *any further.* • *The bus that was involved in the accident was carrying children* **to** *school.* • *The Brooklyn Bridge carries traffic across the East River* **from** *Brooklyn* **to** *Manhattan.* • *The wind was so strong that it lifted the fallen leaves and carried them up in the air.* • *Police think that the body was carried* **down** *the river* (= was transported by the flow of the river). • *Underground cables carry electricity* **to** *all parts of the city.* • *We only had a small suitcase, so we were able to carry it* **onto** *the plane.* • *I've been carrying these letters* **around** *with me for days, and I keep forgetting to post them.* • *Rubbish left on the beach during the day is carried* **away** (= removed) *at night by the tide.* • *Thieves broke the shop window and carried* **off** (= removed) *jewellery worth thousands of pounds.* • *Robson injured his leg in the second half of the match and had to be carried* **off**. • *(fig.) These old photographs really carry me* **back to** *when I was a child* (= make me remember when I was a child). • *(fig.) The balance in our account for June includes £5000 carried* **forward/over from** (= moved from) *May.* • *(Br infml)* If you **carry the can** for something you take the blame for it: *As usual, I was left to carry the can.* • *(infml) Terry has been* **carrying a torch for** (= has been in love with) *Liz for years, but she seems not to notice.* • *All* **carry-on** *luggage* (= bags that you take onto an aircraft with you) *must be stored under your seat or in the overhead compartments.*

car·ri·er /£'kær·i·əʳ, $'ker·i·ɚ/ *n* [C] • A carrier is a person or thing that carries something: *He'd got a job as a hod carrier on a building site.* • A carrier is also a company which operates aircraft: *There is a lot of competition between carriers for the right to fly the route between London and New York.* • Carrier is also a combining form, used esp. in phrases which refer to military vehicles of a type which carry other vehicles or groups of soldiers: *an armoured troop-carrier* ○ *an aircraft carrier* ○ *a freight carrier* • Carrier can be *infml for* **aircraft carrier**, see at AIRCRAFT: *Two American carriers were anchored offshore.* • *(Br)* A **carrier (bag)** (*Am* **shopping bag**) is a large plastic or paper bag with handles which a lot of shops give you free of charge for putting your shopping in. • A **carrier pigeon** is a PIGEON (= a large, usually grey bird) which is trained to return to its home from any place it starts its journey, carrying messages fixed to its leg or neck. • PIC> **Bags**

car·ry *obj* HAVE WITH YOU /£'kær·i, $'ker-/ *v* [T] to have (something) with you all the time • *Police officers in Britain do not usually carry guns.* • *I carry a donor card which says that after my death parts of my body may be used to help other people who are ill.* • *(fig.) He will carry the* **memory** *of the accident with him* (= will remember the accident) *for ever.* • *(fig.) Brendan is very good at carrying numbers* **in** *his* **head** (= remembering numbers). • *"Speak softly (sometimes 'talk softly') and carry a big stick"* (saying used by Theodore Roosevelt, 1903)

car·ry *obj* SPREAD /£'kær·i, $'ker-/ *v* [T] to take (something) from one person or thing and give it to another person or thing; to spread • *Malaria is a disease carried by mosquitoes.*

car·ri·er /£'kær·i·əʳ, $'ker·i·ɚ/ *n* [C] • A carrier is a person who has bacteria or a faulty CHROMOSOME which causes a particular disease and can give that disease to other people without suffering from the disease him- or herself: *Dr Sewards estimates that as many as 1 in every 7 of the community is a carrier of the defective gene.* ○ *At present only about 10% of the US's 1·5 million HIV carriers know that they carry the disease.*

car·ry *obj* HAVE /£'kær·i, $'ker-/ *v* [T] to have (something) as a part, quality or result • *All cigarette packets carry a government health warning.* • *Our cars carry a twelve-month guarantee.* • *His speech carried so much* **conviction** *that I had to agree with him.* • *In some countries, murder carries the death penalty.* • *I'm afraid my opinion doesn't carry any* **weight** *with* (= influence) *my boss.* • *(Am) No, sir, I'm afraid we don't carry* (= regularly sell) *sportswear.* • *(Am)* A **carrying charge** is an extra charge added when you buy goods by making regular small payments for them until the full amount owed has been paid.

car·ry *obj* SUPPORT WEIGHT /£'kær·i, $'ker-/ *v* [T] to support (the weight of something) without moving or breaking • *Do you think the ice is thick enough to carry my weight?* • *The weight of the cathedral roof is carried by two rows of pillars.* • *(fig.) I'm carrying a very heavy workload at the moment* (= I have a lot of work to do).

car·ry *obj* KEEP IN OPERATION /£'kær·i, $'ker-/ *v* [T] to support, keep in operation, or make a success • *The company is currently being carried by its export sales.* • *We can no longer afford to carry people who don't work as hard as they should.* • *I've been carrying this organization for years, and I've just had enough.* • *Luckily they had a very strong actor in the main part and he managed to carry the whole play* (= make a success of it through his own performance).

car·ry *obj* WIN /£'kær·i, $'ker-/ *v* [T] to win the support, agreement or sympathy of (a group of people) • *The President is expected to carry most of the southern states.* • *The management's plans to reorganize the company won't succeed unless they can carry the workforce with them.*

car·ry *obj* APPROVE /£'kær·i, $'ker-/ *v* [T often passive] to give approval, esp. by voting • *The* **motion/proposal/resolution/bill** *was carried* **by** *210 votes to 160.*

car·ry *obj* BROADCAST /£'kær·i, $'ker-/ *v* [T] (of a newspaper, radio or television broadcast) to contain (information) • *This morning's newspapers all carry the same story on their front page.* • *The 9 o'clock news carried an item about a student who'd starved to death.*

car·ry REACH /£'kær·i, $'ker-/ *v* [I] to be able to reach or travel a particular distance • *Even when they were speaking quietly, the actors' voices carried right to the back of the theatre.* • *The sound of the explosion carried for miles.* • *The ball carried high into the air and landed the other side of the fence.*

car·ry *obj* DEVELOP /£'kær·i, $'ker-/ *v* [T always + adv/prep] to develop; to continue • *Lenin carried Marx's ideas a stage further by putting them into practice.* • *If we carry this argument* **to** *its logical conclusion, we realise that further investment is not a good idea.* • *She carries tidiness* **to** *extremes/***to** *its limits* (= She is too tidy). • *We must end here, but we can carry today's discussion* **forward** *at our next meeting.* • *He always carries his jokes too far* (= he continues making jokes when he should have stopped).

car·ry *obj* ADDITION /£'kær·i, $'ker-/ *v* [T] to put (a number) into another column when doing addition • *To add 28 and 15, first add 8 and 5 which makes 13. Write down 3, carry 1. Then add 2 and 1 and the 1 you've carried, which makes 4. The answer is therefore 43.*

car·ry *obj* MOVE BODY /£'kær·i, $'ker-/ *v* [T] to move and hold (your body) in a particular way • *You can tell she's a dancer from the way that she carries herself.*

car·ry *obj* BE PREGNANT WITH /£'kær·i, $'ker-/ *v* [T] to be pregnant with (a child) • *It was quite a shock to Gaile when she learned she was carrying twins.* • *I was enormous when I was carrying Graham.*

car·ry *obj* **a·way** *v adv* [T usually passive] to cause (someone) to become very excited and to lose control • *The crowd were carried away by his passionate speech.* • *I'm sorry, I didn't hear what you said – the music had completely carried me away.* • *He tends to* **get** *a bit carried away when he's dancing and he starts spinning and leaping all over the place.* • *I'm afraid I* **got** *a little carried away when I was decorating the cake and the icing is about two inches thick!* • *I* **got** *rather carried away in one shop and came out with four different garments.*

car·ry off *obj*, **car·ry** *obj* **off** *v adv* [M] to succeed in doing or achieving (esp. something difficult) • *I thought he carried off the part of Hamlet with great skill.* • *She was nervous about giving a talk to her colleagues, but she carried* **it** *off very well.* • *I would dare wear anything so outrageous but Delia carried it off superbly.*

car·ry on *(obj)* CONTINUE, **car·ry** *(obj)* **on** *v adv* to (cause to) continue (to do something) • *Let's carry on this discussion at some other time.* [M] • *We'll carry this conversation on later when we've both calmed down.* [M] • *Carry on* **the good work***!* [T] • *Sorry to interrupt, do carry on* (**with** *what you were saying*). [I] • *You just have to carry on as if nothing's happened.* [I] • *Steve just carried on* **playing** *on his computer.* [+ v-ing] • *Daphne is carrying on the family tradition by becoming a lawyer.* [M] • *The birth of Ian and Diane's son means that the family line will carry on after all.* [I] • *I've run out of space, so I'll have to carry this letter on on another page.* [M]

car·ry on BEHAVE *v adv* [I] to behave in an uncontrolled, excited or anxious way • *If you carry on like this, you'll make yourself ill.* • *The children have been carrying on all day, and have completely worn me out.* • *It's all right, there's no need to carry on* (= cry) *so.* • *I hate hearing people carrying on* **at** (= arguing with) *each other* • *My mother is always carrying on* (= complaining) **about** *my clothes.* • *(infml dated) Is it true that Rachel and Marcus have been carrying on* (**with** *each other*) (= having a sexual relationship)*?*

car·ry–on /£'kær·i·ɒn, $'ker·i·ɑːn, ˌ--'-/ *n* [C] *Br infml* • A carry-on is a show of annoyance, anxiety, dissatisfaction or excitement, usually one which is greater than the situation deserves: *There was a real carry-on when Pat was found kissing Ashley.*

car·ry·ing–on /£ˌkærˌi·ɪŋ'ɒn, $ˌker·i·ɪŋ'ɑːn/ *n pl* **carryings–on** • Carrying-on refers to dishonest or immoral activity: *The company seems to have been involved in some rather dishonest carrying-on.* [U] • *The newspapers were full of the Minister's carryings-on.* [C]

car·ry on with *obj v adv prep* [T] to have for a short time • *I can lend you a few pounds to carry on with till you get paid.* • *We'll have to carry on with this television set for a while, even though it doesn't work very well.*

car·ry out *obj*, **car·ry** *obj* **out** *v adv* [M] to perform or complete (a job or activity); to fulfil • *Nigel is carrying out research on early Christian art.* • *The hospital is carrying out tests to find out what's wrong with her.* • *Our soldiers carried out a successful attack last night.* • *It is hoped that the kidnappers will not carry out their* *threat to kill the hostages.* • *Don't blame me, I'm only carrying out my orders/instructions.*

car·ry o·ver *(obj)*, **car·ry** *(obj)* **o·ver** *v adv* [M] to move to or to come from • *The performance has had to be carried over* **to/till** *next week because the repairs to the theatre aren't finished yet.* [M] • *You can only carry one week's holiday over* **to next year**. [M] • *I try not to let my problems at work carry over* **into** (= influence) *my private life.* [I] • *Her liking for black polo neck jumpers carries over* **from** *when they were fashionable in the sixties.* [I]

car·ry *obj* **through** HELP *v adv* [T] to help in a difficult situation • *Many animals store food in the autumn to carry them through the winter.* • *The soldiers' courage carried them through.*

car·ry through *obj* COMPLETE, **car·ry** *obj* **through** *v adv* [M] to complete; to bring to a successful end • *It is doubtful whether it will be possible to carry through the education reforms as quickly as the government hopes.* • *We are determined to carry our plans through.*

car·ry-all /£ˈkær·i·ɔːl, $ˈker·i·ɑːl/ *n* [C] *Am for* HOLDALL • PIC› **Luggage**

car·ry·cot *Br* /£ˈkær·i·kɒt, $ˈker·i·kɑːt/, *Am trademark* **Port·a·crib** /£ˈpɔː·tə·krɪb, $ˈpɔːr·t̬ə-/, *Aus* **bass·i·net** *n* [C] a container shaped like a rectangular box with two handles in which a baby can be carried

car·ry·out /£ˈkær·i·aut, $ˈker-/ *n, adj* [not gradable] *Am and ScotEng for* TAKEAWAY

car·sick /£ˈkɑː·sɪk, $ˈkɑːr-/ *adj* feeling that you want to vomit because of the movement of a car

car·sick·ness /£ˈkɑːˌsɪk·nəs, $ˈkɑːr-/ *n* [U]

cart VEHICLE /£kɑːt, $kɑːrt/ *n* [C] a vehicle with either two or four wheels, which is pulled by an animal, esp. a horse, or a person, and which is used for carrying goods • *In a field we saw a farmer loading his cart with food for the cattle.* • *My grandfather remembered the time when he would go to the market with his* **horse and cart**. • *Aren't you* **putting the cart before the horse** (= doing things in the wrong order) *by deciding what to wear for the wedding before you've even been invited to it?* • *(Br)* A **cart track** is a narrow road, with a rough surface, usually made of earth. • Cart is *Am for* TROLLEY CARRIER. • PIC› **Supermarket**

car·ter /£ˈkɑː·tər, $ˈkɑːr·t̬ər/ *n* [C] • A carter is a person who drives a cart.

cart *obj* TAKE /£kɑːt, $kɑːrt/ *v* [T always + adv/prep] to take (something or someone) somewhere, esp. using a lot of effort • *We carted all the rubbish to the bottom of the garden and burned it.* • *Council workers have carted* **away** *all the dead leaves that had collected at the side of the road.* • *(infml) I've been carting* (= carrying) *these letters* **around** *with me all week, and I still haven't posted them.* • *(infml) The drunks who had been sleeping in the park were carted* **off** (= taken by force) *to the police station.*

carte blanche /£ˌkɑːtˈblɑ̃ːʃ, $ˌkɑːrtˈblɑ̃ːnʃ/ *n* [U] complete freedom (to do something) • *Her husband has* **given** *her carte blanche* **to** *redecorate the living room.* [+ to infinitive]

car·tel /£kɑːˈtel, $kɑːr-/ *n* [C] a group of similar independent companies who join together to control prices and limit competition • *The seven stainless-steel producers are suspected of forming an illicit cartel to try to control prices.*

Car·tes·i·an /£kɑːˈti·zi·ən, $kɑːrˈti·ʒən/ *adj* [before n; not gradable] *specialized* of or connected with the ideas and theories of the thinker and mathematician René Descartes • *Cartesian doubt/philosophy/geometry*

cart·horse /£ˈkɑːt·hɔːs, $ˈkɑːrt·hɔːrs/ *n* [C] a large strong horse used for pulling CARTS or carriages

car·ti·lage /£ˈkɑː·təl·ɪdʒ, $ˈkɑr·t̬əl/ *n* (a piece of) a strong stretchy type of tissue found in humans in the joints and other places such as the nose, throat and ears • *Although the fall was heavy no serious ligament or cartilage damage was sustained.* [U] • *He has a* **torn** *cartilage in his knee from his collision with another player in yesterday's football match.* [C]

cart·load /£ˈkɑːt·ləud, $ˈkɑːrt·loud/ *n* [C] the amount that a CART holds • *(fig.) We threw out cartloads* (= a large amount) *of rubbish when we moved house.*

car·to·gra·phy /£kɑːˈtɒg·rə·fi, $kɑːrˈtɑː·grə-/ *n* [U] the science or art of making or drawing maps

car·to·graph·er /£kɑːˈtɒg·rə·fər, $kɑːrˈtɑː·grə·fər/ *n* [C] • A cartographer is someone who makes or draws maps.

car·ton /£ˈkɑː·tən, $ˈkɑːr·t̬ən/ *n* [C] a box made from thick cardboard for storing goods, or a container made from cardboard or plastic in which esp. milk or fruit juice is sold • *Discarded hamburger cartons littered the pavements.* • *She was so thirsty that she drank a carton* (= the amount that a carton contains) **of** *orange juice.* • PIC› **Containers** ① Ⓝ

car·toon DRAWING /£kɑːˈtuːn, $kɑːr-/ *n* [C] a drawing, esp. in a newspaper or magazine, that tells a joke or makes an amusing political criticism • *The newspaper cartoon depicted the President as a weasel.* • *(specialized)* In art, a cartoon is a drawing made esp. in preparation for a painting: *Leonardo's cartoon of the Virgin Mary and Saint Anne hangs in the National Gallery.* • **Cartoon strip** is *Br for* **comic strip**. See at COMIC MAGAZINE.

car·toon·ist /£kɑːˈtuː·nɪst, $kɑːr-/ *n* [C] • *Gerald Scarfe, the cartoonist, is best known for his harsh portrayals of politicians.*

car·toon FILM /£kɑːˈtuːn, $kɑːr-/, **an·i·mat·ed car·toon** *n* [C] a film made using characters and images which are drawn rather than real and which is usually amusing • *Toys based on TV cartoons are the top-selling Christmas presents this year.* • *Traditional folk tales have often been made into cartoons.* • *On her T-shirt was a picture of Mickey Mouse, the famous cartoon* **character**.

car·tridge /£ˈkɑː·trɪdʒ, $ˈkɑːr-/ *n* [C] a small part with a particular purpose, used in a larger piece of equipment, which can be easily replaced with another similar part • *Be careful buying a new printer ribbon, each model uses a different size cartridge.* • *My new video game player came with three game cartridges included.* • *The film comes in a cartridge which simply snaps in to the back of the camera.* • A cartridge is also a tube containing an explosive substance and often a bullet for use in a gun: *This rifle only holds one cartridge and so must be reloaded after each shot.* • A **cartridge pen** is a pen in which there is an ink-filled replaceable plastic cartridge: *Do you fill your pen with ink from a bottle or use cartridges?* • PIC› **Writing instruments**

car·tridge pa·per *n* [U] thick, strong paper for drawing or writing on

cart·wheel /£ˈkɑːt·wiːl, $ˈkɑːrt-/ *v, n* (to make) a fast skilful movement like a wheel turning in which you throw yourself sideways onto one hand, then onto both hands with your legs and arms straight and your legs pointing up, before landing on your feet again • *Where did you learn to* **do** *cartwheels?* [C] • *She was* **doing/turning** *a cartwheel across the office floor as the boss walked in.* [C] • *To prove his skill as an acrobat he cartwheeled gracefully into the room.* [I]

carve *(obj)* /£kɑːv, $kɑːrv/ *v* to make (something) by cutting into esp. wood or stone, or to cut into the surface of (stone, wood, etc.) • *The huge heads on Easter Island were carved* **from** *local stone.* [T] • *This totem pole is carved* **from/out of** *a single tree trunk.* [T] • *He carved her name* **on** *the wall.* [T] • *Before Hallowe'en, the children carved a pumpkin* **into** *a frightening mask.* [T] • *The pot was carved* **with** *unusual designs* (= it had patterns cut into its surface). [T] • *We walked up a staircase made of carved oak* (= made of wood with patterns cut into it). [T] • *Some of the tunnels in the cliff are natural, some were carved* **out** (= cut into the rock) *by soldiers for defensive purposes.* [T] • *(fig.) She carved* **out** (= made) *a reputation for herself as an aggressive businesswoman.* [T] • *(fig.) The new airline hopes to carve* **out** (= to obtain by skilful business activities) *a place for itself in the European market.* [T] • *(fig.) The Nazi-Soviet pact carved* **up** (= divided to its own advantage) *the Baltic states in 1939.* [T] • *(fig.) The inner ring road is carved through* (= has been made through) *the city's centre.* [T] • *(fig.) He hopes to carve* **a niche** (= make a position) *for* **himself** *as a leading researcher in his field of study.* [T] • To carve a large piece of cooked meat is to cut thin pieces from it: *Would you like me to carve (the chicken)?* [I/T] • *(infml)* If a suggestion or a plan is **carved in stone**, it cannot be changed: *These proposals are for discussion, they're not carved in stone.*

carv·er /£ˈkɑː·vər, $ˈkɑːr·vər/ *n* [C] • An *(Br)* **electric** carver/*(Am)* **electric knife** is a knife having a blade that is moved very quickly by electricity and is used for cutting cooked meat.

carv·ing /£ˈkɑː·vɪŋ, $ˈkɑːr-/ *n, adj* [not gradable] • *They brought back some wooden/stone carvings* (= decorative objects made from wood/stone) *from India.* [C] • *As a boy he was taught the techniques of carving* (= the art of making patterns in, or objects from, esp. wood or stone) *by his father.* [U] • A **carving knife** is a large knife used for cutting cooked meat. • PIC› **Cutlery**

carve up *obj*, **carve** *obj* **up** *v adv* [T] *Br infml* to drive past (someone in a car) and then suddenly drive in front of them • *Some idiot carved us up on the way over here – I don't know how he missed us!*

carv·e·ry /£'kɑː·vᵊr·i, $'kɑːr·vɚ-/ *n* [C] a restaurant where you eat meat that is cut for you at a special table

Cas·a·no·va /£ˌkæs·ə'nəʊ·və, $ˌkæs·ə'noʊ-/ *n* [C] *infml disapproving* a man who has had a lot of sexual relationships

cas·cade /kæs'keɪd/ *n* [C] a small WATERFALL (=place where a river falls to a lower level), often one of a group • *A series of cascades had been caused by large boulders which had fallen into the stream.* • *(fig.) A cascade* (=a mass that seemed to flow) **of** *golden hair fell down his back.*

cas·cade /kæs'keɪd/ *v* [I always + adv/prep] • *Coins cascaded* (=fell quickly and in large amounts) **from/out of** *the fruit machine.*

case [SITUATION] /keɪs/ *n* [C] a particular situation or example of something • *Over a hundred people were injured, in several cases seriously.* • *Jobs are hard to find but* **in** *his case that's not the problem because he has so much experience.* • *I wouldn't normally agree but I'll make an exception* **in this** *case.* • *The number of new cases* **of** *the illness appears to be declining.* • *Some people think he's mean but that's simply not* **the** *case* (=not true). • *We have lots of applications from people who want to study here and in* **each** *case we consider the candidate very carefully.* • *Lack of communication causes serious problems and their marriage is* **a case in point** (=a situation that shows that this is true). • *When the election is called in April, or June,* **as/whatever the case might be** (=whatever is true), *we shall be ready for it.* • *The law will apply equally to men and women except* **in the case of** (=in situations of) *maternity leave.* • *There's no coffee left?* **In that case** (=Because that is the situation) *I'll have tea.* • *If that* **is/is not the case** (=If that is true/not true) *then I will be very disappointed.* • *I don't want to go and* **in any case** (=and also), *I haven't been invited.* • *Bring a map* **in case** (=because there might be a situation in which) *you get lost.* • *I don't think I'll need any money but I'll bring some* **(just) in case** (=for the possibility that I might). • *(esp. Am)* **In case** (=If) *you need any money I can lend you some.* • *She doesn't want to work full-time,* **it's a case of** (=the situation is one of) *having to.*

case [PROBLEM] /keɪs/ *n* [C] a problem, a series of events or a person being dealt with by police, doctors, lawyers, etc. • *Several social workers have looked into the child's case.* • *The detective* **on** *the case* (=responsible for solving it) *has been suspended from duty.* • *She was suffering from an* **extreme** *case of sunburn.* • *When he first went for treatment at the hospital he seemed to be a* **hopeless** *case* (=a person who could not be cured). • *The article was based on a single* **case history** (=a record of a person's health, development or behaviour by an official such as a doctor). • A **case study** is a detailed account giving information about the development of a person, group or thing, especially in order to show general principles: *This is an interesting psychiatric case study of a child with extreme behavioural difficulties.* • *(law)* In a court of law, a case is a matter to be decided by a judge: *a murder case* ○ *The case will go before the European Court next month.* ○ *She accused her employer of unlawful dismissal and* **won/lost** *her case.* • *(law)* **Case law** is law based on decisions that have been made by judges in the past. • [LP]> **Law**

case [ARGUMENT] /keɪs/ *n* [C] arguments, facts and reasons in support of or against something • *There's a good case* **for/against** *bringing in new regulations.* • *The case* **against** *cigarette advertising is becoming stronger all the time.* • *She's very busy so don't* **overstate** *the case – just give her the essentials.* • To **make (out) a case for/against** something is to give your reasons in support of it or against it: *There's a case to be made for electoral reform.*

case [CONTAINER] /keɪs/ *n* [C] a container or box for storing things in, esp. a SUITCASE • *Could you help me to carry my cases onto the train?* • *Antonio keeps his pet stick insects in a glass case.* • A case of wine or some other types of alcoholic drink is a box holding twelve bottles of it, or the twelve bottles and their contents. • See also BOOKCASE; BRIEFCASE; PILLOWCASE.

cased /keɪst/ *adj* [not gradable] • *The electrical connectors have to be cased in* (=covered in a tight case of) *waterproof plastic.*

cas·ing /'keɪ·sɪŋ/ *n* [C] • *Sheep intestines are sometimes used for sausage casings* (=coverings).

case [GRAMMAR] /keɪs/ *n* [C] *specialized* any of the various types to which a noun can belong, according to the work it does in a sentence, usually shown by a special word ending • *In English, the genitive case is shown by the ending -'s.* • *Latin* hominem *is* **in** *the accusative case.*

case *obj* [LOOK AT] /keɪs/ *v* [T] *infml* to look at (a place) with the intention of stealing from it later • *He looked around shiftily, as if he was casing* **the joint** (=the place).

case·load /£'keɪs·ləʊd, $-loʊd/ *n* [C] the amount of work which someone, esp. a doctor or lawyer has to do in a period of time • *a clinical psychologist's caseload* • *I've got such a heavy caseload this month – I couldn't possibly take on another client.*

case·ment (win·dow) /'keɪ·smənt/ *n* [C] a type of window that is fixed on one side and opens like a door • [PIC]> **Window**

cash /kæʃ/ *n* [U] money in the form of notes and coins, rather than CHEQUES or **credit cards** • *Do you have any cash on you?* • *Will you pay by credit card or* **by/in** *cash?* • *He says he wants cash* **in advance** *before he'll do the job.* • *(infml) I'm a bit* **short of/strapped for** *cash* (=money of any type) *at the moment.* • Goods that are bought **cash-and-carry** are bought for cash and they must be taken away by the customer rather than being delivered: *a cash-and-carry sale* • A **cash and carry** is a business which sells goods in this way: *We bought the bookcases in the new cash and carry at the shopping centre.* • A **cash bar** is a bar at a party or event at which alcoholic drinks can be bought: *Soft drinks and hors d'oeuvres will be served during the reception and a cash bar will be available.* • *(Br)* A **cash card** (*Am* **ATM card**) is a special plastic card given to you by a bank that allows you to take money out of a **cash dispenser**. • A **cash crop** is a crop that is grown mainly to be sold, rather than used by the farmer or those living in the area it is grown in. • *(Br)* A **cash desk** in a shop is the place where you can pay for the things that you buy. • A **cash dispenser/cash machine** (*Br also* CASHPOINT/*Am also* **ATM**/*Aus* **automatic teller**) is a machine, usually in a wall outside a bank, from which you can take money out of your bank account by using a special card. • The **cash flow** of something, esp. a business is the movement of money in and out of it: *Small traders often have short-term cash flow problems.* • A **cash register** is a machine in a shop or other business that records sales and into which money received is put. • See also COD [PAYMENT]. • [LP]> **Money**

cash *obj* /kæʃ/ *v* [T] • *Would you cash a cheque for me?* (=exchange the cheque for money) • To **cash in (on** something) is to try to get as much money as possible by taking advantage of a situation, often unfairly: *They tried to cash in on people's fears by selling them burglar alarms.* • To **cash up** is to count all the money taken by a shop or business at the end of each day: *When she had cashed up she realized there was £10 missing from the till.*

cash·ew (nut) /'kæʃ·uː, kə'ʃuː/ *n* [C] a small edible nut • [PIC]> **Nut**

cash·ier [PERSON] /£kæʃ'ɪəʳ, $-'ɪr/ *n* [C] a person whose job is to receive and pay out money in a shop, bank, restaurant, etc. • [LP]> **Money** [PIC]> **Supermarket**

cash·ier *obj* [DISMISS] /£kæʃ'ɪəʳ, $-'ɪr/ *v* [T] to make (a person who is in the military forces) leave, esp. making them lose their honour at the same time

cash·mere /£'kæʃ·mɪəʳ, $-mɪr, -'-/ *n* [U] very soft, expensive woollen material that is made from the hair of goats from Kashmir • *She wore a cashmere scarf, silk suit and pearls.*

cash·point /'kæʃ·pɔɪnt/ *n* [C] *Br for* **cash dispenser**, see at CASH

cas·ing /'keɪ·sɪŋ/ *n* [C] See at CASE [CONTAINER]

ca·si·no /£kə'siː·nəʊ, $-noʊ/ *n* [C] *pl* **casinos** a building where games, esp. ROULETTE and card games are played for money

cask /£kɑːsk, $kæsk/ *n* [C] a strong round wooden container used for storing liquid • *a cask of water/wine*

cask·et /£'kɑː·skɪt, $'kæs·kɪt/ *n* [C] a small decorative box, esp. one used to keep jewellery in • Casket is also *Am for* COFFIN.

cas·sa·va /kə'sɑː·və/ *n* [U] a S American plant which has large roots, or a type of flour obtained from these roots

cas·se·role /£'kæs·ᵊr·əʊl, $-ə·roʊl/ *n* [C] a dish made by cooking meat, vegetables or other foods in liquid inside a heavy container at low heat, or the heavy deep container with a lid used in cooking such dishes • *a lamb casserole* • *a glass/iron casserole* • (DK) (N)

cas·se·role *obj* /£'kæs·ᵊr·əul, $-ə·roul/ *v* [T] • *Shall we casserole the chicken?*

cas·sette /kə'set/ *n* [C] a flat rectangular device containing a very long strip of magnetic material that is used to record sound and/or pictures, or a machine that plays and/or records on such devices • *a video cassette* • *an audio cassette* • A **cassette player** is a machine that plays cassettes which have been recorded. • A **cassette (recorder)** is a machine that can both play from and record onto cassettes. • ⓘ

cas·sock /'kæs·ək/ *n* [C] a coat-like item of clothing which reaches nearly to the ground, is loose, usually black and is worn esp. by priests

cast *obj* [PUT] /£kɑːst, $kæst/ *v* [T] *past* **cast** to put, cause or direct (a look, thought, feeling or opinion) • *New evidence has cast* **doubt on** *the guilty verdict.* • *Some* **doubt** *has been cast* **on/over** *the future of the business.* • *The tree cast a shadow* **over/on** *his face.* • *(fig.) Her arrival cast* **a shadow over/on** *the party* (=Everyone became less happy when she arrived). • *(fig.) The discovery of the dinosaur skeleton has cast* **light on** (=provided information about) *why they became extinct.* • If someone who is fishing casts something to catch fish with, such as a line, they throw it into the water: *He cast the line to the middle of the river.* • If a snake casts its skin, it leaves its old skin. • *(literary or old use)* Cast can also mean remove or get rid of: *They cast* **off** *their shoes and ran along the beach.* ○ *You must cast* **aside/away/off/** (=get rid of) *all your fears.* ○ *His parents cast him* **out** *and he was forced to fend for himself.* • **Cast-off clothes** or **cast-offs** are clothes you no longer want: *I don't want your cast-offs, thank you.* See also CAST OFF. • To **cast aspersions on** someone or something is to make critical or damaging remarks or judgments about them: *I hope you're not casting aspersions on my taste in clothes.* • *Could you* **cast an eye/a glance over** (=briefly look at) *this report for me?* • *If you* **cast** *your* **mind back** (=try to remember), *you might recall that I never promised to go.* • To **cast** your **net wide** is to include many people or things when you are looking for something: *It's up to the product manager to decide how wide to cast her net in the search for the best team.* • If you **cast pearls before swine** you offer something valuable or good to someone who does not know its value: *Giving him good advice is casting pearls before swine – he never listens to anyone.* • To **cast a spell (on** someone or something) is to seem to use magic: *I was in love – the Caribbean had cast its spell.* • **Cast down** means unhappy. See also DOWNCAST [UNHAPPY]. • *"He that is without sin among you, let him first cast a stone at her"* (Bible, St John 8.7)

cast *obj* [ACTORS] /£kɑːst, $kæst/ *v* [T] *past* **cast** to choose (actors) to play particular parts in (a play, film or show) • *He was often cast* **as** *a pathetic little man because he looked the part.* • *They are casting the musical in New York at the moment.* • *In her latest film she was cast* **against type** (=played a different character than the one she usually played or might be expected to play). See also TYPECAST. • *(fig.) They like to cast the opposing political party* **as** (=to say that they are) *the party of high taxes.* • *(humorous)* If you say that someone has got a good part in a film or play by using the **casting couch**, you mean that they had sex with important people in order to be successful.

cast /£kɑːst, $kæst/ *n* [C] • *After the final performance, the director threw a party for the cast* (=all the actors in a film or play). • *Part of the film's success lies in the strength of the* **supporting** *cast* (=the actors who were not playing the main parts).

cast *obj* [SHAPE] /£kɑːst, $kæst/ *v* [T] *past* **cast** to make (an object) by pouring liquid, such as melted metal, into a shaped container to become hard • *A statue of the general is presently being cast.* • If someone is **cast in the same mould** as someone else, they are very similar to them: *Everyone who works for that firm seems to be cast in the same mould.*

cast /£kɑːst, $kæst/ *n* [C] • A cast is an object made by pouring liquid which then becomes solid into a container. • Cast is another name for **plaster cast**. See at PLASTER [SUBSTANCE]. • **Cast iron** is a type of iron that will not bend easily and is made into shapes by being poured into containers when melted: *a cast iron bracket* ○ *(fig.) She has a cast iron* (=very strong) *will when she wants to.* ○ *(fig.) He has a cast iron* (=impossible to doubt) **alibi** *for where he was on the night of the robbery.* ○ *(fig.) Can you give me a cast iron* (= completely certain) **guarantee/promise** *that the work will be completed on time?* • [PIC〉] **Medical equipment**

cast *obj* [VOTE] /£kɑːst, $kæst/ *v* [T] *past* **cast** to give (a vote) • *All the votes in the election have now been cast and the counting has begun.* • A **casting vote** is a single vote given by the person in charge of a meeting if the number of votes about something is equal and this single vote, therefore, decides the matter.

cast a·round/a·bout *v adv* [I] to look around for (something) • *Fashion editors are always casting around for words to describe colours.*

cast off [LEAVE] *v adv* [I] (of a boat) to leave • *The ship was scheduled to cast off at 8pm.* • See also **cast-off** at CAST [PUT].

cast off *(obj)* [FINISH], **cast** *(obj)* **off** *v adv* [M] *specialized* (in KNITTING) to finish (the item you are making) by using special stitches • See also **cast-off** at CAST [PUT].

cast on *(obj)*, **cast** *(obj)* **on** *v adv* [M] *specialized* (in KNITTING) to make the stitches you need to start an item

cast·an·ets /ˌkæs·tə'nets/ *pl n* an instrument consisting of two small pieces of wood tied together by string and knocked against each other in the hand to make a series of sharp noises

cast·a·way /£'kɑː·stə·weɪ, $'kæs·tə-/ *n* [C] a person who has escaped from a ship that has sunk and managed to get to an island or country where there are few or no other people • A castaway is also something thrown away or no longer wanted or used: *The shed is full of castaways – old toys, broken tools, parts of a bicycle.*

caste /£kɑːst, $kæst/ *n* a system of dividing Hindu society into classes, or any of these classes • *Caste is still very important within Indian society.* [U] • *He was born into the lowest caste.* [C] • *The caste* **system** *is part of daily life in Indian society.*

cas·tel·lat·ed /£'kæs·tɪ·leɪ·tɪd, $-t̬ɪd/ *adj specialized* (of a building) made to look like a castle by having towers and BATTLEMENTS (= a wall with regular spaces in it)

cast·er su·gar /£'kɑː·stə $'kæs·tɚ-/ *n* [U] *Br and Aus* white sugar with very small grains, often used in cooking

cas·ti·gate *obj* /'kæs·tɪ·geɪt/ *v* [T] *fml* to criticize (someone or something) severely • *The report castigates the general failure to make football grounds safe.* • *Health inspectors castigated the kitchen staff* **for** *poor standards of cleanliness.*

cas·tle /£'kɑː·sl̩, $'kæs·l̩/ *n* [C] a large strong building, built in the past by a ruler or important person to protect the people inside from attack • *Nowadays a castle in Scotland can cost almost the same as a flat in London.* • Castle is also *infml for* ROOK [GAME PIECE]. • The phrase **castles in the air** means plans that have very little chance of happening: *He's always* **building** *castles in the air about having a big house and a fast car.* • [PIC〉] **Games**

cas·tle /£'kɑː·sl̩, $'kæs·l̩/ *v* [I] *specialized* • In the game of CHESS, to castle is to make a special move which puts your king in a more protected place at the side of the board: *It is very common to castle in the early part of a game.* ○ *Having castled into safety, Polgar began a powerful attack in the centre.*

ca·stor /£'kɑː·stəʳ, $'kæs·t̬ɚ/, **cast·er** *n* [C] a small wheel, usually one of a set, that is fixed to the bottom (of the leg) of a piece of furniture so that it can be moved easily

ca·stor oil *n* [U] a thick usually yellow oil, used esp. as a medicine to help people excrete the contents of their bowels

cas·trate *obj* /kæs'treɪt/ *v* [T] to remove the TESTICLES (=sex organs that produce sperm) of (a male animal, man or boy) • *Bulls are usually less aggressive if they have been castrated.*

cas·tra·tion /kæs'treɪ·ʃᵊn/ *n* [U]

cas·ual [NOT INTERESTED] /'kæʒ·ju·əl/ *adj* not taking or not seeming to take much interest; not caring • *The psychologist's* **attitude** *seemed far too casual, even brutal.* • *Security around the conference hotel seemed almost casual.* • *Although close to tears, she tried to make her voice sound casual.*

cas·ual·ly /'kæʒ·ju·ə·li/ *adv* • *"How would you kill someone, doctor?" the woman asked casually* (=as if it was not a serious matter).

cas·ual [TEMPORARY] /'kæʒ·ju·əl/ *adj* [before n] not regular or fixed; temporary • *The company is only taking on casual* **labour/labourers/workers**. • *Are you employed permanently or on a casual basis?* • *Casual* **sex/relationships** *can involve serious health risks.* • [LP〉] **Work**

cas·ual·ly /'kæʒ·ju·ə·li/ *adv* • *Eighty per cent of the workforce is employed casually, with no security.*

cas·ual CHANCE /ˈkæʒ·ju·əl/ *adj* [before n] not serious or considered; (done) by chance • *It was just a casual* **comment**, *I didn't mean it to be taken so seriously.* • *To a casual* **observer**, *everything might appear normal.* • *The new law is intended to deter the casual* **user** *of drugs.*

cas·ual·ly /ˈkæʒ·ju·ə·li/ *adv* • *He had information that he could not have acquired casually* (= by chance).

cas·ual INFORMAL /ˈkæʒ·ju·əl/ *adj* (of clothes) not formal or not suitable for special occasions • *For some people casual* **clothes** *means a shapeless T-shirt and old jeans, for others chinos and sweaters.* • LP> **Shopping goods**

cas·ual·ly /ˈkæʒ·ju·ə·li/ *adv* • *She was dressed casually in shorts and a T-shirt.*

cas·ual·ty PERSON /ˈkæʒ·ju·əl·ti/ *n* [C] a person killed or hurt in a serious accident or war, or a person or thing that suffers as a result of something else happening • *The train was derailed but there were no casualties, police said.* • *Casualties* **of/from** *the fighting are being treated in a nearby hospital.* • *The casualty* **toll** *from the invasion was surprisingly low.* • *She lost her job in 1989, a casualty* **of** *the recession.* • *The first casualty* **of** *the reorganization will be the regular bus service, which will either be reduced or stopped altogether.* • *"The first casualty when war comes is truth"* (from a speech by Hiram Johnson, 1917) • Ⓟ

cas·ual·ty HOSPITAL *Br and Aus* /ˈkæʒ·ju·əl·ti/, *Am* **e·mer·gen·cy room** *n* [U] the part of a hospital where people who are hurt in accidents or suddenly become ill are taken for urgent treatment • *She had to be rushed* **to** *casualty.* • *He had to wait for more than an hour* **in** *casualty before seeing a surgeon.* • Ⓟ

cas·u·ist·ry /ˈkæz·ju·ɪ·stri/ *n* [U] *fml* the use of clever arguments to trick people

cat /kæt/ *n* [C] a small four-legged furry animal with a tail and CLAWS (= long sharp nails), usually kept as a pet or for catching mice, or any member of the group of biologically similar animals such as the lion • *a pet/stray cat* • *We'll have to get someone to feed the cat when we're away on holiday.* • When two people or groups of people play **(a game of) cat and mouse** with each other, they try over a long time to defeat each other, esp. when one has more power than the other: *It's a real game of cat and mouse between the multinationals and the small independent companies in the software market at the moment.* • *(Br infml)* If someone hasn't **a cat in hell's chance** *(esp. Am and Aus infml* **a snowball's chance in hell**) of doing something, he or she has no chance of doing it: *They haven't a cat in hell's chance of getting over the mountain in weather like this.* • When you say to someone **has the cat got** your **tongue**, you mean you are annoyed that they are not talking or answering your questions: *Why aren't you answering me, has the cat got your tongue?* • If you **let the cat out of the bag**, you let a secret be known, usually without intending to: *He let the cat out of the bag when he mentioned the party to her – it was supposed to be a surprise.* • Someone who is **like a cat on a hot tin roof**/*(esp. Br dated)* **like a cat on hot bricks** is in a state of nervous anxiety: *She's been like a cat on a hot tin roof ever since she heard he's back in town.* • People who fight **like cat and dog** disagree very strongly and often: *It's awful, my brother and sister are always fighting like cat and dog.* • If someone looks **like something the cat brought/dragged in**, they look very untidy and dirty: *You look like something the cat brought in – go and have a bath and tidy yourself up a bit.* • *(Br and Aus)* To **put/set the cat among the pigeons** is to say or do something that causes trouble or makes a lot of people very angry: *She really put the cat among the pigeons with her comments about our system of government.* • A **cat burglar** is a thief who enters and leaves a building by climbing up walls to an upper window, door, etc. • A **cat-o'-nine-tails**/*(infml)* **cat** is a whip made from rope that has nine ends and was used esp. in the past to hit people with as a punishment. • In children's games, a **cat's cradle** is a special pattern made by weaving string around the fingers of both hands: *The structure was a cat's cradle of wires and supports.* ○ *(fig.) We were stuck in a cat's cradle* (= complicated amount) *of legislation.* • *(Br and Aus)* **Cat's eyes** (*Am* **reflectors**) are small pieces of glass or plastic that are put along the middle and sometimes the sides of a road to reflect the lights of a car in order to show the driver where to drive, esp. when it is dark. • *(Br infml)* If someone is the **cat's whiskers** they are important: *Look at him strutting around like he's the cat's whiskers.* • *(dated slang)* A **cool cat** or a **hep cat** is a fashionable person. • *(saying)* 'While the cat's away, the mice will play' means that when the person who is in charge of a place is not there, people there will behave badly. • *"A cat may look at a king"* (Lewis Carroll in his book *Alice in Wonderland*, 1865) • See also TOMCAT; WILDCAT. • PIC> **Motorway**

cat·te·ry /$ˈkæt·ᵊr·i, $ˈkæţ·ɚ-/ *n* [C] • A cattery is a place where cats are taken care of while their owners are away or where cats are bred for sale.

cat·a·cly·sm /£ˈkæt·ə·klɪ·zᵊm, $ˈkæţ-/ *n* [C] *literary* a great destructive event or sudden violent change • *Only a cataclysm such as a flood or earthquake would stop this football match.* • *Some people are swept into religious faith by a cataclysm in their life.*

cat·a·clysm·ic /£ˌkæt·əˈklɪz·mɪk, $ˌkæţ-/ *adj literary* • *These countries are on the brink of cataclysmic famine.*

cat·a·comb /£ˈkæt·ə·kuːm, $ˈkæţ-/ *n* [C usually pl] a series of underground passages and rooms where bodies were buried in the past • *They went down into catacombs beneath the church.* • *(fig.) The original tape languished in the film studio's catacombs* (= a place where few people ever go) *for many years.*

cat·a·lep·sy /£ˈkæt·ə·lep·si, $ˈkæţ-/ *n* [U] a medical condition in which a person's body becomes stiff and stops moving, as if dead

cat·a·lep·tic /£ˌkæt·əˈlep·tɪk, $ˌkæţ-/ *adj* [not gradable]

cat·a·logue, *Am usually* **cat·a·log** /£ˈkæt·ᵊl·ɒg, $ˈkæţ·ᵊl·ɑːg/ *v*, *n* (to make) a list, usually in the form of a book, esp. of things you can buy or look at, or a series of events or objects that are similar • *I bought some new clothes through a* **mail-order** *catalogue.* [C] • *This is another outrage in a catalogue* **of** *terrorist inhumanity.* [C] • *She recited a catalogue* **of** *the mistakes he had made in the past.* [C] • *Many plants become extinct before they have even been catalogued.* [T] • *This report is the first attempt to catalogue the effects of smoking in a particular community.* [T] • Ⓖⓡ

ca·tal·y·sis /kəˈtæl·ə·sɪs/ *n* [U] the process of making a chemical reaction happen more quickly by using a CATALYST

cat·a·lyst /£ˈkæt·ᵊl·ɪst, $ˈkæţ-/ *n* [C] *(specialized)* something that makes a chemical reaction happen more quickly without itself being changed, or, more generally, an event or person that causes great change • *The spate of suicides* **acted as** *a catalyst* **for** *change in the prison system.*

cat·a·lyt·ic /£ˌkæt·əˈlɪt·ɪk, $ˌkæţ·əˈlɪţ-/ *adj* • *(specialized)* A **catalytic converter** (also **cat**) is a device on a car that reduces the amount of poisonous gas that escapes into the air.

cat·a·ma·ran /£ˈkæt·ə·mə·ræn, $ˈkæţ-/ *n* [C] a sailing boat that has two parallel HULLS (= floating parts) held together by a single DECK (= flat surface) • PIC> **Water sports**

cat·a·pult /£ˈkæt·ə·pʌlt, $ˈkæţ-/ *n* [C] a device which can throw or push objects at a high speed • *In the past, armies used catapults to hurl heavy stones at enemy fortifications.* • *On that type of aircraft carrier, a catapult was used to help launch aircraft.* • *(Br)* A catapult (*Am* **slingshot**, *Aus* **shanghai**) is also a Y-shaped stick or piece of metal with a piece of elastic fixed to the top parts, used esp. by children for shooting small stones

cat·a·pult *obj* /£ˈkæt·ə·pʌlt, $ˈkæţ-/ *v* [T always + adv/prep] • *When the two vehicles collided he was catapulted* (= thrown with great force) **forwards**. • *(fig.) The award for best actress meant that almost overnight she was catapulted* (= suddenly pushed) **into** *the limelight.*

cat·a·ract DISEASE /£ˈkæt·ə·rækt, $ˈkæţ-/ *n* [C] a disease in which an area of the eye becomes cloudy so that a person cannot see correctly, or the area diseased in this way

cat·a·ract WATER FEATURE /£ˈkæt·ə·rækt, $ˈkæţ-/ *n* [C] a large WATERFALL (= place where a river falls to a lower level)

ca·tarrh /£kəˈtɑːʳ, $-ˈtɑːr/ *n* [U] a condition in which a lot of MUCUS (= thick liquid) is produced in the nose and throat, esp. when a person has an infection

ca·tas·tro·phe /kəˈtæs·trə·fi/ *n* [C] a sudden event that causes very great trouble or destruction • *They were warned of the ecological catastrophe to come.* • *(fig.) The emigration of scientists is a catastrophe* (= very bad thing) *for the country.*

cat·a·stroph·ic /£ˌkæt·əˈstrɒf·ɪk, $ˌkæţ·əˈstrɑː·fɪk/ *adj* • *An unchecked increase in the use of fossil fuels could have catastrophic results for the planet.* • *The film 'Raise the Titanic' was a catastrophic box-office flop* (= was very unsuccessful).

cat·a·ton·ic /£ˌkæt·əˈtɒn·ɪk, $ˌkæţ·əˈtɑː·nɪk/ *adj* (of a person) stiff and not moving, as if dead • *In the film, De Niro plays a catatonic patient who is 'awakened' by a doctor.*

cat·call /£'kæt·kɔːl, $-kɑːl/ *n* [C] a loud shout or WHISTLE (= high sound) expressing disapproval, esp. made by people in a crowd

catch *(obj)* TAKE HOLD /kætʃ/ *v past* **caught** /£kɔːt, $kɑːt/ to take hold of (something) • *I managed to catch the glass before it hit the ground.* [T] • *They were happy because they had caught a lot of fish that day.* [T] • *Our dog ran past me and out of the house before I could catch it.* [T] • *We saw the eagle swoop from the sky to catch its prey.* [T] • *Great pressure was put on the police to catch the terrorists as soon as possible.* [T] • *Two armed men were caught* **trying** *to cross the frontier at night.* [T + obj + v-ing] • *The sleeve of my jacket (got) caught* **on** *the door handle and ripped.* [I/T] • *Her hair got caught* **(up) in** (= became stuck in) *her hair dryer.* [T] • If you get **caught up in** something you become involved in it, often without wanting to: *He got caught up in the drugs business.* • *(Br and Aus) The monkey caught* **at** (= took hold of) *her wig and pulled it off.* [T] • *He caught* **hold** (= took hold) **of** *my arm.* [T] • *I felt caught* (= stuck) **between** *two extremes.* [T] • *We placed saucepans on the floor to catch* (= collect) *the drops of water coming through the roof.* [T] • *The photograph catches* (= shows) *the mixture of excitement and fear in the child's face.* [T] • *(Br and Aus specialized) The batsman was caught* (= someone in the other team caught the ball when he hit it) *three short of a century.* • *A movement caught my* **eye** (= I noticed it suddenly). • *Could you try to catch the waiter's* **eye** (= get him to notice you)? • *Something bright had caught the baby's* **attention** (= made the baby very interested in it). • *(Br) You'll have to run if you want to catch* **the post** (= send a letter before the post has been collected). • *The necklace glittered as it caught* **the light** (= as the light hit it and made it shine). [T] • To **catch** your **breath** is to stop breathing for a moment, or to begin to breathe correctly again after running or other exercise: *I caught my breath in amazement when I saw his tattoos for the first time.* ○ *Don't try to talk, sit down and catch your breath.* • *(dated)* If you say to someone that they'll **catch it** you mean that they are likely to be criticized severely by a parent, teacher, etc.: *You'll catch it if your parents find out what you've been up to.* • *(Br)* If you have **caught the sun** the sun has made your skin a slightly darker brown or red colour: *It's not surprising she caught the sun, she was working outside all day.* • *(infml)* To **catch a few/some rays** is to stay outside in the sun for a period of time: *I'm going out to catch a few rays before lunch.* • A **catch-all** is something that is intended to include everything: *The government introduced catch-all legislation to cover a range of offences.*

catch /kætʃ/ *n* [C] • *The fishermen were disappointed with their catch* (= the amount of fish that they had caught) *that day.* • A catch on a door, window, bag, etc. is a small device that keeps it fastened: *I always make sure all the* **window** *catches are tightly closed at night.* • *(infml)* A catch is also a person of the stated type, esp. showing how suitable they are for a relationship: *Her new boyfriend's not much of a catch really, is he?* • PIC **Window**

catch·er /£'kætʃ·əʳ, $'ketʃ·ɚ/ *n* [C] • In baseball, a catcher is a player who stands directly behind the player from the opposing team who is holding the bat, and who attempts to catch the ball when it is thrown if the person with the bat fails to hit it: *Carlton Fisk was one of the best catchers ever to play professional baseball.*

catch *obj* NOTICE /kætʃ/ *v* [T] *past* **caught** /£kɔːt, $kɑːt/ to discover, see or become aware of (something, esp. someone doing something wrong) • *He caught her* **reading** *his old love letters.* [+ obj + v-ing] • *Did you catch the momentary look of surprise on her face?* • *I caught him* (= noticed him without him wanting me to) **looking** *at me fixedly.* [+ obj + v-ing] • *If the virus is caught* (= discovered) *in time, most patients can be successfully treated.* • *I caught* **sight of**/*caught* **a glimpse of** (= saw for a moment) *a red coat in the crowd.* • *He was caught* **red-handed** (= found doing something illegal) *taking money from the till.* [+ obj + v-ing] • *(infml)* If someone is **caught napping**, something happens to them which they are not prepared for: *The sudden attack caught the guards napping.* • If someone is **caught (red-handed)**, they are discovered while in the act of doing something bad or illegal: *He was caught red-handed taking money from the till.* • If you are **caught with** your **trousers**/*(Am usually, Aus also* **pants***)* **down**, you are suddenly discovered doing something which you did not want people to know about, esp. a sexual act: *He was caught with his trousers down when his wife found him kissing the piano teacher.* • To be **caught with** your **trousers**/ *(Am usually, Aus also* **pants***)* **down** can also mean to be unexpectedly asked to do or say something that you are not prepared for: *They were caught with their trousers down when the police asked them where they'd been that night.* • To be **caught without** something is to not have it, esp. when it might be needed: *He doesn't like to be caught* *without any biscuits in the house.* • If you say **you won't catch** someone doing something or at a place, you mean it is extremely unlikely they would do it or be at that place: *You won't catch him having a bath more than once a week.* ○ *You won't catch her at work after four o'clock.*

catch *obj* HEAR /kætʃ/ *v* [T] *past* **caught** /£kɔːt, $kɑːt/ to manage to hear, see, or deal with (something or someone), esp. when there is some difficulty in doing this • *I'm sorry, I didn't quite catch what you said.* • *She just caught the end of the programme when she switched the TV on.* • *I can see you're busy right now, so I'll catch you* (= speak to you) *later.*

catch *obj* TRAVEL /kætʃ/ *v* [T] *past* **caught** /£kɔːt, $kɑːt/ to travel or be able to travel on (an aircraft, train, bus, etc.) • *He always catches the 10.30am train to work.* • *She was worried that she'd arrive too late to catch the last bus home.*

catch *obj* BECOME INFECTED /kætʃ/ *v* [T] *past* **caught** /£kɔːt, $kɑːt/ to get (an illness, esp. one caused by bacteria or a virus) • *He caught* **a** *nasty* **cold** *while on holiday.* • *A lot of children in the school caught measles last term.* • *(fig.) Everyone caught* (= felt and shared in) *the general excitement.*

catch·ing /£ˈkætʃ·ɪŋ, $ˈketʃ-/ *adj infml* • *Flu is catching* (= able to be given to someone else), *so stay away from work.* • *(fig.) Her happiness was catching* (= able to be shared by other people) *and soon we were all laughing.*

catch *obj* HIT /kætʃ/ *v* [T] *past* **caught** /£kɔːt, $kɑːt/ to hit (something), esp. unintentionally • *His head caught the edge of the table as he fell.* • *Medical teams were caught* **in the crossfire** *of the opposing armies.* • *(dated) George caught him* **a blow** *in the stomach with his left fist.* [+ two objects]

catch BURN /kætʃ/ *v* [I] *past* **caught** /£kɔːt, $kɑːt/ (of a fire) to begin to burn • *This wood's too wet, the fire won't catch.* • If something **catches fire**, it starts burning: *For reasons which are not yet known, the factory caught fire late yesterday evening and then burnt throughout the night.*

catch PROBLEM /kætʃ/ *n* [C] a hidden problem or disadvantage • *It sounds too good to be true – free food – what's* **the** *catch?* • *I was sure there had to be a catch* **somewhere/in** *it.* • A **Catch-22** situation is an impossible situation where you are prevented from doing (a) until you have done (b), but you cannot do (b) until you have done (a) first: *In Britain you can't be a professional actor if you don't have an Equity card, but you can't get an Equity card until you have acted first – it's Catch-22/ a Catch-22 situation.* • *"Catch-22"* (title of a book by Joseph Heller, 1961)

catch on BECOME POPULAR *v adv* [I] to become fashionable or popular • *Will helicopters ever catch on as a common mode of transport?*

catch on UNDERSTAND *v adv* [I] *infml* to understand, esp. after a long time • *He doesn't take hints very easily, but he'll catch on* (**to** *what you're saying) eventually.*

catch out *obj* SHOW WRONG, **catch** *obj* **out** *v adv* [M] *infml* to show that (someone) is doing wrong • *I suspected he wasn't telling me the truth, and one day I caught him out when I found some letters he'd written.*

catch out *obj* TRICK, **catch** *obj* **out** *v adv* [M] *infml* to trick (someone) into making a mistake • *The examiner will try to catch you out, so stay calm and think carefully before you speak.*

catch out *obj* MAKE WEAK, **catch** *obj* **out** *v adv* [M] *infml* to put (someone) in a difficult situation • *A lot of people were caught out* **by** *the sudden change in the weather.*

catch *(obj)* **up** *v adv* to reach (someone in front of you) by going faster than them • *I ran after her and managed to catch up* **with** *her.* [I] • *(Br and Aus) Go on to the shops without me, I'll catch you up later.* [T] • *(fig.) She's staying late at the office to catch up* **with/on** *some reports* (= to do something she has not had time to do before). [I] • *(fig.) The police caught up* **with** *the gang* (= found them after a search) *in a disused warehouse.* [I] • *(fig.) Will Western industry ever catch up* **with** (= reach the standard of) *Japanese innovations?* [I]

catch·ment a·re·a /£ˈkætʃ·mənt, $ˈketʃ-/ *n* [C] the area served by a school or hospital

catch·phrase /ˈkætʃ·freɪz/ *n* [C] a phrase which is often repeated by and therefore becomes connected with a particular organization or person, esp. someone famous such as a television entertainer

catch·word /£ˈkætʃ·wɜːd, $-wɜːrd/ *n* [C] a word or phrase which is often repeated by, or becomes connected with a particular organization, esp. a political group

catch·y /£ˈkætʃ·i, $ˈketʃ-/ *adj* **-ier, -iest** (esp. of a tune or song) pleasing and easy to remember • *a catchy tune* • *catchy lyrics* • *a catchy name/slogan for the new product*

cat·e·chi·sm /£ˈkæt·ə·kɪ·zᵊm, $ˈkæt̬-/ *n* [C] an established group of questions and answers, esp. about a set of Christian beliefs • *the Roman Catholic catechism* • *the standard catechism of primitive Marxism-Leninism* • *(fig.) The quiz show involved the usual catechism of easy questions.*

cat·e·gor·i·cal /£ˌkæt·əˈgɒr·ɪ·kᵊl, $ˌkæt̬·əˈgɑːr-/ *adj* without any doubt or possibility of being changed; certain • *a categorical statement/reply/assurance*

cat·e·gor·i·cal·ly /£ˌkæt·əˈgɒr·ɪ·kli, $ˌkæt̬·əˈgɑː·rɪ-/ *adv* • *He categorically refused to take part in the project.*

cat·e·go·ry /£ˈkæt·ə·gri, $ˈkæt̬-/ *n* [C] (in a system for dividing things according to appearance, quality, etc.) a type, or a group of things having some features that are the same • *There are three categories of accommodation – standard, executive and de luxe.* • *Some social scientists try to divide a population into categories according to how much money people earn.* • GR

cat·e·gor·ize *obj, Br and Aus usually* **-ise** /£ˈkæt·ə·gᵊr·aɪz, $ˈkæt̬·ə·gə·raɪz/ *v* [T] • *The books are categorized* **into** *large and small, illustrated and unillustrated, children's and adults'.* • *This type of china is rather hard to categorize, it's very unusual.*

cat·e·gor·iz·a·tion, *Br and Aus usually* **-i·sa·tion** /£ˌkæt·ə·gᵊr·aɪˈzeɪ·ʃᵊn, $ˌkæt̬·ə·gə·raɪ-/ *n* [U]

ca·ter *(obj)* /£ˈkeɪ·təʳ, $-t̬ɚ/ *v* to provide, and sometimes serve, food • *I'm catering* **for** *twelve on Sunday, all the family are coming.* [I] • *Which firm will be catering at the wedding reception?* [I] • *(esp. Am) Who catered your party?* [T]

ca·ter·er /£ˈkeɪ·tᵊr·əʳ, $-t̬ɚ·ɚ/ *n* [C] • *an experienced caterer* • *a firm of caterers*

ca·ter·ing /£ˈkeɪ·tᵊr·ɪŋ, $-t̬ɚ-/ *adj* [before n; not gradable] • *a high-class catering company* • *a catering course*

ca·ter for *obj v prep* [T] to provide what is wanted by (someone or something) • *The organization is trying to cater for a wide range of ethnic groups.*

ca·ter to *obj v prep* [T] to try to satisfy a need, esp. an unpopular or generally unacceptable need • *That type of emotive ranting caters to the most bigoted members of a society.*

cat·er·pil·lar ANIMAL /£ˈkæt·ə·pɪl·əʳ, $ˈkæt̬·ɚ·pɪl·ɚ/ *n* [C] a small long animal with many legs which feeds on the leaves of plants and develops into a BUTTERFLY or MOTH (= insect with wings) • PIC **Insects**

cat·er·pil·lar MACHINE PART /£ˈkæt·ə·pɪl·əʳ, $ˈkæt̬·ɚ·pɪl·ɚ/ *n* [C] *trademark* (a vehicle with) an endless belt of metal plates around the sets of wheels on each side of the vehicle allowing movement over rough ground • *a caterpillar tractor* • *a caterpillar track*

cat·er·waul /£ˈkæt·ə·wɔːl, $ˈkæt̬·ɚ·wɑːl/ *v* [I] (of a person or animal) to make a high unpleasant noise like a cat

cat·fish /ˈkæt·fɪʃ/ *n* [C] an edible fish with a flat head and long hairs around its mouth which lives in rivers or lakes • PIC **Fish**

cat·gut /ˈkæt·gʌt/ *n* [U] strong cord, made from the dried INTESTINES (= tubes which carry food inside the body) of animals, esp. sheep, which is used for the strings of musical instruments

ca·thar·sis /£kəˈθɑː·sɪs, $-ˈθɑːr-/ *n* [C/U] *pl* **catharses** the release of strong emotions by experiencing sympathy or fear, such as that caused by some theatrical performances

ca·thar·tic /£kəˈθɑː·tɪk, $-ˈθɑːr·t̬ɪk/ *adj* • *The sudden loss of their leader was a cathartic* **experience** *for/had a cathartic* **effect** *on the party.*

ca·the·dral /kəˈθiː·drəl/ *n* [C] a very large, usually stone, building for Christian worship, which is the largest and most important church of a DIOCESE (= area) • *Winchester/Washington/Chartres cathedral* • *Exeter is a cathedral* **city**. • *A cathedral contains the throne of the bishop of that area.*

cath·e·rine wheel /£ˈkæθ·rɪn, £-ᵊr·ɪn, $ˈkeθ·ɚ·ɪn/ *n* [C] a circular FIREWORK (= explosive used for entertainment). After being fixed to a stick and set on fire, it spins round giving an attractive show. • PIC **Fires and space heaters**

cath·e·ter /£ˈkæθ·ɪ·təʳ, $-t̬ɚ/ *n* [C/U] *specialized* a long very thin tube, esp. one used medically to take liquids out of or put them into the body • *They* **inserted** *a catheter to empty the patient's bladder.*

cath·ode /£'kæθ·əʊd, $-oʊd/ *n* [C] *specialized* the negative part of an electrical CELL at which ELECTRONS enter a system • *A black wire is often attached to the cathode which is also marked with the negative sign (-).* • Compare ANODE.

Cath·o·lic RELIGIOUS PERSON /'kæθ·əl·ɪk/ *n* [C], *adj* [not gradable] a **Roman Catholic**, see at ROMAN CITY • *Is he (a) Catholic?* • *a Catholic school/church*

Ca·thol·i·ci·sm /£kə'θɒl·ɪ·sɪ·zəm, $-θɑː·lɪ-/ *n* [U] • Catholicism is **Roman Catholicism**. See at ROMAN CITY.

cath·o·lic VARIED /'kæθ·əl·ɪk/ *adj fml* varied or general; including many different types of thing • *He has a catholic* **taste** *in* (= likes many different types of) *music.* • *As a young person he had more catholic* **tastes** (= liked a larger range of things) *than he does now.*

cat·kin /'kæt·kɪn/ *n* [C] a group of small flowers hanging like short pieces of string from the branches of particular trees in the spring • *birch/willow/hazel catkins* • PIC〉 **Tree**

cat·nap /'kæt·næp/ *n* [C] a short sleep

cat·nap /'kæt·næp/ *v* [I] **-pp-** • *I'm not tired – I catnapped on the train.*

cat·suit /'kæt·suːt/ *n* [C] *Br* a tight fitting piece of women's clothing covering the whole body, arms and legs

cat·sup /'kæt·səp/ *n* [C/U] *Am for* KETCHUP

cat·tle /£'kæt·l̩, $'kæt̬-/ *pl n* large farm animals kept for their milk or meat; cows and BULLS • *We used to keep* **beef/dairy** *cattle.* • *They sold twenty* **head** *of cattle* (= twenty cattle) *this week.* • *The cattle are* **lowing** (= making the typical sound of cattle) *in the barn.* • **Cattle cake** is a type of dried food for cattle. • A **cattle grid** is a set of bars over a hole in the road at a gate which allows vehicles but not cattle to cross.

cat·ty /£'kæt·i, $'kæt̬-/ *adj* **-ier, -iest** (of words, esp. speech) unkind because intended to hurt someone • *She's always making catty* **remarks** *about how much some people earn.*

cat·ti·ly /£'kæt·ɪ·li, $'kæt̬·ə-/ *adv*

cat·ti·ness /£'kæt·ɪ·nəs, $'kæt̬-/ *n* [U]

cat·walk /£'kæt·wɔːk, $-wɑːk/ *n* [C] a narrow path built above the ground • *The catwalk along the side of the printing presses was greasy and slippery.* • *As a model, when I walk along the catwalk at a fashion show, I'm expected to look confident and make the clothes I'm wearing look good.*

Cau·ca·sian /£kɔː'keɪ·ʒən, $kɑː-/ *n* [C], *adj* [not gradable] (of) a white person • *The chief suspect for the robbery is (a) Caucasian.*

cau·cus /£'kɔː·kəs, $'kɑː-/ *n* [C] (a meeting of) a small group of people in a political party or organization who have a lot of influence • In the US, caucuses are sometimes held to decide which CANDIDATE (= person trying to win an election) a group will support.

caught /£kɔːt, $kɑːt/ *past simple and past participle of* CATCH

caul·dron, *esp. Am* **cal·dron** /£'kɔːl·drən, $'kɑːl-/ *n* [C] *old use or literary* a large round container for cooking in, usually supported over a fire • *In children's books witches are often shown stirring cauldrons.*

cau·li·flower /£'kɒl·ɪˌflaʊ·əʳ, $'kɑː·lɪˌflaʊr/, *Br infml* **cau·li** /£'kɒl·i, $'kɑː·li/ *n* a firm round white vegetable which is eaten cooked or raw • *Divide the cauliflower into* **florets** *and wash them thoroughly.* [C] • *Do you like cauliflower?* [U] • *(Br)* **Cauliflower cheese** is a dish of cooked cauliflower in a thick sauce made with milk, flour and cheese. • A **cauliflower ear** is a swollen, badly shaped ear caused by repeated hitting which fighters sometimes get in the sport of boxing. • PIC〉 **Vegetables**

cause REASON /£kɔːz, $kɑːz/ *n, v* (to be) the reason why something, esp. something bad, happens • *Heavy snow was the cause* **of** *many delayed trains today.* [C] • *She has been the cause* **of** *all my troubles.* [C] • *One of the causes* **of** *the accident was poor communications.* [C] • *It seems that the* **root/underlying** (= main) *cause of the child's bad behaviour was unhappiness at home.* [C] • *The* **effects** *of poverty are clear to see, but finding its causes is much more difficult.* [C] • *I wouldn't tell you* **without (good)** *cause* (= if there was not a (good) reason). [U] • If something **gives** cause **for concern**, it is a reason for worrying: *Her late arrival gave cause for concern.* [U] • *I believe we have/there* **is just** *cause* (= a fair reason) **for** *taking this action.* [U] • *The difficult driving conditions caused several accidents.* [T] • *Will this deadline for finishing the work cause you any problems?/Will this deadline for finishing the work cause any problems* **for** *you?* [+ two objects] • *The bright light caused her* **to** *blink.* [T + obj + *to* infinitive] • Someone who **causes a disturbance** breaks the law by fighting or behaving extremely noisily in public. • LP〉 **Get: verbs meaning 'cause'**

caus·al /£'kɔː·zəl, $'kɑː-/ *adj fml* • *No causal relationship has been established between violence on television and violent behaviour* (= Violent behaviour has not been shown to be a result of watching violent television programmes).

caus·al·i·ty /£kɔː'zæl·ɪ·ti, $kɑː'zæl·ə·t̬i/ *n* [U] *fml* • Causality is the principle that there is a cause for everything that happens.

cau·sa·tion /£kɔː'zeɪ·ʃən, $kɑː-/ *n* [U] *fml* • Causation is the production of an effect by a cause.

cau·sa·tive /£'kɔː·zə·tɪv, $'kɑː·zə·t̬ɪv/ *adj fml* • A **causative factor** is something such as an action, fact or influence that causes another thing to happen: *Increased public awareness of the health risks associated with smoking is seen as a major causitive factor* **in** *reducing the number of people who smoke.*

cause PRINCIPLE /£kɔːz, $kɑːz/ *n* [C] a socially valuable principle which is strongly supported by some people • *We support the cause of pre-school education.* • *I'll sponsor you for £10 – it's (all) in/for a* **good** *cause.* • *I've tried three times to get my book back from her but it's a* **lost** *cause* (= something that is impossible).

cause cé·lè·bre /£ˌkɔːz·sel'eb·rə, $ˌkɑːz-/ *n* [C] *pl* **causes célèbres** /£ˌkɔːz·sel'eb·rə, $ˌkɑːz-/ an event, such as a famous legal trial, which attracts a lot of esp. disapproving public attention

cause·way /£'kɔːz·weɪ, $'kɑːz-/ *n* [C] a raised path, esp. across a wet area

cau·stic /£'kɔː·stɪk, $'kɑː-/ *adj* (of chemicals) with the ability to damage things, or (of words, esp. speech) hurtful; intentionally unkind • *caustic soda* • *caustic comments/remarks* • *She's famous in the office for her caustic humour/wit.*

cau·stic·ally /£'kɔː·stɪ·kli, $'kɑː-/ *adv*

cau·ter·ize *obj, Br and Aus usually* **-ise** /£'kɔː·tər·aɪz, $'kɑː·t̬ə-/ *v* [T] *specialized* to burn (an injury) to stop bleeding and/or prevent infection

cau·tion CARE /£'kɔː·ʃən, $'kɑː-/ *n* [U] great care and attention • *We need to* **proceed with/exercise** *caution* (= be careful in taking action, making decisions, etc.) • *They* **treated** *the story of his escape* **with** *(some/great/extreme) caution* (= thought that it might not be true). • Ⓕ Ⓘ

cau·tious /£'kɔː·ʃəs, $'kɑː-/ *adj* • A cautious person takes care to avoid risks: *He's a cautious driver.* • Something which is described as cautious is careful, well considered and sometimes slow or uncertain: *a cautious approach* ○ *cautious criticism* • If you feel **cautious optimism**, you are hopeful that a bad situation will develop into a better one because you have a small amount of knowledge about that situation which makes you think it will improve: *Small improvements in the trading figures of some businesses are cause for cautious optimism that the country's economy is generally improving.*

cau·tious·ly /£'kɔː·ʃə·sli, $'kɑː-/ *adv*

cau·tious·ness /£'kɔː·ʃə·snəs, $'kɑː-/ *n* [U]

cau·tion WARNING /£'kɔː·ʃən, $'kɑː-/ *n* [C] a warning • *Let me give you* **a word of** *caution* (= some safety advice) *before you use this machine.* [U] • *(Br and Aus)* A caution is a spoken warning given by a police officer or official to someone who has broken the law: *As it was her first offence, she was only given a caution.* [C] • Ⓕ Ⓘ

cau·tion *obj* /£'kɔː·ʃən, $'kɑː-/ *v* [T] *fml* • *The writer cautioned the newspaper readers* **against/about** *buying* (= warned them not to buy) *shares without getting good advice first.* • *They cautioned* (= warned) *him* **not to** *travel in the war zone.* [+ obj + *to* infinitive] • *(Br and Aus) The policewoman cautioned me* (= gave me a spoken warning) **for** *speeding in a built-up area.* • *(Br and Aus) "I must caution* (= warn) *you* **that** *this interview is being recorded," said the police officer.* [+ obj + *that* clause]

cau·tion·a·ry /£'kɔː·ʃən·ər·i, £-ri, $'kɑː·ʃən·er·i/ *adj slightly fml* • *a cautionary note* • A **cautionary tale** is a story which gives a warning: *She told a cautionary tale about how she paid the builder before the work was completed and now the garage still isn't finished.*

cav·al·cade /ˌkæv·əl'keɪd, '---/ *n* [C] a line of people, vehicles, horses, etc. following a particular route as part of a ceremony

cav·a·lier WITHOUT CARE /£ˌkæv·əlˈɪəʳ, $-ˈɪr/ *adj* without caring about other people's feelings or safety; THOUGHTLESS • *I don't approve of his cavalier* **attitude** *towards expensive equipment.* • *She complained about the shop's cavalier treatment of people with prams.*

Cav·a·lier MAN /£ˌkæv·əlˈɪəʳ, $-ˈɪr/ *n* [C] a supporter of the king in the English Civil War in the 1640s

cav·al·ry /ˈkæv·əl·ri/ *n* [U + sing/pl v] **the cavalry** the group of soldiers in an army who fight in fast vehicles that are protected by a strong covering, or (esp. in the past) the group who fought while riding on horses • *At an early age, he was sent off to join the cavalry.* • *In a modern army, cavalry regiments use armoured vehicles and ride horses only on special public occasions.* • Compare INFANTRY.

cav·al·ry·man /ˈkæv·əl·ri·mən, -mæn/ *n* [C] *pl* **-men**

cave /keɪv/ *n* [C] a large hole in the side of a hill, cliff or mountain, or one that is underground • *They discovered a series of underground caves and passages.* • *There were ancient paintings on the walls and roof of the cave.* • Ⓕ Ⓘ

cav·er *Br and Aus* /£ˈkeɪ·vəʳ, $-vɚ/, *Am* **spe·lunk·er** *n* [C] • A caver is a person who walks and climbs in caves as a sport.

cav·ing *Br and Aus* /ˈkeɪ·vɪŋ/, *Am* **spe·lunk·ing** *n* [U] • Caving is the sport of walking and climbing in caves. • See also **potholing** at POTHOLE UNDERGROUND.

cave in *v adv* [I] to fall down into an empty space • *Because of the explosion, the roof of the building caved in trapping several people.* • *(fig. infml) At first, they refused to sign the agreement, but they caved in* (= agreed, esp. as a result of being persuaded) *when they heard another firm was being approached.*

ca·ve·at /ˈkæv·i·æt/ *n* [C] *fml* a statement which limits a more general statement; PROVISO • *This film can be recommended with the one caveat that it is a little too long.* • *They* **entered** (= made) *the caveat that judges must not comment on their own cases.* • **Caveat emptor** is the principle that buyers must take responsibility for the quality of goods that they are buying.

cave·man (*pl* **-men**), **cave·wo·man** (*pl* **-women**) /ˈkeɪv·mæn/ *n* [C] a person who lived in a cave in the early stages of the development of human society • A caveman is also a modern man who is very rude or violent towards other people, esp. women.

cav·ern /£ˈkæv·ən, $-ɚn/ *n* [C] a large cave

cav·ern·ous /£ˈkæv·ən·əs, $-ɚn-/ *adj* • If something is cavernous, there is a very large open space inside it: *a cavernous 4000-seat theatre* ○ *The lion had a cavernous mouth.*

cav·i·ar, cav·i·are /£ˈkæv·i·ɑːʳ, $-ɑːr, ˌ--ˈ-/ *n* [U] the eggs of various large fish, esp. the STURGEON, salted and eaten as food which is usually very expensive

cav·il /ˈkæv·əl/ *v* [I] **-ll-** or *Am usually* **-l-** *fml* to make annoying, unnecessary or unreasonable difficulties, esp. about things that are not important • *They cavilled* **at** *the price, although many extras had been included.*

cav·il /ˈkæv·əl/ *n* [C] *fml* • *The one cavil I have* **about** *the book is that it is written as a diary.*

cav·i·ty /£ˈkæv·ɪ·ti, $-ə·t̬i/ *n* [C] a hole, or an empty space between two surfaces • *The gold was hidden in a secret cavity in the chimney behind a loose brick.* • *My dentist said I have a cavity* (= holes in a tooth) *which will have to be treated.* • A **cavity wall** is a wall of a building formed from two walls with a space, usually for air, between them. It is made in this way to keep out cold and wetness.

ca·vort /£kəˈvɔːt, $-ˈvɔːrt/ *v* [I] to move about freely or wildly, and sometimes noisily • *Rabbits cavort in the paddock at dawn and dusk.* • *A group of young people were cavorting beside the swimming pool.*

caw /£kɔː, $kɑː/ *v* [I], *n* [C] (to make) the loud, rough cry of a bird like a CROW

cay·enne pep·per /keɪˈen, ˈ--/ *n* [U] a red powder with a hot taste used to give flavour to food, made from a type of PEPPER (= a vegetable)

CB /ˌsiːˈbiː/ *n* [U] *abbreviation for* Citizens' Band (= a local radio system used esp. by drivers to speak to each other)

cc MEASURE /ˌsiːˈsiː/ *n* [C] *pl* **cc** or **ccs** /ˌsiːˈsiːz/ *abbreviation for* cubic centimetre • *a 750cc motorcycle*

cc COPIES *n* [C] *pl* **cc** *abbreviation for* carbon copy (= used, esp. on a letter, to show that the stated people will be sent a copy) • *cc to J. Singh, R. Brown and F. Panthaki* • LP› **Letters**

CD /ˌsiːˈdiː/ *n* [C] *abbreviation for* compact disc (= a small plastic disc with a metallic surface on which information, esp. high quality sound, is recorded) • *The sound quality you get from a CD is generally much higher than you'd get from a record.* • *Most midi systems sold nowadays include a CD player.*

CD-ROM /£ˌsiː·diːˈrɒm, $-ˈrɑːm/ *n* [C] *abbreviation for* compact disc read-only memory (= a compact disc on which information is stored for use by a computer, but which cannot be changed) • *Every three months you will receive a new CD-ROM containing updated information.* • *Several atlases are now available* **on CD-ROM**. • *Most new PCs now come with a CD-ROM* **drive** *as standard.*

cease *(obj)* /siːs/ *v slightly fml* to stop (something) • *Whether the protests will cease remains to be seen.* [I] • *The company has decided to cease all UK operations after this year.* [T] • *Workplace nurseries will cease* **to** *be liable for tax.* [+ *to* infinitive] • *We must cease dumping waste in the sea.* [+ v-*ing*] • *He spoke for three hours without ceasing.* [I] • To **cease fire** means to stop shooting: *If the red flag goes down you must cease fire.* • A **cease-fire** is an agreement, such as between two armies, to stop fighting to allow discussions about peace: *There are hopes here that the fragile cease-fire will hold, allowing peace talks to continue.*

cease /siːs/ *n* [U] *slightly fml* • *It felt like we had walked for days* **without** *cease* (= stopping). • See also CESSATION.

cease·less /ˈsiː·sləs/ *adj* [not gradable] • *There was a ceaseless* (= continuous) *background noise of machines and voices.*

cease·less·ly /ˈsiː·slə·sli/ *adv* [not gradable]

ce·dar /£ˈsiː·dəʳ, $-dɚ/ *n* a tall wide evergreen tree, or (also **cedarwood**) its wood • *The old cedars were badly damaged in the storm.* [C] • *Their linen chest was made from sweet-smelling cedar.* [U] • PIC› **Tree**

cede *obj* /siːd/ *v* [T] *fml* to give (something such as ownership) to someone else, esp. unwillingly or because forced to do so • *Hong Kong was ceded* **to** *Britain after the Opium War.* • *There is no question of us ceding authority/control/sovereignty.* • *The company has ceded* **ground** *over* (= made improvements in) *its policy of no part-time workers.*

ce·dil·la /sɪˈdɪl·ə/ *n* [C] (used when writing some languages) a mark made under a letter, esp. c, which is then written as ç, to show that the letter has a special sound • LP› **Symbols**

Cee·fax /ˈsiː·fæks/ *n* [U] *Br trademark* a TELETEXT service (= a system of giving written information on television) which the BBC provides • See also ORACLE.

cei·lidh /ˈkeɪ·li/ *n* [C] (esp. in Scotland and Ireland) a special event at which people dance in an organized way to traditional music

ceil·ing /ˈsiː·lɪŋ/ *n* [C] the surface of a room which you can see when you look above you • *A light was hanging from the middle of the ceiling.* • *(fig.) There's a low* **cloud ceiling** (= The clouds are low) *today.* • *(fig.) They have* **imposed/set** *a ceiling* (= upper limit) *on pay rises.*

cel·e·brate *(obj)* ENJOY AN OCCASION /ˈsel·ɪ·breɪt/ *v* to take part in special enjoyable activities in order to show that (a particular occasion) is important • *We always celebrate our wedding anniversary/my birthday* **by** *going out to dinner.* [T] • *They celebrated passing their exams* **with** *a party.* [+ v-*ing*] • *If this plan works, we'll celebrate* **in style** (= in a special way). [I]

cel·e·bra·to·ry /£ˌsel·ɪˈbreɪ·təʳr·i, $-t̬ɚ-/ *adj* [not gradable] • *When we heard she'd got the job we all went off for a celebratory* **drink**.

cel·e·bra·tion /ˌsel·ɪˈbreɪ·ʃən/ *n* • *New Year celebrations* [C] • *Such good news* **calls for** (= deserves) *a celebration!* [C] • *This result* **is cause for** *celebration.* [U]

cel·e·brate *obj* PRAISE /ˈsel·ɪ·breɪt/ *v* [T] *fml* to express admiration and approval for (something or someone) • *His work celebrates the energy and enthusiasm of the young.* • *She was celebrated* **as** *one of the finest dancers of her generation.*

cel·e·brat·ed /£ˈsel·ɪ·breɪ·tɪd, $-t̬ɪd/ *adj* • If something or someone is celebrated, they are famous for some special quality or ability: *a celebrated opera singer/city/novel* • *Salisbury is celebrated* **for** *its fine cathedral.* • Compare NOTORIOUS.

cel·e·brate *obj* LEAD A CEREMONY /ˈsel·ɪ·breɪt/ *v* [T] to lead or take part in (a religious ceremony) • *The priest celebrated Mass.*

cel·e·brant /ˈsel·ɪ·brənt/ *n* [C] • A celebrant is a person who takes part in or the priest who leads a religious ceremony.

ce·leb·ri·ty /£sɪˈleb·rɪ·ti, $-t̬i/ *n* someone who is famous, esp. in the entertainment business, or the state of being famous • *Lots of celebrities were at the film première.* [C] •

She said social class in America was largely decided by celebrity. [U]

ce·ler·i·ac /sə'ler·i·æk/ *n* [U] a type of CELERY (= a vegetable) with a large round white root which can be eaten

ce·ler·i·ty /£sə'ler·ɪ·ti, $-t̬i/ *n* [U] *fml* speed or quickness

cel·e·ry /£'sel·ᵊr·i, $'-ɚ-/ *n* [U] a vegetable with long thin whitish or pale green stems which can be eaten raw or cooked • *celery seeds* • *celery soup* • *celery salt* (= salt flavoured with powdered celery seeds) • A **stick**/*(Am also)* **stalk** of celery is one stem of a plant and a **head** of celery is all the stems of one plant when still joined together. • PIC› **Vegetables**

ce·les·ti·al /£sɪ'les·ti·ᵊl, $-tʃᵊl/ *adj fml or poetic* of or from the sky or outside this world • *The moon is a celestial body.* • **Celestial beings** are imaginary creatures that are thought to live in heaven. • **Celestial music** is the type of music thought to be heard in heaven that is therefore very beautiful.

cel·i·bate /'sel·ɪ·bət/ *adj* [not gradable], *n* [C] (a person) not having sexual activity for a long period, esp. because of taking a religious promise to do this

cel·i·ba·cy /'sel·ɪ·bə·si/ *n* [U]

cell ROOM /sel/ *n* [C] a small bare room, esp. in a prison or a MONASTERY or CONVENT (= religious buildings)

cell·mate /'sel·meɪt/ *n* [C] • A prisoner's cellmates are the people with whom he or she shares a prison cell.

cell ORGANISM /sel/ *n* [C] the smallest basic unit of a plant or animal • *In the picture, you can clearly see that each cell is surrounded by a membrane and also that every cell contains a nucleus.* • *"The little grey cells* (= the brain)*"* (phrase used by Hercule Poirot in the books of Dame Agatha Christie, 1890-1976)

-celled /-seld/ *combining form* • *a single-celled life form*

cel·lu·lar /£'sel·jʊ·ləʳ, $-lɚ/ *adj* [not gradable] • *basic cellular functions* • *cellular respiration* • *Changes caused by the radiation first occur at the cellular level.*

cell PART /sel/ *n* [C] a small part of something • *the cells of a honeycomb*

cel·lu·lar /£'sel·jʊ·ləʳ, $-lɚ/ *adj* [not gradable] • *The organization has a cellular structure* (= is made of many small groups that work independently). • A **cellular phone** (*Br also* **cell phone**) is a telephone which operates using radio signals and can be freely moved from one place to another and used in cars, trains, etc.

cell ELECTRICAL DEVICE /sel/ *n* [C] a device for producing electrical energy from chemical energy

cel·lar /£'sel·əʳ, $-ɚ/ *n* [C] a room under the ground floor of a building, usually used for storage • Ⓕ

cel·lo (*pl* **cellos**) /£'tʃel·əʊ, $-oʊ/, *fml* **vi·o·lin·cel·lo** (*pl* **violincellos**) *n* [C] a wooden musical instrument with four strings that is held vertically between the legs and is played by moving a BOW (= stick with hairs fixed to it) across the strings. • PIC› **Musical instruments**

cel·list /'tʃel·ɪst/ *n* [C] • *Her son is a cellist* (= cello player).

cel·lo·phane /'sel·ə·feɪn/ *n* [U] *trademark* thin quite stiff transparent material used for covering goods, esp. flowers and food • *Flowers, still in their cellophane wrapping, lay on the table.*

cel·lu·lite /'sel·jʊ·laɪt/ *n* [U] fat in the human body, esp. in the upper legs, which cannot be removed simply by eating less food • *So why is it mainly women that suffer from cellulite?*

cel·lu·loid /'sel·jʊ·lɔɪd/ *n* [U] a type of plastic used to make many items, esp. in the past cinematic film • *celluloid toys* • *(literary)* Celluloid also means films or the cinema generally: *Critics called it 'The most seductive image of woman ever committed to celluloid'* (= put in a film). ○ *There have been few celluloid attempts* (= attempts in films) *to portray this subject.*

cel·lu·lose /£'sel·jʊ·ləʊs, $-loʊs/ *n* [U] the main substance in the cell walls of plants, also used in making paper, artificial fibres and plastics

Cel·si·us /'sel·si·əs/, **cen·ti·grade**, *abbreviation* **C** *adj* [not gradable] of a measurement of temperature on a standard in which 0° is the temperature at which water freezes and 100° that at which it boils • *Are the temperatures given* **in** *Celsius or Fahrenheit?* • *The sample was heated to (a temperature of) 80°C.* • *All results are given in* **degrees** *Celsius.* • Compare FAHRENHEIT. • LP› **Units**

Celt·ic /'kel·tɪk, 'sel-/ *adj* [not gradable] of an ancient European people whose modern relatives include the Irish, Scots, Welsh and Bretons, or of their language or culture • *Celtic art*

ce·ment BUILDING MATERIAL /sɪ'ment/ *n* [U] a grey powder which is mixed with water and sand to make MORTAR or with water, sand and small stones to make concrete • *a bag of cement* • *a cement factory* • A **cement mixer** is a machine which has a large cylindrical container which turns round and round, in which cement, water and small stones are mixed to make concrete. • Something **set in cement** is fixed and cannot be changed: *These are just proposals, they aren't set in cement.* • PIC› **Building and construction** Ⓘ Ⓟ

ce·ment *obj* /sɪ'ment/ *v* [T] • *They cemented* **(over)** (= put concrete on) *the front garden so that they could park the car.* • *(fig.) The university's exchange scheme for teachers has cemented* (= made stronger) *its links with many other academic institutions.*

ce·ment GLUE /sɪ'ment/ *n* [U] a substance which sticks things together; glue • *polystyrene cement* • *Dentists use cement to hold crowns and bridges in place.* • Ⓘ Ⓟ

ce·ment *obj* /sɪ'ment/ *v* [T] • *To finish the model, cement the wings onto the fuselage.*

cem·e·tery /£'sem·ə·tri, $-ter·i/ *n* [C] an area of ground in which dead bodies are buried, esp. one which is not next to a church • *a municipal cemetery* • *a pet cemetery*

cen·o·taph /'sen·əʊ·tɑːf, -tæf/ *n* [C] a public MONUMENT built in memory of particular people who died in war, often with their names written on it • *Wreaths are laid at the cenotaph on Remembrance Sunday.*

cen·sor /£'sent·səʳ, $-sɚ/ *n* [C] a person whose job is to read books, watch films, etc. in order to remove anything offensive from them, or who reads private letters, esp. sent during war or from prison, to remove parts considered unsuitable • *This film will never* **get past** (= be approved by) *the censors.*

cen·sor *obj* /£'sent·səʳ, $-sɚ/ *v* [T] • *Figures showing the true scale of overspending have been censored* (= removed) **from** *a report published today.*

cen·sor·ship /£'sent·sə·ʃɪp, $-sɚ-/ *n* [U] • *censorship of the press* • *unacceptable censorship*

cen·sure /£'sen·ʃəʳ, $-ʃɚ/ *n, v fml* (to express) strong criticism or disapproval • *His dishonest behaviour came under severe censure.* [U] • *The government survived a censure* **motion**/*a* **vote of** *censure* (= a formal act of criticism). [U] • *The directors were censured* **for** *their lack of decisiveness during the crisis.* [T] • Ⓝⓛ Ⓢ

cen·sus /'sent·səs/ *n* [C] a count for official purposes, esp. one to count the number of people living in a country and to obtain information such as age, type of employment, etc. • *We have a census in this country every ten years.* • *She was stopped in her car at the exit for a traffic census.*

cent /sent/ *n* [C] a unit of money worth 0·01 of the main unit of money of many countries, or a coin with this value • LP› **Money**

cen·taur /£'sen·tɔːʳ, $-tɔːr/ *n* [C] a creature, esp. in ancient Greek stories, which has a human's upper body and the lower body and legs of a horse • PIC› **Imaginary creatures**

cen·te·na·ry /£sen'tiː·nᵊr·i, $-nɚ-, £-'ten·ᵊr-, $'-ɚ-/, *Am usually and Aus also* **cen·ten·ni·al** /sen'ten·i·əl/ *n* [C] (the day or year that is) 100 years after an important event; the 100th ANNIVERSARY • *centenary celebrations* • *Next year is the centenary* **of** *her death.* • See also BICENTENARY; TERCENTENARY.

cen·te·nar·i·an /£ˌsen·tə'neə·ri·ən, $-t̬ə'ner·i-/ *n* [C] • *There are many more centenarians* (= people who are 100 or more years old) *now than there were 30 years ago.*

cen·ter /£'sen·təʳ, $-t̬ɚ/ *n, v Am for* CENTRE

cen·ter·fold /£'sen·tə·fəʊld, $-t̬ɚ·foʊld/ *n* [C] *Am for* CENTREFOLD

cen·ter·piece /£'sen·tə·piːs, $-t̬ɚ-/ *n* [C] *Am for* CENTREPIECE

cen·ti- /£'sen·ti-, $-t̬i-/ *combining form* 0·01 of the stated unit • *a centimetre* • *a centilitre*

Cen·ti·grade /£'sen·tɪ·greɪd, $-t̬ɪ-/ *n, adj* [not gradable] CELSIUS • LP› **Units**

cen·ti·gram /£'sen·tɪ·græm, $-t̬ɪ-/, *Br also* **cen·ti·gramme** *n* [C] a unit of mass equal to 0·01 of a gram

cen·ti·li·tre, *Am usually* **cen·ti·lit·er** /£'sen·tiˌliː·təʳ, $-t̬iˌliː·t̬ɚ/ (*abbreviation* **cl**) *n* [C] a unit of measurement of liquids equal to 0·01 of a litre

cen·ti·me·tre *Br and Aus, Am* **cen·ti·me·ter** /£'sen·tɪˌmiː·təʳ, $-t̬ɪˌmiː·t̬ɚ/ (*abbreviation* **cm**) *n* [C] a unit of length equal to 0·01 of a metre • LP› **Units**

cen·ti·pede /£'sen·tɪ·piːd, $-t̬ɪ-/ *n* [C] a small long thin animal with many legs that eats other animals • PIC **Worm**

cen·tral NEAR THE MIDDLE /'sen·trəl/ *adj* in, at, from or near the centre or most important part (of something) • *There was a central design on the plate, and a pattern around the edge.* • *A central hole had been drilled in the panel.* • *Although the firm has small factories in many locations they're all under central* **control** *from the head office.* • *Of course, you pay more for premises having a central location* (= in or near the centre of a town). • *The new housing development is central* **for** *shops and schools.* • **Central government** is national government from a single important city rather than local government. • **Central heating** is a system of heating buildings by warming air or water at one place and then sending it to different rooms in pipes. • The **central nervous system** is the main system of nerve control in a living thing, consisting of the brain and the main nerves connected to it. • *(Br)* A **central reservation** (*Am and Aus* **median strip**) is the narrow piece of land between the two halves of a large road. • See also CENTRE MIDDLE. • PIC **Motorway** CS NL PL

cen·tral·i·sm /'sen·trə·lɪ·zᵊm/ *n* [U] • Centralism is the principle or action of putting something under central control: *Centralism is a political policy which would be unpopular and would be resisted at the local level.*

cen·tral·ize *obj, Br and Aus usually* **-ise** /'sen·trə·laɪz/ *v* [T] • *Payment of bills is now centralized* (= organized at one place instead of several).

cen·tral·ly /'sen·trə·li/ *adv* • *centrally located/controlled* • *The house is centrally heated.*

cen·tral IMPORTANT /'sen·trəl/ *adj* main or important • *a central role* • *Community involvement is central* **to** *our plan.* • CS NL PL

cen·tral·i·ty /£sen'træl·ɪ·ti, $-ə·t̬i/ *n* [U] • *The centrality* (= importance) *of the family is a feature of both these societies.*

cen·tre MIDDLE *Br and Aus, Am* **cen·ter** /£'sen·təʳ, $-t̬ɚ/ *n* [C] the middle point or part • *Put the vase in the centre* **of** *the table.* • *People used to think that the earth was (at) the centre* **of** *the universe.* • *You can't drive into the centre* **of** *the city/the city centre because it's pedestrianised.* • In politics the centre of a group is the people who hold opinions which are not extreme but are between two opposites: *His political views are known to be* **left of/right of** *centre.* • *She's the* **centre of attention** (= Everyone wants to talk to her) *everywhere she goes.* • In particular sports, a **centre (forward)** in a team is the person who is in the middle of the front row of players who try to score goals. • The **centre of gravity** of an object is the point through which the GRAVITATIONAL forces on it seem to act. • A **centre-spread** is the two pages opposite each other in the middle of a newspaper or magazine which deal only with one particular subject and include many pictures: *Tomorrow's edition will include a centre-spread on the Spanish royal family.* • If someone is at **centre stage**, they are in the middle of a theatre stage, or *(fig.)* are very noticeable to others: *(fig.) She doesn't mind letting some of the younger students* **take** *centre stage from time to time.* • *"Journey to the Centre of the Earth"* (title of a book by Jules Verne, 1864) • See also CENTRAL.

cen·tre *obj Br and Aus, Am* **cen·ter** /£'sen·təʳ, $-t̬ɚ/ *v* [T] • *Centre* (= Put at equal distances from the left and right sides of the page) *all the headings in this document.* • If you centre **around/round/on/upon** something, you make it the main subject of discussion or interest: *The discussion centred around reducing waste.* ○ *She spoke about her travels, centring on the time she had spent in India.*

cen·tre PLACE *Br and Aus, Am* **cen·ter** /£'sen·təʳ, $-t̬ɚ/ *n* [C] a place or building, esp. one where a particular activity happens • *a sports/leisure/health centre* ○ *a garden/shopping centre* ○ *a test centre* ○ *urban centres* (= cities or towns) • *The survey will concentrate on centres* **of population** (= places where many people live) *rather than rural areas.* • *Grants will be given to establish centres* **of excellence** (= places where a particular activity is done extremely well) *in this field of research.*

cen·tre·fold *Br and Aus, Am* **cen·ter·fold** /£'sen·tə·fəʊld, $-t̬ɚ·foʊld/ *n* [C] (a large picture, esp. a photograph, which covers) the two pages opposite each other in the middle of a magazine, or an attractive (and often famous) person who appears in such a picture, esp. without any clothes on • *The week's TV schedule is given in colour across the centrefold of the magazine.* • *This month's centrefold is Tammy Simons.*

cen·tre·piece IMPORTANT PART *Br and Aus, Am* **cen·ter·piece** /£'sen·tə·piːs, $-t̬ɚ-/ *n* [C] the most important or attractive part or feature of something • *The reduction of crime levels is the centrepiece* **of** *the president's domestic policies.* • *Marriage is no longer the centrepiece* **of** *women's lives, she said.* • *A crisply roasted leg of lamb formed the centrepiece* **of** *the meal* • *The centrepiece* **of** *the shopping centre is a giant fountain.*

cen·tre·piece DECORATION *Br and Aus, Am* **cen·ter·piece** /£'sen·tə·piːs, $-t̬ɚ-/ *n* [C] a decorative object put in the centre of a table, esp. for a formal meal • *The centrepiece was a watermelon cut into the shape of a basket and filled with marzipan fruit.*

-cen·tric /-'sen·trɪk/ *combining form* having the stated thing as your central interest • *Eurocentric* • *Afrocentric* • *ethnocentric* • *egocentric* • *He accused the newspaper of being Anglocentric, concentrating on England and ignoring Wales, Northern Ireland and Scotland.*

-cen·tri·sm /-'sen·trɪ·zᵊm/ *combining form* • *ethnocentrism* • *Afrocentrism* • *Politicians are worried by the increasing Eurocentrism of government policies.*

cen·tri·fu·gal /ˌsen·trɪ'fjuː·gᵊl/ *adj* [not gradable] (of a turning object) tending to move away from the point around which it is turning

cen·tri·fuge /'sen·trɪ·fjuːdʒ/ *n* [C] • A centrifuge is a machine which turns a container round very quickly, causing the solids and liquids inside it to separate by centrifugal action.

cen·tri·pe·tal /£ˌsen·trɪ'piː·tᵊl, $-t̬ᵊl/ *adj* [not gradable] (of a turning object) tending to move towards the point around which it is turning • *centripetal force/acceleration*

cen·trist /'sen·trɪst/ *adj, n* [C] (relating to) a person who supports the centre of the range of political opinions

cen·tu·ri·on /£sen'tjʊə·ri·ən, $-'tʊr·i-/ *n* [C] an officer in the army of ancient Rome who was responsible for 100 soldiers

cen·tu·ry /£'sen·tʃᵊr·i, $-tʃɚ-/ *n* [C] a period of 100 years • *The century from 1848 to 1947 saw tremendous political change in Europe.* • *The city centre has scarcely changed in over a century.* • *This sculpture must be centuries old.* • *Her medical career spanned half a century.* • Esp. in Christian society, a century is also a period of 100 years counted from what is believed to be the year of the birth of Jesus Christ: *The twelfth century is the years from 1100 to 1199 and the eighteenth is the years from 1700 to 1799.* • *Rome was founded in the eighth century before Christ.* • *He's an expert on fifteenth century Italian art.* • *How many people have been killed in wars this century?* • *The cathedral was built last century.* • *Queen Victoria died at* **the turn of the** *century* (= the time when one century ends and another begins). • In sport, esp. cricket, a century is a score of 100. • Compare MILLENNIUM. • LP **Periods of time**

ce·ram·ics /sɪ'ræm·ɪks/ *n* [U] the production of objects by shaping pieces of clay which are then hardened by baking

ce·ram·ics /sɪ'ræm·ɪks/ *pl n* • Ceramics are the objects produced by shaping and heating clay, esp. when considered as art: *a collection/exhibition of Indian ceramics*

ce·ram·ic /sɪ'ræm·ɪk/ *adj* [not gradable] • *Our kitchen floor is covered with ceramic tiles.* • *(Br)* A **ceramic hob** is a flat surface on the top of some types of electric cooker on which pans are heated.

ce·re·al /£'sɪə·ri·əl, $'sɪr·i-/ *n* a type of grass which is cultivated to produce grain, or a food made from grain which is eaten esp. in the mornings. There are various types of cereal. • *This region is one in which a lot of cereal is grown.* [U] • *Wheat, rice, barley, oats and maize are cereals.* [C] • *The farm produces cereal crops.* • *Would you like some cereal for breakfast?* [U] • *Cornflakes are a popular breakfast cereal in Britain.* [C]

cer·eb·ral /'ser·ɪ·brᵊl/ *adj* relating to the (front part of the) brain, or demanding careful reasoning and mental effort rather than feelings • *Your left cerebral* **hemisphere** *controls the right-hand side of your body.* • *I couldn't understand that film at all. It was all too cerebral* (= It needed too much thought) *for me.* • **Cerebral palsy** is a physical condition involving permanent tightening of the muscles which is caused by damage to the brain around or before the time of birth.

cer·e·bra·tion /ˌser·ɪ'breɪ·ʃᵊn/ *n* [U] *fml or humorous* the operation of the brain, or the process of thinking

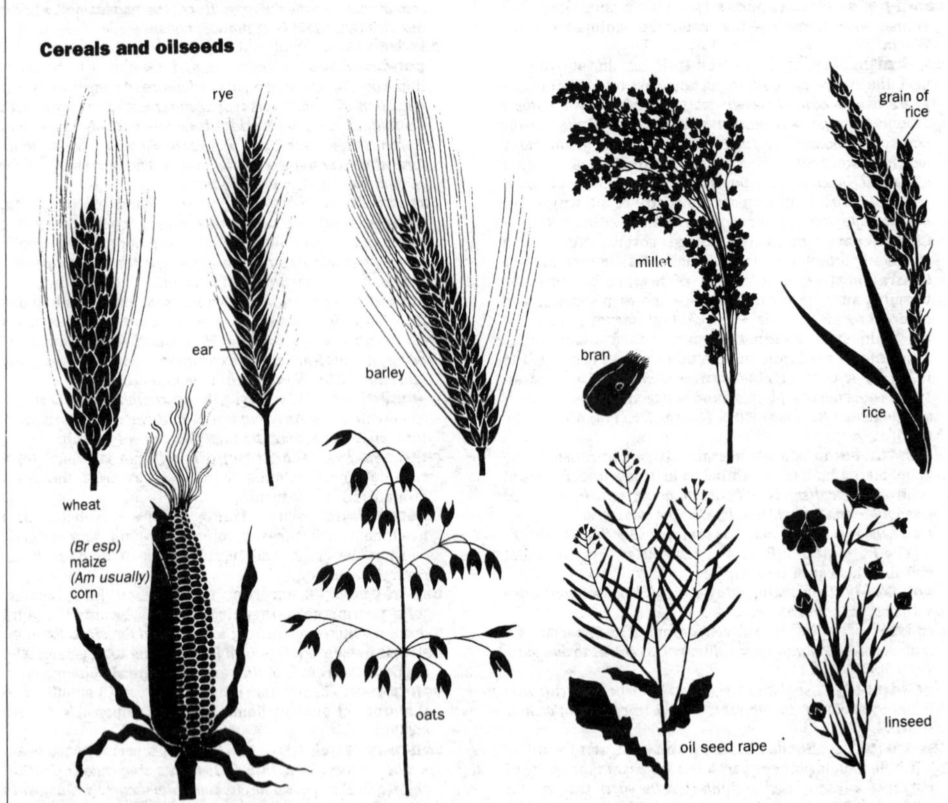

cer·e·brum /sɪ'riː·brəm/ *n* [C] *pl* **cerebrums** or **cerebra** /sɪ'riː·brə/ the front part of the brain, which is involved with thought, decision, emotion and character

cer·e·mo·ny FORMAL ACTS /'ser·ɪ·mə·ni/, *fml* **cer·e·mo·ni·al** *n* (a set of) formal acts, often fixed and traditional, performed on important social or religious occasions • *a marriage/wedding ceremony* [C] • *a degree/graduation ceremony* [C] • *a prize-giving ceremony* [C] • *the opening/closing ceremony at the Olympic Games* [C] • *The coronation ceremony was* **performed** *by the archbishop.* [C] • *The memorial ceremonies* **marked** *the 100th anniversary of the disaster.* [C] • *(fml) Many pagan ceremonials were eventually adopted by the Church.* [C] • *I'd hate to* **go through** *all the ceremony of a church wedding.* [U] • *(humorous) At the end of the meal there was the usual ceremony* (= fixed behaviour) **of** *deciding how much each of us owed.* [C]

cer·e·mo·ni·al /£ˌser·ɪ'məʊ·ni·əl, $-'moʊ-/ *adj* • *ceremonial occasions/duties/processions* • *The President's role is largely ceremonial.* • *The soldiers were in ceremonial dress and carrying ceremonial swords.*

cer·e·mo·ni·al·ly /£ˌser·ɪ'məʊ·ni·ə·li, $-'moʊ-/ *adv* • *The two leaders ceremonially signed the union treaty yesterday evening.* • *The Prime Minister ceremonially opened the new museum.*

cer·e·mo·ny FORMAL BEHAVIOUR /'ser·ɪ·mə·ni/ *n* [U] very formal and polite behaviour • *When we arrived at the hotel, we were received with great ceremony by the owners.* • *She arrived at the airport without the* **pomp and** *ceremony that usually accompanies important politicians.* • *I handed her my letter of resignation* **without** *ceremony* (= in an informal way).

cer·e·mo·ni·ous /£ˌser·ɪ'məʊ·ni·əs, $-'moʊ-/ *adj* • Behaviour which is ceremonious is too formal or polite: *Her ceremonious manner was rather inappropriate for our informal party.*

cer·e·mo·ni·ous·ly /£ˌser·ɪ'məʊ·ni·ə·sli, $-'moʊ-/ *adv* • *He shook hands ceremoniously with each of his supporters as they arrived.*

ce·rise /sə'riːz, -'riːs/ *adj, n* [U] (having) a dark reddish pink colour

cert CERTAIN THING /£sɜːt, $sɜːrt/ *n* [C usually sing] *Br infml* something which is thought to be certain to happen or be successful • *"Do you think Pakistan will win the match?" "Definitely – it's a cert."* • *After such careful planning, the party's success is a* **dead** *cert.* • *With all her experience she's a* **dead** *cert* **for** (= is certain to get) *the job.* • *The Russian team is a dead cert* **to** *win the gold medal.* [+ to infinitive]

cert DOCUMENT /£sɜːt, $sɜːrt/ *n* [C] *abbreviation for* certificate

cer·tain IN NO DOUBT /£'sɜː·tᵊn, $'sɜːr·t̬ᵊn-/ *adj* having no doubt or knowing exactly (that something is true), or known to be true, correct, exact or effective • *"I won't have any more cake, thank you." "Are you certain?"* • *"Are you going to Karl's party?" "I'm not certain yet."* • *I'm certain* **(that)** *he'll go, because he's already bought a ticket.* [+ (*that*) clause] • **It**'*s quite certain* **(that)** *he'll go.* [+ (*that*) clause] • *Are you* **absolutely** *certain* **(that)** *they heard your warning?* [+ (*that*) clause] • *I* **feel** *certain* **(that)** *you're doing the right thing.* [+ (*that*) clause] • *You should* **make** *certain* **(that)** *no one else has already done that.* [+ (*that*) clause] • *The police* **seem** *certain* **(that)** *they will find the people responsible for the attack.* [+ (*that*) clause] • *We're not certain* **wh**ere *they live.* [+ *wh-* word] • *I'm not certain* **how** *much it will cost.* [+ *wh-* word] • **It**'*s not certain* **how** *much it will cost.* [+ *wh-* word] • *I'm not certain* **who** *composed this symphony.* [+ *wh-* word] • **It**'*s not certain* **who** *composed this symphony.* [+ *wh-* word] • *He was quite certain* **about** *the robber's identity.* • *Can we be certain* **about/of** *the truth of what she said?* • If you are certain **about** someone, you have confidence in them and trust them: *The new teacher hasn't been at the school for very long, and no one is quite certain about him yet.* • *Before we offer him the job, we must* **make** *certain* **of** *his reliability.* • *There is no certain* (= known to be effective) *solution to the problem.* • *We shouldn't confuse rumours with certain* (= known to be true) *facts.* • *One thing is certain* (= known to be correct) *– she won't resign willingly.* • *I don't know* **for certain** (= without any doubt) *what I'll do when I leave school.*

cer·tain·ly /£'sɜː·tᵊn·li, $'sɜːr·t̬ᵊn-/ *adv* • *She certainly had a friend called Mark, but I don't know whether he was her boyfriend.* • *"This is rather a difficult question." "Yes,* *it's certainly not easy." • "Do you think more money should be given to education?" "Certainly* (= Yes, without doubt).*"/ "Certainly not! Health is far more important." • "Could you lend me £10?" "Certainly* (= Willingly).*"/"Certainly not! You still haven't paid back the £5 you owe me." • "Had you forgotten about our anniversary?" "Certainly not* (= I definitely have not)*! I've reserved a table at Michel's restaurant for this evening."*

cer·tain·ty /£'sɜː·tᵊn·ti, $'sɜːr·ţᵊn·ţi/ *n* • A certainty is something which cannot be doubted: *There are few absolute certainties in life.* [C] • Certainty is the state of being completely confident or having no doubt about something: *I'm unable to answer that question* **with** *any certainty.* [U]

cer·tain EXTREMELY LIKELY /£'sɜː·tᵊn, $'sɜːr·ţᵊn/ *adj* not avoidable or extremely likely • *The population explosion is certain* **to** *cause widespread famine.* [+ *to* infinitive] • *Oil prices are certain* **to** *rise following the agreement to limit production.* [+ *to* infinitive] • *After all his hard work, he's certain* **to** *pass his exams.* [+ *to* infinitive] • *The team looks* **almost** *certain to win the match.* [+ *to* infinitive] • *The team is certain* **of** *victory/winning.* • **It** *is virtually certain* **(that)** *she will win the gold medal.* [+ (*that*) clause] • *Even if a ceasefire can be agreed, how can they* **make certain (that)** *neither side breaks it?* [+ (*that*) clause] • *Cancer sufferers no longer face certain death as they once did.* • *This scandal will mean certain defeat for the party in the election.*

cer·tain·ly /£'sɜː·tᵊn·li, $'sɜːr·ţᵊn-/ *adv* • *She will certainly win the election if the opinion polls are accurate.*

cer·tain·ty /£'sɜː·tᵊn·ti, $'sɜːr·ţᵊn·ţi/ *n* [C] • A certainty is something which is very likely to happen: *Joan will win – that's a certainty.* ○ *Joan is a certainty* **to** *win.* [+ *to* infinitive]

cer·tain PARTICULAR /£'sɜː·tᵊn, $'sɜːr·ţᵊn/ *determiner* particular but not named or described • *We have certain reasons for our decision, which have to remain confidential.* • *Do you think war is justifiable in certain circumstances?* • *The song has a certain appeal, but I'm not sure what it is.* • *There is a certain level of income below which it is impossible to live in a civilized way.* • *I have a certain actress in mind for the role of Juliet.* • *Certain members of the audience may disagree with what I'm about to say.*

cer·tain /£'sɜː·tᵊn, $'sɜːr·ţᵊn/ *pronoun* [always + *of*] *fml* • *Certain* (= Some) **of** *the candidates were well below the usual standard, but others were very good indeed.*

cer·tain NAMED /£'sɜː·tᵊn, $'sɜːr·ţᵊn/ *adj* [before n; not gradable] *fml* named but neither famous nor known personally • *A certain Jane Smith would like to talk to you.* • *I had lunch today with a certain George Michael – not* **the** *George Michael, I should explain.*

cer·tain LIMITED /£'sɜː·tᵊn, $'sɜːr·ţᵊn/ *adj* [before n; not gradable] limited • *I like modern art to a certain* **extent/ degree***, but I don't like the really experimental stuff.* • *The band enjoyed a certain success a few years ago, but little is heard of them today.* • *We should make a certain profit from the deal, but it won't be very great.*

cer·ti·fi·cate /£sə'tɪf·ɪ·kət, $sɚ-/ (*abbreviation* **cert**) *n* [C] an official document which states that the information on it is true • *a birth/marriage/death certificate* • *You'll need a doctor's/medical certificate to prove that you've been too ill to go to work.* • *My examination certificate* (= document stating that I have passed an exam) *arrived in the post today.* • Certificate sometimes refers to the qualification that you receive when you are successful in an exam: *Jane's a qualified teacher now that she has her Certificate in Education.*

cer·ti·fy *(obj)* /£'sɜː·tɪ·faɪ, $'sɜːr·ţɪ-/ *v* to state (something) officially, usually in writing, esp. that (something) is true or correct • *My accountant has certified last year's tax figures.* [T] • *I hereby certify* **that** *the above information is true and accurate.* [+ *that* clause] • *The driver was certified* **(as)** *dead on arrival at the hospital.* [T + obj + (*as*) n/adj] • *The meat has been certified* **(as)** *fit for human consumption.* [T + obj + (*as*) n/adj] • *The cause of death was certified* **as** *pneumonia.* [T + obj + *as* n/adj] • To certify someone is also to state officially that they are mentally ill: *As a young man, he had been certified and sent to a hospital for the mentally ill.* [T] ○ *In his later years the composer was certified insane.* [T + obj + adj] • *(Am and Aus)* **Certified mail** is post for which proof of delivery is obtained.

cer·ti·fi·ca·tion /£ˌsɜː·tɪ·fɪ'keɪ·ʃᵊn, $ˌsɜːr·ţɪ-/ *n* [U]

cer·ti·fied /£'sɜː·tɪ·faɪd, $'sɜːr·ţɪ-/ *adj* [before n; not gradable] • Certified means having a document that proves that you have successfully completed a course of training: *a certified teacher/nurse* ○ *She is certified* **to** *practise medicine.* [+ *to* infinitive] • **Certified public accountant** (*abbreviation* **CPA**) is *Am for* **chartered accountant**. See at CHARTER.

cer·ti·fi·a·ble /£'sɜː·tɪ·faɪ·ə·bl̩, $'sɜːr·ţɪ-/ *adj* • A person who is certifiable is mentally ill, or *(infml)* behaves in a foolish or stupid way: *(infml) Simon's out washing his car again – I'm telling you the man is certifiable!*

cer·ti·tude /£'sɜː·tɪ·tjuːd, $'sɜːr·ţɪ·tuːd/ *n* [U] *fml* certainty or confidence • *It is impossible to predict the outcome of the negotiations with any degree of certitude.*

cer·vix /£'sɜː·vɪks, $'sɜːr-/ *n* [C] *pl* **cervixes** or **cervices** /£'sɜː·vɪ·siːz, $'sɜːr-/ *specialized* the narrow lower part of the womb which leads into the vagina • *When a woman is in labour, her cervix opens up to allow the baby to be born.*

cer·vi·cal /£sə'vaɪ·kᵊl, £'sɜː·vɪ-, $'sɜːr·vɪ-/ *adj* [not gradable] • *cervical cells/screening* • If a woman has a **cervical smear**, some cells are taken from her cervix and then tested to discover if she has CANCER (= a serious disease).

ce·sar·e·an /£sɪ'zeə·ri·ən, $-zer·i-/ *n* [C], *adj Am for* CAESAREAN

ces·sa·tion /ses'eɪ·ʃᵊn/ *n fml* ending or stopping • *The money saved from the cessation* **of** *the road project will be invested in public transport.* [U] • *Religious leaders have called for a total cessation* **of** *the bombing campaign.* [C] • See also CEASE.

cess·pit /'ses·pɪt/, **cess·pool** /'ses·puːl/ *n* [C] a large underground hole or container which is used for collecting and storing excrement, urine and dirty water • *(fig.) Saying that drug addicts are swirling around in a cesspit* (= unpleasant situation) *of their own making will not help solve the problem.*

c'est la vie /ˌseɪ·læ'viː/ *exclamation* situations like that happen in life, and you cannot do anything about them • *"I can't go to the football match on Saturday because I've got to work." "Oh well, c'est la vie."*

ce·ta·cean /sɪ'teɪ·ʃᵊn/ *adj* [not gradable], *n specialized* (connected with) any of various types of mammal that live in the sea like fish • *Cetaceans include dolphins, porpoises and whales.* [C]

cf /'siː·ef/ *v fml abbreviation for* confer (= Latin for 'compare'). Used to tell the reader that there is something else that is worth thinking about at the same time as the subject already being considered.

CFC /ˌsiː·ef'siː/ *n* [C] *abbreviation for* chlorofluorocarbon (= a type of chemical which is used for cooling air, as a cleaning liquid, for producing plastic FOAM, and for pushing out small drops of liquid from some types of can. There are various types of chlorofluorocarbon.) • *CFCs seem to play a role in depleting the ozone layer.*

PRONUNCIATION OF 'CH'

The letters 'ch' are often found in combination and can be pronounced in three ways: /k/, /tʃ/ and /ʃ/.

/tʃ/	/k/	/ʃ/
church	Christian	chauffeur
charge	psychiatrist	champagne
children	chemical	machine
macho	technology	chef
bachelor	character	moustache
choose	echo	brochure
rich	mechanic	sachet
	ache	

'ch' is silent in yacht /jɒt/

/tʃ/ and /k/ are by far the most common pronunciations and can be checked in the dictionary if a spoken model is not available, as there is no rule to explain which to use. 'ch' is pronounced /ʃ/ in a smaller number of words that have come into English directly from French.

cha–cha(–cha) /'tʃɑː·tʃɑː, ˌtʃɑː·tʃɑː'tʃɑː/ *n* [C] (a piece of music written for) an energetic modern dance, originally from S America, involving small fast steps and movement of the bottom from side to side

chafe BE ANNOYED /tʃeɪf/ *v* to be or become annoyed or lose patience • *Passengers are starting to chafe* **at** *the delay in their flight.* [I] • *We have been chafing* **under** *petty* *regulations for too long.* [I] • *He was a man of vision who chafed* **against** *the cruel practices of his time.* [I] • To chafe is also to be eager: *Although she was prepared for her move to Washington, she was not chafing* **to** *be there.* [+ *to* infinitive]

chafe *(obj)* RUB /tʃeɪf/ *v* to make or become damaged or sore by rubbing, or to warm (a part of the body) by rubbing • *The bracelet was so tight that it chafed my wrist.* [T] • *This lotion should stop your skin from chafing so much.* [I] • *He chafed my hands for me when I'd finished building the snowman.* [T]

chaff /£tʃɑːf, $tʃæf/ *n* [U] the outer layer which is separated by THRESHING (=hitting) from seeds such as wheat before they are used as food, or dried grass and stems when used to feed cattle

chaf·finch /ˈtʃæf·ɪntʃ/ *n* [C] a common small European bird that has black and white wings and, in the male, a bluish-grey head and a reddish-brown body, and which makes musical sounds

chag·rin /ˈʃæg·rɪn/ *n* [U] *fml* disappointment or annoyance, esp. when caused by a failure or mistake • *Imagine my chagrin when I discovered that I'd been wrong all along.* • **(Much) to** *the police's chagrin, the chief suspect for the killing seems to have fled the country.* • **(Much) to** *the chagrin of his children, when he died he left all his money to charity.*

chag·rined /ˈʃæg·rɪnd/ *adj fml* • *I was most chagrined when I heard that Stella had got the job instead of me.*

chain RINGS /tʃeɪn/ *n* (a length of) esp. metal rings that are connected together and used for fastening, pulling, supporting, or limiting freedom, or as jewellery • *The gates were locked with a padlock and a heavy steel chain.* [C] • *Put the chain on the door if you are alone in the house.* [C] • *The chain of a bicycle transfers power from the pedals to the rear wheel.* [C] • *I need half a metre of fine chain to hang up a picture.* [U] • *Don't worry, the dog can't chase you – she's on a chain.* [C] • *Don't forget to* **pull the** *chain when you finish in the toilet.* [C] • *Mary was wearing a beautiful silver chain around her neck.* [C] • *I was given a beautiful chain* **bracelet** *for my birthday.* • *The hostages were kept* **in chains** *for 23 hours a day.* • *(fig.) At last the country has freed itself from the chains* **of** (=limitations on freedom established by) *the authoritarian regime.* [C] • **Chain mail** consists of small metal rings that have been joined together to look like cloth. It was used in the past to protect the body of a soldier from injury when fighting. • A **chain saw** is a large SAW (=a cutting tool) with a motor that has teeth-like parts fitted onto a continuous chain, and which is used esp. for cutting trees. • **Chain stitch** is a decorative sewing method in which each stitch is connected to the next so that they form a chain. • *"Man is born free, and everywhere he is in chains"* (Jean-Jacques Rousseau in *The Social Contract*, 1762) • PIC> **Bicycles, Jewellery, Locks and home security, Plugs, Tools**

chain *obj* /tʃeɪn/ *v* [T always + adv/prep] • *It's so cruel to keep a pony chained* **up** *like that all the time.* • *They chained themselves* **to** *lampposts in protest at the judge's decision.* • *(fig.) I don't want a job where I'm chained* **to** (=limited to working at) *a desk for eight hours a day.*

chain CONNECTED THINGS /tʃeɪn/ *n* [C] a set of connected or related things • *a mountain chain* • *She has built up a chain of 180 bookshops across the country.* • *We witnessed a remarkable chain* **of events** *in eastern Europe in 1989.* • A **chain letter** is a letter promising or asking for something, such as money, which is sent to several people who are each asked to send copies to several others, and which sometimes threatens that bad things will happen if they do not send these copies. • A **chain reaction** is a set of related events in which each event causes the next one: *The explosion crushes the plutonium, thereby increasing its density and starting the chain reaction of nuclear fission.* ○ *The war risked setting off a perilous chain reaction that would endanger the whole of the world.* • A person who **chain-smokes** or is a **chain-smoker** smokes almost continuously, often lighting one cigarette from the end of the previous one: *Joan's under a lot of pressure these days – she's been chain-smoking ever since her divorce.* • A **chain store** is (one of) a group of shops which belongs to a single company, has the same appearance and sells similar goods: *The chain stores are driving the small family-run shops out of business.* ○ *He works for one of the major chain stores.*

chair FURNITURE /£tʃeəʳ, $tʃer/ *n* [C] a movable seat for one person which has a back, usually four legs, and sometimes two arms • *"Is this a private meeting, or can I join you?" "Of course you can.* **Pull up a** *chair."* • **The chair** is the **electric chair**. See at ELECTRICITY. • A **chair lift** is a set of chairs hanging from a moving wire which is powered by a motor, which carries people, esp. SKIERS, up and down mountains and other steep slopes. • See also ARMCHAIR; DECKCHAIR; PUSHCHAIR; WHEELCHAIR. • PIC> **Chair**

chair TITLE /£tʃeəʳ, $tʃer/ *n* [C] (the official position of) a person in charge of a meeting or organization, or a position in an official group, or the person in charge of or having an important position in a college or university department • *Complaints about the procedure of the meeting should be addressed to the chair.* • *Nicky Jones was* **in the** *chair at* (=in charge of) *the debate.* • *Who was elected chair* (=to be in charge) **of** *the committee?* • *Ian has a chair* (=position) *on the board of governors of his daughter's school.* • *She's chair* **of** (=in charge of) *the sociology department this year.* • *At one time, he* **held** *the Montague Burton Chair* **in** *International Relations at the London School of Economics.*

chair *obj* /£tʃeəʳ, $tʃer/ *v* [T] • *Would you like to chair tomorrow's meeting?*

chair·per·son, **chair**, **chair·man** *(pl* **-men**), **chair·wo·man** *(pl* **-women**) /£ˈtʃeəˌpɜː·sᵊn, $ˈtʃerˌpɜːr-/ *n* [C] a person in charge of a meeting or organization • *All the members of the committee take it in turns to act as chairperson.*

chair·man·ship /£ˈtʃeə·mən·ʃɪp, $ˈtʃer-/ *n* [C usually sing] • *The committee met* **under** *the chairmanship of Joan Black* (=with her being in charge). • *His chairmanship* (=The period when he was in charge) *lasted a year.* • *Who do you think will get the chairmanship* (=the position of being in charge) *of the company?*

chaise longue /ˌʃezˈlɔ̃ːŋ/, *Am and Aus also* **chaise lounge** *n* [C] a long low seat, with an arm at one side and usually a low back along half of its length, which is wide enough for a person's legs to rest on • PIC> **Chair**

chal·et /ˈʃæl·eɪ/ *n* [C] a small wooden house found in mountainous areas, esp. in Switzerland, or a house built in a similar style, esp. as used by people on holiday • LP> **'-et' words**

chal·ice /ˈtʃæl·ɪs/ *n* [C] a large decorative gold or silver cup from which wine is drunk in Christian ceremonies

chalk /£tʃɔːk, $tʃɑːk/ *n* a type of soft white rock, or (a stick of) this rock or a similar substance, sometimes coloured, used for writing or drawing • *Chalk was formed in prehistoric times from the shells of tiny sea creatures.* [U] • *The children were drawing with coloured chalks.* [C] • *How can I teach if I don't have any chalk to write on the blackboard/chalkboard?* [U] • *(Br and Aus)* People or things that are **(as different as) chalk and/from cheese** are completely different from each other. *The two sisters are chalk and cheese.* ○ *(humorous) Although the film is supposed to have been based on the book, they're as alike as chalk and cheese* (=are completely different). • *(Br)* Someone who **doesn't know/can't tell chalk from cheese** is unable to understand or judge important differences: *I shouldn't bother asking Hugh's opinion – he doesn't know chalk from cheese.*

chalk *(obj)* /£tʃɔːk, $tʃɑːk/ *v* • *I wish the children would stop chalking (things)* **on** *the classroom walls.* [I/T] • *Every day they chalk the day's menu* **(up) on** *a board on the wall of the restaurant.* [T/M]

chalk·y /£ˈtʃɔː·ki, $ˈtʃɑː-/ *adj* **-ier, -iest** • *The soil in this area is very chalky* (=contains chalk). • *I always have chalky* (=covered with dust from chalk) *fingers after I've been writing on the (Br) blackboard/ (Am and Aus) chalkboard.*

chalk·i·ness /£ˈtʃɔː·kɪ·nəs, $ˈtʃɑː-/ *n* [U]

chalk up *obj*, **chalk** *obj* **up** *v adv* [M] to achieve (a success) or score (points in a game), or to record (a success, points, or money that is owed) • *Today's victory is the fifth that the Irish team has chalked up this year.* • *It was doubtful whether the Conservatives could chalk up a fourth successive election victory, but they did.* • *He's chalked up* (=scored) *ten goals already this season.* • *Carol's generously asked the bar staff to chalk up the drinks* **to** *her* (=record the cost of drinks and she will pay for them). • *"So your new job didn't work out very well?" "No, it didn't, but never mind – chalk* **it** *up* **to experience** (=I will think of it as having been an experience that I can learn from)."

chalk·board /£ˈtʃɔːk·bɔːd, $ˈtʃɑːk·bɔːrd/ *n* [C] *Am and Aus for* BLACKBOARD

chal·lenge INVITATION /ˈtʃæl·ɪndʒ/ *n* [C] an invitation to compete or take part, esp. in a game or argument • *"I bet you can't eat all that food that you've got on your plate." "Is*

that a challenge?" • *Is there going to be a challenge for the position of chairperson when the next election for the committee is held?* • *She* **issued** *a challenge to her rival candidates* **to** *take part in a public debate, but they did not* **accept** *it.* [+ *to* infinitive] • Ⓕ

chal·lenge *obj* /ˈtʃæl·ɪndʒ/ *v* [T] • *Is anyone else going to challenge him for the leadership of the party?* • *Tina has challenged me* **to** *a game of poker* • *Tina has challenged me* **to** *beat her at poker.* [+ obj + *to* infinitive]

chal·leng·er /£ˈtʃæl·ɪn·dʒəʳ, $-dʒɚ/ *n* [C] • A challenger is someone who tries to win a competition, fight or sporting event from someone who has previously won it: *If the challenger wins, he will become the new world heavyweight champion.*

chal·lenge EXPRESSION OF DOUBT /ˈtʃæl·ɪndʒ/ *n* a questioning or expression of doubt about the truth, legality or purpose of something, or the right of a person to have or do something • *The result of the vote* **poses** *a serious challenge* **to** *the government's credibility.* [C] • *Because of the way this research was conducted, its findings are open to challenge.* [U] • Ⓕ

chal·lenge *obj* /ˈtʃæl·ɪndʒ/ *v* [T] • *Children challenge their parents' authority far more nowadays than they did in the past.* • *This new law will challenge the freedom of the press to publish details about people's private lives.*

chal·lenge DIFFICULT JOB /ˈtʃæl·ɪndʒ/ *n* (the situation of being faced with) something needing great mental or physical effort in order to be done successfully and which therefore tests a person's ability • *Finding a cure for this disease is one of the greatest challenges faced by scientists.* [C] • *I'm hoping that my new job will provide me with more of a challenge than my last one.* [C] • *If we give this job to Helga, do you think she will* **rise to** *the challenge?* [U] • Ⓕ

chal·lenge *obj* /ˈtʃæl·ɪndʒ/ *v* [T] • *She prefers films that challenge her, but I just want them to entertain me.* • *Their objections challenged me* **to** *think of better arguments in support of my suggestion.* [+ obj + *to* infinitive]

chal·leng·ing /ˈtʃæl·ɪn·dʒɪŋ/ *adj* • *This challenging book is one of the most thought-provoking that I've ever read.*

chal·lenge INSTRUCTION /ˈtʃæl·ɪndʒ/ *n* [C] an instruction given by a soldier or guard at a border or gate, telling a person to stand still and state their name and reasons for being there • *She was shot in the leg when she ignored the soldier's challenge.* • Ⓕ

chal·lenge *obj* /ˈtʃæl·ɪndʒ/ *v* [T] • *I was challenged by a new security guard who didn't recognize me.*

chal·lenge REFUSAL /ˈtʃæl·ɪndʒ/ *n* [C] *law* a refusal to accept someone as a member of a JURY (= group who decide whether someone is guilty in a trial) • *A challenge* **to** *a member of the jury should be made before the trial begins.* • Ⓕ

chal·lenge *obj* /ˈtʃæl·ɪndʒ/ *v* [T] *law* • *A member of the jury was challenged because she was an employee of the defendant.*

cham·ber BEDROOM /£ˈtʃeɪm·bəʳ, $-bɚ/ *n* [C] *old use* a room in a house, esp. a bedroom • **Chamber music** is music written for a small group of musicians so that it can be performed easily in a small room, or, in the past, in a private home. • A **chamber orchestra** performs chamber music, usually with a single musician playing each instrumental part. • A **chamber pot** is a large round bowl-shaped container, which in the past was kept under a bed and used as a toilet at night or during an illness.

cham·ber ROOM /£ˈtʃeɪm·bəʳ, $-bɚ/ *n* [C] a room used for a special or official purpose, or a group of people who form (part of) a parliament • *The debate finished at midnight and the delegates left the chamber shortly afterwards.* • *Meetings of the council are held in the council chamber.* • *One of the parts of the castle that is most popular with visitors is the old* **torture** *chamber.* • *There are two chambers in the British parliament – the House of Commons is the lower chamber, and the House of Lords is the upper chamber.* • If a trial is **in chambers**, it takes place in a court room without the presence of the public, newspaper reporters, etc. • A **chamber of commerce** is an organization consisting of people in business who work together to improve business in their town or local area. • A **chamber of horrors** is a room which contains a lot of very frightening things.

cham·bers /£ˈtʃeɪm·bəz, $-bɚz/ *pl n* • Chambers are a judge's private office. A judge may have legal discussions with lawyers in private in his or her chambers: *The judge said he would hear the complaint* **in** *chambers.*

cham·ber SPACE /£ˈtʃeɪm·bəʳ, $-bɚ/ *n* [C] an enclosed space in a machine, plant or animal • *the chambers of a gun* • *There are* **inspection** *chambers at various points along the length of the sewer pipe.* • *The human heart has two chambers.* • A **combustion** chamber is the part of an engine where the fuel burns.

cham·ber·maid /£ˈtʃeɪm·bə·meɪd, $-bɚ-/ *n* [C] a woman employed in a hotel to clean and tidy bedrooms

cha·me·le·on /kəˈmiː·li·ən/ *n* [C] a LIZARD (=type of creature) that changes its skin colour to match its surroundings so that it cannot be seen, or *(fig.)* a person who changes their opinions or behaviour to please other people

cham·ois /ˈʃæm·wɑː/ *n* [C] *pl* **chamois** a small animal which looks like a goat and which lives in the mountains of Europe and SW Asia

cham·ois (leath·er), sham·my (leath·er) /ˈʃæm·i/ *n* [C/U] • (A) chamois is (a piece of) soft leather used for cleaning and making things shine, which was originally produced from the skin of a chamois, but is now obtained from sheep and goats, or (a piece of) cotton cloth made to feel like the skin of a chamois .

champ *(obj)* BITE /tʃæmp/ *v* [I/T] to CHOMP

champ CHAMPION /tʃæmp/ *n* [C] *infml for* CHAMPION

cham·pagne /ʃæmˈpeɪn/, *Br and Aus dated infml* **cham·pers** /£ˈʃæm·pəz, $-pɚz/ *n* [U] an expensive white or pink fizzy wine made in the Champagne area of E France, or, more generally, any similar wine from somewhere else. Champagne is often drunk to celebrate something. • *We always celebrate our wedding anniversary with a bottle of champagne.* • *The champagne corks will be popping tonight* (= Bottles of champagne will be opened) *as the team celebrates yet another victory.* • A **champagne flute** (also **flute**) is a tall narrow glass with a stem which is used for drinking champagne. • A **champagne socialist** is a rich person who spends money wastefully but claims to support a fair society in which everyone has equal rights and the rich help the poor. • *"Champagne Charlie"* (title of a song by George Heybourne, 1868)

cham·pi·on WINNER /ˈtʃæm·pi·ən/, *infml* **champ** *n* [C] someone or something, esp. a person or animal, that has beaten all other competitors in a competition • *a tennis champion* • *an Olympic champion* • *a champion tennis player/racehorse* • *She is the world champion for the third year in succession.* • *The defending champion will play his first match of the tournament tomorrow.* • *Who are the reigning European football champions?* • LP› **Sports**

cham·pi·on·ship /ˈtʃæm·pi·ən·ʃɪp/ *n* [C] • A championship is a competition, esp. a sporting one: *the British Diving Championship* ○ *The world championships will be held in Scotland next year.* ○ *He has been playing championship tennis for three years now.* • A championship is also the position of being a champion: *She has held the championship for the past three years.*

cham·pi·on SUPPORT /ˈtʃæm·pi·ən/ *n* [C] a person who enthusiastically supports, defends or fights for a person, belief, right or principle • *She has long been a champion* **of** *prisoners' rights/the disabled/free speech.*

cham·pi·on *obj* /ˈtʃæm·pi·ən/ *v* [T] • *He has championed constitutional reform for many years.*

cham·pi·on·ship /ˈtʃæm·pi·ən·ʃɪp/ *n* [U] • *Their championship* **of** *human rights never weakened, despite the government's threats.*

cham·pi·on GOOD /ˈtʃæm·pi·ən/ *adv, adj Br regional* very good or well; excellent(ly) • *"Hello, how are you?" "Champion, thanks."* • *That was a champion dinner.*

chance LUCK /£tʃɑːnts, $tʃænts/ *n* [U] the force that causes things to happen without any known cause or reason for doing so • *Roulette is a game of chance.* • *I got this job completely* **by** *chance – I happened to be in the right place at the right time.* • *Are you Hungarian* **by any** *chance?* (= Is it possible that you are Hungarian?) • *Could you lend me a fiver* **by any** *chance?* (= Is it possible for you to lend me £5?) • **It** *was* **pure/sheer** *chance* **(that)** *I won the prize.* [+ *(that)* clause] • *We must double-check everything and* **leave nothing to** *chance.*

chance /£tʃɑːnts, $tʃænts/ *v* • *They chanced* **to** *be in the restaurant when I arrived* (= They were there unexpectedly). [+ *to* infinitive] • *I chanced* **on/upon** (= found unexpectedly) *some old love letters in a drawer.* [I] • *Ten years after leaving school, we chanced* **on/upon** (= unexpectedly met) *each other in Regent Street.* [I]

chance LIKELIHOOD /£tʃɑːnts, $tʃænts/ *n* [U] likelihood; the level of possibility (that something will happen) • *You'd have* **a** *better chance/more chance* **of** *passing your exams if you worked a bit harder.* • *There's* **a good** *chance/some chance* **(that)** *I'll have this essay finished by tomorrow.* [+ *(that)* clause] • *There's* **a slim/slight/faint** *chance* **(that)** *I might have to go to Manchester next week.* [+ *(that)* clause] • *If we hurry, there's still* **an outside** *chance* **of** *catching the plane.* • *"Is there any chance* **of** *speaking to him?"* **"Not a/ No** *chance, I'm afraid."* • *I don't think I* **stand/have a** *chance* **of** *winning.* • *(Br) John thinks they're* **in with a** *chance* (= they have a possibility of doing or getting what they want). • *It was* **a** *chance* **in a million** (= There was only an extremely slight possibility) *that we met the way we did.* • *I applied* **on the off chance** (= because there was a small possibility of success), *but I didn't seriously expect to get the job.*

chan·ces /£ˈtʃɑːnt·sɪz, $ˈtʃænt-/ *pl n* • *Her resignation has improved my chances* **of** (= the likelihood that I will get) *promotion.* • *What are her chances* **of** *survival, Doctor?* • *What are the chances* (= How likely is it) **that** *they'll win?* [+ *that* clause] • *I suppose they might possibly win, but the chances are against it* (= it is unlikely). • *(The) chances are* (= It is likely) **(that)** *they'll be late as usual.* [+ *(that)* clause]

chance OPPORTUNITY /£tʃɑːnts, $tʃænts/ *n* [C] an occasion which allows something to be done; an opportunity • *I wish I'd* **had** *the chance* **to** *meet her before she died.* [+ *to* infinitive] • *Would you mind* **giving** *me a chance* **to** *speak, please?* [+ *to* infinitive] • *Society has to* **give** *prisoners a* **second** *chance when they come out of jail.* • *I wanted to say goodbye to him, and now he's gone and I've* **missed** *my chance.* • *I've been waiting for a chance like this all my life.* • *You should* **take** *your chances when they arise, because they'll never be repeated.* • *What do you mean you're not sure? This is your big chance* **to** *do what you've always wanted!* [+ *to* infinitive] • *The opportunity to act in a film with her really is the chance* **of a lifetime.** • *(Br) "Have you ever been to Australia?"* **"Chance would be a fine thing** (= I would really like to go, but I have never had the opportunity.)" • **Given half a** *chance* (= If he had the slightest opportunity), *he'd give up working tomorrow.* • *"Give Peace a Chance"* (title of a song by John Lennon, 1969)

chance RISK /£tʃɑːnts, $tʃænts/ *n* [C] a possibility that something negative will happen; a risk • *They'll have to* **take** *a chance with that old car and pray that it doesn't break down on the way.* • *You don't get anywhere in life without* **taking** *chances.* • *There's a chance* **of** *injury in almost any sport.*

chance *obj* /£tʃɑːnts, $tʃænts/ *v* [T] • *You'd be a fool to chance* (= risk) *your life savings* **on** *a single investment.* • *"Isn't it too icy to drive home tonight?" "Perhaps, but I'll just have to chance* **it**/*(Br also)* **chance** *my* **arm** (= take the risk)."

chanc·y /£ˈtʃɑːnt·si, $ˈtʃænt-/ *adj* **-ier, -iest** *infml* • *Investing on the Stock Exchange is a chancy* (= risky) *business.*

chan·cel /£ˈtʃɑːnt·səl, $ˈtʃænt-/ *n* [C] the part of a church containing the ALTAR (= special table) where the priests and CHOIR (= singers) sit

chan·cel·lor /£ˈtʃɑːnt·səl·əʳ, $ˈtʃænt·səl·ɚ/ *n* [C] a person in a position of the highest or high rank, esp. in a government or university • *Helmut Kohl became the first Chancellor of a united Germany in 1990.* • *A former politician has been appointed Chancellor of the university.* • The **Chancellor of the Exchequer** is the person in the British Government responsible for deciding tax levels and how much money the Government can spend.

chan·cel·le·ry /£ˈtʃɑːnt·səl·ər·i, $ˈtʃænt·səl·ɚ-/ *n* [C] • A chancellery is the building where a chancellor or their employees work.

chan·de·lier /£ˌʃæn·dəˈlɪəʳ, $-ˈlɪr/ *n* [C] a decorative light which hangs from the ceiling and has several branch-like parts for holding BULBS or, esp. in the past, candles

chand·ler /£ˈtʃɑːnd·ləʳ, $ˈtʃænd·lɚ/ *n* [C] a person who trades in particular goods, esp. in supplies for ships

change *(obj)* BECOME DIFFERENT /tʃeɪndʒ/ *v* to make or become different, or to exchange one thing for another thing, esp. of a similar type • *I almost didn't recognize her – she'd changed so much.* [I] • *Life has/Things have changed a lot this past year – new job, different city, new boyfriend.* [I] • *Nothing changes, does it – I've been away two years and the office still looks exactly the same.* [I] • *People have changed their diets quite a lot over the past few years.* [T] • *I'm going to change my hair style.* [T] • Change sometimes means exchange: *I had to change those trousers I bought* **for** (= take them back to the shop in order to get) *a bigger pair.* [T] ○ *She's just changed* **jobs** (= got a new job) *because she couldn't stand her old boss.* [T] ○ *Let's change* **the subject** (= talk about something different) *otherwise we'll start arguing again.* [T] • To change **(over) from** one thing **to** something else is to stop being/doing/using one thing and start being/doing/using another: *The traffic lights changed from red to green.* [I] ○ *We've just changed (over) from gas central heating to electric.* [I] ○ *We changed to driving an automatic last year.* [I] ○ See also CHANGEOVER. • The **wind** and **tide** change when they start to move in a different direction: *Suddenly the wind changed (***from** *south* **to** *west).* [I] • *I'm going to change my room* **about/around/round** (= change the way it is arranged) *and put the bed over by the window.* [T] • *Since she went away to school, her attitude has* **changed for the better** (= improved). • Something is said to **change hands** if it goes from one owner to another: *That Italian restaurant is nowhere near as good since it changed hands.* • If you **change** your **mind (about** something), you form a new opinion or make a new decision about something which is different from your oid one: *You're still not coming out tonight? – well, if you change your mind, give me a call.* ○ *When I first met him I didn't like him but I've changed my mind.* • *I wouldn't* **change places with** (= be in the same situation as) *him for the world!* • If you **change tack**, you try a different method to deal with the same problem: *When there was no reply to their letters they changed tack and phoned the company several times a week.* • *(esp. disapproving)* A person who has a strong opinion on a subject and then unexpectedly forms the opposite opinion might be said to **change** his/her **tune**: *She's always been against the new supermarket, but she soon changed her tune when she realized how much money they would give for her land.* • If you **change** your **ways**, you improve the bad parts of your behaviour: *If he wants to carry on living here, he's going to have to change his ways.*

change /tʃeɪndʒ/ *n* • *Let me know if there's any change* **in** *the situation.* [U] • *Change in this country is always met with fear and suspicion.* [U] • *We're living in a time of great change.* [U] • *We need a change* **of** *government.* [C] • *They decided on a change* **in** *lifestyle.* [C] • *The house was almost perfect when we moved in so we didn't have to* **make** *many changes* **(to** *it).* [C] • *The new management will* **make fundamental/radical/sweeping** *changes* (= do things in a (very) different way). [C] • *We'll try to alter the rota – but don't expect* **overnight** (= sudden) *changes.* [C] • **A change** is often used in an approving way to refer to something which is pleasant or interesting because it is unusual or new: *It's nice to see her smile* **for** *a change.* ○ *"Shall we eat in the garden?" "Why not – it'll* **make** *a change."* ○ *We've always had a red car – it's time we had* **a** *change!* ○ *A free evening – what a* **refreshing** *change.* ○ *This new system is a change* **for the better** (= an improvement). • *She'd been with the same company for too many years and felt she needed a* **change of scene** (= a different situation). • *He decided on a* **change of direction** (= a different set of activities) *and gave up his job to travel the world.* • *She was going to sell her house but had a* **change of heart** (= a different opinion) *at the last minute.* • *Her doctor told her she needed a* **change of pace** (= a more peaceful and relaxed way of life). • **The change (of life)** is *infml dated for* the MENOPAUSE: *She's* **going through** *the change.* • *(saying)* 'A change is as good as a rest'.

change·a·ble /ˈtʃeɪn·dʒə·bl̩/ *adj* • Something is described as changeable if it often changes: *The weather in Britain is notoriously changeable.* ○ *His moods are very changeable.*

changed /tʃeɪndʒd/ *adj* [not gradable] • A man or woman can be described as a changed **man/woman** if their behaviour and character has changed to an unusual degree: *She's a changed woman since she found this new boyfriend.* ○ *He's a changed man since he lost his job.*

changing /ˈtʃeɪn·dʒɪŋ/ *adj* • Something which is changing is in a state of becoming different: *the rapidly changing world of politics* ○ *the ever changing nature of contemporary society* ○ *changing attitudes towards childcare* ○ *changing circumstances* ○ *a changing outlook*

change·less /ˈtʃeɪndʒ·ləs/ *adj literary* • Something which is changeless never seems to change: *Surrounded by this changeless landscape, one can imagine the world as it was many thousands of years ago.*

change *(obj)* CLOTHES/BEDS /tʃeɪndʒ/ *v* to remove one set of clothes and put a different set on yourself or a young child, esp. a baby, or to remove dirty sheets from a bed and put clean ones on it • *You don't need to change – you look great as you are.* [I] • *Have I got time to bath/shower/wash and change?* [I] • *How often do you think he changes his shirt?* [T] • *I'll just change* **into** (= get dressed in) *something a bit smarter.* [I] • *Give me five minutes to change* **out of** (= remove) *my work clothes and I'll come out with you.* [I] • *Could you change the* **baby**/*the baby's (Br and Aus)* **nappy** *(Am* **diaper***)* (= put on a clean one)*?* [T] • *I think the* **baby**/*her* **nappy** *needs changing.* [T] • *I'll have to go and change the baby's dress – she's been sick.* [T] • *I've changed the* **sheets**/*the* **bed** (= the sheets on the bed) *in the guest room.* [T] • A **changing room** is a room where people can change their clothes, for example before and after sports or, in a shop, where people can try on clothes to see if they are suitable for buying. • (LP) **Dressing and undressing**

change /tʃeɪndʒ/ *n* [C] • A change **of clothes** is a set of clothes that is additional to the ones that you are wearing: *She took a change of clothes in her suitcase as they were staying overnight.* • A change of clothes can also be the action of putting on different clothes: *It was a 3-day journey without a wash or a change of clothes*

change *obj* MONEY /tʃeɪndʒ/ *v* [T] to get or give (money) in exchange for money, either because you want it in smaller units, or because you want the same value in foreign money • *Could you change a £10 note (***for** *two fives), please?* • *Could you change me a £5 note?/Could you change a £5 note* **for** *me?* [+ two objects] • *I need to change my dollars* **for/into** *English money.* • (LP) **Money**

change /tʃeɪndʒ/ *n* [U] • Change can refer to coins rather than notes: *She gave me £5* **in** *change.* ○ *My dad always used to carry a lot of* **loose/small** *change* (= coins) *in his pocket.* • Change can refer to smaller units of money given in exchange for larger units of the same amount: *Have you got change for a twenty-dollar bill?* • Change also refers to the money which is returned to someone who has paid for something which costs less than the amount that they gave: *Always check your change before you leave the shop.* ○ *I think you've given me the* **wrong** *change.* ○ *You gave me £10 to get you a ticket but it only cost £7, so you need £3 change.*

change *(obj)* TRANSPORT /tʃeɪndʒ/ *v* to get off (a train, bus, etc.) and catch another in order to continue a journey • *I had to change (trains) twice to get there.* [I/T] • *It's an awkward journey because you have to change several times.* [I] • *Change at Peterborough for York.* [I]

change /tʃeɪndʒ/ *n* [C] • *I hate journeys where you've got a lot of changes, especially if you're carrying luggage.*

change *(obj)* SPEED /tʃeɪndʒ/, *Am usually* **shift** *v* to put a vehicle into a different GEAR, usually in order to change the speed at which it is moving • *He wants an automatic car so that he doesn't have to change* **gear** *all the time.* [T] • *You should change* **into** *fourth (gear) at this speed.* [I] • *(Br and Aus) Change* **down** *(Am* **Downshift***) to go round the corner/to overtake.* [I] • *(Br and Aus) Listen to your engine noise to decide when to change* **up** *(Am* **shift up***).* [I]

chan·gel·ing /ˈtʃeɪndʒ·lɪŋ/ *n* [C] (esp. in stories) a baby who is secretly used to take the place of another baby

change·o·ver /£ˈtʃeɪndʒ,əʊ·vəʳ, $-,oʊ·vɚ/ *n* [C usually sing] a complete change from one system or method to another • *The changeover* **to** *the new taxation system has created a lot of problems.*

chan·nel TELEVISION STATION /ˈtʃæn·ᵊl/ *n* [C] a television station • *a cable/satellite/terrestrial channel* • *a commercial/subscription channel* • *a music/movie/news/shopping/sports channel* • *Shall we watch the news* **on** *Channel 4?* • *She* **switched/turned** *to another channel to watch the football.* • **Channel-hopping** is quickly changing from one channel to another to find something you want to watch.

chan·nel PASSAGE /ˈtʃæn·ᵊl/ *n* [C] a passage for water or other liquids to flow along, or a part of a river or other area of water which is deep and wide enough to provide a route for ships to travel along • *We tried digging a channel to lower the water level but that didn't work.* • *There are* **drainage/irrigation** *channels all over this flat agricultural land.* • *The juice is extracted and runs down this channel here into a large container.* • *Wooden posts mark the* **deep-water/navigable** *channel into the harbour.* • *The boats all have to pass through this* **narrow** *channel.* • **The Channel** or **the English Channel** is the stretch of sea which separates England from France and Belgium: *We're going to have a day-trip across the Channel.* ○ *We took the car to France overnight on a* **(cross-)***channel ferry.* ○ *Dover and Portsmouth are two of the channel ports.* • **The Channel Tunnel** (also *infml* **Chunnel**) is the passage built under the English Channel between England and France.

chan·nel ROUTE /ˈtʃæn·ᵊl/ *n* [C] a route or way out of an airport or port where travellers' bags are examined • *If you have nothing to declare, go through the* **green** *channel.* • *Members of EU countries with nothing to declare go through the* **blue** *channel.* • *Goods to declare – use the* **red** *channel.*

chan·nel WAY /ˈtʃæn·ᵊl/ *n* [C] a way of giving, directing or communicating (something) • *One of the difficulties of the present situation of the two countries is the lack of a proper channel* **of communication.** • *Their doctor played a role in* **opening** *channels of communication between the two* *families.* • *A marketing official confirmed that they had established a regular channel* **of distribution** *for these products.* • *The government pursued every* **diplomatic/official** *channel to free the hostages.* • *You should make the complaint through the* **proper** *channels.* • *Nothing could be done about the flights, except to complain quietly through the* **usual** *channels.* • *In his work, he had found a channel* **for** *all his energy and enthusiasm.*

chan·nel *obj* DIRECT /ˈtʃæn·ᵊl/ *v* [T] **-ll-** or *Am usually* **-l-** to direct (something) into a particular place or situation • *These ditches were constructed to channel* **water** *away from the buildings.* • *Fresh* **water** *collected in gutters will be channelled into the pond.* • *If she could only channel all that nervous* **energy into** *something useful.* • *A lot of* **money** *has been channelled* **into** *research in that particular field.*

chant *(obj)* /£tʃɑːnt, $tʃænt/ *v* to repeat or sing (a word or phrase) continuously, or to sing (a religious prayer or song) to a simple tune • *The crowd chanted the name of their football team* **in unison.** [T] • *There was a group of* **demonstrators** *chanting anti-government* **slogans** *in the square.* [T] • *We could hear the monks chanting.* [I] • *Groups of devout worshippers chanted* **and sang** *as they walked in procession.* [I] • *The women were chanting* **mantras/prayers/psalms.** [T]

chant /£tʃɑːnt, $tʃænt/ *n* [C] • *The* **fans** *started to* **sing** *the familiar* **football** *chant, "Here we go, here we go, here we go!".*

chant·euse /ˌʃɑːnˈtɜːz/ *n* [C] *literary* a female singer, esp. one who sings on the stage in a theatre or bar • *Liza Minelli plays a chanteuse in the film 'Cabaret'.*

chan·ty, *Am* **chan·tey** /ˈʃæn·ti/ *n* [C] a SHANTY SONG

Cha·nu·kah /ˈhɑː·nə·kə/ *n* HANUKKAH

cha·os /£ˈkeɪ·ɒs, $-ɑːs/ *n* [U] a state of total confusion and lack of order • *Snow and ice have* **caused** *chaos on the roads.* • *We muddled up the name labels and chaos* **ensued.** • *We had ten children at the party and chaos* **reigned** *all afternoon.* • *Ever since our secretary walked out, the office has been* **in (a state of) total/utter** *chaos.* • **Chaos theory** is a scientific theory about situations that obey particular laws but appear to have little or no order: *The speaker told us that chaos theory says two things, that complex systems like weather have an underlying order and that simple systems can produce complex behaviour.* ○ *A frequent metaphor for one aspect of chaos theory is called the Butterfly Effect – butterflies flapping their wings in the Amazon affect the weather in Chicago.*

cha·ot·ic /£keɪˈɒt·ɪk, $-ˈɑː·t̬ɪk/ *adj* • *The house is a bit chaotic at the moment – we've got all these extra people staying and we're still decorating.* • *He's a chaotic sort of a person – always trying to do twenty things at once.*

cha·ot·ic·al·ly /£keɪˈɒt·ɪ·kli, $-ˈɑː·t̬ɪ-/ *adv*

chap MAN /tʃæp/, **chap·pie** /ˈtʃæp·i/, **chap·py** *n* [C] *Br dated infml* a man or an older boy • *He's a friendly sort of chap.* • *Come on, (you) chaps, let's have a few goals.* [as form of address] • LP **Titles and forms of address**

chap BOOK *n* [C] *abbreviation for* CHAPTER • *Chap. 21*

cha·pa·ti *(pl* **chapatis** or **chapaties**), **cha·pat·ti** *(pl* **chapattis** or **chapatties**) /£tʃəˈpɑː·ti, $-t̬i/ *n* [C] a type of flat round Indian bread made without YEAST

chap·el /ˈtʃæp·ᵊl/ *n* [C] a room within a larger building which is used for Christian worship, or *(esp. Br)* a building which is used for Christian worship by Christians who do not belong to the Church of England or the Roman Catholic Church • *The college/hospital/prison/school has its own chapel.* • *Two of the cathedral's chapels were added later – the Lady Chapel and the Chapel of St Paul.* • *(esp. Br) Sara and Mike were married in a little Methodist/Baptist chapel in Swansea.*

chap·e·rone /£ˈʃæp·ə·rəʊn, $-roʊn/, **chap·e·ron** *n* [C] (esp. in the past) an older person, esp. a woman, who goes with and takes care of a younger woman who is not married when she is in public • *(esp. humorous) She's asked me to go to the cinema with her and Andrew, I think as a sort of chaperone.* • *(Am)* A chaperone is someone, esp. an older person, who is present at an event to encourage correct behaviour: *Several parents acted as chaperones for the school disco.*

chap·e·rone *obj* /£ˈʃæp·ə·rəʊn, $-ə·oʊn/ *v* [T] • *(esp. humorous) Do you trust him on your own or do you want me to chaperone you?* • *(Am) Several parents volunteered to chaperone class bus trips.*

chap·lain /ˈtʃæp·lɪn/ *n* [C] a Christian official who is responsible for the religious needs of an organization • *the college/hospital/prison/military chaplain*

chap·lain·cy /ˈtʃæp·lɪnt·si/ *n* [C] • A chaplaincy is either the position of chaplain or the building or office in which a chaplain works: *Several groups joined together to fund an airport chaplaincy.* ○ *The building plans included a new university chaplaincy.*

chapped /tʃæpt/ *adj* (of skin) sore, rough and cracked, esp. caused by cold weather • *chapped lips* • *She'd been working outside all winter and her hands were red and chapped.*

chap *(obj)* /tʃæp/ *v* **-pp-** • *Wearing gloves stopped his hands from chapping.* [I] • *The cold wind had chapped her lips.* [T]

chap·py /ˈtʃæp·i/ *n* [C] *Br dated infml* a CHAP MAN

chaps /tʃæps/ *pl n* protective leather clothing worn over trousers by COWBOYS when riding a horse

chap·ter BOOK PART /£ˈtʃæp·təʳ, $-t̬ɚ/ *(abbreviation* **chap**) *n* [C] any of the separate parts into which a book or other piece of text is divided, usually numbered or given a title • *Read until the end of chapter 10 for homework.* • *I'm just reading the chapter called 'Misery' which deals with her first marriage.* • Someone who gives something **chapter and verse** states the exact information and says where it comes from: *I think I'm right, though I can't* **cite/quote** *you chapter and verse what the law says on this point.*

chap·ter PERIOD /£ˈtʃæp·təʳ, $-t̬ɚ/ *n* [C] a period which is part of a larger amount of time during which something happens • *That whole period leading up to the revolution is an interesting chapter* **in** *British history.* • *When scientists announced their findings, they opened a new chapter* **in** *the treatment of this disease.* • *The final chapter* **in** *one of the great Hollywood murder mysteries has just unfolded in a California court house.* • *That chapter* **of** *my life closed when I had a serious riding accident.* • *(Br and Aus fml)* A **chapter of accidents** is when several unlucky events happen one after another: *Their trip was a chapter of accidents.*

chap·ter SOCIETY /£ˈtʃæp·təʳ, $-t̬ɚ/ *n* [C] *esp. Am* a local division of a larger organization • *That building is where the Coventry chapter of Freemasons meet on a Thursday.*

char *(obj)* BURN /£tʃɑːʳ, $tʃɑːr/ *v* to burn slightly and become blackened • *I left the waffles under the grill for too long and they've charred.* [I] • *Their forearms were charred in the blast.* [T] • Food that is **char-grilled** is cooked over or under direct heat so that its surface is slightly blackened.

charred /£tʃɑːd, $tʃɑːrd/ *adj* • Charred means burnt and black: *She yanked the charred meat off the barbecue and threw it away.* • *The charred body of a man was found by police in a burnt-out car last night.*

char CLEAN /£tʃɑːʳ, $tʃɑːr/ *v* [I] **-rr-** *dated* to clean and tidy a house or office for payment • *My grandmother charred* **for** *the same family for thirty years.*

char /£tʃɑːʳ, $tʃɑːr/, **char·la·dy** *n* [C] • Char is *Br infml dated for* CHARWOMAN.

char·a·banc /£ˈʃær·ə·bæŋ, $ˈʃer-/, *infml* **cha·ra** /£ˈʃær·ə, $ˈʃer-/ *n* [C] *Br dated* a large old-fashioned bus, esp. one used by groups for visiting places of interest

char·ac·ter QUALITY /£ˈkær·ɪk·təʳ, $ˈker·ɪk·t̬ɚ/ *n* the particular combination of qualities in a person or place that makes them different from others • *Though similar in appearance, the two sisters were entirely different* **in** *character.* [U] • *He was a man* **of** *dubious/irreproachable character* [U] • *Politeness is traditionally part of the British character.* [U] • *It was when she lived with him that she found out the darker side to his character.* [C] • *One of the joys of being a parent is watching the child's character develop.* [C] • *The idea was to modernize various aspects of the house without changing its essential character.* [C] • *It's not* **in** *his character to* (=He wouldn't ever) *hurt anyone.* [C] • *I can't believe he would have smashed the window – it seems so* **out of** *character* (= different from his usual way of behaving and therefore strange). [U] • *The new extension to the museum has been criticized for being* **out of** *character* **with** (=unsuitable for) *the rest of the building.* [U] • Character is often used approvingly to mean qualities which are interesting and unusual: *a house* **of** *character* [U] ○ *If I was buying somewhere to live, I'd prefer an old place with a bit of character.* [U] ○ *Old books are said to give a room character.* [U] ○ *As people grow older, their faces acquire more character.* [U] • Character, or **strength of** character, can also be used approvingly to mean the quality of being determined and able to bear difficult situations: *I don't think I've got the strength of character to refuse to take part – I'm too easily persuaded to do things.* [U] • A **character assassination** is an intentional attempt to spoil the reputation of a person by criticizing them severely, esp. unfairly, in the newspapers or on television. • A **character reference** is a written statement of a person's good qualities, written by someone who knows the person well, which is sent to a future employer. • (DK)(E)

char·ac·ter·is·tic /£ˌkær·ɪk·tə'rɪs·tɪk, $ˌker-/ *adj* • Something which is characteristic is typical of a person or thing: *With the hospitality so characteristic* **of** *these people, they opened their house to over fifty guests.* ○ *She received the bad news with characteristic dignity.* ○ *The creamy richness is characteristic* **of** *the cheese from this region.*

char·ac·ter·is·tic /£ˌkær·ɪk·tə'rɪs·tɪk, $ˌker-/ *n* [C] • A characteristic is a typical or noticeable quality of someone or something: *Unfortunately a big nose is a* **family** *characteristic.* ○ *Sentimentality seems a characteristic* **of** *all the writers of that period.* ○ *The male bird* **displays** (=has) *several characteristics which distinguish him from the female.* • (N)

char·ac·ter·is·tic·ally /£ˌkær·ɪk·tə'rɪs·tɪ·kli, $ˌker-/ *adv* • *She gave a characteristically brilliant performance.*

char·ac·ter·ize *obj, Br and Aus usually* **-ise** /£'kær·ɪk·tə·raɪz, $'ker·ɪk·tə·aɪz/ *v* [T] • Something which characterizes another thing is typical of it: *Bright colours and bold strokes characterize his early paintings.* • To characterize something also means to describe it by stating its main qualities: *In her essay, she characterizes the whole era* **as** *a period of radical change.*

char·ac·ter·i·za·tion, *Br and Aus usually* **-i·sa·tion** /£ˌkær·ək·tə·raɪ'zeɪ·ʃən, $ˌker-, -rɪ'-/ *n* [C] • *The report strengthens the administration's characterization* (=description) *of the purpose of existing aid.*

char·ac·ter·less /£'kær·ɪk·tə·ləs, $'ker·ɪk·tə-/ *adj* • Something or someone described as characterless lacks interest or style and does not possess any unusual qualities: *It's just one of those characterless modern cities.* ○ *She has the sort of perfect but characterless face that you see on the front of countless women's magazines.*

char·ac·ter [PERSON] /£'kær·ɪk·təʳ, $'ker·ɪk·tə/ *n* [C] a person, esp. when you are describing a particular quality that they have • *She's a curious/interesting character – I don't really know what to think of her.* • *There were one or two strange-looking characters hanging around the bar.* • *(infml)* Someone whose behaviour is different from most people's, esp. in a way that is interesting or amusing, is sometimes referred to as a character: *He's* **quite a** *character*/**a real** *character, is Ted – he's seventy now and still riding that motorbike.* • (DK)(E)

char·ac·ter [REPRESENTATION] /£'kær·ɪk·təʳ, $'ker·ɪk·tə/ *n* [C] a person represented in a film, play or story • *The film revolves around three main characters.* • *She had Mickey Mouse or some other* **cartoon/Disney** *character on her sweater.* • *He made his name as a character* **actor** (=an actor who plays unusual and often humorous people). • *Not renowned for her looks, she was usually chosen for character* **parts** (=playing unusual or humorous people). • *"Six Characters in Search of an Author"* (title of a play by Luigi Pirandello, 1921) • (DK)(E)

char·ac·ter·i·za·tion, *Br and Aus usually* **-i·sa·tion** /£ˌkær·ɪk·tə·raɪ'zeɪ·ʃən, $ˌker-/ *n* [U] • Characterization is the way that people are represented in a film, play or book so that they seem real and natural: *The plots in her books are very strong but there's almost no characterization.* ○ *The film's characterization of the artist* **as** *a complete drunk has annoyed a lot of people.*

char·ac·ter [MARK] /£'kær·ɪk·təʳ, $'ker·ɪk·tə/ *n* [C] a letter, number or other mark or sign used in writing or printing, or the space one of these takes • *The paper was covered in* **a string of** *characters* (=a line of marks, esp. one which does not appear to be arranged into words with meanings). • *The envelope was written in* **Chinese/Japanese** *characters* (=system of writing). • *The computer screen is 66 characters* (=spaces) *wide.* • (DK)(E)

cha·rade /£ʃə'rɑːd, $-'reɪd/ *n* [C] an act or event which is clearly false • *Everyone knew who was going to get the job from the start – the interviews were just a charade.*

cha·rades /£ʃə'rɑːdz, $-'reɪdz/ *pl n* a team game in which each member tries to communicate to the others a particular word or phrase that they have been given by expressing each syllable or word using silent actions

char·coal /£'tʃɑː·kəʊl, $'tʃɑːr·koʊl/ *n* [U] a hard black substance similar to coal which can be used as fuel or, in the form of sticks, as something to draw with • *We need to get some more charcoal for the barbecue.* • *I prefer sketching* **in** *charcoal to pencil.* • *I bought a charcoal* **drawing** *of the cathedral.* • *Their uniform is charcoal* **(grey)** (=dark grey) *and red.*

charge *(obj)* [ASK] /£tʃɑːdʒ, $tʃɑːrdʒ/ *v* to ask (an amount of money) for something, esp. a service or activity • **How much/What** *do you charge* **for** *a haircut and blow-dry?* [T] • *The local museum doesn't charge for admission.* [I] • *They charge you $20 just to get in the nightclub, then you have to pay for drinks.* [+ two objects] • *The bank charged* **commission** *to change my traveller's cheques.* [T] • *(Aus) They charge* **like a wounded bull** (=too much) *for the service.* [I] • If you charge something you have bought **to** your **account**, the amount you have spent is recorded and you pay for it at a later time: *Charge the bill to my account, please.* [T] ○ *Shall we charge the flowers to your account?* [T] ○ *The meal had been charged to his account by mistake.* [T] • [LP] **Two objects**

charge /£tʃɑːdʒ, $tʃɑːrdʒ/ *n* • *The beauty salon's charges are rather high.* [C] • *Is there a charge* **for** *children or do they go free?* [C] • *They'll clean the car while you wait for a modest extra charge.* [C] • *There's an* **admission** *charge of £5.* [C] • *The shop fixed my watch* **free of** *charge!* [U] • **Charge account** is *Am for* **credit account**. See at CREDIT [PAYMENT]. • A **charge card** is a small card which you can get esp. in particular large shops which allows you to take goods by signing a piece of paper and pay for them at a later time. • [LP] **Money**

charge·a·ble /£'tʃɑː·dʒə·bl̩, $'tʃɑːr-/ *adj* [not gradable] • Something is chargeable if you have to pay tax on it: *chargeable earnings/income* ○ *earnings/income chargeable* **to** *tax*

charge *obj* [ACCUSE FORMALLY] /£tʃɑːdʒ, $tʃɑːrdʒ/ *v* [T] *law* (esp. of the police) to make a formal statement saying that (someone) is accused of a crime • *She's been charged* **with** *murder.* • *She is charged* **with** *murdering her husband.* • *(fig.) The paper charged her* **with** *using the company's money for her own purposes.* • *(fig. fml) The opposition has charged* **that** *the government altered the figures to suit themselves.* [+ *that* clause] • [LP] **Crimes and criminals, Law**

charge /£tʃɑːdʒ, $tʃɑːrdʒ/ *n* [C] *law* • *The 19-year-old will be appearing in court on Thursday where she will face* **criminal** *charges.* • *He has been arrested* **on** *a charge* **of** *murder.* • *The police* **brought** *a charge of theft* **against** *him.* • *The police have had to* **drop** (=stop) *charges* **against** *her because they couldn't find any evidence.* • *Her refusal to condemn the violence* **laid/left** *her* **open to** *the charge* **of** *positive support for the campaign* (=allowed people to say that she supported it). • *The family decided not to* **press** *charges against the fraudster* (=not to make their complaint official and have it decided in a court of law). • *He claimed he had been arrested on a* **trumped up** (=false) *charge.* • *(fig.) The president responded angrily to the charge* **that** *she had lost touch with her country's people.* [+ *that* clause] • *(Br)* A **charge sheet** is an official document on which a police officer records the details of a crime of which a person is accused.

charge *(obj)* [MOVE FORWARD] /£tʃɑːdʒ, $tʃɑːrdʒ/ *v* to move forward quickly and violently, esp. towards something which has caused difficulty or annoyance • *The bull lowered its horns and charged.* [I] • *The violence began when the police charged* **(at)** *a crowd of demonstrators.* [T; I + adv/prep] • *(infml)* To charge is also to hurry from one place to another: *I'm exhausted – I've been charging* **about/around** *all day.* [I always + adv/prep] • *I'd forgotten it was her birthday and had to go charging* **into** *town to buy her something.* [I always + adv/prep] • *He came charging* **up** *the stairs to tell me the good news.* [I always + adv/prep]

charge /£tʃɑːdʒ, $tʃɑːrdʒ/ *n* [C] • *a charge of buffalo/elephants* • *a police charge* • *a cavalry charge* • *"The Charge of the Light Brigade"* (title of a poem by Alfred, Lord Tennyson, 1854)

charg·er /£'tʃɑː·dʒəʳ, $'tʃɑːr·dʒə/ *n* [C] *old use or literary* • A charger is a soldier's large strong horse.

charge [CONTROL] /£tʃɑːdʒ, $tʃɑːrdʒ/ *n* responsibility for controlling or caring for something • *Her ex-husband* **has** *charge* **of** *the children during the week and she has them at the weekend.* [U] • *The boss asked him to* **take** *charge* **of** *the office for a few days while she was away.* [U] • *They advertised for a nanny to take/have* **sole** *charge of their children while they were at work.* [U] • To be **in** charge is to be the person responsible: *There's a very angry customer in the shop who wants to know who's in charge.* [U] ○ *Who will be in charge* **of** *the department when Sophie leaves?* [U] ○ *I* *left Jack in charge* **of** *the suitcases while I went to get the tickets.* [U] • *(dated)* A charge is a person, esp. a child, who is in your care and for whom you are responsible: *As a governess, she used to take her little charges to the park in the afternoons.* [C] • *(Br and Aus)* A **charge nurse** is a male nurse who is responsible for a department of a hospital. He is the male equal of a SISTER.

charge *obj* ORDER /£tʃɑːdʒ, $tʃɑːrdʒ/ *v* [T] *fml or dated* to order or instruct (someone) to do something • *She's been charged* **to** *say nothing on the matter.* [+ obj + *to* infinitive] • *She was charged* **with** *taking care of*/**with** *the care of the premises.* • *(Am law)* When a judge charges a JURY (= group of people deciding a legal case), the judge explains the details of the law to them.

charge /£tʃɑːdʒ, $tʃɑːrdʒ/ *n* [C] *fml or dated*

charge·a·ble /£ˈtʃɑː·dʒə·bl̩, $ˈtʃɑːr-/ *adj law*

charge *(obj)* SUPPLY ENERGY /£tʃɑːdʒ, $tʃɑːrdʒ/ *v specialized* to put electricity into (an electrical device such as a BATTERY) • *She drove the car round the block to charge* **(up)** *its batteries.* [T/M] • *It's not working – I don't think the battery is charging.* [I]

charge /£tʃɑːdʒ, $tʃɑːrdʒ/ *n specialized* • The charge of an electrical device is the amount of electricity that it stores or carries. [C usually sing] • *(Br)* If something is **on** charge, you are putting an amount of electricity into it: *Is it all right to* **leave/put** *the battery on charge overnight?* [U] • **Electrical** charge is a basic characteristic of matter: *A proton has* **positive** *charge and an electron has* **negative** *charge.* [U]

charged /£tʃɑːdʒd, $tʃɑːrdʒd/ *adj* • *electrically charged particles/ions* • See also CHARGED.

charge EXPLOSIVE /£tʃɑːdʒ, $tʃɑːrdʒ/ *n* [C] the amount of explosive to be fired at one time, or the bullet or other explosive object fired from a gun

charge *obj* /£tʃɑːdʒ, $tʃɑːrdʒ/ *v* [T] • If you charge a gun, you load it with enough explosive to fire it once.

charged /tʃɑːdʒd/ *adj* (of arguments or subjects) causing strong feelings and differences of opinion or, more generally, filled with emotion or excitement • *Abortion is a* **highly** *charged issue.* • *The film is described as a* **highly** *charged thriller with lots of suspense.* • *He spoke in a voice charged* **with** *emotion.* • See also **charged** at CHARGE SUPPLY ENERGY.

char·gé (d'af·faires) /£ˌʃɑː·ʒeɪ·dæfˈeəʳ, $ˌʃɑːr·ʒeɪ·dæfˈer/ *n* [C] *pl* **chargés (d'affaires)** a person who represents the leader of his or her government, either temporarily while the AMBASSADOR is away, or permanently in a country where there is no ambassador • *the Belgian chargé d'affaires/the chargé d'affaires* **for** *Belgium*

char·i·ot /£ˈtʃær·i·ət, $ˈtʃer-/ *n* [C] a two-wheeled vehicle pulled by a horse that was used in ancient times for racing and fighting

char·i·ot·eer /£ˌtʃær·i·əˈtɪəʳ, $ˌtʃer·i·əˈtɪr/ *n* [C] • A charioteer is a person who drives a chariot.

cha·ris·ma /kəˈrɪz·mə/ *n* [U] a special power which some people possess naturally which makes them able to influence other people and attract their attention and admiration • *On screen Garbo had this great charisma so that you couldn't take your eyes off her.* • *I can't understand how a man* **of** *so little personal charisma came to be prime minister.*

cha·ris·ma·tic /£ˌkær·ɪzˈmæt·ɪk, $-ˈmæt̬-/ *adj* • *Few were able to resist this charismatic and persuasive leader.* • *Always charismatic, if he had not become a politician he would have been an entertainer.*

cha·ris·ma·tic /£ˌkær·ɪzˈmæt·ɪk, $-ˈmæt̬-/ *adj* [not gradable] of various groups within the Christian Church who believe that God gives people special powers, such as the ability to heal others and to speak to him in a special language • *a charismatic church* • *the charismatic movement* • *charismatic gifts*

char·it·a·ble /£ˈtʃær·ɪ·tə·bl̩, $ˈtʃer·ɪ·t̬ə-/ *adj* kind; tending to consider others in a positive way in which you do not judge severely • *Some critics said the show was good in parts – those less charitable said the whole thing was a disaster.*

char·it·ab·ly /£ˈtʃær·ɪ·tə·bli, $ˈtʃer·ɪ·t̬ə-/ *adv* • *She described him, rather charitably, as shy whereas I would have said he was unsociable.*

char·i·ty /£ˈtʃær·ɪ·ti, $ˈtʃer·ɪ·t̬i/ *n* [U] • *I try to show a little charity because I know he's lonely, but it's hard because he's so boring.* • *"And now abideth faith, hope, charity, these three; but the greatest of these is charity"* (Bible, 1 Corinthians 13.13)

char·i·ty /£ˈtʃær·ɪ·ti, $ˈtʃer·ɪ·t̬i/ *n* a system of giving money, food or help free to those who are in need because they are ill, poor or homeless, or any organization which is established to provide money or help in this way • *She does a lot of work for charity.* [U] • *People tend to* **give to** (= give money to) *charity at Christmas time.* [U] • *The old man was entitled to receive financial aid from the government, but was too proud to* **accept** *what he regarded as charity.* [U] • *Proceeds from the sale of these cards will* **go to** (= be given to) *local charities.* [C] • *UNICEF is an international charity.* [C] • *They did a charity performance on the first night to raise money for AIDS research.* • A **charity shop** is a shop in which a charity sells all types of used goods which are given by the public, or in which they sell new goods, to make money for the work of the charity. • *(saying)* 'Charity begins at home' means that people should take care of people who are close to them, esp. those living in the same city or country, before they consider helping people who are living further away or in another country.

char·it·a·ble /£ˈtʃær·ɪ·tə·bl̩, $ˈtʃer·ɪ·t̬ə-/ *adj* [before n] • *a charitable* **foundation/organization/trust** • *The entire organization is funded by charitable donations.* • *The school has charitable* **status** (= It is officially a charity).

char·la·dy /£ˈtʃɑːˌleɪ·di, $ˈtʃɑːr-/ *n* [C] *Br for* CHARWOMAN

char·lat·an /£ˈʃɑː·lə·tən, $ˈʃɑːr·lə·t̬ən/ *n* [C] *disapproving* a person who pretends to have skills or knowledge that they do not have, esp. in medicine • *He was a scientist who claimed to have a miracle cure and was then exposed as a charlatan.* • *Some see the religious leader as a charlatan even though his followers are in their thousands.*

Charles·ton /£ˈtʃɑːl·stən, $ˈtʃɑːrl-/ *n* [C/U] a fast energetic dance that was popular in the 1920s

char·ley horse /£ˈtʃɑː·li, $ˈtʃɑːr-/ *n* [C] *pl* **charley horses** *Am infml* a CRAMP (= a sudden painful tightening of a muscle) in your arm or leg • *Auntie Janet sat on the couch rubbing her leg and complaining about the charley horse she had in her thigh.*

charl·ie /£ˈtʃɑː·li, $ˈtʃɑːr-/ *n* [C] *Br dated infml* a foolish person • *He* **looked a proper/real** *charlie in that hat!* • *He's a* **right** *Charlie.*

charm ATTRACTION /£tʃɑːm, $tʃɑːrm/ *n* a quality which makes you like or feel attracted to someone or something • *He's got a lot of charm – he's an instantly likeable guy.* [U] • *She was a woman* **of** *great charm and she knew how to use it.* [U] • *It's a town with a lot of* **old-world** *charm.* [U] • *Even as a young boy he knew how to* **turn on the** *charm* (= be pleasant intentionally) *when he wanted something.* [U] • *I had to use all my charms to get them to lend us the hall.* [C] • A **charm offensive** is an intentional attempt to achieve something by using charm: *The party leader embarked on a charm offensive to persuade voters that their views were being taken seriously.*

charm *obj* /£tʃɑːm, $tʃɑːrm/ *v* [T] • *He's a very effective boss – he somehow charms you* (= easily persuades you by his pleasant manner) **into doing** *what he wants.* • *(infml humorous) "How did your sister's boyfriend get on with your mum?" "Oh, he* **charmed the pants off** *her – she thinks he's great!"*

charmed /£tʃɑːmd, $tʃɑːrmd/ *adj* • *He said he would be charmed* (= very pleased) *if a woman gave him flowers.* • *(disapproving)* Charmed is sometimes used to express anger when someone does something unhelpful or careless, for example if someone allowed a door to swing back on you: *Charmed, I'm sure!*

charm·er /£ˈtʃɑː·məʳ, $ˈtʃɑːr·mɚ/ *n* [C] • A charmer is a person who has attractive qualities: *Ruth's a little charmer – you'll never meet a more likeable child.* • A charmer is also a person who uses their attractiveness to influence other people, usually for their own purposes: *He's a real charmer is Paul – you want to be careful with him!* • A charmer is also a person without attractive qualities: *He let the door swing back on me – what a charmer!*

charm·less /£ˈtʃɑːm·ləs, $ˈtʃɑːrm-/ *adj disapproving* • *I've always found him a most charmless* (= unpleasant and without charm) *individual/person.*

charm·ing /£ˈtʃɑː·mɪŋ, $ˈtʃɑːr-/ *adj* • *(dated approving)* Charming means pleasant: *"What delightful children!" "Yes, they're charming."* ○ *We had dinner with our director and his charming wife.* ○ *What a charming street you live in.* • *(disapproving)* Charming is also used of people who use their attractiveness to influence people or to make other people like them: *He's very charming but I wouldn't trust* *him.* • *(disapproving)* Charming can also express lack of approval, sometimes humorously: *She invited you out for a drink and then ignored you all evening, did she? – well, that's charming!* ○ *"Shut up, will you, I'm trying to study!" "Oh, charming!"*

charm·ing·ly /£ˈtʃɑː·mɪŋ·li, $ˈtʃɑːr-/ *adv approving* • *Your daughter sings charmingly, Mrs Jones.*

charm JEWELLERY /£tʃɑːm, $tʃɑːrm/ *n* [C] a small, esp. gold or silver, object worn on a chain as jewellery • A **charm bracelet** is a chain which is worn round the wrist and to which small esp. gold or silver objects are fixed. • PIC› **Jewellery**

charm LUCKY OBJECT /£tʃɑːm, $tʃɑːrm/ *n* [C] an object or saying which is thought to possess magical powers, such as the ability to bring good luck • *He keeps a rabbit's paw as a* **lucky/good luck** *charm.*

charmed /£tʃɑːmd, $tʃɑːrmd/ *adj* • Someone who is very lucky or someone who escapes dangerous situations without being hurt can be said to **lead/live a charmed life.**

char·nel (house) /£ˈtʃɑː·nᵊl, $ˈtʃɑːr-/ *n* [C] *old use* a building where the bodies or bones of dead people are kept

chart /£tʃɑːt, $tʃɑːrt/ *n* [C] information given in the form of a GRAPH, DIAGRAM or picture, often intended to show the information more clearly • *There is a chart on the classroom wall showing the relative heights of all the children.* • *The sales chart shows a distinct decline in the past few months.* • *The TV* **weather** *chart showed temperatures and wind speeds expected for the region on the following day.* • A chart is also a detailed map of an area of water: *We bought charts showing the navigable stretches of water in this area.*

chart *obj* /£tʃɑːt, $tʃɑːrt/ *v* [T] • To chart means to show on a chart: *We need some sort of graph on which we can chart our* **progress.** ○ *The map charts the course of the river where it splits into two.* ○ *Captain Cook charted the eastern coast of Australia.* • To chart can also mean to watch with careful attention or to record in detail: *A global study has just been started to chart the effects of climate change.* ○ *The biography charts her dramatic ascent through the ranks of the country's socialist party.* • *(esp. Am)* To chart can also mean to arrange a plan of action: *The local branch of the party is meeting to chart their election campaign.*

chart·er OFFICIAL PAPER /£ˈtʃɑː·təʳ, $ˈtʃɑːr·t̬ɚ/ *n* [C] a formal statement of the rights of a country's people, of an organization or of a particular social group which is agreed by or demanded from a ruler or government • *There is a large pressure group demanding a charter of rights from the government.* • *Education is one of the basic human rights written into the United Nations Charter.* • *The Government produced a Citizen's/Parents'/Patients' Charter.* • *The press was granted a royal charter* **to** *print Bibles.* [+ *to* infinitive]

chart·er *obj* /£ˈtʃɑː·təʳ, $ˈtʃɑːr·t̬ɚ/ *v* [T often passive] • *Cambridge University Press was chartered* (= The official papers creating it were signed) *in 1534.*

chart·er *obj* RENT /£ˈtʃɑː·təʳ, $ˈtʃɑːr·t̬ɚ/ *v* [T] to rent (a vehicle, esp. an aircraft) for a special use and not as part of a regular service • *The company chartered a plane to fly him home for the business meeting.*

chart·er /£ˈtʃɑː·təʳ, $ˈtʃɑːr·t̬ɚ/ *n* [U] • *She runs a company that has boats* **for** *charter.* [U] • *We went to Spain* **on** *a charter* **(flight)**. [C] • *The travel company is one of the major charter* **operators.**

chart·ered /£ˈtʃɑː·təd, $ˈtʃɑːr·t̬ɚd/ *adj* [not gradable] • *A small chartered plane crashed into a hillside in Northern England yesterday, killing six people.* • *They spent their annual holiday on a chartered yacht in the Caribbean.*

chart·ered /£ˈtʃɑː·təd, $ˈtʃɑːr·t̬ɚd/ *adj* [not gradable] *Br and Aus* (of people who do particular jobs) having successfully completed the necessary training and examinations • *He's a chartered* **surveyor/accountant.**

Char·treuse /£ʃɑːˈtrɜːz, $ʃɑːrˈtruːz/ *n* [U] *trademark* a strong French green or yellow alcoholic drink

charts /£tʃɑːts, $tʃɑːrts/ *pl n* **the charts** *infml* the numbered lists produced each week of the records with the highest sales • *the dance/heavy metal charts* • *What number did that record get to* **in** *the charts?* • *It's been number one in the charts for six weeks.*

chart /£tʃɑːt, $tʃɑːrt/ *v* [I] *infml* • *The DJ said he liked the group, although their first record didn't even chart* (= enter the charts).

char·wo·man (*pl* **-women**) /£ˈtʃɑːˌwʊ·mən, $ˈtʃɑːr-/, *Br* **char·la·dy**, *Br infml* **char** *n* [C] *dated* a woman whose job is to clean and tidy an office or private house

cha·ry /£ˈtʃeə·ri, $ˈtʃer·i/ *adj* **-ier, -iest** *slightly dated* doubtful and uncertain; unwilling to take action • *I'm a bit chary* **about/of** *using a travel agency that hasn't got official registration.* • *Banks used to lend money to anyone but they've grown chary since the recession.*

chase *(obj)* FOLLOW /tʃeɪs/ *v* to hurry after (someone or something) in order to catch them • *The police car was going so fast, it must have been chasing someone.* [T] • *She was chasing* **(after)** *a man who had snatched her bag.* [T; I + *after*] • *Could you chase* **(after)** *Jessica with these books that she just left?* [T; I + *after*] • *(fig.) She spent her time chasing* **(after)** (= trying to attract) *other women's husbands.* [T; I + *after*] • *(fig.) It's depressing how many people there are chasing* (= trying to obtain) *so few jobs.* [T] • *(fig.) After years of chasing* (= trying to make real) *her* **dreams,** *she finally got a part in a film.* [T] • To chase can be used more generally to mean hurry or run in various directions: *She couldn't study with the children chasing* **about/around/round** *the house.* [I always + adv/prep] • *(slang)* To **chase the dragon** means to take the drug HEROIN, by smoking it. • If you are **chasing** your **tail** you are busy trying to achieve a lot of things but are not completely successful: *I've been chasing my tail all day trying to get everything ready for my trip, but I still haven't finished packing.*

chase /tʃeɪs/ *n* [C] • *It was one of those boring films with endless* **car/police** *chases.* • **The chase** means the sport of hunting animals: *Asked why he went fox-hunting so much, he replied that he loved* **the thrill of** *the chase.* • *If I were robbed in the street I don't think I'd be brave enough to* **give chase** (= follow the thief to try to catch them).

chas·er /£ˈtʃeɪ·səʳ, $-sɚ/ *n* [C] • *(Br and Aus)* A chaser is a small alcoholic drink which is drunk after a weaker alcoholic drink: *beer with a* **whisky** *chaser* • *(Am)* A chaser is also a drink with little or no alcohol in it which is drunk after a small strong alcoholic drink: *whisky with a beer chaser* ○ *tequila with a grapefruit juice chaser*

chase *obj* GET RID OF /tʃeɪs/ *v* [T] to run after (a person or an animal) threateningly in order to make them leave • *Grandad was a miserable old man who used to chase children* **away** *from his apple trees.* • *(fig.) An early night should chase* **away** *this cold of mine.* • *She's always chasing cats* **out** *of the garden to protect the birds which come to the bird table.* • *(Am)* In baseball, if the PITCHER is chased, he or she is removed from the game because players on the opposing team are hitting the ball well: *That's only the second time in his career that Valenzuela has been chased in the first inning.*

chase *obj* TAKE ACTION /tʃeɪs/ *v* [T] *infml* to take action in order to discover something, or to (cause someone to) do something • *If you don't hear from the builders this week, make sure you chase them.* • *We had to chase* **(up)** *the shop* **to** *deliver the bed.* [T/M + obj + *to* infinitive] • *It's three weeks since you applied for the job – you'd better chase* **it up.** [M] • *I must chase my flatmate* **up** *about those bills and see if she paid them.* [M]

cha·sm /ˈkæz·ᵊm/ *n* [C] a very deep narrow opening in rock, earth or ice • *They leaned over the rails and peered down into the dizzying chasm below.* • *(fig.) Her recently published history of music is well-researched, but the exclusion of modern popular music presents a* **gaping** *chasm* (= its absence means that the book does not seem complete). • A chasm **between** two groups of people or two opinions is a very large difference between them: *There is a chasm between what the government admits and the truth about the appalling situation.* ○ *There is still a vast* **economic** *chasm between developing countries and the United States.* ○ *As president, he tried unsuccessfully to* **bridge** *the* **yawning** *chasm between* (= to reduce the very large difference between) *the north and the south.*

chas·sis /ˈʃæs·i/ *n* [C] *pl* **chassis** /ˈʃæs·i, -iz/ the frame of a vehicle, usually including the wheels and engine, onto which the metal covering is fixed • *The car's lightweight chassis is made from aluminium sheets.* • *In the accident, the main body of the bus was ripped from the chassis and landed in an explosion of breaking glass and flying metal.* • A chassis is also the frame of a piece of electronic equipment, such as a radio or television, onto which the electronic parts are fixed.

chaste /tʃeɪst/ *adj fml or literary* not having had sex, or only having a sexual relationship with the person whom you are married to • *In the past, a woman needed to be chaste to make a good marriage.* • *The author instructs married women to be humble, chaste and obedient at all times.* • *They exchanged a few chaste kisses* (= ones which did not express sexual desire). • Decoration or style that is chaste is very simple: *He likes the simple, chaste lines of the town's architecture.*

chas·ti·ty /£ˈtʃæs·tɪ·ti, $-t̬i/ *n* [U] • Chastity is the state of not having sexual relationships or never having had sex: *As a monk, he had taken vows of chastity, poverty and obedience.* ○ *The education program was designed to promote chastity among young people in an attempt to curb the spread of AIDS.* • In the past, a **chastity belt** was a device that some women were forced to wear to prevent them from having sex. It had a part that went between the woman's legs and a lock so that it could not be removed.

chast·en *obj* /ˈtʃeɪ·sᵊn/ *v* [T] *fml* to make (someone) aware that they have failed or done something wrong and make them want to improve • *The president was greatly chastened by a rebellion that he survived only narrowly and he began to show much greater political flexibility.* • *The defeat was a chastening experience for the Prime Minister.*

chas·tise *obj* /tʃæsˈtaɪz/ *v* [T] *fml* to criticize (someone) strongly • *The ambassador was personally chastised by the Secretary of State* **for** *the behaviour of some of the embassy's staff.* • *Charity organizations have chastised the Government* **for** *not* **doing** *enough to prevent the latest famine in Africa.*

chas·tise·ment /tʃæsˈtaɪz·mənt/ *n* [U] *fml* • *She told us that if our dog did something wrong, the best method of chastisement was to grip it by the scruff of its neck and shake it.*

chat /tʃæt/ *v* [I] **-tt-** to talk to someone in a friendly informal way • *She spends hours on the phone chatting* **to** *her friends.* • *We were just chatting* **about** *what we did last weekend.* • *Whenever I walk in, I always find the two of them chatting* **away** (=talking eagerly). • *(Br and Aus infml)* If you **chat up** (*esp. Am* **come on to**) someone or **chat** someone **up** whom you are sexually attracted to, you talk to them in a friendly way and make your sexual interest known to them: *He spent all evening chatting her up and buying her drinks.* • *(Br and Aus infml)* To **chat up** someone/**chat** someone **up** also means to talk to someone in a friendly and persuasive way in order to obtain something from them: *If you need some more money, why don't you chat your mother up?*

chat /tʃæt/ *n* • A chat is a friendly, informal conversation: *Why don't you give me a call and we'll have a chat?* [C] ○ *When my neighbour comes round, we have lovely long chats about our grandchildren.* [C] ○ *I had a chat* **with** *the boss today* **about** *a salary increase.* [C] ○ *He hates gossip and* **idle** *chat* (=conversation about unimportant things). [U] • *(Br)* A **chat show** is an informal television or radio programme on which famous people are asked questions about themselves and their work. Compare **talk show** at TALK. • *(Br and Aus infml)* A **chat-up line** (*Am* **come-on line**) is a remark which someone makes to a person whom they are sexually attracted to in order to make their sexual interest known to them and start a conversation with them: *"Have you been here before?" "That's one of the oldest chat-up lines I've ever heard!"* • See also CHIT-CHAT.

chat·ty /£ˈtʃæt·i, $ˈtʃæt̬-/ *adj* **-ier, -iest** *infml* • If someone is chatty, they like to talk a lot in a friendly informal way: *My neighbour's a friendly, chatty sort of man.* • If a piece of writing is chatty, it is informal: *The book's style of writing is relaxed and chatty.*

chat·eau /£ˈʃæt·əʊ, $ʃætˈoʊ/ *n* [C] *pl* **chateaux** /£ˈʃæt·əʊ, £-əʊz, $ʃætˈoʊ, $-ˈoʊz/ a large house or castle in France

chat·line /ˈtʃæt·laɪn/ *n* [C] *Br* a telephone service where callers can speak to other callers or to employees of the company • *He ran up an enormous phone bill by ringing up chatlines all the time.*

chat·tel /£ˈtʃæt·ᵊl, $ˈtʃæt̬-/ *n* [C] *fml or old use* a personal possession • *He treated his wife as little more than a chattel.* • *The floods had devastating effects on most people's lives, causing famine, the spread of disease and the loss of chattels.*

chat·ter /£ˈtʃæt·əʳ, $ˈtʃæt̬·ɚ/ *v* [I] (of people) to talk continuously and eagerly, or *(fig.)* (of animals or machines) to make quick repeated noises • *She spent the morning chattering* **away** *to her friends.* • *It really irritates me the way he chatters* **on about** *nothing all the time.* • *(fig.) The gun shot made the monkeys chatter in alarm.* • *(fig.) The noise of old-fashioned computer printers chattering* **away** *gave her a headache.* • If your teeth chatter, they knock together repeatedly because you are very cold or frightened: *I could hardly talk, my teeth were chattering so much.* • *(Br infml disapproving)* The **chattering classes** are well-educated middle class people who enjoy discussing political, cultural and social matters and who are willing to express an opinion about almost any subject: *She hates the snobbery of the chattering classes.* ○ *The prevailing view among the chattering classes is that the country has returned to its depressingly familiar path of post-war decline.*

chat·ter /£ˈtʃæt·əʳ, $ˈtʃæt̬·ɚ/ *n* [U] • *Once the teacher left the room, the chatter in the classroom gradually rose to a din.* • *Stop this* **idle** *chatter* (=Stop talking about unimportant things) *you two, there's work to be done.* • *(fig.) He could hear the chatter of birds in the trees overhead.*

chat·ter·box /£ˈtʃæt·ə·bɒks, $ˈtʃæt̬·ɚ·bɑːks/ *n* [C] *infml esp. disapproving* a person, esp. a child, who likes to talk continuously, usually about unimportant things • *Your sister's a real chatterbox!*

chat·ty /£ˈtʃæt·i, $ˈtʃæt̬-/ *adj* **-ier, -iest** *infml* See at CHAT

chauf·feur /£ˈʃəʊ·fəʳ, $ʃoʊˈfɜːr/ *n* [C] a person employed as a driver by a rich or important person who does not want to drive their own car • *As a company director, she has a chauffeur-driven limousine to take her everywhere.* • Ⓕ

chauf·feur *obj* /£ˈʃəʊ·fəʳ, $ʃoʊˈfɜːr/ *v* [T] • To chauffeur someone somewhere is to drive them there: *His mother spoils him terribly and chauffeurs him* **(around/about)** *everywhere.*

chau·vi·nism /£ˈʃəʊ·vɪ·nɪ·zᵊm, $ˈʃoʊ-/ *n* [U] *disapproving* the strong and unreasonable belief that your own country, sex or race is the best or most important • *The war stimulated an intense national chauvinism.* • *Local chauvinism has been the main cause of the fighting.* • *His* **male** *chauvinism led him to believe that women were less intelligent than men.* • LP **Sexist language**

chau·vi·nist /£ˈʃəʊ·vɪ·nɪst, $ˈʃoʊ-/ *n* [C] *disapproving* • *She called him a* **(male)** *chauvinist because of his insistence on calling all women 'girls'.*

chau·vi·nist /£ˈʃəʊ·vɪ·nɪst, $ˈʃoʊ-/, **chau·vi·nist·ic** /£ˌʃəʊ·vɪˈnɪs·tɪk, $ˌʃoʊ-/ *adj disapproving* • *The crowd was enthusiastically singing chauvinistic patriotic songs.* • *It is a deeply chauvinist community where the few women who have jobs are ridiculed.*

chau·vi·nist·ic·ally /£ˌʃəʊ·vɪˈnɪs·tɪ·kli, $ˌʃoʊ-/ *adv disapproving* • *She was shocked that he had behaved so chauvinistically.*

cheap /tʃiːp/ *adj* **-er, -est** costing little money or less than is usual or expected • *The suits in the sale are really cheap – they're reduced from £200 to £95.* • *If there's four of us in the car, it'll be cheaper to drive than to go by train.* • *"How much was your flight?" "I got it at the last moment, so it was* **dirt** *cheap* (=it cost very little money)." • *Children and the elderly are entitled to cheap train* **tickets**. • *The scheme is simple and cheap* **to** *operate.* [+ *to* infinitive] • If a shop or restaurant is cheap, it charges low prices: *I get my hair cut at the cheapest hairdresser's in town.* • *(disapproving)* A cheap service is one which people get for less money than they should because they are taking unfair advantage of people or of a situation: *During times of mass unemployment, there's a pool of cheap* **labour** *for employers to draw from.* • If someone says that a person's life is cheap, they mean that it is unimportant and of little value: *In a war, human life becomes very cheap.* • *(disapproving)* Goods that are cheap are both low in quality and low in price: *"Is that a bottle of good wine that you're using to cook with?" "No, it's only cheap wine."* ○ *I bought a pair of cheap shoes which fell apart after two weeks.* • *(infml disapproving)* If someone is cheap, they are unwilling to spend money: *He's so cheap he didn't even buy me a card for my birthday.* • *(disapproving)* If you describe the way a person is dressed as cheap, you mean that it is very obvious that they are trying to sexually attract other people: *Her mother told her she wasn't allowed to go out wearing a tight skirt and lots of make-up because it made her look cheap.* • *(disapproving)* Cheap behaviour or humour is unpleasant and unkind: *I wish you'd stop making cheap jokes about my friends.* • *(Br) There's a restaurant round the corner that serves* **cheap and cheerful** *food* (=cheap but enjoyable food). • *(Br and Aus)* Something that is **cheap and nasty** costs little to buy and of very bad quality. • *(infml)* If you say that something is **cheap at half the price**, you mean that it is very good value and the price does not seem expensive. • If someone or something makes you **feel** cheap, it makes you feel ashamed or embarrassed: *The way he just left me alone at the disco made me feel so cheap.* • *(infml)* If you get goods **on the cheap**, you obtain them for a low price, often from someone you know who works in the company or business that produces them: *He did a deal with a man he knew in the* *car trade and got his new car on the cheap.* • **Cheap rate** is the amount charged for a service which is lower than usual because there is not so much demand for the service at that time: *Cheap rate for overseas telephone calls is from 8p.m to 8a.m.* • LP> **Expensive**

cheap /tʃiːp/ *adv* **-er, -est** • *I bought some chairs in the market which were* **going** *cheap* (=they were not expensive). • If you say that something **does not come cheap**, you mean that it is of good quality and is therefore expensive: *I'm a well-qualified accountant, so my services don't come cheap.*

cheap·en *obj* /ˈtʃiː·pᵊn/ *v* [T] • If you cheapen goods, you reduce their price: *American steel has been cheapened due to the fall in the dollar.* • *(disapproving)* If a person is cheapened by something or someone, they are made to lose their good reputation and the respect that others feel for them: *She thought that the photos were exploitative and cheapened her.* ○ *Hollywood stars dread cheapening their reputations by appearing in the wrong movie.* • *(disapproving)* If you cheapen something, you make it lose its value or artistic quality: *The film cheapened the story by turning it into a tear-jerking romance.*

cheap·ly /ˈtʃiː·pli/ *adv* • *The shop round the corner does shoe repairs very cheaply.*

cheap·ness /ˈtʃiːp·nəs/ *n* [U] • *The relative cheapness of foreign travel means that more people are going abroad than ever before.* • *The goods were produced using mass-production methods to ensure both cheapness and quality.*

cheap·o /£ˈtʃiː·pəʊ, $-poʊ/ *adj* [before n] *infml* • Something which is cheapo is low in price and often low in quality: *We stayed in a cheapo hotel to save money.* ○ *I bought a cheapo computer because I just needed something for word processing.*

cheap·y, cheap·ie /ˈtʃiː·pi/ *n* [C], *adj* [before n] *infml* • *My new jacket was a cheapie* (=It cost very little money). • Cheapy can also mean low in quality: *It was one of those cheapy movies, which cost very little to make but which are very popular at the box office.*

cheap·skate /ˈtʃiːp·skeɪt/ *n* [C], *adj infml disapproving* (typical of) a person who is unwilling to spend more than the smallest possible amount of money • *My Dad's such a cheapskate that he's put a lock on the telephone.* • *If you hire cheapskate builders* (=builders who use the cheapest possible materials), *you'll regret it in the future.*

cheat *(obj)* /tʃiːt/ *v* to behave in a dishonest way in order to get what you want • *Anyone caught cheating will be immediately disqualified from the exam.* [I] • *Did you know that he cheats* **at** *cards?* [I] • *She cheated* **in** *the test by copying from the boy in front.* [I] • *He's a crooked businessman who cheats the taxman* (=avoids paying taxes by using illegal methods). [T] • *(literary)* If someone cheats **death**, they manage to stay alive when it was likely that they would die: *As a racing driver, he had been involved in many serious crashes and had cheated death on several occasions.* [T] • If you are cheated **(out) of** something which should belong to you, you are unfairly prevented from obtaining or achieving it: *He thought that he had been cheated of some of his wages by his employer.* [T] ○ *She claimed that her cousin had cheated her out of her inheritance.* [T] ○ *The French team feel the weather cheated them of their victory.* [T] • *(infml)* If you cheat **on** your husband, wife or usual sexual partner, you secretly have a sexual relationship with someone else: *He has lots of affairs, but his wife doesn't seem to know that he cheats on her.* [I]

cheat /tʃiːt/ *n* [C] • A cheat is a person who behaves in a dishonest way: *Trouble broke out in the match when one of the players called a member of the other team a cheat.* • A cheat is also something dishonest which makes people believe that something is true when it is not: *I made the cake using cocoa powder rather than chocolate – it's a bit of a cheat, but nobody will notice the difference.*

check *(obj)* EXAMINE /tʃek/ *v* to make certain that (something or someone) is correct, safe or suitable by examining it or them quickly • *You should always check your oil, water and tyres before taking your car on a long trip.* [T] • *I've checked her references and she seems very suitable for the job.* [T] • *Customs stopped us and checked* (=searched) *our bags* **for** *alcohol and cigarettes.* [T] • *After I had finished the exam, I checked* **(through/over)** *my answers* **for** *mistakes.* [T] • *The doctor will call next week to check* **on** *your progress.* [I] • *My wife checks* **on** (=visits) *our elderly neighbour every few days to make sure that he's alright.* [I] • *You should always check* **(that)** *you've shut the windows before you leave the house.* [+ *(that)* clause] • *I rang them yesterday to check* **when** *the party was.* [+ *wh-* word] • *He* **double-checked** *all the doors* (=checked them all twice) *before leaving the house.* [T] • *If you're near the garage, could you check* **to see** (=ask) *if the car's ready?* [+ *to* infinitive] • *If you're unsure of your legal rights, I would check* **with** (=ask) *a lawyer.* [I] • *They always check* **out** (=find information about) *candidates very thoroughly before interviewing them.* [M] • *(infml) Let's go and check* **out** *the disco on Friday night* (=see what it is like). [M] • See also CROSSCHECK.

check /tʃek/ *n* [C] • *The soldiers gave their equipment a final check before setting off.* • *"I can't find my keys." "Have another check* **in/through** *your jacket pockets."* • *A check* **with** *her boss revealed that she hadn't taken a day off for two years.* • **Security** *checks have become really strict at the airport.* • *The police are carrying out* **spot** *checks on* (=quick examinations of a limited number of) *drivers over the Christmas period to make sure they are not drinking and driving.* • *Every week I go round to Aunt Edie to* **have/keep** *a check* **on** *whether* (=make certain that) *she's alright.* • *I'll just* **run** *a check* **on** (=find information about) *that name for you in the computer.*

check·er /£ˈtʃek·əʳ, $-ɚ/ *n* [C] *Am* • A checker is a CASHIER.

check *obj* STOP /tʃek/ *v* [T] to stop (someone) from doing or saying something, or to prevent (something) from increasing or continuing • *The manager checked her in the middle of a torrent of complaints with a request that she be quiet.* • *They have begun to vaccinate children in an attempt to check the spread of the disease.* • *The advance of the rebel forces towards the capital has been checked by a government air bombardment.*

check /tʃek/ *n* • If you **hold/keep** something **in check**, you limit it: *We must find ways of keeping our expenditure in check.* ○ *She tried and failed to hold the enthusiasm of her supporters in check* (=to stop them from being too eager). • **Checks and balances** are laws or rules which make certain that no single person or group within the government or organization has too much power, or that particular things or places that need protecting are not harmed: *Once the system of local government is reorganized, the checks and balances provided by district councils to protect the local countryside will be lost.*

check *obj* LEAVE /tʃek/ *v* [T] to leave (something) at a particular place in the care of someone, so that it can be sent by aircraft to another place • *You will be given a seat number when you check* **(in)** *your bags at the desk.* [T/M] • *I'm stopping in Rome for five hours, but I want my baggage checked* **through** (=sent) *direct to Addis Ababa, please.* • *(Am)* To check something also means to leave it with someone at a particular place, so that they can take care of it for a short time: *It's quite hot in here. Let's check our coats before going round the gallery.* • See also CHECK IN.

check /tʃek/ *n* [C] *Am* • A check is the ticket or small object which you are given when you leave your coat or another personal possession somewhere for a short time.

check PATTERN /tʃek/ *n* [C] a pattern of squares formed by lines of different colours crossing each other • *The shirt has a pattern of blue and yellow checks.* • *He was wearing a grey check suit.* • PIC> **Patterns**

checked /tʃekt/ *adj* [not gradable] • *I've just bought a red and white checked tablecloth.*

check AGREE /tʃek/ *v* [I] *esp. Am* (of information) to agree with other information • *Her statement checks* **with** *most of the eye-witness reports.*

check *obj* THREATEN /tʃek/ *v* [T] *specialized* (in the game of CHESS) to put (the other player's king) under direct attack, so that the other player is forced to defend against the attack in their next move

check /tʃek/ *n* [U] *specialized* • If your king is **in** check, it is being directly attacked by the other player: *Your king is in check* **from** *my knight.* • To **give** check is to directly attack the other player's king: *I think I should have given check at move 23 instead of trying to find a safer square for the rook.* • If you directly attack the other player's king, you usually say 'check'. • See also CHECKMATE.

check *(obj)* MARK /tʃek/ *v* [I/T], *n* [C] *Am for* TICK MARK

check MONEY /tʃek/ *n* [C] *Am for* CHEQUE • **Checking account** is *Am for* **current account**. See at CURRENT NOW.

check RESTAURANT /tʃek/ *n* [C] *Am and Scot Eng for* BILL REQUEST FOR PAYMENT • *The food at the restaurant was* *great, but it took them forever to bring us the check.* • *Waiter! Can I have the check, please?*

check in *v adv* [I] to report your arrival at an airport or hotel so that you can be told the number of your seat in the aircraft, or be given the key to your hotel room • *Because of strict security measures, passengers are requested to check in three hours before the flight.* • *Please would you check in* **at** *the reception desk and sign your names in the book.* • *When we got to Chicago, we checked* **into** *the best hotel in town.*

check-in /'tʃek·ɪn/ *n* [C] • *A representative from the tour company will meet you at the check-in.* • A check-in **desk/counter** at an airport is a place where you report your arrival, leave your bags, and are given your seat number. • *(Br)* A check-in **hall** is the area in an airport where people go to report their arrival and obtain information about flights.

check off *obj*, **check** *obj* **off** *v adv* [M] to mark (names or items on a list) as correct or as having been dealt with • *He checked off their names on the list and then said that they could get on the coach.*

check /tʃek/ *exclamation Am* • Check is used to react positively to someone who is making certain that all the items on a list have been dealt with or included: *"Did you bring your sleeping bag?" "Check* (= Yes)*." "Pillow?" "Check."*

check out *v adv* [I] to leave a hotel, after paying and returning your room key • *We checked out* **of/from** *our hotel at 5a.m. to catch a 7a.m. flight.* • See also CHECKOUT.

check up *v adv* [I] to obtain information about someone in order to discover whether they are suitable for something, or to discover what someone is doing in order to make certain that they are behaving correctly or legally • *My mother used to visit me twice a term at college to check up* **on** *me.* • *If the tax inspector checks up* **on** *you and finds you've been falsifying your statements, you're going to be in trouble.* • See also CHECKUP.

check·ered /£'tʃek·əd, $-ɚd/ *adj Am for* CHEQUERED [PATTERN]

check·ers /£'tʃek·əz, $-ɚz/ *pl n Am for* DRAUGHTS

check·list /'tʃek·lɪst/ *n* [C] a list of things that you must remember to do, or a list of important things which you should consider before making a decision • *I have a checklist of things that I must remember to do before I go away, such as asking my neighbours to feed the cat.* • *The company has prepared a checklist on interviewing skills to help their employees interview candidates for new posts.*

check·mate /'tʃek·meɪt/, *infml* **mate** *n* [U] a winning position in CHESS in which you have put the other player's king under a direct attack from which it cannot escape • *Whichever way you play, it will be checkmate in three moves.* • *He resigned at move 28 when facing inevitable checkmate.* • Checkmate is also a situation in which someone has been defeated or a plan cannot develop or continue: *The no-confidence vote is checkmate* (= defeat) *at last for the prime minister.* • Compare STALEMATE.

check·mate *obj* /'tʃek·meɪt/, *infml* **mate** *v* [T] • *My Dad can always checkmate me/my king within twenty moves.* • *(fig.) The Government's attempt to limit wage increases and so cut the rate of inflation has been checkmated* (= defeated) *by union resistance.*

check·out /'tʃek·aʊt/ *n* [C] the place in a shop, esp. a large food shop, where you pay for your goods • *Your fruit and vegetables will be weighed at the checkout.* • *She spent her holidays working* **on** *the checkout at the local supermarket.* • See also CHECK OUT. • [PIC]> **Supermarket**

check·point /'tʃek·pɔɪnt/ *n* [C] a place where people are stopped and questioned and vehicles are examined, esp. at a border between two countries • *Checkpoints have been established all along the border between the two countries.* • *Checkpoint Charlie used to be the most famous border crossing between East and West Berlin.* • (J) (KOR)

check·room /'tʃek·ruːm, -rʊm/ *n* [C] *Am for* CLOAKROOM or **left-luggage office**, see at LEAVE [NOT TAKE]

check·up /'tʃek·ʌp/ *n* [C] a medical examination to test your general state of health • *She goes to her doctor for regular checkups.* • *You should have a dental checkup once every six months.* • See also CHECK UP.

ched·dar /£'tʃed·əʳ, $-ɚ/ *n* [U] a type of hard cheese which is yellow or white in colour • *Cheddar is the most popular type of cheese in Britain.* • *Do you prefer* **mild** *or* **mature** *cheddar?*

cheek [BODY PART] /tʃiːk/ *n* [C] the soft part of your face which is below your eye and between your mouth and ear • *Tears of joy ran down her cheeks.* • *She has pink, rosy cheeks.* • *He embraced her, kissing her on both cheeks.* • *(infml)* A cheek is also either of the two halves of your bottom: *I lowered my trousers for the injection and the doctor asked me in which cheek I wanted it.* • Something or someone that is **cheek by jowl** with something or someone else is very close to that thing or person: *In the village you will find pretty little cottages cheek by jowl* **with** *huge factories.*

-cheeked /-tʃiːkt/ *combining form* • *He was red-/rosy-cheeked after his early morning run in the park.*

cheek [BEHAVIOUR] /tʃiːk/ *n* [U] rudeness or lack of respect • *He told me off for being late when he arrived half an hour after me. What* **a** *cheek!* • *Your daughter has some cheek* **to** *take your car without asking.* [+ *to* infinitive] • *First he messed up my work and then he had the cheek* **to** *accuse me of being disorganized.* [+ *to* infinitive] • *She's always getting into trouble for* **giving** *her teachers cheek* (= being rude to them).

cheek·y /'tʃiː·ki/ *adj* **-ier, -iest** • Someone or something that is cheeky is rude and shows a lack of respect: *He's a cheeky adolescent.* ○ *That's a bit of a cheeky comment.* ○ *Don't be so cheeky!*

cheek·i·ly /'tʃiː·kɪ·li/ *adv* • *He cheekily asked his sister which of her many boyfriends she was going to see that night.*

cheek·i·ness /'tʃiː·kɪ·nəs/ *n* [U] • *I'm sick and tired of her bad behaviour and cheekiness!*

cheek·bone /£'tʃiːk·bəʊn, $-boʊn/ *n* [C usually pl] one of the two bones at the top of your CHEEKS, just below your eye and towards your ear • *She has a beautiful face with large eyes and* **high** *cheekbones.*

cheep /tʃiːp/ *n* [C] the high weak cry made by a young bird • *I could hear a faint cheep from high up in the tree.* • *(fig. infml) He seemed annoyed about something, but I couldn't get a cheep* **out of** *him* (= he would not say anything).

cheep /tʃiːp/ *v* [I] • *As soon as it stopped raining, the birds began cheeping again.*

cheer *(obj)* /£tʃɪəʳ, $tʃɪr/ *v* to give a loud shout of approval or encouragement • *Everyone cheered as the winners received their medals.* [I] • *We stood behind the goal and cheered madly* **for** *our daughter's team.* [I] • *As the runners went by, we cheered them* **(on)**. [T/M]

cheer /£tʃɪəʳ, $tʃɪr/ *n* [C] • *Her speech was received with cheers and a standing ovation.* • *His victory in the 400m earned him* (= He was given) *the biggest cheer of the afternoon.* • **Three** *cheers for the winning team* (= Let's give them three shouts of approval)*!*

cheers /£tʃɪəz, $tʃɪrz/ *exclamation esp. Br and Aus infml* • Cheers is a friendly expression spoken by people just before they start to drink a usually alcoholic drink. • *(Br infml)* Cheers is also used to mean thank you or goodbye: *"I've booked you a seat on the 5 o'clock coach." "Cheers, mate."* ○ *"I'll see you next week then. Bye." "Cheers, see you."* • [LP]> **Phrases and customs**

cheer up *(obj)*, **cheer** *(obj)* **up** *v adv* to (cause someone to) feel encouraged and happier • *When I was ill, several friends sent me flowers to cheer me up.* [M] • *He cheered up* **at** *the thought that it was nearly the holidays.* [I] • *Cheer up! Everything will turn out okay in the end.* [I]

cheer /£tʃɪəʳ, $tʃɪr/ *n* [U] *fml or dated* • Cheer is a feeling of happiness: *The victory in the by-election has brought great cheer to the Liberal Democrats.* • *(dated)* **Be of good cheer** means be happy.

cheer·ful /£'tʃɪə·fᵊl, $'tʃɪr-/ *adj* • Someone who is cheerful is happy and shows this by their expression and behaviour: *He's a very cheerful person.* ○ *You're in a cheerful mood this morning.* ○ *The promise of brilliant sunshine got the bank holiday weekend off to a cheerful start today.* ○ *She manages to stay cheerful* (= happy and positive) *even in the midst of disaster.* • If a thing or place is cheerful, it is bright and pleasant and is likely to make you feel positive and happy: *The doctor's waiting room was bright and cheerful with a yellow carpet and curtains.* ○ *Turn that dreadful wailing music off and put on something cheerful.* • If someone is cheerful **about** a situation which could be unpleasant or full of problems, they are not worried about it: *She's fairly cheerful about her exam results, although she knows she hasn't done very well.*

cheer·ful·ly /£'tʃɪə·fᵊl·i, $'tʃɪr-/ *adv* • *She walked down the road, whistling cheerfully.* • *"I lose about £2000 a year on gambling," he admitted cheerfully* (= in a way that showed he was not worried).

cheer·ful·ness /£'tʃɪə·fᵊl·nəs, $'tʃɪr-/ *n* [U] • *She said that the qualities which made a good nurse were patience, honesty and, above all, cheerfulness.* • *Midday sun streamed* *into the drab little room which gave it a sudden cheerfulness* (= it became bright and pleasant).

cheer·less /£'tʃɪə·ləs, $'tʃɪr-/ *adj* • If something is cheerless, it is not bright or pleasant: *It was a cold and cheerless winter afternoon and I had no desire to go out for a walk.* ○ *They live in a bare, cheerless apartment in downtown New York.*

cheer·less·ness /£'tʃɪə·lə·snəs, $'tʃɪr-/ *n* [U] • *His early works are bright and optimistic, but his later works are characterized by a gloomy cheerlessness.*

cheer·y /£'tʃɪə·ri, $'tʃɪr·i/ *adj* **-ier, -iest** • Someone or something that is cheery is bright and happy: *They mumbled a hello, but I said a loud and cheery "Good morning!"* ○ *He gave me a cheery wave as I drove past his house.* ○ *She was in an usually cheery mood.* • If a colour is cheery, it is warm and bright and makes you feel happy: *Sally was wearing jeans and a cheery red jumper.* • *(Br infml)* **Cheery-bye** means goodbye.

cheer·i·ly /£'tʃɪə·rɪ·li, $'tʃɪr·ɪ-/ *adv* • *He cheerily told her the good news.* • *Beth lay on the sofa, talking cheerily with her old friend Louise.*

chee·ri·ness /£'tʃɪə·rɪ·nəs, $'tʃɪr·ɪ-/ *n* [U] • *I've just bought a bright red suit because I like the cheeriness of the colour.*

cheer·i·o *Br infml* /£ˌtʃɪə·ri'əʊ, $ˌtʃɪr·i'oʊ/ *exclamation* goodbye • *"Cheerio, Tom" she said. "Have a good trip."* • [LP] **Meeting someone**

cheer·lead·er /£'tʃɪəˌliː·dəʳ, $'tʃɪrˌliː·dɚ/ *n* [C] (esp. in America) a person, usually a woman or girl, who leads the crowd in shouting encouragement and supporting a team at a sports event • *At high school, she was a cheerleader and a straight A student.* • *She was a cheerleader* **for** *the Dallas Cowboys.*

cheers /£tʃɪəz, $tʃɪrz/ *exclamation esp. Br infml* See at CHEER

cheer·y /£'tʃɪə·ri, $'tʃɪr·i/ *adj* **-ier, -iest** See at CHEER UP

cheese [FOOD] /tʃiːz/ *n* a food made from milk, which can either be firm or soft and is usually yellow or white in colour • *I'm a vegetarian, so I eat a lot of cheese and eggs for protein.* [U] • *Would you like a slice/piece of cheese with your bread?* [U] • **Goat's** *cheese* (= Cheese made with goats' milk) *has a very strong flavour.* [U] • *You need 250g of* **grated** *cheese for this recipe.* [U] • *I've bought a large Stilton cheese to eat over the Christmas holidays.* [C] • *Red Leicester and Double Gloucester are two of my favourite* **hard** *cheeses.* [C] • *He likes* **soft** *French cheeses such as Brie and Camembert.* [C] • A **cheese knife** is a small knife with a curved blade that ends in two sharp points which is used to cut and pick up a piece of cheese. • If you are taking a photograph of someone and you want them to smile, you sometimes tell them to **say cheese**: *Come on everyone, say cheese for the camera.* • *(infml)* You say *(Br)***hard/tough/***(Aus)***stiff cheese** to someone who has just failed to do or achieve something in order to express your sympathy with them or to show that you are not upset by their bad luck. • [PIC] **Cutlery**

chees·y /'tʃiː·zi/ *adj* **-ier, -iest** • If food is cheesy, it tastes like cheese: *This is meant to be a meat pie but it has a sort of cheesy taste.* • *(Br and Aus infml)* If someone's feet, shoes or socks are cheesy, they smell unpleasant: *He's got awful cheesy feet.* • *(Br and Aus infml)* A cheesy smile is a wide smile which is not always sincere: *She gave a cheesy* **grin** *to the cameras.* • See also CHEESY.

cheese *obj* [GO AWAY] /tʃiːz/ *v* [T] **cheese it** *Am slang* used as an exclamation to tell someone that they should leave quickly • *Cheese it! The cops are coming!*

cheese off *obj*, **cheese** *obj* **off** /tʃiːz/ *v adv* [M] *Br and Aus infml* to annoy (someone) • *Her attitude to the whole thing really cheeses me off!*

cheesed off /tʃiːzd/ *adj Br and Aus infml* • If someone is cheesed off, they are annoyed and disappointed with something or someone: *I'm really cheesed off* **with** *him – he didn't even let me know he couldn't come to the party!*

cheese·board /£'tʃiːz·bɔːd, $-bɔːrd/ *n* [C] a board on which several different types of cheese are arranged for you to choose from at the end of a meal • [PIC] **Cutlery**

cheese·burg·er /£'tʃiːzˌbɜː·gəʳ, $-ˌbɜːr·gɚ/ *n* [C] meat which has been cut into very small pieces, pressed into a round flat shape and cooked, which is eaten between two halves of a small loaf of bread with a slice of melted cheese • *A cheeseburger and fries, please.*

cheese·cake [FOOD] /'tʃiːz·keɪk/ *n* a cake made from a layer of biscuit, or a sweet pastry base, covered with soft cheese, eggs, sugar and sometimes fruit • *Sarah makes the best cheesecake in Cambridge.* [U] • *Gordon has made a terrific cheesecake for dessert.* [C]

cheese·cake [WOMEN] /'tʃiːz·keɪk/ *n* [U] *esp. Am dated slang* photographs in newspapers and magazines of attractive women who are wearing very few clothes and who are photographed in a way that emphasizes the sexual attractiveness of their bodies, or the women who appear in such photographs • *She was rather shocked to see he had a cheesecake photograph of his girlfriend prominently displayed on his desk at work.* • Compare BEEFCAKE.

cheese·cloth /£'tʃiːz·klɒθ, $-klɑːθ/ *n* [U] thin rough cotton cloth which is woven loosely • *Strain the mixture through cheesecloth or a strainer.* • *She was wearing a long cotton skirt and a cheesecloth shirt.*

cheese·par·ing /£'tʃiːzˌpeə·rɪŋ, $-ˌper·ɪŋ/ *n* [U], *adj disapproving* (involving an) unwillingness to spend money • *The opposition party has called for less cheeseparing on the financing of the committee which supervises electricity companies.* • *The company has such a cheeseparing attitude that it makes all its executives travel by train rather than fly.*

chees·y /'tʃiː·zi/ *adj* **-ier, -iest** *Am infml* cheap or of low quality • *He rented an apartment in a seedy neighborhood and furnished it with a few cheesy chairs and a bed.* • See also **cheesy** at CHEESE.

chee·tah /£'tʃiː·tə, $-t̬ə/ *n* [C] a wild cat-like animal with yellowish brown fur and black spots, which can run faster than any other animal • *Cheetahs are mainly found in Africa.* • *The cheetah can run at a speed of 110 km/h.* • [PIC] **Cats**

chef /ʃef/ *n* [C] a skilled and trained cook who works in a hotel or restaurant, esp. the most important cook • *He is one of the top chefs in Britain.* • *She is* **head**-*chef at the Waldorf-Astoria.* • (CS) (D) (DK) (F) (NL) (P) (PL) (RUS) (S)

chef d'oeuv·re /£ˌʃeɪd'ɜː·vrə, $-'ɜːr-/ *n* [C] *pl* **chefs d'oeuvre** /£ˌʃeɪd'ɜː·vrə, $-'ɜːr-/ *fml* an artist or writer's greatest piece of work • *This painting is widely regarded as the artist's chef d'oeuvre.*

chem·i·cal /'kem·ɪ·kəl/ *n* [C] any basic substance which is used in or produced by a reaction involving changes to atoms or MOLECULES • *The chemicals in those glass bottles are strong acids, so be careful when handling them.* • *Excessive amounts of alcohol damage the liver and affect its ability to break down chemicals in the body.* • *The government has pledged to reduce the amount of chemicals used in food production.* • *Each year, factories release millions of tonnes of* **toxic** (= poisonous) *chemicals into the atmosphere.* • *The event is being sponsored by a major chemicals company.*

chem·i·cal /'kem·ɪ·kəl/ *adj* • *The chemical industry produces such things as petrochemicals, drugs, paint and rubber.* • *The government has said that it will never use a nuclear bomb except against a chemical* **attack** (= an attack using chemical weapons). • **Chemical engineering** is the design and operation of machinery used in industrial chemical processes. • A **chemical equation** is a symbolic representation of the changes which happen in a chemical reaction. • A **chemical formula** is the representation of a substance using the symbols of its elements: *H_2O is the chemical formula for water.* • A **chemical reaction** is a process in which the atomic or MOLECULAR structure of a substance is changed: *When potassium is added to water, a violent chemical reaction takes place.* • **Chemical warfare** is the use of poisonous gases and other harmful chemicals against enemy forces. • **Chemical weapons** are substances such as poisonous gases, rather than explosives, which can be used to kill or injure people: *Almost all countries say they want to ban the use of chemical weapons.*

chem·i·cal·ly /'kem·ɪ·kli/ *adv* • *Molecules of substances that are chemically very different can look surprisingly similar.* • *The fund provides money to clean up chemically polluted industrial sites.*

che·mise /ʃə'miːz/ *n* [C] a loose piece of clothing for women which covers the top part of the body and which is worn under other clothes

chem·ist *Br and Aus* /'kem·ɪst/, *Br and Aus also* **chem·ist's**, **phar·ma·cy**, *Am* **drug·store** *n* [C] a shop where you can buy medicines, including those which can only be ordered for someone by a doctor, make-up and products used for washing yourself • *I bought my mother some perfume at the chemist down the road.* • *I have to go to the chemist's and get my prescription made up.*

chem·ist·ry /'kem·ɪ·stri/ *n* [U] (the part of science which studies) the basic characteristics of substances and the different ways in which they react or combine with other substances • *She studied chemistry and physics at college.* • *A team of scientists has been studying the chemistry* **of** *the ozone layer.* • *a chemistry department/laboratory* • *(infml)* Chemistry is also understanding and attraction between two people: *I went out with him for two years, but the chemistry just wasn't there.* ○ *There was an immediate* **sexual** *chemistry* **between** *us the first time we met.*

chem·ist /ˈkem·ɪst/ *n* [C] • A chemist is a person who studies chemistry or a scientist who works with chemicals or studies their reactions.

chem·o·ther·a·py /£ˌkiː·məʊˈθer·ə·pi, $-moʊ-/ *n* [U] the treatment of diseases using chemicals • *Chemotherapy is often used in the treatment of cancer.* • *He had incurable cancer and was undergoing painful chemotherapy treatment.*

che·nille /ʃəˈniːl/ *n* [U] a thick soft thread which is used for decorating cloth, or the material which is made from this • *a chenille jumper* • *She's bought a new chenille bedspread.*

cheque *Br and Aus, Am* **check** /tʃek/ *n* [C] a printed form, used instead of money, to make payments from your bank account • *When you write a cheque, you write your name on it, the amount of money you are paying and the name of the person to whom your bank will make the payment.* • *I wrote him a cheque* **for** *£50.* • *I don't have enough cash on me, so could I pay* **with a/by** *cheque, please?* • *Who should I* **make out** *this cheque* **to** (=Whose name should I write on it)*?* • *Please make your cheques* **payable to** *The Brighter Toyshop Ltd* (=Please write this name on them). • A *(Br and Aus)* **cheque account**/*(Am)* **checking account** is a bank account from which money can be taken by the customer using a cheque. • A *(Br and Aus)* **cheque book**/*(Am)* **check book** is a book of cheques with your name printed on them which is given to you by your bank to make payments with. • *(disapproving) (Br and Aus)* **Cheque book journalism**/*(Am)* **Check book journalism** is when a newspaper persuades someone involved in a news story to give their report of events by paying them a lot of money: *Over the past few years, cheque book journalism has become an increasingly common way for the popular press to get stories.* • *(Br and Aus)* A **cheque card** (also **banker's card**) is a small plastic card which you have to show when you pay for something by cheque and which is proof that your bank will pay the money you owe: *We only accept cheques that are accompanied by a cheque card.* ○ *My cheque card has a £100 guarantee* (=There is a £100 limit on my cheque card). • LP› **Money**

chequ·ered VARIED *Br and Aus* /£ˈtʃek·əd, $-ɚd/, *Am* **check·ered** *adj* (of a person or organization) having had both successful and unsuccessful periods in your past • *Her business affairs have been remarkably chequered.* • *The company has had a chequered* **history** *of ownership.* • *His chequered business* **career** *meant that he would never able to gain a high position in politics.*

chequ·ered PATTERN *Br and Aus* /£ˈtʃek·əd, $-ɚd/, *Am* **check·ered** *adj* having a pattern of squares in two or more colours • *The café had red and white chequered tablecloths and fresh flowers on every table.* • The **chequered flag** is the black and white flag which is waved to show that a car has won a race: *Three minutes from the chequered flag, Mansell was in the lead by 2·25 seconds.*

cher·ish *obj* /ˈtʃer·ɪʃ/ *v* [T] to love, protect and care for (someone or something that is important to you) • *Although I cherish my children, I do allow them their independence.* • *Her most cherished possession is a 1926 letter from F. Scott Fitzgerald.* • *Freedom of speech is a cherished* (=carefully protected) *right in this country.* • To cherish hopes, memories or ideas is to keep them in your mind because they are important to you and bring you pleasure: *My grandfather cherished his memories of the years he spent in the army as a young man.*

che·root /ʃəˈruːt/ *n* [C] a short thin CIGAR (=a roll of dried tobacco leaves which is smoked) with both ends cut flat

cher·ry /ˈtʃer·i/ *n* [C] a small, round, soft red or black fruit with a single hard seed in the middle, or the tree on which the fruit grows • *Her mother made her a large cake with cherries on the top for her birthday.* • *They have planted 700 new oaks, maples and cherries in the park.* • *"Life is Just a Bowl of Cherries"* (title of a song written by Lew Brown, 1931) • PIC› **Fruit**

cher·ry /ˈtʃer·i/ *adj* [not gradable] • *Their garden was full of cherry trees.* • *The cabinet is made from wild cherry wood.* • *April is my favourite month when the cherry blossom is out.* • Cherry or cherry-**red** means bright red in colour: *She had dark eyes and cherry-red lips.*

cher·ub /ˈtʃer·əb/ *n* [C] *pl* **cherubs** or *fml* **cherubim** /ˈtʃer·ə·bɪm, ˈ-ʊ-/ an ANGEL (=heavenly being) that is represented in art as a beautiful, rather fat naked child with small wings • *The wooden chest was overlaid with gold and painted with cherubs.* • *She has a cherub-***like** *face* (=a round, pretty face like that of a child). • *(infml approving)* A beautiful child is sometimes called a cherub: *My brother had such a sweet, innocent face when he was young that my mother called him her cherub.*

cher·ub·ic /tʃəˈruː·bɪk/ *adj* • If someone is cherubic or has a cherubic face, they have a round, pretty face like that of a child: *The choirboys' cherubic pink faces smiled across the church as they sang.*

cher·vil /£ˈtʃɜː·vɪl, $ˈtʃɜːr-/ *n* [U] a herb used in cooking which has delicate, feathery leaves and a flavour like LIQUORICE • *Serve the soup with chervil or chopped parsley.*

chess /tʃes/ *n* [U] a game played by two people on a square board, in which each player has 16 pieces that can be moved on the board in different ways • *The aim in chess is to win by attacking the other player's king in such a way that it cannot avoid being taken.* • A **chess set** is the pieces used to play chess and the board on which the game is played: *I found an old chess set in the attic, but two of the pieces were missing.* • PIC› **Games**

chess·board /£ˈtʃes·bɔːd, $-bɔːrd/ *n* [C] a square board divided into 64 smaller squares, half of which are light and half dark in colour, which is used for playing the game of CHESS or DRAUGHTS • *Please don't move the chessboard – there's a game set up on it which I'm half way through.*

chest BODY PART /tʃest/ *n* [C] the upper front part of the body of humans and some animals, between the stomach and the neck, enclosing the heart and lungs • *He was shot in the chest at point blank range.* • *She was hospitalized for leg and chest injuries.* • *He folded his arms* **across** *his chest.* • *His shirt was open to the waist revealing a very* **hairy** *chest.* • *She went to the doctor complaining of chest* **pains.** • *(infml)* If a woman is described as having a large or a small chest, she has large or small breasts. • *(infml)* If you **get** something **off** your **chest**, you free yourself of your worries by telling someone about something worrying that you have been keeping secret: *I had spent two months worrying about it and I was glad to get it off my chest.*

-chest·ed /-ˈtʃes·tɪd/ *combining form* • *He was* **bare**-*chested* (=The top half of his body was naked). • *She is rather* **flat**-*chested* (=She has small breasts).

chest·y /ˈtʃes·ti/ *adj* **-ier, -iest** • A chesty **cough** is one which causes difficulty in breathing: *This cough syrup is really good for chesty coughs.* ○ *(esp. Br) I get a bit chesty* (=I start to cough) *when it's foggy.*

chest BOX /tʃest/ *n* [C] a large, strong box, usually made of wood, which is used for storing valuable goods or possessions or for moving possessions from one place to another • *Her books and clothes were packed into chests and shipped across to Canada.* • *You'll find an aspirin in the* **medicine** *chest in the bathroom.* • A **chest of drawers** (*Am also* **bureau**) is a piece of furniture with drawers in which you keep things such as clothes. • PIC› **Beds and bedroom**

chest·nut NUT /ˈtʃest·nʌt/ *n* [C] a large shiny reddish-brown nut, or the tree on which the nuts grow • *A man in the street was selling bags of* **hot** *chestnuts.* • *He added a spoonful of chestnut* **purée** *to the cake mixture.* • *We have a 200-year-old chestnut* **tree** *in the bottom of our garden.* • There are two types of chestnut, **sweet chestnuts**, which can be cooked and eaten, and **horse chestnuts**, which are not edible. • A chestnut is also a brown horse: *The chestnut, Strike It Lucky, is being retired after a 31-race career in which she won six races.* • See also HORSE CHESTNUT. • PIC› **Nut, Tree**

chest·nut /ˈtʃest·nʌt/ *adj* • Chestnut is a deep reddish-brown colour: *Her hair was cut in a short bob and dyed chestnut.*

chest·nut JOKE /ˈtʃest·nʌt/ *n* [C] *infml* a joke, story or situation that is so old and so familiar that it is no longer very amusing or interesting • *Not that old chestnut about the vicar again!*

chev·ron /ˈʃev·rᵊn, £-rɒn/ *n* [C] a shape like a V or an upside down V, used esp. on the sleeve of a police or military uniform to show the wearer's rank, or on road signs in Britain to show a severe bend in the road • PIC› **Patterns**

chew *(obj)* /tʃuː/ *v* to crush (food) into smaller, softer pieces with the teeth so that it is easier to swallow • *You should chew your food well, or you will get indigestion.* [T] •

He made his sandwich last as long as possible by chewing each mouthful over and over again. [T] • To chew something also means to bite it with your teeth, usually in order to taste its flavour: *Would you like some gum to chew?* [I] ○ *She gave the children some sweets to chew* **(on)** *during the long car journey.* [T] ○ *He chewed* **on** (= bit at) *his lower lip, trying to remember where he had left his car keys.* [T] ○ *She sat in the waiting room at the dentist's, nervously chewing* **(at)** (= biting) *her nails.* [T] • *A mouse seems to have chewed* **through** (= bitten a hole in) *the carpet.* [I] • *The missile can travel almost a mile a second and chew* **through** (= pass through) *the world's toughest armour by brute force.* [I] • *We accidentally left the dog in the house while we were out and the living room carpet was all chewed* **(up)** (= the dog had bitten holes in it) *when we got back.* [T] • *(infml) Your tape recorder's just chewed* **up** (= damaged) *my favourite cassette.* [M] • *(infml)* To **chew on/chew over** something is to think carefully about it for a long time: *Why don't you chew on it for a while before making your decision.* ○ *I've been chewing the problem over since last week* • *(infml)* If you **chew the fat** with someone, you talk with them in an informal and friendly way: *John Major has been chewing the fat with Bill Clinton in Washington.* • **Chewing gum** is a sweet that you keep in your mouth and chew to get its flavour, but which you do not swallow: *Would you like a* **piece/stick** *of chewing gum?* ○ *(fig.) Television is sometimes called chewing gum for the mind because it entertains people without teaching them anything.*

chew /tʃuː/ *n* [C] • *The cheese had a mild flavour which disappeared after a couple of chews.* • *Give the dog a bone and let him have a chew* **on** *that.* • A chew is also a hard sweet that gets softer the more you bite it.

chew·y /ˈtʃuː·i/ *adj* **-ier, -iest** • Food that is chewy needs to be chewed a lot before it is swallowed: *The meat was tasteless and chewy.*

chi·ar·o·scu·ro /£kiˌɑː·rəˈskʊə·rəʊ, $-ˌɑːr·əˈskjʊr·oʊ/ *n* [U] *specialized* the use of areas of light and darkness in a painting • *Caravaggio is famous for his use of chiaroscuro.* • *Rembrandt used dramatic chiaroscuro in his paintings to create a feeling of space.*

chic /ʃiːk/ *n* [U], *adj* (the quality of being) stylish and fashionable • *British politicians are not renowned for their chic.* • *She wears chic, expensive clothes with designer labels.*

chi·cane /ʃɪˈkeɪn/ *n* [C] *specialized* a piece of road with severe bends like an 'S', which forces drivers to go more slowly, esp. in motor racing • *Prost claimed his rival had forced him off the track on lap 38 at the first chicane.*

chi·can·er·y /£ʃɪˈkeɪ·nᵊr·i, $-nɚ-/ *n* [U] *fml* clever, dishonest talk or behaviour which is used to deceive people • *The investigation has revealed political chicanery and corruption at the highest levels.*

Chi·ca·no *male* (*pl* **Chicanos**), *female* **Chi·ca·na** (*pl* **Chicanas**) /£tʃɪˈkɑː·nəʊ, $-noʊ, -nə/ *n* [C] *infml* a person living in the US who was born in Mexico or whose parents came from Mexico

chi·chi /ˈʃiː·ʃi/ *adj* **-er, -est** *infml disapproving* trying too hard to be decorated in a stylish or attractive way and therefore lacking any real style or beauty • *She decorated her house with chichi gold ornaments.* • Chichi can also mean fashionable: *They live in a rather chichi, expensive part of town.*

chick [BIRD] /tʃɪk/ *n* [C] a baby bird, esp. a young chicken

chick [WOMAN] /tʃɪk/ *n* [C] *slang* a young woman. This word is considered offensive by many women.

chick·en [BIRD] /ˈtʃɪk·ɪn/ *n* a type of bird kept on a farm for its eggs or its meat, or the meat of this bird which is cooked and eaten • *In battery farms, chickens are kept in tiny cages.* [C] • *A male chicken is called a cock and a female chicken is called a hen.* [C] • *I don't eat red meat like pork or beef, but I do eat fish and chicken.* [U] • *We're having roast/fried chicken for dinner.* [U] • *(infml)* A **chicken and egg** situation or problem is one where it is impossible to say which of two things existed first and which caused the other one: *It's a chicken and egg situation – are they poor because they were badly educated, or were they badly educated because they were poor?* • **Chicken wire** is netting made of metal wire, which was originally used to make enclosures for chickens. • *"Why did the chicken cross the road?"* (well-known joke question) • *"To get to the other side"* (answer) • PIC› **Birds**

chick·en [COWARD] /ˈtʃɪk·ɪn/, *Am also* **chick·en·shit** *n* [C] *slang disapproving* (used esp. by children) a cowardly person who refuses to do something dangerous or difficult • *What a chicken – he won't jump!* • People who **play chicken** play dangerous games in order to discover who is the bravest: *They would play chicken by driving head-on at each other until one of them lost their nerve and swerved out of the way.*

chick·en /ˈtʃɪk·ɪn/ *adj slang disapproving* • *Why won't you jump? Are you chicken?*

chick·en out /ˈtʃɪk·ɪn/ *v adv* [I] *slang disapproving* • If you chicken **out of** (doing) something, you decide not to do it because you are too frightened: *I was going to go bungee jumping, but I chickened out.* ○ *A group of us went hang-gliding, but a couple of people chickened out of (doing) it at the last minute.*

chick·en·feed /ˈtʃɪk·ɪn·fiːd/ *n* [U] *infml* an amount of money which is so small in comparison with other amounts, that it is unimportant and almost without value • *They're losing $200 000 on this deal, but that's chickenfeed* **to/for** *a company with yearly profits of $25 million.*

chick·en·pox /£ˈtʃɪk·ɪn·pɒks, $-pɑːks/ *n* [U] an infectious disease that causes a slight fever and red spots on the skin • *Chickenpox is a very common disease among children.*

chick·en·shit /ˈtʃɪk·ɪn·ʃɪt/ *n* [C], *adj Am slang disapproving for* CHICKEN [COWARD] • *Don't be such a chickenshit. Go ask her to dance.* • *Captain Schall wouldn't stand for any chickenshit behaviour from the recruits.*

chick·pea /ˈtʃɪk·piː/, **gar·banz·o (bean)** *n* [C] a hard pale brown round seed which can be cooked and eaten • *Chickpeas are used to make houmous and felafel.* • *Chickpeas and lentils are pulses and are an important part of a vegetarian diet.*

chi·co·ry [VEGETABLE] /£ˈtʃɪk·ᵊr·i, $ˈ-ɚ-/, *Am usually* **en·dive**, *Aus* **wit·lof** /£ˈwɪt·lɒf, $-ˈlɑːf/ *n* [U] a vegetable with bitter-tasting white leaves eaten raw in salads • PIC› **Vegetables**

chi·co·ry [POWDER] /£ˈtʃɪk·ᵊr·i, $ˈ-ɚ-/ *n* [U] a powder made from the root of a plant and added to or used instead of coffee

chide *obj* /tʃaɪd/ *v* [T] *fml* to speak (to someone) severely because they have behaved badly • *She chided him* **for** *his bad manners.*

chief [PERSON IN CHARGE] /tʃiːf/ *n* [C] the person in charge of a group or organization, or the ruler of a TRIBE • *a police chief* • *He was once the Communist party chief for the area.* • *A new chief* **of** *the security forces has just been appointed.* • *Chiefs of the local tribes meet at the major festivals.* • *(Br humorous) Can you sign this form for me, chief?* [as form of address] • *(saying)* 'Too many chiefs and not enough Indians' means there are too many people in an organization who want to say what should be done, and not enough people doing the work. • LP› **Titles and forms of address**

chief /tʃiːf/ *adj* [before n; not gradable] • *the chief fire officer/accountant* • In Britain a **chief constable** is the police officer in charge of the police in a particular area. • *She's the* **chief executive** *of* (= the person with the most important position in) *one of the country's largest charities.* • *(Am)* The **chief executive** of a country or STATE (= region) is its PRESIDENT or GOVERNOR (= the elected leader of government). • A **chief justice** is the most important judge of a court of law, esp. a very important court in a country. • A chief medical officer is the person with most authority in medical matters: *The government's chief medical officer has said that these foods could be dangerous to pregnant women.* • A **chief of staff** is one of the highest-ranking officers in the armed forces.

chief [MOST IMPORTANT] /tʃiːf/ *adj* [before n; not gradable] most important or main • *The chief problem we have in the area now is the spread of disease.* • *One of the chief reasons for her leaving was his bad temper.* • *Our chief expenditure is on raw materials.*

chief·ly /ˈtʃiː·fli/ *adv* • *The island chiefly* (= mostly) *attracts upmarket tourists.* • *Those chiefly* (= more than others) *responsible were never brought to justice.*

chief·tain /ˈtʃiːf·tᵊn/ *n* [C] the leader of a TRIBE (= a group of families)

chif·fon [CLOTH] /£ˈʃɪf·ɒn, $ʃɪˈfɑːn/ *n* [U] a very thin, almost transparent cloth of silk or NYLON

chif·fon [FOOD] /£ˈʃɪf·ɒn, $ʃɪˈfɑːn/ *adj* [before n; not gradable] *Am* made light, esp. by adding the clear part of eggs which have been beaten • *lemon chiffon pie*

chignon /£ˈʃiː·njɔ̃ː, $-njɑːn/ *n* [C] a woman's hairstyle where the hair is arranged in a knot or roll at the back of her head

Chi·hua·hua /tʃɪˈwɑː·wə/ *n* [C] a very small dog that usually has short hair

chil·blain /ˈtʃɪl·bleɪn/ *n* [C] a painful or ITCHY red swelling on the toes or fingers caused by cold weather

child /tʃaɪld/ *n* [C] *pl* **children** /ˈtʃɪl·drən, ˈtʃʊl-/ a boy or girl from the time of birth until he or she is an adult, or a son or daughter of any age • *When she was a child she was always healthy.* • *A small group of children waited outside the door.* • *I won't allow a child* **of** *mine to go out dressed like that!* • *Both her children are now married with children of their own.* • *Jan is married with three* **young** *children.* • *The minister is reported to have fathered several* **illegitimate** *children.* • *There were people outside the abortion clinic campaigning for the rights of the* **unborn** *child.* • *(disapproving)* An adult can be called a child if they behave the way a child would: *He can't stand not getting his own way – he's such a child.* • If someone is **a child of** something such as a period of recent history they are very influenced by it: *She's always talking about peace and love – she's a real child of the sixties.* • *(infml)* **Child's play** is something that is very easy to do: *Using computers nowadays is child's play compared to how difficult they were to use twenty years ago.* • *(old use)* A woman who is **(great) with child** is (very) pregnant. • **Child abuse** is the act of making a child suffer physically, sexually or emotionally when it is done either by their parents, or by adults who should be taking care of them. • *(Br)* **Child benefit**/*(Am)* **Aid to Families with Dependent Children** is money received regularly by families from the government to help pay for the costs of caring for children. • **Child care** is care for children provided by either the government, an organization or a person, while parents are at work or are absent for another reason: *What child care facilities does your company offer?* ○ *Without the adequate provision of child care, many women who wish to work are unable to do so.* • A **children's home** is a place where children are cared for if their parents are dead or unable to take care of them. • A **child molester** is a person who tries to have sex with children: *Police are trying to catch a child molester who is active in the area.* • *Why shouldn't a woman have a job after years of* **child-rearing** (= caring for children)? • *(saying)* 'Children should be seen and not heard' means that children should behave and should not make any unnecessary noise. • *"When I was a child, I spake* (= spoke) *as a child, I understood as a child, I thought as a child: but when I became a man, I put away childish things."* (Bible, 1 Corinthians 13) • *"Give me the child until he is seven, and I will give you the man"* (traditional saying, often associated with the Jesuits) • *"The Child is father to the Man"* (William Wordsworth in the poem *My Heart Leaps Up*, 1807) • *"Children of a Lesser God"* (title of a play by Marc Medoff taken from a poem by Tennyson, 1979) • See also BRAINCHILD. • LP **Age, Relationships**

child·hood /ˈtʃaɪld·hʊd/ *n* • *She spent most of her childhood* (= the time when she was a child) *living abroad.* [C] • *Childhood is not always a happy time.* [U] • Compare **boyhood** at BOY; **girlhood** at GIRL.

child·ish /ˈtʃaɪl·dɪʃ/ *adj* • *He is only seven – of course his behaviour's childish* (= like a child's). • *(disapproving)* If an adult is childish, they behave in a way that would be expected of a child, but which is unsuitable for an adult: *It was so childish of him to stamp out of the restaurant just because people didn't agree with what he said.*

child·ish·ly /ˈtʃaɪl·dɪʃ·li/ *adv disapproving* • *"I won't go," she said childishly.*

child·ish·ness /ˈtʃaɪl·dɪʃ·nəs/ *n* [U] *disapproving* • *You're in the army now and childishness* (= behaving like a child) *won't get you anywhere.*

child·less /ˈtʃaɪld·ləs/ *adj* [not gradable] • *Couples who are childless* (= without any children) *can feel excluded from the rest of society.*

child·less·ness /ˈtʃaɪld·lə·snəs/ *n* [U]

child·like /ˈtʃaɪld·laɪk/ *adj* • *a childlike innocence/quality* • *All her life she had a childlike* (= similar to a child's) *trust in other people.*

child·bear·ing /£ˈtʃaɪldˌbeə·rɪŋ, $-ˌber·ɪŋ/ *adj* [not gradable], *n* (of) the process of having babies • *The survey is only concerned with women of childbearing* **age**. • *Years of childbearing had not lessened her beauty.* [U]

child·birth /£ˈtʃaɪld·bɜːθ, $-bɜːrθ/ *n* [U] the act of giving birth to a baby • *A great number of women used to die* **in** *childbirth.*

child·mind·er *Br* /£ˈtʃaɪldˌmaɪn·dəʳ, $-dɚ/, *Am and Aus* **bab·y·sit·ter** *n* [C] a person, usually a woman, whose job is to take care of other people's children in her own home • *a registered childminder*

child·mind·ing *Br* /ˈtʃaɪldˌmaɪn·dɪŋ/, *Am and Aus* **ba·by·sit·ting** *n* [U]

child·mind /ˈtʃaɪld·maɪnd/, *Am and Aus* **ba·by·sit** *v* • *She childminds a baby and a toddler.* [T] • *I used to childmind when my own children were small.* [I]

child·proof /ˈtʃaɪld·pruːf/ *adj* (esp. of containers or locks) that cannot be opened or operated by a child • *This bottle of bleach has a childproof lid.*

child·ren /ˈtʃɪl·drən, ˈtʃʊl-/ *pl of* child

chill /tʃɪl/ *v* to (cause to) become cold but not freeze • *We were chilled by our midnight swim on the lake.* [T] • *Allow the chocolate mousse to chill in a fridge for two hours.* [I] • *She compiled a dossier guaranteed to* **chill the marrow of** (= frighten) *those responsible for security.* • *I heard a scream that* **chilled** *me* **to the bone** (= made me suddenly feel great fear).

chill /tʃɪl/ *n* [C] • *There was a chill in the air* (= It was slightly cold) *that day.* • A chill is also a slight fever: *Don't go out with wet hair, you might* **catch** *a chill.* • *(fig.) His words sent a chill down her spine* (= made her feel suddenly very fearful). • *(fig.) Gwen's arrival cast a chill over the gathering* (= made everyone feel anxious and uncomfortable). • *As soon as we arrived we lit the fire to* **take the chill off** *the room* (= make the room slightly warmer).

chil·ly (**-ier**, **-iest**) /ˈtʃɪl·i/, *literary* **chill** *adj* • *The bathroom gets chilly* (= cold) *in the autumn.* • *I felt* **a bit** *chilly so I put on a jacket.* • *(fig.) Their relationship was decidedly chilly* (= unfriendly) *after the argument.* • *(fig.) When I went to see the sales manager I got a chilly* (= unfriendly) *reception.* • *Many more businesses are feeling* **the chill wind of** (= problems caused by) *recession.*

chil·ling /ˈtʃɪl·ɪŋ/ *adj* • *a chilling wind* • *This memorial to victims of the holocaust is a chilling* (= frightening and upsetting) **reminder** *of a tragedy that must never be repeated.* • *New laws could have a chilling* (= harmful) **effect** *on foreign investment.*

chil·ling·ly /ˈtʃɪl·ɪŋ·li/ *adv* • *His words made it chillingly* (= frighteningly) *clear that he would not give up the gun.*

chill out *v adv* [I] *esp. Am slang* to relax • *Yo, chill out, dude!*

chil·li, *Am usually* **chi·li** /ˈtʃɪl·i/ *n pl* **chillies** the small red seed case from particular types of PEPPER plant that is used to make some foods very hot and spicy • *Add a/some chilli to the mixture.* [C/U] • **Chilli powder** is a dark red powder made from dried chillies and other spices that is used for flavouring particular foods. • **Chilli con carne** is a hot-tasting spicy dish of meat, onions and chillies or chilli powder and usually beans. • PIC **Vegetables**

chime *(obj)* /tʃaɪm/ *v* (of bells) to make a clear ringing sound • *Let the church bells chime.* [I] • *The grandfather clock chimed nine o'clock.* [T]

chime /tʃaɪm/ *n* [C] • *I was woken up by the chimes* (= ringing sounds) *of the cathedral bells.* • *"We have heard the chimes of midnight"* (Shakespeare, Henry IV part 2, 3.2)

chimes /tʃaɪmz/ *pl n* • Chimes are a set of small bells, or objects that make ringing sounds: *wind chimes*

chime in *v adv* [I] *infml* to interrupt or speak in a conversation, usually to agree with what has been said • *"It's very difficult," I said. "Impossible," she chimed in.* • *After a few minutes she'll get bored and chime in* **with** *a comment like, "You think you've got problems".*

chime with *obj v prep* [T] *Br* to agree with (someone or something) • *You'll have to chime with the official policy if you want to be promoted.*

chi·me·ra /ˈkɪm·er·ə/ *n* [C] *fml or literary* a hope or dream that is extremely unlikely ever to come true • *Is the ideal of banishing hunger throughout the world just a chimera?*

chi·mer·ic·al /kaɪˈmer·ɪ·kəl/ *adj fml or literary* • *This hope proved to be chimerical* (= imaginary).

chim·ney PIPE /ˈtʃɪm·ni/ *n* [C] a hollow structure that allows the smoke from a fire inside a building to escape to the air outside • *The house had two chimneys, one at each end.* • *Factory chimneys belched dense white smoke into the sky.* • A **chimney breast** is the part of a wall in a room which is built around a chimney and into which a fireplace is built. • PIC **Accommodation, Fires and space heaters** Ⓕ

chim·ney PASSAGE /ˈtʃɪm·ni/ *n* [C] *specialized* a narrow vertical passage in the rock of a cliff or mountain through which a person can climb • Ⓕ

chim·ney·pot /£ˈtʃɪm·ni·pɒt, $-pɑːt/ *n* [C] a short pipe, often made of clay, fixed to the top of a CHIMNEY

chim·ney·stack /ˈtʃɪm·ni·stæk/ *n* [C] *Br* the part of a CHIMNEY that sticks out above a roof

chim·ney·sweep /ˈtʃɪm·ni·swiːp/, *infml* **sweep** *n* [C] a person whose job is to clean the insides of CHIMNEYS, usually using a set of brushes with a very long handle

chimp·an·zee /ˌtʃɪm·pænˈziː/, *infml* **chimp** /tʃɪmp/ *n* [C] a small, very intelligent African APE (= an animal like a monkey) with black or brown fur • PIC **Apes and monkeys**

chin /tʃɪn/ *n* [C] the part of a person's face below their mouth • *White bristles stick out from his* **unshaven** *chin.* • *At the age of fifty Thelma still had a firm chin and a smooth neck.* • *To keep the safety helmet in position, fasten the strap beneath your chin.* • *She sat behind the table, her chin resting in her hands.* • *(infml)* If you say **(keep** your**) chin up!** to someone you are telling them to be cheerful even though they are in a difficult situation. • *(infml)* To **take it on the chin** is to accept unpleasant events bravely and without complaining: *It's no use whining about the pain – you'll just have to take it on the chin and carry on walking.* • A **chin rest** is the part of a VIOLIN or VIOLA (= a wooden musical instrument with four strings) on which a person puts their chin for support while playing. • PIC **Body**

-chinned /-tʃɪnd/ *adj* [not gradable] • *a square-chinned* (= having a chin that looks square and strong) *film star*

chi·na /ˈtʃaɪ·nə/ *n* [U] high quality clay that is shaped and then heated to make it permanently hard, or objects made from this such as cups and plates • *Most of the china that we sell in our shops is glazed.* • *Their best china was only taken out when guests came to dinner.* • *The candlelight glinted on beautiful china plates and silver cutlery.* • LP **Shopping goods**

Chi·na·town /ˈtʃaɪ·nə·taʊn/ *n* [C/U] an area of a city outside China where many Chinese people live and there are a lot of Chinese restaurants and shops

chin·chil·la /tʃɪnˈtʃɪl·ə/ *n* [C] a small S American animal with pale grey fur that is highly valued

Chi·nese che·quers /ˌtʃaɪ·niːz/ *n* [U] a game played on a star-shaped board where small balls are moved from hole to hole

Chi·nese goose·ber·ry /ˌtʃaɪ·niːz/ *n* [C] KIWI (FRUIT)

Chi·nese lan·tern /ˌtʃaɪ·niːz/ *n* [C] a folding decoration made from thin coloured paper

Chi·nese puz·zle /ˌtʃaɪ·niːz/ *n* [C] a game where you have to solve the problem of fitting many different pieces together, esp. boxes inside other boxes • *(fig.) This latest scandal is a Chinese puzzle* (= a difficult problem) *to me – I have trouble figuring out who all the players are and what their roles are supposed to be.*

chink CRACK /tʃɪŋk/ *n* [C] a small narrow crack or opening • *I peered through a chink in the curtains and saw them all inside.* • A **chink in** someone's **armour** is a weakness that they have: *A single chink in our armour at the negotiating table means we could lose out badly.*

chink SOUND /tʃɪŋk/ *v, n* (to make) a light ringing sound; CLINK • *The coins chinked lightly in his pocket as he walked along.* [I] • *On a hot day it's lovely to hear the chink of ice in a glass.* [U] • *I heard a chink as the key hit the tiled floor.* [C]

Chink PERSON /tʃɪŋk/, *Br also* **Chink·y** *n* [C] *taboo slang* (an offensive word for) a Chinese person

Chink·y /ˈtʃɪŋ·ki/ *n* [C] *Br slang* a restaurant serving Chinese food

chin·less *esp. Br* /ˈtʃɪn·ləs/, *Am usually* **weak–chinned** /ˌwiːkˈtʃɪnd/ *adj* with a small CHIN that slopes inwards, sometimes thought of as a sign of a weak character • *(Br infml) Her latest boyfriend's a bit of a* **chinless wonder** (= a foolish man, esp. of high social class).

chin·os /£ˈtʃiː·nəʊz, $-noʊz/ *pl n* cotton trousers, often of a pale colour

chin·strap /ˈtʃɪn·stræp/ *n* [C] a strap that goes around the lower part of a person's head to keep a protective hat, esp. a HELMET in place • PIC **Hats**

chintz /tʃɪnts/ *n* [U] cotton cloth, usually printed with flowery patterns, that has a slightly shiny appearance • *George was sitting on a plump chintz armchair.*

chintz·y /ˈtʃɪnt·si/ *adj* **-ier, -iest** • *I find their house a bit too chintzy* (= decorated with lots of chintz).

chintz·y /ˈtʃɪnt·si/ *adj* **-ier, -iest** *Am* (of things) cheap and poorly made, or (of people) not willing to spend money • *It's a chintzy hat, you can't expect it to last for long.* • *Don't be so chintzy, the whole evening will only cost you 10 bucks.*

chin·wag /ˈtʃɪn·wæg/ *n* [C] *infml* a long and pleasant conversation between friends • *I'm looking forward to having a* **good** *chinwag with you when we next meet.*

chip FRIED POTATO *Br and Aus* /tʃɪp/, *Am and Aus* **french fry** *n* [C] a long thin piece of potato that is fried and usually eaten hot • *fish and chips* • *beans/egg/sausage and chips* • *oven chips* (= chips that are baked in a cooker) • *It was the sort of restaurant that served chips with everything.* • A **chip shop** (also *infml* **chippy**) is a shop where fish, chips and other food are fried in oil and you usually take them away to eat them. • *(Am and Aus)* A chip is a very thin piece of fried potato, MAIZE, banana or other food which is eaten cold: *I ate three bags of chips while I was waiting and now I'm not hungry!*

chip PIECE /tʃɪp/ *n* [C] a small piece that has been broken off a larger object, or the mark left on an object such as a cup, plate, etc. where a small piece has been broken off it • *The ground was covered with wood chips where they'd been chopping logs.* • *Joan fell and knocked a chip* **out of** *her front tooth.* • *I don't want this mug, it's got a chip* **in it/out of** *it.* • *(infml)* If you say that someone is **a chip off the old block** you mean that they are similar in character to their father or mother. • *(infml)* Someone who has **a chip on** their **shoulder** seems angry all the time because they feel they have been treated unfairly or that they are not as good as other people: *He's got a chip on his shoulder about not having been to university.*

chip *(obj)* /tʃɪp/ *v* **-pp-** • *I never wash up without wearing rubber gloves, I don't like to chip my nail varnish.* [T] • *This toughened glass will never crack or chip.* [I]

chipped /tʃɪpt/ *adj* • *a chipped glass* • *All the crockery was old and chipped.*

chip COMPUTER PART /tʃɪp/, **mi·cro·chip** *n* [C] *specialized* a very small piece of SEMICONDUCTOR, esp. in a computer, that contains extremely small electronic CIRCUITS and devices and can perform particular operations • *a silicon chip*

chip PLASTIC COIN /tʃɪp/ *n* [C] a small plastic disc used to represent a particular amount of money in GAMBLING • *The hostages are being held as* **bargaining** *chips by terrorist organizations.* • *(infml) One day* **when the chips are down** (= when you are in great difficulties and you understand the true value of things), *you will know who your true friends are.* • *(Br infml)* If someone **has had** their **chips** they have lost their position, importance or power: *That type of engine has had its chips now – it's noisy and uses a lot of fuel.*

chip in *(obj)* PAY *v adv infml* to give (some money), esp. when several people are giving money to pay for something together • *They all chipped in (fifty pounds) and bought their mother a trip to Greece.* [I/T]

chip in INTERRUPT *Br infml, Am and Aus* **butt in** *v adv* [I] *Br infml* to interrupt (a conversation) in order to say something • *I was trying to explain things to Bill but Mary kept chipping in (***with** *her comments).*

chip·board /£ˈtʃɪp·bɔːd, $-bɔːrd/ *n* [U] hard material made from small pieces of wood mixed with glue, often used instead of wood in making furniture because it is cheaper • *veneered chipboard*

chip·munk /ˈtʃɪp·mʌŋk/ *n* [C] a small furry N American animal with dark strips along its back

chip·o·lat·a, chipp·o·la·ta /£ˌtʃɪp·əˈlɑː·tə, $-t̬ə/ *n* [C] *Br* a small thin SAUSAGE

chip·per /£ˈtʃɪp·əʳ, $-ɚ/ *adj Am infml* very happy • *You seem mighty chipper this morning – what's up?*

chip·ping /ˈtʃɪp·ɪŋ/ *n* [C usually pl] *Br* a small piece of stone, put in road surfaces or under railway tracks

chip·py FOOD /ˈtʃɪp·i/ *n* [C] *Br infml* a **chip shop**, see at CHIP FRIED POTATO

chip·py WOMAN /ˈtʃɪp·i/ *n* [C] *Am slang* a female PROSTITUTE (= person who has sex with someone for money) • *She wasn't anything to me, just some chippy I picked up.*

chi·rop·od·ist /£kɪˈrɒp·ə·dɪst, ʃɪ-, $-ˈrɑː·pə-/ *n* [C] a person whose job is to treat problems and diseases of people's feet • *He goes to the chiropodist to have his bunions treated.*

chi·rop·o·dy /£kɪˈrɒp·ə·di, ʃɪ-, $-ˈrɑː·pə-/ *n* [U]

chi·ro·prac·tor /£ˈkaɪ·rəʊ·præk·təʳ, $-roʊ·præk·tɚ/ *n* [C] a person whose job is to treat diseases by adjusting a person's joints esp. those in the back

chi·ro·prac·tic /£ˌkaɪə·rəʊˈpræk·tɪk, $-roʊ-/ *n* [U] • *Chiropractic* (= the system of treatment used by a chiropractor), *involving manipulation of the spinal column, can give great relief to people with back problems.*

chirp /£tʃɜːp, $tʃɜːrp/, **chir·rup** /ˈtʃɪr·əp/ *v* (esp. of a bird) to make a short high sound or sounds • *The birds, chirping relentlessly, woke us up at daybreak.* [I] • *(fig.) "Hello!" the children chirped* (= said with high voices) *in unison.* [+ clause]

chirp·y /£'tʃɜː·pi, $'tʃɜːr-/ *adj* **-ier, -iest** happy and active • *He's so chirpy all the time, it drives me mad.*

chirp·i·ly /£'tʃɜː·pɪ·li, $'tʃɜːr-/ *adv*

chirp·i·ness /£'tʃɜː·pi·nəs, $'tʃɜːr-/ *n* [U]

chi·sel [CUT] /'tʃɪz·əl/ *v, n Br and Aus* **-ll-** or *Am usually* **-l-** (to use) a tool with a long metal blade that has a sharp edge for cutting wood, stone, etc. • *Camille used a hammer and chisel to carve out a figure from the marble.* [C] • *She chiselled a figure* **out of** *the marble.* [T] • PIC▷ **Tools**

chi·selled, *Am usually* **chis·eled** /'tʃɪz·əld/ *adj* • *An elderly gentleman with finely chiselled* (=clear and sharp) *features opened the door.*

chi·sel *(obj)* [CHEAT] /'tʃɪz·əl/ *v Am* to use very clever or dishonest methods to achieve something • *I won't spend my life with someone who's always chiseling (a living).* [I/T]

chi·sel·er /£'tʃɪz·əl·əʳ, $-ɚ/ *n* [C] *Am* • *Don't be such a chiseler, you can afford to pay your way in.*

chit [NOTE] /tʃɪt/ *n* [C] *infml* an official note giving information or showing a sum of money that is owed or has been paid • *If you're going to be off work for a long time you'll need a chit from your doctor.*

chit [GIRL] /tʃɪt/ *n* [C] *dated disapproving* a young and foolish girl

chit–chat /'tʃɪt·tʃæt/ *n* [U] *infml* informal conversation about unimportant matters • *The new radio station promises to replace chit-chat with more music.* • *Stop this* **idle** *chit-chat and get on with your work!*

chit–chat /'tʃɪt·tʃæt/ *v* [I] *infml* • *We were just chit-chatting about this and that.*

chit·ter·lings /£'tʃɪt·əl·ɪŋz, $'tʃɪţ·ɚ·lɪŋz/, **chit·lins** /'tʃɪt·lɪnz/ *pl n* the INTESTINES of a pig prepared for eating

chi·val·rous /'ʃɪv·əl·rəs/ *adj* (of men) very polite, honourable and kind towards women • *In public he was always chivalrous and would help her on with her coat.*

chi·val·rous·ly /'ʃɪv·əl·rə·sli/ *adv* • *"After you," he said chivalrously, holding open the door.*

chi·val·ry /'ʃɪv·əl·ri/ *n* [U] • Chivalry means very polite and honourable behaviour, especially shown by men towards women: *"Thank goodness," she said, as she willingly handed him her suitcase, "the age of chivalry is not dead".* • In the MEDIEVAL period of history chivalry was the system of behaviour followed by KNIGHTS (=men of high social position) that put a high value on purity, honour, kindness and bravery.

chives /tʃaɪvz/ *pl n* a plant with long thin leaves and purple flowers, or its leaves when cut into small pieces and used in cooking to give a flavour similar to onions • PIC▷ **Herbs and spices**

chiv·vy *obj*, **chiv·y** /'tʃɪv·i/ *v* [T] *infml* to encourage (someone) to do something they do not want to do • *He kept putting off writing the report so I had to chivvy him* **along/up**. • *I had to chivvy him* **into** *writing the report.*

chlo·ride /£'klɔː·raɪd, $'klɔːr·aɪd/ *n* [U] *specialized* a chemical COMPOUND that is a mixture of CHLORINE and another substance • *Sodium chloride is the chemical name for common salt.*

chlo·rine /£'klɔː·riːn, $'klɔːr·iːn/ *n* [U] a poisonous greenish-yellow gas with a strong smell, used in making chemicals that contain a lot of carbon and to purify water • *Her eyes were red and sore because of all the chlorine in the pool.*

chlo·rin·ate *obj* /£'klɔː·rɪ·neɪt, $'klɔːr·ɪ-/ *v* [T] • To chlorinate water is to add chlorine to it in order to kill organisms that might cause infection.

chlo·rin·at·ed /£'klɔː·rɪ·neɪ·tɪd, $'klɔːr·ɪ·neɪ·ţɪd/ *adj* • *chlorinated swimming pools*

chlo·ro·form /£'klɒr·ə·fɔːm, $'klɔːr·ə·fɔːrm/ *n* [U] a colourless liquid with a sweet smell that makes you unconscious if you breathe it in

chlo·ro·form *obj* /£'klɒr·ə·fɔːm, $'klɔːr·ə·fɔːrm/ *v* [T] • *Four of the gang held him down and chloroformed him* (=held a piece of cloth with chloroform on it by his mouth and nose until he became unconscious).

chlo·ro·phyll, *Am and Aus also* **chlo·ro·phyl** /£'klɒr·ə·fɪl, $'klɔːr·ə-/ *n* [U] the green substance in plants that allows them to use the energy from the sun

choc–ice /£'tʃɒk·aɪs, $'tʃɑːk-/ *n* [C] *Br* a small block of **ice cream** (=a sweet food that is eaten very cold) covered in a thin layer of chocolate

chock /£tʃɒk, $tʃɑːk/ *n* [C] a block of wood that can be put under a wheel or a heavy object to prevent it from moving

chock–a–block /£ˌtʃɒk·ə'blɒk, '–, $'tʃɑːk·ə·blɑːk/, **chock–full** /£tʃɒk'fʊl, $tʃɑːk-/, *Br* **chock·er** /£'tʃɒk·ə, $'tʃɑː·kɚ/, **chock·a**, *Aus* **chock·ers** *adj* [after v] *infml* very full of (people or things) • *On New Year's Eve their little house was chock-a-block (***with** *guests).*

choc·o·hol·ic /£ˌtʃɒk·ə'hɒl·ɪk, $ˌtʃɑː·kə'hɑː·lɪk/, **choc·a·holic** *n* [C] *humorous infml* a person who likes chocolate very much and frequently eats it

choc·o·late /£'tʃɒk·əl·ət, £-lət, $'tʃɑː·kə·lət, $-klət/ *n* a usually brown food made from CACAO seeds and usually sugar, eaten on its own or used in other food such as cakes, or a small sweet made from this • *a bar of chocolate* [U] • *chocolate mousse* • *chocolate(-covered) biscuits* • *Do you prefer* **milk, plain** *or* **white** *chocolate?* [U] • *She pounced on the* **box of** *chocolates* (=sweets made from chocolate) *in delight.* [C] • Chocolate is also a drink made from powdered chocolate and sugar, milk and/or water that is usually served warm: *We'd like two coffees and two* **(hot)** *chocolates please.* [C] • Chocolate can also mean a dark brown colour: *She was wearing a chic little suit in chocolate and beige.* [U] • Something that is **chocolate box** is very attractive but rather boring: *a chocolate box village* • PIC▷ **Bar, Containers**

choice [ACT] /tʃɔɪs/ *n* an act or the possibility of choosing • *Choice is never easy, but it's better than having no options at all.* [U] • *If the product doesn't work, you are given the choice of a refund or a replacement.* [C] • *It's a difficult choice to make.* [C] • *It's your choice/The choice is yours* (=only you can decide). [C] • *It was a choice* **between** *pain now or pain later, so I chose pain later.* [C] • *She stressed that people should always* **have freedom of** *choice* (=be allowed to decide for themselves). [U] • *Now you know all the facts, you can make an* **informed** *choice.* [C] • *If asked, my choice would be* **to** *continue as before.* [U + to infinitive] • *We have* **no** *choice* **but to** (=The only choice we have is to) *close the hospital.* [U + *to* infinitive] • If something is **of** your **choice**, you choose it rather than it being chosen for you by someone else: *Parents cannot always have the school of their choice for their children.*

choice [VARIETY] /tʃɔɪs/ *n* the range of different things from which you can choose • *There wasn't much choice on the menu.* [U] • *In the future the public will be offered a wider choice of television programmes.* [C]

choice [PERSON/THING] /tʃɔɪs/ *n* [C] a person or thing that has been chosen or that can be chosen • *A liberal female lawyer was the surprise choice* **as** *the organization's president.* • *This type of nursery care may well be the best choice* **for** *your child.* • *He wouldn't be my first choice as a friend.*

choice [SPLENDID] /tʃɔɪs/ *adj* **-r, -st** of high quality • *In the restaurant I ordered the most expensive dish, a choice fillet of fish.* • *(fig.) When they turned up late again she had a few choice* (=angry) *words to say to them.*

choir /£kwaɪəʳ, $kwaɪr/ *n* [C + sing/pl v] a group of people who sing together, esp. in a church • *John missed the party because he was singing* **in** *the choir.* • *I'd better go now or I'll be late for choir* **practice**! • See also CHORAL; CHORISTER.

choir·boy /£'kwaɪə·bɔɪ, $'kwaɪr-/ *n* [C] a boy who sings in a church CHOIR

choir·mast·er /£'kwaɪəˌmɑː·stəʳ, $'kwaɪrˌmæs·ţɚ/ *n* [C] a person who trains a CHOIR and is in control of their singing when they perform

choke *(obj)* [STOP BREATHING] /£tʃəʊk, $tʃoʊk/ *v* to (cause to) be unable to breathe, esp. because the tube inside a person's throat that they breathe through is blocked • *She didn't swallow her food properly and she began to choke.* [I] • *He choked* **on** *a fish bone.* [I] • *The stench of decay choked him and he had to turn away.* [T] • *An elderly man choked* **to death** *in his home yesterday.* [I] • If a person chokes someone else they put their hands around the other person's neck and press hard to stop them breathing: *"Let me go, you're choking me!" Jake spluttered.* [T] • *(fig.) The climbing plant had grown too quickly and was choking the other plants* (=preventing them from growing). [T] • *(fig.) At lunchtime the streets were choked* (=blocked) **with** *traffic.* [T] • To **choke back** feelings or tears/**choke** them **back** means to force yourself not to show them: *Choking back my anger, I tried to speak in a calm voice.*

choked /£tʃəʊkt, $tʃoʊkt/ *adj* • *He was crying and spoke in a choked voice* (=a voice that was unusually quiet because of difficulties in breathing). • *(fig. Br infml) She was choked* (=unhappy) *about not getting the job.* • *(fig. infml) The surprise farewell party left him all choked* **up** (=unable to speak because of feeling strong emotions).

choke [DEVICE] /£tʃəʊk, $tʃoʊk/ *n* a device in a motor vehicle that changes the amount of air going into the engine, allowing more fuel compared to air to go in and therefore making the engine easier to start • *an automatic choke* [C] • *The choke was* **out** (= The choke was operating) *but the engine wouldn't start.* [C] • *Don't use too much choke, you'll flood the carburettor.* [U] • LP› **Driving**

choke FAIL /£tʃəʊk, $tʃoʊk/ *v* [I] *Am infml* to be unable to do something useful at a time when it is important to do it • *He could score points at will during the qualifying matches, but in the final he completely choked.*

chok·er /£'tʃəʊ·kəʳ, $'tʃoʊ·kɚ/ *n* [C] *Am infml* • *She had a reputation as a choker, someone who couldn't come through when the pressure was on.*

chok·er /£'tʃəʊ·kəʳ, $'tʃoʊ·kɚ/ *n* [C] a narrow strip of cloth or NECKLACE (= piece of jewellery) that fits very closely around a woman's neck • *a pearl choker* • PIC› **Jewellery**

chol·e·ra /£'kɒl·ᵊr·ə, $'kɑː·lɚ-/ *n* [U] a serious infection of the bowels caused by drinking infected water or eating infected food, causing DIARRHOEA, vomiting and often death • *Sanitary conditions in the camps are non-existent and cholera, typhoid and other epidemics could break out any day.* • ⓘ ⓟ

chol·er·ic /£kɒl'er·ɪk, $kə'ler-/ *adj fml* very angry or bad-tempered

cho·les·ter·ol /£kə'les·tᵊr·ɒl, $-tə·rɑːl/ *n* [U] a fatty substance that is found in the body tissue and blood of all animals, and which is thought to be part of the cause of heart disease if there is too much of it • *This sunflower oil is high in polyunsaturates and low in cholesterol.*

chomp /£tʃɒmp, $tʃɑːmp/, **champ** *v infml* to chew (food) noisily • *He was chomping away* **on** *a bar of chocolate.* [I] • *There she sat, happily chomping her breakfast.* [T]

choo–choo /'tʃuː·tʃuː/ *n* [C] *pl* **choo-choos** (used esp. by or to children) a train

chook /tʃʊk/ *n* [C] *Aus infml* a chicken

choose *(obj)* /tʃuːz/ *v past simple* **chose** /£tʃəʊz, $tʃoʊz/, *past part* **chosen** /£'tʃəʊ·zᵊn, $'tʃoʊ-/ to decide (what you want) from a range of things or possibilities • *All the books looked so interesting, I didn't know which one to choose.* [T] • *She was forced to choose* **between** *the two men who loved her.* [I] • *He chose a shirt* **from** *the many in his wardrobe.* [T] • *It was difficult choosing* **where** *to live.* [+ *wh*-word] • *I've chosen Luis a present/I've chosen a present* **for** *Luis.* [+ two objects] • *Yesterday the selectors chose Dales* **as** *the team's new captain.* [T] • *The firm's directors chose Emma* **to** *be the new production manager.* [T + obj + *to* infinitive] • *Katie chose* (= decided) **to** *stay away from work that day.* [+ *to* infinitive] • *You may* **do as** *you* **choose** (= do what you decide to do) *for the rest of the day.* • If you say that there is **little/not much to choose between** two or more things you mean that they are very similar: *There was little to choose between all of the boats for hire so we took the one numbered 16 because it seemed like a lucky number.*

chos·en /£'tʃəʊ·zᵊn, $'tʃoʊ-/ *adj* [not gradable] • *A small group of chosen* (= specially picked) *soldiers were sent ahead of the main army.* • The **chosen few** are the people who have some special quality or who have been very lucky in some way: *The two or three young dancers who are invited to join such a prestigious ballet company really are the chosen few.* • *She wore some well-chosen pieces of jewellery.*

choos·y /'tʃuː·zi/ *adj* **-ier, -iest** *infml* difficult to please because of being very exact about what you like • *She's very choosy* **about** *what she eats and drinks.*

chop *obj* CUT /£tʃɒp, $tʃɑːp/ *v* [T] **-pp-** to cut (something) into pieces with an AXE, knife or other sharp instrument • *He was chopping wood in the yard.* • *Add some fresh parsley, finely chopped.* • *Most of the diseased trees were chopped* **down** *last year.* • *Chop* **(up)** *the onions and carrots roughly.* • *Two of his fingers were chopped* **off** *in the accident but surgeons managed to attach them again.* • *(infml) Laura had her hair chopped* (= cut) *yesterday.* • *(fig. infml) The original opera has been chopped* (= divided) **(up)** *into three shorter pieces to be shown on television on three successive evenings.* • If something is chopped in finance or business, it is stopped or reduced: *Because of lack of funding many long-term research projects are being chopped.* ○ *The company has chopped another 350 people* **from** *its staff.* • PIC› **Food preparation**

chop *esp. Br and Aus* /£tʃɒp, $tʃɑːp/, *Am usually, Aus also* **ax** *n* [C] • If a person gets or is given **the chop** or **is for the chop** they lose or are about to lose their job or position: *It looks like she'll* **get/be given** *the chop if her performance at work doesn't improve.* • If a thing **is for the chop** or has **the chop**, it is going to be or has been stopped: *When the reorganization occurs the smaller shipyards will be the first for the chop.* ○ *Many of these special schools are facing the chop.*

chop MEAT /£tʃɒp, $tʃɑːp/ *n* [C] a small piece of meat with bone still in it • *a lamb chop* • *a pork chop*

chop CHANGE /£tʃɒp, $tʃɑːp/ *v* [I] **-pp- chop and change** *Br and Aus* to keep changing your ideas, opinions, activities or job • *He can never make up his mind, he's always chopping and changing.* • *She's chopped and changed between jobs for as long as I've known her.*

chop–chop /£,tʃɒp'tʃɒp, $,tʃɑːp'tʃɑːp/ *exclamation infml* quickly • *Come on, chop-chop, we haven't much time before the train goes!*

chop·house /£'tʃɒp·haʊs, $'tʃɑːp-/ *n* [C] *pl* **chophouses** /£'tʃɒp,haʊ·zɪz, $'tʃɑːp-/ a restaurant that mainly serves thick slices of meat such as STEAKS and CHOPS

chop·per AIRCRAFT /£'tʃɒp·əʳ, $'tʃɑː·pɚ/ *n* [C] *infml for* a HELICOPTER

chop·per TOOL /£'tʃɒp·əʳ, $'tʃɑː·pɚ/ *n* [C] a small AXE (= tool for cutting wood) held in one hand • PIC› **Axe**

chop·per PENIS /£'tʃɒp·əʳ, $'tʃɑː·pɚ/ *n* [C] *Br taboo slang for* PENIS

chop·per MOTORCYCLE /£'tʃɒp·əʳ, $'tʃɑː·pɚ/ *n* [C] *infml* a motorcycle, esp. a very powerful one which has been changed in appearance after it was built

chop·pers /£'tʃɒp·əz, $'tʃɑː·pɚz/ *pl n slang* teeth, esp. a set of artificial teeth

chop·py /£'tʃɒp·i, $'tʃɑː·pi/ *adj* **-ier, -iest** (of sea, lakes or rivers) with lots of small, rough waves caused by the wind • *Half way through our boat journey the sea began getting choppy and I started to feel ill.*

chops /£tʃɒps, $tʃɑːps/ *pl n infml* the area of the face surrounding the mouth of a person or an animal • *The lions* **licked** *their chops after they had eaten.* • *She playfully pinched the little girl's chops* (= sides of the face). • *(Am slang)* Chops is also the way you hold your mouth when playing a wind instrument such as a SAXOPHONE, or more generally, your ability to play a musical instrument: *She's got great chops for a 14-year-old.*

chop·stick /£'tʃɒp·stɪk, $'tʃɑːp-/ *n* [C usually pl] either of a pair of thin narrow sticks used for eating food, esp. in E. Asia • PIC› **Cutlery**

chop su·ey /£,tʃɒp'suː·i, $,tʃɑːp-/ *n* [U] a Chinese-style dish made from small pieces of meat and vegetables, esp. beansprouts, cooked together

chor·al /£'kɔː·rᵊl, $'kɔːr·ᵊl/ *adj* of (music sung by) a CHOIR or a CHORUS • *choral music* • *a choral society*

chor·ale /£kɒr'ɑːl, kə'rɑːl/ *n* [C] a formal song written to be sung by a CHOIR (= group of singers), esp. in a church

chord /£kɔːd, $kɔːrd/ *n* [C] three or more musical notes played at the same time • PIC› **Music**

chore /£tʃɔːʳ, $tʃɔːr/ *n* [C] a job or piece of work which is often boring or unpleasant but needs to be done regularly • *I'll go shopping when I've done the/my chores* (= jobs in or around the house). • *As a child one of my chores was to feed the animals.* • *I find writing reports a real chore.*

cho·re·og·ra·phy /£,kɒr·i'ɒg·rə·fi, $,kɔːr·i'ɑː·grə-/ *n* [U] the skill of combining movements into dances to be performed • *His style of choreography is flamboyant.*

cho·re·o·graph *obj* /£'kɒr·i·ə·grɑːf, $'kɔːr·i·ə·græf/ *v* [T] • *The ballet was choreographed by Ashton.*

cho·re·og·raph·er /£,kɒr·i'ɒg·rə·fəʳ, $,kɔːr·i'ɑː·grə·fɚ/ *n* [C] • *Ballanchine, the well-known choreographer*

chor·ist·er /£'kɒr·ɪ·stəʳ, $'kɔːr·ɪ·stɚ/ *n* [C] one of a group of people who sing together in a CHOIR, either in a CATHEDRAL or in a special school connected to a university

chor·tle /£'tʃɔː·tl̩, $'tʃɔːr·tl̩/ *v, n* (to give) a laugh showing pleasure and satisfaction, often at someone else's misfortune • *The boys chortled* **with glee/gleefully** *at the success of their trick.* [I] • *He gave a chortle of pure delight when he realised he had won.* [C]

chor·us SONG PART /£'kɔː·rəs, $'kɔːr·əs/ *n* [C] part of a song which is repeated several times, usually after each VERSE (= set of lines), or a piece of music written to be sung by a CHOIR (= large group of trained singers) • *I'll sing the verses and I'd like you all to* **join in** *the chorus.* • *The choir will be performing the Hallelujah Chorus at the concert.* • *They burst into* **a chorus of** (= they sang the song) *Happy Birthday.* • ⓙ

chor·us SINGING GROUP /£'kɔː·rəs, $'kɔːr·əs/ *n* [C + sing/pl v] a group of people who are trained to sing together • *He sings with the Los Angeles Gay Men's Chorus.* • See also CHORAL. • ⓙ

chor·us THEATRE GROUP /£'kɔː·rəs, $'kɔːr·əs/ *n* [C + sing/pl v] a group of performers who, as a team, have a supporting position singing or dancing in a show • *She quickly left the chorus for a starring role.* • *a chorus* **girl** • *a chorus* **line** (= a row of people dancing and sometimes singing in an entertainment) • *(specialized)* In ancient Greek plays, the chorus was a group of male actors who explained or gave opinions on what was happening in the play using music, poetry and dance. • Ⓙ

chor·us SPEAK TOGETHER /£ˈkɔː·rəs, $ˈkɔːr·əs/ *v* [+ clause] (of a group of people) to say similar things at the same time; to speak together • *"Not now," the children chorused* **(in unison)**, *"we're watching a programme."* • Ⓙ

chor·us /£ˈkɔː·rəs, $ˈkɔːr·əs/ *n* [C usually sing] • *The newcomers added their voices to the chorus expressing delight at the result.* • *There was* **a** *chorus* **of** *disapproval/complaint/condemnation at his words* (= everyone complained together).

chose /£tʃəuz, $tʃouz/ *past simple of* CHOOSE

chos·en /£ˈtʃəu·zᵊn, $ˈtʃou-/ *past participle of* CHOOSE

choux pa·stry /ˌʃuː/ *n* [U] a type of pastry made with eggs which forms a hollow case for filling with cream or other thick liquids when cooked • *choux pastry eclairs* • *choux (pastry) buns/balls*

chow /tʃau/ *n* [U] *dated slang* food; something to eat • *It was 10 o'clock before we finally got our chow that night.*

chow·der *esp. Am* /£ˈtʃau·dəʳ, $-dɚ/ *n* [U] a type of thick soup usually made from fish or other sea creatures • *clam chowder*

Christ /kraɪst/ *n* [U] See JESUS (CHRIST) • See also CHRISTIAN.

christ·en *obj* /ˈkrɪs·ᵊn/ *v* [T] to give a name to and make (esp. a baby) a member of the Christian church through the ceremony of wetting its head with water • *She's being christened in June.* • *They christened their second child Maria.* [+ obj + n] • *He was christened John William* **after** *his grandfather* (= he was given the same names as his grandfather). [+ obj + n] • *(fig.) We christened him* (= gave him the name) *'slowcoach' because he took so long to do anything.* • *(fig.) I'm going to christen my new walking boots* (= use them for the first time) *on Saturday.* • Ⓝ

christ·en·ing /ˈkrɪs·ᵊn·ɪŋ/ *n* [C/U] • *We were pleased to receive an invitation to her baby's christening/christening ceremony.*

Christ·en·dom /ˈkrɪs·ᵊn·dəm/ *n* [U] *old use* Christian people or countries as a whole • *The news spread throughout Christendom.* • *All Christendom responded to the call.*

Christ·ian /ˈkrɪs·tʃən, -ti·ən/ *adj* of or belonging to the religion based on the teachings of Jesus Christ • *Christian values/beliefs/churches/books/philosophy* • *a Christian social worker* • If you describe a person or action as christian, you mean that they are good, kind, helpful, etc.: *It wasn't very christian of you to make him walk home in the rain.* Compare UNCHRISTIAN. • **The Christian era** is a system of counting time from the birth of Christ. • In Western countries, a **Christian name** is a personal name not a family name: *'James' and 'Sarah' are Christian names.* ○ *Some people have two or three Christian names.* ○ Compare **first name** at FIRST. • **Christian Science** is a religion which considers that illness can be cured by religious belief, making medicine unnecessary.

Christ·ian /ˈkrɪs·tʃən, -ti·ən/ *n* [C] • A Christian is someone who believes in and follows the teachings of Jesus Christ: *She became a Christian, although she was brought up in a non-Christian family.* • *He's* **a real** *Christian* (= good, kind, helpful, etc.).

Christ·i·an·i·ty /£ˌkrɪs·tiˈæn·ɪ·ti, $-tʃiˈæn·ə·ṭi/ *n* [U] • *Christianity is the religion based on the teachings of Jesus Christ.*

Christ·mas /ˈkrɪs·məs/ *n* [not after *the*] (the period just before and after) 25 December, a Christian holy day which celebrates the birth of Christ • *People usually visit their families* **at** *Christmas.* [U] • *Three Christmases ago there was a power cut.* [C] • **The Twelve Days of** Christmas is the period from 25 December to 6 January and is a time of celebrations. • **Happy** Christmas and **Merry** Christmas are traditional greetings. • *(Br)* A **Christmas box** is a small present, esp. of money, given at Christmas to the people who deliver the post, milk etc. to your house during the year. • *(Br and Aus)* **Christmas cake** is a cake containing a lot of dried fruit and nuts with ICING (= a white sugar covering) made to be eaten at Christmas. • A **Christmas card** is a decorated card sent to someone at Christmas with good wishes. • *(Br)* A **Christmas cracker** (*Am* **bonbon**) is a tube of brightly coloured paper given at Christmas parties which makes a noise when pulled apart by two people and contains a small present, a paper hat and a joke. • *On* **Christmas Day**, *25 December, people have a special meal.* • **Christmas Eve** is 24 December, the day before Christmas Day. • *(Br and Aus)* **Christmas pudding** (*Am, Br also* **plum pudding**) is a type of cake, traditionally dark brown, ball-shaped and made with a lot of dried fruit, which is cooked by steaming and is eaten hot at the end of the meal, esp. on Christmas Day. • A **Christmas stocking** is a type of large sock which children leave out when they go to bed on Christmas Eve so that it can be filled with small presents. • **Christmas-time** (*old use* **Christmastide**) is the period just before and after Christmas Day. • A **Christmas tree** is a real or artificial FIR tree which is decorated with things such as coloured balls and kept esp. in the house at Christmas. • *"Christmas is coming, the geese are getting fat, / Please put a penny in the old man's hat"* (traditional rhyme) • *"'Twas the night before Christmas, when all through the house / Not a creature was stirring, not even a mouse"* (from the poem *A Visit From St Nicholas* by Clement C. Moore, 1823) • *"At Christmas play and make good cheer, For Christmas comes but once a year"* (Thomas Tusser *Five Hundred Points of Good Husbandry*, c.1524-1580) • LP **Holidays** PIC **Bread and cakes**

Christ·mas·sy /ˈkrɪs·mə·si/ *adj* • *The card showed a Christmassy scene of people singing carols* (= Christmas songs) *in a snowy street.* • *It was hot and sunny on Christmas Day – it didn't feel at all Christmassy to those of us used to cold dark winter days.*

chro·mat·ic /£krəuˈmæt·ɪk, $krouˈmæṭ-/ *adj* of colours; coloured

chrome /£krəum, $kroum/ *n* [U] another word for CHROMIUM • *office furnishings in glass, leather and chrome* • *a chrome-plated mower blade* • *chrome trimmings* • **Chrome yellow** is bright yellow.

chrom·i·um /£ˈkrəu·mi·əm, $ˈkrou-/ *n* [U] a hard blue-grey element used in combination with other substances to form a shiny covering on objects

chrom·o·some /£ˈkrəu·mə·zəum, $ˈkrou·mə·zoum/ *n* [C] any of the rod-like structures found in all living cells containing the chemical patterns which control what an animal or plant is like • *mouse chromosomes* • *X and Y chromosomes* • *sex chromosomes* • *a chromosome defect*

chron·ic /£ˈkrɒn·ɪk, $ˈkrɑː·nɪk/ *adj* (esp. of a disease or something bad) continuing for a long time • *chronic diseases/conditions* • *chronic arthritis/pain* • *a chronic effect/alcoholic* • *a chronic invalid* • *There is a chronic* **shortage** *of teachers/housing.* • *(Br and Aus infml)* Chronic can mean very bad: *The pain was chronic.* ○ *The entertainment was chronic.*

chronically /£ˈkrɒn·ɪ·kli, $ˈkrɑː·nɪ-/ *adv* • *chronically ill*

chron·i·cle /£ˈkrɒn·ɪ·kl̩, $ˈkrɑː·nɪ-/ *n* [C] an esp. written record of esp. historical events • *the Anglo-Saxon Chronicle* • *a chronicle* **of** *the French Revolution* • *(infml) We heard the sad chronicle* (= story) **of** *his accidents.* • Chronicle can be part of the name of a newspaper: *the Hampshire Chronicle*

chron·i·cle *obj* /£ˈkrɒn·ɪ·kl̩, $ˈkrɑː·nɪ-/ *v* [T] • To chronicle something is to make a record or give details of it: *The book chronicles the writer's coming to terms with his illness.* ○ *They observed people's behaviour in pubs and chronicled what they saw and heard.* • *"To suckle fools and chronicle small beer* (= unimportant things)*"* (Shakespeare, Othello 2.1)

Chronicles /£ˈkrɒn·ɪ·kl̩z, $ˈkrɑː·nɪ-/ *n* [U] • Chronicles is the name of two books of the Jewish holy writings and Christian Old Testament.

chron·ic·ler /£ˈkrɒn·ɪ·kləʳ, $ˈkrɑː·nɪ·klɚ/ *n* [C]

chron·o·graph /£ˈkrɒn·ə·grɑːf, £ˈkrəu·nə·græf, $ˈkrɑː·nə·græf/ *n* [C] *specialized* a piece of equipment which measures and records periods of time

chron·ol·o·gy /£krəˈnɒl·ə·dʒi, $-ˈnɑː·lə-/ *n* (the study of) the ordering of events by the time at which they happened, or a list of events so ordered • *Does the study of history require an emphasis on chronology, a clear sense of the sequence of events in time?* [U] • *He gave a detailed chronology of the main events of the last three days.* [C]

chron·o·log·ic·al /£ˌkrɒn·əˈlɒdʒ·ɪ·kᵊl, $-ˈlɑː·dʒɪ-/ *adj* • *Give me the dates* **in** *chronological* **order**.

chron·o·log·ic·al·ly /£ˌkrɒn·əˈlɒdʒ·ɪ·kli, $-ˈlɑː·dʒɪ-/ *adv*

chron·om·e·ter /£krəˈnɒm·ɪ·təʳ, $-ˈnɑː·mɪ·ṭɚ/ *n* [C] *specialized* a piece of equipment which measures time very exactly

chry·sa·lis /ˈkrɪs·əl·ɪs/ *n* [C] *pl* **chrysalises** an insect covered by a hard protective case at the stage of development before it becomes a MOTH or BUTTERFLY with wings • PIC› **Insects**

chry·san·the·mum /krɪˈsæntθ·ɪ·məm, -ˈzæntθ-/ *n* [C] any of several types of garden plant, including some with many small flowers and some with few but very large flowers

chub·by /ˈtʃʌb·i/ *adj* **-ier, -iest** (esp. of children) fat in a pleasant and attractive way • *chubby little fingers and toes* • *chubby cheeks* • *a chubby smiling face*

chub·bi·ness /ˈtʃʌb·ɪ·nəs/ *n* [U]

chuck *obj* THROW /tʃʌk/ *v* [T] *infml* to throw carelessly • *Chuck it away/over there/into the corner.* • *Chuck me the keys/Chuck the keys* **to** *me.* [+ two objects] • *I chucked* **out** *all my student notes/I chucked my notes out.* [M] • *The caretaker chucked* **out** *the troublemakers/chucked them* **out** *(of the hall).* [M]

chuck *obj* END /tʃʌk/ *v* [T] *infml* to end, stop or leave (something) • *I'm going to chuck* **(in)** (= leave) *my job.* [T/M] • *(Br dated infml)* If you chuck someone, you end your romantic relationship with them: *He chucked his girlfriend.* ○ *I've just been chucked by my boyfriend.*

chuck *obj* TOUCH /tʃʌk/ *v* [T] **chuck** *someone* **under the chin** to touch (esp. a younger person) in a friendly way under the CHIN • *"Cheer up", she said and chucked the little girl under the chin.*

chuck /tʃʌk/ *n* [U] • *He gave her a chuck* **under the chin.**

chuck PERSON /tʃʌk/, **chuc·kie** *n Br regional infml* used as a form of address for someone you like • *"All right, then, chuck?"* [as form of address]

chuck MACHINE /tʃʌk/ *n* [C] *specialized* a device for holding an object firmly in a machine

chuck (steak) /tʃʌk/ *n* [U] a piece of meat cut from the shoulder area of a cow

chuck·le /ˈtʃʌkl/ *v* [C], *n* (to give) a low or quiet laugh • *She was chuckling as she read the letter.* • *He gave a chuckle in response to her question.*

chuff *Br* /tʃʌf/ *v* [I always + adv/prep] to make the sound of a steam train or to move making this sound; to CHUG • *The engine chuffed slowly out of the station.*

chuffed /tʃʌft/ *adj Br and Aus infml* pleased or happy • *She's very chuffed* **about** *her daughter's success.* • *They were less than chuffed* **with** *the results.* • *He was chuffed* **to** *learn he had come first.* [+ *to* infinitive]

chug /tʃʌg/ *v* [I always + adv/prep] **-gg-** to make the sound of an engine or motor, or to move making this sound • *The lorry chugged up the hill/along the rough track.*

chug /tʃʌg/ *n* • *We heard the chug(-chug) of the boat's engine in the distance.*

chum /tʃʌm/ *n* [C] *dated infml* a friend • *They were old school/college chums.* • *One worry was that bosses were free to appoint their chums or their countrymen rather than the best people for the job.*

chum up /tʃʌm/ *v adv* [I] *Br infml* • *She chummed up* **with** (= became friends with) *some girls from Bristol on holiday.* • *MacGregor and Peters chummed up on the streets of New York.*

chum·my /ˈtʃʌm·i/ *adj* **-ier, -iest** *infml* • *They're very chummy* (= friendly) **with** *their neighbours.* • *I've noticed that she's getting very chummy* (= friendly in a way that is not approved of) **with** *the course tutor.*

chump /tʃʌmp/ *n* [C] *dated infml* a foolish or stupid person but not one who is disliked • *What a chump he is!* • *You chump! Why did you tell her that?* [as form of address] • *(Br slang)* If someone **is/goes off** their **chump** they are/become foolish and do not act in a sensible way.

chump chop /tʃʌmp/ *n Br and Aus* a thick piece of meat, esp. LAMB (= meat from a young sheep), containing bone, cut from the top of a leg

chund·er /£ˈtʃʌn·dəʳ, $-dɚ/ *v* [I] *esp. Aus infml* to vomit • *He rushed out of the bar and chundered in the street.*

chund·er /£ˈtʃʌn·dəʳ, $-dɚ/ *n* [U] *esp. Aus infml* • *I nearly stepped in* **a pool of** *chunder.*

chunk /tʃʌŋk/ *n* [C] a roughly cut lump • *pineapple chunks* • *a chunk of cheese/meat* • *chunks of stone* • *(infml)* A chunk is a part of something, esp. a large part: *a chunk of text* ○ *a substantial chunk of our profits* ○ *Three hours is quite a chunk out of my working day.*

chunk·y /ˈtʃʌŋ·ki/ *adj* **-ier, -iest** • Chunky clothes are thick and heavy and chunky jewellery is made of large pieces: *a chunky sweater* ○ *a chunky necklace* • Chunky **marmalade** has thick pieces of RIND (= outer layer of particular fruits) in it. • *(approving)* A person, esp. a man, who is described as chunky has a wide upper body and looks strong.

Chun·nel /ˈtʃʌn·əl/ *n* [U] **the Chunnel** *infml for* the **Channel Tunnel**, see at CHANNEL PASSAGE

chunt·er /£ˈtʃʌn·təʳ, $-tɚ/ *v* [I] *Br infml* to complain, esp. in a low voice • *He was always chuntering* **(on) about** *being the last to know what was happening.*

chu·pat·ti /£tʃəˈpɑː·ti, $-t̬i/ *n* [C] a CHAPATI

church BUILDING /£tʃɜːtʃ, $tʃɜːrtʃ/ *n* [C] a building for Christian religious activities • *The town has four churches.* • *church buildings* • *a church spire/tower* • *a church hall* (= a building with a large room for meetings) • *"Get me to the Church on Time"* (title of a song written by Alan Jay Lerner, 1956)

church ORGANIZATION /£tʃɜːtʃ, $tʃɜːrtʃ/ *n* an official Christian religious organization • *All the local churches were represented at the memorial service.* [C] • *Christian Aid is an organization through which the Anglican Church, the Catholic Church, the Free Churches and other church groups work together to give aid to developing countries.* • *He went on a walking trip with some of his friends from church.* [U] • Church is also the organization meeting as a group of people: *I'll see her* **before/after** *church.* [U] ○ *They* **go to/attend** *church every Sunday.* [U] • *The times of the church* **services** *were on the noticeboard.* • *She's very involved in church activities.* • *Some people think* **the Church** (= Christian religious organizations) *shouldn't interfere in politics.* • *When he took early retirement, he decided to* **go into/enter the church** (= become a priest). • The **Church of England** (*abbreviation* **C of E**), or the Anglican church, is by law the official church in England, and its leader is the king or queen: *a Church of England priest*

church·go·er /£ˈtʃɜːtʃˌgəʊ·əʳ, $ˈtʃɜːrtʃˌgoʊ·ɚ/ *n* [C] a person who goes regularly to church • *He's never been a regular churchgoer.*

church·go·ing /£ˈtʃɜːtʃˌgəʊ·ɪŋ, $ˈtʃɜːrtʃˌgoʊ-/ *n* [U] • *Churchgoing in Britain is declining.*

church·man (*pl* **-men**), **church·wo·man** (*pl* **-women**) /£ˈtʃɜːtʃ·mən, -mæn, $ˈtʃɜːrtʃ-, -ˌwʊm·ən/ *n* [C] a priest or other official in the church • *Some churchmen are very hostile towards the idea of women priests or of churchwomen in general.*

church·y /£ˈtʃɜː·tʃi, $ˈtʃɜːr-/ *adj* **-ier, -iest** *infml disapproving* too formal or religious • *a churchy atmosphere/voice* • *The music was hypnotic, contemporary, spiritually provocative and never churchy.*

church·yard /£ˈtʃɜːtʃ·jɑːd, $ˈtʃɜːrtʃ·jɑːrd/ *n* [C] an area of land around a church where dead bodies are buried

churl·ish /£ˈtʃɜː·lɪʃ, $ˈtʃɜːr-/ *adj* rude, unfriendly and unpleasant • *Only a churlish person would call this town dull.* • *They invited me to dinner and I thought* **it** *would be churlish* **to** *refuse.* [+ *to* infinitive]

churl·ish·ly /£ˈtʃɜː·lɪʃ·li, $ˈtʃɜːr-/ *adv*

churl·ish·ness /£ˈtʃɜː·lɪʃ·nəs, £ˈtʃɜːr-/ *n* [U]

churn *(obj)* /£tʃɜːn, $tʃɜːrn/ *v* to move (something) energetically in different directions • *She churned the milk until it turned into butter.* [T] • *The pigs churned* **about** *in the mud.* [I] • *The fish churned* **(up)** *the water when we threw in the food.* [T; I + *up*] • *(fig.) My* **stomach** *was churning with worry when the phone didn't ring.* [I]

churn /£tʃɜːn, $tʃɜːrn/ *n* [C] • A churn is a large container for transporting milk or for making milk into butter: *a milk churn* ○ *a butter churn*

churn out *obj*, **churn** *obj* **out** *v adv* [M] *infml* to produce (esp. something of bad quality) repeatedly and in large amounts • *The factory churns out thousands of pairs of these shoes every week.* • *She churns out a new bestselling novel every year.*

chute SLIDE /ʃuːt/ *n* [C] a narrow steep slope down which objects or people can slide • *a (esp. Br) rubbish/(esp. Am) garbage chute* • *a laundry chute* • *Take off your shoes before sliding down the emergency chute.*

chute CLOTH DEVICE /ʃuːt/ *n* [C] *infml for* PARACHUTE

chut·ney /ˈtʃʌt·ni/ *n* [C/U] a mixture containing fruit, spices, sugar and vinegar, eaten cold with esp. meat or cheese • *tomato and apple chutney* • *plum chutney*

chutz·pah /ˈhʊt·spɑː/ *n* [U] *approving* imaginative and shocking behaviour, involving taking risks but not feeling guilt • *Chutzpah is the quality shown by the man who, having killed both parents, throws himself on the mercy of the courts as an orphan.*

CIA /ˌsiː·aɪˈeɪ/ *n* [U] **the CIA** *abbreviation for* Central Intelligence Agency (= the US government organization which secretly collects information about other countries)

ciao *infml* /tʃaʊ/ *exclamation* hello or goodbye

ci·ca·da /sɪˈkɑː·də/ *n* [C] *pl* **cicadas** a large insect found in warm countries which produces a high continuous sound

CID /ˌsiː·aɪˈdiː/ *n* [U] **the CID** *abbreviation for* Criminal Investigation Department (=the part of the UK police which does not wear uniform and which tries to discover who has committed crimes)

ci·der /ˈsaɪ·dər, $-dɚ/ *n* [U] a drink made from apples which sometimes contains alcohol • Ⓙ ⓀⓄⓇ

cig /sɪg/ *n* [C] *infml* a cigarette

ci·gar /£sɪˈgɑːr, $-gɑːr/ *n* [C] a number of dried tobacco leaves rolled into a short stick, which people smoke • *He enjoys an after-dinner cigar and brandy.* • *a cigar-***shaped** *balloon*

ci·gar·ette /£ˌsɪg·əˈret, $-ɚˈ-/, *infml* **cig**, **cig·gy** /ˈsɪg·i/, *Br and Aus infml* **fag** *n* [C] a small paper tube filled with cut pieces of tobacco, which people smoke • *a pack(et) of cigarettes* • *a cigarette smoker* • *Is there a cigarette machine in this bar?* • *She* **lit** *a cigarette,* **dragged on** *it* (=put it to her mouth and breathed in the smoke) *several times and then* **stubbed** *it* **out**. • A **cigarette end** (*Am and Aus* **cigarette butt**) is the part of the cigarette which remains after it has been smoked: *After the party the floor was littered with cigarette ends.* • A **cigarette holder** is a tube into which a cigarette is put to be held between the fingers for smoking. • A **cigarette lighter** is a device which produces a small flame. • A **cigarette paper** is a thin piece of paper used in making a cigarette, esp. by someone who makes their own. • PIC〉 **Containers**

cill /sɪl/ *n* [C] a SILL

C-in-C /ˌsiː·ɪnˈsiː/ *n* [C] *abbreviation for* **commander-in-chief**, see at COMMANDER

cinch /sɪntʃ/ *n* something which is very easy and is therefore a certainty • *Choosing the best shares to buy when the stock market was rising was a cinch* (=it was easy to be right). • *It's a cinch!*

cin·der /£ˈsɪn·dər, $-dɚ/ *n* [C] a small piece of partly burnt coal or wood • *Rake out the cinders before you start a new fire.* • *The cake was* **burnt** *to a cinder* (=burnt black). • *(Am)* A **cinder block** is a small light block made of concrete mixed with burnt coal which is used in building esp. the walls of houses and other buildings.

Cin·der·el·la /£ˌsɪn·dəˈrel·ə, $-dəˈrel-/ *n* [C] someone or something that is given little attention or care, esp. less than they deserve • *Mental health has long been considered the Cinderella of the health service.* • *Many Russians felt that their republic had been the Soviet Union's Cinderella, better endowed than any other but forced to give way to them all.* • The original Cinderella was a girl in a traditional story who was badly treated by her family.

ci·ne·ma /ˈsɪn·ɪ·mə/, *Am usually* **mov·ie the·a·ter**, *Aus usually* **mov·ie the·a·tre** *n* [C] a theatre where people pay to watch films • *The town no longer has a cinema.* • *a cinema ticket/seat* • *(esp. Br) We* **go to** *the cinema (Am, Aus also* **go to the movies**) (=go to watch a film) *every week.* • *(esp. Br) He was well known for his work in* **the cinema** *(Am and Aus usually* **the movies**) (=in films/film-making).

ci·ne·mat·ic *specialized* /£sɪ·nɪˈmæt·ɪk, $-ˈmæṭ-/ *adj* • *The cinematic effects in her films are clearly borrowed from the great film-makers of the past.* • *There is an almost cinematic quality to this novel/play.*

ci·ne·ma·go·er *esp. Br* /£ˈsɪ·nɪ·məˌgəʊ·ər, $-ˌgoʊ·ɚ/, *esp. Br* **film·go·er**, *esp. Am and Aus* **mov·ie·go·er** *n* [C] a person who regularly goes to watch films at the cinema

ci·ne·ma·go·ing *esp. Br* /£ˈsɪ·nɪ·məˌgəʊ·ɪŋ, $-ˌgoʊ·ɪŋ/, *esp. Br* **film·go·ing**, *esp. Am and Aus* **mov·ie·go·ing** *n* [U] • *Cinemagoing is still popular with the young.* • *The cinemagoing public made the film a box-office success.*

ci·ne·ma·to·gra·phy /£ˌsɪn·ɪ·məˈtɒg·rə·fi, $-ˈtɑː·grə-/ *n* [U] *specialized* the art and methods of film photography • *He's studying cinematography.*

ci·ne·ma·to·gra·pher /£ˌsɪn·ɪ·məˈtɒg·rə·fər, $-ˈtɑː·grə·fɚ/ *n* [C] *specialized* • *She's an expert cinematographer who's not afraid to use the camera in new ways.*

cin·na·mon /ˈsɪn·ə·mən/ *n* [U] a piece of BARK (=outer covering) of a tropical tree, or a brown powder made from this, used as a spice to give a particular taste to esp. sweet food • *A cinnamon* **stick** *placed in a container of sugar gives it a pleasant flavour.* • *Sprinkle the top of the cake with cinnamon.* • *The dress is available in cinnamon* (=the colour of cinnamon) *and green.*

ci·pher SECRET LANGUAGE, **cy·pher** /£ˈsaɪ·fər, $-fɚ/ *n specialized* a system of writing that prevents most people from understanding the message; a CODE • *As a former intelligence expert he had information about enemy ciphers.* [C] • *The message was written* **in** *cipher.* [U]

ci·pher PERSON /£ˈsaɪ·fər, $-fɚ/ *n* [C] a person or group of people without power, but used by others for their own purposes, or someone who is not important • *Teachers complained that the new regulations turned them into ciphers.* • *The interim government is a* **mere** *cipher for military rule.* • *In the manager's view she's a cipher.*

ci·pher NUMBER /£ˈsaɪ·fər, $-fɚ/ *n* [C] *Am* a zero • *If you have no children enter a cipher in the space on the form.*

cir·ca /£ˈsɜː·kə, $ˈsɜːr-/ (*abbreviation* **c**, **ca**) *prep fml* (used esp. with years) approximately • *He was born circa 1600.*

cir·cle SHAPE /£ˈsɜː·kl̩, $ˈsɜːr-/ *n* [C] a continuous curved line, the points of which are always the same distance away from a fixed central point, or the area enclosed by such a line • *Coloured paper was cut into circles, squares and triangles.* • *We drew a pattern of interlocking circles.* • *A circle of chairs had been set out in the centre of the room.* • To **go round in circles/a circle** or to **run round in circles** is to keep doing or talking about the same thing without achieving anything: *The discussion kept going round in circles.* ○ *I've been running round in circles trying to get all the reports finished before the meeting.* • See also CIRCULAR (ROUND). • PIC〉 **Shapes** Ⓙ ⓀⓄⓇ

cir·cle *(obj)* /£ˈsɜː·kl̩, $ˈsɜːr-/ *v* • *The plane circled* (=travelled in a circle around the area) *for an hour before receiving permission to land.* [I] • *Security staff circled the grounds of the house with guard dogs every hour.* [T] • *She circled* (=drew a circle round) *the initials at the top of the page.* [T] • *(fig.) Once the leader's position started to look weak, the vultures began to circle looking for any advantage.* [I] • See also ENCIRCLE.

cir·cu·lar /£ˈsɜː·kjʊ·lər, $ˈsɜːr·kjʊ·lɚ/ *adj* • *a circular flowerbed/tablecloth* • *a circular route/walk/tour* • *a circular mark/stain* • A circular **argument** is one which keeps returning to the same points and is not effective. • See also CIRCULAR.

cir·cu·lar·i·ty /£ˌsɜː·kjʊˈlær·ɪ·ti, $ˌsɜːr·kjʊˈler·ɪ·ṭi/ *n* [U] • *the circularity of political arguments* • *You cannot judge psychoanalysis unless you have been analysed – a nice circularity!*

cir·cle GROUP /£ˈsɜː·kl̩, $ˈsɜːr-/ *n* [C] a group of people with family, work or social connections • *We never mention the subject outside the* **family** *circle.* • *She's not one of my close circle* **of friends**. • *It's a technical term commonly used in medical/diplomatic/financial circles.* • *We never meet these days – we* **move in** *different circles* (=do not have the same group of friends). • *They* **move in exalted** *circles* (=have rich or important friends). • Ⓙ ⓀⓄⓇ

cir·cle UPPER FLOOR /£ˈsɜː·kl̩, $ˈsɜːr-/ *n* [U] an upper floor in a theatre or cinema where people sit to watch the performance • *Shall I get seats in* **the** *circle or in the stalls?* • **Dress/Front** *circle seats/tickets are quite expensive – the* **upper** *circle is cheaper.* • Compare GALLERY RAISED AREA; STALLS THEATRE. • Ⓙ ⓀⓄⓇ

cir·cuit CLOSED SYSTEM /£ˈsɜː·kɪt, $ˈsɜːr-/ *n* [C] a closed system of wires or pipes through which electricity or liquid can flow • *A defect was found in the water-cooling/electrical circuit.* • A **circuit breaker** is a safety device which stops the flow of current to an electrical system when there is a fault. Compare FUSE SAFETY PART. • A **circuit diagram** is a plan of an electrical or electronic circuit.

cir·cuit·ry /£ˈsɜː·kɪ·tri, $ˈsɜːr-/ *n* [U] • The circuitry of an electrical or electronic device is the CIRCUITS that it contains, considered as a single system: *The circuitry in this fighter aircraft has been protected against strong magnetic fields.*

cir·cuit TRACK /£ˈsɜː·kɪt, $ˈsɜːr-/ *n* [C] something shaped approximately like a circle, esp. a route, path or sports track which starts and ends in the same place • *They test the car tyres on a motor racing circuit.* • *We* **made a** *leisurely circuit* **of** *the city walls before lunch.* • **Circuit training** is a type of sports training which involves sets of different exercises done in order one after the other.

cir·cuit JOURNEY /£ˈsɜː·kɪt, $ˈsɜːr-/ *n* a regular pattern of visits or the places visited • *They first met each other* **on the** *tennis circuit* (=going to different tennis competitions). [C] • *They were familiar figures* **on the** *lecture/diplomatic/cocktail/after-dinner circuit* (=they went to/spoke at/took part in many events of this type). [C] • *(law) The judge had served for many years on the North-east Circuit* (=in different courts in the north-east). [C] • *(Br law) For several* *months each year the judge is* **on** *circuit.* [U] • *(law) The case was tried by a circuit judge.*

cir·cu·it·ous /£sɜːˈkjuː·ɪ·təs, $sɜːrˈkjuː·ɪ·t̬əs/ *adj fml* not straight or direct; ROUNDABOUT [INDIRECT] • *a circuitous route/path* • *a circuitous explanation*

cir·cu·it·ous·ly /£sɜːˈkjuː·ɪ·tə·sli, $sɜːrˈkjuː·ɪ·t̬ə-/ *adv*

cir·cu·lar /£ˈsɜː·kjʊ·ləʳ, $ˈsɜːr·kjʊ·lɚ/ *n* [C] a letter or notice sent to a large number of people • *I always put circulars and other junk mail straight in the bin.* • *Several circulars advertising new shops in the town were delivered with the local newspaper.* • See also **circular** at CIRCLE [SHAPE].

cir·cu·lar·ize *obj, Br and Aus usually* **-ise** /£ˈsɜː·kjʊ·lə·raɪz, $ˈsɜːr-/ *v* [T] • *To sell the tickets it is usually necessary to circularize local organizations.*

cir·cu·late /£ˈsɜː·kjʊ·leɪt, $ˈsɜːr-/ *v* to (cause to) move round or through • *Hot water circulates through the heating system.* [I] • *The bad news quickly circulated round the office.* [I] • *Don't stay talking to one person all evening – circulate among your guests.* [I] • *They circulated a good luck card for everyone to sign.* [T]

cir·cu·la·tion /£ˌsɜː·kjʊˈleɪ·ʃᵊn, $ˌsɜːr-/ *n* • *They are studying a group of people with poor circulation* (= of the blood round the body). [U] • *Add her name to the circulation* **list** *for this report* (= the people who will be given it to read). • *The old banknotes are being* **taken out of/withdrawn from** *circulation* (= use). [U] • *(infml) I hear she's* **out of** *circulation/back* **in** *circulation* (= taking part/not taking part in social activities) *after her car crash.* [U] • The circulation of a newspaper or a magazine is the number of people to whom it is regularly sold: *The paper has a circulation of 150 000.* [C] • Ⓕ Ⓟ

cir·cum·cise *obj* /£ˈsɜː·kəm·saɪz, $ˈsɜːr-/ *v* [T] to cut the protecting loose skin off a boy's penis or to cut away a girl's CLITORIS and the skin around it, for medical, traditional or religious reasons

cir·cum·ci·sion /£ˌsɜː·kəmˈsɪʒ·ᵊn, $ˌsɜːr-/ *n* [C/U]

cir·cum·fe·rence /£səˈkʌmp·fᵊr·ᵊnts, $sɚˈkʌmp·fɚ-/ *n* the distance around a circle, or the distance around the widest part of a circular or round object; the line enclosing a circular space • *the circumference of a circle/an orange* [C] • *Draw a circle 30 centimetres* **in** *circumference.* [U] • **The circumference** is the outside edge of an area of any size or shape: *When walking dogs, please keep to the circumference of the park.* • PIC〉 **Shapes**

cir·cum·flex /£ˈsɜː·kəm·fleks, $ˈsɜːr-/ *n* [C] a sign (^) over a letter, esp. a vowel, which shows that it has a different pronunciation from the letter without a sign over it • LP〉 **Symbols**

cir·cum·lo·cu·tion /£ˌsɜː·kəm·ləˈkjuː·ʃᵊn, $ˌsɜːr-/ *n fml* (an example of) an indirect way of saying something, esp. something unpleasant • *'Economical with the truth' is a circumlocution for 'lying'.* [C] • *Politicians are experts in circumlocution.* [U]

cir·cum·lo·cu·to·ry /£ˌsɜː·kəm·ləˈkjuː·tᵊr·i, $ˌsɜːr·kəmˈlɑ·kjuː·t̬ɚ-/ *adj fml*

cir·cum·nav·i·gate *obj* /£ˌsɜː·kəmˈnæv·ɪ·geɪt, $ˌsɜːr-/ *v* [T] *fml* to sail all the way around, or *(fig.)* to move around (something) in order to avoid hitting it • *They circumnavigated Cape Horn Island in canoes.* • *(fig.) We carried the picture carefully through to the main exhibition, circumnavigating several obstacles en route.* • *(fig.) Manufacturers and shops circumnavigate* (= avoid) *gun laws by providing realistic models which are unable to discharge missiles.*

cir·cum·nav·i·ga·tion /£sɜː·kəmˌnæv·ɪˈgeɪ·ʃᵊn, $ˌsɜːr-/ *n* [C/U] *fml* • *a circumnavigation of the globe from west to east*

cir·cum·scribe *obj* /£ˈsɜː·kəm·skraɪb, ˌ-ˈ-, $ˈsɜːr-/ *v* [T] *fml* to (severely) limit • *Their room for manoeuvre will be severely circumscribed by current views on taxation.* • *There followed a series of tightly circumscribed visits to military installations.* • *(specialized)* If you circumscribe a triangle, square etc., you draw a circle which encloses it and touches each of its corners.

cir·cum·spect /£ˈsɜː·kəm·spekt, $ˈsɜːr-/ *adj fml* careful and attentive • *Forty years of twists and turns in politics have taught them to remain circumspect.* • *Officials were circumspect* **about** *what the talks had achieved and the minister spoke cautiously of 'action within a year'.*

cir·cum·spec·tion /£ˌsɜː·kəmˈspek·ʃᵊn, $ˌsɜːr-/ *n* [U] *fml* • *All those involved in the negotiations need to display caution, circumspection and self-control.* • *He is not an ordinary political prisoner and his case requires particular circumspection.*

cir·cum·spect·ly /£ˈsɜː·kəm·spekt·li, $ˈsɜːr-/ *adv fml*

cir·cum·stance /£ˈsɜː·kəm·stɑːnts, $ˈsɜːr·kəm·stænts/ *n* an event connected with what is happening or has happened • *They celebrated the remarkable circumstance of the birth of a daughter after five sons.* [C] • *They were victims of circumstance.* [U] • *We were obliged to do it* **by force of/regardless of** *circumstance.* [U] • *It was a town where nothing* **of** *circumstance* (= nothing important) *ever happened.* [U] • *We can't decide until we know all the circumstances.* [C] • *Their actions attracted strong criticism in the present poor economic circumstances.* [C] • *They are opposed to abortion* **in/under** *almost any circumstances.* [C] • **In/under** *no circumstances can we afford bad publicity.* [C] • *The meeting has been cancelled* **due to** *circumstances* **beyond our control.** [C] • *I'm going away next week so* **under the circumstances** (= because of this) *I wouldn't have time to start and finish the job.*

cir·cum·stan·tial /£ˌsɜː·kəmˈstɑːn·tʃᵊl, $ˌsɜːr-, -ˈstæn-/ *adj* • Circumstantial **evidence** is information, esp. about a crime, which is not firm proof but is based on related events: *No-one saw him commit the murder, but the circumstantial evidence is strong, as he was the only person missing when it happened.* ○ *Circumstantial evidence points to a viral agent for the disease, although a virus has not yet been identified.*

cir·cum·vent *obj* /£ˌsɜː·kəmˈvent, ˈ---, $ˌsɜːr-/ *v* [T] *fml* to avoid, esp. cleverly and/or illegally • *Ships were registered abroad to circumvent employment and safety regulations.*

cir·cum·ven·tion /£ˌsɜː·kəmˈven·tʃᵊn, $ˌsɜːr-/ *n* [U] *fml*

cir·cus [ENTERTAINMENT] /£ˈsɜː·kəs, $ˈsɜːr-/ *n* [C] a group of travelling entertainers including ACROBATS (= people skilled in difficult physical movements), or those who work with trained animals, or a performance by such people usually in a large tent • *She ran away to join the circus.* • *The children loved being taken to the circus.* • *The horses trotted into the circus* **ring** (= the large circle, with seats all round, in which a circus performance takes place). • A group of people travelling to different places together as a part of their work is sometimes called a circus: *the media circus* • A noisy uncontrolled occasion might be described as a circus: *The judge was determined not to let his courtroom turn into a circus.*

cir·cus [ROAD] /£ˈsɜː·kəs, $ˈsɜːr-/ *n Br* an open circular area where several roads join • *Piccadilly Circus* • *Oxford Circus*

cir·rho·sis /£sɪˈrəʊ·sɪs, $-ˈroʊ-/ *n* [U] *medical* a serious disease of the LIVER (= an organ in the body) which usually causes death • *The commonest cause of cirrhosis is drinking too much alcohol.* • *He died of cirrhosis of the liver.*

cir·rus /ˈsɪr·əs/ *n* [U] a type of light feathery cloud that is seen high in the sky • Compare CUMULUS; NIMBUS.

cis·sy /ˈsɪs·i/ *n* [C], *adj* SISSY

Cis·ter·cian /£sɪˈstɜː·ʃᵊn, $-ˈstɜːr-/ *n* [C], *adj* [not gradable] (a member) of a Christian ORDER (= a religious group) • *The Cisterican Order was started in France in 1098.* • *He belonged to the Cistercian Order.* • *Cistercian monks and nuns take a vow of silence.*

cis·tern /£ˈsɪs·tən, $-tɚn/ *n* [C] a container in which water is stored, esp. one connected to a toilet or in the roof of a house

ci·ta·del /£ˈsɪt·ə·del, $ˈsɪt̬-/ *n* [C] a strong castle in or near a city, where people can shelter from danger, esp. during a war • *The town has a 14th century citadel overlooking the river.* • A citadel is also a powerful organization in which it is difficult for someone who does not know people who work there, to find a job: *At the age of 32, she managed to enter/storm one of the citadels of high fashion.*

cite *obj* [GIVE EXAMPLE] /saɪt/ *v* [T] *fml* to mention (something) as proof for a theory or as a reason why something has happened, or to speak or write (words taken from a written work) • *She cited three reasons why people get into debt.* • *The company cited a 12% decline in new orders* **as** *evidence that overall demand for its products was falling.* • *A breakdown in law enforcement in the inner cities is frequently cited* **as** *a factor for the increase in crime.* • *He cited a passage from the Koran to support his argument.* • *In the article, she cites T.S. Eliot and Virginia Woolf.*

ci·ta·tion /saɪˈteɪ·ʃᵊn/ *n* [C] • A citation is a word or piece of writing taken from a written work: *All citations are taken from the 1973 edition of the text.* ○ *She assisted me* *during the final stages of the work, proof-reading the text and checking the citations.*

cite *obj* NAME /saɪt/ *v* [T] *law* to officially name or mention (someone or something) in a court of law, or to officially request (someone) to appear in a court of law • *The lawyer cited two similar cases.* • *He has been cited* **as** *the co-respondent in the divorce case.*

ci·ta·tion /saɪˈteɪ·ʃᵊn/ *n* [C] *law* • A citation is an official request for someone to appear in a court of law: *The court issued a contempt citation against city council members who refused to comply with a court order.*

cite *obj* PRAISE /saɪt/ *v* [T] *fml* to praise (someone in the armed forces) publicly because of their bravery • *He was cited* **for** *bravery.*

ci·ta·tion /saɪˈteɪ·ʃᵊn/ *n* [C] • A citation is official praise for a person in the armed forces for bravery: *The four soldiers are to receive citations from the President* **for** *their brave actions.*

ci·ti·zen /£ˈsɪt·ɪ·zᵊn, $ˈsɪt̬-/ *n* [C] a person who is a member of a particular country and who has rights because of being born there or because of being given rights, or a person who lives in a particular town or city • *The interests of British citizens living abroad are protected by the British Embassy.* • *Chris has applied to* **become** *an American citizen.* • *The citizens of Moscow woke up this morning to find they had a new government.* • *"Old people in this country are treated like* **second-class** *citizens* (= unimportant people)*!" she said angrily.* • *"***Law-abiding** *citizens* (= People who do not break the law) *have nothing to fear from our enquiries," said the police inspector.* • **Citizens Advice Bureaux** (also **CABs**) are information offices in the UK where you can get free advice about problems, and which are usually run by people who do not get paid for their work. • **Citizens' Band (radio)** (also **CB (radio)**) is a radio communication system for members of the public: *Long-distance truck drivers often use CB radio to talk to each other.* ○ *My friend's a CB fanatic.* • *"If a man be gracious and courteous to strangers, it shows he is a citizen of the world"* (Francis Bacon *Essays*, 1625) • *"But Paul said I am ...a citizen of no mean city"* (Bible, Acts 21.39) • Compare SUBJECT PERSON.

ci·ti·zen·ry /£ˈsɪt·ɪ·zᵊn·ri, $ˈsɪt̬-/ *n* [U + sing/pl v] *fml or literary* • The citizenry is the group of people who live in a particular city, town, area or country: *The country's citizenry is/are more politically aware than in the past.*

ci·ti·zen·ship /£ˈsɪt·ɪ·zᵊn·ʃɪp, $ˈsɪt̬-/ *n* [U] • Citizenship is the state of being a member of a particular country and having rights because of it: *He was granted Canadian citizenship.* ○ *She applied for French citizenship.* ○ *He holds joint citizenship in Sweden and Peru.* • Citizenship is also the state of living in a particular area or town and behaving in a way and doing the things which others who live there expect of you: *When he discovered holes in the school fence, he reported them to the council in a spirit of good citizenship.*

ci·trus /ˈsɪt·rəs/ *n* [C] *pl* **citrus** or **citruses** any of a group of plants which produce juicy acidic fruits • *All species of citrus are evergreen trees or shrubs.* • *The field was planted with citrus* **trees**. • *Oranges, lemons, limes and grapefruit are types of citrus* **fruit**.

ci·tric /ˈsɪt·rɪk/ *adj* • *The wine has a sharp, fresh citric flavour.* • **Citric acid** is a weak acid found in many types of fruit, esp. oranges and lemons.

ci·ty LARGE PLACE /£ˈsɪt·i, $ˈsɪt̬-/ *n* [C] a place in which there are many houses, shops, places of work, places of entertainment, places of worship etc., and which is bigger than a town • *Many of the world's cities have populations of more than 5 million.* • *Wellington is the* **capital** *city* (= centre of government) *of New Zealand.* • *City life doesn't suit me – I prefer the country.* • *When their team won the European Cup, the whole city was* (= all the people in the city were) *on the streets to welcome the footballers home.* • *(Br and Aus)* The **city centre** is the central part of a city: *It's impossible to park in the city centre.* ○ *The new out-of-town supermarket will take business away from city-centre shops.* Compare DOWNTOWN. • The **city council** is the local government of a city. • **City councillors** are people who form the local government of a city. • *(dated)* The **city fathers** are members of the governing group of a city. • *(esp. Am)* A **city hall** is a building used as offices by people working for a city government: *The nicest buildings in the city are the Federal Court House and the City Hall.* ○ Compare **town hall** at TOWN. • *(esp. Am)* **City Hall** also refers to the government of a city: *You will have to apply to City Hall for a building permit.* • *(infml disapproving)* A **city slicker** is a person who knows how to deal with the problems of living in city and who pretends to know more about fashion and culture than people who live in the countryside. • A **city-state** in the ancient world was a city and the area around it which had an independent government: *Rome, Carthage and Athens were some of the great city-states of the ancient world.*

Ci·ty FINANCIAL CENTRE /£ˈsɪt·i, $ˈsɪt̬-/ *n* [U] **the City** the business centre of London where the large financial organizations are, such as the Bank of England • *Jan works in the City as a stockbroker.* • The City is also used to refer to the financial organizations as a group and the people who work for them: *The City acted swiftly to the news of a fall in the value of sterling.* • *(Aus)* **The city** is also the centre of the regional capitals of Australia such as Sydney or Melbourne: *I live in the suburbs of Melbourne and spend an hour commuting to my office in the city.* • The **City Desk** of a newspaper is *(Br)* the department which deals with financial news, or *(Am)* the department which deals with local news.

ci·ty·wide /£ˈsɪt·i·waɪd, $ˈsɪt̬-, ˌ--ˈ-/ *adj, adv* [not gradable] *esp. Am* existing or happening in all parts of the city • *In recent months there has been a citywide outbreak of crimes against vehicles.* • *This office is one of forty-six citywide.*

ci·vet /ˈsɪv·ɪt/ *n* a small cat-like animal from Africa and S Asia, or a strong-smelling substance obtained from these animals which is used for making PERFUME (= a liquid with a pleasant smell used on the skin) • *There are 17 different species of civet.* [C] • *The company claims that it does not use civet or musk in its perfumes.* [U]

civ·ic /ˈsɪv·ɪk/ *adj* [before n; not gradable] of a town or city or the people who live in it • *The Prime Minister met many civic* **leaders**, *including the mayor and the leaders of the immigrant communities.* • *She felt it was her civic* **duty** (= her duty as a person living in the town) *to give the police the names of the youths who had vandalized the bus shelter.* • *The mayor has tried to foster civic* **pride** *by having a new public library built in the city.*

civ·ics /ˈsɪv·ɪks/ *n* [U] • Civics is the study of the way in which a local government works and of the rights and duties of the people who live in the city.

civ·il ORDINARY /ˈsɪv·ᵊl/ *adj* [before n; not gradable] not military or religious, or relating to the ordinary people of a country • *Helicopters are mainly used for military rather than civil use.* • *After ten years of military dictatorship, the country now has a civil* **government**. • *We weren't married in church, but we had a civil* **ceremony** *in a registry office.* • **Civil defence** is the organizing and training of ordinary people to protect themselves or their property from an enemy attack during a war. • **Civil disobedience** is a refusal by a group of people to obey laws or pay taxes, as a peaceful way of expressing their disapproval of those laws or taxes and in order to persuade the government to change them: *Gandhi and Martin Luther King both led campaigns of civil disobedience to try to persuade the authorities to change their policies.* • **Civil engineering** is the planning and building of things not used for worship or war, such as roads, bridges and public buildings. The person who does this is a **civil engineer**. • **Civil liberties** are the rights of a person to do, think and say what they want if this does not harm other people: *The suggestion to introduce identity cards has been opposed by the campaign for civil liberties.* • *(Br)* The **civil list** is the amount of money allowed by Parliament for the expenses of the king or queen and royal family in doing their duties. • **Civil rights** are the rights that each person has in a society, whatever their race, sex or religion: *Civil rights include freedom, equality in law and in employment, and the right to vote.* • The **Civil Service** consists of the government departments responsible for putting central government plans into action: *The British Civil Service is supposed to be non-political.* • A **civil servant** is a person who works in the Civil Service. • A **civil war** is a war fought by different groups of people living in the same country: *The Spanish Civil War lasted from 1936 to 1939.* ○ *The country looks as though it is going to erupt into civil war.* ○ *Thousands of people have been driven from their homes by civil war.* • (CS) (PL) (RUS)

civ·il POLITE /ˈsɪv·ᵊl/ *adj* polite and formal • *His manner was civil, though not particularly friendly.* • *(fml) "Would you care for a whisky?" "How very civil of you* (= That's very kind of you)*."* • If you tell someone to **keep a civil tongue in their head**, you are telling them not to be rude. • If someone **does not have a civil word to say for** someone else, they can think of nothing good to say about that person: *She doesn't have a civil word to say for her new neighbours.* • (CS) (PL) (RUS)

civ·il·ly /ˈsɪv·ɪl·li/ *adv* • *He nodded civilly* (=politely) *to them and then carried on with his work.*

civ·il·i·ty /£sɪˈvɪl·ɪ·ti, $-t̬i/ *n* • *She greeted them* **with** *civility* (=politeness), *but not much warmth.* [U] • *After a few civilities* (=polite remarks), *they got down to business.* [C]

civ·il LAW /ˈsɪv·ɪl/ *adj* [before n; not gradable] *law* relating to private arguments between people or organizations rather than criminal matters • *The matter would be better dealt with in the civil* **court** *rather than by an expensive criminal proceeding.* • A **civil action** is an official complaint made by a person or company in a law court against someone who is said to done something to harm them, and which is dealt with by a judge: *She* **brought** *a civil action* **against** *her former employer.* • **Civil law** is the part of law which relates to people's private matters, for example marriage and property, rather than criminal matters. • LP> **Crimes and criminals, Law** (CS) (PL) (RUS)

civ·il·ian /sɪˈvɪl·i·ən/ *n* [C], *adj* [not gradable] (relating to) a person who is not a member of the police or the armed forces • *The bomb killed four soldiers and three civilians.* • *When soldiers are on leave, they tend to wear civilian clothes rather than their military uniforms.* • *The army has been criticized for attacking the unarmed civilian* **population**.

civ·il·i·za·tion, *Br and Aus usually* **-i·sa·tion** /ˌsɪv·əl·aɪˈzeɪ·ʃən, ˌ-ɪ·lɪˈ-/ *n* human society with its highly developed social organizations, or the culture and way of life of a society or country at a particular period in time • *Some people think that nuclear war would mean the end of civilization.* [U] • *Cuzco was the centre of one of the world's most famous civilizations, that of the Incas.* [C] • *(esp. humorous)* Civilization also refers to a place that has comfortable living conditions: *How does it feel to be back in civilization after all those weeks in a tent?* [U] • *"A project which would mean the end of civilization as we now know it"* (In the film *Citizen Kane*, 1941) • See also **civilization** at CIVILIZE.

civ·il·ize *obj, Br and Aus usually* **-ise** /ˈsɪv·ɪ·laɪz/ *v* [T] to educate (a society) so that it becomes more socially and culturally developed • *The Romans set out to civilize the Ancient Britons.* • If you civilize someone, you improve their behaviour: *She had a civilizing effect on her younger brother.*

civ·il·i·za·tion, *Br and Aus usually* **-i·sa·tion** /ˌsɪv·ɪ·laɪˈzeɪ·ʃən/ *n* [U] • *The civilization of Britain by the Romans took years to complete.* • See also CIVILIZATION.

civ·il·ized, *Br and Aus usually* **-ised** /ˈsɪv·ɪ·laɪzd/ *adj* • If a society or country is civilized, it has a highly developed system of government, culture and way of life and treats the people who live there fairly: *He believes that a fair justice system and a health service which is available to all are very important parts of a civilized society.* ○ *The terrorist attack on the UN building has shocked the civilized world.* • If a person or their behaviour is civilized, they are polite and behave in a calm and reasonable way: *I had a very civilized conversation with your mother.* ○ *Let's discuss this like civilized people* (= in a polite and calm way). • If a place or thing is civilized, it is pleasant or comfortable: *"I must say, this is all very civilized," he said as he settled down in a chair by the fire.* ○ *She thinks that afternoon tea is a very civilized tradition.* • *"A civilized society is one that exhibits the five qualities of truth, beauty, adventure, art and peace"* (A.N.Whitehead, 1861-1947)

civ·vies /ˈsɪv·iz/ *pl n dated infml* ordinary clothes which are not part of a uniform • *I didn't realize he was a soldier because he was* **in** *civvies.*

civ·vy street /ˈsɪv·i/ *n* [not after *the*] *Br dated infml* ordinary life which is not connected with the armed forces • *How does it feel to be back* **in** *civvy street now that you're no longer in the navy?*

cl *n* [C] *pl* **cl** *abbreviation for* CENTILITRE • *a 75 cl bottle*

clack /klæk/ *n* [C usually sing] a short sharp noise made by two hard objects being hit together • *He could hear the clack of high heels walking past in the corridor.* • *The clack of an old typewriter could be heard coming from the next room.*

clack /klæk/ *v* [I] • *Her typewriter clacked noisily as she typed out the letter.*

clad /klæd/ *adj* [not gradable] *fml or literary* (of people) dressed, or (of things) covered • *You need to be warmly clad in this cold weather.* • *A strange figure appeared in the doorway, clad* **in** *white.* • *an ivy-clad wall* • *a heather-clad hillside* • *an armour-clad vehicle*

clad·ding /ˈklæd·ɪŋ/ *n* [U] • Cladding is protective material which covers the surface of something: *The pipes froze because the cladding had fallen off.* ○ *They've had stone cladding put on their house to improve its appearance.*

clag /klæg/ *n* [U] *Aus* a type of glue

claim *obj* SAY /kleɪm/ *v* [T] to say that (something) is true or is a fact although you cannot prove it and other people might not believe it • *The company claims* **(that)** *it is not responsible for the pollution in the river.* [+ (*that*) clause] • *He claims* **to** *have met the President, but I don't believe him.* [+ *to* infinitive] • *This moisturiser claims* **to** *contain anti-ageing ingredients.* [+ *to* infinitive] • *All parties have claimed* **success** *in yesterday's elections.* • *An unknown terrorist group has claimed* **responsibility** *for this morning's bomb attack.* • *(infml) I don't claim to be* (=I do not try to make people believe that I am) *an expert on cars, but I do know that there's something wrong with your brakes.* • If an organization or group claims a particular number of members, that number of people are believed to belong to it: *The Baptists claim 29 million members worldwide.* • (J)

claim /kleɪm/ *n* [C] • A claim is a statement that something is true or is a fact, although other people might not believe you: *He claims the police assaulted him while he was in custody, a claim which the police deny.* ○ *The government's claim* **that** *it would reduce taxes proved false.* [+ *that* clause] ○ *Can you give any evidence to* **support** *your claim?* ○ *He* **made wild** *claims* **about** *being able to cure cancer.* • *I* **make no claim to** *be* (=I am not trying to make people believe that I am) *a brilliant pianist, but I can play a few tunes.* • *This little town's only* **claim to fame** (=The only reason why it is famous) *is that the President was born here.*

claim *(obj)* DEMAND /kleɪm/ *v* to ask for (something of value) because you think it belongs to you or because you think you have a right to it • *The police said that if no one claims the watch, you can keep it.* [T] • *When King Richard III died, Henry VII claimed the English throne.* [T] • If you claim money **from** the government or an organization, you make a written demand for it because you think you have a right to it: *The number of people claiming* **unemployment benefit** *has risen sharply this month.* [T] ○ *Don't forget to claim* **for** *your travelling expenses after the interview.* [I] ○ *When my bike was stolen, I claimed* **on** *the insurance and got £150 back.* [I] ○ *(Br) My new TV doesn't work, so I'll either ask the shop for a replacement or claim my money back.* [T] • If you claim **damages** after an accident, you make an official request for money from the person who caused your injuries. [T] • If a violent event or fighting **claims** someone's **life**, that person is killed during it: *The war, which has been raging in the country for over three months, has claimed thousands of lives.* • If someone **claims the moral high ground**, they say that they are morally better than someone else: *Both the media and the politicians are trying to claim the moral high ground.* • (J)

claim /kleɪm/ *n* [C] • A claim is a written request to an organization to pay you a sum of money which you believe they owe you: *There has been a sharp increase in the number of claims for industrial injury compensation.* ○ *After her house was burgled, she* **made** *a claim* **on** *her insurance.* ○ *Please* **submit** *your claim* **for** *travelling expenses to the accounts department.* • A claim is also a right to have or obtain something: *She has no rightful claim* **to** *the title.* • *My ex-wife* **has no claims on** *me* (=has no right to any of my money). • *Our neighbours* **have no (rightful) claim to** (=cannot say that they own) *that strip of land between our houses.* • A **claim form** is an official document which you use in order to request a sum of money from an organization which you believe they owe you.

claim·ant /ˈkleɪ·mənt/ *n* [C] • A claimant is a person who asks for something which they believe belongs to them or which they have a right to: *Unemployment offices paid claimants more than £16 million in benefits that they were not entitled to last year.* ○ *After Sir Edward died, there emerged two claimants* **to** *his property.*

clair·voy·ant /£ˌkleəˈvɔɪ·ənt, $ˌkler-/ *adj, n* [C] (of) a person who claims to have powers to see the future or see things which other people cannot see • *She claims she is clairvoyant and can communicate with the dead.* • *I decided to go to a clairvoyant to find out what would happen to me in the future.*

clair·voy·ance /£ˌkleəˈvɔɪ·ənts, $ˌkler-/ *n* [U] • *He claims he has the powers of telepathy and clairvoyance.*

clam /klæm/ *n* [C] a type of sea creature with a shell in two parts that can close together tightly and a soft body which can be eaten • *The restaurant's specialities are fried clams and oysters.* • *He made a clam chowder (= soup) for dinner.* • *(infml)* If someone **shuts up like a clam**, they suddenly become silent or refuse to talk about a particular subject: *She's quite happy to chat to Ruth, but she shuts up like a clam whenever I ask her anything.*

clam up /klæm/ *v adv* [I] *infml* to go silent suddenly, or to refuse to speak about a particular subject • *He used to clam up if you tried to ask him about his childhood.* • *It is difficult to get proper information about the project, because everyone clams up as soon as you start asking questions.*

clam·bake /ˈklæm·beɪk/ *n* [C] *Am* an event in which sea creatures are cooked and eaten outside, esp. by the sea • *Both families joined up for a traditional clambake on the beach.*

clam·ber /£ˈklæm·bəʳ, $-bɚ/ *v* [I always + adv/prep] to climb somewhere with difficulty, often using the hands and feet • *They clambered* **over/up** *the rocks.* • *I clambered* **into/onto** *the bus.* • *She clambered* **into** *bed.*

clam·ber /£ˈklæm·bəʳ, $-bɚ/ *n* [C usually sing] • *I was completely out of breath after my clamber up the hillside.*

clam·my /ˈklæm·i/ *adj* **-ier, -iest** sticky and slightly wet in an unpleasant way • *My hands felt all clammy.* • *It was a hot, clammy day.* • *Her heart was racing and her forehead was clammy.*

clam·mi·ness /ˈklæm·ɪ·nəs/ *n* [U] • *He shook my hand and I could feel the clamminess of his skin against mine.*

clam·our *Br and Aus, Am and Aus* **clam·or** /£ˈklæm·əʳ, $-ɚ/ *v* [I] to make a loud complaint or demand • *Please don't all clamour* **for** *attention at once!* [I] • *The residents are clamouring* **against** *the dumping of chemical waste near their houses.* [I] • *She always clamours* **to** *go home as soon as she gets to school.* [+ *to* infinitive]

clam·our *Br and Aus, Am and Aus* **clam·or** /£ˈklæm·əʳ, $-ɚ/ *n* [U] • Clamour is a loud complaint about something or a demand for something: *After the bombing, there was* **a** *public clamour* **for** *vengeance.* • Clamour is also loud noise, esp. made by people's voices: *He preferred solitary walks in the wilderness to the clamour of the city.* ○ *There was* **a** *clamour of voices outside the office, all demanding to see the manager.*

clam·or·ous /£ˈklæm·ᵊr·əs, $ˈ-ɚ-/ *adj* • Clamorous means making loud demands or complaints: *The newspaper devoted seven pages to a clamorous call for independence.* • Clamorous also means making a lot of noise: *The air was filled with clamorous, excited voices.*

clamp /klæmp/ *n* [C] a device, made of wood or metal, which is used to hold two things together tightly • *Fasten the two pieces of wood together with a clamp while the glue is drying.* • *Carefully tighten the clamp until it firmly supports the pipette in a vertical position.* • *A surgeon uses a clamp to close blood vessels while performing an operation.* • PIC **Laboratory, Tools**

clamp *obj* /klæmp/ *v* [T] • If you clamp one thing to another, you fasten them together using a clamp: *Clamp the two pieces of wood* **together** *for 15 minutes.* [M] • If you clamp something in a particular place, you hold it there tightly: *He clamped his hand over her mouth to stop her from screaming.* ○ *A heavy iron chain was clamped around his wrists and he was led off by one of the prison guards.* • *(fig.) The UN has clamped (= put) economic sanctions* **on** *the country.* • *(esp. Br)* If a car is clamped, a metal device is fixed to the wheel of it by the police or another person in authority, usually because it is parked illegally. The device is usually only removed when the owner pays an amount of money: *She was amazed to find that her car had been clamped after she had left it to go shopping for just 15 minutes.* ○ See also **wheel clamp** at WHEEL ROUND OBJECT. • If you **clamp down on** something, you act to stop or limit it: *The government is clamping down on teenage drinking.* ○ *The Treasury has clamped down on public expenditure.*

clamp·down /ˈklæmp·daʊn/ *n* [C] a sudden action taken by a government or people in authority to stop or limit a particular activity • *Following the military coup, there has been a clampdown* **on** *press reporting in the capital.* • *Cutbacks in public spending and a tough clampdown* **on** *tax evasion will be part of a new package to reduce the country's debt.*

clan /klæn/ *n* [C + sing/pl v] a group of families, esp. in Scotland, who originate from the same family and have the same name • *The Campbell clan is/are one of the largest Scottish clans.* • *(infml)* A clan also refers to a person's family: *Is/Are the whole clan coming to visit you for Christmas?* • A **gathering of the clans** is a gathering of a lot of people who are related or who have similar interests, esp. in order to enjoy themselves. • See also CLANSMAN.

clan·nish /ˈklæn·ɪʃ/ *adj disapproving* • If members of a group of people or society are clannish, they are friendly to each other but not to people outside the group: *We moved to the area two years ago and found the clannish quality of village life hard to cope with.*

clan·nish·ly /ˈklæn·ɪʃ·li/ *adv disapproving*

clan·nish·ness /ˈklæn·ɪʃ·nəs/ *n* [U] *disapproving* • *The government has introduced a policy designed to reduce clannishness and help the country's minorities feel that they have a stake in the country.*

clan·des·tine /klænˈdes·tɪn/ *adj fml* (esp. of something that is not officially allowed) planned or done in secret • *The group held weekly clandestine meetings in a church.* • *He has been having a clandestine affair with his secretary for three years.* • *She is the director of clandestine operations of the CIA.* • *UN diplomats are suspicious that the country's clandestine weapons programme may be broader than reported.*

clan·des·tine·ly /klænˈdes·tɪn·li/ *adv fml* • *Her father had forbidden her from seeing Charles and so the couple had to meet clandestinely.* • *The main evening news programme showed clandestinely-shot film of the prison camp.*

clang *(obj)* /klæŋ/ *v* to (cause to) make a loud deep ringing sound like that of metal being hit • *He woke up to hear the sound of bells clanging in the distance.* [I] • *She clanged the metal gate shut behind her.* [T + obj + adj]

clang /klæŋ/ *n* [C usually sing] • *They heard the clang of the school bell calling them back to classes.*

clang·er /£ˈklæŋ·əʳ, $-ɚ/ *n* [C] *esp. Br infml* a foolish remark which you make by mistake • *You* **dropped** *(= made) a clanger by talking about her old boyfriend in front of her husband!*

clank *(obj)* /klæŋk/ *v* to (cause to) make a short loud sound like that of metal objects hitting each other • *The heavy iron door clanked shut behind me.* [I] • *My bike chain was clanking in an alarming way as I pedalled along.* [I] • *Whenever their team scored a goal, they leapt up and down and clanked their beer cans together.* [T] • *He was dressed in a black leather suit and clanking gold jewellery.*

clank /klæŋk/ *n* [C usually sing] • *The gate shut with a dull clank.* • *I heard the clank of buckets as the farm workers went to milk the cows.*

clans·man *(pl* **-men***)*, **clans·wo·man** *(pl* **-women***)* /ˈklænz·mən, -ˌwʊm·ən/ *n* [C] a member of a Scottish CLAN (= a group of families who originate from the same family)

clap *(obj)* MAKE NOISE /klæp/ *v* **-pp-** to make a short loud noise by hitting your hands together • *"When I clap my hands, you must stand still," said the teacher.* [T] • *The band played a familiar tune which had everyone clapping* **along**. [I] • *The audience clapped* **in time to** *the music.* [I] • *Try to clap* **out** *the rhythm as you listen to this music.* [T] • If you clap a person or a performance, you clap your hands continuously to show that you like or admire them or have enjoyed the performance: *The audience clapped his performance enthusiastically.* [T] ○ *She had to do a second encore because the audience was clapping so much.* [I] ○ *The audience clapped and cheered when she stood up to speak.* [I]

clap /klæp/ *n* • If you give someone a clap, you clap your hands continuously to show that you like or admire them: *Let's give* **a** *big clap* **to/for** *our winning contestant!* [U] • A clap **of thunder**, is a sudden loud noise made by thunder: *There was a sudden clap of thunder and then it started to pour with rain.* [C]

clap *obj* PUT QUICKLY /klæp/ *v* [T always + adv/prep] **-pp-** to put (a person or thing) somewhere quickly or suddenly • *She clapped her hand* **over** *her mouth to try to stop herself from laughing.* • *The police clapped him* **into/in** *prison for possession of drugs.* • If you **clap eyes on** someone or something, you see them or it for the first time: *Everyone keeps talking about Patrick in the accounts department, but I haven't clapped eyes on him yet.*

clap *obj* HIT /klæp/ *v* [T always + adv/prep] **-pp-** to hit (someone) lightly on the shoulder or back in a friendly way, esp. to express pleasure at what they have done • *He clapped his daughter* **on** *the back and told her how proud he was of her for getting her degree.* • *They spent far too much time* **clapping** *each other* **on the backs** (= being pleased with their own achievements), *rather than trying to improve their performance.*

clap /klæp/ *n* [C] • *He gave me a friendly clap* **on** *the shoulder and said, "Well done!"*

clap DISEASE /klæp/ *n* [U] *slang for* GONORRHOEA • *He returned home from service abroad with a nasty dose of* **the** *clap.*

clap·board /£ˈklæp·bɔːd, $-bɔːrd/ *n Am* a series of boards fixed horizontally to the outside of a building, with each board partly covering the one below, in order to protect the building from the weather • *The town of Rockport is full of rows of white clapboard houses.* [U] • Clapboard is also *Am for* CLAPPERBOARD. [C]

clap·om·e·ter /£klæpˈɒm·ɪ·təʳ, $-ˈɑː·mɪ·t̬ɚ/ *n* a device used to measure the popularity of someone or something by the amount that people clap, esp. on television programmes • *The audience loved his performance and the needle on the clapometer shot up.* [C] • *The winner of tonight's talent contest will be decided by clapometer.* [U] • *(fig.) The deputy leader's clapometer* **ratings** *were higher than the Prime Minister's* (=She was more popular than the Prime Minister) *at the conference.*

clapped–out /ˌklæptˈaʊt/ *adj esp. Br and Aus infml* (of things) old and no longer working well, or (of people) very tired • *She drives a clapped-out old Mini.* • *I felt too clapped-out to go to aerobics last night.*

clap·per /£ˈklæp·əʳ, $-ɚ/ *n* [C] a piece of metal which hangs inside a bell and makes the bell ring when it hits the sides

clap·per·board /£ˈklæp·ə·bɔːd, $-ɚ·bɔːrd/, *Am usually* **clap·board** *n* [C] *specialized* a device used by people making films which consists of a board with two parts which are hit together at the start of filming • *The sound made by the clapperboard is to help check that the sound is matched to the picture.*

clap·pers /£ˈklæp·əz, $-ɚz/ *pl n* **like the clappers** *Br infml* extremely fast • *You'll have to run like the clappers if you want to catch your train.*

clap·trap /ˈklæp·træp/ *n* [U] *infml disapproving* foolish, meaningless talk which should not be believed • *Don't believe a word of what he says. It's just* **a load of** *claptrap.*

clar·et /£ˈklær·ɪt, $ˈkler-/ *n* red wine made in the region near Bordeaux in France • *Medoc and St Emilion are both famous clarets.* [C] • *Would you like a glass of claret?* [U] • Claret is also a dark purplish red colour: *Rosemary and Michael have just bought a new claret sofa for their living room.*

clar·i·fy *obj* EXPLAIN /£ˈklær·ɪ·faɪ, $ˈkler-/ *v* [T] to make (something) clear or easier to understand by giving more details or a simpler explanation • *Could you clarify the first point please? I don't understand it completely.* • *Lawyers hope this case will clarify an area of law which was thrown into confusion by a judgment last year.* • *The* **position** *of all shareholders will be clarified next month when the administrators finalise their proposals.* • If you clarify someone's mind, you help to remove any doubts they might have had.

clar·i·fi·ca·tion /£ˌklær·ɪ·fɪˈkeɪ·ʃᵊn, $ˌkler-/ *n* • *Some further clarification* (=explanation) *of your position is needed.* [U] • *The country has sought clarifications from the United States on the plan for peace talks.* [C]

clar·i·ty /£ˈklær·ɪ·ti, $ˈkler·ɪ·t̬i/ *n* [U] • Clarity is the quality of being clear and easy to understand: *Clarity is an essential part of any children's textbook.* ○ *It was a dreadful story, told with simple clarity.* ○ *There has been a call for greater clarity in this area of the law.* • The clarity of a sound or picture is its quality of being clear: *She was phoning from Australia but I was amazed at the clarity of her voice.* • Clarity is also the ability to think clearly and not be confused: *He has shown great clarity of mind.*

clar·i·fy *obj* COOKING /£ˈklær·ɪ·faɪ, $ˈkler-/ *v* [T] *specialized* to remove water and unwanted substances from (fat, such as butter) by heating it • *You can clarify butter by melting it, leaving it to settle and then keeping the clear liquid.*

clar·i·fied /£ˈklær·ɪ·faɪd, $ˈkler-/ *adj* [not gradable] • *You often use clarified butter when you make curries.*

clar·i·net /£ˌklær·ɪˈnet, $ˌkler-/ *n* [C] a tube-shaped musical instrument which is played by blowing through a single REED (=a thin piece of wood) and pressing the metal keys to produce different notes • *The clarinet is a woodwind instrument.* • *She plays the clarinet in a swing band.* • PIC› **Musical instruments**

clar·i·net·tist, **clar·i·net·ist** /£ˌklær·ɪˈnet·ɪst, $ˌkler·ɪˈnet̬-/ *n* [C] • A clarinettist is a person who plays the clarinet: *This year's concert includes New Orleans jazz clarinettist Pete Fountain and his band.*

clar·i·on call /£ˈklær·i·ᵊn, $ˈkler-/ *n* [C] *fml or literary* strong or persuasive encouragement to make people do something • *Has the country responded to the Prime Minister's clarion call* **for** *a return to old-fashioned family values?*

clash FIGHT /klæʃ/ *v* [I] to fight or argue • *The two armies clashed briefly near the border this morning.* • *Students clashed* **with** *police after demonstrations at five universities.* • *The government and the opposition parties have clashed* **over** *the cuts in defence spending.* • If two people or teams clash in a sports competition or race, they compete against each other: *Damon Hill and Michael Schumacher will clash in the German Grand Prix on Saturday.* • If two opinions, statements or qualities clash **with** each other, they are very different from each other: *This latest statement from the White House clashes with important aspects of the United States' foreign policy.*

clash /klæʃ/ *n* [C] • A clash is a fight or argument between people: *Rioters hurled rocks and petrol bombs in clashes with police at the weekend.* ○ *There were violent clashes* **between** *the police and demonstrators in the city centre.* • A clash is also a sports competition: *The long-awaited Becker-Sampras clash will take place next Tuesday.* • A clash of opinions or qualities is one in which those opinions or qualities are very different from and opposed to each another: *a clash of loyalties/personalities* ○ *There is a clash of interests in this project.*

clash NOT MATCH /klæʃ/ *v* [I; not *be clashing*] (of colours or styles) to look ugly or wrong together • *Some people think that red clashes* **with** *orange, but I think they look nice together.*

clash /klæʃ/ *n* [C] • *There's a horrible clash* **between** *the green carpet and the orange curtains.*

clash HAPPEN TOGETHER /klæʃ/ *v* [I not *be clashing*] *Br and Aus* (of two events) to happen at the same time in a way that is inconvenient • *Her party clashes* **with** *my brother's wedding, so I won't be able to go.*

clash /klæʃ/ *n* [C] *Br and Aus* • *There's a clash in my timetable* **between** *history and physics, so I won't be able to study them both.*

clash *(obj)* LOUD NOISE /klæʃ/ *v* to (cause to) make a loud metallic noise • *The saucepans clashed as he piled them into the sink.* [I] • *She clashed the cymbals together.* [T]

clash /klæʃ/ *n* [C] • *One of the saucepan lids fell to the ground with a loud clash.*

clasp *obj* /£klɑːsp, $klæsp/ *v* [T] to hold (someone or something) firmly in your hands or arms • *He clasped the vase, terrified of dropping it.* • *She leaned back in her chair and clasped her hands behind her head.* • *For this exercise, lie down on your back, clasp your knees and pull them down towards your chest.* • *She clasped her son* **in** *her arms.*

clasp /£klɑːsp, $klæsp/ *n* [C] • *She held the child's hand in a firm clasp as they crossed the road.* • A clasp is a small metal device which is used to fasten a belt, bag or a piece of jewellery. • A **clasp knife** (*Am usually* **pocketknife**) is a knife with one or more folding blades. • PIC› **Bags**

class TEACHING GROUP /£klɑːs, $klæs/ *n* [C] a group of students who are taught together at school, college or university, or a short period of teaching of a particular subject • *Which class are you in?* • *She gave the whole class extra homework for a week.* • *My class* (=The people in my class) *was/were rather noisy this morning.* [+ sing/pl v] • *Okay, class, settle down and open your books.* [as form of address] • *My last class ends at 4 o'clock.* • *Classes have been cancelled today because of a staff meeting.* • *He got in trouble with his teachers because he rarely attended classes.* • *I go to an aerobics class every Monday and Thursday evening.* • *I've been going to evening classes to improve my German.* • *Which teacher* **takes/teaches** *your environmental studies class?* • *I was told off for talking* **in** *class.* • *(Am)* The class **of** a particular year is the group of students who successfully completed their studies in that year: *At America's top business schools, the class of 1988 is receiving almost half as many job offers from Wall Street as its predecessors did.* • LP› **Schools and colleges**

class ECONOMIC GROUP /£klɑːs, $klæs/ *n* a group of people within society who have the same economic and social position • *The Labour Party has lost a lot of support among the* **working** *class.* [U] • *She belongs to the rich American* **upper** *class and spends her time having lunch with friends and doing charity work.* [U] • *We live in a* **middle** *class neighbourhood.* • *She comes from an* **upper middle** *class* background. • *He was a member of the* **ruling** *classes.* [C] • *The British are thought to be very aware of class* **distinctions** (= differences). • *Class should not be the sole factor in determining an individual's success in life.* [U] • *She's studying the class* **structure** *of Japan.* • If someone is **class-conscious**, they are very aware of belonging to a particular social class and of the differences between the various social classes: *America is perceived of as being less class-conscious than Britain.* • According to Marxists, **class conflict/struggle** is a continuing fight between the CAPITALIST class and the working class for political and economic power. • *"Like many of the Upper Class / He liked the Sound of Broken Glass"* (from the poem 'About John' in *New Cautionary Tales* by Hilaire Belloc, 1930) • See also UNDERCLASS.

class·less /£ˈklɑːs·ləs, $ˈklæs·ləs/ *adj* • *Her accent is classless* (= It does not belong to a particular social class). • *The prime minister claims that he wants to create a classless* **society** (= a society without different social classes).

class RANK /£klɑːs, $klæs/ *n* [C] an official division of goods or services according to how good they are • *Whenever I travel by train, I always travel first class.* • *Shall I post the letter first or second class?* • *Would you like a business or economy class ticket to New York?* • *All the vegetables we sell are Class A.* • *(Br and Aus)* Class also refers to the standard which someone has reached in their university degree: *"What class degree did you get at university?" "I got a second-class honours degree."* • If someone is **in a class of** their **own** in a particular activity, no one is as good as they are at that activity: *As a long-distance runner, she's in a class of her own.* • If something is **in a class by itself**, it is of very high quality and nothing can be compared to it. • *I can't play chess with him. He's* **out of** *my* **class** (= much better than me)*!*

class *obj* /£klɑːs, $klæs/ *v* [T] • *I'm 17, but I'm still classed* **as** (= considered to be) *a child when I travel by bus.* • *I would class her* **among/with** (= consider her to be one of) *the top ten American novelists.*

class /£klɑːs, $klæs/ *adj* [not gradable] • *He's a class* (= very good) *golfer.* • *She has the potential to be a* **world-***class tennis player* (= one of the best tennis players in the world).

class STYLE /£klɑːs, $klæs/ *n* [U] the quality of being stylish or fashionable • *She's got real class.*

clas·sy /£ˈklɑː·si, $ˈklæs·i/ *adj* **-ier, -iest** • *She's a really classy lady.* • *(Br infml) That's a really classy motor* (= a very fashionable car).

class BIOLOGY /£klɑːs, $klæs/ *n* [C] (used in the CLASSIFICATION of plants and animals) a group of related plants or animals • *A class is above an order.*

clas·sic HIGH QUALITY /ˈklæs·ɪk/ *adj* having a high quality or standard against which other things are judged • *Have you ever read Fielding's classic novel 'Tom Jones'?* • *That was another classic goal from Paul Gascoigne!* • *(infml disapproving)* If you say that someone's actions are classic, you mean that they are extremely foolish: *That was classic! The man in that car signalled right, and then turned left.* • (J) (KOR) (N) (NL)

clas·sic /ˈklæs·ɪk/ *n* [C] • A classic is a piece of writing, a musical recording or a film which is well-known and of a high standard and lasting value: *Jane Austen's 'Pride and Prejudice' is a classic of English literature.* ○ *Eisenstein's 'Battleship Potemkin' is one of the classics of the Russian cinema.* ○ *Many of the Rolling Stones' records have become rock classics.* ○ *Virginia Woolf's 'To the Lighthouse' is a* **modern** *classic.* ○ *I spent my childhood reading* **the classics** (= the most famous works of literature). • *"A classic – something that everybody wants to have read and nobody wants to read"* (Mark Twain in a speech, 1900) • See also CLASSICS.

clas·sic TRADITIONAL /ˈklæs·ɪk/ *adj* having a simple, traditional style which is always fashionable • *She wore a classic navy suit and a straw hat.* • *Are you looking for loose-fit jeans or classic-***cut** (= traditional style) *ones?* • A **classic car** is a car which is still popular although it is no longer produced: *The Triumph Spitfire is a classic car.* • (J) (KOR) (N) (NL)

clas·sic /ˈklæs·ɪk/ *n* [C] • *You should invest in several wardrobe classics* (= pieces of clothing which are always fashionable)*, such as a wool coat and a smart suit.*

clas·sic·al /ˈklæs·ɪ·kᵊl/ *adj* • If something is classical, it is attractive because it has a simple, traditional style: *I love the classical lines of his dress designs.*

clas·sic·al·ly /ˈklæs·ɪ·kli/ *adv* • *She has a classically beautiful face.*

clas·sic TYPICAL /ˈklæs·ɪk/ *adj* having all the characteristics or qualities that you expect • *The building is a classic* **case/example** *of poor-quality housing – it is badly designed and has been built using cheap materials.* • *He had all the classic* **symptoms** *of the disease, including loss of appetite and a high temperature.* • *(infml) That's just classic* (= an unwelcome or unlucky event that is not surprising)*, isn't it! You arrive at the station on time and you find that the train's left early.* • (J) (KOR) (N) (NL)

clas·sic·al·ly /ˈklæs·ɪ·kli/ *adv* • *They were looking for a villa that was classically Mediterranean, with white walls, shutters and orange trees in the garden.* • *The dress combines stylish lines with an attractive floral print for a classically feminine look.*

clas·sic·al CULTURE /ˈklæs·ɪ·kᵊl/ *adj* [not gradable] belonging to or relating to the culture of ancient Rome and Greece • *the classical world* • *He has little knowledge of classical literature.* • *Renaissance architects and artists had a passion for classical architecture.* • *In classical Rome, wheeled traffic was banned from the city streets during the day.* • *In classical Greek theatre, actors wore masks to represent the characters they played: a smiling mask for comedy and a sad one for tragedy.* • See also CLASSICS; CLASSICISM; NEOCLASSICAL.

clas·sic·al MUSIC /ˈklæs·ɪ·kᵊl/ *adj* [not gradable] (of music) considered to be part of a long tradition and of lasting value • *Do you prefer classical music or pop?* • *She loved classical music and would spend hours listening to Verdi's operas.* • *(specialized)* Classical also refers to music written in Europe between about 1750 and 1830: *The mature works of Haydn, Mozart, Beethoven and Schubert belong to the Classical period.*

clas·sic·al TRADITIONAL /ˈklæs·ɪ·kᵊl/ *adj* [not gradable] traditional in style or form, or based on methods developed over a long period of time • *Did she study mostly classical ballet or modern ballet?* • *He is one of our greatest classical actors.* • *Classical scientific theory was completely overturned by Einstein.* • *The classical* **economics** *of Adam Smith were challenged in the 1920's by Keynes.*

clas·sic·al·ly /ˈklæs·ɪ·kli/ *adv* [not gradable] • *She is a classically trained Indian dancer.*

Clas·si·cism /ˈklæs·ɪ·sɪ·zᵊm/ *n* [U] *specialized* a style in painting, SCULPTURE and building, based on particular standards in Greek and Roman art such as regularity, the use of simple forms, and calm expression of the emotions, which was especially popular during the 18th and 19th centuries in Europe • *Ingres and Delacroix were two famous exponents of Classicism.* • See also **neoclassicism** at NEOCLASSICAL. Compare ROMANTICISM.

clas·sics /ˈklæs·ɪks/ *n* [U] the study of ancient Greek and Roman culture, esp. their languages and literature • *Students could choose between studying a second foreign language or classics.* • *She* **studied/read** *classics at Cambridge.* • *She's a classics scholar.* • *He's a lecturer in the classics faculty.* • See also CLASSICAL CULTURE.

clas·si·cist /ˈklæs·ɪ·sɪst/ *n* [C] • A classicist is a person who studies ancient Greek or Roman culture.

clas·si·fied /ˈklæs·ɪ·faɪd/ *adj* [not gradable] (of information) officially stated to be secret • *These documents contain classified material.* • *The papers concerning the negotiations are classified and will not become declassified for 30 years.*

clas·si·fy *obj* /ˈklæs·ɪ·faɪ/ *v* [T] to divide (things) into groups according to type • *The books in the library are classified* **by/according to** *subject.* • *Would you classify this book* **under/as** *sociology or politics?* • *Biologists classify animals and plants* **into** *groups.* • A **classified ad** (*Br also* **small ad**, *Am also* **want ad**) is a small advertisement which is put by someone in a newspaper or a magazine because they want to sell or buy something or to find or offer a job.

clas·si·fi·a·ble /ˈklæs·ɪ·faɪ·ə·bl̩/ *adj* • *This book is not easily classifiable.*

clas·si·fi·ca·tion /ˌklæs·ɪ·fɪˈkeɪ·ʃᵊn/ *n* • *Do you understand the system of classification used in ornithology?* [U] • *Fingerprint classification is based on four groups of ridge patterns on your fingers.* [U] • *There are six classifications of hotel from simple to de luxe.* [C]

class·mate /£ˈklɑːs·meɪt, $ˈklæs-/ *n* [C] someone who is in the same class as you at school • *He was teased by his classmates for not wearing the proper school uniform.*

class·room /£ˈklɑːs·ruːm, £-rʊm, $ˈklæs-/ *n* [C] a room in a school or college where groups of students are taught • *She was behaving so badly that the teacher told her to go and stand outside the classroom.* • *(fig.) Students learning computer studies spend two days each week in a computer lab and four days* **in the** *classroom* (= being taught by a teacher). • *(fig.) There are also no promotions or hierarchies within the school, so that teachers remain* **in the** *classroom* (= they continue teaching) *throughout their careers.*

clat·ter *(obj)* /£ˈklæt·əʳ, $ˈklæṭ·ɚ/ *v* to (cause to) make continuous loud noises by hitting hard objects against each other • *Don't clatter the dishes – you'll wake the baby up.* [T] • *He was clattering* **away** *on his old typewriter.* [I] • *Someone was clattering* **up** *the stairs behind me and I turned to see who it was.* [I]

clat·ter /£ˈklæt·əʳ, $ˈklæṭ·ɚ/ *n* [U] • *She could hear the clatter of horses' hooves trotting down the road.* • *The sounds of cooking and the clatter of dishes came from the kitchen.*

clause GRAMMAR /£klɔːz, $klɑːz/ *n* [C] *specialized* a group of words, consisting of a subject and a FINITE form of a verb (= the form that shows the tense and subject of the verb), which might or might not be a sentence • *In the sentence 'I can't cook very well but I make quite good omelettes', both 'I can't cook very well' and 'I make quite good omelettes' are* **main/independent** *clauses* (= they are of equal importance and could each exist as a separate sentence). • *In the sentence 'I'll get you some stamps if I go to town', 'if I go to town' is a* **subordinate/dependent** *clause* (= it is not equal to the main part of the sentence and could not exist as a separate sentence). • LP› **Clauses, Comma**

clause LEGAL DOCUMENT /£klɔːz, $klɑːz/ *n* [C] *specialized* a particular part of a written legal document, for example a law passed by Parliament or a CONTRACT (= an agreement) • *to add/delete a clause* • *They have amended a clause in the bill to try to get it through Parliament.* • *There is a clause in the contract which says the company can make people redundant for economic reasons.* • *Clause 4 of the constitution is thought to be the most important section.*

clau·stro·pho·bi·a /£ˌklɒs·trəˈfəʊ·bi·ə, $ˌklɑː·strəˈfoʊ-/ *n* [U] *specialized* an extreme fear of being in enclosed spaces • *He* **suffers from** *claustrophobia so he never travels on underground trains.* • Claustrophobia is also an unpleasant feeling which some people get when they are in small, enclosed spaces: *I get claustrophobia whenever I go through a tunnel.* • Compare AGORAPHOBIA.

clau·stro·phob·ic /£ˌklɒs·trəˈfəʊ·bɪk, $ˌklɑː·strəˈfoʊ-/ *n* [C] • A claustrophobic is a person who suffers from a fear of being in enclosed spaces.

clau·stro·phob·ic /£ˌklɒs·trəˈfəʊ·bɪk, $ˌklɑː·strəˈfoʊ-/ *adj* • *If you are claustrophobic, a psychologist may be able to help you.* • If a place is claustrophobic, it is extremely small and makes you feel uncomfortable when you are in it: *My room's a bit claustrophobic.*

clav·i·chord /£ˈklæv·ɪ·kɔːd, $-kɔːrd/ *n* [C] a keyboard instrument in which the strings are hit by pieces of metal when the keys are pressed • *The clavichord was popular from the 15th century to the late 18th century.*

clav·i·cle /ˈklæv·ɪ·kḷ/ *n* [C] *medical for* **collar bone**, see at COLLAR NECK

claw /£klɔː, $klɑː/ *n* [C] one of the sharp curved nails at the end of each of the toes of some animals and birds • *Our cat likes to sharpen her claws on the legs of the dining table.* • *(fig. infml) So she's finally* **got** *her* **claws into** *him* (= has forced him into a (sexual) relationship or marriage). • A claw is also one of the two pointed parts, used for holding things, at the end of the legs of some insects and sea creatures, such as CRABS and LOBSTERS: *Keep your fingers away from the crab's claws when you pick it up.* • PIC› **Birds, Crustaceans**

claw *(obj)* /£klɔː, $klɑː/ *v* • *The lion tamer was seriously injured when one of his lions clawed his back* (= tore his back with its claws). [T] • *When our cat is hungry, she starts clawing* **at** *my legs* (= takes hold of my legs with her claws). [I always + adv/prep] • *The rescuers could hear the sound of the trapped people desperately trying to claw their* **way through** *the rubble* (= to get through it using their hands). [T] • *(fig.) Sidney ruthlessly clawed his* **way (up) from** *the position of junior clerk* **to** *chairman of the company* (= He achieved success with difficulty and by hurting other people). [T]

claw back *obj*, **claw** *obj* **back** *v adv* [M] to obtain possession of (something) again with difficulty, or *(esp. Br)* (of a government) to take back (money) in one way that has already been given in another way • *The airline is beginning to claw back some of the business it lost after the bomb explosion.* • *(esp. Br) We got a grant from the government to help set up our business, but they clawed it all back again in taxes.*

clay /kleɪ/ *n* [U] thick heavy earth that is soft when wet and hard when dry or baked • *Clay is used for making bricks and pots.* • *If you have clay soil in your garden, you have to dig it well and use a fertiliser.* • A **clay pigeon** is a disc made of clay which is fired into the air to be shot at for sport: *clay-pigeon shooting* ○ *a clay(-pigeon) shoot*

clay·ey /ˈkleɪ·i/ *adj* • *clayey soil* (= earth containing a lot of clay)

clean NOT DIRTY /kliːn/ *adj* **-er, -est** not dirty • *Make sure your hands are clean before you have your dinner.* • *The children all looked very smart in their clean white shirts.* • *It's wonderful to come to the seaside and breathe some clean air.* • *Hospitals need to be kept* **spotlessly** (= extremely) *clean.* • *Cats are supposed to be very clean animals and keep themselves and their surroundings free from dirt.* • *In some countries, the tap water is not very clean* (= it contains bacteria). • *(infml)* Something that is **(as) clean as a (new) pin/as a whistle** is extremely clean: *Their house is always as clean as a new pin.* ○ *I want you to eat everything up and leave your plate as clean as a whistle.*

clean *(obj)* /kliːn/ *v* • *I'm going to clean* (= remove the dirt from) *the car this morning.* [T] • *You should always clean your teeth after meals.* [T] • *This carpet doesn't clean* (= become clean) *very well.* [I always + adv] • *We'll have to clean the fish* (= prepare it by removing the inside parts of it that are not eaten) *before we cook it.* [T] • *It's a good idea to clean* **down** (= remove dirt from) *the woodwork before you paint it.* [M] • *Please would you clean* (= remove by rubbing with a cloth) *the fingermarks* **from/off** *the door.* [T] • *Please would you clean* **off** (= remove by rubbing with a cloth) *the fingermarks* **from** *the door.* [M] • *I hope these bloodstains will clean* **off** *my shirt.* [I always + adv/prep] • *He asked her to help him clean* **out** (= remove the dirt from) *the stables.* [M] • *I wish I could find the time to clean* **out** *these cupboards.* [M] • *We'll go out as soon as I've cleaned* **up** (= removed the dirt from) *the kitchen.* [M] • *Clean your***self up** *before you have your dinner.* [T] • *I need to clean* **up** (= I need to remove the dirt from something or somewhere or from myself) *before we go out.* [I always + adv/prep] • *I'm fed up with cleaning* **up after** *you* (= removing dirt that you have made). [I always + adv/prep]

clean /kliːn/, **clean–up** *n* [U] • *These windows need* **a** *really thorough clean* (= to have the dirt removed from them). • *It's time you gave your bedroom* **a good clean-up**. • *Residents have called for a clean-up campaign to keep their streets free from rubbish.*

clean·er /£ˈkliː·nəʳ, $-nɚ/ *n* • *Chris has an evening job as an office cleaner* (= works removing dirt from an office). [C] • *We've run out of floor cleaner* (= the substance that removes dirt from the floor). [U]

clean·er's /£ˈkliː·nəz, $-nɚz/ *n* [C] *pl* **cleaners** or **cleaners'** • *Could you pick up my suit from the cleaner's* (= the shop where clothes that cannot be washed in an ordinary machine are cleaned) *for me, please.* See also **dry-cleaner's** at DRY NOT WET. • *(infml) Paul was really* **taken to the cleaner's** (= was cheated and lost money) *on that deal.* • *(infml) In the second half, United were really* **taken to the cleaner's** (= severely beaten), *and they finally lost the match 6-1.*

clean·ing /ˈkliː·nɪŋ/ *n* [U] • *It's your turn to* **do the** *cleaning* (= to remove the dirt in the house). • *Joan has a cleaning job.*

clean·li·ness /ˈklen·lɪ·nəs/ *n* [U] • *She doesn't have very high standards of cleanliness* (= does not keep things clean).

clean·ness /ˈkliːn·nəs/ *n* [U] • *We were very impressed by the cleanness* **of** *the hotel* (= how clean it was).

clean HONEST /kliːn/ *adj* **-er, -est** honest or fair; not breaking rules or laws • *"Now then, lads," said the referee, "Let's make it a clean* **fight/contest**." • *The judge took the defendant's clean* **record** (= the absence of previous involvement in crime) *into account when passing sentence.* • *I've always had a clean driving licence* (= I've never broken any driving laws). • *(slang) The police busted Pete last night, but he was clean* (= he did not have any illegal drugs). • *(slang) The police are trying to nail him for the post office robbery, but he's clean* (= he has done nothing illegal or has no stolen goods). • *I think you should* **come clean** *(***with** *everybody)* **about** (= admit) *what you've been*

CLAUSES

Many verbs, and some adjectives and nouns, are followed by subordinate clauses. The following clause patterns are labelled in the dictionary:

Clauses introduced by the conjunction 'that'

- The following types of verb are often followed by a *that* clause:

  verbs of saying: admit, advise, agree, answer, apologize, assert, claim, complain, declare, demand, deny, disagree, emphasize, explain, imply, insist, mention, order, object, point out, promise, recommend, remark, repeat, report, request, respond, say, state, suggest

  verbs of knowing or coming to know: discover, find, find out, hear, know, learn, notice, observe, realize, recall, recollect, remember, see

  verbs of believing: agree, assume, believe, conclude, consider, doubt, expect, estimate, feel, guess, imagine, judge, predict, reason, reckon, sense, suppose, suspect, think

  verbs of choosing or desiring: accept, decide, demand, desire, ensure, intend, mean, order, prefer, require, rule

  verbs of feeling emotion: fear, hope, regret

  verbs of appearing or happening (usually with 'it' as the subject): appear, happen, seem

  verbs of suggesting, requesting or ordering advise, ask, demand, insist, order, propose, recommend, request, suggest, urge.

  When 'that' cannot be omitted, this pattern is labelled [+ *that* clause].

  In most cases 'that' can be omitted, especially in informal English: *She implied I was lazy.* • *I can see you're tired.* This pattern is labelled [+ (*that*) clause] and the example shows 'that' in brackets: *The doctor said* **(that)** *I was very lucky to survive the accident.*

- With a few verbs a *that* clause can follow the direct object. These are labelled [+ obj + *that* clause] or [+ obj + (*that*) clause]: *I told the salesman* **(that)** *we wouldn't buy anything.* • **It** *amuses me* **(that)** *you drink so much tea.* Other examples:

  verbs of giving information: inform, persuade, remind, show, teach, tell, warn

  verbs of causing emotion: amaze, annoy, disappoint, please, puzzle, sadden, surprise, worry

- A *that* clause can also follow some adjectives and nouns, especially those referring to emotions or their causes: *I'm so glad* **(that)** *we visited the harbour.* • **It***'s strange* **(that)** *no-one has seen him for months.* • **There** *is little hope* **that** *rescuers will find the climber before night-time.* Other examples:

  state of emotion: afraid, angry, anxious, disappointed, excited, frightened, glad, happy, pleased, proud, sad, scared, surprised, worried

  causing emotion: annoying, disappointing, exciting, frightening, funny, interesting, strange, surprising, worrying

  related to a judgment: certain, clear, confident, good, important, likely, obvious, possible, probable, sure, unfortunate

Clauses introduced by a question word

- The words *how, if, what, when, where, whether, which, who, why* can introduce a clause following some verbs: *I wonder* **if** *I could use your phone?* • *No-one knows* **wh***ere these birds go in winter.* This grammar pattern is labelled [+ *wh-* word].

  verbs of saying: agree, ask, discuss, explain, point out, say, suggest

  verbs of knowing or coming to know: find out, hear, know, realize, remember, see, tell

  verbs of trying to know: examine, inquire, investigate, look, study, watch, wonder

  verbs of believing: believe, doubt, feel, guess, imagine, suspect, think

- With a few verbs the clause follows the object: *Did you ask him* **if** *he needed anything?* [+ obj + *wh-* word]. Other verbs like this are: amaze, show, surprise, teach, tell.

- Some adjectives can be followed by a clause with a question word: *I was uncertain* **how** *to fill in the form.* • **It** *is doubtful* **wh***ether Bridget will be fit enough to run in the race.* Other adjectives like this are: aware, careful, conscious • certain, clear, obvious, sure • doubtful, questionable.

Clauses of direct speech

- When a verb is used to state the exact words spoken, thought or written by someone, the sentence pattern is labelled [+ clause]. The speech clauses are usually separated from the main clause by quotation marks (" " or ' ') and often by a comma (,) as well: *The man leaned forward and whispered "What's your name?"* • *"Sorry I'm late," he mumbled.* • *"Good Lord," she gasped, "I didn't see you there!"*

- When we refer to thoughts we use the same clause pattern but often omit the quotation marks. *These people are really strange, she thought.* • *Is there a safe path down to the beach, I wondered.*

- 'Ask', 'tell' and a small number of other verbs can have an object as well as a clause of direct speech: *Someone asked me "Are you feeling better now, dear?"* • *"Press the green button," he told me, "and wait a few seconds."* Verbs like this are labelled [+ obj + clause].

Sentence patterns in which 'so' and 'not' replace a clause

- The adverb 'so' can be used to refer to a previous sentence or clause: *"Is this the best place for our tent?" "I think* **so** (=I think *that* this is the best place for our tent)." • *I'm sure that Kevin will pass his exams. His teacher told me* **so** (=His teacher told me *that* Kevin will pass his exams). In these sentences 'so' replaces a *that* clause.

  'Not' is used in a similar way, but gives a negative meaning: *"Do you think Robin will show us all his photos?" "I hope* **not** (=I hope *that* Robin will not show us all his photos)."

  This pattern is labelled [+ *not/so*], and the labels [+ *so*] or [+ *not*] are given when only one of the patterns is possible. The following common verbs are used with both 'so' and 'not':

  appear, seem
  assume, believe, expect, guess, imagine, suppose, think
  claim, say, tell
  fear, hope (and also with 'to be afraid')

- 'So' can also be used at the beginning of a sentence to refer to a previous clause. This is not possible with 'not'. *"Larry and Pete have had another argument."* **"So** *it seems."* (=It does seem *that* Larry and Pete have had another argument) • *I need to change my lifestyle and get more exercise.* **So** *my doctor says, anyway* (=My doctor says *that* I need to change my lifestyle). This pattern is used with many of the verbs listed above.

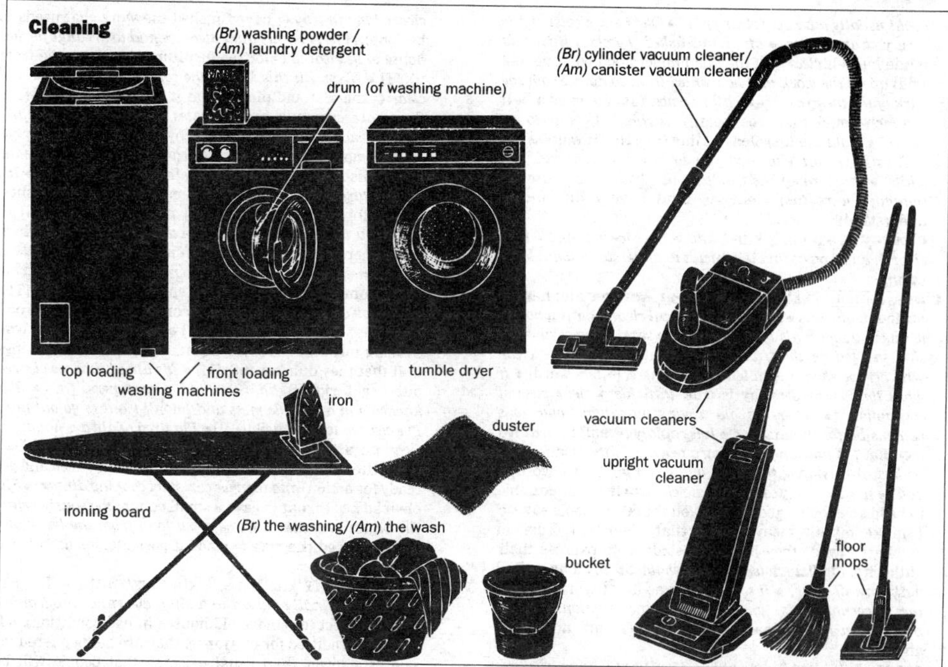

doing on these trips away from home. • *Julia finally* **made a clean breast (of it)** (= told the truth) *and admitted that she had stolen the money.*

clean·ly /ˈkliːn·li/ *adv* • *The election campaign was not conducted very cleanly* (= fairly and honestly).

clean up *obj*, **clean** *obj* **up** *v adv* [M] • *We need a mayor who is tough enough to clean up this town* (= remove illegal or dishonest activity from it).

clean–up /ˈkliːn·ʌp/ *n* [U] • *This town is full of drunks and swindlers – it could really use a good clean-up* (= it needs to have dishonest people and criminals removed from it).

clean MORAL /kliːn/ *adj* **-er, -est** morally acceptable • *It's all* **good** *clean* **fun**. • *You look very healthy – it must be all that clean* **living**. • *I only want to hear your* **joke** *if it's clean* (= not about sex).

clean up *obj*, **clean** *obj* **up** *v adv* [M] • *Some people think that television should be cleaned up* (= that there should be less sex and violence on it). • To **clean up** your **act** is to start to obey certain laws or generally accepted standards of behaviour: *Complaints have dropped significantly this year as a result of holiday companies cleaning up their act to avoid heavy fines.* ○ *You going to have to clean up your act if you're serious about keeping your job.*

clean NO ROUGH EDGES /kliːn/ *adj* **-er, -est** having no rough edges; smooth; straight; even • *What he liked about the car was its clean* (= smooth) **lines**. • *I tried to make a clean* (= smooth) **cut** *in the cake, but the knife wasn't sharp enough.* • *I've broken my leg, but the doctor says that the* **break** *is clean* (= straight), *so it should heal easily.* • *A good clean hit from Botham sent the ball straight out to the boundary.* • *I like the* **clean-cut** (= straight and even) *shapes of classical architecture.* • *(approving) Julie's fiancé is a nice* **clean-cut** *young man* (= is tidy in appearance and behaves well). • *(approving) The school sports field swarmed with* **clean-limbed** (= healthy-looking and active) *young people eager for the day's events.* • *I like a man who is* **clean-shaven** (= who has no hair on the lower part of his face).

clean·ly /ˈkliːn·li/ *adv* • *When I dropped the plate on the floor, it broke cleanly in half* (= the break had no rough edges). • *Opinions on the issue were split cleanly* (= equally) *between men and women.*

clean COMPLETE /kliːn/ *adj* [before n] **-er, -est** complete • *It's better for both of us if we* **make a** *clean* **break (of it)** (= end our relationship completely). • *Sara says she wants to* **make a** *clean* **break with** *the past* (= stop living her life as she has been doing), *and start a new life.* • *The new prime minister is expected to* **make a** *clean* **sweep of** *the government* (= change all the members of it). • *The USA* **made a** *clean* **sweep of** (= won) *all the men's events/The men's events were a clean* **sweep** *for the USA.*

clean /kliːn/ *adv* [not gradable] • *I clean* (= completely) **forgot** *that I was supposed to be meeting Lucy for a drink last night.* • *He's been cheating his customers for years, and getting clean* **away** *with it.* • *The bullet went clean* **through** *his shoulder and out the other side.* • In cricket, if you are **clean bowled** the ball touches the WICKET without you hitting it.

clean NOTHING ON /kliːn/ *adj* [before n] **-er, -est** with nothing on; not yet used • *She sat down with a clean sheet of paper to write a letter to her son.* • *Kevin had been ill for a long time, but the doctor has finally* **given** *him a* **clean bill of health** (= has said that he is healthy again). • *(fig.) Following several cases of food poisoning, the restaurant failed to receive a clean bill of health* (= a report that it is safe) *from the council inspector.* • *(infml) You were very lazy last term, but we'll forget it and start again with a* **clean slate/sheet** (= with past bad behaviour forgotten). See also **wipe the slate clean** at WIPE.

clean out *obj*, **clean** *obj* **out** *v adv* [M] to take or steal all of (someone's) money or goods • *Buying our new house has completely cleaned us out.* • *Richard came home for the weekend and completely cleaned us out* **of** *food.* • *The robbers cleaned out the liquor store.*

clean up *(obj)*, **clean** *(obj)* **up** *v adv esp. Am slang* to win (a lot of money) • *We cleaned up at the roulette table last night.* [I] • *I hear he cleaned up a small fortune in the lottery.* [M]

clean–up /ˈkliːn·ʌp/ *n* [U] *esp. Am slang* • *That was a* **real** *clean-up Joe had* (= He won a lot of money) *at the races yesterday.*

cleanse *obj* /klenz/ *v* [T] to make completely clean or (morally) pure • *You should always make sure a* **cut/wound** *is thoroughly cleansed before you bandage it.* • *The priest asked the congregation to cleanse their thoughts.* • *Roman Catholics go to confession to be cleansed* **of** *their sins.* • *(fig.) The mayor has promised to cleanse the city* **of** *drug dealers* (= to remove them from the city).

cleans·er /£ˈklen·zəʳ, $-zɚ/ *n* • A cleanser is a substance used for cleaning: *Kitchen cleansers are all more or less the same.* [C] • *I use cleanser on my face every night.* [U]

cleans·ing /ˈklen·zɪŋ/ *adj* • **Cleansing creams** and **cleansing lotions** are used for cleaning esp. the skin. • *(Br) The cleansing* **department** *of the town council is responsible for removing household rubbish and keeping the streets clean.*

clear UNDERSTANDABLE /£klɪəʳ, $klɪr/ *adj* **-er, -est** easy to understand, hear, read or see • *We got lost on our way to the theatre because we weren't given very clear* **instructions/directions** *about how to find it.* • *Is what I just said clear?* • *Actors and actresses need to be clear speakers.* • *Children's* *books usually have very clear print.* • *Our new television has a very clear picture.* • *Mr Evans asked the class if he had* **made** *himself* **clear** (=if they had understood what he had said) *about the work that he wanted them to do.* • *From the back of the theatre came a child's voice,* **(as) clear as a bell** (=which could easily be heard), *saying, "I want to go home".* • *I told you* **(as) clear as day** (=so that it was easy to understand) *that I wanted you to buy brown bread, not white.* • *(humorous) His instructions about how to use the computer were* **(as) clear as mud** (=very difficult to understand).

clear·ly /£'klɪə·li, $'klɪr-/ *adv* • *She doesn't speak very clearly, and I often find it difficult to understand what she's saying.*

clear CERTAIN /£klɪəʳ, $klɪr/ *adj* **-er, -est** certain; having no doubt; obvious • *Richard isn't at all clear* **about** *what he wants to do with his life.* • *The police seem quite clear* **that** *she isn't telling the truth.* [+ *that* clause] • *It's not clear* **wh***ether we should turn left or right here.* [+ *wh-* word] • *If what the newspapers say is true, then it's a clear case of corruption.* • *There is no clear indication who was responsible for the accident.* • *It is rapidly becoming clear* **(to** *me)* **that** *I'm not suited to being a teacher.* [+ *that* clause] • *It isn't clear* **how** *long the strike will go on for.* [+ *wh-* word] • *You've* **made** *your* **position** *quite clear* (=It is not possible to have any doubts about what you think). • People say **Do I make myself clear?** or **Is that clear?** in order to emphasize what they have just said, or to express their authority: *I will not tolerate this behaviour any longer. Do I make myself clear?* • *It's* **(as) clear as day** (=certain) *that the government is going to win the election.* • *The prosecution has a* **clear-cut** *case* (=There are no doubts about it).

clear *obj* /£klɪəʳ, $klɪr/ *v* [T] • *After twenty years, the case has finally been cleared* (=there are no longer doubts about it). [T] • *They never cleared* **up** *the mystery of* (=discovered what happened to) *the missing money.* [M] • *We just need to clear* **up** *a few* **loose ends** (=make decisions on a few more points), *and then we'll be ready to submit our report.* [M]

clear·ly /£'klɪə·li, $'klɪr-/ *adv* • *The accident was clearly* (=obviously) *the lorry driver's fault.* • *Clearly,* (=There can be no doubt that) *you should tell her the truth.*

clear NOT CONFUSED /£klɪəʳ, $klɪr/ *adj* **-er, -est** free from confusion; able to think quickly and well • *I won't have another drink, thank you, I need to have a clear* **head***/to be* **clear-headed** *for an important meeting in the morning.* • *Mary is good at making decisions because she's a very clear* **thinker.** • *Simon has a* **clear-sighted** *vision of* (=He is not at all confused about) *the future of the company.*

clear *obj* /£klɪəʳ, $klɪr/ *v* [T] • *It's very hot in here. I think I'll get some fresh air to clear my* **head** (=to make me able to think well).

clear·ly /£'klɪə·li, $'klɪr-/ *adv* • *I had too much to drink last night, and I can't think very clearly* (=well) *this morning.*

clear NOT GUILTY /£klɪəʳ, $klɪr/ *adj* **-er, -est** free from guilt • *She thinks I shouldn't have told her that her son is taking drugs, but I have a clear* **conscience** *about it.* • *The police breathalysed Andy last night, but he was* **in the clear** (=was not guilty).

clear *obj* /£klɪəʳ, $klɪr/ *v* [T] • *After many years in prison, the men were finally cleared* (=were shown to be not guilty) **of** *the bombings.*

clear NOT TROUBLED /£klɪəʳ, $klɪr/ *adj* [after v] **-er, -est** not troubled; without difficulties • *He was relieved to be told that he was clear* **of** *all suspicion.* • *This is the first time in his life that he's been clear* **of** (=without) *debt.* • *The X-rays showed that she's* **in the clear** (=that there's nothing wrong with her).

clear *obj* /£klɪəʳ, $klɪr/ *v* [T] • *After many years, we've finally managed to clear our debts/clear our***selves of** *debt* (=to pay back our debts).

clear NOT BLOCKED /£klɪəʳ, $klɪr/ *adj* **-er, -est** not blocked, covered or interrupted • *We have a clear view of the ocean from our hotel window.* • *Our journey was much quicker than we expected because the road was clear* (=there was not much traffic on it). • *I always like to leave my desk clear* (=with no work on it) *at the end of the day.* • *The only time I have clear* (=not filled by any other planned activity) *next week is Tuesday afternoon.* • *We've got two clear* (=whole) *weeks in which to finish the decorating.*

clear *(obj)* /£klɪəʳ, $klɪr/ *v* • *It took several hours to clear the road after the accident.* [T] • *This nasal spray will help clear a blocked nose.* [T] • *I never leave work until I've cleared my in-tray* (=have finished the work that needs to be done). [T] • *After my aunt died, we had to arrange for her house to be cleared* (=for the furniture to be removed from it). [T] • *If you hit this key on the computer, the screen will clear* (=the text and pictures on it will be removed). [I] • *Shops are currently holding sales in order to clear their summer stock* (=get rid of goods by selling them cheaply). [T] • *I'll make the coffee if you'll clear the table* (=remove the plates, dishes, knives, forks, etc. from the table)*?* [T] • *It's Peter's turn to clear* **away** (=remove the plates, dishes, knives, forks, etc. from the table) *and wash up today.* [I] • *I want you to clear all these toys* **away/up** (=remove them from where they are) *before bedtime.* [M] • *Paul helped his elderly neighbour by clearing her path* **of** *snow/clearing snow* **from** *her path* (=removing snow from her path). [T] • *Could you clear your things* **off/from** (=remove them from) *the sofa so that I can sit down.* [T] • *They spent the weekend clearing* **out** *the attic* (=tidying it and getting rid of things in it that they didn't want). [M] • *It's about time we cleared* **out** (=got rid of) *all those old newspapers.* [M] • *The kitchen's in a terrible mess and I don't want to go out until I've cleared* **up** (=tidied it). [I] • *I'm tired of always having to clear* **up after** *you* (=tidy your things). [I] • *(infml) Let's* **clear the decks** (=remove the things we don't need and get ready for action) *and then we can start cooking dinner.* • *She* **cleared** *her* **throat** (=gave a small cough) *nervously before she began to speak.* • *We've got a loan from the bank and that's* **cleared the way** (=made it possible) *for us to buy a house.*

clear·ance /£'klɪə·rənts, $'klɪr·ᵊnts/ *n* [U] • *The city council has finally agreed to a slum clearance programme* (=to a project to remove old houses in bad condition). • If goods are reduced for clearance, they are being offered for sale at a lower than usual price so that people will be encouraged to buy them and there will be space for new goods: *We bought our new bedroom carpet at a clearance* **sale.**

clear·ing /£'klɪə·rɪŋ, $'klɪr·ɪŋ/ *n* [C] • A clearing is an area in a wood or forest from which trees and bushes have been removed: *As we walked through the forest, we suddenly came upon a small clearing.*

clear–out /£'klɪə·raʊt, $'klɪr·aʊt/ *n* [U] *esp. Br* • *We need to give garage a* **good** *clear-out* (=to tidy it and get rid of the things in it that are no longer wanted).

clear PURE /£klɪəʳ, $klɪr/ *adj* **-er, -est** easy to see through; pure; not marked; not cloudy or foggy • *The water in the lake is so clear that you can see fish swimming around at the bottom.* • *Some of the church windows are made of stained glass and some of clear glass* (=glass which is not coloured). • *She has a beautifully clear* **skin/complexion** (=has no marks or spots on her skin). • *He gazed at her with his clear brown eyes.* • *The clear* (=not rough) *sound of the flute could be heard above the other instruments.* • *He always uses clear* (=bright) *colours in his paintings.* • *The weather is expected to remain clear* (=not cloudy or foggy) *for the next few days.* • *You can see the mountains from here on a clear* **day.** • *We could see hundreds of stars in the clear desert sky.* • *(fig.) I have clear memories of* (=I can easily remember) *visiting my grandfather's farm when I was a child.*

clear *(obj)* /£klɪəʳ, $klɪr/ *v* • *The children enjoyed stirring the mud at the bottom of the pond, then watching the water slowly clear* (=become able to be seen through) *again.* [I] • *Your skin will clear* (=become free of spots) *if you stop eating so many sweets.* [I] • *Using this cream might help clear your skin* (=make it free of spots). [T] • *After the thunderstorm, the sky cleared* (=stopped being cloudy). [I] • *The fog is expected to have cleared* **(away)** (=gone) *by mid-day.* [I] • *I hope the weather clears* **(up)** (=improves) *by this afternoon, because we want to go out.* [I] • *The rain has helped clear* **the air** (=make the air cooler, fresher and more comfortable). [T] • *I had a massive argument with Sue yesterday, but it has* **cleared the air** (=has removed the bad feelings between us).

clear LEFT /£klɪəʳ, $klɪr/ *adj* [not gradable] (of a sum of money) left after all necessary payments have been made • *The school summer fair made a clear* **profit** *of £500.* • *Bill earns a clear $200 a week/earns $200 a week clear.*

clear *obj* /£klɪəʳ, $klɪr/ *v* [T] • *Bill clears $200 a week* (=has $200 a week left after he has paid taxes and made other necessary payments).

clear NOT TOUCHING /£klɪəʳ, $klɪr/ *adj* [not gradable] not touching; away from • *Only one competitor made a clear jump of the highest fence* (=jumped over it without touching it). • *I think we should wait until we're clear* **of** (=away

from) *the main road before we stop for our picnic.* • *His parents warned him to* **keep/stay/steer** *clear* **of** (=avoid) *trouble.* • *The children were saved from the fire only because a neighbour pulled them clear.*

clear /£klɪəʳ, $klɪr/ *adv* [not gradable] • *Stand clear* **of** (=away from) *the doors, please.* • *Make sure you park clear* **of** *the kerb* (=so that your car isn't touching it).

clear *obj* /£klɪəʳ, $klɪr/ *v* [T] • *The horse cleared the fence* (=jumped over it without touching it) *with inches to spare.*

clear·ance /£'klɪə·rənts, $'klɪr·ᵊnts/ *n* [U] • *It was difficult getting the piano through the doorway because we only had a clearance* **of** *a few centimetres* (=there was only a space of a few centimetres as it went through). • *High vehicles are advised to take an alternative route because of low clearance* (=because there is not much space) *under the bridge.*

clear *(obj)* BANKING /£klɪəʳ, $klɪr/ *v* to (cause a CHEQUE to) go from one bank to another through a central organization, so that money can be paid to the person to whom it is owed • *It usually takes four to five working days for a cheque to clear.* [I] • *The bank lost my cheque while they were clearing it.* [T] • A **clearing bank** is a bank which exchanges CHEQUES with other banks through a central organization known as a **clearing house**.

clear·ance /£'klɪə·rənts, $'klɪr·ᵊnts/ *n* [U] • *Clearance of a cheque can take up to a week.*

clear *obj* GIVE PERMISSION /£klɪəʳ, $klɪr/ *v* [T] to give official permission for (something), or to satisfy the official conditions of (something) • *Despite local opposition, the plans for the new supermarket have been cleared by the council.* • *Ladies and gentlemen, air-traffic control has now cleared the plane* **for** *take-off, please fasten your seat belts.* • *I don't know if I can get the car tonight – I'll have to clear it* **with** *Mum.* • *Gail has been cleared* **to** *work* (=has satisfied the official conditions of working) *at the Ministry of Defence.* [+ obj + *to* infinitive] • *Before you can enter the country, you have to clear* (=satisfy the official conditions of) **customs**.

clear·ance /£'klɪə·rənts, $'klɪr·ᵊnts/ *n* [U] • *The plane will be taking off as soon as it gets clearance* (=official permission). • *You can't visit the prison unless you get* **(security)** *clearance* (=satisfy the official conditions) *first.*

clear *(obj)* **off** *v adv, v prep* to (cause someone to) go away (from) • *Clear off and leave me alone.* [I] • *The farmer shouted at the boys to clear off his land.* [I] • *The police used dogs to clear the campers off the village green.* [T]

clear out *v adv* [I] to leave esp. a building • *I hear Daphne's finally told her husband to clear out* (=to leave home). • *My landlord's given me a week to clear out* **of** *my flat.*

clear up *v adv* [I] (of an illness) to go away • *You won't be able to go swimming tomorrow if your cold hasn't cleared up.*

clear·way /£'klɪə·weɪ, $'klɪr-/ *n* [C] *Br* a road on which you are only allowed to stop if your car breaks down

cleat /kliːt/ *n* [C] *Am for* STUD BOOT • Cleats are also boots that are worn for playing football. • PIC〉 **Shoes**

cleav·age /'kliː·vɪdʒ/ *n* the space between a woman's breasts that can be seen when she is wearing a piece of clothing which pushes the breasts together and does not cover the top of them • *Clare was wearing a low-cut dress which showed off her cleavage to its best advantage.* [C] • *It has always troubled Vicky that she doesn't have any cleavage.* [U]

cleave *(obj)* /kliːv/ *v past simple* **cleaved** or **cleft** /kleft/ or *Am also* **clove** /£kləʊv, $kloʊv/, *past part* **cleaved** or **cleft** /kleft/ or **cloven** /£'kləʊ·vᵊn, $'kloʊ-/ *literary or old use* to (cause something to) separate or divide, often violently • *With one blow of the knight's axe, the rock clove* **in twain** (=into two pieces). [I]

cleav·age /'kliː·vɪdʒ/ *n fml* • *There is a marked cleavage* (=division or disagreement) **between** *the parties about the government's defence policy.* [C] • *There are no signs of any cleavage within the union about the strike.* [U]

cleav·er /£'kliː·vəʳ, $-vɚ/ *n* [C] • *A butcher uses a cleaver* (=a knife with a large square blade) *for cutting meat.* • PIC〉 **Axe**

cleave to *obj v prep* [T] *fml or literary* to stick to • *The ancient ivy cleaved to* (=grew up against) *the ruined castle walls.* • *People in the remote mountain villages still cleave to* (=continue to believe in) *their old traditions.*

clef /klef/ *n* [C] a sign put at the beginning of a line of music to show how high or low the notes are • *the bass/treble/alto clef*

cleft /kleft/ *n* [C] an opening or crack, esp. in a rock or the ground • *Eagles often nest in a cleft* **in** *the rocks.*

cleft /kleft/ *adj* • *Bobby was born with a* **cleft lip** *and a* **cleft palate** (=an opening in his lip and in the roof of his mouth which make it difficult for him to speak). • *(Br) We're really* **(caught) in a cleft stick** (=are in a situation in which it is difficult to decide what to do).

cle·ma·tis /£'klem·ə·tɪs, $-ţəs/ *n pl* **clematis** a climbing plant with flat white, pink or purple flowers • *We've got a couple of clematis in our front garden.* [C] • *I'd like to grow clematis up the side of the house.* [U]

clem·en·cy /'klem·ənt·si/ *n* [U] kindness when giving a punishment • *The jury passed a verdict of guilty, with an appeal to the judge for clemency.*

clem·ent /'klem·ᵊnt/ *adj fml* (of weather) not severe; pleasant • *The Mediterranean has a clement climate.* • *It's very clement for the time of year.*

clem·en·cy /'klem·ənt·si/ *n* [U] *fml* • *England is not known for the clemency* **of** *its climate* (=having pleasant weather).

clem·ent·ine /'klem·ən·tiːn/ *n* [C] a fruit like a small orange

clench *obj* /klentʃ/ *v* [T] to close or hold very tightly, often in a determined or angry way • *The old man clenched his* **fist** *and waved it angrily at the girls who had climbed over his fence.* • *"Get out of here," she said through clenched* **teeth.** • *Sam clenched the toy car tightly* **in** *his hands, and wouldn't give it to his brother.* • *The boy climbed the palm tree with a knife clenched* **in/between** *his teeth and began to cut down the coconuts.*

cler·gy /£'klɜː·dʒi, $'klɜːr-/ *pl n* priests, esp. in the Christian Church • **The** *clergy remain divided on the issue of women priests.* • *We were surprised when he announced he wanted to join the clergy* (=become a priest).

cler·gy·man /£'klɜː·dʒɪ·mən, $'klɜːr-/ *n* [C] **-men** • *Thomas has decided to become a clergyman* (=a priest).

cler·ic /'kler·ɪk/ *n* [C] a priest, esp. in the Christian Church • *A leading cleric has criticized the government for its failure to tackle the growing problem of homelessness.*

cler·ic·al /'kler·ɪ·kᵊl/ *adj* [not gradable] • A **clerical collar** (*infml* **dog collar**) is a stiff white circular band worn around the neck by priests. • PIC〉 **Clothes**

clerk /£klɑːk, $klɜːrk/ *n* [C] a person who works in an office, dealing with records or performing general office duties • *Gary has a job as a filing clerk.* • *Joan is a junior office clerk.* • *(Am) When we arrived at the hotel, the* **(desk)** *clerk* (=person who greets guests at a hotel) *checked us in and gave us our key.* • *(Am) Take your purchases to the* **(sales)** *clerk* (=person who sells things in a shop), *and he will wrap them for you.*

clerk /£klɑːk, $klɜːrk/ *v* [I] • *Debbie has a summer job clerking* (=working as a clerk) *in an office.*

cler·ic·al /'kler·ɪ·kᵊl/ *adj* • *David is looking for a clerical job* (=a job performing general office duties). • *We regret that due to a clerical* **error** (=a mistake made in the office) *your application form has been mislaid.*

clev·er /£'klev·əʳ, $-ɚ/ *adj* **-er, -est** having or showing the ability to learn and understand things quickly and easily • *Judy has never been very clever, but she tries hard.* • *He was once called the cleverest man in all England.* • *Fiona is very clever* **at** *physics.* • *Clever girl, well done!* • *Charlie has a clever idea/plan for getting us out of our present difficulties.* • *My mother is very clever* **with** *her hands* (=is skilful at making things with her hands). • *I've got this clever* (=well-designed) *little gadget which opens jars that I can't open myself.* • *That's enough clever talk* (=talk which shows an able mind but is not sincere, polite or serious), *young lady.* • *(Br infml disapproving) If you're such a* **clever dick/clever clogs** (=you have such an able mind), *you finish the crossword puzzle.* • *(infml disapproving) You're* **too clever by half** (=You annoy people by making it too obvious that you have an able mind). • *(Br infml disapproving) I'm sick of his* **clever-clever** *ways* (=his wanting to appear to have an able mind).

clev·er·ly /£'klev·ᵊl·i, $-ɚ·li/ *adv* • *I thought you handled the situation very cleverly* (=skilfully).

clev·er·ness /£'klev·ə·nəs, $'-ɚ-/ *n* [C] • *It's his cleverness* (=ability to understand and learn quickly and easily) *that has got him where he is today.* • *Everyone was impressed by the cleverness* (=intelligent design) **of** *the machine.*

cli·ché /£'kliː·ʃeɪ, $-'-/ *n* a form of expression that has been so often used that its original effectiveness has been lost • *Every time I ask my dad for some money, he always comes out* *with the old cliché, "It doesn't grow on trees, you know."* [C] • *You should always try to avoid the use of cliché.* [U] • *His speeches tend to be boring and cliché*-**ridden** (= contain a lot of clichés).

cli·chéd /ˈkliː·ʃeɪd/ *adj* • *What she says is always dreadfully clichéd* (= contains a lot of clichés).

click [SOUND] /klɪk/ *n, v* (to (cause something to) make) a short sharp sound • *You'll know your seat belt is fastened properly when you hear a click.* [C] • *Tap dancers make loud clicks with their shoes.* [C] • *The soldier gave a click* **of** *his heels as he saluted the Queen.* [C] • *As the door clicked shut behind her, she realized she'd forgotten her key.* [I] • *Can you hear that strange clicking noise?* [I] • *Paul clicked his fingers* (= moved his thumb against his middle finger to make a short sharp sound) *to attract the waiter's attention.* [T] • *Mrs Wilson clicked her tongue in disapproval at the children's behaviour.* [T] • *Soldiers click their heels* (= bring them sharply together) *when they stand to attention.* [T]

click [BECOME FRIENDLY] /klɪk/ *v* [I] to become friendly or popular • *Liz and I really clicked* (**with** *each other) the first time we met.* • *The new daytime soap opera has yet to show signs that it's clicking* **with** *the television audience.*

click [BECOME CLEAR] /klɪk/ *v* [I] to be understood or become clear suddenly • *It took some time for* **it** *to click, but I do now understand how to use the computer.* • *In the last act of the play, everything clicks* **into place**. • *As he talked about his schooldays,* **it** *suddenly clicked* **where** *I had met him before.* [+ *wh*-word] • *So it's finally clicked* **that** *you're going to have to get yourself a job, has it?* [+ *that* clause]

click *(obj)* [OPERATE] /klɪk/ *v specialized* to (cause a computer instruction to) operate by pressing a button on the MOUSE (= movable control device) of a computer • *When you have selected the file you want, click the 'Open' box.* [T] • *If you want to open a file, click twice* **on** *the icon for it.* [I] • *Click to create a new file.* [I]

cli·ent /ˈklaɪ·ᵊnt/ *n* [C] a person who receives services; a customer • *Would you ask my next client to come in now, please?* • *Mr Black has been a client* **of** *this firm for many years.* • *We always aim to give our clients personal attention.* • A **client state** is a country which gets support and protection from another larger and more powerful country.

cli·ent·ele /£ˌkliː·ɒnˈtel, $-ɑːn-/ *n* [C + sing/pl v] • A clientele is all the customers of a business when they are considered as a group: *The nightclub has a very fashionable clientele.* ○ *The bank's clientele includes/include some of the richest people in the city.*

cliff /klɪf/ *n* [C] a high area of rock with a very steep side, often on a coast • *Don't go too close to the edge of the cliff – you might fall.* • *We walked along the cliff edge for a couple of miles.* • PIC〉 **Edge**

cliff·hang·er /£ˈklɪfˌhæŋ·əʳ, $-ɚ/ *n* [C] a story or a situation which is exciting because its ending or result is uncertain until it happens • *Many of Hitchcock's films are real cliffhangers.* • *It looks as if the election is going to be a cliffhanger.*

cliff·top /£ˈklɪf·tɒp, $-tɑːp/ *n* [C] an area of ground at the top of a cliff • *Their house is in a stunning position on the clifftop.* • *We stayed in a marvellous clifftop hotel.*

cli·mate /ˈklaɪ·mət/ *n* the general weather conditions usually found in a particular place • *In some parts of the world there is an extreme climate, and it is very hot in summer and very cold in winter.* [C] • *The climate* **of** *the Mediterranean is good for growing citrus fruits and grapes.* [C] • *When we retire, we're going to move to a warmer climate* (= an area where the weather tends to be warmer). [C] • *I feel as if I could do with a change of climate* (= going somewhere where the general weather conditions are different). [U] • *(fig.) I don't think we should consider trying to expand our business in the current economic climate* (= the existing economic conditions). [C] • *(fig.) The government needs to find out what the climate* **of opinion** *is* (= what people generally think) *before it introduces any further changes in the health service.* [C] • *"Love in a Cold Climate"* (title of a book by Nancy Mitford, 1949)

cli·mat·ic /£klaɪˈmæt·ɪk, $-ˈmæṭ-/ *adj* [not gradable] • *Some parts of the world seem to be experiencing climatic changes* (= changes in general weather conditions).

cli·ma·tol·o·gy /£ˌklaɪ·məˈtɒl·ə·dʒi, $-ˈtɑː·lə-/ *n* [U] • Climatology is the scientific study of general weather conditions.

cli·max /ˈklaɪ·mæks/ *n, v* (to reach) the most important or exciting point in a story or situation, which usually happens near the end • *In the film 'Strangers on a Train', the climax is set in a fairground.* [C] • *The climax* **of** *the air show was a daring flying display.* [C] • *The election campaign* **reaches** *its climax next week, when the people finally cast their votes.* [C] • *Do you think it's possible to enjoy sex without reaching/experiencing a climax* (= the highest point of sexual pleasure)*?* [C] • *The show climaxed* **with** (= The most important and exciting part of the show was) *all the performers singing on stage together.* [I] • *The Olympics climaxed* **in** *a spectacular closing ceremony.* [I] • *After they'd both climaxed* (= reached the highest point of sexual pleasure), *they lay silently in each other's arms.* [I] • See also ANTICLIMAX. • GR

cli·mac·tic /klaɪˈmæk·tɪk/ *adj* • *The third movement of the symphony ends in a climactic crescendo* (= has a loud and exciting ending).

climb *(obj)* [RISE] /klaɪm/ *v* to go up (towards the top of) • *The plane climbed quickly* **to** *a height of 30 000 feet.* [I] • *As it leaves the village, the road climbs steeply* **up** *the mountain and* **down** *the other side.* [I] • *It got hotter and hotter as the sun climbed higher and higher.* [I] • *We're going climbing* (= climbing mountains as a sport) *in Scotland next weekend.* [I] • *They climbed the hill* (= went up it using their legs) *with great difficulty.* [T] • *I hate climbing ladders.* [T] • *We have an old ivy climbing* (= growing) **up/over** *the walls of our house.* [I] • *I want to find some climbing plants that will grow on a north-facing wall.* • *Our costs have climbed* (= increased) *rapidly in the last few years.* [I] • *(fig.) She became more and more ruthless as she climbed* **to** (= moved into a position of) *power.* [I] • A person who is **climbing the walls** is having emotional difficulties with a particular situation: *After a week with my mother I was climbing the walls with anger/boredom/frustration.* • *"Climb Every Mountain"* (title of a song by Oscar Hammerstein II in the musical *The Sound of Music*, 1959) • PIC〉 **Garden**

climb /klaɪm/ *n* [C] • *We were very tired after our climb* (= act of climbing). • *The climb* **up** *the mountain took longer than the climb* **down**. • *I've* **made** *three climbs so far this year.* • *The north face of the Eiger is a very difficult climb* (= place to be climbed). • *(fig.) Her climb* **to** (= move into a position of) *power has been very rapid.*

climb·er /£ˈklaɪ·məʳ, $-mɚ/ *n* [C] • *Sir Edmund Hillary became famous as a* **(mountain)** *climber* (= a person who climbs mountains for sport). • A climber is also a plant which grows up a supporting surface.

climb·ing /ˈklaɪ·mɪŋ/ *n* [U] • *Chris has just taken up climbing* (= the sport of climbing mountains). • *He needs some climbing boots.* • *(Br) The children enjoy playing on their* **climbing frame** *(Am and Aus* **jungle gym** *or Am* **climber***)* (= large frames made of bars which children can go up, over and around). • PIC〉 **Frame, Playground**

climb [MOVE] /klaɪm/ *v* [I always + adv/prep] to move into or out of a small space awkwardly or with difficulty or effort • *Then they climbed* **into** *the truck and drove away.* • *We can't stop Tom climbing* **out of** *his cot.*

climb down *v adv* [I] *Br and Aus* to admit to having made a mistake or to change an opinion in an argument • *He'll have to climb down when the facts are published.* • *The management are refusing to climb down and agree to the union's demands.*

climb–down /ˈklaɪm·daʊn/ *n* [C] *Br* • *Saying she was wrong was a difficult climb-down* (= admission of having made a mistake) *for Sarah.*

climes /klaɪmz/ *pl n literary or humorous for* CLIMATE • *We're off to sunnier climes next week.*

clinch *obj* [DECIDE] /klɪntʃ/ *v* [T] to decide (something) after a lot of consideration or discussion • *When she was told that the job would involve travelling to Paris, that clinched* **it (for** *her)* (= that made her certain that she wanted the job). • *I hear he finally clinched the* **deal** *to buy the land he wanted.*

clinch·er /£ˈklɪn·tʃəʳ, $-tʃɚ/ *n* [C] • *It was the offer of a large discount on the TV that was the real clincher* (= the point that made us decide to buy it).

clinch [HOLD] /klɪntʃ/ *n* [C] the position two people are in when they are holding each other tightly in their arms • *The boxers* **got into** *a clinch and had to be separated by the referee.* • *David and Kay were* **locked in** *a tight clinch, unaware of the world around them.*

cling [HOLD] /klɪŋ/ *v* [I] *past* **clung** /klʌŋ/ to hold tightly or to stick; to refuse to stop holding • *They clung* **together** *in terror as the screams grew louder.* • *Cling* **on** *or you might fall over.* • *Small children often sleep clinging* **(on) to** *a cuddly toy.* • *She clung* **to** *the handrail as she walked down the slippery steps.* • *We got so wet that our clothes clung* **to** *us.* • *The two lost children clung tightly* **to** *each other.* • *(fig.)*

The road clings **to** (=closely follows) *the coastline for several miles, then it turns inland.* • *(fig.) He still clings* **to** (=refuses to give up) *his old-fashioned ways.* • *(fig.) She clings* **to** *the hope/belief that her husband will come back to her.* • *(fig.) The smell of paint always clings* (=stays in the air). • Ⓝⓛ Ⓢ

cling STAY CLOSE /klɪŋ/ *v* [I] *past* **clung** /klʌŋ/ to stay close or near, or to be dependent • *Jenny is the kind of child who always clings* (=stays close to the person who is caring for her) *whenever she is taken to a strange place.* • Ⓝⓛ Ⓢ

cling·ing /ˈklɪŋ·ɪŋ/, **cling·y** /ˈklɪŋ·i/ *adj* • *Jimmy is a very clinging child* (=wants to stay close to the person who is caring for him).

cling·film *Br* /ˈklɪŋ·fɪlm/, *Am and Aus* **plas·tic wrap** *n* [U] thin transparent plastic material used for wrapping food to keep it fresh • *Could you put some clingfilm over the salad?*

cli·nic /ˈklɪn·ɪk/ *n* [C] a building, esp. part of a hospital or other place where doctors work, to which people can go for medical care or advice • *Bring your baby to the clinic and we'll take a look at her.* • *I've got an appointment at the ear, nose and throat clinic next week.* • *Antenatal clinics provide care for pregnant women.* • *(Br) Dr Clark* **holds** *a clinic* (=The time when she provides medical care or advice is) *on Tuesday mornings.* • *(fig. Br) Our MP* **holds** *a clinic* (=is available to talk to members of the public) *every Friday evening.*

cli·nic·al MEDICAL /ˈklɪn·ɪ·kəl/ *adj* [not gradable] (of medical work or teaching) relating to the examination and treatment of ill people • *Clinical tests have so far failed to show the cause of the illness.* • *The medical students will begin their clinical training next month.* • *Richard works in the Department of Clinical Medicine.* • *Clinical* **trials** *of the new drug may take five years.* • *(fig.) We were going to paint our kitchen white, but we decided that would look too clinical* (=too cold and plain, like a hospital). • If someone suffers from **clinical depression**, they have a mental illness which causes feelings of sadness and hopelessness, changes in their sleeping and eating habits, a loss of interest in their usual activities, and pains which have no physical explanation: *After a long period of poor health which was eventually diagnosed as clinical depression, she tried to commit suicide.* • A **clinical thermometer** is a device used for measuring the body temperature of a person or animal.

cli·nic·al·ly /ˈklɪn·ɪ·kli/ *adv* [not gradable] • *This toothpaste has been clinically proven* (=has been shown in experiments) *to protect your teeth.* • *Doctors pronounced him clinically* **dead** (=judged him to be dead from the condition of his body) *at the scene of the accident.* • *People who are clinically* (=medically) **depressed** *are often reluctant to talk about how they feel.*

cli·ni·cian /klɪˈnɪʃ·ən/ *n* [C] *specialized* • A clinician is someone, such as a doctor, who is qualified in an area of highly skilled health work: *Psychiatrists, psychologists and other clinicians attended the conference.*

cli·nic·al EMOTIONLESS /ˈklɪn·ɪ·kəl/ *adj disapproving* expressing no emotion or feelings • *She seems to have a very clinical attitude towards her children.* • *He'd be a much better doctor if he weren't so clinical towards his patients.*

cli·nic·al·ly /ˈklɪn·ɪ·kli/ *adv disapproving* • *Should doctors always remain clinically detached from* (=express no emotion towards) *their patients?*

clink *(obj)* SOUND /klɪŋk/ *v* to (cause to) make a short ringing sound like pieces of glass or metal knocking lightly together • *Ice clinks when you drop it into an empty glass.* [I] • *Everyone at the party clinked their* **glasses** *together and drank to a happy new year.* [T]

clink /klɪŋk/ *n* [U] • *He said he hadn't got any money but I could hear* **the** *clink* **of** *coins in his pocket.*

clink·ing /ˈklɪŋ·kɪŋ/ *n* [U] • *There was* **a** *clinking* **of** *chains as the prisoners walked slowly round the yard.*

clink PRISON /klɪŋk/ *n* [C] *infml* prison • *Everyone always said Joe would end up* **in** *(the) clink.*

clink·er /£ˈklɪŋ·kəʳ, $-kɚ/ *n* [U] dusty material containing rough hard lumps that is left after coal has been burned

clip FASTENER /klɪp/ *n* [C] a small usually metal or plastic object used for fastening things together or holding them in position • *a paper/hair/tie clip* • *The wires were fastened together with a plastic clip.* • PIC〉 **Stationery**

clip *(obj)* /klɪp/ *v* [always + adv/prep] **-pp-** • *You can always tell a real bow tie from one that clips* **on** (=fastens with a clip). [I] • *When you've finished your work sheets, clip them together* (=fasten them together with a clip) *and hand them in to me.* [T] • **Clip-on** *sunglasses are worn over* (= fasten with a clip over) *ordinary glasses.* • *"Are these earrings* **clip-on***?* (=Do they fasten with a clip?)*" "Yes, these ones are* **clip-ons** *and those ones are for pierced ears."* • PIC〉 **Jewellery**

clip *obj* CUT /klɪp/ *v* [T] **-pp-** to cut (something) with SCISSORS or a similar sharp tool, esp. to make it tidier • *I'm going to clip the hedge this weekend.* • *We took our dog to the vet yesterday to get his claws clipped.* • *The children were fascinated to see the sheep being clipped* (=having their wool cut off). • *When the guard came to clip my train ticket* (=make a hole in it to show that it had been used), *I couldn't find it.* • *I'm always clipping recipes* **out of** *magazines and never using them.* • *(fig.) Christie has clipped a tenth of a second* **off** *the record* (=has reduced it by that amount). • *If Lynne's parents don't* **clip** *her* **wings** (=stop her doing what she wants), *she's going to get herself into trouble soon.*

clip /klɪp/ *n* [C] • *I'm going to give your hair a clip* (=cut it to make it tidier), *so that it looks nice for the school concert.* • *They showed a clip* **from** (=a short piece of) *a Tina Turner concert on TV last night.*

clipped /klɪpt/ *adj* [not gradable] • *Richard has a neat clipped moustache.*

clip·pers /£ˈklɪp·əz, $-ɚz/ *pl n* • Clippers are tools used for cutting esp. nails, hair, wire and bushes.

clip·ping /ˈklɪp·ɪŋ/ *n* [C] • *Grass clippings* (=Pieces of grass that have been cut) *can be used to make compost.* • *(esp. Am) A friend recently sent me a newspaper clipping (also* **cutting***)* (=an article cut from a newspaper) *about someone we were at school with.*

clip *obj* HIT /klɪp/ *v* [T] **-pp-** to hit with a short sharp movement • *He clipped the edge of the kerb with his front tyre as he turned the corner.* • *I'll clip you* **on the ear***/clip you* **round the ear***/clip your* **ear** *in a minute, if you're not careful.* • *Harry's father clipped him* **one** *when he broke the window.*

clip /klɪp/ *n* • *You do that once more and you'll get a clip* **round the ear** (=will be hit).

clip SPEED /klɪp/ *n* [U] *infml* a fast speed • *We set off at a* **(fast/good)** *clip, but our speed slowed as we went on.*

clip GUN PART /klɪp/ *n* [C] a container which is fastened to a gun, from which bullets go into the gun for firing

clip·board /£ˈklɪp·bɔːd, $-bɔːrd/ *n* [C] a board with a CLIP at the top which holds sheets of paper in position, and which provides a surface for writing on • *While we were out shopping we were stopped by a woman with a clipboard who was doing a survey on washing powder.* • PIC〉 **Stationery**

clip–clop /£ˈklɪp·klɒp, $-klɑːp/ *n* a sound like that of horses' HOOVES (=feet) on a hard surface • *We heard the clip-clop* **of** *horses' hooves along the road.*

clip–clop /£ˈklɪp·klɒp, $-klɑːp/ *v* [I] **-pp-** • *We heard the horses clip-clopping* (=making a sound with their feet) *along the road.*

clip joint *n* [C] a place of entertainment, such as a bar or NIGHTCLUB, where customers are charged too much for food and drink which is low in quality

clipped /klɪpt/ *adj* with words pronounced quickly and sharply, and with parts of them missing, or using as few words as possible • *As I picked up the phone, I heard the clipped tones of George's brisk secretary saying "I have Mr Watson for you."* • *He has a very clipped style of writing.*

clique /£kliːk, $klɪk/ *n* [C + sing/pl v] *disapproving* a small group of people who spend their time only with other members of that group and are unwilling to allow other people to join the group • *Our golf club is run by a very unfriendly clique* **(of** *people).* • *There's a clique at work that never talks/who never talk to anyone else.*

cliqu·ey (**cliquier**, **cliquiest**) /ˈkliː·ki/, **cliqu·ish** /ˈkliː·kɪʃ/ *adj disapproving* • *I decided not to join the tennis club because I found it very cliquey* (=because new members were not made to feel welcome).

cli·to·ris /£ˈklɪt·ər·ɪs, $ˈklɪt̬·ɚ-/ *n* [C] a sexual organ above the vagina which can give a woman sexual pleasure when it is touched

cli·to·ral /£ˈklɪt·ər·əl, $ˈklɪt̬·ɚ-/ *adj* [not gradable]

cloak PIECE OF CLOTHING /£kləʊk, $kloʊk/ *n* [C] a loose outer piece of clothing without sleeves which fastens at the neck and is worn instead of a coat • *The fairy-tale character Little Red Riding Hood wore a red cloak with a hood.* • A **cloak-and-dagger** story is an exciting one, often about SPIES, involving secrecy and mystery: *(fig.) I'm tired of all these* **cloak-and-dagger** (=secret) *meetings – I think these issues should be discussed openly.* • PIC〉 **Coats and jackets**

cloak HIDE /£kləʊk, $kloʊk/ *n* [U] something which hides, covers or keeps something else secret • *The restaurant he owned was just a cloak* **for** (= hid) *his drug-dealing activities.* • *They left the house under the cloak* **of** *darkness.*

cloak *obj* /£kləʊk, $kloʊk/ *v* [T] • *He has always kept his love affairs cloaked* **in** *secrecy* (= kept them secret). • *The river is often cloaked* **in** (= covered by) *mist in the early morning.*

cloak·room /£ˈkləʊk·rʊm, -ruːm, $ˈkloʊk-/, *Am also* **check·room** *n* [C] a room in a public building where coats, bags, etc. can be left while their owners are in the building • *We left our things in the cloakroom while we looked round the gallery.* • *(Br)* Cloakroom is sometimes used to avoid saying toilet when referring to one in a public building: *We all went to the cloakroom during the first interval of the play.*

clob·ber *obj* HIT /£ˈklɒb·əʳ, $ˈklɑː·bɚ/ *v* [T] to hit hard and repeatedly • *If you do that again, I'll clobber you* **(one)**. • *(fig.) The new supermarket is really going to clobber* (= harm) *the small local shops.* • *(fig.) The government is proposing new measures to clobber* (= punish) *tax dodgers.*

clob·ber *obj* DEFEAT /£ˈklɒb·əʳ, $ˈklɑː·bɚ/ *v* [T] to defeat completely • *Germany clobbered Argentina in the final of the World Cup.* • *The government clobbered the opposition's proposals.*

clob·ber POSSESSIONS /£ˈklɒb·əʳ, $ˈklɑː·bɚ/ *n* [U] *Br and Aus infml* possessions, esp. those that you carry around with you, or clothes • *I've got far too much clobber in my handbag.* • *Have you got all your tennis clobber?*

cloche COVER /£klɒʃ, $kloʊʃ/, **cold frame** *n* [C] a piece of clear material, sometimes on a frame, which can be used to cover plants for a short time, esp. in order to help them grow faster or to protect them from very cold weather • *This early variety of lettuce grows well if protected by a cloche until the weather warms up.*

cloche HAT /£klɒʃ, $kloʊʃ/ *n* [C] a woman's hat which is shaped like a bell, fits closely around the head, and was particularly popular in the 1920s

clock TIME /£klɒk, $klɑːk/ *n* [C] a device for measuring and showing time, which is usually found in or on a building and is not worn by a person • *We have an antique clock on our mantlepiece.* • *The town-hall clock* **says** (= shows that the time is) *9 o'clock.* • *I think the clock in the kitchen is* **fast/slow** (= it is showing a later/earlier time than it should). • *As the clock began to* **strike/chime** *twelve, we all wished each other a happy new year.* • *She* **set** *her clock* (= put it to the right time) *by the time signal on the radio.* • *Meet me* **under** *the clock* (= next to the wall on which the clock is hanging) *at Liverpool Street station.* • If you **put/turn** the clock(s) **back**, at a particular time of the year you change the time shown on the clock to an hour earlier. If you **put/turn** the clock(s) **forward/***(Br usually)* **on** (*Am also* **set** the clock(s) **ahead**), at a different time of year you change the time shown on the clock to an hour later. • *Don't forget that the clocks* **go back/forward** (= the time shown on them should be changed to an hour earlier/later) *tonight.* • *(disapproving) The court's decision on this case will* **put/turn the clock back (by)** *fifty years* (= cause a return to the laws, beliefs and customs of fifty years ago). • *Now we're going to* **turn back the clock** (= remember or imagine times in the past) *with some rock 'n' roll from the 1950s.* • *Doctors and nurses worked* **round/around the clock** (= all day and night) *to help those injured in the train crash.* • *The obstacle race in the children's sports day was run* **against** *the clock* (= the time taken to finish it was recorded and the fastest person was the winner). • *Bill always works exactly* **by/according to the clock** (= He is always aware of the time so that he does not work longer than he has to). • *The meeting was so boring that nearly everyone there* **had** *their* **eye**/*was* **keeping** *their* **eye on the clock**/*was* **watching the clock** (= was looking to see what time it was so that they knew how long it was until the meeting ended). • *(disapproving) Stop this* **clock-watching** *and get on with your work.* • *(disapproving) David is a real* **clock-watcher** (= He keeps looking to see what time it is in order to discover how much longer he has to work). • **Clock radio** is another word for **radio alarm (clock)**. See at RADIO. • A **clock tower** is a tower, usually forming part of a building, which has a clock at the top of it. • LP› **Time** PIC› **Clocks and watches**

clock *(obj)* /£klɒk, $klɑːk/ *v* • *He clocked 10 seconds in the 100 metres* (= He ran it in 10 seconds). [T] • *He was clocked* **at** *10 seconds for* (= recorded as taking 10 seconds to run) *the 100 metres.* [T] • *We have to clock* **in/***(Br also)* **on** *when we get to work* (= record the time at which we arrive, usually on a machine with a clock) *and clock* **out/***(Br and Aus also)* **off** *when we leave* (= record the time at which we leave). [I always + adv/prep] • *(fig. infml) I clocked* **in/***(Br also)* **on** (= arrived at work) *a bit late this morning.* [I always + adv/prep] • *(fig. infml) OK, I'm clocking* **out/***(Br and Aus also)* **off** (= leaving work) *now.* [I always + adv/prep] • **Clocking-in** *time is* (= Employees should arrive at work at) *9.00 a.m.*

clock VEHICLE PART /£klɒk, $klɑːk/ *n* [U] **the clock** a SPEEDOMETER (= a device for recording speed) or a MILEOMETER (= a device for recording distance travelled) • *But officer, I was only doing 30 mph according to the clock.* • *I should be able to get a good price for my car because it's only got 10 000 miles* **on** *the clock.*

clock *obj* /£klɒk, $klɑːk/ *v* [T] • *The police clocked him* (= recorded that he was) **doing** *80 mph in a 50 mph area.* [+ obj + v-*ing*] • *This car can clock* (= travel at a speed of) *150 mph.* • *Jim/Jim's car has clocked* **up** (= has travelled) *40 000 miles in less than two years.*

clock *obj* HIT /£klɒk, $klɑːk/ *v* [T] *infml* to hit (someone), esp. on the head or face • *His dad clocked him* **one** (= hit him) *for being so rude.*

clock up *obj*, **clock** *obj* **up** *v adv* [M] *esp. Br* to win or achieve (a large number of similar things) • *The Australians have clocked up three gold medals and two silvers in the swimming events.* • *By the time he was 30, Peter had clocked up a number of successful deals.*

clock·wise /£ˈklɒk·waɪz, $ˈklɑːk-/ *adj, adv* [not gradable] in the direction in which the pointers of a clock move • *Turn the knob clockwise/in a clockwise direction.* • PIC› **Clocks and watches**

clock·work /£ˈklɒk·wɜːk, $ˈklɑːk·wɜːrk/ *n* [U] a system of springs and wheels or other machinery which makes some types of clocks, toys and other devices work • *a clockwork toy/train/mouse* • *(fig.) This office is run with clockwork efficiency* (= is well organized). • *Our bus service has been improved recently and the buses now run* **like/as regular as** *clockwork* (= at the exact times they should do). • *The party went* **like** *clockwork* (= very smoothly and without any trouble). • *My daughter always calls me on Friday evenings,* **(as) regular as** *clockwork* (= very regularly). • PIC› **Clocks and watches**

clod LUMP /£klɒd, $klɑːd/ *n* [C] a lump of earth or clay • *The horses' hooves threw up clods* **of** *earth as they galloped across the field.*

clod PERSON /£klɒd, $klɑːd/ *n* [C] *dated* a stupid person • *Don't be such a clod!*

clod·hop·per PERSON /£ˈklɒdˌhɒp·əʳ, $ˈklɑːdˌhɑː·pɚ/ *n* [C] *infml* an awkward or CLUMSY person • *Look where you're going, you* **great** *clodhopper.*

clod·hop·ping /£ˈklɒdˌhɒp·ɪŋ, $ˈklɑːdˌhɑː·pɪŋ/ *adj* [before n] *infml* • *You trod on my toe, you clodhopping* (= awkward) *idiot!*

clod·hop·per SHOE /£ˈklɒdˌhɒp·əʳ, $ˈklɑːdˌhɑː·pɚ/ *n* [C] *infml* a heavy shoe • *You're not coming in the house in those* **great** *clodhoppers.*

clod·hop·ping /£ˈklɒdˌhɒp·ɪŋ, $ˈklɑːdˌhɑː·pɪŋ/ *adj* [before n] *infml* • *Careful where you're treading in those clodhopping* (= heavy) *shoes.*

clog *(obj)* BLOCK /£klɒg, $klɑːg/ *v* **-gg-** to (cause to) become blocked or filled so that movement or activity is difficult • *If you eat too much fat, your arteries will clog* **(up)**. [I] • *The roads are clogged* **with** *holiday traffic.* [T] • *Can you move those leaves that are clogging the drains* **(up)**? [T/M]

clogged /£klɒgd, $klɑːgd/ *adj* • *We need to find some way of clearing these clogged* (= blocked) *pipes.*

clog SHOE /£klɒg, $klɑːg/ *n* [C] a type of shoe made completely of wood, or with the top part made of leather and the bottom part made of wood • *Clogs are part of the Dutch national costume.* • PIC› **Shoes**

clois·ter /£ˈklɔɪ·stəʳ, $-stɚ/ *n* [C usually pl] a covered stone passage around the four sides of a COURTYARD (= a square or rectangular space), esp. in a religious building such as a church or MONASTERY

clois·ter /£ˈklɔɪ·stəʳ, $-stɚ/ *adj* • *We stood in the cool of the cloistered* (= surrounded by covered passages) *court.* • *(fig.) These academics lead such a cloistered* (= protected) *life, cut off from the problems of the real world.*

clone /£kləʊn, $kloʊn/ *n* [C] a plant or animal which has the same GENES as the original from which it was produced • *Although two clones are identical genetically, they may develop in different ways.* • *(esp. disapproving)* A clone is also someone or something that looks very much like

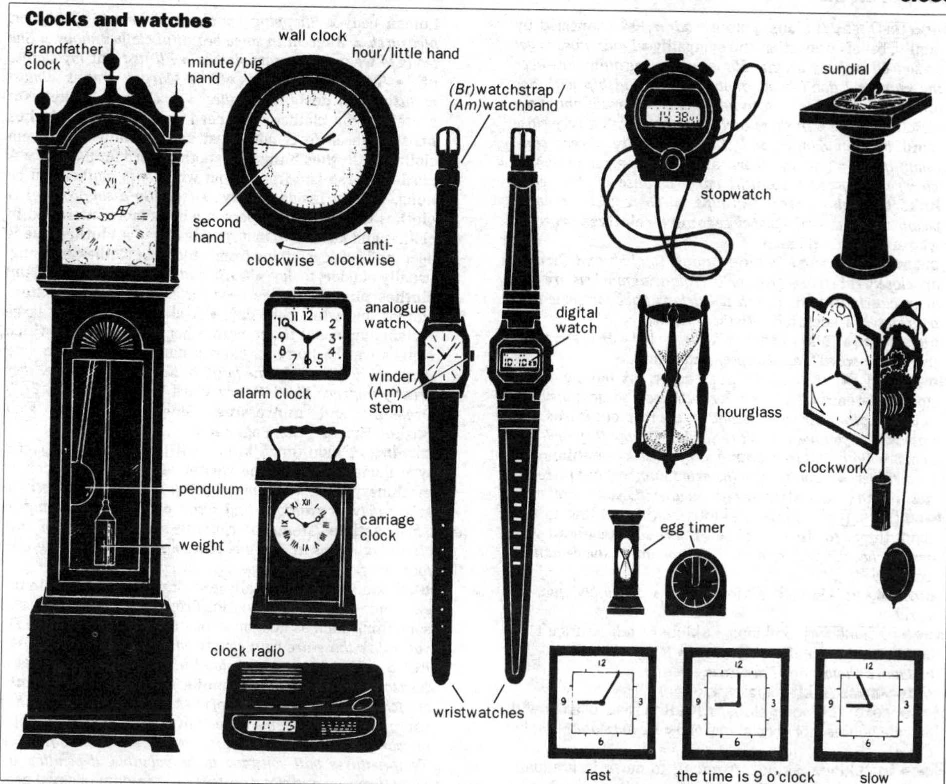

someone or something else: *She's just another blond-haired, red-lipped Marilyn Monroe clone.* • *(specialized)* A clone is also a computer that operates in a very similar way to the one that it was copied from: *There is a market for well-made clone PCs with respected consumer brand names.*

clone *obj* /£kləʊn, $kloʊn/ *v* [T] • *Experiments to try to clone human embryos have met with hostility from some sections of the public.*

close *(obj)* NOT OPEN /£kləʊz, $kloʊz/ *v* to (cause to) change from being open to not being open • *Could you close the* **door**. [T] • *Close your* **eyes** *– I've got a surprise for you.* [T] • *She stopped reading and closed the book.* [T] • *Don't pick at that cut and it will close* **up**. [I] • *(fig.) She closed her eyes* **to** (= intentionally did not deal with or discuss) *the fact that her son was stealing from her company.* [T] • *The banks had closed* **(to** *customers) so I couldn't get any money out.* [I] • *(Br) We can't get a drink! It's after* **(pub)** *closing* **time**. • A group or organization **closes ranks** when its members make an effort to stay united, esp. in order to defend themselves from severe criticism: *The prime minister is thought to have urged his colleagues to close ranks on the issue.* • LP› **Switching on and off**

closed /£kləʊzd, $kloʊzd/ *adj* • *It might be less draughty if the door were closed.* • If something happens **behind closed doors** it is hidden or kept secret from public view: *The issue was considered so controversial that the government held the discussion behind closed doors.* • *(infml)* A **closed book** is a subject about which you know or understand nothing: *I'm afraid physics will always be a closed book to me.* • **Closed circuit television** is a system which sends television signals to a limited number of screens and is often used in shops to stop people stealing. • A **closed shop** is a place of work where you have to belong to a particular **trade union** (= an organization of workers).

close *(obj)* END /£kləʊz, $kloʊz/ *v* to (cause to) end • *I closed that bank* **account** *when I came to London.* [T] • *The* **factory** *closed over ten years ago.* [I] • *The play closed* **with** *the tragic death of both hero and heroine.* [I] • *"The matter is closed," said the health minister.* [T] • *Television and radio stations close* **down** *at the end of a day's broadcasting.* [I] • *The pound closed* **at** (= was worth) *$1·47 at the end of the day's trading.* [I] • *It was a struggle but we closed the* **deal** (= made a successful business arrangement with them). [T] • A **closed season** is a particular period of the year when the killing of animals, for example birds or fish, is not permitted: *Pheasants are safe during closed season.* Compare **open season** at OPEN AVAILABLE. • *(Am)* A **close-out** (*Aus* **sell off**) is when the price of goods in a shop or factory is reduced so they can be sold quickly.

close /£kləʊz, $kloʊz/ *n* [U] • *I was pushed for time so I tried to* **bring** *the conversation* **to a** *close* (= end it). • *"Let's* **draw** *this meeting* **to a** *close* (= end it)*, gentlemen," said the chairman, thinking of his lunch.*

clos·ure /£ˈkləʊ·ʒəʳ, $ˈkloʊ·ʒɚ/ *n* [C] • *The mine-workers' unions are fighting hard to stop the government from implementing its programme of pit closures.* • *Following the factory closure* (= Since the factory stopped operating) *there has been very high unemployment in the surrounding villages.*

close NEAR /£kləʊs, $kloʊs/ *adj, adv* **-r, -st** not distant in position or time • *I wouldn't get too close* **to** *that dog if I were you, Rosie.* • *It worries me when people stand too close* **to** *me.* • *Move closer.* • *The general election is getting close and politicians are smiling for the cameras.* • *As Christmas gets closer the shops get more and more crowded.* • *When you see famous people* **at** *close* **quarters** (= from a short distance) *they always appear much smaller than you imagined them.* • *He was shot* **at** *close* **range**. • *His mother lives in the next street to us which is* **too close for comfort** (= so close it makes me anxious). • *Phil was furious with the manager – I think he* **came close to blows** (= almost hit him). • *He has said he was only joking but his remarks were a bit too* **close to the bone** (= particularly hurtful because they are so close to the truth). • *We should call in on Miranda – she lives* **close-by** (= near). • *Is Polly the one with* **close-cropped** (= very short) *hair?* • *She wears a lot of* **close-fitting** *dresses that leave nothing to the imagination.* • Wood that is **close-grained** has a pattern of narrow rings or lines. • *My mother told me never to trust a man with* **close-set** *eyes* (= eyes that are very near each other). • A **close shave/call** is when you come extremely close to a dangerous or unpleasant situation and only just manage to avoid it: *"I had a close shave this morning. Some idiot in a car almost knocked me off my bike."* • *Ageing Hollywood actors often refuse to have* **close-ups** *taken* (= photographs taken from very near) *for obvious reasons.*

close·ness /£ˈkləʊ·snəs, $ˈkloʊ-/ *n* [U] • *What the hotel lacks in charm is made up by its closeness* **to** *the sea.*

close [RELATED] /£kləʊs, $kloʊs/ *adj* **-r, -st** connected by family, belief or affection and sympathy • *I didn't use to get on so well with my brother but we've become quite close over the years.* • *I don't know about her relationship with her father but she's very close* **to** *her mother.* • *Mira is one of my closest* **friends.** • *In those early months there's a very close* **bond** *between mother and child.* • *They're a very close* **community** (=The members all support each other). • *They're a worrying political party because of their close* **links/ties** *with terrorist groups.* • *There weren't many people at the funeral – just close* **family/relatives** (=people who are directly related).

close·ly /£'kləʊ·sli, $'kloʊ-/ *adv* • *English and German are closely* **related.** • *The world's financial markets are ever more closely* **linked.** • *Both politicians have for some time been closely* **associated** *with the movement.*

close·ness /£'kləʊ·snəs, $'kloʊ-/ *n* [U] • *Between twins there is supposed to exist a special closeness.*

close [SIMILAR] /£kləʊs, $kloʊs/ *adj* **-r, -st** having only a small difference • *The election results were so close they had to vote again.* • *He came second in the race but it was very close.* • *The youngest boys are so close* **in** *age they look like twins.* • *Both children bear a very close* **resemblance** *to their father.* • *I don't know the exact number, but there are close* **on/to** (=almost) *three million unemployed at present.*

close [SECRETIVE] /£kləʊs, $kloʊs/ *adj* unwilling to talk about things to other people • *"You're so close* **about** *your past – what are you trying to hide from me?" she demanded jealously.*

close·ly /£'kləʊ·sli, $'kloʊ-/ *adv* • *a closely guarded secret*

close [LACKING AIR] /£kləʊs, $kloʊs/ *adj* difficult to breathe and uncomfortably warm • *It's so close today – I've just had a shower and I'm already sweaty.*

close·ness /£'kləʊ·snəs, $'kloʊ-/ *n* [U]

close [ROAD] /£kləʊs, $kloʊs/ *n* [C] *Br* a road, usually with private houses, not open at one end • *He lives at 83, Barker Close.*

close in /£kləʊz, $kloʊz/ *v adv* [I] to move in gradually and from all angles • *The advancing soldiers closed in* **on** *the town.* • *The hunt chased the fox until it was too tired and weak to run and then closed in* **for the kill.**

clos·et [CUPBOARD] /£'klɒz·ɪt, $'klɑː·zɪt/ *n* [C] *esp. Am* a cupboard or a small room with a door, used for storing things, esp. clothes • *a bedroom/clothes/linen/storage closet* • A person is said to **come out (of the closet)** when, after a period of secrecy, they admit to their family, their friends or the public that they are homosexual. • (CS) (DK) (N)

clos·et /£'klɒz·ɪt, $'klɑː·zɪt/ *adj* [before n] • A closet belief, activity or feeling is one which is kept secret from the public, usually for fear of the results of it becoming known: *He was a closet alcoholic for most of his life and kept his bottles hidden under his bed.* ○ *a closet homosexual*

clos·et *obj* [STAY] /£'klɒz·ɪt, $'klɑː·zɪt/ *v* [T] to put yourself in a place, esp. an enclosed space, and stay there • *Two weeks before my exams I closeted my***self** *in my room with my books and I didn't speak to anyone.* • *The President is closeted* **with** (=having a private meeting with) *his advisers.* • *The minister remained closeted in meetings much of the day, and didn't return telephone calls.*

clot [LUMP] /£klɒt, $klɑːt/ *n, v* **-tt-** (to form) a half solid lump • *He was rushed into Pemberton Hospital because his blood wasn't clotting properly.* [I] • *A year ago he had a* **blood** *clot removed from his brain.* [C] • *The Institute developed an anti-(blood) clotting agent that stops heart attacks as they are happening.* • **Clotted cream** is a thick cream with soft lumps in it, made esp. in southwest England.

clot [PERSON] /£klɒt, $klɑːt/ *n* [C] *Br dated infml* a stupid person • *You clumsy clot!*

cloth /£klɒθ, $klɑːθ/ *n* (a type of) woven material • *Choose some cloth that you like and I'll make you up a skirt on the machine.* [U] • A cloth is a small piece of material used in cleaning to remove dirt, dust and liquid. [C] • *(Br dated)* **Cloth-ears** is a rude name esp. for a person who has not heard what is being said to them: *Hey, cloth-ears, pay attention!* • LP› **Shopping goods**

clothe *obj* /£kləʊð, $kloʊð/ *v* [T] to provide with clothes • *It costs a lot to* **feed and** *clothe five children.* • *Bathers must be* **fully** *clothed before entering the restaurant.* • *The* **partially** *clothed body of a young man was found by police in the river.*

clothes /£kləʊðz, $kloʊðz/ *pl n* things such as dresses and trousers that people wear to cover, protect or decorate the human body • *Shopping for clothes is one of life's great pleasures.* • *We went in some beautiful clothes shops.* • *She tends to* **wear** *very smart clothes.* • *I'll just* **put** *my clothes* **on.** • **Take** *your clothes* **off.** • *Margot dresses almost exclusively in* **designer** *clothes.* • A **clothes basket** is a container for clothes that need washing. • A **clothes brush** is used to remove dust and unwanted bits from clothes. • **Clothes-hanger** is another word for HANGER. • A **clothes horse** is a frame from which wet clothes can be hung, usually inside, to dry. • *(slightly disapproving)* A **clothes horse** is also a person who is more interested in clothes and fashion than anything else. • A **clothes line** is a length of rope or string from which wet clothes are hung, usually outside, to dry. • A *(Br and Aus)* **clothes peg**/*(Am)* **clothes pin** is a device used for holding clothes onto a clothes line while they dry. • A **clothes rack** is a large rectangular metal frame with a horizontal bar, on which clothes can be hung on clothes hangers. • *"Clothes and manners do not make the man; but when he is made, they greatly improve him"* (Henry Ward Beecher, 1887) • LP› **Dressing and undressing, Shopping goods** PIC› **Basket, Brush, Line, Peg, Rack**

cloth·ing /£'kləʊ·ðɪŋ, $'kloʊ-/ *n* [U] *fml* clothes, esp. of a type made to protect the wearer against heat, water or machinery • *It is sometimes difficult to persuade farmers to take safety precautions and wear* **protective** *clothing.* • *Three* **articles/items of** *clothing only to be taken into changing rooms at any one time.* • *Prices of clothing and footwear fell by almost 4 per cent last month.*

cloud /klaʊd/ *n* [C] a usually grey or white mass seen in the sky made of very small floating drops of water, or a mass of something such as dust or smoke that looks like this • *Do you think those are rain clouds on the horizon?* • *The sky was a perfect blue – not a cloud in sight.* • *On the eastern horizon, a huge cloud* **of smoke** *from burning oil tanks stretched across the sky.* • *Gloria said good night, got in her car, and took off, leaving a cloud* **of dust.** • *The initial cloud of tear gas had hardly cleared before shots were fired.* • *Temperatures will continue to be variable, depending on wind direction and cloud* **cover** (=the amount of sky that is covered by clouds). • *(literary) Dark clouds massed on the horizon.* • A **cloud bank** is a big low mass of cloud. • A **cloud-burst** is a sudden heavy fall of rain. • **Cloud-capped** hills or mountains are surrounded at the top by clouds. • *(specialized)* A **cloud-chamber** is a device containing a gas in which the presence of units of matter smaller than atoms is shown by the small drops of liquid that they produce. • A **cloud hanging over** you is something which makes you worry or be unhappy: *It's awful when you're waiting for an operation, because you feel like there's a cloud hanging over you.* • A **cloud on the horizon** is something that threatens to cause problems or unhappiness in the future: *The only cloud on the horizon is my mother-in-law coming to stay in December.* • If you are **under a cloud**, you are for some reason not trusted or popular: *The cabinet minister left his office under a cloud after a fraud scandal.* • *(disapproving)* Someone is said to live in **cloud-cuckoo-land** if they are not realistic and think that things which are completely impossible might happen. • *(dated)* **On cloud nine** means extremely happy and excited: *"Was Helen pleased about getting that job?" "Pleased? She was on cloud nine!"* • *(saying)* 'Every cloud has a silver lining' means there is a good side to every difficult or unpleasant situation. • *"I wandered lonely as a cloud / That floats on high o'er vales and hills, / When all at once I saw a crowd, / A host of golden daffodils"* (William Wordsworth in the poem *Daffodils*, 1807) • *"Hey! You! Get off of my cloud"* (from the song *Get off of my cloud* by the Rolling Stones, 1965)

cloud *(obj)* /klaʊd/ *v* • *The sky has clouded* **over** *– It looks like rain to me.* [I] • *(fig.) When it came to explaining the lipstick on his collar, he found that drink had clouded* (=confused) *his memory.* [T] • *I don't believe the latest official unemployment statistics – I think they* **cloud the issue** (=are unclear and make people believe something that is not correct). • A person's face **clouds over** when it suddenly shows unhappiness or anxiety: *One mention of her dead husband and her face clouded over.*

cloud·less /'klaʊd·ləs/ *adj* • *a cloudless sky* • *On a cloudless night, you can see a thousand stars.*

cloud·y /'klaʊ·di/ *adj* **-ier, -iest** • *a cloudy day/sky* • *Scotland will be cloudy with wintry showers likely in the north and east.* • *At the bottom of the bottle, the beer was cloudy and dark.*

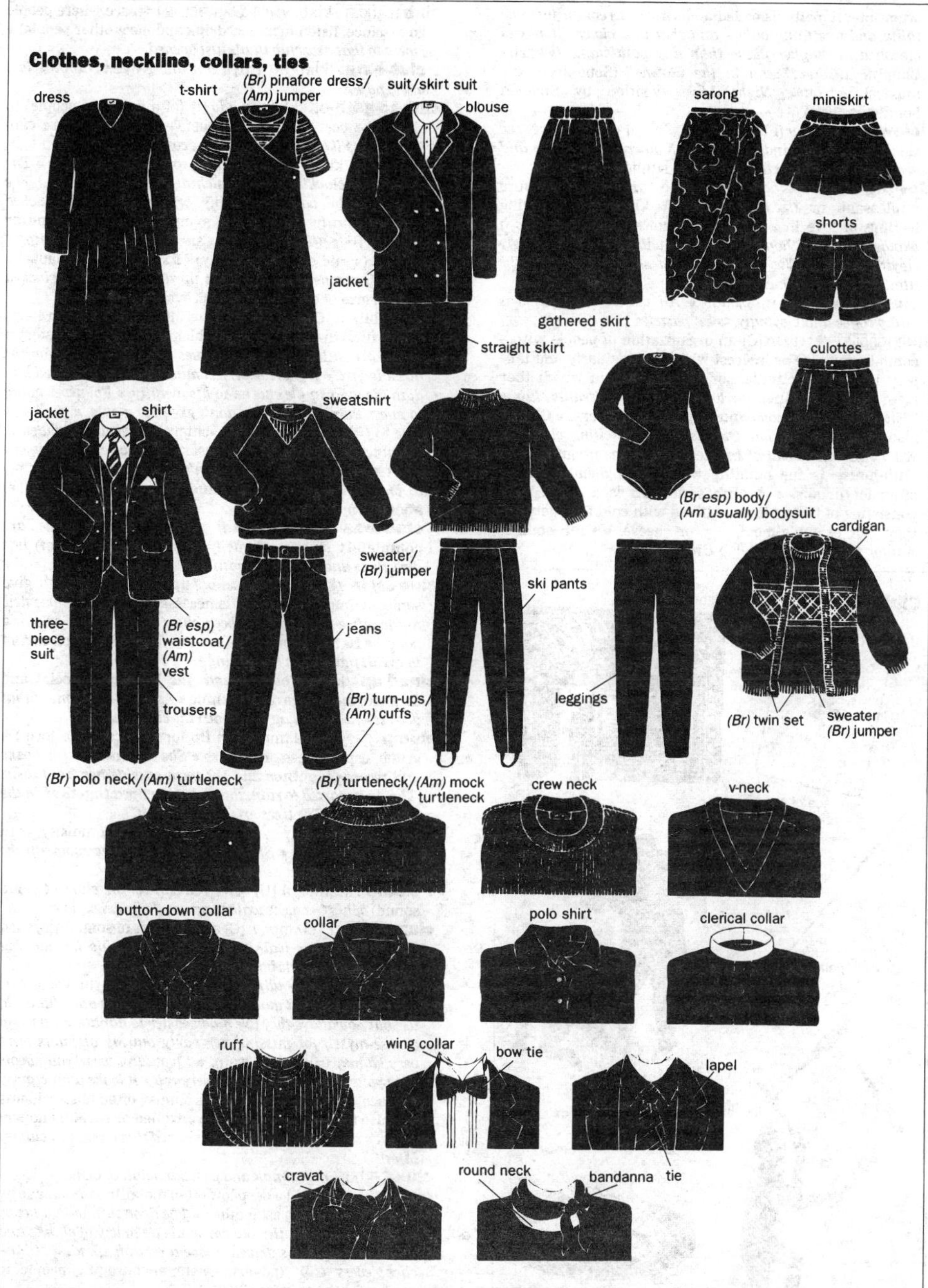

clout HIT /klaʊt/ *n* [C], *v* [T] *infml* (to give) a heavy hit with the hand or a heavy object • *I'll clout you round the head if you say that again!* • *If the photocopier stops working just* **give it** *a* **clout**.

clout POWER /klaʊt/ *n* [U] power and influence over other people or events • *So who* **wields** *the* **clout** (=has the power) *in this organization?* • *The queen may have privilege but she has no real* **political** *clout.*

clove PLANT PART /£kləʊv, $kloʊv/ *n* [C] a small separate part of a GARLIC plant used in cooking to give a strong taste and smell • *This recipe takes four cloves of* **garlic**. • PIC **Vegetables**

clove SPICE /£kləʊv, $kloʊv/ *n* a dried flower of an evergreen tree which is used as a spice • *Cloves add a very pungent flavour to food.* [C] • *I like to put a clove or two in the sauce.* [C] • *Be careful not to add too much* **ground** *clove.* [U] • PIC **Herbs and spices**

clove DIVIDE /£kləʊv, $kloʊv/ *past simple of* CLEAVE

clov·en /£ˈkləʊ·vən, $ˈkloʊ-/ *adj* [not gradable], *past participle of* CLEAVE • If something is cloven it is divided, usually into two parts: *Cows and sheep have cloven* **hooves** (=feet with two separate toes). [T] ○ *The devil is often represented with horns and cloven* **hooves**.

clo·ver /£ˈkləʊ·vər, $ˈkloʊ·vɚ/ *n* [U] a small plant with three round, green leaves often fed to cows • To **live/be in clover** is to enjoy a life of wealth and comfort. • PIC **Flowers and plants** (KOR)

clown /klaʊn/ *n* [C] an entertainer, often of children, who makes people laugh by performing tricks without speech and often wearing amusing clothes • *I used to like the clowns best at the circus.* • Someone who behaves foolishly, often intentionally, is called a clown. • *"I remain just one thing and one thing only – and that is a clown. It places me on a far higher plane than any politician."* (Charlie Chaplin, 1960) • *"Send in the Clowns"* (Song from the musical *A Little Night Music* written by Stephen Sondheim, 1973)

clown /klaʊn/ *v* [I always + adv/prep] • *Left alone, the class threw books and paint at each other, pulled faces and generally clowned* **around** (= acted stupidly).

cloy·ing /ˈklɔɪ·ɪŋ/ *adj literary* too sweet and therefore unpleasant, or *(fig.)* too good or kind or expressing feelings of love in a way that is not sincere • *This is a wonderful wine – honeyed and rich without being remotely cloying.* • *(fig.) She criticized what she described as the film's cloying sentimentality.*

cloy·ing·ly /ˈklɔɪ·ɪŋ·li/ *adv* • *All we were offered was milky coffee and cloyingly sweet pastries.*

club GROUP /klʌb/ *n* [C] an organization of people with a common purpose or interest who meet regularly and take part in shared activities, or the building in which they meet • *I've just* **joined** *the local golf/squash/tennis club.* • *Visitors must be accompanied by club* **members.** • Club is also *Am for* team: *The Orioles are an exciting club this year.* • *(Br dated slang)* **In the club** means pregnant. • A **club-house** is the building where club members meet often for drinks. • A **club sandwich** is a quick meal consisting of three pieces of bread with cold food between them, for example meat, egg, or cheese. • **Club soda** is *Am for* SODA WATER. • PIC **Club**

club GOLF /klʌb/ *n* [C] a long thin stick used in the game of golf to hit the ball • *Jean bought Derrick a set of a* **golf** *clubs for his birthday.* • PIC **Club**

club WEAPON /klʌb/ *n* [C] a heavy stick used as a weapon

club *obj* /klʌb/ *v* [T] **-bb-** • To club a person or an animal is to beat them, sometimes repeatedly, with a heavy object: *Once caught and tied up, the alligators are then clubbed* **to death.** ○ *A number of protesters were then clubbed to the ground and trampled on.*

club CARD /klʌb/ *n* [C] a playing card showing the black three-leaved sign • LP **Cards** PIC **Club**

club DANCE /klʌb/ *n* [C] a NIGHTCLUB (= place where people go to dance, listen to music, drink and meet other people) • *I went to that new club that's just opened.*

club·bing /ˈklʌb·ɪŋ/ *v* [I] • *Roz and I* **went** *clubbing last weekend.*

club to·geth·er /klʌb/ *v adv* [I] (of a group of people) to share the cost of something between them • *If we club together we'll be able to get her the complete dinner set.*

cluck *(obj)* /klʌk/ *v* (of a chicken) to make a low noise • *The* **hens** *were clucking and scratching around.* [I] • *(fig.) The ladies in the bakery saw my broken arm and clucked sympathetically* (= expressed sympathy in words and/or noises). [I] • *(fig.) "Just you sit down, you poor thing," clucked* (= said sympathetically) *Mrs Andrews.* [+ clause] • *(fig.) My mother saw me light up a cigarette and clucked disapproval* (= expressed disapproval). [T]

clue /kluː/ *n* [C] (a sign or some information which helps you to find) the answer to a problem, question or mystery • *Police are still* **looking for** *clues in their search for the missing girl.* • *It was the perfect murder. Whoever killed him didn't leave a single clue* **as to** *his identity.* • *I'm never going to guess the answer if you don't* **give** *me a clue.* • *(fig.) The clue* **to** (= What is needed to achieve) *longevity is evidently happiness.* • *"Who invented algebra?" "I* **haven't a clue** (= I don't know the answer)." • *"Don't ask your father which key to press – he* **hasn't got a clue** (= he has no knowledge) **about** *computers."*

clue·less /ˈkluː·ləs/ *adj infml* • *Most people are* **completely** *clueless* **about** (= have no knowledge of) *tide directions and weather conditions.*

clue *obj* **in** /kluː/, *Aus* **clue** *obj* **up** *v adv* [T] *Am* to give someone information that is necessary or new • *I was new to the office and I hadn't been clued in* **on** *the no-smoking policy.* • *He'd been out of the country for weeks so I clued him in* **on** *all that's been happening.*

clued up /kluːd/ *adj Br and Aus* having a special and detailed knowledge of something • *Ask Ben the name of that actress – he's clued up* **on/about** *the cinema.*

clump GROUP /klʌmp/ *v, n* (to form or cause to form) a group, esp. of trees or flowers • *She clumped all his books and records* **together** *and left them outside her front door.* [T] • *As it started to rain, the crowd clumped* **together** *in the marquee.* [I] • *The trees grew in clumps.* [C]

clump WALK NOISILY /klʌmp/ *v* [I] to walk noisily with heavy, slow steps • *She clumped* **around** *the room/up the stairs in her boots.*

clump /klʌmp/ *n* [U] • *We could hear the clump* (= loud sound) *of his feet as he walked across the wooden floor.*

clump LUMP /klʌmp/ *n* [C] a solid mass of something such as earth • *After walking through the fields he had big clumps* **of** *soil on his boots.*

clum·sy /ˈklʌm·zi/ *adj* **-ier, -iest** awkward in movement or manner • *The first mobile phones were heavy and clumsy to use but nowadays they are much easier to handle.* • *I tried to excuse myself for missing her party but my attempts were very clumsy* (= not said well). • *I wouldn't wear your boots with your white silk skirt if I were you – it looks a bit clumsy* (= graceless). • A person who is clumsy often has accidents because their actions are not controlled or careful enough: *"That's the third glass you've smashed this week, you clumsy idiot!"*

clung /klʌŋ/ *past simple and past participle of* CLING

clunk /klʌŋk/ *n* [C] a deep low often metallic sound made by two objects hitting each other • *The door shut with a heavy satisfying clunk.* • *Her old car made a variety of clunks and rattles when it was driven above a certain speed.* • *"Clunk click, every trip"* (advertisement encouraging people to wear safety belts in cars, 1971 -)

clus·ter /£ˈklʌs·tər, $-t̬ɚ/ *n* [C] a close group of usually similar things, often surrounding something • *They found a cluster* **of** *mushrooms at the bottom of the field.* • *There was a cluster* **of** *fans around the actor, tearing at his clothes.* • *Astronomers are particularly interested in the cluster* **of** *galaxies you can see in this photograph.* • A **cluster bomb** is an explosive device which throws out smaller bombs when it explodes.

clus·ter /£ˈklʌs·tər, $-t̬ɚ/ *v* [I] • *People clustered* **around** *the dead body to get a better look.* • *They clustered* **together** *for warmth.*

clutch *(obj)* HOLD /klʌtʃ/ *v* to take or try to take hold of (something) tightly often in a state of fear or anxiety • *Terrified by the noise, the small child clutched* **(onto)** *her mother's hand.* [T; I + onto] • *Feeling herself fall, she clutched* **at** *a tree branch.* [I] • *With his week's wages clutched tightly* *in his hand, he hurried to the bank.* [T] • A **clutch bag** is a small flat bag without a handle, which is carried by women, esp. on formal occasions. • PIC› **Bags**

clutch·es /'klʌtʃ·ɪz/ *pl n humorous* • If you are **in/fall into the clutches of** something or someone you are in their power: *He's fallen into the clutches of that woman.*

clutch MACHINE PART /klʌtʃ/ *n* [C usually sing] a device which allows turning movement to be sent from one part of a machine to another • *The clutch in my car is* **slipping**. • *Most cars have a clutch to transmit rotary motion from the engine to the gearbox.* • When talking about operating many types of vehicle **the clutch** means the control, such as a bar or handle, that is used to operate the engine's clutch: **Push** *the clutch* **in**, *put the car into gear, rev the engine and then gently* **let** *the clutch* **out**. • LP› **Driving**

clutch GROUP /klʌtʃ/ *n* [C] a small group of eggs laid by a bird, esp. in a nest • *In the hollow we could see a clutch* **of** *beautiful speckled eggs.* • *(fig.) Every year a fresh clutch* (= small group) **of** *students move into the house next door.*

clut·ter /£'klʌt·əʳ, $'klʌt̬·ɚ/ *n* [U] (objects in) a state of untidiness • *Excuse the clutter in the kitchen – I haven't had a chance to clear up yet.* • *He always leaves his office* **in a** *clutter* (= untidy). • *My desk is full of clutter.*

clut·ter *obj* /£'klʌt·əʳ, $'klʌt̬·ɚ/ *v* [T] • *Don't clutter* **(up)** *the living room, kids – I've only just tidied it up!* • *(fig.) She says she deliberately tries not to clutter* **(up)** *her mind* (= fill it with useless information).

clut·tered /£'klʌt·əd, $'klʌt̬·ɚd/ *adj* • *a cluttered desk* • *(fig.) a cluttered mind* • *You can't move in their house – it's cluttered* **with** *kid's toys.*

cm *n* [C] *pl* **cm** *abbreviation for* CENTIMETRE • *The ribbon is 2 cm wide.* • *I need a piece of clear glass 22 cm by 35 cm.* • LP› **Units**

c'mon *infml* /£kə'mɒn, $-mɑːn/ *short form of* come on • *Oh c'mon, you don't really mean that!* • *"Ah c'mon, please take me with you." "C'mon* **then** (= hurry up) *if you're coming."*

CND /ˌsiː·en'diː/ *n* [U] *abbreviation for* Campaign for Nuclear Disarmament (= a British organization which opposes the development and use of nuclear weapons) • *a member of CND* • *Are you going on the CND march this weekend?*

CO OFFICER /£ˌsiː'əʊ, $-'oʊ/ *n* [C] *abbreviation for* Commanding Officer (= person in charge of a military unit)

Co BUSINESS /£kəʊ, $koʊ/ *n* [U] *abbreviation for* COMPANY BUSINESS • *Peters, Stynes & Co* • *Williams Co Ltd* • *(infml)* The phrase **and co** means with other people: *K Brannagh and co have achieved great success in a very short time.* • LP› **Letters**

co– TOGETHER, **con–**, *before l* **col–**, *before b, m or p* **com–**, *before r-* **cor–** /£kəʊ-, $koʊ-, kən-, kəl-, kəm-, kə-/ *combining form* together; with • *co-ownership* • *a co-writer/co-author* • *a political conspiracy* • *a business consortium* • *a combination* • *a close community* • *travelling companions* • *work colleagues* • *to correspond*

c/o CARE OF *abbreviation for* care of (= used in addresses when the person you are writing to is staying at someone else's home) • *Sylvia Mendez c/o Ann Smith* (= Mendez at Smith's house)

Co AREA *n Br and Am abbreviation for* COUNTY, when used in names • *Co Durham* • *Co Wexford*

coach VEHICLE /£kəʊtʃ, $koʊtʃ/, *Am and Aus usually* **bus** *n* [C] a long road vehicle on which people travel • *We're going to the airport* **by** *coach.* • A coach is also an old-fashioned carriage pulled by horses, now used mainly in official or royal ceremonies. • *(dated)* A coach is also a carriage in a train. • *(Br)* A **coach station** is a place where coaches arrive and leave from.

coach *(obj)* TEACH /£kəʊtʃ, $koʊtʃ/ *v* to give special classes in sports or a school subject, esp. privately, to one person or a small group • *Do you know anyone who could coach me in chemistry?* [T] • *She coaches students* **in** *French, usually for exams.* [T] • *By day he's a civil servant but by night he coaches boxing.* [I] • LP› **Sports**

coach /£kəʊtʃ, $koʊtʃ/ *n* [C] • *a tennis coach* • *After six hours of school classes Ben has to do another hour with his geography coach.*

coach·ing /£'kəʊ·tʃɪŋ, $'koʊ-/ *n* [U] • *You're very behind in your English – why don't you get some extra coaching?*

coach·work /£'kəʊtʃ·wɜːk, $'koʊtʃ·wɜːrk/ *n* [U] *Br* the body of a car, esp. its outside surface where covered with paint

co·ag·u·late *(obj)* /£kəʊ'æg·jʊ·leɪt, $koʊ-/ *v* (to cause) to change from liquid to a more solid state • *The sauce coagulated as it cooled down.* [I] • *She quickly wiped the blood away before the air had a chance to coagulate it.* [T]

coal /£kəʊl, $koʊl/ *n* a hard black substance, dug from the earth in lumps which can be burnt to produce heat or power • *A lot of coal used to be* **mined** *in this part of the country.* [U] • *Useful chemicals can be extracted from coal.* [U] • *In her rage she threw a burning hot coal* (= single piece of coal) *at him.* [C] • To **haul/drag** someone **over the coals** is to speak to them severely and often angrily about something they they have done: *He was hauled over the coals* **for** *coming in late for work three times in a week.* • To **carry/take coals to Newcastle** is to supply goods to a place or a person that already has a lot of those particular goods: *Exporting pine to Scandanavia seems a bit like carrying coals to Newcastle.* • **Coal black** means pure black: *She stared into his coal black eyes.* • A **coal bunker** is a large container, esp. outside a house, for storing coal. • The **coal face** is the surface from which coal is cut: *(Br and Aus fig.)* **At the** *coal face* (= In real working conditions) *with thirty-five kids in a class, you sometimes feel under a lot of pressure.* • A **coal field** is an area in which there is a lot of coal. • If something is **coal-fired**, it is fuelled by coal: *a coal-fired boiler* ○ *coal-fired central-heating* • A **coal mine** is the deep hole or system of holes under the ground from which coal is removed. • A **coal miner** is a person who works in a coal mine removing coal from the ground. • A **coal scuttle** is a small container in which coal is kept inside a house. • **Coal tar** is the sticky black substance made from coal which is used to make particular chemical products. • PIC› **Fires and space heaters** Ⓢ

co·a·lesce /£kəʊ·ə'les, $koʊ-/ *v* [I] *fml* (of two or more things) to come or grow together to form one thing or system

co·a·les·cence /£kəʊ·ə'les·ᵊnts, $koʊ-/ *n* [U] *fml* • Coalescence is the process of coalescing.

co·a·li·tion /£kəʊ·ə'lɪʃ·ᵊn, $koʊ-/ *n* the union of different political parties or groups for a particular purpose usually for a limited time • *Government by coalition has its own peculiar set of problems.* [U] • *A government coalition was formed during the war.* [C] • *By forming a coalition, the rebels and the opposition parties defeated the government.* [C]

coarse ROUGH /£kɔːs, $kɔːrs/ *adj* **-r, -st** rough and not smooth or soft • *The sand was so coarse that it was quite painful to walk on.* • *Linen is a coarse-grained fabric.*

coars·en *(obj)* /£'kɔː·sᵊn, $'kɔːr-/ *v* • *A life of working outside in harsh weather coarsened his skin.* [T] • *She sang like an angel until her voice coarsened with age.* [I]

coarse·ness /£'kɔː·snəs, $'kɔːr-/ *n* [U] • *She found that the coarseness of the cloth irritated her skin.*

coarse RUDE /£kɔːs, $kɔːrs/ *adj* **-r, -st** rude and offensive • *a coarse joke* • *He was a coarse man whose manner made him unpopular with some people.*

coarse·ly /£'kɔː·sli, $'kɔːr-/ *adv*

coarse·ness /£kɔː·snəs, $'kɔːr-/ *n* [U] • *No, it's not his coarseness, it's his dishonesty I hate.*

coast LAND /£kəʊst, $koʊst/ *n* [C] the land next to or close to the sea • *Rimini is a thriving holiday resort* **on** *the east coast of Italy.* [C] • *When the tanker sank, fifty thousand gallons of oil went into the sea three miles* **off** *the coast* (= in the sea three miles from land). [U] • *We spent a week* **by/on** *the coast* (= by the sea) *before going inland.* [U] • If you say **the coast is clear**, you mean that there is no (longer) danger because there is no one watching or listening: *He's gone home so the coast is clear, now tell me what he said.* • *We travelled across America* **coast to coast** (= from one side to the other). • **Coast to coast** also means in every part of a country: *The visiting politician received coast-to-coast media attention.*

coast·al /£'kəʊ·stᵊl, $'koʊ-/ *adj* [not gradable] • *a coastal town*

coast MOVE /£kəʊst, $koʊst/ *v* [I] to advance without effort • *At the top of the hill I switched off the engine and then we just coasted down the other side.* • *While I struggled and laboured, my sister coasted through school with top grades in all subjects.*

coast·er BOAT /£'kəʊ·stəʳ, $'koʊ·stɚ/ *n* [C] a ship which sails between ports along a coast

coast·er PROTECTOR /£'kəʊ·stəʳ, $'koʊ·stɚ/ *n* [C] a small piece of material put under a glass or cup to protect a surface such as that of table from heat or liquid

coast·guard /£'kəʊst·gɑːd, $'koʊst·gɑːrd/ *n* [C] an official who is employed to watch the sea near to a coast for ships that are in danger or involved with illegal activities •

The **coastguard** is the official organization which coastguards belong to.

coast·line /£'kəʊst-laɪn, $'koʊst-/ *n* [U] the particular shape of the coast, esp. as seen from above, from the sea, or on a map

coat CLOTHING /£kəʊt, $koʊt/ *n* [C] an outer piece of clothing with sleeves which is worn over other clothes, usually for warmth • *Get/put your coat on if you're coming outside.* • *Do your coat up, Joe, or you'll freeze.* • Coat is often used as a combining form: *an overcoat* • *a raincoat* • *a fur/leather/wool coat* • A **coat-hanger** is a HANGER. • *Hang your jacket on the* **coat-hook** *(Br also* **coat peg***) on the back of the door.* • **Coat-tails** are the long divided pieces of cloth that hang down from the back of an old-fashioned, formal type of man's jacket. See also **tail coat** at TAIL ANIMAL. • *"He made him [Joseph] a coat of many colours"* (Bible, Exodus 37.3) • PIC **Peg**

coat ANIMAL /£kəʊt, $koʊt/ *n* [C] the hair, wool or fur covering an animal • *I was just admiring your dog's glossy coat.* • *My dog is quite old now so his coat's a bit grey.*

-coat·ed /£-kəʊ·tɪd, $-koʊ·t̬ɪd/ *combining form* • *a smooth-coated dog*

coat *obj* COVER /£kəʊt, $koʊt/ *v* [T] to cover (something) with a layer of a substance • *When the biscuits are cool you simply coat them* **in/with** *chocolate.* • *She served us pieces of cheese which had been coated* **in/with** *breadcrumbs and then fried.* • PIC **Food preparation**

coat /£kəʊt, $koʊt/, **coat·ing** /£'kəʊ·tɪŋ, $'koʊ·t̬ɪŋ/ *n* [C] • **Give** *the walls a quick coat* **of paint** *and they'll look all right.* • *He wiped a thin coat* **of** *dust off the plate with his sleeve.* • *They're described on the packet as 'orange-flavoured biscuits with a thick coating of chocolate'.*

coat·ed /£'kəʊ·tɪd, $'koʊ·t̬ɪd/ *adj* • *Your trousers are coated* **in** *mud!* • *Her face was coated* **in** *make-up so that I could scarcely recognise her.* • If your **tongue** is coated, it is covered with a layer of greyish-white substance, often because you are ill.

-coat·ed /£-ˌkəʊ·tɪd, $-ˌkoʊ·t̬ɪd/ *adj* • *plastic-coated wire* • *Have you got any more of those* **sugar***-coated almonds?*

coat of arms *n pl* **coats of arms** a special SHIELD or shield-shaped pattern which is the sign of a family, university or city

coax *obj* /£kəʊks, $koʊks/ *v* [T] to persuade (someone) gently, by being kind and patient or appearing to be so • *I've tried to coax him but he says he's not coming.* • *A mother was coaxing a reluctant child into* (= persuade him/her to go into) *the water.* • *Perhaps you could coax your father* **into** *taking you to the station.* • *Over tea he managed to coax £10* **out of** *his grandmother.* • *He has some information that I want so I'm going to try to coax it* **out of** *him over a drink.* • *This machine is like a sulky child – you have to coax it* **to** *work.* [+ obj + *to* infinitive]

coax·ing /£'kəʊk·sɪŋ, $'koʊk-/ *n* [U] • *A bit of gentle coaxing is all that's required and he'll come, I'm sure.* • *With a little coaxing* (= after a few attempts) *the engine started.* • *She used that coaxing voice on me and I found myself saying yes.*

coax·ing·ly /£'kəʊk·sɪŋ·li, $'koʊk-/ *adv*

co·balt /£'kəʊ·bɒlt, $'koʊ·bɑːlt/ *n* [U] a hard silvery white metal used in metal mixtures and for colouring materials blue • Cobalt **blue** is a dark blue colour.

cob·ber /£'kɒb·əʳ, $'kɑː·bɚ/ *n* [C] *Aus dated infml* a friend

cob·ble *obj* **to·geth·er**, **cob·ble to·geth·er** *obj* /£'kɒb·l̩, $'kɑː·bl̩/ *v adv* [M] to put something together in a hurry, often without good results • *I hope this meal is edible – I just cobbled it together.* • *I had one afternoon to cobble together four essays.*

cob·bled /£'kɒb·l̩d, $'kɑː·bl̩d/ *adj* (of an old-fashioned road surface) made of COBBLESTONES (= naturally rounded stones) • *We walked along the cobbled* **streets** *in the town centre.* • *"Narrow streets of cobbled stone"* (Paul Simon in the song *The Sound of Silence*, 1964)

cob·bler /£'kɒb·ləʳ, $'kɑː·blɚ/ *n old use* a person who repairs shoes

cob·blers /£'kɒb·ləz, $'kɑː·blɚz/ *pl n Br and Aus slang* nonsense or lies • *"So that story he told me about nobody getting a pay-rise?" "Oh, it was* **a load of old** *cobblers!"*

cob(nut) /£kɒb, $kɑːb/ *n* [C] a HAZELNUT • PIC **Nuts**

COBOL, **Cobol** /£'kəʊ·bɒl, $'koʊ·bɑːl/ *n* [U] a computer language designed for business managers

co·bra /£'kəʊ·brə, $'koʊ-/ *n* [C] a poisonous snake from Africa or S Asia which can make itself look bigger and more threatening by spreading the skin at the back of its head • PIC **Reptiles and amphibians**

cob·web /£'kɒb·web, $'kɑːb-/, **spi·der's web**, *Am and Aus also* **spi·der·web** *n* a net-like structure of sticky silk threads made by a SPIDER for catching insects

Co·ca Co·la /£ˌkəʊ·kə'kəʊ·lə, $ˌkoʊ·kə'koʊ·lə/, *trademark* **Coke**, **co·la** *n trademark* a fizzy sweet brown drink which does not contain alcohol • *I'd like three Coca Colas and a lemonade.* [C] • *I've drunk a whole litre bottle of Coca Cola.* [U]

co·caine /£kəʊ'keɪn, $koʊ-/, *infml* **coke** *n* [U] a drug used in medicine to prevent pain and taken illegally for pleasure, often as a powder breathed through the nose

coc·cyx /£'kɒk·sɪks, $'kɑːk-/ *n* [C] *pl* **coccyxes** or **coccyges** /£kɒk'saɪ·dʒiːz, $kɑːk-/ a small triangular bone at the base of the SPINE (= line of bones down the middle of the back) of humans and some APES (= types of monkey)

coch·i·neal /£ˌkɒtʃ·ɪ'niːl, $'kɑː·tʃɪ-/ *n* [U] a bright red substance used as a food colouring, made from the dried body of a type of S American insect

coch·le·a /£'kɒk·li·ə, $'kɑːk-/ *n* [C] *pl* **cochleae** /£'kɒk·li·aɪ, $'kɑːk-/ or **cochleas** a twisted tube inside the inner ear which is the main organ of hearing

cock BIRD /£kɒk, $kɑːk/, *Am and Aus also* **roost·er** *n* [C] an adult male chicken • *At 5 a.m. the cock started to* **crow**. • Cock, used with the name of a bird, refers to the fully-grown adult male of that type: *a cock robin* ○ *a cock sparrow* ○ *a cock pheasant* • *(disapproving infml)* A **cock-and-bull story** is a story which is obviously not true, especially one given as an excuse: *He* **gave me** *some cock-and-bull story about having to be at his cousin's engagement party.* • *(dated disapproving)* A **cock-of-the-walk** is a man who is too confident and thinks himself better than everyone else. • **Cock-a-doodle-doo** is the long call of the cock as copied by children. • **Cock-a-leekie** is a soup, originally from Scotland, made with boiled chicken and vegetables. • A **cock fight** is an activity, illegal in Britain, in which people watch as two chickens with sharp pieces of metal tied to their feet attack each other. • Ⓙ Ⓢ Ⓣ

cock PENIS /£kɒk, $kɑːk/ *n* [C] *taboo slang* a penis • **Cock-teaser** is another word for **prick-teaser**. See at PRICK MAN. • Ⓙ Ⓢ Ⓣ

cock NONSENSE /£kɒk, $kɑːk/ *n* [U] *Br taboo* something said or written which is ridiculous or not true; nonsense • *That's a load of cock.* • *I've never heard so much cock in my life* • Ⓙ Ⓢ Ⓣ

cock *obj* TURN /£kɒk, $kɑːk/ *v* [T] to turn a (part of the body) in a particular direction • *He cocked his* **head** *on one side with a slight frown.* • *The dog cocked its* **leg** *against a tree and urinated.* • *She cocked an* **ear** *towards the door and listened.* • Ⓙ Ⓢ Ⓣ

cocked /£kɒkt, $kɑːkt/ *adj* • *Her hat was cocked* **at a** *jaunty* **angle**.

cock *obj* PREPARE GUN /£kɒk, $kɑːk/ *v* [T] to prepare a gun so that it is ready for firing • *I heard the sound of a rifle being cocked.* • Ⓙ Ⓢ Ⓣ

cock FORM OF ADDRESS /£kɒk, $kɑːk/ *n* [as form of address] *Br dated infml* a friendly and informal form of address, esp. between men • *Wotcher, cock!* • Ⓙ Ⓢ Ⓣ

cock *obj* SHOW LACK OF RESPECT /£kɒk, $kɑːk/ *v* [T] **cock a snook at** show a lack of respect for (someone or something), often in one single action • *He could seldom resist an opportunity to cock a snook at traditional English life.* • Ⓙ Ⓢ Ⓣ

cock PLEASED /£kɒk, $kɑːk/ *n* [U] *Br dated infml* **cock-a-hoop** extremely pleased • *"I bet Julia was pleased about winning that prize." "Oh, she was cock-a-hoop!"* • Ⓙ Ⓢ Ⓣ

cock *obj* **up**, **cock up** *obj v adv* [M] *Br slang* to do something badly or spoil something esp. an arrangement • *David cocked up the arrangements and we ended up being half an hour late for the reception.* • *"Have you filled in that form yet?" "No, I think I've gone and cocked it up."*

cock-up /£'kɒk·ʌp, $'kɑːk-/ *n* [C] • *Gerry's* **made** *a right cock-up* **with/of** *those figures!* • *So, Jamie missed the train because Clive was late?* **What a** *cock-up!*

cock·ade /£kɒk'eɪd, $kɑː'keɪd/ *n* [C] a decorative knot of cloth worn in the hat, often for ceremonial purposes, to show rank

cock·a·too /£ˌkɒk·ə'tuː, $'kɑː·kə·tuː/ *n* [C] *pl* **cockatoos** or **cockatoo** an Australian bird with a decorative CREST (= growth of feathers) on its head and a powerful beak • PIC **Birds**

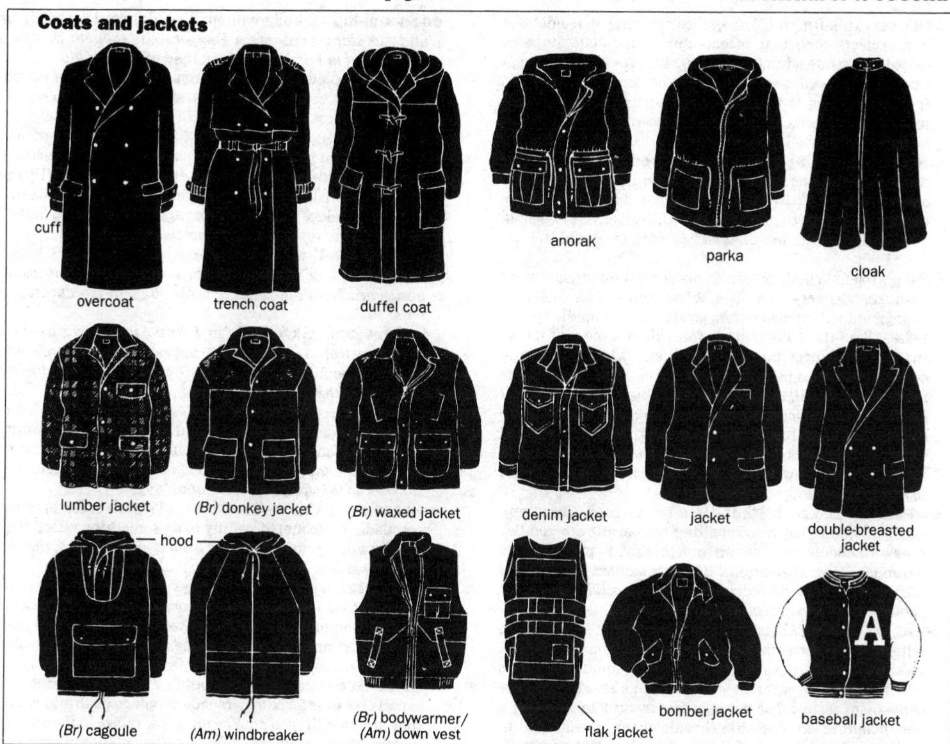

cock·chaf·er /£'kɒkˌtʃeɪ·fəʳ, $'kɑːkˌtʃeɪ·fɚ/ *n* [C] a type of BEETLE (=an insect with hard wing coverings) found in Europe which is active at night and feeds on leaves

cock·er·el /£'kɒk·ᵊr·ᵊl, £-rəl, $'kɑː·kɚ-/ *n* [C] a young COCK (=male chicken)

cock·er span·iel /£'kɒk·əʳ, $'kɑː·kɚ/ *n* [C] a breed of dog with long ears, short legs and hair that is white and black or brown

cock·eyed SLOPING /£ˌkɒk'aɪd, $ˌkɑːk-/ *adj infml* sloping to one side; not straight • *That picture you put up in the dining-room, Guy, I think it's a bit cockeyed.*

cock·eyed RIDICULOUS /£ˌkɒk'aɪd, $ˌkɑːk-/ *adj* (esp. of a plan or idea) unlikely to be successful; ridiculous • *The government has dreamed up some cockeyed scheme for getting unemployed youngsters back into work.*

cock·eyed DRUNK /£ˌkɒk'aɪd, $ˌkɑːk-/ *adj esp. Am infml dated* having had too much alcohol; drunk

cock·le /£'kɒk·l̩, $'kɑː·kl̩/ *n* [C] a small rounded edible sea creature with a shell found commonly in Europe

Cock·ney /£'kɒk·ni, $'kɑːk-/ *n* (the way of speaking of) a person from East London, especially the poorer part • *My father is a Cockney.* [C] • *You won't hear much real Cockney spoken unless you go to the East End of London.* [U]

cock·ney /£'kɒk·ni, $'kɑːk-/ *adj* [not gradable] • *a Cockney accent* • *Cockney humour* • **Cockney rhyming slang** refers to slang which is used instead of a word or phrase and which rhymes with it: *In Cockney rhyming slang, you say 'apples and pears' to mean 'stairs'.*

cock·pit ENCLOSED SPACE /£'kɒk·pɪt, $'kɑːk-/ *n* [C] the small enclosed space where the PILOT sits in an aircraft, or where the driver sits in a racing car • *He climbed into the cockpit of the fighter.* • PIC› **Aircraft**

cock·pit AREA /£'kɒk·pɪt, $'kɑːk-/ *n* [C usually sing] an area in which there is a lot of fighting • *The scene of many a bloody battle, this region was once called the cockpit of Europe.*

cock·roach /£'kɒk·rəʊtʃ, $'kɑːk·roʊtʃ/ *n* [C] a flat brown or black insect sometimes found in the home • *Pregnant and homeless, she was forced to live in a cockroach-infested tower block.* • PIC› **Insects**

cocks·comb /£'kɒks·kəʊm, $'kɑːks·koʊm/, **comb** *n* [C] the red fleshy growth on the head of a COCK (=male chicken)

cock·sure /£ˌkɒk'ʃɔːʳ, $ˌkɑːk'ʃɜːr/ *adj infml disapproving* too confident in a way that is slightly unpleasant or rude • *He's so cocksure I don't think he ever doubts himself for one moment.*

cock·tail DRINK /£'kɒk·teɪl, $'kɑːk-/ *n* [C] a drink, esp. an alcoholic one, made by mixing two or more drinks together • *We were all in the bar* **sipping** *cocktails.* • *I need something to wear to this cocktail* **party** *on Saturday.* • *I left Patrick and Delia in the departure lounge drinking champagne cocktails.* • A **cocktail dress** is a dress worn on a special social occasion such as a party or dance, esp. in the evening. • A **cocktail lounge** is a large room, often inside a hotel, where you can meet people and be served alcoholic drinks. • A **cocktail stick** is a small, pointed, wooden or plastic stick on which small pieces of food such as cheese and fruit or cooked meat are put for people to eat at parties.

cock·tail MIXTURE /£'kɒk·teɪl, $'kɑːk-/ *n* [C] a mixture of different things, often an unexpected, dangerous or exciting one • *Cars produce a* **lethal** *cocktail of gasses.* • *Pop videos offer a* **heady** *cocktail of sex, love, low morals and larger-than-life characters.* • *The twenty-three year old guitarist died from a cocktail of drink and drugs, an inquest heard yesterday.*

cock·tail DISH /£'kɒk·teɪl, $'kɑːk-/ *n* [C] a small dish, eaten at the start of a meal • *a fruit/prawn/shrimp/seafood cocktail*

cock·y /£'kɒk·i, $'kɑː·ki/ *adj* **-ier, -iest** *infml* (esp. of a young person) confident in a way that is unpleasant and sometimes rude • *He's a bit cocky for my liking.*

co·coa /£'kəʊ·kəʊ, $'koʊ·koʊ/ *n* [U] a dark brown powder made from the crushed beans of the tropical CACAO tree, used to make chocolate and give the taste of chocolate to food and drink • Cocoa is also the name of the sweet milky chocolate drink that is made with this powder: *Let's have a nice hot mug of cocoa.* • **Cocoa butter** is a fatty substance from the cocoa bean used in some foods and also various creams for improving the skin and hair.

co·co·nut /£'kəʊ·kə·nʌt, $'koʊ-/ *n* a large nut-like fruit with a hard brown shell, hard white edible flesh and a white milky liquid inside, or the white flesh of this fruit, often used in cooking • *I bought a coconut in the market.* [C] • *He was eating a slice of coconut.* [U] • *Ann, is there coconut in this sponge?* [U] • *I usually put a little* **grated** *coconut in the icing.* [U] • **Coconut butter** is a solid oil taken from the coconut and used in soap, medical creams, etc. • *(Br)* A **coconut shy** is a game at a FAIR where you throw balls at a row of coconuts and try to knock them to the ground, one after the other. • PIC› **Nut**

co·coon /kə'kuːn/ *n* [C] the silky covering that encloses and protects particular insects during the PUPA stage as they develop into adult form • [PIC] **Insects**

co·coon *obj* /kə'kuːn/ *v* [T] • To be cocooned **against/from** something is to be protected against/from pain or unpleasantness: *As a student you're cocooned against the real world.*

cod [FISH] /£kɒd, $kɑːd/ *n pl* **cod** or **cods** a large sea fish which can be eaten • *Cod are found in the North Atlantic and the North Sea.* [C] • *I'd like cod and chips, please.* [U] • **Cod-liver oil** is a thick yellow oil which is given to people as a medicine: *Cod-liver oil is rich in vitamins A and D.* • [PIC] **Fish**

COD [PAYMENT] /£ˌsiː·əʊ'diː, $-oʊ'-/ *n* [U] *abbreviation for* cash on delivery, or *(Am also)* collect on delivery (= payment will be made when goods are delivered)

co·da /£'kəʊ·də, $'koʊ-/ *n* [C] *specialized* a piece of music that ends a longer piece of music and which is usually separate from the basic structure • *The coda is often more technically difficult than the rest of the piece.* • *Her real skill on the piano was evident in the difficult coda.* • *(fig.) The exhibition contains a number of paintings in a coda to* (= as a separate and additional part of) *the main show, works that have been attributed to Rembrandt at some time but were not in fact done by him.*

cod·dle *obj* /£'kɒd·l̩, $'kɑː·dl̩/ *v* [T] to cook (food, esp. eggs) in water just below boiling temperature • *coddled eggs* • To coddle someone or something is to protect them too much: *He was feeling ill and just wanted to be looked after and coddled.* ○ *The steel industry is coddled by trade protection and massive public subsidies.*

code [LANGUAGE] /£kəʊd, $koʊd/ *n* [C] a system of words, letters or signs which is used to represent a message in secret form, or a system of numbers, letters or signals which is used to represent something in a shorter or more convenient form • *The message was written* **in code.** [U] • *She managed to* **decipher/break/crack** (= succeed in understanding) *the code.* [C] • *A person's postal address is identified by their (Br and Aus)* **post**/*(Am)* **zip** *code.* [C] • *Each entry in this dictionary has a* **grammar** *code.* [C] • *What is the (Br)***dialling**/*(Am and Aus)* **area** *code for Birmingham?* • A **code name** is a special word or sign which is used instead of the real name of someone or something to keep the real name secret: *Her code name is 'Running bear'.* ○ *This mission is* **code-named** *'Ice-breaker'.*

code *obj* /£kəʊd, $koʊd/ *v* [T] • To code a message is to represent it in the form of words or symbols so that it can only be understood by the person who is meant to receive it.

code [LAW] /£kəʊd, $koʊd/ *n* [C] a set of rules which are accepted as general principles, or a set of written rules which state how people in a particular organization or country should behave • *From next September, clinics will be subject to a new code* **of conduct** *and stronger controls by local authorities.* • A code **of behaviour/ethics**/*(old use)* **honour** is a set of moral principles accepted and used by society or a particular group of people. • A **code of practice** is a set of standards agreed on by a group of people who do a particular job.

co·deine /£'kəʊ·diːn, $'koʊ-/ *n* [U] a drug made from OPIUM which is used in medicine to kill pain and help people to sleep

co·dex /£'kəʊ·deks, $'koʊ-/ *n* [C] *pl* **codices** /£'kəʊ·dɪ·siːz, $'koʊ-/ an ancient book which was written by hand • *Codices were handwritten on vellum or parchment.*

codg·er /£'kɒdʒ·əʳ, $'kɑː·dʒɚ/ *n* [C] *infml disapproving or humorous* a man, esp. an old one who behaves strangely • *There were a couple of* **old** *codgers sitting on the park bench, grumbling about the children who were playing nearby.*

cod·i·cil /£'kəʊ·dɪ·sɪl, $'kɑː-/ *n* [C] *law* an instruction which is added to a WILL (= an official paper stating what is to be done with a person's property and money when they die) • *She added a codicil to her will to stop her ex-husband from getting all her money.*

cod·i·fy *obj* /£'kəʊ·dɪ·faɪ, $'kɑː-/ *v* [T] to arrange (something such as laws or rules) into a system • *Most of the laws of war are now codified in international agreements, such as the Geneva Convention of 1949.* • *Eisenstein was the first to draw up and codify a formal aesthetics for the cinema.*

cod·piece /£'kɒd·piːs, $'kɑːd-/ *n* [C] a piece of decorative material in the form of a small bag, which was worn by men in the 15th and 16th centuries to cover their sexual organs

cods·wal·lop /£'kɒdzˌwɒl·əp, $'kɑːdzˌwɑː·ləp/ *n* [U] *Br and Aus slang* nonsense • *Everyone else thought that film was great, but I thought it was* **a load of** *codswallop.*

co–ed /£ˌkəʊ'ed, $ˌkoʊ-/ *adj* [not gradable] *infml for* **co-educational**, see at CO-EDUCATION • *Two years after I started at a single-sex school, it went co-ed.*

co–ed /£ˌkəʊ'ed, $ˌkoʊ-/ *n* [C] *Am infml* • A co-ed is a female student in a college with male and female students.

co–ed·u·ca·tion /£ˌkəʊ·ed·jʊ'keɪ·ʃᵊn, $ˌkoʊ-/ *n* [U] the teaching of male and female students together in the same school or college rather than separately • *The city council has a policy of supporting co-education.*

co–ed·u·ca·tion·al /£ˌkəʊ·ed·jʊ'keɪ·ʃᵊn·ᵊl, $ˌkoʊ-/, *infml* **co–ed** *adj* [not gradable] • *Girls tend to do better academically in single-sex schools than in co-educational ones.*

co·ef·fi·cient /£ˌkəʊ·ɪ'fɪʃ·ᵊnt, $ˌkoʊ-/ *n* [C] *specialized* (in mathematics) a value that appears in front of and multiplies another value • *In $2x + 4y = 7$, 2 is the coefficient of x and 4 is the coefficient of y.*

co·e·qual /£ˌkəʊ'iː·kwᵊl, $ˌkoʊ-/ *n* [C], *adj* [not gradable] *fml or dated* (a person or thing that is) equal in rank, ability or power to another person or thing • *She believed that no person, no matter how great, should regard themselves as superior to the state, or even coequal.*

co·erce *obj* /£kəʊ'ɜːs, $koʊ'ɜːrs/ *v* [T often passive] *fml* to persuade (someone) forcefully to do something which they are unwilling to do • *The courts heard that the six defendants had been coerced* **into** *making a confession.*

co·er·cion /£kəʊ'ɜː·ʃᵊn, $koʊ'ɜːr-/ *n* [U] *fml* • *He claimed the police had used coercion, threats and promises to illegally obtain the statement.* • *She said that she had signed the contract* **under** *coercion* (= she had been forced to sign it).

co·er·cive /£kəʊ'ɜː·sɪv, $koʊ'ɜːr-/ *adj* • Something that is coercive uses force to persuade people to do things which they are unwilling to do: *The president relied on the coercive powers of the military and the police to enforce law and order.*

co·e·val /£kəʊ'iː·vᵊl, $koʊ-/ *n* [C], *adj* [not gradable] *fml or literary* (a person or thing) of the same age or existing at the same time as another person or thing • *The Spanish students had clearly been inspired by the protests of their French coevals, which had forced the government to back down on its education reforms.* • *Their research shows that the abundant reef growth on Gotland was coeval* **with** *that in Estonia.*

co·e·xist /£ˌkəʊ·ɪg'zɪst, $ˌkoʊ-/ *v* [I] to live or exist together at the same time or in the same place • *It is a city in which areas of poverty uneasily coexist with areas of great wealth.* • *He does not believe that modern medicine can co-exist with faith-healing.*

co·e·xist·ence /£ˌkəʊ·ɪg'zɪs·tᵊnts, $ˌkoʊ-/ *n* [U] • *After the war, the two countries enjoyed a period of* **peaceful** *coexistence.*

C of E /ˌsiː·əv'iː/ *adj, n abbreviation for* **Church of England**, see at CHURCH [ORGANIZATION] • *a C of E service* • *Are you C of E or Catholic?* • *The C of E has/have appointed local youth workers in several areas.* [U + sing/pl v]

cof·fee /£'kɒf·i, $'kɑː·fi/ *n* a dark brown powder with a strong flavour and smell that is made by crushing the beans of a tropical bush, or a hot drink made from this powder • *Would you get some coffee when you go shopping?* [U] • *Do you prefer caffeinated or decaffeinated coffee?* [U] • *Would you rather have fresh coffee or instant?* [U] • *Would you like a* **cup of** *coffee?* [U] • *Can I get you a coffee* (= cup of coffee)*?* [C] • *If I drink too much coffee, I can't sleep.* [U] • *Do you* **take** (= drink) *your coffee white* (= with milk)*?* [U] • *I'd like a* **black** *coffee* (= a cup of coffee without milk), *please.* [C] • Coffee or **coffee-coloured** is a pale brown colour: *We've just bought a new coffee-coloured rug for the living room.* • **Coffee beans** are the seeds of of a tropical bush which are heated until they are brown and then crushed to make coffee. • A **coffee break** is a short rest from work in the morning or afternoon: *We usually have a coffee break at 11 o'clock.* • *(Br and Aus)* **Coffee cake** is a type of cake made with eggs, sugar, flour and butter that is flavoured with coffee, or *(Am and Aus also)* a type of sweet bread which is made with nuts or fruit. • A **coffee-grinder** (also **coffee mill**) is a machine which crushes coffee beans to make coffee powder. • A **coffee house** is a place found mainly in central and northern Europe where people meet for drinks, cakes and small meals. • *(Am)* A **coffee klatch** is an occasion when people meet socially to talk and drink coffee. • *(Br)* A **coffee-morning** is an organized social event in someone's home which is intended to collect money for organizations that provide help for people who are poor, ill or who have other problems. • A **coffee pot** is a tall thin container, with a handle and SPOUT (= a tube-shaped opening), in which you make coffee and from which coffee is served. • A **coffee shop/bar** is a small informal restaurant where drinks and small meals are served: *Most coffee shops do not serve alcoholic drinks.* • A **coffee table** is a small, low table on which coffee is served or books and magazines are arranged. • A **coffee-table book** is a large expensive book with a lot of pictures, which is meant to be looked at rather than read. • PIC〉 **Bar, Mill, Room, Table**

cof·fer /£ˈkɒf·əʳ, $ˈkɑː·fɚ/ *n* [C] a large strong box in which money or valuable objects are kept • **The coffers** of an organization is the money in its bank accounts that it has available to spend: *There's nothing left in the government's coffers.* ○ *The investigation revealed that town officials regularly dipped into the town's coffers* (= used the town's money) *to finance their own holidays.*

cof·fer·dam /£ˈkɒf·ə·dæm, $ˈkɑː·fɚ-/ *n* [C] a large box filled with air which allows people to work under water, for example while building bridges

cof·fin /£ˈkɒf·ɪn, $ˈkɑː·fɪn/, *Am also* **cask·et** *n* [C] a long box in which a dead person is buried or burnt

cog /£kɒg, $kɑːg/ *n* [C] one of the tooth-like parts around the edge of a wheel in a machine which fits between those of a similar wheel, causing both wheels to move • A cog (also **cogwheel**) is also a wheel with tooth-like parts around its edge which is used to turn another wheel or part in a machine. • *(disapproving)* If someone is described as a **cog in a/the machine**, they are a member of a large organization and their job, although necessary, makes them feel unimportant and powerless: *I decided to set up my own business because I was tired of just being a cog in a machine.*

co·gent /£ˈkəʊ·dʒənt, $ˈkoʊ-/ *adj fml* (esp. of arguments or reasons) clearly expressed and persuasive • *a cogent argument/speech*

co·gent·ly /£ˈkəʊ·dʒənt·li, $ˈkoʊ-/ *adv fml* • *She argued most cogently for a relaxation of the sanctions.*

co·gen·cy /£ˈkəʊ·dʒənt·si, $ˈkoʊ-/ *n* [U] *fml* • *Her writing successfully combines fluency with cogency.*

cog·i·tate /£ˈkɒdʒ·ɪ·teɪt, $ˈkɑː·dʒɪ-/ *v* [I] *fml or humorous* to spend time thinking very carefully about a subject • *I was just cogitating* **about/on/upon** *the meaning of life.*

cog·i·ta·tion /£kɒdʒ·ɪˈteɪ·ʃən, $kɑː·dʒɪ-/ *n* [C/U] *fml or humorous*

cog·nac /£ˈkɒn·jæk, $ˈkoʊ·njæk/ *n* (a glass of) high quality BRANDY (= a strong alcoholic drink) made in W France • *a bottle of cognac* [U] • *Would you like another cognac?* [C]

cog·nate /£ˈkɒg·neɪt, $ˈkɑːg-/ *adj specialized* (esp. of languages or words) having the same origin, or related and in some way similar • *French and Italian are cognate languages.* • *The Italian word 'mangiare'* (= to eat) *is cognate* **with** *the French 'manger'.*

cog·ni·tive /£ˈkɒg·nɪ·tɪv, $ˈkɑːg·nɪ·t̬ɪv/ *adj* [before n] *fml or specialized* connected with thinking or conscious mental processes • *The accident has significantly impaired several of her cognitive* **functions/abilities**. • *(specialized)* **Cognitive psychology** is the study of how people perform mental operations. • *(specialized)* **Cognitive therapy** is a form of treatment used to change someone's habitual patterns of thinking when these thoughts are damaging that person: *She used cognitive therapy on her client to try to inhibit those negative thoughts which were damaging his self-esteem.*

cog·ni·tion /£kɒgˈnɪʃ·ən, $kɑːg-/ *n fml or specialized* • *One of the things we try to do in therapy is to help clients to minimize their negative cognitions* (= thoughts). [C] • *She's writing a book on human learning, memory and cognition* (= mental processes). [U]

cog·ni·zance /£ˈkɒg·nɪ·zənts, $ˈkɑːg-/ *n* [U] **take cognizance of** *fml or law* take notice of and consider, especially when judging • *The lawyer asked the jury to take cognizance of the defendant's generosity in giving to charity.*

cog·ni·zant /£ˈkɒg·nɪ·zənt, $ˈkɑːg-/ *adj fml* • *"Regrettably, we were not cognizant* **of** (= did not know about) *the facts," said the lawyer.*

cog·no·scen·ti /£ˌkɒn·jəʊˈʃen·tiː, $ˌkɑː·njə-/ *pl n fml or literary* a group of people who (seem to) have a great knowledge and understanding of a particular subject, especially one of the arts • *Not being* **one of the** *cognoscenti, I failed to understand the ballet's subtler points.*

cog·wheel /£ˈkɒg·wiːl, $ˈkɑːg-/ *n* [C] a COG

co·hab·it /£kəʊˈhæb·ɪt, $koʊ-/ *v* [I] *fml* (usually of a man and woman who are not married) to live together and have a sexual relationship • *Jim and Ann cohabited for years before getting married.* • *Ann had been cohabiting* **with** *Jim for years before getting married.*

co·hab·it·ant *fml* /£kəʊˈhæb·ɪ·tənt, $koʊˈhæb·ɪ·t̬ənt/, *fml* **co·hab·it·ee** /£ˌkəʊ·hæb·ɪˈtiː, $ˌkoʊ-/ *n* [C] • Someone who lives in the same house, apartment etc. as someone else is officially called a cohabitant or a cohabitee: *Am I right in thinking that Mr Jones is one of the cohabitants at this address?*

co·here CONNECT /£kəʊˈhɪəʳ, $koʊˈhɪr/ *v* [I] *fml* to connect or follow naturally in a way that obeys rules • If an argument or theory coheres all the different stages fit together to form a persuasive whole.

co·her·ence /£kəʊˈhɪə·rənts, $koʊˈhɪr·ənts/ *n* [U] • *There was no coherence* **between** *the first and the second half of the film.*

co·her·ent /£kəʊˈhɪə·rənt, $koʊˈhɪr·ənt/ *adj* • *a coherent argument/speech/set of ideas/plan* • *When she calmed down she was more coherent* (= able to speak clearly and be understood).

co·here UNITE /£kəʊˈhɪəʳ, $koʊˈhɪr/ *v* [I] *fml* to unite or to hold together as a unit • *There are many interesting ideas in the play which unfortunately don't cohere into anything meaningful.* • *As a country of different national groups, Switzerland has achieved the magic trick of cohering where Yugoslavia hasn't.* • *His vision is of a world that coheres through human connection rather than systems of rules.*

co·he·sion /£kəʊˈhiː·ʒən, $koʊ-/, **co·he·sive·ness** /£kəʊˈhiː·sɪv·nəs, $koʊ-/ *n* [U] • *social/national cohesion* • *The* **lack of** *cohesion within the party lost them votes at election time.*

co·he·sive /£kəʊˈhiː·sɪv, $koʊ-/ *adj* • *a cohesive group* • *cohesive forces*

co·hort /£ˈkəʊ·hɔːt, $ˈkoʊ·hɔːrt/ *n* [C] *(specialized)* a group of people who share a characteristic, esp. age, or *(esp. Am disapproving)* a group of people who support a particular person, usually a leader • *(specialized) The company was originally called 13-30 Group for the age cohort it targeted.* • *(specialized) There was less differentiation in 'healthy eating' by social characteristics such as social class, income or sex among the younger cohort compared with the older one.* • *(esp. Am disapproving) The Mayor and his cohorts have abused their positions of power.*

coiffed /£kwʌft, $kwɑːft/ *adj esp. humorous* (of hair) carefully arranged in an attractive style • *How do those TV mothers always manage to look so immaculately coiffed even when they're doing housework?*

coif·feur /£kwʌfˈɜːʳ, $-ˈfɜːr/ *n* [C] (sometimes used in the name of a shop) a HAIRDRESSER, esp. for women • *André – Coiffeur*

coif·fure /£kwʌfˈjʊəʳ, $-ˈfjʊr/ *n* [C] *fml* the style in which someone's hair is cut and arranged • *The star appeared on stage in a black leather outfit and a 1950s coiffure.* • *The wind disturbed the guests' coiffures between door and cab.*

coil CIRCLE /kɔɪl/ *n* [C] a length of rope, hair or wire, arranged into a series of circles, one above the other • *A coil of rope lay on the beach.* • *(fig.) A coil of thick blue smoke rose up from his pipe.* • *(specialized)* A coil is a twisted length of wire through which an electric current travels.

coil *(obj)* /kɔɪl/ *v* • *The snake coiled (itself) tightly* **around** *the deer until it could no longer breathe.* [I/T] • *She coiled her hair* **into** *a neat bun on the top of her head.* [T]

coiled /kɔɪld/ *adj* • *a coiled spring*

coil MEDICAL /kɔɪl/ *n* [C] *infml* an IUD

coin MONEY /kɔɪn/ *n* [U] a small round piece of metal, usually silver or COPPER coloured, which is used as money • *a 10p/ten pence coin* [C] ○ *a pound coin* [C] ○ *a ten-cent coin* [C] ○ *gold coins* [C] • *I asked for ten pounds* **in** *20p coins.* [C] • *I've got too many coins in my pocket.* [C] • *That machine won't* **take** *50p coins.* [C] • *Several shops had been fooled by the* **counterfeit** *coins.* [C] • *The charters granted the royal privilege of* **minting** (= producing) *coins to an ecclesiastical institution in Saxony.* [C] • *Paper money replaced all but smaller* **denominations** (= values) *of coin.* [U] • LP〉 **Money**

coin *obj* /kɔɪn/ *v* [T] • If you are *(Br infml)* **coining it (in)**/ *(Am)* **coining money** you are earning a lot of money quickly.

coin·age /ˈkɔɪ·nɪdʒ/ *n* [U] • Coinage is the set of coins of different values used in a money system: *decimal coinage* • *bronze coinage*

coin *obj* INVENT /kɔɪn/ *v* [T] to invent (a new word or expression) or use one in a particular way for the first time • *The verb 'to escalate' was coined in the 1940s during the Second World War.* • *(humorous)* A person might say **to coin a phrase** to show that they are using an expression which is in popular use at the time of speaking: *I was, to coin a phrase, gobsmacked!*

coin·age /ˈkɔɪ·nɪdʒ/ *n* [C] • Coinage is the act or an occasion of inventing a new expression: *The word 'yuppie' was one of many coinages of the 1980s.*

co·in·cide /£ˌkəʊ·ɪnˈsaɪd, $ˌkoʊ-/ *v* [I] to happen at or near the same time, or to be the same or similar • *I timed my holiday to coincide* **with** *the children's school holiday.* • *His comments coincided* **with** *a survey this week which found that many children begin regular television watching before they are a year old.* • *If the heavy rain had coincided* **with** *an extreme high tide, serious flooding would have resulted.* • *If our schedules coincide we'll go to Spain together.* • *Our views coincide on a range of subjects.* • *A principle does not cease to be a principle because it coincides* **with** *a legitimate interest.*

co·in·cid·ence /£kəʊˈɪnt·sɪ·dᵊnts, $koʊ-/ *n* • A coincidence is an occasion when two or more things happen at the same time, esp. in a way that is unlikely and surprising: *You've had your hair cut in the same style as me –* **what a** *coincidence!* [C] ○ *Is it a coincidence that the wife of the man who designed the competition won first prize?* [C] ○ *We came to be here by a series of* **strange** *coincidences.* [C] • Coincidence also means chance or luck: *Just* **by** *coincidence, I met my old school-mate fifty years later.* [U] ○ **It** *was* **pure/sheer** *coincidence* **that** *I remembered his phone number.* [U + *that* clause]

co·in·cid·ent·al /£kəʊˌɪnt·sɪˈden·tᵊl, $koʊˌɪnt·sɪˈden·t̬ᵊl/ *adj*

co·in·cid·ent·al·ly /£kəʊˌɪnt·sɪˈden·tᵊl·i, $koʊˌɪnt·sɪˈden·t̬ᵊl·i/ *adv* • *The highest scorers, coincidentally, were all women.*

coi·tus /£ˈkɔɪ·təs, $-t̬əs/ *n* [U] *fml or medical* the sexual act in which a man puts his penis into a woman's vagina • **Coitus interruptus** is a method of preventing pregnancy in which the man removes his penis from the woman's vagina before sperm is released: *Coitus interruptus is not a very reliable method of birth control.*

coi·tal /£ˈkɔɪ·tᵊl, $-t̬ᵊl/ *adj* [not gradable]

Coke DRINK /£kəʊk, $koʊk/ *n* [C/U] *trademark abbreviation for* COCA COLA

coke FUEL /£kəʊk, $koʊk/ *n* [U] the solid grey substance that is left after coal is heated and the gas and TAR removed. It is burnt as a fuel to produce heat or power.

coke DRUG /£kəʊk, $koʊk/ *n* [U] *slang for* COCAINE

Col RANK *n* [C] (used in names) *abbreviation for* COLONEL • *Col. (Angus) Ferguson*

col PRINTING /£kɒl, $kɑːl/ *n* [C] *abbreviation for* COLUMN PRINTING

col- TOGETHER /£kɒl-, $kɑːl-/ *combining form* See at CO-

co·la /£ˈkəʊ·lə, $ˈkoʊ-/ *n* [C/U] a sweet fizzy brown drink which does not contain alcohol • *Coke and Pepsi are types of cola.* [U] • *All colas taste pretty much the same to me.* [C]

col·an·der, cul·len·der /£ˈkʌl·ɪn·dəʳ, $ˈkɑː·lən·dɚ/ *n* [C] a bowl with a lot of holes in it, used for washing food or for removing water, esp. that in which vegetables have been cooked • PIC> **Kitchen**

cold LOW TEMPERATURE /£kəʊld, $koʊld/ *adj, n* **-er, -est** (at) a low temperature esp. when compared to the temperature of the human body, and not hot or warm • *cold weather* • *a cold day* • *cold food* • *cold hands* • *a cold house* • *cold water* • *You'll be/get/feel cold if you don't wear a coat.* • *It's* **bitterly** (= extremely) *cold outside.* • *Come and drink your soup or it'll* **go/get** *cold.* • *Feel my toes – they're* **as cold as ice.** • *Look at you! You're blue/shivering* **with** *cold.* [U] • **The cold** is cold temperature or cold weather: *Don't stand out there in the cold, come in here and get warm.* ○ *Old people tend to* **feel** *the cold* (= feel uncomfortable in cold temperatures) *more than the young.* • A person might be said to **get/have cold feet** when they experience a loss of confidence and sometimes unwillingness before doing something risky or difficult. • When children are playing a guessing or searching game they might say "you are **getting colder**" to the person who is guessing or searching to tell them that they are getting further away from the answer or hidden object. • If you **pour/throw cold water on** an idea or suggestion you are not enthusiastic about it and you discourage it by saying that it will not be possible or successful: *His boss is always pouring cold water on his proposals, even when they are very good.* • *(Br)* A **cold bag** (*Br also* **freezer bag**, *Am* **cooler bag**) is a bag in which you transport food and drink, and which has a special thick material inside it to help keep the food and drink cold. PIC> **Bags** • **Cold-blooded** animals, such as snakes, can only control their body heat by taking in heat from the outside or by being very active. See also **cold-blooded** at COLD UNFRIENDLY. • A person in business makes a **cold call** when he or she telephones or visits a possible customer to try to sell them something without being asked by the customer to do so. • If someone says that something is **cold comfort** they mean that it is really not any comfort: *£5000 compensation for an accident is cold comfort when you've lost a leg.* • **Cold cream** is a thick white oily substance used mainly by women to clean the skin and stop it from becoming too dry. • **Cold cuts** are thin flat slices of cold meat. • A **cold frame** is a glass or plastic box, with a top which can be left open, into which young plants are put for a short time, esp. in order to help them grow faster or to protect them from very cold weather: *The cuttings were kept in a cold frame over the winter.* PIC> **Frame, Garden** • A **cold front** is the weather condition in which an advancing mass of cold air pushes into a mass of warm air resulting in a fall in temperature. • *(humorous)* A person might say they need a **cold shower** if something has made them feel sexually excited at a time which is not convenient: *I think I'd better* **take** *a cold shower!* • A **cold snap** is a short period of cold icy weather. • If something, for example food, is kept in **cold storage** it is put in artificially cold conditions, usually to preserve it. • A **cold sweat** is a state of uncontrollable anxiety and fear: **I came out in** *a cold sweat when I realized I had left the house unlocked.* • *The sound of his voice* **put me in** *a cold sweat.* • *(Am and Aus slang)* **Cold turkey** is the period of extreme suffering which comes immediately after a person has stopped taking a drug on which they are dependent: *He* **went through** *cold turkey to cure his heroin addiction.* • *(saying)* 'Cold hands, warm heart' means that if you have cold hands, you are a kind person. • *"A cold coming we had of it, / Just the worst time of the year / For a journey"* (from T.S.Eliot's poem 'Journey of the Magi' in *Ariel Poems*, 1927) • LP> **Measurements** ⓘ

cold UNFRIENDLY /£kəʊld, $koʊld/ *adj* **-er, -est** not showing or influenced by affection, kindness or feeling and not friendly • *His handshake was cold, and his eyes lifeless.* • *He stared into her cold blue eyes.* • *She would never feel welcome in this city with its cold, unsmiling inhabitants.* • If someone **gives** you **the cold shoulder** or **cold-shoulders** you, they are intentionally unfriendly and give you no attention: *I can't understand why you're giving me the cold shoulder – what have I done wrong?* ○ *He cold-shouldered me the next time I saw him.* • If someone kills **in cold blood**, they kill in a way that seems especially cruel because there is no understandable reason: *Both the victims were tied up and no threat to the accused, but he killed them anyway, in cold blood.* ○ *a* **cold-blooded** *murderer* ○ See also **cold-blooded** at COLD LOW TEMPERATURE. • *She gave him a* **cold-eyed** (= unfriendly) *stare.* • Someone might be described as a **cold fish** if their manner is unfriendly and they do not share their feelings. • *The government's decision to shut both the hospital and the clinic was* **cold-hearted** (= not sympathetic). • *The* **cold truth** (= unpleasant fact) *is that she's just not very efficient.* • A **cold war** is a state of extreme unfriendliness existing between countries esp. with opposing political systems which expresses itself not through fighting but through political pressure and threats. • *"Cast a cold eye / On life, on death. / Horseman, pass by!"* (words on W.B.Yeats' grave, from his poem *Under Ben Bulben*, 1939) • ⓘ

cold·ly /£ˈkəʊld·li, $ˈkoʊld-/ *adv* • *"I'd prefer you not to come again", he said coldly.*

cold·ness /£ˈkəʊld·nəs, $ˈkoʊld-/ *n* [U] • *Her coldness of manner and apparent aloofness distressed him greatly.*

cold ILLNESS /£kəʊld, $koʊld/ *n* [C] a common infection esp. in the nose and throat which often causes a cough, a slight fever and sometimes some pain in the muscles • *I've* **got a** *cold – I must have* **caught** *it* **from** *you.* • *(Br and Aus infml) Don't come near me – I've got a* **stinking/streaming** *cold* (= extremely bad cold). • A **cold sore** is a painful red swelling on esp. the lips or nose which is caused by a viral infection. • Ⓘ

cole·slaw /£'kəʊl·slɔː, $'koʊl·slɑː/ *n* [U] thinly cut raw vegetables, esp. CABBAGE leaves, covered in a thick creamy sauce and eaten cold

co·ley /£'kəʊ·li, $'koʊ-/ *n* [U; C] *pl* **coley** or **coleys** (the white or grey flesh used as food of) any of various North Atlantic sea fish

col·ic /£'kɒl·ɪk, $'kɑː·lɪk/ *n* [U] a severe but not continuous pain in the bottom part of the stomach or bowels esp. of babies

col·ick·y /£'kɒl·ɪ·ki, $'kɑː·lɪ-/ *adj*

col·i·tis /£kəʊ'laɪ·təs, $koʊ'laɪ·t̬əs/ *n* [U] an illness of the COLON (=part of the bowels) in which the contents of the bowels are excreted too frequently

col·lab·o·rate WORK WITH /kə'læb·ə·reɪt/ *v* [I] to work with someone else for a special purpose • *Two writers collaborated* **on** *the script for the film.* • *A German company collaborated* **with** *a Swiss firm* **to** *develop the product.* • *The British and Italian police collaborated* **in** *catching the terrorists.*

col·lab·o·ra·tion /kəˌlæb·ə'reɪ·ʃən/ *n* • *The two playwrights worked* **in close** *collaboration* **(with** *each other) on the script.* [U] • *The new airport is a collaboration between two of the best architects in the country.* [C]

col·lab·o·rat·or /£kə'læb·ə·reɪ·tər, $-t̬ər/ *n* [C] • *a new production by Andrew Davies and collaborators*

col·lab·o·rat·ive /£kə'læb·ər·ə·tɪv, $-ər·ə·t̬ɪv/ *adj* • *The presentation was a collaborative effort by all the children in the class.*

col·lab·o·rate SUPPORT AN ENEMY /kə'læb·ə·reɪt/ *v* [I] *disapproving* to work with an enemy who has taken control of your own country • *Anyone who was suspected of collaborating* **with** *the occupying forces was arrested.*

col·lab·o·ra·tion /kəˌlæb·ə'reɪ·ʃən/ *n* [U] *disapproving* • *She is suspected of collaboration.*

col·lab·o·ra·tion·ist /kəˌlæb·ə'reɪ·ʃən·ɪst/ *adj disapproving* • *a collaborationist government*

col·lab·o·rat·or /£kə'læb·ə·reɪ·tər, $-t̬ər/ *n* [C] *disapproving* • *wartime collaborators* • *a Nazi collaborator*

col·lage /£'kɒl·ɑːʒ, $'kɑː·lɑːʒ/ *n* (the art of making) a picture in which various materials or objects, for example paper, cloth or photographs, are stuck onto a larger surface • *The children made a collage of postcards.* [C] • *She frequently uses collage in her work.* [U] • Compare ASSEMBLAGE.

col·lag·en /£'kɒl·ə·dʒen, $'kɑː·lə-/ *n* [U] a substance found esp. in the joints of humans and animals • *Collagen is a protein which helps to hold your body tissues together.* • *A collagen* **implant/injection** *is a medical operation which changes the shape of part of the body in order to make it more attractive.*

col·lapse FALL /kə'læps/ *v* to fall down suddenly because of pressure or lack of strength or support • *Thousands of buildings collapsed in the earthquake.* [I] • *With one mile to go the runner collapsed* **with** *heat and exhaustion.* [I] • *The sofa collapsed* **under** *her enormous* **weight**. [I] • *(fig.) She collapsed* **with laughter** (=became weak with laughing) *at the joke.* [I]

col·lapse /kə'læps/ *n*

col·laps·i·ble /kə'læp·sɪ·bl̩/ *adj* • Collapsible furniture is furniture that can be folded, usually so it can be put or stored in a smaller space: *collapsible chairs*

col·lapse FAIL /kə·læps/ *v* [I] (of people and business) to suffer the sudden inability to continue or work correctly • *Lots of people lost their jobs when the property market collapsed.* • *Talks between management and unions have collapsed.* • *Share prices collapsed* (=became lower suddenly) *after news of poor trading.* • *(fig.) He thought his whole world had collapsed when his wife died.*

col·lapse /kə'læps/ *n* • *Alcohol and unreasonable behaviour caused the collapse* **of** *her marriage.* [U] • *A poor economy has caused the collapse* **of** *thousands of small businesses.* [U] • *Negotiations between the two countries are* **on the brink/verge of** *collapse* (=very near stopping without success). [U] • *The financial community is suffering from a collapse* **of confidence**. [C] • *He* **suffered a mental/nervous** *collapse after ten years' teaching.* [C]

col·lapsed /kə'læpst/ *adj* • A collapsed **lung** or **blood vessel** is one which is no longer able to work in the expected way because of disease.

col·lar NECK /£'kɒl·ər, $'kɑː·lər/ *n* [C] an item, esp. part of a piece of clothing, that goes round the neck • *a tight collar* • *a stiff collar* • *a fur collar* • *a dress with a big collar* • A collar is also a strap made of leather or other strong material which people put around the neck of an animal, esp. a dog or cat: *(Br) "Would you put your dog* **on a** *collar* (=use a piece of rope, etc. tied to a collar to control it), *please?"* • A **clerical** collar (*infml* **dog collar**) is a stiff white circular piece of material worn around the neck of their clothing by priests. • A collar is also a type of NECKLACE (=jewellery worn round the neck): *a diamond collar* • *(specialized)* On an animal a collar is an area around the neck which is coloured differently from the other parts of the body: *The bird has grey feathers with a lighter collar.* • A **collar bone** (*medical* **clavicle**) is a bone between the shoulder and the neck on each side of the body: *She fell off her horse and broke her collar bone.* • PIC› **Clothes**

col·lar *obj* CATCH /£'kɒl·ər, $'kɑː·lər/ *v* [T] *infml* to catch and hold someone so that they can't escape • *She was collared by the police at the airport.* • *(fig.) I was collared on the train by the most boring man on earth!*

col·late *obj* /kə'leɪt/ *v* to bring together (different pieces of written information) so that the similarities and differences can be seen • *When both versions of the story were collated, major discrepancies were found.* • *There are cheap, efficient computers to collate the* **information** *on symptoms, side-effects and cures.* • *According to* **figures** *collated by the council, 640 BMWs and 330 Toyota Crowns were stolen.* • To collate is also to collect and arrange the sheets of a report, book, etc., in the correct order: *Does the new photocopier collate (documents)?* [I/T]

col·la·tion /kə'leɪ·ʃən/ *n* [C/U] • Collation is the act or an example of collating. • See also COLLATION.

col·lat·er·al MONEY /£kə'læt·ər·əl, $-'læt̬·ər-/ *n* [C/U] *specialized* valuable property owned by someone who wants to borrow money which they agree will become the property of the lender if the debt is not paid back • *She* **used/put up/offered** *her house as (a) collateral.*

col·lat·er·al CONNECTED /£kə'læt·ər·əl, $-'læt̬·ər-/ *adj fml* connected but additional and less important, or of the same family although not directly related • *The television showed the bombed military bases but not the collateral* **damage** *to civilian areas.* • *Brothers and sisters are closely related whereas cousins are collateral relatives.*

col·la·tion /kə'leɪ·ʃən/ *n* [C] *fml dated* a meal, esp. one left ready for people to serve themselves • *There will be a* **cold** *collation in the banqueting room.*

col·league /£'kɒl·iːg, $'kɑː·liːg/ *n* [C] one of a group of people who work together • *One of my colleagues will be leaving in August.* • *Maria found it very boring entertaining her husband's colleagues night after night.* • Ⓟⓛ

col·lect GATHER /kə'lekt/ *v* to gather together from a variety of places or over a period of time • *A large crowd of reporters collected outside the Prime Minister's house.* [I] • *After the party I collected* **(up)** *twenty bottles from various parts of the house.* [T/M] • *We're collecting (money)* **for** *the homeless.* [I/T] • *These china ornaments just collect* **dust**. [T] • People sometimes collect one particular type of object, for example stamps or coins, as a hobby: *So when did you start collecting antique glass?* [T]

col·lec·tion /kə'lek·ʃən/ *n* [C] • *We're* **having/holding** *a collection* (=getting money from people who want to give it) **for** *charity/Tom's retirement present.* • *They sold a valuable stamp/coin/art collection and a collection of porcelain at the auction.* • *(fig.) There's quite a collection of* (=a lot of) *toothbrushes in the bathroom.* • A clothes designer shows a collection of the latest styles every season: *Kenzo's* **winter** *collection*

col·lect·or /£kə'lek·tər, $-t̬ər/ *n* • *a* **keen** *stamp/antiques collector* • *a butterfly collector* • A **collector's item/piece** is an object which is very valuable to a person who collects those objects as a hobby because it is so unusual, rare or beautiful.

col·lect·a·ble /£kə'lek·tə·bl̩, $-t̬ə-/, **col·lect·i·ble** *adj* • Something which is collectable is considered to be worth collecting as a hobby: *Comics from the early sixties are highly collectable at the moment.*

col·lect·a·ble, col·lect·i·ble /£kə'lek·tə·bl̩, $-t̬ə-/ *n* [C] • A collectable is any object which people want to collect as a hobby.

col·lect *obj* GET /kə'lekt/ *v* [T] to (go and) get something or someone from a place or a person • *Your shoes will be repaired and ready for you to collect on Thursday.* • *I'll collect you from the station.*

col·lec·tion /kə'lek·ʃən/ *n* • *The photos will be* **ready for** *collection on Tuesday afternoon.* [U] • *Which day is the* *rubbish collection* (= When is the rubbish removed?) *in this street?* [C] • *(Br) There are three collections a day from the post box on the corner* (= the letters are removed three times a day). [C]

col·lect·or /£kə'lek·tər, $-t̬ɚ/ *n* [C] • A debt/ticket/tax/rent collector is someone whose job it is to go to ask people for these things.

col·lect *obj* CONTROL /kə'lekt/ *v* [T] *fml* to get control of your feelings and thoughts esp. after shock, surprise or laughter • *When she introduced this old man as her husband I had to collect* **myself** *before I could say hello.* • *She quickly collected her* **thoughts** *and managed to say something polite but noncommittal.*

col·lect·ed /£kə'lek·tɪd, $-t̬ɪd/ *adj* • *The interviewee appeared* **cool, calm and** *collected despite aggressive questioning.*

col·lect PRAYER /'kɒl·ekt/ *n* [C] a short prayer which is said during some Christian religious ceremonies

col·lect TELEPHONE /kə'lekt/ *adj, adv* [not gradable] *Am* paid for by the person receiving the telephone call • *I'd like to make a collect* **phone call**. • *Could you make this call collect, please?* • LP› **Telephone**

col·lec·tive /£kə'lek·tɪv, $-t̬ɪv/ *adj* of or shared by every member of a group of people • *a collective decision/effort/opinion/action* • *collective leadership* • **Collective bargaining** is the system in which employees talk as a group with their employers to try to agree on matters such as pay and working conditions. • A **collective farm**, originally in countries which had a COMMUNIST system of government, is a large farm or group of farms owned by the state but controlled by the workers. • *(specialized)* A **collective noun** is a noun which describes a group of things or people as a unit but which agrees with a singular verb: *'Family' and 'flock' are examples of collective nouns.*

col·lec·tive /£kə'lek·tɪv, $-t̬ɪv/ *n* [C] • A collective is an organization or business which is owned and controlled by the people who work in it.

col·lec·tiv·i·sm /£kə'lek·tɪ·vɪ·zəm, $-t̬ɪ-/ *n* [U] *specialized* • Collectivism is a theory or political system based on the principle that all of the farms, factories and other places of work in a country should be owned by or for all the people in that country.

col·leen /£kɒl'iːn, $kɑː'liːn/ *n* [C] *(Irish Eng)* a girl or young woman or *(Am)* a girl from Ireland

col·lege EDUCATION /£'kɒl·ɪdʒ, $'kɑː·lɪdʒ/ *n* [C] any place for specialized education after the age of 16 where people study or train to get knowledge and/or skills • *a business college* • *teacher(s') training college* • *secretarial college* • *Naval college* • *(Br) sixth form college* • *She was* **at** *art college but she* **dropped out of** *it* (= stopped before the end of the course) *last year.* • College is also UNIVERSITY: *You have to* **go to** (= study at) *college for a lot of years if you want to be a doctor.* • A college is also one of the separate and named parts into which some universities are divided: *E.M. Forster went to/was at King's College, Cambridge.* ○ *I attended the College* **of** *Arts and Sciences at New York University.* ○ *Cambridge has some very fine old colleges* (= college buildings). ○ *We beat King's College* (= the members of King's College) *at football.* • In Britain and Australia some schools for children, esp. those where education is paid for, use College in their name: *Cheltenham Ladies' College* ○ *Methodist Ladies' College* • LP› **Schools and colleges** (F) (NL)

col·leg·i·ate /£kə'liː·dʒi·ət, $-dʒɪt/ *adj* • Collegiate means of or belonging to a college or its students: *a collegiate theatre* ○ *collegiate sports* • *(Br)* Collegiate also means formed of colleges: *Cambridge is a collegiate* **university**.

col·lege GROUP /£'kɒl·ɪdʒ, $'kɑː·lɪdʒ/ *n* [C] a group of people with a particular job, purpose, duty or power who are organized into a group for sharing ideas, making decisions, etc. • *the Royal College of Medicine* • *an electoral college* • (F) (NL)

col·lide /kə'laɪd/ *v* [I] (esp. of moving objects) to hit (something) violently • *The two vans collided* (**with** *each other) at the crossroads.* • *It was predicted that a comet would collide* **with** *one of the planets.* • *The bike collided* **into** *a tree.* • LP› **Each other**

col·li·sion /kə'lɪʒ·ən/ *n* [C] • *There has been a collision involving a number of cars on the main road into town.* [C] • *Two drivers were killed in a* **head-on** (= direct) *collision* **between** *a car and a taxi last night.* [C] • *Two trains were* **in** *collision at the station.* [U] • *The cyclist was* **in** *collision* **with** *a bus.* [U] • *The cars* **came into** *collision at the traffic lights.* [U] • *(fig.) There was a collision of interests/opinions/principles.* • If two or more people or organizations are **on a collision course** there will probably soon be a fierce disagreement: *The director and his staff are on a collision course.*

col·lie /£'kɒl·i, $'kɑː·li/ *n* [C] any of several breeds of long-haired dog which are bred for controlling sheep

col·li·er·y /£'kɒl·i·ər·i, $'kɑːl·jɚ-/ *n* [C] a coal mine and all the buildings, machines, etc. connected with it

col·li·er /£'kɒl·i·ər, $'kɑːl·jɚ/ *n* [C] • *(fml)* A collier is a **coal miner**. See at COAL. • A collier is also a ship used for carrying coal.

col·lo·cate /£'kɒl·əʊ·keɪt, $'kɑː·lə-/ *v* [I] *specialized* (of words and phrases) to be used frequently together in a way that sounds correct to people who have spoken the language all their lives, but might not be expected from the meaning • *The adjective 'heavy' collocates* **with** *the noun 'rain' but 'strong' doesn't.* • *'Heavy' and 'rain' collocate.* • *You can't always predict from their meanings which words will collocate* **with** *each other.* • LP› **Words used together**

col·lo·ca·tion /£ˌkɒl·əʊ'keɪ·ʃən, $ˌkɑː·lə-/ *n specialized* • A collocation (also **collocate**) is a word or phrase which is frequently used with another word or phrase, in a way that sounds correct to people who have spoken the language all their lives, but might not be expected from the meaning: *In the phrase 'a hard frost', 'hard' is a collocation of 'frost' and 'strong' would not sound natural.* [C] • A collocation can also be the combination of words formed when two or more words are frequently used together in a way that sounds correct: *The phrase 'a hard frost' is a collocation.* [C] • Collocation is also the frequent use of some words and phrases with others, esp. in a way which is difficult to guess: *Awareness of collocation is essential for fluency in a foreign language.* [U]

col·lo·qui·al /£kə'ləʊ·kwi·əl, $-'loʊ-/ *adj specialized* (of words and expressions) informal and conversational, and more suitable for use in speech than in writing • *'He's off his head!' is a colloquial way of saying 'His behaviour is not reasonable'.*

col·lo·qui·al·i·sm /£kə'ləʊ·kwi·əl·ɪ·zəm, $-'loʊ-/ *n* [C] • *'Bananas' is a colloquialism* **for** *silly.*

col·lo·qui·al·ly /£kə'ləʊ·kwi·əl·i, $-'loʊ-/ *adv* • *In the US, the Federal Bureau of Investigation is colloquially called 'the Feds'.*

col·lo·quy /£'kɒl·ə·kwi, $'kɑː·lə-/ *n* [C] *fml or dated* a formal conversation or meeting

col·lude /kə'luːd/ *v* [I] to act together secretly or illegally in order to deceive or cheat someone • *It was suspected that the police had colluded* **with** *the witnesses.*

col·lu·sion /kə'luː·ʒən/ *n* [U] • *They discovered a spy acting* **in** *collusion* **with** *their competitors.*

col·lu·sive /kə'luː·sɪv/ *adj* • *collusive behaviour*

col·ly·wob·bles /£'kɒl·iˌwɒb·l̩z, $'kɑː·liˌwɑː-/ *pl n* **the collywobbles** *infml humorous* an uncomfortable feeling in the stomach caused by feelings of nervousness or slight fear • *I've got the collywobbles* **about** *my exam this afternoon.* • *I'm sorry but driving with you* **gives** *me the collywobbles.*

co·logne /£kə'ləʊn, $-'loʊn/, **eau de co·logne** *n* [U] a type of PERFUME (= a pleasant smelling liquid for putting on the body)

co·lon BODY PART /£'kəʊ·lɒn, $'koʊ·lən/ *n* [C] the lower and bigger half of the bowels in which water is removed from excrement

co·lon SIGN /£'kəʊ·lɒn, $'koʊ·lən/ *n* [C] the sign (:) used in writing esp. to introduce a list of things or a sentence or phrase taken from somewhere else

col·o·nel /£'kɜː·nəl, $'kɜːr-/ (*abbreviation* **Col**) *n* [C] an officer of high rank in the army or air force • *Colonel (Marcus) Furlong* • *Good morning, Colonel.* [as form of address] • *Colonel is the military rank between lieutenant-colonel and brigadier.* • *(esp. Br dated disapproving)* A **Colonel Blimp** is an old man with old-fashioned military principles and an unreasonably high opinion of both himself and his country.

col·on·nade /£ˌkɒl·ə'neɪd, $ˌkɑː·lə-/ *n* [C] a row of columns separated from each other by an equal distance

col·o·ny /£'kɒl·ə·ni, $'kɑː·lə-/ *n* [C] a country or area controlled politically by a more powerful and often distant country • *Australia and New Zealand are* **former** *British colonies.* • A colony is also a group of people who leave their own country to live and work in another one but still officially belong to their own country: *That first winter in America was very hard for the new colony.* ○ *The British*

COLON [:]

Colons are not used very often in informal writing. A colon is used:

- **to introduce a list** (often after 'for example', 'namely', 'i.e.', 'as follows')
  She had three brothers: Joe, Steve and Tony.
  If there is a fire, do the following: ring the alarm, close all windows and leave the building.
  If the items following the colon are long or contain commas they are separated from each other with semicolons (;) – LP **Semicolon**.
- **to introduce an independent part of a sentence which explains the main part or follows from it**
  The doctors ran to his bed: his heart had stopped.
  Kay went white and bit her lip: she was furious.
  We have made a difficult decision: the company will close.
  There is only one important question: how did this happen?
- **esp. in the US following the greeting in a business letter**
  Dear Customer: • *Dear Mr. Stein:*

colony in Spain has its/have their own newspaper. • A colony can also be a group of people with a shared interest or job who live together in a way that is separate from other people: *an artists' colony* ○ *a nudist colony* • *(specialized)* A colony is also a group of animals, insects or plants of the same type that live together: *a colony of ants/termites/bacteria*

co·lo·ni·al /£kəˈləʊ·ni·əl, $-ˈloʊ-/ *adj* • *Turkey was once an important colonial power.* • *Various parts of Africa have suffered* **under** *colonial* **rule**. • A **colonial mentality** is an acceptance of or support for a system in which it is acceptable for one country or group to take control of another. • Colonial is also used to describe furniture or buildings in the style of a period when some countries were colonies: *colonial architecture* ○ *colonial-style houses* ○ *In the US Colonial furniture is of a style which is from the period when America was a British colony.*

co·lo·ni·al /£kəˈləʊ·ni·əl, $-ˈloʊ-/ *n* [C] • A colonial is a person from another country who lives in a colony, esp. as part of its system of government. • *(esp. disapproving)* Colonial also refers to people who lived in a colony in the past and still have the opinions and habits of that period in their lives: *The golf club was run by a bunch of old colonials.*

co·lon·i·al·i·sm /£kəˈləʊ·ni·ə·lɪ·zəm, $-ˈloʊ-/ *n* [U] • Colonialism is the belief in and support for the system of one country controlling another.

co·lo·ni·al·ist /£kəˈləʊ·ni·əl·ɪst, $-ˈloʊ-/ *n* [C] • *Colonialists have taken advantage of less advanced countries throughout the course of history.*

co·lo·ni·al·ist /£kəˈləʊ·ni·əl·ɪst, $-ˈloʊ-/ *adj* • *the colonialist powers* • *colonialist ideology*

col·o·nize *obj, Br and Aus usually* **–ise** /£ˈkɒl·ə·naɪz, $ˈkɑː·lə-/ *v* [T] • *Peru was colonized* (= made into a colony) *by the Spanish in the sixteenth century.*

col·o·ni·za·tion, *Br and Aus usually* **–i·sa·tion** /£ˌkɒl·ə·naɪˈzeɪ·ʃən, $ˌkɑː·lə-/ *n* [U]

Col·o·ra·do bee·tle /£ˈkɒl·ə·rɑː·dəʊ, $-doʊ/, *Am usually* **Col·o·ra·do po·ta·to bee·tle** *n* [C] a type of BEETLE (= an insect with a hard wing covering) with black and yellow lines on its body which attacks potato plants

col·or·a·tion /ˌkʌl·əˈreɪ·ʃən/ *n* [U] the presence of colour on an animal or plant and the pattern which the colour makes • *Many species of insect have bright coloration.* • *A tiger has camouflaged coloration.*

co·los·sus /£kəˈlɒs·əs, $-ˈlɑː·səs/ *n* [C] *pl* **colossuses** or **colossi** /£kəˈlɒs·aɪ, $-ˈlɑː·saɪ/ a very large statue or building • *He compared the statue with an unfinished marble colossus from the island of Naxos.* • *The Colossus of Rhodes was a very large bronze statue of Apollo at the entrance to Rhodes port in ancient times.* • *His office is on the twelfth floor of the Bundesbank colossus* (= building) *with a view over Frankfurt.* • An important or influential person, group or country may also be described as a colossus: *She has been described as the creative colossus of the literary world.* ○ *With his influential friends and extravagant lifestyle, he* **bestrides** *the world of show business* **like** *a colossus* (= he is very important and influential in the world of entertainment).

co·los·sal /£kəˈlɒs·əl, $-ˈlɑː·səl/ *adj* • *In the centre of the hall stood a colossal* (= very large) *wooden statue, decorated in ivory and gold.* • *(infml)* Colossal can also be used to describe things which are extremely large or great: *They were asking a colossal amount of money for the house.* ○ *I think she's got colossal cheek* (= she is very rude) *to suggest such a thing.*

col·our APPEARANCE *Br and Aus, Am and Aus* **col·or** /£ˈkʌl·əʳ, $-ɚ/ *n* the appearance that something has as a result of reflecting light • *Blue, green, red, pink and yellow are colours.* [C] • *Black and white are not considered to be colours.* [C] • *"What colour is her hair?" "It's dark brown."* [C] • *I'd prefer the shirt* **in** *a different colour if possible.* [C] • *Blue, yellow and red are* **primary** *colours* (= They can be mixed together in different ways to make any other colour). [C] • *I like rich jewel colours, such as purple, blue and green.* [C] • *Are the photos* **in** *colour or black and white?* [U] • Colour is also the pleasant effect of a bright colour or of a lot of colours together: *There isn't much colour in this room, is there?* [U] ○ *Add oregano and basil to the sauce to give it colour and flavour.* [U] • *(literary) The whole garden was* **ablaze with/a riot of** *colour* (= full of different bright colours). [U] • A colour is also a substance, such as a paint or DYE, which you add to something to give it a particular colour: *I washed my new green shirt in hot water and the colour* **ran** (= the colour came out of the material). [C] • If you add **(a splash of)** colour to something plain, you add a very strong and noticeable colour: *Tubs of geraniums and begonias add colour to your garden in the early summer.* [U] • If something adds **(some/a little)** colour to something which is boring and uninteresting, it adds some variety and interest to it: *Her lively, brash style of writing will add some colour to the arts pages of the newspaper.* [U] • If a light-skinned person *(Br and Aus)* **has a high colour**/*(Am, Aus also)* **has a lot of color**, the natural colour of their face is pink or reddish. • If something **puts some colour in/brings some colour to** your **cheeks**, it makes you look or feel better or more healthy: *A brisk afternoon walk will put some colour in your cheeks.* • *(infml)* If you look **off-colour**, you look slightly ill: *You look a bit off-colour today. Have you got a temperature?* • If a person is **colour blind**, they have something wrong with their eyes and are unable to see the difference between particular colours, esp. red and green: *People who are colour blind are not allowed to become aircraft pilots.* • If a set of objects such as books or wires are **colour-coded**, they are marked with different colours so that people can recognize them as being different or separate. • If a piece of clothing or material is **colour-fast**, its colour will not change or lose brightness when it is washed. • A **colour scheme** is a combination of colours that has been chosen for a particular room: *We've chosen a peach colour scheme for the living room.* • *(esp. Br)* A **colour supplement** is a magazine with colour pictures which is given free with a newspaper, esp. on Saturdays and Sundays. • *"Any colour – so long as it's black"* (believed to be Henry Ford on the choice of colour for his Model T cars, 1863-1947) • *"The Colour of Money"* (Film title, 1986)

col·our *Br and Aus, Am and Aus* **col·or** /£ˈkʌl·əʳ, $-ɚ/ *adj* [not gradable] • Colour television, photography or printing shows things in all their colours, not just in black and white.

col·our *(obj) Br and Aus, Am and Aus* **col·or** /£ˈkʌl·əʳ, $-ɚ/ *v* • If you colour something, you change its colour using paint or a DYE: *Does he colour his hair, or is that his natural colour?* [T] ○ *If you colour your room blue, it may look rather cold.* [T + obj + adj] • If you colour **in** a particular shape, you fill it with colour: *Rosie drew an elephant and coloured it in.* [M] • If someone colours **(with embarrassment)**, their face becomes red: *She colours with embarrassment every time she sees him.* [I] • If something colours your opinion of something, it influences your opinion in a negative way: *His attitude to marriage has been coloured by his unhappy childhood and his parent's divorce.* [T] ○ *When she found out he had been to prison, it coloured her* **judgment** *of him.* [T]

col·oured *Br and Aus, esp. Am* **col·ored** /£ˈkʌl·əd, $-ɚd/ *adj* • *She drew a picture using crayons and coloured pencils.*

–col·oured *Br and Aus* /£ˈkʌl·əd, $-ɚd/, *esp. Am* **–col·ored** *combining form* • *He was wearing a long multi-*

coloured scarf. • *In June and July, our garden is full of brightly-coloured flowers.* • *She was wearing sandals and flesh-coloured tights.*

col·our·ful *Br and Aus, Am and Aus* **col·or·ful** /£ˈkʌl·ə·fəl, $ˈ-ɚ-/ *adj* • Something that is colourful has bright colours or a lot of different colours: *I like colourful paintings, like Van Gogh's 'Sunflowers'.* ○ *She was wearing a colourful blue and yellow dress.* • Colourful is also used to mean interesting and exciting: *He has a very colourful past.* ○ *The old city around the cathedral is the most colourful part of town.*

col·our·ful·ly *Br and Aus, Am and Aus* **col·or·ful·ly** /£ˈkʌl·ə·fəl·i, $ˈ-ɚ-/ *adv* • *The young girls and boys were dressed very colourfully in their traditional folk costumes.*

col·our·ing *Br and Aus, Am and Aus* **col·or·ing** /£ˈkʌl·ər·ɪŋ, $ˈ-ɚ-/ *n* [U] • Colouring is the combined effect of a person's hair, skin and eye colour: *Their colouring is so totally different that you would never think they were sisters.* • Colourings are substances that are added to food or drink to change its colour artificially: *It says on the label that no preservatives or* **artificial** *colourings have been added.*

col·our·less *Br and Aus* /£ˈkʌl·ə·ləs, $ˈ-ɚ-/, *Am and Aus* **col·or·less** *adj* • Something that is colourless has no colour at all: *Water and glass are colourless.* ○ *Carbon monoxide is a colourless, odourless, poisonous gas.* • Colourless also means boring or uninteresting: *It is a rather grey, colourless city, with few interesting sights or historical monuments.*

col·our RACE *Br and Aus, Am and Aus* **col·or** /£ˈkʌl·ər, $-ɚ/ *n* [U] the natural colour of a person's skin which shows which race they belong to • *She felt she had not been given the job because of her colour.* • *There should be no discrimination on the grounds of colour.* • A **colour bar** (*Am also* **color line**) is a social and legal system in which people of different races are separated, esp. blacks and whites. • **Colour prejudice** is an unreasonable dislike of people who have a different skin colour which results in the unfair treatment of members of different races.

col·oured *Br and Aus, Am and Aus* **col·ored** /£ˈkʌl·əd, $-ɚd/ *adj* • *(dated)* If someone is described as coloured, they belong to a dark-skinned race. This word is considered offensive by many people: *Coloured* **people** *were not allowed to use the same facilities as whites.* • In South Africa, coloured refers to a person of mixed race: *In the recent elections, the National Party was given a lot of support from the coloured population.*

col·oured *Br and Aus, esp. Am* **col·ored** /£ˈkʌl·əd, $-ɚd/ *n* [C] • *(dated)* A coloured is a person who belongs to a dark-skinned race. This word is considered offensive by many people. • In South Africa, a coloured is a person of mixed race: *The majority of officers in the South African police force are now dark-skinned – about 49 000 blacks, 8 500 coloureds and 3 500 Indians, compared to 47 000 whites.*

col·ours *Br and Aus, Am and Aus* **col·ors** /£ˈkʌl·əz, $-ɚz/ *pl n* (at school, college or university) an honour given to people who have been chosen for a sports team, which is often represented by a special symbol on a shirt or tie • *She was awarded her colours* **for** *hockey/her hockey colours at the end of term.* • *He has gained his university colours* **for** *basketball.* • Colours are also the official flag of a country, ship or military group: *The military parade passed through the streets, with each regiment proudly displaying its regimental colours.* • If someone **shows** their **true colours** or you **see** someone **in** their **true colours**, you see their real character for the first time.

col·our·way /£ˈkʌl·ə·weɪ, $ˈ-ɚ-/ *n* [C] *Br* a combination of colours in which cloth or paper is printed

colt HORSE /£kəult, $koult/ *n* [C] a young male horse under the age of four • Compare FILLY.

colt·ish /£ˈkəul·tɪʃ, $ˈkoul-/ *adj* • If a person is coltish, they are young and energetic but rather awkward: *She was young and coltish while her older sister was graceful and self-assured.*

Colt GUN /£kəult, $koult/ *n* [C] *trademark* a small American gun

col·um·bine /£ˈkɒl·əm·baɪn, $ˈkɑː·ləm-/ *n* [C] a plant which has brightly-coloured flowers with five pointed petals that hang down

col·umn BUILDING /£ˈkɒl·əm, $ˈkɑː·ləm/ *n* [C] a tall vertical stone post which is used as a support for a roof or in CLASSICAL buildings for decoration, or which stands alone as a MONUMENT (= a structure built to honour and remember a person or event) • *The roof of the temple was held up by a row of thick stone columns.* • *Nelson's Column is a famous monument in Trafalgar Square in London.* • A column is also used to describe things which have a tall narrow shape: *A column of smoke rose from the chimney.* ○ *All vertebrates have a* **spinal** *column* (= a line of bones down the centre of the back). • A column of people or vehicles is a well-ordered line of them: *People hid inside their houses as columns of tanks rolled down the city streets.* • PIC Columns (PL)

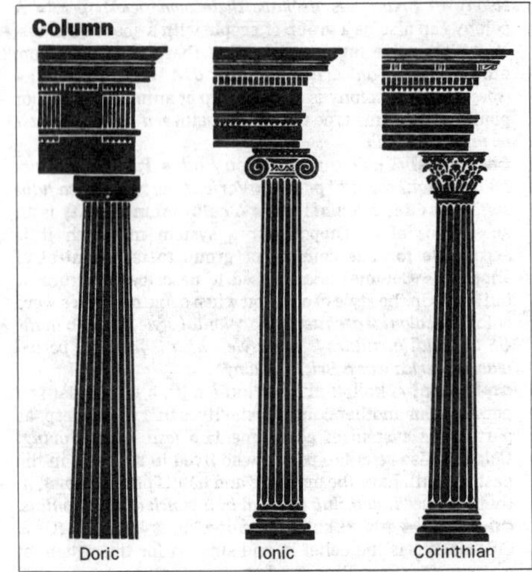

col·umn PRINTING /£ˈkɒl·əm, $ˈkɑː·ləm/ (*abbreviation* **col**) *n* [C] one of several vertical blocks of print into which a page of a newspaper or magazine is divided • *I didn't have time to read the whole article – just the first column.* • A column is also a piece of writing in a newspaper or magazine which is always written by the same person and which appears regularly, usually on a particular subject: *She writes a weekly* **fashion/gossip** *column for the Evening Standard.* • A column is also any vertical block of words or numbers: *Add the column of figures and divide the sum by three.* • PIC **Columns** (PL)

col·umn·ist /£ˈkɒl·əm·nɪst, $ˈkɑː·ləm-/ *n* [C] • A columnist is someone who writes a regular article for a newspaper or magazine: *She's a columnist for USA Today.*

com– /£kɒm-, $kɑːm-/ *combining form* See at CO-

co·ma /£ˈkəu·mə, $ˈkou-/ *n* [C] a state of unconsciousness from which a person cannot be woken, which is caused by damage to the brain after an accident or illness • *He has been in a coma for the past six weeks.* • *She* **went into** *a deep coma after taking an overdose of sleeping pills.*

co·ma·tose /£'kəʊ·mə·təʊs, $'koʊ·mə·toʊs/ *adj* • *(medical)* If someone is comatose, they are in a coma: *She arrived at the hospital in a critical condition and comatose.* • *(infml)* Comatose also means very sleepy or in a deep sleep because of extreme tiredness, hard work or too much alcohol: *He hadn't slept in over 36 hours and he was in a comatose state.*

comb /£kəʊm, $koʊm/ *n* [C] a flat piece of plastic, wood or metal with a thin row of long narrow parts along one side, which you use to tidy and arrange your hair • *Who's been using my comb?* • *(infml) Your hair looks as if it hasn't seen a comb for days* (=Your hair is very untidy). • A comb is also a small comb-shaped object which women put in their hair to hold their hair away from their face or for decoration. • Comb is also another word for COCKSCOMB. • PIC〉 **Comb**

Comb

comb *obj* /£kəʊm, $koʊm/ *v* [T] • If you comb your hair, you tidy it using a comb: *She combed her hair and put on some lipstick.* ○ *The knots in his hair were so bad that he couldn't comb them* **out** (=remove them using a comb). • If you comb a place or an area, you search it very carefully in order to find something: *The police combed the whole area* **for** *evidence.*

com·bat /£'kɒm·bæt, $'kɑːm-/ *n* fighting during a time of war • *a combat aircraft/jacket/zone* • *The new recruits were aged between 17 and 18 and had no experience of combat.* [U] • *There was fierce combat* **between** *the two sides.* [U] • *No one knew how many troops had died* **in** *combat.* [U] • *The soldiers were engaged in* **hand-to-hand** *combat.* [U] • **Armed** combat is fighting with weapons and **unarmed** combat is fighting without weapons. [U] • A combat is a fight between two people or things: *It was a bloody period in history with many combats fought and lives lost.* [C] ○ *The film explores the combat* **between** *good and evil.* [C]

com·bat *obj* /£kəm'bæt, $'kɑːm·bæt/ *v* [T] • To combat something unpleasant or harmful is to try to stop it happening or increasing: *to combat crime/terrorism/inflation/disease* ○ *The government is spending millions of dollars in its attempt to combat drug abuse.* ○ *(infml) I have to combat this constant desire to eat chocolate.*

com·bat·ant /£'kɒm·bə·tᵊnt, $'kɑːm·bə·t̬ᵊnt/ *n* [C] • A combatant is a person who fights in a war: *Hundreds of combatants and civilians were killed in the battle for control of the city.*

com·bat·ive /£'kɒm·bə·tɪv, $'kɑːm·bə·t̬ɪv/ *adj* • Someone who is combative is eager to fight or argue: *The prime minister was in a combative mood and made several verbal attacks on the opposition.*

comb·er /£'kəʊ·məʳ, $'koʊ·mɚ/ *n* [C] a long curling wave • *The beach was wide and flat, so there were no breakers or combers and children could swim there safely.*

com·bine /kəm'baɪn/ *v* to (cause to) exist together, or join together to make a single thing or group • *None of us has much money so let's combine what we've got.* [T] • *The two countries combined* **against** *their common enemy.* [I] • *They are normally harmless substances which combine* **to** *form a highly poisonous gas.* [+ *to* infinitive] • *Sickness,* **combined with** (=together with) *terrible weather, contrived to ruin the trip.* [T] • If someone combines two or more qualities, they possess both of those qualities: *As a writer, he combined wit* **and/with** *cynicism.* [T] • If you combine two activities, you do both at the same time: *She manages to successfully combine family life* **and/with** *a career.* [T] • A **combine harvester** is a large farming machine which cuts the plant, separates the seed from the stem and cleans the grain as it moves across a field. • *(specialized)* A **combining form** is a word or group of letters which is added to the beginning or end of words to change or add meaning: *The combining form 'Anglo', which means English, combines to make various words, including Anglo-American and Anglophile.* • LP〉 **Combining forms, Forms of words (spelling)** PIC〉 **Farming**

com·bine /£'kɒm·baɪn, $'kɑːm-/ *n* [C + sing/pl v] • A combine is a group of people or organizations acting together in business: *They have just established a newspaper combine.*

com·bi·na·tion /£ˌkɒm·bɪ'neɪ·ʃᵊn, $ˌkɑːm-/ *n* [C] • A combination is a mixture obtained when two or more things are combined: *Green is a combination of blue and yellow.* ○ *A combination of tiredness and boredom caused me to fall asleep in the middle of his lecture.* ○ *Her experience and energy are a* **winning** *combination* (=successful mixture) *in business.* • *(specialized)* A combination is also an arrangement in a different order: *From the letters X Y Z, we can get three combinations of two letters: XY, XZ, and YZ* • A combination is also a set of letters or numbers in a particular order which can be used to open some types of locks: *I've been trying to open the safe but I can't remember the combination.* ○ *I have a combination* **lock** *on my locker in the changing room.* • **In combination (with)** means together (with): *We'll be working in combination with another company on this project.* ○ *On their own they work well, but in combination they're a disaster.* • PIC〉 **Luggage** (KOR) (RUS)

com·bo /£'kɒm·bəʊ, $'kɑːm·boʊ/ *n* [C + sing/pl v] *pl* **combos** *infml* a small group of musicians who play dance and jazz music

com·bus·tion /kəm'bʌs·tʃᵊn/ *n* [U] the process of burning • *Air pollutants, such as sulphur dioxide and nitrogen dioxide, are derived mainly from the combustion of fuels in industrial plants and vehicle engines.* • *(specialized)* Combustion is also the chemical process in which substances mix with oxygen in the air to produce heat and light. • A **combustion chamber** is an enclosed space in which combustion happens: *Rockets work by burning fuel inside a combustion chamber.*

com·bust·i·ble /kəm'bʌs·tɪ·bl̩/ *adj fml* • Combustible means able to burn easily: *Wood and coal are both combustible substances.* ○ *The explosion failed to ignite the* **highly** *combustible material held in the storage tanks.* • If a person is combustible, they are easily annoyed or excited: *The government has been combustible since the attempted military coup last December.*

come MOVE TO SPEAKER /kʌm/ *v* [I] *past simple* **came** /keɪm/, *past part* **come** to move or travel towards the speaker or with the speaker • *I'm leaving now – are you coming or staying?* • *Get out of the road – a car's coming!* • *I'm giving a party. I hope you can come* (=be at it). • *(fig.) Christmas is coming* (=It will soon be Christmas). • *(fig.) Tell me when the violent bits of the film are coming* (=when they will soon appear) *and I'll shut my eyes.* • *She's come 500 km* (=has travelled this distance) *to be here with us tonight.* • *I'm going to the Picasso exhibition. Why don't you come* **along** (=with me). • *(fig.) You've come* **a long way** (=improved a lot) *since the early days.* • *Dad, come* **and** *see* (=move towards me in order to see) *what I've done.* • *If you're ever in Penge, come* **and** *visit us.* • *(dated) Come* **away**, *dear! It's dangerous!* • *Come* **back** *and visit us, won't you?* • *(fig.) It's all coming* **back to** *me* (=I've started to remember it all clearly)*!* • *(fig.) I can't think of her name but I'm sure it'll come* **back to** *me later.* • If a person comes **before** a court of law or a judge they are present while their legal case is dealt with. • *Did you come here* **by** *car?* • *If you're ever passing our house you should come* **by** (=enter and visit) *for a coffee.* • *I have to wear a belt or my trousers come* **down**. • *Our plane came* **down** (=landed or fell) *in a field.* • *The snow/rain came* **down** (=fell) *during the night.* • *(fig.) The whole weekend was so wonderful I haven't come* **down** (=started to feel ordinary again after the excitement) *yet.* • *(infml)* If a person comes **down** from a drug, esp. an

COMBINING FORMS

Combining forms are word beginnings or word endings which can be used to make grammatical forms, to give a particular meaning, or to change the part of speech of a word. In English, the most common combining forms are word endings.

• word endings used to make grammatical forms

For example, the past simple of many verbs is formed by adding the ending *-ed*, and the comparative of many adjectives is formed by adding *-er*. For more information LP on **Forms of words** at FORM.

• word endings used to add meanings or change the part of speech

Some word endings, often called suffixes, add or change meaning. For example the ending *-ism* is often used to form nouns which refer to beliefs or ways of behaving: *nationalism, pacifism, Buddhism.* Very often when a word ending is added in this way the part of speech of the word is changed. For example, the ending *-en* changes the adjective *black* into the verb *to blacken* (= cause something to become black). The following table gives the meaning(s) of important word endings and shows how they change the part of speech of the word. See the dictionary for more details.

FORMING VERBS

-EN ADJECTIVE → VERB to cause to have or increase the stated quality

fresh — freshen black — blacken thick — thicken fat — fatten

-IFY ADJECTIVE/NOUN → VERB to cause an increase in the stated quality; to become

simple — simplify pure — purify solid — solidify beauty — beautify

-IZE/-ISE ADJECTIVE → VERB to cause to become
(In British and Australian English these words are usually spelled -ise.)

central — centralize commercial — commercialize modern — modernize standard — standardize

FORMING NOUNS

-AGE VERB → NOUN the action described by the verb, or its result

break — breakage waste — wastage marry — marriage spill — spillage

-AL VERB → NOUN the action described by the verb

approve — approval bury — burial arrive — arrival remove — removal

-AN/-IAN/-EAN NOUN → NOUN a person who studies the stated subject, or who belongs to the stated place or group

history — historian Europe — European Paris — Parisian Mohammed — Mohammedan

-ANCE/-ENCE VERB → NOUN the action or series of actions described by the verb, or the state or quality described

perform — performance disappear — disappearance defy — defiance prefer — preference

ADJECTIVE ENDING -ANT/-ENT → NOUN

brilliant — brilliance distant — distance absent — absence silent — silence

-EE VERB → NOUN the person to whom the action of the verb is being done

employ — employee address — addressee interview — interviewee train — trainee

-ER/-OR VERB → NOUN the person or device that does the activity

(*person*) run — runner employ — employer act— actor collect collector
(*device*) cook — cooker time — timer generate — generator indicate — indicator

-FUL NOUN → NOUN the amount of something needed to fill the stated container or place

spoon — spoonful hand — handful house — houseful bag — bagful

-ION/-ATION / -ITION /-ISION VERB → NOUN the process or condition connected with the verb

educate — education tax — taxation add — addition collide — collision

-ISM ADJECTIVE/NOUN → NOUN social, political or religious beliefs or ways of behaving

modern — modernism consumer — consumerism military — militarism Buddha — Buddhism

-IST ADJECTIVE/NOUN → NOUN a person with a particular set of beliefs or way of behaving, or with knowledge of an area of study

extreme — extremist Marxism — Marxist economy — economist science — scientist

-ITY ADJECTIVE → NOUN the state or quality referred to by the adjective

sincere — sincerity generous — generosity fluid — fluidity acid — acidity

-MENT VERB → NOUN the action or process described by the verb, or its result

govern — government invest — investment develop — development
disappoint — disappointment

-NESS ADJECTIVE → NOUN the quality or condition described by the adjective

happy — happiness ill — illness dark — darkness clever — cleverness

FORMING ADJECTIVES

-ABLE/-IBLE VERB → ADJECTIVE used to add the meaning 'that can be' or 'worth being'

avoid — avoidable bend — bendable desire — desirable admire — admirable

-AL NOUN → ADJECTIVE connected with the stated thing

nation — national culture — cultural emotion — emotional nature — natural

-AN/-EAN / -IAN NOUN → ADJECTIVE connected with or belonging to the stated place, group or type

America — American Rome — Roman suburb — suburban Sagittarius — Sagittarian

-FUL VERB/NOUN → ADJECTIVE having the stated quality to a high degree, or causing it

power — powerful hope — hopeful fear — fearful delight — delightful

-ISH NOUN → ADJECTIVE connected with the stated country

Britain — British Poland — Polish

NOUN → ADJECTIVE (*disapproving*) being like the stated thing

baby — babyish fool — foolish

ADJECTIVE → ADJECTIVE used to add the meaning 'to some degree'

young — youngish red — reddish short — shortish new — newish

-LY NOUN → ADJECTIVE like the stated person or thing

father — fatherly coward — cowardly friend — friendly heaven — heavenly

FORMING ADVERBS

-LY ADJECTIVE → ADVERB in the stated way

loud — loudly happy — happily careful — carefully sudden — suddenly

NOUN → ADVERB/ADJECTIVE happening at the stated regular period of time. (Usually the *-ly* form can also be used as an adjective.)

hour — hourly year — yearly day — daily night — nightly

-WARD(S) PREPOSITION/NOUN → ADVERB towards the stated direction or place. (The *-ward* form can also be used as an adjective.)

down — downwards earth — earthwards home — homeward in — inward

WORD BEGINNINGS

Word beginnings, often called prefixes, are used less frequently than suffixes in English. They do not change the part of speech of the word. Examples of word beginnings include:

number and quantity

kilo-	one thousand	*a two* **kilo***watt heater*
micro-	very small	*a* **micro***organism*
multi-	having many	*a* **multi***-purpose tool*
semi-	partly or half	**semi***-permanent*

relationships

inter-	between or among	*to* **inter***connect*
intra-	within	*an* **intra***family dispute*
post-	after or later than	*a* **post***graduate degree*
pre-	before (a time or event)	*a* **pre***-lunch drink*

opposite and negative meanings (LP on **Opposite and negative meanings** at OPPOSITE)

anti-	against, preventing, or the opposite of	*an* **anti***-war speech*
dis-	not, or the opposite of	*to* **dis***agree*
in-	not, lacking, or the opposite of	**in***complete*
un-	not, lacking, or the opposite of	**un***happy*

OTHER COMBINING FORMS

In addition to suffixes and prefixes, there are other words which act as combining forms to change or add meaning. They are often joined to another word with a hyphen: *a cold*-**hearted** (= unkind) *person* • *It was a light*-**hearted** (= not serious) *discussion*. Other examples:

a Paris-**based** *company*	(= one that does its business from Paris)
*a tooth***brush**	(= a brush used to clean the teeth)
a gas-**filled** *balloon*	(= filled with gas)
chocolate-**flavoured**	(= having the flavour of chocolate)
the **mid***-afternoon*	(= the middle of the afternoon)
a child-**proof** *lock*	(= one that cannot be opened by a child)
*a tea***spoon**	(= a small spoon used to stir tea)
a rubber-**tipped** *pencil*	(= with an end made of rubber)

Combining forms are sometimes joined together to form new words. For example, *Francophile* (= a person who likes France) is formed from the two combining forms *Franco-* (= relating to France) and *-phile* (= someone who enjoys or likes a particular thing or place).

illegal one, they stop feeling its effects: *He likes the high he gets from that stuff, but he's miserable when he comes down* **(from** *it).* See also COMEDOWN. • *(fig.) Selling beefburgers for a living! He's come* **down in the world** (=fallen in rank or importance), *hasn't he?* See also COMEDOWN. • If you come **down** to a place such as a city you come south to visit it: *My boyfriend is coming down* **from** *Scotland this weekend.* ○ *They don't come down* **to** *London much.* • If prices come **down** they are reduced: *I'm waiting for house prices to come down before I buy.* ○ *Inflation is coming down* (=getting less). • *Are you coming* **for** *a coffee or staying here and working?* • *Your father will come* **for** (=to collect) *you at 4 o'clock.* • *Would you like to come* **for** *a walk* (=leave the place where we are in order to walk)*?* • *Come* **forward** *a bit and stand on the line.* • *Have you come straight* **from** *the airport or did you stop on the way?* • *(fig.) England came* **from behind** *to beat Scotland 2-1* (=they were losing 1-0, but in the end they won 2-1). • *Hi, come* **in** *– lovely to see you.* • *(fig.) Can I come* **in on** (=take part in) *your plans for the weekend?* • *The door opened and a nurse came* **into** *the room.* • *(fig.) That's when Peter came* **into** (=became involved with) *my life and all the fun went out of it.* • *(fig.) Love doesn't come* **into** (=is not a part of) *it – I'm marrying for money.* • *Come* **on in***! The water's great.* • *Come* **on over** *and have a drink with us.* • *Can Zoe come* **out** (=come with me) *to play?* • *(fig.) When the facts/information/truth came* **out** (=became known) *there was public outrage.* • *Some valuable finds came* **out of** *those experiments.* • *(fig.) After her death* **it** *came* **out that** (=became known that) *she'd lied about her age.* • People are said to come **out** when after a long period of secrecy they say publicly that they are homosexual: *He didn't come out until his final year at college.* • *Her son is coming* **over from** (=coming here after having been in) *America this summer.* • *Come* **(over) here** *a moment.* • *Are you coming* **round/over** (=to my home) *tonight?* • *(fig.) When you speak in public you mustn't let your nervousness come* **through** (=show). • *Come* **to** *sunny Bridlington for your holidays!* • *"Is he coming* **to** *the cinema tonight?" "No, he can't – he's going to his mother's."* • *If he wants my advice he's going to have to come* **to** *me!* • *The man's coming* **to** *mend the boiler this afternoon.* • *As he came* **towards** *me I could see he'd been crying.* • *A young girl came* **up to** *me* (=moved towards me and spoke) *and asked for money.* • *Are you coming* **with** *me or going with him?* • *Can I come skating too?* [+ v-ing] • *He came rushing over when I fell.* [+ v-ing] • *Don't come running to me* (=asking me to help you with your problems) *every time you're in trouble!* [+ v-ing] • *(fig.) Walking around her old school twenty years later, memories came* **rushing back** *to her.* [+ v-ing] • *(fml)* **It** *has recently come* **to my attention/notice** (=I have noticed) *that some of the younger boys are not using the toilets for the proper purpose!* • If someone or something **comes across** or **comes over**, they can be (easily) understood or seen: *His frustration really comes across/over in his poetry.* ○ *Don't let your politics come across/over in your interview.* ○ *She comes across/over really well* (=creates a positive image) *on television.* ○ *He comes across/over as a bit of a bore in interview.* • *(infml)* People sometimes say **Come again?** if they have not correctly heard or understood what has been said to them: *"Put these papers in the green files, those ones in the red files and any like this keep separate." "Come again?"* • If a person or animal **comes at** or **comes for** you, it attacks you: *This great savage dog came at/for me with its teeth bared.* ○ *He came at me* **with** *a knife.* • To **come forward** is to offer to give help: *No witnesses to the accident have come forward yet, despite the police's appeal.* ○ *If someone would like to come forward* **to** *help with the school trip we should be extremely grateful.* ○ *Nobody has yet come forward* **with** *any information relating to the girl's death.* • If someone **comes into** money, property or a title, they receive it as a result of the death of a relative: *She came into a fortune when her grandfather died.* • If you say that someone **has** something **coming**, you mean that they deserve it: *"He's been sacked!" "Well, he had* **it** *coming* **(to** *him). He was always staying away without permission."* • *(fig.) I don't know* **if/whether** *I'm* **coming or going** (=I'm in state of confusion)*!* • *(saying)* 'It will all come out in the wash' means that something which has until now been kept hidden will at some time become generally known. • *"Come up and see me* *some time (originally 'Why don't you come up, some time, and see me?')"* (Mae West in the film *She Done Him Wrong*, 1933) • *"Come into the garden, Maud"* (from the poem *Maud* by Alfred, Lord Tennyson, 1855)

com·ing /ˈkʌm·ɪŋ/ *adj* [before n] • *We look forward to greater success in the coming year* (= the year that follows from today). • *I'll be back* **this** *coming Friday.*

come MOVE TO LISTENER /kʌm/ *v* [I] *past simple* **came** /keɪm/, *past part* **come** to move or travel in the direction of the person being spoken to • *"Billy, get over here this minute!" "Coming, dad."* • *I thought I'd come* **and** *see your new house.* • *I'll come* **and** *pick you up in the car if you like.* • *I've come* **for** (= come to collect) *your census form.* • *We'll come* **round/over** (= to your house) *at six.* • *I've come* **to** *read the gas meter.*

come ARRIVE /kʌm/ *v* [I] *past simple* **came** /keɪm/, *past part* **come** to get to a particular place • *Has she come yet?* • *How often does the post come?* • *Spring has come early this year – look at all the flowers!* • *(infml) Come Monday morning* (= When Monday morning arrives) *you'll regret staying up all the night.* • *I'm afraid those days are gone and they'll never come* **again** (= return). • *You go now on your own and I'll come* **along** *later and join you.* • *(fig.) I see flared trousers have come* **back** (= are fashionable again). • *Hasn't his train come* **in** *yet?* • When news or information comes **in** it is received: *Reports are just coming in of a major oil spillage in the North Sea.* • Fashions and also some seasonal fruit and vegetables are said to come **in** when they have just arrived in the shops: *Asparagus is best when it's just come in.* • The sea comes **in** when the water reaches further up the beach or coast: *The tide comes in very quickly here.* • *We've got some money coming* **in** (= We're receiving some money) *now that Tim has a job.* • When clothes come **into fashion** they start to be popular. • When performers appear on stage or in a film, they are said to come **on**: *There was great applause when the Russian ballerina came on.* • *I think* **the time** *has come* **to** *do something about this problem.* • *Have the results from the blood test come (Br and Aus)* **through**/*(Am)* **in** (= arrived) *yet?* • *My visa still hasn't come* **through** (= I still haven't got it). • *I was really having trouble with that horse, and was very grateful when Jane came* **to** *my* **rescue** (= saved me). • *If you come* **up against** (= meet and suffer from) *any difficulties let me know and I'll help you.* • *The food didn't come* **up to** *my expectations* (= was not as good as I thought it would be). • *(infml) "How's your toothache?" "Oh, it* **comes and goes** (= sometimes it is present and sometimes it is absent)."

com·ings /ˈkʌm·ɪŋz/ *pl n* • People's movements to and from a particular place over a period of time can be called their **comings and goings**: *With so many comings and goings in this office I just can't seem to concentrate.*

come LEAVE /kʌm/ *v* [I always + adv/prep] *past simple* **came** /keɪm/, *past part* **come** to leave a place • *I had to come* **away from** *the party early.* • *Nightfall is when vampires come* **out**, *thirsty for human blood.* • *The police watched him come* **out of** *the house.* • *When is she coming* **out of** *prison?* • *(fig.) I didn't mean to be rude – it just came* **out** (= it just left my mouth) *that way.* • *(Br dated)* If you come **down (from** a college or university, esp. Oxford or Cambridge University), you leave either permanently or for a short time. • *(Br)* Workers are said to **come out** if they STRIKE (= refuse to work) because of a disagreement: *The postal workers have come out in support of their pay claim.*

come ORIGINATE /kʌm/ *v* [I always + adv/prep] *past simple* **came** /keɪm/, *past part* **come** to be or start from a particular place; to originate • *She comes* **from** *Italy.* • *What sort of background does he come* **from**? • *Some of the best wines come* **from** *France.* • *Does that quote come* **from** *Shakespeare?* • *She could hear banging coming* **from** *the room upstairs.* • *Where did the dog come* **from**? • *Where will the money for the project come* **from**? • *(fml) They will die, and return to the dust* **(from) whence** *they came.* • *A lot of good films/actors/writing came* **out of** *that period.*

come EXIST /kʌm/ *v* [always + adv/prep; not *be coming*] *past simple* **came** /keɪm/, *past part* **come** to exist or be obtainable • *The dress comes* **in** *three sizes – small, medium and large.* • *Do these trousers come* **in** *any other colour?* • *It comes* **in** *an enormous pink box with bows on the top.* • *Surprisingly, runners come* **in** *all shapes and sizes – fat and thin, short and tall.* • *This cuddly baby doll comes* **with** *her own blanket and bottle.* • *They're the best sunglasses you can buy, but they* **don't** *come* **cheap** (= they're expensive). • *He's* **as** *mean* **as they come** (= extremely mean). • *"How would you like your coffee?"* "**As it comes** (= Without anything extra, such as sugar), *please."* • *"I owe you a fiver, don't I?" "Yes, and* **come to that** (= in fact), *you never paid me back the other money I lent you."*

come HAPPEN /kʌm/ *v past simple* **came** /keɪm/, *past part* **come** to happen • *How exactly did you come* **to** *be naked in the first place?* [+ *to* infinitive] • *Christmas only comes* **(round)** *once a year.* [I] • *The office party is coming* **round** *soon.* [I] • *How did the problem/their partnership* **come about** (= happen) *in the first place?* • *(literary) It* **came to pass** (= It happened) *that their love for each other grew and grew.* • *(infml)* **How come** (= How did it happen that) *you missed the train?* • *What are your plans for the year* **to come** (= next year).

come ORDER /kʌm/ *v* [I always + adv/prep] *past simple* **came** /keɪm/, *past part* **come** to be in a particular relation to others in an order • *She (Br and Aus) came second/(Am) came* **in** *second in the 100 m race.* • *He (Br and Aus) came first/(Am) came* **in** *first in the list of the world's richest men.* • *Everyone expected him to do well in the competition but in the end he came nowhere* (= finished in a low position). • *Z comes* **after** *Y in the alphabet.* • *Which king came* **after** *Edward?* • *April comes* **before** *May.* • *I know the first verse of the song, but I don't know what comes* **next**. • In a list or a book, names or contents come **under** particular divisions: *In your recipe book you'll see that soups come under 'starters'.* • If something comes **under** (a particular part of) an official organization, it is controlled or dealt with by them: *Luckily, complaints don't come under our department.* ○ *Playground guidelines come under the Department of Health and Safety.* • *His job always came* **before** (= was more important than) *his wife.*

come CHANGE /kʌm/ *v past simple* **came** /keɪm/, *past part* **come** to change or develop so as to be in a different position or condition • *My boots are coming* **apart** *at the seams* (= the sewing is no longer holding them together). [I always + adv/prep] • *The wallpaper has started to come* **away from** (= it is no longer sticking to) *the wall.* [I always + adv/prep] • *Those pictures will have to come* **down** (= be removed from the wall). [I always + adv/prep] • *A wire has come* **loose** *at the back.* [L only + adj] • *He pulled the knob and it just came* **off** *(in his hand).* [I always + adv/prep] • *My lipstick came* **off** *on the collar of his white jumper.* [I always + adv/prep] • *Is the hood part of the jacket or does it come* **off**? [I always + adv/prep] • *How many times have you come* **off** *that horse?* [I always + adv/prep] • *Hold the horse's saddle or you'll come* **off**! [I always + adv/prep] • *After only two weeks the show came* **off** (= stopped being shown or performed). [I always + adv/prep] • *(esp. Br)* If you come **off** medicine or drugs you stop using them: *He's come off the tablets because they were making him dizzy.* [I always + adv/prep] • *When does the electricity/gas/heating come* **on** (= start working)? [I always + adv/prep] • If you've got an illness or a mood coming **on** it is starting gradually: *Avoid him! He's got one of his headaches/bad tempers coming on.* [I always + adv/prep] • *The door came* **open** *for no apparent reason.* [L only + adj] • *She punched him in the mouth and two of his teeth came* **out**. [I always + adv/prep] • *If you get red wine on that shirt it won't come* **out** (= be able to be removed by washing). [I always + adv/prep] • The colour in clothes is said to come **out** if after washing it loses brightness. [I always + adv/prep] • A book, magazine, stamp, etc. is said to come **out** when it is sold to the public for the first time: *When is her new novel coming out?* [I always + adv/prep] • When the sun, moon or stars come **out** they appear in the sky: *The clouds parted and the sun came out.* [I always + adv/prep] ○ *Which star comes out first at night?* [I always + adv/prep] • Flowers that come **out** open: *Tobacco plants come out in the evening.* [I always + adv/prep] • *Can you get this cork to come* **out of** *the bottle?* [I always + adv/prep] • *Don't worry – everything will come* **right** *in the end.* [L only + adj] • If you come **through** (something), you continue to live after an accident or dangerous situation: *It was a miracle that he came through that car crash.* [I always + adv/prep] ○ *(fig.) Marriage to an alcoholic actor hasn't been easy, but we've come through* (= managed despite a difficult situation). [I always + adv/prep] • *How did that phrase come* **to** *mean* (= develop so that it means) *that?* [+ *to* infinitive] • *It used to be a luxury item, but it's come* **to** *be common nowadays.* [+ *to* infinitive] • *I thought he was an idiot at first, but I've come* **to** *like him.* [+ *to* infinitive] • *It used to hold paper bags, but gradually came* **to** *be used for magazines.* [+ *to* infinitive] • If you come **under** something, you are suddenly caused to experience or suffer it: *Our armies have come under heavy bombardment.* [I always +

adv/ prep] ○ *There have been a lot of thefts, and the caretaker has come under suspicion.* [I always + adv/prep] ○ *The government are coming under pressure to change the law.* [I always + adv/prep] • *Your shoelaces have come* **undone**. [L only + adj] • If something comes **unstuck** it stops sticking and becomes separated: *He opened my letter and pretended it had come unstuck.* [L only + adj] • *(Br and Aus)* If plans or arrangements **come unstuck** they go wrong: *My plans to decorate the house came unstuck when I broke both arms and a leg.* • To **come clean** is to be honest about something secret, esp. something that has made you feel guilty for a period of time: *There's something I'd like to come clean* **about**, *Vicar.*

come [SEX] /kʌm/ *v* [I] *past simple* **came** /keɪm/, *past part* **come** *slang* to have an ORGASM

come /kʌm/ *n* [U] *slang* • Come is SEMEN (= the liquid containing sperm).

come [BE] /kʌm/ *v* [L only + n] *past simple* **came** /keɪm/, *past part* **come** *esp. disapproving* to behave in a way typical of (someone) • *He thinks that by coming* **the** *heavy father he can make them do what he wants.* • *Don't come* **the** *poor little innocent* **with** *me!* • *(dated slang)* If you tell someone not to **come it**, you mean that they should stop being rude or annoying: *Don't come it with me!*

come a·cross *obj v prep* [T no passive] to find (something or someone) by chance • *He came across some of his old love letters in his wife's drawer.* • *If you come across my glasses can you let me have them, please?*

come a·long *v adv* [I] to COME ON • *Come along – we don't want to be late!*

come be·tween *obj v prep* [T] to cause problems between or interrupt • *Don't let one little quarrel come between you!* • *Nothing comes between Jim and his exercise.*

come by *obj v prep* [T] to obtain (something), using effort, by chance or in a way that has not been explained • *A good boss is not so easy to come by.* • *We came by this wonderful little restaurant in a back street.* • *I'd like to know how she came by that black eye/her necklace.*

come down on *obj v adv prep* [T] to punish or blame (someone) for something • *They're coming down* **heavily** *on people* **for** *not paying their licence fees.* • *Do that once more and I'll come down on you* **like a ton of bricks** (= with great force)*!*

come down to *(obj) v adv prep* to have (a particular thing) as the main problem or matter • *What* **it all** *comes down to is your incredible insecurity.* [T] • **It all** *comes down to money in the end.* [T] • *Eventually our choice of hotel will come down to* (= be decided by) **how** *much we can afford.* [+ *wh*-word]

come in *v adv* to be useful for a particular purpose • *Don't throw it away – it might come in later.* [I] • *His money will come in* **handy** *when I want to travel.* [L only + adj] • *Keep it, it might come in* **useful**. [L only + adj]

come in for *obj v adv prep* [T no passive] to receive (blame or criticism) • *The director has come in for a lot of criticism over his handling of the affair.* • *I didn't realize I'd come in for so much abuse.*

come off [SUCCEED] *v adv* [I] *infml* to happen as planned or to succeed • *I thought the funeral came off really well.* • *The property deal was going to make a fortune but it didn't come off.* • *I tried telling a few jokes but they didn't come off* (= no one laughed).

come off [END UP] *v adv* [I always + adv/prep] to finish in a particular position after a fight, argument, etc., esp. compared to someone else • *The little dog actually came off better,* **with** *only a few scratches.* • *In the recent pay increases teachers came off worst.*

come off *obj* [STOP] *v prep* [T] **Come off it** *infml* used to express annoyance with someone who has said something that is obviously not true, or of which you do not approve • *"My dad's a millionaire." "Come off it! We all know that's not true."* • *Come off it, Pete – that's not really fair.*

come off *obj* [COMPLETE] *v adv* [T] *Am* to have completed (something), or to have healed (an injury) • *The company was coming off one of its best years ever.* • *Coming off a back injury, it wasn't clear if she could resume her role as the troupe's principal dancer.*

come on [HURRY], **come a·long** *v adv* [I] to move or act (more) quickly • *Come on/along – we're going to be late if you don't hurry!* • You can also say come on or come along to express annoyed lack of belief: *Oh, come on! You surely don't expect me to give up my bed for him?* • *"Come on (Originally C'mon) Everybody"* (title of a song by Eddie Cochran, 1959)

come on [ADVANCE], **come a·long** *v adv* [I] to advance or improve • *Your piano playing has really come on since I last heard you play.* • *How's your English coming on?* • *"How's your broken leg?" "Oh, it's coming on/along."*

come on *obj* [FIND] *v prep* [T] to COME UPON

come on [MAKE INTEREST KNOWN] *v adv* [I] *esp. Am infml* to make your sexual interest known to someone • *He's not very subtle – he comes on* **to** *women by saying, "I'd like to take a bath with you."* • *She was coming on* **strong** *and I just responded.*

come–on /£ ˈkʌm·ɒn, $-ɑːn/ *n* [C] *esp. Am infml* • *He was giving me the/a come-on.* • A come-on is also something which someone who is selling a product uses to interest a customer: *Offering cash back on a purchase is one of the oldest come-ons in the world.*

come out [GIVE OPINION] *v adv* [I always + adv/prep] to express an opinion • *In the survey politicians came out overwhelmingly* **in favour of** *capital punishment.* • *Some of the members supported the changes, but the majority came out* **against**.

come out [FINISH] *v adv* to be in a particular condition when finished • *However hard I try my cooking always comes out a mess.* [L] • *She came out* **of** *the divorce settlement a rich woman.* [L] • *These figures have come out wrong! I don't understand it.* [L] • *Your painting has come out really well.* [I always + adv/prep] • *He hasn't exactly come out* **of** *the scandal* **with** *his reputation enhanced.* [I always + adv/ prep]

come out [DEVELOP] *v adv* [I] (of a photograph) to produce a successful picture when processed • *My camera was broken and none of the skiing photographs came out.* • *He's in the picture but his face hasn't come out very clearly.*

come out in *obj v adv prep* [T] to get suddenly (a set of spots on the skin) • *This heat has made me come out in an itchy red rash.*

come out with *obj v adv prep* [T] to say (something) unexpectedly or suddenly • *You come out with some strange things/some good ideas/a lot of rubbish sometimes!* • *I asked one innocent question and he came out with all this abuse!*

come o·ver *(obj)* [BE INFLUENCED] *v adv* [L only + adj] *Br and Aus* to be influenced suddenly and unexpectedly by a strange feeling • *I stood up too quickly and came over* **all** *dizzy/faint/peculiar.*

come o·ver *obj* [INFLUENCE] *v prep* [T] to influence (someone) suddenly to behave in a particular way • *I'm sorry! That was a stupid thing to say – I don't know* **what** *came over me.* • *(humorous) He gave you a present!* **What's** *come over him?*

come round/a·round [CHANGE YOUR MIND] *v adv* [I] to change your opinion of something, often influenced by another person's opinion • *He'll come round* **to** *my point of view given a bit of time.* • *Do you still dislike your office, or have you come round* **to thinking** *it's all right?* • *I thought he was a complete idiot at first, but I've come round since then.*

come round/a·round [BECOME CONSCIOUS] *v adv* [I] to become conscious again after an accident or medical operation • *She hasn't come round* **from** *the anaesthetic yet.*

come to *obj* [REACH] *v prep* [T] to reach (a particular point) • *His hair comes right* **down** *to his shoulders.* • *He's tiny, he doesn't even come* **up** *to my chest!* • *That comes to* (= All the items together cost) *£25.* • *"And now I come to* (= I will mention) *my main point," said the speaker.* • *And now, to change the subject, I'd like to come* **on** *to the rather sensitive topic of personal hygiene.* • *We haven't come to* **a decision** (= made a decision) *on the matter yet.* • *The war had just come to* **an end** (= ended) *but for many who had fought, the suffering had just begun.* • *He won't come to any* **harm** (= be in any danger) *so long as Elaine is there.* • *The car spun off the road, turned over twice and came to* **rest** (= stopped moving) *in a field.* • *I've come to* **the conclusion** (= decided after some thought) **that** *you actually enjoy being ridiculed.* • *So much effort and planning and it's all* **come to nothing** (= ended in failure). • *Francine is slowly starting to* **come to terms with** (= learn to accept the fact of) *Pat's death.* • *"What will we do if you lose your job?" "Well,* **if it comes to that** (= if the worst happens) *we'll sell the house."* • **When it comes to** (= When the subject is) *modern jazz, very few people know more than Phil Schaap.*

come to [BECOME CONSCIOUS] *v adv* [I] to become conscious again after an accident or medical operation • *All I can remember when I came to is my mother's anxious face.*

come up [BE MENTIONED] *v adv* [I] to be mentioned or talked about in conversation • *What points came up at the meeting?*

come up HAPPEN *v adv* [I] to happen, usually unexpectedly • *I've got to go – something has just come up at home and I'm needed there.* • *Let me know if anything interesting comes up.*

come up with *obj v adv prep* [T] to suggest or think of (an idea or plan) • *She's come up with some brilliant scheme to double her income.*

come u·pon *obj*, **come on** *v prep* [T] to find or meet, esp. unexpectedly • *I came upon this book in the attic – would you like it?* • *I came upon a little man sitting beside the path.* [+ obj + v-*ing*]

come·back /ˈkʌm·bæk/ *n* [C] a successful attempt to get power, importance or fame again after a period of having lost it • *With ten extra years and ten extra kilos on him, the boxer failed to* **make a** *comeback.*

come·down /ˈkʌm·daʊn/ *n* [U] *infml* something that fails to be as good as you had hoped or expected; an ANTICLIMAX • *I was disappointed with the ending of the film – somehow it was* **such a** *comedown.* • A comedown is also a fall in rank or importance: *From a chauffeur-driven car to public transport – what a comedown!* • See also **come down** at COME MOVE TO SPEAKER.

com·e·dy /£ˈkɒm·ə·di, $ˈkɑː·mə-/ *n* a (type of) film, play or book which is intentionally amusing either in its characters or its action • *She's a director well known for serious films but her latest is a comedy.* [C] • *A lot of Shakespeare's plays are comedies.* [C] • Comedy is also the amusing part of a situation: *The vicar's forgetting his lines in the middle of the speech provided some good comedy.* [U] • A **comedy of manners** is a type of comedy in which the social behaviour of a particular group of people is made to appear foolish. • (NL)

co·med·i·an, *female also* **co·med·i·enne** /kəˈmiː·di·ən, -ˌmiː·diˈen/, **com·ic** *n* [C] • A comedian is a person whose job is to make people laugh by telling jokes and amusing stories or by copying the behaviour or speech of famous people: *a stand-up comedian* • Someone who is amusing and makes other people laugh can be called a comedian even if it is not their job: *Thanks for your comment, Guy, but right now I'm not interested in what the class comedian has to say.* • (E)

come·ly /ˈkʌm·li/ *adj* **-ier, -iest** *dated* (of a woman) attractive in appearance

co·mest·i·bles /kəˈmes·tɪ·bl̩z/ *pl n fml or humorous* anything which is to be eaten • *cheesy comestibles*

com·et /£ˈkɒm·ɪt, $ˈkɑː·mɪt/ *n* [C] an object that moves around the sun, usually at a great distance from it, that is seen only rarely from Earth and then as a bright line in the sky • *"When beggars die, there are no comets seen; / The heavens themselves blaze forth the death of princes"* (Shakespeare, Julius Caesar 2.2)

come–up·pance /kʌmˈʌp·ənts, kəˈmʌp-/ *n* [U] *infml humorous* a person's bad luck that is considered to be a fair and deserved punishment for something bad that they have done • *She'll* **get** *her come-uppance, don't worry.*

com·fort /£ˈkʌm·fət, $-fɚt/ *n* (something that provides) the pleasant and satisfying feeling of being physically or mentally free from pain and suffering • *She loosened her belt* **for** *comfort after such an enormous meal.* [U] • *He's a great comfort* **to** (= by his actions or just his presence he gives strength and hope to) *his mother.* [C] • *It's* **a/some** *comfort to his wife* (= it lessens the pain) *to know that he died instantly and didn't feel a thing.* [U] • *I've got to take an exam too* **if it's** *any comfort* (= if it makes you feel better to know that we share the same problem or bad luck). [U] • *He likes his* **(creature)** *comforts* (= the type of pleasures that are found in the house, for example good food, warmth and television). [C] • If you **take comfort from** something you feel less anxious because of it: *I know she goes out a lot at night but I take comfort from* **the fact that** *she's always with friends.* • **Comfort food** is the type of food which people tend to eat a lot of when they are not happy, for example chocolate. • *(Am)* A **comfort station** is a public toilet. • *(Aus)* A **comfort stop** is a pause in a long car or bus journey to allow passengers to go to a toilet.

com·fort *obj* /£ˈkʌm·fət, $-fɚt/ *v* [T] • *I tried to comfort him* (= make him feel better) *but it was no use.* • *It's a comforting* **thought** *that she'll be in our team.*

com·fort·ing·ly /£ˈkʌm·fə·tɪŋ·li, $-fɚ·t̬ɪŋ-/ *adv*

com·fort·less /£ˈkʌm·fət·ləs, $-fɚt-/ *adj fml*

com·fort·a·ble /£ˈkʌmp·fə·tə.bl̩, $-fɚ·t̬ə-/, *infml* **comf·y** *adj* producing a feeling of physical relaxation because of shape, softness, etc. • *This sofa is really comfortable.* • *Are you comfortable or shall I turn the heat down?* • *Since I've put on all this weight I don't feel comfortable in my clothes.* • *Do sit down and* **make** *yourself comfortable.* • Furniture and clothes might be described as comfortable if they provide a pleasant feeling and do not give you any physical problems: *a comfortable bed/chair/car/dress* • If an ill person in hospital is described by doctors as comfortable then their health is not in a dangerous condition. • Comfortable also means having enough money for a good standard of living: *They're not what you'd call fabulously rich but I think they're quite comfortable.* • In a competition, if you **have a** comfortable **lead over** the other competitors you are winning easily.

com·fort·a·bly /ˈkʌmf·tə·bli/ *adv* • If someone is comfortably **off** they are quite wealthy. • *"Are you sitting comfortably? Then I'll begin"* (Julia Lang introducing the children's stories of BBC radio's *Listen with Mother*, 1950-1982)

com·fort·er /£ˈkʌm·fə·tər, $-t̬ɚ/ *n* [C] *Am for* DUVET or QUILT

comf·y /kʌmp·fi/ *adj* **-ier, -iest** *infml for* COMFORTABLE • *a comfy chair*

com·ic MAGAZINE /£ˈkɒm·ɪk, $ˈkɑː·mɪk/, *Am also* **com·ic book** *n* [C] a magazine, esp. for children, which contains a set of stories told in pictures with a small amount of writing • A **comic strip** (also **cartoon strip** or **strip cartoon**) is a short series of amusing drawings with a small amount of writing which is usually published in a newspaper.

com·ic PERSON /£ˈkɒm·ɪk, $ˈkɑː·mɪk/ *n* [C] a **comedian**, see at COMEDY

com·ic AMUSING /£ˈkɒm·ɪk, $ˈkɑː·mɪk/ *adj* making you want to laugh; amusing • *a comic actor/performance/writer* • *Is it a comic or a tragic play?* • A **comic opera** is a play that is amusing and in which there is a lot of music and singing.

com·ic·al /£ˈkɒm·ɪ·kəl, $ˈkɑː·mɪ-/ *adj* • *Tell me the truth – do I look comical* (= strange or foolish) *in this hat?*

com·ic·al·ly /£ˈkɒm·ɪ·kli, $ˈkɑː·mɪ-/ *adv*

com·i·ty of na·tions /£ˈkɒm·ɪ·ti, $ˌkɑː·mə·t̬i/ *n* [U] *law* the friendship and respect between countries shown in their acceptance of each other's laws, political systems and customs

com·ma /£ˈkɒm·ə, $ˈkɑː·mə/ *n* [C] the mark (,) used in writing to separate parts of a sentence showing a slight pause, or to separate the various single items in a list • LP **Comma**

com·mand ORDER /£kəˈmɑːnd, $-ˈmænd/ *v, n* (to give someone) an order • *The officer commanded his men* **to** *shoot.* [T + obj + *to* infinitive] • *She commanded* **that** *the troops (should) cross the water.* [+ *that* clause] • *The trauma caused by what he experienced made him unable to command.* [I] • *Colonel Sailing commands* (= is in a military position of control over) *the Guards Regiment.* [T] • *Colonel Sailing has command* **over/is in** *command of the Guards Regiment.* [U] • If you command a high **salary/fee** you have the power to demand a lot of money for your work: *She commands one of the highest fees per film in Hollywood.* [T] • *You will run forwards* **at** (= when you hear) *my command.* [C] • *(humorous) "I can't reach my zip – could you unfasten it, please?" "I'm* **at** *your command* (= I will do what you ask)*!"* [U] • *(fig.) As a writer she has both style and humour* **at** *her command* (= she is able to use them effectively). [U] • *"When he* **gives** *the command, fire!" the officer screamed at his men.* [C] • *He hated being in the army because he had to* **obey** *commands.* [C] • *General Haig* **took** *command* **of** *the British Expeditionary Force in 1915.* [U] • *"They retreated?* **Under** *which officer's command?"* [U] • A Command is a group of soldiers or an area controlled by a commander: *Western Command* [C] • In computing, a command is an instruction to a computer to perform a particular action. [C] • If you are **in command (of** yourself or a situation) you are able to control what is happening: *Suntanned and relaxed, looking calmly about the room he appeared completely in command.* • A **command module** is the part of particular types of spacecraft in which the people live and in which they return to Earth. • A **command performance** of a play or film is a special performance which is given because a royal or very important person has requested it. • (RUS)

com·mand·ing /£kəˈmɑːn·dɪŋ, $-ˈmæn-/ *adj* • *a commanding officer* • A commanding **voice/manner/ appearance** is one that seems to have authority and therefore demands your attention.

com·mand KNOWLEDGE /£kəˈmɑːnd, $-ˈmænd/ *n* [U] a great knowledge of a subject and an ability to use that

COMMA [,]

Commas are used:

- **to separate words, phrases or clauses in lists** (before 'and' the comma is often left out)
  Two cokes, three glasses of tonic water and an apple juice, please.
  An absolutely beautiful, relaxing, totally rejuvenating experience.
  I might lose my home, be cut off from my family and end up with no friends.
- **before and after phrases or clauses which add extra or unneccesary information to a sentence**
  Henry, the laziest person in town, was jumping up and down.
  Old castles, which are often poorly insulated, have a special atmosphere about them.
- **to separate adverbial clauses of time** (*often introduced by when, after, before, by the time (that), directly, during the time (that), immediately, the moment (that), now (that), once, since, until/till, whenever*) **and long phrases that come before or in the middle of the main clause**
  After he got married, Andy changed completely.
  Now that it's spring, her mood has improved enormously.
  The book, once you're done with it, can be returned to any branch of the library.
- **to separate from the rest of the sentence words or phrases that suggest if something is likely or suggest other possibilities** (*on the contrary, on the other hand*), **adverbs that act as conjunctions** (*however, consequently*) **and words or phrases that introduce examples** (*namely, for example*)
  On the other hand, we will soon run out of time.
  Most of her friends, however, were rather keen on going swimming.
  He could ask his brother to give them a lift, of course.
  She took everything I had, namely, my watch and my wallet with all my money.
- **before a conjunction** (*and, but, for, or*) **connecting sentences or full clauses, and between very short clauses that are not connected by a conjunction**
  He hadn't worked very hard, but still did well in the exams.
  I came, I went home, I came back again.
- **sometimes in informal sentences when *that* is omitted**
  She runs so fast, no one can catch her.
- **to show that a word or words used earlier in the sentence have been left out**
  Indoor sports are preferred by some; outdoor sports, by many others.
- **to separate direct speech from words identifying the speaker and type of speech**
  "I can bear it no longer," he said.
  "But the options are few," his girlfriend replied anxiously.
  "Still," he continued cautiously, "I don't think I have any choice."
- **to separate the name of a person being addressed, or an interjection**
  You know, Martin, we're the only ones left. • *Damn, I wanted that antique chair.*
- **before phrases that add emphasis to questions**
  They live in Liverpool, don't they? • *I'll just go and get a newspaper, OK?*
- **to separate opposing and contrasting phrases**
  We like his style of writing, not its substance. • *This isn't made from synthetics, it's pure wool.*
- **to avoid confusion when two people's names appear next to each other**
  For Anne, Marie was the most important person in the world.
- **to add emphasis to a phrase at the end of a sentence**
  The higher you fly, the thinner the air.
- **in large numbers (a space can be used instead)**
  The population in 1990 was 8,566,000

A comma should not be used:

- **in *that* clauses**
  It's clear that he would leave a mess. • *That the headmaster is going to retire is only a rumour.* • *She said that "the right word was obscure."*
- **in indirect questions**
  We asked whether he would have the time.
- **in defining relative clauses**
  All those who had voted for him cheered.
- **in *-ing* constructions necessary for the meaning of the sentence**
  We noticed an ape climbing the tree to reach a banana.
- **before most dependent clauses and adverbials in end position**
  I've been a member since I was a student.
- **before 'and' when it is used as a conjunction between phrases**
  She walked out and called a taxi.
- **in decimal numbers like *4.67* (a point is used)**

knowledge • *a command of languages/computers/the sciences* • *She has an* **impressive** *command of the English language.* • (RUS)

com·mand *obj* DESERVE /£kə'mɑːnd, $-'mænd/ *v* [T] *fml* to earn by your character or your particular situation • *As a leader he's hopeless because he doesn't command any respect/admiration/support.* • *Television pictures of the starving millions commanded the nation's sympathy for at least half an hour.* • (RUS)

com·mand VIEW /£kə'mɑːnd, $-'mænd/ *v, n fml* (to give) a view • *The master bedroom commands a* **view** *of rolling green hills.* [T] • *This is a fine castle with its command of the surrounding countryside.* [U] • (RUS)

com·mand·ing /£kə'mɑːn·dɪŋ, $-'mæn-/ *adj* • *The house occupies a commanding* **position** *at the top of the valley.*

com·mand·ant /£'kɒm·ən·dɑːnt, $'kɑː·mən·dænt/ *n* [C] an officer who is in charge of a military organization or establishment such as a prison for soldiers used during war

com·mand·eer *obj* /£ˌkɒm·ən'dɪəʳ, $ˌkɑː·mən'dɪr/ *v* [T] to take possession of or control (private property) by force or for military use

com·mand·er /£kə'mɑːn·dəʳ, $-'mæn·dɚ/ *n* [C] an officer who is in charge of a military operation, or an officer of a particular rank in the British Royal Navy • A **commander-in-chief** (*abbreviation* **C-in-C**) is a commander in charge of all the armed forces of a country or of all the forces fighting in a particular area or operation.

Com·mand·ment /£kə'mɑːnd·mənt, $-'mænd-/ *n* [C] any of the ten very important rules of behaviour which are stated in the **Old Testament** (=first part) of the Bible • *In older churches you sometimes see* **the Ten** *Commandments written on the wall behind the altar.* • *(literary)* A commandment is an order.

com·mand·o /£kə'mɑːn·dəʊ, $-'mæn·doʊ/ *n* [C] *pl* **commandos** or **commandoes** (a member of) a small group of soldiers that are specially trained to make attacks on enemy areas which are particularly difficult to attack or dangerous

comme il faut /£ˌkɒm·ɪl'fəʊ, $ˌkɑː·mɪl'foʊ/ *adj* [after v; not gradable] *fml or humorous* behaving or dressing in the right way in public according to formal rules of social behaviour • *Trust me – it's not comme il faut to wear a pink tie to a funeral.*

com·mem·or·ate *obj* /kə'mem·ə·reɪt/ *v* [T] to remember officially and give respect to (a great person or event) esp. by a public ceremony or by making a statue or special building • *Gathered all together in this church, we commemorate those who lost their lives in the great war.* • *A statue has been built to commemorate the 100th anniversary of the poet's birthday.*

com·mem·or·a·tion /kəˌmem·ə'reɪ·ʃən/ *n* [U] • *A set of stamps has been commissioned* **in** *commemoration* **of** *Independence Day.*

com·mem·or·a·tive /£kə'mem·ər·ə·tɪv, $-ɚ·ə·t̬ɪv/ *adj* • *a commemorative statue/stamp/service/plaque*

com·mence *(obj)* /kə'ments/ *v fml* to begin (something) • *Shall we let the meeting commence, gentlemen?* [I] • *When you've finished your talking I shall commence!* [I] • *Unfortunately, he commenced* **speaking** *before all the guests had finished eating.* [+ v-ing]

com·mence·ment /kə'mentˑsmənt/ *n* [C] *fml* • *Would passengers please put out cigarettes before the commencement of the flight.* • *(Am)* A commencement is a ceremony at which students formally receive their degrees.

com·mend *obj* /kə'mend/ *v* [T] to formally praise (someone or something) • *The judge commended her* **for/on** *her bravery.* • *For a low-budget film it has much to commend it* (=it deserves praise). • *I commend* **to** *all of you his latest production.* • *It says on the back cover of the book '***highly** *commended'.*

com·mend·a·ble /kə'men·də·bl̩/ *adj* • *commendable efforts/behaviour/bravery*

com·mend·a·bly /kə'men·də·bli/ *adv*

com·mend·a·tion /£ˌkɒm·en'deɪ·ʃən, $ˌkɑː·mən-/ *n* • *Several of the firefighters received commendation* (=praise) **for** *their bravery.* [U] • A commendation is an honour such as a prize given to someone because they have done something admirable: *He was very proud when his daughter received a commendation* **for** *her achievement.* [C]

com·men·su·rate /£kə'mentˑsjər·ət, $-sjɚ-/ *adj fml* in a correct and suitable amount compared to something else • *The salary will be commensurate* **with** *age, experience and position.*

com·ment /£'kɒm·ent, $'kɑː·ment/ *v, n* (to express) an opinion • *I don't want any comments* **on/about** *my new haircut, thank you!* [C] • *I suppose his criticism was* **fair** *comment* (=a reasonable opinion). [U] • *She was asked about a pay increase for the factory workers but made* **no** *comment* (=did not give an opinion). [U] • *Asked about his relationship with his former secretary the boss replied* **"No** *comment."* [U] • *The official* **refused to/declined to** *comment (***on** *the matter).* [I] • Sometimes when people comment they are just saying what they have noticed: *He was just commenting* **that** *people were getting married later nowadays.* [+ *that* clause] • *"Comment is free but facts are sacred"* (C.P. Scott writing in *The Manchester Guardian*, 1926)

com·ment·a·ry /£'kɒm·ən·tri, $'kɑː·mən·ter-/ *n* a spoken description of an event on the radio or television that is broadcast as the event happens, or a set of written remarks on an event, book or person which explains its subject or expresses an opinion on it • *The commentary* **on** *the Olympic games was much better on the other channel.* [C] • *There's a good arts coverage in the newspaper but not much political commentary.* [U] • *I don't think literary commentaries offer much insight.* [C] • *(fig.) She never stops talking! She even gives you a* **running** (=continuous) *commentary on brushing her teeth.* [C] • A **commentary box** is a room or place for a radio or television reporter at a special event, esp. a sports competition, from which they report what is happening: *Let's return now to the commentary box to see what's happening in this exciting final.*

com·ment·at·or /£'kɒm·ən·teɪ·təʳ, $'kɑː·mən·teɪ·t̬ɚ/ *n* [C] a reporter for radio or television who provides a spoken description of and remarks on an event, esp. a sports competition, as it happens • *a radio commentator* • *a sports/football commentator*

com·ment·ate /£'kɒm·ən·teɪt, $'kɑː·mən-/ *v* [I] • *She commentates* **on** *the tennis each year at Wimbledon.*

com·merce /£'kɒm·ɜːs, $'kɑː·mɜːrs/ *n* [U] all the activities connected with business; trade • *the world of commerce and industry*

com·mer·cial /£kə'mɜː·ʃəl, $-'mɜːr-/ *adj* • *commercial law/art* • *a commercial organization/venture/success* • *The commercial future of the company looks very promising.* • *(disapproving)* A record, film, book, etc. might be described as commercial if it has been produced with the aim of making money and as a result lacks artistic value. • Television or radio that is commercial is paid for by the advertisements which are broadcast between and during the programmes: *There are more breaks in programmes on commercial TV.* • If a product is commercial it can be bought by or is intended to be bought by the general public.

com·mer·cial·ize *obj* /£kə'mɜː·ʃəl·aɪz, $-'mɜːr-/, *Br and Aus usually* **–ise** *v* [T] • *It's a pity Christmas has become so commercialized* (=involved with buying and selling).

com·mer·cial·iz·a·tion /£kəˌmɜː·ʃəl·aɪ'zeɪ·ʃən, $-ˌmɜːr-/, *Br and Aus usually* **–i·sa·tion** *n* [U] • *The commercialization of football has turned it from a sport into a business.*

com·mer·cial·i·sm /£kə'mɜː·ʃəl·ɪ·zəm, $-'mɜːr-/ *n* [U] • Commercialism is the principles and activity of commerce, esp. those connected with profit and not quality or morality.

com·mer·cial·ly /£kə'mɜː·ʃəl·i, $-'mɜːr-/ *adv* • *Does the market research show that the product will succeed commercially?* • *The drug won't be commercially* **available** (=able to be bought) *until it has been thoroughly tested.*

com·mer·cial /£kə'mɜː·ʃəl, $-'mɜːr-/ *n* [C] an advertisement which is broadcast on television or radio • *a commercial break*

com·mie /£'kɒm·i, $'kɑː·mi/ *n* [C], *adj* [not gradable] *dated disapproving slang for* COMMUNIST

com·mis·er·ate /kə'mɪz·ə·reɪt/ *v* [I] to express sympathy to someone about some bad luck • *I was just commiserating* **with** *Dan* **over** *the loss of his pet rabbit.*

com·mis·er·a·tion /kəˌmɪz·ə'reɪ·ʃən/ *n* [U] • *She gave me a look of commiseration as I entered the room.*

com·mis·er·a·tions /kəˌmɪz·ə'reɪ·ʃənz/ *pl n* • You might say 'commiserations' to someone if you want to express sympathy in a way that is not very serious: *Commiserations* **on** *losing the match!*

com·mis·sar /£'kɒm·ɪ·sɑːʳ, $'kɑː·mɪ·sɑːr, ˌ--'-/ *n* [C] (in the Soviet Union until 1946) the official title of the head of a government department, or an official responsible for political education, esp. in a military group

com·mis·sar·i·at /£ˌkɒm·ɪ'seə·ri·ət, $ˌkɑː·mə'ser-/ *n* [C + sing/pl v] a military department which supplies food and equipment

com·mis·sa·ry /£'kɒm·ɪ·sᵊr·i, $'kɑː·mə·ser-/ *n* [C] *Am* • A commissary is a shop which supplies food and goods, esp. to people in the army or in prison.

com·mis·sion [ARRANGEMENT] /kə'mɪʃ·ᵊn/ *v, n* (to formally choose someone to do) a special piece of work • *The newspaper commissioned a series of articles on the worst excesses of the fashion industry.* [T] • *She's just got a commission* **to** *paint Sir Ellis Pike's wife.* [C + *to* infinitive] • *Do you* **take** *commissions? I'm looking for an artist to paint my dog.* [C] • (RUS)

com·mis·sion [PAYMENT] /kə'mɪʃ·ᵊn/ *n* a (system of) payment to someone who sells goods which is directly related to the amount of goods sold • *Are you paid a regular wage or is it* **on/by** *commission only?* [U] • *She* **gets** *a 15% commission* **on** *every machine she sells.* [C] • (RUS)

com·mis·sion [GROUP] /kə'mɪʃ·ᵊn/ *n* [C] a group of people who have been formally chosen to discover information about a problem or examine the reasons why the problem exists • *a commission on alcohol abuse/racial tension/truancy* • *The government have set up/established/appointed a commission to investigate the problem of inner city violence.* • (RUS)

com·mis·sion [MILITARY] /kə'mɪʃ·ᵊn/ *v, n* (to receive) the official authority to be an officer in the armed forces • *She's got her commission at last and is now a lieutenant.* [C] • *Grandfather was commissioned* **as** *Group Captain in the RAF just before the war.* [T + obj + *as* n; usually passive] • If something, such as a machine or a military ship, is **in commission** it is working and ready for use, and if it is **out of commission** it is broken and not working. • A **commissioned officer** is an officer in the armed forces who has a commission. See also NCO. • (RUS)

com·mis·sion [CRIME] /kə'mɪʃ·ᵊn/ *n* [U] *fml or law* the act of committing a crime • *the commission of the crime/offence/murder* • (RUS)

com·mis·sion·aire /£kəˌmɪʃ·ᵊn'eəʳ, $-'er/ *n* [C] *esp. Br* a person wearing a uniform who stands at the entrance of a hotel, theatre, etc. whose job is to open the door for guests and generally be helpful to them when they arrive

com·mis·sion·er /£kə'mɪʃ·ᵊn·əʳ, $-ɚ/ *n* [C] an important official who has responsibility in a government department or another organization • *There is a commissioner in charge of the London police force.*

com·mit *obj* [CRIME] /kə'mɪt/ *v* [T] **-tt-** to do (something illegal or considered wrong) • *to commit a crime/a sin* • *to commit murder* • *Anyone caught committing an* **offence** *will be punished.* • If a person **commits suicide**, they kill themselves. • [LP> **Crimes and criminals, Law**

com·mit *(obj)* [PROMISE] /kə'mɪt/ *v* **-tt-** to promise or give (your loyalty or money) to a particular principle, person or plan of action • *I think I can come tonight but I won't commit my***self** *till I know for sure.* [T] • *If you want to be an actor you have to really commit your***self to** *it* (= spend all your time trying to fulfil this aim). [T] • *Lots of women complain that the problem with men is that they won't commit them***selves to** *a relationship.* [T] • *The government claimed to commit it***self to** *improving health care.* [T] • *(Am) The president said that once he had committed* **to** *this course of action there was no going back.* [I] • People might be said not to commit themselves if they refuse to express an opinion on a subject: *We don't want to commit our***selves** *to a financial plan until more details are known.* [T] ○ *I can't commit my***self** *on that subject until I've taken legal advice.* [T]

com·mit·ted /£kə'mɪt·ɪd, $-'mɪṭ-/ *adj* • *a committed socialist/Christian/teacher* • *We are committed* **to** *withdraw our troops by the end of the year.* [+ *to* infinitive] • *The party are committed* **to** *(the idea of) helping those who are not able to help themselves.*

com·mit·ment /kə'mɪt·mənt/ *n* • *commitment to left-wing politics/the cause of feminism/the company* • *She is known chiefly for her commitment* **to** *nuclear disarmament.* [U] • *I'd like to thank the staff for having shown such commitment.* [U] • *I don't want children – they're too much of a commitment.* [C] • *Try the product out in the comfort of your own home with absolutely no commitment* **to** *buy!* [U + *to* infinitive] • *I couldn't go to the meeting because I had other commitments* (= other things that had to be done). [C]

com·mit *obj* [SEND] /kə'mɪt/ *v* [T often passive] **-tt-** to send (someone) officially to prison or hospital • *He's been committed* **to** *prison for fraud.*

com·mit·tal /£kə'mɪt·ᵊl, $-'mɪṭ-/ *n* [U] • *The psychiatric team decided that committal* (= sending someone to hospital) *would not be beneficial in her case.*

com·mit *obj* [STORE] /kə'mɪt/ *v* [T] **-tt-** to put (words or ideas) into a particular state so that they can be used in the future • If you commit something **to memory** you make certain that you remember it: *Commit the names to memory then destroy the piece of paper.* • If you commit something **to paper** you write it down: *Perhaps we should commit these ideas to paper before we forget them.*

com·mit·tee /£kə'mɪt·i, $-'mɪṭ-/ *n* [C + sing/pl v] a small group of people chosen to represent a larger organization and either make decisions or gather information for it • *She* **sits on/is on** *the school's development committee.* • *The local council have just* **set up a** *committee to study recycling.* • *What's on the agenda at the next committee* **meeting**?

com·mode /£kə'məʊd, $-'moʊd/ *n* [C] a chair-shaped piece of movable furniture with a container in the seat which people who are ill or old can use as a toilet

com·mod·i·ous /£kə'məʊ·di·əs, $-'moʊ-/ *adj fml or literary* (of rooms or houses) having a lot of space

com·mod·i·ty /£kə'mɒd·ə·ti, $-'mɑː·də·ṭi/ *n* [C] a substance or product that can be traded, bought or sold • *The country's most valuable commodities include tin and diamonds.* • *Today's budget figures caused frantic trading on the international commodities market.* • A commodity is also a valuable quality: *If you're going into teaching, energy is a necessary commodity.* • (F) (P)

com·mo·dore /£'kɒm·ə·dɔːʳ, $'kɑː·mə·dɔːr/ *n* [C] an officer of high rank in the navy, or the person in charge of a sailing organization

com·mon [USUAL] /£'kɒm·ən, $'kɑː·mən/ *adj* **-er, -est** the same in a lot of places or for a lot of people • *It's very common to see daughters who dress just like their mothers.* • *The surname 'Smith' is very common in Britain.* • Common **decency/courtesy** is the basic level of politeness which you expect from a reasonable person. • *You didn't know that they were living together? But it's* **common knowledge** (= something everyone knows). • *How can anyone so privileged have any understanding of the* **common man** (= ordinary people)? • *(Br infml)* If something is described as **common-or-garden** it means it is ordinary and not unusual in any way: *It's a common-or-garden washing machine with just the basic functions but it works perfectly well.* • If someone has **the common touch** it means they are able to deal naturally with and understand ordinary people: *He would be more successful at election campaigning if he didn't lack the common touch.* • If something is done **for the common good** it is done to help everyone: *In the long term a reorganization would be for the common good.* • The **common cold** is a slight illness which a lot of people catch causing a cough, sore throat and blocked nose. • **Common law** in England and most of the US is the legal system which has developed over a period of time from old customs and court decisions rather than laws made in Parliament. A common-law **wife/husband** is someone who is not officially a wife or husband but is considered to be one because she or he has been living with their partner for a long time. • **Common sense** is the basic level of practical knowledge and wisdom that we all need to help us live in a reasonable and safe way: *Don't touch that light switch with wet hands! Use your common sense.* See also COMMONSENSICAL. (J)

com·mon·ly /£'kɒm·ən·li, $'kɑː·mən-/ *adv* • *Elbow injuries are commonly found among tennis players.*

com·mon [SHARED] /£'kɒm·ən, $'kɑː·mən/ *adj* [not gradable] belonging to or shared by two or more people • *We've got a lot of interests in common/common interests* (= We've have many of the same interests). • *Sadly, that large nose is common* **to** *all of the Lewis family.* • **Common ground** is a point on which two or more people or groups agree or understand each other, usually when they disagree about other matters: *We're not really* **on** *common ground when my father and I talk politics.* • *(fml)* If you **make common cause with** someone you act together to achieve something: *Parents with prams have made common cause with the disabled to get easier access to public buildings.* • *(specialized)* A **common denominator** is a number which can be divided exactly by all the

(=numbers under the line) in a group of FRACTIONS: 8 is a common denominator **of** ½ and ¼. • A **common denominator** is also something that is shared by all the members of a group and might bring them together: *Although the groups seem very different the common denominator is their commitment to using renewable sources of energy.* • *(dated)* The **Common Market** is another name for the **European Union** or the **European Community**, see at EUROPEAN. • *(specialized)* A **common noun** is a noun that is the name of a group of similar things such as 'table' or 'book' and not a single person, place or thing. Compare **proper noun** at PROPER [REAL]. • A **common room** (or *Am* **the commons**) is a room esp. in a school or college where students or teachers can sit together and talk when they are not working: *There is a* **senior** *common room and a* **junior** *common room at Nottingham City College, one for the staff and the other for the students.*

com·mon·al·i·ty /£ˌkɒm·əˈnæl·ə·ti, $ˌkɑː·məˈnæl·ə·t̬i/ *n* [C/U]

com·mon [LAND] /£ˈkɒm·ən, $ˈkɑː·mən/ *n* [C] an area of grassy land which everyone is allowed to use, usually near a village

com·mon [LOW CLASS] /£ˈkɒm·ən, $ˈkɑː·mən/ *adj* **-er, -est** *disapproving* lower class • *I've always thought wearing make-up at breakfast was a bit common.*

com·mon·ly /£ˈkɒm·ən·li, $ˈkɑː·mən-/ *adv* • *His father threatened to disown him if he continued behaving so commonly.*

com·mon·er /£ˈkɒm·ən·əʳ, $ˈkɑː·mən·ɚ/ *n* [C] • A commoner is a person who is not born into a position of high social rank: *The princess's children have no titles because their father is a commoner.*

com·mon·place [ORDINARY] /£ˈkɒm·ən·pleɪs, $ˈkɑː·mən-/ *adj* happening frequently or often seen or experienced and so not considered to be special • *Home computers are increasingly commonplace.*

com·mon·place [REMARK] /£ˈkɒm·ən·pleɪs, $ˈkɑː·mən-/ *n* [C] a boring remark which is used very often and does not have much meaning • *We exchanged commonplaces about the weather over countless cups of tea.*

Com·mons /£ˈkɒm·ənz, $ˈkɑː·mənz/ *n* [U + sing/pl v] **the Commons.** See **House of Commons** at HOUSE [POLITICS]

com·mon·sen·si·cal /£ˌkɒm·ənˈsen·sɪ·kᵊl, $ˌkɑː·mən-/ *adj* having or of a practical or reasonable way of thinking or acting • *Commonsensical or not, a decision to call a halt to the arms race will not be easy.* • *I think women are more commonsensical than men.* • See also **common sense** at COMMON [USUAL].

Com·mon·wealth (of Na·tions) /£ˈkɒm·ən·welθ, $ˈkɑː·mən-/ *n* [U] **the Commonwealth (of Nations)** an organization of independent countries which in the past belonged to the British Empire and now still have friendly and practical connections with each other

com·mon·wealth /£ˈkɒm·ən·welθ, $ˈkɑː·mən-/ *n* [C] a country or part of a country that is governed by its people or representatives elected by its the people

com·mo·tion /£kəˈməʊ·ʃᵊn, $-ˈmoʊ-/ *n* a sudden short period of noise, confusion or excited movement • *So much commotion over an actor arriving at a film festival!* [U] • *What a commotion! Can you see what's happening over there?* [C]

com·mun·al /£ˈkɒm·jʊ·nᵊl, £kəˈmjuː-, $ˈkɑː·mjə-/ *adj* belonging to or used by a group of people rather than one single person • *communal facilities/food/property* • *We each have a separate bedroom but share a communal kitchen.* • Communal also means based on racial or religious divisions within a larger social group: *Communal riots/disturbances have once again broken out between the two ethnic groups.* • If a society is communal it is one in which everyone lives and works together and the ownership of property and possessions is shared. • (DK) (S)

com·mun·al·ly /kəˈmjuː·nəl·i/ *adv*

com·mune [GROUP] /£ˈkɒm·juːn, $ˈkɑː·mjuːn/ *n* [C + sing/pl v] a group of families or single people who live and work together sharing possessions and responsibilities, or in some countries the smallest unit of local government • *She ran away from her job and her husband to* **join** *a women's commune.* • (DK) (F) (S)

com·mune [GET CLOSE] /£ˈkɒm·juːn, $ˈkɑː·mjuːn/ *v* [I] *literary* to get very close to someone or something by exchanging feelings or thoughts • *Lying naked in the grass, among the trees and birds, he felt he had communed* **with** *nature.* • (DK) (F) (S)

com·mun·ion /kəˈmjuː·ni·ən/ *n* [U] *literary* • *What he wants is a spiritual communion* **between** *East and West – to bring them to a closer understanding of each other.* • *They wanted no communion* **with** *America – the place or its people.* • *It was her deep communion* **with** *the Sussex countryside and its history that was her true inspiration.* • *He lived* **in** *close communion* **with** *nature/God.* • A communion is a group of people who are united by the same esp. religious beliefs: *The author has a vision of an emerging worldwide Christian communion.* [+ sing/pl v] • *(specialized)* The **communion of saints** is all the people who are part of the Christian church. • Communion is another word for **Holy Communion**. See at HOLY [GOOD].

com·mu·ni·cant /kəˈmjuː·nɪ·kənt/ *n* [C] a person who is involved in **Holy Communion** (=a Christian religious ceremony), and is therefore considered to be an active member of a church • See **Holy Communion** at HOLY [GOOD].

com·mu·ni·cate *(obj)* /kəˈmjuː·nɪ·keɪt/ *v* to give successfully (thoughts, feelings, ideas or information) to others through speech, writing, bodily movements or signals • *I prefer to communicate the results* **by/through/in** *writing rather than by giving them over the telephone.* [T] • *Unable to speak a word of the language, he communicated* **with** (=using) *his hands.* [I] • *As an actor he could communicate a whole range of emotions.* [T] • If two people communicate (**with** each other) they are able to understand each other and have a satisfactory relationship: *I'm afraid we just don't communicate.* [I] • *(specialized)* Diseases are sometimes said to be communicated if they are given by one person to another. [T] • *(fml)* Rooms communicate when they connect with each other through a door: *The bedroom communicates* **with** *both toilet and hall.* [I]

com·mu·ni·ca·ble /kəˈmjuː·nɪ·kə·bl̩/ *adj fml* • Communicable means able to be given from one person to another: *Ideas, emotions or thoughts have to be presented in ways which make them communicable, whether in words, music, graphics, or art forms.* ○ *(specialized) In this period, there were 974 outbreaks of communicable* **disease** *attributed to the consumption of raw milk.*

com·mu·ni·ca·tion /kəˌmjuː·nɪˈkeɪ·ʃᵊn/ *n* • *Television is an increasingly important* **means of** *communication.* [U] • *With an hour's walk to the nearest telephone, communication is not so easy.* [U] • *There's very little communication* **between** *mother and daughter* (=they do not have a good relationship). [U] • *(fml)* A communication is a message or a letter: *We received your communication of 11th March and are sorry to inform you that we won't be attending the conference.* [C] • *(Br)* A **communication cord** (*Am and Aus* **emergency cord**) is a chain in a train carriage which a passenger can pull to stop the train if he/she is in trouble. • (CS) (PL) (RUS)

com·mu·ni·ca·tions /kəˌmjuː·nɪˈkeɪ·ʃᵊnz/ *pl n* • Communications are the various methods of sending information between people and places, esp. official systems such as post systems, radio, telephone, etc.: *Less than 2% of all overseas aid is going to improve communications.* ○ *The emergency communications network was included in the review of emergency planning.* ○ *It is clear from the report that we must invest in more and better communications systems for the company.* • Communications are also the ways which people use to form relationships with each other and understand each other's feelings: *Communications between parents and children are often difficult.* ○ *A* **breakdown in** *communications between staff and the prison governor led to the present unhappy situation.* • Communications are also ways of moving between one place and another: *Its commercial success as a city is partly due to its excellent rail and road communications.* • A **communications satellite** is an artificial object in space used to send out television, radio and telephone signals around the earth's surface.

com·mu·ni·cat·or /£kəˈmjuː·nɪ·keɪ·təʳ, $-t̬ɚ/ *n* [C] • *He is not a natural communicator – he can be shy and remote to all but his closest friends.* • *One of her great merits as a communicator and teacher is the way she shares her own enthusiasm for the subject.*

com·mu·ni·cat·ive /£kəˈmjuː·nɪ·kə·tɪv, $-t̬ɪv/ *adj* • *He wasn't exactly communicative* (=willing to talk) *last night – in fact he only spoke two words to me.* • *The communicative ability of the whale is thought to be highly developed.*

com·mu·ni·qué /kə'mjuː·nɪ·keɪ/ *n* [C] an official piece of news or an announcement esp. to the public or newspapers • *The palace have* **issued** *a communiqué denying the rumour.*

com·mun·i·sm /£'kɒm·jʊ·nɪ·zᵊm, $'kɑː·mjə-/ *n* [U] the belief in a classless society in which the methods of production are owned and controlled by all its members and everyone works as much as they can and receives what they need • Compare CAPITALISM; SOCIALISM.

com·mun·ist /£'kɒm·jʊ·nɪst, $'kɑː·mjə-/, *dated disapproving slang* **com·mie** *adj* [not gradable], *n* • *the Communist party* • *a communist government* • *communist ideology* • *Was she ever a Communist?* [C] • *"Are you now, or have you ever been, a member of the Communist Party?"* (question asked by the House of Representatives Committee on Un-American Activities, 1950s)

com·mu·ni·ty /£kə'mjuː·nə·ti, $-t̬i/ *n* the people living in one particular area or people who are considered as a unit because of their common interests, background or nationality • *He's well-known in the* **local** *community.* [C] • *There's a large* **black/white/Jewish** *community living in this area.* [C] • *Her speech caused outrage among the* **gay** *community.* [C] • *Drug trafficking is a matter of considerable concern for the entire* **international** *community* (= all the countries of the world). [C] • *There's a real* **sense of** *community* (= caring and friendly feeling) *in this neighbourhood.* [U] • **The community** is sometimes used to mean the general public: *Unlike the present government, we believe in* **serving** *the community.* • *(specialized)* A community is a group of animals or plants that live or grow together. [C] • A **community centre** is a place where people who live in an area can meet each other and play sports, take courses, etc. • *(Am)* A **community chest** is an amount of money which has been given and collected by the people of a particular area to help people who are old or ill and in need of help. • **Community service** is work that people do to help other people without payment, and which young criminals whose crime was not serious enough for them to be put in prison are sometimes ordered to do. • **Community spirit** is friendliness and understanding between local people: *The presence of so many outsiders has ruined the community spirit.*

com·mute [TRAVEL] /kə'mjuːt/ *v* [I] to travel regularly a distance between work and home • *It's exhausting commuting* **from** *Brighton* **to** *London (***between** *Brighton* **and** *London) every day.*

com·mute /kə'mjuːt/ *n* [C] *infml* • *It's an hour's commute to work.*

com·mut·er /£kə'mjuː·təʳ, $-t̬ɚ/ *n* [C] • *The train was packed with sweaty complaining commuters.* • A **commuter train** is a train service especially for people travelling between home and work.

com·mut·a·ble /£kə'mjuː·tə·bl̩, $-t̬ə-/ *adj* • *The journey is too long to be commutable.*

com·mu·ta·tion /£ˌkɒm·jʊ'teɪ·ʃᵊn, $ˌkɑː·mjə-/ *n* [U] • **Commutation ticket** is *Am for* **season ticket** used in rail travel. See at SEASON [PART OF YEAR].

com·mute *obj* [CHANGE] /kə'mjuːt/ *v* [T] *fml* to change (one thing into another) • *People used to believe that you could commute base metals* **into** *gold.* • *(specialized)* To commute is also to exchange one type of payment for a different type: *I think I'll commute my life insurance* **into** *an annuity.* • *(law)* To commute a punishment is to change it to one that is less severe: *Her sentence was commuted* **from** *death* **to** *life imprisonment.*

com·mu·ta·tion /£ˌkɒm·jʊ'teɪ·ʃᵊn, $ˌkɑː·mjə-/ *n* [U]

com·mu·ta·tor /£'kɒm·jʊ·teɪ·təʳ, $'kɑː·mjə·teɪ·t̬ɚ/ *n* [C] *specialized* • A commutator is a device used in some types of electric motors to change the direction in which an electric current is flowing.

com·pact [CLOSE TOGETHER] /kəm'pækt/ *adj* consisting of parts that are positioned closely or tidily together, using very little space • *compact soil/sand* • *a compact camera/bag/body* • *What a compact office! How did you fit so much into so little space?* • A **compact disc** is a CD. • Ⓙ

com·pact *obj* /kəm'pækt/ *v* [T] *fml or specialized* • To compact is to press something tightly and solidly together: *Cars had compacted the snow until it was like ice.*

com·pactly /kəm'pækt·li/ *adv* • *He packed all his camping equipment compactly into one backpack.*

com·pact·ness /kəm'pækt·nəs/ *n* [U]

com·pact [CASE] /£'kɒm·pækt, $'kɑːm-/ *n* [C] a small flat case which contains women's face powder • *a powder compact* • [PIC]› **Cosmetics** Ⓙ

com·pact [CAR] /£'kɒm·pækt, $'kɑːm-/ *n* [C] *Am and Aus* a small car • Ⓙ

com·pact [AGREEMENT] /£'kɒm·pækt, $'kɑːm-/ *n* [C] *fml* a formal agreement between two or more people, organizations or countries • *They made a compact not* **to** *reveal any details.* [+ *to* infinitive] • Ⓙ

com·pan·ion [PERSON] /kəm'pæn·jən/ *n* [C] a person you spend a lot of time with either because you are friends or because you are travelling together • *The dog has been her* **constant/close** *companion these past ten years.* • *As a* **travelling** *companion he was terrible – unadventurous, always complaining and dirty.* • In the past a companion was a young woman, who was paid to care for and provide friendship for an old or ill woman especially while she was travelling. • Ⓘ Ⓙ Ⓢ

com·pan·ion·a·ble /kəm'pæn·jən·ə·bl̩/ *adj* • *He's a nice companionable sort of a person* (= He's friendly and pleasant to be with).

com·pan·ion·ship /kəm'pæn·jən·ʃɪp/ *n* [U] • *I lived on my own for a while but I missed the companionship of* (= enjoyment of being with) *others.*

com·pan·ion [OBJECT] /kəm'pæn·jən/ *n* [C] *dated* either of two matching objects • *I've still got one of the candlesticks but I've lost its companion.* • Ⓘ Ⓙ Ⓢ

com·pan·ion [BOOK] /kəm'pæn·jən/ *n* [C] used in the title of the type of book which gives you information on a particular subject or tells you how to do something • *the Music Lover's Companion* • Ⓘ Ⓙ Ⓢ

com·pan·ion·way /kəm'pæn·jən·weɪ/ *n* [C] the steps which lead from one DECK (= level) of a ship to another

com·pa·ny [BUSINESS] /'kʌm·pə·ni/ *n* [C] an organization which sells goods or services in order to make money • *He works for a pet food company/a company that makes pet food.* • *She gets a* **company car** (= a car provided by her employer) *with the job.* • *(esp. disapproving)* A **company man** is a man who puts his company before everything else and does what they want without question. • *No smoking is* **company policy** (= a plan of action chosen by the company). • *(Am and Aus)* A **company town** is a city or town in which most of the workers are employed by a single organization: *Flint had been a company town until the company moved the job overseas.* • *I work for Duggan and Company (abbreviation* **Co***).* • [LP]› **Letters, Work**

com·pa·ny [OTHER PEOPLE] /'kʌm·pə·ni/ *n* [U] (the presence of) a person or a group of people with you • *It was a long journey and I was grateful for his company.* • *It's good he enjoys his* **own** *company* (= he likes being alone) *because he has a very lonely job.* • *I travelled* **in the** *company* **of** (= with) *two teachers as far as Istanbul.* • *Darling, I'd rather you didn't mention my little problem when we're* **in** *company* (= with other people). • *You'll like Rosie – she's* **good/interesting** *company* (= enjoyable to be with). • *He's* **poor/dull** *company* (= not enjoyable to be with) *– he doesn't say much.* • *Everyone here is so badly dressed,* **present** *company* **excepted** (= I'm not criticizing the people I am with). • Company is also used to refer to a person or animal who is present for friendship or to prevent someone feeling alone: *Margot came to stay for a week as company* **for** *my mother while I was away.* • If you do something **for** company, you do it to be with or to have the feeling that you are with other people: *I usually have the radio on* **for** *company.* ○ *When her children left home Eleanor bought two dogs* **for** *company.* • *I'll* **keep** *you company* (= stay with you so that you are not alone) *till the train comes.* • *When I'm alone, I have the TV on* **to keep** *me company* (= so that I don't feel alone). • *Where did you pick up words like that? Is it the company you're* **keeping** (= the influence of the people you spend time with)? • *He's been* **keeping bad** *company* (= spending time with unsuitable people). • *(humorous) "I can't play tennis – I'm hopeless at it!" "Oh well, you're* **in good company** (= we share the same problem)." • *(literary)* **With only** *her* **thoughts for** *company* (= Being alone), *she walked slowly along the seafront.* • See also ACCOMPANY.

com·pa·ny [THEATRICAL GROUP] /'kʌm·pə·ni/ *n* [C] a group of actors, singers or dancers who perform together • *She's in the Royal National Theatre Company.* • *I'd like to thank the director, the choreographer and the other members of the company for being so supportive.*

com·pa·ny [GROUP] /'kʌm·pə·ni/ *n* [C] a large group of soldiers. esp. a division of a BATTALION • A company is also an organized group of young women who are GUIDES: *My cousin and I joined the same Guide company.*

com·par·a·tive /£kəm'pær·ə·tɪv, $-'per·ə·t̬ɪv/ *n* [C] the form of an adjective or adverb that expresses a difference in amount, in number, in degree or quality • *'Fatter' is the comparative* **of** *'fat'.* • *'More difficult' is the comparative* **of** *'difficult'.* • See also **comparative** at COMPARE [EXAMINE DIFFERENCES]. • [LP]› **Comparing and grading**

com·par·a·tive /£kəm'pær·ə·tɪv, $-'per·ə·t̬ɪv/ *adj* [not gradable] • *The comparative form of 'slow' is 'slower'.* • *The comparative form of 'frightened' is 'more frightened'.*

com·pare *obj* [EXAMINE DIFFERENCES] /£kəm'peəʳ, $-per/ *v* [T] to examine or look for the difference between (two or more things) • *If you compare house prices in the two areas it's quite amazing how different they are.* • *That seems expensive – have you compared* **prices** *in other shops?* • *Compare some recent work* **with** *your older stuff and you'll see how much you've improved.* • *This road is quite busy compared* **to/with** *ours.* • *Children seem to learn more interesting things compared* **to/with** *when we were at school.* • To **compare notes** is to exchange information and opinions informally: *As we were getting ready to go out, Becky and I compared notes* **on** *clothes, music, teachers and men.* • Both *compared to* and *compared with* are widely used, although some speakers of British English do not consider *compared to* acceptable.

com·par·a·tive /£kəm'pær·ə·tɪv, $-'per·ə·tɪv/ *adj* • *She's carrying out a comparative study of health in inner cities and rural areas.* • *There's a comparative rise this year in the number of babies born* (=judged by how many were born in previous years). • See also COMPARATIVE.

com·par·a·tive·ly /£kəm'pær·ə·tɪv·li, $-'per·ə·t̬ɪv-/ *adv* • *We're comparatively well-off* (=we are richer than most other people). • *Comparatively* **speaking**, *this computer is easy to use* (=it is easier to use than most other computers).

com·par·i·son /£kəm'pær·ɪ·sᵊn, $-'per-/ *n* • *They* **made a** *comparison of different countries' eating habits/ lifestyles/standards of living* (=showed how they were different). [C] • *We kept a copy of an earlier letter* **for** (=in order to make a) *comparison.* [U] • **By/In** *comparison* **with** *the French, the British eat far less fish.* [U]

com·pare *(obj)* [CONSIDER SIMILARITIES] /£kəm'peəʳ, $-per/ *v* to judge, suggest or consider that (something) is similar or of equal quality (to something else) • *The poet compares his lover's tongue* **to** *a razor blade.* [T] • *Still only twenty-five, she has been compared* **to** *the greatest dancer of all time.* [T] • *People have compared me* **to** *Elizabeth Taylor.* [T] • *You can't compare the two cities – they're totally different.* [T] • *Instant coffee doesn't compare* **with**/*can't be compared* **with** *freshly ground coffee* (=fresh coffee is much better). [I/T] • If some thing compares **favourably** with something else it is better than it: *The hotel compared favourably* **with** *the one we stayed in last year.* [I] • *"Shall I compare thee to a summer's day? / Thou art more lovely and more temperate"* (Shakespeare, Sonnet 18)

com·pare /£kəm'peəʳ, $-per/ *n* [U] • *(literary)* If someone or something is **beyond compare** they are so good that everyone or everything else is of lesser quality.

com·par·a·ble /£'kɒm·pᵊr·ə·bl̩, $'kɑːm·pɚ-/ *adj* • *The girls are of comparable* (=similar) *ages.* • *It was a pleasant beach resort but it wasn't comparable* **with** (=as good as) *the one we stayed at in the Bahamas.* • *The two experiences aren't comparable* (=they have no similarities).

com·par·i·son /£kəm'pær·ɪ·sᵊn, $-'per-/ *n* • *She* **drew a** *comparison* **between** *life in the army and life in prison* (=showed how they were similar in some ways). [C] • *To my mind* **there's no** *comparison between the two restaurants* (=one is much better than the other). [U] • *He's a good writer but he doesn't* **bear/stand** *comparison* **with** *Shakespeare* (=he is not as good as Shakespeare). [U]

com·part·ment /£kəm'pɑːt·mənt, $-'pɑːrt-/ *n* [C] any of the enclosed parts into which a vehicle, a space or an object used for storing things is divided • *a first class compartment (in a train)* • *the sleeping/inner compartment (in a tent)* • *a freezer compartment (in a fridge)* • Ⓟ

com·part·ment·al·ize *obj, Br and Aus usually* **-ise** /£ˌkɒm·pɑːt'men·tᵊl·aɪz, $ˌkɑːm.pɑːrt'men·t̬ᵊl-/ *v* [T] • *His life was carefully compartmentalized* (=divided into separate parts), *with his work in one city and his social life in another.*

com·pass [DEVICE] /'kʌm·pəs/ *n* [C] a device for finding direction which has a freely moving needle which always points to magnetic north • A **compass point** is any of the 32 marks on the compass that show direction. • *They took a* **compass reading** (=looked at the compass to find out where they were). • [LP]› **Directions**

com·pass [LIMIT] /'kʌm·pəs/ *n* [U] *fml or literary* a particular range (of ability, activity, interest, etc.) • *It's a musical instrument made of brass, somewhat like a cornet and with a similar compass.* • *The discussion was* **beyond** *the compass of my brain.* • *In this paper an attempt has been made to explore the compass of contemporary spirituality.*

com·pas·ses /'kʌm·pə·sɪz/ *pl n* [C] a V-shaped device which is used for drawing circles or measuring distances on maps • *He picked up the compasses/***pair of** *compasses.* • [LP]› **Mathematics**

com·pas·sion /kəm'pæʃ·ᵊn/ *n* [U] *approving* a strong feeling of sympathy and sadness for the suffering or bad luck of others and a desire to help them • *"I understand how difficult it must be for you," she said* **with** *compassion.* • *The government hasn't* **shown** *much compassion* **for/ towards** *the sufferers.* • **Compassion fatigue** is unwillingness to give money or care for people in difficulties, as a result of too much discussion of the problem in the media.

com·pas·sion·ate /kəm'pæʃ·ᵊn·ət/ *adj approving* • *The public's response to the crisis appeal was generous and compassionate.* • **Compassionate leave** is a short time spent away from work for personal reasons, such as the death of a close member of your family.

com·pas·sion·ate·ly /kəm'pæʃ·ᵊn·ət·li/ *adv approving* • *He listened compassionately to the account of his brother's accident.*

com·pat·i·ble /£kəm'pæt·ɪ·bl̩, $-'pæt̬-/ *adj* able to exist, live together, or work successfully with (something or someone else) • *Make sure you're compatible* **(with** *him) before you start sharing a house.* • *The computer program isn't compatible* **with** *this operating system.* • *The new laws don't seem compatible* **with** *the government's whole policy on education.* • *Are their two blood groups compatible* (=can blood from one person be given to the other person)? • Compatible also means well matched with: *The curtains aren't compatible* **with** *the carpet* (=they do not look attractive together).

com·pat·i·bil·i·ty /£kəmˌpæt·ə'bɪl·ɪ·ti, $-ˌpæt̬·ə'bɪl·ə·t̬i/ *n* [U]

com·pat·i·bly /£kəm'pæt·ɪ·bli, $-'pæt̬-/ *adv*

com·pat·ri·ot /kəm'pæt·ri·ət, -'peɪ·tri-/ *n* [C] a person who comes from your own country • *(fml) No doubt we will be hearing more of this writer and her Russian compatriots.* • *(fml) National culture is hard to define, but it's something we share with our compatriots.* • *(Am)* A compatriot can also be a companion or someone you work with: *I brought my kids to work with me so they could meet my compatriots.*

com·pel *obj* /kəm'pel/ *v* [T] **-ll-** to force (someone) to do something • *As a school boy he was compelled* **to** *wear shorts even in winter.* [+ obj + *to* infinitive] • *He didn't want to visit her but conscience compelled him* **(to)**. [+ obj (+ *to* infinitive)] • *(fml) The new circumstances compelled a change in policy.* • *(fml)* To compel also means to produce a strong feeling or reaction, sometimes unwillingly: *Over the years her work has compelled universal admiration and trust.* • See also COMPULSION [FORCE].

com·pelled /kəm'peld/ *adj* [after v] • *He* **felt** *compelled* **to** *report the incident.* [+ *to* infinitive] • *She didn't want to make the visit but she* **felt compelled (to)**. [(+ *to* infinitive)]

com·pel·ling /kəm'pel·ɪŋ/ *adj* • *It's a compelling argument* (=forceful and able to persuade). • A performance, painting, film, etc. is compelling if it gets your attention because of its strength and power.

com·pend·i·um /kəm'pen·di·əm/ *n* [C] *pl* **compendiums** or **compendia** /kəm'pen·di·ə/ a short but complete account of a particular subject, esp. in the form of a book • *the Gardener's Compendium*

com·pen·sate *obj* [PAY MONEY] /£'kɒm·pən·seɪt, $'kɑːm-/ *v* [T] to pay (someone) money in exchange for something that has been lost or damaged or for some inconvenience • *The company compensated him* **for** *an injury caused by faulty machinery.*

com·pen·sa·tion /£ˌkɒm·pen'seɪ·ʃᵊn, $ˌkɑːm-/ *n* [U] • *She received £40 000* **in** *compensation* **for** *a lost eye.* • *You should* **claim/seek** *compensation.* • *The airline received hundreds of compensation* **claims** *following the loss of the luggage.*

com·pen·sate [EXCHANGE] /£'kɒm·pən·seɪt, $'kɑːm-/ *v* [I] to be exchanged for or be instead of something of equal or better value • *You'll find my enthusiasm compensates* **for** *my lack of experience.* • *You may need to consider whether you are using work to compensate* **for** *your difficulties in other areas.* • *The fall in the inflation rate* **more than**

COMPARING AND GRADING

If you want to use an adjective to say that something is of a higher degree, you add **-er** to the end of it or qualify it with **more**: *Your hair is* **shorter** *than it was last year.* • *She's* **more intelligent** *than her brother.* This is called the COMPARATIVE.

If you want to say that something is of the highest degree, you add **-est** to the end of it or qualify it with **most**: *the* **longest** *letter I've written.* • *This is the* **most delicious** *ice cream I've ever had.* This is called the SUPERLATIVE.

WHICH COMPARATIVE AND SUPERLATIVE FORMS TO USE

one syllable adjectives usually form their comparative and superlative with -er and -est: *small, smaller, smallest.*
BUT 'real', 'right' and 'wrong' only take more and most.

two syllable adjectives can all take more and most, but some can take -er and -est as well. Adjectives that can take -er/-est include the following:

- **ending in -y and -ow** early, funny, happy, lively, narrow, noisy, pretty, shallow, wealthy
- **ending in -le** able, gentle, noble, simple
- **ending in -er and -ure** clever, mature, obscure
- **a number of other adjectives** common, cruel, handsome, pleasant, polite, quiet, solid, wicked

three syllable adjectives generally form their comparative and superlative only with more and most.
BUT some adjectives with the prefix un- can also take -er and -est, for example: *'unhappy'* and *'untidy'*.

HOW TO ADD -ER AND -EST

In most cases, just put -er or -est on the end of the adjective: *tough, tougher, toughest.* But notice the following adjectives:

- **ending in a single consonant** with the vowel in front of it spelled with a single letter: double the consonant before adding the -er and -est: *big, bigger, biggest.*
- **ending in -y**: change this to 'i' before adding the -er and -est: *happy, happier, happiest.*
- **ending in -e**: drop the 'e' before adding -er and -est: *blue, bluer, bluest.*

GRADABLE AND UNGRADABLE ADJECTIVES

Most adjectives can be used in the comparative and superlative forms, and can be used with words such as 'very' and 'extremely' (LP> **Very, completely**). Adjectives that can do this are called **gradable**:

- **describing action, activity, change and personal qualities** *he's being extremely careful; a very graceful dance; a completely unexpected decrease; terribly proud.*
- **describing unchanging states of affairs** *ten metres longer*

But some adjectives are **not gradable**, usually because the quality they refer to is either completely present or completely absent, with no degrees in between. For example, you would not say 'my most Danish friend' or 'this very steel pan'. Adjectives like this are labelled [not gradable]. The following types of adjectives are often not gradable:

- **describing an extreme limit**: you cannot say 'a more entire accident'. Other examples: *absolute, extreme, utter, total.*
- **restricting the noun completely or mainly to a particular case**: you cannot say 'the most main reason'. Other examples: *same, only, identical.*

  Some people think that this should apply to all such adjectives. They would say that expressions such as 'more perfect' and 'very unique' (which are logically faulty) are bad English. However, such usages are very common, and most teachers regard them as acceptable.
- **formed from nouns by adding -ar, -al, and -ic** You cannot say 'an extremely electronic device'. Other examples: *mathematical, polar.*

compensated **for** *rising unemployment.* • *We were very late and he drove fast to compensate.* • *Her daughter was disappointed that their visit had to be cancelled so, to compensate, he promised her a camping trip.*

com·pen·sat·ing /£ˈkɒm·pən·seɪ·tɪŋ, $ˈkɑːm·pən·seɪ·t̬ɪŋ/ *adj* • *It was a difficult job but there were compensating rewards.* • *Shrinking labour forces will offer partly compensating savings in unemployment benefits.*

com·pen·sa·tion /£ˌkɒm·penˈseɪ·ʃən, $ˌkɑːm-/ *n* • *I have to spend three months of the year away from home – but there are compensations like extra free time and the chance to meet new people.* [C] • *He's lost his hair – so he wears a beard* **in** *compensation.* [U]

com·pere *Br* /£ˈkɒm·peəʳ, $ˈkɑːm·per/, **host**, *Am also* **em·cee** *n, v infml* (a person whose job is) to introduce acts in a television, radio or stage show • *He started his career as a TV compere.* [C] • *She comperes that awful gameshow on Saturday night.* [T] • (F)

com·pete /kəmˈpiːt/ *v* [I] to try to do or be better than someone else • *Both girls compete* **for** *their father's attention.* • *The research groups are competing* **to** *be first to make the breakthrough.* • To compete is also to take part in a race or competition: *Are you competing* **in** *the 100 metres?* ○ *The two athletes are competing* **for** *the gold medal.* • If a company competes **against/with** another it tries to get people to buy its goods or services instead of the other company's. • *(fig.) Turn the music down – I'm not competing* **against/with** *that noise* (=I can't/won't try to speak louder than that music)*!* • LP> **Each other**

com·pe·ti·tion /£ˌkɒm·pəˈtɪʃ·ən, $ˌkɑːm-/ *n* • Competition is the state or activity of competing: *Competition for jobs is fierce/intense/keen* (= there are a lot of people and not many jobs). [U] • *The two companies are* **in** *competition* **with** *each other.* [U] • *There was a competition* **to** *find the prettiest baby.* [C + *to* infinitive] • *There's fierce competition* **to** *join the Special Branch.* [U + *to* infinitive] • **The competition** means the person or people you are trying to be better than: *The competition on the track looked fierce and her heart sank.* • *Foreign competition* (= similar products from other countries) *had reduced their sales.* [U] • *Why are you jealous of her? She's* **no** *competition* (= You're better than her)*!* [U] • A competition is a test of an ability, esp. a sporting ability, and often forms a public event: *a swimming/chess/crossword competition* [C] ○ *I've* **entered** *a beauty competition.* [C] ○ *(humorous) You don't need to eat so quickly! It's not a competition.* [C] • LP> **Sports** (NL)

com·pet·i·tor /£kəmˈpet·ɪ·təʳ, $-ˈpet̬·ɪ·t̬ɚ/ *n* [C] • *We're trying to keep our new product a secret from our competitors.* • *How many competitors took part in the race?*

com·pet·i·tive /£kəm'pet·ɪ·tɪv, $-'peṱ·ə·ṱɪv/ *adj* • *How will such a small firm survive in the competitive world of business?* • *Acting is very competitive – you've got to really push yourself if you want to succeed.* • *You're very competitive! It's meant to be a friendly match.* • *I could never play team sports – I lack the competitive* **spirit** (= strong desire to beat others). • *Their* **prices** *are very competitive* (= as low as any other shop or company). • *With all these foreign imports our product has lost its competitive* **edge** (= advantage over other products).

com·pet·i·tive·ly /£kəm'pet·ɪ·tɪv·li, $-'peṱ·ə·ṱɪv-/ *adv*

com·pet·i·tive·ness /£kəm'pet·ɪ·tɪv·nəs, $-'peṱ·ə·ṱɪv-/ *n* [U]

com·pe·tence /£'kɒm·pɪ·tᵊnts, $'kɑːm·pə·ṱᵊnts/, **com·pe·ten·cy** /£'kɒm·pɪ·tᵊnt·si, $'kɑːm·pə·ṱᵊnt-/ *n* [U] the ability to do something to a level that is acceptable • *Her competence as a teacher is unquestionable.* • *He reached a reasonable level of competence* **in** *his English.*

com·pe·tent /£'kɒm·pɪ·tᵊnt, $'kɑːm·pə·ṱᵊnt/ *adj* • *a competent secretary/horse-rider/cook* • *I wouldn't say he was brilliant but he is competent* **at** *his job.*

com·pet·ent·ly /£'kɒm·pɪ·tᵊnt·li, $'kɑːm·pə·ṱᵊnt-/ *adv* • *The story is competently written, but lacks conviction.* • *I thought she played the role very competently.*

com·pile *obj* GATHER TOGETHER /kəm'paɪl/ *v* [T] to collect (information) from a variety of places and arrange it in a book, report or list • *We're compiling some facts and figures for a documentary on the subject.*

com·pi·la·tion /£ˌkɒm·pɪ'leɪ·ʃᵊn, $ˌkɑːm-/ *n* • *A team of four were involved in the compilation of the book.* [U] • A compilation is also a book, set of records, etc. that has been made from several separate parts: *a compilation of modern poetry* [C] ○ *A new compilation of the band's hit records has just been released.* [C]

com·pil·er /£kəm'paɪ·ləʳ, $-lɚ/ *n* [C] • *She started her career as a compiler of quotations for reference books.*

com·pile *obj* CHANGE INSTRUCTIONS /kəm'paɪl/ *v* [T] to change (a computer program) into a machine language

com·pil·er /£kəm'paɪ·ləʳ, $-lɚ/ *n* [C] • *She ran her code through the compiler* (= program that changes instructions into machine language).

com·pla·cen·cy /kəm'pleɪ·sᵊnt·si/, **com·pla·cence** /kəm'pleɪ·sᵊnts/ *n* [U] *disapproving* a feeling of calm satisfaction with your own abilities or situation that prevents you from trying harder • *What annoys me about these girls is their complacency – they seem to have no desire to expand their horizons.* • *There's no* **room for** *complacency if we want to stay in this competition!*

com·pla·cent /kəm'pleɪ·sᵊnt/ *adj disapproving* • *a complacent smile/attitude*

com·pla·cent·ly /kəm'pleɪ·sᵊnt·li/ *adv disapproving* • *The executive sat back, stuck a fat cigar in his mouth and smiled complacently.*

com·plain /kəm'pleɪn/ *v* to say that something is wrong or not satisfactory • *He complains* **about** *anything – his job, his wife, his back...* [I] • *You're always complaining!* [I] • *He complained* **that** *his boss was useless and he had too much work.* [+ *that* clause] • To complain is also to tell someone formally that something is wrong: *If the service was so bad why didn't you complain* **to** *the manager?* [I] • If you complain **of** a sore throat, back pain, etc., you tell other people what it is that is making you feel ill: *She's been complaining of a bad back recently.* [I]

com·plain·ing·ly /kəm'pleɪ·nɪŋ·li/ *adv* • *"You always walk too fast for me", she said complainingly.*

com·plain·ant /kəm'pleɪ·nənt/ *n* [C] *law* • A complainant is a person who makes a formal complaint in a court of law.

com·plaint /kəm'pleɪnt/ *n* [C] • *Their loud parties have recently caused a number of complaints from the other people in their building.* [C] • *We've received a complaint from one of our listeners* **about** *offensive language.* [C] • *We've* **made a** *complaint* (= formally complained) **to** *the police about the noise.* [C] • *Do you have any* **grounds for** *complaint* (= reason to formally complain)*?* [U] • A complaint is also an illness: *Don't give him any shocks! He's got a heart complaint.* [C] ○ *She loves telling you about all her complaints.* [C]

com·plais·ance /£kəm'pleɪ·zᵊnts, $-sᵊnts/ *n* [U] *fml or literary* a willingness to please others by being polite and fitting in with plans

com·plais·ant /£kəm'pleɪ·zᵊnt, $-sᵊnt/ *adj fml or literary*

com·ple·ment *obj* /£'kɒm·plɪ·ment, $'kɑːm-/ *v* [T] to match two different things together whose combined effect is greater than that of either separately • *Strawberries and cream complement each other perfectly.* • *His dark good looks complement her blonde beauty.*

com·ple·ment·a·ry /£ˌkɒm·plɪ'men·tᵊr·i, $'kɑː·plɪ'men·ṱɚ-/ *adj* • *My family and my job both play an important part in my life, fulfilling separate but complementary needs.* • *A producer of disposable nappies could offer people who buy its product a discount on complementary products such as talcum powder and baby-wipes.* • *Petrol stations offer a range of complementary services, selling food, flowers and everything you need while on the road.* • **Complementary angles** are two angles which add up to 90° when they are put together. • **Complementary medicine** is a wide range of treatments for medical conditions and mental problems which people use as an alternative to ordinary medicine: *Acupuncture, reflexology and homeopathy are all forms of complementary medicine.*

com·plete *obj* PERFECT /kəm'pliːt/ *v* [T] to make whole or perfect • *Just four more china teacups to buy and she'll complete the tea set.* • *All she needed to complete her happiness was a baby or a dog.* • To complete a form is to answer all the questions it has written on it: *Have you completed your application form yet?* • Ⓕ Ⓟ

com·plete /kəm'pliːt/ *adj* • *Sun, sand and romance – her holiday was complete.* • *He wore the whole rabbit outfit, complete* **with** (= including) *teeth.*

com·plete·ness /kəm'pliːt·nəs/ *n* [U] • *China implemented its policies with a speed and completeness that no other country could match.* • *For the sake of completeness* (= So that nothing is omitted), *I should also mention two other minor developments.*

com·plete *obj* FINISH /kəm'pliːt/ *v* [T] to finish (doing something) • *Today we're talking to a director who's just completed filming his 35th feature film.* • *Has the new bridge been completed yet?* • Ⓕ Ⓟ

com·ple·tion /kəm'pliː·ʃᵊn/ *n* [U] • *The road repair work is* **nearing** *completion* (= almost finished). • *You'll be paid* **on** *completion* **of** *the project.*

com·plete VERY GREAT /kəm'pliːt/ *adj* [before n] very great or to the largest degree possible • *The man's a complete fool!* • *I need a break, a complete change of scene.* • *I made a complete* **and utter** *mess of it!* • Ⓕ Ⓟ

com·plete·ly /kəm'pliːt·li/ *adv* • *I agree with you completely.* • *She's completely mad.* • *He'd completely changed – I didn't recognize him.* • *"And now for something completely different"* (phrase used in *Monty Python's Flying Circus* television shows, 1969-74) • LP **Very, completely**

com·plex HAVING MANY PARTS /£'kɒm·pleks, kəm'pleks, $'kɑːm-/ *adj* involving a lot of different but related parts • *a complex molecule/carbohydrate* • *a complex subject/theory* • *a complex network of roads* • *The operation is a very complex procedure.* • *The company has a complex organizational structure.* • Complex can also mean difficult to understand or find an answer to because of having many different parts: *It's a very complex* **issue/problem/matter** *to which there is no straightforward answer.* ○ *The film's plot was so complex that I couldn't follow it.* ○ *She has a very complex personality and sometimes I feel I don't know her at all.* • *(specialized)* In grammar, a **complex sentence** is one which contains a main part and one or more other parts: *'If he asks me, I'll marry him' is a complex sentence containing the main clause, 'I'll marry him', and another clause, 'If he asks me'.* • *(specialized)* A **complex word** is a word consisting of a main part and one or more other parts: *The word 'hopeful' is a complex word of which 'hope' is the main part and 'ful' is an added ending.*

com·plex·i·ty /£kəm'plek·sɪ·ti, $-sə·ṱi/ *n* • *It's a problem of great complexity.* [U] • *There are a lot of complexities surrounding this issue.* [C]

com·plex BUILDING /£'kɒm·pleks, $'kɑːm-/ *n* [C] a large building with various connected rooms or a related group of buildings • *an industrial/arts complex* • *A new shopping/sports and leisure complex is being built on the edge of town.* • *(Am) They live in a large apartment complex.*

com·plex BAD FEELING /£'kɒm·pleks, $'kɑːm-/ *n* [C] a particular anxiety or unconscious fear which a person has, esp. as a result of an unpleasant experience that they have had in the past or because they have a low opinion of their own worth, and which influences their behaviour • *I think he's* **got** *a complex* **about** *being bald.* • *Don't go on about her weight – you'll* **give** *her a complex!* • *She's suffering from a* *guilt persecution complex* (= experiencing those feelings). • *(infml) I've got a real complex* **about** (= do not like) *spiders.*

com·plex·ion FACE /kəm'plek·ʃᵊn/ *n* [C] the natural appearance of the skin on a person's face, esp. its colour or quality • *a dark/fair complexion* • *a good/healthy/clear/smooth complexion* • *a bad/spotty complexion* • *This moisturizing cream is supposed to be good for the complexion.* • (RUS)

com·plex·ion CHARACTER /kəm'plek·ʃᵊn/ *n* [C] the general character of something • *These radical changes are likely to alter the complexion* **of** *the British contemporary dance scene.* • *The election has completely changed the political complexion* **of** *parliament.* • *What Pablo has just said* **puts an** *entirely/completely* **new** *complexion* **on** (= changes) *things.* • *MPs of all complexions* (= types of opinion) *have mounted a fierce campaign against the proposal.* • (RUS)

com·pli·ance /kəm'plaɪ·ənts/ *n* [U] See COMPLY

com·pli·ant /kəm'plaɪ·ənt/ *adj* See COMPLY

com·pli·cate *obj* /£'kɒm·plɪ·keɪt, $'kɑːm-/ *v* [T] to make (something) more difficult to deal with, do or understand • *Three of the dinner guests don't eat meat, two are on a diet and just to complicate matters/things, the sixth is allergic to milk.* • *It will only complicate the situation/issue if we invite his old girlfriend as well.* • *The rescue operation has been complicated by bad weather.* • *The new rules have complicated the tax system even further.* • If something, esp. an illness, complicates another illness, it makes the other illness worse: *His breathing problem has been complicated by a chest infection.*

com·pli·cat·ed /£'kɒm·plɪ·keɪ·tɪd, $'kɑːm·plɪ·keɪ·t̬ɪd/ *adj* • *The relationship is a bit complicated. He's my mother's cousin's daughter's child.* • *This machine looks a bit too complicated for my liking.* • *I had to fill in this really complicated form.* • *The rules are rather complicated to follow.*

com·pli·ca·tion /£ˌkɒm·plɪ'keɪ·ʃᵊn, $ˌkɑːm-/ *n* [C] • A complication is something which makes a situation more difficult: *Dave couldn't find his passport at the airport and then there were* **further** *complications when Fiona lost her baggage.* ○ *Have you thought of the practical complications of doing what you suggest?* ○ *If any complications* **arise**, *let me know and I'll help.* • A complication is also an additional medical problem which makes it more difficult to treat an existing illness: *If there are no complications, the doctor says that she'll be able to come home within two weeks.*

com·plic·i·ty /£kəm'plɪs·ɪ·ti, $-ə·t̬i/ *n* [U] *fml* involvement in a crime or some activity that is wrong • *She is suspected of complicity* **in** *the robbery.*

com·pli·ment /£'kɒm·plɪ·mənt, $'kɑːm-/ *n* a remark that expresses approval, admiration or respect • *She complained that her husband never* **paid** *her any compliments any more.* [C] • *He was being critical when he called me a workaholic, but I* **took it as** *a compliment.* [C] • *She asked us all what we thought of her new hairstyle, but she was really only* **fishing for** (= trying to get) *compliments.* [C] • A compliment can also be an action which expresses approval or respect: *You should* **take it as** *a compliment when I fall asleep in your company – it means I'm relaxed.* [C] ○ *He* **paid** *me* **the** *compliment* **of** *trusting me with his secret.* [U] ○ *Thank you so much for your help. I hope I'll be able to* **return/repay the** *compliment* (= do something for you because you have done something for me) *one day.* [U] • A compliment can also be something that shows the beneficial effect of what someone has done: *That he survived the accident is a compliment* **to** *the skill of the medical team that cared for him.* [U] • A **compliment(s) slip** is a piece of paper printed with the name and address of a company, which is sent with a parcel in place of a letter: *The clothes I had ordered from the catalogue arrived with a compliment slip from the manufacturer.*

com·pli·ment *obj* /£'kɒm·plɪ·mənt, $'kɑːm-/ *v* [T] • To compliment someone is to express to them your approval, admiration or respect for them: *I was just complimenting Robert* **on** *his wonderful food.* • *I must compliment you* **on** *your handling of a very difficult situation.*

com·pli·ment·a·ry /£ˌkɒm·plɪ'men·tᵊr·i, $ˌkɑːm·plɪ'men·t̬ɚ-/ *adj* • *The reviews of his latest film have been highly complimentary.* • *She wasn't very complimentary* **about** *your performance, was she?* • *Our guests said some very complimentary things about the meal I'd cooked.* • If tickets, books, etc. are complimentary, they are given free.

com·pli·ments /£'kɒm·plɪ·mənts, $'kɑːm-/ *pl n fml* • Compliments are the expression of your appreciation or respect: *That was an excellent meal! My compliments* **to** *the chef.* • If you give something to someone **with** your compliments, you give it to them free: *We enclose a copy of our latest brochure, with our compliments.*

com·ply /kəm'plaɪ/ *v* [I] *fml* to act according to an order, set of rules or request • *He's been ordered to have the dog destroyed because it's dangerous, but he refuses to comply.* • *It's difficult to teach if the students won't comply.* • *There are serious penalties for failure to comply* **with** *the regulations.*

com·pli·ance /kəm'plaɪ·ənts/ *n* [U] *fml* • *It is the job of the inspectors to enforce compliance* **with** *the regulations.* • *The company said that it had always acted* **in** *compliance* **with** *environmental laws.* • *(esp. disapproving)* Compliance is also the tendency to be (too) willing to do what other people want you to do: *I don't think punishment is always a good way of getting children's compliance.*

com·pli·ant /kəm'plaɪ·ənt/ *adj fml* • Compliant means (too) willing to do what other people want you to do: *She's a very compliant child, who always does as she's told.*

com·pon·ent /£kəm'pəʊ·nənt, $-'poʊ-/ *n* [C] a part which combines with other parts to form something bigger • *television/aircraft/computer components* • *The factory supplies electrical components for cars.* • *Her job is putting together the component parts of hi-fi systems and other electrical goods.* • *The course has four main components: business law, finance, computing and management skills.* • *Fresh fruit and vegetables are an* **essential** *component* **of** *a healthy diet.* • *The control of inflation is a* **key** *component* **of** *the government's economic policy.*

com·port *obj* /£kəm'pɔːt, $-'pɔːrt/ *v* [T] *fml* to cause (yourself) to behave in a particular way • *She comported* **herself** *with great dignity at her husband's funeral.* • (LP) **Reflexive pronouns and verbs**

com·port·ment /£kəm'pɔːt·mənt, $-'pɔːrt-/ *n* [U] *fml old use*

com·pose *(obj)* PRODUCE ART /£kəm'pəʊz, $-'poʊz/ *v* to produce (music, poetry or formal writing) • *Prokofiev started composing at the age of five.* [I] • *The music was specially composed* **for** *the film.* [T] • *This piece of music was composed* **for** *the flute and the harp.* [T] • *He composed this poem* **for** *his wife.* [T] • *Shakespeare's plays are composed in verse.* [T] • *(fml) My lawyer is going to compose a letter of complaint.* [T]

com·pos·er /£kəm'pəʊ·zəʳ, $-'poʊ·zɚ/ *n* [C] • A composer is a person who writes music, especially CLASSICAL music.

com·pos·i·tion /£ˌkɒm·pə'zɪʃ·ᵊn, $ˌkɑːm-/ *n* • *At music school I studied piano and composition* (= the activity of writing music). [U] • *Is this poem* **of** *your* **own** *composition* (= did you write it)*?* [U] • A composition is a piece of music: *His compositions include six symphonies and three operas.* [C] ○ *This concerto is one of her earlier/later compositions.* [C] • A composition is also the way in which the things represented in a painting, photograph or other piece of art are arranged: *a group composition* [C] ○ *The painting's composition is unusual and arresting.* [C] • A composition can also be a short piece of writing done by students at school in order to improve their writing skills: *a 200-word composition* [C] ○ *Write a composition* **on** *your favourite hobby.* [C] ○ *I hate doing composition* (= producing a short piece of writing). [U]

com·pose *obj* FORM /£kəm'pəʊzd, $-'poʊzd/ *v* [T usually passive] to form • *It takes a baby about two or three months to learn the arrangement of features that compose a face.* • *At the end of the Vietnam war, women composed only 1·6% of the US forces, but the percentage is much higher now.* • *She tried hard to compose her features* **into** *a smile, but it was obvious that she wasn't pleased to see us.* • *Air is composed mainly* **of** *nitrogen and oxygen.* • *The committee is composed* **of** *MPs, doctors, academics and members of the public.* • *The audience was composed largely* **of** *young people.* • *A diet composed entirely* **of** *processed foods is not good for you.*

com·pos·i·tion /£ˌkɒm·pə'zɪʃ·ᵊn, $ˌkɑːm-/ *n* [U] • *The manager has made some changes to the composition of the team.* • *What is the composition of this rock?*

com·pose *obj* CALM /£kəm'pəʊz, $-'poʊz/ *v* [T] to make an effort to cause (esp. yourself or your feelings) to be or seem calm and controlled, esp. after having been upset or angry • *She finally stopped crying and composed* **herself**. • *He took a minute or two to compose his* **thoughts** *before he replied.* • *Danny had composed his* **features**, *but we could* *tell that he was disappointed.* • *(fml)* If two people who disagree about something **compose** their **differences**, they end their argument and become friendly again.

com·posed /£kəmˈpəʊzd, $-ˈpoʊzd/ *adj* • *She looked remarkably composed* (= calm and controlled) *throughout the funeral.* • *He's very composed for a six-year old.*

com·pos·ed·ly /£kəmˈpəʊ·zɪd·li, $-ˈpoʊ-/ *adv*

com·po·sure /£kəmˈpəʊ·ʒəʳ, $-ˈpoʊ·ʒɚ/ *n* [U] • *You may feel nervous but don't* **lose** *your composure* (= calmness and control) *in front of her.*

com·pose *obj* ARRANGE TEXT /£kəmˈpəʊz, $-ˈpoʊz/ *v* [T] to arrange (words, sentences, pages, etc.) in preparation for printing

com·pos·i·tor /£kəmˈpɒz·ɪ·təʳ, $-ˈpɑː·zɪ·t̬ɚ/ *n* [C] • A compositor is a person whose job is to arrange the letters, words, sentences, etc. of a book or a magazine before it is printed. • (CS) (PL) (RUS) (S)

com·pos·ite /£ˈkɒm·pə·zɪt, $kɑːm-/ *n* [C] something which is made of various different parts • *The photograph was a composite* **of** *dozens of pictures put together.* • *The main character in her latest book is a composite* **of** *several of the other characters in her previous works.* • *Scientists have put together a composite picture of what the Earth's crust is like.* • *(specialized)* A composite is a structural material made up of more than one substance: *The bodies of these racing cars are moulded from the same composite that is used for making aircraft fuselage.*

com·pos men·tis /£ˌkɒm·pɒsˈmen·tɪs, $ˌkɑːm·pəs ˈmen·t̬ɪs/ *adj* [after v] *humorous* able to think clearly and be in control of and responsible for your actions; mentally healthy • *He's rarely compos mentis before about ten o'clock in the morning.*

com·post /£ˈkɒm·pɒst, $ˈkɑːm·pɑːst/ *n* [U] decaying plant material which is added to earth to improve its quality • PIC› **Garden**

com·post *obj* /£ˈkɒm·pɒst, $ˈkɑːm·pɑːst, -ˈ-/ *v* [T]

com·pôte /£ˈkɒm·pɒt, $ˈkɑːm·poʊt/ *n* a sweet dish made of cooked fruit • *a fruit compôte* [C] • *The hotel served us compôte and yoghurt for breakfast.* [U]

com·pound COMBINATION /£ˈkɒm·paʊnd, $ˈkɑːm-/ *n, adj* [not gradable] (something) consisting of two or more different parts • *His jokes have been described as a compound* **of** *fears, anxieties and insecurities.* [C] • *Many insects have compound* **eyes.** • *(specialized)* A compound is a chemical substance that combines two or more elements: *Salt is a compound* **of** *sodium and chlorine.* [C] ○ *Many fertilizers contain nitrogen compounds.* [C] • In grammar, a compound (word) is a word which combines two (or sometimes more) different words. Often, the meaning of the compound cannot be discovered by knowing the meaning of the different words that form it. Compounds can be written either as one word or as separate words: *'Bookworm' is a compound noun formed from the words 'book' and 'worm'.* ○ *'Do up' is a compound verb meaning 'fasten'.* LP› **Words used together, Compound verbs** • Compound can be used to refer to a system of paying INTEREST in which interest is paid both on the original amount of money invested or borrowed and on any interest which that original amount has collected over a period of time: *compound interest* ○ *The investment fund has achieved annual compound returns of 18·2%.* ○ *(Am) The seven-day compound yield of the Dawson Dollar Fund was 9·51%.* • A **compound fracture** happens when a bone breaks or cracks and cuts through the surrounding flesh. Compare **simple fracture** at SIMPLE NO MORE THAN. • A **compound leaf** is a type of leaf which is formed from a number of smaller leaves all joined to one stem.

com·pound *obj* /kəmˈpaʊnd, $ˈkɑːm·paʊnd/ *v* [T often passive] • *As she looked at the burning building, her expression was compounded* (= consisted) **of** *interest and horror.* • *Most tyres are made of rubber compounded* (= combined) **with** *other chemicals and materials.*

com·pound *obj* WORSEN /kəmˈpaʊnd, $ˈkɑːm·paʊnd/ *v* [T often passive] to make (something) worse by increasing it • *Severe drought has further compounded the food shortages in the region.* • *Her terror was compounded by the feeling that she was being watched.* • *His financial problems were compounded when he unexpectedly lost his job.*

com·pound AREA /£ˈkɒm·paʊnd, $ˈkɑːm-/ *n* [C] an enclosed area which contains a group of buildings • *The gates opened and the troops marched into their compound.* • *The prisoners are allowed an hour's exercise a day in the compound.* • *When we visited Ghana, we stayed in my cousin's family's compound.* • *The embassy compound has been closed to the public because of a bomb threat.*

com·pre·hend *(obj)* /£ˌkɒm·prɪˈhend, $ˌkɑːm-/ *v* [not *be comprehending*] *slightly fml* to understand (something) completely • *The students seemed to be struggling to comprehend.* [I] • *I just don't comprehend their attitude.* [T] • *His lectures are always so difficult to comprehend.* [T] • *I'll never comprehend* **why** *she did what she did.* [+ *wh-* word] • *I don't think he* **fully** *comprehends* **that** *she won't be here to help him.* [+ *that* clause]

com·pre·hen·si·ble /£ˌkɒm·prɪˈhent·sɪ·bl̩, $ˌkɑːm-/ *adj* • *It's written in clear, comprehensible* (= able to be understood) *English.* • *That film was barely comprehensible* **to** *me.*

com·pre·hen·si·bly /£ˌkɒm·prɪˈhent·sɪ·bli, $ˌkɑːm-/ *adv*

com·pre·hen·si·bil·i·ty /£ˌkɒm·prɪ·hent·sɪˈbɪl·ɪ·ti, $ˌkɑːm·prə·hent·səˈbɪl·ə·t̬i/ *n* [U]

com·pre·hen·sion /£ˌkɒm·prɪˈhen·tʃən, $ˌkɑːm-/ *n* • Comprehension is the ability to understand completely and be aware of a situation, facts, etc.: *He has no comprehension* **of** *the size of the problem.* [U] ○ *How she manages to fit so much into a working day is* **beyond** *my comprehension* (= I cannot understand it). [U] • A comprehension **(test)** is an exercise which tests a student's understanding of written or spoken language by asking them a set of questions about a piece of text that they have read or which has been read to them: *(a)* **listening/reading** *comprehension* [C/U]

com·pre·hen·sive /£ˌkɒm·prɪˈhent·sɪv, $ˌkɑːm-/ *adj* complete and including everything that is necessary • *We offer you a comprehensive training in all aspects of the business.* • *Is this list comprehensive or are there some names missing?* • *He has written a* **fully** *comprehensive guide to Rome.* • If you have **comprehensive insurance** for your car, it financially protects any other vehicles and people that are involved in a car accident with you, in addition to yourself. • (E) (F) (P)

com·pre·hen·sive·ly /£ˌkɒm·prɪˈhent·sɪv·li, $ˌkɑːm-/ *adv* • *a comprehensively illustrated book* • *The plan has been comprehensively rejected.* • *Our local team was comprehensively defeated.*

com·pre·hen·sive (school) /£ˌkɒm·prɪˈhent·sɪv, $ˌkɑːm-/ *n* [C] *Br* a school in Britain for children above the age of eleven in which children of all abilities are taught • *Lucy goes to the local comprehensive.* • *I had a comprehensive (school) education.* • LP› **Schools and colleges**

com·press *obj* PRESS /kəmˈpres/ *v* [T] to press (something) into a smaller space • *Firmly compress the soil in the pot so that the plant is secure.* • To compress (information, a piece of writing, etc.) is to make it shorter: *The course compresses two year's training* **into** *six intensive months.* ○ *I managed to compress ten pages of notes* **into** *four paragraphs.* • **Compressed air** is air which is at a pressure which is greater than ATMOSPHERIC pressure.

com·pres·si·ble /kəmˈpres·ɪ·bl̩/ *adj* • *compressible gas*

com·pres·sion /kəmˈpreʃ·ən/ *n* [U] • *Emmanuel Swedenborg proposed in 1735 that the universe had come into being from an explosion caused by the compression* **of** *gases.* • *The car has a high/low compression engine.* • *He is of the opinion that compression in writing* (= using few words) *is a form of elegance.*

com·press CLOTH /£ˈkɒm·pres, $ˈkɑːm-/ *n* [C] a thick soft piece of cloth which is pressed to a part of a person's body to stop bleeding or to reduce pain or swelling • *a cold/hot compress*

com·pres·sor /£kəmˈpres·əʳ, $-ɚ/ *n* [C] a (part of a) machine which presses gas or air into less space

com·prise *(obj)* /kəmˈpraɪz/ *v* [not *be comprising*] *fml* to have as parts or members, or to be (those parts or members) • *The course comprises a class book, a practice book and an audio tape.* [T] • *The class is comprised mainly* **of** *Italian and French students.* [T] • *Italian students comprise 60% of the class.* [L only + n]

com·pro·mise AGREEMENT /£ˈkɒm·prə·maɪz, $ˈkɑːm-/ *v, n* (to reach) an agreement in an argument in which the people involved reduce their demands or change their opinion in order to agree • *It is hoped that a compromise will be* **reached/agreed/arrived at/worked out** *in today's talks.* [C] • *In a compromise* **between** *management and unions, a 4% pay rise was agreed in return for an increase in productivity.* [C] • *She found that compromise was always the best policy when she got involved in arguments with her mother.* [U] • *The government has said*

COMPOUND (PHRASAL) VERBS AND VERBS FOLLOWED BY AN ADVERB OR PREPOSITION

HOW TO FIND THEM IN THE DICTIONARY

• The adverb or preposition is put in bold print but the verb is not
The basic meaning of the verb is not changed. The adverb or preposition is always or often found with the verb in this meaning.

You usually cut paper and cloth **with** *scissors.* (at **cut** KNIFE)
Where did you get your radio **from**? (at **get** OBTAIN)
Look **at** *all this rubbish on the floor.* (at **look** SEE)

You can find combinations like these in the examples for the meaning of the verb. Sometimes a particular combination also has another related or different meaning (see below). In this case, you can find the combination in the Phrase Index.

• Both the verb and the adverb or preposition are put in bold print
Adding the adverb or preposition gives a more figurative meaning which is related to a basic meaning of the verb.

Dave's so rude: I was just talking to Mary, when he **cut in** (= interrupted us). (at **cut** CROSS)
Her throat was so swollen that she couldn't **get** *the tablets* **down** (= swallow them). (at **get** CAUSE)
I'll **look into** (= try to find out about) *the reasons for the decision.* (at **look** SEARCH)

You can find meanings like this by using the Phrase Index.

• The combination of the verb and the adverb or preposition has a separate definition
Adding the adverb or preposition completely changes the meaning of the verb. Think of it as a new verb which is made up of two or three words.

If this bill is not paid within five days, your gas supply will be cut off. (at **cut off** STOP)
I suspect that her backache was just a way of getting out of the housework. (at **get out of**)
The woman was helping her friend look after the shop. (at **look after**)

Compound verbs like this occur in the alphabetical order of the dictionary and have their own definition. They are listed in the Phrase Index.

GRAMMAR AND WORD ORDER

• Verbs that must be followed by an adverb or a prepositional phrase [always + adv/prep]
If an intransitive verb is marked [I always + adv/prep], it means that you cannot use it on its own. It has to have an adverb or a prepositional phrase after it. For example, you cannot just say 'The old man shuffled', meaning that he moved without lifting his feet. You have to say something like *The old man shuffled* **along** (adding an adverb) or *The old man shuffled* **into** *the room* (adding a prepositional phrase).

In a similar way, a transitive verb marked [T always + adv/prep] must have an adverb or prepositional phrase after its object. You can say *He shunted his parents* **off** (= moved them to get rid of them) *to the seaside* but not simply 'He shunted his parents.'

• Verbs followed by an adverb which goes either before or after the object [M]
Usually the adverb can appear either before or after the object without any change in meaning. When all uses of a verb follow this pattern, the two possible positions of the object are shown before the definition. In other cases, the use is shown in an example, and marked [M].

cross out *obj*, **cross** *obj* **out** *v adv* [M] to draw a line through (writing) because it is wrong
If you think it's wrong, cross it out and write it again. • *He crossed out his name.* (at **cross out**)
Please put your cigarettes **out** (= stop them burning]. [M] (at **put** CONDITION)

Notice that when the object is a pronoun like 'me', 'him', 'it', 'myself' the pronoun is placed before the adverb. *Put out your cigarette* and *Put your cigarette out* are both possible, but with 'it' you can say only *Put it out.*

• Compound verbs
Compound verbs are verbs made up of two or more words. There are four types of compound verbs:

- **transitive verbs with an adverb:** ***v adv*** **[M] or** ***v adv*** **[T]**
  Usually these are [M], as for example 'put away' (= eat): *I don't know how he manages to put so much food away.* • *He put away a whole box of chocolates.* Sometimes the adverb can only go in one position. These verbs are marked [T], for example 'gloss over' (= avoid considering): *She glossed over the company's fall in profits, focussing instead on her plans for modernization.*
- **intransitive verbs with an adverb:** ***v adv*** **[I]**
  For example: *When I opened the office door, I was hit on the head and* **passed out** (= became unconscious). • *Jenny* **set off** *down the road on her new bike.* • *I admired the way she* **soldiered on** (= continued although it was difficult) *when her business ran into trouble.*
- **verbs with a preposition:** ***v prep***
  These are usually [T], for example: *How do you intend to* **deal with** (= manage) *this problem?* • *So, he made a mistake – don't* hold *it* against *him – I'm sure he won't do it again.*
  Some verbs can also be followed by the *-ing* form of another verb: *I've no idea how to* **set about** *changing a tyre on a car.*
- **verbs with an adverb and a preposition:** ***v adv prep***
  These are [T] verbs or followed by an *-ing* form. Notice that they rarely have a passive form. Examples are: *Can I* **come in on** (= join) *your plans for the weekend?* • *I can't seem to* **get down to** (= start to direct efforts to) *writing this letter to Laurie.*

Verbs taking both the ***v adv*** **and the** ***v prep*** **patterns:** Sometimes a verb is followed by an adverb which becomes a preposition if it is followed by an object. Verbs like this are marked *v adv, v prep* and examples show both patterns. For example 'glance off': *The bullets glanced off the car.* [T] • *The arrows struck the protective covering and glanced off.* [I] *that there will be no compromise* **with** *terrorists.* [U] • *Party unity is threatened when members will not compromise.* [I] • *Well, you want $400 and I say $300, so let's compromise* **at/on** *$350.* [I] • Ⓔ Ⓟ

com·pro·mis·ing /£'kɒm·prə·maɪ·zɪŋ, $'kɑːm-/ *adj* • *The government is not in a compromising mood.*

com·pro·mise *obj* LOWER STANDARDS /£'kɒm·prə·maɪz, $'kɑːm-/ *v* [T] *disapproving* to allow (your principles) to be weakened or (your standards or morals) to be lowered • *Don't compromise your* **beliefs/principles** *for the sake of being accepted.* • *If we back down on this issue, our* **reputation** *will be compromised.* • *His political career ended when he compromised* **himself** (= allowed his standards to be lowered) *by accepting bribes.* • Ⓔ Ⓟ

com·pro·mis·ing /£'kɒm·prə·maɪ·zɪŋ, $'kɑːm-/ *adj* • Compromising means causing damage to the reputation of someone, esp. making known that they have had a sexual relationship with someone who is considered unsuitable: *Some compromising details have been revealed about the MP.* ○ *She is in a rather compromising position/situation.*

com·pul·sion DESIRE /kəm'pʌl·ʃən/ *n* [C] a very strong or uncontrollable desire (to do something repeatedly) • *For many people, dieting is a compulsion.* • *I seem to* **have** *a* **constant** *compulsion* **to** *eat.* [+ *to* infinitive]

com·pul·sive /kəm'pʌl·sɪv/ *adj* • *a compulsive liar/thief/eater* • *His compulsive gambling is a serious problem.* • *She is suffering from a compulsive eating disorder.* • Compulsive can also be used to refer to a film, play, sporting event, book, etc. that is so interesting or exciting that you do not want to stop watching or reading it: *His performance in the play was* **utterly** *compulsive.* ○ *I always find programmes about hospitals compulsive* **viewing**. ○ *Her latest book is compulsive* **reading**/*a compulsive* **read**.

com·pul·sive·ly /kəm'pʌl·sɪv·li/ *adv* • *She exercises/cleans/works compulsively. It's become a real obsession.*

com·pul·sive·ness /kəm'pʌl·sɪv·nəs/ *n* [U]

com·pul·sion FORCE /kəm'pʌl·ʃən/ *n* [U] a force that makes you do something • *He seems to be driven by some kind of inner compulsion.* • *Her books have a certain compulsion that makes them hard to put down.* • *I only learnt Latin* **under** *compulsion when I was at school.* • *Are we* **under** *any compulsion* **to** *sign the document?* [+ *to* infinitive] • *Don't feel* **under** *any compulsion* **to** *take me with you. I won't be offended if you don't.* [+ *to* infinitive] • See also COMPEL.

com·pul·so·ry /£kəm'pʌl·sər·i, $-sɚ-/ *adj* • *Swimming was compulsory at my school.* • *Some things are compulsory by law, such as wearing seat belts in cars.* • A **compulsory purchase order** is a demand made by a public authority to buy land or property from a private owner in order to use the land for public purposes.

com·punc·tion /kəm'pʌŋk·ʃən/ *n* [U usually in negatives and questions] *fml* a slight feeling of guilt for something you have done or might do • *I wouldn't have any compunction* **about** *telling him to leave.*

com·pute *obj* /kəm'pjuːt/ *v* [T] *fml* to calculate (an answer or amount) by using a machine • *Compute the ratio of the object's height to its weight.*

com·pu·ta·tion /£ˌkɒm·pjʊ'teɪ·ʃən, $ˌkɑːm·pjə-/ *n* • *Predicting population changes over a period of time involves making a series of computations.* [C] • *Computation involving a large number of variables usually requires a computer.* [U]

com·put·er /£kəm'pjuː·tər, $-t̬ɚ/ *n* [C] an electronic machine which is used for storing, organizing and finding words, numbers and pictures, for doing calculations and for controlling other machines • *Many people now have a personal/home computer.* • *All our customer orders are handled* **by** *computer.* • *The runners' finishing times are recorded* **on** *computer.* • *We need someone who is computer-***literate** (= has had experience working with computers and knows how to use them) *to do this job.* • *She works for a company that produces computer* **software/hardware**. • *Computer* **systems** *can be used to control aircraft.* • *Computer* **graphics** *can produce images on a video screen or directly onto film.* • *You can get computer* **programs** *which check your spelling for you.* • **Computer dating** is a way of helping people find suitable sexual partners by using a computer to match them with people of similar interests. • A **computer game** is a game which is played on a computer, in which the pictures that appear on the screen are controlled by pressing keys or moving a JOYSTICK. • **Computer science** is the study of computers and how they can be used.

com·put·ing /£kəm'pjuː·tɪŋ, $-t̬ɪŋ/ *n* [U] • *Many children are now taught computing at school.* • *Portable computers make it possible for you to do your computing on a train or plane, or in a hotel room.* • *The factory has an elaborate computing system to control its stock.*

com·put·er·ize, *Br and Aus usually* **-ise** /£kəm'pjuː·tər·aɪz, $-t̬ə·raɪz/ *v* • *They've just computerized the whole system* (= caused it to be operated by a computer) *and it's much quicker.* [T] • *I want those records computerized* (= stored on a computer). [T] • *The office hasn't computerized* (= become equipped with a computer) *yet.* [I]

com·put·er·iz·a·tion, *Br and Aus usually* **-i·sa·tion** /£kəmˌpjuː·tər·aɪ'zeɪ·ʃən, $-t̬ɚ-/ *n* [U]

com·rade FRIEND /£'kɒm·reɪd, $'kɑːm-, -ræd/ *n* [C] *slightly dated* a friend or trusted companion, esp. one with whom you been involved in difficult or dangerous, usually military, activities • *Many of his comrades were killed in the battle.* • *They were comrades-***in-arms** *for many years.*

com·rade·ship /£'kɒm·reɪd·ʃɪp, $'kɑːm-/ *n* [U] • *There's a great sense of comradeship among the team.*

com·rade·ly /£'kɒm·ræd·li, $'kɑːm-/ *adj* • *He gave me a comradely slap on the back.*

com·rade POLITICAL MEMBER /£'kɒm·reɪd, $'kɑːm-, -ræd/ *n* [C] a member of the same political group, usually a COMMUNIST or a SOCIALIST one or a **trade union** • *I know my opinion is shared by many of my comrades in the Labour movement.* • *Well, Comrade, are you in favour of the proposal?* [as form of address] • *Welcome to the conference, comrades.* [as form of address]

com·rade·ly /£'kɒm·ræd·li, $'kɑːm-/ *adj* • *They said that he had not behaved in a comradely way towards his fellow members.*

con TRICK /£kɒn, $kɑːn/ *v, n* **-nn-** (to deceive by using) a trick in which someone is cheated into believing something false or giving their money or possessions away • *We are often conned by clever advertising* **into** *think***ing** *that certain products are better than others.* [T] • *The salesman conned us* **out of** *a lot of money.* [T] • *I managed to con £20* **out of** *them* (= get that amount from them by deceiving them). [T] • *It's a con* **(trick)***! You think you're saving money but in fact you're doing the opposite.* [C] • A **con artist/con man** is a person who deceives other people by making them believe something false or making them give money away.

con DISADVANTAGE /£kɒn, $kɑːn/ *n* [C] *infml* a disadvantage or a reason for not doing something • *One of the cons of buying a bigger car is that it will cost more to run.* • *You must* **weigh up/consider** *all the pros and cons* **of** *the matter before you make a decision.*

con PRISONER /£kɒn, $kɑːn/ *n* [C] *slang* a CONVICT • See also **ex-con** at EX.

Con POLITICS /£kɒn, $kɑːn/ *adj abbreviation for* CONSERVATIVE POLITICAL PARTY

con– TOGETHER /kən-/ *combining form* See at CO-

con·cave /£'kɒŋ·keɪv, $'kɑːn-/ *adj* curved inwards • *a concave lens* • *You've lost so much weight. Your stomach is almost concave!* • Compare CONVEX.

con·cav·i·ty /£ˌkɒn'kæv·ɪ·ti, $ˌkɑːn·kæv·ə·t̬i/ *n* [C/U]

con·ceal *(obj)* /kən'siːl/ *v* to prevent (something) from being seen or known about; to hide (something) • *The entrance to the house is concealed behind high gates.* [T] • *I tried to conceal my surprise when she said she was only 22.* [T] • *An accusation has been made that the police concealed vital evidence.* [T] • *Is there something you're concealing* **from** *me?* [T] • *He managed to conceal* **from** *his parents* **where** *he was going.* [+ *wh-* word]

con·cealed /kən'siːld/ *adj* • *The robbery had been recorded on a concealed security camera.* • *He was carrying a concealed weapon.* • *The room had concealed lighting.*

con·ceal·ment /kən'siːl·mənt/ *n* [U] • *They watched what was happening from a place of concealment.* • *The police may search someone if they suspect the concealment* **of** *a knife or other prohibited article.* • *Her concealment* **of** *her true feelings brought her a lot of pain.*

con·cede *(obj)* /kən'siːd/ *v* to admit, often unwillingly, (that something is true), or to allow (something) • *The Government has conceded* **(that)** *the new tax policy has been a disaster.* [+ *(that)* clause] • *I concede* **(that)** *he's clever, but I still think that he's boring.* [+ *(that)* clause] • *"It won't be easy," he conceded.* [+ clause] • *The president is not expected to concede* (= allow) *these reforms.* [T] • *He is not willing to concede* (= allow anyone else to have) *any of his power/authority.* [T] • *Britain conceded* (= allowed) *independence* **to** *India in 1948.* [T] • *With two players injured and three others* *removed from the game, the football team conceded* (=admitted) **defeat**. [T] • If you concede, you admit that you have lost in a competition: *She conceded even before all the votes had been counted.* [I] • If a team or a person concedes a point or a game, it means that they allow the other team or person to win the point or game: *The team conceded two goals* (**to** *the other side*) *in the first five minutes of the game.* [T] • If a country concedes land, it gives it to another country: *After the war, the country was forced to concede a lot of their territory.* [T] • See also CONCESSION.

con·ceit PRIDE /kən'siːt/ *n* [U] too much pride or too much confidence in your general ability to perform particular actions or to achieve particular aims • *She is full of conceit.* • *The conceit of that man is incredible!*

con·ceit·ed /£kən'siː·tɪd, $-t̬ɪd/ *adj disapproving* • *Without wishing to sound conceited, I'm clearly the best salesperson in the company.* • *He's a conceited young man who believes he's always right about everything.*

con·ceit COMPARISON /kən'siːt/ *n* [C] *specialized or literary* a clever comparison made in a piece of writing • *Long stretches of the opera are played in almost total darkness, a conceit that makes the audience work hard to work out what's going on.*

con·ceive *(obj)* IMAGINE /kən'siːv/ *v* to imagine (something); to consider • *A more disgusting expression of racism could hardly be conceived.* [T] • *He conceives* **of** *society* **as** (=thinks that it is) *a jungle where only the fittest survive.* [I always + prep] • *I think my uncle still conceives* **of** *me* **as** *a four-year-old.* [I always + prep] • *The way other people behave towards us influences how we conceive* **of** (=think about) *our***selves**. [I always + prep] • *He couldn't conceive* **of** *a time when he would have no job* (=that was too unlikely for him to imagine). [I always + prep] • *I find it hard to conceive* **of** *such cruelty* (=it is too shocking to imagine). [I always + prep] • *I can't conceive* (=It is too shocking to imagine) **how** *anyone could behave so cruelly.* [+ *wh-* word] • *I find it hard to conceive* (=It is too shocking to imagine) **that** *people are still treated so badly.* [+ *that* clause]

con·ceiv·a·ble /kən'siː·və·bl̩/ *adj* • *I've looked in every conceivable place* (=everywhere that I can think of) *for my keys, but I can't find them anywhere.* • *I can see no conceivable reason for lying to him.* • *It's conceivable* (=possible although difficult to imagine) **(that)** *he stole the money, but I'd be surprised.* [+ (*that*) clause]

con·ceiv·a·bly /kən'siː·və·bli/ *adv* [not gradable] • *I don't see how your idea could conceivably* (=possibly) *work.* • *If we hurry, we might just conceivably catch the train.*

con·ceived /kən'siːvd/ *adj* • *The project did not seem very carefully conceived* (=thought about). • *That's a very well-/***ill***-conceived plan.* • See also PRECONCEIVED.

con·ceive *(obj)* INVENT /kən'siːv/ *v* to invent (a plan or an idea) • *He conceived* **(of)** *the plot for this film while he was still a student.* [I/T] • *French food always seems to be superbly conceived and prepared.* [T] • *The exhibition was conceived by the museum's director.* [T] • See CONCEPT and CONCEPTION.

con·ceive *(obj)* BECOME PREGNANT /kən·siːv/ *v* to become pregnant, or to cause (a baby) to begin to form • *Do you know exactly when you conceived?* [I] • *The baby was conceived in March, so will be born in December.* [T] • See also CONCEPTION BABY.

con·cen·trate *(obj)* GIVE ATTENTION /£'kɒnt·sᵊn·treɪt, $'kaːnt-/ *v* to direct (your mental powers or your efforts) towards a particular activity, subject or problem • *Come on, concentrate! We haven't got all day to do this.* [I] • *Can you turn the music down, please? I can't concentrate* (**on** *my work*). [I] • *If you want to pass your exams, you'll have to concentrate* (*your efforts*) **on** *your listening skills.* [T/I] • *I find running concentrates* **the mind** (=helps me to think). [T] • *You should concentrate more* **on** *saving money rather than spending it.* [I] • *The company is concentrating (its resources)* **on** *developing new products.* [T/I] • *The police are concentrating their search in the area where the missing child was last seen.* [T]

con·cen·trat·ed /£'kɒn·sᵊn·treɪ·tɪd, $'kaːn·sᵊn·treɪ·t̬ɪd/ *adj* • *The company is making a concentrated* (=determined) *effort to broaden its market.* • *His book is a concentrated attack on feminism.*

con·cen·tra·tion /£ˌkɒnt·sᵊn'treɪ·ʃᵊn, $ˌkaːnt-/ *n* [U] • *The noise outside made concentration difficult.* • *There was a look of* **intense** *concentration on her face.* • *I find that yoga improves my* **powers of** *concentration.* • *I found it hard to follow what the teacher was saying, and eventually I* **lost** *concentration.* • *The government's concentration* **on** *tax reduction has won them a lot of support.*

con·cen·trate *(obj)* COME TOGETHER /£'kɒnt·sᵊn·treɪt, $'kaːnt-/ *v* to bring or come together in a large number or amount in one particular area • *Most of the country's population is concentrated in the north.* [T] • *In the dry season, the animals tend to concentrate in the areas where there is water.* [I always + adv/prep] • *(specialized)* If you concentrate a liquid or substance, you make it stronger and reduce its size by removing some of the water from it: *The solution can be concentrated by being boiled.* [T]

con·cen·trate /£'kɒn·sᵊn·treɪt, $'kaːn-/ *n* • Concentrate is a liquid from which some of the water has been removed: *fruit-juice concentrate* [U] ○ *tomato concentrate* [U] • A concentrate is an ORE from which rock has been removed: *a mineral concentrate* [C]

con·cen·trat·ed /£'kɒnt·sᵊn·treɪ·tɪd, $'kaːnt·sᵊn·treɪ·t̬ɪd/ *adj* • Concentrated means having had some liquid removed: *concentrated orange juice/food* ○ *a concentrated solution*

con·cen·tra·tion /£ˌkɒnt·sᵊn'treɪ·ʃᵊn, $ˌkaːnt-/ *n* • *He strongly opposed the concentration* (=existence of a large amount) **of** *power in the hands of so few people.* [U] • *There is* **a (heavy)** *concentration* (=gathering) **of** *troops in the area.* [C] • *Concentrations* (=Groups) **of** *police became apparent as they drove further into the town.* [C] • *(specialized)* Concentration is the exact amount of one particular substance that is found in another substance: *a concentration of one part per million* [C] ○ *High concentrations* **of** *toxic elements were found in the polluted areas of the sea.* [C] ○ *A study is under way to determine the exact concentration* **of** *lead in the local water supply.* [U] • A **concentration camp** is a prison where people are kept in extremely bad conditions, esp. for political reasons: *During World War II, millions of Jews died in Nazi concentration camps.*

con·cent·ric /kən'sen·trɪk/ *adj* (of circles and rings) having the same centre • *a concentric pattern/arrangement* • Ⓙ ⓀⓄⓇ

con·cept /£'kɒn·sept, $'kaːn-/ *n* a principle or idea • *He has written a book about the concepts, values, and arguments used in political science.* [C] • *It is very difficult to define the concept* **of** *beauty.* [C] • *Do you believe in the concept* **of** *the global village?* [C] • *I think I failed to* **grasp** *the film's central concept.* [C] • *When we had the extension to our house built, the concept for it was ours, but we employed an architect to* **realize** *it for us.* [C] • *Kleenbrite is a whole* **new** *concept* **in** *toothpaste!* [C] • *I don't think you have any concept* (=understanding) **of** *what this will mean.* [U] • See also CONCEIVE INVENT. • Ⓓ ⒹⓀ Ⓝ ⓃⓁ Ⓢ

con·cept·ual /kən'sep·tju·əl/ *adj* • *I have no conceptual understanding of computers* (=understanding of the principles on which they operate) – *I just press the keys!* • *The weakness of the proposal is conceptual* (=comes from the ideas on which it is based).

con·cept·ual·ize *(obj), Br and Aus usually* **–ise** /kən 'sep·tju·ə·laɪz/ *v* • *Do you think it's true that men and women conceptualize in different ways?* [I] • *He argued that morality could be conceptualized* (=thought about) *as a series of principles based on human reason.* [T]

con·cep·tion IDEA /kən'sep·ʃᵊn/ *n* an idea (about something), or a basic understanding (of a situation or a principle) • *People from different cultures have different conceptions* **of** *the world.* [C] • *She has a conception* **of** *people as being basically good.* [C] • *Who was responsible for the conception* (=the act of forming) **of** *this plan?* [U] • *I thought the book's writing was dreadful, and its conception* (=the ideas on which it was based) *even worse.* [U] • *He has absolutely no conception* (=understanding) **of** *how a successful business should run.* [U] • See also CONCEIVE INVENT.

con·cep·tion BABY /kən'sep·ʃᵊn/ *n* [U] the process of a sperm and an egg joining which causes a baby to start to form • *She believes that a baby is a person right from the moment of conception.* • *It is now possible for conception to take place outside a woman's body.* • See also CONCEIVE BECOME PREGNANT.

con·cern *obj* INVOLVE /£kən'sɜːn, $-'sɜːrn/ *v* [T] to be important to or to involve closely • *What I have to say to Amy doesn't concern you.* • *Matters of pollution and the environment concern us all.* • *There's no need for you to concern your***self with** *what happened.* • If a story, film or article concerns a particular subject, person, etc., it is written about that person or subject: *The film concerns a* *woman who goes to China as a missionary.* • You write **To whom it may concern** at the start of something such as a formal letter when you do not know exactly to whom the letter should be addressed.

con·cern /£kən'sɜːn, $-'sɜːrn/ *n* • *What were the major concerns* (= interests) **of** *the writers from this period?* [C] • *The results of the election are* **of** *concern* (= importance) **to** *us all.* [U] • *It's no concern* **of** *mine* (= It is not my responsibility or of interest to me)*!* [U] • *"What's happening?" "That's* **none of** *your concern* (= There is no need for you to become involved)*."* [U]

con·cerned /£kən'sɜːnd, $-'sɜːrnd/ *adj* [after v; not gradable] • *I'd like to thank everyone concerned* (= involved) *for making the occasion run so smoothly.* • *It was quite a shock for* **all** *concerned* (= everyone involved). • *Her job is something concerned* **with** (= involving) *computers.* • *Today's lesson is going to be concerned* **with** (= be about) *how to make requests.* • *I'm not very good* **where** *money is concerned* (= I am not good at dealing with money). • **As far as I'm** *concerned* (= In my opinion), *it's a load of rubbish.*

con·cern·ing /£kən'sɜː·nɪŋ, $-'sɜːr-/ *prep slightly fml* • *If you have any information concerning* (= about) *the recent incident at the station, please contact the police.* • *I've had a letter from the tax authorities concerning my tax payments.* • *"Could I speak to Mr James, please?" "May I tell him what it's concerning?"*

con·cern *obj* WORRY /£kən'sɜːn, $-'sɜːrn/ *v* [T] to cause anxiety to • *The state of my father's health concerns us* **greatly**. • **It** *concerns Joe's parents* **that** *he hasn't found himself a job yet.* [+ obj + *that* clause] • *Don't concern* **yourself** *– I'm sure she'll be home soon.*

con·cern /£kən'sɜːn, $-'sɜːrn/ *n* • *I have a matter* **of** *some concern* (= a worrying matter) *that I would like to talk to you about.* [U] • *His concern* (= wish) **to** *appear sophisticated amused everyone.* [+ *to* infinitive] • *The company's* **sole** *concern is* **to** *ensure the safety of its employees.* [+ *to* infinitive] • Concern is anxiety: *Concern* **for** *the safety of the two missing teenagers is* **growing**. [U] ○ *There's a lot of public concern* **about/over** *dangerous toxins recently found in food.* [U] • A concern is a worry: *Community concerns* **about** *the local water supply will be discussed at the meeting.* [C] ○ *My concern is* **that** *you're not getting enough work done.* [C + *that* clause]

con·cerned /£kən'sɜːnd, $-'sɜːrnd/ *adj* • *I'm a bit concerned* **about/for** *your health.* • *Aren't you concerned* **(that)** *she might tell someone?* [+ (*that*) clause] • *He was concerned* **to** *hear that two of his trusted workers were leaving.* [+ *to* infinitive] • *Concerned parents have complained about the dangerous playground.*

con·cern·ed·ly /£kən'sɜː·nɪd·li, $-'sɜːr-/ *adv* • *"Are you sure you're all right?" she asked concernedly.*

con·cern BUSINESS /£kən'sɜːn, $-'sɜːrn/ *n* [C] a company • *a family concern* • *an industrial concern* • *It started slowly, but the company is now a* **going** *concern* (= doing business effectively).

con·cert /£'kɒn·sət, $'kɑːn·sɚt/ *n* [C] a performance of music by one or more musicians or singers • *The school orchestra is playing in a concert this evening.* • *The quartet played to a packed concert hall.* • *I once saw her performing* **in** *concert at Carnegie Hall.* • A **concert-goer** is a person who often goes to concerts. • A **concert grand** is the biggest type of piano, and is the type that is usually played at concerts. • If someone is **at concert pitch**, they are prepared and ready to do something, esp. something important.

con·cert·ed /£kən'sɜː·tɪd, $-'sɜːr·t̬ɪd/ *adj* [usually before n] planned or done together for a shared purpose, or (of an attempt to do something) determined and serious • *She said that the richer countries of the world should take concerted* **action** *to help the poorer countries.* • *The D-Day invasion of Normandy in 1944 was a concerted* **exercise** *by the armed forces of Britain, the US and Canada.* • *There has been a concerted* (= determined) *campaign against the proposals.* • *He's making a concerted* (= determined) **effort/attempt** *to improve his appearance*

in con·cert *adv fml* • *If the various member countries would act in concert* (= together), *the problem might be solved more easily.*

con·cer·ti·na /£ˌkɒn·sə'tiː·nə, $ˌkɑːn·sɚ-/ *n* [C] a small six-sided musical instrument, with a folding middle part, which is played by pushing the instrument inwards with the hands and pressing buttons • *Some folk dances are performed to the music of a concertina.* • *(Br)* A **concertina file** (*Am* **accordion file** or **folding file**, *Aus* **expanding file**) is a box-shaped cardboard container used for storing documents. It has many small folds along two of its sides that allow it to be made larger or smaller as necessary. • PIC **File**

con·cer·ti·na *(obj)* /£ˌkɒn·sə'tiː·nə, $ˌkɑːn·sɚ-/ *v Br and Aus* • *In the accident, several cars concertinaed* (= became crushed) **into** *each other.* [I] • *It might just be possible to concertina the three meetings* (= bring them close together) **into** *one morning.* [T] • *His trousers lay concertinaed* (= in folds) *around his ankles.*

con·cer·to /£kən'tʃeə·təʊ, $-'tʃer·t̬oʊ/ *n* [C] *pl* **concertos** or **concerti** /£kən'tʃeə·ti, $-'tʃer·t̬i/ a long piece of music for one or more SOLO instruments (= those played alone) and an ORCHESTRA (= a large combined group of musicians) • *a violin/piano concerto* • *Mozart's concerto* **for** *flute and harp*

con·ces·sion /kən'seʃ·ᵊn/ *n* something which is allowed or given up, often in order to end a disagreement, or the act of allowing or giving this • *I'm not allowed to play my trumpet in the house, but* **as a** *concession I'm allowed to play it in the garage.* [C] • *Both sides involved in the conflict* **made** *some concessions in yesterday's talks.* [C] • *The prime minister has made it clear that no concessions will be* **made to** *the strikers.* [C] • *He spoke extremely fast,* **making** *no concession to the fact that I understood very little Spanish.* [U] • Concession can also be an act of admitting defeat: *The former president's concession came even before all the votes had been counted, when it was clear that he could not win.* [U] • A concession can also be a special right to property or land, or the right to sell a particular product in a particular area: *The company has bought a concession in Yosemite National Park, which includes hotels, restaurants and camp-grounds.* [C] ○ *He has a concession* **to** *sell hamburgers in the town centre.* [C] • See also CONCEDE.

con·ces·sion·a·ry /£kən'seʃ·ᵊn·ᵊr·i, $-er-/ *adj* • *Tickets are available at a concessionary* (= cheaper) **rate** *for the elderly and the unemployed.*

con·ces·sion·aire /£kənˌseʃ·ᵊn'eəʳ, $-'er/ *n* [C] • A concessionaire is someone who has been given a concession to sell or do something.

con·ces·sive clause /kən'ses·ɪv/ *n* [C] *specialized* a clause, often introduced by '(al)though', expressing an idea which suggests the opposite of the main part of the sentence • *The sentence 'Although he's quiet, he's not shy' begins with a concessive clause.*

conch /£kɒntʃ, £kɒŋk, $kɑːŋk, $kɑːntʃ/ *n* a tropical SNAIL-like sea animal, or its flesh eaten as food, or its shell. There are various different types of conch. • *Conches are abundant in the Caribbean.* [C] • *There was conch on the menu at the restaurant.* [U] • *If you blow into a* **conch(-shell)**, *it produces a deep sound.* [C]

con·chie /£'kɒn·ʃi, $'kɑːn-/ *n* [C], *adj Aus infml* (someone who is) too CONSCIENTIOUS (= using a lot of effort in their work)

con·cil·i·ate *(obj)* /kən'sɪl·i·eɪt/ *v* to end a disagreement or a feeling of anger by acting in a friendly way or slightly changing your opinions, or to satisfy (someone with whom you have had a disagreement) by acting in this way • *An independent adviser has been brought in to conciliate* **between** *the two sides involved in the conflict.* [I] • *These changes have been made in an attempt to conciliate* (= satisfy) *the plan's critics.* [T]

con·cil·i·a·tion /kənˌsɪl·i'eɪ·ʃᵊn/ *n* [U] *fml* • *Their attempts at conciliation had failed and both sides were once again in dispute.*

con·cil·i·at·o·ry /£kən'sɪl·i·ə·tri, $-tɔːr·i/ *adj* • *a conciliatory gesture/remark* • *Her conciliatory smile told him that they were friends again.*

con·cise /kən'saɪs/ *adj* short and clear; expressing what needs to be said without unnecessary words • *Make your answers clear and concise.* • KOR

con·cise·ly /kən'saɪ·sli/ *adv*

con·cise·ness /kən'saɪ·snəs/, **con·ci·sion** /kən'sɪʒ·ᵊn/ *n* [U]

con·clave /£'kɒŋ·kleɪv, $'kɑːn-/ *n* [C] *fml or specialized* a private meeting at which the discussions are kept secret, or a meeting of CARDINALS (= Catholic priests) at which the Pope is elected

con·clude *(obj)* /kəŋ'kluːd/ *v* to end (a speech, meeting or piece of writing), or to judge after some consideration • *She concluded the speech* **by** *reminding us of our responsibility/* **with** *a reminder that we are all responsible.* [T] • *Before I conclude I would like to thank you all for attending this meeting.* [I] • *The soap opera concluded* **with** *the death of the* *entire cast.* [I] • *The jury concluded* **from** *the evidence* **that** *the defendant was innocent.* [+ *that* clause] • *We talked late into the night, but nothing was concluded* (= no decisions were made). [T] • If you conclude a business deal or official agreement, you agree on it finally. [T]

con·clu·sion /kəŋˈkluː·ʒᵊn/ *n* [C] • *I found the conclusion of the film* (= the way the film ended) *rather irritating.* [C] • *Did you* **come to/reach/draw** *any conclusions* (= make any decisions) *at the meeting this morning?* [C] • *What were your conclusions* (= What did you think about the situation) *after you'd been to see the houses?* [C] • *At first I thought he was a bit shy, but I've* **come to the** *conclusion* (= decided after a lot of consideration) **that** *he's simply unfriendly!* [+ *that* clause] • *(fml)* **In conclusion** (= Finally), *I should like to say that I am deeply concerned for the future of British theatre.* • *The conclusion of the deal/treaty will make the world a safer place for all of us.* [U]

con·clu·sive /kəŋˈkluː·sɪv/ *adj* • Facts, proof and arguments that are conclusive end any doubt or uncertainty about a situation: *They had conclusive evidence of her guilt.*

con·clu·sive·ly /kəŋˈkluː·sɪv·li/ *adv* • *It is impossible to* **demonstrate/prove** *conclusively* (= without any doubt) *that the factory is responsible for the pollution.*

con·coct *obj* /£kəŋˈkɒkt, $-ˈkɑːkt/ *v* [T] to make (something, usually food) by adding several different parts together, often in a way that is original or not planned • *He'd concocted the most amazing dish from all sorts of unlikely ingredients.* • If you concoct an excuse, explanation or story you invent one to deceive someone: *He concocted a story about working late at the office, but I knew he was going drinking with his brother.*

con·coc·tion /£kəŋˈkɒk·ʃᵊn, $-ˈkɑːk-/ *n* [C] • *I didn't know what was in the concoction, but I drank it anyway.* [C] • *(humorous) Is this dish* **of** *your concoction* (= Did you create it), *Paul?* [U]

con·com·it·ant /£kəŋˈkɒm·ɪ·tᵊnt, $-ˈkɑː·mə·ţᵊnt/ *n, adj fml* (something) happening together and connected with something else • *Loss of memory is a natural concomitant* **of** *old age.* [C] • *The spread of Arabic outside the Arabian peninsula was concomitant* **with** *the spread of Islam in the 7th and 8th centuries AD.*

con·com·it·ant·ly /£kəŋˈkɒm·ɪ·tᵊnt·li, $-ˈkɑː·mə·ţᵊnt-/ *adv*

con·cord /£ˈkɒŋ·kɔːd, $ˈkɑːŋ·kɔːrd/ *n* [U] *fml* agreement and peace between countries and people • *nations living* **in** *concord* • *His speech did nothing for racial concord.* • *(specialized)* Concord is when the words in a sentence match each other grammatically, for example when the verb is plural because the subject of the sentence is plural. • Compare DISCORD [DISAGREEMENT].

con·cord·ance /£kənˈkɔː·dᵊnts, $-ˈkɔːr-/ *n* [C] *specialized* a book or list which is an alphabetical collection of the words used in a writer's work with information about where the words can be found and in which sentences • *a Shakespeare/Biblical concordance* • *a concordance* **of** *magazine articles* • *(fml) a concordance* **to** *Keats*

con·cord·ance *obj* /£kənˈkɔː·dᵊnts, $-ˈkɔːr-/ *v* [T] *specialized* • *We've got a computer program which will concordance newspaper texts.*

con·cord·at /£kənˈkɔː·dæt, $-ˈkɔr-/ *n* [C] *specialized* a formal agreement, esp. on religious matters, between the Roman Catholic Church and a particular country • *Under the concordat, the state is obliged to maintain Catholic teaching in schools.*

con·course /£ˈkɒŋ·kɔːs, $ˈkɑːn·kɔːrs/ *n* [C] a large space or room in a public building such as a station or airport which people gather in or pass through • *I'll meet you on the station concourse near the paper shop.* • *There's an automatic ticket machine in the main concourse.* • Ⓒⓢ Ⓟ ⓇⓊⓈ

con·crete [HARD MATERIAL] /£ˈkɒŋ·kriːt, $ˈkɑːn-/ *n* [U] a very hard building material made by mixing together CEMENT, sand, small stones and water • *reinforced concrete* • *a concrete floor/path/tower block* • *It's a depressing grey concrete building with tiny windows.* • If something is **set/cast in concrete**, it is fixed and cannot be changed. • A **concrete jungle** is an ugly grey area of a city where people live in closely crowded apartment buildings and there is little space and no trees or grass. • A **concrete mixer** is a **cement mixer**. See at CEMENT [BUILDING MATERIAL].

con·crete *obj* /£ˈkɒŋ·kriːt, $ˈkɑːn-/ *v* [T] • *Why did you concrete* **over** *that nice garden* (= cover the garden in concrete)*?* [M] • *We thought about having a gravel path, but in the end we decided to concrete it.*

con·crete [CERTAIN] /£ˈkɒŋ·kriːt, $ˈkɑːn-/ *adj* clear and certain, or real and existing in a form that can be seen or felt • *They think she killed her husband but they've no concrete evidence/proof.* • *To solve this problem, we'll need concrete facts, not vague ideas.* • *We've got a general idea of what we want, but nothing concrete at the moment.* • A **concrete noun** is a noun which refers to a material object: *'Chocolate' is a concrete noun, whereas 'love' is an abstract noun.* Compare **abstract noun** at ABSTRACT [GENERAL].

con·cu·bine /£ˈkɒŋ·kjʊ·baɪn, $ˈkɑːn-/ *n* [C] (in particular societies) a woman, or one of a group of women, usually of lower social rank, who lives and has sex with a man she is not married to • *(dated humorous)* A woman might be described as a particular man's concubine if she is living and having sex with him but they are not married.

con·cu·pis·cence /kəŋˈkjuː·pɪ·sᵊnts/ *n* [U] *old use or literary* sexual desire

con·cur /£kəŋˈkɜːʳ, $-ˈkɜːr/ *v* [I] **-rr-** *fml* to agree with someone or have the same opinion as someone else • *For once, the politicians concurred* **with** *each other* **on/in** *the matter.* • *Within minutes, the jury had concurred* **that** *he was guilty.* [+ *that* clause] • *"I think you're absolutely right," concurred Chris.* [+ clause] • If two or more events concur, they happen at the same time: *It's extremely unlikely that two such improbable events would concur.*

con·cur·rence /£kənˈkʌr·ᵊnts, $-ˈkɜːr-/ *n* [U] *fml* • *Was there any concurrence of opinion?* • *The unlikely concurrence of these events led many people to believe that they were connected.* • Ⓒⓢ Ⓝ

con·cur·rent /£kənˈkʌr·ᵊnt, $-ˈkɜːr-/ *adj* • *Working on two concurrent* (= happening at the same time) *projects can be very exhausting for an author.* • ⓇⓊⓈ

con·cur·rent·ly /£kənˈkʌr·ᵊnt·li, $-ˈkɜːr-/ *adv* • *Her two dramas are being shown concurrently* (= at the same time) *by rival television stations.*

con·cus·sion /kəŋˈkʌʃ·ᵊn/ *n* [U] temporary damage to the brain caused by a fall or hit on the head or by violent shaking, and resulting in various effects, such as a loss of consciousness and a desire to vomit • *He's been a bit dizzy and confused since the accident. Do you think it's mild concussion?* • Ⓘ

con·cuss *obj* /kəŋˈkʌs/ *v* [T usually passive] • *The boxer was concussed and removed from the ring within three minutes of the fight of starting.*

con·demn *obj* [CRITICIZE] /kənˈdem/ *v* [T] to criticize strongly, usually for moral reasons • *The terrorist action has been condemned* **as** *an act of barbarism and cowardice.* • *The film was condemned by some critics* **for** *its sexist portrayal of women.* • *During that period many people were condemned* **as** *communists.*

con·dem·na·tion /£ˌkɒn·dəmˈneɪ·ʃᵊn, $ˌkɑːn-/ *n* • *The shooting of the policeman on duty late last night has received universal condemnation.* [U] • *It's a real condemnation of* (= reason for criticizing) *the church that they don't accept women as equals.* [C]

con·dem·na·to·ry /£kənˈdem·nə·tri, $kɑːnˈdem·neɪ·ţɚ·i/ *adj* • *a condemnatory speech/tone*

con·demn *obj* [PUNISH] /kənˈdem/ *v* [T] to cause something very bad to happen to (someone) • *The rain condemned her* **to** *an afternoon indoors with her tedious aunt.* • *Poverty had condemned him from birth* **to** *a life of crime.* • Someone might be condemned **to** death or to a long time in prison if their punishment has been formally decided and stated: *She was condemned to death on May 12th and executed two weeks later.* ○ *They were condemned to spend the best years of their lives in prison for a crime they hadn't even committed.* [+ *to* infinitive]

con·demned /kənˈdemd/ *adj* • If someone is condemned, they are going to be killed, esp. as a punishment for having committed a very serious crime, such as murder. • If a building is condemned it has been officially decided that it is not safe for people to live in or to use. • A **condemned cell** is a room in a prison for someone who is going to be punished by death.

con·dens·a·tion /£ˌkɒn·denˈseɪ·ʃᵊn, $ˌkɑːn-/ *n* [U] the drops of water that appear on cold surfaces such as windows as a result of hot air or steam becoming cool • *We get a lot of condensation on the walls in the winter.* • *(specialized)* Condensation is the act or process of changing from a gas to a liquid or solid state.

con·dense *(obj)* /kən'dents/ *v* [I/T]

con·dense *obj* /kən'dents/ *v* [T] to reduce (esp. a text) in size • *I've tried to condense ten pages of comments into two.* • If you condense a liquid you make it thicker by removing some of the water: *condensed soup* • **Condensed milk** is a thick and very sweet milk from which water has been removed and to which a lot of sugar has been added.

con·densed /kən'dentst/ *adj*

con·dens·a·tion /£ˌkɒn·den'seɪ·ʃən, $ˌkɑːn-/ *n* [U]

con·dens·er /£kən'den·səʳ, $-sɚ/ *n* [C] *specialized* a piece of equipment that reduces gases to their liquid or solid form

con·de·scend /£ˌkɒn·dɪ'send, $ˌkɑːn-/ *v* [I] to treat (someone) in a way which shows that you consider yourself to be better or cleverer • *(literary) He condescends to every woman he meets.* • *(usually humorous)* If you condescend to do something, you agree to do something which you do not consider to be good enough for your social position: *I know you're a graduate now, but will you still condescend* **to** *join us for lunch?* [+ *to* infinitive]

con·de·scend·ing /£ˌkɒn·dɪ'sen·dɪŋ, $ˌkɑːn-/ *adj* • *I hate the way he's so condescending to his staff!* • Ⓔ Ⓟ

con·de·scen·sion /£ˌkɒn·dɪ'sent·ʃən, $ˌkɑːn-/ *n* [U]

con·di·ment /£'kɒn·dɪ·mənt, $'kɑːn-/ *n* [C] *fml* a substance such as salt that you add to food to improve its taste

con·di·tion STATE /kən'dɪʃ·ən/ *n* the particular state that something or someone is in • *It's very old but it's been so well kept that it's in perfect condition.* [U] • *The car's in great condition. Believe me, I've never had a day's trouble with it.* [U] • *Her condition* (= state of health) *is improving but we want to keep close watch on her for a few days just to be safe.* [U] • *For a man of sixty-three, Jim's* **in** *pretty good condition.* [U] • *We're looking at an athlete* **in** *peak condition – she's strong, she's fast and she hasn't missed a ball!* [U] • *Her bicycle has never been used and is in* **mint** (= perfect) *condition.* [U] • If you are **out of** condition, you are not physically healthy enough for difficult exercise because you have not been involved in physical activities, such as sport. [U] • *He's* **in no** *condition* (= He's not well enough) **to** *go to work – he has to go to the toilet every five minutes!* [U] • *Don't let him drive home in that condition! He can't even see straight.* [U] • *Be careful with him! Remember he's got a heart condition* (= any of a variety of heart diseases). [C] • *They left the flat in a terrible condition – there was dirt everywhere.* [U]

con·di·tions /kən'dɪʃ·ənz/ *pl n* • The conditions of a situation are all the different influences which have an effect on it: *My* **working** *conditions are terrible: uncomfortable chairs, bad lighting and indescribable food.* ○ *Due to adverse* **weather** *conditions the train service has been slowed down considerably.* ○ *The prisoners were kept* **in/under** *the most appalling conditions.* ○ *What sort of conditions does the plant need to grow in?* ○ *Bacteria multiply* **in** *warm conditions.*

con·di·tion AGREED LIMITATION /kən'dɪʃ·ən/ *n* [C] an arrangement that must exist before something else can happen • *I'll come to the party* **on the** *condition* **that** *you don't wear those ridiculous trousers!* [+ *that* clause] • *One of the conditions in the contract is that we don't build on the land.* • *We're not in a position to make/set any conditions – we'll just have to accept the contracts that are offered to us.* • **Under the conditions of** *the agreement she is obliged to vacate the house on July 12th.* • *"The condition of liberty is eternal vigilance (Originally 'The condition upon which God hath given liberty to man is eternal vigilance')"* (speech by John Philpot Curran, 1790)

con·di·tion·al /kən'dɪʃ·ən·əl/ *adj* • *The offer of a place on the nursing course is conditional* **on/upon** (= dependent on) *my passing all three exams.*

con·di·tion·al·ly /kən'dɪʃ·ən·əl·i/ *adv*

con·di·tion *obj* INFLUENCE /kən'dɪʃ·ən/ *v* [T usually passive] to train or influence (a person or animal) mentally so that they do or expect a particular thing without thinking about it • *a conditioned reflex/response* • *In a series of revolutionary experiments, Pavlov conditioned dogs to salivate at the sound of a bell.* • *As women we've been conditioned* **to** *expect lower wages than men.* [+ obj + *to* infinitive]

con·di·tion·ing /kən'dɪʃ·ən·ɪŋ/ *n* [U] • *Conditioning starts as soon as boys are given guns to play with and girls are given dolls.*

con·di·tion·al SENTENCE FORM /kən'dɪʃ·ən·əl/ *adj* [not gradable], *n specialized* (relating to) a sentence, often starting with 'if' or 'unless', in which one half expresses something which is dependent on the other half • *a conditional clause* • *'If I won a lot of money, I'd go travelling' is an example of a conditional (sentence).* [C] • LP› **Conditionals**

con·di·tion·al VERB FORM /kən'dɪʃ·ən·əl/ *adj* [not gradable], *n* [U] *specialized* (a form of a verb) expressing the idea that one thing is dependent on another thing • *In English,* **the** *conditional is expressed by 'would'.*

con·di·tion·er /£kən'dɪʃ·ən·əʳ, $-ɚ/ *n* [U] a thick often creamy liquid which people put on their hair after washing it to improve its quality and appearance, or a thick liquid which you wash clothes in to soften them

con·di·tion *obj* /kən'dɪʃ·ən/ *v* [T] • If you condition your hair you try to improve its quality or appearance by putting a conditioner on it.

con·dol·enc·es /£kən'dəʊ·lənt·sɪz, $-'doʊ-/ *pl n*,

con·dol·ence /£kən'dəʊ·lənts, $-'doʊ-/ *n* [U] an often written expression of sympathy and sadness for the family or close friends of a person who has recently died • *a letter of condolence* • *(fml) Dignitaries from all over the world came to* **offer** *their condolences to the president's widow.*

con·dom /£'kɒn·dɒm, $'kɑːn·dəm/, **sheath**, *Am slang* **rub·ber** *n* [C] a thin rubber covering that a man can wear on his penis during sex to stop a woman becoming pregnant or to protect him or his partner against infectious diseases

con·do·mi·ni·um BUILDING /£ˌkɒn·də'mɪn·i·əm, $ˌkɑːn-/, *infml* **con·do** /£'kɒn·dəʊ, $'kɑːn·doʊ/ *n* [C] *Am* (an apartment in) an apartment building in which each apartment is owned separately by the people living in it, but the shared areas are owned by everyone

con·do·mi·ni·um COUNTRY /£ˌkɒn·də'mɪn·i·əm, $ˌkɑːn-/ *n* [C] a country which is governed by two or more foreign powers

con·done *obj* /£kən'dəʊn, $-'doʊn/ *v* [T] to approve of (behaviour that some people consider wrong) so that such behaviour is encouraged to happen again in the future • *If the government is seen to condone violence, the bloodshed will never stop.*

con·dor /£'kɒn·dɔːʳ, $'kɑːn·dɔːr/ *n* [C] a type of VULTURE (= a large bird which feeds on dead animals) from S America

con·duc·ive /£kən'djuː·sɪv, $-'duː-/ *adj* providing the right conditions for something good to happen or exist • *Working in such an aggressive environment was not conducive* **to** *her (finding) peace of mind.* • *I prefer to read in the library. I find it more conducive.* • *This is a more conducive atmosphere* **for** *studying.*

con·duce to *obj* /£kən'djuːs, $-'duːs/ *v prep* [T] *fml* • *Managers should be willing to consider any measures which will conduce to* (= help create) *a better working environment.*

con·duct *obj* DIRECT /kən'dʌkt/ *v* [T] to organize and perform (a particular activity) • *We are conducting a survey to find out what our customers think of their local bus service.* • *The experiments were conducted by scientists in New York.* • *The meeting will be conducted by the sales manager.* • If someone conducts you to a place they lead you there so that you know where to go: *May I conduct you to your table, Sir, or would you prefer to have a drink at the bar first?* ○ *I'd like to go on a conducted* **tour** *of the palace.*

con·duct /£'kɒn·dʌkt, $'kɑːn-/ *n* [U] • *He was criticised for his conduct of the meeting.*

con·duct *(obj)* MUSIC /kən'dʌkt/ *v* to direct the performance of (musicians or a piece of music) • *The orchestra was conducted by Mira Shapur.* [T] • *Who's conducting at tonight's concert?* [I]

con·duct·or /£kən'dʌk·təʳ, $-t̬ɚ/ *n* [C] • *The conductor turned to face her audience and the entire concert hall fell silent.*

con·duct *obj* BEHAVIOUR /kən'dʌkt/ *v* [T always + adv/prep] to cause (yourself) to behave in a particular way, esp. in a public or a formal situation, or to organize (the way in which you live) • *For a five-year-old, the prince conducted* **himself** *very well, despite the length of the ceremony.* • *How are you supposed to conduct* **yourself** *at these dinners? I know nothing about etiquette.* • *The way you choose to conduct* (= organize) *your private life is your own business!* • LP› **Reflexive pronouns and verbs**

con·duct /£'kɒn·dʌkt, $'kɑːn-/ *n* [U] • *The president surprised everyone with his unusual conduct* (= behaviour) *at the memorial service.*

CONDITIONALS

A conditional sentence is about the connection between two things, events and so on. It expresses the idea that one thing follows from another, or depends on another:

IF **condition A** THEN **condition B**   **condition B** IF **condition A**

Generally such sentences refer to events or situations that are possible, and not to anything that actually happened or is happening. The meaning of a conditional sentence depends on the tenses of the verbs within it. There are four important patterns:

• zero conditional

IF A (*present tense*) THEN B (*present tense*)

If you add two and two, you get four.
Water boils if you heat it to 100°C.

Expresses a general or scientific truth which is true for the past, present and future. It is a rule that condition (B) always depends on, follows from or is caused by condition (A).

• type 1 conditional

IF A (*present tense*) THEN B (*future tense*)

If she wins the next match, she'll be world champion.
The match will be cancelled if it rains tomorrow.
Unless you book in advance, you won't get a ticket.

States a connection between events or situations which are possible but not certain. Often used to refer to the likely result (B) of a possible event or action (A).

• type 2 conditional

IF A (*past simple*) THEN B (would + *infinitive*)

What would you do if you were a millionaire?
If I was a millionaire, I'd sail round the world.
If Phil was here, he'd know what to do.

States a connection between events or situations which are not likely to happen. Often used to talk now about the likely or imagined result (B) of an imaginary situation or event (A).

In sentences like this the past simple tense does not refer to the past, but shows that (A) is not a really existing condition. In the second and third examples 'was' can be replaced by 'were', though this is more formal. The clause (B) describing the imagined result is sometimes expressed using 'should', but only with 'I' or 'we': *If I needed any help I should ask for it.*

• type 3 conditional

IF A (*past perfect*) THEN B (would have + *past participle*)

If he had asked me, I would have said 'yes'.
What would I have done if you'd got injured?
If I hadn't missed the bus, I wouldn't have been late.

States a connection between imaginary or possible events in the past. Often used to talk about the imagined result (B) of a situation or event (A) that did not happen.

As for type 2 conditionals, 'would' in clause (B) is sometimes replaced by 'should', but only with 'I' or 'we'.

• other conditional sentence patterns

- Although the above patterns are the most frequent, in some situations other combinations of verb tenses are possible. For example:

  If Vince **had** *worked hard, he* **would** *be a doctor.* — Vince did not work hard. As a result he is now not a doctor.

  If you really **liked** *Jane, you* **would***n't* **have** *said that.* — What you said suggests that you did not like Jane, and that you do not like her now.

- Modal auxiliary verbs like 'could' and 'might' can be used in conditional sentences:
  Many crimes **could** *be prevented if the public took more care.*
  You **ought to** *wear a hat if you are out for long in the sun.*
  You really **should***n't do that unless you want to get into trouble.*

- Conditional sentences with 'if' are often used to make requests or to give advice or orders:
  If you need help, just give me a call on 3578.
  If you should meet Sarah, don't ask about her new boyfriend—he's left her.
  If you're stuck, you could try having a rest and then starting again.

• conditional sentences without 'if'

'Unless' is frequently used in conditional sentences, meaning 'except if':
He warned that the company would go bankrupt **unless** *they sold more shares.*
She's almost sure to be world champion **unless** *somehow she loses this match.*

Other words can be used to introduce clauses in conditional sentences, for example: *on condition*, as long as, so long as, provided*, providing*, suppose*, supposing**

*These words can be followed by 'that': *I'd love to have a meal with you* – **provided that** *you don't wear your awful yellow jacket again.* 'Suppose' and 'supposing' are frequently followed by a question clause: *But supposing Brian doesn't finish in time, what will we do then?*

con·duct *obj* [ALLOW THROUGH] /kən'dʌkt/ *v* [T] to allow (electricity or heat) to go through • *Copper conducts electricity but plastic does not.*

con·duc·tion /kən'dʌk·ʃᵊn/ *n* [U] • *the conduction of electricity*

con·duct·ive /£kən'dʌk·tɪv, $-t̬ɪv/ *adj* • *Aluminium is a conductive metal.*

con·duct·iv·i·ty /£ˌkɒn·dʌk'tɪv·ɪ·ti, $ˌkɑːn·dʌk'tɪv·ə·t̬i/ *n* [U] • *We need a material with a high level of conductivity.*

con·duct·or /£kən'dʌk·təʳ, $-t̬ɚ/ *n* [C] • *Metal is a good conductor of heat whereas wood is not*

con·duct·or /£kən'dʌk·təʳ, $-tɚ/ *n* [C] someone whose job is to sell tickets on a bus, train or some other public vehicle • See also **conductor** at CONDUCT [ALLOW THROUGH], CONDUCT [MUSIC]. • Ⓔ Ⓕ

con·duit /£'kɒn·djuː·ɪt, $'kɑːn·duː-/ *n* [C] a pipe or passage for water or electrical wires to go through

cone /£kəʊn, $koʊn/ *n* [C] a solid shape with a round or oval base which narrows to a point, or any of various objects shaped like this, some of which are hollow and open at the end • *I ate the ice-cream but threw away the cone.* • *The police have sectioned off part of the road with* **traffic** *cones.* • A cone is also the hard oval shaped fruit of a CONIFER (= one of various types of evergreen tree). • [PIC] **Cone, Motorway, Shapes**

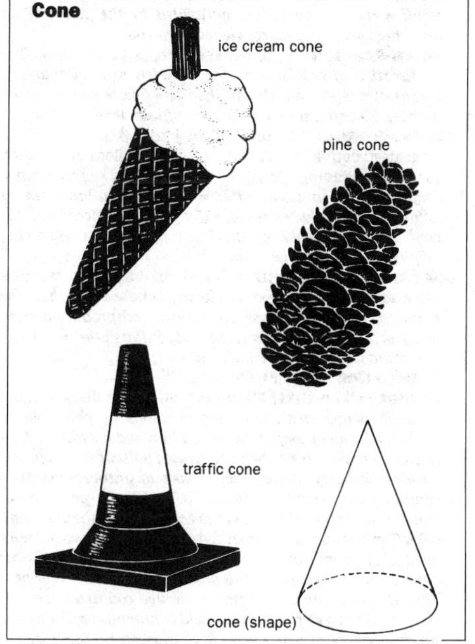

cone off *obj* /£kəʊn, $koʊn/ *v prep* [T] • *Part of the road had been coned off for repair work.*

con·ic·al /£'kɒn·ɪ·kᵊl, $'kɑː·nɪ-/ *adj* • An object which is conical is shaped like a cone: *a conical flask* • [PIC] **Laboratory**

con·ey /£'kəʊ·ni, $'koʊ-/ *n* [C/U] CONY

con·fab /£'kɒn·fæb, $'kɑːn-/ *n* [C] *dated humorous* a conversation in which one particular subject is usually considered • *Why don't we have a quick confab to see what people think about it.*

con·fec·tion /kən'fek·ʃᵊn/ *n* [C] *fml* a decorated cake or unusual sweet dish • Ⓕ

con·fec·tion·e·ry /£kən'fek·ʃᵊn·ri, $-er·i/ *n* [U] small pieces of sweet food; sweets, made mainly of sugar, chocolate or cream • *She stared at the confectionery counter in the shop with an expression of pure desire.* • [LP] **Shopping goods** Ⓒⓢ Ⓟⓛ

con·fec·tion·er /£kən'fek·ʃᵊn·əz, $-ɚz/ *n* [C] • A confectioner is a company or person that makes or sells sweets and chocolates. • **Confectioners' sugar** is *Am for* **icing sugar**. See at ICE [COVER CAKES].

con·fed·er·a·cy /£kən'fed·ᵊr·ə·si, $'-ɚ-/ *n* [C + sing/pl v] a union of STATES (= divisions of a country) or people who have combined together for a particular purpose, esp. one which is political or involves trade • **The Confederacy** was the union of southern American states that fought against the northern states in the American Civil War and were defeated in 1865. • *"A Confederacy of Dunces"* (title of a book by John Kennedy Toole, 1980)

con·fed·er·ate /£kən'fed·ᵊr·ət, $'-ɚ-/ *adj*

con·fed·er·ate /£kən'fed·ᵊr·ət, $'-ɚ-/ *n* [C] a person you are working together with in a secret and sometimes illegal activity

con·fed·er·a·tion /kənˌfed·ə'reɪ·ʃᵊn/ *n* [C + sing/pl v] an organization consisting of different groups of people who are working together for business or political reasons • *the Confederation of British Industry* • *The peace treaty will lay the foundations for a loose confederation of sovereign states.*

con·fer [TALK] /£kən'fɜːʳ, $-'fɜːr/ *v* [I] **-rr-** to exchange ideas on a particular subject, often with the intention of reaching a decision about what action to take • *I should like some time to confer* **with** *my lawyer.* • Ⓟ

con·fer *obj* [GIVE] /£kən'fɜːʳ, $-'fɜːr/ *v* [T] **-rr-** to give (an official title or honour) to someone • *The honour was conferred* **on/upon** *him just after the war.* • Ⓟ

con·fer·ence /£'kɒn·fᵊr·ᵊnts, $'kɑːn·fɚ-/ *n* an event, sometimes lasting a few days, at which there are a group of talks on a particular subject, or a meeting in which esp. business matters are discussed formally • *She spoke at a conference that I went to* **on** *AIDS.* [C] • *That's the room where they hold conferences.* [C] • *I'm attending a conference the whole of next week.* [C] • *Caroline O'Neill isn't available at present. She's* **in** *conference* (= is in a meeting). [U] • *Should I book the conference room for the meeting?* • Ⓔ Ⓕ

con·fess *(obj)* /kən'fes/ *v* to admit that you have done something wrong, esp. when what you have done is secret • *She confessed* **to** *her husband* **that** *she had sold her wedding ring.* [+ *that* clause] • *He confessed* **to** *sleeping/having slept through the second half of the film.* [I] • *Against the advice of his lawyer he confessed* **to** *the murder.* [I] • *I'm afraid I've got something to confess – I've trodden on your hamster.* [T] • *Come on! Confess! You've eaten that entire box of chocolates, haven't you?* [I] • **I have to/must** *confess* **(that)** *when I first met your husband I didn't think he was very bright.* [+ (*that*) clause] • *I confess* **(that)** *I'm a little bit confused by what you said.* [+ (*that*) clause] • *The director has confessed* **himself (to be)** *puzzled by the company's losses.* [+ obj + (*to be*) + adj] • In the Christian religion, esp. the Roman Catholic Church, a person might confess or confess their **sins** if they tell a priest about all the things that they have done wrong so that they can be forgiven. [I/T]

con·fessed /kən'fest/ *adj* [before noun; not gradable] • *He's a (self-)confessed clothes addict and last year admitted to a newspaper that he owned eighty pairs of shoes.* • *a (self-)confessed gambler/alcoholic/man-hater*

con·fes·sion /kən'feʃ·ᵊn/ *n* • *I've got a bit of a confession to* **make**. *You know the book you lent me? Well I've lost it.* [C] • *Is there anything you ought to tell me? Any confessions to make?* [C] • *You actually like housework? Now there's a confession!* [C] • *I can't ask for help. It's such a confession* **of** *failure.* [C] • *A criminal who admits to the police that he or she is guilty of a crime* **makes** *a confession.* [C] • *Confession is the first stage of coming to terms with what you've done.* [U] • Confession is the Christian activity, esp. in the Roman Catholic Church, of formally and privately telling a priest about all the things that you have done wrong so that you can be forgiven: *Have you been to confession recently?* [U] ○ *The priest* **heard** *his confession.* [U]

con·fes·sor /£kən'fes·əʳ, $-ɚ/ *n* [C] • A confessor is the priest to whom someone can confess.

con·fes·sion·al /kən'feʃ·ᵊn·ᵊl/ *n* [C] a small enclosed box-like room in a Christian, esp. Roman Catholic, church in which a person can tell a priest privately about what they have done wrong and be forgiven

con·fet·ti /£kən'fet·i, $-'fet̬-/ *n* [U] small pieces of coloured paper which you throw when celebrating some occasion, esp. over people just after they have married each other • *When they came out of the church, the bride and groom were showered with/in confetti.*

con·fid·ant, *female also* **con·fid·ante** /£kɒn·fɪ'dɒnt, $kɑːn·fɪ'dɑːnt/ *n* [C] a person with whom you can share your feelings and secrets • *a close/intimate confidant* • Ⓒⓢ Ⓟⓛ

con·fide *(obj)* /kən'faɪd/ *v* to tell something secret or personal to someone whom you trust not to tell anyone else • *He confided* **(to her) that** *his hair was not his own.* [+ *that* clause] • *"My husband doesn't know yet, but I'm going to leave him," she confided unhappily.* [+ clause] • If you can confide **in** someone you can share your feelings and secrets with them because you trust them not to tell other people: She's nice but I don't feel I can confide in her. [I]

con·fid·ing /kən'faɪ·dɪŋ/ *adj* • *He's very confiding. He'd tell his secrets to a complete stranger.*

con·fid·ing·ly /kən'faɪ·dɪŋ·li/ *adv* • *She spoke in a low voice, leaning towards him confidingly.*

con·fid·ence SECRET /£'kɒn·fɪ·dənts, $'kɑːn-/ *n* promised secrecy • *I'm telling you this* **in** *confidence* (= in the expectation that you won't tell anyone else). [U] • *They talked endlessly, exchanging confidences* (= secrets) *and sympathies.* [C] • *Once or twice I made the mistake of* **taking** *him* **into** *my confidence and telling him things I shouldn't have.* [U]

con·fid·ent·ial /£ˌkɒn·fɪ'den·tʃəl, $ˌkɑːn-/ *adj* • Something that is confidential is secret, often in a formal, business or military situation: *These documents are confidential. They must not leave this room.* ○ *All information will be treated as* **strictly** *confidential.* ○ *He's got a very confidential* (= secretive) *manner. You always feel that he's telling you something he shouldn't be.*

con·fid·ent·i·al·i·ty /$£ˌkɒn·fɪ·den·tʃi'æl·ɪ·ti, $ˌkɑːn·fɪ·den·tʃi'æl·ə·ṭi/ *n* [U] • *Confidentiality is guaranteed to everyone participating in the survey.*

con·fid·ent·ial·ly /£ˌkɒn·fɪ'den·tʃəl·i, $ˌkɑːn-/ *adv*

con·fid·ence CERTAINTY /£'kɒn·fɪ·dənts, $'kɑːn-/ *n* [U] the quality of being certain of your abilities or of trusting other people, plans or the future • *He's got* **the** *confidence* **to** *walk into a room of strangers and immediately start a conversation.* [+ *to* infinitive] • *She lacks (self-)confidence. I've never known anyone so timid and unsure of themselves.* • *I have* **every** *confidence* **in** *her. She'll be perfect for the job.* • *You don't seem to have much confidence* **in** *your boss. Isn't she very good?* • A **confidence trick** (*infml* **con**) is a trick in which a person is cheated into trusting someone enough to give them their money or possessions which are then stolen. • A **confidence man/trickster** (*infml* **con man**) is a person who performs **confidence tricks**.

con·fid·ent /£'kɒn·fɪ·dənt, $'kɑːn-/ *adj* • *You should be a bit more confident in yourself!* • *They don't seem to be very confident* **about** *the future of the industry.* • *I'm not confident* **of** *his skills as a manager.* • *Are you confident* **that** *enough people will attend the event?* [+ *that* clause] • *The actor gave a confident performance.*

con·fid·ent·ly /£'kɒn·fɪ·dənt·li, $'kɑːn-/ *adv* • *Act confidently in your interview. If you feel nervous, try not to show it.* • *Do you think we can confidently rely on him to improve the image of the company?*

con·fig·u·ra·tion /kənˌfɪg·ə'reɪ·ʃən/ *n* [C] *fml* the particular arrangement or pattern of a group of related things

con·fine *obj* /kən'faɪn/ *v* [T] to limit (someone or something) • *I don't like a job in which I'm confined* **to** *doing only one thing.* • *You are asked to confine your use of the telephone* **to** *business calls alone.* • *Could you confine your discussion* **to** *the matter in question, please!* • *By closing the infected farms we're hoping to confine the disease* (= stop it from spreading). • Something might be confined **to** a particular area or group of people if it appears only to exist there: *It is now known that the illness is not confined* **to** *any one group in society.* • *It's an attitude which seems to be confined* **to** *the upper classes.* • If a person is confined, they are kept, often by force, in an enclosed place: *He had been confined for so long that he couldn't cope with the outside world.*

con·fine·ment /kən'faɪn·mənt/ *n* [U] the situation of being kept somewhere usually by force, or *(medical)* the period during which a woman is in bed for the birth of her child

con·fines /£'kɒn·faɪnz, $'kɑːn-/ *pl n* the outer limits of something • *The narrow confines of a life in the church proved too difficult for him.*

con·firm *(obj)* MAKE CERTAIN /£kən'fɜːm, $-'fɜːrm/ *v* to make (an arrangement or meeting) certain, often by telephone or writing • *I'd like to confirm a reservation for a double room on the first of July.* [T] • *Six people have confirmed* **that** *they will be attending and ten haven't replied yet.* [+ *that* clause] • *I've accepted the job over the phone but I haven't confirmed in writing yet.* [I] • *I'd like to confirm* **when** *you will be arriving on Monday. Will you be here in time for lunch?* [+ *wh-* word]

con·firm·a·tion /£ˌkɒn·fə'meɪ·ʃən, $ˌkɑːn·fɚ-/ *n* • *a letter of confirmation* [U] • *We've had five confirmations for the conference and two refusals so far.* [C]

con·firm *obj* PROVE TRUE /£kən'fɜːm, $-'fɜːrm/ *v* [T] to give certainty to (a belief or an opinion which was previously not completely certain) • *The smell of cigarette smoke confirmed* **what** *he had suspected: There had been a party in his absence.* [+ *wh-* word] • *Her announcement this afternoon confirmed* **(that)** *she would in fact be resigning as Prime Minister.* [+ *(that)* clause] • *The leader's speech was impressive and confirmed her faith in the party.* • *Her husband confirmed* **(that)** *it was he who had crashed her car.* [+ *(that)* clause]

con·firm·a·tion /£ˌkɒn·fə'meɪ·ʃən, $ˌkɑːn·fɚ-/ *n* [U] • *Her confession was no surprise to him. Just the confirmation* **of** *his long-held suspicions.* • *We are still awaiting confirmation* **of** *the reports.*

con·firm *obj* RELIGION /£kən'fɜːm, $-'fɜːrm/ *v* [T usually passive] to accept (someone) formally as a member of the Christian Church at a special ceremony

con·firm·a·tion /£ˌkɒn·fə'meɪ·ʃən, $ˌkɑːn·fɚ-/ *n* [C/U]

con·firmed /£kən'fɜːmd, $-fɜːrmd/ *adj* [before n] having had a particular habit or way of life for a long time so that change seems unlikely • *a confirmed bachelor/sports fanatic/whisky drinker*

con·fi·scate *obj* /£'kɒn·fɪ·skeɪt, $'kɑːn-/ *v* [T] to take (a possession) away from someone when you have the right to do so, usually as a punishment and often for a limited period, after which it is returned to the owner • *Dad, Miss Edwards has confiscated that book you gave me till the end of term!* • *His passport was confiscated by the police in an attempt to prevent him from leaving the country.*

con·fi·sca·tion /£ˌkɒn·fɪ'skeɪ·ʃən, $ˌkɑːn-/ *n* • *The confiscation of his farm by the state left him without any means of supporting his family.* [U] • *There was a record number of confiscations by customs officers last year.* [C]

con·fla·gra·tion /£ˌkɒn·flə'greɪ·ʃən, $ˌkɑːn-/ *n* [C] a large destructive fire, or *(fig.)* a sudden violent event, such as a war, involving a lot of people • *Stratford suffered major conflagrations in 1594 and 1595, with 200 buildings being wholly or partially destroyed.* • *(fig.) There are fears that the civil war will develop into a conflagration involving neighbouring countries.*

con·flate *obj* /kən'fleɪt/ *v* [T] to combine (two or more separate things, esp. texts) to form a whole • *Somehow she managed to conflate these three plays and produce a fresh new work.* • *In his confusion he had conflated the two events and could no longer tell which was which.*

con·fla·tion /kən'fleɪ·ʃən/ *n* [C; U]

con·flict /£'kɒn·flɪkt, $'kɑːn-/ *n* an active disagreement between people with opposing opinions or principles • *There was a lot of conflict* **between** *him and his father.* [U] • *It was an unpopular policy and caused a number of conflicts within the party.* [C] • *I don't wish to* **enter/come into** *conflict* **with** *her on the matter.* [U] • *His outspoken views would frequently* **bring** *him* **into** *conflict* **with** *the president.* [U] • Conflict can also mean fighting between two or more groups of people or countries: *We wish to avoid conflict between our countries if at all possible.* [U] ○ *There have been several minor conflicts between the two countries over the past decade.* [C] • *"Never in the field of human conflict was so much owed by so many to so few"* (Speech by Sir Winston Churchill, 1940)

con·flict /kən'flɪkt/ *v* [I] • *If the two sides conflict* **with** *each other again, it will be disastrous for party unity.* • *The results of the new research would seem to conflict* **with** *existing theories.* • Descriptions of the same thing might conflict if they are different in a way that suggests that one of them must be false: *The statements they gave to the police conflicted* **with** *each other.*

con·flict·ing /£kən'flɪk·tɪŋ, $-ṭɪŋ/ *adj* • *conflicting opinions/ideas/advice* • *She was sometimes troubled by the conflicting* **interests** (= interests which are difficult to combine) *of a career and a home.* • *The jury heard conflicting evidence from three different witnesses.*

con·flu·ence /£'kɒn·fluː·ənts, $'kɑːn-/ *n* [C] *specialized* the place where two rivers flow together and become one larger river

con·form /£kən'fɔːm, $-'fɔːrm/ *v* [I] to behave according to a society's or group's usual standards of behaviour and expectations • *In an age when there was a great pressure on women to conform, she rejected every rule.* • *Originality had no place in the school I went to. You were required to conform.* • If a product conforms **to** or **with** a particular law it has reached the necessary stated standard: *Always check before you buy that your child's pram conforms to the official safety standards.*

con·form·ist /£kən'fɔː·mɪst, $-'fɔːr-/ *n* [C] • *They're just a boring bunch of conformists. Not one of them would step out of line.*

con·form·ist /£kən'fɔː·mɪst, $-'fɔːr-/ *adj* • *He used to be quite interesting as a boy but he's grown really conformist over the years.*

con·form·i·ty /£kən'fɔː·mɪ·ti, $-'fɔːr·mə·t̬i/ *n* [U] • *It's depressing how much conformity there is in such young children.* • *(fml)* **In** *conformity* **with** *your request we have cancelled your club membership.*

con·found *obj* /kən'faʊnd/ *v* [T] to confuse and greatly surprise (someone), causing them to be unable to explain or deal with a situation • *An elderly man from Hull has confounded doctors at the local hospital by living after he was officially declared dead.* • *The dancer confounded the critics who said she was finished by giving the best performance of her life.*

con·found·ed /kən'faʊn·dɪd/ *adj* [before n] *dated infml* • Confounded is used to express annoyance: *It's a confounded nuisance!*

con·front *obj* /kən'frʌnt/ *v* [T] to face, meet or deal with (a difficult situation or person) • *As she left the court, she was confronted by angry crowds who tried to block her way.* • *When he returned to his office he was confronted* **by/with** *a great pile of work.* • *It's an issue we'll have to confront at some point, no matter how unpleasant it is.* • *Pronunciation is just one of the many problems that confront the language learner.* • If you confront someone **with** something you tell them what they do not want to hear, often because it is something bad that they have done or it needs an explanation: *I know she's got a problem, but I daren't confront her with it in case she breaks down.* • *I thought I would remain calm, but when I was confronted* **with/by** *the TV camera, I became very nervous.*

con·front·a·tion /£ˌkɒn·frʌn'teɪ·ʃən, $ˌkɑːn·frən-/ *n* • *She actually enjoys confrontation whereas I prefer a quiet life and tend to avoid it.* [U] • *Violent confrontations between police and demonstrators were reported in the capital.* [C]

con·front·a·tion·al /£ˌkɒn·frʌn'teɪ·ʃən·əl, $ˌkɑːn·frən-/ *adj* • *He's got a rather aggressive, confrontational manner.*

con·fuse *obj* /kən'fjuːz/ *v* [T] to mix up (someone's mind or ideas), or to make (something) difficult to understand • *You're confusing him! Tell him slowly and one thing at a time.* • *You're confusing the issue* (=making the problem unnecessarily difficult)*!* • If someone confuses two separate things or confuses one thing **with** another they mix them up mentally, imagining that they are one: *It's easy to confuse his films because he always uses the same actors.* ○ *You're confusing me with my sister – it was her who was sick on your sofa.*

con·fused /kən'fjuːzd/ *adj* • *I was so confused in today's history lesson. I didn't understand a thing!* • *Grandfather is starting to get really confused. He doesn't even know what day it is sometimes.* • *Your essay gets a bit confused halfway through when you introduce too many ideas at once.* • *I'm a bit confused. Was the man I just met your husband or your son?* • A person might be described as confused if they are unhappy and don't know what they want from life: *The actress had a tragic childhood and as an adult was sad and confused.* • Ⓕ Ⓟ

con·fus·ing /kən'fjuː·zɪŋ/ *adj* • *We've got three people called Paul James working for us, so it's a bit confusing.* • *The instructions are terribly confusing. Could you help me with them, please?* • *What a confusing film. I didn't know what was going on towards the end.*

con·fu·sion /kən'fjuː·ʒən/ *n* • *There seems to be some confusion over who is actually giving the talk. Do you have any idea?* [U] • *To avoid confusion, the twins never wore the same clothes.* [U] • *It is worrying that the document contains many confusions.* [C] • *There was a terrible confusion* (=lack of order) *as everyone struggled madly in the dark to get to some air.* [U] • *In the confusion, I lost my shoe and wasn't able to stop and pick it up.* [U] • Ⓕ

con·fute *obj* /kən·fjuːt/ *v* [T] *fml* to prove (a person or an argument) to be wrong

con·ga /£'kɒŋ·gə, $'kɑːŋ-/ *n* [C] (the music for) a Latin American dance in which a chain of people, holding each other around the waist, follow a leader around using simple steps, sometimes kicking

con·geal /kən'dʒiːəl/ *v* [I] to change from a liquid or soft state to a thick or solid state • *The blood had congealed in thick black clots around his sharp white teeth.*

con·gealed /kən'dʒiːəld/ *adj* • *She felt sick as she looked at the congealed lumps of egg on her plate.*

con·ge·ni·al /kən'dʒiː·ni·əl/ *adj* friendly and pleasant; providing the right conditions for happiness and peace of mind • *congenial company/weather/surroundings*

con·gen·i·tal /£kən'dʒen·ɪ·təl, $-t̬əl/ *adj* [not gradable] *medical* (of diseases) existing at or from birth • *a congenital defect/abnormality/disease/condition* • A congenital **liar** is someone who is always lying.

con·ger eel /£ˌkɒŋ·gə-, $ˌkɑŋ·gɚ-/ *n* [C] a long powerful snake-like sea fish

con·gest·ed /kən'dʒes·tɪd/ *adj* too blocked or crowded and causing difficulties • Roads and towns are described as being congested if there is too much traffic and movement is made difficult. • People might describe themselves as being congested if they cannot breathe through their nose because it is blocked, usually during an infection. • The lungs and the tubes that carry blood might also become congested if they are too full of liquid, esp. blood.

con·ges·tion /kən'dʒes·tʃən/ *n* [U] • *The congestion in the city gets even worse during the summer.* • *This spray helps to ease nasal congestion.*

con·glom·e·rate COMPANY /£kən'glɒm·ər·ət, $-'glɑː·mɚ-/ *n* [C] a company that owns several smaller businesses whose products or services are usually very different • *a financial/industrial conglomerate*

con·glom·e·rate ROCK /£kən'glɒm·ə·rət, $-'glɑː·mɚ·ət/ *n* [C] *specialized* a rock which consists of small rounded stones that are held together by clay and sand and is formed on a beach or at the bottom of a river

con·glom·e·ra·tion /£kənˌglɒm·ər'eɪ·ʃən, $-ˌglɑː·mə'reɪ-/ *n* [C] a large group or mass of different things gathered together as a whole in a way that is unexpected or appears to lack order • *She imagined herself lost in a great conglomeration of ugly concrete buildings.*

con·grat·u·late *obj* /kəŋ'græt·jʊ·leɪt/ *v* [T] to praise (someone) and say that you approve of or are pleased about a special or unusual achievement • *I was just congratulating Ceri* **on** *winning*/**on** *having won her race.* • *I think he expects to be congratulated every time he does the washing up.*

con·grat·u·la·tion /kəŋˌgræt·jʊ'leɪ·ʃən/ *n* [U] • *He sent her a note of congratulation on her election victory.*

con·grat·u·la·tions /kəŋˌgræt·jʊ'leɪ·ʃənz/ *exclamation, pl n* • *"I passed my driving test yesterday." "Did you? Congratulations!"* • *Congratulations* **on** *your marriage! Is it your sixth husband?* • *Do* **give** *him*/**pass on** *my congratulations when you see him.* • LP **Phrases and customs**

con·grat·u·lat·o·ry /£kəŋˌgræt·jʊ'leɪ·tər·i, $-t̬ɚ-/ *adj* • *a congratulatory speech/card/remark*

con·gre·gate /£'kɒŋ·grɪ·geɪt, $'kɑːŋ-/ *v* [I] (of people and animals) to gather together in a large group • *A patient crowd had congregated* **around** *the entrance to the theatre, hoping to catch a glimpse of the stars of the show.*

con·gre·ga·tion /£ˌkɒŋ·grɪ'geɪ·ʃən, $ˌkɑːŋ-/ *n* [C + sing/pl v] a group of people gathered together in a religious building for worship and prayer • *The vicar asked the congregation to kneel.*

con·gress MEETING /£'kɒŋ·gres, $'kɑːŋ-/ *n* [C + sing/pl v] a large formal meeting of representatives from countries or societies at which ideas are discussed and information is exchanged • *an international/medical congress* • *a congress of racial equality*

Con·gress AMERICAN POLITICIANS /£'kɒŋ·gres, $'kɑːŋ-/ *n* [not after *the*] the elected group of politicians in the US who are responsible for making the law, combining the Senate and the House of Representatives • *Congress has rejected the recent presidential proposal on firearms.*

con·gress·man (*pl* **-men**), **con·gress·wo·man** (*pl* **-women**), **rep·re·sent·a·tive** /£'kɒŋ·gres·mən, $'kɑːŋ-, -ˌwʊm·ən/ *n* [C]

con·gres·sion·al /kəŋ'greʃ·ən·əl/ *adj* [before n; not gradable] • *congressional elections* • *a congressional committee* • A Congressional **district** is a place from which a member of the US House of Representatives is elected.

con·gru·ent /£'kɒŋ·gru·ənt, $'kɑːŋ-/ *adj specialized* (of shapes in mathematics) having the same shape and size as another • *congruent triangles*

con·gru·ence /£'kɒŋ·gru·ənts, $'kɑːŋ-/ *n* [U] *specialized*

con·ic·al /£'kɒn·ɪ·kəl, $'kɑː·nɪ-/ *adj* See at CONE

con·i·fer /£'kɒn·ɪ·fər, $'kɑː·nɪ·fɚ/ *n* [C] one of various types of evergreen tree which produce fruit in the form of cones • *Firs, spruces and pines are conifers.* • *Conifers have* *long thin leaves called needles.* • *Conifers are an important source of timber for building and the manufacture of paper and furniture.*

co·nif·er·ous /£kə'nɪf·ər·əs, $'-ɚ-/ *adj* • *a coniferous forest*

conj *n* [C] *abbreviation for* CONJUNCTION CONNECTING WORD

con·jec·ture /£kən'dʒek·tʃər, $-tʃɚ/ *v, n* (to form) a guess or judgment, based on the appearance of a situation rather than on proof • *We'll never know exactly how she died. We can only conjecture.* [I] • *He conjectured* **that** *the company would soon be in financial difficulties.* [+ *that* clause] • *There's been a lot of conjecture in the papers recently* **about** *the royal marriage.* [U] • *It's pure conjecture. Nobody knows the facts.* [U]

con·jec·tur·al /£kən'dʒek·tʃər·əl, $-tʃɚ-/ *adj*

con·joined /kən'dʒɔɪnd/ *adj* [not gradable] *fml* joined together • *The past and the present are conjoined in this author's imagination.*

con·jug·al /£'kɒn·dʒʊ·gəl, $'kɑːn-/ *adj* [not gradable] *fml* connected with marriage or the relationship between husband and wife, esp. their sexual relationship • *conjugal happiness* • *the conjugal bed* • *Some prisoners who want to start a family are to be permitted conjugal* **visits.** • **Conjugal rights** are the right to have sex with the person you are married to: *Men cannot use conjugal rights as an excuse for raping their wives.* ○ *(humorous) What's she going to do about her conjugal rights while her husband's away?*

con·jug·ate *(obj)* /£'kɒn·dʒʊ·geɪt, $'kɑːn-/ *v specialized* (of a verb) to have different forms depending on number, tense etc., or (of a person) to list the various forms of a verb • *The verb 'to be' conjugates irregularly.* [I] • *I used to dread it in French classes when the teacher asked us to conjugate a verb aloud.* [T]

con·jug·a·tion /£ˌkɒn·dʒʊ'geɪ·ʃən, $ˌkɑːn-/ *n* [C] *specialized* • A conjugation is a group of verbs that conjugate in the same way: *The Latin verb 'amare' belongs to the first conjugation.*

con·junc·tion CONNECTING WORD /kən'dʒʌŋk·ʃən/ (*abbreviation* **conj**) *n* [C] a word such as 'and', 'but', 'while' or 'although' that connects words, phrases and clauses in a sentence

con·junc·tion COMBINATION /kən'dʒʌŋk·ʃən/, *fml* **con·junct·ure** /£kən'dʒʌŋk·tʃər, $-tʃɚ/ *n* a combination or happening together of events or conditions • *It was an unfortunate conjunction of circumstances that led to his downfall.* [C] • *There is a team of writers working* **in** *conjunction* **(with** *each other) on the book.* [U] • *For best results use Kissy Blonde shampoo* **in** *conjunction* **with** *Kissy Blonde conditioner.* [U]

con·junct·iv·i·tis /£kənˌdʒʌŋk·tɪ'vaɪ·tɪs, $-t̬ɪs/ *n* [U] a painful and infectious illness of the eyes which makes them red and makes the EYELIDS (= skin covering the eyes) swollen and sticky

con·jure *(obj)* /£'kʌn·dʒər, $-dʒɚ/ *v* to make something appear (as if) by magic • *In an instant the magician had conjured* **(up)** *a perfect white dove from his hat.* [T/M] • *It was claimed she was able to conjure* **up** *the spirits of the dead.* [M] • *The first thing he did when he joined the circus was learn how to conjure.* [I] • A **conjuring trick** is a trick in which something is made to appear as if by magic, often using a quick movement of the hand. • *For some people, the word 'England' may still conjure* **up** (= create in the mind) *images of pretty gardens and tea parties.* [M] • *How am I expected to conjure* **up** (= make quickly and without effort) *a meal for six of his friends with almost nothing in the fridge?* [M] • *Seeing her old school again conjured* **up** (= made her remember) *some horrific memories.* [M]

con·jur·er, con·jur·or /£'kʌn·dʒər·ər, $-dʒɚ·ɚ/ *n* [C] • *I don't know why it's always white rabbits that conjurers produce from their hats.*

conk BODY PART /£kɒŋk, $kɑːŋk/ *n* [C] *Br and Aus humorous slang* a nose

conk *obj* HIT /£kɒŋk, $kɑːŋk/ *v* [T] *humorous infml* to hit (someone) usually on the head with a heavy object

conk out *v adv* [I] *infml* (of vehicles and other machines) to stop working or fail suddenly • *I was just two miles from home when my motorbike conked out!* • *(fig.) After a six-hour flight and a long day of meetings, it's not surprising you conked out* (= became too tired to continue).

conk·er /£'kɒŋ·kər, $'kɑːŋ·kɚ/ *n* [C] *esp. Br* the dark brown, shiny nut of a HORSE CHESTNUT tree • PIC› **Nut, Tree**

con·nect *(obj)* JOIN /kə'nekt/ *v* to join or be joined (with something else) • *Can I connect my printer* **to** *your computer?* [T] • *Where does the cooker connect* **(up) to** *the electricity?* [I] • *Has the telephone/electricity/gas been connected* (= switched on or joined to the main supply) *in your new place yet?* [T] • LP› **Switching on and off**

con·nect·ed /kə'nek·tɪd/ *adj* [not gradable] • *"The TV isn't working." "Have you checked that the aerial's connected?"*

con·nect·ing /kə'nek·tɪŋ/ *adj* [not gradable] • *The houses are detached but there's a connecting garage between them.* • *(specialized)* A **connecting rod** (also *infml* **con rod**) is a rod that joins two particular moving parts in an engine, esp. one joining the PISTON to the CRANKSHAFT in a motor vehicle.

con·nec·tion /kə'nek·ʃən/ *n* • *It's no wonder your shaver isn't working. There's a loose connection* (= a wire is not in the right place) *in the plug.* [C] • *The connection of the two halves of the bridge will take several days.* [U] • *The electricity company guarantees connection within 24 hours.* [U] • *He only got the job because of his connections* (= people who helped him)! [C] • *It's thought that his connections* **with** *the Mafia helped his singing career.* [C]

con·nect·or /£kə'nek·tər, $-tɚ/ *n* [C] *specialized* • A connector is a device at the end of a wire which holds the wire in position in an item of electrical equipment: *electrical connectors* ○ *You'll need to change the connectors if you want to use this cable to link your keyboard to your computer.*

con·nect *obj* RELATE /kə'nekt/ *v* [T] to consider (a person or thing) as related to someone or something else • *She's an actress I connect* **with** *the theatre rather than films.* • *Police are connecting the break-in* **with** *other recent thefts in the area.* • *It's strange that you didn't connect them since they look so alike.*

con·nect·ed /kə'nek·tɪd/ *adj* • *I know he has the same surname but I don't think he's connected* **to** *the family* (= a relative). • *They're not blood relations. They're only connected by marriage.* • *He was connected in some way* **with** *that fraud scandal a couple of years back.* • *Butter is one of a group of foods that are thought to be connected* **with** *heart disease.* • See also WELL-CONNECTED.

con·nec·tion /kə'nek·ʃən/ *n* [C] • *Is there a connection* **between** *your leaving home and my cooking?* • *They're sisters, are they? I knew their surname was the same but I never* **made** (= thought of) *the connection.* • *They say they want to talk to you* **in connection with** (= on the subject of) *an unpaid tax bill.*

con·nect *obj* TELEPHONE /kə'nekt/ *v* [T] (of a telephone operator) to make it possible for (someone) to speak to someone else by telephone • *Could you connect me* **with** *Paris/***to** *a number in Paris, please. I can't seem to get through myself.* • LP› **Telephone**

con·nec·tion /kə'nek·ʃən/ *n* [C] • *I'm always trying to ring you but I can never get a connection.*

con·nect TRANSPORT /kə'nekt/ *v* [I] (of two public transport vehicles) to make it possible for passengers to continue the next part of their journey easily by having the second method of transport leave soon after the first has arrived • *The flight will be arriving in Malaga at ten o'clock where it connects* **with** *a coach service to your hotel.* • *There's a connecting train service between the airport and the city.*

con·nec·tion /kə'nek·ʃən/ *n* [C] • *If the flight is late, we'll miss our connection.* • *The railway connections in the north of the country are fairly poor.*

con·nect·ive tis·sue /kə'nek·tɪv/ *n* [U] *medical* the strong stretchy material that acts as a support around the organs in the body and is also found in the joints

con·nive /kə'naɪv/ *v* [I] to plan secretly and dishonestly for something to happen which will be to your advantage • *The twins were always conniving* **with** *each other when they were young, and I never felt I could trust them.*

con·niv·ing /kə'naɪ·vɪŋ/ *adj* • *He's a conniving bastard!*

con·nive at *obj v prep* [T] to allow (something bad) to happen although you know about it • *The government connive at the problem because it would cost them too much to solve it.*

con·niv·ance /kə'naɪ·vənts/ *n* [U] • *Their appalling treatment of their child could only have happened* **with** *the connivance* **of** *their neighbours.*

con·nois·seur /£ˌkɒn·ə'sɜːr, $ˌkɑː·nə'sɜːr/ *n* [C] a person who has an extremely good knowledge of one of the arts or of food and drink and can judge quality, beauty or skill in that particular subject • *a wine/food/art connoisseur* ○ *a* *connoisseur of ballet/cigars/chocolate/whisky* • *I'm no connoisseur but I know a good champagne when I taste one.*

con·no·ta·tion /£ˌkɒn·əˈteɪ·ʃᵊn, $ˌkɑː·nə-/ *n* [C] a feeling or idea that is suggested by a particular word although not necessarily a part of the word's meaning, or something suggested by an object or situation • *The word 'lady' has connotations of refinement and excessive femininity that some women find offensive.*

con·note *obj* /£kəˈnəʊt, $-ˈnoʊt/ *v* [T] • *To me chocolate connotes pleasure and indulgence.*

con·nu·bi·al /£kəˈnjuː·bi·ᵊl, $-ˈnuː-/ *adj* [not gradable] *fml* connected with marriage • *connubial bliss*

con·quer *obj* /£ˈkɒŋ·kəʳ, $ˈkɑːŋ·kɚ/ *v* [T] to take control or possession of (foreign land or a group of people) by force • *The Spanish conquered the New World in the sixteenth century.* • *The English were conquered by the Normans in 1066.* • *(fig.) In the last minute of the game Spain scored a triumphant goal and conquered* (= defeated) *their rivals.* • You might conquer a problem or an unreasonable fear of something by dealing with or fighting successfully against it: *Efforts must be made to conquer the enormous problem of homelessness.* ○ *You've got to conquer your irrational fear of technology and start using that computer.* ○ *Scientists expect it will be many years before this dreadful disease in conquered.*

con·quer·or /£ˈkɒŋ·kᵊr·əʳ, $ˈkɑːŋ·kɚ·ɚ/ *n* [C] • *William the Conqueror was the first Norman King of England.*

con·quest /£ˈkɒŋ·kwest, $ˈkɑːŋ-/ *n* [U] • *The Battle of Hastings led to the Norman conquest of England.* [U] • *It looks as if the European tennis cup will be the champion's next conquest.* [C] • *(humorous)* A conquest can be someone you have had sex with but probably not a relationship: *I was determined not to become just another of his conquests.* [C]

con·quist·a·dor /£kɒnˈkwɪs·tə·dɔːʳ, $kɑːnˈkiː·stə·dɔːr/ *n* [C] one of the Spanish people who travelled to America in the 16th century and CONQUERED (= took control of) Mexico and Peru

con·science /£ˈkɒn·tʃᵊnts, $ˈkɑːn-/ *n* the tendency to judge the morality of your own actions and feel guilt about the bad things that you have done or for which you feel responsible • *A* **guilty** *conscience was preventing her from sleeping at night.* [C] • *You didn't do anything wrong. You should have a* **clear** *conscience.* [C] • *My conscience would never allow me to wear a fur coat.* [C] • If something is **on** your conscience, it is making you feel guilty: *I ignored an old woman who asked me for money in the street yesterday and it's been on my conscience ever since.* [C] • *If I smoke even one cigarette it* **preys/weighs on** *my conscience all day* (= makes me feel guilty). [C] • *He only gives money to charity to* **salve** *his conscience* (= stop him from feeling guilty.) [C] • *The television coverage of so many starving people was designed to* **prick/stir** *the public conscience* (= make people feel guilty). [C] • *He's got no conscience at all* (= does not feel guilty) *about leaving me to do the housework.* [C] • *There's no obligation to pay. It's a* **question/matter of** *conscience whether you do or not.* [U] • *You couldn't (Br)* **in all conscience**/*(Am)* **in good conscience** (= without feeling guilty) *ask her to pay the whole bill!* • If someone is **conscience-stricken** they regret very much something that they have done wrong. • *"Conscience doth* (= does) *make cowards of us all"* (Shakespeare, Hamlet 3.1)

con·sci·en·tious ob·jec·tor *n* [C] • A **conscientious objector** is a person who refuses to work in the armed forces for moral or religious reasons.

con·sci·en·tious /£ˌkɒn·tʃiˈent·ʃəs, $ˌkɑːn-/ *adj* putting a lot of effort into your work • *She's an excellent student – bright, attentive and conscientious.*

con·sci·en·tious·ly /£ˌkɒnt·ʃiˈent·ʃə·sli, $ˌkɑːnt-/ *adv*

con·sci·en·tious·ness /£ˌkɒnt·ʃiˈent·ʃə·snəs, $ˌkɑːnt-/ *n* [U]

con·scious THINKING /£ˈkɒn·tʃəs, $ˈkɑːn-/ *adj* awake, thinking and aware of what is happening around you • *I'm waiting until the hospital says she's conscious before I visit her again.* • *(fig. humorous) "Can I speak to Isobel, please?" "She's still in bed. I'll just go and see if she's conscious* (= awake) *yet."*

con·scious·ness /£ˈkɒn·tʃə·snəs, $ˈkɑːn-/ *n* [U] • *He* **lost** *consciousness after his accident and never* **recovered/ regained** *it.* • *As she lay on the bed, half asleep and half awake, the smell of gas slowly* **entered into/impinged on** *her consciousness* (= she gradually became able to smell it).

con·scious KNOWING /£ˈkɒn·tʃəs, $ˈkɑːn-/ *adj* [after v] noticing the existence or presence of something particular • *The tooth doesn't exactly hurt but I'm conscious* **of** *it* (= I can feel it) *all the time.* • *She was very conscious* **of** *being stared at as a foreigner.* • *I think she's very conscious* **of** *being the only person in the office who didn't have a university education.* • *He gradually became conscious* (**of** *the fact*) **that** *he was the only man at the party who wasn't wearing a suit.* [+ *that* clause] • See also SUBCONSCIOUS.

con·scious·ness /£ˈkɒn·tʃə·snəs, $ˈkɑːn-/ *n* [U] • *Do you think her consciousness* **that** *she's somehow different makes her feel uneasy?* [+ *that* clause]

con·scious INTENTIONAL /£ˈkɒn·tʃəs, $ˈkɑːn-/ *adj* determined and intentional • *He's obviously making a conscious effort to be nice to me at the moment.* • *It wasn't a conscious decision to lose weight. It just happened.* • *Was it conscious or did you sit down next to him by chance?*

con·scious·ly /£ˈkɒn·tʃə·sli, $ˈkɑːn-/ *adv* • *I don't think she's consciously rude to everyone – she's just got an unfortunate manner.*

con·scious AWARE /£ˈkɒn·tʃəs, $ˈkɑːn-/ *adj* aware of and worried about something • *politically/socially conscious* • *fashion conscious* • *money conscious* • *He's so weight/figure/health conscious – I've never known anyone so careful about what they eat.* • *We have to be very safety conscious with this sort of machine.* • See also SELF-CONSCIOUS.

con·scious·ness /£ˈkɒn·tʃə·snəs, $ˈkɑːn-/ *n* [U] • *Working in an unemployment office had helped to* **raise** *his political consciousness.* • **Consciousness raising** is the attempt to increase people's knowledge of and interest in social and political matters.

con·script *obj* /kənˈskrɪpt/, *Am usually* **draft** *v* [T usually passive] to force (someone) by law to serve in one of the armed forces • *He was conscripted* **into** *the army at the age of 18.*

con·script /£ˈkɒn·skrɪpt, $ˈkɑːn-/, *Am usually* **draf·tee** *n* [C] • *Over half the army was composed of conscripts.* • Compare VOLUNTEER.

con·script /£ˈkɒn·skrɪpt, $ˈkɑːn-/ *adj* [before n; not gradable] • *a conscript army* • *conscript soldiers*

con·scrip·tion /kənˈskrɪp·ʃᵊn/ *n* [U] • *He's been worried that the government will introduce conscription ever since the war began.*

con·se·crate *obj* /£ˈkɒnt·sɪ·kreɪt, $ˈkɑːnt-/ *v* [T] to officially make (something) holy and able to be used for religious ceremonies, or *(fml)* to give (your life or time) completely to a particular esp. religious purpose • *The new cathedral was completed and consecrated in 1962.* • In the Christian Church a BISHOP (= a priest of high rank) is consecrated when he is officially given the title in a ceremony. • *(fml) She consecrated her whole life* **to** *spreading the word of God.*

con·se·crat·ed /£ˈkɒnt·sɪ·kreɪ·tɪd, $ˈkɑːnt·sɪ·kreɪ·t̬ɪd/ *adj* [not gradable] • *consecrated bread/wine/ground*

con·se·cra·tion /£ˌkɒnt·sɪˈkreɪ·ʃᵊn, $ˌkɑːnt-/ *n* [U] • *Inside the cathedral, a thousand white candles were burning for the consecration of the new bishop.*

con·sec·u·tive /£kənˈsek·jʊ·tɪv, $-t̬ɪv/ *adj* (of events) following one after another without an interruption • *This is the fifth consecutive weekend that I've spent working, and I'm a bit fed up with it.*

con·sec·u·tive·ly /£kənˈsek·jʊ·tɪv·li, $-t̬ɪv-/ *adv*

con·sen·sual /£ˌkɒnˈsen·sju·ᵊl, $ˌkɑːn-/ *adj fml* (esp. in legal matters) with the willing agreement of all the people involved • *No criminal charges were brought against him after the police decided that the sexual acts he performed with his neighbour were consensual* (= both people agreed to it).

con·sens·us /kənˈsent·səs/ *n* [U] a generally accepted opinion or decision among a group of people • *The* (**general**) *consensus in the office is that he's useless at his job.* • *Could we* **reach** *a consensus* **on** *this matter? Let's take a vote.* • *There is no consensus* **among** *the experts* **on** *some foods. Advice changes depending on who you listen to.*

con·sent /kənˈsent/ *v, n slightly fml* (to give your) permission or agreement • *Very reluctantly I've consented* **to** *lend her my car.* [+ *to* infinitive] • *My aunt never married because her father wouldn't consent* **to** *her marriage to a cousin.* [I] • *They can't publish your name without your consent.* [U] • *Your organs will only be used after your death if you* **give** *your consent beforehand.* [U] • A **consenting adult** is a person who is considered old enough and therefore responsible enough to decide if they want sex and who they want to have sex with. • *Her latest film,* **by common consent** (= it is generally agreed), *is her best yet.* •

A little while she strove, and much repented, / And whispering 'I will ne'er (=never) *consent' – consented"* (Lord Byron in the poem *Don Juan*, 1819-24)

con·se·quence /£'kɒnt·sɪ·kwənts, $'kɑːnt-/ *n* [C] an often bad or inconvenient result of a particular action or situation • *I missed the bus this morning and* **as a** *consequence was late for work.* • *The government's refusal to put enough money into health care has had* **disastrous** *consequences.* • *I told the hairdresser to do what she wanted to my hair but* **look at the** *consequences!* • *Well, if you insist on eating so much, you'll have to* **suffer/take the consequences** (=live with the results)*!* • *"Was anything interesting said at the meeting?" "Nothing* **of any** *consequence* (=Nothing important)*."* • (NL)

con·se·quent /£'kɒnt·sɪ·kwənt, $'kɑːnt-/, **con·se·quen·tial** /£,kɒnt·sɪ'kwen·tʃəl, $,kɑːnt-/ *adj* • *Our use of harmful chemicals and the consequent(ial) damage to the environment is a very serious matter.* • (PL)

con·se·quent·ly /£'kɒnt·sɪ·kwənt·li, $'kɑːnt-/ *adv* • *I spent most of my money in the first week and consequently* (=as a result) *had very little to eat during the last few days of the holiday.*

con·serv·a·tive [AGAINST CHANGE] /£kən'sɜː·və·tɪv, $-'sɜːr·və·t̬ɪv/ *adj* tending not to like or trust change, esp. sudden change • *It's an extremely conservative society – they're very easily shocked by anything different or daring.* • *I tend to be rather conservative in such matters and a bit suspicious about these supposed advances.* • If you are conservative in your appearance you tend not to like fashionable or modern clothes or hairstyles: *He's such a conservative dresser – he always looks as if he's wearing his father's clothes.* • *I'm a bit conservative in these matters – that's with a small 'c'* (=I'm not referring to politics). • Compare LIBERAL [SOCIETY].

con·serv·a·tive·ly /£kən'sɜː·və·tɪv·li, $-'sɜːr·və·t̬ɪv-/ *adv* • *I dress more conservatively for the office.*

con·serv·a·ti·sm /£kən'sɜː·və·tɪ·zəm, $-'sɜːr·və·t̬ɪ-/ *n* [U] • *He found himself frustrated by the company's deep-seated conservatism.*

Con·serv·a·tive [POLITICAL PARTY] /£kən'sɜː·və·tɪv, $-'sɜːr·və·t̬ɪv/, **To·ry** *adj* belonging to or supporting a political party whose beliefs and ideas tend to oppose sudden social change, high taxation and government involvement in industry • *the Conservative Party* • *Conservative policies* • *a Conservative MP* • *a Conservative government* • *Did you vote Conservative at the last election?*

Con·serv·a·tive /£kən'sɜː·və·tɪv, $-'sɜːr·və·t̬ɪv/, **To·ry** *n* [C] • *She's a* **staunch** (=very loyal) *Conservative.*

Con·serv·a·ti·sm /£kən'sɜː·və·tɪ·zəm, $-'sɜːr·və·t̬ɪ-/ *n* [U] • *The recent revival of Conservatism is due to the weakness of the opposition parties.*

con·serv·a·tive [LOW] /£kən'sɜː·və·tɪv, $-'sɜːr·və·t̬ɪv/ *adj* (of guesses and calculations) likely to be less than the real amount • *If I said there were three million unemployed that would be a conservative* **estimate** *– in fact there are probably a lot more.*

con·serv·a·to·ry [SCHOOL] /£kən'sɜː·və·tri, $-'sɜːr-/, *Br also* **con·serv·a·toire** /£kən,sɜː·və'twɑːr, $-,sɜːr·və'twɑːr/ *n* [C] a school for the teaching of music or sometimes acting or art

con·serv·a·to·ry [ROOM] /£kən'sɜː·və·tri, $-'sɜːr·və·tɔː·ri/, *Am also* **so·lar·i·um** *n* [C] a glass room, usually connected to a house, in which plants are grown and kept • [PIC] **Accommodation**

con·serve *obj* [KEEP] /£kən'sɜːv, $-'sɜːrv/ *v* [T] to keep and protect from damage, change or waste; preserve • *In an attempt to conserve electricity the building's owners are cutting down on their central heating.* • *The nationalists are very keen to conserve their customs and language.* • *I'm not being lazy – I'm just conserving my* **energy/strength** *for later.* • (DK) (NL) (RUS)

con·serv·a·tion /£,kɒnt·sə'veɪ·ʃən, $,kɑːnt·sɚ-/ *n* [U] • Conservation is the protection of plants and animals, natural areas, and interesting and important structures and buildings, esp. from the damaging effects of human activity: *wildlife conservation* ○ *a conservation area* ○ *The group are involved in a conservation battle to save this extraordinary old house.* • Conservation is also the preservation of valuable natural substances that exist in limited amounts: *the conservation of coal/gas/oil reserves* ○ *As well as helping the environment,* **energy** *conservation reduces your fuel bills.*

con·serv·a·tion·ist /£,kɒnt·sə'veɪ·ʃən·ɪst, $,kɑːnt·sɚ-/ *n* [C] • *Conservationists are fighting to stop the fields around here from being built on.*

con·serve [FOOD] /£'kɒn·sɜːv, $'kɑːn·sɜːrv/ *n* [C/U] a type of JAM (=a sweet soft substance made by cooking fruit with sugar) in which the fruit is whole or in large pieces • *apricot conserve* • *strawberry conserve* • *More expensive jams are often called conserves.* • (DK) (NL) (RUS)

con·sid·er *(obj)* [THINK] /£kən'sɪd·ər, $-ɚ/ *v* to spend time thinking about a possibility or making a decision • *Don't make any decisions before you've considered the matter.* [T] • *The director has arranged a meeting to consider the problem and any possible solutions.* [T] • *Have you considered* **what** *you'll do if you don't get the job?* [+ *wh-* word] • *We're considering sell***ing** (=it is possible that we will sell) *the house.* [+ v-*ing*] • *Have you considered France* **for** *a camping trip?* [T] • *She's being considered* **for** *the job.* [T]

con·sid·er·a·tion /kən,sɪd·ə'reɪ·ʃən/ *n* [U] • *After some consideration we've decided to sell the house.* • *The whole matter needs (to be given) careful consideration.*

con·sid·ered /£kən'sɪd·əd, $-ɚd/ *adj* • A **considered opinion** is an opinion that you have reached after a lot of thought: *It is my considered opinion that the man doesn't know what he's talking about.*

con·sid·er *(obj)* [GIVE ATTENTION] /£kən'sɪd·ər, $-ɚ/ *v* to give attention to (a particular subject) when judging something else • *You've got to consider the time factor when planning the whole project.* [T] • *If you consider* **how** *long he's been learning the piano he's not very good.* [+ *wh-* word]

con·sid·er·a·tion /kən,sɪd·ə'reɪ·ʃən/ *n* • *For a big house the price is fairly cheap, but you've got to* **take into** *consideration the money you'll spend on repairs.* [U] • *Comfort is an important consideration when you're deciding how to travel.* [C] • *I've got time to make the visit, but there are other considerations* (=things that influence my decision). [C]

con·sid·er·ing /£kən'sɪd·ər·ɪŋ, $'-ɚ-/ *prep, conjunction, adv* • Considering is used to mention a disadvantageous condition or fact: *Considering the weather, we got here quite quickly.* ○ *Considering what nice parents they've got they're horrible children.* ○ *Her figure is wonderful considering* **(that)** *she eats so much chocolate.* [+ *(that)* clause] ○ *You did very well to lift all those books considering* **how** *small you are!* [+ *wh-* word] ○ *(infml esp. humorous) You look very nice, considering* (=despite conditions which might make you not look nice)*!*

con·sid·er *obj* [CARE ABOUT] /£kən'sɪd·ər, $-ɚ/ *v* [T] to care about or respect (other people or their feelings and wishes) • *Have you considered your mother and how she's going to feel about your leaving the country?* • *She never considers anyone else – she's totally selfish!*

con·sid·er·ate /£kən'sɪd·ər·ət, $'-ɚ-/ *adj* • *It wasn't very considerate of you to drink all the milk when you know I need some for the baby!*

con·sid·er·a·tion /kən,sɪd·ə'reɪ·ʃən/ *n* [U] • *You've got no consideration* **for** *others!* • *Could you turn your music down and* **show** *a little consideration* **for** *the neighbours!* • *The local paper didn't press for an interview* **out of** *consideration* **for** *the victim's family.* • *(dated or humorous)* A **(small)** consideration is also a payment for a service: *For a small consideration, madam, I'll show you the way there myself.*

con·sid·er *obj* [OPINION] /£kən'sɪd·ər, $-ɚ/ *v* [T] to believe to be; to think of as • *He is currently considered* **(to be)** *the best British athlete.* [+ obj + *(to be)* n/adj] • *We don't consider her* **(to be)** *suitable for the job.* [+ obj + *(to be)* n/adj] • *I consider* **myself** *lucky that I only hurt my arm in the accident.* [+ obj + n/adj] • *Do you consider him* **(as)** *a friend or a colleague?* [+ obj + *(as)* n/adj] • *Is he considered* **(as)** *trustworthy?* [+ obj + *(as)* n/adj] • *It is considered* **(as)** *bad manners in some cultures to speak with your mouth full of food.* [+ obj + *(as)* n/adj] • *I think she considers* **(that)** *she has done enough to help already.* [+ *(that)* clause] • *"Do you think you could get this parcel mailed for me, please?"* "**Consider it done** (=Yes, certainly)."

con·sid·ered /£kən'sɪd·əd, $-ɚd/ *adj* • Someone or something that is **highly/well** considered is very much admired: *I've never enjoyed her books but I know she's very highly considered.*

con·sid·er·a·ble /£kən'sɪd·ər·ə·bl̩, $'-ɚ-/ *adj* large or of noticeable importance • *The fire caused considerable damage to the church.*

con·sid·er·a·bly /£kən'sɪd·ᵊr·ə·bli, $'-ə-/ *adv* • *He's considerably fatter than he was when I used to know him.* • [LP] **Very, completely**

con·sign *obj* [SEND] /kən'saɪn/ *v* [T] *fml* to send (something) to someone • *The goods have been consigned* **to** *you by air.*

con·sign·ee /£ˌkɒn·saɪ'niː, $ˌkaːn-/ *n* [C] *fml* • *Goods must be signed for by the consignee* (= the person to whom they are sent).

con·sign·ment /kən'saɪn·mənt/ *n* • *The most recent consignment* **of** *cloth was lost in the post.* [C] • If goods are **on** consignment the person or company that receives them will only pay for them after they have been sold. [U]

con·sign *obj* [PLACE] /kən'saɪn/ *v* [T] *fml* to put or place (someone) into esp. an unpleasant place or situation • *After the financial disaster, she was consigned* **to poverty**. • *After disagreeing with the monarch, he was consigned to* **prison**. • *The book did not sell well and was quickly consigned* **to oblivion** (= forgotten). • *(humorous) I consigned his love letters* **to** *the wastepaper bin* (= got rid of them) *long ago.* • *The child was consigned* **to** *the* **care** *of* (= will be officially taken care of by) *the authorities.*

con·sist of *obj* /kən'sɪst/ *v prep* [L not *be consisting*] to be made of or formed from (something) • *The team consists of four Europeans and two Americans.* • *It's a simple dish to prepare, consisting mainly of rice and vegetables.* • *It was easy to show that the new evidence consisted of lies.*

con·sist in *obj v prep* [L not *be consisting*] *fml* • *The beauty of air travel consists in its speed and ease.* • *For her, happiness consists in watching television and reading magazines.* [+ v-*ing*]

con·sist·en·cy /kən'sɪs·tᵊnt·si/ *n* the physical nature of a substance, esp. a thick liquid, which can be thick or thin, smooth or lumpy, or easy or not to pour • *She loved the cream-like consistency of fresh paint.* [U] • *Melt the chocolate to a pouring consistency.* [C] • See also **consistency** at CONSISTENT [NOT VARYING].

con·sist·ent [NOT VARYING] /kən'sɪs·tᵊnt/ *adj* always behaving or happening in a similar, esp. positive, way • *There has been a consistent improvement in her attitude.* • *Her work is sometimes good but the problem is she's not consistent.*

con·sist·en·cy /kən'sɪs·tᵊnt·si/ *n* [U] • *I'm never quite sure of her political views – they lack a little consistency.* • *It's not good enough to produce a lot of work one day and none the next – we need some consistency.*

con·sist·ent·ly /kən'sɪs·tᵊnt·li/ *adv* • *The occasional mistake doesn't matter, but if you get it consistently wrong you're in trouble.* • *She's been consistently rude to me all week.*

con·sist·ent [AGREEING] /kən'sɪs·tᵊnt/ *adj* [after v] in agreement with principles that do not change or with typical or previous behaviour • *This proposal is not consistent* **with** *our initial aims.* • *What the witness said in court was not consistent* **with** *the statement he made to the police.* • *This is not behaviour that is consistent* **with** (= suitable for) *the holding of a high-ranking job.*

con·sole *obj* [COMFORT] /£kən'səʊl, $-'soʊl/ *v* [T] to make (someone who is sad or disappointed) feel better by giving them comfort or sympathy • *He tried to console her, but she kept saying it was all her own fault.* • *I tried to console her* **with** *a box of chocolates.* • *I was just consoling Liz* **on** *having broken up with her boyfriend.* • *Console* **yourself** *– it could have been worse. What if you'd had your passport stolen as well as your money!*

con·sol·a·tion /£ˌkɒn·sə'leɪ·ʃᵊn, $ˌkaːn-/ *n* • **It** *was some/no consolation* **to** *him* **to** *know that his ex-wife was bitterly unhappy too.* [U + *to* infinitive] • **If it's (of) any** *consolation, you're not the only one he was rude to – he's just told me to shut up!* [U] • *After her husband died she had only the dog* **for** *consolation.* [U] • *As a consolation* **for** *failing her driving test he bought her a bicycle.* [C] • *I didn't know what to say – I just offered a few* **words** *of consolation.* [U] • A **consolation prize** is a small prize given to someone who has taken part in a competition but not won.

con·sol·at·o·ry /£kən'sɒl·ə·tri, $-'saː·lə·tɔːr·i/ *adj fml* • *a consolatory letter/remark*

con·sole [MACHINE] /£'kɒn·səʊl, $-soʊl/ *n* [C] a surface on which you find the controls for a piece of electrical equipment or a machine • *a computer console*

con·sol·i·date /£kən'sɒl·ɪ·deɪt, $-'saː·lɪ-/ *v* to (cause to) become stronger and more certain, or (esp. of businesses) to join together to become more effective • *The recent success of their major product has consolidated the firm's position in this market.* [T] • *The company has been expanding enough recently – I feel it's now time to consolidate* (= stop growing and make our present position stronger). [I] • *She hoped that marriage would consolidate their relationship.* [T] • *The party consolidated its hold* **on** *power/the country during its term of office.* [T] • *The team consolidated their hold* **on** *the premier division with their biggest league win of the season.* [T] • *The two firms consolidated* (= joined) *to form a single company.* [I]

con·sol·i·dat·ed /£kən'sɒl·ɪ·deɪ·tɪd, $-'saː·lɪ·deɪ·t̬ɪd/ *adj* • In Britain **the consolidated fund** is a supply of money collected from taxation which is used esp. to pay the INTEREST on the national debt.

con·sol·i·da·tion /£kənˌsɒl·ɪ'deɪ·ʃᵊn, $-ˌsaː·lɪ-/ *n* [U] • *He is a good administrator and the company is entering a period of consolidation* (= becoming better and stronger at what it does). • *The upheaval in publishing has been mirrored by a similar consolidation* (= joining together) *of book sellers and distributors.*

con·som·mé /£kən'sɒm·eɪ, $ˌkaːnt·sə'meɪ/ *n* [U] a thin clear soup

con·so·nant /£'kɒn·sə·nənt, $'kaːn-/ *n* [C] one of the speech sounds or letters of the alphabet which is not a vowel. They are pronounced by stopping the air from flowing freely through the mouth, esp. by closing the lips or touching the teeth with the tongue. • Compare VOWEL.

con·sort [BE TOGETHER] /£kən'sɔːt, $-'sɔːrt/ *v* [I always + adv/prep] to spend a lot of time in the company of (usually people whose character is not approved of) • *In the dark smoky bar he imagined criminals and businessmen consorting* **together**. • *In prison she found herself consorting* **with** *hardened criminals.*

con·sort [PARTNER] /£'kɒn·sɔːt, $'kaːn·sɔːrt/ *n* [C] a wife or husband, esp. of a ruler

con·sort·i·um /£kən'sɔː·ti·əm, $-'sɔːr·t̬i-/ *n* [C] *pl* **consortiums** or **consortia** /£kən'sɔː·ti·əm, $-'sɔːr·t̬i-/ an organization of several businesses or banks joining together as a group for a shared purpose • *a recently formed consortium* **of** *textile manufacturers*

con·spi·cu·ous /kən'spɪk·ju·əs/ *adj* very noticeable; tending to attract attention, often in a way that is not wanted • *In China, where black hair is the norm, her blonde hair was conspicuous.* • *He tried not to look conspicuous and moved slowly along the back of the room.* • *(esp. humorous) He was conspicuous* **by** *his* **absence** (= absent when he should have been present) *at yesterday's meeting.* • *(disapproving)* Conspicuous **consumption** is when people spend a lot of money intentionally so that people notice and admire them for their wealth.

con·spi·cu·ous·ly /kən'spɪk·ju·ə·sli/ *adv* • *The temple's grand white arches rose conspicuously over the dirty decaying city.*

con·spi·cu·ous·ness /kən'spɪk·ju·ə·snəs/ *n* [U]

con·spire /£kən'spaɪəʳ, $-'spaɪr/ *v* [I] to plan secretly with other people to do something bad, illegal or against someone's wishes • *He felt uneasy with his colleagues, as if they were always conspiring* **together to** *remove him from his job.* [+ *to*-infinitive] • *As girls, the sisters used to conspire* **with** *each other* **against** *their hated brother.* • Events or conditions might be said to conspire if they combine in such a way that they spoil your plans: *The weather had conspired* **to** *ruin their day out – rain, then a raging wind and on the way home a storm.* ◦ *First a broken leg and then a broken heart – circumstances had conspired* **to** *make her thoroughly miserable.* [+ *to*-infinitive]

con·spir·a·cy /kən'spɪr·ə·si/ *n* • *The three men are accused of conspiracy* (= working illegally against the government). [U] • *She has been charged with conspiracy* (= planning with someone else) **to** *murder.* [U] • *(fig.) Fifteen years working for the same firm and she still hadn't been promoted – there was a conspiracy* **against** *her* (= someone did not want her to be successful)*!* [C] • *I think there was a conspiracy* **to** *keep me out of the committee.* [C + *to* infinitive] • *(fig.) When she stepped on the scales she weighed 4 kilograms heavier – it was a conspiracy* (= she thought the machine was intentionally showing the wrong weight)*!* [C] • A conspiracy **of silence** is a general agreement to keep silent about a subject for the purpose of secrecy. [C] • **Conspiracy theory** refers to the belief that unpleasant things which happen, esp. to governments, are planned by people who

CONSONANT DOUBLING

Sometimes a consonant at the end of a word changes to two consonants when the form of the word is changed in certain ways. (For regular verbs these consonants are shown in **bold** print, for example **drop, –pp–**. For adjectives and adverbs, the whole of the changed forms are given, for example **fat, fatter, fattest**.)
Here are the important rules:

- **Adjectives and verbs with one syllable**
  When the word ends with *one* vowel followed by *one* consonant, you double the consonant before **–er –est –ing** and **–ed**

adjectives	*verbs*
big–bigger–biggest	**rob**–robbing–robbed
thin–thinner–thinnest	**stop**–stopping–stopped
hot–hotter–hottest	**plan**–planning–planned

- **Verbs with more than one syllable**
  When the word ends with *one* vowel followed by *one* consonant, you double the consonant only if the last part of the word is *stressed*.

consonant is doubled	*consonant is not doubled*
be'gin–beginning	**'open**–opening–opened
pre'fer–preferring–preferred	**'offer**–offering–offered
re'gret–regretting–regretted	**'visit**–visiting–visited

But notice the following exceptions, esp. in British English:

'cancel–cancelling–cancelled	*(Am)* canceling–cancelled
'dial–dialling–dialled	*(Am usually)* dialing–dialed
'travel–travelling–travelled	*(Am usually)* traveling–traveled
'kidnap–kidnapping–kidnapped	*(Am also)* kidnaping–kidnaped
'worship–worshipping–worshipped	*(Am also)* worshiping–worshiped

- **Verbs ending -ic**
  A 'k' is added before '-ed' and '-ing': **panic**–panicking–panicked
  Other examples: frolic, mimic, picnic, traffic. Adjectives ending in '-ic' are either not gradable (for example *atomic*) or use '*more*' and '*most*' (for example '*basic*').

- **Words ending vowel + -w/-y**
  Notice that **'w'** or **'y'** following a vowel at the end of a word are part of the vowel sound and you do *not* double them:

slow–slower–slowest	**play**–playing–played

want to cause difficulties and do not happen by chance. •
LP> **Crimes and criminals**

con·spir·a·tor /£kən'spɪr·ə·tər, $-t̬ɚ/ *n* [C] • *Guy Fawkes was one of the conspirators who planned to blow up James I and the Houses of Parliament in 1605.*

con·spir·a·tor·i·al /£kən,spɪr·ə'tɔː·ri·əl, $-'tɔːr·i-/ *adj* • *They exchanged conspiratorial glances.*

con·spir·a·tor·i·al·ly /£kən,spɪr·ə'tɔː·ri·əl·i, $-'tɔːr·i-/ *adv* • *She heard them whispering conspiratorially in the bedroom.*

con·sta·ble /£'kʌnt·stə·bl̩, $'kɑːnt-/ *n* [C] (in Britain) a police officer • ⓓⓚ

con·stab·u·la·ry /£kən'stæb·jʊ·lə·ri, $-lə·i-/ *n* [C + sing/pl v] (in Britain) the police force of a particular area

con·stant /£'kɒnt·stənt, $'kɑːnt-/ *adj* staying the same; not getting less or more • *We've kept a fairly constant speed all journey.* • *The fridge keeps food at a constant temperature.* • *I've had this constant headache ever since I woke up this morning.* • Constant can also be used to describe things which happen very frequently: *He's in constant trouble with the police.* ○ *They make constant use of their computers.* • A constant companion/friend/lover is one who is loyal to you.

con·stant·ly /£'kɒnt·stənt·li, $'kɑːnt-/ *adv* [not gradable] • *She has the television on constantly* (=frequently).

con·stant /£'kɒnt·stənt, $'kɑːnt-/ *n* [C] *specialized* • A constant is a particular number or amount that always stays the same.

con·stan·cy /£'kɒnt·stənt·si, $'kɑːnt-/ *n* [U] *fml* • *The constancy of your love for Emma/football/Indian food amazes me.*

con·stel·la·tion /£,kɒnt·stə'leɪ·ʃən, $,kɑːnt-/ *n* [C] any of the groups of stars in the sky which seem from Earth to form a pattern, many of which have name, for example Leo • *(often humorous)* A constellation is sometimes used when describing a group of famous or admired people gathered in one place: *Gathered here tonight at this annual ceremony we have a whole constellation of film stars/actors/acting talent/directors.*

con·ster·na·tion /£,kɒnt·stə'neɪ·ʃən, $,kɑːnt·stɚ-/ *n* [U] a feeling of anxiety, shock or confusion • *The prospect of so much work* **filled** *him* **with** *consternation.* • **To his** *consternation, as he arrived at the airport he realized his passport was at home.*

con·sti·pat·ed /£'kɒnt·stɪ·peɪ·tɪd, $'kɑːnt·stɪ·peɪ·t̬ɪd/ *adj* unable to excrete the contents of the bowels often enough and experiencing pain when attempting to do so • *Are you eating enough fibre? You don't want to* **get** *constipated!* • Ⓔ

con·sti·pa·tion /£,kɒnt·stɪ'peɪ·ʃən, $,kɑːnt-/ *n* [U] • *Constipation is thought to be one of the major causes of bowel cancer.* • Ⓔ

con·sti·tu·en·cy /kən'stɪt·ju·ənt·si/ *n* [C] (the group of voters belonging to) any of the official areas of a country that elect someone to represent them nationally • *The MP's constituency covers the city's poorest areas.*

con·sti·tu·ent /kən'stɪt·ju·ənt/ *n* [C] • A constituent is a voter in a particular area of the country: *As a senator he was excellent – always talking to his constituents and hearing their problems.* • See also **constituent** at CONSTITUTE [FORM PART OF].

con·sti·tute *obj* [FORM PART OF] /£'kɒn·stɪ·tjuːt, $'kɑːn·stɪ·tuːt/ *v* [L not *be constituting*] to form or make (something) • *Women constitute about 10% of Parliament.* • *The under-18s constitute nearly 25% of the town's population.* • *The governing body, as currently constituted, includes two staff members.*

con·sti·tu·ent /kən'stɪt·ju·ənt/ *n* [C] • A constituent is one of the parts that a substance or combination is made of: *What are the basic constituents* **of** *the mixture?* • See also **constituent** at CONSTITUENCY.

con·sti·tu·ent /kən'stɪt·ju·ənt/ *adj* [before n; not gradable] • *Let's consider separately the constituent* **parts** *of this sentence.* • *The council's constituent members include a representative from each country.* • See also **constituent** at CONSTITUENCY.

con·sti·tu·tion /£,kɒn·stɪ'tjuː·ʃən, $,kɑːn·stɪ'tuː-/ *n* [C] • *the constitution* (=structure) *of a chemical compound*

con·sti·tute [BE CONSIDERED AS] /£'kɒn·stɪ·tjuːt, $'kɑːn·stɪ·tuːt/ *v* [L only + n; not *be constituting*] *fml* to be or be considered as • *Over 6440 km in length, the Amazon constitutes the largest river in the world.* • *Nuclear weapons constitute a very real threat to world peace.* • *This* *latest defeat constitutes a major set-back for the government.*

con·sti·tu·tion LAWS /£ˌkɒnt·stɪ'tjuː·ʃən, $ˌkɑːnt·stɪ'tuː-/ *n* [C] (a written document which forms) the set of political principles by which a state or organization is governed, esp. in relation to the rights of the people it governs • *Britain has no written constitution.* • *The Constitution of the United States says that there must be a presidential election every four years.* • **Under** (= As part of) *the union constitution a new committee must be elected each year.*

con·sti·tu·tion·al /£ˌkɒnt·stɪ'tjuː·ʃən·əl, $ˌkɑːnt·stɪ'tuː-/ *adj* • *Such a policy would not be constitutional* (= allowed by the constitution). • *Freedom of speech should be a constitutional* **right**. • In a **constitutional monarchy** the king or queen's power is severely limited, as he or she acts on the advice of the politicians who form the government.

con·sti·tu·tion·al·ly /£ˌkɒnt·stɪ'tjuː·ʃən·əl·i, $ˌkɑːnt·stɪ·tuː-/ *adv* • Constitutionally means according to the rules in the constitution: *There was some doubt as to whether the government were behaving constitutionally.* ○ *The entire committee must be constitutionally elected.*

con·sti·tu·tion·al·i·ty /£ˌkɒnt·stɪ·tjuː·ʃən'æl·ɪ·ti, $ˌkɑːnt·stɪ·tuː·ʃən'æl·ə·ṭi/ *n* [U] *Am* • *The judge chose to ignore questions of the constitutionality of the Senator's actions.*

con·sti·tu·tion HEALTH /£ˌkɒnt·stɪ'tjuː·ʃən, $ˌkɑːnt·stɪ·tuː-/ *n* [C] the general state of someone's health • *He works incredibly hard and yet needs very little sleep – he must have a* **strong** *constitution.*

con·sti·tu·tion·al /£ˌkɒnt·stɪ'tjuː·ʃən·əl, $ˌkɑːnt·stɪ'tuː-/ *adj* • *Because of its constitutional weakness, the dog's stomach just won't accept a lot of food.*

con·sti·tu·tion·al /£ˌkɒnt·stɪ'tjuː·ʃən·əl, $ˌkɑːnt·stɪ'tuː-/ *n* [C] *dated humorous* • A constitutional is a walk that you frequently do to keep yourself healthy: *Nearly 86 years of age and she still goes on her constitutional every morning.*

con·sti·tu·tion·al·ly /£ˌkɒnt·stɪ'tjuː·ʃən·əl·i, $ˌkɑːnt·stɪ'tuː-/ *adv* • *She has no particular illness – she's just constitutionally weak.* • *(humorous) She seems constitutionally unable* (= her character will not allow her) *to make decisions.*

con·straint /kən'streɪnt/ *n* something which controls what you do by keeping you within particular limits • *The constraints of politeness wouldn't allow her to say what she really thought about the dinner he had prepared.* [C] • *Living with a roommate imposed constraints on her – she couldn't play her trumpet or have parties late at night.* [C] • *The financial constraints* **on** *the company mean that they are not employing new staff.* [C] • *(fml)* Constraint is also used to describe the type of awkward behaviour which is sometimes the result of forcing yourself to act in a particular way: *She tried to appear friendly and natural but her constraint was obvious.* [U] • If you do something **under** constraint you do it only because you have been forced to: *They confessed the truth but only under constraint.*

con·strain *obj* /kən'streɪn/ *v* [T] • *The country's progress is being constrained* (= limited) *by a leader who refuses to look forward.* • *The use of solar energy is constrained by the need for sufficient sunshine.* • *Education, he often felt, had constrained his imagination.*

con·strained /kən'streɪnd/ *adj* • *Don't feel constrained* **to** *do what he says – he's got no authority.* [obj + *to* infinitive] • A constrained manner/voice/smile is a forced and unnatural one.

con·strict *obj* /kən'strɪkt/ *v* [T] to make tighter and narrower, or to limit (an action or behaviour) • *He hated wearing a tie – he felt it constricted his breathing.* • *If you're going dancing you don't want to wear anything that constricts your movements.* • *The drug causes the blood vessels to constrict.* • *Too many rules had constricted her lifestyle – she felt trapped in routine.*

con·stric·tion /kən'strɪk·ʃən/ *n* [C] • *The constrictions* (= limitations) *of prison life were inhuman.* • *He felt a constriction* (= a tight feeling) *in the chest – and he couldn't breathe.*

con·struct *obj* /kən'strʌkt/ *v* [T] to build; to put together different parts to form (a whole) • *The company have won the contract to the new bridge/building.* • *The crow constructs its nest* **out of** *sticks.* • *The wall is constructed* **of** *concrete.* • You can also construct a story, a sentence, an argument or a theory: *It's an elegantly constructed theory, but I'm afraid it's not right.*

con·struct /£'kɒn·strʌkt, $'kɑːn-/ *n* [C] *fml* • A construct is an idea or an imaginary situation: *His reputation as an eccentric judge is largely a media construct.*

con·struc·tion /kən'strʌk·ʃən/ *n* • *She works in construction/in the construction* **industry** (= in the building industry). • *The bridge is a marvellous work of engineering and construction.* [U] • *How long has the hotel been* **under** *construction* (= being built)? [U] • *What's that concrete and metal construction* (= building) *over there? Do you suppose people actually live in it?* [C] • The construction of a sentence or a phrase is the way in which the words are arranged. • See also **construction** at CONSTRUE.

con·struct·or /£kən'strʌk·tər, $-ṭɚ/ *n* [C] • *The firm produces kits for amateur car constructors.* • *He was the youngest ever president of the Society of British Aircraft Constructors.* • *The great stone circles were probably of religious as well as practical significance to their constructors.*

con·struct·ive /£kən'strʌk·tɪv, $-ṭɪv/ *adj* (esp. of advice and criticism and also actions) useful and intended to help or improve something • *She criticised my writing but in a way that was very constructive – I learned a lot from her.* • *If you don't have anything constructive to say I'd rather you kept quiet.* • *He didn't offer any constructive* **criticism** *– just complained he didn't like it.*

con·struct·ive·ly /£kən'strʌk·tɪv·li, $-ṭɪv-/ *adv* • *I wish you'd use your energy a bit more constructively. Why don't you take up a sport?*

con·strue *obj* /kən'struː/ *v* [T + obj + *as* adj/n] *fml* to understand the meaning, esp. of other people's actions and statements, in a particular way • *Any change in plan would be construed* **as** *indecision.* • *He construed her blank stare* **as** *boredom and stopped telling her about his new car.*

con·struc·tion /kən'strʌk·ʃən/ *n* [C] • *That's just his construction of the situation – it's not necessarily the truth of the matter.* • *I don't want them to* **put** *the wrong construction* **on** *my actions.* • See also **construction** at CONSTRUCT.

con·sul /£'kɒnt·s·əl, $'kɑːnt-/ *n* [C] an official chosen by a government to live in a foreign city in order to take care of the people from the official's own country who are travelling or living there and to protect the trade interests of that government

con·sul·ar /£'kɒnt·sjʊ·lər, $'kɑːnt·sjə·lɚ/ *adj* [not gradable] • *the consular office* • *consular responsibilities* • *I was in India in a consular capacity.*

con·sul·ate /£'kɒn·sjʊ·lət, $'kɑːn·sjə-/ *n* [C] • *The Spanish consulate is the large white building opposite the bank.*

con·sult *(obj)* /kən'sʌlt/ *v* to get information or advice from (a person or book with special knowledge on a particular subject) • *If the symptoms continue or get worse consult your doctor.* [T] • *I'm going to consult my best friend* **on** *the matter.* [T] • *I don't know how to get there either – perhaps we'd better consult a map.* [T] • *Be patient, consult, and listen to advice before doing anything.* [I] • *This afternoon the Prime Minister was consulting* **with** *his advisors and we are expecting an announcement shortly.* [I]

con·sult·an·cy /£kən'sʌl·tənt·si, $-ṭənt-/ *n* [C] • A consultancy is a business involving a person or a group of people who give specialist advice on a particular subject: *He left the company and he's got his own (engineering/financial) consultancy now.*

con·sult·ant /£kən'sʌl·tənt, $-ṭənt/ *n* [C] • *I think we need to see a computer consultant before we make an expensive mistake.* • *She works for a firm of public relations consultants.* • *(Br medical)* A consultant is a **specialist**. See at SPECIAL PARTICULAR.

con·sult·a·tion /£ˌkɒn·sʌl'teɪ·ʃən, $ˌkɑːn-/ *n* • *After consultations* **with** *our accountants we've decided how to cut costs within the company.* [C] • *He decided on his study course* **in** *consultation* **with** *his parents and teachers.* [U]

con·sult·a·tive /£kən'sʌl·tə·tɪv, $-ṭə·ṭɪv/ *adj* [not gradable] • *She works for the firm in a consultative capacity.* • *We need to set up a consultative committee to advise us on the problem.*

con·sult·ing /£kən'sʌl·tɪŋ, $-ṭɪŋ/ *adj* [before n; not gradable] • *a consulting lawyer/engineer* (= one whose job is to give advice) • A **consulting room** is where a doctor talks to and examines people.

con·sume *obj* /£kən'sjuːm, $-'suːm/ *v* [T] to use (fuel, energy or time), esp. in large amounts • *That's the trouble with those big powerful cars – they consume too much fuel.* • If a fire consumes something, it destroys it completely: *Within a short time, the fire had consumed the whole* *building.* • Someone can be said to be consumed **by/with** a feeling if that feeling is extremely strong and is having a great effect on their lives: *As a teenager, I was consumed by passion for a filmstar I would never meet.* ○ *He was consumed with envy/jealousy/hatred.* • To consume is also to eat or drink a lot: *He consumes vast quantities of chips with every meal.* ○ *"I feel sick." "It's not surprising considering the amount of alcohol you just consumed!"*

con·sum·a·bles /£kən'sjuː·mə·bl̩z, $-suː-/ *pl n* • Consumables are goods, esp. food, or services which people buy regularly because they are quickly used and need to be replaced quite often: *At this hospital we use up bandages, surgical stockings, scalpels, disposable gloves and other consumables at an alarming rate.*

con·sum·er /£kən'sjuː·mər, $-'suː·mɚ/ *n* [C] • A consumer is a person who buys goods or services for their own use: *The new telephone rates will affect all consumers including businesses.* • *consumer rights/advice* • **Consumer durables** are goods that last a long time and are not intended to be bought very frequently, such as televisions and cars. • **Consumer price index** is *Am and Aus for* **retail price index**. See at RETAIL. • **Consumer protection** is the protection of buyers of goods and services against low quality or dangerous products and advertisements that deceive people. • A **consumer society** is one in which people frequently buy new goods, esp. goods which are not essential, and which places a high value on owning many things.

con·sum·er·i·sm /£kən'sjuː·mə·rɪ·zəm, $-'suː·mɚ·ɪ-/ *n* [U] • Consumerism is the state of advanced industrial society in which a lot of goods are bought and sold, or *(disapproving)* the state in which too much attention is given to buying and owning things: *(disapproving) He disliked Christmas time and its* **rampant** (=extreme) *consumerism.*

con·sum·ing /£kən'sjuː·mɪŋ, $-'suː-/ *adj* • *Running is a consuming* (=very strong) *passion with him – it's his whole life.*

con·sump·tion /kən'sʌmp·ʃən/ *n* [U] • Consumption is the amount used or eaten: *Recent health reports have advised us to reduce fat consumption.* ○ *As a nation our consumption of junk food is horrifying.* ○ *We need to cut down on our fuel consumption by having fewer cars on the road.* ○ *Many of the goods they produce are not for national consumption* (=use) *but for export.* • If food or drink is **unfit for human** consumption it is not safe for people to eat or drink. • *(fig.) This memo is for* **internal** *consumption only* (=only to be read by the people in the company). • See also CONSUMPTION.

con·sum·mate [COMPLETE] /£'kɒn·sə·mət, $'kɑːn-/ *adj* [before n] *fml* perfect; complete in every way • *With her he would lead a life of consummate happiness.* • *He's a consummate* (=He has all the qualities of an) *athlete/politician/gentleman/actor/liar.*

con·sum·mate *obj* /£'kɒn·sjʊ·meɪt, $'kɑːn-/ *v* [T] *fml* • *Having agreed a price through the computer, the customer's own machine can then automatically produce an invoice to consummate the* **deal**.

con·sum·ma·tion /£'kɒn·sjʊ·mət, $'kɑːn-/ *n* [U] *fml* • *Becoming Finance Minister was the consummation of his political life.* • *"'Tis a consummation devoutly to be wished"* (Shakespeare, Hamlet 3.1)

con·sum·mate *obj* [HAVE SEX] /£'kɒn·sjʊ·meɪt, $'kɑːn·sə-/ *v* [T] *law* to make (a marriage or romantic relationship) complete by having sex

con·sum·ma·tion /£ˌkɒn·sjʊ'meɪ·ʃən, $ˌkɑːn·sə-/ *n* [U] • *He divorced her for non-consummation of the marriage.*

con·sump·tion /kən'sʌmp·ʃən/ *n* [U] *dated for* TUBERCULOSIS • *The poet Keats died of consumption at the age of 26.* • (NL)

con·sump·tive /£kən'sʌmp·tɪv, $-t̬ɪv/ *adj* [not gradable], *n dated* • *She didn't live very long – she was (a) consumptive.* • See also **consumption** at CONSUME.

cont, contd *adj abbreviation for* **continued**, see at CONTINUE

con·tact [COMMUNICATION] /£'kɒn·tækt, $'kɑːn-/ *n* [U] the act of speaking to someone, either personally, by telephone or radio, electronically or by writing to someone • *"Have you been* **in** *contact* **with** *Andrew recently?" "Only by telephone."* • *I'm still* **in** *contact* **with** *her – we write a couple of times a year.* • *There isn't enough contact* **between** *teachers and parents.* • *I've been shut up in my room for so long – I don't feel I've* **had** *any contact* **with** *the outside world.* • *I'd hate to* **lose** *contact* **with** *my old school friends.* • *After months of trying she finally* **made** *contact* **with** *him in Italy.* • *Air traffic control* **lost** *radio contact* **with** *the pilot of the aircraft ten minutes before the accident.* • *The school likes to have a contact* **number** (=telephone number, esp. for emergencies) *for parents during school hours.*

con·tact *obj* /£'kɒn·tækt, $'kɑːn-/ *v* [T] • *I tried to contact him at his office but he wasn't in.* • *You can contact me (Br)* **on**/*(Am)* **at** (=speak to me by telephoning) *388 9146.* • *If there is any way we can be of assistance please do not hesitate to contact us.* • *Unless the money is returned we shall shortly be contacting our legal department.*

con·tact·a·ble /£kən'tæk·tə·bl̩, $-t̬ə-/ *adj* • *Is he contactable at his home number?*

con·tact [TOUCH] /£'kɒn·tækt, $'kɑːn-/ *n* [U] the act of touching • *Don't let that glue* **come into** *contact* **with** *your skin – it sticks immediately.* • *Your foot should keep contact* **with** *the pedal at all times.* • *Have you been* **in contact with** (=touched or been very near) *anyone with the disease?* • *He hates* **physical** *contact of any sort – he doesn't even like to shake your hand.* • **Contact sports** are sports such as RUGBY and **American football** in which players are allowed to touch each other when, for example, they are trying to get the ball. • **Contact lenses** are small round curved pieces of transparent material, esp. plastic, which fit on the surface of the eye in order to improve the sight and are worn by some people instead of glasses: *I've lost a contact lens.* ○ *I need new contact lenses.* • [LP]〉 **Eye and seeing**

con·tact [PERSON] /£'kɒn·tækt, $'kɑːn-/ *n* [C] a person, esp. in a high position, whom you can use to your advantage in your work or socially to give you useful information or introductions • *If you want to become a successful actor you need contacts.* • *I don't know for sure how she got the job but I suspect her mother's got contacts.* • *If you need more stationery, I've got a good contact in a local printing firm.* • *We're* **building up** (=increasing the number of) *our contacts in the business.*

con·tact [ELECTRICITY] /£'kɒn·tækt, $'kɑːn-/ *n* [C] a part in a CIRCUIT (=an electrical system) which completes the circuit when it is made to touch another part

con·ta·gious /kən'teɪ·dʒəs/ *adj* (of a disease) able to be caught by touching someone with the disease or a piece of infected clothing • *It's a* **highly** *contagious infection, so don't let anyone else use your towel.* • A person who has a contagious disease can also be described as contagious: *Are you contagious or is it alright to kiss you?* • Contagious **laughter/enthusiasm** encourages other people to do or feel the same: *He's got a contagious laugh.*

con·ta·gion /kən'teɪ·dʒən/ *n* [U] • *The doctor says there's no chance of contagion so she can go to school.*

con·tain *obj* [HOLD] /kən'teɪn/ *v* [T not *be containing*] to have inside or include • *How much liquid do you think this bottle contains?* • *I've lost a file containing a lot of important documents.* • *Try to avoid foods which contain a lot of fat.* • *This article contains some useful information.* • *The documents contained* **in** *the old box had crumbled to dust.* • *The allegations contained* **in** *this report are very serious.*

con·tain·er /£kən'teɪ·nər, $-nɚ/ *n* [C] • A container is a hollow object, such as a box or a bottle, which can be used for holding something esp. for the purposes of carrying or storing: *an unbreakable container* ○ *a plastic drinks container* ○ *She kept the buttons in an old ice-cream container.* • *(specialized)* A container is also a very large standard-sized metal box used for transporting goods: *a container ship/lorry/train* • [PIC]〉 **Ships and boats**

con·tain·er·ize *obj, Br and Aus usually* **-ise** /£kən'teɪ·nər·aɪz, $-nə·raɪz/ *v* [T] • To containerize is to put goods in a large standard-sized metal box for transport, or to make a port, ship, etc. suitable for this method of transport: *The goods must be containerized for export.*

con·tain *obj* [CONTROL] /kən'teɪn/ *v* [T not *be containing*] to keep within limits; not to allow to spread • *Farms in the infected area have been closed off in an attempt to contain the disease.* • *More police were sent to the football ground in order to contain the violence.* • If you can't contain an emotion, such as excitement or anger, you cannot hide it because it is so strong: *She was so furious she could no longer contain her anger and shouted at him uncontrollably.* • *(often humorous) Contain yourself! It's not that exciting.*

con·tain·ment /kən'teɪn·mənt/ *n* [U] • *Containment of crowd violence was the police's main concern during the demonstration.* • Containment is also the attempt to keep another country's political power within limits without having a war with them: *The government are said to be pursuing a policy of containment.*

con·tam·in·ate *obj* /kən'tæm·ɪ·neɪt/ *v* [T] to spoil the purity of (something) or make it poisonous • *Much of the coast has been contaminated* **by** *nuclear waste.* • *The food which had been contaminated was destroyed.*

con·tam·in·ant /kən'tæm·ɪ·nənt/ *n* [C] • *Make sure that the equipment is clean and free of contaminants before you start the experiment.*

con·tam·in·at·ed /£kən'tæm·ɪ·neɪ·tɪd, $-t̬ɪd/ *adj* • *Her kidney infection was probably caused by her swimming in contaminated water/water contaminated* **with** *sewage.*

con·tam·in·a·tion /kən,tæm·ɪ'neɪ·ʃən/ *n* [U] • *The water supply is being tested for contamination* (= the presence of unwanted or dangerous substances).

contd, cont *adj abbreviation for* **continued**, see at CONTINUE

con·tem·plate *(obj)* /£'kɒn·təm·pleɪt, $'kɑːn·t̬əm-/ *v* to spend time considering (a possible future action), or to consider (one particular thing) for a long time in a serious and quiet way • *I'm contemplating* **going** *abroad for a year.* [+ v-*ing*] • *You're not contemplating a change of job, are you?* [T] • *She stared into the mirror, contemplating her skin rash.* [T] • *It's* **too** *awful/horrific/dangerous* **to** *contemplate.* [I]

con·tem·pla·tion /£,kɒn·təm'pleɪ·ʃən, $,kɑːn·t̬əm-/ *n* [U] • *This painting depicts a woman staring out over the lake as if* **lost in** *contemplation.* • *The nuns have an hour set aside for silent contemplation every morning.*

con·tem·plat·ive /£kən'tem·plə·tɪv, $-t̬ɪv/ *adj* • *Her mood was calm and contemplative.*

con·tem·plat·ive·ly /£kən'tem·plə·tɪv·li, $-t̬ɪv-/ *adv* • *He lay back and gazed out the window contemplatively.*

con·temp·o·ra·ry EXISTING NOW /£kən'tem·pər·ər·i, $-pə·rer-/ *adj* existing or happening now; MODERN • *contemporary music/literature/art/architecture/fashions* • *Although it was written hundreds of years ago it still has a contemporary* (= modern) *feel to it.* • *I liked the contemporary* (= recently made) *paintings but the classical art display bored me.*

con·temp·o·ra·ry /£kən'tem·pər·ər·i, $-pə·rer-/ *n* [C] • Your contemporaries are people of the same age as you: *She doesn't mix with her contemporaries but prefers the company of older people.*

con·temp·o·ra·ry OF SAME PERIOD /£kən'tem·pər·i, $-pɚ-/ *adj* belonging to the same or a stated period in the past • *Almost all of the contemporary accounts of the event have been lost or destroyed over the years.* • *Most of the writers he was contemporary* **with** *were interested in the same subjects.*

con·temp·o·ra·ry /£kən'tem·pər·i, $-pɚ-/ *n* [C] • Contemporaries are people who live at the same period as each other: *Was he a contemporary of Shakespeare's or did he live a bit later?*

con·temp·o·ra·ne·ous /kən,tem·pə'reɪ·ni·əs/ *adj fml* • Contemporaneous means happening or existing at the same period of time: *The two events were more or less contemporaneous, with only months between them.*

con·temp·o·ra·ne·ous·ly /kən,tem·pə'reɪ·ni·ə·sli/ *adv fml*

con·tempt /kən'tempt/ *n* [U] a strong feeling of combined dislike and lack of respect • *At school she had complete contempt* **for** *all her teachers.* • *She made no attempt to conceal her contempt* **for** *anyone who was of lower social status.* • *He said that criticisms didn't worry him as he* **held** *most of his critics* **in** *contempt anyway.* • *You should* **treat** *those remarks* **with** *the contempt that they deserve – don't give them a second thought!* • *She's* **beneath** *contempt* (= I have no respect for her)*!* • *(law)* **Contempt** or **contempt of court** is the punishable act of disobeying an order made by a judge or court of law or behaving in such a way that the usual process of the courts is interrupted.

con·tempt·i·ble /kən'temp·tɪ·bl/ *adj* • *For a person in a position of such responsibility her behaviour was contemptible* (= deserves contempt).

con·tempt·i·bly /kən'temp·tɪ·bli/ *adv* • *The government have made contemptibly little effort to improve the situation.*

con·tempt·u·ous /kən'temp·tju·əs/ *adj* • *a contemptuous manner/laugh/remark/expression* (= a manner/laugh/remark/expression expressing contempt) • *He was very contemptuous* **of** *'popular' writers whom he described as talentless and worthless.*

con·tempt·u·ous·ly /kən'temp·tju·ə·sli/ *adv* • *The waiter would smile contemptuously at people who didn't know which wine to have with their meal.*

con·tend COMPETE /kən'tend/ *v* [I] to compete in order to win something • *There are three world-class tennis players contending* **for** *this title.* • *He's contending* **against** *someone with twice his experience.*

con·tend·er /£kən'ten·dər, $-dɚ/ *n* [C] • *Now aged 42, he is no longer considered as a serious/leading contender* **for** *the championship title.* • *Who's* **the main** *contender in the* *race?* • *The battle for party leadership grew more intense when a fourth contender was proposed.* • *"I could have been a contender"* (said by Marlon Brando in the film *On the Waterfront*, 1954)

con·tend [ADJUST TO] /kən'tend/ *v* [I] to adjust to a difficult situation or try to solve a problem • *At the age of nine he* **had** *the death of both parents* **to contend with.** • *Right now we don't need a computer failure* **to contend with** *as well as all the other problems we've got.*

con·tend *(obj)* [CLAIM] /kən'tend/ *v* to state as the truth; claim • *The lawyer contended* **(that)** *her client had never been near the scene of the crime.* [+ *(that)* clause]

con·tent [HAPPY] /kən'tent/ *adj* [after v] pleased with your situation and not hoping for change or improvement; SATISFIED • *I think he's fairly content* **with** *(his) life.* • *They seem content* **to** *socialize with a very small circle of people.* [+ *to* infinitive] • *(esp. humorous)* **Not content with** (=In addition to) *having upset my parents with his rudeness he then went and insulted my sister!*

con·tent *obj* /kən'tent/ *v* [T] • *I wanted to take two week's holiday but had to content* **myself with** *one because the office was so busy.* • *As a child she was always easily contented.* • *He was suspicious at first but my explanation seemed to content him.*

con·tent·ed /£kən'ten·tɪd, $-t̬ɪd/ *adj* • *She lay down, stretched her arms out behind her and smiled a contented smile.* • *He won't be contented* (=satisfied) *until he's upset everyone in the office.*

con·tent·ed·ly /£kən'ten·tɪd·li, $-t̬ɪd-/ *adv* • *She finished the last mouthful of her meal and sighed contentedly.*

con·tent·ment /kən'tent·mənt/, **con·tent** *n* [U] • *Once asleep his face wore a look of pure contentment.* • *If you take that job in the chocolate factory you'll be able to eat the stuff* **to** *your* **heart's** *content* (=as much as you want to).

con·tent [SUBJECT] /£'kɒn·tent, $'kɑːn-/ *n* [U] the ideas that are contained in a piece of writing, a speech or a film • *I think it's a very stylish and beautiful film, but it lacks content.* • *We've discussed the unusual form of the book – now, what about the content?*

con·tent [AMOUNT] /£'kɒn·tent, $'kɑːn-/ *n* [U] the amount of a particular substance contained in something • *Chocolate has a* **high** *fat content.* • *This type of steel has a relatively* **low** *carbon content.*

con·ten·tion [DISAGREEMENT] /kən'tent·ʃən/ *n* [U] the disagreement that results from opposing arguments • *There's a lot of contention about that issue – for every person firmly in favour there's someone fiercely against it.* • *The matter has been settled – it's no longer* **in** *contention.* • The phrase **in/out of contention for** is used in sport to mean can/can not achieve something that is stated: *After winning 3-0 the team are still in contention for promotion.* ○ *And that very decisive defeat puts them out of contention for this year's championship finals.*

con·ten·tious /kən'tent·ʃəs/ *adj* • Contentious means causing or likely to cause disagreement: *a contentious decision/policy/question/subject* • *It's currently a very contentious* **issue**. • *She has some rather contentious* **views** *on education.*

con·ten·tious·ness /kən'tent·ʃə·snəs/ *n* [U]

con·ten·tion [OPINION] /kən'tent·ʃən/ *n* [C] *slightly fml* an opinion expressed in an argument • *It is her contention* **that** *exercise is more important than diet if you want to lose weight.* [+ *that* clause]

con·tents /£'kɒn·tents, $'kɑːn-/ *pl n* everything that is contained within something • *He slipped and the contents of his bag spilled all over the floor.* • *The lock had been broken and the drawer emptied of its contents.* • *I bought the caravan* **complete with** *contents – kitchen stuff, bed linen, everything.* • *(fig.) For two whole days he didn't open the letter because he already knew the contents* (=what was written within). • In a magazine or book, the contents is the list of items or parts you will find inside, and on which page each begins.

con·test [COMPETITION] /£'kɒn·test, $'kɑːn-/ *n* [C] a competition to do better than other people, usually in which prizes are given • *a dancing/singing/sports contest* • *She's won a lot of* **beauty** *contests.*

con·test *obj* /kən'test/ *v* [T] • *The championship is being keenly contested by eight athletes.*

con·test·ant /£kən'tes·tənt, $-t̬ənt/ *n* [C] • *In tonight's quiz our contestants have come from all over the country to fight for the title of 'Superbrain'.*

con·test [ATTEMPT] /£'kɒn·test, $'kɑːn-/ *n* [C] an attempt, usually against difficulties, to get power or control • *The contest* **for** *deputy leadership of the party is gathering speed.* • *There's a contest* **for** *a top management job in the company at the moment.*

con·test *obj* /kən'test/ *v* [T] • *She stands a good chance since only two people are contesting the seat and the other candidate is very unpopular.* • If you contest a formal statement or claim or a judge's decision or legal case you argue that it is not right: *We will certainly contest any claims made against the safety of our products.*

con·test·ant /£kən'tes·tənt, $-t̬ənt/ *n* [C] • *Two candidates are emerging as contestants for the presidency.*

con·text [CAUSE OF EVENT] /£'kɒn·tekst, $'kɑːn-/ *n* [C] the influences and events that helped cause a particular event or situation to happen • *Viewed* **in the** *context* **of** *recent political unrest these latest developments make perfect sense.* • *All the fighting and bloodshed in his plays is explained if you see his writing* **in** *a historical context.*

con·text·u·al /kən'tek·stju·əl/ *adj fml*

con·text·u·al·ize *obj, Br and Aus usually* **-ise** /kən'tek·stju·ə·laɪz/ *v* [T] *fml* • *We must contextualize the problem before we can understand its origin.*

con·text·u·al·ly /kən'tek·stju·ə·li/ *adv fml*

con·text [TEXT/SPEECH] /£'kɒn·tekst, $'kɑːn-/ *n* [C] the text or speech that comes immediately before and after a particular phrase or piece of text and helps to explain its meaning • *In this exercise the word itself is blanked out so you have to guess what it is by looking at the context.* • If someone complains that their words have been used **out of context** they mean that only a small, separate part of what they originally said or wrote has been reported and without the surrounding words its meaning is unclear, lost or deceiving: *The papers* **quoted/took** *my remarks completely out of context.*

con·text·u·al /kən'tek·stjʊəl/ *adj* • *It's impossible to understand the nuances of an isolated word without some contextual clues.*

con·text·u·al·ize *obj, Br and Aus usually* **-ise** /kən'tek·stjʊə·laɪz/ *v* [T] *specialized*

con·text·u·al·ly /kən'tek·stjʊə·li/ *adv*

con·ti·gu·ous /kən'tɪg·ju·əs/ *adj* [not gradable] *fml* next to or touching another, usually similar, thing • *The two states are contiguous* **with/to** *each other but the laws are quite different.*

con·ti·gu·i·ty /£ˌkɒn·tɪ'gjuː·ɪ·ti, $ˌkɑːn·t̬ə'gjuː·ə·t̬i/ *n* [U] *fml*

con·ti·nent [LAND] /£'kɒn·tɪ·nənt, $'kɑːn·t̬ən·ənt/ *n* [C] one of the seven large land masses on the Earth's surface, surrounded, or mainly surrounded, by sea and usually consisting of various countries • *the North American continent* • *Asia and Africa are the two biggest continents.* • [LP] **World regions**

con·ti·nent·al /£ˌkɒn·tɪ'nen·təl, $ˌkɑːn·t̬ən'en·t̬əl/ *adj* [not gradable] • *continental waters* • *(specialized)* **Continental drift** is the very slow movement of continents over the Earth's surface. • The **continental shelf** is the area of the bottom of the sea near the coast of a continent where the sea is not very deep.

con·ti·nent [EUROPE] /£'kɒn·tɪ·nənt, $'kɑːn·t̬ən·ənt/ *n* [U] **the Continent** Europe, esp. W Europe but not including the British Isles • *He found driving* **on** *the Continent very different to Britain.* • *"On the Continent people have good food; in England people have good table manners"* (George Mikes in the book *How to be an Alien*, 1946)

con·ti·nent·al /£ˌkɒn·tɪ'nen·təl, $ˌkɑːn·t̬ən'en·t̬əl/ *adj* • *She preferred the continental way of life – the food was better, the cafés stayed open longer and the weather was sublime!* • A **continental breakfast** is a simple meal eaten in the morning that usually consists of coffee and bread with butter and JAM (=a sweet soft substance made by cooking fruit with sugar). • *(Br)* A **continental quilt** is a DUVET.

con·ti·nent·al /£ˌkɒn·tɪ'nen·təl, $ˌkɑːn·t̬ən'en·t̬əl/ *n* [C] • Sometimes people who come from Europe but not including the British Isles are called continentals.

con·ti·nent [CONTROL] /£'kɒn·tɪ·nənt, $'kɑːn·t̬ən·ənt/ *adj* able to control urination and the excretion of the contents of the bowels, or *(old use)* able to control sexual desires

con·tin·ence /£'kɒn·tɪ·nənts, $'kɑːn·t̬ən·ənts/ *n* [U]

con·tin·gen·cy /kən'tɪn·dʒənt·si/ *n* [C] *fml* something that might possibly happen in the future, usually causing problems or making further plans and arrangements necessary • *You must be able to deal with all possible contingencies.* • *Have you made any contingency* **plans?**

con·tin·gent GROUP /kən'tɪn·dʒənt/ *n* [C + sing/pl v] a group of people representing an organization or country, or a part of a military force • *The French contingent certainly made their presence known at this year's conference.* • *There were cries of outrage from the feminist contingent when the speaker referred to the women present as 'girls'.* • *They are strengthening their army with a large contingent of voluntary soldiers.*

con·tin·gent DEPENDING ON /kən'tɪn·dʒənt/ *adj* [after v; always + *on/upon*] depending on something else (in the future) in order to happen • *Outdoor arrangements are, as ever, contingent* **on/upon** *the weather and we have other plans in the event of rain.* • *Our success is contingent* **on/upon** *your support.*

con·tin·ue *(obj)* /kən'tɪn·juː/ *v* to (cause to) keep doing and not stop • *It's said that as the boat went down the band continued* **to** *play.* [+ *to* infinitive] • *Despite my repeated complaints he continues* **to** *leave his dirty clothes on the floor.* [+ *to* infinitive] • *If she continues drinking like that I'll have to carry her home.* [+ v-*ing*] • *Do you intend to continue* **(with)** *your studies?* [T; I + *with*] • *I don't know how long she'll continue work.* [T] • *Continue* **with** *the medicine* (= Keep taking it) *until the symptoms disappear.* [I] • *If the rain continues we'll have to cancel tonight's plans.* [I] • *Sally Palmer will be continuing* **as** *chairperson of the committee this autumn.* [I] • *The article starts on page two and continues/is continued* **on** *page ten.* [I] • You can also continue to do something or continue doing something if you start to do it again after a pause: *After a break for a quick drink they continued* **on** *their way.* [I] ○ *He paused for a moment to listen and then continued eating.* [+ v-*ing*] ○ *The president continued* **by** *saying that his country was a free country and would always remain so.* [I] ○ *"I don't like the weather in this country!" she shouted, "and what's more," she continued, "I don't like the food."* [+ clause] ○ *"May I continue?" she said, clearly irritated by the interruption.* [I]

con·tin·u·al /kən'tɪn·ju·əl/ *adj* [not gradable] • If something is continual it happens repeatedly and often causes trouble or inconvenience: *I've had continual problems with this car ever since I bought the damn thing!* ○ *I'm sorry – I can't work with these continual interruptions.*

con·tin·u·al·ly /kən'tɪn·ju·ə·li/ *adv* • *They're continually arguing – I really don't know how long the relationship will last.* • *"I think continually of those who were truly great"* (title of a poem by Stephen Spender, 1933)

con·tin·u·ous /kən'tɪn·ju·əs/ *adj* [not gradable] • Continuous is used to mean without a pause: *continuous pain* ○ *My computer makes a continuous low buzzing noise.* ○ *The continuous white line* (= line without spaces) *in the middle of the road means no overtaking!* • **Continuous assessment** is the educational system of judging the quality of a student's work by various pieces of work done during their course and not by one final examination.

con·tin·u·ous·ly /kən'tɪn·ju·ə·sli/ *adv* [not gradable] • *You can't work continuously for six hours without a single break – it's impossible!*

con·tin·u·a·tion /kənˌtɪn·ju'eɪ·ʃən/, *slightly fml* **con·tin·u·ance** /kən'tɪn·ju·ənts/ *n* • *The continuation of the miners' strike created a lot of poverty among the local community.* [U] • *It's really just a continuation of the bigger river but called by a different name for a few miles.* [C]

con·tin·ued /kən'tɪn·juːd/, **con·tin·u·ing** /kən'tɪn·ju·ɪŋ/ *adj* [not gradable] • *The continued fighting in the city is causing great concern.* • Continued (*abbreviation* **contd** or **cont**) is often used at the bottom of a page to show that the story, article, etc., is not finished: *continued on page 7* • See also ONGOING. • LP **-ing form of verbs, Tenses**

con·ti·nu·i·ty /£ˌkɒn·tɪ'njuː·ɪ·ti, $ˌkɑːn·tən'uː·ə·ti/ *n* [U] • *There has been no continuity* (= smooth change or development) *in that class – they've had a succession of four different teachers.* • *(specialized)* Continuity is also the way in which film and television broadcasts are joined together so that the action happens smoothly without a pause and, for example, the actor's appearance is the same in a particular part of a recording even if it has been filmed on different days: *a continuity girl/man*

con·tin·u·um /kən'tɪn·ju·əm/ *n pl* **continua** /kən'tɪn·ju·ə/ or **continuums** *fml specialized* something that changes in character gradually or in very slight stages without any clear dividing points • *The spectrum is a continuum of colour from red to violet.*

VERBS RARELY USED IN A CONTINUOUS FORM

- The continuous form of a verb is mainly used to show that an action or event is (or was, or will be) **happening** at a particular point in time—it has reached a stage somewhere **between its beginning and its end.** LP **Tenses**
- Because the continuous form is used to refer to events or actions which **happen**, it is not normally used with verbs referring to **states** (which exist but do not happen).
- The dictionary marks meanings of verbs that are never used in the continuous. For example 'own' is marked [T not *be owning*] because we say *He owns three cars* but never 'He is owning three cars'. These are shown with a * in the following list.
- **verbs of perception and appearance**
  notice*, perceive, see, hear
  seem*, appear*, resemble*
- **verbs of belief and knowledge**
  (These are often followed by a clause.)
  believe, consider, regard, think
  imagine, suppose, suspect*
  know*, realize, recognize, understand*, see
  remember, recall*, remind, forget
- **verbs of emotion, desire and attitude**
  There are many verbs in this group, for example:
  like, love, adore, admire, respect, trust
  please, appeal, amuse, attract, interest
  desire*, need, prefer*, require*, want, wish
  dislike, hate*, detest*, despise*
  care about, mind*, concern
  fear, frighten, shock
  surprise, amaze
  hope, regret
  deserve*, forgive*
- **modal auxiliary verbs**
  can, may, might, ought, should, will, etc.
  Need (MUST DO) and used (IN THE PAST) are also not used in a continuous form.
- **other verbs referring to states**
  exist
  represent, mean*
  belong to, have*, own*, possess*
  include, involve
  (The following verbs can be followed by a particular quantity:)
  contain*, hold*
  cost, count, measure, weigh
  afford, owe*
  equal, consist of*, amount to
- Notice that many of these verbs can be used with other meanings in which the continuous form is possible:
  Are you seeing (= visiting) *your doctor tomorrow?*
  I can't stop thinking about (= imagining) *food.*
  I was just admiring (= looking at with admiration) *your new kitchen.*
  Mother was busy weighing flour for the cakes.

con·tort *(obj)* /£kən'tɔːt, $-'tɔːrt/ *v* to (cause to) twist or bend violently and unnaturally into a different shape or form • *His face had contorted* **with** *bitterness and rage.* [I] • *He must be very supple to be able to contort his body like that.* [T]

con·tort·ed /£kən'tɔː·tɪd, $-'tɔːr·t̬ɪd/ *adj* • *contorted hands/limbs/branches*

con·tor·tion /£kən'tɔː·ʃən, $-'tɔːr-/ *n* • *facial contortions* [C] • *You should have seen me at my yoga class – I performed all sorts of amazing contortions!* [C] • *Repeated loading and unloading* *will eventually cause some contortion of the structure.* [U]

con·tor·tion·ist /£kən'tɔː·ʃᵊn·ɪst, $-'tɔːr-/ *n* [C] • A contortionist is someone who can twist their body into shapes and positions that ordinary people cannot: *You used to be able to see contortionists at the circus or in travelling shows.* • Also, contortionist means someone who can escape from complicated or difficult situations without getting into trouble: *She must be a contortionist to have avoided getting any blame for the mess she caused.*

con·tour /£'kɒn·tɔːʳ, $'kɑːn·tʊr/ *n* [C] the shape of a mass of land or other object, esp. its surface or the shape formed by its outer edge • *the rugged contour of the coast* • *He studied the contour of her face, silhouetted against the darkening sky.* • *The contour of the car has been changed making the new model less boxlike.* • *Her latest collection of swimwear is designed to show off to perfection the contours of the human body.* • The contours (or **contour lines**) on a map are lines drawn joining points of equal height or depth which show how high or low the land is and whether there are hills or mountains: *a 400ft contour (line)* ○ *This map has contours marked at 250m intervals.*

con·tra·band /£'kɒn·trə·bænd, $'kɑːn-/ *n* [U] goods which are brought into or taken out of the country secretly and illegally • *Going through customs, the lorry was found to be carrying thousands of pounds worth of contraband.*

con·tra·band /£'kɒn·trə·bænd, $'kɑːn-/ *adj* [not gradable] • *contraband cigarettes/alcohol/goods*

con·tra·cep·tion /£,kɒn·trə'sep·ʃᵊn, $,kɑːn-/ *n* [U] the use of any of the various methods which are intended to prevent a woman becoming pregnant • *Impartial advice on contraception is available if you feel you need it.* • *What is the most reliable* **form/method of** *contraception?* • *Did you use any* **form of** *contraception?*

con·tra·cept·ive /£,kɒn·trə'sep·tɪv, $,kɑːn·trə'sep·t̬ɪv/ *n* [C] • Contraceptives are any of the various devices or drugs which are intended to prevent pregnancy: *The clinic provides a free supply of contraceptives on request.*

con·tra·cept·ive /£,kɒn·trə'sep·tɪv, $,kɑːn·trə'sep·t̬ɪv/ *adj* [not gradable] • *a contraceptive device/method/pill*

con·tract AGREEMENT /£'kɒn·trækt, $'kɑːn-/ *n* [C] a legal document that states and explains a formal agreement between two different people or groups, or the agreement itself • *a contract of employment* • *a temporary/building contract* • *They might try to take legal action against you if you* **break (the terms of)** *the contract.* • *My solicitor is currently* **drawing up** (=writing) *a contract.* • *Whatever happens don't* **sign/enter into** *any contract before you have examined its conditions in detail.* • *They're the firm of architects who* **won** *the contract* **to** *design the National Museum extension.* [+ *to* infinitive] • If you are **under** contract **to** a company or a person you have formally agreed to work for them on a stated job for a stated period of time. • *"A verbal contract isn't worth the paper it's written on"* (believed to have been said by the film producer Sam Goldwyn who was famous for his mistakes in English, 1884-1974)

con·tract *(obj)* /kən'trækt, $'kɑːn·trækt/ *v* • *The company has just contracted* **to** *build shelters for the homeless.* [T + obj + *to* infinitive] • *We've contracted* **with** *a catering firm for the food at the event.* [I] • *(Br)* If you **contract in** to an official plan or system you formally agree to take part in it: *Have you contracted in* **to** *the scheme?* • If you **contract out** a job or **contract** a job **out**, you formally arrange for other people to do it: *Ever since the government contracted out the job of cleaning* **to** *private companies, the dirt and mess has increased.*

con·tract·ual /kən'træk·tju·ᵊl/ *adj* [not gradable] • *It's one of the contractual obligations/conditions/terms that you work only for this company.* • *Are you* **under a** *contractual* **obligation** *to any other company at this time?*

con·tract·ual·ly /kən'træk·tju·ᵊl·i/ *adv* [not gradable] • *They are contractually* **bound/obliged** *to finish the work.*

con·tract *(obj)* SHORTEN /kən'trækt, $'kɑːn·trækt/ *v* to make or become shorter or narrower or generally smaller • *In spoken English 'do not' often contracts* **to** *'don't.'* [I] • *People often contract word combinations when they are speaking.* [T] • *As it cooled the metal contracted.* [I] • *When a muscle contracts it becomes smaller and tighter.* [I]

con·tract·ile /£kən'træk·taɪl, $-t̬ᵊl/ *adj specialized* • **Contractile tissue** is the tissue in the muscle which allows it to become shorter.

con·trac·tion /kən'træk·ʃᵊn/ *n* • *Cold causes the contraction of the metal.* [U] • *The contraction of this muscle causes the lower arm to be raised.* [U] • In the process of giving birth a contraction is one of the very strong and usually painful movements of the muscles in the womb that help to push the baby out. [C] • A contraction is also a shortened form of a word or combination of words which is often used instead of the full form in spoken English: *'Won't' is a contraction of 'will not'.* [C] • LP> **Short forms**

con·tract *obj* BECOME ILL /kən'trækt, $'kɑːn·trækt/ *v* [T] *slightly fml* to catch or become ill with (a disease) • *He contracted an awful stomach complaint while he was travelling.*

con·tract·or /£kən'træk·təʳ, $-tɚ/ *n* [C] a person or company that arranges to supply materials or workers, esp. for building or moving goods

con·tra·dict *(obj)* /£,kɒn·trə'dɪkt, $,kɑːn-/ *v* (of people) to state the opposite of what someone else has said, or (of one fact or statement) to be so different from another fact or statement that one of them must be wrong • *If you're both going to lie, make sure you get the story the same and don't contradict each other!* [T] • *What's the matter with you today! Everything I say you seem to want to contradict.* [T] • *Did you notice the way he kept contradicting himself when we were arguing? I think he was a bit confused.* [T] • *How dare you contradict (him)!* [I/T] • *Recent evidence has tended to contradict established theories on this subject.* [T]

con·tra·dic·tion /£,kɒn·trə'dɪk·ʃᵊn, $,kɑːn-/ *n* • *You say that you're good friends and yet you don't trust him. Isn't that a bit of a contradiction?* [C] • *There are a few contradictions in recent policies which make you wonder whether the government know what they're doing.* [C] • *The ability to spot contradiction is essential in analytical thought.* [U] • A **contradiction in terms** is a combination of words which is nonsense because some of the words suggest the opposite of some of the others: *He suspected that the notion of an honest politician was a contradiction in terms.*

con·tra·dict·o·ry /£,kɒn·trə'dɪk·tᵊr·i, $,kɑːn·trə'dɪk·t̬ɚ-/ *adj* • *I've been given contradictory advice – someone told me to keep it warm and someone else told me to put ice on it.* • *The evidence given in the trial was contradictory.*

con·tra·flow /£'kɒn·trə·fləʊ, $'kɑːn·trə·floʊ/ *n* [C] *esp. Br* a temporary traffic arrangement, usually on a MOTORWAY (=a type of large road), in which traffic travelling in both directions uses one side of the road while the other side is being repaired • *A contraflow is* **in operation/in force** *between junctions 13 and 14 on the motorway.* • PIC> **Motorway**

con·tra·in·di·ca·tion /£,kɒn·trə,ɪn·dɪ'keɪ·ʃᵊn, $,kɑːn-/ *n* [C] *medical* a sign that someone should not continue with a particular medicine or treatment because it is or might be harmful • *Depression and mood change are recognised contraindications for this particular drug.*

con·tral·to /£kən'træl·təʊ, $-t̬oʊ/ *n* [C], *adj pl* **contraltos** or **contralti** /£kən'træl·tiː, $-t̬iː/ (of) a woman singer with the lowest female singing voice, or (of) such a voice

con·trap·tion /kən'træp·ʃᵊn/ *n* [C] an awkward or old-fashioned looking device or machine, esp. one that you do not know how to use • *Whatever's that weird contraption you've got in the garage?* • *Don't ask me how to use this contraption!*

con·tra·punt·al /£,kɒn·trə'pʌn·tᵊl, $,kɑːn·trə'pʌn·t̬ᵊl/ *adj specialized* (of music) combining two or more separate tunes at the same time

con·tra·ry OPPOSITE /£'kɒn·trə·ri, $'kɑːn·trɚ-/ *n* [U] **the contrary** the opposite • *People say that physical exercise is good for you but I think the contrary – it's dangerous and a waste of valuable time.* • *I was expecting the actress to be loud and aggressive but found the contrary.* • You can use the expression **on the contrary** to show that you think or feel the opposite of what has just been stated: *"Didn't you find the film exciting?" "On the contrary, I nearly fell asleep half way through it!"* • The expression **to the contrary** is used to show that one statement is the opposite of another: *For a long time it was thought to be a harmless substance but there's recently been some proof to the contrary and you're now warned off it.* ○ *If I don't hear to the contrary* (=If I'm not told that the arrangements have been changed) *I'll see you at the station at ten.*

con·tra·ry /£'kɒn·trə·ri, $'kɑːn·trɚ-/ *adj* • *Liz put forward the contrary point of view at the meeting and a lively discussion followed.* • *Contrary* **to** *all our expectations he's actually found a well-paid job and a nice girlfriend.* • *In fact,* **contrary to popular opinion** (=rather than what many people believe to be true), *I* *wasn't crying in my exam yesterday – I had something in my eye!*

con·tra·ri·ly /kən'trer·ɪ·li/ *adv*

con·tra·ry UNREASONABLE /£kən'treə·ri, $-'trer·i/ *adj* (of a person) intentionally wanting to disagree with and annoy other people • *He doesn't really mean it – he's just being contrary!*

con·tra·ri·ness /£kən'treə·ri·nəs, $-'trer·i-/ *n* [U]

con·tra·ri·ly /£kən'treə·rɪ·li, $-'trer·ɪ-/ *adv*

con·trast /£'kɒn·trɑːst, $'kɑːn·træst/ *n* an obvious difference between two or more things • *As little children we made quite a contrast – my brother so blonde, my sister red-haired and me very dark.* [C] • *She couldn't bear going back to work so soon after her holiday – the contrast was too awful.* [C] • *Their economy has expanded enormously in the last five years, whereas ours,* **by/in** *contrast, has declined.* [U] • *The antique furnishing provides an unusual contrast* **to** *the modernity of the building.* [C] • *I like the contrast of the white trousers* **with** *the black jacket.* [C] • *The amount of money spent on defence is* **in stark** (= in very noticeable) *contrast* **to** *the amount spent on housing and health.* [U] • *There's a* **marked** *contrast* **between** *the standard of living in the north of the country and the south.* [C] • *His use of contrast* (= strong differences between light and darkness) *in some of his later photographs is marvellous.* [U]

con·trast *(obj)* /£kən'trɑːst, $'kɑːn·træst/ *v* • *If you contrast some of the early writing* **with** *her later work you can see just how much she improved.* [T] • *As film-makers their two styles contrast quite dramatically.* [I]

con·trast·ing /£kən'trɑː·stɪŋ, $-'træs·tɪŋ/ *adj* • *contrasting colours/flavours/techniques* • *The results of our survey show the contrasting attitudes between different age-groups.*

con·tra·vene *obj* /£ˌkɒn·trə'viːn, $ˌkɑːn-/ *v* [T] *fml* to do something that is not permitted by (a law or rule); to break (a law or rule) • *The penalties for contravening that law are very serious.*

con·tra·ven·tion /£ˌkɒn·trə'ven·tʃən, $ˌkɑːn-/ *n* [C/U] *fml* • *Anyone found acting* **in** *contravention* **of** *these regulations will no longer be allowed club membership.*

con·tre·temps /£'kɒn·trə·tɑ̃ː, $'kɑːn-/ *n* [C] a small argument or unlucky event, often happening in public and causing social embarrassment • *We had* **a slight** *contretemps at the bar because some bloke tried to push in front and Richard got angry.* • *Have you got over your little contretemps* **with** *the neighbour yet or are you still not speaking?*

con·tri·bute *(obj)* /kən'trɪb·juːt, £'kɒn·trɪ·bjuːt, $'kɑːn-/ *v* to give (money, support, help or ideas) towards a particular aim or purpose • *Between all of us at work, we're hoping to contribute £100* **towards** *the new wing of the hospital.* [T] • *If you've anything to contribute* **to** *this year's fair – time, energy, enthusiasm – we'd love to hear from you!* [T] • *I'm not going to contribute* **towards** *someone's leaving present when I don't even like them!* [I] • *He felt he wanted to contribute something* **to** *the community that had given so much to him.* [T]

con·tri·but·or /£kən'trɪb·jʊ·tər, $-jə·t̬ɚ/ *n* [C] • *At the back of the programme, there is a list of contributors* **to** *the theatre appeal.* • Someone who is a contributor to a book/magazine/newspaper writes things such as articles or stories for it.

con·tri·bu·tion /£ˌkɒn·trɪ'bjuː·ʃən, $ˌkɑːn-/ *n* • *This invention* **made a** *major contribution* **to** *road safety.* [C] • *His last novel is his greatest contribution* **to** *Spanish literature.* [C] • *All contributions* (= presents of money), *no matter how small, will be much appreciated.* [C] • *She didn't* **make** *much of* **a** *contribution at the meeting this morning.* [U] • *Contributions* (= articles, stories, etc. to be printed) **for** *the autumn issue of the school magazine should be sent in no later than August 1st.* [C]

con·tri·but·o·ry /£kən'trɪb·jʊ·tri, $-jə·tɔːr·i/ *adj* • *As well as other benefits, the company offers a contributory (Br and Aus)* **pension scheme**/*(Am)* **pension plan** (= one that is paid for by both employer and employee.) • A contributory cause or reason is part of the cause of something: *Too little exercise isn't the only cause of heart disease but it's certainly a contributory* **factor**. • *(Br and Aus law)* **Contributory negligence** is when it is decided in court that a person who has been hurt in an accident was partly responsible for their own injuries because they failed to act in a way that could have prevented the accident or the injuries: *Not wearing seatbelts can be seen as* **(partial)** *contributory negligence.*

con·trite /£'kɒn·traɪt, $'kɑːn-/ *adj fml or literary* feeling great regret and guilt for something bad that you have done • *a contrite apology/expression*

con·trite·ly /kən'traɪt·li/ *adv fml or literary*

con·tri·tion /kən'trɪʃ·ən/ *n* [U] *fml or literary*

con·trive *(obj)* /kən'traɪv/ *v* to arrange (a situation, an event or for something to happen), using clever planning, or to invent and/or make (something such as a device) cleverly and possibly in an unusual way • *Couldn't you contrive a meeting between them? It sounds like they'd be ideally suited.* [T] • *Miraculously, he managed to contrive a supper out of what was left in the cupboard.* [T] • *Somehow she contrived* **to get** (= succeeded in getting) *tickets for the concert.* [+ to infinitive] • *Do you think you could contrive something for hanging my clothes on until I can get a wardrobe?* [T]

con·triv·ance /kən'traɪ·vənts/ *n* [C] • *(disapproving) It might seem like coincidence but because of its timing I'm sure the salary freeze is a contrivance* (= a plan to give someone an advantage usually by causing someone else disadvantage). [C] • *The toilet flusher was broken but he'd made some sort of contrivance* (= device) *using bits of string, wire and an empty bottle.* [C] • *I think the meeting happened more by contrivance than chance.* [U]

con·trived /kən'traɪvd/ *adj disapproving* • *Didn't you think his excuse sounded a bit contrived* (= too reasonable rather than honest)? • A story, film, play, etc. that is contrived is artificial and not believable.

con·trol *obj* /£kən'trəʊl, $-'troʊl/ *v* [T] **-ll-** to order, limit, instruct, or rule (something or someone's actions or behaviour) • *If you can't control your dog put it on a lead!* • *You're going to have to learn to control that temper of yours!* • *Bring your leg slowly up to meet your head, controlling it all the time.* • *The temperature in here is controlled by a thermostat.* • *The laws controlling drugs are very strict in this country.* • *I find this car difficult to control at high speeds.* • *The government have been trying to control spending.* • (CS) (N) (NL) (P) (RUS)

con·trol /£kən'trəʊl, $-'troʊl/ *n* • *She's got no control* **over** *that child of hers – it's terrible.* [U] • *The dictator took control* **of** *the country in 1933.* [U] • *He felt he was* **losing** *control* **of** *his life.* [U] • *Which of the sons is going to* **gain/take** *control* **of** *the company when their father dies?* [U] • *What frightens me about being on horseback is that I don't feel as if I'm* **in** *control.* [U] • *Were you* **in** *control* **of** *your emotions at the time?* [U] • *It seems that the spread of the disease is now* **under** *control.* [U] • *Everything is* **under** *control, sir* (= All problems are being dealt with). [U] • *It took them two hours to* **bring/get** *the fire* **under** *control.* [U] • *There was nothing we could do about it. The situation was* **out of/beyond/outside** *our control.* [U] • *The car skidded on the ice and* **went out of** *control, crashing into an oncoming truck.* [U] • *He thinks the government ought to* **impose** *strict controls* **on** *dog ownership, especially in the case of big dogs.* [C] • *The police's method of* **crowd** *control involved charging on horseback and spraying the demonstrators with tear gas.* [U] • A control of a machine, for example a vehicle, is a device such as a switch used to operate it: *The pilot was surrounded by a mass of controls.* [C] ○ *The main instruments are well located in the centre of the control* **panel**. ○ *When landing it can be very stressful to be* **at the** *controls* **of** *an aircraft.* [C] • In a scientific experiment a control is an object or system that is not changed so that similar objects or systems which are purposely changed can be compared to it: *Do not add glucose to the control but put five milligrams in each of the other test tubes.* [C] • On a computer keyboard the **control key** *(abbreviation* **Ctrl**) is the key that you use together with other keys when you want the keyboard to operate in a particular way: *Press Ctrl+B if you want bold type.* • A **control tower** is a building at an airport from which air traffic is watched and directed. • LP **Switching on and off**

con·trol·ler /£kən'trəʊ·lər, $-'troʊ·lɚ/ *n* [C] • A controller is a person who controls something, or someone who is responsible for what a particular organization does: *Air-traffic controllers are threatening to take industrial action again this weekend.* ○ *He's the controller of Radio 4 so I guess he's a fairly influential man.*

con·trov·er·sy /£'kɒn·trə·vɜː·si, £kən'trɒv·ə-, $'kɑːn·trə·vɜːr-/ *n* (a) strong disagreement about something, esp. (one) that is important to, influences or is of interest to many people • *There was a big controversy* **surrounding/over** *the use of drugs in athletics.* [C] • *I don't know what all* *the controversy was about – it was a dull sort of a film and there was almost no sex in it.* [U] • *There's been (a)* **fierce/ bitter/heated** *controversy over the policy ever since it was introduced.* [C/U]

con·tro·ver·sial /£ˌkɒn·trəˈvɜː·ʃəl, $ˌkɑːn·trəˈvɜːr-/ *adj* • Controversial means causing disagreement or discussion: *a controversial issue/decision/speech/policy/ figure/film* ○ *He wrote a very controversial book but I think he's since regretted it.*

con·tu·sion /£kənˈtjuː·ʒən, $-ˈtuː-/ *n* [C] *medical for* BRUISE • *The victim's left arm was broken and there was a large contusion* **to** *the right shoulder.*

con·tuse *(obj)* /£kənˈtjuːz, $-ˈtuːz/ *v* [I/T] • Contuse is *medical for* **bruise**. See at BRUISE.

co·nun·drum [TRICK] /kəˈnʌn·drəm/ *n* [C] a trick question, esp. one involving an amusing use of words that have two meanings

co·nun·drum [PROBLEM] /kəˈnʌn·drəm/ *n* [C] a problem that is difficult to deal with • *Working parents have to face the conundrum* **of** *who will take care of their children during school holidays.* • If a person is a conundrum, they are difficult to understand or deal with.

con·ur·ba·tion /£ˌkɒn·əˈbeɪ·ʃən, $ˌkɑː·nɚ-/ *n* [C] *fml* a city area containing a large number of people which has been formed by the growth and joining together of various towns • *the conurbations of Tokyo and Osaka*

con·va·lesce /£ˌkɒn·vəˈles, $ˌkɑːn-/ *v* [I] to rest in order to get better after an illness • *After your operation you'll need to convalesce for a week or two.* • *It was while I was convalescing that I managed to read the complete works of Marcel Proust.*

con·va·les·cence /£ˌkɒn·vəˈles·ənts, $ˌkɑːn-/ *n* • *It's an illness which generally requires a fairly long (period of) convalescence afterwards.* [C/U]

con·va·les·cent /£ˌkɒn·vəˈles·ənt, $ˌkɑːn-/ *n, adj* • *Don't do anything too strenuous during this period – remember you're still convalescent* (= getting better after a serious illness or injury). • *She's in a convalescent* **home/ hospital** (= one for people getting better after a serious illness or injury) *for a couple of months where she can be looked after properly.* • *He said that it was better for convalescents* (= people getting better after a serious injury) *to be cared for at home rather than in a hospital.* [C]

con·vec·tion /kənˈvek·ʃən/ *n* [U] *specialized* the flow of heat through a gas or a liquid • *Warm air rises by the process of convection.* • *As warm air rises, cool air is drawn in to replace it, creating a convection* **current**.

con·vect·or /£kənˈvek·təʳ, $-t̬ɚ/ *n* [C] a heating device which warms a room by causing a current of hot air

con·vene /kənˈviːn/ *v fml* to (arrange (a group of people) to) gather together • *The Prime Minister convened (a meeting of) his ministers to discuss the matter.* [T] • *The council will be convening on the morning of the 25th.* [I]

con·ven·or /£kənˈviː·nəʳ, $-nɚ/, **con·ven·er** *n* [C] • In Britain, a convenor is a high-ranking **trade union** official who works in a particular factory. *He's the convenor* **of** *the committee.*

con·ven·i·ent /kənˈviː·ni·ənt/ *adj* suitable for your purposes and needs and causing the least difficulty • *Our local shop has very convenient opening hours.* • *I find my bike a very convenient way of getting around.* • **It's** *very convenient* **that** *you live so close to each other.* [+ *that* clause] • *I find* **it** *convenient* **to** *be able to do my banking by phone.* [+ *to* infinitive] • *What time would* **it** *be convenient* **for me** *to come round?* [+ *to* infinitive] • *I didn't really want to go out, and the fact that it was raining gave me a convenient excuse for not doing so.* • *The new flat is very convenient* **for** (= near to) *the kids' school.* • Shops, transport, etc. are convenient if they are situated near you and are easy to get to: *There's a very convenient bus service near to where we live.* • Ⓟ

con·ven·i·ent·ly /kənˈviː·ni·ənt·li/ *adv* • *The house is conveniently situated near the railway station and five minutes' walk from the shops.* • *(humorous) I asked her to tidy the kitchen before she went out and of course she conveniently forgot* (= she forgot because she did not want to do it).

con·ven·i·ence /kənˈviː·ni·ənts/ *n* • *I like the convenience of living so near work – it only takes me five minutes to get there.* [U] • *Just for convenience, I'm going to live at my mother's place until the repairs have been done on my new house.* [U] • *We chose a modern house for convenience's sake – an old one would have meant too much work.* [U] • *Once the goods have been paid for they will be delivered* **at** *your convenience* (= when you want). [U] • *Please fill in the form attached and send it to the address shown* **at** *your earliest convenience* (= as soon as you can). [U] • A convenience is also a device or machine, usually in the house, which makes life easier for its user because it operates quickly and needs little effort: *He's got every convenience imaginable in that new house of his!* [C] • A convenience is also a **public convenience**. See at PUBLIC. [C] • **Convenience food** is food that is almost ready to eat when it is bought and can be prepared for eating quickly and easily.

con·vent /£ˈkɒn·vənt, $ˈkɑːn-/, *dated or literary* **nun·nery** *n* [C] a building in which NUNS (= a religious group of women) live • *She* **entered** *a convent* (= became a NUN) *at the age of 16.* • A **convent school** is a school in which many of the teachers are NUNS. • Compare MONASTERY. • Ⓘ

con·ven·tion [CUSTOM] /kənˈvent·ʃən/ *n* (an example of) a way of behaving esp. in social situations, which is accepted by most people in a particular society and often follows a way of thinking or a custom belonging to the past • *In some countries, it's a convention that the guests wear black or dark-coloured clothes.* [C + *that* clause] • *Convention* **dictates that** *it is the man who asks the woman to marry him and not the reverse.* [U] • *They* **defied/flouted** *convention by giving up their jobs and producing all their own food and other needs themselves.* [U] • *The British Constitution is founded upon convention, as well as laws.* [U] • A convention is also a common way of showing something in art or writing: *The novelist James Joyce* **broke with** *many of the conventions* **of** *literature.* [C]

con·ven·tion·al /kənˈvent·ʃən·əl/ *adj* • *conventional behaviour/attitudes/opinions/clothes* • *a conventional wedding* • *They're such a conventional family – they must have been horrified when their son died his hair pink.* • *(disapproving) As an artist I find him very dull and conventional – he's not prepared to try anything new.* • *Alternative medicine can sometimes provide a cure where conventional medicine cannot.* • Conventional **weapons/ warfare** are not nuclear.

con·ven·tion·al·i·ty /£kənˌvent·ʃənˈæl·ɪ·ti, $-ə·t̬i/ *n* [U]

con·ven·tion [MEETING] /kənˈvent·ʃən/ *n* [C] a large formal meeting for a group of people who do a particular job or who have a similar interest, or for a political party • *the annual pig breeders' convention* • *a convention of stamp collectors* • *the national Democratic convention* • *They're using that hall to* **hold** *their party convention.*

con·ven·tion [AGREEMENT] /kənˈven·tʃən/ *n* [C] a formal agreement between country leaders, politicians and states on a matter which involves them all • *the Geneva Convention* • *a convention on human rights*

con·verge /£kənˈvɜːdʒ, $-ˈvɜːrdʒ/ *v* [I] (of lines, roads or paths) to move towards the same point and meet there • *All the paths across the park converge at the main gate.* • *Because of repair work on the road, the usual three lanes of traffic are currently converging into two.* • *(fig.) There was once a big difference between the two politicians, but now their ideas seem to be converging* (= becoming similar). • To converge is also to come from other places to meet in a particular place: *Ambulances, police cars and fire engines all converged* **on** *the scene of the explosion.* ○ *100 000 people are expected to converge* **on** *the town for the concert this weekend.* • Compare DIVERGE.

con·verg·ence /£kənˈvɜː·dʒənts, $-ˈvɜːr-/ *n* • *In recent months there seems to have been a/some convergence* **of** *interests and opinions between the two sides involved in the conflict.* [C/U]

con·verg·ent /£kənˈvɜː·dʒənt, $-ˈvɜːr-/ *adj* • *convergent lines/opinions*

con·vers·ant with /£kənˈvɜː·sənt, $-ˈvɜːr-/ *adj fml* familiar with and having knowledge or experience of (facts or rules) • *I'm not conversant with the rules of chess.* • *The barrister asked the judge whether he was conversant with the defendant's family background.*

con·vers·a·tion /£ˌkɒn·vəˈseɪ·ʃən, $ˌkɑːn·vɚ-/ *n* (a) talk between two or more people in which thoughts, feelings and ideas are expressed, questions are asked and answered and news and information are exchanged • *I* **had** *an interesting conversation* **with** *the bloke who lives in the flat below us this morning.* [C] • *We were trying to* **hold/carry on** *a conversation but with all this noise going on it was impossible!* [C] • *I'm afraid my attempts to* **strike up** *(a) conversation* **with** (= start talking to) *the exotic-looking man in black came to nothing!* [C/U] • *He said that because they watch so much television, many people have lost the art of* *conversation* (= talking to each other). [U] • *Every time I've found myself in a social situation with my boss we seem to have* **run out of** *conversation* (= things to say to each other) *after two minutes!* [U] • If you **make** conversation, you try to think of things to say to someone whom you do not know very well because it is polite to do so in that particular situation: *I hate it when you're left alone at a party with a complete stranger and you've got to make conversation.* [U] • A conversation **stopper** is a remark which stops the natural flow of the conversation because it is unexpected and in some way causes embarrassment or shock: *When she told us her son was in prison, it was a real conversation stopper.* • A **conversation piece** is an unusual object which causes people to start talking: *Her collection of Victorian dolls provided a conversation piece for her guests.* • LP **Meeting someone, Phrases and customs**

con·vers·a·tion·al /£ˌkɒn·vəˈseɪ·ʃən·əl, $ˌkɑːn·vɚ-/ *adj* • *He has a relaxed and conversational style of writing, which is very readable.* • *"That's very interesting," she said in a conversational tone.* • *He seems to lack basic conversational skills.*

con·vers·a·tion·al·ist /£ˌkɒn·vəˈseɪ·ʃən·əl·ɪst, $ˌkɑːn·vɚ-/ *n* [C] • *Your sister's not much of a conversationalist is she? She scarcely said a word all evening!*

con·verse /£kənˈvɜːs, $-ˈvɜːrs/ *v* [I] *fml* • *Conducting business with her is fine but I find that actually conversing* **with** *her is quite difficult.* • See also CONVERSE.

con·verse /£ˈkɒn·vɜːs, $ˈkɑːn·vɜːrs/ *adj fml* (esp. of an opinion, statement or situation) opposite • *I wanted to appear friendly and approachable but I think I gave the converse impression.* • See also **converse** at CONVERSATION.

con·verse /£ˈkɒn·vɜːs, $ˈkɑːn·vɜːrs/ *n* [U] *fml* • **The converse** means the opposite: *In the US, cars are driven on the right hand side of the road, but in Britain the converse applies.* ○ *It is possible, of course, that the converse* **of** *this theory may also be true.*

con·verse·ly /£kənˈvɜː·sli, £ˈkɒn·vɜː-, $kənˈvɜːr-, $kɑːn·vɜːr-/ *adv* • *Running can strengthen your heart and muscles, but conversely* (= considering the opposite argument), *it can also damage your knee joints and the bones in your feet.*

con·vert /£kənˈvɜːt, $-ˈvɜːrt/ *v* to (cause to) change in form, character or opinion • *Couldn't we convert the small bedroom* **into** *a second bathroom?* [T] • *They live in a converted windmill.* • *What's the formula for converting pounds* **into** *kilos?* [T] • *He converted* **to** (= starting believing in) *his wife's religion when he got married.* [I] • *I didn't use to like exercise but my sister has converted me* **(to it)** (= persuaded me to enjoy or take part in it). [T]

con·vert /£ˈkɒn·vɜːt, $ˈkɑːn·vɜːrt/ *n* [C] • A convert is someone who changes their beliefs or way of living: *a convert* **to** *Christianity/Buddhism* ○ *a convert* **to** *socialism* ○ *a convert* **to** *healthy living/vegetarianism/wholemeal bread*

con·ver·sion /£kənˈvɜː·ʃən, -ʒən, $-ˈvɜːr-/ *n* • *Her conversion* **to** *Buddhism/Islam was a gradual process which took place over many years.* [C] • *He used to be very right-wing, but he's* **undergone** *something of a conversion recently.* [C] • *What brought about your conversion* **to** *the bicycle after so many years of going around in a car?* [C] • *Solar power is the conversion* **of** *the sun's energy* **into** *heat and electricity.* [U] • *It's 50 000 pesetas – I'm just trying to work out the conversion* **of** *that into dollars.* [U] • *Their apartment is a modernized conversion* (= a place for living in that has been changed from its previous use) *in an old factory building.* [C]

con·vert·i·ble /£kənˈvɜː·tɪ·bl̩, $-ˈvɜːr·t̬ɪ-/ *adj* • *Is this sofa convertible* (= does it open into a bed)*?* • Convertible money is a type of money that can be easily exchanged into other types of money: *The majority of people in the country do not have access to a convertible currency.*

con·vert·i·ble /£kənˈvɜː·tɪ·bl̩, $-ˈvɜːr·t̬ɪ-/ *n* [C] • A convertible (also **soft top**) is a car which has a soft roof which can be folded back: *My boyfriend's got a really great Volkswagen convertible.* • PIC **Vehicles**

con·vert·er /£kənˈvɜː·tər, $-ˈvɜːr·t̬ɚ/, **con·vert·or** *n* [C] • A converter is a number of machines and devices that changes something into a different form.

con·vex /£ˈkɒn·veks, $ˈkɑːn-, kənˈveks/ *adj* curved or swelling out • *a convex lens/mirror* • *(humorous) I wouldn't say your stomach was big – it's just slightly convex.* • Compare CONCAVE.

con·vey *(obj)* COMMUNICATE /kənˈveɪ/ *v* to express (esp. thoughts, feelings and ideas) so that they are understood by other people • *He conveys a great sense of religious devotion in his later poetry.* [T] • *If you see James, do convey my apologies* **(to him)**. [T] • *I tried to convey in my speech* **how** *grateful we all were for his help.* [+ *wh-* word] • *He put his finger to his lips to convey* **to** *me* **that** *I shouldn't say anything.* [+ *that* clause] • *I don't want to convey the wrong impression.* [T]

con·vey *obj* TRANSPORT /kənˈveɪ/ *v* [T] to take or carry (someone or something) to a particular place • *In the event of an accident or breakdown, your car will be conveyed to the nearest garage.* • *The goods are usually conveyed by sea.* • *Could you convey a message* **to** *Mr Merrick for me, please?*

con·vey·ance /kənˈveɪ·ənts/ *n dated* • *By what form of conveyance* (= transport) *did you travel?* [U] • *These pipes are used for the conveyance* (= moving from one place to another) **of** *water.* [U] • A conveyance is a VEHICLE: *a horse-drawn conveyance* [C]

conveyor /£kənˈveɪ·ər, $-ɚ/ *n* [C] • A **conveyor (belt)** is a continuous moving strip or surface that is used for transporting a load of objects from one place to another: *I had to wait an hour at the airport for my suitcase to come round on the conveyor belt.*

con·vey·anc·ing /kənˈveɪ·ənt·sɪŋ/ *n* [U] *law* the moving from one person to another of the legal ownership of (property or land) • *When we bought our house, we did our own conveyancing rather than getting a lawyer to do it for us.*

con·vey·ance /kənˈveɪ·ənts/ *n* [C] • A conveyance is a legal document which officially gives to someone else the rights to land or property.

con·vict *(obj)* /kənˈvɪkt/ *v* to officially decide in a court of law that someone is guilty of a particular crime • *He has twice been convicted* **of** *robbery/theft/arson.* [T] • *She's a convicted murderer.* • *A jury has the power to convict or acquit.* [I] • Compare ACQUIT. • LP **Crimes and criminals**

con·vict /£ˈkɒn·vɪkt, $ˈkɑːn-/ *n* [C] • A convict is someone who is in prison because they are guilty of a particular crime.

con·vic·tion /kənˈvɪk·ʃən/ *n* • *As it was her first conviction* **for** *stealing, she was given a less severe sentence.* [C] • *He has a long record of previous convictions* **for** *similar offences.* [C] • *The conviction* **of** *the three demonstrators has caused outrage amongst members of the local community.* [U]

con·vic·tion /kənˈvɪk·ʃən/ *n* a determined belief or fixed opinion • *He's a man of* **strong** *convictions, is Paul.* [C] • *I wouldn't say I was a non-believer, but I don't have any* **burning** *religious convictions.* [C] • *She had a* **deep/firm/lifelong** *conviction* **(that)** *there would be a better life after death.* [C + *(that)* clause] • **It's** *my personal conviction* **that** *all rapists should be locked away for life.* [U + *that* clause] • *You can't do this kind of work if you don't have conviction* **about** *what you're doing.* [U] • *He claimed he was enjoying his new job, but his voice* **lacked/***didn't* **carry** *much conviction* (= did not sound certain). [U]

con·vince *obj* /kənˈvɪnts/ *v* [T] to make (someone) certain; to persuade • *Your explanation might have convinced Sheila, but it didn't convince me.* • *He managed to convince the jury* **of** *his innocence.* • *It's useless trying to convince her* **(that)** *she doesn't need to lose any weight.* [+ obj + *(that)* clause] • *I hope this will convince you* **to** *change your mind.* [+ obj + *to* infinitive]

con·vinced /kənˈvɪntst/ *adj* • *My boyfriend says I'd enjoy a walking holiday but I'm not convinced.* • *I wasn't convinced* **of** *the truth of what she was saying.* • *I'm convinced* **(that)** *she is lying.* [+ *that* clause] • Convinced also means being certain of your beliefs: *a convinced Christian/Hindu/Muslim* ○ *a convinced socialist*

con·vinc·ing /kənˈvɪnt·sɪŋ/ *adj* • *He gave some excuse or other for not having been at the party but it wasn't very convincing.* • *I didn't find the ending of the film very convincing.* • *She offered a* **totally/utterly** *convincing* **argument/explanation.** • *There is no convincing* **evidence** *that they are guilty.* • *They won a convincing* **victory.**

con·vinc·ing·ly /kənˈvɪnt·sɪŋ·li/ *adv* • *She spoke very convincingly of the need for a more humane prison system.*

con·viv·i·al /kənˈvɪv·i·əl/ *adj* (esp. of social behaviour or occasions) giving a pleasant feeling of happiness and welcome • *a convivial atmosphere/dinner party/host*

con·viv·i·al·ly /kənˈvɪv·i·ə·li/ *adv*

con·viv·i·al·i·ty /£kənˌvɪv·iˈæl·ɪ·ti, $-ə·t̬i/ *n* [U]

con·vo·ca·tion /£ˌkɒn·vəˈkeɪ·ʃən, $ˌkɑːn-/ *n fml* (the act of arranging) a large formal meeting, esp. of church officials or, in some British colleges, of (previous) college members • *They have called for* **an** *early convocation of an international conference to discuss the issue.* [U] • *He has been invited to speak at a university convocation.* [C]

con·vo·lut·ed /£ˈkɒn·və·luː·tɪd, $ˈkɑːn·və·luː·t̬ɪd/ *adj fml* very twisted, or (of sentences, explanations and arguments etc.) unreasonably long and difficult to follow and understand • *The directions he gave us to his house took us along a very convoluted route.* • *His grammar explanations are always so convoluted that I can never follow them.* • *Her book is full of long, convoluted sentences.*

con·vo·lu·tion /£ˌkɒn·vəˈluː·ʃən, $ˌkɑːn-/ *n* [C usually pl] *fml* • *The small child tried to work out exactly how many snakes were hidden amongst the endless convolutions in the pattern.* • *It's a good film but the plot has so many convolutions that you really have to concentrate.*

con·voy /£ˈkɒn·vɔɪ, $ˈkɑːn-/ *n* [C] a group of vehicles or ships which travel together, esp. for protection • *A convoy* **of** *trucks containing food supplies has been sent to the areas worst hit by famine.* • *The killer escaped from a prison convoy which was taking him to jail.* • *Shall we all drive to the party* **in convoy** (= following each other) *so we don't get lost?*

con·voy *obj* /£ˈkɒn·vɔɪ, $ˈkɑːn-/ *v* [T] • *A couple of tanks convoyed the trucks across the border.*

con·vulse *(obj)* /kənˈvʌls/ *v* to (cause to) shake violently with sudden uncontrolled movements • *The injured animal lay by the side of the road, convulsing* **with/in** *pain.* [I] • *(fig.) We were convulsed* **with** *laughter* (= we laughed a lot). [T] • *A racking cough convulsed her whole body.* [T] • *(fig.) Heavy snow has convulsed the entire region* (= caused it to be unable to operate). [T]

con·vul·sion /kənˈvʌl·ʃən/ *n* [C usually pl] • *She went into convulsions several hours after the accident and had to be rushed to a hospital.* • *(fig.) It's such a funny film – I was* **in** *convulsions* (= I laughed a lot)!

con·vul·sive /kənˈvʌl·sɪv/ *adj* • *a convulsive illness* • *convulsive spasms* • *If she forgets to take her tablets, she gets these strange convulsive movements in the whole of her body.*

co·ny /£ˈkəʊ·ni, $ˈkoʊ-/, **con·ey** *n* [C/U] *old use* a rabbit or the fur of a rabbit

coo /kuː/ *v* he/she/it **coos**, **cooing**, *past* **cooed** (esp. of some types of bird, such as DOVES and PIGEONS) to make a low soft call, or (of people) to speak in a soft, gentle and loving way • *Outside we heard the doves cooing.* [I] • *The baby lay in his cot, cooing and gurgling.* [I] • *It's sickening the way she coos* **over** *those cats of hers.* [I] • *"How wonderful to see you again, darling," she cooed.* [+ clause]

cook *(obj)* /kʊk/ *v* to prepare (food) to be eaten by heating in a particular way, such as baking or boiling, or (of food) to be prepared in this way • *I don't cook meat very often.* [T] • *He cooked us an enormous meal./He cooked an enormous meal* **for** *us.* [+ two objects] • *I never bother cooking* **for** *myself – I just eat sandwiches if I'm on my own.* [I] *Let the fish cook for half an hour before you add the wine.* [I] • *How long does this cake take to cook* (= to become ready to eat)? [I] • *(Am infml) "Look! I've found the missing puzzle pieces." "Now we're cooking* (= achieving what we want to achieve)!" [I] • *(Am infml) Jean's new band was really cooking* (= playing well) *at the party last night.* [I] • *(infml)* If EVIDENCE or written facts or records are cooked, they are changed in order to deceive people. [T] • *(infml)* If someone **cooks the books**, they dishonestly change numbers in the accounts in order to steal money from an organization. • *That's* **cooked** *his* **goose**, *hasn't it* (= That's spoilt his chances of success)! • *(infml)* If you **cook up** something or **cook** something **up** you invent something either dishonestly or very imaginatively: *She'd cooked up some weird and wonderful scheme that was going to earn her a fortune.* ○ *I got to work so late this morning I had to cook up some excuse about my car breaking down.* • *(slang)* **What's cooking** means what's happening. *I just saw the police arrive – what's cooking?* • Ⓓ Ⓣ

cook /kʊk/ *n* [C] • *She's a wonderful cook.* • *He works as a cook in a school canteen.* • *(saying)* 'Too many cooks spoil the broth' means if there are too many people doing the same piece of work at the same time, the final result will be spoiled. • *"The Cook, the Thief, his Wife and her Lover"* (title of a film, 1989)

cooked /kʊkt/ *adj* • *cooked food/vegetables* • *a cooked cheesecake* • *I hope that cake is cooked properly in the middle.* • *This food you were describing – do you eat it raw or cooked?* • In Britain, a **cooked breakfast** is a dish usually of fried eggs, BACON and SAUSAGES, served with TOAST and sometimes MUSHROOMS and TOMATOES.

cook·er *esp. Br* /£ˈkʊk·ər, $-ɚ/, *Am* **range**, *Am and Aus* **stove** *n* [C] • A cooker is a large box-shaped device which is used to cook and heat food either by putting the food inside or by putting it on the top: *Is your cooker gas or electric?* • Cooker is also *Br infml for* **cooking apple**. • PIC› **Kitchen**

cook·e·ry /£ˈkʊk·ər·i, $ˈ-ɚ-/ *n* [U] • Cookery is the skill or activity of preparing and cooking food: *cookery classes* • A *(Br and Aus)* **cookery book** or **cookbook** is a book containing RECIPES which tell you how to prepare and cook particular dishes.

cook·ing /ˈkʊk·ɪŋ/ *n* [U] • *My mother always hated cooking* (= preparing and heating food so that it can be eaten). • *Who does the cooking in your house?* • Cooking is used to refer to a particular type of substance that is suitable for use in cooking. *cooking oil* ○ *cooking chocolate* • A **cooking apple** (*Br infml* **cooker**) is a sour and often large apple which is eaten cooked. Compare **eating apple** at EAT HAVE FOOD.

cook·ie BISCUIT, **cook·y** /ˈkʊk·i/ *n* [C] *esp. Am* a sweet biscuit • *Would you like some cookies with your coffee?* • *I've just made some* **chocolate-chip** *cookies.* • *(saying)* 'That's the way the cookie crumbles' means that something slightly unlucky has happened but it could not have been prevented and so must be accepted. • PIC› **Bread and cakes**

cook·ie PERSON /ˈkʊk·i/ *n* [C] *Am infml* a person • *She's a* **smart/tough** *cookie.*

cook·out /ˈkʊk·aʊt/ *n* [C] *infml esp. Am and Canadian Eng* a meal cooked and eaten outside, esp. as part of a party

cool COLD /kuːl/ *adj* **-er, -est** slightly cold; of a low temperature • Cool is often used approvingly of pleasant temperatures: *It was a lovely cool evening.* ○ *Have some nice cool lager.* ○ *She felt so much cooler with her long hair worn up.* ○ *How do you manage to look so cool when I'm all red-faced and sweaty!* ○ *He was dressed in cool white cotton* (= that causing him to feel pleasantly slightly cold). • *(fig.) The bedroom was painted a lovely cool green* (= one giving a feeling of being pleasantly slightly cold). • Less often, cool is used about a temperature which is slightly uncomfortable: *It's a bit cool in here, isn't it? I think I'll close a window.* ○ *He put his hand on her forehead – it was cool and slightly damp.* • *(Br)* A **cool bag** is a **cold bag**. See at COLD LOW TEMPERATURE.

cool *(obj)* /kuːl/ *v* • *After a morning in the sun he liked to cool* **down/off** (= become colder) *in the sea.* [I] • *Let your bath cool* **(down)** *before you get in it – it's very hot.* [I] • *He took off his shoes to cool* (= make colder) *his sweaty feet.* [T]

cool /kuːl/ *n* [U] • *He loved* **the** *cool* (= slight coldness) *of the early morning before the sun had risen.* • *She left the mid-day sun for* **the** *cool of the shade.*

cool·er /£ˈkuː·lər, $-lɚ/ *n* [C] • A cooler is a box-like container with a lid, which is used for making or keeping food and drinks cool: *We can bring a picnic dinner in the small cooler.* • A cooler is also a cold drink, usually of wine, fruit juice and fizzy water: *a wine cooler.* • **Cooler bag** is *Am for* **cold bag**. See at COLD LOW TEMPERATURE.

cool·ing /ˈkuː·lɪŋ/ *adj* • *a cooling drink/breeze/swim* • A **cooling tower** is a tall hollow building or structure which is used in industrial processes to reduce the temperature of esp. water, so that it can be used (again) to cool other parts of the system. • PIC› **Energy**

cool·ness /ˈkuːl·nəs/ *n* [U] • *There's* **a** *slight coolness in the air – do you think it's going to rain?*

cool CALM /kuːl/ *adj* **-er, -est** calm and not anxious or frightened; not influenced by strong feeling of any type • *He was very cool and calm about the mishap, and didn't shout or lose his temper.* • **Stay/Keep** *cool* (= Do not become angry or excited). • *I don't know how you manage to* **keep** *such* **a cool head** (= stay (so) calm) *in such a hectic, stressful office!* • *She walked in* **(as) cool as a cucumber** (= very calmly), *as if nothing had happened.*

cool /kuːl/ *n* [U] *infml* • Your cool is your ability to stay calm and not become angry or excited: **keep** *your cool* ○ *He really* **lost** *his cool when he heard about what happened.*

cool *(obj)* /kuːl/ *v* • If you cool **down**, you stop feeling angry after an argument: *Has your mother cooled down yet or is she still furious?* [I] • *I'm trying to cool her down before Mike comes home and she says something to him that she'll regret.* [T] • If a feeling cools **(off)**, it starts to become less strong: *They were desperately in love to begin with but I think it's starting to cool off now.* [I] ○ *Their interest in the project seems to be cooling.* [I] • *(slang) Just* **cool it** (= become calm) *everyone, fighting won't solve anything.*

cool·ing /ˈkuː·lɪŋ/ *n* [U] • A **cooling-off period** is an agreed length of time in which **trade unions** (=organizations of workers) and management try to end an official argument about pay etc. before a STRIKE (=refusal to work) becomes necessary.

cool UNFRIENDLY /kuːl/ *adj* **-er, -est** unfriendly or not showing affection or interest in something or someone • *Is something the matter? You seem a bit cool* **towards** *me, as if you didn't want to be here.* • *I got a rather cool* **reception/welcome** *this evening. What do you think I've done wrong?* • *Didn't you like my suggestion about going to my mother's for the holidays? You seemed a bit cool* **(about** *it).* • *(infml usually humorous)* A **cool customer** is someone who does not show much personal feeling and whose manner is so calm that it is almost offensive.

cool·ly /ˈkuːl·li/ *adv* • *"How did he receive your suggestion?" "Rather coolly – I don't think he was too keen."*

cool·ness /ˈkuːl·nəs/ *n* [U] • *I noticed a certain coolness between your parents. Is that normal or had they just had an argument?*

cool FASHIONABLE /kuːl/ *adj* **-er, -est** *infml* (of a person's appearance or manner) fashionable, esp. in a way that makes them seem slightly severe • *Are those your new sunglasses? Very cool – very James Dean!* • *Now I know it won't* **look** *very cool, but this hat will keep the sun out of your eyes.* • *Patti's got some cool new jeans.* • *"Cool for Cats"* (title of a song by Squeeze, 1979)

cool GOOD /kuːl/ *adj, exclamation* **-er, -est** *infml* excellent; very good • *"How was the party?" "It was cool!"* • *"Do you want to come to the pool with us?" "Yeah, cool!"*

cool·ant /ˈkuː·lənt/ *n* [C/U] *specialized* (a) specially prepared liquid which is used to stop a machine from getting too hot while it is operating

cool·head·ed /ˌkuːlˈhed·ɪd, ˈ-ˌ--/ *adj* having the ability to stay calm or in control, or to think clearly in difficult situations • *You can trust Samantha – she always manages to remain coolheaded in a crisis.*

cool·ie /ˈkuː·li/ *n* [C] *dated* (in the eastern part of the world) an unskilled and cheaply employed worker. This is considered offensive by many people.

coon /kuːn/ *n* [C] *taboo slang* a black person. This word is generally considered to be very offensive

coop /kuːp/ *n* [C] a cage where small animals and birds are kept, esp. chickens

coop up *obj*, **coop** *obj* **up** /kuːp/ *v adv* [M] • To coop someone or something up is to keep them in an enclosed space: *I think it's wrong to coop animals up in these tiny cages.*

cooped up /kuːpt/ *adj* • If you are cooped up somewhere, you (feel as if you) are in a small, enclosed space from which you cannot escape: *Cooped up in a small dark room, the prisoner hadn't seen daylight for five years.* ○ *It's such a tiny office – don't you ever feel cooped up here?* ○ *The cooped-up animals often fought with each other.*

co·op·e·rate /£kəʊˈɒp·ᵊr·eɪt, $koʊˈɑː·pə·reɪt/ *v* [I] to act or work together for a particular purpose, or to help someone willingly when help is requested • *I find it very hard to dress my two-year-old when she just refuses to cooperate.* • *The two companies have cooperated for the past several years* **in** *joint ventures.* • *The Spanish authorities cooperated* **with** *the British police* **in** *finding the terrorists.* • *He said that he had cooperated* **(fully/closely) with** *the government* **in** *its investigation.* • *(humorous) We're going to have a picnic on Saturday, if the weather cooperates* (=is suitable). • LP **Each other**

co·op·e·ra·tion /£kəʊˌɒp·ᵊrˈeɪ·ʃᵊn, $koʊˌɑː·pəˈreɪ-/ *n* [U] • *The police have thanked the local community for their cooperation* **in** *the search for the missing boy.* • *This documentary was made with the cooperation of British Rail.* • *Could I have a little cooperation* **in** *this matter, please?* • *There's very little cooperation* **between** *the two countries.* • *The company produces computers* **in** *cooperation* **with** *a German firm.*

co·op·e·rat·ive /£kəʊˈɒp·ᵊr·ə·tɪv, $koʊˈɑː·pɚ·ə·t̬ɪv/ *adj* • *I've asked them very politely not to play their music so loudly but they're not being very cooperative.*

co·op·e·rat·ive /£kəʊˈɒp·ᵊr·ə·tɪv, $koʊˈɑː·pɚ·ə·t̬ɪv/ (*abbreviation* **co–op** /£ˈkəʊ·ɒp, $ˈkoʊ·ɑːp/) *n* [C] • A cooperative is a company that is owned and managed by the people who work in it: *The magazine is run by a cooperative.*

co–opt *obj* /£kəʊˈɒpt, $koʊˈɑːpt/ *v* [T] (of an elected group) to make (someone) a member through the choice of the present members • *She was co-opted* **on to** *the committee last June.*

co·or·di·nate *obj* COMBINE /£kəʊˈɔː·dɪ·neɪt, $koʊˈɔːr-/ *v* [T] to make (various different things) work effectively as a whole • *We need someone to coordinate the whole campaign.* • *A number of major charities are coordinating their efforts to send out food to the areas worst affected by the famine.* • *As the disease progresses, the patient loses the ability to coordinate his or her movements* (=make parts of his or her body work together in order to form particular movements).

co·or·di·nat·ed /£kəʊˈɔː·dɪ·neɪ·tɪd, $koʊˈɔːr·dɪ·neɪ·t̬ɪd/ *adj* • *The rebel troops have launched a coordinated attack on government soldiers.* • If a person is coordinated, they move in a very easy and controlled way, especially when playing sports or dancing: *I'm not coordinated enough for doing aerobics – I can't manage to move my arms and my legs in different directions at the same time.*

co·or·di·na·tion /£kəʊˌɔː·dɪˈneɪ·ʃᵊn, $koʊˌɔːr-/ *n* [U] • *There's absolutely no coordination* **between** *the different groups* (=They are not working together) *– nobody knows what anyone else is doing.* • *Gymnastics is a sport that* *requires a considerable level of coordination* (= the ability to make different parts of your body, esp. your arms and legs, move together in order to form particular movements).

co·or·di·nat·or /£kəʊ'ɔː·dɪ·neɪ·təʳ, $koʊ'ɔːr·dɪ·neɪ·t̬ɚ/ *n* [C] • *We've just appointed a coordinator who will oversee the whole project.*

co·or·di·nate POINT /£kəʊ'ɔː·dɪ·nət, $koʊ'ɔːr-/ *n* [C usually pl] one of a pair of numbers and/or letters that show the exact position of a point on a map or GRAPH

co·or·di·nate MATCH /£kəʊ'ɔː·dɪ·neɪt, $koʊ'ɔːr-/ *v* [I] to match; to look attractive together • *He's always wearing clothes that don't coordinate.* • *The bed linen coordinates with the bedroom curtains.* • *She was wearing a coordinating jacket and skirt.*

co·or·di·nat·ed /£kəʊ'ɔː·dɪ·neɪ·tɪd, $koʊ'ɔːr·dɪ·neɪ·t̬ɪd/ *adj* • *You look very coordinated today* (= Your clothes match in colour and style). • *The colour scheme of their living room is carefully coordinated* (= arranged so that the colours match).

co·or·di·nates /£kəʊ'ɔː·dɪ·nəts, $koʊ'oːr-/ *pl n* • Coordinates are clothes, esp. for women, which are made in matching colours or styles so that they can be worn together. • LP **Shopping goods**

coot BIRD /kuːt/ *n* [C] a small dark bird which is found near rivers and lakes

coot PERSON /kuːt/ *n* [C] *Am infml* a person, esp. one who is not very clever • *He's a sweet* **old** *coot.*

cop *obj* PUNISH /£kɒp, $kɑːp/ *v* [T] **-pp-** *Br slang* to ARREST (someone) • *He was copped* **for** *driving without a licence last week.*

cop /£kɒp, $kɑːp/ *n* [U] *humorous* • *Come on, mate, it was* **a fair** (= deserved) *cop – your car wasn't taxed, you were speeding and you weren't wearing a seat belt!*

cop *obj* TAKE /£kɒp, $kɑːp/ *v* [T] **-pp-** *slang* to take or hold • *Cop* **(hold of)** *that, would you – I can't carry both myself.* • *She copped a quick look at the audience from behind the curtain.* • *(Br)He copped a load of trouble from* (= was punished by) *his dad for bunking off school.* • *(Am) I'm just going to cop a few* **Z's** (= have a short sleep). • *(Am)* To **cop a plea** is to admit to having committed a crime in order to avoid being brought to trial for a more serious crime. • *(Br)* To **cop it** is to be punished or spoken to severely because you have done something wrong: *You'll really cop it if your parents find out you've been stealing.*

cop OFFICER /£kɒp, $kɑːp/, **cop·per** *n* [C] *slang* a police officer • *Quick, run – there's a cop coming!* • *I don't much enjoy cops* **and robbers** *films.* • A **cop shop** is a **police station**. See at POLICE.

cop QUALITY *Br* /£kɒp, $kɑːp/, *Aus* **chop** *n* [U usually in negatives] *slang* good quality; worth • *His last book* **wasn't much** *cop – what's his new one like?* • *Was that film you went to see any cop?*

cop *obj* TROUBLE /£kɒp, $kɑːp/ *v* [T] **-pp- cop it** *Br and Aus infml* to be treated and spoken to severely • *You'll really cop it if your parents find out you've been stealing.*

cope /£kəʊp, $koʊp/ *v* [I] to deal (successfully) with a difficult situation or bad luck • *It must be difficult to cope* **with** *three small children and a job.* • *Three staff simply can't cope* **with** *such a heavy work load.* • *Could you give me something to help me cope* **with** *the pain, doctor?* • *The tyres on my car don't cope very well on wet roads.* • *He had so much pressure on him in his job that eventually he just couldn't cope.*

co·pha /£'kəʊ·fə, $'koʊ-/ *n* [U] *Aus* a white wax-like substance, made from COCONUT and used in cooking

co·pi·lot /£'kəʊ,paɪ·lət, $'koʊ-/, **co–pi·lot** *n* [C] the second PILOT (= person who controls an aircraft) who helps the main pilot on an aircraft and shares the controls with him or her

co·pi·ous /£'kəʊ·pi·əs, $'koʊ-/ *adj* in large amounts; more than enough • *He took copious notes during the lecture and then wondered why he had bothered.* • *The book had copious illustrations.* • *The region has had copious snow in the last few days.*

co·pi·ous·ly /£'kəʊ·pi·ə·sli, $'koʊ-/ *adv* • *We ate and drank copiously at the party.*

cop–out /£'kɒp·aʊt, $'kɑːp-/ *n slang* a way of avoiding doing something that is expected of you which you think is too difficult for you or which you are frightened of doing • *She regarded her sister's decision to have a family instead of a career as a sort of cop-out.* • *I thought the end of the film was a bit of a cop-out.*

cop out *v adv* [I] *slang* • *She copped out* **of** *the parachute jump at the last minute with a foot injury or some feeble excuse.*

cop·per METAL /£'kɒp·əʳ, $'kɑː·pɚ/ *n, adj* [not gradable] a common reddish brown metal which is soft and is used in a lot of electrical equipment because it allows heat and electricity to go through it, or the reddish brown colour of this metal • *copper wire/pipes* • *a copper alloy* • *She wears a bracelet made of copper to help her rheumatism.* [U] • *Rosie's hair shone copper* (= reddish brown) *in the sunlight.* • *(Br infml)* Brown coins of low value are sometimes called coppers: *He gave the small child a few coppers.* [C] • *(esp. Br)* A plan, deal or investment which is **copper-bottomed** can be trusted completely because it is safe and certain to succeed.

cop·per·y /£'kɒp·ᵊr·i, $'kɑː·pɚ·i/ *adj* • *The leaves on the trees have started to turn a rich coppery colour.*

cop·per OFFICER /£'kɒp·əʳ, $'kɑː·pɚ/ *n* [C] *infml* a police officer

cop·per·plate /£'kɒp·ə·pleɪt, $'kɑː·pɚ-/ *n* [U] an old-fashioned, decorative style of writing with long flowing letters • *The sign above the shop is written in ornate copperplate.*

cop·pice /£'kɒp·ɪs, $kɑː·pɪs/, **copse** *n* [C] a small area of closely planted trees or bushes

cop·pice *obj* /£'kɒp·ɪs, $'kɑː·pɪs/ *v* [T] *specialized* • To coppice trees or bushes is to cut them back in order to form a small, closely planted area.

co–pro·duc·tion /£ˌkəʊ·prə'dʌk·ʃᵊn, $ˌkoʊ-, '----/ *n* [C] *specialized* a film, television programme or theatrical production organized by a partnership rather than a single person • *The film is a co-production, with input from Disney and the Children's Film Foundation.*

copse /£kɒps, $kɑːps/ *n* [C] a COPPICE

Cop·tic /£'kɒp·tɪk, $'kɑːp-/ *adj* of or connected with the ancient Christian Church of Egypt, which is now based in Egypt and Ethiopia • *a Coptic monastery* • *Coptic art* • *the Coptic Church*

cop·u·la /£'kɒp·jʊ·lə, $'kɑː·pjə-/ *n* [C] *specialized* a type of verb, of which the most common is 'be', which joins the subject of the verb with a COMPLEMENT (= word that describes the subject) • *In the sentence 'You smell nice', 'smell' is a copula.*

cop·u·late /£'kɒp·jʊ·leɪt, $'kɑː·pjə-/ *v* [I] *specialized* to have sex

cop·u·la·tion /£ˌkɒp·jʊ'leɪ·ʃᵊn, $ˌkɑː·pjə-/ *n* [U] *specialized*

cop·y PRODUCE /£'kɒp·i, $'kɑː·pi/ *v* to produce something so that it is the same as (an original piece of work), or to behave, dress, speak etc. in a way that is intended to be like someone else, for example, because you admire them • *They've copied the basic design* **from** *the Japanese model and added a few of their own refinements.* [T] • *He tends to copy his elder brother* **in** *the things he says and the way he dresses.* [T] • *If you've got that cook book with you I'd like to copy* **(down/out)** (= write down for my own use) *a couple of the recipes.* [T/M] • *(disapproving) He was always copying* **from/off** *other children* (= cheating by copying) *in tests and exams but never got caught.* [I] • Ⓣ

cop·y /£'kɒp·i, $'kɑː·pi/ *n* [C] • *This is not an* **exact** *copy, but it's very similar.* • *His copies were so accurate no one could distinguish them from the original paintings.* • *I always* **keep** *a copy* **of** *any official or important letters that I send off.* • *Could you* **make/do** *a copy* **of** (= use a special machine to copy) *this for tomorrow's meeting, please?* • *I'd like a copy* **of** *this photograph if you've still got the negative.* • A copy is also a single book, newspaper, record or other printed or recorded item of which many have been produced: *I bought the last copy left in the whole bookshop.* ○ *Have you got a copy of last Saturday's 'Guardian', by any chance?*

cop·y TEXT /£'kɒp·i, $'kɑː·pi/ *n* [U] written text which is to be printed, or text which is intended to help with the sale of a product • *All copy is carefully checked for mistakes before it is printed.* • *We need someone who can write good copy for our publicity department.* • *Disasters make good copy* (= subjects for articles) *for newspapers.* • Ⓣ

co·py·book /£'kɒp·i·bʊk, $'kɑː·pi-/ *adj* [before n] *approving* agreeing exactly with what is expected or with the rules that are connected with a situation • *a copybook musical performance* • *a copybook military exercise*

cop·y·cat /£'kɒp·i·kæt, $'kɑː·pi-/ *n* [C] *infml* (used esp. by children) someone who lacks their own ideas and does or says exactly the same as someone else • *You're just a copycat!*

cop·y·cat /£'kɒp·i·kæt, $'kɑː·pi-/ *adj* • *In the market you can buy affordable copycat* (=very similar) *versions of expensive perfumes.* • A copycat crime is one that is believed to have been influenced by another, often famous, crime because it is so similar: *copycat murders*

cop·y·right /£'kɒp·i·raɪt, $'kɑː·pi-/ *n* the ownership of and legal right to control all possible ways of producing a copy of an original piece of work, such as a book, play, film, photograph or piece of music • *The publishers* **have/own/hold** *the copyright* **on/for** *the play.* [C] • *His work is no longer protected* **under/by** *copyright.* [U] • *They were sued for* **breach of/infringing** *copyright* (=disobeying copyright laws) *over a text book they'd copied for classroom use.* [U] • *The symbol © is used to show that something is protected by copyright.* [U] • LP› **Symbols**

cop·y·right *obj* /£'kɒp·i·raɪt, $'kɑː·pi-/ *v* [T] • *I copyright all of my poetry.* • *The journalist tried to copyright her article to stop the publisher misusing it.*

cop·y·writ·er /£'kɒp·i,raɪ·təʳ, $'kɑː·pi,raɪ·t̬ɚ/ *n* [C] someone who writes the words for advertisements

co·quette /£kɒk'et, $koʊ'ket/ *n* [C] *esp. literary* a woman whose behaviour is intended to attract sexual attention by being playful and charming

co·quet·tish /£kɒk'et·ɪʃ, $koʊ'ket̬-/ *adj esp. literary* • *She greeted him with a coquettish smile.*

co·quet·tish·ly /£kɒk'et·ɪʃ·li, $koʊ'ket̬-/ *adv esp. literary* • *She lowered her eyes coquettishly.*

co·quet·ry /£'kɒk·ɪ·tri, $'koʊ·kə-/ *n* [U] *esp. literary*

cor EXPRESSING INTEREST /£kɔːʳ, $kɔːr/ *exclamation Br slang esp. humorous* an expression of interest and admiration or surprise • *Cor! Did you see him in the blue swimming trunks?* • *(Br dated slang)* **Cor blimey** is a way, which some people find offensive, of expressing surprise or sometimes annoyance: *Cor blimey guv, I didn't know you were standing behind me!*

cor– TOGETHER /£kəʳ, $kɚ/ *combining form* see at CO-

cor·a·cle /£'kɒr·ɪ·kl̩, $'kɔːr-/ *n* [C] a small round boat which is made by stretching animal skin over a wooden frame

cor·al /£'kɒr·əl, $'kɔːr-/ *n* [U] a rock-like substance, formed in the sea by groups of particular types of small animal, that is often used in jewellery, or the pinkish orange colour that this substance often is • *a coral bracelet/necklace* • *Paul wore pale grey trousers with a coral T-shirt and black jacket.* • A **coral reef** is a bank of coral, the top of which can sometimes be seen just above the sea.

cor an·glais (*pl* **cors anglais**) /£,kɔː·rɒŋ'gleɪ, $,kɔːr·ɑːŋ-/, *Am* **Eng·lish horn** *n* [C] a musical instrument of the WOODWIND family, like an OBOE but with a lower sound

cor·bel /£'kɔː·bəl, $'kɔːr-/ *n* [C] *specialized* a support for an arch or similar heavy structure, which sticks out of a wall and is usually made of stone or brick

cord ROPE /£kɔːd, $kɔːrd/ *n* (a length of) rope or string made of twisted threads, or (a length of) covered wire which connects electrical equipment to an electrical supply or other equipment • *Where's the cord that ties back the curtains?* [C] • *Have you got a bit of cord that I can tie this parcel up with?* [U] • *We need a longer cord for this telephone.* [C] • Cord is *Am and Aus for* LEAD ELECTRICAL. • See also UMBILICAL CORD. • PIC› **Fires and space heaters, Lights** (NL)

cord·less /£'kɔːd·ləs, $'kɔːrd-/ *adj* [not gradable] • A cordless electrical tool or piece of equipment is one that operates without needing to be permanently connected by a wire to an outside electrical supply: *a cordless telephone/drill/iron*

cord CLOTH /£kɔːd, $kɔːrd/ *n* [U] CORDUROY • *a cord shirt/jacket* • See also CORDS.

cor·di·al FRIENDLY /£'kɔː·di·əl, $'kɔːr·dʒəl/ *adj* friendly and/or welcoming • *a cordial smile/greeting/welcome/reception* • *Relations between the two leaders are said to be cordial.*

cor·di·al·ly /£'kɔː·di·ə·li, $'kɔːr·dʒə-·/ *adv* • *The two statesmen shook hands cordially in front of the cameras.* • *(fml) You are cordially* **invited** *to the Young Farmers annual wine-tasting evening.*

cor·di·al·i·ty /£,kɔː·di'æl·ɪ·ti, $,kɔːr'djæl·ə·t̬i/ *n* [U]

cor·di·al DRINK /£'kɔː·di·əl, $'kɔːr·dʒəl/ *n* [U] *Br and Aus* a sweet fruit-based drink to which water is usually added • *lime cordial* • *(Am)* Cordial is also another name for LIQUEUR (=flavoured alcoholic drink).

cor·di·al STRONG /£'kɔː·di·əl, $'kɔːr·dʒəl/ *adj fml* (of a feeling, esp. dislike) strong • *The two statesmen are known to have a cordial* **dislike** *for each other.*

cor·di·al·ly /£'kɔː·di·ə·li, $'kɔːr·dʒə·li/ *adv fml* • *On a personal level they came to be cordially* **disliked**.

cor·dite /£'kɔː·daɪt, $'kɔːr-/ *n* [U] *specialized* a type of explosive, esp. used in bullets

cor·don /£'kɔː·dən, $'kɔːr-/ *n* [C] a line of police, soldiers, vehicles, etc. positioned around a particular area in order to prevent people from entering it • *There was a* **police** *cordon around the building so we assumed someone fairly important was inside.*

cor·don off *obj*, **cor·don** *obj* **off** /£'kɔː·dən, $'kɔːr-/ *v adv* [M] • *They've cordoned off the whole area because of a suspected bomb.*

cor·don bleu /£,kɔː·dɔ̃ːm'blɜː, $,kɔːr·dɔ̃ː'bluː/ *adj* (of food) prepared to the highest standard, or (of people) able to cook food to this standard • *It's not exactly cordon bleu cuisine but it's good, basic food.* • *The restaurant has a cordon bleu chef.*

cords /£kɔːdz, $kɔːrdz/ *pl n* trousers made of CORDUROY material

cord·u·roy /£'kɔː·djuː·rɔɪ, £-drɔɪ, $'kɔːr-/, **cord** *n* [U] a thick cotton material with soft raised parallel lines in one direction, used esp. for making clothes

core /£kɔːʳ, $kɔːr/ *n* [C] the central part of something, esp. the part of some fruits, such as apples, which contains the seeds and is usually not eaten, or more generally, the basic and most important part of something • *Don't throw your apple core on the floor!* • *The earth's core is a hot, molten mix of iron and nickel.* • *She tried a different night-club or bar every week but never felt that she'd got to the core of the city's social scene.* • *Although the acting and script are excellent the real core of the film is its ecological message.* • *The basic lack of government funding is* **at the** *core* (=the main part) *of the problem.* • *He's a Conservative* **to the core** (=completely) *and he's proud of it!* • *He was shocked* **to the core** (=extremely shocked) *– he said he'd never heard such obscene language.* • *(specialized)* The core of a **nuclear reactor** (=a device in which atoms are changed to produce energy) is the place where FISSION (=division of atoms) takes place. • *(specialized)* A core is a long thin cylindrical mass of material taken out of the earth for study: *a core sample* ○ *a core from the Greenland ice cap/the ocean floor* • *(Am and Aus)* The core or **core curriculum** is a group of courses in various subjects which all students in a school must study: *core subject/course/studies* ○ *Many universities no longer require a foreign language as part of the core curriculum.* • PIC› **Fruit**

core *obj* /£kɔːʳ, $kɔːr/ *v* [T] • If you core a piece of fruit you remove the core from it: *Peel and core the pears before cooking them.*

co–re·spon·dent /£,kəʊ·rɪ'spɒn·dənt, $,koʊ·rə'spɑːn-/ *n* [C] *law* the person with whom a married person is said to have committed ADULTERY (=sex outside marriage) • *He was* **cited/named** *as co-respondent in the divorce.* • Compare **respondent** at RESPOND.

cor·gi /£'kɔː·gi, $'kɔːr-/ *n* [C] a breed of dog with a long strong body, short legs and a pointed nose

cor·i·an·der /£,kɒr·i'æn·dəʳ, $'kɔːr·i·æn·dɚ/ *n* [U] a plant grown in many places in the world, or its leaves or seeds which can be added to food to give a special flavour • PIC› **Herbs and spices**

Co·rin·thi·an /kə'rɪnt·θi·ən/ *adj* of or like the most decorated of the three styles of ancient Greek building • *Corinthian columns* • Compare DORIC; IONIC. • PIC› **Column**

cork /£kɔːk, $kɔːrk/ *n* the light soft BARK (=the outer layer) of a Mediterranean tree, or a short solid cylinder of this material (or sometimes of plastic or rubber), esp. one pushed into the top of a bottle in order to close it • *tiles made from cork* [U] • *cork table mats* • *I can't get the cork out of the bottle – can you try?* [C] • *She heard the cheering sound of popping corks from within the room.* [C] • PIC› **Bottles and flasks**

cork *obj* /£kɔːk, $kɔːrk/ *v* [T] • *If you've drunk enough I'll cork* (=push the cork back into the top of) *the bottle and we can have the rest later.* • *(infml)* If someone **corks up** their feelings/**corks** their feelings **up** they do not allow themselves to express their anger, anxiety or sadness.

cork·age /£'kɔː·kɪdʒ, $'kɔːr-/ *n* [U] • Corkage is the charge made by some restaurants for serving wine that has been bought from somewhere else.

corked /£kɔːkt, $kɔːrkt/ *adj* • Wine is described as being corked if its taste has been spoiled by the cork.

cork·er /£'kɔː·kəʳ, $'kɔːr·kɚ/ *n* [C] *infml esp. humorous* a person or thing that is especially good, attractive or amusing • *She told an absolute corker of a story about a priest she'd mistaken for an ex-lover.*

cork·screw /£'kɔːk·skruː, $'kɔːrk-/ *n* [C] a device for removing CORKS from bottles, which consists of a handle with a twisted metal rod to screw into the cork and pull it out

cork·screw /£'kɔːk·skruː, $'kɔːrk-/ *adj* [before n] • *Her daughter's hair is a mass of wonderful red corkscrew* (= twisted) *curls.*

corm /£kɔːm, $kɔːrm/ *n* [C] *specialized* the short underground growth of particular plants from which the new stem grows each year

cor·mo·rant /£'kɔː·mᵊr·ənt, $'kɔːr·mɚ-/ *n* [C] a large sea bird which has dark feathers, a long neck and body and a thin hooked beak • [PIC]> **Birds**

corn [FOOD] /£kɔːn, $kɔːrn/ *n* [U] *esp. Br* (the seeds of) any of various CEREAL plants, such as wheat, MAIZE, OATS and BARLEY, or *(Am)* (the seeds of) the MAIZE **plant** • *a sheaf of corn* • *grains of corn* • *(Am)* **Corn bread** is a type of bread made from maize. • *(Am and Aus)* **Corn chips** are thin, flat pieces of food made from crushed maize: *Would you like a corn chip?* ○ *Buy peanuts and corn chips for the party.* • **Corn oil** is oil made from MAIZE, which is often used for cooking. • **Corn on the cob** is the cylinder-like part of the maize plant which is cooked with the sweet yellow or white grains on it. • **Corn syrup** is a sweet liquid made from maize. • *"The corn is as high as an elephant's eye"* (from the song *Oh what a Beautiful Morning* written by Oscar Hammerstein II, 1943) • [PIC]> **Cereals** (D) (DK) (N) (S)

corn [AREA OF SKIN] /£kɔːn, $kɔːrn/ *n* [C] a small painful area of hard skin that forms on the foot, esp. on the toes • (D) (DK) (N) (S)

corn [EMOTION] /£kɔːn, $kɔːrn/ *n* [U] *esp. Am slang* something which is old-fashioned, boring, or done to cause emotion • *Everyone says it's a great movie but I think it's* **just** *corn.* • (D) (DK) (N) (S)

corn·ball /£'kɔːn·bɔːl, $'kɔːrn·bɑːl/ *n, adj Am* (someone or something) simple and old-fashioned, or CORNY (= lacking new ideas or sincerity) • *cornball ideas* • *a cornball notion* • *cornball humor/jokes* • *My new neighbour's very young but he's quite a cornball.* [C]

corn·cob pipe /£'kɔːn·kɒb, $'kɔːrn·kɑːb/ *n* [C] a pipe for smoking having the tobacco container made from the part of the MAIZE plant on which the grain grows • *Pat always smoked a corncob pipe.*

corn·crake /£'kɔːn·kreɪk, $'kɔːrn-/ *n* [C] a European bird with a loud cry, which is often found in fields

cor·ne·a /£kɔː'ni·ə, $'kɔːr·ni-/ *n* [C] the protective transparent covering of the round area at the front of the eye inside the white part

corned beef /£'kɔːnd, $kɔːrnd/ *n* [U] BEEF (= meat from cattle) which has been cooked in salty water, and often then pressed into metal containers where it can be kept for a long time • *I'd like corned beef hash* (= corned beef mixed with potato) *and a fried egg, please.* • *(Am and Aus)* Corned beef is a large piece of BEEF which has been preserved in salt water: *Corned beef on rye and corned beef and cabbage are popular meals in New York on St. Patrick's Day.*

cor·ner /£'kɔː·nəʳ, $'kɔːr·nɚ/ *n* [C] the point, area or line which is formed by the meeting of two lines, surfaces, roads, etc. • *You drive round corners too fast – just slow down a bit!* • *There's a post-box* **on the corner** (**of** *this street where it joins the main road).* • *Do you think we should put the book-shelf over there* **in** *the corner* (**of** *the room)?* • *What do you think the figure is doing* **in** *the bottom right-hand corner* **of** *the painting?* • *I've got a bruise where I hit my leg against the corner* **of** *the table.* • *A trickle of blood ran out of the corner* **of** *his mouth.* • *They only live* **just around/round the** *corner* (= very close although not in the same road) *– so we see them all the time.* • *Everything is a bit depressing at the moment but I carry on in the belief that good times are* **just around the corner** (= in the very near future). • *They live in a* **remote** *corner* **of** (= place where there are very few people or buildings in) *Scotland, miles from the nearest shop.* • In football or HOCKEY a corner is a kick or shot taken from the corner of the field. • *Heidi sent me a postcard from a* **distant/far** *corner* **of the globe/world/ earth** (= from a place far away where there are very few people). • *She had invited relatives from* **all the corners/the four corners/the far corners of the world/ earth** (= many different, esp. distant places) *to her 80th birthday party.* • *I wasn't looking in that direction but* **out of/from the corner of** *my* **eye** (= without seeing it clearly because it happened to the side of me) *I saw something move.* • If a company has a **corner on** a particular **market**, it is more successful than any other company at selling the particular type of product. • If someone is described as being **in a (tight) corner** or **boxed/forced into a corner**, they are in a difficult situation which they have little control over: *With no money and nowhere to sleep he found himself in a bit of a tight corner.* • *(Br and Aus)* A **corner shop** is a small shop, esp. on a corner of a road, which sells common foods and other objects that are useful in the house: *I'm just going to the corner shop to get a paper – I'll be back in five minutes.* • *"If I should die, think only this of me:/ There is some corner of a foreign field/ That is forever England"* (from Rupert Brooke's poem *The Soldier*, 1915) • (J)

cor·ner *(obj)* /£'kɔː·nəʳ, $'kɔːr·nɚ/ *v* • If a vehicle corners well, badly, etc., it drives around corners in the stated way: *It's a powerful car but it doesn't corner* **well**. [I] • If you corner a person or an animal, you force them into a place or situation from which they cannot easily escape: *Once the police had cornered her at the end of an alley she gave herself up without a fight.* [T] ○ *He once cornered me* (= talked to me alone and made it difficult for me to get away) *at a party and bored me to death about his difficult childhood.* [T] • If a company **corners a/the market** for a particular type of product it is more successful than any other company at selling the product: *They've more or less cornered the fast-food market – they're in every big city in the world.*

-cor·nered /£-ˌkɔː·nəd, $-ˌkɔːr·nɚd/ *combining form* • *a three-cornered hat*

cor·ner·stone /£'kɔː·nə·stəʊn, $'kɔːr·nɚ·stoʊn/ *n* [C] a stone in a corner of a building, esp. one with the day when the building was made or other writing on it, or something of great importance which everything else depends on • *In many countries the family unit is still the cornerstone of society.*

cor·net [CONE] *Br* /£'kɔː·nɪt, $'kɔːr-/, **ice cream cone**, **cone** *n* [C] a cone made of WAFER (= very light thin biscuit), or one of these containing **ice cream** (= a sweet food made from milk and/or cream that is eaten cold) • *Do you want a cornet or a tub of ice-cream?*

cor·net [INSTRUMENT] /£'kɔː·nɪt, $kɔːr-/ *n* [C] a musical instrument made from metal, usually BRASS, that you play by blowing into it

corn·field /£'kɔːn·fiːld, $'kɔːrn-/ *n* [C] a field which is used for growing CEREAL crops • *When the corn is ripe, everyone from the village goes out to help in the cornfields.*

corn·flakes /£'kɔːn·fleɪks, $'kɔːrn-/ *pl n* small thin yellowish-orange pieces made from crushed MAIZE, often eaten with milk and sugar in the morning • *a bowl of cornflakes*

corn·flour *Br and Aus* /£'kɔːn·flaʊəʳ, $'kɔːrn·flaʊr/, *Am* **corn·starch** *n* [U] a white flour made from MAIZE, used in cooking esp. for making liquids thicker

corn·flower /£'kɔːn·flaʊ·əʳ, $'kɔːrn·flaʊ·ɚ/ *n* [C] a small plant that grows in fields and gardens, usually with blue flowers • *We've chosen cornflower* **blue** *as the colour for the bedroom wallpaper and curtains.*

cor·nice /£'kɔː·nɪs, $'kɔːr-/ *n* [C] a decorative border that is sometimes found where the ceiling meets the walls in rooms and also along the top of some walls and buildings

Cor·nish pa·sty /£'kɔː·nɪʃ, $'kɔːr-/ *n* [C] a piece of pastry folded in the shape of half a circle and containing a mixture of meat and vegetables, usually for one person to eat

corn·meal /£'kɔːn·miːl, $'kɔːrn-/ *n* [U] rough yellow flour made from MAIZE, used to make bread, TORTILLAS, etc.

corn·row /£'kɔːn·rəʊ, $'kɔːrn·roʊ/ *v, n esp. Am* (to arrange) strips of hair twisted together close to the head in thin rows • *Tyler likes her hair in cornrows, but braiding it takes a long time.* [C] • *Paul cornrowed her hair.* [T]

corn·starch /£'kɔːn·stɑːtʃ, $'kɔːrn·stɑːrtʃ/ *n* [U] *Am for* CORNFLOUR

cor·nu·co·pi·a /£ˌkɔː·njuˈkəʊ·pi·ə, $ˌkɔːr·njəˈkoʊ-/ *n* [U] *fml or humorous* a pleasingly large amount of something; a great supply • *Laid out on the vast table there was a veritable cornucopia* **of** *every kind of food or drink you could want.*

corn·y /£'kɔː·ni, $'kɔːr-/ *adj* **-ier, -iest** *infml* (esp. of jokes, films, stories etc.) lacking new ideas and sincerity; too often repeated and therefore not amusing or interesting • *He just tells these awful corny* **jokes** *that you've heard a thousand times.*

co·rol·la·ry /£kə'rɒl·ər·i, $'rɑː·lə-/ *n* [C] *fml* something that results from something else • *Unfortunately, violence is the inevitable corollary* **of** *such a revolutionary change in society.*

co·ro·na /£kə'rəʊ·nə, $-'roʊ-/ *n* [C] *pl* **coronas** or **coronae** /£kə'rəʊ·niː, $-'roʊ-/ a circle of coloured light that can sometimes be seen around the moon at night, or a circle of light that can be seen around the sun during an ECLIPSE (= a situation when the moon is positioned exactly between the sun and the Earth)

cor·o·na·ry /£'kɒr·ən·ər·i, $'kɔːr·ə·ner-/, *medical* **cor·o·na·ry throm·bo·sis** (*pl* **coronary thromboses**) *n* [C] an extremely dangerous medical condition in which the flow of blood to the heart is blocked by a blood CLOT (= a lump of blood) • *He's in hospital after having a coronary last week.*

cor·o·na·ry /£'kɒr·ən·ər·i, $'kɔːr·ə·ner-/ *adj* [not gradable] *medical* • Coronary means of the ARTERIES (= tubes carrying blood) that supply blood to the muscles of the heart: *The link established between saturated fats and* **coronary heart disease** (= disease of the coronary arteries) *provides evidence of the modern diet leading to ill-health.*

cor·o·na·tion /£,kɒr·ə'neɪ·ʃən, $,kɔːr-/ *n* [C] a ceremony at which a person is made king or queen

cor·o·ner /£'kɒr·ə·nər, $'kɔːr·ən·ə/ *n* [C] an official who examines the reasons for a person's death, esp. if it was violent or unexpected • *At the inquest the coroner recorded a verdict of accidental death.*

cor·o·net /£'kɒr·ə·nət, $,kɔːr-, --'-/ *n* [C] a small CROWN (= a circular decoration worn on the head and usually made of gold and jewels)

Corp [BUSINESS] /£kɔːp, $kɔːrp/ *n* [C] *abbreviation for* CORPORATION • [LP]> **Letters**

Corp [RANK] *n* [C] *abbreviation for* CORPORAL

cor·po·ra /£'kɔː·pər·ə, $'kɔːr·pə-/ *pl of* CORPUS

cor·po·ral [BODILY] /£'kɔː·pər·əl, $'kɔːr·pə-/ *adj fml* of the body • **Corporal punishment** is the activity of punishing people, esp. children, by hitting a part of their body, often with a stick: *Nowadays, corporal punishment is banned in many schools.*

cor·po·ral [RANK] /£'kɔː·pər·əl, $'kɔːr·pə-/ (*abbreviation* **Corp**) *n* [C] a person of low rank in an army or an air force • *A corporal is an NCO of the rank below a sergeant.*

cor·po·rate /£'kɔː·pər·ət, $'kɔːr·pə-/ *adj* of or shared by a whole group and not just of a single member • *a corporate identity* • *All adults take corporate* **responsibility** *for the upbringing of the tribe's children.* • See also **corporate** at CORPORATION [BUSINESS].

cor·po·ra·tion [BUSINESS] /£,kɔː·pər'eɪ·ʃən, $,kɔːr·pə'reɪ-/ (*abbreviation* **Corp**) *n* [C + sing/pl v] a large company or group of companies that is controlled together as a single organization • *a multinational corporation* • *the British Broadcasting Corporation* • *She didn't want to work for a big corporation where everything was so impersonal.* • *(Br)* **Corporation tax** is tax paid by businesses on profit that they make. • [LP]> **Letters**

cor·po·rate /£'kɔː·pər·ət, $'kɔːr·pə-/ *adj* • *corporate finance* • A company's **corporate image** is the way in which it is seen and understood by people in general. • See also CORPORATE.

cor·po·ra·tion [LOCAL ORGANIZATION] /£,kɔː·pər'eɪ·ʃən, $,kɔːr·pə'reɪ-/ *n* [C + sing/pl v] *esp. Br* the organization in a particular town or city responsible for services such as cleaning roads • *a municipal corporation* • *Coventry corporation* • *The corporation has/have had to cut back on road maintenance.*

cor·po·re·al /£kɔː'pɔː·ri·əl, $kɔːr'pɔːr·i-/ *adj fml or literary* physical and not spiritual; of the body • *His corporeal needs were few – food and physical comforts meant nothing to him.*

cor·po·re·al·ly /£kɔː'pɔː·ri·ə·li, $kɔːr'pɔːr·i-/ *adv*

corps [MILITARY UNIT] /£kɔːr, $kɔːr/ *n* [C + sing/pl v] *pl* **corps** a military unit trained to perform particular duties • *the Royal Army Medical Corps* • *the intelligence corps* • *The officer corps has/have called for the troops to be withdrawn.*

corps [GROUP] /£kɔːr, $kɔːr/ *n* [C + sing/pl v] *pl* **corps** a group of people who are connected because they are involved in a particular activity • *the diplomatic corps* • *the press corps* • *A corps of technicians is/are accompanying the band on their tour.* • The **corps de ballet** are the members of a group of BALLET dancers who dance together rather than on their own as the main dancers do.

corpse /£kɔːps, $kɔːrps/ *n* [C] a dead body, usually of a person • [LP]> **Age**

cor·pu·lent /£'kɔː·pjʊ·lənt, $'kɔːr-/ *adj fml* fat • *a corpulent gentleman*

cor·pu·lence /£'kɔː·pjʊ·lənts, $'kɔːr-/ *n* [U]

cor·pus /£'kɔː·pəs, $'kɔːr-/ *n* [C] *pl* **corpuses** or **corpora** the collection of a single writer's work or of writing about a particular subject, or a large amount of written and sometimes spoken material collected to show the state of a language • *the entire corpus of Baudelaire's works* • *A corpus of spoken language has been gathered from all over the country for the purposes of examining regional differences.*

cor·pus·cle /£'kɔː·pʌs·l̩, $'kɔːr-/ *n* [C] any of the red or white cells in the blood

cor·ral /£kə'rɑːl, $-'ræl/ *n* [C] (esp. in N America) an area surrounded by a fence for keeping horses or cattle in

cor·ral *obj* /£kə'rɑːl, $-'ræl/ *v* [T] **-ll-** • *The horses were swiftly corralled.*

cor·rect /kə'rekt/ *adj* right and not wrong; in agreement with the true facts or with what is generally accepted • *I've made a guess but I don't know if it's the correct answer.* • *"Is that the correct spelling?" "I don't know – look it up in a dictionary."* • **It's** *not correct* **to** *describe them as 'students'.* [+ *to* infinitive] • *(fml) "Your name is Angela Black?" "That is correct."* • Correct also means taking or showing great care to behave or speak in a way that is generally accepted and approved of: *He's very correct* **in** *his dress/speech/manner, isn't he?*

cor·rect *obj* /kə'rekt/ *v* [T] • *Students said it was helpful if the teacher corrected them* (= told them what was right when they had made a mistake). • You can say **correct me if I'm wrong** as a polite and slightly formal way of disagreeing with someone: *Correct me if I'm wrong* **but** *I think we arranged the meeting for the twelfth of December.* • If a medical treatment corrects a particular condition, it cures the condition or makes it easier to manage: *glasses to correct defective vision* ○ *a chair which corrects bad posture*

cor·rect·ly /kə'rekt·li/ *adv* • *Have I pronounced your name correctly?* • *She speaks very correctly* (= in a way that is generally approved of).

cor·rect·ness /kə'rekt·nəs/ *n* [U] • *(slightly fml) It is impossible to question the correctness of the data.* • *He speaks with such correctness* (= care) *that it sometimes sounds very formal.*

cor·rec·tion /kə'rek·ʃən/ *n* • *She was disappointed to see her composition returned with a mass of corrections* (= marks showing mistakes) *in red ink.* [C] • *Correction of speech is very useful to language students.* [U] • The word correction was used in the past to mean punishment of a type that was intended to improve bad behaviour. [U]

cor·rect·ive /kə'rek·tɪv/ *adj* • If something is corrective, it is intended to improve a situation: *corrective measures/action* ○ *He often wondered whether such treatment of criminals was corrective* (= to improve bad behaviour) *or just a punishment.* • Corrective can also mean intended to cure a medical condition: *It is possible to do corrective surgery on the eyes to take care of the problem.*

cor·rec·tions /£kə'rek·tʃənz, $kə-ek-/ *pl n Am fml* the set of methods available to the authorities for punishing and treating people who have committed crimes • *One million dollars has been cut from the city's budget for law enforcement and corrections this year.* • *It's no easy job being a corrections officer.*

cor·rec·tion·al /£kə'rek·tʃən·əl, $kə-ek-/ *adj* [not gradable] *Am and Aus fml* • *a correctional program* • *correctional personnel* • A **correctional center/facility** is another name for a prison.

cor·re·la·tion /£,kɒr·ə'leɪ·ʃən, $,kɔːr-/ *n* a connection between two or more things, often one in which one of them causes or influences the other • *There's a high correlation* **between** *smoking and lung cancer.* [C] • *There's little correlation* **between** *wealth and happiness.* [U]

cor·re·late *obj* /£'kɒr·ə·leɪt, $'kɔːr-/ *v* [T] • *Stress levels and heart disease are strongly correlated* (= connected). • *In some societies a poor diet often correlates* **with** *poverty.*

cor·re·spond [MATCH] /£,kɒr·ɪ'spɒnd, $,kɔːr·ɪ'spɑːnd/ *v* [I] to match or be similar or equal • *The power a political party is allowed to exercise should correspond closely* **to** *the* *proportion of votes it receives.* • *The money corresponds roughly* **to** *the amount I need for my course.* • *The American FBI corresponds* **to** *the British MI5.* • *I can't understand why the date written on her letter doesn't correspond* **with** *the date stamped on the envelope.* • *His story of what happened that night didn't correspond* **with** *the witness's version.*

cor·re·spond·ing /£ˌkɒr·ɪˈspɒn·dɪŋ, $ˌkɔːr·ɪˈspɑːn-/ *adj* • *Company losses were 50 per cent worse than in the corresponding* (=same) *period last year.* • *As the course becomes more difficult and demanding, there's usually a corresponding* (=following as a result) *drop in attendance.*

cor·re·spond·ing·ly /£ˌkɒr·ɪˈspɒn·dɪŋ·li, $ˌkɔːr·ɪˈspɑːn-/ *adv* • *The cost of living in the city is more expensive but salaries are supposed to be correspondingly higher.*

cor·re·spond WRITE /£ˌkɒr·ɪˈspɒnd, $ˌkɔːr·ɪˈspɑːnd/ *v* [I] to communicate by writing • *She's not very good at corresponding – you scarcely ever get a letter from her.* • *"Who have you been corresponding* **with** *in Italy?" he asked examining the envelope.*

cor·re·spond·ence /£ˌkɒr·ɪˈspɒn·dənts, $ˌkɔːr·ɪˈspɑːn-/ *n* [U] • *Any further correspondence* (=letters) *should be sent to my new address.* • *He found her letter at the bottom of a pile of business correspondence.* • Correspondence also means the action of writing, receiving and reading letters, esp. between two people: *Her correspondence* **with** *Jim lasted many years.* • *(fml) Dr. Gillett regrets that she cannot* **enter into** *correspondence* **with** (=will not write personally to) *readers of her column.* • A **correspondence course** is a course of study in which you study at home, receiving and sending off work by post.

cor·re·spond·ent /£ˌkɒr·ɪˈspɒn·dᵊnt, $ˌkɔːr·ɪˈspɑːn-/ *n* [C] *fml* • *I'm a terrible correspondent – I never seem to get the time to write.*

cor·re·spond·ent /£ˌkɒr·ɪˈspɒn·dᵊnt, $ˌkɔːr·ɪˈspɑːn-/ *n* [C] a person employed by a newspaper, a television station, etc. to report on a particular subject or send reports from a foreign country • *a war correspondent* • *our correspondent in/from Baghdad* • *the education correspondent for the Guardian*

cor·ri·dor PASSAGE /£ˈkɒr·ɪ·dɔːʳ, $ˈkɔːr·ɪ·dɚ/ *n* [C] a long passage in a building or train, esp. with rooms on either side • *Her office is at the end of the corridor on the right.* • The **corridors of power** are the higher levels of government where the most important decisions are made.

cor·ri·dor LAND /£ˈkɒr·ɪ·dɔːʳ, $ˈkɔːr·ɪ·dɚ/ *n* [C] a long piece of one country's land which goes through another country • *the Polish corridor*

cor·rob·or·ate *obj* /£kəˈrɒb·ə·reɪt, $-ˈrɑː·bə-/ *v* [T] to add proof or certainty to (an account, statement, idea, etc.) with new information • *Recent research in this field seems to corroborate the theory.* • *Both witnesses corroborated the charge against the driver that he had caused the accident.*

cor·rob·or·a·tion /£kəˌrɒb·əˈreɪ·ʃᵊn, $-ˌrɑː·bə-/ *n* [U] • *Without corroboration from forensic tests, it will be difficult to prove that the suspect is guilty.*

cor·rob·o·rat·ing /£kəˈrɒb·ᵊr·eɪ·tɪŋ, $-ˈrɑː·bə·reɪ·t̬ɪŋ/, *slightly fml* **cor·rob·or·at·ive** /£kəˈrɒb·ᵊr·ə·tɪv, $-ˈrɑː·bɚ·ə·t̬ɪv/ *adj* • *corroborating evidence/reports*

cor·rode /£kəˈrəud, $-ˈroud/ *v* to destroy or be destroyed, esp. by acid or RUST, usually over a long period of time • *Steel tends to corrode faster if it is in a salty atmosphere, such as being by the sea.* [I] • *Rain water had corroded the metal pipes.* [T]

cor·ro·sion /£kəˈrəu·ʒᵊn, $-ˈrou-/ *n* [U] • *There was a lot of corrosion on the body of the car where the paint had come off.* • *(fig.) What we are witnessing now is the corrosion* (=destruction) *of moral standards.*

cor·ro·sive /£kəˈrəu·sɪv, -zɪv, $-ˈrou-/ *adj* • *This acid is highly corrosive so be careful with it.* • Corrosive can also mean harmful and causing bad, bitter feelings: *the corrosive influence of racism* ○ *His corrosive jealousy had ruined their relationship.* ○ *He launched a corrosive* **attack** *on the government* (=He criticized them fiercely).

cor·ro·sive·ly /£kəˈrəu·sɪv·li, -zɪv-, $-ˈrou-/ *adv*

cor·ru·gat·ed /£ˈkɒr·ə·geɪ·tɪd, $ˈkɔːr·ə·geɪ·t̬ɪd/ *adj* [not gradable] (esp. of sheets of iron and cardboard) having parallel rows of folds which look like a series of waves when seen from the edge • *The roof is made from sheets of corrugated iron.* • *Boxes made from corrugated cardboard are light and surprisingly strong.*

cor·rupt IMMORAL /kəˈrʌpt/ *adj* dishonestly using your position or power to your own advantage, esp. for money • *The whole system was corrupt – every official she approached wanted money before helping her.* • *Both companies are under investigation for corrupt practices.* • Corrupt also means morally bad: *When the novel was published some people claimed it was corrupt and said it should be banned.*

cor·rupt *obj* /kəˈrʌpt/ *v* [T] • *When he started his career he was an honest and decent young man but power had corrupted him over the years.* • *So much sex and violence on the television, she claimed, corrupted* (=had a bad moral influence on) *the young, innocent mind.*

cor·rupt·i·ble /kəˈrʌp·tɪ·bl̩/ *adj* • *Perhaps some systems of government are more corruptible than others.*

cor·rup·tion /kəˈrʌp·ʃᵊn/ *n* • *The film is about a young police-officer and his struggle to* **expose** *corruption in the force.* [U] • *Political corruption is widespread throughout the country.* [U] • *In his lifetime he was frequently accused of moral corruption of the young and innocent.* [U] • In language a word whose original form has been changed is sometimes called a corruption: *The swear word 'bloody' is wrongly thought by some to be a corruption of the words 'by our Lady.'* [C] • LP› **Crimes and criminals**

cor·rupt COMPUTER /kəˈrʌpt/ *adj* (of information on a computer) spoilt by the computer making changes to it that should not be there • *corrupt data* • *a corrupt file*

cor·rupt *obj* /kəˈrʌpt/ *v* [T] • *Most of the accounts files on the PC were corrupted by the power cut.*

cor·rup·tion /kəˈrʌp·ʃᵊn/ *n* [U] • *data corruption*

cor·sage /£kɔːˈsɑːʒ, $kɔːr-/ *n* [C] a small decorative group of flowers which a woman pins to her clothes near her neck or chest, usually for a special occasion such as a marriage ceremony

cor·set /£ˈkɔː·sɪt, $ˈkɔːr-/ *n* [C] a tight piece of underwear made from elasticated material, worn on the middle part of a woman's body to make her waist appear smaller

cor·tege /£kɔːˈteʒ, $kɔːr-/ *n* [C] a slowly moving line of people or cars at a funeral

cor·tex /£ˈkɔː·teks, $ˈkɔːr-/ *n* [C] *pl* **cortices** /£ˈkɔː·tɪ·siːz, $ˈkɔːr·t̬ɪ-/ *specialized* the outer layer, esp. of the brain and other organs • *the cerebral cortex*

cor·ti·sone /£ˈkɔː·tɪ·zəun, $ˈkɔːr·t̬ə·zoun/ *n* [U] a particular HORMONE (=chemical produced by some organs of the body) which is used medically, esp. for treating ARTHRITIS (=a painful condition of the joints) and skin problems

cor·u·scat·ing /£ˈkɒr·ə·skeɪ·tɪŋ, $ˈkɒr·ə·skeɪ·t̬ɪŋ/ *adj literary* flashing brightly • *(fig.) He's known for his coruscating* **wit** (=extremely amusing and clever mind).

cor·u·scate /£ˈkɒr·ə·skeɪt, $ˈkɔːr-/ *v* [I] *literary*

cos BECAUSE /£kɒz, $kɑːz/, **'cos** *conjunction not standard for* BECAUSE • *You can cook dinner tonight cos I did it last night.*

cos MATHEMATICS /£kɒz, $kɑːz/ *n* [C] *abbreviation for* COSINE

cosh *Br and Aus* /£kɒʃ, $kɑːʃ/, *Am* **black·jack** *n* [C] a short heavy piece of pipe used as a weapon, esp. for hitting someone on their head

cosh *obj* /kɒʃ, $kɑːʃ/ *v* [T] *Br and Aus* • *He was coshed* (=hit on the head with a cosh) *outside the bank and left unconscious on the pavement.*

co·sign·a·to·ry /£ˌkəuˈsɪg·nə·tᵊr·i, $ˌkouˈsɪg·nə·tɔːr-/ *n* [C] *fml* one of two or more people who sign an official agreement or document • *Both tenants were cosignatories* **of/to** *the lease contract.*

co·si·ly /£ˈkəu·zɪ·li, $ˈkou-/ *adv* See at COSY

co·sine /£ˈkəu·saɪn, $ˈkou-/ (*abbreviation* **cos**) *n* [C] *specialized* (in a triangle that has one angle of 90°) the RATIO of the length of the side next to an angle less than 90° divided by the length of the HYPOTENUSE (=the side opposite the 90° angle • Compare SINE; TANGENT TRIANGLE.

cos (let·tuce) *Br and Aus* /£kɒs, $kɑːs/, *Am* **ro·maine** *n* [C] a LETTUCE (=vegetable used in salads) with long narrow leaves

cos·met·ic BEAUTY SUBSTANCE /£kɒzˈmet·ɪk, $kɑːzˈmet̬-/ *n* [C usually pl] any type of substance for putting on the face or body which is intended to improve its appearance or quality • *We sell a wide range of cosmetics and toiletries at a very reasonable price.* • *The cosmetics industry makes millions of dollars out of people's insecurity and vanity.* • LP› **Shopping goods**

cos·met·ic /£kɒzˈmet·ɪk, $kɑːzˈmet̬-/ *adj* [before n] • *a cosmetic cream* • **Cosmetic surgery** is any medical operation which is intended to improve a person's appearance rather than their health: *She's obviously had some sort of cosmetic surgery, because she's at least 70 but looks about 50.*

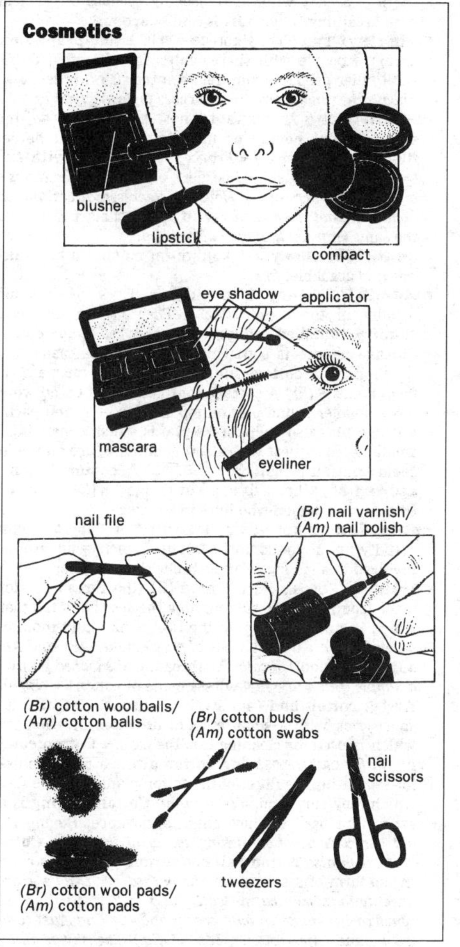

cos·met·ic FALSE /£kɒz'met·ɪk, $kɑːz'meţ-/ *adj disapproving* (esp. of changes and seeming improvements) intended to make you believe that something is better when, in reality, the problem has not been dealt with; SUPERFICIAL • *Social workers have dismissed the government's latest efforts to sort out the homeless problem as purely cosmetic.* • *They were offered a few cosmetic improvements to their working conditions but nothing of significance.*

cos·met·ic·al·ly /£kɒz'met·ɪ·kli, $kɑːz'meţ-/ *adv* • *In the attempt to produce cosmetically perfect fruit* (= fruit that looks perfect), *companies are growing produce that lacks flavour.*

cos·mo·naut /£'kɒz·mə·nɔːt, $'kɑːz·mə·nɑːt/ *n* [C] a Soviet ASTRONAUT (= a person trained to go into space)

cos·mo·pol·i·tan /£ˌkɒz·mə'pɒl·ɪ·tᵊn, $ˌkɑːz·mə'pɑː·lɪ·ţᵊn/ *adj* containing or having experience of people and things from many different parts of the world • *New York is a highly cosmopolitan city.* • *His travels around the world have made him very cosmopolitan.*

cos·mo·pol·i·tan /£ˌkɒz·mə'pɒl·ɪ·tᵊn, $ˌkɑːz·mə'pɑː·lɪ·ţᵊn/ *n* [C] • *Lisa is a real cosmopolitan* (= her opinions, behaviour, etc. shows that she has experience of many different parts of the world).

cos·mos /£'kɒz·mɒs, $'kɑːz·moʊs/ *n* [U] **the cosmos** the universe considered as a system with an order and pattern

cos·mo·log·ic·al /£ˌkɒz·mə'lɒdʒ·ɪ·kᵊl, $ˌkɑːz·mə'lɑː·dʒɪ-/, **cos·mo·log·ic** /£ˌkɒz·mə'lɒdʒ·ɪk, $ˌkɑːz·mə'lɑː·dʒɪk/ *adj* • *Caltech in the fifties was becoming an international centre of cosmological discovery.* • **The cosmological argument** is an argument which attempts to prove the existence of God.

cos·mol·o·gy /£kɒz'mɒl·ə·dʒi, $kɑːz'mɑː·lə-/ *n* [C/U] • Cosmology is a theory about or the study of the nature and origin of the universe.

cos·mic /£'kɒz·mɪk, $'kɑːz-/ *adj* • *Some people believe that what happens in their lives is influenced by cosmic* **forces** (= great powers that come from the universe). • *(infml)* Cosmic means very great: *The earthquake was a disaster* **of** *cosmic* **proportions/scale.**

cos·mic·al·ly /£'kɒz·mɪ·kli, $'kɑːz-/ *adv*

Cos·sack /£'kɒs·æk, $'kɑː·sæk/ *n* [C], *adj* [not gradable] (relating to the customs and fashions of) one of a group of people from Russia with a famous history of fighting and bravery • *a Cossack hat* • *a Cossack dance* • *Cossacks were famous for their horsemanship and their skill with the sword.* • *Trousers in the Cossack style are baggy at the knee but become suddenly tight at the ankle.*

cos·set *obj* /£'kɒs·ɪt, $'kɑː·sɪt/ *v* [T] **-t-** or *Br also* **-tt-** to give a lot of attention to making (someone) comfortable and to protecting (them) from anything unpleasant • *Children need to be cosseted.* • *(disapproving) The country has been cosseted* (= protected) *by the government for so long that people have forgotten how to take responsibility for themselves.*

cos·sie, coz·zie /£'kɒz·i, $kɑː·zi/ *n* [C] *Br and Aus infml for* **swimming costume**, see at SWIM MOVE IN WATER

cost MONEY /£kɒst, $kɑːst/ *n* [U] the amount of money needed to buy, do or make something • *When you buy a new computer, you usually get software included* **at** *no extra cost* (= for the same price). • *The major public industries have been privatized* **at** *huge cost to the taxpayer.* • *For many of these parents, two salaries are essential to* **cover** *the cost of* (= pay for) *school fees.* • *The supermarket chain announced that it was* **cutting** *the cost* (= reducing the price) *of 500 lines by as much as half.* • *(fml) To* **defray** *the cost of* (= pay for) *the expedition, the whales will be sold for meat.* • *The new tax measures mean that the cost* **of** *goods will* **fall/rise** *again.* • *It is an area of* **high/low**-*cost housing.* • *They are planning a cost-***cutting** *exercise/programme/strategy* (= to reduce the cost of what they do). • If an activity is **cost-effective** it is good value for the amount of money paid: *It wouldn't be cost-effective to bring him over from New York just to give the seminar.* ○ *Improving energy efficiency is regarded as the most cost-effective way to reduce the environmental impact of electricity generation.* • The **cost of living** is the amount of money that a person needs to live on: *The increase in interest rates will* **raise** *the cost of living.* ○ *We had a cost of living increase* (= Our pay was increased to cover rising prices of food, housing, etc.) *in January.* • **Cost of living index** is *Am and Aus for* **retail price index**. See at RETAIL. • The **cost price** of an item is the price it cost to make, without a profit being added: *We were able to buy the furniture from a friend* **at** *cost (price).* • LP> **Measurements** (KOR)

costs /£kɒsts, $kɑːsts/ *pl n* • Costs are the cost of something: *We need to* **cut** *our advertising costs.* ○ *The* **estimated** *costs of the building project are well over £1 million.* ○ *Workers fear the costs* **incurred** *in controlling pollution will cost them their jobs.* ○ *(law) The jury found the newspaper guilty of libelling the actress, and she was awarded damages and costs* (= the cost of taking the matter to a law court).

cost *obj* /£kɒst, $kɑːst/ *v* [T no passive] *past* **cost** • *"How much does this book cost* (= What is the price of this book)?" *"It costs £25."* • **It** *costs a lot* **to** *buy a house in this part of London.* • *I'd love to buy a Rolls-Royce but they cost* **an arm and a leg/a bomb/the earth/a packet/a small fortune** (= they are very expensive). • *The trip will cost you $1000.* [+ two objects] • *The repairs to my car cost me a lot of money.* [+ two objects] • *(infml)* **It'll/That'll cost** *you* (= It will be very expensive) *to have your roof mended.* • *Buying that second-hand car without having it checked by a mechanic first* **cost us dear** (= we lost money because of it). • LP> **Two objects**

cost *obj* /£kɒst, $kɑːst/ *v* [T] *past* **costed** • To cost something is to calculate its future cost: *How carefully did you cost the materials for the new fence and gate?* ○ *Has your scheme been properly costed* **(out)**? [T/M]

cost·ing /£'kɒs·tɪŋ, $'kɑː·stɪŋ/ *n* [C] • *We'll need accurate costings* (= calculations of future cost) *before we can agree to fund the scheme.*

cost·ly /£'kɒst·li, $'kɑːst-/ *adj* **-ier, -iest** • Costly means expensive: *Because the fee is calculated on a percentage basis, card holders pay more on costly items than they do on small purchases.* • *(disapproving) Our holiday in Australia* **proved** (= was) *very costly.* • *(disapproving) The project was subject to several costly* **delays/setbacks**. • LP> **Expensive**

cost·li·ness /£ˈkɒst·lɪ·nəs, $ˈkɑːst-/ *n* [U]

cost SOMETHING GIVEN /£kɒst, $kɑːst/ *n* [U] that which is given, needed or lost in order to obtain something • *We were going to paint the house ourselves, but when we considered the cost* **in** *time and effort, we decided to get a painter to do it for us.* • *The driver managed not to hit the child who ran in front of his car, but only* **at the cost of** *injuring himself.* • *She has finally got the job she wanted, but* **at** *great personal* **cost** (=she has had to give up other things that were important to her). • *It's not worth getting into an argument with Tim, as I learned* **to** *my* **cost** (=from my unpleasant experience of having done so). • *He wanted her* **at all cost(s)/at any cost/whatever the cost**, *even if it meant giving up everything he had.*

cost *obj* /£kɒst, $kɑːst/ *v* [T no passive] *past* **cost** • *Drinking and driving costs lives* (=can cause accidents in which people die). • *His relationship with his wife's friend cost him his marriage* (=his marriage ended because of it). [+ two objects] • *It* **cost** *Scotland* **dear** *when they missed that goal* (=they lost the game because of it). • **It cost** *him* **dear** (=It was difficult for him) **to** *apologize.*

cost·ly /£ˈkɒst·li, $ˈkɑːst-/ *adj* **-ier, -iest** • *Building this bridge has already been too costly in terms of lives* (=too many people have been killed while working on it).

cost·li·ness /£ˈkɒst·lɪ·nəs, $ˈkɑːst-/ *n* [U]

co-star /£ˈkəʊ·stɑːʳ, $ˈkoʊ·stɑːr/ *n* [C] a famous actor appearing with another famous actor in a film or a play, both of whom have parts of equal importance • *The co-stars of 'Casablanca' are Ingrid Bergman and Humphrey Bogart.*

co-star *(obj)* /£ˈkəʊ·stɑːʳ, $ˈkoʊ·stɑːr/ *v* **-rr-** • *'Butch Cassidy and the Sundance Kid' co-stars Paul Newman and Robert Redford.* [T] • *Katherine Hepburn co-starred* **with** *Spencer Tracy in many films.* [I]

cos·tume /£ˈkɒs·tjuːm, $ˈkɑː·stuːm/ *n* the set of clothes typical of a particular country or period of history, or suitable for a particular activity • *When we were in Switzerland we saw a group of men and women* **in/wearing national** *costume at a local festival.* [U] • *Singers performing Mozart's operas often* **dress in/wear historical** *costume.* [U] • *The dancers leading the procession were* **in** *colourful and elaborate costumes.* [C] • *The shop has a good selection of bikinis and bathing/swimming costumes.* [C] • A **(fancy-dress)** costume is a set of clothes worn in order to look like someone or something else, esp. for a party or as part of an entertainment: *Our host was wearing a clown costume.* [C] ○ *The children were dressed in* **halloween** *costumes* (=clothes, MASKS and make-up that make the wearers look frightening). [C] • Costume is *Am for* **fancy dress**: *The family was invited to Liz's costume* **party**. [U] • *(esp. disapproving)* A **costume drama** is a film, esp. on television, about a period in history: *A Jane Austen costume drama, Northanger Abbey, is being serialized in six episodes in the autumn.* • **Costume jewellery** is jewellery made from artificial jewels, which look as if they are real. • (NL)

cos·tum·i·er /£kɒsˈtjuː·mi·eɪ, $kɑːˈstuː-/ *n* • A costumier is a person who makes and rents out costumes, esp. for theatrical use.

co·sy (**-ier, -iest**), *Am usually* **co·zy** (**-ier, -iest**) /£ˈkəʊ·zi, $ˈkoʊ-/ *adj* comfortable, pleasant and inviting, esp. (of a building) because small and warm • *He showed me into a* **warm and** *cosy room.* • *They've bought themselves a cosy* **little** *house.* • *This pub has a nice cosy atmosphere.* • *Why don't you come round this evening, and we'll have a nice cosy* (=friendly) **chat**. • *(disapproving)* Cosy also means convenient for those involved but considered by others as too close, esp. when referring to a personal or business relationship: *He has some cosy arrangement/deal with his supplier, which means he's able to sell his goods more cheaply.* ○ *Construction companies are used to a cosy relationship with the government.* ○ *The new rules upset the* **(too-)***cosy world of certain financial institutions.*

co·sy, *Am usually* **co·zy** /£ˈkəʊ·zi, $ˈkoʊ-/ *n* [C] • A cosy is a cover that you put on a TEAPOT or a boiled egg to keep it warm: *a tea cosy* ○ *an egg cosy*

co·si·ly, *Am* **co·zi·ly** /£ˈkəʊ·zɪ·li, $ˈkoʊ-/ *adv* • *The children are cosily* (=warmly and comfortably) *tucked up in bed.* • *We spent the evening cosily* (=in a friendly way) *in front of the fire.*

cot *Br and Aus* /£kɒt, $kɑːt/, *Am* **crib** *n* [C] a small bed for a baby or young child with high bars round the sides so that the child cannot fall out • *The baby is fast asleep in his cot.* • *a cot blanket/quilt* • Cot is also *Am for* **camp bed**. See at CAMP TENTS/BUILDINGS. • (A) **cot death** is the sudden death of a baby while it is sleeping because of problems with breathing. • PIC **Beds and bedroom**

co·te·rie /£ˈkəʊ·tᵊr·i, $ˈkoʊ·t̬ɚ-/ *n* [C + sing/pl v] a small group of people with shared interests who often do not want other people to join them • *a coterie* **of** *writers* • *It's always the same coterie who go/goes to Jean's parties.*

co·term·in·ous /£ˌkəʊˈtɜː·mɪ·nəs, $ˌkoʊˈtɜːr-/ *adj* [not gradable] *fml* having or meeting at a shared border; filling the same space • *France is coterminous* **with** *Italy* (=They meet at a shared border). • *In the US, the terms of office of members of the House of Representatives and the Senate are not coterminous* **with** (=do not start and end at the same time as) *that of the President.*

co·term·in·ous·ly /£ˌkəʊˈtɜː·mɪ·nə·sli, $ˌkoʊˈtɜːr-/ *adv* [not gradable] *fml*

cot·tage /£ˈkɒt·ɪdʒ, $ˈkɑː·t̬ɪdʒ/ *n* [C] a small house, usually in the countryside • *They live in an idyllic* **country/thatched** *cottage, with roses round the door.* • **Cottage cheese** is soft white lumpy cheese made from sour milk. • A **cottage industry** is a small business run from home. • *(Br)* A **cottage loaf** is a loaf of bread which has a smaller round part on top of a larger round part. • **Cottage pie** (also **shepherd's pie**) is a dish consisting of small pieces of meat with a soft potato mixture on the top cooked until it is light brown. • PIC **Accommodation**

cot·tag·er /£ˈkɒt·ɪ·dʒəʳ, $ˈkɑː·t̬ɪ·dʒɚ/ *n* [C] *old use* • A cottager is a person who lives in a cottage.

cot·tag·ing /£ˈkɒt·ɪ·dʒɪŋ, $ˈkɑː·t̬ɪ-/ *n* [U] *Br* sexual activity in a public toilet between men who are not involved in a lasting relationship with each other

cot·ton /£ˈkɒt·ᵊn, $ˈkɑː·t̬ᵊn/ *n* [U] (the thread or cloth made from) the fibre surrounding the seeds of a tall plant which is cultivated esp. in the USA, China and India • *a bale of cotton* • *a shirt made of pure cotton* • *(Br and Aus) a reel (Am* **spool**) *of cotton* (=thread) • *She looked pretty in a simple cotton dress* (=a dress made of cotton). • *(Br and Aus)* A **cotton bud** (*Am* **swab** or *trademark* **Q-tip**) is a short stick with a small amount of cotton on each end, which is used for cleaning esp. the ears. • **Cotton candy** is *Am for* CANDYFLOSS. • A **cotton gin** is a machine used for separating the fibres of the cotton plant from the seeds which they surround. • *(Am infml)* **Cotton-picking** is an expression used to show slight annoyance: *Buying that old car was a cotton-picking waste of money.* • **Cotton wool** (*Am also* **cotton balls** or **cotton batting**) is cotton in the form of a soft mass: *She bathed her child's grazed knee with some warm water and cotton wool.* ○ *She removed her make-up with cream and (Br and Aus) cotton wool* **pads/***(Am) cotton* **pads**. ○ *(fig.) The sky is full of cotton-wool clouds* (=clouds which look like cotton wool) *today.* • PIC **Cosmetics, Reel**

cot·ton·y /£ˈkɒt·ᵊn·i, $ˈkɑː·t̬ᵊn-/ *adj*

cot·ton on to *obj* /£ˈkɒt·ᵊn, $ˈkɑː·t̬ᵊn/ *v adv prep* [T], *Am also* **cot·ton to** *obj v prep infml* to (begin to) understand • *It took me a while to cotton on to what was happening.*

cot·ton on /£ˈkɒt·ᵊn, $ˈkɑː·tᵊn/ *v adv* [I] *Br and Aus infml* • *He'd been talking for at least a quarter of an hour before I finally cottoned on.*

couch SEAT /kaʊtʃ/ *n* [C] piece of furniture that two or more people can sit on at once; a SOFA • *(disapproving)* A **couch potato** is a person who watches a lot of television and does not have an active style of life.

couch BED /kaʊtʃ/ *n* [C] a type of high bed, esp. one in a doctor's office

couch *obj* EXPRESS /kaʊtʃ/ *v* [T always + adv/prep] *fml* to express (something) in a particular way • *I don't understand this form – it's all couched* **in** *legal terminology.* • *You'll have to think carefully about how to couch your reply to his letter.*

couch·ette /kuːˈʃet/ *n* [C] a bed in a train or on a boat which can either be folded away or used as an ordinary seat during the day

cou·gar *esp. Am* /£ˈkuː·gəʳ, $-gɚ/, **moun·tain li·on**, *Br usually* **pu·ma**, *esp. Aus* **pan·ther** *n* [C] a large brown wild cat found in N and S America

cough *(obj)* /£kɒf, $kɑːf/ *v* to force air out of your lungs through your throat with a short loud sound • *The smoke from the bonfire made me cough.* [I] • *She coughed discreetly once or twice to attract his attention.* [I] • *(fig.) The car engine coughed a few times, but wouldn't start.* [I] • *He went to the doctor because he'd been coughing* **(up)** *blood* (=had been bringing blood from his throat by coughing). [T/M] • A **coughing fit** is a sudden period of coughing: *He swallowed a fly accidentally and* **had** *a sudden coughing fit.* • LP› **'-ough' pronunciation**

cough /£kɒf, $kɑːf/ *n* [C] • *a chesty/dry cough* (= one which does/does not produce MUCUS) • *a hacking* (= very bad and loud) *cough* • *a smoker's cough* • *Emily has a very bad/nasty cough* (= has been coughing frequently as part of an illness). • *There are lots of coughs* **and colds** *going around at the moment.* • *The children were full of coughs* **and sneezes** *last winter.* • *When they didn't hear her enter the room, she* **gave** *a quiet cough* (= coughed so that they would know that she was there). • *I need to buy some more* **cough medicine/cough mixture** (= liquid to help a cough get better). • *I've been sucking (Br)* **cough sweets**/*(Am)* **cough drops**/*(Aus)* **cough lollies** (= sweets to help a cough get better) *all day.*

cough up *(obj),* **cough** *(obj)* **up** *v adv slang* to produce (money or information) unwillingly • *I've just had to cough up £10 for a parking fine.* [T/M] • *It's your turn to buy the drinks – come on, cough up* (= produce the money needed to pay for them). [I] • *Which of you broke the window – cough up* (= say who it was). [I]

could CAN /kʊd/ *past simple of* CAN • *When I was younger I could* (= was able to) *stay up all night and not get tired, but I can't do it now.* • *It was so noisy in the pub that we couldn't hear ourselves speak.* • *Peter lifted his small son onto his shoulders so that he could see the procession.* • *You said we could watch television when we've finished our homework.* • *Lyn and Mark asked us if we could go to dinner with them on Friday.* • *I asked him if he could move his chair a bit.* • *I would have phoned if I could.*

could PERMISSION /kʊd/ *v aux* [+ infinitive without *to*; not *be coulding*] he/she/it **could** used as a more polite form of can when asking for permission • *Could I speak to Mr Davis, please?* • *Could I just say something?* • LP› **Auxiliary verbs**

could REQUEST /kʊd/ *v aux* [+ infinitive without *to*; not *be coulding*] he/she/it **could** used as a more polite form of can when making a request • *Could you lend me £5?* • *Could you possibly turn that music down a little, please?*

could POSSIBILITY /kʊd/ *v aux* [+ infinitive without *to*; not *be coulding*] used to express possibility, esp. slight or uncertain possibility • *A lot of crime could be prevented.* • *We could go to the cinema on Saturday.* • *The discovery of the drug could be an important step in our fight against cancer.* • *The baby was due last week, so it could arrive any day now.* • *Sally said she might have to do some shopping on the way home, so that could be why* (= it is possible that that is the reason why) *she's not here yet.* • *I can't collect the book for you today, but I could* **always** *do it tomorrow if it's not too late.* • *Mind what you're doing with that stick – it could* **have** *gone in my eye!* • *(fig.) I was so embarrassed I could've died* (= I felt very unhappy about what had happened). • *(fig.) When she said she'd look after the children for me, I could've kissed her* (= I was so grateful I wanted to give her a kiss). • *"Would you like some more cake?" "Oh no, I couldn't (possibly)* (= I've had enough), *thank you."* • *I couldn't* (= It was unacceptable to) *let her do all the washing up by herself.* • *How could you do such a thing?* (= That was an unacceptable thing to do.)

could SUGGEST /kʊd/ *v aux* [+ infinitive without *to*; not *be coulding*] he/she/it **could** used for making a suggestion • *You could always try painting the wall a paler colour and see if that looks any better.* • *We could go for a drink after work tomorrow, if you like.* • *(infml) I'm very tired – I* **could do with** (= I'd like to have) *a rest.* • *(infml) Your car* **could do with** *a clean* (= I suggest you clean your car).

could SHOULD /kʊd/ *v aux* [+ infinitive without *to*; not *be coulding*] he/she/it **could** used for saying, esp. angrily, what you think someone else should do • *Well, you could try to look a little more enthusiastic!* • *I waited ages for you – you could've said that you weren't coming!*

couldn't /'kʊd·ᵊnt/ *short form of* could not • *She couldn't care less about me.* • *Couldn't you leave on Saturday instead?*

cou·lis /'kuː·li/ *n pl* **coulis** a liquid made by cooking and crushing esp. fruit • *Coulis are made in much the same way as you make purées.* [C] • *For dessert we had bread and butter pudding with* **raspberry** *coulis.* [U]

coun·cil /'kaʊnt·sᵊl/ *n* [C + sing/pl v] a group of people elected or chosen to make decisions or give advice on a particular subject, to represent a particular group of people, or to run a particular organization • *The United Nations Security Council is/are discussing the situation in the Middle East at a meeting in New York today.* • *This play is supported by a grant from the Arts Council.* • A council is the group of people elected to govern a particular area/town/city, and organize services for it: *The* **local** *council has/have decided not to allocate funds for the project.* ○ *The* **town/city** *council is/are responsible for keeping the streets clean.* ○ *This is the third year he's been* **on** (= has been an elected member of) *the* **county** *council.* ○ *Council meetings are held on Thursdays.* ○ *(Br) A new playground has just been built on the (Br) council* **estate** (= an area of houses owned by the council). ○ *They live in a council (Br)* **house/flat** • **Council housing** (*Am* **public housing**) means houses or apartments owned by the council which people pay rent to live in. • A **council of war** is a meeting held by military leaders in order to decide what action to take in a war: *(fig.) Parents are holding a council of war to decide what to do about the threatened closure of the school.*

coun·cil·lor, *Am also* **coun·ci·lor** /£'kaʊnt·sᵊl·əʳ, $-ɚ/, *Am usually* **coun·cil·man** (*pl* **-men**), **coun·cil·wo·man** (*pl* **-women**) *n* [C] • A councillor is an elected member of a local government: *a town/city/county/local councillor* • *Let's now turn to Councillor Moore's question about the provision of services for the elderly.*

coun·sel *obj* /'kaʊnt·sᵊl/ *v* [T] **-ll-** or *Am usually* **-l-** to give advice, esp. on social or personal problems • *The school is now providing a service to counsel students with drug problems.* • *My job involves counselling unemployed people* **on/about** *how to find work.* • *(fml) My doctor has counselled me* **against** *smoking.* • *(fml) The police have counselled caution in dealing with the kidnapper.*

coun·sel /'kaʊnt·sᵊl/ *n fml* • *I should have listened to my father's wise counsel* (= advice), *and saved some money instead of spending it all.* [U] • *If only I'd* **taken** *counsel* **from** *my mother* (= followed my mother's advice), *I wouldn't be in such difficulties now.* [U] • *(law)* Counsel is one or more of the lawyers taking part in a law case: *The judge addressed counsel.* [C] ○ *Counsel* **for the defence** (= the lawyer giving advice to the accused person) *argued convincingly that his client was not guilty.* [C] • *I'd love to know what Anna thinks about things, but she always* **keeps** *her* **own counsel** (= does not say what her opinions are). • A **counsel of despair** is advice which accepts that something is too difficult to achieve: *It is a counsel of despair to say that the task is too big to tackle.* • *(Br)* A **counsel of perfection** is advice that is good, but is difficult or impossible to follow: *Gardening magazines offer a counsel of perfection on the care of lawns – but most people just mow them when they have time.*

coun·sel·ling, *Am usually* **coun·sel·ing** /'kaʊnt·sᵊl·ɪŋ/ *n* [U] • *People who have been involved in serious accidents often need some counselling* (= help or encouragement from a trained person) *afterwards.* • *Relate is an organization which offers a counselling* **service** *to people with marriage difficulties.*

coun·sel·lor, *Am usually* **coun·sel·or** /£'kaʊnt·sᵊl·əʳ, $-ɚ/ *n* [C] • *The college now has a counsellor* (= someone who provides help and encouragement) *to help students with both personal and work problems.* • *Pat has just become a* **marriage-guidance** *counsellor.* • *(Am law) I don't think that question is relevant, counselor* (= lawyer). [as form of address]

count *(obj)* NUMBER /kaʊnt/ *v* to say the names of numbers one after the other in order, or to calculate the number of units in a group • *From outside the classroom, we could hear the children counting* **(out loud)** *– one, two, three, four, etc.* [I] • *If you don't do as I tell you by the time I've counted* **(up) to** *three, there'll be trouble – one, two, three.* [I] • *The teachers counted the students as they got on to the coach.* [T] • *You should always count your change* (= examine the amount of money you are given back if you pay more for an item than it costs). [T] • *We need to count* **who** *'s here, so we can make sure that no one's missing.* [+ *wh-* word] • *Can you count* **how** *many pencils are left for me, please?* [+ *wh-* word] • *There'll be eight for dinner, counting* (= including) *ourselves.* [T] • *When we go to the mountains there'll be six of us, not counting* (= not including) *the baby.* [T] • To count **down** is to count backwards to zero, esp. before sending a spacecraft into space: *Mission control will be starting to count down at 6.00 am.* [I] ○ *The crowd in the square counted down* **to** *midnight.* [I] ○ See also COUNTDOWN. • *The bank clerk counted* **out** (= counted in order to give someone) *$100 in $20 bills.* [M] • *Cooper was* **counted out** *in the final round* (= he was announced as the loser in a boxing competition because he failed to get up from the floor before ten seconds had been counted). • *(infml) "Who wants to come swimming tomorrow?"* **"Count me out/in** (= I won't/ will be involved)." • *"Do we know how many people are coming to the party?" "No, I haven't counted* **(up)** (= added the total number of) *the replies yet."* [T/M] • *We were very upset when someone broke into our house, but we* **counted** *our* **blessings** (= were grateful) *that they didn't steal very much.* • *We're making sure we* **count the cost(s)** (= consider all the likely effects) *before we decide whether or not to move house.* • *Make sure you read the contract carefully before you sign it or you'll* **count the cost** (= might suffer a bad effect). • If you **count heads/***(Am also)* **count noses** you find the total number of people at or planning to be at an event: *I think there are about 25 people, but I'll give you an exact number after I count heads.* See also **head count** at HEAD BODY PART. • If you **could count** something **on the fingers of one hand** it happens very rarely or exists in very small numbers: *I could count the number of times he's been on time on the fingers of one hand.* • *(saying)* 'Don't count your chickens before they're hatched' means don't make plans which depend on something having happened before you know that it has happened.

count /kaʊnt/ *n* • *After several counts* (= after the votes had been counted several times), *a winner was finally declared.* [C] • *We had 450 members* **at** *the last count* (= when they were last counted). [C] • A count is also a scientifically measured amount of something: *a high pollen count* [C] ○ *a low blood/sperm count* [C] • **On the count of** (= After I have counted) *three, start work on the puzzle.* • *Ben has had such a tiring day that he's* **out for the count** (= he is sleeping). • *I'm trying to lose weight, so I'm* **keeping count of** (= recording) *the number of calories I eat every day.* • *I've* **lost count of** (= cannot remember) *how many times she's been late for work this month.* • *(specialized)* A **count noun** (also **countable noun**) is a noun that can be used in the singular and the plural: *Count nouns are marked in this dictionary with a* [C].

count·a·ble /£'kaʊn·tə·bl̩, $-t̬ə-/ *adj* • *(specialized)* A noun that is countable can be counted: *Table is a countable noun* **(count noun)**, *and money is an uncountable noun.* • Compare UNCOUNTABLE.

count·er /£'kaʊn·təʳ, $'kaʊn·t̬ɚ/ *n* [C] • A counter is a person or machine which counts. • See also GEIGER COUNTER.

count *(obj)* CONSIDER /kaʊnt/ *v fml* to consider or be considered as • *(fml) I count* **myself** *fortunate to have had such a good education.* [T] • *(fml) Well, ladies and gentlemen, I think we can count this meeting a great success.* [T] • *I've had three jobs in the last five years, but one of them was unpaid, so that doesn't count* (= cannot be considered as a real job). [I] • *Gail has applied for a job on a newspaper, but I think her inexperience might count* **against** *her* (= might be a disadvantage). [I] • *I hope you won't count it* **against** *me if I don't come to your birthday party.* [I] • *'Cosi fan tutte' has always counted* **among** (= I have always considered it one of) *my favourite operas.* [I] • *I've always counted Lucy* **among** *my closest friends.* [T] • *The Grand Canyon is generally counted* **as** *one of the most spectacular sights in the USA.* [T] • *I didn't think his grudging remarks really counted* **as** *an apology.* [I] • *The work that the students do during the year will count* **towards** (= will be considered part of) *their final degrees.* [I]

count VALUE /kaʊnt/ *v* [I] to have value or importance; to MATTER • *I've always believed that happiness counts more than money.* • *In our school, everybody counts.* • *If people spoil their voting papers, their votes don't count* (= they are ignored). • *My opinion doesn't count* **for** *anything around here* (= nobody values my opinion).

count MAN /kaʊnt/ *n* [C] a European man of the same social rank as an English EARL • See also COUNTESS.

count CRIME /kaʊnt/ *n* [C] a particular crime which a person is accused of • *The prisoner was found guilty* **on** *two counts* **of** *murder.*

count OPINION /kaʊnt/ *n* [C] an opinion in a discussion or argument • *I'm afraid I disagree with you* **on** *all/several counts* (= I disagree with all your opinions in this argument).

count (up)on *obj v prep* to depend on or expect • *You can always count on* (= depend on) *Michael in a crisis.* [T] • *I really need a break, so I'm counting on getting away for a few days next week.* [+ v-ing] • *I'm counting on the meeting finishing on time, or I'll miss my train.* [T + obj + v-ing] • *Anne could always count on Pat* **to** *babysit for her.* [T + obj + to infinitive] • *Sorry I'm late, I didn't count on being held up in the traffic.* [+ v-ing] • *She didn't count on it raining, so she didn't take an umbrella.* [T + obj + v-ing] • *There's never a taxi when you want one – that's the one thing you can count on* (= expect)*!* [T]

count·down /'kaʊnt·daʊn/ *n* [C] the act of counting backwards to zero • *The countdown* **to** *the rocket launch will begin at 9.00 am.* • *(fig.) The countdown* **to** (= the period leading to) *the election has already begun.*

coun·te·nance FACE /£'kaʊn·tɪ·nənts, $-t̬ən·ənts/ *n fml* the appearance or expression of someone's face • *He was of noble countenance.* [U] • *My heart leapt at the sight of her lovely countenance.* [C]

coun·te·nance *(obj)* APPROVE OF /£'kaʊn·tɪ·nənts, $-t̬ən·ənts/ *v* [usually in negatives] *fml* to find acceptable; to approve of or give support to • *The school will not countenance bad behaviour.* [T] • *I just can't countenance killing animals to make fur coats.* [+ v-ing]

coun·te·nance /£'kaʊn·tɪ·nənts, $-t̬ən·ənts/ *n* [U] *fml* • *We will not* **give/lend** *countenance* (= approval) **to** *any kind of terrorism.*

count·er SURFACE /£'kaʊn·təʳ, $-t̬ɚ/ *n* [C] a long flat narrow surface or table in a shop, bank, restaurant, etc. at which people are served • *There was nobody* **behind/on** *the counter when I went into the bank, and I had to wait to be served.* • *You will find sausages* **on** *the meat counter/rolls* **on** *the bread counter.* • **(Kitchen)** counter is *Am for* **worktop**. • **Counter lunch** is *Aus for* **pub lunch**, see at PUB. • Some drugs can be bought **over the counter** or without the permission of a doctor: *You can buy most cold remedies over the counter.* • Things bought **under the counter** are bought secretly and illegally: *He managed to get cigarettes under the counter.* • LP> **Shopping goods** PIC> **Kitchen**

count·er DISC /£'kaʊn·təʳ, $-t̬ɚ/, *Am also* **piece** *n* [C] a small plastic disc used in some games played on boards • *If you throw a six on the dice, you can move the counter six squares.* • PIC> **Games**

count·er *(obj)* OPPOSE /£'kaʊn·təʳ, $-t̬ɚ/ *v* to react to (something) with an opposing opinion or action; to defend yourself against (something) • *The Prime Minister countered the opposition's claims about health service cuts* **by** *saying that the government had increased spending in this area.* [T] • *When criticisms were made of the school's performance, the parents' group countered* **with** *details of its examination results.* [I] • *Argentina scored a brilliant goal in the first half, but Germany countered* (= reacted by also scoring) *immediately, making the score one-all.* [I] • *Extra police have been moved into the area to counter the risk of violence.* [T] • *Something has to be done to counter the recent rise in unemployment* (= to reduce it). [T]

count·er /£'kaʊn·təʳ, $-t̬ɚ/ *adv* [not gradable] • *Acting counter* **to** (= against) *instructions, the soldiers set fire to the rebel camp.* • *Bob's decision not to take the job* **ran** *counter* **to** (= was directly opposite to) *his family's expectations.*

count·er– /£'kaʊn·təʳ-, $-t̬ɚ-/ *combining form* • Counter- means as a reaction to or in opposition to. • The **counter-culture** is a way of life, esp. among young people, in which money, possessions and family life are considered less important than they usually are in most modern Western countries, and personal freedom is emphasized. • When something is said to be **counter-intuitive** it does not happen in the way you would expect it to: *Steering a yacht is counter-intuitive – you push the tiller the opposite way to the way you want to go.* • A **counter-revolution** is a political activity which happens as a reaction or in opposition to an earlier political change. • A **counter-suit** is a legal claim you make as a reaction to a claim made against you. • LP> **Opposites**

count·er·act *obj* /£ˌkaʊn·tə'rækt, $-t̬ɚ·ækt/ *v* [T] to reduce or remove the effect of (something unwanted) by producing an opposite effect • *How can the police counteract this unprecedented rise in crime?* • *Drinking a lot of water counteracts the dehydrating* **effects** *of sweating.*

coun·ter·ar·gu·ment /£ˌkaʊn·tə·rɑː·gju·mənt, $-t̬ɚ·ɑːr-/ *n* [C] an argument against another argument, idea or suggestion • *The traditional counterargument* **to** *a minimum wage is that it would increase unemployment.*

coun·ter·at·tack /£'kaʊn·tə·rə·tæk, $-t̬ɚ·ə-/ *n* [C] an attack intended to stop or oppose an attack by an enemy or competitor • *The Republicans have* **launched** *a strong counterattack against the Democrats' manifesto.*

coun·ter·at·tack *(obj)* /£ˌkaʊn·tə·rə'tæk, $-t̬ɚ·ə-/ *v* • *The air force counterattacked at night.* [I] • *France counterattacked in the second half and won the match.* [I] • *The candidate counterattacked her rival with a powerful speech.* [T]

coun·ter·at·trac·tion /£ˌkaʊn·tə·rəˈtræk·ʃən, $-t̬ɚ-ə-/ *n* [C] a place or type of entertainment which competes with another for visitors or people's attention • *Video rental is now a major counterattraction* **to** *cinema-going.*

coun·ter·bal·ance /£ˈkaʊn·təˌbæl·ənts, $-t̬ɚ-/, *fml* **coun·ter·poise** *n* [C] a weight or force which balances another one

coun·ter·bal·ance *obj* /£ˌkaʊn·təˈbæl·ənts, $-t̬ɚ-/, *fml* **coun·ter·poise** *v* [T] • *(fig.) Regional governments would help to counterbalance the centralized power of the national government.*

coun·ter·blast /£ˈkaʊn·tə·blɑːst, $-t̬ɚ-blæst/ *n* [C] *literary* a forceful reaction to a spoken attack • *The author has since delivered a damning counterblast* **to** *her critics.*

coun·ter·clock·wise /£ˌkaʊn·təˈklɒk·waɪz, $-t̬ɚˈklɑː·kwaɪz/ *adj, adv* [not gradable] *Am for* **anti-clockwise**, see at ANTI-

coun·ter·es·pi·o·nage /£ˌkaʊn·tə·ˈres·pi·ə·nɑːʒ, $-t̬ɚˈes-/ *n* [U] secret action taken by a country to protect itself from the efforts of another country to discover its military, industrial or political secrets

coun·ter·feit *obj* /£ˈkaʊn·tə·fɪːt, $-t̬ɚ-/ *v* [T] to copy (something) exactly in order to make someone believe that the copy is the original • *Two women and a man have been convicted of counterfeiting $100 bills.*

coun·ter·feit /£ˈkaʊn·tə·fɪt, $-t̬ɚ-/ *n, adj* [not gradable] • *counterfeit perfume/jewellery/passports/coins* • *This watch may be a counterfeit, but it looks just like the original.* [C]

coun·ter·feit·er /£ˈkaʊn·təˌfɪ·təʳ, $t̬ɚ·fɪ·t̬ɚ/ *n* [C]

coun·ter·foil *Br* /£ˈkaʊn·tə·fɔɪl, $-t̬ɚ-/, *esp. Am and Aus* **stub** *n* [C] the part of a ticket, CHEQUE, etc. which is kept as a record of payment • [LP]› **Money**

coun·ter·in·sur·gen·cy /£ˌkaʊn·tə·rɪnˈsɜː·dʒənts, $-t̬ɚ·ɪnˈsɜːr-/ *n* [U] military action taken by a government to prevent attacks by small groups of soldiers or fighters that are opposed to it • Compare **insurgency** at INSURGENT.

coun·ter·in·tel·li·gence /£ˌkaʊn·tə·rɪnˈtel·ɪ·dʒənts, $-t̬ɚ·ɪn-/ *n* [U] secret action taken by a country to protect itself from the efforts of another country to discover its military, industrial or political secrets, or information about such efforts

coun·ter·mand *obj* /£ˌkaʊn·təˈmɑːnd, $-t̬ɚˈmænd/ *v* [T] *fml* to change (an order that has already been given), esp. by giving a new order • *As a junior officer you have no right to undermine my authority by countermanding my orders.*

coun·ter·meas·ure /£ˈkaʊn·təˌmeʒ·əʳ, $-t̬ɚˌmeʒ·ɚ/ *n* [C] an action taken against an unwanted action or situation • *The Chancellor's countermeasures* **against** *inflation have been completely ineffective.*

coun·ter·of·fens·ive /£ˌkaʊn·tə·rəˈfent·sɪv, $-t̬ɚ-ə-/ *n* [C] a set of attacks which defend against enemy attacks • *The start of our counteroffensive was the turning point in the war.*

coun·ter·pane /£ˈkaʊn·tə·peɪn, $-t̬ɚ-/ *n* [C] a BEDSPREAD

coun·ter·part /£ˈkaʊn·tə·pɑːt, $-t̬ɚ-pɑːrt/ *n* [C] a person or thing which has the same purpose as another one in a different place or organization • *The Prime Minister is to meet his European counterparts to discuss the war against drugs.* • *Channel 4 is British independent television's counterpart* **to** *BBC2.*

coun·ter·point /£ˈkaʊn·tə·pɔɪnt, $-t̬ɚ-/ *n* [U] the combination of two or more different tunes played at the same time

coun·ter·poise /£ˈkaʊn·tə·pɔɪz, $-t̬ɚ- ˈkaʊn·tə·pɔɪz, $-t-/ *n* [C], *v* [T] *fml* COUNTERBALANCE

coun·ter·pro·duct·ive /£ˌkaʊn·tə·prəˈdʌk·tɪv, $-t̬ɚ·prəˈdʌk·t̬ɪv/ *adj* having an effect which is opposite to the one that is intended or desired • *Improved safety measures in cars can be counterproductive as they encourage people to drive faster.*

coun·ter·sign *obj* /£ˈkaʊn·tə·saɪn, $-t̬ɚ-/ *v* [T] *specialized* to sign (a document which has already been signed), esp. in order to show that the first person really did sign it • *My lawyer countersigned the will after I had signed it.*

coun·ter·sunk /£ˈkaʊn·tə·sʌŋk, $-t̬ɚ-/ *adj* [not gradable] *specialized* (of a screw) put into a hole which is slightly larger at the top, so that the end of the screw is level with or slightly below the surface • [PIC]› **Tools**

coun·ter·ten·or /£ˌkaʊn·təˈten·əʳ, $-t̬ɚˈten·ɚ/, **male al·to** (*pl* **male altos**) *n* [C] a man with a singing voice which is higher than usual for a TENOR and similar to a low female voice

coun·ter·vail·ing /£ˌkaʊn·təˈveɪ·lɪŋ, $-t̬ɚ-/ *adj* [before n; not gradable] *fml* having equal force but an opposite effect • *There was nobody strong enough to lead an effective countervailing force against the dictator.*

count·ess /£ˈkaʊn·tes, $-t̬əs/ *n* [C] a woman of high social rank, or the wife of a COUNT or EARL

count·less /ˈkaʊnt·ləs/ *adj* [not gradable] very many; too many to be counted; INNUMERABLE • *There are countless arguments against this ridiculous proposal.*

coun·try [POLITICAL UNIT] /ˈkʌn·tri/ *n* [C] an area of land which forms or might form an independent political unit with its own government • *Which is the largest country in Europe?* • *France is my native country, but I've been living in Belgium for the past five years.* • *The climate is cooler in the east of the country.* • *The countries of the United Kingdom are Wales, Scotland, Northern Ireland and England.* • *The United Kingdom is one of the countries in the European Union.* • *The separatists are fighting for independence for their country.* • *The whole country* (= All the people living in the country) *celebrated the signing of the peace treaty.* • *(Br slightly fml) The Prime Minister has decided to* **go to the country** (= have an election). • *"The undiscovered country from whose bourn* (= boundry)*/ No traveller returns"* (Shakespeare writing about death, Hamlet 3.1) • *"My country 'tis of thee, / Sweet land of liberty"* (Samuel Francis Smith *America*, 1831) • *"Your country needs you"* (used to encourage people to join the army during The First World War, 1914) • [LP]› **Nations and nationalities, World regions** Ⓙ

coun·try [NATURAL LAND] /ˈkʌn·tri/ *n* [U] land which is not in towns, cities or industrial areas and is either used for farming or left in its natural condition • *Would you prefer to live in* **the** *country instead of a town?* • *I'm spending next weekend in* **the** *country with a friend.* • *Country life isn't always as peaceful as city-dwellers think.* • *She's planning to buy a country cottage for her retirement.* • *It's often quicker to travel* **across** *country and avoid the major roads altogether.* • **Country (and western)** is an emotional style of popular music which is based on the white FOLK music of the western and southern US: *a country(-and-western) singer* • A **country club** is a sporting or social organization based in the countryside, often one which does not allow membership to people who are considered to be unsuitable because of their social position, job or lack of wealth. • **Country dances** are traditional British dances for several pairs of male and female dancers who are arranged in circles, squares or long rows. • A **country house** is a large traditional house in the countryside, esp. one which has belonged to the same family for many years. • A **country seat** is a country house and a large piece of land surrounding it: *Lady Castleton has a flat near Westminster, but her country seat is in Yorkshire.* • Ⓙ

coun·tri·fied /ˈkʌn·trɪ·faɪd/ *adj* • A person or thing that is countrified is more suited to the countryside than to towns or cities: *She is more countrified than her boyfriend from New York.* • *(disapproving) Their house was decorated in a style that was rather tasteless and countrified* (= artificially like the country).

coun·try [LAND] /ˈkʌn·tri/ *n* [U] an area of land considered in relation to a particular feature • *They walked for miles through densely-wooded country.* • *Stratford-on-Avon is the capital of Shakespeare country.* • *The empty roads make this area good cycling country.* • Ⓙ

coun·try·man [FROM YOUR COUNTRY] (*pl* **-men**), **coun·try·wo·man** (*pl* **-women**) /ˈkʌn·trɪ·mən, -ˌwʊm·ən/, *fml* **com·pat·ri·ot** *n* [C] a person from your own country • *Didn't he feel guilty about betraying his* **fellow** *countrymen and women?*

coun·try·man [FROM THE COUNTRYSIDE] (*pl* **-men**), **coun·try·wo·man** (*pl* **-women**) /ˈkʌn·trɪ·mən, -ˌwʊm·ən/ *n* [C] a person who lives in or was raised in the countryside and not in a town

coun·try·side /ˈkʌn·trɪ·saɪd/ *n* [U] land not in towns, cities or industrial areas which is either used for farming or left in its natural condition • *The 200-year-old mansion is set in 90 acres of beautiful, unspoilt countryside.* • *What are the advantages of living in* **the** *countryside?* • **The** *countryside needs greater protection from polluters.*

coun·try·wide /ˌkʌn·triˈwaɪd/ *adj, adv* existing in or involving all parts of a country • *What began as an isolated outbreak of flu has now developed into a countrywide epidemic.* • *The bank has three branches in Norwich, and over three hundred countrywide.*

coun·ty /£ˈkaʊn·ti, $-t̬i/ *(abbreviation* **Co**) *n* [C] a political division of the UK or Ireland, forming the largest unit of local government, or the largest political division of a STATE in the US • *County Antrim* • *A county usually consists of several towns and the rural areas which surround them.* • *Rutland used to be the smallest county in England, but in 1974 it became part of Leicestershire.* • *Texas is divided into 254 counties.* • *(Br)* A **county council** is an elected group of people which forms the government of a county: *Northumberland County Council* • *(Br)* A **county court** is a local law court in England which deals with cases that do not involve crime. • A *(Br)* **county town**/*(Am)* **county seat** is the most important town or city in a county, esp. the one where the local government is based: *Cambridge is the county town of Cambridgeshire.*

coun·ty /£ˈkaʊn·ti, $-t̬i/ *adj* [not gradable] *Br usually disapproving* • Someone who is county behaves in a traditional way that is typical of rich people with a high social position who live in large houses in the countryside.

coun·ty·wide /£ˌkaʊn·tiˈwaɪd, $-t̬i-/ *adj, adv esp. Am* existing in or involving all parts of a COUNTY • *a countywide survey* • *Rockville's mayor has promised to solve countywide trash disposal problems within the next few weeks.* • *Countywide, examination results have improved by an average of eight per cent.*

coup /kuː/ *n* [C] an unexpectedly successful achievement • *It was a tremendous coup for the local paper to get an exclusive interview with Prince Charles.*

coup (d'état) /ˌkuː·deɪˈtɑː/ *n* [C] *pl* **coups (d'état)** /ˌkuː·deɪˈtɑː/ a sudden illegal, often violent, taking of government power, esp. by (part of) an army • *a military coup* • *Gorbachev survived an abortive coup attempt, only to be dethroned a few months later by the breakup of the USSR.*

coup de grâce /ˌkuː·dəˈgræs/ *n* [C] *pl* **coups de grâce** /ˌkuː·dəˈgræs/ an action which ends something that has been gradually worsening or which kills a person or animal in order to end their suffering • *Jane's affair was the coup de grâce* **to** *her disintegrating marriage.* • *He was in tremendous agony and knew he was going to die, so I agreed to* **give/administer** *the coup de grâce to him.*

cou·pé /£ˈkuː·peɪ, $kuˈpeɪ/ *n* [C] a car with a fixed roof, two doors, two or four seats, and usually a sloping back

cou·ple SOME /ˈkʌp·l̩/ *n* [U] two or a few things that are similar or the same, or two or a few people who are in some way connected • *There's* **a** *couple* **of** *gloves in the cupboard, but they can't be a pair because they're both left-handed.* • *"Could you lend me* **a** *couple* **of** *quid?" "Sure, is two pounds enough?"* • *The doctor said my leg should be better in* **a** *couple* **of** *days.* • *It's* **a** *couple* **of** *kilometres to the nearest village.* • *I met* **a** *couple* **of** *interesting journalists at the party.* • **A** *couple* **of** *people objected to the proposal, but the vast majority approved of it.* • *"Have you been drinking?" "Yes, but I've only had* **a** *couple* **(of** *beers)."* • *We'll have to wait* **another** *couple* **of** *hours for the paint to dry.* • *She'll be retiring in* **a** *couple* **more** *years.* • *We usually get together for lunch* **every** *couple* **of** *weeks.* • *We really enjoyed living here for* **the first** *couple* **of** *years.* • *The weather's been terrible for* **the last** *couple* **of** *days.* • *Many economists expect unemployment to fall over* **the next** *couple* **of** *months.* • *I'm sorry I didn't phone you, but I've been very busy over* **the past** *couple* **of** *weeks.* • LP› **Two**

cou·ple TWO PEOPLE /ˈkʌp·l̩/ *n* [C + sing/pl v] two people in a (sexual) relationship, or two people who are together for a particular purpose • *I hope Caroline and Tristan get married – they make such a lovely couple.* • *The couple skated/danced spectacularly throughout the competition.* • *The infertility clinic has brought hope to hundreds of* **childless** *couples.* • *An* **elderly** *couple live next door and they always complain about the noise when we have a party.* • *Only a small proportion of modern households consist of a* **married** *couple with two children.* • *Should the government do more to help* **young** *couples buy their own homes?* • LP› **Relationships**

cou·ple *obj* JOIN /ˈkʌp·l̩/ *v* [T always + adv/prep] to join or combine • *The sleeping car was coupled* **onto** *the restaurant car.* • *The sleeping car and restaurant car were coupled* **together**. • *High inflation coupled* **with** *low output spells disaster for the Government in the election.*

coup·ling /ˈkʌp·lɪŋ/ *n* [C] • A coupling is a device which joins two things together: *The carriage at the end of the train was left stranded when the coupling broke.*

coup·let /ˈkʌp·lət/ *n* [C] two lines of poetry next to each other, esp. ones which RHYME and have the same length and METRE • *a rhyming couplet*

cou·pon /£ˈkuː·pɒn, $-pɑːn/ *n* [C] a piece of paper which can be used to obtain something without paying for it or at a reduced price • *If you save up ten coupons from the cornflakes packet you can get a free teddy bear.* • A coupon is also a piece of paper, esp. a part of an advertisement in a newspaper or magazine, which a reader can send to an organization in order to obtain information about its products or services: *To find out more about our new computers, fill in the coupon and send it to us at the address given below.*

cour·age /£ˈkʌr·ɪdʒ, $ˈkɜːr-/ *n* [U] the ability to control fear and to deal with danger, pain, uncertainty etc.; bravery • *She was a woman of immense courage.* • *They showed great courage when they found out about their baby's disability.* • *People should have* **the** *courage* **to** *stand up for their beliefs.* [+ *to* infinitive] • *It took me ages to* **summon/pluck up** *the courage* **to** *ask for a promotion.* [+ *to* infinitive] • *Although many of his policies were unpopular, he had* **the courage of** *his* **convictions** *to see them through* (= was brave and confident enough to do and say what he believed in). • *"But screw your courage to the sticking-place, / And we'll not fail"* (Shakespeare, Macbeth 1.7)

cou·ra·geous /kəˈreɪ·dʒəs/ *adj* • *She is the most courageous police officer that I have ever met.* • *It was a courageous decision to resign in protest at the company's pollution record.* • *It was courageous* **of** *her to challenge the managing director's decision.*

cou·ra·geous·ly /kəˈreɪ·dʒə·sli/ *adv*

cour·gette *Br* /£kɔːˈʒet, $kʊr-/, *Am and Aus* **zuc·chi·ni** *n* a long thin vegetable with a dark green skin which is cooked before being eaten. It is a type of small MARROW. • *Slice the courgettes, then sauté them lightly with garlic.* [C] • *Would you like some more courgette?* [U] • PIC› **Vegetables**

cou·ri·er /£ˈkʊr·i·əʳ, $ˈkɜːr·i·ɚ/ *n* [C] a person who takes care of a group of people on holiday and shows them the most important things in the place they are visiting, or a person who carries important messages or documents for someone else • *You'll be met by the courier at the airport.* • *I want to have this package delivered by motorcycle courier.* • Ⓟ

course DIRECTION /£kɔːs, $kɔːrs/ *n* [C] the direction in which a vehicle, esp. an aircraft, spacecraft or ship, moves, or the path along which a river flows • *The pilot avoided a collision by* **changing** *course just in time.* • *The air force is trying to change the course of the lava by dropping bombs near the mouth of the volcano.* • *Great environmental damage would be caused by changing the course of the river.* • *(fig.) The new democracies are expected to* **adopt/steer** *a* **middle** *course between communism and capitalism.* • *(fig.) The debate completely changed course after Jane made her persuasive speech.* • *(fig.) The defendants are also accused of attempting to pervert the course of justice.* • *(fig.) Because of the recession we're* **on course for** *(having)*/**on course to** *have record unemployment levels.*

course DEVELOPMENT /£kɔːs, $kɔːrs/ *n* [C] the often gradual development of something, or the way something happens, or a way of doing something • *Throughout* **the** *course* **of** *history people have been dying in pointless wars, and they will doubtless continue to do so.* • *Did the scandal have any effect on the course of the election?* • **In the normal** *course* **of events** (= Usually), *you would be banned from driving, but as you depend on your car for work, I have decided to fine you instead.* • **During/In the** *course* **of** (= During) *the interview it became clear that he was not suitable for the job.* • **In the** *course* **of** *a lifetime's research, she made some very valuable discoveries.* • *What would be an appropriate course* **(of action)** *in such a situation?* • *If our rivals are spending more on advertising, we'll have to follow the same course.* • *When we married, we planned to have children* **in the course of time** (= at some future time), *but Jim's infertility has prevented that.* • **In the course of time** (= Gradually), *I've learned to live with my disability.* • *"Could you possibly lend me a fiver?"* **"Of course** (= Certainly)*."* • *"May I have a look at your newspaper?"* **"Of course** (= Please do)*."* • *"Have you written your English essay yet?"* **"Of course** (= Yes I have, and I don't know how you could doubt that I have). *I finished it last week."* • *"Where did you get the money? Did you steal it?"* **"Of course not/Of course** *I did***n't** (= That's a ridiculous suggestion). *I borrowed it from Carol."* • *The Second World War ended,* **of course** (= as you should know), *in 1945.* • *Professor Howlett's claims are,* **of course** (= I would like you to agree without further proof or argument), *utterly without justification.*

course [CLASSES] /£kɔːs, $kɔːrs/ *n* [C] a set of classes or study periods on a particular subject, consisting of reading, writing or practical activities in addition to teaching, and usually resulting in an exam or qualification • *Guy* **did** *a three-year course* **in** *linguistics at Newcastle.* • *They're going away* **on** *a training course next week.* • *I'd like to* **do** *a cookery course when I retire.*

course [MEDICAL TREATMENT] /£kɔːs, $kɔːrs/ *n* [C] a fixed number of regular medical treatments • *My doctor's* **put** *me* **on** *a course* **of** *antibiotics to get rid of my infection.* • *She needed a six-month course of physiotherapy after she broke her leg.*

course [SPORTS AREA] /£kɔːs, $kɔːrs/ *n* [C] an area of land or water used for a sporting event • *a golf course/cross-country course* • *All the competitors managed to steer their boats around a difficult obstacle course.* • See also RACECOURSE.

course [MEAL] /£kɔːs, $kɔːrs/ *n* [C] a part of a meal which is served separately from the other parts • *a four-course lunch* • *A traditional British* **main** *course consists of a meat dish with potatoes and other vegetables.*

course [LAYER] /£kɔːs, $kɔːrs/ *n* [C] *specialized* a continuous horizontal layer of bricks or other building material

course [FLOW] /£kɔːs, $kɔːrs/ *v* [I always + adv/prep] to flow quickly or in large amounts • *Tears were coursing* **down** *his cheeks.* • *You could almost hear the blood coursing* **through** *her veins as she passed the finishing line.* • *(fig.) A new wave of idealism is coursing* **through** *our schools.*

course·work /£ˈkɔːs·wɜːk, $ˈkɔːrs·wɜːrk/ *n* [U] work set at regular periods as part of an educational course, the marks for the work being included in the student's final result • *The new qualification places much greater emphasis on coursework than on examinations.*

court [LAW] /£kɔːt, $kɔːrt/ *n* (a large room in) a building where trials and other legal cases happen, or the people present in such a room, esp. the officials and those deciding whether someone is guilty • *the European Court of Human Rights* [C] • *The court was rather intimidating.* [C] • *They're building the new law courts down by the river.* [C] • *(fml) Such behaviour is quite inappropriate in a court* **of law**. [C] • *I'm giving evidence in a court* **case** *next week.* • **Silence in** *court!* [U] • *Court* **adjourned**! [U] • *Please describe to* **the** *court exactly what you saw.* [U] • *She's threatening to* **take** *me* **to** *court for not paying the bill on time.* [U] • *The lack of evidence means that the case is unlikely to* **go to** *court.* [U] • *The newspaper has agreed to* **settle (the case) out of** *court* (=without taking legal action). [U] • *(Br)* A **court of inquiry** is a group of people, often with specialist knowledge or skill, who have been brought together in order to examine the causes of an accident: *A court of inquiry is to be set up to investigate what caused the explosion.* • A **court order** is an instruction given by a court telling someone what they can or cannot do: *His wife* **took out** *a court order to stop him from seeing his children.* • See also INNS OF COURT. • [LP] **Law**

court [SPORT] /£kɔːt, $kɔːrt/ *n* [C] a rectangular area marked out on the ground which is used for playing sports such as tennis • *I hate playing on hard courts – I much prefer grass.* • *Tennis players hit the ball over the net which divides the court in two.* • *Squash players hit the ball against the walls of the court.*

court [GROUND] /£kɔːt, $kɔːrt/ *n* [C] an area of ground, such as a short road or a square, which is not covered by a roof and is mostly or completely surrounded by buildings • *Susannah lives in a house at the end of Wintersgill Court.* • *You really should go and see the lovely medieval court in the castle.* • *(Br)* Sometimes apartment buildings are called courts, often to make them sound more pleasant than they really are: *I wasn't expecting somewhere called Meadow Court to be a huge concrete monstrosity.*

court [ROYALTY] /£kɔːt, $kɔːrt/ *n* the official home of a queen or king, or a royal family and the people who take care of them • *the courts of Renaissance Europe* [C] • *He quickly lost his popularity at court.* [U] • A **court correspondent** is someone who reports on the lives of the members of a royal family. • *(Br)* A **court shoe** (*Am* **pump**) is a type of plain shoe with no fastenings which is worn by women. • [PIC] **Shoes**

court *(obj)* [PLEASE] /£kɔːt, $kɔːrt/ *v* to try very hard to please (someone) in the hope of receiving their love or approval, or to have an important personal relationship with (someone) whom you are likely to marry • *Paul was courting Lucy for a couple of years before she agreed to marry him.* [T] • *Brian's been courting his boss in the hope of getting a promotion.* [T] • *She courts* (=tries to get) *publicity by inviting journalists to extravagant parties.* [T] • *They've been courting for six years, but they still have no plans to marry.* [I] • *"Are you courting, then?" asked the hairdresser, trying to start up a conversation.* [I] • Sometimes **courting couple** is used to refer politely to two people involved in sexual activity: *The police are anxious to identify a courting couple who were in a car near the scene of the murder.*

court·ship /£ˈkɔːt·ʃɪp, $ˈkɔːrt-/ *n* • *They had a passionate courtship, but they split up just before they were due to marry.* [C] • *Giselle was wary of accepting Albrecht's courtship at first.* [U] • *These birds have complicated courtship rituals* (=behaviour for attracting a sexual partner). [U]

court *obj* [RISK] /£kɔːt, $kɔːrt/ *v* [T] to risk (something unpleasant), esp. by behaving stupidly or carelessly • *Drinking and driving is simply courting disaster.*

court·ship /£ˈkɔːt·ʃɪp, $ˈkɔːrt-/ *n* [U] • *His courtship of controversy guaranteed him frequent appearances in the headlines.*

cour·te·ous /£ˈkɜː·ti·əs, $ˈkɜːr·t̬i-/ *adj* polite and respectful; WELL-MANNERED • *Although she often disagreed with me, she was always courteous.*

cour·te·ous·ly /£ˈkɜː·ti·ə·sli, $ˈkɜːr·t̬i-/ *adv* • *All the pupils stood up courteously when I went into the classroom.*

court·e·san /£ˌkɔː·tɪˈzæn, ˈ---, $ˈkɔːr·t̬ɪ-/ *n* [C] a woman, usually with a high social position, who in the past had sexual relationships with rich or important men in exchange for money

court·e·sy /£ˈkɜː·tə·si, $ˈkɜːr·t̬ə-/ *n* polite behaviour, or a polite action or remark • *You might get on better with your parents if you showed them some courtesy.* [U] • *He could at least have had the courtesy* **to** *say sorry.* [U + *to* infinitive] • *The President welcomed the Queen with the usual courtesies.* [C] • *Phil Collins appears on the album* **(by) courtesy of** (=by permission of) *Virgin Records.* • *Did the Conservatives win* **(by) courtesy of** (=because of) *the division of the opposition vote between Labour and the Liberal Democrats?*

court·house /£ˈkɔːt·haʊs, $ˈkɔːrt-/ *n* [C] *pl* **courthouses** /£ˈkɔːtˌhaʊ·zɪz, $ˈkɔːrt-/ *Am* a building which contains law courts • *a county/federal courthouse*

court·i·er /£ˈkɔː·ti·əʳ, $ˈkɔːr·t̬i·ɚ/ *n* [C] a companion of a queen, king or other ruler in their official home • *The journalists swarmed around the President like a group of medieval courtiers.* • *(fig.) Her new government is an uninspiring mixture of courtiers and sycophants.*

court·ly /£ˈkɔːt·li, $ˈkɔːrt-/ *adj* **-ier, -iest** polite and graceful in behaviour • *These difficult negotiations require a courtly approach.*

court·li·ness /£ˈkɔːt·lɪ·nəs, $ˈkɔːrt-/ *n* [U]

court mar·tial *n* [C] *pl* **court martials** or *fml* **courts martial** (a trial in) a military court which judges those members of the armed forces who must obey military law

court–mar·tial *obj* /£ˌkɔːtˈmɑː·ʃəl, $ˈkɔːrtˌmɑːr-/ *v* [T] **-ll-** or *Am usually* **-l-** • *She is likely to be court-martialled for disobeying her commanding officer.*

court·room /£ˈkɔːt·rʊm, -ruːm, $ˈkɔːrt-/ *n* [C] a room where a court of law meets • *The accused entered the courtroom handcuffed to two police officers.* • *It was a courtroom drama set in the 1960s.*

court·yard /£ˈkɔːt·jɑːd, $ˈkɔːrt·jɑːrd/ *n* [C] an area of flat ground outside which is partly or completely enclosed by the walls of a building

cous·cous /ˈkuːs·kuːs/ *n* [U] a food, originally from N Africa, consisting of crushed wheat that is cooked by steaming and served with meat or vegetables

cous·in /ˈkʌz·ən/, **first cous·in** *n* [C] a child of a person's aunt or uncle, or, more generally, a distant relative, or a member of a group of people with similar origins • *My brother's wife and I both had babies around the same time, so the cousins are very close in age.* • *Many of our* **distant** *cousins, whom we hadn't seen for years, came to my sister's wedding.* • *We Americans owe a great deal to our European cousins.* • [PIC] **Family tree**

couth /kuːθ/ *adj esp. humorous* (of a person or their behaviour) polite, graceful and with a pleasant appearance; not rude or unpleasant • *Kate's new boyfriend is a very couth youth.*

cou·ture /£kuːˈtʊəʳ, $-ˈtʊr/, **haute cou·ture** /ˌəʊt-/ *n* [U] the designing, making and selling of expensive fashionable clothing • *a couture show/collection/house*

cou·tu·ri·er /£kuː'tʊə·ri·eɪ, $-'tʊr·i-/ *n* [C] • *In 1960, Pierre Cardin became the first couturier to design men's clothes.*

cove COAST /£kəʊv, $koʊv/ *n* [C] a curved part of a coast which partly encloses an area of water; a small BAY

cove MAN /£kəʊv, $koʊv/ *n* [C] *Aus and dated Br slang* a man; a CHAP

cov·en /'kʌv·ən/ *n* [C + sing/pl v] a group of usually 13 WITCHES (= women with magic powers) gathered together

cov·e·nant /'kʌv·ən·ənt/ *n* [C] *specialized* a formal written legal agreement, in Britain esp. one promising to pay regularly a fixed amount of money to esp. a CHARITY • *You can sometimes avoid tax by setting up a covenant to donate money to charity.* • A covenant is also a part of a written legal agreement that gives a particular instruction, usually to prevent something from being done: *The contract contained a* **restrictive** *covenant against building on the land.*

cov·e·nant *obj* /'kʌv·ən·ənt/ *v* [T] • *Regular covenanted donations make our financial planning easier.*

cov·er *obj* PLACE OVER /£'kʌv·əʳ, $-ɚ/ *v* [T] to put or spread something over (something), esp. in order to hide or protect it, or to lie on the surface of (something) • *They laid him on a stretcher and covered him* **(up) with** *a blanket.* • *You should cover that meat* **with** *something to protect it from the flies.* • *The light was so bright that I had to cover my eyes* **with** *my hands.* • *The bandages were covered* **with/in** *blood.* • *Just look at your hands! They're covered* **in** *mud!* • *Fill the pan with water until the carrots are just covered.* • *A bus covered me* **with** *water when it went through a puddle.* • *How much of the Earth's surface is covered* **by/with** *water?* • *London covers 1579 square kilometres (of land).* • *(Am slang)* If you **cover** your **ass** you protect yourself or your interests: *You'll never be promoted if you spend all your time at work covering your ass.* • A **covering letter/note** (*Am also and Aus* **cover letter/note**) is a letter or note which gives information about the thing it is sent with: *Please send a covering letter with your application form.*

-cov·ered /£-'kʌv·əd, $-ɚd/ *combining form* • **snow**-*covered hills* • *an* **ivy**-*covered cottage* • *a* **graffiti**-*covered wall* • PIC> **Coverings**

cov·er /£'kʌv·əʳ, $-ɚ/ *n* [C] • *I keep my computer printer under a protective plastic cover.* • The cover of a book or magazine is the stiff outside part of it, usually made of thick paper or cardboard and often shiny: *Who should we put on the cover of the magazine this month?* ○ *Paperback books have soft covers.* • A **cover girl/boy/model** is an attractive, often famous and usually adult, person whose photograph appears on the front of a magazine. • A **cover story** is a report or article connected with the picture on the front of a magazine. • If you read something **from cover to cover** you read it all the way through from the beginning to the end: *It was so interesting I read it from cover to cover in a single afternoon.* • *Martha threw back the covers* (= sheets etc.) *and bounced out of bed.* • *Shops are using the rise in value-added tax as a cover for increasing prices.* • A **cover charge** is a charge which is sometimes added to the amount that a customer pays for food, drinks and service in a restaurant, or which is added in a NIGHTCLUB to pay for entertainment. • *(fml)* If you send something **under plain/separate cover**, you send it in a plain/separate envelope: *Thankyou for your enquiry. We will be sending you a new brochure under separate cover as soon as it is available.* • PIC> **Coverings**

cov·er·ing /£'kʌv·ər·ɪŋ, $'-ɚ-/ *n* [C] • *There was a light covering* (= thin layer) *of snow when I woke up.* • *We'll need a tough floor covering for the workshop.*

cov·er *obj* TRAVEL /£'kʌv·əʳ, $-ɚ/ *v* [T] to travel (a particular distance) • *We covered 400km in three hours.*

cov·er *obj* DEAL WITH /£'kʌv·əʳ, $-ɚ/ *v* [T] to deal with or direct attention to • *The exam's only a month away and we haven't even covered the whole course, never mind started revising.* • *This leaflet covers what we've just discussed in more detail.* • *Do these parking restrictions cover residents as well as visitors?* • *The new office will cover the whole of Scotland.* • *The new regulations cover precisely* **where** *and* **when** *protest marches can take place.* [+ *wh-* word]

cov·er·age /£'kʌv·ər·ɪdʒ, $'-ɚ-/ *n* [U] • *Cambridge dictionaries give very good grammar coverage* (= They deal with grammar very well).

cov·er *obj* REPORT /£'kʌv·əʳ, $-ɚ/ *v* [T] to report the news about (a particular important event) • *She's covering the American election for BBC television.*

cov·er·age /£'kʌv·ər·ɪdʒ, $'-ɚ-/ *n* [U] • Coverage is the reporting of a particular important event or subject: *What did you think of the BBC's election coverage?* ○ *Sexual abuse has received a lot of media coverage recently.*

cov·er *obj* BE ENOUGH /£'kʌv·əʳ, $-ɚ/ *v* [T] to be enough money to pay for • *The selling price barely covered (the cost of) the raw materials.* • *Would £50 cover your expenses?*

cov·er *obj* PROTECT /£'kʌv·əʳ, $-ɚ/ *v* [T] to protect financially from loss, damage, accident or having something stolen; to INSURE • *Does your travel insurance cover you* **against/for** *the loss or theft of cash?*

cov·er *Br* /£'kʌv·əʳ, $-ɚ/, *Am* **cov·er·age** *n* [U] • *I've got £20 000 worth of cover for the contents of my house.* • *(Br)* A **cover note** is a document which is used temporarily as proof that someone is INSURED until the final official document is available.

cov·er·age /£'kʌv·ər·ɪdʒ, $'-ɚ-/ *n* [U] • Coverage is the highest amount of money that an **insurance policy** will pay, or the risks which it protects against: *You should check that your coverage has kept up with inflation.* ○ *I've only got fire coverage for my car.*

cov·er SHELTER /£'kʌv·əʳ, $-ɚ/ *n* [U] shelter or protection in an unpleasant or dangerous situation • *We* **took** *cover from the storm in a bus shelter.* • *The burglar broke into the house* **under** *cover of darkness.* • *The doctors have agreed to provide* **emergency** *cover, but they are refusing to perform non-essential duties.* • Cover is also plants, esp. bushes, that are used as shelter by animals.

cov·er *obj* GIVE ARMED PROTECTION /£'kʌv·əʳ, $-ɚ/ *v* [T] to aim a gun or shoot at a possible enemy in order to protect (someone), or to aim a gun at (someone) to discourage them from shooting or escaping • *The police officer was covered by her colleagues while she ran towards the gunman's hideout.* • *The security guard covered the robber while the bank manager tied him up.* • A soldier or police officer who is covering a place such as a road or building is in a position which makes it possible to watch and defend it: *We've got all the exits covered, so they've no chance of escape.*

cov·er /£'kʌv·əʳ, $-ɚ/ *n* [U] • *We needed more cover* (= protection) **from** *the enemy aircraft.*

cov·er *(obj)* DO SOMEONE'S JOB /£'kʌv·əʳ, $-ɚ/ *v* to do (someone else's job or duty) when they are absent • *I'm going to the doctor's tomorrow so do you think you could cover my shift for me?* [T] • *Sorry, I'm already covering* **for** *someone else.* [I]

cov·er *obj* RECORD /£'kʌv·əʳ, $-ɚ/ *v* [T] to make a recording of (a song or tune which has already been recorded by someone else) • *I think more singers have covered 'Yesterday' than any other song.*

cov·er (ver·sion) /£'kʌv·əʳ, $-ɚ/ *n* [C] • *How many cover versions have been made of 'My Way'?*

cov·er up *(obj)*, **cov·er** *(obj)* **up** *v adv* to keep (something unpleasant) secret or hidden • *I've discovered a wonderful new cream for covering my spots up.* [M] • *The company tried unsuccessfully to keep these embarrassing pollution statistics covered up.* [M] • *There's no point trying to cover up* **for** *your husband. It's perfectly obvious that he's guilty.* [I]

cov·er–up /£'kʌv·ə·rʌp, $-ɚ·ʌp/ *n* [C] • A **cover-up** is an attempt to prevent the public discovering information about a serious crime or mistake: *Allegations of a cover-up* **of** *the effects of industrial pollution have been strongly denied by the Environment Minister.*

cov·er·alls /£'kʌv·ə·rɔːlz, $-ɚ·ɑːlz/ *pl n* [C] *Am for* **boiler suit**, see at BOILER

cov·er·let /£'kʌv·ə·lət, $'-ɚ-/ *n* [C] a BEDSPREAD

cov·ert /£'kəʊ·vɜːt, $'koʊ·vɜːrt, -'-/ *adj* hidden or secret • *The murdered soldier belonged to an army unit which specializes in covert operations.* • *Should covert action against the dictatorship be considered if overt military action is unacceptable?* • Compare OVERT.

cov·ert /£'kʌv·ə, $-ɚ/ *n* [C] • A covert is a group of bushes and small trees growing close together in which animals can hide esp. from hunters.

cov·ert·ly /£'kʌv·ət·li, $-ɚt-/ *adv* • *Terrorists have been operating covertly in England for several years.*

cov·et *obj* /'kʌv·ɪt/ *v* [T] to desire strongly (esp. something which belongs to someone else) • *The presidency is surely a job that every politician covets.* • *She always coveted power but never quite achieved it.* • *A country can't invade its neighbour just because it covets its wealth and resources.* • *The Booker Prize is the most coveted British literary award.*

cov·et·a·ble /£'kʌv·ɪ·tə·bl̩, $-t̬ə-/ *adj* • If something is covetable it is very desirable: *Some brands of running shoe are far more covetable than others.*

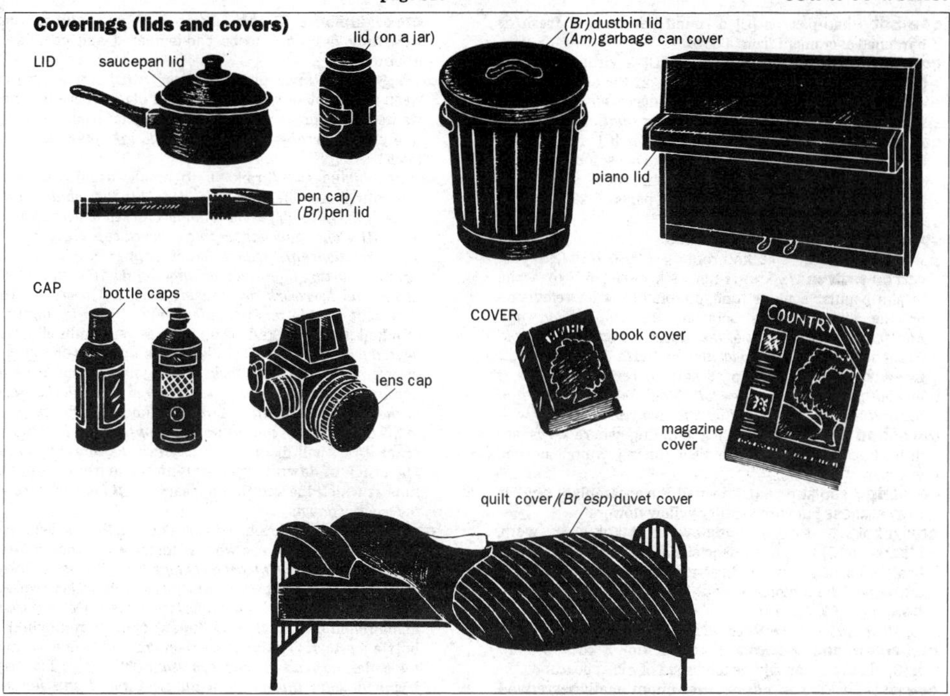

cov·et·ous /£ˈkʌv·ɪ·təs, $-t̬əs/ *adj* • *Western companies are casting covetous eyes on the bargain-priced companies of eastern Europe.* • *My daughters are very competitive and tremendously covetous* **of** *each other's jobs.*

cov·et·ous·ly /£ˈkʌv·ɪ·tə·sli, $-t̬ə-/ *adv* • *The boys looked covetously at the row of expensive cars parked along the street.*

cov·et·ous·ness /£ˈkʌv·ɪ·tə·snəs, $-t̬ə-/ *n* [U] • *Covetousness is one of the Seven Deadly Sins.*

cow ANIMAL /kaʊ/ *n* [C] a large adult female animal, esp. one kept on farms to produce milk and meat, which has four legs and eats plants • *a herd of cows* • *This wine's delicious! I could drink it* **till/until the cows come home** (=for a very long time). • Other large female adult mammals, such as ELEPHANTS, RHINOCEROSES, WHALES and SEALS, are also called cows: *a cow elephant.* • *(Br)* **Cow parsley** (*Am* **Queen Anne's lace**) is a wild plant with delicate white flowers that grows esp. in fields and along the sides of roads in the countryside. • *"The cow jumped over the moon"* (from a children's nursery rhyme) • PIC **Flowers and plants**

cow WOMAN /kaʊ/ *n* [C] *Br slang* a woman or girl who is considered to be unpleasant in appearance or behaviour • *You stupid cow! You've just burnt a hole in my dress with your cigarette.*

cow UNPLEASANT THING /kaʊ/ *n* [U] *Aus infml* something difficult or unpleasant • *It's been* **a cow of a** *day.* • *Painting the ceiling is* **a fair** *cow* (= is very unpleasant).

cow *obj* FRIGHTEN /kaʊ/ *v* [T] to frighten (someone) into doing something using threats or violence • *Fear of unemployment has cowed the workers* **into** *acceptance of the company's plans.* • *The protesters refused to be cowed* **into** *submission by the army.* • *Potential rivals were so cowed by her popularity that no-one dared challenge her for the leadership.*

co·ward /£ˈkaʊ·əd, $ˈkaʊ·ɚd/ *n* [C] *disapproving* a person who is easily frightened or tries to avoid danger, difficulty or pain • *They* **branded** *her a coward for informing on her colleagues during the interrogation.* • *"Cowards die many times before their deaths: / The valiant never taste of death but once."* (Shakespeare, Julius Caesar 2.2)

co·ward·ice /£ˈkaʊ·ə·dɪs, $ˈ-ɚ-/ *n* [U] • *This attack on a defenceless elderly person is an act of pure cowardice.* • *You can accuse me of cowardice, but I still wouldn't volunteer to fight in a war.*

co·ward·ly /£ˈkaʊ·əd·li, $-ɚd-/ *adj* • *This was a particularly brutal and cowardly attack.* • *They are guilty of a cowardly failure to address the problem.*

cow·bell /ˈkaʊ·bel/ *n* [C] a bell which is hung from a cow's neck so that movement of the neck causes the bell to ring and allows a lost cow to be found, or a metal musical instrument which produces a similar sound when hit with a stick

cow·boy FARM WORKER, **cow·girl**, **cow·hand** /ˈkaʊ·bɔɪ, -gɜːrl, -hænd/ *n* [C] a person employed, esp. in the western US, to take care of cattle, usually on a horse, or a similar character in a film • *The ranch employed ten cowboys.* • *He became famous as a cowboy in the movies.* • *He was wearing cowboy boots and a cowboy hat.* • *I don't much like cowboy films/movies.* • *We gave the twins matching cowboy and cowgirl outfits* (= clothes) *for their birthday.* • PIC **Shoes**

cow·boy DISHONEST PERSON /ˈkaʊ·bɔɪ/ *n* [C] *infml* someone who is not honest, careful or skilful in their trade or business, or someone who ignores rules that most people obey and is therefore not considered to be responsible • *Those builders are* **a bunch of** *cowboys – they made a terrible job of our renovations.* • *My first job was with a firm of cowboy solicitors.*

cow·catch·er /£ˈkaʊˌkætʃ·əʳ, $-ɚ/ *n* [C] *Am* a strong metal frame fixed to the front of a train which pushes animals and objects off the railway track as the train moves forward

cower /£ˈkaʊ·əʳ, $ˈkaʊ·ɚ/ *v* [I] to bend down and forward in fear, often while moving backwards • *Do stop cowering! I'm not going to hit you.* • *The dog seemed to realize she'd done something wrong as she cowered* **(down)** *in the corner.*

cow·herd /£ˈkaʊ·hɜːd, $-hɜːrd/ *n* [C] a person employed to take care of cattle

cow·hide /ˈkaʊ·haɪd/ *n* [C; U] (leather made from) the skin of a cow • *a cowhide waistcoat*

cowl /kaʊl/ *n* [C] a large loose covering for the head and sometimes shoulders, but not the face, which is worn esp. by MONKS • A cowl is also a metal cover on the top of a CHIMNEY which helps smoke go up it and prevents wind blowing down it.

cowl·ing /ˈkaʊ·lɪŋ/ *n* [C] • A cowling is a removable metal cover for an aircraft engine which has a smooth shape to help the aircraft move more easily through the air.

cow·lick /ˈkaʊ·lɪk/ *n* [C] a small growth of hair sticking out just above the FOREHEAD

cow·man /ˈkaʊ·mən, -mæn/ *n* [C] *pl* **-men** *(Br)* a male COWHERD, *(Am)* a man who owns cattle, or *(Aus)* a man who owns or manages a large cattle farm

co–work·er /£ˌkəʊˈwɜː·kəʳ, $ˌkoʊˈwɜːr·kɚ/ *n* [C] a person working with another worker, esp. as a partner or helper

cow·pat /'kaʊ·pæt/ *n* [C] a round flat mass of fresh or hardened excrement from a cow

cow·pox /£'kaʊ·pɒks, $-pɑːks/ *n* [U] a viral disease in cattle that results in the formation on the skin of small swellings containing liquid • *The cowpox virus was used in the past to vaccinate humans against smallpox.*

cow·rie, **cow·ry** /£'kaʊ·ri, $'kaʊr·i/ *n* [C] a small sea animal with a soft body, no bone in its back, and a smooth shiny brightly-coloured shell, or the shell of such an animal used in the past as money in parts of Africa and S Asia

co-write *obj* /£'kəʊ·raɪt, $'koʊ-, -'-/ *v* [T] *past simple* **co-wrote** /£'kəʊ·rəʊt, $'koʊ·roʊt/, *past part* **co-written** /£'kəʊ·rɪ·tᵊn, $'koʊ·rɪ·t̬ᵊn/ to write (esp. a popular song or tune, or something for television or the cinema) with someone else • *Lennon and McCartney co-wrote most of the Beatles' songs.* • *The David Bowie song 'Fame' was co-written* **by/with** *John Lennon.*

co-writ·er /£'kəʊˌraɪ·təʳ, $'koʊˌraɪ·t̬ɚ/ *n* [C] • *She is looking for a new co-writer following the sudden death of the partner she had worked with for ten years.*

cow·shed /'kaʊ·ʃed/ *n* [C] a building where cows are milked or where they are kept during winter or bad weather

cow·slip /'kaʊ·slɪp/ *n* [C] a small European plant similar to a PRIMROSE but with smaller yellow flowers

cox /£kɒks, $kɑːks/, *fml* **cox·swain** /£'kɒk·sᵊn, -sweɪn, $'kɑːk-/ *n* [C] the person who sits at the back of a ROWING boat and controls which direction it moves in • *Coxes are often small, light people.* • PIC› **Water sports**

cox *(obj)* /£kɒks, $kɑːks/ *v* • *She coxed* **for** *her college for three seasons.* [I] • *He coxed the winning eight.* [T]

cox·comb, **cocks·comb** /£'kɒks·kəʊm, $'kɑːks·koʊm/ *n* [C] *old use* a man who is too proud of his appearance

coy SECRETIVE /kɔɪ/ *adj* **-er, -est** intentionally secretive • *He called for a change of leadership but remained coy* **about** *his own intentions.* • *The shop assistants were coy* **about** *when the prices would go up.*

coy·ly /'kɔɪ·li/ *adv* • *He refused to comment, saying coyly that he had no first-hand information about the incident and preferred not to speculate.*

coy MODEST /kɔɪ/ *adj* **-er, -est** (esp. of women) being or pretending to be shy, modest, childish or lacking in confidence • *The seventeen-year-old replied in a coy, babyish voice which was quite at odds with her appearance.*

coy·ly /'kɔɪ·li/ *adv* • *She smiled coyly.*

coy·ness /'kɔɪ·nəs/ *n* [U] • *She answered without a hint of coyness in her manner.*

co·yo·te /£kaɪ'əʊ·ti, $-'oʊ·t̬i/ *n* [C] a small dog-like wild animal which lives in N America

coy·pu /'kɔɪ·puː/ *n* [C] *pl* **coypus** or **coypu** an animal that lives by water and is valuable for its fur

co·zi·ly /£'kəʊ·zɪ·li, $'koʊ-/ *adv Am for* **cosily**, see at COSY

co·zy /£'kəʊ·zi, $'koʊ-/ *adj, n* [C] *Am for* COSY

coz·zie /£'kɒz·i, $'kɑː·zi/ *n* [C] *Br and Aus infml for* a **swimming costume**, see at SWIM MOVE IN WATER

CPU /ˌsiː·piː'juː/ *n* [C] *specialized abbreviation for* central processing unit (= the electronic system that performs the basic operations of a computer)

crab /kræb/ *n* a sea animal that has five pairs of legs and a round flat body covered by a shell, or its flesh eaten as food • *We walked along the beach collecting small crabs in a bucket.* [C] • *All the shops on the seafront had crab for sale.* [U] • *This crab* **meat/salad** *is delicious!* • **Dressed** crab is crab prepared for eating: • The Crab can also mean the star sign CANCER: *Sally and Cindy were both born* **under** *the Crab.* • PIC› **Crustaceans**

crab·wise /'kræb·waɪz/ *adv* • If you move crabwise you move sideways or in a careful and indirect manner.

crab (ap·ple) /kræb/ *n* [C] (the small sour fruit of) a small tree which has attractive flowers • *We planted two eating apples and two crabs/crab apples.* • *They bought some homemade crab apple jam.*

crabs /kræbz/, **crab lice** *pl n* a large number of small insects that live in the hair around the sex organs • *She was horrified to discover she* **had** *crabs.*

crabbed /kræbd, 'kræb·ɪd/ *adj dated* (of writing) written too closely together and therefore difficult to read

crab·by (**-ier, -iest**) /'kræb·i/, *dated* **crabbed** *adj infml* bad-tempered and complaining • *You're very crabby today – what's upset you?*

crab·bi·ly /'kræb·ɪ·li/ *adv infml*

crab·bi·ness /'kræb·ɪ·nəs/ *n* [U] *infml*

crab /kræb/ *v* [I] **-bb-** *infml* • *He can always find something to crab* (= to be bad-tempered and complain) **about**.

crab·grass /£'kræb·grɑːs, $-græs/ *n* [U] *Am* a type of WEED (= wild plant which grows in a place where it is not wanted and prevents cultivated plants from growing freely) • *The crabgrass has started to take over our front lawn!*

crack *(obj)* BREAK /kræk/ *v* to break, usually without separating into pieces • *The stone hit the window and cracked the glass.* [T] • *The window cracked when the stone hit it.* [I] • *They gave me tea in a cracked cup.* • *(fig. infml) Their relationship began to crack* **(up)** (= fail) *under the strain of looking after a handicapped child.* [I] • *(fig. infml) Stress and overwork are causing teachers to crack* **(up)** (= become unable to work effectively). [I] • *(fig. infml) I* **cracked up**/*It* **cracked** *me* **up** (= I was very amused) *when he said where he'd been.* See also **crack up** at CRACK GOOD.

crack /kræk/ *n* [C] • *Cracks* (= Long narrow spaces) *had appeared in the dry ground.* • *We peered through the crack in the floorboards.* • *(fig.) Cracks* (= Faults) *began to show in his facade of self- confidence.* • *She opened the door* **just a crack** (= a small distance) *to listen to the conversation.* • The **crack of dawn** is very early in the morning, esp. the time at which the sun first appears: *We'll have to leave* **at** *the crack of dawn.*

crack *(obj)* OPEN /kræk/ *v* to break (something) open, esp. in order to reach or use what is inside • *He cracked three* **eggs** *into a bowl and mixed them together.* [T] • *Dad cracked* **(open)** *the* **nuts** *and we ate them.* [M] • *(infml) They cracked* **(open)** *the* **safe** *and stole important papers.* [M] • *(infml) Come round and we'll crack* **(open)** (= open and drink) *a* **bottle** *together.* [T] • *(fig.) We soon cracked* (= understood) *the* **code** *and read the secret message.* [T] • *(fig.) I've been trying to solve this problem all week but I still haven't cracked it* (= been able to). [T] • *(fig.) The spy cracked* (= lost self-control) *during interrogation and told us what we wanted to know.* [I]

crack *(obj)* SOUND /kræk/ *v* to (cause to) do something with a sudden sharp noise • *The wire swung back and cracked* **against** *the building.* [I] • *Someone cracked him on the back of the head with a stick.* [T] • *The whip cracked* **above/over** *the horses' heads.* [I] • *He's always cracking his* **knuckles** (= pulling the joints of his fingers to make a noise). [T] • *(fig.) Her voice cracked* **with** *emotion* (= started to sound upset) *as she told the story.* [I] • If someone **cracks the whip** they act with authority, esp. to make someone else behave better or work hard: *She decided to crack the whip and shouted, "Will you two be quiet and get on with what you are supposed to be doing?"* • To **get cracking** is to start doing something quickly: *I'd better get cracking* **on** *writing these letters before I go home.* ○ *Get cracking* (= Hurry), *or we'll miss the train.*

crack /kræk/ *n* [C] • *the crack of a rifle/whip/breaking branch*

crack DRUG /kræk/ *n* [U] *slang* a pure and powerful form of the drug COCAINE • *Several kilos of crack were recovered in the raid by officers from the drugs squad.* • *It's a run-down area where a lot of crack addicts hang out.*

crack *obj* JOKE /kræk/ *v* [T] to make (a joke or clever remark) • *He's always cracking* **jokes**. • *That's the first* **joke** *I've ever heard her crack.*

crack /kræk/ *n* [C] • A crack is a WISECRACK.

crack GOOD /kræk/ *adj* [before n; not gradable] excellent, of highest quality • *a crack regiment* • *crack troops*

crack up *obj*, **crack** *obj* **up** *v adv* [M] *infml* • *This new washing powder is* **not all** *it's* **cracked up to be** (= not as good as it is claimed to be). • *They're always* **cracking** *it* **up to be** (= claiming it is) *the best, but I'm not so sure.* • See also **crack up** at CRACK BREAK.

crack·ing /'kræk·ɪŋ/ *adj infml* • *He scored with a cracking shot into the back of the goal.* • *The marathon began at a cracking* (= very fast) *pace.*

crack ATTEMPT /kræk/ *n* [C] *infml* an attempt; a try • *It's not something I've done before, but I'll* **have** *a crack* **at** *it/* **give** *it a crack.* • *It was her first crack at beating the record.*

crack down *v adv* [I] to take strong action to stop something happening • *The library is cracking down* **on** *people who keep their books too long by increasing the fines.* • *Police have been cracking down* **on** *illegal parking – lots of cars have been wheel-clamped.*

crack·down /'kræk·daʊn/ *n* [C] • *There has been a series of government crackdowns* **on** *safety provisions at football stadiums.*

crack·er [FOOD] /£'kræk·əʳ, $-ɚ/ *n* [C] a dry savoury biscuit, esp. one eaten with cheese • [PIC⟩] **Bread and cakes**

crack·er [DEVICE] /£'kræk·əʳ, $-ɚ/, *Aus usually* **bon·bon** *n* [C] a paper tube with small toys, sweets, etc. inside which is covered with bright paper and which makes a short sharp sound when both ends are pulled • *There was a cracker beside every place at the table.* • *The children love* **pulling** *crackers at birthday parties.* • *(Br) I got a ring and a joke in my* **Christmas** *cracker.*

crack·er [GOOD THING] /£'kræk·əʳ, $-ɚ/ *n* [C] *infml approving* a person or thing that is very good or has a special exciting quality • *She's written five books, every one a cracker.* • *The horse ran a cracker* **of** *a race.* • *She's a real cracker.*

crack·ers /£'kræk·əz, $-ɚz/, **cracked** /krækt/ *adj* [after v] *infml* foolish, stupid or slightly mentally ill • *I think she's crackers to take such a boring job.*

crack·le *(obj)* /'kræk·l̩/ *v* to (cause to) make a set of short sharp sounds • *The radio/telephone crackled just then and I missed what was said.* [I] • *He crackled the newspaper, folding it carelessly.* [T]

crack·le /'kræk·l̩/ *n* [C] • *I love the crackle of logs burning in a fireplace.*

crack·ling /'kræk·lɪŋ/ *n* [U] • *There's a lot of crackling on the radio/telephone.* • *We could hear the crackling of a fire.*

crack·ly /'kræk·li/ *adj* • *I turned on the radio but all I could hear was a crackly voice speaking a language I did not understand.*

crack·ling /'kræk·lɪŋ/ *n* [U] the hard skin of cooked meat, esp. PORK (= meat from a pig)

crack·pot /£'kræk·pɒt, $-pɑːt/ *n* [C], *adj infml* (a person who is) foolish or stupid • *He may be a crackpot/have crackpot ideas, but he's persuasive and dangerous.*

cra·dle [BED] /'kreɪ·dl̩/ *n* [C] a small bed for a baby, esp. one with raised sides which can be pushed with a gentle sideways or backwards and forwards movement • *The nurse* **rocked** *the cradle.* • *(slightly literary)* **The cradle of** something means the place or society where it began: *Fossil records indicate that Africa was the cradle of early human evolution.* • The expression **(the) cradle to (the) grave** means all of a person's life: *She lived in the same village* **from** *the cradle to the grave.* • *(humorous)* A **cradle snatcher** is a person whose sexual partner is much younger than they are. • *(saying)* 'The hand that rocks the cradle rules the world' means that women have a strong influence on their children.

cra·dle [EQUIPMENT] /'kreɪ·dl̩/ *n* [C] a frame which supports a ship, aircraft, machine, etc. while it is being built, repaired or transported • *(Br)* A cradle (*Am* **scaffold**) is also a frame which hangs on the side of a building, ship, etc. for people to work from.

cra·dle *obj* [SUPPORT] /'kreɪ·dl̩/ *v* [T] to hold gently, esp. by supporting with the arms • *Mothers tend to cradle babies on their left arms.*

craft [SKILL] /£krɑːft, $kræft/ *n* (a job or activity needing) skill and experience, esp. in relation to making objects • *the craft of furniture making/boat building/glass blowing* [U] • *political/literary craft* [U] • *the craft of management* [U] • *rural/ancient/traditional crafts* [C] • *craft workers* (= skilled workers) • *You can always tell by the quality of a hand-made piece of furniture if it was made by someone who* **knew** (= was good at) *their craft.* [C] • A **craft fair** is an event where people sell decorative objects that they have made by hand. • A **craft shop** is a shop that sells decorative objects that have been made by hand. • A **craft union** is an organization for workers with particular skills. • See also HANDICRAFT; **statecraft** at STATE [COUNTRY]; **witchcraft** at WITCH; WOODCRAFT. • (D) (N)

craft *obj* /£krɑːft, $kræft/ *v* [T usually passive] • *a beautifully crafted silver brooch* • *a cleverly crafted poem*

crafts·man (*pl* **-men**), **crafts·wo·man** (*pl* **-women**) /£'krɑːfts·mən, $'kræfts-, -,wʊm·ən/ *n* [C] • A craftsman is a person who is skilled in a particular craft: *The box was made by one of our finest craftsmen.*

crafts·man·ship /£'krɑːfts·mən·ʃɪp, $'kræfts-/ *n* [U] • *The jewellery showed exquisite craftsmanship* (= skill).

craft [VEHICLE] /£krɑːft, $kræft/ *n* [C] *pl* **craft** a vehicle for travelling on water or through the air • *naval/civilian/patrol/rescue craft* • *Eighteen craft* (= boats) *set out in the race.* • *Small craft* (= boats) *took shelter along the east coast during the storm.* • *The sleek, delta-winged craft* (= aircraft) *flew from Los Angeles to Washington in one hour and four minutes.* • See also AIRCRAFT; HOVERCRAFT; SPACECRAFT. • (D) (N)

craft·y /£'krɑːf·ti, $'kræf·ţi/ *adj* **-ier, -iest** clever, esp. in a dishonest or secretive way • *I've had a crafty idea for getting round the regulations.* • *They were crafty in the way they got us to agree by showing how much money we might lose by saying no.*

craft·i·ly /£'krɑːf·tɪ·li, $'kræf·ţɪ-/ *adv*

craft·i·ness /£'krɑːf·tɪ·nəs, $'kræf·ţɪ-/ *n* [U]

crag /kræg/ *n* [C] a high rough mass of rock which sticks out from the land around it

crag·gy /'kræg·i/ *adj* **-ier, -iest** • *The footpath climbed towards the craggy skyline.* • *(fig.) His craggy* (= attractively strong) *features/profile/face make you feel he's lived a long, interesting life.*

cram *obj* [PUSH] /kræm/ *v* [T always + adv/prep] **-mm-** *infml* to force (a lot of things) into a small space • *She crammed so many clothes* **into** *the suitcase it wouldn't close.* • *Six children were crammed* **into** *the back of the car.* • *I managed to cram three countries* **into** *a week's business trip.* • If you cram **down** food, you eat a lot or eat quickly: *She crammed a sandwich down while she wrote a brief letter.* [M]

crammed /kræmd/ *adj* • *a crammed train/room* • *The hall was crammed* **with**/*crammed* **full of** *people trying book tickets.*

cram [LEARN] /kræm/ *v* [I] **-mm-** to try to learn a lot very quickly before an exam • *She's cramming* **for** *her history exam.*

cram·mer /£'kræm·əʳ, $-ɚ/ *n* [C] *dated infml* • A crammer is a school or a book which helps you to learn quickly.

cramp [PAIN] /kræmp/ *n* a sudden severely painful tightening in a muscle which limits movement, often as a result of extreme exercise • *Several runners needed treatment for sprains, (Br and Aus) cramp/(esp. Am) cramps and exhaustion.* [U/C] • *I've got (Br and Aus) cramp/(esp. Am) a cramp in my foot.* [U/C] • *After swimming for a while he got* **stomach** *cramps.* [C]

cramp *obj* [LIMIT] /kræmp/ *v* [T] to limit (someone), esp. to prevent them from enjoying a full life • *Worry and lack of money cramp the lives of the unemployed.* • *(humorous infml)* To **cramp** someone's **style** means to limit what someone is able to do, esp. what they do for pleasure: *Having his leg in plaster rather cramped his style on the dance floor.*

cramped /kræmpt/ *adj* • *a cramped room/house* • *cramped surroundings/accommodation* • *We have six desks in this room so we're rather cramped* **(for** *space).* • *Meeting you before the end of the month will be difficult, because I have a very cramped schedule until then.*

cramp·on /£'kræm·pɒn, $-pɑːn/ *n* [C] a metal frame with sharp points under and around it which is fixed to the bottom of a boot to make walking on ice or snow easier • *The climbers needed crampons, picks and ropes to make their way up the snow-covered face of the mountain.*

cran·ber·ry /£'kræm·bᵊr·i, $-ber-/ *n* [C] a small red fruit with a sour taste, often cooked and eaten cold with meat, esp. TURKEY, or crushed and mixed with sugar and water to make a drink • *cranberry sauce* • [PIC⟩] **Berries**

crane [MACHINE] /kreɪn/ *n* a tall metal structure with a long movable part to which is fixed a long wire that can be used for lifting and moving heavy objects • *The crane* **lifted** *the container off the ship and swung it onto the back of the lorry.* [C] • *Eventually, the train was put back onto the track by crane.* [U] • [PIC⟩] **Building and construction** (NL)

crane [BIRD] /kreɪn/ *n* [C] a tall bird with long thin legs and a long neck • (NL)

crane *(obj)* [STRETCH] /kreɪn/ *v* to stretch in order to look at something • *She craned* **over** *the heads of the crowd to see what was happening.* [I always + adv/prep] • *He craned* **forward** *to see the procession.* [I always + adv/prep] • *Mike was craning his* **neck** *to get the first glimpse of the car.* [T] • (NL)

crane fly, *infml* **dad·dy long·legs** *n* [C] a flying insect with a narrow body and very long legs

cra·ni·um /'kreɪ·ni·əm/ *n* [C] *pl* **craniums** or **crania** /'kreɪ·ni·ə/ *medical* (in animals and humans) the hard bone case which gives the head its structure and protects the brain; SKULL

cra·ni·al /'kreɪ·ni·əl/ *adj* [not gradable]

crank [STRANGE PERSON] /kræŋk/ *n* [C] *infml* a person who has strange or unusual ideas and beliefs • *He was called a crank at first, the natural fate of all true visionaries.* • A *crank caller is someone who makes unpleasant telephone calls to people whom they do not know.* • (J)

crank·y /ˈkræŋ·ki/ *adj* **-ier, -iest** *infml* • *She's a member of a group that promotes cranky ideas about food and exercise.*

crank UNPLEASANT PERSON /kræŋk/ *n* [C] *Am infml* a bad-tempered person • *I know you don't like it here, but do you have to be such a crank about it?* • (J)

crank·y /ˈkræŋ·ki/ *adj* **-ier, -iest** *Am and Aus infml* • *He'd been up late the night before and was very cranky in the morning.*

crank EQUIPMENT /kræŋk/ *n* [C] a device which allows movement to go between parts of a machine or which changes backward and forward movement into circular movement • *a crank handle* • (J)

crank out *obj*, **crank** *obj* **out** /kræŋk/ *v adv* [M] *infml* to produce (something), esp. in large amounts or like a machine • *The inspectors regularly crank out critical reports, but the system is never improved.*

crank up *obj*, **crank** *obj* **up** /kræŋk/ *v adv* [M] *infml* to increase, develop or improve (something) • *They cranked up the pressure on the company with ads in the press.* • *He cranked* **the volume** *up on the car radio so that we couldn't talk.*

crank·shaft /£ˈkræŋk·ʃɑːft, $-ʃæft/ *n* [C] a rod, esp. one in an engine, having one or more CRANKS that make the rod move around a fixed line along its centre • *a crankshaft bearing*

cran·ny /ˈkræn·i/ *n* [C] a small narrow opening in something solid • *There were small plants growing in every* **nook and** *cranny of the wall.*

crap EXCREMENT /kræp/ *n* [C usually sing] *slightly taboo slang* an act of excreting • *It's no good, I'll have to stop and* **have**/*(Am also)* **take** *a crap*

crap /kræp/ *v* [I] **-pp-** *slightly taboo slang* • *The dog crapped right in the middle of our front lawn.*

crap·per /£ˈkræp·əʳ, $-ɚ/ *n* [C] *slightly taboo slang* • A crapper is a toilet.

crap NO GOOD /kræp/ *n* [U], *adj slightly taboo slang* (something which is) worthless, useless, nonsense or of bad quality • *I can't believe she's trying to pass off this crap as art!* • *That film was awful – I've never seen such* **a load of** *crap!* • *He does crap work.* • *"Books are a load of crap"* (Philip Larkin in the poem *A Study of Reading Habits*, 1960)

crap·py /ˈkræp·i/ *adj slightly taboo slang*

crape /kreɪp/ *n* [U] CREPE

craps /kræps/, **crap** *n* [U] *Am and Aus* a game played with DICE for money

crash *(obj)* MAKE A NOISE /kræʃ/ *v* to (move and) make a sudden loud noise • *Suddenly, cymbals crashed and the spotlight picked out a strangely dressed performer.* [I] • *The dog crashed/***came** *crashing through the bushes.* [I] • *Without warning, the door crashed open.* [I] • *We could hear waves crashing on/against the shore.* [I] • *The driver crashed the gears* (= changed them badly and noisily). [T]

crash /kræʃ/ *n* [C] • *I was woken in the night by a loud crash.* • *There was a crash of cymbals and a roll of drums.* • *The vase landed on the floor with a crash.*

crash·ing /ˈkræʃ·ɪŋ/ *n* [U] • *I could hear crashing* (= loud noises) *in the next room.*

crash *(obj)* ACCIDENT /kræʃ/ *v* to have an accident, esp. one which damages a vehicle • *We skidded on the ice and crashed (***into** *another car).* [I] • *The plane crashed* **into** *a mountainside.* [I] • *Her brother borrowed her motorbike and crashed it.* [T] • *He's the third skier to crash in this race.* [I]

crash /kræʃ/ *n* [C] • *She* **had** *a crash in her car when she was driving to the shops.* • *(Br and Aus)* A **crash barrier** is a strong fence which separates the two sides of a large road or which is built at a dangerous place at the edge of a road, to help prevent accidents. • A **crash helmet** is a hat made from stiff strong material which protects the head of esp. a motorcyclist in an accident. • A **crash-landing** is a situation when an emergency forces an aircraft to land suddenly, sometimes resulting in serious damage or injuries. • PIC> **Hats, Motorway**

crash FAIL /kræʃ/ *v* [I] (esp. of a business) to suddenly fail or become unsuccessful, or (esp. of a computer) to suddenly stop operating • *When the travel company crashed thousands of tourists were stranded.* • *After our computer network crashed for the third time that day, we all went home.*

crash /kræʃ/ *n* [C] • *They lost a lot of money in the Stock Market crash.* • *A computer crash can be very costly, especially if it happens toward the end of processing a large amount of data.*

crash QUICK /kræʃ/ *adj* [before n; not gradable] *infml* quick and complete, or short and difficult • *The company undertook a crash program of machine replacement.* • A **crash course** is a short period of instruction in which a lot is learned: *I did/took a week's crash course* **in** *parachuting before jumping for charity.* • A **crash diet** is a way of losing body weight quickly by eating very little: *The jockey had to go on a crash diet before the race.*

crash SLEEP /kræʃ/ *v* [I] *infml* to sleep, esp. after drinking alcohol • *They crashed* **(out)** *on my floor after the party.*

crash *obj* ENTER WITHOUT PERMISSION /kræʃ/ *v* [T] *infml* to go to (a party or other event) without an invitation • *We tried to crash the party, but the bouncers wouldn't let us in.* • See also GATECRASH.

crash·ing /ˈkræʃ·ɪŋ/ *adj* [before n] *infml dated* (of something bad) very great • *I love his books, but in person he's a crashing* **bore**.

crass /kræs/ *adj* **-er, -est** without consideration for how other people might feel; stupid • *a crass remark* • *crass behaviour/ignorance* • *a crass error of judgment* • *He made crass comments about her worn-out clothes even though he knows she can't afford to buy any more.*

crass·ly /ˈkræs·li/ *adv*

crass·ness /ˈkræs·nəs/ *n* [U]

crate /kreɪt/ *n* [C] a frame like an open box, esp. one divided into parts to hold bottles, or a wooden box • *a milk crate* • *a crate of empty bottles* • *a packing crate* • PIC> **Containers**

crate *obj* /kreɪt/ *v* [T]

cra·ter /£ˈkreɪ·təʳ, $-t̬ɚ/ *n* [C] (a hole like) the round hole at the top of a VOLCANO • *the huge crater of Vesuvius* • *a bomb crater* • *With a good telescope you can see craters on the moon's surface.*

crat·ered /£ˈkreɪ·təd, $-t̬ɚd/ *adj* • *a cratered surface*

cra·vat /krəˈvæt/ *n* [C] a wide straight piece of material worn loosely tied in the open neck of a shirt • PIC> **Clothes** (CS) (PL) (RUS)

cra·ven /ˈkreɪ·vᵊn/ *adj fml* extremely cowardly

crav·ing /ˈkreɪ·vɪŋ/ *n* [C] a strong or uncontrollable desire • *Sometimes she has a craving* **for** *chocolate.*

crave *obj* /kreɪv/ *v* [T] • *Many young children crave* **attention.** • (S)

crawl MOVE /£krɔːl, $krɑːl/ *v* [I] to move slowly or with difficulty, esp. (of a person) with the body stretched out along the ground or on hands and knees • *We watched a caterpillar crawl up the leg of a chair.* • *The child crawled* **across** *the floor.* • *The lorry crawled noisily up the hill.*

crawl /£krɔːl, $krɑːl/ *n* [U] • *The queue of traffic moved forward* **at a** *crawl.*

crawl·er /£ˈkrɔː·ləʳ, $ˈkrɑː·lɚ/ *n* [C] • A crawler is a baby who doesn't yet walk: *Alexander is walking, but his little sister is still a crawler.*

crawl TRY TO PLEASE /£krɔːl, $krɑːl/ *v* [I] *infml disapproving* to try hard to please in order to get an advantage • *He crawled* **(up) to** *the group leader because he wanted a promotion.* • *I don't like people who crawl.*

crawl·er /£ˈkrɔː·ləʳ, $ˈkrɑː·lɚ/ *n* [C] *infml disapproving* • *She has a reputation in the firm for being a real crawler.*

crawl FILL /£krɔːl, $krɑːl/ *v* [usually be crawling] *infml* to be covered or full • *The kitchen floor was crawling* **with** *cockroaches.* • *The airport was crawling* **with** *photographers waiting for the rock star.* • *Cambridge crawls* **with** *tourists in the summer.*

crawl SWIMMING /£krɔːl, $krɑːl/ *n* [U] a way of swimming fast by moving the legs as if walking and raising first one arm then the other out of the water to move yourself forward

cray·fish (*pl* **crayfish** or **crayfishes**) /ˈkreɪ·fɪʃ/, *Am also* **craw·fish** /£ˈkrɔː·fɪʃ, $ˈkrɑː-/ *n* [C/U] a small animal with a hard covering on its body and legs which lives in rivers and streams and is similar to a LOBSTER, or its flesh eaten as food

cray·on /£ˈkreɪ·ɒn, $-ɑːn/ *n* [C] a small stick of coloured wax used for drawing or writing • *wax crayons* • *children's crayons* • PIC> **Writing instruments**

cray·on *(obj)* /£ˈkreɪ·ɒn, $-ɑːn/ *v* • *When I left her she was busy crayoning.* [I] • *The picture had been crayoned by a child.* [T]

craze /kreɪz/ *n* [C usually sing] an activity, object or idea that is very popular, usually for a short time • *Cycling shorts were* **the latest** *craze/***(all)** *the craze that year.* • *The* *craze* **for** *health foods has become big business.* • *She'll soon forget about hitch-hiking to China – it's just a craze.*

crazed /kreɪzd/ *adj* behaving strangely esp. because of strong emotions • *a crazed expression* • *When he heard what had happened he became crazed* **with** *anger/jealousy/pain.*

cra·zy /ˈkreɪ·zi/ *adj* **-ier, -iest** foolish; stupid; interested in or involved with something in an extreme way • *You're crazy* **to** *agree to buy it without seeing it.* [+ *to* infinitive] • *She's the craziest person I've ever met but I like her a lot.* • *The constant whine of the machine nearly* **drove** (= made) *me crazy.* • *I think she'll* **go** *crazy* (= become mentally ill) *if she doesn't have a holiday soon.* • *They're crazy* **about** (= very interested in) *old motorbikes.* • *(infml)* If you do something **like crazy** you do it with a lot of energy: *They were working like crazy to get enough money to go on holiday.* • *(Br and Aus)* **Crazy paving** is a hard surface for paths made with broken pieces of stone or concrete.

cra·zy /ˈkreɪ·zi/ *n* [C] *Am slang* • A crazy is a person who acts in a foolish or stupid way, esp. one who is mentally ill: *Paul's not sure he'll adjust to New York with its beggars and crack-heads and street crazies howling at passers-by.*

cra·zi·ly /ˈkreɪ·zɪ·li/ *adv*

cra·zi·ness /ˈkreɪ·zɪ·nəs/ *n* [U]

creak /kriːk/ *v* [I] to make a noise by moving two things against each other or by standing on something which is not fixed • *The door creaked open.* • *I heard a floorboard creak in the next room.* • *His knees creaked as he stood up.* • *(fig.) It took a long time for the authorities to creak* (= move slowly) *into action.*

creak /kriːk/ *n* [C]

creak·y /ˈkriː·ki/ *adj* **-ier, -iest** • *a creaky hinge/chair/bed* • Also, something which is creaky is not well made or not safe: *a creaky plot/old film* ○ *creaky financial arrangements*

creak·i·ly /ˈkriː·kɪ·li/ *adv*

creak·i·ness /ˈkriː·kɪ·nəs/ *n* [U]

cream /kriːm/ *n* the thick yellowish-white liquid that forms on the top of milk • *strawberries/peaches and cream* [U] • *Do you like cream in your coffee?* [U] • Cream can also mean the colour of cream: *a cream dress.* • A cream is a type of sweet which is soft inside: *chocolate/peppermint creams* [C] • Cream can also mean a smooth thick liquid, esp. one used in make-up or sometimes in cooking: *(a) face/hand/antiseptic cream* [C/U] ○ *salad cream* • A cream **cake** is one which contains cream that has been made stiff by mixing it. • A cream **soup** is one in which all the contents are made into a smooth thick liquid: *cream of tomato/chicken/celery soup* • The phrase **the cream of** means the best of: *The cream of this year's graduates have gone abroad for jobs.* • **Cream cheese** is soft cheese which can be spread rather than cut. • *(Br)* A **cream cracker** is a hard biscuit which is not sweet and is often eaten with cheese. • **Cream of tartar** is a powder made from **tartaric acid** used in making some types of bread. • *(Am)* **Cream soda** is a fizzy drink flavoured with VANILLA. • *(esp. Br)* A **cream tea** is a light meal of SCONES (= a type of bread) with JAM (= a sweet soft substance made by cooking fruit with sugar) and cream.

cream *obj* /kriːm/ *v* [T] • If you cream food you make it into a smooth thick liquid: *Cream the butter and sugar together.* ○ *The main course was served with creamed potatoes, cauliflower and peas.*

cream·y /ˈkriː·mi/ *adj* **-ier, -iest** • *Not everybody likes creamy food.* • *I chose a paint that was more creamy* (= the colour of cream) *than white.*

cream·i·ness /ˈkriː·mɪ·nəs/ *n* [U]

cream off *v adv* [M] to remove (the best part) • *Their policy would be to cream off the brightest children and put them in separate schools.*

cream·er /£ˈkriː·məʳ, $-mɚ/ *n* a powder which is added to hot drinks instead of milk or cream • *I've run out of milk – would you like some creamer instead?* [U] • *(Am and Aus)* A creamer is also a small container for serving cream in. [C]

crease /kriːs/ *n, v* (to make) a mark on paper or material by folding carefully or pressing carelessly • *He ironed a crease down the front of each trouser leg.* [C] • *Some kinds of hat, like panama hats and stetsons, have a crease* (= a hollow), *along their tops.* [C] • *The corner of the page was creased to mark the place.* [T] • *It's a nice dress but it creases very easily.* [I] • *(specialized)* In cricket, the crease is a white line marked on the ground to show the place where a particular activity happens: *The batsman walked out to the crease.* ○ *The bowler ran up to the crease.* • PIC **Mark**

crease *(obj)* **up** /kriːs/ *v adv Br infml* to (cause to) laugh a lot • *The look on his face just creased me up.* [T] • *He creased up at the sight of their clothes.* [I]

cre·ate *obj* MAKE /kriˈeɪt/ *v* [T] to produce or make (esp. something new) • *She cleverly created a job for herself when the company was reorganized.* • *He managed to create a wonderful meal* **from** *a few ingredients.* • *The Bible says that God created the world.* • *Already, the newly created organization is experiencing problems.* • *The visitors created confusion/trouble/a stir/a fuss/difficulties.* • *(fml) She was created* (= given the honour/job of) *Life President of the society.* [+ obj + n] • *It's important to create a good* **impression** *when you meet a client.* • *If we agreed to this request it would create* **a precedent** (= become an example which might be copied.)

creation /kriˈeɪ·ʃᵊn/ *n* • *Huge amounts of money have gone into the creation* **of** *a new exam system.* [U] • *So many people nowadays are obsessed with the creation of wealth.* [U] • *They demanded a* **job**-*creation scheme for areas of high unemployment.* • *These poems are the creations of an unhappy individual.* [C] • *After a serious operation she more fully appreciated the wonders of creation* (= the world, esp. the thing that live in it). [U] • In the Bible **the Creation** is the making of the world by God. [U] • A creation can be an unusual or noticeable piece of clothing and **the latest** creations are clothes in the most recent fashion: *She was wearing a long white creation.* [C] ○ *The magazine was full of photos of the latest Paris creations.* [C]

cre·a·tion·ist /kriˈeɪ·ʃᵊn·ɪst/ *n* [C] • A creationist is a person who believes that the world was made by God exactly as described in the Bible.

cre·at·or /£kriˈeɪ·təʳ, $-t̬ɚ/ *n* [C] • *He's the creator* **of** *a successful cartoon series.* • *Who was the creator* **of** *the miniskirt?* • God is sometimes called the Creator. • (DK)

cre·ate BE ANGRY /kriˈeɪt/ *v* [I] *Br and Aus infml* to be angry • *He really created when he heard where we had been.*

cre·at·ive /£kriˈeɪ·tɪv, $-t̬ɪv/ *adj* producing or using original and unusual ideas • *a creative person/artist/designer/programmer* • *creative talents/powers/abilities* • *a creative solution* • *creative thinking* • *(disapproving)* **Creative accounting** is finding ways of explaining how money has been spent which keep hidden what has really happened to it.

cre·at·ive·ly /£kriˈeɪ·tɪv·li, $-t̬ɪv-/ *adv*

cre·at·i·vi·ty /£ˌkriː·eɪˈtɪv·ɪ·ti, $-ˈt̬ɪv·ə·t̬i/, **cre·at·ive·ness** /£kriˈeɪ·tɪv·nəs, $-t̬ɪv-/ *n* [U] • *Too many rules might deaden creativity.* • *Creativity, ingenuity and flair are the songwriter's real talents.*

creature /£ˈkriː·tʃəʳ, $-tʃɚ/ *n* [C] any large or small living thing which can move independently; an animal • *We could see amazing creatures through the glass in the bottom of the boat.* • *Don't all* **living** *creatures have certain rights?* • Creature is often used to refer to a life form that is unusual, unknown or imaginary: *The unicorn is a mythical creature with a single horn.* ○ *The film was about creatures from outer space.* • Creature can also mean person when an opinion is being expressed about them: *John is a strange/weak/pathetic creature.* • *(dated)* Also a creature can mean a woman. Many people find the word offensive when used in this way: *Through the door came a lovely creature with blonde hair.* • *(fml)* If a person is the creature **of** another person or group, they do everything that is asked without question: *He had become the creature of the secret police.* • *My children are creatures* **of habit** (= always want to do the same things in the same way). • *He was usually very concerned about his* **creature comforts** (= food, clothes and all the things that make life pleasant). • *"All creatures great and small"* (from the hymn *All things Bright and Beautiful* by Mrs C. Alexander, 1848) • (CS) (P) (RUS)

creche /kreʃ/ *n* [C] *esp. Br and Aus* a place where young children are cared for during the day while their parents do something else, esp. work, study or shop • *Does your employer provide a creche?* • *(Am)* A creche is also a model of the people and animals present at the birth of Jesus which is used as a decoration at Christmas. • (F)

cred /kred/ *n* [U] *Br slang* respect; CREDIBILITY • *The publicity campaign has already helped the company's cred.* • *These trainers don't give me much* **street** *cred.*

cre·dence /ˈkriː·dᵊnts/ *n* [U] *fml* acceptance, support or belief that something is true • *I'm not prepared to* **give** *credence* **to** *complaints made anonymously.* • *His bruises* **added/lent** *credence* **to** *his statement that he had been beaten.*

cre·den·tials /krɪˈden·tʃᵊlz/ *pl n* (proof of) abilities and experience which make someone suitable for a particular job or activity • *The candidate emphasized his excellent credentials.* • *He always measured in metres instead of yards to reinforce his credentials as a keen European.*

cre·den·tial *obj* /krɪˈden·tʃᵊl/ *v* [T] *Am* • *The organizers will only credential* (= give official permission to be present to) *journalists who apply in advance.*

cred·i·ble /ˈkred·ɪ·bḷ/ *adj* able to be believed or trusted • *They haven't produced any credible policies for improving the situation.* • *The story of what had happened to her was* **barely** (= only just) *credible.*

cred·i·bly /ˈkred·ɪ·bli/ *adv* • *The family in the television programme could not be credibly compared with a real one.*

cred·i·bil·i·ty /£ˌkred·əˈbɪl·ɪ·ti, $-ə·ţi/ *n* [U] • *He complained that there had been a campaign to undermine his credibility as leader.* • A **credibility gap** is a difference between what is promised and what really happens.

cred·it PRAISE /ˈkred·ɪt/ *n* praise, approval or honour • *She got no credit for solving the problem.* [U] • *Her boss* **took** *credit* **for** *it*/**took** *(all)* **the** *credit instead.* [U] • *The use of Ms for Miss or Mrs has rapidly* **gained** *credit in recent years.* [U] • **To** *her (great) credit, she admitted she was wrong.* [U] • *She has a family, three books and a professorship* **to** *her* **credit** (= has these good achievements). [U] • *I* **gave** *him credit* **for** (= thought that he would have) *better judgment than he showed.* [U] • *She* **is a** *credit* **to** *her family* (= causes her family to receive praise). [C usually sing] • *She* **does** *her family* **credit** (= causes her family to receive praise). • **All credit to** someone means that they deserve a lot of praise for having done something well: *All credit to her, she's certainly improved things here.* • The expression **(give) credit where credit's due** means that you should praise someone who deserves it, although you might dislike other things about them: *She's selfish and unpleasant, but, credit where credit's due, she's very efficient.*

cred·it·a·ble /£ˈkred·ɪ·tə·bḷ, $-ţə-/ *adj* • *Our team came in a creditable* (= deserving of respect) *third.* • *The other, less creditable, reason for their decision was personal gain.*

cred·it PAYMENT /ˈkred·ɪt/ *n* [U] a method of paying for goods or services at a later time, usually paying INTEREST (= extra money) as well as the original money • *They decided to buy the car* **on** *credit.* • *The shop was offering six months'* **(interest-free)** *credit* **on** *electrical goods.* • A *(Br)* **credit account** (*Am and Aus* **charge account**) is a formal agreement between a shop or other business and a customer, in which the customer can take goods and pay the shop or business for them at a later time. • A **credit card** is a small plastic card which can be used as a method of payment, the money being taken from you at a later time. • *(Br and Aus)* A **credit note** is a piece of paper which can be given by a shop when you return something you don't want and allows you to buy other goods of the same value at another time: *They didn't have the larger size, so I got a credit note till the new stock came in.* • **Credit rating** is how much credit someone is considered able to have and pay back: *She has a high salary and a good credit rating.* • A *(Br and Aus)* **credit squeeze** (*Am* **credit crunch**) is a period of economic difficulty when it is difficult to borrow money from banks. • **Credit terms** are the arrangements made for giving credit, esp. the amount of money, the period of borrowing, etc. • Compare DEBIT. • LP **Money**

cred·it·or /£ˈkred·ɪ·təʳ, $-ţɚ/ *n* [C] • A creditor is someone to whom money is owed: *The company couldn't pay its creditors.* • Compare **debtor** at DEBT.

cred·it·wor·thy /£ˈkred·ɪtˌwɜː·ði, $-ˌwɜːr-/ *adj* • Someone who is creditworthy has enough money or property or is considered trustworthy enough for banks and other organizations to lend them money: *The bank refused to give me the loan because they said I wasn't creditworthy.* ○ *Creditworthy clients can demand low interest rates and borrow heavily.*

cred·it HAVING MONEY /ˈkred·ɪt/ *n* **in credit** *esp. Br* having money; not owing money • *I was relieved to see from my statement that my account was in credit.* [U] • *There are only three credits on my bank statement, compared to a whole list of debits.* [C]

cred·it *obj* /ˈkred·ɪt/ *v* [T] • *They credited my account* **with** *$20* (= put $20 into my account) *after I pointed out the mistake.*

cred·it *obj* BELIEVE /ˈkred·ɪt/ *v* [T not *be crediting*] to believe (something which seems unlikely to be true) • *He even tried to pretend he was a film star's son – can you credit it?* • **It** *was hard* **to** *credit some of the stories we heard about her.* • *Her excuse* **took some** *crediting* (= was difficult to believe).

cred·it COURSE UNIT /ˈkred·ɪt/ *n* [C] a successfully completed part of an educational course • *He has already got a credit/three credits in earth science.*

cred·it *obj* **with** *obj* /ˈkred·ɪt/ *v prep* [T] to consider (someone) as (having good qualities or having done something good) • *He'd always been credited with understanding and sympathy for his patients.* • *I credited the company with more concern for its employees than it showed.*

cred·its /ˈkred·ɪts/ *pl n* the list of names of those who took part in or helped to make a film or a television or radio programme, which is shown or given at the beginning or the end of it • *As the credits began to* **roll** (= be shown), *the audience put on their coats and left the cinema.*

cred·u·lous /ˈkred·jʊ·ləs/ *adj slightly fml* too willing to believe what you are told; easily deceived; GULLIBLE • *He was a credulous fool to believe even half of what they promised.*

cred·u·lous·ly /ˈkred·jʊ·lə·sli/ *adv slightly fml*

cre·du·li·ty /£krəˈdjuː·lə·ti, $-ˈduː·lə·ţi/,

cred·u·lous·ness /ˈkred·jʊ·lə·snəs/ *n* [U] *slightly fml* • *I found her story* **stretched/strained** *even my good-natured credulity* **to the limit** (= her story was almost impossible to believe).

creed /kriːd/, **cre·do** (*pl* **credos**) /£ˈkriː·dəʊ, $-doʊ/ *n* [C] *fml* a set of beliefs which expresses a particular opinion and influences the way you live • *(specialized)* **The Creed** is a short formal statement of Christian religious belief said in church.

creek /kriːk/ *n* [C] *(Br)* a usually short narrow length of water flowing into a river, lake, sea, etc., or *(Am and Aus)* a small narrow river • *(infml) If any more people resign, we'll be really* **up the creek** (= in trouble).

creep MOVE SLOWLY /kriːp/ *v* [I always + adv/prep] *past* **crept** /krept/ to move slowly, quietly and carefully, often with the body close to the ground, and usually in order to avoid being noticed • *She crept* **through** *the long grass till she was in a position to fire.* • *When her parents started shouting at each other, Anna used to creep under the table and cry.* • *The traffic was creeping* **along** *at a snail's pace.* • *They crept* **up behind** *her and suddenly yelled "Boo!"* • *(fig.) Over the last year, the rate of inflation has crept* **up** (= slowly increased) *to almost 7%.* • *(fig.) It was only after I turned 60 that old age began to creep* **up on** *me* (= that I began, finally, to experience it). • *(fig. literary) A dangerous tiredness crept* **over** (= began to be felt by) *her as she drove.* • *(fig.) A mistake has crept* **in** (= got in without anyone noticing) *somewhere between sections D and E.* • *(fig.) Doubts began to creep* **into** (= become present in) *people's minds about the likely success of the project.*

creep·er /£ˈkriː·pəʳ, $-pɚ/ *n* [C] • A creeper is a plant that grows along the ground, up walls or trees, etc.

creep·ing /ˈkriː·pɪŋ/ *adj* [not gradable] • *I'll buy a* **creeping plant** (= plant that grows along the ground), *to put where the wall is stained.* • *(fig. disapproving) We are totally against any form of creeping* (= gradually introduced) *Socialism.*

creep PERSON /kriːp/ *n* [C] *infml* an unpleasant person • *What a little creep he is!* • *Leave me alone, you creep!* [as form of address]

creep·y /ˈkriː·pi/ *adj* **-ier, -iest** *infml* giving you an uncomfortable feeling of strangeness and of fear or disgust • *a creepy film* • *creepy reptilian eyes* • *(infml)* A **creepy-crawly** is a small insect that gives you a feeling of fear and disgust. • *(Aus)* A **creepy-crawlie** is also an automatic vacuum cleaner for a home swimming pool.

creeps /kriːps/ *pl n infml* • If someone or something **gives** you **the creeps**, it makes you feel uncomfortable with fear or disgust: *Living next to a graveyard would give me the creeps.*

cre·mate *obj* /£krɪˈmeɪt, $ˈkriː·meɪt/ *v* [T] to burn (a dead person's body), usually as part of a funeral ceremony • *I want to be cremated and scattered from a plane over Long Beach.*

cre·ma·tion /krɪˈmeɪ·ʃᵊn/ *n* • *My Dad's cremation was a sad affair.* [C] • *In his will, he stated that he desired the cremation of his body.* [U]

crem·at·o·ri·um /£ˌkrem·əˈtɔː·ri·əm, $-ˈtɔːr·i-/ *n* [C] *pl* **crematoriums** or **crematoria** /£ˌkrem·əˈtɔː·ri·ə, $-ˈtɔːr·i-/ a building where dead people's bodies are burnt, usually as part of a funeral ceremony

creme de menthe /ˌkrem·dəˈmɑːnθ/ *n* [U] a sweet usually bright green PEPPERMINT-flavoured alcoholic drink

cren·el·lat·ed, *Am usually* **cren·el·at·ed** /£'kren·əl·eɪ·tɪd, $-t̬ɪd/ *adj specialized* having BATTLEMENTS (=castle walls with regular spaces along the top)

cren·el·la·tions, *Am usually* **cren·el·a·tions** /ˌkren·əl 'eɪ·ʃənz/ *pl n*

Cre·ole LANGUAGE /£kri'əʊl, $-'oʊl/ *n* [C] an American or W Indian language, that is a combination of French, Indian and W Indian languages and is now a main language in Louisiana in the US and in Haiti

Cre·ole PERSON /£kri'əʊl, $-'oʊl/ *n* [C] a person who is related to the original group of Europeans who came to the W Indies or the southern US, or a W Indian of mixed African and European origin who speaks creole

Cre·ole /£kri'əʊl, $-'oʊl/ *adj* [not gradable] • *I love Creole cooking, so hot and spicy.*

cre·o·sote /£'kriː·ə·səʊt, $-soʊt/ *n* [U] a thick brown oily liquid, used esp. for preserving wood

cre·o·sote *obj* /£'kriː·ə·səʊt, $-soʊt/ *v* [T] • *The whole place smelled terribly after we'd creosoted the fence.*

crêpe /krep/ *n* [C] a PANCAKE • A **crêpe suzette** is an orange-flavoured PANCAKE, covered with a little LIQUEUR or BRANDY which is set on fire just before you eat it.

crepe, **crape** /kreɪp/ *n* [U] thin cloth with a WRINKLED (=uneven and finely lined) surface • *a black crepe dress* • *a crepe jacket* • Crepe is also a strong type of rubber with an uneven surface, used esp. for making the bottom of shoes: *crepe-soled shoes* • **Crepe paper** is thin, usually brightly coloured paper, used esp. for making party decorations.

crept /krept/ *past simple and past participle of* CREEP

cre·pus·cu·lar /£krɪ'pʌs·kjʊ·lər, $-lɚ/ *adj literary* of or like the time of day just before the sun goes up or just after it goes down; not bright • *the crepuscular gloom of a winter's afternoon* • *a crepuscular church*

cre·scen·do /£krɪ'ʃen·dəʊ, $-doʊ/ *n* [C usually sing] *pl* **crescendos** a gradual increase in loudness, or the moment when a noise or piece of music is at its loudest, or *(specialized)* a place in a piece of music where the music gets louder • *(fig.) There has been a* **rising** *crescendo* **of** (=increase in) *violence/criticism which started last year and is now reaching a climax.*

cres·cent /'kres·ənt/ *n* [C] (something with) a curved shape that has two narrow pointed ends, like the moon when it is less than half of a circle • *The moon was a brightly shining crescent.* • A crescent can also be a row of houses or a road built in a curve: *They live at number 15, Park Crescent.*

cres·cent /'kres·ənt/ *adj* • *the crescent moon*

cress /kres/ *n* [U] any of various plants with small green leaves used esp. in salads • *egg and cress sandwiches* • *Sprinkle some* **mustard and** *cress into the salad.* • See also WATERCRESS. • PIC› **Vegetables**

crest TOP /krest/ *n* [C] the top or highest part of something such as a wave or a hill • *As we came over the crest of the hill we could see the whole town spread out in front of us.* • *The surfers were riding in towards the beach on the crests of the waves.* • *(fig.) Mrs Singh is still* **(riding) on the crest of a wave of** *popularity* (=is very popular at the moment). • A crest is also a growth of feathers, fur or skin along the top of the heads of some animals, esp. birds, or, in the past, a decoration, usually of feathers, on top of a soldier's hat.

crest·ed /£'kres·tɪd, $-t̬ɪd/ *adj* [not gradable] • A crested bird has a growth of feathers on its head: *a crested grebe*

crest PICTURE /krest/ *n* [C] a formal picture that is used by a family, town, organization, etc. as their particular sign • *a coat of arms with the family crest above it*

crest·ed /£'kres·tɪd, $-t̬ɪd/ *adj* [not gradable] • *crested writing paper*

crest·fal·len /£'krestˌfɔː·lən, $-ˌfɑː-/ *adj* disappointed and sad, usually because of having unexpectedly failed in something • *The cricket player strode confidently out on to the pitch, but returned crestfallen a few minutes later, with a score of only two.*

cret·in /£'kret·ɪn, $'kriː·t̬ən/ *n* [C] *infml disapproving* a very stupid person • *What a cretin that boy is – he just can't keep out of trouble.*

cret·in·ous /£'kret·ɪ·nəs, $'kriː·t̬ən-/ *adj infml disapproving*

cre·vasse /krə'væs/ *n* [C] a very deep crack in the thick ice of a GLACIER • *One member of the expedition was lost when she fell down a crevasse.*

crev·ice /'krev·ɪs/ *n* [C] a small narrow crack or space, esp. in the surface of rock • *A lizard darted into a crevice between two stones.* • *(fig.) The harsh light revealed every crevice and wrinkle in his face.*

crew /kruː/ *n* [C + sing/pl v] a group of people who work together, esp. all those who work on and operate a ship, aircraft, etc. • *an ambulance/lifeboat crew* • *a TV/film/camera crew* • *The aircraft* **has/carries** *a crew of seven.* • Crew is also sometimes used to describe the people of low rank who work on a ship, aircraft, etc. who are not officers: *Apart from the 10 officers, a crew of 90 looks after the 300 passengers.* • *(infml esp. disapproving) The President is surrounded by a* **motley** *crew of bad advisers and professional crooks.* • A **crew cut** is a hairstyle in which the hair is cut very short. • A **crew neck** is a round neck hole without a collar on a JUMPER (=a woollen piece of clothing which covers the upper part of the body and the arms), or a jumper with a neck hole in this shape. • See also AIRCREW. • PIC› **Clothes**

crew *(obj)* /kruː/ *v* [I/T] • If you crew a boat or crew for someone on their boat, you are one of the crew on a boat and help to sail it.

crew·mem·ber /£'kruːˌmem·bər, $-bɚ/, **crew·man** *(pl* **-men)** /'kruː·mən, -mæn/ *n* [C] a member of a group of people who work together esp. on a ship • *All crewmembers should return to the ship by 6 a.m.* • *I'd like to welcome on board Ms Catherine Taylor, a new crewmember to our team here at the bank.*

crib BED /krɪb/ *n* [C] *Am or Br dated* a baby's bed with high bars around the sides so that the baby cannot fall out; a COT • *In the local church at Christmas, there's a model of the nativity scene with a tiny baby in a crib, shepherds, animals, and kings bearing gifts.* • PIC› **Beds and bedroom**

crib *(obj)* COPY /krɪb/ *v* **-bb-** *infml disapproving* to copy (someone else's work) esp. dishonestly • *I got chucked out of the exam for cribbing* **from** *the guy in front.* [I] • *It was in 'The Star' first, then all the other newspapers cribbed it the next day.* [T] • *(esp. Am)* **Crib notes** are prepared notes for cheating in an examination.

crib /krɪb/ *n* [C] *infml* • A **crib (sheet)** is a book, paper, etc. that gives some information in a quick simple way. It can also be something used dishonestly by students in an exam. • A crib is also a piece of work copied dishonestly from someone else's work: *Her answers seemed to be full of cribs.*

crick /krɪk/ *n* [C] a painful, usually sudden stiffness in a group of muscles in the neck or back • *I got a crick* **in** *my neck from painting the ceiling.*

crick *obj* /krɪk/ *v* [T] • *I cricked my neck while I was painting the ceiling.*

crick·et GAME /'krɪk·ɪt/ *n* [U] a sport in which two teams of eleven players try to score RUNS (=points) by hitting a small hard leather-covered ball with a BAT (=wooden stick) and running between two sets of small wooden posts • *a cricket ball/bat* • The cricket **net** (*infml* **The nets**) is an area near a cricket field which is surrounded on three sides with netting, where people go to practise BATTING (=hitting the ball). • *(dated or humorous) It's simply* **not cricket** (=not honourable) *to flirt with another man's wife.* • LP› **Sports** PIC› **Net, Sports**

crick·et·er /£'krɪk·ɪ·tər, $-t̬ɚ/ *n* [C] • *The cricketers all looked so elegant in their white clothes, standing about on the green grass.*

crick·et·ing /£'krɪk·ɪ·tɪŋ, $-t̬ɪŋ/ *adj* [before n; not gradable] • *The West Indies have been dominant in the cricketing* **world** *for over ten years, due largely to their seemingly endless supply of pace bowlers.*

crick·et INSECT /'krɪk·ɪt/ *n* [C] a brown jumping insect, the male of which makes short sharp loud noises by rubbing its wings together

cri de coeur /£ˌkriː·də'kɜːr, $-'kɜːr/ *n* [C usually sing] *pl* **cris de coeur** /£ˌkriː·də'kɜːr, $-'kɜːr/ an urgent strongly felt request for help from someone in a very bad or hopeless situation

cried /kraɪd/ *past simple and past participle of* CRY

cri·key /'kraɪ·ki/ *exclamation esp. Br infml dated* an expression of surprise

crime /kraɪm/ *n* an action which is against the law, or, more generally, (an example of) bad or unacceptable behaviour • *a crime* **against** *humanity/the people/property* [C] • *a life of crime* [U] • *rising crime* [U] • *crime prevention* [U] • *He has admitted* **committing** *several crimes, including two murders.* [C] • *The defendant is* **accused of/charged with** *a range of crimes, from theft to murder.* [C] • *A knife was found at the* **scene of the** *crime.* [C] • **Petty** (=Unimportant) *crime is common in this area, but fortunately there isn't much* **serious** *crime* (=very violent crime or the stealing of things of great value). [U] • *Life*

CRIMES AND CRIMINALS

CRIMES INVOLVING STEALING

Generally, crime in which something is stolen is **theft** and the criminal is a **thief**. Here are some more particular words:

Burglars *broke into our office last night and took the computers.*
My house was (Br) **burgled**/ *(Am)* **burglarized** *twice last year, so I put in a burglar alarm.*
Police caught Perry after he broke a window and climbed into the flat. He was found guilty of (Br) **breaking and entering**/ *(Am)* **unlawful entry**.
Don't put your wallet in your back pocket: **pickpockets** *will steal it.*
The **shoplifter** *claimed she had simply forgotten to pay when she left the store with a book.*

CRIMES COMMITTED BY PEOPLE IN BUSINESS OR IN INFLUENTIAL JOBS

The Government promised to fight **bribery** *and* **corruption** *after officials were accused of accepting $1.5 million in bribes from foreign firms.*
She learned to **forge** *the Director's signature and for five years had been* **embezzling** *large amounts of money from her company.*
Stevens was imprisoned for a £60 000 **fraud** *in which he sold holidays that did not really exist.*
The company CCP kept false accounts for six years and were guilty of **tax evasion** *amounting to $75 000.*
Five businessmen were charged with **conspiracy** *to sell illegal weapons.*
Two of Ms Green's employees lied to the judge to protect her. They were both convicted of **perjury**.

CRIMES OF VIOLENCE

In legal language, **assault** is the crime when an attacker threatens or tries to apply violence. In **battery**, (*Br*) **actual bodily harm** or (*Br*) **grievous bodily harm (GBH)**, violence is actually used.
He was **assaulted** *while walking home from a late-night party.*
He was found innocent of **battering** *his two year old son.*
No-one was killed in the robbery, but three men were later charged with causing **grievous bodily harm**.

When someone is killed intentionally this is called **murder**/ *(esp. Am)* **homicide**:
There was a sharp rise in the number of murders/ (esp. Am) homicides last year, especially in killings connected with drugs.
An 18 year old student was **murdered** *by her jealous boyfriend.*

If the killing was not fully intentional, the crime is **manslaughter**:
The drunken driver was convicted of **manslaughter** *after his car left the road and hit three young people.*

Illegally damaging other people's property is called **vandalism** or (*law*) **criminal damage**:
My car was **vandalized** *last night – all its windows were smashed.*

imprisonment is reserved for the most **heinous** (=very serious) *crimes.* [C] • *To have hundreds of homeless people sleeping in the streets of a city like London is a crime* (=an immoral situation). [U] • *(infml)* **It** *would be a crime* (=a waste) **to** *spend such a beautiful day inside – let's go for a long walk somewhere.* [U + *to* infinitive] • A **crime of passion** is a crime committed because of very strong emotional feelings, esp. in connection with a sexual relationship. • A **crime wave** is a sudden increase in the amount of illegal activity. • A **crime writer** is someone who writes stories about esp. murders where the main character tries to solve the mystery of who committed the crime: *Sarah Peretsky is one of the best crime writers of her generation.* • *(saying)* 'Crime doesn't pay' means that criminals almost always receive punishment in the end. • LP **Crimes and criminals, Law**

crim·i·nal /'krɪm·ɪ·nəl/ *n* [C] • *Criminals should be re-educated as well as punished.* • See also CID. • CS

crim·i·nal /'krɪm·ɪ·nəl/ *adj* • *a criminal act/offence* • *criminal behaviour* • *a criminal investigation* • **It's** *criminal* **to** *charge so much for a book.* [+ *to* infinitive] • *Punishing people is the job of the* **criminal courts** (=law courts which deal with criminal law). • *The man was found guilty of causing* **criminal damage** (=serious damage which is against the law) *in a fight in a wine bar.* • *Fraud is dealt with under* **criminal law** (=law which deals with the breaking of a country's laws), *while non-payment of tax is covered by civil law.* • *People with a* **criminal record** (=an official record of having previously committed crimes) *sometimes find it hard to find work.* • *The way we waste this planet's resources is criminal* (=morally wrong). • The **criminal justice system** is the process by which people who are accused of crimes are judged in court.

crim·i·nal·i·ty /£ˌkrɪm·ɪ'næl·ɪ·ti, $-ə·ţi/ *n* [U] • *Once you've stolen something, your criminality is established.*

crim·i·nal·ly /'krɪm·ɪ·nə·li/ *adv* • *a prison for the criminally insane* • *It was criminally stupid* (=stupid in a serious and morally wrong way) *to drive without proper brakes.*

crim·in·al·ize *obj, Br and Aus usually* **-ise** /'krɪm·ɪ·nə·laɪz/ *v* [T] • *Time spent in prison only criminalizes young offenders* (=makes it more likely that they will offend again). • *The law has criminalized* (=made illegal) *prostitution but not got rid of it.*

crim·i·nol·o·gy /£ˌkrɪm·ɪ'nɒl·ə·dʒi, $-'nɑː·lə-/ *n* [U] • Criminology is the scientific study of crime and criminals.

crim·i·nol·o·gist /£ˌkrɪm·ɪ'nɒl·ə·dʒɪst, $-'nɑː·lə-/ *n* [C] • A criminologist is someone who studies crime and criminals.

crimp *obj* /krɪmp/ *v* [T] to press (cloth, paper, pastry, etc.) into small folds along its edges, or to press (hair) into a series of curves or curls

Crimp·lene /'krɪm·pliːn/ *n* [U] *Br trademark* an artificial cloth, used for clothes, that does not easily CREASE (=develop unwanted folds and lines)

crim·son /'krɪm·zᵊn/ *adj, n* [U] (of) a strong, slightly purplish, deep red colour • When a person or their face is crimson, it is a sign that they are feeling a strong emotion, esp. embarrassment or anger: *She went crimson* **with** *embarrassment and hid her face.*

cringe /krɪndʒ/ *v* [I] to move away while trying to make yourself smaller in order to escape from something or someone • *He knows when he's about to be hit and just cringes back in terror.* • *(infml) We all cringed* **(with embarrassment)** (=felt very uncomfortable) **at** *her terrible jokes.* • *(Br infml)* If you describe someone or something as **cringe-making**, you mean that it makes you feel embarrassed because it is so bad: *Isn't he awful – just look at that cringe-making nylon suit!*

crin·kle *(obj)* /'krɪŋ·kl̩/ *v* to (cause to) have many little lines and folds • *When she smiles, her eyes crinkle* **up** *at the corners.* [I] • *She crinkled* **(up)** *her nose in distaste.* [T/M] • **Crinkle-cut** *(Br)* **chips**/*(Am)* **french fries** are potatoes cut in a special uneven shape.

crin·kle /'krɪŋ·kl̩/ *n* [C]

crin·kled /'krɪŋ·kl̩d/ *adj*

crin·kly /'krɪŋ·kli/ *adj* **-ier, -iest** • *What lovely crinkly* (=twisted and curly) *hair he has!*

USE OF VIOLENCE OR THREATS TO GET MONEY AND SO ON

Five **bank robbers** *threatened the cashiers with shotguns.*
A **mugger** *knocked her over and snatched her handbag.*
At first he was afraid to call the police when **kidnappers** *demanded a $10000 ransom for the safe return of his daughter.*
Local businessmen were so terrified of McAllister and his gang that he was able to **extort** *thousands of pounds in protection money from them.*
The **blackmailer** *said he would send the photos to Mr Winter's wife unless he was paid £5 000 hush money.*

CRIMES COMMITTED FOR POLITICAL REASONS

After the politically motivated killings of recent years, most leaders are afraid of **assassination**.
He is on trial for **treason** *for being part of a plot to overthrow the government.*
Two businessmen were **taken hostage** *by* **terrorists** *while travelling in the Middle East. The same terrorist group was responsible for the* **hijacking** *of a passenger plane earlier this year.*
Two men who stole top secret documents were sentenced to life imprisonment for **spying/espionage**.

CRIMES CONNECTED WITH DRUGS/*(esp. Am)* NARCOTICS

Millions of pounds worth of illegal drugs are **smuggled** *into the country every year.*
Mr Shaw seemed a normal businessman, but in fact was a **drug trafficker**, *secretly trading in heroin.*
Many **drug dealers/pushers** *selling narcotics on the streets are addicted themselves.*
Police found 30g of marijuana in her flat, and she was fined for illegal **possession of drugs**.

CAR CRIMES

Some car crimes are not very serious such as **illegal parking**, leaving your car where it should not be. These would usually be called (*law*) **civil offences** rather than crimes.
Some people driving home from parties are over the limit and may be fined for **drink driving** *(also called* **drunk(en) driving**).
Two **joy riders** *stole a car and drove down the High Street at 120 mph. They were later charged with theft and* **dangerous/** *(law)* **reckless driving**.
The first time he drove his new sports car, he was done for **speeding**.
Don't leave your car there, you'll get a **parking ticket**.

If you say something that is damaging and not true about someone, this may be **defamation**. Written defamation is **libel** and when spoken is **slander**:
She decided to sue the newspaper for **defamation** *of character when it carried* **libellous** *articles about her love life.*
What you said about me is nothing but **slander**.

crin·o·line /ˈkrɪn·əl·ɪn/ *n* [C] a woman's very stiff skirt or a long piece of underwear that falls in a very wide circle around the legs, worn esp. in the 19th century

cripes /kraɪps/ *exclamation infml dated* an expression of surprise

crip·ple /ˈkrɪp·l̩/ *n* [C] *dated* a person who because of disease or injury cannot walk or move one or more of their legs or arms correctly • *(fig. disapproving) "Come on, you load of cripples* (= slow-moving people), *you can go faster than that!" yelled the coach.* • An **emotional** cripple is someone who finds it difficult to have or express feelings. • Some people consider this word to be offensive.

crip·ple *obj* /ˈkrɪp·l̩/ *v* [T] • *A heavy piece of machinery fell on him and crippled* (= injured) *him* **for life**. • *(fig.) Our attempts to help these people find jobs have been crippled* (= damaged and limited) *by the withdrawal of government support.*

crip·pled /ˈkrɪp·l̩d/ *adj* • *She's been crippled ever since the car accident.*

crip·pling /ˈkrɪp·l̩ɪŋ, -lɪŋ/ *adj* • *A crippling attack of malaria kept him in bed for months.* • *(fig.) They've got crippling* (= extremely large and therefore damaging) *debts of £2 million.*

crip·pling·ly /ˈkrɪp·lɪŋ·li/ *adv* • *(fig.) They were forced out of business by cripplingly* (= extremely) **high** *interest rates.*

cri·sis /ˈkraɪ·sɪs/ *n* [C] *pl* **crises** /ˈkraɪ·siːz/ a situation that has reached an extremely difficult or dangerous point; a time of great disagreement, uncertainty or suffering • *crisis talks* • *The news reports of the crisis showed tanks in the streets.* • *There is a crisis* **in** *education/Education is* **in** *crisis because of recent spending cuts.* • If there is a cash/energy/housing crisis, there is a severe lack of cash/energy/housing. • *I've got a family crisis on my hands – my 16-year-old sister has got pregnant.* • *The company is facing a crisis* **over** (= caused by) *demands for higher pay.* • *A mediator has been called in to* **resolve/solve** *the crisis.* • A crisis during a serious illness is a moment when there is the possibility of suddenly getting either a lot better or a lot worse: *He's passed the crisis – the fever's started to go down.* • If you have a crisis **in/of confidence**, you lose confidence: *With inflation at 500%, the country* **faces** *a crisis of confidence.* • (GR) (P)

crisp [HARD] /krɪsp/ *adj* **-er, -est** *esp. approving* hard enough to be broken easily • Cooked foods, such as pastry and biscuits, that are crisp are well cooked so that they are just dry and hard enough. • If fresh fruit or vegetables are crisp, they are fresh and firm: *She bit into a crisp apple.* • Paper or cloth that is crisp is stiff and smooth: *a crisp new £5 note/a crisp white tablecloth* • *The crisp snow crunched underfoot as she walked up the path.* • *(fig.) I breathed in deeply the crisp* (= cold, dry and fresh) *mountain air.* • *(fig.) It was a wonderful crisp* (= cold, dry and bright) *spring morning.* • *(fig.) Now that we have cable, we get a wonderfully crisp* (= clear, sharp and exact) *picture, even on our old TV.* • A way of speaking, writing or behaving that is crisp is quick and sharp: *a crisp reply ○ a crisp, efficient manner*

crisp·ly /ˈkrɪs·pli/ *adv* • *"She's not here," he said crisply* (= quickly and sharply) *and shut the door.*

crisp·ness /ˈkrɪsp·nəs/ *n* [U]

crisp·y /ˈkrɪs·pi/ *adj* **-ier, -iest** *approving* • Food that is crispy is hard enough to be broken easily: *crispy bacon*

crisp [POTATO] *Br* /krɪsp/, *Am and Aus* **(po·ta·to) chip** *n* [C usually pl] a very thin, often round piece of fried potato, sometimes flavoured, and sold esp. in plastic bags • *Could I have a packet of salt and vinegar crisps, please?* • [PIC]> **Containers**

crisp [SWEET FOOD] /krɪsp/ *n* [C] *Am for* CRUMBLE

crisp·bread /ˈkrɪsp·bred/ *n* [C/U] a hard dry flat savoury type of food similar to a biscuit. It is often eaten instead of bread by people trying to lose weight.

criss–cross *(obj)* /£ˈkrɪs·krɒs, $-krɑːs/ *v* to move or exist in a pattern of lines crossing (something or each other) • *Hundreds of Greyhound buses criss-cross the United States every day.* [T] • *This area of the city is criss-crossed by railway lines.* [T] • *It is a busy junction where many railway tracks criss-cross.* [I]

criss–cross /£ˈkrɪs·krɒs, $-krɑːs/ *adj* [not gradable] • *a criss-cross grille*

crit /krɪt/ *n* [C] *infml* an article giving the writer's opinion about something, esp. films, books, music, etc. • See also **lit crit** at LIT [LITERATURE].

cri·te·ri·on /£kraɪ'tɪə·ri·ən, $-'tɪr·i-/ *n* [C] *pl* **criteria** /£kraɪ'tɪə·ri·ə, $-tɪr·i-/ a fact or standard by which you judge, decide about or deal with something • *The Health Service should not be judged by financial criteria alone.* • *The criterion I* **apply** *to* (= by which I decide about) *any problem is "What will make me happiest?"*

cri·tic /£'krɪt·ɪk, $'krɪṭ-/ *n* [C] a person whose job is to give their opinion about something, esp. films, books, music, etc., or a person who expresses dislike of or disagreement with something or someone • *She's a film/music/theatre/literary critic for the 'Irish Times'.* • *The play has been well received by the critics.* • *Her critics say she is leading the party to disaster, but she is determined to prove them wrong.* • *He's his own harshest/worst critic* (= He judges himself severely).

cri·tic·al /£'krɪt·ɪ·kəl, $'krɪṭ-/ *adj* • *a critical essay/work* (= one giving opinions or judgments) *on 'Ulysses'* • *a critical examination of the history of psychoanalysis* • *Many of the 'Films on 4' have* **won/received** *critical* **acclaim** (= been praised by film critics). • To be critical **of** someone or something is to make negative judgments about them: *How can I have any self-confidence when you're always so critical of me?* ○ *The report is* **highly/sharply** *critical* **of** *safety standards at the factory.* • See also CRITICAL.

cri·tic·ally /£'krɪt·ɪ·kli, $'krɪṭ-/ *adv* • *The painter stepped back to look critically at the morning's work.* • *The same company produced the critically* **acclaimed** *series 'Family.'* • *You describe my work so critically* (= negatively) *– don't you see any good points at all?*

cri·ti·ci·sm /£'krɪt·ɪ·sɪ·zəm, $'krɪṭ-/ *n* • *He can't take/accept criticism* (= disapproval) *– he just stops listening and starts shouting.* [U] • *The designs for the new mosque have attracted widespread criticism.* [U] • *I have a few criticisms* (= disapproving judgments) *to make* **of/about** *your speech.* [C] • *Apart from the novels and plays, she wrote two books of* **literary** *criticism.* [U] • *If you've got any* **constructive** (= positive) *criticism, I'd be glad to hear it.* [U]

cri·ti·cize *(obj)*, *Br and Aus usually* **–ise** /£'krɪt·ɪ·saɪz, $'krɪṭ-/ *v* • To criticize something or someone is to express disapproval of it or them: *The government is being widely criticized* **for** *its failure to limit air pollution.* [T] ○ *He was heavily criticized* **for** *suggesting that some of the team did not work hard enough.* [T] ○ *We'll get nowhere if all you can do is criticize (my work).* [I/T] ○ *We're a group of artists who meet to discuss things and criticize each other's work.* [T]

cri·tic·al /£'krɪt·ɪ·kəl, $'krɪṭ-/ *adj* of the greatest importance to the way things might happen; dangerous or uncertain • *The President's support is critical* **(to** *this project).* • *The experiment is at a critical point/stage/juncture – we'll know the result in an hour.* • *As long as sales remain above the critical figure of £200 000, we don't need to worry.* • *Both drivers are critical/in a critical* **condition** (= so badly hurt that they might die) *after the 120mph crash.* • If a situation **goes** critical, it suddenly becomes extremely serious: *Union leaders say that the dispute may go critical this week.* • Critical mass is the smallest or largest size that is necessary for something to succeed: *The company has reached a critical mass and is now assured of survival.* ○ *The company has reached a critical mass and must now avoid further growth.* • See also **critical** at CRITIC.

cri·tic·ally /£'krɪt·ɪ·kli, $'krɪṭ-/ *adv* • *The economy is in a critically bad condition.* • *They were both critically* **injured** *in the crash.*

cri·tique /krɪ'tiːk/ *n* [C] a report of something such as a political situation or system or a person's work or ideas, which examines it and provides an often negative judgment • *She has provided us with the first socialist critique* **of** *current economic policy.*

crit·ter /£'krɪt·əʳ, $'krɪṭ·ɚ/, **crit·tur** *n* [C] *Am not standard* a creature

croak *(obj)* [SOUND] /£krəʊk, $kroʊk/ *v* (of animals) to make deep rough sounds such as a FROG or CROW makes, or (of people) to speak with a rough voice because of a sore or dry throat • *I could hear frogs croaking by the lake.* [I] • *"Water, water!" he croaked.* [+ clause] • *(Br slang)* If a criminal croaks, they give information to the police about other criminals.

croak /£krəʊk, $kroʊk/ *n* [C] • *He tried shouting for help but could only manage a weak croak.*

croak *(obj)* [DIE] /£krəʊk, $kroʊk/ *v* [I/T] *slightly dated slang* to die or (more rarely) to murder (someone)

croc /£krɒk, $krɑːk/ *n* [C] *infml for* CROCODILE

cro·chet /£'krəʊ·ʃeɪ, $kroʊ'ʃeɪ/ *n* [U] a method of making things from wool or other thread, using a single large hooked needle, or something being made in this way • A **crochet-hook** is the needle used to do crochet. • [LP]› **'-et' words** [PIC]› **Handicraft**

cro·chet *(obj)* /£'krəʊ·ʃeɪ, $kroʊ'ʃeɪ/ *v* • *Local women were crocheting (cloths) while sitting on their front steps.* [I/T]

cro·cheted /£'krəʊ·ʃeɪd, $kroʊ'ʃeɪd/ *adj* [not gradable] • *She gave me a beautiful crocheted tea cosy.*

crock [CONTAINER] /£krɒk, $krɑːk/ *n* [C] a container, usually one made of clay • *He keeps his coffee in an earthenware crock.*

crock [CAR OR PERSON] /£krɒk, $krɑːk/ *n* [C] *slightly dated humorous* an old person or car which is considered to be worthless • *My Dad is becoming something of an old crock.*

crock [NONSENSE] /£krɒk, $krɑːk/ *n* [U] **a crock** *Am infml* (of ideas, speech or writing) nonsense • *That presentation was just a crock – there wasn't a single useful idea in it!*

crock·ery /£'krɒk·ər·i, $'krɑː·kɚ-/ *n* [U] cups, plates, bowls, etc., used to serve food and drink, esp. made of baked clay • *The sink was full of piles of dirty crockery.* • Compare CUTLERY.

croc·o·dile /£'krɒk·ə·daɪl, $'krɑː·kə-/, *infml* **croc** *n* [C] *pl* **crocodiles** or **crocodile** a large hard-skinned REPTILE (= type of animal) that lives in and near rivers and lakes in the hot wet parts of the world. It usually has a longer and narrower nose than that of an ALLIGATOR. • *a crocodile-infested swamp* • *crocodile-skin shoes* • *(Br infml)* A crocodile is also a row of people, esp. children, who are walking in pairs. • **Crocodile tears** are tears that you cry when you are not really sad or sorry. • [PIC]› **Reptiles and amphibians**

cro·cus /£'krəʊ·kəs, $'kroʊ-/ *n* [C] a small yellow, white or purple spring flower

croft /£krɒft, $krɑːft/ *n* [C] *Br* (esp. in Scotland) a very small farm around a house, or the house itself

croft·er /£'krɒf·təʳ, $'krɑːf·tɚ/ *n* [C] • *Most of the crofters keep sheep and goats on their farms.*

crois·sant /£'kwæs·ɒ̃, $kwɑː'sɑ̃ː/ *n* [C] a piece of light CRESCENT-shaped pastry, usually eaten in the morning • *I've got some real French croissants for breakfast.* • [PIC]› **Bread and cakes**

crom·lech /£'krɒm·lek, $'krɑːm-/ *n* [C] *pl* **cromlechs** a DOLMEN (= an ancient group of stones consisting of one large flat stone supported by several vertical ones)

crone /£krəʊn, $kroʊn/ *n* [C] *disapproving or literary* an old woman, esp. one who is unfriendly or ugly

cron·y /£'krəʊ·ni, $'kroʊ-/ *n* [C] *infml esp. disapproving* a close friend or someone who works with a stated and usually dishonest person in authority • *The General and his cronies are now awaiting trial for drug-smuggling.*

crook [CRIMINAL] /krʊk/ *n* [C] *infml* a very dishonest person, esp. a criminal or a cheat • *Most of these politicians are just a bunch of crooks.*

crook·ed /'krʊk·ɪd/ *adj infml* • *The city is full of crooked police officers taking bribes.*

crook [INSIDE PART] /krʊk/ *n* [C usually sing] the inside part (of something) • The crook **of your arm** is the inside part when it is bent at the ELBOW: *He placed the baby in the crook of his arm.*

crook [STICK] /krʊk/ *n* [C] a long stick with a curved end, esp. one carried by a SHEPHERD or a BISHOP

crook [BAD] /krʊk/ *adj Aus infml* bad or ill

crook·ed /'krʊk·ɪd, krʊkt/ *adj* not forming a straight line; having many sharp bends • *You have to drive slowly on these crooked country roads.*

crook·ed·ly /'krʊk·ɪd·li/ *adv* • *She smiled crookedly at me, turned and left.*

crook *obj* /krʊk/ *v* [T] *dated* • *The English lady delicately crooked* (= bent) *her little finger as she picked up her tea cup.*

croon *(obj)* /kruːn/ *v* to sing or talk in a sweet, low voice full of emotion • *"Are you lonesome tonight?" crooned Elvis from the radio.* [+ clause] • *"One day, one day," he crooned to himself, "I'll be rich and famous."* [+ clause] • *Two men were crooning softly in the corner.* [I]

croon /kruːn/ *n* [C/U] • A croon is either a slow low song or a low soft way of singing.

croon·er /£'kruː·nəʳ, $-nɚ/ *n* [C] *dated* • A crooner is a singer, esp. a man, who sings slow love songs: *Bing Crosby was a well-known crooner.*

crop [PLANT] /£krɒp, $krɑːp/ *n* [C] (the total amount gathered of) a plant such as a grain, fruit or vegetable

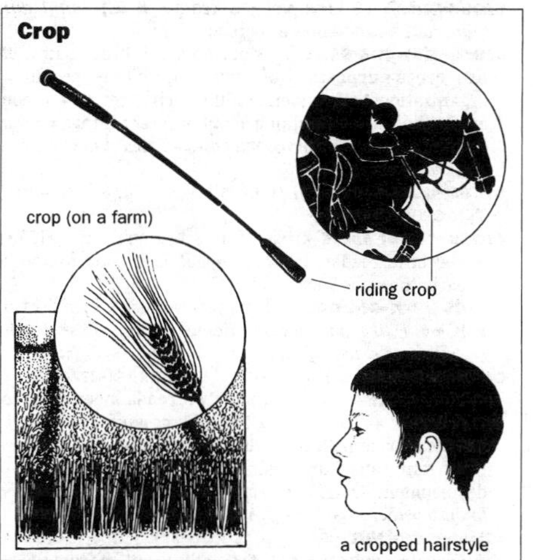

grown in large amounts by farmers • *The main crops grown for export are coffee and rice.* • *The crops are doing well this year.* • *We've got a* **bumper** (= very good) *potato crop this year.* • *(fig.) The judges will select the best from this year's crop* (= group) *of first novels.* • **Crop rotation** is a method of farming where a number of different plants are grown one after the other on a field so that the earth stays healthy and FERTILE. • **Crop spraying** or **crop dusting** is a way of covering crops with chemicals that will kill harmful insects and diseases, sometimes from an aircraft. • PIC› **Crop**

crop *(obj)* /£krɒp, $krɑːp/ *v* **-pp-** • *The land here has been over-cropped* (= too much has been grown on it) *and the soil is exhausted.* [T] • *The carrots have cropped* (= grown) *well this year.* [I always + adv/prep]

crop *obj* CUT /£krɒp, $krɑːp/ *v* [T] **-pp-** to make (something) shorter or smaller, esp. by cutting • *He had his hair cropped when he went into the army.* • When animals such as sheep or horses crop grass or other plants, they eat the top parts. • If you crop a photograph, you cut off some or all of the edges, leaving only the most important part.

crop /£krɒp, $krɑːp/ *n* [C] • A crop is a short hair style or hair cut: *She's had a very short crop.* • PIC› **Crop, Hair**

crop THROAT /£krɒp, $krɑːp/ *n* [C] a bag-like part of the throat in many birds where food is stored before going into the stomach

crop STICK /£krɒp, $krɑːp/ *n* [C] a short stick used to control a horse by hitting it • PIC› **Crop**

crop up *v adv* [I] *infml* to happen or appear unexpectedly • *I'm afraid another program error has cropped up so the printout won't be ready till tomorrow.* • *Her name keeps cropping up* **in** *conversation.*

crop·per /£'krɒp·əʳ, $'krɑː·pɚ/ *n* [U] **come a cropper** *slang* to fail badly, or to fall from a horse or have a bad accident in a vehicle • *Having reached the Final, the British have come a cropper against the more experienced German team.* • *She came an almighty cropper when her back wheels hit an icy patch.*

cro·quet /£'krəʊ·keɪ, $kroʊ'keɪ/ *n* [U] a game in which two, three or four players use MALLETS (= long wooden hammers) to hit wooden balls through small metal HOOPS (= arches) fixed into the grass • *a croquet lawn* • LP› **'-et' words**

cro·quette /£krə'ket, $kroʊ-/ *n* [C] a small rounded mass of food such as meat, fish or potato that has been cut into small pieces, pressed together and fried

cros·i·er, cro·zi·er /£'krəʊ·zi·əʳ, $'kroʊ·zi·ɚ/ *n* a long stick with a decorative end that is curved or in the shape of a cross, carried by BISHOPS (= priests of high rank)

cross *(obj)* GO ACROSS /£krɒs, $krɑːs/ *v* to go across from one side of (something) to the other • *Look both ways before you cross* **(over)**. [I] • *A chicken crossed the road/street.* [T] • *Cross the bridge and turn right at the first set of traffic lights.* [T] • *We crossed (the frontier)* **into** *Germany.* [I/T] • *For two hundred miles, the railway crosses a bare, empty plain.* [T] • In sports, if a ball crosses the **line** it goes out of the playing area: *Serini tried to keep the ball in play, but the referee said it had crossed the line.* [T] ○ *Despite the defender's efforts, the ball just crossed the line* (= went in the goal). [T] • If you **cross** someone's **hand/palm with silver**, you give them money so that they will tell you what will happen to you in the future. • If something **crosses** your **mind**, you think of it: *It crossed my mind yesterday that you must be a bit short of staff – shall I send someone to help out?* • If you say that you will **cross that bridge when you come/get to it**, you mean that you will not worry now about problems that are still in the future.

cross- /£,krɒs-, $'krɑːs-/ *combining form* • *a cross-Channel ferry* (= one that sails between Britain and France, Belgium or Holland) • *a river with a strong cross-current* (= current of water flowing against the main direction of flow) • **Cross-country** sports are those in which competitors travel long distances through the countryside: *cross-country skiing/running* • **Cross-country** also means across the length of a country: *After high school we bought a camper van and travelled cross-country for two months.*

cross·ing /£'krɒs·ɪŋ, $'krɑː·sɪŋ/ *n* [C] • A crossing is a place where something such as a road can be crossed safely, or a place where a road and a railway meet and cross each other: *a pedestrian crossing on a main road* ○ *a border/river crossing* • A crossing can also be a journey across something such as a sea, from one side to the other: • *We had a really rough crossing – I was sick three times.* • PIC› **Road**

cross *(obj)* LIE ACROSS /£krɒs, $krɑːs/ *v* to go, lie or put across each other • *She sat* **with** *her legs/arms* **crossed** (= one on top of the other), *waiting patiently.* • If you **cross** your **fingers** about something, you are showing you hope that it will happen as you want it to happen: *I'm just going to cross my fingers and hope for the best* • If you **cross swords with** someone, you have an argument with them. • If a letter that you have sent to someone and a letter that they have sent to you cross (in the post), they were both sent at about the same time, not as answers to each other. [I] • If you are **cross-legged** you have your feet crossed over each other, but your knees wide apart, usually while sitting on the floor: *Sit cross-legged, rest your hands on your knees and breathe deeply.* • If you get a **crossed line** while you are talking on the telephone, you can suddenly hear what other people are saying on a different line.

cross MARK /£krɒs, $krɑːs/ *n* [C] a mark or object in the shape of two lines across each other, usually + or x • *Put a cross next to the name of the candidate for whom you wish to vote.* • *A red cross on the map showed where the treasure was supposed to be buried.* • *Mark all the wrong answers with a cross (X) and the correct ones with a tick* • *(✓).* • **Cross-stitch** is a decorative style of sewing which uses stitches which cross each other to form X's. • A cross with a † shape is the sign of Christianity because Jesus Christ was left to die on a structure of this shape: *Christ died on the Cross.* ○ *All the graves in the churchyard were marked with a wooden cross.* ○ *She wears a gold cross round her neck.* ○ *The priest* **made the sign of the** *cross* (= moved his or her hand down and then across the chest) *over the dead bodies.* • A cross is also an unpleasant or painful situation or person that you must accept and deal with, although you find it very difficult: *Having my elderly mother to live in my house is a cross I'm not going to find easy to* **bear**. • A cross is also a MEDAL (= special small object given and worn as an official mark of honour) in this shape: *In Britain the Victoria Cross is awarded for acts of great bravery during wartime.* • LP› **Symbols**

cross *obj* /£krɒs, $krɑːs/ *v* [T] • *(Br and Aus specialized)* If you cross a **cheque**, you draw two lines across the middle, which means that it must be paid into a bank account. [T] • When Christians cross themselves, they move their hand down and then across their face or chest, making the shape of a cross. • *(saying)* 'Cross my heart (and hope to die)' means that what you have said or promised is completely true. • See also CROSS OFF; CROSS OUT.

cross ANNOYED /£krɒs, $krɑːs/ *adj* **-er, -est** annoyed or angry • *I'm cross* **about** *you using my bike without asking.* • *She is cross* **at** *being given all the boring jobs.* • *She was cross* **that** *she wasn't given any interesting jobs.* [+ that clause] • *My Dad gets cross* **(with** *me) if I leave the kitchen in a mess.*

cross *obj* /£krɒs, $krɑːs/ *v* [T] • If you cross someone you annoy them by not doing or saying what they want: *I wouldn't cross him if I were you, not if you value your life.*

cross·ly /£'krɒs·li, $'krɑː·sli/ *adv* • *"Get out of here" she said crossly, and stamped her foot.*

cross MIXTURE /£krɒs, $krɑːs/ *n* [C] a mixture of two different things which have been combined to produce something new • *Police dogs are often a cross* **between** *a retriever and an alsatian.* • *Culottes are a cross* **between** *a skirt and shorts.* • *(fig.) She's so gorgeous – She looks like a cross* **between** *Liz Taylor and Sophia Loren.* • See also CROSSBREED.

cross *obj* /£krɒs, $krɑːs/ *v* [T] *esp. specialized* • If you cross a plant or animal **with** another of a different type, you cause them to breed together in order to produce a new variety: *I'm trying to produce a disease-resistant hybrid by crossing several different varieties of maize.*

cross *obj* **off** *(obj) v adv, v prep* [T] to remove (someone or something, such as a name) from (a list) by drawing a line through it • *If you don't want to play in the match, cross your name off.* [M] • *Linda can't come to the barbecue – cross her off the list.*

cross out *obj*, **cross** *obj* **out** *v adv* [M] to draw a line through (writing) because it is wrong • *If you think it's wrong, cross it out and write it again.* • PIC› **Writing**

cross·bar /£ˈkrɒs·bɑːʳ, $ˈkrɑːs·bɑːr/ *n* [C] a horizontal bar, either the part that forms the top of a goal, or the part of a bicycle between the seat and the HANDLEBARS • PIC› **Bar, Bicycles**

cross·bones /£ˈkrɒs·bəʊnz, $ˈkrɑːs·boʊnz/ *n* See **skull and crossbones** at SKULL

cross·bow /£ˈkrɒs·bəʊ, $ˈkrɑːs·boʊ/ *n* [C] a weapon used, esp. in the past, for shooting a short arrow with great force

cross·breed /£ˈkrɒs·briːd, $ˈkrɑːs-/ *n* [C] an animal or plant that is a mixture of breeds, esp. pure breeds, and is therefore a new variety

cross·bred /£ˈkrɒs·bred, $ˈkrɑːs-/ *adj* • *a crossbred dog/bull/sheep*

cross·check *(obj)* /£ˈkrɒs·tʃek, $ˈkrɑːs-, -ˈ-/ *v* to make certain that (information, a calculation, etc.) is correct, by asking a different person or using a different method of calculation • *The school says it's OK, but I'll just crosscheck (that)* **with** *the Education Authority.* [I/T]

cross–dress·ing /£ˌkrɒsˈdres·ɪŋ, $ˌkrɑːs-/ *n* [U] the activity of wearing the clothes of the opposite sex • *There's a lot of cross-dressing in British pantomimes, where men dress up as Dames and a woman plays the part of the young hero.*

cross–ex·am·ine *(obj)* /£ˌkrɒs·ɪɡˈzæm·ɪn, $ˌkrɑːs-/, **cross–ques·tion** *(obj) v* to ask detailed questions of (someone, esp. a WITNESS in a trial) in order to discover if they have been telling the truth • *Both prosecution witnesses were cross-examined* **on** *what exactly they had seen on the night of February 1st.* [T] • *Whenever I ring my Mum to say hello she starts cross-examining me* **about** *my job, my wife, my whole life.* [T]

cross–ex·am·i·na·tion /£ˌkrɒs·ɪɡˌzæm·ɪˈneɪ·ʃən, $ˌkrɑːs-/ *n* • *a two-hour cross-examination* [C] • **Under** *cross-examination, the witness admitted her evidence had been mostly lies.* [U]

cross–ex·am·i·ner /£ˌkrɒs·ɪɡˈzæm·ɪ·nəʳ, $ˌkrɑː·sɪɡˈzæm·ɪ·nɚ/ *n* [C]

cross–eyed /£ˌkrɒsˈaɪd, $ˌkrɑːs-/ *adj* having eyes that look inwards towards the nose; BOSS-EYED • PIC› **Eye**

cross–fer·ti·liz·a·tion, *Br and Aus usually* **–i·sa·tion** /£ˌkrɒs·fɜː·tɪ·laɪˈzeɪ·ʃən, $ˌkrɑːs·fɜːr·t̬ə·lɪ-/ *n* [U] the mixing of the ideas, customs, etc. of different places or groups of people, to benefit all • *These French artists will tour China with the aim of helping cultural cross-fertilization between the two countries.*

cross·fire /£ˈkrɒs·faɪəʳ, $ˈkrɑːs·faɪr/ *n* [U] firing guns from two or more places at the same time, so that their lines of shooting cross • *One boat of refugees was* **caught in** *the naval crossfire and sunk.* • *(fig.) The Health Minister, who resigned today, claims she is an innocent victim* **caught in the crossfire** *of the current battle over inflation.*

cross–hatch·ing /£ˈkrɒsˌhætʃ·ɪŋ, $ˈkrɑːs-/ *n* [U] two groups of parallel lines which are drawn close together across each other, esp. at an angle of 90°, on parts of a picture to show differences of light and darkness

cross–hatched /£ˈkrɒs·hætʃt, $ˈkrɑːs-/ *adj* [not gradable]

cross–hatch /£ˈkrɒs·hætʃ, $ˈkrɑːs-/, **hatch** *v*

cross·ly /£ˈkrɒs·li, $ˈkrɑː·sli/ *adv* See at CROSS ANNOYED

cross·o·ver /£ˈkrɒs·əʊ·vəʳ, $ˈkrɑːs·oʊ·vɚ/ *adj* [not gradable], *n* (mixing) styles, ideas, etc. from different areas or of different origins • *a crossover of popular and classical music* [C] • *We went down to a disco playing reggae crossover.* [U]

cross·patch /£ˈkrɒs·pætʃ, $ˈkrɑːs-/ *n* [C] *infml dated humorous* a bad-tempered person

cross–pur·pos·es /£ˌkrɒsˈpɜː·pə·sɪz, $ˌkrɑːsˈpɜːr-/ *pl n* **at cross-purposes** (of two or more people or organizations) not understanding each other by not being aware that they are talking about different things • *I think we've been talking at cross-purposes – I meant next year, not this year.*

cross–ques·tion *(obj)* /£ˌkrɒsˈkwes·tʃən, $ˌkrɑːs-/ *v* [I/T] to CROSS-EXAMINE

cross–re·fer *obj* /£ˌkrɒs·rɪˈfɜːʳ, $ˌkrɑːs·rɪˈfɜːr/ *v* [T] **-rr-** to direct (a reader) from one place in a book to another place in the same book

cross–ref·er·ence /£ˌkrɒsˈref·ər·ənts, $ˌkrɑːsˈref·ɚ-/ *n* [C] • *I like an encyclopedia which has lots of cross-references* **to** *extra information.*

cross·roads /£ˈkrɒs·rəʊdz, $ˈkrɑːs·roʊdz/ *n* [C] *pl* **crossroads** a place where two roads meet and cross each other • *Turn left at the next crossroads.* • *(fig.)* If someone or something is **at a** crossroads, they are at an important and uncertain stage in their lives or development: *I feel I'm at a crossroads* **in** *my life, and I don't know whether to go back to Africa or not.* • PIC› **Road**

cross–sec·tion DRAWING /£ˈkrɒs·sek·ʃən, $ˈkrɑːs-, ˌ-ˈ--/ *n* [C] (a drawing of) a part of something cut off from the rest at an angle, esp. of 90 degrees • *This cross-section of a human heart shows how it functions.*

cross–sec·tion REPRESENTATIVE GROUP /£ˈkrɒs·sek·ʃən, $ˈkrɑːs-, ˌ-ˈ--/ *n* [C] a small group which is representative of all the different types within the total group • *The demonstrators seemed to be* **from** *a complete cross-section of society – male and female, old and young, rich and poor.*

cross·walk /£ˈkrɒs·wɔːk, $ˈkrɑːs·wɑːk/ *n* [C] *Am for* **pedestrian crossing**, see at PEDESTRIAN • PIC› **Road**

cross·wind /£ˈkrɒs·wɪnd, $ˈkrɑːs-/ *n* [C] a wind blowing at an angle to the direction of travel of a vehicle • *I won't be able to land the plane if this crosswind gets any stronger.*

cross·wise /£ˈkrɒs·waɪz, $ˈkrɑːs-/ *adv, adj* crossing something, esp. at an angle of 90° • *In this city the crosswise streets all go uphill.*

cross·word (puz·zle) /£ˈkrɒs·wɜːd, $ˈkrɑːs·wɜːrd/ *n* [C] a word game of black and white squares in which you have to guess the answers to CLUES and write the words into numbered squares that go across and down • *I do the Times crossword every morning.* • PIC› **Games**

crotch /£krɒtʃ, $krɑːtʃ/, **crutch** *n* [C] the part of your body where your legs join at the top, or the part of trousers or underwear which covers the area between the tops of your legs • *Michael Jackson's dancing involves a lot of strutting and holding his crotch.*

crotch·less /£ˈkrɒtʃ·ləs, $ˈkrɑːtʃ-/ *adj* • Underwear which is crotchless has no part covering the area between the tops of the legs: *He bought her some crotchless panties for her birthday.*

crot·chet /£ˈkrɒtʃ·ət, $ˈkrɑː·tʃət/, *esp. Am* **quar·ter note** *n* [C] *specialized* a musical note with a time value equal to two QUAVERS or half a MINIM

crot·che·ty /£ˈkrɒtʃ·ɪ·ti, $ˈkrɑː·tʃə·t̬i/ *adj infml* bad-tempered and easily annoyed • *By the time the meal began, the youngest children were getting tired and crotchety.*

crouch /kraʊtʃ/ *v* [I] to bend your knees and lower yourself so that you are close to the ground and leaning forward slightly • *She saw him coming and crouched* **(down)** *behind a bush.* • *The lion crouched, ready to attack.*

crouch /kraʊtʃ/ *n* [C usually sing] • *He lowered himself into a crouch, hoping he wouldn't be seen.*

croup /kruːp/ *n* [U] an illness that children sometimes suffer from in which they cough a lot and have difficulty in breathing

crou·pi·er /ˈkruː·pi·eɪ/ *n* [C] a person who works in a CASINO (= a place where people risk money in games) who is responsible for a particular table and whose job is to collect and pay out money and give out playing cards • *The security men were alerted after a player claimed he had put two £25 chips on a winning number when the croupier found just one.*

crou·ton /£ˈkruː·tɔ̃ː, $-tɑːn/ *n* [C usually pl] a small square piece of bread that is fried or TOASTED and which is added to soup or a salad just before you eat it • *Serve the onion soup with grated cheese and croutons.* • PIC› **Bread and cakes**

crow BIRD /£krəʊ, $kroʊ/ *n* [C] a large black bird with a loud unpleasant cry • *As we walked along the path, crows cawed from the poplar trees overhead.* • A place that is a particular distance away **as the crow flies** would be that distance away if you could travel there in a straight line: *As the crow flies, it's about three kilometres, but we'll have to go round by the road, which is about seven kilometres.* • **Crow's feet** are the little lines around the outside corners of a person's eyes: *This moisturising cream will help to smooth away crow's feet.* • A **crow's nest** is a small enclosed space near the top of a ship's MAST from which a person can see in all directions.

crow [CRY] /£krəʊ, $kroʊ/ *v* [I] *past* **crowed** or *Br also* **crew** /kruː/ (of a male chicken) to make a very loud sharp cry, or (of a baby) to make small cries of happiness • *We were woken at dawn by a cock crowing repeatedly.* • *When she saw her father, Olivia crowed with pleasure and waved her arms.* • *(disapproving)* If someone crows **about/over** something, they express too much pride about it: *He never stops crowing over his flashy new car.* ○ *Schools that have achieved good exam results this year have been crowing about it.*

crow·bar /£ˈkrəʊ·bɑːʳ, $ˈkroʊ·bɑːr/ *n* [C] a heavy iron bar with a bent end that is used to help lift heavy objects off the ground or to force things open • *The thieves forced one of the shop windows open with a crowbar and then stole £10 000 worth of jewellery.*

crowd /kraʊd/ *n* [C + sing/pl v] a large group of people who have gathered together • *A crowd of about 15 000 attended the concert.* • *The crowd was/were chanting and holding up banners.* • *When we got to the party, there was quite a crowd of people there already.* • *(infml)* A crowd is also a group of friends or a group of people with similar interests: *She used to go about with a friendly crowd.* ○ *"Who was there?" "Oh, the usual crowd, Dave, Mike and Fiona."* • *(disapproving)* If you **follow/go with/move with** the crowd, you usually do what most other people do: *Think for yourself, don't just follow the crowd.* • A **crowd-puller** is a person or thing that attracts a lot of attention and that people will pay to see: *The toy exhibition is a guaranteed crowd-puller.* • LP› **Sports**

crowd *(obj)* /kraʊd/ *v* • If a group of people crowd **round/about** something or someone, they gather closely around it or them: *As soon as he appeared, reporters crowded round.* [I] • If people crowd **into** a place, they fill it completely: *Hordes of commuters crowded* **into** *the train.* [I] ○ *The soldiers crowded* (=forced) *the demonstrators* **into** *a small hall.* [T] • *(infml)* To crowd someone is to make them feel uncomfortable by standing too close to them or by continually watching them: *I need some time to do this work properly, so don't crowd me.* [T] • To crowd **out** something or someone is to not allow them any space to grow or develop: *By late summer, rampant ivy had crowded out the climbing roses.* [M] ○ *The project's expected $5·9 billion cost could escalate, pushing it far behind schedule and crowding out other projects.* [M]

crowd·ed /ˈkraʊ·dɪd/ *adj* • If a place is crowded, it is full of people: *By ten o'clock the bar was crowded.* ○ *The dance class was crowded* **out** (=very full of people) *last week.* • *(infml)* If you feel crowded, you feel uncomfortably close to other people: *I felt a bit crowded at the party so I went out for a walk.*

crown [HEAD COVERING] /kraʊn/ *n* [C] a circular decoration for the head, usually made of gold and jewels, which is worn by a king or queen at official ceremonies • *For her official portrait, the Queen wore her crown and robes.* • In a sports competition, a crown is a prize or position which you get for beating all the other competitors: *He regained his world crown in Rome in 1991 and went on to win the Olympic gold a year later.* • **The Crown** is the royal governing power of a country that has a king or queen: *All this land belongs to the Crown.* • *(Br law)* In England and Wales, a **crown court** is a law court where criminal cases are judged by a judge and JURY (=a group of people who decide whether a person is guilty or not guilty): *A crown court hears major criminal cases.* LP› **Law** • A **crown colony** is an area or country which is politically controlled by Britain and which has a British governor: *The Crown Colony of Hong Kong returns to Chinese control in 1997.* • **Crown jewels** are the crown and other jewels worn at important official ceremonies by the king or queen: **The** *crown jewels are on display in the Tower of London.* • A **crown prince** is the man who will be king of a country when the ruling king or queen dies. • A **crown princess** is the woman who will be queen of a country when the ruling king or queen dies, or is the wife of a crown prince. • *(Br law)* A **crown prosecutor** is an official who is responsible for trying to prove in a law court that people accused of crimes are guilty. • PIC› **Hats**

crown *obj* /kraʊn/ *v* [T] • *Queen Elizabeth II was crowned* (=made queen in a special ceremony) *in 1953.* • *Elizabeth was crowned queen in 1953.* [+ obj + n] • *She's the newly crowned* (=She has just become) *world champion in the javelin.* • An event or achievement that crowns something else is the best or most successful part of it: *Her exciting acting career was crowned by her performance as Juliet.* • A **crowned head** is a king or a queen who is the ruler of their country: *Most of Europe's crowned heads have been entertained in the palace.* • See also CORONATION.

crown·ing /ˈkraʊ·nɪŋ/ *adj* [not gradable] • *Her performance as Lady Macbeth was the crowning* **achievement** (=the greatest achievement) *of her long career.* • *The astronaut said that walking on the moon was his crowning* **glory** (=his most important achievement).

crown [TOP PART] /kraʊn/ *n* [C] the top part of something, esp. a person's head • *The baby had black hair sticking straight up from her crown.* • *The whole city can be viewed from the crown of the hill.* • The crown of a hat is the part that covers the top of your head: *A pink ribbon had been tied around the crown of the hat.* Compare BRIM [PART OF HAT]. • PIC› **Body, Hats**

crown *obj* /kraʊn/ *v* [T] • *(fml or literary)* If something crowns something else, it is on or around the top of it: *The church was crowned with golden domes.* • *(infml)* To crown someone is to hit them on the head. • *(Br and Aus)* To **crown it all** (*esp. Am* **cap it all**) means to make good or bad luck complete: *I had lost my ticket, was soaked to the skin, and, to crown it all, discovered that my purse had been stolen.*

crown [TOOTH] /kraʊn/ *n* [C] an artificial piece used to cover the top and sides of a broken tooth • *He has had a gold crown fitted on two of his back teeth.*

crown *obj* /kraʊn/ *v* [T] • *She's had her two front teeth crowned* (=fitted with crowns).

crown [COIN] /kraʊn/ *n* [C] a British coin which is no longer used • *A crown was worth five shillings, which is approximately 25 pence.*

cro·zi·er /£ˈkrəʊ·zi·əʳ, $ˈkroʊ·zi·ɚ/ *n* [C] a CROSIER

cru·cial /ˈkruː·ʃəl/ *adj* (of a decision or event in the future) extremely important • *This will be a crucial decision for the education services because it sets the standard for all future years.* • *Wilson's evidence proved crucial* **to** *the legal case.* • *It is crucial* **that** *the problem is tackled immediately.* [+ that clause] • *(Br slang)* If you describe something as crucial, you mean that it is very good: *I've bought some crucial new trainers.*

cru·cial·ly /ˈkruː·ʃəl·i/ *adv* • *This case will be crucially* (=extremely) *important for other people who have suffered mental and physical damage from the drug.*

cru·ci·ble /ˈkruː·sɪ·bl̩/ *n* [C] a container in which metals or other substances can be heated to very high temperatures • *Clay crucibles were used in steel production because they could survive the intense heat which was needed to melt steel.* • A crucible is also a severe test: *This theatre is the crucible of comedy, where fame or failure is found.* • A crucible is also a place in which different cultures or styles can mix together to produce something new and exciting: *A vibrant cultural imagination and sense of community made Los Angeles a crucible for black music in the early 1940s and '50s.*

cru·ci·fix /ˈkruː·sɪ·fɪks/ *n* [C] a model or picture representing Jesus Christ on a cross • *She always wears a small gold crucifix round her neck.*

cru·ci·form /£ˈkruː·sɪ·fɔːm, $-fɔːrm/ *adj fml* in the shape of a cross • *The majority of Christian churches have a cruciform design.*

cru·ci·fy *obj* /ˈkruː·sɪ·faɪ/ *v* [T] to kill (someone) by tying or nailing them to a cross and leaving them there to die • *Calgary is the site just outside Jerusalem where Jesus was said to be crucified.* • *(infml)* To crucify someone or something also means to punish or damage them or it severely: *If they ever find out her secret, they'll crucify her.* ○ *The terrorist threat has made many Americans reluctant to travel to Europe and has crucified the transatlantic air industry.*

cru·ci·fix·ion /ˌkruː·sɪˈfɪk·ʃən/ *n* • *He was executed by crucifixion.* [U] • *Crucifixions were common in the Roman Empire.* [C] • **The Crucifixion** is the death of Christ on a cross: *The Crucifixion was a common subject painted by medieval and Renaissance artists.*

crud /krʌd/ *n* [U] *infml* a sticky substance, such as dirt • *Don't step on my nice clean floor with that crud on your* *boots!* • Crud is also something worthless or bad: *This is just the sort of crud you read in the tabloid press.*

crud·dy /ˈkrʌd·i/ *adj* **-ier, -iest** *infml* • If something is cruddy, it is bad or worthless: *It's a pretty cruddy book, so I didn't bother finishing it.*

crude SIMPLE /kruːd/ *adj* **-r, -st** simple and not skilfully done or made • *The missile is very crude and rather inaccurate.* • *'Keep Out' was painted in crude letters on the door.* • *(disapproving) This is another crude* (=obvious) *attempt to frighten people into silence.* • **Crude** or **crude oil** is oil in a natural state that has not yet been treated: *70 000 tonnes of crude oil has poured out of the damaged tanker into the sea.* • (I)

crude·ly /ˈkruːd·li/ *adv* • *The incendiary device had been crudely made.*

crude·ness /ˈkruːd·nəs/, **crud·i·ty** /£ˈkruː·dɪ·ti, $-də·ṭi/ *n* [U] • *Her ideas were simple to the point of crudity.*

crude RUDE /kruːd/ *adj* **-r, -st** rude and offensive • *Most of his jokes were crude and sexist.* • *Do you have to be so crude?* • (I)

crude·ly /ˈkruːd·li/ *adv* • *There's no need to express yourself so crudely* (=in such a rude way).

crude·ness /ˈkruːd·nəs/, **crud·i·ty** /£ˈkruː·dɪ·ti, $-də·ṭi/ *n* [U] • *She was shocked by the crudity of his remarks.*

crud·i·tés /£ˈkruː·dɪ·teɪ, $ˌkruː·dɪˈteɪ/ *pl n* small pieces of raw vegetables, often served with a DIP (=a cold thick creamy sauce) before a meal

cru·el /ˈkruː·əl, krʊəl/ *adj* **crueller** or **crueler**, **cruellest** or **cruelest** extremely unkind and unpleasant and causing pain to people or animals intentionally • *Don't tease him about his weight, you're being cruel.* • *Children can be very cruel to one another.* • *He was forced to apologise for his cruel remarks.* • *The final stage of the hunt when the fox is dragged out of its hole and killed by the hounds seems particularly cruel.* • *A cruel* (=severe and painful) *wind had been blowing all day.* • *The city's inhabitants were preparing themselves for another cruel* (=extremely cold) *winter without heating or electricity.* • *Not getting the job came as a cruel* (=severe and painful) *disappointment to her.* • To **be cruel to be kind** is to do or say something that causes someone pain because you believe that it will help them later: *I decided to be cruel to be kind, and told her she was wasting her time trying to be an artist.* • *"I must be cruel only to be kind"* (Shakespeare, Hamlet 3.4)

cru·el·ly /ˈkruː·ə·li, ˈkrʊəl·i/ *adv* • *She told him cruelly that she never wanted to see him again.*

cru·el·ty /£ˈkruː·əl·ti, ˈkrʊəl-, $-ṭi/ *n* • *His former wife accused him of beatings, verbal abuse and other cruelties.* [C] • *The farmer was accused of cruelty* **to** *animals.* [U] • *The effects of* **mental** *cruelty* (=unkind words and behaviour) *can be worse than those of physical violence.* [U] • *(Br)* **Cruelty-free** products are developed without being tested on animals: *I always try to buy cruelty-free cosmetics.*

cru·et /ˈkruː·ɪt/ *n* [C] *(Br and Aus)* a container that holds smaller containers of salt and PEPPER etc., used when having a meal, or *(Am)* a glass bottle which holds oil or vinegar for use during a meal

cruise /kruːz/ *n* [C] a journey on a large ship for pleasure, during which you visit several places • *This four-night cruise gives you the opportunity to see the wild beauty of the Shetland Islands and the wonderful Norwegian scenery in Bergen.* • *She has always wanted to go* **on** *a Caribbean cruise.* • *The QE2 is a cruise liner.*

cruise /kruːz/ *v* [I] • To cruise is to travel on ships for pleasure: *We're planning to spend our retirement cruising on luxury liners around the world.* ○ *During your holiday, you can cruise along the Seine and see the famous sights of Paris.* • If a ship or aircraft cruises, it travels at a continuous speed: *The plane is cruising at an altitude of 35 000 feet.* • *(slang)* To cruise is to go around public places looking for someone to have sex with: *He spends the weekends cruising the bars and clubs of Los Angeles.*

cruise (mis·sile) /kruːz/ *n* [C] a winged MISSILE (=flying weapon) which can be directed by a computer during its flight and which sometimes carries nuclear explosives • *The battleship is armed with long range cruise missiles.* • *The government has agreed to reduce its number of cruise missiles.*

cruis·er WAR SHIP /£ˈkruː·zəʳ, $-zɚ/ *n* [C] a large fast ship used in war • *A cruiser often travels in front of a battle fleet to obtain information about what the enemy is doing.* • *The two tankers heading for the war zone were escorted by a cruiser and a destroyer.*

cruis·er PLEASURE BOAT /£ˈkruː·zəʳ, $-zɚ/ *n* [C] a boat with an engine and a CABIN in which people sail for pleasure • *He owns a 30-foot luxury cruiser.* • *There has been concern about the safety of passenger cruisers on the River Thames.*

crumb /krʌm/ *n* [C] a very small piece of bread, cake or biscuit • *The floor was covered with crumbs after breakfast.* • A crumb is also a small amount of something: *Any crumb* **of hope** *was anxiously seized on.* ○ *The team's 2:1 win on Saturday has provided a small crumb* **of comfort** *for their manager after an unsuccessful season.* • See also BREADCRUMB.

crum·ble *(obj)* /ˈkrʌm·bl̩/ *v* to (cause to) break into small pieces • *She nervously crumbled the bread between her fingers.* [T] • *The cliffs on which the houses are built are starting to crumble.* [I] • *(fig.) Support for the government is crumbling* (=becoming gradually weaker). [I]

crum·ble /ˈkrʌm·bl̩/ *n* • A crumble (*Am also* **crisp**) is a sweet dish made from fruit covered in a crumbled mixture of flour, butter and sugar, which is baked and eaten hot: *I've baked three tarts and two crumbles.* [C] ○ *Would you like some apple/rhubarb crumble?* [U]

crum·bly /ˈkrʌm·bli, -bl̩·i/ *adj* **-ier, -iest** • *The cake had just come out of the oven and was warm and crumbly* (=it could easily be broken into small pieces).

crumbs /krʌmz/ *exclamation Br and Aus slightly dated* an expression of surprise or worry • *Crumbs, just look at the time!*

crum·my /ˈkrʌm·i/ *adj* **-ier, -iest** *infml* of very bad quality • *The carpet was pretty crummy so we threw it away.* • *The Smiths live in a crummy little house near the station.* • (NL)

crum·pet BREAD /ˈkrʌm·pɪt/ *n* [C] a small round bread-like cake with holes in one side that is eaten hot with butter • *We sat by the fire, toasting crumpets and drinking tea.*

crum·pet WOMAN /ˈkrʌm·pɪt/ *n* [U] *Br slang* sexually attractive women. Many women consider this word offensive. • *There was some decent crumpet at the party last night.* • *She's a nice bit of crumpet* (=She is a sexually attractive woman).

crum·ple *(obj)* /ˈkrʌm·pl̩/ *v* to (cause to) become full of irregular folds • *You'll crumple that suit if you don't pack it properly.* [T] • *The side of the car had crumpled where it had been hit.* [I] • *Sylvie crumpled* **up** *the letter and threw it in the bin.* [T] • If someone's face crumples, it becomes full of lines because of a strong emotion: *His face crumpled and he started to cry.* [I] ○ *Her face crumpled* **with** *laughter.* [I] • If someone crumples, they fall to the ground suddenly: *When he heard the news, he crumpled* **into a heap** *on the floor.* [I] • *(Br and Aus)* A **crumple zone** is a part of a car that is designed to crumple easily in an accident and so protect the people inside from being hit too hard: *The car has front and rear crumple zones and two side-impact protection bars.*

crunch *(obj)* SOUND /krʌntʃ/ *v* to crush (hard food) loudly between the teeth, or to make a sound as if something is being crushed or broken • *He sat there crunching his cornflakes and reading the newspaper.* [T] • *She was crunching noisily* **on** *an apple.* [I] • *The gravel crunched underfoot as we walked up to the house.* [I] • *The huge machine crunched the car* **up** (=crushed the car noisily) *into a small cube.* [M]

crunch /krʌntʃ/ *n* [C usually sing] • *The woods were silent apart from the crunch of our feet in the snow.* • *We heard the crunch of wheels on the gravel drive.*

crunch·y /ˈkrʌn·tʃi/ *adj* **-ier, -iest** • If food is crunchy, it is firm and makes a loud noise when it is eaten: *I like toast best when it's really crunchy.*

crunch DIFFICULTY /krʌntʃ/ *n* [U] *infml* a difficult situation which forces you to make a decision or act • *New car sales fell by 20% last year and the auto industry has found itself in a severe crunch.* • **If/When it comes to the crunch** means when a situation becomes extremely serious and a decision must be made: *If it comes to the crunch and you and your husband do split up, you can always stay with us.*

cru·sade /kruːˈseɪd/ *n* [C] a long and determined attempt to achieve something which you believe in strongly • *They have long been involved in a crusade* **for** *racial equality.* • *She was a leading light in the crusade* **against** *illiteracy.* • *The President has embarked on a* **moral** *crusade to encourage parenthood within stable marriages.* • The Crusades were the holy wars fought by the Christians against the Muslims, often in Palestine, in the 11th, 12th, 13th and 17th centuries: *The Middle East had become known to Europeans during the 11th-13th century Crusades.*

cru·sade /kruː'seɪd/ *v* [I] • To crusade is to make an effort to achieve something which you believe in strongly: *He has crusaded tirelessly* **for** *women's and gay rights.* ○ *She crusades* **against** *sex and violence on television.*

cru·sad·er /£kruː'seɪ·dəʳ, $-dɚ/ *n* [C] • *He caught the public imagination as a crusader* **against** *corruption.* • *The church contains the tombs of two medieval crusaders* (= soldiers who fought in the holy wars).

crush *obj* PRESS /krʌʃ/ *v* [T] to press (something) very hard so that it is broken or its shape is destroyed • *The package had been badly crushed in the post.* • *Crush three cloves of garlic and then add to the mixture.* • *His arm was badly crushed in the car accident.* • *Crush the almonds* **into** *a fine powder.* • If you crush paper or cloth, you press it so that it becomes full of irregular folds and is no longer flat: *My dress got all crushed in my suitcase.* • If people are crushed against other people or things, they are pressed against them: *Tragedy struck when several people were crushed* **to death** *in the crowd.*

crush /krʌʃ/ *n* [U] • A crush is a crowd of people forced to stand close together: *I had to struggle through the crush to get to the door.* ○ *You can come in our car but it'll be a bit of a crush* (= there will be a lot of people in it). • A **crush barrier** is a strong fence that is used to divide a large crowd, for example at a football game, to stop them from being pressed too close together.

crushed /krʌʃt/ *adj* • *Serve the oysters on a bed of crushed ice.* • If a piece of clothing is crushed, it has a lot of irregular folds in it: *Her dress looked crushed, as though she had slept in it.*

crush *obj* SHOCK /krʌʃ/ *v* [T] to upset or shock (someone) badly • *The news that his wife had been killed in the accident completely crushed him.*

crushed /krʌʃt/ *adj* • *I felt crushed* (= very hurt) *by what she'd said.*

crush·ing /'krʌʃ·ɪŋ/ *adj* • *The news came as a crushing* (= severe) *blow.*

crush *obj* DESTROY /krʌʃ/ *v* [T] to defeat (someone) completely • *The president called upon the army to help crush the rebellion.* • *France crushed Wales by 36 to 3 in last Saturday's match in Paris.* • *The government set out to crush all opposition to the tax.*

crush·ing /'krʌʃ·ɪŋ/ *adj* • *Their army had suffered a crushing* (= severe) *defeat.*

crush ATTRACTION /krʌʃ/ *n* [C] *infml* a strong but temporary attraction for someone • *She has a crush* **on** *one of her teachers at school.*

crust /krʌst/ *n* a hard outer covering of something • *There was a thin crust of dirt around the bath.* [C] • *Pie crust* (= the cooked pastry on top of it) *should be crisp and golden brown.* [U] • The crust on a loaf of bread is the outside layer of it: *Could you cut the crusts off the sandwiches, please?* [C] • A crust is also a small piece of dry bread: *All he had in his pocket was an apple and a dry crust.* [C] • The crust of a planet is its hard outer layer that consists mainly of rock. [C] • PIC> **Bread and cakes**

crust·ed /£'krʌs·tɪd, $-t̬ɪd/ *adj* • *The bath was crusted* **with** *dirt* (= had a line of dirt around it).

crust·y /£'krʌs·ti, $-t̬i/ *adj* **-ier, -iest** • *You can buy freshly baked crusty bread at the shop down the road.* • See also CRUSTY.

crust·a·cean /krʌs'teɪ·ʃən/ *n* [C] any of various types of animal which live in water, have a hard outer shell, long thin organs on the head and many legs • *Crabs, lobsters and shrimps are crustaceans.*

crust·y /£'krʌs·ti, $-t̬i/ *adj* **-ier, -iest** (esp. of older people) bad-tempered and easily annoyed • *He's a crusty old bachelor who lives alone.* • See also **crusty** at CRUST.

crutch /krʌtʃ/ *n* [C] a stick with a piece that fits under the arm which someone leans on for support if they have difficulty in walking because of a foot or leg injury • *Martin broke his leg in a football match and has been* **on** *crutches for the past six weeks.* • A crutch is also something that provides help and support: *When she gave up smoking, she found it hard to concentrate without her nicotine crutch.* ○ *After my husband died, my brother became an emotional crutch for me.* • Crutch is also another word for CROTCH. • PIC> **Medical equipment**

crux /krʌks/ *n* [U] the most important or serious part of a matter, problem or argument • *The crux of the country's economic problems is its foreign debt.* • *The issue of an arms embargo will be at the crux of the negotiations in Geneva.*

cry *(obj)* PRODUCE TEARS /kraɪ/ *v* to produce tears as the result of a strong emotion, such as unhappiness or pain • *I*

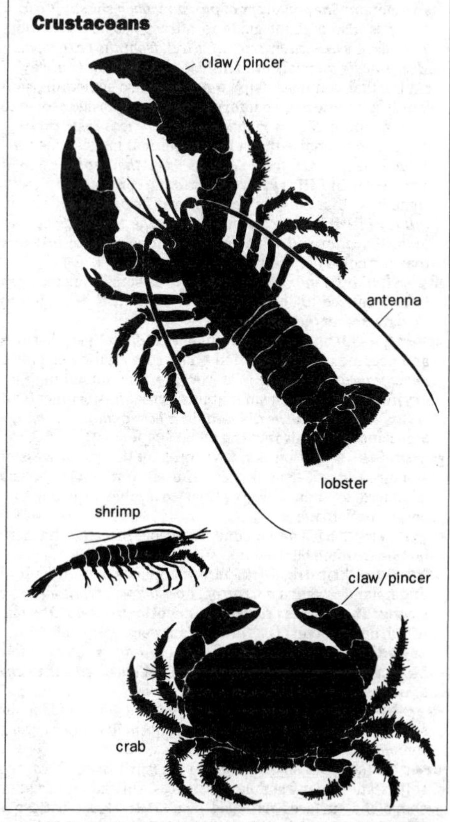

could hear someone crying in the next room. [I] • *"There, there, don't cry," she said.* [I] • *He put his head in his hands and began to cry like a child.* [I] • *We all laughed until we cried.* [I] • *She cried bitter tears when she got the letter.* [T] • *He cried* **for joy** *when he heard that his son had been found alive and well.* [I] • *I was so upset that day, I* **cried** *my* **eyes out** (= cried for a long time). • To cry your**self to sleep** is to cry for a long time until you start to sleep. [T] • *(infml disapproving)* A **cry-baby** is someone, usually a child, who cries a lot without good reason: *Don't be such a cry-baby. You've only got a small scratch on your knee.* • *(saying)* **It is no good/use crying over spilt milk** means that it is useless to regret something which has already happened: *"It's no use crying over spilt milk" she said. "He's spent all the money and there's nothing you can do about it."* • *"Cry, the Beloved Country"* (title of a book about South Africa by Alan Paton, 1948) • *"Don't Cry for Me, Argentina"* (song from the musical *Evita* by Tim Rice and Andrew Lloyd-Webber, 1976)

cry /kraɪ/ *n* [U] • *"Go on, have a good cry", he said.*

cry·ing /'kraɪ·ɪŋ/ *n* [U] • *She could hear sounds of crying coming from the next room.* • See also CRYING.

cry *(obj)* SHOUT /kraɪ/ *v* to call out or speak loudly • *"Help me!" he cried.* [+ clause] • *"Look out!" she cried* [+ clause] • *She cried* **out** *in pain as the bullet grazed her shoulder.* [I] • If you **cry out against** something which you do not approve of, you complain about it loudly: *Women's rights groups have cried out against the proposed cut in benefit paid to single mothers.* • To **cry out for** something is to need it badly: *The country is crying out for a change in leadership.* ○ *The judge said that this sort of crime cries out for a severe punishment.* • *(infml)* You say **for crying out loud** when you are annoyed, and to give force to what you are saying: *Oh, for crying out loud, why won't you listen to me!* • If someone **cries foul**, they say that something which has happened is unfair or illegal: *The opposition parties have cried foul* **at** *the president's act, seeing it as a violation of democracy.* • If someone **cries wolf**, they ask for help when they do not need it: *If you cry wolf too often, people will stop believing that you need help.*

cry /kraɪ/ *n* [C] • A cry is a loud high sound that expresses an emotion: *She gave a cry of pleasure when she saw them.* • A cry is also a shout made to attract people's attention: *They were wakened by cries of 'Fire!' from the next room.* ○ *Most suicide attempts are really a cry* **for help** (= a way of saying that you need help). • A cry is also something said loudly in public to give information or encourage people to do something: *'Equal rights for women' was their cry.* • A cry is also the noise that a bird or animal makes: *The new-born kittens' cries were coming from the cupboard.* • If someone is **in full cry**, they are talking continuously about something in a noisy or eager way: *The opposition was in full cry in Parliament last night* **over** *the proposed changes to the education bill.* • If a group of animals are **in full cry**, they are noisily chasing after something.

cry off *v adv* [I] *infml* to decide not to do something that you have arranged to do • *She usually says she'll be there and then cries off at the last minute.*

cry·ing /ˈkraɪ·ɪŋ/ *adj* [before n; not gradable] very serious and needing urgent attention • *There's a crying* **need** *for a better education system.* • If you say that something is a **crying shame**, you mean that it is a great misfortune: *It's a crying shame* **that** *she didn't have a better chance in life.* [+ *that* clause] • See also **crying** at CRY PRODUCE TEARS.

cry·on·ics /£ˌkraɪˈɒn·ɪks, $-ˈɑː·nɪks/ *n* [U] the process of storing a dead body by freezing it until science has advanced to such a degree that it is able to bring that person back to life

crypt /krɪpt/ *n* [C] a room under the floor of a church where bodies are often buried

cryp·tic /£ˈkrɪp·tɪk, $-t̬ɪk/ *adj* mysterious and difficult to understand • *I found a scrap of paper with a cryptic message saying 'The time has come'.* • A **cryptic crossword** is one which has difficult CLUES and the answers are not obvious.

cryp·tic·ally /£ˈkrɪp·tɪ·kli, $-t̬ɪ-/ *adv* • *The Prime Minister has cryptically hinted at CIA involvement in the affair.*

cryp·to– /£ˈkrɪp·təʊ, $-toʊ-/ *combining form* hidden or secret • *The minister accused his opponent of being a crypto-communist.*

crys·tal REGULAR SHAPE /ˈkrɪs·tᵊl/ *n* [C] *specialized* the solid state of many simple substances, which has a regular shape and surfaces arranged in a SYMMETRICAL pattern • *When seawater is allowed to evaporate, salt crystals are deposited.* • *Cirrus clouds are composed of ice crystals.* • *The exact shape of each snow crystal is determined by the weather conditions.* • *When the liquid cools, the atoms form themselves into a crystal structure.*

crys·tal·line /ˈkrɪs·tᵊl·aɪn/ *adj specialized* • *Crystalline deposits were found on the tip of the needle.*

crys·tal·lize *(obj)*, *Br and Aus usually* **–ise** /ˈkrɪs·tᵊl·aɪz/ *v specialized* • *The liquid mixture will soon start to crystallize* (= turn into crystals). [I] • If something crystalizes your thoughts or opinions, it makes them clear and fixed: *The event helped to crystallize my thoughts.* [T] • **Crystallized fruit** are pieces of fruit that have been covered in melted sugar which has then become hard.

crys·tal·liz·a·tion, *Br and Aus usually* **–i·sa·tion** /ˌkrɪs·tᵊl·aɪˈzeɪ·ʃᵊn/ *n* [U] *specialized* • *To make diamond, the crystallization of carbon must be done at extremely high pressure.*

crys·tal ROCK /ˈkrɪs·tᵊl/ *n* (a piece of) clear transparent rock that looks like ice, which is used in jewellery • *Quartz crystal is found in Brazil.* [U] • *Quartz crystals are widely used in digital watches.* [C] • *She always wears a crystal round her neck because she believes it increases her sense of well-being.* [C] • *I was given a lovely pair of crystal earrings for my 21st birthday.* • *The island has beautiful beaches,* **crystal clear** (= very clear) *water and spectacular countryside.* • Something that is **crystal clear** is very easy to understand: *The evidence is now crystal clear.* ○ *She made it crystal clear* **(that)** *she was speaking with specific instructions from her employer.* [+ *(that)* clause]

crys·tal·line /ˈkrɪs·tᵊl·aɪn/ *adj literary* • Something that is crystalline is clear and bright like crystal: *Her singing voice has a pure, crystalline quality.*

crys·tal GLASS /ˈkrɪs·tᵊl/ *n* transparent glass of very high quality, usually with its surface cut into delicate patterns • *The table had been set with fine china and crystal.* [U] • *They were given a decanter made from lead crystal as a wedding present.* [U] • *The hall was decorated with antique furnishings and had a large crystal chandelier hanging from the ceiling.* • *(Am)* A crystal is a transparent glass or plastic cover for a watch or clock. [C] • A **crystal ball** is a transparent glass ball used by someone who claims they can discover what will happen to you in the future by looking into it. • To **crystal-gaze** is to try to see the future by looking into a crystal ball.

CSE /ˌsiː·esˈiː/ *n* [C/U] *abbreviation for* Certificate of Secondary Education (= in Britain in the past, a system of examinations taken in various subjects at the age of about 16) • Compare GCSE.

CS gas /ˌsiːˈes/ *n* [U] a gas that causes painful breathing and tears, which is used by the army or police to control a person or crowd in a violent situation • *The police sprayed CS gas at the crowd to try and control them.*

cub /kʌb/ *n* [C] the young of particular wild animals that eat meat, such as lions or bears • *a tiger/wolf/bear cub* • A **cub reporter** is a young person being trained to write articles for a newspaper.

cub (scout) /kʌb/ *n* [C] a child aged between 8 and 11 years old who is a member of the international organization called the Scouts • *Is your son in the cubs?* • *My sister runs a cub* **pack** (= group).

cub·by·hole /£ˈkʌb·i·həʊl, $-hoʊl/ *n* [C] a very small room or space for storing things • *My bedroom is really just a cubbyhole.* • *For the first six months of my job, I was stuck in a cubbyhole office writing reports.*

cube SHAPE /kjuːb/ *n* [C] a solid object with six square sides of equal size • *Cut the cheese into small cubes.* • *The* **ice** *cubes in the bottom of her glass clinked as she drank.* • PIC› **Shapes**

cube *obj* /kjuːb/ *v* [T] • *Cube* (= Cut into small cubes) *the potatoes.*

cube NUMBER /kjuːb/ *n* [C] *specialized* the number made by multiplying a number twice by itself • *The cube of 2* (= 2 x 2 x 2) *is 8.* • The **cube root** of a number is another number that when multiplied by itself twice makes the first number: *The cube root of 125 is 5, because 5 x 5 x 5 = 125.* • LP› **Mathematics**

cube *obj* /kjuːb/ *v* [T] *specialized* • If you cube a number, you multiply it twice by itself: *2 cubed* (= 2 x 2 x 2) *equals 8, and is written* 2^3.

cub·ic /ˈkjuː·bɪk/ *adj* [not gradable] *specialized* • Cubic is used in units of volume to show when the length of something has been multiplied by its width and height: *A cubic centimetre is written* cm^3. ○ *A cubic centimetre is equal to something a centimetre high, a centimetre long and a centimetre wide.*

cub·ic·le /ˈkjuː·bɪ·kl̩/ *n* [C] a very small division of a larger room, with three sides and often a door or curtain, which is used for dressing without being seen or for sleeping • *"Can I try this skirt on, please?" "Yes, there's a cubicle free at the end."* • PIC› **Medical equipment**

Cub·i·sm /ˈkjuː·bɪ·zᵊm/ *n* [U] a style of modern art begun in 1907 in which the whole structure of an object and its position in space is represented rather than a single view of it • *Cubism is the most influential of all modern art movements.*

Cu·bist /ˈkjuː·bɪst/ *adj, n* [C] • *Picasso's 'Les Demoiselles d'Avignon' was one of the first Cubist paintings.* • *Picasso and Braque are the best-known Cubists.*

cub·oid /ˈkjuː·bɔɪd/ *adj* [not gradable], *n specialized* (shaped like) a solid object with six rectangular sides • *a cuboid building/greenhouse/structure* • *This brick is a cuboid.* [C]

cuck·old /£ˈkʌk·əʊld, $-oʊld/ *n* [C] *dated disapproving* a man whose wife deceives him by having a sexual relationship with another man

cuck·old *obj* /£ˈkʌk·əʊld, $-oʊld/ *v* [T] *dated disapproving* • If a man or woman is cuckolded, their wife or husband has a sexual relationship with another person: *He came back from a three-month trip abroad to discover that he had been cuckolded.*

cu·ckoo BIRD /ˈkʊk·uː/ *n* [C] *pl* **cuckoos** a grey bird with a two-note call which produces its eggs in other birds' nests • *We were happy to hear the first cuckoo of spring and know that winter was almost over.* • A **cuckoo clock** is a decorative clock that has a little wooden bird inside it which comes out every hour and makes a quick two-note call: *Switzerland is famous for making cuckoo clocks.*

cu·ckoo FOOLISH /ˈkʊk·uː/ *adj infml* foolish • *You must be cuckoo to pay that much for a car.*

cu·cum·ber /£ˈkjuː·kʌm·bəʳ, $-bɚ/ *n* [C] a long thin vegetable which is pale green inside and has a dark green skin • *Cucumbers are usually sliced and eaten raw in salads.* • *We had cucumber sandwiches for tea.* • PIC› **Vegetables**

CZECH FALSE FRIENDS (CS)

English	Czech	Meaning
absolve *v*	absolvovat	graduate
abstinent *adj*	abstinent (n)	teetotaller
accord *n*	akord	musical chord
actual *adj*	aktuální	topical, immediate, current, present
adapt *v*	adaptovat	renovate
advocate *n*	advokát	solicitor, barrister
affect *n*	afekt	emotion, passion
angina *n*	angína	tonsilitis
apartment *n*	apartmá	suite of rooms
approbation *n*	aprobace	qualification to teach
arch *n*	arch	sheet of paper
argument *n*	argument	reasoning
armada *n*	armáda	armed forces; navy
barracks *n*	barák	house
basin *n*	bazén	swimming pool
benzene *n*	benzín	petrol; gasoline
billion *n*	bilión	1 000 000 000 000
blanket *n*	blanket	form
brigade *n*	brigáda	temporary job; volunteer work
calendar *n*	kalendář	diary
central *adj*	centrála	head office; telephone exchange, switchboard
chef *n*	šéf	chief; leader; boss
civil *adj*	civilní	civilian
closet *n*	klozet	lavatory; w.c.
communication *n*	komunikace	road
compositor *n*	komponista	composer of music
concourse *n*	konkurs	competition; bankrupcy
concurrence *n*	konkurence	competition; competitors
confectionery *n*	konfekce	clothes
confidant *n*	konfident	informer
control *n*	kontrola	inspection; supervision; audit; examination
cravat *n*	kravata	tie
creature *n*	kreatura	monster
criminal *n*	kriminál	jail
cylinder *n*	cylindr	top hat
dementia *n*	dementovat (v)	deny officially
desk *n*	deska	board; plaque; tablet; L.P.
disposition *n*	dispozice	aptitude; layout; instructions
divan *n*	divan	couch, sofa
dome *n*	dóm	cathedral
dose *n*	dóza	box, case, container
dress *n*	dres	tracksuit
economic *adj*	ekonomický	economical
emission *n*	emise	issue
eventual *adj*	eventuální	possible
eventually *adv*	eventuálně	possibly
example *n*	exemplář	copy (of book); specimen
expedition *n*	expedice	forwarding, shipping
extravagant *adj*	extravagantní	eccentric
fabric *n*	fabrika	factory
faggot *n*	fagot	bassoon
front *n*	fronta	queue
function *n*	funkce	(official) position
gallantry *n*	galantérie	haberdashery; leatherware; fancy goods
genial *adj*	geniální	brilliant
grenade *n*	granát	garnet
gum *n*	guma	rubber
gymnasium *n*	gymnázium	grammar school
hazard *n*	hazard	gambling; anything risky
history *n*	historie	story
hymn *n*	hymna	national anthem
interpret *v*	interpretovat	explain
justice *n*	justice	judiciary
local *n*	lokál	pub, bar; restaurant
manifestation *n*	manifestace	demonstration; sign
marmalade *n*	marmeláda	jam
maturity *n*	maturita	school-leaving examination
mixer *n*	mixér	blender, liquidiser
nervous *adj*	nervózní	tense
novel *n*	novela	short story; amendment (of a law)
obscure *adj*	obskurní	disreputable
ordinary *adj*	ordinérní	vulgar
ordination *n*	ordinace	doctor's surgery; ordination
pamphlet *n*	pamflet	lampoon
pantomime *n*	pantomima	mime show
paragraph *n*	paragraf	section of text
parapet *n*	parapet	window sill
parcel *n*	parcela	plot of land
pasta *n*	pasta	paste
pathetic *adj*	patetický	full of pathos
pension *n*	penze	retirement
perspective *n*	perspektiva	prospects
pregnant *adj*	pregnantní	pithy
preservative *n*	prezervativ	condom
process *n*	proces	trial
promote *v*	promovat	graduate
promotion *n*	promoce	graduation ceremony
propagate *v*	propagovat	advertise, promote
prospect *n*	prospekt	advertising brochure
protection *n*	protekce	favouritism; patronage
psst! *exclamation*	pst!	sh!
race *n*	rasa	breed
receipt *n*	recept	prescription, recipe
rent *n*	renta	annuity
revenge *v*	revanšovat	to repay
script *n*	skripta	cheap study text
smoking *n*	smoking	dinner jacket
spleen *n*	splín	melancholy
stipend *n*	stipendium	grant, scholarship
stop *v*	stopovat	to hitch-hike; to trace
sympathetic *adj*	sympatický	likeable, pleasant; attractive
technique *n*	technika	technology
transparent *adj*	transparent (n)	banner
vest *n*	vesta	waistcoat, cardigan
wagon *n*	vagon	railway carriage

cud /kʌd/ *n* [U] food that has been eaten by an animal with more than one stomach, such as a cow, and that comes back into the animal's mouth to be chewed again before going into the second stomach • *A cow stood in the middle of the road, calmly* **chewing** *the* **cud.** • *(infml)* If you **chew the cud**, you think slowly and carefully about something: *He sat for a moment chewing the cud before he spoke.*

cud·dle *(obj)* /ˈkʌd·l̩/ *v* to put your arms around (someone) and hold them in a loving way, or (of two people) to hold each other close for affection or comfort • *She cuddled the baby and eventually it stopped crying.* [T] • *They sat in the back row of the cinema kissing and cuddling.* [I] • *(infml)* To cuddle **up (to** someone) is to sit or lie very close to someone and put your arms around them: *We cuddled up together and tried to get warm.* [I]

cud·dle /ˈkʌd·l̩/ *n* [C] • *Come here and give me a cuddle* (= hold me). • *Young children need plenty of cuddles* (= should be held frequently).

cud·dly /ˈkʌd·l̩i/ *adj* **-ier, -iest** *approving* • *He was an adorable, cuddly child* (= the type you would like to cuddle). • *(Br and Aus)* **Cuddly toys** are toy animals which are soft and covered in fur.

cud·gel /ˈkʌdʒ·ᵊl/ *n* [C] a short heavy stick used for hitting people • *Guards armed with cudgels stood on the street corners.* • *(Br and Aus)* To **take up (the) cudgels for/against** someone or something is to argue strongly for or against them: *The union took up the cudgels for the suspended workers.*

cud·gel *obj* /ˈkʌdʒ·ᵊl/ *v* [T] **-ll-** or *Am usually* **-l-** • *The thugs kicked and cudgelled the man to the ground* (= hit him repeatedly with cudgels). • *(fig.) The newspaper cudgelled him into admitting* (= forced him to admit) *the truth.* • To **cudgel** your **brains** is to think very hard or try to remember something you have forgotten: *I cudgelled my brains, trying to remember her name.*

cue [SIGNAL] /kjuː/ *n* [C] a word or action said by a performer in a play or film, which is used as a signal by another performer to begin saying or doing something • *In my first stage appearance, I almost missed my cue.* • *When he turns around, it's her cue* **to** *come out of the wardrobe.* [+ *to* infinitive] • A cue is also a signal for someone to do something: *They started washing up, so that was our cue* **to** *leave the party.* [+ *to* infinitive] • If something happens **on cue**, it happens just after someone has said or thought it would happen: *I was just wondering where Sarah was, when right on cue she came in.* • If you **take** your **cue from** someone, you take notice of their words or behaviour so that you know what you should do: *She watched his lips carefully and took her cue from him.* • If you **take** your **cue from** something, you are greatly influenced by it: *The architects took their cue for the design of the new pub from the nearby Jacobean house, Aston Hall.*

cue *obj* /kjuː/ *v* [T] • If you cue (in) someone, you give them a signal to do something: *With a nod of his head, the drummer cued* **(in)** *the singer.*

cue [STICK] /kjuː/ *n* [C] a long thin wooden pole with a small piece of leather at one end, which is used for hitting the ball in games such as BILLIARDS or SNOOKER

cuff [MATERIAL] /kʌf/ *n* [C] the thicker material at the end of a sleeve nearest the hand, or *(Am and Aus)* the part of a trouser leg that is turned up • *He was dressed like a businessman, with his tie tightly knotted and his cuffs starched.* • *I walked to the sink, rolled back my cuffs and rinsed my hands.* • If you speak **off the cuff**, you say something without having prepared or thought about your words first: *She had to respond to journalists off the cuff, without knowing the details of the report.* ○ *I didn't intend to be taken so seriously, it was just an off-the-cuff suggestion.* • A **cuff link** is a small decorative object used to fasten shirt cuffs: *He has a pair of silver cuff links given to him by his grandfather.* • [PIC] **Clothes, Coats and jackets, Jewellery**

cuffed /kʌft/ *adj* • If trousers are cuffed, they are turned up at the bottom: *She was wearing slim black trousers cuffed just above the ankle.*

cuff *obj* [HIT] /kʌf/ *v* [T] to hit (someone) with your hand in a light, joking way • *His brother cuffed him playfully round the head.*

cuff /kʌf/ *n* [C] • *She gave him a playful cuff on the shoulder.*

cuffs /kʌfs/ *pl n infml for* HANDCUFFS • *Get the cuffs on him, constable!*

cuff *obj* /kʌf/ *v* [T] *infml* • *He was led out of the dock with his hands cuffed* (= in HANDCUFFS) *behind his back.*

cui·sine /kwɪˈziːn/ *n* [U] a style of cooking • *French/Italian/Chinese/Japanese cuisine* • *The cuisine* (= food) *in our restaurant is excellent.* • See also HAUTE CUISINE; NOUVELLE CUISINE.

cul–de–sac /ˈkʊl·də·sæk/ *n* a short road which is blocked off at one end • *We live in a cul-de-sac, so we don't get much traffic noise.* • *(fig.) We have come to a cul-de-sac with our enquiries* (= they are leading nowhere).

cu·lin·ary /£ˈkʌl·ɪ·nᵊr·i, $ˈkʌl·ə·ner-/ *adj* [not gradable] *slightly fml* connected with cooking or kitchens • *culinary implements/equipment/expertise* • *the culinary delights* (= pleasant tasting food) *of Beijing* • *My culinary skills are rather limited, I'm afraid* (= I'm not very good at cooking)*!*

cull *obj* [KILL] /kʌl/ *v* [T] (of people) to kill animals, esp. the weaker members of a particular group, in order to reduce or limit the number of them • *The plan to cull large numbers of baby seals has angered environmental groups.*

cull /kʌl/ *n* [C] • *the annual red deer cull* • *(fig.) She is likely to be one of the few ministers to survive the Prime Minister's annual ministerial cull* (= replacement of one person with another).

cull *obj* [CHOOSE] /kʌl/ *v* [T] to choose or collect (esp. ideas or information) from various places • *Here are a few facts and figures I've culled* **from** *the week's papers.* • *It's a collection of fascinating stories culled* **from** *a lifetime of experience.*

cul·len·der /£ˈkʌl·ɪn·dəʳ, $ˈkɑː·lən·dɚ/ *n* [C] a COLANDER

cul·mi·nate in *obj* /ˈkʌl·mɪ·neɪt/ *v prep* [T] to reach or achieve (a result or a high point) after gradual development and sometimes a lot of effort • *My arguments with the boss got worse and worse, and it all culminated in my deciding to change jobs.* • *Their many years of research have finally culminated in a cure for the disease.*

cul·mi·na·tion /ˌkʌl·mɪˈneɪ·ʃᵊn/ *n* [U] • *Winning first prize was* **the** *culmination* **of** *years of practice and hard work.*

cu·lottes /£kʊˈlɒt, $kjəˈlɑːts/ *pl n* women's short trousers which look like a skirt • *a pair of culottes* • [PIC] **Clothes**

culp·a·ble /ˈkʌl·pə·bl̩/ *adj fml* deserving to be blamed or considered responsible for something bad • *He was* **held** *culpable* (= blamed) **for** *all that had happened.*

culp·a·bil·i·ty /£ˌkʌl·pəˈbɪl·ɪ·ti, $-ə·t̬i/ *n* [U] • *After the accident, the company refused to* **accept** *culpability.* • *Culpability for the terrible state of the economy clearly* **lies** *with the Government.*

culp·a·bly /ˈkʌl·pə·bli/ *adv* • *The doctor's care of the boy was culpably inadequate* (= very bad – and he deserves blame for this.)

cul·prit /ˈkʌl·prɪt/ *n* [C] someone who has done something wrong • *Police hope the public will help them to find the culprits.* • *(humorous) Someone's eaten my piece of cake – which of you is the culprit?* • *(fig.) Children in this country are getting much too fat, and sugar and sweets are the main culprits* (= the bad things that are causing this).

cult /kʌlt/ *n* [C] (a group of people who follow) a particular system of religious belief, or *(fig.)* a strong interest in and liking for a particular person, idea or activity • *the Hindu cult of Shiva* • *(disapproving) He's a member of some strange cult which worships the Devil!* • *Their son has run away from home and joined a* **religious** *cult.* • *(fig.) During the 1980s the personal fitness cult* (= fashion) *spread rapidly.* • *(fig.) There was a* **personality** *cult surrounding Stalin during the 1940s.* • If a singer, writer, etc. has a **cult following** or is a **cult figure**, they have a small number of extremely loyal followers, rather than general popularity.

cul·ti·vate *obj* /£ˈkʌl·tɪ·veɪt, $-t̬ɪ-/ *v* [T] to prepare (land) and grow crops on it, or to grow (a particular crop) • *Most of the land there is too poor to cultivate.* • *The villagers cultivate mostly maize and beans.* • *(fig. fml) At this school we aim to cultivate* (= develop and improve) *the* **minds** *of all the children we teach.* • *She seems to spend her life trying to cultivate her* **career** (= trying to get better jobs and improve her skills). • If you cultivate a **friendship/relationship/contact**, you make a special effort to establish and develop it, because you think it might be useful to you: *The new Prime Minister is cultivating relationships with old Eastern Bloc countries.*

cul·ti·vat·ed /£ˈkʌl·tɪ·veɪ·tɪd, $-t̬ɪ·veɪ·t̬ɪd/ *adj* • *cultivated fields/soil/land* • A cultivated person has had a good education and knows a lot about and likes art, music, painting, etc.

cul·ti·va·tion /£ˌkʌl·tɪˈveɪ·ʃᵊn, $-t̬ɪ-/ *n* [U] • *The new settlers have* **brought** *about half of the island* **under** *cultivation.*

cul·tiv·a·ble /£ˈkʌl·tɪ·və·bl̩, $-t̬ɪ-/, **cul·tiv·at·a·ble** /£ˈkʌl·tɪ·veɪ·tə·bl̩, $-t̬ɪ·veɪ·t̬ə-/ *adj* • *Most of the island isn't cultivable* (= can't be cultivated) *– the soil is too rocky and dry.*

cul·ture [WAY OF LIFE] /£ˈkʌl·tʃəʳ, $-tʃɚ/ *n* the way of life, esp. general customs and beliefs of a particular group of people at a particular time • *youth/working-class/Russian/Roman/mass culture* [U] • *She's studying modern Japanese language and culture.* [U] • *The cultures of Britain and Nigeria are very different.* [C] • *Thatcher's enterprise culture* (= way of thinking and behaving) *of the 1980s brought many changes.* [U] • *There's a* **culture gap** (= difference in ways of thinking and behaving) *between many teenagers and their parents.* • *It was a real* **culture shock** *to find herself in London after living on a small island* (= She felt alone and was confused by the completely different way of life there). • *"The Two Cultures"* (title of a lecture series about the relationship between the arts and the sciences given by C.P.Snow, 1959) • See also SUBCULTURE.

cul·tur·al /£ˈkʌl·tʃᵊr·ᵊl, $-tʃɚ-/ *adj* • *cultural imperialism* • *cultural diversity/differences* • *Australia has its own cultural* **identity**, *which is very different from that of Britain.* • *Is it true that men are better drivers than women, or is this just a cultural* **stereotype**? • *(Br and Aus disapproving)* **Cultural cringe** is the fear that your own country's culture is not as good as that of other countries: *The cultural cringe has faded over the past few decades as Australia has been rethinking its role in the world.*

cul·tur·al·ly /£ˈkʌl·tʃᵊr·ᵊl·i, $-tʃɚ-/ *adv* • *a culturally diverse society* • *The situation in Northern Ireland is religiously, politically and culturally complex.*

cul·ture [ART] /£ˈkʌl·tʃəʳ, $-tʃɚ/ *n* [U] the continuing traditions of art, music, literature etc. of a particular society or group within a society • *She's a person* **of** *culture* (= She likes and knows a lot about literature, music, art, etc.). • *(humorous or disapproving) "Let's have a bit of culture!" he said, turning over to the classical music programme on the radio.* • *You won't find much culture* (= music, art, theatre, etc.) *in this sleepy little town, I'm afraid!* • *(Br disapproving) He's a bit of a* **culture vulture** (= too eager to be in the presence of culture). • *"When I hear the word culture I reach for my pistol (popular version of 'Whenever I hear the word culture ...I release the safety-catch on my Browning')"* (from the play *Schlageter* by Hans Johst, 1933)

cul·tur·al /£ˈkʌl·tʃᵊr·ᵊl, $-tʃɚ-/ *adj* • *Among her many cultural interests/pursuits are opera and classical ballet.* • *(infml) This town's a bit of a* **cultural desert** (= place where there aren't many activities connected with art, music, etc.)*!*

cul·tured /£ˈkʌl·tʃəd, $-tʃɚd/ *adj* • *She's a very cultured woman* (= She's had a good education and knows a lot about art, music, painting, etc.).

cul·ture [GROW] /£ˈkʌl·tʃəʳ, $-tʃɚ/ *n specialized* the growing of a group of MICROORGANISMS for scientific purposes, or the breeding and keeping of particular living things in order to get the substances they produce • *to grow a culture* [C] • *Silkworm culture is practised in order to get silk.* [U]

cul·ture *obj* /£ˈkʌl·tʃəʳ, $-tʃɚ/ *v* [T] • *Scientists have succeeded in culturing these microorganisms in the laboratory.* • A **cultured pearl** is a PEARL that has been formed artificially.

cul·vert /£ˈkʌl·vət, $-vɚt/ *n* [C] a pipe for waste water that crosses under roads, railways etc., or one that carries electricity CABLES under the ground

–cum– [TWO PARTS] /-kʌm-/ *combining form* used to join two nouns, showing that a person or thing does two things or has two purposes; combined with • *This is my bedroom-cum-study.* • *I'm a gardener-cum-handyman.*

cum [SEX] /kʌm/ *v* [I], *n* [U] COME [SEX]

cum·ber·some /£ˈkʌm·bə·səm, $-bɚ-/ *adj* awkward because of being large, heavy or difficult to use • *a cumbersome uniform/overcoat* • *cumbersome luggage* • *a cumbersome style of writing* • *He's got a cumbersome old computer – it's slow and complicated to use.* • *It's rather cumbersome having to carry all these cases around.*

cu·min /ˈkjuː·mɪn/ *n* [U] (a plant with) seeds that smell pleasant and are used as a spice esp. in Indian and Middle Eastern cooking • *cumin seeds* • *ground* (= powdered) *cumin*

cum·mer·bund /£ˈkʌm·ə·bʌnd, $ˈ-ɚ-/ *n* [C] a wide piece of cloth worn round the waist, esp. by men, as part of formal or Middle Eastern clothing

cum·quat /£ˈkʌm·kwɒt, $-kwɑːt/ *n* [C] a KUMQUAT

cu·mu·lat·ive /£ˈkjuː·mjʊ·lə·tɪv, $-t̬ɪv/ *adj* increasing by one addition after another • *a cumulative total* • *cumulative voting* • *The cumulative effect of using so many chemicals on the land could be disastrous.* • *The cumulative impact of these small changes was considerable.*

cu·mu·lat·ive·ly /£ˈkjuː·mjʊ·lə·tɪv·li, $-t̬ɪv-/ *adv*

cu·mu·lus /ˈkjuː·mjʊ·ləs/ *n* [U] a type of tall white cloud with a wide flat base and rounded shape • Compare CIRRUS; NIMBUS.

cu·nei·form /£ˈkjuː·nɪ·fɔːm, $-fɔːrm/ *adj* [not gradable], *n* [U] (of) a form of writing used for over 3 000 years until the 1st century BC in the ancient countries of the Middle East • *cuneiform script/characters*

cun·ni·lin·gus /ˌkʌn·ɪˈlɪŋ·gəs/ *n* [U] the sexual activity of moving the tongue across the CLITORIS and VULVA (= women's sexual organs) in order to give pleasure and excitement • Compare FELLATIO.

cun·ning [CLEVER] /ˈkʌn·ɪŋ/ *adj* (of people) clever at planning something so that you get what you want, esp. by tricking other people, or (of things) cleverly made for a particular purpose • *a cunning plan/plot/idea* • *It was cunning* **of** *the managing director* **to** *sell his shares just before the company went bankrupt!* • *She's invented a cunning little device for catching mice.* • *He is cunning* **as a fox** (= very cunning). • (J) (KOR) (S)

cun·ning /ˈkʌn·ɪŋ/ *n* [U] • *We need to* **show** *a bit of cunning if we want to trick the enemy.*

cun·ning·ly /ˈkʌn·ɪŋ·li/ *adv* • *a cunningly worked-out plan* • *a small but cunningly designed kitchen*

cun·ning [ATTRACTIVE] /ˈkʌn·ɪŋ/ *adj Am* attractive; CUTE • *a cunning little child/puppy/kitten* • (J) (KOR) (S)

cunt [PERSON] /kʌnt/ *n* [C] *taboo slang* a very unpleasant or stupid person • *You (stupid) cunt!*

cunt [SEXUAL ORGANS] /kʌnt/ *n* [C] *taboo slang* the sexual organs on the outside of a woman's body

cup [DRINKING CONTAINER] /kʌp/ *n* [C] a small round container, usually with one handle and used for drinking tea, coffee etc. • *a cup of tea* • *a cup and saucer* • *a coffee cup/teacup* • *(esp. Am)* A cup is a container which holds nearly a quarter of a litre of liquid, used for measuring in cookery. • A **plastic/polystyrene/paper** cup is a round drinking container which does not have a handle and is slightly narrower at the bottom than it is at the top. Such cups are usually thrown away after they have been used. • Something or someone that is **not** your **cup of tea**, is not the type of thing or person that you like: *Thanks for inviting me, but ballet isn't really my cup of tea.* • *"The cup that cheers (originally 'cups that cheer') but not inebriates"* (William Cowper in the poem *The Task*, 1785) • *"My cup runneth over* (= is more than full)*"* (Bible, Psalm 23) • Compare MUG [CONTAINER]. • (KOR)

cup·ful /ˈkʌp·fʊl/ *n* [C] *pl* **cupfuls** or *Am also* **cupsful** • *Add two cupfuls of milk* (= the amount held by a cup) *to the mixture.*

cup [SPORT] /kʌp/ *n* [C] a specially designed cup, usually with two handles and often made of silver, which is given as a prize in a sporting competition, or a game or match in which the winner receives such a cup • *Sheila won this cup in the school squash championship.* • *The Davis Cup is an important international tennis championship.* • A **World** Cup is an international competition, esp. in football: *Who won the 1994 World Cup?* • *(Br)* A **cup final** is the last game in a competition between teams, usually in football or RUGBY, for a cup: *the FA* (= Football Association) *Cup Final* • In a team sport, the **cup holders** are the team which won the cup for the competition held during the previous year or season: *The cup holders began their defence of the trophy in fine style.* • *(Br)* A **cup tie** is a game between two teams trying to win a cup, esp. in football. • (KOR)

cup [CONTAINER] /kʌp/ *n* [C] a bowl-shaped container • *an egg cup* • *the cup of an acorn* • Cup is also used when stating the size of the two parts of a woman's BRA that support the breasts: *"What size bra do you wear?" "A 'C' cup."* • *(Am)* A cup (*Br* **box**) is a curved piece of hard plastic which is worn by men while playing sports to protect their outer sex organs. • (KOR)

cup *obj* /kʌp/ *v* [T] **-pp-** • *She gently cupped the small injured bird* **in her hands** (= held her hands in the shape of a cup around it). • *She cupped her* **hands around** *the mug of hot coffee to warm them.*

cup [DRINK] /kʌp/ *n* [C/U] a mixture of several types of drink, often including one which is alcoholic, which is often drunk at parties and usually served from a bowl • *a strawberry/cider/claret cup* • (KOR)

cup·board /£ˈkʌb·əd, $-ɚd/ *n* [C] a piece of furniture or a small part of a room with a door or doors behind which there is space for storing things, usually on shelves • *a kitchen cupboard* • *a built-in cupboard* • *(Br) an airing cupboard* • *There's a cupboard where you can put your clothes/food/dishes.* • *Is there plenty of cupboard* **space** (= Are there many cupboards) *in your new house?* • *I'm afraid the* **cupboard is bare** (= I haven't anything I can give you). • *(Br) "What's all this* **cupboard love** (= saying you love me in order to make me do something for you)*?" she said to the children, laughing.* • *"But when she got there/ The cupboard was bare"* (from the nursery rhyme *Old Mother Hubbard*)

cup·cake /ˈkʌp·keɪk/ *n* [C] *Am and Aus for* **fairy cake**, see at FAIRY [IMAGINARY CREATURE] • [PIC] **Bread and cakes**

Cu·pid /ˈkjuː·pɪd/ *n* [not after *the*] the ancient Roman god of love, represented by a naked baby boy who has wings and shoots arrows at people to make them start to love each other • If you have a **Cupid's bow**, you have an upper lip with two curves in it which make it look like the BOW (= weapon for firing arrows) carried by Cupid.

cu·pid /ˈkjuː·pɪd/ *n* [C] • A cupid is a statue or painting of a little boy looking like Cupid. • (T)

cu·pid·i·ty /£kjuˈpɪd·ɪ·ti, $-ə·t̬i/ *n* [U] a great desire esp. for money or possessions

cu·po·la /ˈkjuː·pəl·ə/ *n* [C] a small DOME (= part of a roof), shaped like an upside down bowl

cup·pa /ˈkʌp·ə/ *n* [C] *esp. Br infml* a cup of tea • *"Make us a cuppa, will you, love?"*

cur /£kɜːʳ, $kɜːr/ *n* [C] *literary* a bad-tempered, fierce dog, esp. a MONGREL (= dog of mixed type) • A cur is also a person who is thought to be worthless or cowardly.

cur·a·ble /£ˈkjʊə·rə·bl̩, $ˈkjʊr-/ *adj* (of a disease) that can be cured • *Many illnesses which once killed are today curable.*

cur·a·bi·li·ty /£ˌkjʊə·rəˈbɪl·ɪ·ti, $ˌkjʊr·əˈbɪl·ə·t̬i/ *n* [U]

cu·ra·çao /£ˈkjʊə·rə·səʊ, $ˈkjʊr·ə·soʊ/ *n* [U] a golden-coloured orange-flavoured LIQUEUR (= strong alcoholic drink)

cu·rate /£ˈkjʊə·rət, $ˈkjʊr·ət/ *n* [C] a priest of the lowest rank, esp. in the Church of England, whose job is to help the VICAR (= priest of a particular church area) • *(Br) That film was a bit of a* **curate's egg** (= partly good, but mainly bad).

cu·ra·cy /£ˈkjʊə·rə·si, $ˈkjʊr·ə-/ *n* [C] • *He's got a curacy* (= job as a curate) *in the North of England.*

cu·rat·ive /£ˈkjʊə·rə·tɪv, $ˈkjʊr·ə·t̬ɪv/ *adj* able to cure or cause to get better • *Preventive medicine is concerned with preventing disease, whereas curative* **medicine** *is concerned with healing.* • *Do you believe in the curative* **powers** *of the local mineral water?*

cu·rat·or /£kjʊ'reɪ·təʳ, $kjɜːr'eɪ·t̬ɚ/ *n* [C] a person in charge of a MUSEUM, LIBRARY etc. • *the curator of a London museum*

curb [CONTROL] /£kɜːb, $kɜːrb/ *v, n* (to place) a control or limit esp. on something which is not desirable • *The Government should act to curb tax evasion.* [T] • *A child's development can be curbed by poor nutrition.* [T] • *You must try to* **keep/put a** *curb* **on** *your bad temper/spending habits.* [C] • *There will be new curbs* **on** *drink-driving from next week.* [C]

curb [EDGE] /£kɜːb, $kɜːrb/ *n* [C] *Am for* KERB

curb·side /£'kɜːb·saɪd, $'kɜːrb-/ *n* [U], *adj* [before n; not gradable] *Am for* KERBSIDE

curd /£kɜːd, $kɜːrd/ *n* [U] the solid substance which is left when the liquid is removed from milk • *(esp. Br)* **Curd cheese** is a soft, smooth white cheese without a strong taste. • Compare WHEY.

curds /£kɜːdz, $kɜːrdz/ *pl n* • *curds* (= curd) *and whey* (= separated solid and liquid parts of milk) • *"Little Miss Muffet sat on a tuffet* (= a tuft of grass)/ *Eating her curds and whey"* (nursery rhyme)

cur·dle *(obj)* /£'kɜː·dḷ, $'kɜːr-/ *v* to (cause to) form CURDS, or to go sour • *I left the milk out in the hot sun and it curdled.* [I] • *Beat the eggs into the cake mixture carefully, so as not to curdle it.* [T] • *The strange sound* **made** *his* **blood curdle** *(***curdled** *his* **blood***)* (= filled him with fear). See also BLOODCURDLING.

cure *obj* [MAKE WELL] /£kjʊəʳ, $kjʊr/ *v* [T] to make (someone) healthy again, or to cause (something bad, esp. an illness) to go away • *At one time the doctors couldn't cure TB/cure people* **of** *TB.* • *After a year, the cancer was cured/ she was cured* **of** *the cancer.* • *(fig.) Finance Ministers meet this week to discuss how to cure inflation.* • If something or someone cures you **of** a bad habit, unwanted behaviour, etc., it causes you to stop it: *Seeing his friend die of an overdose cured him* **of** (= put an end to) *his interest in illegal drugs.* • A **cure-all** is something that people think will solve any problem or cure any illness: *a cure-all wonder drug* • *(saying)* 'What can't be cured must be endured' means if you can't change something, you must bear it patiently. • See also CURABLE.

cure /£kjʊəʳ, $kjʊr/ *n* [C] • *to effect/find/provide a cure* • *They are searching/looking for a cure* **for** (= treatment that will heal) *cancer/AIDS/the common cold.* • *There is* **no known** *cure* **for** *this disease* (= a cure hasn't yet been found). • *(fig.) The best cure* **for** *boredom is hard work!*

cure *obj* [PRESERVE] /£kjʊəʳ, $kjʊr/ *v* [T] to treat (esp. food) in a special way in order to stop it decaying • *to cure tobacco leaves* • *to cure animal skins* • *Fish, meat and other foods can be cured using salt or vinegar or by drying.*

cur·few /£'kɜː·fjuː, $'kɜːr-/ *n* [C] a rule that everyone must stay at home between particular times, usually at night, esp. during a war or a period of political trouble • *to impose/enforce/lift/end a curfew* • *There's a curfew from eleven at night until seven in the morning.* • *What time is the curfew?* • *He was shot for* **breaking** (= not obeying) *the curfew.*

Cu·ri·a /£'kjʊə·ri·ə, $'kjʊr·i-/ *n* [U] **the Curia** *specialized* the government and court of the Roman Catholic Church, with the Pope in the highest position

cu·rie /£'kjʊə·ri, $'kjʊr·i/ *n* [C] a unit, used in the past, for measuring RADIOACTIVITY

cu·ri·o /£'kjʊə·ri·əʊ, $'kjʊr·i·oʊ/ *n* [C] *pl* **curios** an unusual object • *a shop full of antiques and curios*

cu·ri·os·i·ty [INTEREST] /£ˌkjʊə·ri'ɒs·ɪ·ti, $ˌkjʊr·i'ɑː·sə·t̬i/ *n* [U] an eager desire to know or learn about something • *to arouse/excite/satisfy someone's curiosity* • *I'm* **burning with** *curiosity – you must tell me who's won!* • *She decided to call her ex-boyfriend* **out of** *curiosity.* • *"We try to develop the* **natural** *curiosity of each child," said the teacher.* • *"Why do you ask?" "Oh, just* **idle** *curiosity* (= for no particular reason)*."* • (saying) 'Curiosity killed the cat' is said to someone to stop them asking too many questions. • Ⓓ

cu·ri·os·i·ty [STRANGE OBJECT] /£ˌkjʊə·ri'ɒs·ɪ·ti, $ˌkjʊr·i'ɑː·sə·t̬i/ *n* [C] something that is interesting because it is rare and unusual • *Cars like mine are curiosities nowadays.* • *I kept this old pot because I thought it would have* **curiosity value** (= be valuable because it was strange) *one day.* • Ⓓ

cu·ri·ous [INTERESTED] /£'kjʊə·ri·əs, $'kjʊr·i-/ *adj* interested in learning about people or things around you • *Babies are curious* **about** *everything around them.* • *She felt the parcel, curious* **to** *know what it contained.* [+ to infinitive]

cu·ri·ous·ly /£'kjʊə·ri·ə·sli, $'kjʊr·i-/ *adv* • *He leaned over curiously, trying to see what she was writing.*

cu·ri·ous [STRANGE] /£'kjʊə·ri·əs, $'kjʊr·i-/ *adj* strange and unexpected; PECULIAR • *There was a curious-***looking** *old man standing outside.* • *A curious thing happened to me yesterday.* • *How curious! When I went to the door, no one was there!* • *It's curious* **(that)** *Brian hasn't phoned when he promised he would.* [+ (*that*) clause] • *"Curiouser and curiouser"* (Lewis Caroll in his book *Alice in Wonderland*, 1865)

cu·ri·ous·ly /£'kjʊə·ri·ə·sli, $'kjʊr·i-/ *adv* • *Curiously, there didn't seem to be a bank in the town.*

curl /£kɜːl, $kɜːrl/ *n* a piece of hair which grows or has been formed into a curving shape, or something that is the same shape as this • *tight/loose curls* [C] • *The little boy's face was framed by golden curls.* [C] • *Her hair fell* **in** *curls over her shoulders.* [C] • *As he got older, his hair* **lost** *its curl* (= became straighter). [U] • *Curls of smoke were rising from the chimney.* [C] • Compare WAVE [HAIR CURVES].

curl *(obj)* /£kɜːl, $kɜːrl/ *v* • *Does your hair curl* **naturally** (= grow in curls)*, or is it permed?* [I] • *You can buy lots of devices for curling hair.* [T] • *Some plants curl* (= wind) **round** *tree trunks.* [I] • *The narrow river curled* **through** *the valley.* [I] • *If the leaves on your apple tree curl* **(up)**, *then it probably has greenfly.* [I] • *A new baby will automatically curl its fingers* **round** *any object it touches.* [T] • *The cat was curled* **up** *on the hearth rug.* [I] • *I just want to* **curl up** (= sit comfortably) *in an armchair* **with** *a book.* • *(Br) They all* **curled up** (= began to laugh uncontrollably) *when they saw his amazing new hat.* • *I just wanted to* **curl up and die** (= I felt very ashamed and sorry) *when I spilt coffee on their new carpet!* • *She* **curled** *her* **lip**/ *Her* **lip curled at** *what he said* (= She showed by a movement of her mouth that she felt no respect for it).

curl·y /£'kɜː·li, $'kɜːr-/ *adj* **-ier, -iest** • *curly hair* • *curly leaves*

curl·i·ness /£'kɜː·lɪ·nəs, $'kɜːr-/ *n* [U]

curl·er /£'kɜː·ləʳ, $'kɜːr·lɚ/, **roll·er** *n* [C] a small, often electrically heated, object in the shape of a tube, used to make your hair curl • *to put curlers in/take curlers out* • [PIC] **Hair**

cur·lew /£'kɜː·ljuː, $'kɜːr-/ *n* [C] a large brownish coloured bird with long legs and a very long curved beak, which is usually seen near water • [PIC] **Birds**

curl·ing /£'kɜː·lɪŋ, $'kɜːr-/ *n* [U] a game played on ice esp. in Scotland and Canada in which special flat round stones are slid towards a mark

cur·mud·geon /£kə'mʌdʒ·ən, $kɚ-/ *n* [C] a bad-tempered old person • *You're turning into a complaining old curmudgeon!*

cur·mud·geon·ly /£kə'mʌdʒ·ən·li, $kɚ-/ *adj* • *curmudgeonly behaviour* • *a curmudgeonly manner*

cur·rant [DRY FRUIT] /£'kʌr·ənt, $'kɜːr-/ *n* [C] a small black dried GRAPE without seeds used esp. in cakes • *currant buns* • *a currant loaf*

cur·rant [FRUIT] /£'kʌr·ənt, $'kɜːr-/ *n* a small round fruit which grows on bushes and is eaten fresh or cooked • *Blackcurrants, redcurrants and whitecurrants are all kinds of currants.* • *We've got lots of currant* **bushes** *in the garden.*

cur·ra·wong /£'kʌr·ə·wɒŋ, $'kɜːr·ə·wɑːŋ/ *n* [C] *Aus* a large black and white bird with a loud musical cry

cur·ren·cy [MONEY] /£'kʌr·ənt·si, $'kɜːr-/ *n* the money in use in a particular country at a particular time • *to sell/ buy currency* [U] • *Brazil and Peru have different currencies.* [C] • [LP] **Money, Nations and nationalities**

cur·ren·cy [ACCEPTANCE] /£'kʌr·ənt·si, $'kɜːr-/ *n* [U] the state of being commonly known or accepted, or of being used in many places • *His ideas* **enjoyed wide** *currency during the last century.* • *Many informal expressions are* **gaining** *currency in serious newspapers.*

cur·rent [NOW] /£'kʌr·ənt, $'kɜːr-/ *adj* of the present time • *Who's your current girlfriend?* • *Have you seen the current* **issue** *of* (= the most recently published) *Vogue magazine?* • *The word 'thou'* (= you) *is no longer* **in** *current* **use.** • **Current affairs** is political news about events happening now: *In some schools children study current affairs as a subject.* • A **current account** (*Am* **checking account**) is a bank account which usually earns little or no profit and which you can take money out of at any time. • [LP] **Money**

cur·rent·ly /£'kʌr·ənt·li, $'kɜːr-/ *adv* [not gradable] • *The Director is currently having talks in the USA.* • [LP] **Periods of time**

cur·rent MOVEMENT /£ˈkʌr·ᵊnt, $ˈkɜːr-/ *n* [C] a movement of water, air or electricity, in a particular direction • *to swim against/with the current* • *a direct/alternating (electric) current* • *(fig.) a current of opinion/thought/fashion* • *He was swept out to sea/away by the* **strong** *current.* • *Which way does the current* **flow** *on this coast?* • *Birds fly by catching* **upward** *and* **downward** *currents of air.* • *Switch off the electric current before touching that machine.* • If you **swim/drift/go with the current**, you follow the ideas of most people.

cur·ric·u·lum /kəˈrɪk·jʊ·ləm/ *n* [C] *pl* **curricula** /kəˈrɪk·jʊ·lə/ or **curriculums** the group of subjects studied in a school, college etc., or a particular course of study in one subject • *curriculum planning/development* • *the history/chemistry/music curriculum* • *Is Russian* **on** *the curriculum* (= Can you study it) *at your school?* • *All state schools in Britain* **follow** *a* **national** *curriculum.* • Compare SYLLABUS.

cur·ric·u·lar /£kəˈrɪk·jʊ·ləʳ, $-lɚ/ *adj* [before n; not gradable] *specialized* • **Extra**-curricular **activities** are organized events or activities which take place at school but which are not part of the curriculum: *The school offers a wide range of extra-curricular activities, including swimming, drama, cycling and archery.*

cur·ric·u·lum vi·tae (*pl* **curriculum vitaes**) /kəˌrɪk·jʊ·ləmˈviː·taɪ/ *n* [C] *pl* **curricula vitae** a CV

cur·ry FOOD /£ˈkʌr·i, $ˈkɜːr-/ *n* a dish, originally from India, consisting of meat or vegetables cooked in a spicy sauce • *a hot* (= strong) *curry* [C] • *a medium/mild* (= not strong) *curry* [C] • *vegetable/chicken/lamb curry* [U] • *curry sauce* • **Curry paste** is a mixture of spices and oil, used to flavour curries. • **Curry powder** is a mixture of spices used to flavour curries.

cur·ried /£ˈkʌr·id, $ˈkɜːr-/ *adj* [not gradable] • *curried eggs/fish/beef*

cur·ry *obj* /£ˈkʌr·i, $ˈkɜːr-/ *v* [T] • *Let's curry* (= make a curry with) *the leftover meat.*

cur·ry *obj* CLEAN /£ˈkʌr·i, $ˈkɜːr-/ *v* [T] *specialized* to clean and brush a horse with a special COMB

cur·ry *obj* OBTAIN /£ˈkʌr·i, $ˈkɜːr-/ *v* [T] *(Br and Aus)* **curry favour**/*(Am and Aus)* **curry favor** *disapproving* to praise esp. someone in authority in a way that is not sincere, in order to obtain some advantage for yourself • *He's always trying to curry favour* **with** *the boss.*

curse SPEAK ANGRILY /£kɜːs, $kɜːrs/ *v, n* (to say) a word or expression which is not polite and shows that you are very angry with someone or something • *He cursed violently when he broke the glass bowl.* [I] • **With a** *curse, she picked the papers up out of the puddle.* [C] • *I could curse her* **for** *losing my key!* [T] • *We could hear him cursing and swearing as he tried to get the door open.* [I] • *(infml dated) Curse this dreadful traffic!* [T] • *He* **cursed the day** *he* **was born** (= was very angry with himself) *when he saw what a mess he was in.*

cursed /£kɜːst, £ˈkɜː·sɪd, $ˈkɜːrst/ *adj* [before n] • *It's a cursed* (= annoying) *nuisance, having to work late every evening!* • See also ACCURSED.

curse *obj* PERFORM MAGIC /£kɜːs, $kɜːrs/ *n* [C], *v* [T] (to say) a word or sentence asking a magical power to cause something unpleasant to happen to something or someone • *In the story, a wicked witch* **put a** *curse* **on** *the princess/* **put** *the princess* **under** *a curse for 100 years.* • *(fig.) Noise is the curse of modern city life* (= It makes it extremely unpleasant). • *(infml dated or humorous)* If a woman has **the curse**, she is experiencing her monthly PERIOD (= bleeding from the womb). • See also ACCURSED.

cursed /£kɜːst, $kɜːrst/ *adj* • *(humorous) I'm sure this car is cursed – it never starts when I really need it.* • *(fig.) In recent years I've been cursed* **with** (= I've been unlucky to have) *worsening eyesight.*

cur·sive /£ˈkɜː·sɪv, $ˈkɜːr-/ *adj specialized* (of writing) written with rounded letters that are joined together

cur·sor /£ˈkɜː·səʳ, $ˈkɜːr·sɚ/ *n* [C] a movable marker on a computer screen which shows the point where the work is being done • *You can* **move** *the cursor either by using the mouse or by using the arrow keys on the keyboard.*

cur·so·ry /£ˈkɜː·sᵊr·i, $ˈkɜːr·sɚ-/ *adj* quick and probably not detailed • *a cursory glance/look* • *a cursory check/inspection/examination*

cur·sor·i·ly /£ˈkɜː·sᵊr·ᵊl·i, $ˈkɜːr·sɚ-/ *adv* • *He glanced cursorily at the letter, then gave it to me.*

curt /£kɜːt, $kɜːrt/ *adj* **-er, -est** *disapproving* (of a person's manner or speech) rude as a result of being very brief • *to give a curt nod/refusal/reply* • *The boss was rather curt* **with** *him.* • (D) (I)

curt·ly /£ˈkɜːt·li, $ˈkɜːrt-/ *adv* • *Steve answered curtly and turned his back on me.*

curt·ness /£ˈkɜːt·nəs, $ˈkɜːrt-/ *n* [U] • *Claire's curtness made him wonder what he'd done wrong.*

cur·tail *obj* /£kəˈteɪl, $kɚ-/ *v* [T] to stop (something) before it is finished, or to reduce or limit (something) • *to curtail your holiday/spending* • *to curtail a speech* • *The last government* **severely** *curtailed trade union rights/freedom of speech/public spending.*

cur·tail·ment /£kəˈteɪl·mənt, $kɚ-/ *n* [C; U]

cur·tain /£ˈkɜː·tᵊn, $ˈkɜːr·t̬ᵊn/ *n* [C] a piece of material, esp. cloth, which hangs across a window or opening to make a room or part of a room dark or private • *heavy/thick/thin curtains* • *floor-length curtains* • *lace/net curtains* • *curtain hooks* • *a fire/safety curtain* • *We need a new* **pair of** *curtains/some new curtains in the living room.* • *Would you* **draw** (= open or close) *the curtains for me, please?* • *I suspected something might be wrong when I noticed his bedroom curtains were still drawn* (= closed) *in the middle of the afternoon.* • *We'll have to get a* **shower** *curtain to stop the bathroom floor getting wet.* • *(fig.) They could see nothing through the curtain of* (= the very heavy or thick) *rain/smoke.* • A **curtain rail** is a fixed strip of plastic or metal, usually hidden from view, from which a curtain hangs. • A **curtain rod** is a fixed pole with a set of loose rings from which a curtain hangs. It is usually made of wood and often has a decorative purpose. • In a theatre, the curtain is the large screen of heavy material which separates the stage from the area where people are watching: *The curtain* **rises/goes up** *at 8 pm and* **falls** *at 10 pm.* • *Most New York theatres have a 7.30 curtain/***curtain time** (= Most performances begin at 7.30). • When actors **take a curtain call**, they come to the front of the stage at the end of a performance and the people watching clap to show their enjoyment. • A **curtain raiser** is a short play sometimes performed before the main play: *(fig.) This evening's meeting was a curtain raiser for* (= a preparatory stage before) *the main meetings tomorrow.* • *(infml) It'll* **be curtains for** *him* (= He'll experience a lot of trouble or difficulty), *if he doesn't do what I tell him!* • *The Royal Opera House's longest-running show could be facing* **the final curtain** (= could be performed for the last time) *at the end of this month.* • *As* **the final curtain** *descended on the longest match in the history of the championship* (= As the match ended), *it was Becker who emerged victorious.* • PIC **Net, Window**

cur·tain *obj* /£ˈkɜː·tᵊn, $ˈkɜːr·t̬ᵊn/ *v* [T] • *It'll cost a fortune to curtain* (= provide curtains for) *the new house.* • *The nurse curtained* **off** *the bed* (= pulled a curtain around it) *so that the doctor could see the patient in private.* [M]

curt·sy, curt·sey /£ˈkɜːt·si, $ˈkɜːrt-/ *v* [I] (of girls and women) to bend quickly at the knees, with one foot in front of the other, while holding the skirt, esp. to show respect to kings, queens etc. • *She curtseyed* **to** *the Queen.* • Compare BOW BEND.

curt·sy, curt·sey /£ˈkɜːt·si, $ˈkɜːrt-/ *n* [C] • **to make/drop/***(Br)* **bob a curtsy to** *someone*

cur·va·ceous /£kɜːˈveɪ·ʃəs, $kɜːr-/ *adj* (of a woman) having a body with attractive curves

cur·va·ture /£ˈkɜː·və·tʃəʳ, $ˈkɜːr·və·tʃɚ/ *n* [U] the state of being curved or bent • *the curvature of the earth's surface* • *(medical)* If you suffer from curvature **of the spine** your backbone curves in an unnatural way and may cause health problems.

curve /£kɜːv, $kɜːrv/ *v, n* (to form or move in the direction of) a line which bends continuously and has no straight parts • *a curve* **in** *a river/road/railway* [C] • *(specialized) the curve of a graph* [C] • *The road curves* **(round** *to the left).* [I] • *The golf ball curved* **through** *the air and landed on the green.* [I] • *(Am)* When you throw a **curve ball** in the sport of baseball, the ball curves as it moves towards the player with the bat.

curved /£kɜːvd, $kɜːrvd/ *adj* • *a curved surface*

curv·y /£ˈkɜː·vi, $ˈkɜːr-/ *adj* **-ier, -iest** • Something that is curvy contains a lot of curves: *a curvy line* ○ *That line should be straight but you've drawn it curvy.*

cu·shion /ˈkʊʃ·ᵊn/ *n* [C] a bag made of cloth, plastic or leather which is filled with soft material, often has an attractive cover, and is used esp. on chairs for sitting or leaning on • *She sank back* **against/into** *the cushions.* • *(fig.) A hovercraft travels on a cushion* (= layer) *of air.* • See also PINCUSHION. Compare PILLOW. • (I)

cu•shion *obj* /ˈkʊʃ·ᵊn/ *v* [T] • *The soft grass cushioned his* **fall** (= made it hurt less). • *He has lost his job, but he's got a lot of money in the bank, so that will* **cushion the blow** (= make a bad situation less serious).

cu•shioned /ˈkʊʃ·ᵊnd/ *adj* • *a cushioned* (= soft) *seat*

cush•y /ˈkʊʃ·i/ *adj* **-ier, -iest** *infml disapproving* very easy • *a cushy job* • *He* **has a** *really cushy* **time**/*(Br) He* **is on to a** *cushy* **number** (= He's found an easy job to do), *only working three days a week!*

cusp /kʌsp/ *n* [U] the dividing line between two very different things • *a country* **on the** *cusp* **of** *change/recession/success*

cus•pi•dor /£ˈkʌs·pɪ·dɔːʳ, $-dɔːr/ *n* [C] *Am for* SPITTOON

cuss SWEAR /kʌs/ *v* [I] to say words which are not polite because you are angry; to CURSE • *She was cussing* **and swearing** *at the old car because it wouldn't start.*

cuss /kʌs/ *n* [C] • *(Br) I* **don't give a (tinker's) cuss** *(Am* **don't give a (tinker's) damn/a good goddamn***)* (= I don't care) *what she thinks – I'll do what I want!*

cuss PERSON /kʌs/ *n* [C] a person of the bad type mentioned • *Tom's an* **awkward/stupid/irritable** *(old) cuss!*

cuss•ed /ˈkʌs·ɪd, kʌst/ *adj disapproving* (of people) unwilling to be helpful, or (of things) annoying • *He's just* **plain** *cussed: he's only doing it because I asked him not to!* • *It's a cussed nuisance.*

cus•sed•ly /ˈkʌs·ɪd·li/ *adv*

cus•sed•ness /ˈkʌs·ɪd·nəs/ *n* [U] • *He refused to help* **out of sheer/pure** *cussedness.*

cus•tard /£ˈkʌs·təd, $-tərd/ *n* [U] a (usually warm) sweet sauce made from eggs, milk, flour and sugar or from a special powder, milk and sugar, and poured over sweet dishes • *apple pie/stewed fruit* **and** *custard* • *cold custard* • A **custard pie** is a flat open pastry container filled with artificial custard, thrown at people's faces on the stage to make people laugh. • *(Br and Aus)* **Custard powder** is a yellowish powder used instead of eggs and flour to make custard. • A **custard tart** (also **baked custard**) is a pastry container filled with custard, baked and usually eaten cold.

cus•to•di•an /£kʌsˈtəʊ·di·ən, $-ˈtoʊ-/ *n* [C] a person with responsibility for the care, protection or maintenance of something • *the custodian* **of** *a museum/castle* • *the custodian* **of** *the Queen's jewels* • *(fig.) Mary Whitehouse sees herself as the custodian* **of** *public morals.* • Custodian is also *Am for* CARETAKER BUILDING WORKER.

cus•to•dy CARE /ˈkʌs·tə·di/ *n* [U] the right or duty to care for someone or something, esp. a child after its parents have separated or died • *The court* **awarded/granted/gave** *custody* **of** *the child to the father.* • *The mother* **got/received** *custody (of the child).* • *The parents were given* **joint** *custody (of the child).* • *She left her valuables* **in the** *custody* **of** *her mother* (= She asked her to look after them) *while she was abroad.* • *The ex-President has been* **taken into protective** *custody* (= given police/army protection) *because his life is in danger.*

cus•to•di•al /£kʌsˈtəʊ·di·əl, $-ˈtoʊ-/ *adj* [not gradable] • *custodial care* • *custodial duties* • *custodial staff*

cus•to•dy PRISON /ˈkʌs·tə·di/ *n* [U] the state of being kept in prison esp. by the police, usually while waiting to go to court for trial • *The police have* **taken** *the suspect* **into** *custody/are* **holding** *the suspect* **in** *custody.* • *You will be* **remanded in** *custody until your trial.*

cus•to•di•al /£kʌsˈtəʊ·di·əl, $-ˈtoʊ-/ *adj* [not gradable] • If you are given a custodial **sentence**, you are sent to prison.

cus•tom TRADITION /ˈkʌs·təm/ *n* a way of behaving or a belief which has been established for a long time • *a local/national/old/ancient/strange custom* [C] • *She's studying the manners and customs of the Hopi Indians.* [C] • **According to (ancient)** *custom, their house was built facing the east.* [U] • *In my country, it's* **the** *custom* **(for** *women)* **to** *get married in white.* [U + *to* infinitive] • LP **Holidays, Phrases and customs**

cus•tom•a•ry /£ˈkʌs·tə·mᵊr·i, $-mer-/ *adj* • *In China, it is customary* **for** *a girl* **to** *take her mother's name.*

cus•tom USUAL ACTIVITY /ˈkʌs·təm/ *n* [C] something you usually do • *It is my custom always* **to** *tell the absolute truth.* [+ *to* infinitive] • *He left the house at nine exactly,* **as is** *his custom.*

cus•tom•a•ry /£ˈkʌs·tə·mᵊr·i, $-mer-/ *adj* • *She's not her customary* (= usual) *cheerful self today.*

cus•tom•ar•i•ly /kʌs·təˈmer·ɪ·li/ *adv* [not gradable] • *He had a casual and relaxed manner that is customarily found in the typical Californian.*

cus•tom TRADE /ˈkʌs·təm/ *n* [U] the support given to a business, esp. a shop, by the people who buy things or services from it • *Most of our custom comes from tourists nowadays.* • *If we don't give good service, people will* **withdraw** *their custom/* **take** *their custom* **elsewhere.** • If a car, machine, etc. is **custom-built**, it is made according to the needs of a particular buyer. • If an article of clothing is **custom-made**, it is specially made for a particular buyer: *custom-made shoes*

cus•tom•er /£ˈkʌs·tə·məʳ, $-mɚ/ *n* [C] a person who buys goods or a service • *a satisfied customer* • *Mrs. Wilson is one of our* **regular** *customers.* • *There were two assistants to* **serve** *the customers.* • *(infml esp. disapproving) He's an awkward/strange/odd/cool customer* (= person). • **Customer services** is the part of an organization which answers customers' questions, exchanges goods which have faults, etc.: *Customer services are constantly reviewing shoppers' preferences.* ○ *Ask at the customer service* **counter.** ○ *I phoned the customer service* **department.** • *(saying)* 'The customer is always right' means that someone who is serving in a shop should try very hard not to disagree with the customer.

cus•tom•ize *obj, Br and Aus usually* **-ise** /ˈkʌs·tə·maɪz/ *v* [T] to make or change (something) according to the buyer's or user's needs

cus•tom•ized, *Br and Aus usually* **-ised** /ˈkʌs·tə·maɪzd/ *adj* • *The company specializes in customized computer systems.*

cus•toms /ˈkʌs·təmz/ *pl n* money paid to the government when you take particular goods from one country to another • *You have to* **pay** *customs* **(duty) on** *imported cars.*

cus•toms /ˈkʌs·təmz/ *n* [U] • Customs is the place at a port, airport or border where travellers' bags are looked at to find out if any goods are being carried illegally: *It took us ages to* **pass/go/get through** *Customs.* • **Customs and Excise** is a British government department which collects taxes, esp. on goods going into or out of Britain. • A **customs officer** looks at travellers' bags to make certain they are not taking goods into a country without paying taxes.

cut *(obj)* KNIFE /kʌt/ *v* **cutting**, *past* **cut** to break the surface of (something), or to divide or make (something) smaller, using a sharp tool, esp. a knife • *You usually cut bread, meat and cheese* **with** *a knife, but you usually cut paper and cloth* **with** *scissors.* [T] • *Could you cut me a slice of bread?/Could you cut a slice of bread* **for** *me?* [+ two objects] • *I've cut myself/my hand* **on** *that glass/***with** *that knife.* [T] • *Could you cut my meat* **up** (= cut it all into small pieces) *for me please, Daddy?* [M] • *This knife doesn't cut very well, it's not sharp enough.* [I] • *This material cuts easily* (= It is easy to cut this material). [I] • *I* **had** *my* **hair cut** *at Croppers last time.* [T] • *Which of you children cut this hole* **in** *my best tablecloth?* [T] • *Firefighters had to cut the trapped driver* **loose/free** (= cut the metal, etc. to allow the driver to get out of the car) *using special equipment.* [T + obj + adj] • *He fell off the swing and cut his head* **open** (= got a deep cut in his head). [T + obj + adj] • *Her face was cut* **to pieces/shreds** (= badly cut in many places) *by flying glass.* [T] • *Please don't cut my hair too* **short***!* [T + obj + adj] • *He cut the cake* **in/into** *six (pieces) and gave each child a slice.* [T] • *I've just cut* **through** *two layers of cloth by mistake!* [I] • *I'll cut* **away/out** (= remove completely) *all the dead wood from those rose bushes.* [M] • *Cut your roses* **back** (= shorten their stems) *in February before they start to grow.* [M] • *We'll cut those two trees* **down** (= remove them) *to make room for the swimming pool.* [M] • *Don't cut* **into** (= start) *that cake specially for me.* [I] • *I don't like doing the shopping on a Saturday afternoon because it* **cuts into** *my weekend* (= it stops me doing other things). • *Remember to cut* **off** *the fat before you fry the steak.* [M] • *The children cut the pictures* **out** (= removed them by cutting) *and stuck them in their scrapbooks.* [M] • *I'm not* **cut out** (= I'm not the right type of person) *to be a politician/***for** *politics!* • If you say something **cuts both/two ways**, you think it has both a good and a bad side. • *The storm* **cut a swath through** (= destroyed a large part of) *the village.* • *She always manages to* **cut through** (= understand what is behind) *the complex theory and get at the facts.* • Something which can be **cut with a knife** is very obvious in an unpleasant way: *The tension was so thick in the air you could cut it with a knife.* • *All her talk about her rich friends* **cuts no/very little ice with** *me* (= doesn't make me feel any respect)*!* • *It's silly to* **cut off** *your* **nose to spite** *your* **face** (= hurt yourself more than the person you're trying to hurt) – *if you* *stop using the local shop because you've quarrelled with the owner, you'll have nowhere to buy things!* • If you **cut it/things fine**, you allow very little time or money to do something: *She arrived ten minutes before her flight, so she was cutting it* **a bit** *fine.* • If you are at the **cutting edge** of something, you are involved in its most recent stage of development: *The company is* **at the** *cutting edge* **of** *television miniaturization.* • *(Br saying)* 'You should cut your coat according to your cloth' means you should do the best you can with the limited money you have.

cut /kʌt/ *n* [C] • *She had a horrible/deep/long cut across her cheek.* • *I don't like* **the** *cut* (= shape) **of** *these jeans.* • *Sirloin is the most expensive cut* (= piece) **of** *beef.* • *(infml) When am I going to get my cut* (= share of the money)? • *She thinks she's* **a cut above** (= socially better than) *her neighbours.* • *She enjoys/hates* **the cut and thrust** (= the lively arguments) *of party politics.* • *"The unkindest (originally 'the most unkindest') cut of all (=the most cruel act)"* (Shakespeare, Julius Caesar 3.2)

cut /kʌt/ *adj* [not gradable] • *I'll buy a plant in a pot rather than cut flowers – it'll last longer.* • If something is **cut-and-dried**, it is decided and unlikely to be changed: *We need a cut-and-dried decision by the end of the week.* • A **cut-and-dried** solution to a problem is clear and simple, and removes any further difficulty or confusion: *There is no cut-and-dried answer to this problem.* • **Cut glass** is glass with patterns cut on the surface: *a cut-glass bowl* • **Cut lunch** is *Aus for* **packed lunch**. See at PACK [PUT INTO].

cut·ting /£ˈkʌt·ɪŋ, $ˈkʌt̬-/ *n* [C] • A cutting (*Am also* **clipping**) is an article which has been cut from a newspaper: *The noticeboard was covered with press cuttings.* • A cutting can also be a piece cut off from a plant which can be used to grow another plant of the same type in a different place: *Would you like a cutting from my rose bush/apple tree?*

cut *obj* [REDUCE] /kʌt/ *v* [T] **cutting**, *past* **cut** to make something shorter, lower, smaller etc. • *to cut prices/costs/losses/working hours/overtime/wages* • *They have cut* **(down)** *the cost of cleaning the hospital by lowering standards.* • *They'll have to cut their film* **(down)** *– it's far too long.* • *The Government should cut class sizes* **to** *30 by next year.* • *Our company is cutting its workforce* **by** *20 per cent by the end of the month.* • *The President had to cut* **short** *his visit/cut his visit* **short** (= shorten it) *because of the crisis back home.* [+ obj + adj] • If you **cut back/down** on something, you do less of it or use it in smaller amounts: *The firm has cut back/down* **(on)** *wastage/production/labour.* ○ *The President wants to cut back* **(on)** *defence spending by 10% next year.* ○ *I've decided to cut back on cigarettes/alcohol/sweets.* • *Mum* **cut down** *my big sister's old dress* (= changed it to make it smaller) *to make one for me.* • *Someone should* **cut** *that man* **down to size** (= show him he's not as important or clever as he thinks he is)! • *Let's* **cut** *our* **losses** (= avoid losing even more money than we have already) *and sell the business before prices drop even further.* • **To cut a long story short** means not to tell all the details: *To cut a long story short, I got the job.* • If you buy a **cut-price** article, you pay less than the usual price for it: *cut-price petrol/clothes/airline tickets* • A **cut-price** shop sells things at lower prices than other shops. • *We get* **cut-rate** *electricity* (= charged at a lower rate than usual) *for six hours each night.*

cut /kʌt/ *n* [C] • *a cut* (= reduction) **in** *income/expenditure/interest rates/hospital waiting lists* • *Many people have had to* **take** *a cut* **in** *their living standards.* • *Students and workers were out on the streets protesting against* **the cuts** (= government reductions in public spending).

cut *obj* [REMOVE] /kʌt/ *v* [T] **cutting**, *past* **cut** to take (something) out of something completely; to ELIMINATE • *The film makers have cut the love scene* **from/out of** *the English version.* • *If you cut sugar* **from/out of** *your diet you should lose weight.* • *Since my heart attack I've cut fatty foods* **out** *altogether.* • If someone **cuts** you **out of** their **will**, or **cuts** you **off without a penny**, they decide not to leave you any of their money or possessions when they die, because they are angry with you. • *(Br) If you're thinking of breaking the law, you can* **cut** **(***Br also and Am* **count) me out** (= I won't join you). • If you **cut and paste** text or a picture on paper or on a computer screen, you remove it from one place and put it somewhere else. • *In deciding to lower taxes, the Socialists* **cut the ground from under** *the Conservative Party's* **feet** (= made it difficult for them to succeed, by taking their ideas, or doing something before them).

cut /kʌt/ *n* [C] • *The film contains some very violent scenes, so some cuts were made* (= some parts were removed) *when it was shown on television.*

cut *obj* [MISS] /kʌt/ *v* [T] **cutting**, *past* **cut** to not go, esp. to a place where you should be • *Your son has been cutting* **classes/school/lessons**. • *She decided to cut some of her meetings and spend more time relaxing.*

cut /kʌt/ *n* [C] *Am* • *In Mr Feinstein's class, you fail if you have more than two cuts* (= miss more than two classes) *a term.*

cut *obj* [MAKE SAD] /kʌt/ *v* [T] **cutting**, *past* **cut** to hurt someone's feelings • *Her thoughtless remark* **cut** *him* **to the quick/heart** (= greatly hurt his feelings). • *(Br) Philip was very* **cut up** (= upset) **about** *his grandmother's death.*

cut·ting /£ˈkʌt·ɪŋ, $ˈkʌt̬-/ *adj* • *a cutting* (= unkind) *remark/comment* • *He can be very cutting when he chooses to be!*

cut *(obj)* [STOP SUDDENLY] /kʌt/ *v* **cutting**, *past* **cut** to stop or interrupt something, or (of machines) to stop working suddenly • *to cut an engine/a motor* [T] • *One of the plane's engines cut* **out**, *so they had to land with only one.* [I] • *The heating cuts* **out** *automatically when the temperature rises above 30 degrees.* [I] • *He started to explain, but she cut him* **short** (= stopped him before he had finished), *saying she had to catch a bus.* [T] • *I was just talking to Jan, when Dave* **cut in (on** *our conversation*/**on** *us)* (= interrupted us). • *She was dancing with Jack, when Tom suddenly* **cut in** (= took Jack's place). • *"Cut!* (= Stop filming!)*" shouted the director.* [I] • *(infml)* **Cut (out)** (= Stop) *all this silly behaviour/nonsense/noise will you, children, I've got a headache!* • *(infml)* **Cut it/that out!** means stop talking or behaving in an annoying way: **Just** *cut it out! I've had enough of your silly jokes.* • *(Br and Aus infml humorous)* **"Cut the cackle** (= Stop talking) *and get on with some work!" shouted the boss.* • *(slang) Let's just* **cut the crap** (= stop saying things which are meaningless or not true) *and get straight to the point.* • LP〉 **Driving**

cut *obj* [IGNORE] /kʌt/ *v* [T] **cutting**, *past* **cut** to pretend you do not know someone in order to show you are angry • *I said "Good Morning" to Mr. Jones, but he just cut me* **dead**.

cut *obj* [GROW TEETH] /kʌt/ *v* [T] **cutting**, *past* **cut** (of a baby) to grow a new tooth • *The baby's cutting a tooth. That's why she's crying all the time.* • *The Prime Minister* **cut** *her political* **teeth on** (= got her first political experience from) *student debates.*

cut [CROSS] /kʌt/ *v* [I always + adv/prep] **cutting**, *past* **cut** to go through or across a place, esp. in order to get somewhere quickly • *to cut* **through/across/over** *a field* • *to cut* **through** *an alleyway/passage* • *If we cut* **across country**, *taking the small roads, we'll get there faster.* • *The criminals first went in the London direction, then they* **cut back** (= suddenly went in the other direction) *and headed north.* • *Did you see that white car* **cut in (on us/in front of** *us)* (= go past without leaving enough room)? See also CUT UP [DRIVE BADLY]. • *If you're standing in a queue and someone* **cuts in (on** *you*)/**cuts in front of** *you* (= pushes in front of you), *tell them to go to the back!* • *(Am) Don't* **cut out** (= leave a line of traffic) *when everyone is going fast.* • *(Br and Aus)* If you **cut a corner**, you fail to keep to your own side of the road when going round a corner. • If you **cut corners**, you do something in the easiest, cheapest or fastest way. • If you **cut and run**, you do something in order to escape a difficult situation: *The Government had obviously decided to cut and run when they called an election six months early.*

cut *(obj)* [CARDS] /kʌt/ *v* **cutting**, *past* **cut** to choose a playing card by dividing a pile of cards into two parts • *Let's cut* **for** *dealer*/**to** *see who starts.* [I] • *Who's going to cut the cards?* [T] • *(fig.) Shall we cut you* **in** *(on the deal/game)* (= Do you want to play with us)? [T]

cut *obj* [RECORD] /kʌt/ *v* [T] **cutting**, *past* **cut** to record music or speech on a record • *When did Elvis cut his first record?*

cut *(obj)* [BEHAVE] /kʌt/ *v* **cutting**, *past* **cut** to behave in a particular way • *(dated)* If you **cut a fine figure** or you **cut quite a figure**/*(Br)* **dash** you cause people to admire you: *The young soldier cut a fine figure in his smart new uniform.* • *(Am and Aus)* If people **cut loose**, they behave in an uncontrolled, wild way. • *(Br)*If you **cut up rough**, you become very angry, and often violent.

cut *obj* [DEAL WITH] /kʌt/ *v* [T] **cut it/cut the mustard** *Am* to be able to deal with problems or difficulties satisfactorily • *If he can't cut it, then we'll get someone else to do the job.*

cut *obj* **a·cross**, **cut a·cross** *obj v adv* [T] to have an effect on or be important to different groups which are usually divided • *Support for environmental issues cuts across traditional party lines.*

cut off *obj* STOP, **cut** *obj* **off** *v adv* [M] to stop something, esp. speech or the supply of electricity, gas, water, etc. • *If this bill is not paid within five days, your gas supply will be cut off.* • *If you are having a phone conversation and you are cut off* (=lose communication with the person you were speaking to), *phone the operator.* • *If you speak for too long, the chairwoman will cut you off.* • *The aim was to cut off the enemy's escape route/supplies.* • *She was just explaining the problem, when she was cut off* **in mid-flow/in mid-sentence** *by a loud bang.* • *(Am)* If someone serving drinks in a bar cuts you off, they stop serving you alcoholic drinks because they think you've drunk too many: *I'm glad the bartender cut Tommy off – he's already had too much to drink.* • See also CUTOFF. • LP› **Telephone**

cut off *obj* SEPARATE, **cut** *obj* **off** *v adv* [M] to cause (a person or place) to become separate or cause (someone) to be or feel alone; to ISOLATE • *When his wife died, he cut himself off* **from** *other people.* • *Living out in the country, she felt very cut off* (**from** *her city friends).* • *Many villages have been cut off* **by** *the heavy snow.* • *We were walking along the bottom of the cliffs, and got cut off by the incoming tide* (=the sea covered our path). • See also CUTOFF.

cut up *obj* DRIVE BADLY *Br*, **cut** *obj* **up**, *Am* **cut off** *obj*, **cut** *obj* **off** *v adv* [M] (of drivers) to move in front of another car which was in front of you, leaving too little space • *I* **got/was** *cut up several times on the motorway this morning – I've never seen such dangerous driving!*

cut up BEHAVE STRANGELY *v* [I] *Am* to behave in a very active and silly way in order to make people laugh • *I hate it when Jane cuts up in class.* • See also CUTUP.

cut·back /ˈkʌt·bæk/ *n* [C] a reduction in something made in order to save money • *The closure of the Manchester printing factory is the company's biggest single cutback so far.* • *Cutbacks* **in** *public spending are expected in the next budget.* • *Many of the redundancies resulted from cutbacks* **in** *manufacturing and high technology industries.*

cute CHARMING /kjuːt/ *adj* **-r, -st** (esp. of something or someone small or young) charming and attractive • *He's got a really cute baby brother.* • *'Bambi' is a typical Walt Disney film with cute wide-eyed cartoon animals.* • Ⓘ

cutely /ˈkjuːt·li/ *adv* • *She smiled at the kitten playing cutely with a ball of string.*

cute·ness /ˈkjuːt·nəs/ *n* [U] • *With its combination of womanly beauty and childlike cuteness, Marilyn Monroe's charm was irresistible.*

cute CLEVER /kjuːt/ *adj* **-r, -st** *Am* wishing to seem clever, sometimes in a rude or unpleasant way • *Don't be cute with me, Vicki.* • *He thinks* **it**'*s cute* **to** *tell these real sexist jokes.* [+ *to* infinitive]

cute·sy /ˈkjuːt·si/, **cut·sie** *adj infml disapproving* artificially attractive and charming, esp. in a childlike way • *She sent me one of those awful birthday cards with a cutesy kitten asleep on a lace pillow on it.*

cu·ti·cle /£ˈkjuː·tɪ·kl̩, $-t̬ɪ-/ *n* [C] the thin skin at the base of the nails on the fingers and toes

cut·ie, cute·y /£ˈkjuː·ti, $-t̬i/, **cut·ie·pie** /£ˈkjuː·ti·paɪ, $-t̬i-/, **cut·sie·pie** /ˈkjuːt·si·paɪ/ *n* [C] *esp. Am infml* a woman or girl whom you consider attractive or feel affection for • *His daughter is a real cutie.* • *Hi there, cutie, we were just talking about you.* [as form of address]

cut·lass /ˈkʌt·ləs/ *n* [C] a curved, single-edged sword, esp. as used in the past by PIRATES

cut·le·ry /£ˈkʌt·lə·ri, $-lɚ·i/, *Am also* **sil·ver·ware, flat·ware** *n* [U] knives, forks and spoons used for eating food • Compare CROCKERY. • LP› **Shopping goods**

cut·let PIECE OF MEAT /ˈkʌt·lət/ *n* [C] a small piece of meat still joined to the bone, esp. from the animal's neck or RIBS • *We had* **lamb** *cutlets for dinner.* • *We're having grilled chicken/seafood cutlets for lunch.*

cut·let SAVOURY FOOD /ˈkʌt·lət/ *n* [C] small pieces of vegetables and nuts, or meat or fish, which have been pressed into a round flat shape • *Some people think that all that vegetarians eat is* **nut** *cutlets, but it's not true.*

cut·off LEVEL /£ˈkʌt·ɒf, $ˈkʌt̬·ɑːf/ *n* [C] a fixed point or level at which you stop including people or things • *We have a cutoff of 20 students in each class.* • *I find older men attractive, but there's a cutoff* **point** *at about 50.* • *March 31 is the cutoff* **date** *for applications to be accepted.* • See also CUT OFF STOP; CUT OFF SEPARATE.

cut·off STOP /£ˈkʌt·ɒf, $ˈkʌt̬·ɑːf/ *n* [C] the act of stopping the supply of something • *The US has announced a cutoff* **of** *military aid to the country.* • See also CUT OFF STOP; CUT OFF SEPARATE.

cut·offs /£ˈkʌt·ɒfs, $ˈkʌt̬·ɑːfs/, **cut·off jeans** *pl n* a pair of JEANS which has had parts of the legs removed • *He was wearing ragged cutoffs and a T-shirt.*

cut·out DEVICE /£ˈkʌt·aʊt, $ˈkʌt̬-/ *n* [C] a device which, for safety reasons, stops or interrupts a CIRCUIT (=an electrical system), used, for example, in a motor or engine • *a cutout* **fuse/switch**

cut·out SHAPE /£ˈkʌt·aʊt, $ˈkʌt̬-/ *n* [C] a shape that has been cut out from something, esp. a flat one that can stand vertically • *There's a life-size cutout* **of** *the president that you can stand next to to have your photograph taken.* • *She was wearing a dress with an attractive cutout design round the neck.* • *(fig.) He doesn't want a real woman – just a* **cardboard** *cutout* (=a person without a strong character) *who'll sit opposite him at a dinner table!*

cut·throat /£ˈkʌt·θrəʊt, $-θroʊt/ *adj* fierce; not involving consideration or care about any harm caused to others • *He did not enjoy working in the cutthroat* **world** *of journalism.* • *Graduates trying to find jobs are facing cutthroat* **competition**. • *The advertising world can be a very cutthroat* **business**. • *(Br and Aus)* A **cutthroat razor** (*Am* **straight razor**) is a type of old-fashioned RAZOR (=a device for removing hair, esp. from the face) with a long blade which can be opened.

cut·tle·fish /£ˈkʌt·l̩.fɪʃ, $ˈkʌt̬-/ *n* [C] *pl* **cuttlefish** or **cuttlefishes** a sea animal which has a wide flattened shell inside its body and which lives in coastal waters near the bottom of the sea • PIC› **Mollusc**

cut·up /£ˌkʌtˈʌp, $ˌkʌt̬-/ *n* [C] *Am* someone who behaves in an active and silly way in order to make people laugh • *It's hard to believe Sally was a cutup in school – she's so quiet now.* • See also CUT UP BEHAVE STRANGELY.

CV /ˌsiːˈviː/, *Am and Aus usually* **ré·sum·é** *n* [C] *abbreviation for* curriculum vitae (=a short written description of your education, qualifications, previous employment and sometimes also your personal interests, which you send to a future employer when you are trying to get a job) • *Send a letter and CV to the above address.* • In the US, CV is used to refer to the written description of the previous employment of someone who is looking for a job at a college or university: *Applicants interested in the Assistant Dean's position should submit CVs no later than February 15.*

cwt *n* [C] *pl* **cwt** or **cwts** *abbreviation for* HUNDREDWEIGHT

cy·an /ˈsaɪ·ən/ *adj, n* [U] (of) a deep greenish blue colour, one of the three main colours that are used in colour printing and photography

cy·an·ide /ˈsaɪə·naɪd/ *n* [U] an extremely powerful poison

cy·ber·net·ics /£ˌsaɪ·bəˈnet·ɪks, $-bɚˈnet̬-/ *n* [U] the scientific study of how information is communicated in machines and electronic devices in comparison with how information is communicated in the brain and nervous system

cy·cla·men /ˈsɪk·lə·mən/ *n* [C] a small plant with white, pink, purple or red flowers, whose petals turn backwards, and green and silver leaves

cy·cle BICYCLE /ˈsaɪ·kl̩/ *n* [C] a bicycle • *The shop sells a large range of cycles.* • *Do you know where there's a good cycle shop* (=shop which sells and repairs bicycles)? • **Cycle clips** are thin straps which you wear around the bottom of your trousers when you are riding a bicycle to prevent the trousers from becoming caught in the bicycle's chain. • A **cycle/cycling helmet** is a hard hat which you wear on your head to protect it if you have an accident while you are riding a bicycle. • **Cycle/Cycling shorts** are short tight trousers which are sometimes worn by people riding bicycles, or are worn informally. • A **cycle lane/path/way** is a part of the road or a special path for the use of people riding bicycles. • A **cycle rack** (also **bike rack**) is a row of holders that a bicycle wheel fits into, where bicycles can be left. • *(Br)* A **cycle shed** (also **bike shed**) is a small building for storing bicycles. • PIC› **Bicycles, Road**

cy·cle /ˈsaɪ·kl̩/ *v* [I] • *Shall we cycle into town or go by bus?*

cy·cling /ˈsaɪ·klɪŋ/ *n* [U] • *We did a lot of cycling in France last year.*

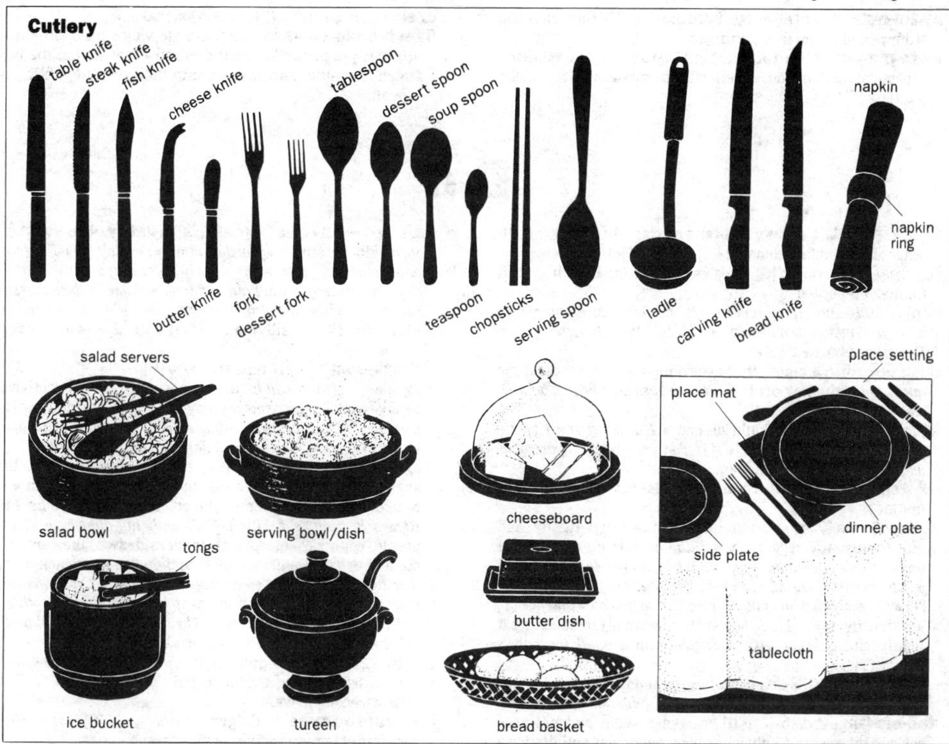

cy·clist /ˈsaɪ·klɪst/ *n* [C] • A cyclist is a person who rides a bicycle: *There's a special lane for cyclists.* ○ *I'm not much of a cyclist really – I'd always rather go on foot.*

cy·cle SERIES /ˈsaɪ·kl̩/ *n* [C] a group of events which happen in a particular order, one following the other, and which are often repeated • *I enjoy the cycle* **of** *the seasons.* • *She complained about the* **endless** *cycle* **of** *getting up, going to work and coming home, day after day.* • *The council holds its elections* **on** *a four-year cycle.* • A cycle is also one in a series of movements that a machine performs: *I took the clothes out before the washing machine had finished its spin cycle.*

cy·clic·al /ˈsaɪ·klɪ·kᵊl, ˈsɪk·lɪ-/, **cy·clic** /ˈsaɪ·klɪk/ *adj* • *Changes in the economy have followed a cyclical pattern.* • *The whole thing is cyclical – people who come from violent homes then make violent homes.*

cy·cle PLAYS/POEMS /ˈsaɪ·kl̩/ *n* [C] a group of plays, poems, etc. written by one person and connected with each other by dealing with the same characters or ideas • *It's one in a cycle of plays that are being performed on successive evenings.*

cy·clone /£ˈsaɪ·kləʊn, $-kloʊn/ *n* [C] a violent tropical storm or wind in which the air moves very fast in a circular direction • *A tropical cyclone brought heavy rain to western Australia last week.* • *(Am and Aus trademark)* A **Cyclone fence** is a **chain-link fence**. See at CHAIN RINGS.

Cy·clops /£ˈsaɪ·klɒps, $-klɑːps/ *n* *pl* **Cyclopes** /£saɪˈkləʊ·piːz, $-ˈkloʊ-/ or **Cyclopses** (in ancient Greek stories) a GIANT (= very big person) with one eye

cyg·net /ˈsɪg·nət/ *n* [C] a young SWAN

cy·lin·der SHAPE /£ˈsɪl·ɪn·dəʳ, $-dɚ/ *n* [C] a solid or hollow tube with long straight sides and two equal-sized circular ends, or an object shaped like this, often used as a container • *Inside a roll of toilet paper there's a cardboard cylinder.* • *There's no gas/hot water left in the cylinder* (= container). • *Deep-sea divers carry cylinders* (= containers) **of** *oxygen on their backs.* • PIC **Laboratory, Shapes** Ⓒⓢ ⓇⓊⓈ

cy·lin·dric·al /sɪˈlɪn·drɪ·kᵊl/ *adj* • *Are those cylindrical structures part of the gasworks?*

cy·lin·der ENGINE PART /£ˈsɪl·ɪn·dəʳ, $-dɚ/ *n* [C] the tube-shaped device, found esp. in an engine, inside which the part of the engine which causes the fuel to produce power moves up and down • *He's just bought himself a powerful new car with a six-cylinder engine.* • *The engine isn't firing on all its cylinders.* • Ⓒⓢ ⓇⓊⓈ

cym·bal /ˈsɪm·bᵊl/ *n* [C usually pl] a flat round musical instrument which is made of BRASS (= a metal) which when hit with a stick or against another cymbal makes a loud noise • *The piece of music ended with a loud* **clash of** *cymbals.* • PIC **Musical instruments**

cy·nic /ˈsɪn·ɪk/ *n* [C] *disapproving* someone who does not trust or respect the goodness of other people and their actions, believing that people are interested only in themselves • *I'm too much of a cynic to believe that he'll keep his promise.* • *A cynic might say that the government has only taken this measure because it is concerned about its declining popularity.* • *"What is a cynic? A man who knows the price of everything and the value of nothing"* (from the play *Lady Windermere's Fan* by Oscar Wilde, 1892)

cy·nic·al /ˈsɪn·ɪ·kᵊl/ *adj disapproving* • *I think she takes a rather cynical* **view** *of men.* • *I've always been* **deeply** *cynical* **about** *politicians.* • Cynical can also be used more generally to describe a tendency to use the weaknesses or feelings of others to your own advantage: *She works in that most cynical of industries, the advertising industry.* ○ *Saying I was a good cook was just a cynical ploy to get me to cook a meal for him.*

cy·nic·al·ly /ˈsɪn·ɪ·kli/ *adv disapproving*

cy·nic·i·sm /ˈsɪn·ɪ·sɪ·zᵊm/ *n* [U] *disapproving* • *He's often been accused of cynicism in his attitude towards politics.* • Ⓔ

cy·no·sure /£ˈsaɪ·nə·sjʊəʳ, $-ʃʊr/ *n* [C] *literary* a person or thing which attracts a lot of attention because of having a quality of excellence or great beauty • *The princess, dressed head to foot in gold, was the cynosure* **of all eyes** (= person everyone was looking at).

cy·pher /£ˈsaɪ·fəʳ, $-fɚ/ *n* [C/U] *specialized* a CIPHER SECRET LANGUAGE

cy·press /ˈsaɪ·prəs/ *n* [C] a type of CONIFER (= evergreen tree)

Cy·ril·lic /sɪˈrɪl·ɪk/ *adj* [not gradable], *n* [U] (of) the alphabet used in some Slavonic languages, such as Russian

cyst /sɪst/ *n* [C] a round growth, just under the skin or deeper in the body, which contains liquid • *He had a cyst removed from near his eye.*

cyst·ic fi·bro·sis /ˈsɪs·tɪk/ *n* [U] a serious disease which causes blockages in the lungs and other organs, such as the PANCREAS and LIVER

cyst·i·tis /£sɪˈstaɪ·tɪs, $-t̬ɪs/ *n* [U] a disease, esp. of women, in which the BLADDER (= the organ in which urine is held) becomes infected and there is pain when urinating

cy·tol·o·gy /£saɪ'tɒl·ə·dʒi, $-'tɑː·lə-/ *n* [U] the scientific study of cells from living things

cy·to·plasm /£'saɪ·təʊ·plæz·ᵊm, $-t̬ə-/ *n* [U] *specialized* the substance inside a cell which surrounds the cell's NUCLEUS

czar /£zɑːʳ, $zɑːr/ *n* [C] *esp. Am for* TSAR

Czech·o·slo·va·ki·an /£ˌtʃek·ə·slə'væk·i·ən, $-oʊ·sloʊ-/ *adj, n* [C] (a person) from the country that was in the past Czechoslovakia, now divided into the Czech Republic and Slovakia

D d

D LETTER (*pl* **D's** or **Ds**), **d** (*pl* **d's** or **ds**) /diː/ *n* [C] the 4th letter of the English alphabet • LP> **Silent letters**

D NUMBER, **d** /diː/ *n* [C] the sign used in the Roman system for the number 500

d. DIED *adj* [after n] *abbreviation for* **died** (= *past simple of* DIE) • *John Winston Lennon (b. 9 October 1940, Liverpool, d. 8 December 1980, New York).*

D MUSIC /diː/ *n* a note in Western music • *At this point the music is in* **(the key of)** *D.* [U] • *The bass part begins on a D.* [C]

'd /əd/ *short form of* would or had • *I asked if she'd* (= she would) *like to come tonight.* • *If you'd* (= you had) *told me what was wrong I could have helped.*

DA /ˌdiː'eɪ/ *n* [C] *Am abbreviation for* **district attorney**, see at DISTRICT

dab *(obj)* /dæb/ *v* **-bb-** to touch (something) lightly and quickly, usually repeatedly • *Dabbing* **(at)** *his eyes with a handkerchief, he left the cinema.* [T; I + *at*] • *I always like to dab a little perfume behind my ears before I go out for the evening.* [T] • *She dabbed a bit of powder* **on** *her nose to hide the spot.* [T] • *Hurriedly, she dabbed the food* (= removed it by touching it lightly and quickly with a cloth) **from** *around the baby's mouth.* [T]

dab /dæb/ *n* [C] • *Can't you just put* **a dab of** *paint over the mark and cover it up?* • *She put* **a dab of** *butter on the potatoes.*

dab·ble TRY /'dæb·l̩/ *v* [I] to take a slight and not very serious interest in a subject or try a particular activity for a short period • *If you want to make any money from investing in stocks and shares, there's no point in dabbling, you have to do it properly.* • *He first dabbled* **in** *politics when he was at law school.* • *She dabbled* **with** *several careers before finally becoming a computer programmer.*

dab·ble /'dæb·l̩/ *n* [U] • *After a brief dabble* **in** *politics, he returned to the world of business.*

dab·bler /£'dæb·ləʳ, $-lɚ/ *n* [C] • *She said that she was only a dabbler* **in** *the art of novel writing, and that her real interest was in poetry.*

dab·ble *obj* MOVE IN WATER /'dæb·l̩/ *v* [T] to put (esp. your feet or toes) in a pool, stream, etc. and move them about • *She would sit by the stream with her babies while they dabbled their feet* **in** *the water.*

dab hand *n* [C] *Br infml* someone who is very good at a particular activity • *Binns was a dab hand* **at** *cricket and played for his county in his youth.* • *Let's get my parents to help us with the decorating – they're dab hands* **at** *painting.* • *You're a bit of a dab hand in the kitchen* (= good at cooking), *aren't you?*

dachs·hund /£'dæk·sᵊnd, £'dæks·hʊnd, $'dɑːks·hʊnd/, *infml* **sau·sage dog**, *Am infml* **hot dog** *n* [C] a small dog with a long body and short legs • PIC> **Dogs**

Dac·ron /£'dæk·rɒn, $-rɑːn/ *n* [U] *Am trademark* TERYLENE

dad /dæd/ *n* [C] *infml* a father • *Can you give me a lift back from the cinema tonight, Dad?* [as form of address] • *I'll have to ask Dad if he'll lend me the money.* • *My dad's car is bigger than that!* • *Simon is really enjoying being a dad.* • *It was lovely to see your (Br and Aus)* **mum and dad**/*(Am)* **mom and dad** at the school concert last night. • LP> **Titles and forms of address**

dad·dy /'dæd·i/ *n* [C] *infml* (used esp. by or to children) a father • *Why haven't you got any hair on your head, Daddy?* [as form of address] • *Do you think Daddy will let me have a dog if I promise to look after it myself?* • *My daddy's a police officer.* • *On Saturday my (Br)* **mummy**/*(Am)* **mommy** *and daddy are taking me to the circus.* • *"My Heart Belongs to Daddy"* (title of a song written by Cole Porter, 1939) • LP> **Titles and forms of address**

dad·dy long·legs FLY /£ˌdæd·i'lɒŋ·legz, $-'lɑːŋ-/ *n* [C] *pl* **daddy longlegs** *infml for* CRANE FLY

dad·dy long·legs SPIDER /£ˌdæd·i'lɒŋ·legz, $-'lɑːŋ-/ *n* [C] *pl* **daddy longlegs** *Am infml for* HARVESTMAN

daf·fo·dil /'dæf·ə·dɪl/ *n* [C] a yellow bell-shaped flower with a long stem which is commonly seen in the spring • PIC> **Flowers and plants**

daft (**-er**, **-est**) /£dɑːft, $dæft/, *infml* **daf·fy** (**-ier**, **-iest**) *adj infml* silly or stupid • *You daft idiot!* • *Driving the wrong way down a one-way street was a fairly daft thing to do.* • *Don't be daft – let me pay – you paid last time.* • *Some of the suggested solutions to the problem were unusual – others were* **just plain** *daft* (= very silly)*!* • *He's* **(as) daft as a brush** (= very silly)*!*

daft·ness /£'dɑːft·nəs, $dæft-/ *n* [U]

dag /dæg/ *n* [C] *Aus infml* a person who looks unattractive or behaves in an unattractive way • *He's such a dag no girl would accept a lift with him.* • *(dated)* A dag is also an amusing person: *She's quite a dag with all those stories.*

dag·ger /£'dæg·əʳ, $-ɚ/ *n* [C] a short pointed knife which is sharp on both sides, used esp. in the past as a weapon • *In Shakespeare's 'Romeo and Juliet', when Juliet finds that Romeo is dead, she kills herself with his dagger.* • If two people, countries, etc. are **at daggers drawn**, they are in a state of extreme unfriendliness and do not trust each other: *The two sides have been at daggers drawn for some months now with no sign of improvement in relations.* • *"Is this a dagger which I see before me, / The handle toward my hand?"* (Shakespeare, Macbeth 2.1) • PIC> **Knife**

da·go /£'deɪ·gəʊ, $-goʊ/ *n* [C] *pl* **dagoes** or **dagos** a person from Spain, Portugal, Italy or S America. This is considered offensive.

da·guer·reo·type /də'ger·ə·taɪp/ *n* [C] the first successfully produced type of photograph

dah·li·a /£'deɪ·li·ə, $'deɪl·jə/ *n* [C] a brightly coloured garden flower with long thin petals in a circular or ball-like shape

Dáil /dɔɪl/ *n* [U] **the Dáil** one of the two law-making bodies which together make up the parliament in the Republic of Ireland

dai·ly EVERY DAY /'deɪ·li/ *adv, adj* [not gradable] happening on or relating to every day, or every working day • *Take the tablets twice daily.* • *Our post is delivered daily, except for Sundays.* • *Exercise has become part of my daily routine.* • *We back up our computer files at work on a daily basis.* • *She's looking forward to retiring and ending the daily* **grind** (= hard, boring work or duty) *of working in an office.* • *(infml) A hard worker, he earned his* **daily bread** (= money) *cleaning offices in the evenings.*

dai·ly PERSON /'deɪ·li/ *n* [C] *Br infml dated* a person who is employed to go to someone else's home in order to clean it • *Our daily comes on Tuesdays and Fridays.*

dai·ly (news·pap·er) /'deɪ·li/ *n* [C] a newspaper which is published every day of the week except Sunday • *Monday's dailies were full of the story.* • *(Br) The story was covered in all the* **national dailies**.

dain·ty /£'deɪn·ti, $-t̬i/ *adj* **-ier**, **-iest** small and graceful • *She was a small, dainty child, unlike her sister who was large and had big feet.* • *We were given tea, and some dainty little cakes.* • *"Wasn't that a dainty dish to put/set before the king"* (from the children's song *Sing a Song of Sixpence*)

dain·ti·ly /£'deɪn·tɪ·li, $-t̬ɪ-/ *adv* • *She skipped daintily down the street, holding her father's hand.* • *He handed round a plate of tiny sandwiches, daintily arranged in rings.*

dain·ti·ness /£'deɪn·tɪ·nəs, $-t̬ɪ-/ *n* [U]

dai·qui·ri /£'dæk·ɪ·ri, $'dæk·ɚ·i/ *n* [C] an alcoholic drink made with RUM, LIME juice, sugar and ice • *a banana/strawberry daiquiri*

dai·ry /£'deə·ri, $'der·i/ *n* [C] a place on a farm where milk and cream are kept and cheese and butter are made, or a company which supplies milk and products made from milk • *While we were camping we bought our milk from a nearby farm dairy.* • *The single supplier of milk for the region was a giant dairy* (= company) *near St Petersburg.* • *(esp. Am)* A dairy is also a farm which only produces milk and products made from milk. • Dairy is used to refer to the use of cows for producing milk, rather than meat, or to foods which are made from milk, such as cream, butter and cheese: *dairy cattle* ○ *a dairy herd* ○ *the dairy industry* ○ *dairy farmers* ○ *dairy products/goods*

GERMAN FALSE FRIENDS (D)

English	German	Meaning
actual *adj*	aktuell	relevant; topical; fashionable
afterthought *n*	Nachdenken	reflection, meditation; thought
all day *adj*	alltäglich	daily; common, ordinary
allure *n*	Allüren	behaviour; affectations, airs
also *adv*	also	so, thus; in that
announce *v*	annoncieren	to advertise
become *v*	bekommen	to obtain, receive, get
benzene *n*	Benzin	petrol; gasoline
blank *adj*	blank	shiny, bright; clean
blink *v*	blinken	to sparkle, glitter, gleam, twinkle
brave *adj*	brav	good; well-behaved; honest
bright *adj*	breit	wide, broad
bring *v*	bringen	to take, convey, put
cabin *n*	Kabine	telephone booth, cubicle
card *n*	Karte	postcard; map; menu; list; ticket
chef *n*	Chef	chief; leader; boss
chips *n*	Chips	potato crisps
concept *n*	Konzept	rough draft, outline, plan
conjunctive *adj*	Konjunktiv	subjunctive mood (grammar)
cook *v*	kochen	to boil
corn *n*	Korn	grain, granule
craft *n*	Kraft	effort; resistance; power; personnel
curiosity *n*	Kuriosität	peculiarity, oddity
curt *adj*	kurz	short; brief; quick; sudden
delicatessen *n*	Delikatessen	table delicacies
energetic *adj*	energisch	resolute, determined, firm,
eventual *adj*	eventuell	possible; contingent; if any
eventually *adv*	eventuell	possibly; perhaps; if necessary
fabric *n*	Fabrik	factory, works, plant, mill
fabrication *n*	Fabrikation	manufacture, production
faggot *n*	Fagott	bassoon
fail *n*	Fehler	mistake; fault; failing
familiar *adj*	familiär	family, familial
famous *adj*	famos	(old use) splendid, capital
fasten *v*	fasten	to fast
fatal *adj*	fatal	embarrassing, awkward
flick *v*	flicken	to mend, darn, patch
floor *n*	Flor	gauze; crepe; veil; carpet pile
floor *n*	Flur	corridor
formula *n*	Formular	form
gage *n*	Gage	salary, fee
genial *adj*	genial	brilliant, inspired; ingenious
geniality *n*	Genialität	genius, ingenuity
genie *n*	Genie	genius
gift *n*	Gift	poison, toxin, venom
glance *v*	glänzen	to gleam, shine, glare, sheen
glance *n*	Glanz	gleam, shine, sparkle, glitter
gracious *adj*	graziös	graceful, charming
hall *n*	Hall	sound; resonance; echo
impregnate *v*	imprägnieren	to waterproof; to creosote
inconsequential *adj*	inkonsequent	inconsistent
insert *v*	inserieren	to advertise
instance *n*	Instanz	court; authority; agency
irritate *v*	irritieren	to confuse (someone)
island *n*	Island	Iceland
kind *n*	Kind	child; baby, infant; minor
labour *n*	Labor	laboratory, lab
labourer *n*	Laborant	laboratory technician
lack *n*	Lack	varnish; paint; lacquer
land *n*	Land	country, state
lemon *n*	Limone	lime
list *n*	List	cunning; trick
local *n*	Lokal	pub, bar; restaurant; meeting place
lust *n*	Lust	pleasure, joy; inclination
man *n*	Mann	husband
map *n*	Mappe	folder, briefcase, school bag
marmalade *n*	Marmelade	jam
mass *n*	Maß	ruler; measurement; litre (of beer)
meaning *n*	Meinung	opinion; view; judgement
middle *n*	Mittel	average; method; device; funds, medicine; agent
middle-aged *adj*	mittelalterlich	medieval
mimic *n*	Mimik	facial expression
mode *n*	Mode	fashion; custom
motif *n*	Motiv	motive; grounds; purpose
necessary *n*	Necessaire	make-up bag; sewing bag
noble *adj*	nobel	(informal) generous, extravagant; posh
notice *n*	Notiz	note; item
novel *n*	Novelle	novella, short story; (political) amendment
novelist *n*	Novellist(in)	short-story writer
obscure *adj*	obskur	dubious, suspect
ordinary *adj*	ordinär	vulgar, common, base
oven *n*	Ofen	heater, fire, boiler
overhear *v*	überhören	to ignore; to be tired of hearing something
oversee *v*	übersehen	to overlook, miss, fail to notice
oversight *n*	Übersicht	overall view, survey; table
packet *n*	Paket	pile, bundle; dossier
party *n*	Partie	section; role; game; trip; batch; good catch (e.g. marriage)
patent *adj*	patent	ingenious; clever; neat; handy
pathetic *adj*	pathetisch	emotional, dramatic, histrionic
pathos *n*	Pathos	emotiveness; emotionalism
patron *n*	Patron	patron saint; (informal) chap, fellow
petrol *n*	Petroleum	oil, paraffin
photograph *n*	Fotograf	photographer
physician *n*	Physiker/in	physicist; physics student
pickle *n*	Pickel	spot, pimple; (pick)axe
plane *v*	planen	to plan, plot
plane *n*	Plane	tarpaulin, hood (on car); canopy
plate *n*	Platte	record; (informal) bald head; panel, sheet of glass/metal etc.; low/flat land; plaque; computer disc
plump *adj*	plump	awkward; obvious; crude
plunder *n*	Plunder	junk, rubbish
police *n*	Police	insurance policy
politics *n*	Politik	policy
pony *n*	Pony	fringe (hair)
principal *adj*	prinzipiell	in principle; on principle
promotion *n*	Promotion	doctorate
proper *adj*	proper	(informal) trim, neat, clean & tidy
pudding *n*	Pudding	blancmange
quit *v*	quittieren	to give a receipt, answer, sign
rash *adj*	rasch	quick, rapid, swift
rate *n*	Rate	instalment
ratio *n*	Ratio	reason
rational *adj*	rationell	efficient
real *adj*	reell	honest; solid, sound; realisic; fair
receipt *n*	Rezept	prescription, recipe
reclaim *v*	reklamieren	to complain, make a complaint
reclamation *n*	Reklamation	query; complaint
rector *n*	Rektor	headteacher, principal
rent *v*	rentieren	to be worthwhile; to pay
representative *adj*	repräsentativ	prestigious; presentable; personable
rudder *n*	Ruder	oar; helm
rusty *adj*	rüstig	sprightly
salad *n*	Salat	lettuce
sauce *n*	Soße	gravy; gunge
scheme *n*	Schema	diagram, plan, pattern, schema
scrupulous *adj*	skrupellos	unscrupulous
sea *n*	See	lake, loch; pond
secret *n*	Sekret	secretion
sensible *adj*	sensibel	sensitive, delicate
serious *adj*	seriös	respectable; reputable
slip *n*	Slip	briefs, panties
slipper *n*	Slipper	slip-on shoe
small *adj*	schmal	narrow, thin; meagre
smoking *adj*	Smoking (n.)	dinner jacket, tuxedo
solid *adj*	solid(e)	sound; respectable; reasonable
spanner *n*	Spanner	peeping tom
spend *v*	spenden	to donate; to offer, give
spender *n*	Spender	dispenser; donator; contributor
spot *v*	spotten	to mock, ridicule, deride
stay *v*	stehen	to stand; to be; to appear
still *adj*	still	quiet; silent; secret; hidden
stool *n*	Stuhl	chair; throne
strand *n*	Strand	beach; shore
stream *n*	Strom	(large) river; current; electricity
sympathetic *adj*	sympathisch	likeable, pleasant; attractive
sympathy *n*	Sympathie	liking; fellow-feeling
tablet *n*	Tablett	tray
taste *n*	Taste	key, button (on machine, etc.)
textbook *n*	Textbuch	script; song-book
tramp *n*	Tramper(in)	hitch-hiker
unsympathetic *adj*	unsympathisch	unpleasant, disagreeable
vest *n*	Weste	waistcoat
warehouse *n*	Warenhaus	department store, emporium
wonder *v*	(sich) wundern	to surprise; to be surprised

da·is /£ˈdeɪ·ɪs, £deɪs, $ˈdaɪ-/ *n* [C] a raised surface at one end of a meeting room which can be used by people speaking to a group

dai·sy /ˈdeɪ·zi/ *n* [C] a type of flower with a round centre and a lot of thin petals in a circular arrangement. There are various types of daisy, the most common of which is small, has white petals with a yellow centre and grows in short grass • PIC **Flowers and plants**

dai·sy·wheel /ˈdeɪ·zi·wiːl/, **print·wheel** *n* [C] a part of particular types of computer printers and TYPEWRITERS which consists of a wheel-shaped piece with letters around the edge

Da·lai La·ma /ˌdæl·aɪˈlɑː·mə/ *n* [U] **the Dalai Lama** the leader of the Tibetan Buddhist religion

dale /deɪl/ *n* [C] *poetic or regional* a valley • *We walked all day, over hill and dale.* • **The Dales** usually refers to the area of N England in which there are a lot of hills and valleys: *the* **Yorkshire** *Dales* ○ *We're going cycling in the Dales.*

dal·li·ance RELATIONSHIP /ˈdæl·i·ənts/ *n esp. humorous* (involvement in) a short sexual relationship with someone for whom your feelings are not lasting or strong • *It seemed that life had been a series of meaningless dalliances before she met Nigel.* [C] • *He admitted that he had had a brief dalliance* **with** *a work colleague.* [C] • *There seemed to be a lot of dalliance going on at the office party.* [U]

dal·ly with *obj v prep* [T] • *It's cruel the way she just dallies with him/his affections* (= is romantically or sexually involved with him without really caring about him).

dal·li·ance INVOLVEMENT /ˈdæl·i·ənts/ *n* an interest or involvement in an activity or belief which only lasts for a very short period • *The 1970s witnessed the first of the pop-star's dalliances* **with** *communism, Buddhism and mysticism.* [C] ○ *The prime minister has firmly said that there will be no dalliance by the government* **with** *any alternative policies.* [U]

dal·ly /ˈdæl·i/ *v* [I] *dated* to waste time or do something slowly • *He always dallies* **over** *tasks that he doesn't like doing.* • See also DILLYDALLY.

dal·ly with *obj v prep* [T] • To dally with esp. ideas, plans, etc. is to consider or imagine them, but not seriously or as a real possibility. *He had occasionally dallied with the idea of starting his own business, but he had never actually done anything about it.*

dal·ma·tian /dælˈmeɪ·ʃᵊn/ *n* [C] a big white dog with short fur and dark spots

dam /dæm/ *n* [C] a wall built across a river which stops the river's flow and collects the water, esp. to make a RESERVOIR (= an artificial lake) which provides water for an area • *The Aswan High Dam is on the river Nile in Egypt.* • Compare DYKE WALL. • PIC **Energy** N

dam *obj* /dæm/ *v* [T] **-mm-** • To dam a river is to build a dam across it in order to store the water: *They're going to dam* **(up)** *the river and build a reservoir.* [T/M] • If you dam **up** your feelings, esp. anger or sadness, you do not allow yourself to express or show your feelings in a healthy way. [M]

dam·age *obj* /ˈdæm·ɪdʒ/ *v* [T] to harm or spoil (something) • *Many buildings were badly damaged during the war.* • *Running on hard road surfaces can damage your knee joints.* • *It was a political scandal which damaged a lot of reputations.* • *Many chemicals have a damaging* **effect** *on the environment.*

dam·age /ˈdæm·ɪdʒ/ *n* [U] • *It is estimated that it will cost about £2 million to repair the damage* **to** *the factory that was caused by the fire.* • *Recent discoveries about corruption have* **done** *serious damage* **to** *the company's reputation.* • *The doctors were worried that he might have suffered* **brain** *damage in the accident.* • *(infml humorous)* If you ask someone **What's the damage?**, you are asking them the price of something, esp. a service. • If someone says **the damage is done**, they mean that it is too late to improve a bad situation. • **Damage limitation** is the process of limiting the damaging effects of an action or mistake, or the attempt in war to use careful planning to avoid unnecessary death: *The government is involved in a damage limitation* **exercise** *to minimize the effects of the scandal.*

dam·aged /ˈdæm·ɪdʒd/ *adj* • *The shop is selling off damaged goods at reduced prices.* • *Both the cars involved in the accident looked badly damaged.*

dam·ag·es /ˈdæm·ɪ·dʒɪz/ *pl n law* money which is paid to someone by a person or organization who has been responsible for causing them some injury or loss • *The politician was* **awarded** *£50 000 damages over false allegations made by the newspaper.* • *The police have been ordered to* **pay** *substantial damages to the families of the two dead boys.*

dam·ask /ˈdæm·əsk/ *n* [U] a type of heavy cloth which has a pattern woven into it that is the same colour as the background • *a white damask tablecloth*

dame WOMAN /deɪm/ *n* [C] *Am dated slang* (esp. said by men) a woman • *a fast-talking dame* • DK NL

Dame TITLE /deɪm/ *n* [C] a title in front of a woman's name which is given in Britain as a special honour, usually for valuable work done over a long period, or a woman having this honour • *Dame Peggy Ashcroft* • *Dame Peggy* • *Congratulations, Dame Peggy!* [as form of address] • *The 60-year-old writer has been* **made** *a dame in the New Year's Honours list.* • Compare KNIGHT.

dame CHARACTER /deɪm/ *n* [C] *Br* (in Britain) the amusing character of an older woman in a PANTOMIME (= musical play for children) who is usually played by a man • DK NL

dam·mit /ˈdæm·ɪt/ *exclamation slang* DAMN

damn EXPRESSION /dæm/, **damn it**, **dam·mit** *exclamation slang* an expression of anger or annoyance which is not strong and is not usually considered offensive • *Damn, I've spilt coffee down my blouse!* • *Damn! I forgot to get any money out and now the banks are closed.* • See also GODDAMN. • LP **Phrases and customs**

damn /dæm/ *n* [U] *slang* • *He can think what he likes about me – I don't* **give/care a damn** (= I'm not interested)*!*

damn /dæm/, **damned** /dæmd/, **god·damn** *adj* [before n; not gradable] *slang* • *I can't get the damn* (= annoying) *thing to work!* • *Some damn* **fool/idiot** *spilt water all over the floor and I slipped on it!* • *"Life is just one damned thing after another"* (Elbert Hubbard in *Philistine*, 1909)

damn *obj* /dæm/ *v* [T] *slang* • *You got the last ticket – damn* (= I'm annoyed with) *you, I wanted that!* • *Damn Peter – he's borrowed my bike without asking and I need it.* • *I'm polite to his ex-wife when I meet her but I'm* **damned if** *I'm going to* (= I certainly will not) *invite her round for dinner.* • *She's marrying that man that she met two months ago? – Well* **I'm damned /I'll be damned** (= I'm extremely surprised)*!*

damn·able /ˈdæm·nə·bl̩/ *adj dated* • *This damnable car! It just won't start on cold mornings!*

damn·ab·ly /ˈdæm·nə·bli/ *adv dated*

damned·est /ˈdæm·dɪst/ *n* [U] *infml* • *I don't know if I'll succeed but I'll* **do my damnedest** (= try very hard).

damned·est /ˈdæm·dɪst/ *adj* [before n; not gradable] *esp. Am* • Damnedest means very surprising or unusual: *Well that's the damnedest excuse I've ever heard!*

damn VERY /dæm/ *adv, adj* [before n; not gradable] *slang* very; great • *You were damn lucky not to have been killed in the accident!* • *He knew damn* **well** *how much trouble it would cause, and he still went ahead and did it.* • *It's* **a damn sight** (= much) *hotter in July.* • *(Br)I know* **damn all** (= nothing) *about computers.*

damn *obj* BLAME /dæm/ *v* [T usually passive] to blame or strongly criticize • *The novel has been unanimously damned by the critics.* • *No matter what decision you make, you're* **damned if** *you* **do and damned if** *you* **don't** (= criticized whatever you decide). • *The inquiry into the disaster damns the company* **for** *its lack of safety precautions.* • If you **damn** someone **with faint praise**, you praise them so slightly and unwillingly that it suggests that you do not mean what you are saying.

damn·ing /ˈdæm·ɪŋ/ *adj* • A damning report, finding, remark, etc. is one which is very critical or which shows clearly that someone is wrong, guilty or has behaved very badly: *He made some fairly damning remarks about the government's refusal to deal with the problem.* ○ *The two men were convicted on some extremely damning* **evidence.**

damn *obj* PUNISH /dæm/ *v* [T usually passive] (esp. of God) to force (someone) to stay in hell and be punished forever • *As a child she was taught that she would be damned for her sins.*

dam·na·tion /dæmˈneɪ·ʃᵊn/ *n* [U] • *He believed that he would be condemned to* **eternal** *damnation for what he had done.*

damned /dæmd/ *pl n* • **The damned** are the people who have been sent to hell after their death.

Dam·o·cles /ˈdæm·ə·kliːz/ *n* [U] **sword of Damocles**, see at SWORD

damp /dæmp/ *adj* **-er, -est** slightly wet, esp. in a way that is not pleasant or comfortable • *Don't sit on the grass – it's damp!* • *Did you dry the clothes properly? – this shirt still feels a bit damp.* • *It was a damp, misty morning.* • *(Br and Aus)* A **damp squib** is an event which people feel excited about in advance but when it happens is found to be extremely disappointing: *After all that media attention, the whole event turned out a bit of a damp squib with almost nobody attending.* • N

damp /dæmp/ *n* [U] *Br and Aus* • *Do you think that's a patch of damp* (= slight wetness) *on the wall?* • A **damp course** or **damp proof course** is a layer of material which is put in the bottom of a wall in order to stop wetness rising through the bricks. To **damp proof** a wall is to put such a layer into it.

damp *obj* /dæmp/ *v* [T] • If you damp something, you make it a little bit wet, usually intentionally: *If the shirts are too dry to iron properly just damp them a little.*

damp·en *obj* /ˈdæm·pən/ *v* [T] • *Rain had dampened the tent so we left it to dry in the afternoon sun.* • To dampen feelings, esp. of excitement or enjoyment, is to make them less strong: *The government has been trying to dampen expectation of a quick economic recovery.* ○ *I think the accident dampened his enthusiasm for the sport for a while.*

damp·ness /ˈdæmp·nəs/, *Br and Aus also* **damp** *n* [U] • *It's not the cold so much as the dampness* (= slight wetness) *in the air that is bad for your lungs.*

damp down *obj*, **damp** *obj* **down** *v adv* [M] to make (a fire) burn more slowly • *Water was pumped from a nearby lake in an attempt to damp down the flames from the burning building.* • *(fig.) The singer has tried to damp down* (= reduce) *speculation about the state of his marriage.*

damp·er /£ˈdæm·pəʳ, $-pɚ/ *n* [C] *infml* something which stops an occasion from being as enjoyable as it was intended to be • *Both the kids were ill while we were on holiday and that rather* **put a** *damper* **on** *things.*

dam·sel /ˈdæm·zəl/ *n* [C] *dated literary* a young woman who is not married • *The film was one of those tales of gallant knights rescuing damsels* **in distress**.

dam·son /ˈdæm·zən/ *n* [C] the sour, dark blue fruit of a type of PLUM tree • *damson* **jam**

dance *(obj)* /£dɑːnts, $dænts/ *v* to move the body and feet to music • *They danced all night at the ball.* [I] • *We* **went** *dancing at a nightclub.* [I] • *What sort of music do you like dancing* **to**? [I] • *Who was she dancing* **with** *at the party last night?* [I] • *They danced* (= performed the particular series of movements that form) *a calypso.* [T] • *He grabbed her arm and danced* (= moved to music with) *her around the room.* [T] • *The children danced* (= moved lightly with small jumping steps) *along the street.* [I] • If something dances, it moves quickly and lightly: *The daffodils were dancing in the breeze.* [I] ○ *She watched the sunlight dancing on the water's surface.* [I] • *(Br and Aus)* If you **dance attendance on** someone, esp. a person in a position of authority, you do everything they ask you to and treat them as if they are special: *I can't stand the way she has to have someone dancing attendance on her the whole time!* • If you **dance to** someone's **tune**, you do what they want. • *"Dances with Wolves"* (film title, 1990) • *"Dancing in the Street"* (title of a song written by William Stevenson and Marvin Gaye, 1969)

dance /£dɑːnts, $dænts/ *n* • *Shall we have a dance* (= an act of dancing)*?* [C] • *On Thursday night I've got my dance* **class**. • A dance can be a particular series of movements which you perform to music or the type of music which is connected with it: *The next dance will be a waltz, ladies and gentlemen.* [C] ○ *The band played a slow dance.* [C] • A dance is also a social occasion at which people dance, esp. a formal occasion in a large room: *Will you come to the dance with me?* [C] ○ *They're having an end-of-term dinner-dance.* [C] • Dance is the art of performing dances, esp. as a form of entertainment: *I've always been interested in the performing arts, especially dance.* [U] ○ *The performers tell the story through song and dance.* [U] • A **dance floor** is an area of a DISCO, restaurant, etc. which is specially for dancing. • A **dance hall** is a special building or large room where people go to dance or take part in dancing competitions: *We enjoy going to the dance hall on a Wednesday evening because they play all the old tunes we love so much.* • A **dance studio** is a place where people can pay for dance classes. • *"A Dance to the Music of Time"* (title of a series of books by Anthony Powell, 1951-75) • *"Dance of the Seven Veils"* (said to be the dance used by Salome to make Herod kill John the Baptist)

dan·cer /£ˈdɑːnt·səʳ, $ˈdænt·sɚ/ *n* [C] • A dancer is someone who dances either as a job or for pleasure: *He's a dancer in the Royal Ballet.* ○ *I never knew you were such a good dancer.*

D and C /ˌdiː·ənd'siː/ *n* [C] *medical abbreviation for* dilation and curettage (= an operation in which the inside surface of a woman's womb is removed for medical reasons)

dan·de·li·on /£ˈdæn·dɪ·laɪ·ən, $-də-/ *n* [C] a common small bright yellow wild flower which has a lot of long thin petals arranged in a circular pattern around a round centre • PIC **Flowers and plants**

dan·dle *obj* /ˈdæn·dl̩/ *v* [T] *dated* to hold (a baby or child) on your knee and move it up and down in a playful way

dand·ruff /£ˈdæn·drʌf, $-drəf/ *n* [U] small white bits of dead skin which sometimes gather in the hair or fall on the clothes, esp. on the shoulders • *I hate the way his jacket is always covered in dandruff.* • *This shampoo is supposed to stop you from* **getting** *dandruff.*

dan·dy MAN /ˈdæn·di/ *n* [C] a man, esp. in the past, who dressed in expensive, fashionable clothes and was very interested in his own appearance • *an upper-class dandy*

dan·di·fied /£ˈdæn·dɪ·faɪd, $-də-/ *adj disapproving or humorous* • *An embroidered silk waistcoat contributed to his dandified appearance.*

dan·dy GOOD (**-ier**, **-iest**) /ˈdæn·di/, **jim-dan·dy** (**-ier**, **-iest**) /ˌdʒɪmˈdæn·di/ *adj dated esp. Am* very good • *"Shall we meet at six?" "Sure, that's just dandy."* • *We had a dandy time over at Elise's house last weekend.*

dan·ger /£ˈdeɪn·dʒəʳ, $-dʒɚ/ *n* the possibility of harm or death to someone, or of something unpleasant happening • *Danger! Keep out!* [U] • *Before we start, can I make sure that you are all fully aware of the dangers* **of** *mountain-climbing* [C] • *He drove so fast that I really felt my life was* **in** *danger.* [U] • *I'm not taking part in any sport that involves danger* **to** *life and limb.* [U] • If an ill person in hospital is described as **out of** danger, it means that they are not expected to die although they have been extremely ill. [U] • *If there's any danger* **of** *seeing him at the party, I'm not going!* [U] • A danger is also a harmful influence: *the dangers of drugs* [C] ○ *The judge described him as a danger* **to** *society.* [C] • *(esp. humorous) "Bye – don't work too hard!" "There's* **no danger of** *that* (= I won't)*!"* • If you are on the **danger list**, you are extremely ill, usually in hospital, and might die: *"How's your father?" "Still* **on** *the danger list, I'm afraid."* ○ *She's finally been taken* **off** *the danger list* (= is no longer extremely ill). • *(Br and Aus)* **Danger money** (*Am* **Hazardous-duty pay**) is extra money which is paid to someone because their job involves danger.

dan·ger·ous /£ˈdeɪn·dʒər·əs, $-dʒɚ-/ *adj* • *I've never played ice hockey – it's far too dangerous.* • **It's** *dangerous* **to** *take more than the recommended dose of tablets.* [+ *to* infinitive] • *"Dangerous Liaisons"* (title of a book by Choderlos de Laclos, 1792)

dan·ger·ous·ly /£ˈdeɪn·dʒər·ə·sli, $-dʒɚ-/ *adv* • *She drives dangerously.* • *The small child was playing dangerously near to the edge of the swimming pool.* • *I think she likes to* **live** *dangerously – look at all those fast cars she owns.* • See also ENDANGER.

dan·gle *(obj)* /ˈdæŋ·gl̩/ *v* to (cause to) hang loosely • *She had big earrings dangling* **from** *her ear.* [I] • *A loose electric wire was dangling* **from** *the wall.* [I] • *He dangled the puppet in front of the children.* [T] • If you dangle something desirable **before/in front of** someone, you offer it in order to persuade them to do something: *I've tried dangling all sorts of offers in front of him to get him to work harder at school, but nothing works.* [T]

dang·ly /ˈdæŋ·gli/ *adj* • *dangly earrings*

Dan·ish pa·stry /ˌdeɪ·nɪʃ/, *Am usually* **Dan·ish** *n* [C] a type of cake for one person, consisting of sweet pastry and often having some fruit inside

dank /dæŋk/ *adj* **-er, -est** (esp. of buildings and air) wet, cold and unpleasant • *For years they have had to live in a dank, dark basement flat with peeling walls and a dripping tap.* • *In the cathedral vaults the air was dank and stale.*

dank·ness /ˈdæŋk·nəs/ *n* [U]

Dao·i·sm /ˈdaʊ·ɪ·zəm/ *n* [U] TAOISM

dap·per /£ˈdæp·əʳ, $-ɚ/ *adj* **-er, -est** (of a man, esp. a small man) stylishly and tidily dressed • *Hercule Poirot is the dapper detective of the Agatha Christie novels.*

dap·pled /ˈdæp·l̩d/ *adj* marked with spots of colour that are lighter or darker than the main colour that something is, or marked with areas of light and darkness • *a dappled pony* • *The dappled sunlight fell across her face as she lay beneath the tree.*

dare BE BRAVE/RUDE /£deəʳ, $der/ *v* [usually in negatives or questions; not usually *be daring*] he/she/it **dares** or **dare** to be brave enough to do something difficult or dangerous, or to be rude or foolish enough to do something that you have no right to do • *I was going to ask if his dog was any better, but I didn't dare in case it had died.* • *Everyone in the office complains that he smells awful but nobody dares actually* **(to)** *mention it to him.* [+ *(to)* infinitive] • *Dare you tell him the news?* [+ infinitive without *to*] • *Do you dare* **(to)** *tell him the news?* [+ *(to)* infinitive] • *Would you dare* **(to)** *jump out of an aeroplane?* [+ *(to)* infinitive] • *I wouldn't dare have a party in my flat in case the neighbours complain.* [+ infinitive without *to*] • *I showed him my new blouse but I didn't dare/(fml) I dared not tell him how much it cost.* [+ infinitive without *to*] • *I daren't/(fml) dare not think how much it's going to cost.* [+ infinitive without *to*] • *I don't dare* **(to)** *think how much it's* *going to cost.* [+ (*to*) infinitive] • *I'd never dare* **(to)** *talk to my mother the way Ben talks to his.* [+ (*to*) infinitive] • *I don't know how he dares* **(to)** *say that I'm lazy, when he's been in bed all day!* [+ (*to*) infinitive] • *He was under attack for daring* **to** *criticize the Prime Minister.* [+ *to* infinitive] • *(dated or humorous)* **Dare I say (it)**, *you're looking particularly lovely today, my dear.* • If you say **How dare** someone do a particular thing, you mean that you are very angry with them for having done it: *How dare you use my car without asking.* ○ *How dare he tell me what to do!* • *(esp. humorous)* If you say **Don't/Just you dare** to someone, you mean that they should not do something that they have said they are going to do, because it will make you angry: *"I think I'll just walk my dirty shoes over your nice clean floor." "Don't you dare!"* • *"I dare do all that may become a man; / Who dares do more is none"* (Shakespeare, Macbeth 1.7) • *"Who dares wins"* (motto of the Special Air Service (SAS), 1942-) • When followed by 'to' + infinitive, the he/she/it form of 'dare' is 'dares'. When used on its own, or followed by an infinitive without 'to', the he/she/it form is either 'dare' or 'dares': "Why doesn't she admit what she did?" "I don't think she dare/dares." In questions and negative sentences, you can follow 'dare' with either 'to' + infinitive or with an infinitive without 'to'. But in ordinary positive sentences, it can only be followed by 'to' + infinitive. • See also DARESAY. • LP **Auxiliary verbs**

dar·ing /£'deə·rɪŋ, $'der·ɪŋ/ *adj* • *In a daring rescue operation* (=one showing bravery and willingness to risk danger), *police entered the building and liberated the hostages.* • *This is a daring new film* (=one showing willingness to risk severe criticism) *by one of our most original modern directors.* • *She was wearing a rather daring* (=sexually exciting) *skirt that only just covered her bottom.*

dar·ing·ly /£'deə·rɪŋ·li, $'der·ɪŋ-/ *adv* • *She rather daringly asked the boss for a pay-rise.*

dare *obj* ASK /£deəʳ, $der/ *v* [T] to ask (someone) to do something which involves risk • *Wear the low-cut blouse with your pink shorts – go on, I dare you!* • *I dare you* **to** *ask him to dance.* [+ obj + *to* infinitive] • *She waved her fist at him, daring him* **to** *come any closer.* [+ obj + *to* infinitive]

dare /£deəʳ, $der/ *n* [C] • *He jumped in the river at twelve o'clock last night (Br)* **as***/(Br and Aus)* **for***/(Am)* **on** *a dare.*

dare·dev·il /£'deəˌdev·əl, $'der-/ *n* [C] *infml* a person who does dangerous things and takes risks • *She's a bit of a daredevil on ice – I've never seen anyone skate so fast.*

dare·dev·il /£'deəˌdev·əl, $'der-/ *adj* [before n] • *A huge crowd gathered to watch the racing-car drivers doing daredevil stunts.*

daren't /£deənt, $dernt/ *short form of* dare(s) not • *I daren't tell him – he'll be so angry.* • *He daren't complain in case they dismiss him.*

dare·say /£ˌdeə'seɪ, $ˌder-, '–/ *v* **I daresay/I dare say** I agree or think (that something is true) • *"She's got a lot of admirers." "I daresay – she's very beautiful."* • *He gets paid a lot of money, but I daresay* **(that)** *he earns it.*

dark WITHOUT LIGHT /£dɑːk, $dɑːrk/ *adj* **-er, -est** with little or no light, or having little brightness • *It was too dark to see properly.* • *What time does it get dark in the summer?* • *Our bedroom was very dark until we put a larger window in.* • *It's very dark in here – open the curtains, will you?* • *All the furniture had very distinctive dark blue upholstery.* • *Their daughter has dark* (=brown or black) *hair/skin/eyes.* • *What's so special about* **tall**, *dark* **and handsome** *men?* • *I'm looking for a dark-coloured outfit that would be suitable for interviews.* • The **Dark Ages** were the period in European history from the end of the Roman empire in AD 476 to about AD 1000: *In spite of the name, the Dark Ages saw some considerable achievements in religion, learning and government.* ○ *(fig.) This repressive law takes gay rights back to the dark ages* (=a time when homosexual people were treated badly). • **Dark chocolate** is *Am and Aus for* **plain chocolate**. See at PLAIN WITH NOTHING ADDED. • A pair of **dark glasses** is a pair of SUNGLASSES. • *(saying)* 'The darkest hour is just before the dawn' means that things often seem worse just before they get better. • *"The Dark Side of the Moon"* (title of album by Pink Floyd, 1973) • *"In a real dark night of the soul it is always three o'clock in the morning, day after day"* (F. Scott Fitzgerald in *Esquire* magazine, 1936)

dark /£dɑːk, $dɑːrk/ *n* [U] • *If you eat carrots does it really help you to see in* **the** *dark?* • *I've always been afraid of* **the** *dark.* • *It isn't safe to leave the house* **after** *dark* (=after the sun has gone down). • *I want to be back home* **before** *dark.* • *(fig.) I'm amazed to hear they're getting a divorce, I was completely* **in the dark** (=I knew nothing at all) *about their problems.*

dark·en *(obj)* /£'dɑː·kən, $'dɑːr-/ *v* • *The sky darkened as thick smoke billowed from the blazing oil well.* [I] • *We crept slowly along the darkened corridor.* [T] • *(fig.) The course of history changed irrevocably the moment nuclear weapons darkened* (=threatened) *our planet.* [T] • *(literary)* **Never darken these doors/my door again!** (=Don't ever come back here again!)

dark·ly /£'dɑː·kli, $'dɑːr-/ *adv* • *His figure could be seen darkly on the foggy moor.* • *"For now we see through a glass, darkly; but then face to face"* (Bible, 1 Corinthians 13)

dark·ness /£'dɑːk·nəs, $'dɑːrk-/ *n* [U] • *The city centre was* **plunged into** *darkness by the power cut.*

dark SAD /£dɑːk, $dɑːrk/ *adj* [before n] **-er, -est** sad or GLOOMY • *Her husband's sudden death was the start of a dark chapter in her life.* • *Chris always manages to find a dark side to any good news of mine.* • *This environmental report contains more dark predictions about the future of the Earth.*

dark EVIL /£dɑːk, $dɑːrk/ *adj* **-er, -est** evil or threatening • *She has a darker side which only her closest friends ever see.* • *He gave me a dark look when I criticized his work.*

dark·ly /£'dɑː·kli, $'dɑːr-/ *adv* • *"Don't come any closer," she said darkly.*

dark SECRET /£dɑːk, $dɑːrk/ *adj* **-er, -est** secret or hidden • *I've just been promoted, but* **keep it** *dark – I don't want everyone to know just yet.* • *(Br and Aus)* A **dark horse** is a person who keeps their interests and ideas secret, esp. someone who has a surprising ability or skill: *Anna's such a dark horse – I had no idea she'd published a novel.* • *(Am)* A **dark horse** is a horse or a politician who is a surprise winner in a competition.

dark·ie, *Am usually* **dark·y** /£'dɑː·ki, $'dɑːr-/ *n* [C] *dated slang* an offensive word used to refer to a person with brown or black skin

dark·room /£'dɑːk·rum, -ruːm, $'dɑːrk-/ *n* [C] a specially lit room where photographic film is processed

dar·ling /£'dɑː·lɪŋ, $'dɑːr-/ *n, adj* [not gradable] (a person who is) greatly loved or liked • *(to someone you love) Oh darling, I do love you.* [as form of address] • *(to someone you are being friendly to, but not used between men) Here's your change, darling.* [as form of address] • *In spite of his unpopularity in the USSR, Gorbachev remained* **a/the** *darling* **of** (=very popular with) *the West right to the end.* [C] • *(in a letter to someone you love) Darling Martha, It was lovely to see you at the weekend.* [before n] • *We've just bought a darling* (=charming) *little cottage in the country.* [before n] • LP **Titles and forms of address**

darn *obj* REPAIR /£dɑːn, $dɑːrn/ *v* [T] to repair (a hole or a piece of clothing) with long stitches across the hole and other stitches woven across them • *Schools should teach boys how to darn (the holes in) their socks.*

darn /£dɑːn, $dɑːrn/ *n* [C] • *You can't wear that cardigan to the party – it's full of darns* (=repairs).

darn·ing /£'dɑː·nɪŋ, $'dɑːr-/ *n* [U] • *I don't think I'll ever finish that darning* (=collection of things needing to be darned). • A **darning needle** is a special large needle used for darning, or for sewing thick cloth. • PIC **Pins and needles**

darn EXPRESSION /£dɑːn, $dɑːrn/ *exclamation infml* used instead of DAMN to express annoyance • *Darn* **it**! *There goes my bus – there isn't another one for a whole hour.*

darn /£dɑːn, $dɑːrn/, **darned** /£dɑːnd, $dɑːrnd/ *adj* [before n], *adv* [not gradable] *infml* • *Getting off the bus while it was moving was a darn stupid thing to do.* • *That's a darn/darned* (=extremely) *fine horse you got there.*

dart WEAPON /£dɑːt, $dɑːrt/ *n* [C] a small thin object with a sharp point which is thrown by hand in a game, or fired from a gun or blown from a tube when used as a weapon • Compare ARROW.

darts /£dɑːts, $dɑːrts/ *n* [U] • Darts is a game in which darts are thrown at a circular board. The number of points won depends on where the darts land on the board: *Do you feel like a* **game of** *darts?* ○ *Who won the darts tournament?*

dart *(obj)* MOVE QUICKLY /£dɑːt, $dɑːrt/ *v* [always + adv/prep] to (cause to) move quickly or suddenly • *I darted behind the sofa as my father stormed into the living room.* [I] • *The lizard darted* **out** *its tongue but the fly escaped just in time.* [M] • *She darted an angry look* (=looked angrily) *at me as I almost revealed her secret.* [T]

dart /£dɑːt, $dɑːrt/ *n* [C usually sing] • *They* **made** *a dart* **for** (=moved quickly towards) *the fire escape as the guard entered the warehouse.*

dart SEWN FOLD /£dɑːt, $dɑːrt/ *n* [C] a small fold becoming narrower towards one end which is sewn into a piece of clothing to make it fit better

dart·board /£'dɑːt·bɔːd, $'dɑːrt·bɔːrd/ *n* [C] a circular board which DARTS are thrown at in a game

dash [MOVE QUICKLY] /dæʃ/ *v* [I] to move quickly, esp. when in a hurry • *We dashed* **along** *the platform and just managed to catch the train.* • *No wonder he's tired – he's been dashing* **around** *all day.* • *I'm afraid I must dash* **(off)** *– I'm seeing my doctor in half an hour.* • If you **dash** something **off** you do it quickly without putting much effort into it: *You can't expect to learn much if you always dash your essays off at the last minute.*

dash /dæʃ/ *n* [C usually sing] • *The car wouldn't start at first, so it was a mad dash* **to** *the airport, but we made it just in time.* • *We* **made** *a dash* **for** *the exit as soon as we smelt smoke.* • If you **make a dash for it** you run quickly esp. to avoid something: *I know it's raining hard – we'll just have to make a dash for it* (=hurry through the rain). • *(esp. Am)* A dash is also a race over a short distance: *Who won the 50 yard dash?*

dash *(obj)* [HIT] /dæʃ/ *v* to hit with great force, esp. causing damage • *The tidal wave dashed the ship* **against** *the rocks.* [T] • *Waves dashed* **against** *the cliffs.* [I] • *She dashed the vase* **against** *the wall.* [T] • *(fig.)* **Hopes** *of an economic recovery have been dashed* (=destroyed) *by the latest unemployment statistics.* [T]

dash [SMALL AMOUNT] /dæʃ/ *n* [C] a small amount of something added to or mixed with something else • *"Would you like cream with your coffee, madam?" "Yes please – just* **a** *dash."* • *Bring the water to the boil and add the rice and* **a** *dash* **of** *salt.* • *A glass of whisky will bring* **a** *dash* **of** *colour to your cheeks.* • *(fig.)This car has* **a** *dash more style than the average family model.*

dash [LINE] /dæʃ/ *n* [C] a short horizontal line used to separate parts of sentences • *In the following sentence, the dashes function as brackets: The kiwi – a type of bird – is threatened with extinction.* • *In the following sentence, the dash functions as a colon, with the second part of the sentence explaining or developing the first part: I'm not surprised they look alike – they're cousins.* • Dashes are also long bursts of sound or light which are used with DOTS (=short bursts) to send messages in MORSE CODE. • Compare HYPHEN.

dash [STYLE] /dæʃ/ *n* [U] style mixed with self-confidence and bravery • *The situation would have embarrassed most people, but Chris carried it off with considerable dash.*

dash·board /£'dæʃ·bɔːd, $-bɔːrd/, **dash**, *Br dated* **fas·cia** *n* [C] the part of a car which contains some of the controls used for driving and the devices for measuring esp. speed and distance

dashed /dæʃt/ *adj* [before n], *adv* [not gradable] *esp. Br dated infml* extremely • *Dashed decent of you, old boy!*

dash·ing /'dæʃ·ɪŋ/ *adj dated* attractive and stylish through being energetic, exciting and confident • *She'd got engaged to a dashing* **young** *soldier.* • *Jane always wears such dashing hats.* • *He enjoyed a dashing and glamorous career in television.*

dash·ing·ly /'dæʃ·ɪŋ·li/ *adv*

dash it *exclamation esp. Br dated infml* used instead of DAMN to express annoyance • *Oh dash it! I've left my umbrella in the office.*

das·tard·ly /£'dæs·təd·li, £'dɑː·stəd-, $'dæs·tɚd·li/ *adj literary* intentionally harmful in a cowardly way • *The bombing of the houses is yet another dastardly attack on innocent people.* • *The film recounts the story of a woman who plots a dastardly revenge on her unfaithful lover.*

DAT /dæt/ *n* [C/U] *abbreviation for* **digital audio tape**, see at DIGITAL

da·ta /£'deɪ·tə, $-t̬ə/ *n* [U + sing/pl v] information, esp. facts or numbers, collected for examination and consideration and used to help decision-making, or information in an electronic form that can be stored and processed by a computer • *The data was/were collected by various researchers.* • *Now the data is being transferred from magnetic tape to hard disk.* • A **data bank** is a large collection of information which can be searched through quickly, esp. by a computer. • The process of **data capture** is any method of collecting information and then changing it into a form which can be processed by a computer. • **Data processing** is the use of a computer to perform calculations on data: *a data-processing bureau*

da·ta·base /£'deɪ·tə·beɪs, $-t̬ə-/ *n* [C] a large amount of information stored in a computer system in such a way that it can be easily looked at or changed • *We're linked to the on-line database at our head office.*

da·ta·glove /£'deɪ·tə·glʌv, $-t̬ə-/ *n* [C] a GLOVE which records information about the hand movements of the operator and sends it to a computer

> **DASH [–]**
>
> Dashes are used:
>
> • **to mean 'to'**
>
> *During the years 1975–1985 our prices increased by only 5–10%.*
>
> *The London–Edinburgh train leaves every morning at eight.*
>
> • **in informal writing to give extra information or an additional thought.** In formal writing, round brackets ( ) or commas , are generally used instead.
>
> *John's gone on a trip to Nanjing – near Shanghai – for a couple of weeks.*
>
> *It's easy to find the house – past the shops, then first on the right.*
>
> *I saw Dave – you remember him, don't you? – waiting in the post office.*
>
> • **in informal writing to separate an independent part of a sentence which follows from the main part, or explains it.** A colon (:) or semicolon (;) is generally used in formal writing.
>
> *We had our tickets, our bags were packed – we were ready to go.*
>
> *The small packet started to smoke – it was a bomb!*
>
> *Local businesses in financial trouble – hundreds of jobs will go.*
>
> • **to show that a speaker paused, was interrupted, or changed what they wanted to say**
>
> *"Helen left about three years ago and went to – er – Bristol, I think".*
>
> *" I'm sorry I'm late, but – " "Look, let's go now, shall we?"*
>
> *"Sam, take this to – no, don't bother, I'll take it myself".*
>
> • **to avoid writing a swear-word or taboo word in full**
>
> *Tim told them to b–r off* (to bugger off = go away).
>
> *"Turn that — music down!"*

date [DAY] /deɪt/ *n* [C] a numbered day in a month, often given with a combination of the name of the day, the month and the year • *What's the date (today)?/What date is it?/What's today's date?* • *Today's date is (Friday) the 24th of June/June the 24th (1994).* • *What is your date* **of birth***?* • *The* **closing** *date for applications is January 31st 1993.* • *We've agreed to meet again at a later date.* • *I'd like to fix a date for our next meeting.* • *I've* **made a** *date* (=agreed a date and time) *to see her about the house.* • A date is sometimes a particular year: *The date on the coins is 1789.* ○ *Albert Einstein's dates are 1879 to 1955* (=he was born in 1879 and died in 1955). • A date can sometimes be a month and a year: *The (Br and Aus)* **expiry***/(Am)* **expiration** *date of this certificate is August 2005.* • If food is **in date** it is still edible, but if it is **out of date**, it is no longer safe to eat. • If information is **out of date** it is no longer useful because a situation has changed: *Your dictionary's terribly out of date – it hasn't got any of the latest words.* • **Out of date** also means old-fashioned: *That radio looks so out of date.* • *(fml) I wrote to you two months ago, but I have not received any response* **to date** (=up to now). • A date can be a performance: *The band would like to play more club dates.* ○ *They've just finished an exhausting 75-date European tour.* • [LP] **Dates**

date *(obj)* /deɪt/ *v* • *Archaeologists have been unable to date these fossils* (=say how old they are). [T] • *My antique dealer has dated the vase* **at** (=said that it was made in) *1734.* [T] • *Thank you for your letter dated August 30th* (=with that date written on it). [T + obj + n] • *This tradition dates* **from/back to** (=has existed since) *medieval times.* [I always + adv/prep]

date [MEETING] /deɪt/ *n* [C] a social meeting planned in advance, such as one between two people who are or might become sexual partners • *I thought Chris and Kim didn't like each other, but they're out* **on** *a date tonight.* • *I've got a date* **with** *some friends at the opera on Monday evening.* • *(Am) She*

COMMON WAYS OF GIVING THE DATE

WRITTEN	SPOKEN
July 18, 1992	*(Br) July the eighteenth, nineteen ninety-two* *(Am) July eighteenth, nineteen ninety-two*
18 July 1992	*the eighteenth of July, nineteen ninety-two*

Dates may be written using numbers only (notice the difference between British and American styles). They are spoken as above, and also:

(Br) **18/7/92** or 18/07/92 or 18.7.92 DAY-MONTH-YEAR	*the eighteenth of the seventh, ninety-two* *eighteen, seven, ninety-two*
(Am) **7/18/92** or 07/18/92 MONTH-DAY-YEAR	*seven, eighteen, ninety-two*

- Sometimes when writing the full date people use the forms 1st, 2nd, 3rd, 18th, 31st and so on. This is becoming old-fashioned.
- The year is usually read two numbers at a time: *1950– nineteen fifty • 1809– eighteen o nine*. But notice: *1900 – nineteen hundred • 2001 – two thousand and one*. The first two numbers of the year are sometimes omitted: *Where were you in '82?*
- Some months may be written in a short form: Jan, Feb, Mar, Apr, Jun, Jul, Aug, Sept, Oct, Nov, Dec.
- Dates before the year 0 are followed by BC (*abbreviation for* before Christ). For dates after 0 the letters AD (*abbreviation for* anno Domini) are put before or after the number, when this is necessary: *The Roman poet Ovid (43BC–18AD)*

LP› **Calendar**, and **Periods of time** at PERIOD

had a **hot** *date* (= an especially exciting meeting) *with the new boy in her class.* • *(Am)* A date is also a person you have such meetings with: *Have you found yourself a date* (= partner) *for the dance tomorrow night?* • *"I can't make it at seven o'clock. How about nine-thirty?" "Sure,* **it's a date** (= that time is suitable for me)*."* • *"I'm free first thing on Tuesday morning – shall we* **make it a date** (= agree to meet or do something on that day)*?"* • **Date rape** is (a case of) RAPE which takes place during a date or social event in which the attacker is already known to the person who is attacked.

date *(obj)* /deɪt/ *v esp. Am and Aus* • *They were dating* (= were sexual or romantic partners) *for five years before they got married.* [I] • *How long have you been dating* (= been the romantic or sexual partner of) *Nicky?* [T] • A *(Br)* **dating agency**/*(Am and Aus)* **dating service** is an organization which introduces people with similar interests to each other, esp. people who want to start a personal or sexual relationship with someone: *She met her husband through a dating agency.*

date *(obj)* AGE /deɪt/ *v* to stop being fashionable or become old-fashioned, or to show the age of (a person or thing) • *I'm looking for a jacket that will last me a long time and won't date quickly.* [I] • *Some James Bond films have dated more quickly than others.* [I] • *She can remember watching live TV coverage of the first lunar landing, so that dates her* (= shows how old she is). [T]

dat·ed /£'deɪ·tɪd, $-t̬ɪd/ *adj* • *A few years ago that hairstyle was considered dated* (= old-fashioned)*, but now it seems to be back in fashion.* • *Spy thrillers with plots based on the Cold War look particularly dated nowadays.*

date FRUIT /deɪt/ *n* [C] the sweet fruit of various types of PALM tree

date·line /'deɪt·laɪn/ *n* [C] the line in a newspaper article which tells the place and date of writing • Compare **by-line** at BY CAUSE; HEADLINE.

da·tive /£'deɪ·tɪv, $-t̬ɪv/ *n* [U] the form of a noun, pronoun or adjective which in some languages marks the **indirect object** of a verb that has two objects • *This should be* **in the** *dative because it's the indirect object of the verb.*

da·tive /£'deɪ·tɪv, $-t̬ɪv/ *adj* [not gradable] • *the dative case*

daub *obj* /£dɔːb, $dɑːb/ *v* [T always + adv/prep] to spread (a thick or sticky liquid) on something or to cover (something) with a thick or sticky liquid, often quickly or carelessly • *It doesn't need to be perfect – just daub the paint* **on** *as quickly as possible.* • *Just daub it* **with** *paint as quickly as possible.* • *The baby had daubed butter all* **over** *its hair and face.* • *(fig.) Graffiti had been daubed* (= carelessly written) **on** *the tombstones.*

daub /£dɔːb, $dɑːb/ *n* [C] • *Vandals have covered the church with daubs of red paint.* • A daub is also a badly-painted picture: *The exhibition was a disappointing collection of daubs by talentless artists.*

daugh·ter /£'dɔː·tər, $'dɑː·t̬ɚ/ *n* [C] someone's female child • *Liz and Phil have a daughter and three sons.* • *(fig.) Monserrat Caballe is probably Barcelona's most famous daughter* (= the most famous woman to have come from there). • *(fig.) She was a daughter of* (= Her political opinions were formed by) *the feminist movement.* • *(fig.) Italian, Spanish, Portuguese, Romanian and French are daughter languages of* (= languages which originate from) *Latin.* • See also STEPDAUGHTER. • LP› **Relationships** PIC› **Family tree**

daugh·ter–in–law /£'dɔː·tər·ɪn·lɔː, $'dɑː·t̬ɚ·ɪn·lɑː/ *n* [C] *pl* **daughters-in-law** or *Br also* **daughter-in-laws** • Someone's daughter-in-law is their son's wife: *Our son and daughter-in-law are staying with us for the weekend.* • PIC› **Family tree**

daunt *obj* /£dɔːnt, $dɑːnt/ *v* [T usually passive] to make (someone) feel slightly frightened or worried about their ability to achieve something; to discourage • *She was not at all daunted by the size of the problem.* • *(esp. Br) She was not accepted by Newcastle University the first time she applied, but,* **nothing daunted** (= not discouraged)*, she reapplied the following year.*

daunt·ing /£'dɔːn·tɪŋ, $'dɑːn·t̬ɪŋ/ *adj* • *In spite of unification the country was still faced with the daunting prospect of overcoming four decades of division.*

daunt·less /£'dɔːnt·ləs, $'dɑːnt-/ *adj literary* • *In spite of the scale of the famine, the relief workers struggled on with dauntless optimism and commitment.*

daw·dle /£'dɔː·dl̩, $'dɑː-/ *v* [I] to do something very slowly, esp. when taking more time than is necessary • *Stop dawdling and try to finish your homework before bedtime.* • *Some people like to spend an afternoon just dawdling around the shops.*

daw·dler /£'dɔːd·lər, $'dɑːd·lɚ/ *n* [C] • *Don't be such a dawdler, Georgina, just get on with it!*

dawn EARLY MORNING /£dɔːn, $dɑːn/ *n* the period in the day when light from the sun begins to appear in the sky • *We'll have to leave before dawn if we're going to get there by ten o'clock.* [U] • *I've never seen a dawn as beautiful as the one this morning.* [C] • *The ball ended as dawn was* **breaking**. [U] • *The ball ended at the* **break of** *dawn.* [U] • *(fig.) The fall of the Berlin Wall marked the dawn* (= beginning) **of** *a new era in European history.* [U] • *(esp. Br and Aus) Twenty-three people were arrested and large quantities of heroin were seized in a dawn* **raid** (= a sudden entering of a building by police officers, in an attempt to catch people involved in illegal activities) *this morning.* • *(Br)* A **dawn raid** is also an unexpected attempt to buy a large number of a company's shares at the start of a day with the intention of controlling or owning the company: *The company launched a dawn raid* **on** *its rival, snapping up around 10 per cent of its shares, and it is expected to make a full takeover bid soon.* • **(From) dawn to dusk** means all of the time in a day that it is light or, more generally, for as long as possible: *No food or drink may be taken from dawn to dusk.* ○ *He was a lifelong workaholic, who painted dawn to dusk seven days a week.* • *(esp. Br and Aus)* The **dawn chorus** is the singing of birds together which happens just before dawn. • *"On the road to Mandalay,/ Where the flyin'-fishes play, / An' the dawn comes up like thunder outer* (= out of) *China 'crost* (= across) *the Bay!"*

(Rudyard Kipling in the poem *Mandalay*, 1892) • *"O say, can you see, by the dawn's early light, / What so proudly we hailed at the twilight's last gleaming"* (beginning of *The Star-Spangled Banner*, the American National Anthem, 1814) • Compare DUSK.

dawn /£dɔːn, $dɑːn/ *v* [I] • *Winston left his house just as the day was dawning.* • *(fig.) As 1990 dawned* (= began), *few people could have predicted the dramatic changes that were to take place in eastern Europe during that year.* • *"This is the dawning of the age of Aquarius"* (song from the musical *Hair* by James Rado and Gerome Ragni, 1967)

dawn [BECOME KNOWN] /£dɔːn, $dɑːn/ *v* [I] to become known or obvious • *The President declared a state of emergency as soon as the full horror of the disaster dawned.* • *We had trusted him for many years, but gradually the truth about him dawned.* • **It** *eventually dawned* **that** *they would never be coming back.* [+ *that* clause] • *I was about to pay for the shopping when* **it** *suddenly dawned* **on** *me* **that** *I'd left my cheque book at home.* [+ *that* clause]

day /deɪ/ *n* [C] a period of 24 hours, esp. from 12 o'clock one night to 12 o'clock the next night, or the part of this between the time when the sun rises and the time it goes down, or the part of this spent at work • *There are 365 days in a year and 366 in a leap year.* • *It took us almost a day to get here – we left at midday on Thursday and arrived on Friday morning at eleven o'clock.* • *Do not take more than ten tablets in any one day.* • *I'm available every day this week.* • *Today is Friday, so the day* **before yesterday** *was Wednesday and the day* **after tomorrow** *will be Sunday.* • *He was last seen alive five days* **ago**. • *They haven't been seen* **for** *days* (= for several days). • *I'll be seeing Pat* **in a few days/in a few days' time**. • *How's your day been* (= Has the day been pleasant for you)? • Day can be used to refer to the period in 24 hours when it is naturally light: *In the northern hemisphere, the shortest day is just a few days before Christmas Day.* ○ *It rained* **all** *day today and most of the evening yesterday.* ○ *I'm such a slob – I've done nothing* **all** *day.* ○ *During the summer we used to laze around in the sun* **all day long**. ○ *I hate working nights, I'd much rather work days.* • A day can also be a usual period of working, esp when that is during the period when it is naturally light: *Can I phone you on this number during the day?* ○ *What's your normal working day like?* ○ *I work a seven-hour day.* ○ *We're having to work a six-day week to cope with demand.* ○ *"Is Annie at work today?" "No, she's having a day* **off**.*"* ○ *The bank is closed* **all** *day Wednesday this week.* • **One** *day* (= On a particular but not named day) *a man came up to me and threatened to stab me if I didn't give him my briefcase.* • *I'd love to go to China* **some/one** *day* (= at a point in the future). • *Tomorrow's* **a big** *day* (= an important day) *for her – she's getting married.* • *Today's the* **big** *day* (= Today is important because it is the day when) – *I find out whether I've got the new job.* • *He's remembered as an important international statesman but few people know he began his days* (= life) *in a small country town.* • *When you're a nurse, talking with the relatives of people who are ill is* **all in a day's work** (= something that has to be done as part of your job or duty, even though it might be difficult, unpleasant or unusual). • *The baby's due* **any day now** (= very soon, esp. within the next few days). • *I prefer travelling* **by day** (= when it is naturally light) *rather than by night.* • *The same problems keep coming up* **day after day** (= repeatedly). • *The noise is absolutely dreadful – you can hear the traffic* **day and night** (= all the time) • *The latest opinion polls suggest that his* **days** (*as leader*) **are numbered** (= he will not be leader for much longer). • *The popularity of compact discs ensured that the* **days of** *vinyl records* **were numbered** (= they would soon become rare). • *He grew weaker* **day by day** (= Every day he became weaker than he had been the day before). • *I have to do the same boring jobs* **day in day out** (= every day). • *The symptoms of the disease change* **(from) day to day** (= each day they are different). • *Ever since he found out that he has cancer, he's been living a* **day-to-day** (= without planning for the future) *existence.* • *Your* **day-to-day** (= ordinary and regular) *responsibilities will include sorting the mail and making appointments.* • *It's impossible to arrange anything with Carol – she never knows what she's doing* **from one day to the next** (= in advance). • *(Am)* **Have a good/nice day** means I hope (the rest of) your day will be pleasant. • *They used to be very popular, but now they* **have had** *their* **day** (= they are no longer popular). • *I can honestly say that* **in all** *my* **(born) days** (= during the whole of my life) *I've never seen anything so strange.* • *Children take so much for granted nowadays –* **in** *my* **day** (= at the time when I was young), *a new bike was really special.* • **In** *her* **day** (= During her most successful period), *she was the best sportswoman around, but now younger women have taken her place.* • *You can't afford to run businesses inefficiently* **in this day and age** (= at the present time). • **In those days** (= In the past) *people used to write a lot more letters.* • If you **make** someone's **day**, you make them happy: *Seeing Adrian again after such a long time really made my day.* • *This really* **isn't** *my* **day** (= I'm having an unpleasant day) – *my wallet was stolen this morning and now I've lost my car keys.* • *You're going to get into serious trouble* **one of these days** (= some time in the near future). • *It's just been* **one of those days** (= a day full of problems). • *Things have changed a lot* **since my day** (= since I was involved) – *we worked mainly on paper and few people had typewriters, let alone computers.* • *"Mike says he's going to give up smoking."* **"That'll be the day** (= I think that's extremely unlikely.)*!"* • *Didn't I see you in the post office* **the other day** (= a few days ago)? • *How did people communicate in* **the days** (= the period in history) *before the telephone (had been invented)?* • *Vegetarianism is very popular* **these days** (= now). • *"I can remember when you could buy a cinema ticket and a big bag of popcorn and still have change from a pound." "Ah,* **those were the days** (= life was better then).*"* • *She died ten years ago* **to the day** (= exactly). • **To this day** (= Until now) *nobody has discovered the real reason for the assassination.* • **Day care** is the provision of education and physical care for young children, esp. while their parents are at work. • A **day nursery** is a public centre for looking after young children, esp. while their parents are working. • The **Day of Atonement** is YOM KIPPUR. • The **Day of Judgment** is the **Final/Last Judgment**. See at JUDGE [DECIDE]. • **The day of reckoning** is a time when the effect of a past mistake is experienced or when a crime is punished: *The day of reckoning has finally arrived for a man who murdered two children ten years ago.* • A *(Br)* **day pupil**/*(Am and Aus)* **day student** (also **day girl/boy**) is a student who sleeps at home and studies at a school where some of the other students live. Compare **boarder** at BOARD [STAY]. • *(Br)* **Day release** is a way of organizing training so that people can study part-time instead of going to work and still be paid by their employers: *My boss wants me to do a day-release course in computing.* • *(Br)* A **day return** is a ticket which can only be used for travelling to a place and back to where you started in a single day: *Day returns are cheaper than ordinary returns.* ○ *How much is a day return to London, please?* • A **day school** is a private school whose students return home in the evening. • If you make a **day trip** to a place, you visit it and return home on the same day: *Do you fancy coming* **on** *a day trip to London next Saturday.* ○ *Two per cent of the people on the beach were residents, 57 per cent were on holiday, and 41 per cent were* **day-trippers**.

day·break /ˈdeɪ·breɪk/ *n* [U] DAWN

day·care /£ˈdeɪ·keəʳ, $-ker/ *n* [U] care provided during the day, esp. for young children or old people, which allows the people who usually take care of them to go to work or have a holiday • *a daycare centre for the elderly* • *Inadequate daycare facilities are preventing many people with young children from returning to work.*

day·dream /ˈdeɪ·driːm/ *n* [C] a set of pleasant thoughts about something you would prefer to be doing or something you would like to achieve in the future • *Chris never pays attention in class and seems to be in a permanent daydream.* • *I was just enjoying a daydream* **about** *winning the Nobel Prize for literature.*

day·dream /ˈdeɪ·driːm/ *v* [I] • *Stop daydreaming and get on with your work!*

day·dream·er /£ˈdeɪˌdriː·məʳ, $-mɚ/ *n* [C]

Day–Glo /£ˈdeɪ·gləʊ, $-gloʊ/ *adj* [before n; not gradable] *trademark* in or of a colour which seems to shine unusually brightly in ordinary light • *Day-glo swimsuits/tracksuits/cycling shorts* • *We stock a wide range of beachwear in dayglo pink, orange and green.*

day·light /ˈdeɪ·laɪt/ *n* [U] (the period when there is) natural light from the sun • *I'd prefer to walk home in daylight.* • *The colours look much better in daylight.* • *We were ready to leave before daylight* (= before light from the sun appeared in the sky). • *More and more crimes are being committed* **in broad daylight** (= where they can be seen easily). • *(infml)* **Daylight robbery** (*Am also* **highway robbery**) is charging an unreasonably high price for something: *£5 for an orange juice is just daylight robbery – how dare they charge so much?* • *(Br and Am)* **Daylight saving time**/*(Aus)* **Daylight saving** is the time set usually one hour later in summer so that there is a longer period of daylight in the evening: *It's useful to change to daylight saving time because it saves energy and enables people to spend more time in outdoor activities.*

day·lights /'deɪ·laɪts/ *pl n infml* • If you beat, knock, etc. **the (living) daylights out of** someone, you hit them with great force: *I'll* **knock** *the living daylights out of him if he says that again!* • If something frightens, scares, etc. **the (living) daylights out of** you, you are very frightened by it: *That explosion* **scared** *the living daylights out of me.*

day·time /'deɪ·taɪm/ *n* [U] the period between the time when the sun rises and the time it goes down, or the part of the day which is neither evening nor night • *I tend to sleep* **in/during** *the daytime and study at night.* • *Chris hasn't been able to find a regular daytime job.* • *Daytime temperatures tomorrow will be average for the time of year.* • *Remember to write your daytime telephone number on the entry form.* • *The style of daytime television is completely different from what is shown in the evening.*

daze *obj* /deɪz/ *v* [T usually passive] to make confused or unable to think clearly, esp. as a result of being hit or of a very good or bad piece of unexpected news • *The collision dazed me for a while, but I soon recovered.* • *Everyone was dazed by the news of her sudden death.* • *You're looking rather dazed – is anything wrong?*

daze /deɪz/ *n* [U] • *The driver was discovered staggering around* **in a** *daze* (= in a confused state) *a short distance from her wrecked car.* • *She was wandering around* **in a** *daze* (= unable to think clearly) *after she got the highest mark in the university.*

daz·ed·ly /'deɪ·zəd·li/ *adv*

daz·zle *obj* /'dæz·l̩/ *v* [T] to make (someone) partly and temporarily blind because too much light is shining in their eyes, or *(fig.)* to cause (someone) to greatly admire or respect you • *Bright sunlight is thought to have dazzled a woman who drove into a train at a railway crossing.* • *I was dazzled by the spotlights as I walked onto the stage.* • *(fig.) He's a skilled politician who has dazzled both his opponents and the voters.* • *(fig.) She's a fascinating speaker who really dazzles you with her intellect.* • LP› **Eye and seeing**

daz·zle /'dæz·l̩/ *n* [U] • *The rabbit froze in the dazzle* (= sudden brightness) *of the car's headlights.* • *(fig.) This film combines the dazzle* (= attractiveness) *of Hollywood with the style of British cinema.*

daz·zling /'dæz·lɪŋ/ *adj* • *The laser system temporarily blinds enemy pilots with rays of dazzling light.* • *(fig.) She was never seen in public without her dazzling jewellery.* • *(fig.) They had never seen such a dazzling array of electronic goods before.* • *(fig.) His second film has been a dazzling success.* • *(fig.) Her dazzling intellect has won her an international reputation.*

daz·zling·ly /'dæz·lɪŋ·li/ *adv* • *(fig.) The prince smiled dazzlingly at the photographers.* • *(fig.) She is a dazzlingly inventive/creative/talented author.*

DBMS /ˌdiː·biː·em'es/ *n* [C] *abbreviation for* database management system (= a set of computer programs for allowing large amounts of information to be put into a computer and for organizing it so that it can be searched, examined or printed easily and quickly)

DC ELECTRICITY /ˌdiː'siː/ *n* [U] *specialized abbreviation for* direct current (= electrical current which always flows in the same direction) • Compare AC ELECTRICITY.

DC UNITED STATES /ˌdiː'siː/ *n* [U] *abbreviation for* the District of Columbia (= an area of the eastern US which has the same borders as the US capital, Washington, and which is not part of a US state) • *Summer in DC can be brutally hot.* • *In 1986 the estimated population of* **Washington, DC** *was 626 000.*

D–Day /'diː·deɪ/ *n* [U not after *the*] the day during the Second World War when the Allies began their INVASION of Europe by attacking the coast of N France, or *(fig.)* the day on which something important is planned • *The D-Day landings began on 6 June 1944, when Allied forces invaded Normandy.* • *(fig.) After four hectic weeks of electioneering, candidates are preparing themselves for D-Day* (= election day) *tomorrow.*

DDT /ˌdiː·diː'tiː/ *n* [U] a poisonous chemical for killing insects • *Nowadays, DDT is not used much because some insects have become immune to it, and also because it does not break down naturally into harmless substances and can therefore harm other living things.*

de– /diː-, dɪ-/ *combining form* used to add the meaning 'opposite', 'remove' or 'reduce' to a noun or verb • *The deforestation of the rainforests is a serious threat to the global environment.* • *The denationalization of the coal industry is expected to increase its competitiveness.* • *Once you've written a computer program, you have to debug* (= remove the faults from) *it.* • *Devaluation* (= Reduction in the value) *of the pound may help exports, but it will also increase inflation.* • LP› **Opposites**

dea·con /'diː·kən/ *n* [C] (in some church groups) a church official, either male or female, who is below a priest in rank and who performs some of the duties of a priest

dea·con·ess /£ˌdiː·kə'nes, $'diː·kᵊn·əs/ *n* [C] • In some church groups a deaconess is a woman who carries out certain duties in a church but who is not a deacon.

de·ac·ti·vate *obj* /ˌdi'æk·tɪ·veɪt/ *v* [T] to cause (something) to be no longer active or effective • *All chemical weapons facilities will be deactivated.*

de·ac·ti·va·tion /£ˌdiː·æk·tɪ'veɪ·ʃᵊn, $diˌæk-/ *n* [U]

dead NOT LIVING /ded/ *adj* [not gradable] no longer living • *You really should throw those dead flowers out.* • *The motorcyclist was dead* **on arrival** *at the hospital.* • *Three of the soldiers were* **shot** *dead* (= killed by shooting), *but one escaped with minor injuries.* • *(fig.) By the end of the week I'm usually dead* (= very tired). • *(fig.) The ashtray was full of cigarette ends and dead* (= used) *matches.* • *(fig.) Are these glasses dead* (= Have you finished your drinks)? • *(fig.) Are car phones more likely to* **go** *dead* (= stop working) *in the middle of a call?* • *(fig.) The city centre's quite lively during the day, but it's totally dead* (= nothing happens there) *at night.* • *(fig.) I've been sitting with my legs crossed for so long that they've gone dead* (= I cannot feel them). • If a performance is dead, it is boring: *The band's latest recording has a very dead sound.* • In some sports if a ball is dead, it is outside the area of play. • *I forgot to water your plant before I went on holiday, and now it's* **as dead as a doornail** (= completely dead). • *The artistic styles of the 1950s now seem* **as dead as the/a dodo** (= very old-fashioned). • *After working as a waiter all day, he's usually* **dead on** *his* **feet** (= very tired) *by the evening.* • *"Is Susannah up yet?" "I doubt it – she was* **dead to the world** (= sleeping) *when I took her some coffee half an hour ago."* • *"Dad, I was thinking of going to an all-night party at Steve's on Friday night."* "**Over** *my* **dead body** (= If I can prevent it I will)*!"* • **Dead bolt** is *Am for* **mortise lock**. See at MORTISE. • *(infml)* A **dead duck** is someone or something that is very unlikely to be successful, esp. because of a mistake or bad judgment: *Thanks to the lack of market research, the project was a dead duck right from the start.* • A **dead language** is a language which is no longer spoken by anyone as their main language: *Latin is a dead language.* • A **dead letter** is a law or agreement which is no longer effective: *The ceasefire treaty was a dead letter as soon as it was signed, as neither side ever had any intention of keeping to it.* • A **dead letter** is also a letter that cannot be delivered to the address written on it and cannot be returned to its sender: *the dead-letter office* • **Dead reckoning** is a way of calculating the position of a ship or aircraft using only information about the direction and distance it has travelled from a known point. • **Dead weight** is the heaviness of a person or object that cannot or does not move by itself: *My daughter may seem small, but when I have to carry her upstairs after she's fallen asleep she is a dead weight/(Am and Aus also) she is dead weight.* • **Dead wood** is people or things which are no longer useful: *She cleared out the dead wood as soon as she took over the company.* • *(saying)* 'Dead men tell no tales' means people who are dead cannot tell secrets. • *"Dead Poets Society"* (title of a film, 1989) • *"Let the dead bury their dead"* (Bible, Matthew 8.22) • LP› **Age** PIC› **Locks and home security**

dead /ded/ *pl n* • *A ceasefire has been called to allow the survivors to bury their dead* (= dead people). • *The government has decided to erect a monument to* **the** *dead of the civil war.*

dead /ded/ *n* [U] • *It would indeed be a miracle if someone* **rose from the** *dead* (= became alive again after being dead). • *In an exciting match Brazil* **came back from the dead** (= dealt with what seemed like a hopeless situation) *to beat their opponents 3-2.* • **Dead of night/Dead of winter** is the middle of night or winter when it is very dark or cold: *The bank was raided* **at** *dead of night.* ○ *We used to go for walks in the forest* **in the** *dead of winter.*

dead·en *obj* /'ded·ᵊn/ *v* [T] • *Morphine is often used to deaden* (= reduce) *the pain of serious injuries.* • *Double glazing has helped to deaden the noise from the motorway.* • *Rubber insulation is used to deaden the vibrations of the motor.* • *Alcohol can have a dangerously deadening effect on the senses.*

dead·ness /'ded·nəs/ *n* [U] • *There was a certain deadness* (= appearance of death) *in the eyes of all the starving children.*

dead·ly /'ded·li/ *adj, adv* **-ier, -iest** • *Cars turn into deadly* (= able to kill) **weapons** *when they are driven dangerously.* • *She fired the rifle with deadly* (= complete and so as to kill) *accuracy.* • *Her aim was deadly accurate.* • **Deadly nightshade** (also **belladonna**) is a very poisonous plant with small black shiny fruits, which grows in Europe, N Africa and W Asia.

dead·li·ness /ˈded·lɪ·nəs/ *n* [U]

dead COMPLETE /ded/ *adj* [before n], *adv* [not gradable] complete(ly) • *The braking system enables the car to come from 100 km an hour to a dead* **halt/stop** *in under five seconds.* • *The conductor waited for dead* **silence** *before commencing the performance.* • *(infml) I'm dead* **certain** *I left my purse on the desk.* • *You won't be able to change his mind – he's dead* **against** *the plan.* • *(infml) Let's stop for something to eat – I'm dead* (= very) *hungry.* • *(infml) The exam was dead* (= very) **easy**. • *(infml) I was dead* **beat** (= very tired) *after running the marathon.* • *(Br infml) Have you seen 'Annie Hall'? It's a dead* (= very) **good** *film.* • *The post office is dead* (= straight) **ahead**. • *Aim for the dead* (= exact) *centre of the target.* • *All your answers were dead* (= exactly) **on target**. • *I always try to arrive dead* (= exactly) **on time**. • *Martha's dead* **set on** *(having)* (= very much wants to have) *a new bike for her birthday.* • *He's dead* **set against** (= completely opposed to) *living in the city.* • *Even a slight hand injury can* **stop/halt** *a guitarist's career dead* **in its tracks** (= stop it suddenly and completely). • *Her imitation of Madonna is* **dead-on** (= exactly right). • *(Am)* **Dead air** is an unintentional time of silence during a radio or television broadcast: *The engineers worked to fix the problem while the station broadcast dead air instead of the program.* • A **dead end** is a road which is closed at one end, and therefore does not lead anywhere: *This road seems to be a dead end – we'll have to turn back.* ○ *(fig.) Negotiators have reached a dead end* (= have not been successful and cannot go further) *in their attempts to find a peaceful solution.* ○ *(fig.) He's in a dead-end* **job** (= one with no hope of improving his position). • A **dead heat** is a competition in which two or more competitors finish at exactly the same time or with exactly the same result: *The race ended* **in** *a dead heat.* ○ *The opinion polls show the three election candidates* **in** *a dead heat* **(with** *each other).* • *Nothing was decided at the meeting – it was just a* **dead loss** (= totally useless). • A **dead ringer** is someone or something which looks very similar to someone or something else: *Of course Pat's a dead ringer* **for** *Rachel – she's her twin sister.* • *(Am)* If someone catches, gets or has you **dead to rights**, they have found you doing something wrong or against the law: *I'd been driving above the speed limit and the police radar caught me dead to rights.* ○ *She said I had her dead to rights when I found her with a slice of cake in front of her.*

dead·ly /ˈded·li/ *adj, adv* **-ier, -iest** • *She was deadly* (= completely) **serious** *when she said what had happened.* • *They have been deadly* (= extreme) **enemies** *ever since she accused him of stealing her chequebook.* • *(infml) Professor Petersen's lectures are deadly* (= very) **boring/dull**. • *(infml)* If an event or situation is deadly, it is extremely bad or unpleasant: *The party was deadly – I'd never seen so many boring people in one place before.* • *She made incredible accusations* **in deadly earnest** (= totally seriously).

dead·beat PERSON /ˈded·biːt/ *n* [C] *esp. Am and Aus infml* a person who is not willing to work or does not behave responsibly or does not fit into ordinary society • *He's a* **real** *deadbeat who's never had a proper job.* • *Come off it, deadbeat, you're never going to get anywhere.* [as form of address]

dead·beat IN DEBT /ˈded·biːt/ *adj* [before n; not gradable], *n* [C] *esp. Am infml* (a person or company) not willing to pay debts • *The new law is aimed at deadbeat landlords who owe $22 million.*

dead·head /ˈded·hed/ *n* [C] *infml* a person who is boring or stupid

dead·line /ˈded·laɪn/ *n* [C] a time or day by which something must be done • *I want the report ready for the three o'clock deadline.* • *There's no way I can* **meet** *that deadline.* • *We're working to a* **tight** *deadline* (= We do not have much time to finish the work). • *The deadline* **for** *applications is May 30th.* • *I'm afraid you've* **missed** *the deadline, so your application cannot be considered.*

dead·lock /£ˈded·lɒk, $-lɑːk/ *n* [U] a situation in which agreement in an argument cannot be reached because neither side will change its demands or accept any of the demands of the other side; STALEMATE • *Somebody will have to compromise if we are to* **break/resolve** *the deadlock* **between** *the two warring factions.* • *Once again the talks have* **ended in** *deadlock.* • *Deadlock* **over** *wage levels has prevented an agreement being reached.*

dead·locked /£ˈded·lɒkt, $-lɑːkt/ *adj* • *deadlocked negotiations/discussions/peace talks* • *The dispute has now been deadlocked for several months.*

dead·ness /ˈded·nəs/ *n* [U] See at DEAD NOT LIVING.

dead·pan /ˈded·pæn/ *adj, adv* without expressing any feelings; without emotions • *Her deadpan face really fooled me when she said she'd lost my bag – I didn't realize she was joking.* • *Their deadpan humour/wit is too subtle for some audiences.* • *The deadpan tone of the police report did not reflect the full horror of the accident.* • *"Come any closer and I'll shoot," she said, completely deadpan.*

deaf /def/ *adj* **-er, -est** unable to hear either completely or partly, or *(fig.)* unwilling to listen • *He's been totally/partially deaf since birth.* • *(fig.) The local council has remained deaf* **to** *all the objections to its proposals.* • *My Grandad's* **deaf as a post** (= completely deaf) • *(Br)* A **deaf aid** is a **hearing aid**. See at HEAR RECEIVE SOUND. • A **deaf-mute** is a person who can neither hear nor speak. • *(saying)* 'There's none so deaf as those who will not hear'. • LP **Sound**

deaf /def/ *pl n* • *Many of the TV programmes are broadcast with subtitles for* **the deaf** (= deaf people).

deaf·en *obj* /ˈdef·ᵊn/ *v* [T] • *The explosion permanently deafened her* (= made her unable to hear) *in her right ear.* • *The music was deafening* (= very loud, esp. so loud that it was impossible to hear anything else).

deaf·ness /ˈdef·nəs/ *n* [U] • *Has listening to loud music increased deafness amongst young people?*

deal *(obj)* SHARE OUT /dɪəl/ *v past* **dealt** /delt/ to give or share out (esp. playing cards) • *Whose turn is it to deal?* [I] • *Would you like to deal* **(out)** *the cards?* [T/M] • *Deal them five cards each./Deal five cards* **to** *each of them.* [+ two objects] • *We have only a small amount of food and clothing to deal* **out to** *each refugee.* [T] • *(fig.) The latest trade figures have dealt a severe* **blow to** (= damaged) *hopes of an early economic recovery.* [T] • LP **Cards**

deal /dɪəl/ *n* [C] • *It's your deal* (= turn to deal).

deal·er /£ˈdiː·ləʳ, $-lɚ/ *n* [C] • *Casino dealers have to dress very smartly.*

deal *(obj)* DO BUSINESS /dɪəl/ *v past* **dealt** /delt/ to do business • *We only deal* **with** *companies which have a good credit record.* [I] • *They mainly deal* **in** (= buy and sell) *cruelty-free cosmetics.* [I] • *(slang) How long had she been dealing* (= selling drugs) *before she was arrested?* [I] • *(esp. Am slang) He was suspected of dealing* (= selling) *cocaine.* [T]

deal /dɪəl/ *n* [C] • A deal is an agreement or an arrangement, esp. in business. • *Firefighters are looking for a new deal with increased pay and reduced hours.* • *It was a* **fair** *deal so both the buyer and the seller went away happy.* • *The unions and management have* **made** *a two-year pay and productivity deal.* • *I'll* **make/do** *a deal* **with** *you – you wash the car and I'll let you use it tonight.* • *The president refused to* **make** *any deal (Br)* **on**/*(Am)* **for** *the hostages.* • *She got* **a good** *deal/***quite a** *deal* (= paid a low price) **on** *her new house.* • *This agreement is a* **great** *deal* (= is very advantageous) *for the Japanese electronics industry.* • *Is industry* **getting** *a* **raw/rough** *deal from* (= being unfairly/badly treated by) *the EU?* • *(Am infml) "You haven't been to work all week – what's the deal* (= what has happened)?"

deal·er /£ˈdiː·ləʳ, $-lɚ/ *n* [C] • *Can you recommend a reputable second-hand car dealer?* • *She used to be an antiques dealer.* • *The police have called for more resources to help their fight against drug dealers.* • LP **Crimes and criminals**

deal·er·ship /£ˈdiː·lə·ʃɪp, $-lɚ-/ *n* [C] • *Their company has just won the dealership* **for** *Rolls-Royce* (= permission from Rolls-Royce to sell their products).

deal·ings /ˈdiː·lɪŋz/ *pl n* • If you **have** dealings **with** someone, you are involved in a personal or formal relationship with them. • *I should never have had any dealings with him – he never loved me and was only after my money.* • *I've never had any business dealings with them.*

deal AMOUNT /dɪəl/ *n* [U] **a deal** a large amount; much • *(dated) I've got a deal* **(of** *work) to do this week.* • *She used to talk a* **good** *deal about her childhood in Glasgow.* • *A* **great** *deal* **of** *time and effort has gone into making the software reliable.* • *(dated) "How are you today, Mrs Cox?" "I'm a deal better than I was yesterday, doctor."* • *They still need a* **great** *deal more money to finish the project.*

deal with *obj* TAKE ACTION *v prep* [T] to take action on; to manage • *How do you intend to deal with this problem?* • *General enquiries are dealt with by our head office.* • *One of our secretaries deals exclusively with customers' complaints.* • *Bank staff are to be given more training to help them deal with armed robbers.*

deal with *obj* BE ABOUT *v prep* [T] to be about or be on the subject of • *Her new film deals with the relationship between a woman and her ill daughter.* • *Do you have any books that deal with rail travel in France?* • *The author has tried to deal with* (= write about) *a very difficult subject.*

dean COLLEGE /diːn/ *n* [C] a high-ranking official in a college or university who is responsible for the organization of a department or departments • *She is the new dean of the Faculty of Social Sciences.* • *The Dean of Medicine will be taking all first-year students on a tour of the department this afternoon.* • *(Am)* A dean is also someone among group of people who has worked the longest in the particular job or activity they share, and who is their unofficial leader: *Parsons is the dean of the TV news correspondents at Channel Nine.*

dean CHURCH /diːn/ *n* [C] a high-ranking priest in the Church of England or the Roman Catholic Church, who is in charge of managing a large church or CATHEDRAL

dear LOVED /£dɪəʳ, $dɪr/ *n, adj* **-er, -est** (a person who is) loved or greatly liked • *She was a very dear friend.* • *He was very dear* **to** *me.* • *This place is very dear* **to** *me – we came here on our honeymoon.* • *Annie's such a dear – she's brought me breakfast in bed every morning this week.* [C] • *Her husband was the dearest, kindest man I've ever met.* • *What a dear* (= lovely) *little kitten!* • *Why don't you go and relax in a nice warm bath, dear?* [as form of address] • **My** *dear Martha/Martha* **my** *dear – how lovely to see you!* [as form of address] • Dear is also used at the beginning of a letter to greet the person you are writing to: *Dear Kerrie/Mum and Dad/Ms Smith/Mr Jones/Madam/Sir/Customer* • Dear is used to address someone you are being friendly to, but is not used between men: *Here's your receipt, dear.* [as form of address] • If you do something **for dear life**, you do it with as much effort as possible, usually to avoid danger: *As the ship began to tilt more and more we clung on for dear life.* • A **Dear John (letter)** is a letter written to end a relationship: *I wouldn't talk to him just now, he got a Dear John this morning from his girlfriend.* • LP **Letters, Titles and forms of address**

dear·ly /£ˈdɪə·li, $ˈdɪr-/ *adv* • *We would dearly love* (= very much like) *to sell our flat and move to the country.* • *She will be dearly* (= very much) *missed by her family and friends.*

dear EXPENSIVE /£dɪəʳ, $dɪr/ *adj, adv* **-er, -est** costing too much; expensive • *That dress is too dear – I'll take the cheaper one.* • If something, esp. a mistake **costs** you **dear** you will suffer a lot because of it: *Missing the train cost me dear – it meant I missed an extremely important meeting.* • LP **Expensive**

dear·ly /£ˈdɪə·li, $ˈdɪr-/ *adv* • *(fig.) If you refuse to cooperate with us, you will* **pay** *dearly* (= suffer greatly) *for it.*

dear EXPRESSION /£dɪəʳ, $dɪr/, **dear·ie** /£ˈdɪə·ri, $ˈdɪr·i/ *exclamation infml* used in expressions of annoyance, disappointment, sadness or surprise • **Oh** *dear! I've lost my keys again.* • *Dear* **me**, *It's already four-thirty and I said I'd be home by five!* • *Dearie* **me**, *that really is a very sad story, isn't it?* • *Dear! Dear! That's terrible. Now just sit down, blow your nose and tell me what happened.*

dear·est /£ˈdɪə·rɪst, $ˈdɪr·ɪst/ *n* [U], *adj* (someone who is) loved a lot • *Would you mind doing the washing-up,* **(my)** *dearest.* [as form of address] • Dearest can be used at the beginning of a letter to greet the person you are writing to if you know them very well or like them a lot: *Dearest Rosalind/* **My** *dearest Rosalind* • LP **Titles and forms of address**

dearth /£dɜːθ, $dɜːrθ/ *n* [U] an amount or supply which is not large enough; a lack • *The factory's closure has been blamed on the dearth* **of** *orders for its products during the recession.* • *The university used to* **suffer** *from a dearth* **of** *facilities for handicapped students.*

dear·y, dear·ie /£ˈdɪə·ri, $ˈdɪr·i/ *n* [as form of address] *dated* a friendly form of address, not usually used between men • *Now then, deary. What can I do for you?* • *Here's your change, dearie. Should I put it in your wallet for you?* • LP **Titles and forms of address**

death /deθ/ *n* the end of life • *She lived here for four years before her death.* [C] • *Their sudden deaths in a car crash shocked everyone.* [C] • *He died a* **natural** *death, peacefully at home in the night.* [C] • *It was a traditional picture of Death in the form of a skeleton.* [U] • *Famous people often receive death* **threats** (= letters or telephone calls from people who threaten to kill them). • **To death** means until you die, or *(fig.)* a lot: *The animals burned to death in the barn.* ○ *He choked to death on a sweet.* ○ *(old use) The traitor was* **put** *to death* (= killed as a punishment). ○ *(fig.) It was really funny. We laughed ourselves to death.* ○ *(fig.) The film* **frightened/scared/worried** *the children to death.* ○ *(fig.)They worked her to death* (= made her work very hard). ○ *(fig.) That subject has been discussed/***done** *to death* (= it has been discussed so much that it is no longer interesting). ○ *I am* **sick** *to death* **of it/bored** *to death* **with** *it.* • **The death of** means the cause of the end of life, or the end or destruction of something: *The failure of the family business was the death of him.* ○ *The court case signalled the death of his hopes for public office.* ○ *That child* **will be** *the death of me* (= is always doing something which upsets me)! • *If you don't put some warm clothes on, you'll* **catch** *your* **death (of cold)** (= become ill). • *(infml)* If you are **at death's door**, you are very ill. • *(infml)* If you **look/feel like death** (*Br and Aus* **warmed up**/*Am* **warmed over**), you do not look/feel well. • *(Br)* To be **in at the death** is to be present at the important time when something comes to an end. • *The girl made a* **death-defying** (= very dangerous) *leap to the ground/dash across the road.* • *(Br)* **Death duty/duties** (*Am* **death tax**/*Aus also* **probate**) is the informal name for a government tax paid on the property that a dead person has left. • A **death's head** is a picture of a human SKULL (= the hard structure of the head) used as a warning of danger or to frighten. • A **death knell** is a warning of the end of something: *Some workers saw the machines as a death knell* **for** *traditional skills.* • If something **sounds/tolls the death knell**, it will soon stop another thing: *The court case sounded the death knell* **of/for** *his political ambitions.* ○ *The opening of the superstore will toll the death knell* **for** (= cause the failure of) *hundreds of small independent shops.* • A **death mask** is made by pressing wax onto the face of a dead person to get the shape from which a model of the face is produced. • **The death penalty** is the legal punishment of particular crimes by death: *The death penalty has been* **abolished** *in Britain – several votes in parliament have failed to* **reintroduce** *it.* • *(esp. Am)* Prisoners **on death row** are waiting in prison to be legally punished by being killed. • A **death sentence** is a legal punishment of a crime by death: *In some countries people caught smuggling drugs are given the death sentence.* • A **death squad** is an unofficial armed group who look for and illegally kill particular people, esp. the enemies of a political party: *The family lived in fear of the death squads.* • *We watched the* **death throes** (= process of dying) *of the bird which had flown into the window.* • The **death toll** is the number of people who died on a particular occasion: *The day after the explosion the death toll had risen to 90.* • A **death trap** is something that is very dangerous and could cause death: *The car he met me in was a death trap.* ○ *Empty bottles thrown carelessly away can become death traps for small creatures.* • A **death warrant** is an official document which says that someone must be killed as a punishment, or *(fig.)* something that causes the end of an activity: *(fig.) The cancellation of a large order was a death warrant* **for** *the company/***signed** *the company's death warrant* (= caused the business to fail). ○ *(fig.) By refusing to take on extra responsibility he signed his own death warrant* (= lost his chance of a better job). • A **death wish** is a desire for death: *The chances he takes, you'd think he had a death wish.* • *"Til death do us part"* (from the marriage service in *The Book of Common Prayer*, 1662) • *"Yea, though I walk through the valley of the shadow of death, I will fear no evil for thou art with me"* (Bible, Psalm 23) • *"Death in Venice"* (title of a book by Thomas Mann, 1912) • LP **Age**

death·less /ˈdeθ·ləs/ *adj literary or humorous* • Something that is deathless is so good that it will last forever and never be forgotten. Deathless is often used humorously about writing that is not of high quality: *The trouble with a diary is that when something exciting happens I haven't time to capture the event in deathless* **prose**.

death·ly /ˈdeθ·li/ *adj, adv* • *After he had spoken, a deathly* **silence/hush** *fell on the room.* • *She went deathly* **pale**. ○ *She felt deathly* **cold**.

death·bed /ˈdeθ·bed/ *n* [C] *old use* the bed that someone dies in or is dying in • *She spoke to her family* **from** *her deathbed.* • *(fig.) There are rumours that the singer is* **on** *his deathbed* (= dying). • *It's a book of famous deathbed statements.*

death·watch bee·tle /£ˈdeθ·wɒtʃ, $-wɑːtʃ/ *n* [C] an insect which eats wood, esp. in old houses, and causes serious damage

deb /deb/ *n* [C] *infml for* DEBUTANTE

de·ba·cle /deɪˈbɑː·kl̩/ *n* [C] a complete failure, esp. because of bad planning and organization • *The collapse of the company was described as the greatest financial debacle in US history.*

de·bar *obj* /£dɪˈbɑːʳ, $ˌdiːˈbɑːr/ *v* [T usually passive] **-rr-** *fml* to stop (someone) from doing something by law or by official agreement • *If you have been declared bankrupt you are debarred* **from** *holding certain public offices.* • *He was debarred* **(from** *the club)* **for** *unacceptable behaviour.*

de·base *obj* /dɪˈbeɪs/ *v* [T] to reduce in quality or value • *The word 'sale' has been debased by shops who hold sales at all times of the year.* • *Our world view has become debased. We no longer have a sense of the sacred.* • *The kebab and hamburger* *have become debased fast-food versions of their original selves.* • To debase **the coinage/currency** is to lower the value of a coin by making it from a less valuable metal.

de·base·ment /dɪˈbeɪ·smənt/ *n* [U]

de·bat·able /£dɪˈbeɪ·tə·bl̩, $-t̬ə-/ *adj* not clear, not certain, not fixed; possibly not true • **It**'*s debatable* **whether** *that is what was originally intended.* [+ *wh*-word] • *I agreed with their first choice but the second choice was slightly more debatable.* • *The value of some of the experiments is debatable.*

de·bate /dɪˈbeɪt/ *n* (a) serious discussion of a subject in which many people take part • *Education is the current focus of public debate.* [U] • *How we proceed from here is a matter* **for** *debate.* [U] • *Over the year we have had several debates about future policy.* [C] • *In a formal debate, two people speak for a subject and two speak against it.* [C]

de·bate *(obj)* /dɪˈbeɪt/ *v* • *In Parliament today, MPs debated the Finance Bill.* [T] • *They had been debating for several hours without reaching a conclusion.* [I] • *The authorities debated* **whether** *to build a new car park.* [+ *wh*-word] • *We debated* (= considered) **wh***ether to take the earlier train.* [+ *wh*-word]

de·bat·er /£dɪˈbeɪ·tər, $-t̬ɚ/ *n* [C] • *She was a good speaker and an excellent debater.* • *He was a poor television debater, being inclined to repeat the same points.*

de·bauched /£dɪˈbɔːtʃt, $-ˈbɑːtʃt/ *adj* weakened or destroyed by bad sexual behaviour, drinking too much alcohol, taking drugs, etc. • *His family were distressed by his increasingly debauched lifestyle.*

de·bauch·ee /£ˌdeb·ɔːˈtʃiː, $-ɑːˈʃiː/ *n* [C] • *He gave a convincing stage performance as the unpleasant young debauchee* (= debauched person).

de·bauch·er·y /£dɪˈbɔː·tʃər·i, $-ˈbɑː·tʃɚ-/ *n* [U] • *It is a society where debauchery has become the answer to conformity.*

de·bil·i·tate *obj* /dɪˈbɪl·ɪ·teɪt/ *v* [T] *fml* to make weak • *Chemotherapy exhausted and debilitated him.* • *It is a debilitating* **disease** *which does not affect the mind but damages muscle control.*

de·bil·it·y /£dɪˈbɪl·ɪ·ti, $-ə·t̬i/ *n* [U] *fml* • Debility is physical weakness: *near-fatal debility*

deb·it /ˈdeb·ɪt/ *n* (a record of) money taken out of a bank account • *What are these debits on 24 February? I didn't sign any cheques that day.* [C] • *The account was* **in** *debit at the end of the month* (= more money had been spent than was in the account at that time). [U] • A **debit card** is a small plastic card which can be used as a method of payment, the money being taken from your bank account automatically: *I paid with my debit card.* • The **debit column** is the list of numbers which shows amounts of money which have been spent from an account. • Compare CREDIT [PAYMENT].

deb·it *obj* /ˈdeb·ɪt/ *v* [T] • *The bank debited my account./ The bank debited the money* **from** *my account.* • LP> **Money**

de·bon·air /£ˌdeb·əˈneər, $-ˈner/ *adj slightly dated* (esp. of men) charming, confident and carefully dressed • *a debonair appearance/manner* • *debonair charm/style* • *a debonair young management consultant*

de·brief *obj* /ˌdiːˈbriːf/ *v* [T] to question (someone) in detail about work they have done for you • *The pilots were thoroughly debriefed after every mission.* • *We'll have a debriefing* **session** *after you have all completed your programme of visits.*

deb·ris /£ˈdeɪ·briː, £ˈdeb·riː, $dəˈbriː/ *n* [U] broken or torn pieces of something larger • *The storm tore down trees, damaged houses and littered the village with debris.* • *The child was killed by* **flying** *debris after the bomb exploded.* • *The car was buried in the debris which the landslide had swept down the hill.*

debt /det/ *n* something, esp. money, which is owed to someone else, or the state of owing something • *He managed to* **pay (off)** *his debts in two years.* [C] • *They are* **in debt to** (= owe money to) *the bank.* [U] • *When he lost his job, he* **ran/got into** *debt* (= borrowed money). [U] • *The firm* **ran up** *huge debts.* [C] • *I'm* **out of** *debt at last* (= no longer owe money). [U] • *A debt-***counselling** *service has been set up to advise those who are finding it hard to repay what they owe.* • *Should the Third World be giving the West more in debt* **repayments** *than we give them in aid?* • A **bad** debt is one which is unlikely ever to be **recovered** (= paid back). [C] • *(fml)* A debt **of honour** is something which you feel you must do or pay although there is no legal need to: *He believed that giving the man a job* **discharged** *a debt of honour.* [C] • *(fml) I* **owe** *all those who offered me support a debt* **of gratitude** (= I am very grateful). [C] • *(fml) Thank you for helping. I'm* **in** *your debt* (= I am very grateful). [U] • See also INDEBTED [GRATEFUL]; INDEBTED [OWING]. • LP> **Borrow**

debt·or /£ˈdet·ər, $ˈdet̬·ɚ/ *n* [C] • *Student loans will cause students to graduate as debtors* (= people who owe money). • *The company was regarded as a reliable debtor* (= one which always pays what it owes). • *Many debtor countries may have to reschedule their loans because of financial difficulties.* • Compare **creditor** at CREDIT [PAYMENT].

de·bug *obj* [REMOVE MISTAKES] /ˌdiːˈbʌg/ *v* [T] **-gg-** to remove BUGS (= mistakes) from (a computer program) • *I'll need a couple of hours to debug this program.*

de·bug *obj* [REMOVE DEVICES] /ˌdiːˈbʌg/ *v* [T] **-gg-** to look for and remove BUGS (= hidden listening or recording devices) from (a place) • *The security officers debugged the room before the meeting.*

de·bunk *obj* /ˌdiːˈbʌŋk/ *v* [T] *infml* to show that (something) is less important, less good or less true than it has been made to appear • *They sought to debunk the widespread belief that taxes would be reduced.* • *The writer's aim was to debunk the* **myth** *that had grown up around the actress.*

deb·ut /ˈdeɪ·bju/ *n, v* (to make) a first public appearance or activity • *She* **made** *her professional stage debut in Swan Lake.* [C] • *He started as an actor,* **making** *his debut* **as** *a director in 1990.* [C] • *The video will* **make** *its debut at a seminar in June.* [C] • *The concert is timed to coincide with the release of her debut* (= first) *album.* • *I debuted in primary school* **as** *third shepherd in the Nativity play.* [I always + adv/ prep] • *The new player is expected to debut in tonight's game.* [I always + adv/prep]

deb·u·tante /£ˈdeɪ·bjuː·tɒnt, £ˈdeb·juː-, $-tɑːnt/, *infml* **deb** *n* [C] a rich young woman who, esp. in the past in Britain, went to a number of social events as a way of being introduced to other young people of high social rank • *a debutantes' ball* • *(fig.) The newcomer, with the joyfulness of a debutante* (= a person who is new to a situation or activity), *beat the older woman in straight sets.*

Dec *n* [C/U] *abbreviation for* DECEMBER

dec·ade /ˈdek·eɪd, -ˈ-/ *n* [C] a period of ten years, esp. a period such as 1860 to 1869 or 1990 to 1999 • *I wasn't in the country much during the seventies. I spent that decade travelling abroad on various assignments.* • LP> **Periods of time** (F)

dec·a·dence /£ˈdek·ə·dənts/ *n* [U] a state of low standards in social and moral behaviour • *The film depicts capitalist decadence, with champagne flowing into glasses, smoky rooms, promiscuity and corrupt leaders.*

dec·a·dent /ˈdek·ə·dənt/ *adj* • *a decadent society* • *the decadent court surrounding the king* • *The writer described the highly decorative style of architecture as decadent.* • *(humorous) Champagne and chocolates for breakfast – how decadent!*

de·caf·fein·a·ted /£ˌdiːˈkæf·ɪ·neɪ·tɪd, dɪ- $-t̬ɪd/, *infml* **de·caf** /ˈdiː·kæf/ *n, adj* [not gradable] (a drink) that has had the CAFFEINE (= a chemical substance) removed • *I only drink decaffeinated coffee/tea/Coke these days.* • *I'm sorry I can't offer you decaffeinated.* [U] • *I'll have a decaffeinated* (= a glass, cup, etc. of such drink), *please.* [C]

de·cal /£ˈdiː·kæl, $-ˈ-/ *n* [C] *esp. Am and Aus* a picture or design printed on special paper, that can be put onto another surface, such as metal or glass; a TRANSFER [PATTERN]

Dec·a·logue /£ˈdek·ə·lɒg, $-lɑːg/ *n* [U] **the Decalogue** *specialized* the rules of behaviour God gave to Israel through Moses on Mount Sinai; the **Ten Commandments**, see at TEN

de·camp /ˌdiːˈkæmp/ *v* [I] *infml* to leave suddenly and unexpectedly, usually without telling anyone • *His father decamped to pursue other interests abroad.* • *He decamped* **from** *the hotel with someone else's luggage.*

de·cant *obj* /dɪˈkænt, ˌdiː-/ *v* [T] to pour (a liquid) from one container into another, or *(fig. Br infml)* to move (a person or thing) from one place to another • *Wines like port and sherry are often decanted* **from** *their bottles* **into** *more attractive containers for serving.* • *(fig. Br infml) Visitors have to decant themselves from the buses* **into** *small boats for the tour.* • (I)

de·cant·er /£dɪˈkæn·tər, $-t̬ɚ/ *n* [C] • *They were given a cut-glass sherry decanter* (= container) *as a wedding present.* • PIC> **Bottles and flasks**

de·cap·i·tate *obj* /dɪˈkæp·ɪ·teɪt/ *v* [T] to cut off the head of (a person or animal) • *The bodies had been decapitated.*

de·cap·i·ta·tion /dɪˌkæp·ɪˈteɪ·ʃən/ *n* [U]

dec·ath·lon /£dɪˈkæθ·lɒn, $-lɑːn/ *n* [C] a competition in which a male ATHLETE competes in ten sporting events • *He was first in the high jump section of the decathlon but was third in the overall competition.* • Compare BIATHLON; HEPTATHLON; PENTATHLON.

de·cath·lete /dɪˈkæθ·liːt,/ *n* [C] • A decathlete is a man who competes in a decathlon.

de·cay *(obj)* /dɪˈkeɪ/ *v* to (cause to) become gradually damaged, worse or less • *They claimed that the plastics would not decay if they were buried.* [I] • *Facilities built in the 1960s have started to decay.* [I] • *The role of the extended family has been decaying for some time.* [I] • *Pollution has decayed the surface of the stonework on the front of the cathedral.* [T] • *She smelt the unpleasantly sweet smell of decaying meat.*

de·cay /dɪˈkeɪ/ *n* [U] • *environmental/industrial/moral/urban decay* • *dental/tooth decay* • *The buildings had started to* **fall into** *decay.* • *This industry has been* **in** *decay for some time.*

de·cease /dɪˈsiːs/ *n* [U] *fml* death • **Upon** *my decease my children will inherit everything.*

de·ceased /dɪˈsiːst/ *n* [C] *pl* **deceased** *fml* • **The deceased** is a person or people who has or have recently died. • *The family of the deceased were the first to be told.* • *All the deceased were completely innocent victims of the bomb.* • [LP]> **Age**

de·ceased /dɪˈsiːst/ *adj* [not gradable] *fml* • *the recently deceased Member of Parliament* • *His parents are recently deceased.* • *The painting formerly belonged to William Cooper, deceased (abbreviation* **decd***).*

de·ceit /dɪˈsiːt/ *n* (an act of) keeping the truth hidden, esp. to get an advantage • *When the newspapers published the full story, all his earlier deceits were revealed.* [C] • *The story is about theft, fraud and deceit on an incredible scale.* [U] • *Espionage is, by definition, an activity which trades in deceit.* [U]

de·ceit·ful /dɪˈsiːt·fᵊl/ *adj* • *It was a deceitful attempt to persuade people that they would make a large profit.*

de·ceit·ful·ly /dɪˈsiːt·fə·li/ *adv* • *The advertisement deceitfully suggested that the product would quickly help you lose weight.*

de·ceit·ful·ness /dɪˈsiːt·fᵊl·nəs/ *n* [U]

de·ceive *obj* /dɪˈsiːv/ *v* [T] to persuade (someone) that something false is the truth; to keep the truth hidden from (someone) for your own advantage; to trick • *I was deceived by his uniform – I really thought he was a police officer.* • *The sound of the door closing deceived me* **into** *thinking they had gone out.* • If you deceive your**self**, you refuse to accept the truth: *She thinks he'll come back, but she's deceiving herself.* • If your **eyes** deceive you, you cannot believe what you see: *Is that snow in June, or are my eyes deceiving me?* ○ *Unless my eyes deceive me, that's your cousin.* • See also DECEPTION. • (F)

de·ceiv·er /£dɪˈsiː·vəʳ, $-vɚ/ *n* [C]

de·cel·er·ate /£ˌdiːˈsel·ᵊr·eɪt, $-ə·reɪt/ *v* [I] to go more slowly; to reduce speed • *The car/driver decelerated at the sight of the police car.* • *Consumer spending is predicted to decelerate rapidly this year.* • Compare ACCELERATE.

De·cem·ber /£dɪˈsem·bəʳ, $-bɚ/ *(abbreviation* **Dec***) n* the twelfth and last month of the year, after November and before January • *23(rd) December/December 23(rd)/23(rd) Dec/Dec 23(rd)* [U] • *We went to Mexico* **on** *the twelfth of December/December the twelfth/(esp. Am) December twelfth.* [U] • *Their baby was born* **last**/*is expected* **next** *December.* [U] • *My parents got married* **in/during** *December.* [U] • *It was one of the coldest Decembers ever.* [C] • [LP]> **Dates**

de·cent /ˈdiː·sᵊnt/ *adj* socially acceptable or good • *Everyone should be entitled to a decent wage/standard of living and a decent home.* • *I thought he was a decent sort of person.* • *They went to visit him after a decent* **interval** (=one that was not too short, esp. after something bad has happened). • **It** *was very decent* (=kind) **of you** *to help.* [+ *to* infinitive] • *It made quite a decent-sized* (=large) *hole.* • *After the recent scandal, the priest is expected to* **do the** *decent* **thing** *and resign from his position.* • *(infml)* Decent can also mean dressed or wearing clothes: *Are you decent yet?* ○ *You can come in now, I'm decent.*

de·cen·cy /ˈdiː·sᵊnt·si/ *n* [U] • *His sense of decency and fair play made him refuse the offer.* • *They showed a shameless contempt for human rights and the norms of human decency.* • *She didn't even* **have the** *decency* **to** *apologize.* [+ *to* infinitive]

de·cen·cies /ˈdiː·sᵊnt·siz/ *pl n* • **The decencies** are the acceptable or expected ways of doing something: • *I hate going to funerals, but you must* **observe** *the decencies* (=it is something you should do).

de·cen·tral·ize *(obj), Br and Aus usually* **-ise** /ˌdiːˈsen·trə·laɪz, dɪ-/ *v* to (cause to) move from a single place to several smaller ones • *We decentralized our operations last year and opened several regional offices.* [T] • *Modern technology has made it easy for us to decentralize.* [I]

de·cen·tral·iz·a·tion, *Br and Aus usually* **-i·sa·tion** /ˌdiː·sen·trə·laɪˈzeɪ·ʃᵊn/ *n* [U] • *"Our party is committed to the decentralization of power," said the minister.*

de·cep·tion /dɪˈsep·ʃᵊn/ *n* (an act of) hiding the truth, esp. to get an advantage • *His wife was a victim of deception.* [U] • *The judge said there had been a misunderstanding rather than a calculated deception.* [C] • *(Br) Their crimes include shoplifting, burglary and credit card deceptions.* [C] • See also DECEIVE. • (E) (F) (NL)

de·cep·tive /dɪˈsep·tɪv/ *adj* • *My first impression of him was deceptive – he was older than he looked.* • *(saying)* 'Appearances can be deceptive' means that you should not always believe what you see.

de·cep·tive·ly /dɪˈsep·tɪv·li/ *adv* • *The plan sounded deceptively simple* (=It was really very hard).

de·cep·tive·ness /dɪˈsep·tɪv·nəs/ *n* [U]

dec·i·bel /ˈdes·ɪ·bel/ *n* [C] a unit for measuring the loudness of sound • *The typical lawn mower makes about 90 decibels of noise.* • *the decibel count/level/scale/limit(s)*

de·cide *(obj)* /dɪˈsaɪd/ *v* to (cause to) choose, esp. after careful thought about several possibilities • *They have to decide by next Friday.* [I] • *I don't mind which one we have – you decide.* [I] • *We decided* **on** *a beige carpet for the dining room.* [I] • *In the end, we decided* **to** *go to the theatre.* [+ *to* infinitive] • *She decided* **(that)** *she would retire to the country.* [+ *(that)* clause] • *I can't decide* **what** *to do.* [+ *wh-* word] • *He can't decide* **whether** *to buy it.* [+ *wh-* word] • *The committee decided* **on/for/in favour of** (=made a formal judgment to choose) *the cheapest option.* [I] • *The weather decided the outcome of the cricket match* (=the weather had an effect on the result). [T] • *The mistake decided the game* (=caused the person or side which made the mistake to lose). [T] • *The environmental argument was the* **deciding factor** (=the most important matter in choosing a plan of action). • *The chairperson always has the* **deciding vote** (=the vote which chooses the winner when the other votes have not made this clear). • (P)

de·ci·sion /dɪˈsɪʒ·ᵊn/ *n* [C] • *We have some difficult decisions to* **make**. • *The company will* **reach/come to/make** *a decision shortly.* • *Let me have a/your decision* (=Tell me what you have decided) *by next week.* • *Their decision not* **to** *take part baffled everyone.* [+ *to* infinitive] • *The decision* **about/on** *whether he is innocent or guilty rests with the jury.* • *The decision* **whether** *he is innocent or guilty rests with the jury.* [+ *wh-* word] • *We need to take a lot of factors into account in our decision-***making**. • *The decision-making* **process** *can take several weeks.* • See also DECISION.

de·cis·ive /dɪˈsaɪ·sɪv/ *adj* • *a decisive role/test* (=one which is important in deciding) • *These results could prove decisive in establishing the criminal's identity.*

de·cis·ive·ly /dɪˈsaɪ·sɪv·li/ *adv*

de·cid·ed /dɪˈsaɪ·dɪd/ *adj fml* clear; certain • *There was a decided need for a change.* • *She holds a very decided view of the world.*

de·cid·ed·ly /dɪˈsaɪ·dɪd·li/ *adv* • *He was decidedly* (=very obviously) *careful about what he told me.* • *An agreement is looking decidedly difficult according to the newspapers.*

de·cid·er /£dɪˈsaɪ·dəʳ, $-dɚ/ *n* [C] a final game or competition which allows one person or team to win, or the winning point scored • *They lost what was regarded as the championship decider at Leeds.* • *Jones scored the decider in the final minute.*

de·cid·u·ous /dɪˈsɪd·ju·əs/ *adj* [not gradable] *specialized* (of a tree) losing its leaves in autumn and growing new ones in the spring • Compare EVERGREEN.

dec·i·mal /ˈdes·ɪ·məl/ *n, adj* [not gradable] (a number expressed in the form) of a system of counting based on the number ten • *Three fifths expressed as a decimal/(specialized) as a* **decimal fraction** *is 0·6.* [C] • *The course will help students develop mathematical skills including the use of decimals, fractions, percentages and simple statistics.* [C] • *In 1971 Britain changed from the imperial system with 240 pence in the pound to the decimal system with 100 pence in the pound.* • The **decimal point** is the · between the two parts of a decimal. In some countries a comma is used instead: *To divide by ten, move the decimal point one place to the left.* • *If you calculate the result* **to** *two decimal* **places** (=give two numbers after the decimal point, as in 3·65, *that should minimize any possible errors.)* • A **decimal currency** is a money system in which a smaller unit can be multiplied by ten to make up a bigger unit: *Great Britain and the United States both have decimal currencies.*

dec·im·a·liz·a·tion, *Br and Aus usually* **-i·sa·tion** /ˌdes·ɪ·mə·laɪˈzeɪ·ʃᵊn/ *n* [U] • Decimalization is the changing of a system or number to a decimal form : *Decimalization of the clock has been tried before, but people seemed to prefer the 24 hour system.* • *Many people in Britain can still remember the days before decimalization* (=before money was changed to a decimal system).

dec·i·mate *obj* /ˈdes·ɪ·meɪt/ *v* [T] to kill a large number of (something), or to reduce (something) severely • *If the disease spreads it will decimate the cattle herds in this country.* • *The population has been decimated by a cholera epidemic.* • *Imports have continued to decimate the shoe industry.*

de·ci·pher *obj* /£dɪˈsaɪ·fəʳ, $-fɚ/ *v* [T] to discover the meaning of (something written badly or in a difficult or hidden way) • *Can you decipher the writing on this envelope?* • *They were part of a team whose job was to decipher (messages written in) code.*

de·ci·sion /dɪˈsɪʒ·ᵊn/ *n* [U] *approving* the ability to decide quickly and positively, with a clear result • *She* **acted with** *decision, closing the bank account and phoning the police.* • *"I certainly won't," he replied with decision.* • See also **decision** at DECIDE.

de·cis·ive /dɪˈsaɪ·sɪv/ *adj* • *a decisive reply* • *decisive action/progress/intervention*

de·cis·ive·ly /dɪˈsaɪ·sɪv·li/ *adv* • *If we had acted earlier and more decisively it might not have come to this.*

de·cis·ive·ness /dɪˈsaɪ·sɪv·nəs/ *n* [U] • *During his 29 years in power he has shown a decisiveness and far-sightedness that puts most other politicians, anywhere, to shame.*

deck [FLOOR] /dek/ *n* [C] a flat area for walking on, esp. one built across the space between the sides of a boat or a bus; a type of floor • *The waves washed over the ship's deck in the stormy sea.* • *When we've eaten, let's go up* **on deck** *and get some air.* • *We sat* **on deck** *until it was dark.* • *Our cabin was* **below decks** (= on a level of the ship below the main deck). • *The upper/top deck of the bus was always full of people smoking.* • *(Am and Aus)* A deck is also a raised roofless area built sticking out from a house, similar to a BALCONY. • See also QUARTERDECK; SUNDECK. • PIC> **Ships and boats** (J) (S)

-deck·er /£-ˈdek·əʳ, ˌ--, $-ɚ/ *combining form* • A **double-decker** (bus) has an upper and a lower deck, while a **single-decker** (bus) has only one. • *(fig.)* A **double-/triple-**decker SANDWICH has two or three layers.

deck [SET OF CARDS] /dek/, **pack** *n* [C] *esp. Am* a set of cards used for playing card games • *We played our game of bridge with a new deck* **(of** *cards).* • LP> **Cards** (J) (S)

deck *obj* [DECORATE] /dek/ *v* [T usually passive] to decorate or add something to (something) to make an effect • *The room was decked* **with** *flowers.* • *The statement was decked* **out with** *grand visions of the future and good intentions.* • *The wedding guests were decked* **out in** *their finery/decked* **in** *their best* (= wearing their best clothes). • *"Deck the halls with boughs of holly"* (traditional Christmas song) • See also BEDECK. • (J) (S)

deck *obj* [HIT] /dek/ *v* [T] *slang* to hit, esp. to hit and knock down • *If you do that again I'll deck you.* • (J) (S)

deck·chair /£ˈdek·tʃeəʳ, $-tʃer/ *n* [C] a folding chair for use outside, esp. on the beach, on a ship or in a park, with a long strip of material which forms a low seat when the chair is open • If you say an activity is like **moving/rearranging the deckchairs on the Titanic** you mean it is not worth doing because it will have no effect. • PIC> **Chair**

deck·hand /ˈdek·hænd/ *n* [C] a person, usually unskilled, who works on a ship, but who does not serve the passengers or work in the engine room • *He worked his passage to South America as a deckhand on a cargo ship.*

de·claim *(obj)* /dɪˈkleɪm/ *v fml* to express with strong feeling, esp. in a loud voice or with forceful language • *"The end of the world is at hand!" the poster declaimed.* [+ clause] • *These lines make far more sense when declaimed than when simply read out.* [T] • *He declaimed with force and authority to his companion about the state of the book trade.* [I]

de·clam·a·tion /ˌdek·ləˈmeɪ·ʃᵊn/ *n fml* • *He subjected us to half an hour of impassioned declamation* **against** *the new motorway.* [U] • *Declamations* **against** *the press are common enough.* [C]

de·clam·a·to·ry /£dɪˈklæm·ə·tᵊr·i, $-tɔːr-/ *adj fml* • *a declamatory style* • *(fig.) The blues and pinks of the painting are muted rather than declamatory.*

dec·lare *(obj)* [EXPRESS] /£dɪˈkleəʳ, $-ˈkler/ *v* to announce clearly, firmly, publicly or officially • *They declared their support for the proposal* [T] ○ *They declared their intention of supporting the proposal.* [T] • *She declared* **(that)** *it was the best chocolate cake she had ever tasted.* [+ (*that*) clause] • *The pamphlet declared* **(that)** *parents would have more influence in schools.* [+ (*that*) clause] • *The company declared themselves (to be) equal opportunity employers.* [T + obj + (*to be*) n/adj] • *They declared themselves (to be) bankrupt.* [T + obj + (*to be*) n/adj] • *"I won't do it!" he declared.* [+ clause] • *America declared* **war on** *Japan in 1941* (= announced officially that it was at war). [T] • *(fig.) The government declared* **war on** *the drug dealers* (= said that they would try to stop them). [T] • *The country declared* **independence** *in 1952* (= announced that it was not longer under the control of another country). [T] • When you go through customs you have to declare (= say if you have) particular goods you have bought in another country: *Nothing to declare.* [T] ○ *Goods to declare.* [T] ○ *Anything to declare?* [T] • *(dated) Well,* **I declare** (= I am surprised)*!* • If you **declare for/against** something or someone, you give/do not give them your public support: *She declared for the new airport plan.* • *"I have nothing to declare except my genius"* (believed to have been said to the Customs Officers when arriving in New York by Oscar Wilde, 1854-1900)

dec·la·ra·ble /£dɪˈkleə·rə·bl̩, $-ˈkler·ə-/ *adj* [not gradable] *fml* • *declarable income for tax purposes* • *goods which are declarable* (= which must be made known) *at customs*

dec·la·ra·tion /ˌdek·ləˈreɪ·ʃᵊn/ *n* [C] • *Members of Parliament must* **make** *a declaration of their business interests.* • *As witnesses to the accident, we were asked to* **make** *written declarations of what we had seen.* • *The company made a declaration* **of intent** *to follow an equal opportunities policy.*

dec·lared /£dɪˈkleəd, $-ˈklerd/ *adj* [not gradable] • *He is a declared supporter of* (= publicly supports) *the scheme.* • *It has always been my declared intention* (= I have always said I intend) *to sail round the world.*

dec·lare [STOP] /£dɪˈkleəʳ, $-ˈkler/ *v* [I] (of a cricket team) to stop BATTING (= taking its turn to hit the ball) because it thinks it already has enough RUNS (= points) to win • *Pakistan declared at 350 for 7, leaving Australia to make an unlikely 5 runs an over to win.*

dec·la·ra·tion /ˌdek·ləˈreɪ·ʃᵊn/ *n* [C] • *a cleverly timed declaration*

de·clas·si·fy *obj* /ˌdiːˈklæs·ɪ·faɪ/ *v* [T] to say officially that (esp. political or military information) is no longer secret • *Many government documents are declassified after 50 years.*

de·clas·sif·i·ca·tion /ˌdiː·klæs·ɪ·fɪˈkeɪ·ʃᵊn/ *n* [U]

de·cline [GO DOWN] /dɪˈklaɪn/ *v* [I] to go, often slowly, from a higher or better position to a lower or worse one • *His interest in the project declined after his wife died.* • *The party's popularity has declined in the opinion polls.* • *(fml) The land declines sharply away from the house.* • *We are struggling to manage on declining resources.* • Your **declining years** are the last years of your life: *He became very forgetful in his declining years.*

de·cline /dɪˈklaɪn/ *n* • *She seemed to be recovering and then she went into a decline.* [C] • *We are pleased by the decline* **in** *the number of unemployed.* [C] • *The town is a victim of industrial decline.* [U] • *Home cooking seems to be* **on the/in** *decline* (= not so many people are doing it). [U]

de·cline *(obj)* [REFUSE] /dɪˈklaɪn/ *v fml* to refuse • *I invited him to the meeting but he declined.* [I] • *The offer of a job in France was declined.* [T] • *They declined* **to** *tell me how they had got my address.* [+ *to* infinitive]

de·code *(obj)* /£ˌdiːˈkəʊd, $-ˈkoʊd/ *v* to discover the meaning of (information given in a secret or complicated way) • *Decoding the paintings is not difficult once you know what the component parts symbolise.* [T] • *(specialized)* To decode (a word or phrase in a foreign language) is to understand its meaning in the correct way: *Grammatical information helps learners to decode (sentences).* [I/T] • Compare ENCODE.

de·col·le·tage /£ˌdeɪ·kɒl·ɪˈtɑːʒ, $-ˌkɑː·ləˈtɑːʒ/ *n* [C; U] (the shoulders and chest of a woman's body shown by) the low top edge of a dress

de·co·lon·iz·a·tion, *Br and Aus usually* **-i·sa·tion** /diːˌkɒl·ə·naɪˈzeɪ·ʃᵊn/ *n* [U] the giving of political independence to a country that was previously a COLONY (= controlled by another country) • *The decolonization* **of** *Africa by white Europeans was largely welcomed by the indigenous people.*

de·com·mis·sion *obj* /ˌdiː·kəˈmɪʃ·ᵊn/ *v* [T] to take (equipment, etc.) out of use • *The government has decided to decommission two battleships.* • *It would cost $300 million to decommission the nuclear installation.*

de·com·pose *(obj)* /£ˌdiː·kəmˈpəʊz, $-ˈpoʊz/ *v* to (cause to) decay or *(specialized)* break into smaller parts • *The body must have been decomposing for several weeks.* [I] • *(specialized) Microbes decompose organic waste into a mixture of methane and carbon dioxide.* [T] • *There was a smell of decomposing vegetable matter.*

de·com·pos·i·tion /£ˌdiː·kɒm·pəˈzɪʃ·ᵊn, $-kɑːm-/ *n* [U] • *The corpse was in an advanced stage of decomposition.*

de·com·press *(obj)* /ˌdiː·kəmˈpres/ *v* to (cause to) return to the original size or air pressure • *The computer chip compresses and decompresses a colour image in less than a second.* [T] • *If a plane window breaks the cabin will rapidly* decompress. [I] • *(fig. Am infml) After relocating to Britain we'll need a few days off to decompress* (= relax). [I]

de·com·pres·sion /ˌdiː·kəmˈpreʃ·ən/ *n* [U] • *The pilot was almost sucked from the cockpit by decompression when the window broke.* • *(specialized)* A DIVER who comes too quickly to the surface of the sea from a great depth suffers from **decompression syndrome/sickness** (also **the bends**), when NITROGEN which has dissolved under pressure forms air bubbles in the blood and can prevent it flowing correctly. This can be avoided by coming to the surface more slowly or treated by spending time in a **decompression chamber**, which is a small room where the air pressure is controlled.

de·con·ges·tant /ˌdiː·kənˈdʒes·tənt/ *n* [C] a medicine which helps you to breathe more easily, esp. when you have a COLD [ILLNESS]

de·con·tam·in·ate *obj* /ˌdiː·kənˈtæm·ɪ·neɪt/ *v* [T] to remove dangerous substances from • *Estimates of the amount of money needed to decontaminate the heavily polluted chemical installations vary.*

de·con·tam·in·a·tion /ˌdiː·kən·tæm·ɪˈneɪ·ʃən/ *n* [U] • *These special suits give 24 hours' protection against radiation/chemical weapons before needing decontamination.* • *A decontamination programme to rid the island of anthrax spores released in a germ warfare experiment was completed recently.*

de·con·trol *obj* /£ˌdiː·kənˈtrəʊl, $-ˈtroʊl/ *v* [T] **-ll-** to remove official control on (esp. prices and businesses) • *Prices have been decontrolled and markets are flourishing.*

dec·or /£ˈdeɪ·kɔːʳ, £ˈdek·ɔːʳ, $deɪˈkɔːr/ *n* [U] the colour, style and arrangement of the objects in a room • *They decided not to modernize the Victorian decor.* • *Red seats and cream walls may not be the most elegant decor, but it's a friendly pub.* • *I've never liked her taste in decor.* • Ⓘ

dec·o·rate *(obj)* [MAKE ATTRACTIVE] /ˈdek·ə·reɪt/ *v* to add something to (an object or place), esp. in order to make it more attractive • *They decorated the wedding car* **with** *ribbons and flowers.* [T] • *The birthday cake was made and decorated* (= covered with ICING) *by her aunt.* [T] • To decorate is also to paint the inside or outside of a house and/or put paper on the inside walls: *We're going to decorate the kitchen next week.* [T] ○ *I hate the smell of paint when I'm decorating.* [I] • Ⓔ Ⓟ

dec·o·ra·tion /ˌdek·əˈreɪ·ʃən/ *n* • *Christmas/party/table/cake/street decorations* [C] • *He's good at cake decoration.* [U] • *He advises on home decoration.* [U]

dec·o·ra·tive /£ˈdek·ər·ə·tɪv, $-ɚ·ə·t̬ɪv/ *adj* • Something decorative is (made to look) attractive: *a decorative display of plants and flowers* ○ *a mirror in a decorative frame* ○ *(humorous) She made a decorative addition to the group.* ○ *Just sit there and look decorative while I finish this.*

dec·o·ra·tive·ly /£ˈdek·ər·ə·tɪv·li, $-ɚ·ə·t̬ɪv-/ *adv* • *The shawl was arranged decoratively over the back of the chair.*

dec·o·ra·tor /£ˈdek·ər·eɪ·təʳ, $-ɚ·eɪ·t̬ɚ/ *n* [C] • A decorator is a person whose job is to paint the inside or outside of buildings and to do other related work: *a firm of painters and decorators.*

dec·o·rate [HONOUR] /ˈdek·ə·reɪt/ *v* [often passive] to reward or honour a person by giving them esp. a MEDAL • *They were decorated* **for** *their part in the rescue.* • Ⓔ Ⓟ

dec·o·ra·tion /ˌdek·əˈreɪ·ʃən/ *n* [C] • *The Victoria Cross and George Cross are British decorations* **for** *bravery.*

dec·o·rous /£ˈdek·ə·rəs, $ˈ-ɚ·əs/ *adj fml* controlled, calm, not wild or excited; behaving well • *a decorous production/performance* • *He explained the problem in his careful and decorous way.*

dec·o·rous·ly /£ˈdek·ə·rə·sli, $-ɚ·ə-/ *adv*

de·co·rum /£dɪˈkɔː·rəm, $-ˈkɔːr·əm/ *n* [U] *fml* behaviour that is controlled, calm and polite • *The meeting was a model of self-restraint and decorum.* • *The film, though risqué, did not offend their sense of decorum.* • *As young ladies we were expected to* **act/behave with** *proper decorum.*

de·coy /ˈdiː·kɔɪ/ *n* [C] something or someone used to trick or confuse other people or animals into doing something, esp. something dangerous • *They used a girl hitch-hiker as the decoy to get him to stop.* • A **decoy duck** is a model duck used to get the attention of wild duck and bring them near to the hunters.

de·coy *obj* /dɪˈkɔɪ/ *v* [T] • *The missiles were decoyed* **into** *going off course by long metal strips which confused their radar.*

de·crease *(obj)* /dɪˈkriːs, $ˈdiː·kriːs/ *v* to (cause to) become less • *Our share of the market has decreased sharply this year.* [I] • *We have decreased our involvement in children's books.* [T] • Compare INCREASE.

de·crease /ˈdiː·kriːs/ *n* • *There has been a steady decrease* **in** *the number of visitors.* [C] • *I haven't noticed much decrease* **in** *interest.* [U]

de·cree /dɪˈkriː/ *n fml* an official statement that something must happen • *The decree stopped short of a full declaration of independence.* [C] • *He said it was an official, judicial command, not a religious decree.* [C] • *More than 200 people were freed* **by** *military decree.* [U] • *(law)* A **decree nisi** is the first stage of the legal agreement to end a marriage and is followed by a **decree absolute**, when the people become free to marry again.

de·cree *obj* /dɪˈkriː/ *v* [T] • *They decreed an end to discrimination on grounds of age.* • *The local council has decreed* **that** *the hospital should close.* [+ *that* clause] • *They decreed the practice barbaric.* [+ obj + adj]

de·cre·pit /dɪˈkrep·ɪt/ *adj* in very bad condition because of being old, or not having been cared for, or having been used a lot • *A decrepit old man sat on a park bench.* • *No one should have to live in a house that's so run-down and decrepit.* • *The President's main task is to do something about the country's decrepit economy.*

de·cre·pi·tude /£dɪˈkrep·ɪ·tjuːd, $-tuːd/ *n* [U] *fml* • *As he grew older, he realized that he was beginning to slide into physical decrepitude.*

de·crim·in·al·ize *obj, Br and Aus usually* **-ise** /ˌdiːˈkrɪm·ɪ·nə·laɪz/ *v* [T] to stop (something) from being illegal • *He argued that the crime rate would be reduced if drugs were to be decriminalized, but few people agreed with him.*

de·crim·in·al·iz·a·tion, *Br and Aus usually* **-i·sa·tion** /ˌdiː·krɪm·ɪ·nə·laɪˈzeɪ·ʃən/ *n* [U]

de·cry *obj* /dɪˈkraɪ/ *v* [T] *fml* to criticize (something) as bad, worthless or unnecessary; to CONDEMN [CRITICIZE] • *She decried the appalling state of the British film industry.*

ded·i·cate *obj* /ˈded·ɪ·keɪt/ *v* [T] to give completely (your energy, time, etc.) • *He has dedicated his life* **to** *scientific research.* • *The new President said she would dedicate her***self to** *protecting the rights of the old, the sick and the homeless.* • If you dedicate a book, play, performance, etc. **to** someone or something, you publicly say that it is in their honour: *The book is dedicated to the author's husband.* • *(fml)* When a building, esp. a religious building, is dedicated, there is a ceremony at which it is formally opened for use and its particular purpose is stated: *The church was dedicated on 1st March 1805* **(to** *the local Saint Jude).* • *"This is dedicated to the one I love"* (The Mamas and the Papas in the song *Dedicated to the One I love*, 1967)

ded·i·cat·ed /£ˈded·ɪ·keɪ·tɪd, $-t̬ɪd/ *adj* • Someone who is dedicated **to** an activity or an idea believes that that activity or idea is important and gives a lot of energy and time to it: *He's a very dedicated father/golfer/teacher.* ○ *She's completely dedicated to her work.* ○ *The Green Party is dedicated to protecting the environment.* • *He's a wonderful doctor – he's very dedicated* (= works very hard). • *(specialized)* Dedicated can also mean having only one use: *a dedicated word processor* • *a dedicated telephone line* • *a dedicated sports channel* • *"Dedicated Follower of Fashion"* (title of a song by The Kinks, 1966)

ded·i·ca·tion /ˌded·ɪˈkeɪ·ʃən/ *n* • *He has always shown great dedication* **(to** *the cause).* [U] • *It was thanks to the dedication* (= hard work) **of** *the medical staff that she recovered from her injuries.* [U] • A dedication is a statement which says in whose honour something has been written, made, performed, etc.: *The dedication at the front of the book read 'For my Father.'* [C] • A dedication is also a ceremony in which a building, esp. a religious building, is opened for use and its purpose is stated. [C]

de·duce *(obj)* /dɪˈdjuːs, $-ˈduːs/ *v* to reach (an answer or a decision) by thinking carefully about the known facts • *We cannot deduce very much* **from** *these figures.* [T] • *The police have deduced* **that** *he must have left his apartment yesterday evening.* [+ *that* clause] • *I couldn't deduce* **whether** *he thought the idea was a good one or not.* [+ *wh-* word]

de·duc·ib·le /£dɪˈdjuː·sɪ·bl̩, $-ˈduː-/ *adj fml* • *The meaning of 'agoraphobia' is deducible* (= can be reached by thinking carefully) *if you know that the Greek words 'agora' and 'phobia' mean 'open space' and 'fear'.*

de·duc·tion /dɪˈdʌk·ʃən/ *n* • *Through a process of deduction* (= thinking carefully about the known facts), *the detectives discovered the identity of the killer.* [U] • *All we can do is make deductions* **from** (= form answers by thinking carefully about) *the available facts.* [C] • See also **deduction** at DEDUCT.

de·duc·tive /dɪˈdʌk·tɪv/ *adj* • *a deductive argument* • *deductive logic/reasoning*

de·duct *obj* /dɪˈdʌkt/ *v* [T] to take away (an amount or part) from a total • *The player had* **points deducted (from** *his score) for arguing with the referee.* • *We made a small profit on the sale of our house, but after we'd deducted our* **expenses**, *it turned into loss.*

de·duct·ib·le, *Aus also* **de·duc·tab·le** /£dɪˈdʌk·tɪ·bl̩, $-t̬ə-/ *adj* [not gradable] • *Expenses like office telephone bills are* **tax** *deductible* (= you do not have to pay tax on them).

de·duc·tion /dɪˈdʌk·ʃən/ *n* • *The interest I receive on my savings account is paid after the deduction* **of** *tax.* [U] • *Deductions* **of** *points will be made if competitors do not follow the rules.* [C] • *After deductions* (= expenses on which tax does not have to be paid), *his taxable income is $30 000.* [C] • See also **deduction** at DEDUCE.

deed ACTION /diːd/ *n* an intentional act, esp. a very bad or very good one • *It seems to me that a lot of* **evil** *deeds are* **done** *in the name of religion.* [C] • *The President always gets someone else to* **do** *his* **dirty** *deeds for him.* [C] • *She's always helping people and* **doing** *other* **good** *deeds.* [C] • *(esp. humorous) So you've finally* **done the** *deed and asked her to marry you.* [C] • *The government must repudiate terrorism* **in word and** *deed.* [U]

deed DOCUMENT /diːd/ *n* [C] *law* a legal document which is an official record of an agreement or official proof of ownership of land or of a building • *I keep the deeds* **to** *my house in a special* **deed box** (= a lockable metal box in which documents are kept). • In Britain, a **deed poll** is a legal document which is signed by only one person, esp. in order for them officially to change their name: *He changed his name* **by** *deed poll.*

dee·jay /ˈdiː·dʒeɪ/ *n* [C] *infml* a **disc jockey**, see at DISC.

deem *obj* /diːm/ *v* [T not *be deeming*; often passive] *fml or law* to consider or judge • *The area has now been deemed safe.* [+ obj + n/adj] • *We will provide help whenever you deem* **it** *appropriate.* [+ obj + n/adj] • *Anyone not paying the registration fee by 31 March will be deemed* **to** *have withdrawn from the scheme.* [+ obj + *to* infinitive]

deep DOWN /diːp/ *adj, adv* **-er, -est** going or being a long way down from the top or surface, or being of a particular distance from the top to the bottom • *a deep well/mine/cave* • *a deep lake/river/sea* • *The hole is so deep you can't see the bottom.* • *The water's not deep here – look, I can touch the bottom.* • *If the wound had been any deeper, you would have had to go to hospital.* • *Drill 20 holes, each 5 cm deep.* • *The water's only* **ankle/knee/waist-deep**, *so we'll be able to get across the river easily.* • *The knife cut deep into her flesh.* • *He thrust his hands deep* **in(to)** *his pockets.* • *The submarine sailed deep* **under** *the ice cap.* • *Take a few deep* **breaths** (= breaths that fill the lungs with air) *and calm down.* • *(fig.) She sat, not listening, but deep* **in thought** (= thinking very hard). • *(fig.) The company is deep* **in debt** (= has many debts) *and is likely to go bankrupt soon.* • *(fig.) It's a story set deep* **in the (distant) past** (= a very long time ago). • To **be in/get into deep water** is to be in serious trouble: *The government is in deep water* **over** *its plans for tax increases.* • If you **go off the deep end** about something, you get very angry about it or lose control of yourself. • If you **jump/plunge in at the deep end** or **are thrown/chucked/pitched in at the deep end**, you start doing something new and difficult without any help or preparation. • *Her fear of forming relationships with other people* **runs/goes deep** (= is an important and basic part of her character). • **Deep-down (inside you)** (= In your true feelings), *I know you love me really.* • A **deep-freeze** is a **freezer**. See at FREEZE. • To **deep-fry** food is to fry it in a lot of oil or fat: *deep-fried chicken/chips* • *They had a* **deep-laid** (= carefully and secretly made) **plan** *to blow up the Houses of Parliament.* • Something that is **deep-seated** or **deep(ly)-rooted** is very strong and so much a part of something else that it cannot be changed or got rid of: *She has a deep-seated faith in God.* • **Deep-set** eyes are far back in the bones of the face. • The **Deep South** is the part of the US that is furthest to the south and east, including Alabama, Georgia, Louisiana, Mississippi and S and N Carolina. • *"When the snow lay round about / Deep and crisp and even"* (from the Christmas song *Good King Wenceslas* by John Mason Neale, 1818-1866) • *"Deep Throat"* (title of a sex film, later used to refer to an unknown person giving secret information, 1971) • See also DEPTH DISTANCE DOWN. • LP **Measurements** PIC **Cooking**

deep /diːp/ *n literary* • **The deep** is the sea or the OCEAN.

deep·en *(obj)* /ˈdiː·pən/ *v* • *One way of preventing further flooding would be to deepen* (= make deeper) *the river bed.* [T] • *The sea bed deepens* (= becomes deeper) *here* **to** *5000 metres.* [I]

deep FRONT TO BACK /diːp/ *adj* **-er, -est** having a large distance between its edges, esp. between its front and back edges • *Is the alcove deep enough for bookshelves?* • *The wardrobe is 2 m high, 1 m wide and 60 cm deep.* • *By midnight, there were customers standing six deep* (= in six rows) *at the bar.* • If you say that something is deep **in/inside/within** something else you mean that it is near the middle of it, and a long distance from the edges: *Little Red Riding Hood's grandmother lived in a house deep in the forest.* • See also DEPTH DISTANCE BACKWARDS.

deep STRONGLY FELT /diːp/ *adj* **-er, -est** very strongly felt or experienced and usually lasting a long time; PROFOUND EXTREME or INTENSE • *His feelings for her are very deep.* • *Their son has been a deep disappointment to them.* • *She has a deep mistrust of men.* • *We're in deep trouble.* • *As I listened to what he was saying, I felt a deeper and deeper sense of irritation.* • *She fell into a lovely deep sleep.* • See also DEPTH STRENGTH.

deep·en *(obj)* /ˈdiː·pən/ *v* • If something deepens, it becomes more strongly felt or experienced: *Over the years, her love for him deepened.* [I] ○ *They felt a deepening sense of despair.* [I] ○ *The economic crisis is deepening.* [I] • *We must try not to deepen* (= make more strongly felt) *existing splits within the party.* [T]

deep·ly /ˈdiː·pli/ *adv* • *I'm deeply* (= very) *grateful to you.* • *He found her comments deeply irritating/offensive.* • *We don't want to get too deeply* (= much) *involved with these people.* • *After 20 years of marriage, they're still deeply* (= very much) *in love with each other.* • LP **Very, completely**

deep COMPLICATED /diːp/ *adj* **-er, -est** showing or needing serious thought; not easy to understand • *Quantum physics is a bit deep for me.* • *(infml) Hey, that was a really deep film.* • See also DEPTH SERIOUSNESS.

deep·en *(obj)* /ˈdiː·pən/ *v* • *If you want to deepen* (= make more serious) *your knowledge of world affairs, you should read a newspaper every day.* [T] • *As I listened to what she said, my understanding of how she felt slowly deepened* (= became more serious). [I]

deep LOW /diːp/ *adj* **-er, -est** (of a sound) low • *a wonderfully deep voice* • See also DEPTH LOW SOUND. Compare HIGH SOUND.

deep·en /ˈdiː·pən/ *v* [I] • *Boys' voices deepen* (= become lower) *in their early to mid-teens.*

deep DARK /diːp/ *adj* **-er, -est** (of a colour) strong and dark • *The sky was deep blue.* • *There was a deep red flush on his cheeks.* • See also DEPTH DARKNESS.

deep·en /ˈdiː·pən/ *v* [I] • *The shadows deepened* (= got darker) *as the evening drew on.*

deer /£dɪəʳ, $dɪr/ *n* [C] *pl* **deer** a quite large four-legged animal which eats grass and leaves. The male has ANTLERS (= wide branch-like horns). The female is called a HIND or a DOE and the male a STAG or BUCK • *Deer are found throughout the world, except in Africa and Australia.* • *A* **herd** *of deer was peacefully grazing between the forest and the river.* • See also REINDEER. • PIC **Wild animals in Britain**

deer·stalk·er /£ˈdɪəˌstɔː·kəʳ, $ˈdɪrˌstɑː-/ *n* [C] a soft hat with two PEAKS (= flat curved parts that stick out), one at the back and one at the front, and coverings for the ears which are usually worn turned up • *The fictional detective, Sherlock Holmes, wore a deerstalker and smoked a pipe.* • PIC **Hats**

de–es·ca·late *(obj)* /ˌdiːˈes·kə·leɪt/ *v* to (cause to) become less dangerous or difficult • *The government has taken these measures in an attempt to de-escalate the conflict.* [T] • *There are signs that the confrontation is beginning to de-escalate.* [I]

de·face *obj* /dɪˈfeɪs/ *v* [T] to damage and spoil the appearance of (something) by writing or drawing on it • *She's been given 20 days in prison for defacing a poster of the President.* • *He was fined for defacing library books.* • *These banknotes have been defaced.*

de fac·to /£ˌdeɪˈfæk·təʊ, $-t̬oʊ/ *adj* [before n], *adv* [not gradable] *fml* existing in fact, although not necessarily intended, legal or accepted • *The city is rapidly becoming the de facto centre of the financial world.* • *He's her de facto husband, though they aren't actually married.* • *English is de facto the common language of much of the world today.* • Compare DE JURE.

de fac·to /£ˌdeɪˈfæk·təʊ, $-t̬oʊ/ *n* [C] *Aus* • A de facto is a person with whom someone lives as a wife or a husband, although they are not married: *They've invited Joanne and her de facto for lunch on Sunday.*

de·fame *obj* /dɪˈfeɪm/ *v* [T] *fml* to damage (a person's or group's reputation) by saying or writing bad things about them which are not true • *Mr Turnock claimed the editorial had defamed him.* • *Many people thought that the book defamed Islam.* • *She said that the article had defamed her* **as** *a liar.* • Compare LIBEL; SLANDER. • LP **Crimes and criminals**

de·fam·a·tion /ˌdef·əˈmeɪ·ʃən/ *n* [U] *fml* • *He is suing for defamation* **of** character.

de·fam·a·to·ry /£dɪˈfæm·ə·tᵊr·i, $-tɔːr-/ *adj fml* • *He claims the remarks/statements were* **highly** *defamatory.* • *"The article is* **grossly** *defamatory* **of** *our client," said her lawyer.* • *When a newspaper prints a defamatory story, the victim can sue for libel.*

de·fault FAIL /£dɪˈfɒlt, $-ˈfɑːlt/ *v* [I] to fail to do something, such as pay a debt, that you legally have to do • *People who default* **on** *their mortgage repayments may have their home repossessed.*

de·fault /£dɪˈfɒlt, $-ˈfɑːlt/ *n* • *Defaults* **on** *loan repayments have reached 52 000 a month.* [C] • *Any default* **on** *your mortgage repayments may mean you will lose your house.* [U] • *The default* **rate** (= the number of people failing to do something) *is estimated at 1 in 10 of tax payers.* • *Since they refuse to reply, I think we've won the argument* **by default** (= because of their failure to act). [U]

de·fault RESULT /£dɪˈfɒlt, $-ˈfɑːlt/ *n* [U] what exists or happens if you do not change it intentionally by performing an action • *Unless something else happens, the default is to meet at the hotel at 7.00 p.m.* • *The computer will take '0' as the default* **value**, *unless you type in something different.* • *The default paper size is US letter, so change it to A4.* • *(fml)* **In default of** (= Because there is not) *any better alternative, we will have to proceed with the original plan.*

de·fault to *v prep* [T] • If a computer defaults to a way of operating, it automatically uses it, unless you intentionally change it: *My word processor has several different page settings, but it defaults to this one.*

de·feat *obj* /dɪˈfiːt/ *v* [T] to win a victory over (someone) in a fight, war or competition, or to cause (someone or something) to fail • *Napoleon was defeated by the Duke of Wellington at the battle of Waterloo.* • *If we can defeat the Italian team, we'll be through to the final.* • *The proposal to change the rules was* **narrowly** (= only just) *defeated by 201 votes to 196.* • *They were* **soundly/resoundingly/roundly** (= completely) *defeated.* • *Our hopes and ambitions for this tournament have been defeated* (= caused to fail) *by the weather.* • *I'm afraid anything that involves language learning has always defeated me* (= I have been unable to do it). • See also SELF-DEFEATING. • LP› **Sports**

de·feat /dɪˈfiːt/ *n* • *After their defeat in battle, the soldiers surrendered.* [U] • *At the last General Election, they* **suffered** *a* **crushing/humiliating** *defeat.* [C] • *She* **admitted/conceded** *defeat well before all the votes had been counted, when it had become obvious that she would lose.* [U] • *I thought I could mend my broken radio myself, but I've had to* **admit** *defeat* (= I cannot do it). [U] • Compare VICTORY.

de·feat·i·sm /£dɪˈfiː·tɪ·zᵊm, $-t̬ɪ-/ *n* [U] *disapproving* • Defeatism is a way of thinking or behaving that shows that you lack any hope or expectation of being successful: *There is a spirit of defeatism among some members of the party.*

de·feat·ist /£dɪˈfiː·tɪst, $-t̬ɪst/ *adj, n disapproving* • *Being defeatist will get us nowhere.* • *That's enough of that defeatist attitude.* • *Why am I surrounded by defeatists with no belief in themselves?* [C]

de·fe·cate /ˈdef·ə·keɪt/ *v* [I] *fml* to excrete the contents of the bowels

de·fe·ca·tion /ˌdef·əˈkeɪ·ʃən/ *n* [U] *fml*

de·fect FAULT /ˈdiː·fekt/ *n* [C] a fault, problem or lack in something or someone that spoils them or causes them not to work correctly • *I bought these shoes cheaply because they have slight defects* (**in** *them).* • *All R45 aircraft have been grounded, after a defect* **in** *the engine cooling system was discovered.* • *I think that there are a lot of defects* **in** *our education system.* • *It's a* **character** *defect* **in** *her that she can't ever accept that she's in the wrong.* • A defect is also a physical condition in which something is wrong with a part of someone's body: *She suffers from a heart/sight/speech defect.* ○ *The drug has been shown to cause* **birth** *defects.* ○ *Cystic fibrosis is caused by a* **genetic** *defect.*

de·fec·tive /dɪˈfek·tɪv/ *adj* • Something that is defective has a fault in it and does not work correctly: *defective brakes* ○ *a defective telephone line* ○ *defective hearing/eyesight* ○ *a defective gene* ○ *a defective design* ○ *I think that argument/theory is defective.*

de·fect LEAVE /dɪˈfekt/ *v* [I] to leave a country, political party, etc., esp. in order to join an opposing one • *When the national hockey team visited America, half the players defected.* • *The British spy, Kim Philby, defected* **to** *the Soviet Union/defected* **from** *Britain in 1963.*

de·fec·tion /dɪˈfek·ʃən/ *n* • *Over the years there were hundreds of defections* **to** *the West/defections* **from** *the East.* [C] • *Recent changes in policy have resulted in large-scale defection* **from** *the party.* [U]

de·fec·tor /£dɪˈfek·tər, $-tɚ/ *n* [C] • *She was one of many Communist Party defectors.* • *Defectors from the British Labour and Conservative Parties formed the Social Democratic Party.*

de·fend *(obj)* /dɪˈfend/ *v* to protect against attack or criticism • *How can we defend our homeland if we don't have an army?* [T] • *I'm going to karate lessons to learn how to defend* **myself**. [T] • *White blood cells help defend the body* **against** *infection.* [T] • *They are fighting to defend their* **beliefs/interests/rights.** [T] • *He* **staunchly/stoutly/vigorously** *defended his point of view.* [T] • *The Bank of England intervened this morning to defend the pound* (= stop it from losing value). [T] • *The Prime Minister was asked how he could defend* (= explain his support for) *a policy that increased unemployment.* [T] • *I can't afford a lawyer so I shall defend myself* (= argue my own case in a law court). [T] • *He will be defending* (= trying not to lose) *his title at the European Championships next week.* [T] • To defend in a sporting event is to try to prevent the opposing player or players from scoring points, goals, etc.: *The team we were playing against in the match defended badly and we scored easily.* [I] ○ *The defending champion will play her first match of the tournament tomorrow.* • *"I disapprove of (or 'disagree' with) what you say, but I will defend to the death your right to say it"* (believed to have been Voltaire, 1694-1778) • Compare ATTACK. • Ⓟ

de·fen·ce *Br and Aus, Am* **de·fen·se** /dɪˈfents/ *n* • *The rebels' only form of defence* (= protection) **against** *the soldiers' guns was sticks and stones.* [U] • *The war has ended but government spending on defence* (= the country's army, navy and air force) *is still increasing.* [U] • *The wall was once an important part of the city's defences* (= things that provide protection against attack). [C] • *When Helen criticized me, Chris* **came/rushed to** *my defence* (= supported me). [U] • *The book is a closely argued defence* **of** (= something that supports) *Keynesian economic theory.* [C] • A defence is also an argument or explanation which you use to prove that you are not guilty of something: *The judge remarked that ignorance was not a valid defence.* [C] ○ *She said that she didn't want a lawyer and was going to* **conduct** *her own defence.* [C] ○ *All I can say,* **in** *defence* **of** *my actions, is that I did it for a just cause, not for my personal advantage.* [U] • *(law)* **The defence** is also the person or people in a law case who have been accused of doing something illegal, and their lawyer(s): *a witness for the defence* [U] ○ *a defence lawyer* • In some sports, the defence is the part of a team which tries to prevent the other team from scoring goals or points: *The team has a strong defence.* [C] ○ *I play (Br)* **in**/*(Am)* **on** *defence.* [U] • In the game of CHESS, a defence is a particular set of moves used by the person playing with the black pieces: *the French defence* [U] ○ *the Sicilian defence* [U] ○ *What defence did you use in that last game?* [C] • A defence **(mechanism)** is also an automatic way of behaving or thinking by which you protect yourself from something, esp. from feeling unpleasant emotions: *Even if his arrogance is only a defence mechanism to cover up his insecurity, I still can't stand him.* • See also SELF-DEFENCE.

de·fen·ce·less /dɪˈfent·sləs/ *adj* • People, animals, places or things that are defenceless are weak and unable to protect themselves from attack: *a small defenceless child* • *a defenceless city* ○ *They were quite defenceless* **against** *the enemy bombs.*

de·fen·ce·less·ness /dɪˈfent·slə·snəs/ *n* [U]

de·fen·dant /dɪˈfen·dᵊnt/ *n* [C] *law* • A defendant is a person in a law case who is accused of having done something illegal. • Compare PLAINTIFF. • LP› **Law**

de·fen·der /£dɪˈfen·dər, $-dɚ/ *n* [C] • *The city's defenders* (= people protecting it from attack) *were outnumbered by the besieging army.* • *There are no longer many defenders* **of** *Stalinist economics.* • A defender is also someone in a sports team who tries to prevent the other team from scoring points, goals, etc.: *The Brazilian attack put France's defenders under pressure.*

de·fen·sib·le /dɪˈfent·sɪ·bl̩/, *Am, Aus also* **de·fend·able** /dɪˈfen·də·bl̩/ *adj* • *A city built on an island is easily defensible* (= able to be protected against attack). • *High petrol taxes are defensible* (= able to be supported) *on ecological grounds.* • *That's not really a defensible* (= able to be supported) *argument.*

de·fen·sive /dɪˈfent·sɪv/ *adj* • *These are purely defensive* (= relating to protection) *weapons, not designed for attack.* • If someone is defensive (**about** something), they are quick to try to protect themselves from criticism: *She's rather defensive about her family background – when you ask her about it, she* *never gives you a direct answer* . • *He's currently the best* *defensive player* (= one who prevents opposing players from scoring points, goals, etc.) *on the team.*

de·fen·sive /dɪˈfent·sɪv/ *n* [U] • **On the defensive** means prepared to protect yourself against attack or criticism: *Now that we have American support, the enemy will* **be/go** *on the defensive.* ○ *George* **was** *rather on the defensive during the meeting.*

de·fen·sive·ly /dɪˈfent·sɪv·li/ *adv*

de·fen·sive·ness /dɪˈfent·sɪv·nəs/ *n* [U]

de·fer *obj* /£dɪˈfɜːr, $-ˈfɜːr/ *v* [T] **-rr-** to delay (something) until a later time; to POSTPONE • *My bank has agreed to defer the* **repayments** *on my loan while I'm still a student.* • *The judge deferred* **sentence** *pending further medical reports on the defendant.* • *Can we defer making a decision until next week* [+ v-*ing*]

de·fer·ment /£dɪˈfɜː·mənt, $-ˈfɜːr-/, **de·fer·ral** /£dɪˈfɜː·rəl, $-ˈfɜːr·əl/ *n* [C/U]

de·fer to *obj v prep* [T] **-rr-** to allow (someone or something) to make decisions for you or tell you what to do, even if you disagree with them, because of your respect for them and/or because of their higher rank, authority, knowledge, etc. • *She said that she wasn't willing to defer to her husband.* • *I have to defer to my boss* **on** *important decisions.* • *I defer to* (= accept) *your judgment.*

def·er·ence /£ˈdef·ər·ənts, $ˈ-ɚ-/ *n* [U] *fml* • *He* **treats** *his mother* **with** *as much deference* (= respect and politeness) *as if she were the Queen.* • *She covered her head* **out of/in** *deference* **to** (= because of a polite respect for) *Muslim custom.*

def·e·ren·tial /ˌdef·əˈren·tʃəl/ *adj* • *She is always extremely deferential* (= respectful and polite) **to/towards** *anyone in authority.*

def·e·ren·tial·ly /ˌdef·əˈren·tʃəl·i/ *adv* • *They bowed deferentially as she came into the room.*

de·fi·ance /dɪˈfaɪ·ənts/ *n* See at DEFY.

de·fi·ant /dɪˈfaɪ·ənt/ *adj*

de·fib·ril·lator /£ˌdiːˈfɪb·rɪ·leɪ·tər, $-t̬ɚ/ *n* [C] *specialized* a machine used esp. in hospitals which uses an electric current to stop any irregular and dangerous activity of the heart's muscles • *Defibrillators are used to restore normal rhythm to the heart.*

de·fi·cien·cy /dɪˈfɪʃ·ənt·si/ *n* (a) lack of what is needed • *Pregnant women often suffer from iron deficiency.* [U] • *There's a deficiency* **of** *really good books on this subject.* [C] • *The deficiency is not* **in** *the quality of women in positions of power, but in the quantity.* [C] • *Deficiencies* (= weaknesses) **in** *the education system have been much in the news.* [C] • A **deficiency disease** is a disease which is caused by not eating enough of particular kinds of food that are necessary for good health: *Scurvy is a deficiency disease which you can get if you don't eat enough Vitamin C.*

de·fi·cient /dɪˈfɪʃ·ənt/ *adj* • *A diet deficient* (= lacking) **in** *vitamin D may cause the disease rickets.* • If something is deficient, it is not as good as it should be: *I thought the book had a very deficient index.* ○ *The team was deficient* **in** *several important areas.*

de·fi·cient·ly /dɪˈfɪʃ·ənt·li/ *adv*

def·i·cit /ˈdef·ɪ·sɪt/ *n* [C] the total amount by which money spent is more than money received • *The country is* **running** *a* **balance-of-payments/budget/trade** *deficit* **of** *$250 million.* • *The UK's deficit* **in** *manufactured goods fell slightly in the last three months.* • *In the year to February, Australia's current-account deficit* **narrowed/widened** *slightly to 9·2 billion dollars.* • *Congress has passed a budget plan intended to help* **reduce/cut** *the federal deficit.*

de·file *obj* SPOIL /dɪˈfaɪl/ *v* [T] *fml* to spoil the beauty, importance, purity, etc. of (something or someone) • *It's a shame that such a beautiful area has been defiled by a rubbish dump.* • *The city has been defiled by ugly buildings.* • *The soldiers deliberately defiled all the holy places.* • *She said that when her house was burgled, it made her feel defiled.*

de·file·ment /dɪˈfaɪl·mənt/ *n* [U] *fml or literary*

de·file VALLEY /dɪˈfaɪl, ˈdiː·faɪl/ *n* [C] *esp. literary* a very narrow valley between two mountains

de·fine *obj* EXPLAIN /dɪˈfaɪn/ *v* [T] to say what the meaning of (something, esp. a word) is, or to explain and state the meaning and exact limits of (something) • *In this dictionary 'reality' is defined* **as** *'the state of things as they are, rather than as they are imagined to be'.* • *Before I answer your question, could you define your* **terms** *a little more* (= explain what you mean by the words you have used)? • *It's impossible to define* (= know and state) *exactly what makes him so attractive.* • *Your rights and responsibilities are defined* (= their limits are stated) *in the citizens' charter.* • *Your role in the project will be strictly defined* (= limited to particular areas). • *I'd hate to feel that I was defined* **by** (= that my life got its meaning and importance only from) *my job.* • See also WELL-DEFINED.

de·fin·ab·le /dɪˈfaɪ·nə·bl̩/ *adj* • *definable rules of grammar/syntax* • *The recession is now perhaps definable* **as** *a slump.*

def·in·i·tion /ˌdef·ɪˈnɪʃ·ən/ *n* [C] • A definition is a statement that explains the meaning of a word or phrase: *In this dictionary, definitions have been written using words from a specially chosen list.* [C] ○ *Can you give me a good definition* **of** *'harsh'?* [C] • *What's the definition* (= meaning) **of** *'plywood'?* [U] • A definition is also a description of the features and limits of something: *The legal definition* **of** *what is and what is not pornography is very unsatisfactory.* • *Psychology is* **by definition** (= because of its own features) *an inexact science.*

de·fine *obj* CLEARLY SHOW /dɪˈfaɪn/ *v* [T] to show clearly the edge of (something) • *The outline of the castle on the hill was* **clearly/sharply** *defined* **against** *the evening sky.* • A **defining moment** is the point at which a situation is clearly seen to start to change: *The end of the Cold War was a defining moment for the world in more ways than one.* ○ *The crisis was the defining moment of his Presidency.*

def·in·i·tion /ˌdef·ɪˈnɪʃ·ən/ *n* [U] • Definition means clearness of shape, sound, colour, etc.: *The photograph rather lacks definition.* ○ *We admired the definition* **of** *the violinist's playing.* ○ *(fig.) I sometimes feel her ideas lack definition* (= are not clear).

def·i·nite /ˈdef·ɪ·nət/ *adj* fixed, certain or clear • *The date for the meeting is now definite: 5th March.* • *She has very definite opinions.* • *The trip is now definite – I've got confirmation and we're going after all!* • *"Are you sure I'm invited too?" "Yes, Roger was quite definite* **about** *it on the phone."* • *There's been a definite improvement in your English since you arrived.* • *There's a definite smell of gas – did you turn the oven off?* • *(specialized)* **Definite article** is the grammatical name for the word 'the' in English, or the words in other languages which have a similar use. Compare **indefinite article** at INDEFINITE. • *(infml)* A **definite maybe** is something that you want to do or are very likely to do, although you are not yet certain that you will be able to do it: *"Are you going to Helen's party?" "It's a definite maybe, but it depends on whether we can get a baby-sitter."* • LP **Articles**

def·i·nite /ˈdef·ɪ·nət/ *n* [C] *infml* • *Let's make the 9th a definite – we'll have a curry and then go to the movies.* • *Smith and Chrysler are definites* **for** *the Olympics team.*

def·i·nite·ly /ˈdef·ɪ·nət·li/ *adv* • *Have you definitely decided to* (= decided that you certainly will) *go to America?* • *He definitely said* (= There is no doubt that he said) *that the film started at 7.30 p.m.* • *"Are you going to have children?" "Oh, definitely* (= without any doubt)*."* • *"Is there any chance of a discount price?" "Definitely* (= Certainly) *not, I'm afraid."*

de·fin·i·tive /£dɪˈfɪn·ɪ·tɪv, $-ə·t̬ɪv/ *adj* not able to be questioned or improved; final, complete, or best • *a definitive decision/judgment/ruling* • *There are no definitive* **answers/solutions** *to this problem.* • *The police have no definitive* **proof** *of her guilt.* • *The document is the most definitive* (= complete) **statement** *of party policy ever.* • *He's written the definitive* (= best and most complete) *guide to Britain's Lake District.* • *For me, the definitive* (= best) *production of 'Hamlet' was one I saw in 1985.*

de·flate *(obj)* MAKE SMALLER /dɪˈfleɪt/ *v* to (cause to) become smaller or weaker • *The party's ambitions have been rather deflated by the two recent by-election defeats.* [T] • *The discovery that he has been involved in illegal trading has seriously deflated his reputation.* [T] • If you deflate someone, you reduce their confidence: *I was quite deflated by her lack of interest in my suggestions.* [T] • If something which has air or gas inside it deflates, or is deflated, it becomes smaller because it loses the air or gas: *If the boat starts to deflate, come back to shore.* [I] ○ *This tyre is too hard – you need to deflate it a bit.* [T]

de·flat·ed /£dɪˈfleɪ·tɪd, $-t̬ɪd/ *adj* • *Her criticism left me feeling very deflated* (= having had my confidence reduced). • *After he'd heard the news, he had a deflated look about him.*

de·flate *obj* REDUCE MONEY SUPPLY /dɪˈfleɪt/ *v* [T] to reduce the supply of money in (an economy) • *If the government deflates the* **economy**, *that will cause a reduction in the country's economic activity, which will lead to lower prices.*

de·fla·tion /dɪˈfleɪ·ʃən/ *n* [U] • Deflation is a reduction of the supply of money in an economy, and therefore a reduction of economic activity, which is often part of an intentional government plan to reduce prices. • Deflation can also mean a reduction (in value): *There has been a deflation* **in/of** *property* *values.* • Compare **inflation** at INFLATE MAKE LARGER; **reflation** at REFLATE.

de·fla·tion·a·ry /£dɪˈfleɪ·ʃᵊn·ᵊr·i, $-er·i/ *adj* • *a deflationary budget/policy* • *These measures are intended to be deflationary.*

de·flect *(obj)* /dɪˈflekt/ *v* to (cause to) change direction • *The crowd cheered as the goalkeeper deflected the* **shot**. [T] • *One of our players stuck his foot out and deflected the ball* **away (from** *the goal).* [T] • *The ball deflected* **off** *my hockey stick, straight into the goal.* [always + *off*] • *The Prime Minister deflected mounting* **criticism** *today by announcing tax cuts.* [T] • *The child's bad behaviour is often no more than a way of trying to deflect his mother's attention* **away from** *his sister.* [T] • *Nothing is going to deflect* (= prevent) *me* **from** *achieving my ambitions.* [T]

de·flec·tion /dɪˈflek·ʃᵊn/ *n* • *The second goal was from a deflection* (= a change of direction) **off** *the Liverpool captain.* [C] • *The goalkeeper's excuse was that ball* **took** *a* **deflection** *(***off** *a defender's leg).* [C] • *The journalists were frustrated by her constant deflection* (= avoidance) **of** *their questions.* [U]

de·flow·er *obj* /£ˌdiːˈflaʊ·əʳ, $-ɚ/ *v* [T] *literary* to have sex with (a woman who has never had sex before)

de·fog *obj* /£ˌdiːˈfɒg, $-ˈfɑːg/ *v* [T] **-gg-** *Am for* DEMIST

de·fo·li·ate *obj* /£ˌdiːˈfəʊ·li·eɪt, $-ˈfoʊ-/ *v* [T] to make the leaves drop off (a plant), esp. by using strong chemicals

de·fo·li·ant /£ˌdiːˈfəʊ·li·ənt, $-ˈfoʊ-/ *n* • *During the Vietnam war, thousands of hectares of forest were destroyed with chemical defoliant* (= substance which causes the leaves to drop off trees). [U] • *Agent orange is a powerful defoliant.* [C]

de·fo·li·a·tion /£ˌdiː·fəʊ·liˈeɪ·ʃᵊn, $-foʊ-/ *n* [U]

de·for·es·ta·tion /£diːˌfɒr·ɪˈsteɪ·ʃᵊn, $-ˌfɔːr-/ *n* [U] the cutting down of trees in a large area; the destruction of forests by people • *Deforestation by local people needing firewood has left these hills bare and empty.* • *Deforestation is destroying large areas of tropical rain forest.*

de·for·est *obj* /£ˌdiːˈfɒr·ɪst, $-ˈfɔːr-/ *v* [T]

de·form *(obj)* /£dɪˈfɔːm, $-ˈfɔːrm/ *v* to spoil the usual and true shape of (something) • *Sitting badly for long periods of time can deform your spine.* [T] • *His face and hands had been badly deformed in a fire.* [T] • *(specialized)* If something deforms, its usual shape changes and becomes spoiled: *These plastics deform at temperatures of over 90°C.* [I]

de·formed /£dɪˈfɔːmd, $-ˈfɔːrmd/ *adj* • *High levels of radioactivity in the sea have led to increasing numbers of deformed and diseased fish.* • *Under American law, a child born deformed can sue the doctor for negligence.*

de·for·ma·tion /£ˌdef·əˈmeɪ·ʃᵊn, $ˈ-ɚ-/ *n* [U] • *Deformation* **of** *her bones was caused by a very poor diet.* • *Fifty years of dictatorship has led to a sad deformation* **of** *political culture.*

de·for·mi·ty /£dɪˈfɔː·mɪ·ti, $-ˈfɔːr·mə·t̬i/ *n* • *Mothers who took the drug Thalidomide in the 1960s gave birth to babies with terrible deformities, such as hands without fingers, or feet without legs.* [C] • *Deformity* **of** *fingernails and toenails was common among people who drank the polluted water.* [U]

de·fraud *obj* /£dɪˈfrɔːd, $-ˈfrɑːd/ *v* [T] to take something illegally from (a person, company, etc.), or to prevent (someone) from having something that is legally theirs by deceiving them • *He was found guilty of defrauding the Internal Revenue Service.* • *The company has been accused of defrauding its customers.* • *They are both charged with conspiracy to defraud an insurance company* **of** *$20 000.* • LP **Crimes and criminals**

de·fray *obj* /dɪˈfreɪ/ *v* [T] *fml* (esp. of an organization) to pay (the cost of something) • *The company will defray all your expenses, including car hire.* • *The cost of the project will be defrayed by a government grant.*

de·frock *obj* /£ˌdiːˈfrɒk, $-ˈfrɑːk/ *v* [T] *old use or humorous* to dismiss (a priest), usually because of bad behaviour • *(humorous)* Defrock can also be used more generally to mean dismiss: *The former England captain has been defrocked.*

de·frost *(obj)* /£ˌdiːˈfrɒst, $-ˈfrɑːst/ *v* to (cause to) become free of ice, or to (cause to) become no longer frozen • *When you get a build-up of ice in your freezer, you know it's time to defrost it.* [T] • *Defrost the chicken* (= cause it to be no longer frozen) *thoroughly before cooking.* [T] • *Leave the chicken to defrost* (= become no longer frozen). [I]

de·frost·er /£dɪˈfrɒs·təʳ, $-ˈfrɑː·stɚ/ *n* [C] • Defroster is *Am for* **demister**. See at DEMIST.

deft /deft/ *adj* **-er, -est** effortlessly skilful, clever or quick • *Her movements were deft and quick, as she assembled the radio.* • *His piano-playing is extremely deft.* • *The way she answered the journalist's questions showed that she has a deft touch.* • *He's very deft* **at** *handling awkward situations.*

deft·ly /ˈdeft·li/ *adv* • *He deftly removed his glasses before she sat on them.* • *Wilson deftly caught the ball.*

deft·ness /ˈdeft·nəs/ *n* [U]

de·funct /dɪˈfʌŋkt/ *adj fml or humorous* no longer existing, living, or working correctly • *They used to be members of a* **now** *defunct communist organization.* • *(humorous) I think this kettle is defunct!*

de·fuse *obj* /ˌdiːˈfjuːz, dɪ-/ *v* [T] to make (a difficult or dangerous situation) calmer by reducing or removing its cause, or to prevent (a bomb) from exploding • *The two groups will meet next week to try to defuse the crisis/row/situation/tension/violence.* • *The minister will need to find a way of defusing* (= answering and reducing the effect of) *public* **criticism** *of her policies.* • *Bomb disposal experts have defused a 110-pound bomb at Victoria Station.*

de·fy *obj* /dɪˈfaɪ/ *v* [T] to refuse to obey, or to act or be against (a person, decision, law, situation, etc.) • *Dad will be really angry if you defy him again.* • *A few workers have defied the majority decision and gone into work despite the strike.* • *The fact that aircraft don't fall out of the sky always seems to me to defy* (= act against) *the* **law** *of gravity.* • *The teams defied the snow to play the semi-final match* (= they played despite the snow). • *A forest fire raging in the south of France is defying* (= is not changed by) *all attempts to control it.* • *(fig.) The chaos at the airport defies* **description** (= is impossible to describe). • If you defy someone **to** do something, you tell them to do something that you think will be impossible: *I defy you to prove your accusations.* [+ obj + *to* infinitive] ○ *I defy you to tell where I've painted over the scratch on my car.* [+ obj + *to* infinitive]

de·fi·ance /dɪˈfaɪ·ənts/ *n* [U] • *The demonstration is a pointless* **act/gesture** *of defiance* **against** (= refusal to obey) *the government.* • **In** *defiance* **of** *the cease-fire, rebel troops are again firing on the capital.* • *The machine seemed to be working* **in** *defiance* **of** (= against) *every known law of physics.*

de·fi·ant /dɪˈfaɪ·ənt/ *adj* • Defiant means proudly refusing to obey authority: *a defiant attitude/gesture/response* ○ *Some teachers find it difficult to deal with defiant children.* ○ *The protesters blocking the entrance to the offices remained defiant this morning.* • Defiant can also mean not willing to accept criticism or disapproval: *The Prime Minister was in defiant mood in the House of Commons yesterday.* ○ *They have taken a defiant stand.*

de·fi·ant·ly /dɪˈfaɪ·ənt·li/ *adv* • *The prisoners stood on the roof, defiantly waving banners and throwing stones.* • *She defiantly refused to eat her food.*

de·ge·ne·rate /dɪˈdʒen·ə·reɪt/ *v* [I] to become worse in quality • *Educational standards are degenerating year by year because of a lack of funds.* • *Her behaviour has degenerated a lot recently.* • *What was intended as a peaceful demonstration rapidly degenerated* **into** *violence.* • *The debate quickly degenerated* **into** *a shouting match.*

de·ge·ne·rate /£dɪˈdʒen·ᵊr·ət, $ˈ-ɚ-/ *adj* • Degenerate means having low standards of behaviour: *He's a degenerate young man, who's never done a day of honest work.*

de·ge·ne·rate /£dɪˈdʒen·ᵊr·ət, $ˈ-ɚ-/ *n* [C] *fml* • *They're just moral degenerates* (= people with low standards of behaviour) *with no sense of decency.*

de·ge·ne·ra·tion /dɪˌdʒen·əˈreɪ·ʃᵊn/ *n* [U] • *There has been a gradual degeneration* **of** *the judicial system in the last few years.* • *High blood pressure can cause degeneration* **of** *the heart muscles.*

de·ge·ne·ra·tive /£dɪˈdʒen·ᵊr·ə·tɪv, $-ɚ·ə·t̬ɪv/ *adj* • A degenerative **condition/disease/disorder/illness** is one in which the body or a part of the body increasingly loses its ability to function.

de·grade *obj* MAKE WORTHLESS /dɪˈgreɪd/ *v* [T] to cause (people) to feel that they or other people are worthless and do not have the respect or good opinion of others • *I believe pornography degrades women.* • *She said that she felt degraded by the stories about her in the newspapers.*

de·grad·ing /dɪˈgreɪ·dɪŋ/ *adj* • *It is so degrading* **to** *have to ask for money.* [+ *to* infinitive] • *No one should have to suffer such degrading treatment.*

de·gra·da·tion /ˌdeg·rəˈdeɪ·ʃᵊn/ *n* [U] • *An increasing number of people are being reduced to the degradation* **of** *having to beg on the streets.*

de·grade *(obj)* SPOIL /dɪˈgreɪd/ *v* to spoil or destroy the beauty or quality of • *Every day the environment is further degraded by toxic wastes.* [T] • *Large areas of tropical forest have been seriously degraded.* [T] • *(specialized)* If the quality of something electrical or electronic degrades or is degraded, it becomes less good or less correct: *The* *information will degrade if there are any system errors.* [I] ○ *The radio signal gets degraded by atmospheric interference.* [T]

de·gra·da·tion /ˌdeg·rəˈdeɪ·ʃən/ *n* [U] • *He said that environmental degradation should be a matter of concern to us all.*

de·grade CHANGE STRUCTURE /dɪˈgreɪd/ *v* [I] *specialized* (of a substance) to change into a more simple chemical structure • *These chemicals quickly degrade* **into** *harmless compounds.* • See also **biodegrade** at BIODEGRADABLE.

de·grad·a·ble /dɪˈgreɪ·də·bl̩/ *adj* • *These bags are made of degradable plastic.* • See also BIODEGRADABLE.

de·gree AMOUNT /dɪˈgriː/ *n* (an) amount or level of something • *This job demands a high degree* **of** *skill.* [C] • *There isn't the slightest degree* **of** *doubt that he's innocent.* [C] • *I have to warn you that there's* **a degree of** (= some) *danger involved in this.* [C] • *We're all involved in this, but* **to/in** *different degrees.* [C] • *The number of terrorist attacks has increased* **to** *a terrifying degree.* [C] • *There was some degree* **of** *truth in what she said.* [U] • **To what** *degree do you think we will be providing a better service than our competitors?* [U] • *"That's really bad." "Well, it's all a* **matter/question of** *degree* (= there are other things better and other things worse)." [U] • *The economy seems to be improving* **by degrees** (= gradually). • *I agree with you* **to a/some degree** (= not completely).

-de·gree /-ˌdɪ·gri/ *combining form* • *She suffered first-/second-/third-degree* (= least serious/serious/very serious) *burns on her legs.* • *(Am) He's being charged with first-degree* (= the most serious type of) *murder.*

de·gree UNIT /dɪˈgriː/ *n* [C], **deg.** *abbreviation* any of various units of measurement, esp. of temperature or angles, usually shown by the symbol ° written after a number • *212°* **Fahrenheit** *is 100°* **Celsius/Centigrade.** • *I hate it when the temperature gets above about 30°.* • *A right angle is an angle of 90°.* • *For this exercise you need to lift your left leg up by about 45°.* • *New York is on a* **latitude of** *41°N and a* **longitude of** *74°W.* • LP **Mathematics**

de·gree COURSE /dɪˈgriː/ *n* [C] a course of study at a college or university, or the qualification given to a student who has completed this • *"What degree did you* **do** *at York?" "Geography."* • *She's* **got** *a physics degree/a degree* **in** *physics* **from** *Oxford.* • *(esp. Am and Aus) She's* **got** *a* **bachelor's/master's** *degree* **in** *history* **from** *Yale.* • *I've* **got** *an* **honorary** *degree* **in** *literature.* • LP **Schools and colleges**

de·hu·man·ize *obj, Br and Aus usually* **-ise** /ˌdiːˈhjuː·mə·naɪz/ *v* [T] to remove from (a person) the special human qualities of independent thought, feeling for other people, etc. • *It's a totalitarian regime that reduces and dehumanizes its population.* • *He said that disabled people are often treated in a dehumanizing way.*

de·hy·drate *(obj)* /ˌdiː·haɪˈdreɪt/ *v* to (cause to) lose water • *These packet soups contain vegetables that have been dehydrated/dehydrated vegetables.* [T] • *Air travel dehydrates the body.* [T] • *You'll dehydrate* (= lose water from your body) *very quickly in this heat, if you don't drink lots of water.* [I]

de·hy·dra·tion /ˌdiː·haɪˈdreɪ·ʃən/ *n* [U] • *More than 11 000 children die every day around the world because of dehydration caused by diarrhoea.*

de-ice *obj* /ˌdiːˈaɪs/ *v* [T] to remove ice from • *On frosty mornings it can take me ten minutes to de-ice my car.*

de-ic·er /£ˌdiːˈaɪ·sər, $-sɚ/ *n* [U] • *In the winter we use de-icer* (= a substance for removing ice) *on the wings of aircraft shortly before takeoff.*

de·i·fy *obj* /ˈdeɪ·ɪ·faɪ/ *v* [T] to make (someone or something) into a god • *The Romans used to deify their emperors.* • *(fig.) Elvis Presley was deified* (= considered to be like a god) *by his fans.* • *(fig.) The 1980s were a decade in which the profit motive was deified* (= valued extremely highly).

de·i·fi·ca·tion /£ˌdeɪ·ɪ·fɪˈkeɪ·ʃən, $ˌdiː·ə-/ *n* [U]

deign /deɪn/ *v* [+ *to* infinitive] *disapproving* to do something unwillingly and in a way that shows that you think you are too important to do it • *If she deigns* **to** *reply to my letter, I'll be extremely surprised.*

de·in·du·stri·al·iz·a·tion, *Br and Aus usually* **-i·sa·tion** /ˌdiː·ɪnˌdʌs·tri·əl·aɪˈzeɪ·ʃən/ *n* [U] the process by which a country or an area within a country comes to stop having industry as its main supplier of work or income • *the deindustrialization* **of** *America/the North East of England* • *As deindustrialization sweeps across Europe, governments are looking to the service industries to provide new employment opportunities.*

de·i·sm /ˈdeɪ·ɪ·zəm/ *n* [U] the belief in a single god who does not act to influence events, and whose existence has no connection with religions, religious buildings, or religious books, etc.

de·i·ty /£ˈdeɪ·ɪ·ti, $ˈdiː·ə·t̬i/ *n* [C] a god or goddess • *Zeus and Aphrodite were ancient Greek deities.*

De·i·ty /£ˈdeɪ·ɪ·ti, $ˈdiː·ə·t̬i/ *n* [U] *fml* • **The Deity** is God.

déjà vu /ˌdeɪ·ʒɑːˈvuː/ *n* [U] the strange feeling that in some way you have experienced already what is happening now • *When I met her, I had a strange/weird* **feeling of** *déjà vu.* • *(disapproving) The movie has a strong* **sense of** *déjà vu about it* (= is similar to other films and does not contain new ideas).

de·ject·ed /£dɪˈdʒek·tɪd, $-t̬ɪd/ *adj* unhappy, disappointed or lacking hope • *"I made too many mistakes in the last game," said a dejected Vazna, after losing the semi-final.* • *She looked very dejected when she was told that she hadn't got the job.*

de·ject·ed·ly /£dɪˈdʒek·tɪd·li, $-t̬ɪd-/ *adv*

de·jec·tion /dɪˈdʒek·ʃən/ *n* [U]

de jure /£ˌdeɪˈdʒʊə·reɪ, £ˌdiː-, $-ˈdʒʊr·i/ *adv, adj* [not gradable] *fml* (as) having legal existence • *The country has de facto independence now, and it will soon be recognized de jure by the world's governments.* • *The President aims to create a de jure one-party state.* • Compare DE FACTO.

dek·ko /£ˈdek·əʊ, $-oʊ/ *n* [U] **have/take a dekko (at)** *Br and Aus dated slang* to have a look (at) • *Here, come and take a dekko at this.*

de·lay *(obj)* /dɪˈleɪ/ *v* to cause to be late or to cause to happen at a later time, or not to act quickly or immediately • *My plane was delayed (an hour) because of a suspected bomb in the luggage compartment.* [T] • *He wants to delay the meeting a few days. Is that OK with you?* [T] • *I think we should delay deciding about this until next year.* [+ v-*ing*] • *If you delay* (= fail to act quickly) *now, the opportunity might be lost.* [I] • *They're delaying* (= intentionally not acting quickly) *in the hope that we might improve our offer.* [I]

de·lay /dɪˈleɪ/ *n* • *Any delay* (= failure to act quickly) *could be disastrous.* [U] • *This situation needs to be tackled* **without** *delay.* [U] • *Long delays* (= Situations in which something cannot happen quickly) *are likely on the motorway because of an accident.* [C] • *There has been a delay in the book's publication* (= it will happen later than expected). [C]

de·layed /dɪˈleɪd/ *adj* [before n] • Delayed means happening at a later time than expected or intended: *Officials said that the reason for the large number of delayed trains was the bad weather conditions.* ○ *The protests are a delayed reaction to last week's announcement.* ○ *The bomb had a delayed-***action** *fuse which had been set to go off ten hours after it was planted.* ○ *He's suffering from delayed* **shock.**

de·lay·ing /dɪˈleɪ·ɪŋ/ *adj* [before n] • Delaying means intended to prevent something from happening quickly: *They're taking delaying* **action**/*They're employing delaying* **tactics** *to try and slow the project down or get it stopped.*

de·lec·ta·ble /dɪˈlek·tə·bl̩/ *adj* beautiful; giving great pleasure • *What a delectable-looking cheesecake!* • *Janet Swale was delectable as the young heroine of the play.*

de·lec·tab·ly /dɪˈlek·tə·bli/ *adv*

de·lec·ta·tion /ˌdiː·lekˈteɪ·ʃən/ *n* [U] *fml or humorous* • *And now,* **for** *your delectation* (= great pleasure and enjoyment), *we present the beautiful Margaret, famous fire-eater.*

del·e·gate CHOSEN PERSON /ˈdel·ɪ·gət/ *n* [C] a person chosen or elected by a group to speak, vote, etc. for them, esp. at a meeting • *Delegates have voted in favour of the motion.* • *Each union elects several delegates* **to** *the annual conference.*

del·e·gate *obj* /ˈdel·ɪ·geɪt/ *v* [T + obj + *to* infinitive] • *A group of four teachers were delegated* (= chosen) **to** *represent the school at the union conference.*

del·e·ga·tion /ˌdel·ɪˈgeɪ·ʃən/ *n* [C + sing/pl v] • *A delegation* (= group of delegates) *from Spain has/have arrived for a month.* • PL

del·e·gate *(obj)* GIVE /ˈdel·ɪ·geɪt/ *v* to give (a particular job, duty, right, etc.) to (someone else) so that they do it for you • *The boss doesn't know how to delegate (responsibilities* **to** *her staff).* [I/T] • *Authority to make financial decisions has been delegated* **to** *a special committee.* [T] • *(humorous) It seems I've been delegated* **to** *feed and walk the dog!* [T + obj + *to* infinitive]

del·e·ga·tion /ˌdel·ɪˈgeɪ·ʃən/ *n* [U] • *Delegation of responsibility is a key part of a manager's job.*

de·lete *(obj)* /dɪˈliːt/ *v* to remove or draw a line through (esp. a written word or words) • *All references to Marxism-Leninism were deleted* **from** *the history books.* [T] • *They insisted that all the* **expletives** *were deleted* **from** *the article.* [T] • *On this computer keyboard, this is the key for deleting* (= removing text). [I] • *Here is a list of possible answers. Please delete* (= draw a line through them) *as appropriate.* [I]

de·le·tion /dɪˈliː·ʃᵊn/ *n* • *In 1982, the management ordered the deletion* (=removal and loss) *of all computer files on this subject.* [U] • *There have been some deletions* (=words have been removed) **from** *this text.* [C]

del·e·te·ri·ous /£ˌdel·ɪˈtɪə·ri·əs, $-ˈtɪr·i-/ *adj fml* harmful • *These drugs have a proven deleterious* **effect** *on the nervous system.*

del·e·te·ri·ous·ly /£ˌdel·ɪˈtɪə·ri·ə·sli, $-ˈtɪr·i-/ *adv fml*

de·li /ˈdel·i/ *n* [C] *infml for* DELICATESSEN

de·lib·e·rate INTENTIONAL /£dɪˈlɪb·ᵊr·ət, $ˈ-ɚ-/ *adj* (often of something bad) intentional or planned • *a deliberate attack/insult/lie* • *We made a deliberate decision to live apart for a while.* • If someone moves, acts or thinks in a deliberate way, they move, act or think slowly and usually carefully: *From her slow, deliberate speech I guessed she must be drunk.*

de·lib·e·rate·ly /£dɪˈlɪb·ᵊr·ət·li, $ˈ-ɚ-/ *adv* • *I'm sure he says these things deliberately* (=intentionally) *to annoy me.* • *Calmly and deliberately* (=slowly and carefully), *she poured petrol over the car and set it alight.*

de·lib·e·ra·tion /dɪˌlɪb·əˈreɪ·ʃᵊn/ *n* [U] • *Slowly and with deliberation she turned to me and told me to get out.*

de·lib·e·rate *(obj)* CONSIDER /dɪˈlɪb·ə·reɪt/ *v fml* to think or talk seriously and carefully about (something) • *I've been deliberating all morning and I still can't decide what to do.* [I] • *The jury took five days to deliberate* **on** *the case.* [I] • *The committee has deliberated the question at great length.* [T] • *He's deliberating* **whether** *or not to accept the new job that he's been offered.* [+ *wh-* word]

de·lib·e·ra·tion /dɪˌlɪb·əˈreɪ·ʃᵊn/ *n fml* • *After much deliberation, she decided to accept their offer.* [U] • *After five days of deliberations, the jury decided on a verdict of not guilty.* [C]

del·i·ca·cy /ˈdel·ɪ·kə·si/ *n* [C] something esp. rare or expensive that is good to eat • *In some parts of the world, sheep's eyes are considered a* **great** *delicacy.* • See also **delicacy** at DELICATE EASILY DAMAGED, DELICATE SOFT.

del·i·cate EASILY DAMAGED /ˈdel·ɪ·kət/ *adj* needing careful treatment, esp. because easily damaged • *Peaches have delicate skins which are easily bruised.* • *Delicate plants need to be kept in a greenhouse during the winter.* • *I'm not going to let anyone else pack my china, it's much too delicate.* • *Molly has always been a delicate person./Molly's* **health** *has always been delicate* (=She becomes ill easily). • *We have a rather delicate* **situation** (=one that needs to be dealt with carefully in order to avoid trouble) *on our hands because my parents don't approve of my sister's fiancé.* • *I'd offer to pay for her if I thought she wouldn't be offended, but it's a rather delicate* **issue/matter/question/subject** (=one that needs treating carefully in order to avoid causing offence). • *The pay negotiations have reached a delicate* **point/stage** (=a point or stage at which care is needed to avoid causing offence). • *Repairing damaged nerves is a very delicate* **operation/process** (=needs to be done carefully). • *Teachers need to strike a delicate* (=carefully achieved) **balance** *between instructing their pupils and letting them discover things for themselves.* • *Weather-forecasters have extremely delicate equipment* (=equipment that can measure very small changes) *which helps them predict what the weather is going to be like.* • (N) (RUS) (S)

del·i·cate·ly /ˈdel·ɪ·kət·li/ *adv* • *I thought you handled the situation very delicately* (=in a way that avoided causing offence). • *We received a delicately worded refusal of our invitation.*

del·i·ca·cy /ˈdel·ɪ·kə·si/ *n* [U] • *I have a matter of some delicacy* (=needing to be handled carefully in order not to cause trouble or offence) *that I'd like to raise.* • *I don't think you quite appreciate the delicacy* **of** *the situation.* • *She always behaves with great delicacy* (=care not to cause offence). • See also DELICACY.

del·i·cate SOFT /ˈdel·ɪ·kət/ *adj* pleasantly soft or light; not strong • *This rose has a very delicate scent.* • *The bridesmaids wore dresses of a delicate pastel shade of pink.* • *We chose a delicate floral pattern for our bedroom curtains.* • *He was struck by her delicate beauty.* • *This wine has a delicate fruity flavour.* • (N) (RUS) (S)

del·i·ca·cy /ˈdel·ɪ·kə·si/ *n* [U] • *This region produces wines of great delicacy.* • See also DELICACY.

del·i·cate·ly /ˈdel·ɪ·kət·li/ *adv* • *The pudding was delicately flavoured with vanilla.*

del·i·ca·tes·sen /ˌdel·ɪ·kəˈtes·ᵊn/ *n* [C] a shop that sells high quality foods, such as types of cheese and cold cooked meat, which often come from other countries • In the US, a delicatessen (*infml* **deli**) also sells food and drink to eat as a light meal or to take away and eat between meals. • (D) (N) (NL)

de·li·cious /dɪˈlɪʃ·əs/ *adj* having a very pleasant taste or smell • *Could I have some more of that delicious cake, please?* • *The delicious smell/aroma of freshly-made coffee came from the kitchen.* • *This wine tastes delicious.* • *(fig.) I've got some delicious gossip* (=some information about someone that will give pleasure or amusement) *for you.*

de·li·cious·ly /dɪˈlɪʃ·ə·sli/ *adv* • *We had some deliciously thick cream with our strawberries.* • *(fig.) As she dived into the pool, the water felt deliciously* (=very pleasantly) *cool on her hot skin.*

de·li·cious·ness /dɪˈlɪʃ·ə·snəs/ *n* [U]

de·light /dɪˈlaɪt/ *n* (something or someone that gives) great pleasure, satisfaction or happiness • *My sister's little boy is a real delight.* [C] • *Her piano-playing is a delight.* [C] • *I read your letter* **with** *great delight.* [U] • *The children squealed* **in** *delight when they saw all the presents under the Christmas tree.* [U] • *Alex* **takes** *delight* **in** (=enjoys) *teasing his sister.* [U] • *We're just discovering* **the delights of** (=how enjoyable it is) *being retired.* • (P)

de·light *(obj)* /dɪˈlaɪt/ *v* • *Peter's success at college delighted* (=gave great pleasure to) *his family.* [T] • *Some people delight* **in** (=get pleasure from) *the misfortunes of others.* [I always + *in*] • *My brother always delights* **in** *telling me when I make a mistake.* [I always + *in*]

de·ligh·ted /£dɪˈlaɪ·tɪd, $-t̬ɪd/ *adj* • *The delighted audience applauded loudly.* • *We're delighted* **with** *our new house.* • *I was delighted* **at/by** *your news.* • *I'm* **absolutely** *delighted* **that** *you can come.* [+ *that* clause] • *We'd be delighted* **to** *come to dinner on Friday.* [+ *to* infinitive] • *"It was very kind of you to help." "Delighted, I'm sure* (=I was pleased to help)*."*

de·ligh·ted·ly /£dɪˈlaɪ·tɪd·li, $-t̬ɪd-/ *adv*

de·light·ful /dɪˈlaɪt·fᵊl/ *adj* • *Our new neighbours are quite delightful* (=very pleasant). • *Thank you for a delightful* (=very enjoyable) *evening.*

de·light·ful·ly /dɪˈlaɪt·fᵊl·i/ *adv* • *She told me a delightfully funny story.*

de·li·mit *obj* /ˌdiːˈlɪm·ɪt/ *v* [T] *fml* to mark or describe the limits of • *Police powers are delimited by law.*

de·li·ne·ate *obj* /dɪˈlɪn·i·eɪt/ *v* [T] to describe or mark the edge of • *The main characters are clearly delineated in the first chapter of the book.* • *A good manager should be able to delineate tasks in a structured way.* • *The boundary of the car park is delineated* (=its edges are marked) *by a low brick wall.*

de·li·ne·a·tion /dɪˌlɪn·iˈeɪ·ʃᵊn/ *n* [C/U]

de·lin·quent /dɪˈlɪŋ·kwᵊnt/ *n* [C] a person, usually young, who behaves in a way that is illegal or unacceptable to most people • *People disagree over whether* **juvenile** *delinquents should be punished or helped.*

de·lin·quen·cy /dɪˈlɪŋ·kwᵊnt·si/ *n* • *Her difficult childhood set her on the path to delinquency* (=illegal or unacceptable behaviour). [U] • *There is a high rate of* **juvenile** *delinquency in this area.* [U] • *His past delinquencies* (=acts of behaving illegally or unacceptably) *have made it difficult for him to get a job.* [C] • *(fml) It was delinquency* (=failure to act in the right way) *on the part of the managing director that led to the collapse of the company.* [U]

de·lin·quent /dɪˈlɪŋ·kwᵊnt/ *adj* • *They are carrying out research on the causes of delinquent* (=illegal or unacceptable) *behaviour among young people.* • *(Am fml)* Delinquent also means late (in paying money owed): *She has been delinquent* **in** *paying her taxes.*

de·lir·i·ous /dɪˈlɪr·i·əs/ *adj* unable to think or speak clearly because of fever, excitement or mental confusion • *Sophie had a high temperature and was delirious all last night.* • *Ellen has been quite delirious* **with** *joy* (=extremely happy and excited) *since Jim asked her out.*

de·lir·i·ous·ly /dɪˈlɪr·i·ə·sli/ *adv* • *He's been* **raving** *deliriously for days, and we can't understand what he's saying.* • *Kate and Peter are deliriously* **happy** *together.*

de·lir·i·um /dɪˈlɪr·i·əm/ *n* [U] • *We're very worried about Paul because he's been in a state of delirium* (=has been unable to think or speak clearly because of fever) *for so long.* • *I've never seen such delirium* (=excited happiness) *at a football match before.* • **Delirium tremens** *is formal for* DTS.

de·liv·er *obj* TAKE /£dɪˈlɪv·əʳ, $-ɚ/ *v* [T] to take (goods, letters, parcels etc.) to people's houses or places of work • *Mail is delivered* **to** *our office twice a day.* • *The shop is delivering our new bed on Thursday.* • *We're having pizza delivered for dinner tonight.*

de·liv·e·ry /£dɪˈlɪv·ᵊr·i, $ˈ-ɚ-/ *n* • *We get two deliveries* **of** *mail* (=it is delivered twice) *a day.* [C] • *You can pay for the carpet* **on** *delivery* (=when it is delivered). [U] • *This box of* *groceries is* **for** *delivery* **to** *Mrs Doyle.* [U] • *We expect to* **take** *delivery* **of** (=receive) *our new car next week.* [U] • *A large delivery* **van** *has just stopped outside the house next door.* • See also DELIVERYPERSON.

de·li·ver *obj* GIVE /£dɪˈlɪv·əʳ, $-ɚ/ *v* [T] to give, direct or aim • *The priest delivered* (=gave) *a passionate* **sermon/speech** *against war.* • *Professor Jones will be delivering a* **lecture/talk** *on Roman architecture at 5:00 p.m.* • *The jury delivered a* **verdict** *of not guilty.* • *He delivered* (=directed) *a sharp* **rebuke to** *his son.* • *The police said that it was the* **blow** *that had been delivered* (=given) **to** *her head that had killed her.* • *The bowler tripped as he was delivering the ball* (= throwing it towards the person with the bat).

de·li·ve·ry /£dɪˈlɪv·ᵊr·i, $ˈ-ɚ-/ *n* • *The actor's delivery* (= the way he spoke) *was so faint that he couldn't be heard at the back of the theatre.* [U] • In some sports, such as cricket or baseball, (a) delivery is the act of throwing the ball towards the person with the bat, in order for that person to try to hit the ball: *That was a good delivery from Thompson.* [C] ○ *The pitcher is famous for the speed of his delivery.* [U]

de·li·ver *obj* GIVE BIRTH /£dɪˈlɪv·əʳ, $-ɚ/ *v* [T] to (help) give birth to (a baby) • *She delivered her third child at home.* • *The baby was delivered by a midwife.* • *(fml) The princess has been delivered* **of** (=has given birth to) *a healthy baby boy.*

de·li·ve·ry /£dɪˈlɪv·ᵊr·i, $ˈ-ɚ-/ *n* [C] • *She always has easy deliveries* (=births). • *(Br and Aus) We arrived at the* **delivery room/suite/unit** *(esp. Am* **maternity ward***)* (=the part of the hospital in which babies are born) *at 2.30 and our baby was born at 3.30.*

de·li·ver *obj* SAVE /£dɪˈlɪv·əʳ, $-ɚ/ *v* [T] *fml or literary* to save (someone) from a painful or bad experience • *Is there nothing that can be done to deliver these starving people* **from** *their suffering?* • *My brother has been seriously ill for so long that we're hoping he will be delivered soon* (=that his suffering will soon be ended by death). • *"Deliver us from evil"* (Bible, *The Lord's Prayer* Matthew 6.9)

de·li·ver·ance /£dɪˈlɪv·ᵊr·ᵊnts, $ˈ-ɚ-/ *n* [U] *fml or literary* • *The people in the church prayed for deliverance* **from** *their sins.*

de·li·ver·er /£dɪˈlɪv·ᵊr·əʳ, $-ɚ·ɚ/ *n* [C] *fml or literary* • *Moses was the deliverer* **of** *the Israelites from Egypt.*

de·li·ver *(obj)* PRODUCE /£dɪˈlɪv·əʳ, $-ɚ/ *v* to achieve or produce; to fulfil (something promised) • *The government has failed to deliver all the things it promised.* [T] • *(esp. Am) The Republicans are relying on their agricultural policies to deliver the farmers' vote* (=to persuade farmers to vote for them). [T] • *The telephone company has promised to mend our phone by tomorrow, but I'll be very surprised if they're able to deliver* **on** (=fulfil) *that.* [I]

de·liv·er·a·ble /£dɪˈlɪv·ᵊr·ə·bl̩, $ˈ-ɚ-/ *adj*

de·li·ve·ry·per·son *(pl* **-people***),* **de·li·ve·ry·man** *(pl* **-men***)* /£dɪˈlɪv·ᵊr·iˌpɜː·sᵊn, $-ɚ·iˌpɜːr-, -mæn/ *n* [C] a person who delivers goods to people's houses or places or work

de·louse *obj* /ˌdiːˈlaʊs/ *v* [T] to remove LICE (=a type of very small insect) from the body, hair or clothing of (a person) or the fur of (an animal)

del·phin·i·um /delˈfɪn·i·əm/, **lark·spur** /£ˈlɑːk·spɜːʳ, $ˈlɑːrk·spɜːr/ *n* [C] a tall garden plant with blue flowers growing all the way up its branching stems

del·ta /£ˈdel·tə, $-t̬ə/ *n* [C] an area of low flat land, sometimes shaped approximately like a triangle, where a river divides into several smaller rivers before flowing into the sea • *the Mississippi delta* • *the delta* **of** *the Nile*

de·lude *obj* /dɪˈluːd/ *v* [T] to make (someone) believe something that is not true; to deceive • *He's deluding him***self** *if he thinks he's going to be promoted this year.* • *The thieves deluded the old lady* **into** *thinking that they were telephone engineers.* • *Poor deluded girl, she thinks he's going to marry her.* • Ⓘ

de·lu·sion /dɪˈluː·ʒᵊn/ *n* • *She is* **suffering from** *the delusion* (=a false belief) **that** *he will marry her.* [C + *that* clause] • *John is* **under** *the delusion* **that** *he will be promoted this year.* [C + *that* clause] • *Unfortunately, he is* **labouring under** *the delusion* (=believes wrongly) **that** *his students enjoy his lessons.* [C + *that* clause] • *I think that it's delusion* (= deceit) *on the part of the government to promise that they won't increase taxes.* [U] • *Diane has always suffered from* **delusions of grandeur** (=has always thought that she is more important than she is). • Ⓘ

de·lu·sive /dɪˈluː·sɪv/, **de·lu·so·ry** /£dɪˈluː·sᵊr·i, $-sɚ-/ *adj* • *The results of the survey gave the delusive* (=false and deceiving) *impression that local people were in favour of a new supermarket being built in their area.*

de·lu·sive·ly /dɪˈluː·sɪv·li/ *adv*

de·luge /ˈdel·juːdʒ/ *n, v* (to cover with) a very large amount of rain or water • *I'm soaked because I got caught in a deluge without an umbrella.* [C] • *This little stream can become a deluge when it rains heavily.* [C] • A deluge **of** something is a lot of it: *I can't come out tonight because I've got a deluge of work to do.* [C] ○ *The newspaper received a deluge of* **complaints/letters/phone calls** *about the article.* [C] • *The city was deluged when the river burst its banks.* [T] • *We've been deluged* **with** (=have received a lot of) *replies to our advertisement.* [T]

de luxe /dɪˈlʌks/ *adj* of very high quality • *We've booked a week's holiday in a de luxe* **hotel** *in Paris.*

delve /delv/ *v* [I] to search, esp. as if by digging, in order to find a thing or information • *I can probably find Jill's address for you, but I'll have to delve* **for** *it.* • *She delved* **in** *her pocket to find some money to buy sweets for the children.* • *We need to delve more* **deeply** *to find the reasons for Alex's present behaviour.* • *It's not always a good idea to delve too deeply* **into** *someone's past.* • *She said she was tired of journalists* **digging and** *delving* **into** *her private life.*

dem, Dem /dem/ *n* [C], *adj* [not gradable] *abbreviation for* **democrat(ic)**, see at DEMOCRACY

dem·a·gogue, *Am also* **dem·a·gog** /£ˈdem·ə·gɒg, $-gɑːg/ *n* [C] *disapproving* a person, esp. a political leader, who wins support by exciting people's emotions rather than by having good ideas • *Many people regard Hitler as having been a demagogue.*

dem·a·go·gic /£ˌdem·əˈgɒg·ɪk, £-ˈgɒdʒ-, $-ˈgɑː·dʒɪk/ *adj*

dem·a·go·gi·cally /£ˌdem·əˈgɒg·ɪ·kli, £-ˈgɒdʒ-, $-ˈgɑː·dʒɪ-/ *adv*

dem·a·gog·ue·ry /£ˌdem·əˈgɒg·ə·ri, $-ˈgɑː·gɚ·i/ *n* [U]

de·mand *(obj)* /£dɪˈmɑːnd, $-ˈmænd/ *v* to ask for forcefully, in a way that shows that a refusal is not expected, or to need • *The headteacher demanded an explanation of why the boys had behaved badly during lessons.* [T] • *The car workers' union is demanding a 7% pay rise this year.* [T] • *He has always demanded the highest standards of behaviour* **from** *his children.* [T] • *"And where do you think you're going?" demanded the police officer.* [+ clause] • *I demand* **to** *see the person in charge.* [+ *to* infinitive] • *She demanded* **that** *he return the books he borrowed from her.* [+ *that* clause] • *This is a very difficult piece of music to play – it demands* (=needs) *a lot of concentration.* [T] • *He seems to lack many of the qualities demanded* **of** (=needed by) *a successful politician.* [T] • Ⓕ Ⓘ Ⓟ

de·mand /£dɪˈmɑːnd, $-ˈmænd/ *n* • *You shouldn't give in to children's demands* (=forceful requests) *all the time.* [C] • *The government is unlikely to agree to the rebels' demands* **for** *independence.* [C] • *The French representative at the meeting made a demand* **that** *part of the international trade agreement be changed.* [C + *that* clause] • *(Br) We've just received a* **final** *demand* (=a last request for payment before legal action is taken) **for** *the electricity bill.* [C] • *My new job is* **making (great/heavy)** *demands* **on** (=takes up a lot of) *my time.* [C] • *The demands* **of** *nursing are too great* (=the work is too difficult) *for a lot of people.* [C] • *The concert has been cancelled because there has been little demand* **for** (=not many people have wanted to buy) *tickets.* [U] • *Babies should be fed* **on** *demand* (=every time they ask). [U] • *Good teachers are always* **in (great)** *demand* (=are always needed). [U] • *His heart has become so weak that it cannot* **meet/satisfy** *his body's demand* (=need) **for** *blood.* [U]

de·mand·ing /£dɪˈmɑːn·dɪŋ, $-ˈmæn-/ *adj* • *Emily is a very demanding child* (=needs a lot of attention). • *I'm trying to learn Spanish, and I find it quite demanding* (=it needs a lot of effort). • *Liz's new job has turned out to be very demanding* **of** (=it takes a lot of) *her time.*

de·mar·cate *obj* /£ˈdiː·mɑː·keɪt, $diːˈmɑːr·keɪt/, *Am also* **de·mark** /£dɪˈmɑːk, $-ˈmɑːrk/ *v* [T] to show the limits of • *Parking spaces are demarcated by white lines.* • *The responsibilities of the different people working in our office are clearly demarcated.*

de·mar·ca·tion /£ˌdiː·mɑːˈkeɪ·ʃᵊn, $-mɑːr-/, *Am also* **de·mark·a·tion** *n* • *The river serves as the* **line** *of demarcation* (=the line showing the separation) **between** *the two counties.* [U] • *In some schools, there is little demarcation* **between** *subjects* (=subjects are not taught separately). [U] • *On this map, demarcations* **between** (=the limits of) *regions are shown with dotted lines.* [C] • *There is a clear demarcation* **line** (=separation) *between the responsibilities of doctors and nurses.* • *(Br and Aus)* A **demarcation dispute** is a disagreement between **trade unions** (=organizations of workers) about what types of work should be done by the members of each of them.

de·mean *obj* /dɪˈmiːn/ *v* [T] to cause to become less respected • *The entire family was demeaned by George's behaviour.* • *I wouldn't demean* **myself** *by asking my father for money.*

de·mean·ing /dɪˈmiː·nɪŋ/ *adj* • *That advertisement is demeaning* **to** *women.* • **It** *was very demeaning* **to** *be criticized in front of all my colleagues.* [+ *to* infinitive]

de·mean·our *Br and Aus, Am and Aus* **de·mean·or** /£dɪˈmiː·nəʳ, $-nɚ/ *n* [U] *fml* a way of looking and behaving • *There was nothing* **in** *his demeanour that suggested that he was anxious.* • *She* **has** *the demeanour* **of** *a woman who is contented with her life.* • *My bank manager* **is of (a)** *rather unfriendly demeanour.*

de·ment·ed /£dɪˈmen·tɪd, $-t̬ɪd/ *adj infml or dated* mentally ill • *Her poor demented sister had killed herself by jumping off a bridge.* • *(fig.) The children have been driving me demented* (= I have found it difficult to deal with them). • (I)

de·ment·ed·ly /£dɪˈmen·tɪd·li, $-t̬ɪd-/ *adv*

de·men·tia /£dɪˈmen·tʃə/ *n* [U] *medical* a gradual worsening in memory and other mental abilities as a result of brain damage, rather than as the natural result of ageing • *The most common form of dementia is Altzheimer's disease.* • (CS)

de·me·ra·ra (su·gar) /£ˌdem·əˈreə·rə, $-ˈrɑːr·ə/ *n* [U] rough pale brown sugar • *Would you like white sugar or demerara in your coffee?*

de·me·rit /ˌdiːˈmer·ɪt/ *n* [C] a fault or disadvantage • *We need to consider the merits and demerits* **of** *the plan.* • *(Am)* A demerit is a mark given to someone, esp. a student in a school, because they have done something wrong or broken a rule: *She got three demerits* **for** *lateness on this term's report.*

dem·i·god, *female also* **dem·i·god·dess** /£ˈdem·i·gɒd, $-gɑːd, £-ˌgɒd·es, $-ˌgɑː·des/ *n* [C] (in ancient stories) a being who is partly human and partly a god • *Some football players become like demigods to their fans.*

de·mil·i·tar·ize *obj, Br and Aus usually* **-ise** /£ˌdiːˈmɪl·ɪ·tᵊr·aɪz, $-t̬ɚ-/ *v* [T] to remove military forces from (an area) • *At the end of the war, the area was demilitarized.* • *A demilitarized* **zone** *has been created on the border between the two countries involved in the conflict.*

de·mil·i·tar·iz·a·tion, *Br and Aus usually* **-i·sa·tion** /£diːˌmɪl·ɪ·tᵊr·aɪˈzeɪ·ʃᵊn, $-t̬ɚ-/ *n* [C/U]

de·mise /dɪˈmaɪz/ *n* [U] *fml* death • **On** *the demise* **of** *my father, the family house will go to myself and my brother.* • *(fig.) The demise* (= closing) **of** *the company was sudden and unexpected.*

de·mist *obj Br* /ˌdiːˈmɪst/, *Am* **de·fog**, **de·frost** *v* [T] to remove the MIST (= thin covering of small drops of water) from (the window of a car), usually by blowing air over it

de·mist·er *Br* /£ˌdiːˈmɪs·təʳ, $-tɚ/, *Am* **de·fog·ger**, **de·frost·er** *n* [C] • A demister is a device for removing MIST (= a thin covering of small drops of water) from a car window.

de·mo /£ˈdem·əʊ, $-oʊ/ *n* [C] *pl* **demos** *infml for* **demonstration**, see at DEMONSTRATE [MARCH], DEMONSTRATE [SHOW] • *When my dad was a student, he went on lots of demos.* • *The band have just made their first demo disc.*

de·mob *obj* /£ˌdiːˈmɒb, $-ˈmɑːb/ *v* [T] **-bb-** *infml for* DEMOBILIZE

de·mob /£ˌdiːˈmɒb, $-ˈmɑːb/ *n* [U] *infml*

de·mo·bil·ize *(obj), Br and Aus usually* **-ise** /£ˌdiːˈməʊ·bɪ·laɪz, $-ˈmoʊ-/ *v fml* to release (someone) or to be released from one of the armed forces, esp. at the end of a war • *At the end of the war, Jack was demobilized and went back to his job as a train driver.* [T] • *As soon as the peace treaty was signed,* **soldiers/troops** *began demobilizing.* [I]

de·mo·bil·iz·a·tion, *Br and Aus usually* **-i·sa·tion** /£diːˌməʊ·bɪ·laɪˈzeɪ·ʃᵊn, $-ˌmoʊ-/ *n* [C/U]

de·moc·ra·cy /£dɪˈmɒk·rə·si, $-ˈmɑː·krə-/ *n* the belief in freedom and equality between people, or a system of government based on this belief, in which power is either held by elected representatives or directly by the people themselves • *The government has promised to uphold the principles of democracy.* [U] • *The early 1990s saw the spread of democracy in Eastern Europe.* [U] • A democracy is a country in which power is held by elected representatives: *Few of the Western democracies still have a royal family.* [C] ○ *(fig.) This company is a democracy – all the employees are equal, and share in making decisions.* [C] • (GR)

dem·o·crat /ˈdem·ə·kræt/ *n* [C] • A democrat is a person who believes in democracy.

Dem·o·crat /ˈdem·ə·kræt/ (*abbreviation* **Dem**) *n* [C] • A Democrat is a member or supporter of the American **Democratic Party**.

dem·o·cra·tic /£ˌdem·əˈkræt·ɪk, $-ˈkræt̬-/ *adj* • *We must accept the results of a democratic election* (= an election in which all people can vote). • *Do you think Australia is a more democratic country* (= there is greater social equality there) *than Britain?* • The **Democratic Party** is one of the two main political parties in the US.

dem·o·crat·i·cally /£ˌdem·əˈkræt·ɪ·kli, $-ˈkræt̬-/ *adv* • *We need to decide this democratically* (= based on the wishes of most of the people). • *Boris Yeltsin was Russia's first democratically elected president.*

de·mo·crat·ize *obj, Br and Aus usually* **-ise** /£dɪˈmɒk·rə·taɪz, $-ˈmɑː·krə-/ *v* [T] • *It's about time we democratized* (= made (more) democratic) *the organization of this company.*

de·mo·crat·iz·a·tion, *Br and Aus usually* **-i·sa·tion** /£dɪˌmɒk·rə·taɪˈzeɪ·ʃᵊn, $-ˌmɑː·krə·t̬ɪ-/ *n* [U]

de·mog·ra·phy /£dɪˈmɒg·rə·fi, $-ˈmɑː·grə-/ *n* [U] the study of changes in the number of births, marriages, deaths, etc. in a particular area during a period of time • *historical demography* • **The** demography **of** an area is the number and characteristics of the people, in relation to their age, sex, whether they are married or not, etc., who live in the area: *The increase in the number of young people leaving to work in the cities has had a dramatic impact on the demography of the villages.*

de·mog·raph·er /£dɪˈmɒg·rə·fəʳ, $-ˈmɑː·grə·fɚ/ *n* [C] • A demographer is a person who studies changes in numbers of births, marriages, deaths, etc. in an area over a period of time.

de·mo·gra·phic /ˌdem·əˈgræf·ɪk/ *adj* [not gradable] • *There have been monumental social and demographic changes in the country.* • *Current demographic* **projections/trends** *suggest that there will be fewer school-leavers coming into the workforce in ten years' time.*

de·mo·gra·phics /ˌdem·əˈgræf·ɪks/ *pl n* • Demographics are the quantity and characteristics of the people, esp. in relation to their age, how much money they have and what they spend it on, who live in a particular area: *The staggering growth in the sale of rock music cannot be explained by simple demographics.* ○ **The** *demographics* **of** *the country have changed dramatically in recent years.* • *No one has exact demographics on* (= information about the quantity and characteristics of the people who live in) *the area.*

de·mol·ish *obj* /£dɪˈmɒl·ɪʃ, $-ˈmɑː·lɪʃ/ *v* [T] to destroy • *I think it's very sad that those houses have had to be demolished so that a supermarket can be built.* • *He completely demolished all her arguments* (= He showed that her arguments were wrong). • *(fig.) She demolished* (= easily defeated) *her opponent in the first round in under half an hour.* • *(fig.) The children demolished* (= ate quickly) *an enormous plateful of sausages and chips.*

dem·o·li·tion /ˌdem·əˈlɪʃ·ᵊn/ *n* • *A large area has been cleared in preparation for the demolition* (= destruction) **of** *the block of flats.* [U] • *Because of the work of several charities and historical societies, the number of church demolitions* (= churches destroyed) *has gone down in recent years.* [C] • *The demolition workers are starting tomorrow.* • *(fig.) His demolition* **of** *her arguments* (= His showing that her arguments were wrong) *was very convincing.* [U] • A **demolition derby** is a car race in which the drivers drive their cars into other cars intentionally, with the winner being the last car still able to move.

de·mon /ˈdiː·mən/ *n* [C] an evil spirit • *They believed that the rabbi would be able to* **exorcise/drive out** *the demons that were* **possessing** *her.* • *I don't know what kind of demon got into me that made me be so unkind.* • *(fig.) James is a real little demon* (= he behaves very badly). • *(fig.) Ellen works like a demon/is a demon worker/is a demon* **for** *work* (= works very hard). • *(fig.) Stefan has a demon serve* (= he hits the ball in tennis very powerfully). • *(Br humorous) It was* **the demon drink** *(Am humorous* **demon alcohol***)* (= too much alcohol) *that made me behave as I did.*

de·mon·i·a·cal /ˌdiː·məˈnaɪ·ə·kᵊl/, **de·mon·i·ac** /£dɪˈməʊ·ni·æk, $-ˈmoʊ-/ *adj fml* • *The police have no idea who is responsible for these demoniacal* (= evil) *killings.* • *The demoniacal* (= uncontrolled) *behaviour of the crowd frightened me.*

de·mon·i·a·cally /ˌdiː·məˈnaɪ·ə·kli/ *adv fml*

de·mon·ic /£dɪˈmɒn·ɪk, $-ˈmɑː·nɪk/ *adj* • *Several cases of demonic* **possession** (= people being controlled by evil spirits) *have been reported in recent months.* • *He had a demonic* (= cruel) *gleam in his eye.*

de·mon·i·cally /£dɪ'mɒn·ɪ·kli, $-'mɑː·nɪ-/ *adv*

demonize *obj, Br and Aus usually* **demonise** /'dɪː·mə·naɪz/ *v* [T] • If you demonize someone or a group of people, you try to make them seem as if they are completely evil: *During the 1930s and 40s, the Nazis used racist propaganda in an attempt to demonize the Jews.*

de·mon·ol·o·gy /£ˌdiː·mə'nɒl·ə·dʒi, $-'nɑː·lə-/ *n* [U] • Demonology is the study of demons and other evil creatures, such as WITCHES: *The most influential work of demonology is the 'Hammer of the Witches' by Kramer and Sprenger, which was published at Cologne in 1484.*

de·mon·strate *(obj)* SHOW /'dem·ən·streɪt/ *v* to show; to make clear • *These figures* **clearly** *demonstrate the size of the economic problem facing the country.* [T] • *Research has demonstrated* **that** *babies can recognize their mother's voice very soon after birth.* [+ *that* clause] • *The connection between smoking and lung cancer has been* **conclusively** *demonstrated* (=proved). [T] • To demonstrate something is also to show it and explain how it works: *Martin has a new job demonstrating vacuum cleaners* **to** *people in their own homes.* [T] ○ *The teacher demonstrated* **how** *to use the equipment.* [+ *wh-* word]

de·mon·strab·le /£dɪ'mɒnt·strə·bl̩, $-'mɑːnt-/ *adj* • *The report contains numerous demonstrable* (=able to be proved) *errors.*

de·mon·stra·bil·i·ty /£dɪˌmɒnt·strə'bɪl·ɪ·ti, $-ˌmɑːnt·strə'bɪl·ə·t̬i/ *n* [U]

de·mon·strab·ly /£dɪ'mɒnt·strə·bli, $-'mɑːnt-/ *adv* • *That's demonstrably untrue!*

de·mon·stra·tion /ˌdem·ən'streɪ·ʃən/, *infml* **de·mo** *n* • *The outcome of the war was a convincing demonstration* **of** (=made clear) *the superior forces of the US army.* [C] • *Let me give you a demonstration* **of** (=show and explain to you) *how the camera works.* [C] • *She told us how easy it was to use the computer, then by way of demonstration* (= showing and explaining) *simply pressed a few keys on the keyboard.* [U] • *We're going to a cookery demonstration* (=a meeting at which ways of cooking will be shown) *tonight.* [C] • *John bought his car cheaply because it was a demonstration* **model** (=it had been used to show customers what that particular type of car was like).

de·mon·stra·tive /£dɪ'mɒnt·strə·tɪv, $-'mɑːnt·strə·t̬ɪv/ *adj fml* • *The findings of this survey are demonstrative* **of** *the need for further research.* • See also DEMONSTRATIVE.

de·mon·stra·tor /£'dem·ən·streɪ·tər, $-t̬ɚ/ *n* [C] • A demonstrator is a person who explains how something works or how to do something: *There was a special stand in the shop where a demonstrator was showing how the food processor worked.*

de·mon·strate *obj* EXPRESS /'dem·ən·streɪt/ *v* [T] to express or show that you have (a feeling, quality, ability) • *She doesn't seem to demonstrate very much affection for him.* • *The surgeon demonstrated great skill in carrying out the operation.* • *His answer demonstrated a complete lack of understanding of the question.*

de·mon·stra·tion /ˌdem·ən'streɪ·ʃən/ *n* • A demonstration of a feeling or quality is a way of expressing it: *She gave him a hug as a demonstration* **of** *her affection.* [C] ○ *Huge crowds followed the funeral procession in a public demonstration* **of** *grief.* [C] • *There has been little demonstration* (=expression) **of** *support for the proposal so far.* [U]

de·mon·stra·tive /£dɪ'mɒnt·strə·tɪv, $-'mɑːnt·strə·t̬ɪv/ *adj* • If you are demonstrative, you show your feelings or behave affectionately: *We're a very demonstrative family.* • See also DEMONSTRATIVE.

de·mon·stra·tive·ly /£dɪ'mɒnt·strə·tɪv·li, $-'mɑːnt·strə·t̬ɪv·li/ *adv* • *I hate it when people behave so demonstratively* (=show their feelings or behave affectionately) *in public.*

de·mon·stra·tive·ness /£dɪ'mɒnt·strə·tɪv·nəs, $-'mɑːnt·strə·t̬ɪv·nəs/ *n* [U]

de·mon·strate MARCH /'dem·ən·streɪt/ *v* [I] to make a public expression of dissatisfaction, esp. by marching or having a meeting • *In 1968, a lot of students demonstrated in the streets of Paris.* • *There will be a march on Sunday, demonstrating* **against/in support of** *the government's plans to reduce the armed forces.* • *Local people are demonstrating* **for** *a road to be built taking traffic away from their village.* • *Protesters* **staged** *an anti-war demonstration in front of the US embassy.*

de·mon·stra·tion /ˌdem·ən'streɪ·ʃən/, *infml* **de·mo** *n* [C] • *The students are holding a demonstration* (=a public expression of dissatisfaction) *to protest about/against the increase in their fees.*

de·mon·stra·tor /£'dem·ən·streɪ·tər, $-t̬ɚ/ *n* [C] • *The police arrested several of the demonstrators* (=people involved in a public expression of dissatisfaction).

de·mon·stra·tive /£dɪ'mɒnt·strə·tɪv, $-'mɑːnt·strə·t̬ɪv/ *adj* being a word such as *'this'*, *'that'*, *'these'* and *'those'* which shows which person or thing is being referred to • *In the sentence 'This is my brother', 'this' is a demonstrative pronoun.* • See also **demonstrative** at DEMONSTRATE SHOW, DEMONSTRATE EXPRESS.

de·mo·ral·ize *obj, Br and Aus usually* **-ise** /£dɪ'mɒr·ə·laɪz, $-'mɔːr-/ *v* [T] to weaken the confidence of • *Losing several matches in succession had completely demoralized the team.* • *Being out of work for a long time is very demoralizing.*

de·mo·ral·iz·a·tion, *Br and Aus usually* **-i·sa·tion** /£dɪˌmɒr·əl·aɪ'zeɪ·ʃən, $-ˌmɔːr-/ *n* [U]

de·mote *obj* /£dɪ'məʊt, $-'moʊt/ *v* [T] to lower in rank or position • *The captain was demoted* **(to** *sergeant) for failing to fulfil his duties.* • Compare PROMOTE RAISE.

de·mo·tion /£dɪ'məʊ·ʃən, $-'moʊ-/ *n* [C/U]

dem·o·tic /£dɪ'mɒt·ɪk, $-'mɑː·t̬ɪk/ *adj fml* (of or in a form of language) used by ordinary people

de·mo·t·ivate *obj* /£ˌdiː'məʊ·tɪ·veɪt, $-'moʊ·t̬ɪ-/ *v* [T] to make (someone) less enthusiastic about a job • *She was very demotivated by being told she had little chance of being promoted.* • *Constant criticism can be very demotivating.*

de·mur /£dɪ'mɜːr, $-'mɜːr/ *v* **-rr-** *fml* to express disagreement or refusal to do something • *The lawyer requested a break in the court case, but the judge demurred.* [I] • *Old Mrs Taylor demurred* **at** *her doctor's suggestion that she needed someone to help her at home.* [I] • *"Not for me," demurred Lennie, when I offered him another drink.* [+ clause]

de·mur /£dɪ'mɜːr, $-'mɜːr/ *n* [U] • *She agreed* **without** *demur when asked if she would work late on Friday.*

de·mure /£dɪ'mjʊər, $-'mjʊr/ *adj* (esp. of women and children) quiet and well behaved • *The two demure little girls sat quiet and still next to their mother in church.* • *She gave him a demure smile.*

de·mure·ly /£dɪ'mjʊə·li, $-'mjʊr-/ *adv* • *She sat with her hands folded demurely in her lap.*

de·mure·ness /£dɪ'mjʊə·nəs, $-'mjʊr-/ *n* [U]

de·mys·ti·fy *obj* /ˌdiː'mɪs·tɪ·faɪ/ *v* [T] to make (something) easier to understand • *What I need is a book that will demystify the workings of a car engine for me.*

de·myth·ol·o·gize *obj, Br and Aus usually* **-ise** /£ˌdiː·mɪ'θɒl·ə·dʒaɪz, $-'θɑː·lə-/ *v* [T] to provide an explanation of something, or to present something, in a way which removes any mystery surrounding it • *Freud's attempt to demythologize religion has been criticized on the basis that he simply replaced one set of myths with another.*

den /den/ *n* [C] the home of particular types of wild animal • A den is also a rough structure built esp. outside, usually from pieces of wood, cardboard, etc., in which children play. • *(esp. Am)* A den is also a room in a house or apartment, which is used for activities not involving work: *The kids are watching television in the den.* • *(sometimes humorous)* A den is also a place where immoral or illegal activities happen secretly: *a den* **of thieves** ○ *a den* **of iniquity** ○ *a* **vice den** • *"They brought Daniel and cast him into a den of lions"* (Bible, Daniel 6.16)

de·na·tion·al·ize *obj, Br and Aus usually* **-ise** /ˌdiː'næʃ·ən·əl·aɪz, -'næʃ·nə·laɪz/ *v* [T] to change (an industry) from public to private ownership • *In the 1980s, the British government denationalized many industries.*

de·na·tion·al·iz·a·tion, *Br and Aus usually* **-i·sa·tion** /diːˌnæʃ·ən·əl·aɪ'zeɪ·ʃən, -ˌnæʃ·nə·laɪ-/ *n* [C/U]

de·ni·ab·le /dɪ'naɪ·ə·bl̩/ *adj* See at DENY NOT TRUE

de·ni·al /dɪ'naɪ·əl/ *n* See at DENY

den·ier /£'den·i·ər, £-eɪ, $-jɚ/ *n* [U] a measure of the thickness of the weave of NYLON (=an artificial fibre), silk, etc. thread, esp. that which is used in making STOCKINGS or TIGHTS • *15 denier tights are quite fine, while 70 denier ones are quite thick.*

den·i·grate *obj* /'den·ɪ·greɪt/ *v* [T] to say that (someone or something) is not good or important • *I was very hurt when he denigrated my efforts.* • *You shouldn't denigrate people just because they have different beliefs from you.*

den·i·gra·tion /ˌden·ɪ'greɪ·ʃən/ *n* [U]

den·im /'den·ɪm/ *n* [U] a thick strong cotton cloth, often blue in colour, used esp. for making JEANS (=informal trousers) • *He wore a denim jacket and denim jeans.*

den·ims /ˈden·ɪmz/ *pl n infml* • *Most of the people at the rock concert were wearing denims* (= clothes, esp. JEANS, made of denim).

den·i·zen /ˈden·ɪ·zᵊn/ *n* [C] *literary or humorous* an animal, plant or person which lives in or is often in a particular place • *Deer, foxes and squirrels are among the denizens* **of** *the forest.* • *(humorous) Douglas is one of the longer-serving denizens* **of** *the accounts department.*

de·nom·in·a·tion RELIGIOUS GROUP /£dɪˌnɒm·ɪˈneɪ·ʃᵊn, $-ˌnɑː·mə-/ *n* [C] a religious group which has slightly different beliefs from other groups which share the same religion • *Protestantism and Roman Catholicism are both denominations of the Christian faith.* • Ⓙ

de·nom·in·a·tion·al /£dɪˌnɒm·ɪˈneɪ·ʃᵊn·ᵊl, $-ˌnɑː·mə-/ *adj* [not gradable] • *Members of different denominational groups joined together for a service yesterday.* • *We want our children to go to a denominational school* (= a school controlled by a particular denomination).

de·nom·in·a·tion VALUE /£dɪˌnɒm·ɪˈneɪ·ʃᵊn, $-ˌnɑː·mə-/ *n* [C] a unit of value, esp. of money • *It always takes time to get used to the different denominations* **of** *coins when you go to a foreign country.* • Ⓙ

de·nom·in·a·tor /£dɪˈnɒm·ɪ·neɪ·təʳ, $-ˈnɑː·mə·neɪ·t̬ɚ/ *n* [C] the number below the line in a FRACTION (= a division of a whole number) • *In the fraction ¾, 4 is the denominator.* • Compare NUMERATOR.

de·note *obj* /£dɪˈnəʊt, $-ˈnoʊt/ *v* [T] to represent (something) • *His angry tone denoted extreme displeasure.* • *The low turn-out for the election denotes a lack of interest on the part of the public.*

de·noue·ment /deɪˈnuː·mɑ̃ː/ *n* [C] the end of a story, in which everything is explained, or the end result of a situation • **In** *the film's unexpected denouement, the woman who was thought to have been murdered was found to be still alive.* • *The match had an exciting denouement.*

de·nounce *obj* CRITICIZE /dɪˈnaʊnts/ *v* [T] to criticize strongly and publicly • *The government's economic policy has been denounced on all sides.* • *We must denounce injustice and oppression.* • *He denounced President Eisenhower* **as** *"Dopey Dwight".*

de·nun·ci·a·tion /dɪˌnʌnt·siˈeɪ·ʃᵊn/ *n* • *The minister's speech contained a strong denunciation* (= public criticism) **of** *the policies of the opposing parties.* [C] • *Denunciation* **of** *the government's failure to help lower-paid workers is not enough – we need to take action.* [U]

de·nounce *obj* ACCUSE /dɪˈnaʊnts/ *v* [T] to accuse (someone) publicly of being (something bad); to give information against • *His former colleagues have denounced him* **as** *a spy.*

de·nun·ci·a·tion /dɪˌnʌnt·siˈeɪ·ʃᵊn/ *n* • *Their denunciation* **of** *him* **as** (= saying that he was) *a traitor was well rewarded.* [U] • *The denunciation came as a great shock to everyone.* [C]

dense THICK /dents/ *adj* **-r, -st** thick; close together; difficult to go or see through • *A dense crowd waited for the arrival of the President.* • *There will be dense* **fog** *in northern parts of the country tomorrow.* • *The body was found hidden in dense* **undergrowth**. • *Books with dense print* (= with the words printed small and close together) *can be difficult to read.* • *It took me a long time to read that philosophy book because it was rather dense* (= contained a lot of information and ideas and was difficult to understand). • *(fig. infml) We've got some really dense* (= stupid) *people in our class.*

dense·ly /ˈdent·sli/ *adv* • *England was once a densely wooded country* (= a lot of trees grew close together there). • *Mexico City is one of the most densely* **populated** *cities in the world* (= a lot of people live close together there). • *His books tend to be rather densely written* (= contain a lot of information and ideas and are difficult to understand).

den·si·ty /£ˈdent·sɪ·ti, $-sə·t̬i/, **dense·ness** /ˈdent·snəs/ *n* • *The area has a* **high/low** *population density.* [C] • *We were unable to move because of the density* **of** *the crowd.* [U] • *The density* **of** *the fog made it difficult to see where we were going.* [U] • *This new film seems to lack the density* **of** (= it is easier to understand than) *some of the director's earlier work.* [U]

dense MATTER /dents/ *adj* **-r, -st** *specialized* (of a substance) containing a lot of matter in a small space • *Plutonium is very dense.*

den·si·ty /£ˈdent·sɪ·ti, $-sə·t̬i/ *n specialized* • Density is the relationship between the mass of a substance and its size: *Lead* **has a high** *density.* [C] ○ *The density* **of** *aluminium is fairly* **low**. [C] ○ *Aluminium is* **low in** *density.* [U]

dent /dent/ *v, n* (to make) a small hollow mark in the surface of something caused by pressure or being hit • *Somebody* **made** *a large dent* **in** *the back of my car while it was parked outside the house.* [C] • To **make** or **put** a dent **in** an amount, esp. of money, is to reduce it: *Buying a new television has made a big dent in our savings.* [C] ○ *Tax increases this year have put a huge dent in the company's profits.* [C] • *I dropped a hammer on the floor, and it dented the floorboard.* [T] • *(fig.) His confidence/ego/pride was dented* (= reduced) *when he didn't get into the football team.* [T]

den·tal /£ˈden·tᵊl, $-t̬ᵊl/ *adj* [not gradable] relating to the teeth • *Fluoride can help reduce dental decay.* • A **dental dam** is a piece of rubber which is used to keep the teeth dry during dental treatment, or which is used to prevent HIV infection during sexual activity in which someone touches someone else's sexual organs with their mouth or tongue. • **Dental floss** is a type of thread which is used for cleaning between the teeth. • A **dental hygienist** (also **hygienist**) is a person who works with a DENTIST and cleans people's teeth to keep them healthy. • A **dental practitioner** or **dental surgeon** is a DENTIST.

den·tist /£ˈden·tɪst, $-t̬ɪst/ *n* [C] a person whose job is treating people's teeth • *You should have your teeth checked by a dentist at least twice a year.*

den·ti·stry /£ˈden·tɪ·stri, $-t̬ɪ-/ *n* [U] • Dentistry is the work of a dentist.

den·tist's /£ˈden·tɪsts, $-t̬ɪsts/ *n* [C] *pl* **dentists** or **dentists'** • *I've got to go to the dentist's* (= the place where a dentist works) *on Friday.*

den·tures /£ˈden·tʃəz, $-tʃɚz/ *pl n* false teeth fixed to a small piece of (usually) plastic, which fits inside the mouth of a person who does not have his or her own teeth • *a set of dentures*

de·nude *obj* /£dɪˈnjuːd, $-ˈnuːd/ *v* [T] to remove the covering of (esp. land) • *The countryside has been denuded by war.* • *Drought and years of heavy grazing by sheep have completely denuded the hills* **of** *grass.* • *(fig.) Any further cuts in the country's armed forces would leave its* **defences** *dangerously denuded* (= unable to provide protection).

de·ny *(obj)* NOT TRUE /dɪˈnaɪ/ *v* to say that (something) is not true • *The prime minister has* **categorically/strenuously/vehemently** *denied reports that she is about to resign.* [T] • *He will not confirm or deny the* **allegations**. [T] • *The three defendants deny all* **charges**. [T] • *Neil denies* **that** *he broke the window, but I'm sure he did.* [+ *that* clause] • *Neil denies breaking the window, but I'm sure he did.* [+ v-*ing*] • *(fml) They denied the accusation* **to** *be true.* [T + obj + *to* infinitive] • **There's no denying** (= It is true) *that this has been a difficult year for the company.*

de·ni·ab·le /dɪˈnaɪ·ə·bl̩/ *adj* • Something that is deniable can be said to be not true: *The facts are simply not deniable.*

de·ni·al /dɪˈnaɪ·əl/ *n* [C] • A denial (**of** something) is a statement that it is not true: *The prime minister has* **issued** *a denial of the reports that she is about to resign.* ○ *Officials did not believe the runner's denial* **that** *he had taken drugs.* [+ *that* clause]

de·ny *obj* REFUSE /dɪˈnaɪ/ *v* [T] not to allow; to refuse • *Her request for time off work was denied.* • *No one should be denied a good education./A good education should be denied* **to** *no one.* [+ two objects] • *The goalkeeper denied him his third goal.* [+ two objects] • *I would have liked to have learnt French, but I was denied* (= not given) *the opportunity/the opportunity was denied* **(to)** *me at school.* [+ two objects] • *Many parents deny* **themselves** (= do not allow themselves to have or do things) *in order to do as much as they can for their children.*

de·ni·al /dɪˈnaɪ·əl/ *n* [U] • *Discrimination on grounds of race or sex is the most basic denial* **of** (= refusal to allow) *equal opportunities.* • *Their imprisonment for a crime they didn't commit was a gross denial* **of** *justice.* • See also SELF-DENIAL.

de·ny *obj* NOT ADMIT /dɪˈnaɪ/ *v* [T] not to admit that you have (knowledge, responsibility, feelings, etc.) • *She denied any knowledge of where he had gone.* • *He denied all responsibility for the rumours which have been circulating about the minister's relationship with an actress.* • *You mustn't deny your true feelings.* • *Even under torture, he refused to deny his beliefs/faith.* • *(fml)* To deny something is also not to admit that you have any connection with it: *She has denied her family and refuses to have any contact with them.* • *"Before the cock crow, thou shall deny me thrice"* (Bible, Luke 22.61)

de·ni·al /dɪˈnaɪ·əl/ *n* [C] • *No one was convinced by their repeated denials* **of** *guilt* (= acts of saying that they were not guilty). • *His denial* **of** *responsibility for the accident was unconvincing.* • *For me to do as you ask would be a denial* **of**

(= an act of saying that I have no connection with) *everything I stand for.*

de·o·do·rant /£di'əʊ·dər·ənt, $-'oʊ·dɚ-/ *n* a substance that is used to prevent or hide unpleasant smells, esp. those of the body • *Someone should tell him that he needs a deodorant.* [C] • *I always use deodorant after I've had a shower.* [U]

dep *v, n abbreviation for* **departs** or **departure** (used in TIMETABLES to show the time at which a bus, train or aircraft leaves a place) • *Flight BA174, dep. Heathrow 07.45.*

de·part /£dɪ'pɑːt, $-'pɑːrt/ *v* [I] to go away, esp. on a journey; to leave • *The plane departs at 6.00 a.m.* • *The train for London departs* **from** *Platform 2.* • *The last guests didn't depart till well after midnight.* • People say **depart this life** in order to avoid saying die: *This is in loving memory of my dear husband, who departed this life on May 5, 1978.* • (J)

de·par·ted /£dɪ'pɑː·tɪd, $-'pɑːr·t̬ɪd/ *adj* [not gradable] • *The old man talked for hours about the departed* (= gone forever) *triumphs of his youth.* • *We will always remember our* **dear** *departed* (= dead) *friends.*

de·par·ted /£dɪ'pɑː·tɪd, $-'pɑːr·t̬ɪd/ *pl n* • **The departed** are people who have died: *Let us remember the departed who are no longer with us.* • LP **Age**

de·par·ture /£dɪ'pɑː·tʃər, $-'pɑːr·tʃɚ/ *n* • *There are several departures* (= buses, trains, ships or aircraft leaving) **for** *Paris every day.* [C] • *Our departure* (= leaving) *was delayed because of bad weather.* [U] • *The departure time has been changed to 3.30 p.m.* • *Everyone in the office was surprised by Graham's sudden departure* (= leaving his job). [U] • *The president's departure* **from** *office was marked by a special ceremony.* [U] • *The plane was delayed and we had to wait for hours in the* **departure lounge** (= the area in an airport in which you wait before getting on an aircraft). • See also **departure** at DEPART FROM.

de·part from *obj v prep* [T] to do something different from (a usual or intended action, way of thinking, way of behaving, etc.) • *Due to unforeseen circumstances, we had to depart from our plans.* • *I see no reason for us to depart from our usual practice.* • *The minister said that in making his speech, he would be departing from his prepared text.*

de·par·ture /£dɪ'pɑː·tʃər, $-'pɑːr·tʃɚ/ *n* • *This decision represents a radical departure* (= change) **from** *our usual policy.* [C] • *To allow these changes would be a significant departure* **from** *tradition.* [C] • *There can be no departure* **from** *the rules.* [U] • *Selling men's clothing is a new departure* (= type of activity) *for the shop.* [C] • See also **departure** at DEPART.

de·part·ment /£dɪ'pɑːt·mənt, $-'pɑːrt-/ (*abbreviation* **dept**) *n* [C] any of the divisions or parts of esp. a school, university, business or government • *Mrs Wilson is the new head of the geography department/the department* **of** *geography.* • *There will be a meeting of the accounts department on Friday.* • *The furniture department is/are having a sale this week.* [+ sing/pl v] • *In Britain, the Department* **of** *Health and Social Security is/are responsible for paying money to the unemployed.* [+ sing/pl v] • *(fig. infml) I thought that buying the tickets was your department* (= area of responsibility), *Brian.* • *(humorous) He's a bit lacking* **in the** *brain/looks* **department** (= is not intelligent/attractive). • A **department store** is a large shop divided into several different parts, each of which sells different things. • *"'Once the rockets are up, who cares where they come down? / That's not my department,' says Wernher von Braun"* (in the song *Wernher von Braun* by Tom Lehrer, 1965) • LP **Shopping goods**

de·part·men·tal /£ˌdiː·pɑːt'men·təl, $-pɑːrt'men·t̬əl/ *adj* [not gradable] • *Janet is now a departmental head/manager.* • *We have weekly departmental meetings.*

de·pend /dɪ'pend/ *v* to be decided by or to vary according to the stated thing • *Whether or not we go to Spain for our holiday depends* **on** *the cost.* [I] • *The result of the competition will depend* **entirely/largely/partly/solely** *on the opinion of the judges.* [I] • *I might go to the cinema tomorrow –* **it** *depends* **what** *time I get home from work.* [+ *wh-* word] • *"Are you going to Emma's party?" "I don't know,* **it/that (all) depends** (= we haven't yet decided) *– we might be going away that weekend."*

de·pen·dent /dɪ'pen·dənt/ *adj* [after v; always + *on/upon*] • *Whether I go to university or not is dependent* **on** (= decided by) *what grades I get in my exams.*

de·pend on/u·pon *obj* TRUST *v prep* [T] to trust; to have confidence in • *You can always depend on Michael in a crisis.* • *I'm depending on you* **to** *keep your promise.* [+ obj + *to* infinitive] • *You can't depend on the trains always arriving on time.* [+ obj + v-*ing*] • *(humorous) You can depend on Jane* **to** *be late* (= she is always late). [+ obj + *to* infinitive] • *You haven't heard the last of this, (you can)* **depend (up)on it** (= you can be certain).

de·pend·able /dɪ'pen·də·bl/ *adj* • If someone or something is dependable, you can trust them or have confidence in them: *I need someone dependable to look after the children while I'm at work.* ○ *It's important for me to have a dependable car.*

de·pend·ab·ly /dɪ'pen·də·bli/ *adv* • *She has never behaved very dependably.*

de·pen·da·bil·i·ty /£dɪˌpen·də'bɪl·ɪ·ti, $-ə·t̬i/ *n* [U] • *The car offers value for money, comfort and dependability.*

de·pen·dence /dɪ'pen·dənts/ *n* [U always + *on/upon*] • *The company is* **placing** *considerable dependence* **on** *its new product as a way of increasing its profits.*

de·pend on/u·pon *obj* SUPPORT *v prep* [T] to need the support of; to be supported by • *Charities depend on people supporting their activities.* • *Children depend on their parents.* • *The country depends* **heavily** *on foreign aid.* • *Pollution of the sea has killed thousands of the fish on which many fishermen depend* **for** *their livelihoods.* • *Elaine depends completely on Bob* **for** *her happiness.*

de·pen·dant, *esp. Am* **de·pen·dent** /dɪ'pen·dənt/ *n* [C] • *Jack has four dependants* (= people who are financially supported by him, such as his wife and children).

de·pen·dence, *Am also* **de·pen·dance** /dɪ'pen·dənts/, **de·pen·den·cy** *n* [U] • Dependence is a state of needing something or someone, esp. in order to continue existing or operating: *The company needs to reduce its dependence* **on** *just one particular product.* ○ *His liking for alcohol quickly turned into* **(a)** *dependence* **on** *it.* ○ *Drug dependence led to her early death.* ○ *She has developed* **a deep** *dependence* **on** *him* (= she needs him emotionally).

de·pen·den·cy /dɪ'pen·dənt·si/ *n* [C] • A dependency is a country which is supported and governed by another country.

de·pen·dent /dɪ'pen·dənt/ *adj* • Dependent means needing the support of something or someone in order to continue existing or operating: *He has three dependent children.* ○ *All life is dependent* **on** *the sun.* ○ *It's very easy to become dependent* **on** *sleeping pills.* • In grammar, dependent can also be used to refer to a clause which cannot form a separate sentence, but can form a sentence when joined to a main clause. • LP **Clauses**

de·per·son·al·ize *obj, Br and Aus usually* **-ise** /£ˌdiː'pɜː·sən·əl·aɪz, $-'pɜːr-/ *v* [T often passive] to remove from (a person, organization, object, etc.) the things that make them particular or special • *He said that he thought wearing school uniform depersonalizes children.* • *I hated visiting my grandmother in that depersonalized hospital ward.*

de·pict *obj* /dɪ'pɪkt/ *v* [T] *fml* to represent or show (something) in a picture, story, etc.; to PORTRAY • *Her paintings depict the lives of ordinary people in the last century.* • *In the book he depicts his father* **as** *a tyrant.* • *Many people were shocked by the advertisement which depicted a man suffering* **from** *AIDS.* [obj + v-*ing*]

de·pic·tion /dɪ'pɪk·ʃən/ *n* • *The painter's depictions* **of** *the horror of war won her a worldwide reputation.* [C] • *I don't approve of the depiction* **of** *violence on television.* [U]

de·pil·a·tor·y /£dɪ'pɪl·ə·tər·i, $-tɔːr-/ *n, adj* [not gradable] (a substance) used for removing unwanted hair, esp. from the human body • *She used a depilatory on her legs.* [C] • *Some women use a depilatory cream to remove the hair from under their arms.* [before n]

de·pil·at·or /£'dep·ɪ·leɪ·tər, $-t̬ɚ/ *n* [C] • A depilator is a device which is used to remove hair from the body, esp. the legs and under the arms.

de·plane /ˌdiː'pleɪn/ *v* [I] *Am* to leave an aircraft • *Would all passengers please deplane by the rear doors.* • *We will be deplaning shortly. Thank you for your patience.*

de·plete *obj* /dɪ'pliːt/ *v* [T] to reduce (esp. supplies, energy, money) in size or amount • *These chemicals are thought to deplete the ozone layer.* • *If we continue to deplete the Earth's natural resources, we will cause serious damage to the environment.* • *The country's coal* **reserves/supplies** *were rapidly depleted when the miners were on strike.* • *(humorous) That last holiday has* **seriously** *depleted my bank account!* • *The illness depletes the body* **of** *vitamins.*

de·ple·ted /£dɪ'pliː·tɪd, $-t̬ɪd/ *adj* • *The heavy rain in the last few days has helped make the reservoirs less depleted.* • *Measures have been taken to protect the world's depleted elephant population.* • *The soil was too depleted* (= lacking in substances needed for plants to grow) *for anything to grow in it.* • *We returned home from the funeral feeling physically and emotionally depleted* (= weakened).

de·ple·tion /dɪˈpliː·ʃᵊn/ *n* • *Steps must be taken to stop the depletion* **of** *the ozone layer/the world's tropical forests.* [U] • *Staff depletion has led to people having to work longer hours.* [U] • *A high level of expenditure has caused a depletion* **in** *our capital/funds.* [C]

de·plore *obj* /£dɪˈplɔːʳ, $-ˈplɔːr/ *v* [T not *be deploring*] to say or think that (something) is very bad; to CONDEMN [CRITICIZE] • *He said that he deplored all violence.* • *Even though I deplore the decision, I'll have to accept it.* • *What is the trait you most deplore in yourself?* • *(Br and Aus) The attitude of the Minister is* **to be** *deplored* (= is very bad).

de·plor·a·ble /£dɪˈplɔː·rə·bl̩, $-ˈplɔːr·ə-/ *adj* • Deplorable means very bad: *I think smoking is a deplorable habit.* ○ *No one should have to live in such deplorable conditions.* ○ **It** *is deplorable* **that** *force should have been used against innocent children.* [+ *that* clause] ○ **It** *seems deplorable* **to** *allow this state of affairs to continue to exist.* [+ *to* infinitive]

de·plor·ab·ly /£dɪˈplɔː·rə·bli, $-ˈplɔːr·ə-/ *adv* • *Tim behaves deplorably when he's drunk.*

de·ploy *obj* /dɪˈplɔɪ/ *v* [T] to use, or to put into position ready to be used, esp. in an effective way • *The company is reconsidering the way in which it deploys its* **resources/staff**. • *She deployed a powerful* **argument** *against the proposal.* • *My job doesn't really allow me fully to deploy my skills/talents.* • *The decision has been made to deploy* (= put into position ready to be used) *extra* **troops**/*more powerful* **weapons**.

de·ploy·ment /dɪˈplɔɪ·mənt/ *n* [U] • *The Chief of Police ordered the deployment* (= use) **of** *2000 troops to try to stop the rioting.* • *The deployment* (= putting into position ready for use) of *nuclear weapons in nearby countries poses a serious threat to peace.*

de·po·li·ti·cize *obj, Br and Aus usually* **-ise** /£ˌdiː·pɒlˈɪt·ɪ·saɪz, $-pɑːˈlɪt̬-/ *v* [T] to cause to have no political connections • *The first job of the new democratic government should be to depoliticize the civil service/judiciary/police force.* • *He said that he wanted to depoliticize the issue.*

de·po·li·ti·ciz·a·tion, *Br and Aus usually* **-i·sa·tion** /£ˌdiː·pɒl·ɪ·tɪ·saɪˈzeɪ·ʃᵊn, $-pɑː·lɪ·t̬ɪ-/ *n* [U]

de·pop·u·late *obj* /£ˌdiːˈpɒp·jʊ·leɪt, $-ˈpɑː·pjə-/ *v* [T usually passive] to cause (an area, country etc.) to have fewer people living in it • *The area has been depopulated by disease/famine/war.*

de·pop·u·la·tion /£diːˌpɒp·jʊˈleɪ·ʃᵊn, $-ˌpɑː·pjə-/ *n* [U] • *The war in Vietnam led to rural depopulation/depopulation* **of** *the rural areas.*

de·port *obj* /£dɪˈpɔːt, $-ˈpɔːrt/ *v* [T] to force (a person) to leave a country, esp. because they have no legal right to be there or because they have broken the law • *Thousands of illegal immigrants are caught and deported every year.* • *The refugees have been deported back* **to** *the country they came from.* • *The escaped prisoner was captured in Spain and deported* **from** *there.*

de·por·ta·tion /£ˌdiː·pɔːˈteɪ·ʃᵊn, $-pɔːr-/ *n* • *Their applications for political asylum were rejected and they now face deportation.* [U] • *There were* **mass** *deportations in the 1930s, when thousands of people were forced to leave the country.* [C] • A **deportation order** is an official document stating that someone must be deported.

de·por·tee /£ˌdiː·pɔːˈtiː, $-pɔːr-/ *n* [C] • A deportee is a person who has been, or is waiting to be, deported.

de·port·ment /£dɪˈpɔːt·mənt, $-ˈpɔːrt-/ *n* [U] *fml* the way someone behaves, esp. the way they walk and stand • *The actors were given lessons in speech and deportment* (= moving well). • *Throughout the ordeal of her husband's funeral, Mrs Kennedy was a model of deportment* (= behaved in a controlled, various and calm way).

de·pose *obj* /£dɪˈpəʊz, $-ˈpoʊz/ *v* [T] to remove (someone important) from a powerful position • *Margaret Thatcher was deposed* **as** *leader of the British Conservative Party in 1991.* • *King Charles I was deposed* **from** *the English throne in 1646.*

de·po·si·tion /ˌdep·əˈzɪʃ·ᵊn, ˌdiː·pə-/ *n* [U] *fml* • *Crowds were celebrating in the streets following the deposition* **of** *the dictator* **from** *power.* • See also DEPOSITION.

de·po·sit *obj* [LEAVE] /£dɪˈpɒz·ɪt, $-ˈpɑː·zɪt/ *v* [T always + adv/prep] to leave (something) somewhere • *The flood waters fell, depositing mud over the whole area.* • *The bus deposited me* (= left me unexpectedly and suddenly) *miles from anywhere.* • *The cuckoo deposits* (= produces) *her eggs in other birds' nests.* • *I deposited my luggage* (= left it in safety) *at the station so I didn't have to carry it around all day.* • Ⓟ

de·po·sit /£dɪˈpɒz·ɪt, $-ˈpɑː·zɪt/ *n* • *Decant the wine carefully, so that you leave the deposit* (= material which has separated out from the liquid) *in the bottom of the bottle.* [U] • *In hard-water areas, a chalky deposit* (= layer) *often forms in pipes and kettles.* [C] • *The flood left a thick deposit* (= layer) **of** *mud over the whole of the ground floor of the house.* [C] • *(specialized)* A deposit is a layer which has formed under the ground, esp. over a long period: *The area has rich mineral and oil deposits.* [C] ○ *There is a huge coal deposit/deposit* **of** *coal in the valley.* [C]

de·po·si·tory /£dɪˈpɒz·ɪ·tᵊr·i, $-ˈpɑː·zə·tɔːr-/ *n* [C] • A depository is a place, esp. a large building, for storing things: *an arms/book/furniture depository* ○ *The Tower of London is the depository* **for/of** *the crown and jewels which are used in British coronations.* • *The Government are having difficulty finding a safe depository* **for** (= somewhere to store) *nuclear waste.*

de·po·sit *obj* [STORE MONEY] /£dɪˈpɒz·ɪt, $-ˈpɑː·zɪt/ *v* [T] to put (something valuable, esp. money) in a bank or SAFE (= a strong box or cupboard with locks) • *There's a night safe outside the bank, so you can deposit money whenever you wish.* • *I deposited £500* **in** *my account this morning.* • *Most of my money is deposited* **with** *a bank/building society.* • If you deposit a sum of money when you make an agreement with someone to pay for or buy something, you pay them that sum, which either will be returned to you later if the agreed arrangement is kept, or forms part of the total payment: *When we moved into our apartment, we had to deposit $1000* **with** *the landlord in case we broke any of his things.* ○ *If you deposit 20% now, you can pay the rest when the car is delivered.* • [LP] Money Ⓟ

de·po·sit /£dɪˈpɒz·ɪt, $-ˈpɑː·zɪt/ *n* • *To open an account, you need to* **make** *a minimum deposit* (= payment) **of** *$500.* [C] • A deposit is also a sum of money which is given in advance as part of a total payment for something: *"If you* **leave** *a deposit* **of** *£10/***leave** *£10* **as** *a deposit, we'll keep the dress for you," said the shop assistant.* [C] ○ *We* **paid/put** *a deposit* **of** *£10 000* **on** *the house, and paid the balance four weeks later.* [C] • A deposit is also a sum of money which you pay when you rent something, and which is returned to you when you return the thing you have rented: *A deposit* **of** *£20 must be paid* **on** *hired boats, which you will* **forfeit/lose** *if the boat is damaged.* [C] ○ *The cost for hiring the yacht was £1000 for a week, plus a £120* **refundable/returnable** *deposit.* [C] ○ *You pay a 10p deposit* **on** *the bottle, which we return to you when you bring the empty bottle back.* [C] • If you have money **on** deposit, you have it saved, esp. in a bank: *I've got £5000 on deposit in my bank/building society.* [U] • A *(Br)* **deposit account** (*Am* **savings account**) is a bank account in which you usually leave money for a long time and which gives you INTEREST (= an amount of profit). • *(Am)* A **deposit bottle/can** is a container for drinks for which a small amount of money is given back to you if you return the container to a shop when it is empty: *If you bring the deposit bottles back, you'll have money for chewing gum.*

de·po·si·tor /£dɪˈpɒz·ɪ·təʳ, $-ˈpɑː·zə·t̬ɚ/ *n* [C] • *Depositors* (= customers, esp. of a bank) *will be informed of any change in interest rates.*

de·po·si·tion /ˌdep·əˈzɪʃ·ᵊn, ˌdiː·pə-/ *n* [C] *law* a formal written statement made in, or for use in, a court of law • *Before the court case, we had to* **file/give** *a deposition.* • *Our lawyer* **took** *a deposition from us.* • *He had received none of the profits, Mr Shaw stated in a* **sworn** *deposition.* • See also **deposition** at DEPOSE.

de·pot /£ˈdep·əʊ, $ˈdiː·poʊ/ *n* [C] a building where supplies or vehicles, esp. buses, are kept • *an arms/weapons depot* • *a fuel/storage/supply depot* • *a bus depot* • *(Am)* A depot is also a bus station or train station.

de·praved /dɪˈpreɪvd/ *adj* morally bad or evil • *a depraved character/mind/personality* • *Someone who can kill a child like that must be totally depraved.*

de·prave *obj* /dɪˈpreɪv/ *v* [T] *slightly fml* • *The British Obscene Publications Act prohibits publication of material which tends 'to deprave* (= cause to be morally bad) *and corrupt those likely to read, see or hear it'.*

de·pra·vi·ty /£dɪˈpræv·ə·ti, $-t̬i/ *n* [U] • *The judge said that the background to the case was one of violence, depravity* (= the state of being morally bad) *and abuse.*

dep·re·cate *obj* [DISAPPROVE] /ˈdep·rɪ·keɪt/ *v* [T not *be deprecating*] *fml* to (say that you do) not approve of (something) • *We deprecate this use of company funds for political purposes.*

dep·re·cat·ing /£ˈdep·rɪ·keɪ·tɪŋ, $-t̬ɪŋ/, **dep·re·ca·to·ry** /£ˌdep·rɪˈkeɪ·tᵊr·i, $-kəˈtɔːr-/ *adj* • *The teacher gave the boys a deprecating stare and told them to be quiet.*

dep·re·cat·ing·ly /£ˈdep·rɪ·keɪ·tɪŋ·li, $-t̬ɪŋ-/ *adv*

dep·re·ca·tion /ˌdep·rɪˈkeɪ·ʃᵊn/ *n* [U] *fml*

dep·re·cate *obj* NOT VALUE /ˈdep·rɪ·keɪt/ *v* [T] to say that you think (something) is of little value or importance • *He is always deprecating my achievements.*

dep·re·cat·ing /£ˈdep·rɪ·keɪ·tɪŋ, $-ṭɪŋ/, **dep·re·ca·to·ry** /£ˌdep·rɪˈkeɪ·tᵊr·i, $-kəˈtɔːr-/ *adj* • *Her deprecating smile clearly showed that she thought I'd said something stupid.* • *He has a very deprecating sense of humour.* • *deprecating wit* (=that involving laughing at someone or something, often unkindly) • Deprecating can also mean showing that you feel embarrassed, esp. by praise: *She reacted to his compliments with a deprecating laugh.* • See also SELF-DEPRECATING.

dep·re·cat·ing·ly /£ˈdep·rɪ·keɪ·tɪŋ·li, $-ṭɪŋ-/ *adv*

dep·re·ca·tion /ˌdep·rɪˈkeɪ·ʃᵊn/ *n* [U]

de·pre·ci·ate *(obj)* /dɪˈpriː·ʃi·eɪt, -si-/ *v* to (cause something to) lose value, esp. over time • *Our car depreciated* **(by)** *£1500/20% in the first year after we bought it.* [I] • *The value of our house has depreciated because of the new factory that has been built next to it.* [I] • *The new factory that has been built next to us has depreciated the value of our house.* [T] • Compare APPRECIATE INCREASE.

de·pre·ci·a·tion /dɪˌpriː·ʃiˈeɪ·ʃᵊn, -si-/ *n* [U] • *I thought I'd get £6000 for my car, but I didn't allow for depreciation, and I only got £4500.*

dep·re·da·tion /ˌdep·rəˈdeɪ·ʃᵊn/ *n* (an act causing) damage or destruction • *The crops have been destroyed by the depredations* **of** *insects.* [C] • *The entire area has suffered the depredations* **of** *war.* [C] • *It will take months to clear up the depredations* **of** (=damage done by) *the storm.* [C] • *Depredation* **of** (=Damage done to) *the environment is destroying hundreds of species each year.* [U]

de·press *obj* CAUSE SADNESS /dɪˈpres/ *v* [T] to cause (a person) to feel unhappy and without hope • *Bad weather depresses me.* • **It** *depresses me* **knowing** *that I'll probably still be doing exactly the same job in ten years' time.* [+ obj + *to* infinitive] • **It** *depresses me* **to** *think that I'll probably still be doing exactly the same job in ten years' time.* [+ obj + *to* infinitive] • **It** *depresses me* **that** *I'll probably still be doing exactly the same job in ten years' time.* [+ obj + *that* clause]

de·pres·sant /dɪˈpres·ᵊnt/ *n* [C] • A depressant is a substance which causes you to feel unhappy and without hope: *Alcohol is a depressant.* ○ *These drugs may have a depressant effect.*

de·pressed /dɪˈprest/ *adj* • *He was depressed* **about/by/over/***(Br)* **at** *his awful exam results.* • *She became* **deeply/profoundly/severely** *depressed when her husband died.* • *Jo has been diagnosed as* **clinically** *depressed* (=as suffering from a mental illness which makes her feel unhappy and without hope).

de·press·ing /dɪˈpres·ɪŋ/ *adj* • *What depressing weather we're having!* • *Spending another evening at home on my own is a very depressing prospect.* • *Her letter made depressing reading.* • **It** *was very depressing* **watching** *the news on television tonight.* [+ v-*ing*] • **It's** *depressing* **to** *think that we've got five more years of this government!* [+ *to* infinitive] • **It** *is* **deeply/profoundly depressing** *that we're making so little progress.* [+ *that* clause]

de·press·ing·ly /dɪˈpres·ɪŋ·li/ *adv* • *My score was depressingly low.* • *By midnight, it was depressingly clear/obvious that we'd lost the election.* • *The story was depressingly* **familiar**.

de·pres·sion /dɪˈpreʃ·ᵊn/ *n* [U] • *I'm only just beginning to get over the* **deep/severe** *depression* (=unhappiness) *I felt about losing my job.* • *(medical)* Depression is a type of mental illness, characterized by a person's having long periods of low mood: *Tiredness, apathy, loss of appetite, lack of energy and sleeping problems are classic symptoms of depression.* ○ *If you* **suffer from** *depression, it's best to get professional help.* ○ *He killed himself while suffering from* **clinical** *depression.* ○ *She had* **postnatal** *depression after the birth of her first child.* • See also DEPRESSION WEATHER, DEPRESSION HOLE.

de·pres·sive /dɪˈpres·ɪv/ *n* [C] *medical* • A depressive is a person who often suffers from depression.

de·pres·sive /dɪˈpres·ɪv/ *adj medical* • *She's suffering from a depressive* **disorder/illness**.

de·press *obj* REDUCE /dɪˈpres/ *v* [T] to reduce the value of (esp. money), or to reduce the amount of activity in (esp. a business operation) • *A surplus of corn has helped depress the grain* **market/***grain* **prices**. • *The rise in the value of the dollar has depressed the company's* **earnings/profits** *this year.* • *High interest rates are continuing to depress the* **economy**. • *This drug helps depress* (=make lower) *high hormone levels.*

de·pressed /dɪˈprest/ *adj* • *In a depressed market, it's difficult to sell goods unless you lower your prices.* • *This is a severely economically depressed area.*

de·pres·sion /dɪˈpreʃ·ᵊn/ *n* [C] • A depression is a period in which there is very little business activity and not many jobs: *a serious/widespread depression* ○ *The depression in the 1930s was called the Great Depression, or, in Britain, also the Slump.* • See also DEPRESSION WEATHER; DEPRESSION HOLE.

de·press *obj* PRESS DOWN /dɪˈpres/ *v* [T] *slightly fml* to press down or lower • *Slowly depress the accelerator pedal/brake pedal.* • *To operate the mechanism, depress this button/lever.*

de·pres·sion WEATHER /dɪˈpreʃ·ᵊn/ *n* [C] *specialized* an area where the air pressure is low • *The deep depression* **over** *the mid-Atlantic will gradually move eastwards during the day, bringing rain and wind to most areas of Britain.* • See also **depression** at DEPRESS CAUSE SADNESS, DEPRESS REDUCE.

de·pres·sion HOLE /dɪˈpreʃ·ᵊn/ *n* [C] a part in a surface which is slightly lower than the rest • *There was a depression in the sand where he'd been lying.* • *We hid in a slight depression in the ground as the enemy soldiers marched past.* • See also **depression** at DEPRESS CAUSE SADNESS, DEPRESS REDUCE.

de·pres·sur·ize *(obj), Br and Aus usually* **-ise** /ˌdiːˈpreʃ·ə·raɪz/ *v specialized* to (cause (an enclosed space, esp. the inside of an aircraft) to) become lower in air pressure • *The explosion instantly depressurized the cabin.* [T] • *If the cabin depressurizes,* (=If the air pressure within it becomes lower), *oxygen masks will automatically drop down.* [I]

de·pres·sur·iz·a·tion, *Br and Aus usually* **-i·sa·tion** /£diːˌpreʃ·ᵊr·aɪˈzeɪ·ʃᵊn, $-ə·rɪ-/ *n* [U]

de·prive *obj* **of** *obj* /dɪˈpraɪv/ *v prep* [T] to take (something, esp. something necessary or pleasant) away from (someone) • *He claimed that he had been deprived of his freedom/rights.* • *No one can function properly if they are deprived of adequate sleep.* • *She said that the treatment she had received in the hospital had completely deprived her of her dignity.* • *(humorous) We've been deprived of your company* (=We have not seen you) *for far too long!*

de·pri·va·tion /ˌdep·rɪˈveɪ·ʃᵊn/ *n* • *There is awful deprivation* (=There are very bad living conditions) *in the shanty towns.* [U] • *There were food shortages and other deprivations* (=lack of the things that are usually considered necessary for a pleasant life) *during the Civil War.* [C]

de·prived /dɪˈpraɪvd/ *adj* • Deprived means not having the things that are necessary for a pleasant life, such as enough money, food or good living conditions: *He's a deprived child.* ○ *She had a deprived childhood/comes from a deprived background.* ○ *They live in a deprived area of London.*

dept *n* [C] *abbreviation for* DEPARTMENT

depth DISTANCE DOWN /depθ/ *n* the distance down either from the top of something to the bottom, or to a distance below the top surface of something • *What is the depth* **of** *this lake/pond/river/part of the sea?* [U] • *There are very few fish* **at** *depths* (=distances below the surface) *below 3000 metres.* [C] • *The swimming pool is 3 metres* **at** *its greatest depth* (=distance below the surface). [C] • *The river froze* **to** *a depth* (=distance below the surface) **of** *over a metre.* [C] • *If you're not a good swimmer, don't go* **out of** *your depth* (=into water which would cover your head if you stood up in it). [U] • *(fig.) I was in the advanced class, but I was* **beyond/out of** *my depth* (=it was too difficult for me), *so I changed to the intermediate class.* [U] • *(fig.) How could you* **sink to** *such* **a** *depth* (=behave so badly)? [U] • A **depth charge** is a bomb which explodes under water. • See also DEEP DOWN.

depths /depθs/ *pl n* • *(literary)* **The depths** are the lowest part of esp. the sea: *The ship sank slowly to the depths* **of** *the ocean.* • *(fig.) How could you sink to such depths* (=behave so badly)?

depth DISTANCE BACKWARDS /depθ/ *n* [U] the distance from the front to the back of something • *I'll just measure the depth* **of** *this cupboard/shelf.* • If something is **in the depth(s) of** somewhere, it is in the middle of it, and a long distance from the edges of it: *The house is in the depths of the forest.* ○ *They live in the depth of the countryside.* ○ *You're crazy to go out in the depth of winter without a coat.* • See also DEEP FRONT TO BACK.

depth STRENGTH /depθ/ *n* [U] (esp. of a feeling or state) the quality of being strong, extreme or detailed • *He spoke with great depth* **of** *feeling about how kind they had been to him.* • *Ann's depth of* **experience/knowledge** *will be of great value to the department.* • *No one realized that she* **had such a** *depth* **of** *courage.* • If you are **in the depth(s) of** a negative feeling, you feel it extremely strongly: *He was in the depth of* **despair**

about losing his job. • If something happens **in the depth(s)** of a situation, it happens when the situation is being most strongly experienced: *The company was started in the depth of the recession of the 1930s.* • See also DEEP STRONGLY FELT.

depths /depθs/ *pl n* • *No one realized that she* **had** *such depths* (= depth) **of** *courage/feeling.*

depth SERIOUSNESS /depθ/ *n* the ability to think seriously about something • *Terry lacks depth – he's a very superficial sort of person.* [U] • *Her writing shows* **an** *astonishing depth.* [U] • If you do something **in** depth, you do it in a serious and detailed way: *I'd like to look at this question in some depth.* [U] • See also DEEP COMPLICATED.

depths /depθs/ *pl n* • *Her writing shows astonishing depths* (= depth). • *She* **has** *depths* (= serious qualities) *her friends would never guess at.* • *Jo has* **hidden** *depths* (= serious qualities that you do not see immediately).

depth LOW SOUND /depθ/ *n* [U] the quality of sounding low • *The depth* **of** *his voice makes him sound older than he is.* • See also DEEP LOW.

depth DARKNESS /depθ/ *n* [U] the quality of being dark and strong (esp. in a colour) • *I love the depth* **of** *colour in her early paintings.* • See also DEEP DARK.

dep·u·ta·tion /ˌdep·jʊˈteɪ·ʃən/ *n* [C + sing/pl v] a group of people sent to speak or act for others • *They led/sent a deputation* **to** *Parliament.* • *The deputation* **from** *the EU arrives/arrive tomorrow.* • *The minister has agreed to receive a deputation* **of** *local government officials.* • *She was sent* **on** *a deputation* **to** *see the Pope.*

de·pute *obj* /dɪˈpjuːt/ *v* [T] *fml* • To depute someone is to ask them to act or speak for you: *I've deputed Kate Brown* **to** *speak for me at the conference.* [+ obj + *to* infinitive] • If you depute something **to** someone, you ask them to do it for you: *She's deputing the organization of the exhibition* **to** *Sara.*

dep·u·ty /£ˈdep·jʊ·ti, $-t̬i/ *n* [C] a person who is given the power to act instead of another person, or the person whose rank is immediately below that of the leader of an organization • *I'd like you to meet Ann Gregory, my deputy.* • *I'm* **acting as** *deputy while the boss is away.* • *She's the deputy (head)* **of** *a large school in the East End of London.* • *He is the deputy chairperson/Foreign Minister/manager/mayor/(Am) sheriff.*

dep·ut·ize, *Br and Aus usually* **–ise** /ˈdep·jʊ·taɪz/ *v* [I] • *I'm deputizing* **for** (= doing the job of) *the director during his absence.*

de·rail *obj* /ˌdiːˈreɪl/ *v* [T] to cause (esp. a train) to fall off the tracks it was travelling on • *The train was derailed by a large boulder which had fallen across the track.* • *(fig.) Renewed fighting threatens to derail* (= stop from continuing to advance) *the peace negotiations/talks.*

de·rail·ment /ˌdiːˈreɪl·mənt/ *n* [C] • *There's been a derailment just outside Crewe, and many people are feared dead.*

de·ran·ged /dɪˈreɪndʒd/ *adj* completely unable to think clearly or behave in a controlled way, esp. because of being mentally ill • *a deranged criminal/mind/personality* • *In the book, 'Jane Eyre', Mr Rochester keeps his* **mentally** *deranged wife locked away in an attic.*

de·range·ment /dɪˈreɪndʒ·mənt/ *n* [U] • *Because of lack of food and sleep, many of the prisoners were* **in a state of (mental)** *derangement.*

der·by SPORTING EVENT /£ˈdɑː·bi, $ˈdɜːr-/ *n* [C] a sporting event between teams in the same area, or *(esp. Am)* a sporting event in which any competitor can take part • *There's a* **local** *derby tonight between Manchester United and Manchester City.* • *(esp. Am) He won first prize in the annual New Hampshire fishing derby.*

Der·by HORSE RACE /£ˈdɑː·bi, $ˈdɜːr-/ *n* [U] **the Derby** a famous British horse race that happens every year in June at the town of Epsom • *Our friend owns a horse that's running in the Derby this year.*

der·by HAT /£ˈdɑː·bi, $ˈdɜːr-/ *n* [C] *Am for* BOWLER (HAT)

de·reg·u·late *obj* /ˌdiːˈreg·jʊ·leɪt/ *v* [T] to remove national or local government controls or rules from (esp. business activity) • *The government plans to deregulate the banking industry/the bus system/the economy.*

de·reg·u·la·tion /ˌdiː·reg·jʊˈleɪ·ʃən/ *n* [U] • *There are concerns that the deregulation* **of** *broadcasting could lead to a lowering of standards.*

de·re·lict IN BAD CONDITION /ˈder·ə·lɪkt/ *adj* (esp. of a building) not cared for and in bad condition; DILAPIDATED • *a derelict building/site* • *There are plans to redevelop an area of derelict land near the station.* • *The theatre has been left to* **stand/lie** *derelict.*

de·re·lic·tion /ˌder·əˈlɪk·ʃən/ *n* [U] • *The old railway cottages were in a state of dereliction.* [U] • See also DERELICTION.

de·re·lict PERSON /ˈder·ə·lɪkt/ *n* [C] *fml* a person who has no home or money and often lives outside; a TRAMP

de·re·lic·tion /ˌder·əˈlɪk·ʃən/ *n* (a) failure to do what you should do • *What you did was a* **grave** *dereliction* **of duty**. [C] • *She has been accused of dereliction* **of** *responsibility.* [U] • See also **dereliction** at DERELICT.

de·ride *obj* /dɪˈraɪd/ *v* [T] *fml* to laugh at (someone or something) in a way which shows you think they are ridiculous or of no value • *I was derided* **for** *making such a stupid suggestion.* • *He derided my efforts to sing* **as** *pathetic.*

de·ri·sion /dɪˈrɪʒ·ən/ *n* [U] • *They treated his suggestion* **with** *derision.* • *Her speech was met with* **hoots/howls of** *derision.*

de·ri·sive /dɪˈraɪ·sɪv/, **de·ri·so·ry** *adj* • *derisive laughter* • *a derisive comment/remark/term* • See also DERISORY.

de·ri·sive·ly /dɪˈraɪ·sɪv·li/ *adv*

de ri·gueur /£də·rɪˈgɜːʳ, $-ˈgɜːr/ *adj* [after v] demanded by fashion, custom, etc. • *At the place where I work, smart suits are de rigueur* **for** *the women.* • *Among the kids in my class, it's de rigueur* **to** *be interested in computer games.* [+ *to* infinitive]

de·ri·so·ry /£dɪˈraɪ·sər·i, $-ə·i/ *adj* (of an amount) not worth being considered seriously because of being so small • *They work very hard but they only earn a derisory amount.* • See also **derisory** at DERIDE.

de·rive *obj* /dɪˈraɪv/ *v* [T always + adv/prep] to get or obtain (something) (from something else) • *The institute derives all its money* **from** *foreign investments.* • *She derives great joy/pleasure/satisfaction* **from/out of** *playing the violin.*

de·ri·va·tive /£dɪˈrɪv·ə·tɪv, $-t̬ɪv/ *adj disapproving* • If something is derivative, it is not the product of new ideas, but has been developed from something else: *His music/painting/style is terribly derivative.*

de·rive from *obj v prep* [T] (of things) to come from (something); to originate from • *The English word 'olive' derives from the Latin word 'oliva'.* • *Most of his ideas derive from those of his parents.*

de·ri·va·tive /£dɪˈrɪv·ɪ·tɪv, $-ə·t̬ɪv/ *n* [C] *specialized* • *Romanian is a derivative* **of** *Latin.* • *(specialized) Petrol is a derivative* **of** (= is made from) *coal.*

de·ri·va·tion /ˌder·ɪˈveɪ·ʃən/ *n* • *I'm very interested in the derivations of words* (= where they come from). [C] • *New ideas are often formed by a process of derivation* **from** *existing ideas.* [U]

der·ma·ti·tis /£ˌdɜː·məˈtaɪ·tɪs, $ˌdɜːr·məˈtaɪ·t̬əs/ *n* [U] *medical* a disease in which the skin is red and painful

der·ma·tol·o·gy /£ˌdɜː·məˈtɒl·ə·dʒi, $ˌdɜːr·məˈtɑː·lə-/ *n* [U] the scientific study of the skin and its diseases

der·ma·tol·o·gist /£ˌdɜː·məˈtɒl·ə·dʒɪst, $ˌdɜːr·məˈtɑː·lə-/ *n* [C] • A dermatologist is a doctor who studies and treats skin diseases.

de·rog·a·tory /£dɪˈrɒg·ə·tər·i, £-tri, $-ˈrɑː·gə·tɔːr-/ *adj* showing that you have a low opinion of something; critical; PEJORATIVE • *She complained that he was always making derogatory* **comments/remarks** *about her.* • *His statements were very derogatory* **of/to/towards** *his colleagues.*

der·rick /ˈder·ɪk/ *n* [C] a type of CRANE (= machine with an arm-like part) used for moving things on and off ships, or a tower above an **oil well** (= a hole in the ground for the removal of oil)

der·ring–do /ˌder·ɪŋˈduː/ *n* [U] *dated* brave action, without any consideration of the danger involved • *The film shows the spy's brave* **acts/deeds/feats of** *derring-do.*

derv /£dɜːv, $dɜːrv/ *n* [U] *Br* a type of liquid fuel, used esp. in a truck or car; DIESEL

der·vish /£ˈdɜː·vɪʃ, $ˈdɜːr-/ *n* [C] a member of a Muslim religious group which has an energetic dance as part of its worship • *The children were dancing like* **whirling** *dervishes* (= in an uncontrolled way).

de·sal·in·ate *obj* /ˌdiːˈsæl·ɪ·neɪt/ *v* [T] to remove salt from (esp. sea water)

de·sal·in·a·tion /£ˌdiː·sæl·ɪˈneɪ·ʃən, $diːˌsæl-/ *n* [U] • *The Canary Islands rely on desalination for much of their water.* • *The desalination* **plant** (= factory) *can process up to 20m gallons of water a day.*

de·scale *obj* /ˌdiːˈskeɪl/ *v* [T] to remove SCALE (= a layer of hard white material) from • *What's the best way to descale these pipes?* • *This kettle needs descaling.*

des·cant /ˈdes·kænt/ *n* [C] a part of a piece of music which is sung or played at the same time as the main tune, but higher • *One group of children sang the theme, and another sang the* *descant.* • A **descant recorder** is a RECORDER (=wind instrument) with a high PITCH (=sound).

de·scend *(obj)* /dɪˈsend/ *v* to go or come down (something) • *The path descended steeply into the valley below.* [I] • *(slightly fml) Jane descended the stairs.* [T] • *(fig.) Darkness/night descended* (=It became dark/night). [I] • *(fig.) The situation rapidly descended* **into** (=became worse so that it was) *chaos.* [I] • *(fig.)* If someone descends (**to** something), they do something bad: *I never thought she would descend so far as to steal.* [I] ○ *I never thought she would descend to illegal behaviour.* [I] ○ *I never thought she would descend to* **the level of** *stealing.* [I] ○ *I never thought she would descend to stealing.* [I]

de·scent /dɪˈsent/ *n* • *The plane began (to* **make***) its* **final** *descent* (=journey down) *into the airport.* [U] • *There is a steep descent* (=way down, such as a path) *down the hillside/mountain to the village below.* [C] • *(fig.)* Descent can also be used to refer to a change in someone's behaviour, or in a situation, from good to bad: *His descent* **into** *crime was rapid.* [U] ○ *The economy's descent* **into** *recession began several months ago.* [U]

de·scend from *obj v prep* [T] (esp. of a living thing) to have developed from • *All living creatures are thought to descend from an organism that came into being three billion years ago.* • *(fig.) His ideas descend from those of Confucius.*

de·scend·ant /dɪˈsen·dᵊnt/ *n* [C] • *He has no descendants* (=children, or children of his children, etc.) • *They claim to be descendants* (=children, or children of the children, etc.) **of** *a French duke.* • *We owe it to our descendants* (=people younger than us who will live after we have died) *to leave them a clean world to live in.* • Compare ANCESTOR.

de·scend·ed /dɪˈsen·dɪd/ *adj* [after v; always +*from*; not gradable] • *He says he is descended* **from** (=is related to) *William the Conqueror.* • *Humans are descended* **from** (=developed from) *ape-like creatures.*

de·scent /dɪˈsent/ *n* [U] • *She's a woman* **of** *mixed/Scottish/Thai descent.* • *The king claims* **direct** *descent* **from** *Mohammed.* • *They trace their* **line of** *descent back to a French duke.*

de·scend on/u·pon *obj v prep* [T] to visit (someone) or arrive (somewhere) suddenly, without warning, or without being invited • *Sorry to descend on you like this, but we had no time to phone.* • *The police descended on the house in the early morning and caught the whole gang.* • *(fig.) A feeling of despair descended upon* (=was felt by) *us as we realized that we were completely lost.* • *(fig.) Silence descended on the room* (=The people in the room became quiet).

de·scent /dɪˈsent/ *n* [U] • *Local people are preparing for the descent* **of** (=(unwanted) arrival of) *thousands of visitors* **on** *their village for the yearly pop festival.*

de·scribe *obj* /dɪˈskraɪb/ *v* [T] to say or write what (someone or something) is like • *In about 350 words, describe the perfect parent, politician or teacher.* • *Could you describe your attacker, miss?* • *He described the painting* **in detail**. • *After they were released, the hostages* **graphically** *described their experiences.* • *The book* **vividly** *describes the area's mountain scenery.* • *Let me describe* (**to** *you*) **how** *it happened.* [+ *wh-*word] • *She described Gary* **as** (=said he was) *shy, but I'd say he was just rude.* • *Would you describe yourself* **as being** (=Do you think you are) *a hard worker?* • *(dated)* If you describe a shape, you draw it or move in a direction that follows the line of it: *He used compasses to describe a circle.* ○ *They watched as the missile described a* **curve** *across the night sky.*

de·scrip·tion /dɪˈskrɪp·ʃᵊn/ *n* • *Write a description* **of** *your favourite seaside resort.* [C] • *A customer has* **given** *the police a very* **accurate/detailed/full/precise** *description* **of** *the men who robbed the post office.* [C] • *A girl* **answering** *the description* **of** *missing teenager, Angela Jones, was last night spotted in Hull.* [C] • *The hotel we stayed in didn't* **fit** *the description that we'd been given of it.* [C] • *Your essay contains too much description, and not enough discussion of the issues.* [U] • *Boats* **of every** *description* (=of all types) *were entering the harbour.* [U] • If something **defies** or **is beyond** description, there is so much of it, or it has a particular quality to such a degree, that it is impossible to describe it accurately: *Her beauty is beyond description.* [U] ○ *The state of Bart's room defies description* (=is very bad)! [U]

de·scrip·tive /£dɪˈskrɪp·tɪv, $-t̬ɪv/ *adj* • *In the exam we had to write one descriptive essay and one discussion essay.* • A descriptive area of study is one that is based on saying what its subject is really like, rather than on providing theories about it: *descriptive linguistics/sociology/statistics*

de·se·crate *obj* /ˈdes·ɪ·kreɪt/ *v* [T] to damage or show a lack of respect towards (esp. something holy) • *The mosque/shrine/temple had been desecrated by vandals.* • *It's a crime to desecrate the country's flag.*

de·se·cra·tion /ˌdes·ɪˈkreɪ·ʃᵊn/ *n* [U] • *People were horrified at the desecration* **of** *the cemetery.*

de·seg·re·gate *obj* /ˌdiːˈseg·rɪ·geɪt/ *v* [T] to end **segregation** (=separation) between races (or sexes) in (an organization) • *President Truman desegregated the American armed forces in 1948.* • *The plans to desegregate the schools/universities were met with opposition.*

de·seg·re·ga·tion /ˌdiː·seg·rɪˈgeɪ·ʃᵊn/ *n* [U] • *Martin Luther King Jr led a campaign aimed at the desegregation* **of** *all public services, including schools, restaurants, stores, and transport.*

de·se·lect *obj* /ˌdiː·səˈlekt/ *v* [T] *specialized* (in British politics, of a local political party) to choose not to have the person who already represents your party as your CANDIDATE (=a person competing for an elected position) at the next election • *He was deselected by his local constituency party because he didn't support the Prime Minister.*

de·sen·si·tize *obj, Br and Aus usually* **-ise** /ˌdiːˈsent·sɪ·taɪz/ *v* [T] to cause (someone) to experience esp. an emotion or a pain less strongly than before • *Seeing too much violence on television can desensitize people* **to** *it.* • *People who suffer from allergies can sometimes be given injections to help desensitize them.* • *Where I had the operation, the skin has* **become** *completely desensitized.*

de·sen·si·tiz·a·tion, *Br and Aus usually* **-i·sa·tion** /diˌsent·sɪ·taɪˈzeɪ·ʃᵊn/ *n* [U]

de·sert *(obj)* RUN AWAY /£dɪˈzɜːt, $-ˈzɜːrt/ *v* to leave (the armed forces) without permission and with no intention of returning • *During the war, if soldiers deserted and were caught, they were shot.* [I] • *Many soldiers deserted* **to** *the enemy.* [I] • *How many people desert* **(from)** *the army each year?* [I +*from*]

de·sert·er /£dɪˈzɜː·tər, $-ˈzɜːr·t̬ɚ/ *n* [C] • A deserter is a person who leaves the army, navy or air force without permission.

de·ser·tion /£dɪˈzɜː·ʃᵊn, $-ˈzɜːr-/ *n* • *During the war, desertion was punishable by death.* [U] • *There were thousands of desertions in the last weeks of the war.* [C] • *(fig.) There have been* **mass** *desertions* **from** (=a lot of people have left) *the party in recent months.* [C]

de·sert *obj* LEAVE BEHIND /£dɪˈzɜːt, $-ˈzɜːrt/ *v* [T] to leave (someone) without help or in a difficult situation • *Please don't desert me: I can't do this on my own!* • *He deserted* (=stopped living with) *his wife and child* **for** *another woman.* • If something, such as a quality, deserts you, you temporarily lose it: *Faced with the exam paper, all my confidence/courage deserted me!*

de·sert·ed /£dɪˈzɜː·tɪd, $-ˈzɜːr·t̬ɪd/ *adj* • *a deserted building/street/town* (=one with no people in it) • *I like to go swimming early in the morning, when the pool is* **largely** *deserted.* • *The town is crowded now, but the place is completely deserted* (=does not have many visitors) *in winter!*

de·ser·tion /£dɪˈzɜː·ʃᵊn, $-ˈzɜːr-/ *n* [U] • *Roger got his divorce on the grounds of desertion* (=because his wife had stopped living with him). • *She found it hard to come to terms with her father's desertion* **of** (=stopping living with) *his family.*

de·sert SANDY AREA /£ˈdez·ət, $-ɚt/ *n* (a large area of) land covered with sand or rocks, where there is very little rain and not many plants • *The Gobi, Kalahari and Sahara Deserts are all deserts, but they don't all have the same features.* [C] • *It is often very hot in* **the desert**. [U] • *They were lost* **in** *the desert for nine days.* [U] • *We had to cross a large area of arid, featureless desert.* [U] • *Not many plants are able to survive in the strong desert sun.* • *(fig.) This town is a cultural/intellectual desert* (=a place with little art, music, serious thinking, etc.). [C] • **Desert boots** are boots made usually of SUEDE (=a type of leather) which reach the ANKLE and are tied with LACES (=strings). • A **desert island** is an island, esp. in the tropics, where no people live: *Robinson Crusoe was* **marooned on** *a desert island.*

de·ser·ti·fi·ca·tion /£dɪˌzɜː·tɪ·fɪˈkeɪ·ʃᵊn, $-ˌzɜːr·t̬ə-/ *n* [U] *specialized* • Desertification is the process by which land changes into desert.

de·serts /£dɪˈzɜːts, $-ˈzɜːrts/ *pl n* the thing you deserve • *We all* **get** *our deserts in the end.*

de·serve *(obj)* /£dɪˈzɜːv, $-ˈzɜːrv/ *v* [not *be deserving*] to have earned or to be given (something) because of the way you have behaved or the qualities you have • *After all that hard work you deserve a break/holiday/rest.* [T] • *She does such a good job that she deserves every penny she earns.* [T] • *The charity deserves better support than it is currently* *receiving.* [T] • *You shouldn't have been so mean to your mother – she* **deserves better** (=should be given better treatment). [T] • *Chris deserves our special* **thanks** *for all his efforts.* [T] • *I hope they get the* **punishment** *they deserve.* [T] • *Your proposals deserve serious* **consideration**. [T] • *Your proposals deserve* **to** *be considered seriously.* [+ *to* infinitive] • *They certainly deserved* **to** *win that match.* [+ *to* infinitive] • *One or two points about this report deserve* **being** *discussed in more detail.* [+ v-*ing*] • *(esp. humorous) What have I done to deserve (all) this?* (=The way in which I am being treated is not fair or not what I expected.) [T] • If someone says that you **deserve a medal**, they mean that they admire you for something you have done. • If you say that someone **deserves whatever/everything** they **get**, you mean that they should have to suffer the results of their bad behaviour: *After all the harm he's done to other people, he deserves whatever he gets.* • *(saying)* 'One good turn deserves another' means if someone does something to help you, you should do something to help them.

de·served /£dɪ'zɜːvd, $-'zɜːrvd/ *adj* • *a* **well-***deserved holiday/rest* • *Their victory was* **richly/thoroughly** *deserved.* • *He has a highly deserved* **reputation** *as a cook.*

de·ser·ved·ly /£dɪ'zɜː·vɪd·li, $-'zɜːr-/ *adv* • *She was deservedly praised for her quick thinking during the accident.* • *He won the award for best actor,* **(and)** *quite deservedly* **(so)** (=it was right that he did).

de·serv·ing /£dɪ'zɜː·vɪŋ, $-'zɜːr-/ *adj* • Someone or something that is deserving should be helped because they have good qualities: *a deserving* **cause/charity** • *(fml) His efforts are certainly deserving* **of** (=should get) *praise.* • **The deserving poor** are people who are poor but have good qualities and are not responsible for having little money.

de·sic·ca·ted /£'des·ɪ·keɪ·tɪd, $-t̬ɪd/ *adj* [not gradable] dried • *The old sailor's skin had become wrinkled and desiccated from years of being out in the sun and the wind.* • *Add 100g of desiccated* (=dried and cut into small pieces) **coconut** *to the cake mixture.* • *(fig.) All the party seems to have to offer is the same desiccated* (=old-fashioned) *old ideas.*

de·sic·ca·tion /ˌdes·ɪ'keɪ·ʃᵊn/ *n* [U] • *Varnish was applied to the wood to protect it from desiccation* (=the process of becoming completely dried).

de·sign *(obj)* PLAN /dɪ'zaɪn/ *v* to make or draw plans for (something) • *Who designed this building/dress/furniture?* [T] • *It is now possible to design books/cars by computer.* [T] • *This range of clothing is* **specially** *designed* **for** *shorter women.* [T] • *An architect is designing us a house/An architect is designing a house* **for** *us.* [+ two objects] • *She has a job designing* (=drawing plans for clothes) *for a big fashion house in Paris.* [I]

de·sign /dɪ'zaɪn/ *n* • A design is a plan: *Have you seen the designs* **for** *the new shopping centre?* [C] ○ *They won a prize for their design* **for** *a new type of luggage trolley.* [C] • Design (also **designing**) is the art of making plans or drawings for something: *She's an expert on dress/kitchen/software design.* [U] ○ *He's studying design at college.* [U] • Design is also the way in which something is arranged: *I don't like the design of this kettle.* [U] ○ *The building was originally Victorian* **in** *design.* [U] ○ *This can opener has* **a** *good/poor design.* ○ *There's a design* **fault** *in this folding table – it doesn't open out properly.* ○ *The car has some excellent design* **features**.

de·sign·er /£dɪ'zaɪ·nəʳ, $-nɚ/ *n* [C] • A designer is a person who imagines how something could be made and draws plans for it: *a fashion/menswear/software/theatrical designer* ○ *She was wearing designer jeans/shoes/sunglasses* (=those which are marked to show that they were made by a famous designer). ○ *I can't afford designer* **labels**/*designer* **label** *clothes* (=clothes marked to show that they were made by a famous designer.) • A **designer drug** is a strong illegal drug. There are different types of designer drug. • *(humorous or disapproving)* If someone is a **designer socialist**, or follows **designer socialism**, they are powerful or wealthy but claim to believe that people are equal and should have equal shares in the wealth of the country. • *(often humorous)* If a man has **designer stubble** he lets his BEARD (=facial hair) grow for one cr two days, then keeps it at this length in order to look fashionable.

de·sign *obj* INTEND /dɪ'zaɪn/ *v* [T always passive] to intend • *This dictionary is designed* **for** *advanced learners of English.* • *These measures are designed* **to** *reduce pollution.* [+ obj + *to* infinitive] • *The hospital was originally designed* **to** *take 1000 patients, but now has 2500.* [+ obj + *to* infinitive]

de·sign /dɪ'zaɪn/ *n* [U] • *Did you phone me on my birthday by accident or* **by** *design?*

de·sign PATTERN /dɪ'zaɪn/ *n* [C] a pattern used to decorate something • *a floral/geometrical/abstract design* • *I like the design* **on** *your sweatshirt.*

des·ig·nate *obj* /'dez·ɪg·neɪt/ *v* [T] to choose (someone) officially to do a particular job or to state officially that (something or a place) has a particular character • *The president traditionally has the right to designate his or her successor.* • *Thompson has been designated* **(as/to be)** *captain of the team.* [+ obj (+ *as/to be*) + n] • *She has been designated* **to** *organize the meeting.* [+ obj + *to* infinitive] • *This area of the park has been* **specially** *designated* (=officially stated as being) **for** *children.* • *They* **officially** *designated the area around the nuclear power station* **(as)** *a disaster area/***(as)** *unsuitable for human habitation.* [+ obj (+ *as*) + n/adj]

des·ig·nate /'dez·ɪg·nət, -neɪt/ *adj* [after n; not gradable] • Designate is used after the title of a particular job, esp. an official one, to refer to the person who has been chosen to do that job, but has not yet started doing it: *the Governor/Prime Minister/Secretary General designate.* • Compare ELECT.

des·ig·na·tion /ˌdez·ɪg'neɪ·ʃᵊn/ *n* • *What's her official designation* (=title)? [C] • *On the basis of the plants that grow there, the area qualifies for designation* **as** (=to be called) *a site of special scientific interest.* [U]

de·sign·er /£dɪ'zaɪ·nəʳ, $-nɚ/ *n* See at DESIGN

de·signs /dɪ'zaɪnz/ *pl n infml* plans, often ones which are not honest, to get something or someone for yourself • *Adolf Hitler* **had** *territorial designs* **(on** *neighbouring countries).* • *(humorous) I think Alan* **has** *designs* **on/upon** *your job/wife!* • *The team* **has** *designs* **on** (=is making an effort to win) *the Championship this year.*

de·sign·ing /dɪ'zaɪ·nɪŋ/ *adj* [before n] *disapproving* • A designing person is someone who tries to get what they want for themselves, usually not in an honest way.

de·sire *(obj)* WANT /£dɪ'zaɪəʳ, $-'zaɪr/ *v* [not *be desiring*] to want (something), esp. strongly • *I desire nothing other than to be left in peace.* [T] • *The hotel we stayed in had everything you could possibly desire.* [T] • *Tom's angry words achieved the desired* **effect**. [T] • *(fml) What does her Ladyship desire me* **to** *do?* [T + obj + *to* infinitive] • *(fml)* Desire can also mean make a request: *The President desires* **to** *meet the new Prime Minister.* [+ *to* infinitive] ○ *The President desires* **that** *the new Prime Minister (should) visit him.* [+ *that* clause]

de·sire /£dɪ'zaɪəʳ, $-'zaɪr/ *n* • *He doesn't* **have** *much desire* **for** (=strong feeling of wanting) *wealth.* [U] • *She's trying to find a way of* **satisfying** *her desire* **for** *revenge.* [U] • *Sara* **had** *a* **burning/strong** *desire* **to** *go back to her home country before she died.* [C + *to* infinitive] • *They* **have** *a* **consuming/insatiable** *desire* **to** *make money.* [C + *to* infinitive] • *Several people have* **expressed** *a desire* **to** *see the report.* [C + *to* infinitive] • *Several people have* **expressed** *a desire* **that** *they should see the report.* [C + *that* clause] • A desire is also something that you want: *I don't have many desires.* [C] ○ *At long last, he had his* **heart's** *desire* (=the thing he most wanted). [C]

de·sir·able /£dɪ'zaɪə·rə·bl̩, $-'zaɪr·ə-/ *adj* • If something is desirable, it is worth having and is wanted: *Reducing the size of classes in schools is a desirable aim.* ○ *I think that smoking is one of your less desirable habits.* ○ *He has a* **highly** *desirable job.* • Desirable also means necessary or useful: **It** *is desirable* **that** *you should be computer-literate for this job.* [+ *that* clause] • Desirable can also mean wanted because of being popular or fashionable: *The house is in a very desirable area of the city.* ○ **It** *is not* **socially desirable** *to live in this part of Los Angeles.* [+ *to* infinitive] ○ **It** *is desirable* **to** *be computer-literate for this job.* [+ *to* infinitive]

de·sir·ab·ly /£dɪ'zaɪə·rə·bli, $dɪ'zaɪr·ə-/ *adv* • *a desirably situated house* (=one in a popular or fashionable area)

de·sir·ab·il·i·ty /£dɪˌzaɪə·rə'bɪl·ɪ·ti, $-ˌzaɪr·ə'bɪl·ə·t̬i/ *n* [U] • *Members of the government seem to disagree about the desirability* **of** *the reforms* (=the degree to which they are wanted). • *A lot of emphasis is placed on the desirability* (= importance) **of** *being thin.*

de·sir·ous /£dɪ'zaɪə·rəs, $də'zaɪr·əs/ *adj* [after v] *fml* • *The duke is desirous* **of** *meeting* (= wants to meet) *you.*

de·sire SEXUAL NEED /£dɪ'zaɪəʳ, $-'zaɪr/ *n* the strong feeling that you want to have sex with someone • *After many years of marriage, they still* **feel/have** *a strong desire* **for** *each other.* [C] • *Some people* **satisfy** *their* **sexual** *desires through reading magazines.* [C] • *Beatrice was the* **object of** *Dante's desire.* [U]

de·sir·able /£dɪ'zaɪə·rə·bl̩, $dɪ'zaɪr·ə-/ *adj* • *Most women think Mike is a* **highly** *desirable* (=sexually attractive) *man.*

de·sir·ab·il·i·ty /£dɪˌzaɪə·rə'bɪl·ɪ·ti, $dɪˌzaɪr·ə'bɪl·ə·ṭi/ *n* [U] • *She need have no doubts about her desirability* (= sexual attractiveness).

de·sire *obj* /£dɪ'zaɪəʳ, $dɪ'zaɪr/ *v* [T not *be desiring*] *esp. literary* • *As soon as he saw her, he desired her.*

de·sist /dɪ'zɪst, -'sɪst/ *v* [I] *fml* to stop (doing esp. something that someone else does not want you to do) • *They have been told that their protest has no chance of being successful, but they refuse to desist.* • *The soldiers have been ordered to desist* **from** *firing their guns.* • *The high* **winds** *are expected to desist tomorrow.*

desk [TABLE] /desk/ *n* [C] a type of table that you can work at, often one with drawers • *a computer/office/school desk* • *She sat* **at** *her desk writing letters.* • *He was sitting in his office, with a pile of papers* **on** *his desk.* • *The report* **arrived on/landed on/reached** *my desk* (= I received it) *this morning.* • *Many of the* **desk-bound** (= who have to work sitting at a desk) *staff would prefer a more active job.* • *His work used to involve a lot of travelling, but now he has a* **desk job** (= a job working in an office). • [PIC] **Office** (CS)

desk [SERVICE AREA] /desk/ *n* [C] a place, often with a COUNTER (= a long flat narrow surface), esp. in a hotel or airport, where you can get information or service • *a check-in/enquiries/information/reception desk* • *Helen's working* **on** *the desk until 5 pm.* • *(Am)* A **desk clerk** is a hotel employee who welcomes people arriving to stay there. • (CS)

desk [NEWSPAPER OFFICE] /desk/ *n* [C] an office which deals with a particular type of news for a newspaper • *the arts/foreign/sports desk* • *Jane works* **on** *the foreign desk on a big London newspaper.* • (CS)

desk·top [COMPUTER] /£'desk·tɒp, $-tɑːp/ *adj* (of computer equipment) small enough to fit on the top of a desk • *a desktop computer/machine/printer/system* • **Desktop publishing** (also **DTP**) is the production of finished page designs for books or other printed material, using a small computer and printer. • Compare LAPTOP, NOTEBOOK, PALMTOP.

desk·top [SCREEN] /£'desk·tɒp, $-tɑːp/ *n* [C] *specialized* the image that appears on a computer when you use the type of computer program which makes it possible for you to perform several activities at the same time • *The menu bar with its windows is one of the features of the desktop.*

des·o·late [EMPTY] /'des·əl·ət/ *adj* (of a place) unattractive and empty; not containing any people or anything pleasant • *The house looked out over a bleak and desolate landscape.*

des·o·la·tion /ˌdes·əl'eɪ·ʃən/ *n* [U] • *It was difficult to describe the emptiness, the loneliness, the desolation* **of** *the area.* • *He gazed out of his window at* **the scene of** *desolation outside.*

des·o·late [SAD] /'des·əl·ət/ *adj* (of a person) extremely sad and feeling alone • *She felt desolate when her closest friend moved away to live in another town.*

des·o·lat·ed /£'des·əl·eɪ·tɪd, $-ṭɪd/ *adj* [after v] • *David felt utterly desolated* **at** *losing his job.* • *She was desolated* **to** *discover that she had lost her wedding ring.* [+ *to* infinitive]

des·o·late·ly /'des·əl·ət·li/ *adv* • *He desolately re-read her letter, unable to believe that she was leaving him.*

des·o·lat·ing /£'des·əl·eɪ·tɪŋ, $-ṭɪŋ/ *adj* • *Caring for a dying relative is a desolating business.*

des·o·la·tion /ˌdes·əl'eɪ·ʃən/ *n* [U] • *A feeling of utter desolation came over them, as they realised there was no hope of being rescued.*

de·spair /£dɪ'speəʳ, $-'sper/ *n* [U] The feeling that there is no hope and that you can do nothing to improve a difficult or troubling situation • *They're* **in (the depths of)** *despair* **over/about** *the money they've lost.* • **To** *the despair* **of** *her teachers, Nicole never does the work that she's told to do.* • *After six defeats in a row, a* **mood/sense of** *despair seems to have settled on the team.* • *He was filled with* **deep/utter** *despair* **at** *the prospect of never seeing her again.* • *Their fourth year without rain* **drove** *many farmers* **to** (= caused them to feel) *despair.* • If someone is **the despair of** someone else, they cause difficulties to that person, who does not know how to deal with them: *He's the despair of his parents because he shows no interest in getting a job.*

de·spair /£dɪ'speəʳ, $-'sper/ *v* [I] • *Don't despair! We'll find a way out!* • *I despair* **at/over** *the policies of this government.* • *She despairs* **of** *her son* (= feels that there is no hope that he will improve) *because he shows no interest in getting a job.* • *They began to despair* **of** *ever finding* (= to think they would never find) *their way back through the forest.*

de·spair·ing /£dɪ'speə·rɪŋ, $-'sper·ɪŋ/ *adj* • *a despairing attitude/gesture/glance* • *His voice sounded despairing.*

de·spair·ing·ly /£dɪ'speə·rɪŋ·li, $-'sper·ɪŋ-/ *adv* • *He spoke despairingly of the increase in the number of people who are unemployed.*

des·patch /dɪ'spætʃ/ *n, v* DISPATCH

des·patch·es /dɪ'spætʃ·ɪz/ *pl n* DISPATCHES

de·spe·ra·do /£ˌdes·pə'rɑː·dəʊ, $-doʊ/ *n* [C] *pl* **desperados** or **desperadoes** someone who willingly does risky, dangerous and often criminal things • *a gang of desperados*

de·spe·rate [RISKY] /£'des·pər·ət, $-pɚ-/ *adj* showing a willingness to take risks, esp. because you are in a bad situation that you want to change • *The doctors made one last desperate* **attempt/effort** *to save the boy's life.* • *Desperate* **measures** *are needed to deal with the growing drug problem.* • *They made a desperate* **plea** *for help.* • *The seriousness of the situation fully justifies these desperate* **remedies/solutions.** • *They are involved in a desperate* **struggle** *for freedom.* • *Don't do anything desperate* (= foolishly risky)*!* • Desperate can also mean being willing to be violent, and therefore dangerous: *Members of the public are warned not to approach the man – he is desperate and may be carrying a gun.*

de·spe·rate·ly /£'des·pər·ət·li, $-pɚ-/ *adv* • *They fought desperately for their lives.*

de·spe·ra·tion /ˌdes·pə'reɪ·ʃən/ *n* [U] • Desperation is the feeling that you have when you are in such a bad situation that you are willing to take risks in order to change it: *There was a note of desperation in his voice.* ○ **In** *desperation, they jumped out of the window to escape the fire.* ○ *She turned to crime* **out of** *sheer desperation.* ○ *This sudden change in policy was* **an act of** *desperation on the part of the government.* • *"The mass of men lead lives of quiet desperation"* (Henry Thoreau, in the book *Walden*, 1854)

de·spe·rate [SERIOUS] /£'des·pər·ət, $-pɚ-/ *adj* very serious or bad; extreme • *Something must be done to save the industry from its current desperate* **plight.** • *They are living in desperate* **poverty.** • *There's a desperate* **shortage** *of food in the area.* • *The* **situation** *is desperate – we have no food, very little water and no medical supplies.* • *We're in desperate* **straits** (= have no money). • Desperate can also mean extreme or very great: *I'm in a desperate hurry.* ○ *The earthquake survivors are in desperate need of help.* ○ *He has a desperate desire to succeed.*

de·spe·rate·ly /£'des·pər·ət·li, $-pɚ-/ *adv* • Desperately means extremely or very much: *He was desperately ill.* ○ *She always seems to be desperately busy!* ○ *I'm not desperately keen on watching football.* ○ *He was desperately in love with her.* ○ *They desperately wanted a child.* • *"Desperately Seeking Susan"* (film title, 1985)

de·spe·rate [WANTING] /£'des·pər·ət, $-pɚ-/ *adj* [usually after v] experiencing great need; wanting very much • *They are desperate* **for** *help.* • *(humorous) I'm desperate* **for** *a drink!* • *He was desperate* **to** *tell someone his good news.* [+ *to* infinitive]

de·spe·ra·tion /ˌdes·pə'reɪ·ʃən/ *n* [U]

de·spise *obj* /dɪ'spaɪz/ *v* [T not *be despising*] to feel a strong dislike for (someone or something) because you think they are bad or worthless • *He despises the present government.* • *I hate and despise that kind of cruel behaviour.* • *She despised him* **for** *the way he treated her sister.* • *He despised him***self** *for being such a coward.* • *That's an offer not* **to be** *despised* (= one worth considering seriously).

de·spi·cab·le /dɪ'spɪk·ə·bl̩/ *adj* • If you say that something or someone is despicable, you mean that you strongly dislike them because they are very unpleasant: *despicable behaviour* ○ *a despicable attitude* ○ *He's a despicable human being!* ○ *That was a despicable film.* ○ **It** *was despicable* **of her** *to lie about her friend.* [+ *to* infinitive]

de·spi·cab·ly /dɪ'spɪk·ə·bli/ *adv* • *I think you behaved despicably* (= very badly) *in being so unkind to Harriet.*

de·spite /dɪ'spaɪt/ *prep* without taking any notice of or being influenced by; not prevented by • *Despite the cold wind, they went out without their coats.* • *Despite repeated assurances that the product is safe, many people have stopped buying it.* • *Despite* **the fact that** *there was almost no hope of finding the missing boy, the search party still went on looking.* • *He managed to eat a big lunch despite hav***ing** *eaten an enormous breakfast.* [+ *v-ing*] • If you do something despite your**self**, you do it, although you do not want to do it or know that you should not do it: *Despite himself, he laughed when she teased him about his tie.* ○ *She took the money from her mother's purse, despite herself.*

de·spoil *obj* /£dɪ'spɔɪl, $ˌdiː-/ *v* [T] *fml* to make (a place) less attractive esp. by taking things away from it by force •

Many of the graves had been despoiled. • *Industrial waste is despoiling the environment.*

de·spon·dent /£dɪˈspɒn·dᵊnt, $-ˈspɑːn-/ *adj* unhappy and discouraged because you feel you are in a difficult situation • *He* **became/got/grew** *increasingly despondent when she failed to return his phone calls.* • *She* **felt** *despondent* **about** *ever finding a proper job.* • *A despondent young man stood by the side of the road in the rain, hoping that someone would give him a lift.*

de·spon·dent·ly /£dɪˈspɒn·dᵊnt·li, $-ˈspɑːn-/ *adv* • *"I don't think there's any hope that things will improve," he said, shaking his head despondently.*

de·spon·den·cy /£dɪˈspɒn·dᵊnt·si, $-ˈspɑːn-/ *n* [U] • *There was a mood of despondency among the members of the defeated team.*

des·pot /£ˈdes·pɒt, $-pɑːt/ *n* [C] a person, esp. a ruler, who has unlimited power over other people, and often uses it unfairly and cruelly • *The people are fighting to bring an end to the rule of the evil despot.* • *The king was generally regarded as having been a benevolent/enlightened despot.* • *(humorous) My dad's a bit of a despot!* • See also **tyrant** at TYRANNY.

des·po·tic /£dɪˈspɒt·ɪk, $desˈpɑː·t̬ɪk/ *adj* • *a despotic government/regime/ruler/state*

des·po·ti·cal·ly /£dɪˈspɒt·ɪ·kli, $desˈpɑː·t̬ɪ-/ *adv* • *For years the president ruled despotically.*

des·po·ti·sm /£ˈdes·pə·tɪ·zᵊm, $-t̬ɪ-/ *n* [U] • *After years of despotism, the country is now moving towards democracy.* • *In the French Revolution, the Bastille was a symbol of the despotism* **of** *the monarchy.*

des res /ˌdezˈrez/ *n* [C] *Br humorous infml* a very desirable house or apartment; a desirable RESIDENCE • *She's got a nice little des res in Chelsea.*

des·sert /£dɪˈzɜːt, $-ˈzɜːrt/ *n* sweet food eaten at the end of a meal • *a dessert fork/spoon* • *There's apple pie, ice-cream, cheesecake or fruit* **for** *dessert.* [U] • *If you make the main course, I'll make a dessert.* [C] • *Would you like to see the dessert menu?* • A **dessert wine** is a sweet wine, drunk esp. with a dessert. • PIC Cutlery

des·sert·spoon /£dɪˈzɜːt·spuːn, $-ˈzɜːrt-/ *n* [C] a medium-sized spoon, used esp. for eating sweet food at the end of a meal, or for measuring food in cooking • *Add one dessertspoon* (= the amount that a dessertspoon holds) **of** *sugar.* • Compare TEASPOON; TABLESPOON.

des·sert·spoon·ful /£dɪˈzɜːtˌspuːn·fʊl, $-ˈzɜːrt-/ *n pl* **dessertspoonsful**, **dessertspoonfuls** • A dessertspoonful is the amount that a dessertspoon holds: *Add one dessertspoonful* **of** *sugar.*

de·sta·bil·ize *obj, Br and Aus usually* **-ise** /ˌdiːˈsteɪ·bᵊl·aɪz/ *v* [T] to make (esp. a government, a political unit, or a political or economic situation) less strong or safe, by intentionally causing problems • *A plot to destabilize the government/president/regime has been uncovered.* • *The conflict has had the effect of destabilizing the whole area/country/region.* • *The recent rioting has destabilized the reform process.* • *If imports increase any further, it could destabilize the country's economy.*

de·sta·bil·iz·a·tion, *Br and Aus usually* **-i·sa·tion** /diˌsteɪ·bᵊl·aɪˈzeɪ·ʃᵊn/ *n* [U] • *The president said that he would do everything he could to prevent the destabilization* **of** *the state.*

des·ta·biliz·ing, *Br and Aus usually* **-is·ing** /ˌdiːˈsteɪ·bᵊl·aɪ·zɪŋ/ *adj* [before n] • *The conflict has had a seriously destabilizing effect on the region.*

des·tin·a·tion /ˌdes·tɪˈneɪ·ʃᵊn/ *n* [C] the place to which a person is going or to which a thing is being sent or taken • *We* **arrived at** *our destination tired and hungry.* • *His letter never* **reached** *its* **(final/ultimate)** *destination.* • *The Caribbean is a popular* **tourist***/(Br and Aus)* **holiday***/(Am)* **vacation** *destination.* • Ⓟ

des·tined /ˈdes·tɪnd/ *adj* intended (for a particular purpose) • *The money was destined* **for** *the relief of poverty, but was diverted by corrupt officials.* • *These cars are destined* **for** *the European market.* • Destined also means travelling or being sent to: *This train is destined* **for** *Birmingham.* ○ *Customs officers have seized nearly a ton of heroin destined* **for** *New York.* • If something or someone is destined, they are controlled by the force which some people believe controls what happens, and which cannot be influenced by people: *She is destined* **for** *an extremely successful career.* ○ *He had always felt that he was destined* **to** *lead his country.* [+ to infinitive] ○ *These plans are destined* **to** *fail.* [+ to infinitive] • *(fml or humorous) Do you think* **it** *was destined* **that** *we should one day meet?* [+ *that* clause] • See also **predestined** at PREDESTINATION.

des·ti·ny /ˈdes·tɪ·ni/ *n* the things that will happen in the future • *The destiny* **of** *our nation depends on the result of this vote!* [C] • *She felt that her destiny had been* **shaped** *by her gender.* [C] • *People want to be able to* **control/determine/take charge of** *their own destinies.* [C] • *I don't believe that you can* **escape** *your destiny.* [C] • *What do you think will be the destiny* **of** *the government's new housing legislation* (= What do you think will happen to it)*?* [C] • Destiny is the force that some people think controls what happens in the future, and which cannot be influenced by people: *You can't fight against Destiny.* [U not after *the*] ○ *He is a tragic victim of destiny.* [U not after *the*]

des·ti·tute /£ˈdes·tɪ·tjuːt, $-t̬ɪ·tuːt/ *adj* without money, food, a home or possessions • *The floods have left thousands of people in the area destitute.* • *Destitute families were living in appalling conditions.*

des·ti·tute /£ˈdes·tɪ·tjuːt, $-t̬ɪ·tuːt/ *pl n* • **The destitute** are people who do not have money, food, a home or possessions: *The destitute receive financial aid from the government.*

des·ti·tu·tion /£ˌdes·tɪˈtjuː·ʃᵊn, $-ˈtuː-/ *n* [U] • *Destitution has become a major problem in the capital city.*

de·stroy *obj* /dɪˈstrɔɪ/ *v* [T] to cause, esp. in a violent way, to exist no longer; to cause damage to • *Most of the old part of the city was destroyed by bombs during the war.* • *Many of the documents have been destroyed for purposes of confidentiality.* • *By the 1900s, hunters had* **systematically** *destroyed most of Africa's vast herds of elephants.* • *The car accident seemed to have* **completely/totally** *destroyed his confidence.* • *She was* **utterly** *destroyed* (= She lost all her confidence and her hope) *when her boyfriend left her.* • To destroy an animal is to kill it because it is ill, in pain or dangerous.

de·stroy·er /£dɪˈstrɔɪ·əʳ, $-ɚ/ *n* [C] • A destroyer is a small, fast military ship which carries weapons. • A destroyer can also be a person or a thing that destroys: *War is a great destroyer.* ○ *The former leader was described by his successor as 'the destroyer* **of** *his people'.*

de·struc·tion /dɪˈstrʌk·ʃᵊn/ *n* [U] • *Many people are very concerned about the destruction* **of** *the rainforests.* • *Unusually high winds have left a* **trail of** *destruction over southern Britain.* • *There is a danger that weapons of* **mass destruction** (= those which kill or hurt large numbers of people) *will be used in the conflict.*

de·struc·tive /dɪˈstrʌk·tɪv/ *adj* • *Modern weapons have an extremely high destructive* **force/power**. • *They are very concerned about the destructive effects that violent films may have on children.* • *Lack of trust is very destructive in a relationship.* • *She is behaving in a very* **self-destructive** *way, drinking too much and taking drugs.*

de·struc·tive·ly /dɪˈstrʌk·tɪv·li/ *adv* • *In the company of other children he behaves very destructively.*

de·struc·tive·ness /dɪˈstrʌk·tɪv·nəs/ *n* [U] • *Some groups of football fans have a reputation for destructiveness.*

des·ul·to·ry /£ˈdes·ᵊl·tᵊr·i, ˈdez-, $-tɔːr-/ *adj fml or literary* without a clear plan or purpose and showing little effort or interest • *She made a desultory attempt at conversation but I could tell she had no real interest in talking to me.* • *We played a desultory game of cards.*

des·ul·to·ri·ly /£ˈdes·ᵊl·tᵊr·ᵊl·i, ˈdez-, $-tɔːr-/ *adv fml or literary* • *The audience applauded desultorily at the end of the concert.*

de·tach *obj* /dɪˈtætʃ/ *v* [T] to separate or remove (something) from something else that it is connected to • *You can detach the hood if you prefer the coat without it.* • *Detach the lower part of the form* **from** *this letter and return it to the above address.* • Compare ATTACH CONNECT.

de·tach·ab·le /dɪˈtætʃ·ɪ·bl̩/ *adj* [not gradable] • *The coat has a detachable fur collar.* • *The curtain linings are detachable so you can wash them separately.*

de·tached /dɪˈtætʃt/ *adj* • *The parcel could not be delivered because the label became detached* (= separated) **from** *it in the post.* • A detached **house** is one that is not connected to any other building. Compare **semi-detached** at SEMI- HALF. • If a person is described as detached, it means that they do not show any emotional involvement or interest in a situation: *She seemed a bit detached, as if her mind were on other things.* ○ *Throughout the novel, the whole story is seen through the eyes of a detached observer.* • PIC **Accommodation**

de·tach·ment /dɪˈtætʃ·mənt/ *n* [U] • *She has an air of detachment* (= not being involved) *as if nothing that happens around her could ever touch her.* • See also DETACHMENT.

de·tach·ment /dɪˈtætʃ·mənt/ *n* [C] a group of soldiers who are separated from the main group in order to perform a particular duty • *The military detachment would total 700 men.* • *A detachment* **of** *Italian soldiers has been sent on a peace-keeping mission to the area.* • See also **detachment** at DETACH.

de·tail [INFORMATION] /£'diː·teɪl, $-'-/ *n* a single piece of information or fact about something, or the small features of something that you only notice when you look carefully • *She insisted on telling me every single detail* **of** *what they did to her in hospital.* [C] • *I've sent off for the details* **of** *a job I saw advertised in the paper.* [C] • *I know they've had some sort of argument but I don't know the* **full** *details yet.* [C] • *(humorous) She was telling me all the* **gory** (=interesting and usually personal) *details* **about** *her various marriages.* [C] • *I've forgotten the* **precise** *details* **of** *what he said.* [C] • *So far we only have* **sketchy** *details* **about** *the accident.* [C] • *She has refused to* **disclose/divulge** *the details* **of** *the plan.* [C] • *The newspaper article did not* **give/provide** *any details* **about** *how he died.* [C] • *A police officer* **took down** *the details* **of** *what happened.* [C] • *Can I have your details* (=name and address, etc.), *please?* [C] • A detail is also an unimportant part of something: *Tony has made up his mind to buy a sports car, and as far as he's concerned, finding the money to pay for it is just a detail.* [C] • *Michael is obsessive about detail* (=the small features of things). [U] • *I was just admiring the detail* (=the way in which small features are carefully shown) *in the doll's house – even the tins of food have labels on them.* [U] • *It's his* **eye for** (=ability to notice) *detail* (=small features of things) *that distinguishes him as a painter.* [U] • If you describe or consider something **in detail**, you do it by giving a lot of attention to all the information about it: *We haven't yet had a chance to discuss the matter in detail.* ○ *The book described her sufferings in* **graphic** *detail.* ○ *He went on in* **great** *detail about the curtains and paper he's just chosen for his lounge.* • *I won't* **go into detail** (=tell you everything) *over the phone but I've been having a few little problems with my health recently.*

de·tail *(obj)* /£'diː·teɪl, $-'-/ *v* • *Mr Richards issued a brief statement detailing who attended the meeting.* [T] • *We need to detail* (=give exact information about) **what** *we've spent so far so that we can budget for the rest.* [+ *wh*- word]

de·tailed /£'diː·teɪld, $-'-/ *adj* • *A witness has given a detailed description of the suspect to the police.*

de·tail *obj* [ORDER] /£'diː·teɪl, $-'-/ *v* [T] to order (someone or a small group, esp. of soldiers) to perform a particular duty • *Four soldiers were detailed* **to** *check the road for troops.* [+ obj + *to* infinitive]

de·tail /£'diː·teɪl, $-'-/ *n* [C] • *A detail* (=group which has been given a particular job) **of** *five police officers accompanied the diplomat to his hotel.*

de·tain *(obj)* /dɪ'teɪn/ *v* to force (someone) officially to stay in a place, or *(fml)* to delay (someone) for a short length of time • *A suspect is being detained by the police for further questioning.* [T] • *He was forcibly detained under federal immigration law.* [T] • *They were arrested and detained* **in custody**. [T] • *In many countries, the police cannot detain people* **without trial**. [T] • *Several of the people injured in the accident were detained overnight in hospital.* [T] • *Their army still have the right to detain, arrest and interrogate.* [I] • *(fml) I'm sorry I'm late – I was* **unavoidably** *detained.* [T] • *(Br law or humorous)* If someone **is detained at His/Her Majesty's pleasure**, they are kept in prison for as long as the authorities feel is necessary.

de·tai·nee /ˌdiː·teɪ'niː/ *n* [C] • A detainee is a person who has been officially ordered to stay in a place, such as a prison, esp. for political reasons: *a political detainee*

de·ten·tion /dɪ'ten·tʃᵊn/ *n* • *He claimed that his detention for anti-government activities was unlawful.* [U] • *They were arrested under a law which allows for indefinite detention without trial.* [U] • *Concern has been expressed about the death* **in** *detention* **of** *a number of political prisoners.* [U] • (A) detention is also a form of punishment in which school children are made to stay at school for a short time after classes have ended: *She's had four detentions this term.* [C] ○ *We were kept late in detention.* [U] • A **detention centre** is a type of prison where young people can be kept for short periods of time or *(Am also)* a place where people who have entered the country without the necessary documents can be kept for short periods of time.

de·tect *obj* /dɪ'tekt/ *v* [T] to notice (something that is partly hidden or not clear) or to discover (something) esp. using a special method • *Some sounds cannot be detected by the human ear.* • *Financial experts have detected signs that the economy is beginning to improve.* • *(esp. humorous) Do I detect a note of irritation in your voice, Ann?* • *High levels of lead have been detected* (=discovered using special equipment) *in the atmosphere.* • *Radar equipment is used to detect* (=find the position of) *enemy aircraft.*

de·tec·tab·le /dɪ'tek·tə·bl̩/ *adj* • *The drug is detectable in the body for up to three months after it has been taken.* • *There has been no detectable change in the patient's condition for several days.*

de·tec·tion /dɪ'tek·ʃᵊn/ *n* [U] • *Early detection* **of** *the cancer improves the chances of successful treatment.* • *Special bomb detection equipment has been installed at the airport.* • Detection also means the solving of crimes by police: *The crime detection rate in the area is particularly low.*

de·tec·tor /£dɪ'tek·təʳ, $-tɚ/ *n* [C] • A detector is a device used for finding particular substances or things, or measuring their level: *a lie/metal/smoke detector*

de·tec·tive /dɪ'tek·tɪv/ *n* [C] a police officer whose job is to discover information about crimes and find out who is responsible for them • *Detectives have finally tracked down the killer.* • *I enjoy reading detective stories.* • Detective can be used as part of the title of particular ranks in the police force: *Detective Sergeant Lewis* • **Detective work** is the activity of finding out information about something, which often takes a long time: *After a lot of detective work, I managed to find out where my old school friend was living.*

de·tente /£deɪ'tɒnt, $-'tɑːnt/ *n* [U] *fml* an improvement in the relationship between two countries which in the past were not friendly and did not trust each other • *East-West/global detente* • *The talks are aimed at furthering detente* **between** *the two countries.*

de·ter *obj* /£dɪ'tɜːʳ, $-'tɜːr/ *v* [T] **-rr-** to prevent or discourage (someone) from doing something by making it difficult for them to do it or by threatening bad results if they do it • *The government is bringing in stricter laws to deter drunken drivers.* • *These measures are designed to deter an enemy attack.* • *High prices are deterring a lot of young couples* **from** *buying houses.* • Ⓟ

de·ter·rent /dɪ'ter·ᵊnt/ *n* [C] • *There is disagreement about whether the country needs to maintain a* **nuclear** *deterrent.* • *It is hoped that the severe prison sentences will* **act/serve as** (=be) *a deterrent* **to** *other would-be offenders.* • *The high fines are designed to be an* **effective/powerful** *deterrent* **against** *fraud.*

de·ter·rent /dɪ'ter·ᵊnt/ *adj* • *One of the arguments in defence of the death penalty is its deterrent* **effect/function/value**.

de·ter·gent /£dɪ'tɜː·dʒᵊnt, $-'tɜːr-/ *n* a chemical substance in the form of a powder or a liquid for removing dirt from clothes or dishes etc. • *Put 120 ml of detergent into the washing machine.* [U] • *The release of industrial detergents into the river has caused the death of thousands of fish.* [C]

de·te·ri·o·rate /£dɪ'tɪə·ri·ə·reɪt, $-'tɪr·i·/ *v* [I] to become worse • *The country's economy has been deteriorating for some time.* • *She was taken into hospital last week when her* **condition** *suddenly began to deteriorate.* • *The political* **situation** *in the region has deteriorated* **markedly/sharply/steadily**.

de·te·ri·o·ra·tion /£dɪˌtɪə·ri·ə'reɪ·ʃᵊn, $-ˌtɪr·i·/ *n* [U] • *There has been a continuing deterioration* **in** *the relations between the two countries.*

de·ter·mine *(obj)* [DECIDE] /£dɪ'tɜː·mɪn, $-'tɜːr-/ *v* to control or influence directly; to decide • *The people who live in the area should be allowed to determine their own future.* [T] • *The number of staff we can take on will be determined by how much money we're allowed to spend.* [T] • *Your health is determined in part by what you eat.* [T] • *Eye colour is* **genetically** *determined.* [T] • *(fml) An early morning inspection of the pitch will determine* **whether** *or not the match will be played.* [+ *wh*- word] • *(fml)* **It** *has yet to be determined* **when** *the meeting is to be held.* [T + obj + *wh*- word] • See also **determine** at DETERMINED.

de·ter·mine *(obj)* [DISCOVER] /£dɪ'tɜː·mɪn, $-'tɜːr-/ *v* to find out or make certain (facts and information) • *The police never actually determined the cause of death.* [T] • *I've been completely unable to determine* **why** *my car is making such a strange noise.* [+ *wh*- word] • *It is the responsibility of the court to determine* **whether** *the men are innocent or guilty.* [+ *wh*-word] • *The jury determined* **that** *the men were guilty.* [+ *that* clause] • *Once the medical examination had determined* **that** *there was nothing seriously wrong with me, I felt much better.* [+ *that* clause] • See also **determine** at DETERMINED.

de·ter·mined /£dɪ'tɜː·mɪnd, $-'tɜːr-/ *adj* certain that you are going to do something, esp. when what you want to do is difficult; with your mind clearly decided on a particular plan of action • *I think she'll get the job that she wants – she's very determined/she's a very determined person.* • *I'm determined* **to**

get this piece of work finished today. [+ *to* infinitive] • *He's determined not* **to** *let his parents stop him from doing what he wants to do.* [+ *to* infinitive]

de·ter·mined·ly /£dɪ'tɜː·mɪnd·li, $-'tɜːr-/ *adv* • *He kept on determinedly running despite an injured toe.* • *He was determinedly polite despite the interviewer's aggressive questioning.*

de·ter·mine /£dɪ'tɜː·mɪn, $-'tɜːr-/ *v slightly fml* • *At the age of ten she sat in the darkened theatre and determined* **that** *one day she would act on its stage.* [+ *that* clause] • *It's a story about a man who leaves jail and determines* **to** *reform.* [+ *to* infinitive] • See also DETERMINE.

de·ter·min·a·tion /£dɪˌtɜː·mɪ'neɪ·ʃᵊn, $-ˌtɜːr-/ *n* [U] • *They are pursuing their aims with* **dogged/relentless** *determination.* • *He is a man of* **fierce/ruthless** *determination.* • *She has* **a** *great determination* **to** *succeed.* [+ *to* infinitive] • See also SELF-DETERMINATION.

de·ter·mi·ner /£dɪ'tɜː·mɪ·nəʳ, $-'tɜːr·mɪ·nɚ/ *n* [C] *specialized* in grammar, a word which is used before a noun to show which particular example of the noun you are referring to • *In the phrases 'my first boyfriend' and 'that strange woman', the words 'my' and 'that' are determiners.* • LP **Articles, Determiners**

de·ter·min·i·sm /£dɪ'tɜː·mɪ·nɪ·zᵊm, $-'tɜːr-/ *n* [U] the theory which states that everything that happens must happen the way it does and could not have happened any other way

de·ter·rent /dɪ'ter·ᵊnt/ *n, adj* See at DETER

de·test *(obj)* /dɪ'test/ *v* [not *be detesting*] to hate; dislike a lot • *She said that she detests any kind of cruelty.* • *I detest warm milk – it makes me feel sick.* • *The country is ruled by a detested dictator.* • *I detest having to get up when it's dark outside.* [+ *v-ing*]

de·tes·tab·le /dɪ'tes·tə·bl/ *adj fml* • *a detestable coward*

de·tes·tab·ly /dɪ'tes·tə·bli/ *adv fml*

de·tes·ta·tion /ˌdiː·tes'teɪ·ʃᵊn/ *n* [U] *fml* • *The country's president is regarded with detestation.* • *Most people have* **a** *detestation* **of** *war.*

de·throne *obj* /£di'θrəʊn, $-'θroʊn/ *v* [T] to remove (a king or queen) from their position of power, or *(fig.)* to beat (a sportsperson who is the best in their particular sport) and in doing so become the best yourself • *(fig.) The world champion was dethroned last night by a young challenger.*

det·o·nate *(obj)* /£'det·ᵊn·eɪt, $'det̬-/ *v* to (cause to) explode • *The terrorists were killed when their bomb detonated unexpectedly.* [I] • *A remote control device was used to detonate the bomb.* [T]

det·o·nat·or /£'det·ᵊn·eɪ·təʳ, $'det̬·ᵊn·eɪ·t̬ɚ/ *n* [C] • A detonator is a small amount of explosive which explodes first in a bomb, causing a larger explosion to happen, or an electrical device which is used from a distance to cause a bomb to explode.

det·o·na·tion /£ˌdet·ᵊn'eɪ·ʃᵊn, $ˌdet̬-/ *n* • *The bomb was prepared so that detonation was delayed for 12 hours.* [U] • *The aircraft blew apart after the detonation* **of** *a bomb disguised as a radio.* [U] • *Underground nuclear detonations are believed to have been carried out.* [C] • *The device involves two successive detonations.* [C]

de·tour /£'diː·tɔːʳ, $-tʊr/ *n* [C] a way of getting to a place which is indirect and longer than the usual one, and which is taken in order to avoid a particular problem, such as a lot of traffic, or in order to do something special • *You'd be best advised to* **make**/*(Am and Aus also)* **take** *a detour to avoid the road works.* • *We* **made**/*(Am also)* **took** *a little detour to drop Sarah off on the way home.*

de·tour /£'diː·tɔːʳ, $-tʊr/ *v* [I] • *We had to detour around the town centre so it took us a little longer to get here.*

de·tox·i·fi·ca·tion /£diːˌtɒk·sɪ·fɪ'keɪ·ʃᵊn, $-ˌtɑːk-/, *infml* **de·tox** /£'diː·tɒks, $-tɑːks/ *n* [U] *specialized* the process of giving medical treatment to someone in order to remove the effects of poisoning from drinking too much alcohol or taking too many drugs • *Detoxification following heroin addiction can be a long and painful process.* • *She has joined a detoxification* **programme.** • A **detoxification centre** is a special place similar to a hospital where people go to receive treatment for drinking too much alcohol or taking too many drugs.

de·tract *(obj)* **from** *obj* /dɪ'trækt/ *v prep* [not *be detracting*] to make (something) seem less valuable or less deserving of admiration, or to take away • *She wears so much make-up that I think it actually detracts from her prettiness.* • *I don't want to detract (at all/one bit) from his achievements, but having a famous father did undoubtedly help his career.* • *These tax-cutting measures are designed to detract* (= take away) *public* **attention** *from the government's past economic failures.*

DETERMINERS

Determiners are words that go in front of a noun and identify what the noun refers to. For example, *bread* is just a general term for the stuff we eat, but if someone says *this bread* or *my bread*, we know which particular bread they are talking about, and if they say *more bread*, we know how much bread they are talking about.

Adjectives can come between a determiner and a noun (*my old coat*), but not before a determiner. Determiners can, however, be qualified by some other determiners: **all** *my money*; **both** *those letters*; **half** *its length*; **twice** *her age*. Words like these are called predeterminers.

- **my, her, his, its, our, your,** and **their** show who the thing belongs to:
  Is this **your** *coffee?* • *They haven't received* **our** *letter.*

- **this, these, that** and **those** show which one is referred to:
  Put it in **this** *bag (pl* **these** *bags).*
  My grandfather built **that** *house (pl* **those** *houses).*

- **what, which** and **whose** in questions ask which one is referred to:
  Whose *photo is this?* • **What** *colour is her hair?*
  Which *dress do you like?*

- **which** and **whose** in statements show which one is referred to:
  The man **whose** *coat you took wants it back.*
  He can't remember **which** *years he visited us.*

- **whichever** and **whatever** refer to items selected from a group:
  Listen to **whatever** *kind of music you like.*
  He's a brilliant footballer in **whichever** *position he plays.*
  ('Whichever' suggests a more limited choice than 'whatever'.)

- **either** and **neither** refer to a choice between two items. The following noun is singular.
  She can write well using **either** *hand.*
  Neither *parent wants to visit the school.*

- **other** and **another** refer to something different, additional or remaining:
  There are **other** *things you could do.*
  Look in the **other** *drawer in my desk.*
  Is there any **other** *news?*
  Give me **another** *apple.* (noun is singular)

- **Determiners that show what quantity is referred to:**
  Every, all, each, both, some, any, many, most, much, lots of, few, several, a little, enough, no.
  LP **Quantity Words** at QUANTITY.

de·trac·tor /£dɪ'træk·təʳ, $-tɚ/ *n* [C] someone who criticizes something or someone, often unfairly • *His detractors claim that his fierce temper makes him unsuitable for party leadership.*

det·ri·ment /'det·rɪ·mənt/ *n* [U] *slightly fml* harm or damage • *Are you sure that I can follow this diet* **without** *detriment* **to** *my health?* • *She was very involved with sports at college, sadly* **to the** *detriment* **of** (= harming) *her studies.*

det·ri·men·tal /£ˌdet·rɪ'men·tᵊl, $-t̬ᵊl/ *adj* • *These chemicals have a detrimental* **effect/impact** *on the environment.* • *They are worried that their decision might prove to be detrimental* **to** *the future of the company.*

de·tri·tus /£dɪ'traɪ·təs, $-t̬əs/ *n* [U] *slightly fml* a loose mass of decaying material, or, more generally, waste material or rubbish, esp. that left after a particular event • *The stadium was littered with bottles and hamburger wrappers – the detritus* **of** *yesterday's rock concert.*

de trop /£də'trəʊ, $-'troʊ/ *adj* [after v; not gradable] *fml or humorous* unnecessary or unwanted; more than is needed or suitable • *(fml) I thought her remarks about Roger's recent problems were rather de trop.* • *(humorous) When I went out to dinner with Helen and Rick, I felt somewhat de trop.*

deuce [NUMBER] /£djuːs, $duːs/ *n* [U] (in tennis) the word used to give the score when both players have 40 points, or (in card and DICE games) the word used to mean two

deuce [EXPRESSION] /£djuːs, $duːs/ *n* [U] **what the deuce** *dated slang* an expression of slight annoyance or anger • *What the deuce is going on here? You kids were sent to bed an hour ago.*

deus ex mach·in·a /£ˌdeɪ·əs·eks'mæk·ɪ·nə, $-'mɑː·kɪ-/ *n* [C] *fml or literary* an artificial or very unlikely end to an event, in which any problems that still exist are dealt with, esp. in too easy a manner • *Shakespeare produces a very unsatisfying deus ex machina in 'The Winter's Tale', when, at the very end of the play, a statue turns out to be a real woman.* • *There has been no deus ex machina to bring down either the president or his government.*

de·val·ue *obj* [MONEY] /ˌdiː'væl·juː/ *v* [T] to reduce the rate at which money can be exchanged for foreign money • *The Chancellor made it clear that he would not hesitate to devalue the currency if it became necessary.*

de·val·u·a·tion /ˌdiː·væl·ju'eɪ·ʃən/ *n* • *The recent devaluation* **of** *the dollar has had a strong effect on the financial markets.* [U] • *There have been several European currency devaluations this year.* [C]

de·val·ue *obj* [NOT VALUE] /ˌdiː'væl·juː/ *v* [T] to cause to be not valued or considered not important • *I don't want to devalue your achievement, but you seem to have passed your exam without doing any work for it.* • *The championships will be seriously devalued if the top athletes refuse to take part in them.* • *Women often devalue them***selves**, *she said.*

dev·as·tate *(obj)* /'dev·ə·steɪt/ *v* to destroy completely or cause great damage to (esp. a place), or to cause emotional suffering or pain to (a person) • *The fire swept through the theatre, devastating the entire building.* [T] • *The earthquake devastated the whole region.* [T] • *The closure of this factory could devastate* (= cause suffering to) *the lives of thousands of families in the area whose incomes depend on it.* [T] • *Divorce can devastate* (= cause suffering) *emotionally.* [I]

dev·as·tat·ed /£'dev·ə·steɪ·tɪd, $-t̬ɪd/ *adj* • *Thousands of people in the areas worst affected by the fighting have left their devastated villages and fled to the mountains.* • *She was utterly devastated when her husband died.*

dev·as·tat·ing /£'dev·ə·steɪ·tɪŋ, $-t̬ɪŋ/ *adj* • *If the bomb had exploded in the main shopping area, it would have been devastating.* • *The team's hopes of winning the championship suffered a devastating* **blow** *last night, when they were defeated in the second round.* • *The drought has had devastating* **consequences/effects.** • *We just heard the devastating news about her son's death.* • Devastating is sometimes used of people's qualities to mean that they have a great effect: *She had a devastating beauty/charm/smile that few men could resist.* ○ *Oscar Wilde was a writer famous in his day for his devastating wit.*

dev·as·tat·ing·ly /£'dev·ə·steɪ·tɪŋ·li, $-t̬ɪŋ-/ *adv* • *(fig.) a devastatingly beautiful boy* (= a boy whose beauty has a great effect)

dev·as·ta·tion /ˌdev·ə'steɪ·ʃən/ *n* [U] • *If disease is allowed to spread among the crops, it will cause widespread devastation.* • *The storm left behind it a* **trail of** *devastation.* • *There was a look of utter devastation on her face when she was told that she had failed her exam.*

de·vel·op *(obj)* [GROW] /dɪ'vel·əp/ *v* to (cause to) grow or change into a more advanced form • *It was soon apparent that something was wrong with him – he wasn't developing like all the other little boys.* [I] • *The fear is that these minor clashes may develop* **into** *all-out confrontation.* [I] • *What started out as a short story eventually developed* **into** *a full-scale novel.* [I] • *Their casual acquaintance developed over time* **into** *a lasting friendship.* [I] • *The whole project developed* **out of** *an idea that I had while I was in the States.* [I] • *This exercise is designed to develop* (= make stronger) *the shoulder and back muscles.* [T] • *I'm looking for a job which will enable me* **fully** *to develop* (= make stronger) *my skills/talents.* [T] • *You've mentioned all the major points in your essay but one or two ideas need developing* (= need to be made more detailed). [T]

de·vel·oped /dɪ'vel·əpt/ *adj* • *Sharks have a* **highly** *developed* (= effective) *sense of smell.* • *He's very highly developed for his age – are you sure he's only twelve?* • See also WELL-DEVELOPED.

de·vel·op·er /£dɪ'vel·ə·pər, $-pɚ/ *n* [C] • If you describe someone, esp. a child, as a particular type of developer, you mean that their physical or mental growth is happening in that way: *Tom was a* **late** *developer, but now he's one of the brightest children in the class.*

de·vel·op·ing /dɪ'vel·ə·pɪŋ/ *adj* [before n; not gradable] • *Many pregnant women are given scans so that the developing fetus can be seen.* • **The developing world/developing countries/less developed countries/developing nations** are the poorer countries of the world, which include many of the countries of Africa, Latin America and Asia, which have less advanced industries.

de·vel·op·ment /dɪ'vel·əp·mənt/ *n* • *A good diet is essential for a child's healthy growth and development* (= growing and becoming more advanced). [U] • *These books are designed to help children with the acquisition and development* **of** (= making more advanced) *the vital skills of reading and writing.* [U] • *The programme traced the development* **of** *popular music* (= the way in which it has changed) *throughout the ages.* [U] • *The region is suffering from under-/over-development* (= having too little/much industry). [U] • *She's working on a development project* (= one to help improve industry) *in Pakistan.* • A development is a recent important event which is the latest in a series of related events: *This week has seen important developments in the crisis.* [C] ○ *Telephone me tomorrow and I'll let you know if there have been any new developments.* [C]

de·vel·op·men·tal /£dɪˌvel·əp'men·təl, $-t̬əl/ *adj* • *They are doing research on the developmental processes in the embryo.* • *She teaches developmental psychology.*

de·vel·op *(obj)* [START] /dɪ'vel·əp/ *v* to invent, or to bring or come into existence • *The government is going to have to develop a new policy/strategy to deal with the problem.* [T] • *They've just developed a new drug which will cure the illness if it's caught in the earliest stages.* [T] • *The company is spending $650 million to develop new products/technology.* [T] • *She's developed some very strange habits since she started living on her own.* [T] • *Large cracks have begun to develop in the wall of the house.* [I] • If an area of land is developed, it is built on, usually by a company which hopes to make a profit in this way: *They're planning to develop that whole site* **into** *some sort of shopping complex.* [T] • If an illness develops, or you develop an illness, you catch it or start to suffer from it: *The virus was discovered in him four years ago, but no symptoms have so far developed.* [I] ○ *The study showed that one in twelve women is likely to develop breast cancer.* [T]

de·vel·op·er /£dɪ'vel·ə·pər, $-pɚ/ *n* [C] • A **(property)** developer is a person or company who makes money from buying land, building new houses, shops or offices, or by changing existing buildings so that they can be sold or rented for profit.

de·vel·op·ment /dɪ'vel·əp·mənt/ *n* • *Mr Berkowitz is in charge of* **product** *development* (= inventing new products) *for the company.* [U] • *There's been a lot of* **housing** *development* (= building of houses) *in the area.* [U] • A development is also an area of new buildings which have been built in order to make a profit: *Quality homes of character and distinction on a new development by Lloyds.* [C] • *(Br)* A **development area** is an area of high unemployment in which the government encourages new industries to start so that more jobs will be created: *This economically depressed region has been designated a special development area.*

de·vel·op *(obj)* [PROCESS FILM] /dɪ'vel·əp/ *v* to make (photographs or NEGATIVES) (from a film) • *I haven't had my holiday photos developed yet.* [T] • *For some reason, the last film I took didn't develop properly.* [I]

de·vel·op·er /£dɪ'vel·ə·pər, $-pɚ/ *n* [C/U] • Developer is the chemical used for developing photographs or films.

de·vi·ant /'diː·vi·ənt/, *Am also* **de·vi·ate** *adj* (esp. of people or behaviour) not usual, and generally considered to be unacceptable • *Deviant behaviour is one of the features of certain types of mental illness.* • *In his speech, the politician criticized what he called 'the deviant minorities' in society.*

de·vi·ant /'diː·vi·ənt/ *n* [C] • A deviant is a person whose behaviour, esp. their sexual behaviour, is not usual and is considered to be unacceptable: *a* **sexual** *deviant*

de·vi·ance /'diː·vi·ənts/ *n* [U]

de·vi·ate /'diː·vi·eɪt/ *v* [I] to do something which is different from the usual or common way of behaving; to go in a different direction • *As children, they were expected to do exactly what their parents told them, and not deviate in any respect.* • *They belong to a branch of the church which deviates in some ways* **from** *other branches.* • *The pattern of weather that we have been experiencing in the last few weeks deviates* **from** *the norm for this time of year.* • *The path follows the river closely, occasionally deviating* (= going in a different direction) *round a clump of trees.*

de·vi·a·tion /ˌdiː·viˈeɪ·ʃən/ *n* • *What we're having for dinner is a slight deviation* **from** *what I'd originally planned.* [C] • *Any deviation* **from** *the party's faith is seen as betrayal.* [U] • (F)

de·vice OBJECT /dɪˈvaɪs/ *n* [C] an object or machine which has been invented to fulfil a particular purpose • *a bugging device* • *a contraceptive device* • *an electronic hearing device* • *The rescuers used a special device* **for** *finding people trapped in collapsed buildings.* • LP **Switching on and off**

de·vice METHOD /dɪˈvaɪs/ *n* [C] a method which used to produce an effect that you want to produce • *a linguistic/literary/rhetorical device* • *The first-person narrator is a stylistic device that has been used by many novelists and poets throughout the ages.* • *A trademark creates an image for a product and can be a powerful marketing device.* • *That rather cool manner of hers is just a device to avoid having to talk to people.* [+ *to* infinitive]

de·vice BOMB /dɪˈvaɪs/ *n* [C] a bomb or other explosive • *an explosive/incendiary/nuclear device* • *The device was detonated in a controlled explosion.*

dev·il /ˈdev·əl/ *n* [C] an evil being, often represented in human form but with a tail and horns • *Hieronymus Bosch was a sixteenth century painter famous for his pictures of devils, freaks and monsters.* • In Christianity and Judaism, **the Devil** is the originator of evil and the enemy of God: *I* **renounce** *the Devil and all his works.* ○ *People were shocked by the horror film about a young child being* **possessed by** *the Devil.* • *(infml)* Devil is also used to refer to someone, esp. a child, who behaves badly: *Those* **little/young** *devils broke my window with their ball.* • *(infml humorous)* Devil is sometimes used to mean a person who enjoys doing things that might be considered to be unacceptable in some way: *"I'm going to wear my short black skirt and my thigh-length leather boots." "Ooh, you devil!"* ○ *"Have another slice of cake – go on,* **be a** *devil!"* • *(infml)* You can also call a person a devil when you are expressing your opinion about something that has happened to them: *I hear you've got a new car, you* **lucky** *devil!* ○ *He's been ill for weeks, the* **poor** *devil.* • *(dated)* **A/the devil of** means extremely difficult or serious: *We've got a devil of a decision/mess/problem facing us here, Pete.* ○ *We had the devil of a* **job/time** *trying to find the place!* • *(humorous or dated)* **Devil-may-care** means not worrying or caring about the results of your actions: *He has a rather devil-may-care* **attitude** *to his studies.* • *(dated, esp. literary)* If you tell someone to **go to the devil** you are annoyed with them and want them to go away: *You can go to the devil, young man, and I hope I never see your face again!* • People sometimes say **speak/talk of the devil** when the person they were talking about appears unexpectedly: *Did you hear what happened to Anna yesterday – oh, speak of the devil, here she is.* • **The devil** can be used to give emphasis to a question: **What** *the devil are you doing?* ○ **Where** *the devil has Jeremy put that paper?* ○ *I haven't seen you for ages!* **How** *the devil are you?* • *(dated) If he catches you doing that there'll be* **the devil to pay** (= a lot of trouble)*!* • **The devil's own** means extremely difficult or bad: *We had the devil's own* **job/time** *finding the place!* ○ *She's had the devil's own luck finding a job.* • If you are **between the devil and the deep blue sea**, you have two choices but both of them are equally unpleasant or inconvenient. • *(saying)* 'Give the devil his due' means admitting that someone you do not like or admire still has particular good qualities: *I don't like the man but – give the devil his due – he works incredibly hard.* • In an argument or discussion, a **devil's advocate** is a person who supports an unpopular or opposite argument in order to make people think seriously about the matter, and question the truth of the most widely held belief: *Joe didn't really believe the things he was saying in the meeting, he was just* **playing** *devil's advocate.* • *(esp. Am)* **Devil's food cake** is a strong-tasting dark chocolate cake. • *(saying)* 'The devil finds work for idle hands' means that if you have nothing to do, you are more likely to get involved in trouble or crime. • *"Why should the Devil have all the good tunes? (Originally 'He did not see why the devil should have all the good tunes')"* (The Reverend Rowland Hill, 1744-1833)

dev·il·ish /ˈdev·əl·ɪʃ/ *adj* • *a devilish* (= evil or morally bad) *plot* • *a young lad with a devilish* (= morally bad but in an attractive way) *grin* • Devilish can also mean extremely difficult or clever: *a devilish problem* • *devilish cunning*

dev·il·ish·ly /ˈdev·əl·ɪʃ·li/ *adv* • Devilishly means extremely: *That's a devilishly* **difficult** *question.* • *What a devilishly* **clever** *plan!*

dev·il·ment /ˈdev·əl·mənt/, **dev·il·ry** /ˈdev·əl·ri/ *n* [U] *dated* • Devilry or devilment is behaviour that intentionally causes a little trouble but is usually intended to be playful or amusing: *The children rang his doorbell, then ran away, purely out of devilment.* ○ *He's* **up to** *some kind of devilment again, I bet.*

de·vi·ous /ˈdiː·vi·əs/ *adj* (of people or plans and methods) dishonest, often in a complicated way, but often clever and successful, or (of roads etc.) indirect, not going the straight way • *You have to be a bit devious if you're going to succeed in business.* • *He has some kind of a devious scheme for avoiding taxes.* • *You'd better watch him – he's a devious bastard!* • *He took a rather devious* (= indirect) *route which avoids the city centre.*

de·vi·ous·ly /ˈdiː·vi·ə·sli/ *adv*

de·vi·ous·ness /ˈdiː·vi·ə·snəs/ *n* [U]

de·vise *obj* /dɪˈvaɪz/ *v* [T] to invent (a plan, system, object, etc.), esp. cleverly or imaginatively • *He's very good at devising language games that you can play with students in class.* • *The cartoon characters Snoopy and Charlie Brown were devised by Charles M. Schultz.*

de·void /dɪˈvɔɪd/ *adj* [after v; always + *of*] *fml* lacking or without (something that is necessary or usual) • *Their apartment is devoid* **of** *all comforts.* • *He seems to be devoid* **of** *any compassion whatsoever.* • *The film was completely/entirely/wholly devoid* **of** *interest.*

de·volve *obj* /£dɪˈvɒlv, $-ˈvɑːlv/ *v* [T] to (cause (power or responsibility) to) be given to other people • *To be a good manager, you must know how to devolve responsibility downwards.* • *The local education authorities have devolved financial control* **to** *individual schools.* • *While my boss is away, most of his work will devolve* **on/upon** *me.*

dev·o·lu·tion /£ˌdiː·vəˈluː·ʃən/ *n* [U] • Devolution is the moving of power or responsibility from a main organization to a lower level, or from a central government to a regional government: *The majority of people in the province are in favour of devolution.*

de·vote *obj* **to** *obj* /£dɪˈvəʊt, $-ˈvoʊt/ *v prep* [T] to give (your time or your effort or your love) wholly to (something you believe in or a person), or to use (a particular amount of time or energy) doing (something) • *The Cabinet minister left government to devote more* **time** *to his young family.* • *She has devoted all her* **energies/life** *to the care of homeless people.* • *At the age of 25 he decided to devote* **himself** *to God.* • *Over half his speech was devoted to the issue of unemployment.* • *Three whole pages of today's paper are devoted to reporting yesterday's bomb explosion.* [+ obj + v-*ing*] • *The report recommends that more* **resources** *be devoted to* (= used for) *teaching.* [+ obj + v-*ing*]

de·vot·ed /£dɪˈvəʊ·tɪd, $-ˈvoʊ·t̬ɪd/ *adj* • *a devoted* (= extremely loving and loyal) *fan/husband/mother* • *Lucy is absolutely devoted* **to** *her cats.*

de·vo·tion /£dɪˈvəʊ·ʃən, $-ˈvoʊ-/ *n* [U] • *He is a teacher who* **inspires** *respect and devotion* (= loyalty and affection) *from his pupils.* • *She will be remembered for her selfless/unstinting devotion* **to** (= work for) *the cause.* • *Ann has a deep devotion* **to** (= love of) *God.* • *He knelt* **in** *devotion* (= in religious worship).

de·vo·tion·al /£dɪˈvəʊ·ʃən·əl, $-ˈvoʊ-/ *adj* • Devotional writing, music, etc. or devotional behaviour are those which are connected with the act of religious worship: *devotional music/poems/practices*

de·vo·tions /£dɪˈvəʊ·ʃənz, $-ˈvoʊ-/ *pl n* • Devotions are acts of religious worship, esp. prayers.

dev·o·tee /ˌdev·əˈtiː/ *n* [C] a person who strongly admires a particular person or is extremely interested in a subject • *He is a great devotee* **of** *the Prime Minister/one of the Prime Minister's greatest devotees.* • *Devotees* **of** *this unusual sport gather monthly at this track to watch the spectacle.*

de·vour *obj* /£dɪˈvaʊəʳ, $-ˈvaʊɚ/ *v* [T] to eat eagerly and in large amounts so that nothing is left • *The young cubs hungrily devoured the deer that the lion had killed.* • *He's just devoured the most enormous plateful of spaghetti.* • *(fig.) She's a very keen reader – she just devours* (= reads quickly and eagerly) *one book after another.* • *(fig.) The flames quickly devoured* (= destroyed) *the building.* • *(fig.)* If you are devoured **by** an emotion, esp. a bad feeling, you feel it very strongly and it strongly influences your behaviour: *He was devoured by jealousy.*

de·vour·ing /£dɪˈvaʊə·rɪŋ, $-ˈvaʊɚ·ɪŋ/ *adj* [usually before n] *literary* • *(fig.) She is driven by a devouring* (= extremely strong and sometimes destructive) *ambition/hatred/passion.*

de·vout /dɪˈvaʊt/ *adj* (of people) believing in a religion in a strong manner and obeying all the rules or principles of that religion • *a devout Buddhist/Christian/churchgoer/Muslim*

de·vout·ly /dɪ'vaʊt·li/ *adv* • *She came from a devoutly Catholic family* • *(fml)* Devoutly also means sincerely and strongly: *He said that he devoutly hoped that an agreement could be reached peacefully.*

de·vout·ness /dɪ'vaʊt·nəs/ *n* [U]

dew /£dju:, $du:/ *n* [U] small drops of water which form on the ground and other surfaces outside esp. during the night

dew·y /£'dju:·i, $'du:-/ *adj* • *a dewy morning* • If someone is **dewy-eyed**, they look young, trusting and not experienced.

dew·drop /£'dju:·drɒp, $'du:·drɑ:p/ *n* [C] a drop of DEW

Dew·ey dec·i·mal sys·tem /£ˌdju:·i-, $ˌdu:·i-/ *n* [U] a system of organizing books and magazines, etc. in LIBRARIES, by which a book is given three numbers for each main subject and another number or numbers, after a **decimal point** (= a small solid circle), for its division within that subject

dew·lap /£'dju:·læp, $'du:-/ *n* [C] a fold of loose skin which hangs under the throat, either of an old person or of an animal such as a cow or some types of dog

dex·ter·i·ty /£dek'ster·ə·ti, $-t̬i/ *n* [U] the ability to perform a difficult action quickly and skilfully with the hands so that it seems easy, or the ability to think quickly and effectively • *The ball was caught* **with** *great dexterity.* • **With** *all the dexterity* (= ability to think quickly) **of** *a politician, he answered the journalists' questions to his own advantage.*

dex·terous, **dex·trous** /£'dek·stᵊr·əs, $-stɚ-/ *adj* • *With one dexterous movement, he flicked the omelette over in the pan.* • *She's very dexterous with her hands.*

dex·terous·ly, **dex·trous·ly** /£'dek·stᵊr·ə·sli, $-stɚ-/ *adv*

dex·trose /£'dek·strəʊs, $-stroʊs/ *n* [U] *specialized* a type of sugar which is found in fruit, HONEY and the blood of animals

DfE /ˌdi:·ef'i:/ *n* [U] **the DfE** *abbreviation for* the British government's Department for Education • *I'm writing to the DfE.*

dho·ti /£'dəʊ·ti, $'doʊ·t̬i/ *n* [C] a loose piece of clothing wrapped around the lower half of the body, worn by men in India

di·a·be·tes /ˌdaɪə'bi:·ti:z, $-t̬əs/ *n* [U] a disease in which the body cannot control the level of sugar in the blood

di·a·be·tic /£ˌdaɪə'bet·ɪk, $-'bet̬-/ *adj* • *diabetic chocolate/jam/soups* (= food made for diabetic people)

di·a·be·tic /£ˌdaɪə'bet·ɪk, $-'bet̬-/ *n* [C] • A diabetic is a person who has diabetes.

di·a·bol·i·cal /£ˌdaɪə'bɒl·ɪ·kᵊl, $-'bɑ:·lɪ·kᵊl/, *Am also* **di·a·bol·ic** /$ˌdaɪə'bɑ:·lɪk/ *adj* extremely bad and shocking • *(infml) Conditions in the prison were said to be diabolical.* • *(infml) His driving is diabolical!* • Diabolical also means evil, or caused by **the Devil** (= in Christianity and Judaism, the originator of evil and the enemy of God).

di·a·bol·i·cal·ly /£ˌdaɪə'bɒl·ɪ·kli, $-'bɑ:·lɪ-/ *adv* • *a diabolically* (= extremely) *clever scheme* • *a diabolically wicked man*

di·a·dem /'daɪ·ə·dem/ *n* [C] a small CROWN with jewels in it

di·ag·nose *(obj)* /£'daɪ·əg·nəʊz, $ˌdaɪ·əg'noʊz/ *v* to recognize and name (the exact character of a disease or a problem) by making an examination • *They've diagnosed cancer.* [T] • *His condition was diagnosed* **as** *some sort of blood disorder.* [T] • *She was diagnosed* **as** *having diabetes/being diabetic.* [T] • *The doctor diagnosed* **that** *the child had an ear infection.* [+ *that* clause] • *It is not possible to diagnose precisely* **which** *of the people who show symptoms will go on to develop the disease.* [+ *wh-* word] • *Failure to diagnose correctly is one of the biggest criticisms made of doctors in a report out this month.* [I] • *The electrician has diagnosed a fault in the wiring.* [T]

di·ag·no·sis /£ˌdaɪ·əg'nəʊ·sɪs, $-'noʊ-/ *n pl* **diagnoses** /£ˌdaɪ·əg'nəʊ·si:z, $-'noʊ-/ • A diagnosis is a judgment about what a particular illness or problem is, made after making an examination: *"What was the diagnosis?" "Arthritis in both joints."* [C] ○ *The doctor has* **made** *an initial diagnosis, but there'll be an additional examination by a specialist.* [C] ○ *The mechanic's diagnosis was that my car needs a new engine.* [C] • *Diagnosis* **of** *the disease* (= saying what it is) *is extremely difficult in the early stages.* [U]

di·ag·nos·tic /£ˌdaɪ·əg'nɒs·tɪk, $-'nɑ:·stɪk/ *adj* • *Diagnostic* **methods/techniques/tests** *for the condition are improving all the time.*

di·ag·o·nal /daɪ'æg·ᵊn·ᵊl/ *adj* (of a line) joining two opposite corners of a four-sided flat shape such as a square or, more generally, going in a sideways direction • *The book has a diagonal black stripe on the cover.* • *Peters received a diagonal pass from Woodford and headed the ball into the net.*

di·ag·o·nal·ly /daɪ'æg·ᵊn·ᵊl·i/ *adv* • *It's quickest if you cut diagonally across the park.*

di·ag·o·nal /daɪ'æg·ᵊn·ᵊl/ *n* [C] *specialized* • A diagonal is a straight line which joins two opposite corners of a four-sided flat shape, such as a square.

di·a·gram /'daɪ·ə·græm/ *n* [C] a simple plan which is drawn to represent a machine, system or idea, etc. whose purpose is often to explain how what is being represented works • *The teacher drew a diagram showing how the blood flows through the heart.* • Ⓙ

di·a·gram·ma·tic /£ˌdaɪ·ə·grə'mæt·ɪk, $-'mæt̬-/ *adj* • *The structure of the engine was explained in diagrammatic form.*

di·a·gram·ma·ti·cal·ly /£ˌdaɪ·ə·grə'mæt·ɪ·kli, $-'mæt̬-/ *adv* • *She explained it diagrammatically* (= using diagrams).

di·al *(obj)* TELEPHONE /'daɪ·əl/ *v* **-ll-** or *Am usually* **-l-** to operate a telephone or make a telephone call to (someone) by pressing a particular series of numbered buttons, or moving a numbered disc, on the telephone • *She picked up the phone and dialled slowly.* [I] • *You've dialled your mother's house three times today.* [T] • *Can I dial this number* **direct**, *or do I have to go through the operator?* [T] • *(Br)* A **dialling code** (*Am and Aus* **area code**) is a particular group of numbers that are dialled before the main number in order to be connected to a particular area, town or country. • *(Br)* A **dialling tone** (*Am and Aus* **dial tone**) is the continuous sound which you hear when you pick up the telephone, letting you know that you can now dial the number that you want. • *"Dial M for Murder"* (film title, 1954) • LP **Telephone**

di·al /'daɪ·əl/ *n* [C] • A dial is the numbered disc on some types of telephone which you move around when you make a telephone call.

di·al MEASURING DEVICE /'daɪ·əl/ *n* [C] the part of a machine or device which shows you a measurement of something such as speed or time, or the device which you move in order to control the instrument • *Can you read what it says on the dial?* • *On my first flying lesson I was horrified by the number of dials in front of me.* • *The dial* **of/on** *his watch* (= the part of it which has the numbers on it) *had a picture of Mickey Mouse on it.* • *I never know where to find any radio station so I just move the dial* (= the device which you move in order to choose what to listen to) *around until I hear what I want.* • LP **Switching on and off**

di·a·lect /'daɪ·ə·lekt/ *n* a form of a language which is spoken in a particular part of a country and contains some different words, grammar and PRONUNCIATION (= the way in which words are said) from other forms of the same language • *a regional dialect* [C] • *A rich variety of dialects still exists throughout the country.* [C] • *The poem is written* **in** *northern dialect.* [U] • LP **Varieties of English**

di·a·lec·tic /£ˌdaɪ·ə'lek·tɪk, $-t̬ɪk/ *n* [U] *specialized* a way of discovering what is true by considering opposite theories • **The** *dialectic is a formal method of argument, in which new positions are reached by testing opposing views against one another.*

di·a·lec·ti·cal /£ˌdaɪ·ə'lek·tɪ·kᵊl, $-t̬ɪ-/ *adj specialized* • *There is a pronounced dialectical quality to her films* (= Her films develop and then try to solve an argument between two opposing opinions).

di·a·logue, *Am also* **di·a·log** /£'daɪ·ə·lɒg, $-lɑ:g/ *n* (a) conversation which is written for a book, play or film, or formal talks between opposing countries, political groups, etc. who have previously not had good relationships • *The play contained some very snappy/witty dialogue.* [U] • *Act Two begins with a short dialogue* **between** *father and son.* [C] • *The two sides involved in the conflict have at last begun to* **engage in** *a* **constructive/fruitful** *dialogue* (= formal talks). [C] • *The rebel leaders have stated that they are now willing to* **enter into** *dialogue* (= formal talks) **with** *the government.* [U]

di·al·y·sis /daɪ'æl·ə·sɪs/ *n* [U] *specialized* a process of separating dissolved substances by putting them through a thin piece of skin-like material, used esp. to make pure the blood of people whose KIDNEYS are not working correctly

di·a·man·té /£daɪ·ə'mɒn·teɪ, $-'mɑ:n·t̬eɪ/ *n* [U] artificial jewels which shine brightly • *The frames of her glasses were encrusted with diamanté.* • *She was wearing a diamanté brooch/diamanté earrings.* • *She was clad from head to foot in shimmering diamanté* (= clothes with artificial jewels fixed to them).

di·a·me·ter /£daɪ'æm·ɪ·təʳ, $-ə·t̬ɚ/ *n* [C] the (length of a) straight line which goes from one side of a round object to another, through the centre of the object • *The diameter* measures twice the radius. [C] • *The pond is six feet* **in diameter**. [U] • PIC› **Shapes**

di·a·me·tri·cal·ly /ˌdaɪ·əˈmet·rɪ·kəl·i/ *adv* completely • *The two politicians have diametrically* **opposite** *points of view/are diametrically* **opposed**. • *They come from diametrically* **different** *backgrounds.*

dia·mond /ˈdaɪə·mənd/ *n* an extremely hard, valuable stone which is used in jewellery, and in industry for cutting hard things, or a shape with four straight sides of equal length but with two opposite angles which are wide and two which are narrow • *Her ring was set with a large diamond.* [C] • *I was given a diamond brooch/necklace for my birthday.* • *She was wearing a diamond-***encrusted** *bracelet.* • *Diamond is the hardest material known.* [U] • *He had worked in the diamond mines of South Africa.* • *The rock is cut from the ground using diamond-tipped saw blades.* • *Joe's socks had diamond* (= four-sided) *patterns on them.* • A diamond is also a card which belongs to one of the four SUITS (= groups) in a set of playing cards. It has a red diamond shape on it: *the six of diamonds* [C] • A **baseball** diamond is the square part of the field on which baseball is played, which is marked off by four equally spaced BASES, or the whole field on which the game is played: *The fielders warmed up for the game by tossing the ball around the diamond.* [C] • **Diamond in the rough** is *Am for* **rough diamond**. See at ROUGH UNEVEN. • *(esp. Br)* A **diamond jubilee** is (a special event which celebrates) the date which happens exactly 60 years after an important occasion. • A **diamond wedding (anniversary)** is the date which happens exactly 60 years after a marriage and is often an occasion for a party or other type of celebration. • *"A Diamond as Big as the Ritz"* (title of a short story by F. Scott Fitzgerald, 1922) • *"Diamonds are a Girl's Best Friend"* (title of a song written by Leo Robin, 1937) • *"Diamonds are forever"* (title of one of the James Bond books by Ian Fleming, based on an earlier advertisement for diamonds, 1956) • LP› **Cards** PIC› **Diamond**

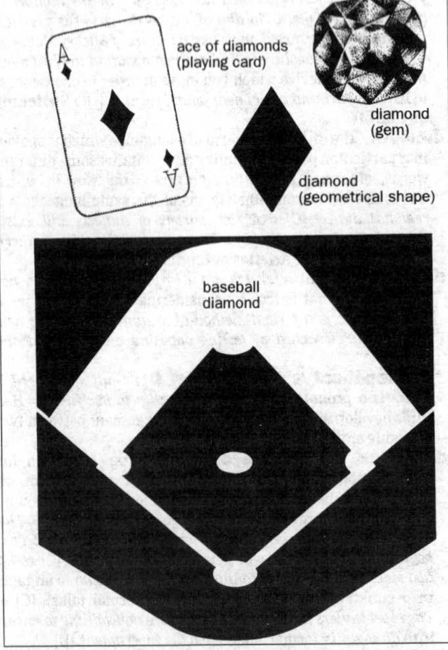

dia·monds /ˈdaɪə·məndz/ *pl n* • Diamonds are jewellery made from diamonds: *Shall I wear the diamonds or the pearls with this dress?*

dia·per /£ˈdaɪ·pəʳ, $-pɚ/ *n* [C] *Am for* NAPPY CLOTHING

di·aph·a·nous /daɪˈæf·ən·əs/ *adj literary* (esp. of cloth) so delicate and thin that you can see through it • *a diaphanous silk veil*

di·aph·ragm /ˈdaɪ·ə·fræm/ *n* [C] a thin piece of material which is stretched across an opening, esp. the muscle which separates the chest from the ABDOMEN (= the stomach and bowels etc.) • *Professional singers learn how to control their breathing using the diaphragm.* • A diaphragm is also a CAP BIRTH CONTROL.

di·ar·rhoe·a, *esp. Am* **di·ar·rhe·a** /ˌdaɪ·əˈriː·ə/ *n* [U] a condition in which the contents of the bowels are emptied too often and in a form which is more liquid than usual, esp. causing pain • *diarrhoea and sickness* • **an attack of** *diarrhoea* • *Many thousands of small children in this devastated area are dying of dehydration as a result of diarrhoea.*

dia·ry /£ˈdaɪə·ri, $ˈdaɪr·i/ *n* [C] a book with a separate space or page for each day, in which you write down your future arrangements, meetings, etc. or in which you record anything of interest that has happened to you during the day, together with your thoughts or feelings that you have at the time • *I'd better note the date of the meeting down in my diary or I'll forget it.* • *I've never* **kept** (= written about what has happened to me in) *a diary.* • LP› **Calendar**

dia·rist /ˈdaɪə·rɪst/ *n* [C] • A diarist is a person who is known for writing or having written a diary: *Anne Frank was a famous diarist of the Second World War.*

di·as·po·ra /£daɪˈæs·pər·ə, $-pɚ-/ *n* [U] *fml* the spreading of people from one original country to other different countries • *the African diaspora* • **The Diaspora** usually refers to the Jews living in different parts of the world outside Israel, or the various places outside Israel in which they live: *the Jews of the Diaspora*

di·a·tribe /ˈdaɪ·ə·traɪb/ *n* [C] *fml* an angry speech or piece of writing which severely criticizes something or someone • *After dinner he* **launched into** *a long diatribe* **against** *the government's policies.*

dib·ble /ˈdɪb·l̩/ *v* [T], *n* [C] (to use) a small tool which makes holes in the ground for planting seeds and small plants

dice GAME /daɪs/, *Am also or old use* **die** *n pl* **dice** a small CUBE (= square box-shaped solid) with a different number of spots on each of its six sides, used in games involving chance • *You need a dice/two dice to play the game.* [C] • **Roll/Throw** *the dice – the highest score wins the first go.* [C] • Dice is also any game involving chance in which the dice are thrown: *Let's play dice.* [U] • *(Am) I asked Mom if we could go to the party, but she said* **no dice** (= no, certainly not). • *"I cannot believe that God plays dice with the cosmos (sometimes 'God does not play dice...')"* (Albert Einstein in a letter, 1926) • PIC› **Games**

dice /daɪs/ *v* [I] • To **dice with death** is to do something extremely dangerous and foolish: *You're dicing with death if you drive at that sort of speed on icy roads.*

dice *obj* CUT /daɪs/ *v* [T] to cut (food) into small squares • *Peel and dice the carrots.* • *Add the diced potatoes to the pan.* • PIC› **Food preparation**

dice·y /ˈdaɪ·si/ *adj* **dicier**, **diciest** *infml esp. Br and Aus* slightly dangerous or uncertain • *The company's finances are looking a bit dicey.* • *The roads are a bit dicey for driving.*

di·cho·to·my /£daɪˈkɒt·ə·mi, $-ˈkɑː·t̬ə-/ *n* [C] *fml or literary* a division between two opposing things, esp. one which is so great that it can never be removed • *There is often a dichotomy* **between** *what politicians say and what they do.*

dick PENIS /dɪk/ *n* [C] *taboo slang for* PENIS

dick STUPID MAN /dɪk/ *n* [C] *taboo slang* a stupid man • *The man's a complete dick! He managed to mess up all my computer files.*

dick·ens /ˈdɪk·ɪnz/ *pl n* **what the dickens** *dated infml* used to express surprise or annoyance • *What the dickens are you doing with that paint!*

Dick·en·si·an /dɪˈken·zi·ən/ *adj* (of living or working conditions) like those described by the 19th century British writer, Charles Dickens, esp. being of below acceptable standard, or (of books and writing) written by or in the style of Charles Dickens • *Dickensian housing/slums/working conditions* • *The bathrooms in this hotel are positively Dickensian – no hot water and grime everywhere.* • *Her latest novel is very Dickensian, and is full of Dickensian characters.*

dick·er /£ˈdɪk·əʳ, $-ɚ/ *v* [I] *Am* to argue with someone, esp. about the price of goods • *She dickered* **with** *the driver until he was willing to drive them for a reasonable fare.*

dick·ey, **dick·y**, **dick·ie** /ˈdɪk·i/ *n* a piece of clothing worn around the neck to fill the space left by an open collar • *The yellow dickey will go nicely with that shirt.*

dick·ey (bow), **dick·ie (bow)**, **dick·y (bow)** /ˈdɪk·i/ *n* [C] *Br infml for* **bow tie**, see at BOW KNOT

dick·head /ˈdɪk·hed/ *n* [C] *taboo slang* a stupid person • *You dickhead – you've dented the back of my car!*

dick·y /ˈdɪk·i/ *adj Br and Aus infml* (esp. of parts of the body) weak and likely to suffer from problems or fail • *Grandad has to be careful going up stairs – he's got a dicky heart.*

dick·y·bird [BIRD] /£ˈdɪk·i·bɜːd, $-bɜːrd/ *n* [C] *Br* (used esp. by or to children) a small bird • *Aah, look at the little dickybird.*

dick·y·bird [ANYTHING] /£ˈdɪk·i·bɜːd, $-bɜːrd/ *n* [U] **a dickybird** *infml* anything • *I promise I won't* **say** *a dickybird to Jan about the party.* • *We haven't* **heard** *a dickybird from* (=spoken to or received a letter from) *Riza recently.*

dic·ta /ˈdɪk·tə/ *pl of* DICTUM

Dic·ta·phone /£ˈdɪk·tə·fəʊn, $-foʊn/ *n* [C] *trademark* a machine used in an office to record spoken words and later repeat them aloud so that they can be written down

dic·tate *(obj)* [GIVE ORDERS] /£dɪkˈteɪt, $ˈ--/ *v* to give orders, or state exactly, with total authority • *The President has so much power within the country that he is able to dictate* **to** *the government.* [I] • *I will not be dictated* **to** *in this manner!* [I] • *The UN will dictate* (=state exactly) *the terms of the withdrawal of troops from the region.* [T] • *He argued that the government should not be allowed to dictate* (=state exactly) **what** *children are taught in schools.* [+ *wh-* word] • *My mother is always trying to dictate* (=state exactly) **what** *I wear.* [+ *wh-* word] • *The tennis club rules dictate* (=state) **that** *suitable footwear must be worn on the courts.* [+ *that* clause] • Dictate can also mean influence or make necessary: *The party's change of policy has been dictated by its need to win back the support of voters.* [T] ○ *The design of the house was dictated by the small size and irregular shape of the plot of land on which it was built.* [T] ○ *I wanted to take a year off to travel when I left college, but my financial situation dictated* **that** *I got a job.* [+ *that* clause]

dic·tate /ˈdɪk·teɪt/ *n* [C usually pl] • A dictate is an order which should be obeyed, esp. one which comes from within yourself: *the dictates* **of** *conscience* ○ *I would have thought the dictates* **of** *common sense would tell you not to go out in this cold weather without a coat.* ○ *He is a slave to the dictates* **of** *fashion* (=He only wears clothes that are extremely fashionable). • Compare DIKTAT.

dic·ta·tor /£dɪkˈteɪ·təʳ, $ˈdɪk·teɪ·t̬ɚ/ *n* [C] *esp. disapproving* • A dictator is someone with complete power in a country, esp. when the power is achieved by force: *The country is ruled by a ruthless dictator.* • *(fig.) My boss is a bit of a dictator* (=acts as if he or she has complete power).

dic·ta·to·ri·al /£ˌdɪk·təˈtɔː·ri·əl, $-ˈtɔːr·i-/ *adj disapproving* • *a dictatorial ruler/government* • *Her father is very dictatorial.*

dic·ta·tor·ship /£dɪkˈteɪ·tə·ʃɪp, $-t̬ɚ-/ *n* • *The island is a military dictatorship* (=a country ruled by a dictator). [C] • *After many years of dictatorship* (=rule by a dictator), *the country is now moving towards democracy.* [U] • *The dictatorship* (=state of being a dictator) **of** *General Franco lasted for nearly 40 years.* [U]

dic·tate *(obj)* [SPEAK] /£dɪkˈteɪt, $ˈ--/ *v* to speak (something) aloud for another person or for a machine to record the words said, so that they can then be written down • *I dictated my order over the phone.* [T] • *She spent the morning dictating letters* **to** *her secretary.* [T] • *When my boss dictates, he speaks so quickly that it's difficult for me to take down everything he says.* [I]

dic·ta·tion /dɪkˈteɪ·ʃᵊn/ *n* • *The secretary took down a letter from dictation* (=the act of someone speaking). [U] • *I'll ask my assistant to* **take** *dictation* (=write down what I say). [U] • A dictation is a test in which a piece of writing is read out to people who are learning a foreign language. The aim of it is to test their ability to hear and write the language correctly: *Our French dictation lasted half an hour.* [C]

dic·tion /ˈdɪk·ʃᵊn/ *n* [U] the manner in which words are pronounced • *It is very helpful for a language teacher to have good diction.*

dic·tion·a·ry /£ˈdɪk·ʃᵊn·ᵊr·i, $-er·i/ *n* [C] a book in which words are listed alphabetically and their meanings, either in the same language or in another language, and other information about them, are given • *a French-English/English-French dictionary* • *a dictionary* **of** *science* • *Many dictionaries are now available on CD-ROM.* • *If you want to know how a word is spelt,* **look it up** *in a dictionary.* • A dictionary can also be a book which gives information about a particular subject, in which the entries are given in alphabetical order: *a biographical dictionary* ○ *a dictionary* **of** *quotations*

dic·tum /ˈdɪk·tᵊm/ *n* [C] *pl* **dicta** /ˈdɪk·tə/ or **dictums** a short statement, esp. one expressing advice or a general truth • *He has always followed the famous American dictum, 'don't get mad, get even'.*

did /dɪd/ *past simple of* DO

di·dac·tic /daɪˈdæk·tɪk/ *adj esp. disapproving* intended to teach, esp. in a way that is too determined or eager and is often fixed and not showing a willingness to be changed • *In some schools, traditional didactic teaching has been replaced by an approach which allows children to discover things for themselves.* • Didactic also means intended to teach people a moral: *didactic literature* ○ *a didactic play*

di·dac·ti·cally /daɪˈdæk·tɪ·kli/ *adv* • *It was supposed to be an informal talk, but he spoke rather didactically.*

did·dle *obj* [CHEAT] /ˈdɪd·l̩/ *v* [T] *infml* to obtain, esp. items of small value, from (someone) in a way which is not honest; to cheat • *He diddled me! He said that there were six in a bag but there were only five.* • *I realized the restaurant had diddled me* **out of** *£5 when I checked the bill.*

did·dle *(obj)* [PLAY] /ˈdɪd·l̩/ *v Am* to work with (something) in a way which is not serious, or to play with (something) • *He diddled with the washing machine, but it still wouldn't work.* [T] • *I'm not much of a musician, I just like to diddle around.* [I]

did·dly /ˈdɪd·l̩.i/, **did·dly–squat** /£ˈdɪd·l̩.i·skwɒt, $-skwɑːt/, **squat** *n* [U] *Am infml* nothing • *He's done diddly all day.* • *There's no point in asking Ellen – she doesn't know diddly.*

did·dums *Br* /ˈdɪd·ᵊmz/ *exclamation humorous* an expression which seems sympathetic but which really means the opposite • *"I hurt my finger." "Ah diddums!"*

didg·er·i·doo /£ˌdɪdʒ·ə·riˈduː, $-ɚ·i-/ *n* [C] *pl* **didgeridoos** a wind instrument which is played by Australian Aborigines, and which produces long deep notes

did·n't /ˈdɪd·ᵊnt/ *short form of* did not • *We didn't arrive at our hotel until after midnight.* • *Didn't you know that she had been ill?* • *"Who broke this cup?" "I didn't."*

die *(obj)* [STOP LIVING] /daɪ/ *v* [no passive] **dying**, *past* **died** to stop living or existing, either suddenly or slowly • *Twelve people tragically died in the accident.* [I] • *His burns were so severe that he died before reaching hospital.* [I] • *She died* **of/from** *hunger/cancer/a heart attack/her injuries.* [I] • *It is a brave person who will die* **for** *their beliefs.* [I] • *When the time comes I should like to die* **in my sleep** (=while I am sleeping). [I] • *She died* **by** *her* **own hand** (=killed herself). [I] • *Olaf has taken time off work because his father is dying* (=is very ill and is likely not to live for much longer). [I] • If someone dies a particular type of **death**, they die in that way: *I'm afraid of dying a violent death.* [T] ○ *My grandmother died a natural death* (=did not die of illness or because she was killed), *as she would have wanted.* [T] ○ *(Br) The play* **died a death** (=was a failure). • If you say that you **nearly/almost/could have** died **of** a particular feeling, you mean that you felt the feeling very strongly: *I almost died of embarrassment/laughter/boredom.* [I] ○ *It was so embarrassing/funny/boring, I could have died.* [I] • *Our love will never die* (=end). [I] • *She will not tell anyone – the secret will die* (=stop existing) *with her.* [I] • *(fig.) The engine just died* (=stopped working) **(on** *us).* [I] • *(fig. Am) He wore his jeans until they died* (=wore out). [I] • If something, esp. a sound, dies **away**, it gradually becomes reduced until it stops existing or disappears: *Jill's sobs eventually died away.* [I] ○ *Many old buildings are dying away through neglect.* [I] • If a sound or activity dies **down**, it becomes quieter or less obvious: *It was several minutes before the applause died down.* [I] • If something dies **out**, it becomes less common until it stops existing: *Dinosaurs died out millions of years ago.* ○ *The custom/idea is dying out.* • *She said she would finish the race* **or die in the attempt** (=she would do anything to achieve what she wanted to achieve). • To **be dying** to do something, or for something, is to be eager to do or to have it: *I'm dying* **to** *hear the news.* [+ *to* infinitive] ○ *I'm dying* **for** *a cup of tea.* • To **do or die** is to do everything possible to succeed. • If a belief or way of behaving **dies hard**, it takes a long time to disappear, and is not given up easily: *Old habits die hard.* See also DIEHARD. • *(saying)* 'Never say die' means do not give up. • *"Men have died from time to time, and worms have eaten them, but not for love"* (Shakespeare, As You Like It 4.1) • See also DEATH. • [LP] **Age**

dy·ing /ˈdaɪ·ɪŋ/ *adj* [not gradable] • *She nursed her dying* (=very ill and likely to die soon) *husband for months.* • Dying means happening at the time someone dies, or connected with that time: *Beethoven's dying* **words** *are said to have been "I shall hear in heaven".* ○ *I'll remember your kindness to/until my dying* **day** (=as long as I live). • A dying tradition/industry is one which is becoming noticeably less common or important.

dy·ing /ˈdaɪ·ɪŋ/ *n* [U] • *Many people have a fear of dying.*

dy·ing /ˈdaɪ·ɪŋ/ *pl n* • *The nurse specialized in the care of* **the dying** (=people who are about to die).

die TOOL /daɪ/ *n* [C] a shaped piece of metal or other hard material used to form metal, plastic etc., or a MOULD (=a hollow container) used for forming liquid metal or plastic into a particular shape • If you **die-cast** an object, or it is die-cast, you make it by pouring liquid metal, plastic, etc., usually under pressure, into a MOULD.

die GAME /daɪ/ *n* [C] *old use or Am also* DICE GAME • If **the die is cast**, a situation is certain to develop in a particular way because particular decisions have been taken and cannot be changed: *It was too late to back out of the project – the die was already cast.* • *"The die is cast"* (Julius Caesar, on crossing the Rubicon, 49 BC)

die·hard /£ˈdaɪ·hɑːd, $-hɑːrd/ *n* [C] *disapproving* someone who is unwilling to change or give up their ideas or ways of behaving, even when there are good reasons for them to do so • *Only a few diehards on the right of the party object to the proposed changes.* • *He's a diehard conservative/reformer/cynic.* • See also **die hard** at DIE STOP LIVING.

die·sel FUEL /ˈdiː·zəl/ *n* [U] a type of heavy oil used as fuel • *My new car* **runs on** (= uses) *diesel.* • *Many trucks have diesel engines/use diesel power/are diesel-powered.*

die·sel VEHICLE /ˈdiː·zəl/ *n* [C] any vehicle, esp. a train, which has a diesel engine

di·et /ˈdaɪ·ət/ *n* the food and drink usually taken by a person or group, or a limiting, for medical or personal reasons, of what you eat or drink • *Diet varies between different countries in the world.* [U] • *It's important to have a* **healthy/balanced/varied** *diet.* [C] • *Rice is the* **staple** *diet* (= most important food) *of many people in China.* [C] • *The children seem to exist on a diet* **of** *burgers and chips.* [C] • *The doctor has put me* **on** *a low-salt diet* (= a limiting, for medical reasons, of what I eat) *to reduce my blood pressure.* [C] • A diet is often a limiting of what you eat and drink in order to lose weight: *I will* **go on** *a diet next week and hope to lose five pounds before Christmas.* [C] ○ *Going on a* **crash/strict** *diet can make you ill.* [C] ○ *This product can only help you lose weight when taken as part of a* **calorie-controlled** *diet.* [C] • *(fig.) All the television seems to offer every evening is a diet* (= limited range) **of** *comedies and old movies.* [C]

di·et /ˈdaɪ·ət/ *v* [I] • If you diet, you limit the food and/or drink which you take, esp. in order to lose weight: *I must lose weight so I'm going to diet.* ○ *Are you still dieting?* ○ *You should be able to reduce your weight by careful dieting.*

di·et /ˈdaɪ·ət/ *adj* [not gradable] • If food or drink is described as being diet, it contains much less sugar than usual and is often sweetened artificially, or contains less fat than usual: *"What would you like to drink?" "A diet cola, please."*

di·e·tary /£ˈdaɪ·ə·tər·i, £-tri, $-ter-/ *adj* [not gradable] • *Dietary* (= eating) **habits** *can be very difficult to change.* • *Do you have any special dietary* **requirements.** • **Dietary fibre** is FIBRE FOOD.

di·et·er /£ˈdaɪ·ə·tər, $-tɚ/ *n* [C] • *Cottage cheese is popular with dieters* (= people who are trying to lose weight by limiting what they eat) *because it is low in calories.*

di·et·i·cian, di·et·i·tian /ˌdaɪ·əˈtɪʃ·ən/ *n* [C] a person who scientifically studies, and gives advice about, food and eating • *I'm going to talk to a dietician to see if he or she can help with my allergies.*

di·et·e·tics /£ˌdaɪ·əˈtet·ɪks, $-ˈteṭ-/ *n* [U] • Dietetics is the scientific study of diet and its effects on health.

dif·fer /£ˈdɪf·ər, $-ɚ/ *v* [I] to be not like something else, either physically or in another way • *These two shirts are a similar style, although they differ in that one has short sleeves and one has long.* • *Interpretations of what this painting really represents differ.* • *The twins look alike, but they differ* **in** *temperament.* • *Your taste in music differs* **from** *hers.* • *His views differ considerably* **from** *those of his parents.* • *The findings of the study differ* **significantly/markedly/radically** *from those of previous research.* • *The incidence of the illness differs greatly* **between** *men and women.* • *The children in the class come from* **widely** *differing backgrounds.* • To differ is also to disagree: *Lisa and her husband rarely differ* **(with** *each other).* ○ *My sister and I differ* **about/over/on** *most things.*

dif·fer·ence /£ˈdɪf·ər·ənts, $ˈ-ɚ-/ *n* • (A) difference is the way in which two or more things which you are comparing are not the same: *The difference* **between** *the three balloons is that one is blue, one is red and one is yellow.* [C] ○ *There is a great difference* **between** *theory and practice.* [C] ○ *Is there any significant difference* **in** *quality* **between** *these two shirts?* [U] • *They have a difference* **of opinion** (= disagree) *over the subject.* [C] • A difference is also a disagreement: *We've had our differences in the past, but we've now learnt to respect each other's points of view.* [C] ○ *They had an awful row several years ago but now they've* **settled/resolved** *their differences.* [C] • If something **makes a (big) difference/makes all the difference (in the world)/makes a world of difference**, it improves a situation (greatly): *Exercise can make a big difference* **to** *your state of health.* ○ *Putting up some new wallpaper in the bedroom has made all the difference* **to it.** • If something does **not make any/the slightest difference** or **makes no difference**, it does not change a situation in any way: *You can ask him again if you like, but it won't make any difference – he'll still say no.* ○ *It makes no difference* **where** *you put the aerial, the TV picture's still lousy.* [U + *wh-* word] • If you do something **for all the difference** it **will make**, you do it although you know it will not change the situation: *Well, you could try apologizing to her – for all the difference that will make.* • **With a difference** means unusual, and more interesting or better than other things of the same type: *Try new Cremetti – the ice cream with a difference.*

dif·fer·ent /£ˈdɪf·ər·ənt, $ˈ-ɚ-/ *adj* • Different means not the same: *She seems to wear something different every day.* ○ *He's different now that he's been to college.* ○ *Are you reading a different book this week or is it still the same one?* ○ *These two cakes are different* **(from** *each other).* ○ *Emily is* **very/completely/entirely** *different* **from** *her sister.* ○ *Emily and her sister are quite* (= completely) *different.* ○ *There are many different* **types/kinds** *of bacteria.* • If you say something or someone is different, you might mean that they are unusual, but you can also mean that you think they show bad judgment: *What do I think of your purple shoes? Well, they're certainly different.* ○ *Do you dare to be different?* • *The two sisters are (Br and Aus)* **(as) different as chalk and/from cheese**/*(esp. Am)* **(as) different as night and day** (= very dissimilar).

dif·fer·ent·ly /£ˈdɪf·ər·ənt·li, $ˈ-ɚ-/ *adv* • *They behave so differently – you'd never believe they were brothers.*

dif·fer·en·tial /ˌdɪf·əˈren·tʃəl/ *adj, n* (showing) an amount of difference between things which are compared • *He thinks it's wrong that people from different social classes have differential access to housing, education and jobs.* • *The department has a differential salary structure which takes into account an employee's experience as well as other factors.* • *The workers maintain that the* **pay** *differentials* **between** *themselves and the management are too great.* [C] • *There is a* **price** *differential* **between** *different types of oil.* [C] • A differential **(gear)** is a device fitted to the AXLE of a vehicle to let the wheels turn at different rates when going round a corner. [C] • *(specialized)* **(The) differential calculus** is the branch of CALCULUS in which rates of change and connected quantities are calculated.

dif·fer·en·tial·ly /ˌdɪf·əˈren·tʃəl·i/ *adv* • *The study showed that students are differentially skilled* (= have different amounts of skill) *in taking exams and that this influenced their results.*

dif·fer·en·ti·ate *(obj)* /ˌdɪf·əˈren·tʃi·eɪt/ *v* to show or find the difference between (things which are compared) • *We do not differentiate* **between** *our workers on the basis of their background or ethnic origin.* [I] • *I'm not very good at differentiating* **between** *wines.* [I] • *Its slate roof differentiates this house* (= makes it different) **from** *others in the area.* [T]

dif·fer·en·ti·a·tion /£ˌdɪf·ər·en·tʃiˈeɪ·ʃən, $-ə·ren-/ *n* • *In the past, no differentiations* (= acts of showing differences) *were* **made** *between mental illness and mental handicap.* [C] • Differentiation is also the process of becoming different: *The differentiation of the fetal organs occurs in the first few weeks after fertilization.* [U] ○ *Product differentiation is essential to the future of the company.* [U]

dif·fi·cult /ˈdɪf·ɪ·kəlt/ *adj* needing skill or effort; not easy • *a difficult problem/choice/task/language/book* • *Diagnosis of the illness is* **notoriously/fiendishly** *difficult.* • **It** *will be very difficult* **to** *prove that they are guilty.* [+ *to* infinitive] • *The manager is difficult* **to** *deal with/a difficult person* **to** *deal with.* [+ *to* infinitive] • *Many things make* **it** *difficult* **for** *women to reach the top in US business.* [+ *to* infinitive] • *He finds* **it** *extremely difficult being a single parent.* [+ v-*ing*] • *His wife is a very difficult person* (= behaves in a way that makes it not easy to have a relationship with her). • *Please children, don't be so difficult* (= badly behaved)*!* • *"Difficult things take a long time; the impossible takes a little longer"* (Fridtjof Nansen and others, 1861-1930)

dif·fi·cult·y /£ˈdɪf·ɪ·kəl·ti, $-ṭi/ *n* • *We finished the job but only* **with** *great difficulty* (= effort). [U] • *The difficulty* **of** *the task* (= amount of skill it needed) *excited them.* [U] • *People with asthma have difficulty* **in** *breathing* (= need to use effort to breathe because it is not easy). [U] • *She has been* **having**

great difficulty (= having to use effort because it is not easy) *finding a job.* [U + v-*ing*] • A difficulty is a problem: *He has been* **having** *financial/personal difficulties recently.* [C] ○ *His work involved assessing the special educational needs of children with* **learning** *difficulties.* [C] ○ *We seem to have some apparently* **insuperable** *difficulties* **facing** *us.* [C] ○ *People who are learning a new language often* **encounter** *some difficulties at first.* [C] ○ *An unforeseen difficulty has* **arisen**. [C] ○ *The situation is* **fraught with** *difficulties.* [C] ○ *A ship is* **in** *difficulties* (= is having problems) *off the coast of Ireland.* [C] • *(Br and Aus) This isn't the first time that she's been* **in** *difficulties* (= trouble) **with** *the police.* [C]

dif·fi·dent /ˈdɪf·ɪ·dᵊnt/ *adj* unwilling to speak or act with confidence because of having a low opinion of your own abilities • *It's a shame she's so shy and diffident, because she really is very clever.* • *He has a politely diffident manner.* • *There's no need to be so diffident* **about** *your achievements – you've done really well!*

dif·fi·dence /ˈdɪf·ɪ·dᵊnts/ *n* [U] • **With** *great diffidence, he asked her if she would go to the dance with him.*

dif·fi·dent·ly /ˈdɪf·ɪ·dᵊnt·li/ *adv* • *The child behaves very diffidently.*

dif·frac·tion /dɪˈfræk·ʃᵊn/ *n* [U] *specialized* (a pattern caused by) a change in the direction of light, water or sound waves • *The colours you see when you look at a CD are made by diffraction.*

dif·fract *obj* /dɪˈfrækt/ *v* [T] • *The beam (of light) was diffracted into several light and dark bands.*

dif·fuse *(obj)* /dɪˈfjuːz/ *v* to (cause to) spread in many directions • *Television is a powerful means of diffusing knowledge.* [T] • *Someone made a joke, which diffused the tension in the room.* [T] • *Oxygen diffuses from the lungs into the bloodstream.* [I] • *The drop of red dye diffused until it was evenly spread out in the glass of water.* [I]

dif·fuse /dɪˈfjuːs/ *adj* • Diffuse means spread out and not directed in one place: *a diffuse light* ○ *I could hear diffuse murmuring coming from the next room.* ○ *The illness is characterized by diffuse muscle pains.* ○ *The company has become large and diffuse.* • *(esp. disapproving)* Diffuse also means not clear and easy to understand: *a diffuse speech* ○ *a diffuse literary style*

dif·fuse·ly /dɪˈfjuː·sli/ *adv*

dif·fus·er, dif·fu·sor /£dɪˈfjuː·zəʳ, $-zɚ/ *n* [C] • A diffuser is a device which is used to make light less direct, esp. one used with a FLUORESCENT light.

dif·fu·sion /dɪˈfjuː·ʒᵊn/ *n* [U] • *The diffusion of new technologies in 19th century Britain varied from industry to industry.* • *(specialized) He was one of the first scientists to study the process of diffusion in gases/liquids/solids.*

dig *(obj)* MOVE EARTH /dɪg/ *v* **digging**, *past* **dug** /dʌg/ to move and break up (earth) using a tool, a machine or your hands • *If these moles carry on digging, there will soon be no grass left.* [I] • *She spent all afternoon digging* **(in/up)** *the garden.* [T; I + prep] • To dig some type of hole is to form it by moving earth: *The tunnel was dug with the aid of heavy machinery.* [T] ○ *The dog was* **furiously** *digging a hole to hide its bone in.* [T] • If you **dig yourself (into) a hole**, you get yourself into a difficult situation: *The government has really dug itself into a hole with its economic policies.* ○ *We need to find a way of digging ourselves out of this hole* (= getting out of the difficult situation that we are in). • *Farmers often dig* **in** *fertilizer* (= mix it into the earth) *before they plant their crops.* [M] • If you tell someone to **dig in** at a meal, you ask them to start eating: *The food is going cold, dig in!* • If soldiers **dig** (themselves) **in**, they make preparations, such as by digging TRENCHES, to protect themselves from an attack by the enemy. • To **dig** yourself **in** means to establish yourself in a place: *We've lived in this house for twenty years, so we're well dug in.* • *Firefighters helped to dig* **out** *the people trapped in the snowdrift.* [M] • *(fig.) The doctor had to dig* **out** (= remove) *a piece of glass that had got stuck in my finger.* [M] • *I spent all morning digging* **out/up** *weeds* (= removing them from the earth) *in the garden.* [M] • *They're digging* **up** *the road outside in order to repair electricity cables.* [M] • If you **dig** your **own grave**, you do something which causes you harm, sometimes seriously: *You're digging your own grave by eating so much fatty food.* ○ *She dug her own grave when she made fun of the boss.*

dig /dɪg/ *n* [C] • A dig is the careful removal of earth and objects from an area of historical interest: *There's an archaeological dig going on at the site of a 4000-year-old settlement.* • See also DIGS.

dig·ger /£ˈdɪg·əʳ, $-ɚ/ *n* [C] • A digger is a machine used for digging, or sometimes a person who digs: *a mechanical digger* • *(Aus)* A digger is also a person who MINES for gold. • *(Aus infml)* A digger is an Australian soldier, esp. one who fought in World War I. • PIC› **Building and construction**

dig *(obj)* SEARCH /dɪg/ *v* **digging**, *past* **dug** /dʌg/ to search for or find after looking (an object or information) • *The plumber dug* **into** *her bag and pulled out a wrench.* [I always + adv/prep] • *He dug* **into** *his pocket and took out a few coins.* [I always + adv/prep] • To **dig (deep/deeper) into** your **pocket(s)/resources/savings**, is to give money: *Richer countries must dig deeper into their pockets if global problems, such as pollution, are to be solved.* • *I thought I knew him well, but as I dug* **deeper** (= found out more), *I realized that there was a lot about him that I didn't know.* [I always + adv/prep] • *After a lot of searching, I've managed to dig* **out** (= find) *those photographs you wanted.* [M] • *I've been doing some research on our family history and I've dug* **up** (= found) *some interesting information.* [M] • *She's one of those journalists who's always trying to dig* **the dirt on**/*dig* **up (the) dirt on** (= find embarrassing facts about the private lives of) *famous people.* [T]

dig *(obj)* PRESS /dɪg/ *v* **digging**, *past* **dug** /dʌg/ to press strongly • *She held his hand so tightly that her nails dug* **into** *his palm.* [I always + adv/prep] • *I've got a stone or something in my shoe and it's digging* **into** *my foot.* [I always + adv/prep] • If you dig someone **in the ribs**, you push the side of their body with your ELBOW (= the central joint of the arm), esp. to make it clear that you wish to share a joke with them or want their attention for another reason. [T] • If you **dig** your **heels in**, you will not change your plans or ideas, esp. when someone is trying to persuade you to do so.

dig REMARK /dɪg/ *n* [C] a remark which is intended to criticize, embarrass or make a joke about someone • *He's always* **having/taking/making** *digs* **at** *me.* • *I couldn't resist a dig* **at** *Pablo when his team lost the match, after he'd been saying that they'd win easily.* • See also DIGS.

dig *(obj)* APPROVE /dɪg/ *v* **digging**, *past* **dug** /dʌg/ *dated slang* to like or understand (something) • *Hey, I* **really** *dig those shoes!* [T] • *You dig (my meaning), man?* [I/T]

di·gest *(obj)* EAT /daɪˈdʒest/ *v* to break (food) down inside a living creature so that it can be used within its body • *Certain people find that they cannot digest meat easily.* [T] • *Some foods digest* (= are broken down) *much more quickly than others.* [I]

di·gest·ion /daɪˈdʒes·tʃᵊn/ *n* • *He always likes to sit for a while after a meal to allow digestion* (= the process of digesting food) *to take place.* [U] • *Ever since her illness, her digestion* (= the ability of her body to digest food) *has been* **poor**. [C]

di·gest·ive /£daɪˈdʒes·tɪv, $-t̬ɪv/ *adj* • *the digestive process* • *a digestive enzyme* • The **digestive system** is the organs of a body which digest food.

di·gest *obj* UNDERSTAND /daɪˈdʒest/ *v* [T] to understand and remember (information) • *This chapter is so difficult to digest, I shall have to read it again later.* • *Having digested the lessons of the past, we must now find new ways with which to face the future.*

di·gest /ˈdaɪ·dʒest/ *n* [C] • A digest is a short written report which provides the most important parts of a larger piece of writing, or a short written report containing recent news: *A digest* **of** *the findings of the research has been made available to the press.* ○ *A monthly digest is published giving details of the company's activities.*

di·gest·ive (bis·cuit) /ˌdaɪˈdʒes·tɪv/ *n* [C] *Br and Aus* a slightly sweet biscuit made from WHOLEMEAL flour • *I like digestive biscuits with cheese.* • *He bought a packet of chocolate* (= covered with a layer of chocolate) *digestives.*

dig·it NUMBER /ˈdɪdʒ·ɪt/ *n* [C] any one of the ten numbers 0 to 9 • *The number 770345 contains six digits, five of them different.*

dig·i·tal /£ˈdɪdʒ·ɪ·tᵊl, $-t̬ᵊl/ *adj* [not gradable] • *Digital compact cassettes are one of several digital recording media.* • Digital means showing information in the form of numbers which can change: *a digital clock/watch/display* • *(specialized)* Digital also means being or using information recorded as a series of the numbers zero and one: *digital data* ○ *a digital recording* ○ *Most computers now are digital computers.* • A **digital audio tape** (*abbreviation* **DAT**) is a **magnetic tape** used to record sound using information stored as a series of the numbers zero and one: *The quality of sound from a digital audio tape is truly excellent.* See **magnetic tape** at MAGNET. • Compare ANALOGUE. • PIC› **Clocks and watches**

dig·i·tal·ly /ˈdɪdʒ·ɪ·tᵊl·i/ *adv* [not gradable] • *My watch shows the time digitally* (= in the form of numbers which can change). • *Sound and pictures can be stored digitally* (= in the form of a series of the numbers zero and one), *as on a CD.* •

The Beatles' recordings have been digitally remastered and issued on CD.

dig·i·tize *obj, Br and Aus usually* **-ise** /ˈdɪdʒ·ɪ·taɪz/ *v* [T] • When information is digitized, it is put into the form of a series of the numbers zero and one, usually so that it can be processed by a computer.

dig·it FINGER /ˈdɪdʒ·ɪt/ *n* [C] *specialized* a finger, thumb or toe

dig·ni·fy *obj* /ˈdɪg·nɪ·faɪ/ *v* [T] to cause (something) to be valued and respected • *The presence of the mayor dignified the occasion.* • *You won't dignify the house just* **by** *painting it.* • *You surely don't intend to dignify that heap of junk* **by** *calling it a car!* • To dignify something can also be to cause it to be valued and respected when that is not deserved: *It would be a crime to dignify this rhyme* **with** *the label poetry.*

dig·ni·fied /ˈdɪg·nɪ·faɪd/ *adj* • Someone or something that is dignified deserves respect because of being controlled, graceful, serious and calm: *He was followed into the room by a tall dignified woman.* ○ *He has maintained a dignified silence about the rumours.* ○ *The defeated candidate in the election gave a dignified speech in which he congratulated his rival.*

dig·ni·ta·ry /£ˈdɪg·nɪ·tᵊr·i, £-tri, $-nə·ter-/ *n* [C] a person who has an important position in a society • *Several foreign dignitaries attended the opening ceremony.*

dig·ni·ty /£ˈdɪg·nɪ·ti, $-ə·ṭi/ *n* [U] the quality or state of deserving respect, esp. because of being controlled, serious and calm • *He is a man of dignity and calm determination.* • *She has a quiet dignity about her.* • *Even though they're poor, they still have a sense of dignity.* • *He said that he wanted to see a society in which the dignity* **of** *all people was recognized.* • *I think everyone should be able to die with dignity.* • *The way the prisoners were treated was an affront to human dignity.* • *She said that she felt as if she had been stripped of her dignity when she was in hospital.* • *Throughout her dreadful ordeal, she behaved with great dignity* (= control, seriousness and calmness). • Your dignity is the opinion that you have of the standard of your own importance and value: *How could you wear something so indecent? Have you no dignity?* ○ *The pupil felt it* **beneath his** *dignity* (= felt himself too important) *to collect the books.*

di·gress /daɪˈgres/ *v* [I] to move away from the main subject when you are writing or talking about something, and write or talk, usually briefly, about something else • *Let me digress for a moment and explain what had happened previously.* • *But I digress. To get back to what I was saying before, this poem reflects both the poet's love of nature and his religious beliefs.* • *The lecturer temporarily digressed* **from** *what she was saying to answer a question from a member of the audience.* • *May I digress* **from** *our discussions for a moment and remind you that the train leaves at three o'clock.*

di·gres·sion /daɪˈgreʃ·ᵊn/ *n* • *Talking about money now would be a digression* **from** *the main purpose of this meeting.* [C] • *Digression might be a useful tactic at this stage of the negotiations.* [U]

digs /dɪgz/ *pl n esp. Br infml for* **lodgings**, see at LODGE STAY • *Many students in London have to live* **in** *digs because their colleges don't have enough accommodation for them.*

dike /daɪk/ *n* [C] a DYKE WALL or a DYKE WOMAN

dik·tat /ˈdɪk·tɑːt, -tæt/ *n disapproving* (the act of giving) an order which must be obeyed • *The occupying force ruled by diktat.* [U] • *The coach has issued a diktat that all members of the team must attend practice on Tuesday.* [C] • Compare **dictate** at DICTATE.

di·lap·i·dat·ed /£dɪˈlæp·ɪ·deɪ·tɪd, $-ṭɪd/ *adj* (of objects) in poor condition because of age and/or lack of care • *The hotel we stayed in was really dilapidated.* • *You're not going to drive all the way to Denmark in that dilapidated old car, are you?* • *The room had no furniture in it apart from a dilapidated old bed.*

di·lap·i·da·tion /dɪˌlæp·ɪˈdeɪ·ʃᵊn/ *n* [U] • *The farmhouse had fallen into a state of dilapidation.*

di·late *(obj)* /£daɪˈleɪt, $ˈ--/ *v esp. medical* to become or make wider or further open • *The pupils of the eyes dilate as darkness increases.* [I] • *This drug will dilate the arteries.* [T]

di·la·tion /daɪˈleɪ·ʃᵊn/ *n* [U] *esp. medical*

di·late on/u·pon *obj v prep* [T] *fml* to write or speak about a subject at length • *He likes to dilate upon what he thinks is wrong with the world.*

dil·a·tory /£ˈdɪl·ə·tri, $-tɔːr·i/ *adj fml* slow and likely to cause delay • *His behaviour is generally dilatory, so it's not surprising he's late.* • *The dilatory actions of the government have not helped the situation.* • *We apologize for being so dilatory* **in** *dealing with your enquiry.*

dil·do /£ˈdɪl·dəʊ, $-doʊ/ *n* [C] *pl* **dildos** an object shaped like and used in place of a penis for giving sexual pleasure • *(esp. Am)* Dildo can also be used to mean a stupid person, esp. a man: *He acts like a real dildo after he's had a few drinks.*

di·lem·ma /daɪˈlem·ə/ *n* [C] a situation in which a difficult choice has to be made between two possibilities, both of which are often unpleasant • *The President is clearly* **in** *a dilemma* **over** *how to tackle the crisis.* • *Two of my friends are having parties on the same day, and I'm* **in** *a real dilemma* **about** *which to go to.* • *The poor girl is* **caught in/facing** *the dilemma* **of** *obeying her father or marrying the man she loves.* • *He is* **faced/confronted** *with the* **moral/ethical** *dilemma* **of** *whether to steal a drug he can't afford so that he can save his wife's life.* • *The Court will have to* **resolve** *the agonizing dilemma* **of** *whether parents can refuse medical treatment for their children on religious grounds.*

dil·et·tan·te /ˌdɪl·ɪˈtæn·ti/ *n* [C] *pl* **dilettantes** or **dilettanti** /ˌdɪl·ɪˈtæn·ti/ *usually disapproving* a person who is or seems to be interested in a subject, but whose understanding of it is not very deep • *Because of her reputation as a dilettante, the art teacher has problems in finding serious students.* • *He's a bit of a dilettante as far as wine is concerned.* • NL

dil·i·gent /ˈdɪl·ɪ·dʒᵊnt/ *adj* careful and using a lot of effort, or done in a careful and detailed way • *a diligent student* • *diligent work* • *Leo is very diligent* **in/about** *his work.* • *Their lawyer was extremely diligent* **in** *preparing their case.* • *The discovery was made after years of diligent research.*

dil·i·gence /ˈdɪl·ɪ·dʒᵊnts/ *n* [U] • *She hoped that her diligence would be noticed at work.* • *The diligence with which the police conducted the investigation was highly praised.*

dil·i·gent·ly /ˈdɪl·ɪ·dʒᵊnt·li/ *adv*

dill /dɪl/ *n* [U] a herb whose seeds and thin feathery leaves are used in cooking • *dill pickles* • *Dill is often used to flavour fish, particularly in Scandinavia.* • PIC **Herbs and spices**

dil·ly·dal·ly /ˈdɪl·iˌdæl·i, ˌ--ˈ--/ *v* [I] *infml dated* to waste time, esp. by being slow, or by not being able to make a decision • *Don't dillydally – just pack your things and then we can go!* • *Stop dillydallying, and make up your mind what kind of ice cream you want.*

di·lute *obj* /daɪˈluːt/ *v* [T] to make (a liquid) weaker by mixing in something else • *Dilute the juice* (**with** *water) before you drink it.* • *(fig.) These measures are designed to dilute* (= make less strong) *public fears about the product's safety.* • *(fig.) He plans to dilute* (= reduce) *his investment in the company.*

di·lute /daɪˈluːt/, *Am usually* **di·lut·ed** /£daɪˈluː·tɪd, $-ṭɪd/ *adj* • *dilute hydrochloric acid* • *The drink is very dilute – it won't hurt the child to have a little.*

di·lu·tion /daɪˈluː·ʃᵊn/ *n* • *The effectiveness of the drug is increased by dilution.* [U] • *Make a dilution of the substance by adding one litre of water.* [C] • *(fig.) There is no good reason for this dilution* **in/of** *the party's health policies.* [U]

dim /dɪm/ *adj* **dimmer, dimmest** not bright; not giving or having much light • *The lamp gave out a dim light.* • *There was someone sitting in a dim corner of the waiting room.* • *We could see the dim* (= not easily seen) *shape of a person in the fog.* • *It's not surprising her eyesight is dim* (= she cannot see very well) *– she's very old.* • *(fig.) I had a dim* (= not clear) **memory/recollection** *of having met her once before, many years ago.* • *(fig.) The company's prospects for the future are rather dim* (= bad). • *(fig.) I* **take a dim view** (= do not approve) *of this kind of behaviour.* • *(fig.) Mina is a hard-working child, but she's a little dim* (= slow to understand). • *He played the part of a* **dim-witted** (= stupid) *police officer.* See also DIMWIT.

dim *(obj)* /dɪm/ *v* **-mm-** • *When the music started, someone dimmed the lights.* [T] • *When the music started, the lights dimmed.* [I] • *Hopes are dimming that any more survivors will be found alive.* [I]

dim·ly /ˈdɪm·li/ *adv* • *The room was dimly lit.* • *I dimly remembered having seen the film before.*

dim·mer (switch) /£ˈdɪm·əʳ, $-ɚ/ *n* [C] • A dimmer is a device used to vary the brightness of an electric light, often found combined with a switch to turn the light on and off. • PIC **Lights**

dim·ness /ˈdɪm·nəs/ *n* [U]

dime /daɪm/ *n* [C] an American or Canadian coin which has the value of ten cents • *Ten dimes make a dollar.* • *(Am) Books like this are* **a dime a dozen** *(Br* **two/ten a penny***)* (= common and/or of very little value). • LP **Money**

di·men·sion /ˌdaɪˈmen·tʃᵊn/ *n* [C] a measurement (of something) in a particular direction, esp. its height, length or width, or a part or feature or way of considering • *Please specify the dimensions* (= the height, length and width) **of** *the* room. • *It will be a building of vast dimensions* (=size). • *His personality has several different dimensions* (=parts). • *These weapons add a new dimension* (=feature) *to modern warfare.* • *There is a spiritual dimension* (=way of considering a situation) *in her poetry.*

-di·men·sion·al /-daɪ'ment·ʃən·əl/ *combining form* • *Space is considered to be three-dimensional* (=having three measurements in different directions) *and time is thought of as the fourth dimension.* • *The two groups form part of a larger multi-dimensional* (=having many parts) *organisation.*

di·min·ish *(obj)* /dɪ'mɪn·ɪʃ/ *v* to reduce or be reduced in size or importance • *There is nothing you can say that will diminish her resolve.* [T] • *I don't want to diminish her achievements, but she did have a lot of help.* [T] • *The memory of them will not be diminished by time.* [T] • *What he did has seriously diminished him in many people's eyes.* [T] • *He says that in his opinion the influence of the church has been slowly diminishing for many years.* [I] • *We have seen the value of our house diminish* **greatly/sharply/substantially** *in value over the last six months.* [I] • *(law)* If someone is in a state of **diminished responsibility** /*(Am)* **diminished capacity**, it means that something, esp. their mental state, has caused them not to be in full control of their actions: *Because the accused had been under great stress at the time of the crime, he pleaded not guilty* **on grounds of** *diminished responsibility.* • The law of **diminishing returns** refers to a situation in which a smaller result is achieved for an increasing amount of effort. • *"Any man's death diminishes me, because I am involved in Mankind"* (John Donne *Devotions*, 1624)

dim·in·u·tion /£ˌdɪm·ɪ'njuː·ʃən, $-ə'nuː-/ *n* • *Some people say that you can achieve a general diminution* **in** *your stress level by taking regular exercise.* [U] • *If your company does expand in the way you propose, there will be a diminution in profits for at least the next two years.* [C]

di·min·u·tive /£dɪ'mɪn·ju·tɪv, $-t̬ɪv/ *adj* very small • *She has diminutive hands for an adult.* • *He's a diminutive figure, less than five feet tall.* • *(esp. humorous) I don't expect you with your diminutive brain to understand what I mean!*

dim·ple /'dɪm·pl̩/ *n* [C] a small hollow place, esp. one which appears on a person's face when they smile and which is generally thought of as being attractive • *Despite dimples, curly hair, and angelic features, Freddie was never very lovable.* • *The pane of glass had a small dimple in it.*

dim·pled /'dɪm·pl̩d/ *adj* • *dimpled cheeks*

dim·wit /'dɪm·wɪt/ *n* [C] *infml* a stupid person • *I came in here to get something and I can't remember what it was – I'm such a dimwit!* • *Look where you're going, dimwit!* [as form of address]

din /dɪn/ *n* [U] a loud unpleasant confused noise, which lasts for a long time • *I had to shout to make myself heard above the din.* • *Even though it was so hot, we closed all the windows to shut out the din* **of** *the traffic.* • *There was a terrible din in the classroom.*

din *obj* **into** *obj v prep* [T] to say (something) forcefully and repeatedly to (someone) so that they remember it • *It was well dinned into me at my last job that I mustn't be late.*

dine /daɪn/ *v* [I] *fml* to eat the main meal of the day, usually in the evening • *I hate dining alone.* • *We dined by candlelight.* • *He claims to have once dined* **with** *the President of France.* • *It's Jan's birthday today, so we're dining* **out** (= having an evening meal away from home) *tonight* **at** *a special little restaurant we know.* • *(esp. Br)* If you **dine out on** an experience or a situation, you entertain people by telling them about it, esp. when you are eating a meal with them: *I've been dining out for months on the story of what happened when my house got flooded.* • *We dined very well* **on/upon** (=ate) *salmon and strawberries.* • A **dining car** (*Br also* **restaurant car**) is a part of a train in which passengers are served meals. • A **dining room** is a room in which meals are eaten. • A **dining hall** is a large room attached to a building such as a school in which many people can eat at the same time. • A **dining table** is a table at which meals are eaten. Compare **dinner table** at DINNER.

din·er /£'daɪ·nəʳ, $-nɚ/ *n* [C] • A diner is someone who is eating a meal, esp. in a restaurant. • *(Am)* A diner is a (small) restaurant at the side of the road, esp. one with a long table at which people sitting in fixed seats are served, and with the appearance of the part of a train in which passengers are served meals.

ding·bat /'dɪŋ·bæt/ *n* [C] a stupid or easily confused person • *Edith may seem like a dingbat, but she's quite clever really.* • *"Get lost, dingbat!", she cried.* [as form of address]

ding–dong SOUND /£'dɪŋ·dɒŋ, $-dɑːŋ/ *n* [U] the sound made by a bell • *The ding-dong of bells greeted them as they approached the church.*

ding–dong /£'dɪŋ·dɒŋ, $-dɑːŋ/ *adv* • *Ding-dong went the doorbell.*

ding–dong ARGUMENT /£'dɪŋ·dɒŋ, $-dɑːŋ/ *adj, n esp. Br and Aus infml* (being) an argument or fight from which there is a lot of noise • *They had a ding-dong argument in the middle of a crowded restaurant.* [before n] • *Be careful, there's a real ding-dong* **(of a fight)** *going on outside.* [C]

din·ghy /'dɪŋ·gi/ *n* [C] a small boat, usually open, which is powered by either sails, a motor or OARS • *They crossed the narrow stretch of sea between the mainland and the island in a dinghy.*

din·go /£'dɪŋ·gəʊ, $-goʊ/ *n* [C] *pl* **dingoes** a type of wild dog found in Australia

din·gy /'dɪn·dʒi/ *adj* **-ier, -iest** dark and often also dirty • *The room was very dingy.* • *We waited in a dingy corridor.* • *Her hair was a dingy brown colour.*

din·gi·ly /'dɪn·dʒɪ·li/ *adv* • *He was dingily dressed in an old jumper and shabby trousers.*

din·ky SMALL /'dɪŋ·ki/ *adj* **-ier, -iest** small • *(Br and Aus approving) 'She's got dinky little* (=small and charming) *feet', he said, 'I love her feet!'* • *(Am disapproving) They live in a dinky* (=small and without charm) *one-room apartment.*

din·ky PEOPLE /'dɪŋ·ki/ *n* [C] *abbreviation for* double income no kids yet (=a husband and wife, or a man and woman who live together as husband and wife, who both earn a lot of money but who have no children yet, and therefore have a lot of money to spend) • *This area of London is too expensive for most people to live in, but it's particularly popular with dinkies.*

din·ner /£'dɪn·əʳ, $-ɚ/ *n* the main meal of the day. In Britain, some people use dinner to refer to the meal that they eat in the evening, and others use it to refer to the meal that they eat in the middle of the day. • *We were having dinner when there was a knock at the door.* [U] • *Whose turn is it to make dinner?* [U] • *We've invited some friends around for dinner on Saturday.* [U] • *They had a romantic* **candlelit** *dinner for two.* [C] • *I'm having/giving a dinner* **party** (=a formal evening meal to which a small number of people are invited) *next week.* • A dinner is also a formal social occasion in the evening at which a meal is served: *A dinner was held to celebrate the opening of the new hotel.* [C] • A **dinner dance** is a social occasion in the evening, often in a hotel, at which there is a meal and dancing. • A **dinner jacket** (*abbreviation* **DJ**) (*Am* **tuxedo**) is a man's black jacket worn with a **bow tie** at formal social events, esp. in the evening. • A **dinner service/dinner set** is a complete set of plates and dishes needed in order for several people to eat a meal at the same time: *They were given a porcelain dinner service as a wedding present.* • The **dinner table** is the table at which the main meal of the day is served, or the occasion at which the main meal of the day is served: *They sat round* **the** *dinner table, arguing about politics.* ○ *No reading at the dinner table!* ○ *We usually talk about the day's events over the dinner table.* Compare **dining table** at DINE. • Compare LUNCH.

din·ner·time /£'dɪn·ə·taɪm, $'-ɚ-/ *n* [U] the time at which the main meal of the day is eaten • *My train was late, and I didn't get home till after dinnertime.*

di·no·saur /£'daɪ·nə·sɔːʳ, $-sɔːr/ *n* [C] a large REPTILE (= type of animal) which stopped existing about 60 000 000 years ago. There were many different types of dinosaur, some of which were extremely large. • *The brontosaurus was one of the largest of all dinosaurs.* • *(fig.) This typewriter's a bit of a dinosaur* (=very old-fashioned), *isn't it?*

dint /dɪnt/ *n* [U] **by dint of** *old use* using • *She got what she wanted by dint of pleading and threatening.*

di·o·cese /'daɪ·ə·sɪs/ *n* [C] *pl* **dioceses** /£daɪ'ɒs·ɪ·siːz, $-'ɑː·sɪ-/ (in the Roman Catholic and Anglican Churches) the area that is under the control of a BISHOP

di·o·ces·an /£daɪ'ɒs·ɪ·zən, $-'ɑː·sə-/ *adj* [not gradable]

di·ode /£'daɪ·əʊd, $-oʊd/ *n* [C] *specialized* a device which controls an electric current so that it can only flow in one direction • *A diode is a type of semiconductor which is used in circuits to convert alternating current into direct current.*

di·o·ra·ma /ˌdaɪə'rɑː·mə, $-'ræm·ə/ *n* [C] *specialized* a model which shows a situation, such as an historical event or animals in their natural surroundings, in a way that looks real because the height, length and width of what is being shown are accurately represented in comparison with each other • *Dioramas are three-dimensional.* • *At the museum there was a diorama of the Last Supper/local wildlife.*

di·ox·ide /£daɪˈɒk·saɪd, $-ˈɑːk-/ *n* [U] a chemical substance consisting of two atoms of oxygen combined with one atom of another element • *carbon dioxide* • *sulphur dioxide*

di·ox·in /£daɪˈɒk·sɪn, $-ˈɑːk-/ *n* a poisonous chemical, produced when substances used for killing plants are made. There are many different types of dioxin. • *A factory explosion in northern Italy in 1976 polluted the town of Seveso with dioxin.* [U] • *Highly toxic dioxins have been released into the air.* [C]

dip *(obj)* [PUT INTO] /dɪp/ *v* **-pp-** to put (something) briefly (into esp. liquid) • *Dip the fish* **in** *the batter, then drop it into the hot oil.* [T] • *He dipped his brush* **in** *the paint.* [T] • *She dipped her toe* **into** *the swimming pool to see how cold the water was.* [T] • *(fig.) The company is dipping its toe* **in** (= taking action to find out about) *the German market.* [T] • If you dip (your hand) **in/into** a container, you put your hand into the container and take something out: *We all dipped into the box of chocolates.* [I always + adv/prep] ○ *He dipped his hand in his pocket and brought out a few coins.* [T] • If people **dip in**, they share something, esp. food: *Wanda set a large bowl of strawberries on the table, and told us all to dip in.* • To **dip into** a book or a subject is to spend short periods of time reading or studying parts of it: *I've only dipped into the book – I haven't read it from cover to cover.* ○ *I've been dipping into our family history recently.* • If you **dip into** your **savings/reserves/pocket/wallet**, you spend your money, esp. money that you have been saving or keeping. • To dip sheep is to put them briefly into a container of liquid which contains chemicals which kill harmful insects on the sheep's bodies. [T]

dip /dɪp/ *n* [C] • A dip is a cold thick creamy sauce which you eat by briefly putting pieces of raw vegetable or biscuits, etc. into it: *Mixing together yoghurt, cucumber and mint makes a refreshing dip.* • A dip is also a quick swim: *I'm just going for a dip* **in** *the sea.* • A dip is also a special liquid used for cleaning: *a silver dip* ○ *a sheep dip* • A dip is also a brief consideration of a subject: *We begin our dip* **into** *local history by examining the town's origins.*

dip *(obj)* [DROP] /dɪp/ *v* **-pp-** to (cause to) go down to a lower level • *As you turn the corner, the road dips suddenly.* [I] • *Seagulls wheeled and dipped on the warm currents of air.* [I] • *The company's profits dipped steeply last month.* [I] • *House prices dipped in the first three months of the year.* [I] • *The sun dipped below the horizon.* [I] • *(Br and Aus)* If you dip the lights on a vehicle, you make the beam of light point down: *I was dazzled when the oncoming driver did not dip his headlights.* [T]

dip /dɪp/ *n* [C usually sing] • *They did not see the dip* **in** *the road.* • *The sudden dip* **in** *the temperature caused snow on the roads to freeze.* • A **dip-switch** is the device that you use to dip the lights on a vehicle.

diph·the·ri·a /£dɪfˈθɪə·ri·ə, dɪp-, $-ˈθɪr·i-/ *n* [U] a serious infectious disease that causes fever and difficulty in breathing and swallowing

diph·thong /£ˈdɪf·θɒŋ, ˈdɪp-, $-θɑːŋ/ *n* [C] *specialized* a vowel sound in which the tongue changes position to produce the sound of two vowels • *English people pronounce 'eye' as a diphthong.*

di·plo·ma /£dɪˈpləʊ·mə, $-ˈploʊ-/ *n* [C] a document given by a college or university to show that you have passed a particular examination or completed a course • *a diploma* **in** *business studies* • *(Am) a high school diploma* • (GR) (PL)

di·plo·ma·cy /£dɪˈpləʊ·mə·si, $-ˈploʊ-/ *n* [U] the management of relationships between countries, or *(fig. approving)* skill in dealing with people without making them angry or unhappy, or offending them • *Diplomacy has so far failed to bring an end to the fighting.* • *Thanks to frantic behind-the-scenes diplomacy, the international agreement has now been signed.* • *(fig. approving) It took all her tact and diplomacy to persuade him not to resign.*

di·plo·mat /ˈdɪp·lə·mæt/, *dated* **di·plo·ma·tist** /£dɪˈpləʊ·mə·tɪst, $-ˈploʊ·mə·t̬ɪst/ *n* [C] • A diplomat is an official of high rank whose job is to represent one country in another, and who usually works in an EMBASSY: *Western diplomats are meeting in Geneva this weekend.* • *(fig. approving) When Anna asked us what we thought of her unattractive new hairstyle, Karin, always a diplomat* (= a person who is skilled at dealing with difficult situations in a way which does not offend people), *said "It makes you look completely different!"*

di·plo·mat·ic /£ˌdɪp·ləˈmæt·ɪk, $-ˈmæt̬-/ *adj* • *The two leaders have been involved in lengthy diplomatic* (= involving the management of the relationships between countries) *negotiations.* • *(fig. approving) Ask him nicely – be diplomatic* (= act in a way that does not cause offence). • *Britain threatened to break off* **diplomatic relations** (= the arrangement between two countries by which each has representatives in the other country). • A **diplomatic bag/diplomatic pouch** is a container in which letters are sent between countries' representatives in other countries, and which is not examined by officials who control what goods are allowed into a country: *The guns were smuggled into the embassy in the diplomatic bag.* • The **diplomatic corps** are all the people who work in one country as representatives of another country. • **Diplomatic immunity** means the special rights that diplomats have while working in a country that is not their own, such as freedom from legal action: *He did not have to pay his speeding fine because he pleaded diplomatic immunity.* • The **diplomatic service** is the government department that employs people to represent their country in other parts of the world.

di·plo·mat·i·cally /£ˌdɪp·ləˈmæt·ɪ·kli, $-ˈmæt̬-/ *adv*

dip·py /ˈdɪp·i/ *adj* **-ier, -iest** *infml* foolish; not clever • *You dippy thing!* • *That's the dippiest thing I ever heard!*

dip·so·ma·ni·a /ˌdɪp·səˈmeɪ·ni·ə/ *n* [U] an uncontrollable need to drink alcohol

dip·so·ma·ni·ac /ˌdɪp·səˈmeɪ·ni·æk/, *infml* **dip·so** /£ˈdɪp·səʊ, $-soʊ/ *n* [C] • A dipsomaniac is a person who has an uncontrollable need to drink alcohol.

dip·stick /ˈdɪp·stɪk/ *n* [C] a long thin stick for measuring the amount of liquid in a container, esp. the oil in a car engine

dire /£daɪəʳ, $daɪr/ *adj* very serious or extreme, or *(infml)* very bad • *The family was living in dire poverty.* • *These people are in dire* **need** *of help.* • *He gave a dire* **warning** *about the likelihood of there being an earthquake.* • *The business is in dire* **straits**. • *This decision will have dire* **consequences** *for local people.* • *(infml) I thought that film was dire!*

di·rect [STRAIGHT] /daɪˈrekt/ *adj* going in a straight line towards somewhere or someone without stopping or changing direction and without anything coming in between • *Is there a direct train to Edinburgh or do we have to change?* • Direct also means without anyone or anything else being involved: *She decided to take direct control of the project.* ○ *He denied that he had any direct involvement in the deal.* ○ *Have you any direct experience of this kind of work?* ○ *There is a direct link between smoking and lung cancer.* ○ *As a direct* **result/consequence** *of what she said, he decided to leave his job.* • *Diana is a direct* **descendant** *of Robert Peel* (= she is a relative of his through one of her parents, not through an aunt or uncle, etc.) • *This plant should be kept out of direct* **sunlight** (= strong light with nothing in between to protect it). • *She's very thoughtful – the direct* (= complete) *opposite of her selfish husband.* • A direct person is someone who says what they think in a very honest way without worrying about other people's opinions: *I like her open and direct manner.* • **Direct action** is the use of STRIKES, violence, etc. as a way of trying to get what you want from an employer, the government, etc., instead of talking. • *(Br)* **Direct debit** is a way of paying money that you owe, to esp. an organization, by which your bank moves money from your account into the organization's account at regular times: *I pay my electricity bill* **by** *direct debit.* Compare **standing order** at STANDING [PERMANENT]. (LP) **Money** • *(Am) I get paid by* **direct deposit** (= the money is paid by electronic transfer into a bank account). • A **direct hit** is when a bullet, bomb etc. hits an object accurately: *The house suffered a direct hit.* • *(esp. Am)* **Direct mail** is a way of selling a product, or trying to obtain money for CHARITY (= people who are ill, or who need help for other reasons), by writing to people to try and persuade them to buy the product or give money. • A **direct tax** is the money that a person has to pay to the government, such as income tax, rather than a tax which is paid through someone else, such as sales tax, which is paid through the seller. • *(specialized)* If you use **direct speech**/*(Am also)* **direct discourse**, you repeat what someone has said using exactly the words they used: *'She said, "If it rains, I won't go out"' is an example of the use of direct speech.* Compare **indirect speech** at INDIRECT [NOT STRAIGHT]. • *(specialized)* The **direct object** of a TRANSITIVE verb is the word or phrase naming who or what the action of the verb is done to. Compare **indirect object** at INDIRECT [NOT STRAIGHT]. • (LP) **Clauses, Quotation marks, Say, Two objects**

di·rect /daɪˈrekt/ *adv* • *Does this train go direct* (= without stopping) *to Edinburgh or do we have to change?* • *Can I dial this number direct* (= without anything or anyone else being involved) *or do I have to go through the operator?* • (LP) **Telephone**

di·rect·ly /daɪˈrekt·li/ *adv* • *Our hotel room was directly above* (= there was nothing between it and) *a building site.* •

The sun shone directly (= in a way not blocked by anything else) *in my eyes.* • *The disease is directly* (= in a way not influenced by other causes) *linked to poor drainage systems.* • *(fig.) She told me quite directly* (= honestly) *that my work wasn't good enough.* • *(fig.) "Did you tell him to go?" "Not directly, no* (= Not using those words)."

di·rect·ness /daɪˈrekt·nəs/ *n* [U] • *(fig.) Her directness* (= very honest way of speaking or behaving) *embarrassed him.*

di·rect *obj* AIM /daɪˈrekt/ *v* [T always + adv/prep] to aim in a particular direction • *Was that remark directed* **at** *me?* • *Strong criticism was directed* **against/at** *the manufacturers of the product.* • *Their efforts were directed* **towards** *helping the homeless.* • *Could you direct me* **to** *the airport* (= tell me how to get there)?

di·rect *(obj)* CONTROL /daɪˈrekt/ *v* to control or be in charge of (an activity, organization etc.) • *She is responsible for directing a large charity.* [T] • *There was a police officer directing the traffic.* [T] • When someone directs a film, play, etc., they tell the actors how to play their parts: *He wanted to give up acting and start directing (his own films).* [I/T] ○ *'Jaws' was one of the first films directed by Steven Spielberg.* [T] • Compare PRODUCE MAKE.

di·rec·tion /daɪˈrek·ʃᵊn/ *n* [U] • *The project was* **under** *the direction* (= control) **of** *a well-known academic.* • *His direction* **of** *the play* (= His telling the actors how to play their parts) *has been strongly criticized.*

di·rec·tor /£daɪˈrek·təʳ, $-t̬ɚ/ *n* [C] • *All the company's cheques have to be signed by two directors* (= people in charge). • *She has become the director* **of** *the new information centre.* • *The decision has yet to be approved by the* **board of** *directors.* • A director is also a person who tells actors in a film or play how to play their parts: *He used to be one of Hollywood's biggest (film/movie) directors.* Compare **producer** at PRODUCE MAKE. • *(Am)* A director is also someone in charge of a school for very young children. • The **director general** of a big organization is the person who is in charge of it. • *(Br)* The **Director of Public Prosecutions** is the lawyer who works for the government and who decides whether a person who has committed a particular type of serious crime should be made to appear in a court of law. • (PL) (RUS)

di·rec·tor·ate /£daɪˈrek·tᵊr·ət, $-t̬ɚ-/ *n* [C] • A directorate is a department or organization which is responsible for one particular thing: *the Norwegian fish and game directorate* ○ *the Department of the Environment's directorate* **on** *environmental pollution* • A directorate is also a group of directors.

di·rec·tor·i·al /£ˌdɪr·ekˈtɔː·ri·əl, $-ˈtɔːr·i-/ *adj* [not gradable] • *Is she ready for directorial responsibility?* • *The actress has left the play because she doesn't like the director's directorial style.* • *The film was the actor's directorial* **debut** (= the first film he had directed).

di·rec·tor·ship /£daɪˈrek·tə·ʃɪp, $-t̬ɚ-/ *n* [C] • *He holds several company directorships* (= the position of being a director).

di·rect *obj* ORDER /daɪˈrekt/ *v* [T + obj + *to* infinitive] *fml* to order, esp. officially • *The judge directed the defendant* **to** *remain silent.*

di·rec·tions /daɪˈrek·ʃᵊnz/ *pl n* • *I couldn't understand* **the** *directions* (= information telling you what to do) *on the back of the packet.* • *She* **gave/issued/left** *directions* **that** *she was not to be disturbed.* [+ *that* clause]

di·rec·tive /£daɪˈrek·tɪv, $-t̬ɪv/ *n* [C] *fml* • *We all received a directive* (= official instruction) *from our boss* **about** *not using the fax machine.*

di·rec·tion /daɪˈrek·ʃᵊn/ *n* the position towards which someone or something moves or faces • *"No, go that way," I said, pointing* **in** *the opposite direction.* [C] • *He was going* **in** *the direction* **of** *the bedroom.* [C] • *They heard laughter coming* **from** *the direction* **of** *the kitchen.* [C] • *They drove away in opposite directions.* [C] • *I have no/a good* **sense of** *direction* (= I am bad/good at finding places). [U] • *(fig.) She seems to lack direction in her life* (= She does not know what she really wants to do). [U]

di·rec·tions /daɪˈrek·ʃᵊnz/ *pl n* • *Can you give me directions* **to** (= tell me how to find) *your house?*

di·rec·tion·al /daɪˈrek·ʃᵊn·ᵊl/ *adj specialized* • Directional radio equipment receives or gives stronger signals in particular directions.

di·rec·tion·less /daɪˈrek·ʃᵊn·ləs/ *adj* • *Sam seems so directionless* (= does not know what he wants to do) *since he left school.*

di·rect·ly /daɪˈrekt·li/ *adv* [not gradable] very soon or immediately • *Dr Schwarz will be with you directly.* • *I'm so tired that when I get home I'm going directly* (= immediately) *to bed.*

di·rect·ly /daɪˈrekt·li/ *conjunction* • *Directly* (= Immediately after) *he was paid, he went out to buy clothes.* • *I'll be with you directly I've finished writing this letter.*

DIRECTIONS OF THE COMPASS

- **Referring to directions:**
  Do you know which way **is west***?*
  This room **faces northeast***.*
  Our office has a **south facing** *window.*
  The station's about a mile **north of** *here.*
  Sri Lanka lies **to the south of** *India.*
  Texas is **in the south of** *the US.*
  It's **due east** (= exactly to the east).
- **Referring to places in general:**
  There will be heavy rain **in the east***.*
  I think she's **from the south***.*
  He walked all along the **western** *coast.*
  An expert on **southern** *Africa.*
  (infml) She lives **down south***.*
  (infml) He's gone **up north** *to visit an aunt.*
  The **northernmost** *island of Japan.*
  The more **southerly** *cities attract tourists.*
- **Referring to particular places.**
  The directions are used to name particular areas of a country or of the world (LP **World regions** at WORLD)
  The countries of **South East** *Asia*/**Southeast** *Asia.*
  She buys and sells **Eastern** *clothes.*
  Most pollution is caused by **the West***.*
  (Am) They moved **out West** *to San Francisco.*
  (Notice the use of capital letters: LP **Capital letters** at CAPITAL.)
- **Referring to movement:**
  The following adjective forms are common:
  All **northbound** *traffic will be delayed.*
  It flew **in a westerly/westward direction***.*
  an **east/easterly wind** (= from the east)

  Adverb forms (notice the ending in *-wards* is also possible):
  We travelled **south/southward/southwards** *for an hour.*

di·rec·tory /£dɪˈrek·tᵊr·i, daɪ-, $-tɚ·i/ *n* [C] a book which gives a list of names, addresses, facts etc. • *a business directory* • *a directory* **of** *hotels* • *Look up their number in the* **telephone** *directory.* • *(Br)* **Directory Enquiries**/*(Am and Aus)* **Directory Assistance** is a service which you can telephone in order to find out someone's telephone number. • LP **Telephone**

dirge /£dɜːdʒ, $dɜːrdʒ/ *n* [C] a slow sad song or piece of music, sometimes played because someone has died

dirk /£dɜːk, $dɜːrk/ *n* [C] a knife used as a weapon in Scotland in the past

dirn·dl (skirt) /£ˈdɜːn·dl̩, $ˈdɜːrn-/ *n* [C] a wide skirt tightly brought in at the waist

dirt /£dɜːt, $dɜːrt/ *n* [U] dust, earth or any substance that prevents a surface from being clean • *I can't get the dirt off these shoes.* • *His coat was covered with dirt.* • *Our cream-coloured rug really* **shows** *the dirt.* • *Footprints were visible in the dirt* (= earth). • *(esp. Am and Aus)* Dirt is also loose earth on the ground: *After I'd finished gardening, there was dirt from the flower beds all over the path.* • *(infml)* Dirt is also excrement: *I got some* **dog** *dirt on my shoes.* • *(infml)* Dirt can also mean the details of people's private lives: *She'll tell you all the dirt* **about/on** *everyone.* ○ *These journalists are always* **digging for** *dirt.* • *They're selling umbrellas* **dirt cheap** (= very cheaply) *on the market.* • *Umbrellas are* **dirt cheap** (= very cheap) *on the market.* • *He comes from a* **dirt poor** (= very poor) *background.* • A **dirt road**/*(Br and Aus also)* **dirt track** is a road in the countryside made from earth: *We drove up a narrow dirt track to their house.*

dirt·y /£'dɜː·ti, $'dɜːr·t̬i/ *adj* **-ier, -iest** • *Her face was dirty* (= marked with dust, earth, etc.) *and tear-stained.* • *I can't wear this shirt, it's dirty.* • *Cleaning the fireplace is a dirty job* (= one that makes your clothes, hands, etc. dirty). • *I put my shirts in the washing machine, and they came out a dirty* (= not clean-looking) *grey colour.* • *(infml)* Dirty can also mean particularly unfair, dishonest or unkind: *She played a dirty* **trick** *on me by telling me Diane was having a party when she wasn't.* ○ *The airline admitted being involved in a dirty* **tricks** *campaign to win customers from their rival.* ○ *Robbing that old man was certainly a dirty* **deed**. ○ *You're a dirty cheat!* ○ *That's a dirty lie!* • *(infml)* Dirty also means connected with sex, in a way that many people think is offensive: *a dirty* **magazine/film/joke** ○ *You've got a really dirty* **mind**! ○ *My dad doesn't approve of dirty* **language/words** *on television.* • If a word or an expression is a **dirty word**, it refers to something that many people do not approve of: *For the environmentally conscious, 'disposable' has become a dirty word.* • *He gave me a really* **dirty look** (= looked at me disapprovingly). • *(disapproving or humorous)* A **dirty old man** is an old or older man who has an unpleasantly strong interest in sex. • *(esp. Br)* A **dirty weekend** is when two people, who are usually not married to each other, go away for a weekend in order to have sex together. • To **do** someone's **dirty work (for** them) is to do for them the unpleasant things that they would prefer not to do themselves: *Tell her yourself – I'm not going to do your dirty work for you.*

dirt·y *obj* /£'dɜː·ti, $'dɜːr·t̬i/ *v* [T] • *Don't sit on the floor – you might dirty your dress* (= make it dirty). • *(fig.) He refused to dirty his hands* (= become involved in something unfair or immoral) *by lying about what had happened.*

dir·ti·ness /£'dɜː·ti·nəs, $'dɜːr·t̬i-/ *n* [U] • *I don't mind untidiness – it's dirtiness I can't stand.*

dirt·y /£'dɜː·ti, $'dɜːr·t̬i/ *adv* [not gradable] • *(fig. infml) Dez likes football but he plays dirty* (= unfairly). • *(Br and Aus slang)* **Dirty great/big** means extremely large: *The puppy turned out to be a dirty great rottweiler.* ○ *There was a dirty big hole in the middle of a road.*

dirt·y /£'dɜː·ti, $'dɜːr·t̬i/ *n* [U] *Br and Aus* • If you **do the dirty on** someone, you behave unfairly towards them, usually without their knowledge: *He can't forgive her for doing the dirty on him and having an affair with his best friend.*

dis– /dɪs-/ *combining form* added to the front of some words to form their opposites • *to disagree* • *to disconnect* • *an expression of disbelief* • *a dishonest person* • Compare IN-; NON-; UN-. • LP **Opposites**

dis·ab·led /dɪ'seɪ·bl̩d/ *adj* lacking one or more of the physical or mental abilities that most people have • *Disabled from birth, she spent her life in a wheelchair.* • *The accident left him severely disabled.* • *He has spent all his life working with mentally disabled people.* • *The library lacks access for disabled people*/**disabled access** (= a way in which people unable to walk or unable to walk well can go into buildings, vehicles, etc.).

dis·ab·led /dɪ'seɪ·bl̩d/ *pl n* • **The disabled** are people who lack some type of physical ability: *It is often very difficult for the disabled to find jobs.*

dis·a·bil·i·ty /£,dɪs·ə'bɪl·ɪ·ti, $-ə·t̬i/ *n* • *She is deaf, but refuses to let her disability* (= the ability she lacks) *prevent her from doing what she wants to do.* [C] • *Trying to change attitudes to disability* (= the state of lacking some physical ability) *is an uphill struggle.* [U] • Compare INABILITY.

dis·ab·le *obj* /dɪ'seɪ·bl̩/ *v* [T] • *Traffic accidents disable* (= cause to lack some type of physical ability) *thousands of children a year.* • *These guns will destroy or disable* (= stop from working) *any incoming missile.* • *(fig.) She suffered from a disabling shyness* (= a shyness that stopped her doing things).

dis·a·buse *obj* /,dɪs·ə'bjuːz/ *v* [T] *fml* to cause (someone) no longer to have (a wrong idea) • *I hate to disabuse you, but we haven't been given the afternoon off work, after all.* • *He thought that all women liked children, but she soon disabused him* **of** *that (idea/notion).*

dis·ad·van·tage /£,dɪs·əd'vɑːn·tɪdʒ, $-'væn·t̬ɪdʒ/ *n* a condition or situation which causes problems, esp. one which causes something or someone to be less successful than other things or people • *One disadvantage of living in the town is the lack of safe places for the children to play.* [C] • *We need to consider whether the disadvantages of the plan outweigh the advantages.* [C] • *Their enthusiasm might work* **to** *their disadvantage* (= cause them to be less successful than others). [U] • *She argued that social disadvantage* (= lacking good living conditions, a good standard of education, etc.) *is a major cause of crime.* [U] • If you are **at a disadvantage**, you are in a situation in which you are less likely to succeed than others: *Companies not using this process risk being at a disadvantage.* ○ *This new law* **places/puts** *poorer families at a* **distinct** *disadvantage.*

dis·ad·van·tage *obj* /£,dɪs·əd'vɑːn·tɪdʒ, $-'væn·t̬ɪdʒ/ *v* [T] • *Teachers claim such measures could unfairly disadvantage* (= cause to be less successful) *ethnic minorities.*

dis·ad·van·taged /£,dɪs·əd'vɑːn·tɪdʒd, £-'væn·t̬ɪdʒd/ *adj* • Disadvantaged means lacking the standard of living conditions, education, etc. that most people have: *Special attention will be paid to people from disadvantaged areas.* ○ *A new educational programme has been set up for economically disadvantaged children.*

dis·ad·van·taged /£,dɪs·əd'vɑːn·tɪdʒd, $-'væn·t̬ɪdʒd/ *pl n* • **The disadvantaged** are people who do not have good living conditions, a good standard of education, etc., considered as a group: *These measures are intended to help the disadvantaged.*

dis·ad·van·ta·geous /£,dɪs·æd·vɑːn'teɪ·dʒəs, $dɪs ,æd·vən'-/ *adj* • *An advantage for one group might prove disadvantageous* **to** *others.*

dis·af·fect·ed /,dɪs·ə'fek·tɪd/ *adj* no longer supporting or being satisfied with an organization or idea • *The party needs to take steps to attract disaffected voters.* • *The fire at the factory is believed to have been started by two disaffected former employees.* • Disaffected young people are those who are no longer satisfied with society's values: *The teacher said that he found it difficult to cope with a class of disaffected teenagers.*

dis·af·fec·tion /,dɪs·ə'fek·ʃᵊn/ *n* [U] • *Disaffection* **with** *the major banks has grown in recent years.*

dis·af·for·est *obj* /£,dɪs·ə'fɒr·ɪst, $-'fɔːr-/ *v* [T] to DEFOREST

dis·a·gree /,dɪs·ə'griː/ *v* not to have the same opinion, idea, etc.; not to agree • *Some say intensive work is bad for a child. Others disagree.* [I] • *I'm afraid I have to disagree* **with** *you* **(on** *that issue).* [I] • *Sometimes we disagree* **on** *what film to see.* [I] • *Few people would disagree* **that** *something should be done to reduce the level of crime in the area.* [+ *that* clause] • *Experts disagree* **whether** *this is the best course of action to take.* [+ *wh-* word] • *I* **profoundly/strongly** *disagree* **with** (= do not accept) *the decision that has been taken.* [I] • If two or more statements, ideas, sets of numbers, etc. disagree, they are not the same: *The witnesses' statements about what time the suspect was seen leaving the building disagreed.* [I] ○ *I've added these figures up three times, and the answers all disagree* **with** *each other.* [I] ○ *Recent surveys disagree* (= produce different findings) **on** *unemployment figures.* [I]

dis·a·gree·ment /,dɪs·ə'griː·mənt/ *n* • *We had a disagreement* (= argument) **about/over** *the fee for the work.* [C] • *Literary critics were* **in** *total disagreement* (= did not have the same opinions) **(about** *the value of the book).* [U] • *It was the only way they could express their disagreement* **with** (= lack of approval of) *government policy.* [U] • *There was clear disagreement* (= difference) **between** *the results of the polls.* [U]

dis·a·gree with *obj v prep* [T] to cause to feel ill • *My stomach really hurts – I must have eaten something that disagreed with me.*

dis·a·gree·ab·le /,dɪs·ə'griː·ə·bl̩/ *adj* unpleasant • *What a disagreeable young man!* • *She said some very disagreeable things.* • *He described the meeting as having been a very disagreeable experience.*

dis·a·gree·ab·ly /,dɪs·ə'griː·ə·bli/ *adv*

dis·al·low *obj* /,dɪs·ə'laʊ/ *v* [T] to state officially that (something) cannot be accepted because it has not been done in the correct way; not to allow • *The England team had two goals disallowed for pushing.* • *The judge disallowed the defendant's application for bail.*

dis·ap·pear /£,dɪs·ə'pɪəʳ, $-'pɪr/ *v* [I] (of a person or thing) to go somewhere where they cannot be seen or found; to VANISH • *The search was called off for the sailors who disappeared in the storm.* • *This is a way of life that is fast disappearing.* • *I can't find my keys anywhere – they've completely disappeared.* • *The ancient city is in danger of disappearing* **beneath** *the sands of the desert.* • *The sun* *disappeared* **behind** *a cloud.* • *We looked for her but she had disappeared* **into** *the crowd.* • *The car turned the corner and disappeared* **from** *view/***out of** *sight.* • *The film is about a girl who* **mysteriously** *disappeared while on a picnic at Hanging Rock.* • *Our chances of winning the competition have* **virtually** *disappeared.* • *This problem won't just disappear* **overnight.** • *I don't know how it's possible for a person to disappear* **without trace.**

dis·ap·pear·ance /£ˌdɪs·əˈpɪə·rᵊnts, $-ˈpɪr·ᵊnts/ *n* [U] • *A man was being questioned in connection with her disappearance.*

dis·ap·point *(obj)* /ˌdɪs·əˈpɔɪnt/ *v* to fail to satisfy (someone or their hopes, expectations etc.); to cause to feel sad • *I'm sorry to disappoint you, but I'm afraid I can't come after all.* [T] • *The hotel did not disappoint our* **expectations** *of it.* [T] • *The view from the top of the mountain did not disappoint – it was spectacular.* [I]

dis·ap·point·ed /£ˌdɪs·əˈpɔɪn·tɪd, $-t̬ɪd/ *adj* • *If you're expecting that Dad will let you borrow his car, you're going to be* **sorely** *disappointed.* • *We were* **deeply** *disappointed* **at/about** *the result.* • *His parents were* **bitterly** *disappointed* **in/with** *him.* • *She was disappointed* **(that)** *they hadn't phoned.* [+ *(that)* clause] • *You must have been disappointed* **to** *find they'd gone.* [+ *to* infinitive]

dis·ap·point·ed·ly /£ˌdɪs·əˈpɔɪn·tɪd·li, $-t̬ɪd-/ *adv*

dis·ap·point·ing /£ˌdɪs·əˈpɔɪn·tɪŋ, $-t̬ɪŋ/ *adj* • *He should have done better – what a disappointing result!* • *The response to our advertisement has been somewhat disappointing.* • *We've just had some extremely disappointing news.*

dis·ap·point·ing·ly /£ˌdɪs·əˈpɔɪn·tɪŋ·li, $-t̬ɪŋ-/ *adv* • *The team played very disappointingly.*

dis·ap·point·ment /ˌdɪs·əˈpɔɪnt·mənt/ *n* • *Book early to avoid disappointment* (=not being satisfied). [U] • **To** *my* **(great)** *disappointment* (=sadness), *he decided to leave.* [U] • A disappointment is something or someone that is not what you were hoping it would be: *The party turned out to be a huge disappointment.* [C] ○ *I'm afraid I've been rather a disappointment* **to** *my parents.* [C]

dis·ap·pro·ba·tion /£ˌdɪs·æp·rəˈbeɪ·ʃᵊn, $dɪsˌæp-/ *n* [U] *fml* strong feelings of not approving of something or someone; disapproval • *He expressed his disapprobation* **of** *what they had done.*

dis·ap·prove /ˌdɪs·əˈpruːv/ *v* [I] to feel strongly that something or someone is bad, wrong etc.; not to approve • *The survey showed that 32% of respondents approve, 54% disapprove and the rest are undecided.* • *Do you disapprove* **of** *advertisements for cigarettes?* • *I* **strongly** *disapprove* **of** *lying.*

dis·ap·pro·val /ˌdɪs·əˈpruː·vᵊl/ *n* [U] • *Although they said nothing, she could sense their disapproval.* • *There was a note of disapproval in the teacher's voice.* • *He expressed his disapproval* **of** *what they had done.* • **A chorus of** *disapproval greeted my suggestion.*

dis·ap·prov·ing /ˌdɪs·əˈpruː·vɪŋ/ *adj* • *Ignoring their disapproving glances, she continued to speak.*

dis·ap·prov·ing·ly /ˌdɪs·əˈpruː·vɪŋ·li/ *adv* • *They looked at her disapprovingly.*

dis·arm *(obj)* REMOVE WEAPONS /£dɪˈsɑːm, $-ˈsɑːrm/ *v* to take weapons away from (someone), or to give up weapons or armies • *With one movement she disarmed the man and pinned him against the wall.* [T] • *They intended to disarm paramilitary groups.* [T] • *Many politicians argued that this was no time to disarm* (=give up the country's weapons and army). [I] • *The terrorist group has shown no signs of being willing to disarm* (=give up its weapons). [I] • *Experts successfully managed to disarm the* **bomb** (=stop it from exploding). [T] • *(fig.) The prime minister has succeeded in disarming most of the criticism against her* (=stopping it from causing her any harm). [T]

dis·ar·ma·ment /£dɪˈsɑː·mə·mənt, $-ˈsɑːr-/ *n* [U] • *The presidents discussed disarmament* (=the act of reducing or giving up weapons) *and human rights.* • *She said she supported* **nuclear** *disarmament* (=the act of reducing or giving up these weapons.)

dis·arm·er /£dɪˈsɑː·məʳ, $-ˈsɑːr·mɚ/ *n* [C] *Br* • *A group of disarmers* (=people who want a government to give up weapons, esp. nuclear ones) *set up camp near the base.*

dis·arm *obj* CHARM /£dɪˈsɑːm, $-ˈsɑːrm/ *v* [T] to make (someone) like you, esp. when they had not expected to • *His frankness completely disarmed her.*

dis·arm·ing /£dɪˈsɑː·mɪŋ, $-ˈsɑːr-/ *adj approving* • *He displayed a disarming honesty by telling them about his father's bankruptcy.* • *What she said about herself was quite disarming.*

dis·ar·range *obj* /ˌdɪs·əˈreɪndʒ/ *v* [T] *fml* to make untidy • *He sprawled on the disarranged bed.*

dis·ar·ray /ˌdɪs·əˈreɪ/ *n* [U] *fml* the state of being confused and lacking in organization or of being untidy • *The unpopularity of the tax has caused complete disarray in the government.* • *There is general disarray* **among** *the organizers of the event.* • *The news had thrown his plans* **into** *disarray.* • *The industry is* **in a state of** *disarray.* • *His clothes and hair were* **in** *disarray* (=were untidy).

dis·as·so·ci·ate *obj* /£ˌdɪs·əˈsəʊ·si·eɪt, $-ˈsoʊ-/ *v* [T] to DISSOCIATE

dis·as·ter /£dɪˈzɑː·stəʳ, $-ˈzæs·tɚ/ *n* (an event which results in) great harm, damage or death, or serious difficulty • *Scientists have warned of the looming global disaster.* [C] • *An inquiry was ordered into the recent rail disaster* (=a serious train accident). [C] • *It would be a disaster* **for** *me if I lost my job.* [C] • *This is one of the worst* **natural** *disasters ever to* **befall** *the area.* [C] • *Disaster was* **averted** *when the pilot took action to stop the plane from crashing.* [U] • *Heavy and prolonged rain can* **spell** *disaster* **for** *many plants.* [U] • *Everything was going smoothly until suddenly disaster* **struck.** [U] • *The club's difficulties edged closer to disaster* (=serious difficulty) *yesterday.* [U] • *Inviting James and Ivan to dinner on the same evening was a* **recipe for** *disaster* (=caused a very difficult situation) – *they always argue with each other.* [U] • *Aid has been flown in to the disaster* **area** (=the place where a very serious accident, such as an EARTHQUAKE, has happened). • *(fig. humorous) After the party, the house was a disaster area* (=was extremely untidy). • *(infml)* If something or someone is a disaster, they are very unsuccessful: *The evening was a complete disaster.* [C] ○ *As a teacher, he was a disaster.* [C]

dis·as·trous /£dɪˈzɑː·strəs, $-ˈzæs·trəs/ *adj* • *Such a war would be disastrous* **for** *the human race* (=it could cause many deaths). • *This decision will have a disastrous impact on* (=will cause great difficulties in) *foreign policy.* • *After a disastrous* (=very unsuccessful) *attempt to be a farmer, he returned to the city.*

dis·as·trous·ly /£dɪˈzɑː·strə·sli, $-ˈzæs·trə-/ *adv* • *Things began to go disastrously wrong.*

dis·a·vow *obj* /ˌdɪs·əˈvaʊ/ *v* [T] *fml* to say that you know nothing about, have no responsibility for or have no connection with (something) • *They were quick to disavow the rumour.* • *She tried to disavow her past.* • *He publicly disavowed any connection with terrorist groups.*

dis·a·vow·al /ˌdɪs·əˈvaʊ·ᵊl/ *n* [C]

dis·band /dɪsˈbænd/ *v* [I] to stop being a group • *She formed a political group which disbanded a year later.*

dis·bar *obj* /£dɪsˈbɑːʳ, $-ˈbɑːr/ *v* [T] **-rr-** to make someone unable to continue working as a lawyer, esp. because they have done something wrong • *An eminent judge has been disbarred* **for** *accepting bribes.*

dis·be·lief /ˌdɪs·bɪˈliːf/ *n* [U] the refusal to believe that something is true • *His response was one of complete disbelief.* • *The world reacted with disbelief to the news of his death.* • *She shook her head* **in** *disbelief.* • *It is said that when you go to the theatre, you have to be willing to* **suspend** *disbelief* (=to believe in something that you know is not real).

dis·be·lieve *obj* /ˌdɪs·bɪˈliːv/ *v* [T] *fml* • *Do you disbelieve* (=not believe) *me?* [T] • *They said that they disbelieved the evidence.* [T] • *As a scientist, he disbelieves* **in** *things that can't be explained.* [I] • *How can you disbelieve* **that** *he killed her?* [+ *that* clause]

dis·burse *obj* /£dɪsˈbɜːs, $-ˈbɜːrs/ *v* [T] *fml* to pay out (money), usually from an amount that has been collected for a particular purpose • *The local authorities annually disburse between £50m and £100m on arts projects.* • *The World Bank and the IMF have agreed to disburse financial aid to the country.*

disc, *Am also* **disk** /dɪsk/ *n* [C] a circular flat object • *The dog had its name engraved on a little metal disc attached to its collar.* • *The orange disc of the sun sank towards the horizon.* • A disc in your back is a small piece of CARTILAGE (=a strong elastic body tissue) between the bones. • Disc is also another name for a musical record or a **compact disc**: *This recording is available* **on** *disc and on cassette.* • *(Br)* A disc is also a DISK (=a device on which computer information is stored). • **A disc brake** is a type of BRAKE (=a device for making a vehicle stop) where two pieces of material are pressed against a metal disc which is fixed to a wheel. • **A disc jockey** (*abbreviation* **DJ**) is someone who plays records and talks on the radio or at an event where people dance to recorded popular music, such as a DISCO. • In American English the spelling 'disc' is used for a musical record, a **compact disc**, a **disc brake**, and a **video-disc**. • See also CD; DISK.

dis·card *obj* /£dɪˈskɑːd, $-ˈskɑːrd/ *v* [T] to throw (something) away or get rid of it because you no longer want or need it • *Remove the skins from the tomatoes and discard them.* • *We've got a cupboard full of discarded toys.* • *Discarded food containers and bottles littered the streets.* • *This popular theory must now be discarded in the light of new findings.* • When you discard during a card game, you get rid of a card you are holding: *After you discard, you can draw three new cards from the deck.*

dis·card /£ˈdɪskɑːd, $-skɑːrd/ *n* [C] • A discard is a card in a card game that you have got rid of: *Once you've put the card in the discard pile, you can't pick it up again.*

dis·cern *obj* /£dɪˈsɜːn, $-ˈsɜːrn/ *v* [T] *fml* to see, recognize or understand (something that is not clear) • *I could just discern a figure in the darkness.* • *A plant's foliage can discern the difference between light and dark.* • *It is difficult to discern any pattern in these figures.*

dis·cern·i·ble, *Am also* **dis·cern·a·ble** /£dɪˈsɜː·nɪ·bl̩, $-ˈsɜːr-/ *adj fml* • *The influence of Rodin is discernible* (=can be seen) *in the younger artist.* • *There are no discernible differences between these two pairs of shoes, but one of them is much more expensive than the other.* • *There is no discernible reason* (=one that can be understood) *why this should be the case.*

dis·cern·i·bly /£dɪˈsɜː·nɪ·bli, $-ˈsɜːr-/ *adv fml*

dis·cern·ing /£dɪˈsɜː·nɪŋ, $-ˈsɜːr-/ *adj fml approving* • Discerning means knowing when things are of good quality: *This shop sells clothes for the discerning customer, Madam.* ○ *These are wines for the discerning palate.* • Discerning also means good at noticing things: *Discerning readers will have noticed that the photograph on page 5 of this newspaper yesterday had the wrong caption.*

dis·cern·ment /£dɪˈsɜːn·mənt, $-ˈsɜːrn-/ *n* [U] *fml approving* • *It's clear that you are a person of discernment* (=have the ability to decide what is of good quality and what is not).

dis·charge *obj* ALLOW TO LEAVE /£dɪsˈtʃɑːdʒ, $-ˈtʃɑːrdʒ/ *v* [T] to allow (someone) to leave esp. a hospital or a court of law • *Patients were discharged* **from** *hospital because the beds were needed by other people.* • *A peace protester was* **conditionally** *discharged for twelve months* (=allowed to go free only if they do not commit a crime again for this period of time). • *More than half of all prisoners discharged* (=allowed to leave prison) *are reconvicted within two years.* • *Because of the recession, half our staff were discharged* (=dismissed).

dis·charge /£ˈdɪs·tʃɑːdʒ, $-tʃɑːrdʒ/ *n* • *The judge* **gave** *him an* **absolute/unconditional** *discharge.* [C] • *The soldier* **received** *a* **dishonourable** *discharge for a disciplinary offence.* [C] • *You shouldn't go back to work for at least two weeks after your discharge* **from** *hospital.* [U]

dis·charge *(obj)* SEND OUT /£dɪsˈtʃɑːdʒ, $-ˈtʃɑːrdʒ/ *v* to send out (esp. waste matter); to EMIT • *Large amounts of dangerous waste are discharged daily by the factory.* [T] • *The oil which discharged* **into** *the sea seriously harmed a lot of birds and animals.* [I] • *The tanker discharges* (=delivers) *its cargo of oil at the port every month.* [T] • *The wound is still discharging* (=producing liquid matter, esp. that which is infected). [I]

dis·charge /£ˈdɪs·tʃɑːdʒ, $-tʃɑːrdʒ/ *n* • *Discharges from the nuclear plant are entirely safe, it has been claimed.* [C] • *Thousands of fish were killed as a result of a discharge* **of** *poisonous chemicals from a nearby factory.* [C] • *The athletes discussed the discharge* **of** *energy that occurs in a race.* [U] • (A) discharge is also liquid matter, which is often infected, that comes from a part of the body: *nasal discharge* [U] ○ *vaginal discharge* [U] ○ *There was a discharge from the cut on her hand.* [C]

dis·charge *obj* PERFORM /£dɪsˈtʃɑːdʒ, $-ˈtʃɑːrdʒ/ *v* [T] *fml* to perform (a duty, esp. an official one) • *If the authority is to discharge its legal* **duty** *to house the homeless, it needs government support.* • *Teachers have certain* **responsibilities** *which they must discharge.* • To discharge a **debt** is to pay it completely.

dis·charge *obj* FIRE /£dɪsˈtʃɑːdʒ, $-ˈtʃɑːrdʒ/ *v* [T] *fml* to fire (a gun or shots from a gun) • *The police stated that some fifty rounds had been discharged.*

dis·charge /£ˈdɪs·tʃɑːdʒ, $-tʃɑːrdʒ/ *n* [C] • *The evidence pointed to an accidental discharge of the gun.*

dis·ci·ple /dɪˈsaɪ·pl̩/ *n* [C] a person who believes in the ideas and principles of someone famous and tries to live the way they do or did • *One of James Joyce's disciples had translated the poem.* • *He's a* **loyal/ardent** *disciple* **of** *the prime minister.* • **The** Disciples were the twelve men who followed Jesus Christ during his life.

dis·ci·pline TRAINING /ˈdɪs·ə·plɪn/ *n* [U] training which produces obedience or self-control, often in the form of rules and punishments if these are broken, or the obedience or self-control produced by this training • *parental/prison/school discipline* • *Good teachers know that children need and enjoy* **firm** *discipline.* • *The army was criticized for its* **harsh** *discipline.* • *Studying a foreign language is* **a** *good discipline* **for** *the mind.* • If someone or a group of people have (good) discipline, they are in control of themselves or other people, even in difficult situations: *The soldiers' discipline* (=calm self-control) *was remarkable.* ○ *Maintaining classroom discipline* (=control of the students) *is the first task of every teacher.*

dis·ci·pline *obj* /ˈdɪs·ə·plɪn/ *v* [T] • *I'm trying* **to** *discipline my***self to** *eat less chocolate.* [+ obj + *to* infinitive] • *Those children are well disciplined.* • To discipline someone also means to punish them: *A senior civil servant has been disciplined* **for** *revealing secret government plans to the media.*

dis·ci·pli·nar·i·an /£ˌdɪs·ə·plɪˈneə·ri·ən, $-ˈner·i-/ *n* [C] *esp. disapproving* • A disciplinarian is someone who believes in keeping complete control of the people he or she is in charge of, esp. by giving strong punishments: *a strict disciplinarian*

dis·ci·pli·na·ry /£ˌdɪs·əˈplɪn·ər·i, $ˈdɪs·ə·plɪ·ner-/ *adj* [not gradable] • *disciplinary problems in the classroom* • *disciplinary measures/action* (=punishment)

dis·ci·pline SUBJECT /ˈdɪs·ə·plɪn/ *n* [C] a particular area of study, esp. a subject studied at a college or university • *I didn't enjoy studying Philosophy – I found it too much of a theoretical discipline.*

dis·claim *obj* /dɪˈskleɪm/ *v* [T] *fml* to say that you do not have (esp. knowledge or responsibility); to DENY NOT ADMIT • *We disclaim all responsibility for this disaster.*

dis·claim·er /£dɪˈskleɪ·mər, $-mɚ/ *n* [C] *fml* • A disclaimer is a statement that something is not true or intended: *The book bore the disclaimer 'Any resemblance to any person, living or dead, is purely coincidental'.* ○ *The President's public disclaimers about tax increases have not convinced anyone.*

dis·close *(obj)* /£dɪˈskləʊz, $-ˈskloʊz/ *v fml* to make (something) known publicly, or to show (something that was hidden) • *Several companies have disclosed profits of over £200 million.* [T] • *The police have disclosed* **that** *two officers are under internal investigation.* [+ *that* clause] • *The door swung open, disclosing* (=showing) *a dead body lying in a pool of blood.* [T]

dis·clo·sure /£dɪˈskləʊ·ʒər, $-ˈskloʊ·ʒɚ/ *n fml* • *Any public disclosure* **of** *this information would be very damaging to the company.* [U] • *The newspaper made damaging disclosures* **of** *management incompetence.* [C]

dis·co (*pl* **discos**) /£ˈdɪs·kəʊ, $-koʊ/, **dis·co·the·que** *n* [C] an event where people dance to modern recorded music for entertainment, or a place where this often happens • *The pub has a disco on Saturday nights.* • *They're opening a new disco in town.* • *(Br)* A disco is also the equipment necessary for playing recorded music, making special lights, etc.: *We've hired a disco for the party tonight.* • *We could hear loud disco music coming from the hall.* • *The disco lights were flashing on and off with the beat of the music.*

dis·col·our *(obj) Br and Aus, Am and Aus* **dis·col·or** /£dɪˈskʌl·ər, $-ˈskʌl·ɚ/ *v* to (cause to) change from the original colour and therefore to look unpleasant • *The covers of the books had discoloured from their exposure to the sun.* [I] • *My new blue shirt discoloured the rest of my clothes in the wash.* [T]

dis·col·o·ra·tion /dɪˌskʌl·əˈreɪ·ʃən/ *n* • *We were concerned by the patches of discoloration on the walls.* [U] • *There are several small discolorations on the fabric.* [C]

dis·com·fit *obj* /dɪˈskʌmp·fɪt/ *v* [T] *fml* to make (someone) feel uncomfortable, esp. mentally • *I felt regret that I had inconvenienced and discomfited whoever was bumped off the plane so that I could have my seat.* • *The bus swerved around tight curves, greatly discomfiting the foreign tourists in the back seats.* • *Her courage in reporting these issues has discomfited the powers-that-be.* • *He is interviewed rarely and clearly finds it a discomfiting experience.*

dis·com·fi·ture /£dɪˈskʌmp·fɪ·tʃər, $-tʃɚ/ *n* [U] *fml* • *She turned away to hide her discomfiture.* • *He noticed the obvious discomfiture* **of** *the woman as the child tried to sit on her lap.*

dis·com·fort /£dɪ'skʌmp·fət, $-fɚt/ *n* a feeling of being uncomfortable physically or mentally, or something that causes this • *"Do you feel any pain or discomfort* **from/in** *the knee?" asked the doctor.* [U] • *You may feel* **a little** *discomfort as I drill into the tooth.* [U] • *Don't you have a feeling of discomfort* **at** *being so rich in such a poor country?* [U] • *The discomforts of a long motorcycle journey are the cold and cramp.* [C]

dis·con·cert *(obj)* /£ˌdɪs·kən'sɜːt, $-'sɜːrt/ *v* to make (someone) feel suddenly uncertain and worried • *His visit to his mother in hospital disconcerted him.* [T] • *They were disconcerted by his strange replies.* [T] • *The family was disconcerted* **at** *the unexpected news.* [T] • *The reply disconcerts, causes awkwardness.* [I] • *We were disconcerted* **to** *be told, "You can't be trusted".* [+ to infinitive]

dis·con·cert·ing /£ˌdɪs·kən'sɜː·tɪŋ, $-'sɜːr·t̬ɪŋ/ *adj* • *a disconcerting experience* • *I find late-night phone calls most disconcerting.*

dis·con·cert·ing·ly /£ˌdɪs·kən'sɜː·tɪŋ·li, $-'sɜːr·t̬ɪŋ-/ *adv* • *He looked so elegant, but spoke with a disconcertingly vulgar accent.*

dis·con·nect *obj* /ˌdɪs·kə'nekt/ *v* [T] to unfasten (something), esp. to break the connection between a supply of electricity, gas, water, etc. and a device or piece of equipment • *Never try to mend a broken machine without disconnecting it* **from** *the electricity supply.* • To disconnect (also *infml* **cut off**) a customer or a service is to stop supplying electricity/gas/water/telephone services, esp. because money has not been paid: *Does the electricity/gas/water industry publish the number of customers it disconnects for non-payment of bills?* [T] ○ *The phone has been disconnected while the house is empty.* • If you are disconnected (also *infml* **cut off**) while speaking on the telephone, the telephone connection is suddenly broken and you can no longer continue your conversation. • LP **Switching on and off**

dis·con·nect·ed /ˌdɪs·kə'nek·tɪd/ *adj* [not gradable] • *a disconnected power supply* • *disconnected customers* • *(fig.) The green lobby's proposal appears disconnected* **from** *scientific reality.* • If things such as ideas or remarks or the different parts of something are disconnected, they are not well joined together and it is difficult to see their purpose or pattern: *disconnected thoughts*

dis·con·nec·tion /ˌdɪs·kə'nek·ʃən/ *n* • *Both gas and electricity suppliers maintain that the rate of disconnection has gone down in recent years.* [U] • *There were 20 000 gas disconnections and around 70 000 from electricity last year.* [C] • *(fig.) Young single mothers admitted to a sense of disconnection* **from** *society.* [U]

dis·con·so·late /£dɪ'skɒnt·sᵊl·ət, $-'skɑːnt-/ *adj* extremely sad and disappointed • *Steve, who finished last, was disconsolate.* • *They tried to comfort the disconsolate widow.*

dis·con·so·late·ly /£dɪ'skɒnt·sᵊl·ət·li, $-'skɑːnt-/ *adv*

dis·con·tent /ˌdɪs·kən'tent/, **dis·con·tent·ment** /ˌdɪs·kən'tent·mənt/ *n* [U] a feeling of wanting better treatment or an improved situation • *Discontent* **among** *junior ranks was rapidly spreading.* • *Food rationing has been abandoned following* **popular/public** *discontent.* • *There was* **widespread** *discontent* **at/about/over/with** *the plan.* • *As he stopped speaking there were audible* **murmurs of** *discontent.* • *Managers fear* **rumblings of** *discontent from shareholders if the new head-office project comes in spectacularly over budget.*

dis·con·tent·ed /£ˌdɪs·kən'ten·tɪd, $ˌdɪs·kən'ten·t̬ɪd/ *adj* • *a discontented expression* • *The girls are discontented* **with** *their present situation.*

dis·con·tent·ed·ly /£ˌdɪs·kən'ten·tɪd·li, $ˌdɪs·kən'ten·t̬ɪd-/ *adv*

dis·con·tin·ue *obj* /ˌdɪs·kən'tɪn·juː/ *v* [T] *fml* to stop doing or providing (something) • *The bank is discontinuing its Saturday service.*

dis·con·tin·u·a·tion /ˌdɪs·kənˌtɪn·ju'eɪ·ʃən/, **dis·con·tin·u·ance** /ˌdɪs·kən'tɪn·ju·ᵊnts/ *n* [U] *fml* • *We demand the discontinuation* **of** *sanctions against our country.*

dis·con·tin·ued /ˌdɪs·kən'tɪn·juːd/ *adj* • A discontinued product or service is one that is no longer being offered: *a discontinued line of software* ○ *a discontinued model*

dis·con·ti·nu·i·ty /£ˌdɪs·kɒn·tɪ'njuː·ɪ·ti, $-kɑːn·tə'nuː·ə·t̬i/ *n fml* • *If all the older workers leave at one time, there will be a period of discontinuity.* [U] • *There are discontinuities* (= breaks) *in their account of what happened during those weeks.* [C]

dis·con·tin·u·ous /ˌdɪs·kən'tɪn·ju·əs/ *adj* • Discontinuous means with breaks, or stopping and starting again: *a discontinuous line* ○ *a discontinuous process*

dis·cord DISAGREEMENT /£'dɪs·kɔːd, $-kɔːrd/ *n* [U] *fml* a lack of agreement or shared opinions • *ethnic/family/marital/international discord* • *The letter caused discord* **between** *uncle* **and** *nephew.* • *Merlyn* **sounded** *the only* **note of** *discord, demanding "Why should Mark get it all?"* • Compare CONCORD.

dis·cor·dant /£dɪ'skɔː·dᵊnt, $-'skɔːr-/ *adj fml* • *The two leaders made a show of unity at the press conference, though they had notably discordant messages.* • *The book, however, records the discordant voice of one young woman who feels she has not experienced discrimination.* • *The only discordant element was a group of parents who felt their views were being ignored.* • *The nurse was the only one to* **strike a** *discordant* **note**, *saying that her group were unhappy with aspects of security.*

dis·cord SOUND /£'dɪs·kɔːd, $-kɔːrd/ *n* [C; U] *specialized* a group of musical notes which give a unpleasant sound when played together

dis·cor·dant /£dɪ'skɔː·dᵊnt, $-'skɔːr-/ *adj* • *Modern classical music just sounds discordant to me.*

dis·co·the·que /'dɪs·kə·tek/ *n* [C] a DISCO

dis·count REDUCTION /'dɪs·kaʊnt/ *n* [C] a reduction in the usual price • *Unlike normal health-insurance schemes there is no discount* **for** *group membership.* • *Discounts* **on** *the price of travel, meals, home furnishings, car parts, etc. are available to club members.* • *I bought these shoes* **at a** *40%* **discount** (= the price was 40% less than the full price). • *The shop assistant said they could* **give** *me a big discount if I bought three at once.* • *Will you* **give** *me a discount* **for quantity** (= if I buy a large number)? • A **discount card** is a document which allows you to pay a cheaper price because you belong to a particular organization or group: *She produced a senior citizen's discount card.* • A **discount store** is a shop which sells its goods at cheap prices. • A **discount warehouse** is a large shop, usually not in the centre of a town, which sells at cheap prices esp. large goods or large quantities: *a discount furniture warehouse* ○ *a discount wine warehouse*

dis·count *obj* /dɪ'skaʊnt/ *v* [T] • *If we have to discount our prices/these cars we aren't going to make a profit.*

dis·count *obj* NOT CONSIDER /dɪ'skaʊnt/ *v* [T] to decide that (something or someone) is not worth consideration or attention • *We can discount Liverpool – they have three injured players.* • *Mr. Allsburg does not discount* **the possibility** *that the stress he was under affected his decisions* (= he thinks the stress he felt influenced them).

dis·cou·rage *obj* MAKE LESS CONFIDENT /£dɪ'skʌr·ɪdʒ, $-'skɜːr-/ *v* [T] to make (someone) feel less confident, enthusiastic and positive about something, or less willing to do something • *Don't be discouraged* **by** *their attitude – you're doing very well.* • *The thought of how much work she had to do discouraged her.*

dis·cou·rag·ing /£dɪ'skʌr·ɪ·dʒɪŋ, $-'skɜːr-/ *adj* • *Why are you always so discouraging* **about** *my chances of getting a job?* • *Your first batch of results may be discouraging, but never mind, they'll improve.* • *It's been a long and very discouraging year, without many bright spots.*

dis·cou·rage·ment /£dɪ'skʌr·ɪdʒ·mənt, $-'skɜːr-/ *n* • *Despite the discouragement* **of** *playing to a very small audience, we soon began to enjoy ourselves.* [U] • *The group has experienced a series of discouragements in the last six months.* [C]

dis·cou·rage *obj* PREVENT /£dɪ'skʌr·ɪdʒ, $-'skɜːr-/ *v* [T] to prevent or try to prevent (something happening or someone doing something) by making things difficult or unpleasant, or by showing disapproval • *The authorities have put tanks on the streets to discourage any protest.* • *Her parents discouraged her from applying for drama courses because they thought she'd never get a job.* • *What discourages me* **from going** *camping is all the insects!*

dis·cou·rage·ment /£dɪ'skʌr·ɪdʒ·mənt, $-'skɜːr-/ *n* [U] • *Recently there has been official discouragement of smoking in public places.*

dis·course /£'dɪs·kɔːs, $-kɔːrs/ *n fml* communication in speech or writing • *Voters in three states were given the opportunity to make English the language of official discourse in those states.* [U] • *Civilized discourse between the two countries has become impossible.* [U] • A discourse is also a speech, piece of writing, or discussion about a particular, usually serious, subject: *a discourse* **on/upon** *the nature of life after death* [C]

dis·course on/u·pon /£dɪ'skɔːs, $-'skɔːrs/ *v prep* [I] *fml*

dis·cour·te·ous /£dɪ'skɜː·ti·əs, $-'skɜːr·ţi-/ *adj fml* rude and not considering other people's feelings; not polite • *According to the customer survey carried out in the past three months, 6% said employees were unhelpful and discourteous.* • *How discourteous* **(of them)** *to leave without saying goodbye.*

dis·cour·te·sy /£dɪ'skɜː·tə·si, $-'skɜːr·ţə-/ *n fml* • *If the story is true it would seem to be the most deplorable act of discourtesy.* [U] • *The exchange of insults went far beyond the usual discourtesies that pass between opponents on television shows.* [C]

dis·co·ver *(obj)* /£dɪ'skʌv·əʳ, $-ɚ/ *v* to find (information, a place or an object), esp. for the first time • *I went to the library but I couldn't discover anything about water rats.* [T] • *Gravity was discovered by Newton when an apple fell on his head.* [T] • *Did Columbus discover America in 1492 or were the Vikings there 500 years before?* [T] • *We searched all morning for the missing papers and finally discovered them in a drawer.* [T] • *Scientists have discovered* **how** *to predict an earthquake.* [+ *wh-* word] • *She discovered* **that** *her husband was having an affair.* [+ *that* clause] • *Following a routine checkup, Mrs Mason was discovered* **to** *have heart disease.* [+ obj + *to* infinitive] • *The boss discovered him* (=unexpectedly found him) *steal***ing** *money from the till.* [+ obj + v-*ing*] • If a person with special abilities is discovered, someone else helps them to become successful: *Los Angeles is full of beautiful girls working as waitresses, hoping to be discovered by a movie agent.* [T]

dis·cov·er·er /£dɪ'skʌv·əʳ·əʳ, $-ɚ·ɚ/ *n* [C] • *Wilhelm Röntgen was the discoverer* **of** *X rays.* • *Jim Watson and Francis Crick were the discoverers* **of** *DNA.* • *Explorers of the New World such as John Cabot, discoverer* **of** *Newfoundland and Nova Scotia, sailed from Bristol.*

dis·cov·er·y /£dɪ'skʌv·əʳ·i, $'-ɚ-/ *n* • *the discovery* **of** *electricity* [U] • *Leonardo made many scientific discoveries.* [C] • *the discovery* **of** *America* [U] • *a journey/voyage of discovery* [U] • *The discovery* **of** *a body in the undergrowth started a murder enquiry.* [U]

dis·cred·it *obj* /dɪ'skred·ɪt/ *v* [T] *fml* to cause people to stop respecting (someone) or believing in (an idea or person) • *Evidence of links with drug dealers has discredited the President.* • *Scientific investigation has discredited her claim to be a mind-reader.*

dis·cred·it /dɪ'skred·ɪt/ *n* [U] *fml* • *The stupid behaviour of one pupil has* **brought** *discredit* **on/upon** *the whole school.* • *The existence of poverty is* **a** *discredit* **to** *our country.* • *It is* **to** *her discredit* (=It lowers our opinion of her) *that she never visits her mother in hospital.*

dis·cred·it·able /£dɪ'skred·ɪ·tə·bḷ, $-ə·ţə-/ *adj fml*

dis·cred·it·ably /£dɪ'skred·ɪ·tə·bli, $-ə·ţə-/ *adv fml*

dis·creet /dɪ'skriːt/ *adj* intentionally not attracting attention by noticeable behaviour or appearance, often in order to hide something • *Most church leaders have kept a discreet silence during this war.* • *There were discreet signs of wealth all over the house.* • *The family made discreet enquiries about his background.* • *They asked me to be discreet when requesting the application form, "since we don't want everyone to ask".* • To be discreet is also to keep information secret or to share it with only a few trusted people: *They are very good assistants, very discreet – they wouldn't go shouting to the press about anything they discovered while working for you.* • *"The discreet charm of the bourgeoisie"* (title of a film by Luis Buñuel, 1972)

dis·creet·ly /dɪ'skriːt·li/ *adv* • *"I don't think she paid for that book," he whispered to me discreetly.*

dis·cre·tion /dɪ'skreʃ·ᵊn/ *n* [U] • *I hope I can rely on your discretion?* (=I do not expect you to tell other people.) • *"Can you trust him with this?" "Yes, he's* **the soul of** *discretion* (=he will not tell other people)." • See also DISCRETION.

dis·crep·an·cy /dɪ'skrep·ᵊnt·si/ *n fml* (a) difference between two things that should be the same • *There are several discrepancies* **between** *the original estimates of the cost* **and** *the actual bills.* [C] • *There is some discrepancy* **between** *the two accounts.* [U] • *The committee is reportedly unhappy about the discrepancy* **in** *numbers.* [C]

dis·crep·ant /dɪ'skrep·ᵊnt/ *adj* • *discrepant figures* • *discrepant opinions/views*

dis·crete /dɪ'skriːt/ *adj* having a clear independent shape or form; separate • *These small companies now have their own discrete identity.*

dis·cre·tion /dɪ'skreʃ·ᵊn/ *n* [U] good judgment • *I* **leave** *the decision* **to** *your discretion.* • *The granting of visas is* **at the** *discretion* **of** (=depends on the decision of) *the immigration officials.* • *(saying)* 'Discretion is the better part of valour' means that it is wise to be careful and avoid unnecessary risks. • See also **discretion** at DISCREET.

dis·cre·tion·ary /£dɪ'skreʃ·ᵊn·ᵊr·i, $-er-/ *adj fml* • Discretionary **powers/grants** are controlled by officials who can act on their own authority.

dis·crim·i·nate TREAT DIFFERENTLY /dɪ'skrɪm·ɪ·neɪt/ *v* [I] to treat a person or particular group of people differently, esp. in a worse way from the way in which you treat other people, because of their skin colour, religion, sex, etc. • *(disapproving) She felt she had been discriminated* **against** *because of her age.* • *(approving) In order to increase the number of female representatives, the selection committee decided to discriminate* **in favour of** *women for three years.*

dis·crim·i·na·tion /dɪˌskrɪm·ɪ'neɪ·ʃᵊn/ *n* [U] • *race/sex/age discrimination* • *Until 1986 most companies would not even allow women to take the examinations but such* **blatant** *discrimination is now disappearing.* • **Positive/Reverse** discrimination means acting in a way which will give special benefit to those who frequently fail to get jobs and other positions in society because they are black, female, etc.

dis·crim·i·na·to·ry /£dɪ'skrɪm·ɪ·nə·tᵊr·i, £-tri, £dɪˌskrɪm·ɪ'neɪ-, $dɪ'skrɪm·ɪ·nə·tɔːr-/ *adj* • *discriminatory language* • *discriminatory legislation/laws/practices/social policy* • *discriminatory treatment*

dis·crim·i·nate SEE A DIFFERENCE /dɪ'skrɪm·ɪ·neɪt/ *v fml* to be able to see the difference between two things or people • *Consider the problem of discriminating one black cat* **from** *another.* [T] • *They reported the discovery that honey bees discriminate* **between** *full and half sisters.* [I]

dis·crim·i·nat·ing /£dɪ'skrɪm·ɪ·neɪ·tɪŋ, $-ţɪŋ/ *adj fml approving* • Discriminating means able to know and act on the difference between good and bad: *He has a discriminating palate for wine.* ○ *They're discriminating shoppers.*

dis·crim·i·na·tion /dɪˌskrɪm·ɪ'neɪ·ʃᵊn/ *n* [U] *fml* • *Discrimination* **between** *these different shades of blue is difficult.* • *(approving) He* **showed** *discrimination* (=good judgment) *in choosing the furniture.*

dis·cur·sive /£dɪ'skɜː·sɪv, $-skɜːr-/ *adj fml esp. disapproving* (of a person, or their style of communicating) talking about or dealing with subjects which are only slightly connected with the main subject for longer than necessary • *a discursive writer/essay/speech/play*

dis·cus /'dɪs·kəs/ *n* [C] a heavy plate-shaped object, made of wood, metal or plastic, which is thrown as part of a sports event • **The discus** is the event or sport in which a discus is thrown as far as possible. • PIC **Sports**

dis·cuss *(obj)* /dɪ'skʌs/ *v* to consider (a subject), esp. by talking about it with others • *Police are meeting local people to discuss recent racist attacks.* [T] • *I don't feel I can discuss anything important* **with** *my parents.* [T] • *This booklet discusses* **how** *to run your own business.* [+ *wh-* word] • *I think we should discuss apply***ing** *for some kind of government help.* [+ v-*ing*] • Ⓔ

dis·cus·sion /dɪ'skʌʃ·ᵊn/ *n* • *Let's have more action, less discussion.* [U] • *I can say nothing – the matter is still* **under** *discussion* (=being considered). [U] • *a discussion group/document* • *Management are* **holding/having** *discussions* **with** *the Union.* [C] • *Discussions* **between** *the two sides produced no solutions.* [C] • Ⓔ Ⓝⓛ

dis·dain /dɪs'deɪn, dɪz-/ *n* [U] *fml* dislike of someone or something that you feel does not deserve your interest or respect • *The local citizens showed their disdain* **of/for** *the foreign artists.*

dis·dain *(obj)* /dɪs'deɪn, dɪz-/ *v fml* • *The older musicians disdain the new, rock-influenced music.* [T] • *Our posh new neighbours seem to be disdaining* **to** *speak to us* (=refusing because they think we do not deserve their attention). [+ *to* infinitive]

dis·dain·ful /dɪs'deɪn·fᵊl/ *adj fml* • *a disdainful expression/stare* • *These book sales are an astonishing development for a country once disdainful* **of** *contemporary foreign authors.*

dis·ease /dɪ'ziːz/ *n* (an) illness of people, animals, plants, etc., caused by infection or a failure of health rather than by an accident • *a contagious/infectious disease* [C] • *a communicable disease* [C] • *a common/rare/incurable/fatal disease* [C] • *a childhood disease* [C] • *They reported a sudden* **outbreak of** *the disease in the south of the country.* [C] • *The first* **symptom of** *the disease is a very high temperature.* [C] • *She has* **caught/contracted** (=began to have) *a lung disease/disease of the lungs.* [C] • *Starvation and disease have killed thousands of refugees.* [U] • *He's got Legionnaire's Disease.* [U] • *Hundreds of thousands of trees died from Dutch Elm Disease.* [U] • *(fig.) The real disease affecting the country is inflation.* [U]

dis·eased /dɪˈziːzd/ *adj* • *a diseased lung/kidney* • *diseased brain tissue* • *Farmers were dumping or burying the diseased animals/carcasses.* • *The bush looked badly diseased, with black marks on all the leaves.* • *(fig.) a diseased mind/imagination* • *(fig.) a diseased society*

dis·em·bark /£ˌdɪs·ɪmˈbɑːk, $-ˈbɑːrk/ *v* [I] *fml* to leave a ship, aircraft, etc. after a journey • *The passengers disembarked* **from** *the ferry/the night flight.*

dis·em·bod·ied /£ˌdɪs·ɪmˈbɒd·id, $-ˈbɑː·did/ *adj* [not gradable] existing without a body • *A disembodied* **voice** *crackled from the radio.* • *A poltergeist is a disembodied* **spirit** *thought to be capable of causing unusual physical disturbances.* • *A pair of seemingly disembodied legs stood on a chair, the upper half of the soldier sticking up through the hole in the roof.*

dis·em·bow·el *obj* /ˌdɪs·ɪmˈbaʊ·əl/ *v* [T usually passive] **-ll-** or *Am usually* **-l-** to remove the stomach and bowels from (a dead animal), or to kill (a person) in this way, sometimes as a punishment • *The animals were disembowelled and the carcasses split down the backbone.* • *The animals had lethal claws – one swipe could disembowel a man, spilling his guts out.* • *He publicly disembowelled him***self** *in 1970 after a failed coup.*

dis·en·chant·ed /£ˌdɪs·ɪnˈtʃɑːn·tɪd, $-ˈtʃæn·t̬ɪd/ *adj* no longer believing in the value of something, esp. having learnt of the faults that it has • *Many* **voters** *have* **become** *disenchanted* **with** *the government.*

dis·en·chant·ment /£ˌdɪs·ɪnˈtʃɑːnt·mənt, $-ˈtʃænt-/ *n* [U] • *Disillusionment and disenchantment have now set in for many people.* • *The latest opinion polls demonstrate the public's deep disenchantment* **with** *social conditions.* • *There is (a) growing disenchantment* **with** *the way the country/school/football club is being run.*

dis·en·fran·chise *obj* /ˌdɪs·ɪnˈfræn·tʃaɪz/, **dis·fran·chise** *v* [T] to take away power or opportunities, esp. the right to vote, from (a person or group) • *Many voters will be disenfranchised because their names did not appear on the electoral register at that date.*

dis·en·fran·chised /ˌdɪs·ɪnˈfræn·tʃaɪzd/ *adj* • Disenfranchised means not having esp. the right to vote or having had that right taken away: *We are a local movement working towards greater democracy and justice for minorities, women, and other disenfranchised groups in this part of the world.*

dis·en·gage *(obj)* /ˌdɪs·ɪŋˈgeɪdʒ/ *v* to (cause to) become separate; to stop being connected • *They recognized that the country would revive only if it thoroughly disengaged* **from** *the chaos of the old regime.* [I] • *The number one rule for being a good person to work with is to disengage your emotions* **from** *the working relationship.* [T] • *Both children, disengaging them***selves from** *their game, came to her side.* [T] • If you disengage **the clutch** of a car, you stop the power produced by the engine being connected to the wheels. [T]

dis·en·gage·ment /ˌdɪs·ɪŋˈgeɪdʒ·mənt/ *n* [U]

dis·en·tan·gle *obj* /ˌdɪs·ɪnˈtæŋ·gl̩/ *v* [T] to separate (things that have become joined or confused) • *I patiently disentangled the wool and rolled it neatly into a ball.* • *She said she'd spent ages disentangling her***self from** *the rose bushes.* • *It's difficult to disentangle hard fact* **from** *myth, or truth* **from** *lies.*

dis·es·ta·blish *obj* /ˌdɪs·ɪˈstæb·lɪʃ/ *v* [T] *fml* to take away official support and position from (esp. a Church)

dis·es·ta·blish·ment /ˌdɪs·ɪˈstæb·lɪʃ·mənt/ *n* [U]

dis·fa·vour *Br and Aus*, *Am and Aus* **dis·fa·vor** /£dɪsˈfeɪ·vəʳ, $-vɚ/ *n* [U] *fml* a feeling of dislike or disapproval • *She regarded the ugly new houses/the tramp* **with** *disfavour.* • If you are **in** disfavour, you are disliked or disapproved of: *His family is holding him in disfavour.* ○ *He's in disfavour* **with** *his family because he refuses to get a job.*

dis·fig·ure *obj* /£dɪsˈfɪg·əʳ, $-jɚ/ *v* [T] to spoil completely the appearance of (esp. a person's face) • *I think the tattoo disfigures him.* • *She was horribly disfigured by burns.* • *This part of the old town has been disfigured by ugly new buildings.* • *(fig.) The history of this century has been disfigured by two world wars.*

dis·fran·chise *obj* /dɪsˈfræn·tʃaɪz/ *v* [T] to DISENFRANCHISE

dis·gorge *obj* /£dɪsˈgɔːdʒ, $-ˈgɔːrdʒ/ *v* [T] to empty or release (the contents) from • *The bus disgorged a crowd of tourists.* • *The pipe was found to be disgorging dangerous chemicals into the sea.* • *(humorous) I've spent days trying to get the bank to disgorge the money I'm owed.*

dis·grace /dɪsˈgreɪs/ *n* [U] (behaviour which causes) embarrassment and the loss of other people's respect • *He* **brought** *disgrace* **on** *his family/him***self** *by falsifying the results.* • *The athlete suffered the disgrace* **of** *being publicly shown to have taken drugs.* • *Brian's* **in** *disgrace* **for** *signing Jack's forms* (=People do not approve of what he did). • If something is **a** disgrace it is considered to be very bad: *Three families living in one room – it's a disgrace!* ○ *You're a disgrace (***to** *the family) – what a way to behave!* ○ *Your clothes are a disgrace – all dirty and untidy!* ○ **It**'s *a disgrace* **that** *the government spends so much on guns and so little on education.* [+ *that* clause] • (E) (P)

dis·grace *obj* /dɪsˈgreɪs/ *v* [T] • *The assistant manager has been disgraced and dismissed for stealing.*

dis·graced /dɪsˈgreɪst/ *adj* • *You shouldn't feel disgraced by finishing last – it was a good effort.* • *The disgraced leader cannot leave the country but is not under arrest.*

dis·grace·ful /dɪsˈgreɪs·fəl/ *adj disapproving* • *disgraceful behaviour/conduct* • *a disgraceful situation* • *She thought that their attitude to the problem was* **absolutely** *disgraceful.* • **It** *is disgraceful* **that** *children can get hold of drugs at school.* [+ *that* clause] • (F)

dis·grace·ful·ly /dɪsˈgreɪs·fəl·i/ *adv* • *You've behaved disgracefully.* • *Unemployment pay is disgracefully low.*

dis·grun·tled /£dɪsˈgrʌn·tl̩d, $-t̬l̩d/ *adj* unhappy, annoyed and disappointed about something • *A disgruntled former employee is being blamed for the explosion.* • *The players were disgruntled* **with** *the umpire.*

dis·guise *obj* /dɪsˈgaɪz/ *v* [T] to give a new appearance to (a person or thing), esp. in order to hide its true form • *He disguised him***self** *by shaving his head and wearing a false beard.* • *We tried to disguise the fact that it was just a school hall by putting up coloured lights and balloons.* • To disguise an opinion, a feeling, etc. is to hide it: *There are important differences of opinion which cannot be disguised.* ○ *I couldn't disguise my terror/disgust/embarrassment.*

dis·guise /dɪsˈgaɪz/ *n* • *He put on a large hat and glasses as a disguise and hoped no one would recognise him.* [C] • *At the end of the play the sisters throw off their male disguises and admit what they have done.* [C] • A person, object or activity **in disguise** appears to be something which it is not, esp. intentionally: *My little brother tells people he's a Martian in disguise* (=he appears to be a ordinary boy but he is not). ○ *He claims that most Western aid to the Third World is just colonialism* **in** *disguise* (=it appears to be money etc. given freely but it is also a method of controlling a situation).

dis·guised /dɪsˈgaɪzd/ *adj* • *In the book, the author gives a* **thinly** *disguised account of his own early teaching experiences.* • *She replied briefly, with* **barely** *disguised anger.*

dis·gust /dɪsˈgʌst/ *n* [U] strong feeling of disapproval and dislike at a situation or person's behaviour, etc. • *We are demonstrating to show our anger and disgust* **at** *this treatment of students.* • *Vic makes no effort to hide his disgust* **at** *Robyn's total ignorance of what factory work is really like.* • *He was filled with disgust* **at** *what he had witnessed in the prisons.* • *She resigned from the committee* **in** *disgust at their lack of power to change things.* • *Beresford,* **(much) to** *his disgust, was fined for illegal parking.* • Disgust is also a feeling of being ill caused by something unpleasant: *The sickly smell of carpets and furniture and scent in the bedroom disgusts me.* ○ *The smell from the carcass was so terrible he stepped back* **in** *disgust.* • (E) (P)

dis·gust *obj* /dɪsˈgʌst/ *v* [T not *be disgusting*] • *Doesn't all this violence on TV disgust you?* • *The way they treat their children disgusts me.* • *I'm disgusted* **at** *the way they treat their children.* • *He was disgusted* **at/with** *his son/him***self** *for having done no work all day.* • *Aren't you disgusted* (= caused to feel ill) *by that awful smell?*

dis·gust·ed·ly /£dɪsˈgʌs·tɪd·li, £-t̬ɪd-/ *adv* • *"There's no point in arguing", he said, and walked off disgustedly.*

dis·gust·ing /£dɪsˈgʌs·tɪŋ, $-t̬ɪŋ/ *adj* • *It's disgusting* (= unacceptable) *that there are no schools or hospitals for these people.* • *Passengers were kept for hours in disgusting* (= unpleasant), *dirty waiting rooms.* • (P)

dis·gust·ing·ly /£dɪsˈgʌs·tɪŋ·li, $-t̬ɪŋ-/ *adv*

dish [CONTAINER] /dɪʃ/ *n* [C] a container, flatter than a bowl and sometimes with a lid, from which food can be served or which can be used for cooking • *Put the beans* **in/on** *a dish.* • *Use an oven-proof dish.* • Dish is also *Am for* PLATE [DISH]. • **The dishes** are all the plates, glasses, knives, forks, etc. that have been used during a meal: *Have you* **done/washed** *the dishes?* • **Dish liquid** is *Am for* **washing-up liquid**. See at WASH [CLEAN]. • **Dish rack** is *Am for* **plate rack**. See at PLATE [DISH]. • **Dish towel** is *Am for* **tea towel**. See at TEA. • [PIC] Rack

dish FOOD /dɪʃ/ *n* [C] food prepared in a particular way as part of a meal • *His favourite dish is fresh ravioli.* • *There were several* **savoury/sweet** *dishes on the menu.*

dish RECEIVING DEVICE /dɪʃ/ *n* [C] *specialized* a device with a curved surface for receiving radio, television, etc. signals • *You have to buy a* **satellite** *dish to get the new TV channels.*

dish ATTRACTIVE PERSON /dɪʃ/ *n* [C] *slang approving* a sexually attractive person • *He's gorgeous – what a dish!* • *That woman in red is a real dish!*

dish·y /ˈdɪʃ·i/ *adj* **-ier, -iest** *Br and Aus slang* • *He's a bit dishy, isn't he?* • *What a dishy guy.*

dish *obj* SPOIL /dɪʃ/ *v* [T] *dated slang* to destroy (someone) or spoil (someone's hopes) • *Accusations of tax evasion have dished his chances of re-election.* • To **dish the dirt** on someone or something is to say publicly what they are really like, esp. when it is unpleasant and kept hidden: *The papers really dished the dirt on the company's shady business deals.*

dish out *obj*, **dish** *obj* **out** *v adv* [M] *infml* to give, esp. too freely • *She dishes money out to anyone who asks.* • *He's one of those people who dish out awards at televised ceremonies.* • *Doctors are short of time to listen and are therefore keen to dish out drugs whenever they can.* • *He's very willing to dish out punishment/criticism.* • *I wouldn't get in a fight with him – he can really* **dish it out** (=fight hard). • If you **can dish it out but** you **can't take it**, you easily criticize or say bad things about other people but don't like it when other people do the same to you: *It's no fun arguing with him, he can dish it out but he can't take it.* • To dish out is also to give or serve food to the people who will eat it: *Jon, could you dish the carrots out for me, please?*

dish up *(obj)*, **dish** *(obj)* **up** *v adv Br infml* to produce and/or serve (a meal) or *(fig.)* to produce (something) • *Come to the table everybody – I'm ready to dish (supper) up.* [I/M] • *What's the canteen dishing up for us today?* [M] • *(fig.) The offer is better than anything the other airlines can dish up.* [M]

dis·har·mo·ny /£dɪsˈhɑː·mə·ni, $-ˈhɑːr-/ *n* [U] *fml* (a state of) unpleasant disagreement • *We're trying to avoid racial disharmony within the organization.*

dish·cloth /£ˈdɪʃ·klɒθ, $-klɑːθ/ *n* [C] a cloth for washing and cleaning dirty plates, cups, forks, etc.

dis·heart·en *obj* /£dɪsˈhɑː·tᵊn, $-ˈhɑːr·t̬ᵊn/ *v* [T] to make (a person) lose confidence, hope and energy; to discourage • *This defeat has really disheartened the team.* • *disheartening news*

di·shev·elled, *Am usually* **di·shev·eled** /dɪˈʃev·ᵊld/ *adj* (of people or their appearance) very untidy • *dishevelled hair/clothes/appearance* • *He ran in looking rather dishevelled.*

dis·hon·est /£dɪˈsɒn·ɪst, $-ˈsɑː·nɪst/ *adj* not honest • *a dishonest lawyer* • *a dishonest way of making money* • *morally dishonest* • *intellectually dishonest* • *He's been dishonest* **in** *his dealings with us/***about** *his past.*

dis·hon·est·ly /£dɪˈsɒn·ɪst·li, $-ˈsɑː·nɪst-/ *adv* • *The money was dishonestly obtained.* • *She's been accused of acting dishonestly.*

dis·hon·es·ty /£dɪˈsɒn·ɪ·sti, $-ˈsɑː·nə-/ *n* [U] • *The court found him guilty of dishonesty.* • *Her dishonesty landed her in prison.*

dis·hon·our *Br and Aus, Am and Aus* **dis·ho·nor** /£dɪˈsɒn·əʳ, $-ˈsɑː·nɚ/ *n* [U] *fml* (a cause of) a feeling of embarrassment and loss of people's respect • *Some of the leaders of the coup took their lives rather than face dishonour.* • *A stay in such an institution should not bring shame or dishonour on the patients.* • *It was no dishonour to finish out of the medals in the most memorable 100 metres race ever seen.*

dis·hon·our *obj Br and Aus, Am and Aus* **dis·ho·nor** *obj* /£dɪˈsɒn·əʳ, $-ˈsɑː·n/ *v* [T] *fml* • *The editor of the newspaper warned her fellow-students not to dishonour their university by joining in demonstrations.* • If you dishonour a promise or agreement you do not do what you said you would do: *We suspect he means to dishonour the* **agreement** *made three years ago.*

dis·hon·our·ab·le *Br and Aus, Am and Aus* **dis·hon·or·ab·le** /£dɪˈsɒn·ᵊr·ə·bl̩, $-ˈsɑː·nɚ-/ *adj* • *dishonourable actions/conduct/life*

dish·wash·er /£ˈdɪʃˌwɒʃ·əʳ, $-ˌwɑː·ʃɚ/ *n* [C] a machine that washes and cleans dirty plates, cups, forks, etc. • *Could you load/unload/empty the dishwasher, please?* • A dishwasher is sometimes a person: *The restaurant employs four people as dishwashers.* • *(esp. humorous) I'd like to get a dishwasher, but my wife says we've already got one – me!* • PIC› **Kitchen**

dish·wa·ter /£ˈdɪʃˌwɔː·təʳ, $-ˌwɑː·t̬ɚ/ *n* [U] water in which dirty plates, cups, forks, etc. have been washed • *(disapproving) This soup/tea tastes* **like** *dishwater* (=tastes weak and unpleasant).

dish·y /ˈdɪʃ·i/ *adj* **-ier, -iest** *slang* See at DISH ATTRACTIVE PERSON

dis·il·lu·sion *obj* /ˌdɪs·ɪˈluː·ʒᵊn/ *v* [T] to disappoint (someone) by telling them the unpleasant truth about something or someone that they had a good idea of, or a respect for • **I hate to/I'm sorry to** *disillusion you, but pregnancy is not always wonderful – I was sick every day for six months.*

dis·il·lu·sion /ˌdɪs·ɪˈluː·ʒᵊn/, **dis·il·lu·sion·ment** /ˌdɪs·ɪˈluː·ʒᵊn·mənt/ *n* [U] • *Disillusion after losing his job has made him a bitter man.* • *There is increasing disillusionment* **with** *the government.*

dis·il·lu·sioned /ˌdɪs·ɪˈluː·ʒᵊnd/ *adj* • *He's become a disillusioned man.* • *All the other teachers are thoroughly disillusioned* **with** *their colleague.*

dis·in·cen·tive /£ˌdɪs·ɪnˈsen·tɪv, $-t̬ɪv/ *n* [C] something that discourages people from doing something or working hard • *High taxes are a disincentive* **to** *industrial investment.*

dis·in·cli·na·tion /ˌdɪs·ɪŋ·klɪˈneɪ·ʃᵊn/ *n* [U] a feeling of not wanting to do something • *I have a strong disinclination* **to** *do any work.* [+ *to* infinitive]

dis·in·clined /ˌdɪs·ɪŋˈklaɪnd/ *adj* [after v] • *I'm disinclined* (=unwilling) **to** *offer him a job if he hasn't got a degree.* [+ *to* infinitive]

dis·in·fect *obj* /ˌdɪs·ɪnˈfekt/ *v* [T] to clean using chemicals that kill bacteria and other very small living things that cause disease • *disinfect the toilets/the drains/a sore/a wound*

dis·in·fec·tant /£ˌdɪs·ɪnˈfek·tᵊnt, $-t̬ᵊnt/ *n* • Disinfectant is a substance which contains chemicals that kill bacteria and is used esp. for cleaning surfaces in toilets and kitchens: *a new brand of disinfectant* [U] ○ *a large range of disinfectants* [C]

dis·in·for·ma·tion /£ˌdɪs·ɪn·fəˈmeɪ·ʃən, $-fɚ-/ *n* [U] false information spread in order to deceive people • *They claimed there was an official disinformation and propaganda campaign by the government.*

dis·in·gen·u·ous /ˌdɪs·ɪnˈdʒen·ju·əs/ *adj fml* (of a person or their behaviour) slightly dishonest; not speaking the complete truth • *a disingenuous manner/smile/look* • *She was carefully disingenuous and told them only what they wanted to hear.*

dis·in·he·rit *obj* /ˌdɪs·ɪnˈher·ɪt/ *v* [T] to prevent (esp. a son or daughter who has made you angry) from receiving any of your property after your death • *Her father said he'd disinherit her if she married Stephen.*

dis·in·te·grate /£dɪˈsɪn·tɪ·greɪt, $-t̬ə-/ *v* [I] to become weaker or be destroyed by breaking into small pieces • *The spacecraft disintegrated as it entered the Earth's atmosphere.* • *The Ottoman Empire disintegrated* **into** *lots of small states.* • *(fig.) The situation/discussion/marriage disintegrated* **into** *chaos.*

dis·in·te·gra·tion /£dɪˌsɪn·tɪˈgreɪ·ʃᵊn, $ˌdɪs·ɪn·t̬ə-/ *n* [U] • *The organization appears to be moving towards disintegration after the retirement of its founder.* • *They observed a gradual disintegration* **of** *the advice and counselling service during the year.*

dis·in·ter *obj* /£ˌdɪs·ɪnˈtɜːʳ, $-ˈtɜːr/ *v* [T] **-rr-** to dig up (a dead body from the ground), or *(fig.)* to find and use (esp. something not seen or used for a long time) • *The body was disinterred and reburied in a specially constructed tomb.* • *(fig.) It is the biographer's task to disinter and present the facts of person's life, leaving the reader to form his/her own opinion.*

dis·in·ter·est·ed /dɪˈsɪn·trə·stɪd/ *adj* having no personal involvement or receiving no personal advantage, and therefore free to act fairly • *a disinterested observer/judgment* • *a piece of disinterested advice* • Disinterested is sometimes used to mean not interested, but many people do not consider this use to be correct.

dis·in·vest /ˌdɪs·ɪnˈvest/, *Am also* **di·vest** *v* [I] to stop investing in a company, activity, etc. • *The director said share holders had always been able to disinvest, but not at a known price.* • *The Swedish company has decided to disinvest* **from** *non-strategic activities in Europe.*

dis·in·vest·ment /ˌdɪs·ɪnˈvest·mənt/, *Am also* **di·ves·ti·ture** /£ˌdaɪˈves·tɪ·tjʊəʳ, $-t̬ɪ·tjʊr/, **di·vest·ment** /ˌdaɪˈvest·mənt/ *n* [U]

dis·joint·ed /£dɪsˈdʒɔɪn·tɪd, $-t̬ɪd/ *adj* (esp. of words or ideas) not well connected or well ordered • *a disjointed account/story/way of speaking*

disk, *Br also* **disc** /dɪsk/, **disk·ette** /dɪˈsket/ *n* [C] a flat circular device, usually inside a square container, which has a magnetic covering and is used for storing computer information • A **disk drive** is a piece of computer equipment that allows information to be stored on and read from a disk. • A **disk operating system** (*abbreviation* **DOS**) is a program which allows the use of information stored on disk. • In American English the spelling 'disk' is also used for the part of your back and when referring to the sun. See DISC. • See also DISC. HARD [SOLID].

dis·like *(obj)* /dɪ'slaɪk/ *v* to not like; to find (someone or something) unpleasant, difficult, etc. • *This painter seems to have actively/heartily/intensely disliked the people he painted.* [T] • *Both counties have had good reason to dislike each other since the last war.* [T] • *I dislike* **walking** *and I hate the countryside.* [+ v-ing] • *The teachers dislike* **the idea of** *testing children in such a narrow way.* [T]

dis·like /dɪ'slaɪk/ *n* • *She has a dislike* **of/for** *cold air.* [U] • *I'm afraid Dad has* **taken** *a dislike* **to** (= decided he doesn't like) *this new boyfriend of yours.* [U] • *She took an* **instant/instinctive** *dislike to the woman.* [U] • *They have a* **mutual** *dislike of each other.* [U] • *His main dislikes about work are the noise and dust in the factory.* [C]

dis·lo·cate *obj* /£'dɪs·ləʊ·keɪt, $dɪ'sloʊ-/ *v* [T] to force (a bone) suddenly out of its correct position, or *(fig.)* to have a negative effect on the working of something • *She dislocated her knee falling down some steps.* • *(fig.) The transport system has been severely dislocated by the bombing.*

dis·lo·cat·ed /£'dɪs·ləʊ·keɪ·tɪd, $-loʊ·keɪ·t̬ɪd/ *adj* • *a dislocated hip*

dis·lo·ca·tion /£ˌdɪs·ləʊ'keɪ·ʃᵊn, $-loʊ-/ *n* [C] • *Dislocations of the shoulder, hip or knee can be very painful.* [C] • *(fig.) Snow has caused serious dislocation* **of/to** *train services.* [U]

dis·lodge *obj* /£dɪ'slɒdʒ, $-'slɑːdʒ/ *v* [T] to remove, esp. by force, from a position • *The earthquake dislodged stones* **from** *the walls and the roof.* • *We need two wins to dislodge the French team* **from** *first place.* • *The army will not find it easy to dislodge* (= defeat and force away) *the enemy* **from** *this town.*

dis·loy·al /ˌdɪs'lɔɪ·əl/ *adj* not loyal; supporting the enemy • *His sisters thought that his autobiography was disloyal* **to** *the family.* • *Two newspapers have been criticized for disloyal reporting of the war.*

dis·mal /'dɪz·məl/ *adj* sad and without hope • *a dismal expression* • *The outlook is dismal – no-one thinks he's going to get better.* • *(infml)* Dismal also means very bad: *The acting/music was dismal, wasn't it?* ○ *We had dismal weather all day.* ○ *The trip was a dismal failure.* ○ *The dismal truth is that we were bored to death.*

dis·mal·ly /'dɪz·mə·li/ *adv*

dis·man·tle *(obj)* /£dɪ'smæn·tl̩, $-t̬l̩/ *v* to take (a machine) apart or to come apart into separate pieces, or *(fig.)* to get rid of (a system or organization) usually over a period of time • *She dismantled the washing machine to see what the problem was but couldn't put it back together again.* [T] • *The good thing about the bike is that it dismantles if you want to put it in the back of the car.* [I] • *(fig.) Bit by bit the government have dismantled the old education system.* [T] • *(fig.) At last apartheid is being dismantled.* [T]

dis·may /dɪ'smeɪ/ *n* [U] a feeling of shock which might be mixed with hopelessness or fear • *As he read the letter his expression changed from disbelief to deep dismay.* • *Aid workers were said to have been* **filled with** *dismay by the appalling conditions that the refugees were living in.* • *The supporters watched* **in/with** *dismay as their team lost 6-0.* • *She discovered,* **to** *her dismay, that her exam was a whole month earlier than she'd expected.*

dis·may *obj* /dɪ'smeɪ/ *v* [T] • *They enjoyed the meal but were a bit dismayed* **by/at** *the bill.*

dis·mem·ber *obj* /£dɪ'smem·bəʳ, $-bɚ/ *v* [T] to cut, tear or pull the arms and legs off (a human body), or to divide (a country or an empire) into different parts • *He used to dismember his victims and hide the pieces under the floorboards of his house.* • *The police found the dismembered body of a young man in the murderer's freezer.* • *The UN protested at the dismembering of Bosnia.*

dis·mem·ber·ment /£dɪ'smem·bə·mənt, $-bɚ·mənt/ *n* [U] • *the dismemberment of the empire*

dis·miss *obj* [FORGET] /dɪ'smɪs/ *v* [T] to decide that (something or someone) is not important and not worth considering • *I think he'd dismissed me* **as** *an idiot within five minutes of meeting me.* • *Let's not just dismiss the idea before we've even thought about it.* • *Just dismiss those thoughts* **from** *your mind – they're crazy and not worth thinking about.*

dis·mis·sal /dɪ'smɪs·ᵊl/ *n* [U] • *I was upset by her dismissal of the plans as a waste of time.*

dis·miss·ive /dɪ'smɪs·ɪv/ *adj* • *I can't stand his air of superiority – he's so dismissive* **of** *anybody else's suggestions.*

dis·miss·ive·ly /dɪ'smɪs·ɪv·li/ *adv* • *"I don't think there's any more to be said about that," he said, waving his hand dismissively.*

dis·miss *obj* [SEND AWAY] /dɪ'smɪs/ *v* [T] to formally ask or order (someone) to leave • *The teacher dismissed the class early because she had a meeting.* • If someone is dismissed **from** their job they are officially told that they are no longer to be employed in that job: *She was dismissed from her job for disobeying the company safety regulations.* • When a judge dismisses a court case he formally stops the trial, often because there is not enough proof of someone's guilt: *The defending lawyer asked that the charge against his client be dismissed.* • [LP]> **Work**

dis·mis·sal /dɪ'smɪs·ᵊl/ *n* [U] • *Her dismissal* **from** *the factory caused considerable outrage among the workforce.* • *The company can't sack you for refusing to sign that form – it would be* **unfair** *dismissal.*

dis·mount /dɪ'smaʊnt/ *v* [I] to get off a bicycle or a horse

dis·o·bed·i·ent /£ˌdɪs·əʊ'biː·di·ənt, $-ə'-/ *adj* (esp. of children) not doing what you are told to do • *At school he was very disobedient* **to/towards** *his teachers.* • *She always used to be a disobedient child.*

dis·o·bed·i·ent·ly /£ˌdɪs·əʊ'biː·di·ənt·li, $-ə'-/ *adv*

dis·o·bed·i·ence /£ˌdɪs·əʊ'biː·di·ənts, $-ə'-/ *n* [U]

dis·o·bey *(obj)* /£ˌdɪs·əʊ'beɪ, $-ə'-/ *v* to not do something that you are told to do; not obey • *She had disobeyed her parents' instruction to leave the party at ten o'clock and they were very angry.* [T] • *I didn't dare disobey – she was a big woman and looked a bit aggressive.* [I]

dis·o·blig·ing /ˌdɪs·ə'blaɪ·dʒɪŋ/ *adj fml* unwilling to help or do what you are asked to do • *He wouldn't get much help from them – they were such rude and disobliging people.*

dis·or·der [CONFUSION] /£dɪ'sɔː·dəʳ, $-'sɔːr·dɚ/ *n* [U] a state of untidiness and lack of organization • *The whole office was in a state of disorder – she couldn't find a thing that she looked for.* • *The opposition party have been in such disorder for so long that they pose no real threat to the present government.*

dis·or·der·ly /£dɪ'sɔː·dᵊl·i, $-'sɔːr·dɚ·li/ *adj* • *It's a disorderly sort of a house with books and papers lying around everywhere.*

dis·or·der [ILLNESS] /£dɪ'sɔː·dəʳ, $-'sɔːr·dɚ/ *n* an illness of the mind or body • *He's got some sort of blood disorder/disorder of the blood – I don't know the exact details.* [C] • *The family have a history of mental disorder.* [U]

dis·or·der [ANGRY SITUATION] /£dɪ'sɔː·dəʳ, $-'sɔːr·dɚ/ *n* [U] an angry, possibly violent, expression of dissatisfaction by crowds of people, esp. about a political matter • *The trial was kept secret because of the risk of* **public** *disorder.* • *The government are very concerned over the recent spate of* **civil** *disorder in the inner cities.*

dis·or·der·ly /£dɪ'sɔː·dᵊl·i, $-'sɔːr·dɚ·li/ *adj* • *The police feared that the crowd were becoming disorderly and so they moved in with horses.*

dis·or·gan·ized, *Br and Aus usually* **-ised** /£dɪ'sɔː·gə·naɪzd, $-'sɔːr-/ *adj* badly planned and lacking order • *He's impossible to work for – he's so disorganized.* • *The whole conference was totally disorganized – nobody knew where they were supposed to be or what they were supposed to be doing.*

dis·or·gan·i·za·tion, *Br and Aus usually* **-i·sa·tion** /£dɪˌsɔː·gə·naɪ'zeɪ·ʃᵊn, $-ˌsɔːr-/ *n* [U] • *I've never known such disorganization in a working environment – I don't know how they cope.*

dis·o·ri·en·tate *obj* /£dɪ'sɔː·ri·ən·teɪt, $-'sɔːr·i-/, *Am usually* **dis·o·ri·ent** /£dɪ'sɔː·ri·ənt, $-'sɔːr·i-/ *v* [T usually passive] to make (someone) confused about where they are and where they are going • *It's very easy to get disorientated because all the streets look the same.*

dis·o·ri·en·tat·ing /£dɪ'sɔː·ri·ən·teɪ·tɪŋ, $-'sɔːr·i-/, *Am usually* **dis·o·ri·ent·ing** /£dɪ'sɔː·ri·ən·tɪŋ, $-'sɔːr·i·ən·t̬ɪŋ/ *adj* • *I find this building really disorientating – I'm always going through the wrong door.* • *(fig.) She found it somehow disorientating* (= strange and confusing) *to see friends from her past mixing with more recent friends.*

dis·own *obj* /£dɪ'səʊn, $-'soʊn/ *v* [T not be disowning] to make it known that you no longer have any connection with (someone that you used to be closely connected with) • *The political party publicly disowned him when his terrorist links became known.* • *It's a story set in the last century about a girl whose parents disowned her when she married a foreigner.* • *(humorous) If you dye your hair pink I'll disown you!*

dis·par·age *obj* /£dɪ'spær·ɪdʒ, $-'sper-/ *v* [T] to criticize (someone or something) in a way that shows you do not respect or value them • *The actor's work for charity has recently been disparaged in the press* **as** *an attempt to get publicity.*

dis·par·ag·ing /£dɪˈspær·ɪ·dʒɪŋ, $-ˈsper-/ *adj* • *She made several rather disparaging* **remarks** *about the director whom she evidently dislikes.*

dis·par·ag·ing·ly /£dɪˈspær·ɪ·dʒɪŋ·li, $-ˈsper-/ *adv* • *He spoke very disparagingly of the firm's environmental policy which he described as 'a disgrace'.*

dis·par·age·ment /£dɪˈspær·ɪdʒ·mənt, $-ˈsper-/ *n* [U]

dis·par·ate /£ˈdɪs·pᵊr·ət, $-pɚ·ət/ *adj fml* different in every way • *The two cultures were so utterly disparate that she found it hard to adapt from one to the other.*

dis·par·i·ty /£dɪˈspær·ə·ti, $-ˈper·ə·t̬i/ *n slightly fml* a lack of equality and similarity, esp. in a way that is not fair • *There was such disparity* **in** *the standards of living between rich and poor.* [U] • *In the competition there was a huge disparity* **between** *the best and the worst performances.* [C]

dis·pas·sion·ate /dɪˈspæʃ·ᵊn·ət/ *adj* able to think clearly or make good decisions because not influenced by emotions • *In all the media hysteria there was one journalist whose comments were clear-sighted and dispassionate.*

dis·pas·sion·ate·ly /dɪˈspæʃ·ᵊn·ət·li/ *adv* • *We need someone who can look at the problem dispassionately.*

dis·patch *obj*, **des·patch** /dɪˈspætʃ/ *v* [T] to send (esp. goods or a message) somewhere for a particular purpose • *Two loads of woollen cloth were dispatched to the factory on December 12th.* • *(humorous)* If food is dispatched it is all eaten quickly and eagerly: *Well, we dispatched that pizza without too much trouble!* • *(humorous)* If a person is dispatched he or she is killed: *In the film's last five minutes our handsome hero manages to dispatch another five baddies.*

dis·patch, **des·patch** /dɪˈspætʃ/ *n* • *Temporary staff have been employed to help with the dispatch* **of** *extra mail.* [U] • *A special dispatch* **of** *food and clothing was flown to the refugees this morning.* [C] • A dispatch can be a newspaper report sent by someone in a foreign country, often communicating war news, or it can be an official, often military report: *In her latest dispatch Clare Duggan, our war correspondent, reported an increase in fighting.* [C] ○ *Sergeant Havers was* **mentioned in dispatches** (= highly praised) *for his courage.* • *(fml dated)* If someone does something **with dispatch** they do it quickly and effectively. • In Britain, the **dispatch box** is the box on a table in the House of Commons which important politicians stand next to when they are making speeches. • *(Br)* A **dispatch rider** is someone who travels between companies riding a motorcycle or bicycle, delivering important documents and messages as quickly as possible.

dis·pel *obj* /dɪˈspel/ *v* [T] **-ll-** to remove (fears, doubts and false ideas), usually by proving them wrong or unnecessary • *The quantity of food that she ate at dinner soon dispelled any fears that he previously had about her health.* • *In his latest novel he aims to dispel the myth that real men don't cry.* • *I'd like to start the speech by dispelling a few rumours that have been spreading recently.*

dis·pens·ab·le /dɪˈspent·sə·bl̩/ *adj* additional to your needs and therefore not necessary; that can be got rid of • *It seemed the soldiers were regarded as dispensable – their deaths just didn't matter.*

dis·pen·sa·tion PERMISSION /ˌdɪs·penˈseɪ·ʃᵊn/ *n fml* a special permission, esp. from the Church, to do something that is not usually allowed • *The couple have requested (a)* **special** *dispensation* **from** *the church to allow them to marry.* [C/U] • *Dispensation has been given* **by** *the authorities to allow the immigrants to enter the country.* [U]

dis·pen·sa·tion SYSTEM /ˌdɪs·penˈseɪ·ʃᵊn/ *n* [C] *fml* a political or religious system controlling a country at a particular time • **Under** *the old dispensation people were not allowed so much freedom.*

dis·pense *obj* PROVIDE /dɪˈspents/ *v* [T] *slightly fml* to provide (esp. money or a service) for several people • *They've been given a budget of two million pounds to dispense* **to** *developing countries.* • *My aunt has gained a reputation for dispensing* **advice/wisdom.**

dis·pens·er /£dɪˈspent·səʳ, $-sɚ/ *n* [C] • *a cash/soap/drinks dispenser* (= a machine from which money/soap/drinks can be obtained) • *The Academy is the major dispenser* **of** *public funds for research in the humanities.*

dis·pense *obj* GIVE OUT MEDICINE /dɪˈspents/ *v* [T] to prepare and give out (medicine) • *(Br, Aus also) a dispensing chemist* • *(Br)* A **dispensing optician** is a person whose job it is to sell people glasses and other things to correct sight problems, but who does not examine people's eyes.

dis·pen·sa·ry /£dɪˈspent·sᵊr·i, $-sɚ·i/ *n* [C] • A dispensary is a place where medicines are prepared and given out, often in a hospital. • ⓘ

dis·pense with *obj v prep* [T] to get rid of (something) or not use it because it is unnecessary or not convenient • *They've had to dispense with a lot of luxuries since Mike lost his job.* • *Having a fierce dog dispenses with* **the need for** (= makes unnecessary) *a burglar alarm.*

dis·perse *(obj)* /£dɪˈspɜːs, $-spɜːrs/ *v* to (cause to) scatter or move away over a large area • *When the rain came down the crowds started to disperse.* [I] • *Security guards dispersed the crowd that had gathered around the building.* [T] • *In the heat of the mid-day sun the clouds had begun dispersing.* [I]

dis·per·sal /£dɪˈspɜː·sᵊl, $-ˈspɜːr-/ *n* [U] • *Police horses and gas were used in the dispersal of the crowds.*

dis·per·sant /£dɪˈspɜː·sᵊnt, $-spɜːr-/ *n* • A dispersant is a chemical which is used to break up large masses of pollutants such as oil esp. when they are in the sea: *an oil dispersant* [C] ○ *Helicopters sprayed dispersant over the oil-slick in an attempt to break it up before it reached the coastline.* [U]

dis·persed /£dɪˈspɜːst, $-spɜːrst/ *adj* • *The friends were widely dispersed when they left university, but they still meet occasionally.*

dis·per·sion /£dɪˈspɜː·ʃᵊn, $-ˈspɜːr-/ *n* [U] *slightly fml* • *The dispersion of emergency supplies to the remotest villages will take another week.* • *(specialized)* Dispersion is the separation of light into different colours.

dis·pir·it·ed /£dɪˈspɪr·ɪ·tɪd, $-t̬ɪd/ *adj* not feeling hopeful about a particular situation or problem • *He was always dispirited on Sunday night because of the prospect of school the next day.*

dis·pir·it·ing /£dɪˈspɪr·ɪ·tɪŋ, $-t̬ɪŋ/ *adj* • *It was a bit dispiriting to see so few people arriving for the meeting.*

dis·place *obj* /dɪˈspleɪs/ *v* [T] to force (something or someone) out of its usual or original position • *The building of a new dam will displace thousands of people who live in this area.* • *Victory in the final could see Seles displace Graf* **as** *the world number one tennis player.*

dis·placed /dɪˈspleɪst/ *adj* • *Our organization tries to assist* **displaced persons** (= people who have had to leave their homes, esp. because of war or very bad weather).

dis·place·ment /dɪˈspleɪs·mənt/ *n* [U] • *The recent famine in these parts has caused the displacement of tens of thousands of people.* • *(specialized)* Displacement is also the weight of liquid that is forced out of position by an object which is floating on or in it. • A **displacement activity** is an unnecessary activity that you only do because you are trying to delay doing a more difficult or unpleasant activity: *When I was studying for my exams I used to clean the house as a sort of displacement activity.*

dis·play *obj* ARRANGE /dɪˈspleɪ/ *v* [T] to arrange (something or a collection of things) so that they can be seen by the public • *Why don't you display your ad* **on** *the notice board where everyone can see it?* • *The permit should be clearly displayed* **in** *the front window.*

dis·play /dɪˈspleɪ/ *n* • *There's an Egyptian art collection* **on** *display* (= being shown) *at the museum at the moment.* [U] • *She spent a whole afternoon in Harrods just looking at the wonderful food displays.* [C] • *There was a (Br)* **firework/***(Am and Aus)* **fireworks** *display to celebrate the occasion.* [C]

dis·play *obj* SHOW /dɪˈspleɪ/ *v* [T] to show (a feeling or an ability) • *The British tend not to display much emotion in public.* • *She displayed her skating skills* **to** *the judges during her performance.*

dis·play /dɪˈspleɪ/ *n* • *There's never much (of a) display* **of** *affection between them.* [C/U]

dis·please *obj* /dɪˈspliːz/ *v* [T] to cause (someone) to be annoyed, often because they are inconvenienced • *The singer is known to have been highly displeased* **by/with/at** *the remarks made in the paper.* • *The team's manager certainly wasn't displeased by their 3-0 victory in last Saturday's football match.*

dis·plea·sure /£dɪˈspleʒ·əʳ, $-ɚ/ *n* [U] • *Employees have publicly criticized the company's plans, much to the displeasure of the management.*

dis·port *obj* /£dɪˈspɔːt, $-ˈspɔːrt/ *v* [T] *old use or humorous* to amuse (yourself), esp. by doing physical activity • *They spent most evenings disporting themselves in night clubs.*

dis·pose *obj* /£dɪˈspəʊz, $-ˈspoʊz/ *v* [T always + adv/prep] *fml* to make (someone) feel a particular, and often bad, way towards someone else, or to influence (someone) in a particular way • *His rudeness when we first met didn't dispose me very kindly* **to/towards** *him.* • *The horrific nature of the crime did not dispose the jury* **to** *leniency.*

dis·posed /£dɪˈspəʊzd, $-ˈspoʊzd/ *adj* [after v] *fml* • *After all the trouble she put me to I didn't feel disposed* **to** (= I did not want to) *help her.* [+ *to* infinitive] • *I don't feel very well disposed* **towards** *my neighbours ever since their dog bit me.* • Compare INDISPOSED [NOT WILLING].

dis·pose of *obj v prep* [T] to get rid of or deal with (something) so that the matter is finished • *Nuclear waste is often disposed of under the sea.* • *They disposed of the dictator during the revolution.* • *That's disposed of the first point, now let's move on to the next matter.* • *Having a salary of $3 million a year I should think he's got a lot of income to dispose of* (= spend). • *It took a mere five minutes for the world's top boxer to dispose of* (= defeat) *his opponent.*

dis·pos·al /£dɪˈspəʊ·zəl, $-ˈspoʊ-/ *n* [U] • *Bins are provided for the disposal* **of** (= to get rid of) *litter.* • *Locals are objecting to the land being used as a disposal* **site** *for household waste.* • A thing or person which is **at** your **disposal** is able to be used by you: *I would take you if I could but I don't have a car at my disposal this week.* ○ *If you want some help preparing for the party I can be at your disposal* (= I am able to help) *all day.* ○ *Having sold the house she had a large sum of money at her disposal* (= to spend as she wanted).

dis·pos·ab·le /£dɪˈspəʊ·zə·bḷ, $-ˈspoʊ-/ *adj* • *disposable* (= intended to be thrown away after use) *cups/cutlery/nappies/razors/contact lenses* • **Disposable income** is the money which you can spend as you want and not the money which is spent on taxes, housing and other basic needs: *Since they don't have any children and their rent is very cheap, they've a lot of disposable income between them.*

dis·pos·ab·le /£dɪˈspəʊ·zə·bḷ, $-ˈspoʊ-/ *n* [C usually pl] *esp. Am* • A disposable is any item that is intended to be thrown away after use: *Many families are giving up disposables and using cloth diapers instead.*

dis·po·si·tion /ˌdɪs·pəˈzɪʃ·ən/ *n* [C] a person's character; whether a person is usually happy, often anxious, etc. • *She* **has** *a*/**is of** *a nervous/cheerful/sunny disposition.* • *As a child he had a very lively, happy disposition.* • Ⓒⓢ Ⓟⓛ

dis·pos·sess *obj* /ˌdɪs·pəˈzes/ *v* [T often passive] *fml* to take property, esp. buildings or land, away from (someone or a group of people) • *A lot of people were dispossessed* **of** *their homes during the civil war.* • Compare REPOSSESS.

dis·pos·sessed /ˌdɪs·pəˈzest/ *adj* [not gradable] *fml* • *dispossessed exiles*

dis·pos·sessed /ˌdɪs·pəˈzest/ *pl n fml* • *the poor and the dispossessed* (= dispossessed people)

dis·pos·ses·sion /ˌdɪs·pəˈzeʃ·ən/ *n* [U] *fml*

dis·pro·por·tion·ate /£ˌdɪs·prəˈpɔː·ʃən·ət, $-ˈpɔːr-/ *adj* unfair and not equal, or not deserving its importance or influence • *The country's great influence in the world is disproportionate* **to** *its relatively small size.* • *Rumours of his resignation attracted a disproportionate* **amount** *of media attention.* • *There are a disproportionate* **number** *of men compared to women in the legal profession.*

dis·pro·por·tion /£ˌdɪs·prəˈpɔː·ʃən, $-ˈpɔːr-/ *n* [U] *fml* • *It would be fair to say that there is* **a** *disproportion* **between** *the responsibility of the job and its low salary.*

dis·pro·por·tion·ate·ly /£ˌdɪs·prəˈpɔː·ʃən·ət·li, $-ˈpɔːr-/ *adv* • *I spend a disproportionately large amount of my salary on clothes.* • *Some might think she has a disproportionately large nose for such a small delicate face.*

dis·prove *obj* /dɪˈspruːv/ *v* [T] to prove that (an idea or fact) is not true • *I ate lots of onions and I didn't feel ill so that disproves my theory that it's onions which make me sick.*

dis·pute /dɪˈspjuːt, ˈdɪs·pjuːt/ *n* an argument or disagreement, esp. an official one between, for example, workers and employers or two bordering countries • *an* **industrial/pay/legal/international** *dispute* [C] • *They've been trying to settle/resolve the dispute* **over** *working conditions for the last three days.* [C] • *The unions are* **in** *dispute* **with** *management over pay.* [U] • *There was a bit of a dispute in the restaurant* **over** *whose turn it was to pay the bill.* [C] • *There's some dispute* **over** *who actually wrote the play – nobody seems to know for sure.* [U] • *He is* **beyond all dispute/without dispute** (= certainly) *the finest actor in Hollywood today.* • *I don't think her ability is* **in dispute** (= being doubted), *what I question is her attitude.* • *He says it's the best musical equipment you can buy but I think that's* **open to dispute** (= not certain). • Ⓕ

dis·pute *(obj)* /dɪˈspjuːt/ *v* • *Few would dispute his status as the finest artist of the period.* [T] • *The legal status of her will was disputed for years after her death.* [T] • *Critics have disputed the official unemployment figures.* [T] • *The two countries have disputed* **(over)** *that stretch of land for years.* [I/T] • *The circumstances of her death have been* **hotly** *disputed.* [T] • *I don't dispute* **(that)** *his films are entertaining but they haven't got much depth.* [+ *(that)* clause] • *They're disputing* **with** *the local council over the proposed new road.* [I]

dis·put·ed /£dɪˈspjuː·tɪd, $-t̬ɪd/ *adj* • *a disputed court case/area/border/goal* • *disputed authorship/ownership/territory* • *The men were convicted on the basis of a disputed confession.*

dis·put·ab·le /£dɪˈspjuː·tə·bḷ, $-t̬ə-/ *adj* • *It's claimed that they produce the best athletes in the world but I think that's disputable.*

dis·put·a·tion /£ˌdɪs·pjʊˈteɪ·ʃən, $-pjuː-/ *n fml or old use* • *Public disputations* (= disagreements) *between directors do nothing to improve the company's image.* [C] • *After much disputation* (= disagreement) *within the government a policy has been agreed.* [U]

dis·put·a·tious /£ˌdɪs·pjʊˈteɪ·ʃəs, $-pjuː-/ *adj fml or dated* • *He's a disputatious young man* (= he argues a lot).

dis·qual·i·fy *obj* /£dɪˈskwɒl·ɪ·faɪ, $-ˈskwɑː·lə-/ *v* [T] to stop (someone), often legally, from doing something because they are unsuitable or they have done something wrong • *He's been disqualified* **from** *driving for a year.* • *Two top athletes have been disqualified* **from** *the championship after positive drug tests.* • *If you're related to anyone in the company it automatically disqualifies you* **from** *entering the competition.* • *She was fined quite heavily for driving while disqualified.*

dis·qual·i·fi·ca·tion /£dɪˌskwɒl·ɪ·fɪˈkeɪ·ʃən, $-ˌskwɑː·lə-/ *n* • *The fans' bad behaviour has resulted in the disqualification of their football team* **from** *the championship.* [U] • *Unusually, there were a number of disqualifications in the games for cheating.* [C]

dis·qui·et·ing /£dɪˈskwaɪə·tɪŋ, $-t̬ɪŋ/ *adj fml* causing anxiety; worrying • *The disquieting situation between these two neighbouring countries looks set to continue.* • *His silence is a little disquieting – I wonder why he hasn't called.*

dis·qui·et /dɪˈskwaɪət/ *n* [U] *slightly fml* • *The leader's decline in popularity is causing disquiet among supporters.* • *There is growing public disquiet* **over** *inadequate food safety regulations.*

dis·qui·et *obj* /dɪˈskwaɪət/ *v* [T] *fml* • *Her unpredictability disquiets me.*

dis·qui·si·tion /ˌdɪs·kwɪˈzɪʃ·ən/ *n* [C] *fml* a long and detailed explanation of a particular subject • *Don't worry – I'm not about to enter into a disquisition* **on** *the evils of eating meat.*

dis·re·gard /£ˌdɪs·rɪˈgɑːd, $-ˈgɑːrd/ *n* [U] lack of consideration or respect for something • *What amazes me is her complete disregard* **for** *anyone else's opinion.* • *It was a reckless military action which showed a flagrant disregard* **for** *human life.* • *He is a criminal with a total disregard* **of** *the law.*

dis·re·gard *obj* /£ˌdɪs·rɪˈgɑːd, $-ˈgɑːrd/ *v* [T] • *He told us to disregard* (= ignore) *everything we'd learned so far and start again.*

dis·re·pair /£ˌdɪs·rɪˈpeəʳ, $-ˈper/ *n* [U] the state of being broken or old and needing to be repaired • *The building has* **fallen into** *disrepair over the years.*

dis·rep·ut·ab·le /£dɪsˈrep·jʊ·tə·bḷ, $-jə·t̬ə-/ *adj* not trusted or respected; thought to have a bad character • *Some of the more disreputable newspapers made false claims about her private life.* • *(humorous) Who's that disreputable looking man with the long hair and sunglasses?*

dis·rep·ut·ab·ly /£dɪsˈrep·jʊ·tə·bli, $-jə·t̬ə-/ *adv*

dis·re·pute /ˌdɪs·rɪˈpjuːt/ *n* [U] • *Involvement with terrorist groups* **brought** *the political party* **into** *disrepute* (= a state of not being trusted). • *The writer's works* **fell into** *disrepute* (= a state of not being respected) *during this period and his plays were not allowed to be performed.*

dis·re·spect /ˌdɪs·rɪˈspekt/ *n* [U] lack of respect • *I didn't* **mean** *(to show)* **any** *disrespect when I criticised her acting technique.* • **No disrespect** (= Not wishing to show any lack of respect) *to your boss but this department worked perfectly well before she started here.*

dis·re·spect·ful /ˌdɪs·rɪˈspekt·fəl/ *adj* • *disrespectful behaviour*

dis·re·spect·ful·ly /ˌdɪs·rɪˈspekt·fəl·i/ *adv*

dis·robe /£dɪsˈrəʊb, $-ˈroʊb/ *v* [I] *humorous or fml* to remove your clothes esp. an outer or ceremonial piece of clothing • *I only went to the doctor with a sore throat and she asked me to disrobe.*

dis·rupt *obj* /dɪsˈrʌpt/ *v* [T] to prevent (esp. a system, process or event) from continuing as usual or as expected • *A heavy fall of snow had disrupted the city's transport system.* • *She sometimes felt frustrated that motherhood had disrupted her career.* • *The meeting was disrupted by a group of protesters who shouted and threw fruit at the speaker.*

dis·rup·tion /dɪsˈrʌp·ʃᵊn/ *n* • *Air travellers continue to face disruptions with more strikes threatened by airport workers.* [C] • *The accident on the main road through town is causing widespread disruption for motorists.* [U]

dis·rup·tive /£dɪsˈrʌp·tɪv, $-t̬ɪv/ *adj* • *His teacher described him as a disruptive* **influence** *in class – always distracting other children and stopping them from working.*

dis·rup·tive·ly /£dɪsˈrʌp·tɪv·li, $-t̬ɪv-/ *adv*

diss *obj* /dɪs/ *v* [T] *Am slang* to show a strong lack of respect for (someone or some group of people) • *In this neighbourhood it isn't a good idea to diss a gang member.* • *Don't diss me man!*

dis·sa·tis·fied /£ˌdɪsˈsæt·ɪs·faɪd, $-ˈsæt̬·əs-/ *adj* not pleased with something; feeling that something is not as good as it should be • *If you're dissatisfied* **with** *the service, why don't you complain to the hotel manager?*

dis·sa·tis·fac·tion /£dɪsˌsæt·ɪsˈfæk·ʃᵊn, $ˌdɪs·sæt̬·əs-/ *n* [U] • *At the moment she's experiencing a lot of dissatisfaction* **with** *her job.*

dis·sect *obj* /£daɪˈsekt, $ˈdaɪ·sekt/ *v* [T] to cut open (esp. a dead body or a plant) and study its structure, or more generally to examine something in detail • *In biology classes at school we used to dissect rats.* • *He's the sort of person who watches a film and then dissects it* (= examines and discusses it) *for hours.*

dis·sec·tion /£daɪˈsek·ʃᵊn, $dɪ-/ *n* • *He objects to the dissection of animals in experiments.* [U] • *She wasn't looking forward to doing her first human dissection.* [C] • *The novel is really a dissection of nationalism.* [C]

dis·sem·ble /dɪˈsem·bl̩/ *v* [I] *literary or fml* to hide your real intentions and feelings or the facts • *Politicians frequently have to dissemble so as not to admit that mistakes have been made.*

dis·sem·i·nate *obj* /dɪˈsem·ɪ·neɪt/ *v* [T] *literary or fml* to spread or give out (esp. news, information, ideas, etc.) to a lot of people • *One of the organization's aims is to disseminate information about the spread of the disease.*

dis·sem·i·na·tion /dɪˌsem·ɪˈneɪ·ʃᵊn/ *n* [U] *literary or fml* • *the dissemination of knowledge/information/new technology*

dis·sen·sion, *Am also* **dis·sen·tion** /dɪˈsen·tʃᵊn/ *n* *slightly fml* arguments and disagreement, esp. in an organization, group, political party, etc. • *There are signs of dissension* **within**/*(Br)* **among** *the ruling political party.* [U] • *Internal dissensions* **between** *members of the group have been increasing since the chairman resigned.* [C]

dis·sent /dɪˈsent/ *n* [U] *slightly fml* strong difference of opinion on a particular subject; disagreement esp. about an official suggestion or plan or a popular belief • *There is some dissent within the committee on this issue.* • *When the time came to approve the proposal there were one or two voices of dissent.* • Compare ASSENT.

dis·sent /dɪˈsent/ *v* [I] *slightly fml* • *Nine people were in favour of the proposal and three dissented* (= were opposed). • *Anyone wishing to dissent* **from** (= to show that they do not agree with) *the motion should now raise their hand.*

dis·sent·er /£dɪˈsen·təʳ, $dɪˈsen·t̬ɚ/ *n* [C] *slightly fml* • *For the sake of party unity he tried to get rid of the dissenters.*

dis·sent·ing /£dɪˈsen·tɪŋ, $-t̬ɪŋ/ *adj slightly fml* • *The jury found it an easy decision to make – in fact there was only one* **dissenting voice** (= person who disagreed).

dis·ser·ta·tion /£ˌdɪs·əˈteɪ·ʃᵊn, $-ɚˈ-/ *n* [C] a long piece of writing on a particular subject, esp. one that is done as a part of a course at college or university • *Ann did her dissertation* **on** *Baudelaire.*

dis·ser·vice /£ˌdɪsˈsɜː·vɪs, $-ˈsɜːr-/ *n* [U] an action which harms something or someone • *She has* **done** *a great disservice* **to** *her cause by saying that violence is justifiable to achieve it.*

dis·si·dent /ˈdɪs·ɪ·dᵊnt/ *n* [C] a person who publicly disagrees with and criticizes their government • *political dissidents*

dis·si·dent /ˈdɪs·ɪ·dᵊnt/ *adj* [not gradable] • *a dissident movement/group/writer/playwright*

dis·si·dence /ˈdɪs·ɪ·dᵊnts/ *n* [U]

dis·sim·i·lar /£ˌdɪsˈsɪm·ɪ·ləʳ, $-lɚ/ *adj* [often in negatives] not similar; different from another thing • *Their faces are not dissimilar* (= are quite similar), *I suppose you could mistake one for the other.* • *The new house is not dissimilar* **to** *our old one except that it's a bit bigger.*

dis·si·pate *(obj)* /ˈdɪs·ɪ·peɪt/ *v slightly fml* to (cause to) disappear or to waste • *After five years in the same job his enthusiasm had finally dissipated.* [I] • *It took months for them to dissipate the oil spill in the North Sea.* [T] • *He's not the first young aristocrat to dissipate his fortune in gambling.* [T]

dis·si·pat·ed /£ˈdɪs·ɪ·peɪ·tɪd, $-t̬ɪd/ *adj fml literary* • *He recalled his dissipated youth spent in nightclubs and bars.*

dis·si·pa·tion /ˌdɪs·ɪˈpeɪ·ʃᵊn/ *n* [U] *fml* • *the dissipation of money/time/energy* • *She'd led a futile life of dissipation.*

dis·so·ci·ate *obj* /£dɪˈsəʊ·si·eɪt, $-ˈsoʊ-/, **dis·as·so·ci·ate** *v* [T] to consider as separate and not related • *I can't dissociate the man* **from** *his political opinions – they're one and the same thing.* • If you dissociate yourself **from** something or someone you make it publicly known that you are not in any way connected to or responsible for them, often to avoid blame or embarrassment: *When he saw how badly it had been made, the writer dissociated himself from the film.*

dis·so·ci·a·tion /£dɪˌsəʊ·ʃiˈeɪ·ʃᵊn, $-ˌsoʊ-/ *n* [U]

dis·so·lute /ˈdɪs·ə·luːt/ *adj literary* (of a person) living in a way that other people strongly disapprove of; immoral

dis·so·lute·ly /ˈdɪs·ə·luːt·li/ *adv literary*

dis·so·lute·ness /ˈdɪs·ə·luːt·nəs/ *n* [U] *literary*

dis·solve *(obj)* BE ABSORBED /£dɪˈzɒlv, $-ˈzɑːlv/ *v* (of a solid) to be absorbed by a liquid, esp. when mixed, or (of a liquid) to absorb a solid • *Dissolve two spoons of powder in warm water.* [T] • *Keep stirring the tea until the sugar has dissolved.* [I] • *Nitric acid will dissolve most animal tissue the notable exception being cartilage.* [T] • If you dissolve **in/into** tears/laughter/giggles, you cry or laugh in an uncontrolled way: *They dissolved into fits of giggles just like silly schoolgirls.* [I]

dis·solve *(obj)* END /£dɪˈzɒlv, $-ˈzɑːlv/ *v* to end (an official organization or a legal arrangement) • *Parliament has been dissolved.* [T] • *The society was dissolved due to lack of members.* [T] • *He became very depressed after their marriage was dissolved.* [T] • *(fig.) The tension in the office just dissolves* (= disappears) *when she walks out.* [I]

dis·so·lu·tion /ˌdɪs·əˈluː·ʃᵊn/ *n* [U] • *the dissolution of parliament/the council/their marriage* • *the dissolution of the Warsaw Pact's military structure*

dis·so·nance /£ˈdɪs·ᵊn·ənts, $-ə·nənts/ *n* [U] *specialized* a combination of sounds or musical notes that are not pleasant when heard together • *the jarring dissonance of Klein's musical score*

dis·so·nant /£ˈdɪs·ᵊn·ənt, $-ə·nənt/ *adj specialized* • *dissonant chords* • *(fig.) dissonant opinions* (= opinions which disagree)

dis·suade *obj* /dɪˈsweɪd/ *v* [T] to persuade (someone) not to do something • *I'm trying to dissuade her* **from** *buying a TV.*

dis·tance /ˈdɪs·tᵊnts/ *n* the amount of space between two places • *What's the distance* **between** *Madrid and Barcelona/* **from** *Madrid* **to** *Barcelona?* [C] • *He travels quite a distance* (= a long way) *to work every day.* [C] • *Does she live* **within walking/driving** *distance of her parents* (= Is she able to walk/drive to them from where she lives)*?* [U] • *He gets very tired driving his lorry over long distances.* [C] • *(fig.) I noticed a certain distance* (= lack of friendliness) **between** *father and son.* [U] • **At/From a distance** (= If you are not too near) *he looks a bit like James Bond.* • If you **go the distance** you manage to continue until the end of a competition: *Surprisingly, he got up after being knocked down early in the fight to go the distance.* ○ *(fig.) The management training course is very tough – do you think he'll be able to go the distance* (= to stay until the end)*?* • *On a clear day you can see the temple* **in the distance** (= at a point which is far away). • To **keep** your **distance** means to not go to near: *I should keep your distance* **from** *the black horse – he tends to bite.* • **Distance learning** is a course of study, esp. for a degree, where you study mostly at home, receiving and sending off work by post: *The Open University runs distance learning courses, teaching you by correspondence packs, summer schools and sometimes video, radio or television.* • *"Distance lends enchantment to the view"* (Thomas Campbell in the poem *Pleasures of Hopes*, 1799) • LP **Measurements, Units**

dis·tance *obj* /ˈdɪs·tᵊnts/ *v* [T] • If you distance yourself from something you (seem to) become less involved or connected with it: *The leader distanced himself from the extremists in the party.* ○ *She prefers to distance herself from the people who are working for her.*

dis·tant /ˈdɪs·tᵊnt/ *adj* • *a distant country/shore* • *distant lands* • *She could hear the distant sound of fireworks exploding.* • A date or event which is in the distant past or future is far away in time: *At some distant point in the future he would have his own house.* ○ *At the reunion she recognised one or two faces from the* **dim and** *distant past* (= a very long time ago). • Someone whose manner is distant does not show much emotion and is not friendly: *At first she might seem very distant but actually she'll be listening to you intently.* • The **not-too-distant future** means quite soon: *They plan to have* *children* **in the** *not-too-distant future.* • A distant **relative** is a person who is related to you but not closely: *She's a distant relative of mine, something like my aunt's husband's great grandmother.*

dis·tant·ly /ˈdɪs·tᵊnt·li/ *adv* • *Bombs exploded distantly* (= far away) *in another part of the city.* • If someone behaves distantly they behave in an unfriendly way: *He looked at me distantly, as if he thought I was threatening him.* • If people are distantly related, they are related but not closely.

dis·taste /dɪˈsteɪst/ *n* [U] a dislike of something which you find unpleasant or immoral • *His distaste* **for** *publicity of any sort is well known.* • *She looked at the advertisement with distaste before walking quickly on.*

dis·taste·ful /dɪˈsteɪst·fᵊl/ *adj* • *He found the subject of their conversation very distasteful.*

dis·taste·ful·ly /dɪˈsteɪst·fᵊl·i/ *adv*

dis·taste·ful·ness /dɪˈsteɪst·fᵊl·nəs/ *n* [U]

dis·temp·er PAINT /£dɪˈstem·pəʳ, $-pɚ/ *n* [U] a type of paint which is mixed with water and can be used for decorating houses

dis·temp·er DISEASE /£dɪˈstem·pəʳ, $-pɚ/ *n* [U] a type of infectious disease that can be caught by animals, esp. dogs

dis·tend /dɪˈstend/ *v* [I] *medical* (usually of the stomach or other part of the body) to swell and become large (as if) by pressure from inside • *In the refugee centres we saw many children whose stomachs were distended because of lack of food.*

dis·ten·sion /dɪˈsten·tʃᵊn/ *n* [U] *medical*

dis·til *obj, Am usually, Aus also* **dis·till** /dɪˈstɪl/ *v* [T] **-ll-** to heat (a liquid) until it changes to a gas and then make it liquid again by cooling • *Sea water can be distilled* (= purified using this method) *to produce drinking water.* • *Some strong alcoholic drinks such as whisky are made by distilling.* • *(fig.) I have distilled* (= reduced to the most important parts) *my eighty page report into five basic recommendations.*

dis·til·la·tion /ˌdɪs·tɪˈleɪ·ʃᵊn/ *n* • *After distillation, the brandy is aged in wooden barrels for at least two years.* [U] • *(fig.) At first sight, the musical seems to be a distillation* (= something that contains only the most important parts) *of all the worst things in modern society.* [C] • *Chemists tried a new distillation process to speed up production.*

dis·til·ler /£dɪˈstɪl·əʳ, $-ɚ/ *n* [C] • A distiller is a person or a company that makes strong alcoholic drinks by the process of distilling.

dis·till·ery /£dɪˈstɪl·ᵊr·i, $-ɚ·i/ *n* [C] • A distillery is a factory where strong alcoholic drinks are produced by the process of distilling: *a whisky distillery*

dis·tinct DIFFERENT /dɪˈstɪŋkt/ *adj* clearly separate and different (from something else) • *The two concepts are quite distinct* **(from** *each other).* • *There are two distinct factions within the one political party.* • *The word 'bow' has two distinct meanings.* • *She's a personal assistant* **as distinct from** (= rather than) *a secretary.*

dis·tinc·tive /£dɪˈstɪŋk·tɪv, $-t̬ɪv/ *adj* • *a distinctive smell/taste* • *She's got a very distinctive* (= unusual) *voice/walk/profile/way of dressing.*

dis·tinc·tive·ness /£dɪˈstɪŋk·tɪv·nəs, $-t̬ɪv-/ *n* [U] • *It's this fragrant lemon-tasting herb that gives the sauce its distinctiveness.*

dis·tinc·tion /dɪˈstɪŋk·ʃᵊn/ *n* • *There's a* **clear** *distinction* **between** *the dialects spoken in the two regions.* [C] • *The politician said he would* **draw/make** *no distinction(s)* **between** *terrorism and murder.* [C/U] • See also DISTINCTION.

dis·tinct NOTICEABLE /dɪˈstɪŋkt/ *adj* [before n] clearly noticeable; that certainly exists • *There's a distinct smell of cigarettes every time he comes into the room.* • *At the moment there's a distinct* **lack** *of enthusiasm in her musical performances.*

dis·tinc·tly /dɪˈstɪŋkt·li/ *adv* • *He was looking distinctly nervous before his interview this morning.* • *I distinctly remember asking him not to tell her.*

dis·tinc·tion HIGH QUALITY /dɪˈstɪŋk·ʃᵊn/ *n* [U] quality which is rare because it is very high • *a writer/scientist/dancer of distinction* • See also **distinction** at DISTINCT DIFFERENT.

dis·tinc·tion HONOUR /dɪˈstɪŋk·ʃᵊn/ *n* [C] an honour in recognition of excellence • *She has the distinction of being one of the few people to have an honorary degree conferred on her by the university this year.* • *(Br) At school she was brilliant and used to get distinctions* (= very high marks) *in most of her subjects.* • See also **distinction** at DISTINCT DIFFERENT.

dis·tin·guish *(obj)* /dɪˈstɪŋ·gwɪʃ/ *v* [not *be distinguishing*] to notice or understand the difference between two things, or to provide an unusual quality which makes something noticeably different from or better than others of the same type • *He's colour-blind and can't distinguish (the difference)* **between** *red and green easily.* [I] • *I sometimes have difficulty distinguishing Spanish* **from** *Portuguese.* [T] • *It's important to distinguish* **between** *business and pleasure.* [I] • *It's not the beauty so much as the range of his voice that distinguishes him* **from** *other tenors.* [T] • You might distinguish, yourself, esp. in a public situation, by doing something so well that you are admired or praised for it: *He distinguished himself in British theatre at a very early age.* [T]

dis·tin·guish·able /dɪˈstɪŋ·gwɪ·ʃə·bl̩/ *adj* • *There are at least twenty distinguishable dialects of the language.* • *On the beach the British were distinguishable* **from** *the Spanish by their paleness and general lack of clothes sense.*

dis·tin·guished /dɪˈstɪŋ·gwɪʃt/ *adj* • A person or their work might be described as distinguished if they or their work are respected because of their extremely high standard: *a distinguished writer/director/politician* ○ *a distinguished career* • *In the evening we were treated to a distinguished performance by this very fine actor.* • A person, esp. an older person, might be described as being distinguished in appearance if they look formal, stylish or wise: *I think grey hair on a man can look very distinguished.*

dis·tin·guish·ing /dɪˈstɪŋ·gwɪ·ʃɪŋ/ *adj* • *The main distinguishing* **feature** *of the new car is its fast acceleration.* • *It's her lovely smile which is her distinguishing feature.*

dis·tort *obj* /£dɪˈstɔːt, $-ˈstɔːrt/ *v* [T often passive] to change (something) from its usual, original, natural or intended meaning, condition or shape • *My original statement has been completely distorted by the media.* • *Unexpected heavy losses this month have distorted the true picture of the company's financial situation.* • *His face was distorted in agony.* • *The wreckage of the plane was distorted almost beyond recognition.*

dis·tort·ed /£dɪˈstɔː·tɪd, $-ˈstɔːr·t̬ɪd/ *adj* • *This report gives a somewhat distorted impression of what actually happened.* • *The music just gets distorted when you play it so loud.*

dis·tor·tion /£dɪˈstɔː·ʃᵊn, $-ˈstɔːr-/ *n* • *These accusations are outrageous distortions* **of** *the truth.* [C] • *Such distortion* **of** *the facts cannot be allowed to go unchallenged.* [U] • *Distortion on compact discs is reduced to an absolute minimum.* [U]

dis·tract *obj* /dɪˈstrækt/ *v* [T] to take (someone or their attention) away from what they should be, or want to be, doing, esp. for a short period • *I hope Mary's new hi-fi won't distract her* **(from** *her studies).* • *The royal scandal has distracted media attention* **(away) from** *the economic crisis.* • *The phone kept ringing and distracting my* **attention.** • *I find studying really difficult because I'm so easily distracted.* • Ⓔ Ⓕ

dis·tract·ing /dɪˈstræk·tɪŋ/ *adj* • *Please turn your music down – it's very distracting.* • Ⓕ

dis·trac·tion /dɪˈstræk·ʃᵊn/ *n* • *I can turn the television off if you find it a distraction.* [C] • *For Jean, the arrival of the coffee was a welcome distraction* **from** *the boring business of the meeting.* [C] • *It's impossible to work with all this distraction.* [U] • *Are there many distractions* (= entertaining activities) *for students at British universities?* [C] • See also **distraction** at DISTRACTED. • Ⓕ

dis·tract·ed /£dɪˈstræk·tɪd, $-t̬ɪd/ *adj* nervous, anxious or confused because you are worried about something • *Gill seems rather distracted at the moment – I think she's worried about her exams.* • Ⓟ

dis·tract·ed·ly /£dɪˈstræk·tɪd·li, $-t̬ɪd-/ *adv* • *"Help! Help!" she cried, waving her arms distractedly in an attempt to attract someone's attention.*

dis·trac·tion /dɪˈstræk·ʃᵊn/ *n* [U] • *They were in a state of extreme distraction* (= mental confusion) *when their daughter went missing.* • *His lessons bore me* **to** *distraction* (= bore me very much). • *That dreadful noise is* **driving** *me* **to** *distraction* (= annoying me so much that it will make me angry). • See also **distraction** at DISTRACT. • Ⓕ

dis·traught /£dɪˈstrɔːt, $-ˈstrɑːt/ *adj* extremely worried, anxious or upset • *The missing child's distraught parents made an emotional appeal on television for information about where he might be.* • *He was distraught* **with** *grief when his wife died.*

dis·tress /dɪˈstres/ *n* [U] great mental or physical suffering such as extreme sadness, worry or pain, or the state of being in great danger and therefore in urgent need of help • *Many of the horses were showing signs of distress at the end of the race.* • *The Red Cross is working hard to relieve the distress caused by the civil war.* • *She claimed that the way she had been treated at work had caused her extreme emotional and psychological distress.* • *Guy has always been a source of considerable disappointment and distress* **to** *his parents.* • *Six people were rescued by helicopter from a fishing boat* **in** *distress off the*

Cornish coast. • *The radio was almost too weak to send out a distress* **signal.** • ①

dis·tress *obj* /dɪˈstres/ *v* [T] • *I hope I haven't distressed you with all these personal questions.* • *She was* **deeply** *distressed by her exam results.*

dis·tressed /dɪˈstrest/ *adj* • *The police said that they had received a phone call from a distressed woman claiming that she had been attacked.* • *He was greatly distressed* **to** *see the damage that the accident had done to his car.* [+ *to* infinitive] • *The government is taking steps to stimulate business development in* **(economically)** *distressed areas* (= those in economic difficulty).

dis·tress·ing /dɪˈstres·ɪŋ/, *Am usually* **dis·tress·ful** /dɪˈstres·fᵊl/ *adj* • *The television reports about the famine were particularly distressing.* • *They had an extremely distressing experience.* • **It** *is very distressing* **that** *so little progress has been made after all this time.* [+ *that* clause] • **It** *was* **deeply distressing for him** *to see his wife in such pain.* [+ *to* infinitive]

dis·tress·ing·ly /dɪˈstres·ɪŋ·li/ *adv* • *Distressingly little aid has reached the people who need it most.*

dis·tri·bute *obj* /£dɪˈstrɪb·juːt, £ˈdɪs·trɪ·bjuːt, $-jʊt/ *v* [T] to share or give (something) out to several people, or to spread, scatter or supply (something) over an area • *Her will contains instructions to sell her house and car and distribute the proceeds* **among** *the poor in her neighbourhood.* • *The world's wealth is not* **fairly** *distributed* **between** *women and men.* • *Several people were arrested for distributing* (= giving) *racist leaflets/pamphlets* **(to** *the spectators).* • *This roller distributes* (= spreads) *paint more* **evenly** *than a brush can.* • *Pollutants like these are now* **widely** *distributed* (= scattered) *across the countryside.* • *The company aims eventually to distribute* (= supply for sale) *its products* **throughout** *the European Union.*

dis·tri·bu·tion /ˌdɪs·trɪˈbjuː·ʃᵊn/ *n* [U] • *We must find a way of achieving* **a more equitable** *distribution* (= sharing) *of resources/wealth.* • *The distribution* (= spread) **of** *cancer cases* **across** *the country is not at all* **even.** • *Has the Channel Tunnel improved the distribution* (= supplying for sale) **of** *goods* **between** *the British Isles and mainland Europe?* • *The company has an extensive international distribution* **network/system.**

dis·tri·but·or /£dɪˈstrɪb·jʊ·təʳ, $-jə·t̬ɚ/ *n* [C] • *a film/record distributor* • A distributor is a person or company which supplies goods to the businesses which sell them: *a film/record distributor* • ○ *If this product should develop a fault, please return it to the distributor, not to your retailer.* • A distributor in a PETROL engine is the device which sends electricity to each of the **spark plugs** (= devices which cause the engine to start) in the necessary order.

dis·trict /ˈdɪs·trɪkt/ *n* [C] an area of a country or town which has fixed borders that are used for official purposes, or which has a particular feature that makes it different from surrounding areas • *South Cambridgeshire District Council* • *Which is the richest district of New York?* • *We're going to the Lake District/the Peak District for the weekend.* • *The Sunday market attracts people from all over the district* (= surrounding area). • A **district attorney** (*abbreviation* **DA**) is a lawyer working in a particular area of the US, who represents the government in a trial in a law court by trying to prove that a particular person has committed a crime. • *(Br)*A **district nurse** is a person who is employed in a particular area to care for people who are ill or injured, often visiting them in their homes. • *(Am)* **The** District is a name used for Washington, D.C.

dis·trust *obj* /dɪˈstrʌst/ *v* [T] to have little or no belief or confidence in; not to trust • *Ever since a property developer cheated her out of £10 000, she's distrusted all business people.* • *In spite of its election success, the government is still* **deeply** *distrusted on key health and education issues.*

dis·trust /dɪˈstrʌst/ *n* [U] • *The two groups have existed in a state of* **mutual** *distrust for centuries.* • *After all those dreadful newspaper articles about her, it's hardly surprising she has* **a (deep)** *distrust* **of** *journalists.*

dis·trust·ful /dɪˈstrʌst·fᵊl/ *adj* • *Many conservationists are* **deeply** *distrustful* **of** *the President's promises on the environment.*

dis·turb *obj* INTERRUPT /£dɪˈstɜːb, $-ˈstɜːrb/ *v* [T] to cause (someone) to stop what they are doing, or to interrupt (something) • *Please don't disturb Georgina – she's trying to do her homework.* • *I'm sorry to disturb you so late, but my car's broken down and I was wondering if I could use your phone.* • *I can call back later if I'm disturbing you.* • *I tried to see you yesterday in your hotel but you had the 'Do Not Disturb'* (= do not knock or enter) sign up on your door. • *My sleep/exam was disturbed* (= the silence was interrupted) *by the noise of the traffic.* • *Only the rustling of the leaves disturbed* (= interrupted) *the tranquillity of the lake.* • Someone who **disturbs the peace** breaks the law by behaving unpleasantly and noisily in public: *Several England supporters were arrested and charged with disturbing the peace after the match.*

dis·tur·bance /£dɪˈstɜː·bᵊnts, $-ˈstɜːr-/ *n* • *Residents are fed up with the disturbance caused by the nightclub.* [U] • *Phone calls are the biggest disturbance at work.* [C] • *There was a minor disturbance* (= violent event in public) *during the demonstration, but nobody was injured.* [C]

dis·turb *obj* WORRY /£dɪˈstɜːb, $-ˈstɜːrb/ *v* [T] to cause (someone) to feel worried or anxious • *Many voters have been disturbed by the party's election tactics.* • *Selma is rather disturbed* **that** *she hasn't had her exam results yet.* [+ obj + *that* clause] • *I'm very disturbed* (= I am not pleased) **to** *hear that you haven't yet done what I asked you to do.* [+ obj + *to* infinitive]

dis·turb·ing /£dɪˈstɜː·bɪŋ, $-ˈstɜːr-/ *adj* • *The Home Secretary described the latest crime figures as 'disturbing'.* • *The revelation about the government's involvement in phone-tapping is an extremely disturbing development.* • *The following programme contains scenes that may be disturbing* **to** *some viewers.* • **It** *is disturbing* **that** *the recommendations of the committee have not been acted upon.* [+ *that* clause] • *I found his letter very disturbing* **to** *read.* [+ *to* infinitive]

dis·turb·ing·ly /£dɪˈstɜː·bɪŋ·li, $-ˈstɜːr-/ *adv* • *Pollution has reached disturbingly high levels in some urban areas.*

dis·turb *obj* MOVE /£dɪˈstɜːb, $-ˈstɜːrb/ *v* [T] to move or change (something) from its usual position, arrangement, condition or shape • *The thief had disturbed the documents in her filing cabinet, but nothing had been taken.* • *The breeze disturbed his hair a little as he strolled down the street.*

dis·turbed /£dɪˈstɜːbd, $-ˈstɜːrbd/ *adj* so mentally confused or ill that special treatment is necessary • *The most* **deeply/seriously/severely** *disturbed patients are kept in a separate part of the hospital.* • *A new centre for* **emotionally/ mentally** *disturbed teenagers was officially opened yesterday.*

dis·u·nite *obj* /ˌdɪs·juːˈnaɪt/ *v* [T] to cause (people) to disagree so much that they can no longer work together effectively • *These economic problems risk disuniting the country's coalition government.* • *A publicly disunited party stands little chance of winning the election.*

dis·un·i·ty /£dɪˈsjuː·nɪ·ti, $-nə·t̬i/ *n* [U] • *This controversy has already caused considerable disunity* **among** *union members/***within** *the union, and may well lead to a permanent split.*

dis·use /dɪˈsjuːs/ *n* [U] the condition of not being used (any longer) • *The church was recently restored after decades of disuse.* • *Muscles can become weak with disuse.* • *They were prosecuted under the terms of an old law which had* **fallen into** *disuse* (= stopped being used), *but has recently been revived.*

dis·used /dɪˈsjuːzd/ *adj* [not gradable] • *Many disused railway lines have become public footpaths.*

di·syl·lab·ic /ˌdaɪ·sɪˈlæb·ɪk/ *adj* [not gradable] *specialized* (of a word) having two syllables • *"Bread" is monosyllabic and "butter" is disyllabic.*

ditch CHANNEL /dɪtʃ/ *n* [C] a long narrow open channel dug into the ground usually at the side of a road or field, which is used esp. for supplying or removing water, or for dividing land • *Ditches can be used for irrigation and drainage.* • *The anti-tank ditch is seven metres deep, twenty metres wide, and filled with oil which can be set alight.*

ditch *(obj)* GET RID OF /dɪtʃ/ *v infml* to get rid of or not continue with (something or someone that is no longer wanted) • *The getaway car had been ditched a couple of kilometres away from the scene of the robbery.* [T] • *The Government has decided to ditch* (= not continue with) *its proposals for a local income tax.* [T] • *I'm afraid we're going to have to ditch* (= dismiss) *Brian – he really isn't suited to the job.* [T] • *(infml) Did you know that Sarah has ditched* (= ended her relationship with) *Max?* [T] • To ditch can also mean to land an aircraft in water in an emergency: *The helicopter has special floats to keep it upright if it has to ditch.* [I] ○ *The pilot had to ditch the plane in the sea after its engine caught fire.* [T]

dith·er /£ˈdɪð·əʳ, $-ɚ/ *v* [I] *disapproving* to be uncertain or unable to make a decision about doing something, or to do something nervously • *Just stop dithering* **(about)**, *Carol, and get on with your essay!* • *She's still dithering* **over** *whether to accept the job she's just been offered.* • *He dithered* (= behaved in a nervous way) *for ages before asking her if she would go out with him.*

dith·er /£'dɪð·əʳ, $-ɚ/ *n* [U] *disapproving* • Someone who is **all of a dither** or **in a dither** is very nervous, excited or confused about something: *Pat is in a bit of a dither about what to wear for the interview.*

dith·er·er /£'dɪð·ə·rəʳ, $-ɚ·ɚ/ *n* [C] *disapproving* • *She has a reputation for being a ditherer who can never make up her mind.*

dith·er·y /£'dɪð·ə·ri, $-ɚ·i/ *adj* **-ier**, **-iest** *disapproving* • *He seems rather dithery but in fact he works very calmly and efficiently.*

di·tran·si·tive /£ˌdaɪ'trænt·sə·tɪv, $-t̬ɪv/ *adj* [not gradable] *specialized* (of a verb) able to be followed by two objects, one of which has the action of the verb done to it and the other of which has the action of the verb directed towards it • *The verb 'send' can be a ditransitive, as in the sentence 'I sent Jane a letter'.* • In this dictionary, ditransitive verbs are labelled "[+ two objects]". • Compare INTRANSITIVE; TRANSITIVE. • [LP] **Two objects**

dit·to (mark) /£'dɪt·əʊ, $'dɪt̬·oʊ/ *n* [C] *pl* **dittos** a symbol which means 'the same' and is used in a list to avoid writing again the word which is written immediately above it • [LP] **Symbols**

dit·to /£'dɪt·əʊ, $'dɪt̬·oʊ/ *adv* [not gradable] • *Local residents are opposed to the proposal. Ditto many members of the council* (=They are also). • *"I love thunderstorms." "Ditto* (=So do I). *They're really exciting."* • *(Am) "I'll have a pizza." "That goes ditto for me."*

dit·ty /£'dɪt·i, $'dɪt̬-/ *n* [C] a short simple song, often one considered to be of low quality • *Why is the Top Twenty full of such appallingly unoriginal ditties?*

di·u·ret·ic /£ˌdaɪ·jʊə'ret·ɪk, $-jə'ret̬-/ *n* [C], *adj specialized* (a substance) causing an increase in the production of urine • *Is alcohol a diuretic?* • *Coffee can often have a diuretic effect.*

di·ur·nal /£ˌdaɪ'ɜː·nəl, $-'ɜːr-/ *adj* [not gradable] *specialized* happening over a period of a day, or being active or happening during the day rather than at night • *Desert plants, faced with severe diurnal temperature fluctuations and acute water shortage, only grow very slowly.* • *Are any owls diurnal* (=active during the day), *or are they all nocturnal?* • Compare NOCTURNAL.

di·ur·nal·ly /£ˌdaɪ'ɜː·nə·li, $-'ɜːr-/ *adv* [not gradable]

di·va /'diː·və/ *n* [C] a very successful and famous female singer, who acts in a way that attracts a lot of attention • *an Italian opera diva* • *a pop diva*

di·van /dɪ'væn/ *n* [C] a bed consisting of a MATTRESS and a base and having no boards at either end • (CS) (PL) (RUS)

dive [MOVE DOWN] /daɪv/ *v* [I] *past simple* **dived** or *Am also* **dove** /£dəʊv, $doʊv/, *past part* **dived** or *Am also* **dove** /£dəʊv, $doʊv/ to jump head first into water, esp. with your arms held straight above your head, or to move down, esp. through water • *Look at those children diving* **for** *oysters over there!* • *They ran to the pool, dived* **in**, *and swam to the other side.* • *Mark dived* **off** *the bridge* **into** *the river.* • *The submarine dived just in time to avoid the enemy attack.* • *What depth can dolphins dive* **to**? • *Carol dived* **under** *the boat and reappeared a few moments later on the other side.* • *The plane dived* (=moved quickly and steeply down) *towards the ground and exploded in a ball of flame.* • *The goal-keeper dived* **for** *the ball* (=tried to catch the ball by jumping towards it and falling on the ground.) • *(fig.) The company's shares dived* (=fell suddenly and by a large amount) **by** *90p* **to** *165p on the stock market yesterday.* • To **dive-bomb** an area is to drop bombs on it from, or in the manner of, a **dive bomber** (= a military aircraft designed to drop its bombs after a steep dive). • *They* **dive-bombed** *the area mercilessly.* • See also NOSEDIVE.

dive /daɪv/ *n* [C] • *She won the prize for the best dive of the competition.* • *The goalkeeper made a valiant dive* **for** (=jump towards) *the ball, but couldn't stop it going in the net.* • *(fig.) The firm's profits* **took** *a dive* (=fell by a large amount) *last month.*

div·er /£'daɪ·vəʳ, $-vɚ/ *n* [C] • Divers are people who dive as a sport, or who work or search for things under water using special breathing equipment: *He was a diver on a North Sea oil rig.*

div·ing /'daɪ·vɪŋ/ *n* [U] • *When I was at school I used to love swimming but I hated diving.* • A **diving bell** is a bell-shaped metal container without a base which is supplied with air so that a person can work in deep water. • A **diving board** is a (high) board, esp. one that sticks out over a swimming pool, from which people can dive into water below.

dive [MOVE QUICKLY] /daɪv/ *v* [I always + adv/prep] *past simple* **dived** or *Am also* **dove** /£dəʊv, $doʊv/, *past part* **dived** to move quickly, often in order to avoid something • *They dived* **for** *cover/safety when they heard the shooting start.* • *The terrified kitten dived* **under** *the armchair when the fireworks started.* • *We dived* **into** *the nearest taxi as soon as the downpour began.* • *The guards dived* (=ran) **after** *her, but she escaped through a hole in the fence.* • *She dived* (=moved her hand quickly) **into** *her jacket pocket and pulled out a gun.* • *(fig.) Everyone has dived* **into** (=become completely involved in) *the project with tremendous enthusiasm.* • *(fig.) Her parents advised her against diving* (=hurrying without thinking) **into** *sexual relationships with people she had only just met.*

dive /daɪv/ *n* [U] • *I* **made** *a dive* **at** *the burglar, but he escaped through the back door.*

dive [PLACE] /daɪv/ *n* [C] *infml* a restaurant, hotel, bar or place for entertainment or social activities that is unpleasant because of the condition of the building or the type of people that go there • *Caroline dragged us to the smokiest, dingiest dive in London.* • *I know this place is a bit of a dive, but the drink's cheap and the food's great.*

di·verge /£ˌdaɪ'vɜːdʒ, $dɪ'vɜːrdʒ/ *v* [I] to follow a different direction, or to be or become different • *They walked along the road together until they reached the village, but then their paths diverged.* • *We suddenly realized that the course the boat was taking diverged markedly/widely* **from** *our intended route.* • *His career has diverged dramatically* **from** *what his parents had hoped for him.* • *Although the two organizations have worked together for many years, their objectives have been diverging recently.* • Compare CONVERGE.

di·ver·gence /£ˌdaɪ'vɜː·dʒᵊnts, $dɪ'vɜːr-/ *n* • *The divergence* **between** *the incomes of the rich and poor countries seems to be increasing.* [U] • *Recently published figures show a divergence* **from** *previous trends.* [C] • *You expect to find wide divergences* **of** *opinion/views in a healthy democracy.* [C]

di·ver·gent /£ˌdaɪ'vɜː·dʒᵊnt, $dɪ'vɜːr-/ *adj* • *Which country's economy is the most divergent* **from** *the European average?* • *They hold* **widely** *divergent opinions on controversial issues like abortion.*

di·vers /£'daɪ·vəz, $-vɚz/ *adj* [before n] *old use* various or several • *At the time of his death in 1642, Sir William was said to own 'many books of divers sorts'.*

di·verse /£daɪ'vɜːs, £'--, $dɪ'vɜːrs/ *adj* varied or different • *This candidate has an impressively diverse range of interests and experience.* • *Students from countries as diverse as Colombia and Lithuania use Cambridge textbooks when they learn English.* • *New York is a very* **culturally/** *ethnically diverse city.*

di·ver·si·fy *(obj)* /£daɪ'vɜː·sɪ·faɪ, $dɪ'vɜːr-/ *v* • *Millions of years ago, changes in the Earth's climate caused animal and plant life to diversify.* [I] • *Many wheat farmers have begun to diversify* **into** *other forms of agriculture.* [I] • *The new director of the television station wants to diversify its programmes.* [T]

di·ver·si·fi·ca·tion /£daɪˌvɜː·sɪ·fɪ'keɪ·ʃᵊn, $dɪˌvɜːr-/ *n* [U] • *Diversification (***into** *new European markets) has helped to protect the company from the worst effects of the recession.*

di·ver·si·ty /£daɪ'vɜː·sɪ·ti, $dɪ'vɜːr·sə·t̬i/ *n* [U] • *Does television adequately reflect the ethnic and cultural diversity of the country?* • *There is* **a** *wide diversity* **of** *opinion on the question of unilateral disarmament.*

di·vert *obj* [CHANGE DIRECTION] /£daɪ'vɜːt, $dɪ'vɜːrt/ *v* [T] to cause (something or someone) to change direction • *Traffic will be diverted through the side streets while the main road is resurfaced.* • *The scandal diverted attention* **from** *the government's problems at a crucial stage in the election campaign.* • *Nothing could divert his thoughts* **from** *his mother's sudden death.* • *Our flight had to be diverted* **to** *Stansted because of the storm.* • To divert something or someone is also to use them for a different purpose: *Should more* **funds/money/resources** *be diverted* **from** *roads* **into** *railways?* ○ *Additional staff have been diverted* **into** *the department to cope with the extra work.*

di·ver·sion /£daɪ'vɜː·ʃᵊn, $dɪ'vɜːr-/ *n* • *The diversion of the railway line is likely to take three years.* [U] • *Traffic diversions will be kept to a minimum throughout the festival.* [C]

di·vert *obj* [TAKE ATTENTION AWAY] /£daɪ'vɜːt, $dɪ'vɜːrt/ *v* [T] to take (someone's attention) away from something, or to entertain them • *My* **attention** *was momentarily diverted* *by the sound of someone singing.* • *The war has diverted* **attention (away) from** *the country's economic problems.* • *It's a marvellous game for diverting* (=entertaining) *restless children on long car journeys.*

di·ver·sion /£daɪˈvɜː·ʃᵊn, $dɪˈvɜːr-/ *n* [C] • *Shoplifters often work in pairs, with one* **creating** *a diversion* (=an action that takes someone's attention away from something) *to distract the shop assistants while the other steals the goods.* • *The arrival of the window cleaner provided a welcome diversion* **from** *the tedium of the meeting.* • *Does this city have any diversions* (=forms of entertainment) *apart from pubs and nightclubs?*

di·ver·sion·a·ry /£daɪˈvɜː·ʃᵊn·ᵊr·i, $dɪˈvɜːr·ʒᵊn·er·i/ *adj* • *The proposal was dismissed as a diversionary* **tactic** *intended to distract attention from the real problems.*

di·vest *obj* **of** *obj* /ˌdaɪˈvest/ *v prep* [T] *fml* to take (something) off or away from (someone) • *There is a growing movement to divest the monarchy of its remaining constitutional power.* • *The Communist Party voted to divest* **itself** *of its incontestable right to rule.* • *She divested* **herself** *of her cumbersome attire.* • *She was unable to divest* **herself** (=get rid) *of the guilt she felt about her husband's death.*

di·vest *(obj)* /ˌdaɪˈvest/ *v esp. Am* to sell (esp. a business or a part of a business) • *One of the directors has announced that he is resigning from the board and divesting* **from** *the company.* [I] • *The company is divesting its less profitable business operations.* [T] • *She has divested* **herself of** (= sold)*some of her share-holdings.* [T]

di·vide *(obj)* SEPARATE /dɪˈvaɪd/ *v* to (cause to) separate into parts, or to cause (people) to disagree strongly • *At the end of the lecture, I'd like all the students to divide* **into** *small discussion groups.* [I] • *Divide the pastry* **into** *four equal parts.* [T] • *After World War Two, Germany was divided* **into** *two separate countries for more than four decades.* [T] • *The independent candidate was accused of dividing the opposition vote and allowing the previous representative to be re-elected.* [T] • *The vote is expected to divide* **equally/ evenly** *for and against the proposal.* [I] • To divide is also to share: *I think we should divide* **(up)** *the costs equally* **among/between** *us.* [T/M] ○ *Britain is to divide the development costs* **with** *Germany and France.* [T] • If something divides two areas, it marks the edge or limit of them: *There's a narrow alley which divides our house* **from** *the one next door.* [T] ○ *This path marks the dividing* **line** *between my land and my neighbour's. / It is not always easy to draw a dividing* **line** *between erotica and pornography.* • To divide something is also to use different amounts of it for different purposes or activities: *She divides her time* **between** *her apartment in New York and her cottage in Yorkshire.* [T] ○ *Greg divides his energies* **between** *running the company and playing tennis.* [T] • To divide a group of people is to cause them to disagree: *When it was first introduced, the ordination of women deeply divided (members of) the Church of England.* [T] • *The party is divided* (=Its members disagree) **on/over** *the issue of capital punishment.* [T] • *(Br)* If representatives in Parliament divide, they vote by separating into two groups, one group who want the law which is being voted on to be accepted and one group who are against it: *After a lengthy debate, MPs/the House of Commons divided.* [I] • **Divide and rule** is a way of acting which a person in a position of power uses to keep himself or herself in power by causing disagreements among other people so that they are unable to question his or her power. • *"England and America are two countries divided by a common language"* (believed to have been said by George Bernard Shaw, 1856-1950)

di·vide /dɪˈvaɪd/ *n* [C] • *Because of debt repayments, the divide* (=large difference) **between** *rich and poor countries is continuing to grow.* • Divide is also *Am for* WATERSHED BIG CHANGE.

di·vid·ed /dɪˈvaɪ·dɪd/ *adj* • If you are divided, you have to make a decision between two or more opposing opinions or actions: *She found herself divided* **between** *her loyalty to her mother and her deeply-ingrained sense of justice.* • **Divided highway** *is Am and Aus for* **dual carriageway**. See at DUAL.

di·vi·sion /dɪˈvɪʒ·ᵊn/ *n* • *The division* (=sharing) **of** *the tasks* **between** *the team members is still to be decided.* [U] • *The division* (=difference) **between** *the rich and the poor has never been greater.* [U] • *A stream marks the division* **between** (=the edge of) *the two farms.* [C] • *Disagreements about defence cuts have opened up* **deep/sharp** *divisions* (= disagreements) **within** *the military.* [C] • *Division* (= Disagreement) **within** *the party will limit its chances at the election?* [U] • A division is also a separate part of an army or large organization: *There is no indication that the 25 foreign divisions* (=military units) *are preparing to withdraw from the region.* [C] ○ *Because of falling sales the company has decided to convert its tobacco division* (= department) *to paper production.* [C] • A division is also a group of teams which play against each other in a particular sport: *Manchester United are currently top of the first division.* [C] LP **Sports** ○ *(fig.) The company prides itself on only hiring people who are in the first division* (= of high quality). [C] • *(Br specialized)* A parliamentary division is a vote during which representatives in parliament go into either of two **division lobbies** (=voting rooms) according to whether they are voting for or against a suggested law. • The **division of labour** is a way of organizing work, esp. making things, so that it is done as a set of separate processes by different (groups of) people: *Society is challenging the traditional sexual division of labour and the idea that men are better suited than women to certain types of work.*

di·vi·sion·al /dɪˈvɪʒ·ᵊn·ᵊl/ *adj* [not gradable] • *the divisional* (=relating to a part of an army or a large organization) *commander/headquarters/representative* • *Rugby/football teams play divisional* (=organized in groups) *competitions.*

di·vis·ive /dɪˈvaɪ·sɪv/ *adj* • If something is divisive, it causes great and sometimes unfriendly disagreement within a group of people: *The Vietnam war was an extremely divisive issue in the US.*

di·vis·ive·ness /dɪˈvaɪ·sɪv·nəs/ *n* [U] • *Some people think that private education is a source of social divisiveness.*

di·vide *(obj)* CALCULATE /dɪˈvaɪd/ *v* to calculate the number of times by which one number fits (exactly) into another, or (of a number) to fit (exactly) into another number • *2 multiplied by 5 is 10, so 10 divided* **by** *5 is/equals 2.* [T] • *5 divided* **by** *10 is/equals 0·5.* [T] • *What is 18 divided* **by** *6?* [T] • *What do you get if you divide 6* **into** *18?* [T] • *2 divides* (=fits) **into** *10 five times.* [I] • *"Does 3 divide* (=fit) **into** *10?" "Yes, but not exactly – there's one left over."* [I] • Compare MULTIPLY; SUBTRACT. • LP **Mathematics**

di·vis·ib·le /dɪˈvɪz·ɪ·bl̩/, *Am also* **di·vid·ab·le** /dɪˈvaɪ·də·bl̩/ *adj* [not gradable] • *A prime number is a whole number greater than 1 which is exactly divisible* **by** *itself and 1 but no other number.* • *5 is divisible* **by** *5 and 1.* • *2 is divisible* **into** *10 five times.*

di·vi·sion /dɪˈvɪʒ·ᵊn/ *n* [U] • *Does everyone find division harder than multiplication?*

di·vis·or /£dɪˈvaɪ·zəʳ, $-zɚ/ *n* [C] • *When you divide 21 by 7, 7 is the divisor.*

div·i·dend /ˈdɪv·ɪ·dend, -dənd/ *n* [C] (a part of) the profit of a company that is paid to the people who own shares in it • *Dividends will be sent to shareholders on March 31.* • *The massive losses have prevented the company from* **declaring** *a dividend this year.* • *(fig.) One dividend* (=additional advantage) *of using recycled materials is that they can be slightly cheaper.* • *(fig.) Studying hard at university and getting good results will* **pay** *dividends* (=produce advantages) *when you start work – you'll earn more and have a wider choice of jobs.*

di·vid·ers /£dɪˈvaɪ·dəz, $-dɚz/ *pl n* a piece of equipment used in mathematics consisting of two movable parts which are joined at one end and have sharp points at the other and which are used for measuring lines and angles and for marking positions along lines • *Don't forget to bring some/***a pair of** *dividers to the next class.* • LP **Mathematics**

di·vine GOD-LIKE /dɪˈvaɪn/ *adj* [not gradable] connected with a god, or like a god • *The Ayatollah described the Iranian earthquake as a divine test.* • *Some fans seem to regard footballers as divine beings.* • *England have fallen so far behind in the championship that their only hope of victory is divine* **intervention** (=help from God). • *Just because you've been promoted that doesn't give you a divine* **right** (= one like that of a god) *to tell us all what to do.*

di·vin·i·ty /£dɪˈvɪn·ɪ·ti, $-ə·t̬i/ *n* • *How can you be a Christian and dispute the divinity* (= state of being a god) *of Jesus?* [U] • *Unlike many superstars she has no delusions of divinity.* [U] • *(dated)* Divinity is the study of religion: *She has a Doctorate in Divinity from York University.* [U] • A divinity is a god or goddess: *Some royalists seem to regard the Queen as a divinity of some sort.* [C]

di·vine SPLENDID /dɪˈvaɪn/ *adj* extremely good, pleasant or enjoyable; splendid • *We had a perfectly divine time in*

Switzerland. • *Their new house is quite divine!* • *"Do you like it?" "Oh darling, of course I do. It's simply divine!"*

di·vine·ly /dɪˈvaɪn·li/ *adv* • *The soprano sang divinely throughout the concert.*

di·vine *(obj)* GUESS /dɪˈvaɪn/ *v* to guess (something), or to find (something) out without being told about it • *Divining someone else's thoughts is a tricky business.* [T] • *I divined* **from** *his grim expression* **that** *the news was not good.* [+ *that* clause] • *She spoke in such a confused way that it was almost impossible to divine* **what** *she wanted to tell me.* [+ *wh*-word] • To divine is also to discover something secret or in the future by using magical powers: *Do you believe that astrologers are able to divine the future?*

di·vin·a·tion /ˌdɪv·ɪˈneɪ·ʃᵊn/ *n* [U] • Divination is the skill or act of saying what will happen in the future or discovering something that is unknown or secret by magical methods: *Palm-reading is a type of divination.*

di·vine *(obj)* SEARCH /dɪˈvaɪn/, **dowse** *v* to search for (water or MINERALS underground) by holding horizontally in your hands a Y-shaped rod or stick, the end of which suddenly points down slightly when water or MINERALS are below it • *What can you divine* **for** *apart from water?* [I] • *Various minerals have been divined in the valley.* [T] • *She found an underground stream using a divining* **rod**.

di·vin·er /£dɪˈvaɪ·nəʳ, $-nɚ/, **dow·ser** *n* [C] • *Diviners sometimes use pendulums instead of rods or sticks.*

div·ing /ˈdaɪ·vɪŋ/ *n* [U] See at DIVE MOVE DOWN

di·vis·ib·le /dɪˈvɪz·ɪ·bl̩/ *adj* See at DIVIDE CALCULATE

di·vis·or /£dɪˈvaɪ·zəʳ, $-zɚ/ *n* [C]

di·vi·sion·al /dɪˈvɪʒ·ᵊn·ᵊl/ *adj* See at DIVIDE SEPARATE

di·vis·ive /dɪˈvaɪ·sɪv/ *adj*

di·vorce *(obj)* /£dɪˈvɔːs, $-ˈvɔːrs/ *v* to end your marriage (to your husband or wife) by an official or legal process • *It was such a shame when Martha and Jamie divorced (each other).* [I/T] • *It's hardly surprising Jane is so stressed at the moment – she's in the middle of divorcing Mike.* [T] • *Chris divorced Pat* **for** *infidelity.* [T] • *They* **got**/*(fml)* **were** *divorced* (**from** *each other) after only six months of marriage.* [T] • *(fig.) How can you divorce* (=separate) *the issues of environmental protection and overpopulation?* [T] • LP **Relationships**

di·vorce /£dɪˈvɔːs, $-ˈvɔːrs/ *n* • *What has caused this dramatic increase in the number of divorces?* [C] • *Mary wants (to get) a divorce* **from** *John, but he won't agree to one.* [C] • *What are the chances of a marriage* **ending in** *divorce?* [U] • *The dispute over custody of the children is likely to make it a complicated divorce case.* • *(fig.) Why is there such a divorce* (=separation) **between** *the arts and the sciences in this country's schools?* [C]

di·vorced /£dɪˈvɔːst, $-ˈvɔːrst/ *adj* [not gradable] • *Please indicate whether you are single, engaged, married, divorced, separated or widowed.* • *The survey reveals that one in four divorced women aged 27 to 34 start new relationships with younger men.* • *(fig.) Sometimes politicians seem to be hopelessly divorced* **from** (=do not understand) *the real world.*

di·vor·cee /£dɪˌvɔːˈsiː, £ˌdɪv·ɔː-, $dəˌvɔːrˈseɪ/ *n* [C] • A divorcee is someone who has got divorced and not married again: *Edward VIII, the British king, had to abdicate because he wanted to marry an American divorcee.* • *The Archbishop stressed that only in exceptional circumstances would divorcees be allowed to become priests.*

di·vulge *(obj)* /daɪˈvʌldʒ/ *v* to make (something secret) known • *Journalists do not divulge their sources.* [T] • *Someone has divulged details of this project* **to** *our competitors.* [T] • *The managing director refused to divulge* **how** *much she earned.* [+ *wh-* word] • *Sources close to the Prime Minister have divulged* **that** *he would like to retire after the next election.* [+ *that* clause]

div·vy up *obj*, **div·vy** *obj* **up** /ˈdɪv·i/ *v adv* [M] *esp. Am infml* to separate (something) into parts; to divide (something) • *They haven't yet decided how to divvy up the proceeds from the sale.* • *We divvied up the cake* **between** *us.*

dix·ie·land /ˈdɪk·si·lænd/ *n* [U] a style of traditional jazz music with a two-beat rhythm, which originally began in New Orleans in the US in the 1920s

DIY /ˌdiː·aɪˈwaɪ/ *n* [U] *Br and Aus abbreviation for* do-it-yourself (=the activity of decorating or repairing your home, or making things for your home yourself, rather than paying someone else to do it for you) • *The popularity of DIY has put a lot of decorators out of business.* • *Guy is a DIY enthusiast.* • *A new DIY superstore has just opened.* • LP **Shopping goods**

diz·zy /ˈdɪz·i/ *adj* **-ier, -iest** having or causing the feeling of spinning round, being unable to balance and being about to fall down • *Going without sleep for a long time makes me feel dizzy and light-headed.* • *She's rather dizzy* **from** *drinking so much wine.* • *I felt quite dizzy* **with** *excitement as I went up to collect the award.* • *Mount Everest reaches the dizzy* **height** *of 8848 metres.* • *(fig.) Do you think Caroline will reach the dizzy* **height** (=important job) *of Senior Editor before she's 30?* • *(fig.) Who could have predicted the dizzy* (=very fast) **pace** *of change in the country?* • *(infml)* If you say that someone is dizzy, you mean that they are foolish or silly: *It's difficult to imagine them bringing up a child – they're such a dizzy couple.* ○ *In the film, she played the part of a dizzy* **blonde** (=a woman with light-coloured hair, who acts as if she is not very intelligent, but in an attractive way). • LP **Feelings and pains**

diz·zi·ly /ˈdɪz·ɪ·li/ *adv* • *The skyscrapers towered dizzily above us.* • *(fig.) The country's economic growth remains dizzily* (=high) *above that of its competitors.*

diz·zi·ness /ˈdɪz·ɪ·nəs/ *n* [U] • *Some artificial sweeteners are thought to cause blurred vision, dizziness, headaches and nausea in some people.*

diz·zy·ing /ˈdɪz·i·ɪŋ/ *adj* • *The acrobats performed a dizzying* (=causing the feeling of spinning round) *display.* • *(fig.) The dizzying* (=very fast) **pace/speed** *of political change in the country caught many people by surprise.* • *(fig.) Consumers are faced by a dizzying* (=confusing) *choice of products.*

diz·zy·ing·ly /ˈdɪz·i·ɪŋ·li/ *adv* • *In spite of its dizzyingly complicated plot, it's one of the best movies I've ever seen.*

DJ PERSON, **dee·jay** /ˌdiːˈdʒeɪ, ˈ--/ *n* [C] *abbreviation for* **disc jockey**, see at DISC

DJ CLOTHING /ˈdiː·dʒeɪ/ *n* [C] *Br abbreviation for* **dinner jacket**, see at DINNER

DMs /ˌdiːˈemz/ *pl n infml abbreviation for* **Dr Martens**, see at DR

DNA /ˌdiː·enˈeɪ/ *n* [U] *specialized abbreviation for* deoxyribonucleic acid (=the chemical at the centre of the cells of living things which controls the structure and purpose of each cell and carries GENETIC information during reproduction)

D–no·tice /£ˈdiːˌnəʊ·tɪs, $-ˌnoʊ·t̬ɪs/ *n* [C] a British government instruction preventing particular information from being made public in order to protect the country • *The D-notice was lifted after news of the computer theft was circulated by an international news agency.*

do FOR QUESTIONS/NEGATIVES /duː/ *v aux* [+ infinitive without *to*; not *be doing*] he/she/it **does** /dʌz/, *past simple* **did** /dɪd/, *past part* **done** /dʌn/ used with another verb to form questions and negative sentences, including negative orders, and sometimes in AFFIRMATIVE sentences for reasons of style • *Do you want to go to London?* • *Where do you work?* • *Why don't we have lunch together on Friday?* • *Doesn't Matthew look old these days?* • *"Didn't you realise she was deaf?" "No I didn't."/"Of course I did."* • *Not only did I speak to her, I even got her autograph!* • *(fml) Never did I hear such a terrible noise.* • *Don't (you) speak to me like that!* • *(Br and Aus) Don't let's argue about it* (=Let's not argue about it). • *(fml) So quietly did she speak* (=She spoke so quietly) *that I could scarcely hear her.* • **Little** *does he know* (=He knows nothing about it), *but we're flying to Geneva next weekend to celebrate his birthday.* • *"I want three cakes, two chocolate bars and an ice cream." "Do you* **now/indeed**?(=That is surprising or unreasonable)." • LP **Auxiliary verbs**

do FOR EMPHASIS /duː/ *v aux* [+ infinitive without *to*; not *be doing*] he/she/it **does** /dʌz/, *past simple* **did** /dɪd/ used to give extra force to the main verb • *Do go to the party – you'll have such a good time!* • *Do shut up, Georgina, and get on with your homework.* • *Do write and let me know how you're getting on.* • *"I wasn't sure whether you liked cheese." "Do I like cheese! – I love cheese!"* • *Boy, did he yell when he hit his thumb with the hammer!* • *I know the smaller one's cheaper, but I do prefer this one.* • *So you do like beer after all – I thought you might if you tried it.* • *"Can I buy stamps here?" "Well, we do sell them, but we haven't got any at the moment."*

do TO AVOID REPEATING /duː/ *v aux* [not *be doing*] he/she/it **does** /dʌz/, *past simple* **did** /dɪd/, *past part* **done** /dʌn/ used to avoid repeating a verb or verb phrase • *She runs much faster than he does.* • *Maria looks much healthier than she did.* • *He said he wouldn't be able to remember, but fortunately he did.* • *"I don't like English food."* "**Nor/ Neither** *do I."* • *"I hate English food."* "**So** *do I."* • *"Excuse*

DANISH FALSE FRIENDS (DK)

English	Danish	Meaning
abortion *n*	abort	miscarriage
acre *n*	ager	field
actual *adj*	aktuel	topical, of current interest
alcove *n*	alkove	box bed
asp *n*	asp	aspen
backbone *n*	bagben	hind leg
barrack *n*	barak	hut
bask *v*	baske	to flap
bassoon *n*	basun	trombone; trumpet
bastard *n*	bastard	mongrel, hybrid
bring *v*	bringe	to take, convey; to put
casserole *n*	kasserolle	saucepan
character *n*	karakter	grade, mark
chef *n*	chef	chief; leader; boss
closet *n*	kloset	lavatory, w.c.
communal *adj*	kommunal	civic; local; municipal
commune *n*	kommune	municipality
concept *n*	koncept	rough draft, outline, plan
conjunctive *adj*	konjunktiv	subjunctive mood (grammar)
conserve *n*	konserves	tinned goods
constable *n*	konstabel	(naval and military) private, 1st class, able seaman
corn *n*	korn	grain, granule
creator *n*	kreatur	head of cattle, livestock
dame *n*	dame	lady; queen; female dance/dinner partner
effects *n*	effekter	stocks, bonds, securities
etiquette *n*	etikette	ticket, label, tag
eventual *adj*	eventuel	possible; if any; prospective
eventually *adv*	eventuelt	perhaps; if necessary; if convenient
fabrication *n*	fabrikation	manufacture
fantasize *v*	fantasere	to rave, be delerious, to improvise
fantasy *n*	fantasi	imagination; hallucination; fantasia
fast *adj*	fast	solid; regular; permanent
feast *n*	fest	celebration; party, fête
foreman *n*	formand	president; chair; speaker; predecessor; person sitting in front of somebody
genial *adj*	genial	brilliant, inspired
geniality *n*	genialitet	genius
gourmand *n*	gourmand	gourmet
gruesome *adj*	grusom	cruel, callous
gymnasium *n*	gymnasium	secondary school, grammar school
history *n*	historie	story, tale; affair; business
inconsequential *adj*	inkonsekvent	inconsistent
island *n*	Island	Iceland
kernel *n*	kerne	fruit pip
learn *v*	lære	to teach
loft *n*	loft	ceiling
marmalade *n*	marmelade	jam
meaning *n*	mening	opinion; object; intention
middle-aged *adj*	middelalderlig	medieval
net *n*	net	rack; string bag; network; system; web
novel *n*	novelle	short story
obligation *n*	obligation	bond, stock, debenture
pantomime *n*	pantomime	mime
pencil *n*	pensel	paint brush
porcelain *n*	porcelæn	china, crockery
port *n*	port	gate; gateway
preservative *n*	præservativ	condom, contraceptive
proper *adj*	proper	clean, tidy
rave *v*	rave	to stagger, totter, reel, lurch
rector *n*	rektor	headmaster; principal; president; vice chancellor
roman *n*	roman	novel
salad *n*	salat	lettuce
sensible *adj*	sensibel	sensitive
simple *adj*	simpel	common, vulgar, low, mean
sky *n*	sky	gravy; stock; jelly; cloud
small *adj*	smal	narrow; slender, slim
speaker *n*	speaker	announcer on TV, radio etc
strand *n*	strand	beach, seashore, seaside
technique *n*	teknik	technology; engineering
Thursday *n*	tirsdag	Tuesday
tin *n*	tin	pewter
tone *n*	tone	musical note
tree *n*	træ	wood, timber
wander *v*	vandre	to hike, walk
wrist *n*	vrist	instep of foot

me, Professor, you left your umbrella." "**So I did.** *I'm becoming so forgetful these days."* • *He said he'd leave the car in the garage, but he didn't.* • *"Would you mind tidying up the kitchen?" (esp. Br) "I have done already./I already have done."* • *Richard suggested I keep all my friends' addresses on my computer, as he does his.* • *"May I join you?" "Please do!"* • *"Should I invite Bill?" "Please don't – he got incredibly drunk at our last party."* • *"Who threw that paper dart?" "I did."* • *"Martha speaks fluent Japanese." "Does she really?"* • *"Do you want to go to London on Saturday?" "Yes, I do/No, I don't/No, I do not."* • *"I thought I'd take a day off school today." "Oh no you don't* (=I'm not going to let you do that)*!"* • *"Give me your handbag." "I shall do nothing of the sort* (=I certainly won't give it to you)*."* • 'Do' can also replace the main verb in questions that are added to the end of a sentence: *You met him at our dinner party, didn't you* (=Did you meet him at our party)*?* ○ *You don't understand the question, do you?* (=I do not think that you understand the question.) ○ *You do understand the question, don't you?* (=I think that you understand the question.) ○ *They live in Tokyo now, don't they* (=Am I right in thinking that they live in Tokyo now)*?* • Sometimes 'do' is used to replace the main verb in questions that are added to the end of a sentence as a way of expressing surprise: *So they finally got married, did they?*

do *obj* PERFORM /duː/ *v* [T] he/she/it **does** /dʌz/, *past simple* **did** /dɪd/, *past part* **done** /dʌn/ to perform, take part in or achieve (something) • *That was a really stupid thing to do.* • *I've finished that job. What shall I do now?* • *Why were you sent home from school early? What have you done now?* • *What are you doing over the weekend?* • *Haven't you got anything better to do?* • *I don't know why she puts up with him – he does nothing but complain.* • *You shouldn't blame yourself. You did everything possible to save him.* • *The only thing we can do now is wait and see what happens.* • *It isn't important whether you win or lose. Just do your* **best** *and try your hardest.* • *She's a real pleasure to do* **business** *with.* • **Justice** *must be done, and I have no choice but to fine you £500.* • *I'm sorry, it simply can't be done* (= achieved) *before next weekend.* • *Well, until the computer's been fixed, you'll just have to do* (=achieve) *what you can without it.* • *You should be able to do* (=achieve) *it by yourself/on your own*. • *(esp. Am) We must do lunch* (=eat it together) *sometime.* • If you do something **about** something, you take action to deal with it: *It's a global problem – what can individuals do about it?* ○ *She knows she drinks too much, but she can't do* **anything** *about it.* ○ **What's to be** (=What can or should be) *done* **about** *all this litter?* • *Would you mind doing* (=performing) *something* **for** *me?* • If someone or something does something **for** you, you like them: *Chopin has never done* **anything** *for me.* • If a doctor of medicine does something **for** someone or their illness, they make them better: *Can you do* **anything** *for my bad back, doctor?* ○ *These pills I've been taking have done* **nothing** *for me.* • *What have you done* (=caused to happen) **to** *her? Why are her arms covered in blood?* • If something or someone does something **to** you, it has a strong effect on you: *Watching that film really did* **something** *to me.* ○ *You really do* **something** *to me* (=I find you sexually attractive), *you know.* • **What (on earth)** *were you doing in the library* (=Why were you there and what action were you performing) *at two o'clock in the morning?* • **What** *are these toys doing here* (=Why are they here)*?* • **What**'*s the front door doing open* (=Why is it open)*?* • **What** *do you do* **(for a living)** (=What is your job)*?* • **What** *can I do* **for** *you* (= How can I help you)*?* • *I've got to look after my nephew next week, and I've no idea what I'm going to do* (=take part in) **with** *him.* • *What have you done* **with** (=Where have you put) *my coat? Have you hidden it?* • *Have you done something* **with** (=touched) *the TV? It's not working properly.* • *She just hasn't known what to do* **with herself** (=how to keep herself busy) *since she retired.* • Sometimes **do it** is used to avoid saying have sex: *How old were you when you first did it?* ○ *There's no way I could do it* **with** *her.* • **That does it** (= That goes beyond the limit of what is acceptable)*! I won't tolerate behaviour like that. Go and report to the head teacher immediately.* • **'That's done it** (=That has caused a problem or difficulty)*!" said Anna as she looked at the damage. "Now I really will have to get a new car."* • **Do-it-yourself** is DIY. • *(esp. disapproving)* A **do-gooder** is

DO: VERBS MEANING 'PERFORM'

- There is a small group of verbs which are often used to mean simply 'to perform an action'.
- When used in this way, the verb has a noun object which provides most of the meaning. For example in the phrases *to take a photograph* or *to have a swim* the verbs 'take' and 'have' mean nothing more than 'perform the action of' (photographing or swimming).
- Phrases like this are often used instead of other more formal verbs, for example 'to photograph' or 'to swim'.

GIVE
help, support, protection
birth
a promise, a warning, permission, an order
attention
a performance, a concert, a party
a cry, a shout, a talk, a speech, a lecture
a smile, a kiss, a hug

HAVE
(esp Br) lunch, *(esp Br)* dinner, a drink, a meal (=eat)
a swim, a walk, a game (of tennis etc.)
a try, a look
a wash, *(Br)* a bath, *(Br)* a shower
an argument, a conversation, a chat
a party

MAKE
lunch, dinner, a drink, a meal (=prepare)
a decision, a choice
an effort, an attempt
changes, arrangements, plans
cuts, payments
a donation, a contribution
progress
a mistake, an error
a suggestion, a request, an offer, a promise
an excuse, an apology
a speech, a statement, a sound, a (phone) call

TAKE
action, a decision
a chance, a risk
a bath, a shower
a look, a breath
a walk, exercise
a holiday, a trip, a break, a rest
a seat
a photograph, a picture

DO*
the shopping, the ironing, the cooking
the housework, the washing/*(Am also)* the wash, the cleaning,
the dishes /*(Br also)* the washing-up
your homework, a job
a painting, a drawing
your exercises
harm, damage

PAY
attention
a visit, a call
a compliment

HOLD
a conversation, talks
an interview, a meeting, a conference
a referendum, an election
a party, a festival

* In informal English 'do' is often used before nouns to refer to a common activity involving the thing mentioned: *She did her face* (= put on make-up). • *We did* (= studied) *Shakespeare at school.* • *I did* (= cooked) *fish for dinner.*

someone who does things that they think will help other people, although the other people might not find their actions helpful. • *(saying)* 'What's done is done'/'What's done cannot be undone' means that you cannot change something that has already happened. • *"Don't just stand there, do something"* (phrase used by the comedians Laurel and Hardy) • *"Why don't we do it in the road?"* (song from The Beatles *White Album*, 1968) • *"If it were done when 'tis done, then t'were well / It were done quickly"* (Shakespeare, Macbeth 1.7)

do·able /ˈduː·ə·bl̩/ *adj* • If something is doable, it can be achieved or performed: *This project may be difficult, but I still think it's doable.*

do·er /£ˈduː·əʳ, $-ɚ/ *n* [C] • A doer is someone who gets actively involved in something, rather than just thinking or talking about it: *There are too many thinkers and not enough doers in this office.*

dos /duːz/ *pl n* • **Dos and don'ts** are rules about actions and activities which people should or should not perform or take part in: *At my school we had to put up with a lot of dos and don'ts that were completely pointless.*

do ACT /duː/ *v* [always + adv/conjunction] he/she/it **does** /dʌz/, *past simple* **did** /dɪd/, *past part* **done** /dʌn/ to act or take action • *Stop arguing with me, Daryl, and do* **as** *you're told!* • *She told me not to ask any questions, just to do* **as** *she did.* • *"Was it wrong of me to go to the police?" "Oh no, I'm sure you did right/did the right thing."* • *You'd do well* **to** *take some professional advice on this matter.* • *"Do as you would be done by"* (Charles Kingsley in the children's book *The Water Babies*, 1863) • *"Do not do unto others as you would they should do unto you. Their tastes may not be the same"* (George Bernard Shaw *Maxims for Revolutionists*, 1907)

do·ing /ˈduː·ɪŋ/ *n* [U] • *Is this your doing?* (=Did you do this?) • *It was none of my doing.* • *Running a marathon takes some/a lot of doing* (= is difficult to do and needs a lot of effort). • See also DEED ACTION.

do·ings /ˈduː·ɪŋz/ *pl n* • *We'd like the doings* (= activities) *of government ministers to be more public.*

do *(obj)* DEAL WITH /duː/ *v* he/she/it **does** /dʌz/, *past simple* **did** /dɪd/, *past part* **done** /dʌn/ to deal with; to be responsible for • *Lucia is going to do the publicity for the school play.* [T] • *Annie does the film reviews for Radio Newcastle.* [T] • *If you do the washing up, I'll do the drying.* [T] • *If they ask any awkward questions, just let me do the talking.* [T] • *Jonathan is doing the catering at the wedding.* [T] • *I'm trying to find someone to do* (=repair) *the garden wall.* [T] • If you say that you **have** done **with** something or someone, or have done performing a particular action, you can mean that you have finished what you were doing with something or someone, or what you were saying to someone, or that you have finished the action: *Have you done with those scissors yet?* [I] ○ *Where the hell are you going? I haven't done with you yet.* [I] ○ *I haven't done talking to you yet.* [+ v-ing] ○ *(esp. regional) Have you done* (=finished talking)*? Can the rest of us get a word in now?*[I]

done /dʌn/ *adj* [after v; not gradable] • *The washing-up's done* (=finished), *but I've left the drying for you.* • If you are done **with** something or someone, or done performing an action, you have finished what you were doing with the thing or person, or what you were saying to the person, or you have finished the action: *Are you done with this saucepan, or are you still using it?* ○ *Where the hell are you going? I'm not done with you yet.* ○ *I want to* **get** *done with the renovations before I start thinking about redecorating.*

do *obj* STUDY /duː/ *v* [T] he/she/it **does** /dʌz/, *past simple* **did** /dɪd/, *past part* **done** /dʌn/ to study or learn • *Today we're going to do Chapter 4.* • *Have you ever done any Chinese?* • *Diane did History at London University.*

do *obj* SOLVE /duː/ *v* [T] he/she/it **does** /dʌz/, *past simple* **did** /dɪd/, *past part* **done** /dʌn/ to solve; find the answer to • *Can you do this sum for me?* • *I've been trying to do this puzzle for hours, but I still haven't managed it.* • *I've never been able to do crosswords.*

do *obj* [MAKE] /duː/ *v* [T] he/she/it **does** /dʌz/, *past simple* **did** /dɪd/, *past part* **done** /dʌn/ to make, produce or create • *Can you do me 20 photocopies of this report/do 20 photocopies of this report* **for** *me?* [+ two objects] • *I can do them* **for** *you by this evening.* • *I can't come out tonight – I've got to do my history essay.* • *(Am) This paper's the worst you've ever done. I think you should do it* **over** (= again).

do *(obj)* [CLEAN] /duː/ *v* he/she/it **does** /dʌz/, *past simple* **did** /dɪd/, *past part* **done** /dʌn/ to clean or tidy • *I want to do* (= clean) *the living room this afternoon.* [T] • *I cooked the dinner so you can do* (= wash) *the dishes.* [T] • *I'll just do* (= make clean and shiny) *my shoes, then I'll be ready.* [T] • *How can I wash up when I've just done my nails* (= put liquid on them to make them shiny)*?* [T] • *Must you do* (= cut) *your nails in the bath?* [T] • *I do* (= brush) *my teeth after every meal.* [T] • *(Br dated) We've got a marvellous cleaner who's been doing* **for** *us* (= cleaning our house) *for the past fifteen years.* [I]

do *obj* [ARRANGE] /duː/ *v* [T] he/she/it **does** /dʌz/, *past simple* **did** /dɪd/, *past part* **done** /dʌn/ to arrange • *You've done those flowers beautifully.* • *Where do you get your hair done?* • *Can anyone here do* (= tie) *bow-ties?*

do *obj* [VISIT] /duː/ *v* [T] he/she/it **does** /dʌz/, *past simple* **did** /dɪd/, *past part* **done** /dʌn/ *infml* to visit the interesting places in (a town or country), or to look around (an interesting place) • *I've always wanted to do India.* • *We didn't manage to do Nice when we were in France.* • *Is it possible to do Oslo in a day?* • *I've been meaning to do* (= look around) *the British Museum for ages.*

do *obj* [TRAVEL] /duː/ *v* [T] he/she/it **does** /dʌz/, *past simple* **did** /dɪd/, *past part* **done** /dʌn/ to travel at a speed of, or to complete (a journey) • *What's the point in having a car that does 200km an hour when the speed limit's only 120?* • *We were doing 150 (km an hour) along the motorway.* • *My new car does 50 miles to the gallon/30 km to the litre* (= uses one GALLON of fuel to travel 50 miles, or one litre to travel 30 km). • *Is it possible to do* (= complete the journey from) *Paris to Bordeaux in five hours?*

do *(obj)* [BE ACCEPTABLE] /duː/ *v* he/she/it **does** /dʌz/, *past simple* **did** /dɪd/, *past part* **done** /dʌn/ to be acceptable, suitable or enough (for) • *Will this room do or would you prefer one with a shower?* [I] • *Will* **it** *do if I get those books to you by Friday?* [I] • *This kind of behaviour just won't do.* [I] • **It** *doesn't* **do to** (= You shouldn't) *criticize your parents.* [+ to infinitive] • *I haven't got any grapefruit juice, but I've got some orange juice. Will that do (you)* (= be acceptable for you)*?* [I/T] • *"Have you got anything I could borrow for my interview?" "Well, I've got a plain green skirt that might do* (= be suitable) *(***for*** you)."* [I] • *"Is that enough potato, or would you like some more?" "That'll do* (= be enough for) *me, thanks."* [T] • **That'll do** (= Stop behaving like that), *Timothy! Please just sit down and keep quiet.* • *"The dinner was excellent except that they served red wine with the chicken." "Dear me!* **That will never do!** (= That is unacceptable.)*"* • *"That'll do nicely"* (advertisement for American Express credit card, 1970s)

do *obj* [CAUSE TO HAVE] /duː/ *v* [T] he/she/it **does** /dʌz/, *past simple* **did** /dɪd/, *past part* **done** /dʌn/ to provide or sell; to cause someone to have (something) • *There's a special offer on and they're doing three for the price of two.* • *Do you do travel insurance as well as flights?* • *I need to find a garage that can do repairs – this one only sells fuel.* • *The pub only does food at lunchtimes, not in the evenings.* • *Could you do me something without fish/do something without fish* **for** *me?* [+ two objects] • *They do you a very nice mixed grill/do a very nice mixed grill* **for** *you at that restaurant.* [+ two objects] • *A good healthy salad would do you (some)* **good**/*do (some)* **good to** *you.* [+ two objects] • *I dropped this apple on the floor. Will it do me any* **harm**/*do any harm* **to** *me if I eat it?* [+ two objects] • *This essay does you no* **credit**/*does no credit* **to** *you whatsoever.* [+ two objects] • *Would you mind doing me a* **favour**/*doing a favour* **for** *me and getting me some milk while you're out?* [+ two objects] • *She did him a really good* **turn**/*did a really good turn* **for** *him, helping him to get that job.* [+ two objects] • *(fml) Would you do me* **the honour** *of accompanying me to the ball?* [+ two objects]

do *obj* [SERVE] /duː/ *v* [T always + adv] he/she/it **does** /dʌz/, *past simple* **did** /dɪd/, *past part* **done** /dʌn/ *esp. Br* to provide (someone) with food, drink, a place to stay or similar service • *"Was your meal at the restaurant good?" "Oh yes, they did us very* **well** *indeed."*

do *obj* [COOK] /duː/ *v* [T] he/she/it **does** /dʌz/, *past simple* **did** /dɪd/, *past part* **done** /dʌn/ to cook or prepare (food) • *How long should the carrots be done for?* • *Who's doing the food for your party?*

done /dʌn/ *adj* [after v] • *Are the vegetables done* (= Have they finished cooking) *yet?* • *"How would you like your steak done?"* "**Well-done** (= Cooked for a long time), *please."* Compare MEDIUM [VALUE]; RARE [COOKED].

do *obj* [PLAY] /duː/ *v* [T] he/she/it **does** /dʌz/, *past simple* **did** /dɪd/, *past part* **done** /dʌn/ to perform (a play) or to play the part of (a character) • *The children are doing a play at the end of term.* • *She's done all the important Shakespearean roles apart from Lady Macbeth.* • *Who did James Bond before Roger Moore?* • *He does a brilliant (impression/impersonation of) Humphrey Bogart.* • *I hope she doesn't do* **a** *Helen* (= do what Helen did) *and get divorced six months after her wedding.*

do *obj* [STEAL] /duː/ *v* [T] he/she/it **does** /dʌz/, *past simple* **did** /dɪd/, *past part* **done** /dʌn/ *infml* to enter illegally and steal from (a building) • *Our house was done while we were away.*

do *obj* [CHEAT] /duː/ *v* [T] he/she/it **does** /dʌz/, *past simple* **did** /dɪd/, *past part* **done** /dʌn/ *infml* to cheat • *Fifty bucks for that old bike! You've been done! I wouldn't give you more than ten.* • *He did me* **for** *a thousand quid for that car.*

do *obj* [PRISON] /duː/ *v* [T] he/she/it **does** /dʌz/, *past simple* **did** /dɪd/, *past part* **done** /dʌn/ *infml* to spend (time) in prison • *He did three years for his part in the robbery.* • *If you're not careful you'll end up doing* **time** *again.*

do *obj* [PUNISH] /duː/ *v* [T] he/she/it **does** /dʌz/, *past simple* **did** /dɪd/, *past part* **done** /dʌn/ *esp. Br infml* to punish • *If you mess with me again I'll do you good and proper.* • *You haven't got away with this – I'll be back to do you.* • *I got done* (= stopped by the police) **for** *speeding on my way home last night.*

do *obj* [TAKE] /duː/ *v* [T] he/she/it **does** /dʌz/, *past simple* **did** /dɪd/, *past part* **done** /dʌn/ *infml* to take (an illegal drug) • *How long have you been doing heroin?* • *(humorous) I've been doing curry for years. I'm addicted to the stuff.*

do [HAPPEN] /duː/ *v* [usually *be doing*] to happen • *This town is so boring in the evening – there's never anything doing.* • *I'm going to Paul's tonight – he said there might be something doing.*

do [MANAGE] /duː/ *v* [I always + adv] he/she/it **does** /dʌz/, *past simple* **did** /dɪd/, *past part* **done** /dʌn/ to develop or continue with the stated amount of success; to manage • **How** *is Mary doing in her new job/school?* • *"***How's** *the patient doing, nurse?" "She's much better today, doctor."* • *"***How** *are you doing?" "I'm doing* **fine** *– I just got a new job."* • *Both the new mother and her baby are doing very* **well.** • *Are your roses doing* **all right** *this year?* • *Many shops are doing* **badly** *because of the economic situation.* • *I did rather* **well** *when I traded in my car – they gave me a good price for it.* • *Alexa has done* **well for herself** (= has achieved great personal success)*, getting that highly paid job.*

do [TREATMENT] /duː/ *n* [C] *pl* **dos** *Br infml* a way of treating people • *There are no special privileges for the managers – we believe in* **fair** *dos all round* (= equal treatment for everyone) *in this company.* • *It's a* **poor** *do* (= a bad/unfair situation) *when a so-called developed country can't even provide homes for all its citizens.* • See also DO BY.

do [PARTY] /duː/ *n* [C] *pl* **dos** *esp. Br and Aus infml* a party or other social event • *What sort of a do was Sophie's wedding?* • *It was one of those dos where nobody really knew each other.*

do [HAIR] /duː/ *n* [C] *pl* **dos** *Am for* HAIRDO

do a•way with *obj v adv prep* [T] to get rid of or destroy • *These ridiculous rules and regulations should have been done away with years ago.* • *Computerization has enabled us to do away with a lot of paperwork.* • *How on earth could they do away with a lovely old building like that and put a car park there instead?*

do by *obj v prep* [T always + adv/prep; usually passive] to treat • *(esp. Br and Aus) He's always complaining that he's so* **hard** (= badly) *done by, but he seems pretty fortunate to me.* • *(fml)* If you do **well** or **badly** by someone, you treat them well or badly. • *(Br saying) 'Do as you would be done by' means that you should treat others as you would like them to treat you.* • See also DO [TREATMENT].

do down *obj*, **do** *obj* **down** *v adv* [M] to cause (someone) to seem unimportant, feel ashamed or lose the respect of other people; to BELITTLE • *She is always doing her brother down* **for** *not having a university degree.*

do for *obj v prep* [T] *infml dated esp. Br* to damage or harm seriously, or to cause the death or destruction of • *I'll do for you, you miserable little bastard.* • *Driving on those rough roads has really done for my car.*

done for *adj* [after v; not gradable] • If you are done for, you are about to die or suffer greatly because of a serious difficulty or danger: *We all thought we were done for when the boat started to sink.* • *(fig.) I'm done for* (= very tired) – *I'm going to bed.*

do in *obj*, **do** *obj* **in** *v adv* [M] *slang* to attack violently or kill • *They threatened to do me in if I didn't pay up by Friday.* • *I heard she did her***self** *in after the scandal was exposed.* • *(fig.) That hockey match really did me in* (= made me very tired). • *(fig.) I was/felt really done in* (= very tired) *after the match.*

do out *obj* [CLEAN], **do** *obj* **out** *v adv* [M] *Br infml* to clean or tidy • *I'd like you to do out your room before Chris comes to stay.*

do out *obj* [DECORATE], **do** *obj* **out** *v adv* [M] to decorate • *They did the room out* **with** *balloons and streamers ready for the party.* • *We've had the bathroom done out* **in** *pale yellow.*

do *obj* **out of** *obj v adv prep* [T] to prevent (someone) from obtaining or keeping (something) by cheating • *That new overtime agreement has done me out of ten bucks a week.* • *Thousands of pensioners have been done out of millions of pounds.*

do o·ver *obj*, **do** *obj* **o·ver** *v adv* [M] *esp. Br and Aus infml* to attack violently • *They said they'd do me over if I refused to drive the getaway car.*

do up *(obj)* [FASTEN], **do** *(obj)* **up** *v adv* to fasten or be fastened • *Can you help me to do up my dress?* [M] • *Do your shoes/laces up before you trip over.* [M] • *These trousers must have shrunk – I can't do the zip up.* [M] • *Why won't this damn zip do up?* [I] • *Where does your dress do up?* [I] • LP› **Dressing and undressing**

do up *obj* [MAKE ATTRACTIVE], **do** *obj* **up** *v adv* [M] to repair or improve the appearance of; to make attractive • *I'd like to buy a run-down cottage that I can do up.* • *How long did it take you to do up your bike?* • *She's bought a load of posters to do her room up with.* • *Don't bother doing yourself up/getting (yourself) (all) done up, we're not going anywhere particularly smart.*

do up *obj* [WRAP], **do** *obj* **up** *v adv* [M] to wrap • *She always does her presents up beautifully* **in** *gold and silver paper.* • *I found the magazines on the doorstep, done up* **in** *brown paper.*

do with *obj* [BEAR] *v prep* [T] **cannot/can't do with** *Br infml* to be unable to bear (something) • *I can't do/be doing with all this shouting and screaming.* • *I really can't do with you behaving like this.* [+ obj + v-*ing*]

do with *obj* [CONNECTED] *v prep* [T] **to be/have** *something* **to do with** to be connected with • *"What's your book about?" "Well, it's to do with human behaviour."* • *"Why did you want to talk to me?" "Well, it's to do with a complaint that's been made about your work."* • *"What do you think causes violence?" "I'd say the way men are brought up has a lot to do with it."* • *"But I didn't have any money." "What has that got to do with it? You still shouldn't have taken my purse without asking me."* • *She's refused to have* **anything (more)** *to do with him since he was arrested for drinking and driving.* • *"I thought I should tell you I saw your son smoking today." "Mind your own business, would you? It has* **nothing** *to do with you what my son does!"* • *"What does Sheila do?" "Oh, she has* **something** *to do with civil engineering."*

do with·out *(obj) v adv, v prep* to manage without • *There's no mayonnaise left, so I'm afraid you'll just have to do without.* [I] • *She simply can't do without at least four weeks holiday a year.* [T] • *Thank you Kate, we can do without language like that* (= we don't want to hear your rude language). [T]

dob *(obj)* /£dɒb, $dɑːb/ *v* **-bb-** *Aus infml* to secretly tell someone in authority that (someone else) has done something wrong • *Who was it who dobbed me* **in** *(***to** *the teacher)?* [T always + *in*] • *I'm dobbing* **on** *you.* [I always + *on*]

dob·ber /£'dɒb·əʳ, $'dɑː·bɚ/ *n* [C] *Aus infml* • A dobber is a person who secretly tells someone in authority that someone else has done something wrong.

dob in *obj*, **dob** *obj* **in** *v adv* [M] *Aus infml* to suggest that (someone who is not present) should be given a usually unpleasant job • *He dobbed me in* **to** *organize the roster.* [+ *to* infinitive]

doc /£dɒk, $dɑːk/ *n* [C] *infml* a medical or university doctor • *You see, doc, I haven't been sleeping at all well recently.* [as form of address] • *Doc Wilson's chemistry lectures used to be so boring.* • **Doc Martens** is *infml for* **Dr Martens**. See at DR. • *"What's up, Doc?"* (phrase from Bugs Bunny cartoons, 1936-)

do·cile /£'dəʊ·saɪl, £'dɒs·aɪl, $'dɑː·sᵊl/ *adj* quiet and easy to influence, persuade or control • *Just because our union is moderate, it doesn't mean we're docile.* • *The once docile population has finally risen up against the ruthless regime.*

do·cil·i·ty /£dəʊ'sɪl·ɪ·ti, $dɑː'sɪl·ə·ṭi/ *n* [U] • *An important consequence of Gorbachev's policies was the destruction of the docility that had made totalitarianism possible.*

dock [ENCLOSED AREA] /£dɒk, $dɑːk/ *n* [C] a specially enclosed area of water in a port that is used for loading and unloading or repairing ships • *The ship will be in the dock for several weeks while it undergoes repairs.* • *(Br and Aus) I'm having to commute by rail at the moment as my car's* **in dock** (= being repaired). • *(Am)* A dock is also a PIER (= raised floor that sticks out at the edge of the sea or a lake or river) where passengers can get on or off a boat or where goods can be loaded and unloaded. • Compare HARBOUR [WATER].

docks /£dɒks, $dɑːks/ *pl n* • *The strike has led to the cancellation of some ferry services and left hundreds of passengers stranded at the docks.*

dock *(obj)* /£dɒk, $dɑːk/ *v* • *Bad weather forced us to dock* (= arrive at a dock) *an hour later than scheduled.* [I] • *Hundreds of people turned up to see the ship dock* **at** *Southampton.* [I] • *The Russians and Americans docked* (= joined together in space) *(their spacecraft) just after one o'clock this morning.* [I/T]

dock·er /£'dɒk·əʳ, $'dɑː·kɚ/, **dock·work·er** /£'dɒk ˌwɜː·kəʳ, $'dɑːkˌwɜːr·kɚ/, *Am also* **long·shore·man** (*pl* **-men**) *n* [C] • A docker is a person who works at a port, loading and unloading ships.

dock [LAW] /£dɒk, $dɑːk/ *n* [U] **the dock** *esp. Br* the place in a criminal law court where the accused person sits or stands during the trial • *The defendant seemed nervous as he left the dock and stepped up to the witness box.* • *The company will find itself* **in the dock** (= in court) *if it continues to ignore the pollution regulations.* • *(fig.) I'll be* **in the dock** (= in trouble) *if I'm late for work again.* • LP› **Law**

dock *obj* [REMOVE] /£dɒk, $dɑːk/ *v* [T] to remove part of (something, esp. money) or remove (a part) from something • *The University has docked lecturers' pay/wages* **by** *20% because of their refusal to mark examination papers.* • *The University has docked 20%* **from** *lecturers' pay/wages.* • *Why are the lambs docked* (= Why are their tails cut short)*?* • *The lambs' tails are docked* (= cut short) *for hygiene reasons.*

dock [PLANT] /£dɒk, $dɑːk/ *n* a common wild plant with large wide leaves which grows in some northern countries such as Britain • *I think this plant is a dock.* [C] • *Dock is sometimes regarded as a weed.* [U] • *Rubbing dock leaves on nettle stings helps to relieve the pain.*

dock·et /£'dɒk·ɪt, $'dɑː·kɪt/ *n* [C] *Br and Aus* an official document describing something that is being delivered or transported and giving details of where it is coming from and where it is going to • *Make sure you get someone to sign the docket when you hand over the package.* • *(Am)* A docket is also a list of cases to be dealt with in a law court or an AGENDA (= a list of things to be done or decided) in business.

dock·et *obj* /£'dɒk·ɪt, $'dɑː·kɪt/ *v* [T] • *Don't forget to docket* (= record the details on an official document) *each consignment before you load it onto the truck.*

dock·land /£'dɒk·lænd, £-lənd, $'dɑːk-/ *n Br* the area that surrounds the DOCKS in a port • *Hundreds of millions of pounds are needed to redevelop large areas of derelict dockland.* [U] • *The new road connects the docklands with the city centre.* [C] • *A dockland community of 2 000 families are planning to build their own housing estate rather than move to other parts of the city.*

dock·side /£'dɒk·saɪd, $'dɑːk-/ *n* [U] **the dockside** the area next to a DOCK where goods can be stored before loading or after unloading • *Crates suspected of containing drugs were secretly inspected by customs officers on the dockside.*

dock·yard /£'dɒk·jɑːd, $'dɑːk·jɑːrd/, **ship·yard** *n* [C] a place where esp. naval ships are built, maintained and repaired • *Hundreds of workers in naval dockyards have* *received large doses of radiation while working on nuclear submarines.*

doc·tor MEDICINE /£'dɒk·tər, $'dɑːk·tɚ/ *(abbreviation* **Dr**) *n* [C] a person with a medical degree whose job is to treat people who are ill or hurt • *he decided to become either a doctor or a vet.* • *The doctor* **prescribed** *these pills but they don't seem to be doing any good.* • *You should* **see** *a doctor about that cough.* • *He went to* **the doctor's** (= the SURGERY where the doctor works) *this morning.* • *Good morning, Doctor Smith/Doctor.* [as form of address] • If something is **just what the doctor ordered**, it is exactly what is wanted or needed: *Ooh thank you, a nice cup of tea, just what the doctor ordered.* • *(esp. humorous)* **Doctor's orders** means you must do something because your doctor has told you to do it: *I have to have a week off work – it's doctor's orders!*

doc·tor EDUCATION /£'dɒk·tər, $'dɑːk·tɚ/ *(abbreviation* **Dr**) *n* [C] a person who has one of the highest-ranking degrees given by a college or university, such as a PHD • LP **Schools and colleges**

doc·tor·al /£'dɒk·tər·əl, $'dɑːk·tɚ-/ *adj* [before n; not gradable] • *This research formed part of her doctoral* **dissertation** (= the written report of the work done in order to obtain the highest degree.)

doc·tor·ate /£'dɒk·tər·ət, $'dɑːk·tɚ-/ *n* [C] • A doctorate is a high-ranking degree, such as a PHD: *She was awarded an* **honorary** *doctorate for her charity work.*

doc·tor *obj* CHANGE /£'dɒk·tər, $'dɑːk·tɚ/ *v* [T] *disapproving* to change (a document) in order to deceive people, or to put poison into (food or drink) • *He was found to have provided the court with doctored evidence.* • *Bottles of lemonade doctored* **with** *rat poison were discovered in the kitchen.* • *(Br and Aus infml)* If an animal is doctored, it has been STERILIZED (= made unable to breed).

doc·trine /£'dɒk·trɪn, $'dɑːk-/ *n* a belief, theory or set of beliefs, esp. political or religious, taught and accepted by a particular group • *Will the Anglican Church break apart over aspects of doctrine?* [U] • *They denounced impractical political doctrines.* [C] • *The president said he would not go against sound military doctrine.* [U]

doc·trin·aire /£ˌdɒk·trɪ'neər, $ˌdɑːk·trə'ner/ *adj fml disapproving* • *These principles are doctrinaire* (= based too much on fixed beliefs that do not consider practical problems).

doc·tri·nal /£dɒk'traɪ·nəl, £'dɒk·trɪ-, $'dɑːk·trɪ-/ *adj* [not gradable] *fml* • *The Bishop made some doctrinal* **statements** (= on matters to do with his Church's teachings) *that many disagreed with.*

doc·u·dra·ma /£'dɒk·jʊˌdrɑː·mə, $'dɑː·kjʊˌdrɑː·mə/ *n* [C/U] **drama documentary**, see at DRAMA THEATRE

doc·u·ment /£'dɒk·jʊ·mənt, $'dɑː·kjʊ-/ *n* [C] a paper or set of papers with written or printed information, esp. of an official type • *Ms. Robbins provided a copy of a* **confidential** *document to a newspaper reporter.* • *They are charged with using* **forged** *documents.* • *The government spokesman stressed that the* **leaked** *document contained proposals and not final government policy.* • *Most of the* **official** *documents are available in the library.* • Your **travel** documents are the important official papers, such as a PASSPORT or VISA, that you need in order to be allowed to travel from one country to another.

doc·u·ment *obj* /£'dɒk·jʊ·mənt, -ment, $'dɑː·kjʊ-/ *v* [T] • *His interest in cricket has been* **well-documented** (= recorded and written about) *by the media.*

doc·u·men·ta·ry /£ˌdɒk·jʊ'men·tər·i, $ˌdɑː·kjʊ'men·t̬ɚ-/ *adj* [before n; not gradable] • *Human rights campaigners have discovered documentary* **evidence** (= written proof) *of torture.* • See also DOCUMENTARY.

doc·u·men·ta·tion /£ˌdɒk·jʊ·men'teɪ·ʃən, $ˌdɑː·kjʊ-/ *n* [U] • *Passengers without proper documentation* (= official papers) *will not be allowed to travel.* • *As yet, no documentation* (= written material which provides proof) *has been found to support the claim.* • *My new computer came with so much documentation* (= written instructions about how to use it) *that I haven't been able to read it all yet.*

doc·u·men·ta·ry /£ˌdɒk·jʊ'men·tər·i, $ˌdɑː·kjə'men·t̬ɚ-/ *n* [C] a film or television or radio programme that gives factual information about a subject • *The documentary took a fresh look at the life of Darwin.* • *They showed a documentary* **on** *animal communication.*

doc·u·men·ta·ry /£ˌdɒk·jʊ'men·tər·i, $ˌdɑː·kjə'men·t̬ɚ-/ *adj* [before n] • *Most of her films have a documentary style* (= consist of facts rather than stories). • See also **documentary** at DOCUMENT.

dod·der /£'dɒd·ər, $'dɑː·dɚ/ *v* [I] *infml* (esp. of an old person) to move in a very slow and shaky way • *The old man doddered down the street.*

dod·der·y (**-ier**, **-iest**) /£'dɒd·ər·i, $'dɑː·dɚ-/, **dod·der·ing** /£'dɒd·ər·ɪŋ, $'dɑː·dɚ-/ *adj infml* • *a rather doddery old man*

dod·dle /£'dɒd·l̩, $'dɑː·dl̩/ *n* [U] *Br infml* something that is very easy to do • *She thought the exam would be a doddle.*

dodge *(obj)* /£dɒdʒ, $dɑːdʒ/ *v* to avoid being hit (by something) by moving quickly to one side, or *(fig.)* to avoid (something unpleasant) • *He dodged to avoid the fist that shot out at him.* [I] • *I had to dodge huge drops of water that fell from the ceiling.* [T] • *(fig.) The minister dodged* (= avoided answering) *almost all the questions that were put to her.* [T] • *(fig.) How did she manage to dodge paying the fine?* [+ v-*ing*]

dodge /£dɒdʒ, $dɑːdʒ/ *n* [C] *infml* • *They bought another car as a* **tax** *dodge* (= a way to avoid paying tax).

dodg·er /£'dɒdʒ·ər, $'dɑː·dʒɚ/ *n* [C] • A dodger is a person who avoids doing what they should do: *a* **tax** *dodger* (= someone who avoids paying tax).

Dodg·em (car) /£'dɒdʒ·əm, $'dɑː·dʒəm/ *n* [C] *trademark for* **bumper car**, see at BUMPER CAR PART • *Shall we go* **on the** *dodgems?*

dodg·y /£'dɒdʒ·i, $'dɑː·dʒi/ *adj* **-ier**, **-iest** *Br and Aus infml* (of things) risky or unable to be depended on, or (of people) dishonest • *The weather might be a bit dodgy at this time of year.* • *They got involved with a dodgy businessman and lost all of their money.* • *"I've just been offered some half-price tickets." "That sounds dodgy* (= risky)."

do·do /£'dəʊ·dəʊ, $'doʊ·doʊ/ *n* [C] *pl* **dodos** or **dodoes** a large bird, unable to fly, that no longer exists

doe /£dəʊ, $doʊ/ *n* [C] the female of animals such as the deer or rabbit • Compare BUCK ANIMAL.

do·er /£'duː·ər, $-ɚ/ *n* [C] See at DO PERFORM

does /dʌz/ *he/she/it form of* DO

does·n't /'dʌz·ənt/ *short form of* does not • *Doesn't she look lovely in that hat?* • *He doesn't want anything to do with me.*

doff *obj* /£dɒf, $dɑːf/ *v* [T] *literary* to remove (esp. your hat), usually to show respect • *The smartly dressed gentleman doffed his hat as he passed the two ladies.* • *(fig.) The song doffs its hat* (= shows its respect) *to the best soul traditions.* • Compare DON PUT ON.

dog ANIMAL /£dɒg, $dɑːg/ *n* [C] a common four-legged animal, esp. kept by people as a pet or to hunt or guard things • *my pet dog* • *hunting dogs* • *wild dogs* • *dog food* • *From the forest came the sound of a dog barking furiously.* • *It is a breed of dog with short legs and long soft hair.* • *More than 20 police dog handlers began the search yesterday afternoon.* • *The sofa was covered in dog hairs.* • *Good dog, come here!* [as form of address] • A **dog in the manger** is someone who, not wanting a particular thing themselves, does not want anyone else to have or enjoy it. • *(infml)* A **dog's breakfast** is something or someone that looks extremely untidy, or something that is very badly done. • *(infml)* If someone hasn't **a dog's chance**, they have no chance . • **A dog's life** is a very unhappy and unpleasant one. • *(infml)* Someone who is **done/dressed/got up like a dog's dinner** is dressed in clothes which make them look silly. • If something or someone is **going to the dogs**, they are gradually changing from being good to being worthless. • *(infml) He has lost a lot of money betting on the dogs* (= risking money on the results of GREYHOUND races). • *(Am and Aus infml)* To **put on the dog** is to act as if you are more important than you are. • A **dog biscuit** is a hard baked biscuit for dogs. • A **dog collar** is a strap worn around a dog's neck, or *(infml)* the stiff white circular piece of material worn around the neck by priests and other religious officials. • **Dog days** are the hottest days of the summer. • A book or paper that is **dog-eared** has the pages turned down at the corners as a result of a lot of use. • A **dog-eat-dog** situation is one where everyone is trying to get the best they can for themselves, not caring about what happens to anyone else. • *(Am slang)* A **dog tag** is the small piece of metal worn round the neck by a soldier with their number on it. • *(infml)* If you are **dog-tired**, you are extremely tired. • *(saying)* 'Every dog has its day' means that everyone is successful or happy at some point in their life. • *(saying)* 'Why keep a dog and bark yourself?' means why do something yourself when someone else is paid to do it. • See also DOGGY.

dog PERSON /£dɒg, $dɑːg/ *n* [C] *slang* a man who is unpleasant or not to be trusted, or an unattractive woman • *He tried to steal my money, the* **dirty** *dog.* • *She's a real dog*

(=She's very ugly). • A dog is also a person of the stated type: *You won $1000? You* **lucky dog!** [as form of address]

dog *obj* FOLLOW /£dɒg, $dɑːg/ *v* [T] **-gg-** to follow (someone) closely and continually • *The child dogged me with her questions for the rest of the day.* • *(fig.) Technical problems dogged our trip* (=We had technical problems) *from the outset.* • See also DOGGED.

dog·cart /£'dɒg·kɑːt, $'dɑːg·kɑːrt/ *n* [C] a light two-wheeled vehicle pulled by a horse, used esp. in the past

dog·catch·er /£'dɒg,kætʃ·əʳ, $'dɑːg,kætʃ·ɚ/ *n* [C] a person whose job is to catch homeless dogs and cats and take them to an official place where they are kept in cages

dog·fight /£'dɒg·faɪt, $'dɑːg-/ *n* [C] a fight between two military aircraft in which they fly very fast and very close to each other, or a fight between dogs, usually organized for illegal entertainment

dog·fish /£'dɒg·fɪʃ, $'dɑːg-/ *n* [C] *pl* **dogfish** or **dogfishes** a type of small SHARK

dog·ged /£'dɒg·ɪd, $'dɑː·gɪd/ *adj* very determined to do something, even if it is very difficult • *Her ambition and dogged determination ensured that she rose to the top of her profession.*

dog·ged·ly /£'dɒg·ɪd·li, $'dɑː·gɪd-/ *adv* • *But I kept at it, doggedly and patiently, and finally I could skate.*

dog·ged·ness /£'dɒg·ɪd·nəs, $'dɑː·gɪd-/ *n* [U] • *Her doggedness and persistence finally paid off.*

dog·ger·el /£'dɒg·ᵊr·ᵊl, $'dɑː·gɚ-/ *n* [U] poetry that is silly or worthless • *This collection of poems is doggerel for the most part.*

dog·go /£'dɒg·əʊ, $'dɑː·goʊ/ *adv* [not gradable] **lie doggo** *infml dated* See at LIE POSITION

dog·gone /£'dɒg·ɒn, $'dɑː·gɑːn/ *adj* [before n; not gradable], *exclamation Am infml* used to express annoyance • *Doggone* **(it)**, *where's that letter?* • *That doggone rabbit ate my lunch.* • *Well, I'll be doggone! He left without even saying goodbye!*

dog·gy, dog·gie /£'dɒg·i, $'dɑː·gi/ *n* [C] (used esp. by or to children) a dog • A **doggy bag** is a small bag that a restaurant provides so that you can take home any food you have not finished. • The **doggy paddle** (*Aus and Am also* **dog paddle**) is a simple swimming action in which a person moves their arms and legs up and down in quick movements under the water. • *"How Much is that Doggy in the Window?"* (title of a song written by Bob Merrill, 1953)

dog·house /£'dɒg·haus, $'dɑːg-/ *n* [C] *pl* **doghouses** /£'dɒg,haʊ·zɪz, $'dɑːg-/ *Am for* KENNEL • *(Br and Am infml)* If you are **in the doghouse**, someone is annoyed with you and shows their disapproval: *I've broken the wife's favourite vase, and now I'm really in the doghouse.*

dog·ie /£'dəʊ·gi, $'doʊ-/ *n* [C] *Am* a CALF that has no mother

dog·leg /£'dɒg·leg, $'dɑːg-/ *n* [C] a sharp bend, esp. in a road or on a **golf course**

dog·ma /£'dɒg·mə, $'dɑːg-/ *n disapproving* a fixed, esp. religious, belief or set of beliefs that people are expected to accept without any doubts • *This is an action born of dogma rather than good sense.* [U] • *Are the churches locked into their separate dogmas?* [C]

dog·mat·ic /£dɒg'mæt·ɪk, $dɑːg'mæt̬-/ *adj disapproving* • If someone is dogmatic, they are certain that they are right and that everyone else is wrong: *Theirs is one of the most dogmatic political parties in Europe.*

dog·mat·i·cal·ly /£dɒg'mæt·ɪ·kli, $dɑːg'mæt̬-/ *adv disapproving* • *He was dogmatically strict about rules and regulations.*

dog·mat·i·sm /£'dɒg·mə·tɪ·zᵊm, $'dɑːg·mə·t̬ɪ-/ *n* [U] *disapproving* • *There is a note of dogmatism in the book* (= The writer states their opinions too strongly and does not accept any others).

dog·mat·ist /£'dɒg·mə·tɪst, $'dɑːg·mə·t̬ɪst/ *n* [C] *disapproving* • A dogmatist is a person who holds their opinions too strongly: *Many dogmatists won't even consider recent developments.*

do–good·er /£,duː'gʊd·əʳ, $-ɚ, '-,--/ *n* [C] See at DO PERFORM

dogs·bo·dy /£'dɒgz·bɒd·i, $'dɑːgz·bɑː·di/ *n* [C] *Br and Aus infml* a person who has to do all the boring or unpleasant jobs that other people do not want to do • *I'm sick of being the* **general** *dogsbody around here!*

dog·wood /£'dɒg·wʊd, $'dɑːg-/ *n* [C] a flowering bush, growing either wild or in gardens

doi·ly, doy·ly, doy·ley /'dɔɪ·li/ *n* [C] a small piece of paper or cloth with a pattern of little holes in it, used as a decoration on a plate or under a cake

do·ing /'duː·ɪŋ/ *n* See at DO ACT

do·ings /'duː·ɪŋz/ *n* [C] *pl* **doings** *Br infml* anything, esp. a small object, the name of which the speaker does not know or wishes to avoid saying because it refers to something embarrassing • *I'm looking for a doings to hold up a curtain* *rail that's fallen down.* • *"Did you remember the doings for the barbecue?" "The charcoal, you mean? Yes, here it is."* • *The streets were filthy and covered with dogs' doings.* • See also **doings** at DO [ACT].

Dol·by /£'dɒl·bi, $'dɑːl-/ *n* [U] *trademark* an electronic system for reducing unwanted noise on sound recordings

dol·drums /£'dɒl·drəmz, $'doʊl-/ *pl n* **the doldrums** *infml* a state of lack of activity or lack of success • *Her career was* **in** *the doldrums during those years.* • The doldrums was originally a name for an area of sea where ships were unable to move because there was no wind.

dole /£dəʊl, $doʊl/ *n* [U] **the dole** *infml* the money that the government gives to people who are unemployed • *Young people* **on** *the dole* (=receiving money because they are unemployed) *are often bored and frustrated.* • To **go on** the dole is to start receiving unemployment payments. • *His family just exist on his dole money.* • *(Br) The government was blamed for lengthening* **dole queues** (=increasing the number of people having to ask for money from the government because they cannot find work). • [LP] **Work**

dole out *obj*, **dole** *obj* **out** /£dəʊl, $doʊl/ *v adv* [M] *infml* to give (money, food, etc.), esp. to several people • *I can't keep doling out money* **to** *you kids.*

dole·ful /£'dəʊl·fəl, $'doʊl-/ *adj* very sad • *The dog looked at me with a doleful expression.*

dole·ful·ly /£'dəʊl·fəl·i, $'doʊl-/ *adv* • *"I can't go with you," she said dolefully.*

doll /£dɒl, $dɑːl/ *n* [C] a child's toy in the shape of a small person or a baby • *The children sat on the floor playing with their dolls.* • *(Br and Aus)* A **doll's house** (*Am* **dollhouse**) is a toy that is a very small house, often with furniture and small dolls in it. • A *(Br and Aus)* doll's **pram**/*(Am)* doll's **carriage** is a vehicle for pushing a doll around in. • *(Am)* A **doll corner** (also **housekeeping corner**) is quiet area or corner of a school room which has dolls and small furniture arranged in it for children to play with. • *(esp. Am infml dated)* Doll is also used by men as a term of address to a woman or a girl, esp. one considered attractive. • [LP] **Titles and forms of address** [PIC] **Toy**

doll up *obj*, **doll** *obj* **up** /£dɒl, $dɑːl/ *v adv* [M] *disapproving* (esp. of a woman) to try to make (yourself) look more attractive by putting on stylish clothes and a lot of make-up • *I'm not going to doll myself up just to go to the shops.*

dol·lar /£'dɒl·əʳ, $'dɑː·lɚ/ *n* [C] a unit of money, used in the US, Canada, Australia, New Zealand and other countries, that is divided into 100 CENTS • *Could you lend me ten dollars?* • *In the financial markets today, the dollar* (=the value of American money) *rose as the pound fell.* • *The suitcase was full of dollar* **bills** (=notes). • The **dollar sign**, $, is put in front of amounts of money in dollars. • *(Am and Aus) When he said he'd marry her he had* **dollar signs in** *his* **eyes** (=he was marrying her because of her wealth). • *"For a Few Dollars More"* (film title, 1965) • *"The sixty-four thousand dollar question"* (phrase from a quiz show, 1941-) • [LP] **Money**

dol·lop /£'dɒl·əp, $'dɑː·ləp/ *n* [C] a small, shapeless amount of something, esp. when served in a careless way • *She put a dollop* **of** *ice-cream in each bowl.*

dol·ly /£'dɒl·i, $'dɑː·li/ *n* [C] (used esp. by or to children) a child's DOLL (=toy in the shape of a small person) • *(Br infml dated)* A **dolly bird** is a young woman who is thought of as attractive but not very intelligent. • *(Br)* A **Dolly mixture** is one of a mixture of small sweets of various shapes and colours.

dol·men /£'dɒl·men, $'doʊl-/, **crom·lech** *n* [C] an ancient group of stones consisting of one large flat stone supported by several vertical ones

dol·or·ous /£'dɒl·ər·əs, $'doʊ·lɚ-/ *adj literary* seeming sad or causing sadness or emotional suffering • *Her music always has a faintly dolorous feel.* • *He has taken to composing dolorous poems which I find extremely self-indulgent.*

dol·phin /£'dɒl·fɪn, $'dɑːl-/ *n* [C] a sea mammal that looks like a large fish with a pointed mouth

dolt /£dəʊlt, $doʊlt/ *n* [C] *disapproving* a stupid person • *Don't be such a dolt!*

do·main /£dəʊ'meɪn, $doʊ-/ *n* [C] an area of interest or an area over which a person has control • *She treated the business as her private domain.* • *Is political reporting a man's domain?* (=Is it only men that do this?) • *These documents should be placed* **in the public** *domain* (=Everyone should be able to see them).

dome /£dəʊm, $doʊm/ *n* [C] a rounded roof on a building or a room • *The dome of St Paul's could be seen in the distance.* • *(fig.) Gerald had a shining dome* (=round hairless top to his head) *and enormous ears.* • *(fig. literary) Clouds drifted across the blue dome of the sky.* • (CS)

domed /£dəʊmd, $doʊmd/ *adj* • *The domed ceiling* (=shaped like a dome) *of the library was its most famous feature.*

do·mes·tic [HOME] /də'mes·tɪk/ *adj* of the home, house or family • *Many women feel they cannot apply for the top jobs because of domestic commitments.* • *She loves going out, but he's very domestic* (=he enjoys being at home with his family). • *For a year they lived in domestic* **bliss** (=they were happy together as husband and wife in their home). • Domestic **violence** is violence that happens between family members in the home. • A **domestic animal** is one that is not wild but is kept in a house as a pet or on a farm to produce food. • **Domestic appliances** are usually large pieces of electrical equipment that are used in the home, esp. in the kitchen: *We stock a wide range of domestic appliances, including fridges, freezers and dishwashers.* • **Domestic science** is the study at school or college of cooking and other skills useful in the home. • [LP] **Shopping goods**

do·mes·tic (help) /də'mes·tɪk/ *n* [C] *dated* • A domestic (help) is someone paid to help with work that needs to be done in a house, such as cleaning and washing.

do·mes·ti·cally /də'mes·tɪ·kli/ *adv* • *She's not really domestically inclined* (=She doesn't enjoy taking care of a home).

do·mes·ti·cate *obj* /də'mes·tɪ·keɪt/ *v* [T] • *Since they had their baby they've both become quite domesticated* (=they enjoy being at home and taking care of a house and family). • *Sheep and cows were two of the most important animals to be domesticated* (=brought under human control in order to produce food).

do·mes·ti·ci·ty /£ˌdəʊ·mes'tɪs·ɪ·ti, £ˌdɒm·es-, $ˌdoʊ·mes'tɪs·ə·ṭi/ *n* [U] • *After her baby was born, she sold her motorbike and settled happily into domesticity* (=the state of being at home with her family).

do·mes·tic [COUNTRY] /də'mes·tɪk/ *adj* relating to a person's own country • *Domestic public opinion had turned against the war.* • *The President's new foreign policy is heavily influenced by domestic factors/considerations.* • *Both international and domestic flights* (=ones flying only within the country itself) *will be disrupted by the strikes.*

do·mes·ti·cally /də'mes·tɪ·kli/ *adv* • *Such a policy would be unacceptable both domestically and internationally.*

do·mi·cile /£'dɒm·ɪ·saɪl, $'dɑː·mə-/ *n* [C] *fml or law* the place where a person lives • *Any change of domicile should be notified to the proper authorities.*

do·mi·ciled /£'dɒm·ɪ·saɪld, $'dɑː·mə-/ *adj* [after v; always + adv/prep; not gradable] *fml or law* • *He was domiciled* (=based) **in** *Saudi Arabia during the 1980s.*

dom·in·ant /£'dɒm·ɪ·nənt, £'-ə-, $'dɑː·mə-/ *adj* more important, strong, noticeable, etc. than anything else of the same type • *It is a country that has long been the dominant military power in the region.* • *Unemployment will be a dominant issue at the next election.* • *No dominant group or personality has emerged.*

dom·in·ance /£'dɒm·ɪ·nənts, £'-ə-, $'dɑː·mə-/ *n* [U] • *Music companies have profited from the dominance* (=greater popularity) *of CDs over vinyl records.* • *During the war both countries struggled for air and sea dominance* (=control over these things).

dom·i·nate *(obj)* /£'dɒm·ɪ·neɪt, £'-ə-, $'dɑː·mə-/ *v often disapproving* to have control over (a place or a person), or be the most important person or thing • *He refuses to let others speak and dominates every meeting.* [T] • *The tree, which had grown too large, dominated the little garden* (=was much bigger than everything else there). [T] • *The group dominated the pop charts during the 1970s.* [T] • *They work as a group – no one person is allowed to dominate.* [I]

dom·i·nat·ing /£'dɒm·ɪ·neɪ·tɪŋ, $'dɑː·mə·neɪ·ṭɪŋ/ *adj often disapproving* • *She has very strong opinions and tends to be quite dominating* (=having or trying to have control over people, situations, etc.)

dom·i·na·tion /£ˌdɒm·ɪ'neɪ·ʃən, $ˌdɑː·mə-/ *n* [U] • *The film was about a group of robots set on world domination* (=control of all countries).

dom·i·na·trix /£ˌdɒm·ɪ'neɪ·trɪks, $ˌdɑː·mə-/ *n* [C] *pl* **dominatrices** /£ˌdɒm·ɪ'neɪ·trɪ·siːz, $ˌdɑː·mə-/ a woman who has a large amount of power or control over other people, esp. men, or a woman who has power or control over her partner in a sexual relationship • *Mrs. Thatcher was often described as a dominatrix by her political enemies.*

dom·i·neer·ing /£ˌdɒm·ɪˈnɪə·rɪŋ, $ˌdɑː·məˈnɪr·ɪŋ/ *adj disapproving* having a strong tendency to try to control other people without taking their feelings into consideration • *She found him arrogant and domineering.*

Do·min·i·can /£dəˈmɪn·ɪ·kən, $doʊ-/ *adj* [not gradable], *n* [C] (a person) of or belonging to a Christian religious group established by Saint Dominic

do·min·ion /dəˈmɪn·jən, ·ɪ·ən/ *n literary* control over a country or people, or the land that belongs to a ruler • *God has dominion* **over** (=controls) *all his creatures.* [U] • *The chief's son would inherit all his dominions.* [C]

dom·i·no /£ˈdɒm·ɪ·nəʊ, $ˈdɑː·mə·noʊ/ *n* [C] *pl* **dominoes** one of a set of small rectangular pieces of wood or plastic marked with a particular number of spots on each half of one surface • A **domino effect** is when one, usually bad, thing happens and causes other similar events to happen, like each of a set of dominoes knocking the next one over.

dom·i·noes /£ˈdɒm·ɪ·nəʊz, $ˈdɑː·mɪ·noʊz/ *n* [U] • *A group of old men sat* **playing** *dominoes* (=a game where you try to match the spots of a domino put down by another player). • PIC〉 **Games**

don TEACHER /£dɒn, $dɑːn/ *n* [C] a LECTURER (=college teacher), esp. at Oxford or Cambridge University in England

don·nish /£ˈdɒn·ɪʃ, $ˈdɑː·nɪʃ/ *adj* • *He was a thin, donnish-looking man* (=He looked like a don) *in a tweed jacket and sandals.*

don *obj* PUT ON /£dɒn, $dɑːn/ *v* [T] **-nn-** *literary* to put on (a piece of clothing) • *He donned his hat and started walking.* • Compare DOFF.

do·nate *(obj)* /£dəʊˈneɪt, $ˈdoʊ·neɪt/ *v* to give without wanting anything in exchange • *An anonymous businesswoman donated one million dollars* **to** *the fund.* [T] • *The appeal for people to donate blood was very successful.* [T] • *Please donate generously.* [I] • See also DONOR.

do·na·tion /£dəʊˈneɪ·ʃən, $doʊˈneɪ-/ *n* • *Charities prefer regular donations* (=money given) *from the public.* [C] • *Is the donation* (=the giving) **of** *food* **to** *the hungry more helpful than giving money?* [U]

done /dʌn/ *past participle of* DO • You can say 'done' to show that you agree to something: *"I'll give you twenty quid for all five of them." "Done!"*

Don Juan /£ˌdɒnˈdʒuː·ən, £-ˈhwɑːn, $ˌdɑːn-/ *n* [C] a man who has had sex with a lot of women • *Keep away from him, Alice, he's a real Don Juan.*

don·key /£ˈdɒŋ·ki, $ˈdɑːŋ-/ *n* [C] a grey or brown animal like a small horse with long ears • *(infml)* **Donkey's years** is a very long time: *She's been in the same job* **for** *donkey's years.* ○ *It's donkey's years since I've seen her.* • *(infml) Why should I* **do (all) the donkey work** (=the hard, boring part of a job) *while you sit around doing nothing?* • *(Br)* A **donkey jacket** is a type of thick jacket, usually dark blue, often worn by men who work outside. • PIC〉 **Coats and jackets**

do·nor /£ˈdəʊ·nəʳ, $ˈdoʊ·nɚ/ *n* [C] a person who gives some of their blood or a part of their body to help someone who is ill, or any person who gives esp. money to an organization • *a blood donor* • *a kidney donor* • *a sperm donor* • *Thanks to a large gift from an anonymous donor, the charity was able to continue its work.* • A **donor card** is a card you can carry that says that if you die you want to let doctors use parts of your body to help ill people. • See also DONATE.

don't /£dəʊnt, $doʊnt/ *short form of* do not • *Don't do that – it hurts!* • *I don't think so.*

do·nut /£ˈdəʊ·nʌt, $ˈdoʊ-/ *n Am and Aus for* DOUGHNUT

doo·dah *Br and Aus* /ˈduː·dɑː/, *Am and Aus* **doo·dad** /ˈduː·dæd/, *Am* **doo·hick·ey** /ˈduːˌhɪk·i/ *n* [C] *infml* anything whose name you cannot remember or do not know • *Have you got the doodah, you know, the thing you clean the bath with?* • *She's* **all of a doodah** (=in a state of confusion) *about the wedding arrangements.*

doo·dle /ˈduː·dl̩/ *n* [C] a drawing or pattern that you make while thinking about something else or when you are bored • *Your doodles can tell you things about your personality.*

doo·dle /ˈduː·dl̩/ *v* [I] • *She'd doodled all over her textbooks.*

doom /duːm/ *n* [U] death, destruction or any very bad situation that cannot be avoided • *A sense of doom hung over the entire country.* • *He wanted to warn the people of their* **impending** *doom* (=that very bad things were going to happen to them). • *The newspapers are always full of doom* **and gloom/gloom and** *doom* (=deep hopelessness) *these days.* • *The* **prophets of** *doom* (=people who always think bad things are going to happen) *were proved wrong again.*

doom *obj* /duːm/ *v* [T] • *Mounting debts doomed the factory* **to** *closure* (=made it unavoidable).

doomed /duːmd/ *adj* • *The project was doomed from the start* (=It had no chance of succeeding). • *This is a city doomed* **to** (=that cannot avoid) *dereliction and despair.* • *This is a doomed city.* • *Are we doomed* **to** *repeat the mistakes of the past?* [+ *to* infinitive]

dooms·day /ˈduːmz·deɪ/ *n* the end of the world, or a time when something very bad will happen • *Ecologists predict a doomsday* **scenario** (=a time when death and destruction will happen) *if the amount of pollution continues to increase at the present rate.* • *You could talk* **till/until** *doomsday* (=for a very long time), *but they will never change their minds.*

door /£dɔːʳ, $dɔːr/ *n* [C] a flat, usually rectangular, object, often fixed at one edge, that is used to close the entrance of something such as a room or building, or the entrance itself • *the front door* • *the back door* • *a car door* • *a sliding door* • *a folding door* • *a revolving door* • *a swing door* • *Shall I meet you at the main door of the library?* • *Mum, there's someone at the door* (=outside the front door) *for you.* • *The door* **to** *his bedroom was locked from the inside.* • *We could hear someone knocking* **at/on** *the door.* • *Could you* **open/close/shut** *the door, please?* • *She asked me to* **answer** *the door* (=go and open the door because someone had just knocked on it or rung the bell). • *He slipped through the door when no one was looking.* • A person **on** the door is someone whose job is to wait by the entrance of a building to collect tickets or to prevent particular people from entering. • *She offered to* **see** *me* **to** *the door* (=to go with me to the door). • Door is also used to refer to a house or other building: *Sam only lives a few doors* **(away/up/down) from** *us.* ○ *My friend lives just two doors* **away**. ○ *Those people* **next door (to us)** (=living in the house beside ours) *are a bit odd.* ○ *The journey takes an hour* **door to door** (=from the very beginning to the very end). ○ *The police made* **door-to-door** *enquiries* (=at every house) *in the area after the murder.* ○ *He took a job as a* **door-to-door salesman** (=selling goods at people's houses). • *These discussions may well* **open the door to/close the door on** *a peaceful solution* (=make this possible/impossible). • Something that happens **out of doors** happens outside in the open air. • To **shut/slam the door in** someone's **face** or **shut/slam the door on** someone is not to allow someone to have an opportunity to do something or to refuse to speak to them or be friendly to them. • To **shut/close the stable/barn door after the horse has bolted/gone** means to be so late in taking action to prevent something bad happening that the bad event has already happened. • PIC〉 **Accommodation, Doors** Ⓟ

door·bell /£ˈdɔː·bel, $ˈdɔːr-/ *n* [C] a bell near the door of a house that you ring to let the people inside know you are there • PIC〉 **Doors**

door·frame /£ˈdɔː·freɪm, $ˈdɔːr-/ *n* [C] the rectangular frame that surrounds an opening into which a door fits

door·knob /£ˈdɔː·nɒb, $ˈdɔːr·nɑːb/ *n* [C] a round handle that you turn to open a door and pull to close it • PIC〉 **Doors**

door·knock·er /£ˈdɔːˌnɒk·əʳ, $ˈdɔːrˌnɑː·kɚ/ *n* [C] a **knocker**, see at KNOCK MAKE NOISE • PIC〉 **Doors**

door·man /£ˈdɔː·mən, £-mæn, $ˈdɔːr-/ *n* [C] *pl* **-men** a person whose job is to stand by the door of a hotel or public building and let people in or out, open their car doors, etc.

door·mat /£ˈdɔː·mæt, $ˈdɔːr-/ *n* [C] a small covering for the floor by a door on which people going into a building can clean their shoes, or *(fig. infml disapproving)* a person who accepts being treated badly and does not complain • *Wipe your feet on the doormat before you come inside.* • *(fig.) He may be selfish and insensitive, but she is a bit of a doormat.* • PIC〉 **Doors**

door·nail /£ˈdɔː·neɪl, $ˈdɔːr-/ *n* [C] See **dead as a doornail** at DEAD NOT LIVING

door·post /£ˈdɔː·pəʊst, $ˈdɔːr·poʊst/, *Am* **door·jamb** /£ˈdɔː·dʒæm, $ˈdɔːr-/ *n* [C] either of the two vertical parts of the rectangular frame surrounding an opening into which a door fits

door·step /£ˈdɔː·step, $ˈdɔːr-/ *n* [C] a step in front of an outside door, or *(fig. Br humorous)* a very thick piece of

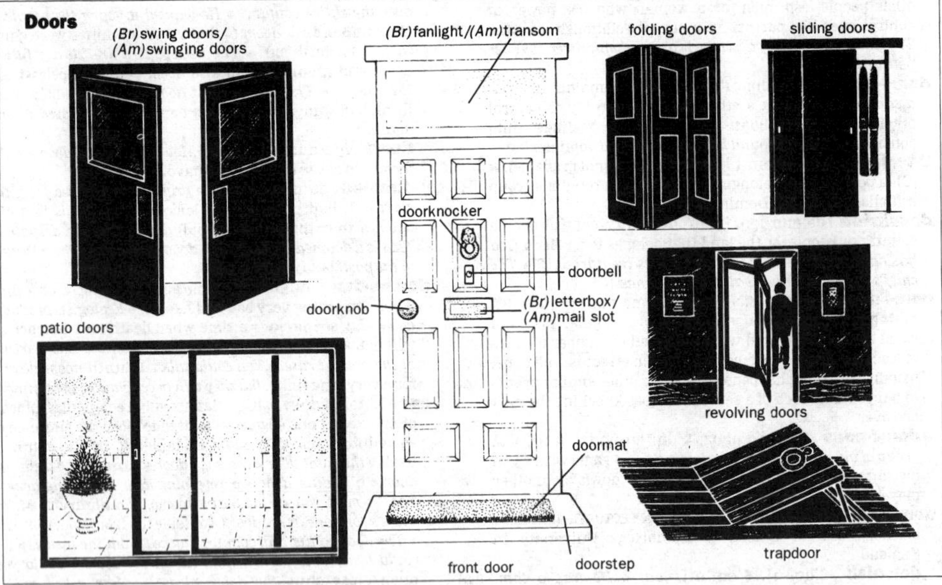

bread. • *Don't keep her* **on** *the doorstep* (=outside the door), *Jamie, invite her in.* • *There's a lovely park right* **on** *our* **doorstep** (=very close to where we live/are staying). • PIC〉 **Doors**

door·step *obj* /£'dɔː·step, $'dɔːr-/ *v* [T] **-pp-** *Br disapproving* • *He complained about being constantly doorstepped by the press* (=about JOURNALISTS causing annoyance by coming to his house to ask him questions).

door·stop /£'dɔː·stɒp, $'dɔːr·stɑːp/ *n* [C] a heavy object that is used to keep a door open

door·way /£'dɔː·weɪ, $'dɔːr-/ *n* [C] the space for a door through which you go into and out of a room or building • *I looked up and saw him standing in the doorway.*

dope DRUG /£dəʊp, $doʊp/ *n* [U] *infml* MARIJUANA, or, more generally, any type of illegal drug • *They were arrested for* **smoking** *dope.* • A **dope test** is an official test to discover whether a person or an animal taking part in a race, game, etc. has had or been given any drugs to make their performance better or worse: *The horse was disqualified when it failed a dope test.*

dope *obj* /£dəʊp, $doʊp/ *v* [T] • To dope a person or an animal about to take part in a competition or sport is to give them drugs to make their performance better or worse. • If someone dopes you or your food or drink, they secretly put a drug in your food or drink that makes you very sleepy: *He must have doped her drink because she woke up with a terrible headache.* • Ⓟⓛ

doped /£dəʊpt, $doʊpt/ *adj* • *They were too doped* **(up)** (=under the influence of drugs) *to notice what was happening.*

dop·ey /£'dəʊ·pi, $'doʊ-/ *adj* **dopier, dopiest** • *He'd taken a sleeping tablet the night before and still felt dopey* (=was sleepy and moving slowly).

dope PERSON /£dəʊp, $doʊp/ *n* [C] a silly person • *You shouldn't have told him, you dope!* [as form of address]

dop·ey /£'dəʊ·pi, $'doʊ-/ *adj* **-ier, -iest** • *He's nice, but a bit dopey* (=silly).

dop·pel·gäng·er /£'dɒp·əlˌgæŋ·əʳ, £-geŋ-, $'dɑː·pəl ˌgæŋ·ɚ/ *n* [C] the spirit of a living person which has exactly the same physical appearance as them • *Seeing your doppelgänger is said to be a sign that your death is imminent.*

Dop·pler ef·fect /£'dɒp·ləʳ, $'dɑː·plɚ/ *n* [U] *specialized* a change that seems to happen in the rate of sound or light wave production of an object when its movement changes in relation to another object • *An everyday example of the Doppler effect is the apparent change in the pitch of an alarm bell as you drive past it.* • *The Doppler effect is used in calculating the size of the universe.*

Dor·ic /£'dɒr·ɪk, $'dɔːr-/ *adj* [not gradable] of or copying the simplest of the CLASSICAL styles of ancient Greek building • *a Doric column* • Compare CORINTHIAN; IONIC. • PIC〉 **Column**

dork /£dɔːk, $dɔːrk/ *n* [C] *esp. Am and Aus slang* a stupid awkward person • *I felt like a real dork when I realized my mistake.*

dor·mant /£'dɔː·mənt, $'dɔːr-/ *adj* (of things) not active or growing, but having the ability to be active at a later time • *The long-dormant volcano has recently shown signs of life.* • *These businesses have remained dormant for several years.* • If something **lies** dormant, it is not active: *Her talent might have lain dormant had it not been for her aunt's encouragement.*

dor·mer (win·dow) /£'dɔː·məʳ, $'dɔːr·mɚ/ *n* [C] a window sticking out from a sloping roof • PIC〉 **Window**

dor·mi·to·ry /£'dɔː·mɪ·tᵊr·i, $'dɔːr·mə·tɔːr-/, *infml* **dorm** /£dɔːm, $dɔːrm/ *n* [C] a large room or *(esp. Am)* building containing many beds, esp. in a **boarding school** or university • A *(Br)* **dormitory town**/*(Aus)* **dormitory suburb** (*Am* **bedroom community**) is a place from which many people travel in order to work in a bigger town or city. • Ⓔ

Dor·mo·bile *Br* /£'dɔː·mə·biːl, $'dɔːr-/, *Aus and Br also* **camp·er van**, *Am* **camp·er** *n* [C] *trademark* a large motor vehicle that is designed to be lived in while travelling. It contains cooking equipment and often has a roof that can be raised to make space for a bed • *The American couple hired a Dormobile for their four-week tour round Europe.*

dor·mouse /£'dɔː·maʊs, $'dɔːr-/ *n* [C] *pl* **dormice** /£'dɔː·maɪs, $'dɔːr-/ a small animal which looks like a mouse with a long furry tail. It is commonly thought of as a very sleepy animal. • PIC〉 **Wild animals in Britain**

dor·sal /£'dɔː·sᵊl, $'dɔːr-/ *adj* [before n; not gradable] *specialized* of, on or near the back of an animal • *The sight of a shark's dorsal* **fin** *above the water is enough to clear the sea of swimmers.*

do·ry /£'dɔː·ri, $'dɔːr·i/ *n* [C] a JOHN DORY

DOS /£dɒs, $dɑːs/ *n* [U] *abbreviation for* **disk operating system**, see at DISK

dose /£dəʊs, $doʊs/ *n* [C] a measured amount of something such as medicine, or *(fig.)* an amount or an experience of something unpleasant • *The label on the bottle says the dose is three of the pills with every meal.* • *Twenty or thirty of these pills would be a* **lethal** *dose* (=enough to kill you). • *Workers at two nuclear power stations are receiving an annual dose* **of** *radiation three times the legal limit.* • *She's got a nasty dose* **of** *flu.* • *(fig.) The government received a hefty dose of bad news this week.* • *She's very nice, but only* **in small doses** (=She is pleasant to be with for short periods of time). • *(dated infml) The medicine went through me* **like a dose of salts** (=very quickly). • *(slang)* A dose is also a case of GONORRHEA (=a sexual disease). • Ⓒⓢ

dose *obj* /£dəʊs, $doʊs/ *v* [T] • *(infml) He dosed himself* **(up) with** (=swallowed a lot of) *valium to calm his nerves.*

do·sage /£'dəʊ·sɪdʒ, $'doʊ-/ *n* [C] *fml* • *"What's the dosage* (=measured amount you must take)*?" "One spoonful three times a day."*

dosh /£dɒʃ, $dɑːʃ/ *n* [U] *Br and Aus slang* money • *I couldn't afford it – I didn't have enough dosh.*

doss /£dɒs, $dɑːs/ *v* [I always + adv/prep] *esp. Br and Aus slang* to sleep and/or live outside or in an empty house, building, etc. because you have no home and no money • *She was dossing in doorways until the police picked her up.* • To doss **down** is to lie down and sleep, esp. on the floor, or in a friend's house: *Don't worry about me – I'll doss down on the camp bed.* • See also DOSSHOUSE.

dos·ser /£'dɒs·əʳ, $'dɑː·sɚ/ *n* [C] *esp. Br slang disapproving* • *A dosser* (=poor homeless person) *was sleeping under the arch of the bridge.*

doss a·round/a·bout *v adv* [I] *Br slang* to do very little work or other activity • *Come on, Peter, stop dossing around and get some work done.*

dos·ser /£'dɒs·əʳ, $'dɑː·sɚ/ *n* [C] *Br slang disapproving* • *There are a couple of dossers in my class who never do any work at all.*

doss /£dɒs, $dɑːs/ *n* [U] *Br slang* • If you describe something as **a** doss, you mean that it is easy or does not need much hard work: *Our geography exams are a doss because the teacher practically tells us what the questions will be.*

doss·house *esp. Br* /£'dɒs·haʊs, $'dɑːs-/, *Am* **flop·house** *n* [C] *pl* **-houses** /-ˌhaʊ·zɪz/ *slang* an extremely cheap hotel for poor homeless people in a city

dos·si·er /£'dɒs·i·eɪ, £-əʳ, $'dɑː·si·eɪ/ *n* [C] a set of papers containing information on a person, often a criminal, or on any subject; a FILE [CONTAINER] • *The secret service probably has a dossier* **on** *all of us.*

dot /£dɒt, $dɑːt/ *n* [C] a very small round mark • *The full stop at the end of this sentence is a dot.* • *Her skirt was blue with white dots.* • *The stars just look like thousands of tiny dots of light.* • *By the time I turned round to wave, Mum and Dad were two dots on the horizon.* • Dots are also the short sounds or flashes of light used with DASHES (= longer sounds or flashes) when sending messages in MORSE CODE. • If someone or something arrives **on the dot**, they arrive or happen at exactly the stated or expected time: *The plane landed on the dot* **(of** *two o'clock).* • *(Br and Aus infml dated) My ancestors left Spain generations ago, back* **in the year dot** (=a very long time ago). • *(specialized)* A **dot-matrix printer** is a computer printer that forms letters, numbers and other symbols from dots.

DOTS [. . .]

Dots are not used very often. They might be used to show that:

- **the writer has omitted some of another person's words**
  He read Hamlet's 'To be or not to be . . . ' with great feeling.
  Carl wrote that 'Every person in this country . . . is dreaming of freedom.'
  'A novel . . . that will change your life . . . stunning . . . ' London Times.
- **a list or an idea has not been completed.**
  In informal writing dots might be used humorously in this way.
  This country has many problems: hunger, disease, war . . . The list seems endless.
  We were miles away from home, with no money, and it started to rain . . .
- **some time passes between a speaker's words**
  Let me introduce you to the others: Mr Hall . . . Miss Mackie . . . Mrs Andrews.
- **a speaker stopped or was interrupted (a dash can be used)**
  "I can't quite remember when we . . . Oh yes, last year."

dot *obj* /£dɒt, $dɑːt/ *v* [T] **-tt-** • *Your handwriting is difficult to read because you don't dot your i's.* • *(infml slightly disapproving) She writes a good report, but she does tend to* **dot** *her* **i's and cross** *her* **t's/dot the i's and cross the t's** (=deal with every possible, even unnecessary, detail). • When an area is dotted **with** things, it has many of them in different places: *The countryside is dotted with beautiful ancient churches.* ○ *We have offices dotted* **about/all over** *the region.* • A **dotted line** is a line of dots, or a line of very small holes on paper which make it easy to tear: *Footpaths are shown on the map as dotted red lines.* ○ *(infml) The car is ready for you, if you'll just* **sign on** *the dotted line* (=formally agree to something, esp. by signing the legal agreement). ○ *Tear along the dotted line.*

do·tage /£'dəʊ·tɪdʒ, $'doʊ·t̬ɪdʒ/ *n* [U] **in** *your* **dotage** *dated humorous* slow, confused and foolish because of old age

dote on/u·pon *obj* /£dəʊt, $doʊt/ *v prep* [T] to love (someone) very much, sometimes foolishly or too much • *He dotes on the new baby.*

dot·ing /£'dəʊ·tɪŋ, $'doʊ·t̬ɪŋ/ *adj* [before n] • *We saw photographs of the doting father with the baby on his knee.*

dot·ty /£'dɒt·i, $'dɑː·t̬i/ *adj* **-ier, -iest** *infml* slightly strange or foolish • *My auntie is getting a bit dotty in her old age.* • *He's got some dotty idea of starting his own religion.* • *(dated)* If you are dotty **about** someone or something, you like or love them very much or are very interested in them: *Jean's dotty about opera.*

dot·ti·ness /£'dɒt·ɪ·nəs, $'dɑː·t̬ɪ-/ *n* [U]

doub·le [TWICE] /'dʌb·l̩/ *adj, adv* [not gradable], *predeterminer, n* (something that is) twice the size, amount, price, etc., or (something) consisting of two similar things together • *We have a double problem because time is short and several staff have recently left.* • *Electrical goods are almost double* **the** *price/what they were a few years ago.* • *She ordered a double (whisky)* (=two standard amounts in one glass). [C] • *I pushed my way through several pairs of double* **doors**. • *He confessed he had been leading a double* **life**, *working in the bank by day and performing at a club by night.* • *Be careful – everything he says has a double* **meaning** (=has two possible meanings). • *The word 'cool' has a double 'o' in the middle.* • *Sabiha's telephone number is double three, one, five, double seven* (= 331577). • *He shook both dice and then threw a double six* (=a six on both DICE). • *I'm sure that idiot in the shop has charged me double* (=twice the correct price). • *They were bent double* (=Their heads and shoulders were bent far forward and down) *from decades of labour in the fields.* • *Fold the blanket double* (=so that it is in two layers) *and then you won't be cold.* • A double flower or plant is a flower with more than the usual number of petals: *a double primrose* • In baseball, if you hit the ball safely so that you reach **second base**, you've hit a double. • If you are **seeing double**, you are seeing two of everything, usually because you are drunk. • *(Br) Arsenal have a chance of winning* **the** *double* (=winning two similar competitions). • *(infml dated)* If you go somewhere or do something **at/on the double**, you go or act very quickly and without any delay. • Esp. in games where money is risked, **double or quits/double or nothing** is an agreement that the player who owes money will owe twice as much if they lose, but will owe nothing if they win. • A **double agent** is a person employed by a government to discover secret information about enemy countries, but who is really working for one of these enemy countries. • A **double-barrelled** gun has two BARRELS (=long tube-like parts). • *(esp. Br)* A **double-barrelled name** is a family name with two joined parts, such as Lloyd-Webber. • *(Am and Aus)* **Double-barreled** can also mean having two purposes: *It was a double-barreled question.* • A **double bass** (also *infml* **bass (fiddle)**) is the largest musical instrument of the VIOLIN type, that plays very low notes. • A **double bed** is a bed big enough for two people to sleep in. • A **double bill** is something such as a cinema or theatre performance that consists of two main items. • A **double bind** is a difficult situation in which, whatever action you decide to take, you cannot escape unpleasant results: *The headteacher is caught in a double bind because whether she expels the boy or lets him off, she still gets blamed.* • A **double-blind** study or TRIAL, esp. in medicine, is one in which two groups of people are studied, for example with one group taking a new drug and one group taking something else, but neither the people in the study nor the doctor knowing which person is in which group. • *(Br)* A **double bluff** is a clever attempt to deceive someone, esp. by telling them the truth when they think you are telling lies. • A **double-breasted** coat has two sets of buttons and two wide parts at the front, one of which covers the other when the buttons are fastened. • To **double-book** a flight, ticket or hotel room is to arrange for two people to pay for it in case one person does not use it: *When we arrived at the airport we were double-booked and couldn't get on the flight.* • If you **double-check** something, you make certain it is correct or safe, usually by examining it again: *I always double-check that I haven't left the gas on.* • A **double chin** is a fold of skin between the face and neck, esp. of older people, which is caused by a layer of fat developing underneath the skin. • In computing, if you **double-click (on)** something, you press the MOUSE (= control device) twice in order to tell the computer to do something or provide a particular piece of information. • *(Br)* **Double cream** *(Am* **heavy cream)** is very thick cream. • *(infml)* If you **double-cross** someone, you deceive them by working only for your own advantage in the usually illegal activities you have planned together: *The diamond thief double-crossed his partners and handed over only worthless fake jewels.* ○ *They set up a* **double-cross** *to cheat him of his money.* • **Double-dealing** is dishonesty and actions intended to deceive: *The local business community has been destroyed by corruption, cheating and double-dealing.* • A **double-decker** is a bus with two levels. • A **double-decker (sandwich)** is a SANDWICH made with three pieces of bread with food such as cold meat or cheese between them. • *(Am)* To **double-dip** is to get two amounts of pay at the same time, for example more than one income from the same employer or pay from an employer as well as money from the government. • *(Aus)* To **double-dip** is to receive two amounts of tax benefit for the same item in two different ways. • *(Br and Aus infml)* If you describe talk or writing as **double Dutch**, you mean that it is nonsense or that you cannot understand it : *When you start talking about economic theory it sounds like double Dutch to me.* • **Double Dutch** is also a game played in the US by jumping over a rope. • Something that is **double-edged** acts in two ways, often with one negative and one positive effect: *The increase in petrol prices is double-edged because it will make life harder for some, but it will reduce congestion and pollution.* ○ *She paid me the double-edged compliment of saying my work was "excellent for a beginner".* ○ *The successful programme to grow cash crops for export is turning out to be a* **double-edged sword** *because it has created a local food shortage.* ○ See also **two-edged** at TWO. • A **double entendre** is a word or phrase that might be understood in two ways, one of which is usually sexual: *The chairperson made a risqué speech full of double entendres which luckily no one quite understood.* • In tennis and some other games, a **double fault** is two mistakes made one after the other by a player who is beginning a game by hitting the ball. • A **double feature** in a cinema is the showing of two different films, one after the other. • A **double-header** is two games of baseball or another sport played one after the other. • *(specialized)* A **double helix** is the structure of a DNA MOLECULE (= basic chemical pattern of living things). • *(Am)* **Double jeopardy** is the act of putting someone on trial twice for the same offence. • If you are **double-jointed** your joints can be moved in an unusual way so that, for example, you can bend your fingers or legs backwards as well as forwards: *She's an amazing acrobat – she must be double-jointed.* • In grammar, a **double negative** is the use of two negatives (= words that mean 'no') in the same sentence: *Don't just do nothing – go and help her.* ○ *I wouldn't be surprised if he didn't apply for the job.* ○ *(not standard) I didn't go nowhere* (= I didn't go anywhere). • To **double-park** is to leave a car along the side of another car, so that it is in the middle of the road rather than at the edge: *He/The car was double-parked and facing the wrong way.* • In baseball, a **double play** is when two players are put out after the ball is hit once. • A **double room** is a room in a hotel for two people. • *(infml)* **Double-quick** or **in double-quick time** means very quick(ly): *She left the room double-quick when I brought the snakes in.* • If a piece of text produced on a TYPEWRITER or printer is **double-spaced**, it has an empty line between each line of writing: *Why have you double-spaced the first paragraph?* ○ *Put it in* **double-spacing**. • In a book, magazine, etc. a **double(-page) spread** is one article, set of photographs, etc. that covers two pages opposite each other. • *The Government is being accused of* **double standards** (= treating one group differently from another) *in having a tough law and order policy but allowing its own MPs to escape prosecution for fraud.* • *(infml)* A **double take** is when you show you have suddenly noticed or understood something surprising, after a moment of delay: *When I saw her in Cairo I* **did a** *double take I couldn't believe it.* • **Double-talk** *(esp. Am also* **Doublespeak)** is talk that has no real meaning or has more than one meaning and is intended to hide the truth: *another example of political double-talk* • To **double-team** a player in BASKETBALL is to have two members of the opposing team trying to prevent that player from scoring. • If you are paid **double time**, you are paid twice the usual amount for the time which you spend working usually at the weekend or on an official holiday. • *(infml) Having twins usually means* **double trouble** (= twice as many problems) *for the parents.* • *The little boy suffered from* **double vision** (= seeing two of everything) *after hitting his head.* • A **double whammy** is a situation when two unpleasant things happen at almost the same time: *Critics claim that the cuts in public spending coupled with a pay freeze is a double whammy which will affect low-paid workers badly.* • Compare SINGLE [ONE]. • [LP] **Two** [PIC] **Coats and jackets, Musical instruments, Road** (T)

doub·le *(obj)* /ˈdʌb·l̩/ *v* • *The government aims to double the number of students in higher education within 25 years.* [T] • *Company profits have doubled since the introduction of new technology.* [I] • *I'll double the blanket* (= fold it into two layers) *so you won't be cold.* [T] • If something or someone doubles **as** something or someone else, they have a second use or job: *The kitchen table doubles as my desk when I'm writing.* ○ *The actress playing the judge also doubles as the victim's sister.* • To **double back** is to turn and go back in the direction you have come from: *Several times we doubled back on ourselves to try and shake off the detectives who were following.* • If you double **up/over**, or if something doubles you **up**, you suddenly bend forwards and down, usually because of pain or laughter: *Most of the crowd doubled up with laughter* **at** *every joke.* ○ *She was doubled up/over* **with** *the pain in her stomach.* • To **double up** is to share something, esp. a room, with someone else: *Terry will have to double up with Bill in the front bedroom.*

doubles /ˈdʌb·l̩z/ *pl n* • Doubles is a game, esp. in tennis, between two people on one side and two people on the other: *mixed doubles* • *the men's doubles* Compare **singles** at SINGLE [ONE].

doub·ly /ˈdʌb·li/ *adv* [not gradable] • *Losing both the Cup and the League is doubly disappointing* (= disappointing in two ways). • *You'd better make doubly* (= very) *sure that everything is switched off.*

doub·le [PERSON] /ˈdʌb·l̩/ *n* [C usually sing] a person who looks the same as someone else • *Hey Tony, I met someone at a party last week who was your absolute double.* • (T)

doub·le·speak /ˈdʌb·l̩.spiːk/ *esp. Am for* **double-talk**, see at DOUBLE [TWICE]

doub·let /ˈdʌb·lɪt/ *n* [C] a short tight jacket worn by men in the 15th, 16th and 17th centuries • *They were in full Elizabethan costume, including doublet* **and hose**.

doubt /daʊt/ *n* (a feeling of) uncertainty about something, esp. about how good or true it is • *Even if your religious faith is strong, it's normal to feel doubt.* [U] • *If there's any doubt* **about** *the rocket's engines, we ought to cancel the launch immediately.* [U] • *The prosecution has to establish his guilt* **beyond (reasonable)** *doubt/(Am)* **beyond a (reasonable)** *doubt.* [U] • *The strength of local opposition has* **cast** *doubt* **on** *the likelihood of a new leisure centre.* [U] • *This latest scandal has* **raised** *doubts* **about** *his suitability for the post.* [C] • *He says he can do it, but I still* **have** *my doubts* **about** *his ability.* [C] • *I'm* **having** *doubts* **about** *going to Africa – maybe I'll stay here.* [C] • *Give a ring if you're* **in (any)** *doubt* (= uncertain) **wh***ere you should go.* [U + *wh-* word] • *There's* **no** *doubt*/**not a shadow of** *doubt* **(in my mind)** *(that) he's guilty.* [U + *(that)* clause] • *I never had any doubt* **(that)** *you would win.* [U + *(that)* clause] • **Wh***ether they can deliver on time is still* **open to** *doubt* (= is not certain). [U + *wh-* word] • *He's the most attractive man in the building,* **no doubt about that/it**. • *The future of the project is* **in doubt** (= at risk) *because of a lack of money.* • *(fml) We will* **no doubt** (= almost certainly) *discuss these issues again at the next meeting.* • *(fml) She is* **without (a) doubt** (= certainly) *the best student I have ever taught.* See also **undoubtedly** at UNDOUBTED. • [LP] **Question mark**

doubt *obj* /daʊt/ *v* [T] • *At first I doubted* (= had little confidence in) *his abilities, but he has done wonderfully.* • *I doubt* **if/whether** (= I think it is unlikely that) *I can finish* *the work in time.* [+ *wh-* word] • *They had begun to doubt* (= to think it unlikely) **that** *it could be completed in time.* [+ *that* clause] • *He may come back tomorrow with the money, but I very much doubt it* (= I think it is very unlikely). • If you doubt someone or doubt someone's **word**, you do not trust them or believe what they say: *"But I did lock the door!" "I'm not doubting it/you, but someone certainly managed to get in."* • A **doubting Thomas** is a person who refuses to believe anything until they are given proof.

doub·ter /£ ˈdaʊ·təʳ, $-t̬ɚ/ *n* [C] • *critics and doubters* • *I urge those of you who are still doubters to have faith and vote with me on this issue.*

doubt·ful /ˈdaʊt·fᵊl/ *adj* • *The expression on her face was doubtful* (= uncertain) *and anxious as I was telling my story.* • *The teacher is doubtful* **about** *having* (= not certain that she wants to have) *parents working as classroom assistants.* • *Having a private education is a doubtful advantage in life.* (= It may not be an advantage.) • **It** *is doubtful* **whether/if** (= unlikely that) *they ever reached the summit before they died.* [+ *wh-* word] • **It** *was doubtful* **that** *the money would ever be found again.* [+ *that* clause]

doubt·ful·ly /ˈdaʊt·fᵊl·i/ *adv* • *"Are you certain of that?" he asked doubtfully.*

doubt·less /ˈdaʊt·ləs/ *adv* [not gradable] • *Doubtless* (= Very probably) *you will have heard the news already.* • *They will doubtless protest, but there's nothing they can do.*

douche /duːʃ/ *n* [C] a stream of water directed onto or into a part of the body, often the vagina, in order to wash it or treat it medically • (NL)

douche *obj* /duːʃ/ *v* [T]

dough FLOUR /£ dəʊ, $ doʊ/ *n* [U] flour mixed with water and often YEAST, fat or sugar so that it is ready for baking • *bread dough* • *biscuit dough* • *pastry dough* • *She kneaded the dough well and left it to rise.* • LP› **'-ough' pronunciation**

dough·y /£ ˈdəʊ·i, $ ˈdoʊ-/ *adj* **-ier, -iest** • If something is doughy, it is soft, thick and sticky, like dough.

dough MONEY /£ dəʊ, $ doʊ/ *n* [U] *dated slang* money • *Have you got enough dough on you, or shall I pay by American Express?*

dough·nut, *Am and Aus also* **do·nut** /£ ˈdəʊ·nʌt, $ ˈdoʊ-/ *n* [C] a small circular cake, fried in hot fat, either with a hole in the middle or filled with JAM • *a* **ring** *doughnut* • *a* **jam/***(Am)* **jelly** *doughnut* • PIC› **Bread and cakes**

dough·ty /£ ˈdaʊ·ti, $-t̬i/ *adj* **-ier, -iest** *literary* determined, brave and unwilling ever to admit defeat • *She has been for many years a doughty campaigner for women's rights.*

dour /£ dʊəʳ, £ ˈdaʊəʳ, $ dʊr/ *adj* **-er, -est** (usually of a person's appearance or manner) unfriendly, unhappy and severe • *The normally dour Mr James was photographed smiling and joking with friends.*

dour·ly /£ ˈdʊə·li, £ ˈdaʊə-, $ ˈdʊr-/ *adv* • *"Oh," she said dourly, "it'll soon start raining again."* • *Their team defended dourly* (= determinedly but uninterestingly) *for most of the game, but lost by letting in a last-minute goal.*

dous·e *obj* MAKE WET /daʊs/ *v* [T] to make (something or someone) wet by putting them into a liquid or by throwing a lot of liquid over them • *We watched as demonstrators doused a car* **in/with** *petrol and set it alight.*

dous·e *obj* PUT OUT /daʊs/ *v* [T] to stop (a fire or light) from burning or shining, esp. by putting water on it or by covering it with something

dove BIRD /dʌv/ *n* [C] a type of usually white bird with short legs, a large body and a small head, that makes a soft singing sound. It is often used as a symbol of peace • *Doves were cooing in the elms.* • A dove is also, esp. in politics, a person who is willing to trust and work with their enemies in order to achieve peace. Compare HAWK PERSON. • *She wore an elegant* **dove-grey** *jacket.*

dove DIVE *esp. Am* /£ dəʊv, $ doʊv/ *past simple of* DIVE

dove·cote, dove·cot /£ ˈdʌv·kəʊt, £-kɒt, $-koʊt, $-kɑːt/ *n* [C] a type of small house built for DOVES or similar birds to live in

dove·tail *(obj)* /ˈdʌv·teɪl/ *v* to (cause to) fit exactly together • *The party is trying to dovetail its industrial strategy* **with** *its policies on regional development.* [T] • *Classic songs such as 'Old Black Eyes' dovetailed neatly alongside the band's own new songs.* [I] • *Their plans for the evening dovetailed conveniently* **with/into** *ours.* [I]

dove·tail (joint) /ˈdʌv·teɪl/ *n* [C] *specialized* • A dovetail (joint) is a type of joint used to fix two pieces of wood firmly together, which you make by fitting the parts that stick out from one piece into the holes cut in the other piece.

Dow Jones (In·dus·tri·al) Av·er·age /£ ˌdaʊˈdʒəʊnz, $-ˈdʒoʊnz/ *n* [U] an INDEX of the prices of shares in the 30 most important companies on the New York Stock Exchange • *On Wall Street, share prices fell back and the Dow Jones Industrial Average was down 22·47 at 2932·18 by the time dealings closed.* • Compare FTSE 100 (INDEX); NIKKEI.

dow·a·ger /£ ˈdaʊə·dʒəʳ, $-dʒɚ/ *n* [C] *specialized* a woman of high social rank whose husband is dead but who has a title and property because of her marriage to him, or *(fig.)* an old woman who is or behaves as if she is of high social rank • *a dowager duchess*

dow·dy /ˈdaʊ·di/ *adj* **-ier, -iest** *disapproving* (esp. of clothes or the person wearing them) unattractive and not stylish, often because of being old-fashioned • *a dowdy brown suit* • *a dowdy conference room* • *She looked a dowdy and very plain young woman.*

down LOWER POSITION /daʊn/ *prep, adv, adj* [not gradable] in or towards a low or lower position, from a higher one • *I walked down the hill to where I'd left my car.* • *My uncle's in hospital after falling down some stairs and breaking his arm.* • *She had spilt ice cream all down her blouse.* • *I ran my eye/finger down the list of ingredients.* • *The space capsule came down in the Pacific Ocean.* • *The leaflet must have slipped down behind the wardrobe – can you see it?* • *I bent down to have a look under the bed.* • *It's a bit smelly – why don't you put some disinfectant down the drain/toilet?* • If something is or has gone **down the drain/toilet/tube(s)/plughole/***(Br also)* **pan/***(Aus)* **gurgler**, it is spoiled or wasted: *We don't want all their hard work to* **go** *down the drain.* ○ *If the factory closes, that will be a million pounds' worth of investment down the toilet.* • *If the dog jumps up at you, just shout "Down!" and she will sit quietly.* • *Come down here* (= Come down the stairs) *this minute and apologize.* • *(fig.) Everyone,* **from** *the Director down* (**to** *the secretaries), was questioned by the police.* • *(fig.) Alfred was dressed completely in black,* (**right**) *down* **to** (= even including such small details as) *black lipstick and a black earring.* • Down also means moving from above and onto or on a chair, a bed, the floor, the ground or the bottom of something: *Just as I was sitting down to watch TV, the phone rang.* ○ *I was sitting down* (= I was in a seated position) *reading a book, when all of a sudden I heard a massive explosion.* ○ *Why don't you lie down on the sofa for a while?* ○ *This box is really heavy – can we put it down (on the floor) for a minute?* ○ *Get down off that table immediately, you silly girl!* ○ *The terrorists forced everybody to lie face down* (= with the front part of the body below) *on the floor.* ○ *The butter's on the fourth shelf down* (= on the shelf three below the top one). • Down also means inside your stomach: *You'll feel better once you've got some hot soup down you.* ○ *He's getting weak because he can't keep anything down.* • If you burn/cut/knock something or someone down, you cause them to fall to the ground, usually damaged or destroyed: *The house burnt down* (= was completely destroyed) *in a terrible fire many years ago.* ○ *These trees will have to be cut down to make way for the new road.* ○ *She was knocked down by a car and killed instantly.* • If you stick/fix something down, you stick/fix it firmly: *I wrapped it in brown paper and stuck the ends down well.* ○ *I put the loose floorboard back and nailed it down.* • If you wash or wipe something down, you clean all parts of it: *He washed the car down with soapy water.* ○ *I wiped the worktop down before preparing supper.* • Down is also used to describe something that has happened over a long period of time: *The necklace has been passed/handed down through seven generations.* ○ *These myths have come down to us from prehistoric times.* ○ *Joan of Arc's fame has echoed down (through) the centuries.* • If someone says/writes/shouts something such as "Down **with** the government!" or "Down **with** Colonialism!", they are showing their opposition to it and demanding its destruction. • *(Br and Am infml)* **Down under** means in or towards Australia or New Zealand: *She was born in Scotland, but she's been living down under for 22 years.* • *It's typical of him to* **kick/hit** *someone* **when** *they're* **down** (= to take unfair advantage of someone when they are in a weak position). • *"Come on down"* (phrase from the television quiz show *The Price is Right*, 1980s) • PIC› **Prepositions of movement** (T)

down *obj* /daʊn/ *v* [T] • *Ali downed* (= knocked down) *his opponent in the second round.* • *We downed* (= shot to the ground) *three enemy planes with our missiles.* • *He'd downed*

(= drunk quickly) *four beers, so I told him he shouldn't drive home.* • *(esp. Br)* To **down tools** is to refuse to carry on working, esp. because of your dissatisfaction with your wages or working conditions: *The printers are threatening to down tools if the pay offer is not increased to 8%.*

down LOWER LEVEL /daʊn/ *adv, adj* [not gradable] in or towards a lower place or level, a smaller amount or a simpler state • *The pay offer is 2% down (Br and Aus)* **on/from** *last year.* • *Milan were three goals down* (= losing by three goals) *at half-time.* • *The number of students in full-time education in the town has* **gone down from** *5000 last year* **to** *4800.* • *When the rescue party found her after two weeks of searching, she was down* **to** *her last bar of chocolate* (= that was all she had left). • *In an hour of bargaining, we got the price down* **(from** *£300)* **to** *£95.* • *Well, if I bring it down* **to** *its simplest level* (= explain it simply), *the sun is just a huge nuclear reactor.* • Down is used with a lot of verbs to show that something is becoming smaller, weaker, slower, etc.: *Let the fire burn down* (= become smaller). ○ *She's slimmed down a lot in the past few months.* ○ *Could you turn the music down a little* (= make it quieter), *please?* ○ *This drink has been watered down – it's got no flavour.* • *(infml)* If you are down **on** someone, you criticize them: *It's not fair of the boss to be so down on a new employee.* • If you **come/go down with** an illness, you start to suffer from it: *Half the people in the office have gone down with this bug that's going around.* ○ *She won't be at work today – she's down with* (= suffering from) *flu.* • If you say that someone has **come/gone down in the world**, you mean that they have lost the money and higher social rank that they used to have: *Fancy her taking a job like that – she's certainly come down in the world!* • *What the problem* **comes down to** (= can be reduced to in its simplest form) *is 'Will the consumer be willing to pay more for a higher quality product?'* • If something *(Br)* **is down to**/*(Am and Aus)* **comes down to** a particular person or organization, it is their responsibility, fault, choice or decision: *We've done all we can – it's all down to you now to make it work.* ○ *I'm sure the problem is down to* (= caused by) *her inexperience, not any lack of intelligence.* • *Well, there are ten lectures in total and we've been to two now, so* **that's** *two* **down,** *eight* **to go** (= two that have happened already and eight that are left). • A **down-and-out** is a person who has no job or home and is unlikely to get either of these: *I met up with a real down-and-out who's been sleeping on the streets for 20 years.* ○ *Nobody loves you when you're down and out.* • Someone or something that is *(Br and Aus)* **down-at-heel**/*(Am)* **down-at-the-heel** is poorly dressed or in bad condition, because of a lack of money: *She had a decidedly down-at-heel appearance.* ○ *He worked in a down-at-heel, decaying 1930s office block.* • Someone or something that is **down-to-earth** is practical, direct or ordinary: *She's a down-to-earth sort of woman with no pretensions.* ○ *Surely there's a more down-to-earth explanation than black magic?* • Ⓣ

down /daʊn/ *n* [U] *Br and Aus infml* • If you **have a down on** someone, you dislike them, often unfairly: *Why do you have a down on him? I think he seems really nice.*

down– LOWER OR WORSE /ˌdaʊn-, ˈdaʊn-/ *combining form* at or towards the end or the lower or worse part • *downhill* • *downriver* • *down-market* • *the downside*

down DISTANT /daʊn/ *adv* [not gradable] used, esp. with prepositions, to emphasize that a place is distant from the speaker or from somewhere considered to be central • *I'll meet you down* **at** *the club after work.* • *He has a house down* **by** *the harbour.* • *My parents live down* **in** *Worcestershire, but they come up to London occasionally.* • *I'll buy it when I go down* **to** *the shops later today.* See also DOWN TO. • Down can also mean in or towards the south: *Things are much more expensive down (in the) south.* ○ *How often do you come down to Cornwall?* • **Down** *our* **way** (= In the (distant) place where we live) *people don't take much interest in politics.* • Ⓣ

down ALONG /daʊn/ *prep* along • *We drove down the motorway as far as Bristol.* • *Her office is down the corridor on the right.* • *They sailed the boat down the river* (= towards the sea). • *We have an idea to develop a talking book, but a marketable product is a long way* **down the road/line/track** (= in the future). • Ⓣ

down TO /daʊn/ *prep Br and Aus not standard* to • *I went down the pub with my mates.* • Compare UP TO. • Ⓣ

down IN WRITING /daʊn/ *adv, adj* [not gradable] in writing or on paper • *I'll write/copy/put it down now in my diary so I won't forget.* • *Are you down (on the list) to help at the Charities Fair?* • *Do you have it down* **in writing/on paper,** *or was it just a verbal agreement?* • *I've* **got/put** *you and Ann down* **for** (= planned that you should take part in) *the costume-making.* • Ⓣ

down UNHAPPY /daʊn/ *adj* unhappy; unable to feel excited or energetic about anything • *She's been really down and depressed since her husband died.* • *I've been* **(feeling) a bit** *down this week, especially after my team lost to Spurs.* • *"Been down so long it looks like up to me"* (saying, used as the title of a book by Richard Farina, 1966) • Ⓣ

down MONEY /daʊn/ *adv* [not gradable] at the time of buying • *If you pay £100 down and the rest within six months, you can have it for £250 in total.* • A **down payment** is an amount of money which is only part of the total cost, paid at the time when you buy something: *I've* **made/put** *a down payment* **on** *a new TV and video.* • Ⓣ

down NOT IN OPERATION /daʊn/ *adj* [after v; not gradable] *specialized* (of a system or machine, esp. a computer) not in operation or not working, usually only for a limited period of time • *The computer will be down for an hour while a new terminal is added to the network.* • *I'm afraid the (telephone) lines/wires are down because of the storm.* • See also DOWNTIME. • Ⓣ

down HAIR /daʊn/ *n* [U] small soft feathers or hair, esp. those of a young bird or on a baby's head • *The highest quality duvets, quilts and pillows are made of down* (= the chest feathers of DUCKS). • **Down vest** is *Am* for BODYWARMER. • PIC Coats and jackets Ⓣ

down·y /ˈdaʊ·ni/ *adj* **-ier, -iest** • *a tiny baby's downy head* • *a downy nest*

down *obj* DEFEAT /daʊn/ *v* [T] *Am and Aus* to defeat, esp. in sport • *The Yankees downed the Red Sox 7-0 last night.* • Ⓣ

down·beat /ˈdaʊm·biːt/ *adj infml* calm and quiet; not energetic; not showing or feeling much excitement or interest • *The actual signing of the treaty was a downbeat affair without any ceremony.* • *The band seemed rather downbeat, even unconcerned about their success.* • Compare UPBEAT.

down·cast UNHAPPY /£ˈdaʊŋ·kɑːst, $-kæst, ˌ-ˈ-/ *adj fml* sad; feeling or showing little hope, energy or confidence; DEJECTED • *I thought you were looking a little downcast this morning.* • See also **cast down** at CAST PUT.

down·cast EYES DOWN /£ˈdaʊŋ·kɑːst, $-kæst, ˌ-ˈ-/ *adj* with the eyes looking down, usually because of shyness or sadness • *She stood with eyes downcast while the doctors examined her.* [after n]

down·er EXPERIENCE /£ˈdaʊ·nəʳ, $-nɚ/ *n* [C] *infml* an event or experience which makes you unhappy and lacking in hope, confidence or energy • *You lost your job? That's a real downer!*

down·er DRUG /£ˈdaʊ·nəʳ, $-nɚ/ *n* [C] *infml* a drug that makes you feel calmer and less active

down·fall /£ˈdaʊn·fɔːl, £-fɑːl/ *n* [C] (something that causes) the usually sudden destruction of a person, organization or government and their loss of power, money or health • *This series of military defeats brought about the downfall of the government.* • *In the end, it was the continual drinking that was his downfall.*

down·grade *obj* /ˌdaʊnˈgreɪd/ *v* [T] to reduce (someone or something) to a lower rank or position; to make less important or less valued • *My job's been downgraded* **to** *that of ordinary editor.* • *Management are trying to downgrade the importance of safety at work.* • Compare UPGRADE.

down·heart·ed /£ˌdaʊnˈhɑː·tɪd, $-ˈhɑːr·t̬ɪd/ *adj* unhappy and lacking in hope, energy or confidence, esp. because of a disappointment or failure • *After hearing the news of the defeat, she told supporters not to be downhearted.*

down·hill /ˌdaʊnˈhɪl, ˈ-ˌ-/ *adv, adj* (moving) towards the bottom of a hill • *It's so much easier running downhill!* • *The route is all downhill from here to the finish.* • **Downhill skiing** is skiing down slopes, rather than along level ground. • *(fig.) The first week was okay, but it's* **all gone** *downhill* (= got worse) *since then.* • *(fig.) Once we get the preparation done, it'll* **be** *downhill* (= easier) **all the way.** • Compare UPHILL.

Down·ing Street /ˈdaʊ·nɪŋ/ *n* [U not after *the*] the road in central London where the official home of the British Prime Minister is situated • *The Prime Minister lives at* **10** *Downing Street.* • Downing Street can also refer to the British government or the British Prime Minister: *The announcement took Washington and Paris by surprise, but Downing Street had been expecting it.*

down·load *obj* /£ˌdaʊnˈləʊd, £ˈ--, $ˈ-loʊd/ *v* [T] *specialized* to copy or move (programs or information) into a computer's memory, esp. from a larger computer

down·mar·ket /£ˌdaʊmˈmɑː·kɪt, $ˈ-ˌmɑːr-/ *adj, adv* relating to or directed at people in the lower social classes, or (of goods and services) low in quality and price • *Once out of prison, he sold his sensational life story to a downmarket tabloid newspaper.* • *It was clear that the shop had moved distinctly downmarket, with very little fresh food on display and the cashiers accepting cash only.* • Compare **up-market** at UP- [COMBINING FORM].

down·play *obj* /ˌdaʊmˈpleɪ/ *v* [T] to make (something) seem less important or less bad than it really is; PLAY DOWN • *The government has been trying to downplay the crisis/the lack of agreement.*

down·pour /£ˈdaʊm·pɔːʳ, $ˈdaʊn·pɔːr/ *n* [C] a lot of rain in a short time • *They were caught in a* **torrential** *downpour and got soaked to the skin.*

down·right /ˈdaʊn·raɪt/ *adj* [before n], *adv* [not gradable] *infml* (esp. of something bad) extremely or very great • *She's being downright difficult and obstructive.* • *I think the way she's been treated is a downright disgrace.* • *These working conditions are unhealthy,* **if not** *downright* (= and probably extremely) *dangerous.*

down·riv·er /£ˌdaʊnˈrɪv·əʳ, $-ɚ/ *adv, adj* DOWNSTREAM

downs /daʊnz/ *pl n esp. Br* low grassy hills, esp. used in the names of two such areas in SE England • *the North Downs* • *the South Downs*

down·side /ˈdaʊn·saɪd/ *n* [U] the negative side of a situation • *Unemployment, inflation and greater inequality are often the downside of a market economy.* • Compare UPSIDE.

down·spout /ˈdaʊn·spaʊt/ *n* [C] *Am* a pipe that carries rain water from the roof of a building; a DRAINPIPE

Down's syn·drome *medical* /£ˈdaʊnzˌsɪn·drəʊm, $-droʊm/, *dated or taboo* **mon·go·li·sm** *n* [U] a condition which some people are born with and which means they have lower than average mental ability, a flat face and nose, and sloping eyes

down·stage /£ˌdaʊnˈsteɪdʒ, $ˈ--/ *adv, adj* towards or at the front of the stage in a theatre • Compare UPSTAGE [THEATRE AREA].

down·stairs /£ˌdaʊnˈsteəz, $-ˈsterz/ *adv, adj* [not gradable], *n* (on or to) a lower floor of a building, esp. the ground floor, or down the stairs • *Would you mind going downstairs and seeing who rang the doorbell?* • *There's a man downstairs who wants to come up and see you.* • *There's a downstairs bathroom as well as the one on this floor.* • *We live in the top half of the house but the downstairs is for sale.* [U] • Compare UPSTAIRS.

down·stream /ˌdaʊnˈstriːm/, **down·riv·er** *adv, adj* in the direction a river or stream is flowing • *The current carried her downstream for 100 metres before she could swim to the bank.* • *The sea is only another few miles downstream from here.* • Compare UPSTREAM.

down·time /ˈdaʊn·taɪm/ *n* [U] the time during which a machine, esp. a computer, is not working or is not able to be used • *An important way of saving time is the reduction of downtime.*

downtown /ˌdaʊnˈtaʊn/ *adj, adv* [not gradable], *n esp. Am* (in or to) the business or central part of a city, or the southern part of Manhattan in New York City, esp. when considered as an important place for art and music • *downtown Los Angeles* • *a downtown address* • *Shall we eat downtown tonight?* • *The hotel is situated two miles north of downtown.* [U] • *Madonna first made it big in the downtown scene.* • Compare UPTOWN.

down·trod·den /£ˈdaʊnˌtrɒd·ən, $-ˌtrɑː·dən/ *adj* badly and unfairly treated and therefore feeling worthless and unable to act independently • *Many of the country's downtrodden black majority feel persecuted by white 'justice'.* • *He leaves his obedient and downtrodden wife for a sexy woman twenty years younger.*

down·turn /£ˈdaʊn·tɜːn, $-tɜːrn/, **down·swing** *n* [C usually sing] a reduction in the amount or success of something, such as a country's economic activity • *the continuing economic downturn* • *There is evidence of a downturn* **in** *the building trade/house prices.* • Compare UPTURN.

down·wards /£ˈdaʊn·wədz, $-wɚdz/, *esp. Am* **down·ward** *adv* [not gradable] towards a lower position • *The road slopes gently downwards for a mile or two.* • *The water filters downwards through the rock for hundreds of feet.* • *He was lying* **face** *downwards on the pavement.* • *Casualty figures were* **revised** *downwards* (= reduced) *after the war had ended.* • Compare **upwards** at UPWARD.

down·ward /£ˈdaʊn·wəd, $-wɚd/ *adj* [not gradable] • *Interest rates in the world economy are generally on a downward trend.* • *At last inflation is on a downward path.* • *The last few months have seen a downward pressure on salaries.* • *The quarterly trend in America's external deficit is still downward.* • *The country's economy is on a downward* **spiral** (= getting worse quickly in a way that cannot be stopped). • Compare UPWARD.

down·wind /£ˌdaʊnˈwɪnd, $daʊnˈwɪnd/ *adv, adj* in the direction in which the wind blows; with the wind behind • *The smoke drifted downwind.* • *They live downwind* **of** *a pig-farm and sometimes the smell is awful.* • Compare UPWIND.

down·y /ˈdaʊ·ni/ *adj* See at DOWN [HAIR]

dow·ry /ˈdaʊ·ri/ *n* [C] an amount of money or property that a woman's parents give to the man she marries in some societies

dowse /daʊz, daʊs/ *v* [I] to DIVINE [SEARCH]

doy·en *male, female* **doy·enne** /ˈdɔɪ·en, dwaɪˈen/ *n* [C] the oldest, most experienced, and often most respected, person of all the people involved in a particular type of work • *Like others of my age, I still think of Stuart Hibberd as the doyen* **of** *radio newsreaders.* • *The party was held in honour of Vivienne Westwood, that doyenne* **of** *British fashion.*

doy·ley, doy·ly /ˈdɔɪ·li/ *n* [C] a DOILY

doze /£dəʊz, $doʊz/ *v, n infml* (to have) a short sleep, esp. during the day • *My cat likes dozing in front of the fire.* [I] • If you doze **off**, you start to sleep, esp. during the day: *The office was so hot I nearly dozed off at my desk.* [I] • *He's just* **having a** *little doze on the settee.* [U]

doz·y /£ˈdəʊ·zi, $ˈdoʊ-/ *adj* **-ier, -iest** *infml* • If you are dozy you feel sleepy, or *(Br infml)* you are mentally slow and tend not to notice what is happening around you: *I think it must be the medicine I'm on – I feel so dozy all the while.* ○ *(Br infml) He'd have driven straight into me if I hadn't seen him first – the dozy idiot!*

doz·i·ly /£ˈdəʊ·zɪ·li, $ˈdoʊ-/ *adv infml*

doz·i·ness /£ˈdəʊ·zɪ·nəs, $ˈdoʊ-/ *n* [U] *infml*

do·zen /ˈdʌz·ən/ *n* [C], *determiner* twelve • *a dozen eggs* • *Could you get me* **half a** *dozen* (= six) *eggs when you go to the shop?* • *The police made a dozen arrests during the demonstration.* • *There were at least two dozen people in the restaurant at the time of the shooting.* • *He was standing on the courthouse steps, surrounded by several dozen cheering supporters.* • *(infml) I've spoken to him dozens* **of** (= many) *times, but I still don't know his name!* • *The refugees arrive* **by the** *dozen*/**in their** *dozens* (= in large numbers), *hungry and cold, all needing food and shelter.* • If you are talking **nineteen/ten to the dozen**, you are talking a lot very quickly and without stopping. • [LP] **Hundred**

DPhil /ˌdiːˈfɪl/ *n* [C] a PHD • [LP] **Schools and colleges**

Dr /£ˈdɒk·təʳ, $ˈdɑːk·tɚ/ *n* [before n] *abbreviation for* Doctor • *An appointment has been made for you to see Dr Fiasco on July 19th at 2.30 p.m.* • *(trademark)* **Dr Martens** (*infml* **Doc Martens, DMs** or **Docs**) are a type of strong, heavy-looking shoe or boot, with LACES and thick rubber bottom parts. • [LP] **Titles and forms of address**

drab /dræb/ *adj* **drabber, drabbest** *disapproving* boring, esp. in appearance; lacking colour and excitement • *She walked through the city centre with its drab, grey buildings and felt depressed.* • *He found himself in the drab surroundings of yet another government building.* • *I feel so drab in this grey uniform.*

drab·ness /ˈdræb·nəs/ *n* [U] • *It's the unrelieved drabness of big industrial cities that depresses me.*

dra·co·ni·an /£drəˈkəʊ·ni·ən, $-ˈkoʊ-/ *adj* (usually of laws, government actions, etc.) unreasonably severe; going beyond what is right or necessary • *He criticized what he called 'the draconian* **measures**' *taken by the police in controlling the demonstrators.* • *Draconian fines keep illegal parking in the city centre to a minimum.* • *The army, which held power at that time, imposed draconian penalties on the non-voters.*

draft [PLAN] /£drɑːft, $dræft/ *n* [C] a piece of text, a formal suggestion or a drawing in its original state, often containing the main ideas and intentions but not the developed form • *Do a* **(first)** *draft of the article and I'll check it before you write up the final copy.* • *I'm drawing up a plan* **in** *draft that we can look over before we make the final decisions.*

draft *obj* /£drɑːft, $dræft/ *v* [T] • *Draft a proposal and we can discuss it at the meeting before any decisions are made.*

draft /£drɑːft, $dræft/ *adj* [before n; not gradable] • *a draft plan/bill/proposal*

draft MILITARY *esp. Am* /£drɑːft, $dræft/, *Br* **con·scrip·tion** *n* [U] **the draft** the system of ordering people by law to join the armed forces • *He avoided the draft because of a foot injury.* • A **draft dodger** is a person who has disobeyed an official order to join the armed forces.

draft *obj esp. Am* /£drɑːft, $dræft/, *Br* **con·script** *v* [T usually passive] • *There's a photo of him in uniform taken just after he was drafted (***into** *the army).*

draf·tee /£ˌdrɑːfˈtiː, $ˌdræfˈţiː/ *n* [C] • A draftee is a person who has been ordered by law to join the armed forces.

draft BANKING /£drɑːft, $dræft/ *n* [C] a written order for money to be paid by a bank, esp. to another bank • *I arranged for some money to be sent from London to Madrid by* **banker's** *draft.* • *A bank cannot refuse to cash a* **banker's** *draft, whereas it can refuse to cash a cheque.*

draft COLD AIR /£drɑːft, $dræft/ *n* [C] *Am for* DRAUGHT COLD AIR

draf·ty /£ˈdrɑːf·ti, $ˈdræf·ţi/ *adj* **-ier, -iest** • Drafty is *Am for* **draughty**.

draft in *obj*, **draft** *obj* **in** *v adv* [M] *Br* to arrange for (people) to go to another place, esp. for a particular period, in order to do a particular job • *Every Christmas thousands of people are drafted in to help with the post.*

drafts·man (*pl* **-men**), **drafts·wo·man** (*pl* **-women**) /£ˈdrɑːfts·mən, $ˈdræfts-, -ˌwʊm·ən/ *n* [C] a person who writes legal papers • Draftsman is also *Am and Aus for* DRAUGHTSMAN.

drag *obj* PULL /dræg/ *v* [T] **-gg-** to move (something heavy) by pulling it along the ground • *Pick the chair up instead of dragging it behind you!* [T] • *I had to drag the child screaming out of the shop.* [T] • *(fig.) I'm ready to go home now but I don't want to drag you* **away** *if you're enjoying yourself.* [T] • *(fig.) All that stress at work had begun to drag him* **down** (= make him feel weak or unhappy) *and he was badly in need of a holiday.* [T] • *(fig.) Don't drag me* **into** *your argument* (= don't force me to take part in the argument)*! It's nothing to do with me.* [T] • *(fig.) She's always dragging sex* **into** *the conversation* (= introducing it although it is not connected with what was being said before). [T] • If you drag **out** an event, you cause it to continue for more time than is necessary or convenient: *I don't want to drag out this meeting, so could we run through the main points quickly?* [M] • *(fig.) You never tell me how you feel – I always have to drag it* **out** *of you* (= force you to tell me). [T] • If a river or area of water is dragged, nets or hooks are pulled along the bottom in order to find something: *They found the man's body when they dragged the canal.* [T] • If you **drag** your **heels/feet**, you do something slowly because you do not want to do it: *I suspect the government is dragging its heels over this issue.* ○ See also **foot-dragging** at FOOT BODY PART. • If you **drag** someone's **name through the mire/mud**, you damage their reputation by saying extremely insulting things about them. • *(Br)* A **drag lift** is a device which takes someone who is SKIING to higher ground and involves the skier holding on to a moving bar while their skis stay flat against the ground. • *"[The Republican Party has to be] dragged kicking and screaming into the twentieth century"* (believed to have been said by Adlai Stevenson, 1900-1965)

drag /dræg/ *n* • *(fig.) She didn't want a husband who would be a drag* **on** (= slow down or limit the development of) *her career.* [C] • *(specialized)* Drag is the force that acts against the forward movement of something which is passing through a gas or a liquid. [U]

drag BORING /dræg/ *n* [U] *slang* something which is inconvenient and boring or unpleasant • *Filling in forms is* **such a** *drag!* • *Travelling by public transport is* **a** *real drag!* • *That's* **a** *bit of a drag – we've run out of coffee.* • *I've got to go to the dentist's again – what* **a** *drag!* • *"What a drag it is getting old"* (Rolling Stones from the song *Mother's Little Helper*, 1966)

drag /dræg/ *v* [I] **-gg-** • *The first half of the film was interesting but the second half dragged* **(on)** (= seemed to go slowly because it was boring).

drag SUCK /dræg/ *n* [C] *slang* the action of taking in a breath of cigarette smoke while holding the cigarette to the mouth • *Taking a deep drag* **of/on** *his cigarette he closed his eyes and sighed.*

drag CLOTHES /dræg/ *n* [U] *infml* (esp. of a man) the action of dressing in clothes of the opposite sex, often for humorous entertainment • *She was speaking to a middle-aged man* **in** *drag with six-inch heels and lipstick.* • *The show is basically a drag* **act** *with a load of men dressed up as women.* • A **drag queen** is a man, often a homosexual, dressed as a woman: *There were prizes for the butchest man and the most beautiful drag queen.*

drag RACE /dræg/ *v* [I] to take part in a **drag race** (= a sport in which people race against each other in specially built cars and motorcycles) • *(Am) Hey, Jim, you wanna drag?* • *I thought we might go and see some drag* **racing** *on Saturday.* • *The first drag* **race** *is usually around midday.*

drag·ster /£ˈdræg·stəʳ, $-stɚ/ *n* [C] • A dragster is a car or motorcycle which has been specially built to take part in **drag races**.

drag·net /ˈdræg·net/ *n* [C] a series of actions taken by the police which are intended to catch criminals • *The police have widened their dragnet in their search for the killer.* • A dragnet is also a heavy net that is pulled along the bottom of a river or area of water when searching for something.

drag·on /ˈdræg·ᵊn/ *n* [C] a large fierce imaginary animal, usually represented with wings, a long tail and fire coming out of its mouth • *I was reading my nephew a story about a handsome prince who rescues a princess from a dragon.* • *(disapproving)* A dragon is also a fierce and frightening woman: *We've got this real dragon in charge of our accounts department – she's terrifying.* ○ *She's a real* **old** *dragon.* • *(Aus)* Dragon also refers to various types of LIZARD. • PIC **Imaginary creatures**

drag·on·fly /ˈdræg·ᵊn·flaɪ/ *n* [C] a large insect with a long thin body and two pairs of big wings • PIC **Insects**

drag·oon *obj* **into** *(obj)* /drəˈguːn/ *v prep* [T] *often humorous* to force or persuade (someone) to do (something unpleasant) • *I've been dragooned into giving the after-dinner speech.* [+ obj + v-ing]

drain *(obj)* /dreɪn/ *v* to (cause to) become dry as liquid flows off, or to (cause a liquid) to flow away • *Drain the rice, making sure that it is quite dry before you return it to the pan.* [T] • *We drained the pond and filled it with fresh water.* [T] • *The soil had got too hard over the summer and it wouldn't drain properly* (= the water couldn't enter the ground). [I] • *The problem with a flat roof is that the water doesn't drain (away) properly.* [I] • *Don't bother drying the pans – just leave them to drain.* [I] • *Drain* **(off)** *any liquid that is left in the rice.* [T/M] • *(fig.) It's time we went – come on, drain your* **glass** (= finish what you are drinking). [T] • *(fig.) Working such long hours had drained him* (= made him extremely tired, physically or emotionally). [T] • *War drains a nation* **of** *its youth and its wealth* (= uses them until they are gone). [T] • *(fig.) Stretching out her tired limbs, she felt the tensions of the day drain* **away***/drain* **out of** *her.* [I] • *(fig.) As she heard the news, her face slowly drained* **of colour/blood** (= she turned pale). [I] • *(Br and Aus)* A **draining board** (*Br also* **drainer**, *Am* **drainboard**) is the place next to a SINK where plates, knives, forks, etc. are put to dry. • PIC **Food preparation, Kitchen**

drain /dreɪn/ *n* [C] • A drain is any of various devices, such as a pipe, which is used to carry away waste matter and water from a building, or an opening in the road which rain water can flow down: *I think the kitchen drain is blocked.* ○ *She accidentally dropped her ring down a drain in the road.* • *(fig.) Having a big mortgage is a real drain* **on** (= uses a lot of) *your earnings.* • *(fig.) I think looking after her elderly mother is quite a drain* **on** *her energy* (= makes her very tired). • PIC **Accommodation**

drains /dreɪnz/ *pl n* • Drains refers to the system of pipes, openings in the ground or other devices that are used for carrying away waste matter and water: *There was an unpleasant smell coming from the drains.* ○ *They're laying sewer drains under the street.*

drained /dreɪnd/ *adj* • *You look completely drained* (= very tired) *– why don't you go to bed?* • *It was one of those films that leaves you* **emotionally** *drained.*

drain·age /ˈdreɪ·nɪdʒ/ *n* [U] • *Clay-rich soils are usually sticky, with poor drainage when wet, or cracked and hard when dry.* • *drainage channels/ditches/systems*

drain·pipe /ˈdreɪm·paɪp/ *n* [C] a pipe that carries waste water or SEWAGE away from buildings • PIC **Accommodation**

drake /dreɪk/ *n* [C] a male DUCK (= common water bird)

dram /dræm/ *n* [C] *esp. Scot Eng* a small amount of a strong alcoholic drink, esp. WHISKY • *Would you care for a* **wee**

dram? ● *There's nothing like a* **wee** *dram* **of** *whisky to get you off to sleep.*

dra·ma [THEATRE] /£ˈdrɑː·mə, $ˈdræm·ə/ *n* plays; writing which is intended to be performed esp. in the theatre, or plays as they are performed in the theatre or on the radio or television ● *She studied English and drama at college.* [U] ● *The bloodthirsty plays of Webster are in many ways typical of the drama* (= plays in general) *of that period.* [U] ● *She's been in several* **television** *dramas.* [C] ● *He's the drama critic for the Times.* ● *Didn't she go to drama* **school**? ● *A new drama* **series** *is starting tonight on TV.* ● Drama can be used in expressions which refer to the type of play or film: *a costume/courtroom/historical drama* ● A **drama documentary** (also **docudrama**) is a television programme whose story is based on an event or situation that really happened although it is not intended to be accurate in every detail. ● (F) (GR) (J)

dra·mat·ic /£drəˈmæt·ɪk, $-ˈmæt̬-/ *adj* ● *She bought me the complete dramatic works* (= texts to be performed) *of Brecht for my birthday.* ● *I once saw a dramatic production of 'The Lady in White'.* ● *She looked rather dramatic with her long flowing cape as if she'd just walked off the set of some period play.* ● (F)

dra·mat·i·cally /£drəˈmæt·ɪ·kli, $-ˈmæt̬-/ *adv* ● *She swept her hair back dramatically* (= as if acting in a play).

dra·mat·ist /£ˈdræm·ə·tɪst, $-t̬ɪst/ *n* [C] ● A dramatist is a person who writes plays: *He was one of the major dramatists of this period.*

dra·ma·tize *obj, Br and Aus usually* **-ise** /ˈdræm·ə·taɪz/ *v* [T] ● If a writer dramatizes a book, story, poem, etc. he or she writes it again in a form which can be performed: *The novel is currently being dramatized* **for** *TV.*

dra·ma·tiz·a·tion, *Br and Aus usually* **-i·sa·tion** /ˌdræm·ə·taɪˈzeɪ·ʃᵊn/ *n* [C] ● *Tonight sees the return of Andrew Davies' award-winning dramatization of the novel 'Mother Love'.*

dra·ma [EXCITEMENT] /£ˈdrɑː·mə, $ˈdræm·ə/ *n* an event or situation, esp. an unexpected one, in which there is anxiety or excitement and usually a lot of action ● *We had a little drama last night when the oil in the pan caught fire.* [C] ● Drama is also the excitement and energy that is created by a lot of action and arguments: *There's always such* **high** *drama in that household – constant arguments and scenes.* [U] ○ *As a lawyer, he positively revelled in the drama of the courtroom.* [U] ● *"We won't make a drama out of a crisis"* (advertisement for General Accident Insurance, 1980s) ● (F) (GR) (J)

dra·mat·ic /£drəˈmæt·ɪk, $-ˈmæt̬-/ *adj* ● *There have been some fairly dramatic* (= sudden and surprising) *developments on the political scene recently.* ● *There's been a dramatic* (= very noticeable) *rise in unemployment recently.*

dra·mat·i·cally /£drəˈmæt·ɪ·kli, $-ˈmæt̬-/ *adv* ● *The new treatment could dramatically* (= very noticeably) *alter the life of people suffering from this disease.* ● *Your life changes dramatically* (= very suddenly and noticeably) *when you have a baby.*

dra·ma·tize *obj, Br and Aus usually* **-ise** /ˈdræm·ə·taɪz/ *v* [T] *disapproving* ● If someone dramatizes an account of what has happened to them, they make the story seem more exciting, important or dangerous than it really is: *She dramatizes everything – she told me she'd cut her head open yesterday and it turns out she'd got a little scratch near her eye.*

dra·mat·is per·son·ae /£drəˌmɑː·tɪs·pɜːˈsəʊ·naɪ, $ˌdræm·ə·t̬ɪs·pɚˈsoʊ-/ *pl n fml* the names of all the characters in a play

drank /dræŋk/ *past simple of* DRINK

drape *(obj)* /dreɪp/ *v* to hang or cover loosely and often decoratively (as if) with folds of cloth ● *She draped the silk scarf loosely* **around** *her bare shoulders.* [T] ● *The coffins were all draped* **in/with** *the national flag.* [T] ● *A Turkish rug lay draped* **over** *the back of the settee.* [T] ● *He designs clothes in soft woollen fabrics because he says they drape so well.* [I] ● *(usually humorous) I saw him last night in the pub with some woman* **draped all over** *him* (= very close and with her arms around him). ● (RUS)

drape /dreɪp/ *n* ● *She liked the heavy drape of velvet* (= the way in which it hangs). [U] ● *The dress hung in artful drapes* (= folds) *around her hips.* [C] ● See also DRAPES.

drapes /dreɪps/, **drap·er·ies** *pl n Am and Aus* ● Drapes are curtains made with thick cloth.

drap·er /£ˈdreɪ·pəʳ, $-pɚ/ *n* [C] *Br dated* ● A draper is someone who owns a shop which sells cloth, curtains, etc. ● LP› **Shopping goods**

drap·er·y /£ˈdreɪ·pᵊr·i, $-pɚ-/ *n* [U] ● *The actor playing the king had some drapery* (= folds of material) *around his neck to suggest the historical era.* ● *(Br dated)* Drapery (*Aus, Br also* **haberdashery**, *Am* **dry goods**) also refers to goods such as cloth and curtains: *You'll find a drapery department in one of the big stores.*

dras·tic /£ˈdræs·tɪk, $-t̬ɪk/ *adj* (esp. of actions) severe and sudden; having very noticeable effects ● *The government have recently taken drastic* **measures** *to control public spending.* ● *Many employees have had to take drastic cuts in pay.* ● *I'm having my hair cut tonight – nothing drastic, just a trim.*

dras·ti·cal·ly /£ˈdræs·tɪ·kli, $-t̬ɪ-/ *adv* ● *Our budget has been drastically reduced.* ● *Rather than changing your diet drastically it's better just to make a few improvements.*

drat /dræt/ *exclamation dated infml* used to express slight annoyance ● *Oh drat! I've gone and lost her telephone number!*

draught [COLD AIR] *Br and Aus, Am* **draft** /£drɑːft, $dræft/ *n* [C] a current of unpleasantly cold air blowing through a room ● *There's a (cold) draught every time that door is opened.*

draugh·ty *Br and Aus* (**-ier**, **-iest**), *Am* **draf·ty** (**-ier**, **-iest**) /£ˈdrɑːf·ti, $ˈdræf·t̬i/ *adj* ● *It's a bit draughty in here – can I shut a window, please?*

draught [BEER] *Br and Aus, Am* **draft** /£drɑːft, $dræft/ *adj* [before n; not gradable] (of drinks such as beer) stored in and served from large containers, esp. BARRELS ● *draught beer/lager/cider*

draught *Br and Aus, Am* **draft** /£drɑːft, $dræft/ *n* [U] ● *Is the lager* **on** *draught or is it bottled?*

draught [ANIMALS] *Br and Aus, Am* **draft** /£drɑːft, $dræft/ *adj* [before n; not gradable] (of animals) used for pulling heavy loads, vehicles, etc. ● *a draught horse*

draught [BOATS] *Br and Aus, Am* **draft** /£drɑːft, $dræft/ *n* [C] *specialized* the depth of water needed for a boat to be able to float ● *A punt has a shallow draught.*

draughts *Br and Aus* /£drɑːfts, $dræfts/, *Am and Aus also* **check·ers** *pl n* a game which is played by two people, each with twelve circular pieces, on a black and white square board ● PIC› **Games**

draughts·man *Br* (*pl* **-men**), *Am and Aus* **drafts·man** (*pl* **-men**), *Br* **draughts·wo·man** (*pl* **-women**), *Am and Aus* **drafts·wo·man** (*pl* **-women**) /£ˈdrɑːfts·mən, $ˈdræfts-, -ˌwʊm·ən/ *n* [C] a person whose job is to do detailed drawings of machines, new buildings, etc. ● Someone might be described as a good draughtsman/draughtswoman if they are skilled at drawing.

draw *(obj)* [PICTURE] /£drɔː, $drɑː/ *v past simple* **drew** /druː/, *past part* **drawn** /£drɔːn, $drɑːn/ to make a picture of (something or someone) with a pencil or pen ● *At school he was very slow at reading and writing but he could draw brilliantly.* [I] ● *The child drew a picture of her mother with an enormous head and tiny legs.* [T] ● *Draw a line at the bottom of the page.* [T] ● If someone says that they **draw the line at** something, it means that they do not do it because they consider it to be unacceptable: *I swear quite a lot but I do draw the line at certain words.* ○ *I can relax with my boss and share a joke or two but I do know where to draw the line.*

draw·ing /£ˈdrɔː·ɪŋ, $ˈdrɑː-/ *n* ● *Rosie loves drawing.* [U] ● *He had on the wall a copy of Dürer's famous drawing* (= picture made using a pen or pencil) **of** *his mother.* [C] ● *(Br and Aus)* A **drawing pin** (*Am* **thumbtack**) is a short sharp pin with a flat round top which can be pushed into wood etc. with the thumb and is used especially for putting up notices. ● A **drawing board** is a large flat wooden board onto which paper is put for drawing or designing something. It is often attached to a metal frame and can be set at an angle or lowered to a horizontal position. ● PIC› **Drawing and painting, Pins and needles, Stationery**

draw [MOVE] /£drɔː, $drɑː/ *v* [I always + adv/prep] *past simple* **drew** /druː/, *past part* **drawn** /£drɔːn, $drɑːn/ to move in a particular direction, esp. in a vehicle ● *As the train approached, the embracing couple slowly and reluctantly drew* **apart** (= separated). ● *She could hear the cars draw* **away/out** (= leave) *as one by one the guests left.* ● *As we drew* **alongside**/*(Br also) drew* **level with/up with** (= reached) *the black Fiat I suddenly recognized my ex-boyfriend at the wheel.* ● *She leaned forward to stroke the dog but quickly drew* **back** *when she saw its teeth.* ● *She looked eagerly along the platform as the train slowly drew* **into** *the station/drew* **in**. See also DRAW IN. ● *Just draw* **up** (= drive to one side and stop) *here and I'll get out.* See also DRAW UP [PREPARE]. ● *As Christmas draws nearer the shops start to*

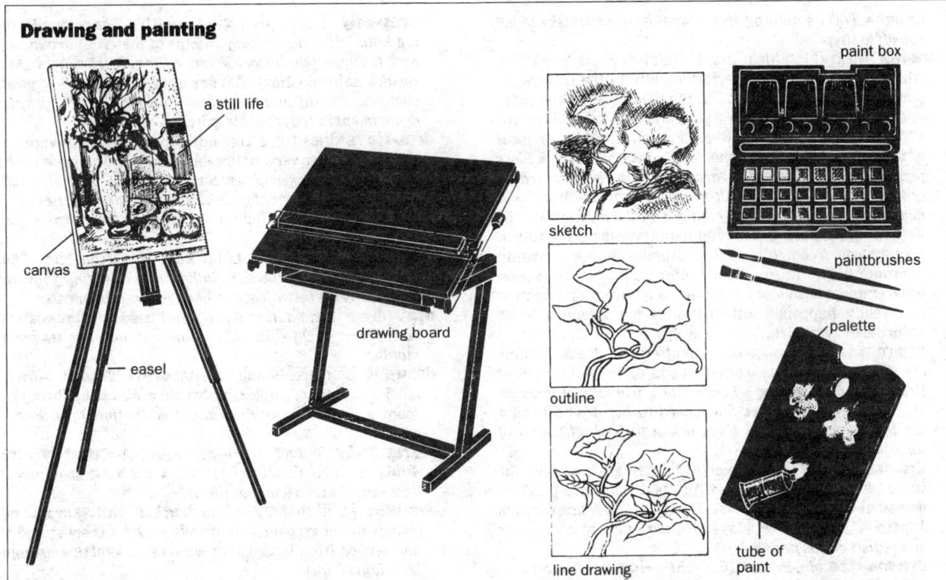

get unbearably crowded. • *(literary) As the evening drew* **to a close/to an end** (= gradually finished) *people started reaching for their coats.* • *(literary) "Ah, Mrs Jones, winter draws* **on** (= it will be winter very soon)." *"Indeed, Vicar!"* See also DRAW ON.

draw *obj* ATTRACT /£drɔː, $drɑː/ *v* [T] *past simple* **drew** /druː/, *past part* **drawn** /£drɔːn, $drɑːn/ to attract (attention or interest) • *He was such a brilliant speaker that he always managed to draw a big crowd.* • *You're drawing a lot of curious looks in that hat.* • *She waved at him across the room to draw his* **attention** *but he wasn't looking in her direction.* • *Does he wear those ridiculous clothes to draw* **attention** *to himself?* • *Her eyes were immediately drawn* **to** *the tall blond man standing at the bar.* • *I felt drawn* **towards** *him from the moment I met him.*

draw /£drɔː, $drɑː/ *n* [C] • *We need someone at the event who'll be a* **big** *draw and attract the paying public.*

draw *obj* PULL /£drɔː, $drɑː/ *v* [T] *past simple* **drew** /druː/, *past part* **drawn** /£drɔːn, $drɑːn/ to pull or direct (something) in a particular direction • *He drew his coat tightly around his shoulders.* [T always + adv/prep] • *The crowd watched as the referee drew the player* **aside/to one side**/*(Br also)* **on one side** *and spoke to him.* [T always + adv/prep] • *Could I draw your* **attention to** *item number three on the agenda?* [T always + adv/prep] • *In her report she draws* **attention to** *the increasing incidence of cancer in the region.* [T always + adv/prep] • If you draw **the curtains**, you pull the curtains so that they are either close together or apart. [T] • If you draw **up** a chair, you put it near a particular place, often a table: *There's going to be another person for dinner – could you draw an extra chair up, please?* [M] • *(fig.) They tried to draw me* **into** (= include me in) *their argument but I refused.* [T always + adv/prep] • *(Br)* If you **draw a veil over** a particular subject, you intentionally do not speak about it because it is unpleasant and you do not want to think about it: *Yes, well I think we'll just draw a veil over what went on last night.*

draw *(obj)* CHOOSE /£drɔː, $drɑː/ *v past simple* **drew** /druː/, *past part* **drawn** /£drɔːn, $drɑːn/ to choose (a number, card, etc.) from several numbers, cards, etc. without first seeing it, in a competition. • *We're about to draw the winning card, ladies and gentlemen, so please look at your raffle tickets.* [T] • *Who's going to go first? Shall we draw* **(for it)**? [I] • *Real Madrid has drawn* (= will play) *Juventus in the football quarter finals.* [T] • *(infml)* If you **draw a blank** you fail to find something that you are looking for: *She had spent all morning looking for his address but had drawn a blank.*

draw /£drɔː, $drɑː/ *n* [C] • *She won a radio in the grand draw at the school fete.*

draw EQUAL /£drɔː, $drɑː/ *n* [C] a situation in which each team in a game has equal points and neither side wins • *Who won the chess? No one – the players* **agreed** *a draw.*

draw /£drɔː, $drɑː/ *v* [I] *past simple* **drew** /druː/, *past part* **drawn** /£drɔːn, $drɑːn/ • *Coventry drew 1-1 with Manchester United in the semi-finals.* • LP **Sports**

draw *obj* SHOW /£drɔː, $drɑː/ *v* [T] *past simple* **drew** /druː/, *past part* **drawn** /£drɔːn, $drɑːn/ to make or show (a comparison, a CONCLUSION or a DISTINCTION) in writing or speaking • *You can't really draw a* **comparison** *between the two cases – they're so entirely different.* • *I'd seen them together so often I drew the logical* **conclusion** *that they were husband and wife.* • *It's sometimes very difficult to draw a clear* **distinction** *between the meanings of different words.*

draw *obj* TAKE OUT /£drɔː, $drɑː/ *v* [T] *past simple* **drew** /druː/, *past part* **drawn** /£drɔːn, $drɑːn/ to remove (something) from somewhere • *Suddenly he drew a* **gun/knife** *and held it to my throat.* • *I'm just going to draw some* **money out**. [M] • You can draw **off** (= remove) a small amount of liquid from a larger amount esp. by letting it flow through a pipe: *She drew off a little of her home-made wine just to taste.* [M] • *I saw a man drawing* **water from** *a well.* • *He bit me so hard that it drew* **blood** (= caused me to bleed). • If you draw **a breath** you breathe in once: *She drew a deep breath, composed her features into a smile and walked into the room.* • If you **draw breath** you pause a moment to let the breathing become calmer and easier: *I had to stop my bike half way up the hill to draw breath.*

draw *(obj)* USE /£drɔː, $drɑː/ *v past simple* **drew** /druː/, *past part* **drawn** /£drɔːn, $drɑːn/ to use (something) as a supply or get (something) from a particular place • *In his later paintings he drew much of his* **inspiration** *from his travels in the Far East.* [T] • *Like most writers, she draws* **from/on/upon** *personal experience in her work.* [I] • *From time to time we tend to draw* **on** *his knowledge of the law.* [I] • *We can draw* **on** *company funds if we need more money for the project.* [I]

draw *obj* CAUSE /£drɔː, $drɑː/ *v* [T] *past simple* **drew** /druː/, *past part* **drawn** /£drɔːn, $drɑːn/ to cause (a sudden reaction) in people • *Her speech last night in the Senate drew an angry* **response**. • *Four times during the dance his performance drew a gasp of amazement* **from** *the audience.*

draw *obj* EARN /£drɔː, $drɑː/ *v* [T] *past simple* **drew** /druː/, *past part* **drawn** /£drɔːn, $drɑːn/ to earn (money) • *She draws a fairly good salary for someone so young.*

draw in *v adv* [I] (of days and nights) to become darker earlier • *The days/nights are beginning to draw in – winter will soon be with us.*

draw on *obj v prep* [T] to take in a breath of cigarette smoke while holding the cigarette to the mouth • *She drew on her cigarette and her green eyes narrowed.*

draw out *obj* LENGTHEN, **draw** *obj* **out** *v adv* [M] to cause (something) to last longer than is usual or really necessary • *The director drew the meeting out for another hour with a series of tedious questions.*

drawn–out /£ˌdrɔːn'aʊt, $ˌdrɑːn-/ *adj* • *This trouble with the unions has been a* **long** *drawn-out affair.*

draw out *obj* ENCOURAGE, **draw** *obj* **out** *v adv* [M] to help (someone) to express their thoughts and feelings more easily by making them feel less nervous • *Like all good interviewers he manages to draw people out of themselves.*

draw up *obj* PREPARE, **draw** *obj* **up** *v adv* [M] to prepare (usually something official) in writing • *We must draw up a contract/list/plan/proposal.* • *I've drawn up a list of candidates that I'd like to interview.*

draw *obj* **up** STRAIGHTEN *v prep* [T] to make (yourself) stand straight with the shoulders back, usually to try to seem bigger and more important • *Like a lot of short men, he tends to draw himself up to his full height in public.*

draw·back /£'drɔː·bæk, $'drɑː-/ *n* [C] a disadvantage or problem; the negative part of a situation • *It is possible that the advantages outweigh the drawbacks.* • *One of the drawbacks* **of** *living with someone is having to share a bathroom.* • *There's a major drawback* **to** *living in any capital city and that's the traffic.*

draw·bridge /£'drɔː·brɪdʒ, $'drɑː-/ *n* [C] a bridge that can be raised or lowered in order to protect a castle from attack or to allow big boats to go under it

draw·er /£'drɔːʳ, $'drɑː/ *n* [C] a box-shaped container without a top which is part of a piece of furniture. It slides in and out to open and close and is used for keeping things in. • *You'll find my address book* **in** *the second drawer down.* • *I keep my socks* **in** *the bottom drawer.* • *I don't like to go rummaging through other people's drawers.*

draw·ers /£drɔːz, $drɑːz/ *pl n dated* KNICKERS or UNDERPANTS

draw·ing room /£'drɔː·ɪŋ-, $'drɑː-/ *n* [C] *fml or dated* a comfortable room in a large house used for relaxing or for entertaining guests • *We had tea in their drawing room.*

drawl /£drɔːl, $drɑːl/ *n* [C] a slow way of speaking in which the vowel sounds are lengthened and words are not separated clearly • *a southern/Texan/mid-Atlantic drawl* • *She speaks* **in/with** *this affected lazy drawl.*

drawl *(obj)* /£drɔːl, $drɑːl/ *v* • *She had had too much to drink and was starting to drawl.* [I] • *"Hey, what's the rush? Slow down baby," he drawled.* [+ clause]

drawn DRAW /£drɔːn, $drɑːn/ *past participle of* DRAW

drawn TIRED /£drɔːn, $drɑːn/ *adj* (usually of the face) very tired and showing suffering • *Seeing her features pale and drawn, he put his arms around her.*

drawn–out /£ˌdrɔːn'aʊt, $ˌdrɑːn-/ *adj* See at DRAW OUT LENGTHEN

draw·string /£'drɔː·strɪŋ, $'drɑː-/ *n* [C] a cord or string which goes through an opening esp. in the top of a bag or the waist of a piece of clothing and can be pulled to fasten, tighten or loosen it

dray /dreɪ/ *n* [C] a large low carriage with four wheels which is pulled by horses • *a dray horse*

dread *obj* /dred/ *v* [T] to feel extremely anxious or unhappy about (something that is going to happen or might happen) • *He's dreading his driving test – he's sure he's going to fail.* • *I'm dreading having to ring her because I know she's going to be furious with me.* [+ v-*ing*] • *He dreads* **that** *if he tells her the truth she'll leave him.* [+ *that* clause] • **I dread to think** *what would happen if he was left to cope on his own.*

dread /dred/ *n* [U] • *She's got this dread* **of** *putting on weight.* • *The prospect of working full-time* **fills me with** *dread.* • **I live in** *dread* **of** *bumping into her in the street.*

dread·ed /'dred·ɪd/ *adj* [before n] *humorous* • *I've got my dreaded cousin coming to stay!* • *(Br and Aus infml)* The **dreaded lurgy** is a humorous way of speaking of any illness which is not very serious but is easily caught.

dread /dred/ *adj* [before n] *literary* • *The dread spectre of civil war looms over the country.*

dread·ful /'dred·fᵊl/ *adj* very bad, of very low quality, or shocking and very sad • *The food was bad and the service was dreadful.* • *I was beginning to think I'd made a dreadful mistake.* • *That was a truly dreadful film.* • *The news report was so dreadful that I just had to switch it off.* • *It's a dreadful* (= very great) *nuisance having to go into work this Saturday!*

dread·ful·ly /'dred·fᵊl·i/ *adv* • *She behaved dreadfully* (= extremely badly) – *there was no excuse for it.* • *He was dreadfully* (= extremely) *upset.* • *I'm dreadfully* (= extremely) *sorry – I really am.*

dread·locks /£'dred·lɒks, $-lɑːks/ *pl n* a hairstyle, esp. of RASTAFARIANS, in which long, tightly twisted lengths of hair hang down • PIC› **Hair**

dream SLEEP /driːm/ *n* [C] an imaginary event or group of events which you experience during sleep • **I had** *a very odd dream* **about** *you last night, Martin.* • **In** *my dreams I'm often performing on stage.* • *He said he'd been having some* **strange** *dreams recently.* • *For some reason, your mother often features* **in** *my dreams.* • *I have this recurring dream* **that** *I'm in public and I've got no clothes on.* [+ *that* clause] • You might be said to be **in a dream** while you are awake if you are not aware of what is happening around you because other thoughts are filling your mind: *I'm sorry, I didn't hear what you were saying – I was in a dream.*

dream *(obj)* /driːm/ *v past* **dreamed** /drempt/ or **dreamt** /drempt/ • *What did you dream* **about** *last night?* [I] • *I often dream* **about/of** *flying.* [I] • *I dreamed* **that** *I was having a baby last night.* [+ *that* clause] • *Did you say that you were going tonight or* **did I dream it** (= am I wrong)? • *I thought I'd bought some polish and it seems I haven't – I* **must have dreamt it.** • If someone says they would **not dream of doing** something, it means they certainly would not do it, often because they consider it to be morally wrong: *My father is very generous, but I wouldn't dream of actually asking him for money!* • *"Last night I dreamt I went to Mandalay again"* (beginning of the novel *Rebecca* by Daphne Du Maurier, 1938)

dream·i·ly /'driː·mɪ·li/ *adv* • If you say or do something dreamily, you do it as if you are not fully awake and are thinking of pleasant things: *"We had the most wonderful evening boating on the lake," she said dreamily.* ○ *She gazed dreamily out of the window.*

dream·less /'driːm·ləs/ *adj* • *I sank into a deep, dreamless sleep.*

dream·like /'driːm·laɪk/ *adj* • *There's a dreamlike* (= as if in a dream) *quality to the final stages of the film.*

dream·y /'driː·mi/ *adj* **-ier, -iest** *approving* • *The film opens with a dreamy* (= beautiful, as if imagined) *shot of a sunset.* • *She gets this dreamy expression on her face* (= looks as if she is not fully awake and is thinking of pleasant things) *when she talks about food.*

dream HOPE /driːm/ *n* [C] an event in the future that would fulfil all your hopes and give you great pleasure or satisfaction • *It's always been his dream to have flying lessons.* • *The first few months of their romance had been* **like a** *dream* (= perfect). • *He let me drive his new car last night – it goes* **like a** *dream* (= extremely well). • *Winning all that money was a dream* **come true** (= so good that they never imagined it would really happen). • *Win the house* **of** *your* **dreams** (= the best that you can imagine) *in our fantastic competition!* • If someone talks about a dream holiday/house/kitchen, they mean the holiday, etc. that they would choose if they had enough money: *My idea of a dream holiday is a desert island with absolutely nobody else around.* • *(disapproving)* If someone is said to be **(living) in a dream world** it means that their hopes and ideas are totally impractical and unrealistic. • *(Br)* A **dream ticket** is two politicians who represent different opinions in their party standing for election as leader and the next in charge, and so getting as much support as possible. • *"I have a dream"* (From a speech by the civil rights leader Martin Luther King, 1963)

dream /driːm/ *v* [I] *past* **dreamed** /drempt/ or **dreamt** /drempt/ • To dream **of/about** a desirable event or situation is to think about it while knowing that it is unlikely to happen: *I dream of one day working for myself and not having a boss.* ○ *When I was little I used to dream about having the money to buy all the sweets that I wanted.* • *"When I've made my money, of course, I'll spend six months of the year on holiday..."* **"Dream on,** (= It's very unlikely) *Dave!"* • *"I'm Dreaming of a White Christmas"* (title of a song written by Irving Berlin, 1942) • *"There are more things in heaven and earth, Horatio, / Than are dreamt of in your philosophy"* (Shakespeare, Hamlet 1.5)

dream·er /£'driː·məʳ, $-mɚ/ *n* [C] • A dreamer is a person who spends a lot of time thinking about or planning enjoyable events that are not likely to happen: *Johnny has always been a bit of a dreamer.*

dream up *obj*, **dream** *obj* **up** *v adv* [M] to invent (something very imaginative and usually silly) • *This is the latest ploy dreamt up by advertising companies to sell their new products.*

dream·boat /£'driːm·bəʊt, $-boʊt/ *n* [C] *dated* a sexually attractive, and usually young, person of the opposite sex • *Have you met Guy yet? Ooh, he's a real dreamboat!*

drear·y /£'drɪə·ri, $'drɪr·i/ *adj* **-ier, -iest** lacking interest and tending to cause a slight feeling of sadness •

Everywhere looked so grey and dreary in the rain. • *She had spent a dreary day in the office sorting out the accounts.*

drear·i·ly /£'drɪə·rə·li, $'drɪr·əl-/ *adv*

drear·i·ness /£'drɪə·rɪ·nəs, $'drɪr·ɪ-/ *n* [U]

dredge *obj* REMOVE /dredʒ/ *v* [T] to remove unwanted things from the bottom of (a river, lake, etc.) using a sucking or other device, or to search (an area of water) for something using this method • *When too much silt accumulates at the canal bottom, they have to dredge the canal.* • *The police are dredging the lake* **for** *his body.* • *They dredged* **up** (= brought to the surface) *the man's clothes but not his body.* [M] • If you dredge **up** something such as a memory or event, you remember it: *Seeing her son after all these years dredged up some painful memories for her.* [M]

dredg·er /£'dredʒ·əʳ, $-ɚ/, **dredge** *n* [C] • *A dredger is a boat or a device which is used to dredge rivers.*

dredge *obj* SCATTER /dredʒ/ *v* [T] to scatter flour, sugar, etc. on (food) • *Lightly dredge the cake* **with** *icing sugar.*

dregs /dregz/ *pl n* the solid bits that sink to the bottom of some liquids, such as wine or coffee, which are not usually drunk, or *(fig.)* a group of people in society whom you consider to be immoral and worthless • *In one swift go, she had drunk her coffee down* **to the** *dregs* (= finished it). • *(fig.) People tend to regard drug addicts as the dregs* **of society**.

drench *obj* /drentʃ/ *v* [T usually passive] to make (someone or something) extremely wet • *A thunderstorm had drenched us* **to the skin**.

drenched /drentʃt/ *adj* • *You're drenched! Why didn't you take an umbrella with you?* • *In the blazing Florida sun the athletes were soon drenched* **in/with** *sweat.*

dress PIECE OF CLOTHING /dres/ *n* [C] a piece of clothing for a woman which covers the top half of the body and some or all of the legs • *a long/short dress* • *a party/wedding dress* • *a sleeveless/strapless dress* • *The little black dress is the classic garment that should be in every woman's wardrobe.* • PIC› **Clothes** (CS) (PL) (RUS)

dress *(obj)* PUT ON CLOTHES /dres/ *v* to put clothes on (someone else, esp. a child, or yourself) • *My husband dresses the children while I make breakfast.* [T] • *She's only four but she can already dress* **herself**. [T] • When you talk about how someone dresses, you mean the type of clothes that they choose to wear: *I have to dress quite smartly for work.* [I] ○ *He always dresses fairly casually.* [I] • If you dress **for dinner**, you put on formal clothes for that meal: *It's the sort of hotel where you're expected to dress for dinner.* [I] • If you dress **down** for an occasion, you intentionally wear informal clothes of the type that will not attract attention: *She always made a point of dressing down on her first date with a man.* [I] • To dress **up** is to put on formal clothes for a special occasion: *You don't need to dress up just to go to the pub – jeans and a T-shirt will do.* [I] ○ *I don't want to go to their wedding because I hate having to dress up.* [I] • To dress **up** is also to put on clothes that are noticeably different from your usual ones, in order to change your appearance: *Small children usually love dressing up* **in** *their mothers' clothes.* [I] • If you **dress up** something/**dress** something **up**, you add something to it in order to make it seem more interesting or pleasing than it really is: *The pizza I bought from the shop didn't look very tasty, so I thought I'd dress it up* **with** *a few extra tomatoes and olives.* • A **dressing gown** (*esp. Am* **bathrobe**) is a long loose piece of clothing, like a coat, which you wear informally inside the house, esp. over the clothes that you wear in bed. • A **dressing room** is a room, esp. in a theatre, in which actors put on clothes and make-up. • A **dressing table** is a small table with a vertical mirror fixed to the top of it, which is usually found in a bedroom, and at which a person can sit to brush their hair, put on make-up, etc. • Most people use 'get dressed' rather than dress. • LP› **Dressing and undressing, Reflexive pronouns and verbs** PIC› **Beds and bedroom** (CS) (PL) (RUS)

dress /dres/ *adj* [before n; not gradable] • Dress is used esp. of men's suits or shirts to refer to the type of clothes that are worn at formal occasions: *a white dress shirt and bow tie*

dress /dres/ *n* [U] • Dress can be used, esp. in combination, to refer to clothes of a particular type, esp. those worn in particular situations: *The young dancers were wearing traditional dress.* ○ *The queen, in full ceremonial dress, presided over the ceremony.* ○ *"You must forgive my casual dress," he apologized.* ○ *Do we have to wear* **formal** *dress for this dinner we're going to on Saturday?* • A **dress code** is an accepted way of dressing at a particular occasion or in a particular social group: *Most evenings there's a party and the dress code is rigid – black tie.* • A **dress rehearsal** is the last time a play, opera, dance, etc. is practised before the real performance and is performed with the clothes, stage and lighting exactly as they will be for the real performance. • **Dress sense** is the ability to dress well in attractive combinations of clothes that suit you: *Julia's never had any dress sense.*

dressed /drest/ *adj* [after v; not gradable] • *Could you answer the door, please – I'm not dressed yet.* • *She'll be down in a moment – she's just* **getting** *dressed.* • *I* **got** *dressed in a hurry this morning and put my jumper on inside-out.* • *Was he the one who was dressed* **in** *that awful yellowy-brown suit?* • *We all* **got** *dressed* **up** (= put on formal clothes) *for the wedding.* • *The room was full of* **smartly/well-***dressed women* (= women wearing stylish clothes). • *(esp. humorous)* Someone who is **dressed to kill** is intentionally wearing clothes that attract sexual attention and admiration. • *"When you're All Dressed Up and Nowhere to Go"* (title of a song written by B.H.Burt, 1916)

dres·sy /'dres·i/ *adj* **-ier, -iest** • Clothes can be described as dressy if they are suitable for formal occasions: *I think it's going to be a rather smart wedding so I need something a bit dressy for it.* • Formal occasions might also be described as dressy if the people who are present wear very formal clothes: *a dressy affair/occasion*

dress·er /£'dres·əʳ, $-ɚ/ *n* [C] • Dresser is used in phrases which describe the type of clothes that someone wears: *Diana was always a very stylish dresser.* ○ *He's a very* **snappy** (= stylish and modern) *dresser.* • A dresser is also a person who works in the theatre or in films, helping the actors to put on their clothes and making certain that the clothes are clean. • See also DRESSER.

dress *obj* SALAD /dres/ *v* [T] to add a liquid, esp. a mixture of oil and vinegar, to a salad for additional flavour • *Dress the salad using an oil and vinegar base together with the herbs of your choosing.* • To dress a CRAB (= sea creature covered by a shell) is to prepare it so it can be eaten. • (CS) (PL) (RUS)

dressed /drest/ *adj* [not gradable] • *Is the salad dressed (with anything)?* • **Dressed crab** is a dish in which the CRAB meat has been specially arranged within the shell.

dress·ing /'dres·ɪŋ/ *n* • Dressing is a liquid mixture, often containing oil, vinegar and herbs, which is added to food, esp. salads, to give flavour: *There's too much French/garlic dressing on this salad.* [U] ○ *I'll make a quick oil and vinegar dressing.* [C]

dress *obj* INJURY /dres/ *v* [T] to treat (an injury) by cleaning it and putting medicine or a protective covering on it • *If you go to the hospital, they'll dress your arm properly for you.* • (CS) (PL) (RUS)

dress·ing /'dres·ɪŋ/ *n* [C] • A dressing is a protective covering which is put on an injury, esp. in which the skin has been cut.

dress *obj* SHOP WINDOW /dres/ *v* [T] to decorate (a shop window) usually with an arrangement of the shop's goods • *They're dressing Selfridges' windows for Christmas.* • (CS) (PL) (RUS)

dres·sage /£'dres·ɑːʒ, $-'-/ *n* [U] the performance by a well-trained horse of special carefully controlled movements as directed by the rider • *a dressage competition*

dress cir·cle *n* [C] the first level of seats above the main floor in a theatre • *We sat* **in** *the dress circle for the ballet.*

dress·er /£'dres·əʳ, $-ɚ/ *n* [C] a large tall piece of furniture with cupboards below and shelves on the top half, or *(Am)* a piece of bedroom furniture with drawers, usually with a mirror on top, used esp. for keeping clothes in • *a kitchen dresser* • See also **dresser** at DRESS PUT ON CLOTHES.

dress·ing–down /ˌdres·ɪŋ'daʊn/ *n* [U] *dated* a spoken attack on someone in which you criticize them severely • *She* **gave** *me a dressing-down for getting there late.*

dress·mak·er /£'dresˌmeɪ·kəʳ, $-kɚ/ *n* [C] someone who makes women's clothes, esp. as a job • *My grandmother was a dressmaker.*

dress·mak·ing /'dresˌmeɪ·kɪŋ/ *n* [U] • *My aunt does a lot of dressmaking.* • *He trained as a tailor, and eventually opened dressmaking and tailoring shops of his own.*

dres·sy /'dres·i/ *adj* See at DRESS PUT ON CLOTHES

drew /druː/ *past simple of* DRAW

drib·ble *(obj)* FLOW SLOWLY /'drɪb·l̩/ *v* to (cause a liquid to) flow very slowly in small amounts • *My three-month-old nephew had dribbled all over my shoulder.* [I] • *She watched, disgusted, as a line of melted butter dribbled* **down** *his chin.*

DRESSING AND UNDRESSING

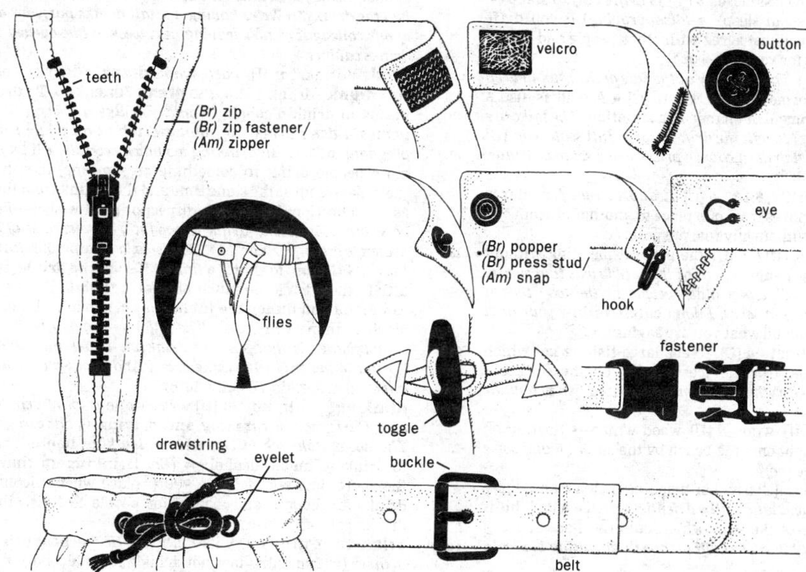

• fastening and unfastening clothes and fasteners

- Generally you **do up** or **fasten** the fasteners shown above, and also articles of clothing with fasteners: *Help me do up this top button, I can't reach it.* • *I must be getting fat – I can hardly do these trousers up.* (The verbs with the opposite meaning are **undo** and **unfasten**.)
- There are some verbs meaning fasten or close which are connected with particular fasteners (notice that 'up' can appear before or after the object): *He* **buttoned** *his shirt* **(up)**. • *I can't* **zip up** *my top, the zip's stuck.* • *You'd better* **zip** *that bag* **shut** *or something will fall out.* • **Tie (up)** *your shoelaces/laces/(Am also) shoestrings, dear, they've come undone again.* (The verbs with the opposite meaning are **unbutton, unzip**, and **untie**.)
- These verbs are used intransitively to describe how clothes fasten: *This dress* **does up** *at the back.* • *Both the pockets* **zip up/closed**. • *My sleeping bag* **ties** *at the neck.*

• verbs of dressing and undressing

get dressed	*I tore my shirt while I was getting dressed this morning.*
get changed	*Have I got time to get changed before the party?*
change	*You're soaking wet! Go and change right away.*
dress*	*She woke up early, dressed and went out.*
put on	*"Goodbye," she said, putting on her coat.*
take off	*Those shoes don't go with* (= match) *your dress: take them off.*
try on	You try on clothes to see if they are suitable: *Try this sweater on and see if it suits you.* • *I'd like to try on this pair of jeans, please.*

* If you use a reflexive pronoun, as in 'she dressed *herself*', this suggests that the person had some difficulty in dressing: *My youngest son can dress himself, but I have to help him with his shoes.*

• verbs of state

wear	*Do you like the trousers I'm wearing today?* • *He never wears green.*
have on	*Jane had on a red blouse and a black skirt.*
be dressed in	*He was dressed in a grey suit.* • *Everyone was dressed in black.*
dress	*She dresses expensively/well/badly/casually/formally.*

[I] • *The water was barely dribbling* **out of** *the tap and it took five minutes to fill the bucket.* [I] • *Dribble the remaining olive oil over the tomatoes.* [T]

drib·ble /ˈdrɪb·l̩/ *n* • *I'd been holding the baby and there was a patch of dribble on my shoulder.* [U] • *I wiped a dribble of saliva off his chin with a handkerchief.* [C]

drib·ble *(obj)* MOVE BALL /ˈdrɪb·l̩/ *v* (in football or HOCKEY) to move (a ball) along the ground with repeated small kicks or hits, or (in BASKETBALL) to move a ball by repeatedly hitting it against the floor with your hand • *She dribbled the ball to the edge of the pitch.* [T] • *He is mobile and quick and has this exciting ability to dribble past defenders.* [I]

drib·ble /ˈdrɪb·l̩/ *n* [C] • *Brinkworth's attempted dribble through the Milan defence was stopped by Ponti's tackle.*

drib·bler /£ˈdrɪb·l̩.əʳ, £ˈ-ləʳ, $-ɚ/ *n* [C] • *He's a good dribbler.*

drib·bling /ˈdrɪb·l̩.ɪŋ, ˈ-lɪŋ/ *n* [U] • *That was a lovely bit of dribbling by Neil Eaves.* • *I've got to practise my dribbling.*

dribs /drɪbz/ *pl n* **in dribs and drabs** in small amounts, a few at a time • *The hostages have been released in dribs and drabs.* • *The crowd trickled into the park in dribs and drabs.*

dried /draɪd/ *past simple and past participle of* DRY NOT WET

dri·er /£ˈdraɪ·əʳ, $-ɚ/ *comparative of* DRY • See also **dryer** at DRY NOT WET.

dries /draɪz/ *pres simple of* DRY NOT WET

dri·est /ˈdraɪ·əst/ *superlative of* DRY

drift MOVE /drɪft/ *v* [I] to move slowly, esp. as a result of outside forces, with no control over direction • *Early that morning, a mist drifted* **in** *from the sea.* • *She watched the balloons as they drifted* **up** *into the sky.* • *Snow had drifted* (= been piled by the wind) **against** *the garage door.* • *After the meeting, people drifted* **away** *in twos and threes.* • *We rested the oars against the side of the boat and let ourselves drift* **downstream**. • *(fig.) The talk drifted* **aimlessly** *from one subject to another.* • *(fig.) There was a time when we *were very close but over the years we've just drifted* **apart** (= gradually become less close). • *(fig.) I drifted* **off to sleep** (= gradually started to sleep). • *(disapproving)* If you **drift with the tide**, you just agree with other people and do not make decisions for yourself. • (NL)

drift /drɪft/ *n* • *The snow lay at the side of the road in deep drifts* (= piles formed by the wind). [C] • A drift is also a general development or change in a situation: *The talks are the latest attempt to halt the drift towards full-scale war.* [U] ○ *The downward drift in copper prices looks set to continue.* [U]

drift·er /£'drɪf·təʳ, $-tɚ/ *n* [C] *disapproving* • A drifter is someone who moves from one place to another or from one job to another without any real purpose.

drift [MEANING] /drɪft/ *n* [U] the general meaning without the details • *The* **general** *drift* **of** *the article was that society doesn't value and respect older people in the way that it should.* • *(infml) I'm sorry, I don't* **catch/follow** *your drift* (= I don't understand what you are saying). • (NL)

drift·net /'drɪft·net/ *n* [C] a very large fishing net which hangs in the sea from devices floating on the surface • *Driftnets catch everything from medium-sized fish to aquatic mammals.*

drift·wood /'drɪft·wʊd/ *n* [U] wood which is floating on the sea or brought onto the beach by the sea • *I found some driftwood on the shore.*

drill [TOOL] /drɪl/ *n* [C] a tool or machine which makes holes • *an electric/pneumatic drill* • *a dentist's drill* • A drill **bit** is the sharp part of the drill which cuts the hole: *A set of removable drill bits* ○ *The drill bit has three cutting blades.* • [PIC] **Tools**

drill *(obj)* /drɪl/ *v* • *Drill three holes in the wall for the screws.* [T] • *They are going to drill* **for** *oil nearby.* [I]

drill [REGULAR ACTIVITY] /drɪl/ *n* [C] an activity which practises a particular skill and involves repetition of the same thing several times, esp. a military exercise intended to train soldiers in the use of weapons • *In some of these centres, army-style drills are still used on the young offenders to instil a sense of discipline.* • *We used to do a lot of spelling drills when I was at school.* • *"Come on, Braithwaite," our drill sergeant would shout, "work harder!"*

drill *(obj)* /drɪl/ *v* • *We watched the soldiers drilling* (= practising movements, marching, etc.) [I] • *The officer drilled the soldiers.* [T] • *(fig.) He drilled the children* **in** (= repeatedly told them) *what they should say.* [T] • *(fig.) We had it drilled* **into** *us* (= We were told repeatedly) *at an early age that we should always say 'please' and 'thank you'.* [T]

dri·ly /'draɪ·li/ *adv* See at DRY [BORING]

drink [LIQUID] /drɪŋk/ *n* (an amount of) liquid which is taken into the body through the mouth • *Would you like a drink* **of** *water/tea/juice?* [C] • *They'd had no food or drink for two days.* [U] • A **drinks machine** is a machine which sells drinks.

drink *(obj)* /drɪŋk/ *v past simple* **drank** /dræŋk/, *past part* **drunk** /drʌŋk/, *Am also* **drank** /dræŋk/ • *He drank three glasses of water.* [T] • *The animals come down to the waterhole to drink.* [I] • *Sit down and drink your tea.* [T] • *Drink* **up** (= Finish drinking). *It's time to go.* [I] • *(fig.) These plants just drink* (= use a lot of) *water.* [T] • *(fig.) They drank* **in** (= listened attentively to) *the words of their leader.* [T]

drink·ab·le /'drɪŋ·kə·bl̩/ *adj* • *Is the water drinkable* (= safe or suitable for drinking)? • *"What's the wine like?" "Oh, it's nice – very drinkable* (= pleasant to drink)."

drink·ing /'drɪŋ·kɪŋ/ *n* [U] • *This water is not for drinking.* [U] • **Drinking water** is water that is suitable for drinking. • A **drinking fountain** *(Am usually* **water fountain**, *Aus also* **bubbler**) *is a device, usually in a public place, which supplies water for drinking.*

drink·er /£'drɪŋ·kəʳ, $-kɚ/ *n* [C] • *Drinkers* **of** *tea may be interested to know that an interesting new blend is now on the market.* • Drinker is often used as a combining form: *I'm a very keen coffee-drinker.* ○ *I'm not much of a milk-drinker.*

drink [ALCOHOL] /drɪŋk/ *n* alcoholic liquid • *We've run out of drink.* [U] • *Drink is a problem amongst some teenagers.* [U] • *I do like a drink occasionally.* [C] • *Have we got time for a quick drink?* [C] • *(dated)* If someone **takes to drink**, they start drinking alcohol frequently, often because of a personal problem: *He took to drink after his wife left him.* • *(Br and Aus) The authorities are campaigning against* **drink-driving** *(Am* **drunk-driving***)* (= driving after drinking alcohol). • *(Br and Aus)* If someone has a **drink problem** *(Am and Aus* **drinking problem**), they regularly drink too much alcohol. • [LP] **Phrases and customs**

drinks /drɪŋks/ *pl n* • Drinks usually means alcoholic drinks: *Come for drinks on Saturday.* ○ *Whose turn is it to buy the drinks?* ○ *We're having a small drinks party for one of our colleagues who's leaving next week.* ○ *She opened the drinks cabinet.*

drink /drɪŋk/ *v* [I] *past simple* **drank** /dræŋk/, *past part* **drunk** /drʌŋk/, *Am also* **drank** /dræŋk/ • To drink means to drink alcohol: *"Would you like a sherry?" "No thanks, I don't drink."* ○ *I didn't drink at all while I was pregnant.* ○ *I've been drinking too much recently.* • If two or more people drink **to** something or someone, they hold their glasses up at the same time and then drink from them as a celebration, or to show respect or good wishes: *"Let's raise our glasses and drink* **to** *the future/the success of the project/absent friends!"* ○ *"Here's to a prosperous future then." "I'll drink to* **that**!" • *(infml)* If someone **drinks like a fish**, they drink too much alcohol. • *(infml)* If someone can **drink** you **under the table**, they can drink a lot more alcohol than you can: *The funny thing about my grandmother is that she can drink me under the table.* • *"Drink to me only with thine eyes / And I will pledge with mine"* (Ben Jonson *To Celia*, 1616)

drink·ing /'drɪŋ·kɪŋ/ *n* [U] • *I've* **done** *a lot of drinking over Christmas.* • *Drinking* **and driving** *is dangerous.* • *The doctor told me to change my drinking* **habits** (= not to drink so much alcohol). • *(Br)* **Drinking-up time** is the short time allowed in a PUB (= place where alcoholic drinks are bought and drunk) for people to finish their drinks before it closes.

drink·er /£'drɪŋ·kəʳ, $-kɚ/ *n* [C] • *He's a* **heavy/light** *drinker* (= He drinks/does not drink a lot of alcohol). • *I'm not much of a drinker* (= I don't drink much alcohol). • *20% of adults describe themselves as moderate drinkers.*

drip *(obj)* [LIQUID] /drɪp/ *v* **-pp-** to fall or let (liquid) fall in drops • *Water dripped* **(down)** *from the umbrella* **onto** *his shoulder.* [I] • *The car dripped oil* **on** *the tarmac.* [T] • *Can you hear a tap dripping?* [I] • *Blood was dripping from a cut above his eye.* [I] • To **drip-dry** a washed piece of clothing is to dry it by hanging it up for the water to run out of it, without the need for IRONING (= making flat): *If I were you, I'd hang that sweater on the line and let it drip-dry.* [I]

drip /drɪp/ *n* • *All I could hear was* **the** *drip(-drip) of the rain from the roof.* [U] • *The drips were being collected in a bucket.* [C] • *(medical)* A drip is a method of slowly giving someone liquid medicine or food through a tube into the body, or a piece of equipment for doing this. [C] • [PIC] **Medical equipment**

drip·ping /'drɪp·ɪŋ/ *adj, adv* [not gradable] • *We've got a dripping tap in the bathroom.* • *It's so hot outside – I'm absolutely dripping* **(wet)**. • *Jim had just been on a run and was standing in the kitchen, dripping* **with** *sweat.* • *(fig. humorous) She was* **dripping with** (= wearing a lot of) *gold/jewels.*

drip [PERSON] /drɪp/ *n* [C] *infml* a boring person without a strong character • *He's pleasant enough, but he's such a drip!*

drip·py /'drɪp·i/ *adj* **-ier, -iest** *infml* • *Where's that drippy brother of yours?*

drip·ping /'drɪp·ɪŋ/ *n* [U], *Am usually* **drip·pings** /'drɪp·ɪŋz/ *pl n* the fat that has come out of meat during cooking • *beef dripping*

drive *(obj)* [USE VEHICLE] /draɪv/ *v past simple* **drove** /£drəʊv, $droʊv/, *past part* **driven** /'drɪv·ᵊn/ to move or travel on land in a motor vehicle, esp. as the person controlling the vehicle's movement • *I learnt to drive when I was seventeen.* [I] • *"Are you going by train?" "No, I'm driving."* [I] • *She drives a red sports car.* [T] • *They're driving to Scotland on Tuesday.* [I] • *We saw their car outside the house and drove* **on/past/away**. [I] • *I got in the car and drove* **off**. [I] • *Someone drove* **into** *the back of his car yesterday.* [I] • *I drove my daughter to school.* [T] • *He drove the van* **at** *the gate* (= in order to hit it). [T] • *He's driving that bus much too fast!* [T] • *(Br)* If someone **drives a coach and horses through** an argument, they destroy it completely. • *(esp. Am and Aus)* A **drive-in** bank, cinema or restaurant etc. is one that you can use or visit while staying seated in your car. • Compare RIDE. • [LP] **Driving**

drive /draɪv/ *n* • *It's a long drive from Glasgow to London.* [C] • *Shall we* **go for a** *drive* **(in** *my new car) this afternoon?* [C] • *I thought we might* **take** *your mother* **out** *for a drive this afternoon.* [C] • *You'll need a car with* **left-hand/right-hand** *drive* (= in which the driver sits in the seat on the left/right). [U] • A drive (also **driveway**) is also a track for vehicles which leads to a house: *I parked* **in** *the drive.* [C] •

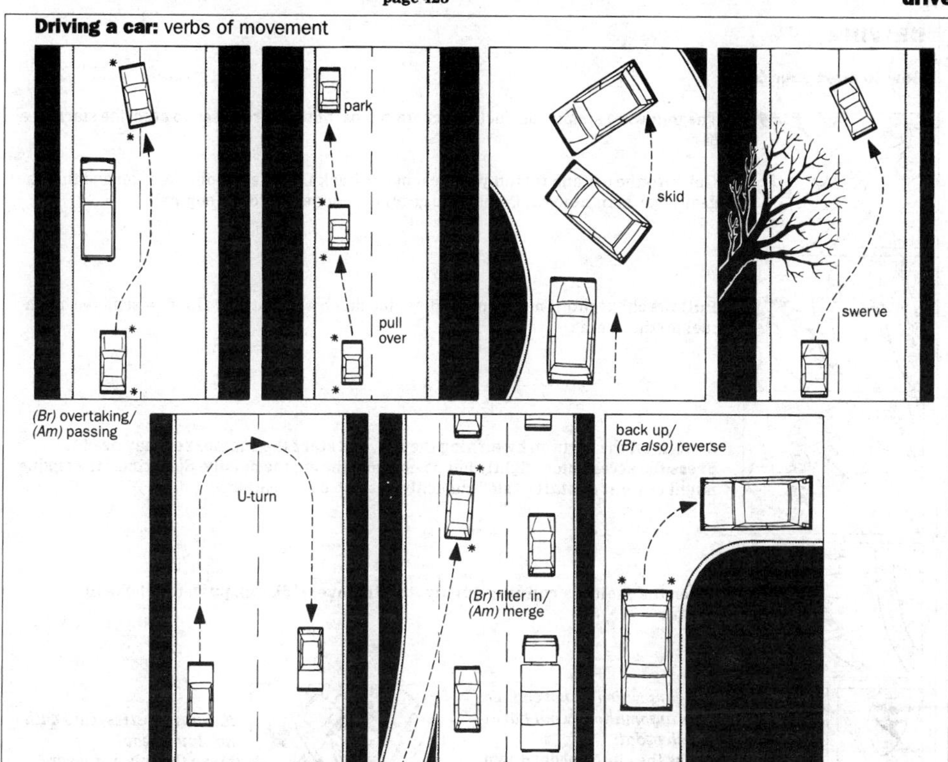

The word Drive is sometimes used in the name of a road, esp. one containing houses: *12, Cotswold Drive* • PIC〉 **Accommodation**

-driv·en /-ˌdrɪv·ən/ *combining form* • *He arrived every morning by* **chauffeur**-*driven car.*

driv·er /£'draɪ·vər, $-vɚ/ *n* [C] • *a bus/lorry/taxi driver* • *The driver of the van was killed in the accident.* • *In my experience, women make better drivers than men.* • (KOR)

driv·ing /'draɪ·vɪŋ/ *n* [U] • *a driving lesson/school/test* • *She has to* **do** *a lot of driving in her job.* • *Devall, a teacher from Surrey, admitted causing death by reckless driving.* • *(Br)* A **driving licence** (*Am* **driver's license**, *Aus* **driver's licence**) is (a document showing) official permission for someone to drive a car, received after passing a driving test: *Have you got a driving licence?* • *(Br)* Someone who is **in the driving seat** (*Am and Aus* **in the driver's seat**) is in charge or in control of a situation. • *(Am law)* If you are **driving under the influence** or **driving while intoxicated** (*abbreviation* **DWI**), you are operating a motor vehicle after having drunk more alcohol than you are legally allowed to.

drive *obj* FORCE /draɪv/ *v* [T] *past simple* **drove** /£drəʊv, $droʊv/, *past part* **driven** /'drɪv·ən/ to force (someone or something) to go somewhere or do something, or to force someone or something into an often unpleasant state • *The dog had driven the sheep into one corner of the field.* • *The rain was driven against the windows by the wind.* • *By the end of the year, most of the occupying troops had been driven from the city.* • *For the second time in ten years, the government has driven the economy into deep and damaging recession.* • *A succession of scandals eventually drove the minister out of office.* • *A post had been driven* (= hit hard) *into the ground near the tree.* • *In the end, it was the arguments that drove her* **to** *leave home.* [+ obj + *to* infinitive] • *In the course of history, love has driven men and women* **to** *strange extremes.* • *According to her biographer it was her husband's infidelity that drove Durante* **to** *suicide.* • *(humorous) These children will* **drive** *me* **to drink** (= They cause me extreme anxiety)*!* • *Of course, banning boxing would simply drive the sport underground* (= cause it to be done illegally). [+ obj + adj] • *(infml)* If something **drives** you **mad/crazy/insane**, it makes you extremely annoyed: *My mother-in-law has been staying with us this past week and she's driving me insane!* ○ *I wish you wouldn't leave your dirty clothes all over the floor – it's driving me mad!* • *(infml approving)* Something might also be said to **drive** you **wild** if it causes you to feel very excited, esp. sexually: *When he runs his fingers through my hair, it drives me wild!* ○ *The smell of that fish is driving the dog wild* (= is making the dog very excited). • *(infml)* If someone **drives a hard bargain**, they expect a lot in exchange for what they pay or do: *You want £2000 for that old car? You certainly drive a hard bargain!* • *(infml) The speaker really* **drove** *his* **message/point home** (= forced people to hear his message/point), *repeating his main point several times.* • To **drive a wedge** between two people or two groups means to damage the good relationship that they have: *It would be silly to let things which have happened in the past drive a wedge* **between** *us now.*

drive *obj* PROVIDE POWER /draɪv/ *v* [T] *past simple* **drove** /£drəʊv, $droʊv/, *past part* **driven** /'drɪv·ən/ to provide the power to keep a (machine) moving or to make something happen • *The engine drives the wheels.* • If you drive a movable object, for example a ball, you hit it hard so that it travels a long way: *Dowell drove the ball across the pitch with typical accuracy.* ○ *Slater drove the ball* **down** *the fairway.* • The **drive shaft** in a vehicle is a rod that spins round and takes the power from the engine to the wheels.

drive /draɪv/ *n* • Drive is a strong feeling which makes you want to do something: *He has the drive* **to** *succeed.* [U + *to* infinitive] ○ *Later on in life the* **sex** *drive tends to diminish.* [U] • *(approving)* Someone who has drive has good ideas and acts energetically to achieve them. [U] • In sport, a drive is a powerful hit which sends the ball a long way. [C]

driv·en /'drɪv·ən/ *adj* • You might describe someone as driven if they are so determined to achieve something or be successful that all their behaviour is directed towards this aim: *Like most of the lawyers that I know, Rachel is driven.*

-driv·en /-ˌdrɪv·ən/ *combining form* • *They have stopped making small, single-engined, propeller-driven aircraft.* • *The new ships, propelled by gas turbines, require less maintenance than older, steam-driven ones.* • *His first car – one of the earliest petrol-driven vehicles – was completed in 1885.* • *The fact remains that there are some public services that cannot be entirely* **market**-*driven* (= controlled by economic forces).

driv·er /£'draɪ·vər, $-vɚ/ *n* [C] • In golf, a driver is a type of CLUB (= long thin stick) which has a wooden head and is used to hit a ball placed on a TEE. • PIC〉 **Sports**

DRIVING

How to start your car

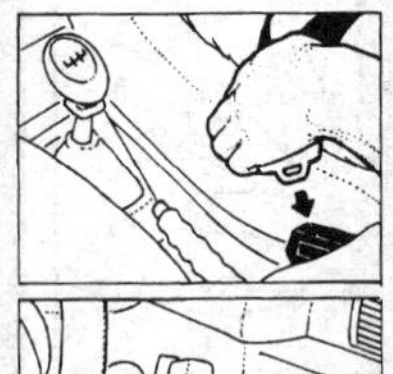

The following simple instructions contain most of the words used to describe starting a car.

Get into the car and **fasten** your seat belt. **Check** that the handbrake is on and that the gear lever is **in neutral** (= with the gears not connected to the engine).

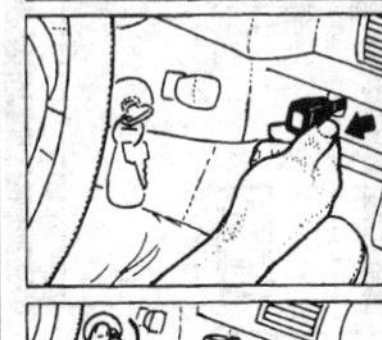

Pull the choke **out** if necessary, but not too much – or you may **flood** (= send too much fuel to) the engine.

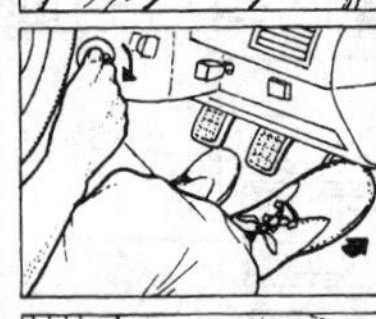

Switch on the ignition by turning the key, and **start** the engine. You may need to **press** the accelerator slightly but do not **race** the engine noisily. Sometimes the engine might **cut out or stall** (= stop suddenly), esp. in cold weather.

When the engine is **running** quietly (**ticking over/idling**), **push** the choke **in**.

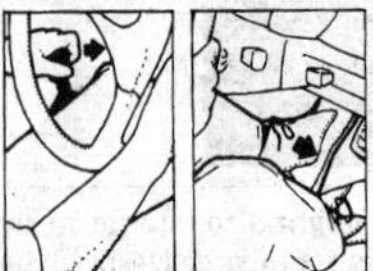

For cars which do not change gear automatically but have a clutch pedal:
Press the clutch pedal **down** and **change** from neutral **into** first gear (**put** the car **in gear**).

*For **automatics**, cars with no clutch pedal:*
Move the selector lever from neutral into drive.

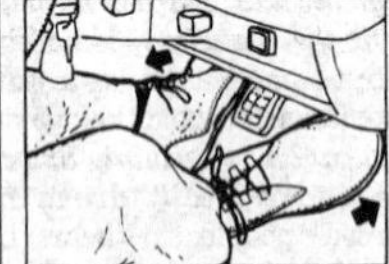

Let the clutch **up** (by **easing** your foot **off** the pedal) until the engine speed drops and press the accelerator down slightly.

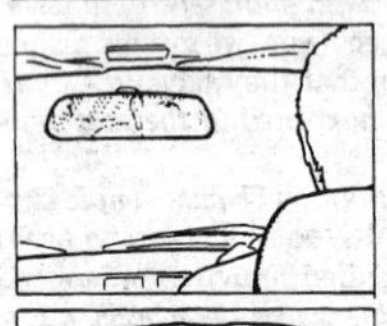

Use your mirrors or **look over your shoulder** (= look behind you) to check that you are **clear** to **move off** (= safe to start to move).

Use your indicators/**Give a signal/Indicate** if you need to **pull out into** (= move nearer the middle of) the road.

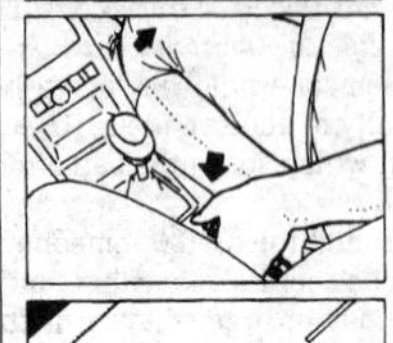

[*Non-automatics only:* **Engage** the clutch (**let** the clutch **out**) a little more.]
Release the handbrake/**Take** the handbrake **off**. The car will move forward.

As you **drive off / away**, you should **pull away from** the side of the road and **steer** (= direct the car) **into** the middle of the correct lane of the road.

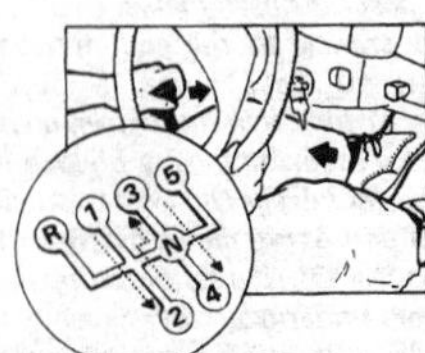

Non-automatics only: (Br) **Change up**/*(Am)* **shift** into higher gears as the car **accelerates**.

driv·ing /ˈdraɪ·vɪŋ/ *adj* [before n] • *Driving* (=Fast and heavy) *rain/snow brought more problems on the roads last night.* • *Driving* (=Powerful) **ambition** *is what most great leaders have in common.* • The **driving force** behind something is the person or thing which has the greatest effect on what happens: *He was the driving force* **behind** *the planning and the building of the theatre.* ○ *As with so many areas of policy, pragmatism not principle is now the driving force.*

drive [PLANNED EFFORT] /draɪv/ *n* [C] a planned effort to achieve something • *I'm meant to be* **on** *an* **economy** *drive at the moment so I'm trying not to spend too much.* • *The latest promotional material is all part of a recruitment drive intended to increase the party's falling numbers.*

drive at *obj v prep* [T usually in negatives] *infml* to try to explain or say something • *I'm sorry, I don't see* **what** *you're driving at.* • *I really don't understand the point she's driving at.*

driv·el /ˈdrɪv·əl/ *n* [U] something written or said which is completely worthless; nonsense • *You don't believe the drivel you read in the papers, do you?* • *You're* **talking** *drivel as usual!* • *Most of what he said was absolute drivel.*

driv·ell·ing /ˈdrɪv·əl·ɪŋ/ *adj* [not gradable] • *Who was that drivelling* **idiot** *on the radio this morning?*

driz·zle [RAIN] /ˈdrɪz·l̩/ *n* [U] rain in very small light drops • *The south will be cloudy with outbreaks of rain and drizzle.*

driz·zle /ˈdrɪz·l̩/ *v* [I] • **It's** *been drizzling all day.*

driz·zly /ˈdrɪz·li/ *adj* • *It was a grey drizzly afternoon.*

driz·zle *obj* [POUR] /ˈdrɪz·l̩/ *v* [T] to pour (liquid, esp. food) in a thin line • *Drizzle any remaining olive oil over the aubergines and grill for five minutes.*

driz·zle /ˈdrɪz·l̩/ *n* [C] • *Add a little water, a touch of lemon juice and finish with a drizzle of olive oil.*

droll /£drəʊl, $droʊl/ *adj* **-er, -est** amusing, esp. in an unusual way • *a droll remark/expression/person*

drol·ly /£ˈdrəʊ·li, $ˈdroʊ·li/ *adv*

drom·e·da·ry /£ˈdrɒm·ə·dər·i, $ˈdrɑː·mə·der-/ *n* [C] a CAMEL (=a large animal that lives in the desert) with one HUMP (=lump) on its back

drone [NOISE] /£drəʊn, $droʊn/ *n* [U] a low continuous noise which does not change its note • *Outside the tent I could hear* **the** *constant drone* **of** *flies.* • **The** *drone* **of** *his voice made me feel sleepy.* • *The loudspeaker gave out orders in a disembodied drone.* • A drone is also a continuous note played by a musical instrument, over which a tune is played: *The bagpipes started up a drone, then began to play a tune over the top of it.*

drone /£drəʊn, $droʊn/ *v* [I] • *Bagpipes droned in the background.* • *(fig. disapproving) He was droning* **on (and on)** (=talking in a boring way) *about house prices.*

drone [BEE] /£drəʊn, $droʊn/ *n* [C] a male bee whose only purpose is to MATE (=have sex) with the **queen bee** (=the large female that produces eggs)

drool /druːl/ *v* [I] to produce too much liquid in the mouth so that it flows out, or *(fig.)* to show extreme and sometimes foolish pleasure • *She brought with her an enormous dog that lay drooling on the mat.* • *(fig.) Roz and I sat by the swimming pool, drooling* **over** *all the gorgeous young men.* • *(fig.) I left Sara in the shop drooling* **over** *a green silk dress.* • *(fig.) I can sit for hours, drooling* **over** *recipes for rich chocolate cakes and desserts.*

droop /druːp/ *v* [I] to bend or hang down heavily • *The flowers were drooping in the heat.* • *I can see you're tired because your eyelids have started to droop.* • *I always worry that if I don't wear a bra my breasts will start to droop.* • *(fig.) My* **spirits** *droop* (=I start to feel unhappy) *at the prospect of work on Monday.*

droop·ing /ˈdruː·pɪŋ/ *adj* [not gradable] • *Blood-red flowers hung down in heavy, drooping clusters.* • *We tied the boat under the drooping branches of the willow tree.*

droop·y /ˈdruː·pi/ *adj* **-ier, -iest** *infml* • *He had a long droopy* **moustache.**

drop *(obj)* [FALL] /£drɒp, $drɑːp/ *v* **-pp-** to fall intentionally or unintentionally or to let (something) fall • *She dropped the tray with a crash.* [T] • *The flag dropped and the race started.* [I] • *The book dropped* **from/off** *the shelf.* [I] • *Warning leaflets were dropped on the town.* [T] • *The parachutists dropped* (=jumped down) *one by one* **from** *the plane.* [I] • To drop **behind/back/away** is to get further behind or away from something or someone: *The runners kept together for a while and then a few started to drop back.* [I] ○ *She dropped behind in her schoolwork because she was ill for several weeks.* [I] • *(infml)* If you drop someone or something **(off)** somewhere you take them to a particular place, usually by car: Shall I drop you (off) at the station? [T/M] ○ *Will you be able to drop off my case for me?* [M] • *(infml)* To drop **(with exhaustion/tiredness)** is to be so tired that you cannot continue: *After two hours' gardening, she was nearly dropping with exhaustion.* [I] ○ *She was so tired, she was* **ready to** *drop.* [I] • *(infml)* If someone **drops dead**, they die suddenly and unexpectedly: *He dropped dead on the squash court at the age of 43.* • If you **drop off (to sleep)**, you begin to sleep: *I'm afraid I dropped off in the middle of the film, so I never saw the ending.* • *(slang)* **Drop dead** is a rude way of expressing disagreement or annoyance: *Oh, just drop dead!* • *(infml)* To **drop** someone **a line** is to write to them: *Drop me a line when you've decided on a date.* • *(infml)* If you **drop** (someone) **a hint**, you tell someone something in an indirect way: *She dropped (him) a hint that they would like to come to the wedding.* ○ *I've been dropping hints that I would like to be taken out for dinner on my birthday.* • To **drop a brick/***(Br also)* **a clanger** is to do or say something which makes you feel embarrassed: *I dropped a real clanger asking about her boyfriend – I had no idea they weren't going out any longer!* • *(esp. Br and Aus)* Someone who **drops** their **aitches/h's** does not say the letter *h* at the beginning of words in which it should be pronounced.

drop /£drɒp, $drɑːp/ *n* [C] • A drop **of** supplies, letters, etc. is a delivery, often made by dropping something from an aircraft: *The helicopter made a drop of food to the stranded animals.* • A drop is also a place where something can be left and later collected by someone else, esp. as used by SPIES (=people who secretly gather information about another country or organization). • *She expected me to find the book for her* **at the drop of a hat** (=unreasonably quickly). • A **drop kick** is an attempt to score a goal in particular team sports such as RUGBY or **American football**: *Andrew aimed a high drop kick at the goal and slotted it between the posts.*

drop *(obj)* [LOWER] /£drɒp, $drɑːp/ *v* **-pp-** to move to a lower level • *The water level in the river has dropped considerably because there has been so little rain.* [I] • *The temperature drops at night.* [I] • *Prices have dropped since there has been more competition between suppliers.* [I] • *Just behind the house the land drops* **(away)** *sharply* (=slopes steeply down). [I] • *Interest in the project seems to have dropped* **away/off** (=become less). [I] • *We've had to drop our prices because of the recession.* [T] • *Drop your voices* (=Speak more quietly) *– she's in next room!* [T] • A **drop-leaf table** is a table whose sides can be folded down so that the table fits into a smaller space when it is not being used.

drop /£drɒp, $drɑːp/ *n* [U] • *There's a drop* (=distance straight down) **of** *2 metres from the window to the ground.* • *There's a* **sheer** (=extremely steep) *drop from the balcony to the sea below.* • *You really notice the drop* (=reduction) **in** *temperature in the evenings.* • *The recent drop* **in** *magazine subscriptions is causing some concern.*

drop *obj* [STOP] /£drɒp, $drɑːp/ *v* [T] **-pp-** to stop doing or stop (someone) doing (something) • *They've dropped the plan for a new railway line.* • *I'm going to drop yoga next year and do aerobics instead.* • *Can you drop what you're doing and help me with this report?* • *I don't want to talk about it anymore – let's drop* **it/the subject.** • *He dropped the idea/plan/business deal* **like a hot potato** (=quickly stopped being interested) *when he realized how much it would cost him.* • *(infml) She asked me what she should do about her boyfriend and I told her to just drop him* (=stop seeing him). • *He's been dropped* **from** (=stopped from playing for) *the team because of injury.* • *(infml) We just* **dropped everything** (=stopped what we were doing) *and rushed to the hospital.* • Someone who **drops out** of an activity stops taking part in it: *Several students dropped out* **of** *the course after three weeks.* See also DROPOUT.

drop [SMALL AMOUNT] /£drɒp, $drɑːp/ *n* [C] a very small amount of liquid • *I thought I felt a drop* **of** *rain.* • *There were little drops* **of** *paint on the kitchen floor.* • A drop also refers to a small amount of something: *I'll have a drop* **more** *juice, please.* ○ *"Would you like some more?"* **"Just** *a drop, please."* • *(infml)* If someone has had **a drop too much (to drink)**, they have drunk too much alcohol: *I think I've had a drop too much – the room is starting to spin.* • A **drop in the ocean** is something very small and unimportant: *My letter of protest was just a drop in the ocean.* • Some sweets are called drops: *chocolate/fruit/pear drops*

drop·let /£'drɒp·lət, $'drɑːp-/ *n* [C] • *Droplets* (=Small drops) **of** *rain appeared on the window.*

drop·per /£'drɒp·əʳ, $'drɑː·pɚ/ *n* [C] • A dropper is a small tube with a rubber container at one end which is filled with air and allows liquid to be given out in separate drops.

drops /£drɒps, $drɑːps/ *pl n medical* • Drops are medicine given in liquid form in very small amounts: *eye/nose/ear drops* ○ *Use drops twice daily.*

drop VISIT /£drɒp, $drɑːp/ *v* [I always + adv/prep] **-pp-** *infml* to visit someone • *Why don't you drop* **in (on** *me)* (= come and see me) *sometime?* • *If you're in this area you should drop* **by** (= come and see me).

drop-out /£'drɒp·aʊt, $'drɑːp-/ *n* [C] a person who leaves school, college or university before finishing a course, or a person who lives in an unusual way • *A school dropout at 14, he worked as a cleaner and waiter before finding his first acting job.* • *If everything fails, I might just give up my job and become a dropout.* • *Many schools in the region have appallingly high dropout* **rates**.

drop·pings /£'drɒp·ɪŋz, $'drɑː·pɪŋz/ *pl n* excrement produced by animals and birds • *There were bird droppings all over the car parked under the tree.* • *I found mouse droppings behind the settee.*

dross /£drɒs, $drɑːs/ *n* [U] something useless or worthless • *So much of what's on TV is pure dross.* • *We read all the manuscripts but 95% are dross.*

drought /draʊt/ *n* a long period when there is little or no rain • *There was a prolonged drought last autumn.* [C] • *In recent years, drought has damaged the harvest, increasing the amount of grain the country needs to import.* [U] • LP **'-ough' pronunciation**

drove DRIVE /£drəʊv, $droʊv/ *past simple of* DRIVE

drove *obj* TAKE ANIMALS /£drəʊv, $droʊv/ *v* [T] *past* **drove** to take (farm animals) on foot over long distances to market or to better land for feeding • *In the past, this path would be used for droving sheep to the summer pastures.* • *The droving routes beside the road are littered with the bodies of dead animals.*

drove /£drəʊv, $droʊv/ *n* [C] • A drove **of** cattle or sheep is a large group being moved from one place to another on foot.

drov·er /£'drəʊ·vəʳ, $'droʊ·vɚ/ *n* [C] • *A drover* (= person who moves animals on foot from one place to another) *walks alongside the oxen, gently tapping them on their backs with his stick.*

droves /£drəʊvz, $droʊvz/ *pl n* a large group, esp. of people, moving towards a place • *Football fans came* **in** *droves/(Br also)* **in their** *droves* (= Lots of them came). • *(humorous) Football fans stayed away from the match* **in** *droves/(Br also)* **in their** *droves* (= Lots of them did not go to the game). • *We walked through the museum without a guide and found ourselves amid droves of American tourists.*

drown *(obj)* DIE /draʊn/ *v* to (cause to) die by being unable to breathe under water • *He drowned in a boating accident.* [I] • *Many animals were drowned by the tidal wave.* [T] • If you **drown** your **sorrows (in drink)**, you drink alcohol to try to forget your problems. • *(infml)* If you look like a **drowned rat**, you are extremely wet: *Neither of us had taken an umbrella and we arrived at the party looking like a pair of drowned rats.* • *(saying)* 'A drowning man will clutch at a straw' means that when you are in a very difficult situation, you will take any opportunity that you can to improve it.

drown *(obj)* COVER /draʊn/ *v* to cover or be covered, esp. with a liquid • *A whole village was drowned* (= covered with water) *when the valley was made into a reservoir.* [T] • *(disapproving) He drowned his food* (= covered it completely) **in/with** *tomato sauce.* [T] • *(fig.) The noise of drilling drowned* **(out)** (= covered) *the sound of the telephone.* [T/M] • *(fig. infml) I'm drowning* **in** (= I've got too many) *unmarked exam papers.* [I]

drow·sy /'draʊ·zi/ *adj* **-ier, -iest** being in a state between sleeping and being awake, often as a result of heat or drinking alcohol • *The room is so warm it's making me feel drowsy.*

drow·si·ness /'draʊ·zɪ·nəs/ *n* [U] • *Seasickness tablets often cause drowsiness.*

drub·bing /'drʌb·ɪŋ/ *n* [C usually sing] *infml* a beating or serious defeat, esp. in a sports competition • *Nottingham Forest* **got/received/took** *a severe drubbing at the hands of Manchester United at Old Trafford last night.* • *Lander was subjected to a thorough drubbing* **by** *Lewis.*

drudg·er·y /£'drʌdʒ·ᵊr·i, $'-ɚ-/ *n* [U] hard boring work • *I thought feminism was about liberating women from enforced domestic and maternal drudgery.* • *Electronic information retrieval will remove much of the drudgery of research and leave time for the more interesting bits.*

drudge /drʌdʒ/ *n* [C] • *I feel like a real drudge – I've done nothing but clean all day!* • *"Lexicographer. A writer of dictionaries, a harmless drudge."* (Samuel Johnson in *A Dictionary of the English Language*, 1755)

drug MEDICINE /drʌg/ *n* [C] any natural or artificially made chemical which is used as a medicine • *anti-cancer/fertility/pain-killing drugs* • *Unfortunately, the tumour failed to respond to drugs/drug therapy.* • *At the time, some 500 000 patients were receiving the drug on prescription.* • *Perhaps drug companies should spend less on product promotion and more on research and development.* • *He* **takes** *drugs for his high blood pressure.*

drug *obj* /drʌg/ *v* [T] **-gg-** • If you drug someone or something you give them a chemical which causes a loss of feeling or unconsciousness: *Dahmer confessed that he often drugged his victims before he killed them.* ○ *She was heavily drugged to ease the pain.* ○ *(infml) We visited her in hospital but she was drugged* **to the eyeballs** (= had been given a lot of drugs and was almost unconscious) *and I don't think she even knew we were there.*

drug·gist /'drʌg·ɪst/ *n* [C] • Druggist is *Am for* PHARMACIST.

drug ILLEGAL SUBSTANCE /drʌg/ *n* [C] any natural or artificially made chemical which is taken for pleasure, to improve someone's performance of an activity, or because a person cannot stop using it • *It was in November of last year that she began to suspect that her son was* **on/taking/doing** *drugs.* • *Broadbent had a history of mental illness and serious drug and alcohol dependency.* • *The report shows an alarming increase in recreational drug use in the under 20s category.* • *The association strongly believes that sport must be free of drug* **abuse** (= the illegal use of drugs). • *His older sister is a drug* **addict**. • *He was arrested on drug* **charges**. • *Drug* **dealers**/*(Br also) Drugs* **dealers** (= People who sell drugs) *are threatened with the death penalty, but the risk of discovery is slight.* • *His son died of a drug/(Br also) drugs* **overdose** *in 1978 at the age of 27.* • *Drug* **trafficking** (= Trading in illegal drugs) *is an international problem, and one which requires an international solution.* • Any activity that you cannot stop doing can also be described as a drug: *Work is a drug* **for** *him.* • LP **Crimes and criminals**

drugged /drʌgd/ *adj* • *(infml) The actress spent the last few years of her life in an apartment in Paris, alone and drugged* **to the eyeballs** (= almost unconscious because of having taken so many drugs).

drug·gie /'drʌg·i/ *n* [C] *slang* • A druggie is a person who frequently uses illegal drugs: *His biography reveals him to be a wife beater and a druggie.*

drug·store /£'drʌg·stɔːʳ, $-stɔːr/ *n* [C] *Am for* CHEMIST • *A drugstore sells both medicines and a range of other goods, such as cigarettes and newspapers.*

dru·id /'druː·ɪd/ *n* [C] a priest of a religion followed in Britain, Ireland and France, esp. in ancient times

drum INSTRUMENT /drʌm/ *n* [C] a musical instrument, esp. one made from a skin stretched over the end of a hollow tube or bowl, played by hitting with the hand or a stick • *a bass drum* • *a snare drum* • *They could hear the regular* **beat** *of the drum* (= sound of the drum being hit). • *There was* **a roll of** *drums* (= several quick hits on a drum or drums), *then the band started to march.* • *Suddenly there was* **the** *drum* **of** (= repeated sound of) *hooves in the distance.* • *(infml)* If someone **bangs/beats the drum**, they speak enthusiastically about a principle that they support, esp. one that they have frequently spoken about in the past: *Once again, she banged the drum* **for** *pre-school nurseries.* ○ *He's always beating the environment drum.* • A **drum kit** (*Am also* **drum set**) is a group of drums and CYMBALS played by one person. • A **drum machine** is an electronic machine which produces the sound of drums. • A **drum major** is the person who leads a marching musical group. • *(esp. Am)* A **drum majorette** is a girl or young woman who wears a uniform and leads a marching musical group. • PIC **Drum, Musical instruments**

drum /drʌm/ *v* [I] **-mm-** • *She drummed impatiently* **on** *the table* (= hit it with her fingers). • *The rain drummed loudly* (= made a noise) **on** *the tin roof.*

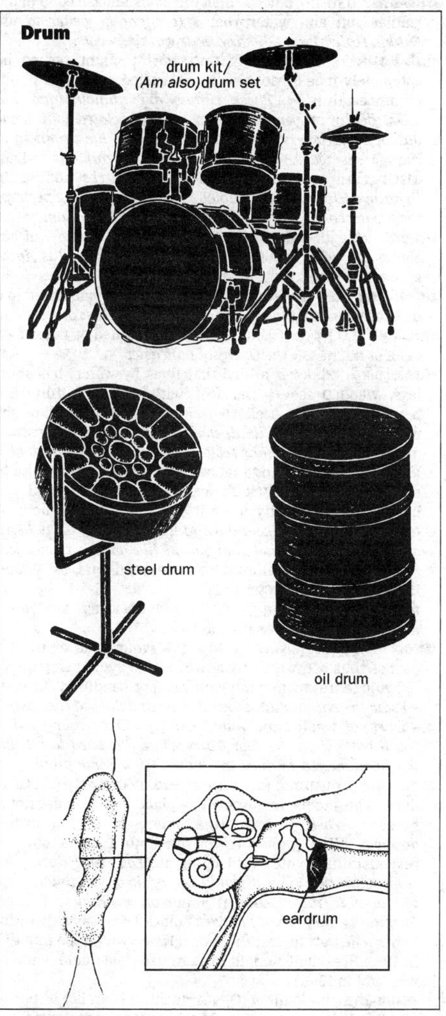

drum·mer /£ˈdrʌm·əʳ, $-ɚ/ *n* [C] • *Roger Taylor was the drummer* (= person who played the drums) *with the rock-group Queen.*

drum CONTAINER /drʌm/ *n* [C] a large tube-like container • *an oil drum* • *a five-gallon plastic drum* • *a drum* **of** *waste/fungicide* • The drum of a washing machine is the hollow metal cylinder into which clothes and other items are put for washing. • PIC **Cleaning, Drum**

drum *obj* **into** *obj v prep* [T] to teach (something) to (someone) by frequent repeating • *We had the importance of careful organization drummed into us.*

drum *obj* **out of** *obj v adv prep* [T] to remove (someone from a job, group, etc.) with disapproval • *The chairman was drummed out of office for incompetence.*

drum up *obj*, **drum** *obj* **up** *v adv* [M] to encourage the development of (something) • *We'll have to drum up more support/enthusiasm/business.*

drum·beat /ˈdrʌm·biːt/ *n* [C] (the sound of) a single hit on a drum

drum·stick MUSIC /ˈdrʌm·stɪk/ *n* [C] a stick for beating a drum • PIC **Musical instruments**

drum·stick FOOD /ˈdrʌm·stɪk/ *n* [C] the lower part of the leg of a chicken or similar bird eaten as food • *chicken drumsticks*

drunk DRINK /drʌŋk/, *Am also* **drank** /dræŋk/ *past participle of* DRINK

drunk TOO MUCH ALCOHOL /drʌŋk/ *adj* **-er, -est** unable to speak or act in the usual way because of having had too much alcohol • *I'd had a couple of glasses of wine but I certainly wasn't drunk.* • *I was a bit drunk at the time so I don't remember much.* • *His father used to get violent and abusive when he was drunk.* • *You're always* **getting** *drunk!* • *She came home last night* **blind** (= extremely) *drunk.* • *(law)* Someone who is drunk **and disorderly** is behaving in a violent way because they are drunk: *The arrests were for possession of drugs, assault and being drunk and disorderly.* • Someone who is drunk **with power** has a strong and unreasonable feeling of being able to control other people.

drunk /drʌŋk/, **drunk·ard** /£ˈdrʌŋ·kəd, $-kɚd/ *n* [C] *disapproving* • A drunk is a person who drinks large amounts of alcohol very frequently and is unable to give up the habit: *I was pestered by a couple of drunks as I left the hotel.* ○ *She had a very unhappy childhood with a drunk for a father.*

drunk·en /ˈdrʌŋ·kən/ *adj* [before n] *disapproving* • Drunken means (often) under the influence of alcohol: *She was convicted of murdering her drunken and allegedly violent husband.* • *Just before midnight, the square filled up with drunken revellers.* • *(infml) At the start of the film, he's just another drunken* **bum** *asking for money in the street.* • Drunken can describe a situation in which a lot of alcohol has been drunk: *There was a drunken* **brawl** (= fight) *outside the nightclub as we were leaving.* ○ *He came home and fell into a drunken* **stupor** (= sleep) *in the lounge.* ○ *(Am law) She was charged with drunken* **driving** (= operating a vehicle after having more alcohol than is legally allowed).

drunk·en·ly /ˈdrʌŋ·kən·li/ *adv* • *On one occasion, he climbed drunkenly into a bus and woke up, with a shock, twenty miles from home.*

drunk·en·ness /ˈdrʌŋ·kən·nəs/ *n* [U] • *The study concluded that alcohol abuse in Scotland had neither risen nor fallen, but that people noticed less public drunkenness.*

dry NOT WET /draɪ/ *adj* **drier** or **dryer**, **driest** or **dryest** without water or liquid in, on, or around something • *Is the washing dry yet?* • *Make sure your hair is dry before you go out.* • *These plants grow well in dry soil/a dry climate.* • *I've got a really dry throat – perhaps I'm getting a cold.* • *My eyes feel dry and prickly.* • *This cake's a bit dry – I think I overcooked it.* • If something **boils/runs** dry, there is no water left: *The kettle boiled dry.* ○ *They found that the well had run dry.* • Dry **bread** or **toast** has no butter or JAM, etc. on it: *All I was offered was a piece of dry bread and a bit of cheese!* • If hair or skin is dry, it lacks the natural oils that make it soft and smooth: *My skin gets very dry in the winter.* ○ *Do you have a shampoo for dry hair?* • **The dry** is a place where the conditions are not wet, esp. when compared to somewhere where the conditions are wet: *You're soaked – come into the dry.* • *(infml)* Something that is **(as) dry as a bone** (also **bone-dry**) is extremely dry: *I don't think he's been watering these plants – the soil is as dry as a bone.* • **There wasn't a dry eye in the house** means that most or all of the people at a particular gathering felt very emotional about what they had seen or heard and a lot of them had tears in their eyes: *The actress then went on to thank her recently deceased father and, by the end of the speech, there wasn't a dry eye in the house.* • If someone **dry-cleans** clothes they clean them with chemicals, not water: *The only bad thing about this jacket is that it has to be dry-cleaned.* ○ *Could you take my suit to the* **dry-cleaner's** (= the shop where clothes are cleaned with chemicals)*?* • A **dry dock** is an enclosed area of water which can be emptied and used for repairing ships: *The Sea Rose, badly in need of repairs, faces a year in dry dock.* • If someone is **dry-eyed**, they are not crying, esp. in a situation in which you might expect them to be crying: *She accused me of being unfeeling because I left the cinema dry-eyed.* • **Dry goods** is *Am for* **drapery**. See at DRAPE. • **Dry ice** is frozen **carbon dioxide**. It is used for preserving things by keeping them very cold and for producing a smoky effect in musical and theatrical performances. • *It was three days before we saw* **dry land** (= land and not sea or water). • **Dry rot** is a disease caused by a FUNGUS (= organism which obtains its food from decaying matter) which destroys wood in houses and boats, etc. • A **dry stone wall** is a low wall around a field made with layers of stones which fit together firmly without being stuck together. • (KOR)

dry *(obj)* /draɪ/ *v* he/she/it **dries**, **drying**, *past* **dried** • *Dry your hair by the fire.* [T] • *Will this paint dry by tomorrow?* [I] • *Hang the clothes up to dry.* [I] • *Drying* (= Removing liquid from) *fruit, vegetables and milk is one way of preserving them for long periods.* [T] • *Come on, Rosie, dry your* **eyes** (= stop crying) *and we'll go and find daddy.* [T] • *Here, dry yourself* **(off)** *with this towel.* [T] • *If you don't keep food covered, it dries* **out**. [I] • Something which dries **up** becomes completely dry, often when this is inconvenient: *The pond had dried up over the long hot summer.* [I] • If a supply of information or food dries **up**, there is none left: His main source of work had dried up, leaving him short of money. [I] • To **dry the dishes** (*Br also* **dry up (the dishes)** or **do the drying up**) is to dry plates, knives, forks, etc. after they have been washed.

dried /draɪd/ *adj* [not gradable] • *dried apricots/bananas/mushrooms* • *There was a stall selling dried* **flowers** *in the market.* • *Johnny doesn't eat anything that has dried* **fruit** *in it.* • *Add a pinch of dried* **herbs**. • *Do you mind having dried* **milk** *in your coffee?*

dry·er, dri·er /£ˈdraɪ·əʳ, $-ɚ/ *n* [C] • A dryer is a machine that dries things: *a hair dryer* ○ *a grain dryer* ○ *Put those damp clothes in the (tumble) dryer.* • [PIC] **Cleaning**

dry·ness /ˈdraɪ·nəs/ *n* [U] • *Despite last summer's dryness, there is no shortage of water.* • *The meat was juicy with no hint of dryness.*

dry [BORING] /draɪ/ *adj* **-ier, -iest** *disapproving* (esp. of writing) not interesting or exciting in any way; boring • *I didn't really enjoy his last book – I found it a bit dry.* • *All the facts are there, but it's a bit dry.* • (KOR)

dry·ness /ˈdraɪ·nəs/ *n* [U] *disapproving*

dry [NO ALCOHOL] /draɪ/ *adj* [not gradable] without alcoholic drinks • *a dry wedding* • *a dry bar* • *a dry state* (= a part of a country which does not allow alcohol) • (KOR)

dry out *v adv* [I] • Someone who dries out learns to stop being dependent on alcohol: *She was in her late thirties when she finally dried out and stopped taking the drugs.*

dry [NOT SWEET] /draɪ/ *adj* **-ier, -iest** (of drinks) not tasting sweet • *dry cider/martini/sherry/wine* • *On the whole, I prefer dry wines to sweet ones.* • (KOR)

dry·ness /ˈdraɪ·nəs/ *n* [U] • *The wine has just enough dryness to balance its fruitiness.*

dry [HUMOUR] /draɪ/ *adj* **-ier, -iest** *approving* (of humour) clever and showing a slightly cruel awareness of other people's faults • *He has a very dry sense of humour.* • *a dry wit* • (KOR)

dri·ly, dry·ly /ˈdraɪ·li/ *adv* • *"I know it sounds silly, but when I get to the beach I feel like a kid again." "We noticed," she said drily.*

DTs /ˌdiːˈtiːz/ *n* [U] **the DTs** *infml abbreviation for* delirium tremens (= a state of mental confusion, including seeing imaginary things, caused by drinking too much alcohol over a long period) • *He's got a bad case of the DTs.*

du·al /£ˈdjuː·əl, $ˈduː·ᵊl/ *adj* [before n; not gradable] with two similar parts or combining two things • *This room has a dual* **purpose**, *serving as both a study and a dining room.* • *The dual* **role** *of chairman and chief executive is not unusual in the publishing business.* • A car with dual **controls** has two sets of controls such as BRAKES, one for the person who is learning to drive and one for the teacher. • Someone with dual **nationality/citizenship** has the nationality of two countries at the same time: *dual British and American nationality* • *(Br)* A **dual carriageway** (*Am and Aus* **divided highway**) is a road which has an area of land in the middle, dividing the rows of traffic which are moving in opposite directions. • If something is **dual-purpose**, it can be used to do two things: *a dual-purpose lawn-raking and leaf-collecting machine.* • [LP] **Two**

du·al·i·ty /£djuːˈæl·ə·ti, $duːˈæl·ə·t̬i/ *n* [U] *fml* • *His poems reveal the duality of his nature, the joy and hope, the fear and despair.*

du·al·i·sm /£ˈdjuː·ə·lɪ·zᵊm, $ˈduː·ᵊl·ɪ-/ *n* [U] *fml* • Dualism is the belief that things are divided into two often very different or opposing parts: *Western dualism values mind over body.* ○ *The old dualism of God and the Devil is sometimes replaced by the idea that God contains both good and evil.*

dub *obj* [NAME] /dʌb/ *v* [T + obj + (*as*) n] **-bb-** to give (something or someone) a particular name, esp. describing what you think of them • *The newspapers dubbed the nurse who murdered several children* **(as)** *'The Angel of Death'.*

dub *obj* [CHANGE] /dʌb/ *v* [T] **-bb-** to change the sounds and speech on (a film or television programme), or to change (the original voices) on a film or television programme, esp. to a different language • *I'd rather watch a film with subtitles than one dubbed* **into** *English.* • *To conceal his identity, the man's voice has been dubbed* **over** (= an actor speaks his words).

dub [MUSIC] /dʌb/ *n* [U] a style of music connected with REGGAE in which the main part of the tune is removed and various special effects are added, or a style of poetry connected with this type of music

dub·bin /ˈdʌb·ɪn/ *n* [U] a thick oily substance used to make leather soft and waterproof • *It might be better to use dubbin rather than polish on your walking boots.*

dub·i·ous /£ˈdjuː·bi·əs, $ˈduː-/ *adj* thought not to be completely true or not able to be trusted, or feeling doubt or uncertainty • *These claims are dubious and not scientifically proven.* • *He has been associated with some dubious characters.* • *I'm dubious* **about** *his promises to change his ways.* • *Ruth Ellis has the dubious* (= bad) **distinction** *of being the last woman to be hanged in Britain.* • *Blake has the dubious* **privilege** *of being perhaps the greatest artist not to be represented in the museum.*

du·cal /£ˈdjuː·kᵊl, $ˈduː-/ *adj* [not gradable] of or connected with a DUKE • *This town is part of his ducal estates* (= which a duke owns).

duch·ess /ˈdʌtʃ·ɪs, -es/ *n* [C] a woman who is married to a DUKE or who is of the rank of duke • *the Duchess of Kent*

duch·y /ˈdʌtʃ·i/ *n* [C] the area of land owned or ruled by a DUKE or DUCHESS • *the Duchy of Lancaster*

duck [BIRD] /dʌk/ *n* a bird that lives by water, has short legs, WEBBED feet (= flat feet with areas of thin skin between the toes), a short neck and a large beak, or the meat of this bird • *Wild ducks flew in a V-shape formation above the trees.* [C] • *The restaurant's speciality was duck* **à l'orange** (= with orange sauce). [U] • *(infml)* If you **take to** something **like a duck to water**, you discover that you have a natural ability to do it and like it very much: *He took to fatherhood like a duck to water.* • *"If it looks like a duck, walks like a duck and quacks like a duck, then it just may be a duck"* (believed to have been said by Walter Reuther, 1950s) • [PIC] **Birds**

duck·ling /ˈdʌk·lɪŋ/ *n* [C/U] • A duckling is a young duck, or its flesh when used as food.

duck *(obj)* [MOVE] /dʌk/ *v* to move (your head or the top part of your body) quickly down, esp. to avoid being hit, or to avoid (a hit) by moving your head or bending your body • *I saw the ball hurtling towards me and ducked* **(down)**. [I] • *Duck, or you'll bang your head.* [I] • *Duck your head or you'll bang it on the door-frame.* [T] • *She tried to hit him but he managed to duck the blows.* [T] • *Some people hate ducking* (= pushing) *(their head)* **under/in** *water.* [I/T] • To duck is also to move quickly to a place, esp. in order not to be seen: *When he saw them coming, he ducked* **into** *a doorway.* [I] • *(infml)* If you duck **(out of)** a duty or responsibility, you avoid doing it: *You can't duck your responsibilities.* [T] ○ *It would be unfair of you to duck* **out of** *going to the cinema.* [I + *out of*] • *"Honey, I forgot (originally 'just forgot') to duck"* (Jack Dempsey explaining to his wife how he lost the World Heavyweight boxing title in 1926. President Ronald Reagan used the quote when he was shot in 1981.)

duck·ing /ˈdʌk·ɪŋ/ *n* [C] • A ducking is an act or period of going below the surface of water: *The boat turned over and we all* **got/had** *a ducking.*

duck [PERSON] /dʌk/, **ducks, duck·y, duck·ie** *n* [C] *Br dated infml* someone you like • *Come and sit beside me, duck.* [as form of address] • **Be a** *duck and* (= Please) *get me a glass of water.* • See also DUCKY.

duck–billed plat·y·pus /ˈdʊk·bɪld/ *n* [C] a PLATYPUS

duck·weed /ˈdʌk·wiːd/ *n* [U] a plant that grows on the surface of some pools

duck·y /ˈdʌk·i/ *adj esp. Am infml* very satisfactory or excellent; pleasant and charming • *Life has been ducky since she got out of the hospital.* • *What a ducky* **little** *room!* • See also DUCK [PERSON].

duct /dʌkt/ *n* [C] a tube or pipe that carries liquid or air, esp. in and out of buildings or through the body • *Most office buildings have dozens of* **air** *ducts and vents.* • *People with blocked* **tear** *ducts cannot cry.*

duc·tile /£ˈdʌk·taɪl, $-tɪl/ *adj specialized* (esp. of metals) able to be bent easily

duct·less gland /ˈdʌkt·ləs-/ *n* [C] an ENDOCRINE GLAND

dud /dʌd/ *n, adj* [not gradable] (something) of no value or that does not work • *Not one of the books she has written has been a dud.* [C] • *Of the many bombs that were found, several turned out to be duds.* [C] • *There is a growing trade overseas in dud medicines.* • *One of the customers tried to pass off a dud* **cheque** (= one for which a bank will not give money) *today.*

dude /duːd/ *n* [C] *esp. Am infml* any man, or one who comes from a city and dresses stylishly • *There were some* **cool** *dudes* (= stylish men) *in sunglasses standing about.* • *It's a school where pupils greet their teachers with 'Hey dude'.* [as form of address] • In the US, a **dude ranch** is a holiday farm that offers activities such as riding horses and CAMPING.

dudg·eon /ˈdʌdʒ·ən/ *n* [U] **in high dudgeon**, see at HIGH [ABOVE AVERAGE]

due [OWED] /£djuː, $duː/ *adj* [not gradable] owed as a debt or as a right • *The rent is due* (= should be paid) *at the end of the month.* • *Fifty pounds is (esp. Br and Aus) due* **to** *me/ (esp. Am) due me by the people I worked for last month.* • *I am due a refund for the dress I took back which was faulty.* • *Our thanks are due* **to** *everyone who gave so generously.* • *He felt that he should be treated with* **the respect** *(esp. Br and Aus) due* **to** *his/(esp. Am) due his senior position.* • *(Br and Aus law) He was found to have been driving without due* (= the necessary) **care and attention**. • **With (all) due respect** is used to express polite disagreement: *I've been thinking about what you said and, with (all) due respect, I think you're wrong.* • See also DULY. • (I)

due /£djuː, $duː/ *n* [U] • To **give** someone their **due** is to praise them when they have done something good, even if you dislike other things about them: *He failed again, but to give him his due, he did try hard.*

dues /£djuːz, $duːz/ *pl n* • Dues are the official payments you make to an organization that you belong to: *Members of the society pay $1000 in annual dues.*

due [EXPECTED] /£djuː, $duː/ *adj* [not gradable] expected (to happen, arrive, etc.) at a particular time • *What time is the next bus due?* • *The next meeting is due* **to** *be held in three months' time.* [+ to infinitive] • *Their first baby is due* (= expected to be born) *in January.* • *We're not due* **to** *arrive for another two hours.* [+ to infinitive] • *(slightly fml) You will receive notification of the results* **in due course/at the due time** (= in the future at a suitable time). • (I)

due [STRAIGHT] /£djuː, $duː/ *adv* [before adv; not gradable] (of north, south, east or west) exactly, straight • *From here, you go due east until you get to a forest.* • [LP] **Directions** (I)

due [RESULTING] /£djuː, $duː/ *adj* [not gradable] **due to** as a result of, caused by; because of • *The fire was due to a faulty wire in a plug.* • *A lot of her unhappiness is due to boredom.* • *Due to wet leaves on the line, this train will arrive an hour late.* • (I)

du·el /£ˈdjuː·əl, $ˈduː·əl/ *n* [C] a formal fight, using guns or swords, arranged esp. in the past between two people to decide an argument • *The two men* **fought** *a duel* **over** *a quarrel about a lady.* • *The composer Strauss was once* **challenged to** *a duel by a jealous officer.* • *(fig.) The two yachts are* **locked in** *a duel* **for** (= competing hard with each other for) *the championship title.*

du·ell·ing, *Am usually* **du·el·ing** /£ˈdjuː·ə·lɪŋ, $ˈduː-/ *adj* [not gradable] • *(fig.) Eventually, the duelling* (= arguing) *politicians agreed to end their quarrel.*

du·el·list, *Am usually* **du·el·ist** /£ˈdjuː·əl·ɪst, $ˈduː-/ *n* [C]

du·et /£djuˈet, $duː-/ *n* [C] a song or other piece of music sung or played by two people

duff [BAD] /dʌf/ *adj* **-er, -est** *Br infml* bad, useless or not working • *He's directed so many films that you might expect a few duff ones.*

duff [BOTTOM] /dʌf/ *n* [C] *Am infml* a person's bottom • **Get off** *your duff and start working – we've only got a few hours to finish.*

duff *obj* [STEAL] /dʌf/ *v* [T] *Aus* to steal (farm animals) by changing the BRAND (= owner's mark) on them, or to steal (goods) by changing their appearance

duff up *obj*, **duff** *obj* **up** /dʌf/ *v adv* [M] *Br infml* to hit (someone) repeatedly in order to hurt them • *Two of the robbers threatened to duff the witness up if he went to the police.*

duf·fel bag, duf·fle bag /ˈdʌf·l̩/ *n* [C] a strong bag with a round bottom and thick string at the top that is used to close it and to carry it • [PIC] **Bags**

duf·fel coat, duf·fle coat /ˈdʌf·l̩/ *n* [C] a coat made of thick wool which has TOGGLE (= tube-shaped) fasteners and usually has a HOOD (= loose covering for the head) • [PIC] **Coats and jackets**

duf·fer /£ˈdʌf·əʳ, $-ɚ/ *n* [C] *dated* a person who lacks skill or ability or is slow to learn • *I was a bit of a duffer* **at** *physics.*

dug /dʌg/ *past simple and past participle of* DIG

dug·out (ca·noe) *Am and Aus* /ˈdʌg·aʊt/ *n* [C] a small light boat that is made by cutting out the middle of a tree trunk

dug·out /ˈdʌg·aʊt/ *n* [C] a shelter, usually for soldiers, made by digging a hole in the ground and covering it • A dugout is also a shelter for the manager, trainer, etc. beside a football field, or *(Am)* a shelter for players along a baseball field.

duke /£djuːk, $duːk/ *n* [C] a man of very high rank in a country, or the ruler of a small independent country • *the Duke of Westminster* • See also DUCAL; DUCHESS.

duke·dom /£ˈdjuːk·dəm, $ˈduːk-/ *n* [C] • A dukedom is the rank of a duke or the land owned by a duke. • See also DUCHY.

dul·cet /ˈdʌl·sət/ *adj literary or humorous* (esp. of sounds) soft and pleasant to listen to • *(literary) We could hear the pilot's dulcet voice encouraging passengers to relax.* • *(humorous) She makes the most awful noise when she sings and I had to put up with her dulcet* **tones** *all evening!*

dul·ci·mer /£ˈdʌl·sɪ·məʳ, $-mɚ/ *n* [C] a musical instrument, consisting of a wooden box with wire strings stretched over it, that is played by hitting the strings with a pair of light hammers

dull [BORING] /dʌl/ *adj* **-er, -est** not interesting or exciting in any way; boring • *She wrote dull, respectable articles for the local newspaper.* • *He's very pleasant, but* **deadly/ terribly** *dull* (= very boring) *I'm afraid.* • *(infml)* Something or someone that is **(as) dull as ditchwater** is very boring.

dul·ly /ˈdʌl·li/ *adv* • *The orchestra plays competently, but dully.*

dull·ness /ˈdʌl·nəs/ *n* [U] • *Their attempts at painting are mechanical to the point of dullness.*

dull [NOT BRIGHT] /dʌl/ *adj* **-er, -est** not clear, bright or shiny; dark • *If your cat's coat is dull, feed it Catto cat food!* • *We could just see a dull* **glow** *given off by the fire's last embers.* • *The first day of our holiday was dull* (= cloudy).

dul·ly /ˈdʌl·li/ *adv* • *The car lights glowed dully through the mist.*

dull [NOT SHARP] /dʌl/ *adj* **-er, -est** (esp. of sound or pain) not sharp or clear • *I heard a dull* **thud** *from the kitchen and realized she must have fainted.* • *The dull rumble of traffic woke her.* • *She felt a dull* **ache** *at the back of her head.* • *(esp. Am) Your knives need never have dull* (= not sharp) *blades again!* • *(dated)* A person who is dull is not very intelligent and has difficulty learning: *He was put into a class for dull children.*

dull *obj* /dʌl/ *v* [T] • *Homeless children in the street sniffed glue to dull their hunger pains* (= make the pains less severe).

dul·ly /ˈdʌl·li/ *adv* • *My arm still ached dully.*

dul·lard /£ˈdʌl·əd, £-ɑːd, $-ɚd/ *n* [C] *dated* a stupid person • *Unlike some sporting heroes, Smith is no dullard – he has a university degree.*

du·ly /£ˈdjuː·li, $ˈduː-/ *adv* [not gradable] in the correct way or at the correct time; as expected • *He knew he had been wrong, and duly apologized.* • *I know you wanted to help, and I'm duly grateful.* • *She asked for his autograph and he duly* **obliged** *by signing her programme.* • *Emma ordered a catalogue, and it duly arrived the following week.*

dumb [SILENT] /dʌm/ *adj* [not gradable] permanently or temporarily unable to speak • *He's been deaf and dumb since birth.* • *She was* **struck** *dumb by what she had seen.* • *Although she doesn't get on very well with people, she's very kind to dumb* **animals** (= animals). • *(Br infml) Unable to speak Chinese, I had to describe what I needed using* **dumb show** (= hand actions and movements but not speech). • A **dumb waiter** is a small LIFT (= device used to move things from one level of a building to another) used esp. in restaurants to deliver food from the kitchen.

dumb·ly /ˈdʌm·li/ *adv* [not gradable] • *She stared dumbly* (= without speaking) *into space.*

dumb·ness /ˈdʌm·nəs/ *n* [U]

dumb [STUPID] /dʌm/ *adj* **-er, -est** *infml* stupid and annoying • *Are they brave or just dumb?* • *What a dumb idea!*

dumb·bell /ˈdʌm·bel/ *n* [C] a short bar with a weight on each end that you lift up and down to strengthen your muscles, esp. those in your arms and shoulders • Dumbbell is also *Am for* DUMMY [STUPID PERSON].

dumb·found·ed /ˌdʌmˈfaʊn·dɪd/, **dumb·struck** /ˈdʌm·strʌk/ *adj* so shocked and surprised that you cannot speak • *He said he was dumbfounded* **by** *the allegations.*

dum–dum (bul·let) /ˈdʌm·dʌm/ *n* [C] a bullet with a soft front that breaks into many pieces when it hits someone, causing serious injuries

dum·my [MODEL] /ˈdʌm·i/ *n* [C] a large model of a human, esp. used to show clothes in a shop • *a ventriloquist's dummy* • *A* **shop** *dummy lay among the rubble on the street.*

dum·my NOT REAL /ˈdʌm·i/ *n* [C], *adj* [before n; not gradable] (something that is) not real or used to deceive • *The police suspect that the device is not a real bomb but a dummy.* • *In the shop window, there was an enormous dummy perfume bottle on display.* • *The buyer of the painting used a dummy name to keep their identity secret.*

dum·my RUBBER OBJECT *Br and Aus* /ˈdʌm·i/, *Am* **pac·i·fi·er** *n* [C] a smooth rubber or plastic object that is given to a baby to suck in order to comfort it and make it stop crying

dum·my STUPID PERSON /ˈdʌm·i/, *Am also* **dumb·bell** *n* [C] a stupid or silly person • *Only a dummy would ignore the safety warnings.* • *Don't touch it, you dummy!* [as form of address]

dump *obj* /dʌmp/ *v* [T] to put down or drop (something heavy) in a careless way, or to get rid of (something you no longer want) • *He came in with four shopping bags and dumped them on the table.* • *Several old cars had been dumped near the beach.* • *Toxic chemicals continue to be dumped in the North Sea.* • *They accused the West of dumping out-of-date medicines* **on** *Third World countries.* • *The tax was so unpopular that the government decided to dump* (= get rid of) *it.* • *(infml)* To dump a person with whom you are having a romantic relationship is to suddenly end your relationship with them: *If he's so awful, why don't you just dump him?* • *(specialized)* If you dump information that is stored in a computer, you move it from the computer's memory to a storage device. • **Dump truck** is *Am for* DUMPER (TRUCK).

dump·ing /ˈdʌm·pɪŋ/ *n* [U] • *The company has promised to limit (the) dumping* **of** *sewage sludge in the sea.* • A **dumping ground** is a place where something unwanted is left: *Most people do not want this country to become a dumping ground* **for** *toxic waste.*

dump /dʌmp/ *n* [C] • A **(rubbish) dump** is a place where people are allowed to leave their rubbish: *I'm going to clear out the shed tomorrow and take everything I don't want to the dump.* ○ *(fig. infml) His room is a dump* (= a very unpleasant and untidy place)*!* • A dump is also a place where things of the stated type are stored, esp. by an army: *an ammunition/arms/weapons/food dump* • *(taboo slang)* To **have/take a dump** is to excrete the contents of the bowels.

dump·er /£ˈdʌm·pəʳ, $-pɚ/ *n* [C] *Aus* a wave which throws SURFERS (= people who ride on the sea on special boards) off their boards

dump·er (truck) *Br* /£ˈdʌm·pəʳ, $-pɚ/, *Am* **dump truck**, *Aus* **tip truck** *n* [C] a small, strong vehicle with a container at the front that can be raised at an angle so that its load of stones, bricks, dirt, etc. falls out

dump·ling /ˈdʌm·plɪŋ/ *n* [C] a small ball of DOUGH (= flour and water mixed together) cooked and eaten with meat and vegetables, or fruit covered in a sweet dough and baked

dumps /dʌmps/ *n* [U] **(down) in the dumps** *infml* unhappy and sad • *She's a bit down in the dumps because she's got to take her exams again.*

Dump·ster /£ˈdʌmp·stəʳ, $-stɚ/ *n* [C] *Am trademark for* SKIP CONTAINER

dump·y /ˈdʌm·pi/ *adj* **-ier, -iest** short and fat • *The film is about a man who falls in love with a dumpy housewife.*

dun /dʌn/ *adj* [not gradable] of a greyish brown colour

dunce /dʌnts/ *n* [C] *disapproving* a person who is slow to learn or stupid, esp. at school • *He was such a dunce in school but now he's very successful in banking.* • *I'm afraid I'm a bit of a dunce* **at** *arithmetic.* • A **dunce's cap** (*Am usually* **dunce cap**) is a tall paper hat with a pointed end that in the past a child who had made many mistakes in their work had to wear in school.

dun·der·head /£ˈdʌn·də·hed, $-dɚ-/ *n* [C] *infml dated* a stupid person

dune /£djuːn, $duːn/ *n* [C] a small hill of sand beside a beach or in a desert

dung /dʌŋ/ *n* [U] solid excrement from animals, esp. cattle and horses; MANURE

dun·ga·rees *Br* /ˌdʌŋ·gəˈriːz/, *Am and Aus* **o·ver·alls** *pl n* a pair of trousers that has an extra piece of cloth that covers the chest and is held in place by a strap over each shoulder • *(Am)* Dungarees are also clothes, esp. trousers and coats, made of DENIM (= a thick strong cotton cloth).

dun·geon /ˈdʌn·dʒᵊn/ *n* [C] an underground prison, esp. in a castle • *Throw him into the dungeon and leave him there.*

dung·hill /ˈdʌŋ·hɪl/ *n* [C] a small pile of solid animal excrement, or *(fig.)* an unpleasant place

dunk *obj* /dʌŋk/ *v* [T] to put (a biscuit, bread, etc.) into a liquid such as tea or soup for a short time before eating it, or *(infml)* to put (anything) into liquid for a short time • *She dunked a biscuit* **in** *her tea thoughtfully.* • *(infml) Dunk the sponge* **in** *water every now and then to stop it from drying out.* • To dunk is also to **slam dunk**. See at SLAM.

dun·no /£dəˈnəʊ, $-ˈnoʊ/ *v slang not standard* (I) don't know • *"Where are we exactly?" "Dunno."* [I] • *Quit pushing him around – he dunno nothing.* [T]

dunny /ˈdʌn·i/ *n* [C] *Aus infml for* TOILET CONTAINER

du·o /£ˈdjuː·əʊ, $ˈduː·oʊ/ *n* [C] *pl* **duos** a pair, esp. of singers, musicians or other performers • *the comedy duo Laurel and Hardy*

du·o·de·num /£ˌdjuː·əʊˈdiː·nəm, $ˌduː·ə-/ *n* [C] *pl* **duodenums** or **duodena** /£ˌdjuː·əʊˈdiː·nə, $ˌduː·ə-/ *medical* the first part of the bowel just below the stomach

du·o·de·nal /£ˌdjuː·əʊˈdiː·nəl, $ˌduː·ə-/ *adj* [not gradable] *medical* • *Drugs have been developed to cure some duodenal* **ulcers**.

dupe *obj* /£djuːp, $duːp/ *v* [T often passive] to deceive (someone), usually making them do something they did not intend to do • *The girls were duped by drug smugglers* **into** *carrying heroin for them.* • *He claimed it was a put-up job and that he'd been duped.*

dupe /£djuːp, $duːp/ *n* [C] • A dupe is someone who has been tricked: *She was an innocent dupe who had been tricked into carrying a bag containing a bomb.* ○ *They were the dupes* **of** *a clever but dishonest salesman.*

dup·lex ROOMS /£ˈdjuː·pleks, $ˈduː-/ *n* [C] *Am* a set of rooms for living in that are on two floors of a building

dup·lex TWO HOUSES /£ˈdjuː·pleks, $ˈduː-/ *n* [C] *Aus* a pair of small houses on a single floor that are joined together

dup·li·cate *obj* /£ˈdjuː·plɪ·keɪt, $ˈduː-/ *v* [T] to make an exact copy of (something) • *Parenthood is an experience nothing else can duplicate.* • *We were anxious not to duplicate* (= repeat) *work already done.* • *Can you duplicate* (= use a special machine to copy) *this document for me?* • LP **Two**

dup·li·cate /£ˈdjuː·plɪ·kət, $ˈduː-/ *adj* [before n; not gradable] • *The thieves were equipped with duplicate keys to the safe.*

dup·li·cate /£ˈdjuː·plɪ·kət, $ˈduː-/ *n* [C] • *I lost the original form so they sent me a duplicate.*

dup·li·ca·tion /£ˌdjuː·plɪˈkeɪ·ʃᵊn, $ˌduː-/ *n* [U] • *Lack of communication between the two offices led to* **a** *wasteful duplication* **of effort**.

du·pli·ci·ty /£djʊˈplɪs·ɪ·ti, $duːˈplɪs·ə·t̬i/ *n* [U] *fml* lack of honesty, esp. by saying different things to two people • *They were accused of duplicity* **in** *their dealings with both sides.*

dur·ab·le /£ˈdjʊə·rə·bl̩, $ˈdʊr·ə-/ *adj* able to last a long time without being damaged • *The parts of the machine which experience a lot of friction have to be made from durable materials.* • *The resolution calls for a just and durable peace settlement in the area.*

dur·a·bil·i·ty /£ˌdjʊə·rəˈbɪl·ɪ·ti, $ˌdʊr·əˈbɪl·ə·t̬i/ *n* [U] • *A point that strikes an outsider is the durability* **of** *political compromise.* • *The way a vehicle is welded has a lot to do with its durability.*

dur·a·tion /£djʊəˈreɪ·ʃᵊn, $duː-/ *n* [U] the length of time that something lasts • *He planned a stay of two years' duration.* • *I suppose we're stuck with each other* **for the duration** (= as long as this situation lasts). • *(dated) Rationing was to last* **for the duration** (= as long as the war lasted). • LP **Measurements**

dur·ess /£djʊˈres, $duː-/ *n* [U] *fml* threats used to force a person to do something • *He claimed that he signed the confession* **under** *duress.*

Dur·ex /£ˈdjʊə·reks, $ˈdʊr·eks/ *n* [C] *Br trademark* a type of CONDOM

dur·ing THROUGH /£ˈdjʊə·rɪŋ, $ˈdʊr·ɪŋ/ *prep* from the beginning to the end of (a particular period); THROUGHOUT • *They work during the night and sleep by day.* • *There were huge advances in aviation technology during World War Two.* • Compare WHILE.

dur·ing AT SOME POINT IN /£ˈdjʊə·rɪŋ, $ˈdʊr·ɪŋ/ *prep* at some time between the beginning and the end of (a period) • *I woke up several times during the night.* • *The programme will be shown on television during the weekend.* • Compare WHILE.

dusk /dʌsk/ *n* [U] the time before night when it is not yet dark • *As dusk* **fell**, *bats began to fly between the trees.* • Compare DAWN EARLY MORNING.

dusk·y /ˈdʌs·ki/ *adj* **-ier, -iest** *slightly literary* dark in colour • *In autumn, the leaves turn a dusky red.* • *The tabloids reported that he had been seen with a dusky* (= dark-skinned) *young woman.* Some people consider this use offensive.

dust /dʌst/ *n* [U] dry dirt in the form of powder that covers surfaces inside a building, or dry very small pieces of earth, sand or other substances • *The furniture was covered in dust and cobwebs.* • *A cloud of dust rose in the air as the car roared past.* • *Many miners have suffered from the effects of coal dust in their lungs.* • *For several days we drove across an arid wasteland of dust and stones.* • *(fig. literary) Every promise they have made has* **turned to** *dust* (= has become worthless). • If you **allow the dust to settle** or **let the dust settle** or **wait until the dust has settled**, you wait for a situation to become calm before doing anything: *We thought we'd let the dust settle before discussing the other matter with them.* • A **dust jacket** on a book is a removable paper cover for it, usually with the book's title and the name of the writer printed on it. • *(infml)* A **dust-up** is a physical fight or noisy argument.

dust *(obj)* /dʌst/ *v* • *I was dusting* (= removing dust from) *the mantelpiece when I noticed the piece of paper.* [T] • *Would you prefer to dust or wash up?* [I] • *The cake should be dusted* (= thinly covered) **with** *icing sugar.* [T] • *After her car had been broken into, it was dusted* **for** *fingerprints* (= special powder was put on its surfaces so that marks made by fingers could be seen) *by the police.* [T] • To **dust off** (*Br and Aus also* **dust down**) something is to prepare it for use, esp. after it has not been used for a long time: *They brought out the old ambulances, dusted them down and put them back into service.*

dust·er /£ˈdʌs·təʳ, $-t̬ɚ/ *n* [C] • A duster is a piece of cloth that is used for removing dust from furniture, books, surfaces, etc. • PIC› **Cleaning**

dust·ing /£ˈdʌs·tɪŋ, $-t̬ɪŋ/ *n* [U] • *There was a dusting* (= a thin layer) *of snow on the lawn.*

dust·y /£ˈdʌs·ti, $-t̬i/ *adj* **-ier, -iest** • *Heaps of dusty books lay on the floor.* • *We drove along the dusty* (= covered in dry earth) *road.* • A dusty colour is one that is slightly grey: *The floor is covered by a dusty pink carpet.*

dust·bin *Br* /ˈdʌst·bɪn/, *esp. Br* **bin**, *Am and Aus* **gar·bage can**, *Am also* **trash can** *n* [C] a large container for rubbish from a house or other building, usually kept outside • *The dustbins are emptied on Wednesdays.* • *Put the dustbin* **lid** *on properly or the cats will get into the bin and cause a mess.* • *(fig.) This exam* **consigned** *many children* **to** *the dustbin* (= The children who failed were considered to be stupid). • *(fig.) Trotsky wrote that his enemies belonged in the dustbin* **of history** (= would be forgotten about). • *(Br)* A **dustbin bag/liner** (*Am and Aus* **garbage bag**, *Am* **trash can liner** or **trash bag**) is a plastic bag put inside a container for waste, esp. one which is used inside a house to hold the waste and keep the container clean. • *(Br)* A **dustbin lorry** (*Br also* **dustcart**, *Am and Aus* **garbage truck**) is a large vehicle that drives from one house to another collecting rubbish from the dustbins outside. • PIC› **Bags, Coverings, Vehicles**

dust·bowl /£ˈdʌst·bəʊl, $-boʊl/ *n* [C] an area of land from which the earth is easily removed by wind and where there are strong winds carrying large amounts of dust

dust·cart /£ˈdʌst·kɑːt, $-kɑːrt/ *n* [C] *Br* a **dustbin lorry**, see at DUSTBIN

dust·man *Br* (*pl* **-men**) /ˈdʌst·mən/, *Am and Aus* **gar·bage·man** (*pl* **-men**), *Br infml* **bin man** (*pl* **-men**), *Br fml* **re·fuse col·lect·or** *n* [C] a person whose job it is to empty people's DUSTBINS and take the rubbish away

dust·pan /ˈdʌst·pæn/ *n* [C] a flat container with a handle into which you brush dust and dirt • *a dustpan and brush* • PIC› **Brush**

dust·sheet /ˈdʌst·ʃiːt/ *n* [C] a large piece of cloth that is put over furniture to protect it from dust

dust·y /£ˈdʌs·ti, $-t̬i/ *adj* See at DUST

Dutch /dʌtʃ/ *adv* **go Dutch** to agree to share the cost of something, esp. a meal • *"Will you let me take you out to dinner tonight?" "As long as we go Dutch."*

Dutch cap /dʌtʃ/ *n* [C] a CAP BIRTH CONTROL

Dutch cour·age *Br and Aus* /dʌtʃ/, *Am* **liq·uid cour·age** *n* [U] the confidence some people get from drinking alcohol before they do something that they are frightened of doing

Dutch elm dis·ease /dʌtʃ/ *n* [U] a disease that slowly kills ELM trees

du·ty RESPONSIBILITY /£ˈdjuː·ti, $ˈduː·t̬i/ *n* something that you have to do because it is part of your job, or something that you feel is the right thing to do • *The duty of the agency is to act in the best interests of the child.* [C] • *I felt it was my duty* **to** *tell them the truth.* [C + *to* infinitive] • *He has a duty* **to** (= It is right that he should) *visit his mother more than once a year.* [C + *to* infinitive] • *You have a duty* **to** *yourself to take a holiday now and then.* [C] • *He only went to see her* **out of** *duty* (= because he thought he should). [U] • *You should* **report for** *duty* (= work) *on Monday morning.* [U] • *(slightly fml) What time are you* **off/on** *duty* (= When do you finish/start work) *tomorrow?* [U] • *The chief of police has been* **suspended from** *duty* (= is not allowed to work) *until the claims against him have been investigated.* [U] • *We are* **duty bound** (= It is necessary for us) *to justify how we spend our funds.*

du·ti·ful /£ˈdjuː·tɪ·fəl, $ˈduː·t̬ɪ-/ *adj* • *When our trainer stopped speaking, there were a few dutiful* (= given because expected rather than from excitement) *cheers.*

du·ti·ful·ly /£ˈdjuː·tɪ·fəl·i, $ˈduː·t̬ɪ-/ *adv* • *The people stood dutifully* (= obediently) *in line waiting to vote.*

du·ty TAX /£ˈdjuː·ti, $ˈduː·t̬i/ *n* a tax paid to the government, esp. on things that you bring into a country • *We had to pay duty* **on** *a rug we brought back from India.* [U] • *Returning soldiers have to pay heavy* **customs** *duties* **on** *tax-free cars bought abroad.* [C] • *There's a high duty* **on** *alcohol.* [C] • **Duty-free** goods are luxury goods bought in special shops (**duty-free shops**) in airports, on ships, etc. on which you do not pay government tax: *He bought his wife some duty-free perfume.* ○ *We can* **buy** *our* **duty-frees** (= duty-free goods) *while we're waiting at the airport.* ○ *Don't buy whiskey here – you can get it duty-free on the ferry.*

du·ti·able /£ˈdjuː·ti·ə·bl̩, $ˈduː·t̬i-/ *adj* [not gradable] • Dutiable goods are those on which duty (= tax) must be paid.

du·vet *esp. Br* /£ˈduː·veɪ, $-ˈ-/, **quilt**, *Br also* **con·ti·nent·al quilt**, *Am* **com·fort·er**, *Aus trademark* **doo·na** /ˈduː·nə/ *n* [C] a large soft flat bag filled with feathers or artificial material used on a bed, esp. instead of sheets and woollen covers to keep you warm • A **duvet cover** (also **quilt cover**) is a washable cover for a duvet. • LP› **'-et' words** • PIC› **Beds and bedroom, Coverings**

dwarf /£dwɔːf, $dwɔːrf/ *n* [C] *pl* **dwarfs** or **dwarves** /£dwɔːvz, $dwɔːrvz/ a person who is much smaller than the usual size, or (in stories for children) a creature like a little man, esp. one having magical powers • *They have campaigned for many years against the discrimination experienced by dwarfs.* • *"Snow White and the Seven Dwarfs"* (title of a children's story)

dwarf /£dwɔːf, $dwɔːrf/ *adj* [before n; not gradable] • *You can grow dwarf* (= small) *conifers in pots on the patio.*

dwarf *obj* /£dwɔːf, $dwɔːrf/ *v* [T] • If one thing dwarfs another, it makes it seem small by comparison: *The new skyscraper will dwarf all those near it.* ○ *This new financial crisis may well dwarf most that have gone before.*

dwell /dwel/ *v* [I always + adv/prep] *past* **dwelt** /dwelt/ or **dwelled** *fml* to live (in a place or in a particular way) • *She dwelt* **in** *remote parts of Asia for many years.* • *He no longer lives alone but now dwells* **with** *his family.* • *"She dwelt among the untrodden ways / Beside the springs of Dove, / A maid whom there were none to praise / And very few to love"* (William Wordsworth in the poem *She Dwelt among the Untrodden Ways*, 1800) • NL

dwell·er /£ˈdwel·əʳ, $-ɚ/ *n* [C] • *city/town/cave dwellers* (= people who live in cities/towns/caves)

dwell·ing /ˈdwel·ɪŋ/ *n* [C] *fml* • *There is such a housing crisis in the country that there is a shortfall of some five million dwellings* (= places where people can live).

dwell on *obj v prep* [T] to think or talk about (something) a lot of the time • *In his speech, he dwelt on the plight of the sick and the hungry.* • *The report dwells rather too much on guns and violence.*

DWI /ˌdiːˌdʌb·l̩.juːˈaɪ/ *Am law abbreviation for* **driving while intoxicated**, see at DRIVE USE VEHICLE

dwin·dle /ˈdwɪn·dl̩/ *v* [I] to become less in number or smaller • *The community has dwindled* **to** *a tenth of its former size in the last two years.* • *Her hopes of success in the race dwindled last night as the weather became worse.*

dwin·dling /ˈdwɪn·dl̩·ɪŋ/ *adj* • *The magazine's circulation was dwindling before our new editor came.*

dye *obj* /daɪ/ *v* [T] **dyeing**, *past* **dyed** to change the colour of (something) using a special liquid • *He's dyed his hair black/a different colour.* [+ obj + n/adj] • *I'm getting bored with these T-shirts – I think I'll dye them.* • If someone has **dyed-in-the-wool** opinions, they hold them strongly and will not change them: *He's a dyed-in-the-wool traditionalist* *about cooking – he won't have any modern gadgets in the kitchen.*

dye /daɪ/ *n* • *She dipped the material into the dye* (= liquid substance for changing the colour of things). [U] • *There are dozens of different dyes to choose from.* [C]

dyke [WALL], **dike** /daɪk/ *n* [C] a wall built to prevent the sea or a river from flooding an area, or a channel dug to take water away from an area • Compare DAM.

dyke [WOMAN], **dike** /daɪk/ *n* [C] *slang* a homosexual woman; a LESBIAN. Many people consider this word offensive.

dyn·am·ic /daɪˈnæm·ɪk/ *adj* having a lot of ideas and enthusiasm; energetic and forceful • *She's young and dynamic and will be a great head of the department.* • *We need a dynamic expansion of trade with other countries.*

dyn·am·ic·al·ly /daɪˈnæm·ɪ·kli/ *adv*

dyn·am·i·sm /ˈdaɪ·nə·mɪ·zᵊm/ *n* [U] • *She keeps a freshness and dynamism about her while others grow stale.*

dyn·am·ics /daɪˈnæm·ɪks/ *pl n* forces that produce movement • *This software is used for modelling atmospheric dynamics.* • *(fig.) The fight for the leadership gave a fascinating insight into the group's dynamics* (= forces that produce change in the group). • *(fig.) The President said he wanted to have talks with the leaders to advance the dynamics* (= processes) *of peace.* • *(specialized)* In music, dynamics are changes in loudness: *Dynamics are indicated in this piece by the Italian words 'piano' and 'forte'.*

dyn·am·ics /daɪˈnæm·ɪks/ *n* [U] *specialized* • Dynamics is the scientific study of the forces that produce movement.

dyn·am·ic /daɪˈnæm·ɪk/ *adj* • *a dynamic force*

dyn·am·ic·al·ly /daɪˈnæm·ɪ·kli/ *adv* • *dynamically stable*

dyn·a·mite /ˈdaɪ·nə·maɪt/ *n* [U] a type of explosive, or *(fig. infml)* something that will cause great shock or excitement • *a stick of dynamite* • *(fig. infml) The issue of unemployment is* **political** *dynamite* (= could cause big problems) *for the government.* • *(fig. infml) Their studio recordings are boring, but on stage the band is dynamite* (= very exciting).

dyn·a·mite *obj* /ˈdaɪ·nə·maɪt/ *v* [T] • *The rebels had dynamited the railway line* (= destroyed it with dynamite).

dyn·a·mo /£ˈdaɪ·nə·məʊ, $-moʊ/ *n* [C] *pl* **dynamos** a device which changes energy of movement into electrical energy • *A dynamo on a bicycle will power a pair of lights while the wheels are going round.* • *(fig.) She's been a real dynamo* (= energetic force) *at this company – always making things happen.* • [PIC] **Bicycles**

dyn·a·sty /ˈdɪn·ə·sti, ˈdaɪ·nə-/ *n* [C] (a period when a country is ruled by) a series of rulers or leaders who are all from the same family • *The Mogul dynasty was founded by Babur and ruled over India for centuries.*

dyn·as·tic /£daɪˈnæs·tɪk, $-t̬ɪk/ *adj* [not gradable] *fml* • *The dynastic union of Norway, Denmark and Sweden was built on shaky foundations.*

d'you *infml* /djuː/ *short form of* do you • *D'you come here often?*

dys·en·tery /£ˈdɪs·ᵊn·tᵊr·i, £-tri, $-ter-/ *n* [U] a disease of the bowels which causes the contents to be excreted much more often and in a more liquid form than usual. It is caused by an infection which is spread by dirty water or food.

dys·func·tion /dɪsˈfʌŋk·ʃᵊn/ *n* [C] *medical or specialized* a problem or fault in an organ, part of the body or any physical system such as a machine • *There appears to be a dysfunction in the patient's respiratory system.*

dys·func·tion·al /dɪsˈfʌŋk·ʃᵊn·əl/ *adj medical or specialized* • *a dysfunctional family*

dys·lex·i·a /dɪˈslek·si·ə/ *n* [U] a difficulty with reading and writing caused by the brain's inability to see the difference between some letter shapes

dys·lex·ic /dɪˈslek·sɪk/ *adj*

dys·pep·si·a /dɪˈspep·si·ə/ *n* [U] *medical* pain in the stomach; INDIGESTION

dys·pep·tic /£dɪˈspep·tɪk, $-t̬ɪk/ *adj medical* • Someone who is dyspeptic has problems with their digestion. • *(literary)* Dyspeptic can also describe someone who is bad-tempered.

E e

E [LETTER] (*pl* **E's** or **Es**), **e** (*pl* **e's** or **es**) /iː/ *n* [C] the 5th letter of the English alphabet • An **E number** is any of a variety of numbers with the letter E in front of them which are used on containers of food in the European Union to show which particular approved chemical has been added to the food: *Have you seen how many E numbers there are in this drink!* ○ *All the E numbers were listed on the packet.* • [LP] **Silent letters**

E [EAST] *n* [U], *adj abbreviation for* EAST or EASTERN

E [MUSIC] /iː/ *n* a note in Western music • *The piece is in* **(the key of)** *E.* [U] • *The bottom string on a guitar is an E.* [C]

E [MARK] /iː/ *n* [C] (in some systems of marking work) a mark in an exam or for a piece of work that shows that the work is considered to be very bad • *You might have to take the course again if you get many more Es.* • *(Am)* (In other systems of marking work) a mark of E in an exam or for a piece of work shows that the work is considered to be excellent.

E [DRUG] /iː/ *n abbreviation for* ECSTASY [DRUG] • *She's stopped taking E.* [U] • *Simon did/took three E's last night.* [C]

each /iːtʃ/ *pronoun, determiner* every thing, person, etc. in a group of two or more, considered separately • *When you run, each foot leaves the ground before the other comes down.* • *There are five leaflets – please take one of each.* • *Each* **of** *the five satellites have their own orbit.* • *He said he'd loved each* **(one) of** *his five wives in different ways.* • *Each* **and every one (of** *the flowers)* *has its own colour and smell.* • *We each* (= Every one of us) *wanted the bedroom with the window, so we decided who'd get it by tossing a coin.* • *The bill comes to £79, so that's about £10 each.* • *It's 490 miles each* **way** *so it'll be almost a 1000-mile trip.* • *(Br) I'm sorry you hate my music, but* **each to his/their own** *(esp. Am* **to each his own***)* (= different people like or do different things). • If you put a sum of money **each way** on something like a horse race, you will win money if your horse comes first, second or third. • [LP] **Quantity words**

each oth·er, **one an·oth·er** *pronoun* (not used as the subject of a sentence) the other person, or all the other people in a group, who each act(s) on the others • *The couple kept looking at each other and smiling.* • *They're always wearing each other's clothes.* • *Everyone in my family tries to help each other when times are hard.* • *Why are you always arguing with each other?* • *Stop shouting at each other.* • *My sister and Tom are so happy together – they were* **made for** *each other* (= are perfectly matched).

eag·er /£ˈiː·gəʳ, $-gɚ/ *adj* wanting very much to do or have esp. something interesting or enjoyable • *eager children's faces* • *Lots of eager volunteers responded to the appeal for help.* • *She sounded very eager* **to** *meet you.* [+ *to* infinitive] • *They crowded round the spokesperson, eager* **for** *any news.* • *(infml)* If you describe someone as an **eager beaver** you mean that they are willing to work very hard.

eag·er·ly /£ˈiː·gə·li, $-gɚ-/ *adv* • *The dog wagged its tail eagerly when I picked up its lead.*

eag·er·ness /£ˈiː·gə·nəs, $-gɚ-/ *n* [U] • *In their eagerness* **to** *find a solution they may have overlooked certain financial difficulties.* [+ *to* infinitive]

eag·le /ˈiː·gl̩/ *n* [C] a (very) large strong bird with a curved beak which eats meat and can see very well • If you describe someone as **eagle-eyed** or say that they have an **eagle eye**, you mean that they notice everything, even very small details: *We sat down and started the exam under the eagle eye of the teacher.* • *"The Eagle has Landed"* (Neil Armstrong landing on the moon, 1969) • *"Where Eagles Dare"* (title of a book by Alistair Maclean, 1967) • [PIC] **Birds**

-ean /·i·ən/ *combining form* See at -AN [BELONG TO]

ear [BODY PART] /£ɪəʳ, $ɪr/ *n* [C] either of the two organs, one on each side of the head, by which people or animals hear sounds, or the piece of skin and tissue outside the head connected to this organ • *The hearing in my left ear's not so good – can you sit on my other side?* • *Van Gogh cut off part of one of his ears after a quarrel.* • *(fig.) I tried to* **close** *my ears* **to** (= tried not to listen to) *the sounds coming from next door.* • *I'm* **all ears** (= eagerly waiting to hear) *– tell us what they had to say.* • If you **have an/your ear to the ground** or **keep an/your ear to the ground**, you pay attention to all that is happening round you and to what people are saying. • If you say that someone's **ears are burning** you

SPANISH FALSE FRIENDS (E)

English	Spanish	Meaning
abortion *n*	aborto	miscarriage
actual *adj*	actual	current, topical, fashionable, up-to-date
actually *adv*	actualmente	at present, currently, nowadays
alcove *n*	alcoba	small bedroom
anticipate *v*	anticipar	to bring forward (an event); to look forward to something
argument *n*	argumento	story, plot
assist *v*	asistir	to be present, attend; to witness
assistance *n*	asistencia	audience, gathering, congregation, attendance
assistant *n*	asistenta	daily help, cleaning (wo)man
asylum *n*	asilo	old people's home
audience *n*	audiencia	court hearing, trial; readership
batter *v*	batir	to strike, hit; to fight, defeat; to tap lightly
cabaret *n*	cabaret	night club
cabin *n*	cabina	telephone booth, kiosk, cubicle; cockpit
cabinet *n*	gabinete	study, library; private sitting room; office; laboratory; museum; studio
cafe *n*	café	coffee
candid *adj*	cándido	white; naïve, disarming, innocent, sincere
career *n*	carrera	run; running; race course; road, path; row; course; conduct; route; travel; course of studies
character *n*	carácter	characteristic, trait
comedian *n*	comediante	actor, player; hypocrite (fig.)
comprehensive *adj*	comprensivo	understanding
compromise *n*	compromiso	promise; appointment, date; commitment; engagement
condescending *adj*	condescendiente	compliant, acquiescent
conductor *n*	conductor	driver; leader; guide; conveyor
conference *n*	conferencia	lecture, speech, address; long distance phone call
constipated *adj*	constipado	suffering from a cold
constipation *n*	constipación	common cold, catarrh
cynicism *n*	cinismo	shamelessness, impudence; lack of principle
deception *n*	decepción	disappointment, disenchantment
discuss *v*	discutir	to argue, agitate, stir, dispute
discussion *n*	discusión	argument
disgrace *n*	desgracia	misfortune, calamity, adversity, trouble
disgrace *v*	desgraciar	to spoil, ruin (appearance of); to displease
disgust *n*	disgusto	annoyance; sorrow; repugnance, boredom; trouble; bother; misfortune; quarrel, upset
disgust *v*	disgustar	to displease, irritate, disgruntle; to grieve
distract *v*	distraer	to amuse, entertain; to embezzle, misappropriate money
dormitory *n*	dormitorio	bedroom
edit *v*	editar	to publish
edition *n*	edición	publication, issue; publishing
editor *n*	editor	publisher
escapade *n*	escapada	escape; flying visit; quick trip
eventual *adj*	eventual	possible; temporary, casual (of work)
eventually *adv*	eventualmente	by chance, possibly, depending on circumstances
evidence *n*	evidencia	obviousness
excite *v*	excitar	to incite, urge on
extravagance *n*	extravagancia	whim; peculiarity, eccentricity
extravagant *adj*	extravagante	eccentric, outlandish, crazy
fantasy *n*	fantasía	imagination; fancy, whim
genial *adj*	genial	inspired, brilliant; characteristic, typical
geniality *n*	genialidad	brilliant idea; genius; eccentricity
gent *n*	gente	people, nation; troops
genteel *adj*	gentil	pagan; Gentile; heathen
gentle *adj*	gentil	elegant; charming; pretty; fine; pagan; heathen; Gentile
honest *adj*	honesto	fair, reasonable; modest, chaste; decent, proper
honestly *adv*	honestamente	decently, properly, modestly, purely, fairly, reasonably
honesty *n*	honestidad	decency, modesty; purity
ignore *v*	ignorar	to not know, be unaware of
illusion *n*	ilusión	excitement, anticipation
inconvenient *adj*	inconveniente	unsuitable; inadvisable; impolite; wrong; (n.) obstacle, drawback, objection
indignant *adj*	indignante	outrageous, infuriating; humiliating
indignity *n*	indignidad	unworthiness
industrious *adj*	industrioso	skilful, resourceful; versatile; handy
inhabitable *adj*	inhabitable	uninhabitable
inhabited *adj*	inhabitado	uninhabited
intend *v*	intentar	to try, attempt
intoxicated *adj*	intoxicar	to poison; mislead
intoxication *n*	intoxicación	poisoning; political disinformation
just *adj*	justo	exact, correct; tight
large *adj*	largo	lengthy, (too) long; full; good; generous, abundant; sharp; shrewd; quick
largely *adv*	largamente	for a long time, at length; fully; comfortably, at ease; generously
librarian *n*	librero	book-seller
library *n*	librería	bookshop; book-selling, book-trade
manifestation *n*	manifestación	political demonstration, mass meeting, rally
mascara *n*	máscara	mask, disguise; masked person
miserable *adj*	miserable	mean, miserly; rotten, despicable; squalid
misery *n*	miseria	poverty; fleas; meanness
molest *v*	molestar	to annoy; to upset; to be a nuisance
morbid *adj*	mórbido	soft, delicate
morose *adj*	moroso	slow, sluggish; dilatory
navigation *n*	navegación	sea voyage, crossing
notice *n*	noticia	news item; knowledge; notion
notorious *adj*	notorio	well-known; acknowledged; famous; obvious, blatant
ordinary *adj*	ordinario	coarse, vulgar; rude, crude
ostensible *adj*	ostensible	obvious, evident
pamphlet *n*	panfleto	satire, lampoon
panties *n*	pantis	tights, panty-hose
parent *n*	pariente/a	relative; (infml) the hubby, the missus
particular *adj*	particular	private, personal
particularly *adv*	particularmente	privately, personally
patio *n*	patio	pit of theatre; garage forecourt
periodical *n*	periódico	newspaper
petrol *n*	petróleo	oil; (L. Am.) paraffin
petulant *adj*	petulante	vain, self-satisfied; opinionated
phrase *n*	frase	sentence
precious *adj*	precioso	pretty, lovely, beautiful; charming
precise *adj*	preciso	necessary, essential; (Carib.) conceited
professor *n*	profesor	teacher, master
realize *v*	realizar	to carry out; bring about
relevant *adj*	relevante	outstanding, important
reparations *n*	reparaciones	repairs, restorations
retribution *n*	retribución	payment; reward; compensation
rude *adj*	rudo	unpolished, rough, coarse, common; stupid
sensible *adj*	sensible	sensitive, sore; responsive; impressionable; emotional, easily hurt; appreciable, noticeable; capable (of); regrettable
slips *n*	slips	briefs, pants; (L. Am.) bathing trunks
stranger *n*	extranjero	foreigner, alien; foreign country
suburb *n*	suburbio	slum quarter, shanty-town
sympathetic *adj*	simpático	likeable, pleasant; attractive
sympathise *v*	simpatizar	to get on well, hit it off
sympathy *n*	simpatía	fellow feeling, affection, warmth, friendliness; attractiveness
topic *n*	tópico	platitude, cliché, catchphrase
tremendous *adj*	tremendo	terrible, dreadful; (person) inventive, witty, entertaining
villa *n*	villa	small town, borough, municipality
virtual *adj*	virtual	potential; future; possible

EACH OTHER

- If we say *Sam and Mike helped each other before their exams* this means Sam helped Mike and Mike helped Sam. The phrase *(Br) one another* means the same but is more formal: *James and I work in the same building but we seldom see one another.*
- More than two people can be involved: *The four brothers were always hitting each other.*
- Sometimes a preposition is needed: *People were shouting* **at** *each other.*
- Notice the possessive form: *The two sisters borrowed each other's clothes.*

Some verbs describe situations like this without needing *each other* (although this can be used for emphasis). Common examples are:

They **met/parted** *in front of the town hall.*
The ships **passed/collided** *during the night.*
Be careful that those wires don't **touch**.
We **shook hands** *and* **said hello**.
Sally and her friend **talked** *for hours.*
"Have you met Ms Langley?" "No, but we've **spoken** *on the telephone."*
They **kissed**, **hugged**, *and within two months they* **married**.
John and Sheila's marriage didn't work out, so they **separated/divorced**.
The teams **fought/competed** *fairly.*
The government and private companies **cooperated** *in the project.*

Be careful about the use of REFLEXIVE pronouns such as 'themselves', 'ourselves'. They do not mean the same as 'each other'. Compare *They bought each other presents* (each gave something to the other) and *They bought themselves presents* (each person kept the present they had bought). Sometimes the action would be unusual – *We kissed ourselves* – or impossible – *They married themselves.* [LP] **Reflexive pronouns** at REFLEXIVE.

mean that they feel as if they are being talked about: All this talk about the boss – her ears must be burning! • *(infml)* If you say that someone's **ears are flapping** you mean that they are trying to hear what you are saying, although they are not part of your conversation. • *If I have to listen to something I don't understand, it just* **goes in one ear and out the other** (= is immediately forgotten and has no effect). • *You must have* **good ears** (= be able to hear well), *if you can hear high-pitched sounds like that.* • If someone **has an ear for** music or languages, they are good at hearing, repeating or understanding these sounds: *She's never had much of an ear for languages.* • If someone **has the ear of** an important and powerful person, their ideas are listened to and given importance by that person: *Now that he has* **gained/lost** *the ear of the Director, he's going to have/lose a lot of influence on policy.* • *(slang) One minute I was in a good job and the next I was* **out on** *my* **ear** (= suddenly dismissed). • *I'm afraid I won't be able to help you – I'm* **up to** *my* **ears in** (= very busy with) *work.* • *She's* **up to** *her* **ears in** *debt* (= very much in debt). • An **ear-splitting/ear-piercing** sound is one that is so loud/high that it hurts your ears: *an ear-splitting explosion* ○ *ear-piercing screams.* • See also AURAL. • [LP] **Sound**

-eared /£-ɪəd, $-ɪrd/ *combining form* • *a long-eared rabbit* (= a rabbit with long ears)

ear [PLANT PART] /£ɪəʳ, $ɪr/ *n* [C] the top part of grass-like plants such as wheat, which contains the seeds or grains which are used as food • *an ear of corn* • [PIC] **Cereals**

ear·ache /£ˈɪə·reɪk, $ˈɪr·eɪk/ *n* [C/U] (a) pain in the inside part of your ear • *When I was a child I used to get terrible earache(s).* • [LP] **Feelings and pains**

ear·drops /£ˈɪə·drɒps, $ˈɪr·drɑːps/ *pl n* liquid medicine put into the ears, usually to cure an ear infection

ear·drum /£ˈɪə·drʌm, $ˈɪr-/ *n* [C] a thin piece of skin inside the ear that moves backwards and forwards very quickly when sound waves reach it, allowing you to hear sounds • [PIC] **Drum**

ear·flaps /£ˈɪə·flæps, $ɪr-/ *pl n* the two pieces of material or fur on some hats which can be pulled down to cover the ears • [PIC] **Hats**

ear·ful /£ˈɪə·fʊl, $ˈɪr-/ *n* [U] angry complaining speech • *I'd better not be late or my granny will* **give** *me* **an** *earful about my laziness and thoughtlessness.*

earl /£ɜːl, $ɜːrl/ *n* [C] a British man of high social rank, between a VISCOUNT and a MARQUIS • *the Earl of Northumberland* • *Security is quite tight because several earls and a duke will be in the audience.*

earl·dom /£ɜːl·dəm, $ɜːrl-/ *n* [C] • An earldom is the rank or lands of an earl or COUNTESS.

ear·lobe /£ˈɪə·ləʊb, $ˈɪr·loʊb/, **lobe** *n* [C] the soft round part at the bottom of the ear

ear·ly /£ˈɜː·li, $ˈɜːr-/ *adj, adv* **-ier**, **-iest** near the beginning of (a period of time), or before the usual, expected or planned time • *If you finish early* (= before the end of the allowed time) *you can go home.* • *I like arriving/being a little early for interviews.* • *The team captain scored two wonderful goals early* **(on) in** *the game.* • *I hate having to get up too early* **(in** *the morning).* • *You should drive very early in the morning, to avoid the traffic.* • *We left in the early* **hours** (= early in the day) *of the 29th of June, before dawn.* • *I'm going to* **have/get** *an early* **night** (= go to sleep before my usual time). • *She was a poet living* **in** *the early fifteenth century.* • *(fml) Ms Perkin learned to read at the early* **age** *of three.* • **It's** *rather early* **to** *be sowing carrot seeds, isn't it?* [+ *to* infinitive] • *Your daughter seems to have recovered but it's a bit too early to be absolutely sure.* • *Mercedes were pioneers during the early* **days/years** (= the beginning time) *of car manufacture.* • *(fml) I think an early decision* (= a decision made without delay) *would be wise.* • *These are some of my early* (= first) *attempts at sculpture.* • Early flowers and vegetables are ones that are ready before ordinary ones. • *Clarke took the lead* **as** *early* **as** (= at the surprisingly soon time of) *the fourth minute.* • *(Br) Although we've lost the first match, it's* **early days** (= a lot might still happen or change) *and I think we can still win the competition.* • *Sometimes I feel my children are going to drive/send me* **to an early grave** (= cause me a lot of worry and annoyance). • *(Am)* **Early Childhood Education** (*abbreviation* **ECE**) is the study of the education of children from two to seven years of age: *She has a Masters in Early Childhood Education.* • Esp. in Britain in the past, **early-closing day** was the one day in the middle of the week when most shops closed very early in the afternoon. • **Early music** is Western music of the **Middle Ages** or RENAISSANCE, written before about 1600: *an expert on early music* ○ *an early-music consort/orchestra* • An **early warning system** is a military system of RADAR stations intended to give a warning as soon as enemy aircraft or bombs approach. • *(saying)* 'Early to bed and early to rise makes a man healthy, wealthy and wise' means that you will be well, successful and intelligent if you get enough sleep and start work early in the day. • *(humorous)* An **early bird** is a person who gets up or arrives early. • *(saying)* 'The early bird gets/catches the worm' means the person who gets up early or arrives first is the one who is successful. • Compare LATE [NEAR THE END]; LATE [AFTER].

ear·li·er /£ˈɜː·li·əʳ, $ˈɜːr·li·ɚ/ *adj, adv* [not gradable] • *If you arrived earlier, you'd have more time.* • *Earlier in the day, the two Presidents had a discussion on nuclear weapons.* • *Here's a dish I prepared earlier* (= I made a short time ago). • *This is an earlier and inferior model.*

ear·li·est /£ˈɜː·li·ɪst, $ˈɜːr-/ *adj, adv* [not gradable] • *My earliest* (= first) *memory is of being held up as a baby to watch Neil Armstrong landing on the moon on TV.* • *I'm very busy, so I won't be with you till 4 o'clock* **at the earliest** (= not before 4 o'clock, and probably after it).

ear·li·ness /£ˈɜː·lɪ·nəs, $ˈɜːr-/ *n* [U]

ear·mark *obj* /£ˈɪə·mɑːk, $ˈɪr·mɑːrk/ *v* [T often passive] to keep or intend (something) for a particular purpose • *Five billion dollars of this year's budget is already earmarked* **for** *hospital improvements.*

ear·muffs /£ˈɪə·mʌfs, $ˈɪr-/ *pl n* a pair of small pieces of furry material worn over the ears and joined by a curved strip which goes over the head to hold them in place • *Put your earmuffs on, it's freezing out there.* • [PIC] **Hats**

earn *(obj)* /£ɜːn, $ɜːrn/ *v* to receive (money) as payment for work that you do, or to (cause to) get (something) that you deserve because of your qualities or actions • *This month's pay increase means that I'll be earning $30 000 a year.* [T] •

How much do you earn, if you don't mind me asking? [T] • *Now that you're earning, how about taking me out to dinner!* [I] • *You can't expect to earn* **a living** (=be paid enough money to live on) *from your painting.* [T] • *At 10% interest, £10 000 in the bank will earn* (=give) *you £1000 a year.* [+ two objects] • *Coffee exports earn* (=give) *Brazil many millions of pounds a year./Brazil earns many millions of pounds a year* **from** *coffee exports.* [+ two objects] • *It's been a tough six months and I feel I've earned a few weeks off.* [T] • *The release of Nelson Mandela earned de Klerk praise from around the world.* [+ two objects] • See also WELL-EARNED. • LP› **Money**

earn·er /£'ɜː·nəʳ, $'ɜːr·nɚ/ *n* [C] • *In most of these cases, the woman is the sole earner in the family.* • *(infml) That hamburger stand is a nice little earner.*

earn·ings /£'ɜː·nɪŋz, $'ɜːr-/ *pl n* • Your earnings are the amount of money that you are paid for the work you do: *Average earnings for skilled workers are rising.*

earn·est /£'ɜː·nɪst, $'ɜːr-/ *adj* serious or determined, esp. too serious and unable to find your own actions amusing • *At school he was very earnest but he's more relaxed now.* • *She made an earnest attempt to convert me to her point of view.* • *These fanatics are* **in/in deadly** *earnest* (=completely serious) *when they say they want to destroy all forms of government.* • If something is done **in** earnest, it is done with seriousness and attention: *After sharpening all his pencils and making a cup of tea, he started drawing in earnest.* • When something begins **in** earnest, it has already started but is now being done in a serious and complete way: *The election campaign has begun in earnest, with both parties severely criticizing the other.* • *"The Importance of Being Earnest"* (title of a play by Oscar Wilde, 1895)

earn·est·ly /£'ɜː·nɪst·li, $'ɜːr-/ *adv* • *They sit for hours, earnestly discussing the state of the economy.*

earn·est·ness /£'ɜː·nɪst·nəs, $'ɜːr-/ *n* [U] • *He explained* **in all** *earnestness* (=very seriously) *how the world was on the brink of ecological disaster.*

ear·phone /£'ɪə·fəʊn, $'ɪr·foʊn/ *n* [C] a small device that changes electrical signals into sound and is held inside or near to the user's ear • *a pair of earphones* • *an earphone socket*

ear·phones /£'ɪə·fəʊnz, $'ɪr·foʊnz/ *pl n* a piece of equipment made from two small devices that change electrical signals into sounds which are held together by a curved strip. The devices then stay next to a person's ears allowing them, but not the people around them, to hear the sounds • *a pair/set of earphones*

ear·piece /£'ɪə·piːs, $'ɪr-/ *n* [C] the part of a telephone that you hold near to your ear and which produces sound

ear·plug /£'ɪə·plʌg, $'ɪr-/ *n* [C usually pl] a small piece of soft material such as wax, cotton or plastic which you put into your ear to keep out noise or water

ear·ring /£'ɪə·rɪŋ, $'ɪr·ɪŋ/ *n* [C] a piece of jewellery, usually one of a pair, worn in a hole in the ear or fixed to the ear by a fastener that does not go through the ear • *gold earrings* • *a stud/clip-on earring* • *a pair of dangly earrings* • *He was* **wearing** *an earring in his left ear.* • PIC› **Jewellery**

ear·shot /£'ɪə·ʃɒt, $'ɪr·ʃɑːt/ *n* [U] the range of distance within which it is possible to be heard or to hear what someone is saying • *I nervously reminded her that the boss was sitting well* **within** *earshot.* • *I don't think you should say anything while she's still* **in** *earshot.* • *Wait till she's* **out of** *earshot before you say anything.*

earth PLANET /£ɜːθ, $ɜːrθ/ *n* [U] the planet third in order of distance from the Sun, between VENUS and MARS; the world on which we live • *The Earth takes approximately 365¼ days to go round the Sun.* • *Earth looks incredibly beautiful from space.* • *Blunkett's Circus is the greatest show on earth* (=in the world). • If you are **brought back/down/back down to earth** or you **come back/down/back down to earth** you suddenly stop thinking about pleasant but probably impossible things and are aware instead of the practical or unpleasant facts of real life: *The realization of how little work I'd done for the exams brought me abruptly back down to earth.* • If something or someone is/looks/sounds/tastes **like nothing (else) on earth**, it seems very strange, unusual or unpleasant: *With the black make-up and strange clothes he looked like nothing on earth.* • *(infml)* **On earth** is used after the question words how, what, when, where, who and why to suggest that the expected answer is extreme, unlikely or unpleasant: *How on earth did this happen?* ○ *What on earth is that terrible noise?* • **The earth** means a lot of money: *What a beautiful coat! It must have* **cost** *(you) the earth!* ○ *I* **paid** *the earth for this leather bag.* ○ *They* **charged** *me the earth for a cup of coffee.* • *(infml)* If someone says **the earth moved** or asks **did the earth move for you?** they are joking about how good or special a sexual experience was. • *(infml)* If you describe a woman as an **earth mother** you mean she seems full of emotional and spiritual awareness, and seems particularly suited to having and loving children. • An **earth science** is one of several sciences, such as GEOLOGY, which deals with the structure, age, etc. of the Earth. • If you describe something as **earth-shattering** or **earth-shaking**, you mean that it is extremely important or very surprising: *an earth-shattering discovery* • *"Earth has not anything to show more fair"* (William Wordsworth in the poem *Sonnet Composed upon Westminster Bridge*, 1807) • LP› **Nations and nationalities**

earth SUBSTANCE /£ɜːθ, $ɜːrθ/ *n* [U] the usually brown, heavy and loose substance of which a large part of the surface of the ground is made, and in which plants can grow; the land surface of the Earth rather than the sky or sea • *The ploughed earth looked rich and dark and fertile.* • *They piled the earth and stones from the hole against the wall.* • *A huge crack appeared in the earth in front of us.* • An **earth tone** or **earth colour** is a rich dark colour which contains some brown: *She went through a phase where she wore nothing but earth tones.* • *"Earth to earth, ashes to ashes, dust to dust"* (Book of Common Prayer, burial service, 1662) • See also EARTHEN.

ear·thy /£'ɜː·θi, $'ɜːr-/ *adj* • *an earthy smell* • Compare EARTHY.

earth WIRE *Br and Aus* /£ɜːθ, $ɜːrθ/, *Am* **ground** *n* [C usually sing] (a wire that makes) a connection between a piece of electrical equipment and the ground, so the user is protected from feeling an electric shock if the equipment develops a fault

earth *obj Br and Aus* /£ɜːθ, $ɜːrθ/, *Am* **ground** *v* [T] • *You could get a nasty shock from that water heater if it isn't earthed properly.*

earth HOLE /£ɜːθ, $ɜːrθ/ *n* [C] a hole in the ground where an animal such as a FOX lives

earth·bound /£'ɜːθ·baʊnd, $'ɜːrθ-/ *adj* unable to leave the surface of the earth, or *(fig.)* not special, not exciting or not spiritual • *The space shuttle remained earthbound because of a technical fault.* • *(fig.) On the whole it was an uninspired and earthbound performance.*

earth·en /£'ɜː·θən, £-ðən, $'ɜːr-/ *adj* [not gradable] made of earth or of baked clay • *The hut had an earthen floor and a thatched roof.*

earth·en·ware /£'ɜː·θən·weəʳ, £-ðən-, $'ɜːr·θən·wer/ *n* [U], *adj* [not gradable] (dishes, bowls, etc.) made of quite rough clay, often shaped with the hands

ear·thi·ness /£'ɜː·θɪ·nəs, $'ɜːr-/ *n* [U] See at EARTHY

earth·ling /£'ɜːθ·lɪŋ, $'ɜːrθ-/ *n* [C] (esp. in stories) a human being, esp. when talked to or talked about by a creature from another planet • *The aliens laughed when they discovered that earthlings have only two legs.*

earth·ly /£'ɜːθ·li, $'ɜːrθ-/ *adj* [not gradable] happening in or related to this world and this physical life, not in heaven or a spiritual life • *He's worshipped as a god who performed many miracles during his earthly existence.* • *The Seychelles islands are an earthly* **paradise**. • *(infml)* Earthly is also used in questions or negatives to mean possible: *What earthly* **reason** *can she have for being so horrible to me?* ○ *At this rate, we haven't got an earthly* **chance** *of finishing on time* (=are almost certain to be late).

earth·quake /£'ɜːθ·kweɪk, $'ɜːrθ-/ *n* [C] a sudden violent movement of the Earth's surface, sometimes causing great damage • *In 1906 an earthquake destroyed much of San Francisco.*

earth·wards /£'ɜːθ·wədz, $'ɜːrθ·wɚdz/, **earth·ward** *adv* [not gradable] towards the Earth, from the air or from space • *Because of ice on the wings, the plane began to spiral earthwards.*

earth·ward /£'ɜːθ·wəd, $'ɜːrθ·wɚd/ *adj* [not gradable] • *an earthward descent*

earth·work /£'ɜːθ·wɜːk, $'ɜːrθ·wɜːrk/ *n* [C usually pl] a bank of earth made, esp. in the past, for defence against enemy attack

earth·worm /£'ɜːθ·wɜːm, $'ɜːrθ·wɜːrm/ *n* [C] a common type of WORM (=small animal with a long narrow soft body), which moves through the earth

ear·thy /£'ɜː·θi, $'ɜːr-/ *adj* **-ier, -iest** enjoying and being honest and clear about subjects that are usually avoided by many people, such as the body and emotions • *an earthy* *sense of humour* • *an earthy film* • Compare **earthy** at EARTH [SUBSTANCE].

ear·thi·ness /£'ɜː·θɪ·nəs, $'ɜːr-/ *n* [U] • *I like the earthiness of the novel.*

ear·wig /£'ɪə·wɪg, $'ɪr-/ *n* [C] a small insect with two PINCERS (= curved pointed parts) at the back end of its body • [PIC]› **Insects**

ease *(obj)* [LESSEN] /iːz/ *v* to make or become less severe, difficult, unpleasant, painful, etc. • *To ease the problem of overcrowding which exists in many prisons, new prisons will be built.* [T] • *After the arrival of the United Nations soldiers, tension in the area began to ease.* [I] • *The doctor promised that these pills would ease the pain.* [T] • *If it will ease your* **mind** (= stop you from worrying), *I'll speak to the boss for you.* [T] • *At last the rain began to ease* **(off/up)** (= gradually stop or become less). [I] • *The police are under political pressure to ease* **up on** (= be less active about) *their investigation.* [I] • *If the professors don't ease* **up on** *her* (= treat her more gently), *she's going to have a nervous breakdown.* [I]

ease *obj* [MOVE] /iːz/ *v* [T always + adv/prep] to move (something) slowly and carefully in a particular direction or into a particular position • *I eased myself* **through** *the crowd to the stage.* • *She eased the key* **into** *the lock, anxious not to wake the family.* • If someone tries to **ease** you **out (of** something such as a job), they try to force you to leave: *It gradually became clear that his political enemies were trying to ease him out of power.*

ease [EASINESS] /iːz/ *n* [U] freedom from difficulty, effort, pain, etc. • *She won the 400m race* **with** *ease* (= without difficulty). • *The doors are extra-wide* **for** *ease* **of** *access* (= so that people can get in without difficulty). • *She retired from her job at 35 and now lives* **a life of** *ease in Barbados.* • *He immediately felt completely* **at (his)** *ease* (= relaxed and able to talk freely). • *She soon* **put/set** *me* **at** *(my) ease* (= made me relaxed and able to talk freely). • If someone such as a soldier is **at ease** or **standing at ease**, they are standing with their feet apart and their hands behind their back. • See also EASY [NOT DIFFICULT].

eas·el /'iː·zəl/ *n* [C] a wooden frame, usually with three legs, that holds a picture, esp. one which an artist is painting or drawing • [PIC]› **Drawing and painting**

eas·i·ly /'iː·zɪ·li/ *adv* See at EASY [NOT DIFFICULT]

eas·i·ness /'iː·zɪ·nəs/ *n* [U] See at EASY [COMFORTABLE]

east /iːst/ *(abbreviation* **E**) *n* [U] the direction from which the sun rises in the morning, opposite to the west, or the part of an area or country which is in this direction • *The points of the compass are North, South, East and West.* • *Can you show me which way is east, please?* • *Most of the country, except the east, is rural.* • *Her home is* **in the** *east* **of** *France.* • *According to the map, the village* **is/lies** *about 10 km* **to the** *east* **of** *here.* • *The house has an east-***facing** *terrace.* • East also refers to those countries in Europe which had COMMUNIST governments before the 1990s: *The collapse of Communism changed East-West relations for ever.* • **The East** is Asia, esp. its eastern and southern parts: *She spent her childhood in the East – mostly in China and Japan.* • *"Oh, East is East, and West is West, and never the twain shall meet"* (Rudyard Kipling in the poem *The Ballad of East and West*, 1892) • [LP]› **Directions**

east /iːst/ *(abbreviation* **E**) *adj, adv* [not gradable] • *Cambridge is in East Anglia.* • *The East wall of the mosque is covered with a beautiful mosaic.* • An east **wind** is a wind coming from the east. • *We'll drive east for a few more miles, then turn south.* • *They were the first people to travel east* **of** *the mountains* (= into the area beyond and to the east of the mountains). • *We walked* **due** (= directly) *east for two kilometres.* • *The garden* **faces** *east, so we'll get the morning sun.* • *I have to go back East, to visit my father.* • In the US, the **East Coast** is the part of the country near the Atlantic Ocean, including cities such as New York, Boston and Philadelphia. • In Britain, the **East End** is an area in the east of London and an **East Ender** is a person who lives or was born in this part of London.

east·bound /'iːst·baʊnd/ *adj* [not gradable] • Eastbound means going or leading towards the east: *an eastbound train* ○ *eastbound flights* ○ *the eastbound lanes of road*

east·er·ly /£'iː·stəl·i, $-stɚ·li/ *adj, n* [C] • *They were travelling in an easterly* (= towards the east) *direction.* • *The town is in the most easterly* (= nearest the east) *part of the country.* • *We had an easterly* **(wind)** (= wind from the east) *today.*

east·ern /£'iː·stən, $-stɚn/ *(abbreviation* **E**) *adj* • *The eastern part of the country is very mountainous.* • *Buddhism and other Eastern* (= Asian) *religions fascinate me.* • *1989 saw the transformation of Eastern Europe.* • *Until about 1991, the Eastern* **bloc** *was the Soviet Union and the communist countries of Eastern Europe.*

east·ern·er /£'iː·stən·əʳ, $-ɚ/ *n* [C] • An easterner is a person born or living in the eastern part of a country, esp. the US.

east·ern·most /£'iː·stən,məʊst, $-stɚn,moʊst/ *adj* [not gradable] • *Lowestoft is the easternmost* (= furthest towards the east) *town in Great Britain.*

east·ward /£'iːst·wəd, $-wɚd/ *adj* [not gradable] • *The eastward* (= towards the east) *route might be quicker.*

east·wards /£'iːst·wədz, $-wɚdz/, **east·ward** *adv* [not gradable] • *The storm is moving slowly eastwards* (= towards the east).

East·er /£'iː·stəʳ, $-stɚ/ *n* [C usually sing; not after *the*] a Christian religious holiday to celebrate Jesus Christ's death and return to life • *I get two weeks off school* **at** *Easter.* • An **Easter egg** is either chocolate in the shape of an egg or an egg with a painted shell. • **Easter Sunday** is the day on which Easter is celebrated. • [LP]› **Holidays**

eas·y [NOT DIFFICULT] /'iː·zi/ *adj, adv* **-ier, -iest** not difficult; not needing much effort • *She looked through the exam paper trying to find an easy question to answer.* • *The book is called 'Ten Easy Ways to Health and Fitness'.* • *Getting into the film business is not easy*/**far from** *easy*/**no** *easy* **matter**. • *Would a ten o'clock appointment be easier* **for** *you?* • *Let's run the last two miles at an easy* (= not fast) *pace.* • **It**'*s easy* **to** *find the house./The house is easy* **to** *find.* [+ *to* infinitive] • *She is very easy* **to** *talk to.* [+ *to* infinitive] • *The easiest thing* **(to** *do) is for us to take the train home.* • **It** *isn't easy* **being** *a student these days, you know.* [+ v-*ing*] • *The French team came an easy first in both races.* • *(disapproving) I don't believe a word, when politicians come out with their easy* (= too simple) *answers.* • *I don't trust that easy* (= relaxed) *charm of his.* • *The two off-duty police officers were an easy target for the bombers.* • *(slang) My car can do 250kph, easy.* • *(infml)* If you think that something is extremely easy, you can say that it is **as easy as ABC/ anything/pie/winking/falling off a log**. • *(infml) It's easy* **(for** *you)* **to** *laugh/criticize/say* (= It's unfair of you to laugh/criticize/state an opinion, because you don't understand the situation), *but you won't get blamed if anything goes wrong.* [+ *to* infinitive] • *(infml) "Why don't you just ask the government to pay?" "That's* **easier said than done** (= easy to suggest but much more difficult to make happen)." • *(infml) Making bread is* **the easiest thing in the world** (= extremely easy) *after you've had some practice.* • *(infml) Until he was caught, he used to say that stealing cars was* **easy money** (= money that you get from only a little, usually dishonest, work). • *(infml) I like her paintings/songs – they're* **easy on the eye/ear** (= very pleasant to look at/listen to). • Clothes that are **easy-care** do not need special treatment when they are washed. • *(esp. Br slang)* If you describe someone as **easy game** or **easy meat** (*Am usually* an **easy mark**), you mean that they can be easily deceived: *Old ladies living alone are easy game* **for** *con-men.* • The type of music that is described as **easy listening** is music that is not very complicated, serious or difficult. • *(Br infml)* The expression **easy-peasy** is used esp. by children about something to mean that it is very easy. • *(infml)* An **easy touch** is someone whom you can easily persuade or deceive into giving you something, usually money. • See also EASE [EASINESS].

eas·i·ly /'iː·zɪ·li/ *adv* • *I can easily* (= without difficulty) *be home early tonight, if you want.* • *Ever since the illness I get tired very easily* (= more quickly than usual). • *I think Venice is easily* (= without doubt) *the most beautiful city in Europe.*

eas·i·ness /'iː·zi·nəs/ *n* [U]

eas·y [COMFORTABLE] /'iː·zi/ *adj, adv* **-ier, -iest** comfortable or calm; free from worry, pain, etc. • *They both retired and went off to lead an easy life in the Bahamas.* • *I don't feel easy* **about** *leaving him alone in the house all day.* • *She won't be easy* **in** *her* **mind** *until I ring her to say I'm OK.* • *With the harvest finished, I was able to relax* **with an** *easy* **mind/conscience**. • *(infml) "Shall we go to the Indian restaurant, or would you prefer Chinese food?" "I'm easy* (= I don't care which is chosen)." • *(infml) I lost £500 in a card game last night, but that's life –* **easy come, easy go** (= Because I got it easily I'm not worried about losing it). • *(infml) "Can I put it down now?" "Yes, but it's fragile so* **easy does it** (= do it slowly and carefully)." • *(infml)* **Go easy on/with** (= Don't take too much of) *the cream – I haven't* *had any yet.* • *(infml)* **Go easy on** *the new students* (= Don't treat them too severely). • *(infml) If you've got a weak heart, you'd better* **take it/things easy** (= not be too active). • *(infml) When we go on holiday we're just going to* **take it/things easy** (= have a relaxing time) *and not do too much sightseeing.* • *(infml)* **Take it easy** (= Relax and do not get upset)! *Let's not start any trouble.* • An **easy chair** is a big soft comfortable chair with arms. • *(approving)* Someone who is **easy-going** manages usually to accept and stay calm about things that other people might get angry or worried about: *an easy-going attitude/manner* ○ *a friendly, easy-going type of guy* • *(infml dated)* If you are **on easy street**, you are rich enough to live comfortably without having to work too hard. • *"Easy Rider"* (title of film, 1969) • See also EASE [LESSEN].

eas·i·ness /ˈiː·zɪ·nəs/ *n* [U]

eat *(obj)* [HAVE FOOD] /iːt/ *v past simple* **ate** /et, eɪt/, *past part* **eaten** /£ˈiː·tᵊn, $-t̬ᵊn/ to put or take (food) into the mouth, chew it, and swallow it • *People who are vegetarian don't eat meat.* [T] • *When I've got a cold, I don't feel like eating.* [I] • *We usually eat* (= have a meal) *at about 7 o'clock.* [I] • *(Am infml)* If you eat a cost or expense, you accept that you will not profit from it: *The agency paid a lot to sign the celebrity to a contract, and now that he's dead they'll just have to eat it.* [T] • *I'm really tired of restaurants – shall we eat* **in** (= have a meal at home) *tonight?* [I] • *We eat* **out** (= have a meal at a restaurant, or at someone else's house) *several times a week.* [I] • *I gave my dog some pasta and she ate it* **up** (= ate it all) *eagerly.* [M] • *(infml esp. humorous)* If you say **(I am so hungry) I could eat a horse**, you mean that you are extremely hungry. • *(infml)* If someone **eats like a horse**, they always eat a lot of food: *You'd better cook plenty of food if your brother's coming to dinner – you know he eats like a horse!* • *(infml)* If a person **eats** someone **for breakfast**, they can very easily control or defeat the other person: *Our boss eats* **people like you** *for breakfast.* • If you **eat for comfort**, you eat because you are feeling anxious or upset and not because you are hungry. • *(infml esp. humorous)* If you **eat** someone **out of house and home**, you eat a lot of the food they have in their house, usually while you are staying with them. • *(infml)* If you have someone **eating out of** your **hand**, they always eagerly do what you ask them to do: *Within two minutes of walking into the classroom, she had the kids eating out of her hand.* • *(infml humorous)* If someone says **eat your heart out** followed by the name of a famous person, they are joking that they are even better than that person: *I'm singing in the village production of Tosca next month – eat your heart out Pavarotti!* • *(infml)* If you **eat humble pie/eat** your **words**/*(Am and Aus also)* **eat crow**, you are forced to admit you were wrong: *You'd better be sure you've got the sales figures right, otherwise you'll be eating humble pie for a long time.* • *If she marries him* **I'll eat my hat** (= I will be extremely surprised). • An **eating apple** is an apple that can be eaten raw, rather than cooked. Compare **cooking apple** at COOK. • *"You are what you eat"* (saying used as the title of a film, 1968) • *"Eating people is wrong"* (from the song *The Reluctant Cannibal* written by Flanders and Swann, 1956) • *"Eat, drink and be merry, for tomorrow we die"* (saying, based on several passages in the Bible) • [LP] **Phrases and customs**

eat·ab·le /£ˈiː·tə·bl̩, $-t̬ə-/ *adj* • If food is eatable it is of just good enough quality for a person to enjoy eating it: *"What was the food like?" "It wasn't excellent but it was certainly eatable."* • Compare EDIBLE.

eat·er /£ˈiː·təʳ, $-t̬ɚ/ *n* [C] • *She's a* **big/small** *eater* (= she eats a lot/a little).

eat·er·y /£ˈiː·tᵊr·i, $-t̬ɚ·ri/ *n* [C] *infml esp. humorous* • *We met in a little eatery* (= restaurant) *just off the main road.*

eats /iːts/ *pl n infml* • *Would you like some eats* (= food, esp. small amounts of special prepared food)?

eat *(obj)* [DAMAGE] /iːt/ *v past simple* **ate** /et, eɪt/, *past part* **eaten** /£ˈiː·tᵊn, $-t̬ᵊn/ to damage, destroy or use (something) • *The metal was eaten* **away** *where the acid had dripped.* [T] • *Dry rot had eaten* **into** *the chair legs.* [I] • *The high cost of living in London is eating* **into** *my savings.* [I] • *A big old car like that eats* **up** (= uses a lot of) *petrol.* [T] • *(infml)* If something **is eating** you it is making you anxious or annoyed: *You've been very quiet – tell me what's eating you.* • *(infml)* If someone **is eaten up with/by** a particular emotion they are experiencing it very strongly: *He was so eaten up with guilt he became ill.*

eau de co·logne /£ˌəʊ·də·kəˈləʊn, $ˌoʊ·də·kəˈloʊn/, **co·logne** *n* [U] a pleasant smelling liquid, less strong than PERFUME, which you put on your body to make yourself feel and smell fresh

eaves /iːvz/ *pl n* the edge of a roof that sticks out over the top of a wall • *There's an old bird's nest* **under** *the eaves.* • [PIC] **Accommodation**

eaves·drop /£ˈiːvz·drɒp, $-drɑːp/ *v* [I] **-pp-** to listen to someone's private conversation without them knowing • *They've been eavesdropping* **on** *all conversations in the Embassy using secret microphones.*

eaves·drop·per /£ˈiːvz·drɒp·əʳ, $-drɑː·pɚ/ *n* [C]

ebb /eb/ *v* [I] (of the sea or its TIDE) to move away from the coast and fall to a lower level, or, more generally, (of something) to become less or disappear • *The tide is ebbing so we'll soon be able to walk further down the beach.* • *He could feel his strength ebbing* **(away)**.

ebb /eb/ *n* [U] • *We'll sail* **on the** *ebb* (= when the TIDE is moving away from the coast). • *(fig.) Consumer confidence is currently* **at a low** *ebb* (= in a bad state). • *The* **ebb and flow** (= frequently changing situation) *of politics in Washington goes on as usual.* • *The* **ebb tide** (= general movement of the sea away from the coast) *will take us out of the bay.* Compare **flood tide** at FLOOD [COVER WITH WATER].

eb·o·ny /ˈeb·ᵊn·i/ *n* [U] a very hard dark-coloured wood of a particular tropical tree, used esp. for making furniture • *(literary)* Ebony is also used to mean very dark.

e·bul·li·ent /ɪbˈʊl·i·ᵊnt/ *adj* (of a person) very energetic, positive and happy • *Our ebullient host couldn't stop laughing and talking.*

e·bul·li·ent·ly /ɪbˈʊl·i·ᵊnt·li/ *adv*

e·bul·li·ence /ɪˈbʊl·i·ᵊnts/ *n* [U]

EC /ˌiːˈsiː/ *n* [U] **the EC** *abbreviation for* **European Community**, see at EUROPEAN

ec·cen·tric [STRANGE] /ɪkˈsen·trɪk, ek-/ *adj* strange or unusual, sometimes in an amusing way • *eccentric behaviour* • *eccentric clothes* • *Don't you think it's eccentric to keep a pet crocodile in the bath?*

ec·cen·tric /ɪkˈsen·trɪk, ek-/ *n* [C] • *She's a real eccentric – she does the strangest things.*

ec·cen·tri·cal·ly /ɪkˈsen·trɪ·kli, ek-/ *adv*

ec·cen·tri·ci·ty /£ˌek·senˈtrɪs·ɪ·ti, $-t̬i/ *n* • *His eccentricity now extends to never washing or changing his clothes.* [U] • *Her eccentricities get stranger by the day.* [C]

ec·cen·tric [NOT CIRCULAR] /ɪkˈsen·trɪk, ek-/ *adj* not perfectly circular

ec·cle·si·as·ti·cal /ɪˌkliː·ziˈæs·tɪk·ᵊl/, **ec·cle·si·as·tic** *adj* [not gradable] *slightly fml* belonging to or connected with the Christian religion • *ecclesiastical history*

ec·cle·si·as·tic /ɪˌkliː·zi·ˈæs·tɪk/ *n* [C] *fml or dated* • An ecclesiastic is a Christian priest or other Christian official.

ECE /ˌiː·siːˈiː/ *n* [U] *Am abbreviation for* **Early Childhood Education**, see at EARLY

ECG /ˌiː·siːˈdʒiː/ *n* [C] *abbreviation for* electrocardiograph (= equipment that records the electrical activity of the heart as it beats), or electrocardiogram (= drawing that is made by an electrocardiograph)

ech·e·lon /£ˈeʃ·ə·lɒn, $-lɑːn/ *n* [C] a particular level or group of people within an organization such as an army or company, or a special formation of soldiers, aircraft or ships • *These salary increases will affect only the highest echelons of local government.*

e·chid·na /ɪˈkɪd·nə/ *n* [C] a small Australian mammal which has a protective covering of SPINES (= long sharp points), a long nose and eats ANTS and TERMITES

ech·o /£ˈek·əʊ, $-oʊ/ *n* [C] *pl* **echoes** a sound that is heard after it has been reflected off a surface such as a wall or a cliff • *The echoes of his scream sounded in the cave for several seconds.* • *Putting down some thick carpet would reduce the echo in this hallway.* • *(fig.) There are echoes* **of** (= details causing you to remember) *Mozart in her first piano compositions.* • An **echo sounder** is a piece of equipment, esp. on a ship, which uses sound waves to discover water depth or the position of an object in the water such as a group of fish. • (J)

ech·o *(obj)* /£ˈek·əʊ, $-oʊ/ *v* **echoes, echoing**, *past* **echoed** • *The sound of footsteps echoed* **round** *the hall.* [I] • *Suddenly, the building echoed* **with** *the sound of gunfire.* [I] • *"She earns £90 000 a year." "£90 000 a year!" echoed* (= repeated) *Sylvia in amazement.* [+ clause] • *(fig.) I've heard the Prime Minister's view echoed* (= repeated in agreement) *throughout the party.* [T] • *(fig.) The design of the church echoes* (= repeats details that cause you to think of) *that of St. Paul's Cathedral.* [T] • *(fig.) The ideas of Plato have echoed* **down/through the ages** (= continued to be very important during history).

éclair /£ɪ'kleəʳ, $-kler/ *n* [C] a small thin cake made of pastry, with cream inside and usually chocolate on top • *Is that your second* **chocolate** *éclair, Elaine?* • PIC› **Bread and cakes**

ec·lec·tic /ɪ'klek·tɪk/ *adj fml* (of methods, beliefs, ideas, etc.) combining whatever seem the best or the most useful things from many different areas or systems, rather than following a single system • *an eclectic style/approach* • *an eclectic taste in literature*

ec·lec·ti·cal·ly /ɪ'klek·tɪ·kli/ *adv fml*

ec·lec·ti·ci·sm /ɪ'klek·tɪ·sɪ·zᵊm/ *n* [U] *fml*

e·clipse /ɪ'klɪps/ *n* the disappearance from view, either completely or partly, of the sun while the moon is moving between it and the Earth, or the darkening of the moon while the SHADOW (=darkness) of the Earth moves over it • *a solar/lunar eclipse* [C] • *On Wednesday there will be a* **total/partial** *eclipse* **of** *the sun* [C] • *(fig.) Many people felt that the eclipse* (=reduced importance and probably replacement) **of** *the ruling political party was inevitable.* [U] • *(fig.) The ideas of that movement in literature are* **in** *eclipse/have* **gone into** *eclipse* (=are no longer important). [U]

e·clipse *obj* /ɪ'klɪps/ *v* [T] • *The moon will be totally eclipsed at 12.10 pm.* • *(fig. fml) The economy has eclipsed* (=been much more important and noticeable than) *all other issues during this election campaign.*

e·co– /£'iː·kəʊ-, $-koʊ-; £'ek·əʊ-, $-oʊ, $-ə/ *combining form* connected with the environment • *I try to buy eco-friendly washing powder that doesn't harm the environment.*

e·col·og·y /£ɪ'kɒl·ə·dʒi, $-'kɑː·lə-/ *n* [U] (the relationships between) the air, land, water, animals, plants, etc., usually of a particular area, or the scientific study of this • *The oil spill caused terrible damage to the fragile ecology* **of** *the coastline.* • *She hopes to study ecology at college.*

e·co·log·i·cal /£ˌiː·kə'lɒdʒ·ɪ·kᵊl, $-'lɑː·dʒɪ-/ *adj* • *The destruction of the rain forests is an ecological disaster that threatens the future of life on Earth.*

e·co·log·i·cal·ly /£ˌiː·kə'lɒdʒ·ɪ·kli, $-'lɑː·dʒɪ-/ *adv* • *It's an ecologically* **friendly/sound** (=not harmful) *means of transportation.*

e·col·o·gist /£ɪ'kɒl·ə·dʒɪst, $-'kɑː·lə-/ *n* [C] • An ecologist is a person who studies the natural relationships between the air, land, water, animals, plants, etc.

e·con·o·met·rics /£ɪˌkɒn·ə'met·rɪks, $-ˌkɑː·nə-/ *n* [U] *specialized* the testing of the performance of economies and economic theories using mathematical methods • *Her pioneering work in the field of econometrics has relied heavily upon computer modelling and advanced statistics packages.*

e·co·no·met·ric /£ɪˌkɒn·ə·'met·rɪk, $-ˌkɑː·nə-/ *adj* [not gradable] *specialized* • *econometric modelling* • *An econometric* **analysis** *of the data reveals some startling conclusions.*

e·co·no·my SAVING MONEY /£ɪ'kɒn·ə·mi, $-'kɑː·nə-/ *n* the intentional saving of money or, less commonly, the saving of time, energy, words, etc. • *They've had to* **make** *economies since Colin lost his job.* [C] • *This can be done by machines with more speed and economy.* [U] • *For the purposes of economy you may prefer to use half the recommended number of eggs in this recipe.* [U] • An **economy class** aircraft ticket is cheaper than other tickets and does not provide such a high degree of comfort. • An **economy drive** is an attempt to save money by spending as little as possible: *I don't think we'll be going anywhere expensive – Guy's* **on** *an economy drive.* • If something is sold in an **economy pack** or is **economy-sized** it contains a larger amount of the goods that you are buying for a lower price. • *She writes with such economy – I've never known a writer say so much in so few words.* [U] • *It's the economy of his running style that strikes you – it looks so effortless.* [U]

e·co·no·mic /£ˌiː·kə'nɒm·ɪk, $-'nɑː·mɪk, ek·ə-/ *adj* • *We had to close our office in central London – with the rent so high it just wasn't economic* (=it wasn't profitable). • (CS)

e·co·nom·i·cal /£ˌiː·kə'nɒm·ɪ·kᵊl, $-'nɑː·mɪ-, ek·ə-/ *adj* • *There's an increasing demand for cars which are more economical* **on** *fuel.* • *What's the most economical way of heating this building?* • *She's very economical – saving money seems to come naturally to her.* • *(humorous)* Someone who is described as being **economical with the truth** is either avoiding stating the true facts of a situation or lying about it. • LP› **Expensive**

e·co·nom·i·cal·ly /£ˌiː·kə'nɒm·ɪ·kli, $-'nɑː·mɪ-, ek·ə-/ *adv* • *As a student she lived very economically, rarely going out and buying very few clothes.*

e·con·o·mize, *Br and Aus usually* **–ise** /£ɪ'kɒn·ə·maɪz, $-'kɑː·nə-/ *v* [I] • If you economize you try to save money by intentionally reducing the amount that you are spending: *You could economize* **on** *food by not eating in restaurants all the time.* ○ *A lot of companies are trying to economize by not taking on new staff.* ○ *If I lived and worked in the same town that would economize* **on** *train fare.*

e·co·no·my SYSTEM /£ɪ'kɒn·ə·mi, $-'kɑː·nə-/ *n* [C] the system of trade and industry by which the wealth of a country is made and used • *a weak/strong economy* • *Tourism contributes millions of pounds to the country's economy.* • *The country's economy has been in a state of decline ever since this government came to power.*

e·co·no·mic /£iː·kə'nɒm·ɪk, ek·ə-, $-'nɑː·mɪk/ *adj* • *The country has been in a very poor economic state ever since the decline of its two major industries.* • *The government's economic* **policies** *have led us into the worst recession for years.*

e·co·nom·i·cal·ly /£ˌiː·kə'nɒm·ɪ·kli, ek·ə-, $-'nɑː·mɪk-/ *adv* [not gradable] • *Economically the country has been improving steadily these past ten years.*

e·co·no·mics /£ˌiː·kə'nɒm·ɪks, ek·ə-, $-'nɑː·mɪks/ *n* [U] • *Many of the party's ideas sound fine in principle but they haven't worked out the economics behind the policies.* • Economics is also the scientific study of the system by which a country's wealth is made and used: *the London School of Economics* ○ *She's in her third year of economics at York university.* • See also MICROECONOMICS.

e·con·o·mist /£ɪ'kɒn·ə·mɪst, $-'kɑː·nə-/ *n* [C] • An economist is a person who studies or has a special knowledge of economics.

e·co·sys·tem /£'iː·kəʊˌsɪs·təm, $-koʊ-/ *n* [C] the plants, animals and people living in an area together with their surroundings, such as earth and weather, considered as a system of relationships • *Pollution can have disastrous effects on the delicately balanced ecosystem.*

ec·sta·sy EMOTION /'ek·stə·si/ *n* a state of extreme happiness, esp. when feeling pleasure • **sexual** *ecstasy* [U] • *The photographer told her to throw her head back as if* **in** *ecstasy.* [U] • *The opera ends when* **in** *an ecstasy* **of** *jealousy the main character kills his lover and then himself.* [C] • *(infml)* If you are **in** ecstasies about something or you **go into** ecstasies over it, you are very excited about it: *She went into ecstasies about a meal that she'd eaten in a restaurant the night before.* [C]

ec·sta·tic /£ɪk'stæt·ɪk, $-'stæt̬-/ *adj* • *The new president was greeted by an ecstatic crowd.* • *(infml) I wasn't exactly ecstatic* (=I was not pleased) **about/at/over** *being woken up at four o'clock in the morning.*

ec·sta·ti·cal·ly /£ɪk'stæt·ɪ·kli, $-'stæt̬-/ *adv* • *The 16-year-old rock stars were received ecstatically by a crowd of waiting fans.*

ec·sta·sy DRUG /'ek·stə·si/, **E** *n* [U] *slang* a powerful drug which makes you feel very active and can cause you to HALLUCINATE (=see or hear things that do not exist)

ECT /ˌiː·siː'tiː/ *n* [U] *abbreviation for* ELECTROCONVULSIVE THERAPY

ec·to·pic preg·nan·cy /£ek'tɒp·ɪk, $-'tɑː·pɪk-/ *n* [C] the development of the EMBRYO outside the usual position within the womb, usually inside one of the FALLOPIAN TUBES

ec·to·pla·sm /£'ek·tə·plæz·ᵊm, $-toʊ-/ *n* [U] *specialized* the outer layer of particular types of cell, or a substance which is believed to surround GHOSTS and other creatures that are connected with spiritual activities • *People who communicate with the dead are supposed to produce ectoplasm when they are in touch with the spirit world.*

ECU /'ek·ju, 'eɪ·kju/ *n* [C] *abbreviation for* European Currency Unit (=a unit of money used in the European Community for trading between countries) • Compare EMS; EMU; ERM.

ec·u·men·i·cal /ˌiː·kjʊ'men·ɪk·ᵊl, ˌek·jʊ-/ *adj fml* tending to support and encourage unity between the various divisions of the Christian religion • *an ecumenical service*

ec·u·men·i·ci·sm /ˌiː·kjʊ·'men·ɪ·sɪ·zᵊm, ˌek·jʊ-/ *n* [U] *fml*

ec·zema /'ek·sɪ·mə/ *n* [U] a skin condition in which areas of the skin become red, rough and sore and make

ADJECTIVES ENDING IN *-ED* AND *-ING*

This group of pairs of adjectives can cause confusion because the two forms are so similar:

Learners get confus**ed** because these adjectives are confus**ing**.

The **-ed** form expresses how you feel. The **-ing** form describes the thing (or person) that made you feel like that.

something or someone is **-ing**	→ causes	someone is **-ed**
It is amaz**ing**	It amazes me	I am amaz**ed**

*Peter's job is bor***ing***. Peter is bor***ed** *(with his job).*
*Helen was terrifi***ed**, *it was the most frighten***ing** *film she had ever seen.*

Some adjectives of this type are:

amazed/amazing
annoyed/annoying
astonished/astonishing
bored/boring
confused/confusing
depressed/depressing
disappointed/disappointing
discouraged/discouraging
disgusted/disgusting
embarrassed/embarrassing
encouraged/encouraging
excited/exciting
exhausted/exhausting
fascinated/fascinating
frightened/frightening
frustrated/frustrating
fulfilled/fulfilling
horrified/horrifying
interested/interesting
irritated/irritating
puzzled/puzzling
revolted/revolting
satisfied/satisfying
shocked/shocking
surprised/surprising
terrified/terrifying
tired/tiring
worried/worrying

you want to rub them • *As a young boy he suffered from eczema.*

-ed /-t, -d, -ɪd, -əd/, **-d** *combining form* used to form the past simple and past participle of regular verbs • *called* • *asked* • *looked* • *started* • *played* • *returned* • *worked* • [LP]> **Pronunciation**

E·dam /ˈiː·dæm/ *n* [U] hard, yellow cheese from the Netherlands which is sold in spherical pieces covered with red wax

ed·dy /ˈed·i/ *v* [I] (of water, wind, smoke, etc.) to move fast in a circle • *The water eddied around in a whirlpool.*

ed·dy /ˈed·i/ *n* [C] • *The bend in the river had caused an eddy of fast swirling water.*

E·den /ˈiː·dᵊn/, **Gar·den of E·den** *n* [U] in the Bible, the garden where the first human beings, Adam and Eve, lived in perfect happiness before they disobeyed God and were ordered by him to leave

edge [OUTER POINT] /edʒ/ *n* [C usually sing] the outer or furthest point of something, or *(fig.)* the point just before something very different and noticeable happens • *He'd piped fresh cream around the edge* **of** *the cake.* • *There are fences to stop you from getting too near the edge of the cliff.* • *They built the church on the edge of the village.* • *A man was standing at the water's edge with a small boy.* • *I caught* (=hit) *my leg on the edge of the table as I walked past.* • *(fig.) It was reported in this morning's papers that the company is* **on** *the edge of collapse.* • *(fig.) The opposition leader claimed that the government had* **brought** *the country* **to** *the edge of a catastrophe.* • An **edge trimmer** is a STRIMMER. • [PIC]> **Edge, Garden**

edged /edʒd/ *adj* [not gradable] • *He bought a white table cloth edged* **with** *a pretty pattern.* (=with a pattern around the outside) • *a lace-edged collar*

edg·ing /ˈedʒ·ɪŋ/ *n* • (An) edging is something which is put around the outside of something, usually to decorate it: *a tablecloth with (a) dark edging* [C/U] • [PIC]> **Edge**

edge [BLADE] /edʒ/ *n* [C] the side of a blade which cuts, or any sharp part of an object which could cut • *You need to sharpen the edge of your knife – it won't cut anything.* • *Careful with that open tin – it's got a very sharp edge.* • *If I eat between meals it really* **takes the edge off** (=reduces) *my appetite.* • *His apology* **took the edge off** (=reduced) *her anger.* • [PIC]> **Edge**

-edged /-edʒd/ *combining form* • *a* **double/two**-*edged blade*

edge *(obj)* [MOVE] /edʒ/ *v* [always + adv/prep] to move slowly with gradual movements or in gradual stages • *A long line of traffic edged* **its way** *forward.* [T] • *Inflation has edged* **up** *to 5% over the last two years.* [I] • *The leader has been criticized for edging her party* **towards** *extremist right-wing policies.* [T] • *Those who disagreed with the director's viewpoint were gradually edged* **out** *of* (=forced/encouraged to leave) *the company.* [T]

edge [ANGER/NERVOUSNESS] /edʒ/ *n* [U] a small but noticeable amount of annoyance in someone's voice • *There's a definite edge* **to/in** *her voice when she talks to her husband.* • If you are **on edge** you are nervous and not relaxed: *Is something wrong? – You seem a bit on edge this morning.*

edgy /ˈedʒ·i/ *adj* **-ier, -iest** *infml* • Someone who is feeling edgy is feeling nervous or anxious.

edg·i·ly /ˈedʒ·ɪ·li/ *adv* • *"Why haven't they arrived yet?" she said, edgily* (=nervously) *looking out the window.*

edge [ADVANTAGE] /edʒ/ *n* [U] **the edge** an advantage over other people • *Because of her experience she* **had** *the edge* **over** *the other people that we interviewed.*

edge·ways /ˈedʒ·weɪz/ *adv* [not gradable] **get a word in edgeways**, see at WORD [LANGUAGE UNIT]

ed·i·ble /ˈed·ɪ·bl̩/ *adj* suitable or safe for eating • *Only the leaves of the plant are edible.* • Compare **eatable** at EAT [HAVE FOOD].

e·dict /ˈiː·dɪkt/ *n* [C] *fml* an official order, esp. one which is given in a forceful and unfair way • *Most shops are ignoring the government's edict against Sunday trading.*

ed·i·fi·ca·tion /ˌed·ɪ·fɪˈkeɪ·ʃᵊn/ *n* [U] *humorous or fml* the improvement of the mind and understanding, esp. by learning • *I tend to watch the television for pleasure rather than edification.*

ed·i·fy *obj* /ˈed·ɪ·faɪ/ *v* [T] *humorous or fml*

ed·i·fy·ing /ˈed·ɪ·faɪ·ɪŋ/ *adj humorous or fml* • *Being left in a bar all afternoon with a load of football supporters is not the most edifying of experiences* (=not an enjoyable experience).

ed·i·fice /ˈed·ɪ·fɪs/ *n* [C] *fml* a large building, esp. a splendid one, or *(fig.)* a system which has been established for a long time • *The town hall is the only edifice surviving from the fifteenth century.* • *(fig.) It looks as if the whole political edifice of the country is about to collapse.*

ed·it *obj* /ˈed·ɪt/ *v* [T] to prepare (a text or film) for printing or viewing by correcting mistakes and deciding what will be removed and what will be kept in, etc., or to be in charge of (the reports in a newspaper or magazine, etc.) • *Janet fixed copy and edited books for a variety of publishers.* • *He edits the local newspaper.* • *The film's 129 minutes were edited* **down** *from 150 hours of footage.* • If you edit something **out** or edit **out** something, you remove it before it is broadcast or printed: *They edited out the most violent scenes when they showed the film on television.* • (I)

ed·it·ing /£ˈed·ɪ·tɪŋ, $-t̬ɪŋ/ *n* [U] • *Doing the filming for the documentary took two months but editing took another four.*

ed·i·tor /£ˈed·ɪ·təʳ, $-t̬ɚ/ *n* [C] • An editor is either a person who corrects and makes changes to texts or films before they are printed or shown, or a person who is in charge of a newspaper or magazine and responsible for all of its reports: *She's a senior editor in the reference*

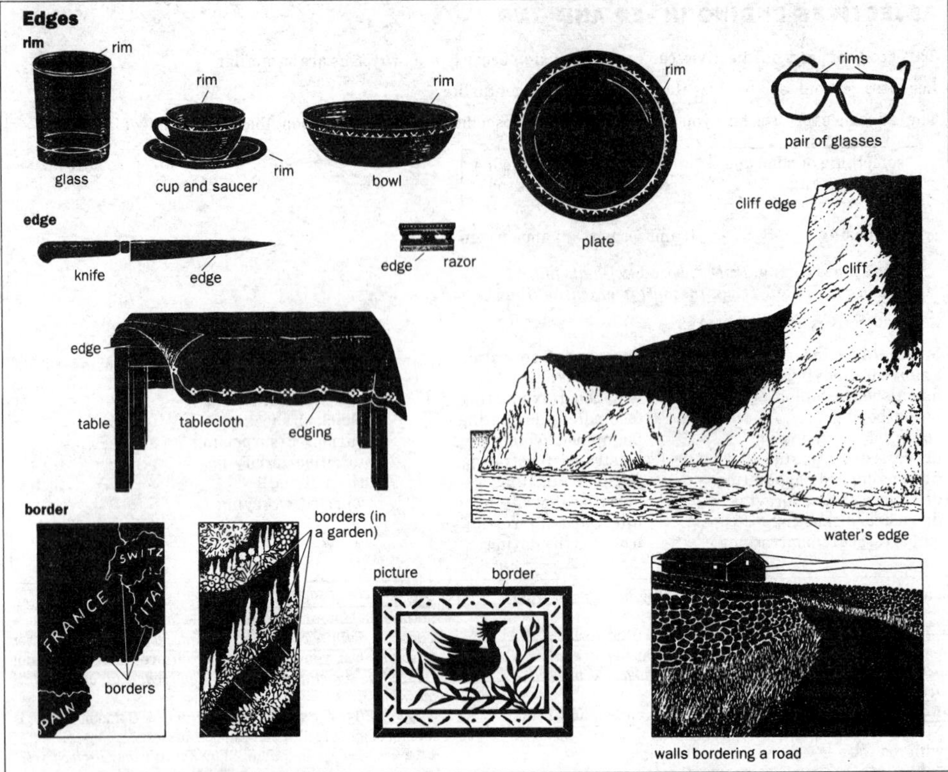

department of a publishing company. ○ *Who is the current editor of the Times?* • Ⓔ Ⓕ Ⓟ

ed·i·tor·i·al /£ˌed·ɪˈtɔː·ri·əl, $-əˈtɔːr·i-/ *adj* • *editorial staff* • *Editorial decisions are generally made by senior editors.* • *It's plain reporting of the facts – there's not much editorial content* (=opinion). • *The government should not exercise any editorial control over what is shown on television.*

ed·i·tor·i·al /£ˌed·ɪˈtɔː·ri·əl, $-əˈtɔːr·i-/, *Br* **lead·er, lead·ing ar·ti·cle** *n* [C] • An editorial is an article in a newspaper which expresses the editor's opinion on a subject of particular interest at the present time: *All the papers deal with the same subject in their editorials – the new tax system.*

ed·i·tor·i·al·ize, *Br and Aus usually* **-ise** /£ˌed·ɪˈtɔː·ri·ə·laɪz, $-əˈtɔːr·i-/ *v* [I] • To editorialize is to express a personal opinion, esp. when you should be giving a report of the facts only.

ed·i·tion /ɪˈdɪʃ·ən/ *n* [C] a particular form in which a book, magazine or newspaper is published, or a single broadcast of a series of radio or sometimes television programmes • *I've ordered the paperback/hardback edition of their dictionary.* • *The regional editions of the paper contain specific information for that area.* • *This morning's edition of 'Women's Hour' is at the earlier time of a quarter to ten.* • Edition also refers to the total number of copies of a particular book, newspaper, etc. that are published at the same time: *She collects* **first** *editions of nineteenth century authors.* ○ *It was published in a leather-bound* **limited** *edition.* • *(Am)* An edition can also be one occasion on which something that is done repeatedly is presented: *The 77th edition of the Indianapolis 500 was held before an estimated 450 000 fans.* • Ⓔ Ⓕ

e·du·cate *obj* /ˈed·jʊ·keɪt/ *v* [T] to teach (someone), esp. using the formal system of school, college or university, or to give knowledge or understanding of a particular subject to (someone) • *The form says he was educated in Africa.* • *There was an article in the paper about how much it costs to educate a child privately.* • *The government say they are trying to do more to educate the public* **in/on/about** *the consequences of drug abuse.* • *She keeps taking me to foreign films and art galleries in an attempt to educate me.* • *"Educating Rita"* (title of a play by Willy Russell, 1981)

ed·u·cat·ed /£ˈed·jʊ·keɪ·tɪd, $-t̬ɪd/ *adj* • *She was probably the most* **highly** *educated prime minister of this century.* • *It says on the form that she was Oxford-educated.* • An educated voice or writing suggests that the person who has or produces it has been taught to a high level or is of a high social class. • An **educated guess** is a guess which is made using judgment and a particular level of knowledge and is therefore more likely to be correct.

ed·u·ca·tion /ˌed·jʊˈkeɪ·ʃən/ *n* [U] • *As a child he* **received** *most of his education at home.* • *It's a country which places great importance on education.* • *We need to increase the quality and quantity of science education in schools.* • *She lectures in education* (=the study of education) *at the teacher training college.* • *"Education is what survives when what had been learnt has been forgotten"* (B.F.Skinner in *New Scientist*, 1964) • LP> **Schools and colleges**

ed·u·ca·tion·al /ˌed·jʊˈkeɪ·ʃən·əl/ *adj* • *Reducing the size of classes may improve educational standards.* • *She seems to have spent all her life studying in educational* **establishments**. • *My father has never been to a rock concert before – it'll be an educational* **experience** *for him* (=a new experience from which he can learn).

ed·u·ca·tion·al·ly /ˌed·jʊˈkeɪ·ʃən·əl·i/ *adv* • *It was reported in the newspapers that the woman who committed the crime was educationally disadvantaged.*

ed·u·ca·tion·ist /ˌed·jʊˈkeɪ·ʃən·ɪst/, **ed·u·ca·tion·al·ist** /ˌed·jʊˈkeɪ·ʃən·əl·ɪst/ *n* [C] • An educationist is a person who has a special knowledge of the principles and methods of teaching.

ed·u·ca·tive /£ˈed·jʊ·kə·tɪv, $-keɪ·t̬ɪv/ *adj* • *Most toys for young children are designed to be educative in some way.*

ed·u·ca·tor /£ˈed·jʊ·keɪ·tər, $-t̬ɚ/ *n* [C] *esp. Am* • An educator is a person who teaches people.

Ed·war·di·an /£edˈwɔː·di·ən, $-ˈwɔːr-/ *n, adj* [not gradable] (a British person) of the period 1901-10 in which Edward VII was king • *Edwardian architecture/clothes* • *She wears the sort of dresses that Edwardians used to wear.* [C]

-ee OBJECT /-iː, -eɪ/ *combining form* added to a verb to form a noun which refers to the person to whom the action of the verb is being done • *an employee* (=someone who is employed) • *the payee* (=a person to whom money is paid) • *an interviewee* (=someone who is being INTERVIEWED for a job) • *a detainee* (= someone who has been DETAINED) • [LP] **Combining forms, Stress in pronunciation**

-ee [CONDITION] /-iː, -eɪ/ *combining form* added to an adjective, noun or verb to refer to a person who is in that condition or state • *an absentee* (= someone who is absent) • *a refugee* (= someone who has taken REFUGE) • *an escapee* (= someone who has escaped)

EEC /ˌiː·iː'siː/, **Com·mon Mar·ket** *n* [U] an organization formed in 1958 by a group of European countries in order to establish agreed aims, esp. in farming and trade, and therefore encourage good relations between its member countries. This organization developed into the European Community, which became the European Union in 1994.

EEG /ˌiː·iː'dʒiː/ *n* [C] *abbreviation for* electroencephalogram or electroencephalograph (= a test in which the electrical activity of the brain is recorded in the form of a drawing, or the machine which does this) • *The specialist said that she should* **have** *an EEG.*

eek /iːk/ *exclamation infml esp. humorous* an expression of anxiety or slight fear

eel /iːl/ *n* [C] a long, thin snake-like fish, some types of which are eaten • *jellied eels* • [PIC] **Fish**

ee·rie /£'ɪə·ri, $'ɪr·i/ *adj* **-r, -st** strange in a frightening and mysterious way • *In bed at night she heard the eerie noise of the wind howling through the trees.* • *He had the eerie* **feeling** *that he had met this stranger before.*

ee·ri·ly /£'ɪə·rɪ·li, $'ɪr·ɪ-/ *adv* • *Her voice was eerily similar to her dead grandmother's.*

ee·ri·ness /£'ɪə·rɪ·nəs, $'ɪr·ɪ-/ *n* [U]

eff /ef/ *v* [I] **eff and blind** *Br slang* to swear, using words that are considered offensive by some people • *(esp. humorous) Some people have complained about the programme because of all the effing and blinding that goes on.*

ef·fing /'ef·ɪŋ/ *adj* [before n; not gradable] *Br slightly taboo slang* • Effing can be used to add force to an expression: *That boy is such an effing nuisance!*

eff off /ef/ *v adv slightly taboo slang* • **Eff off** is used to avoid saying **fuck off**: *If he comes round here again just tell him to eff off!*

ef·face *obj* [REMOVE] /ɪ'feɪs/ *v* [T] to remove intentionally • *The whole country had tried to efface the memory of the old dictatorship.*

ef·face *obj* [BEHAVE MODESTLY] /ɪ'feɪs/ *v* [T] to behave (yourself) in a modest way and treat as unimportant the admirable things that you have achieved, often because you lack confidence • *For an actor he's very shy and tends to efface himself in interviews.* • See also SELF-EFFACING.

ef·fect [RESULT] /ɪ'fekt/ *n* the result of a particular influence • *The radiation leak has had a disastrous effect* **on/upon** *the environment.* [C] • *I tried taking tablets for the headache but they didn't have any effect.* [U] • *That drink has had quite an effect on me – I feel light-headed!* [C] • *I think I'm suffering from the effects of too little sleep.* [C] • *They had to wait ten minutes for the anaesthetic to* **take** *effect* (= produce results) *before they stitched up the cut.* [U] • *Separately his features are rather strange, but the* **overall** *effect is somehow very attractive.* [C] • *As a dancer she combined technique with grace and style* **to** (= with a) *stunning effect.* [U] • *She has a lot of confidence which she uses* **to** *good effect* (= to her advantage) *in interviews.* [U] • *(esp. disapproving)* If you say or do something **for** effect, you intentionally do it to shock people or attract their attention: *I get the impression that she uses bad language in meetings for effect.* [U] • You can use the phrase **in effect** to mean 'in fact' or 'in practice': *So in effect the government have lowered taxes for the rich and raised them for the poor.* • You can use the phrase **to that effect** or **to the effect that** to express that what you are reporting is only a short and general form of what was really said: *She said she was unhappy, or* **words** *to that effect.* ○ *He said something to the effect that he would have to change jobs if the situation continued.* • See also AFTEREFFECT.

ef·fec·tive /£ɪ'fek·tɪv, $-t̬ɪv/ *adj* • Something can be described as effective if it produces the results that it was intended to: *It's a very effective cure for a headache.* ○ *The lighting for the production made a very effective use of shadow.* • A person can also be described as effective if they are skilled in a particular way: *She's a very effective teacher.* • You can also use effective to mean in fact, although not officially: *Although she's not officially our boss, she's in effective control of the office.* • See also **effective** at EFFECT [USE]. • (P)

ef·fec·tive·ly /£ɪ'fek·tɪv·li, $-t̬ɪv-/ *adv* • *The tablets work more effectively if you take a hot drink after them.* • *His wife left him when the children were small, so he effectively* (= in fact) *brought up the family himself.* • *Effectively, we have to start again from scratch.*

ef·fec·tive·ness /£ɪ'fek·tɪv·nəs, $-t̬ɪv-/ *n* [U] • *There are doubts about the effectiveness of the new drug in treating the disease.*

ef·fec·tu·al /ɪ'fek·tju·əl/ *adj fml* • Effectual means effective and successful: *They wish to promote a real and effectual understanding between the two countries.*

ef·fec·tu·al·ly /ɪ'fek·tju·əl·i/ *adv fml*

ef·fect [USE] /ɪ'fekt/ *n* [U] use • *The present system of payment will remain* **in** *effect* (= be used) *until the end of the rental agreement.* • *When do the new driving laws come* **into** *effect?* • *The new salary increases will* **take** *effect* (= begin) *from January onwards.*

ef·fec·tive /£ɪ'fek·tɪv, $-t̬ɪv/ *adj* • *The new laws will become effective next month.* • See also **effective** at EFFECT [RESULT]. • (P)

ef·fect *obj* [ACHIEVE] /ɪ'fekt/ *v* [T] to achieve (something) and cause it to happen • *As a political party they are trying to effect a change in the way that we think about our environment.*

ef·fects [FILM] /ɪ'fekts/, **spe·cial ef·fects** *pl n* lighting, sounds and objects which are specially produced for the stage or a film and are intended to make something which does not exist seem real • *The movie is worth seeing for its effects alone.* • (DK)

ef·fects [POSSESSIONS] /ɪ'fekts/ *pl n specialized* a person's possessions, esp. after their death • *It says on the form that the insurance covers all* **personal** *effects.* • (DK)

ef·fem·i·nate /ɪ'fem·ɪ·nət/ *adj disapproving* (of a man) behaving or appearing in a way that is similar to a woman and lacking in manly qualities • *He's got a very effeminate manner/voice/walk.*

ef·fem·i·na·cy /ɪ'fem·ɪ·nə·si/ *n* [U]

ef·fer·ves·cent [FIZZY] /£ˌef·ə'ves·ᵊnt, $-ɚ'-/ *adj* (of a liquid) producing bubbles of gas • *You can buy effervescent vitamin C tablets which you put in water.*

ef·fer·vesce /£ˌef·ə'ves, $-ɚ'-/ *v* [I] *specialized*

ef·fer·ves·cence /£ˌef·ə'ves·ᵊnts, $-ɚ'-/ *n* [U]

ef·fer·ves·cent [ACTIVE] /£ˌef·ə'ves·ənt, $-ɚ'-/ *adj* (of a person) full of energy; positive and active • *She's one of those effervescent personalities that you often see presenting TV game shows.*

ef·fete /ɪ'fiːt/ *adj disapproving literary* weak and powerless, or (of a man) behaving and appearing in a way that is similar to a woman • *With nothing to do all day except amuse themselves, the aristocracy had grown effete and lazy.* • *Ballet used to be considered an effete career for a young man.*

ef·fi·ca·cy /'ef·ɪ·kə·si/ *n* [U] *fml* an ability, esp. of a medicine or a method of achieving something, to produce the intended result; effectiveness • *They recently ran a series of tests to measure the efficacy of the drug.*

ef·fi·ca·cious /ˌef·ɪ'keɪ·ʃəs/ *adj fml or humorous*

ef·fi·cient /ɪ'fɪʃ·ᵊnt/ *adj* working or operating quickly and effectively in an organized way • *The city's transport system is one of the most efficient in Europe.* • *We need someone really efficient who can organize the office and make it run smoothly.*

ef·fi·cient·ly /ɪ'fɪʃ·ᵊnt·li/ *adv* • *She runs the business very efficiently.*

ef·fi·cien·cy /ɪ'fɪʃ·ᵊnt·si/ *n* [U] • *What is so impressive about their society is the efficiency of the public services.* • *Increased use of public transport would doubtless increase energy efficiency* (= using only what is needed). • *(specialized)* The efficiency of a machine or an engine is the difference between the amount of energy that is put into it in the form of fuel, effort, etc. and the amount that comes out in the form of movement.

ef·fi·gy /'ef·ɪ·dʒi/ *n* [C] a model or other object which represents someone, esp. one made to represent a disliked person which is hung or burnt in a public place • *Crowds marched through the streets carrying burning effigies of the president.*

ef·flor·es·cence /ˌef·lə'res·ᵊnts/ *n* [U] *specialized or literary* the period when flowers start to appear on a plant, or *(literary)* the production of a lot of art, esp. of a high quality • *This period witnessed the efflorescence of ornate architecture.*

ef·flu·ent /'ef·lu·ənt/ *n specialized* liquid waste that is sent out from factories or places where SEWAGE (= human waste) is dealt with, usually flowing into the sea or rivers • *Something must be done to control the amount of effluent in our water supplies.* [U] • *Effluents from various local factories are finding their way into the river.* [C]

ef·fort /£'ef·ət, $-ɚt/ *n* great physical or mental activity needed to achieve something • *It's such an effort to get up on these dark winter mornings.* [C] • *If we could all* **make** *an effort* **to** *keep this office tidier it would help.* [C + *to* infinitive] • *You can't expect to have any friends if you don't* **make** *any effort with people.* [U] • *Despite all my efforts* **to** *improve his life-style he's still smoking twenty cigarettes a day.* [C + *to* infinitive] • **In** *their efforts* **to** *reduce crime the government expanded the police force.* [C + *to* infinitive] • *He's jogging round the park every morning in an effort* **to** *get fit for the football season.* [C + *to* infinitive] • *It takes a long time to prepare the dish but the results are so good that it's* **worth the** *effort.* [U] • An effort can also be the result of an attempt to produce something, esp. when its quality is low or uncertain: *Do you want to have a look at his exam paper? – it's a fairly poor effort.* [C]

ef·fort·less /£'ef·ət·ləs, $-ɚt-/ *adj approving* • An action or activity which is described as effortless is done with such natural ability that it seems not to need any effort: *When you watch her dance it looks so effortless.* ○ *He was an actor of effortless charm.*

ef·fort·less·ly /£'ef·ət·lə·sli, $-ɚt-/ *adv* • *She runs so effortlessly as if it's the easiest thing in the world.*

ef·fort·less·ness /£'ef·ət·lə·snəs, $-ɚt-/ *n* [U]

ef·front·er·y /£ɪ'frʌn·tᵊr·i, $-t̬ɚ-/ *n* [U] *fml* extreme rudeness and lack of ability to understand that your behaviour is not acceptable to other people; NERVE [BRAVERY] • *He arrived late, was silent all evening and then had the effrontery to complain that I looked bored!*

ef·fu·sion /ɪ'fjuː·ʒᵊn/ *n* [C] *literary* a sudden and uncontrolled expression of strong emotion • *an effusion* **of** *anger and despair*

ef·fu·sive /ɪ'fjuː·sɪv/ *adj fml* expressing welcome, approval or pleasure in a way that shows very strong feeling • *They gave us such an effusive welcome it was quite embarrassing.*

ef·fu·sive·ly /ɪ'fjuː·sɪv·li/ *adv fml*

EFL /ˌiː·ef'el/ *n* [U] *abbreviation for* English as a Foreign Language (= the teaching of English to people whose first language is not English) • *Zita teaches EFL in Sárospatak.* • *Which bookshop has the largest selection of EFL materials?*

e.g. /ˌiː'dʒiː, '--/ *abbreviation for* exempli gratia (= Latin for 'for example') • *We're encouraged to eat food which contains a lot of fibre, e.g. fruit, vegetables and bread.* • In spoken English people often say 'for example' or 'such as' instead of 'e.g.'.

e·gal·i·tar·i·an /£ɪˌgæl·ɪ'teə·ri·ən, $-'ter·i-/ *n* [C], *adj fml* (a person) believing that all people are equally important and should have the same rights and opportunities in life • *an egalitarian society* • *The party's principles are basically egalitarian.*

e·gal·i·tar·i·an·i·sm /£ɪˌgæl·ɪ'teə·ri·ən·ɪ·zᵊm, $-'ter·i-/ *n* [U] *fml* • Egalitarianism is the belief in and actions taken according to egalitarian principles.

egg [REPRODUCTION] /eg/ *n* [C] a rounded object, often with a hard shell, which is produced by female birds and particular REPTILES and insects, and contains a baby animal which comes out when it is developed • *The cuckoo* **lays** *her egg in another bird's nest.* • *After fourteen days the eggs* **hatch**, *the young using their hard beaks to break open the shell.* • An egg is also a cell produced by a woman or female animal from which a baby might develop if it combines with sperm from a male: *Identical twins develop from a single fertilized egg which then splits into two.* • PIC> **Insects**

egg [FOOD] /eg/ *n* the oval or rounded object with a hard shell which is produced by female birds, esp. chickens, and which is eaten as food before a baby bird develops inside it • *a hard-boiled/soft-boiled egg* [C] • **half a dozen** (= six) *eggs/a* **dozen** (= twelve) *eggs* [C] • *How do you like your eggs – fried or boiled?* [C] • *Take a slice of bread and dip it in beaten egg.* [U] • *Have you ever tried quails' eggs? – they're smaller and richer than normal eggs.* [C] • An egg can also be an object which is especially made in the shape of a bird's egg: *a chocolate/marble egg* [C] • *(infml)* If someone is described as having **egg on** their **face**, it means that they have been made to look stupid because of something that they have done: *This latest scandal has left the government with egg on its face.* • *(infml)* If you **put all** your **eggs in one basket**, you depend on a single plan of action or person for success: *I'm applying for several jobs because I don't really want to put all my eggs in one basket.* • An **egg cup** is a small container used to hold a boiled egg while you eat it. • **Egg roll** is *Am for* **spring roll**. See at SPRING [SEASON]. • An **egg-and-spoon-race** is a race in which the people taking part run with an egg balanced on a spoon. • An **egg timer** is a device which helps you judge when a boiled egg has been cooked long enough to be eaten. • **Egg white** or the **white of an egg** is the transparent part of an egg which turns white when it is cooked. • **Egg yolk** or the **yoke of an egg** is the round yellow part of an egg. • PIC> **Clocks and watches**, **Outdoor games for children**

eg·gy /'eg·i/ *adj* **-ier, -iest** *infml* • *Something smells eggy – have you been cooking an omelette?*

egg on *obj*, **egg** *obj* **on** /eg/ *v adv* [M] to strongly encourage someone to do something which might not be a very good idea • *Don't egg him on! He gets himself into enough trouble without your encouragement.* • *She's always egging on her friends to skip classes with her.*

egg·head /'eg·hed/ *n* [C] *humorous disapproving* a person, esp. a man, who is very clever and interested only in studying and other mental activities

egg·plant /£'eg·plɑːnt, $-plænt/ *n* [C] *Am and Aus for* AUBERGINE • PIC> **Vegetables**

egg·shell /'eg·ʃel/ *n* [C; U] the hard outside covering of an egg

e·go /£'iː·gəʊ, $'iː·goʊ/ *n* [C] *pl* **egos** *esp. disapproving* your idea or opinion of yourself, or a great feeling of your own importance and ability • *That man has got such an enormous ego – I've never known anyone so full of themselves!* • *I'm glad she got the job – she needed something to* **boost/bolster** *her ego.* (= give her confidence) • *(specialized)* In PSYCHOANALYSIS, the ego is the part of a person's conscious self which tries to match the blind desires of the ID with the demands of reality. • *(disapproving)* An **ego trip** is something that you do because it makes you feel important and also shows other people how important you are: *He was* **on** *another one of his ego trips, directing and taking the main part in a film.* • See also ALTER EGO; SUPEREGO. • Ⓙ

e·go·cen·tric /£ˌiː·gəʊ'sen·trɪk, $-goʊ-/ *adj esp. disapproving* • Someone who is egocentric is selfish, thinking only of themselves: *Babies are entirely egocentric, concerned only with how warm or cold they are and when they will next be fed.*

e·go·cen·tri·cal·ly /£ˌiː·gəʊ'sen·trɪ·kli, $-goʊ-/ *adv esp. disapproving*

e·go·cen·tri·ci·ty /£ˌiː·gəʊ·sen'trɪs·ɪ·ti, $-goʊ-/ *n* [U] *esp. disapproving*

e·go·ma·ni·a /£ˌiː·gəʊ'meɪ·ni·ə, $-goʊ-/ *n* [U] *disapproving* • Egomania is an extreme case of when a person considers themselves to be very important and able to do anything that they want to do.

e·go·ma·ni·ac /£ˌiː·gəʊ'meɪ·ni·æk, $-goʊ-/ *n* [C] *disapproving* • An egomaniac is a person who considers themselves to be extremely important and able to do anything that they want to do.

e·go·ti·sm /£'iː·gəʊ·tɪ·zᵊm, $-goʊ-/, **e·go·i·sm** /£'iː·gəʊ·ɪ·zᵊm, $-goʊ-/ *n* [U] *disapproving* • Egotism is the tendency to think only about yourself and consider yourself better and more important than other people: *Finding herself world-famous by the time she was eighteen only encouraged the actress's egotism.*

e·go·tist /£'iː·gəʊ·tɪst, $-goʊ-/, **e·go·ist** /£'iː·gəʊ·ɪst, $-goʊ-/ *n* [C] *disapproving* • *Politicians are notorious egotists, interested only in promoting themselves.*

e·go·tis·ti·cal /£ˌiː·gəʊ'tɪs·tɪ·kᵊl, $-goʊ-/ *adj*

e·gre·gi·ous /ɪ'griː·dʒəs/ *adj fml disapproving* (often of mistakes) extremely and noticeably bad • *It was an egregious error for a statesman to show such ignorance.* • Ⓘ

eh /eɪ/ *exclamation infml* used to express surprise or confusion, to ask someone to repeat what they have said, or as a way of getting someone to give some type of reaction to a statement that you have made • *"Janet is leaving her husband." "Eh?"* • *"Did you hear what I said?" "Eh? Say it again – I wasn't listening."* • *Going overseas again, eh? – it's a nice life for some!*

ei·der·down /£'aɪ·də·daʊn, $-dɚ-/ *n* [C] a thick covering for on top of the bed, filled with soft feathers or warm material, used esp. in the past • PIC> **Beds and bedroom**

eight /eɪt/ *determiner, pronoun, n* (the number) 8 • *six, seven, eight, nine, ten* • *"How many people are coming to* *dinner?" "Eight (people)." • Is that number a five or an eight?* [C]

eigh·th /eɪtθ/ *determiner, pronoun, adj, adv* [not gradable], *n* • *the eighth batsman in the team* • *the eighth of December/December the eighth* • *He was/finished eighth in the race.* • *Cut the cake into eighths* (= eight equal parts). [C] • **Eighth note** is *Am for* QUAVER [MUSICAL NOTE].

eight·een /eɪ'tiːn, '--/ *determiner, pronoun, n* (the number) 18 • *seventeen, eighteen, nineteen* • *"How many glasses are in the cupboard?" "Eighteen (glasses)."* • *Is the number on that house an eighteen?* [C]

eight·eenth /eɪ'tiːnθ, '--/ *determiner, pronoun, adj, adv* [not gradable], *n* • *the eighteenth floor of the building* • *"How many Christmas cards have you written?" "This is my eighteenth."* • *He currently is/ranks eighteenth in the world.* • An eighteenth is one of eighteen equal parts of something. [C]

eight·y /£'eɪ·ti, $-t̬i/ *determiner, pronoun, n* (the number) 80 • *seventy, eighty, ninety* • *They've invited eighty (guests) to the wedding.* • *Is the number on that gate a fifty or an eighty?* [C]

eight·ies /£'eɪ·tiz, $-t̬iz/ *pl n* • **The** eighties is the range of temperature between 80° and 89°: *The temperature is expected to be* **in** *the eighties tomorrow.* • **The** eighties is also the period of years between 80 and 89 in any century: *Margaret Thatcher was the British Prime Minister for most of the eighties* (= between 1980 and 1989). • A person's eighties are the period in which they are aged between 80 and 89: *My grandmother is* **in** *her eighties.*

eigh·ti·eth /£'eɪ·ti·əθ, $-t̬i-/ *determiner, pronoun, adj, adv* [not gradable], *n* • *She's having a big party for her eightieth (birthday).* • *They were/finished eightieth out of hundred.* • An eightieth is one of eighty equal parts of something. [C]

ei·ther [ALSO] /£'aɪ·ðəʳ, £'iː-, $-ðɚ/ *adv* [not gradable] used in negatives instead of also or too • *I don't eat meat and my husband doesn't either.* • *"I've never been to the States." "I haven't either."* • *They do really good food at that restaurant and it's not very expensive either.*

ei·ther [CHOICE] /£'aɪ·ðəʳ, £'iː-, $-ðɚ/ *determiner, conjunction* one or the other of two • *Either person would be fine for the job.* • *You can get there by train or bus – either* **way/in** *either* **case** *it'll take an hour.* • *We can either eat now* **or** *after the show – it's up to you.* • *I either left it at home* **or** *in the car – I can't remember which.* • *Either you leave now* **or** *I call the police!* • You can also use either to mean both: *Unfortunately I was sitting at the table with smokers on either side of me.* • An **either-or** situation is one in which there is a choice between two different plans of action but both together are not possible: *It's an either-or* **situation** *– we can buy a new car this year or we can go on holiday but we can't do both.* • [LP] **Determiners, Two**

e·jac·u·late [SPERM] /ɪ'dʒæk·jʊ·leɪt/ *v* [I] (of a man or male animal) to push out sperm

e·jac·u·la·tion /ɪˌdʒæk·jʊ'leɪ·ʃᵊn/ *n* [C; U]

e·jac·u·late *obj* [SAY] /ɪ'dʒæk·jʊ·leɪt/ *v* [T] *dated or humorous* to shout or say something suddenly, sometimes unexpectedly • *"You've got my umbrella!" he ejaculated.* [+ clause]

e·jac·u·la·tion /ɪˌdʒæk·jʊ'leɪ·ʃᵊn/ *n* [C] *dated or humorous*

e·ject *obj* /ɪ'dʒekt/ *v* [T] to force (someone) to leave a particular place, or to send out (something) quickly and often with force • *A number of football fans had been ejected* **from** *the bar for causing trouble.* • *The coffee machine suddenly ejected a handful of coins.* • Eject is *Am for* **send off**, see at SEND [CAUSE TO GO].

e·jec·tion /ɪ'dʒek·ʃᵊn/ *n* [U] • An **ejection seat** or **ejector seat** is a seat which can throw out the person flying an aircraft if they suddenly have to leave it because of a particular danger.

eke out *obj*, **eke** *obj* **out** /iːk/ *v adv* [M] to try to make a small supply of (something) enough for your needs • *He managed to eke out* **a living** (= earn just enough to live on) *one summer by selling drinks on a beach.* • *There wasn't much food left but we just managed to eke it out over four people.*

EKG /ˌiː·keɪ·'dʒiː/ *n* [C] *Am for* ECG

e·lab·or·ate [DETAILED] /£ɪ'læb·ᵊr·ət, $'-ɚ-/ *adj* containing a lot of careful detail or many detailed parts • *You want a plain blouse to go with that skirt – nothing too elaborate.* • *They're making the most elaborate preparations for the wedding.* • *He came out with such an elaborate excuse that I didn't quite believe him.*

e·lab·or·ate·ly /£ɪ'læb·ᵊr·ət·li, $'-ɚ-/ *adv* • *It was the most elaborately decorated cake – all sugar flowers and bows.*

e·lab·or·ate [EXPLAIN] /ɪ'læb·ə·reɪt/ *v* [I] *slightly fml* to add more information to or explain something that you have said • *The minister said he was resigning but refused to elaborate* (**on** *his reasons for doing so*). • *Introduce your main points to begin with and elaborate* **on** *them later in the essay.*

e·lab·or·a·tion /ɪˌlæb·ə'reɪ·ʃᵊn/ *n* [C/U] • *This theory needs much greater elaboration to be clear, let alone convincing.* [U] • *His elaborations are even more confusing than his initial statements.* [C]

élan /ɪ'læn/ *n* [U] *literary approving* a combination of style and energetic confidence, esp. in performances or manner • *She dances the role with such élan.* • *As a prime minister, she had a certain élan.*

e·lapse /ɪ'læps/ *v* [I] *fml or literary* (of time) to go past • *Four years had elapsed since he left college and still he hadn't found a job.*

e·las·tic /ɪ'læs·tɪk/ *adj* (esp. of material) able to stretch and be returned to its original shape or size, or *(fig.)* (of arrangements, ideas, etc.) not fixed and able or likely to be changed • *A lot of sports wear is made of very elastic material.* • *(fig.) The project has only just started so any plans are still very elastic.* • *(fig.) In this country, where time is an elastic concept, there is no such thing as a timetable.* • **Elastic band** is *Br for* **rubber band**. See at RUBBER [SUBSTANCE]. • [PIC] **Stationery**

e·las·ti·cat·ed *Br* /£ɪ'læs·tɪ·keɪ·tɪd, $-t̬ɪd/, *Am* **e·las·ti·cized** /ɪ'læs·tɪ·saɪzd/, *Aus* **e·las·ti·cised** *adj* • Clothes or parts of clothes that are elasticated have stretchy threads of elastic in them: *a dress with an elasticated waist* ○ *an elasticated swimming costume*

e·las·ti·ci·ty /£ˌɪl·æs'tɪs·ɪ·ti, $-ə·t̬i/ *n* [U] • *As the skin grows older it loses its elasticity and starts to hang off the face.* • *(fig.) There is some elasticity in our plans – nothing has been firmly decided yet.*

E·las·to·plast /ɪ'læs·tᵊp·lɑːst, -'lɑː·stᵊp-/ *n* [U] *Br trademark* a common type of PLASTER (= a small piece of sticky material to cover and protect a cut in the skin)

e·lat·ed /£ɪ'leɪ·tɪd, $-t̬ɪd/ *adj* extremely happy and excited, often because something has happened or been achieved • *The prince was reported to be elated* **at/by** *the birth of his new daughter.* • *The parents of the child were elated* **to** *hear that she had been found safe and well.* [+ to infinitive]

e·la·tion /ɪ'leɪ·ʃᵊn/ *n* [U] • *There's a sense of elation at having completed a race of such length.*

el·bow /£'el·bəʊ, $-boʊ/ *n* [C] the bony point at which the arm bends, or the part of a piece of clothing which covers this area • *Her arm was bandaged from the elbow to the fingers.* • *The sleeve of his shirt was torn* **at the** *elbow.* • *During the visit, the interpreter was always* **at** *her* **elbow** (= close beside and a little behind her). • *(fig.) He retired after three years* **at** *the Minister's* **elbow** (= after three years working closely with the Minister). • *(Br infml)* If you **give** someone **the elbow**, you end your relationship with them: *When she discovered what had happened, she soon gave him the elbow.* • If you use **elbow grease**, you put a lot of effort into doing something: *The polish needs a certain amount of elbow grease to apply.* ○ *They now need to* **put some real** *elbow grease* **into** *promoting the product.* • **Elbow room** is space to move around in: *There were so many people at the exhibition that you couldn't find any elbow room.* ○ *(fig.) At first the management gave the new director plenty of elbow room* (= freedom of action). • [PIC] **Body**

el·bow *obj* /£'el·bəʊ, $-boʊ/ *v* [T always + adv/prep] *disapproving* • *He elbowed his way to the front of the crowd.* • *They elbowed the onlookers* **aside/out of the way.** • *The woman elbowed me* **in the ribs** (= pushed her elbow against my side).

eld·er /£'el·dəʳ, $-dɚ/ *n* [C] an older person, esp. one with a respected position in society • *You should listen to the advice of your elders* (= people older than you). • *They consulted the* **village** *elders.* • *(fml) She is my* **elder by** *three years* (= three years older than me). • A **church** elder/Elder is an official of a religious group.

eld·er /£'el·dəʳ, $-dɚ/ *adj* [before n; not gradable] • Elder is used for people in the same family: *an elder sister/brother/son/daughter.* • *There were two British prime ministers called William Pitt, and the father is usually known as William Pitt* **the elder.** • An elder **statesman/stateswoman** is an older person who is respected and asked for advice because of their past experience, esp. in politics.

el·der·ber·ry /£'el·dəˌber·i, $-dɚ-/, **eld·er (tree)** *n* [C] a small tree which grows wild or in gardens and has large flat groups of white flowers, or its nearly black fruit which can be used in cooking or making wine • *a row of elderberries* (= trees) • *a basketful of elderberries* (= fruit) • *elderberry wine* • PIC> **Berries**

el·der·ly /£'el·dəl·i, $-dɚ·li/ *adj* (used to avoid saying) old • *elderly relatives/parents* ○ *a well-used and rather elderly bike* • LP> **Age**

el·der·ly /£'el·dəl·i, $-dɚ·li/ *n* • **The elderly** are old people considered as a group: *The city is building new housing for the elderly.*

eld·est /'el·dɪst/ *adj* [not gradable], *n* [U] oldest (of three or more people, esp. within a family) • *She left all her money to my eldest brother.* [before n] • *He was the eldest of a large family.* • *Her eldest (child) is nearly 14.*

e·lect *(obj)* /ɪ'lekt/ *v* to decide on or choose, esp. to choose (a person) for a particular job by voting • *The Government is elected for a five-year term of office.* [T] • *We elected him* **as** *our representative.* [T + obj + *as* n] • *She was elected Chair of the Board of Governors.* [T + obj + n] • *The group elected one of its members* **to** *be their spokesperson.* [T + obj + *to be* n] • *(fml) They elected* **to** *take early retirement instead of moving to the new location.* [+ *to* infinitive]

e·lect /ɪ'lekt/ *pl n fml* • In the Bible, **the elect** are people chosen by God. More generally, they are any group of people who have been specially chosen for their particular qualities.

–e·lect /-ɪ'lekt/ *combining form* • *The President-elect* (= person voted to be President) *has been preparing to take office in January.* • Compare DESIGNATE.

e·lec·tab·le /£ɪ'lek·tə·bl̩, $-t̬ə-/ *adj* • *Clinton's youthful image made him an extremely electable candidate.*

e·lec·tion /ɪ'lek·ʃən/ *n* • *The Government is expected to* **call** *an election* (= allow the country to vote) *very soon.* [C] • *Local government elections will take place in May.* [C] • *These posts will be filled by election.* [U] • *The first election results have started to come in.* • *(fml) A married couple may* **make** *an election* (= choose) **to** *share their tax relief.* [C + *to* infinitive] • An **election campaign** is the period of weeks immediately before an election when politicians try to persuade people to vote for them. • See also BY-ELECTION

e·lec·tion·eer·ing /£ɪˌlek·ʃə'nɪə·rɪŋ, $-'nɪr·ɪŋ/ *n* [U] *esp. disapproving* • Electioneering is the activity of trying to persuade people to vote for a particular political party. *The M.P.'s speech was dismissed by her opponents as crude electioneering.*

e·lec·tive /£ɪ'lek·tɪv, $-t̬ɪv/ *adj* [not gradable] *fml* • *an elective office* (= chosen by voting) • *elective politics/democracy* (= based on voting) • *elective* (= chosen but not necessary) *surgery* • *(Br disapproving)* An **elective dictatorship** is a government which is elected but which has won so many votes that it can do what it likes.

e·lec·tor /£ɪ'lek·tər, $-t̬ɚ/ *n* [C] • *At this election many eighteen-year-olds will become electors* (= voters) *for the first time.*

e·lec·tor·al /£ɪ'lek·tər·əl, $-t̬ɚ-/ *adj* [before n; not gradable] • *the electoral system* • *electoral law/reform/gains/defeat* • *electoral unpopularity/consequences/impact* • An **electoral college** is a group of people whose job is to choose a political or religious leader. • The **electoral register/roll** is the official list of people who are allowed to vote.

e·lec·tor·al·ly /£ɪ'lek·tər·ə·li, $-t̬ɚ-/ *adv* [not gradable] • *electorally damaging/unpopular*

e·lec·tor·ate /£ɪ'lek·tər·ət, $-t̬ɚ-/ *n* [C + sing/pl v] • *The present voting system distorts the wishes of* **the** *electorate* (= the people who are allowed to vote).

e·lec·tri·ci·ty /£ˌɪl·ek'trɪs·ɪ·ti, $-ə·t̬i/ *n* [U] a form of energy, produced in various ways, which provides power to devices that create light, heat, etc. • *an electricity generating company* • *lit/powered/heated by electricity* • LP> **Switching on and off**

e·lec·tric /ɪ'lek·trɪk/ *adj* • *an electric blanket/car/kettle/lawnmower/light* • Something might be described as electric if it is very exciting and produces strong feelings: *an electric performance/atmosphere* • **The electric chair** is used in some parts of the US to kill a criminal with a current of electricity. • An **electric fence** produces a small electric current, usually to keep animals in a particular area. • An *(Br)* **electric fire**/*(Am and Aus)* **electric heater** is a small heater with two metal bars which become red when hot. • An **electric razor** is a device for removing hair which has different types of blades which turn or move backwards and forwards. • An **electric shock** (*infml* **shock**) is a current of electricity going through the body, which can kill if it is strong enough. • PIC> **Fires and space heaters**

e·lec·trics /ɪ'lek·trɪks/ *pl n Br* • *I think the fault is in* **the electrics** (= the electrical system, esp. of a car).

e·lec·tri·cal /ɪ'lek·trɪ·kəl/ *adj* [not gradable] • Something electrical uses electricity for power, is involved in the production or movement of electricity, or is related in some way to electricity: *electrical equipment/goods/devices* ○ *an electrical fuse/circuit/current/meter/fault* ○ *an electrical business/store/shop* • An **electrical engineer** is a trained specialist in electrical systems, esp. those which power and control machines or are involved in communication. • An **electric(al) storm** is a storm with thunder and lightning.

e·lec·tri·cal·ly /ɪ'lek·trɪ·kli/ *adv* [not gradable] • *an electrically powered car*

e·lec·tri·cals /ɪ'lek·trɪ·kəlz/ *pl n specialized* • *Electricals* (= Companies which produce electronic goods) *made big gains in this afternoon's trading on Wall Street.* • *The Japanese electricals giants have cornered the market in TVs and videos.*

e·lec·tri·cian /ˌɪl·ek'trɪʃ·ən/ *n* [C] • *The electrician* (= a person who puts in and maintains electrical wiring) *is coming to do the rewiring on Tuesday.*

e·lec·tri·fy *obj* /ɪ'lek·trɪ·faɪ/ *v* [T] • *The east coast railway line has been electrified* (= now uses electricity for power). • *(fig.) She electrified* (= excited) *her audience with her vivid stories.* • *(fig.) It was an electrifying* (= exciting) *performance.*

e·lec·tri·fi·ca·tion /ɪˌlek·trɪ·fɪ'keɪ·ʃən/ *n* [U] • *the electrification of the railways* • *rural electrification* • *electrification technology*

e·lec·tro·cute *obj* /ɪ'lek·trə·kjuːt/ *v* [T] • *He was electrocuted* (= killed by electricity) *when he touched the bare wires.*

e·lec·tro·cu·tion /ɪˌlek·trə'kjuː·ʃən/ *n* [C/U]

e·lec·tro·con·vul·sive ther·a·py /£ɪˌlek·trəʊ·kən'vʌl·sɪv, $-troʊ-/ (*abbreviation* **ECT**, *Am also* **e·lec·tro·shock ther·a·py** /£ɪ'lek·trəʊ·ʃɒk, $-troʊ·ʃɑːk/) *n* [U] *medical* the treatment of particular mental illnesses which involves sending an electric current through the brain • *Electroconvulsive therapy is usually reserved for cases of very severe depression.*

e·lec·trode /£ɪ'lek·trəʊd, $-troʊd/ *n* [C] the point at which an electric current enters or leaves something, for example, a BATTERY

e·lec·tro·ly·sis /£ˌɪl·ek'trɒl·ə·sɪs, $-'trɑː·lə-/ *n* [U] the use of an electric current to cause chemical change or to destroy living matter, esp. hair roots

e·lec·tro·lyte /ɪ'lek·trə·laɪt/ *n* [C] *specialized* a substance, usually a liquid, which electricity can go through or which breaks into its parts when electricity goes through it

e·lec·tro·mag·net·i·sm /£ɪˌlek·trəʊ'mæg·nə·tɪ·zəm, $-troʊ-/ *n* [U] *specialized* the science of magnetism and electrical currents

e·lec·tro·mag·net·ic /£ɪˌlek·trəʊ·mæg'net·ɪk, $-troʊ·mæg'net̬-/ *adj* [not gradable] • *an electromagnetic* (= having magnetic and electrical parts) *wave* • *electromagnetic radiation*

e·lec·tro·mag·net /£ɪˌlek·trəʊ'mæg·nə·tɪ·zəm, $-troʊ'mæg·nə·t̬ɪ-/ *n* [C] • An electromagnet is a device made from a piece of iron that becomes magnetic when a changing current is passed through the wire that goes round it.

e·lec·tron /£ɪ'lek·trɒn, $-trɑːn/ *n* [C] an extremely small piece of matter with a negative electrical charge • An **electron microscope** is a device which sends electrons through objects which are too small to be seen easily, to produce a picture which is more detailed than that produced by ordinary microscopes. • Compare NEUTRON; PROTON.

e·lec·tron·ic /£ˌɪl·ek'trɒn·ɪk, $-'trɑː·nɪk/ *adj* [not gradable] (esp. of equipment) using, based on or used in a system of operation which involves the control of electric current by various devices • *an electronic keyboard/game* • *electronic surveillance/publishing* • *electronic components/devices* • *Most electronic components use silicon chips these days.* • **Electronic mail** (*abbreviation* **e-mail**) is a system of using computers for sending messages from one place to another. An **electronic mailbox** is the place where the computer stores the messages.

e·lec·tron·ics /£ˌɪl·ek'trɒn·ɪks, $-'trɑː·nɪks/ *n* [U] • *a degree in electronics* • *the electronics industry*

e·lec·tron·i·cal·ly /£ˌɪl·ek'trɒn·ɪ·kli, $-'trɑː·nɪ-/ *adv* [not gradable] • *electronically generated graphics* • *electronically stored information*

e·lec·tro·stat·ic /£ɪˌlek·trəʊ'stæt·ɪk, $-troʊ'stæţ-/ *adj* [not gradable] *specialized* connected with or caused by electricity which does not move in a current but is attracted to the surface of some objects • *an electrostatic charge* • *Electrostatic* **attraction** *causes the balloon to stick to the ceiling.*

el·e·gant /'el·ɪ·gᵊnt/ *adj* graceful and attractive in appearance or behaviour • *an elegant person/figure/profile* • *an elegant gesture/wave* • An elegant idea/plan/solution is attractive because it is clever but simple.

el·e·gant·ly /'el·ɪ·gᵊnt·li/ *adv* • *elegantly dressed*

el·e·gance /'el·ɪ·gᵊnts/ *n* [U] • *He was famous for his elegance and wit.*

el·e·gy /'el·ə·dʒi/ *n* [C] a sad poem or song, esp. remembering someone who has died or something in the past • *Gray's 'Elegy in a Country Churchyard' is a famous English poem.*

el·e·gi·ac /ˌel·ɪ'dʒaɪ·ək, $ɪ'liː·dʒi·æk/ *adj*

el·e·ment [PART] /'el·ɪ·mənt/ *n* [C] a part; a COMPONENT • *List the elements which make up a perfect dinner party.* • *The film had all the elements of a good thriller.* • *An unruly element causes/Unruly elements cause* (=particular badly behaved people create) *trouble for the others in the school.* • *We weren't even taught the elements of* (=basic information about) *physics at school.* • The element is the part of an electrical device which produces heat: *The kettle needs a new element.* • Element is also *Am for* **ring** (=a circular piece of material that is heated to cook things on). See at RING [CIRCLE]. • [PIC]〉 **Ring**

el·e·ment [AMOUNT] /'el·ɪ·mənt/ *n* a particular, esp. a small, amount of an emotion or quality • *an element* **of** *truth/risk/jealousy/caution* [C] • *We walked quietly up to the door to preserve the element* **of surprise**. [U]

el·e·ment [SIMPLE SUBSTANCE] /'el·ɪ·mənt/ *n* [C] a simple substance which cannot be reduced to smaller chemical parts • *Aluminium is an element.* • *There are more than 100 elements.* • *(old use)* In the past, the elements were thought to be earth, air, fire and water from which people believed everything else was made. • If you are **in** your **element**, you are happy because you are doing what you like or can do best: *If you ask Kate to organize the party, she'll be in her element.* • If you are **out of** your **element**, you are unhappy and feel uncomfortable: *He was out of his natural element in such a formal gathering.*

el·e·men·tal /ˌel·ɪ'men·tᵊl/ *adj fml or literary* showing the strong power of nature or *(fig.)* basic or most simple but strong • *elemental force/fury/strength* • *(fig.) elemental needs/desires/feelings/ideas*

el·e·men·tary /£ˌel·ɪ'men·tᵊr·i, $-ţə-/ *adj* simple or easy; basic • *Millions of travellers fail to take elementary precautions.* • *Many adults seem to know little about some of the most elementary science.* • *Elementary services have been provided for the refugee camps.* • *The group had made some elementary mistakes.* • *This book contains a series of elementary exercises for learners.* • *(specialized)* **Elementary particles** are the most simple parts of all matter, such as ELECTRONS, PROTONS and NEUTRONS. • *(Br dated or Am)* An **elementary school** is a school which provides the first part of a child's education, usually for children between five and eleven years old. • *"Elementary* (=it's simple to understand), *my dear Watson"* (Sherlock Holmes in the films based on the books of Sir Arthur Conan Doyle, 1930s-) • [LP]〉 **Schools and colleges**

el·e·ments /'el·ɪ·mənts/ *pl n* **the elements** *esp. humorous* (bad) weather conditions • *We decided to* **brave** *the elements and go for a walk* (=go for a walk despite the bad weather).

el·e·phant /'el·ɪ·fənt/ *n* [C] a very large grey mammal which has a TRUNK (=long nose) with which it can pick things up

el·e·phan·tine /ˌel·ɪ'fæn·taɪn/ *adj* • *She's so tiny she makes me feel elephantine* (=very large).

el·e·vate *obj* /'el·ɪ·veɪt/ *v* [T] *fml* to raise or lift up, or *(fig.)* to make more important or to improve • *The platform was elevated by means of hydraulic legs.* • *(fig.) They want to elevate the status of teachers.* • *(fig.) These factors helped to elevate the town into the list of the ten most attractive in the country.* • If someone is elevated they are given a higher rank or social position: *She was elevated* **to** *the peerage* (=was given the title 'Lady').

el·e·vat·ed /£'el·ɪ·veɪ·tɪd, $-ţɪd/ *adj* • *There is an elevated* (=raised) *area at the back of the building.* • *(fig.) She gives no impression of holding such an elevated* (=high or important) *position in the company.* • *(fig.) He has an elevated idea of his own importance* (=he thinks he is more important than he is). • *(fig.) The report uses rather elevated* (=literary or formal) *language.*

el·e·va·tion /ˌel·ɪ'veɪ·ʃᵊn/ *n fml* • *Atmospheric pressure varies with elevation* (=height) *and temperature.* [U] • *The crop is not grown at high elevations/above an elevation of 1000 metres.* [C] • *The flagpole stands on a small elevation* (=hill) *in front of the building.* [C] • *His elevation to the presidency* (=being made President) *of the new republic was generally popular.* [U]

el·e·va·tion /ˌel·ɪ'veɪ·ʃᵊn/ *n* [C] the front or side of a building as shown on a drawing • *This plan shows the front, side and back elevations of the new supermarket.*

el·e·vat·or /£'el·ɪ·veɪ·tər, $-ţə/ *n* [C] a piece of equipment which moves things from one level to another • *(Am)* An elevator *(Br and Aus)* **lift** is a small room which carries people or goods up and down in tall buildings. • An elevator can be a moving strip which can be used for unloading goods from a ship, putting bags onto an aircraft, moving grain into a store etc. • *(Am)* **Elevator music** is pleasant but not very interesting or exciting recorded music played in public places.

e·lev·en /ɪ'lev·ᵊn/ *determiner, pronoun, n* (the number) 11 • *nine, ten, eleven, twelve* • *There are eleven girls in my class and fifteen boys.* • *"How many children are there?" "Eleven".* • An eleven is a team of eleven players: *The school's first eleven* (=The school's best team for football or cricket) *has/have won every game so far this year.* [C + sing/pl v] ○ *He's a first-eleven player.* • *(Br)* The **eleven-plus** is an exam taken by children aged eleven in some parts of Britain to decide what type of school they will go to next.

e·lev·en·ses /ɪ'lev·ᵊn·zɪz/ *pl n* • *(Br infml)* Elevenses is a drink and a small amount to eat between the morning and the middle of the day: *I always have a cup of coffee and a cake for (my) elevenses.*

e·lev·enth /ɪ'lev·ᵊnθ/ *determiner, pronoun, adj, adv* [not gradable], *n* • *my eleventh visit to Rome* • *the eleventh of June* • *She was/came eleventh.* • An eleventh is one of eleven equal parts of something. [C] • **The eleventh hour** is the last moment or almost too late: *We only received the official signatures* **at** *the eleventh hour.* ○ *They welcomed the eleventh-hour decision by the union to call off the strike.*

elf /elf/ *n* [C] *pl* **elves** /elvz/ a small imaginary person, usually shown in pictures as male and dressed in green with pointed ears and a tall hat, and often described in stories as playing tricks and having magical powers

el·fin /'el·fɪn/ *adj* • *Her elfin* (=small and delicate) *face was surrounded by masses of dark hair.*

e·lic·it *obj* /ɪ'lɪs·ɪt/ *v* [T] *fml* to obtain (esp. information or a reaction), or produce • *No criticism/explanation/promise/reply could be elicited* **from** *her family.* • *They were able to elicit the support/cooperation of the public.* • *The questionnaire was intended to elicit information on eating habits.* • *The parasites that cause malaria elicit an immune response in the body.*

el·i·gib·le /'el·ɪ·dʒə·bl̩/ *adj* having the necessary qualities or fulfilling the necessary conditions • *Are you eligible* **for** *early retirement/promotion/maternity leave?* • *Are you eligible* **to** *vote/enter the competition/claim a refund?* [+ *to* infinitive] • If someone who is not married is eligible, they are desirable as a marriage partner, esp. because they are rich and attractive: *an eligible* **bachelor**

el·i·gi·bil·i·ty /£ˌel·ɪ·dʒə'bɪl·ɪ·ti, $-ə·ţi/ *n* [U] • *I'll have to check her eligibility to take part.* • *The eligibility rules prevent under-18s being in the team.*

e·lim·i·nate *obj* /ɪ'lɪm·ɪ·neɪt/ *v* [T] to remove or take away • *A move towards healthy eating could help eliminate heart disease.* • *We eliminated the possibility that it could have been an accident because it was so well timed.* • *He was eliminated* (=defeated and so unable to continue) *in/after the third round of the competition.* • *The police eliminated him* **from** *their enquiries* (=decided that he was not guilty). • *(slang)* To eliminate can mean to murder: *A police officer was accused of helping a drug gang eliminate rivals.* • [LP]〉 **Sports**

e·lim·i·na·tion /ɪˌlɪm·ɪ'neɪ·ʃᵊn/ *n* [U] • *elimination of disease/pain* • *elimination from the competition* • *We found the answer by* **a process of** *elimination* (=by removing from several possible answers the ones which were unlikely to be correct until only one is left). • **Elimination tournament** is *Am for* KNOCKOUT COMPETITION.

e·lim·i·nat·or /£ɪ'lɪm·ɪ·neɪ·tə^r, $-t̬ɚ/ *n* [C] *Br* • An eliminator is a part of a competition in any game or sport where one person or team plays against another to decide which of them will continue to the next stage and which will be removed from the competition: *After this series of eliminators only sixteen people will remain in the tournament.*

e·lite /ɪ'liːt, eɪ-/ *n* [C + sing/pl v], *adj esp. disapproving* the richest, most powerful, best educated or most highly trained group in a society • *The elite has/have been badly frightened by the revolution.* • *He said that any changes to the tax system should be in order to benefit the workers, not the wealthy and influential elite.* • *Elite troops were airlifted to the trouble zone.*

e·lit·i·sm /ɪ'liː·tɪ·zᵊm, eɪ-/ *n* [U] *esp. disapproving* • Elitism is organizing things for the benefit of a few people with special interests or abilities: *The accusation of elitism seems unfair as the festival presents a wide range of music, with something to please everyone.*

e·lit·ist /ɪ'liː·tɪst, eɪ-/ *adj disapproving* • *They have ruled out extra pay for these skills as elitist and divisive.* • *Many remember sport at school as elitist, focusing only on those who were good at it.*

e·lix·ir /£ɪ'lɪk·sɪə^r, $-sjɚ/ *n* [C] a substance, usually a liquid, with a magical power to cure, improve or preserve • *The soaring sales of bottled water reflect an unscientific search for an elixir.* • *It's another health product claiming to be the elixir* **of life/youth** (=something to make you live longer/stay young).

E·liz·a·beth·an /ɪ,lɪz·ə'biː·θᵊn/ *adj* [not gradable], *n* from the period when Queen Elizabeth I was the ruler of England (1558-1603), or a person living at that time • *Elizabethan furniture* • *Sir Francis Drake was a famous Elizabethan.* [C]

elk (*pl* **elks** or **elk**) /elk/, *Am also* **moose** *n* [C] a type of large deer with large flat horns • *(esp. Am)* An Elk is also a number of the Benevolent and Protective Order of Elks, a men's social organization.

el·lipse /ɪ'lɪps/ *n* [C] an oval; a flattened circle • *An ellipse is the closed figure obtained when a cone is cut by a plane.* • *The planets move around the Sun in ellipses, and the shape is much used in art and architecture.*

el·lip·ti·cal /ɪ'lɪp·tɪ·kᵊl/, **el·lip·tic** /ɪ'lɪp·tɪk/ *adj* • *The comet is in an elliptical orbit which brings it close to the earth at regular intervals.*

el·lip·ti·cal /ɪ'lɪp·tɪ·kᵊl/ *adj fml* (of language) with parts missing, so sometimes difficult to understand • *His message was written in a deliberately elliptical style.*

el·lip·ti·cal·ly /ɪ'lɪp·tɪ·kli/ *adv fml*

el·lip·sis /ɪ'lɪp·sɪs/ *n* [C] *pl* **ellipses** /ɪ'lɪp·siːz/ *specialized* • *An example of ellipsis is "What percentage was left?" "Twenty"* (=20 per cent). • An ellipsis is also the three dots in a printed text which show where one or more words have been intentionally omitted. • LP **Dots**

elm /elm/ *n* a large tree which loses its leaves in winter • *Many elms died from Dutch elm disease.* [C] • *Water pipes used to be made out of elm* (=wood from an elm tree), *because it does not decay easily.* [U]

el·o·cu·tion /,el·ə'kjuː·ʃᵊn/ *n* [U] the art of careful public speaking, using clear pronunciation and good breathing to control the voice • *classes in elocution* • *an elocution teacher*

e·lon·gate *(obj)* /£'iː·lɒŋ·geɪt, $ɪ'lɑːŋ-/ *v* to (cause to) become longer, or longer and thinner • *The cells elongate as they take in water.* [I] • *Sometimes hormones are used to elongate apples so that they look more attractive.* [T]

e·lon·gat·ed /£'iː·lɒŋ·geɪ·tɪd, $ɪ'lɑːŋ·geɪ·t̬ɪd/, *specialized* **e·lon·gate** /£'iː·lɒŋ·geɪt, $ɪ'lɑːŋ-/ *adj* • *The painter's style is characterized by elongated* (=long and thin) *faces.* • *The plants had weak elongated stems.* • *The incubation period of the disease is unusually elongated.*

e·lon·ga·tion /£,iː·lɒŋ'geɪ·ʃᵊn, $ɪ,lɑːŋ-/ *n* [C/U]

e·lope /£ɪ'ləʊp, $-'loʊp/ *v* [I] to leave home secretly in order to get married without parental agreement • *They decided to elope.* • *She eloped* **with** *an Army officer.*

e·lope·ment /£ɪ'ləʊp·mənt, $-'loʊp-/ *n* [C]

el·o·quent /'el·ə·kwᵊnt/ *adj* giving a clear, strong message • *She made an eloquent appeal for action before it was too late.* • *The pictures were an eloquent reminder of the power of the volcano.*

el·o·quent·ly /'el·ə·kwᵊnt·li/ *adv* • *He spoke eloquently with the self-effacing humour that has endeared him to the American press.*

el·o·quence /'el·ə·kwᵊnts/ *n* [U] • *She was renowned for her eloquence and beauty.*

else /els/ *adv* [not gradable] (after words beginning with any-, every-, no- and some-, or after how, what, where, who, why but not which) other, another, different, additional • *Everybody else has* (=All the other people have) *agreed except for you.* • *If it doesn't work, try something else* (=something different/another way or thing). • *Let's go before they ask us to visit anyone else* (=another/an additional person). • *It's not my bag. It must be someone else's* (=it must belong to another person). • *Has anyone else* (=any other person) *got a bag like this?* • *The book isn't here. Where else* (=In what other place) *should I look?* • *He came to see you. Why else* (=For what other reason) *would he come?* • *After I'd thanked them I didn't know what else* (=what other/additional things) *to say.* • **Or else** is a stronger way of saying 'or': *We must be there by six or else we'll miss the beginning.* • *(infml)* **Or else** is also used as a threat, sometimes humorously: *He'd better find it quickly, or else* (=or I will punish him in some way)*!*

else·where /£els'weə^r, $-'wer, '--/ *adv* [not gradable] (at, in, from, or to) another place or other places; anywhere or somewhere else • *We have examples from Britain and elsewhere.* • *They couldn't find what they wanted and decided to look elsewhere.* • *It's hot and sunny in the north-west but not elsewhere.*

ELT /,iː·el'tiː/ *n* [U] *abbreviation for* English Language Teaching (=teaching English to speakers of other languages)

e·lu·ci·date *(obj)* /ɪ'luː·sɪ·deɪt/ *v fml* to explain or make clear • *I don't understand. You'll have to elucidate.* [I] • *The possible reasons for the change in weather conditions have been elucidated by several scientists.* [T]

e·lu·ci·da·tion /ɪ,luː·sɪ'deɪ·ʃᵊn/ *n* [U] • *These figures need elucidation.*

e·lude *obj* /ɪ'luːd/ *v* [T] *fml* to escape from, esp. by a clever trick, or (of information) to be difficult for someone to find or remember • *They eluded the police by fleeing to the United States.* • *Leaving home was just a way of eluding his responsibilities.* • *I know who you mean but her name eludes me* (=I can't remember her name). • *They had minor breakthroughs but real success eluded them* (=could not be achieved).

e·lu·sive /ɪ'luː·sɪv/ *adj* • *an elusive person* • *elusive memories* • *elusive success*

e·lu·sive·ly /ɪ'luː·sɪv·li/ *adv*

e·lu·sive·ness /ɪ'luː·sɪv·nəs/ *n* [U]

el·ves /elvz/ *pl of* ELF

E·ly·si·um /ɪ'lɪz·i·əm/ *n* [U], **the E·ly·si·an fields** /ɪ'lɪz·i·ən/ *pl n literary* a state of great happiness • *Everything was perfect. She was in Elysium.*

em– /im-, em-/ *combining form* See at EN-

'em *infml* /əm/ *short form of* them • *Can you think of anything that might help us find 'em?'* • *Tell 'em not to worry about the money.*

e·mac·i·at·ed /£ɪ'meɪ·si·eɪ·tɪd, $-t̬ɪd/ *adj fml* (esp. of people and animals) very thin and weak, usually because of illness or extreme hunger • *There were pictures of emaciated families on the cover of the magazine.*

e·mac·i·a·tion /ɪ,meɪ·si'eɪ·ʃᵊn/ *n* [U] • *Chronic diarrhoea leads to dehydration and emaciation.*

e–mail /'iː·meɪl/ *n* [U] *abbreviation for* **electronic mail**, see at ELECTRONIC

e·man·ate *(obj)* /'em·ə·neɪt/ *v fml* (esp. of things which have no physical shape or form) to come from or out of • *Angry voices emanated* **from** *the room.* [I always + adv/prep] • *Steam emanated* **through** *cracks in the ground around the hot springs.* [I always + adv/prep] • *Her face emanates sadness.* [T]

e·man·a·tion /,em·ə'neɪ·ʃᵊn/ *n* [C/U] *fml*

e·man·ci·pat·ed /£ɪ'mænt·sɪ·peɪ·tɪd, $-t̬ɪd/ *adj* not limited socially or politically • *We live in more emancipated times.* • *The twenties and sixties are often regarded as the most emancipated decades, when women got the vote and the pill respectively.*

e·man·ci·pate *obj* /ɪ'mænt·sɪ·peɪt/ *v* [T]

e·man·ci·pa·tion /ɪ,mænt·sɪ'peɪ·ʃᵊn/ *n* [U] • *women's/female emancipation* • *black emancipation* • *political emancipation*

e·mas·cu·late *obj* /ɪ'mæs·kjʊ·leɪt/ *v* [T usually passive] *fml* to weaken or to reduce the effectiveness of, or *(specialized)* to remove the male parts of • *They were accused of trying to emasculate the report's recommendations.* • *(specialized) Most male farm animals are emasculated when they are young.* • *(specialized) The flowers are emasculated to prevent self pollination.*

e·mas·cu·la·tion /ɪˌmæs·kjʊˈleɪ·ʃᵊn/ *n* [U] *fml*

em·balm *obj* /ɪmˈbɑːm/ *v* [T] to use chemicals to prevent (a dead body) from decaying • *They asked for the body to be embalmed.*

em·bal·mer /ɪmˈbɑː·məʳ/ *n* [C]

em·bank·ment /ɪmˈbæŋk·mənt/ *n* [C] an artificial slope made of earth and/or stones • *a river/road/railway embankment*

em·bar·go /£ɪmˈbɑː·gəʊ, $-goʊ/ *n* [C] *pl* **embargoes** an order to temporarily stop esp. trading or giving information • *They have* **put** *an embargo* **on** *imports of clothing.* • *The police asked for a* **news** *embargo while they tried to find the kidnapper.*

em·bar·go *obj* /£ɪmˈbɑː·gəʊ, $-goʊ/ *v* [T] he/she/it **embargoes**, **embargoing**, *past* **embargoed** • *They are planning to embargo oil imports.*

em·bark /£ɪmˈbɑːk, $-bɑːrk/ *v* [I] to go on to a ship • *We embarked at Liverpool for New York.*

em·bark·a·tion /£ˌem·bɑːˈkeɪ·ʃᵊn, $-bɑːr-/ *n* • *You'll be asked for those documents* **on** *embarkation.* [U] • *He came home on embarkation leave.* • *A series of embarkations was planned over a three-week period.* [C]

em·bark on/u·pon *obj v prep* [T] to start (esp. something large or important) • *We're embarking upon a new project later this year.*

em·bar·rass *obj* /£ɪmˈbær·əs, $-ˈber-/ *v* [T usually passive] to cause (someone) to feel anxious or uncomfortable • *I was really embarrassed when I knocked the cup of tea over my teacher.* • *He embarrassed everyone by saying the picture was dreadful.* • *(humorous)* You might say you or someone else is **financially** embarrassed to avoid saying that you/they do not have enough money: *I'll have to pay you next week – I'm financially embarrassed at present.*

em·bar·rass·ing /£ɪmˈbær·ə·sɪŋ, $-ˈber-/ *adj* • *an embarrassing situation/person/story/remark* • *Their behaviour was extremely embarrassing.* • **It**'*s embarrassing* **to** *be caught telling a lie.* [+ *to* infinitive] • *My* **most** *embarrassing* **moment** *was when I tried to introduce her but couldn't remember her name.*

em·bar·rass·ing·ly /£ɪmˈbær·ə·sɪŋ·li, $-ˈber-/ *adv* • *an embarrassingly poor performance/loud voice*

em·bar·rass·ment /£ɪmˈbær·ə·smənt, $-ˈber-/ *n* • *She blushed with embarrassment.* [U] • *The day began badly with a series of embarrassments and misunderstandings.* [C] • *My parents are* **an** *embarrassment* **to** *me* (=Their behaviour embarrasses me)*!* [U] • **Financial** *embarrassment made her sell her car.* [U]

em·bas·sy /ˈem·bə·si/ *n* [C] the group of people who represent their country in a foreign country, or the building they work in • *We used to be friendly with some people who worked* **at** *the Swedish Embassy.* • *He's an embassy official.* • *The Ambassador held a reception at the embassy.*

em·bat·tled /£ɪmˈbæt·l̩d, $-ˈbæt̬-/ *adj* having a lot of problems or difficulties • *an embattled government* • *embattled teachers* • *an embattled position*

em·bed *obj*, *Am also* **im·bed** /ɪmˈbed/ *v* [T] **-dd-** to fix (something) firmly into a substance • *The children embedded themselves* **in** *the sand.*

em·bed·ded, *Am also* **im·bed·ded** /ɪmˈbed·ɪd/ *adj* • *The thorn was embedded* **in** *her thumb.* • *I can't move it. It's firmly embedded.*

em·bel·lish *obj* /ɪmˈbel·ɪʃ/ *v* [T] to make more beautiful or interesting by adding something, esp. details which are not true to a story or statement • *The ceiling was embellished* **with** *flowers and leaves.* • *He couldn't resist embellishing the story of his accident a little.*

em·bel·lish·ment /ɪmˈbel·ɪʃ·mənt/ *n* [C; U]

em·bers /£ˈem·bəz, $-bɚz/ *pl n* [C usually pl] pieces of wood, coal, etc. which are burning without flames • *They poked the* **glowing** (=red and hot) *embers and the fire burst into flames.* • *We sat by the* **dying** *embers of the fire.*

em·bez·zle *obj* /ɪmˈbez·l̩/ *v* [T] to secretly take money that is in your care or that belongs to an organization or business you work for • *She embezzled thousands of dollars* **from** *the charity while appearing to be its best fundraiser.* • LP **Crimes and criminals**

em·bez·zle·ment /ɪmˈbez·l̩.mənt/ *n* [U] • *They were arrested for embezzlement* **of** *company funds.*

em·bez·zler /£ɪmˈbez·ləʳ, $-lɚ/ *n* [C]

em·bit·ter *obj* /£ɪmˈbɪt·əʳ, $-ˈbɪt̬·ɚ/ *v* [T usually passive] to make (someone) feel angry and unhappy for a long time • *Losing their home when their business failed embittered them* **towards** *the banks.*

em·blaz·on *obj* /ɪmˈbleɪ·zᵊn/, **bla·zon** *v* [T always + prep; usually passive] to make very noticeable • *Her name was emblazoned* **across** *the front of the theatre.* • *Cars emblazoned* **with** *the company logo were parked in rows.* • *A clenched fist was emblazoned* **on** *the tee-shirts.*

em·blem /ˈem·bləm/ *n* [C] (a picture of) an object which is used to represent a particular person, group or idea • *A rose is the national emblem* **of** *England.* • *A dove is often used as an emblem* **of** *peace.*

em·ble·ma·tic /£ˌem·bləˈmæt·ɪk, $-ˈmæt̬-/ *adj fml* • *A sword is emblematic* **of** *power gained by violence.*

em·ble·mat·i·cally /£ˌem·bləˈmæt·ɪ·kli, $-ˈmæt̬-/ *adv fml*

em·bo·dy *obj* /£ɪmˈbɒd·i, $-ˈbɑː·di/ *v* [T] to include as part of something, or include, show or represent in behaviour • *The book is still in the bestseller lists despite the complex theories it embodies.* • *Ashe always embodied good sportsmanship on the playing field.* • *Kennett embodied in one man an unusual range of science, music and religion.*

em·bo·di·ment /£ɪmˈbɒd·ɪ·mənt, $-ˈbɑː·dɪ-/ *n* [U] • *The car is* **the** *embodiment* **of** (=It includes) *all the latest ideas on safety.* • *She is* **the** *embodiment* **of** (=She always behaves with) *patience and calmness.*

em·bol·den *obj* /£ɪmˈbəʊl·dᵊn, $-ˈboʊl-/ *v* [T] *fml* to make brave • *The children were emboldened by the lack of movement and took a few more steps toward the animal.* • *Their encouragement emboldened him* **to** *accept the challenge.* [+ obj + *to* infinitive]

em·bol·i·sm /ˈem·bə·lɪ·zᵊm/ *n* [C] *specialized* (a bubble of air, a lump of hardened blood or small pieces of fat which cause) a blockage in a tube carrying blood around the body

em·boss *obj* /£ɪmˈbɒs, $-ˈbɑːs/ *v* [T usually passive] to decorate or mark an object, esp. with letters, using special tools which make a raised mark on its surface • *With this device I can emboss my address at the top of all my letters.* • *She handed me a business card with her name neatly embossed on it.*

em·brace *(obj)* HOLD /ɪmˈbreɪs/ *v* to hold (someone) tightly with both arms to express love, liking or sympathy, or when greeting or leaving someone • *They were oblivious to the outside world as they embraced (each other) on the station platform.* [I/T]

em·brace /ɪmˈbreɪs/ *n* [C] • *They greeted each other with a* **warm** (=friendly) *embrace.*

em·brace *obj* INCLUDE /ɪmˈbreɪs/ *v* [T] to include (something which forms an important part) • *Linguistics embraces a diverse range of subjects such as phonetics and stylistics.* • *We're trying to develop an* **all-embracing** *policy which tackles every aspect of education.*

em·brace *obj* ACCEPT /ɪmˈbreɪs/ *v* [T] to accept enthusiastically • *You'd be a fool not to embrace an opportunity as good as that.* • *How old were you when you embraced feminism?*

em·bro·ca·tion /£ˌem·brəʊˈkeɪ·ʃᵊn, $-broʊ-/ *n* [C] *esp. Br* a liquid that is rubbed onto the body to reduce pain or stiffness in muscles caused by a lot of exercise or by being hit

em·broid·er *(obj)* DECORATE /£ɪmˈbrɔɪ·dəʳ, $-dɚ/ *v* to decorate (cloth or clothing) with patterns or pictures consisting of stitches that are sewn directly onto the material, or to create (a pattern or picture) using such stitches • *I am embroidering this picture for my mother.* [I] • *They've embroidered the bedspread* **with** *a map of England.* [T] • *They've embroidered a map of England* **on** *the bedspread.* [T]

em·broid·er·y /£ɪmˈbrɔɪ·dᵊr·i, $-dɚ-/ *n* • *Let me show you Pat's embroideries of birds and animals.* [C] • *I'm no good at embroidery.* [U] • PIC **Handicraft**

em·broid·er *obj* ADD /£ɪmˈbrɔɪ·dəʳ, $-dɚ/ *v* [T] to make (a story) more entertaining by adding imaginary details to it • *Caroline's stories are always interesting because she embroiders the basic facts* **with** *half-truths.*

em·broid·er·y /£ɪmˈbrɔɪ·dᵊr·i, $-dɚ-/ *n* [U] • *Just cut the crap, Caroline, and tell us what happened without all your usual embroidery!*

em·broil *obj* /ɪmˈbrɔɪl/ *v* [T] to cause (someone) to become involved in an argument or a difficult situation • *The Prime Minister is anxious to avoid embroiling the Queen* **in** *an embarrassing row.* • *She has no desire to embroil herself*

in *lengthy lawsuits with the tabloid newspapers.* • *In spite of the civilian misery, the United Nations was reluctant to get its forces embroiled* **(in** *civil war).*

em·bry·o /£'em·bri·əʊ, $-oʊ/ *n* [C] *pl* **embryos** an animal that is developing either in its mother's womb or in an egg, or a plant that is developing in a seed • *embryo research/experimentation* • *a* **seed** *embryo* • *Between the eighth week of development and birth a human embryo is called a foetus.* • *A human embryo up to the age of 14 days is sometimes called a pre-embryo.* • *The department's plans for enlargement are still* **in embryo** (=haven't been put into action yet) *because of the university's spending cuts.*

em·bry·o·nic /£,em·bri'ɒn·ɪk, $-'ɑː·nɪk/ *adj* • *The embryonic phase begins when the egg is fertilized and ends when the animal hatches or is born.* • *(fig.) The project is still in its embryonic* (= developing) **stage** *at the moment.*

em·bry·ol·o·gy /£,em·bri'ɒl·ə·dʒi, $-'ɑː·lə-/ *n* [U] • Embryology is the study of animal development between the FERTILIZATION of the egg and the time when the animal is born or breaks out of its shell.

em·bry·ol·o·gist /£,em·bri'ɒl·ə·dʒɪst, $-'ɑː·lə-/ *n* [C] • *Are embryologists likely to agree to a lowering of the age limit of embryos used for research?*

em·cee /,em'siː/ *n* [C], *v Am for* MC (=Master of Ceremonies; see at MASTER [CONTROL])

e·mend *obj* /ɪ'mend/ *v* [T] to correct or improve (a text) • *The text is currently being emended and the second edition will be published as soon as this has been completed.*

e·men·da·tion /,iː·men'deɪ·ʃᵊn/ *n* [C/U]

em·er·ald /'em·ə·rəld/ *n* a bright green transparent precious stone which is often used in jewellery • *The colour of emerald is caused by small amounts of chromium oxide.* [U] • *The finest emeralds come from Colombia.* [C] • *She was wearing a beautiful emerald necklace.*

em·er·ald (green) /'em·ə·rəld/ *n* [U], *adj* • *He was wearing a stunning emerald (green) shirt.* • *My favourite green is emerald.* • **The Emerald Isle** is a literary name for Ireland.

e·merge [APPEAR] /£ɪ'mɜːdʒ, $-'mɜːrdʒ/ *v* [I] to appear by coming out of something or out from behind something • *She emerged* **from** *the sea cold but exhilarated.* • *They emerged* **from** *the bushes looking rather embarrassed.* • *He had forgotten to do up his trousers before he emerged* **from** *behind the wall.* • *(fig.) The Prince has emerged unscathed* **from** *the scandal.* • *(fig.) She is the most exciting British singer to emerge since Lloyd Cole.*

e·mer·gence /£ɪ'mɜː·dʒᵊnts, $-'mɜːr-/ *n* [U] • *The emergence of small Japanese cars in the 1970s challenged the US and European manufacturers in their own countries.*

e·mer·gent /£ɪ'mɜː·dʒᵊnt, $-'mɜːr-/ *adj* [before n] • *Western governments should be giving more aid to the emergent democracies of the Third World.* • *How can the British film industry prevent emergent talent ending up in Hollywood?*

e·merge [BECOME KNOWN] /£ɪ'mɜːdʒ, $-'mɜːrdʒ/ *v* [I] to become known esp. as a result of consideration, examination or questioning • *The facts behind the scandal are sure to emerge eventually.* • **It** *has emerged* **that** *secret talks had been going on between the two companies before the takeover was announced.* [+ *that* clause]

e·mer·gen·cy /£ɪ'mɜː·dʒᵊnt·si, $-'mɜːr-/ *n* something dangerous or serious, such as an accident, which happens suddenly or unexpectedly and needs immediate action in order to avoid harmful results • *How will disabled people escape* **in** *an emergency?* [C] • *Is the emergency* **exit** *suitable for wheelchairs?* • *How violent must the rioting become before the government declares* **a state of** *emergency* (= gives itself special powers to help deal with a dangerous situation)*?* [U] • *The pilot of the aircraft was forced to make an emergency* **landing** *on Lake Geneva.* • *The emergency* **services** *are the fire brigade, the police, the coastguard, and the ambulance service.* • *(esp. Br)* If you make an emergency **stop** in your car or another vehicle you stop suddenly to avoid hitting someone or something: *If she hadn't made that emergency stop that child would've been killed for sure.* • **Emergency brake** is *esp. Am for* HANDBRAKE. • **Emergency room** is *esp. Am for* CASUALTY [HOSPITAL].

e·me·ri·tus /£ɪ'mer·ɪ·təs, em'er-, $-ţəs/ *adj* [before or after n; not gradable] no longer having a position, esp. in a college or university, but keeping the title of the position • *She became Emeritus Professor of Linguistics when she retired.* • *He is the university's only surviving professor emeritus.*

em·er·y /£'em·ᵊr·i, $'-ɚ-/ *n* [U] a very hard dark grey substance, usually in the form of a powder, which is used to smooth or shape things • *emery paper/cloth* (= paper/cloth with emery on its surface) • *She was filing her fingernails with an emery* **board** (= a piece of cardboard covered with emery which is used to shape nails).

e·me·tic /£ɪ'met·ɪk, $-'meţ-/ *n* [C], *adj specialized* (a substance, esp. a medicine) that causes vomiting • *If you accidentally swallow any of this liquid, take an emetic to induce vomiting.*

em·i·grate /'em·ɪ·greɪt/ *v* [I] to leave a country permanently and go to live in another one • *Millions of Germans emigrated* **from** *Europe* **to** *America in the nineteenth century.* • *How long ago did your parents emigrate?*

em·i·gra·tion /,em·ɪ'greɪ·ʃᵊn/ *n* • *Jim's depression began shortly after his daughter's emigration.* [C] • *Many people saw emigration* **from** *their poor country* **to** *a rich one as a solution to their poverty, and for a long time they were encouraged to hold this view.* [U]

em·i·grant /'em·ɪ·grənt/ *n* [C] • *The number of emigrants* **from** *the UK* **to** *other EU countries is set to rise dramatically over the next few years.* • Compare IMMIGRANT; **migrant** at MIGRATE.

émigré, em·i·gré /'em·ɪ·greɪ/ *n* [C] someone who has had to leave their country permanently, usually for political reasons • *Now that democracy has returned to the former dictatorship, thousands of émigrés are thinking about going back home.*

em·i·nence [RESPECT] /'em·ɪ·nənts/ *n* [U] the state of being respected, of high rank or famous in a particular area of interest or activity which is achieved by having great experience, knowledge or skill • *Having* **achieved/won** *eminence* **as** *an actress she now intends to perform a comparable feat* **in** *politics.*

em·i·nent /'em·ɪ·nənt/ *adj* • *She has been eminent* **in** *philosophy/***as** *a philosopher for many years.* • *A thousand eminent scientists have signed the declaration supporting responsible experiments on animals in medical research.* • See also EMINENT.

Em·i·nence [PRIEST] /'em·ɪ·nənts/ *n* [C] the title of a CARDINAL • *People who are addressed as "***Your** *Eminence" are senior Roman Catholic priests whose rank is immediately below that of the Pope.* • **Their** *Eminences will meet tomorrow to elect a new pope.*

éminence grise /'em·ɪ·nɒ̃s,griːz/, **grey em·i·nence** /,greɪ'em·ɪ·nənts/ *n* [C] *pl* **éminences grises** /'em·ɪ·nɒ̃s,griːz/ someone without an official position who has (secret) power or influence over rulers or people who make decisions • *Civil servants are the ones who really have the power – they are the éminences grises behind the government ministers.*

em·i·nent /'em·ɪ·nənt/ *adj* [before n] noticeable or worth remarking on, or very great • *You have demonstrated eminent good sense in reporting this incident to me.* • See also **eminent** at EMINENCE [RESPECT].

em·i·nent·ly /'em·ɪ·nənt·li/ *adv* • Eminently is used to add force to the adjective which follows, being stronger than *very* but weaker than *extremely*: • *The police handled the crisis in an eminently sensible manner.* • *This is an eminently readable book that no holiday bag should be without.* • *The film is eminently forgettable and certainly not worth the admission price.*

e·mir /£em'ɪəʳ, $-'ɪr/ *n* [C] a ruler of particular Muslim countries in the Middle East • *the Emir of Kuwait*

e·mir·ate /'em·ɪ·rət/ *n* [C] • An emirate is a country ruled by an emir: *The emirate is little more than a city state, with a population of 1·7m and vast oil wealth.* ○ *The United Arab Emirates is a country consisting of seven emirates on the Persian Gulf.*

e·mis·sa·ry /£'em·ɪ·sᵊr·i, $-ser-/ *n* [C] a person sent by one government or political leader to another to deliver messages or to take part in discussions • *The Foreign Secretary has flown to China for a three-day visit as the personal emissary of the Prime Minister.*

e·mit *obj* /ɪ'mɪt/ *v* [T] **-tt-** to send out (a beam, noise, smell or gas) • *The alarm emits infra-red rays which are used to detect any intruder.* • *He emitted a peculiar screech which startled everyone in the audience.*

e·mis·sion /ɪ'mɪʃ·ᵊn/ *n* • *The Green Party conference has called for a substantial reduction in the emission of greenhouse gases by the UK.* [U] • *The increased use of natural gas will help reduce carbon dioxide emissions.* [C] • (CS) (PL)

Emergency services

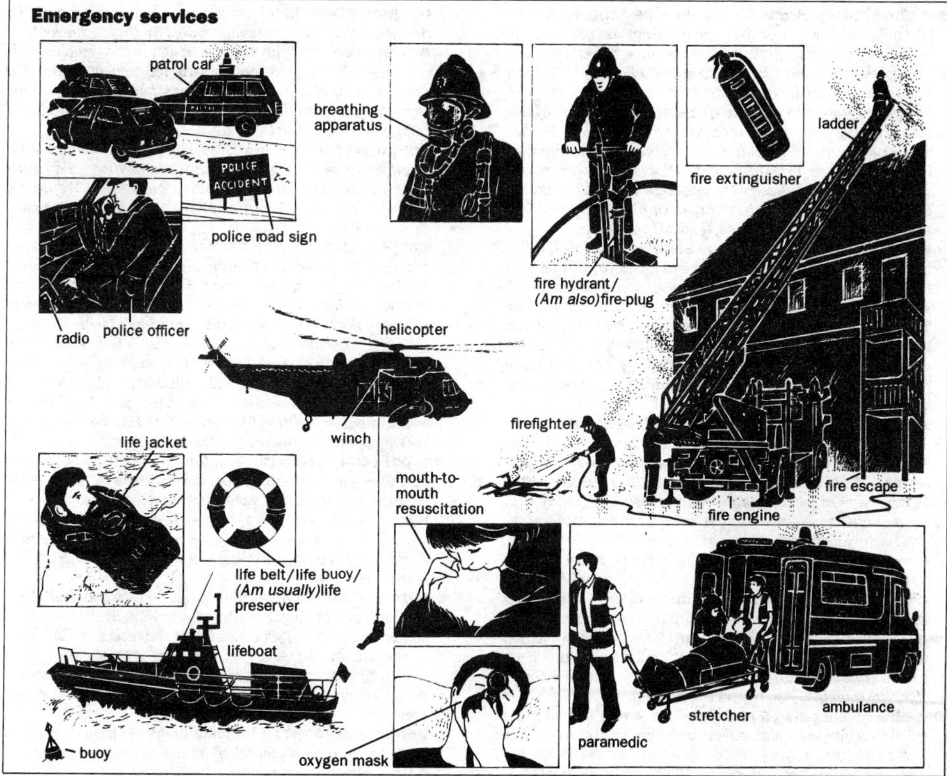

Em·my /ˈem·i/ *n* [C] *trademark* one of a set of American prizes given each year to actors and other people involved in making television programmes • *She won this year's Emmy for best screenplay for a mini-series.*

e·mol·li·ent /£ɪˈmɒl·i·ənt, $-ˈmɑː·li-/ *n* [C], *adj* (a cream or liquid) which makes dry or sore skin softer or less painful • *Dr Jackson gives patients an emollient and tells them to avoid dairy products, red meat and shellfish.* • *(fig.) The Prime Minister admits that he ought to have been less abrasive and more emollient* (=calming and avoiding argument) *in his speech.*

e·mol·u·ment /£ɪˈmɒl·jʊ·mənt, $-ˈmɑːl-/ *n* [C] *Br fml* a payment in money or some other form that is made for work that has been done • *The clearest example of a taxable emolument is the remuneration paid by an employer to an employee.*

e·mo·tion /£ɪˈməʊ·ʃən, $-ˈmoʊ-/ *n* (a) strong feeling • *Human emotions are things like hatred, anger, sadness and happiness.* [C] • *He's always been driven by his emotions – he rarely considers the consequences of his actions.* [C] • *Do you think we'll ever have robots capable of showing emotion?* [U] • *My parents were* **overcome by/with** *emotion at our wedding.* [U] • *She announced her resignation in a voice* **filled with** *emotion.* [U] • *She spurred the candidates on to another election victory with an emotion-***charged** *speech* (=a speech causing strong feelings). [U]

e·mo·tion·al /£ɪˈməʊ·ʃən·əl, $-ˈmoʊ-/ *adj* • *My doctor said the problem was more emotional* (=connected with feelings) *than physical.* • *Both parents should take equal responsibility for the emotional needs of their children.* • If someone uses emotional **blackmail**, they try to control your emotions in order to make you do something, esp. by making you feel guilty. • *Counselling is increasingly recommended to people suffering mental, physical or emotional* **distress**. • *He will have to live with the physical and emotional* **scars** *of the attack for the rest of his life.* • *Amnesia can be caused by emotional* **trauma**. • An emotional person is someone who often has strong feelings and expresses them: *Gerald was such an emotional man that life with him was always exciting.* • Some people only **become** emotional at particular times: *He became very emotional when I told him I was pregnant.* • *The President has made an emotional* (=full of emotion) *plea for the killing to stop.* • *That music's so emotional* (=causing emotion) *– it always brings a tear to my eye.*

e·mo·tion·al·ly /£ɪˈməʊ·ʃən·əl·i, $-ˈmoʊ-/ *adv* • *She spoke emotionally about her experiences as a war correspondent.* • *Many children have become emotionally* **disturbed** *as a result of the abuse they have suffered.* • *an emotionally* **charged** *issue* (=an issue causing strong feelings)

e·mo·tion·al·ism /£ɪˈməʊ·ʃən·əl·ɪ·zəm, $-ˈmoʊ-/ *n* [U] • If you accuse someone of emotionalism, you mean that they allow their emotions to control what they do, or that they feel or express too much emotion: *Unfortunately the catchy tune fails to make up for the shallow emotionalism of the lyrics.*

e·mo·tion·less /£ɪˈməʊ·ʃən·ləs, $-ˈmoʊ-/ *adj* • *Her face remained quite emotionless so it was impossible to tell what she thought of my news.*

e·mo·tive /£ɪˈməʊ·tɪv, $-ˈmoʊ·t̬ɪv/ *adj* causing strong feelings • *Animal experimentation is a highly emotive issue.*

e·mo·tive·ly /£ɪˈməʊ·tɪv·li, $-ˈmoʊ·t̬ɪv-/ *adv*

em·pan·el *obj*, **im·pan·el** /ɪmˈpæn·əl/ *v* [T] *Br and Aus* **-ll-** or *Am usually* **-l-** (in a law court) to choose the people who will form the JURY for a trial • *Judges have the discretion to empanel a new jury if evidence has been heard which might make the trial unfair.*

em·path·y /ˈem·pə·θi/ *n* [U] the ability to share someone else's feelings or experiences by imagining what it would be like to be in their situation • *You've lived in other countries so I'd expect you to have some sort of empathy* **with** *people who've just arrived here.* • Compare SYMPATHY [UNDERSTANDING]. • (P)

em·path·et·ic /£ˌem·pəˈθet·ɪk, $-ˈθet̬-/ *adj* • *My doctor is such an empathetic listener – I feel that she really understands how I feel.*

em·path·ize, *Br and Aus usually* **-ise** /ˈem·pə·θaɪz/ *v* [I] • *Do you really expect these white middle-class men to be able to empathize* **with** *working-class women from ethnic minorities?* • Compare **sympathize** at SYMPATHY [UNDERSTANDING].

em·per·or /£ˈem·pər·ər, $-pə·ə/ *n* [C] a male ruler of an empire • *"The Emperor's New Clothes"* (title of a story by Hans Christian Andersen in which the emperor is tricked into appearing naked, 1805-75) • See also EMPRESS.

em·phas·ize *obj, Br and Aus usually* **-ise** /ˈemp·fə·saɪz/ *v* [T] to show or state that (something) is particularly important or worth giving attention to • *She emphasized her disapproval with a long slow shake of her head.* • *I'd just like to emphasize* **how** *important it is for people to learn foreign languages.* [+ *wh*- word] • *He emphasized* **that** *all the people taking part in the research were volunteers.* [+ *that* clause] • *When "record" is a noun you should emphasize* (= say with extra force) *the first syllable, but when it is a verb you should emphasize the second.* • *You can use italics, bold type, capitals or underlining to emphasize a word in a piece of writing.* • LP **Italics, Quotation marks**

em·phas·is /ˈemp·fə·sɪs/ *n pl* **emphases** • *Jo's English teacher* **puts/places/lays great** *emphasis* **(up)on** *written work and grammar.* [U] • *I think we should put as much emphasis* **on** *preventing disease as we do on curing it.* [U] • *The new government policy places* **(far) greater** *emphasis* **on** *recycling and energy-efficiency.* [U] • *Where do you put the emphasis in the word "controversy"?* [U] • *The split arose from their differing emphases* **on** *controlling inflation and unemployment.* [C]

em·phat·ic /£empˈfæt·ɪk, $-ˈfæṭ-/ *adj* • *The minister has issued an emphatic rejection of the accusation.* • *She was emphatic* **in** *her rejection of the accusation.* • *He is most emphatic* **that** *he should talk to you.* [+ *that* clause] • *(fig.) Poland reached the final of the championship yesterday with an emphatic* (= so great that it is beyond doubt) *5-0 semi-final victory over Italy.*

em·phat·i·cal·ly /£empˈfæt·ɪ·kli, $-ˈfæṭ-/ *adv* • *Jackson has emphatically denied the allegations against him.* • *I emphatically support the proposals for reform.* • *Residents emphatically do not want a new car park on their doorstep.*

em·phy·se·ma /ˌemp·fəˈsiː·mə/ *n* [U] a condition in which the small bags in the lungs become filled with too much air causing breathing difficulties and heart problems • *Heavy cigarette smoking often causes emphysema.*

em·pire /£ˈem·paɪəʳ, $-paɪr/ *n* [C] a group of countries ruled by a single person, government or country • *the Holy Roman Empire* • *(fig.) In the space of just ten years her company has grown from one small shop to a multi-million-pound empire* (= big business). • *(fig.) He established his reputation as an empire-***builder** *when he purchased several overseas companies last year.* • *(fig.) Her empire-***building** *came to an abrupt end when her bankers refused to lend her any more money.* • *"The Empire Strikes Back"* (film title, 1980) • See also IMPERIAL [EMPIRE].

em·pi·ri·cal /ɪmˈpɪr·ɪ·kᵊl/ *adj* based on what is experienced or seen rather than on theory • *This theory needs to be backed up with solid empirical* **data/evidence**. • *Empirical* **studies** *show that some forms of alternative medicine are extremely effective.*

em·pi·ri·cal·ly /ɪmˈpɪr·ɪ·kli/ *adv* • *Philosophy differs from science, in that its questions cannot be answered empirically, by observation or experiment.* • *We all intuitively know this to be the case, but how can we demonstrate it empirically?*

em·pi·ri·ci·sm /ɪmˈpɪr·ɪ·sɪ·zᵊm, em-/ *n* [U] • *If ecology is to improve our lives it must be based on empiricism* (= empirical methods) *not political dogma.*

em·pi·ri·cist /ɪmˈpɪr·ɪ·sɪst, em-/ *n* [C] • *Like any good empiricist, she has based her scientific theories entirely upon the observable facts rather than mere supposition.*

em·place·ment /ɪmˈpleɪ·smənt/ *n* [C] a position specially prepared for large pieces of military equipment • *Missile launchers and radar emplacements were clearly visible on either side of the road.*

em·ploy *obj* /ɪmˈplɔɪ/ *v* [T] to have (someone) work or do a job for you and pay them for it • *How many people does your company employ?* • *We really need to employ someone* **as** *an assistant to help with all this paperwork.* • *I tried putting up the shelves myself, but I'll have to employ a carpenter to get the job done properly.* • *We've employed a market researcher* **to** *find out what people really want from a cable TV system.* [+ obj + *to* infinitive] • *More people are now employed in service industries than in manufacturing.* • *Penny became* **self-***employed* (= worked independently of a single company) *after several years on staff.* • *(fig.) He was intelligent, well-educated, healthy and active, but did not know how to employ* (= use) *his energy.* • *(fig.) Sophisticated statistical analysis was employed* (= used) *to obtain these results.* • *He didn't look up for some time while employed* **in** (= busy) *lacing up his shoes.* • LP **Work**

em·ploy /ɪmˈplɔɪ/ *n* [U] *fml or dated* • If you are **in** someone's employ, you are working for them.

em·ploy·ab·le /ɪmˈplɔɪ·ə·bl̩/ *adj* • *I hope this computing course will make me more employable* **(in** *the job market).*

em·ploy·ee /ɪmˈplɔɪ·iː, ˌ--ˈ-/ *n* [C] • An employee is someone who is paid for working for someone else: *The number of employees in the company has increased tenfold over the past decade.* • *She's a former council employee/employee of the council.*

em·ploy·er /£ɪmˈplɔɪ·əʳ, $-ɚ/ *n* [C] • *I wouldn't want my employer to be a big bureaucratic organization – I'd rather work for an individual or a small business.* • *We need a reference from your former employer before we can give you a definite job offer.*

em·ploy·ment /ɪmˈplɔɪ·mənt/ *n* [U] • *Employment levels are unlikely to rise significantly before the end of next year.* • *(Br fml) Are you* **in** *employment* (= Do you have a job) *at the moment?* • *How long have you been looking for employment?* • *During the first six years of my employment with Sandoz, I shared a laboratory with two colleagues.* • *(esp. Am) This is the first time I've tried to get work through an employment* **agency** (= a business that finds suitable people to work for other businesses). • *How long have you been* **in** *her employment* (= working for her)? • *(fig.) How can you justify the employment* (= use) **of** *capital punishment?*

em·por·i·um /£ɪmˈpɔː·ri·əm, $-pɔːr·i-/ *n* [C] *pl* **emporia** /£ɪmˈpɔː·ri·ə, $-ˈpɔːr·i-/ or **emporiums** a large shop selling a large range of goods, or a shop selling a particular type of goods • *a video/ice cream/antiques emporium* • *Make sure you go to the KaDeWe emporium when you're in Berlin – if you can't find what you want there, you won't find it anywhere.*

em·pow·er *obj* /£ɪmˈpaʊəʳ, $-ˈpaʊr/ *v* [T] to give (someone) the official or legal authority or the freedom to do something • *This 13th amendment empowers the president* **to** *declare an emergency, in any part of the country, for a wide range of reasons.* [+ obj + *to* infinitive] • *The first step in empowering the poorest sections of society is making sure they vote.*

em·pow·er·ment /£ɪmˈpaʊə·mənt, $-ˈpaʊr-/ *n* [U] • *We'll be running a workshop on women's empowerment, a form of assertiveness training, next Monday.*

em·press /ˈem·prəs/ *n* [C] a female ruler of an empire, or the wife of a male ruler of an empire • See also EMPEROR.

emp·ty /ˈemp·ti/ *adj* **-ier, -iest** with nothing inside • *Shall I take those empty bottles for recycling?* • *An optimist is someone who says a half-drunk bottle of wine is half full* • *a pessimist is someone who says it's half empty.* • *The house next door has* **stood** *empty* (= No one has lived in it) *ever since a woman murdered her husband there and was sentenced to life imprisonment.* • *The trains wouldn't be so empty* (= There would be more passengers) *if the fares weren't so high.* • *The village is far from empty* **of** *people who would be willing to help with the appeal.* • *(fig.) He says his life has been completely empty* (= without purpose, value or meaning) *since his wife died.* • *(fig.) I'd never imagined someone's life could be so empty* **of** (= lacking) *happiness.* • *(fig.) I'm fed up with all your empty* (= not sincere) *promises and gestures – I want to see some action!* • *(fig.) He just gave me an empty* (= expressionless) *look when I asked where he'd been all night.* • *You shouldn't go to work* **on an empty stomach** (= having had nothing to eat). • If someone is **empty-handed** they have not brought anything with them: *They always arrive at parties empty-handed, even when it says "Please bring a bottle" on the invitation.* ○ *(fig.) The union's leaders have promised their members that they will not return from the wage negotiations empty-handed.* • Someone who is **empty-headed** is silly, foolish or lacking good judgment: *That is probably the most empty-headed idea I've ever heard you come up with.* ○ *How can anyone be so empty-headed that they leave broken bottles on the beach?*

emp·ty *(obj)* /ˈemp·ti/ *v* • *I emptied* (= took out all the things inside) *the closet and folding my belongings into the black overnight case.* [T] • *I'm sure you're carrying nothing illegal, but would you mind emptying* **(out)** *your pockets?* [T] • *The place emptied pretty quickly when the fight started.* [I] • *The motorways are expected to have emptied* **of** *holiday traffic by late evening.* [I] • *Empty the soup* (= Remove the soup from its container and put it) **into** *a saucepan and simmer gently for ten minutes.* [T] • *She quickly emptied her glass* (= drank its contents) *and ordered another drink.* [T] • *I've almost finished packing – I've just got to empty* (= put the contents of) *that drawer* **into** *my suitcase.* [T] • If a river empties into a larger area of water, the water in the river flows into that larger area: *The River Tees empties into the North Sea.* [I]

emp·ty /ˈemp·ti/ *n* [C usually plural] • *Don't forget to take the empties* (= empty bottles) *to the bottle bank.* • *a crate of empties*

emp·ti·ly /ˈemp·tɪ·li/ *adv*

emp·ti·ness /ˈemp·tɪ·nəs/ *n* [U] • *Forty years of the totalitarian system have left behind a material and spiritual emptiness.*

EMS /ˌiː·emˈes/ *n* [U] **the EMS** *abbreviation for* European Monetary System (= an international financial system intended to bring balance to the rates of exchange between member countries) • Compare ECU; EMU; ERM.

e·mu [BIRD] /ˈiː·mjuː/ *n* [C] *pl* **emu** or **emus** a large Australian bird with a long neck and grey or brown feathers. It cannot fly but has long legs and can run quickly. • *Emus grow to almost two metres and can run at nearly 50 kph.*

EMU [MONEY] /ˌiː·emˈjuː/ *n* [U] *abbreviation for* (European) Economic and Monetary Union or European Monetary Union (= the process within the European Community which is intended to result in a single form of European money and a central European bank) • Compare ECU; EMS; ERM.

em·u·late *obj* /ˈem·jʊ·leɪt/ *v* [T] to copy something achieved by (someone else) and try to do it as well as or better than they have • *People often try to emulate their favourite pop singers or movie stars.*

em·u·la·tion /ˌem·jʊˈleɪ·ʃᵊn/ *n* [U] • *Today's desktop publishing systems offer a very good emulation* **of** *conventional printing methods.*

e·mul·sion /ɪˈmʌl·ʃᵊn/ *n* the mixture resulting when one liquid is added to another and is mixed with it but does not dissolve into it • *Mixing oil and vinegar together produces an emulsion.* [C] • *An emulsion of very small grains of silver bromide and gelatin is used to make the surface of photographic film sensitive to light.* [C] • *Cream is a yellowish oil-in-water emulsion which forms when milk is allowed to stand.* [C] • Emulsion (paint) is water-based and not shiny when it is dry: *Use emulsion for the walls and ceiling and gloss for the doors and window frames.* [U]

e·mul·si·fy *(obj)* /ɪˈmʌl·sɪ·faɪ/ *v* • *It is now a week since the accident and most of the oil seems to have evaporated or emulsified.* [I]

e·mul·si·fi·er /ɪˈmʌl·sɪ·faɪəʳ, $-ɚ/ *n* [C] • An emulsifier is a substance which forms or preserves an emulsion and is often added to processed foods to prevent particular parts separating.

en– [PROVIDE] /ɪn-, en-/, *before b or p* **em–** *combining form* used to form verbs which mean put into or onto, or to cause to be, or to provide with • *to embed/encase/encircle/endanger/engulf/enshrine/enshroud/ensnare* • *to enable/endear/enfeeble/enlarge/enliven/enrich/enslave* • *to empower*

–en [INCREASE] /-ᵊn/ *combining form* used to form verbs which mean to increase the stated quality • *You can sweeten your drink with honey or brown sugar.* • *If your belt is too tight then loosen it.* • [LP] **Combining forms, Stress in pronunciation**

en·ab·le *obj* /ɪˈneɪ·bl̩/ *v* [T] to make (someone) able to do something by providing them with whatever is necessary to achieve it, or to make (something) possible • *Computerisation should enable us* **to** *cut production costs by half.* [+ obj + *to* infinitive] • *An early cut in Germany's interest rates would enable a reduction in British mortgage rates before next January.* • *(specialized) More and more enabling* **legislation** *is giving ministers discretion to act without the scrutiny of Parliament.*

en·abl·er /£ɪˈneɪ·bləʳ, $-blɚ/ *n* [C] • An enabler is an individual or an organization which allows other people to do things themselves rather than doing things for them: *The Prime Minister said that the state should be an enabler for its citizens, rather than spoon-feeding them with jobs, benefits and services.*

en·act *obj* [MAKE LAW] /ɪˈnækt/ *v* [T] to put (something) into action, esp. to change (something) into a law • *Parliament has enacted a plan under which children can give evidence at a trial via a television link.* • *A package of economic sanctions is to be enacted against the country.*

en·act·ment /ɪˈnækt·mənt/ *n* • *The enactment of this decision is likely to take several months.* [U] • *The Queen is not legally liable to pay particular types of tax because the relevant enactments do not apply to the crown.* [C]

en·act *obj* [PERFORM] /ɪˈnækt/ *v* [T] to perform (a part in a play) • *The actors, in stylized make-up and costume, enact dramas using music, song, dance and mime.*

en·act·ment /ɪˈnækt·mənt/ *n* [C/U]

en·a·mel /ɪˈnæm·ᵊl/ *n* a glass-like substance used for decoration or protection which is melted onto clay, metal and glass objects and then left to cool and harden, or an object covered with this substance • *"This used to be beautiful – all enamel," he said, pointing at the sink.* [U] • *The exhibition features paintings, photographs, ceramics and enamels.* [C] • Enamel is also a type of paint which forms a shiny surface when dry. • Enamel is also the hard white shiny substance which forms the covering of a tooth. • (J)

en·a·mel *obj* /ɪˈnæm·ᵊl/ *v* [T] **-ll-** or *Am usually* **-l-** • *This vase has been enamelled beautifully.*

en·am·oured *Br, Am* **en·am·ored** /£ɪˈnæm·əd, $-ɚd/ *adj* [after v] liking a lot • *I have to say I'm not exactly enamoured* **with/of** *this part of the country.*

en bloc /£ˌɒmˈblɒk, $ˌɑːmˈblɑːk/ *adv* [not gradable] all together in a united group • *The right wing of the party is supporting her en bloc.* • *Some ruling committees have resigned en bloc to make way for secret elections to choose their successors.*

en·camp·ment /ɪŋˈkæmp·mənt/ *n* [C] a group of tents or temporary shelters put in one place • *Many people are living in encampments around the city with no electricity or running water.* • *The police said they were monitoring the encampment of 1000 or so people who have gathered on the common for a free music festival.*

en·camp *(obj) esp. Br* /ɪŋˈkæmp/, *Am usually* **camp** *v* • *Many of the fans were afraid to return to their hotels and had to encamp* (= set up tents) *in the station.* [I] • *The protesters have now been encamped outside the embassy for two weeks.* [T]

en·cap·su·late *obj* /ɪŋˈkæp·sjʊ·leɪt/ *v* [T] to express the most important facts about (something) in a short and clear form, or to possess all the necessary qualities of (something) • *It was very difficult to encapsulate the story of the revolution* **in** *a single one-hour documentary.* • *She encapsulates the stereotyped image that the British have of Americans.*

en·cap·su·la·tion /ɪŋˌkæp·sjʊˈleɪ·ʃᵊn/ *n* [C/U]

en·case *obj* /ɪŋˈkeɪs/ *v* [T usually passive] to cover or enclose completely • *The nuclear waste is encased* **in** *concrete before being sent for storage in disused mines.* • *The tower, which dates from the 15th century, was encased* **in** *sandstone in the 1860s.*

–ence [ACTION], **–ance** /-ᵊnts/ *combining form* used to form nouns which refer to an action or series of actions • *a campaign of violence* (= violent actions) • *a great performance* (= act of performing) • [LP] **Combining forms**

–ence [STATE], **–ance** /-ᵊnts/ *combining form* used to form nouns which describe a state or quality • *her long absence* (= period during which she was absent)

en·chant *obj* [PLEASE] /£ɪnˈtʃɑːnt, $-ˈtʃænt/ *v* [T] to charm or please greatly • *At Camp David President Nixon enchanted Leonid Brezhnev with the gift of an armoured Lincoln limousine.* • *The audience was clearly enchanted by her performance.*

en·chant·ing /£ɪnˈtʃɑːn·tɪŋ, $-ˈtʃæn·t̬ɪŋ/ *adj* • *Carcassonne is an enchanting medieval city in southern France.* • *On a summer evening it is enchanting to hear the sound of the shepherd's flute floating across the valley.*

en·chant·ment /£ɪnˈtʃɑːnt·mənt, $-ˈtʃænt-/ *n* [C/U]

en·chant *obj* [MAGIC] /£ɪnˈtʃɑːnt, $-ˈtʃænt/ *v* [T often passive] to have a magical effect on (someone or something) • *To me, Central Park has an atmosphere of mystery, as if it were enchanted with fairies and goblins.*

en·chant·ed /£ɪnˈtʃɑːn·tɪd, $-ˈtʃæn·t̬ɪd/ *adj* • *They met in a Parisian café one enchanted afternoon in early autumn.* • *Kathmandu, the capital of Nepal, is one of the most enchanted places in the world.* • *"Some Enchanted Evening"* (title of a song written by Oscar Hammerstein II, 1948)

en·chant·ress *female, male* **en·chant·er** /£ɪnˈtʃɑːn·trəs, $-ˈtʃæn-, £-təʳ, $-t̬ɚ/ *n* [C] • An enchantress is a woman with magical powers: *In the Odyssey, Circe was an enchantress who detained Odysseus and his followers on the island of Aeaea.* ○ *(fig.) Judith is an enchantress* (= an extremely attractive and interesting woman).

en·chant·ment /£ɪnˈtʃɑːnt·mənt, $-ˈtʃænt-/ *n* [U] • *Falling in love is like a kind of enchantment.*

en·chil·a·da /ˌen·tʃɪˈlɑː·də/ *n* [C] a type of food originally from Mexico consisting of a thin PANCAKE that is fried, filled with meat and covered with a very spicy sauce

en·cir·cle *obj* /£ɪn'sɜː·kḷ, $-'sɜːr-/ *v* [T] to surround or form a circle around or enclose within a circle • *Villaverde is one of the high-rise districts that encircle Madrid.* • *The trawlers use large nets to encircle shoals of mackerel and other fish that swim near the surface.* • *Moscow is encircled* **by/with** *an eight-lane ring road that was built by Stalin.*

en·clave /£'eŋ·kleɪv, $'ɑːŋ-/ *n* [C] a part of a country that is surrounded by another country, or a group of people who are different from the people living in the surrounding area • *Campione d'Italia is an Italian enclave in Switzerland.* • *A few years ago I was in India and visited both the Canadian and American enclaves in New Delhi.*

en·close *obj* SURROUND, *Am also* **in·close** /£ɪŋ'kləuz, $-'klouz/ *v* [T] to surround • *The park that encloses the monument has recently been enlarged.* • *The Health Minister has proposed that smoking should be banned in enclosed* (= inside) *public places.*

en·clo·sure, *Am also* **in·clo·sure** /£ɪŋ'kləu·ʒəʳ, $-'klou·ʒɚ/ *n* • *I'm afraid you're not allowed in here – this enclosure* (= enclosed area) *is for members only.* [C] • *An early example of privatization was the enclosure* **of** *public land for private use by wealthy landlords.* [U]

en·close *obj* SEND /£ɪŋ'kləuz, $-'klouz/ *v* [T] to send (something) in the same envelope or parcel as something else • *I enclose some money, which you may need for your expenses.* • *Please enclose a curriculum vitae with your letter of application.* • *(fml) Please find enclosed a cheque in settlement of your invoice dated May 30th.*

en·clo·sure /£ɪŋ'kləu·ʒəʳ, $-'klou·ʒɚ/ *n* [C] • *Details of my proposals are given in the accompanying enclosure* (= enclosed item).

en·code *(obj)* /£ɪŋ'kəud, $-'koud/ *v* to change (something) into a system for sending messages secretly, or to represent (complicated information) in a simple or brief way • *Two genes that encode eye-pigment proteins have been found on this chromosome.* [T] • *Many satellite broadcasts are encoded so that they can only be received by people who have paid to see them.* [T] • *Some music CDs are now encoded with information about the performers and their music, but you need a special player to use them.* [T] • *(specialized)* To encode (a word or phrase in a foreign language) is to use it in the correct way: *Grammatical information helps learners to encode (sentences).* [I/T] • Compare DECODE.

en·co·mi·um /£ɪŋ'kəu·mi·ᵊm, $-'kou-/ *n* [C] *pl* **encomiums** or **encomia** /£ɪŋ'kəu·mi·ə, $-'kou-/ *fml dated* an expression of very high praise • *He paid tribute to Muhammad Ali with the encomium "He didn't have fights, he gave recitals".*

en·com·pass *obj* /ɪŋ'kʌm·pəs/ *v* [T] to include (esp. a variety of things) • *The festival is to encompass everything from music, theatre and ballet to literature, cinema and the visual arts.* • *The US proposed the creation of a free trade zone encompassing the entire Western hemisphere.* • *There were warnings that this problem was going to be huge and* **all-** *encompassing* (= involving everything).

en·core /£'ɒŋ·kɔːʳ, $'ɑːŋ·kɔːr/ *n, exclamation* (a request for) the performance of an additional song or piece of music after a show has formally finished when people ask for it by clapping or calling out loudly • *They did the whole of their new album, and then one of their old hits* **as/for** *an encore.* [C] • *The audience was still calling "Encore! Encore!" even after the fourth one.* • *(fig.) He accidentally poured the wine over his trousers and then* **as/for** *an encore he dropped our pizzas on the carpet!* [C]

en·count·er *obj* /£ɪŋ'kaun·təʳ, $-t̬ɚ/ *v* [T] to experience (esp. something unpleasant) or to meet (someone) unexpectedly • *The army is reported to be encountering considerable resistance in some remote rural areas.* • *When did you first encounter these problems/difficulties?* • *Before they had gone very far, they encountered a woman selling flowers.*

en·count·er /£ɪŋ'kaun·təʳ, $-t̬ɚ/ *n* [C] • *He once had a very frightening encounter* **with** *a wild pig.* • *This meeting will be the first encounter* **between** *the party leaders since the election.* • *As the search for the attacker continues, police warned gay men against* **sexual** *encounters with strangers.* • *While the German moved into the third round Connors won a first-round encounter* (= game) *with Udo Riglewski of Germany 6-4, 6-4.* • *"Close Encounters of the Third Kind* (= meeting creatures from space)*"* (title of a film by Steven Spielberg, 1977)

en·cou·rage *obj* /£ɪŋ'kʌr·ɪdʒ, $-'kɜːr-/ *v* [T] to strongly advise (someone) to do something or make (someone) believe they are able to do something, or to support (something) or make (something) more likely • *Were you encouraged* **to** *move away from home by your parents?* [+ *to* infinitive] • *We were encouraged* **to** *learn foreign languages at school.* [+ *to* infinitive] • *They've always encouraged me* **in** *everything I've wanted to do.* • *The tax incentive has encouraged many motorists* **to** *start using trains.* [+ *to* infinitive] • *The council is encouraging the development of the property for both employment and recreation.* • *Decay is far more likely to occur with gooey sweets which stick to your teeth and encourage plaque* **to** *form.* [+ *to* infinitive] • *"In [England] it is considered good to kill an admiral from time to time, to encourage the others (sometimes used in the original French 'pour encourager les autres')"* (Voltaire *Candide*, 1759)

en·cou·raged /£ɪŋ'kʌr·ɪdʒd, $-'kɜːr-/ *adj* • *Encouraged* **by** *her school report, Jane decided to apply to Cambridge University.* • *We were encouraged* (= felt supported) **to** *learn that you will be making such a generous donation to our campaign.* [+ *to* infinitive] • *She* **felt/seemed** *encouraged by their promise of support.*

en·cou·rag·ing /£ɪŋ'kʌr·ɪ·dʒɪŋ, $-'kɜːr-/ *adj* • *Every so often my girlfriend gave me an encouraging squeeze on the arm.*

en·cou·rag·ing·ly /£ɪŋ'kʌr·ɪ·dʒɪŋ·li, $-'kɜːr-/ *adv* • *My mother smiled encouragingly at me as I went up on stage to sing my song.*

en·cou·rage·ment /£ɪŋ'kʌr·ɪdʒ·mənt, $-'kɜːr-/ *n* [U] • *I could never have achieved this without the encouragement* **of** *my husband and family.* • *The armed forces are now* **giving** *positive encouragement to applications from Asians and black people.* • *Your comments have been a great encouragement* **to** *us.*

en·croach /£ɪŋ'krəutʃ, $-'kroutʃ/ *v* [I] to approach or take control of (something) gradually or without being noticed • *He rejected the charge that his troops had encroached* **(up)on** *foreign territory.* • *The National Trust has recently bought the farm to save it from the threat of encroaching building development.* • *Her new play is a political mystery set against a background of encroaching revolution.*

en·croach·ment /£ɪŋ'krəutʃ·mənt, $-'kroutʃ-/ *n* • *The new censorship laws are serious encroachments* **on** *freedom of expression.* [C] • *We must defend individual freedoms against encroachment by government.* [U]

en·crus·ta·tion /ˌɪŋ·krʌs'teɪ·ʃᵊn/ *n* [C] *Am and Aus for* INCRUSTATION

en·crust·ed /£ɪŋ'krʌs·tɪd, $-t̬ɪd/ *adj* covered with something hard or decorative • *She arrived home with her knees encrusted* **with** *mud.* • *The manuscript is bound in gold and silver and encrusted* **with** *jewels.* • *They presented a gold-encrusted baton to the conductor.*

en·crypt *obj* /ɪŋ'krɪpt/ *v* [T usually passive] to put (electronic information such as television broadcasts) into a form which can only be used by special equipment • *The movie channel is encrypted so you'd need a decoding device to watch it.*

en·cryp·tion /ɪŋ'krɪp·ʃᵊn/ *n* [U] • *The high-security encryption systems ensure that only paid-up subscribers can watch.*

en·cum·ber *obj* /£ɪŋ'kʌm·bəʳ, $-bɚ/ *v* [T usually passive] to weigh down, or to make it difficult for (someone) to do something • *Today, thankfully, women tennis players are not encumbered* **with/by** *long, heavy skirts and high-necked blouses.*

en·cum·brance /ɪŋ'kʌm·brᵊnts/ *n* [C] • *He decided that a winter coat in the Sahara was a useless encumbrance.*

–en·cy, –an·cy /-ᵊnt·si/ *combining form* used to form nouns showing a state or quality • *her long presidency* (= time during which she was President) • *a difficult pregnancy* (= time during which a woman is pregnant) • *his hesitancy* (= quality of pausing before speaking or acting)

en·cy·clo·pe·di·a, en·cy·clo·pae·di·a /ɪnˌsaɪ·klə'piː·di·ə/ *n* [C] a book or set of books containing many articles arranged in alphabetical order which deal either with the whole of human knowledge or with a particular part of it • *The Cambridge Encyclopedia of Language* • *My parents have an encyclopedia that was published in the 1930s.*

en·cy·clo·pe·dic, en·cy·clo·pae·dic /ɪnˌsaɪ·klə'piː·dɪk/ *adj* • *Modern dictionaries often include encyclopedic information about famous people and important places.* • If something is encyclopedic it covers a large range of knowledge, often in great detail: *Muriel has an encyclopedic knowledge of France.*

end LAST POINT /end/ *n* [C] the point in space or time beyond which something no longer exists, or a part of something that includes this point • *This cable should have a plug* **at** *one end and a socket at the other.* • *We damaged* **the** *end* **of** *the piano when we moved it.* • *Get to* **the** *end* **of** *the queue and wait your turn like everyone else.* • *Our house is the third from the end on the left.* • *They've just bought the house at the end of the road.* • *There is no point continuing with these negotiations as they have clearly reached* **the end of the road** (=cannot continue). • *Austria's ski runs would circle the globe if they were joined end to end.* • *Is it safe to stand the computer on (its) end?* • *He used to lock himself in his bedroom for hours* **on end** (=continuously for several hours) *and refuse to talk to anyone.* • *The end of the film was much more exciting than I'd expected.* • *Some people were in tears at the end of the film.* • *This woman is innocent –* **end of story** (=I am so certain about it that it is not worth talking about it any more.) • *The project will be completed towards the end of the year.* • *I'm going to Berlin at the end of next week.* • *Of course I will be taking advice on this matter, but* **in the end**/*(Br and Aus also)* **at the end of the day** (=finally), *it is up to me to decide what to do.* • *This latest injury must surely mean that her tennis career is now* **at an** *end* (=finished). • *We were thinking about going to Switzerland, but* **in the end** (=the final result was) *we went to Austria.* • *Everyone wishes the war would* **come to an end** (=finish) *soon.* • If you **put an end to** something, you stop it existing or happening any longer: *The government intends to put an end to inflation once and for all.* ○ *How can we put an end to the fighting?* • *Are dental charges* **the beginning of the end** (=the first sign showing the finish) *of free health care?* • *If there were a nuclear war, it would be* **the end of the world (as we know it)**. • *(fig.) I'm really hoping to win, but it won't be* **the end of the world** (=extremely serious) *if I don't.* • *The statement said there would be no end* **to** *the violence until the terrorists demands were met.* • *If you don't want the job, there's* **no end of** (=unlimited) *people willing to take your place.* • *It would please Granny* **no end** (=very much) *if you wrote to her occasionally.* • *I'm afraid we've got some serious problems here. How do things look* **at your end** (=from where you are)? • *(fig.) You take care of the business end of things* (=matters connected with business) *and I'll deal with the publicity.* • Sometimes end is used to avoid saying death: *We were all by her bedside when the end finally came.* ○ *He* **met** *his end* (=died) *in a shoot-out with the police.* • An end is also either of the two halves of a sports field: *The teams change ends at half-time so that neither side has an unfair advantage.* • *(Am)* An end is also one of the two players in American football who begin play furthest from the ball. • *(Br)* If you **keep/hold** your **end up**, you continue to deal with difficulties bravely and successfully: *She's going to be in a wheelchair for another three months, but she's managing to keep her end up in spite of all the problems.* • *At present it's hard to* **make ends meet** (=manage on our income), *but we'll be better off when Helen starts her new job.* • An **end product** is what is produced by an activity, esp. by an industrial process: *Every stage of production from obtaining raw materials to recycling end products is monitored for its environmental effects.* • *The* **end result** *of these changes will be more bureaucracy and fewer resources.* • The **end user** of something is the person or organization that uses it rather than an organization which trades in it: *The software can easily be modified to suit the particular needs of the end user.* • *"Now this is not the end. It is not even the beginning of the end. But it is, perhaps, the end of the beginning."* (speech by Sir Winston Churchill, 1942)

end *(obj)* /end/ *v* • *When is your meeting due to end?* [I] • *Her resignation ends months of speculation about her future.* [T] • *Their marriage ended in 1991.* [I] • *Their marriage ended* **in** *divorce.* [I] • *The match ended* **in** *a draw.* [I] • *I'd like to end* (=finish the performance) **with** *a song from my first album.* [I] • *She ended (her speech)* **on** *an optimistic note.* [I/T] • If you end **up** in a particular place or situation, that is the place or situation that you are in finally: *They're travelling across Europe by train and are planning to end up in Moscow.* [I] ○ *Much of this meat will probably end up* **as** *dog food.* [I] ○ *She'll end up penniless if she carries on spending as much as that.* [L] • *After working her way around the world, she ended up teaching English as a foreign language.* [+ v-ing] • *He tried to* **end it all** (=kill himself) *when he failed all his exams.*

end·ing /ˈen·dɪŋ/ *n* [C] • *People want to be entertained – they want love stories with* **happy** *endings.* • An ending can be a part added to the end of a word to show what job it does in a sentence: *To make the plural of 'dog', you add the plural ending '-s'.*

end·less /ˈend·ləs/ *adj* • If something is endless, it never finishes or seems never to finish because it continues for so long: *Is the universe really endless?* ○ *We used to have endless arguments about politics.* ○ *The running machine basically consists of an endless belt and a set of motorized rollers.*

end·less·ly *adv* • *I find myself endlessly repeating the same phrases.*

end SMALL PART /end/ *n* [C] a small unwanted part of something that is left after most of it has been used • *The floor was covered in cigarette ends.*

end AIM /end/ *n* [C] an aim, intention or purpose • *Do you have a particular end in mind?* • *He wanted science students to take an interest in the arts, and* **to this end** (=to help achieve this) *he ran literature classes at his home on Sunday afternoons.* • *(saying)* 'The end justifies the means' means that the final aim is so important that any way of achieving it is acceptable.

en·dan·ger *obj* /£ɪnˈdeɪn·dʒəʳ, $-dʒɚ/ *v* [T] to put (someone or something) at risk or in danger of being harmed, damaged or destroyed • *The police must deal with criminals without endangering the lives of passers-by.* • *There can be no doubt whatsoever that smoking endangers your health.* • *We must be careful not to do anything that might endanger the economic recovery.* • *Endangered* **species** *are animals that are in danger of dying out completely, often because of exploitation by humans.*

en·dear *obj* **to** *obj* /£ɪnˈdɪəʳ, $-ˈdɪr/ *v prep* [T] to cause (someone) to be liked by (someone) • *She is unlikely to endear herself to her colleagues with such an aggressive approach to the problem.*

en·dear·ing /£ɪnˈdɪə·rɪŋ, $-ˈdɪr·ɪŋ/ *adj* • *She is a funny, determined and endearing woman who laughs at herself more than anyone else does.*

en·dear·ing·ly /£ɪnˈdɪə·rɪŋ·li, $-ˈdir·iŋ-/ *adv*

en·dear·ment /£ɪnˈdɪə·mənt, $-ˈdɪr-/ *n* [U] • *"Terms of Endearment"* (title of film, 1983)

en·dea·vour *Br and Aus, Am and Aus* **en·dea·vor** /£en ˈdev·əʳ, $-ɚ/ *v* [+ *to* infinitive] to try (to do something) • *Engineers are endeavouring* **to** *locate the source of the problem.*

en·dea·vour *Br and Aus, Am and Aus* **en·dea·vor** /£en ˈdev·əʳ, $-ɚ/ *n* • *In spite of our best endeavours, it has proven impossible to contact her.* [C] • *Crossing the North Pole on foot was an amazing feat of human endeavour.* [U]

en·de·mic /enˈdem·ɪk/ *adj* (esp. of disease or a condition) regularly found and very common among a particular group or in a particular area, so that it is part of the general situation • *Malaria is endemic* **in** *many of the hotter regions of the world.* • *The disease is endemic* **among** *British sheep/* **to** *many British flocks.* • *He said that corruption was endemic* **in** *parts of the police force.* • *There is endemic* **racism/poverty/violence** *in many of the country's cities.*

end·game /ˈend·geɪm/ *n specialized* the last stage in a game of CHESS when only a few of the pieces are left on the board • *This section of the book is devoted entirely to the endgame.* [U] • *In the fourth game, Yusupov levelled the score with some clever endgame tactics.* • *(fig.) A fevered diplomatic endgame* (=last stage of a process, esp. one involving discussion) *is now under way to find a peaceful solution to the crisis.*

en·dive /ˈen·daɪv/ *n* [C/U] a plant with curly green leaves which are eaten raw in salads • Endive is *Am for* CHICORY. • PIC **Vegetables**

end·less /ˈend·ləs/ *adj* See at END LAST POINT

en·do·crine gland /ˈen·də·kraɪn/, **duct·less gland** *n* [C] *specialized* any of the organs of the body, such as the PITUITARY GLAND or the OVARIES, which produce and release HORMONES (=substances which control the way the organs of the body operate) into the blood to be carried around the body

en·dor·phin /£enˈdɔː·fɪn, $-ˈdɔːr-/ *n* [C] *specialized* a chemical naturally released in the brain to reduce pain, and which in large amounts can make you feel relaxed and/or energetic

en·dorse *obj* SUPPORT /£ɪnˈdɔːs, $-ˈdɔːrs/ *v* [T] to make a public statement of your approval or support for (something or someone) • *The National Executive is expected to endorse these recommendations.* • *Several senior ministers will be at the meeting, to endorse the party's candidate in the by-election.* • *(fml) I fully endorse* (=agree with) *everything the Chairperson has said.* • *They paid $2* *million to the World Champion to endorse their new aftershave* (= say that it is good) *on television, and watched their sales double.*

en·dorse·ment /£ɪn'dɔː·smənt, $-'dɔːr-/ *n* • *These latest proposals have failed to achieve the Cabinet's endorsement.* [U] *Endorsements from central party officials have helped the local campaign.* [C]

en·dorse *obj* GIVE PERMISSION /£ɪn'dɔːs, $-'dɔːrs/ *v* [T] to write something, esp. your signature, on the back of (esp. a CHEQUE), in order to make it payable to someone else

en·dorse·ment /£ɪn'dɔː·smənt, $-'dɔːr-/ *n* [U]

en·dorse *obj* PUNISH /£ɪn'dɔːs, $-'dɔːrs/ *v* [T usually passive] *Br* (of a law court) to record (on a **driving licence**) that the driver has been found guilty of driving in an illegal way • *She was fined £300 and her licence was endorsed.*

en·dorse·ment /£ɪn'dɔː·smənt, $-'dɔːr-/ *n* • *He's got a couple of endorsements* **on** *his licence already.* [C] • *One of the things that can happen if you get caught speeding is the endorsement* **of** *your licence.* [U]

en·do·scope /£'en·dəʊˌskəʊp, $-doʊˌskoʊp/ *n* [C] *medical* a long thin medical device which is used to examine the hollow organs of the body such as the lungs • *The endoscope enables doctors to examine internal organs without resorting to major surgery.*

en·dos·co·py /£en'dɒs·kə·pi, $-'dɑː·skə-/ *n medical* • (An) endoscopy is a medical examination of the hollow organs of the body. [C/U]

en·dow *obj* /ɪn'daʊ/ *v* [T] to give money to pay for creating, or for providing an income for, (a college, hospital, etc.) • *The state of Michigan has endowed three institutes to do research for industry.* • *This hospital was endowed by the citizens of Strasbourg in the 16th century.* • *The National Gallery in Washington was endowed by Andrew W Mellon.*

en·dowed /ɪn'daʊd/ *adj* • *This university is one of the best endowed* (= having the most money) *in the world.* • *This is one of the best-endowed universities in the world.* • If someone or something is endowed **with** a particular quality or feature, they have that quality or feature: *Why is it that some lucky people are endowed with both brains and beauty?* ○ *Sardinia is generously endowed with prehistoric sites.* • See also WELL-ENDOWED.

en·dow·ment /ɪn'daʊ·mənt/ *n* [C] • *The school has received an endowment* (= present) *of £50 000 to buy new books for the library.* • *(fml) There are tests that can establish a baby's genetic endowment* (= what types of the chemicals that control its development it has received from its parents). • An **endowment mortgage** is an arrangement in which you have an endowment policy which provides the money you need to pay back the amount that you have borrowed in order to buy a house. • An **endowment policy** is an agreement where you pay money regularly so that you will receive a large agreed sum of money at an agreed later date or when you die.

end·point /'end·pɔɪnt/ *n* [C usually sing] a final position or finishing point • *I think we've reached the endpoint of this discussion now, so we should move on to other matters.*

en·dure *(obj)* EXPERIENCE /£ɪn'djʊəʳ, $-'dʊr/ *v* to experience and bear (something painful or unpleasant) calmly for a long time • *We had to endure a nine-hour delay at the airport.* [T] • *The little boy found it difficult to endure spending his summer holidays with his Uncle.* [+ v-ing] • *The country is enduring the worst recession since the 1930s.* [T]

en·dur·ab·le /£ɪn'djʊə·rə·bl̩, $-'dʊr·ə-/ *adj* • *When the pain became no longer endurable, he took some pain-killers.*

en·dur·ance /£ɪn'djʊə·rᵊnts, $-'dʊr·ᵊnts/ *n* [U] • *Running a marathon is a test of human endurance and the power of mind over body.* • *The pain was bad beyond endurance.*

en·dure CONTINUE /£ɪn'djʊəʳ, $-'dʊr/ *v* [I] *fml* to continue to exist for a long time • *The political system established in 1400 endured until about 1650.*

en·dur·ing /£ɪn'djʊə·rɪŋ, $-'dʊr·ɪŋ/ *adj* • *I shall be left with many enduring memories of the time I spent in India.* • *This type of music has an enduring appeal.*

end·ways /'end·weɪz/, *Am also* **end·wise** /'end·waɪz/ *adv* [not gradable] with the end, rather than the side, facing or touching • *Looking at the sofa endways* **(on)**, *I don't think it'll go through the door.*

en·e·ma /'en·ɪ·mə/ *n* [C] *specialized* cleaning or treatment of the bowels by filling them with a liquid through the RECTUM (= the opening in your bottom)

en·e·my /'en·ə·mi/ *n* [C] a person who hates or opposes another person and tries to harm them, or (the armed forces of) a country which is at war with another country • *I'm glad I've got her as a friend, not an enemy.* • *He* **has/has made** *many enemies because of his arrogance.* • **The** *enemy* (= opposing armed forces) *has/have succeeded in stopping our supplies from getting through.* [C + sing/pl v] • *The city has been the victim of an enemy attack/an attack by enemy aircraft.* • *The soldiers are advancing into enemy* **territory**/*behind enemy* **lines**. • *(fig.) The main enemy* **of** (= person or thing that prevents or fights against) *progress in the country is the people's refusal to see change as an opportunity rather than a threat.*

en·er·gy STRENGTH /£'en·ə·dʒi, $'-ɚ-/ *n* [U] the power and ability to be physically and mentally active • *Since I started eating more healthily, I've felt so* **full of** *energy.* • *The children were* **bursting with** *energy.* • *I was going to go out this evening, but I haven't got the energy.* • *These days I just seem to lack* **the** *energy* **to** *do anything.* [+ to infinitive] • *(approving) We need someone with energy* (= eagerness) *and enthusiasm to do this job.* • *(approving) Her writing is full of passion and energy* (= enthusiasm).

en·er·gies /£'en·ə·dʒiz, $'-ɚ-/ *pl n* • Your energies are the total of all your power and ability to be mentally and physically active: *He said that we must* **turn/direct/channel** *all our energies into protecting the environment.*

en·er·ge·tic /£ˌen·ə'dʒet·ɪk, $-ɚ'dʒet̬-/ *adj* • *She's such an energetic* (= very active) *little girl!* • *Jan is an energetic* (= active and determined) *campaigner for animal rights.* • *I tried aerobics but it was too energetic* (= needed too much effort) *for me.* • Ⓓ

en·er·ge·ti·cal·ly /£ˌen·ə'dʒet·ɪ·kli, $-ɚ'dʒet̬-/ *adv*

en·er·gize *obj, Br and Aus usually* **-ise** /£'en·ə·dʒaɪz, $'-ɚ-/ *v* [T] • *I felt very energized* (= more energetic and eager) *after my holiday.*

en·er·gy POWER /£'en·ə·dʒi, $'-ɚ-/ *n* [U] the power from something such as electricity or oil, which can do work, such as providing light and heat • *The energy generated by the windmill drives all the drainage pumps.* • *He said that it would be better if we made more use of the energy provided by the sun.* • *I think the government should do more to promote energy conservation/efficiency.* • *There are fears about rising energy costs/prices.*

en·er·vat·ing /£'en·ə·veɪ·tɪŋ, $'-ɚ·veɪ·t̬ɪŋ/ *adj literary* causing you to feel weak and lacking in energy • *In August, New York often has hot, humid and enervating weather.* • *The production of the play was enervating rather than inspiring.*

en·er·vate *obj* /£'en·ə·veɪt, $'-ɚ-/ *v* [T often passive] *literary*

en·fant ter·ri·ble /ˌɑ̃ː·fɑ̃ː·ter'iː·blə/ *n* [C] *pl* **enfants terribles** /ˌɑ̃ː·fɑ̃ː·ter'iː·blə/ *literary* an annoying or shocking, but interesting and successful, person • *She is an enfant terrible among the traditionalists of the banking world.* • *As a young man, he was the enfant terrible* **of** *the theatre.*

en·fee·ble *obj* /ɪn'fiː·bl̩/ *v* [T] *fml* to make very weak • *Critics have argued that cuts in spending have enfeebled the country's defences.* • *Internal conflicts are enfeebling the government.*

en·fee·bled /ɪn'fiː·bl̩d/ *adj fml* • *an enfeebled economy* • *When her father became enfeebled by age and illness, she gave up her job to care for him.*

en·fold *obj* /£ɪn'fəʊld, $-'foʊld/ *v* [T] *literary* to hold closely or cover completely • *She lovingly enfolded the cat* **in** *her* **arms**. • *As I entered the kitchen, the warm smell of baking bread enfolded me.*

en·force *obj* /£ɪn'fɔːs, $-'fɔːrs/ *v* [T] to cause (a rule, law, etc.) to be obeyed, or to cause (a particular desired situation) to happen or be accepted, esp. when people are unwilling to accept it • *It isn't always easy for the police to enforce speed limits.* • *The regulations should always be strictly enforced.* • *The new teacher totally failed to enforce* (= cause to happen) *any sort of discipline.*

en·force·ab·le /£ɪn'fɔː·sə·bl̩, $-fɔːr-/ *adj*

en·force·ment /£ɪn'fɔː·smənt, $-'fɔːrs-/ *n* [U] • *She's looking for a career in law enforcement.*

en·fran·chise *obj* /ɪn'fræn·tʃaɪz/ *v* [T] *fml* to give (a person or group of people) the right to vote in elections • *Women in Britain were first enfranchised in 1918.*

en·fran·chise·ment /ɪn'fræn·tʃaɪz·mənt/ *n* [U] *fml*

en·gage *obj* INTEREST /ɪŋ'geɪdʒ/ *v* [T] *fml* to cause (someone) to be interested in something and to keep thinking about it, or to attract and keep (someone's interest) • *The programme had some interesting moments, but I wasn't really engaged by it.* • *The puzzle game engaged the children all afternoon.* • *The puzzle game engaged the*

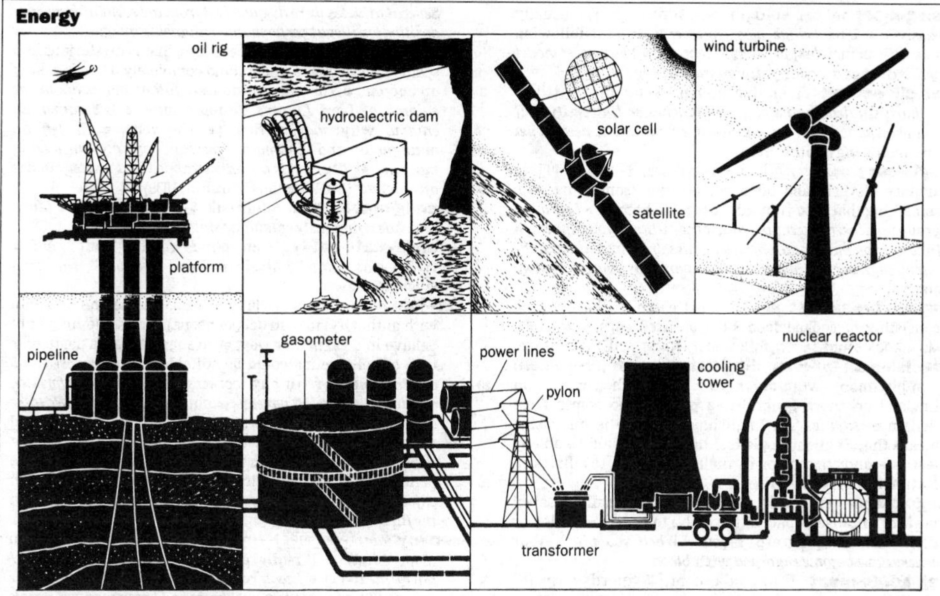

children's **interest** *all afternoon.* • *If a book doesn't engage my* **interest** *in the first few pages, I don't usually carry on reading it.*

en·gage *(obj)* FIT TOGETHER /ɪŋˈgeɪdʒ/ *v* to (cause to) fit into and move together (with another part of a machine) • *When the large cog wheel engages (***with** *the smaller one), the mill stone will start to go round.* [I] • *(slightly fml) Don't engage second gear too soon, or the engine will stall.* [T] • LP **Driving**

en·gage *(obj)* BEGIN FIGHTING /ɪŋˈgeɪdʒ/ *v fml* to attack or begin to fight (with) • *Enemy planes engaged the troops as they advanced into the mountains.* [T] • *We are too weak to engage* **with** *such a strong force.* [I]

en·gage·ment /ɪŋˈgeɪdʒ·mənt/ *n* • *The engagement* (=act of beginning to fight) **with** *the enemy will begin at dawn.* [U] • *The general insisted that his troops had acted within the UN* **rules of** *engagement* (=the rules which say how and when the armed forces are allowed to fight during a war). [U] • An engagement is a particular period of fighting in a war. [C] • See also **engagement** at ENGAGE IN; ENGAGED PROMISED.

en·gage *obj* EMPLOY /ɪŋˈgeɪdʒ/ *v* [T] *esp. Br fml* to arrange to employ (someone), or to use (someone's skills) • *Why don't you engage a carpenter* **to** *make you some kitchen units?* [+ obj + *to* infinitive] • *We're engaging* **the services of** *a professional administrator.*

en·gage *obj* ARRANGE /ɪŋˈgeɪdʒ/ *v* [T] *esp. Br dated* to arrange (something such as a hotel room) to be kept free • *I've engaged a room at the High Point Hotel in Birmingham for you.*

en·ga·gé /ˌɑ̃ˈgæʒ·eɪ, ˌ--ˈ-/ *adj fml* (esp. of a writer, musician, artist, etc.) interested in and taking part in politics

en·gage *(obj)* **in** *obj v prep* [T] to (cause to) take part in or do (something) • *A group of dissidents have been demanding the right to engage in politics.* • *In his spare time, he engages in voluntary work.* • *Once Mrs Kirkpatrick engages you in* **conversation**, *you're stuck with her for at least half an hour.*

en·gaged /ɪnˈgeɪdʒd/ *adj* [after v] • *They've been engaged* **in** *a legal battle with the council for several months.* • *She's part of a team of scientists who are engaged* **on/upon** *cancer research.* • *(fml)* If you are engaged, you are busy doing something: *"Could you come to a meeting on Tuesday morning?" "No, I'm sorry, I'm* **otherwise** *engaged then."* • See also ENGAGED PROMISED; ENGAGED IN USE.

en·gage·ment /ɪŋˈgeɪdʒ·mənt/ *n* [C] • An engagement is an arrangement to meet someone or do something at a particular time: *a dinner engagement* ○ *I'm afraid I'll have to refuse, because of a* **previous/prior** *engagement* (=another arrangement already made). ○ *The band have engagements* (=agreed performances) *in New York this month.* • See also **engagement** at ENGAGE BEGIN FIGHTING; ENGAGED PROMISED.

en·gaged PROMISED /ɪŋˈgeɪdʒd, eŋ-/ *adj* [not gradable] having formally agreed to marry • *Did you know that Eleanor is/has* **got** *engaged* **to** *Philip?* • *They're engaged* **to be married** *in June.* • See also **engaged** at ENGAGE IN. • LP **Relationships**

en·gage·ment /ɪŋˈgeɪdʒ·mᵊnt, eŋ-/ *n* [C] • *We're going to* **announce** *our engagement at the party on Saturday.* • An **engagement ring** is a ring, usually with precious stones in it, which a man might give to a woman as a formal sign that they have decided to get married. • See also **engagement** at ENGAGE BEGIN FIGHTING; ENGAGE IN.

en·gaged IN USE /ɪŋˈgeɪdʒd, eŋ-/ *adj* [after v; not gradable] (of a telephone or a public toilet) already in use by someone else • *Every time I try and ring her, she/the phone/the number is engaged (Am usually* **busy**). • *(Br) I've been trying to call him all evening, but I keep* **getting** *the engaged* **tone**/*(Aus) engaged* **signal** *(Am* **busy signal**) (=the sound you hear when you try to telephone someone but their telephone is in use). • *The sign on the toilet door at the back of the aircraft said 'Engaged'* (=being used) *all the way from New York to London.* Compare VACANT EMPTY. • See also **engaged** at ENGAGE IN. • LP **Telephone**

en·gag·ing /ɪŋˈgeɪ·dʒɪŋ/ *adj approving* pleasant, attractive and charming • *an engaging smile/manner/person*

en·gend·er *obj* /£ɪnˈdʒen·dəʳ, $-dɚ/ *v* [T] *fml* to cause to happen • *Her latest book has engendered a lot of controversy.* • *The minister's speech didn't exactly engender confidence in his judgment.* • *War engenders corruption, he said.*

en·gine /ˈen·dʒɪn/ *n* [C] a machine that uses the energy from liquid fuel or steam to produce movement • *a petrol engine* • *a jet engine* • *a car engine* • *My car's been having engine trouble/problems recently.* • *A fire has been reported in the ship's engine room.* • An engine (also **locomotive**) is also the part of a railway train which pulls it along. • *(Br and Aus)* An **engine driver** (also **train driver**, *Am usually* **engineer**) is a person whose job is to drive railway trains. • LP **Driving, Switching on and off**

-en·gined /-ˈen·dʒɪnd, ˌ-‐/ *combining form* • *twin-engined* • *jet-engined*

en·gin·eer PERSON /£ˌen·dʒɪˈnɪəʳ, $-ˈnɪr/ *n* [C] a person whose job is to design or build machines, engines or electrical equipment, or things such as roads, railways or bridges, using scientific principles • *She is a civil/mechanical/electrical/software engineer.* • An engineer is also a person whose job is to repair or control machines, engines or electrical equipment: *a computer engineer* ○ *a ship's engineer* ○ *The engineer is coming to repair our phone tomorrow morning.* • *(Am)* An engineer is also an **engine driver**. See at ENGINE.

en·gin·eer *obj* /£ˌen·dʒɪˈnɪəʳ, $-ˈnɪr/ *v* [T usually passive] • *This bridge was engineered* (=built following scientific principles) *in the 19th century.* • *The newest model of this car has a wonderfully engineered engine.*

en·gin·eer·ing /£ˌen·dʒɪˈnɪə·rɪŋ, $-ˈnɪr·ɪŋ/ *n* [U] • *Richard studied engineering at Manchester University.* • *If you want to work in an engineering firm, you'll need to get an engineering qualification.*

en·gin·eer *obj* ARRANGE /£ˌen·dʒɪˈnɪəʳ, $-ˈnɪr/ *v* [T] to arrange cleverly and often secretly for (something, esp. something that is to your advantage) to happen • *Left-wing groups engineered a coup against the military government.* • *How did you manage to engineer yourself an invitation to the party/engineer an invitation to the party* **for** *yourself?* [+ two objects]

Eng·lish break·fast *n* [C] a meal eaten in the morning consisting of cooked food such as fried eggs, TOMATOES, MUSHROOMS and BACON, followed by TOAST with MARMALADE

Eng·lish·man (*pl* **-men**), **Eng·lish·wo·man** (*pl* **-women**) /ˈɪŋ·glɪʃ·mən, -ˌwʊm·ən/ *n* [C] a person who comes from England or, more generally, a person who comes from Britain • *(saying)* 'An Englishman's home is his castle' means that English people feel that they should be able to feel safe and in control in their homes. • LP **Britain, Nations and nationalities**

en·gorge *obj* /£ɪŋˈgɔːdʒ, $-gɔːrdʒ/ *v* [T usually passive] *medical* to cause (a part of the body) to become swollen or filled with a liquid, esp. blood • *When you blush, your cheeks have become engorged* **with** *blood.*

en·gorge·ment /£ɪnˈgɔːdʒ·mənt, $-ˈgɔːrdʒ-/ *n* [U] *medical*

en·grave *obj* /ɪŋˈgreɪv/ *v* [T] to cut (words, pictures or patterns) into (the surface of metal, stone, etc.) • *The jeweller skillfully engraved the initials* **on** *the ring.* • *The names of the 58 000 American military personnel who died in Vietnam are engraved* **on** *the Vietnam Veterans Memorial in Washington.* • *The bracelet was engraved* **with** *his name and date of birth.* • *She was presented with an engraved silver cup for winning the championship.* • If something is engraved **on/in** your memory, mind or heart, it is something you will never forget: *The final talk I had with her is engraved on my memory for ever.*

en·grav·er /£ɪŋˈgreɪ·vəʳ, $-vɚ/ *n* [C] • An engraver is a person whose job is to cut words, pictures or patterns into the surface of metal, stone, etc.

en·grav·ing /ɪŋˈgreɪ·vɪŋ/ *n* • *Rembrandt House displays the range of techniques used in engraving.* [U] • An engraving is a picture printed onto paper from a piece of wood or metal into which the design had been cut: *Come up to my room and I'll show you my engravings.* [C] ○ *On the wall hung an engraving* **of a young girl.** [C]

en·grossed /£ɪŋˈgrəʊst, $-ˈgroʊst/ *adj* giving all your attention to something; absorbed • *She was so engrossed* **by/in** *the book that she forgot the cakes in the oven.* • *They were so engrossed* **with** *what they were doing that they didn't hear me come in.* • *The film was so interesting that before long I was* **deeply/completely** *engrossed.* • Ⓘ

en·gross·ing /£ɪŋˈgrəʊ·sɪŋ, $-ˈgroʊ-/ *adj* • *an engrossing book/story*

engulf *obj* /ɪŋˈgʌlf/ *v* [T] to surround and cover completely • *The flames rapidly engulfed the house.* • *A tidal wave completely engulfed the village.* • *Northern areas of the country were engulfed* **by/in** *a snowstorm last night.* • *The prime minister was engulfed by a mob of demonstrators.* • *The war is threatening to engulf the entire region.*

en·hance *obj* /£ɪnˈhɑːnts, $-ˈhænts/ *v* [T] to improve the quality, amount or strength of (something) • *These scandals will not enhance the organization's* **reputation/image.** • *What can we do to enhance our chances of victory?* • *Security at the airport has been enhanced following the discovery of a bomb there.* • *I need to find some way of enhancing my income.* • *Cobalt is used to enhance* (=improve the strength of) *steel.*

en·hance·ment /£ɪnˈhɑːnt·smənt, $-ˈhænt-/ *n* [C/U]

en·han·cer /£ɪnˈhɑːnt·səʳ, $-ˈhænt·sɚ/ *n* [C] • An enhancer is something which is used to improve the quality of something. Enhancer is usually used as a combining form: *The drug is sold as an enhancer of the oxygen-carrying facility of the blood.* ○ *Music can be a* **mood** *enhancer.* ○ *I don't like to use artificial* **flavour** *enhancers in my cooking.* ○ *This* **image** *enhancer allows us to see a lot of detail in the picture which was previously hidden.*

-en·hanc·ing /£-ɪnˌhɑːnt·sɪŋ, $-ˌhænt-/ *combining form* • *mood-enhancing music* • *a life-enhancing experience* • *Several athletes were disqualified from the event after testing positive for illegal performance-enhancing drugs.*

en·ig·ma /ɪˈnɪg·mə/ *n* [C] something that is mysterious and seems impossible to understand completely • *She is a bit of an enigma.* • *The newspapers were full of stories about the enigma of Lord Lucan's disappearance.* • **It's** *rather an enigma* **why** *she left him.* [+ *wh-* word] • *He left an ambiguous and enigmatic message on my answering machine.* • *"[Russia] is a riddle wrapped in a mystery inside an enigma"* (Sir Winston Churchill, 1939)

en·ig·mat·ic /£ˌen·ɪgˈmæt·ɪk, $-ˈmæţ-/ *adj* • *The Mona Lisa has a famously enigmatic smile.*

en·ig·mat·i·cal·ly /£ˌen·ɪgˈmæt·ɪ·kli, $-ˈmæţ-/ *adv* • *"Who was that?" "Just a man I know," she said enigmatically.*

en·join *obj* /ɪnˈdʒɔɪn/ *v* [T] *fml* (esp. of a person or group with authority) to instruct (someone) to do something or to behave in a particular way, or to suggest that (a particular type of behaviour) would be suitable • *The proposed law enjoins employers* **to** *give workers time off to care for sick children and ageing parents.* [+ obj + *to* infinitive] • *We were all enjoined* **to** *be on our best behaviour.* [+ obj + *to* infinitive] • *He enjoined* (=suggested) *caution about believing what they told us.* • *(Am law)* In a court of law, to enjoin someone is to give them an official instruction: *Judge Sporkin enjoined both companies from engaging in such practices in the future.*

en·joy *(obj)* PLEASURE /ɪnˈdʒɔɪ/ *v* to get pleasure from (something) • *I really enjoyed that film/book/concert/party/meal.* [T] • *I was really surprised that I enjoyed the exams!* [T] • *I want to travel because I enjoy meeting people and seeing new places.* [+ *v-ing*] • *(esp. Am) Come on guys! Get yourselves a drink! Enjoy!* (=Have a pleasant time!) [I] • To enjoy your**self** is to get pleasure from the situation which you are in: *I don't think Marie is enjoying herself very much at school.* [T] ○ *Come on, why aren't you dancing? Enjoy yourselves!* [T] • Ⓟ

en·joy·ab·le /ɪnˈdʒɔɪ·ə·bl̩/ *adj* • *That was a very enjoyable game/film.* • *Thank you for a most enjoyable evening.*

en·joy·ment /ɪnˈdʒɔɪ·mənt/ *n* [U] • *Knowing the ending already didn't spoil my enjoyment of the film.*

en·joy *obj* BENEFIT /ɪnˈdʒɔɪ/ *v* [T] *fml* to have the benefit of (something) • *She has always enjoyed a lot of support/a good reputation.* • *Even though he's 86, he's still very active, and enjoys excellent health.* • Ⓟ

en·large *(obj)* /£ɪnˈlɑːdʒ, $-ˈlɑːrdʒ/ *v* to (cause to) become bigger • *They have enlarged the kitchen by building over part of the garden.* [T] • *In this new model, the car's engine has been enlarged from 5·3 to 6·0 litres.* [T] • *The company is looking for new ways of enlarging its market.* [T] • *Symptoms of the disease include an enlarged spleen and/or liver.* • *I've heard that exercise causes your heart to enlarge, but I don't know whether it's true or not.* [I] • If you enlarge a **photograph**, you print a bigger copy of it. [T] • If you **enlarge on/upon** something, you speak or write about it in (more) detail: *Ms Spencer enlarged on the need for tough anti-pollution laws.* ○ *Would you care to enlarge on what you've just said?*

en·large·ment /£ɪnˈlɑːdʒ·mənt, $-ˈlɑːrdʒ-/ *n* • *I am pleased to announce the enlargement of the History Department by three new teachers.* [U] • *I had an enlargement of my graduation photo done for my grandparents.* [C]

en·larg·er /£ɪnˈlɑː·dʒəʳ, $-ˈlɑːr·dʒɚ/ *n* [C] • An enlarger is a piece of equipment used esp. by photographers to make pictures or photographs bigger: *If we use the enlarger to blow up this photo we may get a better idea of the identity of the man in the background.*

en·light·en *(obj)* /£ɪnˈlaɪ·tᵊn,, $-ţᵊn/ *v* to provide (someone) with information and understanding; to explain the true facts about something to (someone) • *Should the function of children's television be to entertain or to enlighten.* [I] • *I don't understand this paragraph that you've written here. Could you enlighten me?* [T] • *The show tries to enlighten us* **about** *ethnic stereotypes by reversing them.* [T]

en·light·ened /£ɪnˈlaɪ·tᵊnd, $-ţᵊnd/ *adj approving* • Enlightened means showing understanding, acting in a positive way, and not following old-fashioned or false beliefs: *The school has an enlightened policy of teaching boys to cook.* ○ *These days she's much more enlightened in her views on education.* ○ *The company's sponsorship of the arts festival was clearly a case of* **enlightened self-interest** (=something advantageous to them as well as to others), *because they got a lot of publicity out of it.* • Enlightened can also mean knowing the truth about existence: *Buddha was an enlightened being.*

en·light·en·ing /£ɪn'laɪ·tᵊn·ɪŋ, $-t̬ᵊn-/ *adj* • *That was a very enlightening* (=informative in a way that produces understanding) *programme.* • *The instruction manual that came with my new computer wasn't very enlightening* **about** *how to operate it.* • **It** *is enlightening* **to** *compare the playwright's later plays with his earlier works.* [+ *to* infinitive]

en·light·en·ment /£ɪn'laɪ·tᵊn·mənt, $-t̬ᵊn-/ *n* [U] • *Can you give me any enlightenment* **on** (=information that will help me understand) *what happened?* • In Hinduism and Buddhism, enlightenment is the highest spiritual state that can be achieved. • **The Enlightenment** was the period in the 18th century in Europe, when particular thinkers began to emphasize the importance of science and of people using their own reason, rather than religion and tradition.

en·list JOIN /ɪn'lɪst/ *v* [I] to (cause to) join something, esp. the armed forces • *They both enlisted* (**in** *the navy) a year before the war broke out.* • *(Am)* An enlisted man/woman is a person in the armed forces who is not an officer.

en·list·ment /ɪn'lɪst·mənt/ *n* [C/U]

en·list *obj* ASK FOR HELP /ɪn'lɪst/ *v* [T] to ask (someone) for help or support, or to ask for and obtain (help and support) • *We've got to enlist some people to help prepare the food.* • *The organization has enlisted the support of many famous people in raising money to help homeless children.*

en·liv·en *obj* /ɪn'laɪ·vᵊn/ *v* [T often passive] to make more interesting or energetic • *The game was much enlivened when both teams scored within five minutes of each other.*

en masse /£ˌɒm'mæs, $ˌɑːm-/ *adv* [not gradable] (of a large group of people) together and at the same time • *The shop's 85 workers have resigned en masse.* • *The soldiers surrendered en masse.*

en·mesh *obj* /en'meʃ/ *v* [T usually passive] to catch or involve (someone) in something esp. unpleasant or dangerous from which it is difficult to escape • *The whales are caught by being enmeshed* **in** *nets.* • *He is* **deeply** *enmeshed* **in** *a political power struggle.* • *She has become enmeshed* **in** *a tangle of drugs and petty crime.* • *Our lives have become increasingly enmeshed* (=involved with each other).

en·mi·ty /£'en·mɪ·ti, $-t̬i/ *n* (a) feeling of hate • *She denied any personal enmity* **towards** *him.* [U] • *Bitter historical enmities underlie the present violence.* [C]

en·nob·le *obj* /£ɪ'nəʊ·bl̩, $-'noʊ-/ *v* [T] to make (someone) a member of the NOBILITY (=highest social rank) or *(literary)* to make (something or someone) more admirable • *The newspaper editor is expected to be ennobled by the Prime Minister.* • *(literary) He has this theory that suffering can ennoble a person's character.*

en·nui /£ˌɒn'wiː, $ˌɑːn-/ *n* [U] *literary* a feeling of boredom and mental tiredness caused by having nothing interesting or exciting to do • *The whole country seems to be affected by the ennui of winter.*

e·nor·mi·ty LARGENESS /£ɪ'nɔː·mɪ·ti, $-'nɔːr·mə·t̬i/ *n* [U] very great size or importance • *Nobody fully understands the enormity and complexity* **of** *the task of reviving the country's economy.* • *You have to fly over the area of the earthquake to appreciate the enormity* **of** *the damage.* • *I don't think you really realize the enormity* **of** *your mistake/error.*

e·nor·mi·ty EVIL ACT /£ɪ'nɔː·mɪ·ti, $-'nɔːr·mə·t̬i/ *n fml* an extremely evil act or the quality of being extremely evil • *His paintings depict the enormities of war.* [C] • *They should be severely punished for the enormity* (=evil quality) **of** *their crimes.* [U]

e·nor·mous /£ɪ'nɔː·məs, $-'nɔːr-/ *adj* extremely large • *an enormous dog/fish/tree/mountain* • *I had an enormous steak/sandwich/lunch.* • *He earns an enormous salary, so he can afford to live in an enormous house and drive an enormous car.* • *I was absolutely enormous when I was pregnant.* • *It gives me enormous pleasure to welcome Professor Hall.*

e·nor·mous·ly /£ɪ'nɔː·mə·sli, $-'nɔːr-/ *adv* • Enormously means extremely or very much: *It's an enormously long book.* ○ *She has worked enormously hard on this project.* ○ *I liked her enormously.* • LP **Very, completely**

e·nor·mous·ness /£ɪ'nɔː·mə·snəs, $-'nɔːr-/ *n* [U]

e·nough /ɪ'nʌf/ *determiner, pronoun, adv* as much as is necessary; in the amount or to the degree needed • *Is there enough cake/Are there enough cakes* **for** *everyone?* • *He had cooked enough food* **to** *feed an army!* [+ *to* infinitive] • *"Can we join you?" "Yes, there's enough room/ (fml) room enough for everybody."* • *There are 25 textbooks per class. That should be enough.* • *Have you had enough* (**to** *eat)?* [+ *to* infinitive] • *I know enough about art* **to** *recognize a masterpiece when I see one.* [+ *to* infinitive] • Enough can also mean as much as or more than is wanted: *I've got enough work* **to** *do at the moment, without being given any more.* [+ *to* infinitive] ○ *She's always willing to help other people, even though she's got problems enough of her own.* ○ *Half an hour in his company is* **quite** *enough!* ○ *Don't ask me for any more cake. You've had* **quite** *enough* **to** *eat already.* [+ *to* infinitive] ○ *Stop. You've made enough* **of a** (=a lot of) *mess already.* ○ *You've drunk* **more than** *enough* (=too much) *already.* ○ *I've* **seen/heard** *enough now* (=I do not want to see/hear any more). ○ *I've* **had** *enough* **of** *your excuses* (=I want them to stop). ○ *Enough* **of this**/*(Am) Enough* **already** (=Stop)! *I don't want to discuss it any more.* • Enough can be used after an adjective, adverb or verb to mean to the necessary degree: *Is the water hot enough yet?* ○ *I don't think he's really experienced enough for this sort of job.* ○ *She told me it was brand new and I was stupid enough* **to** *believe her.* [+ *to* infinitive] ○ *(fml) Would you be* **good** *enough* **to** *take my bag upstairs for me?* [+ *to* infinitive] ○ *I can't run fast enough* **to** *keep up with you.* [+ *to* infinitive] ○ *Make sure that you cook the meat enough.* • Enough can also be used after an adjective or adverb to mean quite: *He's bad enough, but his brother is far worse.* ○ *I suppose Florence is pretty enough, but I really love Venice.* ○ *She's gone away for six months, but strangely/oddly/ funnily enough* (=surprisingly), *her boyfriend doesn't seem too unhappy about it.* • *"I forgot to bring any lunch." "You can share mine if you want to – I've got* **enough and to spare** (=a lot)." • **Enough is enough** (=I want what is happening to stop) – *I don't want to argue with you any more.* • *"Someone has to explain the situation to her."* "**Enough said** (=I understand)." • *The government seems to be* **giving** *the unions* **enough rope to hang** *them***selves** (=allowing them so much freedom that they get into difficulties). • *I've* **had enough** (=I want what is happening to stop) – *I'm going home.* • **That's enough** (=Stop what you are doing), *Peter. Give those toys back to your brother.* • LP **Quantity words, '-ough' pronunciation**

en pas·sant /£ˌɒm'pæs·ɑ̃ː, $ˌɑːn·pæs'ɑːn/ *adv* [not gradable] *slightly fml or slightly literary* used to introduce something extra that you want to say quickly, while you are in the middle of talking about something else • *I feel I must say en passant that your failure to be punctual is still a problem.*

en·quire *(obj), Br dated and Am* **in·quire** /£ɪŋ'kwaɪəʳ, $-'kwaɪr/ *v* to ask for information • *Shall I enquire* **about** *the price of tickets?* [I] • *She rang up to enquire* **when** *her car would be ready.* [+ *wh-* word] • *"Where are we going?" he enquired politely.* [+ clause] • *(fml) "So what happens now?" she enquired* **of** *nobody in particular.* [+ clause] • *(Br fml) He enquired the time from a passer-by.* [T] • If you enquire **after** someone, you ask for information about them, esp. about their health: *Robert enquired* **after** *his father.* [I] ○ *She enquired* **after** *his grandfather's health.* [I] • If you enquire **into** something, you try to discover the facts about it: *When the authorities enquired* **into** *his background, they found he had a criminal record.* [I] • If a notice on a room or building says **enquire within**, it means that information can be found inside: *Saturday staff needed – Enquire within.*

en·quir·er, *Br dated and Am* **in·quir·er** /£ɪŋ'kwaɪə·rəʳ, $-'kwaɪr·ɚ/ *n* [C] • *There's an information officer who will answer the questions any serious enquirer may have.*

en·quir·ing, *Br dated and Am* **in·quir·ing** /£ɪŋ'kwaɪə·rɪŋ, $-'kwaɪr·ɪŋ/ *adj* • *You have a very enquiring* **mind**, *don't you* (=You are very eager to learn new things). • *He gave her an enquiring look* (=a look which showed he was asking a question).

en·quir·ing·ly, *Br dated and Am* **in·quir·ing·ly** /£ɪŋ'kwaɪə·rɪŋ·li, $-'kwaɪr·ɪŋ-/ *adv* • *She* **looked** *at her mother enquiringly.*

en·quir·y, *Br dated and Am* **in·quir·y** /£ɪŋ'kwaɪə·ri, $'ɪŋ·kwɚ·i/ *n* • *I've been* **making** *enquiries* **about/into** *the cost of a round-the-world ticket.* [C] • *Enquiry* **into** *the matter is pointless – no one will tell you anything.* [U] • An enquiry is also an official attempt to discover the facts about something: *a judicial enquiry* [C] ○ *Before the council starts building the new development, they will have to* **hold** *a* **public** *enquiry.* [C]

en·rage *obj* /ɪnˈreɪdʒ/ *v* [T] to cause (someone) to become very angry • *Plans to build a new nightclub in the neighbourhood have enraged local residents.* • *An enraged passenger demanded to know what had happened to her luggage.* • *He was so enraged* **at** *the article about him that he sued the newspaper.*

en·rap·tured /£ɪnˈræp·tʃəd, $-tʃɚd/ *adj literary* filled with great pleasure or extremely pleased by something • *The audience was enraptured by the young soloist's performance.* • *He gazed at her enraptured.*

en·rich *obj* /ɪnˈrɪtʃ/ *v* [T] to improve the quality of (something) by adding something else, or to make (something or someone) richer • *Fertilizer helps to enrich the soil.* • *Uranium is enriched for use in nuclear reactors.* • *Our culture has been enriched by immigrants from many other countries.* • *My life was greatly enriched by knowing her.* • *You should enrich your diet* **with** *more fresh fruit and vegetables.* • *Reading is an excellent way of enriching your* **experience**. • *He claimed that the large stores were enriching themselves* (=making themselves richer) *at the expense of their customers.*

en·rich·ment /ɪnˈrɪtʃ·mənt/ *n* [U]

en·rol *(obj) Br and Aus, Am and Aus usually* **en·roll** /£ɪnˈrəʊl, $-ˈroʊl/ *v* **-ll-** to put (yourself or someone else) onto the official list of members of a course, college or group, or to accept (someone) onto such a list • *Is it too late to enrol* **at** *the college?* [I] • *I enrolled* **for/in/on** *the modern art course.* [I] • *She has just enrolled in the Navy.* [I] • *He is enrolled as a part-time student.* [T] • *They want to enrol their children in their local school.* [T] • *The college will enrol* (=accept) *male students for the first time this September.* [T]

en·rol·ment *Br and Aus, Am and Aus usually* **en·roll·ment** /£ɪnˈrəʊl·mənt, $-ˈroʊl-/ *n* • *The deadline for enrolment* (=the act of enrolling) *is three days before the class.* [U] • *Student enrolments* (=the number of people enrolled) *at the university have increased steadily in recent years.* [C]

en route /£ˌɒnˈruːt, $ˌɑːn-/ *adv* [not gradable] on the way (to or from somewhere) • *I stopped at a shop en route* (**to** *the party) and bought some wine.* • *The bomb exploded while the plane was en route* **from** *Paris* **to** *Tokyo.*

en·sconce *obj* /£ɪnˈskɒnts, $-ˈskɑːnts/ *v* [T always + adv/prep; usually passive] *literary or humorous* to place (yourself) firmly in a particular place for a length of time • *After dinner, I ensconced* **myself in** *a deep armchair with a book.* • *The missing child is now* **safely** *ensconced at home.* • *The Prime Minister is now* **firmly** *ensconced* **in** *Downing Street with a large majority.* • *For over two years, she has been ensconced* (=involved) **with** *lawyers fighting for her rights in the case.*

en·semb·le /£ˌɒnˈsɒm·bl̩, $ˌɑːnˈsɑːm-/ *n* [C] a group of things or people acting or taken together as a whole, esp. a group of musicians who regularly play together • *The Mozart Ensemble is/are playing at the Wigmore Hall tonight.* [+ sing/pl v] • *He's a member of a jazz/orchestral/singing ensemble in New York.* • *There was some wonderful ensemble acting from the all-star cast.* • *She bought a dress and matching hat, gloves and shoes – in fact the whole ensemble.*

en·shrine *obj* /ɪnˈʃraɪn/ *v* [T always + adv/prep; often passive] *fml* to contain or keep (as if) in a holy place, or to contain and protect (esp. a political or social right) • *Almost two and a half million war dead are enshrined at Yasukuni.* • *A lot of memories are enshrined* **in** *this photograph album.* • *A Bill of Rights enshrines the rights of citizens.* • *The right of freedom of speech is enshrined* **in** *law/***in** *the constitution.* • *These practices are enshrined* **in** *tradition.*

en·shroud *obj* /ɪnˈʃraʊd/ *v* [T often passive] *literary* to cover (something) so that it can not be seen clearly • *Thick cloud enshrouded the tops of the mountains.* • *The planet Venus is enshrouded* **in** *thick clouds.* • *(fig.) The talks have been enshrouded* **in** (=have been not known about because of) *secrecy.*

en·sign /ˈen·saɪn, -sᵊn/ *n* [C] a flag on a ship that shows which country the ship belongs to

en·slave *obj* /ɪnˈsleɪv/ *v* [T often passive] to control and keep (someone) forcefully in a bad situation, or to make a SLAVE of (someone) • *Generations of women in this region were enslaved by poverty, by religion and by tradition.* • *The early settlers enslaved or killed much of the native population.* • *(fig.) He was totally enslaved by her* (=He was in love with her and therefore completely controlled by her).

en·slave·ment /ɪnˈsleɪv·mənt/ *n* [U]

en·snare *obj* /£ɪnˈsneəʳ, $-ˈsner/ *v* [T often passive] *literary* to catch or get control of • *Spiders ensnare flies and other insects in their webs.* • *They wanted to make a formal complaint about their doctor, but ended up ensnared* **in** *the complexities of the legal system.* • *It was a sad fairy story about a prince who was ensnared by a beautiful but evil witch.*

en·sue /£ɪnˈsjuː, $-ˈsuː/ *v* [I] *fml* to happen after something else, esp. as a result of it • *The police officer said that he had placed the man under arrest and that a scuffle had ensued.* • *Soldiers began firing on each other and a gun battle ensued.* • *Boredom often ensues* **from** *inactivity.*

en·su·ing /£ɪnˈsjuː·ɪŋ, $-ˈsuː-/ *adj* [before n; not gradable] • *He lost his job and in the ensuing* (=following) *months became more and more depressed.* • *An argument broke out and in the ensuing* (=result) *fight, a gun went off.*

en suite /£ˌɒnˈswiːt, $ˌɑːn-/ *adj, n* (being or having) a bathroom directly connected to a bedroom • *I want a hotel room with an en suite bathroom.* • *The bathroom is en suite.* • *Two of the bedrooms in the house have en suites.* [C]

en·sure *(obj), Am also* **in·sure** /£ɪnˈʃɔːʳ, $-ˈʃʊr/ *v* to make (something) certain to happen • *Following the plane crash, the airline is taking further steps to ensure public safety on its aircraft.* [T] • *The role of the police is to ensure* **(that)** *the law is obeyed.* [+ *(that)* clause] • *Safeguards are necessary to ensure* **(that)** *people are not wrongfully put in prison.* [+ *(that)* clause] • *Their 2-0 victory today has ensured the Italian team a place in the Cup Final/ensured a place in the Cup Final* **for** *the Italian team.* [+ two objects]

en·tail *(obj)* /ɪnˈteɪl/ *v fml or specialized* to make (something) necessary, or to involve (something) • *Such a large investment inevitably entails some risk.* [T] • *For many parents, having children entails certain sacrifices.* [T] • *Repairing the roof will entail spend***ing** *a lot of money.* [+ v-*ing*]

en·tan·gle *obj* /ɪnˈtæŋ·gl̩/ *v* [T usually passive] to catch and cause (something) to become mixed or involved with something else, esp. so that it is difficult to escape from it • *The dolphin had become entangled* **in/with** *the fishing nets.* • *He went to the shop to buy bread, and got entangled* **in/with** *a carnival parade.* • *The bill is sure to entangle parliament* **in** *endless debate.* • *The mayor and the city council are anxious to avoid getting entangled* **in** *the controversy.* • *They are entangled* **in** *a fierce struggle for independence.* • *She seems to be romantically entangled* **with** *some artist in Rome.*

en·tan·gle·ment /ɪnˈtæŋ·gl̩·mənt/ *n* [C] • An entanglement is a situation or relationship that you do not completely want, in which you are involved with other people or things in a way that is difficult to understand, deal with or escape: *The government can no longer afford these expensive entanglements abroad in other countries' wars.* ○ *The book describes the complex emotional and sexual entanglements between the members of the group.* • *(Br specialized)* An entanglement *(also* **barbed wire entanglement**) is a fence made of wire with sharp points on it, intended to make it difficult for enemy soldiers to go across an area of land.

en·tente (cor·di·ale) /£ɒnˈtɒnt, $ɑːnˈtɑːnt/ *n* [C] a friendly agreement or relationship between two countries

enter *(obj)* GO IN /£ˈen·təʳ, $-t̬ɚ/ *v* to come or go into (a particular place) • *The police entered (the building)* **through/by** *the side door.* [I/T] • *You will begin to feel sleepy as the drug enters the* **bloodstream**. [T] • *The River Dart enters the sea at Dartmouth.* [T] • **The thought/It** *hadn't entered my* **mind/head** (=I had not thought of the possibility) **(that)** *she might not want me in the house.* [T + obj + *(that)* clause] • *The project is entering* (=reaching) *its final* **stages**. [T] • *The doctor says she's entering* (=beginning to go through) *a critical* **stage**. [T] • See also ENTRANCE WAY IN; ENTRY WAY IN.

enter *(obj)* INCLUDE /£ˈen·təʳ, $-t̬ɚ/ *v* to (cause to) become included in, involved in, a member of, etc. • *A sense of excitement has entered the proceedings.* [T] • *Both men have been entered* **for/in** *the 100 metres in Paris next month.* [T] • *Let the race organizer know by July if you wish to enter.* [I] • *All three companies have entered the* **race** *to develop a new system.* [T] • *Are you going to enter the* **competition/contest**? [T] • *Ms Doughty entered* **politics/Parliament** *after a career in banking.* • *We've hired him to enter* (=key in) *all the new data* **into** *the computer.* [T] • *Have you entered* (=written) *today's results* **in** *your score book?* [T] • *(fml)* If you enter some type of statement, you state it officially: *The prisoner entered a* **plea** *of not guilty.* [T] • If you enter **into**

something, such as an **agreement** or exchange of letters, you begin to become involved in it: *We have entered into a* **correspondence** *with the company.* [I] ○ *They refuse to enter into any* **discussion** *on this matter.* • *She said she didn't really like Christmas, but she entered into* **the spirit of** (=allowed herself to take part in and enjoy) *the occasion.* [I] • If something enters **into** something else, it is an important or necessary part of it: *The matter of how much they will pay me enters into whether or not I will take the job.* [I] ○ *The Council's opinion does not enter into* **it** *– it is up to us to make the decision.* [I] • *(fml)* If you enter **on/upon** something, you begin to do it or become involved in it: *He first entered on a career in banking over 40 years ago.* [I] • See also ENTRY COMPETITION; ENTRY INFORMATION.

enter COMPUTER /£ˈen·təʳ, $-tɚ/ *n* [U] the key on a computer keyboard which is used to say that the words or numbers on the screen are correct, or to say that an instruction should be performed, or to move down a line on the screen • *Move the cursor to where it says 'New File' and press enter.*

en·ter·i·tis /£ˌen·təˈraɪ·təs, $-ţəˈraɪ·ţəs/ *n* [U] See GASTROENTERITIS

en·ter·prise /£ˈen·tə·praɪz, $-ţɚ-/ *n* an organization, esp. a business, or a difficult and important plan, esp. one that will earn money • *Don't forget this is a* **commercial** *enterprise – we're here to make money.* [C] • *Those were the years of* **private** *enterprise* (=businesses being run privately, rather than by the government), *when lots of small businesses were started.* [U] • *The original enterprise* (=plan) *was to raise the money by giving a concert.* [C] • *Her latest enterprise* (=plan) *is to climb Mount Everest.* [C] • Enterprise is also eagerness to do something new and clever, despite any risks: *They've showed a lot of enterprise* **in** *setting up this project.* [U] ○ *We need someone with enterprise and imagination to design a marketing strategy.* [U] • An **enterprise culture** is a society in which personal achievement, the creation of wealth and the development of private business is encouraged: *The dreams encouraged by the enterprise culture have turned to despair for a large number of people whose businesses have now failed.* • An **enterprise zone** is an area with economic problems that has been given financial help by the government to encourage the growth of new businesses: *The administration has decided to attract businesses and jobs to inner cities by designating certain neighbourhoods enterprise zones.*

en·ter·pris·ing /£ˈen·tə·praɪ·zɪŋ, $-ţɚ-/ *adj* • Someone who is enterprising is good at thinking of and doing new and difficult things, esp. those that will make money: *The business was started by a couple of enterprising young women.* ○ *That was very enterprising* **of** *you, Vijay!*

en·ter·tain *(obj)* AMUSE /£en·təˈteɪn, $-ţɚ-/ *v* to keep (esp. a group of people) interested or amused • *We hired a magician to entertain the children at the party.* [T] • *This children's television programme aims to both educate and entertain at the same time.* [I]

en·ter·tain·er /£en·təˈteɪ·nəʳ, $-ţɚˈteɪ·nɚ/ *n* [C] • *They were entertainers who sang, danced and told jokes for a living.*

en·ter·tain·ing /£en·təˈteɪ·nɪŋ, $-ţɚ-/ *adj* • If you describe someone or something as entertaining, you mean that they are amusing and that you enjoy them: *an entertaining story* ○ *an entertaining film* ○ *His books aren't particularly well-written, but they're always entertaining.*

en·ter·tain·ing·ly /£en·təˈteɪ·nɪŋ·li, $-ţɚ-/ *adv*

en·ter·tain·ment /£en·təˈteɪn·mənt, $-ţɚ-/ *n* • *There's not much in the way of entertainment* (=public shows, performances or other ways of enjoying yourself) *in this town – just the cinema and a couple of pubs.* [U] • *(fml) This season's entertainments include five new plays and several concerts of Chinese and Indian music.* [C] • *"That's Entertainment"* (title of film, and a song by The Jam, 1974)

en·ter·tain *(obj)* INVITE /£en·təˈteɪn, $-ţɚ-/ *v* to invite (someone) to your house and give food and drink to them • *We entertain a lot of people, mainly business associates of my wife's.* [T] • *Now that I live on my own, I don't entertain much.* [I] • *"Be not forgetful to entertain strangers: for thereby some have entertained angels unawares (usually found in the expression 'to entertain an angel unawares')"* (Bible, Hebrews 13.2)

en·ter·tain·ing /£en·təˈteɪ·nɪŋ, $-ţɚ-/ *n* [U] • *The annual budget that I have for my job includes an amount for travel and entertaining.* • *We do a lot of entertaining.*

en·ter·tain *obj* THINK ABOUT /£ˌen·təˈteɪn, $-ţɚ-/ *v* [T not *be entertaining*] *fml* to hold in your mind or to be willing to consider or accept • *The General refused to entertain the possibility of defeat.* • *Would you entertain our proposal if we lowered the cost by £2000?*

en·thral *obj Br and Aus, Am usually* **en·thrall** /£ɪn·ˈθrɔːl, $-ˈθrɑːl/ *v* [T often passive] **-ll-** to keep (someone) completely interested • *The baseball game completely enthralled the crowd.* • *The audience was enthralled for two hours by a sparkling, dramatic performance.* • *They listened enthralled to what he was saying.*

en·thrall·ing /£ɪnˈθrɔː·lɪŋ, $-ˈθrɑː-/ *adj* • *I found your book absolutely enthralling!*

en·throne *obj* /£ɪnˈθrəʊn, $-ˈθroʊn/ *v* [T usually passive] *fml* to put (a king, queen, etc.) through the ceremony of sitting on a THRONE (=ceremonial chair) in order to mark the official beginning of their period in power • *The Archbishop will be enthroned in Westminster Abbey next month.* • *(fig.) She was sitting in the dining room, enthroned* (=sitting) **in/on** *an old high-backed chair.*

en·throne·ment /£ɪnˈθrəʊn·mənt, $-ˈθroʊn-/ *n* [C/U]

en·thus·i·asm /£ɪnˈθjuː·zi·æz·ᵊm, $-ˈθuː-/ *n* a feeling of energetic interest in a particular subject or activity and an eagerness to be involved in it • *One of the good things about teaching young children is their enthusiasm.* [U] • *After the accident he lost his enthusiasm* **for** *the sport.* [U] • *I just can't* **work up** (=start to feel) *any enthusiasm for the whole project.* [U] • *One of his greatest enthusiasms* (=interests) *was yoga.* [C]

en·thuse *(obj)* /£ɪnˈθjuːz, $-ˈθuːz-/ *v* • If you enthuse **about/over** a particular subject, you express excitement or interest in it: *He was enthusing over a wonderful restaurant he'd been to.* [I] • *"She's the best leader that this country has ever known!" he enthused.* [+ clause] • To enthuse also means to give your feeling of excitement and interest in a particular subject to other people: *He was passionately interested in classical music but failed to enthuse his children* (**with** *it*). [T]

en·thus·i·ast /£ɪnˈθjuː·zi·æst, $-ˈθuː-/ *n* [C] • An enthusiast is a person who is very interested in and involved with a particular subject or activity: *a keep-fit enthusiast* ○ *a model-aircraft enthusiast*

en·thus·i·as·tic /£ɪnˌθjuː·ziˈæs·tɪk, $-ˌθuː-/ *adj* • *You don't seem very enthusiastic* **about** *the party – don't you want to go tonight?*

en·thus·i·as·ti·cal·ly /£ɪnˌθjuː·ziˈæs·tɪ·kli, $-ˌθuː-/ *adv* • *The President was welcomed enthusiastically by a cheering crowd.*

en·tice *obj* /ɪnˈtaɪs/ *v* [T] to attract (someone) to a particular place or activity by offering something pleasant or advantageous, often causing them to leave something else • *People are being enticed* **away from** *the profession by higher salaries elsewhere.* • *In the story, the wicked witch entices the children* **into** *her cottage with sweets and cakes.* • *I hadn't intended going to the party, but she managed to entice me.* • *A smell of coffee in the doorway entices people* **to** *enter the shop.* [+ obj + *to* infinitive]

en·tice·ment /ɪnˈtaɪ·smənt/ *n* • *One of the enticements of the job is the company car.* [C] • *They tried to persuade me to go to Florida with them for a visit, but hot weather is not much of an enticement if you don't like the sun.* [U]

en·tic·ing /ɪnˈtaɪ·sɪŋ/ *adj* • Something which is enticing attracts you to it by offering you advantages or pleasure: *an enticing smile* ○ *an enticing job offer* ○ *The enticing sound of laughter drew her into the next room.*

en·tic·ing·ly /ɪnˈtaɪ·sɪŋ·li/ *adv* • *The smell of garlic drifted enticingly out from the kitchen.*

en·tire /£ɪnˈtaɪəʳ, $-ˈtaɪr/ *adj* [before n; not gradable] whole or complete, with nothing missing • *Between them they ate an entire cake.* • *He'd spent the entire journey asleep.* • *They got an entire set of silver cutlery as a wedding present.*

en·tire·ly /£ɪnˈtaɪə·li, $-ˈtaɪr-/ *adv* [not gradable] • *I admit it was entirely my fault.* • *The company is run almost entirely by middle-aged men.* • LP **Very, completely**

en·ti·re·ty /£ɪnˈtaɪə rɪ·ti, $-ˈtaɪr·ɪ·ţi/ *n* [U] *fml* • *I've never actually read the book* **in its** *entirety – just small parts of it.*

en·tit·le *obj* ALLOW /£ɪnˈtaɪ·tḷ, $-ţḷ/ *v* [T usually passive] to give (someone) the right to do or have something • *Being unemployed entitles you* **to** *free medical treatment.* • *A membership card entitles you* **to** *take a guest with you free.* [+ obj + *to* infinitive] • *The employer is entitled* **to** *ask for references.* [+ obj + *to* infinitive]

en·tit·led /£ɪn'taɪ·tl̩d, $-t̬l̩d/ *adj* • *I felt entitled* (=I felt I had the right) **to** *know how my own money is being spent!* [+ *to* infinitive]

en·tit·le·ment /£ɪn'taɪ·tl̩·mənt, $-t̬l̩-/ *n* [U] • *Managers have generous leave entitlement.*

en·tit·le *obj* GIVE TITLE /£ɪn'taɪ·tl̩, $-t̬l̩/ *v* [T usually passive] to give (a title) to (a book, film, etc.) • *Her latest novel, entitled 'The Forgotten Sex', is out this week.*

en·ti·ty /£'en·tɪ·ti, $-t̬ə·t̬i/ *n* [C] *fml* something which exists apart from other things, having its own independent existence • *The museums work closely together, but are separate legal entities.* • *They proposed treating all the company's pension funds as a single entity.* • *He regarded the north of the country as a separate cultural entity.*

en·tomb *obj* /ɪn'tuːm/ *v* [T] *fml or literary* to bury (something) so that it is completely covered, or less commonly, to put (a dead body) in a GRAVE or TOMB • *The nuclear waste has been entombed* **in** *concrete many metres under the ground.*

en·to·mol·o·gy /£,en·tə'mɒl·ə·dʒi, $-t̬ə'mɑː·lə-/ *n* [U] *specialized* the scientific study of insects

en·to·mol·o·gist /£,en·tə'mɒl·ə·dʒɪst, $-t̬ə'mɑː·lə-/ *n* [C] *specialized* • *Entomologists study insects.*

en·tour·age /£'ɒn·tʊ·rɑːʒ, $,ɑːn-/ *n* [C + sing/pl v] the group of people who travel with and work for an important or famous person • *The rock-star arrived in London with her usual entourage of dancers and backing singers.*

en·trails /'en·treɪlz/ *pl n* the INTESTINES and other inside organs of an animal or person, when they are outside the body • *pig entrails* • *(fig.) The sofa's entrails* (=pieces of material from inside) *were sticking out in places.* • In the past, when people **consulted the** entrails they asked esp. a priest to tell them what would happen in the future by examining the inside organs of an animal.

en·trance WAY IN /'en·trənts/ *n* a door, gate, etc. by which you can enter a building or place • *There are two entrances – one at the front and one round the back of the building.* [C] • When an actor or dancer comes onto a stage it is called an entrance: *He* **makes** *a spectacular entrance in act two draped in a gold sheet.* [C] • Entrance can also refer to the act of a person coming into a room in an ordinary situation, although often because there is something noticeable about it: *I noticed her entrance because she slipped and fell in the doorway.* [C] • Entrance can also be the right to enter a place: *The management reserve the right to* **refuse** *entrance.* [U] • An **entrance exam** is an exam which you take to decide if you can be accepted into a school, etc. • An **entrance fee** is an amount of money that you pay in order to be allowed into a cinema, theatre, etc. • See also ENTER GO IN; ENTER INCLUDE; ENTRY WAY IN. Compare EXIT.

en·trant /'en·trənt/ *n* [C] • An entrant is a person who becomes a member of a group or organization: *new entrants to the school/company* • An entrant is also a person who takes part in a competition or an examination: *All entrants complete two three-hour papers.*

en·trance *obj* INTEREST /£ɪn'trɑːnts, $-'trænts/ *v* [T often passive] *slightly poetic* to keep the attention of, filling with pleasure and great interest • *The children sat silent on the carpet, entranced* **by** *the cartoon.*

en·tranc·ing /£ɪn'trɑːnt·sɪŋ, $-'trænt-/ *adj slightly poetic* • *A walk through this countryside will provide you with some of the most entrancing views.*

en·trap *obj* /ɪn'træp/ *v* [T often passive] **-pp-** *fml* to catch (someone) or persuade (someone) to do something by deceiving them • *I firmly believe my son has been entrapped by this cult.* • *The story centres around a man who hires a detective to entrap his unfaithful wife.*

en·trap·ment /ɪn'træp·mənt/ *n* [U] *fml* • *The police have been accused of using entrapment to bring charges against suspects.*

en·treat·y /£ɪn'triː·ti, $-t̬i/ *n* [C] a serious and sincere attempt to persuade someone to do or not to do something • *She refused to become involved with him despite his passionate entreaties.*

en·treat *obj* /ɪn'triːt/ *v* [T] • *We would spend every meal time entreating the child* **to** *eat her vegetables.* [+ obj + *to* infinitive]

en·trée FOOD /£'ɒn·treɪ, $'ɑːn-/ *n* [C] the main dish of a meal, or at very formal meals, a small dish served just before the main part

en·trée ENTRY /£'ɒn·treɪ, $'ɑːn-/ *n* [U] the right to join a particular group of people or enter an organization that will be advantageous to you • *By marrying an aristocrat, he* **gained** *entrée* **into/to** *higher social circles.* • NL

en·trench *obj* /ɪn'trentʃ/ *v* [T usually passive] *esp. disapproving* to establish (something, esp. an idea or a problem) firmly so that it cannot be changed • *The government's main task was to prevent inflation from entrenching itself.* • *The guerillas have entrenched themselves in the mountains.*

en·trenched /ɪn'trentʃt/ *adj esp. disapproving* • *It's very difficult to change* **attitudes** *that have become so* **deeply** *entrenched over the years.* • *It was an enormous struggle to overthrow such an entrenched dictator.* • *The organization was often criticized for being too entrenched* **in** *its views.* • *He's an entrenched conservative/left winger.* • *(usually humorous) She sat entrenched behind an enormous pile of papers and didn't leave her desk all morning.*

en·trench·ment /ɪn'trentʃ·mənt/ *n* [U] *esp. disapproving* • *There has been a shift in opinion on the issue after a decade of entrenchment.* • *The* **legal** *entrenchment of apartheid has been lifted.*

en·tre nous /£,ɒn·trə'nuː, $,ɑːn-/ *adv* [not gradable] *fml or humorous* (used in conversation) between ourselves; in secret and not to be told to anyone else • *He told me – and this is* **strictly** *entre nous – that she was the reason he was leaving his job.*

en·tre·pre·neur /£,ɒn·trə·prə'nɜːʳ, $,ɑːn·trə·prə'nɜːr/ *n* [C] a person who attempts to make a profit by starting their own company or by operating alone in the business world, esp. when it involves taking risks • *He was one of the entrepreneurs of the eighties who made their money in property.*

en·tre·pre·neur·i·al /£,ɒn·trə·prə'nɜː·ri·əl, $,ɑːn·trə·prə'nɜːr·i-/ *adj* • *She'll make money – she's got that entrepreneurial* **spirit**.

en·tre·pre·neur·ship /£,ɒn·trə·prə'nɜː·ʃɪp, $-'nɜːr-/ *n* [C] • *The government needs to promote entrepreneurship and inventiveness, by ending high taxes and other disincentives.*

en·tro·py /'en·trə·pi/ *n* [U] *specialized* the amount of order or lack of order in a system

en·trust *obj* /ɪn'trʌst/ *v* [T always + adv/prep] to give (someone) (a thing or a duty) for which they are responsible • *He didn't look like the sort of man you should entrust your luggage* **to**. • *He's entrusted his precious cat* **to** *me/I've been entrusted* **with** *his precious cat for the week while he's away.* • *She entrusted her violin* **to** *me.* • *Two senior officials have been entrusted* **with** *organizing the auction.* • *The teacher entrusted my son* **with** *the class hamster for the holidays.*

en·try WAY IN /'en·tri/ *n* the act of entering a place or of joining a particular society or organization • *A flock of sheep blocked our entry* **to** *the village.* [U] • *I can't go down that street – there's a 'No entry' sign.* [U] • *The actress's entry* **into** *the world of politics surprised most people.* [U] • *She* **made** *her entry to* (=entered) *the ceremony surrounded by a group of photographers.* [C] • *The burglars* **gained** *entry* (=entered the building) *by a top window.* [U] • An entry is also a door, gate, etc. by which you enter a place: *I'll wait for you at the entry to the park.* [C] • See also ENTRANCE WAY IN; ENTER GO IN; ENTER INCLUDE.

en·try COMPETITION /'en·tri/ *n* [C] a piece of work that you do in order to take part in a competition, or the act of taking part in a competition • *There have been a fantastic number of entries for this year's under 10s poetry competition.* [C] • *Let's have a look at the* **winning** *entries.* [C] • *Entry* **to** *the competition is restricted to those who have a ticket for the exhibition.* [U] • *Have you filled in your entry* **form** *for the competition yet?* • See also ENTER INCLUDE.

en·try INFORMATION /'en·tri/ *n* [C] a separate piece of information that is recorded in a book, computer, etc. • *They've updated a lot of the entries in the most recent edition of the encyclopaedia.* • *As his illness progressed he* **made** *fewer entries in his diary.* • *The database entry for each student records name, address and telephone number.* • See also ENTER INCLUDE.

en·try·i·sm /'en·tri·ɪ·zəm/ *n* [U] *Br disapproving* the activity of joining a political party with the secret intention of changing its principles and plans • *She's been accused of entryism by some members of the party.*

en·try·phone /£'en·tri·fəʊn, $-foʊn/ *n* [C] *Br* a telephone at the entrance to large buildings which people speak into when they want to speak to someone who is inside the building • *My friends in London have a video entryphone in their flat so they can see who is visiting before deciding whether or not to let them in.*

en·try·way /ˈen·tri·weɪ/ *n Am for* PASSAGE [CONNECTING WAY]

en·twine *obj* /ɪnˈtwaɪn/ *v* [T usually passive] to twist together or around (something) • *Put a stick in the plant pot and the plant will entwine* **itself** *around it as it grows.* • *The bride had flowers entwined* **in** *her hair.* • *(fig.) The picture captures the two lovers entwined* (= with their arms around each other) *on a balcony.* • *(fig.) The fates of both countries seem somehow entwined* **(together)**.

e·num·er·ate *obj* /£ɪˈnjuː·mə·reɪt, $-ˈnuː·mər·eɪt/ *v* [T] *fml* to name (things) separately, one by one • *The sales representative enumerated the benefits of the insurance scheme.*

e·num·er·a·tion /£ɪˌnjuː·məˈreɪ·ʃən, $-ˌnuː-/ *n* [U] *fml*

e·nun·ci·ate *(obj)* [PRONOUNCE] /ɪˈnʌnt·si·eɪt/ *v fml* to pronounce (words or parts of words) clearly • *He doesn't enunciate (his words) very clearly – I can't understand what he says.* [I/T]

enunciation /ɪˌnʌn·siˈeɪ·ʃən/ *n* [C/U] *fml* • *He has (a) very clear enunciation.*

e·nun·ci·ate *obj* [EXPLAIN] /ɪˈnʌnt·si·eɪt/ *v* [T] *fml* to state and explain (esp. a plan or principle) clearly or formally • *In the speech, the leader enunciated his party's proposals for tax reform.*

en·ve·lop *obj* /ɪnˈvel·əp/ *v* [T] *literary or fml* to cover or surround (something) completely • *The graveyard looked ghostly, enveloped* **in** *mist.* • *She was enveloped* **in** *a jacket that looked two sizes too big for her.* • *(fig.) Gloom enveloped him.*

en·vel·ope /£ˈen·və·ləʊp, $ˈɑːn·və·loʊp/ *n* [C] a flat, usually square or rectangular, paper container for a letter • *He bought a pad of notepaper and a packet of envelopes.* • *The prices were very roughly calculated – it looked as though he'd done them* **on the back of an envelope** (= in a quick and hurried way). • [PIC]› **Stationery**

en·vi·abl·e /ˈen·vi·ə·bl̩/ *adj* See at ENVY

en·vi·ous /ˈen·vi·əs/ *adj* See at ENVY

en·vir·on·ment [SURROUNDINGS] /£ɪnˈvaɪə·rən·mənt, $-ˈvaɪr·ən-/ *n* [C] the conditions that you live or work in and the way that they influence how you feel or how effectively you can work • *The office is quite bright and airy – it's a pleasant* **working** *environment.* • *As a parent you try to create a stable* **home** *environment for your children to grow up in.*

en·vir·on·ment [NATURE] /£ɪnˈvaɪə·rən·mənt, $-ˈvaɪr·ən-/ *n* [U] **the environment** (the quality of) the air, water and land in or on which people, animals and plants live • *Certain chemicals have been banned because of their damaging effect on the environment.* • *We're not doing enough to protect the environment from pollution.*

en·vir·on·men·tal /£ɪnˌvaɪə·rən·ˈmen·təl, $-ˌvaɪr·ənˈmen·t̬əl/ *adj* [not gradable] • *People are becoming far more aware of environmental* **issues**.

en·vir·on·men·tal·ly /£ɪnˌvaɪə·rənˈmen·təl·i, $-ˌvaɪr·ənˈmen·t̬əl-/ *adv* [not gradable] • When people claim that a product or activity is environmentally **friendly**, they either mean that it will not harm the land, sea or air, or that it will do less damage than other similar products or activities.

en·vi·ron·men·tal·i·sm /£ɪnˌvaɪə·rəˈmen·təl·ɪ·zəm, $-ˌvaɪr·əˈmen·t̬əl-/ *n* [U] • Environmentalism is an interest in or the study of the environment, in order to protect it from damage by human activities.

en·vir·on·men·talist /£ɪnˌvaɪə·rənˈmen·təl·ɪst, $-ˌvaɪr·ənˈmen·t̬əl-/ *n* [C] • An environmentalist is a person who is interested in or studies the environment and who tries to protect it from being damaged by human activities.

en·vir·ons /£ɪnˈvaɪə·rənz, $-ˈvaɪr·ənz/ *pl n fml* the area surrounding a place, esp. a town • *The environs* **of** *the city are even more beautiful than the city itself.*

en·vi·sage *(obj)* /ɪnˈvɪz·ɪdʒ/, *esp. Am* **en·vi·sion** /ɪnˈvɪʒ·ən/ *v slightly fml* to imagine or expect as a likely or desirable possibility in the future • *Train fare increases of 5% are envisaged for the next year.* [T] • **It**'*s envisaged* **that** *the building will start at the end of this year.* [+ *that* clause] • *We envisage* **that** *we will be ready to sign the contract in October.* [+ *that* clause] • *When do you envisage finish***ing** *the project?* [+ v-*ing*] • *I can't envisage anyone buy***ing** *it.* [T + obj + v-*ing*] • **It**'*s hard to envisage* **how** *it could have happened.* [+ *wh*- word] • To envisage is also to form a mental picture of something or someone you have never seen: *He wasn't what I'd expected – I'd envisaged someone much taller and more impressive-looking.* [T]

en·voy /ˈen·vɔɪ/ *n* [C] someone who is sent as a representative from one government or organization to another • *A United Nations special envoy has been sent to discuss the refugee problem with the government.*

en·vy *obj* /ˈen·vi/ *v* [T] to wish that you had (a quality or possession) that another person has • *I envy her ability to start conversations with people she's never met before.* • *He's got the sort of physique that many top athletes would envy.* • *I don't envy you the job of cooking for all those people.* [+ two objects] • *She envied him* **(for)** *his freedom to travel.* [+ two objects] • [LP]› **Two objects** Ⓟ

en·vy /ˈen·vi/ *n* [U] • *They felt a lot of envy* **towards** *the youngest sister because she was so pretty and popular.* • *The family enjoys living standards that are* **the envy of** (= liked and wanted by) *visitors to their estate.* • *"What do people at work think of your new car?" "They're* **all** *envy/ They're* **green with** *envy* (= They would like to have it)*".* • Compare **jealousy** at JEALOUS [UNHAPPY].

en·vi·abl·e /ˈen·vi·ə·bl̩/ *adj* • *She has an enviable* (= desirable) *slimness despite having had three children.*

en·vi·ab·ly /ˈen·vi·ə·bli/ *adv* • *At school he was always enviably good at sports.*

en·vi·ous /ˈen·vi·əs/ *adj* • Envious means wishing you had what another person has: *I'm very envious* **of** *your new coat – it's lovely.* • Compare JEALOUS [UNHAPPY].

en·vi·ous·ly /ˈen·vi·ə·sli/ *adv* • *He looked enviously at his friend's new car.*

en·vi·ous·ness /ˈen·vi·ə·snəs/ *n* [U]

en·zyme /ˈen·zaɪm/ *n* [C] any of a group of chemical substances which are produced by living cells and which cause particular chemical reactions to happen while not being changed themselves • *An enzyme in the saliva of the mouth starts the process of breaking down the food.*

e·on, *Br and Aus also* **ae·on** /£ˈiː·ɒn, $-ɑːn/ *n* [C] a period of time which is so long that it cannot be measured • *The last dinosaur became extinct eons ago.* • *(infml) I've been waiting eons for my new computer.* • [LP]› **Periods of time**

ep·aul·et, **ep·aul·ette** /ˌep·əˈlet/ *n* [C] a decorative part on the shoulder of a piece of clothing, esp. on a military coat, shirt, etc.

e·pée /£ˈep·eɪ, $epˈeɪ/ *n* [C] a thin sword used in the sport of FENCING (= sword fighting) which is heavier than a FOIL (= light, bendable sword) and has a larger, rounded part for protecting the hand of the user

eph·e·me·ral /£ɪˈfem·ər·əl, $-ə·/ *adj* lasting for only a short time • *Fame in the world of rock and pop is largely ephemeral.*

eph·e·me·ra /£ɪˈfem·ər·ə, $-ə·/ *pl n* • Ephemera refers to the type of objects which, when they were produced, were not intended to last a long time or were specially produced for one occasion: *Amongst other pop ephemera, the auction will be selling off rock-stars' stage clothes.*

ep·ic /ˈep·ɪk/ *n* [C] a film, poem or book which is long and contains a lot of action, usually dealing with a historical subject • *It's one of those old Hollywood epics with a cast of thousands.* • *I'm reading a real epic at the moment – it's over a thousand pages long.*

ep·ic /ˈep·ɪk/ *adj* • *an epic film about the Roman Empire* • Epic can also be used of events that happen over a long period and involve a lot of action and difficulty: *an epic journey/struggle* • *(infml)* Epic sometimes means extremely large: *an epic banquet in honour of the president* ○ *The problem of inflation has reached epic* **proportions**.

ep·i·cene /ˈep·ɪ·siːn/ *adj fml* belonging to both sexes or characteristic of the opposite sex • *She noted his epicene features – the long eyelashes, the full lips.*

ep·i·cen·tre *Br and Aus, Am* **ep·i·cen·ter** /£ˈep·ɪ·sen·tər, $-t̬ə·/ *n* [C] *specialized* the point on the Earth's surface directly above an EARTHQUAKE or atomic explosion

ep·i·cure /£ˈep·ɪ·kjʊər, $-kjʊr/, **ep·i·cur·e·an** *n* [C] *fml or literary* a person who enjoys food and drink of a high quality, often having great knowledge of the subject; a GOURMET

ep·i·cur·e·an /£ˌep·ɪˈkjʊə·ri·ən, $-ˈkjʊr·i-/ *adj fml or literary* • *Hamburgers and fries were not really suited to his epicurean tastes.*

ep·i·de·mic /ˌep·ɪˈdem·ɪk/ *n* [C] the appearance of a particular disease in a large number of people in the same period of time • *The flu epidemic has struck down thousands of people in the south of England.* • *They're predicting an AIDS epidemic in the next ten years.* • *(fig.) The capital is suffering from an unemployment epidemic* (= a serious lack of jobs, affecting many people) *that it* *cannot control.* • *(fig.) Poverty in this country has reached epidemic* **proportions** (= has an effect on many people).

ep·i·der·mis /£ˌep·ɪˈdɜː·mɪs, $-ˈdɜr-/ *n* [C/U] *specialized* the thin outer layer of the skin

ep·i·dur·al /£ˌep·ɪˈdjʊə·rəl, $-ˈdʊr·əl/ *n* [C] *medical* the putting of an ANAESTHETIC (= substance which blocks feelings) into the nerves in a person's lower back with a special needle in order to prevent feelings of pain • *They gave my wife an epidural when she was giving birth.*

ep·i·glot·tis /£ˌep·ɪˈglɒt·ɪs, $-ˈglɑː·t̬ɪs/ *n* [C] *specialized* a small flat part at the back of the tongue which closes when you swallow to prevent food from entering the tube which goes to the lungs

ep·i·gram /ˈep·ɪ·græm/ *n* [C] a short saying or poem which expresses an idea cleverly and amusingly, often containing a surprising combination of ideas • *One of Oscar Wilde's most frequently quoted epigrams is "I can resist everything except temptation".*

ep·i·gram·ma·tic /£ˌep·ɪ·grəˈmæt·ɪk, $-ˈmæt̬-/ *adj* • *The play contains a lot of epigrammatic humour.*

ep·i·graph /£ˈep·ɪ·grɑːf, $-græf/ *n* [C] *specialized* a saying or a part of a poem, play or book put at the beginning of a piece of writing to give the reader some idea of what the piece is about • *At the start of 'Zen and the Art of Motorcycle Maintenance' there appears the epigraph 'And what is good, Phaedrus, And what is not good – Need we ask anyone to tell us these things?'*

ep·i·lep·sy /ˈep·ɪ·lep·si/ *n* [U] a condition of the brain which causes a person to lose consciousness for short periods or to move in a violent and uncontrolled way • *She can't drive because she* **suffers from/has** *epilepsy.*

ep·i·lep·tic /ˌep·ɪˈlep·tɪk/ *adj* [not gradable], *n* • *an epileptic fit* • *He takes medication because he's epileptic.* • An epileptic is a person who suffers from epilepsy. [C]

e·pi·logue, *Am also* **ep·i·log** /£ˈep·ɪ·lɒg, $-lɑːg/ *n* [C] a speech or piece of text which is added to the end of a play or book, often giving a short statement about what happens to the characters after the play or book finishes • Compare PROLOGUE.

E·pi·pha·ny HOLY DAY /ɪˈpɪf·ən·i, epˈɪf-/, **e·pi·pha·ny** *n* January 6th, a Christian holy day which, in the Western Church, celebrates the coming of the three MAGI (= important visitors) to see the baby Jesus Christ, and in the Eastern Church, the baptism of Christ

e·pi·pha·ny UNDERSTANDING /ɪˈpɪf·ən·i, epˈɪf-/ *n* [U] *literary* the experience of suddenly understanding or becoming aware of something that is very important to you • *The moment of epiphany happens in the last scene when our hero suddenly realizes who his mother is.*

e·pis·co·pal /ɪˈpɪs·kə·pəl/ *adj* [not gradable] *fml* of a BISHOP (= high ranking priest), or of a church which is directed by bishops • The **Episcopal Church** refers to part of the Anglican Church, esp. in Scotland and the US.

E·pi·sco·pa·li·an /ɪˌpɪs·kəˈpeɪ·li·ən/ *adj* [not gradable], *n* [C] • *He is (an) Episcopalian* (= belongs to the Episcopal church).

ep·is·ode EVENT /£ˈep·ɪ·səʊd, $-soʊd/ *n* [C] a single event or group of related events • *This latest episode in the fraud scandal has shocked a lot of people.* • *The drugs, the divorce and the depression – it's an episode in his life that he wants to forget.* • Ⓙ

ep·is·od·ic /£ˌep·ɪˈsɒd·ɪk, $-ˈsɑː·dɪk/ *adj fml* • Something which is episodic happens only occasionally and not regularly: *The war between these two countries has been long drawn out and episodic.*

ep·is·ode PART OF STORY /£ˈep·ɪ·səʊd, $-soʊd/ *n* [C] one of the single parts into which a story is divided, esp. when it is broadcast on the television or radio • *Tonight at 9 o'clock we have the first of five episodes of a new serial called 'The Londoner'.* • Ⓙ

ep·is·od·ic /£ˌep·ɪˈsɒd·ɪk, $-ˈsɑː·dɪk/ *adj fml* • *The film uses an episodic structure to show us various stages in the poet's life.*

e·pis·tle /ɪˈpɪs·l̩/ *n* [C] *fml or humorous* a letter • *(humorous) Many thanks for your* **lengthy** *epistle which arrived in this morning's post.* • An Epistle is one of the letters written to the early Christians by the APOSTLES (= the first followers of Jesus Christ).

e·pis·to·la·ry /£ɪˈpɪs·təl·ər·i, $-t̬əl·er-/ *adj fml or literary* • *Laclos' 'Les Liaisons Dangereuses' is an epistolary* **novel** (= a book in the form of a group of letters).

ep·i·taph /£ˈep·ɪ·tɑːf, $-tæf/ *n* [C] a short piece of writing or a poem about a dead person, esp. one written on their GRAVESTONE (= the stone which shows the place where they were buried) • *The epitaph read 'Loving father of Emily, Jane and Charlotte'.* • *(fig.) "You just can't say 'no' to a request for help, can you!" "I know, 'Yes, I'll do it' will be my epitaph* (= what I will be remembered for)*!"*

ep·i·thet /ˈep·ɪ·θet/ *n* [C] *fml or literary* an adjective added to a person's name or a descriptive phrase used instead of it, usually to criticize or praise them • *The opera-singer's 104-kilo frame has earned him the epithet of 'Man Mountain' in the press.* • *Few people would apply the epithet 'dynamic' to the new project leader.*

e·pi·to·me /£ɪˈpɪt·ə·mi, $-ˈpɪt̬-/ *n* [U] **the epitome** the typical or highest example of a stated quality, as shown by a particular person or thing • *Her parents regard flying first-class as the epitome* **of** *extravagance, even though they can afford it.*

e·pi·tom·ize *obj, Br and Aus usually* **-ise** /£ɪˈpɪt·ə·maɪz, $-ˈpɪt̬-/ *v* [T] • *With little equipment and unsuitable footwear, she epitomizes* (= is a typical example of) *the inexperienced and unprepared mountain walker.*

e·poch /£ˈiː·pɒk, $-pɑːk/ *n* [C] *pl* **epochs** *fml or literary* a long period of time, esp. one in which there are new advances and great change • *The president said that his country was moving into a new epoch which would be one of lasting peace.* • An event might be described as **epoch-making** if it has a great effect on the future: *The landing on the moon was regarded as epoch-making/an epoch-making event but somehow failed to be as significant as was expected.* • LP **Periods of time**

ep·on·y·mous /£ɪˈpɒn·ɪ·məs, $-ˈpɑː·nɪ-/ *adj* [before n; not gradable] *literary* (esp. of characters in books, plays, etc.) having the same name as the title, or (of titles and names of objects) having the same name as the person who produced them • *Tom Jones is the eponymous* **hero** *of Henry Fielding's novel 'Tom Jones'.* • *He took the role of the eponymous detective in long-running series Columbo.* • *The Australian rock-star released his eponymous debut album earlier this month.*

ep·o·nym /ˈep·ə·nɪm/ *n* [C] *fml* • An eponym is the name of an object or activity which is also the name of the person who first produced the object or did the activity: *Boycott, braille and diesel are examples of eponyms.*

e·pox·y (res·in) /£ɪˈpɒk·si, $-ˈpɑːk-/ *n* [U] a type of strong glue for sticking things together and covering surfaces • *I need a very strong glue so I'm using epoxy (resin).*

e·pox·y *obj* /£ɪˈpɒk·si, $-ˈpɑːk-/ *v* [T] *Am infml* • *I epoxied* (= stuck together) *the broken chair.*

Ep·som salts /ˈep·səm/ *n* [U] a bitter white powder which people mix with water and drink so that they can excrete the contents of their bowels more easily, or *(esp. Am)* which is used to wash an injury to help reduce swelling

eq·uab·le /ˈek·wə·bl̩/ *adj* not changing suddenly; always being pleasant • *Graham has a fairly equable* **temperament** – *I haven't often seen him really angry.* • *The south of the country enjoys an equable* **climate** *where it is rarely too hot and never too cold.*

eq·uab·ly /ˈek·wə·bli/ *adv* • *As a manager she deals with problems reasonably and equably, never losing her temper.*

e·qual SAME /ˈiː·kwəl/ *adj* the same in amount, number or size, or the same in importance and deserving the same treatment • *All people are equal, deserving the same rights as each other.* • *Both political parties have equal reason to be concerned, since neither is popular with the people.* • *They've got a long way to go before they achieve equal* **pay/status** *for men and women.* • *When the company closed, she lost her job and was given a pay-off equal* **to** *one year's salary.* • *One litre is equal* **to** *1·76 imperial pints.* • *One box may look bigger than the other, but in fact they are roughly* (= almost) *equal* **in** *volume.* • **Equal opportunity** (also **equal opportunities**) refers to the principle of treating all people the same, and not being influenced by a person's sex, race, religion, etc. when education, jobs, etc. are being decided on: *We arrange for girls and boys to have equal opportunity/opportunities to study all subjects.* ○ *The advert said 'We are an equal opportunities employer'.* ○ *We have an equal opportunities policy.* • *"All animals are equal but some are more equal than others"* (George Orwell *Animal Farm*, 1945) • *"We hold these truths to be self-evident, that all men are created equal, that they are endowed by their creator with certain inalienable rights ..."* (from the American Declaration of Independence, 4th July 1776)

e·qual /ˈiː·kwəl/ *n* [C] • *The good thing about her as a boss is that she treats us all as equals.* • *Throughout her* *marriage she never considered her husband as her intellectual equal.* • *As an all-round athlete he* **has no equal** (= no-one else is as good).

e·qual /ˈiː·kwəl/ *v* [not *be equalling*] **-ll-** or *Am usually* **-l-** • *We raised over $500 for charity last year and we're hoping to equal that this year.* [T] • *Sixteen ounces equals one pound.* [L only + n] • *In mathematics, equals can be written as the symbol (=): 10 + 10 = 20 means ten plus ten equals twenty.* [L only + n] • LP› **Mathematics**

e·qual·i·ty /£ɪˈkwɒl·ɪ·ti, $-ˈkwɑː·lə·t̬i/ *n* [U] • Equality often refers to the right of different groups of people to have a similar social position and receive the same treatment, regardless of their apparent differences: *I believe in equality between the sexes.* ○ *He fought very hard in his lifetime to achieve* **racial equality**.

e·qual·ize *(obj), Br and Aus usually* **-ise** /ˈiː·kwə·laɪz/ *v* • *They are putting pressure on the government to equalize* (= bring to the same level) *state pension ages between men and women.* [T] • *(Br and Aus)* In a sport such as football, to equalize (*Am* **tie**) is to get the point that brings your score to the same as that of the other team: *Italy were winning 3-2 until the last minute of the game when Spain managed to equalize.* [I]

e·qual·iz·a·tion, *Br and Aus usually* **-i·sa·tion** /ˌiː·kwə·laɪˈzeɪ·ʃən/ *n* [U]

e·qual·iz·er, *Br and Aus usually* **-iser** /£ˈiː·kwə·laɪ·zər, $-zɚ/ *n* [C] *Br and Aus* • In sports such as football, an equalizer refers to a point which gives both teams the same score: *He* **scored** *an equalizer during the closing minutes of the match.*

e·qual·ly /ˈiː·kwə·li/ *adj* • *You looked equally nice in both dresses – I wouldn't know which one to advise you to buy.* • *The inheritance money was shared equally among the three sisters.* • *(fml) The teacher must provide for the quick learners in the class but equally* (= also to the same degree) *she or he must teach those who learn at a slower rate.* • (I)

e·qual ABLE /ˈiː·kwəl/ *adj* [after v; always + *to*] *fml* skilled or brave enough for a difficult duty or piece of work • *It's a challenging job but I'm sure you'll* **prove** *equal* **to** *it.* • *Is he equal* **to the task**?

e·qua·ni·mi·ty /£ˌek·wəˈnɪm·ɪ·ti, $-t̬i/ *n* [U] *fml* calmness and self-control, esp. after a shock or disappointment or in a difficult situation • *He received the news of his mother's death* **with** *remarkable equanimity.* • *He did not view the prospect of three years working abroad* **with** *equanimity.* • *Three years after the tragedy she has only just begun to regain her equanimity.*

e·quate *(obj)* /ɪˈkweɪt/ *v* to consider as the same, or to connect in your mind • *He complained that there was a tendency to equate right-wing politics* **with** *self-interest.* [T] • Equate **to** means to be the same in amount, number or size: *The price of such goods in those days equates* **to** (= is the same as) *about $50 a kilo at current prices.* [I]

e·qua·tion /ɪˈkweɪ·ʒən/ *n* [U] • *There is a tendency in films to* **make** *the equation* **between** (= to connect) *violence and excitement.*

e·qua·tion /ɪˈkweɪ·ʒən/ *n* [C] a mathematical statement that two amounts, or two symbols or groups of symbols representing an amount, are equal, or *(fig.)* a difficult problem which can only be understood if all the different influences are considered • *In the equation 3x – 3 = 15, x = 6.* • *(fig.) Managing the economy is a complex equation* **of** *controlling inflation and reducing unemployment.* • *(fig.) Closing the factory would reduce pollution, but* **the other side** *of the equation is that* (= the other result is that) *a lot of people would lose their jobs.* • LP› **Mathematics**

e·qua·tor /£ɪˈkweɪ·tər, $-t̬ɚ/ *n* [U] an imaginary line drawn around the middle of the Earth an equal distance from the North Pole and the South Pole • **The** *equator runs through parts of South America and Africa.* • *Singapore* **is/lies on** *the Equator.*

e·qua·tor·i·al /£ˌek·wəˈtɔː·ri·əl, $-ˈtɔːr·i-/ *adj* • *equatorial Africa* • *The equatorial climate of the Amazonian rain forests is hot and wet.*

e·quer·ry /£ˈek·wə·ri, $-wɚ·i/ *n* [C] an officer who works for a particular member of a royal family to help them in their official duties • *He was appointed as an equerry* **to** *the Queen Mother.*

e·ques·tri·an /ɪˈkwes·tri·ən/ *adj* [not gradable] connected with the riding of horses • *They plan to hold the Olympics' equestrian* **events** *in another part of the city.* • *They erected an equestrian* **statue** *of the Prince* (= a statue of the Prince on a horse.)

e·ques·tri·an /ɪˈkwes·tri·ən/ *n* [C] *fml* • An equestrian is a person who rides horses, esp. as a job or very skilfully: *an experienced equestrian*

e·qui– /ˈek·wɪ-/ *combining form* equal or equally

e·qui·dis·tant /ˌek·wɪˈdɪs·tənt, ˌiː·kwɪ-/ *adj* [not gradable] equally distant or close • *London is roughly equidistant* **from** *Oxford and Cambridge.* • *I don't mind which of the three routes we take – they're equidistant anyway.*

e·qui·lat·er·al /£ˌiː·kwɪˈlæt·ər·əl, £ˌek·wɪ-, $-læt̬-/ *adj* [not gradable] (esp. of triangles), having all sides the same length • *an equilateral triangle* • PIC› **Shapes**

e·qui·lib·ri·um /ˌiː·kwɪˈlɪb·ri·əm, ˌek·wɪ-/ *n* [U] *slightly fml* a state of balance • *The disease destroys much of the inner-ear, disturbing the animal's equilibrium.* • *The resignation of the president upset the country's economic equilibrium.* • Equilibrium can also be a state of mental calmness: *Yoga is said to restore one's inner* (= mental) *equilibrium.*

e·quine /ˈek·waɪn/ *adj fml* connected with horses, or appearing similar to a horse • *equine flu* • *The portraits showed an aristocratic family with long equine faces.*

e·qui·nox /£ˈek·wɪ·nɒks, $-nɑːks/ *n* [C] either of the two occasions in the year when day and night are of equal length and the sun is directly above at the equator • *the spring/autumn equinox* • Compare SOLSTICE.

e·qui·noc·ti·al /£ˌek·wɪˈnɒk·ʃəl, $-ˈnɑːk-/ *adj* [not gradable] *specialized* • *equinoctial gales*

e·quip *obj* PROVIDE /ɪˈkwɪp/ *v* [T] **-pp-** to provide (a person or a place) with objects that are necessary for a particular purpose • *It's going to cost $4 million to equip the hospital.* • *All the police officers were equipped* **with** *shields to defend themselves against the rioters.* • *You'll need to equip yourselves* **with** *some warm clothes and waterproof shoes to walk in this weather!*

e·quipped /ɪˈkwɪpt/ *adj* • *He's got the best equipped kitchen I've ever seen – there's every imaginable cooking utensil.* • *Their schools are very poorly equipped.*

e·quip·ment /ɪˈkwɪp·mənt/ *n* [U] • Equipment is the set of necessary tools, clothing etc. for a particular purpose: *office equipment* ○ *camping equipment* ○ *kitchen equipment* ○ *a basic piece of household equipment* ○ *electrical equipment* • *The soldiers had to carry their equipment on their backs for miles.* • *(fml)* Equipment is also the act or an occasion of providing a person or a place with the objects necessary for a particular purpose: *We received a price estimate for alteration and equipment of the building.* • LP› **Switching on and off**

e·quip *obj* PREPARE /ɪˈkwɪp/ *v* [T] **-pp-** to prepare (someone) for dealing with a particular situation by educating them, giving them skills or strengthening them mentally • *The course aims to equip people* **with** *the skills necessary for a job in this technological age.* • *A degree in the history of art is very nice but it doesn't exactly equip you* **for** *many jobs.*

e·quipped /ɪˈkwɪpt/ *adj* • *Many consider him the leader best equipped* **to** *be prime minister.* [+ to infinitive] • *Not being a specialist in the subject I don't feel very well-equipped* **to** *answer such questions.* [+ *to* infinitive]

e·qui·ta·ble /£ˈek·wɪ·tə·bl̩, $-t̬ə-/ *adj fml* fair and reasonable; treating everyone in the same way • *There's a great need for a more equitable tax system.*

e·qui·tab·ly /£ˈek·wɪ·tə·bli, $-t̬ə-/ *adv fml* • *If the law is to be effective it must be applied equitably.*

e·qui·ty /£ˈek·wɪ·ti, $-t̬i/ *n* [U] *fml* • *Ultimately, their aim is for a society based on equity and social justice.* • *(law)* In English-speaking countries, equity is also a system of justice which allows a fair judgment of a case where the laws that already exist are not satisfactory.

e·qui·ty /£ˈek·wɪ·ti, $-t̬i/ *n specialized* one of the equal parts into which the value of a company is divided; (a set of) shares • *He sold his equity in the company last year.* [U] • *He was prepared to commit $1 billion in equity to a purchase.* [U] • *There was shift in investments out of equities and into more liquid assets.* [C] • *The rights give holders the opportunity to purchase additional equity interests in the company at a big discount under certain conditions.* • *NBC had agreed to be an equity partner in the purchase of the movie studio.* • *It has a 40% equity stake in a huge and expanding shopping centre.*

e·qui·va·lent /ɪˈkwɪv·əl·ənt/ *adj* having the same amount, value, purpose, qualities, etc. • *She's doing the equivalent job in the new company but for more money.* • *Is $50 equivalent* **to** *about £30?* • *This whole sandwich has the equivalent number of calories as a small chocolate bar.*

e·qui·va·lent /ɪ'kwɪv·ᵊl·ᵊnt/ *n* [C] • *There is no English equivalent* **for** *'bon appetit' so we have adopted the French expression.* • *Ten thousand people a year die of the disease – that's the equivalent* **of** *the population of this town.* • *What's the equivalent* **of** *fifty pounds in dollars?*

e·qui·va·lence /ɪ'kwɪv·ᵊl·ᵊnts/ *n* [U] *fml* • *There's a general equivalence between the two concepts.*

e·qui·vo·cal /ɪ'kwɪv·ə·kᵊl/ *adj fml* (of statements) unclear and seeming to have two opposing meanings, or (of actions or ways of behaving) confusing and able to be understood in two different ways • *His words to the press were deliberately equivocal – he didn't deny the reports but neither did he confirm them.*

e·qui·vo·cal·ly /ɪ'kwɪv·ə·kli/ *adv fml*

e·qui·vo·cate /ɪ'kwɪv·ə·keɪt/ *v* [I] *fml* • Someone who equivocates speaks in a way that is intentionally unclear and confusing to other people, esp. to hide the truth: *She accused the minister of equivocating, claiming that he had deliberately avoided telling the public how bad the problem really was.* • ⓘ

e·qui·vo·ca·tion /ɪˌkwɪv·ə'keɪ·ʃᵊn/ *n* [U] *fml* • *He answered openly and honestly without hesitation or equivocation.*

ER [THE QUEEN] /'iːˌɑːʳ/ *n* [U] *abbreviation for* Elizabeth Regina, Queen Elizabeth II of England (1952-)

ER [HOSPITAL] *n* [U] *Am abbreviation for* **emergency room**, see at EMERGENCY • *Your wife's in ER right now.*

er [SOUND] /£ɜːʳ, $ɜːr/ *exclamation* the sound that people frequently make when they pause in the middle of what they are saying or pause before they speak, often because they are deciding what to say • *"What time shall we meet this evening?" "Er, eightish, is that all right?"* • *"Is he handsome?" "Er, well – he's got a nice friendly sort of face though he's not exactly handsome."*

–er [PERFORMER] /£-əʳ, $-ɚ/, **–or** *combining form* added to some verbs to form nouns which refer to people or things that do that particular activity • *a singer* (= a person who sings) • *a swimmer* (= a person who swims) • *a teacher* (= a person who teaches) • *an office worker* (= a person who works in an office) • *a hairdryer* (= a machine that dries hair) • *a dishwasher* (= a machine or person that washes dishes) • *an actor* (= a person who acts) • *a navigator* (= a person who shows the way) • *a prospector* (= a person who searches for esp. gold) • [LP]› **Combining forms**

–er [SPECIALIST] /£-əʳ, $-ɚ/ *combining form* added to the names of particular subjects to form nouns which refer to people who have knowledge about or are studying that subject • *a philosopher* (= a person who knows about/studies PHILOSOPHY) • *an astronomer* (= a person who knows about/studies ASTRONOMY) • *a geographer* (= a person who knows about/studies GEOGRAPHY)

–er [FROM A PLACE] /£-əʳ, $-ɚ/ *combining form* added to the names of particular places to form nouns referring to people who come from those places • *a Londoner* (= a person who comes from London) • *a northerner* (= a person who comes from the north) • *the islanders* (= the people who live on an island)

–er [INVOLVED WITH] /£-əʳ, $-ɚ/ *combining form* added to nouns or adjectives to form nouns referring to people who are connected or involved with that particular thing • *a pensioner* (= a person who receives a PENSION) • *first graders* (= children who are in the first GRADE of an American school)

–er [CHARACTERISTICS] /£-əʳ, $-ɚ/ *combining form* added to nouns to form nouns or adjectives referring to people or things which have those particular characteristics • *a double-decker* (= a bus with two DECKS) • *a big-spender* (= someone who spends a lot of money)

e·ra /£'ɪə·rə, $'ɪr·ə/ *n* [C] a period of time that is marked by particular events or developments • *the Reagan era* • *a* **bygone** (= past) *era* • *the post-war era* • *The president is taking his country into a new political era with a package of radical reforms.* • *They had worked for peace during the long era* **of** *conflict.* • *These songs* **ushered in** *a new musical era.* • *The fall of the Berlin wall marked* **the end of an era.** • [LP]› **Periods of time**

e·ra·di·cate *obj* /ɪ'ræd·ɪ·keɪt/ *v* [T] *fml* to get rid of completely or destroy (a disease, problem or anything bad) • *The government claims to be doing all it can to eradicate corruption.* • *The disease which once claimed millions of lives in the country has now been eradicated.*

e·ra·di·ca·tion /ɪˌræd·ɪ'keɪ·ʃᵊn/ *n* [U] • *The ultimate aim, stressed the leader, was the complete eradication of social injustice.*

e·rase *obj* [DESTROY] /£ɪ'reɪz, $-'reɪs/ *v* [T] to destroy or remove completely • *Time had caused his* **memories/doubts** *to fade but it hadn't erased them.* • *All trace of the deal has been erased* **from** *the record.* • *Share prices closed little changed, although some early* **gains** *were erased.* • *The city sold property to erase a huge budget* **deficit**.

e·ra·sure /£ɪ'reɪ·ʒəʳ, $-ʒɚ/ *n* [C] *esp. Am* • *There are a few gaps in the text where I* **made** *some erasures.* • [PIC]› **Stationery**

e·rase *obj* [RUB AWAY] *esp. Am* /ɪ'reɪz/, *Br usually* **rub out** *v* [T] to remove (esp. a pencil mark) by rubbing • *It's written in pencil so you can just erase anything that is incorrect.*

e·ras·er /£ɪ'reɪ·zəʳ, $-'reɪ·sɚ/, *Br and Aus usually* **rub·ber** *n* [C] • An eraser is a small piece of rubber used to remove the marks made by a pencil: *If you draw or write in pencil you can always rub out your mistakes with an eraser.*

ere /£eəʳ, $er/ *prep, conjunction poetic or old use* before • *I shall be back ere nightfall.*

e·rect *obj* [BUILD] /ɪ'rekt/ *v* [T] *fml* to build (a building, wall or other structure) • *The war memorial was erected in 1950 in the centre of the park.* • *The soldiers had erected barricades to protect themselves from gunfire.*

e·rec·tion /ɪ'rek·ʃᵊn/ *n* • *(fml)* Erection is the act of building or making a structure: *They approved the erection of an electrified fence around the prison.* [U] ○ *the Walden Erection Company* • *(esp. humorous)* An erection can also be a building: *This splendid if extraordinary erection from the last century is a local landmark.* [C]

e·rect *obj* [MAKE VERTICAL] /ɪ'rekt/ *v* [T] *fml* to put up or raise to a vertical position (a tent, flag or other esp. temporary structure) • *It takes us about half-an-hour to erect our big tent.* • *They erected a marquee to accommodate 500 wedding guests.*

e·rect /ɪ'rekt/ *adj* • If a person is described as erect it means that they stand with their back and neck very straight: *He's very tall and erect for his 78 years.* • When a part of the body, esp. soft tissue, is erect, it is harder and bigger than usual, often pointing out or up: *an erect penis* ○ *erect nipples*

e·rec·tile /£ɪ'rek·taɪl, $-tl̩/ *adj specialized* • Body tissue or parts of the body which are erectile are able to be filled with blood, making them larger and harder than usual: *erectile tissue*

e·rec·tion /ɪ'rek·ʃᵊn/ *n* [C] • When a man has an erection, his penis is temporarily harder and bigger than usual and points up: *to get/have/lose an erection*

er·go /£'ɜː·gəʊ, $'er·goʊ/ *adv* [not gradable] *fml* therefore • *Cars cause pollution, ergo we must find other methods of transport.*

er·go·no·mics /£ˌɜː·gə'nɒm·ɪks, $ˌɜːr·gə'nɑː·mɪks/ *n* [U] the scientific study of people and their working conditions, esp. done in order to improve effectiveness • *A specialist in ergonomics will work with the team designing the production line in our new factory.* • *The ergonomics* (= design and comfort) *of the new office furniture have reduced eyestrain and back problems among the computer users.*

er·go·no·mic /£ˌɜː·gə'nɒm·ɪk, $ˌɜːr·gə'nɑː·mɪk/ *adj* • *ergonomic design/features*

er·go·no·mi·cally /£ˌɜː·gə'nɒm·ɪ·kli, $ˌɜːr·gə'nɑː·mɪ-/ *adv*

ERM /£ˌiː·ɑː'rem, $-ɑːr'em/ *n* [U] **the ERM** *abbreviation for* **Exchange Rate Mechanism**, see at EXCHANGE • Compare ECU; EMS; EMU.

er·mine /£'ɜː·mɪn, $'ɜːr-/ *n* [U] expensive white fur with black spots that is the winter fur of the STOAT (= a small mammal) and is used to decorate formal clothes worn by kings, queens, judges, etc.

e·rode *(obj)* /£ɪ'rəʊd, $-'roʊd/ *v* to rub or be rubbed away gradually • *Wind and rain have eroded the statues into shapeless lumps of stone.* [T] • *The cliffs are eroding* **by/at** *several feet a year.* [I] • *(fig.) His behaviour over the last few months has eroded* (= slowly reduced or destroyed) *my confidence in his judgement.* [T]

e·ro·sion /£ɪ'rəʊ·ʒᵊn, $-'roʊ-/ *n* [U] • *soil erosion* • *coastal erosion*

e·ro·ge·nous /£ɪ'rɒdʒ·ɪ·nəs, $ɪ'rɑː·dʒə-/ *adj* (of areas of the body) especially able to feel sexual pleasure • *erogenous zones*

e·ro·tic /£ɪ'rɒt·ɪk, $-'rɑː·t̬ɪk/ *adj* related to sexual desire and pleasure • *an erotic film* • *erotic feelings* • *an erotic urge* • *erotic dreams*

e·ro·ti·ca /£ɪ'rɒt·ɪ·kə, $-'rɑː·t̬ɪ-/ *n* [U] • *The museum houses a famous collection of nineteenth century erotica*

(= books, pictures, etc. which produce sexual desire and pleasure).

e·ro·ti·cal·ly /£ɪ'rɒt·ɪ·kli, $-'rɑː·t̬ɪ-/ *adv*

e·ro·ti·ci·sm /£ɪ'rɒt·ɪ·sɪ·zᵊm, $-'rɑː·t̬ə-/ *n* [U] • Eroticism is the quality of a picture, book, film, etc. being erotic: *The play's eroticism shocked audiences when it was first performed.*

e·ro·ti·cize *obj, Br and Aus usually* **-ise** /£ɪ'rɒt·ɪ·saɪz, $-'rɑː·t̬ə-/ *v* [T] • *He has a tendency to eroticize* (= consider in a sexual way) *everything.*

err /£ɜːʳ, £eəʳ, $ɜːr, $er/ *v* [I] *fml* to make a mistake or to do something wrong • *He erred in agreeing to her appointment.* • To **err on the side of caution** is to be careful: *Twenty-five people have replied to the invitation but I've erred on the side of caution and put out 30 chairs.* • *(saying)* 'To err is human (to forgive divine)' means it is natural for people to make mistakes.

er·rand /'er·ənd/ *n* [C] a short journey either to take a message or to deliver or collect something • *I'll meet you at six, I've got some errands to* **do/run** *first.* • *The children are old enough now to* **run/go on** *errands* **to** *the shops.* • *(dated)* An **errand boy** is a boy or young man employed by a shop or business to take messages, deliver goods, etc.: *(fig.) "Return those books to the library yourself," she shouted, "I'm not your errand boy* (= servant)*!"* • *(literary)* An **errand of mercy** is an act of bringing help: *They set out on their errand of mercy laden with blankets and hot soup.*

er·rant /'er·ənt/ *adj* [before n] *fml or humorous* behaving wrongly in some way, esp. by leaving home • *an errant husband* • *errant children*

er·ra·ta /£ɪ'rɑː·tə, $-t̬ə/ *pl of fml* ERRATUM • *a list of errata*

er·ra·tic /£ɪ'ræt·ɪk, $-'ræt̬-/ *adj* irregular, uncertain or without organization in movement or behaviour • *He drove in an erratic course down the road.* • *She can be very erratic, one day she is friendly and the next she'll hardly speak to you.* • Ⓘ

er·ra·ti·cal·ly /£ɪ'ræt·ɪ·kli, $-'ræt̬-/ *adv* • *He ran erratically through the building.* • *In her study, books were arranged erratically on chairs, tables and shelves.* • *The machine is working erratically – there must be a loose connection.*

er·ra·tum /£ɪ'rɑː·təm, $-t̬əm/ *n* [C] *pl* **errata** /£ɪ'rɑː·tə, $-t̬ə/ *fml* a mistake in something printed such as a book • An **erratum slip** is a piece of paper put into a published book, or something else that is printed, which corrects a single mistake.

er·ro·ne·ous /£ɪ'rəʊ·ni·əs, $-'roʊ-/ *adj fml* wrong or false • *He held the erroneous belief/made the erroneous statement/had the erroneous impression that the more it cost the better it must be.*

er·ro·ne·ous·ly /£ɪ'rəʊ·ni·ə·sli, $-'roʊ-/ *adv*

er·ror /£'er·əʳ, $-ɚ/ *n* a mistake • *He admitted that he'd made an error.* [C] • *The letter contains a number of typing errors, which I must correct.* [C] • *Human error has been blamed for the air crash.* [U] • *I'm sorry – I took your umbrella* **in** *error* (= by mistake). [U] • *With something as delicate as brain surgery, there is little* **margin for** *error* (= you must not make mistakes). [U] • *(fml or humorous) He was always trying to borrow money, but now he* **sees the error of** *his* **ways** (= understands that his behaviour was wrong). • An **error of judgment** is a wrong decision: *Not telling the staff before they read the bad news in the papers was an error of judgment.*

er·satz /£'eə·zæts, $'er·zɑːts/ *adj* [not gradable] *disapproving* used instead of something else, usually because the other thing is too expensive or rare • *I'm allowed to eat ersatz chocolate made from carob beans, but it's a poor substitute for the real thing.*

Erse /£ɜːs, $ɜːrs/ *n* [U] the GAELIC language esp. as spoken in Ireland

erst·while /£'ɜːst·waɪl, $'ɜːrst-/ *adj* [before n; not gradable] *fml* previous • *My erstwhile employer has now gone out of business.*

e·ru·dite /'er·ʊ·daɪt/ *adj fml* having or containing a lot of specialist knowledge • *He's the author of an erudite book on Scottish history.*

e·ru·di·tion /ˌer·ʊ'dɪʃ·ᵊn/ *n* [U] *fml* • *a work of great erudition* • *a display of erudition*

e·rupt /ɪ'rʌpt/ *v* [I] to explode or burst out suddenly • *At the end of a hot summer, violence erupted in the inner cities.* • *A new political party erupted onto the scene.* • *Since the* **volcano** *last erupted, many houses have been built in a dangerous position on its slopes.* • *Two days after he'd been exposed to the substance, a painful rash erupted* (= suddenly appeared) *on his neck.* • *Her back erupted* **in** *small red spots.* • *(specialized) Your* **wisdom teeth** *are starting to erupt* (= grow through the skin).

e·rup·tion /ɪ'rʌp·ʃᵊn/ *n* [C] • *a volcanic eruption* • *Because of the imposition of martial law there was a violent eruption of anti-government feeling.*

es·ca·late *(obj)* /'es·kə·leɪt/ *v* to make or become greater or more serious • *The decision to escalate UN involvement has been taken in the hopes of a swift end to the hostilities.* [T] • *His financial problems escalated after he became unemployed.* [I] • *Social problems have been escalating in the town since the steel works closed.* [I] • *The escalating rate of inflation will almost certainly bring escalating prices.*

es·ca·la·tion /ˌes·kə'leɪ·ʃᵊn/ *n* • *It's difficult to explain the recent escalation* **in/of** *violent crime.* [U] • *Taking battleships into the area is another escalation in what seems to be a build-up to war.* [C]

es·ca·la·tor /£'es·kə·leɪ·təʳ, $-t̬ɚ/ *n* [C] a set of stairs moved up or down by electric power on which people can stand and be taken from one level of a building to another, esp. in shops, railway stations and airports • *I'll meet you by the* **up/down** *escalator on the second floor.* • *(law)* In a legal agreement, an **escalator (clause)** is a part that provides for the rise or fall of pay, prices, etc.: *Under the escalator clause of my mortgage agreement, my payments decreased when interest rates were lowered.* ○ *The new contract has an escalator tying pay increases to the cost-of-living index.*

es·ca·lope /£'es·kæ·ləp, $ˌes·kə'loʊp/ *n* [C] a thin boneless piece of meat • *veal/turkey escalopes*

es·ca·pade /'es·kə·peɪd/ *n* [C] an act involving some danger, risk or excitement because it is different from usual or expected behaviour • *One of their escapades was to paint anti-war symbols onto a nuclear submarine.* • *Her latest escapade was to camp outside a department store on the night before the sale.* • Ⓔ

es·cape *(obj)* /ɪ'skeɪp/ *v* to get free (from), or to avoid • *Two prisoners have escaped.* [I] • *A lion has escaped* **from** *its cage.* [I] • *She was lucky to escape serious injury.* [T] • *He* **narrowly** (= only just) *escaped a fine.* [T] • *I'm afraid your* **name** *escapes me/has escaped me* (= I have forgotten your name). [T] • *Nothing important escapes her* **notice/attention.** [T] • *We won't escape paying the commercial rate.* [+ v-*ing*] • **There's no escaping the fact that** (= It is certain that) *we won't be able to complete these orders without extra staff.* • *(specialized)* If you escape **from/out of** a particular screen on a computer or a computer process, you leave it or interrupt it: *Escape out of this window and return to the main menu.* ○ *The program was doing strange things, so I escaped from it.* • Ⓙ

es·cape /ɪ'skeɪp/ *n* • *He* **made** *his escape* (= He escaped) *on the back of a motorbike.* [C] • *They* **had a narrow** *escape* (= only just avoided injury or death) *when their car crashed.* • *"You will never get away," said the prison-camp commander. "Escape is impossible."* [U] • An escape is also an accidental loss: *an escape of radioactivity* [C] • *(fig.) Romantic novels provide an escape* **from** *reality.* [C] • *We carefully planned our escape* **route.** • **There's no escape** means that there is no way to get out of a place or avoid a situation: *You'll have to do the exam again – there's no escape if you want to continue the course.* • *(specialized)* The **escape key** (*abbreviation* **Esc**) is the key on a computer keyboard which allows you to leave a particular screen and return to the previous one or to interrupt a process: *Press Esc to return to the main menu.* • An **escape hatch** is the part of a SUBMARINE (= a boat that can travel under water) through which people can leave when the submarine is under water. • *(specialized)* The **escape velocity** of an object is the lowest speed it must have to escape from the GRAVITY (= the force which attracts objects of any mass) of a planet such as the Earth, and fly out into space.

es·ca·pee /ɪˌskeɪ'piː/ *n* [C] • *The escapees* (= people who have escaped) *were recaptured after three days on the run.*

es·cap·i·sm /ɪ'skeɪ·pɪ·zᵊm/ *n* [U] the avoidance of an unpleasant or boring life, esp. by thinking, reading, etc. about more exciting but impossible activities • *These adventure films are pure escapism.* • *For many people going on holiday is a form of escapism.*

es·ca·pist /ɪ'skeɪ·pɪst/ *n* [C], *adj* • *escapist literature*

es·ca·pol·o·gy /£ˌes·kə'pɒl·ə·dʒi, $-'pɑː·lə-/ *n* [U] the activity of escaping from chains, boxes, etc. usually as part of an entertainment

es·ca·po·lo·gist /ˌes·kə'pɒl·ə·dʒɪst, $-'pɑː·lə-/, *Am usually* **es·cape art·ist** *n* [C]

es·carp·ment /£ɪ'skɑːp·mənt, $-'skɑːrp-/ *n* [C] a steep slope or cliff, such as one which marks the edge of a range of hills

es·cha·tol·o·gy /£ˌes·kə'tɒl·ə·dʒi, $-'tɑː·lə-/ *n* [U] *specialized* (the study of) religious beliefs connected with the end of the world

es·chew *obj* /ɪs'tʃuː/ *v* [T] *fml* to avoid (something) intentionally, or to give up (something) • *We won't have discussions with this group unless they eschew violence.*

es·cort /£'es·kɔːt, $-kɔːrt, -'-/ *v, n* (to go with someone or something as) a helper, guard or companion • *People on the tour will be escorted by an expert on archaeology.* [T] • *The police escorted her to the airport.* [T] • *Several little boats escorted the sailing ship into the harbour.* [T] • *Do you know who will be escorting her to the ball?* [T] • *He left the court* **under** *police escort.* [U] • *My escort during my visit was one of the research workers.* [C] • *Soldiers and police officers often have to undertake escort* **duty***, such as guarding important people.* • An escort is also someone, often a young woman, who is paid to go out socially with other people, esp. to be friendly to them: *She describes herself as an escort, but really she's a prostitute.* [C] • An **escort agency/service** is a business that supplies people who work as escorts.

es·crow /£'es·krəʊ, $-kroʊ/ *n* [U] *specialized* an agreement between two people or organizations in which money or property is kept by a third person or organization until a particular condition is completed • *The money was placed* **in** *escrow.* • *Details of the escrow* **agreement** *haven't yet been finalized.*

Es·ki·mo /£'es·kɪ·məʊ, $-kə·moʊ/ *n pl* **Eskimos** or **Eskimo** a member of a group of people who live in the very cold northern areas of N America, Russia and Greenland, or the language they speak • *He lived with/among Eskimos for ten years.* [C] • *She speaks Eskimo.* [U] • *The museum does have an expert in Eskimo customs.* • In Canada, Eskimos are called INUIT. • Compare INUIT.

ESL /ˌiː·es'el/ *n* [U] *abbreviation for* English as a second language (=English as taught to people whose main language is not English and who live in a country in which English is an official or important language)

e·so·pha·gus /£ɪ'sɒf·ə·gəs, $-'sɑː·fə-/ *n* [C] *esp. Am for* OESOPHAGUS

e·so·ter·ic /£ˌiː·səʊ'ter·ɪk, $ˌes·ə-/ *adj* very unusual; understood or liked by only a small number of people, esp. those with special knowledge • *He has an esoteric collection of old toys and games.* • *(disapproving or humorous) She has a rather esoteric* **taste** *in clothes.*

ESP /ˌiː·es'piː/ *n* [U] *abbreviation for* **extrasensory perception**, see at EXTRASENSORY

esp /esp/ *adv abbreviation for* ESPECIALLY

es·pe·cial /ɪ'speʃ·ᵊl/ *adj* [before n] *fml* special • *an especial friend of mine* • *especial difficulties*

es·pe·cial·ly /ɪ'speʃ·ᵊl·i/, **spe·cial·ly** *adv* very (much); particularly; for a particular reason • *I'm especially pleased to meet you because I've heard so much about you.* • *She's not especially interested in sport.* • *I chose this especially for your new house.* • *They invited her to speak especially because of her experience in inner cities.* • [LP]〉 **Very, completely**

Es·pe·ran·to /£ˌes·pᵊr'æn·təʊ, $-pə'ræn·toʊ/ *n* [U] an artificial language, made by combining features of several European languages, intended as a form of international communication

es·pi·on·age /'es·pi·ə·nɑːʒ/ *n* [U] the discovering of secrets, esp. political or military information of another country or the industrial information of a business • *military/industrial espionage* • See also SPY [SECRET PERSON]. • [LP]〉 **Crimes and criminals**

es·pla·nade /£'es·plə·neɪd, $-nɑːd/ *n* [C] *dated* a wide level path for walking along, often by the sea

es·pouse *obj* /es'paʊz/ *v* [T] *fml* to become involved with or support (an activity or opinion) • *Vegetarianism is one cause she does not espouse.*

es·pous·al /es'paʊ·zᵊl/ *n* [U] *fml* • *The council's espousal* **of** *a nuclear-free policy has met with a mixed response.* • *Espousal* **of** *such liberal ideas won't make her very popular around here.*

es·pres·so /£es'pres·əʊ, $-oʊ/ *n pl* **espressos** (a cup of) strong coffee made by forcing steam through crushed coffee beans and served without milk • *Do you like espresso?* [U] • *Would you prefer an espresso* (=a cup of this coffee) *or a cappuccino?* [C]

es·prit de corps /£esˌpriː·də'kɔːʳ, $-'kɔːr/ *n* [U] *fml* the feelings, such as pride and loyalty, shared by members of a group of people • *His leadership kept the team's esprit de corps intact during difficult periods.*

e·spy *obj* /es'paɪ/ *v* [T] *fml or dated* to see (esp. something a long distance away) suddenly or unexpectedly • *She suddenly espied someone waving at her from the window.*

Esq *n* [after n] *esp. Br dated or fml abbreviation for* ESQUIRE (=a title added after a man's name on documents, envelopes, etc., instead of putting 'Mr' before it) • *This envelope is addressed to P. J. Ellis Esq.* • *(Am)* Esq. is usually used only after the full name of a man or woman who is a lawyer: *Address it to my lawyer, Steven A. Neil, Esq./Gloria Neil, Esq.*

-esque /-esk/ *combining form* like or in the style of • *Dali-esque* • *Leonardo-esque* • *Working there was like being trapped in a Kafkaesque nightmare.* • [LP]〉 **Stress in pronunciation**

es·say [WRITING] *Br and Aus* /'es·eɪ/, *Am* **pa·per** *n* [C] a short piece of writing on a particular subject, esp. one done by students as part of the work for a course • *For homework I want you to write an essay* **on** *endangered species.* • *His last book was a collection of literary/political essays.*

es·say·ist /'es·eɪ·ɪst/ *n* [C] • *a political essayist*

es·say *obj* [ATTEMPT] /e'seɪ/ *v* [T] *dated* to attempt (something); to try to do (something) • *The procedure was first essayed in 1923.*

es·sence [SMELL/TASTE] /'es·ᵊnts/ *n* [C] a chemical or group of chemicals which produce the strong smell or taste of particular plants and which can be removed and used to flavour food or make medicines, PERFUME, etc. • *vanilla essence* • *essence of violets*

es·sence [IMPORTANCE] /'es·ᵊnts/ *n* [U] the main feature or most important quality • **The** *essence* **of** *his argument was that education should continue throughout life.* • **In essence** means that what follows is a brief statement of the main features of a subject: *What he said, in essence, was that he can't support our actions and will resign.* • If something **is of the essence**, either there is not much of it or it is important that the stated thing should be used: *You must apply at once – time is of the essence – next week will be too late.* ○ *In all these negotiations, tact will be of the essence.*

es·sen·tial /ɪ'sen·tʃᵊl/ *adj* necessary; needed • *Government support will be essential if the project is to succeed.* • *Only the ambassador and five essential staff will remain in the embassy.* • *There is essential work to be done before the building can be re-occupied.* • *Maintaining standards is essential* **to** *our good reputation.* • *Water is essential* **for/to** *living things.* • **It** *is essential* **(that)** *our prices remain competitive.* [+ (*that*) clause] • *For the experiment to be valid, it is essential* **to** *record the data accurately.* [+ *to* infinitive] • *Cooperation is an essential* **element/ingredient** *in any marriage.* • *Some theorists would say that exams are not an essential* **part** *of education.* • An **essential oil** is an oil, usually with a strong smell, which is taken from a plant and is used to make PERFUME, or for rubbing into a person's body during MASSAGE: *Lavender, peppermint, and jasmine are essential oils which are widely available.* ○ *Essential oils are used in aromatherapy to improve physical and mental well-being.* • **Essential services** are basic public needs, such as water, gas and electricity, which are often supplied to people's houses.

es·sen·tial /ɪ'sen·tʃᵊl/ *n* [C usually pl] • Essentials or **the bare** essentials, are basic things, either things you cannot live without or necessary knowledge about a particular subject: *Because I live in a remote village, I regard my car as an essential.* ○ *When we go on holiday, we only take (the bare) essentials.* ○ *This leaflet will give you the essentials* **of** *how to use the word processor.*

es·sen·tial·ly /ɪ'sen·tʃᵊl·i/ *adv* [not gradable] • *He's essentially* (=mainly) *a farmer but he also writes novels.* • *Essentially I need to know* (=What I need to know is) *how many people will be needed and for how long.*

est [JUDGED] *adj abbreviation for* ESTIMATED • *the town of Brownford (est population 14 000)*

Est [STARTED] *adj abbreviation for* ESTABLISHED • *P. R. Jones & Co, Est 1920*

es·tab·lish *(obj)* [START] /ɪ'stæb·lɪʃ/ *v* to start (an activity which will last a long time); to create (something) • *We have decided to establish a new department/system.* [T] • *These methods of working were established in the last century.* [T] • *The company established a close working relationship with a similar firm in France.* [T] • *Some plants take a long time to establish* (=to start growing well after being planted). [I] • *He has established* **himself** *as the leading candidate in the* *election.* [T] • *A* **link** *has been established between violent films and real-life violence.* [T] • In British law, to establish **a precedent** (*Am usually* **set a precedent**) means that when a decision about a particular case has been made it is then likely that other similar cases will be decided in the same way: *The judgment on pension rights has established a precedent.* [T] • An **old-established** or a **long-established** company is one that was started many years ago.

es·tab·lish·ment /ɪˈstæb·lɪʃ·mənt/ *n* [U] • *Since its establishment two years ago, the advice centre has seen over 500 people a week.* • *The establishment* **of** *new areas of employment is a priority.* • See also ESTABLISHMENT.

es·tab·lish *obj* ACCEPT /ɪˈstæb·lɪʃ/ *v* [T] to cause to be accepted in or familiar with a place, position, etc. • *His reputation for carelessness was established long before the latest problems arose.* • *He's established him***self as** *a dependable source of information.* • *After three months we were well established* **in/at** *our new house/new jobs.* • *There are established* (=standard) *procedures for dealing with emergencies.* • The **established church/religion** of a country is its official religion: *In Britain, the Queen is the head of the established church.*

es·tab·lish *obj* DISCOVER /ɪˈstæb·lɪʃ/ *v* [T] *fml* to discover or get proof of (something) • *Before we take any action we must establish the facts/truth.* • *Can you establish* **what** *time she left home/***whether** *she has left home.* [+ *wh-* word] • *We have established* **(that)** *she was born in 1900.* [+ (*that*) clause]

es·tab·lish·ment /ɪˈstæb·lɪʃ·mənt/ *n* a business or other organization, or the place where an organization operates • *an educational/financial/religious establishment* [C] • *We do not permit smoking in this establishment.* [C] • **The establishment** is the important and powerful people who control a country or an organization, esp. those who support the existing situation: *Critics said judges were on the side of the establishment.* [+sing/pl v] ○ *He's an important figure in the local/political establishment.* [+ sing/pl v] • See also **establishment** at ESTABLISH (START).

es·tate PROPERTY /ɪˈsteɪt/ *n* [C] a large area of land in the country which is owned by a family or an organization and is often farmed • *the owner of estates in Scotland* • *estate management* • *It's a typical* **country** *estate with a large house for the owner, farm buildings and estate workers' houses.* • *(law)* A person's estate is everything they own when they die: *She* **left** *her entire estate to her niece.* • *(Br)* An **estate agent** (*Am and Aus* **real estate agent**, *Aus* **real estate broker** or **realtor**) is a person who works for an **estate agency** (*Am* **real estate office/realty office**) which is a business that arranges the selling, renting or management of houses, land and buildings for their owners.

es·tate BUILDINGS /ɪˈsteɪt/ *n* [C] *Br* a group of houses or factories built in a planned way • *a housing estate* • *an industrial estate* (= a group of factories) • *a council estate* (= a large group of houses built by the local government for rent) • PIC〉 **Accommodation**

es·tate STATE /ɪˈsteɪt/ *n* [U] *old use* a state of being • *the holy estate of marriage* • *man's estate* (= adulthood)

es·tate (car) *Br* /ɪˈsteɪt/, *Am and Aus* **sta·tion wag·on** *n* [C] a car with a lot of space behind the back seat and an extra door at the back for loading large items • *I'll bring my bike in the estate.*

es·teem /ɪˈstiːm/ *v* [not *be esteeming*], *n fml* (to have) respect for, or a good opinion of (someone) • *Her work is highly esteemed by all her colleagues.* [T] • *(dated) We did not esteem* (= consider) *him experienced enough for the post.* [T + obj + adj] • *(dated) I would esteem* (= consider) **it a favour** *if you would accompany me.* [T + obj + n/adj] • *There has been a drop in public esteem* **for** *teachers.* [U] • *Relatively low esteem is given in this country to vocational education.* [U] • *Because of their achievements they were* **held in** (= given) *(high) esteem.* [U] • *The generous donations were a measure of the* **high** *esteem in which they were held.* [U]

es·the·tic /£esˈθet·ɪk, $-ˈθeṭ-/ *adj esp. Am for* AESTHETIC

es·thete /ˈiːs·θiːt/ *n* [C] *esp. Am*

es·tim·ab·le /ˈes·tɪ·mə·bl̩/ *adj fml* (of a person or their behaviour) producing a good opinion; very good • *He writes estimable poetry under a pseudonym.* • *Her performance under such stressful conditions was estimable.*

es·ti·mate /£ˈes·tɪ·mət, $-ṭɪ-/ *n* [C] an approximate calculation or judgment of the size, value, amount, cost, etc. of something • *The number of people who applied for the course was 120 compared with an initial estimate* **of** *between 50 and 100.* • *We'll accept the lowest of three estimates* **for** *the building work.* • *Their* **conservative** (= low) *estimate was 30 to 40 acceptances.* • *As/At a* **rough** (= not exact) *estimate we'll be finished on Thursday.* • LP〉 **Approximate numbers**

es·ti·mate *(obj)* /£ˈes·tɪ·meɪt, $-ṭɪ-/ *v* • *Government sources estimate a long-term 50% increase in rail fares.* [T] • *They estimate* **(that)** *the journey will take a week.* [+ (*that*) clause] • *The journey is estimated* **to** *have taken a week.* [T + obj + *to* infinitive] • **It** *was difficult to estimate* **how** *many trees had been destroyed.* [+ *wh-* word]

es·ti·ma·tion /ˌes·tɪˈmeɪ·ʃᵊn/ *n* [U] • **In** *my estimation* (= By my calculation) *a lot of other banks are going to have the same problem.*

e·stranged /ɪˈstreɪndʒd/ *adj* [not gradable] (of a husband or wife) not living with the person they are married to • *She's been estranged* **from** *her husband for several years.* • *(fml)* If you are estranged from your family or friends then you have seriously argued with them and are no longer friendly with each other: *It's sad to see someone estranged* **from** *their parents.*

es·trange·ment /ɪˈstreɪndʒ·mənt/ *n* [U] *fml*

es·tro·gen /ˈiː·strə·dʒən/ *n* [U] *esp. Am for* OESTROGEN

es·tu·a·ry /£ˈes·tjʊə·ri, $-tu·er·i/ *n* [C] the wide part of a river at the place where it joins the sea • *the Thames estuary* • *the Rance estuary*

es·tu·ar·ine /£ˈes·tjʊə·riːn, $-tjʊr·iːn/ *adj specialized* • *estuarine species*

ETA /£ˌiː·tiːˈeɪ/ *n* [U] *abbreviation for* estimated time of arrival (= the time you expect to arrive) • *Our ETA is 5.45, but you should allow an extra hour for bad weather conditions.*

et al. /etˈæl/ *adv specialized abbreviation for* et alii (= and other people). It is used, esp. in writing, after a name or list of names. • *The method is described in an article by Feynman et al.* (= and other writers).

PRONUNCIATION OF WORDS ENDING IN *-ET*

In most words ending in 'et' the final 't' is pronounced: *bullet* /ˈbʊl·ət/ *supermarket* /£ˈsuː·pə·mɑː·kɪt/ /$ˈsuː·pɚ·mɑːr·kɪt/. However, some words ending in 'et' are borrowed from French: in these words, 'et' is pronounced /eɪ/.

ballet	crochet
beret	croquet
bidet	duvet
bouquet	gourmet
buffet	parquet
cabaret	ricochet
cachet	sorbet
chalet	

In British English, the first syllable of these words is stressed; in American English, the final syllable with 'et' is stressed /£ˈbæl·eɪ/ /$bæˈleɪ/ • /£ˈber·eɪ/ /$bəˈreɪ/

Bouquet does not follow this rule: some British speakers stress the second syllable.

There are a few other words with a silent final t:

debut /£ˈdeɪ.bjuː/ /$deɪˈbjuː/
rapport /£ræˈpɔːʳ/ /$ræˈpɔːr/

etc. *adv abbreviation for* et cetera (= and other similar things). It is used, esp. in writing, after a list. • *We saw lions, tigers, elephants, etc.* • *Put this one here, this one next to it, then another one, etc., etc.* (= and so on).

etch *obj* /etʃ/ *v* [T] to cut (a pattern, picture, etc.) into (a smooth surface, esp. on metal or glass), using acid or sometimes a sharp instrument • *A design is cut into the wax covering the copper plate and the acid then etches the plate.* • *He etched his name on the window with a diamond ring.* • *The prints were made from an etched metal plate.* • *(fig.) The scene will be etched* **on** *my* **memory/mind** (= I will remember it) *forever.*

etch·er /£ˈetʃ·əʳ, $-ɚ/ *n* [C] • An etcher is a person who makes etchings.

etch·ing /ˈetʃ·ɪŋ/ *n* • *The design on the glass bowl was produced by etching.* [U] • An etching is a picture produced by printing from a metal plate which has been etched with acid. [C]

e·ter·nal /ɪˈtɜː·nəl, $-ˈtɜːr-/ *adj* [not gradable] lasting forever or for a very long time; never ending • *The company is engaged in the eternal search for a product that will lead the market.* • *In some religious views, life is seen as an eternal conflict between the forces of good and evil.* • *Will you two never stop your eternal arguing!* • *(humorous)* An **eternal student** is someone who tries to avoid getting a job for as long as possible by taking more educational courses. • *(Br)* An **eternal triangle** (*Am and Aus* **triangle** or **love triangle**) is a situation where two people both love a third person, usually of the opposite sex. • *(saying)* 'Hope springs eternal' means you are hopeful that something will happen even though it seems unlikely: *I don't think I'll get the job, but hope springs eternal.*

e·ter·nal·ly /ɪˈtɜː·nəl·i, $-ˈtɜːr-/ *adv* [not gradable] • *the eternally changing seasons* • *eternally weary/sad/cheerful* • *(fml) I'd be eternally* (= very or always) *grateful if you could arrange it.*

e·ter·ni·ty /ɪˈtɜː·nɪ·ti, $-ˈtɜːr·nə·t̬i/ *n* [U] endless time; time without limits • *They haven't been given these rights* **for (all)** *eternity – they should justify having them just like most other people have to.* • *The film went on for what* **seemed like an** *eternity.* • *Nine months is a long time for anyone, but it's* **an** *eternity* (= a very long time) *for the very young.* • *Religions gain some of their worldly power by claiming they have the key to eternity* (= a state of existence outside normal life). • If you **send** someone **to eternity** you kill them. • LP **Periods of time**

eth·a·nol /ˈeθ·ə·nɒl, $-nɑːl/, **eth·yl al·co·hol** *n* [U] a chemical compound which is a type of alcohol

eth·er MEDICAL /ˈiː·θər, $-θɚ/ *n* [U] a colourless liquid used, esp. in the past, as an ANAESTHETIC to make people sleep before a medical operation

eth·er SKY /ˈiː·θər, $-θɚ/ *n* [U] **the ether** *old use* the clear sky; the upper air, or the AIRWAVES

eth·e·re·al /ɪˈθɪə·ri·əl, $-ˈθɪr·i-/ *adj* light and delicate, esp. in an unnatural way • *an ethereal being* • *ethereal beauty* • *She composed music which had a spiritual, ethereal quality.*

eth·ic /ˈeθ·ɪk/ *n* [C usually pl] a system of accepted beliefs which control behaviour, esp. such a system based on morals • *the (Protestant) work ethic* • *The ethic of some people in business seems to be to maximize profit and it doesn't matter how.* • *The ethics of journalism are much debated.* • *He said he was bound by a scientist's* **code of** *ethics.* • *Publication of the article was a* **breach of** *ethics.* • *As a result of advances in medical research a national ethics committee has been set up.*

eth·i·cal /ˈeθ·ɪ·kəl/ *adj* • *ethical problems* • *ethical standards* • *ethical practice* • *an ethical committee* • *The ethical argument was that righting wrongs should be a priority in itself.* • *We are a moral, ethical people and therefore we do not approve of their activities.*

eth·i·cal·ly /ˈeθ·ɪ·kli/ *adv* • *This action is ethically questionable and borders on the obscene.*

eth·ics /ˈeθ·ɪks/ *n* [U] • Ethics is the study of what is morally right and what is not.

eth·nic /ˈeθ·nɪk/ *adj* of a national or racial group of people • *A question on ethnic origin was included in the census.* • *The exhibition celebrated ethnic differences.* • *The factory's workforce reflects the ethnic mix from which it draws its labour.* • An ethnic **minority** is a national or racial group living a country or area which contains a larger group of people of a different race or nationality: *Ethnic minorities are frequently faced with prejudice and sometimes violence.* • Ethnic also means from a different race or interesting because characteristic of an ethnic group which is very different from those that are common in western culture: *ethnic food* ○ *ethnic costume* ○ *The shop display had an ethnic feel.* • **Ethnic cleansing** is the organized attempt by one racial or political group to completely remove from a country or area anybody who belongs to another particular racial group, using violence and often murder to achieve this: *Each side in the conflict accused the other of ethnic cleansing.*

eth·nic /ˈeθ·nɪk/ *n* [C] *Am and Aus* • An ethnic is a person of an ethnic group.

eth·ni·cal·ly /ˈeθ·nɪ·kli/ *adv* • *ethnically related communities*

eth·ni·ci·ty /eθˈnɪs·ɪ·ti, $-ə·t̬i/ *n* [U] *fml*

eth·no·cen·tric /ˌeθ·nəʊˈsen·trɪk, $-noʊ-/ *adj* believing that the people, customs and traditions of your own race or nationality are better than those of other races • *I'm very concerned about the ethnocentric tone of this leaflet/novel.*

eth·no·graph·y /eθˈnɒg·rə·fi, $-ˈnɑː·grə-/ *n* the description and study of a particular society or culture, produced by someone who has spent some time living in the society, or a book containing this description • *One of the aims of ethnography is to contribute to an understanding of the human race.* [U] • *The famous anthropologist, Malinowski, wrote several ethnographies* **of** *the Trobriand Islands.* [C]

eth·no·graph·ic /ˌeθ·nəʊˈgræf·ɪk, $-noʊ-/, **eth·no·graph·i·cal** /ˌeθ·nəʊˈgræf·ɪ·kəl, $-noʊ-/ *adj* [not gradable] • *ethnographic fieldwork* • *an ethnographic essay*

eth·no·graph·i·cal·ly /ˌeθ·nəʊˈgræf·ɪ·kli, $-noʊ-/ *adv* [not gradable]

eth·no·graph·er /eθˈnɒg·rə·fər, $-ˈnɑː·grə·fɚ/ *n* [C]

eth·nol·o·gy /eθˈnɒl·ə·dʒi, $-ˈnɑː·lə-/ *n* [U] the comparative and historical study of different societies and cultures

eth·no·log·ic /ˌeθ·nəʊˈlɒdʒ·ɪ·kəl, $-noʊˈlɑː·dʒɪ-/, **eth·no·log·i·cal** /ˌeθ·nəʊˈlɒdʒ·ɪ·kəl, $-noʊˈlɑː·dʒɪ-/ *adj* [not gradable]

eth·no·log·i·cal·ly /ˌeθ·nəʊˈlɒdʒ·ɪ·kli, $-noʊˈlɑː·dʒɪ·kli/ *adv* [not gradable]

eth·nol·o·gist /eθˈnɒl·ə·dʒɪst, $-ˈnɑː·lə-/ *n* [C]

e·thos /ˈiː·θɒs, $-θɑːs/ *n* [U] the set of beliefs, ideas, etc. about social behaviour and relationships of a person or group • *national ethos* • *working-class ethos* • *They were as far removed from the ethos* **of** *terrorism as you could imagine.* • *The ethos* **of** *the traditional family firm is under threat.* • GR

eth·yl al·co·hol /ˈeθ·ɪl/ *n* [U] ETHANOL

e·ti·o·lat·ed /ˈiː·ti·əʊ·leɪ·tɪd, $-ə·leɪ·t̬ɪd/ *adj specialized* (esp. of plants) pale and weak • *These plants are etiolated and too tall because they have been grown while being kept in the dark.*

e·ti·ol·o·gy /ˌiː·tiˈɒl·ə·dʒi, $-ˈɑː·lə-/ *n* [U] the scientific study of the cause of diseases

et·i·quette /ˈet·ɪ·ket, $ˈet̬·ɪ·kət/ *n* [U] the set of rules or customs which control accepted behaviour in particular social groups or social situations • **(Social)** *etiquette dictates that men cannot sit while women are standing.* • *Court life was governed by the most precise form of etiquette.* • *Diplomatic etiquette forbids calling for the death of a national leader.* • DK

et·y·mol·o·gy /ˌet·ɪˈmɒl·ə·dʒi, $-ˈmɑː·lə-/ *n* (the study of) the origin and history of words, or of a particular word • *At university she developed an interest in etymology.* [U] • *A list of selected words and their etymologies is printed at the back of the book.* [C]

et·y·mol·o·gi·cal /ˌet·ɪ·məˈlɒdʒ·ɪ·kəl, $-ˈlɑː·dʒɪ-/ *adj* [not gradable]

et·y·mol·o·gi·cal·ly /ˌet·ɪ·məˈlɒdʒ·ɪ·kli, $-ˈlɑː·dʒɪ-/ *adv* [not gradable]

et·y·mol·o·gist /ˌet·ɪˈmɒl·ə·dʒɪst, $-ˈmɑː·lə-/ *n* [C]

EU /ˌiːˈjuː/ *n* [U] **the EU** *abbreviation for* **European Union**, see at EUROPEAN

eu·cal·yp·tus /ˌjuː·kəlˈɪp·təs/, **euc·a·lypt** /ˈjuː·kəl·ɪpt/, **gum**, **gum tree** *n* [C] *pl* **eucalyptuses** or **eucalypti** /ˌjuː·kəlˈɪp·tiː, -taɪ/ any of several types of tree, found esp. in Australia, which produce an oil with a strong smell used in medicine and industry • *eucalyptus oil*

Eu·cha·rist /ˈjuː·kər·ɪst/ *n* [U] (the holy bread and wine used in) the Christian ceremony based on Jesus Christ's last meal with his DISCIPLES (= people who believed in his power) • *to receive/celebrate the Eucharist* • See also **Holy Communion** at HOLY GOOD.

eu·cha·ris·tic /ˌjuː·kərˈɪs·tɪk/ *adj* [not gradable]

Eu·cli·de·an /juˈklɪd·i·ən/ *adj* [not gradable] relating to the GEOMETRY (= the study of angles and shapes formed by the relationships between lines) described by the ancient Greek thinker Euclid

eu·gen·ics /juːˈdʒen·ɪks/ *n* [U] *specialized* the study of methods of improving humans by allowing only carefully chosen people to reproduce • *Eugenics was the central, and most controversial, part of his social philosophy.*

eu·gen·ic /juˈdʒen·ɪk/ *adj specialized*

eu·log·y /ˈjuː·lə·dʒi/ *n fml* (a speech, piece of writing, poem, etc. containing) great praise, esp. for someone who recently died or stopped working • *He was the most self-effacing of men – the last thing he would have relished was a eulogy.* [C] • *The song was a eulogy* **to** *the joys of travelling.* [C] • *He is a writer with a tendency to eulogy.* [U]

eu·log·ist /ˈjuː·lə·dʒɪst/ *n* [C] *fml*
eu·log·is·tic /ˌjuː·ləˈdʒɪs·tɪk/ *adj fml*
eu·log·ize *(obj), Br and Aus usually* **–ise** /ˈjuː·lə·dʒaɪz/ *v fml* • *Critics everywhere have eulogized her new novel.* [T] • *They eulogized* **over** *the breathtaking views.* [I always + adv/prep]

eu·nuch /ˈjuː·nək/ *n* [C] *pl* **eunuchs** a man who has been CASTRATED (=had the sex organs that produce sperm removed)

eu·phem·i·sm /ˈjuː·fə·mɪ·zᵊm/ *n* (the use of) a word or phrase used to avoid saying another word or phrase that is more forceful and honest but also more unpleasant or offensive • *'Senior citizen' is a euphemism* **for** *'old person'.* [C] • *The article made so much use of euphemism that often its meaning was unclear.* [U]
eu·phem·is·tic /ˌjuː·fəˈmɪs·tɪk/ *adj*
eu·phem·is·ti·cal·ly /ˌjuː·fəˈmɪs·tɪ·kli/ *adv*

eu·pho·ni·um /£ juːˈfəʊ·ni·əm, $-ˈfoʊ-/ *n* [C] a large musical instrument made from BRASS (= a metal), that you play by blowing into it

eu·pho·ni·ous /£ juːˈfəʊ·ni·əs, $-ˈfoʊ-/ *adj fml* sounding pleasant

eu·pho·ri·a /£ juːˈfɔː·ri·ə, $-ˈfɔːr·i-/ *n* [U] extreme happiness, sometimes more than is reasonable in a particular situation • *They were in* **a state of** *euphoria for days after they won the prize.*
eu·pho·ric /£ juːˈfɒr·ɪk, $-ˈfɑːr-/ *adj* • *a euphoric mood* • *He described his experience in euphoric terms.*
eu·pho·ri·cal·ly /£ juːˈfɒr·ɪ·kli, $-ˈfɑːr-/ *adv*

Eu·ras·i·an /£ jʊəˈreɪ·ʒᵊn, $ jʊ-/ *n* [C], *adj* (a person) with a European and an Asian parent • Eurasian also means of or connected with Europe and Asia considered as a unit: *Eurasian languages*

eu·re·ka /jʊəˈriː·kə/ *exclamation humorous* used to show that you have been successful in something you were trying to do • *He twisted it and turned it and then, eureka, the top came off.* • *"Eureka!" she shouted as the engine started.*

Eu·ro– /£ˈjʊə·rəʊ-, $ˈjʊr·oʊ-/ *combining form* of or connected with Europe, esp. of the European Union • *Euro-policy* • *Euro-business* • *Euro-partners* • *a Euro-MP* (= Member of the European Parliament)

Eu·ro·cheque /£ˈjuː·rəʊ·tʃek, $-roʊ-/ *n* [C] a CHEQUE (= a form used to make payments from your bank account) that can be used in particular banks or shops in Europe

Eu·ro·crat /£ˈjuː·rəʊ·kræt, $-roʊ-/ *n* [C] an official, esp. an important one, of the European Union

Eu·ro·pe·an /£ˌjʊə·rəˈpiː·ən, $ˌjʊr·ə-/ *n* [C], *adj* of or (a person coming) from the continent of Europe • The **European Community** (*abbreviation* **EC**) was the organization through which particular European governments made decisions and agreed on shared action in social and economic matters until November 1993: *The European Community used to be known as the European Economic Community or EEC.* • Since November 1993 the **European Union** (*abbreviation* **EU**) has been the organization through which European governments who choose to be members make decisions and agree on shared action in social and economic matters. • LP **World regions**

eu·than·a·si·a /ˌjuː·θəˈneɪ·ʒə/ *n* [U] the act of painlessly killing someone who is very ill or old, esp. to reduce their suffering • *Although some people campaign for the right to euthanasia, it is still illegal in most countries.*

e·vac·u·ate *(obj)* /ɪˈvæk·ju·eɪt/ *v* to empty (a dangerous place) of the people who live there, or to remove (everyone) from a dangerous place • *The police evacuated the village shortly before the explosion.* [T] • *A thousand people were evacuated* **from** *their homes in Perth last Sunday night following the floods.* [T] • *When toxic fumes from the factory fire/chemical spill began to drift toward our homes, we were told to evacuate.* [I]
e·vac·u·a·tion /ɪˌvæk·juˈeɪ·ʃᵊn/ *n* • *The evacuation of civilians remains out of the question while the fighting continues.* [U] • *The first warnings and evacuations came ten days after the disaster.* [C]
e·vac·u·ee /ɪˌvæk·juˈiː/ *n* [C] • An evacuee is someone who is evacuated from a dangerous place, esp. during a war: *Thousands of evacuees crossed the border to safety this morning.*

e·vade *obj* /ɪˈveɪd/ *v* [T] to avoid (something unpleasant or unwanted), or to manage not to do (something which should be done) • *Just give me a straight answer, won't you, and stop evading the question!* • *Elmar can't evade* **doing** *his military service forever.* [+ v-*ing*] • *The police have assured the public that the escaped prisoners will not evade recapture for long.* • *She leant forward to kiss him but he evaded her by pretending to sneeze.* • *An Olympic gold medal is the only thing that has evaded her* (= that she has not managed to achieve) *in her remarkable career.*
e·va·sion /ɪˈveɪ·ʒᵊn/ *n* • *Her speech was full of excuses and evasions and never properly addressed the issue.* [C] • **Tax** *evasion* (= intentionally and illegally not paying taxes) *and a massive black economy lie at the heart of the country's economic problems.* [U] • *Fare evasion is estimated to cost railway companies £36 million a year.* [U]
e·vas·ive /ɪˈveɪ·sɪv/ *adj* • *By the time the pilot realised how close the plane was to the pylon, it was too late to take evasive* **action**. • *The Minister was her usual evasive self, skilfully dodging reporters' questions about her possible resignation.*
e·vas·ive·ly /ɪˈveɪ·sɪv·li/ *adv*
e·vas·ive·ness /ɪˈveɪ·sɪv·nəs/ *n* [U]

e·val·u·ate *(obj)* /ɪˈvæl·ju·eɪt/ *v* to judge or calculate the quality, importance, amount or value of (something) • *It's impossible to evaluate these results without knowing more about the research methods employed.* [T] • *Banks have been advised to pay more attention to personal circumstances when evaluating loans to private customers.* [T] • *We shall need to evaluate* **how** *the new material stands up to wear and tear.* [+ *wh*- word]
e·val·u·a·tion /ɪˌvæl·juˈeɪ·ʃᵊn/ *n* • *This book offers a critical evaluation of the LSD experience from the viewpoint of Freud and Jung.* [C] • *Evaluation of this new treatment cannot take place until all the data has been collected.* [U]
e·val·u·a·tive /£ɪˈvæl·ju·ə·tɪv, $-eɪ·t̬ɪv/ *adj fml* • *evaluative terms/discourse* • *Rigorous evaluative research should be carried out before this product goes on the market.*

ev·an·es·cent /£ˌiː·vəˈnes·ᵊnt, $ˌev·ə-/ *adj fml* lasting for only a short time, then disappearing quickly and being forgotten • *The evanescent post-war economic boom was quickly followed by a deep recession.*
ev·an·es·cence /£ˌiː·vəˈnes·ᵊnts, $ˌev·ə-/ *n* [U] *fml*

e·van·gel·i·cal /ˌiː·vænˈdʒel·ɪ·kᵊl/ *n, adj* (someone) belonging to one of the Protestant Churches or Christian groups which believe biblical teaching and persuading other people to join them to be extremely important • *The Evangelical Alliance has warned anyone dressing up as a witch that they could be endangering their sanity or even their lives.* • *The new Archbishop is an evangelical who gives priority to scripture while interpreting it in relation to daily life.* [C] • *(fig.) Why is it that people who've given up smoking become so evangelical and intolerant of other smokers?*
e·van·gel·i·cal·i·sm /ˌiː·vænˈdʒel·ɪ·kᵊl·ɪ·zᵊm/ *n* [U] • *Dr Carey said that evangelicalism tended to distrust critical scholarship, preferring to cling to traditional interpretations of the Bible.*

e·van·gel·ist RELIGIOUS PERSON /ɪˈvæn·dʒə·lɪst/ *n* [C] a person who tries to persuade people to become Christians, often by travelling around and organizing religious meetings • See also **televangelist** at TELEVANGELISM.
e·van·gel·i·sm /ɪˈvæn·dʒə·lɪ·zᵊm/ *n* [U]
e·van·gel·is·tic /ɪˌvæn·dʒəˈlɪs·tɪk/ *adj*
e·van·gel·ize *(obj), Br and Aus usually* **–ise** /ɪˈvæn·dʒə·laɪz/ *v* • *St Pancras of Taormina is reputed to have been sent by St Peter to evangelize Sicily.* [T] • *(fig.) I wish she would stop evangelizing about the virtues of free market economics.* [I]

E·van·gel·ist WRITER /ɪˈvæn·dʒə·lɪst/ *n* [C] one of the writers of the four books in the Bible about Jesus Christ

e·vap·or·ate *(obj)* /£ɪˈvæp·ᵊr·eɪt, $ˈ-ɚ-/ *v* to (cause a liquid to) change to a gaseous form, esp. by heating, or *(fig.)* to disappear • *The high concentration of sugars forms a syrup when the sap evaporates.* [I] • *Plants keep cool during the summer by evaporating water from their leaves.* [T] • *(fig.) Halfway through the film reality evaporates and we enter a world of pure fantasy.* [I] • **Evaporated milk** is milk which has been thickened by evaporating some of the water from it, and it is used in sweet dishes.
e·vap·or·a·tion /ɪˌvæp·əˈreɪ·ʃᵊn/ *n* [U] • *More heat causes more evaporation and therefore more clouds, thus increasing the temperature near the Earth's surface.*

e·va·sion /ɪˈveɪ·ʒᵊn/ *n* See at EVADE
e·vas·ive /ɪˈveɪ·sɪv/ *adj*

eve DAY BEFORE /iːv/ *n* [U] the period or day before an important event, or *(old use)* an evening • *Mr Hurd was speaking to Arab journalists in London* **on the eve of** *his visit to Jordan and Saudi Arabia.* • **Christmas** *Eve is on*

December 24th. • *Are you doing anything exciting on* **New Year's** *Eve* (= the last day of the year)?

Eve WOMAN /iːv/ *n* [not after *the*] the first woman, according to the biblical story of how the world was made, or *(fig.)* all women considered together

ev·en SURPRISE /ˈiː·vᵊn/ *adv* [not gradable] used to show that something is surprising, unusual, unexpected, or extreme • *Everyone I know likes the smell of bacon – even Mike does and he's a vegetarian.* • *Everyone was on time for the meeting – even Chris, who's usually a quarter of an hour late for everything.* • *After the accident he couldn't even feed himself without help (never mind walk about on his own).* • *It's a very difficult job – it might even take* (= take as much as) *a year to finish it.* • *"I never cry." "Not even when you hurt yourself really badly?"* • *Even with* (= Whether or not you have) *a load of electronic gadgetry, you still need some musical ability to write a successful song.* • *I tried to reason with him, but* **even as** (= at exactly the same time as) *I started to explain how the mistake happened he stood up to leave.* • **Even if** (= Whether or not) *you take a taxi, you'll still miss your train.* • **Even now** (= Although it is true and I have had a lot of time to think about it) *I can't believe how lucky I was to survive the accident.* • *I had a terrible headache, but* **even so** (= despite that) *I went to the concert.* • *An immediate interest cut might give a small boost to the economy.* **Even so** (= Despite this), *any recovery is likely to be very slow.* • *I gave Jim very clear instructions, but* **even then** (= despite the instructions) *he managed to make a mess of it.* • **Even though** (= Despite the fact that) *he left school at 16, he still managed to become prime minister.*

ev·en EMPHASIS /ˈiː·vᵊn/ *adv* [not gradable] used to emphasize a comparison • *The next 36 hours will be even colder with snow showers becoming more widespread.* • *Any devaluation of sterling would make it even more difficult to keep inflation low.*

ev·en MORE EXACTLY /ˈiː·vᵊn/ *adv* [not gradable] used when you want to be more exact or detailed about something you have just said • *I find some of his habits rather unpleasant, disgusting even.* • *She has always been very kind to me, even generous on occasion.*

ev·en FLAT /ˈiː·vᵊn/ *adj* flat and smooth, or on the same level • *We resurfaced the kitchen floor because it wasn't even enough for Dad's wheelchair.* • *We couldn't make the living room floor even* **with** *the dining room so we put a ramp over the step.* • If something is **on an even keel** it is regular and well-balanced and not likely to change suddenly: *The new manager succeeded in putting the business back on an even keel.*

ev·en CONTINUOUS /ˈiː·vᵊn/ *adj* continuous or regular • *You should try to work at an even rate instead of taking it easy one day and working flat out the next.* • *(approving)* If someone is **even-tempered**, they are always calm and never get angry or excited about anything.

ev·en·ly /ˈiː·vᵊn·li/ *adv* • To say something evenly is to speak without emotion showing in your voice although you are angry or not satisfied in some way: *"We are not terrorists," he said evenly. "We are freedom fighters."*

ev·en EQUAL /ˈiː·vᵊn/ *adj* equal or equally balanced • *At half-time it was still an even game, but a single goal in the second half gave Italy their victory.* • *Both sides played well – it was a very even contest.* • *The weather forecast said that there's an even chance of thunderstorms tonight* (= that it is equally likely that there will or will not be storms). • *She scratched the door of my car so I* **got** *even* **with** *her* (= did something equally bad to her) *and let the air out of her tyres.* • If someone is **even-handed**, they deal fairly and equally with everyone: *Several broadcasters have been criticized for failing to give even-handed treatment to all the parties during the election campaign.* • LP> **Sports**

ev·en·ly /ˈiː·vᵊn·li/ *adv* • *Divide the mixture evenly between the baking pans.* • *Congress is still evenly divided on the issue.* • *It's impossible to identify a high risk area as the cases of infection seem to be evenly distributed across the country.*

ev·ens *Br* /ˈiː·vᵊnz/, *Am* **ev·en** *adj, adv* [not gradable] • An evens **bet** is one which will pay back twice the amount that is paid, if it is successful: *(fig.) The chances of her getting the job are about evens* (= It is equally likely that she will or will not get the job).

ev·en *(obj)* /ˈiː·vᵊn/ *v* • *Sheila was awarded a scholarship in Chemistry, and now her brother has evened* **the score** *with a scholarship in Economics.* [T] • *The whisky industry is campaigning for the taxes on different alcoholic drinks to be evened* **up** (= made equal or fairer). [M] • *The university has a system designed to even* **out** (= make equal) *the differences between rich and poor colleges.* [M] • *After their dramatic falls over the past few years, house prices are at last beginning to even* **out** (= become level). [I]

ev·en NUMBER /ˈiː·vᵊn/ *adj* [not gradable] forming a whole number which is exactly divisible by two • *6 is an even number and 7 is an odd number.* • *Is 11 odd or even?* • *The examples are on the even pages* (= pages on which the numbers are even) *and the exercises are on the odd ones.*

eve·ning /ˈiːv·nɪŋ/ *n* the part of the day between the end of the afternoon and night • *a chilly evening* [C] • *It's a hard life working in a restaurant – I only get one evening* **off** *a week.* [C] • *Have a good evening, but don't stay out too late.* [C] • *Thank you for such a lovely evening – dinner was wonderful.* [C] • *I always go to see a film* **on** *Friday evenings.* [C] • **In the** *evenings, I like to relax.* [C] • *"Do you fancy a drink after work?" "Thanks but I'm working late* **this** *evening."* [U] • *"What are you doing* **tomorrow** *evening?" "The same as* **yesterday** *evening – preparing for my English exam."* [U] • *It poured down* **all** *evening and most of the night as well.* [U] • *What time do you usually get home* **in the** *evening?* [U] • An **evening class** is a class intended for adults rather than children which happens in the evening and usually is a subject that cannot usually be studied at school: *Pat teaches evening classes* **in** *yoga and relaxation.* ○ *She prepared for one exam at an evening class and another by correspondence course.* • **Evening dress** is special clothing worn by women or men for formal events, such as special evening meals: *The invitation says we should wear evening dress.* • An **evening dress/evening gown** is a long, often expensive, dress that is worn for formal events in the evening. • The **evening primrose** is a plant with pale yellow flowers that open in the evening. Its seeds are used to make **evening primrose oil** which is used to treat various medical conditions. • The **evening star** is a planet, esp. Venus, which can be seen shining brightly in the west just after the sun has gone down. • LP> **Time** Ⓙ

eve·nings /ˈiːv·nɪŋz/ *adv* [not gradable] *esp. Am* • *What time do you get home evenings* (= in the evening)? • *I work evenings.* • *Our softball team plays evenings in Central Park.*

ev·en·song /£ˈiː·vənˌsɒŋ, $-ˌsɑːŋ/ *n* [U] the evening ceremony of the Church of England or the Roman Catholic Church

e·vent /ɪˈvent/ *n* [C] anything that happens, esp. something important or unusual • *This year's Olympic Games will be the biggest ever sporting event.* • *Susannah's party was the* **social** *event of the year.* • *The police are trying to determine the* **series of** *events that led up to the murder.* • An event is also one of a set of races or competitions: *The women's 200 metre event will be followed by the men's 100 metres.* • *(Br) We had expected to arrive an hour late, but* **in the event** (= what happened was that) *we were half an hour early.* • **In the event of** *a strike* (= If that happens), *the army will take over responsibility for firefighting.* • *I might go home next month, but* **in any event** *(Br also* **at all events**) (= whatever happens) *I'll be home for Christmas.* • *I can't decide whether to accept the Cambridge or the London job, but* **in either event** (= whatever happens) *I'll have to move house.* • *There's a possibility of my flight being delayed.* **In that event** (= If that happens) *I'll phone to let you know.* • (KOR)

e·vent·ful /ɪˈvent·fᵊl/ *adj* • *Her time at university was the most eventful* (= full of important or interesting events) *period of her life.* • *We had quite an eventful journey – the police stopped us twice.*

ev·en·tide /ˈiː·vᵊn·taɪd/ *n* [C] *poetic* evening

e·ven·tual /ɪˈven·tju·ᵊl/ *adj* [before n; not gradable] happening or existing at a later time or at the end • *Although the original budget for the project was $1 billion, the eventual cost is likely to be 50% higher.* • *There are still many problems to be resolved, but we remain optimistic about an eventual agreement.* • (CS) (D) (DK) (E) (I) (P) (PL) (S)

e·ven·tu·al·ly /ɪˈven·tju·ᵊl·i/ *adv* [not gradable] • *Although she had been ill for a long time, it still came as a shock when she eventually died.* • *Don't worry, he'll do it eventually, but he might take a long time to get round to it.* • (CS) (D) (DK) (E) (F) (PL)

e·ven·tu·al·i·ty /£ɪˌven·tjuˈæl·ɪ·ti, $-ə·t̬i/ *n* [C] something unpleasant or unexpected that might happen or exist in the future • *We've tried to anticipate the most likely problems, but it's impossible to be prepared for all eventualities/every eventuality.* • *I'm looking for a travel insurance policy that will cover me for any eventuality*

ev·er AT ANY TIME /£ˈev·əʳ, $-ɚ/ *adv* [not gradable] at any time • *Nothing ever happens here in the evenings.* • *"Do you ever go to London?" "Yes, usually once a month."* • *"Have you ever been to London?" "No, never, but I'm hoping to go next year."/"Yes, I was a student there for a year."* • *Can you remember ever seeing anyone of this description in the area?* • *If you're ever/If ever you're in Cambridge, do give me a ring.* • *He* **hardly** *ever* (= almost never) *washes the dishes and he* **rarely, if** *ever,* (= probably never) *does any cleaning.* • *When there's a James Bond film on TV, I* **never** *ever miss it.* • **If** *ever there was a cause for celebration, this peace treaty was it.* • *It was a brilliant performance* **if ever there was one** (= It was certainly a very good performance). • *The smell is worse* **than** *ever.* • *We are spending more money on education than* **ever before** (= than at any time in the past). • *This is the biggest oil slick the world has ever known.* • *I thought she was famous, but none of my friends have ever heard of her.* • *The restaurants are* **as** *good* **as ever** (= as good as they have been at any time) *and no more expensive than when I was last here.* • *(dated)* **Ever and anon** means occasionally.

ev·er ALWAYS /£ˈev·əʳ, $-ɚ/ *adv* [not gradable] always • *Manchester United's record in cup competitions grows ever* **more** *impressive.* • *The ever-***increasing** *demand for private cars could be halted by more investment in public transport.* • *AIDS is an ever-***present** *threat for anyone who practises unsafe sex and changes partners frequently.* • *It's a mistake to think that we would all live* **happily** *ever* **after** *if we could get rid of dictators like him.* • *He's been depressed* **ever since** (= continuously since) *he got divorced two years ago.* • **As ever** (= As always happens), *the last people to know what is happening in this war are the poor people who are fighting it.* • *(Br)* Finishing a letter with **Yours ever** or **Ever yours** is a friendly way of saying goodbye to someone you know well: *I'm looking forward to seeing you all next month. Yours ever, Chris.*

ev·er EMPHASIS /£ˈev·əʳ, $-ɚ/ *adv* [not gradable] used for emphasizing a question or an adjective • *The orchestra is to perform its last ever concert/last concert ever tomorrow night at the Albert Hall.* • *Yesterday the company announced its first ever fall in profits.* • *In questions, ever means the same as the commoner expression 'on earth'.* • **How ever** *could anyone do such a dreadful thing?* • **What ever** *have you done to him?* • **When ever** *are we/***when** *are we* **ever** *going to get this finished?* • **Where ever** *have I put my pen? I had it just a moment ago.* • **Who ever** *was that strange man you were talking to at the bar?* • **Why ever** *would anyone/* **Why** *would anyone* **ever** *want to watch a film like that?* (= I really can't believe anyone would want to.) • **Ever so** and **ever such** are slightly informal ways of saying "very" or "extremely": *Mark got ever so drunk last night.* ○ *Mary's ever such a clever girl.* • *(Am and Aus) Was she ever a fast runner* (= She was a very fast runner)*!* • *(Am and Aus) "Are you looking forward to your vacation?" "Am I ever!"* (= Yes, very much)

ev·er·green /£ˈev·ə·griːn, $ˈ-ɚ-/ *n* [C], *adj* [not gradable] (a plant, bush or tree) having leaves for the whole year • *The leaves of evergreens/evergreen trees are often shaped like needles.* • *(fig.) She is one of those evergreen* (= always popular) *performers who appeal to several generations of music lovers.* • Compare DECIDUOUS.

ev·er·last·ing /£ˌev·əˈlɑː·stɪŋ, $-ɚˈlæs·tɪŋ/ *adj* [not gradable] lasting forever or for a long time • *I wish someone would invent an everlasting light bulb.* • *What is the key to everlasting happiness?* • *Their contributions to science have earned them an everlasting place in history.*

ev·er·more /£ˌev·əˈmɔːʳ, $-ɚˈmɔːr/ *adv* [not gradable] *literary* always in the future • *Their name will live on* **for** *evermore.*

ev·ery ALL /ˈev·ri/ *determiner* used when referring to all the members of a group of three or more • *The police want to interview every employee about the theft.* • *The show will be broadcast every weekday morning between 9 and 10.* • *Every Friday evening we go shopping at the late-night supermarket.* • *We're open every day except Sunday.* • *I've been out every night this week.* • *Every week she went to the cemetery and put fresh flowers on his grave.* • *Every time I go to London I get caught in a traffic jam.* • *Ten pence is donated to charity for every bottle sold.* • *For every pound raised, 95 pence goes directly to the poor.* • *These paintings may look like the real thing, but* **(each and)** *every* **one** *of them is a fake.* • *Every passenger* **but** (= except for) *one was killed in the accident.* • *That salmon was very expensive so make sure you eat up every* **(single) bit**. • *We were shot at from every* **side** (= from all directions). • *Opponents of the war are considered* **every bit as** (= equally as) **patriotic as** *supporters.* • *After the match, police were stationed* **on/at every corner** (= in as many places as possible). • *"Did you like the concert?" "Yes, I enjoyed* **every minute** *of it* (= all of it, very much)*."* • *We can catch the vast majority of people, but hunting down* **every last** (= every) *tax dodger is virtually impossible.* • *(Am) The game was hindered by a fierce wind that swept the ball* **every which way** (= in all directions). • *This movie is* **in every way** *a masterpiece of cinematography.* • *She is devoted to her patients and sees to their* **every need** (= everything they need). • *She's such a fascinating lecturer – I was hanging on to her* **every word** (= everything she said). • *I'd hate to be someone really famous with the press reporting my* **every move** (= everything I do). • LP› **Quantity words**

ev·ery REPEATED /ˈev·ri/ *determiner* used to show that something is repeated regularly • *Computers can perform millions of calculations every second.* • *Every four minutes a car is stolen in this city.* • *During 1990, the police registered more than 500 crimes every hour.* • *Every day in the United States 25 people are murdered with handguns.* • *Every* **few** *days we'd rent a new car so the police wouldn't recognise us.* • *Every* **few** *kilometres we passed a burnt out jeep or truck at the side of the road.* • *The conference used to be held annually but now it takes place every* **other/second** *year.* • *In many areas of these countries every third child* (= one child in three) *is thought to be facing severe malnutrition.* • *The discussion group meets every other Friday.* • *On the first Friday of the month, the group meets in the morning, but on every other Friday it meets in the evening.* • **Every now and again/then** (= Occasionally) *they'll have a beer together.* • **Every once in a while** (= Occasionally) *you meet some really interesting people, but most of the time they're fairly ordinary.* • **Every so often** (= Occasionally) *I treat myself to a meal in an expensive restaurant.* • *"Every day, in every way, I am getting better and better"* (Emile Coué, 1857-1926)

ev·ery GREATEST /ˈev·ri/ *determiner* the greatest possible or imaginable • *I'd like to wish you every success in your new job/happiness in your new home.* • *She has every reason to be unhappy after losing her job and her home.* • *You had every opportunity to make a complaint, so why didn't you?* • *There is every possibility/hope of an agreement between the two sides.* • *Every effort is being made to minimise civilian casualties.* • *I have every intention of paying these bills, but I'm still waiting to be paid.* • *This new drug has every chance/prospect of success.* • *She has every right to be proud of her tremendous achievements.* • *I'm afraid she's showing every sign of having the disease.* • *I have every confidence in her ability to do the job.*

ev·ery·bod·y /£ˈev·riˌbɒd·i, $-ˌbɑː·di/ *pronoun* EVERYONE

ev·ery·day /ˈev·ri·deɪ/ *adj* ordinary, typical or usual • *The documentary offers an insight into the everyday lives of millions of ordinary Russian citizens.* • *Death was an everyday occurrence during the Civil War.* • *"An everyday story of country folk"* (introduction to the radio programme *The Archers*, 1950-)

ev·ery·one /ˈev·ri·wʌn/, **ev·ery·bod·y** *pronoun* every person • *Would everyone who wishes to attend the dinner let me know by Friday afternoon.* • *Everyone in favour of this proposal please raise their hand.* • *Everyone has their own ideas about the best way to bring up children.* • *Everybody has to make up their own mind about this difficult problem.* • *I've received replies from everybody but Jane.* • *Do you agree with the principle that everyone should pay something towards the cost of health care?* • *Everyone knows who stole it, but they're all afraid to tell anyone.* • *Surely everyone agrees that peace is preferable to war?* • *Everybody at the meeting wanted to sign the petition.* • *Everyone involved in the accident has been questioned by the police.* • *Everyone connected with the project is highly qualified.* • *Everybody had expected her to get the leading role in the film.* • *You are, like everyone* **else** (= every other person), *entitled to your opinions on this war.* • *Goodbye, everybody – I'll see you next week.* [as form of address] • *I'm sorry, but you'll just have to wait your turn like everybody* **else**. • LP› **Quantity words, Titles and forms of address**

ev·ery·thing /ˈev·ri·θɪŋ/ *pronoun* all things • *He may be responsible for many of the problems, but you can't* **blame** *everything on him/blame him for everything.* • *She's obsessed with Elvis Presley and collects* **anything and** *everything connected with him.* • *Jane's been unfaithful to Jim three times, but he still loves her* **in spite of** *everything.* • *Everything now* **depends** *on what happens at next week's* *meeting.* • *Money isn't everything* (= the most or the only important thing). • *His children are everything* **to** *him* (= the most important part of his life). • *I will* **do** *everything* **in** *my* **power** *to prevent a war.* • *Have you been crying? Is everything all right?* • *Why do you always have to* **reduce** *everything* **to** *sex? Don't you ever think about anything else?* • *Closing down sale. Everything must go!* • *The thieves* **took** *everything.* • *They* **lost** *everything in the fire.* • *How on earth do you choose a present for the Queen, I mean, what can you give the woman who has everything?* • *We did everything we could to save her but she died.* • *The doctors did everything* **possible** *to save her life.* • *We shall do everything* **necessary** *to bring the murderer to justice.* • *This decision has* **nothing to do with** *raising standards* **and** *everything* **to do with** *saving money.* • *They're very busy with their new house and everything* (= all the things connected with it). • *Everything from caviar to cut glass was on sale.* • *(humorous) We're only going on vacation for a week, but John will insist on taking* **everything but/except the kitchen sink** (= a much larger number of things than is necessary). • LP **Quantity words**

ev·ery·where /£'ev·ri·weə^r, $-wer/, *Am infml* **ev·ery·place** /'ev·ri·pleɪs/ *adv* [not gradable], *n* (to, at or in) all places, or the whole of a place • *His children go everywhere with him.* • *Everywhere looks so grey and depressing in winter.* • *I looked everywhere for my keys – I searched the entire office.* • *Reasonable people everywhere will be outraged by this atrocity.* • *There's pollution almost everywhere these days.* • *Nowadays you can hear English spoken almost everywhere in the world.* • *We had to stay in the sleaziest hotel in town as everywhere* **else** (= all other places) *was fully booked.*

e·vict *obj* /ɪ'vɪkt/ *v* [T] to force (someone) to leave somewhere • *Tenants who fall behind in their rent risk being evicted.* • *He was evicted* **from** *the pub for drunken and violent behaviour.*

e·vic·tion /ɪ'vɪk·ʃ^ən/ *n* • *They had to obtain a court order for the eviction of the squatters.* [U] • *After falling behind with his mortgage repayments he now faces eviction* **from** *his home.* [U] • *In this economically depressed area, evictions are common.* [C]

ev·i·dence /'ev·ɪ·d^ənts/ *n* [U] one or more reasons for believing that something is or is not true • *The police have found no evidence* **of** *a terrorist link with the murder.* • *According to a recent study, there is no scientific evidence* **to** *suggest that underwater births are dangerous.* [+ *to* infinitive] • *Is there any scientific evidence* **that** *a person's character is reflected in their handwriting?* [+ *that* clause] • *Several experts are to* **give** *evidence on the subject to a parliamentary committee.* • *How can they expect me to* **give** *evidence* **against** *my own mother* (= give information about her in court)*?* • *There is only* **circumstantial** *evidence against her, so she is unlikely to be convicted.* • *Campaigners now have compelling* **documentary** *evidence of the human rights abuses that they had been alleging for several years.* • **Fresh** *evidence suggests that the statement had been fabricated.* • *The traces of petrol found on his clothing provided the* **forensic** *evidence proving that he had started the fire deliberately.* • *The charge against her was dropped because of insufficient evidence.* • **All the** *evidence points to a substantial rise in traffic over the next few years.* • *The Census Bureau yesterday provided* **further** *evidence of the widening gulf between rich and poor.* • *There is growing/mounting/increasing evidence* **that** *people whose diets are rich in vitamins are less likely to develop some types of cancer.* [+ *that* clause] • *A new spirit of cooperation was* **much in** *evidence* (= clear to see) *at the meeting.* • **Queen's evidence/King's evidence** is evidence given by someone who has been accused of committing a crime, against the people who were accused with them, in order to have their own punishment reduced: *to* **turn** (= give) *Queen's evidence* • LP **Crimes and criminals, Law** Ⓔ

ev·i·denced /'ev·ɪ·d^əntst/ *adj* [not gradable] *esp. Am* • *His desire to win an Olympic medal is evidenced* **by** *his performances throughout this season.*

ev·i·dent /'ev·ɪ·d^ənt/ *adj* easily seen or understood; obvious • *The full extent of the damage only became evident the following morning.* • *The audience waited with evident excitement for the performance to begin.* • **It** *is evident* **that** *the robber knew the building well.* [+ *that* clause] • **From** *the smell* **it** *was evident* **that** *the drains had been blocked for several days.* [+ *that* clause] • *Harry's courage during his illness was evident* **to** *everyone.* • *Her love for him was evident* **in** *all that she did.* • See also SELF-EVIDENT.

ev·i·dent·ly /'ev·ɪ·d^ənt·li/ *adv* • *She should have been here two hours ago so she's evidently decided not to come after all.* • *He was evidently upset by the news of the accident.*

e·vil /'iː·vəl/ *adj* immoral, or cruel, or very unpleasant • *We must do everything necessary to overthrow this evil dictator.* • *He was a narrow-minded, sadistic, thoroughly evil little man.* • If someone has an evil **tongue**, they tend to say unpleasant things about other people. • If the weather or a smell is evil, it is very unpleasant. • **The evil eye** is the magical power to injure or harm people by looking at them.

e·vil /'iː·vəl/ *n* • *Each new leader would denounce his predecessor, blaming him for all the evils of the past.* [C] • *Drug addiction is perhaps the greatest social evil that confronts Western society today.* [C] • *There are certain circumstances when war is justifiable, when, for the sake of long-term peace, the military option is the* **lesser** *evil/the* **lesser of two** *evils.* [C] • *This novel is just another story about the battle between good and evil.* [U]

e·vil·do·er /£'iː·vəl,duː·ə^r, $-ɚ/ *n* [C] someone who does something evil • *The government has blamed the protests on a handful of evildoers.*

e·vince *obj* /ɪ'vɪnts/ *v* [T] to make obvious or show clearly • *They have never evinced any readiness or ability to negotiate.* • *In all the years I knew her, she never evinced any desire to do such a thing.*

e·vis·cer·ate *obj* /ɪ'vɪs·ə·reɪt/ *v* [T] *specialized* to remove one or all of the organs from (the inside of a body) • *(fig.) The hearts of many old towns have been eviscerated and replaced with anonymous shopping centres.*

e·vis·cer·a·tion /ɪ,vɪs·ə'reɪ·ʃ^ən/ *n* [U]

e·voke *obj* /£ɪ'vəuk, $-'vouk/ *v* [T] to cause (something) to be remembered or expressed • *That smell always evokes memories of my old school.* • *This detergent is intended to evoke "the fresh smell of summer meadows."* • *Fragments of songs and poems evoke the human emotions at the heart of his story.*

e·voc·a·tion /£,ev·əʊ'keɪ·ʃ^ən, £,iː·vəʊ-, $,ev·ə-/ *n* • *An ingenious plot combines with a powerful evocation of rural life between the wars to produce a highly enjoyable film.* [C] • *It is the ability of the great artist to make each artistic creation a unique act of evocation.* [U]

e·voc·a·tive /£ɪ'vɒk·ə·tɪv, $-'vɑː·kə·t̬ɪv/ *adj* • *She mixes imaginative lyrics with evocative melodies to create some quite unforgettable songs.* • *The pebbled streets and traditional shops are evocative* **of** *a completely different era.*

e·voc·a·tive·ly /£ɪ'vɒk·ə·tɪv·li, $-'vɑː·kə·t̬ɪv-/ *adv* • *She spoke evocatively of her work with AIDS sufferers in London.*

e·volve *(obj)* /£ɪ'vɒlv, $-'vɑːlv/ *v* to (cause to) develop gradually • *How do we know that humans evolved* **from** *apes?* [I] • *The company has evolved over the years* **into** *a multi-million dollar organization.* [I] • *Bacteria are evolving resistance to antibiotics faster than new chemicals are being invented.* [T]

e·vol·u·tion /,iː·və'luː·ʃ^ən, ,ev·ə-/ *n* [U] • *Research on insects suggests that bacteria play a vital part in animal evolution.* • *This decision marks yet another change of direction in the evolution of the country's education policy.* • *The programme traced India's evolution since independence.*

e·vol·u·tion·a·ry /£,iː·və'luː·ʃ^ən·^ər·i, ,ev·ə'-, $-er-/ *adj* • *The Prime Minister declared that change should be evolutionary rather than revolutionary.*

ewe /juː/ *n* [C] a female sheep, esp. an adult one • *ewe's milk*

ex– /eks-/ *combining form* used to show that someone is no longer what they were; FORMER EARLIER • *Hundreds of unemployed ex-prisoners could be pushed back towards crime by the closure of job training programmes.* • *Did you know that she'd decided to remarry her ex-husband?* • *A lot of people working as security guards are ex-policemen.*

ex /eks/ *n* [C] *infml* • An ex is someone who is no longer a person's wife, husband, lover, etc.: *Is she still in touch with her ex?* ○ *It was a bit embarrassing because two of my exes were at the party.* • LP **Relationships**

ex·a·cer·bate *obj* /£ɪg'zæs·ə·beɪt, $'-ɚ-/ *v* [T] to make (something which is already bad) worse • *This attack will exacerbate the already tense relations between the two communities.* • *The effects of the drought have been exacerbated by a history of agricultural problems.*

ex·a·cer·ba·tion /£ɪg,zæs·ə'beɪ·ʃ^ən, $-ɚ'-/ *n* [U]

ex·act CORRECT /ɪg'zækt/ *adj* in great detail, or complete or correct or true in every way; PRECISE • *The exact distance is 1·838 metres.* • *The exact time of the accident was 2.43 pm.* • *"I still owe you £7, don't I?" "Actually, it's £7·30* **to be exact***."* • *The exact location of the factory has yet to be* *decided, but it is likely to be in an area of high unemployment.* • *Do the police know the exact circumstances of his death?* • *We arrived at the exact (same) moment that they were leaving.* • *Unlike astronomy, astrology cannot be described as an exact science.*

ex·act·ly /ɪg'zækt·li/ *adv* • *The journey took exactly three hours.* • *That'll be £15 exactly, please.* • *We started going out with each other exactly four years ago today.* • *Make sure you measure the window frame exactly otherwise the glass won't fit properly.* • *Stay exactly where you are and no-one will get hurt!* • *Where exactly can you draw the line between military and civilian targets?* • *What exactly do you want from life?* • *Exactly how do you propose to achieve this?* • *If I had my life to live again, I'd do exactly the same things.* • *It tastes exactly the same as the real thing, but has half the fat.* • *The theatre has been completely restored and now looks exactly as it did when it first opened in 1877.* • *This song is completely unoriginal and sounds exactly like all his other songs.* • *He promised me he wouldn't watch any more soap operas, but he was doing exactly that last night.* • *He's not exactly* (= not what I would describe as) *good-looking, but he has a certain attraction.* • *"So you gave her your Walkman?" "Not exactly* (= That is not completely true), *she said she'd give it back to me when she can afford her own."* • *"What you seem to be saying is that more should be invested in the road system and less in the railways." "Exactly* (= That is completely correct)*."*

ex·act·ness /ɪg'zækt·nəs/, *fml* **ex·ac·ti·tude** /£ɪg'zæk·tɪ·tju:d, $-tu:d/ *n* [U] • *It's impossible to say with exactitude what the eventual cost will be.*

ex·act *obj* OBTAIN /ɪg'zækt/ *v* [T] to demand and obtain (something), sometimes using force, threats or persuasion, or to make (something) necessary • *The blackmailers exacted a total of $100 000 from their victims.* • *This is the story of how a woman exacts grim revenge on the man who murdered her husband.* • *She will exact a high price* **from** *her colleagues for agreement to these proposals.* • *How can the economic toll exacted by sickness be reduced?* • *Heart surgery exacts tremendous skill and concentration.*

ex·act·ing /£ɪg'zæk·tɪŋ, $-t̬ɪŋ/ *adj* • Someone or something that is exacting demands a lot of effort, care or attention: *Chris is the most exacting director that I've ever worked with.* ○ *The trains used in the Channel Tunnel have to conform to exacting fire safety standards.*

ex·ag·ger·ate *(obj)* /£ɪg'zædʒ·ə·reɪt, $-ə·eɪt/ *v* to make (something) seem larger, more important, better or worse than it really is • *The threat of attack has been* **greatly** *exaggerated.* [T] • *A spokeswoman said that the pollution caused by the factory had been* **grossly/wildly** *exaggerated by environmentalists.* [T] • *The recovery in oil sales has exaggerated the improvement on last month's trade deficit.* [T] • *I've told you a million times not to exaggerate.* [I]

ex·ag·ger·at·ed·ly /£ɪg'zædʒ·ə·reɪ·tɪd·li, $-ə·eɪ·t̬ɪd-/ *adv* • *I kissed him on the cheek, exaggeratedly far from his mouth so that no misunderstanding could ever arise.*

ex·ag·ger·a·tion /ɪg,zædʒ·ə'reɪ·ʃən/ *n* • **It's** *not an exaggeration* **to** *say that her work has saved lives.* [+ *to* infinitive] • **It** *is* **no** *exaggeration* **to** *say that without the press none of these issues would have acquired the importance they have.* [+ *to* infinitive] • *There are people so addicted to exaggeration that they can't tell the truth without lying.* [U] • *"The report of my death was an exaggeration"* (Mark Twain to the *New York Journal* after it had reported his death, 1897)

ex·alt *obj* /ɪg'zɒlt, $-'zɑ:lt/ *v* [T] to praise (someone) a lot, or to raise (someone) to a higher rank or more powerful position

ex·alt·ed /£ɪg'zɒl·tɪd, $-'zɑ:l·t̬ɪd/ *adj* • *She rose to the exalted post of Foreign Secretary after only three years in the government.* • (I)

ex·al·ta·tion /£,eg·zɒl'teɪ·ʃən, $-zɑ:l-/ *n* [U] a very strong feeling of happiness • *They played well but missed out on the exaltation of a victory over their Spanish opponents.*

ex·alt·ed /£ɪg'zɒl·tɪd, $-'zɑ:l·t̬ɪd/ *adj* • *We were absolutely exalted when we learned of your success.* • (I)

ex·am /ɪg'zæm/, *fml* **ex·am·i·na·tion** *n* [C] a test of a student's knowledge or skill in a particular subject which results in a qualification if the student is successful • *How many pupils are taking the geography exam this term?* • *I failed my physics exam, but I passed chemistry.* • *Please do not turn over your examination* **paper** *until I instruct you to do so.* • *When do your exam* **results** *come out?* • LP› **Schools and colleges**

ex·am·ine *obj* /ɪg'zæm·ɪn/ *v* [T] • *I wish they'd examine us* **on** *what we've actually studied instead of what they're interested in.* • *(Br) 15 students are being examined* **in** *linguistics this year.* • *All the examining* **boards** (= organizations controlling exams) *have denied that the increased number of passes is due to a fall in standards.* • See also EXAMINE.

ex·am·i·ner /£ɪg'zæm·ɪ·nər, $-nə/ *n* [C] • *The candidates listed below have failed to satisfy the examiners* (= people judging and marking exams).

ex·am·ine *obj* /£ɪg'zæm·ɪn, eg'-, £ɪk'sæm-, £ek'-, $ɪg'zæm-/ *v* [T] to look at or consider (a person or thing) carefully and in detail in order to discover something about the person or thing • *Forensic scientists are examining the wreckage* **for** *clues about the cause of the explosion.* • *Women should examine their breasts regularly* **for** *signs of cancer.* • *The council is to examine ways of reducing traffic in the city centre.* • *They are examining the possibility of a complete ban on private cars.* • *Dr Scott's research examined the effects of alcohol on long-term memory.* • *We need to examine* **how** *an accident like this can be avoided in the future.* [+ *wh-* word] • *A psychiatrist was examined* (= asked questions) **on** *the mental state of the defendant.* • See also **examine** at EXAM.

ex·am·i·na·tion /£ɪg,zæm·ɪ'neɪ·ʃən, eg,-, £ɪk,sæm-, £ek,-, £-ə'-, $ɪg,zæm-/ *n* • *The police said that the post-mortem examination had found no suspicious circumstances.* [C] • *I had to* **have/undergo** *a medical examination when I started my pension scheme.* [C] • *It will be several weeks before the examination* **of** *all the evidence is complete.* [U] • *The evidence is still* **under** *examination* (= being examined). [U] • *I thought it was paint at first, but* **on closer** *examination I realised it was dried blood.* [U] • See also **examination** at EXAM. • LP› **Schools and colleges**

ex·am·ple TYPICAL CASE /£ɪg'zɑ:m·pl̩, $-'zæm-/ *n* [C] something which is typical of the group of things that it is a member of • *Could you give me an example* **of** *the improvements you have mentioned?* • *This painting is a marvellous example* **of** *her work.* • *Offices can easily become more environmentally-friendly by,* **for example** (= doing something like), *using recycled paper.* • **For example** *is sometimes shortened to the Latin abbreviation e.g.* • An example is also a way of helping someone to understand something by showing them how it is used: *Study the examples first of all, then attempt the exercises on the next page.* ○ *This sentence is an example of how the word 'example' is used.* • See also EXEMPLIFY. • (CS) (PL) (RUS) (S)

ex·am·ple BEHAVIOUR /£ɪg'zɑ:m·pl̩, $-'zæm-/ *n* [C] a person or their behaviour when considered for their suitability to be copied • *She was a guiding light and a shining example for generations of ballet dancers.* • *He has decided to* **follow** *the example of* (= do the same thing as) *his father and study law.* • *I wish you'd* **set** *a good example* **to** *your brother instead of coming home drunk every night.* • *Their bravery and perseverance in the face of tremendous adversity is an example* **to** *everyone.* • (CS) (PL) (RUS) (S)

ex·am·ple PUNISHMENT /£ɪg'zɑ:m·pl̩, $-'zæm-/ *n* [C] (a person who receives) a punishment which is intended to warn others against doing the thing that is being punished • *The judge* **made an** *example* **of** *him and gave him the maximum possible sentence in order to discourage similar offences.* • (CS) (PL) (RUS) (S)

ex·as·per·ate *obj* /£ɪg'zɑ:·spə·reɪt, $-'zæs·pə·eɪt/ *v* [T] to cause anger or extreme annoyance in (someone), sometimes mixed with surprise, or disappointment • *Employers are increasingly exasperated* **by/at** *the poor literacy of some young job applicants.*

ex·as·per·at·ed /£ɪg'zɑ:·spə·reɪ·tɪd, $-'zæs·pə·eɪ·t̬ɪd/ *adj* • *Exasperated families and friends of drug victims have begun calling for government action.*

ex·as·per·at·ed·ly /£ɪg'zɑ:·spə·reɪ·tɪd·li, $-'zæs·pə·eɪ·t̬ɪd-/ *adv* • *"But why are you arresting me? I haven't done anything wrong," he spluttered exasperatedly.*

ex·a·sper·at·ing /£ɪg'zɑ:·spə·reɪ·tɪŋ, $-'zæs·pə·eɪ·t̬ɪŋ/ *adj* • *The way he never lets anyone finish what they're saying is really exasperating.*

ex·as·per·at·ing·ly /£ɪg'zɑ:·spə·reɪ·tɪŋ·li, $-'zæs·pə·eɪ·t̬ɪŋ-/ *adv* • *All this bureaucracy is exasperatingly inefficient.*

ex·as·per·a·tion /£ɪg,zɑ:·spə'reɪ·ʃən, $-'zæs·pə-/ *n* [U] • *There is growing exasperation within the government* **at** *the failure of these policies to reduce unemployment.* •

After ten hours of fruitless negotiations, he stormed out of the meeting **in** *exasperation.*

ex ca·the·dra /ˌeks·kəˈθiː·drə/ *adj, adv* [not gradable] *fml* with complete authority, or said by the Pope to be true and so accepted by all members of the Roman Catholic Church • *This MP speaks ex-cathedra – particularly about Europe, which he seems to believe was invented by him.*

ex·ca·vate *(obj)* /ˈek·skə·veɪt/ *v* to remove earth that is covering (very old objects buried in the ground) in order to discover things about the past, or to look for old objects by removing earth from (an area of land) • *Tintagel Castle, the reputed birthplace of King Arthur, is being excavated professionally for the first time in more than 50 years.* [T] • *Three dinosaurs have already been found on the excavated site.* [T] • *They spent seven years excavating in the Middle East.* [I] • *(fig.) She has become famous enough for hordes of journalists to go around excavating her past and unearthing details of her private life.* [T] • To excavate is also to dig a hole or channel in the ground for other purposes: *In tin mining today, workers excavate tunnels horizontally from a vertical shaft.*

ex·ca·va·tion /ˌeks·kəˈveɪ·ʃᵊn/ *n* • *The excavation of the site is likely to take several years.* [U] • *She has taken part in several excavations of Roman settlements across Europe.* [C]

ex·ca·vat·or *Br and Aus* /£ˈek·skə·veɪ·təʳ, $-t̬ɚ/, *Am* **steam shov·el** *n* [C] • An excavator is a large powerful machine with a container connected to a long arm that is used for digging up the ground.

ex·ceed *obj* /ɪkˈsiːd/ *v* [T] to be greater than (a number or amount), or to go beyond (a permitted limit) • *The final cost should not exceed $5000.* • *The total current must not exceed 13 amps.* • *The success of our campaign has exceeded our wildest expectations.* • *She was found guilty on three charges of exceeding the speed limit.*

ex·ceed·ing·ly /ɪkˈsiː·dɪŋ·li/ *adv* to a very great degree; extremely • *Pat is an exceedingly unpleasant person.* • *"Mr Kipling makes exceedingly good cakes"* (advertisement, 1980s-)

ex·cel *(obj)* /ɪkˈsel, ek-/ *v* **-ll-** to be extremely good • *The whole band performed well, but the lead guitarist in particular excelled throughout the concert.* [I] • *I've never excelled* **at/in** *diving, although I've always been a good swimmer.* [I] • *Jane really excelled* **herself** (= did even better than she usually does) *in her exams and got top marks in all her subjects.* [T] • *(humorous or disapproving) You really excelled yourself last night, didn't you? I've never seen you so drunk before.*

Ex·cel·len·cy /ˈek·sᵊl·ənt·si/ *n* [C] (the title of) someone in an important official position, esp. someone, such as an AMBASSADOR, who represents their government in a foreign country • *I do not want to argue with you,* **(Your)** *Excellency.* • **His** *Excellency will be pleased to see you now.*

ex·cel·lent /ˈek·sᵊl·ᵊnt/ *adj* extremely good • *We had an excellent meal but the music was dreadful.* • *Her car is in excellent condition.* • *The fall in interest rates is excellent news for borrowers.* • *"Our sales are up for the third year in a row." "Excellent.* (= I'm extremely pleased)*".*

ex·cel·lent·ly /ˈek·sᵊl·ᵊnt·li/ *adv* • *This computer's been working excellently since Andy fixed it.*

ex·cel·lence /ˈek·sᵊl·ᵊnts/ *n* [U] • *The school is noted for its academic excellence.*

ex·cept /ɪkˈsept/ *prep, conjunction* not including; but not • *The government has few options except to keep interest rates high.* • *It's cool and quiet everywhere except in the kitchen.* • *Upon arrival, the crew discover that all of the inhabitants have been killed except* **for** *one couple.* • *Except* **for** *her lack of experience she would be the ideal person for the job.* • *There is nothing to indicate the building's past, except* **(for)** *the fireplace.* • *The two brothers look exactly the same except* **that** *one has a birth mark on his left arm.* • *We can do nothing except appeal to their conscience.* • *The museum is open daily except Monday(s).*

ex·cept *obj* /ɪkˈsept/ *v* [T] *fml* • *Why should anyone be excepted* **from** (= not have to pay) *this tax?* • *I can't stand academics –* **present company** *excepted* (= not including those who are being talked to).

ex·cept·ing /£ɪkˈsep·tɪŋ, $-t̬ɪŋ/ *prep, conjunction* • *All the people who were on the aircraft have now been identified excepting one.*

ex·cep·tion /ɪkˈsep·ʃᵊn/ *n* • *Mary always leaves home at eight o'clock but today is an exception, she's going later.* [C] • *You must report here every Tuesday* **without** *exception.* [U] • *We don't usually accept late applications but in this case we can* **make an** *exception* (= accept it) *because of the circumstances.* • **With the** *exception of the weather it was a perfect holiday.* [C] • If someone **takes exception (to)** something or someone they are offended or made angry by it: *Why did you take exception to what he said? – he was only joking.* • *(saying)* 'The exception proves the rule' means the existence of some exception(s) shows a (limited) rule exists or that it works in all other cases.

ex·cep·tion·a·ble /ɪkˈsep·ʃᵊn·ə·bl̩/ *adj fml* offensive or upsetting • *Many people find that sort of newspaper article highly exceptionable.*

ex·cep·tion·al /ɪkˈsep·ʃᵊn·ᵊl/ *adj approving* much greater than usual, esp. in skill, cleverness, quality, etc. • *She has exceptional abilities as a pianist.* • *The company has shown exceptional growth over the past two years.*

ex·cep·tion·al·ly /ɪkˈsep·ʃᵊn·ᵊl·i/ *adv* • *an exceptionally fine portrait*

ex·cerpt /£ˈek·sɜːpt, $-sɜːrpt/ *n* [C] a short part taken from a speech, book, film, etc. • *An excerpt* **from** *her new thriller will appear in this weekend's magazine.* • *The excerpts contain the essential points of the report.*

ex·cerpt *obj* /£ekˈsɜːp·tɪd, $-ˈsɜːrp·t̬ɪd, ˈ---/ *v* [T usually passive] *esp. Am* • *This passage of text has been excerpted* **from** *her latest novel.*

ex·cess /ekˈses, ˈ--/ *n* [U], *adj* [not gradable] (an amount which is) more than acceptable, expected or reasonable • *An excess* **of** *enthusiasm is not always a good thing.* • *They both eat* **to** *excess* (= a lot more than they need). • *There will be an increase in tax for those earning* **in** *excess* **of** (= more than) *twice the national average wage.* • *We might seem to be carrying excess supplies but they would be necessary in the case of an emergency.* [before n] • *Because our suitcases were so heavy we he had to pay* **excess luggage/baggage** (= the money charged because your bags weigh more than the allowed amount).

ex·ces·ses /ekˈses·ɪz, ˈ---/ *pl n* • Excesses are actions far beyond the limit of what is acceptable: *For many years people were trying to escape the excesses* (= cruel actions) *of the junta.* ○ *As for shoes, her excesses* (= the large amount she owned) *were well known.*

ex·ces·sive /ekˈses·ɪv/ *adj* • *Excessive exercise can sometimes cause health problems.* • *It's very kind of you to offer, but any more pudding would simply be excessive.*

ex·ces·sive·ly /ekˈses·ɪv·li/ *adv* • *The salesman was excessively persistent.*

ex·change *obj* /ɪksˈtʃeɪndʒ/ *v* [T] to change (something) for something else of a similar value or type • *My uncle bought me this shirt as a present but I don't like the colour, so is it possible to exchange it* **for** *a different one?* • *Every month the group meets so its members can exchange their views/opinions* (= have a discussion). • *Exchanging houses* (= going to live in someone else's house while they live in yours) *for a few weeks is a good way of having a holiday.* • *They* **exchanged words** (= argued) *but now they seem to be talking normally.*

ex·change /ɪksˈtʃeɪndʒ/ *n* • *He gave me some tomatoes* **in** *exchange* **for** *a lift into town.* [U] • *She proposes an exchange of contracts at two o'clock.* [C] • *There was a brief exchange* (= short discussion) *between the two leaders.* [C] • *A bitter exchange* (= bad argument) *occurred between the brothers.* [C] • *Several people were killed during the exchange (of gunfire).* [C] • *It looked as if there would be an exchange of blows* (= a fight) *but they both calmed down.* [C] • An **exchange rate** (or **rate of exchange**) is the rate at which the money of one country can be changed for the money of another country. • The **Exchange Rate Mechanism** (*abbreviation* **ERM**) is the agreement by which some member countries of the European Union willingly control the rate of exchange of their money in relation to the ECU (= European Currency Unit): *The pound left the ERM when its value fell below its required level.*

ex·chan·ge·able /ɪksˈtʃeɪn·dʒə·bl̩/ *adj* [not gradable] • *The cardigan is certainly exchangeable as long as you return it in good condition.*

ex·che·quer /£ɪksˈtʃek·əʳ, $-ɚ/ *n* [U] **the exchequer** (in Britain and some other countries) the department of the Treasury which receives and gives out public money

ex·cise [TAX] /ˈek·saɪz/ *n* [U] a tax made by a government on some types of goods produced and used within their own country • *Government sources have said that the excise* **(duty) on** *beer will probably be increased under the next budget.*

ex·cise *obj* [REMOVE] /£ekˈsaɪz, $ˈ--/ *v* [T] *fml* to remove, esp. by cutting • *During the operation the surgeon excised several tumours* **from** *the wall of the patient's stomach.* •

The official censors have excised the controversial sections of the report.

ex·ci·sion /ek'sɪʒ·ᵊn/ *n* [C/U]

ex·cite *obj* MAKE HAPPY /ɪk'saɪt/ *v* [T] to make (someone) have strong feelings, esp. of happiness and enthusiasm • *The thought of their holiday excited them greatly.* • *Theatre production companies are under continuous pressure to come up with new ideas that will excite today's audiences.* • *At first the classes were excited by this exercise, but as time went on they became bored.* • Ⓔ

ex·cit·a·ble /£ɪk'saɪ·tə·bl̩, $-t̬ə-/ *adj* • If a person or an animal is excitable they are easy to excite: *As a child she was highly excitable – the slightest thing could make her laugh or cry.*

ex·cit·ed /£ɪk'saɪ·tɪd, $-t̬ɪd/ *adj* • *An excited crowd waited for the group to arrive outside the theatre.* • *The progress made in controlling pollution levels is* **nothing to get excited about** (= not much).

ex·cit·ed·ly /£ɪk'saɪ·tɪd·li, $-t̬ɪd-/ *adv* • *She ran excitedly down the hall to greet her cousins.*

ex·cit·ing /£ɪk'saɪ·tɪŋ, $-t̬ɪŋ/ *adj* • *The film had an exciting soundtrack.* • *Both teams played well – it was a really exciting match.* • *The situation has been changed by several exciting new developments.*

ex·cit·ing·ly /£ɪk'saɪ·tɪŋ·li, $-t̬ɪŋ-/ *adv* • *The book is excitingly written.*

ex·cite·ment /ɪk'saɪt·mənt/ *n* • *Robin's heart was pounding with excitement.* [U] • *If you want excitement you should try parachuting.* [U] • *After the initial excitements of planning, the project has entered a calmer phase now that building has begun.* [C]

ex·cite *obj* CAUSE FEELINGS /ɪk'saɪt/ *v* [T] *fml* to cause (strong feelings) in someone • *Such wildness in the landscape excited feelings of terror within her which she had never felt before.* • *The statement excited new speculation that a senior minister may be about to resign.* • Ⓔ

excl *abbreviation for* **excluding** or **exclusive**, see at EXCLUDE • This abbreviation is used mainly in advertisements.

ex·claim *(obj)* /ɪk'skleɪm/ *v* to say or shout something suddenly because of surprise, fear, pleasure, etc. • *"You can't leave so soon!" she exclaimed.* [+ clause] • *"Bah!" he exclaimed in disgust.* [+ clause] • *She exclaimed* **in** *delight upon hearing the news.* [I]

ex·cla·ma·tion /ˌek·sklə'meɪ·ʃᵊn/ *n* [C] • *"Ouch!", "Not now!", "Yes!" and "No!" are all exclamations.* • *They embraced with exclamations* (= saying words to each other) *of happiness.* • An **exclamation mark** (*Am* **exclamation point**) is the mark '!', used in writing immediately after an exclamation. • LP **Phrases and customs** PIC **Mark**

ex·clude *obj* /ɪk'skluːd/ *v* [T] to keep out or omit (something or someone) • *They exclude people* **from** *their club for the most petty of reasons.* • *Microbes must, as far as possible, be excluded* **from** *the room during an operation.* • *Tom has been excluded* **from** *school* (= he is not allowed to go to school) *for bad behaviour.* • *The price excludes local taxes.* • *I don't think we can exclude the possibility that he may have been murdered.* • Compare INCLUDE.

ex·clud·ing /ɪk'skluː·dɪŋ/ *prep* • *The aircraft carries 461 people excluding* (= apart from) *the crew and cabin staff.*

ex·clu·sion /ɪk'skluː·ʒᵊn/ *n* • *Her exclusion* **from** *the list of Oscar nominees put her in a foul mood.* [U] • *There are several noticeable exclusions from the names put forward to be considered for the job.* [C] • *He was obsessed with art – he spent all of his time painting* **to the exclusion of** *his family* (= he never saw his family because he was always painting).

ex·clu·sive /ɪk'skluː·sɪv/ *adj* • *Is the total exclusive* **of** *service charge* (= does it include this charge)*?* • *Some people think that uncontrolled economic growth and environmental stability are* **mutually** *exclusive* (= are not possible at the same time).

ex·clu·sive /ɪk'skluː·sɪv/ *adj* limited to only one person or group of people • *This room is for the exclusive use of guests.* • *The hostage gave an exclusive interview to our reporter* (= to only this one reporter). • *Singing is not her exclusive* (= only) *interest outside work, she does many other things as well.* • A place that is exclusive can only be used by a limited number of people, esp. those who are rich: *The restaurant/shop/hotel is very exclusive* (= provides goods and services for the wealthy). • *The golf club has an exclusive membership.*

ex·clu·sive /ɪk'skluː·sɪv/ *n* [C] • An exclusive is a story which is printed in one newspaper or magazine and no others: *The newspaper published an exclusive about the escape.*

ex·clu·sive·ly /ɪk'skluː·sɪv·li/ *adv* • *This offer is available exclusively* (= only) *to our established customers.* • *Almost all of the surrounding land is owned exclusively* (= completely) *by a few very rich farmers.*

ex·clu·sive·ness /ɪk'skluː·sɪv·nəs/ *n* [U] • *The group's exclusiveness* (= unwillingness to allow others to join it) *offends a lot of people.*

ex·clu·siv·i·ty /£ˌek·skluː'sɪv·ɪ·ti, $-ə·t̬i/ *n* [U] • *Their exclusivity is really annoying.*

ex·com·mu·ni·cate *obj* /ˌek·skə'mjuː·nɪ·keɪt/ *v* [T] (of the Christian Church, esp. the Roman Catholic Church) to refuse (someone) COMMUNION and not allow them to be involved in the Church • *Despite being excommunicated he kept his faith in God.*

ex·com·mu·ni·ca·tion /ˌek·skəˌmjuː·nɪ'keɪ·ʃᵊn/ *n* • *At a time when the Church is especially sensitive about its image, the excommunications have done little more than attract unwelcome publicity.* [C] • *Roman Catholic politicians risk excommunication if they support a woman's right to an abortion.* [U]

ex·co·ri·ate *obj* /£ek'skɔː·ri·eɪt, $-'skɔːr·i-/ *v* [T] *fml* to state the opinion that (a play, a book, a political action, etc.) is very bad • *His latest novel received excoriating reviews.* • *The President excoriated the Western press for their biased views.*

ex·cres·cence /ek'skres·ᵊnts/ *n* [C] *fml* an unusual growth on an animal or one of its organs or on a plant • *Increasing numbers of fish are being caught with excrescences on various parts of their body.* • *(fig.) The new office development is an excrescence* (= ugly growth) **on** *the city.*

ex·crete *(obj)* /ɪk'skriːt/ *v fml or specialized* (of humans, animals or plants) to get rid of (waste material such as excrement or urine) from the body • *Most toxins are naturally excreted from the body.* [T] • *Some people excrete more often than others.* [I]

ex·cre·tion /ɪk'skriː·ʃᵊn/ *n fml or specialized* • *Excretion is one of several activities common to both*

EXCLAMATION MARK [!]

Many writers do not like to use exclamation marks. They are used in informal writing and when writing down something that has been said with a lot of emotion. An exclamation mark may be used:

- **at the end of of a sentence expressing strong feelings, and with exclamations and interjections**

  "This song's great!"
  But that's a terrible thing to happen!
  She's a professor, and she's only 18!
  "Damn!"
  "Hi!"

- **to show that a speaker is shouting, or that a noise is loud**

  "Dave, where are you? Dave!"
  Bang! She slammed the door.

- **at the end of a forceful order**

  "Don't open that parcel, it might be a bomb!"
  (BUT *"Open your book at page 102."*)
  "Stop, there's a car coming!"
  (BUT *"Stop playing with the cat now, Jamie."*)

- **in informal or humorous writing, !! or?! are sometimes used to show strong emotion or loud sounds**

  "Help!!"
  "Terry's been arrested by the police." "Arrested?!"
  Tess made a hell of a noise – Splash!!!

Notice that an exclamation mark is not used at the beginning of letters

Dear Ms Simmonds
Dear Mom and Dad,

plants and animals. [U] • *The patient's excretions have been quite regular.* [C]

ex·cre·ment /ˈek·skrɪ·mənt/ *n* [U] *fml or specialized* • Excrement is the waste material excreted from a body through the bowels: *It was disgusting, there was excrement all over the floor.*

ex·cre·ta /£ɪkˈskriː·tə, $-t̬ə/ *n* [U] *fml or specialized* • Excreta is the waste material produced by a body, esp. solid waste material.

ex·cru·ci·at·ing /£ɪkˈskruː·ʃi·eɪ·tɪŋ, $-t̬ɪŋ/ *adj* (of pain) extreme • *She often suffers from excruciating pain in her hands as a result of what was done to her during her imprisonment.* • *(fig.) The embarrassing facts were explained in excruciating detail.*

ex·cru·ci·at·ing·ly /£ɪkˈskruː·ʃi·eɪ·tɪŋ·li, $-t̬ɪŋ-/ *adv* • *excruciatingly painful/difficult* • *(fig.) excruciatingly boring/funny*

ex·cul·pate *obj* /ˈek·skəl·peɪt/ *v* [T] *fml* to remove blame from (someone) • *The pilot of the aircraft will surely be exculpated when all the facts are known.* • Compare INCULPATE.

ex·cul·pa·to·ry /£ekˈskʌl·peɪ·tᵊr·i, $-tɔː·ri/ *adj* [not gradable] • *His evidence, although damning to the others, was exculpatory* (= freeing him from blame) *concerning his own actions.*

ex·cur·sion /£ɪkˈskɜː·ʃᵊn, £-ʒᵊn, $-ˈskɜːr-/ *n* [C] a short journey usually made for pleasure, often by a group of people • *This year's annual excursion will be* **to** *Lincoln.* • *Next week we're going* **on** *an excursion.* • *An optional excursion has been organised for every day of your holiday* **to** *a nearby place of interest.* • *(fig.) Having produced only novels before she has now made an excursion* **into** *writing for the theatre.*

ex·cuse *obj* FORGIVE /ɪkˈskjuːz/ *v* [T] to forgive (someone) • *Please excuse me* **for** *arriving late – the bus was delayed.* • *You'll have to excuse the interruption caused by the building work.* • *Apologising does not excuse your awful behaviour.* • *No amount of financial recompense can excuse the way in which the company carried out its policy.* • *We cannot excuse him* **(for)** *these crimes.* [+ two objects] • *May I be excused* **from** *cricket practice? My knee still hurts.* • *You must excuse me* **from** *the rest of the meeting as I've just received a telephone call which requires my immediate attention.* • The expression **excuse me** is a polite way of attracting the attention, esp. of someone you don't know, and it can also be used to show respect before disagreeing with someone: *Excuse me* (= I would like to go past). ○ *Excuse me, where is the theatre?* ○ *Excuse me but aren't you forgetting something?* • Excuse me is also *Am for* **pardon me**. See at PARDON. • The question **May I be excused?** is used, esp. by children, to ask permission to go to the toilet: *Please may I be excused, Mr Davies?* • LP› **Phrases and customs, Two objects**

ex·cus·ab·le /ɪkˈskjuː·zə·bl̩/ *adj* • *Considering her difficult childhood her behaviour is excusable* (= can be forgiven).

ex·cuse EXPLANATION /ɪkˈskjuːs/ *n* the explanation given for bad behaviour, absence, etc. • *They have a good excuse* **for** *being late – their car wouldn't start.* [C] • *Your alarm clock didn't go off? That's a poor excuse – you could have asked someone else to check you were awake.* [C] • *She needs only the slightest excuse* (= reason) **to** *go on holiday.* [C + *to* infinitive] • *Admittedly the legislation is not clearly written but* **by way of** *excuse it did go through Parliament very quickly.* [U] • *Please* **make** *my* **excuses** *at Thursday's meeting* (= explain why I am unable to go). • *You're always* **making excuses** (= giving reasons for not doing things). • *It was a miserable* **excuse for** (= example of) *a meal – the portions were very small and everything tasted foul.*

ex–di·rec·tory *Br* /£ˌeks·daɪˈrek·tri, $-tɔːr·i/, *Am and Aus* **un·list·ed** /£ʌnˈlɪs·tɪd, $-t̬ɪd/ *adj* [not gradable] (of a telephone number) not in the public telephone DIRECTORY (= book that lists numbers) and not given to people who ask for it from the telephone company • *We've gone ex-directory because we were receiving so many unwanted calls.*

ex·e·cra·ble /ˈek·sə·krə·bl̩/ *adj fml* very bad • *I've never heard such an execrable performance of the concerto.*

ex·e·crab·ly /ˈek·sə·krə·bli/ *adv* • *He treated her execrably.*

ex·e·cute *obj* DO /ˈek·sɪ·kjuːt/ *v* [T] *fml* to do or perform (something), esp. in a planned way • *Now that we have approval we may execute the scheme as previously agreed.* • *Executing the stunt will require split-second timing.* • *The whole play was executed with great precision.* • *(law)* If you execute someone's **will**, you deal with their money, property, etc., according to the instructions in it.

ex·e·cu·tion /ˌek·sɪˈkjuː·ʃᵊn/ *n* [U] • *Although the original idea was good, its execution has produced a disappointing result.* • *Sometimes in the execution of their duty the police have to use firearms.* • *The guitarist's execution of the sonata was superb.*

ex·e·cu·tive /£ɪɡˈzek·jʊ·tɪv, $-jə·t̬ɪv/, *infml* **ex·ec** /ɪɡˈzek/ *n* • An executive is someone (or sometimes a group) in a high position, esp. in business, who makes decisions and acts according to them: *She is now a senior executive having worked her way up through the company.* [C] • The executive of a group or government is the part responsible for its rules or POLICIES (= intended actions): *The Executive of the union asked for more funds to enable it to enforce the new legislation.* [C + sing/pl v]

ex·e·cu·tive /£ɪɡˈzek·jʊ·tɪv, $-jə·t̬ɪv/ *adj* [before n] • *an executive suite* • *In the US there is a large gap between the legislative and executive branches of government.* • *His executive skills will be very useful to the company.* • *We sell executive cars* (= cars which people in business would use).

ex·e·cut·or /£ɪɡˈzek·jʊ·tər, $-jə·t̬ɚ/ *n* [C] *law* • An executor is a person who executes the wishes expressed in a WILL (= document stating what should happen to a dead person's property): *His uncle is the executor of his mother's will.*

ex·e·cute *obj* KILL /ˈek·sɪ·kjuːt/ *v* [T] to kill (someone) as a legal punishment • *It now seems certain that the prisoner will be executed tomorrow.*

ex·e·cu·tion /ˌek·sɪˈkjuː·ʃᵊn/ *n* • *Execution is still the penalty in some states for murder.* [U] • *The executions will be carried out by a firing squad.* [C]

ex·e·cu·tion·er /£ˌek·sɪˈkjuː·ʃᵊn·ər, $-ɚ/ *n* [C] • An executioner is someone who performs executions.

ex·e·ge·sis /ˌek·sɪˈdʒiː·sɪs/ *n* [C/U] *specialized* an explanation of a text, esp. from the Bible, after its careful study

ex·em·plar·y /£ɪɡˈzem·plə·ri, $-plɚ·i/ *adj* showing a (good) example • *His tact was exemplary, especially considering the circumstances.* • *(fml) The judge awarded exemplary damages* (= ruled that a lot of money would have to be paid) *to dissuade others from committing the same crime.*

ex·em·plar /£ɪɡˈzem·plər, £-plɑːr, $-plɚ/ *n* [C] • *It is an exemplar* (= good example) **of** *a house of the period.*

ex·em·pli·fy *obj* /ɪɡˈzem·plɪ·faɪ/ *v* [T] to be or give an example of (something) • *This painting perfectly exemplifies the naturalistic style which was so popular at the time.* • *I shall exemplify the approach by solving this equation.*

ex·em·pli·fi·ca·tion /ɪɡˌzem·plɪ·fɪˈkeɪ·ʃᵊn/ *n* [C/U]

ex·empt *obj* /ɪɡˈzempt/ *v* [T] to excuse (someone or something) from a duty, payment, etc. • *Exempting small businesses* **from** *an increase in tax should be a popular move.*

ex·empt /ɪɡˈzempt/ *adj* [not gradable] • *Goods exempt* **from** *this tax include books and children's clothes.* • *Pregnant women are exempt* **from** *dental charges under the current health system.*

ex·emp·tion /ɪɡˈzemp·ʃᵊn/ *n* [C/U]

ex·er·cise HEALTHY ACTIVITY /£ˈek·sə·saɪz, $-sɚ-/ *v, n* (to perform) physical actions to make or keep (someone's body) healthy • *She exercises every evening by running.* [I] • *Now he's retired he spends most afternoons exercising his dogs.* [T] • *Grappling with fundamental concepts in mathematics exercises the mind in a most expansive way.* [T] • *(fig.) The whole situation is exercising us/our minds* (= worrying us) *greatly.* [T] • *You really should take more exercise now that your job keeps you in the office so much.* [U] • *Some people do exercises before they go to work each day.* [C] • An **exercise bike** is a machine for taking exercise which looks similar to and is used like a bicycle but does not move from one place. • PIC› **Bicycles**

ex·er·cise PRACTISING /£ˈek·sə·saɪz, $-sɚ-/ *n* [C] an action or actions intended to improve something or make something happen • *Daily exercises can strengthen musical technique.* • *Ships from eight navies will be taking part in an exercise in the Pacific (to improve their efficiency in combat).* • *Getting so many people to such a remote site was a challenging exercise.* • *It would be a useful exercise for you to say the speech aloud several times. The United Nations attempt to end the civil war has been* **an** *exercise* **in** *futility/compromise.* • An exercise can be a short piece of written work which you do to practise something you are learning: *The book has exercises at the end of every chapter.*

ex·er·cises /£'ek·sə·saɪ·zɪz, $-sə-/ *pl n Am fml* • Exercises are a ceremony which includes speeches and usually traditional music or activities: *commencement/ graduation/inaugural exercises*

ex·er·cise *obj* USE /£'ek·sə·saɪz, $-sə-/ *v* [T] *fml* to use (something) • *I exercised my democratic right by not voting in the election.* • *Always exercise* **caution** *when handling radioactive substances.* • *We've decided to exercise the* **option** (= use the part of a legal agreement) *to buy the house we now lease.*

ex·er·cise /£'ek·sə·saɪz, $-sə-/ *n* [U] • *The exercise* **of** *restraint may well be difficult.*

ex·ert *obj* USE /£ɪg'zɜːt, $-'zɜːrt/ *v* [T] to use (an ability or skill) • *By exerting all of his strength he could just move the crate.* • *If you were to exert your* **influence** *they might change their decision.* • *Some managers exert considerable* **pressure** *on their staff to work extra hours without being paid.*

ex·er·tion /£ɪg'zɜː·ʃən, $-'zɜːr-/ *n* [U] • *Exertion of authority does not come easily to everyone.*

ex·ert *obj* MAKE AN EFFORT /£ɪg'zɜːt, $-'zɜːrt/ *v* [T] to cause (yourself) to make an effort • *She'll have to exert* **herself** *more than she does now if she wants to succeed in sales.* • *(fig.) Please don't exert* (= hurt) **yourself***, I can carry some things too.*

ex·er·tion /£ɪg'zɜː·ʒən, $-'zɜːr-/ *n* • *Physical exertion isn't always a good thing in a hot climate.* [U] • *He's so lazy! Getting out of bed is a major exertion for him.* [C] • *We were exhausted after our exertions.* [C]

ex·fo·li·ate *(obj)* /£ɪks'fəʊ·li·eɪt, $-'foʊ-/ *v* to remove dead skin • *For a cleaner, healthier-looking complexion, you should exfoliate (the skin) twice a week.* [I/T]

ex·fo·li·a·tion /£eks,fəʊ·li'eɪ·ʃən, $-,foʊ-/ *n* [U]

ex gra·ti·a /eks'greɪ·ʃə/ *adj* [not gradable] *fml* (of a payment) not necessary, esp. legally but made to show good intentions • *Although the suppliers were shown not to have been negligent ex gratia payments were made to all those who had been affected by the spillage.*

ex·hale *(obj)* /eks'heɪl, $'--/ *v* to send out (gas), esp. from the lungs • *Take a deep breath in then exhale into the mouthpiece.* [I] • *This machine records the ratios of various gases exhaled during exercise.* [T] • Compare INHALE.

ex·hal·a·tion /,eks·*h*ə'leɪ·ʃən/ *n* [C/U]

ex·haust *obj* TIRE /£ɪg'zɔːst, $-'zɑːst/ *v* [T] to tire (a person or an animal) greatly • *The long journey exhausted the children.* • *They exhausted themselves in a day of difficult climbing.*

ex·haust·ed /£ɪg'zɔː·stɪd, $-'zɑː-,/ *adj* • *Exhausted, they fell asleep.* • *By the time they reached the summit they were exhausted but they were also relieved to be there.*

ex·haust·ing /£ɪg'zɔː·stɪŋ, $-'zɑː-/ *adj* • *Most people find the test exhausting but few find it to be impossible.*

ex·haus·tion /£ɪg'zɔːs·tʃən, $-'zɑː-/ *n* [U] • *She felt ill with/from exhaustion.*

ex·haust *obj* USE /£ɪg'zɔːst, $-'zɑːst/ *v* [T] to use (something) completely • *His bad behaviour nearly exhausted her patience.* • *The administrative problems quickly exhausted any enthusiasm I had for the scheme.* • *We seem to have exhausted this topic of conversation* (= we have nothing new to say about it).

ex·haus·ti·ble /£ɪg'zɔː·stɪ·bl̩, $-'zɑː-/ *adj* • *It is clear that many of the Earth's resources are exhaustible* (= will be used completely and disappear).

ex·haus·tive /£ɪg'zɔː·stɪv, $-'zɑː-/ *adj* • If something is exhaustive it is complete: *an exhaustive study/report*

ex·haus·tive·ly /£ɪg'zɔː·stɪv·li, $-'zɑː-/ *adv* • *The survey was exhaustively documented.*

ex·haust GAS /£ɪg'zɔːst, $-'zɑːst/ *n* the waste gas from an engine, esp. a car's, or the pipe the gas flows through • *Car exhaust is the main reason for the city's smog problem.* [U] • *(Br and Aus) The* **exhaust (pipe)** *(Am usually* **tailpipe***) needs replacing.* [C] • PIC› **Car**

ex·hi·bit *(obj)* /ɪg'zɪb·ɪt/ *v* to show (something) publicly • *In the summer the academy will exhibit several prints which are rarely seen.* [T] • *He frequently exhibits at the art gallery.* [I] • *He exhibited great self-control considering her rudeness.* [T]

ex·hi·bit /ɪg'zɪb·ɪt/ *n* [C] • *The museum has a fascinating collection of exhibits* (= objects) *ranging from Iron Age pottery to Eskimo clothing.* • *(law)* An exhibit is an item used as EVIDENCE (= proof) in a trial: *Is exhibit C the weapon which you say was used?*

ex·hi·bi·tion /,ek·sɪ'bɪʃ·ən/ *n* • *There's a marvellous exhibition* (= show of items) **(on)** *at the moment* **about** *Albert Einstein.* [C] • *The photographs will be* **on** *exhibition until the end of the month.* [U] • *The athlete's third, and winning, jump was an exhibition of skill and strength.* [C] • *(disapproving)* If you **make an exhibition of** yourself, you behave badly in a way that other people will notice: *Edward, stop dancing on that table – you're making such an exhibition of yourself!* • An **exhibition match** is a single sports game that is not part of a larger competition, in which the players show their skills.

ex·hi·bi·tion·i·sm /,ek·sɪ'bɪʃ·ən·ɪ·zəm/ *n* [U] • *(disapproving)* Exhibitionism is behaviour which tries to attract attention: *It's exhibitionism to flaunt wealth so blatantly.* • *(fml)* Exhibitionism is also when someone shows their sexual organs in public.

ex·hi·bi·tion·ist /,ek·sɪ'bɪʃ·ən·ɪst/ *n* [C] • *She's an exhibitionist wearing clothes like those when everyone else is so formally dressed.* • *The police have just arrested an exhibitionist* (= person who shows their sex organs in public) *in the supermarket.*

ex·hi·bit·or /£ɪg'zɪb·ɪ·tər, $-t̬ə/ *n* [C] • An exhibitor is someone who has made or owns something, esp. a work of art, shown in an exhibition: *Many of the exhibitors will be at the gallery to meet the public.*

ex·hil·a·rate *obj* /ɪg'zɪl·ə·reɪt/ *v* [T] to give (someone) strong feelings of happiness and excitement • *They were both exhilarated by the motorbike ride.*

ex·hil·a·rat·ing /£ɪg'zɪl·ə·reɪ·tɪŋ, $-t̬ɪŋ/ *adj* • *We came back from an exhilarating* (= very exciting) *walk in the mountains.*

ex·hil·a·ra·tion /ɪg,zɪl·ə'reɪ·ʃən/ *n* [U]

ex·hort *obj* /£ɪg'zɔːt, $-'zɔːrt/ *v* [T] *fml* to strongly encourage or try to persuade (someone) to do something • *The governor exhorted the prisoners not* **to** *riot.* [+ obj + *to* infinitive]

ex·hor·ta·tion /£,eg·zɔː'teɪ·ʃən, $-zɔːr-/ *n* • *Despite the exhortations of the union leaders the workers voted to strike.* [C] • *The book is essentially an exhortation* **to** *religious tolerance.* [U]

ex·hume *obj* /£eks'*h*juːm, $eg'zuːm/ *v* [T] to remove (a dead body) from the ground after it has been buried • *They exhumed the body after the funeral because of evidence that suggested she may have been murdered.*

ex·hum·a·tion /,eks·*h*juː'meɪ·ʃən/ *n* [C/U] *fml*

ex·i·gen·cy /'ek·sɪ·dʒən*t*·si/ *n fml* the difficulties of a situation, esp. one which causes urgent demands • *the exigencies of war* [C] • *Economic exigency obliged the government to act.* [U] • ⓘ

ex·i·gent /'ek·sɪ·dʒənt/ *adj fml* • Something which is exigent needs urgent attention, or demands too much from other people: *an exigent problem* ○ *an exigent manager*

ex·ile /'ek·saɪl, 'eg·zaɪl/ *n* the condition of someone being sent or kept away from their own country, village, etc., esp. for political reasons, or the person who is sent or kept away • *The Dalai Lama went* **into** *exile in 1959 because of the political situation in his own country.* [U] • *The deposed leaders are currently* **in** *exile in the neighbouring country.* [U] • *After many years of exile thousands of families will now be able to return to their homeland.* [U] • *The island is a haven for* **tax** *exiles* (= people who leave their own country because they think they pay too much tax there). [C]

ex·ile *obj* /'ek·saɪl, 'eg·zaɪl/ *v* [T] • *The monarch was exiled because of the coup.*

ex·ist /ɪg'zɪst/ *v* [I] to be; to be real; to live, or to live in difficult conditions • *Do you think God really exists?* • *The realities of poverty exist for a great many people across the globe.* • *Some species exist in this small area of forest and nowhere else on Earth.* • *No-one can be expected to exist* **on** *such a low salary.* • *Few people can exist without water for more than a week.*

ex·is·tence /ɪg'zɪs·tənts/ *n* • *Many people question the existence* **of** *God.* [U] • *Modern cosmology believes the Universe to have* **come into** *existence about fifteen billion years ago.* [U] • *The existence of yetis has yet to be proven conclusively.* [U] • *She has a miserable existence living with him.* [C]

ex·ist·ent /ɪg'zɪs·tənt/ *adj* [not gradable] • If something is existent it is in a state of existence: *This carving is believed to be the only existent image of Saint Frideswide.*

ex·ist·ing /ɪg'zɪs·tɪŋ/ *adj* [before n; not gradable] • *The existing laws* (= laws which exist at the present time) *covering libel in this country are thought by many to be inadequate.* • *Under the existing* (= present) *conditions many children are going hungry.*

ex·is·ten·tial·i·sm /ˌeg·zɪˈsten·tʃəl·ɪ·zəm/ *n* [U] *specialized* the modern system of belief made famous by Jean Paul Sartre in the 1940s in which the world is meaningless and each person is alone and completely responsible for their own actions, by which they make their own character

ex·is·ten·tial /ˌeg·zɪˈsten·tʃəl/, **ex·is·ten·tial·ist** *adj specialized* • *an existential/existentialist argument/philosopher*

ex·is·ten·tial·ist /ˌeg·zɪˈsten·tʃəl·ɪst/ *n* [C] *specialized*

ex·it /ˈek·sɪt, ˈeg·zɪt/ *n* [C] the door through which you might leave a building or large vehicle, or the act of leaving esp. a theatre stage • *a fire exit* (= a door you can escape through if there is a fire) • *There are two* **emergency** *exits, one at the back and one at the front of the hall.* • *He* **made** *a quick exit when he heard strange noises in the house.* • *She* **made** *her exit from the stage to rapturous applause.* • An exit can also be a smaller road used to leave main road: *Come off the motorway at the Duxford exit.* • An **exit poll** is the organized questioning of people as they leave a **polling station** (= place at which people vote) about how they voted, to try to discover who will win the election. • *She has finally got her* **exit visa** (= official permission to leave the country). • Compare ENTRANCE [WAY IN]. • Ⓟ

ex·it *(obj)* /ˈek·sɪt, ˈeg·zɪt/ *v* • *He exited hastily when the crowd realised who he really was.* [I] • *Please exit the theatre by the side doors.* [T] • *"Exit, pursued by a bear"* (stage direction, Shakespeare's Winter's Tale 3.3)

Ex·o·cet /£ˈek·sə·set, $-soʊ-/ *n* [C] *trademark* a MISSILE (= flying bomb) which can be accurately directed over short distances, used esp. against enemy ships

ex·o·dus /ˈek·sə·dəs/ *n* [C usually sing] the movement of a lot of people from a place • *The famine is causing a* **mass** *exodus of people* **from** *the affected country areas to the aid centres.* • *There is always an exodus* **to** *the coast at holiday times.* • Exodus is the second book of the Bible telling of Moses and the journey of the Israelites out of Egypt.

ex of·fi·ci·o /£ˌeks·əˈfɪʃ·i·əʊ, $-oʊ/ *adj, adv* [not gradable] because of a person's position in a formal group • *She is an ex officio member* (= automatically a member) *of the finance committee because she is head of the design department.* • *The cabinet will also attend the meeting ex-officio.*

ex·on·er·ate *obj* /£ɪgˈzɒn·ə·reɪt, $-ˈzɑː·nə·eɪt/ *v* [T] to show or state (someone or something) to not have blame • *The report exonerated the crew* **from** *all responsibility for the collision.*

ex·on·er·a·tion /£ɪgˌzɒn·əˈreɪ·ʃən, $-ˌzɑː·nə-/ *n* [C/U]

ex·or·bi·tant /£ɪgˈzɔː·bɪ·tənt, $-ˈzɪːɔr·bə·ţənt/ *adj* (of prices, demands, etc.) much too large • *The bill for dinner was exorbitant.*

ex·or·cise *obj* /£ˈek·sɔː·saɪz, $-sɔːr-/ *v* [T] to force out (an evil spirit) from (a person or a place) by praying or magic • *After the priest exorcised the spirit/house/child the strange noises stopped.* • *(fig.) It will take a long time to exorcise* (= remove the bad effects of) *the memory of the accident.*

ex·or·ci·sm /£ˈek·sɔː·sɪ·zəm, $-sɔːr-/ *n* [C/U]

ex·or·cist /£ˈek·sɔː·sɪst, $-sɔːr-/ *n* [C]

ex·o·tic /£ɪgˈzɒt·ɪk, $-ˈzɑː·ţɪk/ *adj* unusual and often exciting because of coming (or seeming to come) from a distant, esp. tropical country • *exotic flowers/food/designs* • An **exotic dancer** is a performer who removes her or his clothes in a sexually exciting way. • Ⓖⓡ

ex·o·ti·ca /£ɪgˈzɒt·ɪ·kə, $-ˈzɑː·ţɪ-/ *pl n* • *Collectors of eighteenth century exotica* (= unusual objects, esp. works of art) *are our main customers.*

ex·o·ti·ci·sm /£ɪgˈzɒt·ɪ·sɪ·zəm, $-ˈzɑː·ţɪ-/ *n* [U]

ex·pand *(obj)* [INCREASE] /ɪkˈspænd/ *v* to increase (something) in size, number or importance • *The air in the balloon expands when heated.* [I] • *They expanded their retail operations significantly during the 80's.* [T] • **Expanded polystyrene** is a light plastic containing gas used for wrapping things in before putting them in boxes.

ex·pand·ab·le /ɪkˈspæn·də·bl̩/ *adj* • *The garment is made with expandable material to give extra comfort.*

ex·pan·sion /ɪkˈspæn·tʃən/ *n* • *Free expansion* **of** *a gas causes it to cool.* [U] • *Expansion* **into** *new areas of research might be possible.* [U] • *Figures like these have led to one of the few expansions in the economy – the fear industry.* [C]

ex·pan·sion·i·sm /ɪkˈspæn·tʃən·ɪ·zəm/ *n* [U] *disapproving* • Expansionism is increasing the amount of land ruled by a country, or the business performed by a company: *As a consequence of expansionism by some European countries many ancient cultures have suffered.* ○ *His policy of expansionism is seen by some in the firm to be unnecessary.*

ex·pan·sion·ist /ɪkˈspæn·tʃən·ɪst/ *n* [C], *adj*

ex·pand *(obj)* [GIVE DETAILS] /ɪkˈspænd/ *v* to give more details in (a story, argument, etc.) • *You'll have to expand your reasoning if you want to persuade the panel.* [T] • *The professor expanded* **(up)on** *his experimental methods.* [I]

ex·pan·sion /ɪkˈspæn·tʃən/ *n* [C] • *The novel is little more than a protracted expansion of a short medieval poem.*

ex·pan·sive /ɪkˈspænt·sɪv/ *adj* • *an expansive critique*

ex·pan·sive·ly /ɪkˈspænt·sɪv·li/ *adv*

ex·pan·sive·ness /ɪkˈspænt·sɪv·nəs/ *n* [U]

ex·pand [BECOME FRIENDLY] /ɪkˈspænd/ *v* [I] (of a person) to become more friendly, esp. by talking more • *He expanded quite a lot after he'd given the presentation.*

ex·pan·sive /ɪkˈspænt·sɪv/ *adj* • *You'll find she's very expansive after the initial formality has worn off.*

ex·pan·sive·ly /ɪkˈspænt·sɪv·li/ *adv*

ex·pan·sive·ness /ɪkˈspænt·sɪv·nəs/ *n* [U]

ex·panse /ɪkˈspænts/ *n* [U] a very large area • *She gazed at the immense expanse* **of** *the sea.*

ex·pan·ses /ɪkˈspænt·sɪz/ *pl n* • *vast expanses* (= a very large area) **of** *sand and pine*

ex·pan·sive /ɪkˈspænt·sɪv/ *adj* • *There was an expansive view from the window.* • An expansive **gesture** is one which involves big movements, esp. of the arms: *The artist answered the specific question about her work with nothing but an expansive gesture.*

ex·pan·sive·ly /ɪkˈspænt·sɪv·li/ *adv* • *Dooley gestured expansively with his cigar and caught the ash with his other hand.*

ex·pa·ti·ate /ekˈspeɪ·ʃi·eɪt/ *v* [I] *fml disapproving* to speak or write about something in great detail or for a long time • *She expatiated* **on/upon/about** *her own work for the whole afternoon.*

ex·pa·tri·ate /£ekˈspæt·ri·ət, $-ˈspeɪ·tri-/, *infml* **ex·pat** /ˌekˈspat/ *n* [C] someone who does not live in their own country • *A large community of expatriates has settled there.*

ex·pa·tri·ate /£ekˈspæt·ri·ət, $-ˈspeɪ·tri-/ *adj* [not gradable] • *an expatriate Tibetan*

ex·pa·tri·ate *obj* /£ekˈspæt·ri·eɪt, $-ˈspeɪ·tri-/ *v* [T] *fml* • *The new leaders expatriated the ruling family* (= used force or law to remove from their own country).

ex·pect *obj* [THINK] /ɪkˈspekt/ *v* [T] to think or believe (something) will happen, or (someone) will arrive • *I expect* **(that)** *you'll find it somewhere in your bedroom.* [+ (*that*) clause] • *We were expecting a lot of applicants for the job, but nowhere near the number who actually applied.* • *So, we may expect* **to** *see you next Tuesday.* [+ *to* infinitive] • *We expected the letter* **(to** *arrive) yesterday.* [+ obj + *to* infinitive] • *We expect* **(that)** *it was an accident.* [+ (*that*) clause] • *I expect* **(that)** *it will all be alright in the end.* [+ (*that*) clause] • *It is widely expected* **(that)** *a statement will be issued in the morning.* [+ (*that*) clause] • *The financial performance of the business is* **fully** *expected* (= almost certain) **to** *improve.* [+ obj + *to* infinitive] • *We were* **half** *expecting you* **to** *not come back* (= thinking you might not come back). [+ obj + *to* infinitive] • *It's* **(only) to be expected that** *your health is suffering since you've been working such long hours.* • If someone is **expecting (a baby)**, they are pregnant: *She shouldn't be lifting those boxes if she's expecting.*

ex·pec·tan·cy /ɪkˈspek·tənt·si/ *n* [U] • *There was a general state/air of expectancy in the crowd.* • See **life expectancy** at LIFE.

ex·pec·tant /ɪkˈspek·tənt/ *adj* • *The expectant audience waited in silence for the show to begin.* • An **expectant mother** is a woman in a late stage of pregnancy.

ex·pec·tant·ly /ɪkˈspek·tənt·li/ *adv* • *Roland heard the rustle of biscuit wrappers and looked up at John expectantly.*

ex·pec·ta·tion /ˌek·spekˈteɪ·ʃən/ *n* • *Considering the problems he's had there can be little expectation* **of** *him winning the race.* [U] • *She was constantly* **in** *expectation* **of** *being arrested.* [U] • *Now that our two groups have merged we can all have great expectations* **for** *the future.* [C] • *The size of the bequest was* **beyond all** *(of) our expectations/* **beyond (all)** *expectation* (= much greater than expected). [C/U] • If something is **against/contrary to (all)** expectation(s) it is very different to what is expected: *Contrary to all expectations she was accepted by the academy.* [C/U] • If something **does not come/live up to expectation(s)** it is not as good as expected.

ex·pect *obj* [DEMAND] /ɪkˈspekt/ *v* [T] to believe (someone) will do something because it is their duty • *This country* *expects every member of the armed forces* **to** *do whatever is necessary in the approaching conflict.* [+ obj + *to* infinitive] • *You're expecting too much* **from** *someone if you ask them to work every weekend without pay.* • *Borrowers are expected* **to** (= should) *return books on time.* [+ obj + *to* infinitive] • *"England expects every man will do his duty"* (signal at the Battle of Trafalgar by Horatio Nelson, 1805)

ex·pec·to·rant /£ɪk'spek·tᵊr·ᵊnt, $-t̬ɚ-/ *n* [C] a type of cough medicine used to loosen PHLEGM (= thick liquid) from the lungs

ex·pec·to·rate /£ɪk'spek·tᵊr·eɪt, $-t̬ɚ-/ *v* [I] • To expectorate is to bring up liquid from the throat or lungs and force it out of the mouth.

ex·pe·di·ent /ɪk'spiː·di·ᵊnt/ *adj* helpful or useful in a particular situation, but sometimes not morally acceptable • *We thought it expedient not to pay the builder until he had finished the work.* • *The management has taken a series of expedient measures to improve the company's financial situation.* • (PL)

ex·pe·di·ence /ɪk'spiː·di·ᵊnts/ *n* [U] **expediency** /ɪk 'spiː·di·ᵊnt·si/ • *As a matter of expedience* (= in order to help the present situation), *we will not be taking on any new staff this year.* • *I think this government operates on the basis of expediency, not of principle* (= they do what they think will help them, not what they think they should do).

ex·pe·di·ent /ɪk'spiː·di·ᵊnt/ *n* [C] • *Before choosing a dentist, we took the expedient* (= the useful action) *of asking friends which one they recommended.* • *The company is having to cut jobs as an expedient.*

ex·pe·di·ent·ly /ɪk'spiː·di·ᵊnt·li/ *adv*

ex·pe·dite *obj* /'ek·spə·daɪt/ *v* [T] *fml* to cause to be done more quickly; to hurry • *I'd be grateful if you could do something to expedite a reply to my query.*

ex·pe·di·tion /ˌek·spə'dɪʃ·ᵊn/ *n* [U] *fml* • *We will deal with your order with the greatest possible expedition* (= as quickly as possible).

ex·pe·di·tious /ˌek·spə'dɪʃ·əs/ *adj fml* • *The bank was expeditious* (= quick) *in replying to my letter.*

ex·pe·di·tious·ly /ˌek·spə'dɪʃ·ə·sli/ *adv fml*

ex·pe·di·tion /ˌek·spə'dɪʃ·ᵊn/ *n* [C] (the people, vehicles, animals, etc. taking part in) an organized journey for a particular purpose • *Scott died while he was* **on** *an expedition to the Antarctic in 1912.* • *The British expedition* **to** *Mount Everest is/are leaving next month.* [+ sing/pl v] • *(humorous) We're* **going on** *a shopping expedition on Saturday.* • (CS) (S)

ex·pe·di·tion·a·ry /£ˌek·spə'dɪʃ·ᵊn·ᵊr·i, $-er-/ *adj* [before n] • Expeditionary **forces** are soldiers sent to other countries to fight in a war.

ex·pel *obj* /ɪk'spel/ *v* [T] **-ll-** to force to leave; to remove • *The new government has expelled all foreign diplomats.* • *My brother was expelled* (**from** *school*) *for bad behaviour.* • *When you breathe out, you expel air* **from** *your lungs.* • *We've just installed a fan to expel cooking smells* **from** *the kitchen.* • See also EXPULSION.

ex·pend *obj* /ɪk'spend/ *v* [T] to use or spend (esp. time, effort or money) • *The council is voting on whether to expend the large amounts of money needed to repair the town hall.* • *After expending all that effort on training to be a doctor, Chris has decided that she wants to do something else.* • *We've expended all our resources.*

ex·pend·ab·le /ɪk'spen·də·bl̩/ *adj* • *Expendable materials* (= materials that can be thrown away) *are often used for packaging goods.* • *No one likes to think that they're expendable* (= that other people can deal with things without them).

ex·pen·di·ture /£ɪk'spen·dɪ·tʃəʳ, $-tʃɚ/ *n* • *You will recover more quickly if you keep your expenditure* **of** *energy as low as possible* (= if you are not very active). [U] • *It will not be possible to repair the school buildings without considerable expenditure* (= spending a lot of money) **on** *them.* [U] • *Having to have my car repaired was an expenditure* (= an amount of money I had to spend) *I hadn't expected this month.* [C]

ex·pense /ɪk'spents/ *n* (a cause of) spending of or using money, time or effort • *Our biggest expense this year was our summer holiday.* [C] • *We need to save money by cutting down on our expenses.* [C] • *Buying a bigger car has proved to be well* **worth** *the expense.* [U] • *The government needs to consider the expense* **of** *its policies* **to** *the taxpayer.* [U] • *We've just had a new garage built* **at great** *expense.* [U] • *My employer wouldn't pay for a computer for me to use at work, so I bought one* **at** *my own expense* (= I paid for it myself). [U] • *It's silly to* **go to** *the expense* **of** (= spend money on) *buying*

EXPENSIVE

- **Expensive** and **costly** are used to refer to money and also more generally: *My trip was terribly expensive.* • *an expensive mistake* • *a costly war* • *costly in time and resources*
  Dear, pricey: informal, used of money: *The coffee was good but rather dear.* • *St Tropez is a pricey place to stay.*
  When referring to money, the opposites of these words are **cheap** or, more formally, **inexpensive** and **economical**: *I need some cheap shoes for work.* • *Southdown sheep are very economical to keep.* (Notice that *cheap* is often used disapprovingly in American use.)
  Shops and businesses often use **economy**, **bargain** and **budget** to describe cheap goods and services. These adjectives come before the noun: *coats from our economy range; bargain holidays; budget car hire.*
- **Cost** is common as a verb and noun: *How much does it cost?* • *It cost me £30.* • *Can we afford the high cost of a new space project?*
- **Expense** is used only as a noun: *A new highway was built* **at great** *expense.*
- **Price:** the cost of things in shops etc.: *The price is rather high, can't you drop* (=reduce) *it a bit?* • *What price did he ask?* It is also used more generally: *James was famous, but he paid a high price for his success.*
- The **value** of something is what it is **worth**, and might be different from its cost: *I bought this record for $5 and now it's worth $100.* • *A man who knows the price of everything and the value of nothing* (Oscar Wilde's definition of a CYNIC)
- A **valuable** thing is worth a lot of money or has great value for some other reason: *She made some very valuable suggestions.*
  The common opposite of valuable is **worthless**: *What he writes is completely worthless rubbish.* **Valueless** is more formal: *I'm sorry to tell you these paintings are valueless.*
  Something that is **priceless** has a value so high that you cannot express it in terms of money: *a collection of priceless paintings.* **Invaluable** is used more generally to mean extremely useful: *Thank you for your invaluable help.*

Notice that **valid** and its opposite **invalid** do not refer to the value of something, but to whether it is correct or legally acceptable: *a valid ticket; an invalid argument.*

new clothes when you don't really need them. [U] • *I don't want to* **put** *you* **to** *the expense* **of** *coming to the airport to meet me.* [U] • *We can go wherever you like for dinner this evening,* **no expense(s) spared** (= it isn't important how much it costs). • *His business was very successful, but it was* **at** *his family's* **expense** (= his family suffered because of it). • *I think it's very unkind to make jokes* **at the expense of** *other people* (= which make other people look foolish). • *I can* **put** *this lunch* **on** *my* **expense account** (= my employer will pay for it as forming part of my work).

ex·pen·ses /ɪk'spent·sɪz/ *pl n* • *I need to get my expenses* (= money spent while doing my job, which my employer will pay back to me) *approved.* • *(Br)Don't worry about the cost of lunch – it's* **on** *expenses.* • If something is **all expenses paid**, it means that you do not have to pay for anything yourself: *She's going on a trip to New York,* **all expenses paid**. ○ *She's going on an* **all expenses paid** *trip to New York.*

ex·pen·sive /ɪk'spent·sɪv/ *adj* • *Rolls Royces are very expensive* (= cost a lot of money). • *Big houses are expensive* **to** *maintain.* [+ *to* infinitive] • *She has expensive tastes* (= she likes things that cost a lot of money). • *Going to the* *cricket match when he should have been at work was an expensive mistake for George – he lost his job because of it.* • LP› **Expensive**

ex·pen·sive·ly /ɪk'spent·sɪv·li/ *adv* • *We've found a shop where we can buy carpets not too expensively* (= without spending a lot of money). • *Sarah is always very expensively dressed* (= she wears clothes that cost a lot of money).

ex·pe·ri·ence /£ɪk'spɪə·ri·ᵊnts, $-'spɪr·i-/ *n* (the process of getting) knowledge or skill which is obtained from doing, seeing or feeling things, or something that happens which has an effect on you • *Do you have any experience* **of** *working* (= have you ever worked) *with children?* [U] • *The best way to learn is* **by** *experience* (= by doing, seeing or feeling things). [U] • *I know* **from** *experience* (= things that have happened to me) *that Tony never keeps his promises.* [U] • *I don't think she has the experience* **for** (= enough knowledge and skill suitable for doing) *the job.* [U] • *No experience* (= knowledge and skill) *needed!* [U] • *The experience* **of** *pain* (= what pain feels like) *varies from one person to another.* [U] • *There's nothing we can do about it now, we'll just have to* **put it down to** *experience* (= consider it as a mistake we can learn from). [U] • *Our round-the-world cruise was an experience* (= something that happened) *we'll never forget.* [C] • *Having a tooth removed can be a painful experience.* [C] • *It was interesting hearing about his experiences as a policeman.* [C] • *Enjoy the real coffee experience* (= what it really feels and tastes like). [C] • *"A gentleman who had been very unhappy in marriage, married immediately after his wife died; it was the triumph of hope over experience"* (Samuel Johnson in the book *Boswell's Life of Johnson,* 1770) • *"Experience is the name every one gives to their mistakes"* (From *Lady Windermere's Fan* by Oscar Wilde, 1892) • Ⓟ

ex·pe·ri·ence *obj* /£ɪk'spɪə·ri·ᵊnts, $-'spɪr·i-/ *v* [T] • *We experienced great difficulty in selling* (= we found it difficult to sell) *our house.* • *New companies often experience a loss* (= do not make a profit) *in their first few years.* • *Come and experience* (= see and feel) *the golden sands and clear waters of the Caribbean.*

ex·pe·ri·enced /£ɪk'spɪə·ri·ᵊntst, $-'spɪr·i-/ *adj approving* • *Martin is a very experienced teacher* (= has a lot of skill and knowledge from having been a teacher for a long time). • *I didn't get the job because they were looking for someone more experienced.* • *Frank is very experienced* **at/in** *painting.*

ex·pe·ri·en·tial /£ɪkˌspɪə·ri'en·tʃᵊl, $-ˌspɪr·i-/ *adj* • Experiential knowledge is knowledge that you get from experience.

ex·per·i·ment /ɪk'sper·ɪ·mənt/ *n* a test done in order to learn something or to discover whether something works or is true • *Scientists are* **conducting/performing/carrying out/doing** *an experiment* **to** *test the effectiveness of the new drug.* [C + *to* infinitive] • *Some people believe that experiments* **on** *animals should be banned.* [C] • *The students are conducting an experiment* **in** *communal living* (= trying it to see what it is like). [C] • *I've bought a different kind of coffee this week* **as an experiment** (= in order to see what it is like). [C] • *We can only find the best solution* **by** *experiment.* [U] • Ⓟ

ex·per·i·ment /ɪk'sper·ɪ·ment/ *v* [I] • *Things would never change if people weren't prepared to experiment* (= to try doing something different). • *The school is experimenting* **with** (= trying) *new teaching methods.* • *Peter is learning to cook so he has been experimenting* **on** *his family.*

ex·per·i·men·tal /£ɪkˌsper·ɪ'men·tᵊl, $-ţᵊl/ *adj* • *The drug is still at the experimental stage* (= is still being tested). • *The changes to the distribution system are purely experimental at the moment.* • *Charles works in the department of experimental* **psychology** (= the department in which ideas about how the mind works are tested).

ex·per·i·men·tal·ly /£ɪkˌsper·ɪ'men·tᵊl·i, $-ţᵊl-/ *adv* • *The red light cameras were tried experimentally in Nottingham with considerable success.*

ex·per·i·men·tal·ist /£ɪkˌsper·ɪ'men·tᵊl·ɪst, $-ţᵊl-/ *n* [C]

ex·per·i·men·ta·tion /ɪkˌsper·ɪ·men'teɪ·ʃᵊn/ *n* [U] • *Children need the opportunity for experimentation* (= for trying things). • *Extensive experimentation* (= testing) *is needed before new drugs can be sold.*

ex·per·i·ment·er /£ɪk'sper·ɪ·men·təʳ, $-ţɚ/ *n* [C] • *Van Gogh greatly influenced Matisse and other experimenters of 20th century art.*

ex·pert /£'ek·spɜːt, $-spɜːrt/ *n, adj* (a person) having a high level of knowledge or skill; (a) specialist • *Experts have been* **called in** *to establish the cause of the plane crash.* [C] • *I enjoy radio programmes in which gardening experts give advice.* [C] • *My mother is an expert* **at** *dress-making* (= she does it very well). [C] • *William is an expert* **in/on** (= has studied and knows a lot about) *early Christian art.* [C] • *She's an expert swimmer.* • *I thought your handling of the situation was expert.* • *Gwen is expert* **at** *finding bargains.* • An **expert system** is a computer system which asks questions and gives answers that have been thought of by a human expert.

ex·per·tise /£ˌek·spɜː'tiːz, $-spɜːr-/ *n* [U] • *We admired the expertise* (= skill) *with which he prepared the meal.* • *I have no expertise* **in** *sewing/sewing expertise.* • *Mary has considerable expertise (Br)* **on**/*(Am and Aus)* **in** (= knowledge about) *French history.*

ex·pert·ly /£'ek·spɜːt·li, $-spɜːrt-/ *adv* • *Adults are quite capable of learning to ski expertly, if they are serious enough.*

ex·pi·ate *obj* /'ek·spi·eɪt/ *v* [T] *fml* to show regret for (bad behaviour) by doing something to express that you are sorry and by accepting punishment • *He bought her a bunch of flowers to expiate his* **guilt** *about forgetting her birthday.*

ex·pi·a·tion /ˌek·spi'eɪ·ʃᵊn/ *n* [U] *fml* • *He bought the flowers* **in** *expiation* **for/of** *his guilt.*

ex·pire END /£ɪk'spaɪəʳ, $-'spaɪr/ *v* [I] (of something which lasts for a fixed length of time) to come to an end; to stop being in use; to RUN OUT FINISH • *Our television license expires next month.* • *The contract between the two companies will expire at the end of the year.*

ex·pi·ra·tion /ˌek·spɪ'reɪ·ʃᵊn/, **ex·pi·ry** /£ɪk'spaɪə·ri, $-'spaɪr·i/ *n* [U] • *Of the 2 million foreigners who enter Japan each year, several thousand stay on past the expiration of their tourist visas.* • *What is the expiration/expiry* **date** *of your credit card* (= What is the last date on which it can be used)*?*

ex·pire DIE /£ɪk'spaɪəʳ, $-'spaɪr/ *v* [I] to die • *(fml) We regret to inform you that Mr Jones expired early this morning.* • *(infml) I thought I was going to expire after that run!*

ex·plain *(obj)* /ɪk'spleɪn/ *v* to make (something) clear or easy to understand by describing or giving information about it • *If there's anything you don't understand, I'll be happy to explain.* [I] • *The teacher explained the rules* **to** *the children.* [T] • *Our guide explained* **where** *the cathedral was.* [+ *wh-* word] • *Bill explained* **how** *the computer works, but I didn't understand him.* [+ *wh-* word] • *Please could you explain* **why** *you're so late.* [+ *wh-* word] • *Dad explained* **that** *we have to go to bed now because we need to get up very early in the morning.* [+ *that* clause] • *"Someone must have hit the wrong button," an official explained.* [+ clause] • *Rachel asked the teacher if she could explain* **herself** *a bit more clearly* (= say more clearly what she meant). [T] • *No one has been able to explain* (= give the reason for) *the accident.* [T] • *Sam's mother asked him to explain* **himself** *when he didn't go* (= give the reasons for not going) *to school.* [T] • *I don't know how you're going to explain* **away** *that dent you made in your dad's car* (= avoid blame for it by making it seem unimportant or not your fault). [M]

ex·plan·a·tion /ˌek·splə'neɪ·ʃᵊn/ *n* • *Sarah* **gave** *me a very clear explanation* **of** (= explained very clearly) *how to find her house.* [C] • *I was provided with no explanation* **of** *how the camera worked when I bought it.* [U] • *He said,* **by way of** *explanation* **(for)/in** *explanation* **(of** *what happened), that he hadn't seen the traffic light change to red.* [U] • *I can* **give** *you an explanation* (= a reason) **for/of** *why I'm late.* [C] • *The judge didn't believe his explanation* (= reason) **that** *he had stolen the money in order to give it to charity.* [C + *that* clause]

ex·plan·a·to·ry /£ɪk'splæn·ə·tri, $-tɔːr·i/ *adj* • *The structure of the heart was described in the book with the help of an explanatory diagram.* (= a picture which explained it). • See also SELF-EXPLANATORY.

ex·ple·tive /£ɪk'spliː·tɪv, $'ek·splə·ţɪv/ *n* [C] a swear word used to express anger or pain • *She* **let out** *a row/string of expletives when she dropped a book on her foot.* • Expletive **deleted** means that a swear word has not been included in a report of what someone said.

ex·plic·ab·le /ek'splɪk·ə·bl̩/ *adj* able to be explained • *Under the circumstances, what he said was quite explicable.*

ex·plic·ab·ly /ek'splɪk·ə·bli/ *adv*

ex·pli·cate *obj* /'ek·splɪ·keɪt/ *v* [T] *fml* to explain (esp. a piece of writing or an idea) in detail • *This is a book which clearly explicates Marx's later writings.*

ex·pli·ca·tion /ˌek·splɪ'keɪ·ʃᵊn/ *n* [U]

ex·pli·cit /ɪk'splɪs·ɪt/ *adj* clear and exact • *Sheila shouldn't get lost because I gave her very explicit* (= clearly expressed) *directions how to get here.* • *She was very explicit* **about** (= said very clearly and exactly) *what she thought was wrong with the plans.* • *Some people think that magazines with sexually explicit pictures* (= pictures showing clear and full details of sexual activity) *should not be on public display.*

ex·pli·cit·ly /ɪk'splɪs·ɪt·li/ *adv* • *I told you quite explicitly* (= clearly) *to be home by midnight.*

ex·pli·cit·ness /ɪk'splɪs·ɪt·nəs/ *n* [U] • *Thanks to the explicitness* (= clearness) *of your instructions, we found our way easily.* • *The film has been banned because of its sexual explicitness* (= the details of sexual activity that it contains).

ex·plode *(obj)* BURST /£ɪk'spləʊd, $-'sploʊd/ *v* to (cause to) burst violently • *A* **bomb** *exploded at one of London's busiest railway stations this morning.* [I] • *He was driving so fast that his car tyre exploded.* [I] • *Experts were called in to explode the bomb that was found under the minister's car.* [T] • *(fig.) The resentment that had been building up inside him finally exploded* (= he expressed it suddenly and strongly). [I] • *(fig.) She exploded* **with/in** (= showed sudden and strong) **anger/rage/fury** *when she learned that the airline had lost her luggage.* [I] • *(fig.) The children exploded* **into** *giggles* (= suddenly started laughing uncontrollably). [I] • *(fig.) "What on earth do you think you're doing?" exploded* (= said angrily) *Sam's mother.* [+ clause] • *(fig.) The meeting began as a peaceful protest, but it exploded* (= developed suddenly) **into** *a riot.* [I] • *(fig.) London's parks have exploded* **into** *colour in the last week* (= the flowers in the parks have suddenly opened). [I] • Compare IMPLODE.

ex·plo·sion /£ɪk'spləʊ·ʒᵊn, $-'sploʊ-/ *n* • *The fire was thought to have been caused by a gas explosion.* [C] • *The bomb explosion* (= the noise caused by the bomb exploding) *was heard a long way away.* [C] • *The explosion* (= the intentional exploding) **of** *nuclear devices in the Bikini Atoll was stopped in 1958.* [U] • *(fig.) There was an explosion* **of** *applause from the audience* (= they expressed their approval suddenly and loudly) *at the end of the performance.* [C] • *(fig.) I don't know what caused his sudden explosion* **of** (= strong expression of) *anger.* [C] • *(fig.) The government is facing an unexpected explosion* (= a sudden strong expression) **of** *public protest about its economic policy.* [C]

ex·plos·ive /£ɪk'spləʊ·sɪv, £-zɪv, $-'sploʊ·sɪv/ *n* • *The bomb consisted of explosives* (= substances which explode) *packed into a suitcase.* [C] • *The warheads contain around 1 000 lb of high explosive.* [U]

ex·plos·ive /£ɪk'spləʊ·sɪv, £-zɪv, $-'sploʊ·sɪv/ *adj* • *Certain gases are* **highly** *explosive* (= able to explode easily). • *There was an explosive* (= loud) *clap of thunder overhead.* • *(fig.) She has an explosive* **temper** (= she is likely suddenly to become angry). • *(fig.) Capital punishment is an explosive* **issue** (= causes strong feelings). • *(fig.) The* **situation** *in the poorer parts of some of America's major cities has become very explosive* (= is likely to cause violent behaviour). • *An* **explosive device** (= a bomb) *was found at one of London's busiest stations this morning.*

ex·plos·ive·ly /£ɪk'spləʊ·sɪv·li, £-zɪv-, $-'sploʊ·sɪv-/ *adv* • *Some chemicals react explosively with* (= explode when they touch) *water.* • *(fig.) I was astonished that he reacted so explosively* (= suddenly and violently) *to what I said.*

ex·plos·ive·ness /£ɪk'spləʊ·sɪv·nəs, £-zɪv-, $-'sploʊ·sɪv-/ *n* [U] • *(fig.) We need to do something about the explosiveness of the situation* (= the fact that it is likely to cause violent behaviour).

ex·plode INCREASE /£ɪk'spləʊd, $-'sploʊd/ *v* [I] to increase very quickly • *The rapidly exploding population in some countries is a serious problem for their governments.*

ex·plo·sion /£ɪk'spləʊ·ʒᵊn, $-'sploʊ-/ *n* [C] • *The government has had to take measures to halt the* **population** *explosion.* • *There has been an explosion* **of/in** *demand for computers in the last few years.*

ex·plos·ive /£ɪk'spləʊ·sɪv, £-zɪv, $-'sploʊ·sɪv/ *adj* • *The last few years have seen an explosive increase in the number of homeless people on our streets.*

ex·plode *obj* PROVE FALSE /£ɪk'spləʊd, $-'sploʊd/ *v* [T] to show to be wrong • *This book finally explodes some of the* **myths** *about the origin of the universe.*

ex·plo·sion /£ɪk'spləʊ·ʒᵊn, $-'sploʊ-/ *n* • *What he suggested in his lecture was an explosion* **of** *existing ideas about the causes of heart disease.* [C] • *It's his book's explosion* **of** *existing theories* (= its showing that they are wrong) *that makes it so interesting.* [U]

ex·ploit *obj* USE WELL /ɪk'splɔɪt/ *v* [T] to use for advantage • *We need to make sure that we exploit our* **resources** *as fully as possible.* • *Lendl is fully exploiting his opponent's weak backhand in this tennis match.*

ex·ploit·ab·le /£ɪk'splɔɪ·tə·bḷ, $-t̬ə-/ *adj* • *The coal mine is no longer commercially exploitable* (= can no longer be used for profit). • *Charlotte has a very exploitable talent for drawing* (= she can use it for her advantage).

ex·ploit·a·tion /ˌek·splɔɪ'teɪ·ʃᵊn/ *n* [U] • *Britain's exploitation* (= its use of) **of** *its natural gas reserves began after the Second World War.*

ex·ploit·er /£ɪk'splɔɪ·təʳ, $-t̬ɚ/ *n* [C] • An exploiter is someone who uses other people or things for his or her own profit or advantage.

ex·ploit *obj* USE UNFAIRLY /ɪk'splɔɪt/ *v* [T] to use unfairly for your own advantage • *Laws exist to stop companies exploiting their employees.*

ex·ploit·ab·le /£ɪk'splɔɪ·tə·bḷ, $-t̬ə-/ *adj* • *The lack of jobs in this area means that the workforce is easily exploitable* (= employers can use workers unfairly for their own advantage).

ex·ploit·a·tion /ˌek·splɔɪ'teɪ·ʃᵊn/ *n* [U] • *Marx wrote about the exploitation* **of** *the workers* (= their being used unfairly for their employers' advantage).

ex·ploit·a·tive /£ɪk'splɔɪ·tə·tɪv, $-t̬ə·t̬ɪv/ *adj* • *His behaviour towards her was very exploitative* (= he used her unfairly for his own advantage).

ex·ploit·er /£ɪk'splɔɪ·təʳ, $-t̬ɚ/ *n* [C] • An exploiter is someone who uses other people or things unfairly for his or her own profit or advantage.

ex·ploit ACT /'ek·splɔɪt/ *n* [C] a brave, interesting or humorous act • *We were intrigued to hear about Richard's exploits when he went mountain-climbing.* • *Did she tell you about her exploits during the holiday weekend?*

ex·plore *(obj)* /£ɪk'splɔːʳ, $-'splɔːr/ *v* to search and discover (about) • *Some people think it's wrong to spend money on exploring space* (= going into space in order to discover more about it). [T] • *If we have time on this summer, I'd like to explore some of the less well-known parts of the country.* [T] • *The children have gone exploring in the woods.* [I] • *Let's explore this* **question/issue/topic/idea** *more fully* (= examine it carefully in order to discover more about it). [T] • *Psychotherapists explore* (= ask questions about) *people's pasts in order to help them understand their present feelings and behaviour.* [T] • *She gently explored her new baby's face with her fingers* (= felt it in order to discover more about it). [T] • *"The Treasure of the Sierra Madre" is a film about three men exploring* (= searching) **for** *gold.* [I] • Ⓟ

ex·plo·ra·tion /£ˌek·splə'reɪ·ʃᵊn, $-splɚ'reɪ-/ *n* • *Livingstone was the first European to make an exploration* **of** *the Zambezi river* (= to travel to it in order to discover more about it). [C] • *In 1492, Columbus set out on the* **voyage of** *exploration which led to his discovery of the New World.* [U] • *We need to carry out a full exploration* (= examination) **of** *all the alternatives.* [C] • *The doctor made a careful exploration* **of** *the child's injuries* (= felt them carefully). [C] • *The exploration* (= search) **for** *new sources of energy is vital for the future of our planet.* [U]

ex·plo·ra·tory /£ek'splɒr·ə·tri, $-'splɑː·rə·tɔːr·i/ *adj* • *Brian is going on an exploratory expedition to Antarctica* (= is travelling there in order to discover more about it) *next month.* • *We're having an exploratory meeting next week to talk about* (= a meeting in order to examine) *the possibility of merging the two companies.* • *I'm having some exploratory tests done to find out what's causing my illness.* • *An exploratory well has been dug to look for oil.*

ex·plor·er /£ɪk'splɔː·rəʳ, $-rɚ/ *n* [C] • *Magellan was a famous sixteenth-century explorer* (= he travelled in order to discover and learn about new places).

expo /£'ek·spəʊ, $-spoʊ/ *n* [C] an EXPOSITION SHOW

ex·po·nent PERSON /£ɪk'spəʊ·nənt, $-'spoʊ-/ *n* [C] a person who supports (an idea or belief) or performs (an activity) • *Adam Smith was an exponent* **of** *free trade.* • *Jaqueline du Pré was a leading exponent* **of** *cello-playing.*

ex·po·nent NUMBER /£ɪk'spəʊ·nᵊnt, $-'spoʊ-/ *n* [C] *specialized* a number or sign which shows how many times another number is to be multiplied by itself • *In* 6^4 *and* y^n, *4 and n are the exponents.*

ex·po·nen·tial /£ˌek·spəʊ'nen·tʃᵊl, $-spoʊ-/ *adj* • *(specialized) 6^4 is an exponential expression* (= contains an exponent). • *(fml) We are looking for exponential growth in our investment* (= very fast growth achieved by multiplying the amount of money by itself). • *(fml) There has been an exponential* (= very fast) *increase in world population this century.*

ex·po·nen·tial·ly /£ˌek·spəʊ'nen·tʃᵊl·i, $-spoʊ-/ *adv fml* • *Malthus wrote about the risks involved in the world's population increasing exponentially.*

ex·port *(obj)* /£ɪk'spɔːt, $'ek·spɔːrt/ *v* to send (goods) to another country for sale • *French cheeses are exported* **to** *many different countries.* [T] • *Our clothes sell so well in this country that we have no need to export.* [I] • *(fig.) American culture has been exported* (= the American way of life has been introduced into other countries) *all over the world.* [T] • *(specialized)* To export information from a computer is to copy a large amount of it either to a different part of the computer's storage space or to another form of storage such as a **floppy disk**, so that it can be used for a different purpose. • Compare IMPORT [BRING IN].

ex·port /£'ek·spɔːt, $-spɔːrt/ *n* • *Coffee is one of Brazil's main exports* (= goods it sells in other countries). [C] • *We plan to increase our exports over the next five years* (= to sell more of our goods in other countries). [C] • *The export* (= selling to other countries) **of** *ivory is now strictly controlled.* [U] • *India grows tea* **for** *export.* [U] • *We are planning to develop our export* **market/trade**. [U]

ex·port·ab·le /£ɪk'spɔː·tə·bl̩, $-'spɔːr·t̬ə-/ *adj* • *The value of the new television technology to the company is that it is highly exportable* (= can be sold in other countries).

ex·por·ta·tion /£ˌek·spɔː'teɪ·ʃᵊn, $-spɔːr-/ *n* [U] • *These crates have been packed* **for** *exportation* (= to be sent for sale in other countries).

ex·port·er /£ɪk'spɔː·təʳ, $-'spɔːr·t̬ɚ/ *n* [C] • *Japan is a major exporter* **of** *cars* (= it sells cars in other countries). • *He has become an exporter* **of** *Mexican art.*

ex·pos·é /£ek'spəʊ·zeɪ, $ˌek·spə'zeɪ/ *n* [C] a public report of the facts about a situation, esp. one that is shocking or has been kept secret • *Today's newspaper contains a searing exposé* **of** *police corruption.*

ex·pose *obj* /£ɪk'spəʊz, $-'spoʊz/ *v* [T] to make able to be seen; to leave without protection; to UNCOVER • *The plaster on the walls has been removed to expose the original bricks underneath.* • *He damaged his leg so badly in the accident that the bone was exposed* (= could be seen). • *The soldiers were exposed* **to** (= left without protection against) *considerable danger.* • *It is feared that people living near the power station may have been exposed* **to** (= left without protection against and harmed by) *radiation.* • *(fig.) His beliefs expose him* **to** (= make him likely to experience) *ridicule, but he won't give them up.* • *The newspaper story exposed him* **as** (= showed that he was) *a liar.* • *Investigators have exposed a plot to kill the president.* • *When she went to college, Kate was exposed* (= introduced) **to** *a lot of new ideas.* • *He was found guilty of exposing him***self** (= showing his sexual organs in public) **to** *schoolgirls.* • *This photograph was* **under-/over-***exposed* (= too little/too much light was allowed to reach the film).

ex·posed /£ɪk'spəʊzd, $-'spoʊzd/ *adj* • *The house is in a very exposed position* (= a position which is not protected from bad weather).

ex·po·sure /£ɪk'spəʊ·ʒəʳ, $-'spoʊ·ʒɚ/ *n* • *You should always limit your exposure* **to** (= the amount of time you leave your skin without protection against) *the sun.* [U] • *Even a brief exposure* **to** *radiation is very dangerous.* [C] • *All the members of the expedition to the South Pole died of exposure* (= from being without protection against the cold). [U] • *The exposure* (= discovery and reporting) **of** *the minister's love affair forced him to resign.* [U] • *Spielberg's new film is getting a lot of exposure* (= is being reported) *in the media at the moment.* [U] • *Greg's parents are worried about his exposure* **to** (= that he will be influenced by) *the kind of people they don't approve of while he's at college.* [U] • *There are twenty-four exposures on this film* (= the film can take that many photographs). [C] • *When it is dark, you need a slow exposure* (= need to allow more time for light to enter the camera) *in order to take a photograph.* [C] • *Our dining room has a northern exposure* (= faces north), *so it's rather cold.* [C]

ex·pos·i·tion [EXPLANATION] /ˌek·spə'zɪʃ·ᵊn/ *n fml* (the process of giving) a clear explanation • *The minister's speech included a clear exposition* **of** *the government's policies.* [C] • *She presented the accounts without any exposition* **of** *what they meant in terms of the company's financial position.* [U] • Ⓕ

ex·pos·i·tion [SHOW] /ˌek·spə'zɪʃ·ᵊn/, **expo** *n* [C] a show in which industrial goods, works of art, etc. are shown to the public • *the San Francisco exposition* • *Expo 92* (= a show that happened in 1992) • Ⓕ

ex·pos·tu·late /£ɪk'spɒs·tjʊ·leɪt, $-'spɑː·stjʊ-/ *v* [I] *fml* to express disagreement or complaint • *Walter expostulated* **with** *the waiter* **about** *the size of the bill.* • *The minister expostulated angrily* **on/about/against** *the terrorist bombings.*

ex·pos·tu·la·tion /£ɪkˌspɒs·tjʊ'leɪ·ʃᵊn, $-ˌspɑː·stjʊ-/ *n fml* • *Despite the expostulations/expostulation* (= expressions of complaint) *of the children, we went to visit their aunt on Saturday instead of going to the park.* [C/U]

ex·pound *(obj)* /ɪk'spaʊnd/ *v fml* to give a detailed explanation (of) • *We had to listen for hours to my uncle expounding* **on** *what's wrong with the world.* [I] • *John's expounding his theories about why they lost the football match again.* [T]

ex·press *obj* [SHOW] /ɪk'spres/ *v* [T] to show (a feeling, opinion or fact) • *Her eyes expressed deep sadness.* • *I would like to express my thanks for your kindness.* • *Bill expressed his disagreement with the rest of the committee by voting against the proposal.* • *Words can't express* **how** *happy I am.* [+ *wh-* word] • *These figures are expressed* **as** *a percentage of the total.* • *She has a problem with her speech which makes it difficult for her to express her***self** (= talk) *clearly.* • *Children often express them***selves** (= show their feelings) *in painting.*

ex·pressed /ɪk'sprest/ *adj* [before n; not gradable] • *It was my mother's expressed* **wish** (= she stated) *that after her death, her jewellery should be given to my sister.*

ex·pres·sion /ɪk'spreʃ·ᵊn/ *n* • *He wrote her a poem as an expression* **of** (= in order to show) *his love.* [C] • *We're delighted to have received so many expressions* **of** *support for* (= people have shown that they support us in) *our fight against the planned closure of our local hospital.* [C] • *Freedom of expression is a basic human right* (= people should be allowed to say what they think). [U] • *This school encourages the expression* **of** *individuality in its pupils.* [U] • *It's better to* **give** *expression* **to** (= show) *your anger, rather than hiding it.* [U] • *His sadness at the death of his wife* **found** *expression* (= was shown) *in his music.* [U] • *She plays the violin with great expression* (= feeling). [U] • *He showed no expression* (= he did not show any feeling) *as the judge sentenced him to life imprisonment.* [U] • *I could tell from her expression* (= the appearance of her face) *that something serious had happened.* [C] • *Mark always has such a glum expression (on his face)* (= looks unhappy). [C] • See also EXPRESSION [WORDS].

ex·pres·sion·less /ɪk'spreʃ·ᵊn·ləs/ *adj* • *He has such an expressionless* **face/voice** (= he shows no feeling in his face/voice). • *We thought her reading of the poem was quite expressionless.*

ex·pres·sion·less·ly /ɪk'spreʃ·ᵊn·lə·sli/ *adv*

Ex·pres·sion·i·sm /ɪk'spreʃ·ᵊn·ɪ·zᵊm/ *n* [U] • Expressionism is a style of art, music or writing, found particularly in the 1900s, which expresses people's states of mind: *contemporary American expressionism* ○ *Expressionism was founded in Europe, particularly Germany, in the early part of the twentieth century.*

Ex·pres·sion·ist /ɪk'spreʃ·ᵊn·ɪst/ *adj, n* • *Edvard Munch's "The Scream" is a famous Expressionist painting.* • *Max Beckmann was one of several German Expressionists forced to flee by the Nazis.* [C]

ex·pres·sive /ɪk'spres·ɪv/ *adj* • *A great actor needs to have an expressive* **face/voice** (= a face/voice which shows a lot of feeling). • *The final movement of Beethoven's Ninth Symphony is expressive* **of** *joy.*

ex·pres·sive·ly /ɪk'spres·ɪv·li/ *adv* • *She danced the part of Giselle very expressively.*

ex·pres·sive·ness /ɪk'spres·ɪv·nəs/ *n* [U] • *The performance lacked expressiveness* (= did not show any feeling).

ex·press [FAST] /ɪk'spres/ *adj* [before n; not gradable] moving or being sent fast • *Please send this letter by express* **delivery**. • *We caught the express* **bus/train**. • *The dry cleaners offer a normal or an express* **service**.

ex·press /ɪk'spres/ *n* • *The quickest way to get here is to take the uptown express* (= the fast train). [C] • *I'd love to travel on the Orient Express.* [C] • *This parcel needs to be sent* **by** *express* (= a service which delivers fast). [U]

ex·press /ɪk'spres/ *adv* [not gradable] • *Send this parcel express* (= by a service which delivers fast).

ex·press *obj* /ɪk'spres/ *v* [T] • *Your order will be expressed* (= delivered fast) **to** *you within 24 hours.*

ex·press CLEAR /ɪk'spres/ *adj* [before n] clearly and intentionally stated • *I've given everyone express instructions how to get to our house.* • *It is my express wish that after my death, my books be given to my old college library.* • *The lawyer argued that the accused had gone to the victim's house with the express purpose of killing her.*

ex·press·ly /ɪk'spres·li/ *adv* • *I expressly* (= clearly) *told you to be home by midnight.* • *The farmer put up the fence expressly to stop* (= with the intention of stopping) *people walking across his field.*

ex·pres·sion WORDS /ɪk'spreʃ·ᵊn/ *n* [C] a word or group of words used in a particular situation or by particular people • *He uses a lot of unusual expressions.* • *"Can of worms" is an expression meaning a difficult situation.* • See also **expression** at EXPRESS SHOW. • LP› **Words used together**

ex·pres·sion NUMBERS /ɪk'spreʃ·ᵊn/ *n* [C] (in mathematics) a symbol or group of symbols which represent an amount • $4xy^2$ *is an expression.*

ex·pres·so /£es'pres·əʊ, $-oʊ/ *n* [C/U] ESPRESSO

ex·press·way /ɪk'spres·weɪ/ *n* [C] *Am and Aus* a wide road built for fast moving traffic travelling long distances, with a limited number of points at which drivers can enter and leave it • *Traffic was light on the expressway, and I cleared the suburbs to the northbound Milwaukee toll road in forty-five minutes.* • PIC› **Motorway**

ex·pro·pri·ate *obj* /£ɪk'sprəʊ·pri·eɪt, $-'sproʊ-/ *v* [T] to take away (money or property) especially for public use without payment to the owner, or for personal use illegally • *During the war, the government expropriated land to grow food for the troops.* • *He was discovered to have been expropriating company funds.*

ex·pro·pri·a·tor /£ɪk'sprəʊ·pri·eɪ·təʳ, $-'sproʊ·pri·eɪ·t̬ɚ/ *n* [C]

ex·pro·pri·a·tion /£ɪkˌsprəʊ·pri'eɪ·ʃᵊn, $-ˌsproʊ-/ *n* [C/U]

ex·pul·sion /ɪk'spʌl·ʃᵊn/ *n* (the act of) forcing someone, or being forced, to leave somewhere • *The punishment for this kind of behaviour is expulsion* (**from** *school*). [U] • *The new government has ordered the expulsion* **of** *all foreign journalists* **from** *the country.* [U] • *This is the second expulsion* **of** *a club member this year.* [C] • See also EXPEL.

ex·punge *obj* /ɪk'spʌndʒ/ *v* [T] *fml* to rub off or remove (information) from a piece of writing • *His name has been expunged* **from** *the list of members.* • *(fig.) She has been unable to expunge the details of the accident* **from** *her memory.*

ex·pur·gate *obj* /£'ek·spə·geɪt, $-spɚ-/ *v* [T] to remove parts of (a piece of writing) that are considered likely to cause offence • *The book has been expurgated to make it suitable for children to read.*

ex·pur·gat·ed /£'ek·spə·geɪ·tɪd, $-spɚ·geɪ·t̬ɪd/ *adj* • *Only an expurgated* **version** *of the novel has been published so far* (= the parts of it likely to cause offence have been removed).

ex·pur·ga·tion /£ˌek·spə'geɪ·ʃᵊn, $-spɚ-/ *n* • *This is an expurgation* **of** *the original film* (= the parts of it likely to cause offence have been removed). [C] • *Generally, I don't approve of the expurgation* **of** *books.* [U]

ex·qui·site BEAUTIFUL /ɪk'skwɪz·ɪt/ *adj* very beautiful; delicate • *I've just bought an exquisite piece of china.* • *Look at this exquisite painting* • *She has exquisite taste.*

ex·qui·site·ly /ɪk'skwɪz·ɪt·li/ *adv* • *Their house is exquisitely* (= beautifully) *furnished.* • *Rachel is an exquisitely behaved child* (= she behaves very well).

ex·qui·site·ness /ɪk'skwɪz·ɪt·nəs/ *n* [U] • *I've never heard music of such exquisiteness* (= such beautiful music) *before.*

ex·qui·site SHARP /ɪk'skwɪz·ɪt/ *adj fml* (esp. of pleasure or pain) sharply felt; great; ACUTE • *exquisite joy* • *The pain in my tooth is quite exquisite.* • *A comedian needs to have exquisite* (= very good) *timing.*

ex·qui·site·ly /ɪk'skwɪz·ɪt·li/ *adv* • *The human ear is exquisitely* (= very) *sensitive.*

ex·qui·site·ness /ɪk'skwɪz·ɪt·nəs/ *n* [U]

ex–ser·vice·man (*pl* **-men**), **ex–ser·vice·wo·man** (*pl* **-women**) /£ˌeks'sɜː·vɪs·mən, $-'sɝ-, -ˌwʊm·ən/ *n* [C] a person who was in the past a member of one of the armed forces

ex·tant /ɪk'stænt/ *adj fml* (of something very old) still existing • *We have some extant parish records from the sixteenth century.* • *Medieval customs are extant in some parts of Europe.*

ex·tem·po·ra·ne·ous /ekˌstem·pə'reɪ·ni·əs/ *adj* done or said without any preparation or thought in advance • *When she opened the new school, the minister gave an extemporaneous speech on the government's education policy.*

ex·tem·po·re /ekˌstem·pəri/ *adj, adv* [not gradable] • *an extempore performance* • *At the audition, the actors were asked to perform extempore* (= without any preparation or thought in advance).

ex·tem·po·rize, *Br and Aus usually* **–ise** /£ɪk'stem·pᵊr·aɪz, $-pɚ·aɪz/ *v* [I] • *Because he had lost his notes, the lecturer had to extemporize* (= speak without them).

ex·tend *(obj)* REACH /ɪk'stend/ *v* to (cause to) reach, stretch or continue; to add to in order to make bigger or longer • *From our window we have a view of fields extending* (= reaching) **into** *the distance.* [I always + adv/prep] • *The Sahara Desert extends* (= reaches) **for** *miles.* [I always + adv/prep] • *The path extends* (= continues) **beyond** *the end of the road.* [I always + adv/prep] • *Rain is expected to extend* **to** (= reach) *all parts of the country by this evening.* [I always + adv/prep] • *His concern about saving the rain forest doesn't extend* (= reach) *as far as actually doing anything about it.* [I always + adv/prep] • *The effects of this legislation will extend* (= reach) *further than the government intends.* [I always + adv/prep] • *Parking restrictions do not extend* **to** (= include) *disabled people.* [I always + adv/prep] • *The last party we went to extended* (= lasted) *throughout the night.* [I always + adv/prep] • *The doctor asked me if I could extend* (= stretch out) *my fingers.* [T] • *We've extended a washing line* (= made it reach) *between two trees in the garden.* [T] • *We're planning to extend our publishing of children's books* (= increase it). [T] • *The government has produced a series of leaflets designed to extend* (= increase) *public awareness of the dangers of AIDS.* [T] • *The bank has said that it cannot extend* (= increase) *its commitment to the business any further.* [T] • *We have plans to extend our house* (= to make it bigger). [T] • *This sofa can be extended* **into** (= made bigger so that it forms) *a bed.* [T] • *The pub has recently extended its opening hours* (= made them longer). [T] • *I would like to stay in Britain a bit longer, but I will need to extend my visa* (= make it last longer). [T]

ex·tend·able /ɪk'sten·də·bl̩/ *adj* • *We've bought an extendable ladder* (= one that can be made longer) *so that we can mend our roof.* • *The lease on the office is extendable* (= can be made longer).

ex·tend·ed /ɪk'sten·dɪd/ *adj* [before n] • *They're going on an extended* (= long) *holiday to Australia.* • *There will be an extended* (= longer than usual) *news bulletin tonight because of the plane crash.* • An **extended family** is a family unit which includes grandmothers, grandfathers, aunts and uncles, etc. in addition to parents and children. Compare NUCLEAR FAMILY.

ex·ten·sion /ɪk'sten·tʃᵊn/ *n* • *Martin Luther King, Jr, campaigned for the extension* **of** *civil rights* **to** (= for them to include) *black people.* [U] • *This kidnapping represents an extension* **of** *terrorist activity* (= makes it reach) **to** *innocent children.* [C] • *The article is an extension* **of** (= takes further) *the ideas Professor Fox developed in an earlier book.* [C] • *The extension* (= increasing) **of** *police powers in the province has been heavily criticized.* [U] • *His report contained serious criticisms of the finance director, and,* **by extension** (= therefore), *of the entire board of management.* [U] • *If you want to use the lawnmower, you'll need an (Br)* **extension lead**/*(Am and Aus)* **extension cord** (= an additional wire which takes electricity to something further away). • *I think you have the wrong number – Jackie's on a different extension* (= telephone line within a building). [C] • *We're building an extension* (= adding a new room or rooms) **to/on** *our house.* [C] • *I've applied for an extension* **to** *my visa* (= asked for it to last longer). [C] • *They are hoping to get an extension* **of** *their loan.* (= to be given a longer period of time in which to pay it back). [C] • LP› **Telephone**

ex·tend *obj* OFFER /ɪk'stend/ *v* [T] to offer or give • *I should like to extend my thanks* **to** *you for your kindness.* • *The chairperson extended a warm welcome* **to** *the guest speaker.* • *He extended his hand as a greeting* (= held out his hand for someone to shake it). • *The government is extending* (= giving) *aid to people who have been affected by the earthquake.* • *The bank has agreed to extend us money/extend money* **to** *us* (= lend us money) *to buy our house.* [+ two objects]

ex·ten·sion /ɪk'sten·tʃᵊn/ *n* [U] • *After the extension* **of** *a welcome to the guests, the meeting began.*

ex·tend *obj* USE ABILITY /ɪk'stend/ *v* [T] to cause (esp. a person or animal) to use all its ability • *Ellen's job doesn't really extend her very much.* • *The horse really had to extend itself to win the race.*

ex·ten·sion /ɪk'sten·tʃᵊn/ *n* [C] any of two or more telephones in the same house which share the same number, or any of a number of telephones connected to a SWITCHBOARD in a large building such as an office • *We have an extension in our bedroom.* • *When you call, ask for extension 3276.* • See also **extension** at EXTEND.

ex·ten·sive /ɪk'stent·sɪv/ *adj* covering a large area; having a great range • *The school has extensive grounds.* • *The city of Dresden suffered from extensive bombing during the Second World War.* • *The extensive repairs to the motorway are causing serious traffic problems.* • *Her knowledge of music is extensive* (= she knows a lot about music). • *The royal wedding received extensive coverage in the newspapers.*

ex·ten·sive·ly /ɪk'stent·sɪv·li/ *adv* • *The house was extensively* (= a large part of it was) *rebuilt after the fire.* • *The side effects of the new drug are being extensively researched* (= are being studied in detail).

ex·tent /ɪk'stent/ *n* area or length; amount • *From the top of the Empire State Building, you can see* **the** *full extent* **of** *Manhattan* (= the area it covers). [U] • *We don't yet know* **the** *extent* **of** *his injuries* (= how bad his injuries are). [U] • *Rosie's teacher was impressed by* **the** *extent* **of** *her knowledge* (= how much she knew). [U] • *Marathon runners often have to push themselves beyond* **the** *extent* (= limits) **of** *their endurance.* [U] • *The River Nile is over 6500 kilometres* **in** *extent* (= length). [U] • *People are affected* **to** *different extents by what they see on television.* [C] • *The company is in debt* **to the extent of** (= to the amount of) *several thousand pounds.* • *Some people hold their beliefs very strongly, even* **to the extent of** *being* (= so strongly that they are) *prepared to go to prison for them.* • *Apes are like people* **to the extent that** *they have some human characteristics* (= because they have some of the same characteristics as people) • *Sales have fallen so badly this year,* **to the extent that** (= we have reached the stage where) *we will have to close some of our shops.* • **To a great extent/a large extent** (= Mostly) *people go on holiday there to enjoy the good weather.* • *The rich will not benefit from the proposed changes to the tax system* **to the same extent as** (= as much as) *the lower paid.* • **To some extent/a certain extent** (= Partly), *she was responsible for the accident.* • *The car was damaged* **to such an extent** (= so much) *that it could not be repaired.* • *Straightening the road has reduced the risk of accidents and* **to that extent** (= that being so) *has made it safer, but it is still dangerous.* • **To what extent** (= How much) *will the budget have to be modified?*

ex·ten·u·ate *obj* /ɪk'sten·ju·eɪt/ *v* [T] *fml* to cause (a wrong act) to be judged less seriously by giving reasons for it • *He was unable to say anything that might have extenuated his behaviour.* • Ⓘ

ex·ten·u·at·ing /£ɪk'sten·juː·eɪ·tɪŋ, $-ţɪŋ/ *adj* [before n] *slightly fml* • *She was found guilty of theft, but because of extenuating* **circumstances** *was not sent to prison.*

ex·ten·u·a·tion /ɪkˌsten·ju'eɪ·ʃᵊn/ *n* [U] *fml* • *Her plea of ignorance of the law* **in** *extenuation* **of** (= as an excuse for) *her crime was not accepted.*

ex·te·ri·or /£ɪk'stɪə·ri·əʳ, $-'stɪr·i·ɚ/ *adj* [not gradable] outer; on or from the outside • *In some of the villages the exterior walls of the houses are painted pink.* • *Exterior* **to** *the main house there is a small building that could be used as an office or studio.* • See also EXTERNAL. Compare INTERIOR.

ex·te·ri·or /£ɪk'stɪə·ri·əʳ, $-'stɪr·i·ɚ/ *n* [C] • *The Palace of Fontainebleau has a very grand exterior* (= outside). • *The exterior* (= outside) **of** *the house needs painting.* • *There are shutters* **on** *the exterior* **of** *the windows.* • *She has a tough exterior/She is tough* **on** *the exterior* (= She appears to be strong), *but is really quite gentle.*

ex·ter·mi·nate *obj* /£ɪk'stɜː·mɪ·neɪt, $-'stɜːr-/ *v* [T] to kill (all the animals or people in a particular place or of a particular type) • *Once cockroaches get into a building, it's very difficult to exterminate them.* • *Millions of Jewish people were exterminated in concentration camps in the Second World War.* • *"Exterminate! Exterminate!"* (Said by the imaginary creatures The Daleks in the television series *Dr Who*, 1964-)

ex·ter·mi·na·tion /£ɪkˌstɜː·mɪ'neɪ·ʃᵊn, $-ˌstɜːr-/ *n* [U] • *International measures have been taken to prevent the extermination* **of** *the whale* (= all of them being killed).

ex·ter·mi·nat·or /£ɪk'stɜː·mɪ·neɪ·təʳ, $-'stɜːr·mɪ·neɪ·ţɚ/ *n* [C] • *Mr Clark, the exterminator* (= the person whose job it is to kill unwanted animals), *is coming on Friday to destroy the rats in the cellar.*

ex·ter·nal /£ɪk'stɜː·nəl, $-'stɜːr-/ *adj* [not gradable] of, on, for or coming from the outside • *The external walls of the house are in need of repair.* • *Female kangaroos carry their young in pouches that are external* **to** *their bodies.* • *The doctor thinks her injuries are all external* (= the inside of her body has not been damaged). • *This skin cream is* **for** *external* **use** *only* (= it must not be put inside the body). • *In later years, his paintings began to show a number of external influences* (= influences coming from other people). • *Children must learn to live in the external world outside their families.* • *Most news magazines have a section devoted to external affairs* (= foreign news). • *You shouldn't judge people solely by their external appearances* (= what they appear to be like). • An **external examination** is one arranged by people outside a student's own school, college or university, and in which the student's work is judged by an **external examiner**. • An **external student** is one who is connected with a college or university but does not study the usual courses. • See also EXTERIOR. Compare INTERNAL.

ex·ter·nal·ize *obj*, *Br and Aus usually* **-ise** /£ɪk'stɜː·nə·laɪz, $-'stɜːr-/ *v* [T] • *It's better to externalize your anger* (= express it in words or acts) *than to hide it.*

ex·ter·nal·iz·a·tion, *Br and Aus usually* **-i·sa·tion** /£ɪkˌstɜː·nə·laɪ'zeɪ·ʃᵊn, $-ˌstɜːr-/ *n* • *His music is an externalization* (= expression) **of** *his feelings.* [C] • *The hospital encourages the externalization* (= expression) **of** *feelings among its mentally ill patients.* [U]

ex·ter·nal·ly /£ɪk'stɜː·nə·li, $-'stɜːr-/ *adv* [not gradable] • *The inside of the house is in good condition, but externally it needs repairing.* • *Externally, she appeared calm, but inside she was furious.*

ex·ter·nals /£ɪk'stɜː·nəlz, $-'stɜːr-/ *pl n* • *It's easy to be misled by externals* (= appearances).

ex·tinct /ɪk'stɪŋkt/ *adj* [not gradable] no longer existing • *There is concern that the giant panda will soon* **become** *extinct.* • *Many tribes* **became** *extinct when they came into contact with Western illnesses.* • *The practice of sending children to work in coal-mines is fortunately now extinct.* • *Any love that she once had for him is now extinct.* • An extinct **volcano** is one that is no longer active.

ex·tinc·tion /ɪk'stɪŋk·ʃᵊn/ *n* [U] • *The extinction* **of** *the dinosaurs occurred* (= they stopped existing) *millions of years ago.* • *Many species of plants and animals are* **in danger of/threatened with** *extinction* (= being destroyed so that they no longer exist). • *Some people predict the extinction* **of** *family life as we know it today.*

ex·tin·guish *obj* /ɪk'stɪŋ·gwɪʃ/ *v* [T] to stop (a fire or light) burning • *It took the firefighters hours to extinguish the flames.* • *(fml) The theatre lights have been extinguished, ready for the performance.* • *(fig.) Nothing could extinguish* (= stop) *his love for her.* • *(fig.) We must try to extinguish* (= get rid of) *the memory of what has happened, and look to the future.*

ex·tir·pate *obj* /£'ek·stɜː·peɪt, $-stɚ-/ *v* [T] *fml* to remove or destroy (something) completely • *The country must extirpate the evils of drug abuse.* • *The military rulers have tried to extirpate all opposition.*

ex·tir·pa·tion /£ˌek·stɜː'peɪ·ʃᵊn, $-stɚ-/ *n* [U]

ex·tol *obj* /£ɪk'stəʊl, $-'stoʊl/ *v* [T] **-ll-** to praise highly • *His book extolling the benefits of vegetarianism has proved to be very popular.* • *I'm tired of listening to her extolling the virtues of her children.* • *He was extolled* **as** *a hero when he scored the winning goal.*

ex·tort *obj* /£ɪk'stɔːt, $-'stɔːrt/ *v* [T] to obtain by force or threat, or with difficulty • *He had been extorting money* **from** *the old lady for years.* • *Police have not so far been able to extort a confession* **from** *the people accused of the bombing.* • *They finally succeeded in extorting a reaction* **from** *the audience.* • LP **Crimes and criminals**

ex·tor·tion /£ɪk'stɔː·ʃᵊn, $-'stɔːr-/ *n* [U] • *He was found guilty of obtaining the money by extortion* (= by forceful methods).

ex·tor·tion·ate /£ɪk'stɔː·ʃᵊn·ət, $-'stɔːr-/ *adj disapproving* • *The price of books nowadays is extortionate* (= too high). • *I think he makes extortionate* (= extreme) *demands of you.*

ex·tor·tion·ate·ly /£ɪk'stɔː·ʃᵊn·ət·li, $-'stɔːr-/ *adv* • *These shoes are extortionately expensive.*

ex·tor·tion·er /£ɪk'stɔː·ʃᵊn·əʳ, $-'stɔːr·ʃᵊn·ɚ/, **ex·tor·tion·ist** *n* [C], *adj* • An extortioner/extortionist is a person who obtains something by force or threat. • *Police use of extortionist methods has been criticized.*

ex·tra MORE /'ek·strə/ *adj, adv* [not gradable], *n* (something) added, additional or more • *I'll need some extra help/clothes/time/money.* • *Recently he's been working an extra two hours a day.* • *We agreed on a price but afterwards they wanted £10 extra* (= more). • *The price includes travel and accommodation but meals are extra* (= there is an additional charge for meals). • *They pay her extra to work nights.* • *In her new job she has to work extra long days.* • *He helped us so much we gave him* **a (little) bit** *extra* (= gave more, esp. money, than expected or agreed). • In a game of football *(Br and Aus)* **extra time** (*Am* **overtime**) is the period of time in which play continues if neither team has won in the usual time allowed for the game. • *Seat belts are included as standard but electric windows are an* **(optional)** *extra.* [C] • In a film, extras are people who do not have speaking parts and who are usually part of the background, for example, in a crowd. [C] • In cricket, an extra is a point given to one team if the other team makes an illegal mistake (when **bowling**). [C] • Ⓕ

ex·tra– OUTSIDE /ˌek·strə-, '--/ *combining form* outside or in addition to • *extraterrestrial beings* (= imaginary creatures which come from outside the planet Earth) • *an extramarital affair* (= a sexual relationship of a married person with someone other than their husband or wife) • *extracurricular activities* (= activities which are not part of the usual school or college course)

ex·tract *obj* /ɪk'strækt/ *v* [T] to remove or take out (something) • *They used to extract iron ore* **from** *this site.* • *The oil which is extracted* **from** *olives is used for cooking.* • *I'll have to have this tooth extracted.* • *(fig.) After much persuasion they managed to extract the information/ details/plans* **from** *him* (= although he was unwilling).

ex·tract /'ek·strækt/ *n* • *malt extract* [U] • *yeast extract* [U] • *The cream contained extracts* **of/from** (= chemical substances extracted from) *several plants.* [C] • *She showed me an extract* **from** (= separately printed part taken from) *a book that will be published next year.* [C]

ex·trac·tion /ɪk'stræk·ʃᵊn/ *n* • *The extraction* **of** *minerals has damaged the countryside.* [U] • An extraction is the removal of a tooth: *She had two extractions.* [C] ○ *This is part of the extraction process.* [U] • If someone is **of** a particular extraction, their family originally came from another country: *She's of German/Welsh/Korean extraction.* [U] • *The college has many students of foreign extraction* (= from other countries). [U]

ex·trac·tor /£ɪk'stræk·təʳ, $-tɚ/ *n* [C] • *a juice extractor* • *an extractor fan*

ex·tra·cur·ri·cu·lar /£ˌek·strə·kə'rɪk·jʊ·ləʳ, $-jə·lɚ/ *adj* [not gradable] (of activities or subjects) which are not part of the usual school or college course • *Available* **extracurricular activities** *include pottery, chess, choir, badminton and a series of visits to historic houses.* • *(humorous)* **Extracurricular activities** is also sometimes used to mean sexual activity.

ex·tra·dite *obj* /'ek·strə·daɪt/ *v* [T] to make (someone) return for trial to another country where they have been accused of doing something illegal • *He will be extradited* **to** *Britain* **from** *France.* • *In the US, criminals must be extradited from one state to another state.*

ex·tra·dit·ab·le /£'ek·strə·daɪ·tə·bl̩, $-t̬ə-/ *adj* [not gradable] • An **extraditable crime** is a crime for which someone could be extradited.

ex·tra·di·tion /ˌek·strə'dɪʃ·ᵊn/ *n* [U] • *They have applied for his extradition* **to** *Ireland.* • *Do these two countries have an* **extradition treaty** (= an agreement to send back criminals)*?*

ex·tra·ma·ri·tal /£ˌek·strə'mær·ɪ·tᵊl, $-ə·t̬ᵊl/ *adj* [not gradable] (of a sexual relationship) with a person other than your marriage partner • *extramarital affairs/ adventures*

ex·tra·mu·ral *esp. Br* /£ˌek·strə'mjʊə·rᵊl, $-'mjʊr·ᵊl/, *Am and Aus usually* **ex·ten·sion** *adj* [not gradable] organized esp. by a college or university, etc. for people who are not students there • *extramural classes/courses*

ex·tra·ne·ous /ɪk'streɪ·ni·əs/ *adj* not directly connected with or related to (something) • *These questions are extraneous* **to** *the main business of advanced level study.* • *If no extraneous matters/issues are introduced, we should be able to keep the report to ten pages.*

ex·tra·or·di·na·ry /£ɪk'strɔː·dɪn·ᵊr·i, £ˌek·strə'ɔː-, $ɪk 'strɔːr·dᵊn·er-/ *adj* very unusual, special, unexpected or strange • *He told the extraordinary story of his escape.* • *Her voice had an extraordinary hypnotic quality.* • An extraordinary **meeting** is a special meeting which happens between regular meetings.

ex·tra·or·di·na·ri·ly /£ɪk'strɔː·dɪn·ᵊr·ᵊl·i, £ˌek·strə'ɔː-, $ɪk'strɔr·dᵊn·er-/ *adv* • *She has an extraordinarily* (= unusually, very) *loud voice.* • LP **Very, completely**

ex·tra·po·late *(obj)* /ɪk'stræp·ə·leɪt/ *v* to guess or think about what might happen from information that is already known • *Anyone who has read Moby Dick would find it irresistible to extrapolate* **from** *that great novel* **to** *the real world today.* [I] • *We need to extrapolate trends* **from** *the published figures.* [T]

ex·tra·pol·a·tion /ɪkˌstræp·ə'leɪ·ʃᵊn/ *n* [U]

ex·tra·sen·so·ry /£ˌek·strə'sent·sᵊr·i, $-sɚ-/ *adj* [not gradable] without the use of hearing, seeing, touch, taste and smell • **Extrasensory perception** (*abbreviation* **ESP**) is the ability to know things without using hearing, seeing, touch, taste or smell.

ex·tra·ter·re·stri·al /ˌek·strə·tə'res·tri·ᵊl/ *adj* [not gradable] (coming from) outside the planet Earth • *extraterrestrial beings*

ex·tra·ter·ri·to·ri·al /£ˌek·strəˌter·ɪ'tɔː·ri·ᵊl, $-'tɔːr·i-/ *adj* [not gradable] outside (the laws of) a country • *extraterritorial possessions*

ex·trav·a·gant /ɪk'stræv·ə·gᵊnt/ *adj* spending, using or doing more than necessary in an uncontrolled way • *Executives at the company enjoyed an extravagant lifestyle of free gifts, fine wines and exceptionally high salaries.* • *It was extravagant* **of** *you to buy strawberries out of season.* • *He seldom hailed taxis, which he regarded as extravagant, but travelled by bus and tube.* • *His children made extravagant* (= very great) *demands on his time and money.* • *The product does not live up to the extravagant* (= very great and not realistic) *claims of the advertisers.* • Ⓒⓢ Ⓔ

ex·trav·a·gant·ly /ɪk'stræv·ə·gᵊnt·li/ *adv*

ex·trav·a·gance /ɪk'stræv·ə·gᵊnts/ *n* • *I'm tired of all his extravagance.* [U] • *Chocolate is my greatest extravagance* (= something I don't need which I spend a lot of money on). [C] • Ⓔ

ex·trav·a·gan·za /ɪkˌstræv·ə'gæn·zə/ *n* [C] a very colourful, exciting and decorative event, esp. an expensively produced entertainment • *a musical/film/ dance extravaganza* • *The Opera Ball is an extravaganza that has been held annually for 40 years.* • *The church is a baroque extravaganza built in the sixteenth century.*

ex·treme GREAT /ɪk'striːm/ *adj* very great • *extreme distress/pleasure/relief/caution/pain/difficulties/old age* • *The film was unpleasant* **in the extreme** (= very unpleasant). • Ⓟ

ex·treme·ly /ɪk'striːm·li/ *adv* • *She was very serious, disciplined and hard-working, but extremely dull.* • *I'm extremely sorry I wasn't here to meet you.* • LP **Very, completely**

ex·treme FURTHEST /ɪk'striːm/ *adj, n* [C] (at) the furthest point; (to) the greatest degree • *in the extreme north of the country* • *at the extreme end of the peninsula* • People with extreme **views** have opinions which are outside the usual range of opinion: *He has extreme views/He's extreme* **in** *his views on foxhunting.* • Extreme **weather** is either very good or very bad weather. • **At the furthest** *extreme of the field is a patch of orchids.* • **At one** *extreme there are people who have two homes while* **at the other** *(extreme) there are those who sleep on the streets.* • *Somewhere between the two extremes is a happy medium.* • *This is a crisis which* **at the extreme** (= in the worst situation) *could lead to war.* • *His moods* **go from one extreme to the other** (= first he is very happy then he is very unhappy). • *His unhappiness* **drove** *him* **to extremes** (= made him behave in an unsuitable way). • Ⓟ

ex·trem·i·sm /ɪk'striː·mɪ·zᵊm/ *n* [U] • *political extremism* (= extreme political opinions)

ex·trem·ist /ɪk'striː·mɪst/ *n* [C], *adj* • *a group of extremists* (= people with extreme opinions) • *extremist tendencies*

ex·trem·i·ty /£ɪk'strem·ɪ·ti, $-ə·t̬i/ *n* [C] • *The wood lies on the southern extremity of the estate.* • *A decision of that type is at the extremity of a judge's powers.*

ex·trem·i·ties /£ɪk'strem·ɪ·tiz, $-ə·t̬iz/ *pl n* • Extremities are the parts of the human body furthest from the heart, for example, the fingers, toes and nose: *The patient's breathing was faint and the extremities were very cold.*

ex·tri·cate *obj* /ˈek·strɪ·keɪt/ *v* [T] *fml* to remove or set free (something) with difficulty • *It took hours to extricate the car* **from** *the sand.* • *In an attempt to extricate himself* **from** *a personal disaster he blamed his colleagues.*

ex·tri·ca·tion /ˌek·strɪˈkeɪ·ʃən/ *n* [U] *fml* • *Unskilled extrication of victims who have suffered neck injury can cause serious damage.*

ex·tro·vert, ex·tra·vert /£ˈek·strə·vɜːt, $-vɜːrt/ *adj, n* [C] (of) an energetic, happy person who enjoys being with other people • *a noisy group of extroverts* • *extrovert* **behaviour** • Compare INTROVERT.

ex·tro·vert·ed /£ˈek·strə·vɜː·tɪd, $-vɜːr·t̬ɪd/ *adj* • *His writing shows an extroverted desire to expose his inner self.*

ex·trude *obj* /ɪkˈstruːd/ *v* [T] *specialized* to form (something) by forcing or pushing it out, esp. through a small opening • *extruded aluminium rods* • *There is a strong market for extruded snacks – potato or maize paste made into the strange shapes that children enjoy.*

ex·tru·sion /ɪkˈstruː·ʒən/ *n* [U]

ex·u·ber·ant /£ɪgˈzjuː·bər·ənt, $-ˈzuː·bɚ-/ *adj* (esp. of people and their behaviour) very energetic • *He is a classical dancer with an exuberant, flamboyant style.* • *Young and exuberant, he symbolises Italy's new vitality.* • *(fig.) The path was blocked by the exuberant* (= strong and spreading) *growth of wild blackberry bushes.*

ex·u·ber·ance /£ɪgˈzjuː·bər·ənts, $-ˈzuː·bɚ-/ *n* [U] • *Her exuberance is quite astonishing.*

ex·ude *obj* /£ɪgˈzjuːd, $-ˈzuːd/ *v* [T] to produce from inside yourself • *Some trees exude* **from** *their bark a sap that repels insect parasites.* • *(fig.) Few people exude such* **confidence** *as Sam.*

ex·ult /ɪgˈzʌlt/ *v* to express great pleasure or happiness, esp. at someone else's defeat or failure • *They exulted* **in/at/over** *their victory.* [I] • *"Things will be different now," they exulted.* [+ clause]

ex·ul·tant /ɪgˈzʌl·tənt/ *adj* • *an exultant cheer* • *an exultant crowd*

ex·ul·tant·ly /ɪgˈzʌl·tənt·li/ *adv*

ex·ul·ta·tion /ˌeg·zəlˈteɪ·ʃən/ *n* [U] • *Everyone joined in the exultation* **at** *his release.*

eye /aɪ/ *n* [C] one of the pair of organs of seeing in the faces of humans and animals • *They hoped the operation would restore the sight to his left eye.* • *She's got beautiful green eyes.* • The eye of a needle is the hole through which you put the thread. • The eye of a storm is its calm, quiet centre. • On a potato, or other similar plant part, an eye is a dark spot from which a new stem and leaves will grow. • If something is at eye-**level**, it is positioned at approximately the same height as your eyes. • When you **roll** your eyes, you move them around to express surprise. • *When we took them to the puppet show, the children were* **all eyes** (= watched with great interest). • *The road stretched into the distance* **as far as the eye can/could see.** • *They drove off in my car* **before/under** *my* **very eyes** (= although I was watching). • *(infml)* If you have or need **eyes in the back of** your **head,** you are able or need to give attention to everything, even things you cannot easily see: *Small children are always doing dangerous things. You need eyes in the back of your head!* • *(Br)* In games such as cricket or tennis, a player has to **get/keep** their **eye in** (= develop the ability to judge the way the ball is moving). • *She* **has a** *good/keen/sharp* **eye for** (= a good ability to notice) *detail.* • *(infml) She's* **had** *her* **eye on** (= wanted) *a new bike for some time.* • *(Br and Aus infml)* Someone who **has an eye to/for the main chance** is always ready to use a situation to their own advantage. • *Although I'm forty,* **in** *my parents'* **eyes/in the eyes of** *my parents* (= in my parents' opinion), *I'm still a young person.* • *(infml) Will you* **keep an/***your* **eye on** (= watch carefully) *my suitcase while I go to get the tickets?* • To **clap/lay/set eyes on** something or someone is to see it or them: *Where's Jane? I haven't set eyes on her for weeks.* • *(infml)* To **make eyes at** someone means to look at them in a way that makes it obvious that you are sexually interested in them: *She was making eyes at him all evening.* • *(Br infml) His promotion was* **one in the eye for** (= a disappointment/defeat for) *his rivals.* • *(infml) She couldn't* **take** *her* **eyes off** (= stop looking at) *the wonderful display of food.* • **There's more to** this **than meets the eye** means that something is more difficult to understand than you thought at the beginning. • **To my** *amateur* **eye** (= In my opinion), *it looks like an expensive antique.* • *(infml) I'm* **up**

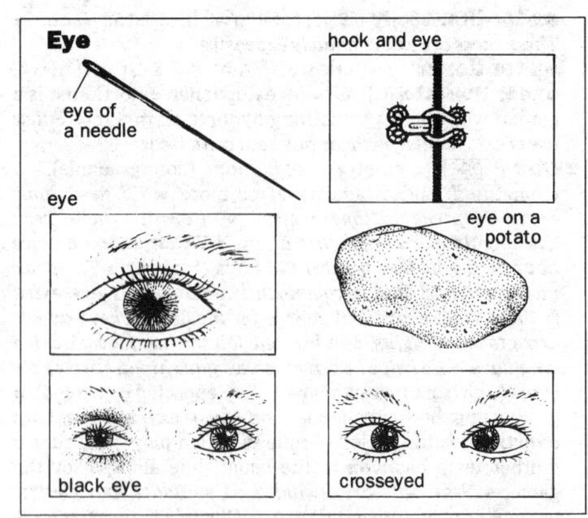

to *my* **eyes in** (= very busy with) *school reports this week.* • *(infml) I could do that journey* **with** *my* **eyes shut** (= easily or automatically) *now, I've done it so many times.* • *(infml) You go around* **with** *your* **eyes shut** (= without noticing what is happening) *half the time, so I'm not surprised you were the last to hear the news about Becky.* • *(infml)* If you **keep an/**your **eye out for** something, or if you **keep** your **eyes open/peeled/***(Br)* **skinned for** something, you look for it: *When you're shopping, keep your eye out for something we can give John as a birthday present.* • *(infml) She went into it* **with** *her* **eyes open** (= knowing what was likely to happen). • *(humorous)* If someone's **eyes are too big for** their **stomach,** they take more food than they can eat. • *She's wearing an* **eye-catching** (= attractive, noticeable) *red dress, you can't miss her.* • **Eye contact** is when two people look at each other at the same time: *If you're telling the truth, why are you* **avoiding** *eye contact* **with** *me?* • *When you are in an interview, it is very important to* **keep/make** *eye contact* **with** (= look into the eyes of) *the person who is interviewing you.* • If something is an **eye-opener,** it surprises you, esp. by giving you information which you did not have before: *That newspaper article on homelessness was a real eye-opener.* • An **eye-patch** is a covering worn over the eye to protect it if it is damaged or sore: *In story books, pirates usually wear eye-patches and have parrots on their shoulders.* • **Eye shadow** is a coloured cream or powder which is put around the eyes to make them look larger or more attractive. • An **eye socket** is one of the two hollows on each side of the nose which contain the eyes. • *(saying)* 'An eye for an eye (and a tooth for a tooth)' means that if someone does something bad to you, it is all right to do something bad to them in return. • *"The Eye of the Tiger"* (title of a book by Wilbur Smith, and later a song title, 1975) • *"For Your Eyes Only* (= secret)*"* (title of one of Ian Fleming's 'James Bond' novels, 1960) • PIC **Cosmetics, Eye**

eye *obj* /aɪ/ *v* [T] **eyeing** or *Am also* **eying,** *past* **eyed** • *She eyed* **(up)** (= looked closely at) *the other passengers warily/suspiciously.* • *The guests were eyeing* **(up)** (= looking with desire at) *the food and drink.* • *Those two blokes over there are eyeing us up* (= looking at us in a way which shows sexual interest).

eye·ful /ˈaɪ·fʊl/ *n* [C] • An eyeful is an amount of dust, dirt etc. which has entered the eye: *As the lorry went past, I got an eyeful* **of** *grit.* • *(fig. infml) She's quite* **an eyeful** (= an attractive sight). • *(fig. infml)* **Get an eyeful of** (= look at) *this.*

-eyed /-aɪd/ *combining form* • *cross-eyed* • *black-eyed* • *wide-eyed*

eye·ball /£ˈaɪ·bɔːl, $-bɑːl/ *n* [C] the whole eye, including the part that cannot usually be seen • If you face someone **eyeball to eyeball** you are angry and speak to them directly. • If you are **up to your eyeballs in** something you are very busy with it: *I'm up to my eyeballs in unanswered letters.* • Someone who is **drugged to** the eyeballs has taken a lot of drugs and is not very aware of what is happening.

eye·ball *obj* /£ˈaɪ·bɔːl, $-bɑːl/ *v* [T] *infml* • *He eyeballed* (= looked closely at) *me across the bar.*

eye·brow /ˈaɪ·braʊ/ *n* [C] the line of short hairs above each eye in humans • *Some women* **pluck** *their eyebrows* (= remove some of the hairs to make them tidy or change their shape). • **Bushy** eyebrows are long and thick. • If you **raise** your eyebrows you are showing surprise.

EYE, EYESIGHT AND SEEING

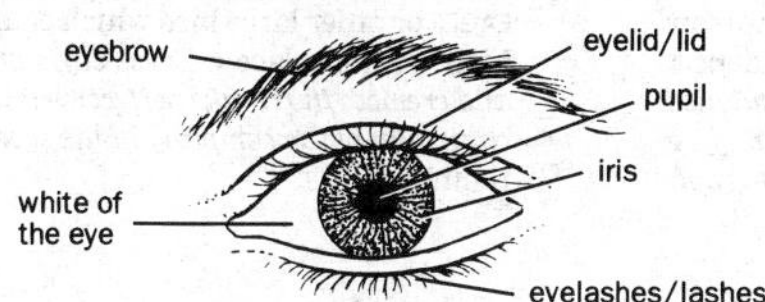

- Your ability to see is called your **eyesight**, **sight** or **vision**: *Airline pilots need to have good eyesight.* • *After his car crashed, Sam lost the sight of his left eye.* • *Sarah's over seventy and she's still got perfect vision.*
- Some common problems with eyesight: *I'm getting* **long-sighted**/*(Am also)* **far-sighted**: *I can't read a newspaper now if it's too close to me.* • *She's so* **short-sighted**/*(esp. Am)* **near-sighted** *she can't find her glasses if she takes them off.* • *Alice is* **blind**/*has* **lost her sight** *and needs a guide dog to help her.* • *Drivers may be temporarily* **blinded**/**dazzled** *by the lights of approaching cars.* • *I wear* **contact lenses** *but I always carry a spare pair of spectacles.*

look = to direct your eyes in order to see
watch = to look at something for a period of time, esp. something that is moving
see = to be aware of what is around you by using your eyes

		look	watch	see
Look **at** *all this rubbish on the floor.* *I* **can't** *see very well without my glasses.* *They all watched as I opened my presents.*	used without an object	●	●	●
I watched TV for a couple of hours. *I* **can** *see three or four empty seats.* *He says he's seen 'Jaws' ten times.*	used with an object		●	●
She sat looking through the window. *Wait a minute – I'm watching the news.* *I can't believe what I'm seeing.*	used in continuous tenses (*be seeing* is not common in this meaning)	●	●	●
Look **how** *beautifully she dances.* *Watch carefully* **where** *the ball lands.* *I can't see* **what**'*s happening.*	+ *wh-* word	●	●	●
Can't you see (**that**) *he's annoyed?*	+ (*that*) clause			●
Hazel watched him open the letter. *She saw the van park outside her house.*	T + obj + infinitive without *to* (esp. referring to a completed action)*		●	●
*I like to watch people walk***ing** *past.* *We could see children play***ing** *outside.*	T + obj + v-*ing* (esp. referring to an incomplete activity)		●	●
*His parents saw him award***ed** the prize.	T + obj + v-*ed*			●

* Notice that when 'see' is used in this way in passive sentences, 'to' is required: *Someone saw Mr Kerry enter the building alone. / Mr Kerry was seen* **to** *enter the building alone.* The pattern with 'watch' is not used in the passive.

These verbs are also used in other meanings – see the dictionary.

eye·glas·ses /£ˈaɪˌglɑː·sɪz, $-ˌglæs·ɪz/ *pl n Am* glasses or SPECTACLES

eye·hole /£ˈaɪ·həʊl, $-hoʊl/ *n* [C] *Am for* **peephole**, see at PEEP [LOOK]

eye·lash /ˈaɪ·læʃ/ *n* [C] any of the short hairs which grow along the edges of the eye • *long eyelashes* • *false eyelashes*

eye·let /ˈaɪ·lət/ *n* [C] a small hole in material, the edge of which is protected by a ring of metal, through which a piece of string, a LACE, etc. is put to fasten something • *a 3-eyelet shoe* • An eyelet is also a small hole edged with thread as part of a design used to decorate material: *an eyelet bedspread*

eye·lid /ˈaɪ·lɪd/ *n* [C] either of the two pieces of skin which can close over each eye

eye·lin·er /£ˈaɪˌlaɪ·nəʳ, $-nɚ/ *n* a coloured substance, usually contained in a pencil, which is put in a line just above or below the eyes in order to make them look more attractive • *The application of (a) traditional liquid eyeliner with a fine brush demands the steadiest of hands.* [C/U] • [PIC] **Cosmetics**

eye·piece /ˈaɪ·piːs/ *n* [C] the part of a piece of equipment, for example a MICROSCOPE, through which you look

eye·sight /ˈaɪ·saɪt/ *n* [U] the ability to see • *good/bad/poor eyesight* • *You need to have your eyesight tested.* • *Many of those aged 75 or over will have failing eyesight.*

eye·sore /£ˈaɪ·sɔːʳ, $-sɔːr/ *n* [C] an unpleasant or ugly sight in a public place • *They think the new library building is an eyesore.*

eye·strain /ˈaɪ·streɪn/ *n* [U] tired or painful eyes as a result of too much reading, looking at a computer screen, etc.

Eye·tie /ˈaɪ·taɪ/ *n* [C] *slang* (an offensive word for) an Italian

eye·tooth /ˈaɪ·tuːθ, ˌ-ˈ-/ *n* [C] *pl* **eyeteeth** /ˈaɪ·tiːθ, ˌ-ˈ-/ either of the two pointed teeth which are found one on each side at the top of the mouth; a CANINE (TOOTH) • *(infml) He said he'd* **give** *his* **eyeteeth for** *a ticket to Saturday's match* (=he wanted one very much).

eye·wash [LIQUID] /£ˈaɪ·wɒʃ, $-wɑːʃ/ *n* a liquid used to clean the eyes • *The doctor prescribed an eyewash to clear up my eye infection.* [C] • *Do you have some eyewash? I think I have some grit in my eye.* [U]

eye·wash [NONSENSE] /£ˈaɪ·wɒʃ, $-wɑːʃ/ *n* [U] *infml* nonsense or something which is not true • *He gave me*

a lot/load of *eyewash about how he needed my support, but it was just to keep me from leaving.*

eye·wit·ness /ˈaɪˌwɪt·nəs, ˌ-ˈ--/ *n* [C] a person who saw something happen, for example a crime or an accident • *According to an eyewitness* **account**, *the thieves abandoned their vehicle near the scene of the robbery and then ran off.* • *Does an eyewitness have a moral obligation to society to come forward?*

ey·ing *Am also* /ˈaɪ·ɪŋ/ *pres part of* EYE

ey·rie /£ˈɪə·ri, $ˈɪr·i/, *esp. Am* **aer·ie** *n* [C] the nest of an EAGLE or other large bird which eats meat, usually built in a high, distant place • *These cliffs are full of cavities, ledges and crevices that make perfect eyries.* • *(fig.) I interviewed the chairman of the company in his seventh-floor eyrie* (= office/room).

F f

F [LETTER] (*pl* **F's** or **Fs**), **f** (*pl* **f's** or **fs**) /ef/ *n* [C] the 6th letter of the English alphabet • People use **f-word** to avoid saying FUCK . *Entertainment Research reports that there are 245 mentions of* **the** *f-word in this movie.*

F [MUSIC] /ef/ *n* a note in Western music • *The song is in* **(the key of)** *F.* [U] • *Play an F followed by a G.* [C]

F [TEMPERATURE] *n* [after n] *abbreviation for* FAHRENHEIT • *Yesterday the temperature was 90°F.* • (LP) **Units**

FA /ˌefˈeɪ/ *n* [U] **the FA** *abbreviation for* Football Association (= the national organization for football in England) • The **FA Cup** is a competition for teams that belong to the Football Association, or the silver cup which is given as a prize in this competition: *Manchester United are hoping to win the FA Cup this year.* ○ *It's the FA Cup* **final** *next week.* ○ *Liverpool will play Nottingham Forest, last season's FA Cup* **finalists.**

fab *esp. humorous* /fæb/ *adj* [not gradable] *infml for* FABULOUS • *You look really fab in those flares!*

fa·ble /ˈfeɪ·bl̩/ *n* a short story which tells a general truth or is only partly based on fact, or literature of this type • *In the fable of the race between the tortoise and the hare, the tortoise wins, even though he is slow, because he keeps going with determination.* [C] • *Even adults have a taste for fable, fantasy and magic.* [U]

fa·bled /ˈfeɪ·bl̩d/ *adj* [before n; not gradable] *approving* • If something or someone is fabled, they have been made very famous, esp. by having many stories written about them: *the fabled film director Cecil B. De Mille* ○ *the fabled gold of the Incas*

fab·ric [CLOTH] /ˈfæb·rɪk/ *n* (a type of) cloth or woven material • *dress fabric* [U] • *seats upholstered in hard-wearing fabric* [U] • *cotton/woollen fabrics* [C] • *high-quality/fine fabrics* [C] • (LP) **Shopping goods** (CS)(D)(RUS)(S)

fab·ric [STRUCTURE] /ˈfæb·rɪk/ *n* [U] **the fabric** the structure or parts esp. of a social unit or a building • *the fabric* **of** *society* • *There has been a systematic dismantling of the fabric of civilized life by the regime.* • *We must invest in the fabric of our hospitals and start rebuilding them.* • *Unhappiness was woven into the natural fabric of people's lives.* • (CS) (D) (RUS) (S)

fab·ri·cate *obj* /ˈfæb·rɪ·keɪt/ *v* [T] to invent or produce (something false) in order to deceive • *He was late, so he fabricated an excuse to avoid trouble.* • *Sometimes patients fabricate illnesses in order to be admitted to hospital.* • *When Ian asked Amy out she fabricated a boyfriend rather than say 'no' directly.* • *Jackson was accused of fabricating banknotes.* • (NL)

fab·ri·ca·tion /ˌfæb·rɪˈkeɪ·ʃən/ *n* • *The evidence he gave in court was* **complete** *fabrication.* [U] • *The report submitted by the police officer was a clear fabrication.* [C] • *Immigration officers at the airport saw immediately that the passport was a fabrication.* [C] • (D) (DK)

fab·u·lous [GOOD] /ˈfæb·jʊ·ləs/ *adj* very good; excellent • *They tempt potential customers with 'fabulous prizes'.* • *She looked* **absolutely** *fabulous in her cycling clothes.* • *There was an exhibition of the fabulous jewelled eggs made by Fabergé.* • *We had a fabulous time at the party.*

fab·u·lous·ly /ˈfæb·jʊ·lə·sli/ *adv* • *fabulously* (= extremely) *rich/wealthy*

fab·u·lous [NOT REAL] /ˈfæb·jʊ·ləs/ *adj* [not gradable] imaginary, not existing in real life • *The unicorn is a fabulous* **creature/beast**. • *The line between the real and the fabulous is very blurred in the film world.*

fa·çade, fa·cade /fəˈsɑːd/ *n* [C] the front of a building, esp. a large or attractive building • *The building has nine large arches along the length of its façade.* • *(fig.) Behind his amiable façade* (= false appearance) *is insincerity and indecision.*

face [HEAD] /feɪs/ *n* [C] the front of the head • *She had a smile/a puzzled expression* **on** *her face.* • A **happy/sad/smiling/fierce** face is a face with an expression of that type: *I was greeted by smiling faces.* • *She's got a face like the back end of a bus* (= She's very ugly). • *His face was* **like thunder**/*He had a face* **like thunder** (= He looked very angry). • If someone's face **drops/falls**, their expression shows their disappointment: *Her face fell when she opened the letter.* • If you speak to someone **face-to-face** or **come face-to-face with** someone or something, you speak to them, or experience something personally: *I'd like to talk to you face-to-face instead of on the phone.* ○ *I came face-to-face with pain for the first time.* • If you do something **to** someone's **face**, you do it obviously without worrying what they will think: *I don't like the plans but I'd find it hard to tell him to his face.* • *She left home* **in the face of** (= despite) *strong opposition from her parents.* • *(Br infml)* If your **face fits** you seem to be suitable for a particular job or activity. • *(Am)* To be **in** someone's **face** is to speak to them in a very critical way: *One of the managers is always in my face.* • **Get out of my face** (= stop annoying me) • *(slang)* **In-your-face** means rudely confident and willing to argue. • **Face cream** is cream which you can rub onto your face to make it smoother. • A **face pack** is a cream-like substance which is left on the face to dry and is then removed, in order to clean and tighten the skin. • **Face powder** is skin-coloured powder used on the face to make it look less shiny and more attractive. • *"Was this the face that launch'd a thousand ships?"* (from the play *Doctor Faustus* by Christopher Marlowe, 1604) • *"I never forget a face, but in your case I'll be glad to make an exception"* (believed to have been said by Groucho Marx, 1895-1977)

-faced /feɪsd/ *combining form* • *round-faced* (= having a round face) • *sad-faced* (= having a sad face) • *red-faced* (= embarrassed) • *purple-faced* (= angry) • *po-faced* (= showing no emotion) • *She was talking to a mean-looking thin-faced man with short blond hair.*

fa·cial /ˈfeɪ·ʃəl/ *adj* [not gradable] • *facial expression* • *facial injuries* • *facial hair* • *Their new products include facial cleansers and moisturizers for sensitive skin.* • *The human infant is strongly attracted to facial as well as vocal movements. My cousin bears a strong facial* **resemblance** *to my father* (= he looks like my father in the features of his face).

fa·cial /ˈfeɪ·ʃəl/ *n* [C] • A facial is a beauty treatment which cleans and improves the skin of the face with creams, gentle rubbing, etc. *Beauty treatments range from an eyelash tint at £8 to a deep cleansing facial costing £58.* • *A basic facial is extremely effective for brightening the complexion and skin tone.*

face·less /ˈfeɪ·sləs/ *adj* [not gradable] • *(disapproving)* Faceless means lacking any clear characteristics and therefore uninteresting: *faceless bureaucrats* ○ *The town's shopping centre consists of rows of faceless high street chain stores.*

face [FRONT] /feɪs/ *n* [C] the front or surface (of an object) • *the north face* **of** *a mountain* • *the west face* **of** *the building* • The face **of** a clock or a watch is the front of it which has the numbers or marks on it which show what time it is: *The face of my watch has Roman numerals on it.* • The face **of** something is also what you can see of it or what shows: *Poor quality is the unacceptable face of increased productivity.* • *The whole tribe seem to have* **disappeared off/been wiped off the face of the earth** (= disappeared completely or been completely got rid of). • **On the face of it** (= It seems that) *the plot is very simple* (= but in fact it is quite difficult). • A **face value** is the value or price which is shown on, for example, a stamp, a coin or a bank note: *The note has a face value of £20, but part of the design is missing so it is worth much more to a collector.* • If you **take** something **at face value** you accept it for what it appears to be rather than studying it more closely: *I took the offer at face value. I didn't think they might be trying to trick me.*

FRENCH FALSE FRIENDS

accommodate *v*	accommoder	to prepare a meal; to arrange, put right; to reconcile (enemies); to give harsh treatment to; to focus
actual *adj*	actuel	present, current, topical
actually *adv*	actuellement	at present, currently, nowadays
advertise *v*	avertir	to warn, notify, advise, inform
agenda *n*	agenda	diary
appreciate *v*	apprécier	to evaluate, estimate, appraise
blouse *n*	blouse	overall; smock; medical white coat; pocket on snooker, billiard table
bouquet *n*	bouquet	clump; crowning piece; prawn
boutique *n*	boutique	small shop
brassiere *n*	brassière	baby's vest; life jacket
cabinet *n*	cabinet	toilet; surgery, consulting room; study
car *n*	car	coach; bus; van
cargo *n*	cargo	cargo boat, freighter
caution *n*	caution	guarantee; bail; backing, support
cave *n*	cave	cellar; nightclub; basement
cellar *n*	cellier	storeroom
challenge *n*	challenge	contest, tournament (for trophy)
chauffeur *n*	chauffeur	driver; fireman; stoker
chef *n*	chef	chief; leader; boss
chimney *n*	cheminée	open fireplace, hearth
chips *n*	chips	potato crisps
circulation *n*	circulation	traffic
college *n*	collège	state secondary school
commodity *n*	commodité	convenience, conveniences, WC
commune *n*	commune	municipality, parish
compere *n*	compère	accomplice; old crony, comrade
complete *adj*	complet, complète	full up, full, no vacancies
comprehensive *adj*	comprehensif/ve	understanding
conductor *n*	conducteur	driver; leader; guide
confection *n*	confection	making-up, the clothing industry
conference *n*	conférence	lecture
confused *adj*	confus	ashamed; embarrassed
confusion *n*	confusion	embarrassment
creche *n*	crèche	Christmas crib
decade *n*	décade	period of ten days
deceive *v*	décevoir	to disappoint
deception *n*	déception	disappointment; disenchantment
demand *n*	demande	request; application; question
demand *v*	demander	to request, apply for; to need
deviation *n*	déviation	diversion (on road), detour
disgraceful *adj*	disgracieux	inelegant; unsightly
dispute *n*	dispute	academic debate, polemic
distract *v*	distraire	to entertain; to misappropriate funds
distracting *adj*	distrayant	entertaining, diverting
distraction *n*	distraction	absentmindedness; misappropriation of funds
drama *n*	drame	tragedy
dramatic *adj*	dramatique	having an unhappy ending, tragic
edit *v*	éditer	to publish
edition *n*	édition	publishing; record-making; editing
editor *n*	éditeur	publisher
eventually *adv*	éventuellement	possibly
exposition *n*	exposition	aspect, orientation (of house)
extra *adj*	extra	first-rate, special, terrific
fete *n*	fête	holiday; feast day celebration
figure *n*	figure	face, countenance
flipper *n*	flipper	pinball machine
formally *adv*	formellement	positively, definitely
formidable *adj*	formidable	super, terrific, incredible
genial *adj*	génial	inspired, fantastic, brilliant
genie *n*	génie	genius; (military) engineers
genteel *adj*	gentil	kind, good; pleasant; Gentile
gentle *adj*	gentil	kind; good; pleasant; Gentile
gratuity *n*	gratuité	gratuitousness, wantonness
herb *n*	herbe	grass
ignore *v*	ignorer	to not know, be unaware of
impotent *adj*	impotent	disabled, crippled
incomprehensible *adj*	incompréhensif	lacking in understanding, unsympathetic
information *n*	informations	news; item of news
inhabitable *adj*	inhabitable	uninhabitable
inhabited *adj*	inhabité	uninhabited
island *n*	Islande	Iceland
issue *n*	issue	exit; outcome, result
jolly *adj*	joli	pretty; large; (ironic) nasty
journal *n*	journal	newspaper; magazine

(F)

journey *n*	journée	day
lard *n*	lard	bacon
large *adj*	large	wide, broad; extensive; generous
lecture *n*	lecture	reading; reading matter
librarian *n*	libraire	book-seller
library *n*	librairie	bookshop; book-selling; book-trade
liquid *n*	liquide	cash, ready money
location *n*	location	renting, hiring; lease; reservation
lunatic *adj*	lunatique	quirky; whimsical; temperamental
manifest *v*	manifester	(politics) to demonstrate
massive *adj*	massif/ve	solid, robust
money *n*	monnaie	currency; coin; loose change
nervous *adj*	nerveux/euse	energetic; sinewy; irritable
offer *v*	offrir	to give (a present)
pass an exam *v*	passer un examen	to take/sit an exam
perfume *n*	parfum	flavour; aroma
personage *n*	personnage	character (in fiction etc.)
petrol *n*	pétrole	oil
photograph *n*	photographe	photographer; camera dealer
phrase *n*	phrase	sentence
piece *n*	pièce	paper; document; (sewing) patch; room; (theatre) play; coin
pocketbook *n*	livre de poche	paperback
pork *n*	porc	pig; pigskin
preservative *n*	préservatif	condom, contraceptive
press *v*	presser	to squeeze; to hurry; to be urgent
professor *n*	professeur	teacher; master
propriety *n*	propriété	ownership; property; land; estate
prune *n*	prune	plum (fruit & colour)
public schools *n*	écoles publiques	state schools
radio *n*	radio	x-ray (photograph)
raisin *n*	raisin	grape
rape *n*	rape	grater; rasp; grinder
raped *adj*	rapé	threadbare; grated
realisation *n*	réalisation	achievement; (film) production
regime *n*	régime	diet; speed (of motor); (grammar) object; (fruit) cluster, bunch
relation *n*	relation	relationship; acquaintance; report
relax *v*	relaxer	to acquit, discharge, release
repertoire *n*	répertoire	index notebook; (alphabetical) list; catalogue
resume *v*	résumer	to summarise; to epitomise
route *n*	route	road
salad *n*	salade	lettuce, endive; tangle; muddle; (fig., pl.) stories, tall tales
sauce *n*	sauce	salad dressing; gravy; (infml) padding
savage *adj*	sauvage	wild; unauthorized; unfair
scotch *n*	scotch	Sellotape
seance *n*	séance	meeting; session; performance
sensible *adj*	sensible	sensitive
slip *n*	slip	briefs, underpants (men's); trunks; (naut.) slipway
smoking *n*	smoking	dinner jacket, tuxedo
solid *adj*	solide	sound, robust, healthy (of a person)
souvenir *n*	souvenir	memory, recollection
spectacle *n*	spectacle	(theatre, etc.) show; show business, entertainment
spot *n*	spot	spotlight; commercial; advertisement
standing *adj*	standing	luxury, de luxe, high quality (of buildings)
starter *n*	starter	choke (in car)
sympathetic *adj*	sympathique	likeable, pleasant; attractive
sympathise *v*	sympathiser	to get on well, hit it off
sympathy *n*	sympathie	liking; fellow feeling
temple *n*	temple	(Protestant) church
terrible *adj*	terrible	terrific, fantastic, great
traffic *n*	trafic	(fig., pl., infml) dealings, funny business, goings-on
transpire *v*	transpirer	to sweat; (infml) to work hard
travel *v*	travailler	to work, practise, train
trespass *v*	trépasser	(literary) to pass away, die
valid *adj*	valide	fit; able-bodied
valour *n*	valeur	value; price; security; bill; merit
vest *n*	veste	jacket
voluntary *adj*	volontaire	headstrong, determined
waters *n*	waters	lavatory, WC

face *obj* /feɪs/ *v* [T always + prep] • If you face a building you put an extra layer in front of what is already there: *The house was built of wood but faced* **in/with** *brick.*

fac·ing /ˈfeɪ·sɪŋ/ *n* • A facing is an outer layer covering a wall, etc.: *The wall was built of rubble with a facing of stone.* [C] • Facing is an extra layer of material sewn to the inside edge of a piece of clothing to strengthen it, or to the outside, esp. of collars and the ends of sleeves for decoration: *A blue jacket with white facing(s)* [C/U]

face *(obj)* DEAL WITH /feɪs/ *v* to (cause or force to) recognize, think about, accept or deal with (a problem or difficulty) • *The dilemma facing ambulance and emergency personnel is poor communication.* [T] • *They face/are faced* **with** *financial penalties.* [T] • *We were faced by a flooded cellar.* [T] • *The main question that faces us at present is how to avoid job losses.* [T] • *We'll have to face her* **with** (= give her) *this new information and see what she has to say.* [T] • *I can't face climbing those stairs again.* [+ v-*ing*] • *We'll have to face* **(the) facts** *and start cutting costs.* [T] • *I've faced* **up to** *the knowledge that I'll never be a great writer.* [I] • *(infml) He'll have to* **face the music** (= he'll be in trouble) *when his parents find out he's been missing school.*

face *(obj)* TURN TOWARDS /feɪs/ *v* to turn or be turned towards (something) physically, to be opposite • *Their houses face each other across the street.* [T] • *The terrace faces towards the sea/faces south.* [I always + adv/prep]

-fac·ing /ˈfeɪ·sɪŋ/ *combining form* • *Most avalanche accidents occur on north- and east-facing slopes.*

face RESPECT /feɪs/ *n* [U] the respect and honour of others • *He thinks he would* **lose** *face if he admitted the mistake.* • *She tried to* **save** *face by inventing a story about being overseas at the time.* • A **face-saving** exercise/gesture/compromise/concession/solution is one which allows someone who disagrees with it, or who will suffer as a result of it, to appear happy about it in public: *They gave him the title of company president as a face-saving gesture, although he no longer had any power.* ○ *They agreed that there should be no attempts at face-saving.*

face·cloth *Br* /£ˈfeɪs·klɒθ, $-klɑːθ/, *Br* **flan·nel**, *Am* **wash·cloth**, *Aus* **face wash·er** *n* [C] a small cotton cloth used to wash the body, esp. the face and hands

face·lift /ˈfeɪs·lɪft/ *n* [C] a medical treatment which tightens loose skin to make the face look younger • *The hospital charges £4000 for a full facelift.* • *(fig.) The bank is planning to give its 1930s building a complete facelift* (= improve it/make it more attractive).

fac·et /ˈfæs·ɪt, -et/ *n* [C] one of the sides, parts, or opinions (of something) • *One facet* **of** *his role in the film is that of stern father.* • *The facets of a precious stone are the small flat surfaces cut on to it.*

-fac·et·ed /£ˈfæs·ɪ·tɪd, $-t̬ɪd/ *combining form* • *His personality is many-faceted/multi-faceted.*

fa·ce·tious /fəˈsiː·ʃəs/ *adj* unsuitably humorous and jokey • *We grew tired of his frequent facetious* **remarks**.

fa·ce·tious·ly /fəˈsiː·ʃə·sli/ *adv*

fa·ce·tious·ness /fəˈsiː·ʃə·snəs/ *n* [U]

fa·cile /ˈfæs·aɪl/ *adj* easy or too easy, not needing effort • *It would be easy, but facile, to dismiss this as a problem which industry should be left to solve.* • *It is facile of reviewers to point out every misprint in a book.* • *We must avoid facile recriminations about who was to blame.* • *In both speech and writing, his use of language is fluid and facile.*

fac·il·i·tate *obj* /fəˈsɪl·ɪ·teɪt/ *v* [T] *fml* to make possible or easier • *The new ramp will facilitate the entry of wheelchairs.* • *The company offered to facilitate an international conference in the following year.* • *The current structure does not facilitate efficient work flow.*

fac·il·i·tat·or /£fəˈsɪl·ɪ·teɪ·tər, $-t̬ɚ/ *n* [C] • *I see my role as that of a facilitator, enabling other people to work in the way that suits them best.*

fac·il·i·ty ABILITY /£fəˈsɪl·ɪ·ti, $-ə·t̬i/ *n* [C] an ability, feature or quality • *His facility* **for** *memorizing dates was astonishing.* [U] • *This phone has a memory facility.* [C]

fac·il·i·ty BUILDING /£fəˈsɪl·ɪ·ti, $-ə·t̬i/ *n* [C] a place, esp. including buildings, where a particular activity happens • *a nuclear research facility* • *a military facility* • *a new sports facility* • *The hospital spokesperson said a temporary ten-bed facility would open this month.* • *What kind of deterrent is prison if it is to be run as an upmarket holiday facility?*

fac·il·i·ties /£fəˈsɪl·ɪ·tiz, $-ə·t̬iz/ *pl n* • Facilities are the buildings, equipment and services provided for a particular purpose: *shopping facilities* ○ *catering facilities* ○ *medical facilities* ○ *sports facilities*

-fac·ing /-ˌfeɪ·sɪŋ/ *combining form* See at FACE TURN TOWARDS

fac·si·mi·le /fækˈsɪm·ɪ·li/ *n* [C] an exact copy, esp. of a document • *It is a facsimile* **of** *the original manuscript.* • *It is on display* **in a** *facsimile version/***in** *facsimile.* • A facsimile of a document sent over the telephone system is called a FAX.

fact /fækt/ *n* something which is known to have happened or to exist, esp. something for which proof exists, or about which there is information • *I'm not interested in hopes and plans, I just want you to tell me the* **(plain/bare)** *facts.* [C] • *Can I regard what you have just told me as fact?* [U] • *The play was closely based on fact.* [U] • **The** *fact* **(of the matter) is that** *they are the stronger team and are sure to win.* [U + *that* clause] • **As a matter of fact**, **In (actual) fact** and **In point of fact** are used to add emphasis to what you are saying, or to show that it is the opposite of or different from what went before: *No I don't work. In fact, I've never had a job.* ○ *Have you always lived here? As a matter of fact* (= The truth is) *I've only lived here for the last three years.* • **A fact of life** is something unpleasant which cannot be avoided: *Going bald is a fact of life.* • The **facts of life** are the details about sex and reproduction. • A **fact-finding mission/visit/study** is one which is planned in order to discover information. • *We are getting some* **facts and figures** (= exact, detailed information) *together and we will then have a full board meeting, and hopefully make a decision.* • *(saying)* 'Fact is stranger than fiction' means that real things are sometimes stranger than imaginary things.

fac·tu·al /ˈfæk·tjuəl/ *adj* • *She gave a clear, factual account of the attack* (= based only on what happened, without expressing personal feelings).

fac·tu·al·ly /ˈfæk·tjuə·li/ *adv* • *factually accurate*

fac·tion /ˈfæk·ʃən/ *n* [C] *esp. disapproving* a group within a larger group, esp. one with slightly different ideas from the main group • *The party split on that issue and is now in danger of breaking into two or more factions.*

fac·tion·al /ˈfæk·ʃən·əl/ *adj* • *factional leaders*

fac·tion·al·i·sm /ˈfæk·ʃən·əl·ɪ·zəm/ *n* [U] • *Factionalism was tearing the party and the country apart.*

fac·ti·tious /fækˈtɪʃ·əs/ *adj fml* false or artificial • *He has invented a wholly factitious story about his past.* • *An expensive advertising campaign has led to a factitious* **demand** *for bottled water.*

fac·tor FACT /£ˈfæk·tər, $-t̬ɚ/ *n* [C] a fact or situation which influences the result of something • *People's voting habits are influenced by political, social and economic factors.* • *Heavy snow was a* **contributing** *factor* **in** *the accident.* • *Price will be a* **crucial** *factor* **in** *the success of this new product.* • *The patients' confidence in the treatment was a* **major** *factor* **in** *contributing to the treatment's success.* • *The economy is regarded as the* **decisive/key** *factor which will determine the outcome of the general election.* • *(infml) The film's success is partly due to its happy ending and its* **feel-good** *factor* (= its ability to make people feel happy). • *The weather is the one* **unknown** *factor which could ruin the whole plan.*

fac·tor NUMBER /£ˈfæk·tər, $-t̬ɚ/ *n* [C] *specialized* (in mathematics) any whole number which is produced when you divide a larger number by another whole number • *Two, three, four and six are all factors of twelve.* • If an amount becomes larger or smaller **by a factor of** a particular number, it becomes that number of times larger or smaller: *Cases of leukemia in the area near the nuclear reactor have risen by a factor of four.* • The word factor can also show a particular level on some systems of measurement: *A factor 4 suntan cream means that you can stay in the sun four times longer than if you did not have any cream on.* ○ *I have a very sensitive skin and so I use a factor 15 suntan oil.*

fac·tor·ize *obj*, *Br and Aus usually* **-ise** /£ˈfæk·tər·aɪz, $-t̬ə·raɪz/ *v* [T] • If you factorize a number, you divide it into factors: *You can factorize twelve* **as** *12 x 1, 6 x 2, or 3 x 4, but you can only factorize seven as 7 x 1.*

fac·tory /£ˈfæk·tər·i, $-t̬ɚ·i/ *n* [C] a building or set of buildings where large amounts of goods are made using machines • *a car/munitions/shoe/textile factory* • *a factory worker/manager/inspector* • *She works* **in/at** *a factory.* • *(Br and Aus)* **Factory farming** is a system of farming in which a lot of animals are kept in a small enclosed area, in order to produce a large amount of meat, eggs or milk as cheaply as possible: *They have launched a campaign* *against factory farming.* ○ *She says that free-range chickens taste much better than* **factory-farmed** *ones.* • The **factory floor** is the area where the ordinary workers in a factory work: *The company has been criticized for the lack of safety measures on the factory floor.* ○ *(fig.) That sort of decision should be taken* **on** *the factory floor* (=by the ordinary workers). • *(Br specialized)* **Factory gate** prices are the prices which a factory sells its goods for: *Factory gate prices have risen by 5% over the past year.* • A **factory ship** is a large ship which has equipment for preserving the fish caught by other smaller ships, usually by freezing them.

fac·to·tum /£fæk'təʊ·təm, $-'toʊ·t̬əm/ *n* [C] *fml or humorous* a person employed to do all types of jobs for someone • *He was a factotum* **for** *the Director, rather than just a secretary.* • *She was a* **general** *factotum at the restaurant – washing dishes, cleaning the floors and polishing the furniture.*

fact·sheet /'fækt·ʃiːt/ *n* [C] a written document containing information for the public • *If you would like a copy of the factsheet which accompanies this programme, please write to us.* • *A free factsheet* **on** *children's healthcare is available at your doctor's.*

fac·ul·ty [COLLEGE] /£'fæk·əl·ti, $-t̬i/ *n* [C] a group of departments in a college which specialize in a particular subject or group of subjects, or *(Am)* the people who teach in a department in a college • *the Arts/Science/Law Faculty* • *the Faculty of Arts/Science/Law* • *The Department of Chemistry is part of the Faculty of Science.* • *(Am) The faculty* (=people who teach in the faculty) *is meeting tomorrow at 10am.*

fac·ul·ty [ABILITY] /£'fæk·əl·ti, $-t̬i/ *n* [C] any of our natural abilities • *Computers may one day be able to compensate for some of the missing faculties of disabled people.* • *Even at the age of 100, she still* **had** *all her faculties.* • *Is he* **in command/possession of** *all his* **(mental)** *faculties* (= Can he still hear, speak, see and think clearly)*?* • A faculty is also a special ability to do a particular thing: *She has a faculty* **for** *inspiring confidence in people.* ○ *A school's job is to* **sharpen** *pupils'* **critical** *faculties* (=to teach them to think carefully about things using their judgment).

fad /fæd/ *n* [C] *infml esp. disapproving* a style, activity or interest which is very popular for a short period of time • *A mobile fax machine is the latest fad among young executives.* • *Wholefood, such as brown rice, was the food fad of the 70s.* • *There was a fad* **for** *wearing ripped jeans a few years ago.* • *Do you know what the latest fad* **in** *cosmetic surgery is?*

fad·di·sm /'fæd·ɪ·zəm/ *n* [U] *infml esp. disapproving* • Faddism is a tendency to like a style, activity or interest for a very short period of time: *Some people confuse food faddism with healthy eating and base their diets on the latest fashionable ingredients.*

fad·dist /'fæd·ɪst/ *n* [C] *infml esp. disapproving* • *She's a health-food faddist.*

fad·dy /'fæd·i/, **fad·dish** /'fæd·ɪʃ/ *adj infml esp. disapproving* having a tendency to like or dislike particular things, esp. food, for no good reason • *I was a really faddy eater when I was young.* • *Stop being so faddy* **about** *what you eat!*

fad·di·ly /'fæd·ɪ·li/, **fad·dish·ly** /'fæd·ɪʃ·li/ *adv infml esp. disapproving* • *He has a very poor diet because he eats so faddily.*

fad·di·ness /'fæd·ɪ·nəs/, **fad·dish·ness** /'fæd·ɪʃ·nəs/ *n* [U] *infml esp. disapproving* • *I'm sick and tired of your faddiness!*

fade *(obj)* /feɪd/ *v* to (cause to) lose colour, brightness or strength gradually • *You'll fade that tablecloth if you wash it in hot water.* [T] • *If you hang your clothes out in the bright sun, they will fade.* [I] • *He had a lovely suntan when he got back from his holiday, but it soon faded.* [I] • *They arrived home just as the light was fading* (= as it was going dark). [I] • *After his girlfriend left him, Bill faded* **from the picture/scene** (=stopped being part of the group of friends). [I] • *The horse riders gradually faded* **from view/sight** (=disappeared in the distance). [I] • If something fades **into** something else, you cannot see the border between them: *Day slowly faded into night.* [I] • If something fades **away/out**, it becomes less clear and then disappears: *The voice on the radio faded out.* [I] ○ *The children's memories of their father slowly faded away.* [I] ○ *Hopes of saving the trapped miners are fading away fast.* [I] • *(literary)* If a person is **fading (away)/fading fast**, they are growing weaker and will probably die soon. • *(specialized)* If the picture or sound of a film or recording **fades in**, or someone **fades** it **in**, it becomes gradually stronger. • *(specialized)* If the picture or sound of a film or recording **fades out** or someone **fades** it **out**, it becomes gradually weaker. • *(saying)* 'Old soldiers never die, they only fade away' means that the qualities soldiers have stay with them forever.

fad·ed /'feɪ·dɪd/ *adj* • *faded curtains/wallpaper* • *He was wearing a pair of faded* **jeans** *and an old T-shirt.* • A faded **beauty** is a woman who was beautiful in the past.

fae·ces, *esp. Am* **fe·ces** /'fiː·siːz/ *pl n fml or specialized* the solid waste excreted from the body of a human or animal through the bowels • *Cholera is spread by the contamination of food and water by faeces.* • *Sheep have been introduced onto the land to add nutrients to the soil in the form of their urine and faeces.*

fae·cal, *esp. Am* **fe·cal** /'fiː·kəl/ *adj* [not gradable] *fml or specialized* • *faecal matter* • *The virus is spread by faecal contamination.* • *During the experiment, food intake and faecal output were measured.*

faff a·bout/a·round /fæf/ *v adv* [I] *Br infml disapproving* to spend your time doing a lot of unimportant things instead of the thing that you should be doing • *I wish you'd stop faffing about and do something useful!*

fag [CIGARETTE] /fæg/ *n* [C] *Br and Aus slang* a cigarette • *She's gone out to get a packet of fags.* • *He smokes 40 fags a day.* • *She's gone outside for a quick fag.* • A fag **end** is the part of the cigarette left after you have smoked it: *He dropped his fag end in the gutter and walked off.* • The **fag end of** something is the last, and often worst, part of something: *We always used to go on holiday at the fag end of the holiday season.*

fag [TROUBLE] /fæg/ *n* [U] *esp. Br and Aus infml* something which is tiring and boring and which you do not want to do • *It's a real fag to have to make your bed every morning.* • *I can't be bothered to write this essay out a second time – it's too much of a fag.*

fagged /fægd/ *adj esp. Br and Aus infml* • If you are fagged **(out)**, you are tired and bored. • If you **can't be fagged** to do something, you are unwilling to make the effort that is needed to do it: *"Are you going to the pub tonight?" "No, I can't be fagged."* ○ *I can't be fagged* **to** *change for the party – I'll just go as I am.* [+ *to* infinitive]

fag [YOUNG BOY] /fæg/ *n* [C] *Br dated* (at some large British private schools) a younger boy who has to do jobs for an older boy

fag /fæg/ *v* [I] **-gg-** *Br dated* • If a younger boy fags **for** an older boy at a British private school, he does jobs for him: *I used to fag for him when I was at Harrow.*

fag·got [HOMOSEXUAL] /'fæg·ət/, *infml* **fag** /fæg/ *n* [C] *esp. Am slang* a homosexual man. This word is considered offensive when it is used by people who are not homosexual. • A **fag hag** is a woman who likes to spend time with homosexual men. • (CS) (D) (I) (RUS)

fag·got [WOOD], *Am also* **fag·ot** /'fæg·ət/ *n* [C usually pl] *dated* sticks of wood, tied together, which are used as fuel for a fire • *The children collected faggots for the fire while their parents set up tables and chairs in a secluded spot.* • *In the past, faggots were used to make the fires on which heretics, witches and homosexuals were burned.* • (CS) (D) (I) (RUS)

fag·got [FOOD] /'fæg·ət/ *n* [C usually pl] *Br* a ball of meat mixed with bread and herbs, which is fried or cooked in sauce • *faggots in gravy* • (CS) (D) (I) (RUS)

Fah·ren·heit /'fær·ən·haɪt/ (*abbreviation* **F**) *adj* [not gradable] of a measurement of temperature on a standard in which 32° is the temperature at which water freezes and 212° that at which it boils • *Shall I give you the temperature in Celsius or* **in** *Fahrenheit?* • *It was 80°F in the shade.* • *Data are recorded in* **degrees** *Fahrenheit.* • Compare CELSIUS. • [LP] **Units**

fail [NOT SUCCEED] /feɪl/ *v* [I] to not succeed in what you are trying to achieve or are expected to do • *I tried to persuade him to come, but I failed.* • *She moved to London in the hope of finding work as a model, but failed.* • *This method of growing tomatoes never fails.* • *He failed dismally/miserably* **in** *his attempt to break the record.* • *The two sides in the negotiations have failed* **to** *come to an agreement.* [+ *to* infinitive] • *She failed* **to** *reach the Wimbledon Final this year.* [+ *to* infinitive] • *The reluctance of either side to compromise means that the talks are* **doomed to** (=will certainly) *fail.* [+ *to* infinitive] • **If all else fails** (= If none of our plans succeed), *we can always spend the holidays at home.* • (D) (NL)

failed /feɪld/ *adj* [not gradable] • *He's a failed* (=unsuccessful) *writer.* • *After two failed marriages, he is* *planning to marry for a third time.* • *She has been given the task of sorting out the government's failed taxation policy.*

fail·ure /£ˈfeɪ·ljəʳ, $-ljɚ/ *n* • Failure is a lack of success in doing something: *The meeting was a* **complete/utter/total** *failure.* [C] ○ *I'm a bit of a failure* **at** *making* (= I cannot make) *cakes.* [C] ○ *I* **feel such a** *failure* (= so unsuccessful). [C] ○ *Their attempt to climb the Eiger* **ended in** *failure.* [U] ○ *The whole project was* **doomed to** *failure right from the start* (= It could never have succeeded). [U] • See also **failure** at FAIL [NOT DO], FAIL [STOP].

fail [NOT DO] /feɪl/ *v* [I] to not do something which you should do • *He promised to help, but he failed* **to** *arrive on time.* [+ *to* infinitive] • *Her parents failed* **to** *understand that there was a problem.* [+ *to* infinitive] • *The club had been promised a grant from the council, but the money failed* **to** (= did not) *materialize.* [+ *to* infinitive] • *He* **never** *failed* **to** *take* (= He always took) *a disapproving stance on people who got divorced.* [+ *to* infinitive] • *You couldn't fail* **to** *be* (= It is impossible that you would not be) *saddened by the distressing report on the famine victims.* [+ *to* infinitive] • *I'd be failing* **in** *my duty if I didn't tell you about the risks involved in the project.* • You say **I fail to see** when you do not understand what someone means: *I fail to see* **what** *you're getting at* (= what you mean). [+ *wh-* word] ○ *I fail to see* **what** *this has to do with the argument.* [+ *wh-* word] • *Be there by ten o'clock,* **without fail** (= You must be there)*!* • *Every morning,* **without fail** (= without exception), *she used to sit in the park and read her newspaper.* • (D) (NL)

fail·ure /£ˈfeɪ·ljəʳ, $-ljɚ/ *n* [U + *to* infinitive] • *His failure* **to** (= The fact that he did not) *return her phone call told her that something was wrong.* • *Failure* **to** *keep the chemical* (= Not keeping it) *at the right temperature could lead to an explosion.* • See also **failure** at FAIL [NOT SUCCEED], FAIL [STOP].

fail *obj* [NOT HELP] /feɪl/ *v* [T] to not help (someone) when they expected you to • *He failed her when she most needed him.* • *When I looked down and saw how far I had to jump, my* **courage** *failed me* (= I began to feel frightened). • (D) (NL)

fail *(obj)* [EXAMINATION] /feɪl/ *v* to be unsuccessful, or to judge that (someone) has been unsuccessful in (a test or examination) • *"Did you pass?" "No, I failed."* [I] • *I passed in history but failed* **in** *chemistry.* [I] • *A lot of people fail their driving test the first time.* [T] • *The examiners failed him because he hadn't answered enough questions.* [T] • (D) (NL)

fail /feɪl/ *n* [C] • A fail is an unsuccessful result in a course, test or examination: *John* **got** *three passes and four fails in his exams.*

fail [STOP] /feɪl/ *v* [I] to become weaker or stop working completely • *If my eyesight fails, I'll have to stop doing this job.* • *The brakes failed and the car crashed into a tree.* • *After talking non-stop for two hours, her voice failed.* • *The wheat failed* (= did not grow) *last year because of the lack of rain.* • *The old man was failing* **fast** (= He was dying). • If a business fails, it is unable to continue because of money problems: *They had a track record of success and they never imagined the business could fail.* • If something is **fail-safe**, it has been designed so that if one part of it does not work, the whole thing does not become dangerous: *a fail-safe device/mechanism/system* • (D) (NL)

fail·ing /ˈfeɪ·lɪŋ/ *adj* [not gradable] • *a failing business* • *She suffers from failing* **eyesight/hearing**. • *In the failing light, it was hard to read the signposts.* • See also FAILING [WEAKNESS], FAILING [WITHOUT].

fail·ure /£ˈfeɪ·ljəʳ, $-ljɚ/ *n* • *He died of* **heart/liver** *failure.* [U] • *The accident was caused by the failure of the reactor's cooling system.* [U] • *The number of* **business** *failures rose steeply last year.* [C] • *After three* **crop** *failures in a row, the people face starvation.* [C] • See also **failure** at FAIL [NOT SUCCEED], FAIL [NOT DO].

fail·ing [WEAKNESS] /ˈfeɪ·lɪŋ/ *n* [C] a fault or weakness • *My car's main failing is its heavy petrol consumption.* • *His one big failing is that he can't say he's sorry.* • *"Did you hear that I've started smoking again?" "Well, we all have our little failings."* • See also **failing** at FAIL [STOP].

fail·ing [WITHOUT] /ˈfeɪ·lɪŋ/ *prep* used to show what will happen if something is not possible or available • *Failing a serious change in attitudes, I do not see how the peace talks can possibly succeed.* • *Give her a book, or failing* **that**, *buy her something to wear.* • See also **failing** at FAIL [STOP].

faint [SLIGHT] /feɪnt/ *adj* **-er, -est** not strong or clear; slight • *a faint sound/noise/smell* • *My memories of my grandfather are very faint.* • *The lamp gave out a faint glow.* • *She gave me a faint smile of recognition when she saw me.* • *The government claims there are faint signs of recovery in the economy.* • *There's not the faintest* **hope** *of ever finding him.* • *You bear a faint* **resemblance** *to my sister.* • *I have a faint* **suspicion** *that you may be right!* • *(infml)* If you say **I haven't the faintest (idea)**, you mean that you do not know the answer to the question which someone has just asked you: *"Is she going to stay?" "I haven't the faintest idea."* • A **faint-hearted** person is not confident or brave and does not like to take unnecessary risks: *The terrorist threat in the region has kept faint-hearted tourists away.* ○ *The drive along the winding coast road is not for* **the** *faint-hearted* (= people who are not brave). • *(saying)* 'Faint heart never won fair lady' means that you must be brave if you want to achieve anything. • [LP> **Sound**]

faint·ly /ˈfeɪnt·li/ *adv* • *She seemed faintly* (= slightly) *embarrassed to see us there.* • *It was faintly* (= slightly) *amusing to see them together again.* • If something happens faintly, it happens with very little strength: *A light flickered faintly in the distance.* ○ *The room smelled faintly of disinfectant.* ○ *He could hear them talking faintly in the other room.*

faint·ness /ˈfeɪnt·nəs/ *n* [U] • Faintness is the quality of not being strong or clear: *The faintness of the handwriting made the manuscript difficult to read.*

faint [LOSE CONSCIOUSNESS] /feɪnt/ *v* [I] to lose consciousness unexpectedly for a short time • *He faints at the sight of blood.* • *I nearly fainted in the heat.* • *When they arrived at the camp, the refugees were almost fainting* **from** (= because of) *hunger.* • *She took one look at the hypodermic needle and fainted* **(dead) away** (= lost consciousness immediately). • If you have a **fainting fit**, you lose consciousness unexpectedly.

faint /feɪnt/ *adj* **-er, -est** • If you **feel** faint, you feel as though you are about to lose consciousness: *He felt faint, standing there for hours under the hot sun.* • If you are faint **from/with** something, you are very weak because of it: *He hadn't eaten for over twelve hours and was faint with hunger.* ○ *They were faint from lack of air.* • [LP> **Feelings and pains**]

faint /feɪnt/ *n* [U] • *On receiving the news, she* **fell into a (dead)** *faint* (= she lost consciousness completely).

faint·ness /ˈfeɪnt·nəs/ *n* [U] • Faintness is the feeling that you are about to lose consciousness: *Faintness and morning sickness can be signs that you are pregnant.*

fair [RIGHT] /£feəʳ, $fer/ *adj* **-er, -est** treating someone in a way that is right or reasonable, or treating a group of people equally and not allowing personal opinions to influence your judgment • *Do you think we live in a fair society?* • *Why should I have to do all the washing up? It's not fair!* • *It's not fair* **on** *Joe* (= It is not right) *to make him do all the work!* • *It's not fair* **that** *she's allowed to go and I'm not!* [+ *that* clause] • *It's not fair* **to** *blame me for everything!* [+ *to* infinitive] • *She tries to be* **scrupulously** *fair* **with** *all her employees* (= to treat them all equally). • *(Br) Complaints about the company's dealings have been sent to the Office of Fair* **Trading** (= the government department which protects people against unfair or illegal business). • *There is too much prejudice in his hometown for him to have a fair* **trial** *there.* • *She claims her article was a fair* **comment** *on* (= a reasonable thing to say about) *a matter of public interest.* • *He offered to do all the washing up if I did all the cooking, which seemed like a fair* (= reasonable) **deal**. • *That's a fair* (= reasonable) **question**. • If something, such as a price or share, is fair, it is reasonable and is what you expect or deserve: *She offered me a fair* **price** *for my record collection.* ○ *I'm willing to do my fair* (= equal) **share** *of the work.* ○ *Poor Fred's had more than his fair* **share** *of trouble* (= more than he expected or deserved) *this week.* ○ *All the workers want is a fair* **wage** *for the work that they do.* • If a game or competition is fair, it is done according to the rules: *It was a fair fight.* • **It is only fair** *to* (= It would be wrong not to) *tell you that we have had over 300 applications for this job.* • *I think* **it's fair to say** (= it is true to say) *that you've done less of the work than I have.* • *He's done the job badly but,* **to be fair** (= considering everything that has an effect on the situation), *I gave him very little time to do it.* • *They are determined to win,* **by fair means or foul** (= either honestly or dishonestly). • *(Br and Aus infml)* You say **it's a fair cop** when someone has caught you doing something wrong and you agree that you were wrong. • If a group of people are given a **fair crack of the whip** (*infml* **fair shake**), they are all given an equal chance: *It's only right that all the candidates should be given a fair crack of the* *whip.* • *(infml)* **Fair enough** means that you agree with what someone has suggested or think that what they have said is reasonable: *"This stereo's in perfect condition and is worth at least £75." "Fair enough, I'll give you £80 for it."* ○ *His criticisms were fair enough but it's too late to change things now.* • *(infml)* If you say **fair's fair/fair do's** to someone, you want them to behave reasonably or treat you the same as other people: *Come on, fair's fair, it's my turn now!* • If someone gets, or you give someone **a fair hearing**, they have the opportunity to explain something or give their opinions, without other people trying to influence the situation: *We'll make sure you get a fair hearing in court.* ○ *Rachel has some ideas about the project, so why don't we give her a fair hearing before we make a decision?* • If you beat someone **fair and square**, you beat them honestly and according to the rules. • *(Br and Aus) He hit me* **fair and square** *(Am* **squarely***)* (=directly) *on the nose.* • *(Aus infml)* **Fair dinkum** means honest(ly) or real(ly): *Are all their promises fair dinkum?* ○ *In rugby league the British beat us fair dinkum!* • If someone or something is **fair game**, it is considered reasonable to criticize them: *Many journalists consider the royal family fair game.* • *(Aus infml)* If you say **fair go** to someone, you want them to act in a reasonable way: *Fair go mate, let the others have a turn!* • If you are **fair-minded**, you treat everyone equally: *She is deeply prejudiced and makes no pretence about being fair-minded.* ○ *The judge acquitted the man, saying he believed any fair-minded person would have had their doubts about the man's guilt.* • In sport, **fair play** is when the players or teams play according to the rules and no one has an unfair advantage: *The referee's job in a football match is to see that there is fair play.* ○ *It is not considered fair play* **to** *distract your opponent during a game.* [+ *to* infinitive] ○ *(fig.) The committee's job is to ensure fair play between all the political parties and candidates during the election.* See also **play fair** at PLAY [ENJOY]. • *(saying)* 'All's fair in love and war' means that in love and war you do not have to obey the usual rules about reasonable behaviour.

fair·ly /£'feə·li, $'fer-/ *adv* • If you do something fairly, you do it in a way which is right and reasonable and treats people equally: *Share the cake out fairly – give everyone a slice.* ○ *Officials will ensure that the election is carried out fairly.* ○ *Councils are finding it hard to allocate the limited number of houses fairly as so many people are desperate for accommodation.* ○ *He claims that he was not* **treated** *fairly by his employers.* • *(Br and Aus) She lays the blame for the recession* **fairly and squarely** *(Am* **squarely***)* (=completely) *on the government.* • See also **fairly** at FAIR [QUITE LARGE].

fair·ness /£'feə·nəs, $'fer-/ *n* [U] • Fairness is the quality of treating people equally or in a way that is right or reasonable: *He had a real sense of fairness and hated injustice.* ○ *There is no fairness in paying female workers a third less than male workers.* ○ *The ban on media reporting during the election has made some people question the fairness of the election* (=ask whether it was fair). ○ *The judge asked the prosecution to disclose all their evidence,* **in** *fairness* **to** *the accused* (=so that the person accused of the crime could have a fair trial). • **In (all) fairness** (=It should be accepted that) *he has been a hard worker.* • **In fairness to** *Diana* (=It should be accepted that) *she has at least told you the truth.* • See also **fairness** at FAIR [BEAUTIFUL].

fair [PALE] /£feəʳ, $fer/ *adj* **-er, -est** (of skin) pale, or (of hair) pale yellow or golden • *She's got fair hair and blue eyes.* • *I've got a fair complexion, so I've got to be careful not to stay out in the sun.* • *My sister's dark and my brother's fair* (=He has fair hair). • *He's tall, thin and fair-***haired**. • *All my family are fair-***skinned**. • **Fair-haired boy** is *Am for* **blue-eyed boy**. See at BLUE [COLOUR].

fair [AVERAGE] /£feəʳ, $fer/ *adj* [after v; not gradable] neither very good nor very bad • *I've rated the films on a scale of poor, fair, good and excellent.* • *He's good at chemistry and fair* **at** *physics.* • **Fair to middling** means not very good but not bad: *"What's your French like?" "Oh, fair to middling."*

fair [QUITE LARGE] /£feəʳ, $fer/ *adj* [before n; not gradable] quite large • *We've had a fair* **amount** *of rain this week.* • *A fair* **number** *of people wrote in to complain about the programme.* • *They have a fair-***sized** *vegetable garden.* • *We've come a long way, but there's still a fair* **way** (=quite a long distance) *to go.*

fair·ly /£'feə·li, $'fer-/ *adv* [not gradable] • Fairly means quite: *The film was fairly good, but not brilliant.* ○ *I saw her fairly recently.* ○ *I'm fairly sure that this is the right address.* ○ *He's not a very good friend, but I know him fairly well.* ○ *We could see fairly easily what the problem was.* ○ *It's a fairly painless operation.* • *(literary)* Fairly can also mean almost when it is used to emphasize figurative expressions which describe what people or objects are doing: *The answer fairly jumps off the page at you!* ○ *The dog fairly flew out of the door to greet him.* • See also **fairly** at FAIR [RIGHT].

fair [PROBABLE] /£feəʳ, $fer/ *adj* [before n; not gradable] (of an idea, guess or chance) likely to be correct or to come into existence • *I think I've got a fair* **idea** *of* (=I understand reasonably well) *what you want.* • *She's got a fair* **chance** *of winning* (=There is a reasonable chance that she will win) *the title this year.*

fair [WEATHER] /£feəʳ, $fer/ *adj* **-er, -est** (of weather) pleasant and dry • *Fair weather was forecast for the following day.* • *(disapproving)* A **fair-weather friend** is someone who is a good friend when it is easy for them to be one and who stops when you are having problems.

fair [BEAUTIFUL] /£feəʳ, $fer/ *adj* **-er, -est** *old use* (of a woman) beautiful • *She was known to be as wise as she was fair.* • *(dated or humorous)* **The fair sex** is used to mean women in general. • *(esp. humorous) I made these shelves* **with** *my* **own fair hand** (=myself). • A **fair copy** of a piece of written work is the final, corrected copy: *Do you always* **make** *a fair copy of your essays?* • *"Mirror, mirror on the wall/ Who is the fairest of them all"* (The wicked stepmother in the fairy story *Snow White and the Seven Dwarfs*)

fair·ness /£'feə·nəs, $'fer-/ *n* [U] *old use* • *She had an exquisite fairness* (=beauty), *with features that were classically beautiful.* • See also **fairness** at FAIR [RIGHT].

fair [PUBLIC EVENT] /£feəʳ, $fer/ *n* [C] a large public event where goods are bought and sold, usually from tables which have been specially arranged for the event, and where there is often entertainment • *I bought a wooden box and a ceramic bowl at the local craft fair.* • A fair (*Br and Aus also* **funfair**, *Am also* **carnival**) is also a form of entertainment in a large outside area where you can ride on large brightly lit machines and win prizes in games of skill or luck. • A fair is also a large show at which producers, sellers and buyers in a particular industry meet, and sell and advertise their products: *a book/ antiques/toy fair* ○ *a trade fair* • In the countryside, a fair is a public event where farm animals and farm products are sold: *a cattle/agricultural fair* ○ *(Am) a county/state fair* • Fair is also *esp. Am for* FETE.

fair·ground /£'feə·graʊnd, $'fer-/ *n* [C] a large outside area used for a FAIR (=public event) • *There was a small fairground just by the river, with a carousel, a roller coaster and a Ferris wheel.*

fair·isle /£'feə·raɪl, $'fer-/, **Fair Isle** *adj* [not gradable] (of KNITTED clothing) made with a special pattern typical of one of Scotland's Shetland Islands • *a fairisle cardigan/ jumper/sweater*

fair·way /£'feə·weɪ, $'fer-/ *n* [C] *specialized* (in golf) the area of short grass between the TEE (=place where you first hit the ball) and the GREEN (=place where the ball should enter a hole) • *He completely missed the fairway from his tee shot, and his ball ended up in the bushes.*

fair·y [IMAGINARY CREATURE] /£'feə·ri, $'fer·i/ *n* [C] an imaginary creature with magical powers which looks like a small person with wings • *Do you believe in fairies?* • *She used to think there were fairies at the bottom of her garden.* • *In the story of Sleeping Beauty, the* **good** *fairies give the baby the gifts of beauty and goodness and the* **wicked** *fairy casts an evil spell on her.* • *(Aus)* **Fairy bread** is a slice of buttered bread covered with very small, brightly coloured sugary balls. • *(Br)* A **fairy cake** (*Am and Aus* **cupcake**) is a small light cake made with eggs, sugar and flour. • A **fairy godmother** is a magical character in some children's stories who helps someone who is in trouble: *Cinderella's fairy godmother helped her go to the ball.* ○ *(fig.) I've got so many money problems that I could do with a fairy godmother* (=someone to arrive unexpectedly and solve all my problems). ○ *(fig.) The company has* **played** *fairy godmother to the club by deciding to sponsor them for a further five years.* • *(Br and Aus)* **Fairy lights** are small coloured electric lights used as decoration: *Fairy lights are often used to decorate Christmas trees.* • A **fairy story/fairy tale** is a traditional story written for children which usually involves imaginary creatures and magic: *Hans Christian Andersen wrote many fairy stories for children,* *such as The Little Mermaid.* ○ *Cinderella, Little Red Riding Hood and Sleeping Beauty are fairy tales.* • *(approving)* If something has a fairy-tale quality, it has a special, charming quality: *Eight chapels surround the main church, and the spires and brightly coloured exteriors create a fairy-tale effect.* ○ *They had a fairy-tale* (=beautiful and romantic) **wedding.** • *(disapproving)* If you describe something that someone has said as a **fairy story** or a **fairy tale**, you think that it is false and is intended to deceive people: *I've had enough of your fairy stories – why don't you just tell me the truth!* • *"There are fairies at the bottom of our garden"* (Rose Fyleman in the poem *Fairies*, 1917) • PIC〉 **Bread and cakes, Imaginary creatures**

fair·y HOMOSEXUAL /£ˈfeə·ri, $ˈfer·i/ *n* [C] *infml disapproving* a homosexual man. Many people find this word offensive.

fair·y·land /£ˈfeə·ri·lænd, $ˈfer·i-/ *n* the place where FAIRIES (=imaginary creatures) are said to live • *She imagined herself living in fairyland.* [U] • *(approving)* A fairyland is also a beautiful place with a charming or special quality: *It had snowed heavily during the night and in the morning the garden was a white fairyland.* [C] • *(disapproving)* If you say that someone's ideas or remarks are from fairyland, they are not practical or wise: *The Minister's argument belongs to fairyland.* [U]

fait ac·com·pli /£ˌfet·ə·kɒmˈpliː, $ˌfeɪ·tə·kɑːmˈ-/ *n* [C] *pl* **faits accomplis** /£ˌfet·ə·kɒmˈpliː, $ˌfeɪ·tə·kɑːm-/ an action which has already been done and which cannot be changed • *With its new system of testing students, the Department of Education has been accused of trying to impose a fait accompli on schools.* • *The sudden change of policy was* **presented to** *the party* **as** *a fait accompli, without any prior consultation or discussion.*

faith TRUST /feɪθ/ *n* [U] great trust or confidence in something or someone • *She says she* **has** *no faith* **in** *modern medicine.* • *I have* **great** *faith* **in** *you – I'm sure you'll manage!* • *Their* **absolute/unshakable** *faith* **in** *their leader helped them at a time of crisis.* • *After the trial, his family said they had* **lost** *all faith* **in** *the judicial system.* • *It will be hard to* **restore** *faith* **in** *the government unless ministers start making promises they can keep.* • *She hasn't got much faith* **in** *human nature* (=She does not expect people to be morally good). • If you tell someone to **have faith**, you do not want them to lose confidence: *Have faith! It'll be all right in the end.* • If you **accept/take** something **on** faith, you are willing to believe it without proof. • If you **put/place** your faith **in** something or someone, you make a decision to trust it or them: *He placed complete faith in the abilities of his old friend.* ○ *Some people put their faith in strong leaders rather than sound policies.* • If you **keep faith with** something or someone, you continue to support it or them, or you do what you promised to do: *Despite the continuing recession, the government has asked people to keep faith with its reforms.* ○ *The company has not kept faith with its promise to invest in training.* • If you **break faith with** someone or something, you do not stay loyal to them or do not do what you promised.

faith·ful /ˈfeɪθ·fᵊl/ *adj* • If a person or animal is faithful, they are loyal: *She was a close and faithful* **friend.** ○ *They are faithful supporters of the Labour Party.* ○ *His faithful old dog always accompanied him wherever he went.* ○ *The company risks alienating its faithful customers with its new modern image.* • If something, such as a copy or record, is faithful, it is true or follows the original exactly: *She gave a faithful account of what had happened on that night.* ○ *Compact discs offer more faithful sound reproduction than records.* ○ *I have tried to keep my translation as faithful as possible* **to** *the original.* • If a person is faithful to their husband, wife or usual sexual partner, they do not have a sexual relationship with anyone else: *Was your wife faithful during your marriage?* ○ *He was faithful* **to** *his wife throughout their 30-year marriage.* • If you are faithful **to** something, you continue to support or follow it: *He has remained faithful to the president's regime when so many others have spoken out against it.* ○ *Despite persecution, she remained faithful to her beliefs.*

faith·ful /ˈfeɪθ·fᵊl/ *n* [C] • A faithful is someone who continues to support someone or something: *She's an* **old** *faithful – she never misses a single match.* ○ *He gave a rousing speech to a room full of* **party** *faithfuls.* • **The faithful** are people who are always loyal to a particular group or organization, esp. a political party: *They asked for donations from the* **party** *faithful to fund the election campaign.*

faith·ful·ly /ˈfeɪθ·fᵊl·i/ *adv* • *He has served the family faithfully* (=in a loyal way) *for 40 years.* • *I always faithfully* (=exactly) *follow the instructions on medicine bottles.* • *She* **promised** *faithfully* (=made a firm promise) *that she would never leave him.* • *(esp. Br and Aus)* You write **Yours faithfully** at the end of a formal letter beginning with 'Dear Sir' or 'Dear Madam'. • LP〉 **Letters**

faith·ful·ness /ˈfeɪθ·fᵊl·nəs/ *n* [U] • *She was given a top government position because of her faithfulness* (=loyalty) **to** *the party.* • *In his sermon, the priest stressed the need for faithfulness* **in** *marriage* (=having a sexual relationship only with your husband or wife).

faith·less /ˈfeɪθ·ləs/ *adj* • A faithless person is someone who is not loyal and cannot be trusted. • If your husband, wife or usual sexual partner is faithless, they are having a sexual relationship with someone else: *She finally decided to leave her faithless husband.*

faith·less·ly /ˈfeɪθ·lə·sli/ *adv*

faith·less·ness /ˈfeɪθ·lə·snəs/ *n* [U] • *He divorced his wife on the grounds of her faithlessness* (=because she was having a sexual relationship with someone else).

faith RELIGION /feɪθ/ *n* a particular religion, or a strong belief in God or a particular religion • *the Muslim/ Christian/Jewish/Buddhist faith* [C] • *They were persecuted for their faith.* [C] • *He was isolated from any contact with other Christians and practised his faith alone.* [C] • *We live in a* **multi-***faith society.* [U] • *They were brought up* **in the true** *faith* (=to believe in the religion which the speaker believes is the only true one). [C] • *During the revolution, he was forced to* **renounce** *his faith* (=to say that he no longer believed in his religion.) [C] • *Her faith* (=belief) **in** *God was shattered when her baby died.* [U] • *I* **lost** *my faith* (=stopped believing in God) *at the age of 15.* [U] • If you **keep the faith**, you continue believing in or supporting something or someone: *Science fiction has lost some of the popularity it once enjoyed, but there are a few authors who still keep the faith* (=who still write that type of book). • **Faith healing** is the activity of trying to cure people who are ill using the power of belief and prayer: *Faith healing has become an important part of the service in the Christian Pentecostal and Charismatic churches.* ○ *After several doctors failed to find a cure for her illness, she decided to go to a* **faith healer** (=a person who heals using the power of prayer and belief). • *(saying)* 'Faith will move mountains'.

faith·ful /ˈfeɪθ·fᵊl/ *adj* • If someone is faithful, they follow a particular religion: *They were faithful* **followers** *of Buddhism.*

faith·ful /ˈfeɪθ·fᵊl/ *pl n* • **The faithful** are the followers of a particular religion: *We heard bells calling the faithful to prayer.* ○ *To gain entry to the temple, the faithful must donate 10% of their income to the church.*

faith·less /ˈfeɪθ·ləs/ *adj* • A faithless person does not believe in God.

faith·less·ly /ˈfeɪθ·lə·sli/ *adv*

faith·less·ness /ˈfeɪθ·lə·snəs/ *n* [U] • *He spoke of his anger with God after the accident and the resulting faithlessness which he experienced.*

fake OBJECT /feɪk/ *n* [C] an object which is made to look real or valuable in order to deceive people • *Experts have revealed that the painting is a fake.* • *I had no way of knowing if the gun in his hand was a fake or was real.* • If a person is a fake, they are not what or whom they say they are: *After he had worked for ten years as a doctor, he was exposed as being a complete fake.*

fake /feɪk/ *adj* • *He was charged with possessing a fake passport.* • *"Is that real fur on your coat?" "No, it's fake."* • *Her suntan must be fake – she couldn't have gone that brown in one day!* • *The actors are covered in fake blood to make it look as though they are injured.*

fake *obj* /feɪk/ *v* [T] • If you fake an object, you make it look real or valuable in order to deceive people: *to fake a document/report* ○ *He admitted to faking famous paintings and selling them around the world.*

fak·er /£ˈfeɪ·kəʳ, $-kɚ/ *n* [C] • *She is a talented faker of great European paintings, and even the experts cannot always tell her work from the originals.*

fake *(obj)* FEELING /feɪk/ *v* to pretend that you have (a feeling or illness) • *to fake surprise/grief/disbelief* [T] • *to fake an orgasm* [T] • *She didn't want to go out, so she faked a headache.* [T] • *He managed to escape from prison after faking a heart attack and persuading prison staff to take him to hospital.* [T] • *He isn't really crying, he's just faking.* [I]

fak·ir /£'feɪ·kɪəʳ, £'fæk·ɪəʳ, $'feɪ·kɪr/ *n* [C] a member of an Islamic religious group, or a Hindu holy man

fa·la·fel /£fə'læf·ᵊl, $-'lɑː·fᵊl/ *n* [C/U] FELAFEL

fal·con /£'fɒl·kᵊn, $'fɑːl-/ *n* [C] a bird with pointed wings and a long tail which can be trained to hunt other birds and small animals • *The falcon is a bird of prey.* • *The kestrel is a type of falcon.*

fal·con·er /£'fɒl·kᵊn·əʳ, $'fɑːl·kə·nɚ/ *n* [C] • A falconer is a person who keeps and often trains falcons for hunting.

fal·con·ry /£'fɒl·kᵊn·ri, $'fɑːl-/ *n* [U] • Falconry is the sport of hunting small animals and birds using falcons: *There were displays of falconry and dog-handling at the fair.*

fall [ACCIDENT] /£fɔːl, $fɑːl/ *v* [I] *past simple* **fell** /fel/, *past part* **fallen** /£'fɔː·lən, $'fɑː-/ to move down unintentionally or accidentally onto or towards the ground from a higher place • *The path's very steep, so mind you don't fall.* • *He fell badly and broke his leg.* • *How do cats always manage to fall on their feet?* • *Athletes have to learn how to fall without hurting themselves.* • *The picture's fallen behind the piano and I can't reach it.* • *She fell under a bus and was killed instantly.* • *The horse fell* **at** *the first fence.* • *I fell* **down** *the stairs and injured my back.* • *The dead woman looked as though she'd fallen* **from** *a great height.* • *The water's deep here, so don't fall* **in!** • *Ten miners were trapped underground when the roof of the tunnel fell* **in** (= dropped down because of lack of support). See also FALL IN. • *He fell* **into** *the river and drowned.* • *She fell head first* **into** *a ditch.* • *(fig.) We fell right* **into** *the enemy's trap* (= We were completely deceived by the enemy). • *(fig.) Don't fall* **into the trap of** (= make the mistake of) *thinking you can learn a foreign language without doing any work.* • *If you fall* **off** *that roof, you could injure yourself badly.* • *She nearly* **fell off** *her* **chair** (= She was very surprised) *when she heard her exam result.* See also **fall off** at FALL [LOWER]. • *He fell* **on** *his arm and hurt it badly.* See also FALL ON. • *The child was leaning out of the window and fell* **out**. • *As he opened the book, a couple of pages fell* **out**. • *(fig. infml) She was almost falling* **out** *of her dress* (= She was showing a large amount of her breasts intentionally). See also FALL OUT [ARGUE], FALL OUT [MOVE]. • *He fell* **through** *a hole onto the floor below.* See also FALL THROUGH. • *She fell five metres* **to** *the bottom of the ravine.* • *He fell* **to** *his* **death** *climbing the Matterhorn.* See also FALL TO [DUTY], FALL TO [START]. • *Kathy fell* **flat on** *her* **face** (= fell and landed with her face) *in the mud.* • If a joke, idea or suggestion **falls flat**, it does not have the intended effect: *Whenever he tries to tell a joke, it always falls flat.* ○ *The Government's new scheme fell flat* **on its face** (= It was completely unsuccessful). • If a person or object falls **down/over**, they move down from a standing or vertical position to a horizontal position on the ground: *Our apple tree fell down in the storm.* ○ *Many buildings fell down when the cyclone hit Darwin.* ○ *There was a single shot, and the stag fell down* **dead**. ○ *When I was learning to ski, I kept falling over.* ○ *She tripped on the pavement and fell over.* • If a building is falling **down**, it is in a very bad condition and there is a risk that it will break into pieces and drop to the ground: *Those apartment blocks must have been built badly because they're starting to fall down already.* • If a plan **falls down**, it fails: *Where do you think the plan falls down?* • *I'm quite good at speaking Chinese, but I* **fall down on** (= I am not very good at) *the written work.* • *(Br and Aus)* If you **fall over yourself**/*(Am)* **fall all over yourself** to do something, you are very eager to do it: *Publishers are falling over themselves* **to** *produce non-fiction for five to seven-year-olds.* [+ to infinitive] • *(Br and Aus infml)* If you **fall about (laughing)**, you laugh uncontrollably: *We fell about when we heard her reply.* • If someone **falls by the wayside**, they fail to complete something: *Ten per cent of last year's students fell by the wayside and never completed their course.* ○ *The company has managed to survive the recession while some of its competitors have fallen by the wayside.* • If you **fall to** your **knees/fall down on** your **knees**, you go down on your knees to show respect: *The people all fell to their knees and began to pray.* • *"The bigger they come (or 'are'), the harder they fall"* (believed to have been the boxer Robert Fitzsimmons, 1902) • *"Jack fell down and broke his crown/ And Jill came tumbling after"* (from the nursery rhyme *Jack and Jill*)

fall /£fɔːl, $fɑːl/ *n* [C usually sing] • *He* **had** *a nasty fall and hurt his back.* • *She* **took** (= had) *a nasty fall in her first race of the season.* • *East and West Germany were reunited after the fall* (= destruction) *of the Berlin Wall.* • *The Finance Minister's* **fall from grace** (= loss of popularity) *gave the tabloid press great satisfaction.* • According to the Bible, **the Fall (of Man)** was the occasion when Adam and Eve (= the first man and woman) disobeyed the rules of God and were sent away from the garden of Eden. • *(Am infml)* If you **take a/the fall for** someone, you accept the blame for something they did: *He tried to make me take the fall for something he'd done.* • *(esp. Am slang)* A **fall guy** is a person who is falsely blamed for something that has gone wrong, or for a crime that they have not committed: *The governor is looking for a fall guy to take the blame for the corruption scandal.* ○ *In his book he claims that President Kennedy was the victim of a conspiracy and that Lee Harvey Oswald was set up as a fall guy.* • See also **fall** at FALL [MOVE DOWN], FALL [LOWER], FALL [BE DEFEATED].

fal·len /£'fɔː·lən, $'fɑː-/ *adj* [before n; not gradable] • *A fallen tree was blocking the road.* • A **fallen idol** is a person who was admired in the past but is no longer admired because of something they have done. • *(dated disapproving)* A **fallen woman** is a woman who has lost her good reputation by having sex with someone before she is married. • See also **fallen** at FALL [MOVE DOWN], FALL [BE DEFEATED].

fall [MOVE DOWN] /£fɔːl, $fɑːl/ *v* [I] *past simple* **fell** /fel/, *past part* **fallen** /£'fɔː·lən, $'fɑː-/ to move down onto the ground or from a high position to a lower position • *The snow had been falling steadily all day.* • *You can tell it's autumn because the leaves have started to fall.* • *The bomb fell* **on** *the church and totally destroyed it.* See also FALL ON. • *A huge meteor has fallen* **to** *earth in the middle of the desert.* See also FALL TO [DUTY], FALL TO [START]. • *In the corner of the room, pieces of plaster had fallen* **away** (= broken off). • *(literary) As she looked at him, the years* **fell away** (= it seemed as if they had not gone past), *and she saw him again as a young boy.* See also **fall away** at FALL [LOWER]. • If land falls **away**, it slopes down steeply: *On the other side of the hill, the land falls away* **sharply**. • *(literary) He begged for mercy as the blows fell* **on** *him* (= as he was being hit). • *(fig.) The Treasury has still not decided where the cuts will fall* (= where government spending will be reduced). • *(fig.) The* **axe** *looks likely to fall* **on** *500 jobs* (= 500 jobs will probably be lost) *at the factory.* See also FALL ON. • *(fml or literary) Not a single sound fell* **from** *my* **lips** (= I said nothing). • *(fig.) She fell* (= moved quickly) **into** *bed, completely exhausted.* • *(fig.) They fell* **into** *each other's arms* (= They began to hold each other tightly with their arms). • *(fig.) He was the last person to see the woman alive, and suspicion immediately fell* **on** *him* (= people thought he was guilty). • *(fig.) Her gaze fell* **on** (= She noticed) *a small box at the back of the shop.* • *(fig.) In the word 'table', the accent falls* **on** (= you emphasize) *the first syllable.* See also FALL ON. • *(fig.) The bottom has fallen* **out** *of the coal market* (= There is no longer a demand for coal). • If teeth or hair fall **out**, they become loose and separate from your mouth or head: *She's at the age when her baby teeth are starting to fall out.* ○ *One of the side effects of the treatment is that your hair starts to fall out.* ○ See also FALL OUT [ARGUE], FALL OUT [MOVE]. • *(fig.) A shadow fell* **over** (= covered) *her work and she looked up to see who was there.* • When the curtain falls in the theatre, it means that the play or performance has ended: *The audience was still laughing as the curtain fell.* ○ *Many of the songs from the musical will still be popular long after the final curtain has fallen* (= when the show is no longer being performed). ○ *(fig.) Although the curtain has now fallen on the Republican era* (= Although the period in which the Republicans had political power has now ended), *many of its values still remain.* • If something **falls between two stools**, it fails to achieve either of two aims: *This grammar guide falls between two stools – it's too difficult for a beginner but not detailed enough for an advanced student.* • If you **fall into** a habit, you begin to do something regularly: *We've fallen into the habit of getting up late on Saturday mornings.* • *If you plan the project well, then everything should* **fall into place** (= operate satisfactorily). • *Once I discovered that the woman whom he had been dancing with was his daughter, everything* **fell into place** (= became clear). • *The last piece of the jigsaw* **fell into place** (= The mystery was solved) *when the blood-stained knife was found in his apartment.* • If something **falls into the hands/clutches of** someone, it is obtained or starts to be controlled by that person: *This is a very dangerous chemical and we must not let it fall into the* **wrong** *hands* (= let someone obtain it who will not use it responsibly). • If a suggestion or warning **falls on deaf ears/falls on stony ground**, no one listens to it: *Their appeals to release the hostages fell on deaf ears.* • If you have

fallen on hard times, you have lost all your money and are starting to have a difficult life: *The scheme is designed to help children whose parents have fallen on hard times.* • **Falling star** is *infml for* METEOR. • *"A Hard Rain's A Gonna* (= is going to) *Fall"* (title of a song by Bob Dylan, referring to nuclear fall-out, 1963)

fall /£fɔːl, $fɑːl/ *n* [C usually sing] • *There was a heavy fall of snow during the night.* • See also RAINFALL. See also **fall** at FALL ACCIDENT, FALL LOWER, FALL BE DEFEATED.

falls /£fɔːlz, $fɑːlz/ *pl n* • Falls, often used in place names, refers to a very wide WATERFALL, often consisting of many separate waterfalls: *They went on a day trip to the Niagara Falls.*

fal·len /£'fɔː·lən, $'fɑː-/ *adj* [before n; not gradable] • *fallen leaves* • See also **fallen** at FALL ACCIDENT, FALL BE DEFEATED.

fall LOWER /£fɔːl, $fɑːl/ *v* [I] *past simple* **fell** /fel/, *past part* **fallen** /£'fɔː·lən, $'fɑː-/ to become lower in size, amount or strength • *Demand for new cars has fallen due to the recession.* • *The standard of his work has fallen steadily during the year.* • *Average salaries in the public sector are expected to fall* **back** *by 15% this year.* See also FALL BACK. • *It will be extremely cold this evening and the temperature could fall* **below** *zero.* • *This work falls* **below** (= is not as good as) *your usual high standard.* • *The temperature fell* **by** *ten degrees during the night.* • *If it doesn't rain soon, water supplies will fall* **to** *danger levels.* • *The pound has fallen* **to** *its lowest-ever level against the Deutschmark.* • *The teacher walked in and the children's voices fell* **to a whisper** (= they became very quiet). See also FALL TO DUTY, FALL TO START. • *Church attendance has fallen* **dramatically** *in Britain.* • *Share prices have fallen* **sharply** *this week.* • *(fig.) She looked at her exam results and her* **face** *fell* (= she suddenly looked very unhappy). • *(fig.) His* **spirits** *fell* (= He felt unhappy and disappointed) *when he saw the distance he still had to go.* • *(fig.) He fell* **in my estimation** (= I thought less well of him) *when he deserted his family.* • *One by one, the prime minister's supporters* **fell away** (= stopped supporting him/her). • *Membership of the club has* **fallen away/off** (= Members have been leaving) *in recent months.* • *Sales have* **fallen off** (= gone down in quantity) *in the past few months.* See also **fall away** at FALL MOVE DOWN.

fall /£fɔːl, $fɑːl/ *n* [C usually sing] • *We could hear the rise and fall of voices from the other room.* • *There has been a slight fall* **in** *the price of petrol.* • *There has been a further fall* **in** *the unemployment rate this month.* • *There was a fall* **in** *support for the Republican party at the last election.* • *The strong winds will accompanied by a* **sharp** *fall* **in** *temperature.* • See also **fall** at FALL ACCIDENT, FALL MOVE DOWN, FALL BE DEFEATED.

fall·ing /£'fɔː·lɪŋ, $fɑː-/ *adj* [not gradable] • *falling birth rates/interest rates* • *Parents have been complaining about falling standards in the school.*

fall·ing-off /£ˌfɔː·lɪŋ'ɒf, $ˌfɑː-/ *n* [C] • *Travel agencies have recorded a falling-off in* (= a lower rate of) *bookings this summer.*

fall BECOME /£fɔːl, $fɑːl/ *v past simple* **fell** /fel/, *past part* **fallen** /£'fɔː·lən, $fɑː-/ used to show a change from one state to another • *He always falls* **asleep** *after drinking red wine.* [L] • *I am writing to confirm that your rent falls* **due** (= must be paid) *on the first of the month.* [L] • *She fell* **ill** *suddenly and was dead within a week.* [L] • *The book fell* **open** (= opened by chance) *at the page on Venice.* [L] • *He fell* **prey/victim to** (= suddenly began to suffer from) *a feeling of extreme terror.* [L] • *As soon as a room falls* **vacant** (= becomes free), *I'll let you know.* [L] • *The government has fallen strangely* **silent** *on the subject of tax cuts after all its promises at the last election.* [L] • **Silence** *fell* **on** *the group of men* (= They became silent) *as they received the news.* [I always + adv/prep] • *She fell* **out of favour** *with* (= She was no longer liked or supported by) *her union over a dispute about contracts.* [I always + adv/prep] • *He has fallen* **under** *her spell* (= He is attracted by her charm and beauty). [I always + adv/prep] • *She fell* **under** *the influence of* (= began to be influenced by) *an older student.* [I always + adv/prep] • If a building falls **into disrepair/decay**, it gets into a bad condition because no one takes care of it: *The house had fallen into decay and needed a new roof and new plumbing.* [I always + adv/prep] • If something falls **into disuse**, people stop using it: *The old school had fallen into disuse.* [I always + adv/prep] • If an organization or system, such as a marriage, family or business **falls apart**, it fails: *The deal fell apart because of a lack of financing.* ○ *Their marriage fell apart when she found out her husband was having an affair with another woman.* • *(infml)* If someone **falls apart**, they experience serious emotional problems and are unable to think or act in the usual way: *After his wife died, he began to fall apart.* • If you **fall foul of** a rule or law, you break it, esp. unintentionally: *Manufacturers may fall foul of the new government guidelines.* • If you **fall foul of** someone, you have a disagreement with them: *People who fall foul of her are never forgiven.* • If you **fall in love** with someone, you are attracted to them and begin to love them: *He is very prone to falling in love.* ○ *She fell deeply/madly in love* **with** *a friend of her brother's.* • If a person in an organization **falls in/into line**, they start to follow the rules and behave according to expected standards of behaviour: *The chief executive of the newspaper group has been told by his fellow directors to fall into line, and stop interfering in editorial matters.* ○ *The two women's colleges are expected to fall into line* **with** *the rest of the university, now that all the other colleges accept both male and female students.* ○ *Teachers who fail to fall in line* **with** *the new regulations may face dismissal.* • If something **falls short of** expectations or hopes, it fails to reach a desired amount or standard and is disappointing: *August car sales fell short of the industry's expectations.* ○ *This essay falls considerably short of your usual standard.* • *"Things fall apart; the centre cannot hold"* (W.B.Yeats in the poem *The Second Coming*, 1920) • *"Falling in love again, never wanted to, What am I to do? I can't help it."* (song made famous by Marlene Dietrich in the film *The Blue Angel*, 1930)

fall BE DEFEATED /£fɔːl, $fɑːl/ *v* [I] *past simple* **fell** /fel/, *past part* **fallen** /£'fɔː·lən, $fɑː-/ to be beaten or defeated • *The Government finally fell after losing the support of the centre parties.* • *The president fell* **from power** *during the military coup.* • *Her suggestion will stand or fall* **on** (= succeed or fail because of) *its merits.* • If a place falls in a war or an election, an enemy army or a different political party obtains control of it: *The city finally fell after a three month siege.* ○ *Rome fell* **to** *the Vandals in 455 AD.* ○ *After ten years of Conservative rule, Basildon finally fell* **to** *Labour at the last election.* • *(literary)* A soldier who falls while fighting is killed: *Many soldiers fell in the fight to save the city.* ○ *During the war, he saw many of his comrades fall* **in battle.** • In cricket, if a WICKET falls, the turn of the player who is hitting the ball has finished: *It was a very slow moving game, with not a single wicket falling in the first hour.* ○ *Ten wickets fell in 22 overs.*

fall /£fɔːl, $fɑːl/ *n* [C usually sing] • *The fall of the city is expected within days.* • *The army took control of the city after the president's fall from power.* • See also **fall** at FALL ACCIDENT, FALL MOVE DOWN, FALL LOWER.

fal·len /£'fɔː·lᵊn, $'fɑː-/ *adj* [before n; not gradable] • *The Education Minister will now join the ranks of other fallen politicians* (= politicians who have lost their government positions). • See also **fallen** at FALL ACCIDENT, FALL MOVE DOWN.

fal·len /£'fɔː·lᵊn, $'fɑː-/ *pl n* • *(dated or literary)* **The fallen** are soldiers who have died in a war: *They have erected a statue in memory of the fallen in the two world wars.*

fall HAPPEN /£fɔːl, $fɑːl/ *v* [I] *past simple* **fell** /fel/, *past part* **fallen** /£'fɔː·lən, $fɑː-/ to happen at a particular time • *Easter falls late this year.* • *My birthday will fall* **on** *a Friday this year.* • **Darkness** *falls* (= comes) *early in the Tropics.* • **Night** *had fallen* (= It had become dark) *by the time we got back to the camp.*

fall BELONG TO /£fɔːl, $fɑːl/ *v* [I always + adv/prep] *past simple* **fell** /fel/, *past part* **fallen** /£'fɔː·lən, $'fɑː-/ to belong to a particular group • *The material falls* **into** *three categories.* • *This matter falls* **outside** (= does not belong to) *the area which we are responsible for.* • *That area falls* **under** *your jurisdiction* (= You are responsible for it).

fall HANG DOWN /£fɔːl, $fɑːl/ *v* [I always + adv/prep] *past simple* **fell** /fel/, *past part* **fallen** /£'fɔː·lən, $'fɑː-/ (of hair or cloth) to hang down loosely • *Her long dark hair fell* **to** *her waist* • *The boy's hair fell* **around** *his shoulders in golden curls.*

fall AUTUMN /£fɔːl, $fɑːl/ *n Am* the season after summer and before winter, when fruits and crops ripen and the leaves fall off the trees • *I first met him three years ago in the fall.* [U] • *Next fall we'll be back in New York.* [C] • *They met* **in the** *fall* **of** *1992.* [C]

fall a·mong *obj v prep* [T] *old use* to meet (a group of esp. bad people) by chance • *"A certain man went down from Jerusalem, and fell among thieves"* (Bible, Luke 10.30)

fall back *v adv* [I] to move away from someone • *She fell back* **in** *horror/disgust.* • If an army falls back, it moves away from an enemy army in order to avoid fighting them: *The army fell back* **in** *disarray.*

fall back on *obj*, **fall back u·pon** *obj v adv prep* [T] to use (something) for help because no other choice is available • *When the business failed, we had to fall back on our savings.* • *If I lose my job, I'll have nothing to fall back on.*

fall·back /£ˈfɔːl·bæk, $ˈfɑːl-/ *adj* [before n; not gradable] • A fallback plan or position is one which can be used if other plans do not succeed or other things are not available: *We must have a fallback* **position** *in the negotiations.* ◦ *Their first choice for the job is Amanda Martin, with Paul Davies as* **the** *fallback.*

fall be·hind *(obj) v prep* to fail to do (something) fast enough or on time • *We have fallen hopelessly behind schedule.* [T] • *He was ill for six weeks and fell behind* **with** *his schoolwork.* [I] • *I've fallen behind* **with** *the mortgage payments.* [I]

fall for *obj* LOVE *v prep* [T] *infml* to be attracted to (someone) and start to love them • *She always falls for unsuitable men.* • *Alex has fallen for Helen in a big way.*

fall for *obj* BE TRICKED *v prep* [T] *infml* to be deceived by (something or someone) • *She fell for the sales talk and agreed to buy a set of encyclopedias.* • *I might have known she'd try a trick like this and that you'd fall for it.* • You say 'I'm not falling for that one' when you recognize a trick and refuse to be deceived by it: *"Lend me a fiver and I'll buy you a drink." "Oh no, I'm not falling for that one."*

fall in *v adv* [I] (of soldiers) to move into a line, one beside the other • *"Company, fall in!" shouted the sergeant-major.* • *He started to march away, and the others fell in* **behind** *him.* • Compare FALL OUT MOVE.

fall in with *obj* PERSON *v adv prep* [T] *infml* to become friendly with (someone) • *He fell in with a friendly group of people when he was travelling in Europe.* • *She fell in with a strange crowd of people at university.*

fall in with *obj* PLAN *v adv prep* [T] *infml* to accept and support (a plan or suggestion) • *Her suggestion was perfectly good, so the rest of us fell in with it.*

fall on *obj*, **fall u·pon** *obj v prep* [T] to attack suddenly and unexpectedly • *The soldiers fell on the villagers and seized all their weapons.* • *(literary)* If you fall on/upon food, you start to eat it eagerly: *They fell upon the bread and cheese as if they had not eaten for days.*

fall out ARGUE *v adv* [I] *infml* to argue with someone and stop being friendly with them • *He left home after falling out* **with** *his parents.* • *She fell out* **with** *her boyfriend* **over** *where to go on holiday.*

fall·ing–out /£ˌfɔː·lɪŋˈaʊt, $ˌfɑː-/ *n* [C] *infml* • A falling-out is an argument: *Rachel and Fiona have had a falling-out and they aren't speaking to each other.*

fall out MOVE *v adv* [I] (of soldiers) to move out of a line • *"Fall out, men!" shouted the sergeant-major.* • Compare FALL IN.

fall through *v adv* [I] to fail to happen • *Our holiday fell through at the last minute because the travel firm went bankrupt.* • *We found a buyer for our house, but then the sale fell through.*

fall to *obj* DUTY *v prep* [T] to be or become the duty or job of (someone) • *The worst job fell to me.* • *(fml)* **It** *falls to me* (= It is my duty) **to** *thank you for all you have done for the association.* [+ *to* infinitive]

fall to START *v adv* [I] *literary* to begin doing something • *There was a lot of work to do, so they fell to immediately.* • *She fell to thinking about the past.* [+ v-*ing*]

fal·la·cy /ˈfæl·ə·si/ *n* [C] *fml* an idea that a lot of people think is true but which is false • *It is a common fallacy* **that** *women are worse drivers than men.* [+ *that* clause] • *The notion that the disease is only prevalent among children is* **exposed** *as a complete fallacy in the report.*

fal·la·cious /fəˈleɪ·ʃəs/ *adj fml* • Fallacious means not correct: *His argument is based on fallacious reasoning.* ◦ *It is quite fallacious* **to** *argue that traffic congestion will be reduced by building more roads, because it will simply encourage people to use their cars more.* [+ *to* infinitive]

fal·la·cious·ly /fəˈleɪ·ʃə·sli/ *adv fml* • *She claims that the Government has fallaciously presented the privatization of public services as increasing their efficiency.*

fal·la·cious·ness /fəˈleɪ·ʃə·snəs/ *n* [U] *fml* • *In his book, he attempts to expose the fallaciousness of some of the arguments supporting nuclear power.*

fal·li·ble /ˈfæl·ɪ·bl̩/ *adj* (of a person) able or likely to make mistakes, or (of an object or system) likely not to work satisfactorily • *The more fallible a politician seems to be, the more honest people think he is.* • *The country's democracy is in danger because of its dependence on its fallible and vulnerable ruler.* • *This method is more fallible than most because it depends on careful and accurate timing.*

fal·li·bil·i·ty /£ˌfæl·ɪˈbɪl·ɪ·ti, $-ə·t̬i/ *n* [U] • *The play deals with the fallibility of human nature.* • *This case has alerted the public to the fallibility of the judicial system.*

fal·lo·pi·an tube /£fəˈləʊ·pi·ən, $-ˈloʊ-/, *infml* **tube** *n* [C usually pl] either of the two tubes in a woman's body along which eggs travel from the OVARIES to the womb • *When a woman is sterilized, clips are put on her fallopian tubes to block them, which stops eggs from travelling to the womb.*

fall·out /£ˈfɔːl·aʊt, $ˈfɑːl-/ *n* [U] the RADIOACTIVE dust in the air after a nuclear explosion • *Fallout from the Chernobyl accident caused contamination thousands of kilometres away from the site of the explosion.* • *Experts say that the number of cancer deaths caused by the fallout from weapons testing could rise to 2·4 million over the next few centuries.* • Fallout is also the unpleasant results or effects of an action or event: *The political fallout of the revelations has been immense.* ◦ *His fortune will largely depend on the legal fallout from the scandal in New York.* • A **fallout shelter** is a strong building, usually under the ground, intended to keep people safe from the dust in the air after a nuclear explosion.

fal·low /£ˈfæl·əʊ, $-oʊ/ *adj* [not gradable] (of land) not planted with crops in order to improve the quality of the earth • *Farmers have been told they cannot be eligible for government support unless they leave a certain amount of land fallow.* • *It is a good idea to let a field* **lie** *fallow* (= to plant nothing in it) *to improve the quality of the soil and restore its fertility.* • If a period of time is described as fallow, very little happens in it: *August is a fallow* **period** *in British politics.* ◦ *She wrote her autobiography during a fallow* **period** *in her acting career.*

fal·low deer /£ˈfæl·əʊ, $-oʊ/ *n* [C] *pl* **fallow deer** a small deer which is grey in winter and pale brown with white spots in summer, and lives esp. in forests in Europe and Asia • *The park has a herd of 24 fallow deer, which are kept in a large enclosure on the western side of the park.*

false NOT NATURAL /£fɒls, $fɑːls/ *adj* (of things) not real or natural; artificial • *Most office buildings are now designed with false floors, under which computer and telephone wires can be laid.* • *She was heavily made-up, with false* **eyelashes** *and bright red lipstick.* • *Both my grandparents have false* **teeth**.

false NOT REAL /£fɒls, $fɑːls/ *adj disapproving* (of things) made to look real, or (of information) made to seem true in order to deceive • *The thieves wore false beards and thick glasses so that they wouldn't be recognized.* • *She was charged with giving false* **evidence** *in court.* • *He assumed/took on a false* **identity** (= pretended he was someone else) *in order to escape from the police.* • *Some officials in the company knew they were selling prohibited equipment and gave false* **information** *to try to conceal what it was.* • *When she was stopped by the police for speeding, she gave them a false* **name** *and* **address**. • If someone does something **under false colours**, they pretend to be someone or something which they are not in order to deceive. • If someone does something **under false pretences**, they pretend to be someone else or have particular qualifications in order to obtain something: *He was deported for entering the country under false pretences.* ◦ *If you're not going to offer me a job, then you've brought me here under false pretences* (= you have deceived me in order to make me come here). • *(specialized)* **False accounting** is the crime of changing or destroying records to obtain money: *He faces 18 charges of fraud and false accounting.* • If a case has a **false bottom**, it has two bottoms with a hiding place between them: *Customs officers found £277 000 worth of cannabis concealed in the false bottom of the suitcase.*

fal·si·fy *obj* /£ˈfɒl·sɪ·faɪ, $ˈfɑːl-/ *v* [T] *disapproving* • To falsify something, such as a document, is to change it in order to deceive: *The certificate had clearly been falsified.*

fal·si·fi·ca·tion /£ˌfɒl·sɪ·fɪˈkeɪ·ʃən, $ˌfɑːl-/ *n* [U] • *the falsification of evidence/information*

false NOT CORRECT /£fɒls, $fɑːls/ *adj* [not gradable] (of information or an idea) not correct or true • *"Three plus three is seven. True or false?" "False."* • *The news report about the explosion turned out to be false.* • *I don't want to raise any false* **hopes** (= to give you hopes about something that might not be true), *but I believe your son is still alive.* • *I* *think you've got a rather false* **idea** *of what I'm like – I'm really rather shy.* • *You'll get a false* **impression** *of the town if you only visit the university.* • *(specialized) Her whole theory is based on a false* **premise** (= an idea which is not correct). • A **false alarm** is when something dangerous or unpleasant does not happen after it was genuinely believed that it would happen: *Three fire engines rushed to the school only to discover it was a false alarm and the alarm system had been set off by a cigarette.* ○ *She thought she was pregnant, but it turned out to be a false alarm* (= she discovered she was not). • A **false dawn** is when something makes you think that things are improving when really they are not: *The increase in sales at the end of the year proved to be a false dawn.* ○ *The government is hoping that this is not a false dawn* **for** *economic recovery.* • A **false economy** is an action which saves money at the beginning but which, over a longer period of time, results in more money being wasted than being saved: *It's a bit cheaper than other washing powders, but if you have to use twice as much of it, then it's a false economy.* • *(law)* **False imprisonment** is the limiting of someone's freedom without the authority or right to do so: *A person who is wrongly arrested can bring civil proceedings against the police for false imprisonment.* ○ *The men are charged with false imprisonment and conspiracy to murder Mr Smith.* • A **false move/step** is an unwise action which is likely to have an unpleasant or dangerous effect: *"One false move and you're dead!" threatened the gunman.* ○ *These negotiations could affect the lives of thousands, so we mustn't* **make** *any false moves.* ○ *You can't afford to* **take** *any false steps once you're in enemy territory.* • In a race, a **false start** is when one competitor starts too early, before the starter has given the signal: *If an athlete* **makes** *a false start in a race, the race must be restarted.* • A **false start** is also an attempt to do something which fails because you are not ready or not able to do it: *We had a couple of false starts because of computer problems, and the project didn't really get going until last month.*

fal·se·hood /£ˈfɒls·hʊd, $ˈfɑːls-/ *n* • Falsehood means lying. It is often used, esp. by politicians, to avoid accusing people of lying: *She doesn't seem to understand the difference between truth and falsehood.* [U] • *(fml)* A falsehood is a lie or a statement which is not correct: *What he told us was a* **blatant/malicious** *falsehood.* [C]

fal·se·ly /£ˈfɒl·sli, $ˈfɑːl-/ *adv* • *She was falsely accused of shoplifting.* • *He claimed, falsely, that he was married.*

fal·si·ty /£ˈfɒl·sə·ti, $ˈfɑːl·sə·t̬i/, **fal·se·ness** *n* [U] • *If we can prove the falsity of the forensic tests* (= If we can prove that the results are false), *the case against him will have to be dropped.*

false NOT SINCERE /£fɒls, $fɑːls/ *adj disapproving* (of a person or their manner) dishonest or not sincere • *a false smile/laugh* • *I don't like her – she always seems very false.* • *He has a rather false, affected voice and I just don't trust him.* • If you **put on a false front**, you do not act naturally because you want to deceive. • **False modesty** is when a person pretends to have a low opinion of their own abilities or achievements: *She claims that her new book lacks originality, but this is false modesty as she has spent years researching her subject.* ○ *He shows great pride in his work and has no false modesty about his success.*

fal·se·ly /£ˈfɒl·sli, $ˈfɑːl-/ *adv disapproving* • *She tends to adopt a falsely cheerful tone when she's upset about something.*

fal·se·ness /£ˈfɒl·snəs, $ˈfɑːl-/, **fal·si·ty** *n* [U] *disapproving* • *There was a note of falseness in his voice which made me distrust him.* • *She left television after five years as a presenter, saying she hated the falsity of it all.*

false NOT LOYAL /£fɒls, $fɑːls/ *adj esp. literary disapproving* (of a friend) not loyal or able to be trusted • *She turned out to be a false friend and abandoned me when I needed her most.* • A **false friend** is a word which learners often confuse with a word in another language because the two words look or sound similar, but have different meanings: *The French word 'actuellement' and the English word 'actually' are false friends.*

fal·set·to /£fɔːlˈset·əʊ, $fɑːlˈset̬·oʊ/ *n* [C] *pl* **falsettos** a form of singing or speaking by men using an extremely high voice • *His voice rose to a high-pitched falsetto.* • *For his role as a young boy, he had to speak in a high falsetto.*

fal·set·to /£fɔːlˈset·əʊ, $fɑːlˈset̬·oʊ/ *adj, adv* • *The lead singer of the band has a falsetto voice.* • *In this piece, he has to sing the highest notes falsetto.*

fal·sies /£ˈfɒl·siːz, $ˈfɑːl-/ *pl n infml* soft round thick pieces of material which are worn by women to make their breasts look bigger

fal·ter /£ˈfɒl·təʳ, $ˈfɑːl·t̬ɚ/ *v* [I] to lose strength or purpose and (almost) stop • *The dinner party conversation faltered for a moment.* • *Her friends never faltered in their belief in her.* • *Nigel's voice faltered and he stopped speaking.* • To falter is also to move uncertainly as if you might fall: *The nurse saw him falter and made him lean on her.*

fal·ter·ing /£ˈfɒl·tᵊr·ɪŋ, $ˈfɑːl·t̬ɚ-/ *adj* • *This legislation is aimed at stimulating the faltering economy.* • *The child's faltering words were sometimes hard to understand.*

fal·ter·ing·ly /£ˈfɒl·tᵊr·ɪŋ·li, $ˈfɑːl·t̬ɚ-/ *adv*

fame /feɪm/ *n* [U] the state of being very well known • *I'm glad to see that fame hasn't spoilt him and made him abandon his old friends.* • *The town's fame rests on its beautiful 14th-century abbey.* • *She moved to London in search of fame* **and fortune** (= success and money). • See also FAMOUS. • Ⓘ

famed /feɪmd/ *adj* [not gradable] • *The town is famed* **for** (= well known because of) *its large number of pubs.* • *His famed calmness seemed to have temporarily deserted him.*

fa·mil·i·ar WELL KNOWN /£fəˈmɪl·i·əʳ, $ˈ-jɚ/ *adj* easy to recognize because experienced previously • *I didn't see any familiar* **faces** (= people I knew). • *The house looked strangely familiar, though she knew she'd never been there before.* • To be familiar **with** something is to know it well: *I'm sorry, I'm not familiar with your poetry.* • *We had met before, but we were hardly* **on familiar terms** (= we did not have a close and informal relationship). • Ⓓ

fa·mil·i·ar·i·ty /£fəˌmɪl·iˈær·ə·ti, $-ˈer·ə·t̬i/ *n* [U] • *The familiarity of her favourite chair* (= the fact that she knew it so well) *was reassuring to her.* • *Ellen's familiarity* **with** *pop music* (= the fact that she knows so much about it) *is astonishing.* • *(saying)* 'Familiarity breeds contempt' means that if you know something or someone too well you are no longer able to see its or their true value.

fa·mil·i·a·rize *obj, Br and Aus usually* **–ise** /fəˈmɪl·i·ᵊr·aɪz/ *v* [T] • *I bought a guidebook to familiarize my***self with** (= to learn something about) *the country before I went there.*

fa·mil·i·ar INFORMAL /£fəˈmɪl·i·əʳ, $ˈ-jɚ/ *adj* informal and friendly, sometimes in a way that shows a lack of respect if it is not between family and close friends • *"That'll be five pounds, dear", he said in an irritatingly familiar way.* • *It doesn't do to let the servants be too familiar* **with** *you.* • Ⓓ

fa·mil·i·ar·ly /£fəˈmɪl·i·ə·li, $ˈ-jɚ·li/ *adv* • *Henry Channon, known familiarly as 'Chips'*

fa·mil·i·ar·i·ty /£fəˌmɪl·iˈær·ə·ti, $-ˈer·ə·t̬i/ *n* [U] • *His excessive familiarity offended her.*

fa·mil·i·ar COMPANION /£fəˈmɪl·i·əʳ, $ˈ-jɚ/ *n* [C] *old use* a close friend, or a spirit in the shape of a cat, bird or other animal that is the close companion of a WITCH (= woman with magic powers) • Ⓓ

fam·i·ly SOCIAL GROUP /ˈfæm·ᵊl·i/ *n* [C + sing/pl v] a social group of people consisting of a parent, or parents, and their children, or your husband/wife and children, or your parents, brothers and sisters and sometimes grandparents, uncles, aunts, etc. • *A new family has/have moved in next door.* • *Bill only sees his family at weekends, so he isn't close to his children.* • *I come from a large family: I have three brothers and a sister.* • *Women should not have to choose between career and family* (= their children). [U] • *He hasn't any family.* [U] • *He's American but his family* (= relatives in the past) *come/comes from Ireland.* • *This film is good family entertainment* (= something that can be enjoyed by parents and children together). • *How does family* **life** (= being married, having children, etc.) *suit you?* • *(fig.) We've got a family* (= group of parents and young) **of** *squirrels living in our garden.* • *(dated infml)* A woman **in the family way** is pregnant. • In Britain, **family allowance** is the old name for **child benefit**. See at CHILD. • Your **family circle** are your close relatives. • In Britain, **family credit** is a payment made by the government to families with a low income. • A **family doctor** is a GP. • A **family man** is a man who has a wife and children, or who enjoys spending a lot of time with them. • Your **family name** is your SURNAME. • **Family planning** means the use of CONTRACEPTION to control how many children you have and when you have them: *a family- planning clinic* • A **family tree** is a drawing that shows the relationships between the different members of a family, especially over a long period of time. • *"We Are Family"* (title of a song by Sister Sledge, 1979) • LP **Relationships**

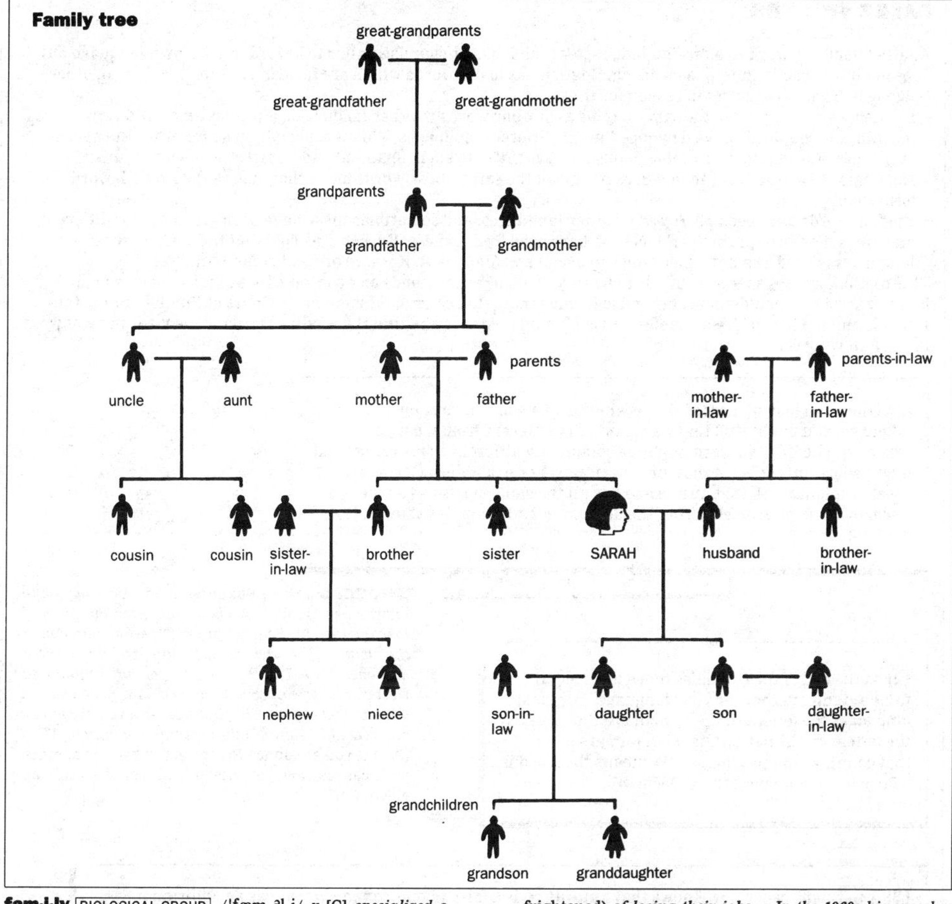

fam·i·ly BIOLOGICAL GROUP /ˈfæm·əl·i/ *n* [C] *specialized* a large group of related types of animal or plant • *The lion is a member of the cat family.*

fam·ine /ˈfæm·ɪn/ *n* a very serious lack of food for a great number of people, causing illness and death • *Another crop failure could result in widespread famine.* [U] • *Thousands died or emigrated during the Irish famine.* [C]

fam·ished /ˈfæm·ɪʃt/ *adj infml* very hungry • *Have some dinner with us – you must be famished!*

fa·mous /ˈfeɪ·məs/ *adj* very well known • *a famous film star/building/city* • *Marie Curie is famous* **for** *her contribution to science.* • *(infml)* If you say **famous last words**, you mean that you think that what someone has said will turn out to be untrue: *"It seems to be fairly well balanced," he said ... famous last words!* • See also FAME. • Ⓓ

fa·mous·ly /ˈfeɪ·mə·sli/ *adv* • *He's designed dresses for many celebrities, most famously the Queen.*

fa·mous·ly /ˈfeɪ·mə·sli/ *adv infml slightly dated* excellently • *The two pandas* **got on** *famously* (=had a very good friendship).

fan DEVICE /fæn/ *n* [C] a device to provide a flow of air, either an object made of folded paper, cloth, plastic, etc. that you wave in front of your face with your hand, or an electric device that has wide blades that turn around • *There was no air conditioning, just a ceiling fan turning slowly.* • A **fan belt** is a belt that makes a fan turn to keep an engine cool. • *We have an* **(electric) fan heater** (=a device which uses an electrically powered fan to push heated air into a room) *in our bedroom.* • PIC〉 **Fires and space heaters** Ⓣ

fan *obj* /fæn/ *v* [T] **-nn-** • To fan yourself or your face is to wave a fan, or something that acts as a fan, in front of your face: *It was very hot in the car, and I tried to fan myself* **with** *the road map.* • You fan a fire to make it burn more brightly. • *(fig.) The newspapers deliberately fanned the public's fears* (=encouraged them to feel frightened) *of losing their jobs.* • *In the 1960s his speeches* **fanned the flames** *of racial tension* (=made it worse).

fan ADMIRER /fæn/ *n* [C] a person who has a great interest in and admiration for a person, sport, sports team, etc. • *Having an ardent football fan as a boyfriend can be a strain.* • *I'm pleased to meet you – I'm a great fan* **of** *your work.* • A **fan club** is an organization for people who admire the same music star, football team, etc. • **Fan mail** is letters that are sent to a famous person from his or her admirers. • LP〉 **Sports** Ⓣ

fa·na·tic /£fəˈnæt·ɪk, $-ˈnæt̬-/ *n* [C] a person whose strong admiration for something is considered to be extreme and unreasonable • *a fitness/film fanatic*

fa·na·ti·cal /£fəˈnæt·ɪ·kəl, $-ˈnæt̬-/ *adj* • *The bombing was carried out by fanatical elements in the animal-rights movement.* • *His enthusiasm for aerobics was almost fanatical.*

fa·na·ti·cal·ly /£fəˈnæt·ɪ·kli, $-ˈnæt̬-/ *adv* • *Although the band is American, it has a fanatically loyal British following.*

fa·na·ti·cism /£fəˈnæt·ɪ·sɪ·zəm, $-ˈnæt̬-/ *n* [U]

fan·cy *obj* LIKE /ˈfænt·si/ *v* [T] *esp. Br* to like or wish for • *Do you fancy a drink this evening?* • *Diana fancied an after-lunch nap.* • *I didn't fancy swimming in that water.* [+ v-ing] • *(Br) I* **don't** *fancy his* **chances** *of ever publishing his novel* (=I think it is very unlikely that he will). • *(Br) She is the most fancied candidate for* (=Most people expect her to win) *the next election.* • To fancy a person is to be sexually attracted to them: *He could tell she fancied him.* • *(Br disapproving) That Dave really fancies himself, doesn't he?* (=he thinks he is very important/attractive).

fan·cy /ˈfænt·si/ *n* [U] • *For me, wanting to learn to parachute was no passing fancy* (=not something I wanted for just a short time). • To **take a fancy to** something or someone, is to start liking it or them very much, without any obvious reason: *Laura's taken a fancy to Japanese food.* • If something **catches/takes/tickles** your **fancy**, you like it a lot: *The thought of getting married again at 70 tickled his*

FALSE FRIENDS

A false friend is a word in a foreign language which looks or sounds similar to a word in your own language but does not have exactly the same meaning. English has many words which are false friends for speakers of other languages. There are two main reason for this:

- English words often have the same *origins* as similar words in other languages, but sometimes different meanings of the words have developed in the different languages. This is especially true for other European languages. For example, 'sensible' looks like '*sensible*' (French, Spanish) and '*sensibel*' (German, Danish, Norwegian, Swedish), but in fact does not mean the same: these words mean the same as the English word 'sensitive'.
- English words have been *borrowed* by other languages, and sometimes these have been given new or different meanings. For example, 'super' has been borrowed by Japanese, Korean and Thai, but the word in these languages is used as a noun meaning 'supermarket' (Japanese, Korean) or 'leaded fuel' (in Thai).

This dictionary uses special symbols to warn you about false friends and contains lists of false friends for 16 languages. These include important false friends that often cause confusion for learners of English. Using these symbols and the lists of false friends, you can avoid mistakes and find the English word for the meaning you want in the following way:

(1) When you look up a word that is similar to a word in your own language, you might find that its meaning is different from what you expected. The English word might be completely different in meaning, or it might share only some of the same meanings. For example, a German speaker might think that **announce** has all the same meanings as the German word '*annoncieren*', but the definition and examples show that it does not.

announce (*obj*) /ə'naʊnts/ *v* to state or make known, esp. publicly • *They announced the death of their mother in the local paper.*[T] • *She announced the winner of the competition* **to** *an excited audience.*[T] • *The Prime Minister has announced* **that** *public spending will be increased next year.* [+ *that* clause] • (*fig.*) *The first few leaves in the gutter announced* (= showed) *the beginning of autumn.*[T] • (*Am*) If you announce **for** the PRESIDENCY or another political position, you intend to be a CANDIDATE in an election.[I]
(D)

(2) At the end of the examples there is a special **false friend symbol** for your language. For most languages the letters in the symbol are the same as the letters on the nationality sign for cars from that country. In the example, 'D' means the word is a false friend for speakers of German.

(3) A German reader now knows that **announce** is a false friend: '*annoncieren*' has an additional meaning other than 'announce'. But what is the English word for this additional meaning? The lists of false friends give this type of information. To find the list for your language, look in the dictionary at the page for the letter(s) in the symbol. For example, German false friends are listed at 'D'.

GERMAN FALSE FRIENDS

actual *adj*	aktuell	relevant, topical, fashionable
afterthought *n*	Nachdenken	reflection, meditation, thought
all day *adj*	alltäglich	daily, common, ordinary
allure *n*	Allüren	behaviour, affectations, airs
also *adv*	also	so, thus, in that
announce *v*	annoncieren	to advertise
become *v*	bekommen	to obtain, receive, get
benzene *n*	Benzin	petrol, gasoline
blank *adj*	blank	shiny, bright, clean

(4) Look for the English word that you know is a false friend. The similar word in your own language is given next to it. This is followed by the English word(s) with the other meaning(s) that you want to know. In the example, the list tells you that **advertise** is the other important meaning of '*annoncieren*'.

advertise (*obj*) /'æd·və·taɪz, $-vɚ-/ *v* to make (something) known generally or in public, esp. in order to sell it • *We decided to advertise our car* (= to publish a description of it together with the price we wanted for it) *in the local newspaper.*[T] • *He advertises his services on the company noticeboard.*[T] • *I'm going to advertise* **for** (= put a notice in the newspaper, local shop, etc., asking for) *someone to clean my house.*[I] • *The extended news bulletin means that the remainder of this evening's programmes will be running twenty minutes later than advertised.*[T] • *He has always advertised* (= made generally known) *his willingness to talk to the press.*[T] • *There's no harm in applying for other jobs but if I were you I wouldn't advertise the fact* (= make it generally known) *at work.*[T]

(5) You can now find the correct English word in the dictionary and look at the definition and examples. A German reader now knows when to use 'announce' and when to use 'advertise'. They can now avoid mistakes such as 'Martha announced her bicycle in the paper but no-one wanted to buy it' (*advertise* is the correct word).

False friend symbols and languages

The list of false friends for a language can be found in the dictionary at the letters in the symbol.

CS	Czech	333	F	French	491	KOR	Korean	788	PL	Polish	1073
D	German	343	GR	Greek	616	N	Norwegian	936	RUS	Russian	1244
DK	Danish	404	I	Italian	699	NL	Dutch	957	S	Swedish	1246
E	Spanish	435	J	Japanese	758	P	Portuguese	1015	T	Thai	1484

fancy. • If you are **(footloose and) fancy-free**, you are free to do whatever you like, esp. because you are not in love with anyone. • *(dated disapproving)* A **fancy man/woman** is a lover.

fan·ci·er /£'fænt·si·əʳ, $-ɚ/ *n* [C] • A fancier is someone who has an interest in and breeds a particular plant or animal: *a pigeon fancier*

fan·cy *obj* [IMAGINE] /'fænt·si/ *v* [T] to imagine or think that something is so • *(Br) I fancy that if we attempted such a thing, we would be unlikely to achieve it.* [+ (*that*) clause] • *(Br) I fancied I saw something moving in the corner.* [+ (*that*) clause] • *When she was young she fancied herself* (= she imagined that she was) *a rebel.* [+ obj + n] • *Dick really fancies himself* **as** *a singer, but he's useless.* [+ obj + *as* n/adj] • *Who do you fancy* **to** *win the Cup this year?* [+ obj + *to* infinitive] • *Fancy (him) saying that to you of all people* (= how surprising that he should do that)*!* [+ obj + v-*ing*] • *"She has fifteen children."* **"Fancy!/Fancy that!"** (= How surprising!). • *(Br dated) This isn't the first time this has happened, I fancy* (= I think). [+ (*that*) clause]

fan·cy /'fænt·si/ *n* [U] • A **flight of** fancy is an idea that cannot be made real: *Buildings should not just be architects' flights of fancy.* • *"Tell me where is fancy bred ...in the heart or in the head?"* (Shakespeare, Merchant of Venice 3.2)

fan·ci·ful /'fænt·sɪ·fᵊl/ *adj* • *He has some fanciful notion* (= not based on reality) *about building a flying boat.*

fan·ci·ful·ly /'fænt·sɪ·fᵊl·i/ *adv*

fan·cy [DECORATIVE] /'fænt·si/ *adj* **-ier, -iest** decorative or complicated, or (of restaurants, shops, etc.) very expensive • *I wanted a simple black dress, nothing fancy.* • *Never mind all these fancy phrases – just tell us the plain facts.* • *We stayed in a fancy* (= expensive) *hotel near the Champs-Élysées.* • *(fig. infml) The Prime Minister showed some fancy* **footwork** (= clever avoidance) *in not answering the question.* • *(esp. Br and Aus)* **Fancy dress** (*Am usually* **costume, masquerade**) is what you wear for a party where everyone dresses in special clothes as a particular type of character or thing: *They came to the fancy-dress* **party** *dressed as two policewomen.*

fan·dan·go /£fæn'dæŋ·gəʊ, $-goʊ/ *n* [C] *pl* **fandangos** a fast Spanish dance performed by a man and a woman dancing close together

fan·fare /£'fæn·feəʳ, $-fer/ *n* [C] a loud short piece of music played, usually on a TRUMPET, to introduce the arrival of someone important or a special event • *"Fanfare for the Common Man"* (title of a piece by Aaron Copland, 1942)

fang /fæŋ/ *n* [C] a long sharp tooth • *The dog growled and bared its fangs.*

fan·light /'fæn·laɪt/, *Am usually* **tran·som (win·dow)** *n* [C] a small window over the top of a door • *Dublin is famed for its beautiful Georgian doors and fanlights.* • PIC **Doors**

fan·ny /'fæn·i/ *n* [C] *taboo (Br and Aus)* a woman's sexual organs or *(Am and Aus)* a person's bottom • **Fanny pack** is *Am for* BUMBAG. • PIC **Bags**

fan·ta·si·a /fæn'teɪ·zi·ə/ *n* [C] a piece of music with no fixed form, or one consisting of well-known tunes

fan·tas·tic [GOOD] /fæn'tæs·tɪk/ *adj infml* very good • *You look fantastic in that outfit!* • *They've won a holiday? Fantastic!*

fan·tas·ti·cally /fæn'tæs·tɪ·kli/ *adv* • *We were treated fantastically* (= extremely well) *by our hosts.*

fan·tas·tic [NOT REAL] /fæn'tæs·tɪk/, **fan·tas·ti·cal** /fæn'tæs·tɪ·kᵊl/ *adj* strange and imaginary, or not reasonable • *He drew fantastic animals with two heads and large wings.* • *(fig.) It seemed fantastic that they still remembered her 50 years later.* • *These plans of yours are quite fantastic – they can never work.* • *He wrote novels and fantastical tales* (= about imaginary things).

fan·tas·ti·cally /fæn'tæs·tɪ·kli/ *adv* • *We saw fantastically painted cycle rickshaws* (= painted with imagined things).

fan·tas·tic [LARGE] /fæn'tæs·tɪk/ *adj* (of an amount) very large • *She must be earning a fantastic amount of money.*

fan·tas·ti·cally /fæn'tæs·tɪ·kli/ *adv* • *Her husband is fantastically* (= extremely) *arrogant.*

fan·tas·y /'fæn·tə·si/ *n* a pleasant situation that you enjoy thinking about, but which is unlikely to happen, or the activity of thinking itself • *Steve's favourite fantasy was* **about** *owning a big house and a flashy car.* [C] • *He looked so respectable, but she couldn't help wondering what his private* **sexual** *fantasies might be.* [C] • *She retreated into a world of fantasy where she could be anything she wanted.* [U] • (DK) (E) (NL)

fan·tas·ist /'fæn·tə·sɪst/ *n* [C] • *A few years ago only a wishful fantasist would have imagined that the Berlin Wall would come down so suddenly.*

fan·tas·ize, *Br and Aus usually* **-ise** /'fæn·tə·saɪz/ *v* • To fantasize is to think about something very pleasant that is unlikely to happen: *He fantasized* **about** *winning the Nobel Prize.* [I] ○ *As a child Emma fantasized* **that** *she would do something heroic.* [+ *that* clause] • (DK)

fan·zine /'fæn·ziːn/ *n* [C] a magazine written by admirers of a sports team, musicians, etc., for other people with the same special interest • See also FAN [ADMIRER].

far [DISTANCE] /£fɑːʳ, $fɑːr/ *adv* **farther** /£'fɑː·ðəʳ, $'fɑːr·ðɚ/ or **further** /£'fɜː·ðəʳ, $'fɜːr·ðɚ/, **farthest** /£'fɑː·ðɪst, $'fɑːr-/ or **furthest** /£'fɜː·ðɪst, $'fɜːr-/ at, to or from a great distance in space or time • *How far is it* **from** *Australia to New Zealand?* • *One day, perhaps far in the future, you'll regret what you've done.* • *"Shall we walk to the station?" "How far* **away** *is it?"* • *She doesn't live far* **from** *here.* • *(fml) He felt lonely and far* (= a long way) **from** *home.* • *(fig.) Jane's a very talented writer – she'll* **go** *far* (= will be successful). • *(fig.) Sometimes you* **go too** *far* (= do something unacceptable) *and say hurtful things.* • *He isn't coming today,* **as/so far as** *I know* (= I believe that this is true). • *She can come whenever she likes,* **as/so far as** *I'm concerned* (= that is my opinion, which other people might not share). • *There's been no change,* **as/so far as** *I can tell* (= I have not noticed any change). • *I wouldn't trust him* **as far as I could throw** *him* (= I don't trust him at all). • *It's a good essay* **as far as it goes** (= it has good qualities but it could be improved). • *We were* **far from** *happy with the situation* (= we were not happy). • *Jim, selfish?* **Far from it** (= The truth is very different)*! He's terribly generous.* • **Far be it from me to** *advise you what to do* (= I certainly would not want to do this). • *People came* **from far and wide** (= from a large number of places) *to see the house.* • *Only one of the escaped prisoners has been captured* **so far** (= until now). • *I found a tin of beans in the cupboard.* **So far so good** (= Things were going well up to now), *but where is the opener?* • Something that is **far-fetched** seems very unlikely to be true, and is difficult to believe: *Their claim to have invented a solar-powered car seems far-fetched.* • A **far-flung** place is a great distance away, and **far-flung** connections are spread over a very large area: *The news spread quickly to all corners of their far-flung empire.* • Someone or something that is **far-gone** is in an advanced state of something considered to be unpleasant: *After three whiskies he was so far-gone* (= very drunk) *that he could hardly walk.* • A time that is **far-off** is a long way from the present, in the past or the future, and **far-off** places are a great distance away. • *(infml) They had some* **far-out** (= strange and unusual) *ideas about everyone living in communes.* • *(dated slang) You got the job?* **Far-out** (= Very good)*!* • Something **far-reaching** has a great influence on many people or things: *These new laws will have far-reaching benefits for all working mothers.* • *(fig. Br and Aus)* Someone who is **far-sighted** is able to see what will be needed in the future and make wise decisions based on this: *Buying shares in Ford all those years ago was a very far-sighted move – they must be worth ten times their original value now.* • *(Am and Aus)* **Far-sighted** (*Br* **long-sighted**) can also refer to people who have problems seeing things which are close to them: *I'm so far-sighted I can't* *read the newspaper without my glasses.* • *"Far from the Madding Crowd"* (title of a book by Thomas Hardy in 1874, taken from the poem *Elegy in a Country Churchyard* by Thomas Gray) • See also INSOFAR AS. • LP› **Eye and seeing, Measurements**

far /£fɑːʳ, $fɑːr/ *adj* **farther** /£'fɑː·ðəʳ, $'fɑːr·ðɚ/ or **further** /£'fɜː·ðəʳ, $'fɜːr·ðɚ/, **farthest** /£'fɑː·ðɪst, $'fɑːr-/ or **furthest** /£'fɜː·ðɪst, $'fɜːr-/ • *"Let's walk back." "Is it far* (=very distant), *because my feet are hurting?"* • *The children ran to the far* (=more distant) *side of the room.* • Supporters of the far **left** or far **right** have the most extreme views in these groups. • *This flat is* **a far cry from** *the house they had before* (=it is completely different from it). • The **Far East** is the countries of East Asia, including China, Japan, N and S Korea and Indonesia. Compare **Middle East** at MIDDLE. • LP› **World regions**

far AMOUNT /£fɑːʳ, $fɑːr/ *adv* [not gradable] very much • *This car is far better than our old one.* • *It cost far more money than I could afford.* • *He loses his temper far* **too** *often.* • *They are* **by** *far*/*far* **and away** (= by a great amount) *the best students in the class.* • *I'd far* **rather/sooner** *go to the theatre than watch a video.* • *(Br) I'd far* **prefer** *to go with you.* • *"It is a far, far better thing that I do, than I have ever done"* (from the novel *A Tale of Two Cities* by Charles Dickens, 1859) • LP› **Very, completely**

far·a·way /£ˌfɑː·rə'weɪ, £'---, $ˌfɑːr·ə-/ *adj* [before n; not gradable] distant • *They travelled to faraway lands.* • If a person has a faraway expression, it looks as if they are thinking about something very far from where you are: *He had a faraway look in his eyes.*

farce PLAY /£fɑːs, $fɑːrs/ *n* a humorous play or film where the characters become involved in unlikely situations, or the style of writing or acting in this type of play • *It's a farce about a man with two pregnant wives.* [C] • *The play changes from farce to tragedy.* [U] • GR

farce SITUATION /£fɑːs, $fɑːrs/ *n disapproving* a ridiculous or meaningless situation or action • *The meeting turned out to be a farce since no one had prepared anything.* • GR

far·ci·cal /£'fɑː·sɪ·kᵊl, $'fɑːr-/ *adj disapproving* • *This is all getting a trifle farcical* (= silly).

far·ci·cal·ly /£'fɑː·sɪ·kli, $'fɑːr-/ *adv disapproving* • *The authorities are farcically inept.*

fare PAYMENT /£feəʳ, $fer/ *n* [C] the money that you pay for a journey on a vehicle such as a bus or train • *Train fares are going up again, unfortunately.* • A fare is also someone who pays to be driven somewhere in a TAXI: *Taxis arrived outside the station to wait for fares.* • Ⓘ

fare MANAGE /£feəʳ, $fer/ *v* [I always + adv/prep] *slightly dated* to succeed or be treated in the stated way • *How did you fare in your exams?* • *Low-paid workers will fare* **badly/well** *under this government.* • Ⓘ

fare FOOD /£feəʳ, $fer/ *n* [U] *slightly dated* (in a restaurant) the type of food that is served • *It's a pub that serves traditional British fare.* • Ⓘ

fare·well /£ˌfeə'wel, $ˌfer-/ *exclamation, n fml* goodbye • *Farewell! I will never see you again!* • *We* **said** *our farewells to our dear friends.* [C] • **Bidding** *us both* **fond** *farewells, they left.* [C] • LP› **Meeting someone**

farm /£fɑːm, $fɑːrm/ *n* [C] an area of land, together with house and buildings, used for growing crops and keeping animals to be sold • *Small farms are being taken over and turned into golf courses.* • *We bought fresh farm produce in the market.* • *Farm* **workers** *often have to work very long days.* • A farm can also be a place where the stated type of animal is raised in large numbers to be sold: *a fish farm* ○ *a mink farm*

farm *obj* /£fɑːm, $fɑːrm/ *v* [T] • *Their family have farmed this land* (=used it for growing crops and raising animals to sell) *for a hundred years.*

farm·er /£'fɑː·məʳ, $'fɑːr·mɚ/ *n* [C] • A farmer is a person who owns or takes care of a farm: *Farmer Giles lives up on the hill.*

farm·ing /£'fɑː·mɪŋ, $'fɑːr-/ *n* [U] • *Sheep farming* (= the activity of raising and selling sheep) *is a major business in Australia and New Zealand.*

farm out *obj*, **farm** *obj* **out** *v adv* [M] to give (work or children) to other people to do or take care of • *Magazines often farm out articles* **to** *freelance journalists.* • *Almost since birth their baby has been farmed out* **to** *nannies and nurseries.*

farm·hand /£'fɑːm·hænd, $'fɑːrm-/ *n* [C] a person who is paid by a farmer to work on a farm

farm·house HOUSE /£'fɑːm·haʊs, $'fɑːrm-/ *n* [C] *pl* **farmhouses** /£'fɑːmˌhaʊ·zɪz, $'fɑːrm-/ the main house on a farm where the farmer lives • PIC› **Farming**

farm·house FOOD /£'fɑːm·haʊs, $'fɑːrm-/ *adj* [before n; not gradable] (esp. of cheese) made in a traditional way, (as if) on a farm • *farmhouse cheddar*

farm·land /£'fɑːm·lænd, $'fɑːrm-/ *n* [U] land that is used for or is suitable for farming • *a house set in rolling farmland*

farm·stead /£'fɑːm·sted, $'fɑːrm-/ *n* [C] *Am* the house belonging to a farm and the buildings around it

farm·yard /£'fɑːm·jɑːd, $'fɑːrm·jɑːrd/, *Am usually* **barn·yard** *n* [C] an area surrounded by or near farm buildings • *farmyard smells* • *Hens and a pet sheep wandered about the farmyard.* • PIC› **Farming**

far·ra·go /£fə'rɑː·gəʊ, $-goʊ/ *n* [C] *pl* **farragos** or *Am* **farragoes** *disapproving* a confused mixture • *He accused them of telling a farrago* **of** *lies.* • *This play is an incoherent farrago.*

far·ri·er /'fær·i·əʳ, $-ɚ/ *n* [C] *specialized* a person who makes and fits metal plates for horses' feet

fart GAS /£fɑːt, $fɑːrt/ *v* [I] *taboo* to allow gas from the bowels to escape through the bottom, esp. loudly

fart /£fɑːt, $fɑːrt/ *n* [C] *taboo* • A fart is an escape of gas from the bowels.

fart PERSON /£fɑːt, $fɑːrt/ *n* [C] *slightly taboo slang* an unpleasant person • *He's a pompous* **old** *fart.*

fart a·bout/a·round *v adv* [I] *Br taboo* to waste time doing silly or useless things • *I wish you'd stop farting about and help me tidy up.*

far·ther /£'fɑː·ðəʳ, $'fɑːr·ðɚ/ *adv, comparative of* FAR DISTANCE; to a greater distance • *How much farther is it to the airport?* • *I can't see any farther than about ten metres because of the fog.* • *Now that they live farther away we don't see them so often.* • See Usage note at FURTHER GREATER DISTANCE.

far·ther /'fɑː·ðəʳ, $'fɑːr·ðɚ/ *adj* • *It was farther than I expected to the shops.* • *Birds from farther north appeared in the garden.* • *He swam to the farther side of the lake.*

far·thest /£'fɑː·ðɪst, $'fɑːr-/ *adv, superlative of* FAR DISTANCE • *What's the farthest you've ever run in your life?* • See Usage note at FURTHEST.

far·thest /'fɑː·ðɪst, 'fɑː-/ *adj* • *The farthest landmark visible is about thirty kilometres away.*

far·thing /£'fɑː·ðɪŋ, $'fɑːr-/ *n* [C] a coin worth a quarter of a PENNY in old British money

fas·cia /'feɪ·ʃə/ *n* [C] *Br dated for* DASHBOARD

fas·ci·nate *obj* /'fæs·ɪ·neɪt/ *v* [T] to have (someone's) complete interest and attention • *Anything to do with aeroplanes and flying fascinates him.* • *I was fascinated by/with her stories.*

fas·ci·nat·ed /£'fæs·ɪ·neɪ·tɪd, $-t̬ɪd/ *adj* • *She watched, fascinated, as the glass fell and shattered.* • *I was fascinated* **to** *hear the story of his travels in Bhután.* [+ *to* infinitive]

fas·ci·nat·ing /£'fæs·ɪ·neɪ·tɪŋ, $-t̬ɪŋ/ *adj* • *The book offers a fascinating glimpse of the lives of the rich and famous.* • **It** *was fascinating* **to** *watch the glass being made.* [+ *to* infinitive]

fas·ci·na·tion /ˌfæs·ɪ'neɪ·ʃᵊn/ *n* [U] • *Miller's fascination* **with** *medieval art dates from her childhood.* • *Mass murders* **hold** *a gruesome fascination* **for** *the public.*

fas·cism /'fæʃ·ɪ·zᵊm/ *n* [U] a political system based on a very powerful leader, state control and extreme pride in country and race, and in which political opposition is not allowed • *Mussolini played a key role in the rise of fascism in Italy in the 1920s.*

fas·cist /'fæʃ·ɪst/, **fas·cis·tic** /fæʃ'ɪs·tɪk/ *adj* [not gradable] • *Democratic leaders in Europe are worried by the rise of fascist groups.*

fas·cist /'fæʃ·ɪst/ *n* [C] • *He left Germany when the fascists took over.* • *(disapproving)* A person of the far RIGHT in politics, or who does not allow any opposition, is sometimes called a fascist: *He reckons all policemen are fascists and bullies.*

fash·ion CLOTHING /'fæʃ·ᵊn/ *n* a style that is popular at a particular time, esp. in clothes, hair, make-up, etc. • *Long, curly hair is* **the** *fashion*/**in** *fashion this summer.* [U] • *Are good manners going* **out of** *fashion?* [U] • *For women in the 1920s,* **it** *was* **the fashion** *to wear the hair short.* [U + *to* infinitive] • *The programme has features on pop music, sport and fashion.* [U] • *She's mad on clothes, and buys all the fashion magazines.* • *Museums should not just cater for* **the latest** *fashion, but have more long-term aims.* [C] • *Owners of fierce dogs are often just* **following** *a fashion*

(= doing what is popular at the time). [C] • *He spends a lot of money on clothes – he's very* **fashion-conscious** (= aware of what clothes are considered as stylish). • A **fashion victim** is someone who is always buying new clothes because they think they must wear the type of clothes that are popular. • LP> **Shopping goods**

fash·ion·ab·le /ˈfæʃ·ən·ə·bl/ *adj* • *a fashionable young man* • *a fashionable night club* • *fashionable ideas* • **It's** *not fashionable* **to** *wear short skirts at the moment.* [+ to infinitive] • *A fashionable couple* (= those wearing clothes that are in fashion) *posed elegantly at the next table.* • *She created a strong female image in films long before it was fashionable* (= before it was popular to do this).

fash·ion·ab·ly /ˈfæʃ·ən·ə·bli/ *adv* • *fashionably dressed*

fash·ion [MANNER] /ˈfæʃ·ən/ *n* [U] a way of doing things • *The rebel army behaved in a brutal fashion.* • *She held the fork in her right hand, American fashion* (= as Americans do). • *I can cook,* **after a** *fashion* (= but not very well).

fash·ion *obj* [MAKE] /ˈfæʃ·ən/ *v* [T] *fml* to make (something) using your hands • *She fashioned hats for them* **out of** *newspapers.* • *(fig.) They are trying to fashion a new approach to teaching English.*

fast [QUICK] /£fɑːst, $fæst/ *adj* **-er, -est** moving or happening quickly or able to move or happen quickly • *They like fast cars and expensive restaurants.* • *The fast train* (= one that stops at fewer stations and travels quickly) *to London takes less than an hour.* • If your watch or clock is fast, it is in advance of the real time. • A fast film in a camera is able to take pictures when there is not much light. • *The action in the last scene of the film is* **fast and furious** (= full of speed and excitement). • **Fast food** is hot food that is already prepared and so is served quickly. • The **fast lane** on a MOTORWAY is the outside part of it where vehicles can travel at the fastest speed: *(fig.) Life* **in the** *fast lane* (= A risky and competitive way of living) *had taken its toll on him by the time he was 30.* • A **fast link** is a road or railway that allows you to travel directly and quickly between two or more places. • The **fast track** is the quickest, but usually most competitive, route to success or advancement: *A degree in computer science offers a fast track to the top/fast-track opportunities.* • LP> **Measurements** PIC> **Motorway** (DK) (P)

fast /£fɑːst, $fæst/ *adv* **-er, -est** • *The accident was caused by people driving too fast in bad conditions.* • *This type of rural village is disappearing fast.* • *The number of flights in and out of the airport is fast approaching saturation point.* • *Children's publishing is a fast-growing business.* • *He scuttled back into the house* **as fast as** *his* **legs would carry** *him* (= as quickly as possible). • The **fast-forward** on a **cassette recorder** or **video recorder** is a device that allows you to move quickly to the end of a CASSETTE (= magnetic strip used to record music or film): *Press the fast-forward.* ○ *I'll just* **fast-forward** *the tape to the end.* • *(esp. Am disapproving) He* **fast-talked** *his way into a powerful job* (= He got the job by persuading people, usually in a dishonest way). • *(disapproving)* A **fast-talker** is someone who is good at persuading people to do what he or she wants.

fast [FIXED] /£fɑːst, $fæst/ *adv, adj* [not gradable] firmly fixed • *The glue had set and my hand was* **stuck** *fast* (= it could not be moved). • **Make** *the rope fast to a tree before you climb down.* • *(fig.) The rebels are* **standing** *fast* (= will not be moved) *and refuse to be defeated.* • Fast colours are ones where the colour does not come out of the cloth when washed. • Someone who is **fast asleep** is sleeping very deeply. • (DK) (P)

fast·ness /£ˈfɑːst·nəs, $ˈfæst-/ *n* [U] • *Before washing, test clothes for* **colour** *fastness* (= the ability of the colour not to come out of the cloth when washed).

fast [NOT EAT] /£fɑːst, $fæst/ *v, n* (to have) a period of time when you eat no food • *Hundreds of prisoners have begun a fast in protest about prison conditions.* [C] • *He is fasting for a week for religious reasons.* [I] • See also BREAKFAST. • (DK) (P)

fast [BAD] /£fɑːst, $fæst/ *adj* **-er, -est** *dated disapproving* considered to be without any moral principles • *a fast crowd* • *a fast woman* • *a fast way of life* • (DK) (P)

fast·ball /£ˈfɑːst·bɔːl, $ˈfæst·bɑːl/ *n* [C] *Am* a type of high-speed throw in baseball • *The pitcher wound up and let loose a fastball.*

fas·ten *(obj)* /£ˈfɑː·sən, $ˈfæs·ən/ *v* to make or become firmly fixed together or in position, or closed • *Make sure your seat belt is securely fastened.* [T] • *This shirt fastens at the back.* [I] • *I fastened the sticker* **to** *the windscreen.* [T] • *The tabloid newspapers have* **fastened on** *popular psychology* (= have suddenly taken a great interest in this). • (D) (S)

fas·ten·er /£ˈfɑːs·ən·ər, $ˈfæs·ən·ɚ/ *n* [C] • A fastener is a button, ZIP or other device for firmly fixing together the separate parts of something, esp. clothes. • LP› **Dressing and undressing** Ⓙ

fas·ten·ing /£'fɑː·sᵊn·ɪŋ, £'fɑːs·nɪŋ, $'fæs-/ *n* [C] • A fastening on a window, door, box, etc. is a device for keeping it closed.

fas·tid·i·ous /fæs'tɪd·i·əs/ *adj* difficult to please and giving too much attention to small details, or having a strong dislike of anything dirty or unpleasant • *He is very fastidious* **about** *how a suitcase should be packed.* • *They were too fastidious to eat in a fast-food restaurant.* • *She's so fastidious that she cleans her teeth after every meal.*

fas·tid·i·ous·ly /fæs'tɪd·i·ə·sli/ *adv* • *She stared fastidiously at the dirty table.*

fas·tid·i·ous·ness /fæs'tɪd·i·ə·snəs/ *n* [U]

fast·ness /£'fɑːst·nəs, $'fæst-/ *n* [C] *literary* a safe place, such as a FORTRESS • *a mountain fastness*

fat BIG /fæt/ *adj* **fatter, fattest** having a lot of flesh on the body • *Her weight's normal, but she thinks she's fat.* • *I wish I didn't have such fat thighs.* • *The story of her life would fill a few fat* (= thick) *volumes.* • *Some producers of mineral water have made fat* (= very large) *profits.* • *(esp. Am infml)* A **fat cat** is someone who is very rich and has a lot of influence. • *"Who's your fat friend?"* (Beau Brummel talking about the Prince of Wales, 1813) • *"Inside every fat man is a thin one trying to get out (originally 'Imprisoned in every fat man is a thin one wildly signalling to be let out')"* (Cyril Connolly in the book *The Unquiet Grave*, 1944) • *"The opera ain't over until the fat lady sings* (= it is not over yet)*"* (saying created by Dan Cook, 1975) • Ⓟ

fat·ness /'fæt·nəs/ *n* [U] • *Fatness* (= the state of being fat) *often runs in families.*

fat·ten *obj* /£'fæt·ᵊn, $'fæt̬-/ *v* [T] • To fatten an animal or *(humorous)* a person is to feed more food to them because you want them to be heavier or fatter: *These cattle are being fattened* **(up)** *before being sold.* ○ *My mum gives me so much food I think she wants to fatten me* **up**. [M]

fat·ten·ing /£'fæt·ᵊn·ɪŋ, $'fæt̬-/ *adj* • Food which is fattening contains a lot of fat, sugar, etc. that would quickly make you fatter if you ate a lot of it: *I don't eat much chocolate any more – it's too fattening.*

fat·ty /£'fæt·i, $'fæt̬-/, **fat·so** *n* [C] *infml disapproving or humorous* • A fatty is a person who is (too) fat: *Come on fatty, can't you run any faster?* [as form of address] ○ *Good news for fatties – this new no-exercise, no-diet regime will change your life permanently.*

fat SUBSTANCE /fæt/ *n* the substance under the skin of humans and animals that stores energy and keeps them warm, or a solid or liquid substance obtained from animals or plants and used esp. in cooking • *An unusually thick layer of fat in the man's body had prevented him from dying of cold.* [U] • *This product contains no animal fat.* [U] • *Doctors recommend the use of vegetable fats in cooking.* [C] • If someone is living off **the fat of the land**, they are rich enough to enjoy the best of everything. • *(infml)* If you say that **the fat is in the fire**, you mean that something has been said or done that will cause a lot of trouble. • **Fat-free** foods are ones without any fats in them. • *"Fat is a Feminist Issue"* (title of a book by Susie Orbach, 1978) • *"Ye shall eat the fat of the land"* (Bible, Genesis 45.18) • Ⓟ

fat·ty /£'fæt·i, $'fæt̬-/ *adj* **-ier, -iest** • *The ham in the sandwiches was too fatty* (= contained too much fat) *for her.* • A **fatty acid** is any of a group of chemicals, most of which are involved in cell operation in the body.

fat NO /fæt/ *adj* [before n; not gradable] *infml* very little or none at all • *"Perhaps they'll invite you." "Fat* **chance** *of that!"* • *A fat* **lot** *of use you are* (= You are not useful in any way)*!* • *He knows how much trouble it causes, but a fat* **lot** *he cares* (= he doesn't care at all). • Ⓟ

fa·tal /£'feɪ·tᵊl, $-t̬ᵊl/ *adj* [not gradable] very serious and having an important bad effect in the future or (of illness, accidents, etc.) causing death • *He made the fatal mistake of believing what they told him.* • **It's** *fatal* **to** *say how well she's playing – she's bound to make a mistake.* [+ *to* infinitive] • *This illness is in almost all cases fatal.* • *"Fatal Attraction"* (film title, 1987) • Ⓓ (PL)

fa·tal·ly /£'feɪ·tᵊl·i, $-t̬ᵊl·i/ *adv* [not gradable] • *Several people were injured, two fatally* (= they died as a result). • Ⓘ

fa·tal·i·ty /£fə'tæl·ə·ti, $-t̬i/ *n* [C] • A fatality is a death caused by an accident or by violence, or a person who has died in either of these ways: *Britain has thousands of road fatalities* (= deaths on roads) *every year.* ○ *The first fatalities of the war have been (among) civilians.* • Ⓟ

fat·al·i·sm /£'feɪ·tᵊl·ɪ·zᵊm, $-t̬ᵊl-/ *n* [U] the belief that people cannot change the way events will happen and that esp. bad events cannot be avoided

fat·al·ist /£'feɪ·tᵊl·ɪst, $-t̬ᵊl-/ *n* [C] • *If you are a fatalist, what can you do about it?*

fat·al·is·tic /£ˌfeɪ·tᵊl'ɪs·tɪk, $-t̬ᵊl-/ *adj* • *Being fatalistic about your chances will do no good.*

fat·al·is·ti·cal·ly /£ˌfeɪ·tᵊl'ɪs·tɪ·kli, $-t̬ᵊl-/ *adv*

fate /feɪt/ *n* [C usually sing] the things that happen to a particular person or thing, esp. something final or negative, such as death or defeat • *We demand the right to vote and* **decide** *our own fate.* • *British companies are trying to avoid the fate that has already* **befallen** *their American counterparts.* • If you say that something is, or would be, **a fate worse than death**, you mean that it is something you do not want to experience because it is so unpleasant, boring, etc.: *A week with my Aunt would be a fate worse than death.* • Fate is also a power that is considered to cause and control all events, so that people cannot change or control the way things will happen: *When we met again by chance in Cairo, she said "It must be fate."* ○ *It seemed that a trip to France was what Fate* **had in store** *for me* (= was what was certain to happen next). • **The Fates** were three goddesses whom the ancient Greeks believed controlled people's lives and decided when people must die.

fat·ed /£'feɪ·tɪd, $-t̬ɪd/ *adj* [after v; not gradable] • *We fell in love immediately and it seemed fated* **that** *we would get married.* [+ *that* clause] • *She seemed fated* **to** *become a writer* (= it seemed planned by a power that controls events and was therefore not avoidable). [+ *to* infinitive]

fate·ful /'feɪt·fᵊl/ *adj* • A fateful day/decision/step is one that is very important because of its, often negative, effect on the future: *the fateful day of President Kennedy's assassination* ○ *I well remember that fateful day we met.*

fat·head /'fæt·hed/ *n* [C] *infml* a stupid person

fat·head·ed /'fæt·hed·ɪd, -'--/ *adj infml*

fa·ther PARENT /£'fɑː·ðəʳ, $-ðɚ/ *n* [C] a male parent • *My father used to take me to watch the football every Saturday.* • *She had a child when she was 15, but she never told her family who the father was.* • *(slightly fml) Can we go and stay with Auntie Doris in New York please, father/Father?* [as form of address] • *The puppies looked just like the neighbour's dog, so we assumed it was the father.* • If you describe a man as the father of something, you mean that he began it, or first made it important: *Freud was the father of psychiatry.* ○ *George Washington was the father of his country.* • *(esp. Br)* **Father Christmas** is SANTA CLAUS. • A **father figure** is an esp. older man whom you treat as a father by asking for their advice, help or support. • **(Old) Father Time** is an image of an old man who represents time going past. • *"And when did you last see your father?"* (title of a painting by W.F.Yeames, 1878) • LP› **Titles and forms of address** PIC› **Family tree**

fa·ther *obj* /£'fɑː·ðəʳ, $-ðɚ/ *v* [T] • To father a child is to become the father of a child by making a woman pregnant: *He's never been married, but he's fathered at least three children.*

fa·ther·hood /£'fɑː·ðə·hʊd, $-ðɚ-/ *n* [U] • *Fatherhood is a lifelong responsibility.*

fa·ther–in–law /£'fɑː·ðəʳ·ɪn·lɔː, $-ðɚ·ɪn·lɑː/ *n* [C] *pl* **fathers-in-law** /£'fɑː·ðəz-, $-ðɚ·ɪn·lɑːz/ or *Br also* **father-in-laws** • Someone's father-in-law is the father of the person they are married to.

fa·ther·less /£'fɑː·ðə·ləs, $-ðɚ-/ *adj* [not gradable] • *I had a fatherless childhood, because my mother never remarried after my father died.*

fa·ther·ly /£'fɑː·ðᵊl·i, $-ðɚ·li/ *adj* • *He keeps giving me ridiculous fatherly warnings* (= those coming from a father) *about going out late at night.* • *He was fatherly* (= kind and caring) *towards the little boy.*

Fa·ther PRIEST /£'fɑː·ðəʳ, $-ðɚ/ *n* [C] (the title of) a Christian priest, esp. a Roman Catholic or Orthodox priest • *Father O'Reilly* • *Are you giving a sermon, Father?* [as form of address] • Father is also a name for the Christian God: *I believe in God the Father.* • *"In my Father's house are many mansions"* (Bible, John 14.2)

fa·ther·land /£'fɑː·ðə·lænd, $-ðɚ-/, **moth·er·land**, **moth·er coun·try** *n* [U] the country in which you are born or the country with which you are spiritually or historically connected • *People often talk of the fatherland when they feel that their country is under threat from an external power.*

fath·om MEASUREMENT /'fæð·əm/ *n* [C] a unit of measurement of the depth of water • *A fathom is a depth of* six feet or 1·8 metres. • The channel into the harbour is twenty fathoms (deep).

fath·om·less /ˈfæð·əm·ləs/ *adj esp. literary* • *a fathomless* (= too deep to be measured) *ocean* • *(fig.) Paula gazed into the fathomless* **depths** *of his perfect blue eyes.*

fath·om *obj* UNDERSTAND /ˈfæð·əm/ *v* [T] to discover the meaning of • *Professor Hake has been trying to fathom* **(out)** *the mysteries of the whale's song.* [M] • *I can't fathom her* (= I do not understand her or why she acts as she does).

fath·om·less /ˈfæð·əm·ləs/ *adj* • *I'm afraid it's a fathomless* (= impossible to understand) *mystery.*

fa·tigue /fəˈtiːg/ *n* [U] *fml* extreme tiredness, or *(specialized)* weakness in something such as a metal part or structure, often caused by repeated bending • *Increasing numbers of people in high-powered jobs are* **suffering from** *fatigue and stress-related illnesses.* • *(humorous)* If someone has **compassion** fatigue, they feel that they have done enough already, and do not want to do any more to help people in a worse situation than themselves: *After making donations for earthquake relief, famine relief and war relief, even the most generous donors are beginning to suffer compassion fatigue.* • *(specialized) The crash was caused by* **metal** *fatigue* (= repeated pressure in opposite directions) *in one of the propeller blades.* • Ⓟ

fa·tigue *(obj)* /fəˈtiːg/ *v fml* • *When there is little to do, the work feels even more fatiguing.* [I]

fa·tigues /fəˈtiːgz/ *pl n specialized* the brownish green uniform worn esp. by soldiers when doing work such as cleaning or cooking, or when fighting • *The young burglar in the back of the police car was wearing a mask and dirty army fatigues.*

fat·ness /ˈfæt·nəs/ *n* [U] See at FAT BIG

fat·so /£ˈfæt·səʊ, $-soʊ/ *n* [C] *infml disapproving or humorous* a **fatty**, see at FAT BIG

fat·ted /£ˈfæt·ɪd, $ˈfæt̬-/ *adj* **kill the fatted calf**, see at KILL

fat·ten *obj* /£ˈfæt·ən, $ˈfæt̬-/ *v* [T] See at FAT BIG

fat·u·ous /ˈfæt·ju·əs/ *adj fml* stupid, not correct or not carefully thought about • *a fatuous person/idea/remark* • *He made some sort of fatuous suggestion about standing on a chair to do it.*

fat·u·ous·ly /ˈfæt·ju·ə·sli/ *adv fml*

fat·u·i·ty /£fəˈtjuː·ə·ti, $fəˈtuː·ə·t̬i/, **fat·u·ous·ness** /ˈfæt·ju·ə·snəs/ *n* [U] *fml*

fat·wa /ˈfæt·wɑː/ *n* [C] an official statement or order from an Islamic religious leader • *The death sentence was issued in the form of a fatwa, or religious decree.*

fau·cet /£ˈfɔː·sɪt, $ˈfɑː-/ *n* [C] *Am for* TAP DEVICE • PIC **Bathroom**

fault MISTAKE /£fɒlt, $fɑːlt/ *n* a mistake, esp. something for which you are to blame, or (esp. in a person's character or a machine) a weakness or broken part • *"Whose fault was the crash?" "Well, it wasn't mine!"* [U] • *Profits are down and the fault* **is/lies in** *bad management.* [U] • *The fault* **was/lay with** *the organizers, who failed to make the necessary arrangements for dealing with so many people.* [U] • **Through no** *fault* **of** *his* **own** *he spent a week in jail after the police mistakenly arrested him.* [U] • *I've found a couple of faults* **in** *the instruction booklet.* [C] • *He's got many faults* (= weaknesses), *but dishonesty isn't one of them.* [C] • **Despite (all)/For all/With all** *its faults* (= weaknesses), *our transport system is better than that in many other countries.* [C] • *Don't touch it if you think it's got an electrical fault* (= broken part). [C] • *I can't phone my Dad – there seems to be a fault* **on the line** (= the connection between the two telephones is not working). [C] • In tennis and other similar games, a fault is a mistake made when hitting the ball over the net in order to begin a game. [C] • *Her doctor was* **at fault** (= was wrong) *in not sending her straight to a specialist.* • To **find fault with** something or someone is to criticize or complain even about small mistakes: *It's depressing to have someone always finding fault with your work.* • If you say that someone is generous/kind/etc. **to a fault**, you mean that they are extremely generous/kind/etc.: *Generous to a fault, she took all her friends out for a lavish dinner.*

fault *obj* /£fɒlt, $fɑːlt/ *v* [T usually in negatives] • *Daniel couldn't fault* (= could find nothing to criticize in) *her/her arguments.* • *I can't fault you* **on** *your logic.* • *That's the fourth serve he's faulted* **on** (= made a mistake in hitting) *today.*

fault·less /£ˈfɒlt·ləs, $ˈfɑːlt-/ *adj approving* • Something that is faultless is perfect and without any mistakes: *a faultless performance* ○ *speaking faultless French*

fault·less·ly /£ˈfɒlt·lə·sli, $ˈfɑːlt-/ *adv*

faul·ty /£ˈfɒl·ti, $ˈfɑːl·t̬i/ *adj* **-ier, -iest** • A faulty machine or device is not perfectly made or not working correctly: *I think it's the ignition that is faulty.*

fault CRACK /£fɒlt, $fɑːlt/ *n* [C] *specialized* a crack in the Earth's surface where the rock has divided into two parts which move against each other • A **fault line** is a line of weakness in the rocks of the Earth's surface, where an EARTHQUAKE is most likely to happen. • A **fault line** within a society, a political party or another organization is a division or disagreement within it that divides it into different groups: *The party is still divided* **along** *the same fault lines that split it in the past.*

faun /£fɔːn, $fɑːn/ *n* [C] an imaginary creature which is like a small man with a goat's back legs, tail, ears and horns

fau·na /£ˈfɔː·nə, $ˈfɑː-/ *n* [U + sing/pl v] *specialized or literary* all the animals that live wild in a particular area • *She took part in an expedition to explore and describe the* **flora and** *fauna of Hornchurch Wood.*

faux pas /£ˌfəʊˈpɑː, $ˌfoʊ-/ *n* [C] *pl* **faux pas** words or behaviour that are a social mistake or not polite • *I realized I'd* **committed/made** *a serious faux pas by joking about his wife's family.*

fave /feɪv/ *n, adj* [not gradable] *infml for* FAVOURITE • *"Does anyone want a sweet?" "Ooh thanks, they're my faves."* [C]

fa·vour SUPPORT *Br and Aus, Am and Aus* **fa·vor** /£ˈfeɪ·vəʳ, $-vɚ/ *n* [U] support or approval of something or someone • *These plans are unlikely to* **find** *favour* **(with** *the management) unless the cost is reduced.* • *The Council has voted/decided/come down/come out* **in** *favour* **of** *a £200 million housing development.* • *Workers have rejected a pay offer of 8%* **in** *favour* **of** *a 4% increase linked with a shorter working week* (= they have accepted the second instead of the first). • *She is* **out of/in** *favour* (= unpopular/popular) **(with** *her colleagues) at the moment.* • *Her economic theories are* **out of/in** *favour* **(with** *the current government)* (= disagreed with/agreed with by the present government). • If something is **in** someone's **favour**, it gives them an advantage: *It was less tiring running on the way back, because we had the wind in our favour.* ○ *She has a lot in her favour, especially her experience of teaching.* • If someone speaks or makes a judgment **in** someone's or something's **favour**, they state their support or say that they are not guilty: *The jury* **found** *in his favour and awarded him $400 compensation.* • *He kept sending her presents in a vain attempt to* **win** *her favour* (= approval).

fa·vour *obj Br and Aus, Am and Aus* **fa·vor** /£ˈfeɪ·vəʳ, $-vɚ/ *v* [T] • *In the survey, a majority of people favoured* (= supported and wanted) *higher taxes and better public services, rather than tax cuts.* • *Personally, I favour* (= prefer) *travelling by night when the roads are quiet.* [+ v-ing] • *A strong wind will favour* (= give an advantage to) *the bigger boats.* • *He has this annoying habit of favouring the women* (= treating them better than the men) *when he gives out work.* • *(fml or humorous) I'm afraid I can't tell you what is happening because Alfred has not* **favoured me with** (= given me) *any explanation either.*

favourable *Br and Aus, Am and Aus* **fa·vor·able** /£ˈfeɪ·vər·ə·bl̩, $-vɚ-/ *adj* • *People's reactions to the proposal have been very favourable* (= they have liked it). • *We have had a favourable response to* (= an answer expressing approval) *of the plan so far.* • *She made a favourable impression on me* (= I liked her) *when I first met her.* • *We ought to set sail soon, while the weather is still favourable* (= to our advantage).

fa·vour·ab·ly *Br and Aus, Am and Aus* **fa·vor·ab·ly** /£ˈfeɪ·vər·ə·bli, $-vɚ-/ *adv* • *She impressed me rather favourably* (= well) *at the interview.* • *Our products* **compare** *favourably with* (= are as good as, or better than) *all the leading brands.*

fa·voured *Br and Aus, Am and Aus* **fa·vored** /£ˈfeɪ·vəd, $-vɚd/ *adj*

fa·vour KIND ACT *Br and Aus, Am and Aus* **fa·vor** /£ˈfeɪ·vəʳ, $-vɚ/ *n* [C] a kind action that you do for someone • *She rang up to* **ask** *me a favour, but I told her I'll be away all this month.* • *Could you* **do** *me a favour – would you lend me your pink dress for this evening?* • *(infml) "Why don't you tell the police what happened?" "Oh,* **do me a favour** (= that is a ridiculous and impossible suggestion)*!"* • *Several elected politicians have been accused of* **dispensing** *favours* (= giving money, power, etc.) *to people who voted for them.* •

(AM) He handed out the **party** *favors* (=small presents given to guests at a party) *as we were leaving.* • *(dated)* A person's **favours** is their willingness to have sex: *She has the reputation of being rather* **free with** *her favours* (=of being willing to have sexual relationships with lots of people).

fa·vour·ite *Br and Aus, Am and Aus* **fa·vor·ite** /ˈfeɪ·vᵊr·ɪt/ *adj* [before n; not gradable] best liked or most enjoyed • *"What's your favourite colour?" "Green."* • *Oh, this is one of my favourite restaurants/books/songs.*

fa·vour·ite *Br and Aus, Am and Aus* **fa·vor·ite** /ˈfeɪ·vᵊr·ɪt/ *n* [C] • *"Which is your favourite?" "The little picture of apples and pears in a bowl."* • *How clever of you to buy chocolate chip cookies – they're my favourites.* • *Brazil are favourites* **to** *win this year's World Cup.* [+ *to* infinitive] • A person who is a favourite of someone in authority is treated with special kindness by them. • *Great Gold is* **(the)** *favourite in* (=the one expected to win) *the 2.00 race at Epsom.*

fa·vour·i·ti·sm *Br and Aus, Am and Aus* **fa·vor·i·ti·sm** /ˈfeɪ·vᵊr·ɪ·tɪ·zᵊm/ *n* [U] *disapproving* • Favouritism is unfair support shown to one person or group, esp. by someone in authority: *The BBC is careful not to* **show** *favouritism* **towards** *any one political party.*

fawn DEER /£fɔːn, $fɑːn/ *n* [C] a young deer

fawn BROWN /£fɔːn, $fɑːn/ *adj, n* [U] **-er, -est** (having) a pale yellowish brown colour

fawn PRAISE /£fɔːn, $fɑːn/ *v* [I always + prep] *disapproving* to praise too much and give a lot of attention which is not sincere to someone, esp. in order to get a positive reaction • *The journalists all fawn* **on/upon** *her like she's some sort of queen.* • *They are mostly ambitious local politicians willing to fawn* **over** *anyone with money and influence.* • If an animal such as a dog fawns **on/upon** you, it is very friendly towards you and rubs itself against your legs and jumps up at you. • If you fawn **over** someone or something, you praise them a lot and show a lot of attention to them: *I hate it when those girls start fawning over the baby.*

fawn·ing /£fɔː·nɪŋ, $fɑː-/ *adj* [not gradable] *disapproving* • *a fawning young man* • *a fawning film review*

fax /fæks/ *v, n* (to send) a copy of a document that travels in electronic form along a telephone line and is then printed on paper, and which arrives in a few seconds • *I'll fax it (through/over/across)* **to** *you.* [T] • *Fax me your reply/Fax your reply* **to** *me* (=send your answer to me). [+ two objects] • *I'll send you a fax with the details of the proposal.* [C] • A **fax (machine)** is the device used to send and receive documents in electronic form along a telephone line: *I'll send you the agenda* **by** *fax.* • PIC› **Office**

faze *obj* /feɪz/ *v* [T usually passive; not *be fazing*] *esp. Am and Aus infml* to surprise and worry (someone) • *No one is fazed by the sight of guns here – life has become cheap in the ghetto.*

FBI /ˌef·biːˈaɪ/ *n* [U] **the FBI** *abbreviation for* the Federal Bureau of Investigation (=one of the national police forces in the US controlled by the central government)

fe·ar /£fɪəʳ, $fɪr/ *n* an unpleasant emotion or thought that you have when you are frightened or worried by something dangerous, painful, unpleasant or bad that is happening or might happen • *Trembling with fear, she handed over the money to the gunman.* [U] • *Even when the boat was rocked by bigger waves, the boy showed no (signs of) fear.* [U] • *I can't go up the tower with you because I have* **a** *fear* **of** *heights.* [U] • *She has* **a** *fear* **of going** *out in the dark.* [U] • *There is a fear among government MPs* **that** *tax increases will prove very unpopular.* [C + *that* clause] • *The low profit figures simply confirmed my* **worst** *fears.* [C] • *The climbers are a day late in coming down from the mountain and the authorities are beginning to* **have fears for** (=are very worried about) *their safety.* • *Lakisha sat inside,* **in fear of her life** (=frightened that she might be killed) *until the police came.* • *They wouldn't let their cat run around outside* **for fear that** (=because they were worried that) *it would get run over by a car.* • *Malcolm knows the city well, so* **there isn't any fear of/there's no fear of** *us getting lost* (=we will not get lost). • If something or someone **puts the fear of God into/in** you, they frighten you a lot. • *(Br and Aus slang) "Are you going to come to the concert with me?"* "**No fear** (=No, certainly not)!" • *The appointments are supposed to be made* **without fear or favour** (=in an equal and fair way). • *"The only thing we have to fear is fear itself"* (speech by President F.D.Roosevelt, 1933) • *"Fear and Loathing in Las Vegas"* (title of a book by Hunter S. Thompson, 1971)

fe·ar *(obj)* /£fɪəʳ, $fɪr/ *v* [not *be fearing*] • *What do you fear most?* [T] • *He wouldn't say anything to the Press because he feared* **being** *misreported.* [+ v-*ing*] • *Fearing* (=Being afraid) **to** *go herself, she sent her son to find out the news.* [+ *to* infinitive] • *(fml) Do you ever fear* **for** (=are you ever worried about) *your children/your children's safety?* [I] • *(fml) I fear* (=I think it likely) **(that)** *few passengers can have survived the crash.* [+ (*that*) clause] • *(fml)* If you say you fear that something bad has happened or might happen, you mean you are sorry that you have to give this bad news: *I fear* **(that)** *your train has already left.* [+ (*that*) clause] • *(dated fml) "Sometimes I worry about Jason."* "**Never fear/Fear not** (=Do not worry). *I will take good care of him."*

fe·ar·ful /£ˈfɪə·fᵊl, $ˈfɪr-/ *adj slightly literary* • *He hesitated before ringing her, fearful* **of** (=frightened about) *what she might say.* • *I get the feeling he's fearful* **of** (=unwilling and frightened of) *committing himself to a real relationship.* • *She's fearful* (=worried) **(that)** *she may lose custody of her children.* [+ (*that*) clause] • *(dated)* If you say that something bad is fearful, you mean that it is very bad: *There was a fearful argument when he demanded his money back.*

fe·ar·ful·ly /£ˈfɪə·fᵊl·i, $ˈfɪr-/ *adv* • *Fearfully, he walked closer to the edge.* • *(dated) These cakes are fearfully* (=extremely) *good.*

fe·ar·ful·ness /£ˈfɪə·fᵊl·nəs, $ˈfɪr-/ *n* [U]

fe·ar·less /£ˈfɪə·ləs, $ˈfɪr-/ *adj* • *She was a fearless* (=not frightened) *and outspoken woman who condemned all violence.*

fe·ar·less·ly /£ˈfɪə·lə·sli, $ˈfɪr-/ *adv* • *They fought fearlessly against the invading armies.*

fe·ar·less·ness /£ˈfɪə·lə·snəs, $ˈfɪr-/ *n* [U]

fe·ar·some /£ˈfɪə·səm, $ˈfɪr-/ *adj fml or humorous* • Fearsome means causing fear: *a fearsome reputation as a disciplinarian* ○ *a fearsome display of violence* ○ *fearsome chemical weapons*

fe·ar·some·ly /£ˈfɪə·səm·li, $ˈfɪr-/ *adv*

fea·si·ble /ˈfiː·zə·bl̩/ *adj slightly fml* able to be made, done or achieved; possible or reasonable • *Now that we have the extra resources, the scheme seems politically/financially/technically feasible.* • *The Government wants a 3% inflation rate, but is this a feasible objective?* • **It's** *quite feasible* (=possible) **(that)** *we'll get the money.* [+ (*that*) clause]

fea·si·bly /ˈfiː·zə·bli/ *adv slightly fml* • *He has already hurt two people and therefore he could quite feasibly attack someone else, perhaps more viciously.*

fea·si·bil·i·ty /£ˌfiː·zəˈbɪl·ɪ·ti, $-ə·t̬i/ *n* [U] • *We're studying the feasibility of building a new shopping centre outside town.* • *The council is making/doing a* **feasibility study** (=examining the situation to decide about the possibility) *of/on the shopping centre proposals.*

feast FOOD /fiːst/ *n* [C] a special meal with very good food or a large meal for many people • *"What a feast!" she said, as she surveyed the dishes on the table.* • *(fig.) The new art gallery is a visual feast/a feast* **for the eyes** (=is very enjoyable to look at). • *(fig.) The new art gallery contains a feast* **of** *good paintings* (=a lot of paintings that are very enjoyable to look at). • (DK) (N) (NL)

feast /fiːst/ *v* [I] • To feast **on/off** a particular food, esp. a special or very good food, is to eat a lot of it: *We feasted off smoked salmon and champagne.* • If you **feast** your **eyes (up)on** something or someone, you look at them with great enjoyment: *She feasted her eyes on the gorgeous display of exotic fruit.*

feast CELEBRATION /fiːst/ *n* [C] a day on which a religious event or person is remembered and celebrated • *the Feast of St James/the Passover* • *a Muslim feast day* • (DK) (N) (NL)

feat /fiːt/ *n* [C] something difficult needing a lot of skill, strength, bravery, etc. to achieve it • *The backward dive from such a great height was quite a feat.* • *She has performed remarkable feats of organization for the office.* • *Getting the job finished in under a week was* **no mean** *feat* (=was a great achievement).

feath·er /£ˈfeð·əʳ, $-ɚ/ *n* [C] one of the many very light objects with hair-like material along each side of a long thin central part which cover a bird's body • *a brightly coloured peacock feather* • *The bird* **ruffled** *its feathers.* • *I like to have feather* **pillows** (=those containing feathers) *on my bed.* • *She was wearing a feather* **boa** (=long thin decorative piece of clothing, worn around the neck by women). • *(fig.) Delicate feathers* (=light hair-like lines) *of* *ice covered the metal framework* • *The little baby rabbit was* **(as) light as a feather** (= very light) *in her hand.* • *If they win both races, it will be a real* **feather in** *their* **cap** (= an achievement to be proud of). • A **feather duster** is a stick with feathers fixed to one end, used for cleaning dust esp. from delicate objects.

feath·er *obj* /£'feð·əʳ, $-ɚ/ *v* [T] • *(esp. disapproving)* Someone who **feathers** their **(own) nest** makes themselves rich, esp. selfishly or dishonestly. • *(specialized)* If you feather your **oars** (= poles with flat ends used to move a boat), you turn them so that the flat parts are horizontal above the water while you prepare for the next pull.

feath·ered /£'feð·əd, $-ɚd/ *adj* [not gradable] • *(humorous) our* **feathered friends** (= birds)

feath·er·y /£'feð·ᵊr·i, $-ɚ·i/ *adj* • *feathery* (= soft or delicate) *leaves/clouds/ice-crystals*

feath·er·bed *obj* /£ˌfeð·ə'bed, $-ɚ'-/ *v* [T] **-dd-** *disapproving* to protect (people, esp. workers, or something such as a company) too much and make things easy for them • If a government featherbeds an industry, it gives it a lot of help, such as lower taxes, esp. so that jobs will not be lost.

feath·er·bed·ding /£ˌfeð·ə'bed·ɪŋ, $-ɚ'-/ *n* [U] • *The featherbedding of inefficient companies will lead to disaster.*

feath·er·brained /£'feð·ə·breɪnd, $'-ɚ-/ *adj slightly dated infml* silly or forgetful

feath·er·weight /£'feð·ə·weɪt, $'-ɚ-/ *n* [C] a boxer who weighs more than a BANTAMWEIGHT but less than a LIGHTWEIGHT

fea·ture QUALITY /£'fiː·tʃəʳ, $-tʃɚ/ *n* [C] an esp. typical quality or important part • *One of the key features* **of** *the deal is the £30 million from government funds.* • *High stress levels are a feature* **of life** (= a part of the situation that is not avoidable) *for business executives.* • A feature can also be a part of a building or an area of land: *The most obvious landscape feature south of the river is the volcano and its crater lake.*

fea·ture *(obj)* /£'fiː·tʃəʳ, $-tʃɚ/ *v slightly fml* • *A really good salary features highest/lowest* (= is the most/least important item) *on her list of what she wants from a job.* [I always + adv/prep] • *The film features* (= includes as a special performer) *James Dean as a disaffected teenager.* [T] • *This week's broadcast features* (= includes as a special item) *a report on victims of domestic violence.* [T] • *It's an Australian company whose logo features* (= shows) *a red kangaroo.* [T]

fea·ture·less /£'fiː·tʃə·ləs, $-tʃɚ-/ *adj* • Something, esp. an area of land, that is featureless looks the same everywhere and is usually considered uninteresting: *a featureless desert* ○ *a succession of featureless suburbs* ○ *(fig.) a featureless* (= boring) *Cup Final game*

fea·tures /£'fiː·tʃəz, $-tʃɚz/ *pl n* • Your features are the parts of your face: *He has wonderful strong features.* ○ *She has very regular* (= even and attractive) *features.* • The features of a place are its physical characteristics or the things you can do there: *When you think of Switzerland's features, you think of mountains.*

fea·ture ARTICLE /£'fiː·tʃəʳ, $-tʃɚ/ *n* [C] a special article in a newspaper or magazine about a particular, subject, usually not the news, or a part of a television or radio broadcast that deals with a particular subject • *There's a very informative feature* **(article) on** *AIDS in today's paper.*

fea·ture (film) /£'fiː·tʃəʳ, $-tʃɚ/ *n* [C] a film that is usually 90 or more minutes long

fea·ture–length /£'fiː·tʃə·leŋkθ, $-tʃɚ-/ *adj* [not gradable] • A feature-length film or broadcast is usually 90 or more minutes long.

feb·rile /£'fiː·braɪl, $'feb·rɪl/ *adj literary* extremely active; almost too excited, imaginative or emotional • *Share prices tumbled on a febrile British stock exchange.* • *She sang with febrile intensity.*

Feb·ru·ar·y /£'feb·ru·ᵊr·i, £-ruːr-, $'feb·ruː·er·i/ (*abbreviation* **Feb**) *n* the second month of the year, after January and before March • *28(th) February/February 28(th)/28(th) Feb/Feb 28(th)* [U] • *I was born* **on** *the fifth of February/February the fifth/(esp. Am) February fifth.* [U] • *I started this job* **last** *February/am starting a new job* **next** *February.* [U] • *Work on the new building is expected to start sometime* **in/during** *February.* [U] • *It was one of those dull, cold Februaries that seem to last forever.* [C] • LP› **Dates**

fe·ces /'fiː·siːz/ *pl n esp. Am fml* FAECES

feck·less /'fek·ləs/ *adj fml* (of people or their behaviour) without energy and enthusiasm • *In those days he was a feckless and poverty-stricken young drop-out.*

fec·und /'fek·ənd, -kʌnd/ *adj fml* able to produce a lot of crops, fruit, babies, young animals, etc.; FERTILE REPRODUCTION • *a fecund pig/field* • *(fig.) a fecund imagination*

fe·cund·i·ty /£fe'kʌn·də·ti, $-ṭi/ *n* [U] *fml*

fed FEED /fed/ *past simple and past participle of* FEED

Fed OFFICER /fed/ *n* [C] *Am infml* a police officer or other representative of the central government • *The Feds completely screwed up the arrest.*

fed·er·a·tion /£ˌfed·ᵊr'eɪ·ʃᵊn, $-ə'reɪ-/ *n* a group of regions or STATES united with a central government which has control over some things such as defence, but with each region having its own local government and laws, or the act of forming such a group • *The United States is a federation of 50 individual states.* [C] • *The Federation of the six original Australian states took place in 1901.* [C] • *He's against European federation* (= the joining together of a group of regions). [U]

fed·er·al /£'fed·ᵊr·ᵊl, $-ɚ·ᵊl/ *adj* [not gradable] • *a federal system* • *a federal republic* • *The proposal must be acceptable at both the state and federal levels.* • *The central federal government decides federal taxes and laws for all the areas within the federation.* • See also FBI.

fed·er·al·i·sm /£'fed·ᵊr·ᵊl·ɪ·zᵊm, $'-ɚ-/ *n* [U] • *She's a great believer in federalism* (= the system of giving power to a central authority).

fed·er·al·ist /£'fed·ᵊr·ᵊl·ɪst, $'-ɚ-/ *n* [C] • A federalist is someone who believes that a federation is a good system of government.

fed·er·ate *(obj)* /£'fed·ᵊr·eɪt, $-ə·reɪt/ *v* [T/I]

fed·o·ra /£fə'dɔː·rə, $-'dɔːr·ə/ *n* [C] a man's hat, like a TRILBY but with a wider BRIM (= edge around the bottom), worn esp. in the first half of the 20th century in the US • *I like to think I look like Humphrey Bogart when I wear my fedora.* • PIC› **Hats**

fed up /ˌfed'ʌp/ *adj infml* bored, annoyed or disappointed, esp. by something that you have experienced for too long • *Tiffany says she's totally fed up – she's going to give up this awful job and move back to New York.* • *Are you fed up* **about** *not getting the job?* • *(esp. Br and Aus) I'm fed up* **to the back teeth** (= very fed up) **with/of** *being criticized by people who know nothing about my work.*

fee /fiː/ *n* [C] an amount of money paid for a particular piece of work or for a particular right or service • *doctors'/lawyers'/legal fees* • *a $30 fee for providing the information* • *an entrance/registration/licence/consultancy fee* • *(Br and Aus)* A **fee-paying** school is a school where parents pay the school directly for their children's education.

fee·ble /'fiː·bl/ *adj* **-r, -st** weak; without energy, strength or power, or not effective or good • *a feeble, helpless old man* • *The little lamp gave only a feeble light.* • *The opposition to the plan has been rather feeble.* • *Martin told me a really feeble* **joke.** • *She had another feeble* **excuse** *for being late.* • Someone who is **feeble-minded** has less than ordinary intelligence or behaves stupidly and without thinking: *Some feeble-minded idiot thought it was funny to put salt in the sugar bowl.*

fee·bly /'fiː·bli/ *adv* • *The dog whimpered feebly and held up its injured paw.* • *Feebly written and directed, this is one film everybody can afford to miss.*

feed *(obj)* GIVE FOOD /fiːd/ *v past* **fed** /fed/ to give food to, or (of an animal or baby) to eat • *I was too tired to lift the spoon, so he took it from me and fed me mouthful by mouthful.* [T] • *I think it's disgusting that some chickens are fed meat/that meat is fed* **to** *some chickens.* [+ two objects] • *If you feed your dog* **on** (= give him only) *cakes and biscuits, it's not surprising he's so fat.* [T] • *When I was a boy I loved to feed the ducks* **with** *bits of bread/feed bread* **to** *the ducks.* [T] • *This amount of pasta is not going to feed* (= be enough food for) *ten people.* [T] • *If agriculture were given priority, the country would easily be able to feed* **itself** (= produce enough food for its people). [T] • *Most babies can feed* (= give food to) **themselves** *by the time they're a year old.* [T] • *The baby only feeds* (= eats) *once a night at the moment, thank goodness.* [I] • If you feed a person or animal **up**, you make them healthier or fatter by giving them lots of food. [M] • If you feed a plant, you give it substances that will help it grow. [T] • *(fig.) Why don't you feed the fire* **with** *some of the big logs* (= put some on the fire)*?* [T] • If something **feeds off/on** something else, it increases because of it: *Fascism feeds off poverty.* • If someone is **fed to the lions**, they are forced to do something unpleasant or dangerous that they do not want to do. • *Tea-time in our house is like* **feeding time at the zoo** (= very noisy and not under control)*!*

feed /fiːd/ *n* • *The baby had a feed* (= was fed) *an hour ago, so she can't be hungry.* [C] • Feed is food eaten by animals: *bags of cattle/animal feed* [U] • *(infml)* A feed is also a meal: *I could do with a decent feed.* [C] • See also CHICKENFEED.

feed·er /£ˈfiː·dəʳ, $ˈfiː·dɚ/ *n* [C] • *a messy/noisy/slow/picky feeder* (= eater) • A feeder is a BIB (= something that is used to cover the clothes of very young children when feeding them).

feed *obj* PUT /fiːd/ *v* [T always + adv/prep] *past* **fed** /fed/ to put (into), or supply, esp. continually • *Feed the string* **through** *the hole and then tie a knot in it.* • *The vegetables are fed* **into** *the machine at one end and soup comes out the other.* • *The images are being fed* **over** *satellite networks to broadcasters throughout the world.* • *Several small streams feed* **into** (= join) *the river near here.* • *The editor admitted that a secretary of the princess had been feeding the newspaper information on her whereabouts/feeding information on her whereabouts* **to** *the newspaper.* [+ two objects] • If you **feed someone a line**, you give them a false explanation or story which allows you to obtain some advantage: *The journalist got her story by feeding the manager a line about being on government business.*

feed /fiːd/ *n* [C] • The feed in a machine is the part through which it is supplied with fuel, or through which something which is operated by the machine is supplied to it: *a blockage in the car's oil feed/the printer's paper feed*

feed·er /£ˈfiː·dəʳ, $ˈfiː·dɚ/ *n* [C] • A feeder road/air route/school/company is one that leads to or supplies a larger one.

feed·back OPINION /ˈfiːd·bæk/ *n* [U] information or statements of opinion about something, such as a new product, that provide an idea of whether it is successful or liked • *The feedback from the customers who have tried the new soap is very positive.*

feed·back RETURN /ˈfiːd·bæk/ *n* [U] the return of part of what a machine or system produces back into the machine or system, esp. to improve what is produced, or the sudden, high, unpleasant noise sometimes produced by an AMPLIFIER when sound it produces is put back into it • *Feedback* **from** *the sensors ensures that the car engine runs smoothly.* • *Jimi Hendrix loved to fling his guitar around to get weird and wonderful sounds from the feedback.*

feed·bag /ˈfiːd·bæg/ *n* [C] *Am for* NOSEBAG

feel *(obj)* EXPERIENCE /fiːl/ *v past* **felt** /felt/ to experience (something physical or emotional) • *"How are you feeling?" "Oh, not so bad – I've still got a slight headache."* [L] • *How would you feel about moving to a different city?* [L] • *He's still feeling a bit weak after his operation.* [L] • *I feel so hungry all the time – I don't know what's wrong with me.* [L] • *My eyes feel really sore with all this smoke.* [L] • *I think he feels a bit annoyed that he wasn't told at the time of the schedule change.* [L] • *I never feel safe when I'm being driven by Richard.* [L] • *Never in her life had she felt so happy.* [L] • *I feel so helpless – I just don't know what to do.* [L] • *After carrying his bags for some time, they began to feel heavy.* [L] • *Robin just didn't feel up to arguing about walking the dog again.* [L] • *I felt* (= thought that I was) *a right idiot when I sat on the cat.* [L] • *She saw me fall flat on my face – I feel* (= think that I am) *such a fool.* [L] • *I really felt my* **age** (= became aware that I am no longer young) *last night – I was in a night-club where almost everybody was under twenty.* [L] • *He felt* (= experienced) *her hot breath on his neck and nearly fainted.* [T] • *I could feel* (= experience) *the drops of sweat trickling down my back.* [T + obj + v-ing] • *I felt* (= experienced) *something snap inside my knee, and I just collapsed to the ground.* [T + obj + infinitive without *to*] • *"Did it hurt?" "Not at all – I didn't feel* **a thing** (= was not aware of anything)*."* [T] • *By mid-day we'd really begun to feel* (= suffer from) *the heat.* [T] • Someone who feels **the cold** (a lot) gets cold quicker and more often than most people: *As you get older, you tend to feel the cold more.* [T] • If you feel **for** someone, you experience sympathy and sadness for them because they are suffering: *I know what it's like to be lonely, so I do feel for her.* [I] • If someone tells you to **feel free** to do something, they are telling you that you can do that thing if you wish to: *Do feel free to help yourself to coffee.* • *It's going to be a good summer – I can* **feel it in** *my* **bones** (= I strongly believe it although I cannot explain why). • *"Did you (originally 'thee') feel the earth move?"* (Ernest Hemingway in the book *For Whom the Bell Tolls*, 1940) • LP› **Feelings and pains**

feel·ing /ˈfiː·lɪŋ/ *n* • *What sort of feeling is it – a sharp pain or more of a dull ache?* [C] • *I've got this strange feeling* **in** *my stomach – I think I'm going to be sick.* [C] • *My toes were so cold that I'd lost all feeling in them.* [U] • *The feeling* **of** *loneliness overwhelmed him.* [C] • *Wearing so few clothes gave her a marvellous feeling* **of** *freedom.* [C] • *There's a general feeling* **of** *dissatisfaction with the government.* [C] • *I got the feeling* **that** *I was definitely not welcome.* [C + *that* clause] • *I'd like to complain to the neighbours about the noise but I don't want to cause any* **bad** *(Br) feeling/(Am) feelings.* (= upset them or make them angry). [U/C] • *"Once More with Feeling"* (film title, 1960)

feel·ing·ly /ˈfiː·lɪŋ·li/ *adv* • If you say something feelingly, you say it with deep and sincere emotion: *"I've just had enough!" she said feelingly.*

feel·ings /ˈfiː·lɪŋz/ *pl n* • Your feelings are your emotions, especially as influenced by other people: *I didn't tell him what she'd said about him – I wanted to* **spare** *his feelings* (= not to upset him). ○ *Some people say that dogs have feelings.* • If you **hurt** someone's feelings, you upset them by criticizing them or by refusing something that they have offered you.

feel *(obj)* TOUCH /fiːl/ *v past* **felt** /felt/ to touch (something) in order to discover something about it • *He ran his fingers gently down the baby's cheek, feeling the softness of her skin.* [T] • *Just feel* **how** *cold my hands are!* [+ *wh*- word] • *Feel* **(around)** (= search with your hands) *in the bottom of the drawer* **for** *the keys.* [I] • If you feel your **way**, you judge where you are going by touching with your hands instead of looking: *The room was so dark that I had to feel my way* **along** *the wall to get to the door.* [T] ○ *(fig.) She was clearly feeling her way yesterday, as it is the first time she has had to deal with a dispute of this kind.* [T] • *(slang)* To feel someone **up**, esp. someone you do not know, is to

FEELINGS AND PAINS

- **Describing how your body feels as a whole**

Often 'to be' can be used instead of 'feel':

How do you **feel***? / How* **are** *you?*
I feel *okay, thanks.*/**I'm** *okay, thanks.*
They **felt/were** *cold, tired and hungry.*

With some adjectives 'to be' is not normally used, or would change the meaning:

I **feel** *wonderful/great.*
He was **feeling** *terrible/awful/dreadful and couldn't sleep.*
When the plane started to shake **I felt** *dizzy and faint.*

- **Feelings in parts of your body**

In this list the most painful feelings come first.

When I broke my arm it was **agony/agonising/** *terribly* **painful**.
Liz was **in agony/in** *a lot of* **pain** *with a bad tooth.*
I've got a really bad **pain** *in my leg where Chas kicked it.*
My back **hurts** *a lot every time I bend down.*
I burned my hand and it feels/is **sore**.
Cheryl has got **backache/earache/a headache/(a) toothache/(a) stomach ache**.
My left knee always **aches** *after I play football.*
This soap makes your eyes **sting/smart** *if it gets in them.*
The sun is so hot today, my head is **burning**.
Alcoholic drinks give me a **burning sensation** *in my stomach.*
The kids are **nauseous/feel sick** *when we travel by ship.*
Roy stood up too quickly and felt **dizzy/light-headed**.
After walking nine miles, our legs felt **tired** *and* **heavy**. *Next day we were really* **stiff**.
My arm has **gone to sleep** (= I cannot control or feel it) – *I must have been lying on it.*
This injection will make your lips **numb**.
An insect bit my arm and now it's **itching** – *I must scratch it.*
Her hair fell across her face and **tickled** *her nose.*

touch their sexual organs for your own sexual excitement: *It was the second time that she had been felt up on the Metro and she was angry.* [M]

feel /fiːl/ *n* • *I can't stand the feel of wool* (= the way that it feels). [U] • *She loved the feel of silk against her skin.* [U] • *(esp. Br infml)* A feel can also be the action of touching: *Is that shirt silk? Ooh, let me* **have a** *feel!* [C]

feel·er /£ˈfiː·ləʳ, $-lɚ/ *n* [C usually pl] • An insect's feelers are the two long parts on its head with which it touches things in order to discover what is around it. • To **put out feelers** is to make informal suggestions as a way of testing other people's opinions on a matter before any decisions are made.

feel *obj* OPINION /fiːl/ *v* [T] *past* **felt** /felt/ to have the opinion, or consider • *I feel* **(that)** *I should be doing more to help her.* [+ (*that*) clause] • *I feel* **(that)** *it's very important that everyone is informed about the matter.* [+ (*that*) clause] • *I can't help feeling* **(that)** *she would be happier without him.* [+ (*that*) clause] • *For whatever reason he had always felt* **himself (to be)** *inferior to his brothers.* [+ obj + (*to be*) n/adj]

feel·ing /ˈfiː·lɪŋ/ *n* [C] • *My feeling on this matter is that we had better act quickly or it will be too late.*

feel CHARACTER /fiːl/, **feel·ing** /ˈfiː·lɪŋ/ *n* [U] the character of a place or situation • *They've decorated this bar really well, haven't they – it's got that real Spanish feel* **to** *it.* • *There was* **a** *feel of mystery about the place.* • *We were in the city for such a short time that we didn't really* **get** *the feel* **of** (= get to know) *the place.*

feel UNDERSTANDING /fiːl/, **feel·ing** /ˈfiː·lɪŋ/ *n* [U] a natural understanding or ability, esp. in a subject or activity • *I tried to learn to play the piano but I never really got a feel* **for** *it.* • *She has such great feel* **for** *language that her books are a pleasure to read.* • To **get the feel of** something such as a new activity, is to learn how to do it: *Using a new computer is a bit difficult to begin with but you soon get the feel of it.*

feel like *obj v prep* [T] to have a desire for (something) or to want to do (something) at a particular moment • *I feel like* **(going** *for) a swim – do you want to come?* [(+ v-*ing*)] • *I feel like (hav***ing***) a nice cool glass of lemonade.* [(+ v-*ing*)] • *"Are you coming to aerobics?" "No, I don't feel like* **it** *– I'm being lazy."* • People often say they felt like doing something when they wanted to do it but for some reason did not: *He was so rude I felt like slap***ping** *his stupid face.* [+ v-*ing*]

feel·good /ˈfiːl,gʊd/ *adj* [before n; not gradable] causing happy and positive feelings about life • *the feelgood* **factor** • *Disney can always be relied upon to come up with a decent feelgood* **movie**.

feet /fiːt/ *pl of* FOOT

feign *obj* /feɪn/ *v* [T] *literary* to pretend to feel (esp. an emotion) • *You know how everyone feigns surprise when you tell them how old you are.* • *For the sake of politeness she responded to his remarks with feigned amusement.* • *I don't want to go tonight – I think I shall feign a headache.*

feint *(obj)* /feɪnt/ *v* (esp. in football or boxing) to pretend to move or make (a move) in a particular direction in order to deceive a competitor • *Callas feinted* **to** *pass the ball and then shot it into the net.* [+ *to* infinitive] • *He feinted a shot to the left.* [T] • *He did what a lot of politicians do. He feinted one way and intended to go the other.* [I]

feint /feɪnt/ *n* [C] • *He sent two English players off one way with a feint and then rolled the ball into the opposite corner of the net.*

fei·sty /ˈfaɪ·sti/ *adj* **-ier, -iest** (esp. of people) active, forceful and full of determination • *She was a feisty lady, my grandma, who campaigned vigorously for prison reform well into her seventies.* • *The opposition leader this morning launched a feisty attack on the government in parliament.*

fe·la·fel, fa·la·fel /£fəˈlæf·əl, $-ˈlɑː·fəl/ *n* (an example of) fried balls of spicy food made with CHICKPEAS (= pale brown round seeds) • *Place four felafels (warm or cold) on a bed of green salad, arranging them around the edge of a dish.* [C] • *For lunch we had felafel in hot pitta bread.* [U]

fe·li·ci·ta·tions /fə,lɪs·ɪˈteɪ·ʃənz, fel,ɪs-/ *pl n humorous* an expression used to praise someone and say you approve of or are pleased about something they have done. The more usual way of saying this is CONGRATULATIONS • *May I offer my felicitations on your engagement.*

fe·li·ci·ty HAPPINESS /£fəˈlɪs·ɪ·ti, £felˈɪs-, $-ə·t̬i/ *n* [U] *literary or fml* happiness or luck; a condition which produces positive results • *the dubious felicity of marriage* • *Wealth is for most people a prospect of unimaginable felicity.*

fe·li·ci·ty SUITABILITY /£fəˈlɪs·ɪ·ti, £felˈɪs-, $-ə·t̬i/ *n literary or fml* a word or remark which is suitable or right and expresses well the intended thought or feeling, or (of words or remarks) the quality of being suitable and expressing what was intended • *Her article contained one or two verbal felicities which will stay in my mind for years.* [C] • *As a song-writer he combined great linguistic felicity with an ear for a tune.* [U]

fe·li·ci·tous /£fəˈlɪs·ɪ·təs, £felˈɪs-, $-t̬əs/ *adj literary or fml* • *'Light-weight' may describe his books but it is hardly the most felicitous* (= suitable) *of adjectives for this hunky six-foot novelist.* • *He thanked the retiring director for his contribution, summing up his achievements in one or two felicitous* **phrases**.

fe·li·ci·tous·ly /£fəˈlɪs·ɪ·tə·sli, £felˈɪs-, $-t̬ə-/ *adv literary or fml* • *a felicitously phrased speech*

fe·line /ˈfiː·laɪn/ *adj* belonging to the cat family or, *(esp. approving)*, appearing or behaving like a member of the cat family • *(infml) In this week's issue we take a closer look at our* **feline friends** (= pet cats). • *(approving) She's very feline in the way that she moves.* • *(approving) She's got those long green feline eyes.*

fe·line /ˈfiː·laɪn/ *n* [C] *specialized or fml* • A feline is a member of the cat family: *They have a wild-life park with tigers and various other felines.*

fell FALL /fel/ *past simple of* FALL

fell *obj* CUT DOWN /fel/ *v* [T] to cut down (a tree) or, esp. in sports, to knock (someone) down • *A great number of trees are felled to make new ground for cattle to graze on.* • *The boxer was felled by a punch to the head.* • If you do something **at/with one fell swoop**, you do it all at the same time: *While we've got so many extra hands why don't we move all the books in one fell swoop.*

fel·la·ti·o /£fəˈleɪ·ʃi·əʊ, $-oʊ/ *n* [U], *slang* **blow job** *n* [C] the sexual activity of moving the tongue across or sucking the penis in order to give pleasure and excitement • Compare CUNNILINGUS.

fel·late *obj* /felˈeɪt/ *v* [T] • To fellate a man is to perform fellatio on him.

fel·low MAN /£ˈfel·əʊ, $-oʊ/, **fel·la** /ˈfel·ə/, **fel·ler** /£ˈfel·əʳ, $ˈfel·ɚ/ *n* [C] *infml* a man • *(Br dated)* Fellow was used esp. in the past by people in a higher social class: *He seems a jolly decent sort of a fellow.* ○ *I say, old fellow, where have you been hiding these past few weeks?* • Fella is used in modern English: *There were a couple of fellas leaning up by the bar.* ○ *Hey, fellas! What do girls really like in a guy? Turn to page six to find out.* • Feller is also used in modern English, although less commonly: *I'm an honest sort of a feller – I tend to say what I think.* • *(Br)* Fellow, fella or feller are sometimes used to mean a male sexual partner or BOYFRIEND: *Was she with her fella?* • LP **Age**

fel·low MEMBER /£ˈfel·əʊ, $-oʊ/ *n* [C] a member of a ruling or teaching group of particular colleges or of particular ACADEMIC societies • *Georgia's a fellow of Clare College, Cambridge.* • *Simon's a fellow of the Royal Institute of Chartered Surveyors.*

fel·low SHARED /£ˈfel·əʊ, $-oʊ/ *adj* [before n; not gradable] used of people or a person with whom you share something, for example the same job, a particular interest or experience • *She introduced me to a few of her fellow students.* • *One of my fellow passengers on the train that morning smelt strongly of garlic.* • *This is Anna, a work colleague, or should I say 'fellow sufferer'.* • *Our fellow travellers were mostly Spanish-speaking tourists.* • A **fellow traveller** is someone who agrees with the beliefs of an organization but does not join it: *Fellow travellers who acted as apologists for the Soviet Union were badly treated here.* • **Fellow feeling** is an understanding or sympathy that you feel for another person because you have a shared experience: *There was a fellow feeling between those who had been through the war together.* • Your **fellow men** are people generally: *As a writer he was extremely clever and witty but I don't think he had much love for his fellow men.*

fel·low·ship GROUP /£ˈfel·əʊ·ʃɪp, $-oʊ-/ *n* a group of people or an organization with the same purpose, or *(dated)* a friendly feeling that exists between people who have a shared interest or are doing something as a group • *the Christian fellowship* [U] • *the National Schizophrenia Fellowship* [C] • *the American Fellowship of Reconciliation* [C] • *(dated) He enjoyed the fellowship of other actors in the company.* [U]

fel·low·ship EDUCATION /£ˈfel·əʊ·ʃɪp, $-oʊ-/ *n* [C] the position of a FELLOW MEMBER at a college, or an amount of money that is given to POSTGRADUATES in order to allow them to study a subject at an advanced level • *He's just been* **elected to** *a fellowship at Merton College.* • *She's applied to various foundations for a research fellowship.*

fells /felz/ *pl n Br regional* mountains, hills or other areas of high land, esp. in NW England

fell /fel/ *adj* [before n] *Br regional* • *We went fell walking/running last weekend.*

fel·on·y /ˈfel·ə·ni/ *n Br dated or Am law* (an example of) serious crime which can be punished by one or more years in prison • *a felony charge* • *She pleaded guilty to both felonies.* [C] • *He was convicted of felony.* [U]

fel·on /ˈfel·ən/ *n* [C] *law* • A felon is a person who is guilty of felony.

felt FEEL /felt/ *past simple and past participle of* FEEL

felt CLOTH /felt/ *n* [U] a thick, often firm, cloth made from a pressed mass of wool and hair • *a felt hat* • A **felt-tip (pen)** (*Br also* **fibre-tip (pen)**) is a pen which has a writing point made of felt. • PIC› **Writing instruments**

fem / / *adj abbreviation for* FEMININE GRAMMAR or FEMALE • *In French, the word for cousin has two forms: cousin (masc) and cousine (fem).*

fe·male SEX /ˈfiː·meɪl/ (*abbreviation* **fem**) *adj* [not gradable] (typical) of the sex that can give birth to young or produce eggs • *She was voted the best female vocalist for the second year running.* • *The female lion is smaller than the male and lacks the long brown mane.* • *Do you agree that not being aggressive is a female characteristic?* • In plants and flowers, female refers to a plant which produces flowers which will later develop into fruit. • See also FEMININE FEMALE. Compare MALE SEX. • LP› **Sexist language**

fe·male /ˈfiː·meɪl/ *n* [C] • *Females represent 40% of the country's workforce.* • *You don't see many lone females walking around that area after dark.* • Female is sometimes used to refer to a woman in a way that shows a lack of respect: *It was my third doctor's appointment in two weeks and I think he dismissed me as just a hysterical female.* • *"The female of the species is more deadly than the male"* (from the poem *The Female of the Species* by Rudyard Kipling, 1919)

fe·male·ness /ˈfiː·meɪl·nəs/ *n* [U] • *Deciding not to have children was not, she stressed, a rejection of her femaleness.*

fe·male CONNECTING PART /ˈfiː·meɪl/ *adj* [not gradable] *specialized* (of a piece of equipment) having a hole or space into which another part can be fitted • *a female plug/connector* • Compare MALE CONNECTING PART.

fem·i·dom /£ˈfem·ɪ·dɒm, $-dɑːm/ *n* [C] *Br trademark* a type of CONDOM (=thin rubber covering that prevents pregnancy) which a woman puts in her vagina before having sex

fem·i·nine FEMALE /ˈfem·ɪ·nɪn/ *adj* having qualities which are traditionally considered to be suitable for a woman • *This year the fashion is for long, flowing dresses in feminine flower-prints.* • *He had big eyes with lashes so long they were almost feminine.* • Compare MASCULINE MALE. • LP› **Sexist language**

fem·in·in·i·ty /£ˌfem·əˈnɪn·ɪ·ti, $-ə·t̬i/ *n* [U] *usually approving* • *Long hair has traditionally been regarded as a sign of femininity.*

fem·in·ize *obj*, *Br and Aus usually* **-ise** /ˈfem·ɪ·naɪz/ *v* [T often passive] • If something is feminized, it is is changed so that it either possesses more of the qualities that are traditionally connected with women or is more interesting to and involves more women: *Under a woman editor, the magazine had been feminized, with more articles on women's issues and more female writers.*

fem·in·iz·a·tion, *Br and Aus usually* **-i·sa·tion** /ˌfem·ɪ·naɪˈzeɪ·ʃən/ *n* [U] • *The increase in the number of women in Parliament, she hoped, would bring about the feminization of politics* (= the greater involvement of women in politics).

fem·i·nine GRAMMAR /ˈfem·ɪ·nɪn/ (*abbreviation* **fem**) *adj* [not gradable] (in some languages) belonging to the group of nouns which are not MASCULINE or NEUTER • *In French, is 'table' feminine or masculine?* • In English there are masculine and feminine forms of some nouns, for example actor and actress, but the feminine forms are now being used less often.

fem·in·i·sm /ˈfem·ɪ·nɪ·zəm/ *n* [U] the belief that women should be allowed the same rights, power and chances as men and be treated in the same way, or the set of activities intended to achieve this state • *As a writer she was chiefly noted for her lifelong commitment to feminism.*

fem·in·ist /ˈfem·ɪ·nɪst/ *n* [C] • A feminist is a person who believes in feminism, often being involved in activities that are intended to achieve change: *All her life she was an* **ardent** *feminist.* • Ⓙ

fem·in·ist /ˈfem·ɪ·nɪst/ *adj* [not gradable] • *the feminist movement* • *feminist issues/literature* • *a feminist perspective on Shakespeare's tragedies* • *Her beliefs are strongly feminist.*

femme fa·tale /ˌfæm·fəˈtɑːl/ *n* [C] *pl* **femmes fatales** /ˌfæm·fəˈtɑːl/ (often in films) a woman who is very attractive in a mysterious way, usually leading people into danger or causing their destruction • *With her dark good-looks and slightly wicked charm, she was the femme fatale in many early Hollywood films.*

fe·mur /£ˈfiː·məʳ, $-mɚ/ *n* [C] *pl* **femurs** or **femora** /£ˈfem·ər·ə, $-ɚ·ə/ *specialized* the long bone in the upper part of the leg

fen /fen/ *n* an area of low flat wet land • *This whole area used to be marsh and fen before it was drained.* [U] • *From Cambridge we took the road to Ely which led us immediately to the fens.* [C]

fence STRUCTURE /fents/ *n* [C] a structure which divides two areas of land, similar to a wall but made usually of wood or wire and supported with posts • *He'd built a fence to keep the neighbour's dog out of his precious garden.* • PIC› **Garden**

fence *obj* /fents/ *v* [T] • If you fence **in** an area, you build a fence around it: *She would need to fence in the field if she was to keep a horse there.* [M] • (*fig. disapproving*) *I feel a bit fenced in* (= limited in my activity) *at work because my boss won't let me apply for promotion.* • To fence **off** an area is to separate it with a fence in order to stop people or animals from entering it: *The hill had been fenced off to stop animals grazing on it.* [M] • *"Don't Fence Me In"* (title of a song written by Cole Porter, 1934)

fenc·ing /ˈfent·sɪŋ/ *n* [U] • Fencing is either the materials used to make fences or the fences themselves: *They use fencing around the football ground as a method of crowd control.*

fence FIGHT /fents/ *v* [I] to fight as a sport with a long thin sword • *You wear a protective mask when you fence.*

fen·cer /£ˈfent·səʳ, $-sɚ/ *n* [C] • A fencer is a person who fences as a sport: *Ted is a keen fencer.*

fenc·ing /ˈfent·sɪŋ/ *n* [U] • *a fencing tournament/mask* • *I did a bit of fencing while I was at college.*

fence CRIMINAL /fents/ *n* [C] *dated slang* a person who buys and sells stolen goods

fend for *obj* /fend/ *v prep* [T] to take care of and provide for (yourself), without depending on anyone else • *Now that the children are old enough to fend for them***selves**, *we can go away on holiday alone.*

fend off *obj*, **fend** *obj* **off** /fend/ *v adv* [M] to push or send away (an attacker or other unwanted person), or to avoid answering (questions) which are too difficult to answer • *He managed to fend off his attackers with a stick.* • *She'd spent the entire evening fending off unwanted admirers.* • *Somehow she managed to fend off the awkward questions.*

fend·er FIRE /£ˈfen·dəʳ, $-dɚ/ *n* [C] a low metal frame around an open fireplace which stops the coal or wood from falling out

fend·er CAR /£ˈfen·dəʳ, $-dɚ/ *n* [C] *Am for* WING PART OF CAR or MUDGUARD • PIC› **Bicycles, Car**

fen·nel /ˈfen·əl/ *n* [U] a plant whose large rounded base can be eaten as a vegetable and whose seeds and small pale leaves are used as a herb • PIC› **Herbs and spices, Vegetables**

fen·u·greek /ˈfen·ʊ·griːk/ *n* [U] a plant whose hard yellowish brown seeds are one of the main spices used in Indian cooking

fe·ral /ˈfer·əl/ *adj* [not gradable] (usually of animals) existing in a wild state, esp. after being kept by people • *Feral dogs behave very much like wolves.*

fer·ment (*obj*) CHANGE CHEMICALLY /£fəˈment, £fɜː-, $fɚ-/ *v* to (cause to) change chemically through the action of living substances, such as YEAST or bacteria • *Yoghurt is obtained by fermenting milk with bacteria.* [T] • *You make wine by leaving grape juice to ferment until all the sugar has turned to alcohol.* [I]

fer·men·ta·tion /£ˌfɜː·menˈteɪ·ʃən, $ˌfɜːr-/ *n* [U] • *Sugar is added to the wine during fermentation to increase the alcohol level.*

fer·ment CONFUSION /£ˈfɜː·ment, $ˈfɜːr-/ *n* [U] *fml* a state of confusion and lack of order in which there is much change, fierce arguing or sometimes fighting; UNREST • *Proposed changes to the electoral system have* *caused ferment in Parliament this week.* • *The resignation of the president has left the country* **in** *ferment.*

fer·ment *(obj)* /£fə'ment, £fɜː-, $fɚ-/ *v fml* • *He accused the leader of fermenting* (=causing or encouraging) **disorder.** [T] • **Trouble** *has been fermenting* (= developing) *in the prison for some weeks now.* [I]

fern /£fɜːn, $fɜːrn/ *n* [C] a green plant with long stems, feathery leaves and no flowers

fe·ro·cious /£fə'rəʊ·ʃəs, $-'roʊ-/ *adj* fierce and violent • *a ferocious dog* • *Last night saw some of the most ferocious battles in this region for months.* • *She's got a ferocious* (= very bad) *temper!* • *The president has come in for some ferocious criticism from the opposition.*

fe·ro·cious·ly /£fə'rəʊ·ʃə·sli, $-'roʊ-/ *adv* • *The mother lion will defend her young ferociously from attack.* • *(humorous) I'm knitting ferociously* (= very fast) *every evening to get the sweater finished.*

fe·ro·ci·ty /£fə'rɒs·ə·ti, $-'rɑː·sə·ṭi/, **fe·ro·cious·ness** /£fə'rəʊ·ʃə·snəs, $-'roʊ-/ *n* [U] • *The ferocity of the attack has shocked a lot of people.* • *She leapt on him with such ferocity in her eyes that he stumbled backwards.*

fer·ret ANIMAL /'fer·ɪt/ *n* [C] a small yellowish white animal with a long body, bred for hunting rabbits and other small animals

fer·ret SEARCH /'fer·ɪt/ *v* [always + adv/prep] *infml* to search, using the hands to move things around, esp. in a drawer, bag or other enclosed space, or to find (esp. information) after searching • *I was just ferreting* **around/about** *in my drawer for my passport.* [I] • *I know his name but I haven't yet managed to ferret* **out** (= find) *his address.* [M]

Fer·ris wheel /'fer·ɪs/ *n* [C] *esp. Am and Aus for* **big wheel**, see at BIG LARGE

fer·rous /'fer·əs/ *adj* [not gradable] *specialized* containing or relating to iron • *ferrous metals/compounds*

fer·ry (boat) /'fer·i/ *n* [C] a boat or ship for taking passengers and often vehicles across an area of water, esp. as a regular service • *a car ferry* • *We're going across to France by/on the ferry.* • *"Ferry 'cross* (= across) *the Mersey"* (song written by Gerry Marsden, 1965) • PIC **Ships and boats**

fer·ry *obj* /'fer·i/ *v* [T always + adv/prep] • To ferry people or goods is to transport them on a vehicle, esp. regularly and often: *I seem to spend most of my time ferrying the children about.*

fer·tile LAND /£'fɜː·taɪl, $'fɜːr·ṭəl/ *adj* (of land) able to produce a large number of good quality crops • *The Nile's regular flooding meant that the surrounding land was very fertile.* • Fertile **ground** can be used more generally to mean something which produces good results or a lot of ideas: *British politics remains very fertile ground* **for** *comedy.* ○ *Such middle-class districts are very fertile ground* **for** *the Republicans.* • Compare BARREN.

fer·til·i·ty /£fə'tɪl·ɪ·ti, £fɜː-, $fɚ'tɪl·ə·ṭi/ *n* [U] • *the fertility of the soil*

fer·til·ize *obj, Br and Aus usually* **-ise** /£'fɜː·tɪ·laɪz, $'fɜːr·ṭəl·aɪz/ *v* [T] • To fertilize land is to spread a natural or chemical substance on it in order to make the plants grow well: *Land that has been fertilized is richer in nutrients.*

fer·til·iz·er, *Br and Aus usually* **-iser** /£'fɜː·tɪ·laɪ·zər, $'fɜːr·ṭəl·aɪ-/ *n* • A fertilizer is a natural or chemical substance which is spread on the land to make plants grow well: *organic fertilizer* [U] ○ *a chemical fertilizer* [C]

fer·tile REPRODUCTION /£'fɜː·taɪl, $'fɜːr·ṭəl/ *adj* (of animals or plants) able to produce (a lot of) young or fruit, or (of seeds or eggs) able to develop into a new plant or animal • *People get less fertile as they get older.* • *Rabbits are notoriously fertile, producing vast numbers of offspring.* • *The eggs which are not fertile are selected to be eaten.*

fer·til·i·ty /£fə'tɪl·ɪ·ti, £fɜː-, $fɚ'tɪl·ə·ṭi/ *n* [U] • *a fertility symbol* • *There's a lot of concern over declining fertility* **rates.** • *You can take special drugs to increase your fertility.*

fer·til·ize *obj, Br and Aus usually* **-ise** /£'fɜː·tɪ·laɪz, $'fɜːr·ṭəl·aɪz/ *v* [T] • To fertilize the sexual cells in a female animal or plant is to join with them so that young begin to be produced: *The male sperm fertilizes the female egg.* ○ *The flower is fertilized by the pollen which is carried by the bee.*

fer·til·iz·a·tion, *Br and Aus usually* **-i·sa·tion** /£ˌfɜː·tɪ·laɪ'zeɪ·ʃən, $ˌfɜːr·ṭəl·aɪ-/ *n* [U] • *In humans, fertilization is more likely to occur at certain times of the month.* • *Fertilization occurs as the eggs are laid.*

fer·tile IMAGINATIVE /£'fɜː·taɪl, $'fɜːr·ṭəl/ *adj esp. literary* (of a person's mind or imagination) active and inventive; producing a lot of interesting and unusual ideas • *It takes a fertile imagination to direct a film as bizarre and original as this.*

fer·til·i·ty /£fə'tɪl·ɪ·ti, £fɜː-, $fɚ'tɪl·ə·ṭi/ *n* [U] *literary* • *the amazing fertility of her imagination*

fer·vent /£'fɜː·vənt, $'fɜːr-/, **fer·vid** /£'fɜː·vɪd, $'fɜːr-/ *adj fml* (of beliefs) strongly and sincerely felt, or (of people) having strong and sincere beliefs • *a fervent supporter of the communist party* • *It was a debate which aroused fervent ethical arguments.* • *The bishop said it was his fervent* **hope** *that a peaceful solution to the problem would soon be found.*

fer·vent·ly /£'fɜː·vənt·li, $'fɜːr-/ *adv fml* • *The nationalists believe fervently in independence for their country.* • *It's a cause for which she has campaigned fervently these past two years.*

fer·vour *Br and Aus, Am and Aus* **fer·vor** /£'fɜː·vər, $'fɜːr·vɚ/, *fml* **fer·ven·cy** /£'fɜː·vənt·si, $'fɜːr-/ *n* [U] *fml* • *There is growing sense of nationalist fervour in the state.*

fes·ter /£'fes·tər, $-tɚ/ *v* [I] (of an injury such as a cut) to become infected and form PUS (= a thick yellow liquid), or *(fig.)* (of an argument or bad feeling) to continue so that feelings of hate or dissatisfaction increase • *a festering sore* • *(fig.) It was better that she expressed her anger than let it fester inside her.* • *(fig.) The talks are aimed at resolving the festering conflict between the two countries.*

fes·ti·val /'fes·tɪ·vəl/ *n* [C] a special day or period, usually in memory of a religious event, with its own social activities, food or ceremonies, or an organized set of special events, such as musical performances or plays, usually happening in one place • *Diwali, or 'the festival of lights', is a major festival in the Hindu calendar.* • *The Brighton Festival* (= set of performances) *is* **held** *every year around May time.* • *I'd love to go to the Cannes Film Festival.* • *We're going to an outdoor* **folk/pop/rock** *festival at the weekend.* • LP **Holidays**

fes·tive /'fes·tɪv/ *adj* • Something which is festive produces a feeling or appearance which is suitable for a festival or other special social occasion: *The hall was looking very festive with its coloured lights.* ○ *Inside the room she could hear the festive sound of glasses clinking and people laughing.* • **The festive season** (*Am usually* **holiday season**) is the period around Christmas.

fes·ti·vi·ty /£fes'tɪv·ɪ·ti, $-ə·ṭi/ *n* • *In the spirit of festivity he came along to the party in a hat and false nose.* [U] • Festivity is another word for festival: *For American children Hallowe'en may be the second biggest festivity after Christmas.* [C]

fes·ti·vi·ties /£fes'tɪv·ɪ·tiz, $-ə·ṭiz/ *pl n* • Festivities are the parties, meals and other social activities with which people celebrate a special occasion: *"Come in and* **join the** *festivities – what will you have to drink?"*

fes·toon /fes'tuːn/ *n* [C] a decorative chain made of coloured paper, flowers, etc., hung in a curve between two points, or the curve that is made when something is loosely hung between two points • *She was standing on a stool putting up festoons that the children had made.* • *Lights hung from the ceiling in bright festoons* (= curves).

fes·toon *obj* /fes'tuːn/ *v* [T] • To festoon a room or other place is to decorate it for a special occasion by hanging coloured paper, lights or flowers around it, esp. in curves: *The hall was festooned* **with** *Christmas lights and holly.*

fe·tal /£'fiː·təl, $-ṭəl/ *adj* [not gradable] *esp. Am for* **foetal**, see at FOETUS

fetch *obj* GET /fetʃ/ *v* [T] to go to another place to get (something or someone) before bringing it or them back • *Could you fetch me my glasses/fetch my glasses* **for** *me from the other room, please.* [+ two objects] • *I'm just going to fetch my mother from the station.* • If you **fetch and carry** for someone, you do uninteresting and unskilled jobs for them, as if you were their servant.

fetch *obj* SELL /fetʃ/ *v* [T] to be sold for (the highest price that a buyer is willing to pay) • *Between them the paintings fetched over a million dollars.* • *The house didn't fetch as much as she was hoping it would.*

fetch *obj* HIT /fetʃ/ *v* [T] *dated infml* to hit (someone) with (the hand) • *If I'd heard that I should have fetched him a swift* **blow** *about the ears!* [+ two objects]

fetch up *v adv* [I always + adv/prep] *esp. Am infml* to arrive somewhere, esp. unintentionally or without planning • *After a whole hour of driving round, we fetched up at some tiny village in the middle of nowhere.*

fetch·ing /ˈfetʃ·ɪŋ/ *adj dated or slightly humorous* (of a person or a piece of clothing) attractive in appearance • *a rather fetching off-the-shoulder dress* • *You look very fetching in your green shorts.*

fetch·ing·ly /ˈfetʃ·ɪŋ·li/ *adv slightly humorous* • *Fetchingly dressed in a pair of gold swimming trunks, he posed by the side of the pool.*

fête [EVENT] *Br and Aus* /feɪt/, *esp. Am* **fair** *n* [C] an event, often held outside, at which the public can take part in competitions and buy food and other small items from STALLS, often organized to collect money for a particular purpose • *the summer fête* • *They're holding the village fête on the green.*

fête *obj* [PRAISE] /feɪt/ *v* [T usually passive] to praise or to welcome (someone) publicly because of the great things that they have achieved • *Fêted in her own country and abroad, she is met by cheering crowds wherever she goes.* • (F)

fe·tid, foe·tid /£ˈfet·ɪd, $ˈfet̬-/ *adj fml* smelling extremely bad and STALE (as if) from decay • *The fetid air of the prison cell made her want to vomit.*

fe·tish [INTEREST] /£ˈfet·ɪʃ, $ˈfet̬-/ *n* [C] a sexual interest in an object or a part of the body other than the sexual organs, or an activity or object which someone is interested in to an extreme degree and to which they give an unreasonable amount of time or thought • *a rubber/foot fetish* • *He has a fetish* **about/for** *high-heels so sometimes as a treat I wear them in bed.* • *She has a well-publicized shoe fetish* (= interest in shoes) *and is reported to own over five hundred pairs.* • *She* **makes a** *fetish* **of** (= gives an unreasonably large amount of attention to) *organization – it's quite obsessive.*

fe·tish·i·sm /£ˈfet·ɪ·ʃɪ·zᵊm, $ˈfet̬-/ *n* [U] • *Among the issues that the programme will deal with are fidelity, homosexuality and fetishism.* • *Ours is a culture of designer fetishism – a society obsessed by style.*

fe·tish·ist /£ˈfet·ɪ·ʃɪst, $ˈfet̬-/ *n* [C] • A fetishist is a person who has a particular fetish: *a foot fetishist*

fe·tish·is·tic /£ˌfet·ɪˈʃɪs·tɪk, $ˌfet̬-/ *adj* • *fetishistic black plastic boots*

fe·tish [RELIGIOUS OBJECT] /£ˈfet·ɪʃ, $ˈfet̬-/ *n* [C] *specialized* an object which is worshipped in some societies because it is believed to possess a spirit or special magical powers

fe·tish·i·sm /£ˈfet·ɪ·ʃɪ·zᵊm, $ˈfet̬-/ *n* [U] *specialized*

fe·tish·is·tic /£ˌfet·ɪˈʃɪs·tɪk, $ˌfet̬-/ *adj specialized* • *fetishistic religions*

fet·lock /£ˈfet·lɒk, $-lɑːk/ *n* [C] the part of a horse's leg at the back, just above the foot, which has long hair growing from it

fet·ter *obj* /£ˈfet·əʳ, $ˈfet̬·ɚ/ *v* [T usually passive] to keep (someone) within limits or stop their advance or, less commonly, to tie (someone) to a place by putting chains around their legs, just above their feet • *(literary) Fettered* **by** *a nine-to-five office existence, he was unable to fulfil his ambition.*

fet·ter /£ˈfet·əʳ, $ˈfet̬·ɚ/ *n* [C] • A fetter is one of a pair of chains which were used, esp. in the past, to tie prisoners to a place, by the legs, and so prevent them from escaping.

fet·ters /£ˈfet·əz, $ˈfet̬·ɚz/ *pl n esp. literary* • *Freed from the fetters of a mortgage, she could once again spend her money as she pleased.*

fet·tle /£ˈfet·l̩, $ˈfet̬-/ *n* [U] *infml* degree of health or strength; condition • *"How was Jane when you saw her?" "Oh, very well –* **in fine** *fettle."*

fe·tus /£ˈfiː·təs, $-t̬əs/ *n* [C] *esp. Am for* FOETUS

feud /fjuːd/ *n* [C] an argument which has existed for a long time between two (groups of) people and has caused a lot of angry feeling or violence • *a family feud* • *Negotiations are taking place aimed at ending the 10-year-old feud* **between** *the two countries.* • *The feud* **over** *two or three miles of land has so far cost over a thousand lives.*

feud /fjuːd/ *v* [I] • *We've been feuding* **with** *our neighbours for years* **over** *an area of our garden which they insist belongs to them.*

feud·al /ˈfjuː·dᵊl/ *adj* [not gradable] of the social system which developed in Western Europe in the 8th and 9th centuries in which people served a Lord by working and fighting for him and in exchange were supported and given land and protection, or of other societies with a similar social system • *the feudal system* • **It** *seems somehow feudal* **to** *have so much land in the hands of a privileged few.* [+ to infinitive]

feud·al·i·sm /ˈfjuː·dᵊl·ɪ·zᵊm/ *n* [U] • Feudalism is another way of referring to the feudal system.

fe·ver /£ˈfiː·vəʳ, $-vɚ/ *n* a medical condition in which the body temperature is higher than usual and the heart beats very fast, or *(fig.)* a state of great excitement • *He's got a headache and a slight fever.* [C] • *After a couple of days the fever went down but I was left with a sore throat.* [C] • *(fig.) With England in the finals of the World Cup, the whole nation seems to be in the grip of football fever.* [U] • *(fig.) By the time the princess emerged on the balcony, excitement among the waiting crowd was at fever* **pitch** (= there was a lot of excitement).

fe·vered /£ˈfiː·vəd, $-vɚd/ *adj* • *The nurse wiped my fevered brow.* • *(fig.) The film is clearly the product of a fevered* (= extremely excited or active) *brain/imagination.*

fe·ver·ish /ˈfiː·vᵊr·ɪʃ/ *adj* • *I'm feeling a bit feverish – I hope it's not the start of flu.* • *(fig.) Have you seen the feverish* (= extremely busy) **activity** *going on in the kitchen! Exactly how many is he cooking for?*

fe·ver·ish·ly /ˈfiː·vᵊr·ɪ·ʃli/ *adv* • *We're working feverishly* (= in an extremely active way) *hard to meet the deadline.*

few [SOME] /fjuː/ *determiner, pronoun* **a few** some; a small number (of) • *There are a few cakes left over from the party – would you like one?* • *I'm going to town – I've got to get a few things.* • *We've been having a few problems with the new computer.* • *I'd like to have a few words with you when you've got a moment.* • *If more people turn up to go on the trip I can take a few in the van.* • *"How many potatoes do you want?" "Oh, just a few, please."* • People also use **a few** to mean quite a large number, often in expressions such as **quite** a few or, less commonly, a **good** few: *I know a few people who have had the same problem with those cars.* ○ *I saw quite a few people with that hair-cut – it must be fashionable.* ○ *A lot of people at the club are under twenty but there are a good few who aren't.* • If someone has **had a few (too many)**, they have drunk quite a large number (or too many) alcoholic drinks: *She'd had a few even before we arrived at the party, judging by the way that she was speaking.* • 'A few' is used with countable nouns. Compare LITTLE. • [LP> **Quantity words**]

few [NOT MANY] /fjuː/ *determiner, pronoun, n, adj* **-er, -est** a small number, not many or not enough • *So few people attended the party that it was embarrassing.* • *He is among the very few people that I can trust with such information.* • *Politics, she said, was concerned with giving too few people too much power.* • *Very few (people) can afford to pay those prices for clothes.* • *There are only a few days left before we leave for France.* • *As a working mother she felt she had all the problems of motherhood with* **precious** (= very) *few of the benefits.* • *There are few things in this world that give me more pleasure than a long bath.* • *Fewer people smoke these days than used to.* • *As a country they have the fewest deaths through cancer in the whole of Europe.* • *The party was a disaster – not many people went and the few who did left early.* • *As few as 10% of people are happy with their jobs, according to a recent survey.* [U] • *The benefits of this scheme are few, he said.* • *Flats which are both comfortable and reasonably priced are* **few and far between** (= there are not many). • *He was a man* **of few words,** *my father, but when he spoke it was worth listening to.* • *(fml) The conference was attended by* **no fewer than** *five hundred delegates* (= it was surprising that that many people went). • *"We few, we happy few, we band of brothers"* (Shakespeare, Henry V 3.1) • 'Few' is used with countable nouns. Compare LITTLE. • [LP> **Approximate numbers**]

fey /feɪ/ *adj literary* mysterious and strange, or trying to appear like this in a way that is not natural or sincere • *The poet is depicted in the film as a rather fey and otherworldly young man.* • *He dismissed her later poems as fey and frivolous.*

fey·ness /ˈfeɪ·nəs/ *n* [U]

fez /fez/ *n* [C] *pl* **fezzes** a high round hat made of stiff, usually red, material with a flat top, no BRIM and often with threads hanging from the top, esp. as worn in the past by men in some Muslim countries • [PIC> **Hats**]

ff *pl n abbreviation for* (and) the following pages

fi·an·cé *male, female* **fi·an·cée** /fiːˈɑːn·seɪ/ *n* [C] the person to whom you are ENGAGED to be married • *I didn't talk to her fiancé – he looked a bit dull.* • [LP> **Relationships**]

fi·as·co /£fiˈæs·kəʊ, $-koʊ/ *n* [C] *pl* **fiascos** or *esp. Am* **fiascoes** something planned that has gone very badly wrong and been a complete failure • *The whole show was a fiasco – the lights wouldn't work, one actor forgot his lines and another fell off the stage.*

fi·at /ˈfiː·æt/ *n* [C] *fml* an order given by a person in authority • *The decision was arrived at not by reasoned argument but* **by** *prime ministerial* **fiat**.

fib /fɪb/ *v* [I] **-bb-** *infml* to tell an unimportant and harmless lie, sometimes playfully • *I can tell he's fibbing because he's smiling!*

fib /fɪb/ *n* [C] *infml* • *I don't believe him – I think he's* **telling** *fibs.*

fib·ber /£ˈfɪb·əʳ, $-ɚ/ *n* [C] *infml* • A fibber is a person who tells fibs: *Fibber! You've never even run ten kilometres let alone a marathon!*

fi·bre MATERIAL, *Am usually* **fi·ber** /£ˈfaɪ·bəʳ, $-bɚ/ *n* any of the thread-like parts which form plant or artificial material and which can be made into cloth by processes such as SPINNING (= twisting fibres together) and weaving • *The fibres in cheaper woollen cloth tend to be shorter.* [C] • Fibre can also refer to these or other threads when they are in a mass that can be used for making products such as cloth and rope: *Natural fibres, such as cotton, tend to be used in sportswear because they are cooler.* [C] ○ *It's sometimes hard to tell artificial from natural fibre these days.* [U] • *(specialized)* **Fibre optics** is the use of very thin glass or plastic fibres through which light can travel to carry information, esp. in telephone, television and computer communications.

fi·brous /ˈfaɪ·brəs/ *adj*

fi·bre BODY, *Am usually* **fi·ber** /£ˈfaɪ·bəʳ, $-bɚ/ *n* (an example of) thread-like structures in the body, such as those found in muscle, or *(fig.)* used in expressions that refer to a person's character or its strength • *muscle fibre(s)* [U/C] • *(fig.) He lacked the* **moral** *fibre* (= strength of character) *to be leader.* [U] • *(fig.) She wanted to win the race with* **every** *fibre* **of** *her* **being** (= very much). [U]

fi·bre FOOD, *Am usually* **fi·ber** /£ˈfaɪ·bəʳ, $-bɚ/, **di·e·tary fi·bre**, **rough·age** *n* [U] a substance in foods such as fruit, vegetables and brown bread which travels through the body as waste, making digestion and the excretion of the contents of the bowels quicker and more effective • *A lot of the fibre in fruit is found in the skin.* • *It's reckoned that an increased intake of fibre in the diet can reduce the risk of bowel cancer.*

fi·brous /ˈfaɪ·brəs/ *adj* • Food which is fibrous contains fibre: *Brown rice is more fibrous than white.*

fi·bre·glass *Br and Aus, Am* **fi·ber·glass** /£ˈfaɪ·bəˌglɑːs, $-bɚˌglæs/, **glass fi·bre**, *Am* **glass fi·ber** *n* [U] a material made from small fibres of glass twisted together, which is used for keeping buildings warm, or a plastic strengthened by these fibres and used for making structures such as the outsides of cars and boats • *a fibreglass speedboat*

fi·bro /£ˈfaɪ·brəʊ, $-broʊ/ *n* [U] *Aus* a type of building material made from ASBESTOS and CEMENT • *fibro houses*

fib·u·la /ˈfɪb·jʊ·lə/ *n* [C] *pl* **fibulas** or **fibulae** /ˈfɪb·jʊ·liː/ *specialized* the outer of the two bones in the lower part of the human leg

fick·le /ˈfɪk·l̩/ *adj disapproving* likely to change your opinion or your feelings suddenly and without a good reason • *She's so fickle – she's never been interested in the same man for more than a week!* • *The world of popular music is notoriously fickle.* • The weather is described as fickle if it tends to change suddenly and without warning: *Fickle winds made sailing conditions difficult.*

fick·le·ness /ˈfɪk·l̩.nəs/ *n* [U] • *The fickleness of children's taste in food is well recognised.*

fic·tion /ˈfɪk·ʃən/ *n* the type of book or story which is written about imaginary characters and events and not based on real people and facts, or a false report or statement which you pretend is true • *The author insists that the book is a* **work of** *fiction and not intended as a historical account.* [U] • *Roald Dahl was an extremely successful writer of children's fiction.* [U] • *At work she managed to keep up the fiction* (= false report) **that** *she had a university degree.* [C + *that* clause] • *All these promising statistics that the government puts out are complete fictions* (= false statements). [C] • *You never really know what's fact and what's fiction* (= false) *when he tells you something.* [U]

fic·tion·al /ˈfɪk·ʃən·əl/ *adj* • *The film is based on a fictional story set in wartime.* • *The problem with fictional characters is that their lives are so much more dramatic than those of real people.*

fic·tion·al·ize *obj, Br and Aus usually* **-ise** /ˈfɪk·ʃən·əl·aɪz/ *v* [T] • If a writer fictionalizes a real event or a real character, he or she writes about the subject adding imaginary details and changing the real facts: *The real-life politician is fictionalized in the film into a womanizing alcoholic.*

fic·tion·al·iz·a·tion, *Br and Aus usually* **-i·sa·tion** /ˌfɪk·ʃən·əl·aɪˈzeɪ·ʃən/ *n* [C/U]

fic·ti·tious /fɪkˈtɪʃ·əs/ *adj* false; invented and not true or existing • *The actor has dismissed the recent rumours about his private life as fictitious and malicious.* • *Roz keeps inventing these fictitious weekends away so that she doesn't have to see her Aunty Ann.* • Fictitious can also mean characters and events in films and stories to mean imaginary.

fid·dle *obj* CHEAT /ˈfɪd·l̩/ *v* [T] *infml* to act dishonestly in order to get (something) for yourself, or to change (something) dishonestly, esp. to your advantage • *She managed to fiddle a free trip to America.* • *He had been fiddling* **the accounts/books/finances** *for several years before he was discovered.*

fid·dle /ˈfɪd·l̩/ *n infml esp. Br* • *It's a (big) fiddle – people think they are getting designer clothes cheaply but they're just copies.* [C] • *Everyone suspected they were* **on the** *fiddle* (= cheating). [U]

fid·dle MOVE ABOUT /ˈfɪd·l̩/ *v* [I] to move things about or touch things without a particular purpose • *Put your papers down and stop fiddling!* • *Don't fiddle* **with** *my computer/desk/books while I'm out.* • *He stood there fiddling* **(about/around) with** *the things on my desk.* • *He loves fiddling* **(about/around) with** (= separating into pieces, making small changes or trying to repair) *radios and clocks, or anything with little pieces.* • *There's no point in fiddling* **(about/around) with** (= changing) *the format because the whole report will have to be altered.* • *(fig.) She fiddled* **about/around** *in the kitchen, keeping out of the way* (= doing unnecessary things in order to seem busy). • *(fig.) I spent all morning fiddling* **about/around** (= doing several different things but completing nothing). • *(fig.) Let's go, we haven't got time to fiddle* **about/around** (= we cannot waste time) *queueing for tickets.*

fid·dle INSTRUMENT /ˈfɪd·l̩/ *n* [C] *infml* a VIOLIN (= stringed musical instrument) • *We need someone to play the fiddle.*

fid·dle /ˈfɪd·l̩/ *v* [I] *infml* • *He plays the piano and fiddles* (= plays VIOLIN) *a bit.* • To **fiddle while Rome burns** means to enjoy yourself and not give attention to something important and unpleasant that is happening: *Environmentalists claimed governments were fiddling while Rome burned.*

fid·dler /£ˈfɪd·l̩.əʳ, £-ləʳ, $-l̩·ɚ/ *n* [C] *infml* • *The fiddler started to play a dance tune.*

fid·dle DIFFICULTY /ˈfɪd·l̩/ *n* [U] *Br infml* something difficult to do, esp. because the things involved are small or need careful use of the fingers • *I find threading a needle* **a** *terrible fiddle.* • **It's a** *real fiddle* **to** *assemble because of all the small parts.* [+ *to* infinitive]

fid·dly /ˈfɪd·l̩.i, ˈfɪd·li/ *adj* **-ier, -iest** *infml* • *Be careful when you paint that fiddly* **bit** *in the corner.* • *Repairing something as small as a watch is a very fiddly job.*

fid·dle·sticks /ˈfɪd·l̩.stɪks/, *Am also* **fid·dle** /ˈfɪd·l̩/, **fid·dle–fad·dle** /ˈfɪd·l̩ˌfæd·l̩/ *exclamation old use* nonsense; I disagree

fid·dling /ˈfɪd·l̩.ɪŋ, ˈfɪd·lɪŋ/ *adj* [before n] unimportant; of no real interest; PETTY • *fiddling little details* • *fiddling restrictions*

fi·del·i·ty /£fɪˈdel·ə·ti, $-ţi/ *n* [U] *fml* honest or lasting support; loyalty • *They had shown great fidelity* **to** *Brighton, spending their holidays there for twenty years.* • *(fig.) Her paintings show her remarkable fidelity* **to** *detail* (= the careful attention that she gives to detail). • *The play was Somerset Maugham's 1920s comedy of* **marital** *fidelity, 'The Constant Wife'.* • *How important do you think* **sexual** *fidelity* (= having a sexual relationship only with your partner) *is in a marriage?*

fidg·et /ˈfɪdʒ·ɪt/ *v* [I] to make continuous small movements which annoy other people • *Children can't sit still for long without fidgeting.* • *I watched him fidgeting* **with** *the packets on the shelf.* • *Stop fidgeting* **about**.

fidg·et /ˈfɪdʒ·ɪt/ *n* [C] • A fidget is a person who is always fidgeting: *Tim's a terrible fidget.*

fidg·ets /ˈfɪdʒ·ɪts/ *pl n* • *She's got (a bad case of)* **the fidgets** (= is moving around a lot) *today – she can't concentrate on anything for long.*

fidg·e·ty /ˈfɪdʒ·ɪ·ti/ *adj* • *The audience looked very fidgety and bored.*

field LAND /fiːld/ *n* [C] a limited area of land with grass or crops growing on it, which is usually surrounded by fences or closely planted bushes when it is part of a farm • *We* *drove past fields of ripening wheat.* • *The cows were all standing in one corner of the field.* • Your field **of vision** is the whole area that you can see. • **The field** is an area of land in which you are working or studying: *Relief aid workers who had recently returned from the field* (= the area where they were working) *had sad stories to tell.* ○ *They are reviewing village healthcare provision* **in** *the field* (= by visiting the villages). • *(Am and Aus)* A **field day** is a special day of organized sports or other outside activities for students. • If you **have a field day** you enjoy yourself very much or take advantage of an opportunity: *No-one else liked strawberries, so we had a field day* (= we ate a lot of them). ○ *The newspapers had a field day when the wedding was announced* (= they wrote a lot about it and printed many photographs of it). • **Field glasses** are BINOCULARS. • A **field marshal** is a British army officer of the highest rank. • A **field trip** is a visit made by students to study something away from their school or college: *a geography field trip* ○ *a field trip to an Iron Age settlement.*

-field /fiːld/ *combining form* • *an oilfield* (= area of land containing oil) • *an airfield* (= area of land where small aircraft can land and take off)

field [SPORT] /fiːld/ *n* [C] a grassy area used for playing sport • *The school playing/football/hockey/rugby field was a windy, uninviting place.* • To **take** the field is to go onto the field at the start of a game: *There were loud cheers as the Irish team took the field.* • To **leave the field clear for** someone means you are no longer competing against them in any way: *John's transfer left the field clear for Judy to be given the job.* • A **field event** is a sporting event in which competitors take part one after the other rather than race or compete against each other at the same time: *High jump and javelin throwing are field events.* • **Field hockey** is *Am for* HOCKEY.

field *(obj)* /fiːld/ *v* • To field in games such as cricket or baseball is to catch or pick up the ball after it has been hit, and to try to prevent the other team from scoring. *He fielded the ball well.* [T] • *Our team is fielding first.* [I] • To field also means to have or produce a group of people to play something: *The college fields several football teams.* [T] ○ *(fig.) The company fielded a group of experts to take part in the conference.* [T]

field·er /£ˈfiːl·dəʳ, $-dɚ/ *n* [C] • A fielder is a person in the team that are fielding in a game such as cricket or baseball who tries to prevent the opposition from scoring: *A well-placed fielder can win matches.*

field [COMPETITORS] /fiːld/ *n* [C +sing/pl v] all the (other) competitors taking part in a race or activity • *The race started with a field of eleven, but two horses fell.* • *We have a strong field this afternoon.* • *Once again Jones finished ahead of* **the field** (= Jones won).

field [AREA OF INTEREST] /fiːld/ *n* [C] an area of activity or interest • *the field* **of** *history/science/medicine/law* • *Are you still in the same field* (= Are you still working in the same business)? • *Our product is the best in the field.* • *That's not my field/That's* **outside** *my field* (= That's not something I know much about).

field *obj* [ANSWER] /fiːld/ *v* [T] to answer cleverly or to avoid giving a direct answer • *The chairperson skilfully fielded several awkward questions.*

field [COMPUTER] /fiːld/ *n* [C] *specialized* a division of a DATABASE (= collection of similar information on a computer) which contains a particular type of information, such as names or numbers

field·work /£ˈfiːld·wɜːk, $-wɜːrk/ *n* [U] study which consists of practical activities that are done away from a school, college, etc. • *Our fieldwork included taking a survey of shoppers in the middle of Cambridge.*

fiend /fiːnd/ *n* [C] a cruel, unpleasant person • *Their father was a fiend, violent when he was drunk.* • *The newspaper report portrayed the car driver as a fiend, without a single good quality.* • A fiend can also be a person who likes something in an extreme way: • *a health/fresh-air/racing fiend* ○ *She's a fiend* **for** *chocolate/exercise.* • Ⓝ

fiend·ish /ˈfiːn·dɪʃ/ *adj* • *a fiendish* (= very bad and cruel) *gang/attacker* • *a fiendish* (= clever and difficult, and possibly bad) *plot/scheme/plan/policy* • *(Br dated) I'm in a fiendish* (= very great) *hurry.* • *(Br dated) We abandoned the scheme because of the fiendish* (= very great) *costs.*

fiend·ish·ly /ˈfiːn·dɪʃ·li/ *adv dated* • *a fiendishly* (= extremely) *difficult decision*

fiend·ish·ness /ˈfiːn·dɪʃ·nəs/ *n* [U] • *The fiendishness* (= cruelty) *of the plan horrified us.*

fierce /£fɪəs, $fɪrs/ *adj* **-r**, **-st** physically violent and frightening, or strong and powerful, or showing strong feeling or energetic activity • *a fierce attack* • *a fierce battle* • *The two men had been shot during fierce* **fighting** *last weekend.* • *The cats lived wild and had become very fierce.* • *Fierce* (= Strong) *winds/seas/weather prevented the race from taking place.* • *The fire fighters had to retreat from the fierce* (= strong) *heat.* • *But any expansion plans will face fierce* **opposition/resistance** (= that showing strong feeling) *from environmentalists.* • *There is fierce* (= great) **competition** *to join the Special Branch, which investigates terrorist and political crime.* • *(Am infml) The chemistry exam was fierce* (= difficult)*!* • *(Am infml) I need a cold drink* **something** *fierce* (= very much). • Ⓝⓛ

fierce·ly /£ˈfɪə·sli, $ˈfɪr·sli/ *adv* • *The two countries have battled fiercely over their frontier.* • *The fiercely* (= extremely) **competitive** *school system has been known to drive young schoolchildren to suicide.* • *She is fiercely* (= extremely) **independent**.

fierce·ness /£ˈfɪə·snəs, $ˈfɪr·snəs/ *n* [U]

fi·er·y /ˈfaɪə·ri/ *adj* **-ier**, **-iest** bright red or very hot like fire, or *(fig.)* showing very strong feeling • *a fiery sky/sunset* • *fiery or spicy foods like curry* • *(fig.) a fiery temper/speech/manner* • *(fig.) fiery passions*

fi·es·ta /fiˈes·tə/ *n* [C] a public celebration in Spain or South America, esp. one on a religious holiday, with entertainments and activities • *We were lucky enough to be there for the Easter fiesta.* • *The town was clearly in fiesta mood.*

fif·teen /ˌfɪfˈtiːn, ˈ--/ *determiner, pronoun, n* (the number) 15 • *thirteen, fourteen, fifteen* • *a fifteen-storey building* • *"How many books were returned?" "Fifteen (books)."* • *(Br)* A fifteen is a RUGBY team: *He plays in the first fifteen* (= the best of several RUGBY teams belonging to one organization). [C]

fif·teenth /ˌfɪfˈtiːnθ, ˈ--/ *determiner, pronoun, adj, adv* [not gradable], *n* • *the fifteenth lap* • *Her birthday is on the fifteenth of May.* • *You're fifteenth on the list.* • *He's ranked fifteenth in the world.* • A fifteenth is one of fifteen equal parts of something. [C]

fifth /fɪfθ/ *determiner, pronoun, adj, adv, n* [C] See at FIVE

fif·ty /ˈfɪf·ti/ *determiner, pronoun, n* (the number) 50 • *forty, fifty, sixty* • *fifty pounds* • *the fifty states of the Union* (= the United States of America) • *How fast were they driving? They were doing fifty (miles an hour).* • *There are two fifties in a hundred.* [C] • **Fifty-fifty** means (into) equal halves: *They divided the cake fifty-fifty.* ○ *Let's* **go** *fifty-fifty* (= We'll share esp. the cost equally). ○ *We could share the work* **on a** *fifty-fifty* **basis**. ○ *There's only* **a** *fifty-fifty* **chance** *that she'll survive the operation.*

fif·ties /ˈfɪf·tiz/ *pl n* • **The** fifties is the range of temperature between 50° and 59°: *It's been* **in** *the fifties all week.* • **The** fifties is also the period of years between 50 and 59 in any century: *Rock and roll first became popular* **in** *the fifties* (= between 1950 and 1959). • A person's fifties are the period in which they are aged between 50 and 59: *My dad is* **in** *his fifties.*

fif·ti·eth /ˈfɪf·ti·əθ/ *determiner, pronoun, adj, adv* [not gradable], *n* • *That's the fiftieth Christmas card I've written.* • *She was the fiftieth of the applicants we interviewed.* • *He is/is ranked fiftieth in the world.* • A fiftieth is one of fifty equal parts of something. [C]

fig [FRUIT] /fɪg/ *n* [C] a tree which grows in warm places or its edible fruit • *fresh/dried figs* • *a fig tree* • *(dated)* If you **don't care/give a fig** for something, or if something is **not worth a fig**, it is not important to you. • A **fig leaf** is the type of leaf sometimes used in paintings to cover a naked person's sex organs. • A **fig leaf** is also used to mean something that hides something else, esp. something that is dishonest or embarrassing: *The spokesperson said the information campaign was a fig leaf to hide the most regressive tax in history.*

fig [PICTURE] /fɪg/ *n* [C] *abbreviation for* FIGURE [PICTURE]

fig [LANGUAGE] *adj* [not gradable] *abbreviation for* FIGURATIVE

fight *(obj)* /faɪt/ *v past* **fought** /£fɔːt, $fɑːt/ to use force against (esp. another person or group of people) • *The children were fighting in the playground.* [I] • *The soldiers fought from house to house under constant artillery fire.* [I] • *In the English Civil War, the Roundheads fought the Cavaliers.* [T] • *He's a famous American boxer who fought in the fifties.* [I] • *They fought* **with** (= on the side of) *the North* **against** *the South.* [I] • *It doesn't look encouraging, but we are determined to fight* **on** (= continue fighting). [I] • *The birds were fighting* **over** (= competing for) *the crusts of* *bread we had thrown for them.* [I] • *I could hear them fighting* (=arguing) **about** *who had left the lights on.* [I] • *He fought* (=argued angrily) *for years* **with** (=against) *his neighbours* **over** *who owned the fence.* [I] • *They were fighting* **like cats and dogs** (=fighting or arguing very angrily and violently). [I] • *They fought* **to the bitter end/ to the death** (=until everyone on one side was dead or completely defeated). [I] • If someone fights something, it can also mean that they use a lot of effort to defeat it or stop it happening: *The firefighters spent three days fighting the warehouse* **fire**. [T] ○ *He fought the disease bravely for three years.* [T] ○ *We need the public's help in fighting* **crime**. [T] ○ *They had to fight hard* **for** *improvements to the road system.* [I] ○ *The child fought* **(back/down)** (=tried hard not to show or produce) *its tears/its fear/its rude reply/the impulse to run away.* [T/M] ○ *The bank fought* **off** (=successfully prevented) *a takeover by another bank recently.* [M] ○ *I managed to fight* **off** (=quickly get rid of) *the sore throat/feeling of depression.* [M] • To fight (something) can also mean to try to win it: *The battle was fought and won in the air.* [T] ○ *They fought the* **case** *in/ through the (law) courts.* [T] ○ *She successfully fought the* **seat** (=the position of Member of Parliament) *at the last election.* [T] ○ *She successfully fought* **(at/in)** *the last* **election**. [T; I + prep] • *(infml) There's only one free ticket – you'll have to* **fight it out between** *you* (=make a decision/ come to an agreement). • *He* **couldn't fight** *his* **way out of a (brown) paper bag** (=he is not a person with energy and ability). • *(Br)* To **fight** your **corner** is to fight hard for something or defend it: *They nearly stopped the project but she fought her corner well and persuaded them to extend it.* • To **fight fire with fire** means to use the same methods as someone else to defeat them. • If you **fight a losing battle** you are trying to do something that is not possible: *We were fighting a losing battle trying to get him to keep his bedroom tidy.* • Someone who **fights shy of** something tries to avoid it: *I'd always fought shy of computers/flying, but after a recent experience I've changed my mind.* • *(saying)* 'He that fights and runs away, lives to fight another day.' • *"Fight for your Right to Party"* (title of a song by The Beastie Boys, 1987) • *"We shall fight on the beaches, we shall fight on the landing grounds, we shall fight in the fields and in the streets, we shall fight in the hills; we shall never surrender"* (speech by Sir Winston Churchill, 1940) • *"Fight the good fight / With all thy might"* (from a hymn by J.S.B.Monsell, 1811-1875) • LP› **Each other**

fight /faɪt/ *n* • *The older boys* **broke up** (=stopped)/ *started the fight.* [C] • *Have you got tickets for* **the** *big fight* (=boxing competition)? [C] • *I had a* **stand-up** *fight* **with** *her* (=we argued strongly) **about** *the telephone bill.* [C] • *We must continue* **the** *fight* **against** (=effort to defeat or prevent) *inflation/homelessness/crime.* [C] • If you **put up a (good)** fight, you fight or work hard against a stronger person or group: *He put up a fight when the police tried to arrest him.* ○ *They put up a good fight* (=played well) **against** *a more experienced football team.* ○ *The commuters put up a fight* (=complained/argued) **about** *the fare increases.* [C] • Fight can also mean desire or ability to fight or act energetically: *The team came out on the court full of fight.* [U] ○ *The news* **knocked/took** *all the fight out of him.* [U] ○ *There wasn't* **much/any** *fight left in the thieves after their car crashed.* [U] • **Fight or flight** is the ability of an animal or human to quickly use extra energy to fight or escape from danger: *Stress can occur if you are unable over a long period to release anger or tension by fight or flight.*

fight·er /£'faɪ·tər, $-t̬ɚ/ *n* [C] • *She's a fighter* (=someone who tries hard and will not easily give up). • *He made his name as a fighter* **against** *royal privilege.* • A **fighter (plane/aircraft)** is a small fast military aircraft used for chasing and destroying enemy aircraft: *He used to be a fighter pilot.* • See also FIREFIGHTER; PRIZEFIGHTER. • PIC› **Aircraft**

fight·ing /£'faɪ·tɪŋ, $-t̬ɪŋ/ *n* [U], *adj* [not gradable] • *Fierce fighting has continued all day on the outskirts of the town.* • Fighting ships are ships built for war. • A **fighting chance** is a small but real possibility that something can be done: *If we can raise enough money, there's a fighting chance* **(that)** *we can save the newspaper.* • *You look* **fighting fit** (=very healthy) *after your holiday.* • If you have **fighting spirit**, you are willing to compete/fight or to do things which are difficult: *Don't take no for an answer – where's your fighting spirit?* • If you use **fighting talk/words**, you show by your speech that you are willing to fight if necessary: *In a further display of fighting talk, the Government said today, "There will be no compromise on this issue."*

fig·ment /'fɪg·mənt/ *n* [C] **figment of** *someone's/the* **imagination** something which seems real but is not • *Was it just a figment of my imagination or did I hear John's voice in the other room?* • *Ghosts are just figments of the imagination.*

fig·ur·a·tive LANGUAGE /£'fɪg·ər·ə·tɪv, $-ɚ·ə·t̬ɪv/ *adj* (of words and phrases) used not with their basic factual meaning but to suggest part of that meaning • *The sentence 'He scored a goal' uses the basic meaning of 'score' as 'to win or obtain a point', but the sentence 'She has scored a success with her latest novel' makes figurative use of 'score' to mean 'achieve something desirable'.* • Compare LITERAL. • LP› **Labels**

fig·ur·a·tive·ly /£'fɪg·ər·ə·tɪv·li, $-ɚ·ə·t̬ɪv·/ *adv* • *In the sentence 'There's trouble brewing', 'brewing' is used figuratively to mean 'about to start'.* • *Figuratively speaking, it was a blow right between the eyes* (=it was a bad shock).

fig·ur·a·tive ART /£'fɪg·ər·ə·tɪv, $-ɚ·ə·t̬ɪv/ *adj* (of a painting, drawing, etc.) representing something as it really looks, rather than in an ABSTRACT way • *As early as 1915 she pioneered abstract art in America but later moved towards a more figurative style.*

fig·ure SHAPE /£'fɪg·ər, $-jʊr/ *n* [C] the shape of the human body, or a person • *I could see two figures/a tall figure* (=these human shapes) *in the distance.* • *A strange bearded figure* (=person) *entered the room.* • *She was a* **central/key/leading** *figure* **in** (=was an important person in) *the movement for constitutional reform.* • In art, a figure is a painting, drawing or model of a person: *There are few figures in the street scene and most are children.* • A woman's figure is her body shape: *She has (got) a lovely figure.* ○ *She* **got** *her figure* **back** (=returned to her usual shape) *quite quickly after the baby was born.* ○ *She has* **kept** *her figure well* (=is still an attractive shape despite being older or having had children). • *(humorous or dated)* A **fine figure of a man/woman** is a person who is tall, with a large physically attractive body. • A **figure of fun** is someone who is laughed at unkindly: *His old-fashioned clothes made him a figure of fun.* • A **figure of speech** is an expression which uses words to mean something different from their ordinary meaning: *'Get up with the lark' is a figure of speech, meaning 'Get out of bed early'.* ○ *(infml) It's just a figure of speech* (=I didn't mean to offend you by the word or phrase I used). • Ⓕ

fig·ure NUMBER /£'fɪg·ər, $-jʊr/ *n* [C] the symbol for a number or an amount expressed in numbers • *Can you read this figure? Is it a three or an eight?* • *Write the amount in both words and figures.* • *I looked quickly down the* **column of** *figures.* • *I* **haven't got a head for** *figures* (=I can't do mathematics very well). • *I'm not sure we can afford it. We'll have to* **look at the** *figures* (=the accounts, costs, etc.). • *The job vacancies are now in* **single/double figures** (=less than 10/10-99). • *Her salary is* **in** *four/five/ six* **figures** (=more than £1000/£10 000/£100 000)/*She earns a four/five/six-figure salary.* • *They're asking a high/large figure /They've put a high/large figure on* (=they want a high price for) *the antique table.* • *I'm sure we'll have a good crowd/make a reasonable profit but I couldn't* **put a figure on it** (=say exactly how many/how much). • A *(Br and Aus)* **figure of eight**/*(Am)* **figure eight** is the shape made when drawing an 8: *She skated a perfect figure of eight.* • **Figure skating** is a type of SKATING in which the skater moves in circular patterns based on the shape of the number 8. • Ⓕ

fig·ure PICTURE /£'fɪg·ər, $-jʊr/ (*abbreviation* **fig** /fɪg/) *n* [C] a picture or drawing, often numbered, in a book or other document • *The illustration/graph/diagram shown in Figure 2 needs to be better labelled.* • Ⓕ

fig·ure APPEAR /£'fɪg·ər, $-jʊr/ *v* [I always + adv/prep] to be, appear, take part or be included in something • *Their names did not figure* **in** *the passenger list/***as** *potential helpers.* • *Visiting Britain does not figure* **in** *my travel plans.* • *They denied that violence and intimidation had figured* **prominently in** *achieving the decision.* • Ⓕ

fig·ure EXPECT /£'fɪg·ər, $-jʊr/ *v esp. Am* to expect or think that something will happen • *We figured* **(that)** *you'd want to rest after your journey.* [+ *(that)* clause] • *We figured* **on** *being there at about eight.* [I] • *They'd figured* **on** *about twenty people (being there).* [I] • **That/It figures** (=That/It is what I expected). • Ⓕ

fig·ure *(obj)* UNDERSTAND /£ˈfɪg·əʳ, $-jʊr/ *v infml* to understand (someone or something), or to find the answer to (something) by thinking • *I can't figure* **(out) why** *he did it.* [+ *wh*- word] • *Can you figure* **(out) how** *to open this box?* [+ *wh*- word] • *I've never been able to figure her* **out**. [T] • (F)

fig·ure·head PERSON /£ˈfɪg·ə·hed, $-jə-/ *n* [C] someone who has the position of leader in an organization but who has no real power • *He would be a popular figurehead – a head of state who represented France ceremonially to the rest of the world.* • *The President of this company is just a figurehead – the Chief Executive has day-to-day control.*

fig·ure·head MODEL /£ˈfɪg·ə·hed, $-jə-/ *n* [C] a painted model, usually of a person, which in the past was fixed to the front of a ship

fig·ur·ine /£,fɪg·əˈriːn, $-jəˈ-/ *n* [C] a small model of a human, usually made of clay or PORCELAIN

fil·a·ment /ˈfɪl·ə·mᵊnt/ *n* [C] a thin thread or wire, esp. that inside an electric **light bulb** • PIC> **Lights**

fil·bert /£ˈfɪl·bət, $-bət/ *n* [C] a HAZELNUT

filch *obj* /fɪltʃ/ *v* [T] *infml* to steal (something of little value, esp. in small amounts) • *Who has filched my pencils?*

file CONTAINER /faɪl/ *n* any of several different types of container used to store papers, letters and other documents in an ordered way, esp. in an office • *a box/envelope file* [C] • *a concertina file* [C] • *secret/confidential files* [C] • *You'll find it* **in the** *files under C.* [C] • *We keep your records* **on** *file for five years.* [U] • If you have or **open** a file **(on** someone or something), you have or start to keep records about that person or subject: *Here's the file on Mr Jones.* [C] ○ *The police have opened a file on local incidents of this type.* [C] • *Government files are usually* **opened** (= the information they contain is made available) *to the public after 50 years.* [C] • A computer file is a collection of information stored on a computer as one unit with one name: *What's the file name?* [C] ○ *I'm going to copy/save this file.* [C] • PIC> **File, Office, Stationery** (I)

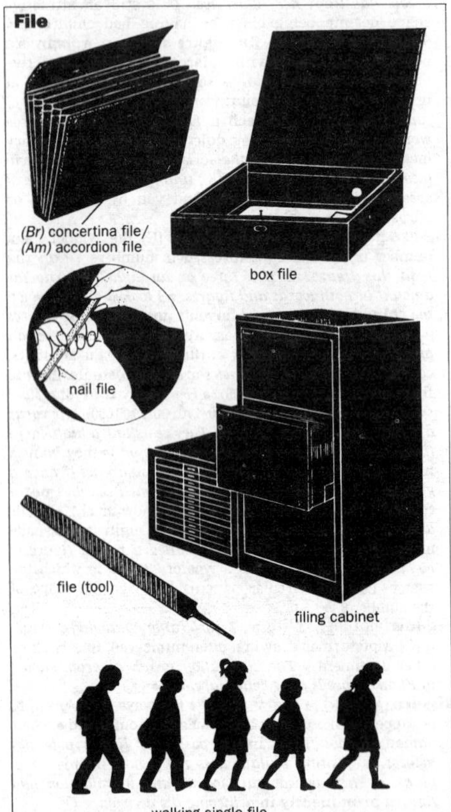

file *obj* /faɪl/ *v* [T] • *We file these reports* (= put them in a file) **under** *country of origin.* • *(law)* To file something can mean to make an official record of it: *Immigration papers were filed last year.* • *(law)* To file **for** something can mean to make an official request for it: *She has filed for divorce.* • News reporters file a story by sending or telephoning it to their office: *Kate Adie filed this report earlier today – some viewers may find the pictures distressing.*

fil·ing /ˈfaɪ·lɪŋ/ *n* [U] • *Her job involves filing and other general office work.* [U] • *(law) The firm has been racing to complete the transaction by its Oct. 15 deadline to avoid a* **bankruptcy** *filing* (= official order). [C]

file LINE /faɪl/ *v, n* (to walk as) a long line of people, one behind another • *A file* **of** *children carrying chairs has just gone past the entrance.* [C] • *They were horrified to see files* **of** *ants converging on the house.* [C] • *They walked* **in (single)** *file* (= one behind another). [U] • *The visitors filed* **through** *the entrance to the ticket offices.* [I always + adv/prep] • PIC> **File** (I)

file TOOL /faɪl/ *v, n* (to use) a long thin flat or rounded metal tool, which has rough surfaces for rubbing esp. wooden or metal objects to make them smooth or to change their shape • *Smooth the rough edges down with a file.* [C] • *First file the stick* **(down)** *to a point/until it fits into the hole.* [T/M] • *The surface had been filed smooth.* [T + obj + adj] • *Her hands were long and slim with* **nails** *which had been carefully filed.* [T] • The prisoner filed **through** (= cut) the bars on his window and made his escape. [I always + adv/prep] • PIC> **File, Tools** (I)

fil·ings /ˈfaɪ·lɪŋz/ *pl n* • Filings are small pieces of metal which are removed from a larger piece by filing: *iron filings.*

fi·let /£ˈfɪl·eɪ, $fɪˈleɪ/ *n* [C], *v* [T] *Am for* FILLET

fil·i·al /ˈfɪl·i·əl/ *adj fml* of a son or daughter • *filial duty/respect/affection* • (S)

fil·i·bus·ter /£ˈfɪl·ɪ·bʌs·təʳ, $-tə/ *v, n* to make a long speech in order to delay or prevent (a new law) being made, or the act of doing this • *Republican senators have announced that they may yet again filibuster a bill.* [T] • *They deny that they're filibustering, even as they refuse to consent to a time for a vote.* [I] • *The filibuster began three days ago.* [C]

fil·i·gree /ˈfɪl·ɪ·griː/ *n* [U] delicate jewellery made from twisted esp. silver wire, or *(fig.)* decorative open patterns • *a beautiful filigree brooch* • *The filigree ironwork lent an elegant air to the bandstand.* • *(fig.) The sunlight shining through the branches made a filigree pattern on the tiles.*

fill *(obj)* /fɪl/ *v* to make or become full; to use (empty space) • *I filled the bucket* **with** *water.* [T] • *I could hear the cistern filling.* [I] • *Fill the bottle half full.* [T + obj + adj] • *I went to the library to fill* **(in) time/an hour/the afternoon** (= use that period of time) *until the meeting.* [T] • *Please fill* **in/out** (= write the necessary information on) *the form/your cheque and sign it.* [M] • *The seats in the hall were filling* **(up)** *fast* (= many people were coming to sit on the seats). [I] • To fill can also mean to make or become completely full: *As she read the poem, their eyes filled* **(up) with** *tears.* [I] ○ *That sandwich filled me* **up**. [T] ○ *I want to fill* **up** *the fuel tank before returning the car.* [M] • *Happy sounds/A bright light filled the room* (= could be heard/seen everywhere in the room). [T] • *A strong sweet smell filled the air* (= could be smelt everywhere). [T] • *The thought of it fills me* **with** (= makes me feel) *dread/anger/pleasure/surprise.* [T] • To fill a job or position is to give it to someone: *I'm sorry, the* **job/post/vacancy** *has already been filled.* [T] ○ *We would prefer to fill the post* **with** (= give it to) *a recent graduate.* [T] • To fill an empty space is to put esp. a substance into it: *Before painting, fill* **(in)** *all the cracks in the plaster.* [T/M] ○ *A dentist fills (holes in)* **teeth**. [T] ○ *These cakes are filled* **with** *cream.* [T] ○ *The product clearly filled a* **need/gap in the market**. [T] • If you **fill** someone **in (on** something), you give them extra or missing information: *We filled them in on the gossip.* ○ *You have ten minutes to fill me in.* • To **fill in (for** someone) is to replace them because they are unable or unwilling to work, play or perform: *Substitute teachers and volunteers would fill in for teachers in the event of a strike.* • To **fill out** is to become larger: *When John is a little older and fills out more, he'll be an outstanding athlete.* • **Filling station** is *esp. Am for* **petrol station**. See at PETROL.

fill /fɪl/ *n* • If you **eat/drink** your **fill**, you eat/drink as much as you need/want: *He took only a few minutes to eat his fill.* • To **have** your **fill of** something means to have had enough of it: *I've had my fill of commuting everyday, I'm going to get a job locally.*

-filled /-fɪld/ *combining form* • *a smoke-filled room* • *a fun-filled weekend*

fil·ler /£ˈfɪl·əʳ, $-ə/ *n* • A filler is a substance that is used to fill small holes and cracks, esp. in wood and walls. [C/U] • A filler is also something such as a short text or drawings used to fill extra space in a magazine or newspaper, or talk, music, etc. used to fill extra time in a radio or television broadcast: *The station always has a filler ready in case the speech/ceremony/tennis match ends earlier than expected.* [C]

fill·ing /ˈfɪl·ɪŋ/ *n* • Filling is any material used to fill something: *Have these pillows got feather or synthetic filling?* [U] • Cakes, pastry dishes and SANDWICHES can have (a) filling inside them: *pies with sweet or savoury fillings* [C] ○ *six different sandwich fillings* [C] ○ *What kind of filling have they got?* [U] • A filling can also be the artificial substance put into holes in teeth to repair them: *I need a filling.* [C] ○ *The dentist gave me two fillings/fillings in two teeth* [C]

fill·ing /ˈfɪl·ɪŋ/ *adj* • If food is filling, you feel full after you have eaten only a little of it: *This chocolate cake is very filling.*

fil·let /ˈfɪl·ɪt/, *Am* **fi·let** *n* a piece of meat, or the flesh of one side of a fish, without bones • *a piece of cod fillet* [U] • *fillet of plaice/beef* [U] • *small trout fillets* [C] • *fillet steak*

fil·let *obj* /ˈfɪl·ɪt/, *Am* **fi·let** *v* [T] • *Would you fillet the fish* (=cut the flesh from the bones) *for me, please?* • *I prefer filleted fish.*

fil·lip /ˈfɪl·ɪp/ *n* [C usually sing] something which causes a sudden improvement • *The athletics win* **provided** *a much-needed fillip* **to/for** *national pride.* • *The news* **gave** *the stock market a* **(big)** *fillip.*

fil·ly /ˈfɪl·i/ *n* [C] a young female horse under the age of four • Compare COLT [HORSE].

film [MOVING PICTURES] /fɪlm/, *esp. Am and Aus* **mov·ie** *n* a series of moving pictures, usually shown in a cinema or on television and often telling a story • *a recently released* (=shown to the public for the first time) *film* [C] • *a career in films/film* (=the business of making films) [C/U] • *the film industry* • *a film star/producer/director/critic* • *a film-maker* • *Her last film was* **shot** (=made) *on location in South America.* [C] • *The film was made specially for television/was a wild-life documentary.* [C] • *We took the children to* **(see)** *a film.* [C] • *I hate people talking while I'm* **watching** *a film.* [C] • *Andy's a real film* **buff** (=enjoys and knows a lot about films). • *Andy knows a lot about film* (=films). [U]

film /fɪlm/ *v* • *They filmed for a week in Spain.* [I] • *We filmed the children's school play.* [T]

film·ing /ˈfɪl·mɪŋ/ *n* [U] • *Gerard claims that after three weeks of filming* (=the making of a film) *there is not a great deal more that a director can teach the actors.*

film [MATERIAL] /fɪlm/ *n* (a length of) dark plastic-like material which can record images as photographs or as a moving picture • *a* **roll of** *film* [U] • *a 24 exposure/16mm/high-speed film* [C] • *A passer-by recorded the incident* **on** *film.* [U] • *I'm getting my film* **developed** *at the chemist's.* [C] • A **film strip** is a length of film with a set of pictures which are shown one at a time: *a health education film strip*

film [LAYER] /fɪlm/ *n* [C] a thin layer of something light • *a film of dust/oil/grease* • *a film* **of** *smoke*

film·y /ˈfɪl·mi/ *adj* • *filmy material* • *a filmy dress* • *filmy cloud/smoke/mist*

fil·mi·ness /ˈfɪl·mɪ·nəs/ *n* [U]

film o·ver *v adv* [I] • If something films **over**, it becomes lightly covered with a thin layer: *Her eyes filmed over* **(with** *tears) at the news.*

film·go·er *esp. Br* /£ˈfɪlmˌɡəʊ·əʳ, $-ˌɡoʊ·ɚ/, *esp. Br* **ci·ne·ma·go·er**, *esp. Am and Aus* **mov·ie·go·er** *n* [C] a person who regularly goes to the cinema

film·go·ing *Br* /£ˈfɪlmˌɡəʊ·ɪŋ, $ˌɡoʊ-/, *esp. Br* **ci·ne·ma·go·ing**, *esp. Am and Aus* **mov·ie·go·ing** *n* [U] • *the filmgoing public*

filo (pa·stry), phyl·lo (pa·stry) /£ˈfiː·ləʊ, $-loʊ/ *n* [U] a type of pastry made in thin, almost transparent layers • *We saw the filo being made, rolled out, then pulled gently, getting thinner and thinner until almost transparent.* • *A samosa might be made with filo pastry, then baked instead of fried.*

fi·lo·fax *trademark* /ˈfaɪ·lə·fæks/, **per·son·al or·gan·iz·er** *n* [C] a small book in which a record can be kept of telephone numbers, future plans and visits, business meetings, etc. • *The details of Sue's entire business and personal lives are held between the black leather covers of her Filofax.*

fil·ter /£ˈfɪl·təʳ, $-t̬ɚ/ *v, n* (to use or act as) any of several types of equipment or devices for removing solids from liquids or gases, or for removing particular types of light, or *(fig.)* a way of removing part of something • *an oil/water filter* [C] • *a dust filter* [C] • *I like to experiment with different*

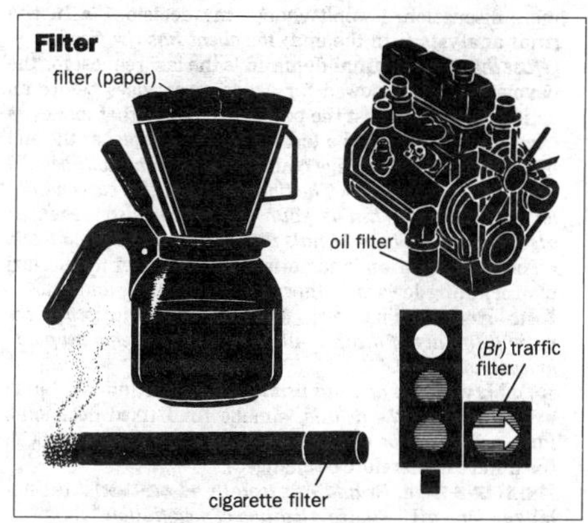

light filters on my camera. [C] • *Ozone is the earth's primary filter for ultraviolet radiation.* [C] • *(fig.) The interviewers would act as a filter and see that urgent cases received attention first.* [C] • A filter **bed** is an area of stones and sand through which water flows to be cleaned. • *(Br)* A **traffic** filter (*Am and Aus* **right/left turn lane**) is one row of traffic, controlled by a green arrow-shaped light, which turns left or right while other rows do not move: *a left/right filter* [C] ○ *You'll have to get into the left filter at the lights.* [C] ○ *Filter left* (=move in this row of traffic). [I always + adv/prep] • *Mussels filter 50 litres of water daily to extract food.* [T] • *Devices in the two chimneys would filter* **(out)** *radioactive dust from smoke released into the air.* [T] • To filter **down**, **in**, **out** and **through** means to appear or happen gradually or to a limited degree: *News filtered down to us during the day.* [I always + adv/prep] ○ *Reports about an accident began to filter in.* [I always + adv/prep] ○ *Word began to filter out about the changes.* [I always + adv/prep] ○ *Payments have started to filter through to the office.* [I always + adv/prep] ○ *Sunlight filtered through the branches.* [I always + adv/prep] • When driving, to filter **in** (*Am* **merge**) is to join a line of moving traffic without causing other vehicles to slow down. [I always + adv/prep] • **Filter coffee/filtered coffee** is made by hot water flowing through coffee solids in a coffee filter. • A **filter (paper)** is a paper cone which allows only liquid to flow through, and is used to make filter coffee. • A **filter tip/filter-tipped cigarette** is a cigarette with a filter on the end to remove TAR from the tobacco. • [PIC] **Driving, Filter**

fil·tra·tion /fɪlˈtreɪ·ʃᵊn/ *n* [U] • *a filtration unit/plant* (=place for filtering) • *The technology exists to remove all of these contaminants through filtration* (=the act of filtering) *and condensation.*

fil·thy /ˈfɪl·θi/ *adj* **-ier, -iest** extremely or unpleasantly dirty • *The boys were filthy when they came in from football.* • *The door led into a filthy room, full of rubbish and rotting food.* • *I think smoking is a filthy* **habit**. • *That girl just gave me a filthy* **look** (=looked at me in very unpleasant, disapproving way). • *(Br infml) We had filthy* (=bad and unpleasant) **weather** *for the whole holiday.* • *(Br infml) He was in a filthy* **temper/mood** (=very bad-tempered). • *He's got a filthy* **temper** (=gets very angry easily). • Filthy can mean containing esp. sexually offensive words or pictures: *filthy language* • *a filthy joke/book/film* • *a filthy mind* • *"Filthy lucre* (=money)*"* (Bible, 1 Timothy 3.3)

fil·thy /ˈfɪl·θi/ *adv* • *(infml) They're* **filthy rich** (=extremely rich).

filth /fɪlθ/ *n* [U] • *The floor was covered in filth.* • *People complain about the filth* (=esp. sexually offensive material) *on TV and in the press.* • *(Br slang)* **The filth** is a strongly disapproving name for the police.

fil·thi·ly /ˈfɪl·θɪ·li/ *adv*

fil·thi·ness /ˈfɪl·θɪ·nəs/ *n* [U]

fin [THIN PART] /fɪn/ *n* [C] a thin vertical part sticking out of the body of esp. a fish or an aircraft which helps balance and movement • *The pelvic fins of the male catfish are longer and more pointed than those of the female.* • *The aircraft has a long tail fin.* • [PIC] **Fish**

fin [MONEY] /fɪn/ *n* [C] *Am dated slang* a $5 note

fi·nal [LAST] /ˈfaɪ·nəl/ *adj* [not gradable] last • *a final warning/offer* • *the final chapters of a book* • *the final years* • *Her life/The game/The performance is* **in its final stages**. • *(infml) I'm not coming and* **that's final** (=there can be no more discussion, I won't change my decision). • **In the final analysis** (= in the end) *the client has the freedom to refuse the offer.* • A **final demand** is the last request for the payment of money owed for goods or services before an action is taken against the person who owes that money. • *(Am)* A **final (exam)** is a test taken on a subject at the end of a school year or college course: *Final exams will be held the third week in May.* ○ *The final exam for this class will be on May 21st.* ○ *When is your history/chemistry/French/algebra final?* ○ *I have 2 finals this week and three next week.* • The **final solution** is sometimes used to refer to the Nazi plan of killing Jews and others during the 1930s and 1940s.

fi·nal·i·ty /£faɪˈnæl·ə·ti, $-t̬i/ *n* [U] • *Accepting the painful finality of death is ultimately what helps people to grieve and so heal.*

fi·nal·ize *obj, Br and Aus usually* **-ise** /ˈfaɪ·nə·laɪz/ *v* [T] • *We'll finalize the details* (= make final/fixed decisions) *later.* • *Plans have not yet been finalized* (= have not been fixed and can therefore be changed).

fi·nal·iz·a·tion, *Br and Aus usually* **-i·sa·tion** /ˌfaɪ·nə·laɪˈzeɪ·ʃᵊn/ *n* [U] • *the finalization of negotiations*

fi·nal·ly /ˈfaɪ·nə·li/ *adv* [not gradable] • *We finally* (= after some difficulty or delay) *got home at eleven o'clock/collected the parcel and left.* • *Finally* (= As the last item of several), *I would like to tell you a little story.* • *The plan hasn't been finally approved* (= approved in its finished form).

fi·nals /ˈfaɪ·nəlz/ *pl n Br* • Finals are the exams taken at the end of a university or college course, or *(Am)* exams taken at the end of each school year: *I'm* **taking** *my finals in June.* ○ *The finals results have gone up on the noticeboard.* • See also **finals** at FINAL [COMPETITION].

fi·nal [COMPETITION] /ˈfaɪ·nəl/ *n* [C] the last in a series of games, races or competitions, usually the one in which the winner is chosen • *Our team got all the way to/through to the final before being beaten.* • *The men's basketball final will be on Sunday.* • [LP] **Sports**

fin·al·ist /ˈfaɪ·nə·lɪst/ *n* [C] • A finalist is a person or group competing in a final: *All four regional finalists will advance to the state tournament, which begins next week.*

fi·nals /ˈfaɪ·nəlz/ *pl n* • *The tennis finals* (= final) *are on Saturday.*

fi·na·le /fɪˈnɑː·li/ *n* [C usually sing] the last part of esp. a musical or theatrical performance, which is often very exciting or emotional • *All the dancers come on stage during the* **(grand)** *finale.* • *What better finale* **to** *her career than this extravagant gesture.*

fi·nance /ˈfaɪ·nænts, fɪˈnænts/ *n* [U] (the management of) a supply of money • *corporate finance* (= management of a company's money) • *personal finance* (= management of your own money) • *public finance* (= management of public money) • *the minister of finance/the finance minister* • *The Dockland Development scheme has recently sought to bring industry and finance* (= money) *into the area.* • *We've had some difficulty* **raising** *finance* (= money) *for the project.* • *The finance* **committee** *controls the school's budget.* • *He set up a finance* **company/house** *and rapidly expanded from lending to investment in real estate to building golf courses.*

fi·nance *obj* /faɪˈnænts, fɪ-/ *v* [T] • If you finance something, you provide the money needed for it to happen: *The local authority has refused to finance the scheme.*

fi·nan·ces /ˈfaɪ·nænt·sɪz, fɪˈnænt-/ *pl n* • *We keep a tight control on the organization's finances* (= the money it has available to spend). • *(Br and Aus infml) My finances won't* **run to** (= I do not have enough money to buy) *a new car this year.*

fi·nan·cial /faɪˈnæn·tʃᵊl, fɪ-/ *adj* [not gradable] • *financial difficulties/success* • *a financial adviser* • *financial affairs* • The **financial year** is a period of twelve months (not always January to January) for which a business, government, etc. plans its management of money.

fi·nan·cial·ly /faɪˈnæn·t·ʃᵊl·i, fɪ-/ *adv* [not gradable] • *The project is not financially* **viable** (= will not produce enough money). • *It is hard for students to be financially* **dependent on** (= receive all the money they need to live from) *their parents.*

fi·nan·ci·er /£fɪˈnænt·si·əʳ, $-ɚ/ *n* [C] • A financier is a person who has control of a large amount of money and can give or lend it to people or organizations: *An unnamed millionaire financier bought the painting.*

finch /fɪntʃ/ *n* [C] any of various types of small singing bird with a short wide pointed beak • See also BULLFINCH; CHAFFINCH; GOLDFINCH.

find *(obj)* [DISCOVER] /faɪnd/ *v past* **found** /faʊnd/ to discover, esp. where (a thing or person) is, either unexpectedly or by searching, or to discover where to obtain or how to achieve (something) • *I've just found a ten-pound note under my bed.* [T] • *Although a body has not yet been found, the police suspect that he has been murdered.* [T] • *Have you managed to find a replacement for that waiter who left so suddenly?* [T] • *I'm hoping to find somewhere to live near my office.* [T] • *Did you find* **where** *I'd left the key?* [+ *wh-* word] • *Nancy has found us a small flat/found a small flat* **for** *us.* [+ two objects] • *I eventually found her* **reading** *a newspaper in the library.* [T + obj + v-*ing*] • *She was found unconscious 50 metres from the scene of the accident.* [T + obj + adj] • *Surprisingly, the study found* **that** *men who drank no milk were more likely to have a heart attack than those who drank more than a pint a day.* [+ *that* clause] • *Some insects have been found* **to** *live for several years without any water.* [T + obj + *to* infinitive] • *Do you find Clive* (= In your experience is he) *difficult to talk to?* [T + obj + n/adj] • *I don't find him* (= In my experience he is not) *an easy person to get on with.* [T + obj + n/adj] • *Linda found* **living** *in Buenos Aires* (= experienced it as) *a fascinating experience.* [+ v-*ing*] • *Whenever I get home I always seem to find you* (= you always seem to be) *in front of the TV having a little snack.* [T] • *You'll find the knives and forks* (= They are kept) *in the left-hand drawer.* • *You don't find many people* **cycling** (= Not many people cycle) *to work in New York.* [T + obj + v-*ing*] • *Many plant and animal species are found* (= exist) *only in the rainforests.* [T] • *The pound should be left to find* (= gradually reach) *its own level against the other European currencies.* [T] • *We went to sleep soon after we got on the train and woke up to find* **ourselves** (= when we woke up we were) **in** *Calais.* [T] • *(fig.) You'll soon find* **yourself** *without any friends* (= have no friends) *at all if you keep on being so rude to everybody.* [T + obj + n/adj] • *She's hoping to* **find herself** (= learn about her character, desires and abilities) *by doing a degree in philosophy.* • *Ever since the operation his sight has been good enough for him to find his* **way** *about* (= go where he needs to) *by himself.* • *Do you think they'll ever find* (= create) *a way of bringing peace to the region?* • *We must make every effort to find* (= produce) *a diplomatic solution to the crisis – the military option is not a solution.* • *We're really struggling to find* (= obtain) *the/enough money to pay the rent at the moment.* • *After years of suffering beatings from her husband because she did not want to live alone, she eventually found* (= obtained) *the courage to leave him.* • *I wish I could find (the) time* (= have enough time) *to do more reading.* • *Did it take you long to* **find** *your* **feet** (= become familiar with your new surroundings and able to do things on your own with confidence) *when you started your new job?* • *The victim's widow said that her husband was a man who would have* **found it in himself/his heart to** (= been willing to) *forgive the bombers.* • *Those witnesses will* **find** *their* **tongues** (= become willing to talk) *when they hear a reward has been offered.* • To **find fault with** someone is to criticize them: *She's always finding fault with the way he works.* • If someone or something is **nowhere/not anywhere to be found**, you cannot see them: *We looked for her everywhere, but she was nowhere to be found.*

find /faɪnd/ *n* [C] • A find is a good or valuable thing or a special person that has been discovered but was not known about before: *This café's quite a find – I had no idea there was anywhere like it around here.* ○ *She's a real find, you know – singers like her don't grow on trees.* ○ *A find* **of** *some ancient silver brooches by a local man has been valued at £1m.*

find·er /£ˈfaɪn·dəʳ, $-dɚ/ *n* [C] • *The identity of the finder of the treasure and its location are being kept secret, so that treasure hunters do not trespass on the site.* • *(saying)* Children sometimes say 'finders keepers (losers weepers)' which means they will keep something that they have found and that the person who did not find it cannot have or share it.

find·ing /ˈfaɪn·dɪŋ/ *n* [C] • *The report's finding* (= official discovery) *is supported by new figures that show a dramatic rise in car crime over the past year.* • *The government has promised to take the committee's findings into account.*

find *(obj)* [JUDGE] /faɪnd/ *v past* **found** /faʊnd/ *law* to make a judgment in a law court • *In a unanimous verdict, the jury found Smith* **guilty/not guilty** *of the murder.* [T + obj + adj] • *How do you find the accused* (= Is the accused person guilty or not guilty)*?* [T + obj + adv] • *The jury found* **for** (= made a judgment on the side of) *the Duchess, and awarded her £200 000 in libel damages against the newspaper.* [I] • *The judge found* **against** (= made a judgment against) *the Government and declared that the social security rules were hopelessly inadequate.* [I]

find·ing /ˈfaɪn·dɪŋ/ *n* [C usually sing] • A finding is a judgment made at the end of a JUDICIAL INQUIRY (= an official legal attempt to discover the facts about something).

find out *(obj)*, **find** *(obj)* **out** *v adv* to obtain knowledge of (something), or to obtain knowledge of the dishonest or criminal activities of (someone) • *How did you find out my new address/find my new address out?* [M] • *How did you find out* **about** *the party?.* [I] • *To find out more* **about** *these beauty products, please write to us at the address given below.* [T] • *The holiday was a complete surprise – I only found out* **about** *it the day before we left.* [T] • *I'll just go and find out* **what***'s going on outside.* [+ *wh-* word] • *Too late, she found out* **that** *the train had been cancelled.* [+ *that* clause] • *The only way to find out is to ask him how he feels about you.* [I] • *I asked her what she meant and she told me that I would find out soon enough.* [I] • *If the army had found out, I would have been executed.* [I] • *They found her out before she could carry out the bomb attack.* [T] • *The only thing he could do was to hide it somewhere and hope to God he wouldn't be found out.* [T]

fin-de-si·ècle /ˌfæn·də·siːˈek·lə/ *adj* [not gradable] relating to the end of a century, esp. the 1890s, and suggesting an unusual and exciting period or a period of low moral standards esp. as shown in art • *The novel begins with an evocative description of fin-de-siècle Paris* (= Paris in the 1890s). • *A fin-de-siècle feel has crept into fashion recently.*

fine SATISFACTORY /faɪn/ *adj* [after v], *adv* [not gradable] causing no problems; satisfactory or satisfactorily • *I felt terrible last night but I feel fine this morning.* • *The apartments are very small, which is fine if you're a childless couple.* • *"Are you alright? Is something wrong?" "No, no, nothing's wrong. Everything's just fine, thanks."* • *The car's fine for now, but we'll need a bigger one when the baby arrives.* • *"Can you meet me at seven o'clock?" "Seven's fine* **by/for** *me, but I don't know if Tristan can make it then."* • *"I'll come round to your place at eight." "Fine. See you then."* • *"Will a loan of $500 be sufficient?" "That will* **suit** *me fine."* • *When did it break down? It was working fine yesterday.* • *"I Feel Fine"* (song by The Beatles, 1965)

fine GOOD /faɪn/ *adj* **-r, -st** of excellent quality or much better than average • *It's hard to believe that these fine musicians are still only students.* • *The world's finest collection of Impressionist paintings is housed in the Musée d'Orsay in Paris.* • *This building is the finest example of its type.* • *New Zealand has already shown that it can produce some of the finest white wines in the world.* • *Our support for the campaigners should not be confined to fine words but actually turned into positive action.* • *What you've said is all very fine, but what are you going to do about this problem?* • Fine is sometimes used with an opposite meaning for humorous effect or for emphasis: *She really is in a fine mess* (= in a very bad situation) *now that she's lost her house as well as her job.* ○ *That's a fine* (= very unpleasant) *thing to say about your father after all he's done for you.* • **Fine art** consists of drawings, paintings and SCULPTURES that are admired for their beauty and have no practical use: *She's a great lover of fine art.* ○ *How relevant are the fine arts to the modern world?* • If you have something **down/off to a fine art**, you can do or make it extremely well: *This tastes delicious. You've really got (making) pizzas down to a fine art.* • *"This was their finest hour"* (speech by Winston Churchill, 1940)

fi·nest /ˈfaɪ·nɪst/ *n* [U] • *This 100-year old restaurant is popularly reckoned to be among London's finest.* • *(Am infml)* A city's finest is its police force: *New York's finest*

fine·ly /ˈfaɪn·li/ *adv* • *The painting depicts a finely-dressed couple and a man, who is reading, seated on a table.*

fine THIN /faɪn/ *adj* **-r, -st** very thin or in very small grains or drops • *He has lovely fine blond hair just like his father.* • *This brush will do for the outline but you'll need a finer one for the detail.* • *We were almost choked and blinded by the fine desert dust blowing in our faces.* • *The paint comes out of the can in a fine spray.* • *Apply a fine line of highlighter along the middle of your top lip.* • *(fig.) There's a fine* **line** *between love and hate.* • *(approving) She has inherited her mother's fine* (= delicate and beautiful) **features**. • *(fig.) I understood in general what she was talking about, but some of the finer* **points** (= exact details) *were beyond me.* • *I think she's mistaken – in fact* **not to put too fine a point on it** (= to be completely direct and honest) *I think she's completely wrong.* • If you examine something **with a fine-tooth comb**, you examine it in great detail and with great care: *They have promised to examine all the evidence with a fine-tooth comb.* ○ *Holidaymakers should go through their insurance policies with a fine-tooth comb to find out what risks they are not covered for.* • *Make sure you examine the* **fine print** (= the details that are printed in small letters) *before you sign any agreement.* • If you **fine-tune** something, you make very small changes to it in order to make it work as well as possible: *The computer senses how many people are in the room and fine-tunes the air-conditioning accordingly.*

fine·ly /ˈfaɪn·li/, **fine** **(-r, -st)** /faɪn/ *adv* • *Chop the herbs very fine(ly).* • *Make sure the spices are finely ground.* • *The desk is made of beautiful fine-grained wood.* • *Racing car engines have to be very finely tuned to achieve the best possible performance.* • *(fig.) The decision about whether or not to proceed with the project is very finely balanced* (= there are equal reasons for and against it).

fine·ness /ˈfaɪn·nəs/ *n* [U] • *It's the fineness of the thread that makes the cloth so soft.* • *When I look at her paintings I'm always struck by the fineness of the details.*

fine SUNNY /faɪn/ *adj* [not gradable] sunny and dry • *The weather forecast said it would be fine in the morning but cloud over later on.* • *Morning, Harry, it's* **turned out** *fine again, hasn't it?* • *We've only had two fine days all summer.*

fine PUNISHMENT /faɪn/ *n* [C] an amount of money that has to be paid as a punishment for not obeying a rule or law • *I've paid out fifty pounds in parking fines already this year.* • *The* **maximum** *fine* **for** *this offence is £1000.* • *The maximum penalty for the offence is a $1000 fine.* • *If found guilty, he faces six months in jail and a* **heavy** *fine.*

fine *obj* /faɪn/ *v* [T] • *Drivers who exceed the speed limit can expect to be fined heavily.* • *They fined him $100* **for** *using threatening behaviour.* [+ two objects] • *He was fined a total of £450 and ordered to pay £200 costs.* [+ two objects] • LP **Two objects**

fin·er·y /£ˈfaɪ·nᵊr·i, $-nɚ·i/ *n* [U] unusually stylish and beautiful clothing and jewellery worn on a special occasion • *We watched the stars arriving for the awards ceremony dressed up* **in all their finery**.

fines her·bes /£ˌfiːnzˈeəb, $-ˈɜːrb/ *pl n* a mixture of fresh or dried herbs that have been cut into small pieces and are used to flavour some savoury foods • *Fines herbes are used in salads and omelettes and consist of parsley, chives, tarragon and chervil, and sometimes also thyme and rosemary.*

fi·nesse /fɪˈnes/ *n* [U] great skill or style • *It was a disappointing performance which lacked finesse.* • *She has handled these difficult negotiations with tremendous finesse.*

fi·nesse *obj* /fɪˈnes/ *v* [T] • To finesse something is to deal with it by deceiving slightly but skilfully without telling lies: *She finessed the fact that she had no relevant experience and instead talked about her long-standing interest in the field.* ○ *To finesse someone is to defeat them in this way.*

fin·ger /£ˈfɪŋ·gəʳ, $-gɚ/ *n* [C] any of the long thin jointed parts of the hand, esp. those which are not thumbs • *He noticed her long delicate fingers.* • *I cut my finger when I was chopping onions last night.* • *"How many fingers have you got?" "Ten, or eight if you don't count my thumbs."* • A finger is also a part of a GLOVE which covers a finger: *She was wearing black gloves that had had their fingers cut off.* • If you are *(Br and Aus)* **all fingers and thumbs**/*(Am)* **all thumbs**, you move your hands in an awkward or CLUMSY way: *I'm all fingers and thumbs today. That's the third plate I've dropped this morning.* • *(Am)* If you **give** someone **the finger**, you show them in an offensive way that you are angry with them by turning the back of your hand towards them and putting your middle finger up: *I gave him the finger and told him I never wanted to see him again.* • If you have **a finger in every pie**, you are involved in everything that is happening: *Sharon's very busy these days – she's got a finger in every pie at the moment.* • *(Am)* If you **have a finger in the pie**, you are involved in something, often when your involvement is not wanted: *It's my project but he keeps putting his finger in the pie.* • If someone has their **fingers in the till**, they are stealing money from the place where they work: *She lost her job after she was* **caught** **with** *her fingers in the till.* • *We're* **keeping** *our* **fingers crossed** (= hoping strongly) *for a complete recovery.* • *He just watches TV all evening and never* **lifts/raises a finger** (= makes any effort to help) *when it comes to cooking or washing up.* • *(Br and Aus) She's really going to have to* **pull/get** *her* **finger out** (= start working hard, esp. after a period of low activity) *if she wants to finish before Friday.* • *Something seemed to be wrong, but I couldn't* **put** *my* **finger on** (=tell exactly) *what it was.* • A **finger bowl** is a small bowl that is filled with water so that people can wash their fingers if they have food on them, during a meal. • A **finger buffet** is a meal that takes place on a special or formal occasion and consists of a wide choice of usually cold food which can be eaten with the fingers rather than with knives, forks or spoons. The guests serve themselves and often eat standing up. • **Finger food** is food that you can hold and eat in your hand without using knives, forks or spoons. • *"Let your fingers do the walking"* (advertisement for using the telephone, 1960s) • See also FOREFINGER; INDEX FINGER. • (I)

fin·ger *obj* /£'fɪŋ·gəʳ, $-gɚ/ *v* [T] • If you finger something you touch or feel it with your fingers: *"We are all ready to defend our nation," she said as she fingered the handle of her revolver.* ○ *He won't stop fingering his new video-recorder – he's always like that when he gets a new gadget.* ○ *You'd find this tune easier to play if you fingered it correctly* (=played the notes of the tune with the correct fingers). • *(infml)* If you finger someone, you tell the police that they are guilty of a crime: *You don't really expect me to finger my own sister* (**to** *the police), do you?*

-fin·gered /£'fɪŋ·gəd, $-gɚd/ *combining form* • *This is one of the first robots to have a fully functioning five-fingered hand.* • *We expect more than two-fingered typing from our journalists.*

fin·ger·ing /£'fɪŋ·gᵊr·ɪŋ, $-gɚ-/ *n* [U] • The fingering of a piece of music is the way that fingers are used to play particular notes, or the numbers on a sheet of music that show which fingers should play which notes: *The fingering for this song is a bit more complicated.*

fin·ger·board /£'fɪŋ·gə·bɔːd, $-gɚ·bɔːrd/ *n* [C] the long strip of wood on a stringed musical instrument against which the strings are pressed by the fingers in order to vary the note that is played • *Guitars and banjos have fingerboards.*

fin·ger·mark /£'fɪŋ·gə·mɑːk, $-gɚ·mɑːrk/, *Am usually* **fin·ger·print** *n* [C] a mark left by a dirty or oily finger on a clean surface • *I wish you wouldn't leave your fingermarks all over the windows when I've only just cleaned them.*

fin·ger·nail /£'fɪŋ·gə·neɪl, $-gɚ-/, **nail** *n* [C] the hard slightly curved part that covers and protects the top of the end of a finger • *When did you last cut your fingernails?* • *I'm always breaking my fingernails on the strings of my guitar.* • PIC> **Body, Nail**

fin·ger·print /£'fɪŋ·gə·prɪnt, $-gɚ-/, *infml* **print** *n* [C] the pattern of curved lines on the end of a finger or thumb, which is different in every person, or a mark left by this pattern • *He must have fired the gun – his fingerprints are all over it.* • *The police have* **taken** *the fingerprints of every man in the neighbourhood who matched the rapist's description.* • Fingerprint is also another word for FINGERMARK.

fin·ger·print *obj* /£'fɪŋ·gə·prɪnt, $-gɚ-/ *v* [T] • *We would like to fingerprint* (=record the pattern of the fingerprints of) *every one of your employees.*

fin·ger·tip /£'fɪŋ·gə·tɪp, $-gɚ-/ *n* [C] the end of a finger • *He touched the parcel lightly with his fingertips.* • *If you have any problems just ask Phil – he's got the whole system* **at** *his* **fingertips** (=he has a complete knowledge of it). • *(Br and Aus) She's a novelist* **to** *her* **fingertips** (=in every way).

fin·ick·y /'fɪn·ɪ·ki/ *adj disapproving* giving or needing too much attention to detail • *He's terribly finicky about his food and refuses to eat anything that doesn't look perfect.* • *Repairing watches must be a very finicky job.*

fin·ish *(obj)* /'fɪn·ɪʃ/ *v* to come or bring (something) to an end, or to complete or use (something) completely • *The meeting should finish at four o'clock.* [I] • *If you'd let me finish my sentence I'll explain it to you.* [T] • *Let him finish* (=continue speaking), *please – I'm sure we're all interested in what he's got to say.* [I] • *She finished* (=ended) *the concert* **with** *a song from her first album.* [T] • *I'm going to finish* (=end) *with a new song.* [I] • *She may not have won the race but she did finish* (=end the race) *second.* [I] • *He finished* (=ended the race) *last, but finishing at all is quite an achievement.* [I] • *Have you finished* (=completed) *reading that magazine?* [+ v-*ing*] • *Have you finished* **with** (=completed using) *that magazine?* [I] • *She finished* **with** *him* (=ended her personal/sexual relationship with him) *when she discovered he was having an affair with another woman.* [I] • *I want to finish* **(off)** (=complete) *this essay before I go to bed.* [M] • *We may as well finish* **(off)** (=completely use) *this whisky – there's only a little bit left.* [M] • *(Am slang) After testifying in court, he was severely beaten and warned that if he showed up in court again, they'd* **finish** *him* **off** (=kill him). • *He could spar well enough but he couldn't seem to* **finish off** (=defeat completely) *his opponents/***finish** *his opponents* **off**. • *That game of football has really* **finished** *me* **off** (=made me extremely tired). • *They've already run out of money and the building isn't even* **half-finished** (=half of it has not been completed). • *Make sure she finishes* **(up)** (=eats all of) *her vegetables.* [M] • If you finish **up** in a particular place or situation, that is the place or situation that you are in finally: *You'll finish* **up** *dead/in hospital* (=The result will be that you will die/become ill) *if you carry on drinking as much as that.* [L only + adj/I] • *They're working their way around the world and planning to finish up* (=end their journey) *in Australia.* [I] • *(Br and Aus) I originally intended to spend £600 on it, but I finished up spending* (=but by the time I had finished I had spent) *£750.* [+ v-*ing*] • If you finish something made of wood, you give it a last covering of paint, POLISH or VARNISH so that it is ready to be used: *This dining table has been beautifully finished.* • A **finishing school** is a school or college, paid for by parents or relatives, where young women from rich families learn how to behave in high-class society: *Annabelle went to a finishing school in Switzerland for a year before college.* • *She's currently in Hollywood* **putting the finishing touches to**/*(Am and Aus also)* **putting the finishing touches on** (=completing and making perfect) *her new movie.*

fin·ish /'fɪn·ɪʃ/ *n* [C] • *It was a very* **close** *finish* (=end to the race), *but I just managed to win.* • *Most political commentators are predicting a* **close** *finish in this election.* • *The project has been very badly organized* **from start to** *finish* (=all the way through). • *Both sides in the civil war are bent on* **a fight to the** *finish* (=they intend to fight until one side has been defeated). • The finish of a material such as wood is the condition of the surface of the material: *Look at the lovely shiny finish on that piano.* • A finish is also the last covering of VARNISH, POLISH or paint that is put onto something: *Even a clear finish will alter the colour of wood slightly, usually making it darker.* ○ *These cupboards are available in a range of finishes.*

fin·ished /'fɪn·ɪʃt/ *adj* [not gradable] • *Are you finished* **with** *that drill?* • *When do you expect to be finished?* • *The rebels' ammunition is almost finished* (=completely used) *and it is only a matter of time before they surrender.* • *Raw materials make up only a small proportion of the cost of the finished* (=completed) *product.* • *As a result of this latest scandal the minister's career is almost certainly finished* (=at an end). • *This financial crisis means that the government's economic policy is finished* (=destroyed).

fin·ish·er /£'fɪn·ɪ·ʃəʳ, $-ʃɚ/ *n* [C usually pl] • *Although Potter didn't win a medal, she was one of the top ten finishers in the race.*

fi·nite LIMITED /'faɪ·naɪt/ *adj* having a limit or end • *How do we know whether the universe is finite or infinite?* • *The funds available for the health service are finite and we cannot afford to waste money.* • *We only have a finite amount of time to complete this task – we can't continue indefinitely.*

fi·nite GRAMMAR /'faɪ·naɪt/ *adj* [not gradable] in a form that shows the tense and subject of a verb, rather than the INFINITIVE form or a participle • *In the following sentence 'go' is finite: "I often go to the cinema."* • *In the following sentence 'been' is non-finite: "How many times have you been to the cinema?"*

fi·ni·to /£fɪ'niː·təʊ, $-t̬oʊ/ *adj* [after v; not gradable] *infml* brought to an end or unable to continue; finished • *It's taken me three weeks to get this bit of work done but there it is at last, finito!* • *As far as I am concerned the relationship is over – finito – and I can start living again.* • *If you don't finish this on time, you're finito – you won't get a second chance.*

fink /fɪŋk/ *n* [C] *Am and Aus infml* an unpleasant person who has told someone in authority secret and damaging information about someone else • *Martha's such a fink -she's gone and told Mom I was smoking again.*

fink on *obj* /fɪŋk/ *v prep* [T] *Am slang* • If you fink on someone, you tell other people secret and damaging information about them: *Someone must have finked on him.*

fink out *v adv* [I] *Am slang* to fail to do something, esp. something promised • *We'd planned to go camping but at the last minute Ron finked out.*

fi·ord /£fjɔːd, $fjɔːrd/ *n* [C] a FJORD

fir (tree) /£fɜːʳ, $fɜːr/ *n* [C] any of several types of usually pointed, usually evergreen tree that have needle-like leaves and are grown esp. for their wood • *The fir trees on the upper slopes of the mountain were covered in snow.* • *My father had brought a fir tree in from the garden for Christmas.* • *Firs have been badly damaged by acid rain in several areas of Europe and North America.*

fire FLAMES /£faɪəʳ, $faɪr/ *n* (material that is in) the state of burning that produces flames which send out heat and light, and might produce smoke • *The world would be very different if humans had not discovered how to use fire.* [U] • *The factory had to be closed because the risk of fire was too great.* [U] • *The library was badly damaged* **in** *the fire.* [C] • *How many historic buildings are damaged* **by** *fire each year?* [U] • *The library was badly damaged* **by** *fire.* [U] • *I had to be rescued by my neighbours when my house* **caught** *fire* (= started to burn unintentionally). [U] • *There have been a lot of* **forest** *fires because of the drought.* [C] • *Forty people helped to* **put out** (= stop) *the fire.* [C] • If someone's words or their way of speaking is described as **fire and brimstone**, they are connected with the threat of severe punishment in hell after death: *The preacher gave a real fire-and brimstone sermon.* ○ *She was* **breathing** *fire and brimstone, threatening us with eternal damnation of our souls.* • If something is **on fire**, it is burning when it is not meant to be: *If your home was on fire and you could save only one thing, what would it be?* • If you **set** something/someone **on fire** or **set fire to** something or someone, you cause it or them to start burning: *Soldiers chased the protesters into a warehouse and set fire to it.* ○ *Several peace campaigners set themselves on fire in protest at the government's involvement in the war.* • *(dated)* If you **go through fire and water** for someone, you face great difficulties or dangers for them. • A fire is also a small controlled fire that is used for heating or cooking: *It's very cold in here – should I* **light** *the fire?* [C] ○ *We cooked our supper on a fire that we'd* **lit** *on the beach.* [C] • A fire is also a gas or electric heater that is used to warm up a room: *Why don't you* **switch/put/turn** *the fire* **on** *if you're so cold?* [C] ○ *I love* **real** *fires* (= small controlled fires made from wood or coal that produce flames), *but they create a lot more work than gas and electric fires.* [C] • A **fire alarm** is (the switch connected to) a device such as a bell or SIREN that warns the people in a building that the building is on fire: **Sound** *the fire alarm by breaking the nearest fire alarm glass.* ○ *If the fire alarm* **goes off** *leave the building quickly and calmly.* • A **fire blanket** is a type of cover made of a material which does not burn very easily, which you throw over a fire to put it out or stop it from spreading: *He quickly threw the fire blanket over the burning saucepan, which put out the fire immediately.* • *(Br and Aus)* A **fire brigade**/*(Am)* **fire department** is an organization that is in charge of preventing unwanted fires or stopping them burning. • A **fire door** is made of material that will not burn and is used to prevent a fire from spreading within a building: *Fire doors should not be wedged open at any time.* • A **fire drill** is (the practising of) the set of actions that should be performed in order to leave a building such as an office, factory or school safely when it is on fire: *Employers should ensure that all new employees are familiar with the fire drill.* ○ *Don't worry about the alarm – it's probably only a fire drill.* • A **fire-eater** is a performer who entertains people by seeming to swallow the flames on sticks that are burning at one end and also by JUGGLING (= throwing and catching) these sticks. • A **fire engine** is a large vehicle that carries FIREFIGHTERS and their equipment to a fire: *Dozens of ambulances, fire engines and police cars raced to the scene after the explosion.* • A **fire escape** is a set of metal stairs, esp. on the outside of a building, which allows people to escape from a burning building. • A **fire extinguisher** is a device which contains water or a special gas, powder or FOAM that is put onto a fire to stop it burning. • A **fire hydrant**/*(Am also)* **fire-plug** is a device to which FIREFIGHTERS can connect their equipment in order to obtain water from the public supply. • *(Br)* A **fire-raiser** (also **arsonist**) is a criminal who intentionally starts fires in buildings: **Fire-raising** *seems to be increasingly popular with teenagers who have dropped out of the education system.* • A **fire station**/*(Am also)* **fire house** is a building where fire engines and equipment to fight fires are kept and where FIREFIGHTERS are based when they are not stopping fires from burning. • *"Come home to a real fire"* (advertisement by the British coal industry, 1970s) • See also FIERY. • PIC〉 **Emergency services, Fires and space heaters**

fire *obj* /£faɪəʳ, $faɪr/ *v* [T] • If you fire objects made of clay, you heat them in a KILN (= box-like device for heating them to a very high temperature) so that they harden.

-fired /£faɪəd, $faɪrd/ *combining form* • *Our central heating is* **oil**-*fired* (= uses oil for fuel). • **Gas**-*fired* (= using gas for fuel) *power stations are expected to produce cheaper electricity than* **coal**-*fired ones.*

fire *(obj)* SHOOT /£faɪəʳ, $faɪr/ *v* to (cause a weapon to) shoot bullets, arrows or MISSILES • *He fired his gun into the air.* [T] • *Someone started firing* **at** *us.* [I] • *Without warning he started firing* **into** *the crowd.* [I] • *I just prayed that he would stop firing.* [I] • *The ambassador denied that any missiles had been fired across the border.* [T] • *(fig.) The journalists were firing* **questions** (= asking questions that followed quickly one after the other) *at me for two whole hours.* [T] • *(fig.) "I'd like to ask you some questions about your childhood, if I may." "Fire* **away**! (= You can start asking them immediately)*".* [I] • *(fig.) He* **fired off** (= wrote quickly) *an angry letter.* • If something is **in the firing line** (*Am also* **on the firing line**) its existence is threatened: *The new limits on government spending mean that next year's proposed tax cuts are now in the firing line.* • If someone is **in the firing line** (*Am* **on the firing line**), they are being criticized for something they have said or done: *The judge found himself in the firing line* **from** *women's groups after his controversial comments about sexual assault.* • A **firing squad** is a group of soldiers whose job is to shoot and kill someone who has been given the **death sentence** (= who is to be killed as a punishment).

fire /£faɪəʳ, $faɪr/ *n* [U] • *Why didn't you* **cease** *fire* (= stop shooting) *when you were ordered to do so?* • *The city* **came under** *renewed fire* **from** *anti-government forces last night.* • *(fig.) The government has* **come under** *fire* (= is being criticized) **for** *its decision to close the mines.* • *She gave him* **covering** *fire* (= protected him by shooting at the person shooting at him) *as he ran towards the house.* • *We need to* **draw** *their fire away from* (= make them fire at something other than) *the hospital.* • *Three people were injured when the police* **opened** *fire* **on** (= started shooting at) *the protesters.*

fire *obj* DISMISS /£faɪəʳ, $faɪr/ *v* [T] to dismiss (someone) from their job, esp. because they have done something wrong • *She was fired after she was discovered stealing from her employer.* • *You're fired!* • LP〉 **Work**

fire *obj* EXCITE /£faɪəʳ, $faɪr/ *v* [T] to cause a strong emotion in (someone) • *I had a brilliant English teacher who fired me* **with** *enthusiasm for literature at an early age.* • *The stories of their adventures have really fired me* **with** *the urge to travel more myself.* • *Linda's talks always get me fired* **up** (= excited) *about Latin American politics.*

fire /£faɪəʳ, $faɪr/ *n* [U] • *The fire* (= strong emotion) *in her speech inspired everyone to carry on campaigning in spite of the recent setbacks.*

fire·arm /£ˈfaɪə·rɑːm, $ˈfaɪr·ɑːrm/ *n* [C] a gun such as a RIFLE, PISTOL or REVOLVER that can be carried easily • *He was found guilty of possession of an unlicensed firearm.* • *According to US government figures 60 per cent of murder weapons are firearms.*

fire·ball /£ˈfaɪə·bɔːl, $ˈfaɪr·bɑːl/ *n* [C] a ball of fire, esp. one caused by a very powerful explosion • *As the oil refinery exploded, a huge orange fireball leapt hundreds of feet into the sky and lit up the sea for miles around.*

fire·bomb /£ˈfaɪə·bɒm, $ˈfaɪr·bɑːm/ *n* [C] a bomb that causes destruction by starting a fire rather than exploding • *Rioters armed with firebombs set light to several government buildings.* • *Many shops were badly damaged in the firebomb attacks.*

fire·bomb *obj* /£ˈfaɪə·bɒm, $ˈfaɪr·bɑːm/ *v* [T] • *Animal rights extremists have threatened to firebomb any department stores that continue to stock fur coats.* • *The offices of an anti-government newspaper were destroyed by firebombing last month.*

fire·brand /£ˈfaɪə·brænd, $ˈfaɪr-/ *n* [C] a person who causes political or social trouble by opposing authority

fire·break /£ˈfaɪə·breɪk, $ˈfaɪr-/, *Aus also* **fire·trail** *n* [C] a strip of land in a wood or forest from which the trees have been removed to prevent an accidental fire from spreading

fire·brick /£ˈfaɪə·brɪk, $ˈfaɪr-/ *n* [C] a brick that is not damaged by high temperatures and is therefore used

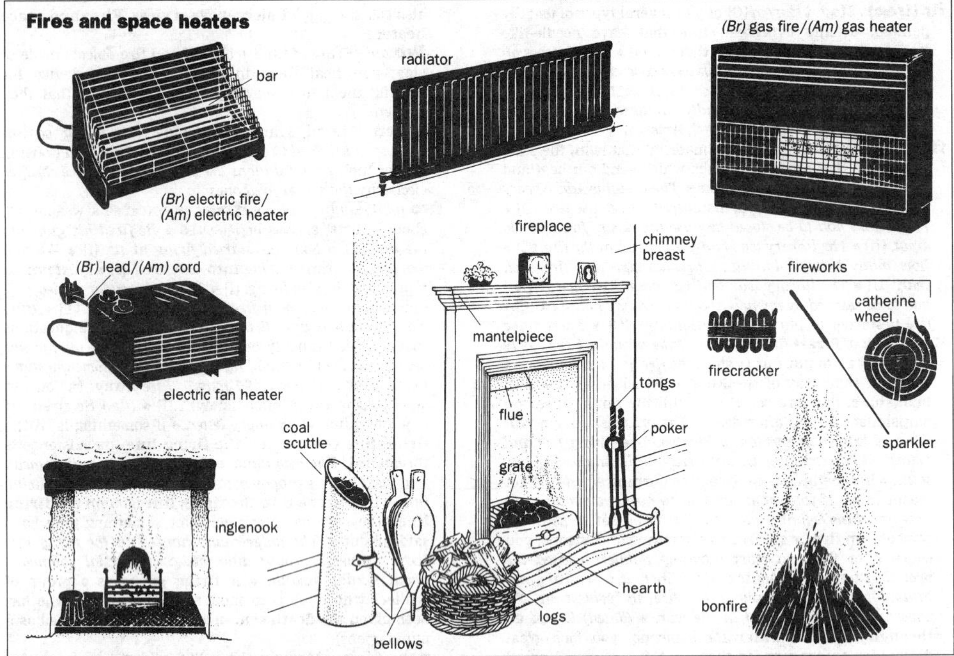

when building things, such as CHIMNEYS and fireplaces, that will reach high temperatures

fire·crack·er /£ˈfaɪəˌkræk·əʳ, $ˈfaɪrˌkræk·ɚ/ *n* [C] a FIREWORK (=small container filled with explosive chemicals) that makes a loud noise or several loud noises when it explodes • PIC› **Fires and space heaters**

fire·fight /£ˈfaɪə·faɪt, $ˈfaɪr-/ *n* [C] a fight, often unexpected, between opposing groups of soldiers in which they shoot at each other • *The opposing units opened fire simultaneously at close range and a 15-minute firefight ensued.*

fire·fight·er, **fire·man** (*pl* **-men**), **fire·wo·man** (*pl* **-women**) /£ˈfaɪəˌfaɪ·təʳ, $ˈfaɪrˌfaɪ·t̬ɚ, -mən/ *n* [C] a person who is employed to stop fires from burning and sometimes also to save people from fires or serious accidents • *The driver of the lorry had to be cut from the wreckage by firefighters.* • PIC› **Emergency services**

fire·fight·ing /£ˈfaɪəˌfaɪ·tɪŋ, $ˈfaɪrˌfaɪ·t̬ɪŋ/ *n* [U] • *The firefighting can't begin until we have an adequate supply of water.* • *An American firefighting team was employed to put out the blaze on the oil rig.*

fire·fly /£ˈfaɪə·flaɪ, $ˈfaɪr-/ *n* [C] an insect which is active during the night and whose tail shines on and off in the dark • *A firefly is a type of beetle.*

fire·guard /£ˈfaɪə·gɑːd, $ˈfaɪr·gɑːrd/, *Am and Aus also* **fire·screen** *n* [C] a metal frame that is put in front of a fire to prevent burning wood or coal from falling onto the floor or prevent children or pets from burning themselves

fire·light /£ˈfaɪə·laɪt, $ˈfaɪr-/ *n* [U] the light produced by a fire, esp. one used for heating a room

fire·light·er /£ˈfaɪə·laɪ·təʳ, $ˈfaɪr·laɪ·t̬ɚ/, *Am usually* **fire start·er** *n* [C] (a small block of) material which burns very easily and is used for helping to start wood or coal fires • *The wood's a bit damp – we'll have to use a firelighter to get it going.*

fire·place /£ˈfaɪə·pleɪs, $ˈfaɪr-/ *n* [C] a space in the wall of a room for a coal or wood fire to burn in, or the decorated part which surrounds this space • *A chimney above the fireplace allows smoke to escape through the roof.* • *I saw a beautiful old fireplace in the antique shop today.* • PIC› **Fires and space heaters**

fire·pow·er /£ˈfaɪə·paʊəʳ, $ˈfaɪr·paʊɚ/ *n* [U] the amount of bullets, bombs, etc. that a military group has available to fire at an enemy • *With our vastly superior firepower we should be able to win this war even though we've got half the number of soldiers.* • *(fig.) The promotion of these young and energetic ministers has dramatically increased the government's firepower.*

fire·proof /£ˈfaɪə·pruːf, $ˈfaɪr-/ *adj* unable to be damaged by the flames or heat of a fire • *She keeps her stamp collection in a fireproof safe.*

fire·screen /£ˈfaɪə·skriːn, $ˈfaɪr-/ *n* [C] *Am and Aus for* FIREGUARD

fire·side /£ˈfaɪə·saɪd, $ˈfaɪr-/ *n* [C] the part of a room which surrounds a coal or wood fire • *There's nothing I like more than curling up* **by the** *fireside with a good book.* • *(fig. dated) We should not forget our servicemen and women as they celebrate Christmas far from their firesides* (=homes). • *(fig.) Do you think the voters will be convinced by the President's fireside address* (=informal talk, usually broadcast on television and filmed in the president's home) *to the nation?*

fire·storm /£ˈfaɪə·stɔːm, $ˈfaɪr·stɔːrm/ *n* [C] a very large uncontrollable fire which is usually started by heavy bombing from aircraft and is kept burning by the violent winds caused by the hot air rising over the burning area

fire·trail /£ˈfaɪə·treɪl, $ˈfaɪr-/ *n* [C] *Aus for* FIREBREAK

fire·trap /£ˈfaɪə·træp, $ˈfaɪr-/ *n* [C] (a part of) a building that would burn easily if a fire started accidentally or would be difficult to escape from during a fire

fire·wat·er /£ˈfaɪəˌwɔː·təʳ, $ˈfaɪrˌwɑː·t̬ɚ/ *n* [U] *infml humorous* a very strong alcoholic drink, esp. WHISKY

fire·wood /£ˈfaɪə·wʊd, $ˈfaɪr-/ *n* [U] wood used as fuel for a fire • *The land allocated to the refugees has been stripped of trees for firewood and building materials.* • *We can use those old shelves as firewood.*

fire·work /£ˈfaɪə·wɜːk, $ˈfaɪr·wɜːrk/ *n* [C] a small container filled with explosive chemicals which produce bright coloured patterns or loud noises when they explode • *Large numbers of fireworks are often (Br)* **let off***/(Am)* **set off** (=lit) *in a fireworks* **display** *to celebrate a special occasion.* • *What time do the fireworks start?* • *(fig.) I'd love to come to the nightclub, but my parents won't let me and* **there'll be** *fireworks* (=they will be very angry) *if I get home late.* • LP› **Holidays** PIC› **Fires and space heaters**

firm FIXED /£fɜːm, $fɜːrm/ *adj* **-er, -est** well fixed in position and unable to slide or fall over • *Check that the ladder's firm before you climb up it.* • *The protesters* **stood** *firm* (=refused to move) *as the riot police tried to disperse them with rubber bullets and water cannons.* • *(fig.) Sometimes it takes more courage to admit you're wrong than to* **stand** *firm* (=continue to defend an opinion). • *(fig.) The government is* **holding** *firm, and refusing to give in to opposition demands for a parliamentary debate on the issue.* • *(fig.) The pound lost four cents against the dollar, falling to $1·79, but it* **held** *firm* (=kept its value) **against** *the Deutschmark at DM2·92.* • Ⓘ Ⓟ

firm·ly /£ˈfɜːm·li, $ˈfɜːrm-/ *adv* • *Make sure the rope is firmly attached before attempting to climb down it.* • *Please seal the envelope firmly before posting it.*

firm SOLID /£fɜːm, $fɜːrm/ *adj* **-er, -est** not soft; quite solid or strong • *I'd rather sleep on a firm mattress than a soft one.* • *Don't forget to give him a firm handshake when you're introduced to him.* • *Keep a firm hold of the handrail as you go down.* • *My body is much firmer than it used to be when I didn't do any exercise.* • *(fig.) Research has shown that children who leave primary school without a firm grounding in* (=a good understanding of) *literacy and numeracy never catch up.* • *(fig.) No one seems to have a firm grip on the company at the moment.* • Ⓘ Ⓟ

firm·ly /£ˈfɜːm·li, $ˈfɜːrm-/ *adv* • *She held me firmly in her arms.* • *He shook my hand firmly and climbed into the taxi.*

firm·ness /£ˈfɜːm·nəs, $ˈfɜːrm-/ *n* [U]

firm CERTAIN /£fɜːm, $fɜːrm/ *adj* **-er, -est** certain or fixed in a belief, opinion, etc. and unlikely to change, or so certain as to be beyond doubt or question • *He is a firm believer in traditional family values.* • *We're appealing to the government for a firm commitment to help these refugees.* • *Some people still claim that there is no firm evidence linking smoking with lung cancer.* • *They've expressed an interest in working with us, but we're still waiting for a firm proposal from them.* • *I was always very firm with my children – they knew the rules and I made sure they kept to them.* • *Firm* **in** *the belief that they could never be caught, they didn't bother to hide the clues which eventually betrayed them to the police.* • Ⓘ Ⓟ

firm *(obj)* /£fɜːm, $fɜːrm/ *v* • *After a turbulent week on the markets, share prices firmed* (= stopped changing) *today.* [I] • *In spite of months of negotiations, they still haven't managed to firm* **up** (= agree the final form of) *a deal.* [M]

firm·ly /£ˈfɜːm·li, $ˈfɜːrm-/ *adv* • *We are firmly committed to reducing unemployment.* • *"There's no way I'm letting you go to the party," she said firmly.*

firm·ness /£ˈfɜːm·nəs, $ˈfɜːrm-/ *n* [U] • *The new teacher has a reputation for firmness and is unlikely to tolerate the misbehaviour that her predecessor put up with.*

firm BUSINESS /£fɜːm, $fɜːrm/ *n* [C] a business partnership, or more generally any company or business • *He works for a law firm called Neil and Vigliano.* • *He's just started working for an accountancy firm/a firm* **of** *accountants in Cambridge.* • *She took over the* **family** *firm when her mother died.* • *Future economic growth depends heavily on the success of* **small** *firms.* • *The agency was set up to privatize the 8000 state-owned firms in the former East Germany.* • LP> **Letters** Ⓘ Ⓟ

fir·ma·ment /£ˈfɜː·mə·mənt, $ˈfɜːr-/ *n* [U] **the firmament** *literary* the sky • *(fig.) She is one of the rising stars in the political firmament* (= in the world of politics).

first /£ˈfɜːst, $ˈfɜːrst/ *adj, adv* [not gradable], *n, pronoun* (a person or thing) coming before all others in order, time, amount, quality or importance • *Who was* **the** *first (person)* **to** *finish?* [+ *to* infinitive] • *Who finished first?* • *She was* **one of the** *first (guests)* **to** *arrive at the party.* [+ *to* infinitive] • *Much of his success, as he is* **the** *first* (=very willing) **to** *acknowledge, is due to his good looks.* [+ *to* infinitive] • *The first we heard about the murder was a news report on the radio.* • *This concert will be her first since the birth of her child a year ago.* • *Tonight sees the first of three documentaries about cancer.* • *When was the first* **(ever)** *radio broadcast made?* • *This is my first visit to New York.* • *This is the first time I've been to New York.* • *The temperature has risen above freezing for the first time in six days/since last Sunday.* • *It won't be the first time that he's changed his mind.* • *I'm always nervous for the first* **few** *minutes of an exam.* • *What's the first thing you think of when you hear that noise?* • *Think carefully before you answer their questions and don't just say the first thing that comes into your head.* • *When did you first meet each other?* • *The company was still very small when I first joined.* • *"Should I put the potatoes in the oven?" "You should chop them up first* (=before you put them in)*."* • *She'll never agree to work for him. She'd die first* (= She would never work for him whatever happened)*!* • *First* **(of all)** *(infml First* **off)** (= Before anything else), *I'd like to ask you a few questions about your childhood.* • *First looking over his shoulder, he took a small box from his pocket.* • *This new surgical technique is a first* **for** (=has never been done before in) *Britain.* [C] • *(Br) She got a first (fml* **first-class degree)** (=best possible qualification in a college degree) **in** *English from Newcastle University.* [C] • **At first** (= In the beginning) *I thought he was joking but then I realized he meant it.* • *South-east England will start cloudy with showers* **at first**, *but it should brighten up by late morning.* • **First come, first served** means that those who ask for something first will receive it first and that there might not be enough for those who ask later: *Tickets for the concert are free and will be distributed on a first come, first served basis.* • A member of a group of people who is described as **first among equals** is officially on the same level as the other members but in fact has slightly more responsibility or power: *The British Prime Minister is first among equals in the Cabinet.* • If you are **in the first flush of** something, you are at the start of it: *You're no longer in the first flush of* **youth**, *you know Dad!* • *In spite of her recent election success, she remains* **first and foremost** (=more than anything else) *a writer, not a politician.* • *Don was,* **first and last** (=as the most important fact), *a good friend.* • *I opposed the proposal* **from the (very) first** (=from the beginning). • *Enquiries about the post should be addressed* **in the first place** *(Br also* **in the first instance***)* (= in the beginning) *to the personnel manager.* • *He said he'd phone back* **first thing** (= very early in the morning) *tomorrow.* • *Don't worry, your car can be repaired, but* **first things first** (=more important things should be done before less important things), *are you sure you're not hurt?* • **First aid** is basic medical treatment which is given to someone as soon as possible after they have been hurt in an accident or suddenly become ill: *Did you learn any first aid at school?* ○ *The government is appealing for supplies of first-aid equipment.* ○ *How many* **first-aiders** (=people who know about first aid) *are there in your office?* • In baseball, **first base** (or **first**) is the place a BATTER runs to after hitting the ball, or the position played by an INFIELDER: *(fig.) Your proposal is so poorly designed, you won't even* **get to/reach** *first base* (= have the first achievement or agreement which is needed for later success) *with the directors.* • The **first-born (child)** in a family is the child who is older than all the other children of those parents: *Do first-borns develop closer relationships with their parents than their brothers and sisters?* • If a service is **first class**, it is the best that is possible or available: *Most first-class mail* (=the more expensive class of post in Britain which is delivered more quickly than second class) *is delivered the day after it is posted.* ○ *How much more would it cost to send it first class?* ○ *First class rail fares are to rise by an average of 6 per cent.* ○ *Is it possible to upgrade to first class once you're on board the plane?* ○ *She used to travel (in) first class but she can't afford it anymore.* • **First class** is also used to mean excellent: *She'd never done any decorating before, but she's made a first-class job of the living room.* ○ *Your work is first class.* • A **first cousin** is a child of someone's aunt or uncle: *(fig.) CD-ROM is a first cousin of* (= is closely related to) *music compact discs – information is stored digitally and read with a laser.* • *(dated)* A **first-degree burn** is the least serious type of burn that needs medical treatment. • *(Am)* **First-degree murder** is the most serious type of murder. • *(Aus)* The **First Fleet** was the ships that brought the first Europeans to Australia. • *(Aus)* A **first fleeter** is someone who is related to a person who travelled in the First Fleet. • In British English, the **first floor** of a building is the floor directly above ground level. In American English, it is the floor at ground level. • In a vehicle, **first gear** (or **first**) is used when starting to move forward or when moving up a steep hill, providing the wheels with a lot of engine power but not much speed: *I failed my driving test because I kept* **putting** *the car* **into** *third instead of first.* [U] • Information that is **first-hand** is obtained directly from its origin: *How can you talk about poverty when you've had no first-hand experience of it?* ○ *These reports of torture have come first-hand from the prisoners.* ○ *It is difficult to appreciate the scale of the problem without seeing the effects of the famine* **at first hand**. • The **first fruit** of something is the first result of it: *The deal to supply each other with car engines is the first fruit of a recent cooperative agreement between the companies.* ○ *These improvements in quality are the first fruits of our investment.* • A **first lady** is a woman whose husband is the political leader of a country or a part of a country. • A person's **first language** is the language they learn from their parents as they are growing up: *Her first language is German, but she has lived in Paris since she was five so she speaks extremely good French.* • **First light** is the time when the sun first appears in the morning: *They had to wait* **till/until** *first light to evacuate the wounded to an army hospital.* ○ *We'll leave* **at** *first light.* • A **first mate** or

first officer is the second most important officer on a ship which is not part of the navy. • A person's **first name** (*fml* **forename** *Am also* **given name**) is the name that they use with people they know well, such as friends and family, and sometimes also to express friendliness or reduce the formality of a situation: *It can be rude to* **call** *someone* **by** *their first name if they are much older or more important than you.* Compare **Christian name** at CHRISTIAN. • If you are **on first-name terms with** (*Am also* **on a first-name basis with**) someone, you call each other by your first names, often when you might not expect to because you don't know them very well: *The meeting was a great success and by the end of it we were all on first-name terms with each other.* • The **first night** (*Am usually* **opening night**) of a play is the first official time it is performed in public (in a particular place): *Our first night in London was a disaster, but New York was much more successful.* • A **first offender** is someone who has been officially judged to be guilty of a crime for the first time: *Are first offenders treated more leniently than criminals with previous convictions?* • *(Br)* **First-past-the-post** is a voting system in which a person is elected by obtaining more votes than anyone else in the area that they want to represent, whether or not their political party obtains more votes than any other party in the whole of the country: *Many people in Britain want to replace first-past-the-post (voting) with proportional representation.* • The **first person** is the form of pronouns and verbs people use when speaking or writing about themselves: *In English, 'I', 'me', 'my, 'myself' and 'mine' refer to the first person singular, and 'we', 'us', 'our', 'ourselves' and 'ours' refer to the first person plural.* ○ *Autobiographies are written* **in the** *first person.* • **First principles** are the basic and most important reasons for doing or believing something: *We seem to have forgotten why we're fighting this campaign – we really need to return to first principles.* • If something is **first-rate** it is extremely good: *The sound quality of compact discs is first-rate.* • If you have **(the) first refusal on** something, you have the chance to buy it before it is offered to anyone else: *My sister's selling her car and she's offered me first refusal on it.* • A **first strike** in a nuclear war is an attack intended to destroy the enemy's ability to fire before they have had an opportunity to do so. • *(Br)* A **first-time buyer** is someone who is buying their own house or apartment for the first time, esp. by borrowing money from a bank or similar organization: *Would tax incentives for first-time buyers help to revive the depressed housing market?* • *The University regrets that it cannot guarantee accommodation to all* **first-year** *students.* • [LP]> **One**

first·ly /£ˈfɜːst·li, $ˈfɜːrst-/, **first** *adv* [not gradable] • First(ly) is used when referring to the first thing in a list: *There are two very good reasons why we can't do it. Firstly, we don't have enough money, and secondly, we don't have enough time.* ○ *He studied economics firstly because he enjoyed it and secondly because he wanted to get a good job.*

firth /£fɜːθ, $fɜːrθ/ *n* [C] *Scot Eng* a long strip of sea reaching into the land • *the Firth of Forth* • *the Firth of Tay*

fis·cal /ˈfɪs·kəl/ *adj* [not gradable] *specialized* connected with (public) money • *fiscal policy* • **Fiscal year** is another word for **financial year**. See at FINANCE.

fis·cal·ly /ˈfɪs·kəl·i/ *adv specialized* • *The proposal is fiscally* **sound/unsound**.

fish [ANIMAL] /fɪʃ/ *n pl* **fish** or **fishes** an animal without legs which lives in water, using its tail to help it swim, and which breathes by taking oxygen from the water • *Several large fish live in the pond.* [C] • *Many people find fish relaxing to look at.* [C] • *Chapter 6 of St John's Gospel contains the parable of the loaves and the fishes.* [C] • Fish is also the flesh of these animals eaten as food: *We usually have fish for dinner on Friday.* [U] • A **odd/strange/queer** fish is a person who behaves strangely. [C] • If someone **has bigger/other fish to fry**, they have something more important or interesting to do. • Someone who is **(like) a fish out of water** is uncomfortable because of the situation or surroundings they are in. • **There are (plenty) more/ (plenty of) other fish in the sea** means that there are (many) other people or possibilities, esp. when one person or thing has been unsuitable or unsuccessful. • *(specialized)* A **fish-eye lens** is a LENS (= shaped piece of glass) for a camera, which gives a view of an extremely wide area in a single picture. • A **fish farm** is an enclosed area of water used for breeding and growing fish. • A *(Br and Aus)* **fish-finger**/ *(esp. Am)* **fish stick** is a piece of fish, rectangular in shape, that is covered in BREADCRUMBS and cooked. • A **fish kettle** is a large metal pan for cooking fish. • A **fish knife** is a knife with a wide blade which has a round edge, used when eating fish. • *(esp. Br)* A **fish-slice** (*Am usually* **(slotted) spatula**) is a kitchen utensil which has a wide flat blade with long holes in it and a handle, used for lifting and turning food while cooking. • A **fish tank** is a container which is usually rectangular and made of glass which is used for keeping fish in, esp. pet tropical fish. • **Fish and chips** is fish covered with BATTER (= a mixture of flour, eggs and milk) and then fried and served with pieces of fried potato. • *"A Fish called Wanda"* (title of film, 1988) • [LP]> **Plurals** [PIC]> **Cutlery**

fish *(obj)* /fɪʃ/ *v* • *We fished* (= tried to catch fish) *every day on our holiday.* [I] • *The sea here has been fished intensely over the last ten years.* [T] • If an area of water has been **fished out**, all or most of the fish in it have been caught: *This branch of the river is pretty much fished out, but you might have some luck a few miles upstream.* • *(Am) You've suggested five possible plans, now it's time to* **fish or cut bait** (= choose an action or admit you are not going to act). • *Some people* **fish in troubled waters** (= try to get an advantage for themselves from a difficult situation).

fish·ing /ˈfɪʃ·ɪŋ/ *n* [U] • *a fishing (Br and Aus) rod/(Am) pole* • *a fishing line/net/boat* • *salmon fishing* • *fishing tackle* (= equipment used for catching fish) • *Let's go fishing today.* • *Fishing is still their main source of income.* • [PIC]> **Line**

fish·y /ˈfɪʃ·i/ *adj* **-ier, -iest** • *This chicken has got a fishy taste.* • See also FISHY.

fish [SEARCH] /fɪʃ/ *v* [I always + adv/prep] to search, esp. in difficult conditions • *She fished* **in** *her toolbox* **for** *the right spanner.* • *The director was fishing* **for** *information about our strategy.* • *He's always fishing* **for compliments** (= trying to make people say good things about him).

fish out *obj*, **fish** *obj* **out** *v adv* [M] *infml* to pull or take (something) out, esp. after searching • *The police fished a body out* **of** *the river this morning.* • *He fished out a sweet* **from** *his pocket.*

fish·bowl /£ˈfɪʃ·bəʊl, $-boʊl/ *n* [C] *Am for* **goldfish bowl**, see at GOLDFISH

fish·cake /ˈfɪʃ·keɪk/ *n* [C] a mixture of fish and potato which has been formed into small flat round shapes, covered with BREADCRUMBS and then cooked

fish·er·man (*pl* **-men**), **fish·er·wo·man** (*pl* **-women**) /£ˈfɪʃ·ə·mən, $ˈ-ɚ-, -ˌwʊm·ən/ *n* [C] someone who catches fish, esp. as their job but sometimes as a sport

fish·er·y /£ˈfɪʃ·ər·i, $-ɚ·i/ *n* [C] an area of water where fish are caught so they can be sold • *an offshore fishery*

fish·mon·ger /£ˈfɪʃˌmʌŋ·gəʳ, $-gɚ/ *n* [C] *esp. Br* a person who sells fish, esp. from a shop • *I'll ask the fishmonger if he can order three dozen oysters for me.*

fish·mon·ger's, **fish·mon·gers** /£ˈfɪʃˌmʌŋ·gəz, $-gɚz/ *n* [C] *pl* **fishmongers'** or **fishmongers** *esp. Br* • A fishmonger's is a place where people who sell fish work: *I'll stop at the fishmonger's on my way home from work.*

fish·net /ˈfɪʃ·net/ *n* [C] a net for catching fish, or a type of material which looks like net • *A pile of fishnets lay on the quay.* • *She was wearing black fishnet stockings.*

fish·wife /ˈfɪʃ·waɪf/ *n* [C] *pl* **fishwives** /ˈfɪʃ·waɪvz/ *dated disapproving* an unpleasant offensive woman • *She was swearing like an old fishwife!*

fish·y /ˈfɪʃ·i/ *adj* **-ier, -iest** *infml* seeming dishonest or false • *There's something fishy going on here.* • See also **fishy** at FISH.

fis·sion /ˈfɪʃ·ən/ *n* [U] *specialized* the dividing into parts of the NUCLEUS (= inner part) of an atom, or of a living cell • *a fission reactor* • *All commercial nuclear power is provided by fission at the present time.* • *The fission* **of** *the cell could be inhibited with certain chemicals.*

fis·sile /£ˈfɪs·aɪl, $-ɪl/ *adj* [not gradable] *specialized* • *Because of its layered structure, mica is fissile* (= divides easily into pieces). • *An amount of fissile material went missing as a result of the accident.*

fis·sure /£ˈfɪʃ·əʳ, $-ɚ/ *n* [C] a narrow deep crack in rock or the earth

fist /fɪst/ *n* [C] a hand with the fingers and thumb held tightly in • *She* **clenched** *her fists because of the pain.* • *The cyclist* **shook** *his fist in anger.* • A **fist-fight** occurs when two or more people have a fight with each other using only their bare hands: *An ugly fist-fight broke out following the argument.* • [PIC]> **Body**

fist·ful /ˈfɪst·fʊl/ *n* [C] • *Joan rummaged in her desk drawer and came up with a fistful of newspaper clippings.* • *(fig.) He won international acclaim for his King Lear and*

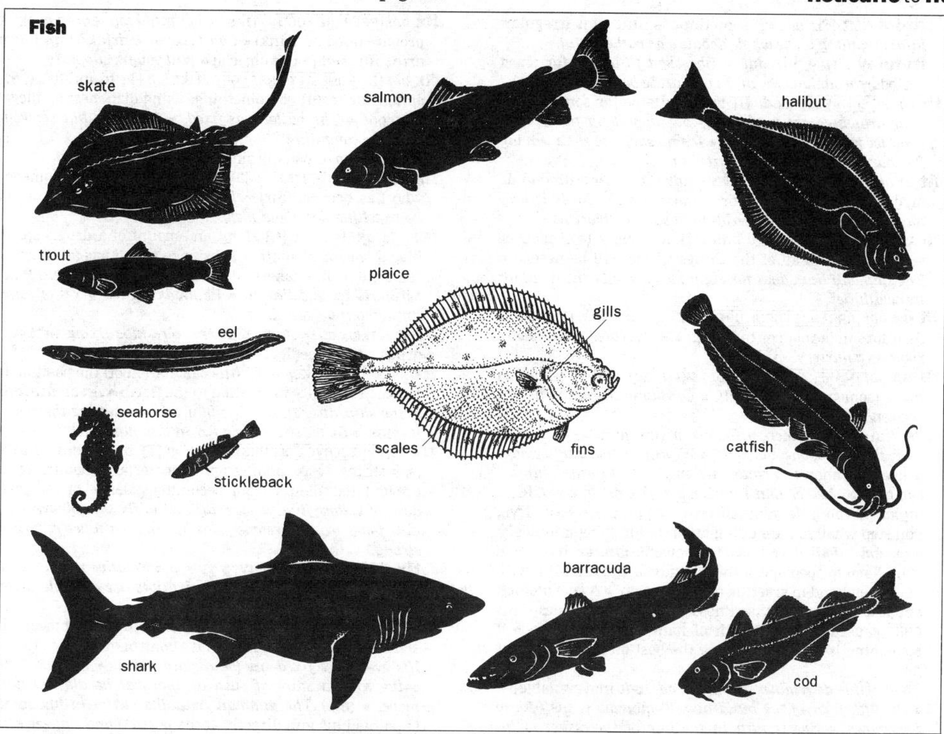

has a fistful (= a large number) *of other acting awards.* • *"A Fistful of Dollars"* (film title, 1964)

fis·ti·cuffs /ˈfɪs·tɪ·kʌfs/ *pl n old use and humorous* fighting in which people hit each other with their FISTS • *We might have to resort to fisticuffs to resolve the problem.*

fit *(obj)* [CORRECT SIZE] /fɪt/ *v* **fitting**, *past* **fitted** or *Am also* **fit** to be the right size or shape for (someone or something) • *The jacket fits you perfectly.* [T] • *I don't think the new fridge will fit* **in(to)** *the kitchen unless we move the furniture around.* [I] • *The wood has rotted so the door doesn't fit properly.* [I] • *You look so good in that dress – it fits you* **like a glove** (= very well). • *(saying)* 'If the cap/hat fits, (wear it)' means that if the way someone has described you seems true to you, then accept it and use it. • (T)

fit /fɪt/ *n* [U] • *These shoes are a good/bad/perfect/poor fit.* • *Check the fit* **of** *the gasket before final assembly.*

fit·ted /£ˈfɪt·ɪd, $ˈfɪt̬-/ *adj* [not gradable] • *a fitted jacket* (= one made to match someone's shape)

fit·ter /£ˈfɪt·əʳ, $ˈfɪt̬·ɚ/ *n* [C] • A fitter is someone who changes clothes while they are being made to make them fit someone well.

fit·ting /£ˈfɪt·ɪŋ, $ˈfɪt̬-/ *n* [C] • *I'm having the final fitting of my wedding dress on Thursday.*

fit *obj* [SUIT] /fɪt/ *v* [T] **fitting**, *past* **fitted** or *Am also* **fit** to be suitable for (something) • *Looking at his CV, he should fit the sales job perfectly.* • *Some people think the punishment should always fit the crime.* • *I'm sure we'll have something to fit your requirements, Madam.* • *What you saw does fit* (= agree with) *the facts we know.* • If something **fits the bill**, it is suitable for its intended purpose: *The new software certainly fits the bill.* • (T)

fit /fɪt/ *adj* **fitter, fittest** • *She's not fit* **for** *the amount of responsibility she has within the group.* • *He's very upset and is in no fit state* **to** *drive.* [+ *to* infinitive] • *Although the food has been stored for a long time it is still* **fit for human consumption** (= safe for humans to eat). • *Do whatever you* **see/think** *fit* (= consider to be correct for the situation). • *After the run they were* **fit to drop** (= so tired they almost could not stand). • *(infml)* If someone is **fit to burst** with an emotion or a feeling, it is very strong within them: *The children were fit to burst with excitement.* • *(Am) When the referee ejected her from the game, she was* **fit to be tied** (= extremely angry). • *"It ain't a fit night out for man nor beast"* (phrase used by the comedian W.C. Fields, c.1929)

fit·ness /ˈfɪt·nəs/ *n* [U] • *His fitness* **for** *the new position is not in question.* • *Many people are concerned about her fitness* **to** *govern.* [+ *to* infinitive]

fit·ting /£ˈfɪt·ɪŋ, $ˈfɪt̬-/ *adj fml* • **It** *is fitting* (= right) **that** *we should remember those who died.* [+ *that* clause]

fit *obj* [POSITION] /fɪt/ *v* [T] **fitting**, *past* **fitted** or *Am also* **fit** to supply (something) and put it in the correct position • *All the carpets we sell are fitted free.* • (T)

fit·ment /ˈfɪt·mənt/ *n* [C] *esp. Br* • A fitment is a removable piece of furniture, such as a cupboard: *kitchen/bathroom fitments*

fit·ted /£ˈfɪt·ɪd, $ˈfɪt̬-/ *adj* [before n; not gradable] • *The bedroom has a fitted carpet* (= one which has been cut to cover the floor completely and is then fixed in position). • *(Br) We're having a new* **fitted kitchen** *put in* (= We're having cupboards that all look the same fixed into position in our kitchen).

fit·ter /£ˈfɪt·əʳ, $ˈfɪt̬·ɚ/ *n* [C] • A fitter is someone who puts together, takes care of or repairs machines or electrical devices: *He's joined the navy as an engine fitter.*

fit·ting /£ˈfɪt·ɪŋ, $ˈfɪt̬-/ *n* [C] • A fitting is a small part or item: *plumbing fittings* ○ *electric light fittings* • *(Br and Aus)* Fittings (*Am* **furnishings**) are also items, such as cookers, washing machines and curtain poles, which are not permanently fixed in or part of the structure of a house and which a person might be expected to take with them when they move to a new home: *The house price, including* **fixtures and** *fittings, is £200 000.* • Compare FIXTURE [FIXED OBJECT].

fit [HEALTHY] /fɪt/ *adj* **fitter, fittest** in good health, esp. as a result of exercise; strong • *She's very fit because she does a lot of ballet dancing.* • *People often find that if they* **keep/stay** *fit, they sleep better.* • *(infml) She said she was* **(as) fit as a fiddle/flea** (= in very good health). • *(Br slang)* If you describe someone as fit, you mean that they are sexually attractive. • (T)

fit·ness /ˈfɪt·nəs/ *n* [U] • *Physical fitness is encouraged for children in most schools.*

fit [ILLNESS] /fɪt/ *n* [C] a sudden attack of an illness, esp. EPILEPSY • *If someone has an* **epileptic** *fit, their body will convulse with severe uncontrolled movements and they will probably become unconscious.* • *(fig. infml) Your mother will* **have/throw a fit** (= be very angry) *when she sees the mess you've made.* • (T)

fit [SHORT FEELING] /fɪt/ *n* [C] a short experience of a slight illness or an emotion • *a coughing fit* • *It was said in a fit* **of** *anger/rage.* • *His stories had them* **in fits (of laughter)** (= made them laugh very much). • **In/By fits and starts** means irregularly or in small groups: *The replies to the advertisement are arriving in fits and starts.* • (T)

fit·ful /ˈfɪt·fᵊl/ *adj* • If something is fitful, it is irregular: *fitful breathing* ○ *The whole debate was rather fitful.*

fit·ful·ly /ˈfɪt·fᵊl·i/ *adv* • *She slept fitfully* (=for short periods) *throughout the night and arose before dawn.*

fit in BE SUITABLE *v adv* [I] to be suitable for something • *Your drawings are marvellous but they don't fit in* **with** *what we're trying to do here.* • *It's no surprise she's leaving the course – she never really fitted in.*

fit in *obj* FIND TIME, **fit** *obj* **in** *v adv* [M] to find time to do or deal with (something or someone) • *Dr Jones is very busy but I'm sure she'll be able to fit you in tomorrow.*

fit out *obj*, **fit** *obj* **out** *v adv* [M] to supply (someone or something) with all of the things which will be needed • *The ship will be in dock for eight months to be fitted out for its new duties.*

fit up *obj* ARRANGE FURNITURE, **fit** *obj* **up** *v adv* [M] to put furniture in (a room or building) • *We've fitted up the spare room* **as** *a nursery.*

fit up *obj* MAKE GUILTY, **fit** *obj* **up** *v adv* [M] *Br slang* to make (someone) seem guilty • *Of course she didn't do it – someone fitted her up.*

five /faɪv/ *determiner, pronoun, n* (the number) 5 • *Five, four, three, two, one, blast-off!* • *We work the usual five days a week, Monday to Friday.* • *Emily is five (years old).* • *I can't read whether that number is a five or an eight.* [C] • *(infml)* If you **give** yourself **five**, or you **take/have five**, you stop what you are doing and rest for a few minutes. • *(esp. Am infml)* If you say to someone **gimme five!**, you want them to open one of their hands so you can hit it with your open hand in greeting or celebration. • A **five o'clock shadow** is the slight darkness on a man's face, esp. his CHIN, caused by the growth of hair during the day. • If something is **five-star**, it is of the best quality: *a five-star hotel*

fifth /fɪfθ/ *determiner, pronoun, adj, adv* [not gradable], *n* • *the fifth floor of the building* • *Tomorrow is the fifth of September.* • *She is fifth in the line of succession to the throne.* • *He came fifth.* • *One fifth is the same as 20%.* [C] • A **fifth column** is a group of people who support the enemies of the country they live in and secretly help them. A member of such a group is a **fifth columnist**.

fiv·er /£ˈfaɪ·vəʳ, $-vɚ/ *n* [C] *infml (Br)* a £5 note, or *(Am)* a $5 note • *It only cost me a fiver.* • See also TENNER. • LP **Money**

fix *obj* FASTEN /fɪks/ *v* [T always + adv/prep] to fasten (something) in position • *Will you fix the shelf* **to** *the wall at the weekend?* • *(fig.) Her heart was beating so violently that she could not fix her thoughts* **on** (=think of) *anything.* • *She was fixed to the spot* **with** (=She could not move because of) *fear.* • If you fix something **in your mind**, you remember it in such a way that it will be difficult to forget it.

fixed /fɪkst/ *adj* [not gradable] • *fixed* (=not changing) *repayment terms* • *(fig.) a fixed* (=not changing) *idea/stare* • *(esp. law)* If someone **is of/has no fixed abode/address**, they do not have a permanent place to live. • A **fixed star** is a star which is so far from the Earth that it seems not to move in relation to other distant stars as the Earth moves through space. • The **fixed assets** of a business are things of value of a permanent type such as buildings.

fix·ed·ly /ˈfɪk·sɪd·li/ *adv* [not gradable] • *She stared fixedly at the setting sun.*

fix *(obj)* ARRANGE /fɪks/ *v* to arrange or agree (a time, place, price, etc.) • *Shall we fix* **(up)** *a time for our next meeting?* [T/M] • *I understand the rent is fixed* **at** *£750 a month.* [T] • *So, can we fix* **(on)** *two o'clock tomorrow for the presentation?* [T; I + on] • *Have you fixed* **(up)** *your trip to Asia for this year?* [T/M] • *Can he fix us* **(up) with** *somewhere to stay?* [T] • *They have not fixed* **(up)on** *a successor for the mayor.* [I always + adv/prep]

fixed /fɪkst/ *adj* [after v; not gradable] *infml* • *How are you fixed* **for** (=Have you already arranged to do anything on) *Saturday evening?*

fix·er /£ˈfɪk·səʳ, $-sɚ/ *n* [C] *infml* • A fixer is someone who arranges for something to happen, esp. by dishonest means: *He's a real fixer – he can get you in to see anyone in the music business.*

fix *obj* REPAIR /fɪks/ *v* [T] to repair (something) • *The right peddle of your bicycle has come loose – you'd better fix it!* • *(fig.) Give me a couple of minutes while I fix my hair* (=make it look better).

fix AWKWARD SITUATION /fɪks/ *n* [C usually sing] *infml* an awkward or difficult situation • *He's* **in** *a real fix – he's got two meetings booked for three o'clock.*

fix *obj* PREPARE FOOD /fɪks/ *v* [T] *infml esp. Am* to cook or prepare (food or drink) • *Can I fix you a drink?/Can I fix a drink* **for** *you?* [+ two objects] • *Will you fix supper?*

fix *obj* DISHONESTLY ARRANGE /fɪks/ *v* [T] to influence the actions or result of (something) using dishonest or illegal methods • *The ballot was fixed.* • *It sounds like someone fixed the committee.*

fix /fɪks/ *n* [C usually sing] • *The result was a fix!*

fix *obj* PUNISH /fɪks/ *v* [T] *slang* to punish (esp. someone who has been unfair) • *I'm gonna fix her one day – she keeps telling lies about me!*

fix DRUG /fɪks/ *n* [C] *slang* an amount of a drug, esp. an illegal one, or of another substance which has an effect on someone if they take it • *The usual way of taking a fix of heroin is by injecting it.* • *He needs regular fixes of coffee throughout the morning.*

fix /fɪks/ *v* [I] *slang* • *There were kids fixing* (=taking drugs with a needle) *in doorways.*

fix POSITION /fɪks/ *n* [C] (the calculation of) the position of a vehicle, usually in relation to the Earth • *An accurate fix of the ship/aircraft can be obtained by detecting the signal it emits.* • *Do we still have a fix* **on** *that jumbo jet?*

fix *obj* PRESERVE COLOURS /fɪks/ *v* [T] *specialized* to treat (something, esp. photographic material) chemically to prevent its colours from becoming paler • *In the early days of colour film, it was difficult to fix the colours – the blue tones would become faint but the red tones remained strong.*

fix·a·tive /£ˈfɪk·sə·tɪv, $-t̬ɪv/ *n* • *Fixative technology is still improving.* [U] • *Several fixatives are suitable under these conditions.* [C]

fix *obj* SIGHT /fɪks/ *v* [T] to keep something or someone in sight, esp. when wishing to have control over the person • *His eyes were fixed* **on** *the distant yacht.* • *She fixed the child* **with** *a stare of such disapproval he did not dare move.* • *(fig.) The gunman fixed the victim in his sights* (=pointed his gun directly at the person) *and squeezed the trigger.*

fix *obj* STOP REPRODUCTION /fɪks/ *v* [T] *Am infml* to remove the reproductive organs of (an animal) • *We had our dog fixed after she gave birth to a litter of six puppies.*

fix·at·ed /£fɪkˈseɪ·tɪd, $ˈfɪk·seɪ·t̬ɪd/ *adj* [after v] (of thoughts or people) unable to stop thinking about • *She is fixated* **on** *the things which happened to her while she was working abroad.* • *The boss is fixated* **with** *automating the office.*

fix·a·tion /fɪkˈseɪ·ʃᵊn/ *n* [C] • A fixation is an inability to stop thinking about something: *a mother fixation* ○ *Such a fixation* **with** *money can't be healthy.*

fix·a·tive /£ˈfɪk·sə·tɪv, $-t̬ɪv/ *n* a substance which holds something in position • *(a) denture fixative* [C/U]

fix·i·ty /£ˈfɪk·sə·ti, $-t̬i/ *n* [U] *fml* the quality of not changing • *Every member of the team displayed great fixity of purpose.*

fix·ture FIXED OBJECT /£ˈfɪks·tʃəʳ, $-tʃɚ/ *n* [C] a permanently fixed item in a house, such as a bath, which would not be taken by someone when they move to a new home • *All fixtures* **and fittings** *are included in the house price.* • *(fig.) They've been together so long he's become a permanent fixture in her life.* • Compare **fitting** at FIT POSITION.

fix·ture SPORTS EVENT /£ˈfɪks·tʃəʳ, $-tʃɚ/ *n* [C] *esp. Br and Aus* a day and usually a time agreed for a sports event • *Next season's fixtures will be published early next month.*

fizz PRODUCE GAS /fɪz/ *v* [I] (of a liquid) to produce gas bubbles • *There'll be a lot of fizzing as soon as you mix the powder into the water.* • *You could hear the liquid fizz as she poured it out of the bottle.*

fizz /fɪz/ *n* [U] • *Who left the top of the bottle loose? The tonic water has lost its fizz.* • *(infml)* Fizz also means a bubbly drink, esp. CHAMPAGNE: *Who'd like some fizz?*

fiz·zy /ˈfɪz·i/ *adj* **-ier, -iest** • *fizzy lemonade/mineral water*

fiz·zi·ness /ˈfɪz·ɪ·nəs/ *n* [U]

fizz SOUND /fɪz/ *v* [I] to make a long sound like the s in 'sing' • *Fireworks fizzed above the crowd.*

fizz /fɪz/ *n* [U]

fiz·zle /ˈfɪz·l̩/ *v* [I] to make a weak sound like the s in 'sing' • *The fire fizzled miserably in the rain.*

fiz·zle out *v adv* [I] to end in a disappointing or weak way • *When the popular interest has fizzled out, the serious debate will begin.*

fjord, fi·ord /£fjɔːd, $fjɔːrd/ *n* [C] a long strip of sea between steep hills, found esp. in Norway

flab /flæb/ *n* [U] *infml disapproving* soft loose flesh on someone's body • *I can feel the flab building up around my waist – I must start doing some exercise.*

flab·by /ˈflæb·i/ *adj* **-ier**, **-iest** *infml disapproving* • *flabby thighs* • *She's become so flabby since she started her job in the office.*

flab·bi·ness /ˈflæb·ɪ·nəs/ *n* [U] *infml disapproving*

flab·by /ˈflæb·i/ *adj* **-ier**, **-iest** *disapproving* weak; lacking force • *a flabby argument*

flab·bi·ness /ˈflæb·ɪ·nəs/ *n* [U] *infml disapproving*

flab·ber·gast *obj* /£ˈflæb·ə·gɑːst, $-ɚ·gæst/ *v* [T usually passive] *infml* to shock (someone) usually by telling them something they were not expecting • *She was flabbergasted when she learned that the test would have to be repeated.*

flac·cid /ˈflæk·sɪd, ˈflæs·ɪd/ *adj fml* soft rather than firm; weak • *The penis is usually in a flaccid state.* • *(fig.) It was a very flaccid* (= bad) *production of the play.*

flack /flæk/ *n* [U] FLAK

flag [SYMBOL] /flæg/ *n* [C] a piece of cloth, usually rectangular or square and fixed to a rope or pole at one edge, that has a pattern which either shows it represents a country or a group or has a particular meaning • *Flags of all the member countries are* **flying** *outside the headquarters.* • *The flag is at half-mast at St. John's College today in respect for a tutor who has just died.* • *Flags were* **flapping/fluttering** *in the breeze.* • *The flag was raised (Br also* **hoisted***) every morning on parade.* • *The guard* **waved** *his flag and the train pulled away from the station.* • *Perhaps we should* **wave/show/fly the flag** (= show support for our country, group or organization). • *(Br)* If someone **puts out the flags** or **puts the flags out**, they show in some way that a person or event is special: *We won – let's put out the flags and have a really good party.* • If someone **keeps the flag flying**, they act or speak for the country or group which the flag represents: *Our sales team keep the flag flying when they go to exhibitions abroad.* • *(Br)* A **flag day** (*Am* **tag day**, *Aus* **button day**) is a day when money is collected for a CHARITY from people in public places. • *(Am)* **Flag Day** is 14 June, the day in 1777 when the US first officially used its flag. • If a ship sails **under a flag of convenience**, it means it is operated or taxed under the laws of a country different from its home country which costs less money: *They always register their ships under a flag of convenience.* • *(disapproving)* **Flag-waving** is the strong expression of support for a country or group, sometimes with military intention: *There wouldn't be so much flag-waving if people thought through what might happen if there was a war.*

flag *obj* [MARK] /flæg/ *v* [T] **-gg-** to put a mark on (something) so it can be found easily among other similar things • *Flag any cards which might be useful later.* • *(specialized)* If you flag computer information, you mark it with one of two possible values so that you can process it later: *We'll flag the records of interest in the database and then we can give you a print-out.*

flag /flæg/ *n* [C] • *Use a paper clip as a flag on any of the sheets which may be of interest.*

flag [BECOME TIRED] /flæg/ *v* [I] **-gg-** to become tired or less interested • *flagging energy/enthusiasm* • *Some people's strength had flagged by the third week of walking.* • *The conversation was flagging.*

flag [STONE] /flæg/ *n* [C] a FLAGSTONE

flag·ged /flægd/ *adj* [not gradable] • *a flagged path* (= a path made of FLAGSTONES)

flag [PLANT] /flæg/ *n* [C] a type of large IRIS [FLOWER]

flag down *obj*, **flag** *obj* **down** *v adv* [M] to cause (a vehicle) to stop by waving at its driver • *A police officer flagged the car down.*

fla·gel·late *obj* /ˈflædʒ·ə·leɪt/ *v* [T] *fml* to whip (someone), esp. as a religious act

fla·gel·la·tion /ˌflædʒ·əˈleɪ·ʃən/ *n* [U] *fml* • *self-flagellation*

fla·gel·lant /ˈflædʒ·ɪ·lənt/ *n* [C] *fml* • A flagellant is someone who whips themself (or someone else) for religious reasons: *Few religious orders encourage flagellants nowadays.*

flag·on /ˈflæg·ən/ *n* [C] *old use* a container for alcoholic drink, either in the form of a large rounded bottle which liquid can be poured from, or a container with a handle and a lid which is used for drinking from • *a flagon of wine*

flag·pole /£ˈflæg·pəul, $-poul/, **flag·staff** *n* [C] a long pole, usually in a position where it can be seen easily, which a flag is fastened to

fla·grant /ˈfleɪ·grənt/ *adj* (of a bad action, situation, person, etc.) shocking because of being so obvious • *a flagrant misuse of funds/privilege* • *Telling the story was a flagrant breach of trust.*

fla·grant·ly /ˈfleɪ·grənt·li/ *adv* • *The organization flagrantly promotes the use of violence.*

flag·ship [BEST PRODUCT] /ˈflæg·ʃɪp/ *n* [C] the product or idea of highest quality or of most importance within a set • *The scheme is seen as the flagship among the batch of new proposals.* • *This is the flagship system in our range of computers.*

flag·ship [SHIP] /ˈflæg·ʃɪp/ *n* [C] the ship within a group on which the most important officer sails

flag·staff /£ˈflæg·stɑːf, $-stæf/ *n* [C] a FLAGPOLE

flag·stone /£ˈflæg·stəun, $-stoun/, **flag** *n* [C] a flat, usually rectangular or square, piece of stone or concrete used for paths, floors, etc. • *Putting flagstones down would make the whole area look much better.*

flail *(obj)* [WAVE] /fleɪl/ *v* (esp. of arms and legs) to wave energetically as if hitting (something) but with little or no control • *She ran from the house in a terrible rage, her arms flailing* **(in)** *the air.* [I/T] • *The prisoner's limbs flailed* **(about)** *violently because of the pain.* [I]

flail [TOOL] /fleɪl/ *n* [C] a tool consisting of a rod which swings from a long handle, used esp. in the past for THRESHING grain

flair /£fleəʳ, $fler/ *n* [U] natural ability to do something well • *The head of the department has a great flair* **for** *public speaking.*

flak [OPPOSITION] /flæk/, **flack** *n* [U] strong criticism or opposition • *She* **took/caught** *some flak from her parents about her new dress.* • *The government's proposal to change the tax rate has* **run into/come into** *a lot of flak.*

flak [FIRING OF GUNS] /flæk/, **flack** *n* [U] firing of guns from the ground aimed at enemy aircraft • *They flew into heavy flak over the target area.* • A **flak jacket** is a piece of clothing made from special material which protects the body from bullets. It is worn esp. by soldiers and police officers. • [PIC]› **Coats and jackets**

flake [SMALL PIECE] /fleɪk/ *n* [C] a small thin piece of something, esp. if it has come from a layered surface • *flakes of snow* • *soap flakes* • *This room needs decorating – flakes of paint keep coming off the walls.*

flake /fleɪk/ *v* [I] • *The skin on the back of his hands flakes* **(off)** *in hot dry weather.*

flak·y /ˈfleɪ·ki/ *adj* **-ier**, **-iest** • **Flaky pastry** is pastry consisting of many very thin layers.

flake [UNUSUAL PERSON] /fleɪk/ *n* [C] *infml esp. Am* a person whose behaviour is not usual or expected • *Nigel's such a flake – you can't rely on him ever getting anything done properly.*

flak·y /ˈfleɪ·ki/ *adj* **-ier**, **-iest** *infml esp. Am* • *The central character of the play is a flaky neurotic* (= a person whose behaviour is unusual). • *a flaky computer/program* (= one which does not behave as expected)

flake out *v adv* [I] *infml* to sleep or feel weak because of extreme tiredness • *The children flaked out on their beds after their exhausting day.* • *You must be flaked out after all that exercise.*

flam·bé *obj*, **flam·bée** /£ˈflɒm·beɪ, $flɑːmˈbeɪ/ *v* [T] to pour BRANDY (= a strong alcoholic drink) over (food) and set fire to it during cooking • *flambéed pancakes*

flam·bé /£ˈflɒm·beɪ, $flɑːmˈbeɪ/ *adj* [after n; not gradable] • *steak flambé*

flam·boy·ant /flæmˈbɔɪ·ənt/ *adj* very confident in behaviour, or intended to be noticed, esp. by being brightly coloured • *a flamboyant gesture* • *The writer's flamboyant lifestyle was well known.* • *His clothes were rather flamboyant for such a serious occasion.*

flam·boy·ance /flæmˈbɔɪ·ənts/ *n* [U] • *Her flamboyance annoys some people but delights others.*

flam·boy·ant·ly /flæmˈbɔɪ·ənt·li/ *adv*

flame /fleɪm/ *n* burning gas (from something on fire) which produces usually yellow light • *The flames of the fire were comforting on such a cold day.* [C] • *It's been dry for so long that the forest could* **burst into** *flame* (= start burning) *at any moment.* [U] • *When the fire engine arrived the house was already* **in** *flames* (= burning). [C] • *Don't hold a* **naked** *flame* (= one which is open to the air instead of separated from it by glass, etc.) *near the fuel.* [C] • *The factory* **went up in flames** (= was destroyed by fire). • *(fig.) Flames of* (= Strong feelings of) *passion swept through both of them.* [C] • A **flame-thrower** is a device which produces a stream of burning liquid and is used for military purposes or for clearing wild land. • If a substance is **flame retardant**, it will slow down the spread of fire.

flame /fleɪm/ *v* [I] • *The coals flamed when she blew over them.* • *(fig.) His face flamed* **(red)** (=quickly coloured) *with anger.* • *(fig.) Seeing the damage made hatred flame* (=become quickly and strongly felt) *within her.*

flam·ing /ˈfleɪ·mɪŋ/ *adj* [before n] • *(fig.) They usually get along well but last night they had a flaming* (=angry and severe) *row.*

flam·ing /ˈfleɪ·mɪŋ/ *adj* [before n; not gradable] *slang* used to add force, esp. anger, to something which is said • *Put that down you flaming idiot!*

fla·men·co /£fləˈmeŋ·kəʊ, $-koʊ/ *n* [C/U] *pl* **flamencos** a type of Spanish dance music, or the dance performed to this music • *flamenco music/dancers*

flame·proof /ˈfleɪm·pruːf/ *adj* not likely to burn or be damaged by fire • *flameproof clothing*

fla·min·go /£fləˈmɪŋ·gəʊ, $-goʊ/ *n* [C] *pl* **flamingos** or **flamingoes** a bird with pink or red feathers that lives on lakes in hot or warm countries, has long thin legs, a long neck and a beak that curves down

flam·ma·ble /ˈflæm·ə·bl̩/ *adj Am or specialized for* INFLAMMABLE • *This solvent is highly flammable* (=burns very easily), *so don't use it near a naked flame.* • Flammable is often used on official warnings because people might wrongly think that 'inflammable' means 'will not burn'.

flan /flæn/ *n* [C] a case of pastry or cake without a top, which contains fruit or something savoury such as cheese • *a pear flan* • *a flan dish* • *(Am)* A flan is also CUSTARD (=sweet thick liquid made from milk and eggs) with a layer of CARAMEL (=sticky brown cooked sugar) on top. • PIC› **Kitchen**

flange /flændʒ/ *n* [C] a flat surface sticking out from an object, which is used to fix it to something or to make it stronger • *The flange around the wheels on railway trains and carriages helps to keep them on the rails.*

flank /flæŋk/ *v, n* (to be at) the side of someone or something • *The president was flanked on both sides by senior ministers.* [T] • *Police motorcyclists flanked the car.* [T] • *The general concentrated his attack on the left flank of the opposing army.* [C] • *A small group of houses clings to the eastern flank of the mountain.* [C] • The flank of an animal or a person is the area of the body between the RIBS and the hips. [C]

flan·nel PIECE OF CLOTH /ˈflæn·əl/ *n* [C] *Br for* FACECLOTH • PIC› **Bathroom**

flan·nel TYPE OF CLOTH /ˈflæn·əl/ *n* [U] a light cloth usually made from wool, used esp. for making clothes • *grey flannel trousers*

flan·nels /ˈflæn·əlz/ *pl n* • Flannels are trousers made of flannel: *Traditionally, white flannels are worn when playing cricket.* • *(Am)* Flannels are also underwear made of flannel.

flan·nel UNNECESSARY WORDS /ˈflæn·əl/ *n* [U] *Br infml* speech containing a lot of words which is used to avoid telling the truth or answering a question, and is frequently intended to deceive • *Leave out the flannel and answer the question!*

flan·nel *(obj)* /ˈflæn·əl/ *v* **-ll-** *Br and Aus infml* • *She flannelled the entire committee and they didn't realise until after the vote had been taken.* [T] • *Don't flannel in the interview.* [I]

flan·nel·ette /ˌflæn·əlˈet/ *n* [U] a soft cloth made of cotton • *flannelette sheets/pyjamas* • *a flannelette nightdress*

flap *(obj)* WAVE /flæp/ *v* **-pp-** to wave (something, esp. wings) when or as if flying • *A small bird flapped its wings furiously and flew upwards.* [T] • *The shopkeeper ran forwards flapping his arms.* [T] • *The geese flapped* (=flew by waving their wings) *slowly out of sight.* [I] • *Flags flapped in the breeze above their tents.* [I]

flap /flæp/ *n* [C] • *With a few flaps of its long wings, the bird took off.* • *In the dark, we could hear the flap of the sails above us.*

flap ADDITIONAL PIECE /flæp/ *n* [C] a piece of cloth or other material fixed along one edge, esp. used for covering or closing something • *a pocket flap* • *a tent flap* (=a piece of cloth which acts like a door) • *The extra flap behind the zip on the coat gives added protection against the wind.* • *A small flap of skin can be seen above the wound.*

flap ANXIOUS STATE /flæp/ *n* [U] *infml* a state of anxious excitement • *You're* **getting in(to) a** *flap for no reason!* • *She's* **in a** *great flap because her parents are coming to visit.*

flap /flæp/ *v* [I] **-pp-** *infml* • *Don't flap – there's plenty of time to cook before they arrive.* • *Stop flapping* **about/around**!

flap AIRCRAFT PART /flæp/ *n* [C] *specialized* part of the back of an aircraft wing which can be moved up or down to give greater control when landing and taking off

flap·jack /ˈflæp·dʒæk/ *n* [C] *(esp. Br and Aus)* a type of sweet chewy cake made from OATS, or *(esp. Am)* a PANCAKE

flap·per /£ˈflæp·əʳ, $-ɚ/ *n* [C] *old use infml* (in the 1920s) a fashionable young woman, esp. one showing independent behaviour

flare BURN BRIGHTLY /£fleəʳ, $fler/ *v* [I] to burn brightly either for a short time or irregularly • *The flame above the oil well flared* **(up)** *into the dark sky.* • *(fig.) Violence flared* **up** (=happened suddenly) *again last night in many areas with armed gangs taking to the streets.*

flare /£fleəʳ, $fler/ *n* [C] • *There was a sudden flare when she threw the petrol onto the fire.* • A flare is also a very bright light or coloured smoke which can be used as a signal, or a device which produces this: *The dinghy is equipped with flares to attract the attention of nearby ships or aircraft.* • *(fig.) A further* **flare-up** *of rioting occurred later in the day.*

flare *(obj)* MAKE WIDER /£fleəʳ, $fler/ *v* to (cause to) become wider • *The horse's nostrils flared.* [I] • *She made the skirt fit tightly over the hips and flared it just below the knees.* [T]

flare /£fleəʳ, $fler/ *n* [C usually sing] • *This skirt has a definite flare.*

flared /£fleəd, $flerd/ *adj* • *flared trousers*

flares /£fleəz, $flerz/ *pl n Br and Aus* • Flares are trousers that widen below the knee.

flash *(obj)* SHINE /flæʃ/ *v* to shine (a light) suddenly and usually brightly, but only for a short time • *Stop flashing that light* **in** *my eyes!* [T] • *The lightning flashed and distant thunder rolled.* [I] • *You'd better slow down, that car was flashing (its lights)* **at** *you.* [I/T] • *(fig.) Christopher's eyes flashed* (=looked bright) *with sudden rage.* [I] • (KOR)

flash /flæʃ/ *n* [C] • *A flash of lightning lit the sky.* • *(fig.) The answer came to her in a flash of* (=with sudden) *inspiration.* • *(infml)* If something happens **quick as/like/ in a flash**, it happens quickly or suddenly: *The ceremony was over in a flash.* ○ *The idea came in a flash.* • If something was a **flash in the pan**, it happened only once or for a short time and will not be repeated: *Let's hope the group's overnight rise to stardom will not be a flash in the pan.* • A **flash point** is the place or stage at which violence might be expected to begin: *Because of the army's presence, the city is seen to be the flash point of the area.* ○ *The whole situation is nearing flash point with widespread acts of civil unrest.* • *(specialized)* The **flash point** of a liquid is the lowest temperature at which the VAPOUR it produces will burn in air. • *The unusually heavy rain caused* **flash floods** (=sudden and severe floods) *in several mountain villages.*

flash MOVE FAST /flæʃ/ *v* [I always + adv/prep] to move very fast • *They flashed past/by on the motorcycle.* • *We're having such a good trip, the time is just flashing* **by/past**. • *(fig.) A strange thought flashed through/across her mind.* • *(fig.) Her mind flashed* **back** (=suddenly returned) *to the day of their divorce.* • *A good way to cook a thin steak is to* **flash-fry** *it* (=fry it quickly on both sides in very hot oil). • (KOR)

flash *(obj)* SHOW QUICKLY /flæʃ/ *v* to show (something) for a short time • *She flashed her credit cards and the salesperson suddenly became very helpful.* [T] • *(fig.) Now she's got her new job, she certainly flashes her money* **about/around** (=acts in a way which shows everyone she has money to spend). [T] • *(infml)* If someone flashes, they show their sexual organs in public: *She was very upset because a man flashed* **at** *her on the train.* [I] • (KOR)

flash /flæʃ/ *n* [C] *infml* • *I know the design is secret but you can give me a quick flash – I won't tell anybody what it looks like.* • A **flash card** is a card with a word written on it which is shown to a child for a short time to help them learn the word.

flash·er /£ˈflæʃ·əʳ, $-ɚ/ *n* [C] *infml* • A flasher is someone who shows their sexual organs in public.

flash SEEMING EXPENSIVE /flæʃ/ *adj* **-er, -est** *infml esp. disapproving* seeming expensive and modern, but usually lacking style • *That's a very flash suit he's wearing.* • (KOR)

flash·y /ˈflæʃ·i/ *adj* **-ier, -iest** *infml esp. disapproving* • *flashy clothes* • *a flashy car*

flash·i·ly /ˈflæʃ·ɪ·li/ *adv infml esp. disapproving* • *flashily dressed*

flash·i·ness /ˈflæʃ·ɪ·nəs/ *n* [U] *infml esp. disapproving*

flash [PHOTOGRAPHY] /flæʃ/, *specialized* **flash·light** *n* the device or system used to produce a bright light for a short time when taking a photograph when it is dark • *Where's the flash for the camera?* [C] • *It's quite dark in here, I'll have to use flash.* [U] • (KOR)

flash *obj* [COMMUNICATE] /flæʃ/ *v* [T always + adv/prep] to communicate (something) quickly, esp. using radio or light waves • *Within moments of an event happening, the news can be flashed around the world.* • (KOR)

flash [MILITARY SIGN] /flæʃ/ *n* [C] *Br* a small object or piece of material worn on a military uniform as a sign of rank, or (on clothing) a strip or mark of colour different from the main colour • (KOR)

flash·bulb /ˈflæʃ·bʌlb/ *n* [C] *specialized* a small electric light that can be fixed to a camera and which makes a bright flash so that photographs can be taken inside

flash·gun /ˈflæʃ·gʌn/ *n* [C] *specialized* a device usually held away from a camera which automatically makes a flash when a camera is taking a picture

flash·light /ˈflæʃ·laɪt/ *n* [C] *esp. Am for* TORCH

flask /£flɑːsk, $flæsk/ *n* [C] a container for liquids, usually having a wide base and a narrow neck • *The cupboard held a collection of glass bottles and flasks of different shapes and sizes.* • *(specialized) As part of their chemistry lesson, the children were told to heat different liquids in a* **conical** *flask.* • A flask is also a **hip flask**: *a flask of whisky* ○ See at HIP [BODY PART]. • *(Br)* A flask is also a **vacuum flask**: *a flask of coffee* ○ See at VACUUM. • [PIC⟩ **Bottles and flasks** (N)

flat [LEVEL] /flæt/ *adj* **flatter, flattest** level and smooth; not rounded and having little or no height • *An ice rink needs to be completely flat.* • *Roll out the pastry on a flat surface.* • *Much of the countryside in East Anglia is very flat* (= has no hills). • *People used to believe that the earth was flat* (= not ball-shaped). • Flat **bread** is bread that is made without YEAST: *Pitta and naan are two types of flat bread.* • A flat **cap** or **hat** is one which is not rounded on top and has little height. • *I got a flat (Br and Aus)* **tyre**/*(Am)* **tire** (= The air went out of it) *when I drove over a nail.* • *(infml) We rolled the lawn until it was* **as flat as a pancake** (= very level). • *(esp. disapproving)* A woman who is **flat-chested** has small breasts. • *Several people in our family have* **flat feet** (= the bottom parts of their feet are level instead of being curved). • *He has become more* **flat-footed** (= the bottom parts of his feet have become more level) *as he has got older.* • **Flat racing** is a type of horse racing where the horses do not jump over fences. • (T)

flat /flæt/ *n* [C] • *The* **(mud/salt)** *flats* (= area of low level ground, often near water) *attract large numbers of birds.* • *(esp. Am and Aus) I think we've got a flat* (= The air has gone out of one of the car's tyres). • *He hit me with* **the flat of** (= the level inside part of) *his hand.* • *Most of the path is* **on the flat** (= does not go up or down a hill). • *(specialized)* A flat is also a movable level board on which background pictures for a play or other type of performance are painted.

flat /flæt/ *adv* **flatter, flattest** • *He injured his spine falling from his horse, and had to spend weeks lying flat on his back* (= with all of his back touching the surface on which he was lying). • *These garden chairs will fold flat* (= can be folded into a narrow shape) *for storage.* • *The bulldozer* **knocked/laid** *the building flat* (= knocked it down) *in minutes*.

flat·ness /ˈflæt·nəs/ *n* [U] • *The flatness* **of** *the desert was broken only by a few large piles of rocks.*

flats /flæts/ *pl n* • *I find it more comfortable to wear flats* (= shoes without high heels).

flat·ten *(obj)* /£ˈflæt·ᵊn, $ˈflæṭ-/ *v* • To flatten something is to cause it to be level: *Several trees were flattened* (= knocked down) *by the storm.* [T] ○ *We flattened ourselves against* (= made ourselves level with) *the hedge to allow a car to pass us on the narrow country road.* [T] ○ *He folded the bag and flattened it before placing it on the pile.* [T] ○ *I need to get the dents in my car flattened* **out** (= get the surface of my car made level). [M] ○ *The path flattens* **(out)** (= does not go up or down so much) *as it reaches the top of the hill.* [I]

flat [NOT ACTIVE] /flæt/ *adj* **flatter, flattest** not active; not interesting or lacking emotion • *After the excitement of the party, life seems very flat now.* • *We thought the leading lady was excellent, but the rest of the performances were rather flat.* • *She answered his questions in a completely flat tone* (= her voice expressed no emotion or interest). • *Business is always a bit flat at this time of year* (= not much is being sold). • *I think the colours in this painting are rather flat* (= not varied or bright). • *(Br and Aus) I left my car lights on all night and now the battery is flat (Am* **dead***)* (= has no electrical power left in it). • A drink which is flat has stopped being fizzy: *If you don't put the top back on that bottle of beer, it will* **go** *flat.* Compare STILL [NOT MOVING]. • *The joke* **fell** *flat – no one laughed.* • *"How weary, stale, flat, and unprofitable / Seem to me all the uses of this world"* (Shakespeare, Hamlet 1.2) • (T)

flat·ly /ˈflæt·li/ *adv* • *The witness responded flatly* (= without emotion or interest) *to the judge's questions.* • *I thought the pianist played rather flatly* (= without any emotion or interest).

flat·ness /ˈflæt·nəs/ *n* [U] • *All the critics remarked on the flatness of the performance* (= said that it lacked emotion and interest).

flat [COMPLETE] /flæt/, *Am also* **flat–out** *adj* [before n; not gradable] complete or certain, esp. without an explanation being given and not likely to change • *His request for time off work was met with a flat* **refusal**. • *The minister has issued a flat* **denial** *of the accusations against her.* • *I'm not coming,* **and that's flat** (= that decision will not change)*!* • (T)

flat /flæt/ *adv* [not gradable] *infml* • Flat means completely or to the greatest degree possible: *She told him flat/(Am also)* **flat out** *that she would not go to the show.* ○ *Going out of the school grounds without permission is flat (Am also flat* **out***) against the rules.* ○ *Could you lend me some money, I'm flat* **broke** (= I have no money). ○ *My car only does about 60 mph, even when it's going* **flat out** (= as fast as it can).

flat·ly /ˈflæt·li/ *adv* [not gradable] • Flatly means completely or to the greatest degree possible: *The child sat in the middle of the floor and flatly* **refused** *to move.* ○ *He flatly* **denied** *that he saw what had happened.*

flat [FIXED] /flæt/ *adj* [before n; not gradable] (esp. of an amount of money) fixed; not likely to vary • *There is a flat* **fare** *of 60p on all buses in the city.* • *We charge a flat* **fee/rate** *of $25 per hour.* • A flat-rate **contribution** is a payment made to an organization, such as a trade union, that is the same for everyone whatever they earn.

flat /flæt/ *adv* [after n; not gradable] • *(infml) We managed to get to the station in five minutes flat* (= in exactly five minutes).

flat [MUSIC] /flæt/ *adj, adv* **flatter, flattest** (in music) lower than a particular or the correct note • *The top string on your violin is flat.* • *Sibelius' 5th symphony is written in the key of E flat major* (= the set of musical notes a SEMITONE lower than the one based on the note E). [after n] • *She sang flat throughout the song* (= all the notes she sang were too low). • Compare NATURAL [MUSIC]; SHARP [MUSIC]. • [PIC⟩ **Music** (T)

flat /flæt/ *n* [C] • A flat is also a symbol for a note that is a SEMITONE lower than a stated note.

flat·ten *obj* /£ˈflæt·ᵊn, $ˈflæṭ-/ *v* [T] • *You need to flatten the D string* (= make it play a lower sound) *on your guitar a little.*

flat [HOME] *Br and Aus* /flæt/, *esp. Am* **a·part·ment** *n* [C] a set of rooms for living which are part of a larger building and are usually all on one floor • *a basement flat* • *a furnished flat* • *a penthouse flat* • *They have a house in the country and a flat in London.* • *Turn right at the* **block of** *flats (Am* **apartment house***) on the corner.* • See also FLATMATE. • [PIC⟩ **Accommodation**

flat·let *Br* /ˈflæt·lət/, *Am* **ef·fi·cien·cy (a·part·ment)** *n* [C] • A flatlet is a small flat.

flats /flæts/ *pl n Br and Aus* • *A lot of the children in the school live in* **the** *flats* (= building containing flats) *at the end of the road.*

flat·fish /ˈflæt·fɪʃ/ *n* [C] *pl* **flatfish** or **flatfishes** any thin flat sea fish, such as a PLAICE or a SOLE

flat·head /ˈflæt·hed/ *n* [C] *Aus* a thin flat sea fish which can be eaten

flat·mate /ˈflæt·meɪt/ *n* [C] *Br* a person who shares an apartment with another person

flat·ter *obj* /£ˈflæt·əʳ, $ˈflæṭ·ɚ/ *v* [T] to make (someone) feel or appear important, attractive or pleased, esp. by praising them • *His remarks about her new dress flattered her.* • *I knew he was* **only** *flattering me* (= praising me without being sincere) *because he wanted to borrow some money.* • *Short skirts don't flatter me* (= do not make me look attractive) *at all.* • *You're flattering* **yourself** *if you think* (= You are wrong to think that) *she'll go out with you.* • *Clive flatters* **himself** (= is proud of the fact) **that** *he never* *forgets a name.* [+ obj + *that* clause] • *I flatter my***self on** (=take pride in) *always paying bills on time.* • To **flatter to deceive** is to give the appearance of being better than the true situation: *The figures flatter to deceive – only one in five of these new jobs is genuine full-time employment, most are part-time or seasonal.* • *"What really flatters a man is that you think him worth flattering"* (George Bernard Shaw in *John Bull's Other Island*, 1907)

flat·tered /£'flæt·əd, $-t̬ɚd/ *adj* • *The town was flattered* **to** *hear that its beach was one of the cleanest in the country.* [+ *to* infinitive] • *They were flattered* (=pleased and proud) **to** *be invited to dinner by the mayor.* [+ *to* infinitive] • *We felt flattered* **that** *so many people came to our party.* [+ *that* clause]

flat·ter·er /£'flæt·ᵊr·ər, $'flæt̬·ɚ·ɚ/ *n* [C] • *You can't believe a word Tony says, he's a real flatterer* (=he praises people without really meaning it).

flat·ter·ing /£'flæt·ᵊr·ɪŋ, $'flæt̬·ɚ-/ *adj* • *That suit is very flattering* (=makes you look attractive). • *Emma's school photograph isn't very flattering* (=does not make her look attractive). • *He's always making flattering* **remarks** (=remarks praising people), *but he doesn't really mean them.*

flat·ter·y /£'flæt·ᵊr·i, $'flæt̬-/ *n* [U] • *I was really pleased when he said how well I'd done, because he isn't known for flattery.* • *(saying)* 'Flattery will get you nowhere' means that praise which is not sincere will not persuade someone to do what you want them to do.

flat·u·lence /'flæt·jʊ·lᵊnts/ *n* [U] *fml* (the uncomfortable feeling caused by having) gas in the stomach and bowels • *Eating beans can cause flatulence.*

flat·u·lent /'flæt·jʊ·lᵊnt/ *adj fml*

flat·ware /£'flæt·weəʳ, $-wer/ *n* [U] *Am for* CUTLERY

flat·worm /£'flæt·wɜːm, $-wɜːrm/ *n* [C] any of various types of WORM with a flat body, that can live inside the bodies of people and animals and often cause disease • *A tapeworm is a type of flatworm.*

flaunt *obj* /£flɔːnt, $flɑːnt/ *v* [T] *esp. disapproving* to show or make obvious (something you are proud of) in order to get admiration • *They flaunt their wealth by driving around in a Rolls-Royce.* • *Ever since he started working out, he likes to flaunt him***self** (=show his body) *at every opportunity.* • To flaunt something, such as a rule or tradition, is to intentionally ignore it: *The company continues to flaunt* **convention/tradition.** • *"When you got it, flaunt it. (Often used in the form 'If you've got it – flaunt it')"* (In the film *The Producers*, 1968)

flaut·ist /£'flɔː·tɪst, $'flɑː·t̬ɪst/, *Am also* **flut·ist** *n* [C] a person who plays the FLUTE

fla·vour *Br and Aus, Am and Aus* **fla·vor** /£'fleɪ·vəʳ, $-vɚ/ *n* a taste or *(fig.)* quality • *The soup needs to be simmered for at least half an hour to bring out the flavour* **of** *the herbs.* [U] • *The fish we had for dinner last night had no flavour* (=did not taste of anything) *at all.* [U] • *This wine has a light, fruity flavour* (=the particular taste of fruit). [C] • *We sell 32 different flavours* (=particular types of taste) *of ice cream.* [C] • *(fig.) The restaurant has* **a** *nautical flavour* (=the particular quality of being like a ship). [U] • *(fig.) This brief description should give you* **a** *flavour* **of** (=show you a little) *what the book is like.* [U] • *(Br and Aus infml) Andy is certainly* **flavour of the month** (=the most popular person at the moment) *with the boss.* • *This sauce contains a* **flavour enhancer** (=a substance used to improve its taste).

fla·vour *obj Br and Aus, Am and Aus* **fla·vor** /£'fleɪ·vəʳ, $-vɚ/ *v* [T] • *I like to use cinnamon to flavour* (=give a particular taste to) *coffee.* • *He always flavours roast lamb* **with** (=gives it the taste of) *rosemary.*

-fla·voured *Br and Aus, Am and Aus* **-fla·vored** /£'fleɪ·vəd, $-vɚd/ *combining form* • *The children like chocolate-flavoured ice-cream* (=ice-cream with the taste of chocolate).

fla·vour·ing *Br and Aus, Am and Aus* **fla·vor·ing** /£'fleɪ·vᵊr·ɪŋ, $-vɚ-/ *n* • *I try not to buy foods with too many artificial flavourings* (=substances added to improve the taste). [C] • *A little vanilla flavouring improves the taste of the dessert.* [U]

fla·vour·less *Br and Aus, Am and Aus* **fla·vor·less** /£'fleɪ·və·ləs, $-vɚ-/ *adj* • *These grapes are completely flavourless* (=do not taste of anything).

fla·vour·some *Br and Aus, Am and Aus* **fla·vor·some** /£'fleɪ·və·səm, $-vɚ-/, *Br and Aus* **fla·vour·y**, *Am and Aus also* **fla·vor·y**, *Am usually* **flav·or·ful** /£'fleɪ·və·fᵊl, $-vɚ-/ *adj* • *flavoursome wine* • *a nice flavoury casserole* • *The meat nearest the bone is often the most flavoursome.*

flaw /£flɔː, $flɑː/ *n* [C] a fault, mistake or weakness, esp. one that happens while something is being planned or made or which causes something not to be perfect • *I should like to return this coat because it has a flaw* **in** *it.* • *If this washing machine has a flaw, it's the way it's noisy when spinning.* • *The toy was withdrawn from sale because there was a flaw in the design.* • *This report is full of flaws.* • *There is a* **fatal** *flaw* **in** *your argument.* • *His inability to admit that he's wrong is a flaw* **in** *his character.*

flaw *obj* /£flɔː, $flɑː/ *v* [T] • To flaw something is to cause it not to be perfect: *A tiny mark flawed the otherwise perfect silk shirt.* ○ *Our evening out was flawed by having to wait a long time in the rain for a taxi home.*

flawed /£flɔːd, $flɑːd/ *adj* • *Diamonds are still valuable, even when they are flawed* (=not perfect). • *His argument is deeply flawed* (=contains a lot of mistakes).

flaw·less /£'flɔː·ləs, $'flɑː-/ *adj* [not gradable] • *The audience applauded the pianist's flawless* (=perfect) *playing.* • *You can't help noticing her flawless beauty.*

flax /flæks/ *n* [U] (thread made from) a plant with blue flowers grown for its stems or seeds • *Flax is used for making linen.*

flax·en /'flæk·sᵊn/ *adj literary* (of hair) pale yellow • *a flaxen-haired/-headed beauty*

flay *obj* /fleɪ/ *v* [T] to remove the skin from (a person's or animal's body) • *In prehistoric times, people used flint to flay the animals they killed.* • To flay a person or animal is to whip them so hard that some of their skin comes off: *(fig.) The critics really flayed* (=severely criticized) *his new book.* ○ *(fig. infml) My dad'll* **flay** *me* **alive** (=punish me severely) *for crashing his car.*

flea /fliː/ *n* [C] a very small jumping insect without wings which feeds on the blood of animals and people • *Our cat wears a special collar so it doesn't* **get** *fleas.* • *(infml) You'll get* **a flea in** *your* **ear** (=an annoying or angry remark) *if you do that again.* • *I bought this coat at our local* **flea market** (=an outside market selling old or used goods at low prices). • *"So, naturalists observe, a flea / Hath smaller fleas that on him prey; / And these have smaller fleas to bite 'em / And so proceed ad infinitum"* (Jonathan Swift *On Poetry: A Rhapsody*, 1733) • See also FLEABITE. • PIC **Insects**

flea·bag PERSON OR ANIMAL /'fliː·bæg/ *n* [C] *Br slang* a dirty and/or disliked person or animal • *The old man who lives in the house down the road from us is a* **real** *fleabag.*

flea·bag HOTEL /'fliː·bæg/ *n* [C] *Am* a cheap dirty hotel • *We stayed in a* **real** *fleabag when we went to New York.*

flea·bite /'fliː·baɪt/ *n* [C] the bite of a FLEA • *When we woke in the morning, we were covered in fleabites.* • *(fig. infml) The initial protests at the court's decision were only a fleabite* (=a small problem) *compared to the major rioting that followed.*

flea·bit·ten /£'fliː·bɪt·ᵊn, $-bɪt̬-/ *adj esp. Br infml* dirty and in bad condition • *I'm not going to stay in that fleabitten old place.*

flea·pit /'fliː·pɪt/ *n* [C] *Br infml dated* a cinema or theatre, esp. one that is old, dirty, in bad condition and cheap

fleck /flek/ *v, n* (to cover or mark with) a small mark or piece, esp. of a different colour • *Blackbirds' eggs are pale blue with brown flecks on them.* [C] • *He wore a light grey suit with* **a** *dark grey fleck* (=with dark grey threads in the material). [U] • *I got a few flecks* **of** *paint on the window when I was painting the frames.* [C] • *(literary) The years have flecked her hair* **with** *grey.* [T]

flecked /flekt/ *adj* • *She was wearing a flecked coat* (=a coat with threads of a different colour from the main colour of the material). • *At this time of year, the hedgerows are beginning to be flecked* **with** *blossom.*

fled /fled/ *past simple and past participle of* FLEE

fledged /fledʒd/ *adj* [not gradable] See **fully fledged** at FULLY.

fledg·ling, fledge·ling /'fledʒ·lɪŋ/ *n* [C] a young bird that has grown feathers and is learning to fly • *(fig.) The current economic climate is particularly difficult for fledgling* (=new and not experienced) *businesses.*

flee *(obj)* /fliː/ *v past* **fled** /fled/ to escape by running away, esp. because of danger or fear • *Everyone fled* **(from)** *the building when the fire alarm sounded.* [T; I + *from*] • *She fled* **(from)** *the room in tears.* [T; I + *from*] • *In order to escape capture, he fled* **to** *the country.* [I] • *It is thought that the robbers have* **fled the country** (=gone to another country) *by now.* • *(fig. literary) All our dreams have fled* (= our hopes have quickly disappeared). [I]

fleece SHEEP /fliːs/ *n* the woolly fur of a sheep • *In the winter, sheep have thick fleeces.* [C] • A fleece is the fur of a sheep cut off in one piece. [C] • *My jacket is lined with fleece/ is fleece-***lined** (= has sheep's fur inside it). [U]

fleece *obj* /fliːs/ *v* [T] • *Sheep are usually fleeced* (= The fur is cut from them) *in the summer.*

flee·cy /ˈfliː·si/ *adj* **-ier, -iest** • *The children's boots have a fleecy lining* (= have material like sheep's fur inside them). • *(fig.) The sky is full of fleecy clouds today* (= clouds looking like sheep's fur).

fleece *obj* CHEAT /fliːs/ *v* [T] *infml* to take someone's money, by charging too much money or by cheating them • *That restaurant really fleeced us!*

fleet SHIPS /fliːt/ *n* [C] a number of ships under the control of one person, country or organization, or organized for a particular purpose • *a fleet* **of** *20 ships* • *A peace-keeping fleet has been sent to the area.* • **The** *(British) fleet is sailing from Southampton early this morning.* • *Fishing fleets are not allowed inside another country's territorial waters.* • A **fleet admiral** is an officer of the highest rank in the US Navy.

fleet VEHICLES /fliːt/ *n* [C] a number of buses, aircraft, etc. under the control of one person or organization • *All the bus fleets in the city are controlled by the council.* • Fleet **cars** are cars which belong to a company and are used by people it employs.

fleet QUICK /fliːt/ *adj* **-er, -est** quick or moving fast • *She's pretty fleet* **of foot**/*fleet-***footed**.

fleet·ing /£ˈfliː·tɪŋ, $-t̬ɪŋ/ *adj* • Fleeting means brief or quick: *We caught a fleeting* **glimpse** *of the queen as she drove past.* ○ *This is just a fleeting visit.*

fleet·ing·ly /£ˈfliː·tɪŋ·li, $-t̬ɪŋ-/ *adv* • *I wondered fleetingly* (= briefly) *if Jill was as old as she said she was.*

fleet·ness /ˈfliːt·nəs/ *n* [U] • *He was saved from disaster only by the fleetness* (= speed) *of his horse.*

Fleet Street /fliːt/ *n* [U] the road in London where most of Britain's national newspapers were produced in the past, often used to refer to British national newspapers in general • *There are rumours* **in** *Fleet Street* (= among people working for British national newspapers) *that the company is about to be taken over.* • *Fleet Street is obsessed with these stories of killer dogs.* • *He's a Fleet Street journalist* (= He works for a British national newspaper).

flesh /fleʃ/ *n* [U] the soft part of the body of a person or animal which is between the skin and the bones, or the soft inner part of a fruit or vegetable • *The thorn went deep into the flesh of my hand.* • *Vegetarians don't eat animal flesh* (= meat). • *To make tomato sauce, you have to remove the skins from the tomatoes and use only the flesh.* • Your **bare** flesh is your skin: *He stripped down to his bare flesh.* ○ *(fig.) In the summer, this beach will be covered with bare flesh* (= people wearing few clothes). • *I've seen her perform on television, but never* **in the flesh** (= in real life). • **The** flesh sometimes refers to sex: *This part of the city is well known as being somewhere people can indulge in the* **desires/ pleasures/sins of** *the flesh.* ○ See also FLESHPOT. • *I can't possibly do that, I'm only* **flesh and blood** (= I have human limits). • *Some of these cartoon characters are more famous than many* **flesh and blood** (= human) *celebrities.* • *Spiders always* **make** *my* **flesh crawl/creep** (= I am frightened by them). • *I think you need to provide some more data to* **add flesh to** *your* **argument/put flesh on** *your* **argument** (= make your argument stronger). • If something is *(Br and Aus)* **flesh-coloured**/*(Am)* **flesh-tone**, it is approximately the colour of white people's skin: *I'd like a pair of flesh-coloured tights, please.* • *He cut his head when he fell off his bicycle, but it was only a* **flesh wound** (= his bones and inner organs were not damaged). • PIC> **Fruit**

flesh·ly /ˈfleʃ·li/ *adv fml or literary* • *He is someone who finds it difficult to curb his fleshly* (= sexual) **desires**.

flesh·y /ˈfleʃ·i/ *adj* **-ier, -iest** • *The women in many of Rubens' paintings are rather fleshy* (= fat). • *Make sure you buy nice fleshy peaches* (= ones with a lot of flesh). • *We've decided to paint the walls a fleshy colour* (= a colour like white people's skin).

flesh·i·ness /ˈfleʃ·ɪ·nəs/ *n* [U]

flesh out *obj*, **flesh** *obj* **out** *v adv* [M] to add more details or information to (something) • *These plans need to be fleshed out* **with** *some more figures before the committee votes on them.*

flesh·pot /£ˈfleʃ·pɒt, $-pɑːt/ *n* [C usually pl] a place which supplies sexual entertainment and food and drink

fleur-de-lis (*pl* **fleurs-de-lis**), **fleur-de-lys** (*pl* **fleurs-de-lys**) /£ˌflɜː·dəˈliː, $ˌflɜːr-/ *n* a pattern representing a flower with three branching parts joined at the bottom, used in **coats of arms**

flew /fluː/ *past simple and past participle of* FLY

flex *obj* BEND /fleks/ *v* [T] to bend (esp. a muscle, arm or leg) in order to exercise it • *Sit down, straighten your legs and flex your feet.* • *(fig.) The new director is flexing his* **muscles** (= testing or showing his power) *by making a lot of changes in the company's organization.*

flex WIRE *Br* /fleks/, *Am* **wire**, *Br and Aus also* **lead**, *Aus also* **cord** *n* (a length of) wire with a plastic cover used for connecting a piece of electrical equipment to a supply of electricity • *The flex on this iron isn't long enough to reach the socket.* [C] • *I need to buy a new piece of flex for my hairdryer.* [U] • PIC> **Fires and space heaters, Lights**

flex·i·ble ABLE TO BEND /ˈflek·sɪ·bl̩/ *adj* able to bend or to be bent easily without breaking • *Rubber is a flexible substance.* • *Dancers need to be flexible* (= able to bend their bodies easily).

flex·i·bil·i·ty /£ˌflek·sɪˈbɪl·ɪ·ti, $-ə·t̬i/ *n* [U] • *These shoes are uncomfortable because the soles have no flexibility.* • *You can increase your flexibility by exercising.*

flex·i·ble CHANGEABLE /ˈflek·sɪ·bl̩/ *adj* able to change or be changed easily according to the situation • *We've arranged to go to the cinema on Thursday, but we can be flexible and go another day if necessary.* • *I have a very flexible arrangement with my employer so I can work whatever hours suit me.* • *The Prime Minister is not prepared to be flexible* **about** *the government's economic policy.* • *"Your flexible friend"* (British advertisement for Access credit cards, 1981-)

flex·i·bil·i·ty /£ˌflek·sɪˈbɪl·ɪ·ti, $-ə·t̬i/ *n* [U] • *The advantage of this system is its flexibility.*

flex·i·bly /ˈflek·sɪ·bli/ *adv* • *Today's schedule of events is organized flexibly so that people can decide for themselves what they want to do.*

flex·i·time /ˈflek·si·taɪm/, *Am also* **flex·time** /ˈfleks·taɪm/ *n* [U] a system of working according to which people work a set number of hours within a fixed period of time, but can vary the time they start or finish work • *Everyone in the office* **is on/works** *flexitime.*

flib·ber·ti·gib·bet /£ˌflɪb·ə·tiˈdʒɪb·ɪt, $-ɚ·t̬i-/ *n* [C] *dated* a person, often a woman, who talks too much, is foolish, and cannot be serious

flick *(obj)* /flɪk/ *v* to (cause to) move with a short sudden movement, or to hit quickly and lightly • *Horses flick their tails to make flies go away.* [T] • *You hit a squash ball by flicking your wrist.* [T] • *Windscreen wipers flick from side to side.* [I always + adv/prep] • *"Don't move," he said, flicking his knife open.* [T + obj + adj] • *The boys ran round the swimming pool, flicking* (= hitting) *each other with their towels.* [T] • *Could you flick the light switch* **(on/off)** *for me, please.* [T/M] • *It really annoys me the way you keep flicking* **channels** (= turning from one television station to another) *all the time.* [T] • *The lizard flicked* **out** *its tongue at a fly.* [M] • *Before he went into the interview, he carefully flicked the loose hairs* **from** *the shoulders of his jacket* (= removed them by hitting them sharply with the back of his finger). [T] • *Could you just flick the dust* **off** *the windowsills, please* (= remove it by hitting it lightly)? [M] • *She flicked idly* **through** *the pages of a magazine* (= turned them quickly) *while she was waiting for the bus.* [I always + adv/prep] • *(Br and Aus)* A **flick knife** (*Am* **switchblade**) is a knife with a blade hidden inside its handle which springs out when a button is pressed. • PIC> **Knife** Ⓓ Ⓝ

flick /flɪk/ *n* [C] • *Cows* **give** *flicks* **of** (= quick movements with) *their tails to brush away flies that are annoying them.* • *With a flick* **of** *a switch, the room was in darkness.* • *The horse went faster when it was* **given a** *quick flick* **of** (= a light blow with) *the whip.* • *(infml) Could you have a quick flick* **through** *this report* (= read it quickly) *for me, and let me know what you think of it?*

flick·er *(obj)* /£ˈflɪk·əʳ, $-ɚ/ *v* to burn, shine or (cause to) move with small quick shaking movements • *Candles flickered on all the tables in the restaurant.* [I] • *He'd been in a coma for weeks, when all of a sudden he flickered an eyelid.* [T] • *She tried not to laugh at what he said, but she couldn't stop a smile flickering across her face.* [I] • *(fig.) The thought flickered into my head* (= I had the sudden thought) *that I'd met him before.* [I]

flick·er /£ˈflɪk·əʳ, $-ɚ/ *n* [C] • *There's a flicker on our television* (= The picture is shaking). • *They could see a flicker* **of** *light* (= a quickly moving light) *at the end of the* *tunnel.* • *(fig.) There was a flicker* (= a slight and short expression) **of** *fear in his eyes.* • *(fig.) He didn't show a flicker* **of** (= any) *interest in what I was saying to him.*

flick·er·ing /£ˈflɪk·ər·ɪŋ, $ˈ-ɚ-/ *adj* • *We sat comfortably by the flickering fire, reading our books.* • *(fig.) I still have a flickering* (= slight) *hope that I'll find the bracelet I lost.*

flicks /flɪks/ *pl n* **the flicks** *dated infml* the cinema • *What's on at the flicks this week?*

flick /flɪk/ *n* [C] *dated infml* • *Do you fancy seeing a flick* (= film) *tonight?*

fli·er TRAVELLER, **fly·er** /£ˈflaɪ·əʳ, $-ɚ/ *n* [C] See at FLY TRAVEL

fli·er INFORMATION, *Am usually* **fly·er** /£ˈflaɪ·əʳ, $-ɚ/ *n* [C] a piece of printed information about a product or event

flies TROUSERS *Br* /flaɪz/ *pl n*, *Am and Aus usually* **fly** *n* [C] the opening at the front of a pair of trousers • *Your flies are undone.* • LP› **Dressing and undressing**

fly [before n] • *These jeans fasten with fly* **buttons**. • See also **button-fly** at BUTTON.

flies THEATRE /flaɪz/ *pl n* the space above the stage in a theatre, used for lights and for storing and moving SCENERY

flight FLYING /flaɪt/ *n* (an act or the process of) flying • *The young birds hovered on the edge of the nest, preparing themselves for flight.* [U] • *Certain birds spend most of the day* **in** *flight.* [U] • *Modern missiles are so accurate because their flight* (= the direction in which they fly) *is controlled by computer.* [U] • *Some people thought that too much money was spent on space flight.* [U] • A flight of birds, aircraft, etc. is a group flying together: *a flight of geese/swans* [C] • *I shall never forget my first flight* (= the first time I flew in an aircraft). [C] • *How was your flight* (= What was your aircraft journey like)? [C] • *All flights* (= journeys by aircraft) *to New York today are delayed because of bad weather.* [C] • *We'll be arriving back on Tuesday on flight number 147* (= the stated aircraft journey). [C] • *(fig.) Young people don't appreciate the flight* **of** *time* (= how quickly time goes past). [U] • *His latest* **flight of fancy** (= unusual and probably impossible idea) *is for us to walk across America.* • *The stage design for this production of 'The Magic Flute' is a real* **flight of fancy** (= shows a lot of imagination). • *(Br) We need to recruit more young people* **in the top flight** (= of the highest quality). • *She asked the* **flight attendant** (= a person who serves passengers on an aircraft) *to bring her some more coffee.* • A **flight deck** is the part of an aircraft where the PILOT sits and where the controls are. • A **flight deck** is also a flat open surface on a ship from which aircraft take off. • A **flight lieutenant** is an officer in the British air force. • *When they bought their house, they didn't realise that it was* **in/under the flight path** (= the route followed by aircraft) *to the airport.* • *The people investigating the plane crash have not yet recovered the aircraft's* **flight recorder** (= a device which records information about an aircraft while it is flying). • **Flight sergeant** is the next rank above SERGEANT in the British air force. • *For your* **in-flight entertainment** (= entertainment provided while travelling on an aircraft) *today, we are showing the film 'Ghost'.* • *"Goodnight, sweet prince, and flights of angels sing thee to thy rest!"* (Shakespeare, Hamlet 5.2) • *"All at once my heart took flight"* (from the song *I could have danced all night* written by Alan Jay Lerner, 1956)

flight·less /ˈflaɪt·ləs/ *adj* [not gradable] • *The ostrich is a flightless bird* (= one which cannot fly).

flight ESCAPE /flaɪt/ *n* [U] (an act or example of) escape, running away or avoiding something • *They lost all their possessions during their flight* **from** *the invading army.* • *The robbers were* **in full** *flight* (= escaping) *when they were caught.* • *(fig.) The government needs to take steps to stop the flight* **of** *investment/capital* (= money being sent) *out of the country.* • *(dated) During the civil war, rebel villagers were* **put to flight** (= forced to run away) *by government troops.* • *The burglars* **took flight** (= ran away) *when the alarm sounded.*

flight STAIRS /flaɪt/ *n* [C] a set of steps or stairs, usually between two floors of a building • *We live up three flights of stairs.*

flight·y /£ˈflaɪ·ti, $-t̬i/ *adj* **-ier, -iest** *disapproving* (esp. of a woman) not responsible or serious; likely to change activities, jobs, lovers, etc. frequently • *These flighty young women never stick at a job for more than a few weeks at a time.*

flight·i·ly /£ˈflaɪ·tɪ·li, $-t̬ɪ-/ *adv disapproving*

flight·i·ness /£ˈflaɪ·tɪ·nəs, $-t̬ɪ-/ *n* [U] *disapproving*

flim flam /ˈflɪm·flæm/ *n* [U] *infml* talk which deceives others, esp. in order to benefit the speaker • *The union complained that when they asked the management about their future plans, all they got was flim flam.*

flim·sy /ˈflɪm·zi/ *adj* **-ier, -iest** very thin; easily broken or destroyed • *You won't be warm enough in that flimsy dress.* • *The storm flattened the flimsy wooden huts that the villagers lived in.* • *When I asked him why he hadn't come to the meeting, he gave the flimsy* (= weak and not believable) **excuse** *that he'd forgotten what time it was.*

flim·si·ly /ˈflɪm·zɪ·li/ *adv*

flim·si·ness /ˈflɪm·zɪ·nəs/ *n* [U]

flinch /flɪntʃ/ *v* [I] to make a sudden small movement because of pain or fear • *He flinched as the doctor touched his wounded leg.* • *She listened to the teacher's criticisms without flinching.* • *(fig.) We must not flinch* **from** *doing our duty* (= avoid it because it is unpleasant). • *(fig.) These are people who wouldn't flinch* **from** *harming* (= are willing to harm) *innocent children.*

fling *obj* THROW /flɪŋ/ *v* [T always + adv/prep] *past* **flung** /flʌŋ/ to throw suddenly using force, or to throw violently and without care • *He was so cross when he couldn't make the radio work that he flung it across the room.* • *"And you can take your ring back too!" she cried, flinging it down on the table.* • *She tried to run away from him, but he grabbed hold of her and flung her to the ground.* • *In 'Anna Karenina', Anna kills herself by flinging* **herself** *in front of a train.* • *(fig.) He's always flinging insults at people* (= attacking them with rude remarks). • *(infml) It's embarrassing the way she* **flings herself at** *him* (= clearly shows sexual interest in him).

fling *obj* ACT /flɪŋ/ *v* [T always + adv/prep] *past* **flung** /flʌŋ/ to do (something) quickly and energetically, esp. without care • *The players flung their arms round each other when they scored the winning goal.* • *They flung the door open wide* (= opened the door quickly) *to greet their friends.* • *(infml) Let me just fling* (= quickly put) *a few things into my bag, and I'll be right with you.* • *(infml) Could you fling the paper over here* (= give me the paper)? • *(infml) I don't think the police should have flung* (= quickly put) *the protesters into prison like that.* • *Tom has really flung* **himself into** *his work* (= worked hard and enthusiastically) *this year.* • *We were so hot we flung* **off** *our* **clothes** (= took our clothes off quickly and without care) *and dived into the swimming pool.* [M] • *I overslept his morning, so I had to fling* **on** *some* **clothes** (= get dressed quickly and without care) *and rush off to work without having any breakfast.* [M] • *(infml) I think it's about time we flung* **out** (= got rid of) *these old magazines.* [M] • *They* **flung up** *their* **hands** *in horror* (= were very shocked) *when they discovered how much the meal cost.*

fling *(obj)* ANGRILY /flɪŋ/ *v* [always + adv/prep] *past* **flung** /flʌŋ/ to move or say angrily • *She flung* **out** *of the room.* [I] • *He flung* **off** *in a temper.* [I] • *"I don't care what you think", she flung* **(back) at** *him.* [+ clause] • *They were flinging* **(out)** *bitter accusations* **at** *each other.* [T/M]

fling PERIOD /flɪŋ/ *n* [C usually sing] *infml* a short period of enjoyment • *The students are* **having a final/last** *fling before they leave university and start work.* • *Did you know that she's been* **having a fling** (= having a short, not serious sexual relationship) **with** *her next-door neighbour?*

flint /flɪnt/ *n* (a piece of) very hard grey or black glassy stone • *Houses in this part of the country are built of flint.* [U] • *People in early times used flint tools.* • *Archaeologists have discovered several flints* (= pieces of flint used as tools) *on the site.* [C] • A flint is also a piece of stone or metal used in a MUSKET (= gun) to make it fire or in a cigarette LIGHTER to produce a flame. [C] • *The morning air was* **sharp as** *flint against their faces.* [U] • *He has a heart* **like** *flint*/**as hard as** *flint* (= He is very unkind). [U]

flint·y /£ˈflɪn·ti, $-t̬i/ *adj* **-ier, -iest** • *The church is built of a flinty material* (= a material like flint). • *(fig.) The head teacher has a rather flinty* (= severe) *manner.*

flip *(obj)* TURN QUICKLY /flɪp/ *v* **-pp-** to (cause to) turn over quickly one or more times, often with a short quick movement • *All the reporters flipped their notebooks open as the prime minister began his speech.* [T + obj + adj] • *When one side is done, flip the pancake* **over** *to cook the other side.* [M] • *She flipped* **over** *the pages of a magazine* (= turned them over quickly), *not really concentrating on them.* [M] • *I lost my place in my book when the pages flipped* **over** *in the wind.* [I always + adv/prep] • *I'll be with you in a minute, I just need to flip* **through** *these papers* (= read them quickly) *first.* [I always + adv/prep] • *You turn the television on by* *flipping* (= operating) *the* **switch** *at the side.* [T] • *The captains flipped a* **coin** *(into the air)* (= made it turn over in the air to see which side it landed on) *to decide which side would bat first.* [T] • *(slang) My father really flipped/* **flipped** *his* **lid** (= became very angry) *when I told him I'd been in trouble with the police.* • *(infml) 'The Fisher King' is a film about a man who flips/***flips** *his* **lid** (= becomes mentally ill) *after his wife is killed.* • A **flip chart** is a board standing on legs with large pieces of paper fixed to the top which can be turned over: *He usually writes the agenda for the meeting on the flip chart.*

flip /flɪp/ *n* [C] • *The children settled their argument about whose turn it was by the flip* **of a coin** (= they made it turn several times in the air to see which side it landed on). • The **flip side** (also **B side**) of a record is one that does not have the main song on it: *(fig.) We're now starting to see the* **flip side** (= the less good side) *of the government's economic policy.*

flip NOT SERIOUS /flɪp/ *adj* **flipper**, **flippest** *infml for* FLIPPANT

flip EXPRESSION /flɪp/ *exclamation Br slang* used to express slight annoyance • *Oh, flip, I've missed the bus.*

flip–flop /£ˈflɪp·flɒp, $-flɑːp/, *Aus and Am also* **thong** *n* [C usually pl] a type of open shoe, often made of rubber, with a V-shaped strap which goes between the big toe and the toe next to it and is fixed to the SOLE (= the flat bottom piece) • *a pair of flip-flops* • PIC> **Shoes**

flip·pant /ˈflɪp·ᵊnt/, *infml* **flip** *adj* not serious about a serious subject, in an attempt to be amusing or to appear clever • *It's easy to be flippant, but we have a serious problem to deal with.* • *I'm tired of your flippant remarks/ comments/attitude – please take the matter more seriously.*

flip·pant·ly /ˈflɪp·ᵊnt·li/ *adv*

flip·pan·cy /ˈflɪp·ᵊnt·si/ *n* [U] • *Your flippancy* (= not being serious about a serious subject) *isn't appreciated here.*

flip·per PART OF CREATURE /£ˈflɪp·əʳ, $-ɚ/ *n* [C] the arm-like part of particular sea creatures, such as SEALS and PENGUINS, used for swimming • (F) (I)

flip·per SHOE /£ˈflɪp·əʳ, $-ɚ/, *Am also* **fin** *n* [C] a type of large flat rubber shoe, used for swimming, esp. under water • PIC> **Water sports** (F) (I)

flip·ping /ˈflɪp·ɪŋ/ *adj, adv esp. Br slang* used to emphasize what is being said, or to express annoyance • *What a flipping awful film!* • *It's a flipping nuisance!* • *You'll do as you're flipping well told!*

flirt /£flɜːt, $flɜːrt/ *v* [I] to behave as if sexually attracted to someone, although not seriously • *She left him because he was always flirting* (**with** *other women*). • *(fig.) I'm flirting* **with** (= considering, although not seriously) *the* **idea** *of taking a year off and travelling round the world.* • *(fig.) He loves to flirt* **with danger** (= to take risks). • (NL)

flirt /£flɜːt, $flɜːrt/ *n* [C] • *He's a dreadful flirt* (= he behaves as if he is sexually attracted to a lot of people).

flir·ta·tion /£flɜːˈteɪ·ʃᵊn, $flɜːr-/ *n* • *Did you know that Polly has been* **having a** *flirtation* (= a short, not serious sexual relationship) **with** *her boss?* [C] • *A lot of flirtation goes on in this office.* [U] • *(fig.) We had a brief flirtation* **with** *the* **idea** *of starting our own business* (= we considered it for a short while), *but decided against it.*

flir·ta·tious /£flɜːˈteɪ·ʃəs, $flɜːr-/ *adj* • *They maintain an easy, joking, flirtatious relationship with one another* (= they pretend to behave as if they are sexually attracted to each other).

flir·ta·tious·ly /£flɜːˈteɪ·ʃə·sli, $flɜːr-/ *adv*

flir·ta·tious·ness /£flɜːˈteɪ·ʃə·snəs, $flɜːr-/ *n* [U]

flit /flɪt/ *v* [I always + adv/prep] **-tt-** to fly or move quickly and lightly • *As it began to grow dark, we could see bats flitting* **around/about** *in the garden.* • *Sara finds it very difficult to settle – she's always flitting* **from** *one thing* **to** *another* (= changing her activities). • *(fig.) The* **thought** *flitted* **across/into/through** *my mind* (= I had the sudden thought) *that I'd met her somewhere before.*

flit /flɪt/ *n* [C] • *(Br) When he discovered the police were after him, he* **did a (moonlight)** *flit* (= he secretly left the place where he had been living).

float NOT SINK /£fləʊt, $floʊt/ *v* [I] to stay on the surface of a liquid • *An empty bottle will float* (**on** *water*) (= stay on the surface of water, without sinking). • *People can float very easily* (= lie at the surface without sinking) **in/on** *the Dead Sea because it is so salty.* • *Have you heard the rumours* **floating around/about** (= being frequently talked about) *that the shop is going to close.* • *(fig. infml) I can't find my purse, but it must be* **floating around/about** *somewhere* (= it must be somewhere, but I don't know exactly where). • *When he got his results he was* **floating on air** (= very happy). • (J)

float /£fləʊt, $floʊt/ *n* [C] • A float is a piece of wood or other light material that stays on the surface of water: *Fishing nets are often held in position by floats.* ○ *Timmy is learning to swim holding on to a float.* • A float is also a drink with ice cream on the top of it: *I'll have a cola float, please.*

float·a·tion /£fləʊˈteɪ·ʃᵊn, $floʊ-/ *n* • See FLOTATION.

float *(obj)* MOVE /£fləʊt, $floʊt/ *v* to (cause to) move easily through, or along the surface of, a liquid, or to (cause to) move easily through air • *At high tide there was enough water to float the boats (off the rocks).* [T] • *The killer had tied stones to the body before throwing it into the river to stop it from floating* **to the surface** (= moving up through the water). [I always + adv/prep] • *We spent a lazy afternoon floating* **down/along** *the river.* [I always + adv/prep] • *He tossed the bottle over the side of the boat, and watched it float* **out to** *sea.* [I always + adv/prep] • *The children enjoy floating their boats* **on** *the pond in the park.* [T] • *They transported the logs by floating them down the river.* [T] • *Fluffy white clouds were floating across the sky.* [I always + adv/prep] • *The leaves floated down from the tree.* [I always + adv/prep] • *The sound of piano-playing floated* (= could be heard, but not loudly) *from the open window.* [I always + adv/prep] • *(fig.) All eyes were on Emma as she floated* (= came gracefully) **into** *the room.* [I always + adv/prep] • *(fig.) The idea floated* **into/through/across** *my mind* (= I suddenly thought) *that it would be nice to have a weekend in the country.* [I always + adv/prep] • To float is also to move or act without purpose: *Beth's parents are worried because she just seems to float* **from** *place* **to** *place, and is unable to settle.* [I always + adv/prep] ○ *Since he lost his job, Mike has just floated* **around/about** *doing nothing.* [I always + adv/prep] • (J)

float·ing /£ˈfləʊ·tɪŋ, $ˈfloʊ·t̬ɪŋ/ *adj* [before n; not gradable] • *The city has a large floating* **population** (= a lot of people who do not live in a fixed place). • *(specialized)* A part of the body that is floating is out of its usual position, or not connected to another part of the body: *a floating rib* • *The bank has offered us a loan with a floating* **interest rate** (= the charge made for borrowing the money is not fixed). • *(Br)* A **floating voter** is one who does not always vote for the same political party.

float CHANGE VALUE /£fləʊt, $floʊt/ *v* to allow (the value of a country's money) to vary according to the value of other countries' money • *The government has decided to float the pound.* [T] • *The mark has been left to float.* [I] • (J)

float *obj* START A BUSINESS /£fləʊt, $floʊt/ *v* [T] to start (a new business or company) by selling shares in it • *Naturally Yours Cosmetics is being floated* **on** *the Stock Exchange next week.* • (J)

float·a·tion /£fləʊˈteɪ·ʃᵊn, $floʊ-/ *n* • See FLOTATION.

float *obj* SUGGEST /£fləʊt, $floʊt/ *v* [T] to suggest (a plan or an idea) for consideration • *Ian has floated the* **idea** *that we should think about expanding into Europe next year.* • (J)

float MONEY /£fləʊt, $floʊt/ *n* [C] *Br and Aus* a small sum of money, available before any money is received for goods sold, which is used for returning amounts to customers who give more than a particular item costs • *We'll need to have a float for the beginning of the jumble sale.* • (J)

float VEHICLE /£fləʊt, $floʊt/ *n* a large vehicle with a flat surface which is decorated and used in special celebrations • *The football club have entered a float decorated like a pirate ship in the carnival parade.* • (J)

flock GROUP /£flɒk, $flɑːk/ *n* [C + sing/pl v] a group of sheep, goats or birds, or a group of people • *The farmer is bringing his flock* (= sheep/goats) *down from the hills for the winter.* • *Police are warning motorists that a flock* **of** *sheep has/have escaped onto the road.* • *Flocks* **of** *geese often fly in a V-shaped formation.* • *A noisy flock* **of** *tourists/sightseers came into the building.* • *The vicar invited all the members of his flock* (= all the people who go to his church) *to attend the church fête on Saturday.*

flock /£flɒk, $flɑːk/ *v* • To flock is to move or gather together in large numbers: *The swallows are flocking on the telephone wires.* [I always + adv/prep] ○ *Hundreds of people are flocking* **to** *the football match.* [I] • *Crowds of people flocked* **to** *see the Picasso exhibition.* [+ to infinitive]

flock MATERIAL /£flɒk, $flɑːk/ *n* soft material used for filling objects such as CUSHIONS, or soft material that forms a raised pattern on WALLPAPER or curtains

floe /£fləʊ, $floʊ/ *n* [C] a large area of ice floating in the sea • *Ships have been warned to watch out for* **(ice)** *floes.*

flog *obj* PUNISH /£flɒg, $flɑːg/ *v* [T] **-gg-** to beat very hard with a whip or a stick, as a punishment • *Soldiers used to be flogged for disobedience.* • *(infml) I keep trying to get Bob to come dancing with us, but it's just* **flogging a dead horse** (= wasted effort) *because he says he hates dancing.* • *(infml) There's no point in* **flogging yourself to death/into the ground** *like that* (= working so hard and making yourself so tired). • *(infml) That idea has been absolutely* **flogged to death** (= has been repeated so often that it is no longer interesting).

flog·ging /£'flɒg·ɪŋ, $'flɑː·gɪŋ/ *n* • *The many floggings* (= severe beatings with a whip) *that the captain gave his men led to the ship's mutiny.* [C] • *The punishment for breaking the rules is flogging.* [U]

flog *obj* SELL /£flɒg, $flɑːg/ *v* [T] **-gg-** *infml* to sell, esp. quickly or cheaply • *He tried to flog his old car, but no one would buy it.* • *We're flogging our neighbours our lawnmower/flogging our lawnmower* **to** *our neighbours.* [+ two objects]

flood *(obj)* COVER WITH WATER /flʌd/ *v* to (cause to) fill or become covered with water, esp. in a way that causes problems • *There are plans to flood the valley to form a reservoir.* [T] • *Our washing machine broke down yesterday and flooded the kitchen.* [T] • *The whole town flooded when the river burst its banks.* [I] • *Locks on a river flood* **with** *water when the lock gates are opened.* [I] • *The river has flooded* (= the water in it has flowed over its banks) *several times this winter.* [I] • *Several families living on the sea front were flooded* **out** (= forced to leave their houses because they became covered with water) *during the storm.* [T]

flood /flʌd/ *n* • A flood is a large amount of water covering an area that is usually dry: *After the flood it took weeks for the water level to subside again.* [C] ○ *We had a flood in the cellar last week.* [C] • *When the snow melts, this little stream becomes a flood* (= is very full of water and flows very fast). [C] • *The river is* **in** *flood* (= water has flowed over its banks) *again.* [U] • A **flood plain** is an area of flat land beside a river that is frequently flooded when the river becomes too full. • A **flood tide** is the movement of the sea inwards to the coast: *(fig.) In the last year, a* **flood tide** (= a lot) **of** *recycled products has been released into the shops.* Compare **ebb tide** at EBB. • In the Bible, **the Flood** was a flood sent by God as a punishment. • *(humorous)* If something is from **before the Flood** it is very old.

flood·ed /'flʌd·ɪd/ *adj* • *For miles you could see nothing but flooded fields* (= fields covered with water).

flood·ing /'flʌd·ɪŋ/ *n* [U] • *Some roads have been closed because of flooding* (= they are covered with water).

floods /flʌdz/ *pl n* • *The floods* (= a large amount of water that covers an area that is usually dry) *have ruined the farmers' crops.*

flood *(obj)* ARRIVE OR FILL /flʌd/ *v* to come to or from (somewhere) in, or fill (somewhere or someone) with, large numbers or a large amount of something • *Donations are flooding* **into** *the appeal office.* [I always + adv/prep] • *Refugees have been flooding* **from** *the war-torn areas of the country.* [I always + adv/prep] • *We have been flooded* **(out) with** (= have received large numbers of) *responses to our advertisement.* [T] • *She drew back the curtains and the sunlight came flooding* **in** (= a large amount of light from the sun filled the room). [I always + adv/prep] • *Japanese cars have flooded* **(onto/into)** *the* **market** (= a lot of them are on sale). [T; I + prep] • *He was flooded* **with** (= suddenly felt a lot of) *joy when his first child was born.* [T] • *Anger flooded* **(into/over)** *him when he realised he had been cheated.* [T; I + prep] • *For Proust, the taste of a madeleine brought childhood memories flooding* **back** (= suddenly brought him a lot of memories of when he was a child). [I always + adv/prep] • *The* **colour** *flooded* **(into)** *her cheeks* (= Her face went red with embarrassment) *when she realised her mistake.* [T; I + prep] • *It finally all came flooding* **out** (= she talked a lot about) *how unhappy she was.* [I always + adv/prep] • *If you keep turning the ignition like that, you'll flood the* **engine** (= fill it with so much fuel that it will not start). [T]

flood /flʌd/ *n* [C] • *A flood* **of** *cheap imports has come into the shops.* • *I couldn't believe it when he let out such a flood* (= a lot) **of** *abuse.* • *She left the room in a flood* **of tears** (= crying).

flood·ed /'flʌd·ɪd/ *adj* • *The car* **market** *became flooded* **with** *imports* (= a lot of foreign cars were for sale).

floods /flʌdz/ *pl n* • *The BBC has received floods* (= a lot) **of** *complaints about its decision to cancel the programme.* • *She was* **in floods of tears** (= cried a lot) *when she heard the news.*

flood·gate /'flʌd·geɪt/ *n* [C] a gate which can be opened or closed to control a flow of water

flood·light /'flʌd·laɪt/ *n, v past* **floodlit** /'flʌd·lɪt/ (to light with) a large powerful electric light used for lighting outside areas, such as sports grounds or buildings, in the dark • *This evening's match will be played* **under** *floodlights.* [C] • *The square is lit by floodlight.* [U] • *They are going to floodlight the clock tower.* [T] • *Notre Dame cathedral is going to be floodlit at night.* [T]

flood·lit /'flʌd·lɪt/ *adj* [not gradable] • *a floodlit building/stadium*

floor SURFACE /£flɔːʳ, $flɔːr/ *n* [C] the flat surface of a room on which you walk • **The** *floor was partly covered with a dirty old rug.* • *The bathroom floor needs cleaning.* • *The children sat playing* **on** *the floor.* • *We're going to choose some floor tiles for the kitchen tomorrow.* • *In the 1950s, wall-to-wall carpeting became the floor* **covering** *of choice in the suburbs.* • *There's barely enough floor* **space** *to fit a bed in this room.* • *House prices have* **gone through the floor** (= have fallen to very low levels) *this year.* • *Please could you get me a* **floor cloth** (= a piece of cloth for cleaning the floor) *so I can wipe up the coffee I've spilled.* • **Floor lamp** is *Am for* **standard lamp**. • PIC **Lights** (D)(N)

floor *obj* /£flɔːʳ, $flɔːr/ *v* [T] • *We're going to floor the dining room* **with/in** (= make the floor of it from) *pine.*

floored /£flɔːd, $flɔːrd/ *adj* [not gradable] • *Our kitchen is floored* **with** (= has a floor made of) *tiles.*

floor·ing /£'flɔː·rɪŋ, $'flɔːr·ɪŋ/ *n* [U] • *The cellar has stone flooring* (= has a floor made of stone).

floor OPEN SPACE /£flɔːʳ, $flɔːr/ *n* [C usually sing] a public space for activities such as dancing and having formal discussions • *Long after all the others had left the* **(dance)** *floor* (= the area on which people dance), *Donna and Simon were still dancing.* • *The minister's involvement in the arms deal will be discussed* **on the** *floor* **of the** *House of Commons* (= in Parliament) *tomorrow.* • *He spent several years working on the* **factory** *floor* (= in the factory) *before becoming a manager.* • *Business has been brisk on the* **trading** *floor* (= the place where business activity takes place). • *The chairman said that he would now take questions* **from the** *floor* (= from the ordinary people attending the meeting). • *Silence, please, the Prime Minister* **has the** *floor* (= has the right to speak). • *The Prince and Princess were the first to* **take the floor** (= stand up and start to dance). • *The Chancellor of the Exchequer will* **take the floor** (= start speaking) *for his Budget speech at 3.00 p.m.* • *After dinner, we watched the* **floor show** (= the series of performances by singers, dancers, etc. in a restaurant).

floor LEVEL OF BUILDING /£flɔːʳ, $flɔːr/ *n* [C] a level of a building; a STOREY • *Take the elevator to the 51st floor.* • *We live* **on** *the third floor.* • *The ground floor apartment* (= the apartment at road level) *is for sale.* • *The second floor* (= the people who live/work on the second floor) *aren't very friendly.* • In British English the first floor of a building is the level above ground level. In American English the first floor of a building is at ground level. • (D)(N)

floor BOTTOM /£flɔːʳ, $flɔːr/ *n* [U] **the floor** the bottom surface of the sea, a forest, a cave, a valley, etc. • *The wrecked ship has finally been lifted from the floor* **of** *the ocean/the ocean floor.* • *Animal bones were found on the floor* **of** *the cave.* • (D)(N)

floor *obj* CAUSE TO FALL /£flɔːʳ, $flɔːr/ *v* [T] to hit and cause to fall • *It only took a few punches for Taylor to floor his opponent.* • *(fig.) The final question in the exam really floored* (= defeated) *me.* • *(fig.) She was completely floored* (= surprised) *when she heard that he was leaving the country.* • (D)(N)

floor·board /£'flɔː·bɔːd, $'flɔːr·bɔːrd/ *n* [C] one of the long straight pieces of wood used to make a floor • *polished/bare floorboards* • *The stolen goods were found hidden* **under** *the floorboards.* • PIC **Room**

floor·ing /£'flɔː·rɪŋ, $'flɔː-/ *n* [U] the material used to make a floor • *wooden/marble/stone flooring*

floo·zie, floo·sie, floo·zy /'fluː·zi/ *n* [C] *infml disapproving or humorous* an esp. young woman who intentionally wears the type of clothes and make-up that attract sexual attention in a way that is too obvious • *Anthony brought some floozie along to the party.*

flop FALL /£flɒp, $flɑːp/ *v* [I always + adv/prep] **-pp-** to fall or drop heavily • *A new-born baby's head flops* **backwards** *if you don't support it.* • *I just want to flop* **into** *bed and go to sleep!* • *My hair keeps flopping* **over/into** *my eyes – I think I'll tie it back.* • *(infml) When she gets home from school, she's so tired all she can do is flop* **(down) in front of** *the television!*

flop /£flɒp, $flɑːp/ *n* [U] • *He fell* **with a** *flop* (= he dropped heavily) *on the bed.*

flop FAILURE /£flɒp, $flɑːp/ *n* [C usually sing] *infml* a failure • *The concert/play/performance/book was a* **complete/total** *flop.* • *His last musical received a certain amount of critical acclaim but it was a commercial flop.*

flop /£flɒp, $flɑːp/ *v* [I] **-pp-** • *Her first book flopped, but her second became a bestseller.*

flop·house /£ˈflɒp·haʊs, $ˈflɑːp-/ *n* [C] *pl* **flophouses** /£ˈflɒp,haʊ·zɪz, $ˈflɑːp-/ *Am for* DOSSHOUSE

flop·py /£ˈflɒp·i, $ˈflɑː·pi/ *adj* **-ier, -iest** soft and easily bent; not able to maintain a firm shape or position • *She was wearing a big floppy* **hat.** • *He's got a wonderful dog with big floppy ears.* • *He's got floppy blond hair that's always falling in his eyes.* • *(Br infml)* If a person **feels** floppy, they feel weak and tired: *This hot weather makes you feel floppy.* • A **floppy disk** is a round piece of bendable plastic, protected by a plastic cover, used to store computer information. Compare **hard disk** at HARD SOLID.

flop·pi·ness /£ˈflɒp·ɪ·nəs, $ˈflɑː·pɪ-/ *n* [U]

flo·ra /£ˈflɔː·rə, $ˈflɔːr·ə/ *n* [U] *specialized* all the plants of a particular place or from a particular time in history • *the flora of the Balearic Islands* • *Stone Age flora* • The **flora and fauna** of a place are its plants and animals.

flo·ral /£ˈflɔː·rəl, $ˈflɔːr·əl/ *adj* made of flowers, or decorated with a flowery pattern • *floral curtains/print/wallpaper* • *a floral display/tribute*

flo·ret /£ˈflɒr·ɪt, £-et, $ˈflɔːr-/ *n* [C] any of the smaller flowers which together form a larger flower • *Blanche the* **broccoli/cauliflower** *florets in boiling water, removing them as soon as the water returns to a boil.* • PIC **Vegetables**

flo·rid DECORATED /£ˈflɒr·ɪd, $ˈflɔːr-/ *adj* with too much decoration or detail • *a florid architectural style* • *florid prose/rhetoric*

flo·rid·ly /£ˈflɒr·ɪd·li, $ˈflɔːr-/ *adv*

flo·rid RED /£ˈflɒr·ɪd, $ˈflɔːr-/ *adj fml* (of a person's face) too red, esp. in a way that is unhealthy • *He had a florid* **complexion.** • *Mr Higgins was the florid-***faced** *gentlemen in the green jacket.*

flo·rist /£ˈflɒr·ɪst, $ˈflɔːr-/ *n* [C] a person who works in a shop which sells cut flowers and plants for inside the house

flo·rist's /£ˈflɒr·ɪsts, $ˈflɔːr-/ *n* [C] • A florist's is a shop which sells cut flowers and plants for inside the house: *I bought a dozen red roses from the local florist's.*

floss THREAD /£flɒs, $flɑːs/ *n* [U] a mass of soft silky threads esp. produced by particular insects and plants • See also CANDYFLOSS.

floss *obj* CLEAN TEETH /£flɒs, $flɑːs/ *v* [T] to clean between (your teeth) using **dental floss** (= thin thread made especially for this purpose) • *It's important to floss your teeth at least twice a week.*

flo·ta·tion BUSINESS /£fləʊˈteɪ·ʃən, $floʊ-/, **float·a·tion** *n* the act of starting up or financing a new company by selling shares in it to the public • *Flotation on the stock exchange was one way of raising money.* [U] • *The Glasgow-based electrical retail chain is to launch a* **stock-market** *flotation this summer to raise up to £30m.* [C] • See also FLOAT START A BUSINESS.

flo·ta·tion FLOAT, **float·a·tion** /£fləʊˈteɪ·ʃən, $floʊ-/ *n* [U] the action of floating • A flotation chamber/compartment/tank helps something to float because it is filled with gas or air.

flo·til·la /fləˈtɪl·ə/ *n* [C] a large group of boats or small ships, esp. military ships • *A flotilla* **of** *eight Italian warships is also to be sent there.* • See also FLEET SHIPS.

flot·sam /£ˈflɒt·səm, $ˈflɑːt-/ *n* [U] **flotsam and jetsam** pieces of broken wood and other waste materials found on the beach or floating on the sea • *We wandered along the shore, stepping over the flotsam and jetsam that had washed up in the night.* • Flotsam (and jetsam) also refers to anything or anyone that is unwanted or worthless: *The homeless sleep in doorways and stations – we step over their bodies like so much human flotsam.*

flounce WALK /flaʊnts/ *v* [I always + adv/prep] to walk quickly with large noticeable movements, esp. to attract attention or show that you are angry • *"Right, don't expect any help from me in future!" he said and flounced* **out of** *the room.* • *The children were flouncing* **about** *the room pretending they were in a fashion show.*

flounce DECORATION /flaʊnts/ *n* [C] a decoration added to something, esp. a dress or skirt, usually made from a strip of cloth sewn along one side to give a wavy appearance • *I don't want a wedding dress with* **frills and** *flounces.*

floun·cy (**-ier, -iest**) /ˈflaʊnt·si/, **flounced** /flaʊntst/ *adj* • *She was wearing a dreadful pink flouncy skirt.*

flound·er /£ˈflaʊn·dəʳ, $-dɚ/ *v* [I] to experience great difficulties or be completely unable to decide what to do or say next • *He lost the next page of his speech and floundered for a few seconds.* • *Yet even as his business was flourishing, his marriage to Lynne was floundering.* • *In 1986 Richardson resigned as chairman, leaving the company floundering.* • *As Bundy claimed more and more victims the police floundered* **(around)** *in their search for clues.* • *He floundered* **(around)** *in the deep water, trying desperately to reach the bank.*

flour /£flaʊəʳ, $flaʊɚ/ *n* [U] powder made from grain, esp. wheat, used for making bread, cakes, pasta, pastry, etc. • *plain/self-raising flour* • *wheat/rye flour* • *wholemeal/white flour* • *a packet of flour* • See also CORNFLOUR.

flour *obj* /£flaʊəʳ, $flaʊɚ/ *v* [T] • *Grease and flour* (= put a thin layer of flour on) *the tins thoroughly.* • *Roll the pastry out on a well-floured board.*

flour·y /£ˈflaʊə·ri, $ˈflaʊɚ·i/ *adj* **-ier, -iest** • *Can you answer the phone? My hands are all floury* (= covered with flour). • Potatoes may be described as floury if they are dry and break into small pieces when they are cooked.

flour·ish SUCCEED /£ˈflʌr·ɪʃ, $ˈflɜːr-/ *v* [I] to grow or develop successfully • *Nothing seems to flourish in my garden – perhaps the soil's too poor.* • *Watercolour painting began to flourish in Britain around 1750.* • *Rock'n'roll flourished in the 1950s.* • *Four years ago, the country's tourist* **industry** *was flourishing.*

flour·ish·ing /£ˈflʌr·ɪ·ʃɪŋ, $ˈflɜːr-/ *adj* • *To the north of the city lie the charred remains of a once flourishing village.* • *There's a flourishing* **trade** *in second-hand video machines.* • *The Royal Academy aims to demonstrate with its latest show that Britain has a flourishing* **tradition** *of modern art.*

flour·ish *obj* WAVE /£ˈflʌr·ɪʃ, $ˈflɜːr-/ *v* [T] to move (something) in your hand in order to make people look at it • *She came in smiling, flourishing her exam results.*

flour·ish /£ˈflʌr·ɪʃ, $ˈflɜːr-/ *n* [C] • If you do something **with a** flourish, you do it with one big, noticeable movement: *He took off his hat with a flourish.*

flout *obj* /flaʊt/ *v* [T] to disobey intentionally (a rule or law), or to avoid intentionally (behaviour that is usual or expected) • *The research indicates that 4 out of 10 rear passengers flout the law by not wearing their belts.* • *The orchestra decided to flout* **convention/tradition**, *and wear their everyday clothes for the concert.*

flow /£fləʊ, $floʊ/ *v* [I] (esp. of liquids, gases or electricity) to move in one direction, esp. continuously and easily • *Lava from the volcano was flowing* **down** *the hillside.* • *Air flows over an aircraft's wing faster than it flows below it.* • *An electrical current flows* **from** *positive* **to** *negative.* • *Many short rivers flow* **into** *the Pacific ocean.* • *The river flows* **through** *three counties before flowing* **into/to** *the sea just south of here.* • *Your blood flows continuously* **through** *your veins.* • *Which way does the sea's current flow along this coast?* • *With fewer cars on the roads,* **traffic** *is flowing* (= moving forward) *more smoothly than usual.* • Something can be said to flow if it hangs down loosely and often attractively: *Her long red hair flowed down over shoulders.* • *(fig.) After they'd all had a drink or two, the* **conversation** *began to flow* (= people began to find it easy to talk). • *(fig.) By eleven o'clock, the* **beer/drink/wine** *was starting to flow* (= people were being given a lot of it to drink). • *(fig.) My* **thoughts** *flow more easily* (= I can think more easily) *if I work on a word processor.* • *(fig.) Offers of help are flowing* **into** *the disaster area from all over the country.* • *(fig.) Please* **keep** *the money flowing* **in** (= continue to send us money)*!*

flow /£fləʊ, $floʊ/ *n* [C usually sing] • *the flow* **of** *a river* • *the flow* **of** *traffic/goods/supplies* • *(fig.) the flow* **of** *ideas/information* • *A dam is a barrier constructed to control the flow of water.* • *They've threatened to* **cut off** *the flow of oil/water to the country.* • *She acted quickly to* **stem/staunch** *the flow of blood from the boy's injured leg* (= stop it bleeding). • *There's been a* **steady** *flow* (= regular and quite large number) *of visitors to the gardens through the* *summer.* • *(fig.) There's been a flow of funds/money* **away from/into** *the organization* (= it has been losing/receiving money). • *(fig.) In this new film, he is* **going/moving with the flow** (= doing what other people are doing). • *(fig.) With this new book, she is* **going/moving against the flow** (= doing or saying the opposite of what most people are doing or saying).

flow·ing /£'fləʊ·ɪŋ, $'floʊ-/ *adj* • *The wine used to be transported down the* **fast**-*flowing river to Oporto.* • Hair and clothes that are flowing are long: *He is tall with a flowing white* **beard.** ○ *I remember her as a young girl with flowing black hair.* ○ *Everyone on stage was dressed in flowing white* **robes.** • Flowing may also be used, esp. of writing or of movements, to mean smooth and regular: *She dances with beautiful flowing movements.* ○ *I recognized your flowing script.*

flow·chart /£'fləʊ·tʃɑːt, $'floʊ·tʃɑːrt/, **flow di·a·gram** *n* [C] a diagram which shows the stages of a process

flow·er /£'flaʊ·əʳ, $'flaʊ·ɚ/ *n* [C] the part of a plant which is often brightly coloured with a pleasant smell • *wild/cultivated flowers* • *to cut/gather/pick flowers* • *a bunch/bouquet/vase of flowers* • *cut/dried flowers* • *a flower garden/border* • *I always* **send** *my mother flowers on her birthday.* • *Our roses are usually* **in flower** (= there are flowers on the rose bushes) *from April to November, but this year they* **came into flower** (= their flowers first appeared) *late.* • *(fig. literary)* **The flower of** (= the best of) *the nation's youth were killed in the war.* • *(fig. literary) He died* **in the flower of** *(his)* **youth** (= he was very young when he died). • *While she was in Japan Susan did classes in* **flower arranging** (= making beautiful decorations with flowers). • The **flower children** or **flower people** (also **hippies**) were the followers of **flower power**, a young people's movement in the 1960s who believed in peace and love. • *"Say it with flowers"* (advertisement for flower shops, 1917-) • *"Where have all the Flowers Gone?"* (title of a song by Pete Seeger, 1961) • See also FLORAL.

flow·er /£'flaʊ·əʳ, $'flaʊ·ɚ/ *v* [I] • *When does this plant/bush/tree flower* (= When does it have flowers)? • *(fig.) Her talent flowered* (= developed completely) *during her later years.*

flow·ered /£'flaʊ·əd, $'flaʊ·ɚd/, **flow·er·y** (**-ier**, **-iest**) *adj* • *flowered wallpaper/curtains* (= decorated with pictures of flowers) • PIC〉 **Patterns**

flow·er·ing /£'flaʊ·ə·rɪŋ, $'flaʊ·ɚ·ɪŋ/ *adj* [before n; not gradable] • *an autumn-flowering shrub* (= one that has flowers in autumn) • A flowering plant/bush/tree is grown because of the beauty of its flowers: *a flowering cherry*

flow·er·ing /£'flaʊ·ə·rɪŋ, $'flaʊ·ɚ·ɪŋ/ *n* [U] • *(fig. literary) There was a flowering of* (= a lot of activity in) *the arts between the wars.*

flow·er·y /£'flaʊ·ə·ri, $'flaʊ·ɚ·i/ *adj* • *a flowery material/dress* • *flowery curtains/wallpaper* • *(disapproving)* If a speech or writing style is flowery, it uses too many complicated words or phrases in the attempt to sound skilful.

flow·er·bed /£'flaʊ·ə·bed, $'flaʊ·ɚ-/ *n* [C] a part of a garden where flowers are planted • *There's a round flowerbed in the middle of the lawn.* • PIC〉 **Garden**

flow·er·pot /£'flaʊ·ə·pɒt, $'flaʊ·ɚ·pɑːt/ *n* [C] a container usually made of clay or plastic in which a plant is grown • PIC〉 **Containers, Garden**

flown /£fləʊn, $floʊn/ *past participle of* FLY

flu /fluː/, *fml* **in·flu·en·za** *n* [U] an infectious illness which is like a very bad cold, but which causes a fever • *a flu virus* • *(infml) the flu bug* • *to catch/get/have (the) flu* • *They're giving everyone flu* **vaccinations** *at work.* • *There's a new* **strain of** *flu about this year.*

fluc·tu·ate /'flʌk·tju·eɪt/ *v* [I] to change or vary, esp. continuously and between one level or thing and another • *Vegetable prices fluctuate* **according to** *the season.* • *Her wages fluctuate* **between** *£150 and £200 a week.* • *I fluctuate* **between** *feeling really happy and utterly miserable.* • *Her weight fluctuates* **wildly.** • *It is essential for any national health service to be able to respond to fluctuating need.*

fluc·tu·a·tion /ˌflʌk·tju'eɪ·ʃᵊn/ *n* • *fluctuations* **in** *share prices/the exchange rate/temperature* [C] • *A certain amount of fluctuation* **in** *quality is unavoidable.* [U]

flue /fluː/ *n* [C] a pipe which leads from a fire or heater to the outside of a building, taking smoke, gases or hot air away • *It's important to have the flue checked regularly to make sure it's not blocked.* • PIC〉 **Fires and space heaters**

flu·ent /'fluː·ənt/ *adj* (of a person) able to speak a language easily, well and quickly, or (of a language) spoken easily and without many pauses • *She was fluent* **in** *her own language by the age of two, and* **in** *French by the time she was five.* • *He speaks fluent Chinese.* • *He's a fluent Chinese speaker.* • *She's always been a very fluent public speaker.*

flu·ent·ly /'fluː·ənt·li/ *adv* • *I'd like to speak English fluently.* • *She spoke fluently and with great passion about the need to look after the homeless.*

flu·enc·y /'fluː·ənt·si/ *n* [U] • *One of the requirements of the job is fluency* **in** *two or more African languages.* • *He spoke with fluency and directness.*

fluff SOFT MASS /flʌf/ *n* [U] a soft mass of fibres from wool and other materials, esp. when it collects in places where it is not wanted, or the DOWN (= soft new hairs) on a young animal • *He brushed the fluff off his coat.* • *Tess took the biscuit out of her pocket and blew* **a bit of** *fluff off it.* • *I swept up all the dust and fluff from under the sofa.* • *The little chick was covered in yellow fluff.* • *(fig. Am) They're supposed to give the news but mostly they just broadcast fluff* (= unimportant or boring information).

fluff *obj* /flʌf/ *v* • If a bird fluffs **(up/out)** its feathers it puts air between them to keep itself warm. [T/M] • *Make the beds and don't forget to fluff the pillows* **(up/out)** (= shake them so that they fill with air). [T/M]

fluf·fy /'flʌf·i/ *adj* **-ier, -iest** • Fluffy means soft and woolly or furry: *a fluffy mohair jumper* • *a fluffy little kitten* • *fluffy toys* • Fluffy also means light and full of air: *Beat the eggs and sugar together until they are pale and fluffy.*

fluf·fi·ness /'flʌf·ɪ·nəs/ *n* [U]

fluff *obj* FAIL /flʌf/, *Am also* **flub** /flʌb/ *v* [T] *infml* to fail (something) or do it badly • *I fluffed my driving test three times before I finally got it.* • *I tried to tell them that joke that you told me but I fluffed* **it** *because I couldn't remember the punch line.* • If actors fluff their **lines**, they forget them or get them wrong.

flu·id /'fluː·ɪd/ *n, adj* (a substance) which flows and is not solid • *When you have a fever it's best to drink plenty of fluid(s)* (= have a lot to drink). [U/C] • *The doctor drained (off)/removed some fluid* (= unwanted liquid) *from her lung.* [U] • *A loss of* **bodily** *fluids, for example by getting too hot and not drinking enough, can lead to dehydration and death.* [C] • *(specialized)* In chemistry, a fluid is a substance which flows and fills the container it is in, so liquids and gases are both called fluids. [C] • *(fig.) The dancer's movements were beautifully fluid* (= smooth and flowing). • *(fig.)* If situations/ideas/plans are fluid, they are not fixed and are likely to change: *The military situation is still fluid.* • A **fluid ounce** is a measurement of liquid equal to *(Br)* 0·024 or *(Am)* 0·030 of a litre: *There are 20 fluid ounces in a British* PINT *and 16 in an American one.*

flu·id·i·ty /£flu'ɪd·ɪ·ti, $-ə·t̬i/ *n* [U] • *(fig.) Durante dances with such fluidity* (= smooth, flowing movements) *and grace.* • *(fig.) What is remarkable is the fluidity of the political situation* (= it's tendency to change repeatedly and unexpectedly).

fluke /fluːk/ *n* [C usually sing] *infml* something good that has happened that is the result of chance instead of skill or planning • *I didn't even see which way I kicked the ball and it was just a fluke that it went in the net.* • *It was a complete fluke that we just happened to be in the same place at the same time.* • **By** *some amazing fluke the essay that I was required to write in the exam was one that I'd already done at home.*

flu·key, flu·ky /'fluː·ki/ *adj* **flukier, flukiest** *infml* • *a flukey result/outcome* • *a flukey shot*

flume /fluːm/ *n* [C] a narrow channel made for carrying water, esp. to factories that produce electricity

flum·mox *obj* /'flʌm·əks/ *v* [T] *infml* to confuse (someone) so much that they do not know what to do • *I have to say that last question flummoxed me.*

flum·moxed /'flʌm·əkst/ *adj infml* • *She looked completely flummoxed.*

flung /flʌŋ/ *past simple and past participle of* FLING THROW, FLING ANGRILY

flunk *(obj)* /flʌŋk/ *v esp. Am infml* to fail (an exam or course of study) • *I flunked my second year exams and was lucky not to be thrown out of college.* [T] • *He flunked the first* **test** *but fortunately passed the second.* [T] • *(fig. Am humorous) I flunked the parent* **test** – *I forgot my own daughter's birthday!* [T] • *(Am)* If students flunk **out (of** school), they are forced to leave because the standard of their work is not good enough. [I]

flun·key /'flʌŋ·ki/, **flun·ky** *n* [C] a male servant wearing a uniform • *In the old days, when a gentleman left his club, he*

Flowers and plants

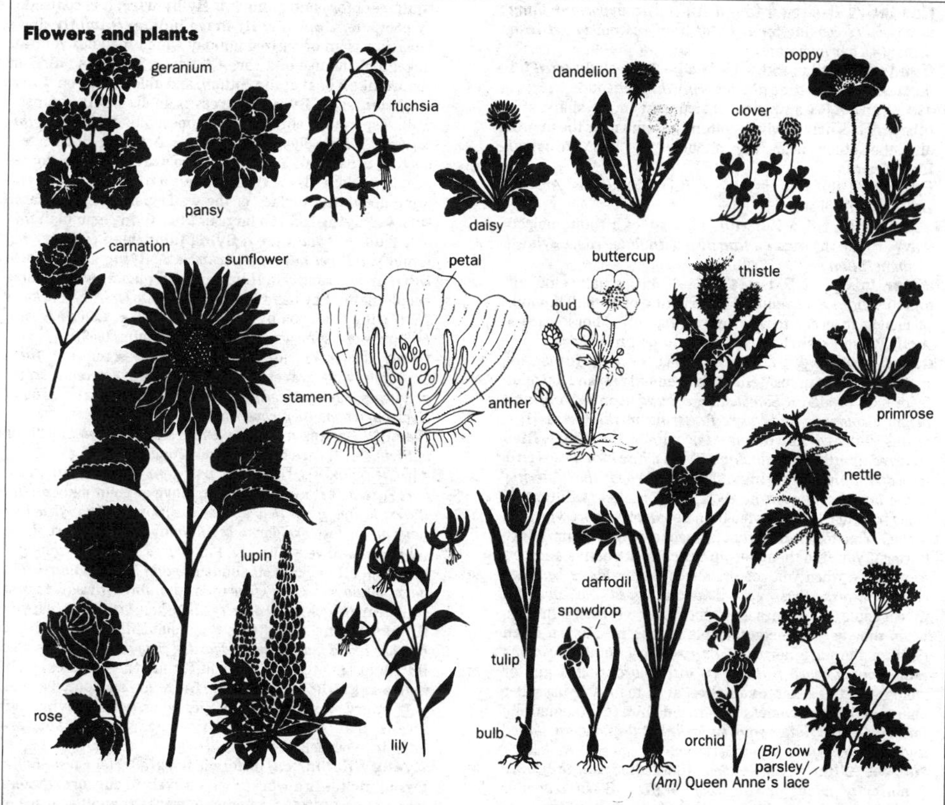

was seen from the door to his carriage by a flunkey carrying his umbrella.

fluor·es·cent /£fluəˈres·ᵊnt, $flʊ-/ *adj* (of a substance) giving off a very bright light when electricity or other waves go through it • *fluorescent lighting* • *a fluorescent tube* • *fluorescent paint* • *Some cyclists wear a fluorescent* **strip** *round their body, or fluorescent* **armbands**, *so that they can be seen at night.*

fluor·es·cence /£fluəˈres·ᵊnts, $flʊ-/ *n* [U]

fluor·ide /£ˈfluə·raɪd, $ˈflʊ-/ *n* [U] a chemical substance sometimes added to water or TOOTHPASTE (=substance for cleaning teeth) in order to help keep teeth healthy • *This toothpaste contains fluoride to help protect against tooth decay.*

fluor·i·date *obj* /£ˈfluə·rɪ·deɪt, $ˈflʊ-/ *v* [T] • *Some water companies in Britain fluoridate* (=add fluoride to) *the drinking water.*

fluor·i·da·tion /£ˌfluə·rɪˈdeɪ·ʃᵊn, $ˌflʊ-/ *n* [U] • *Is artificial fluoridation really safe?*

fluor·ine /£ˈfluə·riːn, $ˈflʊ-/ *n* [U] *specialized* a poisonous pale yellow gas

fluor·o·car·bon /£ˌfluə·rəˈkɑː·bᵊn, $ˌflʊ·roʊˈkɑːr-/ *n* [C] *specialized* a chemical containing FLUORINE and carbon, with various industrial uses • See also CFC.

flur·ry /£ˈflʌr·i, $ˈflɜːr-/ *n* [C] a sudden light fall of snow, blown in different directions by the wind • *There may be the odd flurry* **of snow** *over the hills tonight.* • *A wind picked up and the snow fell* **in** *flurries.* • *(fig.) There was a flurry* (=sudden moment) *of* **excitement/activity** *at the end of the hall, and in walked the President.* • *(fig.) The prince's words on marriage have prompted a flurry* **of** (=have suddenly caused a lot of) *speculation in the press this week.*

flush [BECOME RED] /flʌʃ/ *v* [I] (of a person) to become red in the face, esp. as a result of strong emotions, heat or alcohol • *She flushed* **with** *pleasure as she accepted the prize.* • *The champagne had caused his face to flush and his eyes were bright.* • *She flushed red* **with** *embarrassment at the suggestion.*

flush /flʌʃ/ *n* [C usually sing] • *The thought of Richard with another woman brought a flush* **of** *anger to her cheeks.* • *She daubed a spot of make-up on her cheeks to try to hide an alcohol-induced flush.*

flushed /flʌʃt/ *adj* • *You look flushed* (=red in the face) *– are you hot?* • *Harry came back from his squash match hot and flushed.* • *My face feels hot – have I got flushed* **cheeks**? • *"And you really think I'm stupid enough to believe that, do you?" he said, flushed* **with** *anger.* • *(fig.) Flushed* **with** *success* (=made excited and confident) *after their surprise win against Italy, Belgium are preparing for Saturday's game against Spain.*

flush [LEVEL] /flʌʃ/ *adj* not sticking out, on the same level • *The two sideboard doors aren't quite flush.* • *I want the light fittings to be flush* **with** *the ceiling.* • *A flush* (=flat) **door** *is quicker to paint than a panelled door.*

flush [RICH] /flʌʃ/ *adj* [after v] *infml* having a lot of money • *I've just been paid so I'm feeling flush.* • *Although many private companies are flush* **with cash** *they do not intend to invest it.*

flush [CARD GAMES] /flʌʃ/ *n* [C] a number of playing cards held by one player which are all from the same SUIT

flush *(obj)* [EMPTY] /flʌʃ/ *v* (of a person) to operate a (toilet) after it has been used by pressing a handle or button or by pulling a chain, or (of a toilet) to operate in this way • *Why don't you ever flush* **the toilet/lavatory** *after you?* [T] • *I can't get the toilet to flush.* [I] • If you flush something **down** the toilet you get rid of it by putting it in the toilet and operating it: *I tend to flush old medicines down the toilet.* [T] • You can also flush **(out)** a pipe which is blocked by pouring a large amount of water down it to remove the blockage. [M] ○ *(fig.) You're supposed to drink a lot of water when you're on a diet to flush the toxins* **out** *of* (=remove them from) *your system.* [M]

flush /flʌʃ/ *n* [C] • *They've got one of those notices on the toilet that tells you to press quickly for a short flush and press and hold down for a long flush.* • PIC **Bathroom**

flush out *obj*, **flush** *obj* **out** *v prep* [M] to force (a person or animal) to leave a place where they are hiding • *Planes bombed the guerrilla positions yesterday in an attempt to flush out snipers from underground tunnels.* • *We used a dog to flush out the rabbits.*

flus·ter *obj* /£ˈflʌs·təʳ, $-tɚ/ *v* [T] to make (someone) nervous or upset, esp. when they are trying to do something • *Don't fluster me – I'm trying to concentrate.*

flus·ter /£'flʌs·təʳ, $-tɚ/ *n* [U] • *The important thing when you're cooking for a lot of people is not to get* **in a** *fluster* (= a nervous state).

flus·tered /£'flʌs·təd, $-tɚd/ *adj* • *If I look flustered it's because I'm trying to do about twenty things at once.*

flute /fluːt/ *n* [C] a musical instrument in the shape of a tube which is played while holding one end near the mouth and the other near the shoulder • PIC **Musical instruments**

flut·ist /£'fluː·tɪst, $-t̬ɪst/ *n* [C] • Flutist is *Am for* FLAUTIST (= flute player).

flut·ed /£'fluː·tɪd, $'fluː·t̬ɪd/ *adj* (esp. of a round object) wavy around the edge • *a flan dish with fluted edges* • *fluted columns/pillars*

flut·ter MONEY /£'flʌt·əʳ, $'flʌt̬·ɚ/ *n* [C usually sing] *Br and Aus infml* a small BET (= the risking of a small amount of money in order to win more), esp. on a horse race • *Aunty Paula likes to* **have** *a bit of a flutter* **on** *the horses.*

flut·ter *(obj)* MOVE /£'flʌt·əʳ, $'flʌt̬·ɚ/ *v* to (cause to) make a series of quick delicate movements up and down or from side to side • *Somewhere a band was playing and brightly coloured* **flags** *were fluttering in the breeze.* [I] • *Leaves fluttered* **down** *onto the path.* [I] • **Butterflies** *fluttered* **about** *in the sunshine.* [I] • *A white bird poised on a wire and fluttered its* **wings**. [T] • *I could hear the fluttering of the birds' wings on the roof.* • If your **heart** flutters it beats irregularly and faster than usual for a short while. [I] • *(fig.)* You might say that someone makes your **heart** flutter if you find them very physically attractive and you feel excited when you see or talk to them: *James has been making hearts flutter ever since he joined the company.* [I] • People sometimes say that their **stomach** flutters when they get an uncomfortable feeling in their stomach because they are nervous: *Every time I think about my exams my stomach flutters!* [I] • *(humorous)* If a girl or woman **flutters** her **eyelashes** at a man she uses her charm and attractiveness to persuade him to do something for her: *Go and flutter your eyelashes* **at** *the barman, Janet, and see if you can get him to serve us.*

flut·ter /£'flʌt·əʳ, $'flʌt̬·ɚ/ *n* [C] • *I could hear the flutter* (= noise) *of wings on the roof.* • *(fig.) When economic statistics are first published they grab headlines and put markets* **in a flutter** (= in a confused and excited state). • *(fig.) Peter was coming round for dinner and I was* **all of a flutter** (= in a state of nervous excitement). • *(fig.) The publication of her first novel last autumn caused a flutter* (= brief period) *of excitement which was soon forgotten.*

flu·vi·al /'fluː·vi·əl/ *adj* [not gradable] *specialized* of a river • *a fluvial basin* • *fluvial ice*

flux CHANGE /flʌks/ *n* [U] continuous change • *Our plans are* **in a state of** *flux at the moment.* • *Nature is dynamic, always* **in** *flux, always changing.*

flux CHEMICAL /flʌks/ *n* [U] *specialized* a substance added to a metal to make it easier to SOLDER (= join by melting) to another metal

fly *(obj)* TRAVEL /flaɪ/ *v past simple* **flew** /fluː/, *past part* **flown** /£fləʊn, $floʊn/ (of birds, insects or aircraft) to move through the air, or (of people) to travel by aircraft • *The poor bird couldn't fly because it had a broken wing.* [I] • *The pilot just said that we were flying* **at** *(a height of) 9000 metres.* [I] • *"How are you travelling to Spain?" "We're flying."* [I] • *I usually fly Lufthansa/Japan Airlines/El Al* (= I travel in one of this company's aircraft). [T] • *Who was the first person to fly* **(across)** *the Atlantic* (= to cross it in an aircraft)? [I] • *She has to fly thousands of miles every year for her job.* [I] • *I learned to fly* (= how to control an aircraft) *when I was in Australia.* [I] • *Thousands of bats were flying* **about** *overhead.* [I] • *As soon as it saw us, the bird flew* **away/off**. [I] • *We fly* **from/out from/***(Am also)* **out of** *Heathrow, but fly* **back (in)to** *Gatwick.* [I] • *If we fly* **high**, *we may avoid the storm.* [I] • *(fig. Am) He was really flying* **high** (= extremely excited and happy) *after the birth of his first child.* • *Have you ever flown* **in** *a helicopter/hot-air balloon?* [I] • *The wasp flew* **in/out** *through the open window.* [I] • *My wife's flying* **in** (= coming in an aircraft) *from New York tonight.* [I] • *The restaurant flies its fish* **in** (= transports it by aircraft) *daily from Scotland.* [M] • *He's flying* **out** (= going to a foreign country by aircraft) *(to Australia) next week.* [I] • *We will be flying* (= transporting by aircraft) *100 badly wounded civilians* **out** *(of the battle zone) tonight.* [M] • *Some interesting new ideas are* **flying about/around** (= being talked about) *at work.* • If you **fly in the face of** something, you go against it: *You're flying in the face of* **common sense/reason**. • If an aircraft or the equipment for controlling it is **fly-by-wire**, it is controlled by computers. • A *(Br)* **fly-drive holiday**/*(Am)* **fly-drive vacation** is an organized holiday which includes your air ticket and the use of a car. • A **flying boat** is an aircraft shaped like a boat at the bottom, and able to land on water. • *(specialized)* A **flying buttress** is an arch built against a wall, esp. of a church, to support its weight: *Gothic cathedrals have flying buttresses.* • A **flying doctor** is a doctor, usually in Australia, who travels by air to see people who are ill. • A **flying fish** is a tropical fish that can jump above the surface of the water using its very large FINS. • A **flying fox** is a large BAT (= a flying mammal) that eats fruit. • *If you* **take** *a* **flying jump/leap** (= a very big jump) *you'll get over the stream.* • A **flying saucer** (also **UFO**) is a spacecraft from another planet, which some people claim they have seen. • *"One Flew Over the Cuckoo's Nest"* (title of a book by Ken Kesey, 1962) • *"Come Fly with Me"* (title of a song written by Sammy Cahn, 1958)

fli·er, **fly·er** /£'flaɪ·əʳ, $-ɚ/ *n* [C] • **Frequent** *fliers* (= people who travel by air frequently) *receive travel privileges.* • *It's a large bird, unable to take off from ground level, but a good flier, covering long distances.*

fly·ing /'flaɪ·ɪŋ/ *n* [U] • *Annette's scared of flying.* • *"Fear of Flying"* (title of a book by Erica Jong, 1973)

fly MOVE QUICKLY /flaɪ/ *v* [I] *past simple* **flew** /fluː/, *past part* **flown** /£fləʊn, $floʊn/ to move or go quickly • *With the explosion, glass flew* **across** *the room.* • *Cathy flew* **by/past** *me in the corridor.* • *My holiday seems to have flown* **(by)** (= passed very quickly) *this year.* • *The lid/champagne cork flew* **off** (= came off suddenly) *and hit the lamp.* • *The door/window suddenly flew* **open**. • *(infml) Anyway, I* **must** *fly* (= leave quickly) – *I didn't realize how late it was!* • If you **fly at** someone, you attack them suddenly: *He flew at his brother like a mad thing.* ○ *The dog flew at the cat.* See also **let fly** at LET ALLOW. • If you **fly off the handle**, or **fly into a rage/***(Br also)* **temper/fury**, you suddenly become very angry. • *(saying)* 'Time flies when you're having fun' means that time passes very quickly when you are enjoying yourself.

fly·ing /'flaɪ·ɪŋ/ *adj* [before n; not gradable] • *(esp. Br)* A **flying picket** is a worker who travels to support workers who are on STRIKE (= refusing to work) at another place of work. • A **flying squad** is a small group of police officers which is trained to act quickly, esp. when there is a serious crime. • In a race, a **flying start** is when one competitor starts more quickly than the others: *(fig.) She's* **(got) off to** *a flying start* (= has begun very well) *in her new job.* • A **flying visit** is a very short visit, usually to a person: *I'm afraid this will have to be a flying visit as we've only got an hour before the train leaves.*

fly INSECT /flaɪ/ *n* [C] a small insect with two wings, esp. a HOUSEFLY • **Swat** *that fly before it lands on the food!* • *I could hear the sound of a fly* **buzzing** *around the room.* • *(infml)* If people are **dropping (off) like flies** they are dying or falling down in large numbers: *The heat was overwhelming and people were dropping off like flies.* • *(infml)* Members of a group who meet in order to do a particular activity might also be said to be **dropping off like flies** if a lot of them are stopping doing that activity: *There used to be over twenty of us in our aerobics class but they're dropping off like flies!* • *(infml)* A **fly in the ointment** is a single thing or person that is spoiling a situation which could have been very positive or enjoyable: *I'm looking forward to Sunday, the only fly in the ointment being the fact that I shall have to sit next to my mother-in-law.* • If you say you'd like/love to be a **fly on the wall** on a future occasion you mean that you would like to hear what will be said or see what will happen while not being noticed: *I'd* **like/love to be** *a fly on the wall when those two get home!* • *(Br)* A **fly-on-the-wall documentary/programme** is one in which the people involved forget that they are being filmed. • If you say there are **no flies on** someone, you mean that they cannot easily be deceived. • If you say that someone **wouldn't harm/hurt a fly** you mean they are gentle and would not do anything to injure or offend anyone.

fly FISHING /flaɪ/ *n* [C] a hook with coloured threads fastened to it, fixed to the end of a fishing line to attract fish • If you go **fly-fishing**, you try to catch fish using a fly.

fly TROUSERS /flaɪ/ *n* [C] *Am and Aus for* FLIES TROUSERS

fly·ing /'flaɪ·ɪŋ/ *adj* [after v; not gradable] *dated humorous* • If someone is flying (low) the opening at the front of their trousers is not fastened.

fly *(obj)* WAVE /flaɪ/ *v past simple* **flew** /fluː/, *past part* **flown** /£fləʊn, $floʊn/ to wave or move about in the air while being fixed at one end • *The ship was flying the Spanish flag.* [T] • *The flag was flying* **at half-mast** (= lowered to a point half way down the pole) *to mark the death of the President.* [I] • *There isn't really enough wind to fly a kite today.* [T] • To **fly a kite** is to find out what people's opinions about something new is by informally spreading news about it. See also **kite-flying** at KITE FLYING OBJECT. • *(esp. Am infml)* **Go fly a kite** (= Go away and stop troubling me)*!* • *She passed the test/exam/interview* **with flying colours** (= very well).

fly TENT /flaɪ/ *n* [C] *esp. Am for* FLYSHEET

fly·a·way /ˈflaɪ·ə·weɪ/ *adj* (of hair) soft, light and difficult to keep in place • *It said on the shampoo bottle that it was for flyaway* **hair**.

fly·by /ˈflaɪ·baɪ/ *n* [C] a flight, esp. in a spacecraft, past a particular place • *Modern understanding of Mars dates back to the first spacecraft flyby of the planet in 1965.* • Flyby is also *Am for* FLYPAST.

fly–by–night /ˈflaɪ·baɪ·naɪt/ *adj* [not gradable] *infml disapproving* (of a company) not able to be trusted, likely to avoid debts by closing down • *a fly-by-night company/organization*

fly·catch·er /£ˈflaɪˌkætʃ·əʳ, $-ɚ/ *n* [C] a small bird which catches insects in the air

fly·er /£ˈflaɪ·əʳ, $-ɚ/ *n* [C] See FLIER TRAVELLER and FLIER INFORMATION

fly·leaf /ˈflaɪ·liːf/ *n* [C] *pl* **flyleaves** /ˈflaɪ·liːvz/ an empty page at the beginning or end of a book next to the cover • *She stopped to read the inscription on the flyleaf.*

fly·o·ver BRIDGE *Br* /£ˈflaɪˌəʊ·vəʳ, $-ˌoʊ·vɚ/, *Am and Aus* **o·ver·pass** *n* [C] a bridge that carries a road or railway over another road • *You'll have to use the Chiswick flyover.* • PIC〉 **Motorway**

fly·o·ver AIRCRAFT /£ˈflaɪˌəʊ·vəʳ, $-ˌoʊ·vɚ/ *n* [C] *Am for* FLYPAST

fly·pap·er /£ˈflaɪˌpeɪ·pəʳ, $-pɚ/ *n* [C] a long strip of sticky paper which you hang in a room to catch flies

fly·past *Br* /£ˈflaɪ·pɑːst, $-pæst/, *Am* **fly·by**, *Am also* **fly·o·ver** *n* [C] an occasion of a group of aircraft flying in a special pattern as a part of a ceremony

fly·post·ing /£ˈflaɪˌpəʊ·stɪŋ, $-ˌpoʊ-/ *n* [U] *Br* illegally sticking a political or other POSTER (= notice) on a public wall, fence, etc.

fly·post·er /£ˈflaɪˌpəʊ·stəʳ, $-ˌpoʊ·stɚ/ *n* [C] *Br* • *Someone had pasted a load of flyposters up on the wall during the night.*

fly·screen *Aus* /ˈflaɪ·skriːn/ *n* [C] a frame with fine net fitted over an open window to keep out insects

fly·sheet *Br* /ˈflaɪ·ʃiːt/, *esp. Am* **fly** *n* [C] an extra sheet of CANVAS (= strong cloth) stretched over the outside of a tent to keep the rain out

fly·weight /ˈflaɪ·weɪt/ *n* [C] *specialized* a boxer who is in the lightest weight group, weighing 51 kilograms or less

fly·wheel /ˈflaɪ·wiːl/ *n* [C] *specialized* a heavy wheel in a machine which helps the machine to work at a regular speed

FM /ˌefˈem/ *n* [U] *abbreviation for* frequency modulation (= a radio system, usually on VHF, in which the AMPLITUDE (= strength) of the radio waves does not change, but the FREQUENCY (= number of waves each second) varies, producing a very clear sound) • *Can you get the station* **on** *FM as well as on medium wave?* • *an FM radio*

foal /£fəʊl, $foʊl/ *n* [C] a young horse • *We saw a foal being born.* • *Two of the mares are* **in foal** (= going to give birth).

foal /£fəʊl, $foʊl/ *v* [I] • If a mare foals, she gives birth to a baby horse.

foam /£fəʊm, $foʊm/ *n* [U] a mass of very small bubbles formed on the surface of a liquid • *Further out to sea the waves were a metre high and capped with white foam.* • Foam sometimes refers to a cream-like substance which is filled with bubbles of air: *bath/contraceptive/shaving foam* • Foam also refers to a type of material which is made by adding gas bubbles to a liquid, then letting it cool: *foam rubber/plastic* • *a foam cushion/mattress/pillow*

foam /£fəʊm, $foʊm/ *v* [I] • *Some washing liquids foam too much* (= produce too many bubbles) *to use in an automatic washing machine.* • If a person or an animal foams **at the mouth**, they have bubbles coming out of their mouth as a result of a disease: *A dog staggered towards us, foaming at the mouth, and I immediately thought of rabies.* • If you say a person is **foaming at the mouth** you mean they are extremely angry: *The Almeida theatre's recent staging of the opera had critics foaming at the mouth.*

foam·y /£ˈfəʊ·mi, $ˈfoʊ-/ *adj* **-ier, -iest** • *foamy shampoo/washing-up liquid*

fob /£fɒb, $fɑːb/ *n* [C] a piece of leather or other material to which a group of keys is fastened, or a chain or piece of material used, esp. in the past, to fasten a watch to a man's WAISTCOAT (= clothing for upper body) • *a key fob* • *a fob watch*

fob off *obj*, **fob** *obj* **off** *v adv* [M] to persuade someone to accept something that is of a low quality or different to what he or she really wanted • *If I decide I don't like an expensive piece of clothing that I've bought I can usually fob it off on one of my daughters as a birthday present.* • *My niece wanted me to take her to the zoo but I managed to fob her off* **with** *an afternoon in the park.* • *Well, he wants the report ready by tomorrow but I can always fob him off* **with** *some excuse.*

fo·cus CENTRE /£ˈfəʊ·kəs, $ˈfoʊ-/ *n* [C] *pl* **focuses** or *fml* **foci** /£ˈfəʊ·kiː, $ˈfoʊ-/ the main or central point of something, esp. of attention or interest • *I think Dave likes to be the focus* **of attention**. • *The main focus* **of interest** *at the fashion show was Christian Lacroix's outrageous evening wear.* • *Lately the main focus* **of** *monetary policy has shifted to interest rates.* • *It seems that the focus* **of discontent** *among the party is the leader himself.* • *In tonight's programme, the focus is* **on** (= we'll be giving special attention to) *vegetarian food.* • *The media focus* **on** *politicians' private lives inevitably switches the attention away from the real issues.* • (RUS)

fo·cal /£ˈfəʊ·kᵊl, $ˈfoʊ-/ *adj* • Focal means central and important: *The focal* **figure** *of the film is Annette Corley, a dancer who has boyfriend troubles.* • *The open fire used to be the* **focal point** (= centre) *of the British living room whereas now it's usually the television.* • *(specialized)* **The focal point** is another name for the FOCUS SCIENCE.

fo·cus *(obj)* /£ˈfəʊ·kəs, $ˈfoʊ-/ *v* **-s-** or **-ss-** • To focus **(up)on** something or someone is to direct your attention to it: *Tonight's programme focuses on the way that homelessness affects the young.* [I] ○ *We didn't really focus upon any specific area – we just talked generally about the problem.* [I] ○ *When the kitchen is finished I'm going to focus* **my attention** *on the garden and get that sorted out.* [T] ○ *All her energies are focused upon her children and she seems to have little time for anything else.* [T] • *I find it hard to focus* (= direct my mental powers to a particular activity) *when it's so late at night.* [I]

fo·cus SCIENCE /£ˈfəʊ·kəs, $ˈfoʊ-/ *n pl* **focuses** or **foci** /£ˈfəʊ·kiː, $ˈfoʊ-/ (in physics) the point where waves of light or sound which are moving towards each other meet • *the focus of a lens* [C] • A photograph that is **in** focus has a clear image. [U] • A photograph that is **out of** focus, it is not clear. [U] ○ *(fig.) The recent shootings have brought the whole issue of firearms into much* **sharper** *focus* (= made it more noticeable). [U] • (RUS)

fo·cal /£ˈfəʊ·kᵊl, $ˈfoʊ-/ *adj* [not gradable] • *(specialized)* The distance between a point where waves of light meet and the centre of a LENS is called the **focal length**.

fo·cus *(obj)* /£ˈfəʊ·kəs, $ˈfoʊ-/ *v* **-s-** or **-ss-** • If you focus a device such as a camera or MICROSCOPE, you move a device on the LENS so that you can see a clear picture: *I focused the telescope* **on** *the moon.* [T] • If you focus your eyes, or if your eyes focus, you try to look directly at an object so that you can see it more clearly: *When they first took the bandages off, she/her eyes couldn't focus properly* (= she couldn't see clearly). [I] ○ *(fig.)* **All eyes** *were focused on* (= everyone was looking at) *the young actress who was sitting at the table next to us.* [T]

fo·cused /£ˈfəʊ·kəst, $ˈfoʊ-/, **fo·cussed** *adj* • *a focused* (= clear) *image*

fod·der /£ˈfɒd·əʳ, $ˈfɑː·dɚ/ *n* [U] food that is given to cows, horses and other farm animals, or *(fig.)* people or things that are useful for the stated purpose • *Some root vegetables are grown for fodder.* • *The farmer has two fields planted with fodder crops.* • *(fig.) Politicians are always good fodder* **for** *comedians* (= they make jokes about them). • *(fig.) There's plenty of fodder* **for** (= things that will cause) *nightmares in this film.* • *(fig.) Her books are recommended literary fodder* (= reading) **for** *schoolchildren.*

foe /£fəʊ, $foʊ/ *n* [C] *literary* an enemy • *The two countries have united against their common foe.* • *They were* **bitter** *foes for many years.* • *Foes* **of** *the government will be delighting in its current difficulties.*

FoE /£ˌef·əʊ'iː, $-oʊ'-/ *n* [U] *abbreviation for* **Friends of the Earth**, see at FRIEND [COMPANION]

foe·tid /£'fet·ɪd, $'feṭ-/ *adj* FETID

foe·tus, *Am and Aus also* **fe·tus** /£'fiː·təs, $-ṭəs/ *n* [C] a young human being or animal before birth, after the organs have started to develop • *Women usually have regular checks during pregnancy to make sure that the foetus is developing satisfactorily.* • [LP> **Age**

foe·tal, *Am and Aus also* **fe·tal** /£'fiː·tᵊl, $-ṭᵊl/ *adj* [not gradable] • *The machine is designed for foetal monitoring* (= watching the foetus carefully) *during labour.*

fog /£fɒg, $fɑːg/ *n* a weather condition in which very small drops of water gather together to form a thick cloud close to the land or sea, making it difficult to see • **Thick/Heavy/Swirling** *fog has made driving conditions dangerous.* [U] • *Mists,* **freezing** *fogs and snow are common in this area.* [C] • *Fog came* **rolling in** *from the ocean.* [U] • *It took several hours for the fog to* **lift**. [U] • *(fig. infml) I felt* **in a** *fog* (= confused) *about what to do next.* [U] • Fog can also be used to mean something which makes it impossible to understand or think about something else clearly: *We became completely lost in the fog* **of** *conditions surrounding our application for a loan.* [U] ○ *The origins of Valentine cards are wrapped in a fog* **of** *history.* [U] • A **fog bank** is a thick cloud of fog, esp. at sea. • A **fog light** or **fog lamp** is a special light at the front or back of a vehicle that helps you to see and be seen when driving through fog.

fog *(obj)* /£fɒg, $fɑːg/ *v* **-gg-** • *The airport was fogged* **in** (= could not operate because of fog). [T] • *I couldn't see a thing because my glasses had fogged* **up** (= small drops of water had gathered close together on them). [I] • *(fig.) The minister's speech merely fogged the issue* (= made it less clear), *instead of making it clearer.* [T] • *(fig.) He says that alcohol fogs his brain* (= makes him stop thinking clearly). [T]

fog·gy /£'fɒg·i, $'fɑː·gi/ *adj* **-ier, -iest** • *a cold, foggy day* • *(infml)* If you **haven't the foggiest (idea)** about something, you know nothing about it at all.

fog·bound /£'fɒg·baʊnd, $'fɑːg-/ *adj* [not gradable] prevented from operating as usual because of fog • *Their flight was cancelled because the* **airport** *was fogbound.*

fo·gey, fo·gy /£'fəʊ·gi, $'foʊ-/ *n* [C] *infml* a person who is old-fashioned and likes tradition • *The party is run by a bunch of* **old** *fogies who resist progress.* • *When you're 16, anyone over 25 seems an* **old** *fogey.* • *(esp. Br)* A **young** fogey is a young person, usually a man, who dresses and behaves as if he is much older than he is and likes a very traditional way of life: *The restaurant was full of young fogeys wearing tweed jackets and smoking pipes.*

fo·gey·ish /£'fəʊ·gi·ɪʃ, $'foʊ-/ *adj* • *He has a fogeyish attitude towards contemporary music.* • **It** *would be fogeyish not* **to** *admit that these changes are for the better.* [+ *to* infinitive]

fog·horn /£'fɒg·hɔːn, $'fɑːg·hɔːrn/ *n* [C] a horn that makes a very loud sound to warn ships that they are close to land or other ships • *We heard the blast/blare of a foghorn through the mist.* • *He has a voice like a foghorn/a foghorn voice* (= an unpleasantly loud voice).

foi·ble /'fɔɪ·bl̩/ *n* [C usually pl] a small weakness or foolish habit that is seen as harmless and unimportant • *We all have our little foibles.*

foil [METAL SHEET] /fɔɪl/ *n* [U] a very thin sheet of metal, esp. used to wrap food in to keep it fresh • *tin/silver foil* • *(Br and Aus) aluminium/(Am) aluminum foil* • *The potatoes should be wrapped in foil and placed in a hot oven.*

foil *obj* [PREVENT] /fɔɪl/ *v* [T] to prevent (someone or something) from being successful • *An attempted coup against the country's military ruler was foiled yesterday.* • *The prisoners'* **attempt** *to escape was foiled at the last minute when police received a tip-off.* • *(humorous) Drat! Foiled* **again**! (= My secret plans have not worked!)

foil [COMPARISON] /fɔɪl/ *n* [C] something or someone that makes another's good or bad qualities all the more noticeable • *The older, cynical character in the play is the perfect foil* **for** *the innocent William.* • *Her husband's strength acts as a foil* **to** *her impetuousness.*

foil [SWORD] /fɔɪl/ *n* [C] a thin light sword used in the sport of FENCING

foist *obj* **on/u·pon** *obj* /fɔɪst/ *v prep* [T] to force (someone) to have or experience (something they do not want) • *He said that parents should not try to foist their values on their children.* • *The greengrocer tried to foist some old apples on me, but I wouldn't accept them.*

fold *(obj)* [BEND] /£fəʊld, $foʊld/ *v* to bend (esp. paper or cloth) so that one part of it lies on the other part, or to be able to be bent in this way • *I folded the letter* **(in half)** *and put it in an envelope.* [T] • *Make sure the umbrella is dry before folding it.* [T] • *He had a* **neatly** *folded handkerchief in his jacket pocket.* • *Will you help me to fold* **up** *the sheets?* [M] • *She opened the window and folded* **back** *the shutters.* [M] • *As it was such a nice day, we folded the car roof* **down**. [M] • *These chairs fold* (= can be bent) **flat** *and can be stacked away.* [I] • Fold can also mean wrap: *She folded her baby* **in a** *blanket.* [T] ○ *He folded his arms* **around** *her.* [T] • If you fold your **arms**, you bring them close to your chest and hold them together: *He folded his arms and tried to look stern.* [T] • If you fold another part of your body, you move it into a position where it is close to your body: *She sat with her legs folded* **under** *her.* [T] ○ *Some of the dancers seemed to be able to fold themselves* **in half** (= bend so that the upper part of their bodies lay next to their legs). [T]

fold /£fəʊld, $foʊld/ *n* [C] • *She made a small fold* (= bend) *in the corner of the page of the book she was reading so that she would know how far she had read.* • *Sand had blown into the folds of her newspaper* (= the bends formed where it had been folded). • *The painter captured every fold of the silk dress.* • *(specialized)* A fold is also a bend in a layer of rock under the earth's surface caused by movement there.

fold·ing /£'fəʊl·dɪŋ, $'foʊl-/ *adj* [not gradable] • A folding bed, chair, bicycle, etc. is one that can be folded into a smaller size to make it easier to store or carry. • A folding door is one made of several parts joined together which can be folded against each other when the door is opened. • [PIC> **Beds and bedroom, Bicycles, Chair, Doors**

fold [FAIL] /£fəʊld, $foʊld/ *v* [I] (of a business) to close because of failure • *Many small businesses fold within the first year.*

fold [SHELTER] /£fəʊld, $foʊld/ *n* [C] a small area of a field surrounded by a fence where sheep can be put for shelter for the night, or *(fig.)* your home or an organization where you feel you belong • *The sheepdogs drove the sheep into the fold.* • *(fig.) Her children are all away at college now, but they always* **return** *to* **the** *fold in the holidays.* • *(fig.) "Welcome to* **the** *fold," said my boss on my first day in my new job.* • *(fig.) The party needs to find a way of getting its former supporters to* **go back** *to* **the** *fold.*

fold *obj* [MIX] /£fəʊld, $foʊld/ *v* [T always + adv/prep] (in cooking) to mix (a substance) (into another substance) by turning it gently with a spoon. • *Fold the eggs* **into** *the melted chocolate.* • *Fold* **in** *the flour.* [M]

-fold [NUMBER] /£fəʊld, $foʊld/ *combining form* having the stated number of parts, or multiplied by the stated number • *threefold* • *fourfold* • *The problems are twofold – firstly, economic, and secondly, political.* • *In the last 50 years, there has been a 33-fold increase in the amount of pesticide used in farming.*

fold·a·way /£'fəʊld·ə·weɪ, $'foʊld-/ *adj* [not gradable] able to be folded away out of sight • *a foldaway bed*

fold·er /£'fəʊl·dəʳ, $'foʊl·dɚ/ *n* [C] a thin, folded piece of cardboard used for keeping loose papers in • [PIC> **Stationery**

fol·i·age /£'fəʊ·li·ɪdʒ, $'foʊ-/ *n* [U] the leaves of a plant or tree, or leaves on the stems or branches on which they are growing • *The* **dense** *foliage overhead almost blocked out the sun.* • *She put some dark green foliage in the vase with the roses.*

fo·lic ac·id /£'fəʊ·lɪk, $'foʊ-/ *n* [C] a VITAMIN found in the leaves of plants and in LIVER, which is needed by the body for the production of red blood cells

fo·li·o /£'fəʊ·li·əʊ, $'foʊ·li·oʊ/ *n* [C] *pl* **folios** a book made of paper of a large size, esp. one of the earliest books printed in Europe • *The library holds the first folio of Shakespeare's plays.*

folk [PEOPLE] /£fəʊk, $foʊk/, *esp. Am* **folks** *pl n* people, esp. those of a particular group or type • *What on earth do these folk think they're playing at?* • *The drama follows the lives of farming folk.* • *The bus was full of* **old** *folk on a day trip.* • *Cars like that are much too expensive for* **ordinary** *folk.* • A **folk hero** is someone who is popular with and respected by ordinary people: *The mayor is still a folk hero in Chicago's black community.* • *"The Folks who live on the Hill"* (title of a song written by Oscar Hammerstein II, 1937) • See also FOLKSY.

folks /£fəʊks, $foʊks/ *pl n* • *(infml)* Folks can mean the people you are talking to: *All right, folks, dinner's ready!* [as form of address] • *(esp. Am)* Your folks are your parents: *I'm* *going home to see my folks.* • LP› **Titles and forms of address**

folk TRADITIONAL /£fəʊk, $foʊk/ *adj* [before n; not gradable] traditional to or typical of a particular group or country, esp. one where people mainly live in the countryside, and usually passed on from parents to their children through speech over a long period of time • *folk customs* • *folk culture* • *folk religion* • Folk can be used to refer to art that expresses something about the lives and feelings of ordinary people in a particular group or country, esp. those living in the countryside: *folk art/dance/music* ○ *a folk song* • **Folk medicine** is traditional medicine, which is based esp. on the use of plants instead of on scientific principles. • A **folk memory** is the knowledge that people have about something that happened in the past because parents have spoken to their children about it over many years. • A **folk tale** is a story that parents have passed on to their children through speech over many years. • **Folk wisdom** is knowledge in general that people have because it has been passed on by parents to their children through speech over many years. • See also FOLKSY.

folk /£fəʊk, $foʊk/ *n* [U] • Folk is modern music and songs that are written in a style similar to that of traditional music: *I enjoy listening to folk* **(music/songs)**. ○ *Several well-known folk* **singers** *are performing at the concert.* ○ *We're going to a folk* **club/festival** *in Edinburgh next week.* • Folk **rock** is a mixture of music in a traditional style and modern popular music.

folk·lore /£ˈfəʊk·lɔːʳ, $ˈfoʊk·lɔːr/ *n* [U] the traditional stories and culture of a group of people • *Her books are often based on folklore and fairytales.* • *In Irish folklore, the leprechaun had a large piece of gold.* • *Arguments between directors and stars are part of the folklore of Hollywood.*

folks·y /£ˈfəʊk·si, $ˈfoʊk-/ *adj* **-ier, -iest** having a traditional artistic or musical style, or (pretending to be) simple and informal • *Fashion has a folksy theme this summer.* • *The film evokes a folksy America of apple pies and friendly neighbours.*

fol·li·cle /£ˈfɒl·ɪ·kl̩, $ˈfɑː·lɪ-/ *n* [C] any of the very small holes in the skin, esp. one that a hair grows from

fol·low *(obj)* GO AFTER /£ˈfɒl·əʊ, $ˈfɑː·loʊ/ *v* to come or go after or go in the same direction as (someone or something), or to happen directly after (something else) • *The dog followed us home.* [T] • *She got up and walked out of the room, and her husband followed.* [I] • *The book was delivered yesterday with a note saying the bill for it would follow in a day or two.* [I] • *He had the feeling he was being followed* (= someone was going after him to catch him or see where he was going). [T] • *I could feel them following me with their eyes* (= watching my movements closely). [T] • *His job has taken him all over the world, and his family have had to follow (him)* (= go with him). [I/T] • *Follow* (= Go in the same direction as) *the road for two kilometres, then turn left.* [T] • *Follow* (= Go in the direction shown by) *the arrows to the car park.* [T] • *The path follows* (= goes in the same direction as) *the coastline for several kilometres.* [T] • *Do your own thing, don't just follow* **the crowd** (= do what everyone else does). [T] • *We were not prepared for the events that followed* (= happened next). [I] • *The meal consisted of smoked salmon, followed by guinea fowl* (= with this as the next part). [T] • *The meal consisted of smoked salmon with guinea fowl* **to follow** (= with this as the next part). [I] • *She published a book of poems and followed it* **(up) with** (= next produced) *a novel.* [T/M] • *Following* **on from** *what I said earlier* (= Presenting the next part of what I was saying)... [I] • *She was so good at her job, she'll be difficult to follow* (= it will be difficult to do the same thing as she did). [T] • *Sophie always follows* (= does the same as) *what her sister does.* [T] • To follow a piece of music or writing is to read the notes or words at the same time as they are being played or said. • You say **as follows** to introduce a list of things or to describe how to do something: *The winners are as follows – Woods, Smith and Cassidy.* ○ *Combine the ingredients as follows.* • If you **follow in** someone's **footsteps**, you do the same thing as they did previously: *She followed in her mother's footsteps and started her own business.* • *(infml)* If you **follow** your **nose**, you trust your own feelings rather than obeying rules or letting yourself be influenced by other people's opinions: *Take a chance and follow your nose – you may be right!* ○ *He never reads reviews but follows his nose to find the best new literary talent.* • *(infml)*To **follow** your **nose** is also to go straight on: *Turn left, then* **just** *follow your nose and you'll see the shop on your left.* • To **follow suit** is to do the same thing: *When one airline reduces its ticket prices, the rest usually soon follow suit.* • To **follow through** (something)/**follow** (something) **through** is to continue to develop (it): *The essay started interestingly, but failed to follow through (its argument).* ○ *When you're playing a sport involving hitting or kicking a ball, it's important to follow through (your shot)* (= complete the movement of hitting or kicking by continuing to move your arm or leg in the same direction.) • To **follow** something **up**/*(Am also)* **follow up on** something is to find out more about it, or take further action connected with it: *The idea sounded interesting and I decided to follow it up.* ○ *The police officer took their names, but did not follow them up.* ○ *I've got to go for a* **follow-up** *visit to the doctor next week.* ○ *This meeting is a* **follow-up to** *the one we had last month.* • *(Br and Aus)* **Follow-my-leader**/*(Am)* **Follow-the-leader** is a children's game in which one child is followed by a line of other children, who have to copy everything the first child does.

fol·low·ing /£ˈfɒl·əʊ·ɪŋ, $ˈfɑː·loʊ-/ *adj* [before n; not gradable] • *They arrived late at night, so did not see the garden until the following day* (= the next day). • *The following items* (= those which will now be listed) *have been found – a ring, some money and a watch.* • A following **wind** is one which is blowing in the same direction as the one in which you are going: *Because of the following wind, I did my run much more quickly than usual.*

fol·low·ing /£ˈfɒl·əʊ·ɪŋ, $ˈfɑː·loʊ-/ *pl n* • **The following** are the people or things which are going to be listed: *Will the following please stand up – Woods, Smith and Cassidy.*

fol·low·ing /£ˈfɒl·əʊ·ɪŋ, $ˈfɑː·loʊ-/ *prep* • *The weeks following* (= after) *the riots were extremely tense.* • *Following the dinner, there will be a dance.*

fol·low *obj* OBEY /£ˈfɒl·əʊ, $ˈfɑː·loʊ/ *v* [T] to obey or to act as ordered by • *Follow the* **instructions** *on the back of the packet carefully.* • *I decided to follow her* **advice** *and go to bed early.* • *The people living in this area still follow their ancient* **traditions**. • *Muslims follow the* **teachings** *of the Koran, and Christians follow those of the Bible.*

fol·low·er /£ˈfɒl·əʊ·əʳ, $ˈfɑː·loʊ·ɚ/ *n* [C] • *Be a leader, not a follower* (= someone who does what they are told to do by others)*!* • A follower is also someone who supports, admires or believes in a particular person, group or belief: *a follower of Picasso* ○ *These people are followers* **of** *the Dalai Lama/Buddhism.*

fol·low·ing /£ˈfɒl·əʊ·ɪŋ, $ˈfɑː·loʊ-/ *n* [C usually sing] • *In the 1970s he joined a strange religious sect which had a large following* (= group of people who supported, admired or believed in it) **among** *young people.*

fol·low *(obj)* UNDERSTAND /£ˈfɒl·əʊ, $ˈfɑː·loʊ/ *v* to understand • *I'm sorry, I don't quite follow (you).* [I/T] • *His lecture was complicated and difficult to follow.* [T]

fol·low *obj* HAVE INTEREST IN /£ˈfɒl·əʊ, $ˈfɑː·loʊ/ *v* [T] to have a great interest in (something) or watch (something) closely • *He follows most sports avidly.* • *Do you follow any soap operas on television?* • *They followed her academic progress closely.*

fol·low·er /£ˈfɒl·əʊ·əʳ, $ˈfɑː·loʊ·ɚ/ *n* [C] • *They are keen followers* **of** (= have a great interest in) *their local football team.*

fol·low·ing /£ˈfɒl·əʊ·ɪŋ, $ˈfɑː·loʊ-/ *n* [C usually sing] • *She has* **attracted** *a large following* (= group of people who are interested in her) *among the rich and famous.* • *The shop has a small but* **loyal/devoted** *following* (= group of people who use it).

fol·low *(obj)* BE RESULT /£ˈfɒl·əʊ, $ˈfɑː·loʊ/ *v* [not *be following*] to happen as, or to be a likely, result • *If we were to adopt this proposal, several advantages would follow.* [I] • *This conclusion clearly follows* **from** *the evidence.* [I] • *If he has been violent before,* **it** *follows* **that** *he will be violent again.* [+ *that* clause] • *Just because I agreed last time,* **it** *doesn't* **necessarily follow** *that I will do so again.* [+ *that* clause]

fol·ly STUPIDITY /£ˈfɒl·i, $ˈfɑː·li/ *n* stupidity, or a stupid action, idea, etc. • *She said that the idea was folly.* [U] • **It** *would be folly* **for the country** *to become involved in the war.* [U + *to* infinitive] • *Customers were furious to discover that they had subsidized the bank's follies in investing funds overseas.* [C] • *His latest folly was buying a second-hand car which turned out to have a faulty engine.* [C]

fol·ly BUILDING /£ˈfɒl·i, $ˈfɑː·li/ *n* [C] (esp. in Britain) a building in the form of a small castle, TEMPLE, etc., that has been built as a decoration in a large garden or park • *a Gothic garden folly*

fo·ment *obj* /£fəʊ'ment, $foʊ-/ *v* [T] *fml* to cause (trouble) to develop • *The song was banned on the grounds that it might foment racial tension.*

fond [LIKING] /£fɒnd, $fɑːnd/ *adj* [before n] **-er, -est** having a great liking (for someone or something) • *She was very fond* **of** *horses.* • *"I'm very fond* **of** *you, you know," he said.* • *My brother is fond* **of** *pointing out my mistakes.* • *He gave her a fond smile.* • *Many of us have fond* **memories/recollections** *of our childhoods.* • *We said a fond* **farewell** *to each other* (= We said goodbye in a loving way) *and promised to write.*

fond·ly /£'fɒnd·li, $'fɑːnd-/ *adv* • *He smiled fondly* (= in a loving way) *at the children.*

fond·ness /£'fɒnd·nəs, $'fɑːnd-/ *n* [U] • *George's fondness* (= liking) **for** *pink gins was well known.*

fond [FOOLISH] /£fɒnd, $fɑːnd/ *adj* **-er, -est** foolishly hoped for or believed in • *They sent off their competition entry in the fond* **hope/belief** *that they would win.*

fond·ly /£'fɒnd·li, $'fɑːnd-/ *adv* • *She fondly* (= foolishly) *believed that he would phone her.*

fon·dant /£'fɒn·dᵊnt, $'fɑːn-/ *n* [C] a soft sweet made from sugar that seems to melt in the mouth

fon·dle *obj* /£'fɒn·dl̩, $'fɑːn-/ *v* [T] to touch gently and in a loving way, or to touch in a sexual way • *She fondled the puppies and put them in their basket.* • *He fondled the baby's feet.* • *She accused him of fondling her* (= touching her in a sexual way) *in the back of a taxi.*

fon·due /£fɒn'duː, $fɑːn-/ *n* [C] a hot dish prepared by keeping a container of either hot oil or melted cheese over a flame at the table and putting pieces of meat in the oil to be cooked or pieces of bread into the cheese • *a cheese fondue* • *a meat fondue* • A **fondue set** is the container in which the liquid is kept, together with the device which holds the flame over which it is heated and the forks used for putting the pieces of meat etc. into it.

font [CONTAINER] /£fɒnt, $fɑːnt/ *n* [C] a large, usually stone, container in a church, which holds the water used for BAPTISMS

font [LETTERS] /£fɒnt, $fɑːnt/ *n* [C] a collection of letters, numbers and other symbols that all have the same appearance • *Word processors usually offer a choice of different fonts.*

food /fuːd/ *n* (an example of) the things that are eaten by people and animals, or used by plants, so that they can live and grow • *baby food* [U] • *cat food* [U] • *plant food* [U] • *She's very choosy about what food she eats.* [U] • *There was lots of food* **and drink** *at the party.* [U] • *People can be allergic to certain foods.* [C] • *Food supplies are being exported to the starving refugees.* • Someone who is **off** their food does not want to eat, usually because they are ill. [U] • A **food additive** is an artificial substance added to food to give it taste or colour. • A **food chain** is a series of living things which are connected because each group of things eats the group below it in the series: *Sheep products are being fed to cows, thereby passing into the human food chain.* • **Food poisoning** is an illness usually caused by eating food that contains harmful bacteria. • A **food processor** is an electric machine that cuts, slices and mixes food quickly. • *(Am)* A **food stamp** is a piece of paper which is given to poor people by the government and with which they can then buy food. • If something gives you **food for thought**, it makes you think seriously about particular matters.

food·ie /'fuː·di/ *n* [C] *infml* a person who enjoys preparing and/or eating good food

food·stuff /'fuːd·stʌf/ *n* [C] any substance that is used as food or to make food • *They lack basic foodstuffs, such as bread and milk.*

fool [PERSON] /fuːl/ *n* [C] a person who behaves in a silly way without thinking • *I wouldn't bother asking Jake's opinion – he's such a fool.* • *You fool, you've missed your chance now.* [as form of address] • *He's a fool if he thinks she still loves him.* • *He's a fool* **to** *think she still loves him.* [+ to infinitive] • *He's fool* **enough to** *think she still loves him.* [+ to infinitive] • *My fool* **of a** (= My silly) *husband has gone out and taken my keys!* • In the past, a fool was a person who was employed in the court of a king or queen to make them laugh by telling jokes and doing amusing things. • Someone who **acts/plays the fool** is behaving in a silly way, often intentionally to make people laugh: *Stop acting the fool, I'm trying to talk to you.* • **Any fool** means anyone: *Any fool could tell that she was only joking.* • To **make a fool of** someone is to trick them or make them appear stupid in some way. • If you **make a fool of** yourself, you do something that makes other people think you are silly or not to be respected: *I told him I loved him – I've made a dreadful fool of myself.* • *(esp. Br)* If you say **more fool** you to someone, you mean that you think they are being unwise: *"I lent Rhoda $100 and she hasn't paid me back." "More fool you – you know what she's like!"* • Someone who is **no/no one's/nobody's fool** is not easily deceived: *You'll never get the teacher to believe that you did your essay but lost it – he's no fool.* • A **fool's errand** is a useless effort: *It's a fool's errand trying to get Lena to join in anything.* • **Fool's gold** is a MINERAL that is found in rocks and looks like gold but is worthless: *(fig.) He thought he'd found a sure scheme to make money but it turned out to be fool's gold* (= to be unsuccessful). • If someone is living in a **fool's paradise**, they are happy and are not aware of how bad or serious their situation really is. • *"Fools rush in where angels fear to tread"* (from the poem *An Essay in Criticsm* by Alexander Pope, 1711) • *"What kind of fool am I?"* (title of song written by Leslie Bricusse and Anthony Newley, 1961) • *"A fool and his money are soon parted"* (saying)

fool /fuːl/ *v* • *We weren't fooled* (= tricked) *by his promises.* [T] • *Tim was fooled* **into** *believing* (= wrongly made to believe) *that he'd won a lot of money.* [T] • *I haven't really crashed the car, I was only fooling* (= it is not true, I was just joking). [I] • To fool **about/around** is to behave in a silly way, esp. in a way that might have dangerous results: *Don't fool around* **with** *matches.* [I] • To fool **about/around** is also to behave in an amusing way in order to make other people laugh. [I] • To fool **around** is also to spend your time doing nothing useful: *We spent the afternoon fooling around on the beach.* [I] • *(esp. Am)* If a married person **fools around**, they have sexual relationships with someone other than their husband or wife: *She's fooling around* **with** *one of her colleagues at work.* • *(infml) "Really, I'm very happy." "You* **could have fooled** *me* (= I find that hard to believe)." • *"You can fool all the people some of the time, and some of the people all the time, but you can not fool all the people all the time"* (believed to have been said by Abraham Lincoln, 1809-1865)

fool /fuːl/ *adj* [before n; not gradable] *esp. Am infml* • *You've done some fool* (= silly) *things in your time, but that's the worst.*

fool·er·y /£'fuː·lᵊr·i, $-lə·i/ *n* • *I've had enough of this foolery* (= silly behaviour). [U] • *Stop these fooleries* (= silly actions) *immediately.* [C]

fool·ish /'fuː·lɪʃ/ *adj* • Foolish means unwise, ridiculous or lacking in judgment: *That was an extremely foolish thing to have done.* ○ *She was afraid that she would look foolish if she refused.* ○ **It** *was foolish* **of them** *to hope that he would change his ways.* [+ to infinitive] ○ *You were foolish* **to** *trust a man like Mick.* [+ to infinitive] • *"I am a very foolish, fond* (= silly) *old man"* (Shakespeare, King Lear 4.7)

fool·ish·ly /'fuː·lɪʃ·li/ *adv* • *Foolishly, I didn't write the phone number down.*

fool·ish·ness /'fuː·lɪʃ·nəs/ *n* [U] • *Would they ever forget my foolishness?*

fool [SWEET DISH] /fuːl/ *n* (a) sweet food of soft fruit made into a liquid and mixed with cream • *strawberry fool* [U] • *I've made a* **gooseberry** *fool for dinner.* [C]

fool·hard·y /£'fuːl,hɑː·di, $-,hɑːr-/ *adj* foolishly brave, taking unnecessary risks • *Sailing the Atlantic in such a tiny boat wasn't so much brave as foolhardy.* • *He made a foolhardy attempt to climb the tree in order to rescue the kitten.* • *She is foolhardy* **enough to** *risk all her money on this crazy scheme.* [+ to infinitive] • **It** *would be foolhardy* **to** *try and predict the outcome of the talks at this stage.* [+ to infinitive] • **It** *was foolhardy* **of you** *to try and climb that mountain.* [+ to infinitive]

fool·proof /'fuːl·pruːf/ *adj* (of a plan or machine) so simple and easy to understand that it is unable to go wrong or be used wrongly • *I don't believe there's any such thing as a foolproof scheme for making money.* • *This new video-recorder is supposed to be foolproof.*

fool·scap /'fuːl·skæp/ *n* [U], *adj* [not gradable] (paper) of a standard size, measuring 17·2 centimetres x 21·6 centimetres • *Foolscap is longer and narrower than A4.* • *Have you got a sheet of foolscap I could have?* • *Is this paper foolscap?*

foot [BODY PART] /fʊt/ *n* [C] *pl* **feet** /fiːt/ the part of the body at the bottom of the leg on which a person or animal stands • *I've got a blister on my left foot.* • *What size are your feet?* • *I've been* **on** *my feet* (= standing) *all day and I'm*

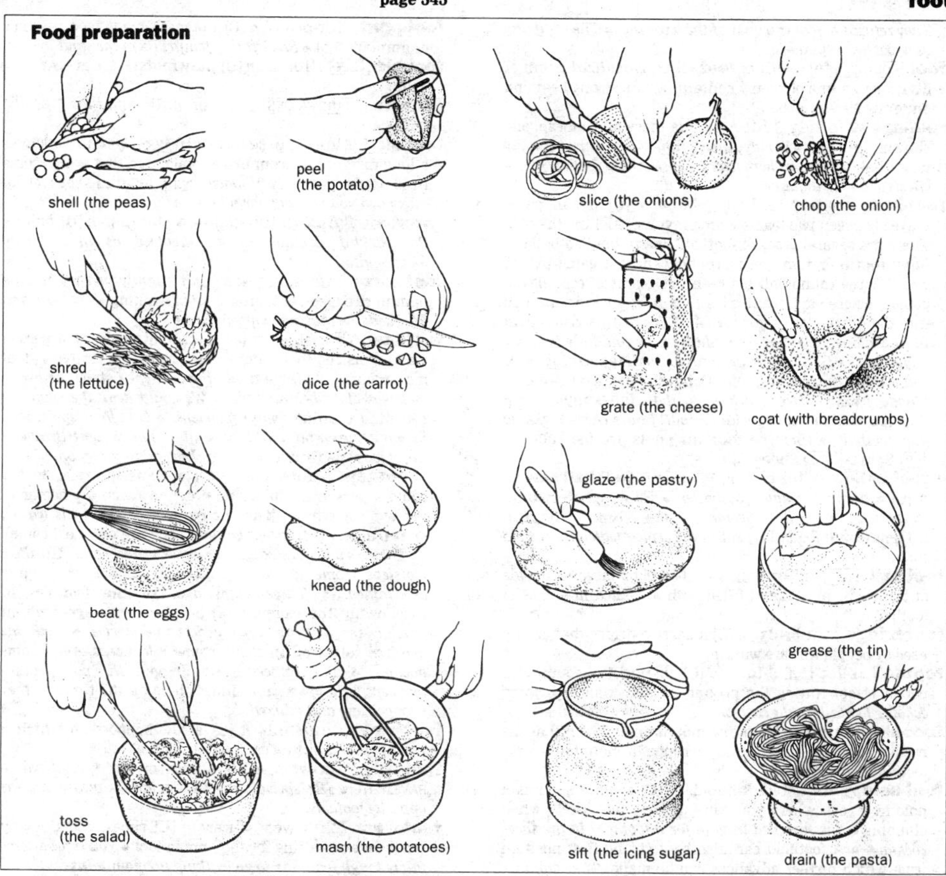

exhausted. • *Are you going by bicycle or* **on foot** (= walking)*?* • *"We'll soon have you* **(back) on** *your* **feet** (= healthy) **again,***" said the nurse.* • *He* **got to/rose to/jumped to** *his feet* (= stood up) *when she walked in.* • *(infml) "You look tired. Why not* **put** *your feet* **up** (= sit or lie down with your feet resting on something)*?"* • *Making contacts can help you get* **a foot in the door** (= be more likely to succeed) *when it comes to getting a job.* • To have **a foot in both camps** is to be connected to two groups with opposing interests. • If you say that **the boot/shoe is on the other foot** you mean that a situation has changed and someone who was previously weak now has power. • If you **have** your **feet on the ground/have both feet on the ground**, you are very practical and see things as they really are. • To **have one foot in the grave** is to be very old and near death. • If you **fall/land on** your **feet**, you are successful or lucky, esp. after a period of not having success or luck: *She's really fallen on her feet with that new job she's got.* • If someone, esp. an important person, or, less commonly, an organization, is described as having **feet of clay**, it means that they have a hidden fault or weakness and are not perfect as was thought in the past: *It was only after his death, when all his debts were discovered, that the financier was found to have feet of clay.* • *(dated)* If you say **my foot**, you mean that you do not believe what another person has just told you: *"He says his car isn't working." "Not working, my foot. He's just too lazy to come."* • To start off or get off **on the right/wrong foot** when doing something new is to make a successful/unsuccessful start: *When I first met him I* **got off** *on the wrong foot by spilling my drink over him.* • Someone who **never puts/sets a foot wrong** does not make any mistakes. • To **put** your **foot down** is to use your authority to stop something happening: *When she started borrowing my clothes without asking, I had to put my foot down.* • If you *(esp. Br)* **put** your **foot down**/*(Am)* **put** your **foot to the floor**, you increase your speed when you are driving: *The road ahead was clear, so he put his foot down and tried to overtake the car in front.* • To **put** your **foot in it**/*(esp. Am)* **put** your **foot in** your **mouth** is to say or do something that you should not have: *I really put my foot in it by asking her when the baby was due and she wasn't even pregnant.* • If you can **hardly/barely put one foot in front of the other**, you are having difficulty walking: *I was so tired that I could hardly put one foot in front of the other.* • If you **rush/run** someone **off** their **feet**, you cause them to be very busy: *I've been rushed off my feet all morning.* • To **set foot** is to go: *He refuses to set foot in an art gallery.* • If someone is **under** your **feet**, their presence prevents you from doing what you want to be doing: *The children were under my feet all day so I couldn't get anything done.* • **Foot-and-mouth disease** is a serious illness of cattle, sheep, PIGS and goats that causes sores in the mouth and on the feet and is very infectious. • A **foot brake** is a BRAKE (= a control device for slowing a vehicle) which you press with your foot. • *(infml)* **Foot-dragging** is failing to take action and delaying matters as much as possible: *The government was accused of foot-dragging* **on** *the issue.* See also **drag** your **feet** at DRAG [PULL]. • In tennis, a **foot fault** is when a player steps over the back line of the COURT while SERVING. • A **foot soldier** is an **infantryman**. See at INFANTRY. • [PIC⟩] **Body**

-foot·ed /£'fʊt·ɪd, $'fʊṭ-/ *combining form* • *our four-footed friends* (= animals having four feet) • *bare-footed children* (= children wearing no shoes)

foot [MEASUREMENT] /fʊt/ *(abbreviation* **ft***) n* [C] *pl* **foot** or **feet** /fiːt/ a unit of measurement, equal to twelve INCHES or 0·348 metres, sometimes shown by the symbol ′ • *The man was standing only a few feet away.* • *She is five feet/foot three inches tall.* • *She is 5′ 3″ tall.* • *The building is about two hundred feet high.* • [LP⟩] **Symbols, Units**

-foot·er /£'fʊt·əʳ, $'fʊṭ·ɚ/ *combining form* • *Our boat's a forty-footer* (= is of this number of FEET in length).

foot [BOTTOM] /fʊt/ *n* [U] the bottom or lower end of a space or object • *They built a house at the foot* **of** *a cliff.* • *She dreamed she saw someone standing at the foot* **of** *her bed.* • *I prefer it when books have their notes at the foot* **of** *the page, rather than at the end.*

foot *obj* [PAY] /fʊt/ *v* [T] *infml* to pay (an amount of money) • *His parents footed* **the bill** *for his course fees.* •

They refused to foot **the cost** *of the wedding.* • *The company will foot her* **expenses.**

foot POETRY /fʊt/ *n* [C] *pl* **feet** /fiːt/ *specialized* a unit of division of a line of poetry containing one strong beat and one or two lesser ones

foot·age /£ˈfʊt·ɪdʒ, $ˈfʊṭ-/ *n* [U] (a piece of) film esp. one showing an event • *Woody Allen's film 'Zelig' contains early* **newsreel** *footage.* • *There was some stunning footage* **of** *the effects of the earthquake.*

foot·ball GAME /£ˈfʊt·bɔːl, $-bɑːl/ *n* [U] a ball game played between two teams which involves kicking the ball. There are several types of football. • *(esp. Br)* Football (*Br infml* **footie** or **footy**, *esp. Am* **soccer**) is a game played with a large round ball between two teams of esp. eleven people, where each team tries to win by kicking the ball into the other team's goal. • *(Am)* Football is **American football.** See at AMERICAN. • *Shall we go and play (a game of) football?* • *He plays for the local football* **team/club.** • *Do you want to come to the football* **match/***(esp. Am)* **game** *on Monday?* • *My sister is a keen football* **fan/supporter.** • *(Br) You need to wear special football* **boots** *(Am* **cleats***) to play football.* • *(Br)* The **football pools** are the POOLS. • LP› **Sports** PIC› **Shoes, Sports**

foot·ball·er /£ˈfʊt·bɔː·ləʳ, $-bɑː·lɚ/, **foot·ball play·er** *n* [C] • *a rugby league footballer* • *He's a* **professional** *footballer.* • *Billy Bremner, the former Scottish* **international** *footballer, sat in the crowd watching his old team.*

foot·ball BALL /£ˈfʊt·bɔːl, $-bɑːl/ *n* [C] a large ball made of leather or plastic and filled with air, used in games of football

foot·bridge /ˈfʊt·brɪdʒ/ *n* [C] a narrow bridge that is only used by people who are walking

foot·fall /£ˈfʊt·fɔːl, $-fɑːl/ *n* [C] *literary* the sound of a person's foot hitting the ground as they walk • *I heard echoing footfalls in the corridor.*

foot·hill /ˈfʊt·hɪl/ *n* [C] a low mountain or low hill at the bottom of a larger mountain or range of mountains • *the foothills of the Pyrenees*

foot·hold /£ˈfʊt·həʊld, $-hoʊld/ *n* [C] a place such as a hole in a rock where you can put your foot safely when climbing • *She searched in vain for a foothold in the sheer rockface.* • A foothold can also be a strong first position from which further advances can be made: *The computer company is trying to* **get/gain** *a foothold in Europe.*

foot·ing FEET /£ˈfʊt·ɪŋ, $ˈfʊṭ-/ *n* [U] a safe position where both feet are on the ground the particular type of position or base that something or someone has • *The girls* **lost** *their footing and fell into the water.*

foot·ing BASE /£ˈfʊt·ɪŋ, $ˈfʊṭ-/ *n* [U] the particular type of base that something or a relationship has • *The council wants to put the bus service on a* **commercial** *footing.* • *The country is on a* **war** *footing.* • *Men and women ought to be able to compete for jobs on an* **equal** *footing, but they often don't.*

foot·lights /ˈfʊt·laɪts/ *pl n* a row of lights along the front of a stage at a theatre

foot·ling /£ˈfuː·tḷ·ɪŋ, $-ṭḷ-/ *adj* unimportant or silly • *When I started in my new job, I was given a lot of footling tasks to do.*

foot·loose /ˈfʊt·luːs/ *adj* free to do what you like and go where you like because you have no responsibilities • *My sister's married but I'm still footloose* **and fancy-free.**

foot·man /ˈfʊt·mən/ *n* [C] *pl* **-men** a male servant whose job includes opening doors and serving food, and who often wears a uniform

foot·note /£ˈfʊt·nəʊt, $-noʊt/ *n* [C] a note printed at the bottom of a page or in a list at the end of a book or article and which gives extra information about something that has been written on that page • *The book is 900 pages long, and has many footnotes.* • *(fig.) As a footnote* (=something extra) **to** *what I was saying before...* • *(fig.) He said that homelessness was no longer a footnote* (=something unimportant) **to** *the political agenda, but had become a matter of central concern.* • *(fig.) The crisis seemed of great importance at the time, but it later became just a footnote* (=something unimportant) **to history**.

foot·path /£ˈfʊt·pɑːθ, $-pæθ/ *n* [C] a path with a hard surface by the side of a road, or a track, esp. in the countryside, for walking on • *While repairs are in progress, please use the other footpath.* • *Keep to the footpath, and don't walk across the farmer's fields.*

foot·plate /ˈfʊt·pleɪt/ *n* [C] the part of a steam railway engine on which the driver stands

foot·print /ˈfʊt·prɪnt/ *n* [C] the mark made by a person's or animal's foot • *She left tiny footprints in the sand.*

foot·sie FEET /ˈfʊt·si/ *n* [U] **play footsie**, see at PLAY ENJOY

Foot·sie SHARE PRICES /ˈfʊt·si/ *n* [U] *infml for* FTSE 100 (INDEX)

foot·slog /£ˈfʊt·slɒg, $-slɑːg/ *v* [I] **-gg-** *infml* to walk over a long distance or from place to place so that you become tired • *After you've been footslogging* **around** *shops for an afternoon you're ready for a long bath.*

foot·slog·ging /£ˈfʊt·slɒg·ɪŋ, $-slɑː·gɪŋ/ *n* [U] *infml* • *Backpacking around Europe involved us in a lot of footslogging.*

foot·sore /£ˈfʊt·sɔːʳ, $-sɔːr/ *adj slightly literary* having painful tired feet, esp. after a lot of walking • *Footsore and fatigued, the soldiers stopped to rest.*

foot·step /ˈfʊt·step/ *n* [C] the sound made by a person walking as the foot touches the ground, or a STEP (=foot movement) • *Walking along the darkened street, he heard footsteps close behind him.* • *We could hear the sound of* **receding** (=going away) *footsteps.* • *Our footsteps echoed through the empty building.* • *(fig.) The Wright Brothers' flight was* **the first** *footstep* **on** *the road to the moon.*

foot·steps /ˈfʊt·steps/ *pl n* • Footsteps refer to the route a person has taken in order to reach a place or to achieve something: *When he realized he'd lost his wallet, he* **retraced** *his footsteps* (=went back the way he'd come). • *These early campaigners were brave, and* **in** *their footsteps come a new generation which is equally determined.* • *Three years ago,* **in the** *footsteps* **of** (=following the example of) *another former government official, she took up writing detective stories.* • *Both the children* **followed in** *their mother's footsteps and became doctors.* • *The camera crew* **dogged** *the pop group's footsteps* (=followed and filmed them all the time) *as they shopped, ate and relaxed.*

foot·stool /ˈfʊt·stuːl/ *n* [C] a low support on which a person who is sitting can place their feet

foot·way /ˈfʊt·weɪ/ *n* [C] a path or *(Br specialized)* a PAVEMENT • *(Br specialized) Pedestrians – please use the opposite footway.*

foot·wear /£ˈfʊt·weəʳ, $-wer/ *n* [U] shoes, boots or any other outer covering for the human foot • *You'll need some fairly tough footwear to go walking up mountains.*

foot·work /£ˈfʊt·wɜːk, $-wɜːrk/ *n* [U] the way in which the feet are used in sports or dancing, esp. when it is skilful, or *(fig. infml)* a group of cleverly planned and performed actions that are intended to result in an advantage or deal with a difficult situation • *And that's a marvellous bit of footwork there from Ponti as he takes the ball from Garcia.* • *(fig. infml) With a bit of* **fancy** *footwork she managed to negotiate a good deal.*

foot·y, foot·ie /£ˈfʊt·i, $ˈfʊṭ-/ *n* [U] *Br slang for* football, or *Aus slang for* RUGBY

fop /£fɒp, $fɑːp/ *n* [C] (esp. in the past) a man who is extremely interested in his appearance and who wears very decorative clothes • *I saw that actor playing the fop in a Restoration play.*

fop·pish /£ˈfɒp·ɪʃ, $ˈfɑː·pɪʃ/ *adj disapproving old use or humorous* • *a foppish young man*

for INTENDED FOR /£fɔːʳ, $fɔːr/ *prep* intended to be given to • *There's a phone message for you.* • *I suppose I'd better buy something for the new baby.* • *Is this for me? Thank you – that's very kind of you!* • *There's a prize for the fastest three runners in each category.* • *Here's a romantic song for the ladies.* • *(disapproving) You spend two hours cooking a meal and they say "it's disgusting" –* **that's** *children* **for you** (=that's typical of children)*!* • *(disapproving) I hold the door open for a man and he doesn't even say thank you –* **there's** *manners* **for you***!* • *Is this cake (up) for* **grabs***?* (=able to be had by anyone?)

for PURPOSE /£fɔːʳ, $fɔːr/ *prep* having the purpose of • *There's a sign there saying 'boats for hire'.* • *This pool is for the use of hotel residents only.* • *I'm sorry, the books are not for sale.* • *They've invited us round for dinner on Saturday.* • *Everyone in the office is contributing money for his leaving present.* • *I need some money for* (=for my activities) *tonight.* • *Which vitamins should you take for* (=in order to cure) *skin problems?* • *She needed to move closer for me* **to** *hear* (=so that I could hear) *what she was saying.* • **What** *do you use these enormous scissors* **for** (=what is their purpose)*?* • **What** *did you do that* **for***?* (=why did you do it?) • *Put those clothes in a pile for* **mending** (=so that they can be mended). [+ v-*ing*]

for BECAUSE OF /£fɔːʳ, $fɔːr/ *prep* because of; as a result of (doing something) • *Bob was back in the office today and looking all the better for his three weeks in Spain.* • *"How are you?" "Fine, and all the better for seeing you!"* [+ v-*ing*] • *Angie was looking a bit the worse for her late night* (= she looked tired). • *She did fifteen years in prison for murder.* • *I don't eat meat for various reasons.* • *I couldn't see for the tears in my eyes.* • *The things you do for love!* • *He's widely disliked in the company for his arrogance.* • *She couldn't talk for coughing* (= she was coughing too much to talk). [+ v-*ing*] • *Scotland is* **famous** *for its spectacular countryside.* • *Graham's best remembered* **for** *his work on disease resistance.* • *I didn't dare say anything for* **fear of** (= because I was frightened of) *offending him.* • **If it weren't for/If it hadn't been for**/*(fml)* **But for** (= Without) *the factor-fifteen sun-cream I'm sure I would have burnt.*

for TIME/DISTANCE /£fɔːʳ, $fɔːr/ *prep* showing amount of time or distance • *We walked (for) miles before we saw anything that we recognized.* • *I'll drive (for) a little longer then you can take a turn.* • *She's out of the office (for) a few days next week.* • *I'm just going to sleep for half an hour.* • *I haven't played tennis for years.* • *He's living with his parents* **for the time being** (= at present but only for a short time). • *They won the trophy* **for the** *third* **year running** (= for a third year out of three).

for OCCASION /£fɔːʳ, $fɔːr/ *prep* on the occasion of or at the time of • *What did you buy him for Christmas?* • *I'd like an appointment with the doctor for some time this week.* • *We're having a party for Jim's 60th birthday party.* • *For the first time in my life I weigh less than 62 kilos.* • *For the hundredth time, will you stop interrupting me when I'm speaking!* • *I've booked a table at the restaurant for nine o'clock.* • If someone invites you to eat with them and they tell you to arrive at 8.00 for 8.30, it means that food will be served at the later of the two times but that you should come half an hour before for drinks and conversation.

for COMPARING /£fɔːʳ, $fɔːr/ *prep* used for comparing one thing with others of the same type • *For every three people in favour of the law there are two or three against.* • *The summer has been quite hot for England.* • *She's very mature for her age.* • *It was a difficult decision, especially for a child.* • *For a man of his wealth he's not exactly generous.* • *(esp. humorous) He's quite thoughtful for a man!* • *(disapproving) You could be the Queen of England,* **for all** *I* **care/know** (= it's not important to me) – *you're not coming in here without a ticket.*

for SUPPORT /£fɔːʳ, $fɔːr/ *prep* in support of or agreement with • *I voted for the Greens at the last election.* • *Those voting for the motion, 96, and those voting against, 54.* • *So let's hear some applause for these talented young performers.* • *Who's for* (= Who wants to play) *tennis?* • *"What do you think about her going to the States?" "Oh, I'm* **(all)** *for it* (= I approve) – *it's such a good career move."* • People sometimes say they are **all** for something and then say something else that suggests the opposite: *I'm* **all** *for sexual equality* **but** *I don't want my wife to work.*

for IN RELATION TO /£fɔːʳ, $fɔːr/ *prep* in relation to (someone or something) • *Her feelings for him had become so strong over the past few weeks that she could no longer contain them.* • *He felt nothing but contempt for her.* • *He has a great liking for sweet food.* • *I've got a lot of admiration for people who do that sort of work.* • *He's quite good-looking but he's a bit too short for me.* • *That jacket looks a bit big for you.* • *I can't run with you – you're far too fast for me!* • *Is this seat high enough for you?* • *36 degrees Celsius! Hot enough for you is it?* • *Jackie's already left and,* **as** *for me, I'm going at the end of the month.* • *Luckily for me* (= I was lucky), *I already had another job when the redundancies were announced.* • *How are you doing for money/time* (= have you got enough money/time)*?* • **For all** (= Despite) *her qualifications, she's still useless at the job.*

for PAYMENT /£fɔːʳ, $fɔːr/ *prep* (getting) in exchange • *How much did you pay for your glasses?* • *I've sponsored her £1 for every mile that she runs.* • *She sold the house for quite a lot of money.* • *They've said they'll repair my car for £300.* • *I wouldn't do his job for* **(all) the world** (= I would hate it)*!*

for REPRESENTING /£fɔːʳ, $fɔːr/ *prep* representing (a company, country, etc.) • *She works for a charity.* • *He used to swim for his country when he was younger.* • *I had to give a talk at a conference for my boss who was ill.*

for TOWARDS /£fɔːʳ, $fɔːr/ *prep* towards; in the direction of • *They looked as if they were heading for the train station.* • *Just follow signs for the town centre.* • *This time tomorrow we'll be setting off for the States.* • *It says this train is for* (= going to stop at) *Birmingham and Coventry only.*

for MEANING /£fɔːʳ, $fɔːr/ *prep* showing meaning • *What's the Spanish word for 'vegetarian'?* • *What does the 'M.J.'* **stand** *for? Maria Jose?*

for TO GET /£fɔːʳ, $fɔːr/ *prep* in order to get or achieve • *I hate waiting for public transport.* • *I had to run for the bus.* • *Did you send off for details of the competition?* • *I've applied for a job with another computer company.* • *He's trying for (Br and Aus) a first/(Am) first honours in his exams.*

for DUTY /£fɔːʳ, $fɔːr/ *prep* the duty or responsibility of • *As to whether you should marry him – that's for you to decide.* • *It's not for me to tell her what she should do with her life.*

for BECAUSE /£fɔːʳ, $fɔːr/ *conjunction dated or literary* because; as • *She remained silent, for her heart was heavy and her spirits low.* • *"Father forgive them for they know not what they do"* (Bible, Luke 23.34)

for IN TROUBLE /£fɔːʳ, $fɔːr/ *prep* **for it** *infml esp. humorous dated* in trouble • *I'll be for it if Hilary finds out I've been late every day this week!* • Compare **for the high jump** at HIGH DISTANCE.

for·age /£ˈfɒr·ɪdʒ, $ˈfɔːr-/ *v* [I] to go from place to place searching, esp. for food • *She could hear him in the kitchen, noisily foraging* **(about/around) for** *dinner leftovers.* • *The children had been living on the streets, foraging* **for** *scraps and sleeping rough.* • *The pigs foraged in the woods* **for** *acorns.*

for·age /£ˈfɒr·ɪdʒ, $ˈfɔːr-/ *n* [U] • Forage is food grown for horses and farm animals: *winter forage* ○ *forage crops.*

for·ay /£ˈfɒr·eɪ, $ˈfɔːr-/ *n* [C] the act of an army suddenly and quickly entering the area belonging to the enemy in order to attack them or steal their supplies, or (by people in general) a brief involvement in an activity which is different from and outside the range of a usual set of activities • *The soldiers* **made** *the first of several forays* **into** *enemy-occupied territory.* • *She* **made** *a brief foray* **into** *acting before starting a career as a teacher.* • *(infml)* A foray to a particular place is a short visit, esp. with a known purpose: *I* **made** *a quick foray* **into** *town before lunch to get my sister a present.*

for·bear STOP YOURSELF /£fɔːˈbeəʳ, $fɔːrˈber/ *v past simple* **forbore** /£fɔːˈbɔːʳ, $fɔːrˈbɔːr/, *past part* **forborne** /£fɔːˈbɔːn, $fɔːrˈbɔːrn/ *fml dated* to prevent yourself from saying or doing something, esp. in a way that shows control, good judgment or kindness to others • *His plan was such a success that even his original critics could scarcely forbear* **from** *congratulating him.* • *The doctor said she was optimistic about the outcome of the operation but forbore* **to** *make any promises at this early stage.* [+ *to* infinitive]

for·bear·ance /£fɔːˈbeə·rᵊnts, $fɔːr-/ *n* [U] *fml dated* • Forbearance is the quality of patience, forgiveness and self-control shown in a difficult situation: *He thanked his employees for the forbearance* **(that)** *they had shown during the company's difficult times.* [+ *(that)* clause]

for·bear·ing /£fɔːˈbeə·rɪŋ, $fɔːrˈber·ɪŋ/ *adj fml dated* • Someone who is forbearing is patient and forgiving: *The vicar praised what he called her "kind and forbearing nature".*

for·bear PERSON /£ˈfɔː·beəʳ, $ˈfɔːr·ber/ *n* [C usually pl] a FOREBEAR

for·bid *(obj)* /£fəˈbɪd, $fɚ-/ *v* **forbidding**, *past simple* **forbade** /£fəˈbæd, $fɚ-/ or *old use* **forbad**, *past part* **forbidden** /£fəˈbɪd·ᵊn, $fɚ-/ to refuse to allow (something), esp. officially, or to prevent (a particular plan of action) by making it impossible • *The law forbids the sale of cigarettes to people under the age of 16.* [T] • *Driving has been forbidden in the town centre.* [+ v-*ing*] • *He's obviously quite embarrassed about it because he forbade me* **to** *tell anyone.* [+ obj + *to* infinitive] • *(fml) She forbade her children television/forbade television* **to** *her children because she thought it was a corrupting influence.* [+ two objects] • *(fml) I should like to do more sightseeing but this hot climate forbids it.* [T] • **God/heaven forbid** means 'I hope it does not happen': *Heaven forbid* **(that)** *his parents should ever hear he lost his wallet with £50 in it.* [+ *(that)* clause] ○ *"Will she find out about it?" "Heaven forbid!"*

for·bid·den /£fəˈbɪd·ᵊn, $fɚ-/ *adj* • Something which is forbidden is not permitted, esp. by law: *Smoking is forbidden in the cinema.* ○ *We don't talk about politics at home – it's forbidden* **territory/ground** *because we all disagree.* ○ *Sport is a forbidden* **subject** *when Marcus is here – he hates it.* • *(literary)* When people talk about **forbidden fruit** they mean something, esp. sexual, which has a greater attraction because it is not allowed: *Other men's wives were irresistible to him – the forbidden fruit that he longed to taste.*

for·bid·ding /£fə'bɪd·ɪŋ, $fə-/ *adj* unfriendly and likely to be unpleasant or harmful • *Concealed by a forbidding row of security guards, the pop-star left the building.* • *With storm clouds rushing over them, the mountains looked dark and forbidding.*

for·bid·ding·ly /£fə'bɪd·ɪŋ·li, $fə-/ *adv* • *The water looked forbiddingly cold.*

for·bore /£fɔː'bɔːʳ, $fɔːr'bɔːr/ *past simple of* FORBEAR (STOP YOURSELF)

for·borne /£fɔː'bɔːn, $fɔːr'bɔːrn/ *past participle of* FORBEAR (STOP YOURSELF)

force PHYSICAL POWER /£fɔːs, $fɔːrs/ *n* physical, esp. violent, strength or power • *The force of the wind had brought down a great many trees in the area.* [U] • *She slapped his face with unexpected force.* [U] • *Sometimes the window gets stuck and you have to use a bit of force to get it open.* [U] • *Teachers aren't allowed to use force in controlling their pupils.* [U] • Force also refers to being present **in** large numbers: *The anti-nuclear protesters had turned up at the meeting* **in** *force.* [U] ○ *The police were able to control the crowd by sheer force* **of numbers** (= because there were more police than there were people in the crowd). [U] • *(specialized)* In scientific use, force is (a measure of) the influence which changes movement: *the force of gravity* [C/U] • If you **combine/join forces (with** someone), you work with them in order to achieve something which you both want. • If you **force-feed** a person or an animal, you make them eat and drink, often sending food to the stomach through a pipe in the mouth: *In those days prisoners who refused to eat were always force-fed.* ○ *(fig.) The whole nation was force-fed government propaganda about how well the country was doing.* • *"May the force be with you"* (phrase from the film *Star Wars*, 1977)

force *obj* /£fɔːs, $fɔːrs/ *v* [T] • *Move your leg up gently when you're doing this exercise but don't force it.* • *If you force the zip it will only break.* • *She forced her way through the crowds, pushing people aside and ignoring their insults.* • To force a lock, door, window, etc. is to break it in order to allow someone to get in: *I forgot my key, so I had to force a window.* ○ *The police had forced* **open** *the door because nobody had answered.* [+ obj + adj] ○ *The burglar forced* **an entry** (= broke a window, door, etc. to get into the house).

for·ci·ble /£'fɔː·sɪ·bl̩, $'fɔːr-/ *adj* • Forcible actions involve the use of physical power or of violence: *The police's forcible entry into the building has come under a lot of criticism.*

for·ci·bly /£'fɔː·sɪ·bli, $'fɔːr-/ *adv* • *Several rioters were forcibly removed from the town square.*

force INFLUENCE /£fɔːs, $fɔːrs/ *n* (a person or thing with a lot of) influence and energy • *Everyone who worked with her was struck by the sheer force of her personality.* [U] • *He was a powerful force in British politics during the war years.* [C] • *A united Europe, he said, would be a great force in world affairs.* [C] • If an organization or a person is described as a **force to be reckoned with** it means that they are powerful and have a lot of influence: *The United Nations is now a force to be reckoned with.* • *Poverty and ignorance, the bishop said, were the* **forces of evil** *in our society today.* • *I always check that I've got money with me when I leave home – just from* **force of habit** *really* (= it is something that I do because I've always done it). • *(literary) Fishermen are always at the mercy of* **the forces of nature** (= bad weather conditions).

force·ful /£'fɔːs·fəl, $'fɔːrs-/ *adj* • *The opposition leader led a very forceful attack on the government in parliament this morning.* • *She has a very forceful personality which will serve her well in politics.*

force·fully /£'fɔːs·fəl·i, $'fɔːrs-/ *adv* • *He argued forcefully that stricter laws were necessary to deal with the problem.*

force·ful·ness /£'fɔːs·fəl·nəs, $'fɔːrs-/ *n* [U] • *They were persuaded by the forcefulness of his argument.*

for·ci·ble /£'fɔː·sɪ·bl̩, $'fɔːr-/ *adj* • *An upturned car by the roadside served as a forcible* (= effective) **reminder** *to me not to drive fast on country roads.*

force *obj* DO UNWILLINGLY /£fɔːs, $fɔːrs/ *v* [T] to (cause to) do something difficult, unpleasant or unusual, esp. by threatening or not offering the possibility of choice • *I really have to force myself* **to** *be pleasant to him.* [+ obj + *to* infinitive] • *You can't force her* **to** *make a decision – she's got to do it on her own.* [+ obj + *to* infinitive] • *Hospitals are being forced* **to** *close departments because of lack of money.* [+ obj + *to* infinitive] • If you force a laugh or a smile you manage, with difficulty, to laugh or smile although it involves a lot of effort: *He had to force a smile as he said goodbye.* • *You could tell he was having to force* **back** *the tears* (= stop himself from crying) *as he gave his resignation speech.* [M] • *I didn't actually want any more dessert, but Julia forced it* **on** *me*(= caused me to accept it). • *I couldn't stay at their flat – I'd feel as if I was forcing* **myself on** *them* (= causing them to allow me to stay). • *"Thank you," he said, forcing* **out** (= saying with difficulty) *the words unwillingly.* [M] • *You never tell me your feelings about anything – I have to force it* **out of** *you* (= cause you to tell me)*!* • If you **force** someone's **hand**, you make them do something they do not want to do, or act sooner than they had intended: *The President will not allow public unrest to force his hand.* • To force an **issue** is to take action to make certain that an urgent problem or matter is dealt with now: *If the management wouldn't listen to their demands they would have to force the issue by striking.* • If plants or vegetables are forced, they are made to grow faster by artificially controlling growing conditions such as the amount of heat and light: *forced strawberries*

forced /£fɔːst, $fɔːrst/ *adj* [not gradable] • An action which is forced is done because it is suddenly made necessary by a new and usually unexpected situation: *The aeroplane had to make a forced* **landing** *because one of the engines cut out.* • Forced **laughter** or a forced **smile** is produced with effort and not sincerely felt: *She tried hard to smile but suspected that it looked forced.*

for·ci·ble /£'fɔː·sɪ·bl̩, $'fɔːr-/ *adj* • *There's a law to protect refugees from forcible return to countries where they face persecution.*

force IN OPERATION /£fɔːs, $fɔːrs/ *n* [U] **in/into force** (of laws, rules or systems) existing and being used; in operation • *The new telephone charges aren't in force yet.* • *The new driving regulations are going to* **come/be brought** *into force later this year.*

force GROUP /£fɔːs, $fɔːrs/ *n* [C often pl] a group of people organized and trained, esp. for military, police or a stated purpose • *the Air Force* • *the security forces* • *the labour force* • *the work force* • *a task force* • *He joined the* **police** *force straight after school.* • **The (armed) forces** are the military organizations for air, land and sea: *Large reductions in the armed forces are planned for the next five years.* ○ *Elvis Presley joined/went into the forces in 1958.*

ford /£fɔːd, $fɔːrd/ *n* [C] an area in a river or stream which is not deep and can be crossed on foot or in a vehicle

ford *obj* /£fɔːd, $fɔːrd/ *v* [T] • *The trucks forded the river* (= crossed at a place where it was not deep) *without any problems, although there was a strong current.*

ford·ab·le /£'fɔː·də·bl̩, $'fɔːr-/ *adj* [not gradable] • *The river wasn't fordable because of all the recent rainfall.*

fore /£fɔːʳ, $fɔːr/ *adj* [before n], *adv* (esp. on ships) towards or in the front • *the fore cabin* • *There was damage from the torpedos both fore and aft.*

fore– /£fɔːʳ, $fɔːr/ *combining form* • *the forelegs of a horse* • *the foreground of a picture*

fore /£fɔːʳ, $fɔːr/ *n* [U] • **The fore** means public attention or a noticeable position: *Various ecological issues have come* **to** *the fore since the discovery of the hole in the Earth's ozone layer.* ○ *The prime minister has deliberately brought* **to** *the fore those ministers with a more caring image.* • See also FOREFRONT.

fore·arm /£'fɔː·rɑːm, $'fɔːr·ɑːrm/ *n* [C] the lower part of the arm, between the wrist and the ELBOW

fore·armed /£fɔː'rɑːmd, $fɔːr'ɑːrmd/ *adj* **forewarned is forearmed**, see at FOREWARN

fore·bear, **for·bear** /£'fɔː·beəʳ, $'fɔːr·ber/ *n* [C usually pl] *fml or literary* a relative who lived in the past; an ANCESTOR • *Many of us conform to the outdated customs laid down by our forebears.*

fore·bod·ing /£fɔː'bəʊ·dɪŋ, $fɔːr'boʊ-/ *n literary* a feeling that something very bad is going to happen soon • *There's a* **sense of** *foreboding in the capital as if fighting might at any minute break out.* [U] • *Her forebodings about the future were to prove justified.* [C] • *He had a strange foreboding* **(that)** *something would go wrong.* [C + *(that)* clause]

fore·cast /£'fɔː·kɑːst, $'fɔːr·kæst/ *n* [C] a statement of what is judged likely to happen in the future, esp. in connection with a particular situation, or of the expected weather conditions • *The government's confident forecast* **that** *inflation would drop this year has proved wrong.* [+

that clause] • *She* **gave** *a very depressing* **economic** *forecast last night on the radio.* • *Have you heard the* **(weather)** *forecast* **for** *this afternoon?* • *The* **(weather)** *forecast says it's going to rain later today.*

fore·cast *obj* /£'fɔː·kaːst, $'fɔːr·kæst/ *v* [T] *past* **forecast** or **forecasted** • *They forecast a large drop in unemployment over the next two years.* • *Snow has been forecast* **for** *tonight.* • *Environmentalists forecast* **(that)** *we will destroy the planet if we carry on polluting it as we are today.* [+ (*that*) clause] • *Oil prices are forecast* **to** *increase by less than 2% this year.* [+ obj + *to* infinitive]

fore·cast·er /£'fɔː·kaː·stəʳ, $'fɔːr·kæs·tɚ/ *n* [C] • A forecaster is a person who tells you what particular conditions are expected to be like: *an economic forecaster* ○ *a weather forecaster*

fore·close *(obj)* TAKE POSSESSION /£fɔː'kləuz, $fɔːr'klouz/ *v specialized* (esp. of banks) to take back property that was bought with borrowed money because the money was not being paid back as formally agreed • *In a recession banks tend to foreclose* **on** *businesses that are in financial difficulty.* [I] • *Their building society has foreclosed their mortgage.* [T]

fore·clo·sure /£fɔː'kləu·ʒəʳ, $fɔːr'klou·ʒɚ/ *n* [U]

fore·close *obj* PREVENT /£fɔː'kləuz, $fɔːr'klouz/ *v* [T] *rather fml* to prevent (something) from being considered as a possibility in the future • *The president said he had not entirely foreclosed the possibility of a military solution.* • *The leader's aggressive stance seems to have foreclosed any chance of diplomatic compromise.*

fore·court /£'fɔː·kɔːt, $'fɔːr·kɔːrt/ *n* [C] a flat area in front of a large building • *the garage forecourt* • *I'll pick you up in the station forecourt.* • *(specialized)* In sports such as tennis the forecourt is the area next to the net.

fore·doomed /£fɔː'duːmd, $fɔːr-/ *adj literary* (esp. of planned activities) going to fail; extremely unlucky from the beginning • *With some actors falling ill and others leaving the company, the whole play seemed foredoomed.* • *The whole project seemed foredoomed* **to** *failure from the start.*

fore·fath·ers /£'fɔːˌfaː·ðəz, $'fɔːrˌfaː·ðɚz/ *pl n literary* relatives who lived in the past • *He went to visit the graves of his forefathers.*

fore·fing·er /£'fɔːˌfɪŋ·gəʳ, $'fɔːrˌfɪŋ·gɚ/, **in·dex fin·ger** *n* [C] the finger next to the thumb

fore·foot /£'fɔː·fʊt, $'fɔːr-/ *n* [C] *pl* **forefeet** /£'fɔː·fiːt, $'fɔːr-/ one of the two front feet of a four-legged animal

fore·front /£'fɔː·frʌnt, $'fɔːr-/ *n* [U] **the forefront** the most noticeable position • *She was one of the politicians* **at/in** *the forefront* **of** *the campaign to free the prisoners.* • *His team are* **at** *the forefront* **of** *scientific research into vaccines.*

fore·go *obj* /£fɔː'gəu, $fɔːr'gou/ *v* [T] he/she/it **foregoes**, **foregoing**, *past simple* **forewent** /£fɔː'went, $fɔːr-/, *past part* **foregone** /£fɔː'gɒn, $fɔːr'gaːn/ to FORGO

fore·go·ing /£fɔː'gəu·ɪŋ, $fɔːr'gou·ɪŋ/ *n* [U] **the foregoing** *fml* what has just been mentioned or described • *I can testify to the foregoing since I was actually present when it happened.*

fore·go·ing /£fɔː'gəu·ɪŋ, $fɔːr'gou·ɪŋ/ *adj* [before n] *fml* • *The foregoing account was written fifty years after the incident.*

fore·gone con·clu·sion /£'fɔː·gɒn-, $'fɔːr·gaːn-/ *n* a result that is obvious to everyone even before it happens • *The results of the general election next week now seem (like) a foregone conclusion.*

fore·ground /£'fɔː·graund, $'fɔːr-/ *n* [C] the people, objects, countryside, etc. in a picture or photograph that seem nearest to you and form its main part • **In the** *foreground of the painting is a horse and cart.* • *(fig.) Celebrated the world over for his writing, he still refused to put himself* **in the** *foreground* (= where he would attract attention). • Compare BACKGROUND.

fore·ground *obj* /£'fɔː·graund, $'fɔːr-/ *v* [T] • *His speech foregrounded* (= gave particular importance to) *the history of the decision.*

fore·hand /£'fɔː·hænd, $'fɔːr-/ *n* [C] (in sports such as tennis) a hit in which the PALM (= fleshy side) of the hand which is holding the RACKET (= piece of equipment used for hitting) faces the same direction as the hit itself, or the player's ability to perform this hit • *Ortega has probably the most powerful forehand of anyone in this tournament.* • *... and what a marvellous forehand that was by Lewis!* • If, in tennis, etc., you send the ball to the other player's forehand, you send it to the side on which they are holding the RACKET. • Compare BACKHAND.

fore·head /£'fɒr·ɪd, £'fɔː·hed, $'faː·rɪd/ *n* [C] the flat part of the face, above the eyes and below the hair • *She's got a* **high** *forehead.* • PIC〉 **Body**

for·eign /£'fɒr·ən, $'fɔːr-/ *adj* [not gradable] belonging or connected to a country which is not your own • *Spain was the first foreign country she had visited.* • *I wish I had learned more foreign languages at school.* • *His work provided him with the opportunity for a lot of foreign travel.* • *She's a former foreign correspondent for the Financial Times newspaper.* • *(literary)* Something can be described as foreign **to** a particular person if it is unknown to them or not within their experience: *The whole concept of democracy, she claimed, was utterly foreign to the present government.* • An object or substance which has entered something else, possibly by accident, and does not belong there is sometimes described as foreign: *a foreign object/substance* ○ *foreign matter* ○ *At the hospital they cleaned the cut thoroughly to stop any foreign bodies from getting into my arm.* • **Foreign affairs** are matters that are connected with other countries: *the minister of foreign affairs* • **Foreign aid** is the help that is given by esp. a richer country to esp. a poorer one, usually in the form of money. • **Foreign exchange** is the system by which the type of money used in one country is exchanged for another country's money, making international trade easier: *On the foreign-exchange markets the pound remained firm.* • In Britain, **the Foreign Office** is the department of the government which deals with Britain's connections with other countries. • *(literary)* **Foreign soil** is another country: *He spent 30 years in exile* **on** *foreign soil.* ○ *I was 28 the first time my feet touched foreign soil.*

for·eign·er /£'fɒr·ə·nəʳ, $'fɔːr·ə·nɚ/ *n* [C] • A foreigner is a person who comes from another country: *With his northerner's blond hair and pale skin he felt such a foreigner in this hot southern country.*

fore·know·ledge /£fɔː'nɒl·ɪdʒ, $fɔːr'naː·lɪdʒ/ *n* [U] *fml* knowledge of an event before it happens • *The ministers who left the government before the scandal obviously had foreknowledge of the affair.*

fore·leg /£'fɔː·leg, $'fɔːr-/ *n* [C] one of the two front legs of a four-legged animal • PIC〉 **Dogs**

fore·lock /£'fɔː·lɒk, $'fɔːr·laːk/ *n* [C] a piece of hair which grows or falls over the FOREHEAD • *a horse's forelock* • To **tug at/touch** one's **forelock** is to show respect to someone in a higher position than you in a way that seems old-fashioned.

fore·man (*pl* **-men**), **fore·wo·man** (*pl* **-women**) /£'fɔː·mən, $'fɔːr-, -ˌwʊm·ən/ *n* [C] a skilled person with experience who is in charge of and watches over a group of workers, or (in a court of law) one of the JURY (= the twelve people giving their decision on the case) who is chosen to be in charge of their discussions and to speak officially for them • (DK)

fore·most /£'fɔː·məust, $'fɔːr·moust/ *adj* [not gradable] most important or best; leading • *This gallery and cinema is described as one of the country's foremost experimental arts centres.* • *She's one of the foremost experts on child psychology.*

fore·name /£'fɔː·neɪm, $'fɔːr-/ *n* [C] *fml* the name which is chosen for you at birth and goes before the family name

fo·ren·sic /fə'ren·zɪk/ *adj* [before n; not gradable] used to discover information about a crime by scientifically examining the objects or substances that are involved in the crime • *forensic* **evidence/medicine/science** • *Forensic examination revealed a large quantity of poison in the dead man's stomach.*

fo·ren·sics /fə'ren·zɪks/ *n* [U] • Forensics is the study of the physical information connected with crime: *She's always been interested in studying forensics.* • *(infml)* Forensics is also the place where physical information about a crime is tested scientifically: *The blood-stained clothing was sent to forensics for examination.*

fore·play /£'fɔː·pleɪ, $'fɔːr-/ *n* [U] sexual activity such as kissing and touching each other, before **sexual intercourse**

fore·run·ner /£'fɔːˌrʌn·əʳ, $'fɔːrˌrʌn·ɚ/ *n* [C] something or someone that acts as a early and less advanced model for what will appear in the future, or a warning or sign of what is to follow • *Germany's Green party was said to be the forerunner* **of** *environmental parties throughout Europe.* • *The drop in share prices in March was a forerunner* **of** *the financial crash that followed in June.*

fore·see *obj* /£fə'siː, $fɚ-/ *v* [T] *past simple* **foresaw** /£fə'sɔː, $fɚ'sɑː/, *past part* **foreseen** /£fɚ'siːn, $fɚ-/ to know about (something) before it happens • *I don't foresee* (=expect) *any difficulties so long as we keep within the project's budget.* • *It's impossible to foresee exactly* **how** *our actions will affect the future.* [+ *wh-* word] • *He foresaw* **that** *the future with Margot was going to be one long battle.* [+ *that* clause]

fore·see·ab·le /£fɔː'siː·ə·bl̩, $fɔːr-/ *adj* • A foreseeable event or situation is one that can be known or guessed about before it happens: *The company can only blame itself for the entirely foreseeable mess that it is now in.* • **The foreseeable future** is as far into the future as you can imagine or plan for: *I don't know about forever but I'll carry on living in this city* **for** *the foreseeable future.* ○ *He asked me if there was any point* **in** *the foreseeable future when I'd like to have children.*

fore·shad·ow *obj* /£fɔː'ʃæd·əʊ, $fɔːr'ʃæd·oʊ/ *v* [T] *esp. literary* to act as a warning or sign of (a future event) • *The recent outbreak of violence was foreshadowed by isolated incidents in the city earlier this year.* • *We have not yet seen proof of the radical reforms that were foreshadowed in the president's speech.*

fore·shore /£'fɔː·ʃɔːʳ, $'fɔːr·ʃɔːr/ *n* [U] **the foreshore** *specialized* the part of the SHORE (=land at the edge of the sea) which is between the limits reached by high and low TIDE (=the sea's natural movement in and out), or any part of the shore that has neither grass on it nor buildings • *birds of the foreshore*

fore·short·ened /£fɔː'ʃɔː·tᵊnd, $fɔːr'ʃɔːr·t̬ᵊnd/ *adj* (of forms represented in pictures), drawn, painted or appearing with part of the form shorter or smaller in order to show that it is further in the distance

fore·short·en *obj* /£fɔː'ʃɔː·tᵊn, $fɔːr'ʃɔːr·t̬ᵊnd/ *v* [T] • *In the fresco, the flying figure is severely foreshortened.* • *(fig.) Smoking was certainly one of the factors that foreshortened* (=reduced/shortened) *his life.*

fore·sight /£'fɔː·saɪt, $'fɔːr-/ *n* [U] the ability to judge correctly what is going to happen in the future and plan your actions based on this knowledge • *She'd had the foresight to sell her house just before house prices came down.*

fore·skin /£'fɔː·skɪn, $'fɔːr-/ *n* [C] the loose skin which covers the end of the penis

for·est /£'fɒr·ɪst, $'fɔːr-/ *n* a large area of land covered with trees and plants, usually larger than a wood, or the trees and plants themselves • *the Black Forest* [C] • *The children got lost* **in** *the forest.* [C] • *Much of the country is covered by forest.* [U] • *Many of our forests have disappeared over the years because we chopped them down for wood.* [C] • *They saw deer in a forest clearing.* • *"Down in the forest something stirred"* (from the song *Down in the Forest* written by Harold Simpson, 1906)

for·est·er /£'fɒr·ɪ·stəʳ, $'fɔːr·ɪ·stɚ/ *n* [C] • A forester is a person who is in charge of taking care of a forest.

for·es·try /£'fɒr·ɪ·stri, $'fɔːr-/ *n* [U] • Forestry is the science of planting and taking care of large areas of trees.

fore·stall *obj* /£fɔː'stɔːl, $fɔːr'stɑːl/ *v* [T] to prevent (something) from happening by acting first • *The government forestalled criticism by holding a public enquiry into the matter.*

fore·taste /£'fɔː·teɪst, $'fɔːr-/ *n* something that gives you an idea of what something else is like by letting you experience a small example of it in advance • *The poet read out a poem as a foretaste* **of** *her new collection, to be published soon.* • *The recent factory closures and job losses are just a foretaste of the recession that is to come.*

fore·tell *obj* /£fɔː'tel, $fɔːr-/ *v* [T] *past* **foretold** /£fɔː'təʊld, $fɔːr'toʊld/ *literary* to state (what is going to happen in the future) • *He was a sixteenth-century prophet who foretold* **how** *the world would end.* [+ *wh-* word] • *I think it's a good thing that we can't foretell* **the future** – *I don't really want to know about disasters waiting to happen!*

fore·thought /£'fɔː·θɔːt, $'fɔːr·θɑːt/ *n* [U] the good judgment to consider the near future in your present actions; planning in advance • *I'm glad I had the forethought to make a copy of the letter, as proof of what had been promised.* • *I wish you'd had the forethought to go to the bank for some money before the weekend.*

for·ev·er, *Br also* **for ev·er** /£fə're·vəʳ, $fɔː'rev·ɚ/ *adv* [not gradable] for all time; without ending • *I like the house but I don't imagine I'll live there forever.* • *Written on the wall were the words, 'Maria + Paul, forever'.* • *(infml)* Forever can be used to mean continually, often in a way that suggests too often: *She's forever telling him she's going to leave him but she never actually does.* • *(infml)* Forever can also mean for an extremely long time or too much time: *We'd better walk a bit quicker – it's going to* **take** *forever if we go at this pace.* • *"Forever Young"* (film title, 1983) • *"On a Clear Day you can see Forever"* (title of a song written by Alan Jay Lerner, 1965) • LP **Periods of time**

fore·warn *obj* /£fɔː'wɔːn, $fɔːr'wɔːrn/ *v* [T] to tell (someone) that something unpleasant is going to happen • *There was no-one left in the village. They had obviously been forewarned* **about** *the raid.* • *The employees had been forewarned* **(that)** *the end-of-year financial results would be poor.* [+ obj + (*that*) clause] • *(saying)* 'Forewarned is forearmed' means that if you know about something before it happens, you can be prepared for it.

fore·word /£'fɔː·wɜːd, $'fɔːr·wɜːrd/ *n* [C] a short piece of writing at the beginning of a book, sometimes praise by a famous person or someone who is not the writer • *The book has a foreword by the President.*

for·feit /£'fɔː·fɪt, $'fɔːr-/ *v*, *n* to give up or lose (something) if something goes wrong, or the thing (to be) given up • *She forfeited her* **chance** *of entering the competition by not posting her form in time.* [T] • *We had to forfeit the deposit on our holiday when we changed our plans.* [T] • If you **pay a** forfeit, you give up something, esp. in a game. [C]

for·feit /£'fɔː·fɪt, $'fɔːr-/ *adj* [after v; not gradable] • *The situation was dangerous and she felt her life* **was**/*might* **be** *forfeit* (=likely to be lost).

for·fei·ture /£'fɔː·fɪ·tʃəʳ, $'fɔːr·fɪ·tʃɚ/ *n* • Forfeiture is the loss of rights, property or money, esp. as a result of breaking a legal agreement: *He was deep in debt and faced with forfeiture of his property.* [U] ○ *Judge Thomas said that he could not rule out the possibility of forfeitures in this case.* [C] ○ *The defendants face stiff forfeiture penalties after having been found guilty of breaking their contractual agreement on several counts.*

for·gave /£fə'geɪv, $fɚ-/ *past simple of* FORGIVE

forge *obj* COPY /£fɔːdʒ, $fɔːrdʒ/ *v* [T] to make an illegal copy of (something) in order to deceive • *She forged his signature on the cheque/painting.* • *They are forging all kinds of documents to a high standard.* • *Immigration control noticed the forged passport.* • *A number of forged works of art have been sold as genuine.* • LP **Crimes and criminals**

forg·er /£'fɔː·dʒəʳ, $'fɔːr·dʒɚ/ *n* [C] • *The paintings had been produced by a clever art forger.*

for·ger·y /£'fɔː·dʒəʳr·i, $'fɔːr·dʒɚ·i/ *n* • *These banknotes are forgeries.* [C] • *He increased his income by forgery.* [U]

forge WORK AREA /£fɔːdʒ, $fɔːrdʒ/ *n* [C] a working area with a fire for heating metal until it is soft enough to be beaten into different shapes • *a blacksmith's forge* • *the heat of the forge* • *the house next to the forge*

forg·ing /£'fɔː·dʒɪŋ, $'fɔːr-/ *n* [C] • A forging is a metal object which has been made in a forge.

forge *obj* MAKE /£fɔːdʒ, $fɔːrdʒ/ *v* [T] to make or produce, esp. with some difficulty • *The accident forged a* **bond/link** *between the two families.* • *She forged a new career for herself as a singer.*

forge MOVE /£fɔːdʒ, $fɔːrdʒ/ *v* [I always + adv/prep] to suddenly and quickly move forward • *She forged round the bend/down the straight/into the water.* • *The visiting team has forged* **into the lead** *with 100 points.* • *Medical science has forged* **ahead** *in the last twenty years.*

for·get *(obj)* /£fə'get, $fɚ-/ *v* **forgetting**, *past simple* **forgot** /£fə'gɒt, $fɚ'gɑːt/, *past part* **forgotten** /£fə'gɒt·ᵊn, $fɚ'gɑː·t̬ᵊn/ to be unable to remember, fail to remember or decide not to remember • *I'm sorry, I've forgotten your name.* [T] • *Let me write down that date before I forget* **(about** *it).* [I] • *Don't forget* **to** *leave a space.* [+ *to* infinitive] • *We had forgotten* **(that)** *she doesn't come on Thursdays.* [+ (*that*) clause] • *I'm sorry, I was forgetting* (=I had forgotten) **(that)** *you would be away in August.* [+ (*that*) clause] • *She never forgot see***ing** *the Himalayas for the first time.* [+ v-*ing*] • *She forgot* **about** *book***ing** *the ticket.* [I] • *I've forgotten* **what** *you do next/***how** *to do it.* [+ *wh-* word] • *He tried to forget* (=not think about) *her.* [T] • *I've forgotten* (=unintentionally not brought) *my keys.* [T] • *I never forget* **a face** (=I'm good at remembering people). [T] • If you forget something you do not continue with it or do it: *It seemed unlikely that the debt would ever be paid so we quietly forgot* **(about)** *it.* [T; I + *about*] ○ *We'll have to forget* **(about) the whole thing** (=we can't continue with the plan). [T; I + *about*] ○ *"I'd like to take a week's holiday."*

Forget it, we're too busy." [T] • **Forget it** also means 'don't worry about it' or it's not important: *"I'm sorry I've broken the cup." "Forget it."* • **And don't you forget it** is a strong way of telling someone how they should behave: *That's the rule and don't you forget it!* • If you **forget** your**self**, you act in a socially unacceptable way: *He was so angry he forgot himself and swore loudly.* • *This is where we keep all the books,* **not forgetting** (= including) *the magazines and newspapers.* • *"Lest we forget"* (Rudyard Kipling in the poem *Recessional*, 1897) • LP› **Memory**

for·get·ful /£fə'get·fəl, $fɚ-/ *adj* • *She worries because her mother's getting very forgetful* (= doesn't remember things). • *(fml) He has become very forgetful* **of** (= he gives no attention to) *his duties.*

for·get·ful·ly /£fə'get·fəl·i, $fɚ-/ *adv*

for·get·ful·ness /£fə'get·fəl·nəs, $fɚ-/ *n* [U]

for·get·ta·ble /£fə'get·ə·bl̩, $fɚ'geṭ-/ *adj* • Forgettable means not important or good enough to be remembered: *a forgettable film/song* ○ *Dennis White scored the only goal in an otherwise forgettable match.*

for·get–me–not /£fə'get·mi·nɒt, $fɚ'get·mi·nɑːt/ *n* [C] a small garden plant with blue or pink flowers which grows from seed every year

for·give *obj* /£fə'gɪv, $fɚ-/ *v* [T not *be forgiving*] *past simple* **forgave** /£fə'geɪv, $fɚ-/, *past part* **forgiven** /£fə'gɪv·ən, $fɚ-/ to stop blaming or being angry with (someone) for something they have done, or to ask someone not to be angry with you • *She never forgave him* **for** *his lies/ruining her holiday.* • *We forgave him* **(for)** *the unpleasantness* (= for causing the unpleasantness) *because he was so young.* [+ two objects] • *(fml disapproving) Forgive me, but I thought you said you were leaving on Sunday (not Saturday).* • *There's nothing to forgive.* • *(saying)* 'Forgive and forget' means to stop being angry and stop remembering something unpleasant which happened. • *"God may forgive you but I never can"* (Queen Elizabeth I of England, 1533-1603) • LP› **Two objects**

for·giv·ab·le /£fə'gɪv·ə·bl̩, $fɚ-/ *adj* • *Handwritten 'n' and 'm' are easily confused – it was a forgivable mistake* (= a mistake which was easy to make).

for·give·ness /£fə'gɪv·nəs, $fɚ-/ *n* [U] • Forgiveness is the act of forgiving or the willingness to forgive: *to deserve/ask for/beg forgiveness*

for·giv·ing /£fə'gɪv·ɪŋ, $fɚ-/ *adj* • Someone who is forgiving is willing to forgive.

for·go *obj*, **fore·go** /£fɔː'gəʊ, $fɔːr'goʊ/ *v* [T] he/she/it **forgoes**, **forgoing**, *past simple* **forwent** /£fɔː'went, $fɔːr-/, *past part* **forgone** /£fɔː'gɒn, $fɔːr'gɑːn/ *fml or humorous* to stop having or not do something • *I'll have to forgo the* **pleasure/opportunity** *of seeing you this week.* • *I'm not forgoing the* **chance** *of a free ticket.* • A **forgone conclusion** is something which is certain to happen: *"She passed her driving test." "Well, it was a foregone conclusion."*

fork TOOL /£fɔːk, $fɔːrk/ *n* [C] any of several types of tool with a handle and an end part divided into two or more usually pointed pieces • *You eat with a* **knife and** *fork.* • *Dig up the plants with a* **(garden)** *fork.* • A **fork-lift (truck)** is a small vehicle which has two strong bars of metal fixed to the front used for lifting piles of goods. • See also PITCHFORK. • PIC› **Cutlery, Fork, Garden, Vehicles**

fork *obj* /£fɔːk, $fɔːrk/ *v* [T] • *She forked a pattern* (= made a pattern with a fork) *on the top of the cake. He forked the fertilizer* (= put it with a fork) *round the shrubs.* • *Fork* **(up)** (= lift with a fork) *the meringue into peaks.* [T/M] • *Fork* **(over)** *the soil* (= break it up with a fork) *lightly.* [T/M]

forkful /£'fɔːk·fʊl, $'fɔːrk-/ *n* [C] • *a forkful of earth* • *He just sat there shovelling forkfuls* **of** *peas into his mouth.*

fork DIVISION /£fɔːk, $fɔːrk/ *n* [C] a division into usually two parts, or one of the parts • *The house is on the left just past the fork* **in** *the road.* • *Take the left/right fork* (= road on the left/right where it divides). • *Stay to the left at the first two forks but go right at the third one.* • *The bird perched near the fork* **in** *the branch.* • The **forks** of a bicycle, motorcycle, etc., are the two metal bars which support the front wheel. • PIC› **Bicycles, Fork**

fork /£fɔːk, $fɔːrk/ *v* [I] • *The pub is near where the road forks.* • *(Br) Fork* **left/right** (= go left/right) *where the road divides.* [always + adv/prep] • *(literary)* Roots and branches of trees are sometimes said to fork: *Where the*

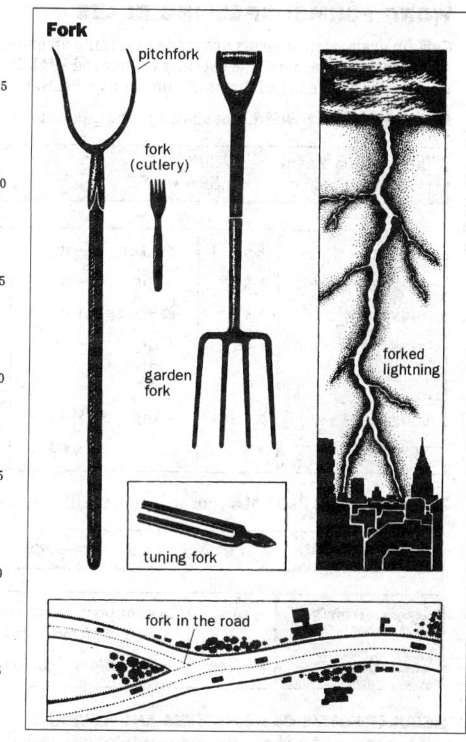

roots of the old oak had forked long ago, she found a shaded place to sit and rest.

forked /£fɔːkt, $fɔːrkt/ *adj* [not gradable] • *a forked tail/stick* • *forked lightning* • *a snake's forked tongue* • If someone speaks with a **forked tongue**, they tell lies or say one thing and mean something else. • PIC› **Fork**

fork out *(obj), Am also* **fork o·ver**, *Aus also* **fork up**, *Am also* **fork up** *v adv infml* to pay, esp. unwillingly • *I forked out ten quid* **for/on** *the ticket.* [T] • *I couldn't persuade him to fork out* **(for** *a new one).* [I] • *Leave him to me. I'll get him to fork up* **(for** *the meal)!* [I] • *Don't be mean. Fork* **(it)** *up/over!* [I/T]

for·lorn /£fə'lɔːn, $fɚ'lɔːrn/ *adj esp. literary* alone and unhappy; left alone and not cared for • *a forlorn look/face* • *a forlorn and forgotten house/garden* • A forlorn **hope/attempt** is one which has little chance of succeeding.

for·lorn·ly /£fə'lɔːn·li, $fɚ'lɔːrn·li/ *adv* • *She sat forlornly watching the sky.*

form SHAPE /£fɔːm, $fɔːrm/ *n* [C] the shape or appearance of something • *A large form blocked the doorway.* • *The large form of the guard came out of the shadows.* • *The moon highlighted the shadowy forms of the houses/hills/fir trees.* • *The lawn was laid out* **in the** *form* **of** (= in the shape of) *the figure eight.* • *The training* **takes the** *form* **of** (= consists of) *one full week and then five days spread over six months.* • Something which **takes** form is gradually seen or gradually develops to a greater degree: *Trees and hedges started to take form as the fog cleared.* ○ *The idea of a holiday together took form as they chatted.* • A form is a part of a verb, or a different but related word: *The continuous form of 'to stand' is 'to be standing'.* ○ *'Stood' is an inflected form of 'stand'.* ○ *The present participle is also called the -ing form.* ○ *'Hers' is the possessive form of 'her'.* ○ *'Isn't' is the short form of 'is not'.* • LP› **Forms of words (spelling)** GR J KOR P

form *(obj)* /£fɔːm, $fɔːrm/ *v* • *A crowd formed around the accident.* [I] • *A way out of the difficulty began to form in her mind as she listened.* [I] • *She formed the clay* **into** *a small bowl.* [T] • *I formed* **the impression/opinion/view** (= the way she behaved suggested to me) *that she didn't really want to come.* [T] • To form **up** is usually used when separate things come together to make a whole: *The children formed (up) into a square.* [I] ○ *The procession formed (up) and moved off slowly.* [I] • To form something is to make or be (a part of) it: *Vegetables and bread form the normal diet.* [L only + n] ○ *The lorries formed a barricade*

WORD FORMS: SPELLING RULES

Certain grammatical forms are made by adding an ending such as **-ing** or **-er** to the basic word: *meet, meeting ; soon, sooner*. Sometimes the spelling is changed slightly: *tie, tying ; lucky, luckier*. This dictionary does *not* show the *regular* grammatical forms of nouns or verbs. Here are the rules of how to form and spell regular forms:

REGULAR VERB FORMS (not shown in the dictionary)

third person singular:	VERB + -S	past simple:	VERB + -ED
present participle:	VERB + -ING	past participle:	VERB + -ED

ending -e	+ s	~~e~~ + ing	+ d	*wipe, wipes, wiping, wiped*
ending -ee/-oe	+ s	+ ing	+ d	*agree, agrees, agreeing, agreed*
ending -ie	+ s	~~ie~~ +ying	+ d	*tie, ties, tying, tied*
-s/ss/sh/ch/x/z	+ es	+ ing	+ ed	*miss, misses, missing, missed* *wash, washes, washing, washed* *watch, watches, watching, watched*
consonant + y	~~y~~ + ies	+ ing	~~y~~ + ied	*apply, applies, applying, applied*
vowel + y	+ s	+ ing	+ ed	*play, plays, playing, played*

REGULAR NOUN PLURALS (not shown in the dictionary)

singular: NOUN	plural: NOUN + S	*one hand, two hands*

-s/ss/sh/ch/x/z	+ es	*bus, buses; mass, masses; wish, wishes; match, matches; box, boxes*
consonant + y	~~y~~ + ies	*baby, babies; university, universities*

REGULAR FORMS OF ADJECTIVES AND ADVERBS

- When the word is short, the comparative and superlative are usually formed using the endings *-er/-est* or *-ier/-iest*. These forms are shown in full: **noisy** /ˈnɔ·ɪzi/ *adj* **noisier**, **noisiest** ; **soon** /suːn/ *adv* **sooner**, **soonest** The spelling rules for these endings are as follows:

ending -e	+ r	+ st	*wide, wider, widest*
consonant + y	~~y~~ + ier	~~y~~ + iest	*dirty, dirtier, dirtiest*
other endings	+ er	+ est	*quick, quicker, quickest* *hot, hotter, hottest**

*See the note below about consonant doubling

- When no separate comparative or superlative forms are shown, this means that the word forms its comparative and superlative by putting *more* and *most* in front: **famous** /ˈfeɪ·məs/ *adj* This is the most common pattern for adjectives.
- Adjectives and adverbs with no comparative or superlative are marked [not gradable]. This is the most common pattern for adverbs.

LP **Comparing and grading** at COMPARE

IRREGULAR FORMS OF WORDS

The dictionary shows all the word forms that do not follow the rules given above. For example:

give (obj) /gɪv/ *v past simple* **gave**, *past part* **given**
bring obj /brɪŋ/ *v* [T] *past* **brought** (this means 'brought' is the past simple *and* the past participle)
life /laɪf/ *n* pl **lives** /laɪvz/
good /gʊd/ *adj* **better**, **best**

For more information on irregular noun plurals LP **Plurals of nouns** at PLURAL.

Words ending in a consonant: When a word ends with one consonant, it might be necessary to *double* it when you add an ending such as **-er** or **-ing** that begins with a vowel: *tap, taps, tapping, tapped; red, redder, reddest.* LP **Consonant doubling** at CONSONANT for the rules. The dictionary shows when a consonant should be doubled:

hop (obj) /hɒp/ *v* **-pp-** (This means: *hop, hops, hopping, hopped*)
get obj /get/ *v* [T] **getting**, *past* **got**
hot /hɒt/ *adj* **hotter**, **hottest**

SPELLING OF WORDS FORMED BY ADDING A COMBINING FORM

Many words are formed by adding a combining form to the end of a word: *sudden* ➡ *suddenly; depend* ➡ *dependable.* The spelling might change: *happy* ➡ *happily; believe* ➡ *believable.* Here are some useful rules to remember:

consonant + y	**-LY** y + ily *noisy* ➡ *noisily; tidy* ➡ *tidily* **-NESS** y + iness *friendly* ➡ *friendliness* The same change is made before other suffixes, except **-ing**. But notice: *shyly, shyness; drily/dryly, dryness; slyly, slyness*
ending -e	**-ABLE** e + able *admire* ➡ *admirable; argue* ➡ *arguable* But notice for words ending **-ce/-ee/-ge** the 'e' is not dropped: *replaceable; agreeable; changeable.* Notice also: *like* ➡ *likeable* **-ISH** e + ish *large* ➡ *largish; blue* ➡ *bluish* **-Y** e + y *ice* ➡ *icy; curve* ➡ *curvy; probable* ➡ *probably* **-LY** + ly *fine* ➡ *finely; wide* ➡ *widely* But notice: *due* ➡ *duly; true* ➡ *truly; whole* ➡ *wholly* **-MENT** + ment *excite* ➡ *excitement; manage* ➡ *management* But the following can drop the 'e': *judgment; acknowledgment; abridgment.* Notice that *argue* always drops the 'e': *argue* ➡ *argument*

Certain words are often spelled differently in British and American English. These differences are always shown in the dictionary. [LP›] **American spelling** at AMERICAN.

across the road. [L only + n] ○ *The party leaders were hoping they would form the next government.* [L only + n] ○ *The families form part of a self-help network.* [L only + n] ○ *Information from our observers formed the basis of the report.* [L only + n]

for·ma·tion /£fɔːˈmeɪ·ʃᵊn, $fɔːr-/ *n* • A formation is the way something is naturally made or the way it has been arranged: *a rock formation* [C] • *cloud formations* [C] • The formation **of** something is the way in which it is made, produced or shaped: *The first sign of the disease is the formation of blisters on the skin.* [U] • Activities which are done **in** formation are done in a pattern by a number of people, vehicles, etc.: *marching in (close) formation* [U]

for·ma·tive /£ˈfɔː·mə·tɪv, $ˈfɔːr·mə·t̬ɪv/ *adj* • Something which has a formative effect, has a big influence on the way things happen: *My aunt's example had a formative effect on my career decisions.* • The formative **years** are those in which a child's knowledge, experience and character are formed.

form·less /£ˈfɔːm·ləs, $ˈfɔːrm-/ *adj* • Formless means without clear shape or expression.

form [DOCUMENT] /£fɔːm, $fɔːrm/ *n* [C] a paper or set of papers printed with marked spaces in which answers to questions can be written or information can be recorded in an organized way • *an application form* (= document used for asking officially for something, for example a job) • *an entry form* (= document used for a competition). • **Fill in/out/up** *one of these forms with all your personal details.* • *When you have* **completed** *the form, hand it in at the desk.* • (GR) (J) (KOR) (P)

form [TYPE] /£fɔːm, $fɔːrm/ *n* [C] a type of (something) • *A tandem is a form* **of** *bicycle.* • *The Cornish language is a form of Celtic.* • *Mice is the plural form of mouse.* • *'I'm' is the short form of 'I am'.* • *We agreed on a* **form of words** (= way of expressing something) *to cover the most likely situations that would arise.* • (GR) (J) (KOR) (P)

form [SCHOOL GROUP] /£fɔːm, $fɔːrm/ *n* [C] in England, a class (of school children, usually aged 11-18), or a group of classes of children of a similar age • *She's in Mrs Leach's form next year.* • *Form 6 are going on an educational visit tomorrow.* • *There are six classes in the third form* (= in the 13-14 age group) *of this secondary school.* • [LP›] **Schools and colleges** (GR) (J) (KOR) (P)

-form·er /£ˈfɔː·məʳ, $ˈfɔːr·mɚ/ *combining form* • *We have a large number of sixth-formers* (= students usually aged 16-18) *this year.*

form [BEHAVIOUR] /£fɔːm, $fɔːrm/ *n* [U] the way in which a person or animal acts • A competitor's form is their ability to be successful over a period of time: *The horse has shown good form over the last season.* ○ *After a bad year, she has regained her form.* • If someone is *(Br)* **on**/*(Am and Aus usually)* **in (great/good/top)** form they are doing something well: *Paul was on good form at the wedding and kept everyone entertained.* • *(Br) We were hoping to raise several thousand pounds, but* **on present** *form* (= judging by what has happened until now) *it seems unlikely.* • *(Br slang)* If someone has form, they are known to the police because they have been found guilty of crimes: *Has he got any form?* • *(dated)* **Bad** form is rude behaviour: *Leaving so early was very bad form.* • (GR) (J) (KOR) (P)

form [SEAT] /£fɔːm, $fɔːrm/ *n* [C] *dated* a long thin seat, usually without a back • (GR) (J) (KOR) (P)

for·mal /£ˈfɔː·məl, $ˈfɔːr-/ *adj* using an agreed way of doing things; well planned and organized • *There are formal procedures for making complaints.* • *We have recently adopted more formal methods of assessment.* • Formal language is not used in relaxed or friendly conversation; it is suitable for serious or official occasions and writing: *The letter of appointment was in very formal language.* ○ *'Reprimand' is a more formal word than 'tell off' although both mean 'to criticize someone for something they have done'.* • A formal meeting/occasion/meal is one at which particular types of behaviour and/or types of clothes (= formal dress) are expected and used. • If someone has a formal manner or acts in a formal way they are (too) serious and careful in what they say or do. • A formal **offer**/refusal/statement or formal **notice** is a way of clearly explaining or making public all the necessary details, often in writing: *We made a formal offer for* (= to buy) *the house.* ○ *They gave formal notice that they were changing the parking arrangements.* • Someone who has had no formal education has not been to school or been taught in the usual way. • A formal garden is carefully designed and kept according to a plan, and it is not allowed to grow naturally. • Formal can mean in appearance or by name only: *I am the formal leader of the project but the everyday management is in the hands of my assistant.* ○ *The visitors took only a formal interest in the classroom activities.* • [LP›] **Labels**

for·mal·ly /£ˈfɔː·mə·li, $ˈfɔːr-/ *adv* • *You will receive a letter formally confirming the appointment.* • *Formally, he has to give approval but there will be no problem.* • (F)

for·mal·ize *obj, Br and Aus usually* **-ise** /£ˈfɔː·mə·laɪz, $ˈfɔːr-/ *v* [T] • If you formalize something you make it official or decide to arrange it according to a fixed structure: *They started as informal gatherings but they have become increasingly formalized in the last few years.* ○ *We need to formalize our initial thoughts about the way to proceed.*

for·mal·i·ty /£fɔːˈmæl·ə·ti, $-t̬i/ *n* • *She found the formality* (= serious and not relaxed behaviour) *of the occasion rather daunting.* [U] • *A note of formality in his voice alerted her to the fact that others were listening.* [U] • Something which is a formality is something which has to be done but which has no real importance: *You'll have to sign the visitors' book but* **it's just a** *formality.* [C]

for·mal·i·ties /£fɔː'mæl·ə·tiz, $-t̬iz/ *pl n* • Formalities are things that must be done: *To get a passport you have to go through a set of formalities such as filling in a form, getting the signature of someone who has known you for many years and sending in your birth certificate and a photo.* ○ *We'll have to observe the formalities* (= do what is expected).

for·mat /£'fɔː·mæt, $'fɔːr-/ *n* a pattern, plan or arrangement • *The meeting will have the usual format – introductory session, group work and then a time for reporting back.* [C] • *We'll produce the leaflet* **in** *large and small formats/***in** *a two-colour format.* [C] • *I think we need a change of format.* [U]

for·mat *obj* /£'fɔː·mæt, $'fɔːr-/ *v* [T] **-tt-** • If you format a text, esp. on a computer, you organize or arrange it according to a chosen pattern: *When you have deleted those lines, format the page.* • To format a computer DISC (= device for storing electronic information), is to prepare it for use with a particular type of computer.

form·er [EARLIER] /£'fɔː·məʳ, $'fɔːr·mɚ/ *adj* [before n; not gradable] of or in an earlier time; before the present time or in the past • *They asked the woman, a former nurse at the hospital, for information.* • *The house, a former barn, has been attractively converted.* • *He was sure he had been a doctor in a former* **existence/life** (= previous existence). • *The painting was restored to its former* **glory** (= returned to its original good condition). • *After the accident it was a long time before he seemed like his former* **self** (= behaved in the way he had done before).

form·er·ly /£'fɔː·mə·li, $'fɔːr·mɚ-/ *adv* [not gradable] *fml* • *She was formerly a nurse.* • *Formerly there were two houses but we made them into one.*

form·er [FIRST] /£'fɔː·məʳ, $'fɔːr·mɚ/ *n, adj* [not gradable] **the former** (the) first of two people, things or groups previously mentioned • *Of the two suggestions, I prefer the former.* • *I visited Naples and Rome but I liked the former city much more.* • Compare LATTER [SECOND].

For·mi·ca /£fɔː'maɪ·kə, $fɔːr-/ *n* [U] *trademark* a type of hard plastic made into a thin sheet which is used to cover table tops and other pieces of esp. kitchen furniture

for·mi·dab·le /£fɔː'mɪ·də·bl̩, $fɔːr-/ *adj* causing fear and respect because of being difficult to do or deal with • *a formidable obstacle/task* • *a formidable adversary/enemy/opponent* • *a formidable intellect/brain* • *(disapproving) the director and his formidable wife* • Ⓕ

for·mi·dab·ly /£fɔː'mɪd·ə·bli, $fɔːr-/ *adv* • *How will he succeed with these forces ranged so formidably against him?* • *He is formidably efficient/intelligent/dangerous.*

for·mu·la /£'fɔː·mjʊ·lə, $'fɔːr-/ *n pl* **formulas** or **formulae** /£'fɔː·mjʊ·liː, $'fɔːr-/ a standard or accepted way of doing or making something, the items needed for it, or a mathematical rule expressed in a set of numbers and letters • *We have changed the formula* **of** *the washing powder.* [C] • *We had to learn chemical formulae at school but I can only remember H_2O for water.* [C] • *(Am and Aus)* Formula is liquid food, like milk, for babies. [U] • *(fig.) The filmstar talked about her formula* **for** *success.* [C] • *The two groups worked out a formula* **for** *sharing the use of the building.* [C] • Formula followed by a number is used to describe different types of racing cars: *A Formula One race is for very high-speed cars.* • Ⓓ Ⓝ

for·mu·late *obj* /£'fɔː·mjʊ·leɪt, $'fɔːr-/ *v* [T] • *to formulate* (= plan) *a new system/programme/solution* • *to formulate legislation* • *The plan was formulated in the days before costs became so great.*

for·mu·la·tion /£,fɔː·mjʊ'leɪ·ʃᵊn, $,fɔːr-/ *n* [C/U]

for·mu·la·ic /£,fɔː·mjʊ'leɪ·ɪk, $,fɔːr-/ *adj fml or specialized* • If something is formulaic, it contains or consists of fixed and repeated groups of words: *The text was dull and formulaic.*

for·ni·cate /£'fɔː·nɪ·keɪt, $'fɔːr-/ *v* [I] *old use* to have sex with someone who you are not married to

for·ni·ca·tion /£,fɔː·nɪ'keɪ·ʃᵊn, $,fɔːr-/ *n* [U]

for·ni·cat·or /£'fɔː·nɪ·keɪ·təʳ, $'fɔːr·nɪ·keɪ·t̬ɚ/ *n* [C]

for·sake *obj* /£fɔː'seɪk, $fɔːr-/ *v* [T] *past simple* **forsook** /£fɔː'sʊk, $fɔːr-/, *past part* **forsaken** /£fə'seɪ·kᵊn, $fɚ-/ *old use literary* to leave forever, esp. when causing the person you leave to be unhappy, or to give up completely; to DESERT or ABANDON • *"Do not forsake me, oh my darling/ On this our wedding day"* (song from the film *High Noon,* 1952) • *"Wilt thou love her ...and, forsaking all others, keep thee only unto her...?"* (from the Marriage Service in the Book of Common Prayer, 1662)

for·sak·en /£fə'seɪ·kᵊn, $fɚ-/ *adj* • *The house and garden had a forsaken look/air/appearance.*

for·swear *obj* /£fɔː'sweəʳ, $fɔːr'swer/ *v* [T] *past simple* **forswore** /£fɔː'swɔːʳ, $fɔːr'swɔːr/, *past part* **forsworn** /£fɔː'swɔːn, $fɔːr'swɔːrn/ *old use or humorous* to make a serious decision to stop doing (something) • *I've forsworn alcohol/smoking now that I'm pregnant.*

for·syth·i·a /£fɔː'saɪ·θi·ə, $fɔːr-/ *n* [C] a medium-sized bush grown in gardens, which has yellow flowers before the leaves appear

fort /£fɔːt, $fɔːrt/ *n* [C] a military building consisting of an area enclosed by a strong wall, in which soldiers live and which is designed to be defended from attack • *The US cavalry rode into the fort and the gates closed behind them.* • *The remains of the Roman fort are well preserved.* • If something is like **Fort Knox**, it is impossible to enter it illegally or steal anything from it: *His shed has so many locks and bolts it should be as safe as Fort Knox.*

for·te /£'fɔː·teɪ, $'fɔːr-/ *n* [C usually sing] a strong ability, something that a person can do well • *I'm afraid sewing isn't one of my fortes.* • *His forte is after-dinner speeches.*

forth /£fɔːθ, $fɔːrθ/ *adv* [not gradable] *fml* (from a place) out, or (from a point in time) forward • *They set forth on their travels in early June.* • *From that day/time forth he never drank cider again.* • To go **back and forth** means to go backwards and forwards several times. • See also HOLD FORTH.

forth·com·ing [SOON] /£'fɔːθ,kʌm·ɪŋ, $'fɔːrθ-/ *adj* [before n; not gradable] about to happen, happening soon • *We have just received the information about the forthcoming conference.*

forth·com·ing [WILLING] /£,fɔːθ'kʌm·ɪŋ, $,fɔːrθ-/ *adj* friendly and helpful, willing to give information or to talk • *a pleasant, forthcoming young woman* • *He was very forthcoming in the interview, but I'm not sure he's right for the job.* • *I had difficulty getting any details. He wasn't very forthcoming.*

forth·com·ing [SUPPLIED] /£,fɔːθ'kʌm·ɪŋ, $,fɔːrθ-/ *adj* [after v; not gradable] produced, supplied, given • *No explanation for his absence was forthcoming.* • *Will financial support for the theatre project be forthcoming?*

forth·right /£'fɔːθ·raɪt, $'fɔːrθ-/ *adj* (too) honest or direct in behaviour • *His forthright manner can be mistaken for rudeness.* • *I admire her forthright way of dealing with people.*

forth·right·ness /£'fɔːθ·raɪt·nəs, $'fɔːrθ-/ *n* [U]

forth·with /£,fɔːθ'wɪθ, $,fɔːrθ-/ *adv* [not gradable] *fml* immediately • *We expect these practices to cease forthwith.*

for·ti·eth /£'fɔː·ti·əθ, $'fɔːr·t̬i-/ *pronoun, n, adj, adv* See at FORTY

for·ti·fy *obj* /£'fɔː·tɪ·faɪ, $'fɔːr·t̬ɪ-/ *v* [T] to strengthen, esp. in order to protect • *They hurriedly fortified the village* **with** *barricades of carts, tree trunks and whatever came to hand.* • *The argument fortified her resolve to prove she was right.* • *He fortified himself* **with** *a drink and a sandwich before driving on.* • *She fortified herself during the winter months* **with** *the thought of the warm sunny weather to come.*

for·ti·fied /£'fɔː·tɪ·faɪd, $'fɔːr·t̬ɪ-/ *adj* • A fortified town has strong walls which can be defended against enemies. • *The fruit drink is fortified* **with** *vitamin C* (= has it added). • A **fortified wine** is a wine that contains more alcohol that usual wines: *Sherry and Martini are fortified wines.*

for·ti·fi·ca·tion /£,fɔː·tɪ·fɪ'keɪ·ʃᵊn, $,fɔːr·t̬ə-/ *n* • *Ditches were a popular means of fortification.* [U] • *The fortifications of the castle were massive and impenetrable.* [C usually pl]

for·ti·tude /£'fɔː·tɪ·tjuːd, $'fɔːr·t̬ə·tuːd/ *n* [U] *fml* bravery over a long period • *Throughout that difficult period of illness and bereavement she showed* **great/commendable** *fortitude.*

fort·night /£'fɔːt·naɪt, $'fɔːrt-/ *n* [C usually sing] *Br and Aus* a period of two weeks • *a fortnight's holiday/stay* (= a holiday/visit of two weeks) • *once a fortnight* (= once in two weeks) • *a fortnight ago* (= two weeks ago) • *He's taking his usual fortnight* (= two weeks holiday) *in July.* • *We visit her every fortnight* (= once every two weeks). • *I'm going in a fortnight's time* (= two weeks from now). • *(dated) It will be ready on Thursday fortnight* (= on Thursday two weeks from now). • [LP] **Calendar**

fort·night·ly /£ˈfɔːt·naɪt·li, $ˈfɔːrt-/ *adj, adv* [not gradable] • *We make a fortnightly check on supplies.* • *The club meets fortnightly on Tuesdays.*

for·tress /£ˈfɔː·trəs, $ˈfɔːr-/ *n* [C] a large strong building or group of buildings which can be defended from attack • *The fortress had massive walls and a heavily fortified gateway.* • *(disapproving)* In the expression 'Fortress Europe' or 'Fortress Britain' the suggestion is that the place mentioned wants to defend itself from outside influences: *to adopt a Fortress Britain policy/mentality*

for·tu·i·tous /£fɔːˈtjuː·ɪ·təs, $fɔːrˈtuː·ə·t̬əs/ *adj fml* (of something that is to your advantage) not planned, happening by chance, or *(not standard)* FORTUNATE • *The extraordinarily convenient timing of the meeting is said to be fortuitous.* • *The collapse of its rivals brought fortuitous gains to the company.* • *The surpluses have not disappeared but have been hidden by fortuitous circumstances.* • *Accepting the job was a fortuitous* (= good) *move and her career blossomed.*

for·tu·i·tous·ly /£fɔːˈtjuː·ɪ·tə·sli, $fɔːrˈtuː·ə·t̬ə·sli/ *adv*

for·tu·i·tous·ness /£fɔːˈtjuː·ɪ·tə·snəs, $fɔːrˈtuː·ə·t̬ə·snəs/ *n* [U]

for·tu·nate /£ˈfɔː·tʃən·ət, $ˈfɔːr-/ *adj approving* having good things happen to you • *You're very fortunate* **to** *have found such a pleasant house.* [+ *to* infinitive] • *I feel I'm a very fortunate person* **having** *so many choices.* [+ v-*ing*] • *He was fortunate* **in** *his choice of assistant.* • **It** *was fortunate* **that** *they had left in plenty of time.* [+ *that* clause]

for·tu·nate·ly /£ˈfɔː·tʃən·ət·li, $ˈfɔːr-/ *adv* [not gradable] • *Fortunately we got home before it started to rain.* • *We were fortunately able to use an alternative route.*

for·tune WEALTH /£ˈfɔː·tʃuːn, £-tjuːn, $ˈfɔːr-/ *n* [C] a large amount of money, goods, property, etc. • *She inherited a/her fortune from her grandmother.* • *He lost a fortune gambling.* • *You can* **make** *a fortune out of junk if you call it 'antiques'.* • *This dress* **cost** *a* **(small)** *fortune/an* **absolute** *fortune* (= a lot of money). • *Any painting by Van Gogh is* **worth** *a fortune.* • *(disapproving)* A **fortune hunter** is someone who tries to marry a person who has a lot of money.

for·tune CHANCE /£ˈfɔː·tʃuːn, £-tjuːn, $ˈfɔːr-/ *n* the set of esp. good events which happen to you and have an effect on your life • *He* **had** *the* **(good)** *fortune* **to** *be chosen to play Hamlet.* [U] • If **Fortune smiles on** you then everything goes well for you. • If you **read/tell** someone's fortune, you discover what will happen to them in the future, for example by looking at the lines on their hands or using a special set of cards. • A **fortune cookie** is a biscuit containing a message, usually about your future, eaten esp. after a Chinese meal. • A **fortune teller** is a person who tells you what they think will happen to you in the future.

for·tunes /£ˈfɔː·tʃuːnz, £-tjuːnz, $ˈfɔːr-/ *pl n* • *His fortunes underwent a drastic change for the worse* (= bad things happened). • *(saying)* 'The fortunes of war' means that some people do well and other people do badly in a particular situation.

for·ty /£ˈfɔː·ti, $ˈfɔːr·t̬i/ *determiner, pronoun, n* (the number) 40 • *thirty-nine, forty, forty-one* • *a forty-seater coach* • *a forty-roomed mansion* • *"How many children are there?" "Forty (children)."* • *I can't read this number – is it a forty?* [C] • *(infml)* **Forty winks** is a short sleep during the day: *He usually has forty winks going home on the train.* • *"Ali Baba and the Forty Thieves"* (title of a traditional story)

fort·ies /£ˈfɔː·tiz, $ˈfɔːr·t̬iz/ *pl n* • **The** forties is the range of temperature between 40° and 49°: *The temperature is expected to be* **in** *the forties tomorrow.* • **The** forties is also the period of years between 40 and 49 in any century: *Our house was built some time* **in** *the forties* (= between 1940 and 1949). • A person's forties are the period in which they are aged between 40 and 49: *I'd never have known she was* **in** *her forties – she looks so young.*

for·ti·eth /£ˈfɔː·ti·əθ, $ˈfɔːr·t̬i-/ *determiner, pronoun, adj, adv* [not gradable] • *in his fortieth year* • *the fortieth in a set of sixty volumes* • *Our group was/came fortieth.* • A fortieth is one of forty equal parts of something. [C]

fo·rum /£ˈfɔː·rəm, $ˈfɔːr·əm/ *n* [C] a place or an occasion for talking about a problem or matter esp. of public interest • *The phone-in programme* **provides**/*is a forum* **for** *the public to express their views on different topics.* • *The World Economic Forum met in Switzerland.* • In ancient Rome the forum was the area in the middle of the town for public business.

for·ward *obj* SEND /£ˈfɔː·wəd, $ˈfɔːr·wɚd/ *v* [T] to send (something), esp. from an old address to a new address • *My parents will forward my mail* **to** *China while I'm teaching there.* • *She asked for any letters that arrived to be forwarded for three months.* • *(fml) We will shortly be forwarding you a cheque/forwarding a cheque* **to** *you to cover the refund.* [+ two objects] • A **forwarding address** is where you want your post sent after you have left the address at which it will arrive.

for·ward SPORT /£ˈfɔː·wəd, $ˈfɔːr·wɚd/ *n* [C] a player who is in an attacking position in a team • Compare BACK SPORT.

for·wards /£ˈfɔː·wədz, $ˈfɔːr·wɚdz/, **for·ward** *adv* [not gradable] to the front, to the direction in which you are facing, to a future time or *(fig.)* to a position of importance or being noticed • *She moved the chair forwards.* • *He stepped forwards three paces.* • *The traffic moved slowly forwards.* • *I reached forwards to take the book off the shelf.* • *We need to move our plans forward quickly.* • *Put your watches forward one hour to continental time.* • *(fml)* **From that day/time forward** (= After that) *they never spoke to each other.* • *(fig.) They brought forward several reasons for not approving the project.* • *(fig.) She's never been the kind of person to push herself forward.* • Compare BACKWARDS.

for·ward /£ˈfɔː·wəd, $ˈfɔːr·wɚd/ *adj* [not gradable] • *a forward movement* • *forward planning* • *forward* (= too noticeable or confident) *behaviour* • Someone who is **forward-looking** always plans for the future.

for·ward·ness /£ˈfɔː·wəd·nəs, $ˈfɔːr·wɚd·/ *n* [U] *disapproving* • *They didn't approve of her forwardness* (= too noticeable and confident behaviour considered socially unacceptable).

for·went /£fɔːˈwent, $fɔːr-/ *past participle of* FORGO

fos·sil /£ˈfɒs·əl, $ˈfɑː·səl/ *n* [C] a bone, a shell or the shape of a plant or animal which has been preserved in rock, ice or earth for a very long period • *a collection of fossils* • *a fossil skeleton* • *a fossil hunter* • **Fossil fuels** are fuels such as gas, coal and oil, which are produced from ancient plant material. • *(infml)* People who are not willing to accept change are sometimes called **(old)** fossils.

fos·sil·ize, *Br and Aus usually* **-ise** /£ˈfɒs·ɪ·laɪz, $ˈfɑː·səl·aɪz/ *v* [I] • *The remains gradually fossilized.*

fos·sil·ized, *Br and Aus usually* **-ised** /£ˈfɒs·ɪ·laɪzd, $ˈfɑː·səl·aɪzd/ *adj* [not gradable] • *fossilized shells/leaves/remains* • Someone who has fossilized **ideas** has opinions which they do not want to change.

fos·sil·iz·a·tion, *Br and Aus usually* **-i·sa·tion** /£ˌfɒs·ɪ·laɪˈzeɪ·ʃən, £-lɪˈ-, $ˌfɑː·səl·aɪ-/ *n* [U] • *a process of fossilization*

fost·er *(obj)* TAKE CARE OF /£ˈfɒs·təʳ, $ˈfɑː·stɚ/ *v* to take care of (a child) as if it were your own, usually for a limited time, without being the child's legal parent • *Would you consider fostering* **(children)** *if you couldn't have children of your own?* [I/T] • Compare ADOPT TAKE CHILD. • LP **Relationships**

fost·er /£ˈfɒs·təʳ, $ˈfɑː·stɚ/ *adj* [before n; not gradable] • *She was taken into care by the local council and placed with a foster* **family**. • *The children lived in different foster* **homes**. • *As a child, he had lived with a succession of foster* **parents**.

fost·er *obj* ENCOURAGE /£ˈfɒs·təʳ, $ˈfɑː·stɚ/ *v* [T] to encourage the development or growth of (ideas or feelings) • *I'm trying to foster an interest in classical music* **in** *my children.* • *They were discussing the best way to foster democracy and prosperity in the former communist countries.*

fought /£fɔːt, $fɑːt/ *past simple and past participle of* FIGHT

foul UNPLEASANT /faʊl/ *adj* **-er, -est** extremely unpleasant • *Those toilets smell foul!* • *The air in Mexico City is some of the foulest* (= most polluted) *in the world.* • *I've had a foul* **day** *at work.* • *What a foul day – I got totally drenched in that thunderstorm.* • *He condemned the death as a foul* (= evil) *murder perpetrated by the forces of racism.* • *Why are you in such a foul* **temper** (= very bad mood) *this morning?* • *Why are so many films full of violence and* **foul language** (= swearing) *these days?* • If someone is **foul-mouthed** they swear a lot and use offensive language: *They are the most impolite and foul-mouthed children I have ever come across.* • **Foul play** is a criminal act which results in serious damage or injury, esp. murder: *The drowned man had been suffering from depression for several months, and the police have* **ruled out** *foul play.* ○ *It is not clear what caused the explosion, but foul play is not* **suspected**. See also **foul play** at FOUL SPORT.

foul SPORT /faʊl/ *n* [C] an act which is against the rules of a sport, often causing injury to another player • *(Br) He was sent off for a foul* **against/on** *the French captain.* • In baseball, a foul or **foul ball** is a ball hit outside the playing field on either side. • In sport, someone is guilty of **foul play** if they have played unfairly or acted against the rules. See also **foul play** at FOUL UNPLEASANT.

foul *(obj)* /faʊl/ *v* • *He was penalized for fouling (the French captain).* [I/T]

foul *obj* MAKE DIRTY /faʊl/ *v* [T] *fml or specialized* to pollute (something) or make it dirty • *The oil slick fouled* (= polluted) *the Kuwaiti shoreline.* • *Penalty for* **dogs** *fouling* (= excreting the contents of their bowels onto) *the footway – £50.*

foul up *(obj)*, **foul** *(obj)* **up** *v adv infml* to spoil (something) by making a mistake or doing something stupid • *I don't want David organizing this party after the way he fouled things up last year.* [M] • If something fouls up it stops working correctly: *Why does this computer system keep fouling up?* [I]

foul–up /ˈfaʊl·ʌp/ *n* [C] *infml* • *This investigation has been mismanaged right from the start – I've never seen such a foul-up.*

found FIND /faʊnd/ *past simple and past participle of* FIND

found *obj* BEGIN /faʊnd/ *v* [T] to bring (something) into existence • *York was founded by the Romans in the year 71 AD.* • *She left a large sum of money in her will to found a wildlife sanctuary.* • *We are planning a dinner to celebrate the fiftieth anniversary of the founding of the company.* • The **founding father/mother** (also **founder**) of an important organization or idea is the person who establishes it: *John Reith was the founding father of the BBC.* ○ *Would you say that Simone de Beauvoir was the founding mother of French feminism?* ○ *The Founding Fathers of the United States were the members of the 1787 Convention which decided the country's constitution.* • *France is a* **founding member** (= one of the original members) *of the European Community.*

foun·da·tion /faʊnˈdeɪ·ʃən/ *n* • *The foundation of the children's home was made possible by a generous donation from an anonymous benefactor.* [U] • *The university is an ancient foundation* (= was established a long time ago). [C] • A foundation is also an organization that has been established in order to provide money for a particular group of people in need of help or for a particular type of study: *the British Heart Foundation* [C] ○ *the Environmental Research Foundation* [C] ○ *He was the principal of the* **arts** *foundation.* [C]

found·er /£ˈfaʊn·dəʳ, $-dɚ/ *n* [C] • *She is the founder and managing director of the company.* • *The United States is a* **founder member** (= one of the original members) *of the United Nations.*

found *obj* BUILD /faʊnd/ *v* [T always + adv/prep; often passive] to build a support in the ground for (a large structure such as a building or road), or *(fig.)* to base (a belief, claim, idea, etc.) on something • *Buildings founded* **on** *clay are the most likely to be damaged when the soil dries out.* • *Her lawyer accused the prosecution of founding its case* **on** *insufficient evidence.* • *I'd like to see the research that these recommendations are founded* **on.** • *You would expect to find more women in an international organization founded* **upon** *egalitarian principles.* • *Make sure your allegations are firmly founded before you make them.* • See also WELL-FOUNDED.

foun·da·tion /faʊnˈdeɪ·ʃən/ *n* [U] • *(fig.) These outrageous allegations are completely* **without** *foundation* (= are completely false). • *(fig.) Such claims are a figment of the imagination and have* **no** *foundation* **in fact.** • *(Br)* A **foundation course** (*Am and Aus* **introductory course**) at a college or university introduces students to a subject and prepares them for studying it at a higher level: *Students with no previous experience of computing are expected to attend a foundation course before starting their degree course.* • A **foundation stone** is a large block of stone that is put in position at the start of work on a public building, often with a ceremony: *The foundation stone of the new theatre was* **laid** *by the Queen in a ceremony attended by many famous figures from the acting profession.* • See also FOUNDATION

foun·da·tions /faʊnˈdeɪ·ʃənz/ *pl n* • The foundations of a building are the structures below the surface of the ground which support it: *The foundations will have to be reinforced to prevent the house from sinking further into ground.* • *(fig.) The two leaders have* **laid** *the foundations* **of** *a new era in cooperation between their countries.* • *(fig.) The scandal has* **shaken/rocked** *the Democratic Party* **to its** *foundations* (= seriously upset the whole party).

foun·da·tion /faʊnˈdeɪ·ʃən/ *n* [U] a type of make-up which is spread over the skin of the face, usually before other make-up is put on, giving it a better and more even colour and hiding unwanted marks • *She* **wears** *a lot of foundation.*

found·er /£ˈfaʊn·dəʳ, $-dɚ/ *v* [I] (esp. of a boat) to fill with water and sink, or *(fig.)* to be unsuccessful • *The ferry foundered in a heavy storm, taking many of the passengers and crew with it.* • *(fig.) The council's plans for new community services have foundered because of budget cuts.* • *(fig.) Teaching computers to read and write has always foundered* **on** (= failed because of) *the unpredictable human element in language.*

found·ling /ˈfaʊnd·lɪŋ/ *n* [C] *dated* a young child who is left forever by its unknown parents and then found and cared for by someone else • *Foundlings were often adopted by local families.*

found·ry /ˈfaʊn·dri/ *n* [C] a factory where metal is melted and poured into specially shaped containers to produce objects such as wheels and bars

fount /faʊnt/ *n* [C] *literary or humorous* the origin of something; SOURCE • *Dr Barrett is renowned as* **the** *fount* **of (all) knowledge** *on the disease.* • *I'm just repeating what I heard from Patrick Campbell,* **the** *fount* **of all** *salacious gossip.*

foun·tain /ˈfaʊn·tɪn/ *n* [C] a stream of water that is forced up into the air through a small hole, esp. for decorative effect, or the structure in a lake or pool from which this flows • *I'll meet you by the Trevi Fountain at seven o'clock.* • *(fig.) This was a very troubled and turbulent period of my life and I regarded Mira very much as a fountain* **of** *calm.* • A **fountain pen** is a pen whose NIB (= point at the end which you write with) is supplied with ink from a container inside it. • PIC› **Writing instruments**

four /£fɔːʳ, $fɔːr/ *determiner, pronoun, n* (the number) 4 • *one, two, three, four, five* • *Most animals have four legs.* • *"How many sides does a square have?" "Four (sides)."* • *Three fours are twelve.* [C] • In ROWING, a four is a team of four people or the boat that they use: *Our four almost sank when we crashed into the riverbank.* [C + sing/pl v] • In cricket, if you **hit** a four you get four RUNS (= points) by hitting the ball to the edge of the field. [C] • If you are **on all fours**, your body is supported on your hands and knees: *You'll have to* **get down** *on all fours to clean behind the toilet.* • *(infml)* **Four-eyes** is an offensive way of addressing someone who wears glasses: *Hey four-eyes, can't you see anything without your specs?* • A **four-leaf/four-leaved clover** is a CLOVER (= small plant) with a leaf which is divided into four parts rather than the usual three, which is thought to bring good luck to anyone who finds it. • A **four-letter word** is a short swear word that is considered to be extremely rude or offensive: *Four-letter words refer to the taboo subjects of sex and excretion.* ○ *Four-letter words are often edited out of films before they are shown on television.* • A **four-pack** is a group of four of the same thing that are sold together: *Could you get me a four-pack* **of** *beer at the supermarket?* ○ *They'll probably be cheaper if you buy them* **in** *a four-pack.* • A **four-poster (bed)** is a large old-fashioned bed with tall posts at each corner which support a frame from which curtains hang. PIC› **Beds and bedroom** • If a building is **four-square**, it is square in shape and solidly built: *What I don't like about modern architecture is that it is four-square and lacks imagination.* ○ *(fig.) With his four-square physique he could be a rugby player.* • If something is **four-square** it is established, determined and unlikely to change: *Public opinion is four-square* **behind** *the government's decision to go to war.* • A **four-star** restaurant or hotel is one of a very high standard. • *(Br)* **Four-star (petrol)** (*Am* **high-test (gas)**, *Aus* **super (petrol)**) is the highest quality LEADED fuel that can be used in cars: *I'd prefer to use unleaded petrol, but my car can only* **run on** (= use) *four-star.* • If a vehicle has **four-wheel drive** (*abbreviation* **4WD**) its engine supplies power to all four wheels rather than the usual two, so that the vehicle can travel easily over ground that is rougher than an ordinary road. • PIC› **Beds and bedroom**

fourth /£fɔːθ, $fɔːrθ/ *determiner, pronoun, adj, adv* [not gradable], *n* • *Inflation increased in the fourth quarter of the year.* • *My birthday is on the fourth of December.* • *Henry was/finished fourth in the race.* • A fourth is a quarter: *The area is three fourths desert.* [C] • The **fourth dimension**

was originally thought of as a direction of measurement in addition to those of length, width and height, but now it generally refers, esp. in **science fiction**, to time: *If you travel in the fourth dimension you travel backwards or forwards through time.* • **The Fourth Estate** is newspapers, magazines, television and radio stations and the people who work for them who are thought to have a lot of political influence. • The **Fourth of July** (*fml* **Independence Day**) is the national holiday in the US which celebrates the 1776 Declaration of Independence from Great Britain: *The Fourth of July is traditionally celebrated with firework displays.* ○ *The anti-aircraft guns lit up the sky like the Fourth of July.* • LP〉 **Holidays**

four·some /£'fɔː·səm, $'fɔːr-/, **four** *n* [C] a group of four people meeting for a social activity, such as playing a game or having a meal • *Why don't we invite Caroline and Mark and* **make up a** *foursome?*

four·teen /£ˌfɔː'tiːn, $ˌfɔːr-, '--/ *determiner, pronoun, n* (the number) 14 • *thirteen, fourteen, fifteen* • *"How many people work in your office?" "Fourteen (people)."* • *Two fourteens are twenty-eight.* [C]

four·teenth /£ˌfɔː'tiːnθ, $ˌfɔːr-, '--/ *determiner, pronoun, adj, adv* [not gradable], *n* • *the fourteenth edition of the book* • *Could we arrange a meeting for the fourteenth (of the month)?* • *Your name is/lies fourteenth on the list.* • A fourteenth is one of fourteen equal parts of something. [C]

4WD *n* [U] *abbreviation for* **four wheel drive**, see at FOUR

fowl /faʊl/ *n* [C/U] *pl* **fowl** or *old use* **fowls** a bird of a type that is used to produce meat or eggs, or *(old use)* any bird • *Since my heart attack, I've eaten more fish and fowl and less red meat.* [U] • See also WATERFOWL; WILDFOWL.

fox ANIMAL /£fɒks, $fɑːks/ *n* a wild mammal belonging to the dog family which has a pointed face and ears, a wide furry tail and often reddish-brown fur • *Foxes are often nocturnal.* [C] • *In Britain foxes are hunted.* [C] • Fox is also the skin of this animal used to make coats and hats: *Artificial fur is increasingly replacing natural furs such as mink and fox.* [U] • Foxes are traditionally thought to be clever and good at deceiving people, so humans are sometimes compared to them: *The President is very crafty, just like a fox.* [C] ○ *Are you sure you can trust him – he's such a cunning/sly/wily old fox.* [C] • A **fox terrier** is a small dog with smooth or rough fur that is white with black or pale brown marks: *In the past, fox terriers were used in hunting to dig foxes out of the ground so that they could be killed by the foxhounds.* • PIC〉 **Dogs, Wild animals in Britain**

fox·y /£'fɒk·si, $'fɑːk-/ *adj* **-ier, -iest** • A foxy person is like a fox in their appearance or character: *He has a foxy, pointed face.* ○ *She can be really foxy at times – she often tricks me into doing things for her when I've already refused.*

fox WOMAN /£fɒks, $fɑːks/ *n* [C] *Am infml* a sexually attractive woman • *John's girlfriend is quite a fox, isn't she?*

fox·y /£'fɒk·si, $'fɑːk-/ *adj* **-ier, -iest** *Am infml* • *That Annie's one hell of a foxy* (= sexy) *chick!*

fox *obj* CONFUSE /£fɒks, $fɑːks/ *v* [T] to confuse (someone) or be too difficult to be understood by (someone) • *This puzzle has well and truly foxed me!*

foxed /£fɒkst, $fɑːkst/ *adj* • *I've done the rest of the crossword but this last clue has got me really foxed!*

fox *obj* DECEIVE /£fɒks, $fɑːks/ *v* [T] to deceive (someone) in a clever way • *She foxed him* **into** *giving her all his money.*

fox·glove /£'fɒks·glʌv, $'fɑːks-/ *n* [C] a tall thin plant with white, yellow, pink, red or purple bell-shaped flowers growing all the way up its stem

fox·hole /£'fɒks·həʊl, $'fɑːks·hoʊl/ *n* [C] a small hole dug in the ground during a war or military attack which is used by a small group of soldiers as a base for firing at the enemy and as a shelter from attack • *Their only protection was the foxholes which were wet from the storm the previous night.* • Compare TRENCH.

fox·hound /£'fɒks·haʊnd, $'fɑːks-/ *n* [C] a type of small dog with ears that hang down and short smooth usually black, white and light brown fur • *Foxhounds are bred and trained to hunt foxes because they have a very good sense of smell and can run fast for a long time without getting tired.*

fox·hunt·ing /£'fɒksˌhʌn·tɪŋ, $'fɑːksˌhʌn·t̬ɪŋ/ *n* [U] the activity of hunting FOXES for entertainment in which people on horses follow dogs which chase a fox and kill it when they catch it • *He* **goes** *foxhunting in the winter.* • *Many people think foxhunting should be banned.*

fox·hunt /£'fɒks·hʌnt, $'fɑːks-/ *n* [C] • *Has attendance at foxhunts fallen because of the campaigns by hunt saboteurs?* • *There are almost two hundred foxhunts* (= organizations of hunters in particular areas) *in Great Britain.*

fox·trot /£'fɒks·trɒt, $'fɑːks·trɑːt/ *n* (a piece of music for) a type of formal BALLROOM dance that combines short quick steps with longer ones in various patterns • *Would you like us to play a foxtrot?* [C] • *Do you know how to dance the foxtrot?* [U]

foy·er /'fɔɪ·eɪ/ *n* [C] a large open area just inside the entrance of a public building such as a theatre or a hotel, where people can wait and meet each other • *I'll see you downstairs* **in** *the foyer in half an hour.* • *(Am)* A foyer (*Br and Aus* **hall**) is also the room in a house or apartment leading from the front door to other rooms, where items like coats and hats are kept. • NL

Fr *n* [before n] *abbreviation for* FATHER when used as a title of a Christian priest, esp. a Roman Catholic or Orthodox priest • *Fr McDonald conducted the mass.*

fra·cas /'fræk·ɑː/ *n* [C] *pl* **fracas** or *Am* **fracases** a noisy argument or fight • *He was injured in a Saturday-night fracas outside a disco.* • *The Prime Minister has joined the fracas* **over** *the proposed changes to the health service.*

frac·tal /'fræk·təl/ *n* [C] *specialized* a complicated irregular line or pattern in mathematics built from simple repeated shapes that are reduced in size every time they are repeated • *Fractals are used in the study of things like forked lightning and to produce some types of computer graphics.* • *The way that the trunk of a tree divides into smaller and smaller branches and twigs is an approximate fractal pattern.*

frac·tion /'fræk·ʃən/ *n* [C] a number that results from dividing one whole number by another, or a small part of something • *¼ and 0·25 are different ways of representing the same fraction.* • *Although sexual and violent crimes have increased by 10%, they remain* **only a tiny/small** *fraction* **of** *the total number of crimes committed each year.* • *They can produce it* **at a** *fraction* **of** *the cost of* (= much more cheaply than) *traditional methods.* • *The shopkeepers are complaining that business has been reduced to* **a** *fraction* **of** (= to much less than) *what it was before the outbreak of war.* • *The five children killed last night* **represent a tiny** *fraction* **of** *those killed in the war over the last year.* • LP〉 **Mathematics**

frac·tion·al /'fræk·ʃən·əl/ *adj* • Fractional means extremely small: *The fall in the value of the yen might result in a fractional increase in interest rates of perhaps a quarter of one per cent.* ○ *At the end of the first round she enjoys a fractional lead over her nearest rival.*

frac·tion·al·ly /'fræk·ʃən·əl·i/ *adv* • *Despite substantial price cuts, sales have increased only fractionally* (= by a very small amount). • *After eight hours of negotiations, the two sides seem to be fractionally* (= by a very small amount) *closer to an agreement.*

frac·tious /'fræk·ʃəs/ *adj* easily upset or annoyed, bad-tempered and tending to complain • *He put his finger to his lips, as if hushing a fractious child.* • *I'm afraid I don't have much patience in dealing with fractious teenagers.*

frac·tious·ness /'fræk·ʃə·snəs/ *n* [U]

frac·ture *(obj)* /£'fræk·tʃər, $-tʃɚ/ *v* to (cause esp. a bone to) crack or break • *She fractured her* **skull** *in the accident.* [T] • *Two of her ribs fractured when she was thrown from her horse.* [I] • *A fractured pipe at a steelworks has leaked 20 tons of oil into the Severn estuary.* • *The pipes will fracture if the temperature drops too low.* [I] • *(fig.) Intense disagreement over economic policy risks fracturing the coalition government.* [T]

frac·ture /£'fræk·tʃər, $-tʃɚ/ *n* [C] • *He suffered/sustained* **multiple** *fractures in a motorcycle accident.* • *He has a* **hairline** *fracture* (= a thin crack in the bone) **of** *the wrist.* • *(fig.) The war has accentuated fractures between neighbouring states.*

frag·ile /£'frædʒ·aɪl, $'frædʒ·əl/ *adj* easily damaged, broken or harmed • *Be careful with that vase – it's very fragile and worth a lot of money.* • *The assassination could do serious damage to the fragile peace agreement that was signed last month.* • *I felt rather fragile* (= weak) *for a few days after the operation.* • *(humorous) No breakfast for me, thanks – I'm feeling rather fragile* (= ill, upset or tired) *after last night's party.*

frag·il·i·ty /£frə'dʒɪl·ɪ·ti, $-t̬i/ *n* [U] • *The collapse of the bank is an ominous reminder of the fragility of the world's banking system.*

frag·ment /'fræg·mənt/ *n* [C] a small piece or a part, esp. when broken from something whole • *The road was covered with fragments* **of** *glass from the shattered window.* •

Literary scholars are piecing together her last unpublished novel from fragments **of** *a recently discovered manuscript.*

frag·ment *(obj)* /frægˈment/ *v* • *The satellite will fragment* (= break into small pieces) *and burn up as it falls through the Earth's atmosphere.* [I] • *The government is planning to fragment the industry before privatizing it.* [T]

frag·ment·ed /£frægˈmen·tɪd, $-t̬ɪd/ *adj* • Fragmented means consisting of several separate parts: *In this increasingly fragmented society, a sense of community is a thing of the past.* ○ *The President has only held onto power because the opposition is so fragmented.* ○ *A new constitution that reflects the fragmented nature of the country is urgently needed.*

frag·men·ta·ry /£ˈfræg·mən·t^{ə}r·i, $ˈfræg·mən·ter-/ *adj fml* • Fragmentary means existing only in small parts and not complete: *Reports are still fragmentary but it is already clear that the explosion has left many dead and injured.* ○ *Early memories of childhood are mostly fragmentary.* ○ *My husband spoke not a word of the language and I had only a fragmentary knowledge.*

frag·men·ta·tion /ˌfræg·menˈteɪ·ʃ^{ə}n/ *n* [U] • *It was partly the fragmentation of the opposition which helped to get the Republicans re-elected.* • A **fragmentation bomb** has a thick outer covering which breaks into a lot of small pieces that are thrown in every direction when it explodes.

fra·grance /ˈfreɪ·gr^{ə}nts/ *n* [C] a sweet or pleasant smell • *The fragrance of coffee and spices fills the store.* • *This shampoo contains a light fragrance of natural herb and plant extracts.* • *They've developed a new range of fragrance-free* (= without a smell) *toiletries for sensitive skin.* • LP› **Shopping goods, Smells**

fra·granced /ˈfreɪ·gr^{ə}nst/ *adj* • *Do you stock fragranced* (= with a fragrance added) *toilet cleaners?*

fra·grant /ˈfreɪ·gr^{ə}nt/ *adj* • *Many species of lily are prized for their beautiful and often fragrant* (= pleasant smelling) *flowers.* • *The sauce itself was light, fragrant* (= pleasant smelling) *and slightly sweet.*

frail /freɪl/ *adj* **-er, -est** weak or unhealthy, or easily damaged, broken or harmed • *I last saw him just last week and thought how old and frail he looked.* • *At 85, Doris, single, diabetic and living alone, was becoming increasingly forgetful and frail.* • *He seems unconcerned by the damage that has been done to the country's economy and to its frail democracy.* • *The evidence against him is too frail for a successful prosecution.*

frail·ty /£ˈfreɪl·ti, $-t̬i/ *n* • *Even during his last few months of considerable frailty he kept up his writing.* [U] • *Though ill for most of her life, physical frailty never stopped her from working.* [U] • Frailty also means moral weakness: *Most of the characters in the novel exhibit those common* **human** *frailties – ignorance and greed.* [C] • *Tolerant of* **human** *frailty in whatever form, she almost never judged people.* [U]

frame BORDER /freɪm/ *n* [C] a border which encloses and supports a picture, door or window • *The door is attached to its frame by two hinges.* • PIC› **Frame, Window**

frame *obj* /freɪm/ *v* [T] • If you frame a picture, photograph etc. you fix a border around it, and often glass in front of it: *We still haven't had our wedding photos framed.* ○ *(fig.) Her new hairstyle frames her face in a much more flattering way.*

framed /freɪmd/ *adj* [not gradable] • *A large framed portrait of the President hangs on the wall behind his desk.* • *She stood, framed in* (= surrounded by) *the doorway, a tall impressive figure in a long tailored coat.* • Sometimes -framed is used as a combining form: *He was wearing a pair of silver-framed spectacles.*

frames /freɪmz/ *pl n* • The frames of a pair of glasses hold the LENSES (= parts that you see through) in position on the head: *Do you think I'd look more intellectual if I got some round frames for my glasses?*

frame STRUCTURE /freɪm/ *n* [C] a structure that holds the parts of an object in position and gives them support • *A tent basically consists of a frame of metal or wooden poles covered by a sheet of cloth or plastic.* • *The bicycle frame was chained to a post, so the thieves could only steal the wheels.* • Because a SKELETON is a type of frame, a person's body can be referred to as a frame when talking about its size or structure: *Robbie plays squash and lifts weights to keep his 6ft 1in frame in good shape.* • A wooden triangular frame is used in SNOOKER and BILLIARDS to put the balls in position at the start of a game, so a game itself can also be called a frame: *In the final frame she drew on her full range of skills to win.* • A person's **frame of mind** is their mood or the way they think about something or feel at a particular time: *I'm sorry but I'm not* **in** *the right frame of mind for going to a party tonight.* ○ *The most important thing is to go into the exam* **in** *a positive frame of mind.* • A **frame of reference** is a set of ideas or facts accepted by a person which explains their behaviour, opinions or decisions: *How can Christians and atheists ever come to understand each other when their frames of reference are so different?* • PIC› **Bicycles, Frame**

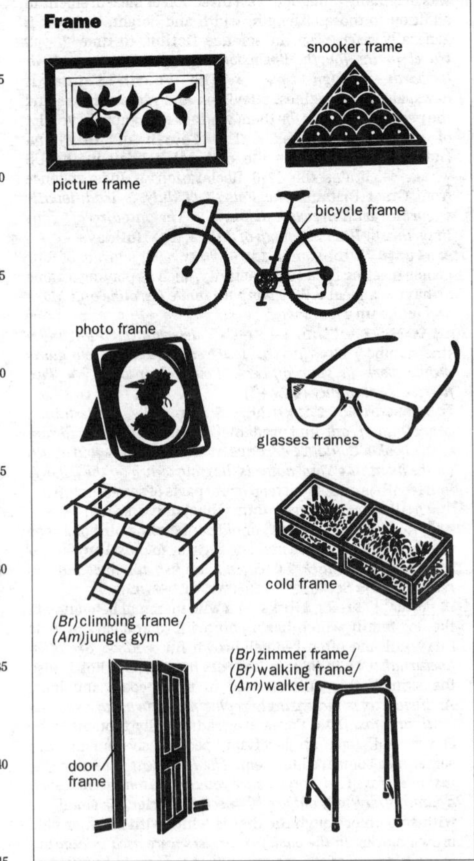

frame PICTURE /freɪm/ *n* [C] *specialized* one of the pictures on a strip of photographic film, or one of the single pictures which together form a television or cinema film

frame *obj* EXPRESS /freɪm/ *v* [T] to express (an idea), esp. after careful consideration, or plan a course of action • *The interview would have been more productive if the questions had been framed more precisely.* • *The peace proposals were framed by the five permanent members of the UN Security Council.* • *This year's budget has been framed to get interest rates down as fast as possible.*

fram·er /£ˈfreɪ·mə^{r}, $-mɚ/ *n* [C] *esp. Am, specialized* • *The framers* **of the Constitution** (= The people who wrote the US Constitution) *would never have thought that one day lawmakers would have to deal with issues surrounding the creation of new life forms.* • *The framers* **of** *the 1986 act sought to eliminate most of the exemptions, deductions and credits that gave some taxpayers an advantage over others.*

frame *obj* MAKE GUILTY /freɪm/ *v* [T] *infml* to make (a person) seem to be guilty of a crime when they are not by producing facts or information which are not true • *He was convicted of armed robbery, but he claims that detectives fabricated crucial evidence against him in order to frame him.* • *He was framed* **for** *murder and conspiracy in 1962.* • *The two civil servants claim they were framed in order to cover up for the minister's mismanagement of the department.*

frame·work /£ˈfreɪm·wɜːk, $-wɜːrk/ *n* [C] a supporting structure around which something can be built • *The chair has a bamboo framework.* • *(fig.) Any changes that you make must fit into the existing framework.* • *(fig.)*

Negotiators are still trying to find a framework for a long-term peace agreement.

fran·chise VOTE /ˈfræn·tʃaɪz/ *n* [U] **the franchise** the right to vote in an election, esp. for representatives in a parliament or similar law-making organization ○ *In 1918 the suffragists* **won the** *franchise for UK women over the age of 29.* • Ⓘ

fran·chise BUSINESS /ˈfræn·tʃaɪz/ *n* [C] a right to sell a company's products in a particular area using the company's name • *They lost the franchise when they failed to meet the required standards of service.* • *The company is planning to expand in Poland with a chain of franchise shops.* • *The company were concerned that the franchise* **holder** *apparently showed little business sense.* • A franchise is also a right to provide a service in a particular area: *Anglia Television has retained the franchise* **for** *the east of England.* • Ⓘ

fran·chise *obj* /ˈfræn·tʃaɪz/ *v* [T] • *He is starting the first school himself, but subsequent ones will be franchised to use the Fujita method.*

fran·chis·ee /ˌfræn·tʃaɪˈziː/ *n* [C] • *Mr Smith was the franchisee of a computer store, and paid the main company a fixed percentage of his total income.*

fran·chis·er /£ˈfræn·tʃaɪ·zəʳ, $-zɚ/ *n* [C] *specialized* • *The company is a shoe distributor and a franchiser of shoe stores.*

fran·chis·ing /ˈfræn·tʃaɪ·zɪŋ/ *n* [U] • *Franchising enables a company to grow rapidly because it does not have to provide all the money necessary for investment in new shops.*

Fran·cis·can /frænˈsɪs·kən/ *n, adj* [not gradable] (a person) belonging to a Christian group originally established by St Francis of Assisi in 1209 • *Franciscans are noted for their charitable work and religious speaking and teaching.* [C]

Fran·co– /£ˈfræŋ·kəʊ, $-koʊ/ *combining form* of or connected with France • *Strasbourg lies on the Franco-German border* (=the border between France and Germany). • *A francophile is someone who greatly admires France and French people and culture.* • *A francophone is someone who speaks French.*

frank HONEST /fræŋk/ *adj* **-er, -est** honest, sincere and truthful, even when this might be awkward or make other people uncomfortable • *I was brought up to be frank and speak my mind.* • *A spokeswoman said there had been a frank exchange of views at the conference.* • *The magazine, which gives frank advice about sex and romance, is aimed at the teenage market.* • **To be perfectly** *frank* **(with you)**, *I don't think she's the woman for the job.*

frank·ly /ˈfræŋ·kli/ *adv* • *She spoke remarkably frankly* (=honestly) *and openly about her experiences.* • *I'm frankly terrified every time I go on stage.* • **(Quite)** *frankly* (=To say what I really think), *I think that suggestion is utterly ridiculous!* • *"Frankly, my dear, I don't give a damn"* (said by Rhett Butler (Clark Gable) to Scarlett O'Hara (Vivien Leigh) in the film *Gone With The Wind*, 1939)

frank·ness /ˈfræŋk·nəs/ *n* [U] • *A lot more frankness is needed in sex education if unwanted pregnancies and diseases such as AIDS are to be dealt with effectively.*

frank *obj* PRINT /fræŋk/ *v* [T] to print a mark on (a postage stamp) so that the stamp cannot be used again, or to print a mark on (an envelope) to show that the cost of sending it has been paid • *Is it illegal to reuse a stamp that hasn't been franked?* • *Many large organizations have their own machine for franking the letters that they send.*

Frank·en·stein /ˈfræŋ·kən·staɪn/, **Frank·en·stein's mon·ster** *n* [C] something evil which damages or destroys the person who made it or who made it important • *In arming the dictator, the US was creating a Frankenstein who threatened their influence in the region.*

frank·furt·er /£ˈfræŋk·fɜː·təʳ, $-fɜːr·t̬ɚ/ *n* [C] a thin red-brown SAUSAGE consisting of BEEF or PORK (=types of meat) cut into extremely small pieces which is cooked when it is being made and is preserved using smoke or chemicals • *Frankfurters are often eaten in a bread roll with mustard or tomato sauce.*

frank·in·cense /ˈfræŋ·kɪn·sents/ *n* [U] a thick sticky liquid that produces a sweet smell when burned and is obtained from a tree that grows in E Africa and Asia

fran·tic EMOTIONAL /£ˈfræn·tɪk, $-t̬ɪk/ *adj* almost out of control because of extreme emotion, such as anxiety • *Where on earth have you been? We've been frantic* **with** *worry.* • *Exams always* **drive** *him frantic – he gets so nervous.*

fran·ti·cal·ly /£ˈfræn·tɪ·kli, $-t̬ɪ-/ *adv* • *As the helicopter flew overhead, they waved frantically, trying to attract its attention.*

fran·tic HURRIED /£ˈfræn·tɪk, $-t̬ɪk/ *adj* done or arranged in a hurry and a state of excitement or confusion • *Share prices have soared to a new all-time high in a day of frantic trading on the stock market.* • *Their frantic diplomatic activity failed to prevent the escalation of hostilities into full-scale war.* • *Rescuers were engaged in a frantic all-night effort to reach the survivors before their supply of air ran out.*

fran·ti·cal·ly /£ˈfræn·tɪ·kli, $-t̬ɪ-/ *adv* • *I've been working frantically all week to get it finished on time.* • *The President is frantically attempting to hold on to power.* • *Air traffic controllers at Cleveland had frantically tried to contact both planes as they approached each other.* • *Both countries are frantically preparing themselves for war.*

frap·pé /£ˈfræp·eɪ, $-ˈ-/ *n* [C] a partly frozen drink made of milk or fruit juice, or a strongly alcoholic drink served with ice • *a chocolate/strawberry/crème de menthe frappé*

frat /fræt/ *n* [C] *Am infml for* FRATERNITY

fra·ter·nal /£frəˈtɜː·nəl, $-ˈtɜːr-/ *adj* relating to brothers, or *(fig.)* friendly, like brothers • *There's always been a lot of fraternal rivalry between my sons.* • *(fig.) The President's official visit marks the start of a more fraternal relationship between the two countries.*

fra·ter·nal·ly /£frəˈtɜː·nə·li, $-ˈtɜːr-/ *adv*

fra·ter·ni·ty /£frəˈtɜː·nə·ti, $-ˈtɜːr·nə·t̬i/ *n* [U] • *He described sport as a symbol of peace and a means of promoting fraternity* (=friendship) *between nations.* • See also FRATERNITY.

fra·ter·ni·ty /£frəˈtɜː·nə·ti, $-ˈtɜːr·nə·t̬i/ *n* [C + sing/pl v] a group of people who have the same job or interest • *She's a member of the television fraternity* (=She works in television). • *The criminal fraternity* (=criminals) *will no doubt welcome the proposed cuts in police funding.* • *The racing world is a pretty* **close-knit** *fraternity.* • A fraternity (*Am infml* also **frat**) is a social organization for male students at an American or Canadian college. Compare SORORITY. • See also **fraternity** at FRATERNAL.

fra·ter·nize, *Br and Aus usually* **–ise** /£ˈfræt·ə·naɪz, $ˈ-ɚ-/ *v* [I] to meet someone socially, esp. someone who belongs to an opposing army or team or has a different social position • *Do the doctors fraternize much* **with** *the nurses here?* • *(disapproving) He accused the England team of fraternizing too much* **with** *the opposition.*

fra·ter·niz·a·tion, *Br and Aus usually* **–i·sa·tion** /£ˌfræt·ən·aɪˈzeɪ·ʃən, $-ɚ·nɪ-/ *n* [U] • *(disapproving) Fraternization between the army and the civilian population is not permitted.*

fra·tri·cide /ˈfræt·rɪ·saɪd/ *n* [U] *fml* the crime of murdering your brother, or killing members of your own group or country • *The life-long rivalry between the brothers ended tragically in fratricide.* • *The crisis might have led to another civil war, but the population was not yet ready for a another round of fratricide.*

fra·tri·cid·al /ˌfræt·rɪˈsaɪ·dəl/ *adj* [not gradable] *fml* • *The civil war is just the latest outbreak of centuries of fratricidal strife in the area.*

fraud CRIME /£frɔːd, $frɑːd/ *n* the crime of obtaining money by deceiving people • *Cheque-card fraud is at its highest level since cards were introduced 20 years ago.* [U] • *Some people tend to regard frauds* **against** *large organizations as unimportant because no single person is a victim.* [C] • *He is fighting extradition to Hong Kong to face trial on fraud* **charges**. • The **Fraud Squad** is a department in the British police force which discovers and takes action against business fraud. • LP› **Crimes and criminals**

fraud·ster /£ˈfrɔːd·stəʳ, $ˈfrɑːd·stɚ/ *n* [C] • A fraudster is someone who obtains money by deceiving people: *New measures are needed to prevent fraudsters opening bank accounts with stolen cheques.*

fraud·u·lent /£ˈfrɔː·djʊ·lənt, $ˈfrɑː-/ *adj* • *A worrying trend for insurers has been a rise in fraudulent* **claims**.

fraud·u·lent·ly /£ˈfrɔː·djʊ·lənt·li, $ˈfrɑː-/ *adv* • *If your credit card is lost or stolen and then used fraudulently, you will be liable for the first £50 of losses.*

fraud FALSE /£frɔːd, $frɑːd/ *n* [C] a person or thing that is not what is claimed • *He told people that he was a serious and well-known musician, but he was a fraud really.* • *She described the minister's proposal as an elaborate fraud that appeared to make radical reforms but in fact changed nothing at all.*

fraud·u·lent /£'frɔː·djʊ·lənt, $'frɑː-/ *adj* • *Bartlett is attacked by the opposition for tolerating, if not directing, several fraudulent local elections.* • *They claim that the fall in unemployment is based on a fraudulent manipulation of statistics.*

fraud·u·lent·ly /£'frɔː·djʊ·lənt·li, $'frɑː-/ *adv* • *She fraudulently claimed she loved him in order to get at his money.*

fraud·u·lence /£'frɔː·djʊ·lənts, $'frɑː-/ *n* [U] • *There was no question of fraudulence – it was just a misunderstanding.*

fraught FULL OF /£frɔːt, $frɑːt/ *adj* [after v] **fraught with** full of (unpleasant things such as problems or dangers) • *These negotiations have been fraught with* **difficulties/ problems** *right from the start.* • *From beginning to end, the airlift was fraught with* **risks**. • *The project had already been criticized, delayed and fraught with financial* **complications**.

fraught ANXIOUS /£frɔːt, $frɑːt/ *adj* causing or having extreme worry or anxiety • *This is one of the most fraught weekends of the year for the security forces.* • *She was clearly fraught as she announced the job losses.* • *I'll certainly meet you for a coffee, if only to escape from the fraught atmosphere in the office for half an hour.*

fray *(obj)* LOOSEN /freɪ/ *v* to become or to cause the threads in (cloth or rope) to become slightly separated, forming loose threads at the edge or end • *The only problem with denim is that it frays so easily.* [I] • *I'd frayed the edges of my jeans as that was the fashion in those days.* [T] • *(fig.) Without the unifying forces of the army and the monarchy, it seems, the nation would begin to fray* **at the edges** (= fall apart). [I] • *(fig.)* **Tempers** *frayed* (= people became angry) *as thousands of motorists began the Christmas holiday with long waits in traffic jams.* [I]

frayed /freɪd/ *adj* • *The edge of the carpet is all frayed and keeps getting tangled up in the vacuum cleaner.* • *(fig.) Moving house can leave you with battered furniture, frayed* **nerves** (= a feeling of nervousness) *and a determination not to do it again.*

fray ACTION /freɪ/ *n* [U] **the fray** an energetic and often not well organized effort, activity, fight or disagreement • *With a third country about to* **enter** (= take part in) *the fray, the fighting looks set to continue.* • *Members of the royal family rarely* **enter** *the political fray* (= involve themselves in arguments about politics). • *Three companies have already lined up to bid for his chemist group and a fourth may* **join** *the fray.* • *A good holiday should leave you feeling refreshed and* **ready for** *the fray* (= ready to work) *again.*

fraz·zled TIRED /'fræz·l̩d/ *adj infml* extremely tired in a nervous or slightly anxious way after a lot of mental or physical effort • *Frazzled commuters have welcomed the introduction of soothing music to relax them as they travel to work on over-crowded trains.* • *Many workers are feeling so frazzled that they would willingly sacrifice some of their salary to spend more time with their families.*

fraz·zle /'fræz·l̩/ *n* [U] *infml* • *A recent drive through downtown Washington left me a frazzle* **of** *tangled nerves* (= very nervous). • *She's* **worn** *herself* **to a** *frazzle* (= made herself very tired and nervous) *trying to meet the deadline for her report.*

fraz·zled BURNED /'fræz·l̩d/ *adj Br infml* burned or dried out after being in the sun or cooking for too long • *Her back was totally frazzled after she fell asleep in the sun.* • *The meat's a bit frazzled, I'm afraid, I shouldn't have left it in the oven for so long.*

fraz·zle /'fræz·l̩/ *n* [U] *Br infml* • *I went to answer the phone and when I came back the eggs were* **burned to a** *frazzle* (= completely burned).

freak STRANGE /friːk/ *n* [C] a thing, person, animal or event that is extremely unusual or unlikely and not like any other of its type • *I was born with black hair all over my back, like some sort of freak.* • *The pearl, valued at £75 000, is so big that it has been described as a freak* **of nature**. • *The surprising by-election result is regarded by many as a freak that will not be repeated throughout the rest of the country.* • *(humorous) At my school you were regarded as a freak if you weren't interested in sport.*

freak /friːk/ *adj* [before n; not gradable] • Freak means very unusual or unexpected: *She was crushed in a freak* (= very unlikely) **accident** *in a cave in France.* ○ *A freak whirlwind has destroyed over 20 caravans in west Wales.* • In the past, a **freak show** was a show in which the items being shown were a collection of people and animals that had not developed as they should have done: *We saw the skeleton of a two-headed goat that had been exhibited at a freak show in the last century.*

freak·ish /'friː·kɪʃ/, *infml* **freak·y (-ier, -iest)** /'friː·ki/ *adj* • Freakish means very unusual or unexpected, esp. in an unpleasant or strange way: *Aged 33 and about the height of your average 6-year old, she resents being labelled as freakish.* ○ *When you're a child you always imagine that your own bodily imperfections are somehow freakish.* ○ *Freakish weather conditions have caused massive traffic hold-ups in the area.*

freak·ish·ly /'friː·kɪʃ·li/ *adv* • *The freakishly cold winter has pushed electricity consumption to a record level.*

freak·ish·ness /'friː·kɪʃ·nəs/ *n* [U]

freak ENTHUSIAST /friːk/ *n* [C] a person who is extremely enthusiastic about the stated thing • *I'm fed up with all these* **health** *freaks telling me how to improve my lifestyle.* • *She's been a jazz freak ever since she went to New Orleans.* • *Last week a gun freak went mad on the metro and killed five people.* • *My aunt's a religious freak.* • *Clare is a control freak – she has to be in charge all the time.* • *Graham's a real speed freak – he loves driving fast.*

freak *(obj)* GET EMOTIONAL /friːk/ *v infml* to become or cause (someone) to become extremely emotional • *My parents freaked when I told them I was pregnant.* [I] • *He just freaked* **out** *when he heard he'd got the job.* [I] • *This song just freaks me* **out** *whenever I hear it.* [M]

freck·le /'frek·l̩/ *n* [C] a small pale brown spot on the skin, usually on the face, esp. of a light-skinned person • *Exposure to sunlight temporarily causes freckles to darken and new ones to appear.* • *He has red hair, green eyes and a face full of freckles.* • A person who is **freckle-faced** has a lot of freckles on their face. • Compare MOLE SPOT.

freck·led /'frek·l̩d/, **freck·ly (-ier, -iest)** /'frek·l̩.i, '-li/ *adj* • *She grinned, wrinkling her freckled nose.* • *She has red hair and a pale, freckly complexion.*

free NOT LIMITED /friː/ *adj, adv* **-r, -st** not limited or controlled • *Am I free* (= Do I have permission) **to** *leave now?* [+ *to* infinitive] • *I'll give you a key then you're free* **to** *come and go as you please.* [+ *to* infinitive] • *Please* **feel** *free* **to** *interrupt me if you don't understand anything.* [+ *to* infinitive] • *The agreement gives companies free* **access** *to the markets of member countries.* • *The accord guarantees free passage between the countries.* • *Free translations read more naturally than strict, literal ones in which each word is translated exactly.* • *In his speech he reminded listeners that a great deal had been achieved, such as free* **elections** (= elections in which people can vote as they wish). • A **free agent** is someone whose actions are not limited or controlled by anyone else: *The minister hinted that she had not been a free agent and that a more senior member of the government was responsible for the decision.* ○ *Once his contract expired he became a free agent and could negotiate with any team.* • **Free association** is a method of trying to see how the human mind works, in which a person says the first word that they think of after hearing a word that is spoken to them: *Psychoanalysts use free association to find out about the unconscious connections between ideas that might be influencing the behaviour of their patients.* • A **Free Church** is a Protestant Church that is not part of a country's officially accepted church. • *(Br)* **Free collective bargaining** consists of formal discussions between workers and employers that are not limited by the law or government, about pay, working hours and conditions at work. See also **collective bargaining** at COLLECTIVE. • A **free country** is one which is not controlled by another country: *After four decades of Soviet domination the Baltic States are at last free countries.* • A **free country** is also one where the government does not control what people say or do for political reasons and where people can express their opinions without punishment: *The transition from a totalitarian state to a free country will be long and slow.* ○ *I can say what I like – it's a free country!* • **Free and easy** means relaxed and informal: *The atmosphere in our office is very free and easy.* ○ *They have a rather free-and-easy relationship so I doubt whether they're ready for the commitment of marriage yet.* • **Free enterprise** is an economic system in which private businesses compete with each other to sell goods and services in order to make a profit, and in which government control is limited to protecting the public and running the economy. • A **free-for-all** is an argument or fight in which anyone can take part and in which there are no limits on what can be said or done: *The row between the Prime Minister and the opposition leader soon developed into a free-for-all between*

MPs from all parties. • A **free-for-all** is also a situation without limits or controls in which people can have or do what they want: *A glorious free-for-all followed when film directors could make anything they wanted for almost any amount they wanted.* • If something is **free-form** it does not have or follow a particular style or structure: *free-form skating* • If someone has a **free hand** they have the right or authority to do anything they consider necessary: *The company's* **given** *me a free hand* **to** *negotiate a deal with the Japanese.* • *(Br)* A **free house** is a type of bar in the UK which is not owned and controlled by a BREWERY (= business which makes beer), so the range of beers and other drinks that it can sell is not limited. Compare **tied house** at TIE [FASTEN]. • **Free jazz** is a type of modern music in which the players do not follow any written structure: *Ornette Coleman and Cecil Taylor were at the forefront of free jazz in the 1960s.* • In football, a **free kick** is an opportunity to kick the ball without opposition from the other team, which is allowed when a player from the other team has not obeyed one of the rules. • *(dated)* **Free love** is sexual activity with several partners which does not involve loyalty to any particular person: *To understand, you need to have taken part in the anti-establishment, free-love drug culture of the 1960s.* • A **free market** is an economic system with only a small amount of government control, in which prices and earnings are decided by the level of demand for, and production of, goods and services: *In a free market, if demand for a product increases then so does its price.* ○ *Government intervention is incompatible with a free-market* **economy**. • A **free pass** is an official document giving the right to travel without limitation: *She managed to obtain a free pass which even allowed her to visit sensitive military areas.* See also **free pass** at FREE [NO CHARGE]. • If a country has a **free press**, its newspapers, magazines and television and radio stations are able to express any opinions they want, even if these criticize the government and other authorities: *How can there be democratic elections without a free press?* • **Free speech** is the right to express your opinions publicly: *Does the right to free speech mean you can say absolutely anything about anybody regardless of how offensive it is?* • A **free spirit** is a person who does what they want with enjoyment and pleasure and does not feel limited by the usual rules of social behaviour. • In BASKETBALL, a **free throw** at the BASKET is given to a member of one team if a player from the other team has not obeyed one of the rules. • **Free trade** is international buying and selling of goods, without limits on the amount of goods that one country can sell to another, and without special taxes on the goods bought from a foreign country: *They are trying to reach a free-trade agreement that will abolish tariffs and quotas on imports and government subsidies on exports.* • **Free verse** is poetry whose lines do not have a regular pattern. • **Free will** is the ability to decide what to do independently of any outside influence: *New evidence shows that she did not sign the confession* **of** *her* **own** *free will, but was coerced into it by police officers.* ○ *Do you believe in free will, or do you think that the outcome of events is predetermined?* • The **free world** is those countries without Communist governments, or more generally, those countries whose governments have been chosen in fair elections and whose people have full human rights: *Wherever tyranny, oppression and brutality have threatened the free world, our two countries have stood for the triumph of good over evil.*

free *obj* /friː/ *v* [T + obj + *to* infinitive] • *Her retirement from politics will free her* (= provide her with enough time) **to** *write her memoirs.*

free·ly /ˈfriː·li/ *adv* • *Better sex education and freely available* (= unlimited) *contraception would help to reduce the number of teenage pregnancies.* • *The animals are allowed to* **move** *freely* (= without being limited) *instead of being kept in small enclosures.* • *She freely* (= willingly) *admits that she's not as fast a runner as she used to be.* • *We encourage the victims to talk freely* (= talk a lot and honestly) *about their experiences.* • *She gave freely of both her time and money to many worthy causes.*

free [NOT IN PRISON] /friː/ *adj, adv* **-r, -st** not a prisoner (any longer), or having unlimited movement • *She left the court a free woman after the case against her collapsed because of a legal technicality.* • *The new government has decided to* **set** *all political prisoners free.* • *She* **went/walked** *free after the charges against her were dropped.* • *Dogs should be kept on their leads and not allowed to run free in the park.* • *(Br)* A criminal who is given a **free pardon** (*Am and Aus* **pardon**) is officially forgiven for their crime and released from prison: *The new government is to grant a free pardon to all political prisoners.* Compare **royal pardon** at ROYAL. • A **free-range** chicken is kept for its meat and eggs but is allowed to move around in an open area: *How much more do free-range eggs cost?*

free *obj* /friː/ *v* [T] • *After a ten-hour siege the gunman agreed to free the hostages.* • *Anti-vivisectionists last night freed a number of animals* **from** *a laboratory involved in cancer research.* • *Her great great grandmother was a slave who was freed* (= became no longer legally owned by another person) *in her forties.*

free [NO CHARGE] /friː/ *adj, adv* [not gradable] costing nothing; not needing to be paid for • *I'm saving up the vouchers for some free cinema tickets.* • *Every member of the association receives a free copy of the monthly newsletter.* • *If people could travel free on public transport there wouldn't be so much traffic congestion.* • *We will install your washing machine free* **of charge/for** *free* (= without charge). • A **free gift** is an item which is given to a customer free when they buy something in order to encourage people to buy more of it: *You get a free gift if you spend more than £20.* • A **free pass** is a document giving the right to travel on public transport or go to a theatre, cinema or MUSEUM without paying: *Annie's the film critic for the local radio station, so she's got a free pass for all the cinemas in the area.* See also **free pass** at FREE [NOT LIMITED]. • A **free port** is an area near a port or airport to which goods from foreign countries can be brought without tax being paid if they are sent to another country when they leave this area. • *(saying)* 'There's no such thing as a free lunch' means that people don't usually do things for others without expecting something in exchange: *"She offered to lend me her car and then expected me to spend the weekend helping her move house." "Well, there's no such thing as a free lunch."*

-free /friː/ *combining form* • *They've agreed to let us live here rent-free while we're redecorating.* • *Many banks are now offering interest-free overdrafts to students.* • *It says the book costs £12, post-free.*

free [NOT BUSY] /friː/ *adj* [not gradable] not doing anything planned or important or not being used • *I do a lot of reading in my free* **time**. • *She's in a meeting at the moment, but she should be free* **to** *see you in ten minutes.* [+ *to* infinitive] • *If he's free could he come to the phone?* • *I'm working in the café all this week, but I've got a free evening next Monday.* • *Excuse me, is this seat free* (= is anyone intending to sit in this seat)*?* • *We queued for half an hour waiting for a free space in the car park.* • *If you take these bags that will give me a free hand to open the door.*

free *obj* /friː/ *v* [T] • *They planned to extend the car park, freeing existing parking spaces for visitors.* • *Can you cancel my meetings – I need to free* **(up)** *the afternoon to write this report.*

free [LOOSE] /friː/ *adj, adv* **-r, -st** not in a fixed position or not joined to anything • *I want the bookcase to stand free* **of** *the wall.* • *He made a loop from one end of the rope, threw it over a hook and grabbed the free end to pull himself up.* • *The bolts have worked (themselves) free because of the vibrations.* • *Rescuers took several hours to cut the survivors free* **of/from** *the wreckage.* • In chemistry, if an element is free, it is not combined chemically with anything else: *free oxygen/nitrogen* • If something is in **free fall** it is moving down under the influence of GRAVITY (= the natural force which attracts things towards the Earth) without any other force acting on it to reduce its speed: *Free fall from an aircraft is the part of a jump that is made before the parachute opens.* ○ *(fig.) Only massive intervention from European central banks will prevent the pound* **going into** *free fall* (= falling quickly in value by a large amount) *against the Deutschmark.* • A person who is **free-floating** does not believe strongly in any particular principle or aim: *The election campaign was livened up by the free-floating independent candidate who was not obliged to adhere to a particular party line.* • If something is **free-standing** it is not fixed to anything and stands alone: *Guy's very proud of the free-standing bookshelf he's just built.* ○ *(fig.) The company's electronics division is to become a free-standing independent company.*

free *obj* /friː/ *v* [T] • *We'll have to call in a plumber to free this tap.* • *In vain he tried to free the rope around his hands.*

free·ly /ˈfriː·li/ *adv* • *Remember to apply plenty of oil so that the wheel can rotate freely.*

free [WITHOUT] /friː/ *adj* [after v/ always + prep] **-r, -st** not having something that is unwanted or unpleasant •

Because the organization is a charitable enterprise it is free **from** *tax worldwide.* • *My doctor told me I would never be completely free* **of** *the disease.* • *Ensure the wound is free* **from/of** *dirt before applying the bandage.* • *Is the Princess ever free* **of/from** *journalists following her around wherever she goes?* • *Organic vegetables are completely free* **of** *preservatives and other chemicals.*

free *obj* /friː/ *v* [T always + prep] • *Not even his complete forgiveness freed her* **from** *her feelings of guilt about her infidelity.* • *She is trying to free* **herself from** *a three-book contract with her publisher.* • *He dedicated his life to freeing the world* **from** *famine and disease.* • *I'd like to free* **myself of** *some of the responsibilities of this job.*

-free /friː/ *combining form* • *The tax on lead-free fuel is likely to go up less than that on leaded fuel.* • *No working environment is entirely stress-free.* • *The journey was surprisingly hassle-free.*

free GENEROUS /friː/ *adj* [after v] **-r, -st free with** giving frequently or in large amounts • *He's rather free with his wife's money.* • *She's very free with advice but she never seems to act on it herself.* • *Mike's always been free with his time so he might be willing to help.* • *She's very free with her criticism!* • *(disapproving)* If you **make free with** something you use it a lot or treat it as if it belongs to you although it doesn't: *Don't her parents mind her making free with their house while they're on holiday?*

free·bas·ing /ˈfriː·beɪ·sɪŋ/ *n* [U] *slang* the activity of smoking a specially prepared form of the drug COCAINE

free·base /ˈfriː·beɪs/ *v* [I] *slang*

free·bie /ˈfriː·bi/ *n* [C] *infml* something which is given to you without you having to pay for it, esp. as a way of attracting your support for or interest in something • *The company's marketing rep was giving out freebies like pens and mugs.* • *All the journalists were given a freebie lunch.*

free·dom /ˈfriː·dəm/ *n* the condition or right of being able or allowed to do, say, think, etc. whatever you want to, without being controlled or limited • *I felt such a sense of freedom, up in the hills alone.* [U] • *If parents don't allow their children any freedom, they will never learn to be independent.* [U] • *At university, she revelled in* **having** *the freedom* **to** *do as she liked.* [U + *to* infinitive] • *Now that the organization has more money, it will have more freedom* **of manoeuvre/movement/action** (= ability able to choose different ways of acting). [U] • *Everyone should be allowed freedom* **of choice** (= the ability to make their own choices). [U] • *Freedom* **of speech** *and freedom* **of thought** (= The ability to say and think whatever you want) *were both denied under the dictatorship.* [U] • *They are campaigning for freedom* **of information** (= for any information to be allowed to be given to anyone who wants it). [U] • *We demand freedom* **from** *injustice/persecution/state control/unfair taxation* (= the condition of not having to suffer these things). [U] • A freedom is a right to act in the way you think you should: *Being able to vote as you want to is an important political/democratic freedom.* [C] • Freedom is also the state of not being in prison: *They regained their freedom after ten years of unjust imprisonment.* [U] • Freedom is also the ability to move: *I hate wearing clothes that limit my freedom* **of** *movement.* [U] • To **give** someone **the freedom of** a particular place is to give them special rights there: *To honour her achievements, she was given the freedom of her native city.* See also FREEMAN. • *(approving)* A **freedom fighter** is a person who uses violent methods to try to remove a government from power: *Do you think it's true that one person's freedom fighter is another person's terrorist?* • *"Freedom's just another word for nothin' left to lose"* (from the song *Me and Bobby McGee* by Kris Kristofferson, 1969) • Compare LIBERTY.

Free·fone /£ˈfriː·fəʊn, $-foʊn/ *n* [U] *Br trademark for* FREEPHONE

free·hand /ˈfriː·hænd/ *adj, adv* [not gradable] (of a drawing) (done) without the help of any special equipment for accurately creating circles, straight lines, symbols, etc. • *She made a quick freehand sketch of the view from the bridge.* • *The plans have only been drawn freehand so far, but they will be prepared to scale next week.*

free·hold /£ˈfriː·həʊld, $-hoʊld/ *n, adj, adv* [not gradable] (with or having) ownership and control of a building or piece of land for an unlimited time • *Who owns the freehold* **of/on** *the property?* [C] • *Are those flats freehold or leasehold?* • *The house is being sold freehold.* • Compare LEASEHOLD.

free·hold·er /£ˈfriː·həʊl·dəʳ, $-hoʊl·dɚ/ *n* [C] • A freeholder is an owner of a particular building or piece of land.

free·lance /£ˈfriː·lɑːnts, $lænts/ *adj, adv* [not gradable] doing particular pieces of work for different organizations, rather than working all the time for a single organization • *Most of the journalists I know are/work freelance.* • *The illustrations for the book were drawn by a freelance artist.*

free·lance /£ˈfriː·lɑːnts, $-lænts/, **free·lanc·er** /£ˈfriː·lɑːnt·səʳ, $-lænt·sɚ/ *n* [C] • *The firm employs several freelances.*

free·lance /£ˈfriː·lɑːnts, $-lænts/ *v* [I] • *I prefer to freelance from home rather than to work in an office,*

free·load·er /£ˈfriː·ləʊ·dəʳ, $-loʊ·dɚ/ *n* [C] *Am and Aus disapproving* a person who uses money, food, a room in a house, etc. given by other people, but who gives nothing to them in exchange

free·load·ing /£ˈfriː·ləʊ·dɪŋ, $-loʊ·dɪŋ/ *n* [U] *Am and Aus disapproving*

free·ly /ˈfriː·li/ *adv* See FREE

free·man (*pl* **-men**), **free·wo·man** (*pl* **-women**) /ˈfriː·mən, -mæn, -ˌwʊm·ən/ *n* [C] *Br* a person who has been given particular special rights in a city, as an honour • *Paul McCartney was made a freeman* **of** *the City of Liverpool.*

Free·ma·son /ˈfriːˌmeɪ·sᵊn/, **Ma·son** *n* [C] a member of a large, old and powerful secret society for men in which all the members help each other and use secret signs to communicate with each other

Free·ma·son·ry /ˈfriːˌmeɪ·sᵊn·ri/, **Ma·son·ry** *n* [U] • Freemasonry is Freemasons considered as a group, or their beliefs and activities. • *(fig.) The two rivals were nevertheless united by the freemasonry* **of** *the acting profession* (= by the friendly understanding between people who are similar or do similar things).

Free·phone *Br, Br trademark* **Free·fone** /£ˈfriː·fəʊn, $-foʊn/, *Am* **800 num·ber**, *Am and Aus* **toll–free num·ber** *n* [U] a system which allows you to telephone particular organizations without paying for the call, because the organizations will pay the cost • *The company has a 24-hour freephone customer ordering service.* • *For further details, call Freephone 0800 123456/call our Freephone number 0800 123456.*

Free·post /£ˈfriː·pəʊst, $-poʊst/ *n* [U] *Br* a system which allows you to send something by post to particular organizations without payment, because the organizations will pay the cost

free·sheet /ˈfriː·ʃiːt/ *n* [C] *Br* a free newspaper in which local shops or other businesses put advertisements telling people about their services, and which often gives details of local entertainment

free·sia /ˈfriː·ʒə/ *n* [C] a plant with pleasant smelling yellow, white, pink or purple flowers

free·style /ˈfriː·staɪl/ *n* [U] a sports competition, esp. a swimming race, in which each competitor can use any style or method they choose, or a style of swimming in which you lie on your front and move first one arm then the other over your head, while kicking your legs

free·think·er /£ˌfriːˈθɪŋ·kəʳ, $-kɚ/ *n* [C] *dated* someone who forms their own opinions and beliefs, esp. about religion or politics, rather than just accepting what is officially or commonly believed and taught

free·think·ing /ˈfrɪːˌθɪŋ·kɪŋ, ˌ-ˈ--/ *adj dated*

free·way /ˈfriː·weɪ/ *n* [C] *Am and Aus for* MOTORWAY • PIC〉 Motorway

free·wheel /ˈfriː·wiːl/, *esp. Am* **coast** *v* [I] *Br and Aus* to travel, esp. down a hill, on a bicycle or in a vehicle without using the legs or engine to provide power

free·wheel·ing /ˈfri·wiː·lɪŋ/ *adj infml* not limited by rules or accepted ways of doing things • *He is the freewheeling chairperson of a freewheeling company.* • *She has an eccentric freewheeling style of painting.* • *The city is a freewheeling* (= exciting) *business and entertainment centre.*

freeze *(obj)* /friːz/ *v past simple* **froze** /£frəʊz, $froʊz/, *past part* **frozen** /£ˈfrəʊ·zᵊn, $ˈfroʊ-/ to (cause to) solidify, esp. into ice, because of very low temperatures, or to (cause to) be very cold • *Water freezes at a temperature of 0°C.* [I] • *The ground had frozen* **hard/solid.** [I] • *When the lake freezes* **(over)** (= turns into ice on the surface), *we can go skating on it.* [I] • *Our pipes froze* **(up)** (= the water in them turned to ice) *several times last winter.* [I] • *(Am)* If something such as an engine or lock freezes **(up)**, it stops working because its parts have become stuck and can no longer move: *My old bicycle was so rusty that the gears had* *frozen.* [I] ○ *If the lock has frozen up, try lubricating it with oil.* [I] • If you freeze food, you preserve it by storing it at a very low temperature so that it solidifies: *Foods like tomatoes lose their texture and taste if they are frozen.* [T] ○ *Food that has been frozen should generally be allowed to thaw completely before it is cooked.* [T] ○ *Most soups freeze* (=can be preserved by being stored at a very low temperature) *well.* [I] • *The weather forecast says that* **it** *is going to freeze tonight* (=that the temperature will be at or below 0°C. [I]) • *Without a tent or sleeping bag, you could freeze* **to death** (=become so cold that you die) *out there on the mountainside.* [I] • If a person or animal that is moving freezes, it stops suddenly and becomes completely still, esp. because of fear: *At the sudden noise of the alarm, she froze* **(to the spot)**. [I] ○ *"Freeze* (=don't move at all) *or I'll shoot", screamed the gunman.* [I] • To freeze something such as pay or prices is to fix them at a particular level and not allow any increases: *The Government has frozen pensions until the end of next year.* [T] ○ *The training programme has been frozen* (=stopped at its present level). [T] • To freeze money or property is to officially and legally prevent it from being used or moved: *When it was obvious the company was going bankrupt, the government ordered all their assets to be frozen.* [T] • If you say that it would, or that it is cold enough to, **freeze the balls off a brass monkey**, you mean that the weather is extremely cold. • To **make** someone's **blood freeze** is to cause them to feel great shock or fear: *Hearing about those murders made my blood freeze.* • To **freeze-dry** something, esp. food, is to preserve it by freezing and then drying it: *freeze-dried coffee* • A **freeze-frame** is a single picture from a film, or the device on a **video recorder** that allows you to stop a film at a particular point and look at a single picture. • **Freezing (point)** is the temperature (0°C) at which water becomes ice: *The temperature was below freezing for most of the day.* • The **freezing point** of a liquid is the temperature at which it freezes: *The freezing point of mercury is -38.9°C.* • Compare MELT; THAW.

freeze /friːz/ *n* [C] • *I was snowed in for a month up at my house during the big freeze* (=period of extremely cold weather) *last winter.* • A freeze is a temporary stopping of something: *The Government has imposed a wage freeze/a freeze* **on** *wage increases.*

freez·ing /ˈfriː·zɪŋ/ *adj* [not gradable] • *It's freezing* **(cold)** (=It is very cold) *in here – can I shut the window, please?* • *I'm freezing* **(cold)** (=I feel very cold) *– have you got a jumper I could borrow?*

freez·er /£ˈfriː·zəʳ, $-zɚ/, **deep freeze** *n* [C] • A freezer is a container, operated by electricity, which preserves food at a very cold temperature so that it becomes solid and can be kept safely for a long time: *a chest/upright freezer* • A **freezer compartment** in a FRIDGE is a small, very cold part of the fridge for preserving and keeping food at a very cold temperature for quite a long time. • A **freezer bag** is a strong, usually clear, plastic bag in which food is preserved and/or stored in a freezer. • A **freezer bag** is also a **cold bag**. See at COLD [LOW TEMPERATURE]. • A **freezer pack** is a plastic container filled with water or other liquid which can be frozen and then put in a container holding food and drink, in order to keep the food and drink cold. • [PIC〉] **Bags**

freeze out *obj*, **freeze** *obj* **out** *v adv* [M] to intentionally prevent (someone) from being involved in an activity • *They turned their backs on me to freeze me out* (**of/from** *the conversation).*

freight /freɪt/ *n* [U] goods, but not passengers, that are carried from one place to another, by ship, aircraft, train or truck, or the system of transporting these goods • *The ship* **carries** *both freight and passengers.* • *He works for a freight company/carrier/shipper.* • *Will the goods be sent by* **air** *or* **sea** *freight?* • *Environmentalists would like to see the expansion of the* **rail** *freight system.* • *This railway line is used mainly by freight* **trains**. • *(Am) The escaped prisoner made his getaway in a freight car/wagon on a train.* • Freight is also the money paid for transporting goods: *Is freight paid by the supplier or the person to whom the goods are being sent?* ○ *Increased freight costs/charges are reflected in higher prices for goods.*

freight /freɪt/ *adv* [not gradable] • *It would be much cheaper to send the goods freight* (=as part of a large group).

freight *obj* /freɪt/ *v* [T usually passive] • *Grapes from this region are freighted all over the world.*

freight·er /£ˈfreɪ·təʳ, $-t̬ɚ/ *n* [C] • A **freighter** is a large ship or aircraft for carrying goods.

French bean /frentʃ-/ *n* [C] *Br for* **green bean**, see at GREEN [COLOUR]

French bread /frentʃ-/ *n* [U] a type of usually white bread in the form of a long thin loaf with a hard outer layer • See also BAGUETTE. • [PIC〉] **Bread and cakes**

French Ca·nad·i·an /frentʃ-/ *n* [C], *adj* [not gradable] a person from Canada whose first language is French, or of or from that part of Canada where French is spoken

French doors /frentʃ-/ *pl n esp. Am for* FRENCH WINDOWS

French dress·ing /frentʃ-/, **vin·ai·grette** *n* [U] a mixture of oil, vinegar and spices, used to flavour salad • *She tossed the lettuce in French dressing.* • In the US, French dressing can also be a mixture of oil, MAYONNAISE and KETCHUP.

French Fo·reign Le·gion /frentʃ-/, **Fo·reign Le·gion** *n* [U] a force of foreign soldiers in the French army

French fries /frentʃ-/, **fries** *pl n Am and Aus for* CHIPS, or *(Br)* long pieces of fried potato cut slightly thinner than chips

French horn /frentʃ-/ *n* [C] a musical instrument which consists of a long metal tube bent into circles, with a wide opening at one end, played by blowing down the tube and moving the fingers on VALVES

French kiss /frentʃ-/ *n* [C] a kiss with the lips apart and the tongues touching

French leave /frentʃ-/ *n* [U] *dated or humorous* absence from work without asking for permission or saying that you are going to be absent • *Is Pat really ill, or is she just* **taking** *French leave?*

French let·ter /frentʃ-/ *n* [C] *Br and Aus dated infml for* CONDOM

French loaf /frentʃ-/ *n* [C] a loaf of FRENCH BREAD

French·man (*pl* **-men**), **French·wo·man** (*pl* **-women**) /ˈfrentʃ·mən, -ˌwʊm·ən/ *n* [C] a person who comes from France

French man·i·cure /frentʃ/ *n* [U] the act of putting a clear liquid onto the pink part of your nails and a white liquid onto the white part, as decoration

French pol·ish /frentʃ-/ *n* [U] *Br and Aus* a type of VARNISH (=liquid brushed onto wood to produce a clear, hard, shiny surface), used on furniture • *The table top looks much better since we put some French polish on it.*

French pol·ish *obj v* [T] *Br and Aus* • *Do you think I should get someone to French polish* (=put this type of varnish on) *the dining-room table?*

French pol·ish·er *n* [C] • A French polisher is a person whose job is to put this type of VARNISH onto furniture.

French stick /frentʃ-/ *n* [C] a loaf of FRENCH BREAD

French toast /frentʃ-/ *n* [U] bread which has been covered in egg and fried • *The children love French toast with their breakfast.*

French win·dows /frentʃ-/, *esp. Am* **French doors** *pl n* a pair of glass doors, usually opening from the back of a house into its garden • [PIC〉] **Window**

fre·ne·tic /£frəˈnet·ɪk, $-ˈnet̬-/ *adj* involving a lot of movement or activity; extremely active, excited or uncontrolled • *She has a very frenetic lifestyle.* • *There was frenetic trading on the Stock Exchange yesterday.* • *After weeks of frenetic* **activity**, *the job was finally finished.*

fre·ne·ti·cal·ly /£frəˈnet·ɪ·kli, $-net̬-/ *adv* • *Everyone is working frenetically to try and meet the deadline.*

fren·zy /ˈfren·zi/ *n* (an example of) uncontrolled and excited behaviour or emotion, which is sometimes violent • *A gunman killed ten people* **in** *a murderous frenzy today in Los Angeles.* [C] • *The audience* **worked/whipped** *themselves* **up into** *a frenzy as they waited for the singer to come on stage.* [C] • *There was a frenzy* **of** *activity on the financial markets yesterday.* [C] • *The kids* **drive me into** *a frenzy sometimes.* [C] • *It's been a week of complete frenzy.* [U] • *In a moment of jealous frenzy, she cut the sleeves off all his shirts.* [U]

fren·zied /ˈfren·ziːd/ *adj* • *frenzied activity* • *frenzied haste* • *frenzied dancing*

fre·quen·cy [HAPPENING] /ˈfriː·kwənt·si/ *n* [U] the number of times something happens within a particular period, or the fact of something happening often or a large number or times • *Complaints about the frequency* **of** *trains rose by 201% in the last year.* • *The frequency* **of** *terrorist attacks seems to have fallen recently.* • *The illness occurs* **with** *increasing frequency in older people.* • *There are concerns about the frequency* **of** *side effects* (=the fact that they happen often) *with this drug.* • *She remarked on the frequency* **of** *his absences from work* (=the fact that he is absent so often). • *The frequency with which* (=The large number of times that) *he is absent from work is remarkable.* • LP> **Measurements**

fre·quen·cy WAVES /ˈfriː·kwᵊnt·si/ *n specialized* the number of times that a wave, esp. a sound or radio wave, is produced within a particular period, esp. one second • *the frequency of light* [U] • *low frequency radiation* • *The human ear cannot hear very high-frequency sounds.* • A frequency is a particular number of radio waves produced in a second at which a radio signal is broadcast: *Do you know what frequency the BBC World Service is* **on***?* [C]

fre·quent COMMON /ˈfriː·kwᵊnt/ *adj* happening often; common • *A frequent criticism of the proposal has been its high cost.* • *Cases of cancer are ten times more frequent among nuclear industry workers.* • *The most frequent cause of death is heart attack.*

fre·quent·ly /ˈfriː·kwᵊnt·li/ *adv* • *The buses run less frequently on Sundays.*

fre·quent *obj* VISIT /frɪˈkwent, $ˈfriː·kwᵊnt/ *v* [T] to be often in or often visit (a particular place) • *It's a famous café which was once frequented by Picasso and his friends.* • *In the summer months, the birds frequent the marshes along the French coast.*

fres·co /£ˈfres·kəʊ, $-koʊ/ *n pl* **frescos** or **frescoes** (a picture made by) painting on wet PLASTER (=mixture of sand, LIME and water) on a wall or ceiling • *Michelangelo's famous frescoes are in the Sistine Chapel in Rome.* [C] • *Painting* **in** *fresco is not a common technique these days.* [U]

fresh NEW /freʃ/ *adj* [before n] **-er, -est** new; different or another • *The original orders were cancelled and I was given fresh instructions.* • *Some fresh evidence has emerged that casts doubts on the men's conviction.* • *We need to take a fresh look at the problem.* • *The tea is cold – let me make you a fresh pot.* • *I've made a mistake – could I have a fresh sheet of paper?* • *There has been fresh fighting between police and demonstrators.* • *Let's stop now, and* **make a fresh start** (=start again (as if) from the beginning) *tomorrow morning.* • *(approving)* Fresh can also mean new and therefore interesting or exciting: *His book offers some fresh insights into the events leading up to the war.* ○ *We have tried to come up with a fresh new approach.* ○ *What the company really needs is some fresh talent* (=new and interesting employees).

fresh·en *obj* /ˈfreʃ·ᵊn/ *v* [T] • To freshen something **up** is to make it different and more interesting: *The Prime Minister has freshened up her Cabinet with a few new faces.* [M] • *(esp. Am)* If you freshen **(up)** someone's esp. alcoholic drink, you add more to it. [T/M]

fresh·ly /ˈfreʃ·li/ *adv* [not gradable]

fresh·ness /ˈfreʃ·nəs/ *n* [U]

fresh RECENT /freʃ/ *adj* **-er, -est** recently made, done, arrived, etc., and esp. not yet changed by time • *The police discovered fresh footprints leading across the flower beds.* • *There was a fresh fall of snow during the night.* • *The house with its fresh coat of paint looked lovely in the sunshine.* • *She's fresh* **out of/from** *university and very bright.* • *The events of last year are still fresh* (=clear) **in** *people's* **minds**. • *(fig.) She has a lovely fresh* (=clear and smooth) **complexion**. • *(esp. Am)* If you are **fresh out** of something, you have just finished or sold all of it, so that there is no more left: *The shopkeeper said she was fresh out of soap.* • **Fresh-faced** means looking young: *fresh-faced 18- and 19-year-old soldiers*

fresh- /freʃ-/ *combining form* • Fresh- means recently done: *fresh-baked bread* ○ *fresh-cut flowers* ○ *fresh-mown hay*

fresh·ly /ˈfreʃ·li/ *adv* [not gradable] • Freshly means recently done: *freshly baked bread* ○ *freshly made sandwiches* ○ *freshly planted seeds* ○ *freshly washed hair*

fresh·ness /ˈfreʃ·nəs/ *n* [U]

fresh NATURAL /freʃ/ *adj* **-er, -est** (of food or flowers) in a natural condition rather than artificially preserved by a process such as freezing, or in good condition because of being recently picked, made or cooked • *fresh fruit and vegetables* • *fresh fish* • *fresh coffee* • *Mrs Jones has stopped buying from the local butchers – she says their meat is not very fresh.* • *There's nothing better than fresh bread, straight from the oven.* • *Elise has gone out to the garden to cut some fresh flowers for the table.*

fresh·ness /ˈfreʃ·nəs/ *n* [U]

fresh COOL /freʃ/ *adj* **-er, -est** (of air) clean and cool; found outside rather than in a room • *The air in the train wasn't very fresh, so she opened a window.* • *He took a deep breath of the fresh mountain air.* • *She sent the children outside to get some fresh air.* • *I'm just going out for a breath of fresh air.* • *I work in an office all week, so I like to get out into the fresh air* (=to go outside) *at weekends.* • If the weather is fresh, it is cool and sometimes windy: *It was a lovely fresh spring morning.* ○ *As it gets closer to autumn, the weather starts to get fresher.* • If the wind is fresh, it is quite strong: *There's quite a fresh breeze today.* ○ *The weather report says the wind will be fresh to moderate.*

fresh·en *(obj)* /ˈfreʃ·ᵊn/ *v* • *She opened a window to freshen* **(up)** *the room* (=make the air in it cleaner and cooler). [T/M] • If a wind freshens, it becomes stronger: *The wind is expected to freshen as it moves in from the east.* [I]

fresh·ly /ˈfreʃ·li/ *adv* • *The wind was blowing rather freshly* (=strongly).

fresh·ness /ˈfreʃ·nəs/ *n* [U]

fresh CLEAN /freʃ/ *adj* **-er, -est** clean and pleasant • *I felt wonderfully clean and fresh after my shower.* • *Using this mouthwash will help keep your breath fresh.* • *This wine has a light, fresh taste.*

fresh·en up *(obj) v adv* • *Would you like to freshen up* (=make yourself clean) *after your journey?* [I] • *I'm just going to have a shower to freshen myself up* (=make myself clean). [T] • *The towels aren't really dirty, but I'm going to give them a quick wash to freshen them up* (=make them pleasant). [M] • *We're going to paint the kitchen to freshen it up* (=make it look cleaner and brighter) *a bit.* [M]

fresh·ness /ˈfreʃ·nəs/ *n* [U]

fresh NOT TIRED /freʃ/ *adj* [after v] **-er, -est** energetic and enthusiastic; not tired • *I'll deal with this problem in the morning when I'm fresh.* • *Try and get some sleep on the plane, then you'll arrive feeling fresh.* • *Give me a cup of tea and I'll soon feel* **(as) fresh as a daisy** (=energetic and enthusiastic).

fresh NOT SALTY /freʃ/ *adj* [before n; not gradable] (of water) not salty • *These fish are only found in fresh water like rivers and lakes.* • *Inland the river water is fresh, but it becomes salty where it joins the sea.* • *Trout are fresh water fish* (=live in water that is not salty). • *These plants are found in fresh water lakes and rivers* (=those containing water that is not salty).

fresh·ness /ˈfreʃ·nəs/ *n* [U]

fresh TOO CONFIDENT /freʃ/ *adj* **-er, -est** *infml* being too confident and showing a lack of respect, or showing by your actions or words that you want to have sex with someone • *Don't you* **get** *fresh* **with** *me, young woman!* • *I'm not having some fresh little kid telling me what to do.* • *He started* **getting** *fresh* (=behaving in a sexual way) *in the cinema, so she slapped his face.*

fresh·er *Br and Aus infml for* /£ˈfreʃ·əʳ, $-ɚ/ *n* [C] FRESHMAN

fresh·man *(pl* **-men***)* /ˈfreʃ·mən/ *n* [C] a student in the first year at college or university (*Br and Aus infml* **fresher**, *Am infml* **frosh**), or *(Am also)* a student in the first year at **high school** (*Am infml* **frosh**) • *He's a freshman at Harvard.* • *Greg and Jody met in their freshman year at college and married soon after they graduated.* • *(Am)* Freshman can also be used to refer to someone who is new to any particular job or activity: *a freshman in Congress* ○ *a freshman football player* • LP> **Schools and colleges**

fret WORRY /fret/ *v* **-tt-** to worry or be unhappy (about something) • *Don't fret – I'm sure he's OK.* [I] • *She spent the day fretting* **about/over** *whether James had missed his plane or not.* [I] • *He's fretting* **that** *he's going to fail his exams.* [+ (*that*) clause] • *"Whatever can have happened?" she fretted.* [+ clause]

fret·ful /ˈfret·fᵊl/ *adj* • *By midnight the children were tired and fretful* (=complaining a lot because they were unhappy).

fret·ful·ly /ˈfret·fᵊl·i/ *adv*

fret MUSIC /fret/ *n* [C] any of the small raised metal bars across the long thin part of a stringed musical instrument such as a guitar, that show you where to put your fingers on the strings in order to produce different notes

fret·ted /£ˈfret·ɪd, $ˈfreṭ-/ *adj* [not gradable] • *Guitars and lutes are fretted musical instruments.*

fret·board /£ˈfret·bɔːd, $-bɔːrd/ *n* [C] a FINGERBOARD (=long strip of wood on a stringed musical instrument against which the strings are pressed) with FRETS, such as on a guitar

fret·saw /£ˈfret·sɔː, $-sɑː/ *n* [C] a SAW (=metal cutting tool) for cutting curves and inside corners in wood

fret·work /£ˈfret·wɜːk, $-wɜːrk/ *n* [U] decorative open patterns esp. cut out of wood or metal or made in EMBROIDERY

Freud·i·an /ˈfrɔɪ·di·ən/ *adj* relating to the ideas or methods of Sigmund Freud, esp. his ideas about the way in which people's hidden thoughts and feelings influence their behaviour • A **Freudian slip** is something which you say accidentally which is different from what you intended to say, and which seems to show your true thoughts.

FRG /£ef·ɑːˈgiː, $-ɑːr-/ *n* [U] *abbreviation for* (the former) Federal Republic of Germany

Fri *n abbreviation for* Friday

fri·ab·le /ˈfraɪ·ə·bl̩/ *adj fml or specialized* easily broken into small pieces

fri·ar /£fraɪəʳ, $fraɪr/ *n* [C] a man belonging to one of several Roman Catholic religious groups, whose members often promise to stay poor

fri·a·ry /£ˈfraɪə·ri, $ˈfraɪɚ·i/ *n* [C] • A friary is a building in which friars live.

fri·cas·see /ˈfrɪk·ə·siː, -seɪ/ *n* a dish made of pieces of meat, esp. chicken or VEAL (=meat from young cows), cooked and served in a white sauce • *a veal fricassee* [C] • *Have some more fricassee.* [U]

fric·tion FORCE /ˈfrɪk·ʃən/ *n* [U] the force which makes it difficult for one object to slide along the surface of another or to move through a liquid or gas • *The friction* **on/against** *the ball's rough surface stopped it going very fast.* • *Friction within the pump caused the metal to become hot.*

fric·tion·al /ˈfrɪk·ʃən·əl/ *adj*

fric·tion DISAGREEMENT /ˈfrɪk·ʃən/ *n* [U] disagreement or unfriendliness caused by people having different opinions • *Politics is a source of friction in our family because we all have different views.* • *Border clashes have led to increased friction* **between** *the two countries.* • *I had a bit of friction* **with** *my teacher yesterday.*

Fri·day /ˈfraɪ·deɪ/ (*abbreviation* **Fri**) *n* the day of the week after Thursday and before Saturday • *Shall we go to the theatre* **on** *Friday?* [U] • *(Br infml and Am) She'll be arriving Friday.* [U] • *I love Fridays because I can usually leave work early.* [C] • *I was born* **on a** *Friday.* [C] • *(esp. Br) She went into hospital on* **the** *Friday* (= on the Friday of that particular week). [U] • LP> **Calendar**

fridge /frɪdʒ/, **re·fri·ge·ra·tor**, *Am dated* **ice–box** *n* [C] a container which uses electricity to preserve food at a cold temperature • *Don't forget to put the milk back in the fridge.* • A **fridge-freezer** (*Am usually* **refrigerator-freezer**) is a container divided into two parts for preserving food, one of which is a fridge and the other a freezer. • PIC> **Kitchen** Ⓟ

friend COMPANION /frend/ *n* [C] a person whom you know well and whom you like a lot, but who is usually not a member of your family • *She's my* **best/oldest/closest** *friend – we've known each other since we were five.* • *He's a* **family** *friend/friend* **of the family**. • *This restaurant was recommended to me by a friend* **of** *mine* (= one of the people I like a lot). • *We've been friends* (= have liked each other) *for many years.* • *José and Pilar are* **(good)** *friends* **of** *ours* (= we like them). • *We're* **(good)** *friends* **with** *José and Pilar* (= we like them). • *She said that she and Peter were* **just (good)** *friends* (= they were not having a serious or sexual relationship). • *I've* **made** *a lot of friends* (= met people whom I like a lot) *in my new job.* • *He's the kind of person who finds it difficult to* **make** *friends* (= form relationships with people he likes a lot). • *Emily has* **made** *friends* **with** (= formed a relationship with and likes) *a new child in her class at school.* • *Now children, can't you* **be** *friends* (= behave in a pleasant way that shows that you like each other) *and play quietly together?* • A friend is also someone who is not an enemy and whom you can trust: *You don't have to pretend anymore – you're among friends now.* • *(dated or humorous)* Friend can also be used when you are addressing or talking about someone, esp. someone who is familiar to you or your listeners: *Well, my friends, I think it's time to go.* [as form of address] ○ *Well, I suppose it's time I went to see my* **old** *friend the dentist again!* • *(fml)* In Britain, lawyers refer to each other when they are in court as **my learned** friend, and Members of Parliament when they are in Parliament refer to each other as **my honourable** friend. • A person or organization that is a friend **to/of** someone or something helps and supports them: *Thank you for being such a good friend to me, when I had all that trouble.* ○ *She's no friend of the Socialists* (= She disagrees with and does not support them). ○ *The Friends of* (= The organization which supports) *the Royal Academy raised £10 000 towards the cost of the exhibition.* • If you have **friends in high places**, you know important people whom you can ask for support and help in getting what you want. • **Friends of the Earth** is an international organization which aims to protect the environment. • *(saying)* 'A friend in need (is a friend indeed)' means a friend who helps you when you really need help is a true friend. • *(saying)* 'With friends like you, who needs enemies' means although you are my friend, you are treating me very badly. • *(saying)* 'What are friends for?/That's what friends are for' means that someone has said or done the particular thing that they have said or done because they are your friend. • *"The little friend of all the world"* (from the novel *Kim* by Rudyard Kipling, 1901) • *"Friends, Romans, countrymen, lend me your ears* (= listen to me)*"* (Shakespeare, Julius Caesar 3.2) • *"I'll get by with a little help from my friends"* (from the song *With a Little Help From My Friends* by The Beatles, 1967) • See also BEFRIEND. • LP> **Relationships**

friend·less /ˈfrend·ləs/ *adj* [not gradable] • *Friendless* (= having no friends) *and jobless, he wondered how he would survive the year ahead.*

friend·ly /ˈfrend·li/ *adj* **-ier, -iest** • *a friendly person* • *a friendly look/manner* • *Our neighbours have always been very friendly* **to/towards** *us.* • *I'm on quite friendly* **terms** *with my daughter's teacher.* • *Are you friendly* **with** (= a friend of) *Graham?* • If you describe a place as friendly, you mean that it is pleasant and makes you feel happy and comfortable: *It's a friendly little restaurant.* ○ *The restaurant has such a friendly atmosphere.* • A friendly game or argument is one which you play or have for pleasure and in order to practise your skills, rather than playing or arguing seriously with the aim of winning: *We were having a friendly argument about Green politics.* ○ *The teams are playing a friendly match on Sunday.* • Friendly countries and friendly soldiers are ones who are not your enemies and who are working positively on your side. • During a war, **friendly fire** is shooting that is hitting you from your own side, not from the enemy: *Three soldiers were killed by friendly fire when a mortar bomb hit their truck.* • In Britain, a **friendly society** is an organization to which members pay small amounts of money over a long period so that when they are ill or old they will receive money back.

friend·ly /ˈfrend·li/ *n* [C] • A friendly is a game which is played for enjoyment and in order to practise, not with the aim of winning points as part of a serious competition: *The rugby club has a friendly next week against the Giants.*

–friend·ly /ˈfrend·li/ *combining form* • A product that is -friendly will not cause damage: *ozone-friendly aerosols* • *dolphin-friendly tuna* (= fish caught without unintentionally killing DOLPHINS). • If a product is **user-friendly**, it is easy to understand how to use it: *The computer manual was supposed to be user-friendly, but I couldn't understand a word of it.*

friend·li·ness /ˈfrend·lɪ·nəs/ *n* [U] • *The friendliness of the people around here is wonderful.*

friend·ship /ˈfrend·ʃɪp/ *n* • *Their friendship* (= relationship of liking each other) *goes back to when they were at school together.* [C] • *Did you* **form** *any close/lasting friendships while you were at college?* [C] • *Germany is holding out the hand of friendship* (= the state of being friendly) *and cooperation.* [U] • *I value her friendship* (= having her as a friend) *above anything else.* [U]

Friend RELIGION /frend/ *n* [C] a QUAKER

fri·er /£ˈfraɪ·əʳ, $-ɚ/ *n* [C] a **fryer**, see at FRY COOK

fries /fraɪz/ *pl n* FRENCH FRIES

Frie·sian *esp. Br and Aus* /ˈfriː·ʒən/, *esp. Am* **Hol·stein** *n* [C] a black and white cow that produces a large amount of milk

frieze /friːz/ *n* [C] a narrow piece of decoration along a wall, either inside a room or on the outside of a building just under the roof • *They put up a frieze with jungle animals on it in the children's bedroom.* • *There is a carved marble frieze all around the walls of the temple.*

frig a·bout/a·round /frɪg/ *v adv* [I] *slang* to behave stupidly • *Stop frigging about, you idiot.*

frig·ate /ˈfrɪg·ət/ *n* [C] a small fast military ship • *The convoy of merchant ships was escorted by several frigates.*

frig·ging /ˈfrɪg·ɪŋ/ *adj* [before n], *adv* [not gradable] *slang* used to give more force to an expression of annoyance or anger. This may be considered offensive. • *You frigging idiot!* ○ *Oh, frigging hell!*

fright FEAR /fraɪt/ *n* the feeling of fear, esp. if felt suddenly, or an experience of fear which happens suddenly • *When the rescue team reached him, he was shaking with fright.* [U] • *I thought you were hurt – what a fright!* [C] • *You* **gave** *her such a fright turning the lights out like that.* [C] • *Hearing the explosion gave me the fright* **of my life** (= a very severe fright). [C] • If someone or something **takes fright**, they feel fear: *Our dog took fright* **at** *the noise of the fireworks and ran indoors.*

fright·en *obj* /ˈfraɪ·tᵊn/ *v* [T] • *An experience like that would be enough to frighten anyone.* • *Some people are frightened* **of** *birds.* • *She was frightened* **by/at** *the way he spoke.* • *Our dog frightens birds* **(away) from** *the garden.* • *Be quiet or you'll frighten the deer* **away**. • *That noise frightened me* **to death/out of** *my* **wits** (=gave me a severe fright). • *The sight of a gun frightened* **the life/the (living) daylights/the wits out of them** (=It gave them a severe fright). • If you frighten someone **into/out of** doing something, you make them so frightened that they do something that they did not want to do or they do not do something which they had intended to do: *His unpleasant manner frightened her* **into** *agreeing with him.* • *"I don't know what effect these men* (=his soldiers) *will have upon the enemy, but, by God, they frighten me"* (believed to have been said by the Duke of Wellington, 1769-1852) • *"It doesn't matter what you do in the bedroom as long as you don't do it in the street and frighten the horses"* (Mrs Patrick Campbell, 1865-1940)

fright·ened /ˈfraɪ·tᵊnd/ *adj* • *The policewoman found a frightened child in the hut.* • *She was quite frightened when she went into the room.* • *They were frightened* **(that)** *the river would burst its banks again and flood their home.* [+ (*that*) clause] • *Don't be frightened* **to** *complain if the service is bad.* [+ *to* infinitive]

fright·en·ing /ˈfraɪ·tᵊn·ɪŋ/ *adj* • *a frightening thought/possibility* • **It** *is frightening* **to** *consider the possible outcome of releasing dangerous chemicals into the environment.* [+ *to* infinitive]

fright·en·ing·ly /ˈfraɪ·tᵊn·ɪŋ·li/ *adv* • *He holds some frighteningly reactionary ideas.*

fright·en·ers /£ˈfraɪ·tᵊn·əz, $-ɚz/ *pl n Br infml* • To **put the frighteners on** someone is to threaten them: *The landlord used threatening letters to put the frighteners on the students to make them pay the rent.*

fright·ful /ˈfraɪt·fᵊl/ *adj* • If something is frightful, it is shocking or extremely unpleasant: *It was a frightful sight.* ○ *There was a frightful smell when I walked into the room.* ○ *It's simply frightful news about James.* • See also FRIGHTFUL.

fright UNATTRACTIVE /fraɪt/ *n* [C usually sing] *infml dated* someone or something that looks unattractive • *Doesn't she* **look** *a fright in that awful dress!*

fright·ful /ˈfraɪt·fᵊl/ *adj infml slightly dated* used to emphasize what you are saying • *I could get into frightful trouble if I borrow her car without asking.* • *He's been getting into a frightful flap about having to move house.* • See also **frightful** at FRIGHT.

fright·ful·ly /ˈfraɪt·fᵊl·i/ *adv infml slightly dated* • *She's frightfully* (=very) *clever.* • *I'm* (=very) *frightfully sorry about the noise last night.*

frig·id DISLIKING SEX /ˈfrɪdʒ·ɪd/ *adj* (usually of a woman) having difficulty in becoming sexually excited

frig·id·i·ty /£frɪˈdʒɪd·ɪ·ti, $-ţi/ *n* [U] • *Frigidity is often difficult to deal with because there are so many taboos attached to human sexuality.*

frig·id UNFRIENDLY /ˈfrɪdʒ·ɪd/ *adj* very formal or unfriendly • *She gave him a frigid look.* • *There's a very frigid atmosphere in the school.*

frig·id·ly /ˈfrɪdʒ·ɪd·li/ *adv* • *Sarah shook his hand frigidly.*

frig·id·i·ty /£frɪˈdʒɪd·ɪ·ti, $-ţi/ *n* [U] • *He was struck by the bareness and frigidity of the room as soon as he walked in.*

frig·id COLD /ˈfrɪdʒ·ɪd/ *adj* physically cold • *She managed to successfully grow plants that were not supposed to be hardy in the frigid Pennsylvania winter.* • *(Am) It's frigid* (=extremely cold) *in here – could you turn down the air conditioning?* • The Earth's **Frigid Zones** are the cold areas inside the **Arctic** and **Antarctic Circles** which receive very small amounts of light from the sun.

frill /frɪl/ *n* [C] a long, narrow strip of cloth with folds along one side which is sewn along the edge of a piece of clothing or material for decoration • *You could always sew a frill or two around the bottom of the skirt if you think it's too plain.* • *(infml)* A frill is also something additional which is not necessary for an object to perform its basic operations: *Forget the frills, I just want a calculator that can do simple things like multiply and divide.* ○ *The company specializes in low-cost,* **no-frills** *travel* (=simple, cheap travel with no additional features).

fril·ly (**-ier**, **-iest**) /ˈfrɪl·i/, **frilled** /frɪld/ *adj* • *She was wearing a white frilly dress.*

fringe EDGE /frɪndʒ/ *n* [C] the outer or less important part of an area, group or activity • *Members* **on** *the radical fringes of the party would like to see more protest marches being organized.* • *Until public attitudes change, these people are destined to remain a fringe organization.* • Fringe theatre is a form of theatre that deals with more unusual or emotional subjects than traditional theatre: *Fringe productions often deal with political and experimental themes and they try to challenge people's expectations.* • A **fringe benefit** is something that you get because of your job which is additional to your pay but is not in the form of money: *Fringe benefits include a company car and free health insurance.* • *"Men who form the lunatic fringe in all reform movements"* (Theodore Roosevelt in his *Autobiography*, 1913)

fringe *obj* /frɪndʒ/ *v* [T] • If something fringes a place or area, it is situated around the edges: *The fields were fringed with beautiful hedgerows.*

fringe DECORATION /frɪndʒ/ *n* [C] a decorative edge of hanging narrow strips of material or threads on a piece of clothing or material • *My aunt used to have a rust-coloured tablecloth with a fringe around it.*

fringed /frɪndʒ/ *adj* [not gradable] • *She was wearing a fringed leather skirt.* • If a piece of clothing is fringed **with** something, it is decorated with it: *The robe is fringed with ermine.*

fringe HAIR *Br and Aus* /frɪndʒ/ *n* [C], *Am* **bangs** *pl n* the hair which hangs above someone's face • *Do you think a fringe would suit me?* • *She's had her hair cut into a bob with a long fringe.* • PIC **Hair**

frip·per·y /£ˈfrɪp·ᵊr·i, $ˈ-ɚ-/ *n* [U] *disapproving* unnecessary additions to something which are added for decoration but which have no purpose • *It was an awful film – all frippery and no real substance.*

frip·per·ies /£ˈfrɪp·ᵊr·iz, $ˈ-ɚ-/ *pl n* • Fripperies are things which are unnecessary: *The council is indulging in fripperies by building a swimming pool rather than using the money to help the city's poor.*

Fris·bee /ˈfrɪz·bi/ *n trademark* a circular piece of plastic with a curved edge which is thrown between people as a game • *Let's play with the Frisbee on the beach.* [C] • *Do you want a game of Frisbee?* [U]

fri·sée, fri·sé /ˈfriː·zeɪ/ *n* [U] a plant which has green leaves with uneven edges which are eaten raw in salads • *He made a salad of spinach, rocket and frisée.*

frisk *obj* /frɪsk/ *v* [T] to use your hands to search (someone's body when they are wearing clothes) for hidden illegal objects or weapons • *I don't mind being frisked before going onto an aeroplane – I feel safer knowing everyone has been.*

fris·ky /ˈfrɪs·ki/ *adj* **-ier**, **-iest** *infml* (of a person or an animal) playful or full of activity • *It's a beautiful horse but a bit too frisky for an inexperienced rider.* • *(slang) He got very frisky* (=sexually playful) *at the party.*

fris·ki·ly /ˈfrɪs·kɪ·li/ *adv*

fris·ki·ness /ˈfrɪs·kɪ·nəs/ *n* [U]

frisk /frɪsk/ *v* [I] • If a person or animal frisks, they move around in a happy, energetic way: *The postcard had a lovely picture of lambs frisking in the fields.*

fris·son /ˈfriː·sɔ̃ː/ *n* [C] a feeling of excitement caused by fear or the expectation that something is going to happen • *As the music grew quieter, a frisson* **of** *excitement ran through the crowd.*

frit·ter FOOD /£ˈfrɪt·əʳ, $ˈfrɪţ·ɚ/ *n* [C] a slice of fruit, vegetable or meat covered with BATTER (=a mixture of flour, egg and milk) and then fried • *banana/apple fritters*

frit·ter *obj* WASTE /£ˈfrɪt·əʳ, $ˈfrɪţ·ɚ/ *v* [T] *disapproving* to waste (money, time or an opportunity) carelessly • *If I've got money in my pocket, I tend to fritter it* **(away)**. • *She fritters so much money* **(away) on** *expensive make-up.*

friv·o·lous /ˈfrɪv·ᵊl·əs/ *adj* behaving in a silly and foolish way when you should be serious • *He is generally a good student but he is inclined to be frivolous in discussion groups.* • *A frivolous attitude won't help you in this profession.* • A frivolous activity or object is one which is silly or unimportant rather than useful or serious: *I feel like doing something completely frivolous today.*

friv·o·lous·ly /ˈfrɪv·ᵊl·ə·sli/ *adv* • *You shouldn't talk so frivolously about his painting – he obviously takes it very seriously.*

friv·o·lous·ness /ˈfrɪv·ᵊl·ə·snəs/ *n* [U] • *She was criticized for her frivolousness.*

friv·o·li·ty /£frɪˈvɒl·ə·ti, $-ˈvɑː·lə·t̬i/ *n* • *You shouldn't treat such a serious subject with frivolity.* [U] • *I'm far too busy to waste time on frivolities* (=unimportant activities) *like going to the cinema.* [C]

friz·zled /ˈfrɪz·l̩d/ *adj* (of food) fried for too long making it burnt and unpleasant to eat • *I can't eat this bacon – it's all frizzled (up)!*

friz·zy /ˈfrɪz·i/ *adj* **-ier, -iest** (of hair) having small wiry curls and not being smooth or shiny • *I've got straight hair but my sister has frizzy hair.* • *Tracy's hair has gone all frizzy because she went out in the rain without a hat on.*

frizz *obj* /frɪz/ *v* [T] *infml* • *She's just had her hair frizzed* (=made curly), *and I didn't recognise her at first.*

frizz /frɪz/ *n* [U] • Frizz is the state in which hair is not smooth or shiny and has lots of small wiry curls: *This hair mousse is designed to eliminate frizz and make hair glossy and easier to manage.*

fro /£frəʊ, $froʊ/ *adv* [not gradable] See TO-AND-FRO

frock /£frɒk, $frɑːk/ *n* [C] *dated* a dress • *She's wearing that horrible pink frock again.* • A **frock coat** is a short coat with a skirt which reaches the knees: *Frock coats were commonly worn by men in the 18th and 19th centuries.*

frog [ANIMAL] /£frɒg, $frɑːg/ *n* [C] a small animal which has smooth skin, lives in water and on land, has long powerful back legs with which it jumps from place to place, has no tail, and is usually greenish-brown in colour • *Frogs make a low noise called a croak.* • *The frog startled Paul when it leaped from the garden into the kitchen.* • If someone has **a frog in** their **throat**, they have difficulty in speaking because their throat feels dry: *"I've got a frog in my throat," he gasped, "could I have a glass of water?"* • See also BULLFROG. • [PIC〉 **Reptiles and amphibians**

Frog [PERSON] /£frɒg, $frɑːg/ *n* [C] *Br and Aus slang* a French person. This word is considered offensive by most people.

frog·man /£ˈfrɒg·mən, $ˈfrɑːg-/ *n* [C] *pl* **-men** someone who swims or works under water for a long time wearing breathing equipment, FLIPPERS (=rubber or plastic shoes which are longer than the feet) and usually a rubber SUIT • *The body of the missing woman was recovered by police frogmen from a lake near her home.*

frog·march *obj* /£ˈfrɒg·mɑːtʃ, $ˈfrɑːg·mɑːrtʃ/ *v* [T always + adv/prep] to force (someone who is unwilling) to move forward by holding the person's arms behind their back and then pushing them forward • *Soldiers frogmarched several protesters* **away** *from the square.* • *He was frogmarched* **off** *by two police officers.*

frog·spawn /£ˈfrɒg·spɔːn, $ˈfrɑːg·spɑːn/ *n* [U] a close group of FROG's eggs, each egg being a small almost transparent ball with a black grain near its centre

fro·lic /£ˈfrɒl·ɪk, $ˈfrɑː·lɪk/ *v* [I] **frolicking**, *past* **frolicked** to behave in a happy and playful way • *We walked down to the sea where a group of suntanned children were frolicking on the beach.*

fro·lic /£ˈfrɒl·ɪk, $ˈfrɑː·lɪk/ *n* [C] • A frolic is happy and playful behaviour: *The two teams were so unevenly matched that the game was little more than a frolic for the winning side.*

fro·lics /£ˈfrɒl·ɪks, $ˈfrɑː·lɪks/ *pl n* • *It was all* **fun and** *frolics until it began to pour down with rain.*

fro·lic·some /£ˈfrɒl·ɪk·səm, $ˈfrɑː·lɪk-/ *adj dated or humorous* • *The game was played in a friendly, high-spirited way, with frolicsome behaviour on both sides.*

from [PLACE] /£frɒm, $frɑːm/ *prep* used to show the place where someone or something starts • *What time does the flight from Amsterdam arrive?* • *When the wind comes from the north, it gets much colder here.* • *She sent me a postcard from Majorca.* • *He took a handkerchief from his pocket.* • *Lisa took her hairbrush from her handbag and began to brush her hair.* • *"From Russia with Love"* (title of a 'James Bond' book by Ian Fleming, later made into a film, 1957) • [PIC〉 **Prepositions of movement**

from [TIME] /£frɒm, $frɑːm/ *prep* used to show the time when something starts or the time when it was made or first existed • *Drinks will be served from seven o'clock.* • *The price of petrol will rise by 5p a gallon from tomorrow.* • *Most of the tapestries in this room date from the seventeenth century.* • **From that day/time on(wards)** means starting at that time and then continuing: *From that day on, she vowed never to trust him again.* ○ *From that time onwards, he was a reformed character.*

from [DISTANCE] /£frɒm, $frɑːm/ *prep* used to show the distance between two places • *It's about two kilometres from the airport* **to** *your hotel.* • *We're about a mile from home.*

from [ORIGIN] /£frɒm, $frɑːm/ *prep* used to show the origin of something or someone • *I wonder who this card is from.* • *You're wanted on the phone by someone from the reference department.* • *The sales executive from Unilever is here to see you.* • *You can never predict the reaction you'll get from him.* • *My mother is from France and my father is from Italy.* (=She is French and he is Italian.)

from [MATERIAL] /£frɒm, $frɑːm/ *prep* used to show the material of which something is made • *The desk is made from pine.* • *Meringues are made from sugar and egg whites.*

from [LEVEL] /£frɒm, $frɑːm/ *prep* used to show the level at which a range of things begins, such as numbers or prices • *Prices start from £2·99.* • *Tickets will cost from $10* **to** *$45.* • *From one (thousand)* **to** *three thousand people visit the museum each day.* • *The number of people employed by the company has risen from 25* **to** *200 in three years.* • *This new tax will affect everyone, from school leavers* **to** *pensioners* (=will have an effect on people of all ages).

from [CHANGE] /£frɒm, $frɑːm/ *prep* used to show a change in the state of someone or something • *Things went from bad* **to** *worse.* • *She has been promoted from deputy manager* **to** *senior manager.* • *He's changed from being cynical about politics* **to** *being very interested in it.* • *Since the success of her first play, she has gone from strength* **to** *strength* (=her success has continued to increase).

from [CAUSE] /£frɒm, $frɑːm/ *prep* used to show the cause of something or the reason why something happens • *He was rushed to hospital but he died from his injuries.* • *She made her fortune from investing in property.* • *You could tell she wasn't lying from the fear in her voice.* • *Wearing the correct type of clothing will reduce the risk from radiation.*

from [CONSIDER] /£frɒm, $frɑːm/ *prep* used to show the facts or opinions you consider before making a judgment or decision • *From looking at the clouds, I would say it's going to rain later.* • *It's difficult to guess what they will conclude from the evidence.*

from [REMOVE] /£frɒm, $frɑːm/ *prep* used to show that someone has left a place, or that something has been removed or taken away • *People who were exiled from their homes during the war are now able to return.* • *She's very upset because her handbag was snatched from her in the street this morning.* • *A refining process is used to extract usable fuel from crude oil.* • If you take a smaller amount from a larger amount, you reduce the larger amount by the smaller one: *Three from sixteen is thirteen.* ○ *Thirty subtracted from fifty equals twenty.*

from [DIFFERENCE] /£frɒm, $frɑːm/ *prep* used to show a difference between two people or things • *His opinion could hardly be more different from mine.* • *The two sisters are so similar that it's almost impossible to tell one from the other.*

from [POSITION] /£frɒm, $frɑːm/ *prep* used to show the position of something in comparison with other things, or the point of view of someone when considering a matter or problem • *From the restaurant there is a beautiful view of Siena.* • *She was talking from her own experience of the problem.* • *From our point of view, we do not see how these changes will be beneficial to the company.*

from [PROTECTION] /£frɒm, $frɑːm/ *prep* used to show what someone is being protected against • *They found shelter from the storm under a large oak tree.*

from [PREVENTION] /£frɒm, $frɑːm/ *prep* used to show what someone is not allowed to do or know, or what has been stopped happening • *For many years, the truth of what happened was kept from the public.* • *The bank loan saved her company from bankruptcy.* • *He has been banned from driving for six months.*

fro·mage frais /£ˌfrɒm·ɑːʒˈfreɪ, $frəˌmɑːʒ-/ *n* a type of soft, pale cheese which is low in fat, and which is often produced with fruit flavours and sugar added • *You can make a low-fat version of the cheesecake using fromage frais instead of cream.* [U] • *Would you like a fromage frais?* [C]

frond /£frɒnd, $frɑːnd/ *n* [C] *specialized* a long thin leaf of a plant • *Ferns and palms have fronds.* • *This type of decorative fern comes from Mexico and has fronds which are two to three metres long.*

front [PLACE] /frʌnt/ *n* [C usually sing] the part of a building, object or person's body which faces forward or which is most often seen or used • *The front of the museum is very impressive.* • *From the front of the house you have a marvellous view over parkland.* • *He spilt soup all down his front.* • *Do you want me to lie on my front or on my back?* • *The* **shop** *front occupies a very prominent position on the* *main street.* • The front of a vehicle is the part nearest to its direction of movement: *If we sit near the front of the bus, we'll have a better view.* ○ *When you travel as a passenger in a car, do you prefer to sit* **in the** *front* (= next to the person driving) *or in the back?* • The front of a book, newspaper or magazine is the outside part or cover: *There was a picture of the Trevi fountain* **on** *the front of the book.* • The front of a book is also one of the first pages: *There is an inscription* **in** *the front of this book.* • If a person is **in front**, they are further forward or more advanced than other people who are doing the same activity: *You walk in front and I'll walk behind you.* ○ *In terms of research, we're six months* **out** *in front* **of** *any other team* (= it will be six months before anyone else knows as much as we do about the subject). • If someone is **in front** in a race or competition, they are winning or are more successful than other people involved: *Of the two companies, it's difficult to say which is in front at the present time.* • If a person or object is **in front of** something, they are in a position close to the front part of it: *There's space to park your car in front of the hotel.* ○ *During the storm, a tree fell in front of the train.* • If you do or say something **in front of** other people, you do or say it when they are present: *You shouldn't discuss that in front of the children.* • *(infml)* In the theatre, if you say that someone is **out front**, you mean they are one of the people watching the performance: *Don't worry about your parents being out front tonight.* • If you give someone an amount of money **up front**, you pay them in advance: *He wants all the money up front or he won't do the job.* • *(specialized)* **Front-of-house** is the area in a theatre which is used by the public: *The theatre has just received a grant to improve front-of-house.* • (CS) (J)

front /frʌnt/ *adj* [before n; not gradable] • *One of his front teeth is missing.* • *I'd like seats on the front row of the stalls.* • *Our dog is so large that it can put its front paws on my shoulders when it's standing up.* • The **front door** of a building, esp. a house, is the door on the side of the building which faces the road or the door which is used most often. • A **front loader** is a washing machine with a door at the front, rather than the top, in which you put your clothes. • A **front man/woman** is a person who has responsibility for explaining the aims or plans of a group or organization to the public. See also **front man/woman** at FRONT APPEARANCE. • *(infml)* Information which is **front-page** is so important that it deserves to be printed on the front page of a newspaper: *This story is front-page news.* • *(esp. Br dated)* The **front room** (*Am usually* **living room**) of a house is the room that faces the road and which is more formally decorated than the other rooms and which is kept for special occasions, such as entertaining guests. • A **front-runner** is the person or idea that seems to be the most likely to succeed: *Is there a front-runner in the race for the new directorship?* ○ *Of the possible options for cutting expenditure, the front-runner seems to be closing down the staff restaurant.* • A **front-wheel drive** vehicle is one in which the power from the engine is put directly to the front wheels rather than the back wheels.

front *obj* /frʌnt/ *v* [T] • If a building or area fronts **(onto)** a particular place, it is near it and faces it: *All the apartments front onto the sea.* • If someone fronts **(up)** an organization, they lead it and are responsible for it: *We're looking for someone with the right experience to front up the new department.* • If a building is fronted **with** something, its surface is covered with it: *Although the house is made of brick, it is fronted on three sides with timber.*

fron·tal /£'frʌn·tᵊl, $-t̬ᵊl/ *adj* [before n; not gradable] • *The government's latest policy has been the subject of frontal* **attacks** (= The main points have been criticized) *by many people.* • *(medical)* A **frontal lobotomy** is a medical operation on the front part of the brain which is used in treating some mental illnesses.

front AREA OF ACTIVITY /frʌnt/ *n* [C usually sing] a particular area of activity • *How are things on the work front* (= Is the situation at work satisfactory)? • *She's very creative on the design front* (= She is a very good designer). • *The government's record has been the least impressive on the employment front* (= The government has not been successful in creating new jobs). • (CS) (J)

Front POLITICS /frʌnt/ *n* [C usually sing] a group of people sharing a political belief who perform actions in public to achieve their aims • *The National Front is an extremely right-wing political party in Britain.* • *The Animal Liberation Front has claimed responsibility for releasing the monkeys from the laboratory.*

front APPEARANCE /frʌnt/ *n* the character or qualities which a person or organization appears to have in public which is different from their real character, and whose purpose is often to deceive people or hide an illegal activity • *Don't be fooled by his kindness and sensitivity – it's just* **a** *front.* [U] • *She presents such* **a** *cheerful front that you would never know she has cancer.* [U] • *Several trading companies were set up in the early 1960's to act as fronts* **for** *money-laundering operations.* [C] • *(Br infml)* If someone has **a lot of front**, they are determined to get what they want and are often rude in order to get it: *She's got a lot of front asking for promotion – she's only been here a week!* • (CS) (J)

front /frʌnt/ *adj* [before n; not gradable] • *The machinery company was a front operation for arms smuggling.* • A **front man/woman** is a person who does something illegal for an organization but who behaves in such a way that people do not think that they are doing anything wrong or illegal: *Large quantities of heroin were brought into the country on several occasions by a front man travelling on chartered flights.* ○ See also **front man/woman** at FRONT PLACE.

front /frʌnt/ *v* [I] • If a person fronts **for** an illegal organization, they help that organization by using their good character or reputation to hide its secret activities: *The police suspect him of fronting for a crime syndicate.*

front WEATHER /frʌnt/ *n* [C] *specialized* the place where two masses of air which have different temperatures meet • *A* **cold/warm** *front is approaching from the west.* • (CS) (J)

fron·tal /£'frʌn·tᵊl, $-t̬ᵊl/ *adj* [before n; not gradable] *specialized* • A **frontal system** is a weather front: *With so many frontal systems so close together, we can expect the weather to be highly changeable over the next few days.*

front LAND /frʌnt/ *n* [C usually sing] land beside the sea or a lake, or the part of a coastal town next to the beach which often has a wide road or path along it • *Let's go for a stroll along the front.* • *She remembers the town in the 1950s when the front (also* **seafront***) was lined with cafés rather than amusement arcades.* • *The company specializes in building lake-front property.* • *They run an ocean-front restaurant.* • (CS) (J)

front (line) /frʌnt/ *n* [C] a place where opposing armies face each other in war and where fighting happens • *After a brief cease-fire, fighting has broken out again along several fronts.* • *More front-line troops will be flown to the battle zone over the next few days.* • *Tens of thousands of soldiers died* **at the** *front (line).* • *Our undercover agents are* **in the front line** *of* (= in a position of direct and important influence on) *the fight against drugs.* • *The opposition party has suffered losses* **on all fronts** (= has experienced problems in everything they were trying to do).

front·age /£'frʌn·tɪdʒ, $-t̬ɪdʒ/ *n* [C] *fml* the front part of a building which faces a road or river, or land beside a road or river • *These apartments all have a delightful dockside frontage.* • *The shop's frontage lines most of the block.* • *Although the building is new, its frontage blends in well with its surroundings.* • *The estate for sale includes two miles of river frontage.*

front·bench /ˌfrʌnt'bentʃ/ *n* [C] (one of the two rows of seats in the British parliament used by) leading members of the government and leading members of the main opposition party • *The Prime Minister's reply was met with howls of laughter from the opposition frontbench.* • *She is a former frontbench Treasury spokeswoman.* • Compare BACKBENCH.

front·bench·er /£ˌfrʌnt'ben·tʃəʳ, $-tʃɚ/ *n* [C] • *He is the government's longest serving frontbencher.* • Compare **backbencher** at BACKBENCH.

fron·ti·er /£frʌn'tɪəʳ, £'--, $-'tɪr/ *n* [C] a border between two countries, or (esp. in the past in the United States) a border between cultivated land where people live and wild land • *Some of the frontier* **between** *Germany and Poland follows the course of the river Oder* • *Nepal has frontiers* **with** *both India and China.* • *Heavy fighting took place last night* **at** *the frontier.* • *There have been reports of an incident which occurred* **on** *the frontier.* • *They lived in a town close to* **the** *frontier.* • A frontier is also a border between what is known and not known: *Many researchers enjoy the exhilaration of working at the frontiers* **of** *knowledge.* • *"Space, the final frontier"* (beginning of the television series *Star Trek* written by Gene Roddenberry)

fron·ti·ers·man *(pl* **-men***),* **fron·ti·ers·wo·man** *(pl* **-women***)* /£frʌn'tɪəz·mən, $-'tɪrz-, -ˌwʊm·ən/ *n* [C] (esp. in the past in the United States) a person who lives on the border between cultivated land and wild land • *The* *book portrays him as a heroic frontiersman of the Wild West.*

fron·tis·piece /£ˈfrʌn·tɪ·spiːs, $-t̬ɪ-/ *n* [C] the picture which faces the page of a book with the title on • *A photograph of the author forms the frontispiece to the book.*

frosh /£frɒʃ, $frɑːʃ/ *n* [C] *Am for* FRESHMAN

frost [COLD] /£frɒst, $frɑːst/ *n* (a period of time in which there is) an air temperature below the freezing point of water, or the white, powdery layer of ice which forms in these conditions, esp. outside at night • *There was a frost last night.* [C] • *Frost can kill young plants, so you should put them indoors on cold nights.* [U] • *The wood looked beautiful – the hedges and paths were covered with frost.* [U] • *There were a lot of* **hard/heavy** (= severe) *frosts that winter.* [C] • *We had several* **late** *frosts* (= happening in the spring) *this year.* [C] • *I wonder if we'll have* **early** *frosts* (= happening in the autumn) *this year.* [C] • *(specialized) There were twelve* **degrees of** *frost* (= The temperature was twelve degrees Celsius below freezing point) *last night.* [U] • See also HOAR FROST.

frost *(obj)* /£frɒst, $frɑːst/ *v* • *Our bedroom window frosted* **up**. [I] • *Our lawn is frosted* **over**. [T] • *A bitter cold frosted trees and land* **with** *white.* [T]

frost·ed /£ˈfrɒs·tɪd, $ˈfrɑː·st̬ɪd/ *adj* [not gradable] • If a plant is frosted, it has been damaged or killed by frost. • See also **frosted** at FROST [GLASS].

fros·ty /£ˈfrɒs·ti, $ˈfrɑː·st̬i/ *adj* **-ier, -iest** • *Be careful – the pavements are very frosty.* • *It was a cold and frosty morning and she stamped her feet to keep warm.* • If someone or their behaviour is frosty, they are unfriendly and not welcoming: *He gave me a frosty look.* ○ *She was frosty to us all evening.*

fros·ti·ly /£ˈfrɒs·tɪ·li, $ˈfrɑː·st̬ɪ-/ *adv* • If someone does or says something frostily, they do it in an unfriendly way: *"I didn't ask you to come," she said very frostily.*

fros·ti·ness /£ˈfrɒs·tɪ·nəs, $ˈfrɑː·st̬ɪ-/ *n* [U] • *It was apparent from the frostiness of his reply that he didn't want to come with us.*

frost *obj* [CAKE] /£frɒst, $frɑːst/ *v* [T] *Am for* ICE [COVER CAKES] • *Leave the cake to cool before frosting it.*

frost·ing /£ˈfrɒs·tɪŋ, $ˈfrɑː·stɪŋ/ *n* [U] • Frosting is *Am for* **icing**, see at ICE [COVER CAKES]

frost *obj* [HAIR] /£frɒst, $frɑːst/ *v* [T] *Am* to make (narrow strips of a person's hair) paler in colour than the surrounding hair • *Gemma has had her hair frosted.*

frost *obj* [GLASS] /£frɒst, $frɑːst/ *v* [T] to give (glass) a roughened surface to stop it being transparent

frost·ed /£ˈfrɒs·tɪd, $ˈfrɑː·st̬ɪd/ *adj* [not gradable] • *They have had frosted glass put in the bathroom windows.* • See also **frosted** at FROST [COLD].

frost·bite /£ˈfrɒst·baɪt, $ˈfrɑːst-/ *n* [U] injury to someone caused by severe cold, usually to their toes, fingers, ears or nose • *Frostbite is very painful and may result in the affected part of the body having to be amputated.*

frost·bit·ten /£ˈfrɒstˌbɪt·ən, $ˈfrɑːst-ˌbɪt̬-/ *adj* • *He suffered from frostbitten toes after crossing the Antarctic on foot.*

froth *(obj)* /£frɒθ, $frɑːθ/ *v* to (cause a liquid to) have or produce a lot of small bubbles which often rise to the surface • *The waves frothed as they crashed onto the beach.* [I] • *Shake the drink before serving it to froth it* **up**. [M] • If a person or animal **froths at the mouth**, a mass of small bubbles appears from their mouth as the result of a disease: *Someone with rabies may froth at the mouth.* • *(infml)* If a person **froths at the mouth**, they are extremely angry: *She was more than annoyed – she was almost frothing at the mouth.*

froth /£frɒθ, $frɑːθ/ *n* [U] • *There'll be a lot of froth if you pour the beer into the glass quickly.* • Froth is also something which is not serious and has no real value but which is entertaining or attractive: *The book is really no more than froth, but it's enjoyable to read.*

froth·y /£ˈfrɒθ·i, $ˈfrɑː·θi/ *adj* **-ier, -iest** • *Beat the mixture until it becomes frothy.*

frou–frou /ˈfruː·fruː/ *n* [C] a large decoration on clothing which is meant to be noticed

frown /fraʊn/ *v* [I] to bring your EYEBROWS together so that there are lines on your face above your eyes to show that you are annoyed or worried • *It takes more muscles to frown than it does to smile.* • *She frowned as she stared at the blank piece of paper, wondering what to write.* • *The teacher frowned* **at** *the class of noisy children but it had no effect.* • If you **frown upon** something, you disapprove of it: *Smoking is frowned upon in many restaurants.* ○ *Many doctors frown upon a diet which contains a lot of fat.*

frown /fraʊn/ *n* [C] • *"Stop doing that," she said with a frown.*

frow·sty /ˈfraʊ·sti/ *adj* **-ier, -iest** *esp. Br infml disapproving* (of a room) having an unpleasant smell because of a lack of fresh air

froze /£frəʊz, $froʊz/ *past simple of* FREEZE

froz·en [FREEZE] /£ˈfrəʊ·zən, $ˈfroʊ-/ *past participle of* FREEZE

froz·en [TURNED INTO ICE] /£ˈfrəʊ·zən, $ˈfroʊ-/ *adj* (of water) turned into ice, or (of food) preserved by freezing • *They skated over the frozen lake.* • *We don't have any fresh vegetables, only frozen peas.* • If you are frozen, you are very cold: *I'm frozen – could you close the window?*

FRS /£ˌef·ɑːˈes, $-ɑːr-/ *n* [C] *abbreviation for* Fellow of the Royal Society (= a member of an English society for scientific study)

fruc·tose /£ˈfrʊk·təʊs, $-toʊs/ *n* [U] a type of sugar found in HONEY and many fruits

fru·gal /ˈfruː·gəl/ *adj* careful when using money or food, or (of a meal) cheap or small in amount • *Judging by their frugal lifestyle, you would never guess they were rich.* • *Although the meal was frugal, we had an enjoyable evening.*

fru·gal·ly /ˈfruː·gəl·i/ *adv* • *We had very little money left, so we ate frugally in cheap cafés and bars.*

fru·gal·i·ty /£fruːˈgæl·ə·ti, $-t̬i/ *n* [U] • *He believes in a life of simplicity and frugality.*

fruit [PLANT PART] /fruːt/ *n* the usually sweet-tasting part of a tree or bush which holds seeds and which can be eaten • *Oranges, apples, pears and bananas are all types of fruit.* [U] • *Would you like some fruit for dessert?* [U] • *What is your favourite fruit?* [C] • *Apricots are the one fruit I don't like.* [C] • *The cherry tree in our garden is* **in** *fruit* (= It has fruit growing on it). [U] • *Do you like* **exotic** *fruit, such as mangoes and papayas?* [U] • *For a healthy diet, you should eat at least one piece of* **fresh** *fruit every day.* [U] • *For this recipe, you need* **summer** *fruits, such as raspberries, redcurrants and blackberries.* [C] • *The cupboard shelves were stocked with* **tinned** *fruit.* [U] • *Our orchard contains mature fruit* **trees**. • *He runs a fruit* **and vegetable** *stall in the market.* • *(specialized)* A fruit is also the part of any plant which holds the seeds: *The fruit of the sycamore is winged and a single fruit can travel a considerable distance if there is a wind.* [C] • A **fruit bat** (also **flying fox**) is a large flying mammal which eats fruit and lives in warm or hot countries. • *(literary)* The **fruits of the earth** are types of food which have come from plants, such as vegetables or wheat. • A **fruit fly** is a small flying insect which feeds on plants and leaves its eggs on the leaves of plants. • *(Br and Aus)* A **fruit machine** is a **slot machine**. See at SLOT [LONG HOLE]. • **Fruit salad** is a mixture of pieces of different types of fruit, which is usually served at the end of a meal: *I made a fruit salad for dessert using strawberries, kiwis and pineapple.* • Compare VEGETABLE.

fruit /fruːt/ *v* [I] *specialized* • *Over the last few years, our apple trees have been fruiting* (= producing fruit) *much earlier than usual.*

fruit·y /£ˈfruː·ti, $-t̬i/ *adj* **-ier, -iest** • *This wine has a delicious fruity flavour.* • See also FRUITY [REMARK]; FRUITY [VOICE].

fruit·ful·ness /ˈfruːt·fəl·nəs/ *n* [U] *literary* • *She loved the beauty and fruitfulness of the autumn, when the whole countryside was ablaze with rich golden autumnal colours.* • *"Season of mists and mellow fruitfulness"* (first line of *To Autumn* by John Keats, 1819)

fruit·i·ness /£ˈfruː·ti·nəs, $-t̬i-/ *n* [U] • *This wine is lively with a refreshing lemon fruitiness.*

fruit [RESULT] /fruːt/ *n* the pleasant or successful result of work or actions • *It's been hard work, but now the business is running smoothly you can sit back and enjoy the fruits of your labours.* [C] • *All your work will* **bear** *fruit* (= Your efforts will be rewarded) *in the end.* [U]

fruit·ful /ˈfruːt·fəl/ *adj* • If something is fruitful, it produces good results: *It was a most fruitful discussion, with both sides agreeing to adopt a common policy.* • *(old use)* If a person is fruitful, they produce a lot of children. • *"Be fruitful and multiply"* (The Bible, Genesis 1.28)

fruit·ful·ly /ˈfruːt·fəl·i/ *adv* • *Your time and effort would be more fruitfully spent on another project.*

fruit·ful·ness /ˈfruːt·fəl·nəs/ *n* [U] • *Ideas such as these need proper thought and consideration, otherwise they lose their fruitfulness.*

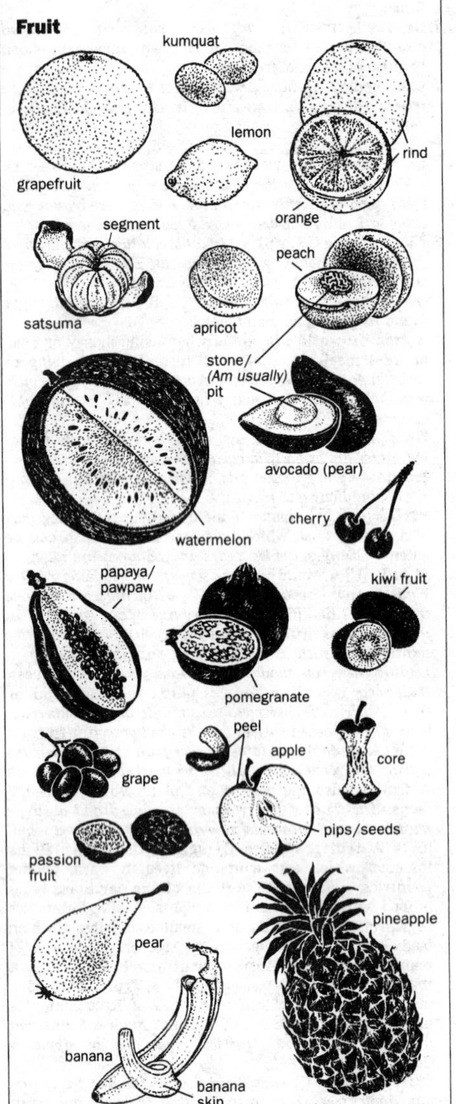

fru·i·tion /fruː'ɪʃ·ᵊn/ *n* [U] *fml* • If a plan or idea reaches fruition, it begins to happen or exist: *The idea came to fruition with an exhibition of students' work.* ○ *None of his grand plans for a TV series ever came to fruition.*

fruit·less /'fruːt·ləs/ *adj* • If an action or attempt to do something is fruitless, it is unsuccessful or produces nothing of value: *All diplomatic attempts at a peaceful solution to the crisis have been fruitless.*

fruit·less·ly /'fruːt·lə·sli/ *adv* • *For years she had been fruitlessly searching for a company to sponsor her research.*

fruit·less·ness /'fruːt·lə·snəs/ *n* [U] • *He was convinced of the fruitlessness of the task he was doing.*

fruit PERSON /fruːt/ *n* [C] *Am and Aus slang* a male homosexual. Many people consider this word offensive.

fruit·cake CAKE /'fruːt·keɪk/ *n* a cake containing small dried fruit • *Do you like fruitcake?* [U] • *My mother always makes a fruitcake for my birthday.* [C]

fruit·cake PERSON /'fruːt·keɪk/ *n* [C] *Br and Aus slang* a person who behaves strangely or foolishly • *My teacher's a bit of a fruitcake.*

fruit·er·er /£'fruː·tᵊr·əʳ, $-t̬ə·ɚ/ *n* [C] *esp. Br* a person who sells fruit in a shop or market

fruit·y REMARK /£'fruː·ti, $-t̬i/ *adj* **-ier, -iest** (of a remark) humorous in a slightly shocking way • *He was well known for making quite fruity jokes.* • See also **fruity** at FRUIT PLANT PART.

fruit·y VOICE /£'fruː·ti, $-t̬i/ *adj* **-ier, -iest** *infml approving* (of a voice) deep and pleasant • See also **fruity** at FRUIT PLANT PART.

frump /frʌmp/ *n* [C] *disapproving* a person, esp. a woman, who is old-fashioned and boring • *She looked like a frump, dressed in a thick woollen cardigan and a green tweed skirt.*

frump·y /'frʌm·pi/ *adj* **-ier, -iest** *disapproving* • *She always wears really frumpy clothes.*

frum·pish /'frʌm·pɪʃ/ *adj disapproving* • *I don't like these shoes – they look really frumpish.*

fru·strate *obj* DISCOURAGE /frʌs'treɪt/ *v* [T] to make (someone) feel annoyed or discouraged because of difficulties or problems which they are unable to deal with • *The lack of computing facilities in the office frustrated him.* • *She was deeply frustrated* **by** *the amount of criticism her play received.*

fru·strat·ed /£frʌs'treɪ·tɪd, $-t̬ɪd/ *adj* • *Are you feeling frustrated in your present job?*

fru·strat·ing /£frʌs'treɪ·tɪŋ, $-t̬ɪŋ/ *adj* • *I find talking to him very frustrating because he never listens to anything I say.*

fru·stra·tion /frʌs'treɪ·ʃᵊn/ *n* • *The noise from that pneumatic drill outside the window is one frustration I do not need.* [C] • *You could see the frustration building up inside her.* [U]

fru·stra·tions /frʌs'treɪ·ʃᵊnz/ *pl n* • *She understood the frustrations he was feeling.*

fru·strate *obj* PREVENT /frʌs'treɪt/ *v* [T] to prevent the plans or efforts of (someone or something) being achieved • *The continuing civil war is frustrating the efforts of relief agencies to feed thousands of famine victims.* • *Fear of terrorist activity will frustrate the proposal to decrease security measures.*

fru·strat·ed /£frʌs'treɪ·tɪd, $-t̬ɪd/ *adj* [before n; not gradable] • Someone who is frustrated has been unsuccessful in their job: *Frustrated writers often end up as teachers.*

fru·stra·tion /frʌs'treɪ·ʃᵊn/ *n* [U] • *Strong emotions often arise from the satisfaction or frustration of desires.*

fry *(obj)* COOK /fraɪ/ *v* to cook (food) in hot oil or fat • *Put a little oil into the pan and quickly fry the vegetables.* [T] • *Frying has become less popular as a method of cooking because people are more health conscious.* [I] • *(fig. infml) You'll fry* (= Your skin will get burnt) *if you lie in the sun all day.* [I] • A **frying pan** (*Am and Aus also* **skillet**) is a flat metal pan with a long handle which is used for frying food. • *(Br infml)* A **fry-up** is a meal consisting of fried meat, eggs and vegetables: *Do you want a fry-up for breakfast? I've got some bacon, eggs, sausages and tomatoes.* • *(saying)* 'Out of the frying pan into the fire' means changing from a bad or difficult situation to one which is worse. • PIC **Containers, Cooking, Pan**

fried /fraɪd/ *adj* [not gradable] • *We had fried chicken for supper.* • *Fried food contains more fat than grilled food.*

fry·er, fri·er /£'fraɪ·əʳ, $-ɚ/ *n* [C] • *(Am)* A fryer is a chicken suitable for frying. • A fryer is also a metal pan in which food is fried: *I've just bought a new* **deep-fat** *fryer for frying chips.*

fry FISH /fraɪ/ *pl n* young, small fish • *What's important is not how many eggs hatch into fry, but how many fry grow large enough to be caught.*

FT NEWSPAPER /ˌef'tiː/ *n* [U] **the FT** *abbreviation for* Financial Times (= a British newspaper)

ft MEASUREMENT *n* [C] *pl* **ft** *abbreviation for* FOOT MEASUREMENT • *The main bedroom measures 24ft by 18ft (24' x 18').*

FTSE 100 (In·dex) /ˌfʊt·si·wʌn'hʌn·drəd/, *infml* **Foot·sie** *n* [U] a number which expresses the value of the share prices of the one hundred most important British companies, which is published by the Financial Times (= a British newspaper for people interested in business and finance) • *The FTSE 100 closed 31·6 points down at 2459·3 in today's trading.* • Compare DOW JONES (INDUSTRIAL) AVERAGE; NIKKEI.

fuchs·ia /'fjuː·ʃə/ *n* [C] a small plant, often grown in gardens, which has red, purple or white flowers that hang down • *Their terrace was filled with tubs of geraniums and fuchsias.* • PIC **Flowers and plants**

fuchs·ia /'fjuː·ʃə/ *adj* [not gradable], *n* • Fuchsia is a pinkish-purple colour: *She was wearing a fuchsia dress and silver jewellery.* ○ *Fuchsia is one of my least favourite colours.* [U]

fuck *(obj)* HAVE SEX /fʌk/ *v* [I/T] *taboo slang* to have sex (with someone), esp. when considered to be only physical and without any emotional involvement

fuck /fʌk/ *n* [C] *taboo slang* • A fuck is either the act of having sex or a sexual partner.

fuck EXTREME ANGER /fʌk/ *exclamation taboo* used when expressing extreme anger or annoyance to add force to what is being said • *Fuck – the bloody car won't start!* • *Fuck what he says – I'll do it my own way.* • *Shut the fuck up!* • *Who the fuck does she think she is, telling me what to do?*

fuck·ing /ˈfʌk·ɪŋ/ *adj, adv* [not gradable] *taboo slang* • *That was a fucking waste of time.* • *That was a fucking awful meal.*

fuck *(obj)* **a·bout/a·round** *v adv taboo slang* to waste (someone's) time and energy • *Stop fucking around!* [I] • *You shouldn't fuck him about like that.* [T]

fuck off GO AWAY *v adv* [I] *taboo slang* to go away • *Just fuck off and leave me alone!*

fuck off *obj* ANNOY, **fuck** *obj* **off** *v adv* [M] *taboo slang* to annoy or upset (someone) greatly • *Being spoken to like that really fucked her off.*

fuck up *obj*, **fuck** *obj* **up** *v adv* [M] *taboo slang* to damage, harm or upset (someone or something), or to do (something) very badly • *She's been really fucked up since her parents' divorce.* • *He's worried that he fucked his job interview up.* • *"They fuck you up, your mum and dad./ They may not mean to, but they do."* (first lines of *This be the Verse* by Philip Larkin, 1974)

fuck–up /ˈfʌk·ʌp/ *n* [C] *taboo slang* • *It's been one fuck-up after another since she took charge.*

fuck all /fʌk/ *n* [U] *taboo slang* nothing • *It's not his fault – he had fuck all to do with it.*

fuck all /fʌk/ *adj* • *The wheel's broken, it's fuck all* (= no) *use to anyone now.*

fuck·er /£ˈfʌk·əʳ, $-ɚ/, **fuck·head** /ˈfʌk·hed/ *n* [C] *taboo slang* someone who has done something extremely stupid

fud·dle *obj* /ˈfʌd·l̩/ *v* [T often passive] *infml* to confuse (someone) and make them unable to think clearly • *Aunt Agatha becomes fuddled if she has too many visitors.*

fud·dle /ˈfʌd·l̩/ *n* [C usually sing] *infml* • *Sometimes he gets in a fuddle and then he can't find things.*

fud·dy–dud·dy /ˈfʌd·iˌdʌd·i/ *n* [C] *disapproving* a person who has old-fashioned ideas and dresses in an old-fashioned way • *She's just an old fuddy-duddy!*

fudge SWEET /fʌdʒ/ *n* [U] a soft sweet made from sugar, butter and milk which often has flavouring added • *vanilla/walnut fudge*

fudge *(obj)* DO BADLY /fʌdʒ/ *v esp. disapproving* to do (something) badly in order to hide a dishonest or illegal action, or to avoid making a clear decision or statement • *Each political party is accusing the other of fudging to hide the true level of unemployment.* [I] • *There are complaints that the government has been fudging figures to make it look as though targets have been met.* [T]

fudge /fʌdʒ/ *n* [C usually sing] • *She suspects that this compromise deal will be nothing more than a fudge.* • *It's a bit of a fudge but we could put the cost through on next year's budget.*

fu·el /fjʊəl/ *n* a substance which is used to provide heat or power, usually by being burned • *Wood, coal, oil, petrol and gas are all different kinds of fuel.* [U] • *Plutonium is a fuel used to produce nuclear energy.* [C] • *Fuel bills are usually higher in the winter than in the summer, because fuel* **consumption** *is higher then.* [U] • *To the south of the city is a* **nuclear** *fuel reprocessing plant.* [U] • *There are plans to reduce the tax on* **unleaded** *fuel.* [U] • *The new exhaust system, it is claimed, will reduce noise levels, improve engine power and lower fuel* **consumption**. [U] • Fuel is also anything that keeps people's ideas or feelings active, or makes them stronger: *His unreasonable behaviour only* **gives** *fuel* **to** *his opponents.* [U] ○ *Reports in today's newspapers have* **added** *fuel* **to** *the controversy* (= made it worse). [U] ○ *The discovery that the government was aware of the cover-up has really* **added fuel to the fire/flames** (= made a bad situation worse). • *We've never had a* **fuel-injected** *car* (= a car with a device which puts an exact amount of fuel into the engine) *before.* • A **fuel rod** is part of a device which produces nuclear power.

fu·el *obj* /fjʊəl/ *v* [T] **-ll-** or *Am usually* **-l-** • *Our heating system is fuelled* (= its power is provided) *by gas.* • *We have a gas-fuelled heating system.* • *(fig.) The prime minister's speech fuelled* (= made stronger) **speculation** *that she is about to resign.* • *(fig.) The rapid promotion of the director's son has itself fuelled* (= increased) *resentment within the company.*

fug /fʌg/ *n* [U] a condition which can exist in a small, crowded place when the air is not pure, esp. because of smoke or heat • *There was such a fug in the train carriage, I was very relieved when we reached the station.* • *We smiled at each other through a grey fug of cigarette smoke.*

fug·gy /ˈfʌg·i/ *adj* **-ier**, **-iest** • *This room is dreadfully fuggy* (= it is hot and smoky and the air is not pure)*!*

fug·i·tive PERSON /£ˈfjuː·dʒɪ·tɪv, $-t̬ɪv/ *n* [C] a person who is running away or hiding from the police or a dangerous situation • *After three weeks, the police finally caught the fugitives.* • *Thousands of fugitives are fleeing from the war-torn area.* • *She travelled on a boat full of fugitives* **from** *post-Holocaust Europe.* • *Butch Cassidy and the Sundance Kid were fugitives* **from justice** (= they ran away to avoid being tried in court).

fug·i·tive /£ˈfjuː·dʒɪ·tɪv, $-t̬ɪv/ *adj* [before n; not gradable] • *Fugitive families who have fled* (= families who have run away from) *the fighting in the cities are now trying to survive in the mountains.*

fug·i·tive TEMPORARY /£ˈfjuː·dʒɪ·tɪv, $-t̬ɪv/ *adj fml or literary* (esp. of thoughts or feelings) lasting for only a short time; temporary • *He struggled to capture his fugitive impressions in a poem.*

fugue /fjuːg/ *n* [C] a piece of music consisting of three or more tunes played together • *a Bach organ fugue*

–ful HAVING /fᵊl, fʊl/ *combining form* having the stated quality to a high degree, or causing it • *a colourful picture* (= a picture containing a lot of colours) • *a powerful person* (= someone who has a lot of power) • *a tearful child* (= a child who is crying a lot) • *a painful illness* (= an illness causing pain) • *a truthful person* (= someone who always tells the truth) • LP› **Combining forms, Stress in pronunciation**

–ful·ly /-fᵊl·i, -fʊ·li/ *combining form* • *powerfully* • *tearfully* • *joyfully* • *truthfully*

–ful AMOUNT /-fᵊl, -fʊl/ *combining form* the amount of something needed to fill the stated container or place • *two spoonfuls/spoonsful* **of** *sugar* • *a mouthful* **of** *tea* • *a houseful* **of** *people*

ful·crum /ˈfʊl·krəm/ *n* [C] *pl* **fulcrums** or *specialized* **fulcra** /ˈfʊl·krə/ the point at which a bar, or something that is balancing, is supported or balances • *A pair of weighing scales balances on a fulcrum.* • *A see-saw balances at its fulcrum.* • *(fig.) The fulcrum* (= main subject) **of** *the* **debate/argument** *is the individual's right to choose.*

ful·fil *obj* MAKE HAPPEN, *Am usually and Aus also* **ful·fill** /fʊlˈfɪl/ *v* [T] **-ll-** to do (something that is expected, hoped for or promised) or to cause it to happen • *A school fails if it does not fulfil the* **needs/requirements** *of its pupils.* • *At the age of 45, she finally fulfilled her* **ambition** *to run a marathon.* • *Zoos, it is often claimed, fulfil an important* **function** *in the protection of rare species.* • *That old cupboard isn't fulfilling any* **useful function** *any more, let's get rid of it.* • *He has also sacked his finance minister for 'having failed to fulfil his job* **obligations**'. • *We're looking for a very specific sort of person and this woman seems to fulfil all of our* **criteria**. • *So did the course fulfil all your* **expectations**? • *Do you think the President will be able to fulfil his promise not to raise taxes?* • *Macbeth didn't expect the witches' prophecy to be fulfilled.* • *We're suing our suppliers for failing to fulfil their contract.*

ful·fil·ment, *Am usually and Aus also* **ful·fill·ment** /fʊlˈfɪl·mənt/ *n* [U] • *For many women, the fulfilment of family* **obligations** *prevents the furtherance of their career.* • *Due to circumstances beyond our control, the fulfilment* **of** *your contract will be delayed by* (= what was agreed in it will not be done for) *several weeks.* • *When their son became a doctor, it was the fulfilment* **of** *all their dreams* (= what they had hoped for, happened).

ful·fil *obj* SATISFY, *Am usually and Aus also* **ful·fill** /fʊlˈfɪl/ *v* [T] **-ll-** to satisfy; to make happy • *I don't feel that my present way of life really fulfils me.* • *Sally is looking for a job in which she will be able to fulfil* **herself** (= fully develop her abilities and interests).

ful·filled /fʊlˈfɪld/ *adj* • *For the first time in my life, I feel really fulfilled* (= I am happy with my life).

ful·fill·ing /fʊlˈfɪl·ɪŋ/ *adj* • *Nursing is hard work, but it can be very fulfilling* (= can make you feel happy and satisfied).

ful·fil·ment, *Am usually* **ful·fill·ment** /fʊlˈfɪl·mənt/ *n* [U] • *After trying many different kinds of jobs, Henry finally* **found** *fulfilment* (= happiness. and satisfaction) *as a* *teacher.* • *It's a novel about a woman who demands her right to sexual fulfilment in a society that makes no such allowance.*

full [CONTAINING A LOT] /fʊl/ *adj* **-er, -est** (of a container or a space) holding or containing as much as possible or a lot; filled • *Now this cup is very full so be careful with it, Joe.* • *"More vegetables, anyone?" "No thanks, my plate's already full."* • *I tried to get in the cinema last night but it was full.* • *Don't talk with your* **mouth** *full!* • *He brought home a box full* **of** *books.* • *She looked at him with her eyes full* **of** *tears.* • *I tried to get on the 8.45 train but it was full* **(up)**. • *Don't* **fill** *your glass too full* (= put too much liquid in it) *or you'll only spill it.* • *The theatre was only* **half** *full* (= it contained only half the number of people it was able to contain) *last night.* • *We decided to go to a different restaurant because the one we went to first was too full* (= there were too many people in it). • If something or someone is full **of** something, they have a lot of it: *This sweater is full* **of** *holes.* ○ *Please type this letter again, it's full* **of** *mistakes.* ○ *I'm full* **of** *admiration for you.* ○ *You're always so full* **of** *energy.* ○ *(infml) Your children are* **full of beans** (= very active and energetic), *aren't they?* • *The train was full* **to bursting** *(with people)* (= completely filled with people) *and I had to stand all the way to London.* • *I left the tap running and now the bath is full* **to overflowing** (= completely filled with water). • *She put a jug on the table full* **to the brim** (= completely filled) **with** *cream.* • *(fig.) I've got rather a full week* (= I have a lot of work/activities planned) *next week – could we postpone our meeting?* • *(fig.) Her* **heart** *was so full* (= she was so happy), *she couldn't speak.* • *She's so* **full of** (= she gives attention only to) *what she's doing, she never takes any notice of anyone else.* • *"Did the kids enjoy their trip to the zoo?" "Oh, yes, they were* **full of it** (= very excited and talking a lot about it) *when they got back this afternoon."* • *(disapproving) Since he got his new job, Nick has been very* **full of** *his* **own importance** (= thinks that he is very important). • *(disapproving) I can't bear Sarah – she's so* **full of** *herself* (= thinks that she is very important). • *(Br and Aus) What's made you so* **full of the joys of spring** (= very happy) *this morning?* • *We're expecting to have a* **full house** (= every seat in the cinema/theatre/sports ground to be filled) *tonight.* • Ⓟ

full·ness, ful·ness /ˈfʊl·nəs/ *n* [U]

full [FOOD] /fʊl/ *adj* **-er, -est** having eaten so much food that you cannot eat any more • *I don't want any more pudding, thank you, I'm full* **(up)**. • *Tom ate so much that he was* **full to the brim/full to bursting** (= was unable to eat any more). • *If you go swimming* **on a full stomach** (= after having eaten), *you might get cramp.* • Ⓟ

full·ness, ful·ness /ˈfʊl·nəs/ *n* [U] • *I've always disliked that feeling of fullness* (= of having eaten a lot) *after a large meal.*

full [COMPLETE] /fʊl/ *adj* [before n] **-er, -est** complete; whole; containing a lot of detail • *The headmaster demanded a full explanation from the boys.* • *We do not yet have full details of the bomb explosion.* • *It is likely to be some weeks before the full* **story** *can be told* (= before it will be possible to say what happened). • *Few journalists have managed to convey the full horror of the situation.* • *The full impact of the tax changes is yet to be felt.* • *Write your full name and address at the top of the page.* • *What shall we do on our last full day in Paris?* • *It's been a full six months since I last heard from her.* • *He unwound the rope to its full extent, but it still wasn't long enough.* • *Are you a full* **member** (= do you have all the membership rights) *of the club?* • *She has a very full* (= busy, interesting and satisfying) *life.* • *Some plants need to be in full sun* (= to have the sun shining on them) *all the time.* • **Things have/The wheel has come full circle** (= a situation that existed in the past has come back into existence) *now that long skirts are in fashion again.* • *The minister was* **in full flow** (= in the middle of what he was saying) *when a man at the back started shouting.* • *The yacht was* **in full sail** (= all its sails were open). • *(fig.) Jack was* **in full sail** (= in the middle of saying something) *when there was a sudden knock at the door.* • *The party was* **in full swing** (= was no longer in its early stages and there was a lot of activity) *when we arrived.* • *Andy and Vicki had a furious row outside the front of their house,* **in full view of** (= seen by) *the watching neighbours.* • *He's a* **full-blooded** *Maori* (= is not of mixed race). • *Andy is a* **full-blooded** (= strong and enthusiastic) *Liverpool supporter.* • *It has been confirmed that his illness has developed into* **full-blown** (= fully developed) *AIDS.* • *The price of the hotel room includes* **full board** (= the providing of all meals). Compare **half board** at HALF. • *A* **full-grown**/*(esp. Br)* **fully-grown** *giraffe is 5·5m tall.* • *Steve won the poker game with a* **full house** (= of his five cards, three were of the same type and two were of a different type but the same as each other). • *I don't think that newspapers ought to be allowed to print* **full-frontal pictures/full-frontals** (= pictures of naked people showing the front of their bodies). • *He tripped on the rug, and fell* **full length** (= so that his whole body lay) *on the floor.* • *She likes to look at herself in a* **full-length** *mirror* (= one which shows her whole body) *before she goes out.* • *There are two* **full-length** (= usual length and not made shorter) *films on television tonight.* • *Victoria wore a* **full-length** *evening gown* (= one reaching to her feet) *to the ball.* • *There's a* **full moon** (= the moon is appearing as a complete disc) *tonight.* • *This newspaper has nothing in it but* **full-page** *advertisements* (= those filling a complete page). • *The* **full-scale** *models of* (= models the same size as the original) *dinosaurs are one of the main attractions of London's Natural History museum.* • *The disagreement between the management and the unions has now developed into a* **full-scale** (= very large) *row.* • *(Am) I need to find a good* **full-service** *bank* (= one which provides the complete range of services). • *(Br and Aus)* A **full stop** *(Am* **period***)* is a mark that you put at the end of a sentence, or at the end of a word that has been abbreviated. • *It's no good trying to persuade me – I'm not going to the party,* **full stop** (= and I'm not willing to talk about it any more). • *Our negotiations have* **come to a full stop** (= we are not able to continue with them). • A **full-time** job is done for the whole of a working week: *Derek has finally settled down and got himself a full-time job.* ○ *She went back to work full-time when her youngest child went to school.* Compare **part-time** at PART [SOME]. ○ *(fig.) Keeping our garden tidy is a full-time* **job/occupation** (= takes a lot of time). • *(Br) The score was 2-2 at* **full time** (= the end of the usual period of time during which a game is played). Compare **half-time** at HALF. • [LP] **Sports, Work** Ⓟ

full /fʊl/ *n* • *The bill must be paid* **in full** (= completely) *by the end of the month.*

full /fʊl/ *adv* **-er, -est** • *You know* **full well** (= you are completely aware) *that you're not supposed to go there without asking me!*

full·ness, ful·ness /ˈfʊl·nəs/ *n* [U] • *The fullness* **of** *the research report* (= how much detail it contains) *has been widely praised.* • *I envy him the fullness* **of** *his life* (= how

FULL STOP / PERIOD [.]

A *(Br)* full stop or *(Am)* period is used:

- **to mark the end of a sentence that is not a direct question and does not express a strong feeling**
  I'll meet you outside the cinema. Be there by half past eight.

  Notice that a comma (,) can only mark the end of a sentence which is in quotation marks and followed by a reporting verb:
  "I think this bag is yours," she said.

- **to mark shortened words and in people's titles** (this is becoming dated in Britain)
  e.g. (= for example) • *no.* (= number)
  Feb. 17th (= February 17th)
  Mr. James • *Mrs. Drew* • *Ms. Talbot* • *Dr. Grey*

- **as one way to separate the numbers in dates and times**
  (Br) 13.7.84 or *(Am) 7.13.84* (= 13 July 1984)
  8.30 pm or *20.30* (= half past eight in the evening)

- **as the decimal point in figures and amounts of money.** It is usually read out as "point".
  6.25 metres ("six point two five")

A point is *not* used to separate large numbers or telephone numbers
The city has a population of 4,500,000
Please telephone (071) 565 6821

busy and interesting his life is). • **In the fullness of time** (= After a (long) period of time), *the trees we've planted at the front of the house will grow to form a screen.*

full·y /ˈfʊl·i/ *adv* • *Have you fully* (= completely) *recovered from your illness?* • *I was fully intending to call you last night.* • *If you're not fully satisfied with the trousers, you can return them.* • *I'm sorry, madam, the restaurant is fully booked* (= all the tables are being kept to be used by people who have asked for them in advance). • *Brian is now a fully qualified teacher.* • **Fully fashioned** /*(Am also)* **full-fashioned** clothes, such as STOCKINGS and TIGHTS, are made so that they fit the body exactly. • If something is **fully fledged** /*(Am)* **full-fledged**, it is completely developed: *What started as a small business is now a fully fledged company.* ○ *After years of study, Tim is now a fully fledged* (= completely trained) *architect.* • [LP] **Very, completely**

full [GREATEST POSSIBLE] /fʊl/ *adj* [before n] **-er, -est** the greatest possible; MAXIMUM • *James is very bright, but he doesn't make full use of his abilities.* • *Nobody got full* **marks** (= all the answers right) *in the spelling test.* • **Full marks** *to Mrs Dunn* (= she should be praised) *for alerting the police about the break-in.* • *It doesn't seem likely that we will see a return to full employment* (= that all the people in the country will have a job) *in the near future.* • *It annoys me when our neighbours have their windows open and their television on* **(at) full blast** (= as loudly as possible). • *Tony drove his car* **(at) full speed/tilt/***(Br)* **pelt** (= as fast as possible) *down the motorway to get to the airport on time.* • If you go **full steam ahead** with something you do it with all your energy and enthusiasm: *Now that problem is out of the way it's full steam ahead to get the job finished.* • *(Br) The emergency services are working* **(at) full stretch** (= as hard as possible) *to cope with the accident.* • *The winning team left the football ground in a bus, with crowds of fans* **in full cry** *after them* (= excitedly following them). • *Police have begun a* **full-scale** *investigation* (= one using all possible methods) *into the murder.* • (P)

full /fʊl/ *n* • *Richard always enjoys life* **to the full** (= as much as possible).

full·y /ˈfʊl·i/ *adv* • *Kate has always participated fully* (= as much as possible) *in the life of the school.* • *Students are advised to answer all questions as fully as possible.*

full [LARGE] /fʊl/ *adj* **-er, -est** (of clothing) loose or containing a lot of material, or (of parts of the body) quite large and rounded. • *Charlotte wore a ball gown with a tight bodice and a full skirt.* • *This jacket is rather full across the shoulders, can you alter it?* • *Women often have full* **faces/***become full* **in the face** *when they're pregnant.* • *She's just had an operation to make her breasts fuller.* • *She inherited her mother's full mouth/lips and dark hair.* • Full is sometimes used to avoid saying fat: *I'm sorry, sir, we don't sell clothes for the fuller* **figure**. • (P)

full·ness, ful·ness /ˈfʊl·nəs/ *n* [U] • *I think the fullness* **of** *the sleeves* (= the fact that they have a lot of material in them) *spoils the look of this dress.* • *She emphasized the fullness* **of** *her lips* (= how large and rounded they are) *by wearing bright red lipstick.*

full [STRONG] /fʊl/ *adj* **-er, -est** (of a flavour, sound, smell, etc.) strong or deep • *This wine has a full fruity flavour.* • *A cello has a fuller sound than a violin.* • *The full rich aroma of coffee wafted from the kitchen.* • *Red wines tend to be more* **full-bodied** (= stronger in taste) *than white wines.* • (P)

full·ness, ful·ness /ˈfʊl·nəs/ *n* [U] • *I like this cheese's for the fullness* **of** *its flavour* (= its strong flavour).

full [STRAIGHT] /fʊl/ *adv* [before adv/prep] **-er, -est** straight; directly • *The footballer was carried off the field after he was kicked full* **in** *the stomach.* • *The intruders turned and ran as the police shone their torches full* **on** *them.* • (P)

full·back /ˈfʊl·bæk/ *n* [C] a defending player in games such as football and HOCKEY who plays near the end of the field, or a player in American football whose team has control of the ball

-full·y /-fᵊl·i, -fʊ·li/ *combining form* See at -FUL [HAVING]

ful·mi·nate /ˈfʊl·mɪ·neɪt/ *v* [I always + adv/prep] *fml* to criticize strongly or express strong opposition or opinion • *Last week a British health minister joined her colleagues in other countries to fulminate against 'passive' smoking.* • *Uncle Ted is always fulminating* **about** *the youth of today.*

ful·min·a·tion /ˌfʊl·mɪˈneɪ·ʃᵊn/ *n fml* • *His letter to the local council was a long fulmination* **against** *their plans to change the bus services.* [C] • *The editorials in this newspaper never have anything in them apart from fulmination* **against** *the government.* [U]

ful·some /ˈfʊl·səm/ *adj* extremely and sometimes unnecessarily positive and generous • *Her new book has received fulsome* **praise** *from the critics.* • *We weren't convinced by the salesperson's fulsome words about the car.* • *Simon and Ruth were fulsome* **in** *their compliments about the meal we cooked for them.*

ful·some·ly /ˈfʊl·səm·li/ *adv* • *He thanked her fulsomely for her help.*

ful·some·ness /ˈfʊl·səm·nəs/ *n* [U]

fum·ble *(obj)* /ˈfʌm·bl̩/ *v* to do something awkwardly, esp. when using your hands • *He fumbled* **in** *his pockets* **for** *some change.* [I always + adv/prep] • *When I had to make a speech, I was so nervous that I fumbled* **with** *my notes and dropped them.* [I always + adv/prep] • *She fumbled* **around/about** *in her handbag, looking for her key.* [I always + adv/prep] • *They fumbled* **(around/about)** (= moved awkwardly) *in the dark, trying to find their way out of the cinema.* [I always + adv/prep] • *At night this car park is full of couples fumbling* (= involved in nervous and awkward sexual activity) *in the back seats of cars.* [I always + adv/prep] • *(fig.) Instead of fumbling* **for** (= trying to think of) *the right word to say, why don't you look it up?* [I always + adv/prep] • *If Wilson hadn't fumbled that* **catch** (= failed to catch the ball), *we might have won the match.* [T]

fume *(obj)* /fjuːm/ *v* to be very angry, sometimes without expressing it • *I saw her a week after they'd had the argument and she was still fuming.* [I] • *The whole episode left me fuming* **at** *the injustice of it all.* [I] • *He didn't say anything during the meeting, but sat there silently fuming.* [I] • *"They treat us like this because we're from Naples," he fumed* (= said very angrily). [+ clause]

fumes /fjuːmz/ *pl n* strong, unpleasant and sometimes dangerous gas or smoke • *He killed himself by breathing car* **exhaust** *fumes in a locked garage.* • **Petrol** *fumes always make me feel sick.* • *After the meeting, the room was full of cigar fumes.* • *Some chemical fumes are poisonous.*

fum·i·gate *obj* /ˈfjuː·mɪ·geɪt/ *v* [T] to remove harmful insects, bacteria, disease, etc. from (somewhere or something), using chemicals in a gaseous or smoky form • *We had to fumigate the cellar to get rid of cockroaches.*

fum·i·ga·tion /ˌfjuː·mɪˈgeɪ·ʃᵊn/ *n* [U] • *Two hospital wards have had to be closed for fumigation.*

fum·i·gat·or /£ˈfjuː·mɪ·geɪ·tər, $-t̬ɚ/ *n* [C] • A fumigator is a person who uses chemicals to remove harmful insects or bacteria from buildings.

fun [PLEASURE] /fʌn/ *n* [U] pleasure, enjoyment, amusement • *She rang me last night from Brighton and it sounded as if she was* **having** *a lot of fun.* • *I enjoyed our outing yesterday – it was* **good** *fun.* • *It's not very informative as magazines go but it's fun to read.* • *We* **had** *a lot of fun on the beach.* • *Children* **get** *a lot of fun* **from/out of** *playing with water.* • *Mark broke his leg when we went skiing and that* **took** *all the fun* **out of** *it.* • *It's no fun/not much fun* (= not enjoyable) *having to work on Saturdays.* • **Have** *fun* (= enjoy yourself)*!* • *Liz is a fun-***loving** *sort of person* (= someone who likes to enjoy herself). • *"We're going on a picnic at the weekend." "***What** *fun!* (= how enjoyable)*!"* • *We're going to run the marathon just* **for fun/for the fun of it/for the fun of the thing** (= for pleasure). • If you **make fun of** someone, you laugh at them unkindly or you cause others to laugh at them: *You're always making fun of me!* • *(Am)* A **fun house** is a building at a FAIR containing frightening or amusing objects and devices. • *Hundreds of people are expected to take part in next week's* **fun run** (= an event in which people run for amusement, often to make money for CHARITY) *to raise money for the homeless.* • *(saying)* 'It was fun while it lasted' means an experience or situation was enjoyable while it lasted although now it is finished. • See also FUNNY [AMUSING].

fun /fʌn/ *adj* [before n] *esp. Am, Aus also* • *Going camping would be a really fun thing to do.* • *Say, this is a fun place.*

fun [PLAYFUL ACTIVITY] /fʌn/ *n* [U] playful and often energetic activity • *The children are always* **full of** *fun.* • *I didn't mean what I said, it was only* **in fun** (= as a joke). • **Fun and games** is pleasant playful activity: *It's not* **all** *fun and games* (= it can be difficult) *being a teacher.* • **Fun and games** can also be an activity that is awkward or difficult: *We* **had** *real fun and games trying to bath the dog.*

fun /fʌn/ *adj* [before n] *esp. Am, Aus also* • *Cindy is a real fun person* (= is energetic and enjoyable to be with).

func·tion [PURPOSE] /ˈfʌŋk·ʃᵊn/ *n* [C] the natural purpose (of something) or the duty (of a person) • *The function* **of** *the veins is to carry blood to the heart.* • *Your function* **as** *a sales representative will include dealing with queries from* *customers.* • *A thermostat* **performs** *the function* **of** *controlling temperature.* • *This raincoat isn't very smart, but it* **fulfils/serves** *the function* **of** *keeping me dry.* • (CS)

func·tion as *obj v prep* [T] • *Our spare bedroom also functions as* (=performs the purpose of being) *a study.* • *My mother is ill, so I'm having to function as* (=perform the duties of) *a nurse at the moment.*

func·tion·al /ˈfʌŋk·ʃᵊn·ᵊl/ *adj* • *We want our new kitchen to be functional* (=arranged so that it is easy to use). • *Is this window functional* (=has it a practical purpose) *or is it for decorative purposes only?*

func·tion·al·i·sm /ˈfʌŋk·ʃᵊn·ᵊl·ɪ·zᵊm/ *n* [U] • Functionalism is the principle that the most important thing about an object such as a building is its use rather than what it looks like.

func·tion·al·ist /ˈfʌŋk·ʃᵊn·ᵊl·ɪst/ *adj*

func·tion·al·ly /ˈfʌŋk·ʃᵊn·ᵊl·i/ *adv* • *The office is functionally designed* (=is planned to be easy to use rather than to look attractive).

func·tion WORK /ˈfʌŋk·ʃᵊn/ *v* [I] to work or operate • *You'll soon learn how the office functions.* • *The television was functioning normally until yesterday.* • *I'm so tired today, I can barely function.* • *The lungs function* **to** *supply the body with oxygen.* [+ *to* infinitive] • (CS)

func·tion /ˈfʌŋk·ʃᵊn/ *n* [U] • *Multiple sclerosis is a disease which affects the function* **of** *the nervous system* (=the way in which it works or operates). • *Studies suggest that regular intake of the vitamin significantly improves brain function.* • The **function keys** on a keyboard are the keys at the top of the keyboard which make the computer perform particular operations.

func·tion·al /ˈfʌŋk·ʃᵊn·ᵊl/ *adj* • *Is the central heating functional yet* (=is it working as it should do)*?* • *(specialized) He's suffering from a functional disorder of the ear* (=his ear is not working correctly, although it has not been damaged by a physical injury). • *(specialized, esp. Am) It's time something was done about the number of* **functional illiterates**/*the rates of* **functional illiteracy** (=the number of people who are able to live and possibly work in society, but who cannot read and write) *in this country.*

func·tion·al·ly /ˈfʌŋk·ʃᵊn·ᵊl·i/ *adv*

func·tion CEREMONY /ˈfʌŋk·ʃᵊn/ *n* [C] an official ceremony or a formal social event, such as a party or a special meal, at which a lot of people are usually present • *As a mayor, he has a lot of* **official** *functions to* **attend**. • *I see her two or three times a year, usually at* **social** *functions.* • *I've got to hire a dinner jacket for a function at work.* • (CS)

func·tion RESULT /ˈfʌŋk·ʃᵊn/ *n* [C usually sing] *fml* something which results from something else, or which is as it is because of something else • *His success is a function* **of** *his having worked so hard, as well as* **of** *his natural ability.* • *The low temperatures here are a function* **of** *the terrain as much as* **of** *the climate.* • (CS)

func·tion VALUE /ˈfʌŋk·ʃᵊn/ *n* [C] *specialized* (in mathematics) a value which depends on and varies with another value • *x is a function* **of** *y.* • *The sales tax you pay is a function of the cost of the goods bought.* • (CS)

func·tion·a·ry /£ˈfʌŋk·ʃᵊn·ᵊr·i, $-er-/ *n* [C] *fml* a person who has official duties, esp. in a government or political party • *The visitors were met by a functionary who escorted them to the director's office.* • *A high-ranking* **party** *functionary, he speaks fluent Russian and is said to have many associates in Moscow.* • *The Defence Ministry would have liked a* **government** *functionary to run the company after the founder's death.*

fund /fʌnd/ *n* [C] a sum of money saved, collected or provided for a particular purpose • *In the UK,* **pension** *fund assets account for 70% of personal sector saving.* • *The hospital has* **set up** *a special fund to buy new equipment.* • *Contributions are being sought for the disaster fund.* • *The money from the land sale sits untouched in a* **trust** *fund.* • *(fig.) She has a fund* (=a lot) **of** *knowledge about modern jazz.* • A **fund-raiser** is a person or event which collects money: *He is a fund-raiser* **for** *a major charity.* ○ *The dance is being held as a fund-raiser.* • *The summer fête will be the school's main* **fund-raising** *event* (=event to collect money) *this year.*

fund *obj* /fʌnd/ *v* [T] • *The company has agreed to fund* (=pay for) *my trip to Australia.* • *The new college is being privately funded* (=money for it is not being provided from taxes).

fund·ing /ˈfʌn·dɪŋ/ *n* [U] • *Ian is trying to get funding* (=to find someone to provide money to pay) *for his research.*

funds /fʌndz/ *pl n* • *Following the repairs to the roof, church funds* (=money that the church has for spending) *are now seriously depleted.* • *The President has agreed to allocate further funds to develop the new submarine.* • *(infml) I'd love to come on holiday with you, but I'm a bit* **short of/low on** *funds* (=I haven't got much money) *at the moment.*

fun·da·men·tal /£ˌfʌn·dəˈmen·tᵊl, $-t̬ᵊl/ *adj* forming the base, from which everything else originates; more important than anything else • *The school is based on the fundamental* **principle** *that each child should develop its full potential.* • *We need to make fundamental* **changes** *to the way in which we treat our environment.* • *Psychologist Jane Firbank sees fundamental* **differences** *between male and female approaches to negotiation.* • *Has science really answered any of the fundamental* **questions** *of life?* • *It is one of the fundamental* **flaws** *of our education system that it only caters for a certain type of intelligence.* • *Wherever illiteracy is a problem, it's as fundamental a* **problem** *as getting enough to eat or a place to sleep.* • *Diversity is* **of** *fundamental* **importance** *to all ecosystems and all economies.* • *The commission said yesterday that fundamental* **rights** *for workers should now be written into the treaty.* • *Many officials are becoming convinced that the time is right for a fundamental reappraisal of European strategy.* • *Some understanding of grammar is fundamental* **to** *learning a language.*

fun·da·men·tal·ly /£ˌfʌn·dəˈmen·tᵊl·i, $-t̬ᵊl-/ *adv* • *Many senior legal figures believe the system is fundamentally* **flawed** (=has very serious faults). • *Our new managing director has reorganized the company a bit, but nothing has fundamentally* **changed/altered** (=its basic character has not changed). • *I still believe that people are fundamentally good* (=are basically good). • *I disagree fundamentally* (=in every way that is important) *with what you're saying.*

fun·da·men·tals /£ˌfʌn·dəˈmen·tᵊlz, $-t̬ᵊlz/ *pl n* • *It's important for children to be taught the fundamentals* (=main principles) **of** *science.* • *Let's stop talking about these trivial things and get down to fundamentals* (=the most important matters).

fun·da·men·tal·i·sm /£ˌfʌn·dəˈmen·tᵊl·ɪ·zᵊm, $-t̬ᵊl-/ *n* [U] the belief in old and traditional forms of religion, or the belief that what is written in a holy book, such as the Christian Bible, is completely true • *A deep fundamentalism underlies her religious beliefs.* • *Recent years have witnessed a growth in religious fundamentalism.*

fun·da·men·tal·ist /£ˌfʌn·dəˈmen·tᵊl·ɪst, $-t̬ᵊl-/ *n* [C] • *Fundamentalists do not accept scientific theories about the origins of the world.*

fun·da·men·tal·ist /£ˌfʌn·dəˈmen·tᵊl·ɪst, $-t̬ᵊl-/ *adj* • *There is a strong fundamentalist movement in parts of the US.*

fu·ner·al /£ˈfjuː·nᵊr·ᵊl, $-nɚ·əl/ *n* [C] a (usually religious) ceremony for burying or burning the body of a dead person • *The entire village went to the church for Jim's funeral.* • *She was allowed out of prison to attend her sister's funeral.* • *William Vaughn, 29, was one of the 75 mourners at the funeral.* • *For a lot of people, baptisms, weddings and funerals are the only time they go to church.* • *Passers-by stopped to watch the funeral* **procession**. • *(infml dated) "But if he doesn't come in this afternoon he won't know what we're doing at the meeting next week." "***That's** *his* **funeral** (=that is his fault so it does not worry me if he suffers)." • *(esp. Am and Aus)* A **funeral director** is a person whose job it is to arrange for the bodies of dead people to be buried or burned. • A **funeral parlour** /*(Am also)* **mortuary** or **funeral home** is a place where the bodies of dead people are prepared to be buried or burned.

fu·ner·e·al /£fjuːˈnɪə·ri·əl, $-ˈnɪr·i-/ *adj disapproving* • *This music is rather funereal* (=sad and suitable for a funeral). • *The only problem with walking with my father is that he moves at such a funereal* **pace** (=so slowly).

fu·ner·e·al·ly /£fjuːˈnɪə·ri·ə·li, $-nɪr·i-/ *adv disapproving*

fun·fair *Br* /£ˈfʌn·feəʳ, $-fer/, *Am and Aus* **a·muse·ment park** *n* [C] a place of outside entertainment where there are machines for riding on and games that can be played for prizes

fun·gi·cide /ˈfʌn·dʒɪ·saɪd, ˈfʌŋ·gɪ-/ *n* [C/U] (a) chemical substance used to kill FUNGUS or prevent it from growing

fun·gus /ˈfʌŋ·gəs/ *n pl* **fungi** /ˈfʌŋ·gaɪ, ˈfʌŋ·giː/ or **funguses** any of various types of organism which obtain their food from decaying material or other living things • *Mushrooms and mould are funguses.* [C] • *Fungi usually grow on other plants or on decaying matter.* [C] • *There's fungus growing in the cellar.* [U] • *Fungus can be poisonous.* [U]

fun·gal /ˈfʌŋ·gəl/ *adj* [not gradable] • *Roses are very prone to fungal disease* (= diseases caused by fungus).

fun·goid /ˈfʌŋ·gɔɪd/ *adj* [not gradable] *specialized* • *We have a strange fungoid growth* (= something similar to fungus is growing) *in our lawn.*

fu·ni·cu·lar (rail·way) /£fjʊˈnɪk·jʊ·ləʳ, $-lɚ/ *n* [C] a special type of railway which travels up and down steep slopes, with the carriages being pulled by a strong metal rope • *There's a funicular which goes to the top of the mountain.*

funk UNHAPPY /fʌŋk/ *n* [U] **in a funk** *Am and Aus infml* very unhappy and without hope • *He's been in a real funk since she left him.*

funk MUSIC /fʌŋk/ *n* [U] a style of music, usually for dancing to, with a strong jazz-based rhythm and a tune that repeats itself • *The singer James Brown is a master of funk.*

funk·y /ˈfʌŋ·ki/ *adj* **-ier, -iest** • *Have you heard their new record? It's really funky.*

funk·y /ˈfʌŋ·ki/ *adj* **-ier, -iest** *slang* very fashionable, esp. because not within the established standards of ordinary society • *She has some really funky clothes.*

fun·nel TUBE /ˈfʌn·əl/ *n* [C] an object which has a wide round opening at the top, sloping sides, and a narrow tube at the bottom, used for pouring liquids or powders into containers with narrow necks • *When you've ground the coffee, use a funnel to pour it into the jar.* • *(Aus)* A **funnel-web** is a large poisonous SPIDER (= insect-like creature with eight legs) found in eastern Australia which makes a WEB (= sticky net), with a funnel-shaped entrance. • PIC› **Laboratory**

fun·nel *(obj)* /ˈfʌn·əl/ *v* [always + adv/prep] **-ll-** or *Am usually* **-l-** • *If you funnel the oil* (= put it through a funnel) *into the engine, you're less likely to spill it.* [T] • *The wind funnels down these narrow streets* (= is directed down them by the buildings on each side). [I] • *The children funnelled along the corridor into the school hall.* [I] • *(fig.) No one knows who has been funnelling* (= directing and sending) *weapons to the terrorists.* [T]

fun·nel PIPE /ˈfʌn·əl/, *Am also* **smoke·stack** *n* [C] a vertical metal pipe on the top of a ship or steam train through which smoke comes out • PIC› **Ships and boats**

fun·ny AMUSING /ˈfʌn·i/ *adj* **-ier, -iest** amusing; causing laughter • *Do you know any funny jokes?* • *I've never found Charlie Chaplin very funny.* • *It's an extremely funny film.* • *It's not funny – don't laugh!* • *Breaking your leg isn't funny* (= is serious), *I can assure you.* • *No matter how disastrous the situation there always seems to be a funny* **side to it**. • *(infml) Don't you try to be funny* **with** *me* (= Be serious and show respect), *young man!* • *(infml)* The **funny bone** is the delicate part of the ELBOW (= middle joint of the arm), which hurts if it is knocked. • *(infml) "She's a very funny woman."* "**Funny ha-ha or funny peculiar** (= do you mean that she is amusing or that she is strange)?" • Compare FUN.

fun·nies /ˈfʌn·iz/ *pl n esp. Am* • *I never bother to look at the funnies* (= the series of drawings in a newspaper that tell an amusing story). See also **comic strip** at COMIC MAGAZINE.

fun·ny STRANGE /ˈfʌn·i/ *adj* **-ier, -iest** strange, surprising, unexpected or difficult to explain or understand • *The washing machine is making a funny noise again.* • *He's got some funny ideas about how to bring up children.* • **That's** *funny – I'm sure I left my keys here.* • *A funny* **thing** *happened to me on the way to the crematorium.* • *Was Camilla the dark-haired lady in the funny hat?* • *Do you think this jacket looks* **a bit** *funny with these trousers?* • **It's** *funny* **that** *we don't hear from David any more.* [+ *that* clause] • **It's** *funny* **how** *Pat always disappears whenever there's work to be done.* [+ *wh-* word] • **It** *must be funny* **to** *be famous and have everyone looking at you.* [+ *to* infinitive] • *He's a funny chap* (= he is strange and difficult to understand). • *(Br infml) The television's* **gone** *funny* (= isn't working correctly). • *(saying)* 'It's a funny old world'.

fun·ni·ly /ˈfʌn·ɪ·li/ *adv* • *If I'm talking a bit funnily* (= strangely) *it's because I've just had an injection in my mouth.* • *(Br and Aus)* **Funnily enough** /*(Am)* **funny enough** (= strangely), *I was just thinking about you when you called.*

fun·ny DISHONEST /ˈfʌn·i/ *adj* **-ier, -iest** *infml* dishonest; involving cheating • *I think there's something funny* **going on** *next door.* • *If you try anything funny/ try any* **funny business** (= try to deceive me), *there'll be trouble.* • *There seems to have been some* **funny business** (= dishonest activity) **going on** *with the company's funds.*

fun·ny UNFRIENDLY /ˈfʌn·i/ *adj* [after v] *Br infml* unfriendly or seeming to be offended • *I'm not being funny or anything but I think I'd rather go on my own.* • *She sounded a bit funny with me on the phone last night and I wondered if I'd offended her.*

fun·ny ILL /ˈfʌn·i/ *adj* [after v] **-ier, -iest** slightly physically or mentally ill • *I feel a bit funny today* (= feel slightly physically ill). • *(Br) She doesn't smoke because cigarettes make her* **go** *(all) funny.* • *He seemed to* **go** *a bit funny (in the head)* (= to become slightly mentally ill) *after the car accident.* • *The old man next door is a bit funny* (= behaves strangely). • *(humorous) If things get much worse, I'll soon be carted off to the* **funny farm** (= the hospital for mentally ill people). • LP› **Feelings and pains**

fur HAIR /£fɜːʳ, $fɜːr/ *n* [U] the thick hair that covers the bodies of some animals, or the hair-covered skin(s) of animals, removed from their bodies • *She stroked the rabbit's soft fur.* [U] • *Persian cats have long fur.* [U] • *I think it's wrong to breed animals for their fur.* [U] • *"Is that real fur on your collar?" "Certainly not – I only wear* **fake** *fur."* [U] • *Many of the women wore the sort of elegant fur* **coats** *you associate with Hollywood stars.* • *I'm wearing a fur-lined jacket so I'm fairly warm.* • *Her coat is trimmed with fur.* [U] • *Some people think the sale of furs* (= clothing made from the hair-covered skin of animals) *should be banned.* [C] • *Native Americans traded furs* (= the hair-covered skins of animals) *with early European settlers.* [C] • *When Mum told my sister she couldn't go to the party,* **the fur** *really* **began/ started to fly** (= a fierce argument started). • *The only reason Mark said what he did was to* **make the fur fly**/ *(Br)* **set the fur flying** (= cause a fierce argument). • Ⓢ

fur·ry /£ˈfɜː·ri, $ˈfɜːr·i/ *adj* **-ier, -iest** • *She sat with a small furry* (= with soft thick hair) *kitten curled up in her lap.* • Items that are furry are made from a soft material that looks like fur: *My husband bought me some lovely furry* **slippers** *for the winter.* ○ *Rosie has a massive collection of furry toys.* ○ *Kevin has some of those awful furry dice hanging in the front window of his car.*

fur·ri·er /£ˈfʌr·i·əʳ, $ˈfɜːr·i·ɚ/ *n* [C] • A furrier is a person who makes or sells clothes made from fur.

fur GREY SUBSTANCE /£fɜːʳ, $fɜːr/ *n* [U] a hard pale grey substance which can form on the inside of water pipes, KETTLES etc. • *The water in our area is very hard, so we get a lot of fur in our kettle.* • *Fur consists mainly of calcium carbonate.* • Ⓢ

fur /£fɜːʳ, $fɜːr/ *v* [I] **-rr-** • *Over the years, the pipes in our house have slowly furred* **(up)** (= a hard grey substance has formed in them).

fur TONGUE /£fɜːʳ, $fɜːr/ *n* [U] a greyish covering on the tongue, caused by illness or by smoking cigarettes • *You often get fur on your tongue when you're not well.* • Ⓢ

furred /£fɜːd, $fɜːrd/ *adj* • *You know why your tongue is furred* (= has a greyish covering on it) *-it's because you smoke too much!*

fur·i·ous ANGRY /£ˈfjʊə·ri·əs, $ˈfjɜːr·i-/ *adj* extremely angry • *He's furious because someone drove into his car while it was parked.* • *He was furious* **with** *me.* • *The passengers are furious* **about/at** *being kept waiting.* • *Gordon was furious* **that** *I borrowed his car without asking him.* [+ *that* clause] • *We had a furious row last night.* • *Dad's in a furious temper.* • See also FURY.

fur·i·ous·ly /£ˈfjʊə·ri·ə·sli, $ˈfjɜːr·i-/ *adv* • *"Get out of here!" she shouted furiously* (= in a very angry way) *at him.*

fur·i·ous·ness /£ˈfjʊə·ri·ə·snəs, $ˈfjɜːr·i-/ *n* [U] • See also FURY.

fur·i·ous STRONG /£ˈfjʊə·ri·əs, $ˈfjɜːr·i-/ *adj* using a lot of effort or strength • *There is a furious struggle going on between the two presidential candidates.* • *When you're running a marathon, it's better not to set off at a* *furious pace.* • *The debate about capital punishment continues to be as furious as ever.*

fur·i·ous·ly /£'fjʊə·ri·ə·sli, $'fjɜːr·i-/ *adv* • *Tim pedalled his bike furiously* (=with as much effort as possible) *to try and keep up with the other children.*

fur·i·ous·ness /£'fjʊə·ri·ə·snəs, $'fjɜːr·i-/ *n* [U] • See also FURY.

furl *obj* /£fɜːl, $fɜːrl/ *v* [T] to fold (esp. a flag, sail or UMBRELLA), esp. into a tube shape • *At the end of the day, the soldiers take down the flag and furl it carefully, ready for the next morning.*

fur·long /£'fɜː·lɒŋ, $'fɜːr·lɑːŋ/ *n* [C] a unit of length equal to 201 metres or 1/8 mile, used esp. in horse racing • *a five-furlong race*

fur·nace /£'fɜː·nɪs, $'fɜːr-/ *n* [C] a container which is heated to a very high temperature, so that substances that are put inside it, such as metal, will melt or burn, or *(Am)* a piece of equipment for heating a building • *People who work with furnaces in a steel factory need to wear protective clothing.* • *This room's* **(like)** *a furnace* (=is very hot)! • *(Am) It's cold in here – should I turn on the furnace?*

fur·nish *obj* [ADD FURNITURE] /£'fɜː·nɪʃ, $'fɜːr-/ *v* [T] to provide with furniture; to put furniture in • *We've spent so much money on our new house, we can't afford to furnish it.* • *His house is furnished* **with** *things he's collected on his travels round the world.* • *"Books do Furnish a Room"* (title of a book by Anthony Powell, 1971)

fur·nished /£'fɜː·nɪʃt, $'fɜːr-/ *adj* • *She's looking for a furnished* **flat/apartment** (=one which already has furniture in it). • *Their house is expensively furnished* (=the furniture in it is expensive).

fur·nish·ings /£'fɜː·nɪ·ʃɪŋz, $'fɜːr-/ *pl n* • *We need to think carefully about the furnishings* (=the furniture and other items in the house, room or other area). • *Bathroom furnishings are in the basement of the store, Sir.* • LP› **Shopping goods**

fur·nish *obj* [SUPPLY] /£'fɜː·nɪʃ, $'fɜːr-/ *v* [T] *fml* to supply or provide • *We can furnish everything you need for a successful party.* • *Furnished* **with** *maps, a compass and sandwiches, they set off for a day's hiking.* • *The travel company has furnished us* **with** *all the details of our journey.*

fur·ni·ture /£'fɜː·nɪ·tʃəʳ, $'fɜːr·nɪ·tʃɚ/ *n* [U] items such as chairs, tables, beds, cupboards etc. which are put into a house or other building to make it suitable and comfortable for living or working in • *They have a lot of antique furniture.* • *The only* **piece/item of** *furniture he has in his bedroom is a bed.* • *We've just bought some new garden furniture* (=tables, chairs, etc. for use in the garden).

fu·ro·re *Br, Am* **fu·ror** /£'fjʊ·rɔːʳ, $-rɔːr/ *n* [U] a sudden excited or angry reaction to something by a lot of people • *Her response to the furore* **over** *her new book is measured.* • *The government's decision to raise taxes has caused a great furore.*

fur·phy /£'fɜː·fi, $'fɜːr-/ *n* [C] *Aus slang* a RUMOUR (=unofficial interesting story or piece of news that might be true or invented)

furred /£fɜːd, $fɜːrd/ *adj* See at FUR [GREY SUBSTANCE], FUR [TONGUE]

fur·ri·er /£'fʌr·i·əʳ, $'fɜːr·i·ɚ/ *n* [C] See at FUR [HAIR]

fur·row /£'fʌr·əʊ, $'fɜːr·oʊ/ *n* [C] a long line or hollow which is formed or cut into the surface of something • *Farmers use ploughs to cut furrows into the earth, so that seeds can be sown in them.* • *A deep furrow has formed in the rock, where water has run over it for centuries.* • *Years of anxiety have lined her brow with deep furrows.* • PIC› **Farming**

fur·row *obj* /£'fʌr·əʊ, $'fɜːr·oʊ/ *v* [T] • *The wheels of the heavy tractor furrowed* (=made deep hollows in) *the soft ground.* • *The pain of his headache made him furrow his* **brow** (=make lines in the skin above his eyes).

fur·rowed /£'fʌr·əʊd, $'fɜːr·oʊd/ *adj* • *She sat by her child's hospital bed with furrowed* **brow** (=with lines in the skin above her eyes, caused by anxiety).

fur·ry /£'fɜː·ri, $'fɜːr·i/ *adj* **-ier, -iest** See at FUR [HAIR]

fur·ther [GREATER DISTANCE] /£'fɜː·ðəʳ, $'fɜːr·ðɚ/ *adv, comparative of* FAR [DISTANCE]; to a greater distance or degree; at a more advanced level • *I'm afraid I never got further than the first five pages of 'Ulysses'.* • *We discussed the problem but we didn't get much further in actually solving it.* • *The whole matter is further complicated by the fact that Amanda and Jo refuse to speak to each other.* • *Every day she sinks further and further into depression.* • If you **go** or **take** something further you take it to a more advanced stage: *Before we go any further with the project I think we should check that there's enough money to fund it.* ○ *If you wish to take* **the matter** *further you can file charges against him.* ○ *If you want to take this stretch further, hold the back of your legs with your hands.* ○ *(fig.) These safety schemes for aircraft should be taken further* (=made even more effective). ○ *(fig.) I think he's a nice enough person but I wouldn't go any further than that* (=I couldn't express greater enthusiasm for him). ○ *(fig.) We kissed and fooled around a little, but we didn't go any further* (=we didn't have sex). • Both further and farther are used as adverbs and adjectives. Farther is more commonly used when referring to distances. Further is more often used when the intended meaning is figurative.

fur·ther /£'fɜː·ðəʳ, $'fɜːr·ðɚ/ *adj* [not gradable] • *I'd forgotten how long the journey was and it was much further than I remembered.* • *Get to the shops and you'll see a bit further on there's a bridge.* • *Fourteen miles is further than you'd think once you start to run it.* • *Is that her at the further* (=other) *end of the room?* • If you say that nothing could be, or something could not be, **further from** your **mind/thoughts**, you are saying that what has been suggested is not true: *I certainly wasn't trying to get money off him –* **nothing** *could have been further from my mind!*

fur·ther·most /£'fɜː·ðə·məʊst, $'fɜːr·ðɚ·moʊst/ *adj* [not gradable] *fml* • The furthermost place or places are those at the greatest distance away: *The boats had sailed from the furthermost ports of northern Europe.* ○ *I'd purposely sat in the chair furthermost* **from** *the telephone so that I wouldn't have to get up to answer it!*

fur·ther [EXTRA] /£'fɜː·ðəʳ, $'fɜːr·ðɚ/ *adj, adv* [not gradable] more or additional • *Have you anything further to add?* • *If you have any further problems with the clock just bring it straight back to the shop.* • *It cost me £50 a day and a further £60 for insurance.* • *I thought I'd give my riding hat to Stephanie since I've no further use for it.* • *I got a letter telling me that any further contact we had would be through our solicitors.* • *Please don't hesitate to send any further enquiries to the above address.* • *This shop will be closed until further notice.* • *We need to talk further about this – can we have a meeting after lunch?* • *(esp. Br and Aus fml)* Further **to** is sometimes used in business letters to state what subject it is that you are referring to or which conversation or letter you are answering: *Further to your letter of March 11th, I should like to inform you of a number of recent developments regarding the Saffron Hill site.* • *(Aus fml and Br)* **Further education**/*(Am and Aus)* **Adult education** is education below degree level for people who are older than school age: *She teaches at a college of further education.* • When you're talking about real physical distance, you can use either further/furthest or farther/farthest: How much further/farther is it to where we're staying? But when you're talking about a more advanced level, it's usual to use further/furthest: Do you want to take the matter any further?

fur·ther *obj* [ENCOURAGE] /£'fɜː·ðəʳ, $'fɜːr·ðɚ/ *v* [T] to encourage (something) to succeed; to advance (something) • *He has probably done more to further* **the cause** *of interracial harmony than any other person.* • *The interests of an organization will never be furthered through acts of terrorism.* • *Additional training is probably the best way to further your career these days.*

fur·ther·ance /£'fɜː·ðᵊr·ᵊnts, $'fɜːr·ðɚ-/ *n* [U] *fml* • *The charter states that the press shall be devoted to printing and publishing* **in** *the furtherance and dissemination* **of** *knowledge.*

fur·ther·more /£ˌfɜː·ðə'mɔːʳ, £'---, $'fɜːr·ðɚ·mɔːr/ *adv* [not gradable] *fml* in addition; more importantly • *I suggest we go to the Italian restaurant – it's very good and furthermore it's very cheap.* • *I don't know what happened to Rupert Ford and furthermore I don't care.*

fur·thest /£'fɜː·ðɪst, $'fɜːr-/ *adv, superlative of* FAR [DISTANCE] • *That's the furthest I can see without glasses.* • *Of all the research that's been done in this field, this project has taken it the furthest.* • *I wanted to be an actress but the furthest I ever got was selling ice-creams in a theatre.* • Both furthest and farthest are used as adverbs and adjectives. Farthest is more commonly used when referring to distances. Furthest is more often used when the intended meaning is figurative.

fur·thest /£'fɜː·ðɪst, $'fɜːr-/ *adj* • *The novel explores the furthest extremes of human experience.*

fur·tive /£'fɜː·tɪv, $'fɜːr·t̬ɪv/ *adj* (of people) behaving secretly so that other people do not notice them, or (of actions) done secretly and often quickly so that people do not notice • *I saw him cast a furtive* **glance** *at the woman at the table to his right.* • *He spent the afternoon making furtive phone calls whenever his boss was out of the office.* • *There was something furtive* **about** *his behaviour and I immediately felt suspicious.* • *He had the furtive air of someone on an embarrassing errand, like buying underwear for his mother.*

fur·tive·ly /£ˈfɜː·tɪv·li, $ˈfɜːr·t̬ɪv-/ *adv* • *She glanced furtively at the photo in his wallet.* • *As she turned away I saw him sniff furtively under his arm.*

fur·tive·ness /£ˈfɜː·tɪv·nəs, $ˈfɜːr·t̬ɪv-/ *n* [U]

fur·y /£ˈfjʊə·ri, $ˈfjɜːr·i/ *n* [U] extreme anger • *In a fit of fury he thumped his fists down on the desk.* • *She turned on him with* **(a)** *sudden fury.* • *The minister made no attempt to contain his fury.* • *(dated)* If you do something **like fury** you do it with great energy and determination: *I've been working like fury these past few days to catch up.* • See also FURIOUS [ANGRY].

fuse [SAFETY PART] /fjuːz/ *n* [C] a small safety part in an electrical device or piece of machinery which causes it to stop working if the electric current is too high, and so prevents fires or other dangers • *Many household appliances in Britain use a thirteen-amp fuse.* • *My hairdrier's stopped working – I think the fuse has* **blown/** *(Br and Aus also)* **gone** (= broken). • *Household appliances don't usually have individual fuses in the US.* • A **fuse box** is a container holding several fuses, such as all the fuses for the electrical system of a single house: *The fuse box is on the wall in the kitchen.* • Compare **circuit breaker** at CIRCUIT [CLOSED SYSTEM].

fuse *(obj)* /fjuːz/ *v Br* • When an electrical device or piece of machinery fuses *(Am and Aus* **blows a fuse***)* or someone or something fuses it *(Am and Aus* **blows its fuse***)*, it stops working because the electric current is too high: *Either my headlights have fused or the bulbs have gone.* [I] ○ *The kids were messing around with the switches and they fused the lights.* [T] ○ *(fig.) Your father's brain seems to fuse* (= stop working) *if he has to take in too many new things at once.* [I]

fused /fjuːzd/ *adj* [not gradable] • An electrical device or piece of machinery that is fused has a fuse in it: *It says on the plug that it's fused.* ○ *The computer is fused so if there's a power surge it won't destroy the circuitry.*

fuse [DEVICE ON EXPLOSIVE] /fjuːz/ *n* [C] a string or piece of paper connected to a FIREWORK or other explosive item by which it is lit, or a device inside a bomb which causes it to explode after a fixed length of time or when it hits or is near something • *He* **lit** *the fuse and ran.* • *(fig.) Anti-police feeling was high in the area and an incident in which a local youth died in custody just seemed to light the fuse* (= suddenly start a dangerous situation).

fuse *(obj)* [JOIN] /fjuːz/ *v* to join or become combined • *Genes determine how we develop from the moment the sperm fuses with the egg.* [I] • *The rate at which nuclei fuse is much greater when the plasma is hotter.* [I] • *They're going to remove the damaged disc in her back and fuse the surrounding vertebrae.* [T] • *In Istanbul, East and West fuse together in a way that is fascinating to observe.* [I]

fu·sion /ˈfjuː·ʒᵊn/ *n* [U] • *nuclear fusion* • *Their music is described as 'an explosive fusion of Latin American and modern jazz rhythms'.* • *He describes opera as the glorious fusion of music and high drama.*

fuse *(obj)* [MELT] /fjuːz/ *v* to (cause to) melt (together) esp. at a high temperature • *Iron ore fuses when it is smelted.* [I] • *The heat of the fire fused many of the machine's parts together.* [T]

fu·se·lage /ˈfjuː·zᵊl·ɑːʒ/ *n* [C] the main body of an aircraft • *A close inspection revealed minute cracks in the aircraft's fuselage and wings.*

fu·sil·ier /£ˌfjuː·zɪ·ˈlɪəʳ, $-ˈlɪr/ *n* [C] *Br* a low-ranked British soldier who is in the INFANTRY

fu·sil·lade /ˌfjuː·zɪˈleɪd/ *n* [C] a large number of bullets fired at the same time or one after another very quickly • *Twenty-eight demonstrators were shot dead and 188 wounded in a 5-minute fusillade* **of** *automatic fire.* • *(fig.) A fusillade* (= sudden large amount) **of** *questions greeted the president at this afternoon's press conference.*

fuss [FEELING] /fʌs/ *n* [U] a show of annoyance, anxiety, dissatisfaction or excitement, usually one which is greater than the situation deserves • *You've never seen anything like the fuss she* **made** *when Richard spilt a drop of wine on her blouse!* • *It's all a fuss over nothing if you ask me.* • *Don't* **make** *a fuss, darling, it's only a little cut.* • *I said I might be late for dinner but he* **made such** *a fuss that I thought I'd better arrive on time.* • *The meal wasn't quite as hot as it could have been but I didn't say anything – I don't like to create a fuss.* • *She* **kicked up** (= caused) *such a fuss I think they raised her salary just to shut her up!* • *Everyone's going on about this brilliant young actress and I don't know what all the fuss is about – I really don't think she's anything special.* • *I don't see what the fuss is about – he seems like a fairly ordinary looking guy to me.* • *My mother was* **in a fuss** (= in a nervous state) *this morning because the house was untidy and she had people coming round for dinner.* • If you **make a fuss of**/*(Am also)* **make a fuss over** someone you give them a lot of attention and treat them well: *She doesn't see her grandchildren very often so she tends to make a real fuss of them when she does.*

fuss *(obj)* /fʌs/ *v Am* • *The Democratic Congress and the Republican president are forever fussing* **at** (= being annoying to) *each other, usually over nothing at all.* [I] • If you fuss someone you make them nervous and angry by trying to get their attention when they are very busy: *Don't fuss me, honey, I've got a whole pile of work to do – go ask your mother to help you.* [T]

fuss [GIVE ATTENTION TO] /fʌs/ *v* [I] giving too much attention to small and unimportant matters, usually in a way which shows that you are anxious and not relaxed • *Please, stop fussing – the food's cooking and there's nothing more to do until the guests arrive.* • *I wish he'd relax for a moment instead of fussing all the time!* • *She's always fussing* **over** *that son of hers as if he were a little boy.* • *It irritates me the way she's always fussing* **with** *her hair!*

fuss /fʌs/ *n* [U] • *The article was entitled 'Making up with the minimum of fuss: a five-minute beauty routine that every busy woman should know'.*

fuss·pot /£ˈfʌs·pɒt, $-pɑːt/, *Am also* **fuss·budg·et** /ˈfʌs·bʌdʒ·ɪt/ *n* [C] *infml* a person who is often dissatisfied and complains about things that are not important • *"I can't eat this meat – it's too tough." "You old fusspot – give it here and I'll eat it!"*

fus·sy [NOT EASILY SATISFIED] /ˈfʌs·i/ *adj* **-ier, -iest** *disapproving* not easily satisfied; having very high standards or very fixed standards about particular things • *She's a bit fussy* **about** *people having clean hands.* • *All my children were fussy eaters.* • *He's so fussy* **about** *the house – everything has to be absolutely perfect.* • *"I haven't met a man I've fancied for ages!" "You're too fussy – that's your problem!"* • *If there's the slightest crease in his trousers he just won't wear them – he's so fussy!* • *(Br infml)* If you ask someone to choose between things and they say 'I'm not fussy' or 'I'm not fussed', they mean they do not prefer one rather than another and would be satisfied with either: *"Would you like red wine or white?" "I'm not fussy – either would do fine."*

fus·si·ly /ˈfʌs·ɪ·li/ *adv*

fus·si·ness /ˈfʌs·ɪ·nəs/ *n* [U]

fus·sy [TOO HIGHLY DECORATED] /ˈfʌs·i/ *adj* **-ier, -iest** *disapproving* having too much decoration and too many small details, in a way that is not stylish • *They've got those curtains that tie up with big bows – they're a bit fussy for my taste.* • *She showed me a couple of hats but they were very fussy – I prefer something simpler.*

fus·si·ly /ˈfʌs·ɪ·li/ *adv disapproving* • *fussily decorated*

fus·si·ness /ˈfʌs·ɪ·nəs/ *n* [U] *disapproving*

fus·ti·an /£ˈfʌs·ti·ən, $-tʃᵊn/ *n, adj* [not gradable] (made of) a thick rough cotton cloth that lasts for a long time

fus·ty /ˈfʌs·ti/ *adj* **-ier, -iest** *disapproving* smelling unpleasantly DAMP (= slightly wet) and not fresh, or *(fig.)* old fashioned in ideas and beliefs • *This room smells a bit fusty – I think I'll just open a window.* • *I don't think he lets his clothes dry properly before he puts them away – somehow they always smell fusty.* • *(fig.) As a child I used to have to go and stay with this fusty old aunt of mine who believed that children should be seen and not heard.* • *(fig.) Rupert's father belongs to some fusty old gentleman's club in London where they don't allow women in.*

fu·tile [UNSUCCESSFUL] /£ˈfjuː·taɪl, $-t̬əl/ *adj* (of actions) having no effect or achieving nothing; unsuccessful • *Attempts to get supplies to the region are futile because troops will not allow the aid convoy to enter the city.* • **It's** *quite futile* **trying** *to reason with him – he just won't listen.* [+ v-ing] • *All my attempts to cheer her up* **proved** *futile.* • *It is hoped that the leaders will consider the matter deeply before they embark on a long, bloody and futile war.*

fu·til·i·ty /£fjuː'tɪl·ɪ·ti, $-t̬i/ *n* [U] • *"What's his latest book about?" "Oh, the usual – the transience of love and the futility of life."*

fu·tile SILLY /'fjuː·taɪl, $-t̬əl/ *adj* (esp. of remarks and questions) silly and without meaning • *She made some futile remark that I can't remember.*

fu·til·i·ty /£fjuː'tɪl·ɪ·ti, $-t̬i/ *n* [U]

fu·ton /£'fuː·tɒn, $-tɑːn/ *n* [C] a MATTRESS (= large flat firm bag filled with soft material and used for sleeping on) which is used on the floor or on a wooden frame • *The futon was a Japanese invention.* • *We bought a futon which we can roll up in the daytime (and use as a sofa).* • PIC› **Beds and bedroom**

fu·ture /£'fjuː·tʃəʳ, $-tʃɚ/ *n* time which is to come; not the present or the past • **The** future refers to time that is to come as a period: *Regarding your work situation, what are your plans for the future?* [U] ○ *Sometimes I worry about the future.* [U] ○ *I wonder what the future* **holds** *for* (= what will happen to) *you and me.* [U] ○ *I'm sure at some point* **in** *the future I'll want a baby but I certainly don't at the moment.* [U] ○ *He's always telling me that I don't plan for the future.* [U] ○ *When you talk about moving out of London is that in the* **distant** *future or the* **near** *future?* [U] ○ *You see these kids from really poor families and you think what have they got to look forward to* **in** *the future?* [U] ○ *Well, you never know what the future will bring.* [U] ○ *I can see those two getting married in the* **not too distant** *future* (= quite soon). [U] • Future can also be used to refer to the opportunities for improvement or success that a particular person or thing has: *With unemployment around 70% in this area, a lot of these school-leavers don't have much (of a) future.* [C/U] ○ *Torn apart by war, its economy virtually destroyed, this country now faces a very* **uncertain** *future.* [C] ○ *She's a very talented young singer, Mike and I personally think she's got a* **great** *future ahead of her!* [C] ○ *I'm afraid the future's not looking too rosy for that company.* [C] ○ *The minister will make an announcement this afternoon stating the future of the city's hospitals.* [C] • Future can also mean the chance of continuing success or existence for something: *With falling audiences, the future of this theatre is in doubt.* [U] • In grammar **the** future is the form of a verb which you use when talking about something that will happen or exist: *In the sentence 'Who will look after the dog?' the verb phrase 'will look' is* **in** *the future.* [U] • *(esp. Br and Aus)* The phrase **in future** (*Am usually* **in the future**) is often used at the beginning or end of a sentence in which there is a decision about a plan of action or a warning: *In future I won't bother asking him out anywhere if he's just going to complain that he's bored!* ○ *He wasn't cross with me – he just asked me to be more careful in future.* ○ *In future I'm going to check every single piece of work that you do!* • *"I have seen the future; and it works"* (Lincoln Steffens in a letter describing a visit to Russia, 1919) • *"Back to the Future"* (title of a film, 1985) • *"Future Shock"* (title of a book by Alvin Tofler, 1970) • *"The Once and Future King"* (title of a series of books about King Arthur by T.H.White, 1958-) • LP› **Periods of time, Tenses**

fu·ture /£'fjuː·tʃəʳ, $-tʃɚ/ *adj* [before n; not gradable] • *Of course we'll keep you up to date with any future developments.* • *There's an old superstition that young girls going to bed on this night dream of their future husbands.* • *The success of this product will affect the funding that we receive for any future projects.* • *You perhaps didn't know about this but* **for future reference** (= so that you will know in the future), *could you use the headed paper for any correspondence that leaves this office.* • In grammar the future form of a verb is used when talking about something that will happen or exist: *How do you say that in the future* **tense?** • The **future perfect** is the tense which is used to show that an action will have been performed by a particular time. In English it is formed by 'will have' or 'shall have' and a past participle: *the future perfect tense* ○ *In the sentence 'By that time I will probably have left,' the verb phrase 'will have left'* **is in** *the future perfect.*

fu·tur·i·sm /£'fjuː·tʃəʳr·ɪ·zəm, $-tʃɚ-/ *n* [U] • Futurism was a new way of thinking in the arts that started in the 1920's and 1930's which attempted to express through a range of art forms the characteristics and images of the modern age, such as machines, speed, movement and power: *F.T. Marinetti is said to have founded Futurism, whose first manifesto on the subject was written in 1909.*

fu·tur·ist /£'fjuː·tʃəʳr·ɪst, $-tʃɚ-/ *adj, n* [C] • *a futurist painter* • *The futurists rejected the past and all received artistic traditions.*

fu·tur·is·tic /ˌfjuː·tʃə'rɪs·tɪk/ *adj* • Futuristic means strange and very modern, or intended or seeming to come from some imagined time in the future: *At the unspoiled North Bay, three white pyramids rise like futuristic sails from the sea.* ○ *His winter collection looked weirdly futuristic with massively shoulder-padded jackets and trailing cloaks.* ○ *Her latest novel is a futuristic thriller, set some time in the twenty-first century.*

fu·tures /£'fjuː·tʃəz, $-tʃɚz/ *pl n* agreements for the buying and selling of goods, in which the price is agreed in advance of a particular future time at which the goods will be provided • *the futures market* • *She works in futures.*

fuzz /fʌz/ *n* [U] *infml* a covering of short thin soft hairs, or a mass of tightly curled and often untidy hair • *He's got that bit of adolescent fuzz on his upper lip.* • *I must buy a razor today and get rid of the fuzz on my legs!* • *(Br and Am dated slang and Aus infml)* The fuzz is another word for the police: *Watch out! it's the fuzz.*

fuz·zy /'fʌz·i/ *adj* **-ier, -iest** *infml* • *Oh no, it's raining – my hair will go all fuzzy.* • Fuzzy can describe a surface that feels like short fur: *I have to peel peaches because I don't like their fuzzy skins.* ○ *Feel this fuzzy bit at the back of Ben's neck where the hair is shaved!*

fuz·zy /'fʌz·i/ *adj* **-ier, -iest** (of an image) having shapes that do not have clear edges, or (of a sound, esp. from a television, radio, etc.) not clear, usually because of other unwanted noises making it difficult to hear • *Is the picture always fuzzy on your TV?* • *You can pick up a lot of stations on the car radio but the sound is usually a bit fuzzy.* • *(fig.) The basic facts of the story are starting to emerge though the details are still fuzzy* (= unclear). • *(fig.) My head's a bit fuzzy* (= I cannot think clearly) *this morning after all that wine last night.* • **Fuzzy logic** is a theoretical system used in mathematics, computing and PHILOSOPHY which allows theorists and computers to deal with statements which are neither true nor false: *It is said that fuzzy logic offers computers the best chance of making sense of what people are thinking and then of reproducing their behaviour.* • See also **fuzzy** at FUZZ.

fuz·zi·ly /'fʌz·ɪ·li/ *adv*

fuz·zi·ness /'fʌz·ɪ·nəs/ *n* [U]

-fy /faɪ/ *combining form* See at -IFY

G g

G LETTER (*pl* **G's** or **Gs**), **g** (*pl* **g's** or **gs**) /dʒiː/ *n* [C] the 7th letter of the English alphabet • A **G-spot** is a small area that is believed to be inside the vagina and to increase sexual pleasure when rubbed. • A **G-string** is a narrow piece of cloth worn between a person's legs to cover their sexual organs that is held in place by a piece of string around their waist. • LP› **Silent letters**

G MUSIC /dʒiː/ *n* a note in Western music • *This sonata is in* **(the key of)** *G.* [U] • *Beethoven's 5th symphony starts with three short Gs followed by a long E flat.* [C]

g FORCE /dʒiː/ *n* [C] *specialized* a unit of measurement of the ACCELERATION (= rate of change of speed) of an object caused by GRAVITY (= the force of attraction between objects that contain matter)

g MASS, **gm** *n* [C] *pl* **g** *abbreviation for* gram • LP› **Units**

G FILM /dʒiː/ *adj* (in the US, of a film) considered suitable for children of any age • *'Bambi' is one of the best G movies of all time.*

G MONEY *Am and Aus infml* /dʒiː/, *Br and Aus infml* **K** *n* [C] $1000 • *You've got 6 G's worth of machinery here – you should get it insured.* • LP› **Money**

gab /gæb/ *v* [I] **-bb-** *infml disapproving* to talk continuously and eagerly, esp. about unimportant matters • *I got so bored listening to him gabbing* **on** *about nothing.*

gab·ar·dine, gab·er·dine /£'gæb·ə·diːn, $'-ɚ-/ *n* a thick cloth which is esp. used for making coats, or a long coat made from this cloth • *It says on the label it's made of gabardine.* [U] • *I was wearing my father's beige gabardine.* [C]

gab·ble *(obj)* /ˈgæb·l̩/ *v* to speak quickly and not clearly so that it is difficult to understand • *He gabbled his speech – I found parts of it quite difficult to understand.* [T] • *Your mother gabbles a bit, doesn't she – I don't always catch what she's saying.* [I] • *She started gabbling* **away** *at me in Spanish and I didn't understand a word.* [I] • *Gina, as usual, was gabbling* **away** *on the telephone!* [I]

gab·ble /ˈgæb·l̩/ *n* [U] • Gabble is fast conversation or speech which is difficult to understand, often because many people are talking at the same time: *He phoned me from the party but I couldn't hear what he was saying because of all the gabble in the background.*

ga·ble /ˈgeɪ·bl̩/ *n* [C] the triangular top end of the wall of a building where it meets the sloping parts of a roof • *In his biography he recalls the town as a place of wrought-iron railings and pastel gables.*

ga·bled /ˈgeɪ·bl̩d/ *adj* [not gradable] • *With its narrow cobbled streets and gabled houses, Brugge must be one of the most beautiful cities in Europe.*

gad a·bout/a·round *(obj)* /gæd/ *v adv, v prep* **-dd-** *humorous or dated* to visit or travel to a lot of different places, enjoying yourself and having few worries or responsibilities • *He spent his early twenties gadding about Europe when he should have been establishing himself in his career!* [T] • *We spent the weekend gadding about London and generally enjoying ourselves.* [T] • *We've just been gadding around, enjoying ourselves.* [I]

gad·a·bout /ˈgæd·ə·baʊt/ *n* [C] *humorous or dated* • *Where have you been, you young gadabout!*

gadg·et /ˈgædʒ·ɪt/ *n* [C] a small device or machine with a particular purpose • *Have you seen this handy little gadget – it's for separating egg yolks from whites.* • *She's mad about gadgets, her kitchen is just full of them.* • *America was then the world's biggest market for gadgets like self-sharpening pencils.*

gadg·et·ry /ˈgædʒ·ɪ·tri/ *n* [U] • *We've got a juicer, a blender, a coffee grinder – in fact all manner of kitchen gadgetry.*

Gael·ic /ˈgeɪ·lɪk, ˈgæl·ɪk/ *n* [U], *adj* [not gradable] (relating to) a language spoken in parts of Ireland, Scotland and, in the past, the Isle of Man • LP **Nations and nationalities**

gaffe /gæf/ *n* [C] a remark or action that is a social mistake and not considered polite; FAUX PAS • *I* **made** *a real gaffe – I called his new wife 'Judy' which is the name of his ex-wife.* • *Was that a bit of a gaffe then, starting to eat before everyone else had been served?*

gaf·fer MAN IN CHARGE /£ˈgæf·əʳ, $-ɚ/ *n* [C] *Br infml* a man who is in charge of other workers • *I don't know if there are any jobs going – ask the gaffer, mate, he's over there.*

gaf·fer FILM /£ˈgæf·əʳ, $-ɚ/ *n* [C] *specialized* the most important electrician who works on a film or television programme • *In most productions the gaffer works in close collaboration with the lighting director.*

gaf·fer OLD MAN /£ˈgæf·əʳ, $-ɚ/ *n* [C] *infml* an old man • *Anyway, I was standing at the bar and this old gaffer comes up to me and asks me to buy him a drink.*

gag PIECE OF CLOTH /gæg/ *n* [C] a piece of cloth which is tied around a person's mouth or put inside it in order to stop them from speaking, shouting or calling for help • *Her hands and feet were tied and a gag placed over her mouth.* • *(Am)* A **gag order** or **gag rule** is an official order not to discuss something, esp. a legal case: *The judge* **issued** *a gag order enjoining all parties to the case from speaking to the press.*

gag *obj* /gæg/ *v* [T] **-gg-** • *He was* **bound and** *gagged and left in a cell for three days.* • *(fig.) The media have obviously been gagged* (= prevented from saying anything) *about the incident because nothing has been reported.*

gag ALMOST VOMIT /gæg/ *v* [I] **-gg-** to experience the sudden uncomfortable feeling of tightness in the throat and stomach that makes you feel you are going to vomit • *When I was pregnant I got morning sickness so bad even putting a tooth-brush in my mouth made me gag.* • *I tried my best to eat it but the meat was so fatty I gagged* **on** *it.*

gag JOKE /gæg/ *n* [C] *infml* a joke or story that is intended to amuse, esp. one told by a COMEDIAN • *I did a few opening gags about the band that had been on before me.* • *(Am and Aus)* A gag is also a trick played on someone or an action performed to amuse other people.

ga·ga MENTALLY UNCLEAR /ˈgɑː·gɑː/ *adj infml* unable to think clearly and make decisions because of old age; SENILE • *My granny's 94 and she's a bit gaga.* • *I know I'm seventy-three but I haven't* **gone** *gaga yet!*

ga·ga IN LOVE /ˈgɑː·gɑː/ *adj* [after v] *infml* having a strong but usually temporary love for someone • *She doesn't just like him – she's totally gaga* **about/over** *him!* • *Just standing near her makes him* **go gaga**! • If you **go gaga over** something you are extremely enthusiastic about it: *People went gaga over this model of car when it was first introduced.*

gag·gle /ˈgæg·l̩/ *n* [C + sing/pl v] a group of GEESE or *(fig. disapproving)* a group of people, esp. if they are noisy or silly • *(fig. disapproving) I tried to avoid the gaggle* **of** *women in the kitchen.* • *(fig. disapproving) There were the usual gaggle of journalists waiting for the princess when she got out of her car.*

gai·e·ty /£ˈgeɪ·ə·ti, $-t̬i/ *n* [U] *dated* happiness and excitement • *As the effects of the drink gradually wore off the mood of gaiety evaporated.* • *I felt there was an air of forced gaiety about her manner.*

gai·ly /ˈgeɪ·li/ *adv dated* happily or brightly • *I could hear her gaily singing in her bedroom.* • *The tree lights twinkled gaily across the lake.*

gain *obj* OBTAIN /geɪn/ *v* [T] to obtain (something useful, advantageous or in some way positive), esp. over a period of time • *The Nationalist Party have gained a lot of support in the south of the country.* • *What do you hope to gain* **from** *the course?* • *It was an interesting experience though quite what I gained* **from** *it I don't know.* • *Being with his family for a few days I gained one or two insights into the reason he behaves the way he does.* • *Alternative medicine has only just started to gain respectability in our society.* • *It was her performances in Aida which gained her an international reputation as a soprano.* [+ two objects] • *Like most sports, in squash you can gain the advantage just by being in the right position.* • *After you've gained some experience teaching abroad you can come home and get a job.* • *We only just started up the business last year so we haven't really gained a foothold in the market yet.* • *It took a long time for Charles Darwin's theory of evolution to gain acceptance.* • *At college he gained* **a reputation** *for being a brilliant debater.* • *From the late nineteenth century Britain and other European powers began to gain* **control** *of parts of the Ottoman Empire.* • *You've got nothing to lose and everything to gain.* • *She's certainly gained* **(in)** *confidence over the last couple of years.* • *The data exists all right – the difficulty is in gaining* **access** *to it.* • *The thieves gained entrance through an upstairs window that was left open.* • If a political party or an idea or belief **gains ground** it becomes more popular or accepted: *The Republicans are gaining ground in the southern states.*

gain /geɪn/ *n* • *Whatever the objections to this sort of treatment, the gains in terms of the number of lives saved are substantial.* [C] • *The minister was sacked for abusing power for his* **personal** *gain.* [U]

gain *(obj)* INCREASE /geɪn/ *v* to increase in weight, speed, height or amount • *I gained a lot of weight while I was on holiday.* [T] • *You know when you're gaining altitude because you begin to feel sleepy.* [T] • *The car gained speed going down the hill.* [T] • *Good economic indicators caused the share index to gain* **(by)** *ten points.* [I/T] • *The campaign has been gaining momentum ever since the television appeal.* [T] • If you gain **on** someone or something that you are chasing or trying to get in front of, you get nearer to them: *You're going to have to speed up – they're gaining on us.* [I] ○ *Garcia was gaining on her opponent throughout the race, but only overtook her at the very end.* [I] • If a clock or watch gains it works too quickly and shows a time which is later than the real time: *My watch has gained* **(by)** *ten minutes over the last twenty-four hours.* [I/T]

gain /geɪn/ *n* • *Side effects of the drugs may include tiredness, headaches or weight gain.* [U] • *Having deducted costs we still made a net gain of five thousand pounds.* [C] • *Oil prices rose again today after yesterday's gains.* [C]

gainer /£ˈgeɪ·nəʳ, $-nɚ/ *n* [C] • *The government says there are far more gainers* (= people whose situation has improved) *than losers from its new healthcare scheme.*

gain·ful /ˈgeɪn·fəl/ *adj* [not gradable] *fml* providing money or useful • *Many graduates tell of months spent in search of gainful* **employment**.

gain·ful·ly /ˈgeɪn·fəl·i/ *adv* [not gradable] *slightly fml* • *There's nothing else which can be gainfully said on the matter.* • *His estate continues to keep lawyers gainfully* **employed** *even seven years after his death.*

gain·say *obj* /ˌgeɪnˈseɪ/ *v* [T usually in negatives] *past* **gainsaid** /ˌgeɪnˈsed/ *fml* to refuse to accept (something) as the truth • *There's no gainsaying* (= It is not possible to doubt) *the technical brilliance of his performance but one might have hoped for a little more feeling.*

gait /geɪt/ *n* [C] *fml or humorous* a particular way of walking • *He was tall and portly and walked with a slow stiff gait.* • Gait is also used esp. of the particular way a horse walks or runs: *The pony's gait slowed from a canter to a trot.*

gait·ers /£'geɪ·təz, $-t̬ɚz/ *pl n* a pair of coverings for the lower half of the legs, often worn in the past but worn now mainly by climbers and walkers in order to stop earth and water from entering their boots

gal GIRL /gæl/ *n* [C] *infml or humorous* a girl • *No, I'm sorry, I just ain't that kind of gal.* • *You're just an old-fashioned gal, aren't you, honey!*

gal UNIT OF MEASUREMENT /gæl/, *Br also* **gall** *n* [C] *pl* **gal** or **gals** *abbreviation for* GALLON (= a unit for measuring the volume of a liquid)

ga·la CELEBRATION /£'gɑː·lə, $'geɪ-/ *n* [C] a special public occasion at which there is a lot of entertainment, usually in the form of a variety of performances • *There will be many stars performing in the Royal Ballet's Gala Night, held in aid of children's charities.* • *A number of luminaries from the opera world were performing – it was a real gala affair.*

ga·la SPORTING OCCASION /£'gɑː·lə, $'geɪ-/ *n* [C] *Br* a sports competition, esp. in swimming • *I went to see my niece take part in her school's* **swimming** *gala.*

ga·lah /gə'lɑː/ *n* [C] a medium-sized COCKATOO (= type of bird) common in most parts of Australia that has a grey upper part of its body and a pink lower part, or *(Aus infml)* a stupid person

gal·ax·y /'gæl·ək·si/ *n* [C] one of the independent groups of stars in the universe • *Astronomers at the University of California discovered one of the most distant galaxies known.* • **The Galaxy** (also **the Milky Way**) is the very large group of stars that contains the **solar system** (= the sun and all the planets, including Earth, that go round it). • A gathering of rich and famous people can be referred to as a galaxy: *Present tonight at the long-awaited opening of this film are a whole galaxy* **of** *stars from the acting and musical professions.*

gal·ac·tic /£gə'læk·tɪk, $-t̬ɪk/ *adj* [not gradable] • Galactic means relating to the Galaxy or other galaxies: *We are still many years away from realizing the possibility of inter-galactic travel.*

gale /geɪl/ *n* [C] a very strong wind • *A lot of old oaks were blown down in the gales last year.* • *I heard on the forecast that there are going to be gales on the south coast tonight.* • *I could hear* **gales of laughter** (= a lot of loud laughter) *coming from downstairs.*

gall RUDENESS /£gɔːl, $gɑːl/ *n* [U] rudeness and inability to understand that your behaviour or what you say is not acceptable to other people • *Considering that he never even bothers to visit my parents I'm amazed that Tim* **has the** *gall* **to** *ask them for money!* [+ *to* infinitive] • *I don't know how she can* **have the** *gall* **to** *accuse other people of inefficiency when she's the most incompetent person I know!* [+ *to* infinitive]

gall *obj* ANNOY /£gɔːl, $gɑːl/ *v* [T] to make (someone) feel annoyed • *I think it galls him to take orders from a younger and less experienced colleague.*

gall·ing /£'gɔː·lɪŋ, $'gɑː-/ *adj* • *It was very galling* **to** *have a younger brother who did everything better than me.* [+ *to* infinitive] • *After a galling defeat against France last night, Italy will have to recover their morale for the big match next week.*

gal·lant BRAVE /£'gæl·ənt, $gə'lænt/ *adj fml approving* showing no fear of dangerous or difficult things • *At the centre of the play is O'Neill, a Northern Irish chieftain who made a gallant stand against the English invaders.* • *Despite fierce competition she made a gallant effort to win the first medal of the championships.*

gal·lan·try /'gæl·ən·tri/ *n* [U] • *The speech praised those who had displayed gallantry in the liberation of their country.* • (CS) (RUS)

gal·lant POLITE /£'gæl·ənt, $gə'lænt/ *adj fml* (of a man) polite and kind towards women, esp. when in public • *He was a confirmed bachelor but he was always charming and gallant towards women.* • *That wasn't very gallant of you, Paul, pushing a young lady out of the way like that!*

gal·lan·try /'gæl·ən·tri/ *n* [U] *fml* • (CS) (RUS)

gall blad·der /£gɔːl, $gɑːl/ *n* [C] a small bag-like bodily organ connected to the LIVER which stores BILE (= a bitter liquid that helps to digest food) • *She had an operation to remove a stone from her gall bladder.*

gal·le·on /'gæl·i·ən/ *n* [C] a large sailing ship with three or four MASTS (= poles for supporting sails), used both in trade and war from the 15th to the 18th centuries

gal·ler·y BUILDING /£'gæl·ᵊr·i, $'-ɚ-/ *n* [C] a room or building which is used for showing works of art, sometimes so that they can be sold • *In the afternoon we went to the National Portrait Gallery.* • *There are a couple of contemporary* **art** *galleries in the city that are worth visiting.* • *I bought the picture from a gallery that we went to.*

gal·ler·y RAISED AREA /£'gæl·ᵊr·i, $'-ɚ-/ *n* [C] a raised area around the sides or at the back of a large room which provides extra space for people to sit or stand, or the highest floor in a theatre that contains the cheapest seats • Compare CIRCLE UPPER FLOOR; STALLS THEATRE.

gal·ley KITCHEN /'gæl·i/ *n* [C] a kitchen in a ship or aircraft

gal·ley BOAT /'gæl·i/ *n* [C] (in the past) a long low ship which had sails and was usually ROWED by prisoners and SLAVES (= people who are owned by and work for someone else) • *a galley slave*

Gal·lic /'gæl·ɪk/ *adj* French or typically French • *Catherine Deneuve seemed to typify cool Gallic elegance.*

gal·li·vant /'gæl·ɪ·vænt/ *v* [I] *humorous* to visit or go to a lot of different places, enjoying yourself and having few worries or responsibilities • *Well you won't be able to go off gallivanting* **around** *like this when there's a baby to be taken care of.*

gal·lon /'gæl·ən/ *n* [C] a unit for measuring volume • *An imperial gallon, used in Britain, is equal to 4546 cubic centimetres.* • *A US gallon is equal to 3785 cubic centimetres.* • *(infml) I love milk – I drink gallons* (= a great amount) *of the stuff.* • LP› **Units**

gal·lop *(obj)* /'gæl·əp/ *v* (of a horse) to run fast so that all four feet come off the ground together in each act of forward movement, or (of a person) to ride a horse that is running in this way • *She gallops her horses regularly and they're very fit.* [T] • *We galloped through the woods.* [I] • *(fig.) It is the height of folly and a tragic waste to gallop* (= move quickly) *into war.* [I] • *(fig. infml) I'll just gallop* (= go very quickly) *down to the shops.* [I] • Compare CANTER; TROT.

gal·lop /'gæl·əp/ *n* [C] • *A horse naturally shifts from a trot to a gallop.* • *At the sound of gunfire the horse suddenly* **broke into** *a gallop.* • *We had a good gallop on the shore.* • *(fig.) We had to complete the work* **at a** *gallop* (= very quickly).

gal·lop·ing /'gæl·ə·pɪŋ/ *adj* [before n; not gradable] increasing or developing at a very fast and often uncontrollable rate • *Galloping* **inflation** *and massive unemployment were the two major economic problems at that time.* • *This has been a century of galloping technological innovation.*

gal·lows /£'gæl·əʊz, $-oʊz/ *n* [C] *pl* **gallows** a wooden structure used, esp. in the past, to hang criminals from as a form of EXECUTION (= killing as a punishment) • *New witnesses have cast doubt on some of the evidence that* **sent** *the 19 year old* **to the** *gallows.* • **Gallows humour** refers to jokes or humorous remarks that are made about unpleasant or worrying subjects such as death and illness: *There was a lot of gallows humour about job security on the day the job losses were announced.*

gall·stone /£'gɔːl·stəʊn, $'gɑːl·stoʊn/ *n* [C] a small piece of hard material which sometimes forms in the GALL BLADDER (= a bodily organ) and can cause great pain • *My father had an operation to remove a gallstone a few years ago.*

ga·lore /£gə'lɔːʳ, $-'lɔːr/ *adj* [after n; not gradable] *infml dated* in great amounts or numbers • *And for the sweet-toothed, this café has desserts galore.*

ga·losh·es /£gə'lɒʃ·ɪz, $-'lɑː·ʃɪz/ *pl n dated for* OVERSHOES

ga·lumph·ing /gə'lʌmp·fɪŋ/ *adj Br infml* moving about or behaving in an awkward or graceless manner • *In his galumphing way he somehow managed to sneak over the line to score.* • *Her galumphing entry into the music business has annoyed many of the established stars.*

gal·van·ize *obj, Br and Aus usually* **-ise** /'gæl·və·naɪz/ *v* [T] to cause (someone) to suddenly take action, esp. by shocking or exciting them in some way • *During the previous famine western charities were galvanized by TV pictures of starving people.* • *The prospect of his mother coming to stay galvanized him* **into action** *and he immediately set about cleaning the house.* • *What the team need is a leader who will somehow galvanise them.*

gal·van·ized, *Br and Aus usually* **-ised** /'gæl·və·naɪzd/ *adj* [not gradable] (of iron or steel) covered with a thin layer of ZINC (= a type of metal) for protection • *galvanized iron/steel* • *galvanized nails/rivets*

gam·bit [CLEVER ACTION] /ˈgæm·bɪt/ *n* [C] a clever action in a game or other situation which is intended to achieve an advantage and usually involves taking a risk • *Her clever* **opening** *gambit gave her an early advantage.* • *The government's promise to lower taxes is so obviously an election-year gambit.* • *(specialized)* In chess, a gambit is a way of beginning the game where you intentionally lose a PAWN [GAME PIECE] in order to gain some other form of advantage at a later point.

gam·bit [INTRODUCTORY REMARK] /ˈgæm·bɪt/ *n* [C] a remark that you make to someone in order to start a conversation • *He approached me with that tired old* **conversational** *gambit, "Don't I know you from somewhere?"* • *I met a man at the party last night whose rather charmless* **opening** *gambit was "Is it as boring as it sounds being a librarian?"*

gam·ble *(obj)* /ˈgæm·bl̩/ *v* to do something risky that might result in loss of money or failure, in the hope of making money or achieving success • *Anyone who gambles* **on** *the stock exchange has to be prepared to lose money.* [I] • *In foreign policy, as in other spheres, the president has gambled outrageously during his two terms of office.* [I] • *You're rather gambling* **on** *it being* (= trusting that it will be) *a nice day by holding the party in the garden, aren't you?* [I] • *Further reductions in the armed forces, he said, would be 'gambling* **with** *the nation's defence'.* [I] • *I'm gambling* **that** *he'll have forgotten what I promised last year.* [+ *that* clause] • You might gamble by BETTING money, for example in a game or on a horse race: *When they played cards they always gambled.* [I] ○ *When he gambled he always won, whether he was playing roulette, poker or just the fruit machines in Las Vegas.* [I] ○ *He'd gambled* **away** *most of his inheritance by the time he was thirty.* [M]

gam·ble /ˈgæm·bl̩/ *n* [C usually sing] • *Starting up a newspaper during a recession is a business gamble that Gilmore is not taking lightly.* • *Her publishers knew they were* **taking** *a gamble when they agreed to publish such an unusual novel.* • *The film was very successful – using such an inexperienced director was a gamble which* **paid off**.

gam·bler /£ˈgæm·bləʳ, $-blɚ/ *n* [C] • *He's joined a self-help group for* **compulsive** *gamblers.* • *Horse racing is not the sport of kings but a game for gamblers.*

gam·bling /ˈgæm·blɪŋ/ *n* [U] • *In a quarter of the families in the study at least 10 per cent of the income was spent on drink, gambling and tobacco.* • *He had to borrow money to pay off his gambling debts.*

gam·bol /ˈgæm·bᵊl/ *v* [I] **-ll-** or *Am usually* **-l-** to run and jump happily and playfully • *The lambs were gambolling* **(about)** *in the spring sunshine.*

game [ENTERTAINMENT] /geɪm/ *n* an entertaining activity, esp. one played by children, or (a part of) a competition • *a baseball game* • *a computer game* [C] • *The children were playing a game* **of** *cops and robbers.* [C] • *I told the children to put their toys and games* (= equipment needed for games played inside) *away.* [C] • *Would you like a game* **of** *chess?* [C] • In some activities such as tennis a game is one part of a competition. [C] • A person's game is the way in which they play a particular sport: *Susan is playing golf every day to try to improve her game.* [U] • *(infml) I'm in the stocks and shares game* (= that is my business). [U] • If you say you are **new to this** game, you are saying you have not had experience of this activity or situation before. [U] • *Love is just a game* (= something that is not treated seriously) *to him.* [U] • *Not telling the whole truth is one of the games that people* **play** (= one of the ways in which they behave in order to get an advantage). [C] • *(infml) It's a secret, so don't* **give the game away** (= tell anyone about it), *will you?* • If you tell someone **the game is up** you mean that you know what they are secretly planning to do so they cannot succeed. • *(Br infml)* If you ask someone **"What's your game?"**, you are asking what their secret plan is: *The porter saw me climbing over the wall and shouted "Hey you, what's your game?"* • *(Br)* If you ask whether **the game is worth the candle** you ask whether it is really worth making a great effort to get something. • *(Br)* A woman **on the game** is a PROSTITUTE. • *(Am infml)* Someone who is **on the game** is involved in illegal activities. • A **game plan** is a plan for achieving success: *Cutting the cost of our products is an essential part of our game plan.* • *"Games People Play: the psychology of human relationships"* (title of a book by Eric Berne, 1964) • [LP] **Sports**

games /geɪmz/ *pl n* • *(Br)* Games are organized sports activities that children do at school: *I always hated games.* ○ *Have you met the new games teacher?* • Games are also an organized competition consisting of several different sporting events: *the Olympic Games*

game [WILLING] /geɪm/ *adj* willing to do new or risky things • *It was a difficult challenge but Roberta was game.* • *She's game* **for** *anything.*

game·ly /ˈgeɪm·li/ *adv* • *"I'll look after the baby," he said gamely* (= bravely).

game [ANIMALS] /geɪm/ *n* [U] wild animals and birds that are hunted for food or sport • *Venison and pheasants are types of game.* • *Game* **birds** *have a particularly strong taste.*

gam·ey /ˈgeɪ·mi/ *adj* **gamier, gamiest** • *The pheasant had been hanging in the kitchen and there was a gamey smell* (= having a strong smell of game) *in the air.*

game·keep·er /£ˈgeɪmˌkiː·pəʳ, $-pɚ/ *n* [C] a person whose job is to take care of the wild animals and birds kept on someone's land to be hunted

games·man·ship /ˈgeɪmz·mən·ʃɪp/ *n* [U] *infml* the activity of winning a game by doing things that are not really breaking the rules but are intended to destroy the confidence of the other player

gam·ete /ˈgæm·iːt/ *n* [C] *specialized* a cell connected with sexual reproduction, which is either a male sperm or a female egg • *Each gamete contains one set of chromosomes, and can join with another gamete of the opposite sex to form a zygote.*

ga·mine /ˈgæm·iːn/ *adj approving* (of a girl or young woman) thin, short-haired and attractively like a young boy in appearance • *Her newly cropped hair gives her a fashionably gamine look.*

gam·ing /ˈgeɪ·mɪŋ/ *n* [U], *adj* [not gradable] (of) the risking of money in games of chance esp. at a CASINO • The **gaming tables** are places where you can go to GAMBLE, esp. the tables on which people play cards or ROULETTE.

gam·ma, γ /ˈgæm·ə/ *n* [C] the third letter of the Greek alphabet, sometimes given as a mark for a student's work to show satisfactory quality • **Gamma globulin** is a natural substance in the blood that gives protection against disease: *Gamma globulin injections are often used as a way of protecting you against certain diseases, esp. when travelling abroad.* • **Gamma radiation** is a type of ELECTROMAGNETIC RADIATION of very short wave length, often produced in RADIOACTIVE decay, which goes through most solid objects. • Compare ALPHA; BETA.

gam·mon *esp. Br* /ˈgæm·ən/, *Am and Aus usually* **ham** *n* [U] meat which has been taken from the back leg or side of a pig and been preserved with smoke or salt

gam·my /ˈgæm·i/ *adj* **-ier, -iest** *Br infml* (esp. of a person's leg) damaged or not working correctly • *He can't get about much these days because of his gammy leg.*

gam·ut /ˈgæm·ət/ *n* [U] **the gamut** the whole range of things that can be included in something • *In her stories she expresses the whole gamut of emotions from happiness to sorrow.* • To **run** the gamut of something is to experience all the different things included in it: *Jonson has run the gamut of hotel work, from porter to owner of a large chain of hotels.*

gan·der [BIRD] /£ˈgæn·dəʳ, $-dɚ/ *n* [C] a male GOOSE

gan·der [LOOK] /£ˈgæn·dəʳ, $-dɚ/ *n* [U] **have/take a gander** *infml* to have a quick look • *I heard she had a new car so I went out to take a gander* **at** *it.*

gang /gæŋ/ *n* [C + sing/pl v] a group of criminals or of people, esp. young men who spend time together and cause trouble, or any group of friends or workers • *A gang of armed robbers was involved in a shoot-out with police yesterday.* • *Fights among rival gangs account for most murders in the city.* • *The gang of labourers were digging a hole in the road.* • *A teacher was knocked down by a gang of school pupils.* • *(infml) I went out with the usual gang on Friday night – all my friends from college.* • *Gang* **warfare** (= Gangs fighting other gangs) *is usually drugs-related.* • A **gang-bang** is when a group of men have sex with a woman, esp. by force. • Ⓙ Ⓢ

gang up /gæŋ/ *v adv* [I] *infml* • *(disapproving)* To gang up is to unite as a group against someone: *They ganged up to try and change his decision, but he refused to discuss it.* ○ *The whole class ganged up* **against/on** *her because she was the teacher's pet.*

gang·land /ˈgæŋ·lænd/ *n* [U] people and places involved in violent crime • *The Kray twins were once the scourge of London's gangland.* • *McAuley was shot in a gangland feud.*

gan·gling /ˈgæŋ·glɪŋ/ *adj* (esp. of a boy or young man) very tall, thin and awkward in his movements • *From a gangling boy he had grown into an elegant young man.*

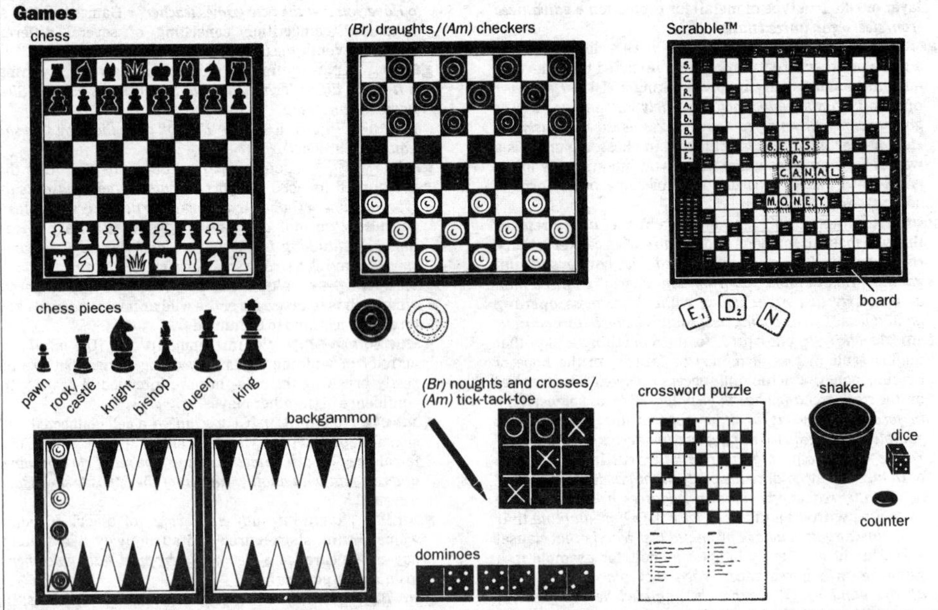

gan·gli·on /ˈgæŋ·gli·ən/ *n* [C] *pl* **ganglions** or **ganglia** /ˈgæŋ·gli·ə/ *medical* a swelling, often on the back of the hand, or a mass of nerve cells, esp. appearing outside the brain or SPINE (= row of bones down the centre of the back)

gang·plank /ˈgæŋ·plæŋk/ *n* [C] a board or similar object put between a ship and the land so that people can get on and off

gang·rene /ˈgæŋ·griːn/ *n* [U] the decay of a part of a person's body because the blood has stopped flowing there • *If you don't treat the cut properly, gangrene might set in.*

gang·ren·ous /ˈgæŋ·grɪ·nəs/ *adj* • *His foot had become gangrenous and had to be amputated.*

gang·ster /£ˈgæŋ*k*·stəʳ, $-stɚ/ *n* [C] a member of an organized group of violent criminals

gang·way /ˈgæŋ·weɪ/ *n* [C] a passage between two rows of seats, for example in a cinema or bus, or another word for GANGPLANK • *His suitcase was blocking the gangway.* • If you shout "gangway!" you are asking people to move so that you can go past quickly.

gan·ja /ˈgæn·dʒə/ *n* [U] *infml* MARIJUANA

gan·net /ˈgæn·ɪt/ *n* [C] a large bird with mainly white feathers and a yellow beak that lives by the sea

gan·try /ˈgæn·tri/ *n* [C] a tall metal frame that supports heavy machines such as CRANES, railway signals or other equipment

ga·ol /dʒeɪl/ *n, v Br dated for* JAIL

gaol·er /£ˈdʒeɪ·ləʳ, $-lɚ/ *n* [C] *Br dated*

ga·ol·bird /£ˈdʒeɪl·bɜːd, $-bɜːrd/ *n* [C] *Br dated for* JAILBIRD

ga·ol·break /ˈdʒeɪl·breɪk/ *n* [C] *Br dated for* JAILBREAK

gap /gæp/ *n* [C] an empty space or opening in the middle of something or between two things • *The children squeezed through a gap* **in** *the wall.* • *She has a small gap* **between** *her front teeth.* • *(fig.) There is a gap* (= something missing) **in** *the magazine market that needs to be filled.* • *(fig.) The gap* **between** *rich and poor is still widening* (= the difference between them is becoming greater). • *(fig.) How can we* **bridge** *the gap* (= make the difference smaller)*?* • *(fig.) After a gap* (= a period of time doing something different) *of five years, Jennifer decided to go back to work full-time.* • A **gap-toothed** person is one with spaces between their teeth.

gape LOOK /geɪp/ *v* [I] to look in great surprise (at someone or something), esp. with an open mouth • *They stood gaping* **at** *the pig in the kitchen.*

gape OPEN /geɪp/ *v* [I] to be or become wide open • *Peter's jacket gaped at the seams.*

gap·ing /ˈgeɪ·pɪŋ/ *adj* • *There were gaping holes in the wall where it had been hit by the bomb.* • *(fig.) The newspaper report of the event had gaping holes in it* (= there were a lot of things missing from it).

gar·age /£ˈgær·ɑːʒ, £-ɪdʒ, gəˈrɑːʒ/ *n* [C] a building where a car is kept, which is built next to or as part of a house • *Have you put the car away in the garage?* • *(Br and Aus)* A garage (*Am* **gas station**) is also a place where you can buy fuel for cars and other vehicles. • A garage is also a place where you can have your car repaired: *The car's still at the garage getting fixed.* • *(Br)* A garage (also **car dealer/showroom**) is also a place where you can buy a car. • A **garage sale** is an occasion when people sell things, often in their garage or outside their house, that they no longer want: *When we moved to Italy, we sold our house contents at a garage sale.* • PIC› **Accommodation**

garb /£gɑːb, $gɑːrb/ *n* [U] *literary* clothes that are in a particular style • *She wore the usual garb of the office worker – smart suit and high heels.* • *He was dressed in nun's garb.*

gar·bage /£ˈgɑː·bɪdʒ, $ˈgɑːr-/ *n* [U] nonsense or worthless ideas or things, or *Am and Aus for* RUBBISH • *He was talking a lot of garbage about education.* • **Garbage bag** is *Am and Aus for* **dustbin bag/liner**. See at DUSTBIN. • **Garbage can** is *Am for* DUSTBIN. Garbage can **cover** is *Am for* **dustbin lid**. • **Garbage collector** is *Am for* DUSTMAN. • **Garbage truck** is *Am and Aus for* **dustbin lorry**. See at DUSTBIN. • PIC› **Coverings, Vehicles**

gar·bag·y /£ˈgɑː·bɪdʒ·i, $ˈgɑːr-/ *adj Am* • *He just reads garbagy novels.*

gar·bage·man (*pl* **-men**) /£ˈgɑː·bɪdʒ·mæn, $ˈgɑːr-/ *n* [C] *Am and Aus for* DUSTMAN

gar·banz·o (bean) /£gɑːˈbæn·zəʊ, $gɑːrˈbæn·zoʊ/ *n* [C] a CHICKPEA

gar·bled /£ˈgɑː·bl̩d, $ˈgɑːr-/ *adj* (of something said) confused and giving a false idea of the facts • *He left a rather garbled* **message** *on my answerphone.*

gar·çon /£ˈgɑː·sɒn, £-ˈ-, $gɑːrˈsoʊn/ *n* [C] *dated* a WAITER (= a man who serves food in a restaurant) in France

gar·den /£ˈgɑː·dᵊn, $ˈgɑːr-/ *n* [C] a piece of land next to a house where flowers and other plants are grown and which often has an area of grass • *garden tools* • *garden furniture* • *a garden shed* • *Shall we go and sit in the garden (Am usually* **yard**, *Aus* **backyard**)*?* • *(esp. Br) The house has a large* **back** *garden, and a small* **front** *garden* (= There is a large garden behind the house, and a small one in front of it). • Gardens are often public parks with flowers, plants and places to sit: *the Botanical Gardens* • *(Am)* A **garden apartment** is (an apartment in) a building containing several apartments which is not very tall and is surrounded by open land with trees and flowers. • A **garden centre** is a place where you can buy things such as plants and equipment for your garden. • *(Br)* A **garden city** is a town or part of a town that has been planned to include lots of trees, plants and open spaces. • *(literary)* In the Bible, the **garden of Eden** was the beautiful garden God made for Adam and Eve. • *(Br)* A **garden flat** is an apartment which has its own garden. • A **garden party**

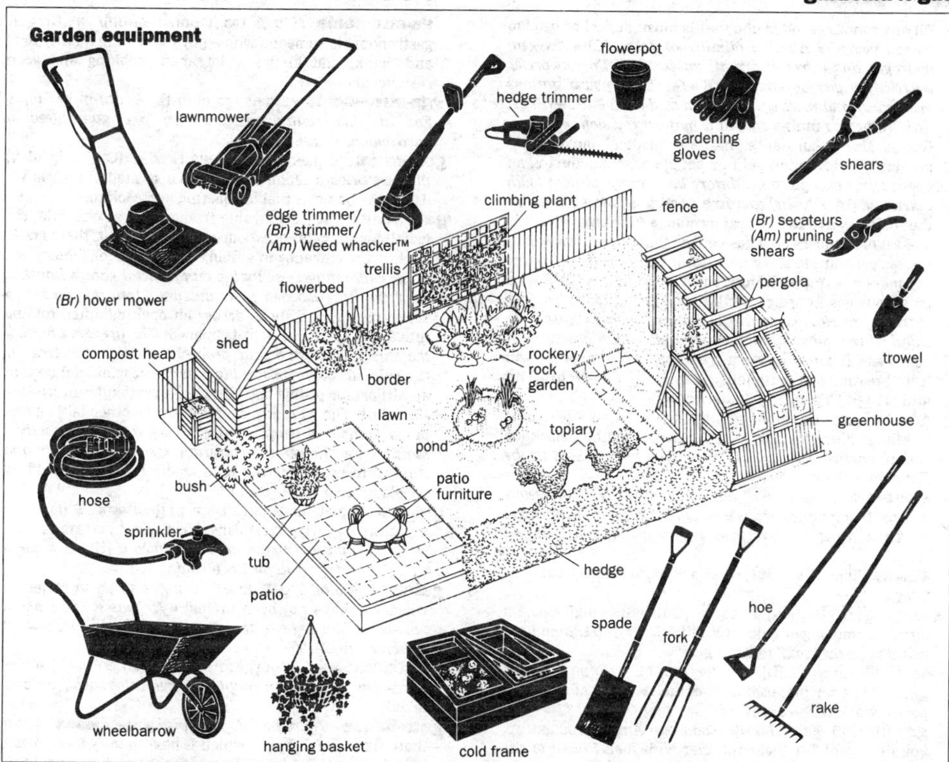

(*Am also* **lawn party**) is a formal party that happens outside in the afternoon, often in a large private garden. • *"Nothing grows in our garden, only washing. And babies."* (from the play *Under Milk Wood* by Dylan Thomas, 1954) • *"Everything in the garden's lovely* (= All is well)*"* (title of a song sung by Marie Lloyd, 1898)

gar·den·er /£'gɑː·dᵊn·əʳ, $'gɑːr·dᵊn·ɚ/ *n* [C] • A gardener is someone who takes care of a garden: *Our new garden is so big that we have had to hire a gardener.* ○ *I'm not much of a gardener* (= not very good at taking care of my garden).

gar·den·ing /£'gɑː·dᵊn·ɪŋ, $'gɑːr-/ *n* [U] • *gardening gloves/equipment* • *Many people in Britain are fond of gardening* (= working in and taking care of their gardens). • PIC〉 **Garden**

gar·de·ni·a /£gɑː'diː·ni·ə, $gɑːr-/ *n* [C] a tropical plant with large white or yellow flowers that have a pleasant smell

gar·gan·tu·an /£gɑː'gæn·tju·ən, $gɑːr-/ *adj* very large • *Many developing countries have gargantuan debts.*

gar·gle /£'gɑː·gḷ, $'gɑːr-/ *v* [I] to wash your mouth or throat with liquid by holding the liquid in your mouth, keeping your head back and breathing out slowly through the mouth • *Gargling with an aspirin solution soothes a sore throat.*

gar·gle /£'gɑː·gḷ, $'gɑːr-/ *n* [U] • *Have a gargle with this mouthwash before you brush your teeth.*

gar·goyle /£'gɑː·gɔɪl, $'gɑːr-/ *n* [C] a stone object in the shape of the head of an ugly creature on the roofs of old churches and other buildings, through whose mouth rain water often flows away • *The gargoyles at the top of Notre Dame look down over Paris.*

gar·ish /£'geə·rɪʃ, $'ger·ɪʃ/ *adj* unpleasantly bright • *He was wearing garish Bermuda shorts and training shoes.*

gar·land /£'gɑː·lənd, $'gɑːr-/ *n* [C] a circle made of flowers and leaves worn around the neck or head as a decoration • *She wore a garland of white roses on her head for her wedding.*

gar·land *obj* /£'gɑː·lənd, $'gɑːr-/ *v* [T] • *They garlanded the visitors* **with** *scented flowers.*

gar·lic /£'gɑː·lɪk, $'gɑːr-/ *n* [U] a plant of the onion family that has a strong taste and smell and is used in cooking to add flavour • A **clove of** garlic is a single part of a garlic **bulb** that is usually crushed or cut before being added to food. • **Garlic bread** is bread that has been spread with a mixture of butter, garlic and herbs before being baked. • A **garlic press** is a small device in which cloves of garlic are crushed. • PIC〉 **Vegetables**

gar·lick·y /£'gɑː·lɪ·ki, $'gɑːr-/ *adj* • *He refuses to eat garlicky food* (= food tasting of garlic).

gar·ment /£'gɑː·mənt, $'gɑːr-/ *n* [C] *fml* a piece of clothing • *He was wearing a strange garment that reached down to his ankles.* • **Garment bag** is *Am for* **suit bag**. See at SUIT SET OF CLOTHES. • PIC〉 **Luggage**

gar·ner *obj* /£'gɑː·nəʳ, $'gɑːr·nɚ/ *v* [T] *literary* to collect (something), often with difficulty • *(fig.) Coppola garnered several Oscar awards for 'The Godfather'.*

gar·net /£'gɑː·nɪt, $'gɑːr-/ *n* [C] a hard dark red stone used in jewellery

gar·nish *obj* /£'gɑː·nɪʃ, $'gɑːr-/ *v* [T] to decorate (food) with a small amount of different food • *Garnish the dish with parsley and serve.*

gar·nish /£'gɑː·nɪʃ, $'gɑːr-/ *n* [C] • *Use some parsley as a garnish.*

gar·ret /'gær·ɪt/ *n* [C] *literary* a very small uncomfortable room at the top of the house • *She doesn't fit the image of an impoverished artist starving in a garret.*

gar·ri·son /£'gær·ɪ·sᵊn, $'ger-/ *n* [C + sing/pl v] a group of soldiers living in or defending a town or building, or the buildings that the soldiers live in • *The 100-strong garrison has/have received no supplies for a week.*

gar·ri·son *obj* /£'gær·ɪ·sᵊn, $'ger-/ *v* [T always + adv/prep] • *British troops are garrisoned in the area.*

gar·rotte *obj*, **ga·rotte**, *Am also* **gar·rote** /£gə'rɒt, $-'rɑːt/ *v* [T] to kill (someone) by putting a metal wire or collar around their neck, so breaking their neck or preventing them from breathing

gar·rotte, ga·rotte, *Am also* **gar·rote** /£gə'rɒt, $-'rɑːt/ *n* [C] • A garrotte is a piece of wire or a metal collar used to kill someone in this way.

gar·ru·lous /£'gær·ᵊl·əs, $'ger-/ *adj* having the habit of talking a lot, esp. about unimportant things • *I had expected her to be fat and garrulous.*

gar·ru·lous·ly /£'gær·ᵊl·ə·sli, $'ger-/ *adv*

gar·ru·lous·ness /£'gær·ᵊl·ə·snəs, $'ger-/, **gar·ru·li·ty** /£gær'uː·lɪ·ti, $-lə·ṭi/ *n* [U]

gar·ter /£'gɑː·təʳ, $'gɑːr·ṭɚ/ *n* [C] a piece of elastic used, esp. in the past, for holding up a STOCKING or sock

gas MATTER /gæs/ *n pl* **gases** or **gasses** a form of matter which is neither solid nor liquid and can increase in size to fill any container, often one that is burnt as fuel or used to poison people • *Air is a mixture of gases.* [C] • *Oxygen, hydrogen and nitrogen are all gases.* [C] • *Do you prefer electricity or gas for cooking?* [U] • *Gas-***fired** *power stations are cleaner and more efficient than coal-fired ones.* • *(Br) A leak in the gas* **mains** *caused a major explosion.* • *(infml)* Gas is also a substance used for medical purposes to prevent people feeling pain or being conscious during an operation: *I was given gas before having my wisdom tooth taken out.* [U] • A *(Br)* **gas fire** *(Am)* **gas heater** is a fire that uses gas as a fuel to heat a room. • *(Br)* A **gas mark** is one set of numbers on a gas cooker that is used instead of the temperature to show how hot it is: *Preheat the oven to gas mark 4.* • A **gas chamber** is a room that is filled with poisonous gas in order to kill people or animals: *The gas chambers at Nazi concentration camps such as Auschwitz stand as reminders of the extremes of human cruelty.* • A **gas mask** is a device worn over the face to prevent you from breathing in poisonous gases. • LP **Switching on and off** PIC **Fires and space heaters**

gas *obj* /gæs/ *v* [T often passive] **-ss-** • To gas a person is to kill or injure them by making them breathe poisonous gas: *Hundreds of thousands of soldiers were gassed in the First World War.*

ga·seous /ˈgeɪ·si·əs/ *adj specialized* • *a gaseous mixture* (=a mixture of gases) • *Condensation is the process by which water changes from a gaseous state to a liquid state.*

gas·sy /ˈgæs·i/ *adj* **-ier, -iest** • *This beer is very gassy* (= fizzy).

gas AMUSING SITUATION /gæs/ *n* [C usually sing] *esp. Am infml* an amusing or enjoyable situation • *You should have heard what they said, it was a* **gas**.

gas FUEL /gæs/ *n* [U] *Am for* PETROL • *(infml)* A **gas guzzler** is a car that uses a lot of fuel. • A **gas station** is a **petrol station**. See at PETROL.

gas up *(obj)*, **gas** *(obj)* **up** *v adv* **-ss-** *Am* • If you gas up, you fill a vehicle's fuel container with fuel: *I want to gas up when we get to the next town.* [I] • *You should gas the car up before you head home.* [M]

gas TALK /gæs/ *v* [I] **-ss-** *infml dated* to talk for a long time about unimportant things • *We sat there gassing for hours and having a great time.*

gas·bag /ˈgæs·bæg/ *n* [C] *infml* a person who always talks too much

gash /gæʃ/ *v, n* (to make) a long deep cut, esp. in the skin • *Sarah had bruises on her legs and a gash in her knee.* [C] • *She gashed her knee when she slipped on a rock.* [T]

gas·ket /ˈgæs·kɪt/ *n* [C] a flat piece of soft material or rubber put between two joined metal surfaces to prevent gas, oil or steam from escaping

gas·light /ˈgæs·laɪt/ *n* [C/U] (esp. used in the past) a light that uses gas as fuel, or the light that is produced by this

gas·man *(pl* **-men***)* /ˈgæs·mæn/ *n* [C] *Br infml* a man whose job is reading gas METERS and repairing gas systems

gas·o·line /ˈgæs·əl·iːn, ˌ--ˈ-/ *n* [U] *Am for* PETROL

gas·o·met·er /£gæsˈɒm·ɪ·təʳ, $-ˈɑː·mə·t̬ɚ/, **gas·hold·er** *n* [C] a large metal container where gas is stored before it is supplied to customers • PIC **Energy**

gasp /£gɑːsp, $gæsp/ *v* to take a short quick breath through the mouth, esp. because of surprise, pain or shock • *When she saw the money hidden in the box she gasped* **in** *surprise.* [I] • *"Help me!" he gasped.* [+ clause] • *(Br infml)* If someone is gasping, or gasping **for** a drink, they are very thirsty: *"Could you give me some water? I'm gasping!"* [I]

gasp /£gɑːsp, $gæsp/ *n* [C] • *He gave a gasp* **of** *amazement.*

gas·ses /ˈgæs·ɪz/ *pl of* GAS MATTER

gas·sy /ˈgæs·i/ *adj* See at GAS MATTER

ga·stric /ˈgæs·trɪk/ *adj* [not gradable] *fml or medical* of the stomach • *gastric juices* • *a gastric ulcer* • *Caffeine can cause gastric* **upset** *in some people.*

ga·stri·tis /£gæsˈtraɪ·tɪs, $-t̬əs/ *n* [U] *medical* • *When you have gastritis* (=a swelling of the stomach walls), *it can eventually lead to ulcers.*

ga·stro·en·ter·i·tis /£ˌgæs·trəʊˌen·təˈraɪ·tɪs, $-troʊˌen·t̬əˈraɪ·t̬əs/ *n* [U] *medical* an illness which causes the stomach and bowels to become swollen and painful

ga·stro·no·my /£gæsˈtrɒn·ə·mi, $-ˈtrɑː·nə-/ *n* [U] *fml* the art and knowledge involved in preparing and eating good food • *The food writer Elizabeth David introduced gastronomy to many Britons.*

ga·stro·nome /£ˈgæs·trə·nəʊm, $-noʊm/ *n* [C] • A gastronome is someone who enjoys very high quality food and drink, and knows a lot about cooking and good restaurants.

ga·stro·nom·ic /£ˌgæs·trəˈnɒm·ɪk, $-ˈnɑː·mɪk/ *adj* • *Eat at this restaurant and you are guaranteed a gastronomic delight.*

gas·works /£ˈgæs·wɜːks, $-wɜːrks/ *n* [C + sing/pl v] *pl* **gasworks** a factory where coal is made into gas for use in the home as fuel for heating and cooking

gate /geɪt/ *n* [C] a movable frame fixed at one side and usually with metal or wooden strips across it, that is used to close the entrance to a field, garden, school, factory etc. • *The children were swinging on the metal gate.* • *I pushed open the little wooden gate and went into the garden.* • Sometimes a gate slides across an opening, often folding into a smaller space as it is opened: *The lift won't move if the safety gate isn't shut properly.* • *All passengers for flight LH103 please proceed to gate 16* (=the official door at an airport for people travelling on a particular aircraft). • *(Br infml)* The gate at a sports event or other large event is the number of people that go to see it: *Gates at football matches were lower than average last season.* • *(Br and Aus)* **Gate money** is the total amount of money paid by people to see a sports event.

gat·eau /£ˈgæt·əʊ, $gæt̬ˈoʊ/ *n pl* **gateaux** /£ˈgæt·əʊz, $gæt̬ˈoʊz/ a large sweet cake, usually with cream or fruit in it • *Would you like some more gateau?* [U] • *I made a rich chocolate gateau for his birthday.* [C]

gate·crash *(obj)* /ˈgeɪt·kræʃ/ *v infml* to go to (a party) when you have not been invited • *He was so cross about not being invited to the wedding that he decided to gatecrash (it).* [I/T]

gate·crash·er /£ˈgeɪtˌkræʃ·əʳ, $-ˌkræʃ·ɚ/ *n* [C] • *The party was ruined by a couple of gatecrashers who got very drunk.*

gate·house /ˈgeɪt·haʊs/ *n* [C] *pl* **gatehouses** /ˈgeɪtˌhaʊ·zɪz/ a small house which is next to the gate into esp. a park or castle and is often where the **park keeper** lives

gate·keep·er /£ˈgeɪtˌkiː·pəʳ, $-pɚ/ *n* [C] *dated* a person whose job is to open and close a gate and to prevent people entering without permission

gate·post /£ˈgeɪt·pəʊst, $-poʊst/ *n* [C] a post to which a gate is fixed, or to which it is fastened when closed

gate·way /ˈgeɪt·weɪ/ *n* [C] an entrance through a wall, fence, etc. where there is a gate, or *(fig.)* a place through which you have to go to get to a particular area • *(fig.) Manchester is known as the gateway* **to** *the north.*

gath·er *(obj)* COLLECT /£ˈgæð·əʳ, $-ɚ/ *v* to collect or obtain (things), esp. from different places • *I went to several libraries to gather information about the scheme.* [T] • *We gathered blackberries from the nearby fields.* [T] • *She gathered* **up** *the newspapers that were scattered around the floor* (=picked them up and put them together). [M] • *He gathered her* **in** *his arms* (=put his arms around her and held her close) *and kissed her tenderly.* [T] • *We gathered our things* **together** *and left quickly.* [M] • *(literary) Storm clouds were gathering* (=becoming thicker and closer). [I] • In sewing, when you gather cloth you pull it into small folds by sewing a thread through it and then pulling the thread tight: *a gathered skirt* • If you gather a piece of clothing or loose cloth **about/around** yourself, you pull it close to your body: *She shivered, and gathered the blanket around her.* [T] • If something is **gathering dust**, it is not being used regularly: *My guitar has just been gathering dust since I injured my hand.* • *Economic recovery is gathering* **pace** (=becoming faster and more obvious). [T] • If something gathers **speed/momentum** it gradually becomes faster or stronger: *The bicycle gathered speed as it went down the hill.* [T] • When a person gathers their **strength/courage** they prepare to make a great effort to be strong or brave: *I spent a week gathering the courage to say no.* [T] • *"Here we go gathering nuts in May"* (traditional children's song) • PIC **Clothes**

gath·ers /£ˈgæð·əz, $-ɚz/ *pl n* • Gathers are small folds that have been sewn into cloth.

gath·er COME TOGETHER /£ˈgæð·əʳ, $-ɚ/ *v* [I] (of people or animals) to come together in a group • *A crowd had gathered to hear her speak.* • *Gather* **(a)round**, *children, and I'll tell you a story.* • *The cows had gathered in a herd by the gate.*

gath·er·ing /£ˈgæð·əʳ·ɪŋ, $ˈ-ɚ-/ *n* [C] • *There will be a gathering* **of** *world leaders in Vienna next month.* • *We're* *having a little social gathering* (=meeting of people) *tonight, can you come?*

gath·er *(obj)* UNDERSTAND /£ˈgæð·ər, $-ɚ/ *v* to understand or believe (something) as a result of something that has been said or done • *Harry's not happy in his job, I gather.* [+ (*that*) clause] • *From the look on their faces, she gathered* **(that)** *they were annoyed with her.* [+ (*that*) clause] • *I never really gathered* **why** *he left his job.* [+ *wh-* word] • *I didn't gather much from his lecture.* [T]

ga·tor /£ˈgeɪ·tər, $-t̬ɚ/ *n* [C] *Am infml for* ALLIGATOR

GATT /gæt/ *n* [U not after *the*] *abbreviation for* General Agreement on Tariffs and Trade (=an international agreement, which more than 100 countries have signed, to end rules which reduce levels of trade between countries) • *The main purpose of GATT is to ensure free trade between nations.* • *The minister said that the GATT settlement preserved inequalities between the First and Third World, rather than doing anything to redress the balance.*

gauche /£gəʊʃ, $goʊʃ/ *adj* awkward and uncomfortable with other people, esp. because young and lacking in experience • *She had grown from a gauche teenager to a self-assured young woman.*

gau·cho /£ˈgaʊ·tʃəʊ, $-tʃoʊ/ *n* [C] *pl* **gauchos** a South American COWBOY

gaud·y /£ˈgɔː·di, $ˈgɑː-/ *adj* **-ier, -iest** having too many bright colours and lacking good judgment about style • *British tourists often wear gaudy shorts and t-shirts.*

gaud·i·ness /£ˈgɔː·dɪ·nəs, $ˈgɑː-/ *n* [U]

gauge *(obj), Am also* **gage** /geɪdʒ/ *v* to calculate (an amount), esp. by using a measuring device, or *(fig.)* to make a judgment about (people's feelings) • *Use a thermometer to gauge the temperature.* [T] • *I tried to gauge* (=guess) *the weight of the box.* [T] • *It's difficult to gauge* **how** *they'll react.* [+ *wh-* word] • *(fig.) A poll was conducted to gauge consumers' attitudes.* [T] • Ⓓ Ⓢ

gauge, *Am also* **gage** /geɪdʒ/ *n* [C] • A gauge is a device for measuring the amount or size of something: *a fuel gauge* • *a rain gauge* • A **tyre** gauge is used to measure the pressure of the air in a tyre. • *(specialized)* On a railway line, the gauge is the distance between the two RAILS: *a narrow-gauge railway* • *(specialized)* A gauge of metal or wire is its thickness. • *(fig.) The tests that the pupils take in January are considered to be a gauge* **of** (=a way of judging) *how well they will do in the proper exams.* • *(fig.) The fact that the play has transferred to New York is a gauge* **of** *its success* (=shows that it has been successful). • PIC› **Meters and gauges**

gaunt /£gɔːnt, $gɑːnt/ *adj* **-er, -est** very thin, esp. because of illness or hunger • *Hunger had made her face gaunt and grey.* • *(fig.) The house looked gaunt* (=bare and unattractive) *and unwelcoming.*

gaunt·ness /£ˈgɔːnt·nəs, $ˈgɑːnt-/ *n* [U]

gaunt·let /£ˈgɔːnt·lət, $ˈgɑːnt-/ *n* [C] a long thick GLOVE, worn for protection • *She put on a helmet and a leather jacket and gauntlets before getting on the motorbike.* • If you **throw down the gauntlet** you invite someone to fight or compete with you or show that you are wrong, and if someone **picks up the gauntlet** they agree to fight or compete with you or show that you are wrong: *I had to pick up the gauntlet he had thrown down and prove I could do the job as well as he could.*

gauze /£gɔːz, $gɑːz/ *n* [U] a very thin light cloth which is used for making clothing and for covering cuts in the skin • *a gauze skirt* • *a piece of sterile gauze ribbon* • Gauze is also a material formed by wires crossing over each other to produce a type of net: *Gauze is used in chemistry for supporting something above a flame while it is being heated.* • PIC› **Laboratory** Ⓙ

gauz·y /£ˈgɔː·zi, $ˈgɑː-/ *adj* **-ier, -iest** • *She was wearing a beautiful gauzy dress.*

gave /geɪv/ *past simple of* GIVE

gav·el /ˈgæv·əl/ *n* [C] a small hammer used by an official in charge of a meeting for hitting a wooden block or table in order to get people's attention • *The judge had to* **bang** *her gavel several times before people were quiet.*

ga·votte /£gəˈvɒt, $-ˈvɑːt/ *n* [C] (a piece of music for) a fast dance from France, popular in the past

Gawd /£gɔːd, $gɑːd/ *exclamation* used to avoid saying God • *"Gawd save us," she cried out.* • *Oh my Gawd! What have you done to the car?*

gawk /£gɔːk, $gɑːk/, *Br also* **gawp** *v* [I] *infml* to look at something or someone in a stupid way without thinking • *Don't stand there gawking* **(at** *her), give her a hand!* • *They stood gawping open-mouthed* **at** *me.*

gawk·y /£ˈgɔː·ki, $ˈgɑː-/ *adj* **-ier, -iest** *infml* tall and awkward • *Ten years ago he was a gawky teenager.*

gawp /£gɔːp, $gɑːp/ *v* [I] *Br for* GAWK

gay HOMOSEXUAL /geɪ/ *adj* [not gradable] *infml* homosexual • *gay rights* • *Mark knew he was gay by the time he was fourteen.* • Sometimes gay refers only to men: *the lesbian and gay community* • A gay **activist** is a person who uses public protests and other methods to try and improve the way homosexuals are treated by society: *Gay activists were demonstrating outside the cinema.* • **Gay liberation** is the idea that homosexuals should be treated equally in society: **The** *Gay Liberation* **movement** *of the late 1960s set out to challenge the stereotyped ideas that many people had about homosexuals.*

gay /geɪ/ *n* [C] *infml* • *Gays and lesbians held a huge rally to promote AIDS awareness.*

gay·ness /ˈgeɪ·nəs/ *n* [U] • *Fiona's parents took a long time to accept her gayness* (=her homosexuality).

gay HAPPY /geɪ/ *adj* **-er, -est** *dated* (of a person) happy, or (of a place) bright and attractive • *She had a gay, lively personality that attracted people to her.* • *At carnival time the streets were gay and full of people.* • See also GAIETY; GAILY.

gaze /geɪz/ *v* [I] to look (at something or someone) for a long time, esp. in surprise, admiration or because you are thinking about something else • *Annette gazed admiringly* **at** *Warren as he spoke.* • *Every day for a week Laura would sit gazing* **at** *the painting.* • *He spends hours gazing* **out of** *the window when he should be working.*

gaze /geɪz/ *n* [U] • *a steady gaze* • *I felt his malevolent gaze on the back of my neck all the way downstairs.*

ga·ze·bo /£gəˈziː·bəʊ, $-boʊ/ *n* [C] *pl* **gazebos** a small decorated building, usually in a garden, designed to give a good view of the surrounding countryside

ga·zelle /gəˈzel/ *n* [C] an animal like a small deer that lives in Africa or Asia, has large eyes and moves quickly and gracefully; a small ANTELOPE

ga·zette /gəˈzet/ *n* [C] a newspaper • Gazette is only used now in the titles of newspapers: *the Montreal Gazette* ○ *Who's going to be the new editor of the Evening Gazette?*

ga·zet·te·er /£,gæz·əˈtɪər, $-ˈtɪr/ *n* [C] a book or part of a book that contains a list of names of places, usually with some additional information, such as which country or region they are in • *the Cambridge Gazetteer of the United States and Canada*

gaz·pach·o /£gæsˈpætʃ·əʊ, $-pɑː·tʃoʊ/ *n* [U] a spicy soup made from raw vegetables and eaten cold

ga·zump *obj* /gəˈzʌmp/ *v* [T] *Br and Aus infml* (of the owner of a house) to refuse to sell your house to (someone you have agreed to sell it to) and sell it instead to someone who offers to pay more for it • *Sally's offer for the house has been accepted, but she's worried she might be gazumped.* • *There have been more reports of gazumping in parts of London where there is not enough property to meet demand from first-time buyers.*

ga·zun·der·ing /£gəˈzʌn·dər·ɪŋ, $-dɚ-/ *n* [U] *Br infml* the unfair activity of demanding a reduction in the price you have agreed to pay for a house just before you buy it • *The lack of activity in the property market, with few people buying houses, has resulted in gazundering and house prices creeping downwards.*

GB /,dʒiːˈbiː/ *n* [U not after *the*] *abbreviation for* Great Britain • LP› **Britain**

GBH /,dʒiː·biːˈeɪtʃ/ *n* [U] *abbreviation for* **grievous bodily harm**, see at GRIEVOUS

GCE /,dʒiː·siːˈiː/ *n* [C] *abbreviation for* General Certificate of Education (=an exam in Britain in various subjects usually taken at the age of 18, or, in the past, an exam at a lower standard usually taken at the age of 16)

GCSE /,dʒiː·siː·esˈiː/ *n* General Certificate of Secondary Education (=in Britain, a system of public examinations taken in various subjects at the age of about 16, or the qualifications obtained) • *I'm taking six subjects for GCSE.* [U] • *Many children leave school after GCSE.* [U] • *Owen is retaking two of his GCSEs.* [C] • *She's got nine GCSEs, all at grade A.* [C]

g'day /gəˈdeɪ/ *exclamation Aus infml* HELLO • LP› **Meeting someone**

GDP /,dʒiː·diːˈpiː/ *n* [U] *specialized abbreviation for* Gross Domestic Product (=the total value of goods and services produced by a country in a year) • *If the GDP continues to shrink the country will be in a recession.* • Compare GNP.

gear ENGINE PART /£gɪər, $gɪr/ *n* a device, often consisting of connecting sets of wheels with teeth around the edge, that controls how much power from an engine goes to the moving parts of a machine • *Does your car have four or five gears?* [C] • *I couldn't find reverse gear.* [U] • *The car should be* **in** *gear* (=with its gears in position, allowing the vehicle to move). [U] • *When you start a car you need to be* **in** *first/(Am also)* **low** *gear.* [U] • *(fig.) After a slow start, the leadership campaign has suddenly shifted into* **top** *gear.* [U] • To **change**/*(Am also)* **shift** gear is to change the position of the gears to make the car go faster or more slowly: *Remember to take your foot off the accelerator when you change gear.* [U] • In sport, if you **step/move up a gear**, you start to play better: *After a disappointing first half, United moved up a gear and took control of the game.* • *(Br and Aus)* A **gear lever/stick** (*Am* **stick shift** or **gearshift**) is a metal rod that you use to change gear in a car or other vehicle. • LP> **Driving** PIC> **Bicycles, Stick**

gear *(obj)* MAKE READY /£gɪəʳ, $gɪr/ *v* [always + adv/prep] to organize, make ready or prepare a person or place for a particular event or type of activity • *Most public places are simply not geared* **to** *the needs of people with disabilities.* [T usually passive] • *The workshops are geared* **toward/towards** *helping people to become more employable.* [T usually passive] • *(infml) Politicians are already gearing* **up** *for the election in two years' time.* [I] • *(infml) I'm gearing myself up* **to** *ask him to give me my money back.* [T + obj + *to* infinitive]

gear EQUIPMENT /£gɪəʳ, $gɪr/ *n* [U], *combining form* the equipment, clothes etc. that you use to do a particular activity • *fishing/camping/walking gear* • *When riding a bicycle you should wear the proper headgear* (=protection for your head). • *Police in* **riot** *gear* (=protective clothing) *arrived to control the protesters.* • *Graham was really keen when he joined the athletics club and he bought all the gear, but now he's lost interest and he's trying to sell everything.* • *(infml) She spends a lot on clothes and is always wearing the latest gear* (=clothes).

gear·box /£'gɪə·bɒks, $'gɪr·bɑːks/ *n* [C] *specialized* a metal box containing the GEARS in a vehicle

gear·shift /£'gɪə·ʃɪft, $'gɪr-/ *n* [C] *Am for* **gear lever**, see at GEAR ENGINE PART

geck·o /£'gek·əʊ, $-oʊ/ *n* [C] *pl* **geckos** or **geckoes** a small LIZARD, found esp. in the tropics, with wide feet that can stick to vertical surfaces such as walls

geddit? /'ged·ɪt/ *exclamation Br infml* used at the end of a statement to attract attention to an obvious joke that has been made with two meanings of a word • *The new series of plays on Channel Four is called 4-Play. Geddit?*

gee SURPRISE /dʒiː/ *exclamation esp. Am infml* an expression of surprise or enthusiasm • *"Gee, honey, is that all your own hair?"* • LP> **Phrases and customs**

gee MONEY /dʒiː/, **G** *n* [C] *pl* **gee** *Am infml for* GRAND MONEY (=$1000 or £1000)

gee up *(obj)*, **gee** *(obj)* **up** *v adv Br infml* to (encourage to) move or do things more quickly • *The new boss tried to gee people up a bit.* [M] • *You say "gee up!" to a horse to make it go faster.* [I]

gee–gee /'dʒiː·dʒiː/ *n* [C] *Br and Aus* (used by or to children) a horse

geek /giːk/ *n* [C] *infml* a person who tends to be disliked because of their stupid appearance or behaviour • *Her new boyfriend's a real geek. I can't understand what she sees in him.*

geese /giːs/ *pl of* GOOSE BIRD

gee–whiz /ˌdʒiː'wɪz/ *exclamation Am and Aus slightly dated* a childish expression of surprise • *The book takes a gee-whiz approach to science* (=It shows too much surprise and enthusiasm for everything).

geez·er /£'giː·zəʳ, $-zɚ/ *n* [C] *infml dated* a man, often an old man who behaves in an unusual way • *Carol and Paul used to live next door to a very peculiar geezer who refused to speak to anyone.*

Gei·ger count·er /£'gaɪ·gəʳ, $-gɚ/ *n* [C] an electronic device for measuring the level of RADIOACTIVITY

gei·sha (girl) /'geɪ·ʃə/ *n* [C] a Japanese woman trained in music and dancing whose job is entertaining men

gel /dʒel/ *n* [U] a thick oily substance, esp. used in some hair styles or in make-up

gel /dʒel/, **jell** *v* [I] **-ll-** • If an idea or thought gels, it starts to become more clear and fixed: *The race issue gelled in the 1960s.*

gel·a·tine, *Am usually and Aus also* **gel·a·tin** /'dʒel·ə·tiːn/ *n* [U] a clear substance, often sold in the form of a powder, made from boiling animal bones and used esp. to make JELLY • *He's a vegetarian and refuses to eat anything with gelatine in it.*

gel·a·tin·ous /£dʒə'læt·ɪ·nəs, $-læṭ-/ *adj* • Something that is gelatinous is thick and like JELLY: *The scrambled eggs were tasteless and gelatinous and made her feel sick.*

geld *obj* /geld/ *v* [T] to CASTRATE (=remove the sexual organs of) (a male animal such as a horse)

geld·ing /'gel·dɪŋ/ *n* [C] • A gelding is a male animal, esp. a horse, that has had its sexual organs removed.

ge·lig·nite /'dʒel·ɪg·naɪt/ *n* [U] a very powerful explosive substance, similar to DYNAMITE

gem /dʒem/, **gem·stone** /£'dʒemˌstəʊn, $-ˌstoʊn/ *n* [C] a jewel, esp. when cut into a particular regular shape • *She inherited £20 000 in gold and gems.* • If you say that someone or something is a gem, you mean that they are very good, pleasing or useful: *You've been an* **absolute** *gem – I couldn't have managed without your help.* ○ *And then he came out with a gem* (=clever remark) *about the absurdity of the situation.*

gem·fish /'dʒem·fɪʃ/ *n* [C/U] *Aus* a sea fish which is common in the sea near SE Australia, or its flesh, which has a delicate flavour, eaten as food

Gem·in·i /'dʒem·ɪ·naɪ/ *n* [not after *the*] the third sign of the ZODIAC, relating to the period 23 May to 21 June, represented by TWINS (=two people born together), or a person born during this period • *Sophie was born* **under** *Gemini* (=during this period). [U] • *Geminis are supposed to have split personalities.* [C]

gen /dʒen/ *n* [U] *Br dated infml* information about a particular subject • *So who's going to give me the gen* **on** *what's been happening while I've been away?*

gen up *obj* /dʒen/ *v adv* [I] **-nn-** *Br dated infml* to find out as much information as possible • *We must all make sure that we gen up before the meeting.* • *Derek genned up* **on** *the history of the country before he visited it.*

genned up *adj*

gen·der /£'dʒen·dəʳ, $-dɚ/ *n specialized or fml* the physical and/or social condition of being male or female, or *(specialized)* the grammatical divisions of MASCULINE, FEMININE and NEUTER into which nouns, adjectives, etc. are divided in some languages • *There are now various tests which can show the gender of a baby long before it is born.* [U] • *Discrimination on the basis of race, gender, age or disability is not allowed.* [U] • *She has never allowed her gender to restrict her in any way.* [U] • *I think both genders* (=sexes) *are equally capable of looking after children.* [C] • *In some societies, gender* **roles** *are very fixed.* • *(specialized) French has two genders.* [C] • *(slang)* A **gender-bender** is a person who wears the clothes and copies the behaviour of the opposite sex. • LP> **Sexist language**

gene /dʒiːn/ *n* [C] information in the form of a pattern of chemicals which is received by children from their parents and which controls one part of the development, behaviour, etc. of an animal or plant • *Scientists are trying to find the gene responsible for the disease.* • *You* **inherit** (= receive from a parent) *half your genes from your mother and half from your father.* • *The illness is believed to be caused by a* **defective** *gene.* • **Gene amplification** is a scientific method which uses a very small amount of GENETIC material to produce enough of it to study. • A **gene pool** is all the genes of a particular POPULATION: *He said that toxic chemicals are having a seriously harmful effect on the human gene pool.* • **Gene therapy** is the science of changing and curing particular genes that are causing a disease to be given from parents to their children.

gen·e·al·o·gy /ˌdʒiː·ni'æl·ə·dʒi/ *n* (the study of) the history of the past and present members of a family, or a drawing showing this with all past and present members joined together by lines • *I've been studying the genealogy* **of** *my family.* [U] • *My father has produced a genealogy* (= drawing showing the members) **of** *our family back to 1732.* [C]

gen·e·al·o·gi·cal /£ˌdʒiː·ni·ə'lɒdʒ·ɪ·kəl, $'lɑː·dʒɪ-/ *adj*

gen·e·al·o·gi·cal·ly /£ˌdʒiː·ni·ə'lɒdʒ·ɪ·kli, $'lɑː·dʒɪ-/ *adv*

gen·e·al·o·gist /ˌdʒiː·ni'æl·ə·dʒɪst/ *n* [C]

gen·e·ra /£'dʒen·ər·ə, $'-ɚ-/ *pl of* GENUS

gen·er·al COMMON /£'dʒen·ər·əl, $'-ɚ-/ *adj* involving or relating to most people, things or places, esp. when these are considered as a unit; not relating to exceptions and details • *The general feeling among people at the meeting was that a vote should be taken.* • *There is general concern about rising crime rates.* • *The general standard of living is very high in Denmark.* • *The general impression she gave* was one of efficient kindness. • It's a general-**purpose** cleaner which you can use anywhere in the house. • In their first year at the college, students take a general (= including a lot of subjects) course. • The book is written in an easy style, intended to interest the general reader (= one who is not a specialist). • I think you'll find that what I have to say is of general **interest** (= of interest to most people). • What he said was very general (= did not include any details). • The school aims to give the children a general (= not detailed) background in a wide variety of subjects. • If you're not quite sure of your facts, then only talk in general **terms** (= without giving any details). • (Br fml) Rain will become general (= common) in the south-east during the afternoon. • If general is used as part of the title of a job, it means that the person who has that job is in charge of the organization or company: the general manager • the General Secretary of the UN • **As a general rule** (= Usually), we don't allow children in the bar. • Do you think it's true that people **in general** (= most people) are against nuclear weapons? • **In general** (= In most cases), men are taller than women. • His book moved from **the general** (= things considered as a unit and without giving attention to details) to the particular. • (fml) The government will only say it is not in **the general interest** (= not good for the public) to reveal any more information. • A **general anaesthetic** is a drug which you are given in hospital to make you sleep during an operation and so not feel any pain. • The **General Assembly** is the main official body of the United Nations where members discuss subjects and which controls much of the work of the United Nations. • **General delivery** is *Am for* POSTE RESTANTE. • A **general election** is an election in which all the voters in a country elect the government: In Britain, a general election must be held at least every five years. • A **general hospital** is a large hospital which deals with all types of ill people. • **General knowledge** is the information that you have about many different subjects that you learn from school, television, reading, etc., rather than detailed information about a particular subject that you know because you have studied it. • (Br and Aus) **General practice** is the work of a GP (= doctor) who treats the ill people who live in a particular area. If the illness is serious, the doctor sends them to a hospital: She worked for several years as a hospital doctor and now she's **in general practice**. • The **general public** means ordinary people, esp. all the people who are not members of a particular organization or who do not have a particular type of knowledge: The shop's lack of fire exits exposed the general public to great potential danger. ○ This is a matter of great concern to the general public. ○ The general public must be able to have confidence in the police force. • A **general store** is a shop which sells a wide range of products, including food, esp. the only shop in a village. • The **general staff** is the group of army officers who work for and give advice to a **commanding officer**. • A **general strike** is a STRIKE in which most people in a country refuse to work, until they are given something that they are demanding, such as higher pay.

gen·er·al·ist /£'dʒen·ᵊr·ᵊl·ɪst, $'-ɚ-/ *adj, n* • Children of this age need specialist rather than generalist teachers. • The generalists and the specialists will always argue about which approach is best. [C]

gen·er·al·i·ty /£ˌdʒen·ə'ræl·ɪ·ti, $-ə·t̬i/ *n* • (slightly fml) A generality is a general statement without any details, and often also without much meaning: We need to get away from generalities and focus on the issues. [C] ○ His reply to the question was just a string of bland generalities. [C] • (slightly fml) What she said was of such generality (= the condition of lacking details) that it was virtually meaningless. [U] • (fml) For **the generality of** young people (= For most young people) university is not an option. [U]

gen·er·al·ly /£'dʒen·ᵊr·ᵊl·i, '-rᵊl·i, $'-ɚ-/ *adv* • The doctor said that my health is generally (= mostly) good, although I do have a few minor problems. • The proposal has received a generally favourable reaction. • The baby generally (= usually) wakes up three times during the night. • He said that more money should be given to the arts generally (= all parts of them). • Does this principle apply more generally (= in more situations) also? • Well, generally **speaking** (= in most situations), it's quicker on public transport. • It was generally believed (= Most people believed) at the time that both men were guilty. • I shall now go on to develop my previous point more generally (= to say more about what it includes).

gen·er·al·ize, *Br and Aus usually* **-ise** /£'dʒen·ᵊr·ə·laɪz, '-rᵊl·aɪz, $'-ɚ-/ *v* [I] • You can't generalize (= make a general statement based on limited facts) **about** a continent as varied as Europe. • It is too soon to generalize **from** these findings.

gen·er·al·ized, *Br and Aus usually* **-ised** /£'dʒen·ᵊr·ə·laɪzd, '-rᵊl·aɪzd, $'-ɚ-/ *adj* • Generalized means involving a lot of people, places or things: He said that there is generalized corruption in the government. ○ The recession is showing signs of becoming generalized over much of the south-east. ○ Isolated showers will give way to more generalized rain later in the day. ○ The school is moving towards a more generalized approach to its teaching.

gen·er·al·iz·a·tion, *Br and Aus usually* **-i·sa·tion** /£ˌdʒen·ᵊr·ᵊl·aɪ'zeɪ·ʃᵊn, ˌ-rᵊl-, $ˌ-ɚ-/ *n* • (esp. disapproving) The survey's conclusions are full of errors and **sweeping** generalizations (= statements extremely lacking in detail). [C] • The research has so far not produced enough evidence to allow for any generalization (= making general statements). [U]

gen·er·al RANK /£'dʒen·ᵊr·ᵊl, $'-ɚ-/ *n* [C] a high ranking officer, esp. in the army

gen·er·al·is·si·mo /£ˌdʒen·ᵊr·ə'lɪs·ɪ·məʊ, $-ɚ·ə'lɪs·ɪ·moʊ/ *n* [C] *pl* **generalissimos** a leader of the armed forces, esp. one who is also the ruler of the country

gen·er·ate *obj* /£'dʒen·ᵊr·eɪt, $'-ɚ-/ *v* [T] *fml or specialized* to cause to exist, or to produce • Her latest film has generated a lot of **interest/excitement**. • I'm afraid I can't generate much **enthusiasm** for the idea. • There has been a lot of **publicity/controversy** generated **by** this event. • The new development will generate 1500 new jobs. • These measures will increase the club's ability to generate **revenue/income**. • The wind farm may be able to generate enough **electricity/power** for 2000 homes. • The equipment generates a **signal**.

gen·er·a·tion /ˌdʒen·ə'reɪ·ʃᵊn/ *n* [U] • Electricity generation from wind and wave power should be encouraged, she said. • Government aid is needed to help boost income generation in the region. • See also GENERATION.

gen·er·a·tive /£'dʒen·ᵊr·ə·tɪv, $-ɚ·ə·t̬ɪv/ *adj fml or specialized* • the generative (= reproductive) organs of the body • the generative (= imaginative) power of the mind • generative (= productive) social forces

gen·er·a·tor /£'dʒen·ə·reɪ·təʳ, $-ɚ·eɪ·t̬ɚ/ *n* [C] • A generator is a machine which produces something, esp. electricity.

gen·er·a·tion /ˌdʒen·ə'reɪ·ʃᵊn/ *n* [C] all the people of about the same age within a society or within a particular family, or the period of time which it usually takes for a human baby to become an adult and have its own children • The generation who were teenagers thirty years ago are now senior business people and politicians. • The **younger** generation smoke/smokes less than their parents did. [+ sing/pl v] • There were at least three generations – grandparents, parents and children – at the wedding. • The disease is transmitted **down** the generations/**from one** generation **to the next**. • Environmental resources must be preserved for **future** generations. • A generation (= That period of time) ago, home computers were virtually unknown. • This painting has been in the family **for** generations (= several periods of time during which babies have become adults). • If someone is a **first/second/third/** etc. generation nationality, they are a member of the first/second/third/etc. group of people of the same age in the family to have been born in that country: She's a second generation American (= her parents were American, although their parents were not). • A particular generation of a product or a machine is a group of them which are all at the same stage in the product's or machine's development: This is one of the **new** generation of low-fat margarines. ○ Scientists are working on developing the **next** generation of supercomputers. ○ The company is launching the second-generation model of this car in March. • A **generation gap** is a lack of understanding between older and younger people that results from them having different opinions, behaviour and experiences of life: She's a young politician who manages to **bridge/cross** the generation gap. • See also **generation** at GENERATE. • LP **Periods of time**

ge·ner·ic /dʒə'ner·ɪk/ *adj fml* shared by, typical of or relating to a whole group of similar things, rather than to any particular thing • The new types of engine all had a generic problem with their fan blades. • It's not a picture of a specific sort of bird – it's intended to be generic. • The plays all fit within the generic definition of 'comedy'. • The band *then slipped into fairly generic* (= ordinary) *heavy rock.* • *(esp. Am and Aus)* Generic can also mean not having a trademark: *a generic drug* ○ *The store sells a wide range of generic products.*

ge·ne·ric /dʒəˈner·ɪk/ *n* [C] • Generics are low-cost medical drugs that do not have trademarks: *Brand-name prescription drugs can be copied as generics once their patents have expired.* • *(esp. Aus)* A generic is also an item sold under the name of a particular group of shops, rather than under a well-known product name, and which is therefore usually cheaper.

gen·er·ous /£ˈdʒen·ᵊr·əs, $ˈ-ɚ-/ *adj* (esp. of a person) willing to give money, help, kindness, etc., esp. more than is usual or expected, or (of an object) larger than usual or expected • **It** *was most generous* **of** *you* **to** *lend me the money.* [+ *to* infinitive] • *She's very generous* **with** *her time – always ready to help other people.* • *He has a very generous* (= kind) **nature**. • *There's a generous* (= kinder than deserved) *review of the book in today's newspaper.* • *He cut me a generous* (= large) *slice of chocolate cake.* • *No one is expecting a very generous* (= large) *pay increase this year.* • *You want the waistband on the trousers to be generous/a generous fit* (= not tight).

gen·er·os·i·ty /£ˌdʒen·əˈrɒs·ɪ·ti, $-ˈrɑː·sə·t̬i/ *n* [U] • *Her friends take advantage of her generosity, and stay in her house for months on end without paying her anything.*

gen·er·ous·ly /£ˈdʒen·ᵊr·ə·sli, $ˈ-ɚ-/ *adv* • *Please give generously to children in need.* • *The farmer generously allowed us to camp on his land.* • *The jacket is very generously cut* (= is made from a large amount of cloth).

gen·e·sis /ˈdʒen·ə·sɪs/ *n* [U] *fml* the time when something came into existence; the beginning or origin • *In her autobiography, she describes the song's genesis late one night in a Dublin bar.* • *Scientists are carrying out research into* **the** *genesis* **of** *cancer.* • In the Bible, Genesis is the first book of the Old Testament, describing how God made the world.

ge·net·ics /£dʒəˈnet·ɪks, $-ˈnet̬-/ *n* [U] the study of how, in all living things, the characteristics and qualities of parents are given to their children by their GENES

ge·net·ic /£dʒəˈnet·ɪk, $-ˈnet̬-/ *adj* • *a genetic defect/disease* • *Each individual has a completely unique set of genetic* **information**. • *Do you think it will ever be possible to alter human genetic* **material** *in order to produce the 'perfect' human being?* • A **genetic code** is the arrangement of GENES which controls the development of characteristics and qualities in a living thing. • **Genetic engineering** is (the science of) changing the structure of the GENES of a living thing in order to make it healthier or stronger or more useful to humans. • **Genetic fingerprinting** is the process of recording and/or examining the pattern of GENES that someone has, which is different from that of anyone else, often in order to prove that they did or did not commit a crime.

ge·net·i·cal·ly /£dʒəˈnet·ɪ·kli, $-ˈnet̬-/ *adv* • *a genetically engineered new type of wheat*

ge·ne·ti·cist /£dʒəˈnet·ɪ·sɪst, $-ˈnet̬-/ *n* [C] • A geneticist is a person whose job is studying GENETICS.

Ge·nev·a Con·ven·tion /dʒəˌniː·və/ *n* [U] **the Geneva Convention** an agreement accepted by most countries of the world which establishes standards for the reasonable treatment of soldiers, and other people involved, in periods of war

ge·ni·al /ˈdʒiː·ni·ᵊl/ *adj esp. literary* friendly and pleasant • *The headteacher is an easy-going genial man/has a genial manner.* • Ⓒⓢ Ⓓ Ⓓⓚ Ⓔ Ⓕ Ⓝ Ⓟⓛ Ⓡⓤⓢ Ⓢ

ge·ni·al·ly /ˈdʒiː·ni·ᵊl·i/ *adv*

ge·ni·al·i·ty /£ˌdʒiː·niˈæl·ɪ·ti, $-ə·t̬i/ *n* [U] • Ⓓ Ⓓⓚ Ⓔ Ⓝ Ⓢ

ge·nie /ˈdʒiː·ni/ *n* [C] *pl* **genies** or **genii** /ˈdʒiː·ni·aɪ/ a magical spirit, originally in Arab traditional stories, who will do or provide whatever the person who controls it asks it to do • *In some stories, genies are found inside a lamp or a bottle, from which they are released when someone rubs the lamp or bottle.* • *(fig.) The party leadership contest let the genie of change out of the bottle* (= caused change to happen). • Ⓓ Ⓕ Ⓢ

gen·i·tals /£ˈdʒen·ɪ·tᵊlz, $-t̬ᵊlz/, **gen·i·ta·li·a** /ˌdʒen·ɪˈteɪ·li·ə/ *pl n specialized* the sex organs, esp. the outer organs such as the penis and the VULVA

gen·i·tal /£ˈdʒen·ɪ·tᵊl, $-t̬ᵊl/ *adj* • *the genital area/organs* • *genital herpes* • See also CONGENITAL.

gen·i·tive /£ˈdʒen·ɪ·tɪv, $-t̬ɪv/ *n* [C] *specialized* the form of a noun, pronoun, etc. in the grammar of some languages, which shows that the noun, pronoun, etc. possesses something • *In English,* **the** *genitive* **of** *nouns is usually formed by adding 's.* • LP **Possessive form**

ge·ni·tive /£ˈdʒen·ɪ·tɪv, $-t̬ɪv/ *adj* [not gradable] • *the genitive form of a noun*

ge·ni·to·u·ri·na·ry /£ˌdʒen·ɪ·təʊˈjʊə·rɪn·ri, $-t̬oʊˈjʊr·ə·ner·i/ *adj* [not gradable] *specialized* to do with (esp. diseases of) the sexual organs and those parts of the body which excrete urine • *Research in the field of genito-urinary* **medicine** *has led to significant health advances in the last decade.*

ge·ni·us /ˈdʒiː·ni·əs/ *n pl* **geniuses** (a person with) very great and rare natural ability or skill, esp. in a particular area such as science or art • *(an) artistic/creative/musical genius* [C/U] • *Einstein was a (mathematical) genius.* [C] • *As a painter, Matisse was an* **absolute** *genius* **with** *colour.* [C] • *She thinks her son is a* **budding** *genius on the piano.* [C] • *From the age of three, she showed signs of genius.* [U] • *Your idea is a real* **stroke of** *genius!* [U] • *He has a* **spark of** *genius that distinguishes him from the other actors.* [U] • *Its simplicity is the genius* (= special quality or skill) **of** *the plan.* [U] • *She has* **a** *genius* (= special skill) **for** *raising money.* [U] • *(humorous) I paid the doctor $200 and all she could say was "Yes, you are a little deaf in your left ear." What a genius* (= The doctor only said what was already obvious)*!* [C] • A genius can also be a person who has an esp. bad influence over someone else: *The film was about an* **evil** *genius who wanted to control the world.* [C]

gen·o·cide /ˈdʒen·ə·saɪd/ *n* [U] the murder of a whole group of people, esp. a whole nation, race, religious group etc. • *The secret police have been accused of a campaign of genocide against the immigrant population.*

gen·o·ci·dal /ˈdʒen·ə·saɪ·dᵊl, ˌ--ˈ--/ *adj* • *This genocidal killing/warfare must be stopped.*

ge·nome /£ˈdʒiː·nəʊm, $-noʊm/ *n* [C] *specialized* the complete set of GENETIC material of a human, animal, plant or other living thing

ge·no·type /£ˈdʒen·əʊ·taɪp, $-oʊ-/ *n* [C] *specialized* the particular type and arrangement of GENES that each organism has • Compare PHENOTYPE.

gen·re /ˈʒɑ̃ː·rə, ˈʒɒn-/ *n* [C] *fml* a particular style, esp. of literature, art, music, etc., recognizable by its particular subject or form • *What genre does the book fall into – comedy or tragedy?* • *Mozart's opera 'The Marriage of Figaro' is a good example of the genre* **of** *comic opera.* • *Most of his movies are* **in** *the horror film genre.*

gen·re /ˈʒɑ̃ː·rə, ˈʒɒn-/ *adj* [not gradable] • Genre means produced according to a particular model: *a genre movie* ○ *This romance is her first attempt at writing genre fiction.*

gent /dʒent/ *n* [C] *infml or humorous for* a GENTLEMAN • *He always behaves like a* **true** *gent.* • *With his striped suit and his briefcase, he looks like a real* **city** *gent* (= a man who works in business, esp. in a high position). • *(Br and Aus)* **The gents** is a public men's toilet: *Pardon me, where's the gents?* Compare **the ladies** at LADY WOMAN. • Ⓔ Ⓘ

gen·teel /£dʒenˈtɪəl, $-ˈtiːl/ *adj* having a high social class, being very polite, etc., or trying too hard to seem of a higher social class than you really are • *a genteel old lady* • *genteel table manners* • *The mansion had an atmosphere of genteel elegance and decay.* • *He took elocution lessons to try to make his accent sound more genteel.* • *After the war they lived* **in** *genteel* **poverty** (= without much money, but still trying to appear of a higher social class). • *(fig.) The game seemed to be a more genteel* (= calmer, less violent) *version of American football.* • Ⓔ Ⓕ Ⓢ

gen·teel·ly /£dʒenˈtɪə·li, $-ˈtiː-/ *adv* • *Genteelly* (= In a polite and graceful way)*, she picked up her cup to take a sip of tea.*

gen·til·i·ty /£dʒenˈtɪl·ɪ·ti, $-ə·t̬i/ *n* [U] • *The family had invented several highly respectable ancestors in order to try and acquire a degree of gentility* (= in order to seem of a higher social class). • *(fml) The gentility* (= politeness) *of her manners is remarkable, even a little suffocating sometimes.*

gen·tile /ˈdʒen·taɪl/ *n, adj* [not gradable] (relating to) a person who is not Jewish • *The war memorial was dedicated to both* **Jews and** *Gentiles.* [C] • *The circumcision performed by a gentile doctor was pronounced unclean.*

gen·tle /£ˈdʒen·tl̩, $-t̬l̩/ *adj* **-r, -st** calm, kind or soft; not violent or severe • *He has a gentle smile and a soft voice.* • *Be gentle with her and try not to frighten her, please.* • *Regular walking is a wonderful form of gentle* **exercise**. • *(literary or humorous) That, gentle* **reader**, *is the subject of our story.* • *It is not by force that she accomplishes things, but by gentle* persuasion. • *The path has a gentle* (= not steep or sudden) **slope/gradient**. • *The gentle* (= not strong) **breeze** *filled the sails.* • *"Do not go gentle into that good night, ...Rage, rage against the dying of the light"* (Dylan Thomas in the poem *Do not go gentle* addressed to his dying father, 1952) • Ⓔ Ⓕ Ⓟ Ⓢ

gen·tly /ˈdʒent·li/ *adv* [not gradable] • *Gently* (= Slowly and carefully), *he lifted the baby out of its cot.* • *She smiled gently* (= kindly) *at me.* • *It's a gently* **rolling** *landscape, without any high hills.* • *(Br)* **Take it gently** *(Am and Aus usually* **Take it easy***)* (= Go slowly and carefully), *because the road may be icy.* • *(Br)* If someone says **gently does it** (*Am* **easy does it**), they are telling you to be slow and careful.

gen·tle·ness /£ˈdʒen·tl̩·nəs, $-t̬l̩-/ *n* [U] • *His gentleness, patience and love were an example to us all.* • *The gentleness of the slope is perfect for those new to skiing.*

gen·tle·man /£ˈdʒen·tl̩·mən, $-t̬l̩-/ *n* [C] *pl* **-men** a man who is polite and behaves well towards other people, or a man of a high social class • *(approving) Gerald is such a* **(perfect)** *gentleman/is a* **real** *gentleman.* • *(approving) He's too much of a gentleman to get involved in a quarrel like this.* • *Just because I didn't hold the door open for her, she told me I was* **no** *gentleman.* • *He belongs to a gentlemen's club in London.* • Gentleman is also used as a polite way of addressing or referring to a man: **Ladies and** *gentlemen, the show is about to begin.* ○ *Excuse me, but this gentleman has a question for you.* • *An elderly gentleman sat reading a newspaper in the corner of the waiting room.* • A **gentleman's agreement** is an agreement which is based on trust and is not written down. • *"Gentlemen Prefer Blondes"* (title of a book by Anita Loos, 1925) • LP〉 **Titles and forms of address**

gen·tle·man·ly /£ˈdʒen·tl̩·mən·li, $-t̬l̩-/ *adj* • *He treated her with an old-fashioned gentlemanly courtesy.*

gen·tle·wo·man /£ˈdʒen·tl̩ˌwʊm·ən, $-t̬l̩-/ *n* [C] **-women** *fml dated* a woman who is kind, polite and honest, or a woman of a high social class

gen·try /ˈdʒen·tri/ *n* [C + sing/pl v] **the gentry** people of high social class, esp. in the past • *The village used to hold an annual cricket match between the gentry and the manual labourers.* • *At the time, the local gentry was/were resisting the changes.* • *The* **rural** *gentry are strong fighters who will resist change.* • *The French Riviera was made into a popular holiday resort by the British* **landed** *gentry* (= those who own a lot of land).

gen·tri·fy *obj* /ˈdʒen·trɪ·faɪ/ *v* [T] • When a part of a town is gentrified, it is changed from being a poor area to a richer one, by people of a higher social class moving to live there: *He told me quite sadly that most of the area in which he had grown up had now been modernized and gentrified, and had lost all its old character.*

gen·tri·fi·ca·tion /ˌdʒen·trɪ·fɪˈkeɪ·ʃᵊn/ *n* [U] • *The increasing gentrification of the neighbourhood has resulted in property values and rents rising and the poorer residents and local stores being driven out.*

gen·u·flect /ˈdʒen·jʊ·flekt/ *v* [I] to bend one or both knees as a sign of respect to God, esp. when entering or leaving a Catholic church • *People were genuflecting* **before/in front of** *the altar.*

gen·u·flec·tion /ˌdʒen·jʊˈflek·ʃᵊn/ *n* • *She bent her knees in genuflection as she entered the cathedral.* [U] • *(fig.) Contemporary Hollywood movies often make subtle genuflections* (= respectful signs or remarks) **to** *the great film-makers of the past.* [C]

gen·u·ine /ˈdʒen·ju·ɪn/ *adj* being what it appears to be; real; not false • *If it is a genuine Michelangelo drawing, it will sell for millions.* • *His suitcase was made of genuine leather.* • *How can these be genuine peace talks if the fighting is still continuing?* • *(infml) Those cowboy boots sure look like* **the** *genuine* **article**. • When used of people or their emotions, genuine also means honest and sincere: *Is she genuine – does she really work for the CIA?* ○ *Do you think you can ever trust a salesperson to be genuine?* ○ *He's a very genuine person.* ○ *Machiko looked at me in genuine surprise – "Are you really going?" she said.*

gen·u·ine·ly /ˈdʒen·ju·ɪn·li/ *adv* • *These will be the first genuinely free elections in the country.* • *I'm genuinely sorry for what I said, I really am.*

gen·u·ine·ness /ˈdʒen·ju·ɪn·nəs/ *n* [U]

ge·nus /ˈdʒiː·nəs, ˈdʒen·əs/ *n* [C] *pl* **genera** /£ˈdʒen·ᵊr·ə, $ˈ-ɚ-/ *specialized* a group of animals or plants, below a FAMILY and above a SPECIES • *Oranges and lemons belong to the same genus.*

ge·o– /£ˈdʒiː·əʊ, $-oʊ-/ *combining form* of or relating to the Earth • *geophysics* • *geology*

ge·o·cen·tric /£ˌdʒiː·əʊˈsen·trɪk, $-oʊ-/ *adj specialized* having the Earth as its centre • *In 1543 Copernicus suggested instead of a geocentric model of the solar system, one in which the sun was central.*

ge·og·raph·y /£dʒiˈɒg·rə·fi, £ˈdʒɒg-, $dʒiˈɑː·grə-/ *n* [U] the study of the systems and processes involved in the world's weather, mountains, seas, lakes, etc. and of the ways in which countries and people organize life within an area • *a degree in geography* • *a geography teacher/lesson* • The geography **of** a place is the way all its parts are arranged within it: *The children were learning about the geography of Australia.* ○ *The region continues to be a prisoner of its own geography, because the mountains prohibit all further expansion.* ○ *The geography of the hospital was impossible to understand without a map.* • **Physical** geography is the study of the earth's features. • **Human** geography is the study of the cultural features of a place. • LP〉 **Nations and nationalities, World regions**

ge·og·raph·er /£dʒiˈɒg·rə·fəʳ, £ˈdʒɒg-, $dʒiˈɑː·grə·fɚ/ *n* [C] • A geographer is a person who studies geography.

ge·o·graph·i·cal /ˌdʒi·əˈgræf·ɪ·kᵊl/, **ge·o·graph·ic** /ˌdʒi·əˈgræf·ɪk/ *adj* • *a geographical region* • *The city's success owes much to its geographical position.*

ge·o·graph·i·cal·ly /ˌdʒi·əˈgræf·ɪ·kli/ *adv*

ge·ol·o·gy /£dʒiˈɒl·ə·dʒi, $-ˈɑː·lə-/ *n* [U] the study of the rocks and similar substances that make up the Earth's surface, esp. in order to understand its structure, origin, etc. • *a geology course/teacher* • The geology **of** an area is the particular rocks and similar substances that form it and their arrangement.

ge·o·log·i·cal /£ˌdʒi·əˈlɒdʒ·ɪ·kᵊl, $-ˈlɑː·dʒɪ-/ *adj* • *a geological survey* • *a geological map*

ge·o·log·i·cal·ly /£ˌdʒi·əˈlɒdʒ·ɪ·kli, $-ˈlɑː·dʒɪ-/ *adv*

ge·ol·o·gist /£dʒiˈɒl·ə·dʒɪst, $-ˈɑː·lə-/ *n* [C] • A geologist is a person who studies geology.

ge·om·e·try /£dʒiˈɒm·ə·tri, £ˈdʒɒm-, $dʒiˈɑː·mə-/ *n* [U] the area of mathematics relating to the study of space and the relationships between points, lines, curves and surfaces • *the laws of geometry* • *Euclidean geometry* • *a geometry lesson* • The geometry **of** an object is the way its parts fit together: *the geometry of a DNA molecule* ○ *the geometry of the spine*

ge·o·met·ric /ˌdʒiː·əˈmet·rɪk/, **ge·o·met·ri·cal** /ˌdʒiː·əˈmet·rɪ·kᵊl/ *adj* • A geometric pattern or arrangement is one which is made up of shapes such as squares, triangles or rectangles: *The wallpaper has a geometric design of overlapping circles.* • A **geometric(al) progression** is an ordered set of numbers, where each is in turn multiplied by a fixed amount to produce the next: *"What is the next number in the geometric progression 1, 3, 9, 27, 81?" "243."*

ge·om·e·tri·cal·ly /ˌdʒiː·əˈmet·rɪ·kli/ *adv* • *The lamps were arranged geometrically to produce a circle of light.*

ge·o·phy·sics /ˌdʒiː·əˈfɪz·ɪks/ *n* [U] *specialized* the study of the rocks and other substances that make up the Earth and the physical processes happening on, in and above the Earth

ge·o·phy·si·cal /ˌdʒiː·əˈfɪz·ɪ·kᵊl/ *adj* [not gradable] *specialized* • *geophysical research* • *This area provides us with a wide range of observable geophysical and geological phenomena.*

ge·o·phy·si·cist /ˌdʒi·əˈfɪz·ɪ·sɪst/ *n* [C] *specialized* • *Their research was presented to a gathering of geophysicists, who were very impressed with the findings.*

ge·o·po·li·tics /£ˌdʒiː·əʊˈpɒl·ə·tɪks, $-oʊˈpɑː·lə·t̬ɪks/ *n* [U] the study of the way a country's size, position, etc. influence its power and its relations with other countries, or political activity as influenced by the physical features of a country or area of the world • *These developments are having a major impact on the geopolitics* **of** (= political activity in) *the region.*

ge·o·po·li·ti·cal /£ˌdʒiː·əʊ·pəˈlɪt·ɪ·kᵊl, $-oʊ·pəˈlɪt̬-/ *adj*

Geor·die /£ˈdʒɔː·di, $ˈdʒɔːr-/ *n Br* (the variety of English spoken by) someone who comes from Tyneside in NE England • *Geordie can be difficult to understand if you're not familiar with it.* [U] • *Jimmy is a real Geordie.* [C]

Geor·die /£ˈdʒɔː·di, $ˈdʒɔːr-/ *adj* • *His accent is pure Geordie.*

Geor·gian /£ˈdʒɔː·dʒən, $ˈdʒɔːr-/ *adj* [not gradable] (esp. of the style of buildings and furniture) of the period when Kings George I, II and III ruled Britain, esp. from 1714 to 1811 • *a Georgian house*

ge·o·ther·mal /£ˌdʒiː·əʊ'θɜː·məl, $-oʊ'θɜːr-/ *adj specialized* of or connected with the heat inside the Earth • *a geothermal power station*

ge·ran·i·um /dʒə'reɪ·ni·əm/ *n* [C] a plant with usually bright red flowers, which is grown in containers and gardens • PIC› **Flowers and plants**

ger·bil /£'dʒɜː·bəl, $'dʒɜːr-/ *n* [C] a small animal with long back legs and a thin tail that is often kept as a pet

ger·i·at·ric /ˌdʒer·i'æt·rɪk/ *adj specialized* of or for old people, esp. those who are ill • *a geriatric hospital/ward/nurse* • *(disapproving) No one would want to elect a geriatric* (= too old and weak) *President.*

ger·i·at·ric /ˌdʒer·i'æt·rɪk/ *n* [C] • *A new clinic for the care of geriatrics is being proposed.*

ger·i·at·ri·cian /ˌdʒer·i·ə'trɪʃ·ən/ *n* [C] • A geriatrician is a doctor who specializes in the care and treatment of old people who are ill.

ger·i·at·rics /ˌdʒer·i'æt·rɪks/ *n* [U] • Geriatrics is the medical care and treatment of old people who are ill.

germ /£dʒɜːm, $dʒɜːrm/ *n* [C usually pl] a very small organism that causes disease • *Wash your hands so you don't get germs on the food.* • *Germs can be* **spread** *by rats.* • *Places where medical operations are carried out should be kept as germ-***free** *as possible.* • *(specialized)* A **germ cell** is either a small part of an organism that can grow into a plant, animal, etc., or a GAMETE. • *(fig.) Although there's a germ* (= small amount) **of** *truth in the story, it's mostly very exaggerated.* • *(fig.) Looking for a way to make money, he found the germ* **of an idea** (= an idea that might later develop into something large and important) *in an old newspaper.* • **Germ warfare** (also **biological warfare**) is the use of germs during periods of war to cause disease among enemy soldiers or among crops in enemy countries. • See also **wheat germ** at WHEAT.

ger·mane /£dʒɜː'meɪn, $dʒɜːr-/ *adj fml* (of ideas, information, etc.) connected with and important to a particular subject or situation; RELEVANT • *I don't think that question is really germane.* • *Her remarks could not have been more germane* **to** *the discussion.*

Ger·man·ic /£dʒə'mæn·ɪk, $dʒɚ-/ *adj* typical of German people or things • *He's very Germanic in his efficiency.* • *(specialized)* Germanic is also used to describe the group of languages that includes German, English and Dutch.

ger·man·i·um /£dʒə'meɪ·ni·əm, $dʒɚ-/ *n* [U] *specialized* an element which has unusual electrical characteristics that allow it to be used in SEMICONDUCTORS

Ger·man meas·les /£'dʒɜː·mən, $'dʒɜːr-/, *specialized* **ru·bel·la** *n* [U] an infectious disease which causes red spots on your skin, a cough and a sore throat • *If a pregnant woman catches German measles, it may damage her unborn child.*

Ger·man shep·herd /£'dʒɜː·mən, $'dʒɜːr-/ *n* [C] *esp. Am for* ALSATIAN • PIC› **Dogs**

ger·mi·cide /£'dʒɜː·mɪ·saɪd, $'dʒɜːr-/ *n* [C/U] (a) substance that kills GERMS

ger·mi·cid·al /£dʒɜː·mɪ'saɪ·dəl, $dʒɜːr-/ *adj*

ger·mi·nate *(obj)* /£'dʒɜː·mɪ·neɪt, $'dʒɜːr-/ *v specialized* to (cause (a seed) to) start growing • *The beans will only germinate if the temperature is warm enough.* [I] • *The seeds were germinated in a greenhouse, then planted outside.* [T] • *(fig.) What he said caused an idea to germinate* (= start developing) *in my head.* [I]

ger·mi·na·tion /£ˌdʒɜː·mɪ'neɪ·ʃən, $ˌdʒɜːr-/ *n* [U]

ger·on·tol·o·gy /£ˌdʒer·ən'tɒl·ə·dʒi, $-'tɑː·lə-/ *n* [U] *specialized* the study of old age and of the problems and illnesses that old people have

ger·on·to·log·i·cal /£ˌdʒer·ən·tə'lɒdʒ·ɪ·kəl, $-lɑː·dʒɪ-/ *adj* [not gradable] *specialized* • *He works at a centre for gerontological* **research**, *where he is studying the experiences of old people in institutions.*

ger·on·tol·o·gist /£ˌdʒer·ən'tɒl·ə·dʒɪst, $-tɑː·lə-/ *n* [C] *specialized* • A gerontologist is a person who studies old age.

ger·ry·man·der·ing /£'dʒer·iˌmæn·dər·ɪŋ, $-dɚ-/ *n* [U] the giving of an unfair electoral advantage to one political party by measures which increase the number of people living in a particular area who will vote for that party • *The boundary changes have been denounced as* **political** *gerrymandering.*

ger·ry·man·der *(obj)* /£'dʒer·iˌmæn·dər, ˌ--'--, $-dɚ/ *v* [I/T]

ger·und /'dʒer·ənd/ *n* [C] *specialized* a word that ends in '-ing' which is made from a verb, and which is used like a noun • *In the sentence 'Everyone enjoyed Tyler's singing', the word 'singing' is a gerund.* • LP› **-ing form of verbs**

ges·talt /gə'ʃtælt, $-'ʃtɑːlt/ *n* [C usually sing] *specialized* something such as a structure or experience which, when considered as a whole, has qualities that are more than the total of all its parts • *This new biography is the first to consider fully the writer's gestalt.* • *In* **gestalt psychology** *and* **gestalt psychotherapy**, *people's thoughts and emotions are seen as complex wholes.*

Ge·sta·po /£ge'stɑː·pəʊ, $-poʊ/ *n* [C + sing/pl v] the secret police of the Nazi period in Germany 1933-45, who used cruel and evil methods and were involved in the killing of a very large number of people

ges·ta·tion /dʒes'teɪ·ʃən/ *n* [U] *specialized* (the period of) the development of a child or young animal while it is still inside its mother's body • *The baby was born prematurely at 28 weeks gestation/at a gestation* **of** *28 weeks.* • *The* **period of** *gestation* **of** *rats is 21 days.* • *(fig.) These ideas have not come from nowhere – there has been a* **long** *gestation* **period**.

ges·tate /dʒes'teɪt/ *v* [I]

ges·ti·cu·late /dʒes'tɪk·jʊ·leɪt/ *v* [I] *fml* to make movements with your hands or arms, esp. to help express something you are trying to communicate • *As he became more excited, he gesticulated more and more* **wildly**.

ges·ti·cu·la·tion /dʒesˌtɪk·jʊ'leɪ·ʃən/ *n* [C/U] *fml*

ges·ture MOVEMENT /£'dʒes·tʃər, $-tʃɚ/ *n* [C] a movement of the hands, arms, head, etc. to express an idea or feeling • *Covering her face in a gesture* **of** *despair, she burst out crying.* • *The prisoner held up his fist in a* **defiant** *gesture/gesture* **of defiance** *as he was led out of the courtroom.* • *She* **made** *a very rude gesture at the other driver.*

ges·ture *(obj)* /£'dʒes·tʃər, $-tʃɚ/ *v* • *When he asked where the children were, she gestured* (= moved part of her body) *vaguely in the direction of the beach.* [I] • *The head of our department gestured* (= directed with part of her body) *me over to the seat next to her.* [T] • *She gestured* (= directed with part of her body) *her son* **to** *be quiet.* [T + obj + *to* infinitive] • *He was gesturing* (= expressing with part of his body) **that** *he needed help.* [+ *that* clause]

ges·ture SYMBOLIC ACT /£'dʒes·tʃər, $-tʃɚ/ *n* [C] an action that you take which expresses your feelings or intentions, although it might have little practical effect • *The Government has donated £500 000 as a goodwill gesture/gesture* **of** *goodwill.* • *The release of the prisoners is being seen as a* **grand** *gesture by the governor of the state.* • *Not having butter on his potatoes was his gesture* **towards** *a healthy diet.*

ges·und·heit /gə'zʊnt·haɪt/ *exclamation esp. Am infml* spoken to someone after they have sneezed • *People often say 'Bless you!' rather than 'gesundheit'.*

get *obj* OBTAIN /get/ *v* [T] **getting**, *past simple* **got** /£gɒt, $gɑːt/, *past part* **got** or *Am, Aus infml* **gotten** /£'gɒt·ən, $'gɑː·t̬ən/ to take (something) into your possession; to obtain • *He's gone down to the corner shop to get some milk.* • *I got quite a surprise when I saw her with short hair.* • *You're getting some very admiring looks in those shorts!* • *I think she gets* (= earns) *about forty thousand pounds a year.* • *When did you get the news about Sam?* • *Which radio stations can you get in your car?* • *We stopped off on the motorway to get some breakfast.* • *What mark did he get in his exam?* • *We don't get much snow* (= It does not often snow) *in this country.* • *I just managed to get a glimpse of him* (= see him for a moment) *through the crowds.* • *I got the impression that they'd rather be alone.* • *If you've already had measles, you can't get it again.* • *If you get a moment* (= have time available), *could you help me fill in that form?* • To get something or someone is also to take them into your possession by force: *That man who shot someone in the bank – have the police got him yet?* ○ *Your cat got a bird this morning!* • *I managed to get all three suitcases* **for** *under $200.* • *What did you get* (= What were you given) **for** *your birthday?* • *If you're going to the shops, could you get me a newspaper/get a newspaper* **for** *me, please?* [+ two objects] • *Can I get you a drink?* [+ two objects] • *How much did he get* **for** *his car* (= How much money did he sell it for)? • *Where did you get your radio* **from**? • *I got a (telephone) call* **from** *an old boyfriend last night.* • *We're getting a load of hassle* **from** *the neighbours for making too much noise.* • *She gets such pleasure* **from/out of** *her garden.* • *He climbed over the wall to get his ball* **back**. • *Could you get the washing* **in** (= bring it from outside)? [M] • *We'll have to get some food* **in** (= provide ourselves with food) *for the weekend if we're* *having visitors.* [M] • If you get an electrician or other trained person **in**, you ask them to visit a place such as your home in order to do some work such as repairing: *We'll have to get a plumber in to look at that water tank.* [M] • *(Br infml) Whose turn is it to* **get in** *the drinks/***get** *the drinks* **in** (= buy the drinks)*?* • *If you can get some time* **off** *from work we could take a much longer holiday.* • *I can never get her* **to myself** (= be alone with her) *because she's always surrounded by people.*

get *obj* DEAL WITH /get/ *v* [T] **getting**, *past simple* **got** /£gɒt, $gɑːt/, *past part* **got** or *Am also* **gotten** /£ˈgɒt·ən, $ˈgɑː·t̬ən/ *Am infml* to deal with or answer (a ringing telephone, knock on the door, etc.) or to pay for (an expense) • *Hey, Ty, someone's at the door – would you get it, please?* • *You bought lunch last time, so I've got it this time.*

get *obj* BECOME ILL WITH /get/ *v* [T] **getting**, *past simple* **got** /£gɒt, $gɑːt/, *past part* **got** or *Am also* **gotten** /£ˈgɒt·ən, $ˈgɑː·t̬ən/ *infml* to become ill with (a disease, virus, etc.) • *I got food poisoning at that cheap little seafood restaurant.* • *Kids get all kinds of bugs at school.*

get BECOME /get/ *v* **getting**, *past simple* **got** /£gɒt, $gɑːt/, *past part* **got** or *Am, Aus infml* **gotten** /£ˈgɒt·ən, $ˈgɑː·t̬ən/ to become or start (to be) • *He gets really upset if you mention his baldness.* [L] • *I think he's getting a bit suspicious.* [L] • *I'm glad to hear you are/your cold is getting better.* [L] • *I'm getting tired now – shall we go?* [L] • *I must be getting fat – these trousers are really tight.* [L] • *Your coffee is getting cold.* [L] • *You work long hours, but after a while you just get used to it.* [L] • *(slang) "I'm going to apply for that job." "Get* **real** (= Be reasonable)*! They'd never appoint you."* [L] • *You're getting quite a big boy now, aren't you!* [L] • *How did you get* **to** *be* (= How did you become) *a belly dancer?* [+ *to* infinitive] • *You're getting* **to** *be just like your mother.* [+ *to* infinitive] • *I used to hate jogging but I'm actually getting* **to** *like it.* [+ *to* infinitive] • If a political party gets **in** it comes to a position of power: *The Republicans are bound to get in at the next elections.* [I always + adv/prep] • To get **in on** an activity that is already taking place is to take part in it because it will be useful or profitable for you: *She was trying to get in on some sort of business deal involving property.* [I always + adv/prep] • If you get **into** a particular activity you start to like and become interested in it: *She's been getting into yoga recently – she does three classes a week.* [I always + adv/prep] • If a group of people or two people get **together** they meet each other having arranged it before: *Shall we get together on Friday and go for a drink or something?* [I always + adv/prep] • To get **up to** something is to do esp. something surprising or disapproved of by others: *She's been getting up to all sorts of* **mischief** *lately.* ○ *What do you think those kids we saw were getting up to?* [I always + adv/prep] • *(infml) We'd better* **get going/moving** (= go now) *or we'll be late.* [+ v-*ing*]

get *obj* CAUSE /get/ *v* [T] **getting**, *past simple* **got** /£gɒt, $gɑːt/, *past part* **got** or *Am, Aus infml* **gotten** /£ˈgɒt·ən, $ˈgɑː·t̬ən/ to cause (something) to be done or persuade (someone) to do something • *The bed is too wide – we'll never get it through the door.* • *Are you trying to get me into trouble?* • *She had to get the kids ready for school.* [+ obj + adj] • *I'm trying to get this article finished for Thursday.* [obj + v-*ed*] • *Haven't you got the photocopier working yet?* [+ obj + v-*ing*] • You might say that you get something stolen or caught somewhere, or that you get two people's names confused when you mean that you do it unintentionally or accidentally: *He got his bag caught in the train doors as they were closing.* [+ obj + v-*ed*] ○ *I always get the two youngest sisters' names confused.* [+ obj + v-*ed*] • *We get our milk delivered.* [+ obj + v-*ed*] • *I can't get my computer* **to** *work!* [+ obj + *to* infinitive] • *Why don't you get Nicole* **to** *come to the party?* [obj + *to* infinitive] • To get **across** an idea or a meaning is to make it understood or believed: *Did you manage to get the message across/get across the message?* [M] • If something gets you **down**, it makes you feel unhappy and dissatisfied: *The chaos in his house was starting to get him down.* ○ *Don't let it get you down.* • *I didn't manage to get* **down** (= write) *every word that she said.* [M] • To **get** something **down** is to succeed in swallowing it although it is difficult: *Her throat was so swollen that she couldn't get the tablets down.* ○ *(infml humorous) Your dinner is on the table and you've got ten minutes to get it down (you).* • To get something **in** by a particular time is to send it so that it arrives by that time: *When do you have to get your application in by?* [M] • To get a letter or parcel **off** is to send it to someone: *I got that letter off this morning.* [M] • If you get an unpleasant but necessary piece of work or duty **over (with)** you do it or finish doing it so that you do not have to deal with it in the future: *I'll be glad to get these exams over (with).* • To get someone **through** something is to make it possible for them to deal successfully with a difficult or painful experience: *It was my friendship with Helen that got me through the bad months.* • *(slang)* If you **get it on** you (start to) have sex: *She hardly thinks about anything but getting it on* **with** *him.* • To **get it together** is to make a decision or take positive action in your life: *Tom has really got it together since I last saw him – he has started a teaching course and lost a lot of weight.* • LP **Get: verbs meaning 'cause'**

get BE /get/ *v* [L + v-*ed*] **getting**, *past simple* **got** /£gɒt, $gɑːt/, *past part* **got** or *Am, Aus infml* **gotten** /£ˈgɒt·ən, $ˈgɑː·t̬ən/ sometimes used instead of 'be' to form the passive • *I got shouted at by some idiot for walking past his house.* • *I got rained on as I was coming to work.* • *They're getting married later this year.* • *This window seems to have got broken.*

get *(obj)* MOVE /get/ *v* [always + adv/prep] **getting**, *past simple* **got** /£gɒt, $gɑːt/, *past part* **got** or *Am, Aus infml* **gotten** /£ˈgɒt·ən, $ˈgɑː·t̬ən/ to move in a particular direction • *(dated) Get* **along** (= Hurry up and go)*, children – we don't want to be late!* [I] • *I just need to get* **away** (= leave the place where I live) *for a few days.* [I] • *I'll get* **away** *from* (= leave) *work as soon as I can.* [I] • *(infml dated)* If you say **get away (with you)!** you mean that you don't believe or agree with what someone is saying: *"They say you're a very aggressive player." "Get away with you!" he laughed.* • *Then he got* **down** *on his knees to ask me to marry him!* [I] • *Once you're in the sea it's fine, but it's the getting* **in** *that is the problem.* [I] • *I hit my head as I was getting* **into** *the car.* [I] • To get **off** a train, bus or aircraft is to leave it: *Get off (the train) at Camden Town.* [I] • *(infml)* To get a part of your body **off** a particular place is to remove it from that place: *Get your feet off the settee – they're dirty!* [T] ○ *(fig.) Get your hands off that wine* (= do not drink it) *– it's for later!* [T] • To get **off** is to leave a place in order to start a journey: *If we can get off by seven o clock the roads will be clearer.* [I] • To get **off** is also to leave work with permission: *How early can you get off this afternoon?* [I] • *The dog managed to get* **out** *of* (= escape from) *the garden by making a hole in the fence.* [I] • *She went for a walk just to get* **out (of)** *the house.* [I] • *If you don't get* **out of** *here now I'm going to call the police.* [I] • If secret information or news gets **out** it becomes known by the public. [I] • *News of someone's pregnancy soon gets* **around/round** (= spreads) *in a small neighbourhood.* [I] • *I got* **up** (= left my bed) *at five o'clock this morning!* [I] • *The whole audience got* **up** (= stood up) *and started clapping.* [I] • *(Br infml) What time do you want getting* **up** (= do you want me to wake you) *tomorrow?* [T] • *Getting* **up** *the ladder was easy enough – it was coming down that was the problem.* [I]

get *obj* TRAVEL /get/ *v* [T] **getting**, *past simple* **got** /£gɒt, $gɑːt/, *past part* **got** or *Am also* **gotten** /£ˈgɒt·ən, $ˈgɑː·t̬ən/ to go into (and travel in) (a train, bus or other vehicle) • *If you want to be sure of getting your plane, you'd better leave now.* • *Shall we get a taxi to the station?* • *I got the train down to the coast.*

get *obj* UNDERSTAND/HEAR /get/ *v* [T] **getting**, *past simple* **got** /£gɒt, $gɑːt/, *past part* **got** or *Am, Aus infml* **gotten** /£ˈgɒt·ən, $ˈgɑː·t̬ən/ to understand or hear • *I didn't get* (= hear) *what he said because the music was so loud.* • *I told that joke to Sophia but she didn't get it.* • *I don't think she got what I was talking about.* • *You've got it all* **wrong** *– it was your boss that she was annoyed with and not you!* [+ obj + adj] • *Don't get me* **wrong** (= Don't misunderstand me and be offended) *– there's nothing wrong with your legs – but I prefer you in trousers to dresses.* [+ obj + adj] • *I never answer his calls and I ignore him every time I see him, so you'd think he'd get* **the message** (= understand the intended meaning). • *(infml) Stanley's in love with Lydia, who's married to his sister's boss-* **get the picture** (= do you understand the situation)*?*

get *obj* PREPARE /get/ *v* [T] **getting**, *past simple* **got** /£gɒt, $gɑːt/, *past part* **got** or *Am, Aus infml* **gotten** /£ˈgɒt·ən, $ˈgɑː·t̬ən/ to prepare (a meal) • *I'll put the kids to bed while you're getting the dinner.*

get *obj* CONFUSE /get/ *v* [T] **getting**, *past simple* **got** /£gɒt, $gɑːt/, *past part* **got** or *Am, Aus infml* **gotten** /£ˈgɒt·ən, $ˈgɑː·t̬ən/ *infml* to confuse (someone) and make them completely unable to understand or explain •

‘GET’, ‘HAVE’ AND OTHER VERBS USED TO MEAN ‘CAUSE’

TO CAUSE SOMEONE TO DO SOMETHING

You **caused** *me* **to** *make a mistake.* [obj + *to*-infinitive]	rather formal; used esp. of actions that are unpleasant, morally wrong etc.
I **got** *the doctor* **to** *come.* [+ obj + *to*-infinitive]	= cause or persuade
We **got** *her singing* [+ obj + v-*ing*]	used esp. of actions taking some time
I **had** *him sign the contract.* [+ obj + infinitive without *to*]	often suggests the other person was unwilling
I **had** *Nita* **helping** *in the kitchen.* [+ obj + v-*ing*]	used esp. of actions taking some time; often suggests the action is unlikely
She **made** *me apologise.* [+ obj + infinitive without *to*] *You'll* **make** *me miss my train.*	= persuade or force = cause
Don't **keep** *Mr Darn* **waiting.** [+ obj + v-*ing*]	= cause to continue
What **led** *the police* **to** *suspect him?* [+ obj + *to*-infinitive]	= influence or cause

These verbs are also used with things as objects, meaning ‘to cause something to happen’: *High temperatures* **caused** *the motor* **to** *burn out.* • *Haven't you* **got** *the photocopier working yet?* *It was you who* **made** *it go wrong.* • *I* **had** *it working okay.*

VERB + OBJECT + PAST PARTICIPLE : [+ obj + v-*ed*]

- *‘Get’* and *‘have’* can be used in this pattern to describe situations where you cause somebody to do something to a particular object, often by paying them: *I* **had** *my car* **repaired**. • *She* **got** *her hair* **cut**.
- When the other verb refers to something that was not wanted, these patterns mean the same as a passive: *Ben* **had** *his watch* **stolen**. (=Ben's watch was stolen) • *I* **got** *my face* **slapped**. (= My face was slapped).
- Especially when a time is mentioned, these patterns mean ‘to finish doing’: *I'll* **have** *these letters* **answered** *by 5 o'clock.* • *Gill will soon* **get** *the work* **done**.
- *Want, need, prefer, like* can also be used in the pattern [obj + v-*ed*]:
  to express an order or the desire for someone else to do something: *They* **want** *the guilty men* **punished**. • *I* **need** *this room* **painted** *by tomorrow.* • **I'd like** *this tree* **taken** *down.*
  to express preferences: *I* **prefer** *my steak* **grilled**.

TO CAUSE A STATE

This plan will **cause** *us trouble.* [+ two objects]
The committee **made** *him chairman.* [+ obj + n]
Her behaviour **got** *him angry.* [+ obj + adj]
This medicine might **make** *you sleepy.* [+ obj + adj]
Here's more work to **keep** *you busy.* [+ obj + adj]

[LP] on *Verbs with two objects* at TWO

You've got me there – you'll have to ask someone else that question.

get *obj* [ANNOY] /get/ *v* [T] **getting**, *past simple* **got** /£gɒt, $gɑːt/, *past part* **got** or *Am, Aus infml* **gotten** /£'gɒt·ᵊn, $'gɑː·t̬ᵊn/ *infml* to cause to feel annoyance • *What really gets me is the way we're expected to actually laugh at his pathetic jokes!*

get *obj* [EMOTION] /get/ *v* [T] **getting**, *past simple* **got** /£gɒt, $gɑːt/, *past part* **got** or *Am, Aus infml* **gotten** /£'gɒt·ᵊn, $'gɑː·t̬ᵊn/ *infml* to cause to feel strongly emotional and often to cry • *That bit in the film when he finds out that his daughter is alive – that always gets me!*

get *obj* [HIT] /get/ *v* [T] **getting**, *past simple* **got** /£gɒt, $gɑːt/, *past part* **got** or *Am, Aus infml* **gotten** /£'gɒt·ᵊn, $'gɑː·t̬ᵊn/ to hit (someone), esp. with a bullet or something thrown • *The bullet got her in the leg.* • *"Did you get him?" "No, I just missed by an inch!"*

get *(obj)* [REACH] /get/ *v* [always + adv/prep] **getting**, *past simple* **got** /£gɒt, $gɑːt/, *past part* **got** or *Am, Aus infml* **gotten** /£'gɒt·ᵊn, $'gɑː·t̬ᵊn/ to reach or arrive at a particular place • *We hadn't even got as far as London when the car broke down.* [I] • *Spain last week and Germany this week – he gets* **around/about** (= goes to many places) *doesn't he!* [I] • *If you get* **back** (= return) *in time you can come with us.* [I] • *(fig.) We're not getting very* **far** (= not advancing) *with conversation, are we?* [I] • *What time is the plane expected to get* **in** (= arrive)? [I] • *What time does he normally get home/***in** *(from work)?* [I] • *If you get* **to** *the restaurant before us just wait at the bar.* [I] • *(infml) If you can get yourself to the station I'll come and pick you up from there.* [T] • *I'm getting to the stage now where I'm so fed up I could leave tomorrow.* [I] • *It's a profession in which you earn a lot if you get to the top.* [I] • *It had got to* (= It was as late as) *Thursday and she still hadn't received any news.* [I] • To get **at** something is to reach it, often in order to use it yourself: *I've put the cake on a high shelf where he can't get at it.* [I] ○ *She's inherited a lot of money but she's not allowed to get at it until she's 21.* [I] • To get **through** to someone on the telephone is to succeed in talking to them: *I tried to telephone her but couldn't get through.* ○ *I got through* **to** *the wrong department.* [I] • To get **through** an examination is to be successful in it: *She got through her exams without too much trouble.* [I] • *(Br)* **Getting on for** (*Am and Aus* **going on**) means ‘almost’ in the following types of phrase: *He must be getting on for* (= nearly) *80 now.* ○ *It must be getting on for midnight.* ○ *There were probably getting on for a hundred people there.* • *I wonder where my glasses have* **got to** (= I don't know where they are).

get [HAVE CHANCE] /get/ *v* [+ *to* infinitive] **getting**, *past simple* **got** /£gɒt, $gɑːt/, *past part* **got** or *Am, Aus infml* **gotten** /£'gɒt·ᵊn, $'gɑː·t̬ᵊn/ to have the chance to do something • *I never get* **to** *see her now that she's left the company.* • *If you ever get* **to** *eat there you must try their fish.*

get *obj* [LOOK] *Am* /get/ *v* [T usually in commands] *infml* to look at or notice (someone), and usually laugh at them • *Get him in his new clothes!*

get a·round/round to *(obj) v adv prep* to do (something that you have intended to do for a long time) • *I was meaning to see that film but I just never got around to it.* [T] • *I finally got around to sorting out that cupboard yesterday.* [+ v-*ing*]

get at *obj* [SUGGEST] *v prep* [T] *infml* to suggest or express (something) in a way that is not direct or clear • *I don't really understand what you're getting at – do you mean I shouldn't come tonight?* • *What do you think the poet is getting at in these lines?*

get at *obj* CRITICIZE *Br and Aus, Am usually* **get on** *v prep* [T] *infml* to criticize (a person) repeatedly in a way that makes them unhappy • *He keeps getting at me and I really don't know what I've done wrong.*

get at *obj* INFLUENCE *v prep* [T often passive] *infml* to influence (a person) illegally, esp. by offering them money • *The accused claimed that the witness had been got at.*

get a·way with *obj v adv prep* [T] to succeed in avoiding punishment for (something), or *(fig.)* to do (something) successfully where there is a risk • *If I thought I could get away with it I wouldn't pay any tax at all.* • *(fig.) It is a close-fitting dress but you're slim enough to get away with it.* • *(infml)* If someone lets you **get away with murder**, they allow you to do what you want without criticizing or punishing you, often because they like you so much and can't see your faults.

get back at *obj v adv prep* [T] *infml* to punish (someone) because they have done something wrong to you • *I think he's trying to get back at her* **for** *those remarks she made in the meeting.*

get by *v adv* [I] to manage to pay for the necessary things in life but nothing extra, or to continue to manage a situation in a way that is satisfactory but not perfect because there is less of something than you would like • *How can he get by* **on** *so little money?* • *We can get by* **with** *four computers at the moment, but we'll need a couple more when the new staff arrive.*

get down to *obj v adv prep* to start to direct your efforts and attention to (esp. a piece of hard work) • *I've got a lot of work to do but I can't seem to get down to it.* [T] • *I must get down to sorting out that pile of papers on my desk.* [+ v-ing]

get in *obj* FIND TIME, **get** *obj* **in** *v adv* [M] *infml* to manage to find time for doing (something) or dealing with (someone) • *I get in a bit of gardening most evenings.* • *Doctor Fiasco is very busy today, but I'm sure we can get you in later this afternoon.*

get in *obj* SAY, **get** *obj* **in** *v adv* [M] to succeed in saying (something), often in a situation where other people talk a lot too • *I couldn't get a word in because she was talking so much.* • *I'll try to get my suggestion in at the start of the meeting.*

get *(obj)* **off** SLEEP *v adv* to start sleeping or to help (a baby) to start sleeping • *It was so hot that I didn't get off* **(to sleep)** *till three o'clock.* [I] • *I've been trying to get the baby off* **(to sleep)** *for an hour!* [T]

get *(obj)* **off** *(obj)* ESCAPE PUNISHMENT *v adv, v prep* (to help someone) to avoid punishment for (something) • *She was charged with fraud, but her lawyer managed to get her off.* [T] • *If you've got the money to pay for top lawyers, they can get you off almost anything.* [T] • *"Was he found guilty?" "No, he got off."* [I] • *She got off* **with** (= her only punishment was) *a small fine.* [I] • *(fig.) I think I got off quite* **lightly** *with one or two cuts, bearing in mind how damaged the car was.* [I]

get *(obj)* **off** PLEASURE *v adv esp. Am* (to help someone) to experience extreme pleasure, esp. to have an ORGASM • *They got off simultaneously.* [I] • *She got him off three times that night.* [T]

get off on *obj v adv prep* [T] *infml* to find (something) exciting and pleasant • *Dave likes power – he gets off on it.*

get off with *obj v adv prep* [T] *Br slang* to kiss and touch (someone) sexually for the first time • *She'd got off with some bloke at the party.*

get on RELATIONSHIP, **get a·long** *v adv* [I] to have a good relationship • *We're getting on much better now that we don't live together.* • *They're not getting on at the moment.* • *He doesn't get on* **with** *his daughter.*

get on MANAGE *esp. Br,* **get a·long** *v adv* [I] to manage or deal with a situation, esp. successfully • *How are you getting on in your new flat?* • *We're getting on quite well* **with** *the decorating.*

get on CONTINUE *v adv* [I] to continue doing something, esp. work • *I thought I'd get on* **with** *some work while I've got some time.* • *I'll leave you to get on then, shall I?*

get on BECOME OLD/LATE *v adv* [I] to grow old or become late • *He's getting on – he'll be seventy-six next birthday.* • *It's getting on – we'd better go soon.* • *Time is getting on and we're meant to be there by eight o'clock.*

get out of *obj* AVOID *v adv prep* to avoid (doing something that you do not want to do), esp. by giving an excuse • *I suspect that her backache was just a way of getting out of the housework.* [T] • *If I can get out of* **going** *to the meeting tonight I will.* [+ v-ing]

get out of *obj* STOP *v adv prep* [T] to give up or stop (a habit or a regular activity) unintentionally or intentionally • *I must get out of the habit of finishing off people's sentences for them.* • *I used to go swimming but I've got out of the habit these past few months.*

get o·ver *obj v prep* [T] to get better after (an illness or an experience that has made you unhappy), or find a solution to a (problem) • *She was only just getting over the flu when she got a stomach bug.* • *It took him years to get over the shock of his wife dying.* • *He's a bit upset that she won't see him any more but he'll get over it.* • *It took her months to get over Rupert when he finished the relationship.* • *We were missing one teacher but got over that little difficulty by combining the two classes.* • *(infml)* People might sometimes say that they **can't get over** something to mean that they are extremely surprised or shocked by it: *I can't get over the way he behaved at your party – it was appalling!*

get round/a·round *obj v prep* [T] to succeed in avoiding or solving (a problem) • *We can get round the problem of space by building an extension.*

get round *obj v prep* [T] *Br* to persuade (someone) to allow you something by charming them • *See if you can get round your father* **to** *give you a lift to the cinema.* [+ obj + to infinitive]

get round to *v adv prep* GET AROUND TO

get through *obj* FINISH *v prep* [T] to use up or finish (something) • *We're getting through a lot of coffee/biscuits/toilet paper.* • *I can get through a lot more work when I'm on my own.*

get *(obj)* **through** BE UNDERSTOOD *v adv* [usually in negatives] to succeed in making someone understand or believe (something) • *We can't get through* **to** *the government just* **how** *serious the problem is!* [+ *wh-* word] • *I don't seem to be able to get through* **to** *him.* [I] • *I can't seem to get* **(it)** *through* **to** *you* **that** *I love you and I'm not going to leave you!* [T + obj + *(that)* clause]

get to *obj v prep* [T] *infml* to cause (someone) to feel suffering • *The heat was beginning to get to me so I went indoors.* • *The smell of her perfume really gets to me after a while!* • See also GET EMOTION.

get up *obj* ORGANIZE, **get** *obj* **up** *v adv* [M] to organize (a group of people) to do something • *He's getting up a small group to go carol-singing for charity.*

get up WIND *v adv* [I] *Br* (of the wind) to start to grow stronger • *The wind is getting up.*

get up *obj* CAUSE *v adv* [T] to cause (a strength or fearlessness) within yourself • *He couldn't get up* **the courage** *to ask her for a date.*

get *obj* **up** DRESS *v adv* [T always + adv/prep] *infml* to dress (someone) in particular clothing, esp. clothing which is strange and unusual and intended to achieve a particular effect • *He'd got* **himself** *up* **as** *a Roman emperor for the fancy-dress party.* • *She appeared at her niece's wedding got up* **like** *a Christmas tree, to everyone's embarrassment.*

get–up /£ˈget·ʌp, $ˈget̬-/ *n* [C] *infml* • *He was in a sort of Mafia get-up with a pin-striped suit and wide tie.*

get·a·way /£ˈget·ə·weɪ, $ˈget̬-/ *n* [C] *infml* an escape; an act of leaving somewhere quickly, usually after committing a crime • *The four* **made** *their getaway in a car parked outside the bank.* • *The two masked men ran across the railway line to be picked up by a getaway* **car**. • See also **get away** at GET MOVE.

get–to·geth·er /£ˈget·təˌgeð·əʳ, $-ɚ/ *n* [C] *infml* an informal meeting or social gathering, often arranged for a particular purpose • *She went home for a family get-together which she'd been dreading.* • *It's time for the* **annual** *get-together of the heads of the seven leading industrial nations.*

get–up–and–go /£ˌget·ʌp·ənˈgəʊ, $get̬·ʌp·ənˈgoʊ/ *n* [U] *infml* the quality of being positive, having a lot of new ideas and the determination and energy to put those ideas into action • *We need someone for the job with a bit of get-up-and-go.*

gey·ser /£ˈgiː·zəʳ, $ˈgaɪ·zɚ/ *n* [C] a hole in the ground from which hot water and steam are sent out, or *(Br)* a device which uses gas to provide a house with hot water

gha·stly /£ˈgɑːst·li, $ˈgæst-/ *adj* **-ier, -iest** *rather infml* unpleasant and shocking or *(infml)* extremely bad • *This morning's newspaper reports all the ghastly details of the murder.* • *(infml) What ghastly* **weather**! • *(infml) It was all a ghastly* **mistake**. • *(infml) She was wearing the most ghastly outfit you've ever seen.* • *(literary)* Ghastly can also be used to mean unhealthily and unpleasantly pale: *She staggered out of the room, her face a ghastly* **white**.

gha·stli·ness /£ˈgɑːst·lɪ·nəs, $ˈgæst-/ *n* [U]

ghee /giː/ *n* [U] a type of clear butter used in Indian cookery

gher·kin /£ˈgɜː·kɪn, $ˈgɜːr-/ *n* [C] a small type of CUCUMBER (=a long green vegetable) which is often PICKLED (= preserved in a vinegar sauce) • *a pickled gherkin* • *cocktail gherkins*

ghet·to /£ˈget·əʊ, $ˈgeţ·oʊ/ *n* [C] *pl* **ghettos** or **ghettoes** a very poor area of a city in which a lot of people, often of the same race or religion, live closely together and apart from the rest of the city, or a part of society or group that is in some way set apart from the others • *As a child she lived in one of New York's poorest ghettos.* • *To the west of the city people are living in almost ghetto conditions.* • *Brought up in what he describes as 'a middle class ghetto' he imagined that all people were as privileged as he was.* • *(slang)* A **ghetto blaster** (*Am also* **boom box**) is a large long TAPE RECORDER that can be carried around by hand.

ghet·to·ize *obj, Br and Aus usually* **-ise** /£ˈget·əʊ·aɪz, $ˈgeţ·oʊ-/ *v* [T often passive] • If groups in society are ghettoized, they are treated as if they are different from the other parts of society and their activities and interests are not important to other people: *Feminist writers, she claimed, had been ghettoized, their books placed on separate shelves in the shops.* • *The TV company is aware of the danger of ghettoizing disability issues by offering 'specialist' programmes.*

ghost [SPIRIT] /£gəʊst, $goʊst/ *n* [C] the spirit of a dead person believed by some to visit the living and sometimes represented as a pale, almost transparent picture of the dead person • *Do you* **believe in** *ghosts?* • *The gardens are said to be* **haunted** *by the ghost* **of** *a dead child who drowned in the river.* • *(fig.) The ghost* (= memory) **of** *the old dictator still lingers on in his monstrous architecture.* • *The priest* **exorcized** *the ghost* (=caused it to stop appearing in a particular place). • *(fig.) His actions* **exorcized/laid** *the ghost* (=removed the memory) *of that unhappy period of their lives.* • *What's the matter? You look* **as though** *you've* **just seen a ghost** (=very shocked)*!* • *(infml) He hasn't got* **a/the ghost of a chance** *of* (= it's not possible he will be) *getting the money from his father.* • To **give up the ghost** is to die or to stop working: *Our TV has given up the ghost.* • A **ghost ship** is an imaginary ship. • A **ghost story** is frightening story about ghosts and their activities. • A **ghost town** is a town or city that in the past was successful and rich and is now poor with fewer people living there and empty buildings. • A **ghost train** is an entertainment for adults and children, which involves moving in a vehicle through a set of exciting and frightening experiences. • *"The ghost in the machine* (=a spiritual mind in a mechanical body)*"* (the philosopher Gilbert Ryle in the book *The Concept of Mind,* 1949) • PIC› **Imaginary creatures**

ghost·ly /£ˈgəʊst·li, $ˈgoʊst-/ *adj* **-ier, -iest** • Ghostly means pale and transparent like a ghost, or not loud and clear: *a ghostly figure/apparition* ○ *Ghostly grey clouds drifted across the moon.* ○ *a ghostly voice/echo*

ghost·li·ness /£ˈgəʊst·lɪ·nəs, $ˈgoʊst-/ *n* [U]

ghost *obj* [WRITE] /£gəʊst, $goʊst/, **ghost-write** /£ˈgəʊst·raɪt, $ˈgoʊst-/ *v* [T] to write (a book or article etc.) for another person so that they can pretend it is their own or use it themselves • *His autobiography was ghosted.*

ghost-writ·er /£gəʊst, $goʊst/ *n* [C] • A ghost writer is a person who writes a book or an article for someone else who can then pretend it is their own or use it themselves.

ghoul /guːl/ *n* [C] an evil spirit • *As a child I was fascinated by the idea of ghosts and ghouls.*

ghoul·ish /ˈguː·lɪʃ/ *adj* • Ghoulish means ugly, unpleasant or frightening: *ghoulish faces* ○ *She smiled a ghoulish smile, her front teeth missing.* • *(disapproving)* Ghoulish often means connected with death and unpleasant things or tending to think about them to an unhealthy degree: *People take such a ghoulish delight in reading about horrific murders.*

ghoul·ish·ly /ˈguː·lɪʃ·li/ *adv*

GHQ /ˌdʒiː·eɪtʃˈkjuː/ *n* [U] *abbreviation for* General Headquarters (=the main centre from which a military operation is controlled)

GI /ˌdʒiːˈaɪ/ *n* [C] *infml* a soldier in the US army, esp. in World War Two • *Janet was a GI bride, marrying an American soldier with whom she then went back the States.*

gi·ant /ˈdʒaɪ·ənt/ *n* [C] an imaginary creature, appearing esp. in children's stories, like a man but extremely tall and powerful and usually cruel, or a very successful and powerful person or organization • *No children's fairy story is complete without a princess, witch or giant!* • *A large powerful man, he was nevertheless a* **gentle giant.** • *The giants who came into the hotel turned out to be a visiting basketball team.* • *He was one of the intellectual/political giants of this century.* • *The takeover battle is between two of America's industrial/retail giants* (=large companies). • *This afternoon's match is between Manchester and those giants of the Italian football league, Juventus.* • *"If I have seen further it is by standing on the shoulders of giants"* (Sir Isaac Newton in a letter, 1676) • See also GIGANTIC. • PIC› **Imaginary creatures**

gi·ant /ˈdʒaɪ·ənt/ *adj* [not gradable] • *a giant earth-moving machine* • *a giant property corporation* • *He's got amazingly long legs and walks with giant steps.* • A **giant panda** is a PANDA. • See also GIGANTIC.

gib·ber /£ˈdʒɪb·əʳ, $-ɚ/ *v* [I] *esp. disapproving* to speak in a way that is fast and cannot be understood, often as a result of great mental confusion or fear • *Stop gibbering, man, and tell us what you saw.*

gib·ber·ing /£ˈdʒɪb·ᵊr·ɪŋ, $ˈ-ɚ-/ *adj esp. disapproving* • *I stood there like a gibbering* **idiot** *– I didn't know what I was saying.*

gib·ber·ish /£ˈdʒɪb·ᵊr·ɪʃ, $ˈ-ɚ-/ *n* [U] *disapproving* • Gibberish is words, spoken or written, which are nonsense and have no meaning: *I couldn't understand what he was saying – it sounded like gibberish.*

gib·bet /ˈdʒɪb·ɪt/ *n* [C] a wooden structure which was used in the past to hang criminals from as a form of EXECUTION (=killing as a punishment) • Compare GALLOWS.

gib·bon /ˈgɪb·ᵊn/ *n* [C] a small long-armed APE (=a monkey-like animal but without a tail) which lives in trees in the forests of S Asia • PIC› **Apes and monkeys**

gibe /dʒaɪb/ *n* [C], *v* [I] JIBE

gib·lets /ˈdʒɪb·ləts/ *pl n* the inside parts of a bird together with its neck, which are removed before the bird is cooked and are sometimes eaten themselves or used to give flavour to sauces etc.

gid·dy /ˈgɪd·i/ *adj* **-ier, -iest** *dated for* DIZZY

gift [PRESENT] /gɪft/ *n* [C] something which is given; a present • *It's her birthday party so I need a gift of some sort to take along.* • *There's a shop in the hospital which sells flowers and fruit and all the usual gifts.* • *They arrived for a week's stay,* **bearing** (=with) *gifts for us all.* • *(infml)* Something which is surprisingly easy or cheap can sometimes be referred to as a gift: *That goal was a gift!* ○ *£100 for a good leather coat? It's a gift!* • *What wonderful weather we've had lately – it's a* **gift from the Gods** (= something very special)*!* • *We got her a pen as a leaving present, all nicely presented in a* **gift box.** • A **gift shop** is one which sells goods which are suitable for giving as presents. • A **gift token** is a card or piece of paper with a particular amount of money printed on it and which can be exchanged in a shop for goods of that value. • A present which is **gift-wrapped** has been put in decorative paper ready for giving. • (D) (N) (S)

gift [ABILITY] /gɪft/ *n* [C] a special ability in something; a TALENT • *He has a gift* **for** *languages – he speaks about five fluently.* • *Her greatest gift as a novelist is* **for** *creating atmosphere.* • *(Br and Aus infml)* **The gift of the gab**/*(Am infml)* **The gift of gab** is the ability to speak easily and confidently in a way that makes people want to listen to you and persuades them that what you are saying is correct: *She's got the gift of the gab – she should work in sales and marketing.* • (D) (N) (S)

gift·ed /ˈgɪf·tɪd/ *adj* • *He's a very gifted* (=he has special ability as a) *dancer/musician.* • Gifted can also be used more generally to mean clever or having a greater range of ability than average: *Schools, he said, were failing to cater for the needs of gifted* **children.** ○ *She's very gifted – she's a wonderful athlete, she writes beautifully and plays the guitar and so on.*

gig [PERFORMANCE] /gɪg/ *n* [C] *infml* a single performance by a musician or group of musicians, esp. playing modern or POP music • *The band are* **doing** *the last gig on their world-tour later this week in Sydney.*

gig /gɪg/ *v* [I] **-gg-** • *Gigging around the London clubs has really helped the band develop their own sound.*

gig [CARRIAGE] /gɪg/ *n* [C] a light two-wheeled carriage with no cover, pulled by one horse and used esp. in the past

gi·ga- /ˈgɪg·ə-/ *combining form* used to form words with the meaning 1 000 000 000 • *gigavolt* • *gigahertz* • *gigajoules* • *gigawatt*

gi·ga·byte /ˈgɪg·ə·baɪt/ *n* [C] *specialized* 1024 MEGABYTES

gi·gan·tic /£ˌdʒaɪˈgæn·tɪk, $-t̬ɪk/ *adj* extremely large • *He built a gigantic New York apartment complex which he named after himself.* • *The cost of the whole operation has been gigantic.*

gi·gan·ti·cal·ly /£dʒaɪˈgæn·tɪ·kli, $-t̬ɪ-/ *adv*

gig·gle /ˈgɪg·l̩/ *v* [I] to laugh repeatedly in an uncontrolled and childish way, often at something silly or something that you know you should not be laughing at • *Once one child starts giggling it starts the whole class off.* • *Every time he went to drink, he spilled wine down his shirt and in the end I'm afraid I just giggled.* • *There's a lot of giggling going on at the back!*

gig·gle /ˈgɪg·l̩/ *n* • *There were a few* **nervous** *giggles from people in the audience.* [C] • *I caught Roz* **having** *a giggle over some of Janet's awful poetry.* [C] • *(Br and Aus infml)* A giggle can also be something which is amusing, often when it involves laughing at someone else: *Just* **for a** *giggle why don't we steal his trousers while he's in the water?* [U] • *(infml)* Someone who has **the giggles** can't stop giggling although they might be trying to: *I often used to* **get** *the giggles in lectures when I was at college.*

gig·gler /£ˈgɪg·ləʳ, $-lɚ/ *n* [C] • A giggler is a person who often giggles: *She's a real giggler.*

gig·gly /ˈgɪg·l̩.i, -li/ *adj* **-ier, -iest** *esp. disapproving* • *A load of giggly school-kids were sitting at the back of the bus.*

gi·go·lo /£ˈdʒɪg·ə·ləʊ, $-loʊ/ *n* [C] *pl* **gigolos** *dated* a man who is paid by a woman to be her lover and companion

gild *obj* /gɪld/ *v* [T] to cover (a surface) with a thin layer of gold or a substance that looks like gold • *The statue, recently gilded, shone brightly in the mid-day sun.* • *(fig.) Sunlight gilded* (=brightly lit) *the children's faces.* • *(disapproving)* If you **gild the lily** you try to improve or decorate something which is already perfect and therefore spoil it.

gild·ed /ˈgɪl·dɪd/ *adj* [not gradable] • *The gilded dome of the cathedral rises above the city.* • Gilded can also mean rich or of a higher social class: *The story revolves around the gilded* **youth** *of the 1920s and their glittering life-styles.* ○ *Both young princes are on the guest-list of this gilded occasion.*

gill [ORGAN] /gɪl/ *n* [C usually pl] the organ through which fish and other water creatures breathe • *(humorous)* If someone is described as **green/pale about the gills**, it means that they are looking ill and pale. • *(infml)* **To the gills** means completely: *By the time the fourth course was served I was* **full/stuffed** *to the gills* (=could not eat any more food). ○ *The restaurant was* **packed** *to the gills* • [PIC] **Fish**

gill [MEASUREMENT] /dʒɪl/ *n* [C] a measure of liquid that is equal to 0·142 litres or a quarter of a PINT

gilt /gɪlt/ *adj* [not gradable] covered with a thin layer of gold or a substance which is intended to look like it • *a gilt picture frame* • *It's not solid gold – it's just gilt.* • **Gilt-edged securities** are GILTS. • See also GILD.

gilt /gɪlt/ *n* [U] • *(Br infml)* Something that **takes the gilt off the gingerbread** spoils something that is otherwise enjoyable: *We had a great trip but our flight home was badly delayed, which took the gilt off the gingerbread.*

gilts /gɪlts/ *pl n Br specialized* a type of investment offered by the government which pays a fixed rate of interest and is considered low-risk

gim·crack /ˈdʒɪm·kræk/ *adj disapproving* attractive on the surface but badly made and of no real or permanent value • *She criticized the gimcrack architecture of the 1970s which she said had already lost its appeal.*

gim·let [TOOL] /ˈgɪm·lət/ *n* [C] a small tool used for making holes in wood • Someone who has **gimlet eyes** looks long and searchingly and doesn't miss anything. • [PIC] **Tools**

gim·let [DRINK] /ˈgɪm·lət/ *n* [C] *Am* an alcoholic drink made with the juice of LIMES (= a fruit) and GIN or VODKA

gim·me /ˈgɪm·i/ *v not standard for* give me • *Gimme that pen, would you?*

gim·mick /ˈgɪm·ɪk/ *n* [C] *esp. disapproving* something temporary whose purpose is to attract attention or interest and which is not serious or of any real value • *Free gifts given away with purchases are just another* **sales** *gimmick.* • *Among the gimmicks in last night's live act were holograms and a revolving stage.*

gim·mick·ry /ˈgɪm·ɪ·kri/ *n* [U] *esp. disapproving* • Gimmickry is the use of or an example of using gimmicks, esp. in order to make a product or activity more successful: *She dismissed the latest software package as just another piece of computer gimmickry.* ○ *Gimmickry is a major feature in the marketing of children's toys.*

gim·mick·y /ˈgɪm·ɪ·ki/ *adj esp. disapproving* • *I don't want any of those running shoes with gimmicky zips and bits of plastic.*

gin /dʒɪn/ *n* a colourless strong alcoholic drink flavoured with **juniper berries** (= small fruits), or a glass of this • *a bottle of gin* [U] • *a gin and tonic* [C] • *a pink gin* [C] • *(Br disapproving)* A **(floating) gin palace** is a large expensive privately owned boat: *It is the marina with the glossiest gin palaces and sleekest racing yachts.* • **Gin rummy** is a card game.

gin·ger /£ˈdʒɪn·dʒəʳ, $-dʒɚ/ *n* [U] the spicy root of a tropical plant which is used in pieces or as a powder in cooking, or is eaten preserved in sugar • *ground ginger* (= ginger powder) • *crystallized ginger* (=hard pieces of ginger covered in sugar) • *preserved ginger* (= ginger pieces in liquid sugar) • The colour ginger is red or orange-brown: *His nickname was Ginger because of his ginger* **hair**. • **Ginger ale** and **ginger beer** are fizzy drinks containing ginger. Ginger ale (*Br also* **ginger** or *Br and Aus* **dry ginger**) is sometimes mixed with an alcoholic drink: *brandy and ginger.* • **Ginger wine** is an alcoholic drink made with ginger. • *(Br and Aus)* A **ginger nut/biscuit/** *(esp. Am)* **snap** is a type of hard biscuit containing ginger. Compare GINGERBREAD. • *(Br and Aus)* A **ginger group** is a group of people who try to encourage other people to follow a new, more interesting or more active way of doing things.

gin·ger·y /£ˈdʒɪn·dʒəʳr·i, $-dʒɚ-/ *adj* • *It has a rather gingery taste* (= It tastes of ginger).

gin·ger up *obj*, **gin·ger** *obj* **up** /£ˈdʒɪn·dʒəʳ, $-dʒɚ/ *v adv* [M] to make more exciting, interesting or active • *They have done things this way for years, we'll have to change them around to ginger them up.* • *They've gingered up the book cover with a new design but the contents are the same.*

gin·ger·bread /£ˈdʒɪn·dʒə·bred, $-dʒɚ-/ *n* [U] a type of cake, often very dark brown, which contains GINGER • A **gingerbread man** is a hard ginger biscuit shaped like a person. • Compare **ginger nut** at GINGER. • [PIC] **Bread and cakes**

gin·ger·ly /£ˈdʒɪn·dʒə·li, $-dʒɚ-/ *adv* in a way that is careful or CAUTIOUS • *She sat down gingerly saying that she ached all over.* • *Gingerly he moved the glass bowl aside.* • *The two governments gingerly sought to prevent the crisis escalating.*

ging·ham /ˈgɪŋ·əm/ *n* [U] a cotton cloth which has a pattern of coloured squares on a white background • *a gingham dress/shirt/tablecloth* • *red gingham curtains* • [PIC] **Patterns**

gin·gi·vi·tis /£ˌdʒɪn·dʒɪˈvaɪ·tɪs, $-t̬əs/ *n* [U] *medical* an infection of the GUMS (= the part of the mouth from which the teeth grow) which makes them red, swollen and painful and can cause bleeding

gi·nor·mous /£ˌdʒaɪˈnɔː·məs, $-ˈnɔːr-/ *adj Br and Aus infml often humorous* extremely large • *a ginormous three-scoop ice-cream cone*

gin·seng /ˈdʒɪn·seŋ/ *n* [U] the root of a tropical plant, esp. from China, used as a medicine and to improve health

gip·py tum·my /ˌdʒɪp·i/ *n Br infml* a medical condition, esp. suffered by people on holiday, which causes stomach pains and sometimes the need to excrete the contents of the bowels frequently • *It's a shame – he had (a) gippy tummy most of the time he was on holiday.* [C/U]

gip·sy /ˈdʒɪp·si/ *n* [C] *esp. Br* a GYPSY

gi·raffe /£dʒɪˈrɑːf, $-ˈræf/ *n* [C] *pl* **giraffes** or **giraffe** a large African animal with a very long neck and long legs

gird *obj* /£gɜːd, $gɜːrd/ *v* [T] *past* **girded** or **girt** /£gɜːt, $gɜːrt/ *old use* to tie something around (your body) • *The knights girded themselves* **for** *battle* (=put on their swords and fighting clothes). • *(fig. humorous) We girded ourselves for the fray* (= We prepared ourselves for the trouble we were expecting). • *(humorous)* If you **gird (up)** your **loins** you get ready to do something.

gird·er /£ˈgɜː·dəʳ, $ˈgɜːr·dɚ/ *n* [C] a long thick piece of esp. steel or concrete which supports a roof, floor, bridge or other large structure • *steel roof girders* • Compare JOIST.

gir·dle /£ˈgɜː·dl̩, $ˈgɜːr-/ *n* [C] *dated* a long strip of cloth worn tied around the waist, or an elastic piece of underwear for women worn around the waist and bottom to shape the body, or *(literary)* something which surrounds something else • *"I'll put a girdle round about the earth/ In forty minutes"* (Shakespeare, A Midsummer Night's Dream 2.1)

gir·dle *obj* /£ˈgɜː·dl̩, $ˈgɜːr-/ *v* [T] *dated or literary* • *a garden girdled* (= surrounded) *by oak trees*

girl /£gɜːl, $gɜːrl/ *n* [C] a young woman, esp. one still at school • *Two girls showed us round the classrooms.* • Girl sometimes means daughter: *We have two girls.* ○ *My little girl is five.* • Adult women consider it offensive to be called girls by other people, esp. men, although this was common in the past, but they might call themselves or their friends girls: *Mum says she's going out with* **the** *girls tonight.* ○ *The girls at work gave it to me.* • Women workers as a group are often called girls: *shop/office girls* • *(Br infml humorous) He's just* **a big/great girl's blouse** (= a weak and cowardly man). • A **girl Friday** is a type of SECRETARY or general helper in an office, usually someone willing to do several different types of work. • *(Br)* **Girl Guide** is *dated for* **Guide**. See at GUIDES. • *(Am)* A **Girl Scout** is a girl or young woman who belongs to a youth organization similar to the GUIDES and SCOUTS. • [LP] **Age, Sexist language, Titles and forms of address**

girl·hood /£'gɜːl·hʊd, $'gɜːrl-/ *n* [U] *dated* • *She lived in India during her girlhood* (= when she was young). • Compare **boyhood** at BOY; **childhood** at CHILD.

gir·lie (-r, -st), **girl·y** (-ier, -iest) /£'gɜː·li, $'gɜːr-/ *adj* • *She told the reporter, "I like to think of myself as feminine without being girlie".* • A girlie **magazine/picture** is one which shows young women wearing few or no clothes to cause sexual excitement.

gir·lish /£'gɜː·lɪʃ, $'gɜːr-/ *adj* • *The nurse gave an unexpectedly girlish laugh.* • *His eyelashes were long and girlish.*

gir·lish·ly /£'gɜː·lɪʃ·li, $'gɜːr-/ *adv*

gir·lish·ness /£'gɜː·lɪʃ·nəs, $'gɜːr-/ *n* [U]

girl·friend /£'gɜːl·frend, $'gɜːrl-/ *n* [C] the close female friend of a man, with whom he has a romantic or sexual relationship, or the female friend of a woman • *I've never met his girlfriend.* • *Susan was going out to lunch with her girlfriends.* • Compare BOYFRIEND. • [LP] **Relationships**

gi·ro /'dʒaɪ·rəʊ, $-roʊ/ *n pl* **giros** a system used between European banks and similar organizations, in which money can be moved from one account to another by a central computer • *The money was* **transferred by** *giro.* [U] • *(Br)* A giro or a giro **cheque** is a CHEQUE for the money given by the government to people who are unemployed, ill or have very little income: *She didn't know how she would manage until she got her next giro.* [C]

girth /£gɜːθ, $gɜːrθ/ *n* the distance around the outside of a thick or fat object, like a tree or a body; CIRCUMFERENCE • *a tree of massive girth* [U] • *large in girth* [U] • *The oak measured 2 metres round the/its girth.* [C] • *(humorous) His* **ample** *girth* (= fatness) *was evidence of his love of good food.* [C] • The girth is also the strap which goes around the middle of a horse to keep the rider's seat or the load in the right position: *Loosen the girth a little.* [C]

gis·mo /£'gɪz·məʊ, $-moʊ/ *n* [C] a GIZMO

gist /dʒɪst/ *n* [U] **the gist** the most important pieces of information, or general information without details • *Don't go into details about the book, just give me the gist.* • *I'll give you the gist* **of** *the meeting over the phone.*

git /gɪt/ *n* [C] *Br slang* a person, esp. a man, considered to be unpleasant • *That mean old git would have me in court tomorrow if he could.* • *You stupid git!* [as form of address]

gite /ʒiːt/ *n* [C] *Br* a holiday house for renting in France • *They've taken a gite in Brittany for the whole of August.* • *a gite holiday*

give *(obj)* [OFFER] /gɪv/ *v past simple* **gave** /geɪv/, *past part* **given** /'gɪv·ən/ to offer (something) to (someone) or to provide them with it • *Sally's getting married next week, and her aunt's giving a set of saucepans as a wedding present.* [T] • *We always try to give* **to** *charity.* [I always + adv/prep] • *We're collecting for the children's home – please give generously.* [I always + adv/prep] • *She gave her nephew five pounds./She gave five pounds* **to** *her nephew.* [+ two objects] • *Give our guest a seat./Give a seat* **to** *our guest.* [+ two objects] • *Can you give me a date for another appointment?* [+ two objects] • *They never gave me a chance/choice.* [+ two objects] • **Given the chance/choice** (= If I were allowed to/If I could choose), *I'd spend all day reading.* • *The visit will give me an excuse for leaving early.* [+ two objects] • *Has the director given you permission to do that?* [+ two objects] • *I gave* (= paid) *£40* **for** *this pump and it's broken already!* [T] • *(fig.) I wouldn't give much* **for** *his chances* (= I do not think he will succeed) *in the next race.* [T] • *If you're found guilty, they'll give you three years* (= you will be put in prison for that period). [+ two objects] • *Look at that old car she's bought – I'll give it two weeks* (= I calculate it will last that long) *before it breaks down.* [+ two objects] • If you give something **away** you give it to someone without asking for payment: *The shop is giving away a sample pack to every customer.* [M] ○ *We gave our old table away when we moved house.* [M] ○ *Nobody wants this type of heater anymore – I can't even give them away!* [M] • *Give me* **back** *my book/Give my book* **back to** *me/Give me my book* **back** (= Return my book to me). [M + two objects] • *Please give* **in** *your homework* (= give it to the person responsible for collecting it) *on Monday morning.* [M] • *The police gave* **(out)** *road-safety booklets* **to** *the children* (= they gave them to all the children). [T/M] • *The winner's name was given* **(out)**/*They gave the winner's name* **(out)** (= the name was announced) *on the news.* [T/M] • *We've given the attic* **over to** *the children* (= only the children use it). [T] • *Please give* **(up)** *your* **seat** *to an elderly or disabled person if they require it.* [T/M] • *"But I was going to let you have it tomorrow."* **"Don't give me that** (= Don't try to deceive me in that way)!" • *(dated)* If you **give** your **all** *(Am also* **give** your **best**) you put a lot of effort into doing something: *We must be finished by tonight, so I want you to give your all.* • If you **would give anything/a lot/the world**/your **eye teeth**/your **right arm for** something or **to** do something, you want it very much: *I'd give anything to see the Taj Mahal.* • **What I wouldn't give for** (= I very much want) *a cold drink!* • *I'll say this for Jill, she always* **gives as good as** *she* **gets** (= fights or argues with equal force as the person she is fighting or arguing against). • *(fml) At the wedding the bride was* **given away** *by her father* (= her father brought her formally to her husband at the ceremony). • If you say **give** someone their **due**, or **give the devil his due**, you are remembering someone's good characteristics, esp. when you don't like some things about the person or when they have done something bad: *The repairs aren't finished, but give him/the devil his due, he was working on the car all weekend.* • **Give me** *the old-style weather forecast* **any day/every time** (= I like it best). • If you **give** your **life to** something, you continue to have a close involvement or interest in it for the whole of your life: *She gave her life to cancer research.* • *(fml)* If you **give of** your **money/time/***(Br also)* **best**, you give it, esp. in a way that seems generous: *We're very grateful to all the people who have given of their time.* ○ *She wasn't feeling well, so I don't think she gave of her best* (= wasn't as good as she could be) *tonight.* • *The gunman* **gave** *himself* **up** (= offered himself as a prisoner) *to the police.* See also GIVE UP. • *(infml)* If you **give** someone **what for** you punish them by shouting at or hitting them: *I'll give you what for, young lady, coming home at 2 o'clock in the morning!* • **Give or take** means a little more or less than the amount or time mentioned: *It cost £200, give or take a few pence.* ○ *It'll be ready at six, give or take a few minutes.* • A **give-away** is an item given free to a customer: *First-class passengers get various give-aways, such as in-flight slippers.* ○ *The furniture shop's offering three-piece suites at* **give-away** (= very low) *prices.* • *(Br saying)* 'Give a dog a bad name' means that when a person has been considered bad in the past, it is difficult to change people's opinion.

give /gɪv/ *n* • **Give-and-take** is willingness to accept suggestions from another person and give up some of your own: *You can't always insist on your own way – there has to be some give-and-take.* • *(Am)* A **Give-and-take** is also an exchange of ideas or statements: *The candidates entered into a lively give-and-take.*

give *obj* [PRODUCE] /gɪv/ *v* [T] *past simple* **gave** /geɪv/, *past part* **given** /'gɪv·ən/ to produce or cause (something), or to do (an action) • *Who is giving the speech/talk/lecture/performance/concert?* • *The wounded ox gave a great below.* • *She gave me a smile/strange look* (= She smiled/looked strangely at me). [+ two objects] • *A TV programme gave her the idea/the idea* **to** *her.* [+ two objects] • *His visit will give me the excuse to discuss these issues.* [+ two objects] • *The fresh air has given us an appetite* (= made us hungry). [+ two objects] • *Whisky gives me a headache.* [+ two objects] • *The children have been giving me a lot of trouble recently.* [+ two objects] • *They had to give the car a* **push** (= push the car) *to start it.* [+ two objects] • *The alarm gave* **(out)** *a high-pitched* **noise/sound**. [T/M] • *Give me a* **call/ring/***(Br infml also)* **bell** (= telephone me) *when you get back from holiday.* [+ two objects] • To give a party, meal, etc. is to organize it: *They're always giving parties.* ○ *The ambassador is giving a banquet for the visiting president.* • If something gives **off** a smell/smoke it produces it: *The fire gave off thick swirling smoke.* • If you **give** something **a go**, you attempt it: *Only a few people are successful as sports professionals, but you have to* *give* **it** *a go because if you make it it's a great life.* • *(fml)* If someone **gives** you **to understand** something, they tell it to you: *I was given to understand she was staying at this hotel, but it appears she's not here.* • LP Do: **verbs meaning 'perform'**

give STRETCH /gɪv/ *v* [I] *past simple* **gave** /geɪv/, *past part* **given** /ˈgɪv·ᵊn/ to stretch (until it breaks) or to become less firm • *The rope gave* **under/with** *the weight of the load.* • *Suddenly her patience gave* **(out)** *and she shouted crossly at the children.* See also **give out** at GIVE OFFER, GIVE PRODUCE; GIVE OUT. • *You can't work so hard all the time – something will have to give* (= change). • *The shoes may feel tight now, but they'll give a little after you've worn them once or twice.*

give /gɪv/ *n* [U] • *A sweater knitted in pure cotton hasn't much give.*

give *obj* DRINK /gɪv/ *v* [T + two objects; no passive] *past simple* **gave** /geɪv/, *past part* **given** /ˈgɪv·ᵊn/ to suggest that (everyone present at a formal occasion, esp. a meal) should drink a TOAST to (= a drink in honour of) (someone) • *Gentlemen, I give you the Queen!*

give *obj* DECIDE /gɪv/ *v* [T + obj + adj] *past simple* **gave** /geɪv/, *past part* **given** /ˈgɪv·ᵊn/ *Br* (in particular sports) to state officially that (a player or the ball) is in a particular condition or place • *The umpire gave the batsman out.* • *The ball was clearly out, but the line judge gave it in.*

give a·way *(obj)*, **give** *(obj)* **a·way** *v adv* to tell people (something secret) • *She wouldn't give away any details of the plan.* [M] • *He refused to give away* **why** *he'd been sent.* [+ *wh-* word] • *I won't give* **the game** (= the information or plan) *away.* [T] • *She really likes him and thinks no one knows, but the look on her face when I mentioned his name gave her away* (= showed her secret feelings). [T]

give–a·way /ˈgɪv·əˌweɪ/ *n* [U] *infml* • *He said he'd given up smoking, but the empty packets in the rubbish bin were* **a dead** *give-away* (= showed the secret truth).

give in *v adv* [I] to decide not to continue; to agree that you have been defeated • *She was determined not to give in until she received compensation for the accident.* • *You'll never guess the answer – do you give in?* • *I gave in* **to** *her repeated requests.* • See also **give in** at GIVE OFFER.

give on to *obj v adv prep*, **give on·to** *obj v prep* [T no passive] to open in the direction of • *The patio doors give on to a small courtyard.* • *The window gives onto the garden.*

give out *v adv* [I] to finish or to not work any longer • *The food supplies will give out at the end of the week.* • *At the end of the race his legs gave out and he collapsed on the ground.* • *She phoned to say her clutch has given out and the car has been taken to a garage.* • See also **give out** at GIVE OFFER, GIVE PRODUCE, GIVE STRETCH. • Ⓢ

give o·ver *v adv Br infml* to stop • *(Do) give over* (= Stop complaining), *it's not my fault!* [I] • *It's time you gave over pretending you were still a teenager.* [+ v-ing] • Give over can be used to show that you do not believe what has been said to you: *They've doubled your salary? Give over!* [I]

give o·ver/up *obj* **to** *obj*, **give** *obj* **o·ver/up to** *obj v adv prep* [M] to spend all your time doing (something); to DEVOTE (yourself) to doing (something) • *After her death he gave him***self** *up to grief.* • *We gave over the afternoon to a discussion of the new project.*

give up *(obj)*, **give** *(obj)* **up** *v adv* to stop doing or having (something) • *He's given up driv***ing** *since his illness.* [+ v-ing] • *We're going to give up our sports club membership after this year.* [M] • *She was working part-time but she suddenly gave up.* [I] • *The garage has given up sell***ing** *petrol – it only does repairs now.* [+ v-ing] • *I've been waiting half-an-hour – I'd almost given you up/***given up on** *you* (= stopped expecting you would arrive). • *The hospital had virtually given her up* **(for dead)**/**given up on** *her after her heart attack* (= stopped expecting that she would live), *but she eventually recovered.* • If you give up a friend you stop being friendly with them: *She seems to have given up all her old friends.* [M] ○ *His girlfriend has given him up.* [M] • To give up also means to stop trying to guess: *You'll never guess the answer – do you give up?* ○ *I give up – how many were there?* • See also **give up** at GIVE OFFER.

giv·en CERTAIN /ˈgɪv·ᵊn/ *n* [C], *adj* [not gradable] (something which is) certain to happen • *You can take it as (a) given that there will be champagne at the wedding.* • *In his novels, reality and morality are not givens.*

giv·en GIVE /ˈgɪv·ᵊn/ *past participle of* GIVE

giv·en KNOWING /ˈgɪv·ᵊn/ *prep* knowing about, considering • *Given his age, he's a remarkably fast runner.* • *Given the time available to us, we'll have to submit the report in draft form.* • *Given* **(the fact) that** *a prospective student is bombarded by prospectuses, selecting a suitable course is not easy.* [+ *that* clause]

giv·en ARRANGED /ˈgɪv·ᵊn/ *adj* [not gradable] already decided, arranged or agreed • *At the given signal, the group rushed forward to the barrier.* • *The procession set off at the given time.* • *The bomb could go off at* **any** *given* (= any) *time and in* **any** *given* (= any) *place.* • A **given name** is a name which is decided on around the time of birth and which is not the family name: *Her family name is Smith and her given names are Mary Elizabeth.*

giv·en DO FREQUENTLY /ˈgɪv·ᵊn/ *adj* **be given to** to do regularly or as a habit • *She was given to staying in bed till lunchtime.*

giz·mo *(pl* **gizmos**), **gis·mo** *(pl* **gismos**) /£ˈgɪz·məʊ, $-moʊ/ *n* [C] *infml* any small device with a particular purpose • *electronic gizmos* • *Her office has a computer, fax, answering machine and a host of other gizmos and gadgets.*

gla·cé /£ˈglæs·eɪ, $glæsˈeɪ/, *Am also* **gla·céed** /£ˈglæs·eɪd, $glæsˈeɪd/ *adj* [before n; not gradable] preserved in liquid sugar and then dried • *glacé fruit/cherries*

glac·i·er /£ˈglæs·i·əʳ, $ˈgleɪ·si·ɚ/ *n* [C] a large mass of ice which moves slowly esp. down the side of a mountain, causing the formation of features on the land such as valleys

gla·ci·al /ˈgleɪ·si·əl/ *adj* [not gradable] • *glacial deposits* (= left by a glacier) ○ *a glacial valley* (= made by a glacier) • A **glacial period** (also **ice age**) is a time in the past when the temperature was very cold and glaciers spread over large parts of the Earth. • Glacial can mean very cold: *glacial temperatures* ○ *a glacial wind.* • *(fig.) She gave me a glacial* (= unfriendly) *look/smile/stare.*

glac·i·at·ed /£ˈgleɪ·si·eɪ·tɪd, $-t̬ɪd/ *adj specialized* • Glaciated means formed by glaciers or covered by them: *the glaciated peaks of the Himalayas*

glad /glæd/ *adj* **gladder, gladdest** pleased and happy • *We were glad* **about** *her success.* • *I'm glad* **(that)** *you came.* [+ *(that)* clause] • *They were glad* **to** *know the parcel had arrived safely.* [+ *to* infinitive] • *I'd be* **(only too)** *glad* (= pleased and willing) **to** *help you.* [+ *to* infinitive] • *We'd be glad* **of** *the chance to meet her.* • *(dated slang)* **The glad eye** is a look of sexual approval: *All the men were giving her the glad eye.* • *(infml)* **To (give the) glad hand** or **glad-handing** is to treat people well for your own advantage: *The politician gave everyone the glad hand.* ○ *It was a big business known for glad-handing and self-promotion.* • *(humorous)* Your **glad rags** are your best clothes: *You'd better put on your glad rags for dinner with the boss!* • *(old use or humorous)* **Glad tidings** are good news: *Let me be the first to give you the glad tidings.* • *"Glad All Over"* (title of a song by The Dave Clark Five, 1963)

glad·ly /ˈglæd·li/ *adv* • *I'd gladly meet her, but I'm on holiday that week.* • *I'll do it gladly.*

glad·ness /glæd·nəs/ *n* [U] • *They returned home with great gladness.*

glad·den *obj* /ˈglæd·ᵊn/ *v* [T] • *The news gladdened his* **heart** (= made him happy).

glade /gleɪd/ *n* [C] *esp. literary* a small area of grass without trees in a wood; a CLEARING

glad·i·at·or /£ˈglæd·i·eɪ·təʳ, $-t̬ɚ/ *n* [C] a man who fought another man or an animal, esp. until one of them died, for public entertainment in ancient Rome

glad·i·at·or·i·al /£ˌglæd·i·əˈtɔː·ri·əl, $-ˈtɔːr·i-/ *adj* [not gradable] • Gladiatorial is used to refer to a fierce fight which only one person or group can win: *gladiatorial combat* • *Can justice be served in the gladiatorial arena of the law courts?*

glad·i·ol·us /£ˌglæd·iˈəʊ·ləs, $-ˈoʊ-/, *Am usually* **glad·i·ol·a** /£ˌglæd·iˈəʊ·lə, $-ˈoʊ-/ *n* [C] *pl* **gladioli** /£ˌglæd·iˈəʊ·laɪ, $-ˈoʊ-/ or **gladioluses** a garden plant which grows each year from a BULB and has long thin leaves and a stem with many brightly-coloured flowers along it

glam *(obj)* **up** /glæm/ *v adv* **-mm-** *Br infml* to dress (yourself) attractively, wear make-up etc. • *Have I got time to glam (myself) up?* [I/T] • *You're all glammed up and looking great, ready for a good night out.* [T]

glam·our *Br and Aus, Am and Aus* **glam·or** /ˈglæm·əʳ, $-ɚ/ *n* [U] the special excitement and attractiveness of a person, place or activity • *Who can resist the glamour* **of** *a theatre premiere/travelling by chauffeur-driven car?* • *Nightclubs have lost their glamour for me.*

glam·or·ous, glam·our·ous /£ˈglæm·ᵊr·əs, $ˈ-ə-/, *esp. Br infml* **glam** /glæm/ *adj* • *a glamorous woman/outfit* • *a* *glamorous job* • *glam clothes* • *She was looking very glam.* • (J)

glam·or·ous·ly /£'glæm·ər·ə·sli, $'-ɚ-/ *adv*

glam·or·ous·ness /£'glæm·ər·ə·snəs, $'-ɚ-/ *n* [U]

glam·or·ize *obj, Br and Aus usually* **–ise** /£'glæm·ə·raɪz, $'-ɚ·aɪz/ *v* [T] • To glamorize something is to make it seem better than it is and therefore more attractive: *The ad glamorized life in the army, emphasizing travel and adventure.* ○ *The film was criticized for glamorizing violence.*

glam·our·puss /£'glæm·ə·pʊs, $'-ɚ-/ *n* [C] *dated* a sexually attractive woman who wears decorative clothes and make-up so that she will be noticed • *She is decorative, larger than life, a terrific glamourpuss.*

glance [LOOK] /£glɑːnts, $glænts/ *n, v* (to give) a quick short look • *She* **took/cast** *a glance* **at** *her watch.* [C] • *He could* **tell at a** *glance* (= saw immediately) *that something was wrong.* [C] • **At first** *glance* (= When first looking) *I thought it was a dog (but I was mistaken).* [U] • *She glanced* **around/round** *the room to see who was there.* [I always + adv/prep] • *He glanced* **up** *from his book as I passed.* [I always + adv/prep] • *Just glance* **over/through** *this letter and see if it's alright.* [I always + adv/prep] • (D) (NL) (S)

glance [SHINE] /£glɑːnts, $glænts/ *v* [I] to shine, reflect light or SPARKLE • *The sunlight glanced* **on** *the lake.* • (D) (NL) (S)

glance off *(obj) v adv, v prep* (of an object) to touch quickly and lightly at an angle rather than go through • *The bullets glanced off the car.* [T] • *The arrows struck the protective covering and glanced off.* [I]

glanc·ing /£'glɑːnt·sɪŋ, $'glænt-/ *adj* [before n; not gradable] • *He received a glancing* **blow** *on his head.*

gland /glænd/ *n* [C] an organ of the body or of a plant which SECRETES (= produces) liquid chemicals that have various purposes • *The glands in my neck are swollen – I must have got some sort of infection.*

glan·du·lar /£'glæn·djʊ·lər, $-dʒə·lɚ/ *adj* [not gradable] • *glandular secretions* • *glandular problems* • **Glandular fever** (*Am usually* **mononucleosis**) is a disease which has an effect on particular glands, which can be given from one person to another and can make a person with the disease feel weak and ill for a long time.

glare [LOOK] /£gleər, $gler/ *n* [C] a long angry look • *After several angry/fierce glares she finally got the message and shut up.*

glare /£gleər, $gler/ *v* [I] • *She glared angrily/crossly* **at** *everyone.* • *He glared round the room/down the hall.* • *We could see the child's eyes glaring up* **at** *us.*

glare [SHINE] /£gleər, $gler/ *v* [I] to shine too brightly • *Car lights glared* **(out)** *at the end of the street.* • *I can't sit here – the sun is glaring* **(down** *on me/in my eyes).*

glare /£gleər, $gler/ *n* [U] • *Tinting the windows will cut down* **the** *glare/the sun's glare.* • *This screen* **gives off** *a lot of glare.* • *I was* **dazzled** *by the glare of the oncoming headlights.* • *(fig.) The actor's wedding took place* **in the (full)/in a** *glare* **of publicity**.

glar·ing /£'gleə·rɪŋ, $'gler·ɪŋ/ *adj* • *glaring light* • *glaring colours* • See also GLARING.

glar·ing /£'gleə·rɪŋ, $'gler·ɪŋ/ *adj* (of something bad) very obvious • *glaring errors/weaknesses* • *a glaring injustice* • See also **glaring** at GLARE [SHINE].

glar·ing·ly /£'gleə·rɪŋ·li, $'gler·ɪŋ-/ *adv* • *glaringly obvious*

glass /£glɑːs, $glæs/ *n* a hard transparent material which is used to make windows, bottles or other containers and objects • *coloured glass* [U] • *broken glass* [U] • *a glass jar/dish/plate/vase/ornament* • *The sculpture was* **made of** *glass.* [U] • *In the wall there was a huge window made from a single* **pane of** *glass.* [U] • *That bin is for broken glass only.* [U] • *In cool climates you have to grow tropical plants* **under** *glass* (= in a GLASSHOUSE). [U] • Glass also means objects made from glass when thought of as a group: *The museum has a fine collection of valuable glass.* [U] • A glass is a small container for drinks, which is usually round, has a flat base and is usually without a handle. It can also be made of plastic: *She poured some milk into a glass.* [C] ○ *We'll need to borrow some* **beer** *glasses and some* **wine** *glasses for the party.* [C] • **Brandy** *glasses are curved so that you can put your hands round them in order to warm the brandy.* [C] • *(Br)* If you are served beer in a **straight** glass, you are given it in a glass with no handle: *"A pint of bitter, please". "Would you like that in a straight glass or a mug, sir?".* [C] • A glass **of** something is the type or amount of drink the glass contains: *Would you like a glass of water?* [C] ○ *Two glasses of lemonade, please.* [C] • *(dated)* A glass (also **looking glass**) is also a mirror: *You've got grease on your face, look* **in** *the glass.* [C] • *(dated)* **The** glass is a BAROMETER (= a device which tells you if the weather is going to change): *The glass has been falling/rising* (= showing a change to bad/good weather) *all day.* [U] • Glass which has been heated until it becomes soft can be shaped into objects by blowing air into it down a tube: *On the shelf there was a beautiful* **blown** *glass vase.* ○ *He is a skilful* **glass-blower**. • Glass can be cut into pieces or have a pattern cut into it for decoration: *Use a* **glass-cutter** (= device for cutting glass) *to cut the window pane to size.* ○ *a* **cut-glass** *sherry decanter* • A **glass ceiling** is a point beyond which you cannot go, for example, in connection with improving your position at work: *A variety of reasons was given for the apparent glass ceiling women hit in many professions.* • **Glass fibre** is FIBREGLASS. • *(saying)* 'People who live in glass houses shouldn't throw stones' means that you should not criticize other people if you have faults yourself. • See also GLAZE [GLASS].

glass *obj* /£glɑːs, $glæs/ *v* [T always + adv] • *We glassed* **in** *the porch* (= put glass in the open spaces) *to make a small conservatory.* [M] • *You used to be able to touch the manuscripts but now they are glassed* **over** (= in glass cases/covered with glass) *to stop them being damaged.* [M]

glas·ses /£'glɑː·sɪz, $'glæs·ɪz/ *pl n* • Glasses (also **spectacles**) are two small pieces of special glass or plastic in a frame worn in front of the eyes to improve sight: *a* **pair of** *glasses* ○ *glasses* **for** *reading/reading glasses* ○ *glasses frames* • BINOCULARS are sometimes called glasses. • *"Men seldom make passes / At girls who wear glasses"* (Dorothy Parker *News Item*, 1937) • See also SUNGLASSES. • [LP] **Eye and seeing** [PIC] **Frame**

glass·ful /£'glɑːs·fʊl, $'glæs-/ *n* [C] • *She's very young – will she be able to drink a whole glassful* **of** *orange juice?*

glas·sy /£'glɑː·si, $'glæs·i/ *adj* **-ier, -iest** • *(literary)* A glassy surface is smooth and shiny like glass: *a glassy sea/lake* • If someone has glassy **eyes** or a glassy **stare** they have a fixed expression and seem unable to see anything: *His eyes were glassy and he was muttering to himself.*

glass·house /£'glɑːs·haʊs, $'glæs-/, *Am and Aus usually* **green·house** *n* [C] *pl* **-houses** /-ˌhaʊ·zɪz/ a building with glass sides and roof for growing plants in; a large GREENHOUSE • *He's a commercial tomato grower with ten glasshouses.*

glass·ware /£'glɑːs·weər, $'glæs·wer/ *n* [U] objects made of glass • *Ornamental glassware was displayed in a wall cabinet.* • [LP] **Shopping goods**

Glas·weg·i·an /glæz'wiː·dʒən/ *n* [C], *adj* [not gradable] (a person) from Glasgow, the largest city in Scotland

glau·co·ma /£glaʊ'kəʊ·mə, $-'koʊ-/ *n* [U] a disease of the eye which can cause a person to gradually lose their sight

glaze *obj* [MAKE SHINE] /gleɪz/ *v* [T] to make (a surface) look shiny, esp. by putting a liquid substance onto it and leaving it or heating it until it dries • *Glaze the pastry with beaten egg.* • *The pottery bowls had been badly glazed.* • *The paper was glazed by rubbing it with a stone.* • [PIC] **Food preparation**

glaze /gleɪz/ *n* [C] • *The cake was finished with a redcurrant glaze.* • *The plates were very old and the glaze had fine cracks across it.*

glaze *(obj)* [GLASS] /gleɪz/ *v* to put a piece of glass into (a window) • *The house is nearly finished but the windows haven't been glazed yet.* [T] • If you **double**-glaze (or **triple**-glaze) a window you use two (or three) PANES (= pieces) of glass instead of one. • *(fig.) Among the audience eyes glazed* **over** (= became fixed, as if unable to see) *with boredom and a few heads started to nod.* [I]

glazed /gleɪzd/ *adj* • *All the rooms have glazed doors.* • If someone has a glazed expression/look they look as if they do not know what is happening around them.

gla·zi·er /£'gleɪ·zi·ər, -ʒər, $-ʒɚ/ *n* [C] • A glazier is a person who sells glass or fits it into windows.

glaz·ing /'gleɪ·zɪŋ/ *n* [U] • Glazing is the glass used for windows: *The new house has central heating and* **double**-*glazing* (= windows with two thicknesses of glass), *so it is very easy to keep warm.* • [PIC] **Window**

gleam /gliːm/ *v* [I] to produce a small, bright light; to reflect • *The diamond gleamed and shone under the display lights.* • *He polished the table until it gleamed.* • *A light was gleaming in the window of the house.* • If your eyes gleam with an emotion, you express the emotion with them: *His eyes gleamed* **with/in** *triumph/pleasure.*

gleam /gliːm/ *n* [C] • *We saw the gleam* **of** *a fire through the curtains.* • *A gleam* **of** *interest/hope/pride appeared in her eyes.*

gleam·ing /ˈgliː·mɪŋ/ *adj* • Gleaming often means that something is bright and shiny because it has been cleaned: *a gleaming kitchen* ○ *gleaming windows*

glean *obj* /gliːn/ *v* [T] to collect (esp. information) in small amounts and often with difficulty • *From what I was able to glean, the news isn't good.* • *They're leaving on Tuesday, I managed to glean that much* (**from** *them).*

glee /gliː/ *n* [U] happiness, excitement or pleasure • *She opened her presents with glee.* • *When the cheque arrived he hugged me in glee.*

glee·ful /ˈgliː·fᵊl/ *adj* • *a gleeful smile/shout*

glee·ful·ly /ˈgliː·fᵊl·i/ *adv*

glen /glen/ *n* [C] a deep narrow valley, esp. among mountains • *the glens of Scotland* • *Ballaglass Glen* • *Glen Maye*

glib /glɪb/ *adj* **glibber, glibbest** speaking or spoken confidently and persuasively but without sincerity, honesty or thought • *He's a glib, self-centred man.* • *Former political rivals started issuing glib tributes as soon as her death was announced.* • *It's easy to make glib generalizations.* • *No one was convinced by his glib* **answers/explanations.** • **It** *is just too glib to blame crime on unemployment and poverty.*

glib·ly /ˈglɪb·li/ *adv* • *He spoke glibly about the economic recovery that was just around the corner.* • *She answered the question too glibly.* • *They glibly assume that we'll do whatever they want us to do.*

glib·ness /ˈglɪb·nəs/ *n* [U]

glide MOVE /glaɪd/ *v* [I always + adv/prep] to move easily without stopping and without effort or noise • *Tourist boats glide* **up and down** *the river all day long.* • *A shiny black limousine glided* **(smoothly) into** *the square.* • *She glided* **(gracefully) into** *the ballroom wearing a long flowing gown.* • *I love my new pen – it just glides* **across/over** *the paper.* • *(fig.) Some people glide* **(effortlessly) through** *life* (=find it easy) *without ever worrying about having enough money.*

glide /glaɪd/ *n* [C] • *She skated across the ice rink and came to a stop with a smooth glide.*

glide FLY /glaɪd/ *v* [I] to fly by floating on air currents instead of using power from wings or an engine • *These birds can glide for hours, circling round and round on the columns of hot air rising from the ground.* • *Unlike other spacecraft, the shuttle can glide back* **through** *the atmosphere, land safely, and be reused.* • *Martha's promised to take me gliding* (=flying in a **glider**) *next Sunday.*

glid·er /£ˈglaɪ·dəʳ, $-dɚ/ *n* [C] • A glider is an aircraft without an engine and with long fixed wings: *To get airborne, gliders either have to be towed into the air by a plane with an engine, or launched into the air by a special machine.* • PIC **Aircraft**

glim·mer /£ˈglɪm·əʳ, $-ɚ/ *v* [I] (of light) to shine weakly or not continuously • *We could see the lights of the village glimmering in the distance.* • *The sky glimmered* **with** *stars.* • *The only light in the room was a faintly glimmering candle.* • *(fig.) The first faint signs of an agreement are starting to glimmer through* (=appear).

glim·mer /£ˈglɪm·əʳ, $-ɚ/, **glim·mer·ing** /£ˈglɪm·ᵊr·ɪŋ, $ˈ-ɚ-/ *n* [C] • *We saw a glimmer* **of light** (=a weak, not continuously shining light) *from their campfire a long way off.* • *(fig.) In spite of the recent pessimism of negotiators, the first glimmer* **of light** (=the first sign of development or understanding) *has appeared in the peace talks.* • *(fig.) This month's consumer sales figures offer a glimmer* (=a slight sign) **of hope** *for the otherwise depressed economy.* • *(fig.) Despite our best efforts to get her to take up an instrument, she didn't show a glimmer* (=any sign) **of interest** *in classical music.*

glimpse *obj* /glɪmps/ *v* [T] to see (something) for a very short time or only partly • *I thought I glimpsed Meg at the station this morning.* • *We glimpsed the ruined abbey from the windows of the train.* • *Observers glimpsed the shooting star as it shot through the sky.* • *Signs that the economy is improving are beginning to be glimpsed.*

glimpse /glɪmps/ *n* [C] • *I* **caught** *a* **(fleeting)** *glimpse* (= a brief sight) **of** *the driver of the getaway car, but I doubt I would recognize her if I saw her again.* • *This biography offers only a few glimpses* **of** *his life* (=briefly shows what it was like) *before he became famous.*

glint /glɪnt/ *v* [I] to produce small bright flashes of light reflected from a surface • *The stream glinted in the moonlight.* • *A large diamond glinted on her finger.* • *(fig.) His eyes glinted* (=were bright) **with** *excitement as he unwrapped the parcel.*

glint /glɪnt/ *n* [C] • *She was distracted by the glint* **of** *a knife that was lying in the undergrowth.* • *(fig.) "I think I can persuade them to cooperate," she said with a cunning glint* (=a brightness expressing that quality) *in her eye.*

glis·ten /ˈglɪs·ᵊn/ *v* [I] to shine by reflecting light from a wet, oily or smooth surface • *The grass glistened in the early-morning dew.* • *Her forehead was glistening* **with** *sweat.* • *Fry the onions in the olive oil until they glisten.* • *He pointed to the glistening veins of gold in the lump of rock.* • *His eyes glistened* (=filled with tears) *as he told her about their mother's death.*

glitch /glɪtʃ/ *n* [C] a small problem or fault that prevents something from being successful or working as well as it should • *(infml) We'd expected a few glitches, but everything's gone remarkably smoothly.* • *(infml) The system was finally withdrawn from sale last week, having been plagued with glitches ever since its launch.* • *(specialized)* A glitch is also a sudden unexpected increase in electrical power, esp. one that causes a fault in an electronic system: *The computer failure was due to a glitch caused by lightning.*

glit·ter /£ˈglɪt·əʳ, $ˈglɪṭ·ɚ/ *v* [I] to produce a lot of small bright flashes of light reflected from a surface • *Her diamond necklace glittered brilliantly under the spotlights.* • *The lake glittered in the sunlight.* • *The harbour was glittering* **with** *lights.* • *His dark eyes glittered* (=were bright and expressed strong feeling) *(***with** *anger) behind his spectacles.* • *(saying)* 'All that glitters is not gold' means that something that seems to be good on the surface may not be when you look at it more closely.

glit·ter /£ˈglɪt·əʳ, $ˈglɪṭ·ɚ/ *n* [U] • *The castle looked magnificent beneath the glitter* **of** *the fireworks.* • *(fig.) He was attracted by the glitter* (=excitement and attractiveness connected with rich and famous people) **of** *Hollywood.* • Glitter is also very small pieces of shiny material used to decorate the skin or, esp. by children, for making pictures: *She was dressed up as a fairy and her face was covered with make-up and glitter.*

glit·ter·ing /£ˈglɪt·ᵊr·ɪŋ, $ˈglɪṭ·ɚ-/ *adj* • *The glittering skyline of Manhattan is an impressive sight.* • Glittering can also mean causing admiration: *She has had a glittering career.* ○ *As a student, he carried off most of the glittering* **prizes** *of his year.* ○ *The Cannes Film Festival is one of the most glittering* (=exciting and causing admiration from being connected with rich and famous people) *occasions in the movie world.*

glit·ter·y /£ˈglɪt·ᵊr·i, $ˈglɪṭ·ɚ-/ *adj* • *She was wearing glittery* (=containing very small pieces of shiny material) *eye-shadow.*

glit·ter·a·ti /£ˌglɪt·əˈrɑː·ti, $ˌglɪṭ·əˈrɑː·ṭi/ *pl n* rich, famous and fashionable people whose activities are of interest to the public and are written about in some newspapers and magazines • *The ball was attended by 7000 glitterati.* • *The restaurant owes its success to its popularity with the glitterati* **of** *the music world.* • Compare LITERATI.

glitz·y /ˈglɪt·si/ *adj* **-ier, -iest** having a fashionable appearance intended to attract attention; SHOWY • *The former president celebrated his birthday at a glitzy party in Beverly Hills.* • *She's bought herself a glitzy new car.* • *Beneath his glitzy surface, he's really a very lonely person.*

glitz /glɪts/ *n* [U] • *There is a danger of the party's electoral message being obscured by the glitz and glamour of its presentation.*

gloam·ing /£ˈgləʊ·mɪŋ, $ˈgloʊ-/ *n* [U] **the gloaming** *literary or Scot Eng* the part of the day after the sun has gone down and before the sky is completely dark • *They sat on a hillside* **in** *the gloaming, watching the lights come on in the houses below.*

gloat /£gləʊt, $gloʊt/ *v* to feel or express great pleasure or satisfaction because of your own success or good luck, or someone else's failure or bad luck • *She won't stop gloating* **over/about** *her new job.* [I] • *I know I shouldn't gloat, but it really serves him right.* [I] • *Some soldiers gloated* **at** *what they saw as the divine punishment of their enemies.* [I] • *"This is our fourth victory in a row," he gloated.* [+ clause] • *They gloated* **that** *their opponents stood no chance of winning the election because they lacked a strong leader.* [+ *that* clause]

gloat /£gləʊt, $gloʊt/ *n* [C] • *He couldn't resist a small gloat when the woman who sacked him lost her own job.*

gloat·ing·ly /£ˈgləʊ·tɪŋ·li, $ˈgloʊ·t̬ɪŋ-/ *adv* • *She smiled gloatingly at her defeated rivals.*

glob /£glɒb, $glɑːb/ *n* [C] *infml* a round mass of a thick liquid or a sticky substance • *A big glob* **of** *chewing-gum had been stuck under the table.*

globe WORLD /£gləʊb, $gloʊb/ *n* [U] **the globe** the world • *His greatest ambition is to sail the globe.* • *Three large satellite dishes were ready to transmit TV pictures* **around** *the globe.* • *She is a superstar* **around** *the globe* (= everywhere in the world) *as well as in her home country.* • *Delegates to the conference came from* **all corners of** (= all parts of) *the globe.* • LP **Nations and nationalities, World regions**

glob·al /£ˈgləʊ·bəl, $ˈgloʊ-/ *adj* • If something is global, it relates to the whole world: *The oil-well fires are a regional but not a global catastrophe.* ○ *The minister blamed the rise in unemployment on the global economic recession.* • Global also means considering all parts of something: *This report gives a global picture of the company's finances.* ○ *We need to take a global view of the situation.* • If you do a **global search** on a computer, you look for every example of a word or phrase in a document: *Do a global search for 'organise' and replace it with 'organize'.* • **The global village** is all the countries of the world when thought of as being closely connected by modern communications and therefore economically, politically, socially and environmentally dependent on each other: *As citizens of the global village, we cannot ignore our obligations to others.* • **Global warming** is a gradual increase in temperature caused by gases collecting in the air and other gases surrounding the Earth, which prevents heat escaping into space: *Reducing the amount of carbon dioxide released into the air by burning fossil fuels would help to limit global warming.*

glob·al·ly /£ˈgləʊ·bəl·i, $ˈgloʊ-/ *adv* • *Many environmental problems can be solved by people thinking globally* (= considering the whole world) *and acting locally.* • *We need to look at this issue globally* (= consider all its parts).

glob·al·i·sm /£ˈgləʊ·bəl·ɪ·zəm, $ˈgloʊ-/ *n* [U] • Globalism is the idea that events in one country cannot be separated from those in another and that a government should therefore consider the effects of its actions in other countries as well as its own. • Compare **isolationism** at ISOLATE.

glob·al·ist /£ˈgləʊ·bəl·ɪst, $ˈgloʊ-/ *n* [C] • *He is a globalist* (= someone who believes that a country should consider the effects of its actions on other countries), *whereas we are nationalists who will put our country first.* • *She has always been critical of the president's globalist foreign policy.*

glob·al·ize *obj, Br and Aus usually* **-ise** /£ˈgləʊ·bəl·aɪz, $ˈgloʊ-/ *v* [T] • *Satellite broadcasting is helping to globalize* (= cause to operate internationally) *television.*

glob·al·iz·a·tion, *Br and Aus usually* **-i·sa·tion** /£ˌgləʊ·bəl·aɪˈzeɪ·ʃən, $ˌgloʊ-/ *n* [U]

globe ROUND OBJECT /£gləʊb, $gloʊb/ *n* [C] a map of the world in the shape of a ball which is fixed to a support so that it can be turned round at the same angle as the Earth turns in space, or any ball-shaped object • *My father wants an antique globe for his birthday.* • *She* **spun** *the globe, and pointed to the Solomon Islands.* • *One of those paper globes* (= ball shapes made of paper) *would make a good lampshade in this room.* • *They keep their goldfish in a glass globe* (= ball-shaped container). • *(Aus)* A globe is also a **light globe**. See at LIGHT BRIGHTNESS. • A **globe artichoke** is a plant which has a round mass of pointed leaf-like parts surrounding its flower, which are eaten as a vegetable.

glob·u·lar /£ˈglɒb·jʊ·ləʳ, $ˈglɑː·bjə·lɚ/ *adj* • *Some goldfish bowls have a globular* (= like a ball) *shape.* • See also **globular** at GLOBULE.

globe·trot·ter /£ˈgləʊbˌtrɒt·əʳ, $ˈgloʊbˌtrɑː·t̬ɚ/ *n* [C] someone who travels frequently to a lot of different countries • *Mary's such a globetrotter – she's just come back from Japan and now she's planning a trip to Brazil.*

globe·trot·ting /£ˈgləʊbˌtrɒt·ɪŋ, $ˈgloʊbˌtrɑː·t̬ɪŋ/ *n, adj* [not gradable] • *The Prime Minister's globetrotting has led to accusations that he is ignoring domestic problems.* [U] • *Globetrotting business people are the target of the airline's new advertising campaign.* [before n]

glob·ule /£ˈglɒb·juːl, $ˈglɑːb-/ *n* [C] a small ball of something, esp. a drop of liquid • *The disease might be caused by fat globules blocking the blood vessels of the nervous system.* • See also GLOB.

glob·u·lar /£ˈglɒb·jʊ·ləʳ, $ˈglɑːb·jə·lɚ/ *adj* • *Egg proteins consist of long molecules like chains that are folded into a globular* (= like a small ball) *shape.* • See also **globular** at GLOBE ROUND OBJECT.

glock·en·spiel /£ˈglɒk·ən·ʃpiːl, $ˈglɑː·kən·spiːl/ *n* [C] a musical instrument consisting of flat metal bars of different lengths that are played by someone hitting them with a pair of small hammers • *The note produced by a glockenspiel depends on the length of the bar that is hit.*

gloom HOPELESSNESS /gluːm/ *n* [U] feelings of hopelessness or great unhappiness; great PESSIMISM • *Bergman's films are often full of gloom and despair.* • *The article about the pollution of the environment that I read painted a picture of* **unremitting/unmitigated** *gloom.* • *The workforce is managing to remain cheerful in spite of all the gloom* **and doom** *about the company's future.* • *There is a sense of gloom* **and despondency** *among the team.* • *As the days went by, her gloom about her exam results* **deepened/lifted**.

gloom·y /ˈgluː·mi/ *adj* **-ier, -iest** • *The vet was rather gloomy about my cat's chances of recovering from his illness.* • *In spite of the gloomy economic forecasts, manufacturing output has risen slightly.* • *The cemetery is a gloomy place to visit.*

gloom·i·ly /ˈgluː·mɪ·li/ *adv* • *He spoke gloomily about his prospects of getting another job now that he's 55.*

gloom·i·ness /ˈgluː·mɪ·nəs/ *n* [U] • *The survey demonstrates deep gloominess in the business community about the prospects for economic revival.*

gloom DARKNESS /gluːm/ *n* [U] near darkness in which it is difficult to see well • *She peered into the gloom, but she couldn't see where the noise was coming from.* • *A figure emerged from the gloom of the corridor.*

gloom·y /ˈgluː·mi/ *adj* **-ier, -iest** • *What gloomy weather we're having!* • *We waited in a gloomy waiting-room.*

glop /£glɒp, $glɑːp/ *n* [U] *infml* liquid, sauce-like food which often tastes unpleasant • *They served up a greyish glop, with bits in it.*

glo·ri·fy *obj* /£ˈglɔː·rɪ·faɪ, $ˈglɔːr·ɪ-/ *v* [T] to make (something) seem splendid or excellent, often when it is really not • *I didn't like the way the film glorified war/violence.* • *It's very easy to glorify the past.* • *The minister was accused of glorifying the proposals* **with** *an important-sounding name to hide the fact that they contained no new ideas.* • *(infml) My word processor's not so much a computer, more a kind of glorified typewriter.* • Glorify can also mean praise and honour: *A statue was erected in the main square of the city to glorify the country's national heroes.* ○ *Prayer beads often have 99 beads on a string – one for each way Allah can be glorified in the Koran.*

glo·ri·fi·ca·tion /£ˌglɔː·rɪ·fɪˈkeɪ·ʃən, $ˌglɔːr·ɪ-/ *n* [U] • *He was a modest man, and strongly resisted any glorification of his many achievements.*

glo·ry ADMIRATION /£ˈglɔː·ri, $ˈglɔːr·i/ *n* great admiration, honour and praise which you earn by doing something successfully, or an important achievement which has earned these • *He revelled in the glory* **of** *scoring three goals in the last 8 minutes of the match.* [U] • *This was to be her final professional tennis match, and she wanted to end her career in* **a blaze of** *glory.* [U] • *The government is* **basking/bathing** *in the* **reflected** *glory* (= glory that it has not earned itself) *of its victorious military forces.* [U] • *He didn't exactly* **cover himself in/with** *glory* (= He was not very successful) *in his last job.* • *The annual reunion is an opportunity for the soldiers to remember their past glories* (= achievements). [C] • Glory can also mean praise and thanks, esp. as given to God: *Glory be to God!* [U] ○ *He dedicated his poetry to the glory of God.* [U] • Someone's **glory days** are a period of time when they were very successful: *Her popularity as a singer has waned since the glory days of the 1980s.*

glo·ry in *obj* /£ˈglɔː·ri, $ˈglɔːr·i/ *v prep* [T] • If you glory in something, you show that you are very happy and proud about it, and believe that it deserves praise or admiration: *He is still glorying in the success of his first Hollywood film.* ○ *She's always gloried in the fact that she's much better qualified than her sister.*

glo·ri·ous /£ˈglɔː·ri·əs, $ˈglɔːr·i-/ *adj* • Glorious means deserving admiration, praise and honour: *This was yet another glorious victory for the team.* ○ *She enjoyed a glorious 40-year career on the stage.* ○ *The monument is a memorial to the glorious dead of two world wars.*

glo·ri·ous·ly /£ˈglɔː·ri·ə·sli, $ˈglɔːr·i-/ *adv*

glo·ry BEAUTY /£ˈglɔː·ri, $ˈglɔːr·i/ *n* great beauty, or something which is splendid or extremely beautiful, which gives great pleasure • *How long will it take to restore the castle to its former glory?* [U] • *The garden* **in all** *its glory is now open to the public.* [U] • *The museum houses many of the artistic glories* (= splendid things) **of** *the ancient world.* [C] • *The ballroom is the* **crowning** *glory* **of** (= most beautiful thing in) *the palace.* [C] • **Glory box** is *Aus for* **bottom drawer**. See at BOTTOM LOWEST PART. • *"The glory that was Greece / And the grandeur that was Rome"* (Edgar Allan Poe in the poem *To Helen*, 1831)

glo·ri·ous /£ˈglɔː·ri·əs, $ˈglɔːr·i-/ *adj* • *The beetroot had turned the soup a glorious* (= beautiful) *pink.* • *Your roses are glorious!* • If weather is described as glorious, it means that it is very pleasant, esp. that it is hot and sunny: *Luckily, they had glorious weather for their wedding.* ○ *It was a glorious winter day – crisp and clear.* • Glorious can also mean very enjoyable or giving great pleasure: *This wine is absolutely glorious.* ○ *We had a glorious time when we went to the south of France last summer.*

glo·ri·ous·ly /£ˈglɔː·ri·ə·sli, $ˈglɔːr·i-/ *adv* • *Her hair is gloriously* (= beautifully) *thick.* • *The weather's been gloriously* (= giving great pleasure) *sunny this week.* • *They looked gloriously happy.*

gloss COVERING /£glɒs, $glɑːs/ *n* [U] (paint or similar substance which produces) a smooth shiny appearance on the surface of something • *We'll need a litre of gloss (paint) to cover the woodwork.* Compare EMULSION. • *I need to buy some* **lip** *gloss.* • *Marble can be polished to* **a** *high gloss.* • *This varnish provides a long-lasting and hard-wearing gloss finish.* Compare MATT. • *(fig.) Bad weather* **took the** *gloss* **off** *our trip to the zoo* (= made it less special and enjoyable).

glos·sy /£ˈglɒs·i, $ˈglɑː·si/ *adj, n* **-ier, -iest** • *How did you manage to get such a glossy finish on this table?* • *She has wonderfully glossy hair.* • If a book or magazine is described as glossy, it means that it has been produced on shiny and expensive paper and usually contains many colour pictures: *a glossy coffee-table book* ○ *She came home with a pile of glossy brochures and announced she had decided to buy a car.* • *(esp. disapproving)* Glossy can also mean looking attractive, but often not having serious value or quality: *This magazine is full of glossy advertisements for after-shave.* • A glossy/**glossy magazine** (*Am* **slick**) is a magazine printed on shiny high-quality paper which contains a lot of colour photographs and advertisements, and is usually about famous people, fashion, beauty, etc. [C] • *(Am and Aus)* A glossy is also a photograph printed on smooth shiny paper: *an 8-by-10 black and white glossy* [C]

glos·si·ly /ˈglɒs·ɪ·li/ *adv*

glos·si·ness /£ˈglɒs·ɪ·nəs, $ˈglɑː·sɪ-/ *n* [U]

gloss EXPLANATION /£glɒs, $glɑːs/ *n, v* (to provide) an explanation for a word or phrase • *There is a special edition of the book for schools, in which the older and more rare words have been glossed.* [T] • *Expressions that are difficult to understand are explained in the glosses at the bottom of the page.* [C] • A gloss is also a way of considering something that has been done which emphasizes the good parts, esp. those which are to your advantage, and avoids the bad ones: *Politics is all about* **putting** *a good gloss* **on** *unpleasant or difficult situations.* [C]

gloss o·ver *obj v adv* [T] • If you gloss over something, such as a mistake or an embarrassing fault, you avoid considering it, esp. in order to make it seem unimportant, and often quickly continue to talk about something more positive: *She glossed over the company's fall in profits, focussing instead on her plans for investment and modernization.* ○ *The film was well researched, but it glossed over the important issues.*

glos·sa·ry /£ˈglɒs·ər·i, $ˈglɑː·sɚ-/ *n* [C] an alphabetical list, with meanings, of the words or phrases in a text that are difficult to understand • *The book would have been more useful if a glossary* **of** *technical terms and abbreviations had been included.*

glot·tis /£ˈglɒt·ɪs, $ˈglɑː·ţɪs/ *n* [C] *medical* the space between the thin strips of muscle inside the throat that produce sound by moving slightly as air travels over them

glot·tal stop /£ˈglɒt·əl, $ˈglɑː·təl/ *n* [C] • A glottal stop is a speech sound produced by closing the **vocal cords** and then opening them quickly so that the air from the lungs is released with force: *Some English speakers use a glottal stop instead of a /t/ sound that occurs after a vowel sound, for example in the word 'butter'.*

glove /glʌv/ *n* [C] a piece of clothing which covers the hand and wrist, with separate parts for each finger, and which provides warmth or protection • *leather/woollen/rubber gloves* • *I need a new* **pair of** *gloves.* • A **glove box** is a closed transparent container in which poisonous or RADIOACTIVE substances can be handled safely using gloves that are firmly fixed to holes in one side of the container. • A **glove compartment/glove box** is a small cupboard or shelf in the front of a car that is used for storing small items such as maps. • A *(Br and Aus)* **glove puppet** (*Am* **hand puppet**) is a toy person or animal which has a soft hollow body into which you put your hand, using your fingers to move its head and arms. • Compare MITTEN. • PIC **Toy**

glove *obj* /glʌv/ *v* [T] • *(Am) She gloved her hands* (= put gloves on) *to protect them from the chemicals.* • *She held out her gloved hand to shake mine.* • *A white-gloved police officer was directing the traffic.* • *(Am)* To glove a ball is to catch it when playing baseball: *He gloved the ball, turned and threw in one motion.*

glow /£gləʊ, $gloʊ/ *v* [I] to produce a continuous light and sometimes heat • *These bullets contain a special chemical which glows brightly as the bullets fly through the air, indicating the path they have taken.* • *A small nightlight glowed dimly in the corner of the children's bedroom.* • *Polonium is so radioactive that it glows in the dark.* • *He lit another cigarette from the glowing stub of the previous one.* • Someone who is glowing is hot or red because of exercise: *When we got back from our walk in the snow, my whole body was glowing.* • To glow is also to look attractive because you are happy or healthy: *Her eyes glowed as he told her how well she had done.* ○ *The children's faces were glowing* **with** *excitement.* ○ *They came back from their week by the sea, glowing* **with** *health.* • A **glow-worm** is a BEETLE (= type of insect), of which the females and young produce a green light from the tail. • See also GLOWING.

glow /£gləʊ, $gloʊ/ *n* [U] • *Neon emits a characteristic red glow.* • *He stared thoughtfully into the glow* **of** *the fire burning in the grate.* • A glow is also a positive feeling: *They felt a glow* **of** *pride as they watched their daughter collect the award.* ○ *She felt a* **warm** *glow* **of** *satisfaction.*

glow·er /£ˈglaʊ·əʳ, $-ɚ/ *v* [I] to look very angry, annoyed or threatening • *There's no point glowering like that just because you can't go to the party.* • *The defendant glowered defiantly* **at** *the judge as she sentenced him to life imprisonment.* • *She gave me a glowering look when I told her that I hadn't done what she'd told me to do.* • *(fig.) Large black rain clouds glowered* (= looked likely to produce rain) *in the sky.*

glow·er /£ˈglaʊ·əʳ, $-ɚ/ *n* [C] • *Her glower turned to a grin as she realized it had all been a joke.*

glow·ing /£ˈgləʊ·ɪŋ, $ˈgloʊ-/ *adj* praising with enthusiasm • *I'm pleased to say we've received a glowing letter of recommendation from your former employer.* • *In her acceptance speech, the new prime minister paid a glowing* **tribute** *to her predecessor.* • *His latest book has received glowing* **reviews**. • *The government's efforts to bring down unemployment have had little effect but it has a glowing* (= successful and therefore worth praising) *record on reducing inflation.*

glow·ing·ly /£ˈgləʊ·ɪŋ·li, $ˈgloʊ-/ *adv* • *She talked glowingly about the school's achievements over the past year.*

glu·cose /£ˈgluː·kəʊs, $-koʊs/ *n* [U] a type of sugar which is found in plants, esp. fruit, and which supplies an important part of the energy animals need • *The body digests carbohydrates down to glucose, which itself is broken down in the muscles to release energy.*

glue /gluː/ *n* [U] a sticky substance which is used for joining things together permanently, and which is often made by boiling animal bones and skins or by a chemical process • *I think we could mend that cup with glue.* • *(fig.) Her father had been the glue holding the family together, and when he died, it quickly fell apart.* • **Glue ear** is a medical condition, which is commonly found in children, where the middle part of someone's ear becomes filled with a liquid which prevents them from hearing correctly: *Over half of all children in Britain get glue ear at some time before they are 16, and it can lead to permanent hearing loss.* • A **glue-sniffer** is someone who breathes in the gases that are produced by some types of glue, in order to produce an excited mental condition which feels pleasant but is very dangerous: *Today sees the launch of a government advertising campaign to discourage* **glue-sniffing**. • See also SUPERGLUE.

glue *obj* /gluː/ *v* [T] **gluing** or **glueing** • *Is it worth trying to glue these pieces of broken plate together again?* • *I've nearly finished making my model aeroplane – I just have to* *glue the wings* **on**. [M] • *(fig.) We were glued* **to** (= could not stop watching) *the television watching the election results come in.* • *(fig.) Have you ever had a dream where you're trying to run away from something but you can't because you're glued* **to the spot** (= unable to move)*?*

glu·ey /ˈgluː·i/ *adj* **gluier, gluiest** • *You'll have to wash those gluey hands of yours before you eat.*

glum /glʌm/ *adj* **glummer, glummest** disappointed or unhappy or without hope, and quiet • *"Why are you so glum?" "I failed my exam."* • *He's very glum* **about** *the company's prospects.* • If a place is glum, it is unattractive and lacks anything that causes pleasure: *They live in one glum little room.*

glum·ly /ˈglʌm·li/ *adv* • *"I've no chance of finding another job at my age," she said glumly.*

glum·ness /ˈglʌm·nəs/ *n* [U] • *There was an air of glumness in the room after the bad news was announced.*

glut /glʌt/ *n* [C] a supply of something that is much greater than can be sold or is needed or wanted • *The fall in demand for coffee could cause a glut* **on/in the market**, *forcing some producers to cut prices.* • *There is a glut* **of** *large, expensive houses lying empty and unsold.* • *The current glut* **of** *graduates means that many of them will not be able to find jobs.* • *There has been a glut* **of** *articles about the World Cup in the papers over the last week.*

glut *obj* /glʌt/ *v* [T] **-tt-** • *A few producers have enough oil to glut* **the market** *and cause an oil-price collapse a few months from now.*

glu·ten /£ˈgluː·tᵊn, $-t̬ᵊn/ *n* [U] a PROTEIN (= a chemical necessary for life) which is contained in wheat • *Gluten enables dough to rise when baking, by trapping bubbles of carbon dioxide produced by the yeast in the mixture.* • *Some people are allergic to gluten, and have to have a gluten-free diet.*

glu·tin·ous /£ˈgluː·tɪ·nəs, $-t̬ɪ-/ *adj* sticky • *Short-grain rice turns into a soft glutinous mass when cooked, making it easy to eat with chopsticks.*

glut·ton /£ˈglʌt·ᵊn, $ˈglʌt̬-/ *n* [C] a person who regularly eats and drinks more than is needed • *Marco's such a glutton – he ate a whole packet of biscuits while he was watching the film.* • If you are a glutton **for** something, you like it very much: *Sophie is a glutton for books.* • If you describe someone as a **glutton for punishment**, you mean that they seem to enjoy doing something that you consider unpleasant: *He's a real glutton for punishment, taking on all that extra work without getting paid for it.*

glut·ton·ous /£ˈglʌt·ᵊn·əs, $ˈglʌt̬-/ *adj* • *Somehow, despite being really gluttonous, he manages to stay thin.* • *(fig.) She said that industrialized countries should reduce their gluttonous* (= greater than is needed) *consumption of oil.*

glut·ton·ous·ly /£ˈglʌt·ᵊn·ə·sli, $ˈglʌt̬-/ *adv*

glut·ton·y /£ˈglʌt·ᵊn·i, $ˈglʌt̬-/ *n* [U] • *San Francisco is famed for its gluttony – more is spent per person there in restaurants than anywhere else in America.* • *Gluttony is one of the seven deadly sins.*

glyc·er·ine, *Am also* **glyc·er·in** /£ˈglɪs·ᵊr·iːn, -ɪn, $-ɚ·rɪn/, *specialized* **glyc·er·ol** /£ˈglɪs·ə·rɒl, $-rɑːl/ *n* [U] a colourless sweet thick sticky liquid which is obtained from animal and vegetable fats and oils, and is used in making explosives and medicines and for sweetening foods • *In spite of its sweetness, glycerine is not a type of sugar.* • Compare NITROGLYCERINE.

gm *n* [C] *pl* **gm** *abbreviation for* GRAM

G–man /ˈdʒiːˌmæn/ *n pl* **-men** a government official in the US, esp. one who works for the FBI

GMT /ˌdʒiː·emˈtiː/ *n* [U] *abbreviation for* GREENWICH MEAN TIME

gnarled /£nɑːld, $nɑːrld/ *adj* rough and twisted, esp. because of old age or a lack of protection from bad weather • *It was a typical old village pub, with gnarled beams and a wood fire.* • *Wisteria plants can reach a considerable age, developing thick, gnarled stems.* • *The old man drew a long gnarled finger across his throat.* • *A gnarled old tramp lay curled up on a park bench.*

gnash *obj* /næʃ/ *v* [T] to bring (teeth) forcefully together because of anger • *In the film there were green monsters which roared and gnashed their teeth.* • If you **gnash** your **teeth** about something, you complain angrily and noisily about it: *Villagers have been gnashing their teeth* **about** *the council's decision to build a car park on the meadow.*

gnash·ing /ˈnæʃ·ɪŋ/ *n* [U] • *There has been much* **gnashing of teeth** (= angry complaining) *about the proposal to close the local hospital.* • *The decision has produced a lot of teeth-gnashing.* • *"There shall be weeping and gnashing of teeth"* (Bible, Matthew 8.12)

gnat /næt/ *n* [C] a very small flying insect that bites animals and people • *Gnats are often found flying in swarms above stagnant water.*

gnaw *(obj)* BITE /£nɔː, $nɑː/ *v* to bite or chew (something) repeatedly, usually making a hole in it or gradually destroying it • *Babies like to gnaw hard objects when they're teething.* [T] • *A dog lay under the table, gnawing* **(on)** *a bone.* [T; I + prep] • *How can I stop my son gnawing* **(at)** *his fingernails all day long?* [T; I + prep] • *(fig.) Bad debts are continuing to gnaw* **(away) at** (= make smaller) *the bank's profits.* [I] • To gnaw something is to form it by biting repeatedly: *A mouse had gnawed a hole in the rug.* [T] ○ *Rats had gnawed* **their way** *into a sack of corn.* [T]

gnaw *(obj)* FEEL ANXIOUS /£nɔː, $nɑː/ *v* to cause (someone) to feel anxious or uncomfortable • *I've been gnawed by guilt about not having replied to the letter I had from Liz some months ago.* [T] • *The feeling that I've forgotten something has been gnawing* **at** *me all day.* [I]

gnaw·ing /£ˈnɔː·ɪŋ, $ˈnɑː-/ *adj* • *I've had gnawing* (= continuously uncomfortable or worrying) *doubts about the viability of this project for some time.* • *I have a gnawing* (= continuously uncomfortable) *pain in my leg.* • *After not eating for three days, we felt an agonizing, gnawing* (= continuously painful) *hunger.*

gnoc·chi /£ˈnɒk·i, £ˈnjɒk-, $ˈnjɑː·ki/ *pl n* small round balls which are made by mixing together potato or wheat flour and water, and served in soup or with a savoury sauce

gnome /£nəʊm, $noʊm/ *n* [C] (in children's stories) an imaginary very small old man with a BEARD (= hair on the face below the mouth) and a pointed hat, who lives underground and guards gold and other valuable objects • A gnome is also a model of a gnome used as a garden decoration: *I don't think* **garden** *gnomes are in very good taste.* • Powerful bankers from Switzerland are sometimes called the **gnomes of Zurich** because they control a lot of money, much of it belonging to foreign governments. • *(Am)* A gnome is also a person who works by using their mind, but does not talk to, and is not known by, the public; a boffin: *The gnomes in the back room are putting the finishing touches on the new software.*

gnom·ic /£ˈnəʊ·mɪk, £ˈnɒm·ɪk, $ˈnoʊ-/ *adj esp. literary* (esp. of something said or written) brief, mysterious and not easily understood, but often seeming wise • *Peter is always coming out with gnomic utterances/pronouncements.*

GNP /ˌdʒiː·enˈpiː/ *n* [U] *abbreviation for* Gross National Product (= the total value of goods and services produced by a country in one year, including profits made in foreign countries) • *GNP is one of the statistics used for judging the state of a country's economy.* • *Although the gross national product grew by 6·4%, real GNP growth after allowing for inflation was only 1·8%.* • Compare GDP.

gnu /£nuː, £gəˈnuː/, **wil·de·beest** *n* [C] *pl* **gnu** or **gnus** an African animal with a long tail and horns that curve to the sides, and which lives in grassy areas • *The gnu is a type of large antelope.*

go TRAVEL /£gəʊ, $goʊ/ *v* he/she/it **goes**, **going**, *past simple* **went** /went/, *past part* **gone** /£gɒn, $gɑːn/ to travel or move to another place • *There's a good film on at the Odeon. Shall we go?* [I] • *Are you going anywhere special for your birthday?* [I] • *Where do you think you're going? Shouldn't you be at school?* [I] • *Don't go any closer – that animal's dangerous.* [I] • *We go* **shopping** *every Friday night.* [+ v-ing] • *I've never been* **skiing**, *but my parents go every year.* [+ v-ing] • *Don't you dare go* **crying** *to your mum about this.* [+ v-ing] • If you go **and** do something, you travel or move to a different place in order to do it: *Would you go and get me some things from the supermarket?* [I] ○ *I just want to go and have a look at that antique shop over there.* [I] ○ *Why don't you children go and play upstairs out of our way?* [I] ○ *Would you wait for me while I go and fetch my coat?* [I] • *(infml)* **Go and** is used to express disapproval of something that is done: *He's gone and lost* (= He has lost) *that wallet I gave him for his birthday.* ○ *I don't want you going and telling Dad what I've bought for him.* ○ *Mike's really gone and* **done it** *now – he'll be in terrible trouble for breaking that window.* • To go **back** is to return: *That restaurant was terrible – I'm never going back there again.* [I] ○ *Bother, I've left my gloves behind. I'll have to go back* **for** *them.* [I] ○ *Do you think you'll ever go back* **to** *London, or will you stay in this area for the rest of your life?* [I] ○ *When do you go back* **to** *school?* [I] ○ *Let's go back* **to** *the beginning and *start again.* [I] ○ *I'd just like to go back* **to** *the question you raised earlier.* [I] ○ *We can always go back* **to** *the original plan if necessary.* [I] ○ *Jenny gave up drinking and smoking for a while, but she soon went back* **to** *her old ways.* [I] ○ *When are these library books due to go back* (= be returned)? [I] ○ *That TV will have to go back* (= be returned) *– it hasn't worked properly ever since I bought it.* [I] • *(fig.) This church goes back further* (= is older) *than any other in the country.* [I] • *(fig.) Our house goes back* **to** (= has existed since) *the 18th century.* [I] • *(fig.) Their relationship goes* **back to** (= has existed since) *when they were at university together.* [I] • *Wouldn't it be quicker to go* **by** *train rather than by car?* [I] • *(fig.) The temperature went* **down** (= became reduced) **to** *minus ten last night.* [I] • *(fig.) The company's shares went* **down** (= became reduced by) *7p* **to** *53p.* [I] • *(fig.) Go* **down to** (= Read as far as) *the bottom of the page and then write a summary of what you've just read.* [I] • *They've gone* **for** *a walk* (= left the place where they were in order to walk), *but they should be back soon.* [I] • *They've gone* (= travelled to another place) **in** *the Land Rover, leaving me the other car.* [I] • *It's really cold out here, why don't you go* **in** (= move inside). [I] • *(fig. esp. Br) No matter how many times you tell him something, it never seems to go* **in** (= be understood). [I] • *(fig.) I reminded her about the meeting this morning, but I don't know if it went* **in** (= if she noticed it). [I] • *The train hooted as it went* **into** (= entered) *the tunnel.* [I] • *Their car was travelling at 50 miles an hour when it went* **into** (= hit) *a tree.* [I] • *(fig.) My son's planning to go* **into** (= get a job in) *journalism/politics/the Navy.* [I] • *(fig.) At the end of the cold war, many armaments manufacturers went* **into** (= started producing) *consumer goods.* [I] • *(fig.) A considerable amount of money, time and effort has gone* **into** (= been used when producing) *this exhibition.* [I] • *He continued to play for a while after the injury, but eventually he had to go* **off** *(the field)* (= leave the field). [I] • *You go* **on (ahead)** (= travel to another place in front of or before other people) *and I'll come along in a minute.* [I] • *Why don't you go* **on** (= travel in front of or before other people) **to** *the post office and I'll see you there when I've finished at the bank?* [I] • *(Br) We're going* **out to** (= travelling to) *Austria for a week's walking in the mountains next month.* [I] • *The broadcast caused a lot of controversy when it first went* **out** (= was broadcast). [I] • *Redundancy notices have gone* **out** (= been sent) **to** *one in five of the company's employees.* [I] • *(fig. fml) Our thoughts go* **out to** (= are sent to) *all the people who cannot be with their families at this special time of year.* [I] • *(fig. fml) Our deepest sympathies go* **out to** (= are expressed to) *her husband and children.* [I] • *(fig.) We're now going* **over to** *our correspondent* (= he or she will now appear in this broadcast) *speaking from the scene of the explosion.* [I] • *(fig.) He couldn't give up smoking altogether, so he went* **over to** (= changed to) *cigars instead of cigarettes.* [I] • *(fig.) Many motorists are going* **over** (= changing) *(***from** *leaded)* **to** *unleaded fuel.* [I] • *(fig.) She went* **over** (= changed her support) *(***from** *the Republicans)* **to** *the Democrats at the last election.* [I] • *I'm just going* **round to** (= making a visit to) *Mario's for half an hour.* • *We don't go* **to** *the cinema very often these days.* [I] • *I went* **to** (= visited) *Paris last summer. Have you ever been there?* [I] • *Does this train go* (= travel) **to** *Newcastle?* [I] • *What time do you usually go* **to** *bed* (= get into bed in order to sleep)? [I] • *She's gone* (= travelled) **to** *meet Brian at the station.* [+ *to* infinitive] • If something **goes to** someone, it is given or sold to them: *Whom did the award for Best Actress go to?* ○ *All the money raised will go to charity.* ○ *She left a considerable fortune which is expected to go to her niece.* ○ *The painting went to the highest bidder.* • To **go to** something difficult or unpleasant is to experience it in order to do something for someone else: *I'd love to come to dinner, but I don't want you going to a lot of* **trouble** (= doing a lot of work) *for me.* ○ *Your parents went to a great deal of* **expense** (= spent a lot of money) *to send you on holiday, so you could at least send them a postcard.* • *(Br dated)* If you go **up (to** a college or university, esp. Oxford University or Cambridge University), you begin studying there, or continue studying after a holiday: *Susannah went up to Cambridge University in 1988.* [I] ○ *I'm planning to go back up the first weekend of January.* [I] • You ask **where** someone or something **has** gone when you cannot find them or you have lost them: *Where have my keys gone? I always seem to be losing them.* • *I've got a dentist's appointment on Friday that I'm rather worried about. Will you go* **with** *me?* [I] • *Follow the road until it ends, go* (= turn) **right/left**, *and we're the first house on your left.* [I] • If a person or animal **goes at** or **goes for** you, they attack you: *Suddenly, he went at me* **with** *a knife.* ○ *She really went for the Prime Minister in a blistering attack on the government's policies.* ○ *(fig.) He went at* (= ate eagerly) *his dinner as if he hadn't anything to eat for weeks.* • When you use 'go' in the perfect tense about someone who has finished or come back from what they went to do, you use 'been' as the past participle, rather than 'gone': Compare 'She's gone skiing' (= and she is still doing it) and 'She's been skiing' (= she has finished and come back).

-go·er /£-gəʊ·əʳ, $-goʊ·ɚ/ *combining form* • A -goer is a person who goes to the stated type of place: *Restaurant-goers ought to complain more about bad food and service.* ○ *The cinema's new season ticket offers substantial discounts to regular filmgoers* • See also **goer** at GO [ENERGY].

-go·ing /£-ˌgəʊ·ɪŋ, $-ˌgoʊ-/ *combining form* • -going means the activity of going to the stated place: *After years of decline caused by the video boom, cinema/movie-going is now enjoying a revival.* ○ *He grew up in a strict church-going family.* ○ *He's just bought himself an ocean-going yacht.*

go [MOVE] /£gəʊ, $goʊ/ *v* [I] he/she/it **goes**, **going**, *past simple* **went** /went/, *past part* **gone** /£gɒn, $gɑːn/ to be in the process of moving • *Don't get off the bus while it's going.* • *Can't we go any faster?* • *When I heard he'd left, I got on my bike and went* **after** (= followed to try to catch) *him.* • *(fig.) Are you planning to go* **after** (= to try to obtain) *Paul's job when he leaves?* • *We were going* (= moving) **along** *at about 50 miles an hour.* • *(fig.) We have a flexible approach to what we're doing that allows us to make any necessary changes as we go* **along** (= as we are doing the activity). • *There's a nasty flu bug going* **around/round/about** *(the school)* (= being passed from one person to another) *at the moment.* • *I wish she'd stop going* **around/round/about** (= moving between places) *telling everyone what to do.* • *We used to see a lot of each other, but we don't go* **around/round/about** (= spend time moving to places and doing things) **together** *much these days.* • *I don't want you going* **around/round/about** (= spending time moving to places and doing things) **with** *people like that.* • *(fig.) I've got a tune going* **around/round** (= I am continually hearing it) *in my head and I just can't remember the name of it.* • *Don't forget that the clocks go* **back** (= will be put one hour earlier in order to change to standard time in the autumn) *tonight.* • *You can watch the trains going* (= moving) **by** *from this window.* • *(fig.) You can't let an opportunity like that go* **by** (= pass) *– it's too good to miss.* • *(fig.) Several weeks had gone* **by** (= passed) *before I realized the necklace was missing.* • *(fig.) Hardly a day goes* **by** (= passes) *when I don't think about her.* • *(fig.) The house was a railway station in* **days** *gone* **by** (= in the past). • *She was going* (= moving) **down** *the road on her bike.* • *He's been a coal miner all his working life, and first went* **down** (= started working in) *the pits when he was 17.* • *On summer evenings we would sit on the verandah and watch the sun go* **down** (= move below the line between the sky and the land or sea). • *Could I have a glass of water to help these pills go* **down** (= help me swallow them). • *(fig.) He went* **down** *in my opinion* (= My opinion of him became lower) *when he started trying to be an actor as well as a singer.* • *The plane went* **down** (= fell to the ground because of an accident, bomb explosion, etc.) *ten minutes after take-off.* • *Three of our fighter planes have gone* **down** (= been shot so that they fell to the ground) *in enemy territory since the war began.* • *Everyone took to the lifeboats when the ship started to go* **down** (= sink). • *The museum houses a memorial to the 2000 sailors who went* **down with** *the Scharnhorst* (= died when that ship sank) *in 1943.* • *He went* **down on** *his knees* (= got into a position with his knees on the ground) *and begged for forgiveness.* • *Tomorrow will start cold but it should get warmer as the day goes* **on** (= continues or passes). • *As the evening went* **on** (= continued or passed) *it became clear that we should never have agreed to see each other again.* • *Trains go* **over** *the bridge to cross the river, but cars go* **through** *the tunnel.* • To go **through** something is to experience it: *The company has been going through considerable changes for the past three years.* ○ *I wouldn't like anyone else to go through what I've been through.* ○ *I've been going through a bad patch recently.* ○ *You'd think his children would be more sympathetic towards him after all he's been through* (= the many bad things he has experienced). • *Oil spurted into the air as the tanker went* **under** (= sank). • *The current was so strong that nothing could have prevented him from going* **under** (= sinking). • *(fig.) The government has refused any financial assistance to prevent the company from going* **under** (= completely failing financially). • *(fig.) The charity* *will go* **under** (=completely fail financially) *unless a generous donor can be found within the next few months.* • *I was going* (=moving) **up** *the stairs when the phone rang.* • *What goes* **up** (=rises) *must come down.* • *Interest rates have been* **up** (=risen) *as high as 15%.* • *The average cost of a new house in this area has gone* **up** (=increased) **by** *5%* **(to** *£60 000).* • If you say that (a period of) time goes, you mean it passes: *I had a wonderful weekend but it went awfully quickly.* ○ *Time seems to go faster as you get older.* ○ *There's only a week* **to go** *before* (=until) *my exam results come out.* ○ *There's still three months* **to go to** (=until) *his wedding, but he's already feeling nervous about it.* • *(esp. Br) We were really* **going it (some)** (=travelling very fast) *along the empty roads.* • If someone or an animal **goes to ground**/*(Br also)* **goes to earth**, they hide in order to escape from their enemies: *America's most wanted criminal is rumoured to have gone to ground in Mexico.* • If you **go with the crowd/the flow/the stream/the times**, you are ordinary and do or think the same things as other people: *George tends to go with the crowd, so we should be able to persuade him without much difficulty.* • A **go-between** is someone who delivers messages between people who are unable or unwilling to meet personally: *Her younger brother was the go-between for her and her secret lover.* ○ *The ambassador has offered to* **act as** *a go-between for the two countries involved in the conflict.*

go·ing /£ˈgəʊ·ɪŋ, $ˈgoʊ-/ *n* [U] • *Cambridge to Newcastle in four hours is good going* (=quick moving) *– you must have been driving flat out all the way.* • *The research is now in progress, but* **the** *going* (=starting and continuing with it) *has been slower than anticipated owing to a reduction in government funding.* • *She's obviously very intelligent, but her lectures are* **heavy** *going* (=they are difficult to understand). • *He found three 400 metre races in two days* **hard** *going* (=difficult). • *(esp. Am) The closures are the latest sign that US car makers could face* **rough** *going* (=difficult conditions) *for the rest of the year.* • *After an inch of rain at the racecourse overnight, the going* (=condition of the ground for racing on) *is described as good to soft.* • *Many people fear that the newly-elected government will be ousted in a military coup and are leaving their country* **while the going is good** (=while they have the opportunity). • *(saying)* 'When the going gets tough, the tough get going' means that when conditions become difficult, strong people take action. • See also **going** at GO LEAVE, GO OPERATE, GO BE SOLD.

go LEAVE /£gəʊ, $goʊ/ *v* he/she/it **goes**, **going**, *past simple* **went** /went/, *past part* **gone** /£gɒn, $gɑːn/ to leave a place, esp. in order to travel to somewhere else • *I don't think much of this play. Shall we go before it finishes?* [I] • *(esp. Br) What time does the last train to Bath go?* [I] • *Is it midnight already? I really must go/must be going.* [I] • *Just go* **away** *and leave me alone.* [I] • *She wasn't feeling well, so she went* **home** (=left where she was and travelled to her home) *early.* [I] • *I'm afraid he'll have to go* (=be dismissed from his job) *– he's far too inefficient to continue working for us.* [I] • *This carpet's terribly old and worn – it really will have to go* (=be got rid of). [I] • Sometimes go is used to avoid saying die: *She went peacefully in her sleep.* [I] • *(Br dated)* If you go **down (from** a college or university, esp. Oxford University or Cambridge University), you leave either permanently or for a holiday: *She published her first novel shortly after going down from Oxford in 1969.* [I] ○ *Are you planning to go down as soon as term finishes?* [I] • *Please would you close the door as you go* **out** (=leave the room). [I] • *She went* **out of** (=left) *the room with a smile on her face.* [I] • *I always go* **out** (=leave my home and travel to another place, esp. for entertainment) *on Saturday evenings.* [I] • *Do you fancy going* **out for** (=leaving your home and travelling to another place in order to have) *a meal after work?* [I] • *It's terribly smoky in here – I'm just going* **out for** (=leaving the room in order to get) *a breath of fresh air.* [I] • *He went* **out** (=left in order to do some) *shopping a couple of hours ago.* [I] • *I wish you'd spend more time at home instead of going* **out** (=leaving home in order to do some) *drinking with your friends every night.* [I] • *A few small boats were left stranded on the beach as the* **tide/sea** *went* **out** (=returned to a lower level and moved away from the beach). [I] • *(fig.) All the life and energy has gone out* **of** *her* (=left her) *since she lost her job.* [I] • *(fig. Br) England went* **out** (=lost) **(to** *France) in the second round of the championship.* [I] • To **go out** is to have a romantic and sometimes sexual relationship with someone else: *How long have you been going out* **with** *him?* ○ *They'd been going out* **(with each other/together)** *for almost five years before he moved in with her.* • *(Am)* In sports, if a team or person wins or loses a competition **going away**, they win or lose it by a lot of points, goals, etc.: *They seemed to score at will in the final period and the Knicks won going away.* • *(esp. Am)* If you ask for some food **to go** at a restaurant, you want it wrapped up so that you can take it away with you instead of eating it in the restaurant: *I'd like a cheeseburger and strawberry milk shake to go, please.* See also TAKEAWAY.

go·ing /£ˈgəʊ·ɪŋ, $ˈgoʊ-/ *n* [U] • *Your going will be a great disappointment to everyone who has had the pleasure of working with you.* • See also **going** at GO MOVE, GO OPERATE, GO BE SOLD.

gone /£gɒn, $gɑːn/ *adj* [after v] • *I don't know how she'll manage with both her parents gone* (=dead). • *Fortunately I'll be* **dead and** *gone long before the money runs out.* • *They did everything they could to save him, but he was already* **too far** *gone* (=too close to death) *when the ambulance arrived.* • *(infml) You were completely gone* (=very drunk) *when you got back from the pub last night. You must have had an awful lot to drink.* • If something is gone, there is none of it left: *All my money is gone and I have nothing to buy food with.* ○ *I can't believe all that milk is gone already – I only bought it yesterday.*

gon·er /£ˈgɒn·əʳ, $ˈgɑː·nɚ/ *n* [C usually sing] *infml* • A goner is a person or thing that has no chance of succeeding or continuing to live or exist: *I thought I was a goner when I saw that car heading towards me.* ○ *He was a goner when he messed up that Japanese contract – he was bound to lose his job after that.* ○ *Your bike's a goner, I'm afraid – there's no way that frame can be fixed.*

go LEAD /£gəʊ, $goʊ/ *v* [I always + adv/prep] he/she/it **goes**, **going**, *past simple* **went** /went/, *past part* **gone** /£gɒn, $gɑːn/ (of a road, path, etc.) to lead in a particular direction • *This road goes* **to** *Birmingham.* • *The path went* **through** *the wood.* • *A huge crack went* **from** *the top* **to** *the bottom of the wall.* • *The path going* **up to** *the back door is very muddy.* • *(fig.) This edition's rather out of date, and only goes* **up to** *1989* (=that is the most recent time that it covers). • If something goes a particular length, it is that long: *The tree's roots go down three metres.*

go BECOME /£gəʊ, $goʊ/ *v* he/she/it **goes**, **going**, *past simple* **went** /went/, *past part* **gone** /£gɒn, $gɑːn/ to become • *I always go red when I'm embarrassed.* [L only + adj] • *The idea of going grey doesn't bother me, but I'd hate to go bald.* [L only + adj] • *I think her father's going senile/blind/deaf.* [L only + adj] • *My parents'll go berserk when they find out I'm pregnant.* [L only + adj] • *We'd better eat these apples before they go* **bad/***(Br and Aus)* **off/***(Br)* **rotten**. [L only + adj] • *I'm fed up with this watch – it's gone* **wrong** *three times already this year.* [L only + adj] • *If anything goes* **wrong** *you can call our emergency hotline free of charge.* [L only + adj] • *Many companies are going bankrupt/out of business because of cripplingly high interest rates.* [L only + adj/I always + adv/prep] • *After 12 years of Republican presidents, the US went Democratic in 1992.* [L only + adj] • *(Br and Aus) One of my books has gone* **missing**. [L only + adj] • *The swelling's gone* **down** (=has got smaller), *but there's still a lot of bruising.* [I always + adv/prep] • *One of the tyres on my car has gone* **down** (=the air has gone out of it). [I always + adv/prep] • *The computer went* **down** (=stopped operating) *twice last week.* [I always + adv/prep] • *The sun went* **in** (=became hidden by clouds) *just as I'd settled down for an afternoon on the beach and it never came out again.* [I always + adv/prep] • To go **into** a state or condition is to start to be in it: *The new regulations will go* **into** *effect/force/action next year.* [I always + adv/prep] ○ *The new trains went* **into** *service last month.* [I always + adv/prep] ○ *The drug is still being tested and will not go* **into** *commercial production for at least two years.* [I always + adv/prep] ○ *Some of the fans seemed to go* **into** *a trance when she appeared on stage.* [I always + adv/prep] • *The lights went* **off** (=stopped operating) *in several villages because of the storm.* [I always + adv/prep] • *It's best to set the video so that it goes* **off** (=stops operating) *five minutes after the programme is scheduled to finish.* [I always + adv/prep] • *The pain's going* **off** (=is becoming less strong) *a bit now.* [I always + adv/prep] • *This bacon smells a bit funny – do you think it's gone* **off** (=become decayed so that it is no longer pleasant or safe to eat). [I always + adv/prep] • *That milk will go* **off** (=become sour and no longer pleasant to drink) *if you don't put it back in the fridge.* [I always + adv/prep] • *(Br) That newspaper's really gone* **off** (=become lower in quality) *since they got that new editor.* [I always + adv/prep] • *(Br) The film starts well, but goes* **off** (= becomes lower in quality) *after the first half-hour.* [I always + adv/prep] • To go **off** is also to stop liking: *I went off beefburgers after I got food poisoning from one.* [I always + adv/prep] ○ *She used to be really keen on tennis, but she's gone off it since she left school.* [I always + adv/prep] ○ *He went off skiing after he broke his leg.* [I always + adv/prep] ○ *I went off Peter when he said those dreadful things about Clare.* [I always + adv/prep] • *The spotlights go* **on** (= start operating) *automatically when an intruder is detected in the garden.* [I always + adv/prep] • *My doctor says I must go* (= start to be) **on** *a diet.* [I always + adv/prep] • *Special chemicals prevent cigarettes from going* **out** (= stopping burning) *once they're lit.* [I always + adv/prep] • *Everyone screamed when the lights went* **out** (= stopped giving light). [I always + adv/prep] • *He's always using old-fashioned words that went* **out** (= became old-fashioned) *years ago.* [I always + adv/prep] • *Records were rapidly going* **out** (= becoming no longer used) *and being replaced by CDs.* [I always + adv/prep] • *I normally go* **to** *sleep* (= start to sleep) *as soon as I get into bed.* [I always + adv/prep] • *Are the two countries likely to go* **to** *war* (= start to fight a war) *over this dispute.* [I always + adv/prep] • *She hates to see good food go* **to** *waste* (= be wasted). [I always + adv/prep] • *A new factory is going* **up** (= being built) *on the old airport.* [I always + adv/prep] • *He described the new regulations as bureaucracy* **gone mad** (= become out of control).

go BE /£gəʊ, $goʊ/ *v* he/she/it **goes**, **going**, *past simple* **went** /went/, *past part* **gone** /£gɒn, $gɑːn/ to be or stay in a particular, esp. unpleasant, condition • *In spite of the relief effort, thousands of people continue to go hungry.* [L only + adj] • *Why do so many rapes go unreported?* [L only + adj] • *It wasn't a bad hospital,* **as** *hospitals go* (= compared with the usual standard of hospitals), *but I still hated being there.* [I] • *"The cook was a good cook, as cooks go; and as cooks go she went"* (Saki in *Reginald on Besetting Sins,* 1904)

go WEAKEN /£gəʊ, $goʊ/ *v* [I] he/she/it **goes**, **going**, *past simple* **went** /went/, *past part* **gone** /£gɒn, $gɑːn/ to become weak or damaged, esp. from being used (too much), or to stop working • *After a gruelling six months singing on a world tour, it is hardly surprising that her voice is starting to go.* • *I really must get a new jacket – this one's starting to go in the elbows.* • *Her hearing is going, but otherwise she's remarkably fit for a 95-year-old.* • *Can you get a 60-watt bulb while you're out? The one in the hall has just gone* (= stopped working).

go START /£gəʊ, $goʊ/ *v* [I] he/she/it **goes**, **going**, *past simple* **went** /went/, *past part* **gone** /£gɒn, $gɑːn/ to start doing or using something • *I'll just connect up the printer to the computer and then we'll be ready to go.* • *We really must* **get** *going* **with** *these proposals or they'll never be ready for the meeting.*

go OPERATE /£gəʊ, $goʊ/ *v* [I] he/she/it **goes**, **going**, *past simple* **went** /went/, *past part* **gone** /£gɒn, $gɑːn/ to operate (in the right way) • *Have you any idea why this watch won't go?* • *Can you help me get my car going?* • *I'm not saying anything as long as your tape recorder is going* (= recording). • *Our company has been going* (= has been in business) *for twenty years.* • If you **go it alone**, you do something without other people: *He's decided to leave the band and go it alone as a singer.* • *(Br and Aus)* To **go slow** is to work more slowly and with less effort than usual to try to persuade an employer to agree to higher pay or better working conditions or arrangements: *Union leaders are advising their members to go slow instead of recommending an all-out strike.* ○ *The two week* **go-slow** *(Am* **slowdown***)* (= act of working slowly) *at the factory has ended after unions agreed a new pay deal with the management.*

go·ing /£'gəʊ·ɪŋ, $'goʊ-/ *adj* [before n; not gradable] • *We hope to avoid any job losses by selling the factory as a going* **concern** (= successful business that will continue to operate). • See also **going** at GO MOVE, GO LEAVE, GO BE SOLD.

go *(obj)* NOISE /£gəʊ, $goʊ/ *v* he/she/it **goes**, **going**, *past simple* **went** /went/, *past part* **gone** /£gɒn, $gɑːn/ to produce (a noise) • *I wish my computer would stop going 'beep' whenever I do something wrong.* [T no passive] • *Crash went the plates as they fell on the floor.* [T no passive] • *Turn down the music for a moment – I think I heard the doorbell go* (= ring) *just now.* [I] • *Ducks go* (= make the noise) *'quack'.* [T no passive] • *(infml)* Go can sometimes mean say, esp. when a story is being told: *"I never want to see you ever again," he goes, and storms out of the house.* [+ clause]

go MOVE BODY /£gəʊ, $goʊ/ *v* [I always + adv/prep] he/she/it **goes**, **going**, *past simple* **went** /went/, *past part* **gone** /£gɒn, $gɑːn/ to move a part of the body in a particular way or the way that is shown • *Can you move your foot at all? Try going backwards and forwards.* • *Go* **like this** *(***with** *your hand) to show that you're turning left.* • *When she showed me what to do, she went* **like so** *first, but I can't remember what she did next.*

go DIVIDE /£gəʊ, $goʊ/ *v* [I not *be going*] he/she/it **goes**, *past simple* **went** /went/, *past part* **gone** /£gɒn, $gɑːn/ (of a number) to fit (into another number) esp. resulting in a whole number • *Does 3 go* **into** *12?* • *3 goes* **into** *12 four times.* • *5* **into** *11 won't go.* • *5 goes* **into** *11 twice with 1 left over.* • *"Divide 5 by 11." "I can't – it won't go* (= it will not fit resulting in a whole number)."

go SITUATE /£gəʊ, $goʊ/ *v* [I always + adv/prep; not *be going*] he/she/it **goes**, *past simple* **went** /went/, *past part* **gone** /£gɒn, $gɑːn/ to be put in a particular place, esp. as the usual place • *The sofa went* **against** *that wall before we had the radiator put in.* • *The TV would go nicely* **in** *that corner, wouldn't it?* • *I'll put it all away if you tell me* **where** *everything goes.*

go HAPPEN /£gəʊ, $goʊ/ *v* [I always + adv/prep] he/she/it **goes**, **going**, *past simple* **went** /went/, *past part* **gone** /£gɒn, $gɑːn/ to happen or be found habitually or typically with each other or another • *Wisdom and maturity don't necessarily go* **together**. • *Researchers have discovered that short-sightedness and high IQs seem to go* **together** *in children.* • *Prostitution often goes* **with** *drug addiction.* • *She knows all about the health problems that go* **with** *smoking.* • *Great wealth often goes* **hand in hand with** *meanness.*

go BE SOLD /£gəʊ, $goʊ/ *v* [I] he/she/it **goes**, **going**, *past simple* **went** /went/, *past part* **gone** /£gɒn, $gɑːn/ to be sold or be available • *The shop is having a closing-down sale – everything must go.* • *The painting is expected to go* **for** *at least a million dollars.* • *They were asking £60 000 for their house, but in the end it went* **for** *£55 000.* • *Things sold at auctions go* **to the highest bidder**. • *I bought a lot of cheese that was going* **cheap**. • *"Going... going... gone!* (= Sold!)*" said the auctioneer, banging down the hammer.* • *I don't suppose there's any left-over pie going* (= available), *is there?* • If someone or something has something going **for** them, that thing causes them to have a lot of advantages and to be successful: *They've got a happy marriage, brilliant careers and wonderful children – in fact they've got* **everything** *going for them.* ○ *Just remember you've got* **a lot** *going for you, so make the most of your opportunities while you can.* ○ *This film is dreadful – it has absolutely* **nothing** *going for it* (= nothing good about it).

go·ing /£'gəʊ·ɪŋ, $'goʊ-/ *adj* [after n; not gradable] • *She's just bought herself one of the most expensive TVs going.* • *I wouldn't trust him if I were you – he's the biggest crook going* (= he's the most dishonest person that exists). • See also **going** at GO MOVE, GO LEAVE, GO OPERATE.

go BE EXPRESSED /£gəʊ, $goʊ/ *v* [not *be going*] he/she/it **goes**, *past simple* **went** /went/, *past part* **gone** /£gɒn, $gɑːn/ to be expressed, sung or played • *I can never remember* **how** *that song goes.* [I always + adv/prep] • *"Doesn't it go something* **like** *this?" said Joan, and played the first couple of bars on her guitar.* [I always + adv/prep] • *The story goes* (= People say) **that** *he was sacked after he was caught stealing company property.* [+ *(that)* clause] • *A headless ghost walks the castle at night – or* **so** *the story goes* (= so people say). [after *so*] • If a story is going **around/round/about**, it is being discussed generally: *I've heard that joke before – it's being going around for ages.* ○ *There are* **rumours** *going around* **that** *the company is going to sack half its workforce.* ○ **It's** *going around* **that** *they're having an affair.* [+ *that* clause] • See also GO ABOUT; GO ROUND.

go BE ACCEPTABLE /£gəʊ, $goʊ/ *v* [I not *be going*] he/she/it **goes**, *past simple* **went** /went/, *past part* **gone** /£gɒn, $gɑːn/ to look or be acceptable or suitable • *That picture would go* **well** *on the wall in the living room.* • *If I wear the orange hat with the blue dress, do you think it will go?* • *Do you think the orange hat and the blue dress go* **together**? • *I'm not sure that this orange hat really goes* **with** *this blue dress.* • *This wine goes particularly well* **with** *seafood.* • *Just remember that I'm the boss and what I say goes* (= you have to accept what I say). • *My parents don't worry too much about what I get up to, and most of the time* **anything** *goes*

(=I can do what I want). • *He blamed the ever-increasing crime rate on the media and the* **'anything** *goes' attitudes of the sixties.* • *"Anything Goes"* (title of a song written by Cole Porter, 1934)

go·ing /£'gəʊ·ɪŋ, $'goʊ-/ *adj* [before n; not gradable] • *What's the going* **rate** (=What are people usually paid) *for this kind of work?* • *The going* (=usual or average) **rate** *for pay increases is currently around 3%.* • See also **going** at GO MOVE, GO LEAVE, GO BE SOLD.

go BE KNOWN /£gəʊ, $goʊ/ *v* [I always + adv/prep] he/she/it **goes going**, *past simple* **went** /went/, *past part* **gone** /£gɒn, $gɑːn/ to be known (by a particular name) • *He had a scruffy old teddy bear which went* **by** *the name of Augustus.* • *In Britain, this flour usually goes* **under** *the name of maize meal.* • *The campaign goes* **under** *the slogan 'Sometimes You've Gotta Break the Rules'.*

go DEVELOP /£gəʊ, $goʊ/ *v* [I always + adv/prep] he/she/it **goes**, **going**, *past simple* **went** /went/, *past part* **gone** /£gɒn, $gɑːn/ to develop or happen • *"How did the interview go?" "It went very* **well**, *thanks."* • *Things have gone badly* **for** *him since his business collapsed.*

go BASE /£gəʊ, $goʊ/ *v* [I always + adv/prep] he/she/it **goes**, **going**, *past simple* **went** /went/, *past part* **gone** /£gɒn, $gɑːn/ to base an opinion, decision, judgment or action (on something) • *What do you go* **by** *when you're deciding whether or not to employ someone?* • *I'm only going* **on** *what I overheard him saying to Frank, but I think he's planning to leave next month.* • *The investigation has only just started, so the police haven't got much to go* **on** *at the moment.* • **If** *past experience* **is anything** *to go* **by**, *he'll completely ignore our suggestions.*

go BE TRUE /£gəʊ, $goʊ/ *v* [I] he/she/it **goes going**, *past simple* **went** /went/, *past part* **gone** /£gɒn, $gɑːn/ **go to prove/show** to prove that (something) is true • *The threats of some owners to drown their dogs* **just** *go to prove* **that** *they are unfit to care for them.* • *Your daughter's attitude* **only** *goes to prove how much society has changed over the last 30 years.*

go OPPORTUNITY /£gəʊ, $goʊ/, *Am usually, Aus also* **turn** *n* [C] *pl* **goes** an opportunity to play in a game, or to do or use something • *Hey, it's Ken's go now! You've just had your go.* • *You carry on playing while I make some coffee and I'll just miss a couple of goes.* • *Please can I* **have a** *go* (=can I ride) *on your bike?* • *I'll* **have a go at** *driving for a while if you're tired.* • *(Br)* If you **have a go at** someone, you criticize them: *My Dad's always having a go at me about getting a proper job.*

go /£gəʊ, $goʊ/ *v* [I] he/she/it **goes**, **going**, *past simple* **went** /went/, *past part* **gone** /£gɒn, $gɑːn/ • *You can't go without shaking the dice.*

go ATTEMPT /£gəʊ, $goʊ/, *Am usually, Aus also* **try** *n* [C] *pl* **goes** an attempt to do something • *Georgina passed her driving test* **(on** *her) first go.* • *"This jar is impossible to open." "Here, let me* **have** *a go."* • *I want to* **have a go at** *finish***ing** *my essay tonight.* • *We can't do it* **all in one** *go* (= all at the same time) – *we'll have to divide it up into stages.* • *These criminals are extremely dangerous, and we would strongly advise members of the public not to* **have a go (at** *them)* (=try to catch them or stop them from committing a crime). • If you **make a go of** something, you are successful at it: *She's really making a go of her new antique shop.* ○ *I can't see him ever making a go of accountancy.*

go ENERGY /£gəʊ, $goʊ/ *n* [U] the condition of being energetic and active • *You're full of go this morning.* • *He doesn't have much go about him, does he?* • A **go-getter** is someone who is very energetic, determined to be successful and able to deal with new or difficult situations easily: *We only recruit go-getters who will be actively involved in the company's development.* ○ *He's a* **go-getting** *high-powered business manager.* • If something is **go-go**, it is energetic, modern and fashionable: *The charity is trying to develop a go-go image that will take it into the future.* ○ *(fig.) They made a fortune during the go-go years* (=years of active development) *of the stock market.* • A **go-go dancer** or **go-go girl** performs in places such as bars, dancing energetically to modern music with a strong beat, often in a sexually exciting manner and while wearing very little clothing: *We ended up in a sleazy nightclub full of middle-aged men leering drunkenly at go-go dancers.* • See also GET-UP-AND-GO.

go·er /£'gəʊ·əʳ, $'goʊ·ɚ/ *n* [C] *infml* • A goer is an energetic person, esp. one who is sexually active with a lot of people: *We should have invited a few more goers to liven the party up a bit.* ○ *Pat and Chris were real goers before they got married.* • If you describe a car as a goer, you mean that it can move very quickly: *My car's not much of a goer, but it's comfortable and reliable.* • See also **-goer** at GO TRAVEL.

go a·bout *(obj) v prep* (to begin) to do (something) • *Of course we're anxious to help, but we're not sure what's the best way of going about it.* [T] • *How can we go about solving this problem?* [+ v-ing] • When you go about your **business** or your work, you continue with it in the usual way: *In spite of last night's terrorist attack most people seem to be going about their business as if nothing had happened.* [T]

go a·gainst *obj v prep* [T] to oppose or disagree with (something) • *Public opinion is going against the government on this issue.* • *What you're asking me to do goes against everything I believe in.* • *He's always going against his father's advice* (=doing things that his father advised him not to do). • *The vote went against her* (=She lost the vote).

go a·head *v adv* [I] to continue (with an action or plan of action), esp. after a period when nothing has happened, or to begin to do something • *We've received permission to go ahead* **with** *the music festival in spite of opposition from local residents.* • *The festival is now going ahead as planned.* • *I got so fed up with waiting for him to do it that I just went ahead and did it myself in the end.* • *All the preparations are complete, but we can't go ahead without more government money.* • *"Could I ask you a rather personal question?" "Of course, go ahead."*

go–a·head /£'gəʊ·ə·hed, $'goʊ-/ *n* [U] • *The government has* **given the** *go-ahead* (=given permission) *for a multi-billion pound road-building project.* • *We're ready to start but we're still waiting to* **get/receive the** *go-ahead from our head office.* • *No official go-ahead has yet been* **given to** *begin the study.* [+ *to* infinitive]

go–a·head /£'gəʊ·ə·hed, $'goʊ-/ *adj Br and Aus* • To be go-ahead is to be enthusiastic about using new inventions and modern methods of doing things: *I went to a very go-ahead school which had all the latest computer equipment.* ○ *We have a flexitime system and crèche facilities and like to think of ourselves as a go-ahead employer.*

go a·long with *obj v adv prep* [T] to agree with, accept or support (something) • *Kate's already agreed, but it's going to be harder persuading Mike to go along with it.* • *They are unlikely to go along with the scheme voluntarily.*

go back on *obj v adv prep* [T] to fail to keep (a promise), or to change (a decision or agreement) • *Gary's hopelessly unreliable and always goes back on his promises.* • *The government looks likely to go back on its decision to close the mines.* • *She's gone back on her word and decided not to give me the job after all.*

go by *obj v prep* [T no passive] to follow or be shown the way by (something) • *I'm sorry, madam, but we have to go by the rules.* • *We went by the lights of the village in the distance to find our way back to the car.*

go down BE REMEMBERED *v adv* [I always + adv/prep] to be remembered or recorded (in a particular way) • *Hurricane Hugo will go down* **in** *the record books* **as** *the costliest storm ever faced by insurers.*

go down BE RECEIVED, **go o·ver** *v adv* [I always + adv/prep] to be received (in a particular way) • *"I think my speech went down rather* **well**, *don't you?" "It would've gone down better if you'd left out those appalling jokes."* • *In spite of going down* **badly with** *the critics, the film has been a tremendous commercial success.*

go down LOSE *v adv* [I] to lose or be defeated • *England's unbeaten run of ten games ended last night when they went down 4-2 to France.* • *Dictators like him rarely go down without a fight.*

go down HAPPEN *v adv* [I] *infml* to happen • *I tried warning Andy about what was going down, but he wouldn't take me seriously.*

go down on *obj v adv prep* [T] *infml* to excite the sexual organs of (someone) with the mouth, lips or tongue

go for *obj* TRY *v prep* [T] to try to have or achieve (something) • *She tripped me as I went for the ball.* • *Are you planning to go for that scholarship to Harvard University?* • *The Russian relay team will again be going for the gold medal at the Olympic Games.* • *If you want something,* **go for it** (=do anything you have to to obtain it). • *Vicki never worried or hesitated about anything, she just* **went for it** *and did whatever she had to do.*

go for *obj* CHOOSE *v prep* [T] to choose • *Instead of butter, I always go for a margarine high in polyunsaturates or a low-fat spread.* • *Many small investors go for the safety of savings accounts.* • *If I were offered the choice between a* *higher salary and a longer contract, I know which one I'd go for.*

go for *obj* LIKE *v prep* [T] to like or admire • *I don't go for war films in a big way.* • *Most borrowers of library books go for romance, mystery and crime.* • *What sort of men do you go for* (= are you attracted to)*?*

go for *obj* BE TRUE FOR *v prep* [T] to be true for or relate to • *You really need to smarten up your appearance, Chris, and I don't know what you lot are smiling about, because the same goes for the rest of you.* • *What Mary's just said goes for me too* (= I agree with what she said).

go in for *(obj)* ENJOY *v adv prep* to do (something) regularly, or to enjoy (something) • *I've never really gone in for classical music, but I love jazz.* [T] • *Have you ever considered going in for medicine* (= becoming a doctor)*?* [T] • *She really goes in for travel***ling** *and sight-see***ing**. [+ v-*ing*]

go into *obj v prep* [T] to discuss, examine, describe or explain (something) in a detailed or careful way • *This is the first book to go into her personal life as well as her work.* • *I'd rather not go into that now. Can we discuss it later?* • *Every aspect of the bank's collapse will be gone into thoroughly by the government investigators.* • *I'm unable to go into* **detail(s)** *at this stage because I still have very little information about how the accident happened.*

go much on *(obj) v adv prep* [always in negatives and questions] *Br infml* to like • *I don't go much on French food – I'd far rather have something Italian.* [T] • *He's never gone much on cycl***ing** *– he's always preferred to walk everywhere.* [+ v-*ing*]

gone /£gɒn, $gɑːn/ *adj* [after v; always + *on*] • *Nicky's really gone* **on** *Marty* (= likes Marty a lot).

go off EXPLODE *v adv* [I] to explode or (of a gun) to fire bullets • *A local radio station received an anonymous warning twenty minutes before the* **bomb** *went off.* • *His gun went off accidentally as he was climbing over a fence.* • If a noise-making device goes off, it starts to ring loudly or make a loud noise: *The* **alarm** *should go off automatically as soon as smoke is detected.* ○ *Didn't you hear your* **alarm clock** *going off this morning?* ○ *The ambulance's* **siren** *was going off.*

go off HAPPEN *v adv* [I always + adv/prep] to happen • *The negotiations went off rather badly at first, but things gradually improved.* • *The protest march went off peacefully with only two arrests.*

go off with *obj* TAKE *v adv prep* [T] to take (something) without obtaining permission from the owner first • *I do wish you'd stop going off with my car without asking me beforehand.*

go off with *obj* LEAVE *v adv prep* [T] to leave a wife, husband or partner in order to have a sexual or romantic relationship with (someone else) • *Did you know that Hugh had gone off with his sister-in-law?*

go on HAPPEN *v adv* [I] to happen • *I'm sure we never hear about a lot of what goes on in government.* • *What on earth's been going on here? This room looks like a bomb's hit it!* • *This war's been going on for years and there seems to be no way of ending it.*

go·ings–on /£ˌgəʊ·ɪŋz'ɒn, $ˌgoʊ·ɪŋz'ɑːn/ *pl n* • Goings-on are strange, unusual, amusing or unsuitable events or activities: *There've been a lot of* **strange/odd** *goings-on in that house recently.* ○ *It was absolute chaos when the Queen visited our school – I've never seen such goings-on.*

go on CONTINUE *v adv* to continue • *"What happened next is very hard to explain." "Please go on if you can."* [I] • *You smoke and drink too much and you can't go on like that indefinitely.* [I] • *Please go on* **with** *what you're doing and don't let us interrupt you.* [I] • *She paused to light another cigarette and then went on* **with** *her account of the accident.* [I] • *We really can't go on liv***ing** *like this – we'll have to find a bigger house.* [+ v-*ing*] • *"What I want more than anything else," he went on, "is a house in the country with a large garden for the children to play in."* [+ clause] • *She admitted her company's responsibility for the disaster and went on* **to** *explain how compensation would be paid to the victims.* [+ *to* infinitive] • *What proportion of people who are HIV-positive go on* **to** *develop* (= later develop) *AIDS?* [+ *to* infinitive] • *If you go on* (= continue behaving) *like this you won't have any friends left at all.* • *"I just wish he'd stop going on* (= talking all the time) **about** *how brilliant his daughter is." "Yes, he does go on* **(a bit)**, *doesn't he?"* • *I wish you'd stop going on* **at** (= criticizing repeatedly) *me about my haircut.*

go on PLEASE DO *v adv* [I always in orders] used when encouraging or asking someone to do something • *Go on, have another drink.* • *"Are you sure you don't want another slice of cake?" "Oh go on then, but just a small one."* • *"I don't really feel like seeing a film tonight." "Oh go on. We haven't been to the cinema for ages."*

go on NOT BELIEVE *exclamation* used when you do not believe someone • *"You know Mary just inherited a million pounds?" "Go on* **(with you)**!*"*

go o·ver *obj* EXAMINE *v prep* [T] to examine or look at (something) in a careful or detailed way • *Forensic scientists are going over the victim's flat in a search for clues about the murderer.* • *Guards go over every vehicle at the border to prevent drugs being smuggled into the country.* • *Remember to go over your essay checking for grammar and spelling mistakes before you hand it in to me.* • *Would you mind going over this form with me to see I've filled it in right?* • *Don't sign anything until you have gone over it thoroughly.* • *I've been over the problem several times, but I can't think of a solution.*

go·ing–o·ver /£'gəʊ·ɪŋˌəʊ·vəʳ, $'goʊ·ɪŋˌoʊ·vɚ/ *n* [C usually sing] *pl* **goings-over** /£'gəʊ·ɪŋzˌəʊ·vəʳ, $'goʊ·ɪnzˌoʊ·vɚ/ • *Detectives have given the flat a thorough going-over* (= examined it carefully). • A going-over is also an activity such as cleaning that is done carefully and completely: *This carpet's filthy! It needs a really good going-over.*

go o·ver *obj* STUDY *v prep* [T] to study or explain (something) • *I always go over my revision notes just before I go into an exam.* • *I've gone over these lines again and again but I still keep forgetting them.* • *Could you go over the main points of your argument again, Professor?*

go o·ver BE RECEIVED *v adv* [I always + adv/prep] to GO DOWN BE RECEIVED

go o·ver *obj* ATTACK *v prep* [T] to attack (someone) violently • *The burglars went over him* **with** *a cricket bat and left him for dead.*

go·ing–o·ver /£'gəʊ·ɪŋˌəʊ·vəʳ, $'goʊ·ɪŋˌoʊ·vɚ/ *n* [C] *pl* **goings-over** /£'gəʊ·ɪŋzˌəʊ·vəʳ, $'goʊ·ɪŋzˌoʊ·vɚ/ • *They said I'd get a real going-over if I didn't pay them by tomorrow.* • *(fig.) My mum gave me a good going-over* (= strongly criticized me) *when I dyed my hair pink.*

go round, go a·round *v adv* [I] to be enough for everyone • *There won't be enough soup to go round if you fill your bowl right to the top.*

go through *obj* USE *v prep* [T] to use (something that cannot be used again) • *Before I gave up smoking I was going through 40 cigarettes a day.* • *I went through a hundred quid on my last trip to London.*

go through BE ACCEPTED *v adv* [I] to be officially accepted or approved • *A council spokeswoman said that the proposals for the new shopping centre were unlikely to go through.*

go through *obj* PRACTISE *v prep* [T] to do (something) in order to practise or as a test • *The director wants us to go through the whole of the third act before we go home.* • *I'd like you to go through that manoeuvre again and then bring the car to a halt next to the kerb.*

go through *obj* EXAMINE *v prep* [T] to examine ((something which contains) a collection of things) carefully in order to organize them or find something • *I'm going through my wardrobe and throwing out all the clothes I don't wear any more.* • *I went through everything but I couldn't find that letter you sent me.* • *Remember to go through the pockets before you put those trousers in the washing machine.*

go through with *obj v adv prep* [T] to do (something unpleasant or difficult that has already been agreed or promised) • *He'd threatened to divorce her but I never thought he'd go through with it.* • *When the auctioneer's hammer falls, the buyer is legally obliged to go through with the deal.* • *The company has decided not to go through with the takeover of its smaller rival.*

go to·geth·er *v adv* [I] *infml* (of two people) to have a romantic and often sexual relationship with each other • *Maria and Francis have been going together for over five years – do you think they'll get married?*

go up *v adv* [I] to burn fiercely or explode • *Several refugee hostels have gone up* **(in flames)** *during firebomb attacks by right-wing extremists.* • *There's a gas leak and the whole building could go up at any moment.*

go with *obj* RELATIONSHIP *v prep* [T no passive] to have sex or a sexual relationship with (someone) • *Did he ever go with anyone else while they were living together?* • *How long has she been going with him?*

go with *obj* ACCEPT *v prep* [T] to accept (an idea) or agree with (a person) • *I think we can go with the advertising* *agency's suggestions, don't you?* • *Your first proposal was fine, but I can't go with you* **on** *this one – it's much more expensive.*

go with·out *(obj) v adv, v prep* to not have (something) or to manage to live despite not having (something) • *If you don't want fish then you'll just have to go without (your dinner).* [I/T] • *She's always in a bad mood when she's gone without sleep.* [T] • *I'd rather go without food than work for him.* [T] • *He had to learn to go without drink***ing** *while he was in Saudi Arabia.* [+ v-*ing*]

goad *obj* /£gəʊd, $goʊd/ *v* [T] to make a person or an animal do something or encourage them to do it by frequently annoying, upsetting or pushing them • *Will the pressure applied by environmentalists be enough to goad the industrialized nations* **into** *us***ing** *less fossil fuels?* • *As a manager, he has an undoubted ability to goad his staff* **to** *ever greater efforts.* • *She was trying to goad him* **to** *buy her a champagne cocktail.* [+ obj + *to* infinitive] • *He refused to be goaded by their insults.* • *The team were goaded* **on** *by their desire to be first to complete the course.* • To goad is also to laugh at or intentionally annoy someone in an unkind way: *A group of children were goading another child in the school playground.*

goad /£gəʊd, $goʊd/ *n* [C] • *The thought of exams next week is a great goad to the students to work hard.*

goal [GAME] /£gəʊl, $goʊl/ *n* [C] (in some sports, such as football or HOCKEY) a point scored when a player gets the ball into an area, usually marked by two posts with a net fixed behind them, on the playing field, or this area itself • *Brazil won by three goals to one.* • *Only one goal was* **scored** *in the entire match.* • *The game was won on a* **penalty** *goal.* • *Black kicked/headed the ball* **into/towards** *the goal.* • *Lanzo kicked the ball high and it went over the goal and into the crowd.* • *(Br) Who is playing* **in** *goal* (= is the player who tries to prevent the other team from scoring goals) *for Milan this evening?* • *For many years, he* **kept** *goal* (= was the player who tries to prevent the other team from scoring goals) *for England.* • A **goal line** is the line between the two posts that mark the goal, over which the ball must pass if a point is to be scored. Compare BYLINE.

goal·less /£'gəʊl·ləs, $'goʊl-/ *adj* [not gradable] • Goalless means no goals were scored: *The match ended in a goalless draw.*

goal [AIM] /£gəʊl, $goʊl/ *n* [C] an aim or purpose • *Our goal is for the country to be fully independent within two years.* • *The department's main goal is to reduce the amount of illegal drugs entering the country.* • *They have set themselves a series of goals to achieve by the end of the month.* • *Do you think I'll be able to* **achieve** *my goal* **of** *losing 5 kilos before the summer?*

goal·keep·er /£'gəʊl,kiː·pəʳ, $'goʊl,kiː·pɚ/, *Am* **goal·tend·er**, *infml* **goal·ie** /£'gəʊ·li, $'goʊ-/, **keep·er** *n* [C] the player who stands in the team's goal to try to stop the other team from scoring • [PIC> **Sports**

goal·mouth /£'gəʊl·maʊθ, $'goʊl-/ *n* [C] the area near to and in front of the goal • *There was a lot of goalmouth action in this thrilling final.* • *The ball passed right across the front of the goalmouth, but no one could get a touch on it to score.*

goal·post /£'gəʊl·pəʊst, $'goʊl·poʊst/, **up·right**, **post** *n* [C] one of the two vertical posts, often painted white, which are connected with a CROSSBAR to form a goal • [PIC> **Sports**

goal·scor·er *esp. Br* /£'gəʊl,skɔː·rəʳ, $'goʊl,skɔːr·ɚ/, *Am usually* **scor·er** *n* [C] a person who scores points or goals for their team in games such as football • *Matthew Le Tissier was Southampton's* **leading/top** *goalscorer that season.*

goal·scor·ing *esp. Br* /£'gəʊl,skɔː·rɪŋ, $'goʊl,skɔːr·ɪŋ/, *Am usually* **scor·ing** *n* [U] • *Jones missed a very simple goalscoring* **opportunity/chance** *in the last seconds of the game.*

goal·tend·er /£'gəʊl,ten·dəʳ, $'goʊl,ten·dɚ/ *n* [C] the person who stands in goal in **ice hockey** (= a game played by two teams on ice) and tries to stop the opposing team from scoring, or *Am for* GOALKEEPER. • *The goaltender wears a lot of protective clothing, including a face-mask, to prevent serious injuries on the ice.*

go·an·na /£gəʊ'æn·ə, $goʊ-/ *n* [C] a type of large LIZARD (= an animal which produces eggs and uses the heat of the sun to keep its body warm) which is common in Australia

goat [ANIMAL] /£gəʊt, $goʊt/ *n* [C] an animal which is related to sheep, which usually has horns, and which lives wild on mountains or is kept on farms to provide milk, meat, wool etc. • *goat's milk* • *goat/goat's cheese* • *(Br infml) Stop* **acting/playing the goat** (= behaving in a silly way)*!* • *(infml) That sort of attitude really* **gets** *her* **goat**/*(Aus)* **gets (on)** *her* **goat** (= annoys her greatly).

goat [MAN] /£gəʊt, $goʊt/ *n* [C] *infml dated usually disapproving* a man who is very active sexually, or would like to be and makes it obvious • *He's a sly* **old** *goat.*

goat·ee /£'gəʊ·tiː, $'goʊ-/ *n* [C] a small pointed BEARD (= the hair on the lower part of a man's face) grown on the middle but not the sides of the lower part of the face

goat·herd /£'gəʊt·hɜːd, $'goʊt·hɜːrd/ *n* [C] a person who takes care of a FLOCK (= group) of goats

goat·skin /£'gəʊt·skɪn, $'goʊt-/ *n* [C/U] the skin of a single goat, or leather made from the skin

gob [MOUTH] /£gɒb, $gɑːb/ *n* [C] *esp. Br and Aus slang* a mouth • *He was stuffing his gob full of chips.* • *You'd better* **keep** *your gob* **shut** (= not say anything) *about what happened.*

gob [EXCRETE] /£gɒb, $gɑːb/ *v* [I] **-bb-** *Br and Aus slang* to SPIT (= push out what is held in the mouth), usually SALIVA (= the liquid made in the mouth) • *Don't gob in the street!*

gob·bet /£'gɒb·ɪt, $'gɑː·bɪt/ *n* [C] *infml* a small piece or lump of something, esp. food

gob·ble *(obj)* [EAT] /£'gɒb·l̩, $'gɑː·bl̩/ *v infml* to eat (food) too fast • *Don't gobble, you'll give yourself indigestion!* [I] • *She gobbled her dinner* **(down/up)** *– she must have been very hungry.* [T/M] • *(fig.) The mounting legal costs quickly gobbled* **up** (= used) *their savings.* [M]

gob·ble [MAKE NOISE] /£'gɒb·l̩, $'gɑː·bl̩/ *v* [I] to make the sound of a male TURKEY (= a large bird)

gob·ble·de·gook, **gob·ble·dy·gook** /£'gɒb·l̩.di·guːk, $'gɑː·bl̩-/ *n* [U] *infml disapproving* language, esp. used in official letters, forms and statements, which seems difficult or meaningless because you do not understand it • *This computer manual is complete gobbledegook.*

gob·let /£'gɒb·lət, $'gɑː·blət/ *n* [C] *esp. old use* a container from which drink, esp. wine, is drunk, usually made of glass or metal, and with a stem and a base but no handles

gob·lin /£'gɒb·lɪn, $'gɑː·blɪn/ *n* [C] (in stories) a small, usually ugly, creature which is harmful to humans • See also HOBGOBLIN. • [PIC> **Imaginary creatures**

gob·smacked /£'gɒb·smækt, $'gɑːb-/ *adj Br infml* shocked by surprise • *He was gobsmacked when he heard of the redundancies.*

gob·stop·per *Br* /£'gɒb,stɒp·əʳ, $'gɑːb,stɑː·pɚ/, *Am* **jaw·break·er** *n* [C] a large round hard sweet which often has different coloured layers

god [SPIRIT], *female also* **god·dess** /£gɒd, $gɑːd, £'gɒd·es, $'gɑː·des/ *n* [C] a spirit or being believed to control some part of the universe or life and often worshipped for doing so, or a representation of the being • *Aphrodite was the ancient Greek goddess* **of** *love.* • *Many ancient civilizations had the same gods but with different names.* • *The Egyptian physician and architect Imhotep was worshipped as a god after he died.* • *Some of his most devoted fans think of Elvis Presley as a god* (= as having qualities that make him better than other people). • *He treats that motorbike of his like a god* (= it is the most important thing to him). • A god can also be someone who is very important to you, whom you admire very much, and who greatly influences you: *Josie's older brother is her god.* • To **make a god of** someone or something is to consider them to be more important than anything else: *Keeping fit is a good idea, but there's no need to make a god of it.* • *(saying)* 'Those whom the Gods love die young'. • *(saying)* 'Those who the Gods would destroy, they first make mad'. • See also GODS.

god·less /£'gɒd·ləs, $'gɑːd-/ *adj* • Godless means lacking a god or gods: *a godless society* • See also GODLESS; see also **godless** at GOD [MAKER].

god·less·ly /£'gɒd·lə·sli, $'gɑːd-/ *adv*

god·less·ness /£'gɒd·lə·snəs, $'gɑːd-/ *n* [U]

god·like /£'gɒd·laɪk, $'gɑːd-/ *adj* • Godlike means like a god in some way: *godlike powers*

God [MAKER] /£gɒd, $gɑːd/ *n* [U not after *the*] (in esp. Christian, Jewish and Muslim belief) the being which made the universe, the Earth and its people and is believed to have an effect on all things • *As a nun, she is a servant of God.* • *Do you believe in God?* • *God* **bless** *this house.* • **God/My God/Oh God/God Almighty** are all used to express surprise or for emphasis: *My God, what a terrible shock that was.* This is sometimes considered offensive. • **God willing** means if everything happens as you hope it will: *We'll be there tomorrow, God willing!* • The expression **to God** is used to emphasize the meaning of a verb: *I* **hope** *to God the talks are successful.* ○ *I* **wish** *to God you hadn't done* *that.* • *(slang)* Something which is **god-awful** is bad, difficult or unpleasant: *That was a god-awful meal.* ○ *He suffered some god-awful injuries.* • *(old use)* Someone who is **God-fearing** is religious and tries to live in the way they believe God would wish them to. • *(disapproving)* If a place is **god-forsaken**, it is unattractive and contains nothing interesting or pleasant: *The town is a god-forsaken place at night.* • *(disapproving)* If a person is said to act as if, or think, they are **God's gift** (to someone or something), they believe that they are better than anyone else: *He* **thinks** *he's God's gift* **to women** (=very attractive to women). • If you say something is **God-given**, you mean that it has not been made by people: *She has a God-given talent as a painter.* • **God-given** can also mean having to be obeyed: *She seems to think she has a God-given* **right** *to tell us all what to do.* • **God's truth** is something which according to the speaker is the complete truth: *I didn't know she would be there – God's truth.* • *(saying)* 'God helps those who help themselves'. • *"With God all things are possible"* (Bible, Matthew 19.26) • *"God save our gracious king/queen"* (first line of the British national anthem) • *"God Bless America"* (title of a song written by Irving Berlin, 1939) • *"If God did not exist it would be necessary to invent him"* (Voltaire *Epîtres*, 1694-1778) • *"God is love"* (Bible, 1 John 4.8)

god·less /£'gɒd·ləs, $'gɑːd-/ *adj* • Godless means not having respect for or belief in God. • See also GODLESS; see also **godless** at GOD [SPIRIT].

god·less·ly /£'gɒd·lə·sli, $'gɑːd-/ *adj*

god·less·ness /£'gɒd·lə·snəs, $'gɑːd-/ *n* [U]

god·like /£'gɒd·laɪk, $'gɑːd-/ *adj* • Godlike means like God in some way: *Godlike powers*

god·ly /£'gɒd·li, $'gɑːd-/ *adj* [not gradable] • Godly means showing obedience to God: *This saint lived a godly life.*

god·li·ness /£'gɒd·lɪ·nəs, $'gɑːd-/ *n* [U] • *(saying)* 'Cleanliness is next to godliness' means the next most important thing after living in a morally right way is being clean.

god·child *(pl* **godchildren**), **god·daught·er**, **god·son** /£'gɒd·tʃaɪld, $'gɑːd-, £-ˌdɔː·tər, $-ˌdɑː·t̬ɚ, -sʌn/ *n* [C] (in the Christian religion) a child whose moral and religious development is partly the responsibility of two or more GODPARENTS (=adults who promise to take this responsibility at a ceremony)

god·damn, **God damn**, **god·damned**, *Am also* **god·dam** /£'gɒd·dæm, $ˌgɑːd'dæm/ *exclamation, adj, adv* [not gradable] *infml* used to add force to what is being said • *Goddamn* **(it)** *(also* **Goddamnit, Godammit***), how much longer will it take?* • *When will that goddamn noise stop?* • *Don't drive so goddamn fast!* • See also DAMN [EXPRESSION].

god·less /£'gɒd·ləs, $'gɑːd-/ *adj* bad or evil • *This godless regime which is torturing and murdering people must be stopped.* • See also **godless** at GOD [MAKER]; See also **godless** at GOD [SPIRIT].

god·par·ent, **god·moth·er**, **god·fath·er** /£'gɒd·peə·rənt, $'gɑːd·per·ᵊnt, £-ˌmʌð·ər, $-ɚ, £-ˌfɑː·ðər, $-ðɚ/ *n* [C] (in the Christian religion) a person who, at a BAPTISM ceremony, promises to help a new member of the religion, usually a child, in religious and moral matters • Godfather can also be used to refer to the leader of a criminal group, esp. a MAFIA family. • See **fairy godmother** at FAIRY [IMAGINARY CREATURE].

gods /£gɒdz, $gɑːdz/ *pl n* **the gods** *Br and Aus infml* (in a theatre) the seats which are at the highest level and the furthest distance from the stage • See also GOD [SPIRIT].

god·send /£'gɒd·send, $'gɑːd-/ *n* [C] *infml* something good which happens unexpectedly, esp. at a time when it is needed • *The grant was a* **real** *godsend, especially considering the theatre was due to close next month.*

god·slot /£'gɒd·slɒt, $'gɑːd·slɑːt/ *n* [C] *Br infml* a period of time on television or radio for religious broadcasts

god·squad /£'gɒd·skwɒd, $'gɑːd·skwɑːd/ *n* [C] *infml usually disapproving* any group of EVANGELICAL Christians whose members are generally thought to be too forceful in trying to persuade other people to believe as they do

go·er /£'gəʊ·ər, $'goʊ·ɚ/ *n* [C], *combining form* See at GO [ENERGY], GO [TRAVEL]

goes /£gəʊz, $goʊz/ *he/she/it form of* GO

go·fer /£'gəʊ·fər, $'goʊ·fɚ/ *n* [C] *Am and Aus infml* someone whose job, or part of whose job, is to be sent to get and carry things such as messages, drinks, etc. for other people.

gog·gle /£'gɒg·l̩, $'gɑː·gl̩/ *v* [I] *infml* to look with the eyes wide open, often when surprised • *He goggled* **at** *her as if she'd said something very strange.* • *They goggled in amazement as about twenty overweight men and women ran past them in track suits, panting and wheezing.* • *The cathedral was full of goggling tourists.* • *(Br dated infml)* **Goggle-box** is another word for television: *What's on* **the** *goggle-box tonight?* ○ *She's bought a new goggle-box.* • *(infml)* If someone is **goggle-eyed**, their eyes are very wide open, usually because of surprise: *He stared in goggle-eyed amazement.*

gog·gles /£'gɒg·l̩z, $'gɑː·gl̩z/ *pl n* special glasses which fit close to the face to protect the eyes from chemicals, wind, water etc. • *ski goggles* • *The steelworker was wearing* **(a pair of)** *safety goggles.* • [PIC] **Water sports**

go·ing on, *Br also* **go·ing on for** *adv* [not gradable], *prep* nearly; almost • *It was going on midnight when we left the party.* • *It must be going on 50 years that they've been married, isn't it?* • *Her new car cost going on £20 000.* • *There were/was going on two hundred people at their wedding.* • *Liesl is 16 going on 17.* • *(fig. esp. humorous) "How old is Brian?" "30 going on* (=but he looks or behaves like he's) *50."* • [LP] **Approximate numbers**

go·ing to /£'gəʊ·ɪŋ, $'goʊ-/ *v aux* [+ infinitive] **be going to** *(infml* **gonna***)* to intend to (do something in the future), or to be certain or expected to (happen in the future) • *Are you going to go to Claire's party?* • *He was going to phone me this morning, but I haven't heard from him yet.* • *Isn't she going to accept the job after all?* • *He wants me to mend his shirt for him, but I'm not going to!* • *They're going to have a baby in the spring.* • *There's going to be trouble when Paul finds out about this.* • *The forecast said it was going to be hot and sunny tomorrow.* • [LP] **Tenses**

go·ing–o·ver /£'gəʊ·ɪŋˌəʊ·vər, $'goʊ·ɪŋˌoʊ·vɚ/ *n* [C] See at GO OVER [EXAMINE]; GO OVER [ATTACK]

go·ings–on /£ˌgəʊ·ɪŋz'ɒn, $ˌgoʊ·ɪŋz'ɑːn/ *pl n* See at GO ON [HAPPEN]

goi·tre *Br and Aus* /£'gɔɪ·tər, $-t̬ɚ/, *Am* **goi·ter** *n* [U] a swelling at the front of the neck caused by the increase in size of the **thyroid gland** (=an organ)

go–kart, *Am usually* **go–cart** /£'gəʊ·kɑːt, $'goʊ·kɑːrt/, **kart** /£kɑːt, $kɑːrt/ *n* [C] a small car used for racing, or a toy car which you operate with your feet • *I had a go-kart when I was a kid, but you had to pedal really hard to get it to go fast.*

go–kart·ing /£'gəʊˌkɑː·tɪŋ, $'goʊˌkɑːr·t̬ɪŋ/, **kart·ing** /£'kɑː·tɪŋ, $'kɑːr·t̬ɪŋ/ *n* [U] • *My dad took us go-karting* (= racing in small cars) *last Saturday.*

gold [METAL] /£gəʊld, $goʊld/ *adj* [not gradable], *n* (made of) a soft, yellow, heavy, metallic element which is quite rare and very valuable • *gold jewellery/bullion* • *In many civilizations, gold objects were buried with important people who had died.* • *There is said to be* **(a crock/pot of)** *gold at the end of the rainbow.* [U] • *It's every prospector's dream to* **strike** (=find) *gold.* [U] • *There are still people who* **pan** *for gold* (=look for it by washing stones from a stream in a pan). [U] • *A legend says there is gold* (=objects made of gold, such as coins and jewellery) *buried somewhere on the island.* [U] • *She was* **dripping with** *gold* (=wearing a lot of gold jewellery). [U] • If a recording of a popular song, or of a collection of popular songs, **goes gold**, it sells a large number of copies. • A **gold card** is a **credit card** (=a card used for paying for things) which you can get if you earn a lot of money. • *(disapproving)* A **gold digger** is someone, usually a woman, who tries to (sexually) attract a rich person, usually a man, in order to obtain presents, money or social advance. • A **gold digger** is also a person who digs for gold. • A **gold disc** is a prize given to the performer(s) of a popular song, or a collection of popular songs, when a large number of copies of the recording of it have been sold. • **Gold dust** is gold in powder form: *(fig. esp. Br) Tickets for the concert are* **(like)** *gold dust* (=very difficult to obtain because a lot of people want them). • **Gold leaf** is gold in the form of very thin sheets which is often used to cover objects, such as decorative details in a building. • A **gold (medal)** is a small disc of gold, or a metal that looks like gold, which is given to the person who wins a competition, esp. in a sport: *He's running so well, surely he'll take the gold.* ○ *What a race she's having – she's really* **going for** *gold* (=trying very hard to win). • If something is **gold-plated**, it has been electrically covered with a very thin layer of gold. • The **gold reserve** is the amount of gold held by a national bank, which is used for dealing with the national banks of other countries. • A **gold rush** is a situation in which a lot of people move to a place to try to find gold because they have heard that gold has been found there. • The **gold**

standard is a system of providing and controlling the exchange of money in a country, in which the value of money (relative to foreign money) is fixed against that of gold.

gold·en /£'gəʊl·dᵊn, $'goʊl-/ *adj* • *a golden* (=made of gold) *necklace* • *(esp. Br)* A **golden jubilee** is (a special event which celebrates) the day exactly 50 years after an important occasion: *The local hospital will be* **celebrating** *its golden jubilee on Thursday.* • A **golden wedding (anniversary)** is the day exactly 50 years after a marriage and is often the occasion for a party or other type of celebration. • *"The Golden Bough"* (title of a book by Sir James Frazer, 1890) • See also GOLDEN.

gold [COLOUR] /£gəʊld, $goʊld/ *adj, n* a yellowish colour, like that of gold • *a gold dome* • *gold ink/paint* • *The lettering on the book's cover was* **in gold**. [U] • *I love the gold(s) of the autumn trees.* [U/C]

gold·en /£'gəʊl·dᵊn, $'goʊl-/ *adj* • Golden means the colour of gold: *golden hair/skin* • *miles of golden beaches* • A **golden eagle** is a large flesh-eating bird with golden brown feathers on its back, which lives in northern parts of the world. • A **golden retriever** is a large dog which has golden or cream-coloured fur. • *(Br and Aus)* **Golden syrup** is a thick golden-coloured sugary liquid used in cooking in Britain to sweeten food. • See also GOLDEN.

gold·ish /£'gəʊld·ɪʃ, $'goʊld-/ *adj* • *She was wearing a goldish-brown dress.*

gold·en /£'gəʊl·dᵊn, $'goʊl-/ *adj* [before n] special, advantageous or successful, or promising success in the future • *the golden days of our youth* • *He's got a place at university which gives him a golden* **opportunity** *to do research in the subject which interests him.* • *I like listening to those radio stations that play all the golden* **oldies** (=old popular songs which people still like or which have become liked again.) • A **golden age** is a period of time, sometimes imaginary, when everyone was happy, or when a particular art, business, etc. was very successful: *Adults often look back on their childhood as a golden age.* ○ *She was an actress from the golden age* **of** *the cinema.* • A **golden boy/golden girl** is a person who is very successful and is much admired, although often only temporarily: *Charles really seems to be the golden boy in the department at the moment.* ○ *She's the current golden girl* **of** *American ice-skating.* • A **golden goose** is something which is to your esp. financial advantage: *Many companies suffering under the recession see the lowering of interest rates as a golden goose.* See also **kill the goose that lays the golden egg** at KILL. • **Golden handcuffs** are payments made to employees, esp. those in a high position, as a way of persuading them not to leave their jobs and go and work somewhere else: *The stock benefits were promised to the company's top executives as golden handcuffs to entice them to stay there.* • *(infml)* A **golden handshake** is a usually large payment made to someone when they leave their job, either when their employer has asked them to leave, or, if they are leaving at the end of their working life, as a reward for particularly long or good service in their job. • *(Am infml)* A **golden parachute** is a large payment made to someone who has an important job with a company when they are forced to leave their job. • **The golden triangle** is the area of SE Asia covering parts of Burma, Laos and Thailand where OPIUM (=a drug) is produced, most of which is made into illegal drugs. • A **golden rule** is an important rule or principle, esp. in a particular situation: *The golden rule for working in any factory is to observe its safety regulations.* • *"The golden rule is that there are no golden rules"* (from *Man and Superman* by George Bernard Shaw, 1903) • See also **golden** at GOLD [METAL]; GOLD [COLOUR].

gold·field /£'gəʊld·fiːld, $'goʊld-/ *n* [C] an area where gold is found in the ground, at the bottom of a river, etc.

gold·fish /£'gəʊld·fɪʃ, $'goʊld-/ *n* [C] *pl* **goldfish** or **goldfishes** a small, shiny, gold or orange-coloured, fish which is often kept as a pet in a bowl or a garden pool • A **goldfish bowl** (*Am also* **fishbowl**) is a bowl which is usually round and made of glass and is used for keeping pet fish in, esp. goldfish: *There are so many windows in the office, it's* **like** *being in a goldfish bowl* (=people can easily see what you are doing)*!*

gold·mine /£'gəʊld·maɪn, $'goʊld-/ *n* [C] a place where gold or rock containing gold is dug from under the ground, or something which produces wealth or information • *If a restaurant were to open here, it would be a real goldmine* (=would produce a lot of money). • *The archive is a goldmine* (=contains a lot of interesting information) *for historians.*

gold·smith /£'gəʊld·smɪθ, $'goʊld-/ *n* [C] someone who makes objects from gold

golf /£gɒlf, $gɑːlf/ *n* [U] a game played outside in which a small ball is hit a long distance into (usually) nine or 18 small holes in a particular order, using as few hits as possible • *Do you play golf?* • *We often play a* **round** (= game) *of golf at the weekend.* • A **golf ball** is a small hard ball used for playing golf which is usually white but is sometimes another bright colour. • A **golf ball** is also a small metal ball with raised letter shapes on it which is used in some types of TYPEWRITER and computer printer. • A **golf club** is one of a set of specially shaped wooden or metal sticks used for hitting a golf ball. • A **golf club** is also an organized group of golf players, or the building in which they meet and the area on which they play. • A **golf course** is an area of land used for playing golf. • [PIC] **Club, Sports** (PL)

golf /£gɒlf, $gɑːlf/ *v* [I] • *Now that she's retired she spends most of her time golfing* (=playing golf).

golf·er /£'gɒl·fəʳ, $'gɑːl·fɚ/ *n* [C] • *He's one of the highest-earning professional golfers in the world.*

golf·ing /£'gɒl·fɪŋ, $'gɑːl-/ *n* [U] • *I've just bought a book on golfing for beginners.* • *He was wearing a golfing sweater and carrying a golfing umbrella.* • *This year they went on a golfing* **holiday**. • *The ability to win big tournaments stayed with her throughout her golfing* **career**.

Go·li·ath /gə'laɪ·əθ/ *n* [C] a very large and powerful person or organization • *The newly formed company will be a Goliath in the insurance sector.* • *The country is being seen as* **the** *Goliath* (=the most powerful) *of the region.* • *This is developing into a* **David and** *Goliath contest/battle* (=one between someone who is not powerful and someone who is very powerful). • In the Bible, Goliath was a GIANT who was killed by the boy David throwing stones at him.

gol·li·wog, **gol·ly·wog** /£'gɒl·ɪ·wɒg, $'gɑː·lɪ·wɑːg/, **gol·ly** /£'gɒl·i, $'gɑː·li/ *n* [C] *Br and Aus dated* a child's toy made of soft material, in the form of a small man with a black face and stiff black hair. Such toys are considered by many people to be offensive and are no longer very common.

gol·ly /£'gɒl·i, $'gɑː·li/ *exclamation dated infml* used to show surprise • *Grandad might be 70 but he said he'd finish the marathon and,* **by golly**, *he did.*

gon·ad /£'gəʊ·næd, $'goʊ-/ *n* [C] *specialized* an organ in either a man or a woman which makes one of the two types of cell needed to produce babies; an OVARY or a TESTICLE

gon·do·la /£'gɒn·dᵊl·ə, $'gɑːn-/ *n* [C] a type of boat which is narrow with a raised point at both ends, which is used on CANALS in Venice and is moved by a man with a pole

gon·do·li·er /£ˌgɒn·də'lɪəʳ, $ˌgɑːn·də'lɪr/ *n* [C] • A gondolier is a man who takes people from one place to another in a gondola.

gone [GO] /£gɒn, $gɑːn/ *past participle of* GO

gone [PAST] /£gɒn, $gɑːn/ *prep Br* later or older than • *I said I'd be home by six and it's already gone seven.* • *I'd never have thought he was gone 60 – he looks amazingly young for his age.* • See also **gone** at GO [LEAVE].

gone [PREGNANT] /£gɒn, $gɑːn/ *adj* [after n; not gradable] *infml* pregnant • *She got married when she was five months gone* (=had been pregnant for five months). • *How far gone is she* (=How long has she been pregnant)*?*

gon·er /£'gɒn·əʳ, $'gɑː·nɚ/ *n* [C usually sing] See at GO [LEAVE]

gong /£gɒŋ, $gɑːŋ/ *n* [C] a round piece of metal which is hung in a frame and hit with a stick to produce a sound, usually for musical purposes but sometimes as a signal • *Ryudo Uzaki's music is a haunting mix of guitar, synthesizer, Oriental gongs and bells.* • *It used to be common among wealthy families who lived in big houses for a gong to be* **sounded** *to let people know that dinner was ready.* • *(Br and Aus infml)* A gong is also an honour that is given to someone for the public service they have done, or a for a particular acting or singing performance: *He wants to see fewer gongs going automatically to senior diplomats and civil servants.* ○ *She picked up the gong for Best Female Vocalist.*

gon·na /£'gə·nə, $'gɑː·nə/ *v aux* [+ infinitive without *to*] *esp. Am infml* GOING TO • *"What you gonna do about it?" "Beats me!"* • *I think I'm gonna throw up.* • *He wants me to lend him some money, but I'm not gonna.* • In written English 'going to' is usually used instead of 'gonna'.

gon·or·rhoea, *esp. Am* **gon·or·rhe·a** /£ˌgɒn·əˈriː·ə, $ˌgɑː·nəˈ-/, *slang* **clap** *n* [U] a disease which causes pain in the sexual organs and which can be given from one person to another during sex

gon·zo /£ˈgɒn·zəʊ, $gɑːn·zoʊ/ *adj Am and Aus slang* (esp. used of pieces of writing in newspapers) strange and unusual

goo /guː/ *n* [U] *infml* a sticky substance • *What's all this goo on the floor? It looks like someone spilt some jam and didn't clear it up.*

goo·ey /ˈguː·i/ *adj* **gooier, gooiest** • *a gooey cake*

good VERY SATISFACTORY /gʊd/ *adj* **better** /£ˈbet·əʳ, $ˈbet̬·ɚ/, **best** /best/ very satisfactory because of being pleasant, enjoyable, of high quality, effective or suitable • *The weather has been unusually good for the time of year.* • *I've just had some very good news.* • *Jo is such a good person to work with.* • **It**'s *so good* **to** *see you after all these years!* [+ *to* infinitive] • **It**'s *so good* **seeing** *you after all these years!* [+ v-*ing*] • *Did they* **have a** *good* **time** *on their trip?* • *There's nothing like a good book.* • *That was a really good story/ joke.* • *I've heard it's a very good school.* • *The author's work, although entertaining, is not particularly good.* • *The teacher wrote 'good' on my science homework.* • *Her cherry pie always looks good and tastes good.* • *Our computers are* **as** *good* **as** *those made by our competitors, if not better.* • *This restaurant has a good* **reputation** *for its food.* • *I wish I'd known we were going out, I haven't brought any good clothes* (= newer and better quality clothes) *with me.* • *Most dogs have a very good* (= effective) *sense of smell.* • *The child had the good sense to tell us she smelled gas in the kitchen.* • *It was a good attempt at the world record but not good* (= effective) *enough.* • *He's a good* (= able and skilful) *runner.* • *He's good* **at running**. • *Is she* **(any)** *good* **at** (= skilful and successful at) *tennis?* • *They have a good* (= successful) *relationship – they can talk about most things.* • *It was a good* (= successful) *year for growing fruit.* • *We got a good deal on our new fridge* (= We bought it at an advantageous price). • *She makes good* **money** *at* (= earns a high income from) *her new job.* • *Our daughter's very good* (= deals well) **with** *children.* • *Now would be a good* (= suitable) *time to talk to Andy about the promotion.* • **It**'s *good* (= valuable) **(that)** *you checked the door – I forgot to lock it.* [+ (*that*) clause] • *Activity holidays are not good* **for** (= suitable for) *everyone.* • *The jumper may be old but it's good* **for** (= can be used for) *another few months.* • *What's put her in such a good* (= happy and pleasant) **mood**? • *Despite being tired she was still good* **tempered** (= calm and relaxed). • *He only has one good* (= healthy) *leg but it doesn't affect his lifestyle.* • Good can sometimes be used for emphasis: *Don't decide now – have a good think about it and let me know tomorrow.* ○ *Now, now – have a good cry and you'll feel better.* ○ *Don't rush her – she'll do it* **in her own** *good* **time**. ○ *You'll get* **a** *good* **talking to** (= be spoken to in an angry way) *by your mother if you're late.* • Good can also mean having a large probability or being able to be accepted: *There's a good chance the operation will be successful.* ○ *I expect there's* **some** *good* **reason** *for them not turning up.* • Good can also mean able to be trusted: *Her credit is good* (= She can be trusted to pay her debts). ○ *This £5 is good* (= not false) *but you can see the other is a forgery if you look closely.* • The word good can also be used to express praise: *Good man! Splendid catch.* ○ *Good old Dad – he's done it again.* ○ *Those were the good old days when not everything had a price.* • **A good deal of** means much: *The new law met with a good deal of opposition at local level.* • **All in good time** means at the suitable time: *Be patient, you'll hear the result all in good time.* • **As good as** means almost: *The house is as good as painted – a few more hours and it'll be done.* • If something is **(as) good as new**, it is in very good condition: *The cobbler fixed my shoes and now they're as good as new.* • If you say that something is **good as** things of that type **go**, you mean that it is better than the average thing of its type, but you do not think any of the type are very good: *It was quite a good film, as horror films go.* ○ *I suppose the concert was OK, as* **these things** *go.* • *(fml)* If you ask someone to **be so good as to/be good enough to** do something, you are making a polite request: *Be so good as to close the door when you leave.* • **For good (and all)** means forever: *She's gone and this time (it's) for good.* • **For good measure** means in addition: *The concert was excellent – there were lots of well-known songs with some new ones* **thrown in** *for good measure.* • If you **give as good as** you **get**, you can argue or fight as well as anyone: *Don't feel too sorry for him – he gives as good as he gets.* • *(infml)* **Good and** means completely: *She won't drink coffee if it's not good and hot.* • *(infml)* **Good and proper** means completely: *The table is broken good and proper.* • Someone who is **good for** something provides, or is willing to provide, it: *Bette is* **always** *good for a laugh.* ○ *Dad will probably be good for a few pounds, if we ask him.* • **Good for nothing** means useless: *He can't do anything, he's completely good for nothing!* • **Good-for-nothing** means a worthless person: *She's a good-for-nothing.* ○ *They're all good-for-nothing* **layabouts**. • The expression **good for** you (*Aus also* **good on** you) is used to show approval for someone's success or good luck: *You passed the exam – good for you!* • *(Br dated infml)* **Good show** is used as an expression of approval: *Good show, chaps, you completed the course in the time allowed.* • *(Am)* **Have a good one** means **have a good/nice day**. See at DAY. • *(esp. Br)* **In good time** means early *We'll be at the airport in good time.* • **It's a good job/thing** means it is lucky: *It's a good job they didn't go camping last weekend – the weather was awful.* • If you **make good**, you make yourself successful and usually rich: *He's a boy from a poor background who made good in the property market.* • When someone **makes good** something, they either pay (for) it, or make it happen: *The shortfall in the budget will be made good by selling further shares.* ○ *The lion stumbled leaving the antelope to make good its escape.* • If you **make good time**, you complete a journey quickly. • If something or someone is **no good/not much good/not any good**, it is useless or of low quality: *The new houses we're being forced to live in are no good.* ○ *Food aid is not much good until the fighting stops.* ○ *The protest was not going to do any good.* • If a situation or possibility is **too good to be true**, it will not happen or continue because it would give too much advantage: *I'm not surprised the offer wasn't genuine, it* **sounded** *too good to be true.* • A situation which is **too good to last** is very enjoyable or pleasant, but must end: *We had a fantastic summer but it was too good to last.* • If something is **too much of a good thing**, it is usually pleasant but becomes unpleasant by having or doing too much of it: *Eating chocolate is nice, but after a while it can become too much of a good thing.* ○ *(saying) 'You can have too much of a good thing'.* • **What good is/What's the good of/What's the good in** something are ways of asking what the purpose of (doing) something is: *What good is sitting alone in your room?* See also **what's the use of/what use is** at USE PURPOSE. • If someone or something is **good-humoured**, they have a friendly and happy personality: *a good-humoured remark* ○ *The walkers were good-humoured despite the bad weather.* • **Good looks** are an especially attractive appearance: *Her good looks should make her very popular with the boys at school.* ○ *She's a* **good looker** (= looks very attractive). • **Good-time** is used to describe someone who eagerly looks for pleasure or something for which pleasure is very important: *a good-time girl* ○ *They're a band with a good-time message.* • A **good word** is a statement of approval: *If you see the captain could you* **put in a** *good word* **for** *me?* ○ *The critics didn't* **have a** *good word* **(to say) for/to say about** *the performance.* • *(Br dated)* **Very good** is a way of saying yes to someone who is in a higher position or rank than you: *"Higgins, you may go now." "Very good, sir."* • *"What's good for the country is good for General Motors, and vice versa"* (Charles E. Wilson to a Congressional Committee, 1953)

good·y /ˈgʊd·i/ *n* [C usually pl] • A goody is something which is desirable or gives pleasure: *electronic goodies* ○ *So what if they do have a nice house and a fast car – there's more to life than acquiring goodies.*

good MORAL RIGHT /gʊd/ *adj* **better** /£ˈbet·əʳ, $ˈbet̬·ɚ/, **best** /best/ morally right or based on religious principles; behaving well; kind and helpful • *May you lead a good life and live long.* • *Try to set a good example to the children.* • *Do a good* **deed** *every day.* • *If you're a good boy* (= If you behave well) *at the doctor's I'll take you swimming afterwards.* • **It**'s *good* (= kind and helpful) *of you to offer but I can carry the shopping.* • *He's always good* (= kind and helpful) **to** *his grandchildren.* • *The college has been very good* (= helpful) **about** *her health problem.* • Good can be used to make particular exclamations stronger: *good gracious/grief/heavens/God/Lord* • Someone, esp. a child, is **as good as gold** if they behave very well: *She's been as good as gold all evening.* • If you are **(as) good as** your **word**, you do what you say you will do: *He was as good as his word* **about** *phoning.* • If you **do** (someone) **a good turn**, you do something which is helpful or kind: *You did grandma a good turn by carrying her bags.* • *(saying)* 'One good turn deserves another' means that it is right to do a helpful or kind act for someone if they have done something for you. • If something is done **in good faith**, it is done sincerely and honestly: *She was* **acting** *in good faith for her client.* • *(dated)* **The good book** is the Bible. • A **good cause** is either something which deserves effort, or a strong reason for doing something: *Please give what you can, it's for a good cause.* ○ *The judge ruled her actions were done without good cause.* • In the Christian religion, **Good Friday** is the day Jesus is believed to have died, the Friday before Easter Sunday. • Someone who is **good-hearted** is kind, helpful and generous. • If someone or something is **good-natured**, they are kind and friendly: *a good-natured child/manner* • *(fml)* **Good offices** are the helpful actions of someone, esp. if they are in authority: *Thanks to the good offices* **of** *the senior administrator, the annual party will be held again this year.* • A **good Samaritan** (also **samaritan**) is a person who is always ready to help someone else. • *(saying)* 'If you can't be good, be careful'.

good /gʊd/ *n* [U] • *There is an eternal struggle between good* (= the force which produces morally right action) *and evil.* • *Ambition can sometimes be a force* **for** *good* (= morally right action). • *The government could* **do** *a lot of good* (= provide help) *by sending aid to the area.* • *Even a small donation can do* **a lot of** *good* (= provide help). • *I'm punishing you* **for** *your* **own** *good* (= to help you). • Someone who is **up to no good** behaves in a dishonest or bad way: *Anyone who spends so much time taking other people to court is up to no good.*

good /gʊd/ *pl n* • **The good** means all the people who are good: *You can't buy your way into the ranks of the good.* • *"The Good, the Bad and the Ugly"* (title of a film, 1966)

good·ness /ˈgʊd·nəs/ *n* [U] • *Mother Teresa's goodness is an example to us all.* • *(fml) Would you* **have the goodness to** (= please) *phone me as soon as they arrive.* • *"'Goodness, what beautiful diamonds!' 'Goodness had nothing to do with it!'"* (Mae West in the film *Night After Night*, 1932)

good·y /ˈgʊd·i/ *n* [C often pl] • A goody is someone who is good: *It's one of those films where you don't know until the last moment who are (the) goodies and who are (the)* **baddies**. ○ *The goodies usually win in the end.*

good GREETING /gʊd/ *adj* [not gradable] used in greetings • **Good afternoon** is often the first thing said when people meet in the afternoon: *Good afternoon, it's so good of you to come.* • The expression **Good day** is used either *(Am)* when people meet, esp. in the morning or the afternoon, or *(Br dated)* when people meet or leave each other. See also G'DAY; **have a good/nice day** at DAY. • **Good evening** is often the first thing said when people meet in the evening. • **Good morning** is often the first thing said when people meet in the morning: *Good morning, how are you?* • **Good night** is said when people leave each other in the evening or before going to bed or to sleep. • LP **Meeting someone**

good HEALTH /gʊd/ *adj, n* **better** /£ˈbet·əʳ, $ˈbet̬·ɚ/, **best** /best/ useful for health or generally improving, or the state of being healthy or in a satisfactory condition • *Make sure you eat plenty of good fresh food.* • *Too much sugar in your diet isn't good* **for** *you.* • **It's** *good* **for old people** *to stay active if they can.* [+ *to* infinitive] • *You should stop smoking* **for** *your* **own** *good* (= the benefit of your health). [U] • *He goes running every day* **for the** *good* (= benefit) **of** *his* **health**. [U] • *Take the medicine – it will* **do** *you* **(a power/world of)** *good* (= improve your health (a lot)). [U] • *You can't work all the time – it* **does** *you good* (= improves your life) **to** *go out and enjoy yourself sometimes.* [U + *to* infinitive] • *The rally has been cancelled* **for the** *good* (= benefit) **of** *all concerned.* [U] • *Modernizing historic buildings can often* **do more harm than** *good* (= improvement). [U] • *Greater international stability can surely only be* **to the good** (= generally helpful). • **To the good** can also mean with a profit: *Property prices increased rapidly so we were £7000 to the good when we sold our house.* ○ *(fig.) He was two gold medals to the good by the end of the day.* • **Good times** are periods of happiness or (esp. financial) success: *As with most married couples, we've had our good times and our bad times.* ○ *Even* **in** *good times, January and February are traditionally slow months for retailers.*

good·ness /ˈgʊd·nəs/ *n* [U] • The goodness is the part of something, esp. of food, which is good for health: *Don't cook vegetables for too long – they'll lose all their goodness.*

good LARGE AMOUNT /gʊd/ *adj* [before n; not gradable] large in amount • *We walked a good distance today.* • *There was a good-sized crowd at the airport waiting for the plane to land.* • *You're looking* **a** *good* **deal** (= much) *better now you've had a few weeks off.* • *There has been* **a** *good* **deal of** (= a lot of) *discussion about the subject.* • *Not all of his films have been successful – there were* **a** *good* **few** (= several) *failures in the early years.* • **A good** means more than: *It's a good half hour's walk to the station from here.* ○ *The police said a good twenty kilos of explosive were found during the raid.* ○ *Driving through the deserted town we saw a good* **many** (= a lot of) *burnt-out houses.* • *(Br infml)* If you say that someone has **had a good innings**, you mean that they have had a long and successful life: *He was 86 when he died so I suppose he'd had a good innings.* • LP **Approximate numbers**

good·bye /ˈgʊd·baɪ, ˈgʊb-, ˌ-ˈ-/, *infml* **bye** *exclamation, n* (the word) used when someone leaves or is left • *Goodbye, Robert, and thank you again for a lovely dinner.* • *See you at work tomorrow. Goodbye!* • *Don't go without* **saying** *goodbye* **to** *me, will you?* [U] • *She* **kissed** *her children goodbye before leaving for work.* [U] • *They* **said** *a tearful goodbye at the airport.* [C] • *We* **said** *our goodbyes, and left.* [C] • *I hate long drawn-out goodbyes* (= acts of leaving). [C] • *It's getting late, so we really should* **say** *goodbye* (= leave). [U] • *She only finished sixth – that surely means goodbye* **to** (= accepting that there is no possibility of) *a place in the final.* [U] • *"Goodbye to all that"* (title of autobiography by Robert Graves, 1929) • *"The Long Goodbye"* (title of a book by Raymond Chandler, 1953) • LP **Meeting someone**

good·ish /ˈgʊd·ɪʃ/ *adj* [before n; not gradable] good but not very good, or quite large • *It was a goodish production of the play: I've seen better but there have also been far worse.* • *You could walk to the bookshop but it's a goodish* (= quite large) *distance from here.*

good·ly /ˈgʊd·li/ *adj* [before n; not gradable] *dated* great or large • *The audience was of a goodly size.*

good·ness (gra·cious) /ˈgʊd·nəs/ *n* [U] used to express any strong emotion, esp. surprise • **(My)** *goodness* **(me)**, *how many more times do I have to tell you!* • **(My)** *goodness gracious* **(me)**, *what a terrible thought!*

good·o /£ˌgʊdˈəʊ, $-ˈoʊ/ *exclamation, adj* [after v], *adv Aus slang* (used to express that things are) in a satisfactory state, way or manner

goods /gʊdz/ *pl n* items for sale, or movable possessions • *There is a 25% discount on all electrical goods until the end of the week.* • *The house insurance will not cover your personal goods.* • Goods (also **freight**) are also items, but not people, which are transported by railway or road: *a goods train/lorry* • *The union is good at talking but they hardly ever* **come up with/deliver the goods** (= produce what is wanted). • *(law)* Someone's **goods and chattels** are their personal possessions other than land and buildings. • LP **Shopping goods**

good·will /gʊdˈwɪl/ *n* [U] friendly and helpful feelings • *The school has to rely on the goodwill of the parents to help it raise money.* • *There was a consistent feeling of goodwill throughout the games.* • *Releasing the hostages has been seen as a* **gesture of** *goodwill/a goodwill* **gesture**.

good·y FOOD /ˈgʊd·i/ *n* [C usually pl] *infml* something pleasant to eat • *She always makes us some goodies for tea.*

good·y EXPRESSION /ˈgʊd·i/, *dated* **good·y gum·drops** /£ˌgʊd·iˈgʌm·drɒps, $-drɑːps/ *exclamation* used, esp. by children, to show pleasure • *Oh goody! Chocolate cake.*

good·y–good·y /ˈgʊd·iˌgʊd·i/ *n* [C] *disapproving* someone who behaves in a way intended to please people in authority • *She's a real goody-goody – who always does exactly as she's told.* • *He's not very popular with the other children in his class because of his goody-goody behaviour.*

goo·ey /ˈguː·i/ *adj* **gooier, gooiest** See at GOO

goof *(obj)* MISTAKE /guːf/ *v infml esp. Am* to make a silly mistake (with); to fail to achieve (something) • *If Tom hadn't goofed and missed that shot, we'd have won the game.* [I] • *She goofed her lines* (= said the words in the play wrong) *again.* [T]

goof /guːf/ *n* [C] *infml esp. Am* • *I* **made** *a real goof by forgetting his name.*

goof·y /ˈguː·fi/ *adj* **-ier, -iest** *infml esp. Am* • *That was a real goofy thing to do* (= a silly mistake to make).

goof PERSON /guːf/ *n* [C] *Am infml* a silly or stupid person • *Don't be such a goof.*

goof·y /ˈguː·fi/ *adj* **-ier, -iest** *Am infml* • *I like Jim, but he's a bit goofy.*

goof a·bout/a·round *v adv* [I] *Am infml* to do nothing important or to behave in a silly way • *The boys spent the whole summer just goofing around.*

goof off *v adv* [I] *Am infml* to avoid work or to waste time instead of working • *They've goofed off and gone to the ball game.*

goon SILLY PERSON /guːn/ *n* [C] *infml* a silly or stupid person • *You can be a real goon sometimes.*

goon CRIMINAL /guːn/ *n* [C] *Am infml* a violent criminal who is paid to hurt or threaten people • *These killings look like the work of hired goons.*

goose BIRD /guːs/ *n pl* **geese** /giːs/ a bird like a DUCK but larger. There are various different types of goose. • *Geese often fly in a V-shaped formation.* [C] • *The goose honked at the farm cat as it went past the pond.* [C] • *Shall we have goose* (= the meat from a goose) *for dinner on Sunday?* [U] • The female bird is called a goose: the male bird is called a GANDER. [C] • **Goose bumps** are GOOSEFLESH. • **Goose-pimples** are GOOSEFLESH. See also **goose-pimply** at GOOSEFLESH.

goose *obj* PUSH FINGER /guːs/ *v* [T] *infml* to push your finger or thumb between (someone's) BUTTOCKS in order to surprise them • *Ted's always going around goosing people just to make them mad.*

goose *obj* MAKE ACTIVE /guːs/ *v* [T] *Am infml* to encourage or cause to be more active • *The company's productivity has been falling, so Anna has called a meeting of her department to try and goose her staff.* • *I'm sure a lot of stores over-charge their customers just to goose* **up** (= increase) *their profits.*

goose PERSON /guːs/ *n* [C] *infml dated* a silly person • *How could you be such a goose as to climb on those sharp rocks with no shoes on?* • *It's all right, you* **silly** *goose, I didn't mean it.* [as form of address]

goose·ber·ry /ˈgʊz·bᵊr·i, ˈguːz-/ *n* [C] a small green fruit covered with short hairs, which grows on a bush and has an acid taste • *Gooseberries are used for making pies and jam.* • **Gooseberry fool** is a DESSERT (= sweet food eaten at the end of a meal) made from gooseberries and cream or CUSTARD (= a sweet sauce). • PIC **Berries**

goose·flesh /ˈguːs·fleʃ/, **goose–pim·ples** /ˈguːs·pɪm·pl̩z/, **goose bumps** *n* [U] a temporary condition in which very small raised swellings appear on the skin because of cold, fear or excitement • *The sudden chilly breeze brought gooseflesh to her arms and legs/brought her arms and legs out in gooseflesh.* • *I* **got** *gooseflesh just thinking about how angry Dad was going to be.*

goose–pimp·ly /ˈguːs·pɪm·pli/, *Aus* **goo·sy** (**-ier, -iest**) /ˈguː·si/ *adj infml* • *When I heard someone downstairs in the middle of the night, I (Br and Aus)* **went**/ *(Am)* **got** *goose-pimply all over.*

goose·step /ˈguːs·step/ *n* [U] a special way of marching with the legs lifted high and straight • *Hitler's soldiers used to* **do (the)** *goosestep.*

goose·step /ˈguːs·step/ *v* [I] **-pp-** • *The soldiers goosestepped through the town.*

GOP /ˌdʒiː· əʊˈpiː/ *n* [U] **the GOP** *abbreviation for* the Grand Old Party (= a name for the Republican political party in the US) • *The symbol of the GOP is an elephant.*

goph·er /£ˈgəʊ·fəʳ, $ˈgoʊ·fɚ/ *n* [C] a N American animal which lives in holes that it makes in the ground

Gor·di·an knot /£ˈgɔː·di·ən, $ˈgɔːr-/ *n* [C] a difficult problem or situation • *We have a real Gordian knot to deal with here.* • *The company has appointed a new managing director to* **cut/untie** *the Gordian knot* **of** *its financial difficulties* (= deal with them by taking forceful action).

Gor·don Ben·nett /ˌgɔː·dᵊmˈben·ɪt/ *exclamation Br dated slang* used to express great surprise or annoyance • *"It's going to cost four hundred quid to get the car fixed." "Gordon Bennett, that's a lot!"* • *Gordon Bennett, Chris, why did you have to do that!*

gore *obj* INJURE /£gɔːʳ, $gɔːr/ *v* [T] (of an animal) to cause an injury with the horns or TUSKS • *A rhinoceros at the city zoo gored a small child yesterday.* • *The bullfighter was almost gored* **to death**.

gore BLOOD /£gɔːʳ, $gɔːr/ *n* [U] blood that has come from an injury and become thick • *The bodies lay in a pool of gore .* • *'Apocalypse Now' is a great film, but there's a lot of* **blood and** *gore in it* (= it contains scenes of people being badly injured).

go·ry /£ˈgɔː·ri, $ˈgɔːr·i/ *adj* **-ier, -iest** • *The television programme about the hospital showed a rather gory operation* (= an operation in which a lot of blood could be seen). • *That was a very gory film* (= it showed people being badly injured). • *He told us all the gory* **details** (= those about people being badly injured) *of the accident he'd seen.* • *(fig.) Come on, I want to know all the gory* (= interesting and usually personal) **details** *about your date with Jon.*

gorge VALLEY /£gɔːdʒ, $gɔːrdʒ/ *n* [C] a deep narrow valley with steep sides, usually formed by a river or stream cutting through hard rock • *The only way to cross the gorge was over a flimsy wooden bridge.* • *Olduvai Gorge is in Tanzania.*

gorge *(obj)* EAT /£gɔːdʒ, $gɔːrdʒ/ *v* to eat until unable to eat any more; to fill (yourself) completely with food • *It was a custom of the ancient Romans to gorge and then make themselves vomit.* [I] • *She sat in front of the television, gorging* **on** *chocolates.* [I] • *If you gorge your***self (on/with** *crisps) like that, you won't eat your dinner.* [T]

gorge STOMACH /£gɔːdʒ, $gɔːrdʒ/ *n* [C] the contents of the stomach • *My gorge* **rose** (= I felt as if I was going to vomit) *at the smell of the rotting fish.* • *The smell of the rotting fish* **made** *my gorge* **rise** (= made me feel as if I was going to vomit). • *(fig.) My gorge* **rose** (= I felt disgusted and angry) *at the reports of how the prisoners had been tortured.* • *(fig.) The reports of how the prisoners had been beaten* **made** *my gorge* **rise** (= made me feel disgusted and angry). • If a feeling such as fear or anger **rises in** your gorge, you feel as if you might vomit because you are frightened or angry.

gor·geous /£ˈgɔː·dʒəs, $ˈgɔːr-/ *adj* beautiful; attractive; pleasant; giving pleasure • *What a gorgeous room/place/dress/flower/colour!* • *The bride looked gorgeous.* • *We had gorgeous weather on our holiday* (= The weather was bright and sunny). • *That was an absolutely gorgeous meal, thank you* (= it tasted very good). • *He gave her a gorgeous* (= very beautiful) *emerald brooch for her birthday.* • *Hello, gorgeous!* [as form of address]

gor·geous·ly /£ˈgɔː·dʒə·sli, $ˈgɔːr-/ *adv* • *She's always gorgeously dressed* (= she wears beautiful clothes).

gor·geous·ness /£ˈgɔː·dʒə·snəs, $ˈgɔːr-/ *n* [U]

gor·gon /£ˈgɔː·gən, $ˈgɔːr-/ *n* [C] a woman whose appearance or behaviour causes fear • *Our teacher is a real gorgon!* • The Gorgons were three sisters in ancient Greek stories who had snakes on their heads instead of hair, and who turned anyone who looked at them into stone.

go·ril·la /gəˈrɪl·ə/ *n* [C] a large APE (= animal like a monkey) that comes from W Africa • *Gorillas are the largest of the apes.* • *King Kong was a gorilla.* • *(fig.) I don't know what she sees in a gorilla* (= a rough and violent man) *like him.* • PIC **Apes and monkeys**

gorm·less /£ˈgɔːm·ləs, $ˈgɔːrm-/ *adj Br infml* foolish; stupid; slow to understand • *He looks really gormless, but I think he's brighter than he seems.* • *That was a very gormless thing to do.*

gorse /£gɔːs, $gɔːrs/, **furze** /£fɜːz, $fɜːrz/ *n* [U] a bush with sharp THORNS (= pointed parts) and small yellow flowers, which grows in the countryside

go·ry /£ˈgɔː·ri, $ˈgɔːr·i/ *adj* **-ier, -iest** See at GORE BLOOD

gosh /£gɒʃ, $gɑːʃ/ *exclamation infml* used to express surprise or strength of feeling • *Gosh, I didn't expect to see you here!* • *Gosh, what a dreadful thing to have happened!* • LP **Phrases and customs**

gos·ling /£ˈgɒz·lɪŋ, $ˈgɑːz-/ *n* [C] a young GOOSE (= bird)

gos·pel /£ˈgɒs·pᵊl, $ˈgɑː·spᵊl/ *n* [C] any of the four books of the Bible which contain details of the life of Jesus Christ • *St Mark's Gospel/the Gospel* **according to** *St Mark* • *Missionaries travel all over the world to* **preach/spread** *the Gospel* (= to tell people about the life of Jesus Christ). • *(fig.) He believes firmly in the gospel* (= principle) **of** *hard work.* • *(fig.) She's always* **spreading** *the feminist gospel* (= principles or ideas).

gos·pel (mu·sic) /£ˈgɒs·pᵊl, $ˈgɑː·spᵊl/ *n* [U] a style of religious music originally performed by black Americans • *Gospel (music) has strong rhythms.* • *I like to listen to gospel* **songs/singers**.

gos·pel (truth) /£ˈgɒs·pᵊl, $ˈgɑː·spᵊl/ *n* [U] the complete truth • *I don't know what happened to the money, that's gospel (truth).* • *I'm telling you the gospel truth.* • *If Mary tells you something, you can* **take it as** *gospel (truth)* (= as being correct).

gos·sam·er /£ˈgɒs·ə·məʳ, $ˈgɑː·sə·mɚ/ *n* [U] the very thin thread that SPIDERS produce to make WEBS • *In the early morning the lawn was covered with gossamer* **(threads)**. • *(fig.) The bride wore a delicate gossamer veil* (= one made of very delicate, light cloth). • *"A trip to the moon on gossamer* (= very delicate and light) *wings,/ Just one of those things"* (from the song *Just One of Those Things* written by Cole Porter, 1935)

gos·sip /£ˈgɒs·ɪp, $ˈgɑː·səp/ *n* (an) informal talk, or (a) talk about other people's private lives which is usually unkind, disapproving or not true • *I always used to enjoy our gossips over the garden fence.* [C] • *Her letter was full of gossip.* [U] • *Jane and Lyn sat in the kitchen* **having** *a good gossip* **about** *their friends.* [C] • *All this talk that she's going to leave her husband is just gossip.* [U] • *I don't like all this* **idle** *gossip.* [U] • *I've got some* **juicy** *gossip for you.* [U] • *Have you heard* **the (latest)** *gossip* (= what is being said about someone)*?* [U] • A gossip is also someone who enjoys talking about other people's private lives: *She's a real gossip.* [C] • *I love reading the* **gossip columns** (= the parts of newspapers in which the private lives of famous people are written about). • *Has that old* **gossip-monger** (= a person who talks a lot about other people's private lives) *been talking about me again?*

gos·sip /£ˈgɒs·ɪp, $ˈgɑː·səp/ *v* [I] • *Stop gossiping* (= having an informal conversation) *and get on with some work.* • *People have started to gossip* **about** *us* (= talk about our private lives).

gos·sip·y /£ˈgɒs·ɪ·pi, $ˈgɑː·sɪ-/ *adj* • *She always writes long gossipy letters* (= letters containing gossip). • *There are too many gossipy people* (= people who enjoy gossip) *in this office.*

got /£gɒt, $gɑːt/ *past simple and past participle of* GET • See also GOTTEN.

got·cha /£ˈgɒtʃ·ə, $ˈgɑːtʃ-/ *exclamation slang* (said in order to surprise or frighten someone you have caught, or to show that you have an advantage over them) I have got you • *"Gotcha, you little thief!" the shopkeeper cried.* • *"Gotcha!" shouted Tom, as he jumped out from behind the door and leapt onto his father's back.*

Goth·ic BUILDING /£ˈgɒθ·ɪk, $ˈgɑː·θɪk/ *adj* of or like a style of building common in Europe between the 12th and the 16th centuries • *Gothic churches and cathedrals have pointed arches and windows, tall thin pillars and high ceilings.* • *Many Victorian buildings in England were built in the Gothic style.*

Goth·ic STORIES /£ˈgɒθ·ɪk, $ˈgɑː·θɪk/ *adj* of or like stories in which strange things happen in frightening places • *Gothic tales are usually set in haunted castles, graveyards or ruins.* • *Gothic* **novels** *were especially popular in the eighteenth century.*

got·ta /£ˈgɒt·ə, $ˈgɑː·t̬ə/ *v* [I + infinitive without *to*] *not standard* used in writing to show a very informal or not standard way of saying '(have/has) got to' • *I gotta go now.* • *He's gotta be kidding.* • *Gotta* (= Have you got a) *cigarette?* • If you say **a man's gotta do what a man's gotta do** you mean that you will do whatever you have to do, even if it is difficult or dangerous: *(humorous) He gave his friends a wink and said "A man's gotta do what a man's gotta do" as he walked towards the toilets.* • *"We Gotta Get Out of this Place"* (title of song by The Animals, 1965)

got·ten *Am, Aus infml* /£ˈgɒt·ən, $ˈgɑː·t̬ən/ *past participle of* GET • *I've gotten* (= I have) *some new shoes.* • *They were so pleased that they'd finally gotten to visit* (= succeeded in visiting) *England.*

gouge *obj* /gaʊdʒ/ *v* [T] to make (a hole) in something, or to remove (something) from a hole using a sharp pointed object or your fingers • *He drove into some railings and gouged a* **hole** *in the back of his car.* • *To make a Halloween lantern, you first have to gouge* **out** (= remove) *the inside of the pumpkin.* [M] • *In Shakespeare's play, 'King Lear', the Earl of Gloucester's eyes are gouged* **out** (= removed). [M]

gouge /gaʊdʒ/ *n* [C] • *There's a great gouge* (= hole) **in** *the side of the hill, where the plane crashed into it.*

gou·lash /ˈguː·læʃ/ *n* [U] a savoury dish originally from Hungary, which consists of meat cooked in a sauce with PAPRIKA (= a hot-tasting spice)

gourd /£gʊəd, £gɔːd, $gɔːrd/ *n* [C] a round or bottle-shaped fleshy fruit which has a hard shell and which cannot usually be eaten, or the shell of this fruit, used as a container • *Dried gourds are sometimes used as ornaments.* • *The villagers use gourds for holding water.*

gour·mand /£gɔːˈmɑ̃ːd, $ˈgʊr·mɑːnd/ *n* [C] a person who enjoys eating large amounts of food • (DK)

gour·met /£ˈgɔː·meɪ, $ˈgʊr·meɪ/ *n* [C] a person who knows a lot about food and cooking, and who enjoys eating high-quality food • *Our speciality foods will appeal particularly to the gourmet.* • *Have you tried that new gourmet restaurant* (= restaurant that has high-quality food)*?* • LP **'-et' words**

gout /gaʊt/ *n* [U] a painful disease which makes the joints, esp. the feet, knees and hands, swell • *He's got gout.*

gout·y /£ˈgaʊ·ti, $-t̬i/ *adj* [not gradable]

gov·ern *(obj)* RULE /£ˈgʌv·ən, $-ərn/ *v* to control and direct the public business of (a country, city, group of people, etc.); to rule • *Military leaders have overthrown the president and are now governing the country.* [T] • *They accused the government of being unfit to govern.* [I]

gov·ern·ing /£ˈgʌv·ən·ɪŋ, $-ər·nɪŋ/ *adj* [before n; not gradable] • *The country is being run by a governing coalition.* • *The king spoke of turning his kingdom into a federation of* **self-governing** *provinces.* • *It has been agreed that there will be a student representative on the college's* **governing body** (= the group of people who control the college).

gov·ern·ment /£ˈgʌv·ən·mənt, $-ərn·mənt/ (*abbreviation* **govt**) *n* • The government is the group of people who control a country: *the government of Israel* [C + sing/pl v] ○ *When President Peron fell from power in Argentina, a provisional military government took office.* [C + sing/pl v] ○ *The Prime Minister is the head of the government.* [C + sing/pl v] ○ *The government is/are expected to announce its/their tax proposals today.* [C + sing/pl v] ○ *All the European governments will be represented at the summit meeting.* [C] ○ *The minister has announced that there will be no change in government policy.* ○ *Prices rose dramatically* **under** *the last government* (= during the time it was in control). [C] • Government can also be used to mean all the departments which operate the decisions made by the group of people who control the country: *In those days, many industries used to be run by the government.* ○ *Senior government officials will be attending a meeting tomorrow.* ○ *Government departments and agencies have been ordered to reduce their spending by 5%.* ○ *Theatre companies are very concerned about cuts in government grants to the arts.* ○ *A government enquiry has been launched.* • Government is also the system of controlling a country, city, group of people, etc.: *The 1990s have seen a shift to democratic government in Eastern Europe.* [U] ○ *What this state needs is really strong government.* [U] • Government can also mean the activities involved in controlling a country, city, group of people, etc.: *The party that was elected to power has no experience of government.* [U] ○ *(Br and Aus) The party was* **in** *government* (= controlled the country) *for four years in the 1960s.* [U] • **Her/His Majesty's Government** is the group of people who control Britain: *Her Majesty's Government is/are making a formal protest about the treatment British citizens have received in another country.*

gov·ern·men·tal /£ˌgʌv·ənˈmen·təl, $-ərnˈmen·t̬əl/ *adj* [not gradable] • *It was a governmental decision* (= a decision of the government) *to change the local taxation system.*

gov·er·nor /£ˈgʌv·ən·əʳ, $-ər·nər/ (*abbreviation* **Gov**) *n* [C] • A governor is a person in charge of a particular political unit *After the independence ceremony, the former governor left the colony.* ○ *Three US state governors have put themselves forward as presidential candidates.* • *(esp. Br)* A governor can also be a person in charge of a particular organization: *She wants to be a prison governor.* ○ *The governor* **of** *the Bank of England is expected to comment this afternoon on the current financial crisis.* ○ *I've just become a governor* **of** *my daughter's school.* ○ *The* **board of** *governors* **of** *the hospital meets every month.* • See also GUBERNATORIAL; GUVNOR.

gov·er·nor–gen·er·al /£ˌgʌv·ən·əˈdʒen·rəl, $-ər-/ *n* [C] *pl* **governor-generals** or **governors-general** • A governor-general is the main representative of a country in another country which is controlled by the first country, esp. the representative of the British king or queen in a country which is a member of the Commonwealth: *He was a former governor-general* **of** *Indochina.* ○ *The Governor-General greeted the Queen on the first day of her official visit to Canada.*

gov·er·nor·ship /£ˈgʌv·ən·ə·ʃɪp, $-ər·nər-/ *n* [U] • *His period of governorship* (= The time during which he is a governor) *finishes at the end of the year.*

gov·ern *(obj)* INFLUENCE /£ˈgʌv·ən, $-ərn/ *v* to have a controlling influence on, to have a direct effect on, or to fix or decide • *The movement of the tides is governed mainly by the moon.* [T] • *Prices of goods are governed by the cost of the raw materials, as well as by the cost of production and distribution.* [T] • *The Geneva Convention laid down* **rules** *governing the treatment of prisoners of war.* [T] • *Most countries have speed limits governing* **how** *fast cars can drive.* [+ *wh-* word] • *They are fighting for the right to govern their own lives.* [T] • *(specialized) The German preposition* *'in' governs both the accusative and the dative case* (= a noun that follows it must be in one of these forms).

gov·ern·ess /ˈgʌv·ən·əs, $-ɚ·nəs/ *n* [C] (esp. in the past) a woman who lives with a family and educates the children at home • *In Charlotte Bronte's book, 'Jane Eyre', Jane worked as a governess* **to** *Mr Rochester's daughter.*

gown /gaʊn/ *n* [C] a woman's dress, esp. a long one worn on formal occasions, or a long loose piece of clothing worn over other clothes for a particular purpose • *She wore a low-cut satin* **ball/evening** *gown.* • *At many universities, students wear black gowns for their degree ceremonies.* • *A* **hospital** *gown is worn by people receiving medical treatment in hospital.* • *Doctors and nurses wear* **surgical** *gowns when they're carrying out operations.* • PIC› **Medical equipment** Ⓙ

gowned /gaʊnd/ *adj* [not gradable] • *The doctors and nurses are gowned* **(up)** (= wearing special gowns) *ready for the operation.*

GP /ˌdʒiːˈpiː/ *n* [C] *esp. Br and Aus abbreviation for* general practitioner (= a doctor who provides general medical treatment and who treats people who live in a particular area) • *He went to see his GP about his bad back.* • *My GP has referred me to a specialist about my lungs.*

grab *(obj)* /græb/ *v* **-bb-** to take hold of (something or someone) suddenly and roughly; to take or have quickly • *A mugger grabbed her handbag as she was walking across the park.* [T] • *He grabbed* **(hold of)** *his child's arm to stop her from running into the road.* [T] • *She grabbed* **at** (= tried to take hold of) *the balloon, but couldn't stop it blowing away.* [I always + *at*] • *Sam grabbed the toy* **from** *his brother.* [T] • *If you don't grab* (= quickly take of) *this opportunity, you might not get another one.* [T] • *We'd better get there early, or someone else will grab the best seats* (= take them first). [T] • *(infml) Let's just grab a quick bite* (= have something to eat quickly). [T] • *(infml) I need to grab* (= have) *a couple of hours' sleep.* [T] • *(fig. infml) Can I just grab you* (= talk to you) *for a minute?* [T] • *(fig. infml) How does that (idea) grab you* (= do you like that idea)*?* [T] • *"Grabbed my coat, grabbed my hat, made the bus in seconds flat"* (from the song *A Day in the Life* by The Beatles, 1967)

grab /græb/ *n* [C] • *The two children both* **made** *a* **grab for** (= made a sudden attempt to take) *the same cake.* • *There are hundreds of prizes* **up for grabs** (= ready to be won or taken) *in our competition.* • *(Am)* A **grab bag** is a type of game played at parties in which you bring a wrapped object which is put into a container from which you pick another wrapped object. • **Grab bag** is also *Aus for* **lucky dip**. See at LUCK. • *(Aus)* A grab bag is also any mixed collection of things.

-grab·bing /-ˌgræb·ɪŋ, ˈ--/ *combining form* • *The company has launched a new* **attention**-*grabbing* (= strongly attracting attention) *advertising campaign.* • *They are involved in a* **headline**-*grabbing court case* (= one which is being written about a lot in newspapers).

grab·by /ˈgræb·i/ *adj* **-ier, -iest** *infml* • *Don't be so grabby* (= trying to take things for yourself), *Shirley. Let the others have their share.*

grace BEAUTY /greɪs/ *n* [U] a quality of simple, natural beauty, esp. of movement or form • *Joanna has natural grace and elegance.* • *The skaters moved over the ice with a smooth, effortless grace.*

grace *obj* /greɪs/ *v* [T] • *A fine porcelain vase graces the table in the hall* (= makes it look beautiful).

grace·ful /ˈgreɪs·fəl/ *adj* • *That Georgian chair is a very graceful piece of furniture* (= it has an attractive form). • *She has a graceful way of moving* (= She moves in an attractive smooth and effortless way).

grace·ful·ly /ˈgreɪs·fəl·i/ *adv* • *The dancers waltzed gracefully across the floor.*

grace·ful·ness /ˈgreɪs·fəl·nəs/ *n* [U]

grace·less /ˈgreɪ·sləs/ *adj* • *She always wears such cheap, graceless* (= unattractive) *clothes.* • *I don't know why you have to slouch around in that graceless way all the time.*

grace·less·ly /ˈgreɪ·slə·sli/ *adv*

grace·less·ness /ˈgreɪ·sləs·nəs/ *n* [U]

grace POLITENESS /greɪs/ *n* [U] a quality of politeness or pleasantness, or a willingness to be fair and honourable • *She always handles her clients with tact and grace.* • *At least he* **had** *the (good) grace* (= was willing) **to** *admit that he was wrong.* [+ *to* infinitive] • *They accepted their defeat* **with (a)** *good/bad grace* (= willingly/unwillingly).

grace *obj* /greɪs/ *v* [T] *fml* • *Many important people will be gracing the opening night of the play* (= honouring it by going to it). • *The flower show was graced by the* **presence** *of the Queen.* • *We are delighted that the mayor will be gracing us* **with** *his* **presence** *at our annual dinner.* • *(humorous) So you've finally decided to grace us* **with** *your* **presence**, *have you?* (= You are late.)

grace·ful /ˈgreɪs·fəl/ *adj* • *He made a graceful* (= polite and pleasant) *speech accepting the nomination.* • *She finally apologized, but she wasn't very graceful about it.*

grace·ful·ly /ˈgreɪs·fəl·i/ *adv* • *They're trying to handle their divorce as gracefully* (= politely and pleasantly) *as possible.*

grace·ful·ness /ˈgreɪs·fəl·nəs/ *n* [U]

grace·less /ˈgreɪ·sləs/ *adj* • *It was rather graceless* (= not polite and pleasant) *of her not to say thank you for all the help he gave her.*

grace·less·ly /ˈgreɪ·slə·sli/ *adv*

grace·less·ness /ˈgreɪ·slə·snəs/ *n* [U] • *It's unlike them to behave with such gracelessness.*

gra·ces /greɪsɪz/ *pl n* • *Ken is sadly lacking in (the)* **social** *graces* (= does not behave in the way considered polite, esp. by people of a high social position).

grace APPROVAL /greɪs/ *n* [U] approval or kindness, esp. (in the Christian religion) that freely given by God to all human beings; FAVOUR SUPPORT • *Betty believed that it was through* **divine** *grace that her husband had recovered from his illness.* • In the CATHOLIC church, after a priest has delivered the last RITES to a dying person (= has said special religious words to them), they are in a **state of** grace (= are believed to be free of evil and have God's approval). • *Rebecca used to be the teacher's favourite but she has* **fallen from** *grace* (= is no longer approved of so much) *recently.* • *His* **fall from** *grace was sudden and unexpected* (= he lost approval suddenly and unexpectedly). • **By the grace of God**, *the pilot managed to land the damaged plane safely.* • *(saying)* 'There but for the grace of God (go I/we)' means something bad that has happened to someone else could have happened to me/us.

grace TIME /greɪs/ *n* [U] a period of time left or allowed before something happens or before something must be done • *The exams have been postponed, so the students have a few days' grace before they start.* • *We're supposed to pay the bill this month, but we've been* **given** *a month's grace.*

grace PRAYER /greɪs/ *n* a prayer said by Christians before and sometimes after a meal to thank God for the food • *The children always* **say** *grace at school.* [U] • *There are several different graces you can* **say**. [C]

Grace TITLE /greɪs/ *n* [C] used to address or refer to a DUKE, DUCHESS or ARCHBISHOP • *His Grace will see you now.* • *Her Grace the Duchess of Kent presented the prizes.* • *This is indeed an honour, your Grace.* [as form of address]

gra·cious PLEASANT /ˈgreɪ·ʃəs/ *adj* (esp. of the behaviour of people towards other people who have a lower social position) polite and pleasant; kind • *The princess always has a gracious smile for everyone she meets.* • *How could you be so rude when they were gracious enough to ask us to dinner?* • *Caroline was very gracious* **to** *all her guests.* • *It was very gracious* **of** *you to invite us.* • *The losing team were gracious* **in** *their defeat.* • *Christians believe that God is gracious* (= that he forgives people who do wrong). • (D) (NL) (P) (S)

gra·cious·ly /ˈgreɪ·ʃə·sli/ *adv* • *She graciously* (= politely and pleasantly) *accepted the flowers that were presented to her.*

gra·cious·ness /ˈgreɪ·ʃə·snəs/ *n* [U]

gra·cious COMFORTABLE /ˈgreɪ·ʃəs/ *adj* having the qualities of great comfort, beauty and freedom from hard work, made possible by wealth • *Visiting the Palace of Versailles gives you an idea of the gracious world the French kings lived in.* • *Our lifestyle isn't particularly gracious, but we're happy.* • *We can't afford gracious* **living**. • (D) (NL) (P) (S)

gra·cious SURPRISE /ˈgreɪ·ʃəs/ *exclamation dated* used to express surprise or to emphasize what is being said • *Gracious* **(me)/Good** *gracious* **(me)/Goodness** *gracious* **(me)**, *I never thought he'd do that!* • *"I'm sorry I'm late." "***Good** *gracious, that doesn't matter."* • (D) (NL) (P) (S)

grad /græd/ *n* [C] *infml for* GRADUATE

gra·da·tion /£grəˈdeɪ·ʃən, $greɪ-/ *n* (a) gradual change, or a stage in the process of change • *The gradation* **in/of** *tempo in this piece of music is very* **subtle.** [U] • *She sees things as being either right or wrong, with no gradations in between.* [C] • *The gradations* (= marks showing units of measurement) *on a ruler are usually marked with different sized lines.* [C]

grade STANDARD /greɪd/ *n* [C] a particular standard, quality or rank • *Which grade* **(of)** *petrol does this car take?*

GREEK FALSE FRIENDS (GR)

English	Greek	Meaning
agenda *n*	ατζέντα	pocket diary
antagonism *n*	ανταγωνισμός	competition; opposition
apathy *n*	απάθεια	callousness; placidity
apology *n*	απολογία	defence against charge; explanation of faith
atomic *adj*	άτομο	of an individual or person
blouse *n*	μπλούζα	overalls
box *n*	μποξ	boxing
camping *n*	κάμπινγκ	a campsite
canteen *n*	καντίνα	mobile snack-bar
catalogue *n*	κατάλογος	(price) list
category *n*	κατηγορία	accusation
climax *n*	κλίμακα	scale (of map, music, or proportion)
crisis *n*	κρίση	decision; fit (of coughing)
democracy *n*	δημοκρατία	republic
diploma *n*	δίπλωμα	driving licence; degree certificate
drama *n*	δράμα	tragedy; (theatre) play
ethos *n*	ήθος	morals, manners, way of life
exotic *adj*	εξωτικός	strange
farce *n*	φάρσα	practical joke
form *n*	φόρμα	overalls; tracksuit
graphic *adj*	γραφικός	striking
gymnasium *n*	γυμνάσιο	high school
history *n*	ιστορία	work of fiction; fuss, trouble
icon *n*	εικόνα	picture
idiotic *adj*	ιδιωτικός	private; individual
logical *adj*	λογικός	reasonable
marmalade *n*	μαρμελάδα	jam
nautical *adj*	ναυτικός	marine, naval, maritime, seafaring
nostalgia *n*	νοσταλγία	homesickness
parking *n*	πάρκινγκ	car park
pathos *n*	πάθος, παθητικός *adj*	passive
phrase *n*	φράση	sentence
physical *adj*	φυσικός	bodily
physiognomy *n*	φυσιογνωμία	personality
political *adj*	πολιτικός	civil
politics *n*	πολιτική	policy
protocol *n*	πρωτόκολλο	file, record; etiquette
scale *n*	σκάλα	ladder, staircase, steps
schism *n*	σχισμή	physical rent, rift, split
scope *n*	σκοπός	sphere of action
slip *n*	σλιπ	briefs, pants
stylus *n*	στύλος	(architecture) column, post
sycophant *n*	συκοφάντης	scandalmonger, slanderer, libeller
sycophantic *adj*	συκοφαντία	libellous
sympathetic *adj*	συμπαθητικός	likeable, nice
sympathise *v*	συμπαθώ	to like
sympathy *n*	συμπάθεια	a liking or weakness for someone or something
syndicate *n*	συνδικάτο	Trade Union; organised group
tavern *n*	ταβέρνα	restaurant
technical *adj*	τεχνικός	skilful; pertaining to science
thesaurus *n*	θησαυρός	treasure; wealth; mine
topical *adj*	τοπικός	local
typical *adj*	τυπικός	formal

• *He's suffering from some kind of* **low**-*grade* (= slight) *infection, which he can't seem to get rid of.* • *There's some really* **high**-*grade* (= high quality) *musicianship on this recording.* • *Factories and offices need to have industrial-grade* (= made for use in industrial places of work) *flooring.* • *These nuclear weapons contain a total of about 100 tonnes of* **weapons**-*grade* (= suitable for making weapons) *plutonium.* • *The planned job losses will mainly affect the lower grades* (= ranks) **of** *staff.* • *Bill has been (Br and Aus)* **on**/*(Am)* **at** *the same grade* (= his job has been of the same level of importance, or he has had the same level of pay) *for several years now.* • *In order to gain university places, British students are required to get certain grades* (= results in an examination) *at A level.* • *Ian wanted to be an actor, but he didn't* **make the grade** (= was not successful). • *(Br) Things seem to be* **on the up/down grade** (= to be getting better/worse). • *(Am and Aus)* A **grade point average** (*abbreviation* **GPA**) is a number which is the average mark received for all the courses a student takes and shows how well the student is doing: *The winners were selected on the basis of their grade point average, SAT scores and answers to essay questions.* ○ *Tulane limits the scholarships to students who have been granted admission and have at least a 2·0 grade point average in high school.* • Ⓘ Ⓝⓛ

grad·ab·le /ˈgreɪ·də·bḷ/ *adj* [not gradable] • A gradable **adjective** or **adverb** is one which can have '-er' and '-est' added to it or be used with 'more' and 'most': *Hot is a gradable adjective, but atomic is not.* • LP **Comparing and grading**

grade *obj* /greɪd/ *v* [T] • *Eggs are usually graded* **into** *different sizes* (= separated into groups according to their size). • *The students' work is graded* (= judged and separated into groups according to quality) *by three examiners.*

grad·ed /ˈgreɪ·dɪd/ *adj* [not gradable] • *The children are learning to read using a graded series of books* (= a series of books in which the level of difficulty gradually increases).

grade SCHOOL /greɪd/ *n* [C] *Am and Aus* a school class or group of classes in which all the children are of a similar age or ability • *Jackie is in the sixth grade.* • *As a child, he had skipped two grades in school.* • *(Am)* **Grade school** is a school for children from the age of five to the age of ten or 14. • LP **Schools and colleges** Ⓘ Ⓝⓛ

-grad·er /£-greɪ·dəʳ, $-greɪ·dɚ/ *combining form Am* • *Shannon is still an eighth-grader* (= in the eighth level of school education) *because she's had to repeat a whole year.*

grade SLOPE /greɪd/ *n* [C] *Am for* GRADIENT • *You'll need to shift to a low gear on your bike on the next hill – it has a real* **steep** *grade.* • **Grade crossing** is *Am for* **level crossing**. See at LEVEL. • PIC **Road** Ⓘ Ⓝⓛ

gra·di·ent /ˈgreɪ·di·ᵊnt/, *Am also* **grade** *n* [C] the amount of slope (of a road, path, railway, etc.) • *This part of the railway track has quite a* **steep** *gradient.* • *The hill is high, but it isn't difficult to climb because the gradient* **of** *the path is very* **gentle** (= the path slopes gradually). • *The gradient* **of** *the road is* **1 in** *6* (= the road rises or falls 1 unit of length in every 6 units of length horizontally).

grad·u·al /ˈgræd·jʊl, ˈgrædʒ·ʊl/ *adj* happening or changing over a long period of time or distance; not sudden • *There has been a gradual improvement in our sales figures over the last two years.* • *As you go further south, you will notice a gradual* **change** *of climate.*

grad·u·al·ly /ˈgræd·jʊ·li, ˈgrædʒ·ʊ·li/ *adv* • *The country's eating habits are gradually shifting towards a healthier diet.* • *She gradually realized that he wasn't telling her the truth.* • *The bank slopes gradually down to the river.*

grad·u·ate PERSON /ˈgrædʒ·u·ət, ˈgræd·ju·ət/, *infml* **grad** *n* [C] a person who has a (first) degree from a university or college • *She's a Cambridge graduate/a graduate* **of** *Cambridge* (= has a degree from Cambridge University). • *Chris is a physics graduate/a graduate* **in** *physics.* • *The company takes on about ten graduates* (= people who have just got degrees) *each year.* • *Levels of graduate unemployment are expected to be higher than ever this year.* • In the US, a graduate is also a person who has completed their PRIMARY or SECONDARY education: *All high-school graduates who wish to do so should have the opportunity of going to college.* • Graduate can also be used to mean POSTGRADUATE: *There are twenty graduate students in the history department this year.* ○ *He became interested in philosophy after completing graduate* **courses/degrees** *in theology and psychology.* • *(Am) Craig hopes to go to* **graduate school** (= a college or college department where students who already have a first degree are taught). • See also POSTGRADUATE; UNDERGRADUATE. • LP **Schools and colleges**

grad·u·ate *(obj)* /ˈgrædʒ·u·ət, ˈgræd·ju·ət/ *v* • *Lorna graduated* (= got her (first) degree) **from** *the University of London.* [I] • *Tom has just graduated (Br and Aus* **with** *first-class* **honours**) **in** *psychology.* [I] • *(Am) After he graduated* (= completed his education at) *high school, he joined the Army.* [T] • *(Am) The college graduates hundreds of students* (= Hundreds of students complete courses at the college) *each year.* [T] • *(fig.) She graduated* (= advanced) **from** *being a secretary* **to** *running her own department.* [I]

grad·u·a·tion /ˌgrædʒ·uˈeɪ·ʃᵊn, ˌgræd·juˈ-/ *n* [U] • *After graduation, she wants to travel round the world.* • *We're all going to Oxford on Saturday for Rob's graduation* **(ceremony)** (= a ceremony at which an official document saying that he has got a degree will be given to him).

grad·u·ate *obj* DIVIDE /ˈgræd·ju·eɪt, ˈgrædʒ·u-/ *v* [T often passive] to divide into levels or measured units • *Our salary scale is graduated* **into** *five levels.* • *This thermometer is graduated* **in/into** *both Centigrade and Fahrenheit.*

grad·u·at·ed /£ˈgræd·ju·eɪ·tɪd, $-t̬ɪd/ *adj* [not gradable] • *The books that the children are using to learn to read are on a graduated* **scale** (= are divided into levels) *of difficulty.* • *I'm paying into a graduated pension scheme* (= one in which the payments I make are related to what I earn).

grad·u·a·tion /ˌgrædʒ·uˈeɪ·ʃᵊn, ˌgræd·juˈ-/ *n* [C] • A graduation is a mark showing a level in a set of measured units.

Graec·o- *Br, Am* **Gre·co-** /£ˈgriː·kəʊ, £ˈgrek·əʊ, $ˈgrek·oʊ/ *combining form* of or connected with (Ancient) Greece • *splendid Graeco-Roman ruins*

graf·fi·ti /£grəˈfiː·ti, $-t̬i/ *pl n* words or drawings, esp. humorous, rude or political, on walls, doors, etc. in public places • *The subway walls are covered in graffiti.* • *'A woman without a man is like a fish without a bicycle' is a well-known* **piece of** *feminist graffiti.* • *Keith Haring was a New York graffiti artist.*

graft PIECE /£grɑːft, $græft/ *n* [C] a piece of healthy skin or bone cut from one part of a person's body and used to repair another damaged part, or a piece cut from one living plant and fixed to another plant so that it grows there • *He has had a* **skin** *graft on his badly burned arm.* • *Plant the roses so that the graft* (= place where one type of rose is joined to another) *is above the surface of the soil.*

graft *obj* /£grɑːft, $græft/ *v* [T] • *Surgeons removed some skin from her leg and grafted* (= fixed) *it* **on/onto** *her face.* • *Are these plants grafted or grown from seed?* • *Roses are usually grafted* **onto** *the stems of wild roses to help them grow strongly.* • *(fig.) The management tried to graft* (= add) *new working methods* **onto** *the existing ways of doing things, but it was unsuccessful.*

graft INFLUENCE /£grɑːft, $græft/ *n* [U] the act of obtaining money or advantage through the dishonest use of (esp. political) power and influence • *The whole government was riddled with graft, bribery, and corruption.*

graft WORK /£grɑːft, $græft/ *n* [U] *Br* hard work • *I've never been afraid of* **hard** *graft.*

graft /£grɑːft, $græft/ *v* [I] *Br* • *It was very sad that after spending all those years grafting* **away** (= working hard), *he died so soon after he retired.*

graft·er /£ˈgrɑːf·təʳ, $ˈgræf·t̬ɚ/ *n* [C]

Grail /greɪl/ *n* [U] See **Holy Grail** at HOLY GOOD

grain SEED /greɪn/ *n* (a) seed from a plant, esp. a grass-like plant such as rice or wheat • *wheat/maize grains* [C] • *This bread is made from whole grains.* [C] • *They didn't have so much as a grain* **of** *rice to eat.* [C] • *Grain* (= the crop from grass-like food plants) *is one of the main exports of the American Midwest.* [U] • *Grain prices have fallen again.* • See also WHOLEGRAIN. • PIC **Cereals**

grain SMALL PIECE /greɪn/ *n* [C] a very small piece (of a hard substance) • *The trouble with having picnics on the beach is that you get grains* **of sand** *in the food.* • The grain **of** a photograph is its appearance of being formed by a pattern of extremely small spots of black and white or colour. • *(fig.) There wasn't a grain* **of truth** (= there was no truth) *in anything she said.* • *"To see a World in a Grain of Sand / And a Heaven in a Wild Flower, / Hold Infinity in the palm of your hand,/ And Eternity in an hour"* (William Blake in the poem *Auguries of Innocence*, c.1803)

-grained /-greɪnd/ *combining form* • *She bought some coarse-grained salt* (= salt in rough pieces).

grain·y /ˈgreɪ·ni/ *adj* **-ier, -iest** • *Old photographs and films are often rather grainy* (= are unclear because of appearing to be made up of a lot of spots of black and white or colour).

grain PATTERN /greɪn/ *n* [U] the natural patterns of lines in the surface of wood, rock, cloth, paper or meat, or the direction in which the fibres that form these substances lie • *Varnishing the wood brings out its grain.* • *This table-top has a beautiful grain.* • *It's easier to split marble* **along** *the grain* (= in the direction of the fibres which form it), *rather than* **across/against** *it* (= at an angle of 90° to the fibres.) • *(fig.) It really* **goes against** *the grain for Sarah* (= it is not typical of her and she does not like) *to admit that she's wrong.* • *(fig.) These actions* **go against** *the grain* (= principles) **of** *the party.*

-grained /-greɪnd/ *combining form* • *a cabinet made of finely-grained wood* (= wood with a pattern of very thin lines on its surface)

grain WEIGHT /greɪn/ *n* [C] *dated* a unit of mass, equal to 0·0648 grams • *The old coins weighed about 54 grains* **of** *gold.*

gram MEASUREMENT, **gramme** /græm/, **g, gm** *n* [C] (a unit of mass equal to) 0·001 kilograms • *This bag of flour weighs 500 grams.* • *Could I have 250 grams* **of** *cheese, please?* • LP **Units**

-gram MESSAGE /-græm/ *combining form* an amusing message sent as a surprise • *a kissogram* (= a message delivered by someone who kisses the person receiving it) • *a strippagram* (= a message delivered by someone who removes their clothes)

gram·mar /ˈgræm·əʳ, $-ɚ/ *n* (the study or use of) the rules about how words change their form and combine with other words to make sentences • *I think it's important for children to be taught grammar.* [U] • *He's finding it difficult to learn Russian grammar.* [U] • *If students' grammar isn't corrected, they'll never learn to use it properly.* [U] • *In English, it's* **bad** *grammar to say "you was".* [U] • A grammar is a book which describes the rules about how words change their form and combine with other words to make sentences in a particular language: *I've just bought a German grammar.* [C] • In Britain, esp. in the past, a **grammar school** is a school for children aged 11-18 who are good at studying. In America, esp. in the past, it is a school for children aged 5-12/14. • LP **Schools and colleges**

gram·mar·i·an /£grəˈmeə·ri·ən, $-ˈmer·i-/ *n* [C] • A grammarian is a person who studies and usually writes books about grammar: *We consulted a leading grammarian.*

gram·ma·ti·cal /£grəˈmæt·ɪ·kᵊl, $-ˈmæt̬-/ *adj* [not gradable] • *This sentence has a simple grammatical structure* (= the words it contains combine in a simple way). • *"I are tired" is not grammatical* (= is not a correct combination of words). • *She speaks good grammatical French* (= she combines the words correctly).

gram·mati·cal·ly /£grəˈmæt·ɪ·kli, $-mæt̬-/ *adv* [not gradable] • *Some people think it doesn't matter if you don't use words in a grammatically correct way* (= follow the rules for combining words) *as long as you can be understood.*

gram·ma·ti·cal·i·ty /£grəˌmæt·ɪˈkæl·ɪ·ti, $-ˌmæt̬·əˈkæl·ə·t̬i/ *n specialized* • *I'm not sure about the grammaticality* **of** *this sentence* (= about whether the words are correctly combined).

Gram·my /ˈgræm·i/ *n* [C] *trademark* (in the US) one of a set of prizes given each year to people involved in many different areas of the music industry • *She won a Grammy (Award) for the most promising female vocalist a couple of years ago, and has hardly been heard of since.* • *The National Academy of Recording Arts and Sciences is the organization which hands out the Grammys.*

gram·o·phone /£ˈgræm·ə·fəʊn, $-foʊn/ *n* [C] *dated for* **record player**, see at RECORD STORE ELECTRONICALLY • **Gramophone record** is *dated for* RECORD.

gran /græn/ *n* [C] *infml for* GRANDMOTHER • *(My) gran's ill.* • *Sit down here, Gran.* [as form of address]

gran·a·ry /£ˈgræn·ᵊr·i, $ˈ-ɚ-/ *n* [C] a large building for storing wheat or other similar crops • *(fig.) The effect of the President's policies is being felt particularly in the granary states* (= the parts of the US where a lot of wheat is grown). • *(Br)* **Granary bread** (*Aus* **wholegrain bread**) or a **granary loaf** is a type of bread containing whole seeds of wheat.

grand SPLENDID /grænd/ *adj* **-er, -est** splendid in style and appearance; attracting admiration and attention • *The Palace of Versailles is very grand.* • *We don't want a grand wedding, just a quiet family affair.* • *They always entertain their guests* **in grand style**. • *All the performers in the show came on stage for the grand* **finale**. • *In the opera 'The Magic Flute', the Queen of the Night makes a grand* **entrance** *in Act I* (= her entrance attracts everyone's attention). • *Tony is someone who always likes making grand* **gestures** (= doing splendid things in order to attract attention). • Grand is sometimes used in the name of a place or building to show that it is splendid or large: *the Grand Hotel* ○ *the Grand Canyon* ○ *the Grand Canal* • If someone or an animal lives to a **grand old age**, they live until they are very old: *Our cat lived to a grand old age.* ○ *He lived to the grand old age* **of** *97.* ○ *(humorous) At the grand old age* **of** *six, Leila had lived in four different European capitals.* • **Grand opera** is a type of serious opera. • *The hotel has a pianist playing at the large white* **grand piano** (= a large piano which has horizontal strings and is used esp. for performances) *in the bar.* • A **grand tour** is a visit to the most important countries and cities of Europe which rich young men made in the past as part of their education: *(fig. humorous) Let me give you a grand tour* **of** (= show you) *the house.* • Ⓟ

grand·ly /ˈgrænd·li/ *adv* • *Their house is very grandly furnished.*

grand·ness /ˈgrænd·nəs/ *n* [U]

grand IMPORTANT /grænd/ *adj* **-er, -est** important and large in degree • *The management has put forward a grand scheme/design for re-organizing the company.* • *She has all kinds of grand ideas/ambitions/hopes for the future.* • *His job has a grand title, but he's little more than a clerk.* • *(disapproving) The Jacksons think they're very grand* (= important and better than other people) *but they're not really.* • *(disapproving) Diane is always acting the grand lady* (= acting as if she is important and better than other people). • Grand can also be used in a disapproving way to mean showing a desire to seem important: *This project is just another one of Leon's grand ideas.* • *He's been called the* **grand old man of** (= He is an important and respected person in) *cricket.* • *(Aus)* The **grand final** is the final game of a sporting competition which decides the winners for that part of the year. • A **grand jury** in the US is a group of people who decide whether a person who has been charged with a crime should be given a trial in a court of law. • *She will be going for the* **grand slam** (= trying to win all of a set of important sports competitions). • A **grand slam** is also the winning of all the cards in a card game, esp. BRIDGE. • In baseball, a **grand slam** is when a player hits the ball so that he is able to run round all the points on the field while other members of the team are already at three of the points. • A **grand sum** or **grand total** is the complete number after everything has been added up: *The school bazaar raised a/the grand total of £550.* • (P)

grand·ly /ˈgrænd·li/ *adv* • *She announced grandly that she was spending Christmas in the Caribbean.*

grand·ness /ˈgrænd·nəs/ *n* [U]

grand EXCELLENT /grænd/ *adj dated infml or Irish Eng* excellent; pleasing • *We had grand weather on our holiday.* • *It would be a grand adventure for the children to go sailing.* • *My grandson is a grand little chap.* • *You've done a grand job.* • (P)

grand MONEY /grænd/, *Am* **G** *n* [C] *pl* **grand** *infml* £ £1000 or $1000 • *John's new car cost him 20 grand!* • LP› **Money** (P)

grand INSTRUMENT /grænd/ *n* [C] *infml for* **grand piano**, see at GRAND SPLENDID • *a* **baby** (= small) *grand* • *a* **concert** *grand* • (P)

gran·dad, grand·dad /ˈgræn·dæd/ *n* [C] *infml for* GRANDFATHER • *Watch me ride my bike, Grandad.* [as form of address] • Grandad can also be used rudely or humorously to address an old man: *Come on, grandad!* [as form of address]

gran·dad·dy, grand·dad·dy /ˈgræn·dæd·i/ *n* [C] *Am infml for* GRANDFATHER • *(Am infml) As my old grandaddy used to say, hard work never hurt no one.* • *(fig.) 'Modern Times' is a classic comedy starring Charlie Chaplin, the grandaddy* **of** (= one of the first, greatest and most influential) *comic film actors.* • *(fig.) There was a grandaddy* **of** *a* (= a very great) *crash when the storm blew down a tree outside our house.*

grand·child /ˈgrænd·tʃaɪld/ *n* [C] *pl* **grandchildren** /ˈgrænd,tʃɪl·drən/ the child of a person's son or daughter • PIC› **Family tree**

grand·daught·er /ˈgrænd·dɔː·tər, $-dɑː·t̬ɚ/ *n* [C] the daughter of a person's son or daughter • PIC› **Family tree**

gran·dee /grænˈdiː/ *n* [C] an important person, esp. in a particular job or area of public life • *All the local grandees attended the opening of the new hospital.* • *The grandees* **of** *film and television will all be at tonight's awards ceremony.*

gran·deur /£ˈgræn·djər, $-dʒɚ/ *n* [U] a quality of great beauty and size, or of attracting attention • *We were struck by the silent grandeur* **of** *the desert.* • *This recording does not bring out the full grandeur* **of** *Wagner's music.* • *Even if you don't like it, you have to admit that the Brighton Pavilion* **has** *(a certain) grandeur.*

grand·fath·er /£ˈgrænd·fɑː·ðər, $-ðɚ/, *infml* **grand·pa, gran·dad**, *Am infml* **gran·dad·dy** *n* [C] the father of a person's mother or father • *(fml) How are you, Grandfather?* [as form of address] ◦ A **grandfather clock** is a tall clock in a wooden case which stands on the floor, and is usually larger than a person. • PIC› **Clocks and watches, Family tree**

gran·dil·o·quent /grænˈdɪl·ə·kwənt/ *adj fml esp. disapproving* in a style that is intended to cause admiration and attract attention, esp. in order to make someone or something seem important • *a grandiloquent style of architecture* • *He was a performer who loved making grandiloquent gesture.* • *Her speech was full of grandiloquent* (= complicated and difficult to understand) *language, but it contained no new ideas.*

gran·dil·o·quence /grænˈdɪl·ə·kwənts/ *n* [U]

gran·dil·o·quent·ly /grænˈdɪl·ə·kwənt·li/ *adv*

gran·di·ose /£ˈgræn·di·əus, £-əuz, $-ous/ *adj disapproving* larger and containing more detail than necessary, or intended to seem important or splendid • *They have some grandiose* **plans/ideas/schemes** *for making money.* • *He is full of grandiose* **ambitions/hopes/dreams** *for the future.* • *The house is decorated in a very grandiose style.*

grand·ma /ˈgrænd·mɑː, ˈgræm-/ *n* [C] *infml for* GRANDMOTHER • *Can I have a drink, please, Grandma?* [as form of address]

grand·master /£ˈgrænd,mɑː·stər, $-,mæs·tɚ/ *(abbreviation* **GM**) *n* [C] (the rank of) a person who plays the game of CHESS with the highest level of skill • *England has more than twenty grandmasters.* • *She has just achieved her second grandmaster* **norm** (= performance at grandmaster standard).

grand·moth·er /ˈgrænd·mʌð·ər, ˈgræm-, $-ɚ/, *infml* **grand·ma, gran·ny, gran**, *Br infml or Am regional* **na·na**, *infml* **nan·ny** *n* [C] the mother of a person's father or mother • *(fml) Would you like to sit here, Grandmother?* [as form of address] • *(saying)* 'Don't teach your grandmother to suck eggs' means that you should not try to tell people who are more experienced than you something they already know. • PIC› **Family tree**

grand·pa /ˈgrænd·pɑː, ˈgræm-/ *n* [C] *infml for* GRANDFATHER • *Will you read me a story, Grandpa?* [as form of address]

grand·par·ent /£ˈgrænd·peə·rənt, $-per·ənt/ *n* [C] the father or mother of a person's father or mother • PIC› **Family tree**

grand prix /£,grɑ̃ːˈpriː, $,grɑːn-/ *n* [C] *pl* **grands prix** an important international race for very fast and powerful cars. There are several different grands prix. • *the Italian Grand Prix*

grand·son /ˈgrænd·sʌn/ *n* [C] the son of a person's son or daughter • PIC› **Family tree**

grand·stand /ˈgrænd·stænd/ *n* [C] a set of seats arranged in rising rows, sometimes covered by a roof, from which people can easily watch sports or other events • *Do you want to come to the match tonight? I've got two tickets for the grandstand/two grandstand tickets.* • *(fig.) From our hotel room window, we had a grandstand* (= very good) **view** *of the parade.*

grand·stand·ing /,grændˈstæn·dɪŋ,li/ *n* [U] *Am infml* acting or speaking in a way intended to attract the good opinion of other people who are watching

grange /greɪndʒ/ *n* [C] a large house in the countryside with farm buildings connected to it • *The main school building is an old grange that has been modernized.* • *Their house is called Chiltern Grange.* • Grange is also *Am for* FARM.

gran·ite /ˈgræn·ɪt/ *n* [U] very hard, grey, pink and black rock, which is used for building • *The cathedral is built on foundations made of granite.* • *The ground has frozen so hard, it's like granite* (= is very hard).

gran·ny, gran·nie /ˈgræn·i/ *n* [C] *infml for* GRANDMOTHER • *Would you like a cup of tea, Granny?* [as form of address] • Granny can also be used of something that you wear, to mean having a style like those worn by old women: *granny glasses* (= those with small round metal frames) ◦ *granny shoes* (= those fastened with small buttons) • *(Br and Aus)* A **granny flat** is a set of rooms, often connected to or part of a relative's house, in which an old person lives.

gran·ny knot /ˈgræn·i/ *n* [C] a type of knot that has not been tied correctly and so can be easily unfastened

gran·o·la /£grəˈnəu·lə, $-ˈnou-/ *n* [U] *Am* a food made of baked grains, nuts and dried fruit which is usually eaten in the morning • *Granola is a lot like muesli, only crunchier.*

grant MONEY /£grɑːnt, $grænt/ *n* [C] a sum of money given esp. by the government to a person or organization for a special purpose • *a student/research grant* • *a local authority/government grant* • *a maternity grant* • *They* **gave/awarded** *her a grant* **to** *study abroad for one year.* [+ *to* infinitive] • *We* **applied for/claimed/got/received** *a grant* **from** *the local council* **for** *roof insulation.* • *They've decided to* **freeze** *the grant* (= pay it) *at last year's level.* • *As a student I* **was/lived on** *a grant of less than £4000 a year.* • If an organization is *(Br)* **grant-aided**, or receives *(Am)* a **grant-in-aid**, it is given part of the money it needs by the government or another organization. See also SUBSIDIZE. •

A **grant-maintained school**(also **GM school**) receives its money directly from central government.

grant *obj* GIVE /£grɑːnt, $grænt/ *v* [T] to give or agree to give or do (something that another person has asked for) • *They granted her an entry visa/They granted an entry visa* **to** *her.* [+ two objects] • *He was granted access to a lawyer/asylum/a pardon.* • *The US agreed to grant the new state diplomatic recognition/grant diplomatic recognition* **to** *the new state).* [+ two objects] • *fml She granted their request/wish.* • *fml I wonder if you could grant me a favour/grant a favour* **to** *me).* [+ two objects] • *fml "Permission to speak?"* "**Granted** (= Yes)."

grant *obj* ACCEPT /£grɑːnt, $grænt/ *v* [T] to accept that something is true, often before expressing an opposite opinion • *I grant* **that** *it must have been upsetting but even so I think she made a bit of a fuss.* [+ *that* clause] • *Granted/***I grant you** (= It is true that), *it's a difficult situation but I feel sure he could have handled it more sensitively.* • *(fml) As reluctant as I was to do so, I had to grant the truth in what Noel said.* • To **take** a fact **for granted** is to believe it to be the truth without even thinking about it: *I know it was silly of me but I just took it for granted* **that** *they were married.* [+ *that* clause] ○ *I didn't realize that Melanie hadn't been to college – I suppose I just took it for granted.* • If you **take** situations or people **for granted** you do not appreciate or show gratitude for how much you benefit from them: *He just takes it for granted* **that** *the house is always tidy.* [+ *that* clause] ○ *Most young people take central heating for granted because they've never lived without it.* • *One of the problems with relationships is that after a while you just take each other for granted.*

grant·ed (that) /£ˈgrɑːn·tɪd, $ˈgræn·tɪd/ *conjunction* • *Granted (that)* (= If you accept that) *the story's true, what are you going to do about it?*

gran·u·lat·ed /£ˈgræn·jʊ·leɪ·tɪd, $-t̬ɪd/ *adj* [not gradable] (esp. of sugar) in small grains • *Granulated* **sugar** *is coarser than caster sugar.*

gran·ule /ˈgræn·juːl/ *n* [C] a small grain-like piece of something • *instant coffee granules* • *a granule of sugar*

gran·u·lar /ˈgræn·jʊ·ləʳ, $-jə·lɚ/ *adj* [not gradable] • If something is granular, it is made of, or seems like, granules: *a granular texture/surface/taste* ○ *granular snow* • *Does it come in granular form or in powder form?*

grape /greɪp/ *n* [C] a small round purple or pale green fruit that you can eat or make into wine • *black/white/red/green grapes* • *a bunch of grapes* • *seedless grapes* • *grape juice* • *wine grapes* • *Different kinds of grape are dried in order to make raisins, sultanas and currants.* • *I'm going grape-***picking** *in France this autumn.* • *(humorous)* People sometimes refer to wine as **the grape**: *Care for a little more of the grape?* • PIC **Fruit** ①

grape·fruit /ˈgreɪp·fruːt/ *n* [C] *pl* **grapefruit** or **grapefruits** a tree fruit which is like a large orange, but has a yellow skin and tastes less sweet • *grapefruit juice/segments* • *a grapefruit knife/spoon* (= a special knife/spoon for eating grapefruit) • *We start breakfast with half a grapefruit.* • PIC **Fruit**

grape·shot /ˈgreɪp·ʃɒt, $-ʃɑːt/ *n* [U] a mass of small iron balls which were fired together from a CANNON (= a big gun) in the past

grape·vine /ˈgreɪp·vaɪn/, *also* **vine** *n* [C] the climbing plant that the GRAPE grows on • If you **hear** something **on/through the grapevine**, you hear it from someone who heard it from someone else: *I heard it on the grapevine that he was leaving – is it true?*

graph /£grɑːf, græf/ *n* [C] a picture which shows how two sets of information or variable amounts are related, usually by lines or curves • *a block graph* • *graph paper* • *To draw a graph you need to plot results along the x and y axes.* • *This graph shows how crime has varied in relationship to unemployment over the last 20 years.* • *There was a temperature graph hanging at the foot of each patient's bed.*

graph·ic /ˈgræf·ɪk/, *esp. Br* **graph·i·cal** /ˈgræf·ɪ·kəl/ *adj* [not gradable] • *a graphic presentation/representation* • See also GRAPHIC CLEAR; GRAPHIC DRAWING.

graph·i·cally /ˈgræf·ɪ·kli/ *adv* [not gradable] • *We can show this information graphically.* • See also **graphically** at GRAPHIC CLEAR.

graph·ic CLEAR /ˈgræf·ɪk/ *adj* very clear and powerful; VIVID • *a graphic description/account/example* • *He insisted on describing his operation* **in** *graphic* **detail** *while we were eating lunch.* • See also **graphic** at GRAPH. • GR

graph·i·cally /ˈgræf·ɪ·kli/ *adv* • *The incident graphically* (= very clearly) *illustrates just how dangerous the situation in the war zone has become.* • See also **graphically** at GRAPH.

graph·ic DRAWING /ˈgræf·ɪk/ *adj* [before n] related to drawing or printing • *the graphic works* (= drawings) *of Rembrandt* • The **graphic arts** are the arts that include drawing, writing and printing: *a graphic artist* • A **graphic designer** deals with the TYPOGRAPHY (= style of printing) of printed work, esp. books: *Nick's a graphic designer.* ○ *Nick works in* **graphic design**. • A **graphic novel** is a book containing a long, single story told mostly in pictures but with some writing: *Art Spiegelman's 'Maus' is a very well-known graphic novel.* • See also **graphic** at GRAPH. • GR

graph·ics /ˈgræf·ɪks/ *pl n* • The pictures and symbols that you can produce with a computer are called **(computer)** graphics. • Graphics are also the pictures and photographs, sometimes with writing on them, used in books, magazines, films and television: *media graphics*

graph·ite /ˈgræf·aɪt/ *n* [U] a soft dark grey form of carbon, used in the middle of pencils, as a LUBRICANT in machines, and in some atomic REACTORS • Graphite is also one of the substances in the material from which a lot of sports equipment is made: *Graphite rackets are lighter than metal ones.*

graph·ol·o·gy /£grəˈfɒl·ə·dʒi, $-ˈfɑː·lə-/ *n* [U] the study of people's writing, esp. in order to discover things about their characters

graph·ol·o·gist /£grəˈfɒl·ə·dʒɪst, $-ˈfɑː·lə-/ *n* [C] • A graphologist is a person who is an expert at studying people's writing.

grap·nel /ˈgræp·nəl/, **grap·pling i·ron/hook** /ˈgræp·lɪŋ/ *n* [C] a device used in sailing which consists of several hooks on the end of a rope

grap·pa /£ˈgræp·ə, $ˈgrɑː·pə/ *n* [U] a type of BRANDY (= a strong alcoholic drink) made from GRAPES • *Annette brought me a bottle of grappa back from Italy.*

grap·ple /ˈgræp·l̩/ *v* [I] to STRUGGLE or fight (with someone) • *The policeman was grappling* **with** *two men.* • *The children grappled* **for** *the ball.* • *(fig.) This is just one of the* **problems** *the council is grappling* **with** (= trying with difficulty to deal with). • A **grappling iron/hook** is a GRAPNEL.

grasp *obj* HOLD /£grɑːsp, $græsp/ *v* [T] to quickly take (something) esp. in your hand(s) and hold it firmly • *Rosie suddenly grasped my hand.* • *She grasped me* **by** *the arm and led me to the window.* • *(fig.) She'll grasp* (= take eagerly) *any opportunity she can to practise her Spanish.* • If you grasp **at** something, you try to hold or touch it: *She grasped at his shirt as he ran past.* • *(fig.) Certainly if the job were offered me I'd grasp at the chance.* • *(Br and Aus)* If you **grasp the nettle**, you force yourself to be brave and do something that is difficult or unpleasant: *You've been putting off making that phone-call for days – I think it's about time you grasped the nettle!*

grasp /£grɑːsp, $græsp/ *n* [U] • *I lost my grasp on the suitcase and it fell open on the road.* • *He shook my hand with a very firm grasp.* • *(fig.) The gold medal* **slipped from** *his grasp* (= He missed winning it) *in the last moments of the race.* • *(fig.) The presidency at last looked* **within** *her grasp* (= It looked possible that she might become president). • *(fig.) Why is success always* **beyond** *my grasp* (= impossible to get)? • *(fig.) I sometimes think that he may be* **losing** *his grasp* **on** *reality* (= He no longer knows what is real and what is not).

grasp *obj* UNDERSTAND /£grɑːsp, $græsp/ *v* [T] to understand (esp. something difficult) • *I think I managed to grasp the main points of the lecture.* • *As a concept, it is intriguing even if I don't fully grasp its logic.* • *The school feels the family has not fully grasped the seriousness of the situation.* • *The Government has acknowledged that homelessness is a problem but it has failed to grasp the scale of the problem.* • *I don't think he grasps* **what** *a serious situation it is.* [+ *wh*-word]

grasp /£grɑːsp, $græsp/ *n* [U] • *I'm afraid my grasp of economics is rather limited.*

grasp·ing /£ˈgrɑː·spɪŋ, $ˈgræs·pɪŋ/ *adj disapproving* (of people) always trying to get and keep more of something, esp. money • *She was portrayed in the press as a grasping sort of character who was only interested in men for their money.*

grass /£grɑːs, $græs/ *n* a low green plant which grows naturally over a lot of the Earth's surface, having groups of very thin leaves which grow in large numbers very close together • *a blade/tuft of grass* [U] • *Cows eat grass.* [U] • *Jim, are you going to* **cut** *the grass this afternoon?* [U] • *Shall we sit on the grass* (=an area of grass)*?* [U] • *She had on the mantelpiece a vase of dried flowers and grasses* (= different types of grass) [C] • *There was a sign saying "Please do not walk on the grass."* [U] • *She prefers playing tennis* **on** *grass (***on** *a grass* **court***) to playing on a hard court. She's a good grass* **player**. [U] • *(Br) We* **put** *most of the garden* **down to** *grass* (=planted grass in it). [U] • *The farmers* **put** *the cows* **out to** *grass* (=put them in a field where they can eat grass) *in April.* [U] • *(fig. infml)* If you **put** a person **out to grass**, you tell them they can no longer work: *A lot of people in their sixties feel much too young to be put out to grass.* • Grass is also slang for MARIJUANA. [U] • A **grass widow** (*male* **grass widower**) is a woman/man who does not live with their husband/wife, or whose husband/wife is away from home for long periods of time. • *(saying)* 'The grass is (always) greener on the other side (of the fence)' means that things always seem to be better somewhere where you are not: *I sometimes think I'd be happier teaching in Spain. Oh well, the grass is always greener on the other side!* • PIC› **Blade**

grass *obj* /£grɑːs, $græs/ *v* [T] • *Let's grass* **(over)** (= grow grass on) *the top of the garden.* • *They covered the rubbish tip with soil, then grassed it* **over** (= covered it with grass to hide it).

gras·sy /£'grɑː·si, $'græs·i/ *adj* **-ier, -iest** • *a grassy slope/hillside*

grass on *obj v prep* [T] *Br and Aus slang* (esp. of a criminal) to secretly give information about (someone who has committed a crime) to the police; INFORM on (someone) • *Dan grassed on them* **to** *the local police.*

grass /£grɑːs, $græs/ *n* [C] *Br slang* • *His friends had begun to suspect that he was a grass.* • See also SUPERGRASS.

grass·hop·per /£'grɑːsˌhɒp·əʳ, $'græsˌhɑː·pɚ/ *n* [C] a plant-eating insect with long back legs that can jump very high and makes a sharp high noise using its back legs or wings • PIC› **Insects**

grass·land /£'grɑːs·lænd, -lənd, $'græs-/ *n* a large area of land covered with grass • *temperate/tropical/sub-tropical grasslands* • *the grasslands of North America* [C] • *It says in my book that the cheetah inhabits dry grassland and scrub.* [U]

grass·roots /£ˌgrɑːs'ruːts, $ˌgræs-/ *pl n* **the grassroots** the ordinary people in a society or an organization, esp. a political party • *The feeling among the grassroots of the Party is that the leaders are not radical enough.*

grass·roots /£'grɑːs·ruːts, $'græs-/ *adj* [before n; not gradable] • *grassroots politics/activity/ideas/opinion* • *a grassroots activist*

grass-tree /£'grɑːs·tri, $'græs-/ *n* [C] a large Australian plant with a woody, trunk-like stem, stiff grass-like leaves and groups of small white flowers

grate FIRE /greɪt/ *n* [C] a metal structure which holds coal or wood in a fireplace • *There was a fire burning* **in** *the grate.* • PIC› **Fires and space heaters**

grate ANNOY /greɪt/ *v* [I] (esp. of an unpleasant noise) to annoy you • *After a while her voice really started to grate* **on** *me.* • *He's got one of those voices that really grates* **on** *your* **nerves***!* • *I can tolerate her voice for a while but then it starts to grate.* • *It's the way she's always talking about herself – it just grates* **on** *me.*

grate *obj* COOKING /greɪt/ *v* [T] to rub (food) against a GRATER (=metal device with sharp holes in it), in order to cut it into a lot of small pieces • *Could you grate the cheese for me?* • PIC› **Food preparation**

grat·ed /£'greɪ·tɪd, $-t̬ɪd/ *adj* [not gradable] • *grated cheese/carrots/nutmeg*

grat·er /£'greɪ·təʳ, $-t̬ɚ/ *n* [C] • A grater is a metal device with holes surrounded by sharp edges used to cut food into small pieces: *a cheese grater* • PIC› **Kitchen**

grate RUB TOGETHER /greɪt/ *v* [I] (of two hard objects) to rub together, sometimes making a sharp unpleasant sound • *After a while the hard ends of the bones grate against each other instead of gliding smoothly over one another.* • *I can't bear the noise of the chair grating on the stone floor.*

grat·ing /£'greɪ·tɪŋ, $-t̬ɪŋ/ *adj* • *There was a horrible grating* **sound** *as she tried to move her leg.*

grate·ful /'greɪt·fəl/ *adj* showing or expressing thanks, esp. to another person • *I'm so grateful* **(to you) for** *all that you've done.* • *If you could get that report finished by Thursday I'd be very grateful.* • *After the earthquake we felt grateful* **to** *be alive.* [+ *to* infinitive] • *I'm just grateful* **that** *I'm not still working for him.* [+ *that* clause] • *I'd be (most) grateful if you would send me the book immediately.*

grate·ful·ly /'greɪt·fəl·i/ *adv* • *She smiled at me gratefully.*

gra·ti·tude /£'græt·ɪ·tjuːd, $'græt̬·ə·tuːd/, **grate·ful·ness** /'greɪt·fəl·nəs/ *n* [U] • *deep/sincere/everlasting gratitude* • *She sent them a present to* **show/express** *her gratitude.* • *Take this* **as a token of** *my gratitude for all your help.* • *How can I show my gratitude* **(to** *him)?*

grat·i·fy *obj* /£'græt·ɪ·faɪ, $'græt̬·ə-/ *v* [often passive] to please (someone), or to satisfy (a wish or need) • *We were gratified* **at/by** *the response to our appeal.* • *He was gratified* **to** *see how well his students had done.* [+ obj + *to* infinitive] • *Judge Pryor said, "You told them lie after lie in order to get their money so that you could gratify your gambler's* **desire***."* • *Her need for intellectual stimulation wasn't gratified until she got to university.*

grat·i·fi·ca·tion /£ˌgræt·ɪ·fɪ'keɪ·ʃən, $ˌgræt̬·ə-/ *n* [U] • *Some people expect* **instant** *gratification* (=to get what they want immediately). • *A former member of the police force, he seemed to get* **sexual** *gratification from beating people up.* • *I learnt with (some) gratification that he'd failed to get the job.* • (NL)

grat·i·fy·ing /£'græt·ɪ·faɪ·ɪŋ, $'græt̬-/ *adj* • *It must be very gratifying* **to** *see all your children grown up and happy.* [+ *to* infinitive] • **It** *is gratifying* **that** *she hasn't lost her job.* [+ *that* clause]

grat·i·fy·ing·ly /£'græt·ɪ·faɪ·ɪŋ·li, $'græt̬-/ *adv* • *The success rate in the exam was gratifyingly high.*

gra·tin /£'græt·æ̃ŋ, $'grɑː·t̬ən/ *n* [C], *adj* [not gradable] used in the names of dishes which have a thin layer of cheese and often bread on top • *I've chosen the aubergine and tomato* **(au)** *gratin.* • *Put the thinly sliced potato into a buttered gratin* **dish** (=cooking container) *and then cover with breadcrumbs and grated cheese.*

grat·ing /£'greɪ·tɪŋ, $-t̬ɪŋ/ *n* [C] a structure made of metal bars which covers a hole, esp. in the ground over a DRAIN • *His ring fell to the ground and rolled through a grating.* • See also **grating** at GRATE RUB TOGETHER.

gra·tis /£'grɑː·tɪs, $'græt̬·əs/ *adv* [after v], *adj* [after v; not gradable] free; not costing anything • *I'll give it to you, gratis!* • *For you, it's gratis!* • *Drinks will be provided gratis.*

gra·tu·i·tous /£grə'tjuː·ɪ·təs, $-'tuː·ə·t̬əs/ *adj disapproving* not necessary; with no cause • *A lot of viewers complained that there was too much gratuitous* **sex** *and* **violence** *in the film.*

gra·tu·i·tous·ly /£grə'tjuː·ɪ·tə·sli, $-'tuː·ə-/ *adv* • *Many scenes in the film have been condemned as excessively and gratuitously violent.*

gra·tu·i·tous·ness /£grə'tjuː·ɪ·tə·snəs, $-'tuː·ə-/ *n* [U]

gra·tu·i·ty /£grə'tjuː·ə·ti, $-'tuː·ə·t̬i/ *n* [C] a sum of money given as a reward for a service • *(fml) The guides sometimes receive gratuities from the tourists which supplement their salaries.* • *(Br) After he was disabled in the accident, he left the army with a one-off gratuity of £5000.* • *(Am) Government regulators were accused of taking* **illegal** *gratuities from the drug companies they oversee.* • (F)

grave DEATH /greɪv/ *n* [C] a place where a dead person or dead people are buried, esp. when under the ground and marked by a stone • *a mass grave* • *an unmarked grave* • *a grave digger* • *He visits his mother's grave every Sunday and lays fresh flowers on it.* • *Do you think there's life* **beyond the grave** (=after death)*?* • *"The Grave's a fine and private place / But none I think do there embrace"* (Andrew Marvell in the poem *To His Coy Mistress*, 1681) • (I)

grave SERIOUS /greɪv/ *adj* **-r, -st** seriously bad • *grave conditions* • *a grave situation* • *a grave political crisis* • *With so little medical equipment, there's a grave risk of infection.* • *It was a grave misjudgment when he accused me of lying.* • *He was standing quietly with a grave face* (= looking serious). • (I)

grave·ly /'greɪv·li/ *adv* • *It was reported on the news that he was gravely ill.* • *She looked at him gravely* (=seriously).

grav·i·ty /£'græv·ɪ·ti, $-ə·t̬i/ *n* [U] • *I don't think you understand the gravity* (=seriousness) *of the situation.* • See also GRAVITY.

grave (ac·cent) /£grɑːv, $greɪv/ *n* [C] a symbol used over a letter in some languages, for example the letter 'è' in French, to show that it is pronounced in a particular way • *There's a grave accent* **on** *the second letter of the French word 'mère'.* • LP› **Symbols**

grav·el /ˈgræv·əl/ *n* [U] small rounded stones, often mixed with sand • *a heap/pile of gravel* • *a gravel path/drive* • A **gravel pit** is a place where gravel is dug out of the ground.
grav·elled, *Am usually* **grav·eled** /ˈgræv·əld/ *adj* [not gradable] • *a gravelled drive/path*
grav·el·ly /ˈgræv·əl·i/ *adj* • *gravelly soil*
grav·el·ly /ˈgræv·əl·i/ *adj* (of a voice, esp. a man's voice) low and rough • *Bob has a gravelly* **voice**.
grav·en /ˈgreɪ·vən/ *adj* [after v; not gradable] *literary* fixed for always • *Nureyev's performance will remain graven* **in** *my* **memory** *as long as I live!*
grav·en im·age /ˈgreɪ·vən/ *n* [C] *disapproving* an object made esp. from wood, stone etc. and used for religious worship; IDOL • *"Thou shalt not make unto thee any graven image"* (Bible *Ten Commandments*, Exodus 20.4)
grave·side /ˈgreɪv·saɪd/ *n* [C usually sing] the area next to a GRAVE (= place where a dead person is buried) • *He made a short speech* **at the** *graveside, then the body was finally buried.*
grave·stone /ˈgreɪv·stəʊn, $-stoʊn/, **head·stone**, **tomb·stone** *n* [C] a stone that shows where a dead person is buried and which usually has their name and the years of their birth and death written on it
grave·yard /£ˈgreɪv·jɑːd, $-jɑːrd/ *n* [C] a place where dead people are buried; CEMETERY • *(infml)* A **graveyard shift** is a period of work, for example in a factory, which begins late at night and ends early in the morning.
grav·i·tas /ˈgræv·ɪ·tæs/ *n* [U] *fml* seriousness and importance of manner, causing feelings of respect and trust in others • *He's an effective enough politician but somehow he lacks the statesmanlike gravitas of a world leader.*
grav·i·tate to·ward/to *obj* /ˈgræv·ɪ·teɪt/ *v prep* [T] to be attracted by or to move in the direction of • *Susie always gravitates towards the older children in her playgroup.* • *I can feel myself gravitating towards the food table!* • *In their search for work, people are gravitating to the cities.*
grav·i·ta·tion /ˌgræv·ɪˈteɪ·ʃən/ *n* [U] • *The gravitation of country people* **to/towards** *the capital began in the 1920s.* • See also **gravitation** at GRAVITY.
grav·i·ty /£ˈgræv·ɪ·ti, $-ə·t̬i/, *specialized also* **grav·i·ta·tion** /ˌgræv·ɪˈteɪ·ʃən/, *abbreviation* **g** *n* [U] the force which attracts any object of any mass towards any other object of any mass • *the laws of gravity* • *Gravity makes something fall if you drop it.* • *Gravity acts within and between stars, planets and spacecraft.* • *Enormous energy is needed to launch a spacecraft* **against** *(the force of) gravity.* • See also **gravity** at GRAVE [SERIOUS].
grav·i·ta·tion·al /ˌgræv·ɪˈteɪ·ʃən·əl/ *adj* [not gradable] • *gravitational forces* • *gravitational attraction* • *The spacecraft was re-entering the Earth's gravitational* **field**.
gra·vy /ˈgreɪ·vi/ *n* [U] a sauce made from meat juices, liquid and flour, and served with meat and vegetables • *thick/thin gravy* • A **gravy boat** is a long low container with a handle, used for serving gravy at the table. • **The gravy train** is a way of making money quickly, easily, and often dishonestly. • [PIC] **Jug**
gray /greɪ/ *adj* **-er, -est** *Am for* GREY
graze *obj* [HURT] /greɪz/ *v* [T] to break the surface of the skin by rubbing against something rough • *He fell down and grazed his* **knee**. • *He was lucky, the bullet just grazed his leg.* • *(fig.) The aircraft's landing gear grazed* (= touched lightly) *the treetops as it landed.*
graze /greɪz/ *n* [C] • *Her legs were covered with cuts and grazes.*
graze *(obj)* [EAT] /greɪz/ *v* to (cause animals to) eat grass • *The cows were grazing* (**in** *the field*). [I] • *The farmer grazes cattle on this land in the summer months.* [T] • *(fig. infml) Some families don't sit down to proper meals nowadays, they just graze* (= eat small amounts repeatedly all day instead of meals). [I]
graz·ing /ˈgreɪ·zɪŋ/ *n* [U] • Grazing or **grazing land**, is land where animals can eat the grass.
grease /griːs/ *n* [U] animal or vegetable fat that is soft after melting, or more generally, any thick oily substance • *The dinner plates were thick with grease.* • *You'll have to put some grease on those ball bearings.* • A **grease gun** is an device used to force grease into special holes in machines with moving parts, to make them work more easily. • *(esp. Am dated slang)* A **grease monkey** is an unskilled person who works on esp. car or aircraft engines.
grease *obj* /griːs/ *v* [T] • *Grease and flour the tins well before adding the cake mixture.* • *You must grease the tractor every day.* • *(disapproving)* If you **grease** someone's **palm**, you secretly give them money in order to persuade them to do something for you. • If someone is, or does something, **like greased lightning**, they do it very fast: *As soon as I mentioned work, he was out of the door like greased lightning!*
greas·er /£ˈgriː·səʳ, $-sɚ/ *n* [C] • *(dated slang)* A greaser is a long-haired man who rides a motorcycle, wears black leather clothes, and is often a member of a GANG (= group): *Greasers were originally so-called because of the grease that they used on their hair and on their bikes.*
grea·si·ness /ˈgriː·sɪ·nəs/ *n* [U]
grea·sy /ˈgriː·si/ *adj* **-ier, -iest** • Something that is greasy is covered with or is full of grease: *greasy food/dishes/skin/hair* • *(slang)* A **greasy spoon** is a small cheap bad restaurant, esp. one which sells a lot of fried food.
grease·paint /ˈgriːs·peɪnt/ *n* [U] make-up as used by actors in the theatre
grease·proof pa·per /£ˌgriːs·pruːfˈpeɪ·pəʳ, $-pɚ/ *n* [U] *Br and Aus* paper which does not allow GREASE through, used esp. in cooking • *Line the tins with greaseproof paper.*
great [BIG] /greɪt/ *adj* **-er, -est** large in amount, or unusually or unexpectedly big • *A great crowd had gathered outside the President's palace.* • *A great rock had fallen onto the road.* • *The improvement in water standards over the last 50 years has been very great.* • *A great many people would agree.* • *I spent a great* **deal of** (= a lot of) *time there.* • *A great* **number of** *people arrived late.* • *(fml) It gives us great* **pleasure** *to announce the engagement of our daughter Maria.* • *There wasn't a great* **quantity/amount of** *food at the party.* • *(fml) It is with great* **sorrow** *that I inform you of the death of our director.* • *I have great* **sympathy** *for you.* • **The** *great* **majority of** (= Almost all) *people would agree.* • *(infml dated) For the first 400 metres he was* **going great guns** (= going fast and successfully), *but then he fell and that lost him the race.* • *(infml) I'm afraid I am* **no great shakes as** *a cook/***at** *cooking* (= I'm not very good at it)*!* • *"Great Expectations"* (title of a book by Charles Dickens, 1861) • *"The great leap forward"* (Mao Zedong on the industrialization of China, 1958) • [LP] **Measurements**
great·ly /ˈgreɪt·li/ *adv* • Greatly means very much and is used esp. to show how much you feel or experience something: *I greatly regret not having told the truth.* ○ *She greatly admires her grandmother.* ○ *Her piano-playing has greatly improved/has improved greatly since I last heard her.* • [LP] **Very, completely**
great [FAMOUS] /greɪt/ *adj* **-er, -est** *approving* famous, powerful, or important as one of a particular type • *a great politician/leader/artist/man/woman* • *This is one of Rembrandt's greatest paintings.* • *Who do you think is the greatest modern novelist?* • *(humorous saying)* You might say 'great minds think alike' to someone just after you have discovered that they have had the same idea as you. • *"I am the greatest"* (the boxer Muhamad Ali, 1962-) • *"The greatest show on earth"* (advertising slogan for Barnum and Bailey's Circus, 1881-)
great /greɪt/ *n* [C] • A great can sometimes mean a famous person in a particular area of activity: *former tennis great Arthur Ashe* ○ *Woody Allen, one of the* **all-time** *greats of the cinema* • *(Br)* **The great and the good** (= Important people) *are calling on the Government to support the arts.*
great·ness /ˈgreɪt·nəs/ *n* [U] • *Her greatness as a writer is unquestioned.*
great [GOOD] /greɪt/ *adj* **-er, -est** *infml* very good; WONDERFUL • *a great surprise/idea/relief* • *We had a great time last night at the party.* • **It**'*s great* **to** *see you after all this time!* [+ to infinitive] • **It** *was great driving over the mountains.* [+ v-*ing*] • **It**'*s great* **that** *you don't have to do all that driving.* [+ *that* clause] • *"I'll lend you the car if you like." "Great! Thanks a lot!"* • *"What's your new teacher like?" "Oh, he's great."* • *"How are you feeling now?" "Great* (= very well/healthy)*!"/"***Not all that** *great* (= I feel quite ill)*."* • *(infml) My sister is great* **at** *(playing) football.* • *This device is great* **for** (= very suitable for) **cleaning** *windows.* [+ v-*ing*] • *He's* **a great one for** (= very good at) *getting other people to do his work for him, old Peter!* • **The** *great* **thing about** *Sue is that* (= I like her because) *she never complains.* • *Oh great* (= That's very bad)*! That's all I need – Karen's not coming in today so there's no one to answer the phone!*
great [EMPHASIS] /greɪt/ *adv* [before n], *adj* [not gradable] *infml* used to strengthen and emphasize the meaning of another word; very • *a great big spider* • *a great long queue* • *a huge/enormous great hole* • *You great idiot/fool!* • *Pat's a great friend of mine* (= I'm very friendly with her). • If you

say someone is a great organiser/story-teller/party-goer etc., it means that they do these things very often or very well.

great– [FAMILIES] /greɪt-/ *combining form* used with a word for a family member to mean one GENERATION away from that member • *great-grandmother* • *great-grandson* • *Great-Uncle Wilfred* • *I'm 14, my mother's 34, my grandmother's 59 and my great-grandmother's 80.* • *One of my great-great-grandfathers, my Grandma Gregory's grandfather, was Italian.* • [PIC]> **Family tree**

great [NAMES] /greɪt/ *adj* [not gradable] **-er** or **-est** used in names, esp. to mean large or important • *a great spotted woodpecker* • *a Great Dane* (= large type of dog) • *Catherine the Great* • *the Great War* (= World War I) • *the Great Wall of China* • *the Great Bear* (= group of stars) • *Great Malvern* • *the Great Lakes* • *the greater black-backed gull*

Great·er /£'greɪ·tər, $-t̬ɚ/ *adj* [before n; not gradable] • Greater is used before names of some cities to refer to both the city itself and the area around it: *Greater Manchester* • *Greater London* • *Greater New York*

great·coat /£'greɪt·kəʊt, $-koʊt/ *n* [C] a long heavy warm coat, worn esp. by soldiers over their uniform • *an army greatcoat*

grebe /gri:b/ *n* [C] any of a family of grey or brown water birds which swims on or under the water

Gre·cian /'gri:·ʃən/ *adj* [not gradable] (esp. of building styles or a person's appearance) beautiful and simple, in the style of Ancient Greece • *a Grecian column/temple* • *She's got Grecian features/a Grecian profile.*

greed /gri:d/, **greed·i·ness** /'gri:·di·nəs/ *n* [U] a very strong wish to continually get more of something, esp. food or money • *I don't know why I'm eating more – it's not hunger, it's just greed!* • *He was unsympathetic with many house sellers, complaining that they were motivated by greed.*

greed·y /'gri:·di/ *adj* **-ier**, **-iest** • *We ate a lot as children but I don't think we were ever greedy.* • *He's greedy* **for** *power/success/victory.* • *This plant is greedy* **for** (= needs a lot of) *water.* • **It** *was greedy of them* **to** *eat all the food up.* [+ *to* infinitive] • *(infml) You mean you've eaten all three slices of cake? You greedy* **pig**! • *(Br and Aus)* The phrase **greedy-guts** is used by or to children to mean someone who eats too much.

greed·i·ly /'gri:·dɪ·li/ *adv* • *He looked greedily at the pile of cream cakes.*

Greek /gri:k/ *adj* [not gradable] of or from Greece • *Greek history/culture/philosophy/drama* • *Greek food/customs* • *She's Greek.* • A **Greek cross** has four arms which are all the same length. • *"For my own part, it was Greek to me"* (Shakespeare, Julius Caesar 1.2) • *"I fear the Greeks even when bearing gifts"* (From the *Aeneid* by the Roman poet Virgil, 70-19 BC) • See also GRECIAN.

Greek /gri:k/ *n* [C] • *Her mother's a Greek.* • **The** Greeks are the people from Greece: *The Greeks have an ancient culture.*

Greek /gri:k/ *n* [U] • *to speak Greek* • *modern/ancient Greek* • *The New Testament of the Bible was written* **in** *Greek.* • *(infml) It's* **all Greek to me** (= I don't understand it at all).

green [COLOUR] /gri:n/ *adj, n* **-er**, **-est** (of) a colour between blue and yellow; the colour of grass • *light/pale green* • *dark/bottle green* • *green vegetables* • *Green is my favourite colour.* [U] • *She's got black hair and green eyes.* • *They painted the room green.* • *We're painting the house in greens and blues.* [C] • *The traffic lights turned green, and the car moved off.* • You sometimes **go/turn** green (= look pale and ill) when you are going to vomit. • If you **give the green light to** something, or you *(infml)* **green-light** it, you say that it can happen: *The council has given the green light to the new shopping development.* • *I was* **green (with envy)** (= very JEALOUS) *when I heard he'd been given the job.* • **Green beans** (also **French beans**) are a type of long, green, edible bean. • A **green card** is a document giving a foreigner permission to live and work in the United States. *He's applied for/been granted his green card.* • A **green card** is also a document which INSURES your car against accidents (= protects you financially if you have a car accident) when travelling in other countries. • A **green paper** is a document prepared by the British Government for anyone interested to study and make suggestions about, esp. before a law is changed or a new law is made. Compare **white paper** at WHITE [COLOUR]. • *"O! beware, my lord, of jealousy;/ It is the green-ey'd monster which doth mock/ The meat it feeds on"* (Shakespeare, Othello 3.3)

green·ish /'gri:·nɪʃ/ *adj* • If something is greenish it is slightly green: *Peter has wonderful greenish blue eyes.*

green·ness /'gri:n·nəs/ *n* [U]

green [POLITICAL] /gri:n/ *n, adj* **-er**, **-est** (someone who cares a lot about matters) relating to the protection of the environment • *green politics/ideas/issues* • *a green campaigner* • *The Green Party is/are campaigning against the dumping of nuclear waste at sea.* • *He used to be a Liberal, but now he's a Green* (= member of the Green Party). [C] • *(Aus)* A **green ban** is when a **trade union** prevents building on any area of land that is of environmental importance.

green·ing /'gri:·nɪŋ/ *n* [U] • *The next ten years, he predicted, would see the greening of* (= having more care for the environment in) *America.* • See also **greening** at GREEN [PLANTS].

green [NOT RIPE] /gri:n/ *adj* **-er**, **-est** (esp. of fruit) not ripe enough to eat, or (of wood) not dry enough to use • *green bananas/plums/tomatoes*

green [NOT EXPERIENCED] /gri:n/ *adj* **-er**, **-est** not experienced or trained; NAIVE • *I was very green when I started working there.*

green [PLANTS] /gri:n/ *adj* **-er**, **-est** covered with grass, trees and other plants • *the green hills of Ireland* • *a beautiful green country churchyard* • If a person has *(Br and Aus)* **green fingers**/*(Am)* **a green thumb**, they are good at making plants grow: *Helen's got green fingers – plants in her care just flourish!* ○ *I'm afraid I'm not very (Br and Aus)***green-fingered**/*(Am)* **green-thumbed**. • A **green belt** is a strip of countryside round a city or town where building is not allowed: *There's a green belt around Coventry.* • A **green pepper** is a shiny green vegetable with a hollow centre which can be eaten raw or cooked: *stuffed green peppers.* • The very big increase in CEREAL production in some developing countries in the 1960s and 1970s, made possible by new scientific methods, was called the **Green Revolution**. • You make a **green salad** with LETTUCE and other green vegetables. • **Green tea** is the light-coloured tea drunk esp. in China and Japan, made from leaves that have been steamed and dried quickly. • *"England's green and pleasant land"* (William Blake in the hymn *Jerusalem*, 1804) • *"How Green was my Valley"* (title of a book by Richard Llewellyn, 1939)

green /gri:n/ *n* [C] • A green is an area planted with grass, esp. for use by the public: *Children were playing on the* **village** *green.* • Green is sometimes used as a part of a name: *We walked across Sheep's Green to Newnham.* • A green is also a flat area of grass surrounding the hole on a golf course.

green·er·y /'gri:·nə·ri/, *Am also* **greens** /gri:nz/ *n* [U] • Greenery refers to green plants or branches cut off plants, esp. when used as decoration: *I put a few leaves in amongst the flowers for a bit of greenery.*

green·ing /'gri:·nɪŋ/ *n* [U] • *Concern about the ugly effects of industrialization has led to* **the** *greening* **of** (= the planting of grass, trees and plants in) *many of our cities.* • See also **greening** at GREEN [POLITICAL].

green·ness /'gri:n·nəs/ *n* [U] • *What first struck her when she arrived in England was the greenness of the countryside.*

greens /gri:nz/ *pl n* • Greens are the leaves of green vegetables such as SPINACH or CABBAGE when eaten as food: *I always make sure the children eat their greens.* • Greens is also *Am for* for **greenery**.

green·back /'gri:m·bæk/ *n* [C] *Am dated slang* a US DOLLAR • *The value of the greenback increased against most currencies yesterday.*

green·field /'gri:n·fɪəld/ *adj* [not gradable] *Br* (of land) not yet built on, or (of factories etc.) built on land not yet used for industry • *a greenfield site* • *greenfield industries* • *a greenfield hi-tech plant*

green·finch /'gri:n·fɪntʃ/ *n* [C] a medium-sized greenish FINCH (= bird), common in Europe

green·fly /'gri:n·flaɪ/ *n* [C] *pl* **greenfly** or **greenflies** a very small pale green insect that often harms plants; a type of APHID • *My roses have got greenfly* (= There are greenfly on my roses).

green·gage /'gri:ŋ·geɪdʒ/ *n* [C] a small greenish yellow PLUM (= tree fruit with a large seed in the middle) • *greengage jam* • *a greengage pie*

green·gro·cer /£'gri:ŋ·grəʊ·sər, $-groʊ·sɚ/ *n* [C] a person who owns or works in a shop that sells fresh vegetables and fruit

green·gro·cer's /£'griːŋ·grəʊ·səz, $-groʊ·sɚz/ *n* [C] • A shop in which fresh vegetables and fruit are sold is called a greengrocer's.

green·horn /£'griːn·hɔːn, $-hɔːrn/ *n* [C] a person who is not experienced • *I'm a bit of a greenhorn when it comes to skiing.* • *As a greenhorn journalist, I made a lot of mistakes.*

green·house /'griːn·haʊs/ *n* [C] *pl* **greenhouses** /'griːn ˌhaʊ·zɪz/ a building with a roof and sides made of glass, used for growing plants that need warmth and protection • *Gladys grows a lot of tomatoes in her greenhouse.* • The **greenhouse effect** is an increase in the amount of **carbon dioxide** and other gases in the ATMOSPHERE which is believed to be the cause of a gradual warming of the surface of the Earth. • A **greenhouse gas** is a gas which causes the greenhouse effect, esp. **carbon dioxide.** • PIC **Garden**

green·ish /'griː·nɪʃ/ *adj* See at GREEN COLOUR

Green·wich Mean Time /ˌgren·ɪtʃ'miːn·taɪm/ (*abbreviation* **GMT**) *n* [U not after *the*] the time (at Greenwich, near London) that world **time zones** are based on • See also **British Summer Time** at BRITISH; **standard time** at STANDARD USUAL.

greet *obj* /griːt/ *v* [T] to welcome (someone) with particular words or a particular action, or to react to (something) in the stated way • *Germans often greet one another* **by** *shaking hands.* • *The teacher greeted each child* **with** *a friendly 'Hello!'* • *The unions have greeted the decision* **with** *delight/anger.* • *(fig.) As we walked into the house, we were greeted by* (= we suddenly smelled/saw/heard) *a wonderful smell of coffee/a scene of chaos/a strange sound.* • LP **Meeting someone**

greet·ing /£'griː·tɪŋ, $-t̬ɪŋ/ *n* [C] • *The usual British greeting amongst friends is 'Hello'.* • *They briskly* **exchanged** *greetings before starting the session.*

greet·ings /£'griː·tɪŋz, $-t̬ɪŋz/ *pl n* • *They sent birthday greetings* (= good wishes for someone's birthday). • *(fml) Greetings* **to** *you, my friends and colleagues.* • A *(Br)***greetings card**/*(Am and Aus)* **greeting card** is a piece of thick paper folded in half with a picture on the outside and a message inside, which you write in and send or give to someone, for example at Christmas or on their BIRTHDAY. • LP **Shopping goods**

gre·gar·i·ous /£grɪ'geə·ri·əs, $-'ger·i-/ *adj* (of people) liking to be with other people, or (esp. of animals) living in groups • *Emma's a gregarious, outgoing sort of person.* • *Pigeons are gregarious birds, but blackbirds tend to be solitary.* • See also **sociable** at SOCIAL.

gre·gar·i·ous·ly /£grɪ'geə·ri·ə·sli, $-'ger·i̯-/ *adv*

gre·gar·i·ous·ness /£grɪ'geə·ri·ə·snəs, $-'ger·i-/ *n* [U]

Gre·go·ri·an cal·en·dar /£grɪ'gɔː·ri·ən, $-'gɔːr·i-/ *n* [U] **the Gregorian calendar** the system used in large parts of the world to divide the 365 days of the **solar year** into weeks and months, and numbering the year starting with the birth of Jesus Christ

Gre·go·ri·an chant /£grɪ'gɔː·ri·ən, $-'gɔːr·i-/ *n* [U/C] a type of Christian church music for voices alone, used since the Middle Ages; PLAINSONG

grem·lin /'grem·lɪn/ *n* [C] an imaginary little creature which gets inside things, esp. machines, and makes them go wrong • *We must have a gremlin in the engine – it isn't working properly.*

gre·nade /grə'neɪd/ *n* [C] a small bomb thrown by hand or shot from a gun • *a hand/rifle grenade* • *There was a gun and grenade* **attack** *on the army offices this morning.* • CS

gre·na·di·er /£ˌgren·ə'dɪəʳ, $-'dɪr/ *n* [C] a member of the Grenadier Guards (= a special part of the British, Canadian or other army), or a soldier who is given GRENADES (= small bombs) as weapons

gre·na·dine /'gren·ə·diːn/ *n* [U] a sweet liquid made from the juice of the POMEGRANATE and used to give colour and sweetness to other drinks

grew /gruː/ *past simple of* GROW

grey (**-ier, -iest**), *Am usually* **gray** (**-er, -est**) /greɪ/ *adj, n* (of) the colour that is a mixture of black and white, the colour of clouds on a rainy day • *grey eyes* • *a grey sky* • *a grey skirt* • *She was dressed in grey.* [U] • *The room was decorated in greys and blues.* [C] • *Her face went/turned grey* (= very pale because of shock) *as she read the letter.* • A person who is grey has hair that has changed from its original colour to grey, usually as they become old: *A tall, grey and distinguished-looking woman stood in the doorway.* ○ *He started to* **go/turn** *grey in his mid-forties.* • *(disapproving)* Grey weather is when there are a lot of clouds in the sky and there is very little light: *Night turned into morning, grey and cold.* ○ *The weather's been very grey and miserable recently.* • *(disapproving)* Grey means uninteresting and unexciting: *He saw a grey future stretch ahead of him.* • *They regarded their father as a grey civil servant working in grey office job.* • A **grey area** is a situation which is not clear or where the rules are not known: *The difference between gross negligence and recklessness is a legal grey area.* • A **grey eminence** is an EMINENCE GRISE. • *(infml)* **Grey matter** is the substance of a person's brain and nervous system and refers to the ability to think: *It's not the sort of movie that stimulates the old grey matter much.*

grey·ing /'greɪ·ɪŋ/, *Am usually* **gray·ing** *adj* • If a person or their hair is greying, their hair is becoming grey: *He is greying now but still elegant.* ○ *A photograph of a greying couple stood on the mantlepiece.*

grey·ish, *Am usually* **gray·ish** /'greɪ·ɪʃ/ *adj* • *There was a greyish* (= slightly grey) *substance in the bottom of the bowl.*

grey·ness /'greɪ·nəs/, *Am usually* **gray·ness** *n* [U] • *The greyness of the afternoon was depressing.*

grey·hound /'greɪ·haʊnd/ *n* [C] a type of dog that has a thin body and long thin legs and can run fast, esp. in races • PIC **Dogs**

grid /grɪd/ *n* [C] a pattern of lines, bars etc. that cross over each other to make a set of squares • *A metal grid had been placed across the hole to stop people falling in.* • *In Barcelona the streets are laid out in/on a grid* **system.** • *The photograph is divided into a grid of small squares.* • A grid is also a system of wires through which electricity is connected to different power stations across a region: *the national grid* • A **grid reference** is a position on a map which has been marked into squares by numbered lines going from one side to the other and from top to bottom so that you can find places easily on it: *What's the grid reference of the village on this map?* • See also GRIDIRON.

grid·dle /'grɪd·l̩/ *n* [C] a round, flat piece of metal used for cooking over a fire or cooker

grid·i·ron /£'grɪd·aɪən, $-aɪrn/ *n* [C] *Am* a field marked with lines for American football

grid·lock /£'grɪd·lɒk, $-lɑːk/ *n* [U] a situation where roads in a town become so blocked by cars that it is impossible for any traffic to move • *A car breaking down at rush hour could cause gridlock across the entire city.* • *(fig.) The programs are swamped with paperwork and paralysed by bureaucratic gridlock* (= an inability to get things done).

grief /griːf/ *n* very great sadness, esp. at the death of someone • *Newspapers should not intrude on people's private grief.* [U] • *You mustn't say "I know how you feel" as each person's grief and sense of loss is unique.* [U] • *The son and mother were unable to communicate their respective griefs.* [C] • *I'd no idea forgetting his birthday would* **cause** *him so much grief* (= make him so unhappy). [U] • *(infml) It* **caused** *him grief* (= He was annoyed) *to see the equipment being used so carelessly.* [U] • If something or someone **comes to grief**, they have an accident or fail in some way: *His plans to be a politician came to grief when he failed to get any votes.* • *(infml) My parents* **gave me (a lot of) grief** (= spoke angrily to me) *about my bad school reports.* • Someone who is **grief-stricken** is extremely sad. • NL

grieve *(obj)* /griːv/ *v* • *He grieved* (= felt great sadness) **for** *the companion he had lost.* [I] • *If someone is grieving, he or she needs to find ways of talking about it.* [I] • *Grieving relatives and friends of the man blamed his death on carelessness.* • *(fml)* **It** *grieves me* (= makes me feel very sad/annoyed) **to** *see how selfish they've become.* [T + obj + *to* infinitive]

griev·ance /'griː·vᵊnts/ *n* [C] a complaint or a strong feeling that you have been treated unfairly • *A special committee has been appointed to handle prisoners' grievances.* [C] • *Bill still* **harbours/nurses** *a grievance* **against** *his employers for not promoting him.* [C] • *The small amount of compensation is a further source of grievance to the people forced to leave their homes.* [U]

griev·ous /'griː·vəs/ *adj fml* having very serious effects or causing great pain • *They are running out of food and are in grievous danger of starvation.* • *She died in hospital of grievous head wounds.* • *(law)* In British law, **grievous bodily harm** (*abbreviation* **GBH**) is a crime in which one person does serious esp. physical injury to another. • LP **Crimes and criminals**

griev·ous·ly /'griː·və·sli/ *adv fml* • *You are grievously* (= very seriously) *mistaken.*

grif·fin /'grɪf·ɪn/, **gry·phon** *n* [C] an imaginary creature with the head and wings of an EAGLE and the body of a lion

grill *obj* [COOK] /grɪl/, *Am also* **broil** *v* [T] to cook (something) by direct heat, esp. under a very hot surface in a cooker • *I decided to grill the sausages rather than fry them.* • [PIC> **Cooking**

grill /grɪl/, *Am also* **broil·er** *n* [C] • A grill in a cooker is the surface which can be heated to very high temperatures and under which you put food to be cooked. • A grill over a fire is a frame of metal bars on which food can be put to be cooked. • *(esp. Am)* A grill is also an informal restaurant: *Everyone in Bayonne loved the steak sandwiches at Frank's Bar and Grill.* • A *(Br)* **grill pan**/*(Aus)* grill tray *(Am* **broiler pan***) is an open rectangular metal container, often with a frame of metal bars inside, on which food is cooked under a grill.* • [PIC> **Kitchen, Pan**

grill *obj* [QUESTION] /grɪl/ *v* [T] *infml* to ask (someone) a lot of questions for a long time • *After being grilled by the police for two days, Johnson signed a confession.* • *She knew her parents would grill her* **about** *where she'd been.*

grill·ing /ˈgrɪl·ɪŋ/ *n* [U] *infml* • *She faced a grilling* (= being asked lots of questions) *when she got home.*

grille /grɪl/ *n* [C] a frame of metal bars used to cover something such as a window or a machine • *a security grille* • *A grille separated the prisoners from their visitors.*

grim [SERIOUS] /grɪm/ *adj* **grimmer, grimmest** very serious • *Her face was grim as she told them the bad news.* • *It has taken ten years of grim* **determination** *to achieve this success.* • *"The situation is pretty grim," he said.* • *(Br)* If you **hang/hold on like grim death**, you hold on very tightly to something, despite great difficulty: *The dog grabbed hold of the suitcase with its teeth and hung on like grim death.* • *The lieutenant was* **grim-faced** (= looked very serious) *as he stared into the camera and answered the question put to him without emotion.* • *(literary)* The **Grim Reaper** is death thought of in the shape of a person with a large curved tool used for cutting crops: *When the Grim Reaper comes for you, there is no escape.* • [PIC> **Imaginary creatures**

grim·ly /ˈgrɪm·li/ *adv* • *"You've got six months to live," the doctor said grimly.*

grim·ness /ˈgrɪm·nəs/ *n* [U] • *The grimness of his expression told me something was wrong.*

grim [UNPLEASANT] /grɪm/ *adj* **grimmer, grimmest** *infml* very unpleasant or unattractive • *They had to live in a grim flat in a high-rise building.* • *We were running out of money and things were looking grim.* • *This year the* **outlook** *for the company is grim.* • *A recently published report by a group of independents paints a grim* **picture** *of Europe's traffic.* • *The occasion was a grim* **reminder** *of the shortcomings of his brother.* • *I felt pretty grim* (= ill), *so I went home to bed.*

grim·ness /ˈgrɪm·nəs/ *n* [U] • *The town has a post-war grimness about it.*

grim·ace /ˈgrɪ·məs, grɪˈmeɪs/ *v, n* (to make) an expression of pain, strong dislike, etc. in which the face twists in an ugly way • *He grimaced* **with** *pain when he tried to stand.* [I] • *Helen made a grimace* **of** *disgust when she saw the raw meat.* [C]

grime /graɪm/ *n* [U] a layer of dirt on skin or a building • *The once-beautiful building is now covered with grime from the city streets.*

gri·my /ˈgraɪ·mi/ *adj* **-ier, -iest** • *The child's face was grimy* (= dirty) *and streaked with tears.*

grin /grɪn/ *n* [C] a wide smile • *He gave a* **broad/sheepish/toothy** *grin when he saw her.* • (N)

grin /grɪn/ *v* [I] **-nn-** • *Janice grinned* **broadly/cheekily/impishly/mischievously** *at him.* • To **grin and bear it** is to accept something without complaining: *I don't want to stay there for a week on my own, but I suppose I'll have to grin and bear it.*

grind *obj* [MAKE SMALLER] /graɪnd/ *v* [T] *past* **ground** /graʊnd/ to make (something) into small pieces or a powder by pressing between hard surfaces • *He always grinds some black pepper over his pizza.* • *For a good cup of coffee use freshly ground beans.* • *They grind the bones* **down** *and make them into a traditional drink that is believed to increase strength and vigour.* [M] • *They grind the grain* **into** *flour* (= make flour by crushing grain) *between two large stones.* • If you grind something **into** something else, you press the first thing hard into the second thing using a twisting movement: *Sara angrily ground her cigarette into the ashtray.* • *(Br literary)* Someone who **grinds the faces of the poor** treats poor people very badly, often to get money from them. • See also GROUNDS.

grind·er /£ˈgraɪn·dəʳ, $-dɚ/ *n* [C] • A **coffee** grinder is a device for breaking coffee beans into smaller grains. • **Meat** grinder is *Am for* **mincer**. See at MINCE [CUT].

grind·ing /ˈgraɪn·dɪŋ/ *adj* • *(literary)* Grinding **poverty** is the condition of being extremely poor.

grind *obj* [RUB] /graɪnd/ *v* [T] *past* **ground** /graʊnd/ to rub (something) against a hard surface, in order to make it sharper or smoother • *She has a set of chef's knives which she grinds every week.* • *He ground* **down** *the sharp metal edges to make them smooth.* [M] • If you **grind** someone **down**, you treat them so badly for such a long time that they are no longer able to fight back: *Ground down by years of abuse, she did not have the confidence to leave him.* • A person who grinds their **teeth** makes a noise by rubbing their teeth together: *She gets headaches because she grinds her teeth during her sleep.* • See also GRINDSTONE.

grind·er /£ˈgraɪn·dəʳ, $-dɚ/ *n* [C] • A (knife) grinder is a device for making knives sharper, or a person whose job is to do this.

grind·ing /ˈgraɪn·dɪŋ/ *n* [U] • A grinding **noise** is an unpleasant noise of moving things being rubbed together: *The car engine was making a strange grinding noise.*

grind [ACTIVITY] /graɪnd/ *n* [U] *infml* difficult or boring activity, which needs a lot of effort and which you do not enjoy • *Having to type up my handwritten work was a real grind.* • *The* **daily** *grind of looking after three children was wearing her down.*

grind *(obj)* /graɪnd/ *v* [always + adv/prep] *infml* • To grind is to do something unpleasant or uninteresting, or to do it in an unexciting way: *The after-dinner speeches ground* **on** *for two hours.* [I] ○ *The orchestra ground* **out** *the same tunes it has been playing for twenty years.* [M] ○ *We ground* **through** *50 pages of closely written text before we found the information we were looking for.* [I] • *The car slowed down and* **ground to a halt** (= stopped slowly) *at the traffic lights.* • *(fig.) If we don't do something soon, the whole theatre industry could* **grind to a halt/standstill** (= slowly come to an end).

grind·stone /£ˈgraɪnd·stəʊn, $-stoʊn/ *n* [C] a large round stone that is turned by a machine and is used to make tools sharper or sharp edges smooth

grin·go /£ˈgrɪŋ·gəʊ, $-goʊ/ *n* [C] *pl* **gringos** *infml disapproving* a foreigner in a Latin American country, esp. one who speaks only English

grip *(obj)* [HOLD] /grɪp/ *v* **-pp-** to hold very tightly • *The baby gripped my finger with her tiny hand.* [T] • *Worn tyres don't grip* (= stay on the surface of the road) *in the rain very well.* [I] • If an emotion or activity grips you, you feel it strongly or are very interested by it: *As the bull ran towards him Jeff was gripped by fear.* [T] ○ *I was gripped by the film from the moment it started.* [T]

grip /grɪp/ *n* [C usually sing] • *She would not loosen her grip* (= tight hold) **on** *my arm.* • *My golf has got better but I still need to improve my grip* (= way of holding the CLUB). • *(fig.) Rebels have tightened their grip* **on** (= their control of) *the city.* • *(fig.) The local economy is* **in the grip of** (= suffering from) *a recession.* • *The government's popularity has dropped alarmingly as it failed to* **come to grips with** *unemployment and bankruptcies* (= deal with them effectively). • *I can't seem to* **get to grips with** *this problem* (= understand it correctly). • If you tell someone to **get/keep a grip on** themselves, you are telling them to control themselves and behave more reasonably: *You're getting hysterical, Henry! Get a grip on yourself!*

grip·ping /ˈgrɪp·ɪŋ/ *adj* • Gripping means interesting or exciting: *I found the book so gripping that I could not stop reading it from start to finish.*

grip [BAG] /grɪp/ *n* [C] *dated* a bag for clothes etc. that is smaller than a SUITCASE; a HOLDALL

gripe /graɪp/ *n* [C] *infml* a strong complaint • *Her main gripe is that she's not being trained properly.*

gripe /graɪp/ *v* [I] • *There's no point griping about the price of things.*

gripe wa·ter /graɪp/ *n* [U] *Br* a medicine given to babies to cure stomach pain

gris·ly /ˈgrɪz·li/ *adj* **-ier, -iest** extremely unpleasant, esp. because dealing with particularly disgusting ways of killing people • *The newspaper described a series of grisly murders where people had been burnt alive or tortured to death.*

grist /grɪst/ *n* [U] *(Br and Aus)* **grist to the mill**/*(Am)* **grist for** *someone's* **mill** anything that can be used to your advantage • *I might as well learn another language,* **it's all** *grist to the mill when it comes to getting a job.*

gris·tle /ˈgrɪs·l̩/ *n* [U] a solid white substance in meat that comes from near the bone and is hard to chew • *Joan won't eat meat if it has any gristle.*

gris·tly /ˈgrɪs·l̩.i, ˈgrɪs·li/ *adj* • *The sandwich was full of gristly ham.*

grit STONES /grɪt/ *n* [U] very small pieces of stone or sand • *The road had been covered with grit to make it less slippery in icy weather.*

grit *obj* /grɪt/ *v* [T] **-tt-** • *The men had been out gritting* (= putting small stones on) *the icy roads the night before.*

grit·ter *Br* /£ˈgrɪt·əʳ, $ˈgrɪṭ·ɚ/, *Am* **sand·er** *n* [C] • A gritter is a special vehicle that spreads grit on the roads when they are icy.

grit·ty /£ˈgrɪt·i, $ˈgrɪṭ-/ *adj* **-ier, -iest** • *The sandwiches we ate on the beach were gritty with sand but delicious.*

grit BRAVERY /grɪt/ *n* [U] bravery and determination despite difficulty • *It takes grit to stand up to a bully as she did.* • *He showed* **true** *grit* (= real courage).

grit·ty /£ˈgrɪt·i, $ˈgrɪṭ·i/ *adj* **-ier, -iest** • *She showed gritty* (= strong) *courage when it came to fighting her illness.* • *We watched a gritty documentary* (= one showing unpleasant things in full detail) *about life in the inner city slums.*

grit *obj* PRESS /grɪt/ *v* [T] **-tt- grit** *your* **teeth** to press your top and bottom teeth together, often in anger, or *(fig.)* to accept (a situation) although it is very difficult • *He gritted his teeth in silent fury.* • *(fig.) We had to grit our teeth and agree with their conditions, because we wanted the contract.*

grits /grɪts/ *pl n Am* a dish of roughly ground HOMINY grain eaten esp. as a morning meal

griz·zle /ˈgrɪz·l̩/ *v* [I] *disapproving* (esp. of a young child) to cry continually but not very loudly, or to complain all the time • *The baby was cutting a tooth and grizzled all day long.* • *They're always grizzling* (= complaining) *about how nobody invites them anywhere.*

griz·zled /ˈgrɪz·l̩d/ *adj slightly literary* having hair that is grey or becoming grey • *Grizzled veterans in uniform gathered at the war monument.*

griz·zly (bear) /ˈgrɪz·li/ *n* [C] a very large greyish brown bear from N America and Canada

groan /£grəʊn, $groʊn/ *n* [C] a deep long sound showing great pain or unhappiness • *She heard faint groans coming from the next room.* • *Susan looked at the untidy room and gave a groan* **of** *dismay.*

groan /£grəʊn, $groʊn/ *v* • *When she tried to stand up she groaned* **in** *pain.* [I] • *"Not again," he groaned* (= said in a low unhappy voice). [+ clause] • *When he heard the delivery hadn't come, he groaned* **inwardly** (= felt unhappy). [I] • When wood or other material groans it makes a deep noise: *The floorboards groaned as I tiptoed across them.* [I] ○ *(fig.) The table groaned under the vast assortment of foods* (= there were a lot of things on it). [I] • *(infml)* To groan is to complain: *What are you* **moaning and** *groaning about now?* [I]

groc·er /£ˈgrəʊ·səʳ, $ˈgroʊ·sɚ/ *n* [C] a person who owns or works in a shop selling food and small items for the house • *I asked the grocer if he could order that brand of pesto for me.* • See also GREENGROCER.

groc·er's /£ˈgrəʊ·səz, $ˈgroʊ·sɚz/ *n* [C] *pl* **grocers** or **grocers'** • A grocer's is the shop where a grocer works: *I popped into the grocer's on the way home from work to get some cheese.*

groc·er·ies /£ˈgrəʊ·sᵊr·iːz, $ˈgroʊ·sɚ-/ *pl n* • Groceries are the food that you buy in a grocer's shop or SUPERMARKET: *I'll need help to carry the groceries home.*

groc·er·y /£ˈgrəʊ·sᵊr·i, $ˈgroʊ·sɚ-/ *n* [C] • A grocery (*Br also* **grocery shop**, *Am also* **grocery store**) is a grocer's.

grog /£grɒg, $grɑːg/ *n* [U] strong alcohol, such as RUM, that has been mixed with water, or *(esp. Aus)* any alcoholic drink

grog·gy /£ˈgrɒg·i, $ˈgrɑː·gi/ *adj* **-ier, -iest** *infml* weak and unable to think clearly or walk correctly, usually because of tiredness or illness • *The seasickness tablets were making Fiona feel groggy.*

groin BODY /grɔɪn/ *n* [C] the place where your legs meet at the front of your body • *Jenkins's strained groin meant he couldn't play in the football finals.* • Groin is also a way of referring to the male sex organs: *As Frank lay on the ground he was kicked in the stomach and groin.*

groin SEA /grɔɪn/ *n* [C] a GROYNE

groom *obj* CLEAN /gruːm/ *v* [T] to clean (an animal), often by brushing its fur • *Polly spends hours in the stables grooming her pet pony.* • *The apes groom each other as part of their social ritual.*

groom /gruːm/ *n* [C] • A groom is a person whose job is to take care of and clean horses.

groomed /gruːmd/ *adj* [not gradable] • *The dog looked well groomed and cared for.* • *His mother was always impeccably groomed* (= very tidy and stylish). • See also WELL-GROOMED.

groom·ing /ˈgruː·mɪŋ/ *n* [U] • *Wearing a stained jacket and trousers, he made even my scruffy brother look a model of good grooming* (= extremely neat and tidy). • *We took the dog to a grooming parlour.*

groom *obj* PREPARE /gruːm/ *v* [T] to prepare (someone) for a special job or activity • *She was being groomed* **for** *leadership.* • *My boss is grooming me* **to** *take over his job next year.* [+ obj + *to* infinitive]

groom MAN /gruːm/ *n* [C] a BRIDEGROOM • *The* **bride and** *groom walked down the aisle together.*

groove /gruːv/ *n* [C] a long narrow hollow space cut into a surface • *The window slides along a* **deep/shallow** *metal groove to open and close.* • To be **in** a **groove** means to do the same things for a long time and therefore to be boring: *Things just go along in the same old groove.* ○ *Don't get* **stuck** *in a groove, do something different.* • *(fig. dated) Things are going well, we're* **in the groove** (= everything is going successfully) *now!*

grooved /gruːvd/ *adj* [not gradable] • *There was a grooved pattern* (= one with grooves in it) *in the wood.*

groov·er /£ˈgruː·vəʳ, $-vɚ/ *n* [C] *infml dated* a person who likes dancing and music • *Seventies disco music has always been popular with the* **movers and** *groovers.*

groov·y /ˈgruː·vi/ *adj* **-ier, -iest** *dated slang* very fashionable and interesting • *That's a groovy hat you're wearing, did you knit it yourself?*

grope *(obj)* /£grəʊp, $groʊp/ *v* to feel with your hands, esp. in order to find or move towards something when you cannot see easily • *She groped* **for** *her glasses on the bedside table.* [I] • *The lights went out and he tried to grope towards the door.* [I] • *I had to grope my* **way** *up the dark stairs.* [T] • *(fig.) He hesitated and groped for* (= thought with difficulty of) *the right words.* [I] • *(fig.) The two countries are groping towards peace* (= trying, with great difficulty, to find peace). [I] • *(infml)* To grope is to touch someone's body in a sexual way: *Teenage couples were busy groping each other in the back of the cinema.* [T]

grope /£grəʊp, $groʊp/ *n* [C] *infml* • A grope often means a sexual touch: *They only had time for a kiss and a quick grope before saying good night.* ○ *She accused the man standing beside her on the train of trying to have a grope.*

grop·er /£ˈgrəʊ·pəʳ, $ˈgroʊ·pɚ/ *n* [C] *infml disapproving* • *I didn't enjoy dancing with him – he was a real groper* (= he touched me in a sexual way). • See also GROPER.

grop·er /£ˈgrəʊ·pəʳ, $ˈgroʊ·pɚ/ *n* [C] *Aus* a large fish with a very wide mouth • See also **groper** at GROPE.

gross UNACCEPTABLE /£grəʊs, $groʊs/ *adj* [before n] **-er, -est** *fml* (esp. in law) unacceptable because clearly wrong • *This child has suffered gross neglect.* • *The court has made a gross error in sending an innocent man to prison.*

gross·ly /£ˈgrəʊ·sli, $ˈgroʊ-/ *adj* • *They grossly mistreated* (= treated very badly) *their pet dog.* • *It was grossly unfair to demand such a high interest rate on the loan.*

gross FAT /£grəʊs, $groʊs/ *adj* **-er, -est** extremely fat or large and ugly • *Their dog does no exercise and has become really gross and unhealthy.* • *The new tower block is gross, an ugly blot on the landscape.*

gross UNPLEASANT /£grəʊs, $groʊs/ *adj* **-er, -est** *infml* extremely unpleasant, very rude or offensive • *He's really gross.* • *"Oh, gross!" she said, looking at the piles of dirty plates, clothes and papers all over the floor.*

gross out *obj*, **gross** *obj* **out** /£grəʊs, $groʊs/ *v adv* [M] *esp. Am infml* • *"His room really grossed me out* (= I found his room extremely unpleasant)*," she said.*

gross TOTAL /£grəʊs, $groʊs/ *adj, adv* [not gradable] (in) total • *A person's gross* **income** *is the money they earn before tax is deducted from it.* • *Once wrapped, the gross* **weight** *of the package is 2kg.* • *She earns £30 000 a year gross.* • Compare NET LEFT OVER.

gross *obj* /£grəʊs, $groʊs/ *v* [T] • To gross a particular amount of money is to earn it before tax is paid or costs are subtracted: *The film has grossed over $200 million this year.*

gross NUMBER /£grəʊs, $groʊs/ *n* [C] *pl* **gross** or **grosses** *dated* (a group of) 144

gro·tesque /£grəʊˈtesk, $groʊ-/ *adj* ridiculous in an unpleasant way, or extremely ugly or unpleasant • *His attempt to appear young was grotesque and embarrassing.* •

The most grotesque story was told by an oil worker who saw a small boy of five or six shot. • *Gothic churches are full of devils and grotesque figures.*

gro·tesque /£grəʊ'tesk, $groʊ-/ *n* [C] • *Spencer's grotesques* (= paintings of ugly and unpleasant subjects) *are his best works.* • *The film exposed us to a terrifying collection of monsters, freaks and grotesques.*

gro·tesque·ly /£grəʊ'tes·kli, $groʊ-/ *adv* • *a grotesquely fat man* • *My views were grotesquely misrepresented.*

grot·to /£'grɒt·əʊ, $'grɑː·t̬oʊ/ *n* [C] *pl* **grottoes** or **grottos** a small cave, esp. one that is attractive

grot·ty /£'grɒt·i, $'grɑː·t̬i/ *adj* **-ier, -iest** *infml* unpleasant or of bad quality • *The students share a grotty little room.*

grouch /graʊtʃ/ *v* [I] *infml* to complain in a bad-tempered way • *He's always grouching* **about** *how boring his job is.*

grouch /graʊtʃ/ *n* [C] • *He's such a grouch* (= a person who is always complaining).

grouch·y /'graʊ·tʃi/ *adj* **-ier, -iest** • *Don't be so grouchy!*

grouch·i·ness /'graʊ·tʃɪ·nəs/ *n* [U]

ground [LAND] /graʊnd/ *n* the surface of the Earth, the floor of a room, or a piece of land esp. used for a particular purpose • *We placed a rug on the ground for the picnic.* [U] • *The vase wobbled from the table and fell to the ground.* [U] • *The factory is to be built on waste ground outside the town.* [U] • *a football ground* [C] • *a training ground* [C] • *(fig.) A country village can be a fertile* **breeding** *ground for prejudice* (= place where this can develop). [C] • The ground is also the earth and rocks that the Earth's surface is made of: **The** *ground was frozen hard and was impossible to dig.* [U] • If something happens **above/below** ground, it happens above or below the Earth's surface: *The badger appears above ground at night.* ○ *The nuclear fallout shelters are built below ground.* • *The whole village was* **burnt/razed to** *the ground* (= completely destroyed by fire with no buildings left). • *She's working so hard that she's* **driving/working** *herself* **into the ground** (= making herself extremely tired and ill because of work). • *Their political ideas have a lot of support* **on the ground** (= among the general public). • When a person or animal **goes/is run to ground**/*(Br also)* **earth**, *they hide in order to escape someone or something following them:* He found the constant media attention intolerable and went to ground abroad for several months. ○ *They ran the fox to ground in a small wood.* • *(Am)* A **ground ball** is a **grounder.** • If something is **ground-breaking**, it is very new and a big change from other things of its type: *His latest film is interesting, but not ground-breaking.* • **Ground cover** is plants which grow thickly and close to the ground, sometimes used in gardens to prevent WEEDS (= unwanted wild plants) from growing: *This plant grows quickly and provides excellent ground cover.* • The **ground crew** at an airport are the people who take care of the aircraft while it is on the ground. • The **ground floor** (*Am usually and Aus also* **first floor**) of a building is the floor that is level with the ground. • **Ground frost** is a temperature at or below freezing point on and near the ground during the night which can damage plants. • **Ground level** is the same level as the surface of the ground: *There are several small holes in the fence at ground level.* ○ *The window is 2 metres above ground level.* • A **ground plan** is the plan that has been drawn of a building or *(fig.)* the basic plan of action for something: *(fig. esp. Am) He doesn't have a ground plan, he just makes decisions as the need arises.* • **Ground rent** is money paid by the owner of a building or apartment to the person who owns the land on which it has been built. • **Ground rules** are rules on which future action is based: *A committee will lay down the ground rules for what the crew can and can't do.* • *(specialized)* An aircraft's **ground speed** is its speed when measured against the ground rather than the air through which it moves. • **Ground staff** are the people whose job is to take care of a sports ground and its equipment. • A **ground stroke** in tennis and similar games is when you hit the ball after it has hit the ground.

ground *obj* /graʊnd/ *v* [T usually passive] • *The oil tanker was grounded* **on** (= hit some ground under the water and could not move off) *a sandbank.* • *The snowstorm meant that all planes were grounded* (= prevented from flying). • *(fig. esp. Am and Aus) My parents have grounded me* (= not allowed me to go out as a punishment) *for a week.*

ground·er /£'graʊn·dəʳ, $-dɚ/, **ground ball** *n* [C] *Am* • A grounder is a ball which moves along the ground rather than through the air when it has been hit in a game of baseball: *Morris hit three grounders in the game, but failed to hit a home-run.*

grounds /graʊndz/ *pl n* • Grounds are the gardens and land that surround a building and are often enclosed by a wall or fence: *We went for a walk around the hospital grounds.* • See also GROUNDS.

ground [AREA OF KNOWLEDGE] /graʊnd/ *n* [U] an area of knowledge or experience; a subject • *When the conversation turns to politics he's* **on** *his own ground*/**on familiar** *ground* (= he knows a lot about this subject). • *Once we'd found some* **common** *ground* (= things we both knew about) *we got on very well together.* • *You'll be* **on safe/dangerous** *ground if you discuss your childhood with a journalist* (= it is a good/bad subject for you to talk about). • *The lectures* **covered a lot of** *ground* (= included information on many different subjects). • *I enjoyed her first novel, but I felt in the second she was* **going over the same** *ground* (= writing about the same area of experience).

ground·ing /'graʊn·dɪŋ/ *n* [U] • *This course is designed to give drivers a grounding* (= a knowledge of the basic facts) **in** *car maintenance.*

ground [CAUSE] /graʊnd/ *n* [C] a reason, cause or argument • *An EU national could not be deported solely* **on the** *ground* **of** *his conviction.* • *She is suing the company* **on** *grounds* **of** *unfair dismissal.* • *Do you have any ground* **for** *suspecting them?* • *We have grounds* **to** *believe that you have been lying to us.* [+ *to* infinitive] • *He refused to answer* **on the** *grounds* **that** *she was unfairly dismissed.* [+ *that* clause]

ground *obj* /graʊnd/ *v* [T usually passive] • *His phobia is grounded* **in** (= based on) *a childhood experience.* • See also WELL-GROUNDED.

ground·less /'graʊnd·ləs/ *adj* • *My fears turned out to be groundless* (= there were no reasons for them).

ground [WIRE] /graʊnd/ *n* [C] *Am for* EARTH [WIRE]

ground [GRIND] /graʊnd/ *past simple and past participle of* GRIND • **Ground beef** is *Am for* MINCE.

ground·cloth /£'graʊnd·klɒθ, $-klɑːθ/ *n* [C] *Am for* GROUNDSHEET

ground·hog /£'graʊnd·hɒg, $-hɑːg/ *n* [C] *Am* a WOODCHUCK

ground·nut /'graʊnd·nʌt/ *n* [C] a PEANUT, esp. as a crop or when used in particular products • *a bottle of groundnut oil* • *The farmers grow sugar cane and groundnuts as cash crops.*

groun·dout /'graʊnd·aʊt/ *n* [C] *Am* (in baseball) the act of hitting a ball along the ground so that it is caught by someone on the other team who then causes the BATTER (= hitter) to be out • *Reynolds went to second base on a Segui groundout.*

grounds /graʊndz/ *pl n* the small bits of coffee left at the bottom of a cup or other container that has had coffee in it • See also GRIND [MAKE SMALLER].

ground·sheet /'graʊnd·ʃiːt/, *Am also* **ground·cloth** *n* [C] a piece of waterproof material which you put on the ground to sleep on when CAMPING

ground·sman *Br and Aus* (*pl* **-men**) /'graʊndz·mən/, *Am* **grounds·keep·er** /£'graʊndz,kiː·pəʳ, $-pɚ/ *n* [C] a man whose job is to take care of a sports ground or park

ground·swell /'graʊnd·swel/ *n* [U] a growth of strong feeling among a large group of people • *There is a groundswell* **of** *opinion against the new rules.*

ground·work /£'graʊnd·wɜːk, $-wɜːrk/ *n* [U] work that is done as a preparation for work that will be done later • *The committee will meet today to* **lay** *the groundwork* **for** *inter-party talks next month.*

group /gruːp/ *n* [C + sing/pl v] a number of people or things that are put together or considered as a unit • *I'm meeting a group* **of** *friends for dinner tonight.* • *The car was parked near a small group of trees.* • *She showed me another group of pictures, this time of children playing.* • *They are hoping to organize a campaign group that will aim to get better conditions for prisoners.* • *Inert gases form one group of the periodic table.* • A group is also a number of people who play music together, especially popular music: *What's your favourite group?* ○ *She began her career by singing in a pop group.* • A **group captain** is an officer in the British air force. • A **group practice** is several doctors who work together in the same place. • The **Group of Seven** (*abbreviation* **G7**) are the seven industrial countries of Canada, France, Italy, Japan, Britain, the United States and Germany which meet together to discuss and make plans. • **Group therapy** is treatment in which people meet in a group to talk about their emotional problems, with a trained leader or doctor present.

group /gruːp/ *v* • *We all grouped together the bride* (= formed a group round her) *for a family photograph.* [I always + adv/prep] • *The relatives of those killed in the crash grouped together* (= organized themselves into a group with an aim) *to seek compensation.* [I always + adv/prep] • *I grouped the children* (= put them in groups) *according to age.* [T] • *The books were grouped* (= put into groups) *by size.* [T]

group·ing /ˈgruː·pɪŋ/ *n* [C] • A grouping is several people or things when they have been arranged into a group or are being considered as a group: *There exist two clearly defined political groupings in the country, the establishment and the dissidents.* ○ *A survey of death trends in Britain shows that the worst grouping for early deaths is Northern men.* ○ *These colleges can offer a broader range of subjects in more varied groupings than anyone else.*

group·ie /ˈgruː·pi/ *n* [C] a person who likes a particular popular singer or other famous people and follows them to try to meet them • *Players' wives must live with the knowledge that groupies await their husbands in every city.*

grouse BIRD /graʊs/ *n* [C] *pl* **grouse** a small fat bird with feathered legs and feet, shot for sport and food • *They went grouse shooting at the weekend.*

grouse COMPLAIN /graʊs/ *v* [I] *infml* to complain, esp. often • *She's always grousing* **about** *her daughter's cooking.*

grouse /graʊs/ *n* [C] • *The high cost of theatre tickets is one of his favourite grouses.*

grout *obj* /graʊt/ *v* [T] to put a thin layer of MORTAR to fill the spaces between TILES, for example in a kitchen or bathroom • *We spent the weekend grouting the bathroom.*

grout /graʊt/, **grout·ing** /£ˈgraʊ·tɪŋ, $-t̬ɪŋ/ *n* [U] • *I used a spatula to put the grout between the tiles.*

grove /£grəʊv, $groʊv/ *n* [C] a group of trees planted close together • *Orange groves grow around the village.* • Grove is also used in some road and place names: *Ladbroke Grove*

grov·el TRY TO PLEASE /£ˈgrɒv·əl, $ˈgrɑː·vəl/ *v* [I] -**ll**- or *Am usually* -**l**- to behave too respectfully towards someone to show that you have a low opinion of yourself and that you are very eager to please them, esp. in the past by bending very low • *I will apologize to him but I won't grovel.* • *They felt obliged to write grovelling notes apologising for and explaining their omissions.*

grov·el MOVE /£ˈgrɒv·əl, $ˈgrɑː·vəl/ *v* [I] -**ll**- or *Am usually* -**l**- to move close to or on the ground • *I grovelled under the sofa to find my contact lens.* • *He grovelled* **on his knees/on all fours** *by the car.*

groves /£grəʊvz, $groʊvz/ *pl n* **the groves of academe** *literary humorous* universities considered as a whole • *It's yet another novel set in the groves of academe.*

grow *(obj)* INCREASE /£grəʊ, $groʊ/ *v past simple* **grew** /gruː/, *past part* **grown** /£grəʊn, $groʊn/ to increase in size or amount, or to become more advanced or developed • *This plant grows best in the shade.* [I] • *She has grown two centimetres taller in the past couple of months.* [L only + adj] • *Football's popularity continues to grow.* [I] • *The labour force is expected to grow by 2% next year.* [I] • *The male deer grows large branching horns called antlers.* [T] • *One aim of psychotherapy is to enable people to grow in all their relationships* (= to develop stronger emotions within relationships). [I] • If you grow your hair, you let it become longer and do not cut it: *She wanted to grow her hair long.* [T + obj + adj] • If a man grows a **beard**, he lets hair develop on the lower part of his face: *I grew a beard so as not to have the bother of shaving every morning.* [T] • If a plant grows in a particular place, it exists and develops there: *The roses grew up against the wall of the cottage.* [I] • If you grow a plant, you put it in the ground and take care of it: *The villagers grow coffee and maize to sell in the market.* [T] • If children **grow into** clothes, they become tall or big enough for the clothes to fit them: *If you buy the shoes half a size larger, she'll have grown into them by next month.* ○ See also **grow into** at GROW BECOME. • If children **grow out of** clothes, they become too tall or big to fit into the clothes: *Tyler has grown out of her sundress.* • If you **grow out of** an interest or way of behaving, you stop having or doing it as you become older: *He wants to join the army when he leaves school, but I hope he'll grow out of it.* • If an idea **grows out of** another one, it develops from it: *The idea for the story grew out of a strange experience I had last year.* • When children **grow up**, they gradually become adults: *I grew up in Scotland* (= I lived in Scotland when I was young). ○ *Taking responsibility for yourself is part of the process of* **growing up** (= becoming an adult). • *(infml)* If you say **grow up** to someone, you are telling them to stop behaving in a silly or foolish way: *Oh, do grow up you two and stop fighting!* • If a town or city **grows up**, it starts to increase in size or importance: *The city grew up originally as a crossing point on the river.* • If you say that something, esp. money, **does not grow on trees**, you mean that it is valuable and should not be wasted: *You shouldn't spend all your money at once – it doesn't grow on trees, you know.* • A **grown-up** is a person who is an adult: *The grown-ups always spoil our fun and tell us to be quiet or play outside.* • If you say that someone is **grown-up**, you mean that they are an adult or that they behave in a responsible way: *She has two grown-up children who work in the family business with her.* ○ *Even at ten years old, he was very grown-up and sensible.* • LP› **Age**

grow·er /£ˈgrəʊ·əʳ, $ˈgroʊ·ɚ/ *n* [C] • A grower is a person who grows large amounts of a particular plant or crop in order to sell them: *There has been a long-running dispute between growers and their distributors.* ○ *Many farmers are also growers.* • A grower is also a plant that grows in a particular way: *The new varieties of wheat are good growers even in poor soil.*

grow·ing /£ˈgrəʊ·ɪŋ, $ˈgroʊ-/ *adj* [not gradable] • Something that is growing is increasing in size or quantity: *A growing percentage of the population are taking holidays abroad.* ○ *There is a growing awareness of the seriousness of this disease.* • **Growing pains** are pains felt by young people in the bones or joints of their legs, which are commonly believed to be the result of some bones growing much faster than others. • **Growing pains** are also emotional difficulties or confusion experienced by a young person nearing adulthood. • If an organization has **growing pains**, it experiences temporary difficulties when it first starts or when it develops a new area of activity.

grown /£grəʊn, $groʊn/ *adj* [before n; not gradable] • A grown woman or man is an adult: *She said it upset her to see a grown man in tears.* ○ *You can't tell her what to do anymore – she's a grown woman.*

-grown /£-grəʊn, $-groʊn/ *combining form* • *The bear cubs are full-grown at two years.*

growth /£grəʊθ, $groʊθ/ *n* • The growth of a person, animal or plant is its process of increasing in size: *Plant growth is most noticeable in spring and early summer.* [U] ○ *You will see new growth* (= newly developing parts of a plant) *sprouting in the spring, even if the plant seems dead at the moment.* [U] ○ *She's written several books on* **personal growth** (= the development of truer and stronger emotions). • The growth of something is its increase in size or importance: *The government is trying to limit population growth.* [U] ○ *The rapid growth of opposition to the plan has surprised the council.* [U] ○ *Electronic publishing is a* **growth area** (= an area of activity that is increasing in size and developing quickly). • A growth is a lump growing on the outside or inside of a person, animal or plant which is caused by a disease: *The doctor says the growth on her arm is not cancerous.* [C] • Growth is also a short beard on a man's face when he has not shaved for a few days: *Graham came back from holiday with a week's growth on his chin.* [U] • **Growth hormones** are chemicals that increase the speed of growth: *Scientists have warned that the use of growth hormones to make cattle grow more quickly may result in a health risk for consumers.*

grow BECOME /£grəʊ, $groʊ/ *v* [L only + adj] *past simple* **grew** /gruː/, *past part* **grown** /£grəʊn, $groʊn/ to develop gradually, or to start to do something gradually • *She has grown much friendlier in the past few months.* • *My grandfather is finding it hard to cope with growing old.* • *She has grown* **to** *hate him.* [+ *to* infinitive] • *It took me a while to grow* **to** *like beer.* [+ *to* infinitive] • If two people in a close relationship **grow apart** or if they **grow away from** each other, they gradually begin to have a less close relationship, usually because they no longer have the same interests and desires. • If something or someone **grows on** you, you begin to like or enjoy it or them increasingly, after not liking it or them originally: *The more times I visit France, the more the French way of life grows on me.* • If you **grow into** a new situation such as a new job, you gradually become familiar with it and confident about dealing with it: *It may take you a few weeks to grow into the work.* ○ See also **grow into** at GROW INCREASE. • *"They shall grow not old, as we that are left grow old:/ Age shall not weary them, nor the years condemn. / At the going down of the sun and in the morning / We will remember them"* (Laurence Binyon **Poems for the Fallen** written about those who died in the First World War, 1914)

growl *(obj)* /graʊl/ *v* to make a low rough sound, usually in anger • *The dog growled and snapped at her ankles as she tried to pass.* [I] • *She has taught her dog to growl* **at** *strangers.* [I] • *The sergeant growled* **out** *his commands to the troops.* [I always + adv/prep] • *He picked up the letter, looked at it angrily, and then growled, "What's this?"* [+ clause]

growl /graʊl/ *n* [C] • *The dog stared at me suspiciously and low growls came from its throat.* • *(fig.) The new proposal has provoked growls of protest from the opposition parties.*

groyne /grɔɪn/, **groin** *n* [C] a low wall built out from the coast into the sea, to prevent the continual movement of the waves from removing parts of the land gradually

grub INSECT /grʌb/ *n* [C] an insect in the stage when it has just come out of its egg • *A grub looks like a short fat worm.*

grub FOOD /grʌb/ *n* [U] *infml* food • *They've got really good grub in the pub near the bridge.* • *OK, everyone, grub's* **up** (= the food is ready).

grub *(obj)* DIG /grʌb/ *v* [always + adv/prep] **-bb-** to search for (something) by digging or turning over earth • *The dog was grubbing* **around/about** *in the mud for a bone.* [I] • *(Am slang)* To grub is also to ask someone for something when you are unable or unwilling to get it yourself: *Could I grub a cigarette* **off** *you?* [T] ○ *Every time I see him, he's looking to grub something* **from** *me.* [T] • If you **grub** something **up/out**, you dig it out of the ground to get rid of it: *The farmer hired a huge mechanical digger to grub up the trees between the two fields.*

grub·by /ˈgrʌb·i/ *adj* **-ier, -iest** *infml* quite dirty • *He was wearing some old shorts and a grubby T-shirt.* • *Don't wipe your grubby hands on my clean towel!* • *(disapproving)* If you describe an activity or someone's behaviour as grubby, you do not think that it is honourable or acceptable: *She sees the business of making money as just grubby opportunism.* ○ *They made a grubby compromise with one of the opposition parties.* ○ *He doesn't want this story to get into the grubby hands of the tabloid press* (= to be obtained by newspapers who are not honourable).

grudge /grʌdʒ/ *n* [C] a strong feeling of anger and dislike for a person whom you feel has treated you badly, which often lasts for a long time • *I don't* **bear** *any grudge against you.* • *Philippa still* **has/holds** *a grudge against me for refusing to lend her that money.*

grudge *obj* /grʌdʒ/ *v* [T] • If you grudge something, you do or give it very unwillingly: *She grudged every hour spent helping a man whom she hated.* • If you grudge someone something, you wish that they did not have it: *I don't grudge you your holiday/I don't grudge your holiday* **to** *you, it's just that you've chosen an unfortunate time to go.* [+ two objects]

grudg·ing /ˈgrʌdʒ·ɪŋ/ *adj* • A grudging action or feeling is one which you do or have unwillingly: *She won the grudging respect of her boss.* ○ *The Government's response to the peace process has been grudging and rather hostile.*

grudg·ing·ly /ˈgrʌdʒ·ɪŋ·li/ *adv* • *She grudgingly admitted that she had been wrong to criticize him.*

gru·el /£grʊəl, $ˈgruː·əl/ *n* [U] a cheap food made by boiling OATS with water or milk • *While he was in prison, he was served a meagre diet of rice, bread and gruel.*

gru·ell·ing, *Am usually* **gru·el·ing** /£ˈgrʊə·lɪŋ, $ˈgruː·lɪŋ/ *adj* extremely tiring and difficult, and demanding great effort and determination • *They have just completed a gruelling 500-mile journey across the desert.* • *Junior doctors often have to work a gruelling 100-hour week.* • *She eventually won the match after five gruelling sets.*

gru·ell·ing·ly, *Am* **gru·el·ing·ly** /£ˈgrʊə·lɪŋ·li, $ˈgruː-/ *adv* • *It was a gruellingly long journey, and they got only three hours sleep in two days.*

grue·some /ˈgruː·səm/ *adj* extremely unpleasant and shocking, and usually dealing with death or injury • *The newspaper article included a gruesome description of the murder.* • *He told me a gruesome tale about the police finding human remains in the wood behind our house.* • (DK)

grue·some·ly /ˈgruː·səm·li/ *adv* • *His death was due to asbestos poisoning and he died very quickly and very gruesomely.*

gruff /grʌf/ *adj* **-er, -est** (of a person's voice) low and unfriendly, or (of a person's behaviour) unfriendly or lacking patience • *She spoke to me in a gruff voice, obviously annoyed that she had been disturbed.* • *He was gruff* **with** *the doctor, afraid to let her see how embarrassed he was.*

gruff·ly /ˈgrʌf·li/ *adv* • *She gruffly ordered him out of the house.*

gruff·ness /ˈgrʌf·nəs/ *n* [U] • *He was an intelligent, amusing man, but this was often masked by his gruffness.*

grum·ble /ˈgrʌm·bl̩/ *v* [I] to complain about someone or something in an annoyed way • *It's no use grumbling* **about** *the hotel – we're only here for one night.* • *She spent the evening grumbling to me* **about** *her job.* • *"Why aren't I allowed a day off?" she grumbled.* [+ clause] • If your stomach grumbles, it makes a low continuous noise, usually because you are hungry: *I didn't have any breakfast and my stomach's been grumbling all morning.* • *(Br infml)* If you say **mustn't grumble**, you mean that what you are doing is not very bad and that you should not complain about it: *"How's your work going?" "Oh, mustn't grumble."* • If you have a **grumbling appendix**, the organ which is connected to the bowels is causing you slight pain.

grum·ble /ˈgrʌm·bl̩/ *n* [C often pl] • A grumble is a complaint: *If I hear any more grumbles about the food, you can learn to cook yourself.*

grum·bler /£ˈgrʌm·bləʳ, $-blɚ/ *n* [C] • A grumbler is a person who complains a lot: *There's always one grumbler in every class who spends the whole time trying to stir up trouble among the others.*

grum·py /ˈgrʌm·pi/ *adj* **-ier, -iest** *slightly infml* bad-tempered because of annoyance or tiredness • *The shopkeeper was a grumpy and rather unfriendly man.* • *I hadn't had enough sleep and I was grumpy all day.* • *She made a grumpy remark about how late I was.*

grump /grʌmp/ *n* [C] *infml* • A grump is a bad-tempered person: *He's only an old grump – don't listen to him.*

grum·pi·ly /ˈgrʌm·pɪ·li/ *adv slightly infml* • *"I suppose you can borrow my car," she said grumpily, "but you'd better not damage it."*

grum·pi·ness /ˈgrʌm·pɪ·nəs/ *n* [U] *slightly infml* • *Her grumpiness is probably due to a lack of sleep.*

grunge /grʌndʒ/ *n* [U] a type of ROCK music, and a fashion for untidy clothes which was popular in the early 1990s • *Grunge music began in the clubs of Seattle and is based on a heavy, distorted guitar sound.* • *Nirvana is one of the most famous grunge bands.* • *The grunge look was based on ordinary, rather shapeless clothes, such as tight-fitting T-shirts and baggy sweaters.*

grun·gy /ˈgrʌn·dʒi/ *adj esp. Am slang* (of a person) feeling tired and dirty, or (of a thing) dirty • *After a 15-hour flight, I felt grungy and desperate for a bath.*

grunt /grʌnt/ *v* [I] (of a pig) to make a low rough noise, or (of a person) to make a short low noise to show that you do not want to talk or are unable to talk because of physical tiredness • *The pigs grunted happily as they ate their food.* • *I asked him if he wanted to go out, but he just grunted and carried on reading his newspaper.* • *"OK," he grunted, "we're almost at the top, and then we can rest."* [+ clause] • *She grunted* **with** *pain.*

grunt /grʌnt/ *n* [C] • *Loud grunts were coming from the pig sty.*

grunt·led /ˈgrʌn·tl̩d/ *adj infml* happy or satisfied • *Although he wasn't actually disgruntled, he was far from being gruntled.*

Gruy·ère /£ˈgruː·jeəʳ, $gruˈjer/ *n* [U] a hard, pale yellow, strong-tasting cheese which was originally made in Switzerland

GTi /ˌdʒi·ti'aɪ/ *n* [C] *abbreviation for* Gran Turismo injection (= a car which is comfortable, expensive and very powerful) • *I hear you've got a GTi now.* • *She drives a white Golf GTi.* • *It's a standard saloon with GTi performance.*

gua·ca·mo·le /£ˌgwæk·əˈməʊ·li, $-ˈmoʊ-/ *n* [U] a thick mixture of AVOCADO (= a savoury green tropical fruit), TOMATO, onion and spices, which is usually eaten cold with bread

gua·no /£ˈgwɑː·nəʊ, $-noʊ/ *n* [U] the excrement of sea birds • *Guano is often used as a fertilizer.*

gua·ran·tee /ˌgær·ənˈtiː/ *n* a promise that something will be done or will happen, esp. a written promise by a company to repair or change a product that develops a fault within a particular period of time • *The system costs £99·95 including postage, packing and a 12-month guarantee.* [C] • *The video recorder* **comes with/has** *a two-year guarantee.* [C] • *The shop said they would replace the television as it was still* **under** *guarantee.* [U] • *The United Nations has demanded a guarantee from the army* **that** *food convoys will not be attacked.* [C + *that* clause] • *There is no guarantee* **(that)** *it will be nice weather tomorrow.* [C + *(that)* clause] • *There is no guarantee* **(that)** *the discussions will lead to a deal.* [C + *(that)* clause] • *A product as good as that is a guarantee* **of** *commercial success* (= It is certain to be successful). [C] ● If a product has a **money-back** guarantee, the company that produced it will give you back the money you paid for it if it develops a fault. [C] ● A guarantee is also a formal acceptance of responsibility for something, such as the payment of someone else's debt: *I will give you a guarantee for the £2000 he owes you.* [C] ● *(specialized)* A guarantee is also something valuable which you give to someone temporarily while you do what you promised to do for them, and which they will keep if you fail to do it. [C] ● Ⓙ (KOR)

gua·ran·tee *obj* /ˌgær·ᵊnˈtiː/ *v* [T] ● If a product is guaranteed, the company that made it promises to repair or change it if a fault develops within a particular period of time: *The fridge is guaranteed* **for** *three years.* ● If someone guarantees something, they promise that that thing will happen or exist: *European Airlines guarantees its customers top-quality service/European Airlines guarantees top-quality service* **for** *its customers.* [+ two objects] ○ *The label on this bread says it is guaranteed* **free of/from** *preservatives* (= it contains no preservatives). ● If something guarantees something else, it makes certain that it will happen: *The £50 deposit guarantees* **(that)** *people return the boats after their hour has finished.* [+ *(that)* clause] ● If something is guaranteed to happen or have a particular result, it is certain that it will happen or have that result: *Just looking at a picture of the sea is guaranteed* **to** *make me feel sick.* [+ *to* infinitive] ● If you guarantee someone's debt, you formally promise to accept the responsibility for that debt if the person fails to pay it: *The company has agreed to guarantee the £10·5 million bank loan.*

gua·ran·tor /£ˌgær·ᵊnˈtɔːʳ, $-tɔːr/ *n* [C] *fml* ● A guarantor is a person who makes certain that something happens or that something is protected: *The armed forces see themselves as the guarantors of free elections in the country.* ● *(law)* A guarantor is a person who formally accepts responsibility for you or for something that belongs to you: *You must have a guarantor in order to get a visa to enter the country.*

guard /£gɑːd, $gɑːrd/ *n* [C] a person or group of people whose job it is to protect a person, place or thing from danger or attack, or to prevent a person such as a criminal from escaping ● *There are guards* **posted** (= standing and watching) *at every entrance.* ● **Armed** *guards are posted around the site.* ● *The frontier is patrolled by* **border** *guards.* ● *He managed to get past two* **prison** *guards and escape.* ● *The company employs* **security** *guards with dogs to patrol the perimeter fence.* ● *(Br and Aus)* A guard (*Am* **conductor**) is a railway official who travels on and is responsible for a train. ● A guard is also a device that protects a dangerous part of something or that protects something from getting damaged: *a trigger guard* ○ *The helmet has a face guard attached.* ● If someone is **under guard**, they are being protected or are being prevented from escaping: *The ex-President was under* **armed** *guard in the Palace.* ● If you **stand/keep guard** or are **on guard**, you are responsible for protecting someone or something, or preventing someone from escaping: *Two of the soldiers kept guard* **over** *the captured guns.* ● Your guard is also your readiness to defend yourself from physical or other types of attack: *He got in* **under** *Paul's guard and punched him on the jaw* (= He hit him despite Paul's attempt to defend himself). ○ *After a few days he* **dropped/lowered** *his guard* (= stopped being so careful and watchful), *and it was then that the kidnap occurred.* ○ *The boxer* **let** *his guard* **slip** (= stopped protecting himself) *for an instant and was knocked out.* ● If you are **on** your **guard**, you are careful and aware because a situation might be dangerous: *It's wise to be on your guard* **against** *people who are trying to con you.* ● If you **catch** someone **off guard**, you surprise them by doing something which they are not expecting and are not ready for: *The bad news caught her off her guard.* ● **The Changing of the Guard** is a ceremony held once a day outside Buckingham Palace in London when one set of soldiers replaces the soldiers who have finished their time on duty standing outside the Palace. ● A **guard dog** is a dog trained to protect a place. ● A **guard of honour** is a group of people, usually soldiers, who are lined up at a special occasion such as a marriage ceremony or an official visit, to honour someone very important. ● A **guard post** is a small building for the soldiers who are protecting a place. ● A **guard rail** is a bar along the edge of something steep, such as stairs or a cliff, to prevent people from falling off. ● *(Br and Aus)* A **guard's van** (*Am* **caboose**) is a small carriage, usually at the back of the train, in which the guard travels. ● *"Who will guard the guards?"* (Juvenal *Satires*, c.60-130 AD)

Guards /£gɑːdz, $gɑːrdz/ *pl n* ● The Guards is the name of several important REGIMENTS (= units) in an army: *the Grenadier Guards* ○ *the Norwegian King's Guards* ○ *He was always proud of having been a Guards officer.* ○ See also GUARDSMAN.

guard *obj* /£gɑːd, $gɑːrd/ *v* [T] ● If you guard a place, you protect it: *Government troops are guarding key buildings in the capital* **against** *terrorist attacks.* ○ *Since the start of last week's attempted coup, the President has hardly left his* **heavily** *guarded headquarters.* ● If you guard a person, you protect them or prevent them from escaping: *The terrorists guarded their prisoners day and night.* ● If you guard information, you keep it secret: *Journalists* **jealously** (= carefully) *guard their sources of information.* ● If you **guard against** something, you take careful action in order to try to prevent it from happening: *The best way to guard against financial problems is to avoid getting into debt.* ○ *Her way to guard against being attacked is never to go out alone at night.* [+ v-*ing*]

guard·ed /£ˈgɑː·dɪd, $ˈgɑːr-/ *adj* ● Someone who is guarded is careful about what they say in order to avoid giving any important or secret information to someone else or because they are not certain about something: *Her remarks about the department were guarded, although slightly negative.* ● See also WELL-GUARDED.

guard·ed·ly /£ˈgɑː·dɪd·li, $ˈgɑːr-/ *adv* ● *Some trading officials are guardedly* **optimistic** *that the market is now on the road to recovery.*

guard·house /£ˈgɑːd·haʊs, $ˈgɑːrd-/ *n* [C] *pl* **guardhouses** /£ˈgɑːdˌhaʊ·zɪz, $ˈgɑːrd-/ a building for the soldiers who are protecting a place

guard·i·an /£ˈgɑː·di·ən, $ˈgɑːr-/ *n* [C] a person who has the legal right and responsibility of taking care of someone who cannot take care of themselves, such as a child whose parents have died ● *The girl's parents or guardians must give their consent before she has the operation.* ● *(fml)* A guardian is also someone who protects something: *These three official bodies are the guardians* **of** *the nation's countryside.* ● A **guardian angel** is a spirit who is believed to protect and help a particular person: *(fig.) The Tourist Protection Unit is a squad of 45 undercover officers who are assigned as guardian angels to protect the city's unwary visitors.*

guard·i·an·ship /£ˈgɑː·di·ən·ʃɪp, $ˈgɑːr-/ *n* [U] ● Guardianship is the state or duty of being a guardian: *During the 1930s in Britain, women campaigned for guardianship rights over their children and pensions for widows.* ○ *(fml) The monument is currently in the guardianship of English Heritage.*

guard·room /£ˈgɑːd·rʊm, -ruːm, $ˈgɑːrd-/ *n* [C] a room for soldiers who are protecting a place

guards·man /£ˈgɑːdz·mən, $ˈgɑːrdz-/ *n* [C] *pl* **-men** a soldier who is a member of the Guards (= a particular army unit)

gua·va /ˈgwɑː·və/ *n* [C] a round yellow tropical fruit with pink or white flesh and hard seeds, or the small tropical tree on which it grows

gub·bins /ˈgʌb·ɪnz/ *n* [U] *Br infml* a collection of unimportant objects; rubbish ● *I've just got to clear all this gubbins off my desk before I start working.*

gu·ber·na·tor·i·al /£ˌguː·bᵊn·əˈtɔː·ri·əl, $-bɚ·nəˈtɔːr·i-/ *adj* [not gradable] *Am specialized* relating to a governor of a STATE in the United States ● *Bill Clinton's first big election victory was the gubernatorial contest in Arkansas.*

guer·ril·la, guer·il·la /gəˈrɪl·ə/ *n* [C] a member of an unofficial military group that is trying to change the government by making sudden, unexpected attacks on the official army forces ● *A small band of guerrillas has blown up a train in the mountains.* ● *The guerrilla army has defeated a much larger force of government soldiers.* ● *His followers are highly trained in the tactics of guerrilla* **warfare.**

guess *(obj)* /ges/ *v* to give an answer to a particular question when you dc not have all the facts and so cannot be certain if you are correct ● *I didn't know the answer, so I had to guess.* [I] ● *On the last question, she guessed* **right/wrong.** [I always + adv] ● *Can you guess* **how** *old this picture is?* [+ *wh-* word] ● *I bet you can't guess* **how** *old she is.* [+ *wh-* word] ● *The police, having guessed* **(that)** *she would return, were waiting for her.* [+ *(that)* clause] ● *He guessed her age* **to be** *48.* [+ obj + *to be* n/adj] ● *The manager guessed the total amount* **to be** *about £50000.* [+ obj + *to be* n/adj] ● To guess can also mean to give the correct answer: *How did you guess?* [I] ○ *She guessed the answer first time.* [T] • *(infml)* To guess also means to think or believe: *My train leaves in an hour, so I guess I'd better be going now.* • *(infml)* You can say **guess what** before telling someone something interesting or surprising: *Hey, guess what? We won the match 4-0.* • If you **keep** someone **guessing**, you do not give them the information that they want and so keep them uncertain of what is really happening: *The idea was to keep the enemy guessing until the attack had actually begun.*

guess /ges/ *n* [C] • A guess is an attempt to give the right answer when you are not certain if you are correct: *Go on –* **have/make/***(Am)* **take** *a guess.* ○ *Both teams made some* **wild** *guesses* (=ones which were made without much thought), *none of which were right.* ○ *"What's the time?" "It's about 5 o'clock,* **at a** *guess* (=without knowing exactly)." • Someone's guess is also their opinion about something which is formed without any knowledge of the situation: *Her parents' guess was that she and David had quarrelled.* ○ *"I don't know why she's so late." "My guess is that her car has broken down."* • If you say that something is **anyone's/anybody's guess**, you mean it is not possible for anyone to really know: *The plan is to double the amount of nuclear power produced, but what the effect will be is anyone's guess.* • If you say **Your guess is as good as mine**, you mean that you do not know what has happened or what will happen: *"What's he up to?" "I don't know. Your guess is as good as mine."*

guess·ti·mate, gues·ti·mate /ˈges·tə·mət/ *n* [C] *infml* an approximate calculation of the size or amount of something when you do not know all the facts • *Current guesstimates are that the company's turnover will increase by 7% this year.* • *Clothing retailers often have to make guesstimates about customer requirements months in advance of the season.*

guess·work /£ˈges·wɜːk, $-wɜːrk/ *n* [U] the process of making a guess when you do not know all the facts • *She had to rely on pure guesswork in calculating her expenditure.* • *Knowing how high the price increase will be is a matter for guesswork.*

guest /gest/ *n* [C] a person who is staying with you, or a person whom you have invited to a social occasion, such as a party or a meal • *150 guests were invited to the wedding.* • *We have guests (Am and Aus* **houseguests***) staying this weekend.* • *You should make a guest* **list** *of who you want to invite.* • *He is a* **paying** *guest* (=He pays for the use of a room in someone's home). • If someone is your guest, you pay for them to do something: *Whenever I go somewhere with my grandmother, she always insists that I'm her guest and won't let me pay.* ○ *The journalists were sent to Paris as guests of a multinational company.* • A person who is staying in a hotel is also called a guest: *We would like to remind all our guests to leave their keys at reception before they depart.* • A guest is also a person, such as an entertainer, who has been invited to appear on a television or radio programme or in a performance: *Our special guest on the programme is Robert de Niro.* ○ *The guest stars on tonight's show are Barbra Streisand and Barry Manilow.* ○ *Madonna made a guest appearance at the concert.* ○ *Simon Rattle will be the guest conductor with the London Symphony Orchestra.* • If you say **be my guest** to someone when they have asked if they can do something, you mean that you allow them to do it: *"Can I try out your new bicycle?" "Be my guest."* • *(Br)* A **guest beer** is a type of beer which is sold in a bar for a short time and which is made by a different company from the one that normally supplies the beer. • A **guest book** is a book in which people write their names and addresses when they have been staying in a friend's house or at a hotel. • A *(Br and Aus)* **guest of honour**/*(Am and Aus)* **guest of honor** is the most important person at a particular social occasion: *The Prime Minister was guest of honour at the dinner.* • A **guest worker** is a person who lives and works in foreign country for a limited period of time, doing low paid and usually unskilled work.

guest /gest/ *v* [I] • If a person, esp. an entertainer, guests on a programme or show, they are invited to appear or perform on it: *He was a famous singer who guested* **on** *several pop videos and even hosted his own TV show.*

guest·house /ˈgest·haus/ *n* [C] *pl* **guesthouses** /ˈgest ˌhau·zɪz/ a small cheap hotel • *We stayed in a guesthouse near the city centre when we visited Oxford.*

guest·room /£ˈgest·rum, $-ruːm/ *n* [C] a bedroom in a house for visitors to sleep in

guff /gʌf/ *n* [U] *infml* (of speech or writing) nonsense • *I've never heard so much guff!* • *Most of what he said was just* **a load of** *guff.*

guf·faw /£gʌfˈɔː, $-ˈɑː/ *v* [I] to laugh loudly, esp. at something stupid that someone has said or done • *He guffawed with delight when he heard the news.* • *I tried very hard to restrain my laughter, but tears started flowing down my cheeks and I began guffawing.*

guf·faw /£gʌfˈɔː, $-ˈɑː/ *n* [C] • *She let out a loud guffaw.* • *His story was greeted with guffaws by his friends.*

guide /gaɪd/ *n* [C] a person whose job it is to show a place or a particular route to visitors, or a book or piece of information which gives advice or help on how to do or understand something • *It would be foolish to go on an expedition into the mountains without taking a guide.* • *The* **tour** *guide took us round the city and told us a lot of interesting historical facts.* • *A new guide* **to** *good hotels in Britain has just been published.* • *I never follow recipes exactly when I cook – I just use them as a* **rough** (= approximate) *guide.* • *Do you sell* **tourist** *guides?* • A guide is also something which helps you form an opinion about someone or something: *What he says is not always a good guide as to how he will act.* • Guide is also another word for GUIDEBOOK: *a guide to the British Isles* • *"Thou wert my guide, philosopher, and friend"* (Alexander Pope in the poem *An Essay on Man*, 1734)

guide *obj* /gaɪd/ *v* [T] • If you guide people round a place, you show it to them: *The curator guided us* **round** *the gallery, pointing out the most famous paintings in the collection.* ○ *We were* **taken** *on a guided tour of the city.* ○ *(fig.) If you want to learn how to use the computer, it has a program that will guide you* **through** *it* (=show you how to use it). • If you guide someone somewhere, you lead them to that place: *The shop assistant guided me to the shelf where the gardening books were displayed.* • If you guide something, you make it move in the right direction: *She guided the child's head and arms into the T-shirt.* ○ *The pilot guided the plane in to land.* ○ *The lights along the runway had been lit to guide the plane in to land.* • To guide someone or something can also mean to control or influence them: *As managing director, she guided company policy for twenty years.* ○ *Don't allow yourself to be guided by your emotions.* • A **guide dog** is a dog that has been specially trained to help a blind person travel around safely. • A **guided missile** is an explosive weapon whose direction is controlled electronically during its flight: *The flight path of a guided missile can be altered after the missile has been launched.* • A **guiding principle** is an idea which influences you greatly when making a decision or considering a matter: *Equality of opportunity has been the government's guiding principle in its education reforms.* • A **guiding spirit/light** is a person who influences you and shows you how something can be done or achieved successfully. • In this dictionary, **guide words** are given to help you find the sense of the word that you are looking for when the word has more than one meaning. They are printed in capital letters, inside a rectangular box at the start of the entry.

guid·ance /ˈgaɪ·dᵊnts/ *n* [U] • Guidance is help and advice about how to do something or about how to deal with problems connected with your work, education, or personal relationships: *My professor gave me a lot of helpful guidance while I was writing up my PhD.* • Guidance also refers to the process of directing the flight of a MISSILE or ROCKET: *a missile guidance system*

guide·book /ˈgaɪd·buk/, **guide** *n* [C] a book which gives information for visitors about a place, such as a city or country • *Have you got a guidebook to Montreal?*

guide·line /ˈgaɪd·laɪn/ *n* [C usually pl] a piece of information intended to advise people on how something should be done or what something should be • *The EU has issued some guidelines on appropriate levels of pay for part-time manual workers.* • *The government is drawing up some new guidelines about health and safety in schools.* • *Opponents of the project say that the company did not adhere to economic guidelines during the planning and construction of the buildings.*

Guides /gaɪdz/ *pl n* **the Guides** an international organization for young women which encourages them to take part in different activities and to become responsible and independent • *The Guides was formed in 1910 by Lord Baden-Powell.* • *Were you ever in the Guides?* • Compare SCOUTS.

guide /gaɪd/ *adj* [before n; not gradable] • *She belongs to the local guide* **company** (= group).

guide /gaɪd/, *dated* **girl guide** *n* [C] • A guide is a girl aged between 10 and 14 years old who is a member of the Guides.

guild /gɪld/ *n* [C] an organization of people who do the same job or have the same interests • *the Writers' Guild* • *the Fashion Designers' Guild*

guild·hall /£ˈgɪld·hɔːl, $-hɑːl/ *n* [C usually sing] (in Britain) a building in the centre of a town in which members of a GUILD met in the past, which is now often used as a place for meetings or performances • *The concert will be held on 27 June in the Guildhall.*

guile /gaɪl/ *n* [U] *fml* the ability to obtain or achieve what you want by indirect and clever but possibly dishonest methods • *The President will need to use all her political guile to stay in power.* • *He is a simple, honest man, totally lacking in guile.*

guile·ful /ˈgaɪl·fᵊl/ *adj fml* • *He was a guileful manipulator who had clawed his way up to the top of the organization.*

guile·less /ˈgaɪl·ləs/ *adj fml* • If someone is guileless, they are honest: *Disillusion with the other candidates and a liking for her guileless campaign style were enough to give her victory in the election.*

guil·le·mot /£ˈgɪl·ɪ·mɒt, $-ə·mɑːt/ *n* [C] a black and white sea bird with a long narrow beak that lives in northern parts of the world

guil·lo·tine [DEVICE] /£ˈgɪl·ə·tiːn, $-t̬iːn/ *n* a device, invented in France, consisting of a sharp blade in a tall frame which was used in the past for killing criminals by cutting off their heads • *A guillotine was erected in the town square and a crowd began to gather around it.* [C] • *King Louis XVI and Marie Antoinette* **went to** *the guillotine* (=were killed by the guillotine) *during the French Revolution.* [U] • *(Br and Aus)* A guillotine is also a device with a long sharp blade which is used for cutting large quantities of paper. [C]

guil·lo·tine *obj* /£ˈgɪl·ə·tiːn, $-t̬iːn/ *v* [T] • *During the French Revolution, thousands of people were guillotined.*

guil·lo·tine [LIMIT] /£ˈgɪl·ə·tiːn, $-t̬iːn/ *n* [C] *Br and Aus specialized* a limit on the amount of discussion allowed about a particular law in Parliament, which is made by setting a fixed time before a final vote must be taken • *The government forced the bill through Parliament by the ruthless application of the guillotine.*

guil·lo·tine *obj* /£ˈgɪl·ə·tiːn, $-t̬iːn/ *v* [T] *Br specialized* • *The bill was guillotined by 318 votes to 236.*

guilt [FEELING] /gɪlt/ *n* [U] a feeling of anxiety or unhappiness that you have because you have done something wrong, such as causing harm to another person • *She was tormented by feelings of guilt and shame over what she had done.* • *There was a sense of collective guilt in the community that the disaster had been allowed to happen.* • *The protagonist in the novel is a guilt-***ridden** *young man* (=he has a strong feeling of guilt) *who is trying to come to terms with his past.* • A **guilt complex** is a very strong feeling of guilt which you cannot get rid of: *She has a guilt complex about inheriting so much money from her father.* • *(infml)* A **guilt trip** is a very strong feeling of guilt for something you have done wrong or forgotten to do: *At first David was reluctant, but his parents had laid such a heavy guilt trip on him for being irresponsible, he agreed to it.* • *(infml)* To **guilt-trip** someone is to make them feel guilty for something that they should have done but have not done: *She claims his idea that young children need the constant supervision of their mothers guilt-tripped a generation of caring and competent mothers.*

guilt·y /£ˈgɪl·ti, $-t̬i/ *adj* **-ier, -iest** • *She must have done something wrong, because she's looking so guilty.* • *I feel so guilty* **about** *forgetting your birthday.* • If someone has a **guilty conscience**, they are unhappy because of something they feel they have done wrong.

guilt·i·ly /£ˈgɪl·tɪ·li, $-t̬ɪ-/ *adv* • *She guiltily took another biscuit from the tin, knowing that she shouldn't be eating in between meals.*

guilt [RESPONSIBILITY] /gɪlt/ *n* [U] the fact of having done something wrong or committed a crime • *Interrogating officers said they were certain of the suspect's guilt before they interviewed him.* • *Both suspects* **admitted** *their guilt to the police.* • *The prosecution's task in a case is to* **establish** *a person's guilt beyond any reasonable doubt.* • Compare **innocence** at INNOCENT.

guilt·y /£ˈgɪl·ti, $-t̬i/ *adj* **-ier, -iest** • *The jury has to decide whether a person is guilty or innocent* **of** *a crime.* • *A person accused of a crime is presumed innocent until* **proven** *guilty.* • *He* **pleaded** *guilty* (= He formally admitted his guilt in court) **to** *the charge of attempted murder.* • *She claims the company is guilty* **of** *falsifying its accounts.* • The guilty **party** is the person who has done something wrong or who has committed a crime: *The judge said although it would be unfortunate for a guilty party to escape justice, it was far more important that an innocent person should not be wrongly punished.* • Compare INNOCENT. • LP> **Crimes and criminals, Law**

guilt·less /ˈgɪlt·ləs/ *adj* • A person who is guiltless is not responsible for doing something wrong or committing a crime: *These men are guiltless and should go free.*

guin·ea /ˈgɪn·i/ *n* [C] an old British gold coin worth £1·05 • *The painting was sold at auction for 100 guineas.*

guin·ea fowl /ˈgɪn·i/ *n* [C] *pl* **guinea fowl** a large grey and white African bird, kept for its eggs and meat

guin·ea pig [ANIMAL] /ˈgɪn·i/ *n* [C] a small furry animal with rounded ears, short legs and no tail, which is often kept as a pet by children • *Guinea pigs make very docile pets.*

guin·ea pig [TEST] /ˈgɪn·i/ *n* [C] a person used in a scientific test, usually to discover the effect of a drug on humans • *They're asking for students to be guinea pigs in their research into the common cold.* • *He was used as a guinea pig to test a new cure for AIDS.*

guise /gaɪz/ *n* [U] the appearance of someone or something, esp. when intended to deceive • *The men who arrived* **in the** *guise* **of** *drug dealers were actually undercover police officers.* • *The company has been accused of trying to sell their products* **under the** *guise* **of** *market research.*

guit·ar /£gɪˈtɑːʳ, $-ˈtɑːr/ *n* [C] a musical instrument with six strings and a long neck which is usually made of wood, and which is played by pulling or hitting the strings with the fingers • *I've been learning how to play the guitar.* • *He sat on the grass, strumming his guitar.* • The two main types of guitar are the **acoustic** guitar (= a hollow wooden guitar) and the **electric** guitar (= a guitar in which the sound is produced electronically). • PIC> **Musical instruments**

guit·ar·ist /£gɪˈtɑː·rɪst, $-ˈtɑːr·ɪst/ *n* [C] • A guitarist is a person who plays the guitar: *a classical/folk/rock guitarist*

gu·lag /ˈguː·læg/ *n* [U] **the gulag** severe work prisons for people found guilty of crimes against their country • *Thousands of people were sent to the gulag in the Soviet Union during Stalin's rule.* • *He was charged with being a spy and spent the next eight years in a prison camp in the Siberian gulag.*

gulch /gʌltʃ/ *n* [C] *Am for* GULLY

gulf [AREA], **Gulf** /gʌlf/ *n* [C] a very large area of sea surrounded on three sides by a curving length of coast • *The ship sailed into the Gulf of Mexico.* • *The storm over Queensland was caused by a depression moving inland from the Gulf of Carpentaria.* • The Gulf is another name for the Persian Gulf and the countries around it: *The Gulf states include Iran, Iraq, Saudi Arabia, Kuwait, Bahrain, Oman, Qatar, and the United Arab Emirates.* • *(fml)* A gulf is also a very large deep hole in the ground. • The **Gulf Stream** is the current of warm water which flows across the Atlantic Ocean from the Gulf of Mexico towards Europe. • LP> **World regions**

gulf [DIFFERENCE] /gʌlf/ *n* [C] an important difference between the ideas and opinions of two groups of people • *There is a widening gulf* **between** *the middle classes and the poorest sections of society.* • *It is hoped that the peace plan will* **bridge** *the gulf* (=reduce the very large difference) **between** *the government and the rebels.*

gull /gʌl/, **sea·gull** *n* [C] a sea bird with black and white or grey and white feathers • *We could hear the cries of gulls as they circled overhead.*

gul·let /ˈgʌl·ət/, *medical* **oe·so·phag·us**, *esp. Am medical* **e·so·pha·gus** *n* [C] the tube which food travels down from the mouth to the stomach • *The gullet squeezes solids and liquids towards the stomach by contracting the muscles.* • If something **sticks in** your **gullet**, you find it unpleasant and you refuse to accept or do it: *The idea that she should have to go on her knees and apologise stuck in her gullet.*

gul·li·ble /ˈgʌl·ə·bl/ *adj* (of a person) easily deceived or tricked, and too willing to believe everything that other people say • *The local tourist guides delight gullible Western tourists with unlikely stories.*

gul·ly, **gul·ley** /ˈgʌl·i/, *Am also* **gulch** *n* [C] a narrow, stony valley or channel with steep sides, made by a fast flowing stream • *Heavy rainfall had cut deep gullies into the side of the hill.*

gulp *(obj)* /gʌlp/ *v* to eat or drink (food or liquid) quickly by swallowing it in large amounts, or to make a swallowing movement because of fear, surprise or excitement • *She gulped* **down** *her drink and made a hasty exit.* [M] • *He gulped* **down** *vast quantities of oysters and champagne at the party.* [M] • *When it was his turn to dive, he gulped and stepped up onto the diving board.* [I] • If you gulp air, you breathe in a large amount of it very quickly. [T] • If you **gulp back** an emotion, you try to stop yourself from showing it, usually by making a swallowing movement: *She gulped back the tears.*

gulp /gʌlp/ *n* [C] • *He swallowed his drink in one gulp.* • *She rose to the surface of the water once every minute to get a gulp of air.* • *He* **took** *a gulp of tea and burnt his mouth because it was far too hot.*

gum MOUTH /gʌm/ *n* [C] either of the two areas of firm pink flesh inside the mouth which cover the bones into which the teeth are fixed • *I've got really sore gums.* • *If you brush your teeth too hard, your gums may start to bleed.* • A **gum shield** is a device which boxers put inside their mouths in order to protect their teeth and gums during fights. • (CS) (J)

gum *obj* /gʌm/ *v* [T] **-mm-** *Am* • *He gave his baby daughter a biscuit to gum* (= to practise chewing with, using her gums).

gum·my /ˈgʌm·i/ *adj* **-ier**, **-iest** • Gummy means showing the gums: *The baby gave her a gummy smile.*

gum STICKY SUBSTANCE /gʌm/ *n* a sticky substance obtained from the stems of some trees and plants, or a type of glue used for sticking together pieces of paper • *Gum arabic is used as a glue, in ink and in the manufacture of sweets and the gum is extracted from the acacia tree.* [U] • Gum is another word for **chewing gum** or **bubble gum** (= a soft sweet that people chew but do not swallow): *She walked down the street chewing a piece of gum.* [U] • Gum is another word for GUMDROP: *fruit gums* [C] ○ *wine gums* [C] • Gum or **gum tree** is another word for EUCALYPTUS. [C] • *(Br infml dated)* If you say that someone is **up a gum tree**, you mean that they are in a difficult situation which they will find it extremely difficult to escape from. • *(Br infml dated)* If you say **by gum**, you are expressing surprise: *By gum, he's a big lad!* • (CS) (J)

gum *obj* /gʌm/ *v* [T] **-mm-** • If you gum one piece of paper to another, you stick them together using glue: *Can you gum these address labels onto these envelopes?* • If something is **gummed up**, it will not work or open and close correctly: *When I woke up, I had gummed up eyelids and a sore throat.* • If something **gums up the works**, it prevents something else from operating correctly.

gummed /gʌmd/, **gum·my** /ˈgʌm·i/ *adj* [not gradable] • If something is gummed, it is sticky or has glue on it: *gummed labels/envelopes*

gum·bo /£ˈgʌm·bəʊ, $-boʊ/ *n pl* **gumbos** a thick soup made with OKRA (= a green vegetable) and meat or fish, which comes from America • *The restaurant had a limited menu – gumbo, Creole rice, a few sandwiches.* [U] • *Gumbos are usually thickened with flour and butter.* [C] • Gumbo is also *Am for* OKRA. [U]

gum·boot /ˈgʌm·buːt/ *n* [C] *Aus or Br dated* a long waterproof boot • PIC› **Shoes**

gum·drop /£ˈgʌm·drɒp, $-drɑːp/, **gum** *n* [C] a chewy sweet that is usually fruit-flavoured

gump·tion /ˈgʌmp·ʃᵊn/ *n* [U] *infml* the ability to decide what is the best thing to do in a particular situation, and to do it with energy and determination • *She had the gumption to write directly to the company manager and persuade him to give her a job.*

gum·shoe /ˈgʌm·ʃuː/ *n* [C] *Am slang for* DETECTIVE

gun /gʌn/ *n* [C] a weapon from which bullets or SHELLS (= explosive containers) are fired • *Have you ever* **used** *a gun before?* • *The British police do not* **carry** *guns.* • *You could hear the noise of the big guns* **firing** *in the distance.* • In sport, a gun is a device which makes a very loud sudden noise as a signal to start a race: **At the** *gun, the runners sprinted away down the track.* • A gun is also be a type of tool. See **grease gun** at GREASE; **staple-gun** at STAPLE WIRE. • *(esp. Am)* A **(hired)** gun is a person whose job it is to carry and use a gun to protect or kill people. • If someone does something **with guns blazing**, they do it in a determined or angry way: *Both sides are determined to get the best deal possible from tomorrow's negotiations and will go in with guns blazing.* • A **gun carriage** is a frame on wheels for a CANNON (= a large powerful gun). • A **gun dog** (*Am also* **bird dog**) is a dog used by hunters to find and gather birds they have shot. • A **gun-runner** is a person who illegally brings guns into a country. • **Gun-running** is the activity of bringing guns and other weapons into a country illegally, esp. for use against the government: *A special police task force has been set up to combat gun-running and drug dealing.* • *"Annie Get Your Gun"* (title of a musical by Irving Berlin, 1946) • See also AIRGUN; FLASHGUN; HANDGUN; SHOTGUN.

gun *obj* /gʌn/ *v* [T] **-nn-** • *(esp. Am dated infml)* If you gun an engine, you make it operate at a higher speed: *You must have been really gunning the engine to get here on time.* • If you **gun** someone **down**, you shoot and kill or badly injure them when they cannot defend themselves: *The police officer was gunned down as he took his children to school.* • *(infml)* If you are **gunning for** someone, you are trying to cause trouble for them: *Ever since she was dismissed from the Cabinet, she has been gunning for the Prime Minister with fiercely critical speeches.* • *(infml)* To **gun for** someone or something also means to support them or to try and achieve something: *Which team are you gunning for?* ○ *I'm gunning for a place in the semi-finals.*

gun·ner /£ˈgʌn·əʳ, $-ɚ/ *n* [C] • A gunner is a member of the armed forces who is trained to use guns.

gun·ner·y /£ˈgʌn·ᵊr·i, $ˈ-ɚ-/ *n* [U] • Gunnery is the skill and activity of shooting with heavy guns.

gun·boat /£ˈgʌn·bəʊt, $-boʊt/ *n* [C] a small military ship with large guns, used esp. in coastal areas • *(disapproving)* **Gunboat diplomacy** is the use of military threats esp. by a stronger power against a weaker state in an attempt to win an argument: *The government has lately been criticized for its increasing reliance on gunboat diplomacy.*

gun·fight /ˈgʌn·faɪt/ *n* [C] a fight using guns between two or more people, esp. COWBOYS • *After the gunfight only one of the cowboys was left alive.* • *The famous gunfight at the O.K. Corral took place in 1881, and several films have been made of the events of that day.* • *A gunfight broke out between the escaped convicts and state police officers.*

gun·fight·er /£ˈgʌnˌfaɪ·təʳ, $-t̬ɚ/ *n* [C] • *He was a gunfighter by trade.*

gun·fire /£ˈgʌn·faɪəʳ, $-faɪr/ *n* [U] the usually repeated firing of one or more guns • *The sound of gunfire echoed into the night.* • *There have been reports of gunfire in the capital.*

gunge /gʌndʒ/, **gunk** /gʌŋk/ *n* [U] any unpleasant esp. sticky soft substance, often one which you can not recognize • *It was amazing how much gunge had accumulated in the pipe.* • *He's always got this revolting gunge in the corner of his eyes.*

gung-ho /£ˌgʌŋˈhəʊ, $-ˈhoʊ/ *adj infml* extremely enthusiastic about doing something, esp. going to war • *The Prime Minister was widely criticized for her gung-ho enthusiasm for the war.* • *The film stars Mark Burgess-Ashton as the gung-ho young fighter pilot.* • *Mrs Parsons had organized the village fete with her customary gung-ho zeal.*

gun·man /ˈgʌn·mən/ *n* [C] *pl* **-men** a man, usually a criminal, who is armed with a gun • *The three men were held hostage for two days by masked gunmen.*

gun·me·tal grey /£ˈgʌnˌmet·əl, $-ˌmet̬-/ *adj* [not gradable] (esp. of clothes) dark grey

gun·nel /ˈgʌn·ᵊl/ *n* [C] a GUNWALE

gun·ner /£ˈgʌn·əʳ, $-ɚ/ *n* See at GUN

gun·ner·y /£ˈgʌn·ᵊr·i, $ˈ-ɚ-/ *n*

gun·point /ˈgʌn·pɔɪnt/ *n* [U] **at gunpoint** experiencing or using a threat of killing with a gun • *The family were held at gunpoint for an hour while the men raided their house.*

gun·pow·der /£ˈgʌnˌpaʊ·dəʳ, $-dɚ/ *n* [U] an explosive mixture of substances in the form of a powder, used for making explosive devices and FIREWORKS

gun·shot /£ˈgʌn·ʃɒt, $-ʃɑːt/ *n* [C] (the sound of) the firing of a gun • *When I heard the gunshot, I looked out of the window and saw a man lying in the middle of the road.* • *Most of the people admitted to the hospital were suffering from gunshot* **wounds**.

gun·sling·er /£ˈgʌnˌslɪŋ·əʳ, $-ɚ/ *n* [C] a type of COWBOY who could be employed for protection or to kill people • *They hired a gunslinger to catch the cattle thieves.* • *(fig.*

Br) Jones has always always been seen as the gunslinger (= strong and determined man) *of his party.*

gun·smith /ˈgʌn·smɪθ/ *n* [C] a person who makes and repairs guns, esp. small guns

gun·wale /ˈgʌn·ᵊl/, **gun·nel** *n* [C] the upper edge of the side of a boat or ship • If something is described as being **full to/up to the gunwales**, it is extremely full, possibly even beyond its limits: *A crowd of fifty thousand packed the stadium almost to the gunwales.*

gur·gle /£ˈgɜː·gl̩, $ˈgɜːr-/ *v* [I] (of babies) to make a happy sound with the back of the throat, or (of water, esp. small streams) to flow with a low, uneven and pleasant noise • *Gail's baby twins lay gurgling* (**with** *pleasure) in their pram.* • *Outside of her window the stream gurgled over the rocks.*

gur·gle /£ˈgɜː·gl̩, $ˈgɜːr-/ *n* [C] • *The water went down the plughole with a loud gurgle.*

gurg·ler /£ˈgɜː·glər, $ˈgɜːr·glɚ/ *n* [C] *Aus infml* • A gurgler is a PLUGHOLE. • If something has **gone down the gurgler**, it is permanently lost: *"Did you find that key you were looking for?" "No, I reckon it's gone down the gurgler."*

gu·ru /ˈgʊr·uː/ *n* [C] a religious leader or teacher in the Hindu or Sikh religion or, more generally, a person who is respected for their knowledge of a particular subject and gives advice • *For the last decade she has acted as the president's economics guru.* • *On philosophical and spiritual matters the prince has often sought guidance from this guru figure.*

gush *(obj)* FLOW /gʌʃ/ *v* to flow or send out quickly and in large amounts • *Oil gushed out from the hole in the tanker.* [I] • *Blood was gushing out of my nose – I thought it would never stop!* [I] • *She would lie in bed at night listening to the gushing of the river.* [I] • *Her arm gushed blood where the knife had gone in.* [T]

gush /gʌʃ/ *n* [U] • *Showers with pumps are more expensive, but they deliver* **a** *really powerful gush* **of** *water.*

gush·er /£ˈgʌʃ·ər, $-ɚ/ *n* [C] • A gusher is an **oil well** from which oil flows without the use of a PUMP (= a piece of equipment used to move liquids).

gush EXPRESS /gʌʃ/ *v* to express a positive feeling, esp. praise, in such a strong way that it does not sound sincere • *She spent most of her time at the party gushing to Jim about how wonderful it was for him to be working in advertising.* [I] • *"It's without a doubt the best play in the West End!" gushed the morning paper.* [+ clause]

gush /gʌʃ/ *n* [U] • *She was quite unprepared for the gush* **of** *praise which her play received.*

gush·ing /ˈgʌʃ·ɪŋ/, **gush·y** (**-ier, -iest**) /ˈgʌʃ·i/ *adj* • *One of the more gushing newspapers described the occasion as 'a fairy-tale wedding'.* • *The reason he's so gushing about her ideas is that he's trying to get a promotion.*

gush·ing·ly /ˈgʌʃ·ɪŋ·li/, **gush·i·ly** /ˈgʌʃ·ɪ·li/ *adv* • *She was gushingly described by one journalist as a legend in her own lifetime.*

gus·set /ˈgʌs·ɪt/ *n* [C] a second layer of cloth which is sewn into a piece of clothing to make it larger, stronger or more comfortable • *silk panties with a cotton gusset*

gust /gʌst/ *n* [C] a sudden brief period of strong wind • *A sudden gust* **of** *wind blew his umbrella inside out.* • *(fig. literary) She could hear gusts* **of** *laughter from within the room.*

gust /gʌst/ *v* [I] • *At one stage winds gusted* (**up**) **to** *95 mph.*

gust·y /ˈgʌs·ti/ *adj* **-ier, -iest** • *a gusty wind* • *The day was cold and gusty.*

gust·a·tor·y /£ˈgʌs·tə·tᵊr·i, $-tɔː·ri/ *adj* [not gradable] *specialized* connected with taste • *The wine produces a whole range of gustatory sensations.*

gust·o /£ˈgʌs·təʊ, $-toʊ/ *n* [U] great energy, enthusiasm and enjoyment that is experienced by someone taking part in an activity, esp. a performance • *The actors sang and danced with such gusto that they managed to compensate for the play's weakness.*

gut BOWEL /gʌt/ *n* the long tube in the body of a person or animal through which food moves during digestion • *Meat stays in the gut longer than vegetable matter.* [U] • Gut is also a strong thread made from an animal's bowel which was used, esp. in the past, for making musical instruments and sports RACKETS: *Steel is often used nowadays instead of gut for the strings of musical instruments.* [U] • *(slang)* Gut can be used to refer to a person's stomach when it is extremely large: *He's got a disgusting* **beer** *gut* (= large stomach caused by drinking a lot of beer) *hanging over his trousers.* [C] • *(infml)* A **gut feeling/reaction** is one which is deeply felt but cannot completely be explained and is not necessarily decided by reasoning: *My gut feeling is that it is not good for children to see a lot of violence on television.* • Something that is **gut-wrenching** is emotionally painful: *The film ends with a gut-wrenching scene where the lovers part forever.*

gut *obj* /gʌt/ *v* [T] **-tt-** • If you gut an animal you remove its inner organs, esp. in preparation for eating it: *She cut the fish's head off and gutted it.*

guts /gʌts/ *pl n* • *(slang)* Guts is sometimes used to mean bowels: *My guts hurt.* • *(Br infml humorous)* If you say you will **have** someone's **guts for garters**, you mean that you will punish them: *If that boy has taken my bike again I'll have his guts for garters!* • *(slang) We've been* **working** *our* **guts out** (= working extremely hard) *for the past month.* • See also GUTS.

gut *obj* DESTROY /gʌt/ *v* [T usually passive] **-tt-** to destroy the inside of (a building) completely, usually by fire • *The whole building was gutted in the fire so that only the charred walls remained.*

guts /gʌts/ *pl n infml* bravery; the ability to control fear and to deal with danger and uncertainty • **It takes** *a lot of guts* **to** *admit to so many people that you've made a mistake.* [+ *to* infinitive]

gut·sy /ˈgʌt·si/ *adj* **-ier, -iest** *infml* • *She gave a very gutsy* (= brave) **performance** *on stage tonight.*

gut·less /ˈgʌt·ləs/ *adj infml* • *Politicians are too gutless* (= lacking in bravery) *to take on the big long-term problems such as pollution.* • *The performance by the two main actors was gutless* (= lacking enthusiasm and determination)*, but the supporting cast did their best to compensate.*

gut·ted /£ˈgʌt·ɪd, $ˈgʌt̬-/ *adj Br slang* extremely disappointed and unhappy • *I was absolutely gutted when I heard he'd been killed in the accident.*

gut·ter CHANNEL /£ˈgʌt·ər, $ˈgʌt̬·ɚ/ *n* [C] a channel between a road and a path whose purpose is to collect and carry away rain, or a plastic or metal channel at the lower edge of a roof which collects and carries away rain • *He dropped his keys in the gutter.* • Gutter is sometimes used to mean the lowest level, esp. of society: *Born to a poverty-stricken family, she dragged herself out of the gutter to become one of the wealthiest people in Britain today.* • *(Br disapproving)* People sometimes refer to **the gutter press** meaning the type of newspapers which pay more attention to shocking stories about crime and sex than serious matters. • PIC〉 **Accommodation**

gut·ter·ing /£ˈgʌt·ᵊr·ɪŋ, $ˈgʌt̬·ɚ-/ *n* [U] • Guttering is the system of channels on a building which collects and carries away rain.

gut·ter BURN WEAKLY /£ˈgʌt·ər, $ˈgʌt̬·ɚ/ *v* [I] *literary* (of a flame or candle) to burn unevenly and weakly, esp. before completely stopping burning • *The light flickered strangely as the candle guttered* (**out**).

gut·ter·snipe /£ˈgʌt·ə·snaɪp, $ˈgʌt̬·ɚ-/ *n* [C] *dated disapproving* a child from a poor area of a town who is dirty and dressed badly and spends a lot of time outside • *a Victorian guttersnipe*

gut·tur·al /£ˈgʌt·ᵊr·ᵊl, $ˈgʌt̬·ɚ-/ *adj* (of speech sounds) produced at the back of the throat and therefore deep • *Two Egyptians were arguing outside the room, their voices loud and guttural.*

guv /gʌv/ *n Br slang dated* used to address a man • *Excuse me, guv, could you spare an old man the price of a cup of tea?* • LP〉 **Titles and forms of address**

guv·nor /£ˈgʌv·nər, $-nɚ/, **guv** *n* [C] *Br slang dated* a man who is in a position of authority over you • *If you want any time off work you'll have to ask the guvnor.* • *He's one of the best guvnors I've ever had.*

guy /gaɪ/ *n* [C] *infml* a man • *He's a great guy.* • *Do you mean the guy with the blonde hair and glasses?* • *(esp. Am and Aus)* In the plural form, **guys** can be used to address a group of people whether they are male or female: *Are you guys coming to lunch?* • In Britain, **Guy Fawkes Night** (also **Bonfire Night**) is the night of November 5th on which models of men, called guys, are burnt on large fires outside and there are FIREWORKS in memory of Guy Fawkes' failed attempt to destroy the Houses of Parliament in London in 1605 with explosives. • LP〉 **Age, Holidays, Titles and forms of address**

guy (rope) /gaɪ/, *Am also* **guy·line** /ˈgaɪ·laɪn/ *n* [C] a rope which at one end is connected to a tent or pole while the other end is fastened to the ground by a PEG, keeping the tent or pole in position

guz·zle *(obj)* /ˈɡʌz·l̩/ *v infml* to eat or drink quickly, eagerly and usually in large amounts • *I'm not surprised you feel sick after guzzling three ice-creams!* [T] • *You're bound to get indigestion if you guzzle like that!* [I]

guz·zler /£ˈɡʌz·l̩əʳ, £-ləʳ, $-l̩ɚ/ *n* [C] *infml* • *She's a real guzzler!*

gym /dʒɪm/ *n* GYMNASTICS, esp. when done as a subject at school, or a GYMNASIUM • *a gym skirt* • *gym shoes* • *Class 3 do gym on a Wednesday afternoon.* [U] • Gym is *Am for* **physical education**: *This term our team will play volleyball and basketball at gym.* [U] • *They've got a really good gym with weights at the local sports centre.* [C]

gym·kha·na /dʒɪmˈkɑː·nə/ *n* [C] *esp. Br* an event at which people ride horses, taking part in various competitions involving horse racing and jumping over special fences

gym·na·si·um /dʒɪmˈneɪ·zi·əm/, **gym** *n* [C] a large room with weights for lifting, horizontal bars and other equipment for exercising the body and increasing strength • (CS) (DK) (GR) (NL) (P) (PL) (RUS)

gym·nas·tics /dʒɪmˈnæs·tɪks/ *n* [U] physical exercises and activities performed inside, often using equipment such as bars and ropes which are intended to increase the body's strength and the ability to move and bend easily • *Olympic arenas have been built for swimming and gymnastics.* • PIC› **Sports**

gym·nas·tics /dʒɪmˈnæs·tɪks/ *pl n* • *(fig.) I'm afraid I can't cope with the mental gymnastics that are required to follow some of his arguments!*

gym·nas·tic /dʒɪmˈnæs·tɪk/ *adj* [before n; not gradable] • *gymnastic skills* • *Are your daughters taking part in the school's gymnastic display?*

gym·nast /ˈdʒɪm·næst/ *n* [C] • A gymnast is a person who is skilled in gymnastics, often someone who competes in gymnastic competitions: *a great Russian gymnast*

gym·slip /ˈdʒɪm·slɪp/ *n* [C] *Br* a plain dress without sleeves usually worn over a shirt, esp. in the past, by girls as a part of their school uniform

gyn·ae·col·o·gy *Br and Aus, Am and Aus* **gyn·e·col·o·gy** /£ˌɡaɪ·nəˈkɒl·ə·dʒi, $-ˈkɑː·lə-/ *n* [U] the area of medicine which involves the treatment of women's diseases, esp. those of the reproductive organs

gyn·ae·co·log·i·cal *Br and Aus, Am and Aus* **gyn·e·col·o·gi·cal** /£ˌɡaɪ·nə·kəˈlɒdʒ·ɪ·kəl, $-ˈlɑː·dʒɪ-/ *adj* [not gradable] • *gynaecological problems*

gyn·ae·col·o·gist *Br and Aus, Am and Aus* **gyn·e·col·o·gist** /£ˌɡaɪ·nəˈkɒl·ə·dʒɪst, $-ˈkɑː·lə-/ *n* [C] • A gynaecologist is a doctor who specializes in the treatment of women's diseases, esp. those of the reproductive organs.

gyp /dʒɪp/ *n* [U] *Br and Aus slang* pain or trouble • *My knee has been* **giving** *me gyp since I started running.* • *If my nephew* **gives** *me any gyp* (= behaves badly towards me) *I hand him back to his parents.*

gyp·sum /ˈdʒɪp·səm/ *n* [U] a hard white substance that is used in making **plaster of Paris** • (PL) (RUS)

Gyp·sy, **Gip·sy** /ˈdʒɪp·si/, **Ro·ma·ny** *n* [C] a member of a race found in parts of Europe and America who travel from place to place in CARAVANS (= homes on wheels) • *a gypsy caravan* • *a Gypsy encampment* • *I had my fortune told by Gypsy Rose at the fair.*

gyr·ate /£dʒaɪˈreɪt, $ˈ--/ *v* [I] to turn around and around on a fixed point, usually quickly or *(fig. usually humorous)* to dance, esp. in a sexual way • *(fig.) A line of male dancers gyrated to the music while the audience screamed their appreciation.*

gyr·a·tion /ˌdʒaɪˈreɪ·ʃən/ *n* [C/U] • *(fig.) Recent gyrations on the stock exchange* (= frequent and sudden changes in the price of shares) *have caused confusion in the financial world.*

gyr·o /£ˈjɪə·rəʊ, £ˈdʒɪə-, $ˈjɪr·oʊ/ *n* [C] *pl* **gyros** *Am* a food consisting of PITTA bread filled with LAMB and vegetables

gyr·o·scope /£ˈdʒaɪ·rə·skəʊp, $-skoʊp/, **gyr·o** /£ˈɡaɪ·rəʊ, $-roʊ/ *n* [C] a device containing a wheel which spins freely within a frame, used on aircraft to help find the aircraft's position, and as a children's toy

H h

H *(pl* **H's** or **Hs**), **h** *(pl* **h's** or **hs**) /eɪtʃ/ *n* [C] the 8th letter of the English alphabet • LP› **Silent letters**

ha, **hah** /hɑː, hæ/ *exclamation esp. humorous* used to express satisfaction that something bad has happened to someone who deserves it, or to express a feeling of victory • *He's left her has he? Ha! That'll teach her to go chasing other women's husbands!* • *Ha! So I am right after all!*

ha·be·as cor·pus /£ˌheɪ·bi·əsˈkɔː·pəs, $-ˈkɔːr-/ *n* [U] *law* a legal order which states that a person in prison must appear before and be judged by a court of law before he or she can lawfully be made to stay in prison • *The applicant sought a writ of habeas corpus for his release.*

ha·ber·dash·er·y *Br and Aus* /£ˌhæb·əˈdæʃ·ər·i, $-ɚˈdæʃ·ɚ-/, *Am* **no·tions**, *Am dated* **dry goods**, *Br dated* **drap·er·y** *n* [C/U] (the cloth, pins and cotton thread etc. sold in) a shop or a department of a large shop which sells items for use in making clothes and sewing • LP› **Shopping goods**

hab·it REPEATED ACTION /ˈhæb·ɪt/ *n* something which you do often and regularly, often without knowing that you are doing it • *I always buy the same brand of toothpaste just* **out of/from** (= because of) *habit.* [U] • *I'm trying not to* **get into** (= start) *the habit of always having biscuits with my coffee.* [C] • *I used to swim twice a week, but I seem to have* **got out of** (= ended) *the habit recently.* [C] • *I was taught to drive by my boyfriend and I'm afraid I've* **picked up** (= caught) *some of his bad habits.* [C] • *His eating habits are extraordinary.* [C] • *I'm trying to get him to* **break** (= end intentionally) *the habit of switching on the TV when he comes home at night.* [C] • *I don't mind being woken up once or twice in the middle of the night by my flatmate so long as she doesn't* **make a habit of it** (= do it frequently). [C] • *I'm not really* **in the habit of** *looking at* (= I don't usually look at) *other people's clothes, but even I noticed that awful suit!* [C] • A habit might be something which other people find slightly annoying: *She's got this irritating habit of finishing off other people's sentences.* [C] • A habit can also refer to the state of being dependent on a drug: *a cocaine habit* [C] • You can describe something as **habit-forming** if it makes you want to have or do it repeatedly: *Smoking is definitely habit-forming.*

hab·it·u·al /həˈbɪtʃ·u·əl/ *adj* [not gradable] *slightly fml* • Habitual means usual or repeated: *a habitual thief* ○ *habitual drug use* ○ *dressed in his habitual black* ○ *her habitual meanness*

hab·it·u·al·ly /həˈbɪtʃ·ʊ·ə·li/ *adv* [not gradable] • *There is something wrong with anyone who is so habitually rude.* • *She smokes habitually.*

hab·it CLOTHING /ˈhæb·ɪt/ *n* [C] special long clothing worn by NUNS and MONKS

hab·it·ab·le /£ˈhæb·ɪ·tə·bl̩, $-t̬ə-/, **in·hab·it·a·ble** *adj* providing conditions which are good enough to live in or on • *A lot of improvements would have to be made before the building was habitable.* • *Some areas of the country are just too cold to be habitable.*

hab·it·at /ˈhæb·ɪ·tæt/ *n* [C] the natural surroundings in which an animal or plant usually lives • *With so many areas of woodland being cut down, a lot of wildlife is losing its natural habitat.*

hab·it·a·tion /ˌhæb·ɪˈteɪ·ʃən/ *n* [U] *fml* the act of living in a building • *The report had described the houses as* **unfit for human** *habitation.*

hab·it·u·at·ed /£həˈbɪtʃ·u·eɪ·tɪd, $-t̬ɪd/ *adj fml* used to something, esp. something unpleasant • *We find children's emotional needs difficult to respond to because we are habituated* **to** *disregarding our own.*

hab·i·tu·é /hæˈbɪt·juː·eɪ/ *n* [C] *fml or literary* a person who regularly visits a particular place • *Habitués* **of** *this gentlemen's club are generally middle-aged, grey-haired and overweight.* • *In the sixties, she was a habitué of all the international night-clubs.*

hack CUT /hæk/ *v* [always + adv/prep] to cut (into pieces) in a rough and violent way, often without aiming exactly • *Three villagers were hacked* **to death** *in a savage attack.* [T] • *Don't just hack* **(away) at** *the bread – cut it properly!* [I] • *The butcher hacked* **off** *a large chunk of meat.* [M] • *The garden was so overgrown that she had to hack her way*

through *the bushes.* [T] • *(fig.) The article had been hacked* **about** (=changed noticeably and carelessly) *by three different editors by the time it was published.* [T] • *(Br)* In some sports, such as football and RUGBY, to hack is either to kick the ball away or to FOUL (=act against the rules) by kicking another player in the leg: *Platt was twice hacked* **down** *in the second half by the other team's sweeper.* [M]

hack WRITER /hæk/ *n* [C] *disapproving or humorous* a JOURNALIST (=writer for newspapers or magazines) whose work is low in quality or lacks imagination • *Fleet Street hacks*

hack POLITICIAN /hæk/ *n* [C] *disapproving or humorous* a politician, esp. an unimportant one • *tired old* **party** *hacks*

hack COMPUTING /hæk/ *v* [I] to get into someone else's computer system without permission in order to find out information or do something illegal • **Computer** *hacking has become very widespread over the last decade.* • *A programmer had managed to hack* **into** *some top-secret government data.*

hack·er /£'hæk·əʳ, $-ɚ/ *n* [C] • A **(computer)** hacker is a person who hacks into other people's computer systems.

hack HORSE /hæk/ *n* [C] a ride on a horse in the countryside

hack /hæk/ *v* [I] • To hack or **go** hacking is to ride a horse in the countryside.

hack DRIVER/CAR /hæk/ *n* [C] *Am infml* (the driver of) a car which is available for rent, esp. a TAXI

hack *obj* MANAGE /hæk/ *v* [T; usually in negatives and questions] *infml Am and Aus* to manage to deal successfully with (something) • *Do you think you'd be able to hack another four years of working with her?* • *I tried working on the nightshift for a while, but I just* **couldn't** *hack it.*

hacked off /hækt/ *adj* [after v] *esp. Br infml* unhappy and dissatisfied, because of the situation you are in; FED UP • *She's getting a bit hacked off* **with** *all the travelling she has to do.*

hack·ing cough /'hæk·ɪŋ/ *n* [C] a loud cough that sounds painful

hack·les /'hæk·l̩z/ *pl n* the hairs on the back of some animals or the feathers on the back of the neck of some birds which rise when the animal or bird is frightened or about to fight • If something **makes** someone's **hackles rise, gets** their **hackles up** or **raises hackles**, it makes them angry: *It really gets my hackles up when government ministers start moralizing.* ○ *The prime minister's speech has raised hackles among the opposition.*

hack·ney (car·riage) /'hæk·ni/ *n* [C] a carriage pulled by a horse that can be rented with a driver for making short journeys, used esp. in the past

hack·neyed /'hæk·nid/ *adj disapproving* used or said so often that it has become meaningless or boring; TRITE • *The plot of the film is just a hackneyed boy-meets-girl scenario.*

hack·saw /£'hæk·sɔː, $-sɑː/ *n* [C] a small SAW (=a cutting tool with a thin flat blade) used esp. for cutting metal • PIC› **Tools**

had HAVE /hæd/, **'d** *past simple and past participle of* have, also used with the past participle of other verbs to form the past perfect • *When I was a child I had a dog.* • *No more food please – I've had enough.* • *I had heard/I'd heard they were planning to move to Boston.* • *(fml) Had I known* (=If I had known), *I would have come home sooner.* • If you **had better/best** do something, you should do it or it would be good to do it: *I had better/I'd better leave a note so they'll know I'll be late.* ○ *You'd best leave the parcel on the table out of the way.* • LP› **Tenses**

had TRICKED /hæd/ *adj* [not gradable] **be had** *infml* to be tricked and given less than you agreed or paid for • *There were only five biscuits instead of six in the packet – I've been had!* • *"I paid £2000 for this car." "You've been had, mate. It's not worth more than £1500."*

had FINISHED /hæd/ *v* **had it** *infml* finished or unwilling to continue because you are tired, have done enough or are angry, or unable to be used because of not working correctly or being broken • *We've been walking all day and we've just about had it.* • *I've had it for today – I'll do the rest tomorrow.* • *I've had it* **(up to here) with** *you – you never make any effort to keep the house tidy.* • *This kettle's had it. It's not worth mending.*

had·dock /'hæd·ək/ *n* [C/U] *pl* **haddock** a fish that can be eaten, which is found in the N Atlantic • *baked haddock*

Ha·des /'heɪ·diːz/ *n* [U not after *the*] (in stories about Ancient Greece) a place under the earth where the spirits of the dead go; the UNDERWORLD SPIRITS

hadj /hædʒ/ *n* [C] a HAJJ

had·n't /'hæd·ᵊnt/ *short form of* had not • *If you hadn't told him he would never have known.*

had up /hæd/ *adj* [not gradable] *Br infml* (forced to appear in a law court because of being) accused of breaking the law • *He was had up* **(in court) for** *speeding.*

hae·ma·tol·o·gy, *esp. Am* **he·ma·tol·o·gy** /£ˌhiː·mə'tɒl·ə·dʒi, $-'tɑː·lə-/ *n* [U] *specialized* the part of medical science which studies (diseases of) the blood and the body tissues which form blood

hae·ma·to·log·i·cal, *esp. Am* **he·ma·to·log·i·cal** /£ˌhiː·mə·tə'lɒdʒ·ɪ·kᵊl, $-'lɑː·dʒɪ-/ *adj* [not gradable] *specialized*

hae·ma·tol·o·gist, *esp. Am* **he·ma·tol·o·gist** /£ˌhiː·mə'tɒl·ə·dʒɪst, $-'tɑː·lə-/ *n* [C] *specialized*

haem·o·glo·bin *Br and Aus, Am* **hem·o·glob·in** /£ˌhiː·mə'gləʊ·bɪn, $-gloʊ-/ *n* [U] *specialized* a substance in the red blood cells which combines with and carries oxygen around the body, and gives blood its red colour

haem·o·phil·i·a *Br and Aus, Am* **hem·o·phil·i·a** /ˌhiː·mə'fɪl·i·ə/ *n* [U] a rare blood disease in which blood continues to flow after a cut or other injury because one of the substances which causes it to thicken does not work correctly

haem·o·phil·i·ac *Br and Aus, Am* **hem·o·phil·i·ac** /ˌhiː·mə'fɪl·i·æk/ *n* [C] • A haemophiliac is a person who suffers from haemophilia.

haem·or·rhage *Br and Aus, Am and Aus also* **hem·or·rhage** /£'hem·ᵊr·ɪdʒ, $'-ɚ-/ *n* [C] a large flow of blood from a damaged **blood vessel** (=tube carrying blood around the body) • *a brain haemorrhage* • Haemorrhage is sometimes used to refer to a sudden or serious loss: *The higher salaries paid overseas have caused a haemorrhage of talent from this country.*

haem·or·rhage *Br and Aus, Am and Aus also* **hem·or·rhage** /£'hem·ᵊr·ɪdʒ, $'-ɚ-/ *v* [I] • *She started haemorrhaging while giving birth to the baby.*

haem·or·rhoids, *esp. Am* **hem·or·rhoids** /£'hem·ᵊr·ɔɪdz, $'-ɚ-/ *pl n specialized* a medical condition in which the VEINS (=tubes carrying blood) at the ANUS (=the hole where solid waste is excreted) become swollen and painful and sometimes bleed; PILES

hag /hæg/ *n* [C] *disapproving* an ugly old woman • *Her greatest fear was that one day she would look in the mirror and an old hag would stare back at her.*

hag·gard /£'hæg·əd, $-ɚd/ *adj* tired and usually old-looking with dark areas around the eyes and skin hanging in folds • *She was looking a bit haggard as if she hadn't slept for days.*

hag·gis /'hæg·ɪs/ *n* [U] a food which comes from Scotland and consists of various sheep's organs cut up with onions and spices and cooked in a sheep's stomach

hag·gle /'hæg·l̩/ *v* to attempt to decide on a price or conditions which are acceptable to the person selling the goods and the person buying them, usually by arguing • *It's traditional that you haggle* **over/about** *the price of things in the market.* [I] • *We haggled the man in the shop* **down** *to eighty Egyptian pounds for the larger of the bags.* [+ obj + adv/prep]

hag·i·og·ra·phy /£ˌhæg·i'ɒg·rə·fi, $-'ɑː·grə-/ *n* a BIOGRAPHY in which the writer represents the person as perfect or much better than they really are, or the tendency to write so admiringly about a person that it is not realistic • *This latest book about the queen is more than just another hagiography.* [C] • *It's a shame that the later chapters of the book degenerate into hagiography.* [U] • *(specialized)* Hagiography is also writings about the lives of holy people such as SAINTS. [U]

hag·i·o·graph·ic /hæg·i·ə'græf·ɪk/ *adj literary* • *The biography has been criticized for being too hagiographic.*

hah /hɑː, hæ/ *exclamation* HA

ha–ha, **ha ha** /hə'hɑː, 'hɑː·hɑː/ *exclamation* used in writing to represent a shout of laughter, or said by children or by adults childishly as a way of making something or someone look foolish

hai·ku /'haɪ·kuː/ *n* [C] *pl* **haiku** a short Japanese poem in 17 syllables

hail ICE /heɪl/ *n* [U] small hard balls of ice which fall from the sky like rain • *Did you get caught in the hail on your way home?* • A hail of things is a lot of them directed towards someone: *The police were met by* **a** *hail* **of** *stones and bottles as they moved in on the rioters.* ○ *The Prime Minister was greeted with* **a** *hail* **of** *insults as she arrived at the students' union.*

hail /heɪl/ *v* [I] • *It's hailing outside.*

hail *obj* CALL /heɪl/ *v* [T] *slightly fml* to call (someone) in order to attract their attention • *Shall we hail a taxi?* • *I tried to hail her from the other side of the street, but she didn't hear me.* • *(dated)* If you are **within hailing distance of** somewhere, you are near it: *(fig.) The negotiators believe they are within hailing distance of reaching an agreement.* • *(dated or humorous)* If a man or his actions are described as **hail-fellow-well-met**, they are enthusiastically friendly, sometimes in a way that is annoying or not suitable for the occasion: *He greeted him with the usual hail-fellow-well-met slap on the back and handshake.* • A **Hail Mary** is a Catholic prayer to Mary, the mother of Jesus Christ.

hail *obj* **as** *obj v prep* [T usually passive] to praise (a person or an achievement) for their greatness • *She's being hailed as one of the best up-and-coming young dancers today.* • *The film was hailed as a masterpiece in its day.*

hail from *obj v prep* [T no passive] *fml or humorous* to come from; be born (somewhere) • *Where do you hail from with an accent like that?*

hail·stone /£'heɪl·stəʊn, $-stoʊn/ *n* [C] a small hard ball of ice which falls from the sky like rain; a piece of HAIL ICE

hail·storm /£'heɪl·stɔːm, $-stɔːrm/ *n* [C] a sudden heavy fall of HAIL

hair /£heəʳ, $her/ *n* the mass of thin threadlike structures on the head of a person, or any of these structures that grow out of the skin of a person or animal • *He's got short dark hair.* [U] • *I'm going to have my hair cut.* [U] • *He watched as she brushed her long red hair.* [U] • *He had lost his hair by the time he was twenty-five.* [U] • *My husband is like a monkey – he's even got hair on his back!* [U] • *He's starting to get a few grey hairs now.* [C] • *I found a hair in my soup.* [C] • *My grandmother has long dark hairs growing out of her nose.* [C] • *The antelope had a tuft of hair on its head.* [U] • *Carl has suffered hair loss* (=hair falling out) *since having radiation therapy.* • *(humorous)* Someone might say as a joke **that'll put hairs on your chest** when you are about to drink something that it is very strongly alcoholic or eat something satisfying that will make your stomach feel full. • People say **it'll make** your **hair curl** to children to persuade them to eat food, esp. the CRUST (= edge) of their bread. • *(infml)* If someone **gets in** your **hair**, they annoy you, usually by being present all the time when you wish they were not: *My flatmate has been getting in my hair a bit recently.* • *(Br and Aus infml often humorous)* If you tell someone who is getting angry to **keep** their **hair on** (*Am* **keep** their **shirt on**), you mean that they should stay calm. • *(infml)* Something which **makes** your **hair stand on end** makes you feel very frightened or anxious: *To be honest, the thought of jumping out of a moving aeroplane makes my hair stand on end.* • *(humorous)* **The hair of the dog** is an alcoholic drink taken as a cure the morning after an occasion when you have drunk too much alcohol. • A **hair dryer** or **hair drier** is an electrical device, usually held in the hand, which blows out hot air and is used for drying and sometimes styling a person's hair. • **Hair gel** is a thick liquid substance which is put in the hair to help the hair keep a particular shape or style. • **Hair mousse** is a light creamy substance which is put in the hair to help the hair keep a particular shape or style: *Hair mousse is usually sold as an aerosol.* • *(infml)* Something which is described as **hair-raising** is very frightening: *She gave a hair-raising account of her escape through the desert.* • A **hair salon** is a shop where people go to have their hair cut and put into a particular style. • *(Br and Aus)* A **hair slide** (*Am* **barrette**) is a small and often decorative fastener which women and girls use in their hair, esp. to hold it back off the face. • **Hair spray** is a liquid which is forced out of a special container in a cloud-like mass of drops onto the hair to keep it in a particular shape. • A **hair's breadth** is a very small distance or amount: *(fig.) She came within a hair's breadth of losing her life.* • *(infml)* Something which is described as **hair-trigger** could change very suddenly with very little cause or warning: *Watch her – she's got a hair-trigger temper!* • PIC› **Hair**

-haired /£-'heəd, $-'herd/ *combining form* • *dark-haired* • *short-haired*

hair·less /£'heə·ləs, $'her-/ *adj* • *His broad chest was hairless and muscular.*

hair·y /£'heə·ri, $'her·i/ *adj* **-ier, -iest** • Hairy means having a lot of hair, esp. on parts of the body other than the head: *hairy armpits/legs* ○ *a hairy chest* ○ *He's very hairy, isn't he? Have you noticed his arms?* • See also HAIRY.

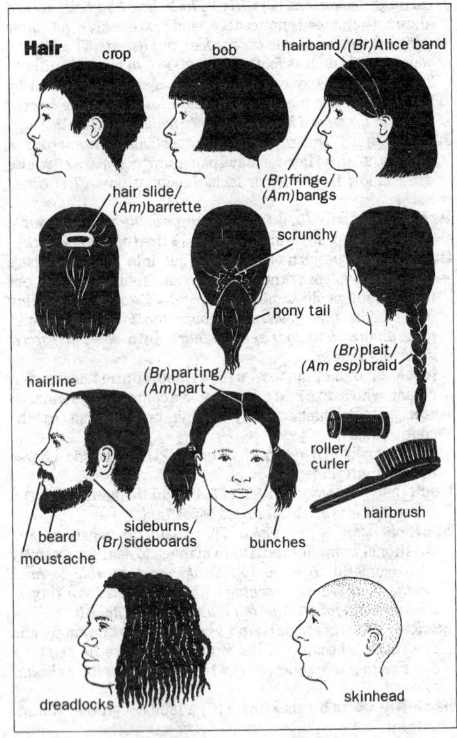

hair·band /£'heə·bænd, $'her-/, **A·lice band** /'æl·ɪs/ *n* [C] a curved plastic strip worn in the hair, which fits closely over the top of the head and behind the ears • PIC› **Hair**

hair·brush /£'heə·brʌʃ, $'her-/ *n* [C] a brush used for making the hair on your head tidy and smooth • PIC› **Brush, Hair**

hair·cut /£'heə·kʌt, $'her-/ *n* [C] the style in which someone's hair is cut, or an occasion of cutting or styling the hair • *She's had a really awful haircut.* • *I wish he'd* **get/have** *a haircut.*

hair·do /£'heə·duː, $'her-/ *n* [C] *pl* **hairdos** *infml often humorous* the style in which a person, esp. a woman, has had their hair cut and arranged, esp. if it is unusual or done for a particular occasion • *She had a most elaborate hairdo, all piled up on top of her head.*

hair·dress·er /£'heəˌdres·əʳ, $'herˌdres·ɚ/ *n* [C] a person who cuts people's hair and puts it into a style, usually working in a special shop, called a hairdresser's or a **hair salon** • *My hairdresser told me to let my hair dry naturally if I wanted it to curl.* • *I've got a four o'clock appointment at the hairdresser's.*

hair·dress·ing /£'heəˌdres·ɪŋ, $'her-/ *n* [U] • *Have you ever thought of hairdressing as a career?* • *My uncle owns a hairdressing salon in Manchester.*

hair·grip *Br* /£'heə·grɪp, $'her-/, *Am and Aus* **bob·by pin** *n* [C] a metal U-shaped pin which is tightly bent and slides into the hair in order to keep it back off the face or to keep part of the hair in the desired position

hair·less /£'heə·ləs, $'her-/ *adj* See at HAIR

hair·line HEAD /£'heə·laɪn, $'her-/ *n* [C] the edge of a person's hair, esp. along the top of the FOREHEAD • *He's got a* **receding** *hairline* (=He's losing his hair at the front of the head). • PIC› **Hair**

hair·line NARROW /£'heə·laɪn, $'her-/ *adj* [before n; not gradable] (of cracks or lines) very narrow • *She's got a hairline* **fracture** *of her lower leg.*

hair·net /£'heə·net, $'her-/ *n* [C] a light net that some women wear over their hair to keep it in place • PIC› **Net**

hair·piece /£'heə·piːs, $'her-/ *n* [C] an artificial covering of hair used to hide an area of the head where there is no hair • *Do you think he wears a hairpiece?*

hair·pin /£'heə·pɪn, $'her-/ *n* [C] a thin metal U-shaped pin which is used to hold part of the hair in the desired position • *(Br and Aus)* A **hairpin bend** (*Am* **hairpin turn**) is a bend in the road which curves so sharply that it almost turns back to go in the opposite direction. • PIC〉 **Pins and needles**

hair·spray /£ˈheə·spreɪ, $ˈher-/ *n* a liquid which is SPRAYED onto the hair to hold it in the desired style or position • *a can of hairspray* [U] • *Remind me to buy another hairspray when I'm in town, would you?* [C]

hair·style /£ˈheə·staɪl, $ˈher-/ *n* [C] the style in which someone's hair is cut and arranged • *She seems to change her hairstyle every week.*

hair·y /£ˈheə·ri, $ˈher·i/ *adj* **-ier, -iest** *infml* frightening or dangerous, esp. in a way that is exciting • *I like going on the back of Laurent's motorbike, though it can get a bit hairy.* • See also **hairy** at HAIR.

hajj (*pl* **hajjes**), **hadj** (*pl* **hadjes**) /hædʒ/ *n* [C] the religious journey to Mecca which all Muslims try to make at least once in their life

ha·ka /ˈhɑː·kə/ *n* [C] a traditional war dance of the Maori people of New Zealand, or a similar performance before a sporting event which is intended to give support to one team while discouraging the opposing team • *The New Zealand rugby team, the All Blacks, perform the haka before they play a match.*

hake /heɪk/ *n* [C/U] *pl* **hake** or **hakes** a big sea fish which is eaten as food

hal·al /həˈlɑːl/ *adj* [not gradable] (of meat) from an animal that has been killed in the way that is demanded by Islamic law • A halal **butcher** sells halal meat.

hal·cy·on days /ˈhæl·si·ən/ *pl n slightly literary* a period in the past which was completely happy and free of worry or trouble • *He would look back on those halcyon days at college when he hadn't a care in the world.*

hale /heɪl/ *adj* [not gradable] **hale and hearty** *slightly literary or dated* (esp. of old people) healthy and strong • *She found her grandfather hale and hearty, walking five miles each day before breakfast.*

half /£hɑːf, $hæf/ *n, pronoun, predeterminer, adj, adv* [not gradable] *pl* **halves** /£hɑːvz, $hævz/ either of the two equal or nearly equal parts that together make up a whole • *"What's half* **of** *ninety-six?" "Forty-eight."* • *Roughly half* **(of)** *the class are Spanish and the others are a mixture of nationalities.* • *Would you like half an apple?* • *Cut the apple* **in** *half/***into** *halves* (= into two equal parts). • *My little brother is half* **as** *tall* **as** *me/half my height.* • *I got half* **a dozen** (= six) *eggs at the shop.* • *Half* **of** *me would just like to give it all up and travel around the world* (= partly I would like to, but partly I would not). • *She was born in the latter half of the eighteenth century.* [C] • *The recipe tells you to use a pound and a half of butter.* [U] • *(Br infml)* A half is half a PINT, esp. of beer: *A pint of lager and two halves, please.* [C] • *(infml)* "I hear things aren't running very smoothly at work." "Oh, you **don't know/haven't heard the half of it** (= The situation is even worse than you realize)". • *(infml) That was a game* **and a half** (= a very good or very long game)*!* • When someone says that something is **half the battle**, they mean that when you have done it, you have solved the most difficult part of the problem: *For jobs like that, getting an interview is half the battle.* • *(infml)* If someone says they would do something **given half a chance**, they mean they would do it willingly if they had the opportunity: *I'd go to India, given half a chance.* • *(infml)* If two people **go halves** when they are paying for something, they share the cost equally: *Shall we go halves* **on** *a bottle of champagne for the party?* ○ *If you can't afford to pay for it on your own, I'll go halves* **with** *you.* • *(humorous)* If you see or discover **how the other half lives**, you learn something about a group of people or a social class who are completely different from you: *They have a huge house with servants – we really saw how the other half lives.* ○ *Walking past the people sleeping in doorways and boxes, we were left in no doubt about how the other half lives.* • *(humorous)* If it is said of someone that they do not **do things by halves**, it means that they make an effort to do things correctly and completely, often doing or providing more than is expected of them. • Half **past** a particular hour is 30 minutes later than that hour: *I'll meet you at half past nine* (= 09.30 or 21.30). • *(Br infml) I'll meet you at half seven* (= half past seven) *outside the theatre.* LP〉 **Time** • Various games are divided into a **first** and a **second** half with a short pause for rest between them. [C] • *(Br)* A half can also be a ticket which is cheaper because it is for a child: *Two adults and three halves to Manchester, please.* [C] • *(infml)* Half is sometimes used to mean a lot: *She invited a lot of people to the party but half of them didn't turn up.* ○ *He's so difficult to understand that half* **(of) the time** *I just nod and smile politely when he's talking to me.* • Half can be used to mean only partly: *The meat must only have been half cooked because it was still bloody.* ○ *He answered the door half naked!* ○ *I was half expecting to see her at the party.* ○ *I'm half inclined to take the job just because it's in London.* ○ *He was being funny but I think he was half serious.* ○ *He was half running along the street to keep up with her.* ○ *The bottle is half empty.* • *"Do you use milk or cream in the recipe?"* "**Half and half** (= Equal amounts of milk and cream)*.*" • *You use 400 grams of butter in the icing and* **half as much again**/*(Am also)* **half again as much** (= 600 grams) *in the cake.* • *(Br infml)* People sometimes use **not half** in spoken English to express a positive statement more strongly: *It wasn't half crowded in the club last night* (= It was very crowded). ○ *He wasn't half handsome* (= He was very attractive). ○ *She didn't half shout at him* (= She shouted a lot at him)*!* ○ *"You enjoyed yourself last night, didn't you?" "Not half* (= Very much)*!"* • *(infml)* If something is **not half as** good/bad/amusing as something else, it is clearly not as good/bad/amusing: *It wasn't half as good as that other restaurant we went to.* ○ *Films these days aren't half as good as they used to be.* • *(infml disapproving)* An idea or plan which is **half-baked** or *(Br slang)* **half-arsed**/*(Am infml)* **half-assed** is stupid or has not been considered carefully enough: *The government has set up some half-baked scheme for training teachers on the job.* • *(esp. Br)* If you stay **(on) half board** (*Am* **Modified American plan**) in a hotel or similar place, you have a room, a morning meal and a meal either in the middle of the day or in the evening: *The hotel only offers half board, but that suits me fine because I can have lunch at work.* Compare **full board** at FULL COMPLETE. • **Half-caste** is a usually offensive way of referring to someone whose parents are from different races: *He said I was a half-caste, but I just ignored him.* ○ *Of course she looks half-caste – her father was white.* • If something **goes off at half cock**/*(esp. Am)* **goes off half-cocked**, it does not happen as completely or successfully as intended because it was badly planned or it started too early: *His schemes always go off at half cock because he never prepares them properly.* • *(Br slang disapproving)* If someone is **half-cut**, they are quite drunk: *He was already half-cut when he arrived at the party.* • *(infml)* Someone who is **half-dead** is extremely tired: *"Phew! I'm half-dead!" "Well, what do you expect after you've been on a three-mile run?"* • *(infml)* **Half-decent** means quite good or skilled: *Any half-decent sprinter can run 100m in 11 seconds.* • A person or action that is **half-hearted** shows a lack of enthusiasm and interest: *He made a rather half-hearted* **attempt** *to clear up the rubbish.* ○ *The audience applauded* **half-heartedly**. • **Half an hour** or a **half-hour** is a period of 30 minutes: *The dollar surged against the yen in the final half-hour of trading.* ○ *Half an hour later, she was smiling and chatting as if nothing had happened.* ○ *She is to host a new half-hour show which will be broadcast every weekday evening.* ○ *Trains for Washington depart* **on the** *half-hour* (= at 10.30, 11.30, etc.). • Something that is **half-hourly** happens twice every hour: *There's a half-hourly train service to London from here.* ○ *I want you to call my office half-hourly and keep me fully informed about what's going on.* • If you say something **half-joking** or **half-jokingly**, you are partly joking and partly serious: *She was only half-joking when she said that dogs were treated better than homeless people.* • *(specialized)* The **half-life** of a RADIOACTIVE substance is the length of time its level of radioactivity takes to fall by half: *The most stable isotope of plutonium has a half-life of almost 25 000 years.* • **Half-light** is the greyness or less than complete darkness that exists in a badly lit room or just after the sun has gone down or just before the sun comes up: *In the dim half-light of evening, I was unable to tell whether it was Mary or her sister.* • A **half-marathon** is a running race over a distance of about 21 kilometres. • If a flag is **(flying) at half-mast** (*Am also* **half-staff**), it has been lowered to a point half the way down the pole as an expression of sadness at someone's death. • A **half-measure** is an action which only achieves part of what it is intended to achieve: *These so-called reforms are just cosmetic half-measures which do nothing to resolve the problem.* • A **half-moon** is (something shaped like) the moon when only half of the surface facing the Earth is lit by light from the sun. • *She peered over her* **half-moon glasses/half-moons** (= glasses in which the glass is shaped like half circles) *at me and asked why I was so late.* • **Half note** is *esp. Am for* MINIM. • Someone's **other half** is their husband, wife or usual partner: *Bring your other half next time you come.* • If someone is **half the** person they **used to be**, they are not as good as they were previously: *She's half the player she used to be.* • Something that is **half-price** costs half its usual price: *I got some half-price pizzas at the supermarket.* ○ *The railcard allows students and young people to travel half-price on most trains.* ○ *If you wait until the January sales, you might be able to get it* **at** *half-price.* • Your **half-sister** or **half-brother** has one of the same parents as you do, but their other parent is different from yours. [LP] **Relationships** • A **half-size** in clothing is a size which is half of the way between two usual sizes: *They're one of the few shops to stock men's slippers in half-sizes.* • **Half step** is *Am for* SEMITONE. • *(Br)* **Half term** (*Am* **midterm**) is a short holiday in the middle of each of the three periods into which the school year is divided: *Some families go on holiday* **at** *half term, but many stay at home.* • A **half-timbered** building has a wooden frame whose spaces are filled with brick or stone to form the walls, so that the wood still shows on the surface. • **Half-time** is a short rest period between the two parts of a sports game: *Italy had a comfortable three-goal lead over France by half-time.* ○ *What was the half-time score?* Compare **full time** at FULL [COMPLETE]. • A **half-truth** is a statement which is intended to deceive by being only partly true: *The book is a jumble of speculation, half-truths and downright lies about what really happened.* • A **half volley** is a shot in a game such as tennis in which the ball is hit just after it has bounced. • *(disapproving)* A **half-wit** is a silly or stupid person: *She really is a half-wit – we all told her she shouldn't marry him.* ○ *You half-wit! I asked you to get me some parsnips, not turnips.* [as form of address] ○ *That was a really* **half-witted** *thing to say – you can be so stupid sometimes.* • [LP] **Two** (J)

halve *(obj)* /£hɑːv, $hæv/ *v* • If you halve something you reduce it by half or divide it into two equal pieces: *In the past eight years, the elephant population in Africa has been halved.* [T] ○ *Hydrofoils run instead of ferries on some routes, halving the journey time but doubling the cost.* [T] ○ *Her jail sentence was halved after her case went to the appeal court.* [T] ○ *The potatoes will cook more quickly if you halve them before you put them in the oven.* [T] • If something halves, it is reduced by half: *Their profits have halved in the past six months.* [I]

half·back /£ˈhɑːf·bæk, $ˈhæf-/, **half** *n* [C] (in football and other sports) a player who plays in the middle of the field, in front of the FULLBACKS and behind the FORWARDS

half·tone [PRINTING] /£ˌhɑːfˈtəʊn, $ˌhæfˈtoʊn/ *n* (a method of printing) a picture built up from a pattern of very small black spots • *Black-and-white pictures in newspapers are printed in halftone.* [U] • *Darker shades of grey are represented in halftones with a greater number of dots.* [C]

half·tone [MUSIC] /£ˌhɑːfˈtəʊn, $ˌhæf·toʊn/, **half step** *n* [C] *Am for* SEMITONE

half·way /£ˌhɑːfˈweɪ, $ˌhæf-/ *adj, adv* [not gradable] in the middle of something, or at a place which is equally distant from two other places • *York is halfway* **between** *Edinburgh and London.* • *I'd like you to look at the diagram which is halfway* **down** *page 27.* • *She started feeling sick halfway* **through** *dinner.* • *The management's proposals don't even* **go** *halfway* **towards** *meeting our demands.* • *He started the final round with a lead of seven shots, but by the halfway stage this had fallen to three.* • *(fig. infml) Any halfway* **decent** (=reasonably good) *teacher should be able to explain the difference between transitive and intransitive verbs.* • A **halfway house** is something which combines particular features of two other things, esp. in order to try to please people who do not like the two things on their own: *The new proposals are a halfway house* **between** *the original treaty and the British government's revised version.*

hal·i·but /ˈhæl·ɪ·bət/ *n* [C] *pl* **halibut** or **halibuts** a large flat edible sea fish • [PIC] **Fish**

hal·i·tos·is /£ˌhæl·ɪˈtəʊ·sɪs, $-ˈtoʊ-/, *infml* **bad breath** *n* [U] breath which smells extremely unpleasant when it comes out of the mouth • *Halitosis can be caused by tooth decay or throat infections.* • *She's* **got** *terrible halitosis.*

hall [ENTRANCE] /£hɔːl, $hɑːl/, **hall·way** *n* [C] the room just inside the main entrance of a house, apartment or other building which leads to other rooms and usually to the stairs • *Just leave your bags* **in the hall** *and I'll take them upstairs later on.* • *Your bike's cluttering up the hallway.* • (D)

hall [BUILDING] /£hɔːl, $hɑːl/ *n* [C] a building or large room used for events involving a lot of people • *This afternoon there was a big demonstration against the job losses outside the* **town/city/county** *hall* (=the building from which these places are controlled). • *I'm playing in a concert at the* **village/church** *hall next weekend.* • *The new complex will include a* **concert** *hall and a (Br)* **sports** *hall.* • *(Br) Many old cinemas have been turned into bingo halls.* • A **hall (of residence)** (*Am also* **residence hall/dormitory**) is a college building where students live: *I want to live in a hall of residence that's close to my department.* ○ *I lived* **in** *hall in the first year but I moved out and shared a house with friends in the second.* • *(Am)* A **hall of fame** is a building which contains images of famous people and interesting things that are connected with them: *You really know you've made it when they enshrine you in the Rock 'n' Roll Hall of Fame.* • (D)

hal·le·lu·jah, al·le·lu·ia /ˌhæl·ɪˈluː·jə/ *exclamation, n* [C] (an emotional expression of) praise and thanks to God • *Hallelujah, praise the lord!* • *The Hallelujah Chorus is probably the best-known part of Handel's Messiah.* • *(fig.) The hallelujahs* (=expressions of praise and pleasure) *which greeted England's victory in the World Cup are just a distant memory.* [C] • *(infml humorous)* Hallelujah is sometimes said to express surprise and pleasure that something positive that you were certain would not happen has really happened: *At last, Richard's found himself a girlfriend – Hallelujah!*

hall·mark [MARK] /£ˈhɔːl·mɑːk, $ˈhɑːl·mɑːrk/ *n* [C] an official mark put in Britain on objects made of gold or silver which shows their place and year of origin and the purity of the metal used to make them

hall·mark *obj* /£ˈhɔːl·mɑːk, $ˈhɑːl·mɑːrk/ *v* [T] • *How can you tell how old this silver cup is if it hasn't been hallmarked?*

hall·mark [CHARACTERISTIC] /£ˈhɔːl·mɑːk, $ˈhɑːl·mɑːrk/ *n* [C] a typical characteristic or feature of a person or thing • *Her hallmark in business is her personal involvement with all her major clients.* • *A free press is one of the hallmarks* **of** *democracy.* • *This explosion* **bears/has all the** *hallmarks* **of** (=is extremely likely to have been) *a terrorist attack.*

hal·lo /£hælˈəʊ, $-ˈloʊ/ *n* [C], *exclamation pl* **hallos** *esp. Br for* HELLO

hallowed /£ˈhæl·əʊd, $-oʊd/ *adj* holy or *(fig.)* very respected and honoured because of great age or importance • *Can atheists be buried in hallowed ground?* • *(fig.) Why are Marilyn Monroe and James Dean such hallowed icons?*

Hal·lo·ween, Hal·lowe'en /£ˌhæl·əʊˈiːn, $-oʊ-/ *n* [not after *the*] the last day of October, when according to Christian tradition the spirits of the dead return to where they lived and WITCHES and DEMONS become active • *To celebrate Halloween children dress up as witches, ghosts and devils.* [U] • *I've spent three Halloweens in England.* [C] • [LP] **Holidays**

hal·luc·in·ate /həˈluː·sɪ·neɪt/ *v* [I] to seem to see, hear, feel or smell something which does not exist • *Mental disorders, drug use and hypnosis can all cause people to hallucinate.* • *(fig.) "I'm sure I saw Mary Tyler in town this morning." "You must have been hallucinating – she emigrated to Australia three years ago."*

hal·luc·in·a·tion /həˌluː·sɪˈneɪ·ʃᵊn/ *n* [U] • *At the beginning of a drug-induced hallucination people report seeing simple, coloured, geometric patterns.* • *Auditory hallucinations* (=Hearing sounds which are not there) *are a symptom of schizophrenia.*

hal·luc·i·na·to·ry /£həˈluː·sɪ·nə·tri, $-tɔːr·i/ *adj* • *In some patients the drug has been found to have hallucinatory side-effects* (=to cause hallucinations unintentionally). • *Computer graphics produce hallucinatory images* (=pictures that look like hallucinations) *which are projected onto the walls of the nightclub.*

hal·luc·in·o·gen /£ˌhæl·uːˈsɪn·ə·dʒᵊn, $həˈluː·sɪ·nə·dʒen/ *n* [C] a drug which causes people to imagine they are seeing or hearing things that do not really exist • *He used to use hallucinogens like acid and ecstasy.*

hal·luc·in·o·gen·ic /həˌluː·sɪ·nəˈdʒen·ɪk/ *adj* • *LSD is a hallucinogenic* **drug**. • *A judge has ruled that it is legal to grow hallucinogenic mushrooms in Britain.*

hall·way /£ˈhɔːl·weɪ, $ˈhɑːl-/ *n* [C] a HALL [ENTRANCE]

ha·lo /£ˈheɪ·ləʊ, $-loʊ/ *n* [C] *pl* **halos** or **haloes** a ring of light around the head of a holy person in a religious drawing or painting • *Artists usually put halos around the heads of saints, angels and Jesus Christ.* • *(fig.) In this photo we positioned him in front of the light to produce a halo* (=

ring of light) *around his head.* • *(humorous) "Aren't I good? I've done all the shopping as well as cleaning the whole house." "Oh yes, I can see your halo growing already."* • A halo is also the ring of light that appears around outside lights and the moon and sun in foggy and wet weather: *Can you see the halo* **effect** *around the street lamps?*

hal·o·gen /ˈhæl·ə·dʒen/ *n* [C] a member of a group of five particular chemical elements • *Chlorine and iodine are halogens.* • *(Br)* If an electric cooker has a **halogen hob** its top surface is heated by tubes containing halogens: *Halogen hobs heat up and cool down much more quickly than normal electric hobs.* • A **halogen lamp** gives a very bright light.

halt *(obj)* /£hɒlt, $hɑːlt/ *v* to (cause to) stop moving or doing something or happening • *"Halt!" called the guard. "You can't go any further without a permit."* [I] • *Security forces halted the demonstrators by blocking the road.* [T] • *Production has halted at all of the company's factories because of the pay dispute.* [I] • *The trial was halted when a member of the jury died.* [T] • *All previous attempts to halt the fighting have failed so why should these proposals be any more successful?* [T] • Ⓢ

halt /£hɒlt, $hɑːlt/ *n* [U] • *The workers are blaming the new computer system for the halt* **in** *production.* • *Severe flooding has* **brought** *trains* **to a** *halt* (= prevented them from moving) *on several lines in Scotland.* • *The bus* **came to a** *halt* (= stopped) *just in time to avoid hitting the wall.* • *If traffic increases beyond a certain level, the city* **grinds to a** *halt*/**comes to a grinding** *halt* (= stops completely). • *The car* **screeched to a** *halt just as the lights turned red.* • If you **call a** halt **to** something you prevent it from continuing: *How many more people will have to die before they call a halt to the fighting?*

halt·ing /£ˈhɒl·tɪŋ, $ˈhɑːl·t̬ɪŋ/ *adj* • If something, esp. speech or movement, is halting, it is slow, stopping and starting repeatedly and often lacking certainty and confidence: *His speech was slow and halting, as if his mind was confused.* ○ *She mumbled out a halting apology.*

halt·ing·ly /£ˈhɒl·tɪŋ·li, $ˈhɑːl·t̬ɪŋ-/ *adv* • *She stood up for the first time since the accident and walked haltingly towards me.* • *He spoke haltingly about his experiences as a hostage.*

hal·ter ROPE /£ˈhɒl·təʳ, $ˈhɑːl·t̬ɚ/ *n* [C] a piece of rope or a leather strap which is tied round an animal's head so that it can be led by someone or tied to something

hal·ter CLOTHING /£ˈhɒl·təʳ, $ˈhɑːl·t̬ɚ/ *n Am for a* HALTERNECK

hal·ter·neck *Br and Aus* /£ˈhɒl·tə·nek, $ˈhɑːl·t̬ɚ-/, *Am* **hal·ter (top)** *n* [C] a piece of women's clothing which is held in position by a strap which goes behind the neck, leaving the upper back and shoulders bare • *a halterneck dress/swimsuit* • *My back's far too spotty to wear a halterneck.*

hal·va /ˈhæl·və/, **hal·vah** *n* [U] a sweet food made of crushed SESAME seeds mixed with a thick sweet liquid such as HONEY (= substance made by bees)

halve /£hɑːv, $hæv/ *v* See at HALF

halves /£hɑːvz, $hævz/ *pl of* HALF

ham MEAT /hæm/ *n* pig's meat from the leg or shoulder, preserved with salt or smoke • *How many slices of ham would you like?* [U] • *Did you notice those delicious-looking hams hanging up in the butcher's window?* [C] • *Could I have another ham sandwich?*

ham ACTOR /hæm/ *n* [C] an actor whose style of acting is artificial and old-fashioned, tending to use movements and emotions that are too obvious • *They had some dreadful* **old** *ham in the main part who kept rolling his eyes and clutching at his heart.* • *They had some old ham* **actor** *playing the part of the king.*

ham /hæm/ *v* **-mm-** *infml* • If you **ham it up** you act in an artificial way which makes it very obvious that you are acting: *There's always a risk of hamming it up if you put too much emotion into a performance.*

ham·my /ˈhæm·i/ *adj* • *I've never seen such a hammy performance in a professional production before.*

ham RADIO /hæm/ *n* [C] a person who operates a radio station as a hobby rather than as a job • *Did you know that the kings of Spain, Morocco and Jordan are all* **radio** *hams?*

ham·burg·er /£ˈhæmˌbɜː·gəʳ, $-ˌbɜːr·gɚ/, **beef·bur·ger**, *infml* **bur·ger** *n* meat crushed or cut into very small pieces and pressed into a round flat shape, or one of these shapes cooked and eaten between two halves of a bread ROLL • *Hamburgers are often eaten with mustard or ketchup.* [C] • *Gimme a hamburger and fries.* [C] • *Hamburgers are named after the German city of Hamburg and don't actually contain any ham – they are made of beef.* [C] • *(Am)* Hamburger can also refer to the crushed meat that is used to make hamburgers: *How many pounds of hamburger will I need to make a meat loaf for six people?* [U]

ham–fist·ed *esp. Br and Aus* /£ˌhæmˈfɪs·tɪd, $-t̬ɪd/, *Am* **ham–hand·ed (-er, -est)** /ˌhæmˈhæn·dɪd/ *adj* doing things in an awkward or unskilled way, esp. when using the hands • *You're far too ham-fisted to become a surgeon!* • *The report criticizes the ham-fisted way in which many complaints are dealt with.*

ham·let /ˈhæm·lət/ *n* [C] a small village, usually without a church • *She used to live in a remote hamlet consisting of eight houses and a pub.*

ham·mer TOOL /£ˈhæm·əʳ, $-ɚ/ *n* [C] a tool consisting of a piece of metal with a flattened end which is fixed onto the end of a long thin usually wooden handle, used for hitting things • *Hammers are used for hitting nails into wood.* • *To sound the fire alarm, break the glass with the hammer.* • *Fortunately her revolver didn't go off because the hammer* (= part which hits the bullet) *jammed.* • If you **go at it hammer and tongs**, you do something very energetically and enthusiastically: *They had a very heated argument about it – they were going at it hammer and tongs all evening.* • *A private collection of her early paintings is expected to* **come/go under the hammer** (= be sold) *at an auction early next year.* • The **hammer and sickle** is a symbol of COMMUNISM, which was based on tools used by workers in factories and on farms: *The Italian Communist Party has changed its name and replaced the red flag and hammer and sickle with a new symbol, an oak tree.* • **Hammer-throwing** is a sport in which a heavy metal ball joined by a wire to a handle is thrown as far as possible. • PIC **Tools**

ham·mer *(obj)* /£ˈhæm·əʳ, $-ɚ/ *v* [always + adv/prep] • *Can you hold this nail in position while I hammer it* **into** *the door/hammer it* **in**? [T] • *The blacksmith hammers the horseshoes* **into** *shape on an anvil.* [T] • *Ask them to stop that noisy hammering next door.* • *My car's got a dent, and I was hoping you'd be able to hammer it* **out** (= remove it by hammering). [T] • *I was woken up suddenly by the sound of someone hammering* **on/at** (= hitting loudly and repeatedly) *the front door.* [I] • *(fig.) Poor Mark's been hammering* **away (at** *his homework)* (= working without stopping and with a lot of effort) *all weekend and he still hasn't finished.* [I] • *(fig.) He hammered* (= kicked with a lot of force) *the ball into the net, giving France a 3-2 win over Italy.* [T] • If you **hammer** something **home** you make certain it is understood by expressing it clearly and strongly: *The advertising campaign will try to hammer home the message that excessive drinking is a health risk.* • If you **hammer** something **in** or if you **hammer** something **into** someone, you force someone to understand something by repeating it a lot: *I always had it hammered into me that you shouldn't lie or steal.*

ham·mer *obj* DEFEAT /£ˈhæm·əʳ, $-ɚ/ *v* [T] *infml* to defeat (someone) completely in a game or a fight, or to damage (something) badly • *France hammered Italy 6-1 in the European Championships.* • *They'll be hammered* **to a pulp** (= defeated completely) *if they declare war on China.* • *Share prices have been hammered* (= caused to fall a lot in value) *by the latest batch of disappointing economic statistics.* • *(fig.) Her new film has been hammered* (= strongly criticized) *by the critics* **for** *its gratuitous violence.* • *(fig. infml) He* **got** *completely hammered* **on** (= got very drunk by drinking) *whisky.*

ham·mer·ing /£ˈhæm·ᵊr·ɪŋ, $ˈ-ɚ-/ *n* [C] • *You should have seen the hammering I* **gave** *her in the second game.* • *Both countries* **took** *a tremendous hammering in the war.* • *The English sausage has come in for a bit of a hammering* (= criticism) *recently because of its low meat content.*

ham·mer out *obj*, **ham·mer** *obj* **out** *v adv* [M] to arrive at (an agreement or solution) after a lot of argument or discussion • *Three years after the accident my lawyer has finally managed to hammer out a settlement with the insurance company.*

ham·mock /ˈhæm·ək/ *n* [C] a net or piece of strong cloth which is tied to a support at each end and used as a bed, esp. outside • *She found him sleeping in a hammock hanging between two trees.*

ham·my /ˈhæm·i/ *adj* See at HAM ACTOR

ham·per *obj* CAUSE DIFFICULTY /£ˈhæm·pəʳ, $-pɚ/ *v* [T] to prevent (something) being done easily or (someone) doing something easily • *Is it always easier working on a* *computer, or does it sometimes hamper you?* • *Fierce storms have been hampering rescue efforts and there is now little chance of finding more survivors.*

ham·per CONTAINER /£'hæm·pəʳ, $-pɚ/ *n* [C] a large rectangular container with a lid • *We packed our hamper with food, crockery and cutlery and set off for our picnic.* • *Shall we use the* **picnic** *hamper?* • In Britain and Australia hampers can also be filled with special things to eat and drink for giving as Christmas presents. • *(Am)* A hamper is used for carrying dirty clothes and bed sheets and for storing them while they are waiting to be washed. • PIC **Basket**

ham·ster /£'hæmp·stəʳ, $-stɚ/ *n* [C] a small furry animal with a short tail and large spaces in each side of its mouth which are used for storing food. It is often kept as a pet. • *"Freddie Starr Ate My Hamster"* (*Sun* newspaper headline, 1986)

ham·string *obj* LIMIT /'hæm·strɪŋ/ *v* [T often passive] *past* **hamstrung** /'hæm·strʌŋ/ to limit the amount of (something) that can be done or the ability or power of (someone) to do something • *A lack of funds has hamstrung restoration work on the church.* • *The company is hamstrung by its traditional but inefficient ways of conducting business.*

ham·string MUSCLE /'hæm·strɪŋ/ *n* [C] a muscle at the back of the upper leg • *He* **pulled** (= injured) *a hamstring in a rugby match at school.* • *She couldn't play because of a strained hamstring/a hamstring* **injury**. • A hamstring is also a cord of tissue at the back of the knee that joins the muscles to the bones.

hand BODY PART /hænd/ *n* [C] the part of the body at the end of the arm which is used for holding, moving, touching and feeling things • *The four fingers, thumb and palm are the main parts of the hand, which is attached to the arm by the wrist.* • *All these toys are made* **by** *hand, not on a machine.* • *Surely we can get a computer to analyse all this data instead of doing it* **by** *hand?* • *You may as well as deliver her invitation* **by** *hand* (= not using the postal service) *since she lives so close.* • *Hey you!* **Get** *your hands* **off** (= Stop touching) *my bike!* • *(fig.) The peace protesters' placards carried slogans such as 'Hands* **off** *the Middle East!'* • *Guy's made a marvellous bookcase – I had no idea he was so* **good with** *his hands.* • *Rosie, remember you should always* **hold** *my hand when we cross the road.* • *They weren't kissing or anything – they were just* **holding** *hands.* • *Hold your fork* **in** *your left hand and your knife* **in** *your right hand.* • *I wish you'd try and look smart instead of just standing there with your hands* **in your pockets**! • *She sat, pen* **in** *hand* (= with a pen in her hand), *searching for the right words.* • *Those two can't* **keep** *their hands* **off** *each other – they never stop kissing and cuddling.* • *(fig.) Susan* **keeps a firm** *hand* **on** (= controls carefully) *everything that goes on in the office.* • *"Congratulations!" she said and* **shook** *me* **by the** *hand/***shook** *my hand/***shook** *hands* **with** *me.* • *She* **took** *me* **by the** *hand and led me into the cave.* • *There's a hand* **towel** *in the bathroom by the washbasin.* PIC **Bathroom** • A person's hand is also their writing: *Most of his letters were typed, but we've found a few personal ones written* **in** *his own hand* (= written by him with a pen). ○ *I've never seen such an untidy hand! Your writing is barely legible.* • If something is **at hand**, it is near in time or position: *An end to illicit trafficking in these drugs may be at hand.* ○ *We want to ensure that* **help** *is at hand* (= easily available) *for all children suffering abuse.* ○ *Remember to keep a first-aid kit* **close/near** *at hand all the time.* • *I have been involved in war and know of its terrible costs* **at first hand** (= from my personal experience of it). • *The report of the attack came* **at second hand** (= through another person). • *How many people have died* **at the hands of** (= because of) *terrorist organizations since the violence began?* • *Welsh has suffered badly* **at the hands of** *the dominant English language.* • If you live **(from) hand to mouth** or if you live a **hand-to-mouth existence**, you have just enough food or money to live without suffering: *We've been living hand to mouth ever since I lost my job.* • *I'll kill him if I ever* **get** *my* **hands on** (= catch) *him.* • *We can't* **get/lay/put** *our* **hands on** (= obtain) *enough of these computers – they've been selling amazingly well.* • *I'd love to help but I've* **got** *my* **hands full** (= I'm very busy) *organizing the school play.* • *We soon realised this was no ordinary singer that we'd* **got on** *our* **hands** (= that we were dealing with). • If you are **hand in glove**/*(Am also)* **hand and glove** with someone, you have a very close business or working relationship with them: *We have been working hand in*

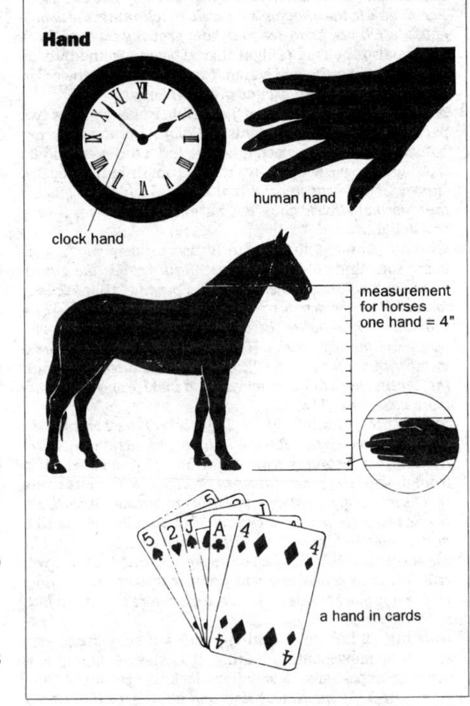

glove **with** *our European partners to beat our American competitors.* • *I saw Pat and Chris walking* **hand in hand** (= holding each other's hand) *through town the other day.* • If something goes **hand in hand** with something else, it is closely related to it and happens at the same time as it or as a result of it: *Prosperity* **goes** *hand in hand* **with** *investment.* ○ *Prosperity and investment* **go** *hand in hand.* • If you make or lose money **hand over fist**, you make or lose a lot of money very quickly and easily: *She's been making money hand over fist since she set up her own business.* • If you have something **in hand**, it is left over and so you can use it: *I've got enough money in hand to buy a new car.* ○ *(esp. Br) Italy are three points behind France in the championship, but they have one game in hand* (= one game more than France still to play). • Something *(Br and Aus)* **in hand**/*(Am)* **at hand** is something that is important at the present moment: *I wish you'd concentrate on the* **job** *in hand instead of worrying about what we might be doing in a year's time.* ○ *I'd like to return to the matter in hand and try to solve the problem that we're supposed to be discussing.* • If preparations are **in hand**, they are being made at the present moment: *They've had plenty of time to prepare, so the arrangements should be* **well** *in hand* (= almost ready). • If something is **put in hand**, it is put into action: *All major hospitals now have disaster plans to put in hand when notified of serious incidents.* • If something is **on hand**, it is present so that it can take action or be used: *A 1200-strong military force will be on hand to monitor the cease-fire and voting.* ○ *My bank always has an advisor on hand to discuss financial problems.* • If you want to compare two opposing opinions or two ways of thinking about the same thing, or if you want to mention the two opposing groups in an argument, you can use the expression **on the one hand...on the other (hand)**: *On the one hand I'd like a job which pays more, but on the other hand I enjoy the work I'm doing at the moment.* ○ *She's caught in a dispute between the city council on the one hand and the education department on the other.* ○ *The country is dominated by a power struggle between the communists on the one hand and the nationalists on the other.* • *She rejected/dismissed my suggestions* **out of hand** (= completely and without any consideration) *and wouldn't even let me explain them properly.* • If you are **bound/tied hand and foot**, your hands and your feet are tied together: *The police discovered the hostage bound hand and foot in a disused warehouse.* ○ *(fig.) New reporting restrictions have bound the country's media hand and foot* (= have greatly limited its freedom). •

I'm always having to **put** *my* **hand in** *my* **pocket** (= pay) *for some new toy or other for the kids.* • *For those of you who don't have an atlas* **to hand** (= within reach of you), *Newcastle is a city in the north-east of England.* • *He's one of those experimental artists who uses whatever materials come* **to hand** (= are easy to find). • *"***Hands up!** (= Put your hands above your head!)*" she said calmly, holding the revolver to his head.* • If you **win** something **hands down** or you **beat** someone **hands down**, you do it completely and very easily: *If we had a race, she'd win hands down.* ○ *They'd beat us hands down if we went to war with them.* • *(Am) He's* **hands down** (= He is certainly) *the best pitcher in the game today.* • A passenger's **hand baggage/luggage** is the small cases or bags that they carry with them onto an aircraft or bus: *How many items of hand luggage am I allowed to take onto the plane?* ○ *Electrical equipment such as radios should be packed in your hand baggage.* • A **hand grenade** is a small bomb consisting of explosive material in a metal or plastic container that can be thrown easily: *The hand grenade will explode a few seconds after you remove the trigger pin.* • Something that is **hand-held** has been designed so that it can be held and used easily with one or two hands: *Credit card purchases are recorded on a hand-held computer and then transmitted to our head office for processing.* • A person who has a **hands-off** way of organizing or dealing with something allows other people to make decisions about how things should be done and avoids becoming personally involved: *Paul has a hands-off style of management.* • Someone with a **hands-on** way of doing things becomes closely involved in managing and organizing things and in making decisions: *She's very much a hands-on manager and likes to know exactly what everyone is doing.* • Someone who has **hands-on** experience of something has done or used it personally rather than just read or learned about it: *All children are expected to have had hands-on experience of computers by the time they leave school.* ○ *Many employers consider hands-on experience to be as useful as academic qualifications.* • Someone who is **hand-picked** has been carefully chosen for a special job or purpose: *He was the Prime Minister's hand-picked choice to lead the investigation into police corruption.* • If people fight **hand-to-hand**, they are very near or touching each other while they are fighting rather than firing guns at each other from a long way away: *Air attacks will severely weaken the enemy, but hand-to-hand* **combat** *will be necessary to clear up the last pockets of resistance.* ○ *Artillery pounded the city while hand-to-hand* **fighting** *continued in the streets.* • *(Am)* A **hand truck** is a frame with two wheels and two handles used to move large or heavy things: *It will be much easier to move the filing cabinets if we use the hand truck.* • *"Hands that do dishes can be soft as your face"* (advertisement for Fairy Liquid washing-up liquid) • *"Hands across the sea"* (title of a poem by Byron Webber, used to refer to friendship with foreign people or countries, c.1890) • PIC **Body, Hand**

hand *obj* /hænd/ *v* [T] • If you hand someone something, you put it into their hand from your own hand: *The waiter smiled politely as he handed me my bill/handed my bill* **to** *me.* [+ two objects] • *"No, I've never seen him before," I said, handing her* **back** *the photograph.* [+ two objects] • *(fig.) My grandmother handed* **down** *this necklace* **to** *my mother* (= gave it to her when she died or no longer needed it). [M] • *You should hand* **in** *your essays* (= give them to the teacher) *by Tuesday.* [M] • *I'm going to hand* **in** *my* **resignation** (= tell my employer that I no longer want my job). [M] • *Please read this memo carefully and hand it* **on** *(***to** *your colleagues).* [M] • *Would you hand the cake* **out** (= give a piece to everyone present) *while I pour the coffee.* [M] • *(fig.) She's always willing to hand* **out** (= give) *advice, but she's not so keen to take it.* [M] • *Could you hand* **over** *the big screwdriver, please?* [M] • *The blackmailer's recordings have been handed* **over** (= given) *to the police.* [M] • *(fig.) If you'll hold the line a moment I'll hand you* **over** *to someone* (= ask someone else to speak to you on the telephone) *who might be able to help.* [M] • *Mrs Briggs handed* **round** *the sandwiches* (= offered them to everyone present). [M] • If you **hand down** a decision or judgment you make it publicly known with an official statement: *Although it was only his first offence, the court handed down an eight-year sentence.* • If you **hand over** to someone, you give control of or responsibility for something to them: *He's getting a bit old to run a shop – I think he'll hand over* **to** *his son soon.* See also HANDOVER. • If you say you **have (got) to hand it to** someone you mean that they have been very successful or skilful: *I mean you've got to hand it to her, she's brought up those three children all on her own.* • A **hand-me-down** is a piece of clothing which someone has given to a younger relative or friend because they no longer want to wear it: *I'm fed up with having to wear my sister's hand-me-downs – I want some new clothes of my own for a change.*

-hand·ed /-ˈhæn·dɪd/ *combining form* • *She's left-/right-handed.* • *Some tennis players use a two-handed grip.*

hand POINTER /hænd/ *n* [C] a narrow pointer on a clock or watch which shows the time • *The* **minute/big** *hand is pointing to the twelve and the* **hour/little** *hand is pointing to the seven, so the time is exactly seven o'clock.* • *Does anyone have a watch with a* **second** *hand?* • PIC **Clocks and watches, Hand**

hand CARDS /hænd/ *n* [C] a (single part of a) game of cards, or the set of cards which a player has in a game • *Who's for a hand* **of** *poker?* (= Who would like to play a game of poker?) • *You* **dealt** *me an appalling hand in that game.* • LP **Cards** PIC **Hand**

hand PERSON /hænd/ *n* [C] a person who does physical work or is skilled or experienced in something • *How many extra hands will we need to help with the harvest?* • *I joined the firm as a* **factory** *hand and gradually worked my way up to the top.* • A hand on a ship is a sailor: *All hands on deck!* • See also FARMHAND.

hand HELP /hænd/ *n* [U] help with doing something that needs a lot of effort • *Would you like* **a** *hand carry***ing** *those bags? They look awfully heavy.* [+ v-ing] • *Could you* **give/lend** *me* **a** *hand* **with** (= help me to move) *the piano, please?* • *Fiona's helping me with the fund-raising and Mike's offered to* **lend a** *hand too.* • *(esp. Am) I could really* **use a** *hand* **with** *these accounts if you could spare a moment.*

hand INVOLVEMENT /hænd/ *n* [U] involvement in or influence over an event • *The security services are suspected of* **having a** *hand* **in** (= being involved with) *the recording of the prince's phone conversations.* • *It is not thought that terrorists* **had a** *hand* **in** *this explosion.* • *I don't have as much time to play the guitar as I used to, but I like to* **keep** *my* **hand in** (= continue to practise).

hand CONTROL /hænd/ *n* [U] control or responsibility • *They were very drunk before the dinner, but things really* **got out of** *hand when they started throwing cream at each other.* • *There's no need to panic. The police have the situation* **in** *hand* (= under control). • *How come there's a problem? I thought you had everything* **in** *hand* (= arranged and organized). • *They should* **take** *their daughter* **in** *hand* (= bring her under control) *before she does something really serious like setting fire to her school.*

hands /hændz/ *pl n* • *I'm worried about confidential information* **falling into the wrong** *hands* (= being received by people who could use it against us). • *Are you sure your money's* **in safe** *hands with that bank?* • *You'll be* **in** *excellent hands with her – she's one of the best surgeons in the country.* • *Unless I receive a satisfactory response from you within a month I shall put this matter* **in(to) the** *hands of* (= make it the responsibility of) *my solicitor.* • *They're trying to* **get** *old stock* **off** *their hands by cutting prices.* • *We* **get** *Daryl* **off** *our hands one evening a week when my mother looks after him for us.* • *The problem's* **out of** *my hands* (= is not mine) *now that Colin's taken over responsibility for the department.* • *Give the job to Smithers – he's got* **a safe pair of hands** (= he can be depended on to do it in a satisfactory way).

hand CLAP /hænd/ *n* [U] clapping for a performer • *Our devoted fans always* **give** *us* **a big** *hand* (= clap enthusiastically) *no matter how good or bad our performance is.* • *So please* **give a big** *hand* **to** (= welcome with clapping) *your host for the evening, Bill Cronshaw!*

hand MEASUREMENT /hænd/ *n* [C] a unit for measuring the height of a horse up to its shoulder • *One hand equals 4 inches* (= 10.16 centimetres). • PIC **Hand**

hand·bag /ˈhæm·bæg/, *Am also* **pock·et·book, purse** *n* [C] a small bag, usually with a handle or a strap going over the shoulder, used for carrying money, keys, travel documents and small personal items such as make-up • *In the UK it is usually women who carry handbags, but in other countries men often do as well.* • PIC **Bags**

hand·ball /£ˈhænd·bɔːl, $-bɑːl/ *n* [U] a game for two or four people in which the players wear special GLOVES (= hand-coverings) and hit a small hard rubber ball against a wall with their hands

hand·book /ˈhænd·bʊk/ *n* [C] a book which contains instructions or advice about how to do something or the most important and useful information about a subject • *The student handbook gives details of all courses.*

hand·brake /ˈhænd·breɪk/, *Am usually* **e·mer·gen·cy brake**, *Am and Aus also* **park·ing brake** *n* [C] a device operated by hand which locks into position and prevents a vehicle from moving • *You're supposed to* **put** *the handbrake* **on** *whenever you stop on a hill.* • *You've forgotten to* **release** *the handbrake.* • *(Am)* A handbrake on a bicycle is the BRAKE (= the device operated by hand that stops it). • LP› **Driving** PIC› **Bicycles**

hand·cart /£ˈhænd·kɑːt, $-kɑːrt/ *n* [C] a small vehicle with two wheels and long handles which is used for carrying goods, esp. in the road, and is pushed or pulled with your hands

hand·clap /ˈhænd·klæp/ *n* [C] See **slow handclap** at SLOW.

hand·craft /£ˈhænd·krɑːft, $-kræft/ *n* [U] *Am for* HANDICRAFTS

hand·crafts /£ˈhænd·krɑːfts, $-kræfts/ *pl n Aus for* HANDICRAFTS

hand·cuffs /ˈhænd·kʌfs/, *infml* **cuffs** *pl n* two metal rings joined by a short chain which lock around a person's WRISTS (= the part of the arms just above the hands) • *Handcuffs can be used to join the hands of a criminal or prisoner together or to join one hand to the hand of a police officer or to an immovable object.* • *She was taken to the police station* **in handcuffs.**

hand·cuff *obj* /ˈhænd·kʌf/, *infml* **cuff** *v* [T] • *The youths forced him to hand over his wallet, watch and car keys and then handcuffed him* **to** *the steering wheel.* • *He arrived in court handcuffed* **to** *two police officers.* • *(fig.) I don't want to be handcuffed* (= limited) *by a contract that stops me working for someone else at the same time.*

hand·ful AMOUNT /ˈhænd·fʊl/ *n* [C] an amount of something that can be held in one hand • *He pulled out* **a** *handful* **of** *coins from his pocket.* • *She picked up* **a** *handful* **of** *snow and threw it at me.* • *"How much rice should I cook?" "Oh, a couple of handfuls should be enough."* • *"I can show you fear in a handful of dust"* (from the poem *The Waste Land* by T.S.Eliot, 1922)

hand·ful A FEW /ˈhænd·fʊl/ *n* [U] a small number of people or things • *There's only* **a** *handful* **of** *people in the country who can do work as sophisticated as this.* • *She invited loads of friends to her party, but only* **a** *handful* **(of** *them)* *turned up.* • *This disease is usually incurable, but in* **a** *handful* **of** *cases the patients have survived.* • LP› **Approximate numbers**

hand·ful PROBLEM /ˈhænd·fʊl/ *n* [U] a person or thing that is difficult to take care of or deal with • *Her older son is fine but the little one is* **a bit of a** *handful.* • *Paul wants you to do all that by this evening? That's* **quite a** *handful for one day, isn't it?*

hand·gun /ˈhænd·gʌn/ *n* [C] a gun which can be held in one hand and which does not need to be supported against the shoulder when it is fired • *The number of people murdered with handguns in Britain was 7, while in the United States it was 8915.*

hand·hold /£ˈhænd·həʊld, $-hoʊld/ *n* [C] a thing you can hold on to with your hand as a support • *The lack of handholds made climbing the cliff very dangerous.*

hand·i·cap CONDITION /ˈhæn·dɪ·kæp/ *n dated* a mental or physical condition usually caused by an accident, illness or a problem at birth which makes ordinary life more difficult than it is for people without such a condition • *The loss of my arm hasn't been as great a handicap as you might have expected.* [C] • *In cases of severe* **mental** *handicap, constant supervision is recommended.* [U]

hand·i·capped /ˈhæn·dɪ·kæpt/ *adj, pl n dated* • *What's the best way of improving theatre access for people who are physically handicapped?* • *The Camphill Village Trust is a charity which cares for* **the** *mentally handicapped.*

hand·i·cap DIFFICULTY /ˈhæn·dɪ·kæp/ *n* [C] something which causes unusual difficulties • *Doesn't she find it a bit of a handicap trying to organize her social life without a phone?*

hand·i·cap *obj* /ˈhæn·dɪ·kæp/ *v* [T] **-pp-** • *Rescue efforts have been handicapped* (= made difficult) *by rough seas and hurricane-force winds.*

hand·i·cap DISADVANTAGE /ˈhæn·dɪ·kæp/ *n* [C] a disadvantage given to a person taking part in a game or competition in order to reduce their chances of winning, or a sporting event in which such disadvantages are given • *Handicaps give people with different abilities an equal chance of winning.* • *My current golf handicap is nine.*

hand·i·crafts /£ˈhæn·dɪ·krɑːfts, $-kræfts/, *Am usually* **hand·i·craft**, *Am also* **hand·craft**, *Aus* **hand·crafts** *pl n* skilled activities in which things are made in a traditional way with the hands rather than being produced by machines in a factory, or the objects made by such activities • *Each village has its own traditional dress, cuisine, folklore and handicrafts.* • *At the Cambridge Craft Market you can buy a wide range of handicrafts which make excellent presents or souvenirs.* • LP› **Shopping goods**

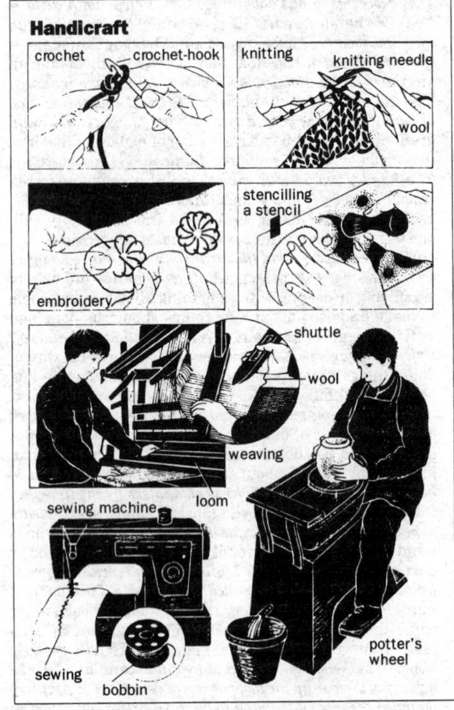

hand·i·craft /£ˈhæn·dɪ·krɑːft, $-kræft/ *adj* [before n; not gradable] • *They've started a new handicraft class at the community centre.* • Ⓢ

hand·i·ly /ˈhæn·dɪ·li/ *adv* See at HANDY USEFUL

hand·i·work /£ˈhæn·dɪ·wɜːk, $-wɜːrk/ *n* [U] work done skilfully with the hands • *Susannah put down the paintbrush and stood back to admire her handiwork.* • *(fig. humorous) "Is this your handiwork?" he asked, pointing at the graffiti on the wall.* • *(fig.) The bombers' handiwork* (= The destruction caused by the bombers) *will take several months to repair.*

hand·ker·chief (*pl* **handkerchiefs**) /£ˈhæŋ·kə·tʃiːf, $-kɚ-/, *infml* **hank·ie, hank·y** *n* [C] a square piece of cloth used for cleaning the nose and drying the eyes when they are wet with tears • *She took out her handkerchief and blew her nose loudly.* • *Sometimes handkerchiefs are worn as a decoration around the neck or sticking out of a jacket pocket.* • Compare TISSUE PAPER.

han·dle PART /ˈhæn·dl̩/ *n* [C] a part of an object designed for holding, moving or carrying the object easily • *I can't pick the kettle up – the handle's too hot.* • *She* **turned** *the handle and slowly opened the door.* • PIC› **Bags, Car, Knife**

han·dle *obj* TOUCH /ˈhæn·dl̩/ *v* [T] to pick (something) up and touch, hold or move it with your hands • *Please don't handle the vases – they're very fragile and very valuable.* • *Do you think it'll do any good if I write "handle with care" on the envelope?* • *Union leaders are advising their members not to handle any more nuclear waste.* • *We do cash cheques for people who bank elsewhere but we have to impose a handling* **charge** *to cover our costs.*

han·dle *obj* DEAL WITH /ˈhæn·dl̩/ *v* [T] to deal with, have responsibility for or be in charge of • *If you can't handle the job I'll get someone else to do it.* • *Who handles the marketing in your company?* • *Some people are brilliant with computers, but have no idea how to handle* (= behave with) *other people.* • *This new biography handles* (=

(=discusses) *his suicide with much more sensitivity and sympathy than previous books about him.*

hand·ler /£'hænd·lər, $-lɚ/ *n* [C] • *More than 30 police officers, including dog handlers, were needed to break up the fighting.* • *(esp. Am) The president's handlers* (=advisers) *are telling him to pull out of the talks.*

han·dling /'hænd·lɪŋ/ *n* [U] • *Her handling* **of** *the economy has come in for severe criticism in a report by a leading financial institution.* • *John F Kennedy made his reputation with his handling* **of** *the Cuban missile crisis.*

hand·le *(obj)* OPERATE /'hæn·dḷ/ *v* to operate or control (something which could be difficult or dangerous) • *Have you ever handled a gun before?* [T] • *Too many young riders have no idea how to handle their motorcycles safely.* [T] • If a car handles well it is easy and pleasant to drive: *Does your new car handle better than your old one?* [I always + adv/prep]

han·dling /'hænd·lɪŋ/ *n* [U] • *Power steering can dramatically improve a car's handling.*

hand·le *obj* SELL /'hæn·dḷ/ *v* [T] to buy and sell (goods) • *We only handle cosmetics which have not been tested on animals.* • *(esp. Br) He's been arrested for handling* (= possessing and selling) *stolen goods.*

hand·le NAME /'hæn·dḷ/ *n* [C] *slang* a title before a name, or a family name that sounds as if it belongs to a person from a high social class • *The people with handles don't always give the biggest tips.* • *"Doesn't she have a double-barrelled name?" "Yeah, Ponsonby-Smythe or some posh handle like that."*

hand·le·bars /£'hæn·dḷ·bɑːz, $-bɑːrz/ *pl n* a bar with curved ends forming handles which turns the front wheel of a bicycle or motorcycle so that it points in a different direction • *I had to brake suddenly and went straight over the handlebars.* • PIC> **Bicycles**

hand·le·bar /£'hæn·dḷ·bɑːʳ, $-bɑːr/ *adj* [not gradable] • A **handlebar moustache** is a thick, wide MOUSTACHE (= hair which grows on the upper lip) with curled ends in the shape of handlebars: *I love Martin's handlebar moustache.*

hand·made /ˌhæm'meɪd/ *adj* [not gradable] made using the hands rather than a machine • *Bren's father bought me some wonderful handmade chocolates at the weekend.* • *I was fed up with all that mass-produced rubbish so I decided to buy some handmade shoes for a change.*

hand·maid·en /'hændˌmeɪ·dən/, **hand·maid** /'hænd·meɪd/ *n* [C] *literary* a female servant • *Many doctors still treat nurses as their handmaidens instead of as qualified professionals in their own right.* • *(fig. fml) Technique is the handmaiden of* (= helps in producing) *art.*

hand·out PRESENT /'hænd·aʊt/ *n* [C] *often disapproving* something such as food, clothing or money that is given free to someone who has a great need for it • *I'm not interested in government handouts – all I want is a job.* • *The theatre owes its survival to cash handouts from the local council.* • See also **hand out** at HAND BODY PART.

hand·out INFORMATION /'hænd·aʊt/ *n* [C] a document given to students or reporters which contains information about a particular subject • *On page two of your handout you will find a list of the books that I have referred to during the lecture.* • *Everything I have to say is contained in the* **press** *handout, and I have no further comment to make.*

hand·ov·er /£'hæn·dəʊ·vər, $-doʊ·vɚ/ *n* [U] the giving of control of or responsibility for something to someone else • *The United Nations is to supervise the handover of the prisoners of war.* • See also **hand over** at HAND BODY PART.

hand·rail /'hænd·reɪl/ *n* [C] a long narrow bar of wood or metal which people can hold on to for support when going up or down stairs or when the ground that they are walking on is much higher than the ground at the side • PIC> **Rail**

hand·set /'hænd·set/ *n* [C] the part of a telephone which is held in front of the mouth and against the ear and used for speaking and listening to other people

hand·shake /'hænd·ʃeɪk/ *n* [C] a greeting or expression of agreement in which two people who are facing each other take hold of each other's right hands and sometimes also move them up and down several times • *Chris welcomed me with a wide smile and a warm handshake.* • *My father says he can tell a lot about a person from their handshake.*

hand·some ATTRACTIVE /'hæn·səm/ *adj* (esp. of a man) physically attractive in a traditional, MASCULINE way • *Whenever I see him in a film he always seems to play the part of the handsome hero.* • *She's dreaming she'll be whisked off her feet by a* **tall, dark (and)** *handsome stranger.* • A woman who is handsome is beautiful but not in a delicate way: *You'd never call her pretty but she's attractive in a handsome sort of way.*

hand·some GENEROUS /'hæn·səm/ *adj* generous or in a large amount • *We've received a handsome donation from an anonymous benefactor.* • *This vase would fetch a handsome price if you were to sell it at auction.*

hand·some·ly /'hæn·səm·li/ *adv* • *Western businesses have a unique opportunity to profit handsomely from the new economic freedom in eastern Europe.*

hand·stand /'hænd·stænd/ *n* [C] an action in which you balance vertically on your hands with your legs pointing straight up in the air • *I've never been able to* **do** *handstands.*

hand·writ·ing /£'hændˌraɪ·tɪŋ, $-ṭɪŋ/ *n* [U] (a person's style of) writing done with a pen or pencil • *We need to ensure that handwriting is properly taught in our primary schools.* • *Two psychologists have cast doubts on whether handwriting analysis really can help employers in their assessment of job applicants.* • *His handwriting is impossible to read.* • **Handwriting on the wall** is *Am for* **writing on the wall**. See at WRITE.

hand·writ·ten /£ˌhænd'rɪt·ən, $-'rɪṭ-/ *adj* [not gradable] • Something that is handwritten is written with a pen or pencil rather than printed or TYPED: *On the wall was a framed handwritten note from the President thanking her for her hospitality.*

hand·y USEFUL /'hæn·di/ *adj* **-ier, -iest** useful or convenient • *A remote control for the TV would be very handy.* • *First-time visitors to France will find this guide particularly handy.* • *Her new book is packed with handy hints and tips about how to get the most from your microwave.* • *Laptop computers offer a handy, compact and portable alternative to desktop machines.* • *He always seems to have a handy excuse for not buying the drinks.* • *Our new house is very handy* **for** *work – it's only ten minutes away by bike.* • *The supermarket might be cheap but the corner shop is handier* (=easier to go to). • *I'm going to put the kitchen shelves up this afternoon, so I want to keep that drill handy* (= in a convenient place). • *Don't throw those bottles away – they'll* **come in** *handy* (= be useful) **for** *the picnic next Sunday.*

hand·i·ly /'hæn·dɪ·li/ *adv* • *An additional power switch for the radio is handily located next to the steering wheel.* • *(Am) The Yankees handily* (= easily) **defeated** *the Boston Red Sox.*

hand·y SKILFUL /'hæn·di/ *adj* [after v] **-ier, -iest** able to use something skilfully • *Jonathan's good at wallpapering but he's not so handy* **with** *a paintbrush.* • *Susannah's very handy* (= good at doing things which need skilled use of the hands) **about** *the house – she's always fixing things which don't work properly.*

hand·y·man /'hæn·di·mæn/ *n* [C] *pl* **-men** • A handyman is a man who is skilled at repairing and making things in his home: *I knew nothing about things like carpentry and plumbing when I started renovating the cottage, but I was a real handyman by the time I'd finished!*

hang *(obj)* FIX AT TOP /hæŋ/ *v past* **hung** /hʌŋ/ to support (something) at the top leaving the other parts free, or (esp. of cloth) to be held in this way • *A heavy gold necklace hung* **around** *her neck.* [I] • *Long creepers hung* **down** *from the trees.* [I] • *There were several aprons hanging* **from** *a hook behind the kitchen door.* [I] • *The curtains hung* **in** *thick folds.* [I] • *Hang your coat and hat* **(up)** *on the rack over there.* [T] • *It's a fact that clothes hang better on thin people.* [I] • *Many of his finest pictures hang/are hung* (= are fixed to the wall so that they can be seen) *in the National Gallery.* [I/T] • *Hang the pheasant/Let the pheasant hang for a few days for the flavour to improve before you cook it.* [I/T] • If you hang **wallpaper** you fix it to the wall. [T] • If a usually serious situation **hangs by a thread** it means that even slight changes can decide what will happen: *The mayor's political future has been hanging by a thread since the fraud scandal.* • *(infml)* **Hang on in there** *(esp. Am and Aus* **hang in there**) means do not give up despite difficulties: *Work can get tough in the middle of a term but hang on in there and it'll be OK.* See also HANG ON. • *So when did you* **hang up** *your boxing gloves/golf-club/ballet shoes* (= stop boxing/playing golf/BALLET dancing)? • A **hang-glider** is a very small aircraft without an engine. It has a wing made of cloth or other material fixed over a frame which someone hangs under: *Mark's just bought a hang-glider.* ○ *Have you ever been* **hang-gliding?** • A **hanging basket** is a light, open container, often in the shape of a half sphere, which holds a variety of flowering plants and hangs above the ground in a garden or outside a building. • *"Any old place I can hang my hat is home sweet home to me"* (title of a song written by William Jerome, 1901) • [PIC]> **Garden, Sports**

hang /hæŋ/ *n* [U] • **The** hang of something, esp. something made of cloth, is the way it looks when it is hanging: *That coat fits you so well – the hang is perfect.* ○ *If you ironed that skirt it might improve the hang* **of** *it.* • See also **get the hang of** at HANG [SKILL].

hang·ings /ˈhæŋ·ɪŋz/ *pl n* • *The castle's great hall was decorated with sumptuous* **(wall)** *hangings* (=pieces of cloth, often with pictures on them).

hang *(obj)* [KILL] /hæŋ/ *v past* **hanged** or **hung** /hʌŋ/ to kill (someone), esp. as punishment for a serious crime, by dropping them with a rope tied around their neck and fixed at the other end • *In the morning they hanged the prisoner from a gibbet.* [T] • *The sentence of the court is that you be hanged by the neck until you are dead.* [T] • *With so little evidence to prove her guilt, few people thought she should hang* (= be killed in this way). [I] • *He hanged* **himself** *in his garage.* [T] • In the past if someone was **hanged/hung, drawn and quartered** they were hanged and their body was cut into pieces. • *(esp. Br and Aus saying)* 'You might as well be hanged/hung for a sheep as (for) a lamb' means that because the punishment for a bad action and an even worse one will be the same, you have no reason not to do the worse one. • The standard past form of the verb is *hanged*, but *hung* is quite commonly used too. • See also HANGMAN.

hang·ing /ˈhæŋ·ɪŋ/ *n* • *Hanging is still legal in some countries.* [U] • *The prosecution of their leaders led to a number of hangings and imprisonments.* [C]

hang [STAY] /hæŋ/ *v* [I] *past* **hung** /hʌŋ/ to stay in the air • *Smoke from the houses hung* **above** *Kit's village on the still air.* • *The falcon seemed to hang (in the air) for a moment before diving onto its prey.* • *(literary) The sound of the bells hung in the midnight air.* • *(fig.) The whole question/issue still hangs* **in the balance** (= is still to be decided). • If a threat or doubt **hangs over** a place or a situation it exists: *The prospect of famine hangs over many areas of the world.* ○ *Uncertainty again hangs over the project.*

hang *(obj)* [CURVE DOWN] /hæŋ/ *v past* **hung** /hʌŋ/ to curve down • *The branches hung heavy with snow.* [I] • *He knew he'd done something wrong and hung his* **head in shame** (= with guilt) *as he entered the room.* [T]

hang *(obj)* [STRONG FEELING] /hæŋ/ *v past* **hanged** *infml dated* used to express strong feeling, esp. annoyance • *She may want the report by tomorrow but she can* **go hang** *for all I care* (= I do not care about what she wants). • **Hang it (all)** is an expression of annoyance: *Hang it all – when is that woman going to arrive!* • **I'll be hanged** *if she's going to do that* (= I'm determined that she will not)*!* • *Just fix the washing machine and* **hang the cost/expense** (= the cost is not important)*!* • *Why ask me –* **I'm hanged if I** (= I don't) *know.* • *Well,* **I'll be/I'm hanged** (= I am very surprised)*! Whatever brings you to a club like this?*

hang [SKILL] /hæŋ/ *n* [U] **get the hang of** *infml* to learn how to do (something), esp. if it is not obvious or simple • *I'll teach you to ride a bicycle – you'll soon get the hang of* **it**. • *"I've never used a word processor before." "Don't worry – you'll soon get the hang of* **it**.*"*

hang *obj* [DELAY] /hæŋ/ *v* [T] *past* **hung** /hʌŋ/ **hang fire** to delay making a decision • *Ideally we would settle the matter now, but I think we should hang fire until the general situation becomes clearer.*

hang a·bout, **hang a·round** *v adv* [I] *infml* to move or do things slowly • *Go and pack but don't hang about – we have to go in an hour.* • *If you hang about much more you're going to miss the train.* • *(Aus) Hang on (Br also* **hang about***)* (= stop for a moment)*, let's just check we've got everything.*

hang a·round *(obj)*, *Br also* **hang a·bout**, **hang round** *v adv prep* to wait at (a place), or to stay near (a place or person), usually for no particular reason • *Her bus was late so I had to hang around the bus station for a whole hour.* [T] • *I spent most of my youth hanging around the bars of Dublin.* [T] • *"So what are you doing here?" "Me, nothing – I'm just hanging around."* [I] • *There's usually a couple of kids just hanging round on street corners.* [I] • *I thought I'd hang around for a while and see if she comes.* [I] • *(infml) The last thing I want is a couple of kids* **hanging round** *my* **neck** (= staying with me and limiting what I do)*!*

hang at *obj v prep* [T] *Am infml* to wait at (a place), usually for no particular reason • *We were hanging at Groncki's house for a couple of hours before going to the party.*

hang back *v adv* [I] to be slow to do something, often because of fear or lack of confidence • *There's no need to hang back – you can sing as well as anyone.* • *Some nations are hanging back more than others in the aid effort.* • *That car ahead seems to be swerving a lot – I think I'll hang back* (= drive a safe distance behind) *for a while.*

hang on [WAIT] *v adv* [I] to wait • *Sally is on the other phone – would you like to hang on?* • *I know you want the toilet but we can't stop the car here – you'll have to hang on a minute/for a while.* • *(infml) Hang on – I'll be with you in a moment!*

hang on [HOLD] *v adv* [I] to hold or continue holding onto something • *Hang on* **tight** (= firmly) *– it's going to be a very bumpy ride.* • *Hang on* **to** *the ledge until I can get help.* • See also HANG ON TO; HANGER-ON;

hang on *obj* [GIVE ATTENTION], **hang u·pon** *v prep* [T] to give careful attention to (esp. something said) • *It's so embarrassing the way he hangs on her* **every word** *as if she were some sort of goddess.*

hang on *obj* [DEPEND ON], **hang u·pon** *v prep* [T] to depend on (something) • *The safety of air travel hangs partly on the thoroughness of baggage checking.*

hang on to *obj v adv prep* [T] to keep (something) • *You should hang on to that painting – it might be valuable one day.* • *Lots of people hang on to their childhood teddy bears.*

hang out *v adv* [I] *infml* to spend a lot of time in a place or with someone, or live in a place • *You still hang out at the pool hall?* • *Where does he hang out these days?*

hang·out /ˈhæŋ·aʊt/ *n* [C] *infml* • A hangout is a place where someone spends a lot of time or where they live: *The café is a favourite hangout of artists.* ○ *Their hangout was a grubby attic.*

hang to·geth·er [STAY TOGETHER] *v adv* [I] to stay together • *If the opposition party can hang together over the next six months, they might just stand a chance of being elected.* • *"We must indeed all hang together, or, most assuredly, we shall all hang separately"* (Benjamin Franklin, 1776)

hang to·geth·er [SEEM TRUE] *v adv* [I] to show clear reasoning; to seem true • *Somehow her story doesn't quite hang together.*

hang up *v adv* [I] to end a telephone conversation, sometimes suddenly, by putting down the RECEIVER (= the part that you hold to the ear and mouth) or switching off the telephone in another way • *Don't you hate it when someone hangs up* **(on you)** *before you've finished speaking?* • *Let me speak to Melanie before you hang up.* • See also HANG-UP.

han·gar /£ˈhæŋ·əʳ, $-ɚ/ *n* [C] a large building in which aircraft are kept

hang·dog /£ˈhæŋ·dɒg, $-dɑːg/ *adj* [before n] (of an expression on a face) unhappy or ashamed, esp. because of feeling guilty • *hangdog look/expression*

hang·er /£ˈhæŋ·əʳ, $-ɚ/, **clothes–hang·er** /£ˈkləʊðz ˌhæŋ·əʳ, $ˈkloʊðzˌhæŋ·ɚ/, **coat–hang·er** /£ˈkəʊtˌhæŋ·əʳ, $ˈkoʊtˌhæŋ·ɚ/ *n* [C] a curved piece of wire, wood or plastic on which clothes can be hung • [PIC]> **Beds and bedroom**

hang·er–on /£ˌhæŋ·ərˈɒn, $-ɚˈɑːn/ *n* [C] *pl* **hangers-on** /£ˌhæŋ·əzˈɒn, $-ɚzˈɑːn/ *disapproving* a person who tries to be friendly and spend time with rich and important people, esp. to get advantage • *Wherever there is Royalty, there are always hangers-on.*

hang·man /ˈhæŋ·mən, -mæn/ *n* [C] *pl* **-men** a person whose job is to operate the device which kills criminals by hanging them from a rope by their necks • See also HANG [KILL].

hang·out /ˈhæŋ·aʊt/ *n* [C] See at HANG OUT

hang·ov·er [ILLNESS] /£ˈhæŋˌəʊ·vəʳ, $-ˌoʊ·vɚ/ *n* [C] a feeling of illness after drinking too much alcohol • *Headache, upset stomach – it sounds like you've got a hangover.* • *Do you know any good hangover cures?* • See also HUNG-OVER.

hang·ov·er [CONTINUATION] /£ˈhæŋˌəʊ·vəʳ, $-ˌoʊ·vɚ/ *n* [C] something that continues from an earlier time • *The present political system is a hangover* **from** *the nineteenth century colonial era.* • *Hating sport is a hangover* **from** *her schooldays.*

hang–up /ˈhæŋ·ʌp/ *n* [C] *infml* a permanent and unreasonable feeling of anxiety about some feature of yourself • *He's one of these men who went bald very young and has a terrible hang-up* **about** *it.* • *I think Melanie's got a bit of a hang-up* **about** *her lack of education.* • *The English are notorious for their* **sexual** *hang-ups.* • *Most women have some sort of hang-up* **about** *their body.* • *She's* *a very insecure person – she's got a lot of hang-ups.* • See also HANG UP.

hung–up /ˌhʌŋˈʌp/ *adj infml* • *Why are so many women so hung-up* **about** *food?* • *To understand why Moreno was so sexually hung-up, you need only look at his childhood.* • If you are hung-up **on** a particular subject, you are extremely interested in or worried by it and spend an unreasonably large amount of time thinking about it: *Why are the British so hung-up on class?*

hank·er af·ter *obj* /£ˈhæŋ·kəʳ, $-kɚ/, **hank·er for** *obj v prep* [T] to have a strong desire for (something), esp. if you cannot or should not have it • *What did you hanker after most when you were in prison?* • *Even after all these years, I still hanker for a motorbike.* • *I'm rather impatient with writers who spend their time hankering* **after** *the past.*

hank·er·ing /£ˈhæŋ·kᵊr·ɪŋ, $-kɚ-/ *n* [C] • *Don't you ever* **have** *a hankering* (= strong desire) **for** *a different lifestyle?*

hank·y /ˈhæŋ·ki/, **hank·ie** *n* [C] *infml* a HANDKERCHIEF

hank·y–pan·ky /ˌhæŋ·kɪˈpæŋ·ki/ *n* [U] *infml dated* dishonest behaviour, esp. involving sexual activity or money • *The senator's career was brought to an abrupt end after revelations of hanky-panky with Ms Ashby, a former model.* • *Allegations of financial hanky-panky have been hotly denied by both chairman and club manager.*

Han·sard /£ˈhæn·sɑːd, $-sɚd/ *n* [U not after *the*] the official record of what is said and done in a parliament, esp. the British, Australian and Canadian parliaments

han·som (cab) /ˈhæn·səm/ *n* [C] a two-wheeled carriage pulled by a horse, used like a TAXI in the past

Han·uk·kah /ˈhɑː·nə·kə/, **Cha·nu·kah** *n* [C/U] a Jewish religious holiday lasting for eight days in December

hap·haz·ard /£ˌhæpˈhæz·əd, $-ɚd/ *adj disapproving* not having an obvious order or plan • *He tackled the problem in a typically haphazard manner.*

hap·haz·ard·ly /£ˌhæpˈhæz·əd·li, $-ɚd-/ *adv disapproving*

hap·less /ˈhæp·ləs/ *adj* [before n] *literary* unlucky and usually unhappy • *Many children are hapless* **victims** *of this war.* • *Jack Stewart plays the part of the hapless minister who finds himself at the centre of a political scandal.*

hap·less·ly /ˈhæp·lə·sli/ *adv literary*

ha'porth /£ˈheɪ·pəθ/ *n* [U] **(not) a ha'porth of difference** *Br dated infml* (not) any difference at all • *You can shout as much as you like but it won't make a ha'porth of difference – you're not going.*

hap·pen [HAVE EXISTENCE] /ˈhæp·ᵊn/ *v* [I] (of a situation or an event) to have existence or come into existence • *No one knows exactly what happened but several people have been hurt.* • *Anything could happen in the next half hour.* • *A funny thing happened in the office today.* • *I don't like to think what might have happened if he'd been driving any faster.* • *Bad weather means the rescue mission won't be happening until the weekend.* • If something happens **to** someone or something, it has an effect on them, and changes them in some way: *I don't know what I'd do if anything happened to him* (= if he was hurt, became ill, or died). ○ *What happened to your jacket! There's a big rip in the sleeve.* ○ *What's happened to my pen* (= Where is it)*? I put it down there a few moments ago.*

hap·pen·ing /ˈhæp·ᵊn·ɪŋ, £ˈhæp·nɪŋ/ *n* [C usually pl] • *Recent happenings* (= things that happened) *on the money markets can be interpreted in various ways.* • In the 1960s and early 1970s a happening was a performance or similar event that happened without preparation. • Ⓙ (KOR)

hap·pen·ing /ˈhæp·ᵊn·ɪŋ, £ˈhæp·nɪŋ/ *adj slang dated* • A happening place is one that is extremely fashionable and exciting: *Ask Caroline – she knows all the happening clubs in town.*

hap·pen *(obj)* [CHANCE] /ˈhæp·ᵊn/ *v* to do or be by chance • *They happened* **to** *look in the right place almost immediately.* [+ *to* infinitive] • *Fortunately* **it** *happened* **(that)** *there was no one in the house at the time of the explosion.* [+ (*that*) clause] • **It just so** *happens* **that** *I have one in my pocket now.* [+ *that* clause] • *She happens* **to** *like swimming* (= She does like swimming, although you might not believe it). [+ *to* infinitive] • *I happen* **to** *think he's right* (= I do think so, although you do not). [+ *to* infinitive] • **As it happened** (= Although it was not planned), *I had a few minutes to spare.* • *(literary)* If you happen **on/upon** something or someone, you find or meet them by chance: *Eventually they happened on a road leading across the desert.* [T] • *(esp. Am)* If someone happens **along/by/past**, they go to a place by chance or without planning to: *We happened by your house last night, but you were out.* [I] • LP› **It**

hap·pen [POSSIBLY] /ˈhæp·ᵊn/ *adv* [not gradable] *Br regional* possibly; I expect that • *Happen it'll rain later on.*

hap·pen·stance /£ˈhæp·ᵊn·stɑːnts, $-stænts/ *n* [C/U] chance or a chance situation, esp. one producing a good result • *By (a strange) happenstance they were both in the room at the same time.*

hap·py [PLEASED] /ˈhæp·i/ *adj* **-ier, -iest** feeling, showing or causing pleasure or satisfaction • *You look happy!* • *It was a very happy marriage.* • *Stella didn't have a very happy childhood.* • *School days are said to be the happiest days of your life.* • *Nicki seems a lot happier since she met Steve.* • *You'll be happy* **to** *know that Jean is coming with us.* [+ *to* infinitive] • *I won't come with you to the cinema, but I'm perfectly happy* **to** (= I will willingly) *pick you up afterwards.* [+ *to* infinitive] • *I'm so happy* **(that)** *everything is working out for you.* [+ (*that*) clause] • *Barry seemed happy enough working 60 hours a week.* [+ v-*ing*] • *Are you happy* **about/with** (= satisfied with) *your new working arrangements?* • *Your mother's not going to be very happy when she sees the mess you've made!* • *(fml) The manager will be happy* (= able) **to** *see you this afternoon.* [+ *to* infinitive] • *(humorous)* A marriage is sometimes referred to as **the happy day**: *So when's the happy day then?* • *(humorous)* The birth of a child is sometimes referred to as **the happy event** (*Am also* **the blessed event**). • If someone is **happy-go-lucky**, they do not plan very much and they accept what happens without being made anxious by it: *You need to be a bit happy-go-lucky in this business.* • A **happy hour** is a period of time, usually in the early evening, when drinks are sold cheaply in a bar or a PUB. • *(approving)* A **happy medium** is a state or way of doing something which avoids being extreme, often combining the best of two opposite states or ways of doing something: *I try to* **strike a** (= achieve a) *happy medium when I'm on holiday, and spend half my time doing things and the other half just relaxing.* • *"Happy Days are Here Again"* (title of a song written by Jack Yellen, 1929)

hap·pi·ly /ˈhæp·ɪ·li/ *adv* • *He was happily married with two young children.* • *She munched happily on her chocolate bar.* • *I'd happily* (= willingly) *offer to help him if I thought it would make any difference.* • *If you're short of time, I'll happily* (= willingly) *take you to the station.* • *"And they all lived happily ever after"* (traditional ending to stories)

hap·pi·ness /ˈhæp·ɪ·nəs/ *n* [U] • *It was only later in life that she found happiness and peace of mind.* • *(fml) Will you join me in wishing the bride and groom* **every** *happiness?*

hap·py [LUCKY] /ˈhæp·i/ *adj* [before n] **-ier, -iest** (of a condition or situation) lucky • *We hadn't planned to be in France at the same time as Ann and Charles – it was just a happy* **coincidence**.

hap·pi·ly /ˈhæp·ɪ·li/ *adv* • *Happily, the weather remained fine throughout the afternoon.*

hap·py [SUITABLE] /ˈhæp·i/ *adj* **-ier, -iest** *literary* (of words or behaviour) suitable • *It wasn't a happy (choice of) phrase for such a formal occasion.*

hap·py [GREETING] /ˈhæp·i/ *adj* [before n; not gradable] (used in greetings for special occasions) full of enjoyment and pleasure • *Happy Birthday/Anniversary!* • *To Norma and John, wishing you a Merry Christmas and a Happy New Year, from Bill and Hilary.* • LP› **Phrases and customs**

ha·ra–ki·ri /ˌhær·əˈkiː·ri/ *n* [U] (in Japan, esp. in the past) a ceremonial way of killing yourself by cutting open the stomach with a sword • *(fig.) If the company raises its prices, it will be* **committing** *economic hara-kiri* (= destroying itself).

ha·ran·gue *obj* /həˈræŋ/ *v* [T] *disapproving* to speak to (someone or a group of people), often for a long time, in a forceful and sometimes angry way, esp. to persuade them • *I listened to him in parliament yesterday haranguing the opposition about the education reforms.* • *A drunk in the station was haranguing passers-by.*

ha·ran·gue /həˈræŋ/ *n* [C] *disapproving* • *The team were given the usual half-time harangue by their manager.*

har·ass *obj* /ˈhær·əs/ *v* [T] to make (someone) anxious and unhappy by causing them problems • *Stop harassing the child with so many difficult questions.* • *Snipers still harass the occupying army from ruined apartment blocks.*

har·assed /ˈhær·əst/ *adj* • *You look harassed – is something the matter?* • *The supermarket was full of harassed-looking mothers with young children.*

har·ass·ment /ˈhær·ə·smənt/ *n* [U] • *There have been some cases of* **sexual** *harassment of/against women in this office.*

har·bing·er /£ˈhɑː·bɪn·dʒəʳ, $ˈhɑːr·bɪn·dʒɚ/ *n* [C] *literary* someone or a thing that shows that something is going to happen soon or in the future • *The blackbird is a welcome sight in the garden, its mellow song* **the** *harbinger* **of** *spring.* • *The latest figures are seen by many to be harbingers* **of** *financial* **doom**.

har·bour WATER *Br and Aus, Am and Aus* **har·bor** /£ˈhɑː·bəʳ, $ˈhɑːr·bɚ/ *n* an area of water next to the coast, often surrounded by thick walls, where ships and boats can be sheltered • *Our hotel room overlooked a pretty little fishing harbour.* [C] • *After being at sea for so long, seeing harbour was wonderful.* [U] • A **harbour-master** is the official who is in charge of a harbour. • Compare DOCK ENCLOSED AREA.

har·bour *obj* HAVE IN MIND *Br and Aus, Am and Aus* **har·bor** /£ˈhɑː·bəʳ, $ˈhɑːr·bɚ/ *v* [T] to have in mind (a thought or feeling), usually over a long period • *Tiffany's been harbouring a* **grudge** *against our boss ever since her transfer was refused.* • *There are those who harbour suspicions about his motives.* • *I'm certainly not harbouring a secret passion for the man, if that's what you're thinking.* • *Powell remains non-committal about any political ambitions he may harbour.*

har·bour *obj* HIDE *Br and Aus, Am and Aus* **har·bor** /£ˈhɑː·bəʳ, $ˈhɑːr·bɚ/ *v* [T] to protect (someone or something bad), esp. by giving them somewhere to hide • *There will be a severe penalty for anyone who harbours traitors.*

hard SOLID /£hɑːd, $hɑːrd/ *adj* **-er, -est** firm and solid; not easy to bend, cut or break • *There was a heavy frost last night and the ground is still hard.* • *Heating the clay makes it hard.* • *The road is much harder than your head, so wear a crash helmet when you're cycling.* • *The ground's impossible to dig – it's* **as** *hard* **as iron/stone/a rock**. • A rule which is **hard and fast** is fixed and can not be changed: *There are no hard-and-fast rules for getting a job in television.* • Information or facts which are **hard and fast** are certain: *We don't have any hard-and-fast information about the number of casualties yet.* • When an egg is **hard-boiled**, it has been heated in its shell in boiling water until both the white and yellow parts are solid. See also **hard-boiled** at HARD SEVERE. • **Hard cash** is money in the form of coins or notes but not CHEQUES or a **credit card**. • **Hard copy** is information from a computer which has been printed on paper. • *(esp. Br)* **Hard core** is the pieces of broken stone, brick, etc. used to make the base under a floor, path or road. See also **hard-core** at HARD SEVERE. • **Hard currency** is money of a type that has a value in countries other than its own. • A **hard disk** is a magnetic device that is fixed inside a computer and stores a very large amount of information. Compare **floppy disk** at FLOPPY. • A **hard hat** is a hat made of a strong substance which is worn to protect someone's head, esp. if they are a builder: *Hard hats must be worn in this area.* • *(taboo slang)* A **hard-on** is an ERECTION (= condition of the penis when it is stiff). • *(Br)* A **hard shoulder** (*Am and Aus* **shoulder**, *Irish Eng* **hard margin**) is the hard area beside a main road, esp. a MOTORWAY, where a driver can stop if there is a serious problem. PIC **Motorway** • NL

hard·en *(obj)* /£ˈhɑː·dᵊn, $ˈhɑːr-/ *v* • *The mixture hardens as it cools.* [I] • *It is thought that high cholesterol levels in the blood can harden the arteries* (= make them thicker and stiffer, causing disease). [T]

hard·ness /£hɑːd·nəs, $hɑːrd-/ *n* [U] • *These alloys are characterized by their extreme hardness.*

hard DIFFICULT /£hɑːd, $hɑːrd/ *adj* **-er, -est** difficult to understand or do • *There were some really hard questions in the exam.* • **It's** *hard* **to say** *which of them is lying.* [+ *to* infinitive] • **It's** *hard* **being** *a single mother.* [+ v-*ing*] • *Her handwriting is very hard* **to** *read.* [+ *to* infinitive] • *He's a hard man* **to please**. [+ *to* infinitive] • *The topics* **get** *hard/harder* (= become difficult/more difficult) *later in the course.* • **The hard way** is a way of doing something which is unnecessarily difficult: *She always* **does things** *the hard way.* See also **the hard way** at HARD SEVERE. • *You're 16? I find that rather* **hard to swallow** (= I do not believe it)*!* • *(infml) I find her books a bit* **hard going** (= difficult and/or tiring to understand). • If someone is **hard of hearing**, they are not able to hear well: *My father is quite old now and he's increasingly hard of hearing.* • NL

hard USING EFFORT /£hɑːd, $hɑːrd/ *adj* **-er, -est** needing or using a lot of physical or mental effort • *Go on – give it a good hard push!* • *It was hard* **work** *on the farm but we all enjoyed it.* • *After three years of hard* **work** *we finally finished the project.* • *The climb* **gets** *hard/harder* (= needs more effort) *near to the summit.* • A **hard drinker** is someone who often drinks a lot of alcohol. See also **hard drink** at HARD DRUG. • NL

hard /£hɑːd, $hɑːrd/ *adv* **-er, -est** • *Work hard, play hard and be happy.* • *I'm not surprised he failed his exam – he didn't exactly try very hard!* • *(infml) That's what I like to see – everybody* **hard at it** (= putting a lot of effort into what they are doing)*!* • If something is **hard-earned**, it is deserved because lots of work was done: *You've done a lot of work for the project, so go and enjoy your hard-earned holiday.* • If something is **hard-won**, it was only achieved after a lot of effort: *The bridge was hard-won, with many deaths in the fighting.* • Someone who is **hard-working** continually does a lot of work: *She deserves a bit of success – she's very hard-working.*

hard SEVERE /£hɑːd, $hɑːrd/ *adj* **-er, -est** not pleasant or gentle; severe • *You have to be quite hard to succeed in the property business.* • *Ooh, you're a hard woman, Elaine!* • *Our boss has been giving us all a hard* **time** *at work* (= making our time at work difficult). • If a person is hard **on** someone, they treat them severely and look for their faults: *Don't be too hard on him – he's new to the job.* • If someone is hard **on** a piece of clothing, they tend to damage it quickly: *I'm very hard on shoes.* • *(Br and Aus)* If you feel **hard-done-by**, you believe that you have not been treated fairly: *No wonder you feel hard-done-by if you wrote the report and she claimed it as her own.* ○ *There's more food here, if anyone feels hard-done-by.* • You might express sympathy for someone over a small misfortune by saying **hard luck** (*infml* **tough luck** or *Br* **hard lines** or *Br dated infml* **hard cheese**): *"We lost again." "Oh, hard luck!"* ○ *It was hard luck you weren't picked for the team.* ○ *Oh, hard lines! You almost got the top score.* • *(infml)* You might say to someone **(that's)** your **hard luck** if you think that it is their fault that something bad has happened to them: *Well, if you missed the presentation because you couldn't be bothered to turn up on time, that's your hard luck!* • Someone who is **(as) hard as nails** does not show or feel emotion: *The supervisor is a sweetie but the boss is hard as nails.* • *She's finding the bad news* **hard to take** (= difficult to accept). • *We may disagree about the subject, but let's not have any* **hard feelings** (= let there be no bad thoughts or feelings between us)*!* • **The hard way** means learning from unpleasant experiences rather than by being taught: *If she won't listen, she'll have to* **learn/find out** *the hard way.* See also **the hard way** at HARD DIFFICULT. • *(sometimes disapproving)* A **hard core** of a group or the **hard-core** members of a group are the people who strongly believe in its principles and usually have a lot of power in it: *The hard core of the party has not lost sight of the original ideals.* ○ *He's a hard-core reactionary.* • **Hard-core** can also mean showing sexual acts clearly and in detail: *a hard-core video* ○ *hard-core pornography* ○ See also **hard porn**. • **Hard-core music** is very fast modern music in which drums and electric guitar are played very loudly. • Someone who is **hard-headed** is not influenced by their emotions: *She has a very practical and hard-headed approach to the problem.* • *(disapproving)* If someone is **hard-hearted**, they are not kind or sympathetic. Compare **kind-hearted** at KIND GOOD; **soft-hearted** at SOFT GENTLE. • *She'll have (to take) a lot of* **hard knocks** (= be in situations which are not pleasant) *now she's left the protection of school and home.* • **Hard labour** is a punishment for criminals, esp. used in the past, which involves a lot of tiring and often useless physical work. • **Hard-line** beliefs or plans are those which are fixed and do not change: *a hard-line manifesto* ○ *The ministers in the cabinet are all* **hard-liners** (= people who are unwilling to change their opinions). • *(infml disapproving)* A **hard-luck story** is a story or piece of information that someone tells you or writes about themselves which is intended to make you feel sad and sympathetic towards them: *She came out with some hard-luck story about never having been loved by her mother.* • **Hard-nosed** means practical and determined: *His hard-nosed business approach is combined with a very real concern for the less fortunate in society.* • *(esp. Br infml)* If someone is a **hard case/nut**, they are difficult to deal with and possibly angry and violent. See also **a hard nut to crack** at NUT FOOD. • **Hard porn** is PORNOGRAPHY (= books, films etc. showing sexual acts) which shows sex in a very detailed and often violent way. Compare **soft porn** at SOFT

[NOT HARMFUL]. • **Hard rock** is a type of ROCK music (= popular music) with a strong beat in which drums and electric guitars are played very loudly. • If someone uses or tries the **hard sell**, they try to sell something to the buyer by being very forceful: *We were interested in buying the fridge until the salesman came on with* **the** *hard* **sell**. Compare **soft sell** at SOFT [GENTLE]. • *"It's been a Hard Day's Night"* (title of a song by The Beatles, 1964) • *"Hard Times"* (title of a book by Charles Dickens, 1854) • (NL)

hard– /£hɑːd, $hɑːrd/ *combining form* • If someone is **hard-bitten**, their character has been made stronger and they are less likely to show emotion as a result of difficult experiences in the past: *This particular murder case was so horrific that it shocked even the most hard-bitten of New York police officers.* • *(infml)* A person who is **hard-boiled** does not seem to have any emotions or weaknesses: *The film stars Kathleen Turner as the hard-boiled detective of Sarah Paretsky's novel.* See also **hard-boiled** at HARD [SOLID]. • **Hard-fought** means achieved after a lot of difficulty or fighting: *But success did not come easily and this has been a hard-fought campaign.* • A speech or piece of writing that is **hard-hitting** is extremely critical of something: *The committee published a hard-hitting report on the bank's management.* • **Hard-pressed** means having a lot of difficulties: *The latest education reforms have put extra pressure on teachers who are already hard-pressed.* ○ *Because of shortages, the emergency services were hard-pressed* (=found it almost impossible) *to deal with the accident.* ○ *(infml) Most people would be hard-pressed* (= would find it difficult) *to name more than half a dozen members of the government.* • If something, esp. clothing or material, is **hard-wearing** it lasts for a long time and looks good even if it is used a lot: *The good thing about denim is that it's quite hard-wearing.*

hard·en *(obj)* /£'hɑː·d^{ə}n, $'hɑːr-/ *v* • *Living rough in the desert hardened the recruits a lot* (=made them stronger). [T] • *As the war progressed, attitudes on both sides hardened* (= became more severe and determined). [I] • *She'd be better at her job if she could* **harden** *her* **heart** (=feel or show less emotion).

hard·ened /£'hɑː·d^{ə}nd, $'hɑːr-/ *adj* • *He was described in court as a hardened* **criminal** (= one who cannot stop his criminal activity). • To become hardened **to** an upsetting situation is to develop a way of dealing with it so that it no longer upsets you: *After a while as an ambulance-driver, you get hardened to what you see at accidents.*

hard·en·ing /£'hɑːd·nɪŋ, $'hɑːrd-/ *n* [U] • *There has been a hardening of government policy since the invasion.*

hard·ness /£hɑːd·nəs, $hɑːrd-/ *n* [U] • *So much hardness is not natural in someone so young.*

hard [DRUG] /£hɑːd, $hɑːrd/ *adj* [before n] **-er, -est** (of a drug) dangerous and ADDICTIVE (=giving you the habit of taking it), or (of alcoholic drink) containing a large amount of alcohol • *She's into hard* **drugs**. • *For those who prefer* **hard drink** *(esp. Am* **hard liquor**), *we have whisky, vodka and gin.* See also **hard drinker** at HARD [USING EFFORT]. • *(infml humorous)* **Hard stuff** is another way of saying hard drink: *Would you like* **a drop of the** *hard stuff* (=some strong alcoholic drink)? • (NL)

hard [WEATHER] /£hɑːd, $hɑːrd/ *adv* **-er, -est** (of weather) strongly, a lot or severely • *It's raining/snowing hard.* • (NL)

hard /£hɑːd, $hɑːrd/ *adj* **-er, -est** • If a season is hard, it causes difficulties because it is very cold: *We had a very hard* **winter** *last year and some of the plants died.*

hard [WATER] /£hɑːd, $hɑːrd/ *adj* **-er, -est** (of water) containing a lot of LIME (=a chemical substance) which prevents soap from cleaning • *We live in a hard water area.* • (NL)

hard·ness /£hɑːd·nəs, $hɑːrd-/ *n* [U]

hard [CLEAR] /£hɑːd, $hɑːrd/ *adj* [before n] **-er, -est** able to be proven • *hard facts/evidence* • *Physics is thought of as a* **hard science** *because of its mathematical nature, but sociology is not.* • (NL)

hard·back /£'hɑːd·bæk, $'hɑːrd-/, *Am and Aus also* **hard·cov·er** *n* a book which has a stiff cover • *Hardbacks are so much nicer to read than paperbacks.* [C] • *His latest novel will be published* **in** *hardback later this month.* [U] • *The hardback edition is more expensive than the paperback.* • Compare PAPERBACK; SOFTBACK.

hard·ball /£'hɑːd·bɔːl, $'hɑːrd·bɑːl/ *n* [U] *Am for* BASEBALL • Compare SOFTBALL.

hard·board /£'hɑːd·bɔːd, $'hɑːrd·bɔːrd/ *n* [U] a substance made of wood fibres mixed with glue and pressed into large thin flat pieces • *We used* **a sheet of** *hardboard to make a base for the toy farm.*

hard by *adv* [not gradable], *prep literary* very near • *The house where he lived as a child is hard by the main plaza.*

hard·cov·er /£'hɑːdˌkʌv·əʳ, $'hɑːrdˌkʌv·ɚ/ *n* [C/U] *Am and Aus for* HARDBACK • *The novel was originally published* **in** *hardcover.* [U]

har·di·ness /£'hɑː·dɪ·nəs, $'hɑːr-/ *n* [U] See at HARDY

hard·ly [ONLY JUST] /£'hɑːd·li, $'hɑːrd-/ *adv* [not gradable] only just; almost not • *Can you speak louder – I* **can** *hardly hear you.* • *The play had hardly started when there was a power cut.* • *My youngest daughter is so excited – she* **can** *hardly wait until tomorrow.* • *You* **could** *hardly stand up because the wind was so strong.* • *He hardly ate anything/ He ate hardly anything – he must be ill.* • *Hardly had a moment passed before the door creaked open.* • *We hardly* **ever** (=almost never) *go to concerts.*

hard·ly [CERTAINLY NOT] /£'hɑːd·li, $'hɑːrd-/ *adv* [not gradable] certainly not • *You* **can** *hardly* (=You cannot) *expect a pay-rise when you've only been working for the company for two weeks!* • *You can hardly* (=You cannot) *blame me for it when I wasn't even there!* • *Well don't be angry with me – it's hardly my fault* (=it's not my fault) *that it's raining!*

hard on *prep* close behind • *The masked man ran from the shop with a police officer hard on* **his heels** (=running closely behind him). • *(fig. fml) It was one piece of bad news hard on* (=soon after) *another.*

hard·ship /£'hɑːd·ʃɪp, $'hɑːrd-/ *n* (something which causes or an example of) difficult or unpleasant conditions of life • *The 1930's was a time of high unemployment and economic hardship in much of the United Kingdom.* [U] • *Hardship is part of life in this war-torn city.* [U] • *The drought is one more hardship in this already ravaged area.* [C] • *An hour's business meeting in Hawaii is a small hardship to endure for a week-long, expenses-paid holiday.* [C]

hard·top /£'hɑːd·tɒp, $'hɑːrd·tɑːp/ *n* [C] a car with a metal roof

hard up *adj* **harder up, hardest up** having very little money • *We're a bit hard up at the moment so we're not thinking in terms of holidays.* • *You're surely not trying to tell me that they're hard up when he gets a company director's salary!* • *(fig.) If you're so hard up* **for** (=haven't got many) *friends, why don't you join a club?*

hard·ware [COMPUTER] /£'hɑːd·weəʳ, $'hɑːrd·wer/ *n* [U] *specialized* the physical and electronic parts of a computer, rather than the instructions it follows • *He works for a firm that makes* **computer** *hardware.* • Compare SOFTWARE.

hard·ware [TOOLS] /£'hɑːd·weəʳ, $'hɑːrd·wer/ *n* [U] metal tools, materials and equipment used in a house or a garden, such as hammers, nails and screws • *a hardware shop/store/department* • **Hardware dealer** is *Am for* IRONMONGER. • **Hardware store** is *Am and Aus for* IRONMONGER. • [LP]> **Shopping goods**

hard·ware [MILITARY] /£'hɑːd·weəʳ, $'hɑːrd·wer/ *n* [U] *infml* equipment, esp. if it is for military use or if it is heavy • *The White House said yesterday that the ship was laden with tank parts, explosives, and other* **military** *hardware.*

hard·wood /£'hɑːd·wʊd, $'hɑːrd-/ *n* strong heavy wood used to make things which will last for a long time, esp. high-quality furniture, or the tree it comes from • *They're trying to persuade the government to stop the import of tropical hardwoods.* [C] • *The most effective type of door is made of solid hardwood or has at least a solid hardwood core.* [U] • Compare SOFTWOOD.

hard·y /£'hɑː·di, $'hɑːr-/ *adj* **-ier, -iest** strong; able to bear extreme conditions; able to work hard for a long time • *You have to be hardy to live in such an inhospitable place.* • *A few hardy souls continue to swim in the sea even in the middle of winter.* • A hardy plant can live through the winter without protection from the weather: *a hardy perennial*

har·di·ness /£'hɑː·dɪ·nəs, $'hɑːr-/ *n* [U]

hare [ANIMAL] /£heəʳ, $her/ *n* [C] *pl* **hares** or **hare** a small animal with fur and long ears that can run very fast and is like a large rabbit • *Hares have longer legs and ears than rabbits.* • *(esp. Br)* **Hare coursing** is the activity of chasing a hare using dogs. • [PIC]> **Wild animals in Britain**

hare [RUN] /£heəʳ, $her/ *v* [I always + adv/prep] *esp. Br* to run or go very quickly, usually in an uncontrolled way • *She was so pleased that she hared* **off** *down the road shouting.*

hare·bell /£ˈheə·bel, $ˈher-/, *Scot Eng also* **blue·bell** *n* [C] a wild plant found in northern parts of the world which has blue cup-shaped flowers

hare·brained /£ˈheə·breɪnd, $ˈher-/ *adj* (of plans or people) not practical; foolish • *That sounds like another of his harebrained* **schemes**!

Hare Krish·na /ˌhɑː·rɪˈkrɪʃ·nə/ *n* [U/C] a modern type of Hinduism in which the god KRISHNA is especially worshipped, or *(infml)* someone who lives by its system of belief

hare·lip /£ˌheəˈlɪp, $ˌher-/ *n* [C; U] (the condition in which someone has) a top lip divided into two parts at the middle because it did not develop in the usual way before birth

ha·rem /ˈhɑː·riːm, ˌ-ˈ-/ *n* [C] esp. in the past in some Muslim societies, the wives or other female sexual partners of a man, or the part of a house in which they live • *(fig. humorous) I noticed that Henry was surrounded by his harem* (= women who are sexually interested in him) *as usual at the party last night.*

har·i·cot (bean) /£ˈhær·ɪ·kəʊ, $-koʊ/ *n* [C] a small usually white bean used for making **baked beans**

hark /£hɑːk, $hɑːrk/, **heark·en** *v literary* to listen • *Hark, I hear a distant trumpet!* • *(humorous)* You might say **hark at him/her** to someone who has just accused you of something that you think they are guilty of themselves: *Hark at him calling me lazy when he never even walks anywhere if he can drive!* • *"Hark! the herald-angels sing"* (Christmas song written by Charles Wesley, 1739)

hark back *v adv* [I] (of someone) to remember something in the past, often repeatedly, or (of something) to suggest something from the past • *He's always harking back* **to** *his childhood and saying how things were better then.* • *The director's latest film harks back* **to** *the early years of cinema.*

har·le·quin /£ˈhɑː·lɪ·kwɪn, $ˈhɑːr-/ *n* [C] a humorous character in plays at the theatre, esp. in the past, who wears brightly-coloured clothes

Har·ley Street /£ˈhɑː·li, $ˈhɑːr-/ *n* [U; not after *the*] (the area around) a road in central London where many medical specialists have their treatment rooms

har·lot /£ˈhɑː·lət, $ˈhɑːr-/ *n* [C] *old use* a female PROSTITUTE (= someone who is paid for sex)

harm /£hɑːm, $hɑːrm/ *n* [U] physical or other injury or damage • *Both deny conspiring to cause actual bodily harm.* • *A mistake like that will* **do** *his credibility a lot of harm.* • *Missing a meal once in a while never* **did** *anyone (any) harm.* • *You could always ask Jim if they need any more staff in his office –* **(there's) no** *harm* **in** *asking* (= nobody will be annoyed and you might benefit). • *She* **meant no** *harm* (= did not intend to offend), *she was joking.* • *Getting involved at this stage will* **do more** *harm* **than good** (= be damaging rather than helpful). • *Cindy had a fright when her car skidded but she* **came to** *no harm* (= was not hurt). • **Out of harm's way** means in a position which is safe from harm or from which harm cannot be done: *The children will be here soon – you'd better put that plate out of harm's way.* • Ⓢ

harm *obj* /£hɑːm, $hɑːrm/ *v* [T] • *The government's reputation has already been harmed by a series of scandals.* • *The local community will be harmed if the factory does close down.* • *It wouldn't harm you to visit your grandma* (= You should visit her) *every now and then.* • **Harm a hair of/on** someone's **head** means to hurt someone even if it is only slightly: *Be warned – if you harm a hair of his head, you'll be sorry!*

harm·ful /£ˈhɑːm·fᵊl, $ˈhɑːrm-/ *adj* • *This group of chemicals is known to be harmful* (= causes harm) **to** *people with asthma.*

harm·ful·ly /£ˈhɑːm·fᵊl·i, $ˈhɑːrm-/ *adv*

harm·ful·ness /£ˈhɑːm·fᵊl·nəs, $ˈhɑːrm-/ *n* [U]

harm·less /£ˈhɑːm·ləs, $ˈhɑːrm-/ *adj* • Harmless means not able or not likely to cause harm: ○ *Ozone is fairly harmless to people, but it hurts plants.* ○ *Peter might look a bit fierce, but actually he's fairly harmless.* ○ *There were those who found the joke offensive, but Jackson insisted it was just a bit of harmless* **fun**.

harm·less·ly /£ˈhɑːm·lə·sli, $ˈhɑːrm-/ *adv*

harm·less·ness /£ˈhɑːm·lə·snəs, $ˈhɑːrm-/ *n* [U]

har·mon·i·ca /£hɑːˈmɒn·ɪ·kə, $hɑːrˈmɑː·nɪ-/, **mouth or·gan** *n* [C] a small rectangular musical instrument which is played by blowing or sucking air through one of the long sides at different places to make different notes

har·mon·y MUSIC /£ˈhɑː·mə·ni, $ˈhɑːr-/ *n* the sound of different notes being played or sung at the same time • *The group specializes in singing* **in (close)** *harmony.* [U] • *It is a simple melody with complex harmonies.* [C]

har·mon·ic /£hɑːˈmɒn·ɪk, $hɑːrˈmɑː·nɪk/ *adj specialized* • *harmonic complexity*

har·mon·ic /£hɑːˈmɒn·ɪk, $hɑːrˈmɑː·nɪk/ *n* [C] *specialized* • A harmonic is one of a special series of notes that a musical instrument can play which sound different from the other notes: *On stringed instruments, harmonics are played by holding your finger lightly on the string at a particular point and pulling and releasing the string.*

har·mon·i·ous /£hɑːˈməʊ·ni·əs, $hɑːrˈmoʊ-/ *adj* • Harmonious means having a pleasant tune or harmony.

har·mon·ize *(obj), Br and Aus usually* **-ise** /£ˈhɑː·mə·naɪz, $ˈhɑːr-/ *v* • To harmonize a tune is to add harmonies to it: *I've harmonized the song in the style of the Beach Boys.* [T] ○ *I can sing a tune but I find it hard to harmonize.* [I]

har·mon·y MATCH /£ˈhɑː·mə·ni, $ˈhɑːr-/ *n* [U] a good match of ideas or feelings, and in the way things are done, happen or appear; complete agreement • *racial harmony* (= good relations between different races) • *domestic harmony* (= good relations in the family or home) • *Imagine a society in which everyone lived together* **in (perfect)** *harmony.* • *Before the recent trouble there was a long period of* **peace and** *harmony.* • *The town's new buildings clash harshly with the medieval harmony of its old churches.* • *We must ensure that tourism develops* **in** *harmony* **with** *the environment.*

har·mon·i·ous /£hɑːˈməʊ·ni·əs, $hɑːrˈmoʊ-/ *adj* • *She seems to have enjoyed a fairly harmonious* (= friendly and peaceful) *relationship with all three of her children.* • *The government is understandably reluctant to do anything which might spoil the harmonious* (= friendly and peaceful) *relations between the country's ethnic groups.* • *In his later paintings he used a more harmonious* (= matching well together) *blend of colours.*

har·mon·i·ous·ly /£hɑːˈməʊ·ni·ə·sli, $hɑːrˈmoʊ-/ *adv*

har·mon·i·ous·ness /£hɑːˈməʊ·ni·ə·snəs, $hɑːrˈmoʊ-/ *n* [U]

har·mon·ize *(obj), Br and Aus usually* **-ise** /£ˈhɑː·mə·naɪz, $ˈhɑːr-/ *v* • *We need to harmonize* (= bring together) *the different approaches into a unified strategy.* [T] • *The plan is to harmonize* (= make similar) *safety standards across all the countries involved.* [T] • *He believes that it is simply not possible to harmonize theology* **with** *modern science.* [T] • *Four per cent of the population wanted summertime to end a month early to harmonize* **with** *European countries.* [I]

har·mon·iz·a·tion, *Br and Aus usually* **-i·sa·tion** /£ˌhɑː·mə·naɪˈzeɪ·ʃᵊn, $ˌhɑːr-/ *n* [U] • *The harmonization of relations between these ethnic groups will be hard to achieve.*

har·ness /£ˈhɑː·nəs, $ˈhɑːr-/ *n* [C] a piece of equipment, with straps and fastenings, used to control or hold in place a person, animal or object • *a safety harness* • *a baby harness* • *a parachute harness* • *a lifting harness* • *She lifted the harness over the horse's head.* • *The guide dog wears a working harness which allows it to lead its blind owner.* • If two or more (groups of) people work **in harness**, they work together to achieve something. • If you are **back in harness**, you have returned to work after a period of absence: *What's it like to be back in harness after your maternity leave?*

har·ness *obj* /£ˈhɑː·nəs, $ˈhɑːr-/ *v* [T] • *A donkey, harnessed* **to** *a long pole, walked round in a circle to draw water.* • *He harnessed the baby* **into** *her car seat.* • *(fig.) There is a great deal of interest in harnessing* (= controlling in order to use) *wind and waves as new sources of power.*

harp INSTRUMENT /£hɑːp, $hɑːrp/ *n* [C] a large musical instrument which has strings stretched across it. It is often triangle-shaped and is played by a seated person who PLUCKS (= pulls with their fingers) the strings.

harp·ist /£ˈhɑː·pɪst, $ˈhɑːr-/ *n* [C]

harp REPEAT /£hɑːp, $hɑːrp/ *v* [I always + adv/prep] *infml esp. disapproving* to talk or esp. complain about something many times • *He's always harping* **(on) about** *lack of discipline.* • *I know you want to go to Paris. Don't keep harping* **on (about** *it)!*

har·poon /£ˌhɑːˈpuːn, $ˌhɑːr-/ *v* [T], *n* [C] (to kill esp. a WHALE by throwing or shooting from a gun) a long heavy SPEAR (= long sharp weapon) fixed to a rope

harp·si·chord /£ˈhɑːp·sɪ·kɔːd, $ˈhɑːrp·sɪ·kɔːrd/ *n* [C] a large musical instrument with a row of keys which the player presses, causing a set of wire strings to be pulled. It was played esp. in the 17th and 18th centuries.

har·py /£'hɑː·pi, $'hɑːr-/ *n* [C] in Greek MYTHOLOGY (= ancient stories), a creature with the head of a woman and the body of a bird, or *(disapproving)* a fierce unpleasant woman who shouts a lot • *(disapproving) Though portrayed by the media as a man-hating harpy, she is nothing of the sort when you meet her.*

har·ri·dan /£'hær·ɪ·dᵊn, $'her-/ *n* [C] *disapproving* a fierce and frightening, esp. older woman, who shouts a lot • *He's got an absolute harridan of a mother-in-law.*

har·row /£'hær·əʊ, $'her·oʊ/ *n* [C] a large piece of equipment which is pulled behind a TRACTOR (= farm vehicle) to break the earth into small pieces ready for planting

har·row *(obj)* /£'hær·əʊ, $'her·oʊ/ *v* [I/T]

har·row·ing /£'hær·əʊ·ɪŋ, $'her·oʊ-/ *adj* extremely upsetting because connected with suffering • *His first novel tells the harrowing story of the death of his youngest child.* • *Last night's news contained some harrowing famine reports.* • *I can't bear to hear first hand accounts of torture – I find it too harrowing.* • *For many women, the harrowing prospect of giving evidence in a rape case can be too much to bear.*

har·rowed /£'hær·əʊd, $'her·oʊd/ *adj* • *She came back from the hospital* **looking** *very harrowed/with a harrowed* **expression** *on her face.*

har·rumph /hə'rʌmpf/ *v infml esp. humorous* to express annoyance and disapproval, often not by speaking but making a noise • *I didn't hear what he said – he sort of harrumphed and walked off.* [I] • *"Absolute nonsense!" harrumphed the colonel.* [+ clause]

har·ry *obj* /'hær·i/ *v* [T] *fml* to repeatedly demand something from (someone), often causing them to feel anxious or angry • *She harried the authorities, writing letters and getting up petitions.*

har·ried /'hær·id/ *adj* • *I saw a harried-looking mother at the checkout trying to manage two small children and a mountain of shopping.*

harsh /£hɑːʃ, $hɑːrʃ/ *adj* **-er, -est** unpleasant, unkind, cruel or unnecessarily severe • *The children had had a harsh upbringing/life/father.* • *We thought the punishment was rather harsh for such a minor offence.* • *"There is no alternative," she said in a harsh voice.* • *He said some harsh* **words** (= spoke unkindly) *about his brother.* • A harsh light or colour is one that is unpleasantly bright and strong.

harsh·ly /£'hɑːʃ·li, $'hɑːrʃ-/ *adv* • *Don't treat him/speak to him too harshly.*

harsh·ness /£'hɑːʃ·nəs, $'hɑːrʃ-/ *n* [C]

ha·rum–sca·rum /£ˌheə·rəm'skeə·rəm, $ˌher·əm'sker·əm/ *adv* [after v] *dated* uncontrolled, in all directions, without a plan • *The fans ran harum-scarum onto the football pitch.*

har·vest /£'hɑː·vɪst, $'hɑːr-/ *n* the time of year when crops are brought in, or the activity of collecting, or the crops which are collected • *the wheat/potato/grape/apple harvest* [C] • *We had a good harvest* **(of** *potatoes) this year.* [C] • *Farmers are reporting a* **bumper** (= very big) *harvest this year.* [C] • *It won't be long now till harvest (time).* [U] • *The grain harvest is set to fall from last year's record level, necessitating large imports of wheat.* [C] • *We were fortunate enough to be visiting the Loire during the grape harvest.* [C] • *Harvest failures had caused famines on a scale not seen for a century.* • A **harvest festival** is a celebration which is held in churches and schools in the autumn, which gives thanks for crops and food. • *"The harvest of a quiet eye"* (William Wordsworth in the poem *Intimations of Immortality,* 1807) • LP› **Holidays**

har·vest *(obj)* /£'hɑː·vɪst, $'hɑːr-/ *v* • *In the US, winter wheat is harvested in the early summer.* [T] • *We'll begin to harvest next week.* [I] • *The ban imposed on harvesting shellfish on the north-east coast has been lifted.* [T]

har·vest·er /£'hɑː·vɪ·stəʳ, $'hɑːr·vɪ·stɚ/ *n* [C] • A harvester is a machine for harvesting crops or *(old use)* a person who harvests crops: *a combine harvester/a root harvester* • PIC› **Farming**

har·vest·man *(pl* **-men***)* /£'hɑː·vɪst·mæn, $'hɑːr-/, *Am infml* **dad·dy long·legs** *n* [C] a small creature with eight legs that looks like a SPIDER

has /hæz/ *he/she/it form of* HAVE

has–been /'hæz·biːn/ *n* [C] *infml disapproving* a person who in the past was famous, important, admired or good at something, but is no longer any of these • *It's every actor's greatest fear that one day people will just regard them as an old has-been.*

hash FAILURE /hæʃ/ *n* [U] *infml* a failure, a bad attempt • *He* **made a** *complete* **hash of** *his last exam.*

hash up *obj,* **hash** *obj* **up** /hæʃ/ *v adv* [M] *infml* • *The first interview was all right but I rather think I hashed up* (= failed) *the second one.*

hash FOOD /hæʃ/ *n* [U] *esp. Am* a mixture of meat, potatoes and vegetables cut into small pieces and baked or fried • *corned beef hash* • *(Am) We stopped at a coffee shop and ordered eggs and hash.* • **Hash browns** are small pieces of potato pressed into flat shapes and fried: *We had eggs, toast, bacon and hash browns for a stunningly cheap $3·50.*

hash DRUGS /hæʃ/ *n* [U] *infml for* HASHISH

hash·ish /hæʃ'iːʃ/ *n* [U] a drug, illegal in many countries, made from the CANNABIS plant and usually smoked

has·n't /'hæz·ᵊnt/ *short form of* has not • *Hasn't he grown!* • *She hasn't even spoken to me yet.*

has·sle /'hæs·l̩/ *n infml* (a situation causing) difficulty or trouble • *I can't face the hassle of moving house again.* [U] • *My boss has been* **giving** *me a lot of hassle this week.* [U] • *It's one of the few bars that women can go to and not* **get** *any hassle from men.* [U] • *I've bought a new computer programme which is supposed to take the hassle out of working out my income tax position.* [U] • *It was such a hassle trying to get my bank account changed that I nearly gave up.* [U] • *I should have taken it back to the shop but I just didn't think it was worth* **(all)** *the hassle.* [U] • *For me it's worth paying extra to travel by train just so that I can avoid all the hassles of driving.* [C]

has·sle *obj* /'hæs·l̩/ *v* [T] *infml* • *I'll do it in my own time – just stop hassling me!* • *The children keep hassling me* (= repeatedly and forcefully trying to persuade me) **to** *take them to Disneyland.* [+ obj + *to* infinitive]

haste /heɪst/ *n* [U] *disapproving* (too much) speed • *Unfortunately the report was prepared* **in** *haste and contained several inaccuracies.* • **In** *her* **haste** *to get up from the table, she knocked over a cup.* [+ *to* infinitive] • *His father had just died and he didn't want to marry with* **indecent/unseemly** *haste.* • *(old use)* **Make haste** (= Hurry up)! • *(Br saying)* 'More haste, less speed' means that if you try to do things too quickly, it will take you longer in the end.

has·ten *(obj)* /'heɪ·sᵊn/ *v fml* • You hasten something by acting in order to make it happen sooner: *I was grateful for his letter which hastened the course of the enquiry.* [T] ○ *There is little doubt that poor medical treatment hastened her death.* [T] • If you hasten **to** do something, you quickly do it: *The president hastened to reassure his people that he was in perfect health.* [+ *to* infinitive] • If you hasten **to say/add** something, you want to make it clear: *It was an unfortunate decision and I hasten to say it had nothing to do with me.* [+ *to* infinitive] ○ *"I detest everyone in this office – except you, Justin." she hastened to add.* [+ *to* infinitive]

hast·y /'heɪ·sti/ *adj* **-ier, -iest** • Hasty means done in a hurry, sometimes without the necessary care or consideration: *He warned against making hasty decisions.* ○ *Now let's not leap to any hasty conclusions.* ○ *We saw the rain and made a hasty retreat into the bar.* ○ *I think perhaps we were a little hasty* **in** *judging him.*

has·ti·ly /'heɪ·stɪ·li/ *adv* • *I ate a hastily prepared sandwich and shot out the door.* • *"He's looks good for his age. Not that 55 is old," she hastily added.*

has·ti·ness /'heɪ·stɪ·nəs/ *n* [U]

hat /hæt/ *n* [C] a covering for the head that is not part of a piece of clothing • *a straw/felt/fur/leather/cotton hat* • *a woolly/knitted hat* • *a wide-brimmed hat* • *Johnny was* **wearing** *a new hat that Angi had made for him.* • When someone says they are wearing a particular hat, they mean they are carrying out only one of the various jobs or responsibilities they have: *"Which hat are you wearing* (= Which is your main responsibility) *at this event?"* ○ *I'll be wearing my parent's hat* (= I'm acting only as a parent) *at the school concert.* • If you say that you **take** your **hat off to** someone, you mean that you admire them for an achievement: *So Emma actually manages to juggle two small children and a full-time job, does she? Well, I take my hat off to her.* • *(dated)* If you say **hats off to** someone you are praising and thanking them for doing something helpful: *Hats off to Connie for finding such a splendid venue for a party!* • If you **throw/toss** your **hat into the ring**, you show your intentions, or *(esp. Am)* you enter a, usually political, competition. • See also BOWLER HAT.

hat·band /'hæt·bænd/ *n* [C] a strip of material which is fixed around the outside of the CROWN (= the part which fits over the head) of a hat • *He tucked the ticket into his hatband.* • PIC› **Hats**

hat·box /£'hæt·bɒks, $-bɑːks/ *n* [C] a round container for storing or carrying hats

hatch *(obj)* EGG /hætʃ/ *v* to (cause an egg to) break in order to allow a young animal to come out • *The eggs/young birds/turtles have started to hatch* **(out)**. [I] • *The children hatched the eggs/the chickens in the warm kitchen.* [T]

hatch·er·y /£'hætʃ·ᵊr·i, $'-ɚ-/ *n* [C] • A hatchery is a place where large numbers of eggs, esp. fish eggs, are hatched and the young are looked after.

hatch *obj* PLAN /hætʃ/ *v* [T] to make (a plan, esp. a secret plan) • *It was in August of '78 that the Bolton brothers hatched their* **plan/plot** *to kill their parents.*

hatch *obj* MARK /hætʃ/, **cross-hatch** *v* [T] to mark with a set of diagonal lines • *The middle part of the road has been hatched with white lines to stop people overtaking.* • *The hatched section of the diagram shows the increase in sales last year.*

hatch OPENING /hætʃ/, **hatch·way** /'hætʃ·weɪ/ *n* [C] an opening through a wall, floor, etc., or the cover for it • *Hand the parcels to me through the hatch.* • *Pick up your food at the serving hatch.* • *The crane swung the box up through the cargo hatch/the hatchway.* • *(saying)* 'Down the hatch!' means I am going to drink this. You say it before swallowing a drink, esp. an alcoholic one.

hatch·back /'hætʃ·bæk/, **hatch** *n* [C] a car which has an extra door at the back which can be lifted up to allow things to be loaded in • PIC› **Vehicles**

hatch·et /'hætʃ·ɪt/ *n* [C] a small tool with a blade which cuts when you hit things with it; a small AXE • Someone who is **hatchet-faced** has a thin, hard and unpleasant or cruel face. • *(infml)* A **hatchet job** is a cruel written or spoken attack on someone or something: *Currie has condemned the profile of the minister as a hatchet job.* ○ *Fleck was certainly not the only critic to* **do a hatchet job on** *his latest novel.* • *(infml)* A **hatchet man** is someone who is used for unpleasant and difficult or violent jobs: *In a recession, the axe is always poised and the company hatchet man works overtime.*

hate /heɪt/ *n* an extremely strong dislike • *She gave him a look of pure hate.* [U] • *The feelings of hate grew stronger every day.* [U] • *One of my* **pet** *hates* (= one of the main things I dislike) *is people who use your name all the while when they're speaking to you.* [C] • If someone receives **hate mail** they get unpleasant or cruel letters from someone who dislikes them. • See also HATRED.

hate *(obj)* /heɪt/ *v* [not *be hating*] • *Kelly hates her teacher.* [T] • *She hated the cold dark days of winter.* [T] • *I hate it when you do that.* [T] • *I have always hated speaking in public.* [+ *v-ing*] • *I hate him telling me what do to all the time.* [+ obj + *v-ing*] • *I hate* (= do not want) **to** *interrupt, but it's time we left.* [+ *to* infinitive] • *I'd hate* (= would not like) *you* **to** *think I didn't appreciate what you'd done.* [+ obj + *to* infinitive] • *In this terrible conflict how can we avoid the children learning to hate?* [I] • *(infml)* Children sometimes say that they hate someone's **guts**, meaning that they really do hate them: *Tell Harry from me that I hate his guts!*

hat·ed /£'heɪ·tɪd, $-t̬ɪd/ *adj* • *He was the most hated teacher in the school.* • *Reluctantly she put on the hated shoes.*

hate·ful /'heɪt·fᵊl/ *adj dated* • Hateful means very unpleasant: *I never wear grey because it reminds me of my hateful school uniform.*

hate·ful·ness /'heɪt·fᵊl·nəs/ *n* [U]

-hat·er /£-'heɪ·təʳ, $-t̬ɚ/ *combining form* • *I may be a feminist, but I'm certainly not some sort of* **man**-*hater.* • *He's a self-confessed* **woman**-*hater.*

hat·red /'heɪ·trɪd/ *n* [U] • Hatred is an extremely strong feeling of dislike: *What is very clear in these letters is Clark's passionate hatred* **of** *his father.* ○ *The motive for this shocking attack seems to be racial hatred.* ○ *Orbach believes that the root cause of the so-called slimmer's disease is self-hatred and fear of rejection.*

hat·pin /'hæp·pɪn/ *n* [C] a long metal pin, often with a decorated end, which is pushed through a woman's hat and hair to keep the hat on the head

hat·stand /'hæt·stænd/ *n* [C] a vertical pole with hooks at the top for hanging hats and coats on

hat·ter /£'hæt·əʳ, $'hæt̬·ɚ/ *n* [C] **mad as a hatter**, see at MAD MENTALLY ILL

hat trick *n* [C] a set of three similar successes, esp. in sport • *I think the crowd are all wondering whether Jackson will score his third goal this match and make it a hat trick.* • *Having already bowled two men out I thought I'd go for the hat trick.* • *After two election victories the government clearly has hopes of a hat trick.*

haugh·ty /£'hɔː·ti, $'hɑː·t̬i/ *adj* **-ier**, **-iest** *disapproving* unfriendly and seeming to consider yourself better than other people • *She has a rather haughty manner which I* *find offputting.* • *Her personality, at times brittle, defensive and haughty, irritated many Canadians.*

haugh·ti·ly /£ˈhɔː·tɪ·li, $ˈhɑː·t̬ɪ-/ *adv*

haugh·ti·ness /£ˈhɔː·tɪ·nəs, $ˈhɑː·t̬ɪ-/ *n* [U]

haul *(obj)* PULL /£hɔːl, $hɑːl/ *v* to pull (something heavy) slowly and with difficulty • *They hauled the boat out of the water.* [T] • *She hauled herself* **up** *into the tree.* [T] • *The tractor hauled* **away** *the barricade.* [M] • *They helped to haul the man's body out of sight.* [T] • *He hauled* **(away) on** *the rope and the door came open suddenly.* [I] • *(fig. infml) He was hauled* **(up)** (= was forced to appear) *in court/in front of a magistrate/before the headteacher.* [T/M] • *(Am infml)* If you **haul ass** you move very quickly: *When the shooting started we hauled ass out of there.*

haul /£hɔːl, $hɑːl/ *n* [C usually sing] • *Give another haul* (= Pull) *on the rope.* • *Give me a haul up* (= Pull me up) *onto the wall.*

haul·age /£ˈhɔː·lɪdʒ, $ˈhɑː-/ *n* [U] • *The firm built up a good business in* **road** *haulage* (= transporting goods by road). • *He owns a haulage company.*

haul·i·er *Br and Aus* /£ˈhɔː·li·əʳ, $ˈhɑː·li·ɚ/, *Am* **haul·er** /£ˈhɔː·ləʳ, $ˈhɑː·lɚ/ *n* [C] • A haulier is a business or a person involved in a business which transports goods by road: *Hauliers are protesting about the new regulations.*

haul AMOUNT /£hɔːl, $hɑːl/ *n* [C] the amount of something obtained • *Fishermen have been complaining of poor hauls* **(of** *fish) all season.* • *The police said it was the largest haul* **of** *illegal drugs this year.*

haul PERIOD OF TIME /£hɔːl, $hɑːl/ *n* [C] the time taken for a journey or for something to happen • *It's quite a haul* (= a long and difficult walk) *up the hill.* • *From there it was a* **long** *haul/only a* **short** *haul* (= long and difficult/short and easy journey) *back to our camp.* • *We broke the longest section of the route into two short hauls.* • *It was a long haul* (= It took a long time and was difficult), *but the alterations to the house are finished at last.* • A **long**-haul/**short**-haul flight is a long/short journey by air.

haunch /£hɔːntʃ, $hɑːntʃ/ *n* [C] the top part of the leg between the knee and the waist • *a haunch* **of** *venison* • If you **sit/squat on** your haunches you bend your knees, keeping your feet on the floor, until your bottom touches the back of your feet.

haunt *obj* SPIRIT /£hɔːnt, $hɑːnt/ *v* [T] (of a GHOST (= spirit of a dead person)) to appear in a place repeatedly • *A ghostly lady haunts the stairway looking for her children.* • *This room is said to be haunted.*

haunt·ed /£ˈhɔːn·tɪd, $ˈhɑːn·t̬ɪd/ *adj* • *There's a haunted* **house** *in the village.*

haunt·ing /£ˈhɔːn·tɪŋ, $ˈhɑːn·t̬ɪŋ/ *n* • *It was not a routine case of haunting.* [U] • *He was asked to investigate the strange haunting* **of** *the family home.* [C]

haunt *obj* REPEATEDLY TROUBLE /£hɔːnt, $hɑːnt/ *v* [T] to cause repeated suffering or anxiety • *Fighting in Vietnam was an experience that would haunt him for the rest of his life* • *Thirty years after the fire he is still haunted by* **images** *of death and destruction.* • *Johnson was haunted by* **memories** *of his unhappy childhood well into his adult life.* • *Our* **imaginations** *were still haunted by the war.* • *It was over five years since their relationship had ended but she still haunted his dreams.* • *For some reason she's still haunted by* **the spectre of** *of his ex-wife.*

haunt·ed /£ˈhɔːn·tɪd, $ˈhɑːn·t̬ɪd/ *adj* • Haunted means showing signs of suffering or severe anxiety: *Then he looked up at her again, with those haunted* **eyes**. ○ *He had a haunted* **look** *about him.*

haunt·ing /£ˈhɔːn·tɪŋ, $ˈhɑːn·t̬ɪŋ/ *adj* • Something which is haunting cannot be forgotten, sometimes in a way that is pleasant and sometimes in a way that makes you anxious: *a haunting memory/melody/refrain* • *haunting beauty* • *a haunting fear*

haunt PLACE /£hɔːnt, $hɑːnt/ *n* [C] a place often visited • *Jamaica has been a* **favourite** *haunt of Americans and Canadians for the last 20 years.* • *This pub used to be one of your* **old** *haunts, didn't it Jim?* • *The village is a favourite* **tourist** *haunt.* • *During those early visits to Bradford, Bren would take me round the haunts of his childhood.*

haunt *obj* /£hɔːnt, $hɑːnt/ *v* [T] • *He haunts* (= visits repeatedly) *the bars where drug dealers are known to operate.*

haute cou·ture /£ˌəʊt·kuˈtjʊəʳ, $ˌoʊt·kuːˈtʊr/ *n* [U] (the business of making) expensive clothes of original design and high quality • *haute couture collections/shows* • *Despite the hard times, haute couture is alive and well and living in Paris.*

haute cui·sine /£ˌəʊt·kwɪˈziːn, $ˌoʊt-/ *n* [U] cooking of a high standard, typically French cooking • *Tony tends to spend his holidays motoring around France, indulging his taste for haute cuisine.* • *It's not haute cuisine by any means but it's good quality basic food.*

hau·teur /£əʊˈtɜːʳ, $hoʊˈtɜːr/ *n* [U] *fml or literary* formal and unfriendly behaviour, with an appearance of being better than other people • *He presided over the first day of the meeting with his customary detached hauteur.*

have PERFECT TENSE /hæv/, **'ve** *v aux* [+ v-ed; not *be having*] he/she/it **has** /hæz/, *past* **had** /hæd/ used with the past participle of other verbs to form the present and past perfect tenses • *I have/I've heard that story before.* • *He hasn't/I haven't* (= He has not/I have not) *visited London before.* • *I would have/I would've/I'd have bought it but it was too small for me.* • *She has had/She's had an unhappy time recently.* • *Have you seen Roz?* • *"Have we been invited?" "Yes, we have/No we haven't."* • *"I've passed my driving test." "Have you? Congratulations!"* • *They still hadn't* (= had not) *had any news when I spoke to them yesterday.* • *(fml) Had I known* (= if I had known) *you were coming, I'd have booked a larger room.* • LP **Auxiliary verbs, Tenses**

have *obj* POSSESS /hæv/, **'ve**, *Br and Aus* **have got** *v* [T not *be having*] he/she/it **has** /hæz/, *past* **had** /hæd/ to own or possess • *We have a dog/a new car.* • *He has plenty of money but no style.* • *The dictionary hasn't got an entry for the word.* • *I've got a French mother/two brothers.* • *"Have you got a cold/a pain/a headache/back trouble?" "No, I haven't."* • *(fml) Have you reason to think he'll refuse?* • *Will you have time/Have you got time to finish the report today?* • *Have you got the time?* (= Please tell me the time.) • *I haven't (got) any sympathy for these troublemakers.* • *I've got a suggestion/a plan/a reason/an idea.* • *I've got several papers* **to** (= which I must) *edit before Wednesday.* [+ obj + *to* infinitive] • *(slang)* To have someone can mean to have sex with them: *He asked me how many men I'd had.* • *(infml) Have we got anything* **on** (= any information about or records for) *this organization?* • *Have you got any money/your keys/a penknife* **on** *you* (= Are you carrying it with you)*?* • If you have esp. clothing **on**, you are wearing it: *She had on a thick sweater, gloves and a hat.* [M] • If you have something **on**, you have planned to do it: *Have you got anything on this week?* [M] ○ *I've got something on this Tuesday but I'm free on Wednesday.* See also HAVE ON. • If you say that someone has **the** honesty/patience/etc. **to** do something, you mean that they are honest, patient etc. enough to do it: *At least he had the good sense to turn the gas off.* [+ obj + *to* infinitive] ○ *He had the gall to tell me that I was fat!* [+ obj + *to* infinitive] • *His speech was really funny – we didn't know he* **had it in** *him* (= possessed this ability). • *(infml) He's a good player, but he'***s got nothing on** (= is not as good as) *his brother.* • *(infml) She's always* **had it in for** *me* (= disliked me). • To *(Br and Aus slang)* **have it off**/*(Br slang also)* **have it away** is to have sex: *He was having it off* **with** *his friend's wife.* • 'Have got' is commonly used, but only in the present tense.

haves /hævz/ *pl n* • *I would like to see a decrease in the gap between the haves* (= people with lots of property and money) *and the* **have-nots** (= poor people) *in our society.*

have *obj* DO /hæv/ *v* [T] he/she/it **has** /hæz/, *past* **had** /hæd/ to do (an action) • *It's so hot I'd love to have a swim* (= to swim). • *We had a short walk* (= We walked) *after lunch.* • *I've never done it before but I'd like to have a try* (= to try). • *Don't disturb him while he's having a snooze* (= is sleeping). • *Would you like to have a wash/bath/shower* (= to wash/bath/shower)*?* • *We're going to have* (= eat) *lunch at Fiona's.* • *I'll have the report ready for you by tomorrow.* [+ obj + adj] • When a woman has a baby, she gives birth to it: *My mother had three boys before she had me.* ○ *I hear his wife's having a baby* (= is pregnant). • LP **Do: verbs meaning 'perform'**

have *obj* RECEIVE /hæv/, *Br and Aus* **have got** *v* [T] he/she/it **has** /hæz/, *past* **had** /hæd/ to receive, accept or allow (something) to happen • *"Here, have some more coffee." "No thanks."* • *I've just had news of my family/a letter from John.* • *My mother's having visitors/the children* **(to** *stay) next week.* [+ obj + *to* infinitive] • *We had his hamster* (= cared for it) *for a week while he was in Mauritius* • *We've got* (= We have been or will be given) *sausages for lunch today.* • *They've got Ian's father staying with them.* [+ obj + v-*ing*] • *Let me have the book* **back** (= Give it back to me) *next week.* • *In the end they solved their problems and she had him* **back** (= allowed him to come and live with her again). • *(infml) I'm afraid this old vacuum cleaner* **has had it** (= no longer works properly and cannot be repaired). • *(infml)* **I've had it with** (= I have suffered because of and can no longer bear) *foreign holidays.* • *I looked in all the shops for string but there was* **none to be** *had* (= none that anyone could obtain). • *I kept telling him that you were French but he* **wouldn't** *have* **it** (= would not accept that it was true). • **I won't** *have those kids running all over my flower beds* (= I refuse to let them do this). [+ obj + v-*ing*] • *(infml) I asked him to help out, but he* **wasn't having any (of it)** (= wasn't willing).

have *obj* CAUSE /hæv/ *v* [T] he/she/it **has** /hæz/, *past* **had** /hæd/ to cause (something) to happen or (someone) to do something • *We have the house painted every three years.* [+ obj + v-*ed*] • *We're having the house painted next month.* [+ obj + v-*ed*] • *If you wait, I'll have someone collect it for you.* [+ obj + infinitive without *to*] • *The film soon had us crying.* [+ obj + v-*ing*] • *Guy'll have it working in no time.* [+ obj + v-*ing*] • *He had my sweater* **off** *before I could say a word of protest.* • *She had her parents* **down** (= invited them to stay) *for a week in the summer.* • *You'll have to have that tooth* **out** (= it needs to be removed) • *We had the boat* **out** (= went out in the boat) *for the first time this week.* See also HAVE OUT. • *We often have friends* **over/round** (= invite them to come) *on a Saturday night.* • You can also use have when something happens to you without you causing it: *She had her car stolen* (= it was stolen) *last week.* [+ obj + v-*ed*] • *(Br infml) He was* **had up** (= taken to court for a trial) **for** *burglary.* • *Why don't you just pull up all the plants and* **have done with it** (= deal with and finish the whole matter in that way). • LP **Get: verbs meaning 'cause'**

have *obj* EXPERIENCE /hæv/ *v* [T] he/she/it **has** /hæz/, *past* **had** /hæd/ to experience (something) • *We're having a wonderful time/holiday/stay in Venice.* • *She had her car stolen last week.* [+ obj + v-*ed*] • *We didn't have any difficulty/problem finding the house.* • *He hasn't been having much luck recently.* • *(saying)* 'A good time was had by all' means everyone enjoyed themselves.

have MUST /hæv/, *Br and Aus* **have got** *v* [+ *to* infinitive] he/she/it **has** /hæz/, *past* **had** /hæd/ to need to or be forced • *I have (got)* **to** *go to Manchester tomorrow.* • *What time have we got* **to** *be there?* • *Do we have* **to** *finish this today?* • *We will have* **to** *start keeping detailed records.* • *They have had* **to** *change their plans suddenly.* • *I'm not going back there unless I have* **to**. • *"Come on now, put your toys away." "Oh, dad, do I have* **to**?"

have *obj* **on** *Br, Am* **put on** *v adv* [T] *infml* to trick (someone) or to persuade (someone) that something is true when it isn't • *That's your new car? You're having me on!* • *We had him on* **that** *he had won a free holiday.* [+ obj + (*that*) clause] • See also **have on** at HAVE POSSESS.

have *obj* **out** *v adv* [T] *infml* to argue or discuss (something) with someone you disagree with • *They had* **it** *out in front of all the guests.* • *Don't keep complaining, just have* **it** *out* **with** *him* **once and for all** (= solve the problem completely by discussing it). • *We'll have* **the whole thing** *out* (= discuss it completely) *tomorrow.*

ha·ven /ˈheɪ·vᵊn/ *n* [C] a safe or peaceful place • *The garden was a haven* **from** *the noise and bustle of the city.* • *They wanted to provide* **safe** *havens for the refugees.* • Haven is an old word for HARBOUR (= safe place for boats) and is sometimes found in place names: *Whitehaven/Peacehaven* • (NL)

ha·ven't /ˈhæv·ᵊnt/ *short form of* have not • *Haven't you heard? He's leaving.* • *I haven't ever been to Australia.*

hav·er·sack /£ˈhæv·ə·sæk, $ˈ-ɚ-/ *n* [C] *dated* a bag, often made from strong rough cloth, with one or two shoulder straps

hav·oc /ˈhæv·ək/ *n* [U] confusion and lack of order, esp. causing damage or trouble • *A scene of havoc met their eyes when they opened the door.* • *The room never looked the same after the havoc* **of** *the fire.* • *The storm* **wreaked** (= caused) *havoc* **on** *the garden, uprooting several trees.* • *The delay* **played** (= caused) *terrible havoc* **with** *their travel arrangements.*

haw SLOW TO ACT /£hɔː, $hɑː/ *v* [I] **hum and haw**, see at HUM

haw LAUGH /£hɔː, $hɑː/ *exclamation* used in writing to suggest a loud rather unpleasant laugh • *"Then he fell over the cat." "Haw haw."*

hawk BIRD /£hɔːk, $hɑːk/ *n* [C] a type of large bird which catches small birds and animals for food • Someone who is **hawk-eyed** watches and notices everything that happens: *You have to be hawk-eyed when there are small children about.* ○ *Hawk-eyed store detectives stood by the doors.*

hawk PERSON /£hɔːk, $hɑːk/ *n* [C] a person who strongly supports the use of force in political relationships rather than discussion or other more peaceful solutions • *The hawks are pressing for a vigorous response to the challenge.* • Compare DOVE BIRD.

hawk·ish /£ˈhɔː·kɪʃ, $ˈhɑː-/ *adj* • *The president is conventionally hawkish on foreign policy.* • *He is on the left of the party and finds their defence stance a little too hawkish.*

hawk·ish·ness /£ˈhɔː·kɪʃ·nəs, $ˈhɑː-/ *n* [U]

hawk *obj* SELL /£hɔːk, $hɑːk/ *v* [T] to sell goods informally in public places • *On every street corner there were traders hawking their wares, everything from plastic sunglasses to 'genuine' antiques at half their usual price.* • *In order to survive, companies have to learn to hawk their products in commercial marketplaces.*

hawk·er /£ˈhɔː·kəʳ, $ˈhɑː·kɚ/ *n* [C] • *As the police approached, the hawkers rolled their goods in a blanket and ran into the crowd.*

haw·ser /£ˈhɔː·zəʳ, $ˈhɑː·zɚ/ *n* [C] a strong thick rope, often made of steel

haw·thorn /£ˈhɔː·θɔːn, $ˈhɑː·θɔːrn/ *n* [U] a type of small wild tree with THORNS (= sharp points) which has white or pink flowers in spring and small red fruits in the autumn

hay /heɪ/ *n* [U] grass which is cut, dried and used as animal food or as covering material • If you **make hay while the sun shines** you make good use of an opportunity. • **Hay fever** is an illness caused by POLLEN (= powder from plants) which gives you watery, ITCHY eyes and makes you sneeze: *Sue suffers from hay fever.*

hay·stack /ˈheɪ·stæk/ *n* [C] a large pile of HAY (= cut dried grass) in a field • PIC **Farming**

hay·wire /£ˈheɪ·waɪəʳ, $-waɪr/ *adj* [after v] *infml* not working correctly, not organized, confused • *The television's* **gone** *haywire.* • *I was pregnant at the time and my hormones were haywire.*

haz·ard DANGER /£ˈhæz·əd, $-ɚd/ *n* something dangerous and likely to cause damage • *A high incidence of lung disease is one of the known hazards of the job.* [C] • *Drivers faced the dual hazards of black ice and frozen snow.* [C] • *Smoking is both a* **health** *hazard and a fire hazard.* [C] • *He compared radiation risks with other kinds of potential daily hazard.* [C] • *They decided to reduce the number of people in the hazard zone round the chemical factory.* • *The busy traffic entrance was a hazard* **to** *pedestrians.* [C] • **Hazard (warning) lights** are orange lights at the front and back of a car which turn on and off repeatedly to warn other drivers of danger. They are also road signs which warn drivers of danger by giving different messages in a pattern of lights. • (CS) (PL) (RUS)

haz·ard·ous /£ˈhæz·ə·dəs, $ˈ-ɚ-/ *adj* • *a hazardous journey/occupation/sport/chemical*

haz·ard·ous·ly /£ˈhæz·ə·də·sli, $ˈ-ɚ-/ *adv* • *He leaned hazardously out of the window.*

haz·ard *obj* RISK /£ˈhæz·əd, $-ɚd/ *v* [T] to risk doing (something, esp. making a guess, suggestion, etc.), or to put (something) at risk • *No-one would hazard a* **guess** *of how long it would take to finish.* • *(fml) He hazarded* **that** (= based his actions on the guess that) *the examiner might be more lenient after a good lunch.* [+ *that* clause] • *The policy hazarded the islands and put the lives of the inhabitants at risk.* • (CS) (PL) (RUS)

haze /heɪz/ *n* (a) thin fog caused by water, smoke or dust, or an effect of heat which prevents things being seen clearly • *A haze* **of** *dust hung over the field.* [C] • *The road shimmered in the* **heat** *haze.* [U]

haze o·ver /heɪz/ *v adv* [I] • *As we got nearer the sea the sky began to haze over with a fine mist.*

haz·y /ˈheɪ·zi/ *adj* **-ier, -iest** • *a hazy day/sky* • *(fig.) a hazy* (= unclear) *thought/picture* • *(fig.) There remained only the haziest memories of that childhood birthday party.* • *(fig.) I'm very hazy* **about** *what happened after we hit the other car.*

haz·i·ly /ˈheɪ·zɪ·li/ *adv* • *(fig.) She only hazily* (= unclearly) *remembered her last visit twenty years ago.*

haz·el TREE /ˈheɪ·zᵊl/ *n* [C] a small tree that produces nuts that can be eaten

haz·el COLOUR /ˈheɪ·zᵊl/ *adj* (esp. of eyes) light brown, greenish brown or yellowish brown in colour

haz·el·nut /ˈheɪ·zᵊl·nʌt/, **fil·bert**, **cob(nut)** *n* [C] the nut of the HAZEL tree which has a hard brown shell • PIC **Nut**

HB /ˌeɪtʃˈbiː/ *n* [C], *adj* [not gradable] *Br abbreviation for* hard black (= printed on pencils to show that the LEAD in the pencil is medium hard)

H–bomb /£ˈeɪtʃ·bɒm, $-bɑːm/ *n* [C] a **hydrogen bomb**, see at HYDROGEN

he /hiː/ *pronoun* used to refer to a man, boy or male animal that has already been mentioned • *Don't ask Andrew, he won't know.* • *There's no need to be frightened – he's a very friendly dog.* • He is sometimes used to refer to a person whose sex is not known. Some people do not like this use because it is offensive to women, and prefer *he/she, s/he* or *they*: *The modern traveller can go where he likes.* ○ *As soon as a baby is born, he often begins to take an interest in the world around him.* • A **he-man** is a man who is very strong and who likes to show everyone how strong he is. • [LP> **Sexist language**

he /hiː/ *n* [C] • *How can you tell whether the fish is a he* (= a male) *or a she?*

head [BODY PART] /hed/ *n* the part of the body that contains the eyes, nose, mouth and ears and the brain • *Put this hat on to keep your head warm.* [C] • *Stephen banged his head on the low ceiling when he stood up.* [C] • *She nodded her head vigorously in agreement.* [C] • A head is a person or animal when considered as a unit: *The dinner cost £20 a/per head* (= for each person). [U] ○ *I did a quick head* **count** (= calculated how many people there were). ○ *They own a hundred head of* (= 100) *cattle.* [U] • A head can also be as a measure of length: *Her horse won by a head.* [U] ○ *Paul is a head taller than Andrew.* [U] • *She's got* **an old/wise head on young shoulders** (= is young but wise). • If you **bang/knock** people's **heads together**, you try to make them understand the situation and change their behaviour. • If you **beat/bang/knock** your **head against a brick wall**, you try to do something that is very difficult to achieve: *I've been banging my head against a brick wall, trying to get her to understand.* • To **bite/snap** someone's **head off** is to speak to them angrily: *I asked what was wrong, but he just bit my head off.* • To **bury/have** your **head in the sand** is to refuse to think about unpleasant facts, although they will have an influence on your situation: *She's burying her head in the sand and ignoring the signs that she may have a serious illness.* • If something **comes to a head** or someone **brings** something **to a head**, a situation reaches a point where something must be done about it: *Things had been going badly in the office, and they were finally brought to a head when six people resigned at once.* • **From head to foot/ From head to toe** means completely: *The dog was covered in mud from head to foot.* • *(Br)* To **get/put** your **head down** is to direct all your efforts to the particular task you are involved in: *I'm going to get my head down and try and finish this report before I go home today.* • To **get/put** your **head down** is also to sleep: *I'm just going to put my head down for a couple of hours.* • *(taboo slang)* To **give head** is to perform FELLATIO or CUNNILINGUS. • To **give** someone their **head** is to allow them to do what they want to do without trying to help them or give them advice. • *(infml)* To **head-butt** someone is to hit them with force on the head or in the face using the front of your head: *Oliver gave his brother a* **head-butt** (= an act of hitting him in this way). • If someone has their **head (buried/stuck) in a book**, they are reading: *Rose always has her head buried in a book.* • If you have your **head in the clouds**, you are foolish because you are not aware of the realities of a situation. • *(infml)* If you laugh, shout, scream etc. your **head off**, you do it very noisily and for a long time: *The dog ran out of the house, barking its head off.* • A **head of hair** is a lot of hair: *Even as a tiny baby, she had a* **good/thick** *head of red hair.* • If someone is **head over heels (in love)**, they are completely and uncontrollably in love. • If you have your **head screwed on**, you are very practical and wise: *Ask Lois to help – she's got her head screwed on* **the right way**. • If someone or something is **head and shoulders above** other people or things, they are a lot better than them: *She is head and shoulders above all the other actors in the film.* • If you say that **heads will roll**, you mean that particular people will be punished if a mistake is made. • *(infml)* If you are **in over** your **head** , you are involved in an unpleasant situation that you cannot get out of: *Sean tried to pay back his gambling debts, but he was in over his head.* • If you **keep** your **head above water**, you are just able to continue doing what you do: *The business is in trouble, but we are keeping our heads above water.* • To **keep** your **head down** is to avoid trouble: *The boss is in a bad mood today, so keep your head down.* • If someone does something **over** your

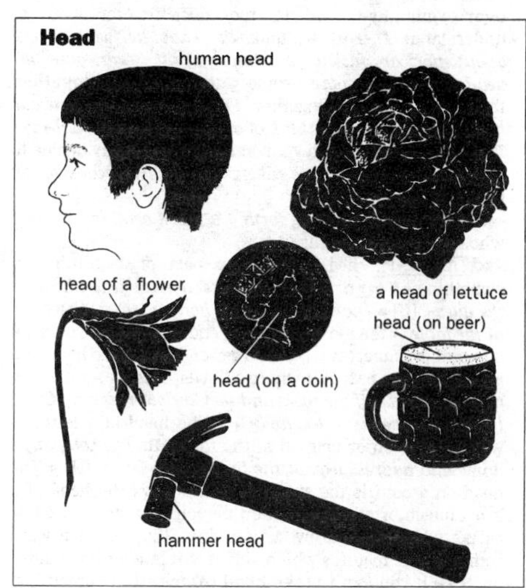

head, they do not tell you about it or ask for permission to do it: *How dare he* **go** *over my head and order this new equipment?* • *(Br)* To **put/stick** your **head above the parapet** is to say or do something risky: *Nobody ever criticized the boss's decisions, because they were all too afraid to put their heads above the parapet.* • A **head cold** is COLD (= illness) which makes you sneeze a lot. • A **head-to-head (contest)** is a direct competition between two people or teams of almost equal ability. • **Head lice** are very small insects that live on the human head. • An accident which is **head-on** is one where two vehicles hit each other with their front parts: *The car crossed the road and hit a truck head-on.* • A **head restraint** is a support for the head that is fixed to a car seat and is intended to stop the head from being forced back too sharply in an accident. • If you have a **head start**, you have an advantage over other people in a competition or race: *You've got a head start* **over/on** *others trying to get the job because you've got relevant work experience.* • *(Am)* **Head Start** is a set of educational courses provided by the US central government for disadvantaged children below school age. • [PIC> **Head**

-head·ed /-ˈhed·ɪd, ˌ-ˈ-/ *combining form* • *a many-headed monster*

head *obj* /hed/ *v* [T] • *Johnson headed the ball* (= hit it with his head) *into the back of the net.*

head·er /£ˈhed·əʳ, $-ɚ/ *n* [C] • In football, a header is an act of hitting the ball with your head. • A header is also an act of jumping or falling with your head going first: *He* **took** *a header into the water.*

head·less /ˈhed·ləs/ *adj* [not gradable] • *The headless body* (= one with the head cut off) *of a sheep was found in a ditch.* • *(humorous) I've been rushing around all day* **like a** *headless* **chicken** (= I've been very busy and active).

head [MIND] /hed/ *n* [C] the mind and mental abilities • *You need a* **clear** *head to be able to drive safely.* • *What put that* **(idea) into** *your head* (= What made you think that)? • *I can't get that tune/that man* **out of** *my head* (= I cannot stop hearing the tune in my mind/thinking about that man). • **Use** *your head* (= Think more carefully)! • *Harriet has a* **(good** *) head* **for** *figures* (= She is very clever at calculating numbers). • *(Br) Do you have* **a** *head* **for heights** (= Are you able to be in high places without fear)? • *(infml)* If you say that you **can't get** your **head around** something, you mean that you cannot understand it: *I just can't get my head around these tax forms.* • To **get** something **into** one's **head** is to believe or decide something: *When will you get it into your head that he's not coming back.* ○ *One day, she got it into her head* (= decided for no reason) *that we all hated her.* • If something **goes to** someone's **head**, it makes them think that they are very important and makes them a less pleasant person: *Don't let fame/success go to your head.* • If alcohol **goes to** your **head**, it makes you feel slightly drunk: *A glass of sherry always goes straight to my head.* • If you **keep** your **head** or **keep a cool head**, you stay calm despite great difficulties. • To be **off** your **head** is to be extremely foolish, or to be experiencing the strong effect of alcohol or drugs: *Ben must be off his head if he thinks Dad'll give him the money to buy a motorbike.* • If something is over your **head,** it is too difficult for you to understand: *I tried to take in what he was saying about nuclear fusion, but most of it went over my head.* • If two or more people **put** their **heads together**, they plan something together: *I'm sure that if we put our heads together, we can think of a solution to the problem.* • To **take** something **into** your **head** is to suddenly decide to do it: *They seem to have taken it into their heads to get married.*

-head /-hed/ *combining form* • *a crack-head* (= someone who depends on the drug CRACK)

head [TOP PART] /hed/ *n* the top part or beginning of something • *They arrived early to get a place at* **the** *head* **of** *the queue.* [U] • *Diana, the guest of honour, sat at* **the** *head* **of** *the table* (= the most important end of it). [U] • The head of a nail, hammer, etc. is its larger end. [C] • The head of a plant is the top part of it where a flower or leaves grow: *Cut the dead heads off the roses and they'll flower again.* [C] ○ *I bought two heads of lettuce.* [C] • The head of a letter is what is written or printed at the top of it: *The company's name and address was at the head of the letter.* [U] • The head on a coin is the side of it that shows the head of a king, queen or other important person. You ask **heads or tails?** when you throw a coin into the air and want someone else to guess which side it will land or has landed on. [C] • If you **can't make head (n)or tail of** something, you cannot understand it at all: *I can't make head or tail of these instructions on the packet.* • *(saying)* 'Heads I win, tails you lose' means that whatever happens I am going to win. • If beer has a head on it, it has a layer of white bubbles on top of it after it has been poured: *You have to pour Guinness slowly so there isn't too big a head on it.* [C] • The head of a river is the upper part of it. [C] • A head **of steam** is the force produced by a large amount of steam in an enclosed space: *(fig.) The investigating team is building up a head of steam* (= preparing for action) *and will soon be ready to put its plans into action.* [C] • The head of a PIMPLE (= small swelling on the skin) is the top part when it contains PUS (= yellowish liquid). [C] • [PIC] **Head**

head *obj* /hed/ *v* [T] • *The Queen's carriage headed* (= was at the front of) *the procession.* • *The article was headed* (= had as its title) *'How to cut your heating bills'.* • **Headed notepaper** (also **Letterhead**) is writing paper with a person's or organization's name and address printed at the top of it.

head [LEADER] /hed/ *n* [C] someone in charge of or leading an organization, group, etc. • *the head of the History department* • *(esp. Br)* A head is a HEADTEACHER: *I stood outside the head's study waiting to speak to her.* • A **head of state** is the official leader of a country, but is often someone who has few or no real political powers: *The King or Queen is the head of state in Britain, but political power is exercised by the Prime Minister and the Cabinet.*

head /hed/ *adj* [not gradable] • *the head* (= most important) *gardener/waiter* • *Our* **head office** (= most important office) *is in London.* • *(esp. Br)* A head **boy** or head **girl** is a boy or girl who is the leader of the other PREFECTS and often represents his or her school on formal occasions.

head *obj* /hed/ *v* [T] • *She heads* (= is in charge of) *one of Britain's leading travel firms.* • *Judge Hawthorne was chosen to head* **up** *the team investigating the allegations of abuse.* [M]

head·ship /'hed·ʃɪp/ *n* [C] • Headship is the position of being in charge of an organization or *(esp. Br)* in charge of a school, or the period during which a particular person holds this position: *(esp. Br) Dozens of well-qualified teachers applied for the headship.* ○ *(esp. Br) A lot of changes have taken place during her headship.*

head [DEVICE] /hed/ *n* [C] the part of a **tape recorder** or **video recorder** which touches the TAPE to record and play music, speech etc. • *You need to keep your tape recorder heads clean by using a special cleaning fluid.*

head [GO] /hed/ *v* [I always + adv/prep] to go in a particular direction • *I was heading* **out of** *the room when she called me back.* • *We were heading* **towards** *Kumasi when our truck broke down.* • *He headed straight* **for** (= went towards) *the fridge.* • *(fig.) They are heading* **for** *disaster* (= Their behaviour is making this situation likely) *if they aren't careful.* • *I think we ought to head* **back/home** (= return to where we started) *now, before it gets too dark.*

head·ed /'hed·ɪd/ *adj* [after v; not gradable] • *Which way are you headed* (= are you going)? • *She is headed* **for** (= likely to have) *trouble if she keeps drinking so much.*

head off *obj*, **head** *obj* **off** *v adv* [T] to force (someone or something) to change direction • *I tried to head the dog off by running towards it.* • *(fig.) The company is putting up wages in an attempt to head off a strike* (= prevent this from happening).

head·ache /'hed·eɪk/ *n* [C] a pain you feel inside your head • *I've* **got** *a* **splitting** (= severe)/**slight** *headache.* • *That noise is giving me a headache.* • A headache is also something that causes you great difficulty and worry: *Finding a babysitter for Saturday evening will be a major headache.* • [LP] **Feelings and pains**

head·ach·y /'hed,eɪ·ki/ *adj* • *I knew I was getting a cold when I started feeling tired and headachy* (= having headaches).

head·band /'hed·bænd/ *n* [C] a narrow strip of material worn around the head, usually to keep your hair or PERSPIRATION out of your eyes

head·bang·ing /'hed,bæŋ·ɪŋ/ *n* [U] the activity of shaking your head up and down with great force to the beat of ROCK music • *Too much headbanging is thought to cause brain damage in young people.*

head·bang·er /£'hed,bæŋ·əʳ, $-ɚ/ *n* [C] • *The place was full of long-haired headbangers playing invisible guitars.* • A headbanger is also a stupid or foolish person.

head·board /£'hed·bɔːd, $-bɔːrd/ *n* [C] a vertical board at the end of a bed behind where your head rests • [PIC] **Beds and bedroom**

head·case /'hed·keɪs/ *n* [C] *infml* a person who behaves strangely or who is very foolish or violent

head·cheese /'hed·tʃiːz/ *n* [U] *Am for* BRAWN [FOOD]

head·dress /'hed·dres/ *n* [C] a decorative covering for the head • *The men going into the mosque were dressed in flowing white robes and headdresses.*

head·first /£,hed'fɜːst, $-'fɜːrst/, *Am and Aus also* **head·long** *adj, adv* [not gradable] with the head going first • *He made a headfirst dive into the lake.* • *She fell headfirst into the muddy pool.* • *(fig.) You shouldn't rush headfirst* (= without thinking or preparation) *into starting your own business without proper advice.*

head·gear /£'hed·gɪəʳ, $-gɪr/ *n* [U] hats or other coverings that are worn on the head • *The department store stocks a wide range of headgear.* • *When riding a bicycle, you should wear the proper headgear.*

head·hunt·er [FIGHTER] /£'hed,hʌn·təʳ, $-t̬ɚ/ *n* [C] a member of a TRIBE that keeps the heads of its enemies whom it kills

head·hunt·er [PERSUADE] /£'hed,hʌn·təʳ, $-t̬ɚ/ *n* [C] *infml* a person who tries to persuade someone to leave their job by offering them another job with more pay and a higher position

head·hunt *obj* /'hed·hʌnt/ *v* [T] • *She was headhunted by a rival firm who offered her a company directorship.*

head·ing /'hed·ɪŋ/ *n* [C] words written or printed at the top of a text as a title • *The article was published under the heading 'Time travel in the 21st century'.*

head·land /'hed·lənd, -lænd/ *n* [C] a piece of land that sticks out from the coast into the sea

head·less /'hed·ləs/ *adj* [not gradable] See at HEAD [BODY PART]

head·light /'hed·laɪt/, **head·lamp** /'hed·læmp/ *n* [C usually pl] a large powerful light at the front of a vehicle, usually one of two • *I could see a car's headlights coming towards me.* • *It was foggy, and all the cars had their headlights* **on** (= so that they were giving out light). • **Dip** *your headlights* (= Change the direction of their light so that it is shining downwards) *when you see another car coming towards you.* • Compare SIDELIGHT [LIGHT]. • [PIC] **Car**

head·line /'hed·laɪn/ *n* [C] a line of words printed in large letters as the title of a story in a newspaper, or the main points of the news that are broadcast on television or radio • *The news of his death was splashed in headlines across all the newspapers.* • *I turned on the radio to get the eight o'clock headlines.* • *The comedian* **hit/made/reached/grabbed** *the headlines* (= became written about a lot) *when he was accused of eating a pet hamster.* • Compare **by-line** at BY [CAUSE]; DATELINE.

head·line *obj* /'hed·laɪn/ *v* [T + obj + n] • *The story was headlined* (= had as its headline) *'Killer dogs on the loose'.*

head·long /£'hed·lɒŋ, $-lɑːŋ, ,-'-/ *adv, adj* [not gradable] with great speed and/or without thinking • *The child ran headlong into a wall.* • *Little did they realize that they were walking headlong into danger.* • *The car skidded and* **plunged** *headlong over the cliff.* • *Thousands of soldiers are* *in headlong retreat.* • *In the headlong* **rush** *to buy houses, many people got into debt.* • Headlong is also *Am and Aus for* HEADFIRST.

head·man /ˈhed·mən, -mæn/ *n* [C] *pl* **-men** the CHIEF or TRIBAL leader of a village

head·phones /£ˈhed·fəʊnz, $-foʊnz/ *pl n* a device with a part to cover each ear through which you can listen to music, radio broadcasts, etc. without other people hearing

head·quart·ers /£ˌhedˈkwɔː·təz, $-ˌkwɔːr·t̬ɚz/ (*abbreviation* **HQ**) *n* [C + sing/pl v] *pl* **headquarters** the main offices of an organization such as the army, police or a business company • *Letter bombs were sent to the army's Southeast district headquarters.* • *The company's headquarters is/are in Amsterdam.*

head·rest /ˈhed·rest/ *n* [C] something that supports the head, esp. a support fixed to the back of the seat of a car

head·room /ˈhed·ruːm, -rʊm/ *n* [U] the amount of space below a roof or bridge • *It's a small car but there's lots of headroom.* • *The bridge is low and there isn't enough headroom for tall vehicles.*

head·scarf /£ˈhed·skɑːf, $-skɑːrf/ *n* [C] *pl* **headscarves** /£ˈhed·skɑːvz, $-skɑːrvz/ a usually square piece of material worn on the head by women • *a silk headscarf* • PIC› **Hats**

head·set /ˈhed·set/ *n* [C] a set of HEADPHONES, esp. one with a MICROPHONE fixed to it

head·ship /ˈhed·ʃɪp/ *n* [C] see at HEAD [LEADER]

head·stone /£ˈhed·stəʊn, $-stoʊn/ *n* [C] a GRAVESTONE • *A headstone was erected in the Garden of Remembrance to commemorate the soldiers who had died.*

head·strong /£ˈhed·strɒŋ, $-strɑːŋ/ *adj* very determined to do what you want without listening to others • *She was a headstrong child, always getting into trouble.* • *He's always so headstrong and never thinks before he acts.*

head·teach·er *esp. Br, female* **head·mi·stress**, *male* **head·mast·er** /£ˌhedˈtiː·tʃəʳ, $ˈhedˌtiː·tʃɚ/, *Am and Aus usually* **prin·ci·pal** *n* [C] someone who is in charge of a school • *My mum used to be a headteacher.* • *Headteachers gathered in Brighton today for their annual conference.*

head·way /ˈhed·weɪ/ *n* [U] **make headway** to advance or get closer to achieving something • *I'm trying to learn to drive, but I'm not making much headway* (**with** *it*). • *The company seems to be making some headway against its competitors.* • *Little headway has been made so far* **in** *the negotiations.*

head·wind /ˈhed·wɪnd/ *n* [C] a wind blowing in the opposite direction to the one you are moving in • *The runners had to battle against a* **stiff/strong** *headwind.*

head·y /ˈhed·i/ *adj* **-ier, -iest** having a powerful effect, making you feel slightly drunk or excited • *a heady wine/perfume* • *He remembered the heady experience of first love.* • *In the heady* **days** *of their youth, they thought anything was possible.*

heal *(obj)* /hɪəl/ *v* to make or become well again, esp. after a cut or other injury • *The wounds were gradually healing* **(up/over)**. [I] • *The plaster cast will help to heal the broken bone.* [T] • *(fig.) His broken heart will take a long time to heal* (= stop feeling pain). [I] • *(fig.) Peace talks were held to try to heal* (= end) *the growing rift between the two sides.* [T]

heal·ing /ˈhɪə·lɪŋ/ *adj, n* • *Doctors are becoming interested in the healing properties of sugar ointments on wounds.* • *Spiritual healing* (= the activity of making someone well again) *is an ancient practice.* [U] • *He'd been involved in exorcisms and healings* (= acts of making someone well again) *in many parts of the region.* [C]

heal·er /£ˈhɪə·ləʳ, $-lɚ/ *n* [C] • A healer is a person who has the power to heal people without using ordinary medicines: *The healer uses the laying on of hands or hands held slightly apart from a person's body to work on its energy field.*

health /helθ/ *n* [U] the condition of the body and the degree to which it is free from illness, or the state of being well • *You must look after your health.* • *How's your health these days?* • *I gave up smoking for health reasons.* • *He gave up work because of* **ill-health**. • *At the age of seventy-three she is still* **enjoying** (= she still has) **good** *health.* • *After a course of antibiotics he was soon restored to health* (= made well again). • *She has been* **in (very) good/bad** *health* (= well/ill) *recently.* • *"Here's to Trevor and Pam!" we said, raising our glasses and* **drinking (to)** *their health* (= drinking as a sign that we hope they will be well and successful). • *(fig.) The health* (= condition) *of the economy is still causing great concern.* • In Britain, a **health authority** is an organization that is responsible for hospitals and medical services in a particular area. • A **health centre** is a building in which several doctors have offices and where people go to visit them. • A **health farm**/*(Am usually)* **health spa** is a place where you go for a holiday and eat healthy food, take exercise, etc. • **Health food** is food that is believed to be good for you because it does not contain chemicals or much sugar or fat. Compare **junk food** at JUNK [RUBBISH]. • **Health insurance** is an arrangement with a special company to which you pay money in exchange for that company paying most or all of your medical expenses. • *(Am)* A **health maintenance organization** (*abbreviation* **HMO**) is an organization which people join so that they can obtain health care. It serves a particular area, offers the service of a limited number of doctors and is paid for by its members or their employers. • *(Br)* A **health visitor** is a person employed to give advice to people, esp. the parents of very young children and older people, about health care, sometimes by visiting them in their own homes. • LP› **Phrases and customs**

heal·thy (**-ier, -iest**) /ˈhel·θi/, *Am also* **health·ful** /ˈhelθ·fəl/ *adj* • *All the children are strong and healthy.* • *Drinking lots of water helps to give you healthy skin.* • *She'll only eat healthy food* (= food that is good for you). • *It's not healthy* (= It is not good for people) *to be so interested in death.* • A healthy amount of something is a large amount of it, that shows success: *The business showed a healthy profit in its first year.* • A healthy **attitude** is one which is reasonable or shows that you have a strong character: *She has a healthy disrespect for authority.*

heal·thi·ly /ˈhel·θɪ·li/ *adv* • *Eat healthily* (= Eat foods that are good for you) *and take plenty of exercise.*

health·care /£ˈhelθ·keəʳ, $-ker/ *n* [U] the set of services provided by a country or an organization for the treatment of the physically and the mentally ill • *Attempts to control the cost of providing healthcare have so far proved unsuccessful.* • *Healthcare workers are some of the lowest paid people in the country.*

heap /hiːp/ *n* [C] an untidy pile or mass of things • *a heap of earth/books/old clothes* • *We piled all the newspapers into a heap.* • *His clothes lay* **in** *heaps on the floor.* • *No, I can't come out with you this evening – I've got* **a (whole) heap of** (= a lot of) *work to do.* • *The woman staggered and collapsed* **in a heap** (= fell heavily and did not move). • People who are at **the bottom of the heap** are poor and unsuccessful and have the lowest position in society. People at **the top of the heap** have money and are successful and have the highest position in society: *The unemployed become* **stuck** *at the bottom of the heap.*

heap *obj* /hiːp/ *v* [T] • *He heaped the leaves* **(up)** *in the corner of the garden.* [T/M] • *They heaped the food* **on** *our plates/They heaped our plates* **with** *food* (= They put a lot of food on our plates). • *(fml)* To heap praise/criticism **on** someone is to give them a lot of praise/criticism: *The press heaped insults on the team's manager after the team had lost six games in a row.*

heaped /hiːpt/ *adj* • *Add a heaped teaspoonful of sugar.*

heaps /hiːps/ *pl n, adv infml* • *Have some more cake – there's heaps* (= a lot). • *Let Sarah pay for dinner, she's got heaps* **of** (= a lot of) *money.* • *Our new house is heaps* (= much) *bigger than our last one.*

hear *(obj)* [RECEIVE SOUND] /£hɪəʳ, $hɪr/ *v past* **heard** /£hɜːd, $hɜːrd/ to receive or become aware of (a sound) using your ears • *She heard a noise outside.* [T] • *My grandfather is getting old and can't hear very well.* [I] • *You'll have to speak up, I can't hear you* (= hear your voice). [T] • *I heard/I could hear someone* (= the sound of someone) *calling my name.* [+ obj + v-*ing*] • *At eight o'clock Jane heard him go out* (= heard the sound he made as he went out). [+ obj + infinitive without *to*] • *(esp. Am infml) Yeah, I hear you/hear what you're saying* (= I understand what you are telling me) *– you don't like my attitude.* [T] • *(infml) She knew that if she brought her boyfriend home her mother would start* **hearing wedding bells** (= expecting them to get married.) • *(infml) He's offered to wash the dishes – I* **must be hearing things** (= I must be imagining this because it is so unlikely). • If you say that you can **not/hardly/barely hear** yourself **think**, you mean that you cannot give your attention to anything: *There was so much noise in the classroom that I could hardly hear myself think.* • LP› **Sound**

hear·er /£ˈhɪə·rəʳ, $ˈhɪr·ɚ/ *n* [C] • *Sound from a fire-engine siren appears to drop in pitch as it moves away from the hearer.*

hear·ing /£'hɪə·rɪŋ, $'hɪr·ɪŋ/ *n* [U] • *He's getting old and his hearing* (=ability to hear) *isn't very good.* • *They were saying things about her* **in/within** *her hearing* (=She was close enough to them to hear what they were saying). • A **hearing aid** is a device worn inside or next to the ear by people who cannot hear well in order to help them to hear better. • Ⓙ

hear *(obj)* BE TOLD /£hɪəʳ, $hɪr/ *v past* **heard** /£hɜːd, $hɜːrd/ to be told or informed (of); receive news • *Have you heard the news?* [T] • *If you haven't heard by Friday, assume I'm coming.* [I] • *Have you heard* **what's happened?** [+ *wh-*word] • *I hear* **(that)** *you're going abroad.* [+ (*that*) clause] • *Have you heard* **about** *Jane getting married* (=Has someone told you this news)? [I] • *I* **have** *heard all these arguments* **before** (=I am already aware of them). [T] • If you hear **from** someone, you get a letter or telephone call from them, or they tell you something: *We haven't heard from her for ages.* [I] ○ *You'll be hearing from my solicitors* (=They will write to you about my complaint). [I] ○ *Martin, perhaps we could hear from you* (=you could tell us) *about what you think.* [I] • To hear **of** something is to receive news about it: *This is the first time I've heard* **of** *the problem.* [I] • To hear something **of** someone is to receive news about them: *We haven't heard anything of Jan for months.* [I] • If you **have** heard **of** someone or something, you have a little knowledge about them or it: *"Do you know Derrida?" "I've heard of him."* [I] ○ *She said she'd* **never** *heard of word processors.* [I] • **Do you hear** is a way of emphasizing that you want people to give their attention to what you are saying: *I won't stand for this rudeness, do you hear?* • *If Mary gets that promotion, we'll never* **hear the end of it** (= she'll never stop talking about it). • If someone says **Hear, hear!**, they are strongly agreeing with what someone else has just said. • If you **hear tell (of)** something, someone tells you about it: *There are fairies at the bottom of the garden, or so I hear tell.* ○ *Have you heard tell of the fairies at the bottom of the garden?* • If you **will not hear of** something, you refuse to allow it: *I tried to give him back the money I owed him, but he wouldn't hear of it.*

hear *obj* LISTEN /£hɪəʳ, $hɪr/ *v* [T] *past* **heard** /£hɜːd, $hɜːrd/ to listen to (someone or something) attentively or officially • *I heard a really interesting programme on the radio this morning.* • *I heard the orchestra play at Carnegie Hall last summer.* [+ obj + infinitive without *to*] • *An audience gathered to hear him speak.* [+ obj + infinitive without *to*] • *(fml) Lord, hear our prayers.* • *The case will be heard* (=officially listened to) *by the High Court.* • To hear someone **out** is to listen to them and let them finish speaking before you start to speak. [M] • LP› **Sound**

hear·er /£'hɪə·rəʳ, $'hɪr·ɚ/ *n* [C] • *In making her speech, she took care not to insult or patronize her hearers.* • *Jokes establish an intimacy between the teller and the hearer.*

hear·ing /£'hɪə·rɪŋ, $'hɪr·ɪŋ/ *n* [C] • A hearing is an official meeting that is held to gather the facts about an event or problem: *A disciplinary hearing will examine charges of serious professional misconduct against three surgeons.* • *I think we should give him a* **(fair)** *hearing* (= we should listen to what he wants to say) • Ⓙ

heark·en /£'hɑː·kᵊn, $'hɑːr-/ *v* [I] *literary* to listen

hear·say /£'hɪə·seɪ, $'hɪr-/ *n* [U] information you have heard, although you do not know whether it is true or not • *They can't be accused of the crime because the evidence against them is all hearsay.*

hearse /£hɜːs, $hɜːrs/ *n* [C] a vehicle used to carry a body in a COFFIN to a funeral • PIC› **Vehicles**

heart ORGAN /£hɑːt, $hɑːrt/ *n* [C] the organ that sends the blood around your body • *I listened to his chest to see if his heart was still* **beating.** • *Her parents took her to the United States for a heart and lung transplant.* • *He's got a weak/bad heart* (=His heart is not healthy). • *My* **heart bleeds for** (=I feel great sadness about) *the children who have lost their parents.* • *(humorous) John complains he only has two cars – my* **heart bleeds for** *him* (=I certainly do not feel sadness about that)! • *Her* **heart skipped/missed a beat** (=She felt excited or nervous) *when he said "There's something I want to ask you".* • A **heart attack** is a serious medical condition in which the heart does not get enough blood, and which causes great pain and often leads to death: *Although John* **had** *a heart attack three years ago, he now has a healthy and active life.* ○ *(fig.) I almost* **had** *a heart attack* (=was very surprised or shocked) *when I found out how much the book cost.* • **Heart failure** is when the heart stops working correctly and sometimes stops completely. *(fig.) Don't come up behind me like that – you*

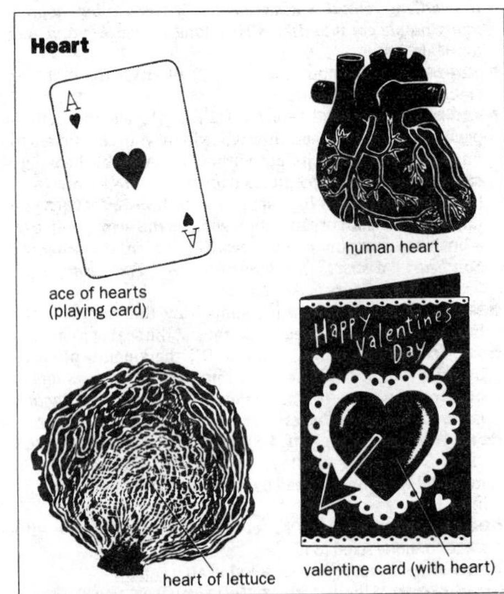

nearly **gave** *me* **heart** *failure* (=made me frightened). • A **heart murmur** is a condition in which unusual sounds can be heard in the heart, sometimes as a result of a fault in its structure. • PIC› **Heart** Ⓙ

heart EMOTIONS /£hɑːt, $hɑːrt/ *n* used to refer to a person's character, or the place within a person where their feelings or emotions are considered to come from • *She has a soft/kind/good heart* (=She is a kind person). [C] • *He has a hard/cold/cruel heart* (=He is an unpleasant person). [C] • *Their gratitude came* **from the** *heart* (=was sincere). [U] • *I love you, and I mean it* **from the bottom of** *my heart* (=very sincerely). [C] • *I love you* **with all** *my heart* (=very much). [C] • *He said he'd never marry but he had a* **change of** *heart* (=his feelings changed) *when he met her.* [U] • *Homelessness is a subject very* **close/dear/near to** *her heart* (=is very important to her and she has strong feelings about it). [C] • *He* **broke** *her heart* (=made her very sad) *when he left her for another woman.* [C] • *It* **breaks** *my heart* (=makes me feel very sad) *to see him so unhappy.* [C] • *They say he died of a* **broken** *heart* (=because he was so sad). [C] • *(dated) It* **does** *my heart* **good** (=makes me very happy) *to see those children so happy.* [C] • *His heart* **leapt** (=He suddenly felt very excited and happy) *when the phone rang.* [C] • *My heart* **sank** (=I felt sad and disappointed) *when I heard the news.* [C] • *She's a woman* **after** *my* **own heart** (=We have similar opinions). • *She's* **all heart** (=She is very kind and generous). • *(humorous) He says that he wants to marry her for her money and you say that's a good enough reason – you're* **all heart** (=you are not very kind)! • *My father can still recite the poems he learned* **(off) by heart** (=in such a way that he could say them from memory) *at school.* • *Don't make me write it again!* **Have a heart** (=Show some kindness and sympathy)! • *(literary) He promised to give his beloved wife her* **heart's desire** (= everything she wanted). • *(Br infml) Their* **hearts were in** *their* **boots** (=they felt worried and anxious) *when they realized that they would have to tell him the bad news.* • *I tried to look interested, but my* **heart wasn't in it** (=I did not feel interested or enthusiastic). • *My* **heart was in** *my* **mouth** (=I was extremely nervous) *when I opened the letter.* • *(literary) She loves those children* **heart and soul** (= completely). • *He is bad-tempered sometimes but his* **heart is in the right place** (=intentions are good). • *She has a* **heart of gold** (=is very generous and kind.) • *Sometimes I think my teacher has a* **heart of stone** (=is unkind or cruel). • *I didn't want to believe it, but* **in my heart of hearts** (=in my most secret and true thoughts) *I knew that it was true.* • *She has* **set** *her* **heart on** *having* (=wants very much to have) *a pony.* • If you do something **to** your **heart's content**, you do something enjoyable for as long as you want to do it: *When I go to the beach I shall read to my heart's content.* • A **heart-to-heart** (talk, discussion, etc.) is a serious conversation between two people, usually close friends, where they talk honestly about their feelings: *I think we should have a heart-to-heart.* • **Heart-searching** is thinking very seriously about your feelings, usually before making an important decision. • *"The Heart is a Lonely Hunter"* (title of a book by Carson McCullers, 1940) • *"There are two tragedies in life. One is not to get your heart's desire. The other is to get it."* (George Bernard Shaw in *Man and Superman*, 1903) • Ⓙ

-heart·ed /£-ˈhɑː·tɪd, $-ˈhɑːr·t̬ɪd/ *combining form* • -hearted means having a character or feelings of the stated type: *a cold-hearted judge* ○ *a light-hearted play* ○ *a kind-hearted nurse*

-heart·ed·ly /£-ˈhɑː·tɪd·li, $-ˈhɑːr·t̬ɪd-/ *combining form* • *cold-heartedly* • *light-heartedly* • *kind-heartedly*

-heart·ed·ness /£-ˈhɑː·tɪd·nəs, $-ˈhɑːr·t̬ɪd-/ *combining form* • *cold-heartedness* • *light-heartedness* • *kind-heartedness*

heart·less /£ˈhɑːt·ləs, $ˈhɑːrt-/ *adj* • *Don't be so heartless* (=cruel)! • *He was evicted on Christmas Day by a heartless landlord.*

heart BRAVERY /£hɑːt, $hɑːrt/ *n* [U] bravery or determination or hope • *You're doing really well – don't* **lose** *heart now.* • **Take** *heart – things can only get better.* • *Emily* **took** *heart* **from** *her tutor's praise and wrote another story.* • *When Sally asked me to look after her pet mouse, I didn't* **have the heart** *to refuse* (=I could not refuse because I felt that would be unkind). • *She's one of those people who* **puts heart and soul into** (=puts a lot of effort into) *their work.* • Ⓙ

heart CENTRE /£hɑːt, $hɑːrt/ *n* the central or most important part • *The demonstrators will march through* **the** *heart* **of** *the capital.* [U] • *A disagreement about boundaries is* **at the** *heart* **of** (=is the most important part of) *of the two countries' dispute.* [U] • *The recession is striking at the heart* **of** *industry* (=is harming the most important part of it). [U] • *Let's get to the heart* **of the matter** (=the most important thing). [U] • The heart of a vegetable, esp. a leafy one, is its firm central part: *artichoke hearts* [C] ○ *the heart of a lettuce* [C] • *"Deep in the Heart of Texas"* (title of a song written by June Hershey, 1941) • *"Heart of Darkness"* (title of a book by Joseph Conrad, 1902) • Ⓙ

heart SHAPE /£hɑːt, $hɑːrt/ *n* [C] a shape, consisting of two half-circles next to each other at the top and a v-shape at the bottom, which is often coloured pink or red, and which represents love, or this shape printed in red on a playing card • *a valentine card with a big red heart on it* • *a box of heart-shaped chocolates* • *She had a heart tattooed on her arm.* • *My queen of Hearts beats your ace of Spades.* • LP› **Cards** PIC› **Heart** Ⓙ

heart·ache /£ˈhɑːt·eɪk, $ˈhɑːrt-/ *n literary* feelings of great sadness • *You've caused me nothing but heartache.* [U] • *She writes about the joys and heartaches of bringing up children.* [C]

heart·beat /£ˈhɑːt·biːt, $ˈhɑːrt-/ *n* the regular movement or sound that the heart makes as it sends blood around your body • *She had been running, and her heartbeat was rapid.* [U] • *I put my head on his chest and listened for a heartbeat.* [C]

heart·break /£ˈhɑːt·breɪk, $ˈhɑːrt-/ *n* [U] feelings of great sadness or disappointment • *The kidnap has caused the family months of heartbreak and suffering.* • *"Heartbreak Hotel"* (title of song by Elvis Presley, 1956)

heart·break·ing /£ˈhɑːtˌbreɪ·kɪŋ, $ˈhɑːrt-/ *adj* • *a heartbreaking report on child poverty* • **It** *is heartbreaking* **(for him)** *that he cannot see his children.* [+ *that* clause] • **It** *was heartbreaking* **to** *hear of the way the animals had been treated.* [+ *to* infinitive] • See also HEARTRENDING.

heart·brok·en /£ˈhɑːtˌbrəʊ·kᵊn, $ˈhɑːrtˌbroʊ-/ *adj* • *If she ever left him he would be heartbroken* (=very sad). • *Sarah was heartbroken* (=very sad) **at** *not being allowed to join the team.*

heart·burn /£ˈhɑːt·bɜːn, $ˈhɑːrt·bɜːrn/ *n* [U] a painful burning feeling in the lower chest caused by the stomach not digesting food correctly

hear·ten *obj* /£ˈhɑː·tᵊn, $ˈhɑːr·t̬ᵊn/ *v* [T usually passive] to encourage and make confident and happy • *Anti-government protesters have been heartened by recent government promises of free and fair elections.* • *I was heartened* **to** *hear reports that the tickets for the show were selling well.* [+ obj + *to* infinitive]

hear·ten·ing /£ˈhɑː·tᵊn·ɪŋ, $ˈhɑːr·t̬ᵊn-/ *adj* • *The most heartening* (=encouraging) *thing* **for** *us has been the reaction of the children.* • **It** *is heartening* **to** *note the emphasis on involving local people in planning the services that they want.* [+ *to* infinitive]

heart·felt /£ˈhɑːt·felt, $ˈhɑːrt-/ *adj* strongly felt and sincere • *With heartfelt relief he saw a car coming towards him through the rain.* • *(fml) Please accept my heartfelt* **apologies/thanks.** • Ⓙ

hearth /£hɑːθ, $hɑːrθ/ *n* [C] the area around a fireplace or the area of floor in front of it • *A bright fire was burning in the hearth.* • *Their slippers were warming on the hearth.* • *A cat was lying on the hearth* **rug.** • *(esp. literary)* Hearth also refers to a home, esp. when seen as a place of comfort and love: *Hearths which once welcomed you will one day turn you away.* ○ *Reluctant to leave hearth* **and home**, *they rarely go on holiday.* • PIC› **Fires and space heaters**

heart·i·ly /£ˈhɑː·tɪ·li, $ˈhɑːr·t̬ɪ-/ *adv* See at HEARTY

heart·land /£ˈhɑːt·lænd, $ˈhɑːrt-/ *n* [C] the central or most important area • *The town of Roermond is in the agricultural heartland of southern Holland.* • *Many job losses are occurring in the Southeast, the heartland of Tory support.*

heart·less /£ˈhɑːt·ləs, $ˈhɑːrt-/ *adj* See at HEART EMOTIONS

heart·rend·ing /£ˈhɑːtˌren·dɪŋ, $ˈhɑːrt-/ *adj* causing great sympathy or sadness • *"Oh please, may I go?" she asked, looking up at me with a heartrending expression.* • *The pictures of the starving children in the newspaper were absolutely heartrending.* • See also HEARTBREAKING.

heart·sick /£ˈhɑːt·sɪk, $ˈhɑːrt-/ *adj literary* very sad or disappointed

heart·strings /£ˈhɑːt·strɪŋz, $ˈhɑːrt-/ *pl n* **pluck/pull/tug/tear at** *someone's* **heartstrings** to cause strong feelings of love or sympathy • *Her pleading look tugged at my heartstrings.*

heart·throb /£ˈhɑːt·θrɒb, $ˈhɑːrt·θrɑːb/ *n* [C] *infml* a very attractive, and usually famous, man with whom many women fall in love • *He wanted to be considered as a serious actor, not just a heartthrob.*

heart·warm·ing /£ˈhɑːtˌwɔː·mɪŋ, $ˈhɑːrtˌwɔːr-/ *adj* (esp. of an event, action or story) seeming to be something positive and good and therefore causing feelings of pleasure and happiness • **It's** *heartwarming* **to** *see the friendship and enthusiasm these kids display on the sports field.* [+ *to* infinitive]

heart·y ENTHUSIASTIC /£ˈhɑː·ti, $ˈhɑːr·t̬i/ *adj* **-ier, -iest** enthusiastic, energetic, and often loudly expressed • *a hearty welcome* • *a hearty laugh* • *The football supporters sang a hearty chorus of the national anthem.* • *His* **hale and** *hearty manner hid a sensitive and shy man.* • *The business community's reaction to the President's re-election was hearty.* • *(Br old use)* **My hearties** was a form of address for a group of men, esp. sailors.

heart·i·ly /£ˈhɑː·tɪ·li, $ˈhɑːr·t̬ɪ-/ *adv* • *She laughed heartily* (=enthusiastically and loudly) *at the joke.*

heart·y LARGE /£ˈhɑː·ti, $ˈhɑːr·t̬i/ *adj* large or (esp. of food) in large amounts • *We ate a hearty breakfast before we set off.* • *She's got a hearty* **appetite** (=she eats a lot). • *(dated)* Hearty can also mean very great: *She has a hearty dislike for any sort of office work.*

heart·i·ly /£ˈhɑː·tɪ·li, $ˈhɑːr·t̬ɪ-/ *adv* • *He ate heartily.* • *(dated)* Heartily also means greatly or extremely: *I'm heartily* **sick** *of his complaints.* ○ *I heartily* **dislike** *cycling in the rain.*

heat TEMPERATURE /hiːt/ *n* [U] (an amount of) warmth or esp. hot temperature • *the heat of the sun/fire* • *She could feel the heat of the dog's body as it sat at her feet.* • Heat is also temperature, esp. a hot temperature: *How do you manage to work in this heat without air conditioning?* ○ *She always wore a coat, even in the heat of summer.* ○ *Turn down the heat.* ○ *Cook the meat* **on a high/low** *heat* (=at a high/low temperature). • *(specialized)* The heat of a substance is the energy it produces because of the amount of movement of the atoms it consists of. • If you **put the heat on** someone, you try to persuade or force them to do something: *Friends of the Earth are putting the heat on the government to reduce sulphur dioxide pollution.* • If you **take the heat off** someone, you protect them from criticism or attack: *The deputy's resignation over the scandal has taken some of the heat off his superior.* • *Stay out of the sun during* **the heat of the day** (=the hottest part of the day). • *The incident occurred during* **the heat of** (=at the busiest period of) *the* **argument/battle/campaign.** • If you say **the heat is on**, you mean that a time of great activity and/or pressure has begun: *Now that IBM have entered the market the heat is really on.* • **Heat exhaustion/** *(Am also)* **heat prostration** is a condition where you feel very weak and ill because of being too long in a very hot place. • *(Br and Aus)* A **heat haze** *(Am* **haze**) is an effect of very hot sun, making it difficult to see objects clearly:

There were poor distant views from the mountains, because of heat haze. ○ *When the heat haze* **lifted**, *the island could be seen clearly.* • **Heat rash** (also **prickly heat**) is a condition where the skin feels uncomfortable and becomes covered by red spots: *His neck was covered in (a) heat rash.* • A **heat-seeking** weapon is one that can direct itself towards something hot esp. the hot engine of an aircraft: *The heat-seeking rockets/missiles will follow the enemy aircraft even if it changes direction.* • The **heat shield** of a spacecraft is the part of its structure which prevents it from getting too hot as it returns to Earth. • **Heat stroke** is a condition which can lead to death, caused by being too long in a very hot place. • If something is described as **heat-treated** it means it has been heated to a high temperature for a short time in order to preserve it: *heat-treated milk/blood* ○ **Heat treatment** *of blood eliminates any diseases it might contain.* • If a person is given **heat treatment**, a part of the body is heated with an electrical device, usually in order to relax it. • A **heat wave** is a period of time such as a few weeks when the weather is much hotter than usual. • *(saying)* 'If you can't stand/take the heat, get out of the kitchen' means if you find an activity or situation too difficult or unpleasant you should stop it or leave it. • *"In the Heat of the Night"* (film title, 1967) • LP **Measurements**

heat *obj* /hiːt/ *v* • *A large house like this must be expensive to heat.* [T] • *Shall I heat* **(up)** *some soup for lunch?* [T/M]

heat·ed /£ˈhiː·tɪd, $-t̬ɪd/ *adj* • *a heated towel rail* • *heated rollers* • *a heated greenhouse* • *a heated swimming pool*

heat·er /£ˈhiː·təʳ, $-t̬ɚ/ *n* [C] • A heater is a device which produces heat: *The room is kept warm by a gas/electric/oil/solar heater* (=one which uses the stated fuel). ○ *The company makes* **water/space/room/etc.** *heaters* (=ones which heat the stated thing or place).

heat·ing /£ˈhiː·tɪŋ, $-t̬ɪŋ/ *n* [U] • *The house has no heating* (=no heating system). • *The heating bills for the new house* (=cost of making it warm) *will be low.*

heat EMOTION /hiːt/ *n* [U] a state of strong emotion, esp. excitement or anger • *"No, I did not do it, and I deny absolutely all your accusations," he replied* **with/without** *heat.* • *John came up and apologised for the remarks he had made* **in the heat of the moment** (=while he was angry/excited).

heat·ed /£ˈhiː·tɪd, $-t̬ɪd/ *adj* • *a heated* (=excited/angry) *discussion* • *Do you always* **get** *so heated* (=feel/speak so strongly, esp. angrily) **about** *politics?*

heat·ed·ly /£ˈhiː·tɪd·li, $-t̬ɪd-/ *adv* • Heatedly means excitedly and strongly: *A similar proposal was heatedly discussed by the faculty of the University of California.* ○ *McGinnis heatedly denied he intentionally ran into the official.*

heat RACE /hiːt/ *n* [C] a less important race or competition in which it is decided who will compete in the final event • *The winner and second fastest runner from each of the five* **qualifying** *heats will run in the finals.*

heat BREED /hiːt/ *n* [U] **on/in heat** (esp. of an animal) in a state of sexual excitement and ready to breed

heath /hiːθ/ *n* [C] an area of land that is not farmed, where grass and other small plants grow, but where there are few trees or bushes

hea·then /ˈhiː·ðᵊn/ *adj old use disapproving* (of people or their way of life, activities and ideas) having no religion, or belonging to a religion that is not Christianity, Judaism or Islam • *a heathen cult* • *heathen practices*

hea·then /ˈhiː·ðᵊn/ *pl n* • **The heathen** are heathen people: *Those who attempted to* **convert** *the heathen were put to death.*

hea·then /ˈhiː·ðᵊn/ *n* [C] *old use disapproving*

heath·er /£ˈheð·əʳ, $-ɚ/ *n* [C] a low spreading bush with small pink, purple or white flowers, which grows wild, esp. on hilly land that has not been farmed

heath·land /ˈhiːθ·lənd/ *n* an area of HEATH • *To the north of the village is a thousand acres of sandy heathland.* [U] • *This heathland and others like it are home to many birds.* [C]

Heath Rob·in·son /£ˌhiːθˈrɒb·ɪn·sᵊn, $-ˈrɑː·bɪn-/ *adj Br humorous* (of a machine) very clever and complicated in a ridiculous and amusing way, but not practical or working well • *a Heath Robinson contraption* • *Each machine was a bizarre mixture of Heath-Robinson-style rubber pulleys, wheels and moving parts.*

heave *(obj)* MOVE /hiːv/ *v* to pull, push or lift (esp. something heavy) using a lot of effort • *They heaved* **(away) at** *the cupboard, but it was much too heavy to move.* [I] • *"Come on, we'll only move it if we all heave together," she said.* [I] • *He cleared a space, heaving boxes out of the way.* [T always + adv/prep] • *Protesting loudly, he heaved him***self (up) out** *of his armchair.* [T always + adv/prep] • *She leaned her weight against the door and heaved it open.* [T + obj + adj] • *(infml)* Heave also means throw: *She picked up a big dictionary and heaved it at him.* [T always + adv/prep] • If something heaves, it makes a single or many large movements up and down: *As the wind increased, the deck of the ship began to heave beneath his feet.* [I] ○ *After the race she was covered in sweat, her chest heaving.* [I]

heave /hiːv/ *n* [C] • *They gave a great heave and rolled the boulder out of the way.* • *(fig.) One more heave* (=big effort) *and we'll have done this month's quota.*

heav·ing /ˈhiː·vɪŋ/ *adj* • *his heaving chest* • *He stood on the heaving deck.*

heave *obj* MAKE A SOUND /hiːv/ *v* [T] **heave a sigh** (of a person) to let out a deep breath slowly so that it makes a sound • *We both heaved a sigh* **of** *relief when she went out, leaving us in peace.*

heave VOMIT /hiːv/ *v* [I] to feel as if you are going to vomit, or to vomit • *Just looking at the revolting food on offer made me/my stomach heave.* • *I could hear the sounds of someone heaving in the bathroom.*

heave ho SHOUT /£ˌhiːvˈhəʊ, $-ˈhoʊ/ *exclamation dated* a phrase which you say or shout when you are making a big effort to pull or lift something

heave ho DISMISS /£ˌhiːvˈhəʊ, $-ˈhoʊ/ *n* [U] **give** *someone* **the (old) heave ho** *infml humorous* to dismiss (someone) from a job • *She's been given the old heave ho.*

heave to *v adv* [I] *past simple* **hove** *specialized* (of a ship) to stop moving and to stay in one place • *The boat hove to in order to receive the visitors.*

heav·en /ˈhev·ᵊn/ *n* [U] in some religions, the place, sometimes imagined to be in the sky, where God or the gods live and/or where good people are believed to go after they die, so that they can enjoy perfect happiness • *In the painting, God and the angels are sitting on clouds in heaven.* • *The children were discussing whether or not you* **go to** *heaven when you die.* • *(infml)* If you say that something is heaven, or that you are **in** heaven, you mean that it gives you great pleasure: *It's heaven to get away from work for a week.* ○ *This ice cream is heaven – did you make it yourself?* ○ *Lying in the sunshine listening to the birds singing – I was in heaven.* • If someone or something is **heaven-sent**, they arrive or happen, usually unexpectedly, at the time when they are most useful: *The medical supplies that arrived in January were heaven-sent.* • *"Heaven can Wait"* (film title, 1943) • *"All this and Heaven Too"* (book and film title, 1940)

heav·en·ly /ˈhev·ᵊn·li/ *adj* **-ier, -iest** • Heavenly means of heaven: *heavenly music* ○ *heavenly light* • Heavenly also means giving great pleasure: *It was a good party and the food was heavenly.* • A **heavenly body** is any object existing in space, esp. planets, moons or stars. • A **heavenly host** is a group of ANGELS (=a spiritual creature).

heav·ens /ˈhev·ᵊnz/ *pl n* • *We stared up at* **the** *heavens* (=the sky) *trying to see the plane.* • *Just when we got to the park,* **the heavens opened** (=it suddenly started to rain a lot). • *(dated)* **Heavens (above)/Good heavens** is used to express surprise or anger.

heav·en·ward /£ˈhev·ᵊn·wəd, $-wɚd/, **heav·en·wards** /£ˈhev·ᵊn·wədz, $-wɚdz/ *adv* [not gradable] • If you you **lift/raise/etc.** your **eyes heavenward**, you show your feeling that a situation is annoying or hopeless.

heav·y WEIGHING A LOT /ˈhev·i/ *adj* **-ier, -iest** weighing a lot; needing effort to move or lift • *The piano's much too heavy for one person to lift.* • *How heavy is that box* (=How much does it weigh)? • *I don't want to do any heavy work/heavy lifting and carrying.* • *The old car had rather heavy* (=difficult to move/turn) **steering**. • *(fig.) Her eyes were heavy* **with** *tiredness.* • *(literary)* If you are **heavy-hearted**, **have a heavy heart** or your heart is heavy, you are unhappy: *With a heavy heart, she turned to wave goodbye.* • *(specialized)* A **heavy metal** is a dense and usually poisonous metal, such as CADMIUM or LEAD. • **Heavy metal** is a style of ROCK (=music) with a strong beat, played very loudly using electrical instruments. • *(specialized)* **Heavy water** is water that contains much more than the usual amount of DEUTERIUM (=type of HYDROGEN). • LP **Measurements**

heav·i·ly /ˈhev·ɪ·li/ *adv* • *She fell heavily and bruised her shoulder.* • *The news she had received* **weighed** *heavily* **on** *her* (=worried her).

heav·i·ness /ˈhev·ɪ·nəs/ *n* [U] • *The child's heaviness surprised him.*

heav·y STRONG /ˈhev·i/ *adj* thick, strong, solid or strongly made • *I need to buy a heavy winter* **coat**. • *You'll need heavy* **shoes** *– the paths are wet and muddy.* • *I don't like to have a heavy* **meal** (= a large amount of solid food) *in the middle of the day.* • *He was a big man with rather heavy* **features** (= large and obvious nose, mouth, etc.) • Heavy earth/ground is thick and difficult to dig or walk through: *My garden is on heavy clay.* • Heavy machines/vehicles are very large and powerful: *heavy artillery/machinery* ○ *(Br) Turn left just after the road sign saying 'Slow – Heavy* **plant** *crossing'.* • *(fig.) The sun disappeared behind heavy* (= thick and solid-looking) *clouds.* • *(fig.) I don't like the design – it's too heavy* (= thick, solid-looking and not delicate). • **Heavy-duty** clothes, machines, vehicles, etc. are strongly made so that they can be used a lot, esp. in difficult conditions: *heavy-duty tools* ○ *heavy-duty shoes* • *(Br)* A **heavy goods vehicle** (*abbreviation* **HGV**) is a large truck used for carrying goods from one place to another. • **Heavy industry** is industry that uses large machines to produce either materials such as steel or large goods such as ships and trains. • Someone who is **heavy-set** has a large, wide, strong body.

heav·y /ˈhev·i/ *n* [C] *slang* • A heavy is a large strong man employed to protect someone else or to frighten other people: *Frank always took a couple of heavies along with him when he went collecting his debts.*

heav·i·ly /ˈhev·ɪ·li/ *adv* • *He's a heavily* **built** (= large and strong) *man.*

heav·y TO A GREAT DEGREE /ˈhev·i/ *adj* **-ier, -iest** (esp. of something unpleasant) of very or unusually great force, amount or degree • *a heavy blow on the head* • *a heavy defeat* • *heavy casualties* • *heavy fighting* • *heavy traffic* • *heavy rain/snow* • *a heavy fine/penalty/prison sentence* • *Heavy* **breathing** *is loud and deep, usually because of tiredness, illness or excitement.* • *I've got a heavy* (= very busy and full of hard work) *day/month/schedule ahead of me.* • *Heavy* **drinking/smoking** (= drinking/smoking a lot) *will damage your health.* • *The heaviest* **gamblers** *are usually men aged 45 to 64.* • *If you slept through the storm, you must be a heavy* **sleeper** (= able to sleep without being awoken by noise). • *Looking after the health of 700 children is a heavy* **responsibility** *to bear.* • A heavy **sea** is rough with large waves. • *(slightly dated slang)* If you say that something such as a situation is heavy, you mean that it is dangerous or unpleasant: *When the police arrived, things got really heavy, you know.* • To **be heavy on** someone is to treat or punish them severely: *I think his parents are being rather heavy on him.* • To **(be) heavy on** also means to use a lot: *The engine is heavy on fuel.* ○ *Not too* **heavy on** *the cream please.* • If something is **heavy with** something else it has a lot of it or is full of it: *The trees were heavy with fruit.* ○ *The atmosphere was heavy with menace.* • *(Br disapproving)* If you say that someone is **making heavy weather of** something, you mean that they are finding it hard to do, although it is not very difficult: *Her report should have been finished today, but she's making heavy weather of it.* • *(Br and Aus)* A **heavy breather** (*Am* **breather**) is a man who gets sexual pleasure from making telephone calls and saying nothing but only breathing noisily. • *(disapproving)* If you do something with **a heavy hand**, you do it with an unnecessarily great amount of force, or in a forceful way which angers other people: *The police investigation has been conducted* **with** *a heavy hand, in ways that have deeply annoyed the local community.* ○ *Their response to the problem was rather* **heavy-handed**. • If something is **heavy going**, you are finding it difficult: *I'm* **finding** *the advanced physics a bit heavy going.* ○ *The book was rather heavy going.* • **Heavy petting** is where two people kiss, hold and touch each other in a sexual way, but do not have sex. • *"He ain't Heavy, he's my Brother"* (title of a song by The Hollies, 1969) • LP **Very, completely**

heav·i·ly /ˈhev·ɪ·li/ *adv* • Heavily means to a great degree: *They were heavily defeated.* ○ *The terrorists are heavily armed.* ○ *The compound is heavily guarded.* ○ *She's heavily involved in* (= doing a lot of work for) *the project.* ○ *They rely heavily on his advice.* • *(infml) When I was younger I was* **heavily into** (= interested in and involved with) *politics.*

heav·i·ness /ˈhev·ɪ·nəs/ *n* [U] • *The heaviness of the prison sentence was a surprise.*

heav·y·weight /ˈhev·ɪ·weɪt/ *n* [C], *adj* a boxer who weighs more than 175 POUNDS (79·5 kilograms) and is therefore in the heaviest group, or *(fig.)* a person or thing that is important or serious and that other people notice • *Mike Tyson was heavyweight champion of the world.* • *(fig.) Her extraordinary intelligence and speaking ability made her a political heavyweight.* • *(fig.) The committee produced a heavyweight report on the global situation.* • Compare LIGHTWEIGHT.

He·brew /ˈhiː·bruː/ *n* a person belonging to a group whose history is connected with the ancient kingdoms of Israel • *It is the ancient capital of the kingdom of the Hebrews, Israel.* [C] • *The history of the Hebrew people is tied to that of other Semitic peoples.* • Hebrew is also the ancient language of the Jewish people and the official language of modern Israel: *Adam in Hebrew means "man" or "mankind"* • *Eve possibly means "living".* [U]

He·bra·ic /hɪˈbreɪ·ɪk/ *adj* [not gradable] • *Hebraic studies*

heck /hek/ *exclamation, n slang* an expression of usually slight annoyance or surprise, or a way of adding force to a statement, question, etc. • *Oh heck! It's later than I thought.* • *Where the heck have you been – we're late?* • *It's* **a heck of a** (= a very) *long way to the nearest shop from here.* • *The doctor said I shouldn't drink, but* **what the heck** (= I'll do it although I know I probably should not). • LP **Phrases and customs**

heck·le *(obj)* /ˈhek·l̩/ *v* to interrupt (esp. a public speech or speaker) with loud unfriendly statements or questions • *A few angry locals started heckling (the speaker).* [I/T]

heck·ler /£ˈhek·ləʳ, $-lɚ/ *n* [C] • *The heckler was ejected from the hall by a couple of police officers.*

hec·tare /£ˈhek·teəʳ, $-ter/ *n* [C] a unit of measurement of an area of land (10 000 m²) • LP **Units**

hec·tic /ˈhek·tɪk/ *adj* full of activity; very busy and fast • *a hectic schedule* • *a hectic week* • *We made a hectic three-day visit to New York.* • *This morning there was hectic trading on the Stock Exchange.* • *The area has become a haven for people tired of the hectic* **pace** *of city life, searching for quiet and inner peace.*

hec·tor *obj* /£ˈhek·təʳ, $-t̬ɚ/ *v* [T] *disapproving* to talk and behave towards (someone) in a loud and unpleasantly forceful way, esp. in order to get them to act or think as you want them to • *Audiences do not want to be hectored by aggressive, unsympathetic speakers.*

hec·tor·ing /£ˈhek·tᵊr·ɪŋ, $-t̬ɚ-/ *adj disapproving* • *He did not take kindly to the hectoring moral tone of the speaker.* • *He had a loud, hectoring manner.* • *She was regarded as rude, haughty, bossy and hectoring.*

hedge BUSHES /hedʒ/ *n* [C] a line of bushes or small trees planted very close together, esp. along the edge of a garden, field or road • *a beech/privet hedge* • *The fields are divided from each other by hedges.* • *Clip/cut/trim your hedge regularly.* • **Hedge-trimmers** are a tool with which you cut a garden hedge to keep it tidy. • PIC **Garden**

hedge PROTECTION /hedʒ/ *n* [C] a means of protection, control or limitation • *Her overseas investments were made as a hedge* **against** *rising inflation in this country.*

hedge *(obj)* /hedʒ/ *v* • *We've got permission, but it's hedged* **about/around/in with** (= is very limited by) *strict conditions.* [T] • To hedge is also to try to avoid giving an answer or taking any action: *Stop hedging and tell me what you really think.* [I] • If you **hedge** your **bets**, you protect yourself against loss by supporting more than one possible result or both sides in a competition: *They're hedging their bets and keeping up contacts with both companies.*

hedge·hog /£ˈhedʒ·hɒg, $-hɑːg/ *n* [C] a small brown mammal with a protective covering of SPINES (= long sharp points) on its back • PIC **Wild animals in Britain**

hedge·row /£ˈhedʒ·rəʊ, $-roʊ/ *n* [C] *Br and Am* a line of different types of bushes and small trees growing very close together, esp. between fields or along the sides of roads in the countryside • PIC **Farming**

he·don·i·sm /ˈhed·ᵊn·ɪ·zᵊm/ *n* [U] living and behaving in ways that mean you get as much pleasure out of life as possible, according to the belief that the most important thing in life is to enjoy yourself

he·don·ist /ˈhed·ᵊn·ɪst/ *n* [C]

he·don·is·tic /ˌhed·ᵊnˈɪs·tɪk/ *adj*

hee·bie–jee·bies /ˌhiː·bɪˈjiː·biz/ *pl n* **the heebie-jeebies** *infml* strong feelings of fear or anxiety • *Don't start talking about ghosts – they* **give** *me the heebie-jeebies.*

heed *obj* /hiːd/ *v* [T] *fml* to listen to and follow (esp. advice or a warning) • *The airline has been criticized for failing to heed* **advice/warnings** *about lack of safety routines.* • *The remaining 140 party members in the union have so far refused to heed the* **call** *to resign.*

heed /hiːd/ *n* [U] *fml* • *In recent years, those setting teachers' salaries have been allowed to* **pay** *some heed* **to** (=

consider) *market pressures.* • *The company* **took** *no* **heed of** (= did not consider) *public opposition to the plans.*

heed·less /ˈhiːd·ləs/ *adj fml* • Heedless means not giving attention to a risk or possible difficulty: • *Heedless destruction of the rainforests is contributing to global warming.* ○ *The journalists insisted on getting to the front line of the battle, heedless* **of** *the risks.* ○ *Heedless* **of** *the terrible noise all around, the boy carried on with his work.*

heed·less·ly /ˈhiːd·lə·sli/ *adv* • *Consumers are heedlessly buying everything in sight and getting into debt.*

hee–haw /£ˈhiː·hɔː, $-hɑː/ *n* [C] the sound that a DONKEY makes

heel BODY PART /hɪəl/ *n* [C] the rounded back part of the foot • *Place your heel on the ground before your toes.* • The heel of a sock or shoe is the part which covers the heel of the foot. • The heel of a shoe is also the raised part at the back, under your heel: *She caught a heel in a crack in the concrete.* • The heel of your hand is the part of your PALM nearest your wrist which you can use to push or hit something very firmly. • The heel of something, esp. of a loaf of bread, is the end part, and is usually the last part that is left after the rest has been eaten or used. • If you describe a building or place as **down at (the) heel**, you mean that it is in bad condition and has not been cared for. • If you bring a dog **to heel** you cause it to come close to you. • If you bring a person or organization **to heel**, you cause them to obey you. • If a dog **comes/walks** to heel it follows close behind the person it is with. If a person or organization **comes to heel**, they agree to obey, usually because they have been forcefully persuaded to do so. • If you are **close/hard/hot on** someone's **heels**, you are following very closely behind them: *As the bank robbers made their getaway, the police were hot on their heels.* • If an event or situation **comes/follows (hard) on the heels of** another, it happens very soon after it: *For Walter, disaster followed hard on the heels of his initial success.* • If you **take to** your **heels**, you quickly run away: *When they saw the soldiers coming, they took to their heels.* • *This country would never submit to living* **under the heel of** (= completely controlled by) *a foreign power.* • *(Br)* A **heel-bar** is a small shop which repairs shoes, esp. while a customer waits. • See also WELL-HEELED. • PIC› **Body**

heel /hɪəl/ *exclamation* • If you say "Heel!" to a dog you are ordering it to come and stand next to you or to walk close beside you as you walk.

heel *obj* /hɪəl/ *v* [T] • *(specialized)* In RUGBY, to heel the ball is to kick it backwards with the heel.

heel·er /£ˈhɪə·ləʳ, $-lɚ/ *n* [C] *Aus* • A heeler is a dog used to collect together cattle or sheep.

heels /hɪəlz/ *pl n* • *She was wearing black stockings and four-inch heels* (= shoes with a part at the back which was four inches high). • *I don't often wear heels (also* **high heels, high-heeled shoes***)* (= shoes with high heels).

heel PERSON /hɪəl/ *n* [C] *dated infml disapproving* a person who treats other people badly and unfairly • *I felt like a real heel when I saw how I'd upset her.*

heft *obj* /heft/ *v* [T always + adv/prep] to lift, hold or carry (something heavy) using your hands • *I watched him heft the heavy sack onto his shoulder.* • *Rose met her at the door, hefting a squalling baby on one hip.*

heft·y /ˈhef·ti/ *adj* **-ier, -iest** large in amount, size, force, etc. • *Her salary will go up by a hefty 10%.* • *There have been several hefty price rises this year.* • *It's a hefty* (= large and heavy) *hardback book of over 1000 pages.* • *A hefty push was enough to knock him over.*

he·gem·on·y /hɪˈgem·ə·ni/ *n* [U] *fml* (esp. of countries) the position of being the strongest and most powerful and therefore controlling others • *The three nations competed for regional hegemony.* • *The country will never regain its political and economic hegemony.*

he·gem·on·ic /£ˌheg·ɪˈmɒn·ɪk, $-ˈmɑː·nɪk/ *adj fml*

heif·er /£ˈhef·əʳ, $-ɚ/ *n* [C] a young cow, esp. one that has not yet given birth to a CALF

heigh–ho /£ˈheɪ·həʊ, $-hoʊ/ *exclamation* an expression of tiredness or of acceptance of something

height /haɪt/ *n* the distance from the top to the bottom of something, the quality of being tall, or the distance from a surface to a position on an object • *His height is about 1·75 metres.* [C] • *The sheer height of New York's skyscrapers is so impressive.* [C] • *She's about average height* (= neither unusually short or tall). [U] • Height also refers to the particular distance that something is above a surface: *At heights of 4000 or 5000 metres above sea level the air gets quite thin.* [C] ○ *The bullet entered the body at chest height.* [U] ○ *You can adjust the height of the chair with this lever.* [U] • **The height of** a situation or event is the time when it is strongest or most full of activity: *August is the height of the tourist season.* ○ *At the height of the storm/riot/violence/crisis we were left without any help.* • **The height of** also means an extreme example of: *It would be the height of stupidity to refuse to answer their questions.* ○ *They were dressed in the height of fashion* (= in extremely modern stylish clothes). • **The height of** is the top of or the highest possible achievement: *She was* **at** *the height of her career when he first met her.* • LP› **Measurements**

heights /haɪts/ *pl n* • Heights are high places, or the top of hills: *Machine guns were mounted along the heights behind the town.* ○ *Don't go up the tower if you're* **afraid of** *heights.* ○ *(fig.) The plan was to take the* **commanding** *heights of the economy and put them under public control.* ○ *(fig. often humorous) Her husband rose to the* **dizzy/giddy/lofty** *heights of transport minister.* ○ *(fig.) Share prices* **scaled** *new heights yesterday.* • *The value of tourism to the country* **attained** *its greatest heights* (= height) *in the late 1980s and later declined.* • *He* **reached** *the heights* (= height) **of** *his profession at the age of 35.*

height·en *(obj)* /£ˈhaɪ·tᵊn, $-t̬ᵊn/ *v* to increase (esp. an emotion or effect) • *The strong police presence only heightened the tension among the crowd.* [T] • *As the feeling of panic heightened, people started to flee towards the exits.* [I] • *She heightened the effect of her costume by wearing black eyeliner and lipstick.* [T]

hei·nous /ˈhɪː·nəs/ *adj fml* (esp. of a crime) extremely wrong or bad • *They admitted to the most heinous crimes/atrocities/murders.*

heir /£eəʳ, $er/ *n* [C] a person who will legally receive money, property or a title from another person, esp. an older member of the same family, when that other person dies • *The guest of honour was the Romanoff heir* **to** *the throne of all Russia.* • *He was the* **rightful** *heir* **to** *the Duke of Marlborough and a £100 million fortune.* • *Their fourth child was the long-awaited* **male** *heir.* • *Despite having a large family, they still had no* **son and** *heir.* • *(fig.) Imam Ali, the prophet's son-in-law, is regarded by Shia Muslims as the heir* **to** *Mohammed's spiritual authority.* • *(fig.) The French finance minister is heir* **to** *a tradition of central control that goes back to Louis XIV's minister, Colbert.* • *(fig.) When we bought the business we were heir* **to** (= received from previous owners) *a lot of administrative problems.* • The **heir apparent** is the person with the automatic right to legally receive all or most of the money, property, titles, etc. from another person when they die, or *(fig.)* a person who seems certain to take the place of someone in power when they stop working: *The Prince of Wales is the heir apparent* **to** *the throne.* • *(fig.) The finance director Maria Braun was the heir apparent* **to** *current chairman Gerhard Benz.* • See also HEIRESS.

heir·ess /£ˈeə·res, $ˈer·es/ *n* [C] a woman or girl who will receive or already has received (a lot of) money, property or a title from another person, esp. an older member of the same family, when that person dies • *the heiress* **to** *the throne* • *a Texan oil heiress* • *a rich heiress* • *He* **married** *Bertha Krupp, heiress* **to** *the Krupp industrial empire.* • See also HEIR.

heir·loom /£ˈeə·luːm, $ˈer-/ *n* [C] a valuable object that has been given by older members of a family to younger members of the same family over many years • *The necklace is a valuable family heirloom.*

heist /haɪst/ *n* [C] *infml* a crime in which property is taken illegally and often violently from a place or person • *a $2 million jewellery heist*

held HOLD /held/ *past simple and past participle of* HOLD

held CARRIED /held/ *adj* carried, kept or maintained • *a* **hand**-*held video game* • *a long-held view* • *firmly held beliefs* • *widely held opinions*

hel·i·cop·ter /£ˈhel·ɪˌkɒp·təʳ, $-ˌkɑːp·tɚ/, *infml* **chop·per** *n* [C] a type of aircraft without wings, that has one or two sets of large blades which go round very fast on top. It can land and take off vertically and can stay in one place in the air • *Two helicopters constantly* **hovered** *near the building.* • *The injured were ferried to hospital by helicopter.* • *a helicopter pilot* • A **helicopter gunship** is a military helicopter armed with guns and other weapons: *Helicopter gunships carry rockets and missiles capable of causing a large amount of damage.* • PIC› **Aircraft, Emergency services**

hel·i·pad /ˈhel·ɪ·pæd/ *n* [C] a place where a single HELICOPTER can take off and land

hel·i·port /£'hel·ɪ·pɔːt, $-pɔːrt/ *n* [C] an airport for HELICOPTERS

he·li·um /'hiː·li·əm/ *n* [U] a gas that is lighter than air, will not burn, is an element and is used in BALLOONS, AIRSHIPS and some types of lights

he·lix /'hiː·lɪks/ *n* [C] *pl* **helices** /'hiː·lɪ·siːz/ *specialized* a curve that goes around a central tube or cone shape in the form of a SPIRAL • *A corkscrew is in the shape of a helix.* • *In 1953 Watson and Crick discovered that DNA is in the form of a* **double** *helix.*

hel·i·cal /'hiː·lɪ·kəl/ *adj* [not gradable] *specialized* • *helical molecules* • *a helical structure*

hell [PLACE] /hel/ *n* [U] in some religions, the place where some people are believed to go after death to be punished forever for the bad things they have done during their lives, or an extremely unpleasant or difficult place, situation or experience • *They believed that some people would* **go to** *hell when they died.* • *Work is* **(sheer)** *hell at the moment, with both computers not working.* ○ *Soldiers who lived through the jungle war described it as hell/(a)* **hell on earth**. ○ *My husband and I* **went through** *hell when we were told the baby might have cancer.* ○ *As the sun went down it became* **as cold as hell** (= extremely cold). • *(infml)* If **all hell breaks loose**, a situation suddenly becomes violent and noisy, esp. with people arguing or fighting: *At the announcement of more tax increases all hell broke loose in Parliament.* ○ *One policeman drew his gun and then suddenly all hell broke loose.* • *(infml)* If you say that you have **been to hell and back**, you mean you have lived through an extremely unpleasant, difficult or painful experience: *I have been to hell and back since the unjust jailing of my two sons.* • *(infml)* If you say that you will do something **come hell or high water**, you mean that you are determined to do it, despite any difficulties that there might be: *I'll get you to the airport by noon, come hell or high water!* • *(infml)* If you do something **for the hell of it**, you do it without having any particular purpose or desire, but usually for amusement: *I didn't know what I wanted to do, so I drove my van round Europe, just for the hell of it.* • *(infml)* If someone or something painful **gives** you **hell**, they criticize you severely, shout at you, hit you or give you pain: *The boss gave me hell* **for** *losing the computer disks.* ○ *These new shoes are giving me hell.* • *(slang)* If you tell someone to **go to hell**, you are swearing at them and angrily telling them to stop talking and go away: *"Listen to me, you're being very stupid." "Oh, go to hell!"* • *(dated infml)* If you go, run, ride, etc. **hell for leather**, you go or travel as fast as you can. • *(infml dated)* If you say that something won't happen until **hell freezes over**, you mean that it will probably never happen: *She'll be waiting until hell freezes over if she's trying to get the boss's permission for a year off.* • *(infml)* If you say that there will be **hell to pay**, you mean that there will be a lot of trouble and severe criticism because of it: *There's going to be hell to pay if these figures are made public.* • *(infml)* If someone or something **makes** your **life hell**, they make a particular situation or length of time very difficult for you and cause you to feel unhappy: *The class bully made her life hell at school.* • **Hell's Angels** are a group of people who ride large motorcycles, wear jackets with the name and symbol of the group on them and are considered by some people to be often noisy, violent and drunk. • *"Hell is other people"* (Jean-Paul Sartre *Huis clos*, 1944) • *"There is many a boy here to-day who looks on war as all glory, but, boy, it is all hell (usually quoted as 'War is hell')"* (speech by General William Tecumseh Sherman, 1880) • See also HELLFIRE; HELLHOLE; INFERNAL.

hel·lish /'hel·ɪʃ/ *adj* • *a hellish* (= very bad or unpleasant) *experience*

hel·lish·ly /'hel·ɪʃ·li/ *adv* • *a hellishly* (= very unpleasantly) *busy week*

hell [EXPRESSION] /hel/ *exclamation, n* [U] used to express anger or to give emphasis to an expression • *Oh hell, I've forgotten my key!* • *It's a/one* **hell of a** *(also* **helluva***)* (= extremely) *big decision to take.* • *The house was in a/one* **hell of a** *(also* **helluva***)* (= a very big) *mess.* • **What the** *hell was that noise?* • *We haven't got a* **chance/hope in hell** (= we have no chance/hope) *of meeting such a tight deadline.* • If you do something **as** confidently/quick/easily **as hell**, you do it very confidently/quickly/easily. • *(infml)* If you **get the hell out of** a place, you leave it quickly: *Let's get the hell out of here, before any shooting starts.* • *(infml)* If you do something **like hell** or if you feel something **like hell**, you do it or feel it very quickly, very hard, very strongly, etc.: *We ran like hell.* ○ *We worked like hell to finish the job.* ○ *The tooth began to hurt like hell.* • *(slang)* **Like hell** is also used to mean certainly not: *"Surely you feel quite rich by now?" "Like hell! I'm only making $10 000 a year."* • *(infml)* If something or someone annoys, frightens, etc. **the hell out of** you, it makes you extremely annoyed or frightened: *He jumped out from behind a wall and* **scared** *the hell out of her.* • To beat, knock, etc. **the hell out of** someone is to hit them with great force: *There are two guys beating the hell out of each other in the street outside.* • *(Am infml)* If you answer someone by saying **the hell** you **do/are** or **the hell it does** you are telling them you do not believe what they have said or will not allow them to do what they want: *"I don't need your advice, I know what's good for me." "The hell you do!"* • *(infml)* If you wish or hope **to hell** that something is true or that it will happen, you are saying how strongly you want it to be true or to happen: *I hope to hell she hasn't missed that plane.* • *(slang)* If you say **what the hell**, you are expressing a feeling that something is suddenly not very important to you: *I was supposed to be working this evening but what the hell – I'll see you in the pub in half an hour.* • *(infml)* If you are **hell-bent on** doing something, you are extremely determined to do it, without caring about risks or possible dangerous results: *hell-bent on revenge/violence/causing trouble* • *(infml)* If you say **hell's bells** or *(Br and Aus also)* **hell's teeth**, you are expressing your anger, surprise or fear: *Hell's bells, man, can't you do anything right?* • [LP] **Phrases and customs**

Hel·len·ic /hə'len·ɪk/ *adj* [not gradable] of or relating to the ancient or modern Greeks, and their history, art, etc.

Hel·len·ist·ic /ˌhel·ə'nɪs·tɪk/ *adj* [not gradable] of or relating to the history, art, etc. of ancient Greece and other countries of the Eastern Mediterranean, esp. during the fourth to the first century B.C.

hell·fire /£'hel·faɪəʳ, $-faɪr/ *n* [U] the punishment that some Christians believe bad people will suffer after they die • *He certainly believed in preaching hellfire* **and damnation**. • *a hellfire preacher*

hell·hole /£'hel·həʊl, $-hoʊl/ *n* [C] *infml disapproving* an extremely unpleasant place • *One prisoner described the jail as "an unbearably filthy hellhole."*

hello /£hel'əʊ, $-'oʊ/, *Br* **hal·lo**, **hul·lo** *exclamation, n pl* **hellos** used when meeting or greeting someone • *"Hello, Paul," she said, "I haven't seen you for a few weeks."* • *"Hello, madam. Can I help you?" said the shop assistant.* • *I know her vaguely – we've exchanged hellos a few times.* [C] • **Come and say** *hello* **to** (= meet for the first time) *my friends.* • *(infml) And a* **big** *hello* (= welcome) *to all the parents who've come to see the show.* • Hello is also said at the beginning of a telephone conversation: *"Hello, I'd like some information about your flights to the USA, please."* ○ *Suddenly the line went dead. "Hello? Hello?" he said, but there was no reply.* • Hello is also used to attract someone's attention: *The front door was open so she walked inside and called out, "Hello! Is there anybody in?"* • *(dated)* Hello can also be an expression of surprise: *"Hello, this is very strange – I know that man."* • *"Hello, good evening and welcome"* (TV personality David Frost, 1966-) • [LP] **Meeting someone**

hel·luv·a /'hel·ə·və/ *adj, adv* [not gradable] *infml* used to give force or emphasis to an expression • *It's a helluva nice place.* • *We're going to have a helluva problem.*

helm /helm/ *n* [C] the handle or wheel which controls the direction in which a ship or boat travels • *Who was* **at** *the helm when the collision occurred?* • *Someone more competent than me had better* **take** *the helm if this wind increases.* • *(fig.) She is the first woman to* **take***/be* **at** *the helm* (= to be officially controlling/leading) *of a national industry.*

hel·met /'hel·mət/ *n* [C] a strong hard hat that covers and protects the head. There are different types for different purposes. • *a soldier's steel helmet* • *a crash helmet* • *a safety helmet* • *(Br) a policeman's helmet* • [PIC] **Hats**

hel·met·ed /£'hel·mə·tɪd, $-t̬ɪd/ *adj* [not gradable], *combining form* • *As onlookers stand behind barricades, helmeted firemen surveyed the collapsing building.* • *Plainclothes officers darted into the crowds to tackle hooligans, assisting helmeted, baton-wielding police.* • *After grabbing the cash, the crash-helmeted gunman jumped into a getaway car.*

helms·man *(pl* **-men***)*, **helms·wo·man** *(pl* **-women***)* /'helmz·mən, -ˌwʊm·ən/ *n* [C] a person who directs a ship or boat, using a handle or wheel

help *(obj)* [MAKE EASIER] /help/ *v* to make it possible or easier for (someone) to do something, by doing part of the work yourself or by providing advice, money, support, etc. • *How can I help you?* [T] • *Is there any way that I can help?* [I] • *I wonder if you could help me – I'd like some information about flights to New Zealand.* [T] • *All the children have calculators to help them* **with** *their addition.* [T] • *My dad said he would help* **with** *the costs of* (= give part of the cost of) *buying a house.* [I] • *Her daughters helped her* **(to)** *carry the table upstairs.* [T + obj + *to* infinitive] • *The £10 000 loan from the bank helped her* **(to)** *start her own business.* [T + obj + *to* infinitive] • *It was very nice of you to help that old gentleman across* (= help him to cross) *the road.* [T] • *Very politely, he helped her* **into/out of** (= to put on/take off) *her coat.* [T] • If you help **out**, you do a part of someone's work or give someone money: *They're employing extra staff to help (us) out on Saturdays when it's busy.* [I/M] ○ *Her parents helped (her) out with a £500 loan.* [I/M] • *I feel that learning English will help* (= improve) *my chances of promotion at work.* [T] • *Nothing can help her now* (= Her situation is too bad for anyone to be able to improve it). [T] • If something helps a difficult or painful situation, it improves it or makes it easier or less painful: *If you're feeling so tired, perhaps a little sleep would help.* [I] ○ *The morphine didn't seem to help (the pain).* [I/T] • If something or someone helps to do something, they are one of several parts that make it happen: *The drought has helped* **(to)** *make this a disastrous year for Somalia.* [+ *(to)* infinitive] • If someone shouts "**Help!**" they are asking for someone to come and save them from or do something about a dangerous situation. • If you **can't/couldn't help** something, such as acting in a particular way or making a particular remark, you are not able to control or stop it: *He can't help his looks, poor thing.* ○ *It's awful, but I couldn't help laughing at her as she fell into the water.* [+ v-*ing*] ○ *I couldn't help* **but** *see the signature on the letter.* ○ *"Stop giggling!" "I can't help it!"* ○ *I can't help thinking* (= My true feeling is that) *she'd be better off without him.* [+ v-*ing*] • If you **give/lend** someone **a helping hand**, you help them: *These tax cuts will give industry a helping hand.* • If you say **it can't be helped**, you mean that an unpleasant or painful situation or unwanted duty cannot be avoided and must be accepted: *I've got to go into London again tonight – it can't be helped.* • If you say **God/heaven help** someone, you are giving force to a statement of the danger or seriousness of a situation or action: *Heaven help us if they attack now while we're still unprepared.* ○ *And then he said "I've killed him, God help me."* • **So help me (God)** is a formal and very serious way of making a promise: *Everything I have said is true, so help me God.* • *"Help! I need somebody"* (from the song *Help!* by The Beatles, 1965) • *"You don't have to be mad to work here, but it helps"* (popular joke, often found as a notice in offices) • See also HELPLINE.

help /help/ *n* • *Do you need any help with those boxes?* [U] • *Her parents gave her some help* **with** *her bank loan* (= paid some of it). [U] • *Having a word processor would be a help.* [U] • *He was a great help* **(to** *me) while my husband was away.* [U] • If you have help **in the house** or if you have help **come in** or *(Am)* have **hired** help, you employ someone, usually a woman, to clean your house and do other small jobs: *Do you have help come in at the moment?* [U] ○ *Unfortunately my help is going to leave.* [C] • *(esp. Br) If she is caught stealing again,* **there'll be no help for it** *(Am usually* **nothing for it***)* **but** (= the only choice will be) **to** *call the police.* • *(specialized)* A **help screen** is information or instructions which you can ask the computer to show you if you are having difficulty using the computer. • *"With a Little Help from my Friends"* (song by the Beatles, 1967)

help·er /£ˈhel·pəʳ, $-pɚ/ *n* [C] • *The teachers made great use of volunteer/parent helpers.* • *I'll need four helpers for this part of the activity.*

help·ful /ˈhelp·fᵊl/ *adj* • *She's such a pleasant, helpful child!* • *I'm sorry, I was only trying to be helpful.* • *He made several helpful suggestions.*

help·ful·ly /ˈhelp·fᵊl·i/ *adv* • *The manufacturers helpfully provide an instruction manual.*

help·ful·ness /ˈhelp·fᵊl·nəs/ *n* [U]

help *obj* GIVE/TAKE /help/ *v* [T] to give something to (someone) or to take something for (yourself) • *"Is there any more bread?" "Please help yourself!"* • *(slightly fml) Shall I help you* **to** *some more soup?* • *(infml) She got six months in jail for helping* **herself to** (= stealing) *$200 from the office safe.*

help·ing /ˈhel·pɪŋ/ *n* [C] • *Would you like another helping* (= single amount of food)? • *You've already had three helpings of dessert!*

help·less·ly /ˈhel·plə·sli/ *adv* • *Unable to swim, she watched helplessly as the child struggled desperately in the water.*

help·less·ness /ˈhel·plə·snəs/ *n* [U] • *We experienced a frightening feeling of helplessness as we saw her wheeled in to the operating theatre.*

help·line /ˈhelp·laɪn/ *n* [C] a telephone service providing advice and comfort to worried or unhappy people • *a telephone helpline* • *a helpline number* • *They have access to 24-hour helplines which give free legal advice.* • *A new helpline is now available for people trying to stop smoking.*

hel·ter–skel·ter HURRIED /£ˌhel·təˈskel·təʳ, $-t̬ɚˈskel·t̬ɚ/ *adj* very hurried and without organization, usually because of anxiety to make something happen as quickly as possible • *We live in a helter-skelter world of congestion, noise and traffic.*

hel·ter–skel·ter /£ˌhel·təˈskel·təʳ, $-t̬ɚˈskel·t̬ɚ/ *adv* • *People were screaming and running helter-skelter down the steps to escape the flames.*

hel·ter–skel·ter STRUCTURE /£ˌhel·təˈskel·təʳ, $-t̬ɚˈskel·t̬ɚ/ *n* [C] *Br and Aus* a tall structure in a FAIRGROUND which you slide down and around for enjoyment

hem EDGE /hem/ *n* [C] the edge of a piece of cloth, such as the bottom edge of a skirt or dress, which is folded over and sewn so that it does not develop loose threads • *If the curtains are too long, you can always* **take the** *hem* **up/let the** *hem* **down** (= make them shorter/longer).

hem *obj* /hem/ *v* [T] **-mm-** • *I'll hem your skirt for you, shall I?*

hem SOUND /hem/ *exclamation* the written form of the sound made when clearing your throat or coughing quietly, in order to get someone's attention

hem in *obj*, **hem** *obj* **in** *v adv* [M usually passive] to surround (someone or something) closely, esp. to prevent movement or action • *The crowd were hemmed in by the police on one side and the railings on the other.* • *The house is hemmed in between a garage and a supermarket.* • *Oh, you can't guess the number of regulations that hem us in.*

he·ma·tol·o·gy /£ˌhiː·məˈtɒl·ə·dʒi, $-ˈtɑː·lə-/ *n* [U] *esp. Am for* HAEMATOLOGY

hem·i·sphere /£ˈhem·ɪ·sfɪəʳ, $-sfɪr/ *n* [C] half of a sphere • *The earth is divided into the northern and southern hemispheres by the equator and into eastern and western hemispheres by some meridians.* • *The main part of the brain is divided into the left and right cerebral hemispheres.*

hem·line /ˈhem·laɪn/ *n* [C] the level at which a skirt or dress hangs, or the lower edge of a skirt or dress • *In the 1960's hemlines suddenly shot up with the introduction of the mini-skirt.* • *The hemline on my dress needs altering because it's slightly too long.*

hem·lock /£ˈhem·lɒk, $-lɑːk/ *n* [U] a type of poison made from a plant which has small white flowers and divided leaves • *After his trial, Socrates ended his life by drinking a cup of hemlock.*

hem·o·glob·in /£ˌhiː·məˈgləʊ·bɪn, $-gloʊ-/ *n* [U] *esp. Am for* HAEMOGLOBIN

hem·o·phil·i·a /ˌhiː·məˈfɪl·i·ə/ *n* [U] *esp. Am for* HAEMOPHILIA

hem·or·rhage /£ˈhem·ᵊr·ɪdʒ, $ˈ-ɚ-/ *n* [C], *v* [I] *Am and Aus for* HAEMORRHAGE

hem·or·rhoids /ˈhem·ᵊr·ɔɪdz, $ˈ-ɚ-/ *pl n esp. Am for* HAEMORRHOIDS

hemp /hemp/ *n* [U] a family of plants, some of which are used to make rope and strong rough cloth and others of which are used to obtain the illegal drug MARIJUANA

hen /hen/ *n* [C] an adult female chicken which is often kept for its eggs, or the female of any bird • *She keeps hens in her back yard and sells their eggs.* • *a hen pheasant* • *(Scot Eng)* Hen is sometimes used as a way of addressing a woman or girl, esp. someone that you like: *"Are you not feeling too good, hen?"* • A **hen night/party** is a party for women only, often one held for a woman in the period just before she is married. Compare **stag night** at STAG ANIMAL.

hence THEREFORE /hents/ *adv* [not gradable] *fml* that is the reason or explanation for; therefore • *His mother was Italian, hence his name – Luca.* • *A better working environment improves people's performance, and hence productivity.*

hence FROM NOW /hents/ *adv* [after n; not gradable] *fml* from this time • *The project will be completed at the end of the decade, two years hence.*

hence·forth /£ˌhentsˈfɔːθ, $-ˈfɔːrθ, ˈ--/, **hence·for·ward** /£ˌhentsˈfɔː·wəd, $-ˈfɔːr·wərd, ˈ-ˌ--/ *adv* [not gradable] *fml or law* starting from this time • *Henceforth, the said building shall be the property of Brendan Duggan.*

hench·man /ˈhentʃ·mən/ *n* [C] *pl* **-men** *esp. disapproving* a person who works for someone in a position of authority or for a criminal, obeying their orders without questioning • *Like other dictators, he tried to distance himself from the dirty deeds carried out by his henchmen.*

hen·na /ˈhen·ə/ *n* [U] a reddish brown DYE made from the powdered leaves of a plant, which is used mainly for colouring the hair and skin • *I use henna to colour my hair.*

hen·na *obj* /ˈhen·ə/ *v* [T] he/she/it **hennas, hennaing,** *past* **hennaed** • *Is her hair hennaed or is that a natural red?* • *Her hands were hennaed with intricate patterns.*

hen·pecked /ˈhen·pekt/ *adj* (of a man) controlled by and a little frightened of a woman, esp. his wife • *My grandfather was the typical henpecked* **husband**, *worn down by my grandmother's constant nagging.*

he·pat·ic /£hepˈæt·ɪk, $-ˈæt̬-/ *adj* [not gradable] *specialized* relating to the LIVER (= an organ in the body) • *During the operation, specialized cell clusters are injected into the patient's hepatic vein, leading to the liver.*

hep·a·ti·tis /£ˌhep·əˈtaɪ·tɪs, $-t̬ɪs/ *n* [U] a disease of the LIVER (= an organ in the body) which causes fever, weakness and JAUNDICE (= yellowing of the skin and eyes) • **Hepatitis A** is a form of the disease which is caused by a virus found in food or drink that has been poisoned by bacteria. • **Hepatitis B** is a more serious form of the disease which is caught from infected blood or dirty HYPODERMIC needles.

hep·ta·gon /£ˈhep·tə·gᵊn, $-gɑːn/ *n* [C] a shape which has seven straight sides

hep·ta·gon·al /hepˈtæg·ᵊn·ᵊl/ *adj* [not gradable]

hep·tath·lon /£hepˈtæθ·lɒn, $-lɑːn/ *n* [C] a competition in which women ATHLETES compete in seven sporting events • *The heptathlon is held over two days and consists of the 100m hurdles, shot put, high jump, 200m, long jump, javelin and 800m.* • Compare BIATHLON; DECATHLON; PENTATHLON.

hep·tath·lete /hepˈtæθ·liːt/ *n* [C]

her /£hɜːʳ, $hɜːr/ *pronoun, determiner* used, usually after a verb or preposition, to refer to a woman, girl or female animal that has just been mentioned or is just about to be mentioned, or used to show that something belongs to or is connected with a woman, girl or female animal that has just been mentioned • *If your flat-mate is around, why don't you bring her to the party?* • *When you go and see Sophia, could you take this package to her?* • *I gave her the letter.* • *Did you give the letter to her?* • *I've never met your sister before. What's her name?* • Her is sometimes used to refer to a country, a boat and, less often, a car: *The boat sank with all her crew.* • Her **own** is used to emphasize that something belongs to or is connected with a particular woman or girl and no-one else: *She got her* **very** *own pony as a birthday present from her parents.* • See also HERS. • LP **Determiners, Sexist language**

her·self /£hɜːˈself, $hɜːr-/ *pronoun* • *She kept telling herself that nothing was wrong.* • *My mother would worry herself to death if she knew what I was doing.* • Herself is sometimes used to give special attention to a female noun or to make clear which female person or animal is being referred to: *She decorated the cake herself.* ○ *She admits herself that she shouldn't have hit him.* ○ *She herself admitted that it was wrong.* • If a woman or girl does something **by** herself, she does it alone or without help from anyone else: *She lives* **(all)** *by herself in an enormous house.* ○ *Holly's only three but she wrote her name* **(all)** *by herself.* • *She's got the whole house* **to** *herself* (= for her own use only) *now that her husband has gone away.* • If a woman or girl **is/seems** herself, she is in her usual mental or physical condition: *Jane hasn't* **been** *herself recently.* • LP **Reflexive pronouns and verbs**

her·ald *obj* /ˈher·ᵊld/ *v* [T] *fml or literary* to be a sign that (something important, and often good) is starting to happen, or to make (something) publicly known, esp. by celebrating or praising it • *The president's speech heralds a new era in relations between these two troubled states.* • *This latest development has been heralded* **as** *a major breakthrough in modern science.* • *This novel comes three years after the writer's* **much** *heralded* (= greatly praised) *first book.*

her·ald /ˈher·ᵊld/ *n* [C] *fml or literary* • *If this first opera of the season is a herald* (= sign) **of** *what is to come, we can expect great things.* • In the past, a herald was a person who delivered important messages and made announcements.

her·al·dry /ˈher·ᵊl·dri/ *n* [U] the study of **coats of arms** and the history of the families which they belong to

her·al·dic /herˈæl·dɪk/ *adj* [not gradable] • *a heraldic banner*

herb /£hɜːb, $ɜːrb/ *n* [C] a type of plant whose leaves are used in cooking to give flavour to particular dishes, or which are used in making medicine • *Basil, oregano, thyme and rosemary are all herbs.* • *A large range of herbs and spices are used in Indian cookery.* • *Do you prefer* **dried** *or* **fresh** *herbs to cook with?* • Ⓕ Ⓟⓛ Ⓡⓤⓢ

herb·al /£ˈhɜː·bᵊl, $ˈɜːr-/ *adj* [not gradable] • Herbal means relating to herbs or made from herbs: *She believes in the beneficial properties of herbal remedies.* ○ *Have you ever smoked herbal cigarettes?* • **Herbal tea** is another word for TISANE.

herb·al·ist /£ˈhɜː·bᵊl·ɪst, $ˈɜːr-/ *n* [C] • A herbalist is a person who grows or sells herbs for medicinal uses.

herb·y /£ˈhɜː·bi, $ˈɜːr-/ *adj* **-ier, -iest** *infml* • *This salad dressing is nice and herby* (= It tastes of herbs).

her·ba·ceous /£hɜːˈbeɪ·ʃəs, $hər-/ *adj* [not gradable] *specialized* (of plants) soft, fleshy and not woody • A **herbaceous border** is a narrow strip of land in a garden which is planted with different types of flowering plants that mainly live for more than two years.

her·bi·cide /£ˈhɜː·bɪ·saɪd, $ˈhɜːr-/ *n* [C] a chemical which is used to destroy plants, esp. WEEDS (= unwanted wild plants) • *There is a lot of concern over the amount of herbicides and pesticides used in farming.* • Compare INSECTICIDE; PESTICIDE.

her·bi·vore /£ˈhɜː·bɪ·vɔːʳ, $ˈhɜːr·bə·vɔːr/ *n* [C] an animal that eats grass and other plants • *Cows and sheep are herbivores.* • Compare CARNIVORE.

her·bi·vor·ous /£hɜːˈbɪv·ᵊr·əs, $hɜːrˈbɪv·ər-/ *adj* [not gradable] • *Kangaroos are herbivorous mammals.*

her·cu·le·an /£ˌhɜː·kjʊˈliː·ən, $ˌhɜːr-/ *adj* needing great strength and determination • *If he's going to hold his party together in this time of crisis, it will require a herculean* **effort**. • *She has had the herculean* **task** *of bringing up four children single-handedly.*

herd /£hɜːd, $hɜːrd/ *n* [C + sing/pl v] a large group of animals of the same type that live and feed together • *a herd* **of** *cattle/elephants/goats* • *(esp. disapproving)* A herd is also a large group of people that is considered together as a group and not separately: *A herd of commuters got off the train.* ○ *She vowed always to do her own thing and never to follow* **the herd** (= not to do what other people were doing). • *(disapproving)* The **herd instinct** is the tendency to act like everyone else without considering the reason why.

herd *obj* /£hɜːd, $hɜːrd/ *v* [T] • To herd animals is to make them move together as a group: *A woman was herding the goats up the mountainside.* • *(esp. disapproving)* If people are herded somewhere, they are made to move there as a group, often with force or against their wishes: *The football fans complained that they had been herded into a police-station forecourt.*

herds·man /£ˈhɜːdz·mən, $ˈhɜːrdz-/ *n* [C] *pl* **-men** a man who takes care of a large group of animals of the same type

here /£hɪəʳ, $hɪr/ *adv* [not gradable] in, at, or to this place • *I've lived here for about two years.* • *I like it here – I wouldn't want to live anywhere else.* • *London is only 50 miles from here.* • *Did you leave your bike here, or is it at home?* • *Come here – I've got something to show you.* • *Shall I come to your place, or do you want to come over here?* • *How long are you* **over** *here* (= in this country)? • *"Where does it hurt?" "Here, just above my ankle."* • *(infml) Give it here* (= to me) *and I'll have a look at it.* • Here can be used at the beginning of a statement to introduce someone or something: *Here's Fiona – let me introduce you to her.* ○ *Here's the book I said I'd lend you.* • Here can also be used to show that someone has arrived or that something has started: *Here they are! We thought you'd never come!* ○ *They're here – I've just seen their car pull in.* ○ *Here we are* (= We have arrived) – *I said it wouldn't take more than half an hour by car.* ○ *Now that Christmas is here* (= has begun), *I might as well give up my diet.* • Here can also be used to refer to someone or something that is near you: *I don't know anything about this, but I'm sure my colleague here can help you.* ○ *It says here* (= in this piece of writing) *that she was born in 1943.* • Here can sometimes refer to the present moment in time: *Shall we break here* (= now) *and have a coffee?* ○ *Where do we*

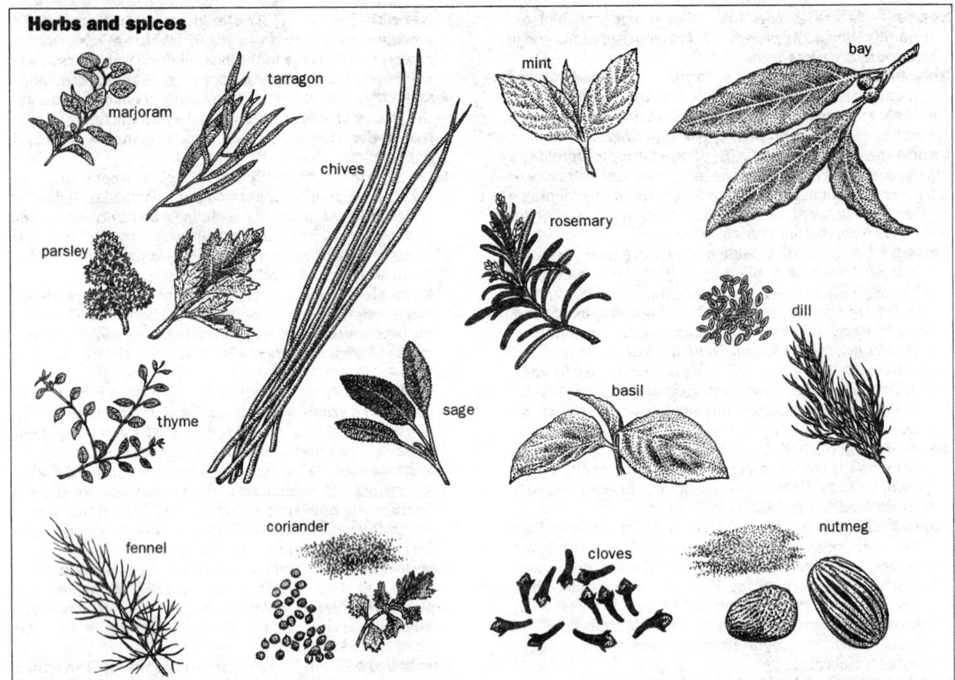

go/ *Where do we take it* **from** *here?* (= What should we do next?) • You can say **here you are** when you are giving something to someone: *"Could you pass the sugar, please?" "Here you are."* ○ *Here you are, try some of this – it should soon sort out your cough.* • *(fml or literary)* **The here and now** can be used to refer to the present time, or to life as it is lived on Earth rather than the spiritual life that might exist after death: *She complained that while most people were interested in what had happened in the past and what would happen in the future, he was only interested in the here and now.* • *There are a few books* **here and there** (= in different places), *but apart from that the room is quite bare.* • *(infml)* People sometimes say **here goes** just before they do something brave or something that they have never done before: *Well, I've never ridden a motorbike before, so here goes!* • *(infml)* **Here we go** is a phrase often sung repeatedly by British football crowds when their team is successful. • *(infml)* People sometimes say **here we go (again)** to express their annoyance when something happens again that always happens in this way: *Oh, here we go again! Claude is in love for the fourth time this month!* • People sometimes say **here's to** a particular person as a way of wishing them happiness or success: *Here's to the happy couple!* • *(saying)* 'Here today and gone tomorrow' is said of something which lasts only a short time: *I don't know what Richard does with his money – it's here today and gone tomorrow.* • *"Here's to you, Mrs Robinson"* (from the Simon and Garfunkel song *Mrs Robinson*, from the film *The Graduate*, 1968) • *"Here's Johnny"* (phrase from The Johnny Carson Show on American television, 1961-)

here·ab·outs *Br and Aus* /£ˌhɪə·rə'baʊts, $ˌhɪr·ə-/, *Am* **here·ab·out** /£ˌhɪə·rə'baʊt, $ˌhɪr·ə-/ *adv* [not gradable] in this area; near this place • *Any trouble hereabouts is swiftly dealt with by the police.*

here·af·ter [IN THE FUTURE] /£ˌhɪə'rɑːf·tər, $ˌhɪr'æf·tɚ/, **here·in·after** *adv* [not gradable] *fml or law* (written in books or legal documents) starting from this time; in the future • *Elizabeth Gaskell's novel 'Ruth' will hereafter be cited within the text as EG.*

here·af·ter [AFTER DEATH] /£ˌhɪə'rɑːf·tər, $ˌhɪr'æf·tɚ/ *n* [U] **the hereafter** *fml or literary* life after death • *She had a firm conviction that they would meet again* **in** *the hereafter.*

here·by /£ˌhɪə'baɪ, $ˌhɪr-/ *adv* [not gradable] *fml or law* (used in official statements) as a result of this statement or law • *I hereby pronounce you man and wife.*

he·red·i·ta·ry /hɪ'red·ɪ·tri/ *adj* [not gradable] (of characteristics or diseases) able to be given through the GENES of a parent to a child, or (of titles and positions in society) given as a right from parent to child • *The disease is hereditary, so there is a chance her daughter may suffer from it too.* • *It is a hereditary* **title**, *so Mark Howard will become Sir Mark Howard on his father's death.* • *She believes that hereditary* **peerages** (= high social ranks) *should be abolished.* • A **hereditary peer** is a person who has received a particular title and who can give it to their child.

he·red·i·ty /hɪ'red·ə·ti/ *n* [U] the process by which characteristics are able to be given from a parent to their child through the GENES • *Diet and exercise can influence a person's weight, but heredity is also a factor.*

here·in /£ˌhɪə'rɪn, $ˌhɪr-/ *adv* [not gradable] *fml or law* in this • *The people have no faith in their government, and herein* **lies** *the root of the problem.*

here·in·after /£ˌhɪə·rɪn'ɑːf·tər, $ˌhɪr·ɪn'æf·tɚ/ *adv* [not gradable] *fml or law* HEREAFTER

her·e·sy /'her·ə·si/ *n* (the act of having) an opinion or belief that is the opposite of or against what is the official or popular opinion, or an action which shows that you have no respect for the official opinion • *Radical remarks like this amount to heresy in the far-right Republican party.* [U] • *She committed the heresy of playing a Madonna song on a classical music station.* [C] • Heresy is also a belief which is against the principles of a particular religion: *He was burned at the stake in the fifteenth century for heresy.* [U]

her·e·tic /'her·ə·tɪk/ *n* [C] • A heretic is a person who is guilty of heresy: *An advocate of Marxism in this age of capitalism is regarded as a heretic.* ○ *She was branded a heretic and burned at the stake.*

he·re·ti·cal /£hə'ret·ɪ·kəl, $-'reṭ-/ *adj* • *Her belief that a split would be good for the party was regarded as heretical.*

here·to /£ˌhɪə'tuː, $ˌhɪr-/ *adv* [not gradable] *fml or law* to this matter or document • *You will find attached hereto the text of the Treaty on European Union.*

here·to·fore /£ˌhɪə·tʊ'fɔːr, $ˌhɪr·tʊ'fɔːr/ *adv* [not gradable] *fml or law* before this point in time; previously • *He argued, with more passion than heretofore, for the abolition of the tax.*

here·up·on /£ˌhɪə·rə'pɒn, $ˌhɪr·ə'pɑːn/ *adv* [not gradable] *fml* at this point in time

here·with /£ˌhɪə'wɪð, -'wɪθ, $ˌhɪr-/ *adv* [not gradable] *fml or law* together with this letter or other official written material • *I enclose three documents herewith.*

her·it·age /£'her·ɪ·tɪdʒ, $-ṭɪdʒ/ *n* [U] features belonging to the culture of a particular society, such as traditions, languages or buildings, which still exist from the past and which have a historical importance • *The charity aims to preserve old churches which it sees as an invaluable part of our* **national** *heritage.* • *She believes that science is as much* *part of our* **cultural** *heritage as art or architecture.* • **Heritage-listed building** is *Aus for* **listed building**. See at LIST [RECORD].

her·maph·ro·dite /£hɜː'mæf·rə·daɪt, $hɜːr-/ *n* [C] a plant, animal or person with both male and female sex organs

her·met·ic [CLOSED] /£hɜː'met·ɪk, $hɚ'met̬-/ *adj* [not gradable] *specialized* (of a container) so tightly closed that no air can leave or enter • *The hermetic* **seal** *on the packet means that the food lasts longer.* • *(literary)* If a particular society is hermetic, the people who live within it rarely communicate with those who live outside it: *He entered the hermetic world of the monastery at a young age.* ○ *Politics, war and the real world rarely threatened to impinge on her hermetic existence.*

her·met·ic·ally /£hɜː'met·ɪ·kli, $hɚ'met̬-/ *adv* [not gradable] *specialized* • *The disk is housed in a hermetically* **sealed** *unit to protect it from dust.* • *(fig.) We drove past a row of squalid shacks to our hotel, where we slept in air-conditioned, hermetically* **sealed** *rooms* (= rooms free from the dust, dirt and noise of the surrounding area).

her·met·ic [MAGICAL] /£hɜː'met·ɪk, $hɚ'met̬-/ *adj* [not gradable] *old use* magical or connected with ALCHEMY • *Her novels explore the hermetic world of wizards and potions.*

her·mit /£'hɜː·mɪt, $'hɜːr-/ *n* [C] a person who lives alone and apart from the rest of society, esp. for religious reasons • *The cave was inhabited by a hermit in the 19th century.* • *(fig.) He leads the life of a hermit, scarcely setting foot outside his New York apartment.*

her·mit·age /£'hɜː·mɪ·tɪdʒ, $'hɜːr·mɪ·t̬ɪdʒ/ *n* [C] • A hermitage is a place where a religious person lives on their own, apart from the rest of society.

her·n·ia /£'hɜː·ni·ə, $'hɜːr-/, **rup·ture** *n* [C] a medical condition in which an organ pushes through a weakness or hole in the wall of muscle which surrounds it, sometimes resulting from the muscle being stretched too much • *He hasn't been able to play football since his hernia operation.*

he·ro [PERSON] (*pl* **heroes**), *female also* **her·o·ine** /£'hɪə·rəʊ, $'hɪr·oʊ, £'her·əʊ·ɪn, $'-oʊ-/ *n* [C] a person who is admired for having done something very brave or having achieved something great, or the main character in a book, film or play, esp. one who is admired for their good qualities • *He was one of the great First World War heroes.* • *The programme recounted the career of one of the greatest sporting heroes of our time.* • *Harrison Ford always seems to play the part of the hero in films.* • *Meryl Streep plays the heroine in the film.* • If someone is your hero, you admire them greatly: *Humphrey Bogart's my hero – I've seen every one of his films!* • *(infml)* If you say that someone is a hero, you mean that you admire them for doing which needs to be done but which is unpleasant: *Antonio says he'll take my parents to the airport at four o'clock in the morning – what a hero!* • **Hero worship** is a feeling of extreme admiration for someone, imagining that they have qualities or abilities that are better than anyone else's: *His hero worship of his largely absent father stayed with him throughout his adulthood.* ○ *He* **hero worships** *his older brother.* • See also **anti-hero** at ANTI-.

he·ro·ic /£hɪ'rəʊ·ɪk, $-'roʊ-/ *adj* • *He was famed for heroic* (= brave) *deeds during the war.* • *(infml)* If you make a heroic attempt or effort to do something, you try very hard to do it: *Despite Roz's heroic efforts to liven it up, the party was a disaster.*

he·ro·ic·ally /£hɪ'rəʊ·ɪ·kli, $-'roʊ/ *adv* • *(infml) The team fought back heroically* (= in a way using a lot of effort) *from 3-1 down to finish the match 3-3.*

he·ro·ics /£hɪ'rəʊ·ɪks, $-'roʊ-/ *pl n esp. disapproving* • Heroics are risky or foolish actions which are only done to make other people admire you: *Mark was in no mood for heroics after his fall and skied very slowly down the mountainside.*

her·o·i·sm /£'her·əʊ·ɪ·zᵊm, $'-oʊ-/ *n* [U] • Heroism is great bravery: *He received the George Cross for his act of heroism.*

he·ro [FOOD] /£'hɪə·rəʊ, $'hɪr·oʊ/, **sub·ma·rine sand·wich** *n* [C] *pl* **heroes** *Am* a long thin SANDWICH filled with cold meat, cheese and salad

her·o·in /£'her·əʊ·ɪn, $-oʊ-/ *n* [U] a powerful drug which is taken illegally for pleasure or is sometimes used as a medicine to reduce extreme pain • *Heroin is obtained from morphine and is extremely addictive.* • *He died from a heroin overdose.* • *She's a heroin* **addict**.

her·on /'her·ᵊn/ *n* [C] *pl* **herons** or **heron** a large long-legged bird with a long neck and grey or white feathers which lives near water • [PIC] **Birds**

her·pes /£'hɜː·piːz, $'hɜːr-/ *n* [U] any of several very infectious diseases which cause painful red sores to appear on the face, the main part of the body, the lips or the sexual organs • *genital herpes* • *People who suffer from the sort of herpes which is around the mouth often refer to it as a 'cold sore'.*

her·ring /'her·ɪŋ/ *n pl* **herrings** or **herring** a long silvery coloured fish which swims in large groups in the sea, or its flesh eaten as food • *Herrings swim in large groups called shoals.* [C] • *Herring is rich in vitamin D.* [U]

her·ring·bone /£'her·ɪŋ·bəʊn, $-boʊn/ *n* [U] a pattern, used esp. in cloth, which consists of rows of V shapes • *herringbone tweed* • *He wore a herringbone jacket.* • [PIC] **Patterns**

hers /£hɜːz, $hɜːrz/ *pronoun* used to show that something belongs to or is connected with a woman, girl or female animal that has just been mentioned • *I'm looking for Sylvia's bag. Is that black one hers?* • *My sister and I both own BMWs – mine is red and hers is black.*

her·self /£hɜː'self, $hɜːr-/ *pronoun* See at HER

hertz /£hɜːts, $hɜːrts/ (*abbreviation* **Hz**) *n* [C] *pl* **hertz** a unit for measuring the number of times something happens every second, esp. in electronics • *Adults usually cannot hear sound of a frequency greater than about 20 000 Hz.* • See also KILOHERTZ; MEGAHERTZ.

hes·i·tate /'hez·ɪ·teɪt/ *v* [I] to pause before you do or say something, often because you are uncertain or nervous about it • *When you reach the pool side, don't hesitate, just jump straight in.* • *He hesitated before he spoke, as if he wasn't sure how his words would be received.* • *"Do you love me?" she asked. He hesitated and then said, "I'm not sure".* • *If you need anything, don't hesitate* **to** *call me.* [+ to infinitive] • *If I were you, I wouldn't hesitate* **to** *buy that jacket – it really suits you.* [+ to infinitive] • *"He who (originally 'the woman that') hesitates is lost"* (Joseph Addison in the play *Cato*, 1713)

hes·i·ta·tion /ˌhez·ɪ'teɪ·ʃᵊn/ *n* • *After a slight hesitation, she began to speak.* [C] • *Any hesitation on the part of the government will be seen as weakness.* [U] • *I'd invite him without hesitation, but I'm just worried that too many people are coming already.* [U] • *(fml) I have no hesitation* **in** *recommending Ms Shapur for the job.* [U]

hes·i·tant /'hez·ɪ·tᵊnt/ *adj* • *She gave me a hesitant smile.* • *He has rather a hesitant manner, as though he's slightly unsure of himself.* • *You seemed a bit hesitant* **about** *recommending that restaurant – is something wrong with it?*

hes·i·tant·ly /'hez·ɪ·tᵊnt·li/ *adv* • *She approached the teacher hesitantly.*

hes·i·tanc·y /'hez·ɪ·tᵊnt·si/ *n* [U] • *The president is not known for his hesitancy in such matters.*

hes·si·an /'hes·i·ən/, *Am usually* **bur·lap** *n* [U] a type of thick rough cloth used for items and coverings which must be strong • *The wheat was transported in large hessian sacks.*

het·er·o /£'het·ᵊr·əʊ, $'het̬·ɚ·oʊ/ *n* [C] *pl* **heteros** *infml for* HETEROSEXUAL

het·er·o·dox /£'het·ᵊr·ə·dɒks, $'het̬·ɚ·ə·dɑːks/ *adj* [not gradable] *fml* (of beliefs, ideas or activities) different and in opposition to generally accepted beliefs or standards • *His opinions have always been distinctly heterodox.* • *They left the country to avoid persecution for their heterodox views.* • Compare ORTHODOX.

het·e·ro·dox·y /£'het·ᵊr·ə·dɒk·si, $'het̬·ɚ·ə·dɑːk-/ *n* [U] *fml*

het·er·og·en·eous /£ˌhet·ᵊr·ə'dʒiː·ni·əs, $ˌhet̬·ə·roʊ-/ *adj fml* consisting of various parts that are very different from each other • *Switzerland is a heterogeneous confederation of 26 self-governing cantons.* • *There was a wonderfully heterogeneous gathering of people at the party.* • Compare HOMOGENEOUS.

het·er·og·en·e·i·ty /£ˌhet·ᵊr·əʊ·dʒə'neɪ·ɪ·ti, $ˌhet̬·ə·roʊ·dʒə'neɪ·ə·t̬i/ *n* [U] *fml* • *Archaeological studies of the tombs have shown the heterogeneity of religious practices in the region.*

het·er·o·sex·i·sm /£ˌhet·ᵊr·əʊ'sek·sɪ·zᵊm, $ˌhet̬·ə·roʊ-/ *n* [U] the dislike, fear, or unfair treatment of people who are sexually attracted to people of the same sex

het·er·o·sex·ist /£ˌhet·ᵊr·əʊ'sek·sɪst, $ˌhet̬·ə·roʊ-/ *adj*

het·er·o·sex·u·al /£ˌhet·ᵊr·əʊ'sek·sjʊ·ᵊl, $ˌhet̬·ə·roʊ-/, *infml* **het·er·o** *n* [C] a person who is sexually attracted to people of the opposite sex • *Many heterosexuals still mistakenly think of AIDS as being a homosexual disease.* • Compare BISEXUAL; HOMOSEXUAL.

het·er·o·sex·u·al /£ˌhet·ᵊr·əʊˈsek·sjʊ·ᵊl, $ˌhet̬·ə·roʊ-/ *adj* [not gradable] • *heterosexual sex/relationships* • *She is heterosexual but has no plans to marry or embark on a sexual relationship with a man.*

het·er·o·sex·u·al·ly /£ˌhet·ᵊr·əʊˈsek·sjʊ·ᵊl·i, $ˌhet̬·ə·roʊ-/ *adv* [not gradable] • *You shouldn't presume that someone is heterosexually inclined.*

het·er·o·sex·u·al·i·ty /£ˌhet·ᵊr·əʊˌsek·sjʊˈæl·ə·ti, $ˌhet̬·ə·roʊˌsek·ʃuˈæl·ə·t̬i/ *n* [U] • *Many young people still regard heterosexuality as an automatic guarantee of protection from the HIV virus.*

het up /£het, $het̬/ *adj infml* anxious or angry and not calm • *There's no need to get so het up about there being a few dirty dishes in the sink!*

heu·ris·tic /hjʊəˈrɪs·tɪk/ *adj specialized* (of a method of teaching) allowing the students to learn by discovering things themselves and learning from their own experiences rather than by telling them things • *He believes in the heuristic approach to teaching.*

hew *obj* /hjuː/ *v* [T] *past simple* **hewed**, *past part* **hewed** or **hewn** /hjuːn/ to cut (a large piece) out of rock, stone or another hard material in a rough way • *The monument was hewn* **out of** *the side of a mountain.* • *He specializes in creating roughly-hewn sculptures out of wood.*

hex /heks/ *n* [C] *Am and Aus infml* an evil SPELL, bringing bad luck and trouble • *Someone's* **put** *a hex* **on** *my computer this morning – it keeps on crashing.*

hex·a·gon /£ˈhek·sə·gən, $-gɑːn/ *n* [C] a shape which has six straight sides • PIC **Shapes**

hex·ag·on·al /hekˈsæg·ᵊn·ᵊl/ *adj* [not gradable] • *a hexagonal building/object* • *The church tower is hexagonal in shape.*

hey /heɪ/ *exclamation infml* used as a way of attracting someone's attention, sometimes in a way which is not very polite • *Hey! What are you doing with my car?* • *Hey, you guys, are you coming to the beach?* • *(Br and Aus infml)* **Hey presto** is said by someone performing a magical trick, at the point when they are producing the results of their trick, or in other situations when something appears or happens quickly like magic: *You put your money in the machine and, hey presto, the coffee comes out!* • LP **Meeting someone**

hey·day /ˈheɪ·deɪ/ *n* [C usually sing] the most successful or popular period of someone or something • *In their heyday, the group sold as many records as all the other groups in the country put together.* • *By the 80s, punk rock had really had its heyday* (= had stopped being very popular).

hi /haɪ/ *exclamation infml* used as an informal greeting, usually to people who you know • *Hi, Rachel!* • *Hi, how are you doing?* • LP **Meeting someone**

hi·a·tus /£haɪˈeɪ·təs, $-t̬əs/ *n* [C usually sing] *fml or literary* a short pause in which nothing happens or is said, or a space where something is missing • *Tourists are once again visiting the country's capital after a brief hiatus caused by the war.* • *The company expects to resume production of the vehicle again after a two-month hiatus.*

hi·ber·nate /£ˈhaɪ·bə·neɪt, $-bɚ-/ *v* [I] (of some animals and insects) to spend the winter months in a sleep-like state, with the body temperature and the rate of breathing lowered, and gradually using up fat which is stored up during the warmer months • *The turtle hibernates in a shallow burrow for six months of the year.*

hi·ber·na·tion /£ˌhaɪ·bəˈneɪ·ʃᵊn, $-bɚ-/ *n* [U] • *The bear* **goes into** *hibernation during the autumn.*

hib·is·cus /hɪˈbɪs·kəs/ *n* [C] a tropical plant or bush with large brightly coloured flowers

hic·cup /ˈhɪk·ʌp/, **hic·cough** /ˈhɪk·ʌp/ *n* [C often plural] the loud sound which is caused by a sudden tightening of a muscle just below the chest, usually happening repeatedly over a short period • *You can usually get rid of hiccups by drinking water very quickly.* • **The** hiccups or **an attack of (the)** hiccups is a situation in which this noise happens repeatedly: *I've* **got** *the hiccups.* • A hiccup is also a problem which delays or interrupts something for a while, but which does not usually cause serious difficulties: *We've had one or two* **slight** *hiccups, but progress has generally been quite steady.* • LP **'-ough' pronunciation**

hic·cup /ˈhɪk·ʌp/ *v* [I] **-p-** or **-pp-** • *I can't stop hiccuping – does anyone know a good cure?*

hick /hɪk/ *n* [C] *Am and Aus infml disapproving* a person from the countryside who does not like or suit life in the city • *Did you think I was some kind of hick just up from the country?* • *It's a bit of a hick* **town** (= a town which is a long way from a city) *– there's not much happening really.*

hick·or·y /£ˈhɪk·ᵊr·i, $ˈ-ɚ-/ *n* a small tree from N America or E Asia which has edible nuts, or the hard wood from this tree • *They planted a hickory in their garden.* [C] • *New England is famous for its forests of oak, maple and hickory.* [U] • **Hickory chips** are small pieces of hickory wood used as a fuel for a BARBECUE (= a method of cooking outside) which give food a smoky taste.

hicks·ville /ˈhɪks·vɪl/ *n* [U] *esp. Am infml disapproving* a small town or village which is not interesting and not modern

hide *(obj)* OUT OF VIEW /haɪd/ *v past simple* **hid** /hɪd/, *past part* **hidden** /ˈhɪd·ᵊn/ to put (something or someone) in a place where they cannot be seen or found, or to put (yourself) somewhere where you cannot be seen or found • *She used to hide her diary under her pillow.* [T] • *A kilo of heroin was found hidden inside the lining of the suitcase.* [T] • *They hid the escaped prisoner in their barn.* [T] • *Rosie wants you to go and look for her – she's hiding somewhere upstairs.* [I] • *I like wearing sunglasses – I feel I can hide* **behind** *them.* [I] • To hide something is also to prevent it from being seen: *He tries to hide his bald patch by sweeping his hair over to one side.* [T] • If you hide an emotion, you do not show it: *The president made no attempt to hide his annoyance at the newspaper's allegations.* [T] • If you hide information from someone, you do not let that person know it: *I feel sure there's something about her past that she's trying to hide* **from** *me.* [T] • **Hide-and-seek** is a children's game in which a group of children hide in secret places and one child, who all this time has had their eyes closed and has been counting up to a particular number, has to go to look for the other children. • *(infml)* A **hidey-hole** or **hidy-hole** is a small place for hiding things in. • *(saying)* 'Don't hide your light under a bushel' means do not keep your good qualities and abilities secret from other people. • *"The Hidden Persuaders"* (title of a book on advertising by Vance Packard, 1957)

hide *Br and Aus* /haɪd/, *Am* **blind** *n* [C] • A hide is a place where people can watch wild animals or birds without being noticed by them.

hid·ing /ˈhaɪ·dɪŋ/ *n* [U] • *The old house was full of cupboards and small rooms that the children could use as hiding* **places.** • Someone who is **in** hiding or has **gone into** hiding has secretly gone somewhere where they cannot be found: *Police believe that the terrorists are in hiding somewhere on the mainland.* • See also HIDING.

hide SKIN /haɪd/ *n* the strong thick skin of an animal which is used for making leather • *What's the bag made of? Is it calf hide?* [U] • *She prepares animal hides for use in the manufacture of walking shoes.* [C]

hide·a·way /ˈhaɪd·ə·weɪ/ *n* [C] *infml* a place where someone goes when they want to relax and get away from their usual surroundings • *They have a country hideaway in the Lake District where they go at weekends.*

hide·bound /ˈhaɪd·baʊnd/ *adj disapproving* limited by having fixed opinions and ways of doing things and not able to be changed or influenced, esp. by new or modern ideas • *It's a very hidebound society and views anything new with suspicion.* • *They're very hidebound in the accounts department – they tend to stick to the rules.*

hid·e·ous /ˈhɪd·i·əs/ *adj* extremely unpleasant or ugly • *They have just built some hideous new apartment blocks on the seafront.* • *She wears the most hideous colour combinations you could ever imagine.*

hid·e·ous·ly /ˈhɪd·i·ə·sli/ *adv* • *He's not hideously ugly, but he's not what you would call handsome.* • *(infml)* Hideously can also be used to emphasize the great degree of something: *It's a wonderful restaurant, and it's not even hideously* (= extremely) *expensive.*

hid·e·ous·ness /ˈhɪd·i·ə·snəs/ *n* [U]

hide·out /ˈhaɪd·aʊt/ *n* [C] a secret place where someone can go when they do not want to be found by other people • *The police discovered the wanted man in a hideout near the airport.* • *The children have a* **secret** *hideout somewhere in the garden.*

hid·ing /ˈhaɪ·dɪŋ/ *n* [C usually sing] *dated or humorous* a punishment by beating repeatedly • *He threatened her with* **a good** (= severe) *hiding if she said another word.* • *(infml)* A hiding is also a total defeat: *"How did the French team get on in their match against Italy?" "They got a real hiding!"* • *(Br infml)* If someone is **on a hiding to nothing**, they are trying to do something when there is no chance that they will succeed: *They're on a hiding to* *nothing trying to get money out of this government.* • See also **hiding** at HIDE [OUT OF VIEW].

hie *obj* /haɪ/ *v* [T] **hying**, *past* **hied** *old use or humorous* to hurry (yourself) to a particular place • *I must hie* **me** *to the sales before all the bargains are gone.*

hier·ar·chy /£ˈhaɪə·rɑː·ki, $ˈhaɪr·ɑːr-/ *n* [C] a system in which people are put at various levels or ranks according to their importance • *There's a very rigid social hierarchy in their society.* • A hierarchy is also the people in the upper levels of an organization who control it: *She is considered to be the most likely candidate for deputy leader in the party hierarchy.*

hier·ar·chi·cal /£ˌhaɪəˈrɑː·kɪ·kəl, $ˌhaɪrˈɑːr-/ *adj* • *It is a very hierarchical organization in which everyone's status is very clearly defined.*

hier·ar·chi·cally /£ˌhaɪəˈrɑː·kɪ·kli, $ˌhaɪrˈɑːr-/ *adv* • *The organization is hierarchically structured.*

hier·o·glyph·ic /£ˌhaɪə·rəˈglɪf·ɪk, $-roʊ-/, *specialized* **hier·o·glyph** /£ˈhaɪə·rə·glɪf, $-roʊ-/ *n* [C usually pl] a picture or symbol which represents a word, and which is used in some writing systems, such as that used in ancient Egypt • *Hieroglyphics are carved into the walls of the temple.*

hi·fal·u·tin /£ˌhaɪ·fəˈluː·tɪn, $-t̬ɪn/ *adj infml* See at HIGHFALUTIN

hi–fi /ˈhaɪ·faɪ/ *n* [C] a set of electronic equipment which is used to play recorded sound, esp. music • *I've just bought a new hi-fi.* • *She works in a shop selling hi-fi equipment.*

hi–fi /ˈhaɪ·faɪ/ *adj* [not gradable] • Hi-fi is used to refer to broadcast or recorded sound of a high quality that is similar as possible to the original sound: *The new television system offers wider pictures and hi-fi sound.*

hig·gle·dy–pig·gle·dy /ˌhɪg·l̩.diˈpɪg·l̩.di/ *adj, adv infml* mixed up and in no particular order • *I still haven't unpacked my clothes – they're all higgledy-piggledy in my suitcase.* • *The project was set up in a rather higgledy-piggledy way, with no overall structure.*

high [DISTANCE] /haɪ/ *adj* **-er, -est** (esp. of things that are not living) being a large distance from top to bottom or a long way above the ground, or having the stated distance from top to bottom • *Everest is one of the highest mountains in the world.* • *The hall has a high elegant ceiling.* • *Could you get that book down, please – the shelf is too high for me to reach.* • *We had to climb over a wall that was three-metres high.* • *It's two and a half metres high and one metre wide.* • *The corn grew waist-high* (= as high as a person's waist) *in the fields.* • *She has very high cheekbones* (= her bones are close to her eyes). • *(infml)* If someone **leaves** you **high and dry**, they do something which is very inconvenient for you and puts you in a very difficult situation: *They pulled out of the deal at the last minute leaving us high and dry.* • *(old use)* **On high** is used to refer to God in heaven: *He looked down from on high.* ○ See also **on high** at HIGH [IMPORTANT]. • A **high chair** is a long-legged chair for a baby or a small child, usually with a small table connected to it for the child to eat from. [PIC> **Chair** • A **high-five** is a greeting or an expression of admiration in which two people each raise a hand above their shoulder and bring the fronts of their hands together with force. • **High heels** or **high-heeled shoes** are shoes usually worn by women that make the person wearing them seem taller: *I find it quite difficult to walk in high heels.* • The **high jump** is a sport in which competitors try to jump over a bar supported on two poles. The height of the bar is gradually raised and the winner is the person who jumps the highest without knocking the bar off the poles: *She is expected to become the first British woman to clear* (= jump higher than) *two metres in the high jump.* ○ *How many* **high jumpers** *are competing today?* [PIC> **Sports** • *(Br and Aus)* Someone who is **for the high jump** is going to be severely punished for something they have done wrong: *She'll be for the high jump when her tutor finds out that she still hasn't done her essay.* • Compare **for it** at FOR [IN TROUBLE]. • **High noon** is exactly twelve o'clock, when the sun should be at its highest point in the sky: *We reluctantly left our air-conditioned hotel and walked out into the stifling heat of high noon.* • The **high noon** of something is the most important stage in its development: *He produced his best-known paintings at the high noon* **of** *his Impressionist phase.* • A roof that is **high-pitched** slopes steeply: *Many of the houses are two storeys tall with wooden frames and high-pitched gable roofs.* ○ See also **high-pitched** at HIGH [SOUND]. • A **high rise** is a tall modern building with a lot of floors: *She lives in a high rise overlooking the river.* ○ *I would hate to work in a high-rise office building.* • **High tide** or **high water** is the time when the sea or a river reaches its highest level and comes furthest up the beach or the bank. • Something's **high tide** is its most successful point: *The signing of the peace treaty was the high tide* **of** *her presidency.* • A **high water mark** is a mark which shows the point furthest up a beach that can be reached by the sea, or which shows the greatest height reached by an area of water during a flood: *(fig.) His 1991 election victory was probably the high water mark* **of** *his popularity* (= the point when he was the most popular). • *"High Noon"* (film title, 1952) • [LP> **Measurements**

high /haɪ/ *adv* **-er, -est** • *You'll have to hit the ball quite high to get it over that net.* • *Concorde flies much higher than most aeroplanes.* • If you say that you have been searching for something **high and low**, you mean that you have been searching everywhere: *I've been searching high and low for that shoe and I still can't find it!*

high [ABOVE AVERAGE] /haɪ/ *adj* **-er, -est** greater than the usual level • *The job demands a high level of concentration.* • *Salaries are high but so is the cost of living.* • *He suffers from high blood pressure.* • *Antique furniture fetches very high prices these days.* • *She got very high marks in her geography exam.* • *It is very dangerous to drive at high speed when the roads are wet.* • *I don't have a very high opinion of Gino after his behaviour last night.* • *He's in a high-security prison.* • *She demands very high* **standards** *from the people who work for her.* • High **standards** or **principles** are also very moral standards: *My mother is a woman of high principles.* • If you do something **in high dudgeon**, you do it angrily, usually because of the way you have been treated: *After waiting an hour for them, he drove off in high dudgeon.* • In the Church of England, **high church** means containing a lot of customary acts and ceremonies, like those of the Roman Catholic Church, or believing that church services should contain a lot of customary acts and ceremonies: *Ceremony plays an important part in high church services.* ○ *Our family has always been high church.* ○ Compare **low church** at LOW [SMALL IN AMOUNT]. • If something is described as **high-class**, it is of good quality: *The hotel offers high-class accommodation in the city centre.* • **High definition television** is a system which produces very good quality television images in greater detail than ordinary systems. • A **high explosive** is a very powerful explosive: *Gelignite is a high explosive.* ○ *Allied planes bombed the road repeatedly with high explosive bombs.* • **High fidelity** (*abbreviation* **hi-fi**) is the production by electrical equipment of very good quality sound that is as similar as possible to the original sound: *The technology used in compact discs offers the ultimate in high fidelity.* ○ *The company is a major manufacturer of high-fidelity audio equipment.* • A **high-flyer** or **highflier** is someone who has a lot of ability and a strong desire to be successful and is therefore expected to achieve a lot: *High-flyers in the industry typically earn 25% more than their colleagues.* ○ *(fig.) The company used to be a stock-market highflier* (= an extremely successful organization), *but its share price has fallen dramatically in recent months.* ○ *They have an international reputation as a* **high-flying** (= extremely successful) *manufacturer of computer equipment.* • A person or thing that is in **high gear** is very active: *As soon as the candidates have been chosen, the presidential campaign will move into high gear.* • Something that is **high-grade** is good quality or better quality than usual: *I'd recommend using high-grade videotape for important recordings that you want to keep for a long time.* • *(specialized)* A **high-level language** is a language for writing computer programs which looks more like human language than computer language and is therefore easier to understand: *LOGO was the first high-level language to be specially written to help children learn about computers.* • **High-level waste** is waste, such as nuclear fuel that has been used to produce electricity, which is very RADIOACTIVE and needs to be kept cool for many years before it can be got rid of without harming the environment. • The **high life** is an exciting way of living in which rich and successful people enjoy themselves by spending a lot of time and money in fashionable places : *Her string of hit singles has earned her millions and enabled her to live the high life in the south of France.* • A person who is **high-minded** has very moral standards of behaviour and expects other people to follow them: *The public is fed up with high-minded newspaper editors telling them what they should and shouldn't do.* • Fuel that is **high-octane** contains a larger than usual amount of the substance used to improve the quality of fuel: *Oil companies claim that high-octane fuel* *keeps engine parts cleaner than regular gasoline.* • Something's **high point** is the time when it is the most successful, enjoyable, important or valuable: *The documentary marks the high point* **in** *a recent campaign to improve the public image of the secret service.* ○ *The high point* **of** *my week is arriving home from work on a Friday evening.* • Something that is **high-powered** has a lot of power or strength: *Are you sure you've got enough experience to be riding a high-powered motorbike like that?* ○ *You'll need a very high-powered computer system to process so much data.* ○ See also **high-powered** at HIGH [IMPORTANT]. • **High-pressure** is used to refer to something that involves pressure which is greater than usual: *Hot water sprayed from high-pressure hoses is being used to wash the oil off the rocks.* • Methods of selling that are **high-pressure** involve persuading people in a forceful way to buy something that they often do not really want: *The high-pressure sales techniques used for selling financial services such as life insurance have been strongly criticized in a new report.* ○ *(esp. Am) The saleswoman tried to* **high-pressure** *me* **into** *buying* (=persuade me to buy) *an extended guarantee which almost doubled the cost of the television.* • Someone who has a **high profile** receives a lot of attention and interest from the public: *Unlike most business people she has a high profile and is rapidly becoming a household name.* ○ *She's a high-profile politician.* ○ *He came to public attention when he started in a high-profile job as economic adviser to the Prime Minister.* • Something that is **high-risk** involves a greater than usual amount of risk: *Only people who can afford to lose their money should make high-risk investments.* ○ *The government is to launch a new AIDS education campaign which will target high-risk groups such as intravenous drug-users.* • *(esp. Am)* A **high roller** is someone who spends a lot of money on things that are not really needed or who GAMBLES (=risks money on the result of games or races) when they have little chance of winning. • **High season** is the period in the year when the greatest number of people visit a place and when the prices are at their highest level: *People on limited budgets should avoid travelling* **in/during/***(Br)***at** *high season if they can.* ○ Compare **low season** at LOW [SMALL IN AMOUNT]. • Something that is **high-speed** moves or operates very quickly: *The proposed high-speed rail link would transport passengers between Houston and Dallas in just 1 hour 45 minutes.* • *(dated)* **High tension** means high VOLTAGE: *a high-tension cable*

high /haɪ/ *n* [C] • *Interest rates have reached an* **all-time/record** *high* (=a greater level than has ever been reached previously).

high·er /£ˈhaɪ·əʳ, $-ɚ/ *adj* [before n; not gradable] • Higher is sometimes used to describe something that is more developed: *The brains of higher animals such as mammals are larger than those of reptiles.*

high·ly /ˈhaɪ·li/ *adv* • *The company's new products have been highly* (=very) *profitable.* • *My daughter has just started work in a highly-***paid** (=very well paid) *job with a television company.* • *The judge will face a tough challenge conducting a fair trial in such an emotional and highly* (=much) **publicized** *case.* • *Japanese cars are highly regarded* (=very much admired) *by American motorists.* • *For our country to remain competitive, we need a highly-skilled, highly-educated workforce.* • If you **speak** highly **of** someone, you praise them: *Your former employer speaks very highly of you in her letter of recommendation.* • If you **think** highly **of** someone, you admire them: *In spite of his recent failure, he is still highly thought of by his colleagues.* • Someone who is *(Br and Aus)* **highly-strung**/*(Am)* **high-strung** worries about things unnecessarily, is easily upset and finds it difficult to relax: *The air force said I was too highly-strung to become a fighter pilot.* • [LP] **Very, completely**

high [IMPORTANT] /haɪ/ *adj* **-er, -est** having an important position, power or great influence • *He is an officer of high rank.* • *She has a lot of friends* **in high places** (=She knows people in positions of power). • *(esp. humorous) I* **have it on the highest authority** (=I have been told by someone who knows the truth) *that they are getting a divorce.* • *(disapproving)* If someone is **high and mighty**, they treat other people as if other people are not as important as themselves. • *(esp. humorous)* If an order comes from **on high**, it comes from someone in a position of authority. See also **on high** at HIGH [DISTANCE]. • A **high commissioner** is an official of high rank who represents the government of a country that is a member of the British Commonwealth in another country that is also a member of the Commonwealth. • The office where a high commissioner works is called the **High Commission**: *The Canadian High Commission is in Trafalgar Square in London.* • A **high commission** is also an international organization that has been established for a particular purpose, and a **high commissioner** is the person in charge of this organization: *According to the United Nations High Commission for Refugees, at least 24 000 people have fled the country.* • The **high court** is the law court in England and Wales for trials of CIVIL rather than criminal cases and where decisions made in regional courts can be considered again: *He intends to appeal against the verdict* **in the** *High Court.* ○ *Two police officers have lost their High Court libel action over a newspaper story which accused them of being liars.* • In the US, the **high court** is the Supreme Court. • The **High Court of Australia** is the law court where decisions that are made in the Supreme Court of each STATE (=a part of the country with its own government) can be considered again. • Something that is **high-flown** or **high-sounding** tries to be much more important than it really is, sometimes seeming silly as a result: *He's full of high-flown ideas about how to save the world.* • Someone who is **high-handed** uses their power or authority more forcefully than is needed without thinking about the feelings or wishes of other people: *The report criticizes their high-handed treatment of customers who have difficulty paying their bills.* ○ *Such* **high-handedness** *will only make her unpopular with her employees – she should try dealing with their problems more sympathetically.* • If you are **on your high horse**, you are annoying people by telling them how something should be done, as if you know the best way of doing it, and as if other people's ideas are not important: *She's always on her high horse* **about** *how the office should be organized.* • If discussions are **high-level**, very important people are involved in them: *This meeting is the first high-level contact between the two countries since diplomatic relations were resumed last April.* • If a person is **high-powered**, the things that they do are important and need a lot of energy, skill, experience, knowledge or responsibility: *I've got a meeting with some high-powered executives from head office this morning.* • If something such as a book is **high-powered**, it is advanced and needs a lot of knowledge to understand it: *This book is more high-powered than the introductory textbook, but it's well worth putting in the extra effort to understand it.* ○ See also **high-powered** at HIGH [ABOVE AVERAGE]. • A **high priest** or **high priestess** is a very important priest or priestess in a religious or spiritual organization: *(fig.) She is widely regarded as the high priestess* **of** (=the most important person working in) *contemporary dance.* • The **high seas** are the seas which are not controlled by any country: *For over 30 days they wandered* **the** *high seas, searching for a port that would accept a cargo of nuclear waste.* • *(Br)* The **high street** (*Am and Aus* **main street**) in a town is the road with the most important shops and businesses: *I see there's a new Italian restaurant opening on the high street.* • *(Br)* The **high street** also refers to the business done at shops: *There are signs of economic recovery in the high street.* ○ *There was a modest rise in high-street spending last month.* • *(Br)* The **high table** in a school or university is the table at which the most important teachers eat their meals. • *(Br)* **High tea** is a meal eaten by some people in the late afternoon or early evening which usually includes cooked food and tea to drink. • **High treason** is the committing of a crime which seriously threatens the safety of a country, its queen or king or its governing organization: *He was sentenced to life imprisonment for high treason and espionage.* • Someone who is **high up** in an organization has an important position in it: *You have to be fairly high up in the company in order to be given a car.* • *(infml)* A **higher-up** is someone with a more important position than you in an organization: *They're still waiting for a decision about the extra money from the higher-ups.*

high /haɪ/ *adv* **-er, -est** • Someone who is **high-ranking** has an important position in an organization: *A number of high-ranking officials have resigned in the wake of the scandal.* ○ *He is a high-ranking officer in the army.* • *(Am infml slightly disapproving)* Someone who is living **high on/off the hog** is living in great comfort with a lot of money.

high·ly /ˈhaɪ·li/ *adv* • *According to one highly*-**placed** *source* (=a person in an important position), *the Prime Minister had threatened to resign over this issue.*

high MENTAL STATE /haɪ/ *n* [C usually sing] a period of extreme excitement or happiness when you feel full of energy, often caused by a feeling of success, or by drugs or alcohol or a religious experience • *Exercise gives you a high.* • *She's been* **on** *a high ever since she got her article published.* • *There are lots of* **highs and lows** *in this job.*

high /haɪ/ *adj* **-er, -est** • *He was high* **on** *drugs and couldn't think straight.* • *(infml) She was* **as high as a kite** (=She was greatly under the influence of drugs). • *(infml)* **High jinks** is energetic behaviour in which people do amusing or entertaining things for their own enjoyment: *Okay, class, settle down. That's enough high jinks for one lesson.* • If someone is in **high spirits**, they are extremely happy and enjoying themselves: *They'd had a couple of drinks and were in high spirits.* • Someone who is **high-spirited** is energetic and happy and likes doing exciting and enjoyable things: *You ought to invite Jackie to your party – she's very high-spirited and always livens things up.* • If a horse is **high-spirited**, it is very active and therefore difficult to control.

high SOUND /haɪ/ *adj* **-er, -est** near or at the top of the range of sounds • *I can't reach that note – it's too high for me.* • *Dog whistles are too high for human beings to hear.* • A voice that is **high-pitched** is higher than usual: *She's got a very high-pitched voice.* • A noise that is **high-pitched** is high and sometimes also loud or unpleasant: *I was almost deafened by the high-pitched scream of the fire alarm.* ○ See also **high-pitched** at HIGH DISTANCE.

high EDUCATION /haɪ/ *adj* [before n; not gradable] relating to the education of children between the ages of approximately 11 and 18 years old in Britain and Australia, and 15 and 18 years old in the United States • In Britain and Australia, a **high school** (*infml* **high**) is a school for children aged between 11 and 18: *She goes to the local high (school).* • In the United States, a **high school** (*infml* **high**) is a school for children aged between 15 and 18, or 16 and 18 if there is also a junior high school: *A high school is for people in grades 9-12 or 10-12.* • LP› **Schools and colleges**

high·er /£ˈhaɪ·əʳ, $-ɚ/ *adj* [before n; not gradable] • Higher refers to an advanced level of education: *A greater proportion of people with first degrees are now going on to study for higher degrees.* • **Higher education** is education at a college or university where subjects are studied in great detail and at an advanced level: *The government wants to double the number of students* **in** *higher education by the year 2015.*

high·er /£ˈhaɪ·əʳ, $-ɚ/ *n* [C] *Scot Eng* • A higher is an official exam that is taken in schools in Scotland, esp. by students who want to study at college or university: *What grades do I need in my highers to get a university place?*

high BAD /haɪ/ *adj* **-er, -est** (of food) smelling bad and no longer good to eat • *This meat is rather high – shall I throw it out?*

high·ball /£ˈhaɪ·bɔːl, $-bɑːl/ *n* [C] *esp. Am* an alcoholic drink made with WHISKY mixed with water or SODA (=fizzy water) and ice, which is served in a tall glass

high·brow /ˈhaɪ·braʊ/ *adj esp. disapproving* (of literature, art, films or plays) serious and intended for intelligent educated people who are knowledgeable about art, literature and films, or (of people) intelligent and knowing a lot about such things • *highbrow entertainment* • *She tries to disprove the highbrow assumption that bestselling novels are shallow and badly written.* • Compare LOWBROW; MIDDLEBROW.

high·brow /ˈhaɪ·braʊ/ *n* [C] *esp. disapproving* • *The TV company specializes in making arts shows for highbrows.*

high·fa·lu·tin /£ˌhaɪ·fəˈluː·tɪn, $-t̬ɪn/, **hi·fal·u·tin** *adj infml* trying to seem very important or serious without having a good reason for doing so and looking foolish as a result • *She's one of those highfalutin art critics who take themselves far too seriously.*

high·flier /£ˌhaɪˈflaɪ·əʳ, $-ɚ/ *n* [C] **high-flyer**, see at HIGH ABOVE AVERAGE

high·lands /ˈhaɪ·ləndz/ *pl n* a mountainous area of a country, esp. in Scotland • *They're spending their holiday in the Scottish Highlands.* • *Most villages in the highlands are now connected to the telephone network.*

high·land /ˈhaɪ·lənd/ *adj* [before n; not gradable] • *The highland landscape is breathtakingly beautiful at any time of year.* • The **Highland fling** is an energetic Scottish dance which is performed without a partner. • The **Highland Games** is an event that happens once every year in Scotland which involves dancing, music and sports competitions.

high·land·er /£ˈhaɪ·lən·dəʳ, $-dɚ/ *n* [C] • *Many Highlanders* (=people who live in the Scottish Highlands) *have moved to the towns and cities in search of work.*

high·light BEST PART /ˈhaɪ·laɪt/ *n* [C] the best or most exciting, entertaining or interesting part • *The highlight* **of** *our trip to New York was going to the top of the Empire State Building.* • *You'll be able to see the highlights* **of** *the TV series in a one-hour special on Christmas Day.*

high·light HAIR /ˈhaɪ·laɪt/ *n* [C usually pl] a narrow strip of hair on a person's head which has been made paler in colour than the surrounding hair • *Do you think Gary's hair looks better with blonde highlights?*

high·light *obj* EMPHASIZE /ˈhaɪ·laɪt/ *v* [T] to attract attention to or emphasize (something important) • *The report on the accident highlights the need for considerable improvements in safety.* • *Could you read through this for me and highlight the important points?*

high·light·er /£ˈhaɪˌlaɪ·təʳ, $-t̬ɚ/ *n* [C] • A highlighter is a pen containing a bright ink which is used to colour parts of a text in a book, magazine, etc. to make it easier to find them later.

High·ness /ˈhaɪ·nəs/ *n* [C] *fml* a title used when referring to an important member of a royal family • *Will that be all,* **Your** *Highness?* [as form of address] • *The building was officially opened by* **Their** *(Royal) Highnesses the Prince and Princess of Wales.* • *The independence ceremony was attended by the Queen and* **His** *Royal Highness The Prince Philip, Duke of Edinburgh.*

high·tail *(obj)* /ˈhaɪ·teɪl/ *v* **hightail (it)** *infml esp. Am* to leave or move somewhere in a great hurry • *We'd better hightail* **out** *of here if we're going to be on time for the film.* [I] • *After the robbery, Cath and Jez hightailed it* **out** *of town.* [T]

high·way /ˈhaɪ·weɪ/ *n* [C] *Am and Aus, Br fml* a public road, esp. an important road that joins cities or towns together • *My new car gets 53 miles per gallon in the city and 58 mpg on the highway.* • *230 of the 712 highway fatalities in Queensland last year were alcohol-related.* • *(fml) Five people have been charged with obstructing the highway during a peace protest in London last weekend.* • *We drove along the* **coastal** *highway from Sydney to Newcastle.* • *Everyone with a car knows that the* **interstate** *highway system needs major repairs.* • *I felt I had travelled along every* **highway and byway** (=every road) *in Yorkshire.* • *(Br)* The **Highway Code** is the set of government rules, published in a small book, which have to be obeyed by drivers using public roads in the UK: *You'll fail your driving test if you don't learn* **the** *Highway Code.* • See also SUPERHIGHWAY.

high·way·man /ˈhaɪ·weɪ·mən/ *n* [C] *pl* **-men** (in the past) a man riding a horse who forced people travelling on public roads to stop and then stole their valuable possessions • *The most famous English highwayman is Dick Turpin, who lived from 1706 to 1739.*

hi·jack *obj* /ˈhaɪ·dʒæk/ *v* [T] to force someone to give you control of (a vehicle, aircraft or ship that is in the middle of a journey) • *A man armed with a pistol hijacked a jet that was travelling to Paris early today and demanded payment of $125 000.* • *400 tons of food was stolen when a convoy of trucks was hijacked in the famine-hit town.* • If a person or group of people hijacks someone else's ideas or plans, they start to use them as their own: *Many Green Party members resent the way in which other political parties have hijacked environmental issues that they originally publicized.* • LP› **Crimes and criminals**

hi·jack /ˈhaɪ·dʒæk/ *n* [C] • *The hijack ended with the release of all the plane's passengers unharmed.*

hi·jack·er /£ˈhaɪˌdʒæk·əʳ, $-ɚ/ *n* [C] • *Government policy is to refuse to negotiate with hijackers.*

hi·jack·ing /ˈhaɪˌdʒæk·ɪŋ/ *n* • *During the two airline hijackings, American passengers were singled out and murdered.* [C] • *Greater international cooperation is required to reduce the risk of hijacking.* [U]

hike WALK /haɪk/ *n* [C] a long walk in the countryside • *People* **go on** *hikes for pleasure and for exercise.* • *(Am infml)* If someone tells you to **take a hike**, they are telling you to leave: *The manager came up to us and suggested we take a hike.*

hike /haɪk/ *v* [I] • *We're going hiking in the Lake District next weekend.* • **Hiking boots** is *Am and Aus for* **walking boots**. See at WALK. • PIC› **Shoes**

hik·er /£ˈhaɪ·kəʳ, $-kɚ/ *n* [C] ● *The hotel is ideally situated for hikers looking for an inexpensive place to stay.*

hike INCREASE /haɪk/ *n* [C] an increase in the cost of something, esp. a large or unwanted increase ● *The recent hike* **in** *train fares is necessary to fund investment in the rail industry.*

hike *obj* /haɪk/ *v* [T] ● *The Chancellor has hiked* **(up)** *interest rates to levels twice as high as those in the United States.* [T/M]

hike up *obj*, **hike** *obj* **up** *v adv* [M] *esp. Am* to lift (something heavy) by putting a lot of energy into a short, powerful movement ● *Do you think we'll be able to hike the piano up over that step?* ● If you hike up a piece of clothing, you raise it with a quick movement: *He hiked up his trouser leg and showed me the bruise.* ○ *My skirt was hiked up on one side.*

hi·la·ri·ous /£hɪˈleə·ri·əs, $-ler·i-/ *adj* extremely amusing and causing a lot of laughter ● *Some of her jokes are absolutely hilarious.* ● *It's hilarious watching him try to flirt with women half his age.*

hi·la·ri·ous·ly /£hɪˈleə·ri·ə·sli, $-ler·i-/ *adv* ● *Her new book's hilariously funny.*

hi·la·ri·ty /£hɪˈlær·ə·ti, $-ler·ə·ṭi/ *n* [U] ● *He came to the party dressed in a yellow suit and pink bow tie, which caused great hilarity among the other guests.*

hill /hɪl/ *n* [C] an area of land that is higher than the surrounding land ● *Hills are not as rocky or high as mountains, and they are usually covered by plants such as grass and trees.* ● *They have built a house on the top of a hill overlooking the town.* ● *In South Australia, wine growers are going up into* **the** *hills* (= an area where there are hills) *in search of cooler sites for their vines.* ● *The railway line runs through* **rolling** (= gently rising and falling) *green hills, out towards the coast.* ● *She enjoys hill-***walking** *and often spends her holidays in Wales.* ● A hill is also a slope in a road: *That hill's far too steep to cycle up.* ○ *One of the manoeuvres you have to perform in your driving test is a hill* **start** (= beginning your journey when your car is parked on a slope in a direction which faces up the slope). ● *(infml disapproving)* Someone who is **over the hill** is considered too old, esp. to do a particular job: *Some companies think that people in their fifties are over the hill and not worth employing.* ● *(dated)* **Up hill and down dale** means everywhere: *Where have you been? We've been searching up hill and down dale for you.* ● A **hill station** is a village or town high up in the hills, esp. in India, where people go in the summer to escape from the heat: *Darjeeling is a hill station in the Himalayan foothills of north east India, which was once the summer residence of the Bengal government.* ● *"The hills are alive with the sound of music"* (song from the Rodgers and Hammerstein musical *The Sound of Music*, 1959) ● *"I will lift up mine eyes unto the hills, from whence cometh my help"* (Bible, Psalm 121.1)

hil·ly /ˈhɪl·i/ *adj* **-ier, -iest** ● *In the hilly areas of Kenya, women spend nine-tenths of their time collecting water.*

hill·bil·ly /ˈhɪlˌbɪl·i/ *n* [C] *Am dated disapproving* a person from a mountainous area of the US who has a simple way of life and is considered to be slightly stupid by people living in towns and cities

hil·lock /ˈhɪl·ək/ *n* [C] a small hill

hill·side /ˈhɪl·saɪd/ *n* [C] the sloping surface of a hill, rather than the level surface at the top of it ● *Rescuers have been hampered by the fact that the plane crashed on a heavily-wooded hillside.*

hill·top /ˈhɪl·tɒp, $-tɑːp/ *n* [C] the top part of a hill, rather than its sloping sides ● *The light green valley pastures contrast dramatically with the dark evergreen trees on the hilltops.* ● *Spello is a beautiful hilltop village in Umbria.*

hilt /hɪlt/ *n* [C] the handle of a sharp pointed weapon such as a sword ● *Charles's body was discovered with an antique dagger thrust to the hilt into his chest.* ● Something that is done **to the hilt** is done completely and without limitation: *The government is already borrowing* **up** *to the hilt, so it can't afford to spend any more.* ○ *I've always supported my wife to the hilt in everything she's done.*

him MALE /hɪm/ *pronoun* used, usually after a verb or preposition, to refer to a man, boy or male animal that has just been been mentioned or is just about to be mentioned ● *I sent Peter a letter last month, but I haven't had a reply from him yet.* ● *Why don't you give him his present?* ● *Why don't you give his present to him?* ● *We've just got a new cat, but we haven't thought of a name for him yet.* ● *"That boy over there looks really nice, doesn't he?" "Who? Him! He's horrible!"* ● *Do you recognise your attacker in any of these photographs? Is this him, perhaps?* ● *A jury has to be convinced beyond all reasonable doubt that a defendant is guilty, otherwise they must find him* **or her** *innocent.* ● *Our duty-free shop stocks a wide range of toiletries for him and her* (= for men and women).

him·self /hɪmˈself/ *pronoun* ● Himself is used to refer to a male object of a verb that is the same person or animal as the subject of the verb: *You ought to give John an electric razor because he always cuts himself when he's shaving.* ○ *Brian's started sending letters to himself because nobody else writes to him.* ○ *Norman said he was so upset that he cried himself to sleep last night.* ● Himself is sometimes used to give special attention to a male noun or to make clear which male person or animal is being referred to: *Did you want to talk to the chairman himself, or could his personal assistant help you?* ○ *Fred has nobody but himself to blame for the financial mess he's in.* ○ *Guy was going to buy a bookcase, but in the end he made one himself.* ● If a man or boy **is/seems** himself, he is in his usual mental or physical condition: *Hugh hasn't* **been** *himself since the accident.* ○ *What's the matter with Tom? He doesn't* **seem** *himself this morning.* ○ *He was very nervous about the interview, so I told him to act naturally and* **be** *himself.* ● If a man or boy does something **by** himself, he does it alone or without help from anyone else: *Isn't Jamie clever? He made that snowman* **(all)** *by himself.* ○ *Mary's father lives* **(all)** *by himself in a very large house.* ● *Tim wants a desk* **(all) to** *himself* (= that he and no one else can use). ● LP **Reflexive pronouns and verbs**

him FEMALE OR MALE /hɪm/ *pronoun* used, esp. in formal situations, usually after a verb or preposition, to refer to a person or animal that has just been mentioned or is just about to be mentioned and whose sex is not known or not considered to be important. Some people consider this offensive to women. ● *Your doctor should know all about the latest treatments, so ask him for more details.* ● *If someone is causing us problems, we should get rid of him.* ● *Man's ability to talk makes him unlike any other animal.* ● *There was a spider in the bath, so I flushed him down the plughole.* ● LP **Sexist language**

him·self /hɪmˈself/ *pronoun* ● *"There's been a nasty accident at the end of the road." "Oh dear, I hope nobody's hurt himself."*

hind BACK /haɪnd/ *adj* [before n; not gradable] at the back of an animal's body ● *As I walked into the house, Phil's dog ran towards me and stood up on her hind* **legs** *to greet me.* ● PIC **Dogs**

hind ANIMAL /haɪnd/ *n* [C] *pl* **hinds** or **hind** a female deer, esp. a red deer more than three years old

hin·der *obj* /£ˈhɪn·dəʳ, $-dɚ/ *v* [T] to limit the ability of (someone) to do something, or to limit the development of (something) ● *Smoking hinders the ability of the heart and lungs to recover quickly from the effects of surgery.* ● *Broken water pipes and gas leaks have hindered firefighters* **in** *their efforts, but the fire is now under control.* ● *I don't want you to do anything that is going to hinder you* **from** *getting the job finished on time.* ● *Her progress certainly hasn't been hindered by her lack of experience.*

hin·drance /ˈhɪn·drənts/ *n* ● A hindrance is something which makes it more difficult for someone to do something or for something to develop: *I've never considered my disability a hindrance, but other people often see it as a big problem.* [C] ○ *Will increasing output be a hindrance* **to** *maintaining quality?* [C] ○ *Tax inspectors are to be given new powers which will allow them to enter business premises without hindrance.* [U]

Hin·di /ˈhɪn·di/ *n* [U] one of the official languages of India, spoken esp. in northern India ● *Do you speak Hindi?*

hind·quart·ers /£ˌhaɪndˈkwɔː·təz, $-ˈkwɔːr·ṭɚz/ *pl n* the back part of a four-legged animal

hind·sight /ˈhaɪnd·saɪt/ *n* [U] an understanding of why or how something has been done in the past and of how it might have been done better ● *At the time it seemed like the best thing to do, but* **with (the benefit/wisdom of)** *hindsight I guess we should have done it differently.* ● **In** *hindsight, it would have been better to wait.*

Hin·du·i·sm /ˈhɪn·duː·ɪ·zᵊm/ *n* [U] an ancient religion with Indian origins whose characteristics include the worship of many gods and goddesses and the belief that when a person or creature dies, their spirit returns to life in another body

Hin·du /ˈhɪn·duː, ˌ-ˈ-/ *adj* [not gradable], *n* [C] • *The most important Hindu gods are Brahma, Vishnu and Shiva.* • *There are more than 500 million Hindus* (=people who follow the religion of Hinduism) *in the world.*

hinge /ˈhɪndʒ/ *n* [C] a folding device, usually made of metal, which fixes a door, window, lid, etc. in place while allowing it to swing freely • *We had to take the front door off its hinges to get this desk into the house.*

hinged /ˈhɪndʒd/ *adj* [not gradable] • *For easy access, the door of your washing machine can be hinged on the right or left.*

hinge on *(obj),* **hinge u·pon** *(obj) v prep* to depend on (something), or to need (something) in order to be successful • *The prosecution's case hinged on the evidence of a witness who died before the trial.* [T] • *The plot of the film hinges on a case of mistaken identity.* [T] • *Completion of the library hinges on finding another $2 000 000.* [+ v-*ing*] • *The success of the play will hinge on* **what** *the theatre critics have to say about it.* [+ *wh-* word]

hint INDIRECT STATEMENT /hɪnt/ *n* [C] a statement or action which expresses indirectly what a person thinks or wants and which allows another person to take no notice of it without causing offence • *He has* **dropped** (= given) *several strong hints to his boss* **that** *he will go and work for someone else if he doesn't get a pay increase.* [+ *that* clause] • *Didn't she even* **give** *you a hint* **where** *she was going?* [+ *wh-* word] • *I coughed politely as she lit her cigarette, but she didn't* **take** (= understand) *the hint, so I had to explain that it was a no-smoking restaurant.* • *You just can't* **take** *a hint, can you? I wish you'd push off and leave me alone!*

hint /hɪnt/ *v* • *Mum's hinted* **(to** *me)* **(that)** *she might pay for my trip to Mexico if I pass all my exams.* [+ *(that)* clause] • *The government has pardoned 200 political prisoners and hinted* **at** *the early release of at least 170 more.* [I always + *at*]

hint ADVICE /hɪnt/ *n* [C] a piece of advice which helps you to do something • *Could you* **give** *us a hint* **about** *how to do this exercise, please?* • *This recipe book is full of* **handy** (= useful) *hints and will be very useful for people who haven't done much cooking before.*

hint SMALL AMOUNT /hɪnt/ *n* [C usually sing] a small amount of something • *There's only a hint* **of** *brandy in the sauce, so I don't think it'll make you drunk.* • *I'd like to paint the bedroom in white with a hint* **of** *blue.* • *I detected a hint* **of** *uncertainty in Rupert's voice.* • **At the** *slightest hint* **of** *trouble, I'll be out of here like a shot.* • *Without the slightest hint* **of** *irony* (= Completely seriously) *he said the accident was the best thing that had ever happened to him.* • *I've heard rumours that Pam and Pat are about to get divorced, but there was* **no** *hint* (= not even a small sign) **(that)** *they were going to when I last saw them.* [+ *(that)* clause]

hin·ter·land /£ˈhɪn·tə·lænd, $-t̬ɚ-/ *n* [U] land behind the coast or beyond the banks of a river, or an area of a country that is far away from cities and not economically developed • *A century ago, eastern Germany was* **an** *agricultural hinterland.* • *Under the 1922 convention, Kuwait lost much of its hinterland to Saudi Arabia.*

hin·ter·lands /£ˈhɪn·tə·lændz, $-t̬ɚ-/ *pl n Am* • The hinterlands are a part of the country away from the big city areas.

hip BODY PART /hɪp/ *n* [C] the area below the waist and above the legs at either side of the human body, or the joint which connects the leg to the upper part of the body • *This exercise is designed to trim your hips and stomach.* • *That dress is a bit too tight for you on the hips.* • *Helen stood* **(with** *her)* **hands on** *(her) hips, waiting for an explanation.* • *Many elderly people in need of a hip* **replacement** *operation have to suffer in pain because there are not sufficient resources.* • A **hip flask** is a small flat glass or metal bottle for strong alcoholic drinks which is designed to be carried in a pocket or joined to a belt: *When we stopped for a rest, he offered me his hip flask.* • PIC› **Bottles and flasks** Ⓙ

hip FRUIT /hɪp/, **rose hip** *n* [C] a small round bright red fruit produced by a wild rose • *Hips contain a lot of vitamin C.* • PIC› **Berries** Ⓙ

hip FASHIONABLE /hɪp/ *adj* **hipper, hippest** *infml* fashionable, or interested in and knowing a lot about the most modern fashions in things such as music and clothes • *Flared jeans have become hip again this year.* • *The bars and cafés in the old part of the town are frequented by hip young students.* • *Roy thinks he looks really hip dancing like that, but he just looks stupid to me.* • Ⓙ

hip APPROVAL /hɪp/ *exclamation* **hip, hip hooray/hurray** an expression that is called out, often by a group of people at the same time, to express approval of someone • *Three cheers for the bride and groom! Hip, hip, hooray!* • Ⓙ

hip-bath /£ˈhɪp·bɑːθ, $-bæθ/ *n* [C] a small bath with a seat built into it which is designed for sitting rather than lying in

hip–hop /£ˈhɪp·hɒp, $-hɑːp/ *n* [U] a type of popular music in which the subject of the songs is often politics or society and the words are spoken rather than sung • *Hip-hop is an aggressive type of music whose origins lie in the ghettos of 1980s New York and Los Angeles.*

hip·pie, hip·py /ˈhɪp·i/ *n* [C] a person, typically young, esp. in the late 1960s and early 1970s, who believed in peace, was opposed to many of the accepted ideas about how to live, had long hair and often lived in groups and took drugs

Hip·po·crat·ic oath /£ˈhɪp·ə·kræt·ɪk, $-kræt̬/ *n* [U] **the Hippocratic oath** a promise made by people when they become doctors to do everything possible to preserve human life and to maintain high working standards • *The Hippocratic oath obliges doctors not to give information about their patients to people who are not involved in treating them.*

hip·po·pot·a·mus /ˌhɪp·əˈpɒt·ə·məs, $-ˈpɑː·t̬ə-/, *infml* **hip·po** *n* [C] *pl* **hippopotamuses** or **hippopotami** /£ˌhɪp·əˈpɒt·ə·maɪ, $-ˈpɑː·t̬ə-/ a very large animal with a large rectangular head, short legs and thick, dark grey skin which lives in river areas in tropical Africa • *Hippopotamuses' skin dries out easily, so they spend the day in water and only come onto land at night.*

hip·sters *Br and Aus* /£ˈhɪp·stəz, $-stɚz/, *Am* **hip·hug·gers** /£ˈhɪpˌhʌg·əz, $-ɚz/ *pl n* trousers which reach as high as the hips but not as high as the waist

hire *obj* /£haɪəʳ, $haɪr/ *v* [T] to pay to use (something) for a short period or to pay (someone) to do a job temporarily, or *(esp. Am)* to start to employ (someone) • *How much would it cost to hire (Am usually* **rent**) *a car for a fortnight?* • *You could always hire (Am usually* **rent**) *a dress for the ball if you can't afford to buy one.* • *I had to hire a gardener for a couple of months when I broke my leg.* • *We ought to hire a public relations consultant* **to** *help improve our image.* [+ obj + *to* infinitive] • *(esp. Am) Our continuing success means that we will need to hire a hundred more staff over the coming year.* • *(Br and Aus)* **Hire purchase** *(Am* **Installment plan**) is a system of paying for something in which the buyer pays part of the cost immediately and then makes small regular payments until the debt is reduced to nothing: *Something bought* **on** *hire purchase is usually more expensive because an interest charge is added to the original price.* • LP› **Borrow, Money** Ⓙ

hire /£haɪəʳ, $haɪr/ *n* [U] • *There's a camping shop in town that has tents* **for** *hire (Am usually* **rent**) *at £10 a week.* • *How much would it cost for the hire (Am usually* **rental**) *of a moped for the weekend?* • *They run a hire* **car** *business* (= a business renting cars to people). • *He had an accident while he was driving a hire* **car** (= a car that had been hired).

hired /£haɪəd, $haɪrd/ *adj* [not gradable] • *a hired car* • *The police believe he was killed by a hired assassin.* • *My mother has a hired help* (= She pays someone to help her in her home).

hir·ing /£ˈhaɪə·rɪŋ, $ˈhaɪr·ɪŋ/ *n* [C usually pl] • *The office has completely changed in the past few weeks because there have been so many hirings* **and firings** (= a lot of new people have been employed and a lot of others have lost their jobs).

hire out *obj,* **hire** *obj* **out** *v adv* [M] to allow someone to use (something or yourself) temporarily in exchange for money • *How much do you charge for hiring out (Am usually* **renting**) *a bicycle for a week?* • *I've decided to go freelance and hire* **myself** *out as a computer programmer.* • LP› **Borrow**

hire·ling /£ˈhaɪə·lɪŋ, $ˈhaɪr-/ *n* [C] someone who has been persuaded by an offer of money to do an unpleasant or unpopular job • *He's not the boss, he's just a hireling employed to do the dirty work.*

hir·sute /£ˈhɜː·sjuːt, $ˈhɜːr·suːt/ *adj literary or specialized* having a lot of hair on the face or body or a lot of hair that is growing untidily • *Do you prefer Jim clean-shaven or hirsute?*

his MALE /hɪz/ *determiner, pronoun* (something) belonging to or connected with a man, boy or male animal that has just been mentioned • *"Jo's got a new boyfriend." "Oh really? What's his name?"* • *Mark just phoned to say he'd left his coat behind. Do you know if this is his?* • *I don't know many John Lennon songs – 'Imagine' was one of his, wasn't* *it?* • His **own** is used to emphasize that something belongs to or is connected with a particular man or boy and no one else: *He got his (very) own computer for Christmas.* • *Dad gave us* **his and hers** (= matching and designed for a man and a woman in a relationship) *dressing gowns for Christmas.* • LP> **Determiners**

his [FEMALE OR MALE] /hɪz/ *determiner, pronoun esp. fml* (something) belonging to or connected with a person or animal that has just been mentioned and whose sex is not known or not considered to be important. Some people think this use of 'his' is offensive to women. • *Anyone who drives his car at 100 miles an hour is asking for trouble.* • *What a lovely dog! What's his name?* • *"Can you tell me where Professor Lee's office is." "Sorry, I don't know which is his."* • LP> **Sexist language**

His·pan·ic /hɪˈspæn·ɪk/ *adj* [not gradable], *n* [C] (connected with) a person who lives in the United States but who originally came from or whose family came from S America, Mexico, Cuba or Puerto Rico • *The United States' Hispanic population totalled more than 22 million in 1990.* • *Hispanics make up a large proportion of the population of Miami.*

hiss *(obj)* /hɪs/ *v* to make a noise which is like the first sound in the word 'sing' but lasts a lot longer • *Why do snakes hiss?* [I] • *If you put a very hot pan into cold water, it will hiss and produce a lot of steam.* [I] • *He's a political extremist who's grown used to being* **booed and** *hissed* (= being shown anger or strong disagreement) *whenever he speaks in public.* [T] • If you hiss something, you say it in an angry way: *"Shut up, Tom!" she hissed. "The concert's just about to begin."* [+ clause]

hiss /hɪs/ *n* • *She silenced him with a glare and a hiss.* [C] • *Hiss on tape recordings can be reduced using the Dolby system.* [U]

hist·a·mine /ˈhɪs·tə·miːn/ *n* [U] a chemical found in almost all body tissue, esp. the skin, lungs and bowels, which increases blood flow and encourages digestion • *In some people, histamine can cause unpleasant reactions such as swelling when they come into contact with things like pollen.*

hist·o·gram /ˈhɪs·tə·græm/ *n* [C] a **bar chart**, see at BAR [POLE]

hist·ol·o·gy /£hɪˈstɒl·ə·dʒi, $-ˈstɑː·lə-/ *n* [U] *specialized* the scientific study of the structure of tissue from plants, animals and other living things • *Histology involves looking at cells under a microscope.*

hist·o·ry [PAST EVENTS] /£ˈhɪs·tᵊr·i, $-t̬ə-/ *n* (the study of or a record or story of) past events considered together, esp. events or developments of a particular period, country or subject • *I studied modern European history at college.* [U] • *Annie's decided to write a history* (= a book about the development) **of** *electronic music.* [C] • *I only asked him for a light, but two hours later he'd told me his whole* **life** *history.* [C] • *(fig.) Tina and Charles went out together for five years, but they're* **(ancient/past)** *history now* (= their relationship is completely finished now). [U] • *(fig.) This ten-year-old report is* **ancient** *history* (= not important any longer) *and totally irrelevant to the current situation.* [U] • If you **make** history, you do something important which has not been done before and which will be recorded publicly and remembered for a long time: *Margaret Thatcher made history when she became the first British woman Prime Minister.* [U] ○ **Legal** *history has been made with a ruling that a husband does not have the right to have sex with his wife against her will.* [U] • *"History repeats itself. Historians repeat each other."* (Philip Guedalla *Supers and Supermen*, 1920) • (CS) (DK) (GR) (P) (PL) (RUS) (S)

hist·o·ri·an /£hɪˈstɔː·ri·ən, $-ˈstɔːr·i-/ *n* [C] • A historian is someone who writes about or studies history, who often has qualifications in the subject.

hist·o·ric /£hɪˈstɒr·ɪk, $-ˈstɔːr-/ *adj* • Something that is historic is (likely to be) important when the period to which it belongs is studied in the future: *In a historic vote, the Church of England decided to allow women to become priests.* ○ *More money is needed for the preservation of historic buildings and monuments.* • *(specialized)* The **historic present** is the present tense when it describes past events, and is used either informally or to produce a special effect: *The historic present is used in this sentence, Anyway, I'm in the pub with my friends and a bloke comes up to me and asks if I want to buy a stereo.*

hist·o·ri·cal /£hɪˈstɒr·ɪ·kᵊl, $-ˈstɔːr-/ *adj* • Something that is historical is connected with the study or representation of things from the past: *Many important historical documents were destroyed when the library was bombed.* ○ *She specializes in historical novels set in eighteenth-century England.*

hist·o·ri·cally /£hɪˈstɒr·ɪ·kli, $-ˈstɔːr-/ *adv* • *The film doesn't try to be historically accurate, but it is based loosely on real events and people.* • *Historically* (= Over a long period in the past), *there have always been close links between France and Scotland.*

hist·o·ry [REPEATED HAPPENINGS] /£ˈhɪs·tᵊr·i, $-t̬ə-/ *n* [C usually sing] something that has been done or experienced by a particular person or thing repeatedly over a long period • *Her family* **has** *a history* **of** *heart problems.* • *The suspect* **has** *a history* **of** *arson attacks on schools.* • *There's a long history* **of** *industrial disputes at that factory.* • *The family has a very good* **credit** *history* (= They have paid what they owed on goods and services regularly and on time). • (CS) (DK) (GR) (P) (PL) (RUS) (S)

hi·stri·on·ic /£ˌhɪs·triˈɒn·ɪk, $-ˈɑː·nɪk/ *adj* very emotional and energetic, but lacking sincerity or real meaning • *For the benefit of the media, she put on a histrionic display of affection for her ex-husband at his funeral.*

hi·stri·on·i·cally /£ˌhɪs·triˈɒn·ɪ·kli, $-ˈɑː·nɪ-/ *adv* • *The way these footballers roll around histrionically on the ground after they've been tackled doesn't convince anyone.*

hi·stri·on·ics /£ˌhɪs·triˈɒn·ɪks, $-ˈɑː·nɪks/ *pl n* • Histrionics are very emotional and energetic behaviour that lacks sincerity and real meaning: *The President's speech introduced no new policies and instead was full of histrionics about patriotism.*

hit *obj* [TOUCH] /hɪt/ *v* [T] **hitting**, *past* **hit** to swing your hand or an object onto (the surface of something) so that it touches it, usually with force or violently • *I'll hit you if you dare talk to me like that again.* • *This type of glass won't shatter no matter how hard you hit it.* • *She hit the ball as hard as she could and it landed in her neighbour's garden.* • To hit something is also to touch it with sudden force: *They were going at about 60 kilometres an hour when their car hit the tree.* • *One journalist was hit* **in** *the leg by a stray bullet.* • *That new shelf in the bathroom is too low – I just hit my head* **on it**. • *The burglars hit him* **on/over** *the head with an iron bar when he refused to tell them where the money was kept.* • In sports such as cricket or baseball, players hit a score by hitting the ball with a BAT (= a specially shaped piece of wood): *He hit a quick 40 before lunch.* • If you **hit the jackpot**, you do something very successfully: *Our company has hit the jackpot with profits nearly doubled to £2·2 million in six months.* • The results of something that is **hit-and-miss/hit-or-miss** depend more on chance than on good planning or organization: *The trains are often late, so getting to work on time is very much a hit-and-miss affair.* • If someone says that you have **hit the nail on the head**, they mean that you have expressed exactly and clearly what they think about something: *You really hit the nail on the head when you said there's no point training people for jobs that don't exist.* • A **hit-and-run** is a road accident in which the driver who caused the accident drives away without helping the other people involved and without telling the police: *Hit-and-runs often involve young male drivers who lose control of their cars.* ○ *a hit-and-run driver/accident* • A **hit-and-run** military attack is one which needs to happen unexpectedly and quickly in order to be successful: *hit-and-run warfare* • In baseball, a **hit-and-run** play is one where a player on first BASE (= one of four points on a square playing field) starts to run as soon as the ball is PITCHED (= thrown) and another player then tries to hit the ball.

hit /hɪt/ *n* [C] • *She gave him a hit* **on** *the head which knocked him flying.* • In baseball, a hit is when the ball is hit and the person hitting the ball safely reaches a BASE (= one of four points on a square playing field).

hit·ter /£ˈhɪt·ər, $ˈhɪt̬·ə/ *n* [C] • In baseball, a hitter is a person whose turn it is to hit the ball: *Henderson is the* **leadoff** *hitter* (= the player who hits first for their team in the game) *for the Athletics this season.* ○ *Davis is expected to see action primarily as a* **designated** *hitter* (= a player who regularly hits instead of another player, usually instead of the PITCHER, each time it is the other player's turn to hit). ○ *In the seventh inning, the manager inserted Trammell as a* **pinch** *hitter* (= a player who hits instead of another player after the other player has appeared in the game).

hit *obj* [EFFECT] /hɪt/ *v* [T] **hitting**, *past* **hit** to have an unpleasant or negative effect on (a person or thing) • *Production has been badly hit by the strike.* • *The tax increases are expected to hit low-earners as well as people on* *high incomes.* • *Demand for transatlantic flights has been hit by fears of terrorist attacks.* • Something that **hits** you **where it hurts** has an unpleasant or negative effect on you by attacking or criticizing your weakest characteristics: *He's always worrying about his weight, so if you want to hit him where it hurts, tell him he's looking a bit fat.* • If something **hits** you **between the eyes**, it has a sudden strong effect on you.

hit *obj* [ARRIVE AT] /hɪt/ *v* [T] **hitting**, *past* **hit** to shoot at or bomb (a place) • *Try to hit the middle of the target.* • *Two schools and a hospital were hit during the air-raid.* • *(fig.) Our profits hit* (=reached) *an all-time high of £20 million last year.* • *(fig.) I just can't hit* (= sing) *those high notes like I used to.* • If you hit a place or position, you arrive at it: *It was past midnight by the time we hit town.* ○ *If we turn left at the next junction, we should hit the main road after five miles or so.* • If you **hit the bottle**, you start to drink too much alcohol: *She hit the bottle soon after her husband died.* • If you **hit the ceiling/roof**, you become extremely angry: *Dad'll hit the roof when he finds out I've left school.* • If you **hit the deck**, you lie down quickly and suddenly so that you are hidden from view or sheltered from something dangerous: *Hit the deck! Someone's coming!* ○ *Everyone hit the deck when he started firing his gun into the air.* • If you **hit the hay/sack**, you go to bed in order to sleep: *I've got a busy day tomorrow, so I think I'll hit the sack.* • To **hit the headlines** is to appear in the news suddenly or receive a lot of attention in news reports: *He hit the headlines two years ago when he made an unsuccessful challenge for the leadership of the party.* • *The full horror of the war only* **hit home** (= became fully understood) *when we started seeing the television pictures of it in our living-rooms.* • If you **hit the road**, you leave a place or begin a journey: *I'd love to stay longer but I must be hitting the road.* • *That bacon sandwich really* **hit the spot** (=was exactly what I needed)*!* • *"Hit the road, Jack"* (song written by Percy Mayfield, 1961)

hit /hɪt/ *n* [C] • *The United Nations headquarters in the city took a* **direct** *hit from a bomb on Thursday night.* • *The hurricane scored a* **direct** *hit on Miami, leaving at least 10 people dead and the city with no electricity.*

hit *obj* [ATTACK] /hɪt/ *v* [T] **hitting**, *past* **hit** *esp. Am infml* to attack violently or kill (someone) • *Three drugs dealers were hit in the city over the weekend.*

hit /hɪt/ *n* [C] *esp. Am infml* • *Rival gangs are competing with each other to score the greatest number of hits* **on** (= murders of) *members of other gangs.* • A **hit list** is a list of people, groups or organizations that someone intends to take unpleasant action against: *His fingerprints were found on the terrorists' hit list of 100 military and political targets.* ○ *The union claims that the management has drawn up a hit list of staff that are to be made redundant.* • A **hit man** is a man who is paid to kill someone: *Her husband's violent behaviour eventually drove her to hiring a hit man to shoot him.*

hit [SUCCESS] /hɪt/ *n* [C] a thing or person that is very popular or successful • *Their unique song-writing talents gave the Beatles a string of number-one hits throughout the sixties.* • *Those pizzas of yours were a real hit.* • *The group has just released a compilation of their* **greatest** *hits* (= their most successful songs). • *Her last film was a* **smash** (=extremely successful) *hit in the States but it was less popular in Britain.* • If you **make a hit with** someone, they start to like you a lot: *She's trying to make a hit with my brother, but he's already going out with someone.* • *(dated)* A **hit parade** is a list of recordings of songs in which the recording which has sold the most copies during a particular period appears first: *This song spent two weeks at the top of the hit parade in 1959.*

hit *obj* /hɪt/ *v* [T] **hitting**, *past* **hit** • People who **hit it off** have a friendly relationship with each other: *Kim and Pat were really hitting it off at the party, weren't they?* ○ *I didn't really hit it off* **with** *his friends.*

hit back *v adv* [I] to attack someone who has attacked you • *To establish air superiority, we have to destroy the enemy's ability to hit back with missiles or aircraft.* • *England were 2-0 down at half-time, but they hit back in the second half to win by four goals to three.* • *In tonight's speech, the attorney general is expected to hit back* **at** *critics who have attacked her handling of the crisis.*

hit on *obj* [SHOW INTEREST] *v prep* [T] *Am slang* to show (someone) that you are sexually attracted to them • *I hate parties where all the men are hitting on you the whole time.*

hit on/u·pon *obj* [DISCOVER] *v prep* [T] *infml* to think of (an idea) unexpectedly or unintentionally • *When we first hit on the idea, everyone told us it would never work.* • *She says she's hit on a way of dealing with this problem.*

hit out *v adv* [I] to attack someone violently or repeatedly, either physically or by speaking against them • *He was hitting out in all directions and had to be restrained by the police.* • *In a passionate speech, she hit out* **at** *the media's coverage of her divorce.*

hit up *obj*, **hit** *obj* **up** *v adv* [M] *Am infml* to ask (someone) for something • *She tried to hit me up* **for** *a contribution to the school appeal, but I said I'd have to think it over.*

hitch [DIFFICULTY] /hɪtʃ/ *n* [C] a temporary difficulty which causes a short delay • *We were told that there was a slight* **technical** *hitch and the concert would be starting half an hour late.* • *The opening ceremony was a great success and went off* **without a** *hitch* (=without any problems).

hitch *(obj)* [RIDE] /hɪtʃ/ *v infml* to get (a free ride in someone else's road vehicle) as a way of travelling, or to HITCH-HIKE • *They hitched* **a lift/ride** *to Edinburgh from a passing car.* [T] • *If we hitch it'll keep the costs down.* [I]

hitch *obj* [FASTEN] /hɪtʃ/ *v* [T always + adv/prep] to fasten (something) to another thing by tying it with a rope or using a metal hook • *You'd better hitch the horse* **to** *that fence.* • *We just need to hitch the trailer* **(on)to** *the car and then we can go.* • *When the horses have been fed you can hitch them* **(up) to** *the plough.*

hitch up *obj*, **hitch** *obj* **up** *v adv* [M] to pull up trousers, a skirt, etc. usually with a quick movement • *He hitched up his trouser leg and showed me his scar.* • *She hitched her skirt up before wading across the stream.*

hitch /hɪtʃ/ *n* [C] • *Nervously she gave her stockings a quick hitch before going into the interview.*

hitched /hɪtʃt/ *adj* **get hitched** *slang* to get married • *Is Tracy really getting hitched?*

hitch-hike /ˈhɪtʃ·haɪk/ *v* [I] to travel by getting free rides in someone else's road vehicle • *In Britain people who hitch-hike show they want a lift by holding up their thumb to passing traffic.* • *Women should never go hitch-hiking on their own.* • See also HITCH [RIDE].

hitch-hik·er /£ˈhɪtʃˌhaɪ·kəʳ, $-kɚ/ *n* [C] • *Jack often* **picks up** *hitch-hikers.*

hi-tech /ˌhaɪˈtek/, **high tech**, **high tech·nol·o·gy** *adj, n* [U] (using) the most advanced and developed machines and methods • *This weapons system is an affordable, hi-tech solution.* • *High technology does give new solutions to old problems.* • Hi-tech or high tech is also a way of decorating houses and buildings using industrial styles and materials. • Compare **low-tech** at LOW [SMALL IN AMOUNT]

hith·er /£ˈhɪð·əʳ, $-ɚ/ *adv* [not gradable] *old use or fml* to or towards this place • *Come hither young sir!* • **Hither and thither** means in many directions: *In clearer water, one usually encounters shoals of tiny fish, which dart hither and thither like flights of arrows.*

hith·er·to /£ˌhɪð·əˈtuː, $-ɚˈ-/ *adv* [not gradable] *fml* until now or until a particular time • *This Saturday sees the first extract from the president's hitherto* **unpublished** *diaries.* • *Mira revealed hitherto* **unsuspected** *talents on the cricket pitch.* • *When the verdict was announced the prisoner, who had hitherto sat silently throughout the trial, started shouting.*

HIV /ˌeɪtʃ·aɪˈviː/ *n* [U] *abbreviation for* human immunodeficiency virus (=the virus which is believed to cause AIDS) • If a person is **HIV-positive**, they are infected with HIV although they might not have AIDS or develop it for a long time.

hive [BEE HOUSE] /haɪv/ *n* [C] the place where bees live, esp. a BEEHIVE (=box-like container), or the group of bees living there • *There are several hives at the end of our garden.* • *The hive* (=the bees in the hive) *is/are getting ready to swarm.* [+ sing/pl v] • [PIC] **Wasps and bees**

hive [PLACE] /haɪv/ *n* [C] **a hive of activity/industry** a place where a lot of people are working very hard • *The whole house was a hive of activity on the day before the wedding.*

hive off *obj*, **hive** *obj* **off** *v adv* [M] *esp. Br and Aus* (esp. in business) to separate a smaller part or parts from a larger organization • *The plan is to hive off individual companies as soon as they are profitable.*

hives /haɪvz/ *n* [U] a condition in which a person's skin develops sore, usually red, areas, esp. because they have eaten a type of food that harms them slightly

hi·ya /ˈhaɪ·jə/ *exclamation infml* an expression said when people who know each other well meet; hello • *Hiya, Pete, how are you doing?* • LP> **Meeting someone**

hmm /həm/ *exclamation* a sound made to express doubt or uncertainty • *Hmm, I'm not sure about that.* • *"He says he's doing it for our benefit." "Hmm, I'm still not convinced."* • *Hmm, how do you suppose this thing works?*

HMO MEDICAL /£ˌeɪtʃ·emˈəʊ, $-ˈoʊ/ *n* [C] *pl* **HMOs** *Am abbreviation for* health maintenance organization (= a group that provides health care to people who pay to join it) • *For a monthly flat fee, paid by the consumer or employer, HMOs provide a specified list of medical services both in and outside the hospital.*

HMO HOUSING /£ˌeɪtʃ·emˈəʊ, $-ˈoʊ/ *n* [C] *pl* **HMOs** *specialized Br abbreviation for* house in multiple occupation (= a house shared by a number of people, esp. those receiving money from the government because they have little or no income) • *Today, the once-grand streets are characterized by decaying HMOs, sorely in need not just of redecoration but more fundamental repair.*

HMS /ˌeɪtʃ·emˈes/ *n* [before n] *abbreviation for* Her/His Majesty's Ship or Service (= that belonging to Britain) • *HMS Ark Royal*

HMSO /£ˌeɪtʃ·em·esˈəʊ, $-ˈoʊ/ *n* [U] *abbreviation for* Her/His Majesty's Stationery Office (= the government department in Britain which prints many official documents)

HNC /ˌeɪtʃ·enˈsiː/ *n* [C] *Br abbreviation for* Higher National Certificate (= a qualification, esp. in a scientific or technical subject, which you can study for at a British college) • LP> **Schools and colleges**

HND /ˌeɪtʃ·enˈdiː/ *n* [C] *Br abbreviation for* Higher National Diploma (= a qualification, esp. in a scientific or technical subject, studied for at a British college) • LP> **Schools and colleges**

hoag·ie /£ˈhəʊ·gi, $ˈhoʊ-/ *n* [C] a SUBMARINE (SANDWICH)

hoard *(obj)* /£hɔːd, $hɔːrd/ *v* to collect (large amounts of something) and keep in a safe, often secret, place • *Because people expected prices to rise rapidly, they started to hoard goods.* [T] • *There would be enough food on a daily basis if people were not hoarding (it).* [I/T] • *Wealthy folk from politically uncertain countries hoard their cash in Switzerland.* [T]

hoard /£hɔːd, $hɔːrd/ *n* [C] • *In the kitchen we found a huge hoard* **of** *tinned food.* • *The electronics company is estimated to have a cash hoard worth $13·4 billion.*

hoard·er /£ˈhɔː·dəʳ, $ˈhɔːr·dɚ/ *n* [C] • *My aunt's a terrible hoarder – she never throws anything away.*

hoard·ing ADVERTISEMENT *Br and Aus* /£ˈhɔː·dɪŋ, $ˈhɔːr-/, *Am and Aus* **bill·board** *n* [C] a very large board on which advertisements are shown, esp. at the side of a road • *an advertising hoarding*

hoard·ing FENCE /£ˈhɔː·dɪŋ, $ˈhɔːr-/ *n* [C] a temporary fence, usually made of boards, put around an area, esp. one where people are building

hoar frost /£ˈhɔːʳ, $ˈhɔːr/ *n* [U] a white layer of needle-like pieces of ice which forms on objects outside when it is very cold

hoarse /£hɔːs, $hɔːrs/ *adj* **-r, -st** (of a voice) sounding rough, often because the speaker has a sore throat or a cold, or (of a person) having a rough-sounding voice • *Paddy smoked so incessantly that he had a hoarse* **voice** *and his hands were yellow.* • *His voice came out in a hoarse* **whisper** *and he cleared his throat.* • *I don't know if she had a cold but she* **sounded** *very hoarse over the telephone.* • *You'll* **make yourself** *hoarse if you keep shouting like that!* • See also HUSKY VOICE.

hoarse·ly /£hɔː·sli, $hɔːr·sli/ *adv* • *"You can't leave now," she* **whispered** *hoarsely.*

hoarse·ness /£hɔː·snəs, $hɔːr·snəs/ *n* [U] • *I thought I detected a little hoarseness in her voice as if she had a cold.*

hoar·y /£ˈhɔː·ri, $ˈhɔːr·i/ *adj* **-ier, -iest** *literary* very old and familiar and therefore not interesting or amusing, or *(literary)* (of a person) very old and white- or grey-haired • *He told a few hoary* **old** *jokes and nobody laughed.* • *He came up with some hoary* **old** *excuse about having to attend his grandmother's funeral.* • *(literary) A hoary* **old** *butler slowly opened the creaking door.*

hoax /£həʊks, $hoʊks/ *n* [C] a plan to deceive someone, such as telling the police there is a bomb somewhere when there is not one, or a trick • *The area was cleared of people but the telephone warning turned out to be a hoax.* • *A* **bomb** *hoax last night forced the evacuation of the City of London's Barbican Centre.* • *The speaker called for the maximum penalty for hoax* **calls** *to be increased to one year.*

hoax *obj* /£həʊks, $hoʊks/ *v* [T] • To hoax means to deceive, esp. to play a trick on someone: *She hoaxed us* **into** *thinking the buses were still running, so we waited for nearly an hour!*

hoax·er /£ˈhəʊk·səʳ, $ˈhoʊk·sɚ/ *n* [C] • *Attempts are made to keep hoaxers on the line while the call is traced.*

hob *Br* /£hɒb, $hɑːb/, *Am and Aus* **stove, stove·top**, *Am* **range** *n* [C] the top part or surface of a cooker on which pans can be heated • *Most domestic hobs have four gas or electric rings.* • In the past a hob was a metal shelf beside a fireplace where pans could be heated. • PIC> **Kitchen**

hob·bit /£ˈhɒb·ɪt, $ˈhɑː·bɪt/ *n* [C] an imaginary small human-like creature described in books by J.R.R. Tolkien

hob·ble WALK /£ˈhɒb·l̩, $ˈhɑː·bl̩/ *v* [I always + adv/prep] to walk in an awkward way, usually because the feet or legs are hurting or damaged • *Civilians and soldiers with missing legs hobbling on crutches are a common sight.* • *The last time I saw Rachel she was hobbling around with a stick, having injured her ankle skiing.*

hob·ble *obj* LIMIT /£ˈhɒb·l̩, $ˈhɑː·bl̩/ *v* [T] *literary* to limit (something) or control the freedom of • *A long list of amendments have hobbled the new legislation.* • If you hobble an animal, esp. a horse, you tie two of its legs together so that it cannot run away.

hob·by /£ˈhɒb·i, $ˈhɑː·bi/ *n* [C] an activity which someone does for pleasure during the time that they are not working in a job • *When she isn't modelling, Sonya's hobbies include hang-gliding, aerobics and scuba-diving.*

hob·by·ist /£ˈhɒb·i·ɪst, $ˈhɑː·bi-/ *n* [C] *esp. Am* • *a computer hobbyist* • *The convention attracted professionals and enthusiastic hobbyists in equal number.*

hob·by–horse SUBJECT /£ˈhɒb·i·hɔːs, $ˈhɑː·bi·hɔːrs/ *n* [C] an opinion on a subject that someone talks about frequently, usually for a long time • *The shortcomings of the British diet is something of a hobby-horse for Elizabeth.*

hob·by–horse TOY /£ˈhɒb·i·hɔːs, $ˈhɑː·bi·hɔːrs/ *n* [C] a toy, more popular in the past than now, consisting of a stick with a shape like a small horse's head at one end, which a child can pretend to ride • PIC> **Toy**

hob·gob·lin /£ˌhɒbˈgɒb·lɪn, $ˈhɑːbˌgɑː·blɪn/ *n* [C] a badly behaved or evil GOBLIN (= a small ugly imaginary creature which is found in stories)

hob·nail (boot) /£ˈhɒb·neɪl, $ˈhɑːb-/, **hob·nailed boot** /£ˈhɒb·neɪld, $ˈhɑːb-/ *n* [C] a heavy boot or shoe that has nails hammered into the bottom to make it last longer

hob·nob /£ˈhɒb·nɒb, $ˈhɑːb·nɑːb/ *v* [I] **-bb-** *infml disapproving* to spend time being friendly with someone who is important or famous • *She often has her picture in the papers, hobnobbing* **with** *the rich and famous.* • *Dave's been hobnobbing* **with** *the directors of the company recently.*

ho·bo /£ˈhəʊ·bəʊ, $ˈhoʊ·boʊ/ *n* [C] *pl* **hobos** or **hoboes** *Am and Aus* a person who does not have a job or a house to live in, or an unskilled worker who moves from one place to another to find employment

Hob·son's choice /£ˈhɒb·sᵊnz, $ˈhɑːb-/ *n* [U] a situation in which there seem to be different things or actions to choose between but in fact there is no choice • *I hadn't intended to buy a chocolate cake but it was* **a case of** *Hobson's choice* (= it was the only type of cake there was)*!*

hock WINE /£hɒk, $hɑːk/ *n* [U] *esp. Br* a type of white wine from Germany • *Hock is a general term applied to white wines which are produced beside the River Rhine.*

hock MONEY /£hɒk, $hɑːk/ *n* [U] **in hock** *infml* in debt; owing or owed • *By 1918 America was no longer in hock* **to** *others, and went on to become the world's biggest creditor.* • *The company's entire assets are now in hock* **to** *the banks.* • Possessions which are in hock are PAWNED (= left temporarily with a person in exchange for an amount of money which must be paid back after a limited time to prevent the item from being sold).

hock *obj* /£hɒk, $hɑːk/ *v* [T] *infml* • *A lot of young couples do not want to be hocked* (= in debt) *up to the neck with a mortgage.*

hock JOINT /£hɒk, $hɑːk/ *n* [C] the middle joint in the back leg of an animal such as a horse, or *(esp. Am)* the meat on the lower leg of an animal

hock·ey /£ˈhɒk·i, $ˈhɑː·ki/, *Am also* **field hock·ey** *n* [U] a game played on a sports field between two teams of eleven players who each have a curved stick with which they try to put a small hard ball into the other team's goal • In America, and sometimes in Britain, hockey can be used to mean **ice hockey**. See at ICE FROZEN WATER. • LP> **Sports**

ho·cus–po·cus /£ˌhəʊ·kəsˈpəʊ·kəs, $ˌhoʊ·kəsˈpoʊ-/ *n* [U] tricks used to deceive, or words used to hide what is happening or make it unclear • *So much of what politicians say is just hocus-pocus.* • *Like so many academics, he hides behind a lot of unfathomable hocus-pocus.*

hod /£hɒd, $hɑːd/ *n* [C] a container for carrying bricks made of an open box on a pole which is held against the shoulder • PIC› **Building and construction**

hodge·podge /£ˈhɒdʒ·pɒdʒ, $ˈhɑːdʒ·pɑːdʒ/ *n* [C] a HOTCHPOTCH

hoe /£həʊ, $hoʊ/ *n* [C] a garden tool with a long handle and a short blade used to remove WEEDS (= unwanted plants) and break up the surface of the ground • PIC› **Garden**

hoe *(obj)* /£həʊ, $hoʊ/ *v* **hoeing**, *past* **hoed** • *They spent the afternoon hoeing (the vegetable patch).* [I/T]

hoe·down /£ˈhəʊ·daʊn, $ˈhoʊ-/ *n* [C] (in the US) an energetic dance with a set of steps, or a party where there are such dances • *(Am slang)* A hoedown is also a noisy argument or fight.

hog ANIMAL /£hɒg, $hɑːg/ *n* [C] *(Am)* a pig, esp. one which is allowed to grow large so that it can be eaten, or *(Br)* a male pig with its sexual organs removed which is kept for its meat • Compare BOAR; SOW ANIMAL.

hog PERSON /£hɒg, $hɑːg/ *n* [C] *infml* someone who takes much more than a fair share of something, esp. by eating too much • *You've eaten it all, (you) hog!* [as form of address]

hog *obj* /£hɒg, $hɑːg/ *v* [T] **-gg-** *infml* • *He's always hogging the newspapers* (= keeping them close to him so that no one else can read them). • *(disapproving)* If someone **hogs the road**, they drive so that other vehicles cannot go past.

hog·gish /£ˈhɒg·ɪʃ, $ˈhɑː·gɪʃ/ *adj* (of people) selfish, dirty or GREEDY (= taking too much for themselves)

Hog·man·ay /£ˈhɒg·mə·neɪ, £ˌ--ˈ-, $ˈhɑːg·mə·neɪ/ *n* [U not after *the*] (in Scotland) the last day of the year and the parties to celebrate it which start in the evening and continue until the next day • See also **New Year's Eve** at NEW DIFFERENT. • LP› **Holidays**

hog·wash /£ˈhɒg·wɒʃ, $ˈhɑːg·wɑːʃ/ *n* [U] *infml* nonsense or words which are intended to deceive • *His answer was pure hogwash.*

ho–ho(–ho) /£ˌhəʊˈhəʊ, $ˌhoʊˈhoʊ/ *exclamation* used in writing or sometimes spoken to represent the sound of laughter

ho–hum /£ˌhəʊˈhʌm, $ˌhoʊ-/ *exclamation* an expression used when someone is not interested or when they accept that something, usually unpleasant, cannot be stopped from happening • *"So there's no more funding for the project and that's final is it?" "I'm afraid so." "Ho-hum, so be it."*

hoi pol·loi /ˌhɔɪ·pəˈlɔɪ/ *pl n* **the hoi polloi** *disapproving or humorous* ordinary people considered as a group, rather than well-educated or rich people of a higher social class • *Anthony will be in the VIP lounge where he doesn't have to mix with the hoi polloi.*

hoist *obj* /hɔɪst/ *v* [T] to lift something heavy, usually using ropes • *Tomorrow the final section of the bridge will be hoisted into place.* • *I was the last crew member to be hoisted to safety by helicopter.* • *They hoisted placards saying "War's no solution" and presented the minister with a white dove.* • *With some difficulty he managed to hoist her onto his shoulders.* • *I scrabbled for a handhold and hoisted myself up.* • If you hoist a **flag**, you raise it to the top of a pole using a rope: *The island was renamed Prince of Wales Island when the British flag was hoisted on 11 August 1786.* ○ *(fig.) On how many more days will the occupying forces hoist their flag* (= be present) *here?* • *(Am)* To **hoist a few** is to drink several glasses of beer or other alcoholic drink. • If someone is **hoist(ed) with/by** their **own petard**, they suffer the harm from a plan by which they had intended to harm someone else.

hoist /hɔɪst/ *n* [C] • A hoist is a device used for lifting heavy things: *The hoist has broken so we can't get the sacks upstairs.*

hoi·ty–toi·ty /£ˌhɔɪ·tiˈtɔɪ·ti, $-ṭiˈtɔɪ·ṭi/ *adj infml dated disapproving* behaving as if you are better or more important than other people • *I thought she was rather hoity-toity.*

hok·ey /£ˈhəʊ·ki, $ˈhoʊ-/ *adj Am* too emotional or artificial and not believable • *Some of the songs on Wayne's latest recording seem sentimental, contrived and hokey.*

ho·kum /£ˈhəʊ·kəm, $ˈhoʊ-/ *n* [U] *infml esp. Am* a film, play or television programme which is of little real value or interest, although possibly entertaining • *As a whole the series was never less than watchable – hokum, perhaps, but entertaining.*

hold *(obj)* SUPPORT /£həʊld, $hoʊld/ *v past* **held** /held/ to take and keep (something) in your hand or arms • *Can you hold the bag while I open the door?* [T] • *We have witnesses who saw you holding a gun.* [T] • *The little girl held her mother's* **hand**. [T] • *He held the coin tightly* **in** *his hand.* [T] • *The nurse held the dying child* **in** *her arms.* [T] • *When the prisoner was on the ground one police officer held him* **down** *while the other handcuffed him.* [T] • *Please hold* **(on to)** *the rail if you stand while the bus is moving.* [T; I + *on to*] • *Hold* **on**/*Hold* **tight**/*Hold* **on tight** (= Hold something which is fixed) – *we're going to hit a bump!* [I always + adv/prep] • *Could you hold the door* **open** *for me please?* [T + obj + adj] • *Rosie held* **out** *an apple and the horse gently took it from her palm.* [M] • *Close your eyes and hold* **out** *your hand – I've got a present for you.* [M] • *All those who agree please hold* **up** *their hand* (= raise their arm). [M] • *When a dog swims, it holds its head* **up** *to keep it out of the water.* [M] • If you hold your **nose**, you press your nose tightly between thumb and finger to close it: *I have to hold my nose when I put my head under the water.* [T] • To hold something is also to support it: *Will the rope be strong enough to hold the weight?* [T] ○ *I can't fasten this skirt unless I hold my stomach* **in** (= support it with my muscles so that it does not stick out). [M] ○ *Each wheel is held* **on** *by/with four bolts.* [T] ○ *Individual parts are held* **together** *with glue.* [M] ○ *The marquee is held* **up** *with/by poles and ropes.* [M] • When two people **hold hands**, one person holds the other person's hand in their hand, esp. to show that they love each other: *They walked along holding hands.* See also **hand in hand** at HAND BODY PART. • *(Br)* If a person or group of people **hold out the hat** (*Aus* **pass round the hat**), they ask for money: *Issuing more bonds is a sly way for the government to hold out the hat.* • When someone **holds** their **head (up) high** they are confident and proud: *If you know that you did your best, you can hold your head high.* • *Her latest book is enjoyable, but it does* **not hold a candle to** (= is of much lower quality than) *her earlier, less commercial work.*

hold /£həʊld, $hoʊld/ *n* • *If you can get* **(a)** *hold* **of** (= can hold) *that end of this box, I'll take this end and we'll lift it.* [U] • *Don't worry if you* **lose** *hold* **of** *the reins – the horse won't wander off.* [U] • *Babies often have* **a** *strong hold* (= they close the hand with a lot of force). [C] • In fighting sports, a hold is a position in which one person holds another person so that they cannot move part of their body: *In this martial art there are several simple holds which are taught to beginners.* [C] • A hold is also a place to put the hands and feet, esp. when climbing: *It's a difficult mountain to climb as there aren't many holds.* [C] • If you **take/grab** hold **of** something or someone, you take them firmly and hold them: *He took hold of one end of the carpet and tugged.* [U] ○ *I just managed to grab hold of Lucy before she fell in the pool.* [U] • *(infml)* If you **get hold of** someone or something, you find or obtain them: *Where can I get hold of Jeff/some stamps?* • If you **get hold of** information, you understand it: *This is a very difficult concept to get hold of.* • **No holds barred** means nothing is omitted or not allowed: *The book is an account of the actor's life with no holds barred.* • See also FOOTHOLD; HANDHOLD; TOEHOLD.

hold·er /£ˈhəʊl·dəʳ, $ˈhoʊl·dɚ/ *n* [C] • A holder is a device for putting objects in or for keeping them in place: *a toilet-roll holder* • *a toothbrush holder* • *a cigarette holder*

hold *(obj)* KEEP /£həʊld, $hoʊld/ *v past* **held** /held/ to keep (something), esp. when it might have been lost • *I told the manageress of the shop I didn't have enough money and asked her to hold the dress for me until this afternoon.* [T] • *The champion held* **(on to)** *the lead until the last lap.* [T; I + *on to*] • *The councillor held* **(on to)** *her* **seat** (= official position) *in the election.* [T; I + *on to*] • If someone is held **(in custody)**, they are kept guarded in a police station: *A man is being held in connection with the murder.* [T] ○ *The police are holding several people (in custody) for questioning.* [T] • *He was held* **hostage** *by the terrorists for 18 months.* [T + obj + n] • *I was held* **prisoner** *in a tiny attic room.* [T + obj + n] • *You have to be a fairly good speaker to hold an audience's* **attention/interest** *for over an hour.* [T] • *Don't feel you have to hold the pain* **in** (= feel pain without talking about it or showing it) – *cry if you want to.* [M] • *Don't* **hold** *(anything)* **back** (= keep information secret) – *tell us everything that happened.* • *(disapproving)* If you **cannot hold** your **drink**/*(Am usually)* **liquor**, you become ill easily if you drink too much alcohol. • If you **hold on to** something, you keep it and do not throw it away: *I should* *hold on to that drawing – it might be valuable one day.* ○ *(fig.) She holds on to the hope* (= continues to hope, although it is difficult) *that her son will return some day.*

hold·ing /£'həʊl·dɪŋ, $'hoʊl-/ *adj* [not gradable] • A holding **operation** is a temporary way of dealing with a situation until a new and better way can be introduced: *This is just a holding operation until we get the new management structure sorted out.* • See also HOLDING.

hold *(obj)* CONTINUE /£həʊld, $hoʊld/ *v past* **held** /held/ to (cause to) stay or continue in the same way as before • *Let's hope our good luck holds.* [I] • *(esp. Br and Aus) The special price holds until the end of the month.* [I] • *If the weather holds* (= continues to be good) *we could have a picnic.* [I] • *The law on speeding holds* **for** (= is the same for) *everyone regardless of who they are.* [I] • *I hope the repair holds* **(up)** *until we get the car to a garage.* [I] • *The arguments for reducing pollution still hold* **(true)**, *even though there may be disagreement on how to go about it.* [I] • *It is unlikely the group will hold* **together** (= stay as a group) *after such a failure.* [I] • *The government is committed to holding exports at their present level.* [T] • *The ship/aircraft held its course.* [T] • *Amazing! She held the note she was singing for over a minute.* [T] • *The soldiers are holding them***selves** *in readiness* (= are ready) *to attack.* [T] • *A great diplomat will be required to hold the country* **together** (= keep it as one country so that it does not become divided or get into a state of confusion). [M] • *We believe wage settlements must be held* **down** (= kept at a low level) *to avoid inflation.* [T] • *He's never been able to* **hold down** (= stay and work in) *a steady* **job**. • If something **holds good**, it continues to be true: *Their arguments were valid a hundred years ago and they still hold good today.* • If you **hold on/tight**, you make yourself continue to do what you are doing or stay where you are although it is difficult or unpleasant: *If you can just hold on I'll go and get some help.* See also HOLD SUPPORT; **hold on** at HOLD DELAY. • *They won't be able to* **hold out** (= continue to do what they were doing without being defeated) *much longer under this sort of bombardment.* • *The air supply will* **hold out** (= last) *for another two hours.* • *The workers are* **holding out for** (= continuing to demand) *a 10% pay rise and have threatened to strike.* • *(Am)* If a film, play, etc. is **held over**, it is shown or performed more times than was originally planned, usually because it is very popular with the public: *That show's been held over for another six weeks.* See also HOLD DELAY. • When someone **holds** their **own/holds** their **(own) ground**, they maintain their opinions or position despite difficulties: *She held her ground under severe criticism.* ○ *Josie can hold her own in any argument.* • *(dated)* To **hold** your **own** also means to not become more ill or more weak: *He was very ill after the accident but now he's holding his own.* • If a vehicle **holds the road**, its wheels stay firmly on the road and do not slide while moving: *The latest model holds the road well when cornering.* ○ *It has poor* **road-holding** *in wet conditions.* • *Defensive play allowed the home team to* **hold** *the challengers* **to a draw** (= to make certain that neither side won). • *Will the evidence* **hold up** (= continue to seem true) *under thorough scrutiny?*

hold *(obj)* DELAY /£həʊld, $hoʊld/ *v past* **held** /held/ to stop (something) happening, or to wait or delay (something) temporarily • *They've decided to hold all future deliveries until the invoice has been paid.* [T] • *Don't worry, we'll hold lunch* (= stop it from being served) *till you get here.* [T] • *How long can you hold your* **breath** (= stop breathing)? [T] • *She said she'd get back to us, but* **don't hold your breath** (= don't expect it to happen for a very long time)! • *Hold (your)* **fire** (= Do not shoot) *until they're closer.* [T] • *Will you hold my calls* (= not connect telephone calls to me) *for the next half hour please?* [T] • *She's on the phone at the moment – will you hold* **(the line)** (= wait on the telephone until she can speak to you)? [I/T] • *(Am)* If you hold something, you do not include it: *I'd like a fruit salad, but hold the apples please.* [T] • If you hold something **back**, you stop it coming or advancing: *It is not clear if the army will be able to hold back the invaders.* [M] ○ *Sandbags will hold the flood waters back for a while.* [M] ○ *You shouldn't let other people's opinions hold you back* (= stop you from doing what you want to do). [M] ○ *Hold back your tears* (= do not cry) *– there's good news as well.* [M] • To hold something **back** is also to delay its development: *It's a good plan, but the lack of money has been holding it back for months.* [M] ○ *Farmers say the cold weather is holding their vegetables back.* [M] • If you **hold back**, you do not do something for as long as possible, often because of fear or because you do not want to make a bad situation worse: *She held back* **from** *interfering in their arguments.* ○ *He held back, terrified of going into the dark room.* ○ *She holds back in lessons* (= is unwilling to answer questions) *because she's shy.* • If **there is no holding** someone **(back)**, they do what they want to do eagerly and cannot be stopped: *Once she gets a promotion, there'll be no holding her.* • **Hold everything** means wait or stop because of something important: *We should hold everything until the building is made safe.* • **Hold it** (= Stop and do not do anything else)! *Let's take some of the books out of the boxes before we move them.* • If you **hold** something **off**, you stop something unpleasant happening for as long as possible: *How much longer will the resistance fighters be able to hold off the enemy/hold the enemy off?* • If something **holds off** or is **held off**, it is delayed: *I hope the rain holds off* (= I hope it does not rain) *while we walk home.* ○ *The board has decided to hold off (making) its decision.* • *Will you* **hold on** (= wait) *while I see who's at the door?* • **Hold on!** (= Pause for a moment) *What's that strange noise?* • *There's been a problem – can we* **hold** *the presentation* **over** (= delay it) *until next week?* • **Hold still** (= Don't move), *this won't hurt.* • **Hold tight** (= Stop) *a minute, I don't agree with what you're saying at all!* • If you **hold** your **tongue**, you do not speak: *Hold your tongue, young man!* ○ *I'm going to have to learn to hold my tongue* (= not upset people by what I say). • *Traffic was* **held up** (= delayed) *for several hours by the accident.* • *Sorry to* **hold** *you* **up** (= make you wait) *– my train was late.* • *There was a short* **hold-up** (= delay) *while the choir moved on to the stage.* • *(dated)* **Hold your horses!** means pause, esp. for thought, before doing or deciding something: *Hold your horses! We might get this cheaper somewhere else.*

hold /£həʊld, $hoʊld/ *n* [U] • If you are **on hold** when using the telephone, you are waiting to speak to someone: *Mr Briggs is on hold.* ○ *His phone is engaged – can I* **put** *you on hold?* • If something is **on hold**, it is intentionally delayed: *The project is on hold for a while.* ○ *We've* **put** *the plans on hold until the financial situation improves.*

hold *obj* CONTAIN /£həʊld, $hoʊld/ *v* [T; not *be holding*] *past* **held** /held/ to contain or be able to contain (something) • *This jug holds exactly one pint.* • *One bag won't hold all of the shopping – we'd better take two.* • *Modern computers can hold* (= store) *huge amounts of information.* • *(fig.) She's very religious, so death holds no fear for her.* • *(fig.) Politics is a turbulent profession which holds many surprises.* • If a reason, argument or explanation **holds water**, it is true: *Her alibi seems to hold water.* • LP **Measurements**

hold *obj* CONTROL /£həʊld, $hoʊld/ *v* [T] *past* **held** /held/ to have (something, esp. a position or money) or to control (something) • *He currently holds the position of technical manager.* • *Can she be trusted to hold the office of treasurer if she can't pay her own bills?* • *The bank holds large reserves of gold.* • *He holds three different accounts with the same building society.* • *She holds 100 British Telecom shares and thirty shares in British Gas.* • *After many days of severe fighting the rebels now hold the town.* • *It will require a huge military presence to hold* **down** (= control) *public unrest.* [M] • If someone **holds all the cards**, they have a big advantage: *Management holds all the cards when it comes to the negotiations over job cuts.* • *(esp. humorous)* When someone **holds court**, they receive a lot of attention from other people who gather round to listen to them, esp. on social occasions: *Patrick is holding court at the end table.* • If someone **holds the stage**/*(Br and Aus also)* floor, they speak to a group of people, often for a long time, without letting anyone else speak: *The rest of us sat there impatiently while the chairman held the floor.* • If a person **holds the fort**, they have responsibility for something while someone is absent: *I'll be out of the office for a few hours – will you hold the fort until I get back?* • *Because the two main parties have won almost the same number of votes, the minority group* **holds the key to** (= has control of) *the result.* • *She's the boss, but her secretary* **hold the reins** (= is in control) *of the department's operation.* • *Fundamentalist beliefs* **hold sway over** (= have a very strong influence over) *whole districts, ensuring the popularity of religious leaders.*

hold /£həʊld, $hoʊld/ *n* [U] • *For many years the guerillas have been increasing their hold* (= control) *in the hills.* • *This student already has* **a good hold of** *the subject* (= understands it well). • *She* **has a** *strong hold* (= large influence) **over/on** *her daughters.*

hold·er /£ˈhəʊl·dər, $ˈhoʊl·dɚ/ *n* [C] • *an account/licence/passport-holder* (=someone who has an account/licence/passport) • *The current holder of the record will be competing.* • *Holders of shares in the company receive various benefits.* See also SHAREHOLDER. • *All office-holders* (=people with official positions) *should attend.*

hold *obj* [CAUSE TO HAPPEN] /£həʊld, $hoʊld/ *v* [T] *past* **held** /held/ to make (something, esp. a meeting or an election) happen • *Could we hold a meeting to discuss this tomorrow afternoon?* • *The election will be held on the 8th of August.* • *Why don't we hold a party to celebrate the news?* • *I find it's almost impossible to hold a sensible conversation with her.* • *Peace talks will continue to be held until an agreement is reached.* • LP› **Do: verbs meaning 'perform'**

hold *(obj)* [BELIEVE] /£həʊld, $hoʊld/ *v* [not *be holding*] *past* **held** /held/ to believe (an idea or opinion) to be correct • *He holds unusual views/opinions on many subjects.* [T] • *Very few people still hold ideas like that.* [T] • *She still holds* **that** *he's alive.* [+ *that* clause] • *Murphy's law holds* (=states) **that** *if you drop a piece of bread it will land with the buttered side down.* [+ *that* clause] • *Small amounts of alcohol are held* **to** *be good for the heart.* [+ obj + *to* infinitive] • *You sold it to me, so if it breaks I'll hold you* **responsible** (=make you take responsibility). [+ obj + adj] • *I* **don't hold with** *that sort of behaviour* (=I don't find it acceptable).

hold [SPACE] /£həʊld, $hoʊld/ *n* [C] the space in a ship or aircraft in which goods are carried

hold *obj* **a·gainst** *obj v prep* [T] to allow (something) to make you have a bad opinion about (someone or something) • *He made a mistake but I don't hold* **it** *against him – we all make mistakes.* • *She's a little older than we are but I don't think we should hold that against her.*

hold forth *v adv* [I] *usually disapproving* (when speaking) to express opinions for a long time • *She held forth all afternoon* **about/on** *a variety of subjects.* • *I have no wish to sit on Michael's table if he's just going to hold forth all throughout lunch.*

hold out *obj v adv* [T] to offer (a possibility, solution, hope etc.) • *The proposals hold out a real prospect for settling the dispute.* • *Few people hold out any* **hope** *of finding more survivors.* • (N)

hold out on *obj v adv prep* [T] *infml* to refuse to give help, information or *(Am)* money to (someone) • *Don't hold out on me – I need to know who did it.* • *(Am) Pat was holding out on us, refusing to pay his share of the rent, but we finally convinced him to hand it over.*

hold *(obj)* **to** *obj v prep* [T] to (cause (someone) to) act on (a promise or agreement) • *Will the new president hold to his election promises?* • *We'll hold him to the exact terms of the contract.*

hold up *obj* [STEAL], **hold** *obj* **up** *v adv* [M] to steal or try to steal from (something, esp. a shop, bank or vehicle) using violence or the threat of violence • *The gang held a security van up using shotguns.* • *They held the same bank up twice in one week.*

hold–up /£ˈhəʊld·ʌp, $ˈhoʊld-/ *n* [C] • *In the hold-up at the bank a masked youth threatened staff with a gun.* • See also **hold-up** at HOLD [DELAY].

hold up *obj* [GIVE EXAMPLE], **hold** *obj* **up** *v adv* [M] to offer (something) as an example • *Corelli is often held up* **as** *a composer to be admired.*

hold·all *esp. Br and Aus* /£ˈhəʊld·ɔːl, $ˈhoʊld·ɑːl/, *Am usually, Aus also* **car·ry·all** *n* [C] a soft bag or small case used for carrying clothes and personal items when travelling • PIC› **Luggage**

hold·ing /£ˈhəʊl·dɪŋ, $ˈhoʊl-/ *n* [C] something owned such as shares in a company or buildings, or land which is looked after and owned or rented • *To ensure security the investment fund has holdings in many companies.* • A **holding company** is a company whose main purpose is to control another company or companies through owning shares in it or them.

hole [SPACE] /£həʊl, $hoʊl/ *n* [C] an empty space in an object, usually with an opening to the object's surface, or an opening which goes completely through an object • *Large holes appeared* **in** *the field when sections of a disused mine collapsed.* • *We* **dug** *a hole to plant the tree.* • *We'll make a hole through the wall then we can put a window in.* • *My jumper's got a hole* **in** *it where it caught on a nail.* • *Cut different shaped holes* **in** *your piece of paper.* • In golf, a hole (*Am also* **cup**) is one of the small hollow spaces in the ground into which the ball is hit. • In golf, a hole is also one of the usually 18 areas of play: *The famous 18-hole Old Course is at St. Andrews.* • If someone says you have a **hole in** your **head**/*(Am also)* **holes in** your **head**, they think you have done something stupid: *You must have a hole in your head if you're willing to do all that work for free.* • If something **makes a hole in** an amount of money, it reduces it a lot: *The holiday made a (large) hole in our savings but I'm glad we went.* • In golf, if someone has a **hole in one**, their ball goes into the hole the first time they hit it, which is rare. • A **hole in the heart** is a medical condition in which there is an additional opening between the main parts of the heart. • *(infml)* A **hole-in-the-wall** is a machine into which you put a special plastic card to take your money from a bank when the bank is closed. See also **hole-in-the-wall** at HOLE [PLACE]. • A **hole punch(er)** is a device used for making two holes in the side of pieces of paper so that they can be fastened together easily or stored in a FOLDER (=a folded piece of cardboard used for keeping loose papers in). • PIC› **Stationery**

hole *obj* /£həʊl, $hoʊl/ *v* [T] *specialized* • *The second mortar attack severely holed* (=made holes in) *the road.* • *A torpedo holed* (=made a hole in) *the ship below the water and it quickly sank.*

hole [PLACE] /£həʊl, $hoʊl/ *n* [C] a place in the ground where a small animal lives, or *(infml)* a small unpleasant place where someone lives • *a mouse/rabbit/fox hole* • *(infml) What a hole that place was – I'm so pleased we don't live there anymore.* • *(Am)* A **hole in the wall** is a small simple shop, house or restaurant: *We went to dinner at this little hole in the wall where the food is terrific.* • See also **hole in the wall** at HOLE [SPACE].

hole [FAULT] /£həʊl, $hoʊl/ *n* [C] a fault in the use of reason or LOGIC in an argument, discussion, plan, etc. • *The new proposal has several holes* (**in** *it*). • *Be careful when you give your talk – some people will try to* **pick holes in** (=find faults in) *everything you say.*

hole [DIFFICULTY] /£həʊl, $hoʊl/ *n* [C] *infml* a difficult situation • *Because we lost the order we're* **in a bit of a** *hole.* • *(Am)* If someone is **in the hole**, they are in debt: *After selling all its assets and paying its depositors, the bank was still half a million dollars in the hole.*

hole up *v adv* [I always + adv/prep] *infml* to stay in a safe place, often as a way of escape • *After the robbery the gang holed up for a few days in an old warehouse.* • *We'd better find some shelter and hole up until the storm passes.*

hol·i·day *Br and Aus* /£ˈhɒl·ɪ·deɪ, $ˈhɑː·lɪ-/, *Am* **va·ca·tion** *n* a time, often one or two weeks, when someone does not go to work or school but is free to do what they want, such as travel or relax • *a camping/skiing holiday* [C] • *Have you decided where you're going* **for** *your holiday this year?* [C] • *Bren and I had a brilliant holiday in Egypt.* [C] • *Patricia is* **on** *holiday next week.* [U] • *I haven't had any holiday so far this year.* [U] • *How many days' holiday do you get with your new job?* [U] • *We thought we'd go to France for our* **summer** *holiday.* [C] • *She showed me her holiday* **snaps** (=photographs). • A holiday is also a day for which it is officially agreed that everyone does not need to work, or a period of time for which it is agreed that someone or a group of people do not need to work: *St Patrick's Day is a holiday in Ireland.* [C] ○ *There are eight* **public** *holidays during the year in both Britain and the US.* [C] • A **holiday camp** is a place where people on holiday can stay and entertainments are provided for them: *Zoe* **went on** *holiday camp last summer.* • LP› **Holidays, Work**

hol·i·days /£ˈhɒl·ɪ·deɪz, $ˈhɑː·lɪ-/, *Br infml* **hols** *pl n* • *Have you decided where you're going* **for** *your holidays* (=holiday) *this year?* • *Wayne is* **on** *his holidays next week.* • *Surely the* **school** *holidays start soon.*

hol·i·day *Br and Aus* /£ˈhɒl·ɪ·deɪ, $ˈhɑː·lɪ-/, *Am* **va·ca·tion** *v* [I always + adv/prep] • *My parents are holidaying in Spain this year.*

hol·i·day·mak·er *Br and Aus* /£ˈhɒl·ə·diˌmeɪ·kər, -deɪ-, $ˈhɑː·lə·deɪˌmeɪ·kɚ/, *Am* **va·ca·tion·er** *n* [C] a person who is on holiday away from where they usually live • *The strike has left thousands of British holidaymakers stranded at Spanish airports.*

Ho·li·ness /£ˈhəʊ·lɪ·nəs, $ˈhoʊ-/ *n* See at HOLY [GOOD]

hol·i·sm /£ˈhəʊ·lɪ·zəm, $ˈhoʊ·lɪ-/ *n* [U] the belief that anything natural is in some way connected to everything else and that each thing, such as a person, is a whole which is more important than the parts that make it up • *More and more people are taking holism seriously because they find materialism unsatisfying.*

hol·is·tic /£həʊˈlɪs·tɪk, £hɒlˈɪs-, $hoʊlˈɪs·t̬ɪk/ *adj* [not gradable] • *Ecological problems usually require holistic*

HOLIDAYS AND SPECIAL DAYS IN BRITAIN AND THE US

About 8 days of the year are public holidays, also called *(Br)* **bank**/*(Am)* **national** holidays. Many days of the year are given a special name, e.g. 1st May is called *May Day*. Some of these are traditionally connected with particular activities and customs. **Festivals** are usually days with a special religious meaning. **Anniversaries** celebrate the date of an important past event. Here are some special days with a name:

JAN	1	New Year's Day	People say *Happy New Year!* to anyone they meet in the first few days of the New Year, and make New Year's resolutions (= plans to improve their behaviour). *I'm giving up smoking for the New Year.*
FEB	14	Valentine's Day	(Not a holiday) People send Valentines (= unsigned cards) or give presents to someone they love, such as their girlfriend or boyfriend.
	*	Pancake Tuesday, Pancake Day; also *(Br)* Shrove Tuesday,	(Not a holiday) The day before the Christian period of Lent (= the 40 days before Easter). In Britain people make and eat pancakes, a type of thin flat cake. *The Mardi Gras festivities in New Orleans last several days,with parades, costume parties and music.*
MARCH	*	Mother's Day, Mothering Sunday	(Britain; not a holiday) Children give cards and presents to their mothers. In the US this is held in May.
	*	Easter = Good Friday Easter Sunday Easter Monday	On Good Friday, Christians remember the death of Jesus and on Easter Sunday/ Easter Day they celebrate his return to life. People in Britain eat hot cross buns (= small round cakes marked with a cross), and on Easter Day children receive chocolate Easter eggs.

* The date of these special days is fixed by the date of Easter, which is different in different years. Sometimes Easter is in April. Mother's Day is two Sundays before Easter in Britain.

APR	1	April Fool's Day	(Not a holiday) People play tricks on each other and say *"April fool!"* afterwards to show it was a joke. Even some newspapers and television programmes contain silly news items.
MAY	1	May Day	(Britain has a May Day holiday on the first Monday of May) Traditionally a celebration of spring, it is now often a time for political marches and meetings connected with the Labour Party.
		Mother's Day	(US; not a holiday) The third Sunday in May. Children give cards and presents to their mothers.
JUN		Father's Day	(Not a holiday) The third Sunday in June. Children give cards and presents to their fathers.
JULY	4	the Fourth of July, Independence Day	(US) The US national day, celebrating the signing of the Declaration of Independence in 1776: *Fireworks and parades are traditional Fourth of July celebrations. Over the Fourth there are many family reunions, picnics and barbecues.*
SEP		Labor Day	(US) The first Monday in September. A national holiday honouring workers and marking the end of summer.
OCT		Harvest Festival	(Britain; not a holiday) In schools and churches, people give thanks for a successful harvest (= collection of crops), with displays of flowers, fruit and vegetables.
	31	Halloween	(Not a holiday) Esp. in US, children 'trick or treat', (= wear frightening clothes and face masks, and visit people's homes to get *(Br)* sweets/*(Am)* candy). Adults might go to *(Br)* fancy dress/*(Am)* costume parties.
NOV	5	Guy Fawkes' Night	(Britain; not a holiday) Remembering the failure of the 'Gunpowder Plot', a plan by Guy Fawkes and others to blow up the Houses of Parliament in 1605. *We're not having a bonfire* (= large fire outside) *this year – I'm taking the kids to the fireworks display in the park.*
		Thanksgiving (Day)	(US) The fourth Thursday in November. Celebrating the survival in 1621 of early English travellers to America, who nearly died of hunger: *Every Thanksgiving all our family come over and Mom cooks turkey, corn, sweet potatoes and pumpkin pie.*
DEC	24 25 26	Christmas = Christmas Eve Christmas Day *(Br)* Boxing Day	The main public holiday, celebrating the birth of Jesus. People sing carols (= religious songs), houses, offices and public places are decorated, and people send Christmas cards, give presents and wish each other *Merry/Happy Christmas!* Families gather at home and eat Christmas dinner (in Britain this is traditionally turkey and Christmas pudding).
	31	New Year's Eve	(Not a public holiday) Called Hogmanay in Scotland. People go to parties or gather in public places to let in (= welcome) the New Year.

solutions. • *Shapur's latest book, written with Dr Ellis Pike, offers a more positive and holistic* **approach** *to the menopause.* • **Holistic medicine** is treatment which deals with the whole person, not just the injury or disease.

hol·is·ti·cally /£həʊ'lɪs·tɪ·kli, $hoʊ'lɪs·t̬ɪ-/ *adv* [not gradable]

hol·ler /£'hɒl·əʳ, $'hɑː·lɚ/ *v esp. Am infml* to shout or call, esp. because of pain or in order to attract a person's attention • *By the time the ambulance arrived she was really hollering.* [I] • *Ma's been hollering for you!* [I] • *"What's the time?" he hollered.* [+ clause]

hol·ler /£'hɒl·əʳ, $'hɑː·lɚ/ *n* [C] *esp. Am infml* • *He* **let out** *a holler when he fell.*

hol·low [EMPTY] /£'hɒl·əʊ, $'hɑː·loʊ/ *adj* [C], *n* **-er, -est** having an empty space inside, or (having) a space in the surface of an object • *Hollow blocks are used because they are lighter.* • *The dog found a hollow (in the ground) to hide in from the wind.* [C] • *He was* **hollow-cheeked** (= His face was too thin) *and pale, almost unearthly.* • *When I last saw her she was pale and* **hollow-eyed** (= her eyes seemed to have sunk into her face because of illness or tiredness). • *(Am)* A hollow (also **holler**) is a valley: *We used to go for long walks in the hollow.* ○ *Sleepy Hollow* [C]

hol·low *obj* /£'hɒl·əʊ, $'hɑː·loʊ/ *v* • *Sand carried by the wind has hollowed* **(out)** *the base of the cliff.* [T/M] • *Sometimes a colony of ants will completely hollow* **out** *a tree trunk leaving just the bark.* [M]

hol·low·ness /£'hɒl·əʊ·nəs, $'hɑː·loʊ-/ *n* [U]

hol·low [WITHOUT VALUE] /£'hɒl·əʊ, $'hɑː·loʊ/ *adj* **-er, -est** *disapproving* (of situations, feelings or words) lacking value; not true or sincere • *It was something of a hollow victory – she won the case but lost all her savings in legal fees.* • *After many years of promiscuity she felt that sex had become a hollow pleasure.* • *Will their good intentions become realities or hollow promises?* • *There's a rather* **hollow ring** *to her profession of complete contentment* (= it does not sound sincere).

hol·low·ness /£'hɒl·əʊ·nəs, $'hɑː·loʊ-/ *n* [U]

hol·low [SOUND] /£'hɒl·əʊ, $'hɑː·loʊ/ *adj* **-er, -est** (of sound) as if made by hitting an empty container • *We could hear the hollow sound of a bell through the fog.*

hol·low·ly /£'hɒl·əʊ·li, $'hɑː·loʊ·li/ *adv* • *Her footsteps echoed hollowly in the quiet streets.*

hol·ly /£'hɒl·i, $'hɑː·li/ *n* [C/U] a small evergreen tree which has shiny leaves with points on their edges and sometimes small red fruit • *Birds feed on holly berries in winter.* • [PIC] **Berries**

hol·ly·hock /£'hɒl·i·hɒk, $'hɑː·li·hɑːk/ *n* [C] a garden plant which has very tall stems covered with brightly coloured flowers

hol·o·caust /£'hɒl·ə·kɔːst, $'hɑː·lə·kɑːst/ *n* [C] a large amount of destruction, esp. by fire or heat; the killing of large numbers of people • *A* **nuclear** *holocaust* (= destruction caused by nuclear weapons) *would leave few survivors.* • **The Holocaust** was the killing of many Jews and others by Nazis before and during the second World War.

hol·o·gram /£'hɒl·ə·græm, $'hɑː·lə-/ *n* [C] a special type of photograph or image made with a LASER beam in which the objects shown can look solid, as if they are real, rather than flat

hol·o·graph·y /£hɒl'ɒg·rə·fi, $hoʊ'lɑː·grə-/ *n* [U] • *Holography* (= making holograms) *is used to make security figures on credit cards.*

hol·o·graph·ic /£ˌhɒl·ə'græf·ɪk, $ˌhɑː·lə-/ *adj* [not gradable] • *a holographic picture/image/projection*

hols /£hɒlz, $hɑːlz/ *pl n Br infml for* **holidays**, see at HOLIDAY

Hol·stein /£'hɒl·staɪn, £'həʊl-, $'hoʊl·stiːn/ *n* [C] *Am for* FRIESIAN

hol·ster /£'həʊl·stəʳ, $'hoʊl·stɚ/ *n* [C] a stiff bag-like container for a gun, esp. a PISTOL (= a small gun fired with one hand), usually made of leather and fixed on a belt or a strap

ho·ly [GOOD] /£'həʊ·li, $'hoʊ-/ *adj* **-ier, -iest** related to God and religion and therefore thought to be morally good • *holy scriptures/rites* • *a holy city/person/well* • *As a nun, she led a holy life humbly attending to the needs of the sick.* • *(disapproving)* If a person is **holier-than-thou**, they think that they are morally better than anyone else: *Her holier-than-thou* **attitudes** *make her very unpopular.* • **Holy Communion** (also **Communion, the Eucharist, the Lord's Supper** or **Mass**) is the Christian religious ceremony based on Jesus Christ's last meal with his friends. See also COMMUNICANT. • **The Holy Grail** (also **the Grail**) is a bowl believed to have been used by Jesus Christ at the meal before his death. Some of his blood is believed to have been collected in it and it therefore became a holy thing which many people looked for: *(fig.) Sustained nuclear fusion is the holy grail* (= the thing which is most wanted and which people try to discover) *of the power industry.* • The **holy of holies** is the most special part of a religious building, esp. a Jewish TEMPLE. • *(humorous)* A **holy of holies** is also any place which is very special: *This football stadium is the holy of holies to many fans.* • **Holy orders** are the ceremony by which someone becomes a priest in some parts of the Christian Church: *Will you be* **taking** *holy orders?* • **The Holy See** is the government of the Roman Catholic Church, under the POPE. • The **Holy Spirit** (also **Holy Ghost**) is God in the form of a spirit in the Christian church. • A **holy war** is a war fought to defend a religion, to force others to follow a different religion, or for other religious beliefs. See also CRUSADE; jihad. • **Holy Week** is the week before Easter Sunday. [not after *the*]

ho·li·ness /£'həʊ·lɪ·nəs, $'hoʊ-/ *n* [U] • *This temple is a place of great holiness for the religion's followers.*

Ho·li·ness /£'həʊ·lɪ·nəs, $'hoʊ-/ *n* • **His/Your Holiness** is a title used of or to the POPE: • *What are the views of His Holiness on the subject?* ○ *Yes, Your Holiness.* [as form of address]

ho·ly [EMPHASIS] /£'həʊ·li, $'hoʊ-/ *adj* **-ier, -iest** *infml* (used to emphasize another word, sometimes to avoid swearing) • *Holy mackerel! What a noise!* • *Holy cow! How did you get that black eye?* • *(taboo) Holy shit – what was that?*

hom·age /£'hɒm·ɪdʒ, $'hɑː·mɪdʒ/ *n* [U] deep respect and often praise shown for a person or god • *On this occasion we* **pay** *homage (***to** *him) for his achievements.* • *Many people* **came in** *homage to the place where the miracle/tragedy had happened.*

hom·burg /£'hɒm·bɜːg, $'hɑːm·bɜːrg/ *n* [C] a man's hat with a wide curled BRIM (= the bottom part of a hat that sticks out all round) and a fold in the middle of the top

home [HOUSE/APARTMENT] /£həʊm, $hoʊm/ *n* a building or structure in which a person lives, esp. a house or apartment • *The family has three homes – an apartment in New York, a country house in Pine Plains and a beach house in the Hamptons.* [C] • *Our new house doesn't feel like a home yet.* [C] • *He was living on the streets for three months, and his home was a cardboard box.* [C] • *Phone me* **at** *home after four o'clock.* [U] • *He left the letters* **at** *home.* [U] • *She was elderly and needed help* **in the** *home* (= in her house). [U] • *He decided to* **leave** *home* (= stop living with his parents) *when he was 23.* [U] • *More and more couples are* **setting up** *home together without getting married.* [U] • *They wanted to* **give** *the child* **a home** (= wanted the child to live with them). [U] • If you **are/feel at home** you feel comfortable and relaxed: *By the end of the week she was beginning to feel at home in her new job.* • To **make** yourself **at home** you behave informally and in a relaxed way as if in your own house: *She was shocked to find he had made himself at home in the lounge and showed no signs of leaving.* (J) • Home is used to mean done or made at home: *home-made cakes/wine* • *home-grown vegetables* • *home baking* • *home-brewed beer.* • As home suggests pleasant things like comfort and safety, people selling new houses or apartments often call them homes: *luxury/starter homes* [C] • Home can mean the type of family you come from: *We had a happy home.* [C] ○ *The children were from a* **broken** *home* (= the parents had separated). [C] • A home is also a place where a group of people or animals live and are cared for by people who are not their relatives or owners: *a children's home/an old people's home/a dogs' home* [C] ○ *He spent his early years in a home.* [C] • Your **home address** and **home (phone) number** are the address and telephone number of the house or apartment you live in. • A **home buyer** is a person who is buying a house or an apartment. • **Home economics** is the study of all matters relating to the management of a home. • **The home front** means the people at home, esp. those staying behind during war: *(humorous) How are things* **on** *the home front* (= How is your family)? • A *(Br)* **home from home**/*(Am and Aus usually)* **home away from home** is a place where you feel as comfortable as you are in your own house: *The hotel was a real home from home.* • *(Br)* A **home help** is someone who is paid to help someone else with the cleaning of their home. • A **home loan** is money borrowed from a bank or similar organization in order to buy a house or apartment. • A **home movie** is a film made for personal enjoyment, esp. one of family or holiday activities. • 'House' is the more usual word for describing a building that one family lives in. The word 'home' also refers to the life that goes on in that building. • LP> **Shopping goods**

home·less /£'həʊm·ləs, $'hoʊm-/ *adj* [not gradable] • *Accommodation needs to be found for thousands of homeless families.*

home·less /£'həʊm·ləs, $'hoʊm-/ *pl n* • *We need to address the problem of* **the** *homeless* (=people who do not have a place to live).

home·less·ness /£'həʊm·lə·snəs, $'hoʊm-/ *n* [U] • *Surveys show the most common causes of homelessness among women to be domestic violence and the breakdown of a relationship.*

home ORIGIN /£həʊm, $hoʊm/ *n* someone's or something's place of origin, or the place where a person feels they belong • *Britain has been my home for ten years* (=I have lived in Britain for ten years). [C] • *I live in London, but my home* (= where I was born) *is in Yorkshire.* [U] • *I was actually born in New Zealand, but I've lived in England for so long that it* **feels like** *home now.* [U] • *Australia is* **the** *home* **of** *the kangaroo.* [U] • If you are *(Br)* **home and dry**/*(Aus)* **home and hosed**, you have successfully completed something: *We just have to finish this section, then we're home and dry.* • *(Am infml)* If you **home free**, you are certain that what you are trying to do will be finished or successful: *Once you leave the main road and cross the bridge, you're home free – we live just three houses further on.* • *(Am)* A **home run** or a **homer** is a point scored in baseball by hitting the ball so far that you have time to run all the way round the four corners of the playing field before it is returned. • The **home stretch** is the last part of something which is being done: *It's taken three months so far, but we're on the home stretch now.* • A **home truth** is a piece of information which is not pleasant or welcome, but is true: *He decided it was time to tell her a few home truths.* • *"Home, Sweet Home"* (title of a song written by J.H.Payne, 1823) • *"Home Alone"* (film title, 1990) • *"Home is the place where, when you have to go there / They have to take you in"* (Robert Frost in the poem *The Death of the Hired Man*, 1914) • *"Keep the home fires burning ... Till the boys come Home"* (from the song *Till the Boys Come Home!* written by Lena Guilbert Ford, 1914) • *"You can't go Home Again"* (title of a book by Thomas Wolfe, 1940) • *"Won't You Come Home, Bill Bailey?"* (song written by Hughie Cannon, 1902)

home /£həʊm, $hoʊm/ *adv* [not gradable] • If something **comes home** to you or you **bring** something **home to** someone, you (cause someone to) understand something: *The danger really came home to me when I saw the pictures on TV.* ○ *The TV pictures really brought the crisis home to me.* • To **drive** something **home** is to state something strongly: *She really drove home the message that we need to economize.*

home COUNTRY /£həʊm, $hoʊm/ *adj* [before n], *adv* [not gradable], *n* (connected with or done in) your own country or your own area • *The book was published* **at** *home and abroad but it sold better in the home market* (= in the country in which it was produced). • Sports matches can be played **at** home (=on your own sports field) or away: *the home* **team** ○ *a home* **game** Ⓙ ○ *Is a team more likely to win a match when playing on its home* **ground**? LP> **Sports** • **The Home Counties** are the COUNTIES around London in south-east England. • The **Home Office** is the British government department, under the control of the **Home Secretary**, which deals with matters inside Britain that are not the responsibility of other departments. • **Home rule** is a political arrangement in which a part of a country governs itself partly or completely independently of the central government of the country, possibly becoming an independent country: *Would home rule for Scotland mean an additional parliament in Edinburgh or complete independence from the UK?*

home in *v adv* [I] *infml* to aim for, find or choose • *The missile homed in* **on** *the ship.* • *She homed in* **on** *the word 'early'. "How early?" she asked.* • *High above, a seabird was homing in to take another fish.*

home·boy /£'həʊm·bɔɪ, $hoʊm-/ *n* [C] *Am* a boy or man from your own town or general area, or *(slang)* a close friend or member of the same GANG (=a group of esp. young men who spend time together and often cause trouble) • *They were really pleased when their homeboy won a medal at the winter Olympics.*

home·com·ing /£'həʊm,kʌm·ɪŋ, $'hoʊm-/ *n* [C] a person's arrival home after being away for a long time • *They planned a special celebration for her homecoming.* • *(Am)* A homecoming is also an occasion when a group of people who have spent some time together at a place, esp. people who went to a college or university together, return to that place: *Cindy was chosen to be the homecoming* **queen** (=female student who leads the celebration) *for this year's alumni reunion.*

home·land /£'həʊm·lænd, $'hoʊm-/ *n* [C] the country you were born in • *They spent many years hoping to return to their homeland.* • In South Africa, homelands were areas of the country in which black people were separated from whites under the political system of APARTHEID.

home·ly PLAIN *esp. Br and Aus* (**-ier**, **-iest**) /£'həʊm·li, $'hoʊm-/, *Am usually and Aus also* **home·y** (**-ier**, **-iest**) *adj* plain or ordinary, but pleasant • *The hotel was homely and comfortable.* • *We were welcomed by a homely lady who said she was the caretaker.*

home·li·ness /£'həʊm·lɪ·nəs, $'hoʊm-/ *n* [U] *esp. Br and Aus*

home·ly UGLY /£'həʊm·li, $'hoʊm-/ *adj* **-ier**, **-iest** *Am and Aus disapproving* (esp. of people) not attractive • *She thought she was too homely to get a date.*

home·li·ness /£'həʊm·lɪ·nəs, $'hoʊm-/ *n* [U] *Am and Aus disapproving*

home·mak·er /£'həʊm,meɪ·kəʳ, $'hoʊm,meɪ·kɚ/ *n* [C] a person who manages a home and often raises children instead of earning money from employment • *I was earning more money than Ian, so we agreed that he would be the homemaker when Mary was born.*

ho·me·o·path·y, **hom·oeo·pa·thy** /£,həʊ·mi'ɒp·ə·θi, $,hoʊ·mi'ɑː·pə-/ *n* [U] a way of treating diseases in which sufferers are given very small amounts of natural substances which, in healthy people, would produce the same effects as the diseases produce

ho·me·o·path, **ho·moe·o·path** /£'həʊ·mi·əʊ·pæθ, $'hoʊ·mi·oʊ-/ *n* [C] • A homeopath is a person who treats ill people by homeopathy.

ho·me·o·path·ic, **ho·moe·o·path·ic** /£,həʊ·mi·əʊ'pæθ·ɪk, $,hoʊ·mi·oʊ-/ *adj* [not gradable] • *homeopathic medicine*

home·own·er /£'həʊm,əʊ·nəʳ, $'hoʊm,oʊ·nɚ/ *n* [C] a person who owns the house or apartment that they live in • *Being a homeowner involves a lot more responsibility than being a tenant.* • *Homeowners were badly hit by the fall in house prices last year.*

hom·er /£'həʊ·məʳ, $'hoʊ·mɚ/ *n* [C] a **home run**, see at HOME ORIGIN

home·sick /£'həʊm·sɪk, $'hoʊm-/ *adj* unhappy because of being away from home for a long period • *In her first month at college she was/felt very homesick.*

home·sick·ness /£'həʊm·sɪk·nəs, $'hoʊm/ *n* [U]

home·spun /£'həʊm·spʌn, $'hoʊm-/ *adj* (of beliefs, theories, etc.) simple and ordinary • *homespun philosophy/wisdom*

home·stead /£'həʊm·sted, $'hoʊm-/ *n* [C] *esp. Am and Aus* a house and the surrounding area of land, esp. land obtained for little or no money from the government which is lived on and used for farming

home·town /£,həʊm'taʊn, $,hoʊm-, '--/ *n* [C] *esp. Am* the town or city that a person is from, esp. the one in which they were born and lived while they were young • *He was born in Pittsburgh, but he considers Chicago his hometown since he's lived there most of his life.* • *She worked on her hometown newspaper for several years while she was trying to get a job in television.*

home·wards /£'həʊm·wədz, $'hoʊm·wɚdz/, **home·ward** *adv* [not gradable] towards home • *After three hours cycling we decided to turn homeward(s).*

home·ward /£'həʊm·wəd, $'hoʊm·wɚd/ *adj* [not gradable] • *We stopped twice on the homeward journey.*

home·work /£'həʊm·wɜːk, $'hoʊm·wɜːrk/ *n* [U] studies done by children who have been told to do them at home by their school teacher • *I'm always having to help my son with his history homework.* • *You can't watch TV until you've* **done** *your homework.* • *(fig.) It was obvious that she had* **done** *her homework* (=made a lot of preparations) *and thoroughly researched the backgrounds of her interviewees.* • Compare HOUSEWORK.

home·y /£'həʊ·mi, $'hoʊ-/ *adj* **-ier**, **-iest** *Am and Aus for* HOMELY PLAIN

hom·i·cide /£'hɒm·ɪ·saɪd, $'hɑː·mə-/ *n Am and Aus fml or law* (an act of) murder • *He was convicted of homicide.* [U] • *The number of homicides in the city has risen sharply.* [C] • LP **Crimes and criminals**

hom·i·cid·al /£ˌhɒm·ɪ'saɪ·dᵊl, $ˌhɑː·mə'-/ *adj Am and Aus* • Someone who is homicidal is likely to murder: *He has homicidal tendencies.* ○ *He is a homicidal* **maniac**.

hom·i·ly /£'hɒm·ɪ·li, $'hɑː·mə-/ *n* [C] *disapproving* a piece of spoken or written advice about how someone should behave • *He launched into a homily* **on** *family relationships.*

hom·ing /£'həʊ·mɪŋ, $'hoʊ-/ *adj* [before n; not gradable] relating to the ability of some animals to find their way home, or (of electronic devices) producing a special signal so that it can be found using electronic equipment • *Migrating birds and fish have a strong homing* **instinct** *and return to their place of birth to produce their own young.* • *The signal from the homing* **device** *was getting fainter as the car drove further away.* • A homing **pigeon** is trained to return to its home from any place that it starts its journey.

hom·i·ny /£'hɒm·ə·ni, $'hɑː·mə-/ *n* [U] *Am* MAIZE from which the outer covering had been removed

ho·mo·er·o·tic /£ˌhəʊ·məʊ·ɪ'rɒt·ɪk, $ˌhoʊ·moʊ·ɪ'rɑː·t̬ɪk/ *adj* (of art, literature, etc.) connected to or causing homosexual desire or pleasure • *Mapplethorpe's homoerotic photographs of naked men still cause much controversy.*

ho·mo·gen·eous /£ˌhɒm·ə'dʒiː·ni·əs, £ˌhəʊ·mə-, $ˌhoʊ·moʊ'dʒiː-/, **ho·mo·gen·ous** *adj* consisting of parts which are similar to each other • *The population of the village has remained remarkably homogeneous.* • Compare HETEROGENEOUS.

hom·o·ge·ne·i·ty /£ˌhɒm·ə·dʒə'neɪ·ɪ·ti, $ˌhɑː·mə·dʒə'neɪ·ə·t̬i/ *n* [U] • *cultural/racial homogeneity*

ho·mo·gen·ized, *Br and Aus usually* **-ised** /£hə'mɒdʒ·ɪ·naɪzd, $hə'mɑː·dʒə-/ *adj* [not gradable] *specialized* • Homogenized milk has had the cream mixed into the other parts of the liquid so that all the milk is the same.

ho·mo·graph /£'hɒm·əʊ·grɑːf, $'hɑː·mə·græf/ *n* [C] *specialized* a word which is spelled the same as another word and might be pronounced the same or differently but which has a different meaning • *'Bow' meaning the front of a ship, 'bow' meaning a loop made in a string or ribbon and 'bow' meaning a device used to shoot arrows are all homographs.* • *Homographs in this dictionary are given guide words so you can tell them apart.* • LP **Homophones and homographs**

ho·mo·pho·bi·a /£ˌhəʊ·mə'fəʊ·bi·ə, $ˌhoʊ·mə'foʊ-/ *n* [U] a fear or dislike of homosexuals

ho·mo·pho·bic /£ˌhɒm·ə'fəʊ·bɪk, $ˌhoʊ·mə'foʊ-/ *adj* • *a homophobic attitude*

hom·o·phone /£'hɒm·ə·fəʊn, $'hɑː·mə·foʊn/ *n* [C] *specialized* a word which is pronounced the same as another word but has a different meaning or a different spelling • *The words 'so' and 'sew' are homophones.* • LP **Homophones and homographs**

Ho·mo sap·i·ens /£ˌhəʊ·məʊ'sæp·i·enz, $ˌhoʊ·moʊ-/ *n* [U not after *the*] *specialized* human beings considered together as a type of animal • *He will probably be best remembered for his work on the origin of Homo sapiens.*

ho·mo·sex·u·al /£ˌhəʊ·məʊ'sek·sju·ᵊl, ˌhɒm·əʊ'-, $ˌhoʊ·moʊ'sek·ʃu·ᵊl/ *n, adj* [not gradable] (a person who is) sexually attracted to people of the same sex and not to people of the opposite sex • Compare BISEXUAL; HETEROSEXUAL.

ho·mo·sex·u·al·i·ty /£ˌhəʊ·məʊˌsek·sju'æl·ə·ti, £ˌhɒm·əʊ-, $ˌhoʊ·moʊ·sek·ʃu'æl·ə·t̬i/ *n* [U] • *I've never been ashamed of my homosexuality.*

hon /£ɒn, $ɑːn/ *adj* [before n; not gradable] *abbreviation for* HONORARY, when used as part of a title • *the hon. treasurer* • *Alistair Cooke, hon. KBE*

Hon /£ɒn, $ɑːn/ *adj* [before n; not gradable] *abbreviation for* HONOURABLE, when used as a title • *The report was written by a recently appointed judge, the Hon. Mr. Justice Carlton.* • *The Hon./hon. member for Crawley* (= The member of the British Parliament representing Crawley) *spoke next.* • *The Hon. P. O'Neill, Speaker of the House of Representatives, will present the award.* • *The Hon. Angus Ogilvy was present at the dinner.*

hone *obj* /£həʊn, $hoʊn/ *v* [T] to sharpen (an object), or *(fig.)* to make (something) perfect or completely suitable for its purpose • *The bone had been honed* **to a point**. • *(fig.) Her debating skills were honed in the students' union and the council chamber.* • *(fig.) Life in the desert has been honed* **(down) to** *its bare essentials.*

hon·est /£'ɒn·ɪst, $'ɑː·nɪst/ *adj* truthful or able to be trusted; not likely to steal, cheat or lie; typical of a person of this type • *She was poor but honest.* • *I'd like you to give me an honest answer/your honest opinion.* • *He had an honest face* (= He looked like he could be trusted). • *To be honest* **(with you)**, *I don't think it will be possible.* • *He's* **as honest as the day (is long)** (= completely honest). • *(infml)* **Honest (to God)** means honestly: *I tried to be nice to him, honest (to God)/honest I did* (= I'm being completely honest when I say that I tried). • *The book is an* **honest-to-goodness** (= simple, plain or natural) *account of her early life.* • *(humorous) When are you going to* **make an honest woman of** (= marry) *her?* • *(humorous) Isn't it time you stopped being a student and* **made an honest living** (= got a job and earned money)*?* • An **honest broker** is someone who speaks to both sides involved in an argument or disagreement and tries to help them to agree. • *"An honest politician is one who when he is bought, will stay bought"* (Simon Cameron, 1789-1889) • Ⓔ

hon·est·ly /£'ɒn·ɪst·li, $'ɑː·nɪst-/ *adv, exclamation* • *They have always dealt honestly and fairly with their customers.* • *I'll do it tomorrow, honestly I will* (= I promise I will do it). • *I can't honestly* (= With certainty) *say what time I'll be home.* • Honestly can be used to emphasize disapproval: *Honestly, I'd have thought she'd tell me she was leaving.* ○ *"She didn't even say thank you." "Honestly!"* • Ⓔ

hon·est·y /£'ɒn·ə·sti, $'ɑː·nə-/ *n* [U] • *We appreciated her honesty/the honesty* **of** *her reply.* • *I must tell you* **in all honesty** (= truthfully and hiding nothing) *that there is little chance of the scheme being approved.* • *(saying)* 'Honesty is the best policy' means it is best to be honest. • Ⓔ

hon·ey SWEET SUBSTANCE /'hʌn·i/ *n* [U] the sweet sticky substance made by bees and used as food • **Set** *honey is firm and cloudy, and* **runny** *honey is a thick transparent liquid.* • *heather/clover honey* (= made by bees that mostly visit these flowers) • *They crowded round the display like bees round a honey-***pot** (= a container of honey). • *(Br)* A **honey trap** is a big attraction: *The Tower of London is a honey trap* **for** *tourists.* • *"A land flowing with milk and honey"* (Bible, Exodus 3.8) • *"Stands the church clock at ten to three?/ And is there honey still for tea?"* (from *The Old Vicarage, Grantchester* by Rupert Brooke, 1915) • PIC **Containers**

hon·eyed /'hʌn·id/ *adj* • Honeyed **speech** or a honeyed **voice** is made to sound pleasant intentionally, especially in order to deceive.

hon·ey PERSON /'hʌn·i/ *n* [C] *esp. Am* a pleasant person • *She's/He's a real honey.* • *It's great to see you, honey/John honey/Mary honey.* [as form of address] • LP **Titles and forms of address**

hon·ey·bee /'hʌn·i·biː/ *n* [C] a type of bee which lives with others in a HIVE and makes HONEY

hon·ey·comb /£'hʌn·i·kəʊm, $-koʊm/ *n* a wax structure containing many small holes which is made by bees to store their HONEY, or *(fig.)* something with a similar structure • *The jar contains pieces of whole honeycomb.* [U] • *The stall was selling jars of honey and whole honeycombs.* [C] • *(fig.) The hotel complex was a honeycomb* **of** *rooms and courtyards* (= there were many small rooms and passages). [C] • *a honeycomb pattern/appearance* • PIC **Comb, Wasps and bees**

hon·ey·combed /£'hʌn·i·kəʊmd, $-koʊmd/ *adj* [after v] • *The hill was honeycombed* **with** *passages and chambers.*

hon·ey·dew /£'hʌn·i·djuː, $-duː/ *n* [U] a sticky substance left on leaves by some types of insect • A **honeydew (melon)** is a type of MELON (= a large round fruit) with whitish, greenish or yellow skin and green flesh.

hon·ey·eat·er /£'hʌn·iˌiː·tər, $-t̬ɚ/ *n* [C] an Australian bird whose beak and tongue are specially shaped for taking honey from flowers

hon·ey·moon /'hʌn·i·muːn/ *n* a short holiday taken by a man and a woman immediately after their marriage • *Where are you going* **on** *(your) honeymoon?* [C/U] • *They couldn't afford to have a honeymoon.* [C] • *a honeymoon couple/hotel*

hon·ey·moon /'hʌn·i·muːn/ *v* [I always + adv/prep] • *They are honeymooning* **in the Bahamas**.

hon·ey·moon·ers /£'hʌn·iˌmuː·nəz, $-nɚz/ *pl n* • *The hotel is popular with honeymooners.*

hon·ey·moon (pe·ri·od) /'hʌn·i·muːn/ *n* [usually sing] a short period at the beginning of a new job, government, etc. when relationships are good • *The arguments made it clear that the honeymoon (period) was over.*

hon·ey·suck·le /'hʌn·iˌsʌk·l̩/ *n* a climbing plant with flowers that smell sweet, which grows wild and in gardens

HOMOPHONES AND HOMOGRAPHS

A homophone is a word with the same pronunciation as another word, but with a different spelling and meaning. For example, *son* and *sun* are both pronounced /sʌn/. Usually the meaning of words like this is clear from the sentences they are in: *My son is a doctor.* • *The sun is really hot today.* Homophones are sometimes used humorously, for example in newspaper headlines. For example *The cent of success* might be the headline of a story of a successful perfume and cosmetics business.

The following table lists some common words that are homophones in both British and American pronunciation. They are grouped according to the sound (usually a vowel) that is differently spelled:

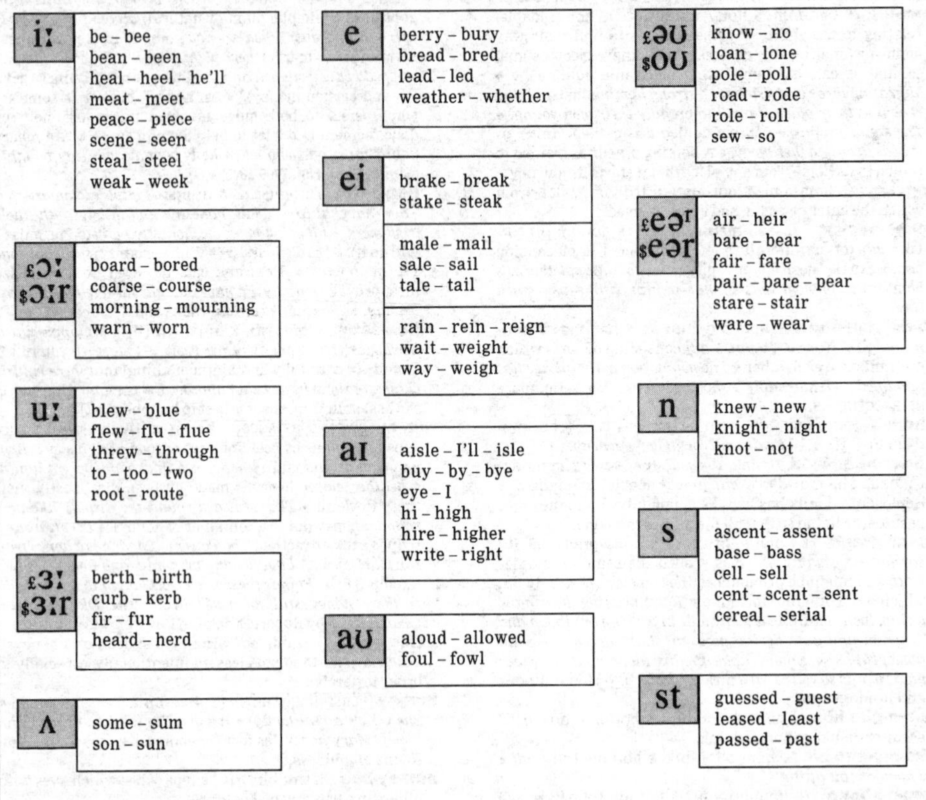

Sound	Homophones
iː	be – bee bean – been heal – heel – he'll meat – meet peace – piece scene – seen steal – steel weak – week
£ɔː $ɔːr	board – bored coarse – course morning – mourning warn – worn
uː	blew – blue flew – flu – flue threw – through to – too – two root – route
£ɜː $ɜːr	berth – birth curb – kerb fir – fur heard – herd
ʌ	some – sum son – sun
e	berry – bury bread – bred lead – led weather – whether
ei	brake – break stake – steak male – mail sale – sail tale – tail rain – rein – reign wait – weight way – weigh
aɪ	aisle – I'll – isle buy – by – bye eye – I hi – high hire – higher write – right
aʊ	aloud – allowed foul – fowl
£əʊ $oʊ	know – no loan – lone pole – poll road – rode role – roll sew – so
£eər $eər	air – heir bare – bear fair – fare pair – pare – pear stare – stair ware – wear
n	knew – new knight – night knot – not
s	ascent – assent base – bass cell – sell cent – scent – sent cereal – serial
st	guessed – guest leased – least passed – past

• *She picked a large bunch of honeysuckle.* [U] • *It's an unusual honeysuckle with long orange flowers.* [C]

honk SOUND /£hɒŋk, $hɑːŋk/ *v, n* (to make) a short loud unpleasant noise, like that of a GOOSE or a car horn • *The noise of traffic and cars honking (their horns) drifted up to our sixth-floor window.* [I/T] • *He gave us a honk on his horn as he drove off.* [C]

honk *(obj)* VOMIT /£hɒŋk, $hɑːŋk/ *v Br slang* to vomit • *He honked* **(up)** *all over the floor.* [I] • *He honked up his tea.* [M]

honk·y /£ˈhɒŋ·ki, $ˈhɑːŋ-/ *n* [C] *Am slang disapproving* a word used by black people to refer to a white person

honk·y–tonk /£ˈhɒŋ·ki·tɒŋk, $ˈhɑːŋ·ki·tɑːŋk/ *adj* [before n] connected with an informal type of jazz piano-playing • *a honky-tonk piano* • *honky-tonk music*

honk·y–tonk /£ˈhɒŋ·ki·tɒŋk, $ˈhɑːŋ·ki·tɑːŋk/ *n* [C] *Am* • A honky-tonk is a NIGHTCLUB (=place where people listen to music and drink alcohol), esp. one that is not very stylish: *She was first introduced to country music at one of those West Texas honky-tonks.*

hon·or·ar·i·um /£ˌɒn·əˈreə·ri·əm, $ˌɑː·nəˈrer·i-/ *n* [C] *pl* **honorariums** or **honoraria** /£ˌɒn·əˈreə·ri·ə, $ˌɑː·nəˈrer·i-/ *fml* a usually small sum of money paid to someone for a service for which no official charge is made • *We usually offer our visiting lecturers an honorarium of £50.*

hon·or·ar·y /£ˈɒn·ər·ə·ri, $ˈɑː·nə·rer·i/ *adj* [not gradable] (esp. of a degree) given as an honour to someone who has not completed a course of study • *She received an honorary doctorate from Oxford University in recognition of her work for the homeless.* • An honorary position in an organization is one for which no payment is made: *Charities often have a well-known person as their honorary treasurer.*

hon·o·rif·ic /£ˌɒn·əˈrɪf·ɪk, $ˌɑː·nəˈrɪf-/ *adj* [before n] *fml* showing or giving honour or respect • *an honorific post/title*

hon·our RESPECT *Br and Aus, Am and Aus* **hon·or** /£ˈɒn·ər, $ˈɑː·nɚ/ *n* [U] a quality that combines respect, pride, honesty and truthfulness • *They are fighting for things like honour, reputation and pride.* • *The dinner was held* **in** *honour* **of** (=arranged specially for) *a colleague who was leaving.* • *I felt* **(in) honour bound** (=I believed it was right) *to tell him that his wife was having an affair with his best friend.* • If you are **on your honour** to do something, you have made a promise to act as you have said you will: *The children were on their honour to go to bed at ten o'clock.* • *(humorous or fml) Would you* **do** *me* **the honour of** (=make me proud and happy by) *accompanying me to the New Year Ball?* • **Your Honour** is the way to address a judge: *May I have a word in private, Your Honour?* • *"All is lost save honour"* (popular version of saying by Francis I of France after his defeat at the battle of Pavia, 1525)

hon·our *obj Br and Aus, Am and Aus* **hon·or** /£ˈɒn·ər, $ˈɑː·nɚ/ *v* [T] • To honour a promise/agreement/contract is to do what you said you would: *They decided not to honour an existing order for aircraft.* • *(fml) We are honoured* (=proud and happy) *that you chose our company.*

hon·our·able *Br and Aus, Am and Aus* **hon·or·able** /£ˈɒn·ər·ə·bl̩, $ˈɑː·nɚ-/ *adj* • *an honourable person* • *an honourable agreement* • *(dated or humorous)* If you say a man has honourable **intentions** you are saying he is going to marry the woman he has a sexual relationship with: *I'm not sure he has honourable intentions.*

HOMOGRAPHS

Homographs are words with different meanings and origins which have the same spelling. The pronunciation is usually the same: *We saw a polar* **bear** *at the zoo* • *I just can't* **bear** *the excitement.* But some homographs differ in their pronunciation, for example 'lead' can be pronounced /led/ as in *Gold is heavier than* **lead** or /liːd/ as in *You* **lead** *and I'll follow you.* Other examples are:

close	£kləʊz, $kloʊz	*v*	**Close** *your eyes and count to ten.*
	£kləʊs, $kloʊs	*adj*	*Please keep* **close** *to the path, it's easy to get lost.*
minute	'mɪn·ɪt	*n*	*Can I speak to you for a* **minute**, *Mr Trent?*
	£maɪ'njuːt, $maɪ'nuːt	*adj*	*We've got a small house with a* **minute** *garden.*
row	£rəʊ, $roʊ	*n*	*I looked quickly along the* **row** *of books.*
	raʊ	*n*	*I had a blazing* **row** *with my girlfriend last night.*
tear	£tɪəʳ, $tɪr	*n*	*She noticed a* **tear** *in the corner of his eye.*
	£teəʳ, $ter	*v*	*To open the packet,* **tear** *along dotted line.*
used to	'juːs·tuː	*v*	*There* **used to** *be a farm here, years ago.*
	'juːzd·tuː	*v*	*Explosives were* **used to** *enter the building.*
wind	wɪnd	*n*	**Wind** *speeds reached 102 mph yesterday.*
	waɪnd	*v*	*You have to* **wind** *the handle to the left.*
wound	waʊnd	*v*	*He* **wound** *the rope round his arm.*
	wuːnd	*n*	*In the fight one young man received a knife* **wound**.

Sometimes the pattern of stress is the main difference between homographs. Notice that nouns are usually stressed on the first syllable and verbs are stressed on the second syllable. Some common examples are:

content	kən'tent	*adj*	*I won't be* **content** *until you give me an answer.*
	£'kɒn·tent, $'kɑːn·tent	*n*	*Meat usually has a high protein and fat* **content**.
contract	£'kɒn·trækt, $'kɑːn·trækt	*n*	*The new export* **contract** *is worth £16 million.*
	kən'trækt	*v*	*Your muscles will* **contract** *if you get cold.*
object	£'ɒb·dʒekt, $'ɑːb·dʒekt	*n*	*This small stone* **object** *is over 5000 years old.*
	əb'dʒekt	*v*	*I strongly* **object** *to these cuts in public spending.*
project	£'prɒdʒ·ekt, $'prɑː·dʒekt	*n*	*The housing* **project** *will create 5000 new homes.*
	prə'dʒekt	*v*	*We* **project** *a 10% increase in sales next year.*

hon·our·ab·ly *Br and Aus, Am and Aus* **hon·o·ra·bly** /£'ɒn·ᵊr·ə·bli, $'ɑː·nɚ-/ *adv* • *They acted honourably and returned the wallet.*

hon·our REWARD *Br and Aus, Am and Aus* **hon·or** /£'ɒn·əʳ, $'ɑː·nɚ/ *n* [C] a reward that publicly expresses admiration or respect • *She received an honour for her services to the community.* • *It's an honour to be asked to speak at this meeting.*

hon·our *obj Br and Aus, Am and Aus* **hon·or** /£'ɒn·əʳ, $'ɑː·nɚ/ *v* [T] • If you honour someone, you give them public praise or a reward: *We are here to honour their heroism.* ○ *He was honoured* **with** *a knighthood.*

hon·our·ab·le *Br and Aus, Am and Aus* **hon·or·ab·le** /£'ɒn·ᵊr·ə·bl̩, $'ɑː·nɚ-/ *adj* • An **honourable mention** in a competition is given to work of high quality which did not receive first, second or third prize.

hon·ours *Br and Aus, Am and Aus* **hon·ors** /£'ɒn·əz, $'ɑː·nɚz/ *pl n* • *He was buried with* **full (military)** *honours* (= marks of public respect). • *(humorous)* If you are asked to **do the honours**, you are being asked to pour drinks or serve food: *John, will you do the honours?* • *(Am)* An honors **course** or **program** is one or more courses for students whose work is of a very high standard. • An **honours degree** (also *fml* **degree with honours**) is a first degree, based esp. on one subject, which is taken in Britain. • An **honors degree** (also *fml* **degree with honors**) is a degree from an American school, college or university which shows that a student has done work of a very high standard. • The **honours list** or the **New Year/Birthday honours** in Britain is the list of people who receive public praise and an reward for things they have done: *She became a baroness/received an MBE in the New Year honours.*

Hon·our·ab·le, *esp. Am* **Hon·or·ab·le** /£'ɒn·ᵊr·ə·bl̩, $'ɑː·nɚ-/ (*abbreviation* **Hon**) *adj* [before n; not gradable] used with the first name and family name of the younger children of particular British ARISTOCRATS (= people of high social rank), members of the Privy Council (= politicians who give advice to the Queen), in particular phrases used by Members of Parliament to each other, and in the titles of some elected officials in the US • *the Honourable Christina Jameson* • *the Right Honourable Tony Blair, Privy Councillor* • *Is the honourable lady/gentleman/member for Basildon* (= Member of Parliament) *prepared to give evidence for that claim?* • *The chair recognizes the Honorable Daniel P. Moynihan of New York.*

hooch /huːtʃ/ *n* [U] *Am slang* strong alcohol, esp. WHISKY

hood CLOTHING /hʊd/ *n* [C] part of a piece of clothing which can be pulled up to cover the top and back of the head, or something like a bag, with or without holes to see through, which is put over the whole head • *The coat has a detachable hood.* • *The prisoners had been tortured and made to wear hoods.* • PIC〉 **Coats and jackets**

hood·ed /'hʊd·ɪd/ *adj* [not gradable] • *a hooded jacket* • *armed and hooded intruders* • Hooded **eyes** are eyes partly covered by the EYELIDS.

hood COVER /hʊd/ *n* [C] a part which covers or shelters a piece of equipment • *a pram hood* • *a cooker hood* • *The hood over the air vent is loose.*

hood CAR /hʊd/ *n* [C] *Am for* BONNET METAL COVER • PIC〉 **Car**

hood PLACE /hʊd/ *n* [C] *Am infml* a NEIGHBOURHOOD (= area of a city with recognizable characteristics that make it different from other areas) • *Me and my friends respected him even though he wasn't from the hood.*

hood·lum /'huːd·ləm/, **hood** *n* [C] *slightly dated* a violent person, esp. one who is member of a group of criminals • *You're a smart kid, Chris, and I don't want to see you end up like those hoodlums out on the streets.*

hood·wink *obj* /'hʊd·wɪŋk/ *v* [T] to deceive or trick • *He hoodwinked us* **into** *agreeing.*

hoof /huːf/ *n* [C] *pl* **hooves** /huːvz/ or **hoofs** the hard part on the bottom of the feet of animals such as horses, sheep and deer • If an animal which is used for meat is **on the hoof**, it is still alive: *He's a bit squeamish about seeing his* *veal on the hoof.* • *(Br)* If you do something **on the hoof**, you do it while you are moving about or doing something else, often without giving it the attention it deserves: *Educational policies made on the hoof by successive secretaries of state are the main reason for low teacher morale.* • Compare PAW.

hoof *obj* /huːf/ *v* [T] *infml* • If you **hoof it**, you walk, esp. unwillingly: *We missed the bus so we had to hoof it.*

hoo–ha /ˈhuː·hɑː/ *n* [U] *infml* (a case of) too much interest esp. in something unimportant • *There was a lot of/a great hoo-ha about the pictures that the paper published, but it was soon forgotten.*

hook DEVICE /hʊk/ *n* [C] a curved device used for catching or holding things, esp. one fixed to a surface for hanging things on • *a coat hook* • *a picture hook* • *a boat hook* • *a fish hook* • If you leave the telephone **off the hook**, you do not put the part of it that you talk with back correctly and it will not ring. • If you are **off the hook**, you have escaped from a difficult situation: *I'll be out of town when the managing director visits us, so that* **lets/gets** *me off the hook.* • *You're off the hook – they've found out who really stole the money.* • *He* **fell for/swallowed** *the story* **hook, line and sinker** (= completely believed it). • **By hook or by crook** means by any method possible: *I'll find out where she lives by hook or by crook.* • A **hook and eye** is a device for fastening clothes consisting of a small bent piece of metal into which a hook fits. • Someone who is **hook-nosed** has a large nose which curves out from the face. • To **get** your **hooks on/into** someone is to hold or influence them strongly: *This product has really got its hooks into the American market.* ○ *Why are you agreeing with her? Has she got her hooks on you too?* • PIC〉 **Beds and bedroom, Eye, Tools**

hook *(obj)* /hʊk/ *v* • *How many salmon did you hook* (= catch) *this afternoon?* [T] • *He hooked the trailer* (= joined it with a hook) *to his car.* [T] • *She hooked the shoe* (= lifted it with a hook) *out of the water.* [T] • *(fig.) Can we hook* **up** (= get connected) *to the electricity at the campsite?* [I always + adv/prep]

hook–up /ˈhʊk·ʌp/ *n* [C] • A hook-up is a connection between two or more things, places or people using electronic equipment: *We hope to bring you a live report from Ouagadougou via our* **satellite** *hook-up.* ○ *(fig.) I hope to arrange a hook-up* (= meeting) *with her associates the next time I'm in town.* ○ *Each campsite has electric, water and sewage hook-ups* (= connections).

hooked /hʊkt/ *adj* • A hooked **nose** is large and curved. • *She's hooked* **on** (= physically dependent) *drugs.* • *(fig.) He's hooked* **on** (= very interested in) *the idea of going on a round-the-world trip.*

hook HIT /hʊk/ *n* [C] a way of hitting in boxing, cricket or golf • *a right/left hook* • *a hook shot*

hook·ah /ˈhʊk·ə, ˈhuː·kə/ *n* [C] a type of pipe which brings smoke through a container of water before it is breathed in by the smoker

hook·er SEX /£ˈhʊk·əʳ, $-ɚ/ *n* [C] *esp. Am and Aus infml for* PROSTITUTE

hook /hʊk/ *v* [I] *Am infml* • To hook is to have sex for money: *She was hooking at night to help pay for her studies.*

hook·er SPORT /£ˈhʊk·əʳ, $-ɚ/ *n* [C] a RUGBY player who pulls the ball out of the SCRUM with his foot

hook·y /ˈhʊk·i/ *n* [U] **play hooky** *Am and Aus infml* to stay away from school without permission

hool·i·gan /ˈhuː·lɪ·gᵊn/ *n* [C] a person who acts in a violent way without thinking and causes damage • *Hooligans had sprayed paint all over the car.*

hool·i·gan·i·sm /ˈhuː·lɪ·gᵊn·ɪ·zᵊm/ *n* [U] • *football/soccer hooliganism*

hoop /huːp/ *n* [C] a ring of wood, metal or plastic, or sometimes a half ring • *The dogs had been trained to jump through hoops.* • *The bride walked under an arch of hoops* (= half rings) *covered with flowers.* • A **hoop (earring)** is a ring-shaped earring: *She wore large gold hoops and a thin gold necklace.* • If you **put** someone **through (the) hoop(s)**, you make them do something difficult. • PIC〉 **Jewellery**

hoop·la GAME *Br and Aus* /ˈhuːp·lə/, *Am* **ring toss** *n* [U] a game in which a ring is thrown so that it falls over an object • *a game of hoopla*

hoop·la EXCITEMENT /ˈhuːp·lɑː, ˈhʊp-/ *n* [U] *Am* exciting noise and activity in celebration of an event • *A lot of hoopla surrounded the arrival of the pop star.* • *In spite of all the media hoopla, the public has shown little interest in the space program this year.*

hoop·la NONSENSE /ˈhuːp·lɑː, ˈhʊp-/ *n* [U] *Am* nonsense • *Charlene is really talking a lot of hoopla about Dave.*

hoo·ray /hʊˈreɪ, hə-/ *exclamation, n* HURRAY • *(Br disapproving)* A **Hooray Henry** is a young man from a high social class who speaks loudly and behaves in a noticeable way in public: *The pub was full of Hooray Henrys.*

hoo·roo /hʊˈruː/ *exclamation Aus infml for* GOODBYE

hoot /huːt/ *v, n* (to make) a short loud high sound • *She gave three short hoots on the car horn.* [C] • *She hooted her horn* **at** *the dog in the road.* [T] • *He gave a hoot* **of** *laughter/derision.* [C] • *He hooted* **with** *laughter.* [I] • The sound an OWL makes is called a hoot: *We could hear owls hooting.* • *(infml)* If you say something or someone is **a** hoot, you mean they are amusing: *The film was an absolute hoot.* ○ *He's a real hoot.* • *(infml)* If you **don't care/give a hoot/two hoots** about something, you do not think it is important: *She doesn't give two hoots* **about** *being in debt.*

hoot·er /£ˈhuː·təʳ, $-t̬ɚ/ *n* [C] • A hooter is an electrical device which makes a loud noise, often to mark the start or end of work at a factory. • *(Br and Aus dated)* If you say someone has a big hooter you mean they have a big nose. • *(Am slang) He says she's a good-looking woman with enormous hooters* (= breasts).

hoo·ver /£ˈhuː·vəʳ, $-vɚ/ *n, v Br and Aus trademark* (to use) a **vacuum cleaner** • *"We've just bought a new hoover." "Really? What make is it?"* [C] • *He was busy hoovering (the bedroom carpet) when I arrived home from work.* [I/T] • In British English, hoover is used to mean '(to clean with) any **vacuum cleaner**'; in American English it is only used as a trademark for machines made by the Hoover company. • See **vacuum cleaner** at VACUUM.

hooves /huːvz/ *pl of* HOOF

hop *(obj)* /£hɒp, $hɑːp/ *v* **-pp-** to make small jumps on one or two feet, or to move along in this way • *The rabbit/bird hopped up to the fence.* [I] • *Her left foot hurt so much she had to hop over to the car.* [I] • *(infml) Hop into/out of* (= Get quickly into/out of) *the car.* [I] • *(infml) He hopped off/on* (= got quickly off/on) *the bus at the traffic lights.* [I] • *(Am infml) They hopped* (= got onto) *a plane for Chicago.* [T] • *(Br infml)* **Hop it** (= Go away), *I'm too busy to play with you just now.* • *(Br infml) When the police started asking questions, he decided to* **hop it** (= go away) **to** *Scotland.* • *(infml) When I saw her she was* **hopping (mad)** (= very angry).

hop /£hɒp, $hɑːp/ *n* [C] • *With his feet tied together he could only move in little hops.* • *(Br infml)* If you **catch** someone **on the hop**, they are not prepared for you: *I'm afraid you've caught me on the hop – I wasn't expecting you home till next week.* • *(infml)* A **short hop** is a short journey, esp. in an aircraft: *London to Edinburgh is just a short hop.*

hope /£həʊp, $hoʊp/ *n* a desire for the future to be as good as you want it to be • *My best/last/only hope is to see if the bank will lend me the money.* [C] • *I have great hopes/no hope* **of** *getting financial support for the project.* [C] • *His reply* **dashed** (= destroyed) *our hopes.* [C] • *They have* **pinned (all)** *their hopes* **on** (= They are depending for success on) *their new player.* [C] • *She's very ill, but there's still hope/we* **live in** *hope* (= we think she might be cured). [U] • *The situation is now* **beyond/past** *hope* (= unlikely to produce the desired result). [U] • *We never* **gave up** *hope* (= stopped hoping) *that she would be found alive.* [U] • *The letter offered us* **a glimmer/ray of** (= a little) *hope.* [U] • *Is there any hope* **that** *they will be home in time?* [U + *that* clause] • *I didn't phone till four o'clock* **in the hope that** *you'd be finished.* [U + *that* clause] • ***I don't hold out much*** *hope* **of** *getting* (= I don't expect to be able to get) *a ticket.* [U] • *(infml)* If you do not have **a hope in hell**, you have no possibility at all of doing something: *The other team scored three goals in the first two minutes, so we didn't have a hope in hell of winning!* • **Hope chest** is *Am for* **bottom drawer**. See at BOTTOM LOWEST PART. • *"Hope springs eternal in the human breast"* (Alexander Pope in the poem *Essay on Man*, 1732)

hope /£həʊp, $hoʊp/ *v* • If you hope **for** something, you want something to happen and usually have some reason to expect that it will happen: *I'm hoping* **for** *an interview next week.* ○ *The* **hoped-for** *interview didn't happen.* • If you hope **for the best**, you want the best results even if it seems unlikely: *I've repaired it as well as I can – we'll just have to hope for the best.* [I] • *She's hoping* **(that)** *she won't be away too long.* [+ *(that)* clause] • *I hope* **(that)** *she'll win.* [+ *(that)* clause] • *She was* **hoping against hope** (= hoping although she knew it was unlikely) **(that)** *she would arrive in time.* •

We have to hope **and pray (that)** *the operation will go well.* [+ (*that*) clause] • *They hope* **to** *visit us next year.* [+ *to* infinitive] • *It's good news, I hope.* [+ (*that*) clause] • *"Will you be at the meeting tomorrow?" "I hope* **not/so***".* [+ *not/so*] • *"Hope I die before I get old"* (from the song *My Generation* by The Who, 1965) • Compare WISH.

hope·ful /£ˈhəʊp·fᵊl, $ˈhoʊp-/ *adj* • If you are hopeful you have hope: *He was hopeful* **about** *the outcome of the meeting.* ○ *They were hopeful* **of** *a successful agreement.* ○ *I'm hopeful* **(that)** *we can reach a compromise.* [+ (*that*) clause] • If something is hopeful it gives hope: *The green shoots were hopeful signs of spring.*

hope·ful /£ˈhəʊp·fᵊl, $ˈhoʊp-/ *n* [C usually pl] • *Over a thousand* **young** *hopefuls* (=people hoping to achieve something) *went to the Theatre Royal today to audition for a part in Peter Cook's new musical.*

hope·ful·ly /£ˈhəʊp·fᵊl·i, $ˈhoʊp-/ *adv* • *Hopefully* (=I hope that) *we'll be in Norwich by early evening.* • *"Do you have a cigarette?" he asked hopefully* (=wishing the answer to be 'yes').

hope·less /£ˈhəʊ·pləs, $ˈhoʊ-/ *adj* • *a hopeless situation/case/cry/effort* (=without hope of a good result) • *(infml) I'm hopeless* (=very bad) **at** *cooking.*

hope·less·ly /£ˈhəʊ·plə·sli, $ˈhoʊ-/ *adv* • *He's hopelessly* (=very much) *in love with Pat.*

hope·less·ness /£ˈhəʊ·plə·snəs, $ˈhoʊ-/ *n* [U] • *I find the hopelessness of the situation very depressing.*

hop·per /£ˈhɒp·əʳ, $ˈhɑː·pɚ/ *n* [C] *specialized* a large tube, wide at one end, through which large amounts of small separate items, for example seeds, can be moved from one container to another

hops /£hɒps, $hɑːps/ *pl n* the dried fruits of a climbing plant which are used to give a bitter flavour to beer

hop /£hɒp, $hɑːp/ *adj* [before n] • *a hop plant* • *the hop fields of Kent*

hop·py /£ˈhɒp·i, $ˈhɑː·pi/ *adj* **-ier, -iest** • *a hoppy aroma/flavour*

hop·scotch /£ˈhɒp·skɒtʃ, $ˈhɑːp·skɑːtʃ/ *n* [U] a game played by children, who throw a stone onto a set of joined squares drawn on the ground and jump on one leg and then on two legs into each square in turn to get the stone • PIC **Playground**

horde /£hɔːd, $hɔːrd/ *n* [C] a large noisy and excited crowd • *A horde* **of** *students on bikes made crossing the road difficult.* • *There were* **hordes of** (=very many) *fans waiting outside the theatre.* • *When they heard the concert was free, they came* **in (their) hordes** (=a lot of them came).

hor·i·zon /həˈraɪ·zᵊn/ *n* [U] **the horizon** the furthest thing which you can see and the place at which the sky and the Earth seem to join • *The moon rose slowly above the horizon.* • *They scanned the horizon with their binoculars.* • *We could see a row of camels silhouetted on the horizon.* • Something **on the horizon** is about to happen: *The new threat on the horizon is unemployment.*

hor·i·zons /həˈraɪ·zᵊnz/ *pl n* • If you **broaden/expand/widen** your **horizons** you increase your knowledge and experience: *The visit to the Far East certainly broadened our horizons.*

hor·i·zon·tal /£ˌhɒr·ɪˈzɒn·tᵊl, $ˌhɔːr·ɪˈzɑːn·t̬ᵊl/ *adj* [not gradable] flat or level; parallel to the ground or to the bottom or top edge of something • *Draw a horizontal line across the bottom of the page.* • *Horizontal lines are at right angles to vertical ones.* • *Keep the patient horizontal with the feet slightly raised.* • Compare VERTICAL.

hor·i·zon·tal /£ˌhɒr·ɪˈzɒn·tᵊl, $ˌhɔːr·ɪˈzɑːn·t̬ᵊl/ *n* [U] *specialized* • **The horizontal** is a horizontal line, surface or position: *Rotate it slowly from the horizontal into a vertical position.*

hor·i·zon·tal·ly /£ˌhɒr·ɪˈzɒn·tᵊl·i, $ˌhɔːr·ɪˈzɑːn·t̬ᵊl-/ *adv* [not gradable]

hor·mone /£ˈhɔː·məʊn, $ˈhɔːr·moʊn/ *n* [C] any of various chemicals made by living cells which influence the development, growth, sex, etc. of an animal and are carried around the body in the blood • *male and female hormones* • *growth hormones* • **Hormone replacement therapy** (*abbreviation* **HRT**) is the giving of additional amounts of female hormones to women who have low amounts because they are getting older.

hor·mo·nal /£hɔːˈməʊ·nəl, $hɔːrˈmoʊ-/ *adj* [not gradable] • *He's suffering from a hormonal* **imbalance** *which is caused by the drugs he's taking.*

horn ANIMAL /£hɔːn, $hɔːrn/ *n* a hard, pointed, often curved part that grows from the top of the head of some animals • *Cattle, sheep and goats have a pair of horns, but the Indian rhinoceros only has one.* [C] • *Horn* (=the substance animals' horns consist of) *is sometimes used to make decorative objects such as knife handles or jewellery.* [U] • If you **draw/pull in** your **horns**, you spend less or do less than you did in the past: *He'll have to draw in his horns now he's lost his job.* • If you are **on the horns of a dilemma**, you can not decide which of two unpleasant things to do. • **Horn-rimmed** glasses have frames that are coloured with a mixture of dark and light brown.

horned /£hɔːnd, $hɔːrnd/ *adj* [not gradable] • A horned animal has horns: *horned cattle* ○ *a rare breed of four-horned sheep*

horn·y /£ˈhɔː·ni, $ˈhɔːr-/ *adj* **-ier, -iest** • *Birds have horny* (=hard) *beaks.* • See also HORNY.

horn MUSIC /£hɔːn, $hɔːrn/ *n* [C] a musical instrument, usually made of metal, which is narrow at the end you blow down to make a sound, and gets wider towards the other end • *She plays the horn.* • *He's a horn-player.* • PIC **Musical instruments**

horn VEHICLE /£hɔːn, $hɔːrn/ *n* [C] a device on a vehicle that is used to make a loud noise as a warning or signal to other people • *The driver* **blew/sounded/***(infml)* **honked** *her horn.* • See also FOGHORN.

horn in *v adv* [I] *infml disapproving* to become involved in something when you have not been invited to • *Whenever we have a private conversation, she tries to horn in.* • *Another company's trying to horn in* **on** *our export markets, which will be bad for our profits.*

hor·net /£ˈhɔː·nɪt, $ˈhɔːr-/ *n* [C] a large WASP (=type of flying insect) which can give you a bad sting • A **hornet's nest** is a very difficult or unpleasant situation, esp. in which lots of people get very angry and complain: *His remarks about the low quality of women tennis players* **stirred up** *a* **(real)** *hornet's nest.* • PIC **Wasps and bees**

horn·y /£ˈhɔː·ni, $ˈhɔːr-/ *adj* **-ier, -iest** *infml* (always) sexually excited; RANDY • *He's a horny little so-and-so – can't keep his hands off the women.* • *She'd had a couple of drinks and was* **feeling** *fairly horny.* • See also **horny** at HORN ANIMAL.

hor·ni·ness /£ˈhɔː·nɪ·nəs, $ˈhɔːr-/ *n* [U] *infml*

ho·ro·scope /£ˈhɒr·ə·skəʊp, $ˈhɔːr·ə·skoʊp/ *n* [C] a description of what is going to happen to you, based on the position of the stars and planets at the time of your birth • *A lot of people* **read** *their horoscope every day in newspapers or magazines.* • *What does your horoscope say?*

hor·ren·dous /həˈren·dəs/ *adj* shocking and frighteningly bad, or extremely unpleasant • *a horrendous accident/tragedy/crime* • *horrendous suffering/damage* • *Conditions in the refugee camps were horrendous.* • *The firm made horrendous* (=very big) **losses** *last year.*

hor·ren·dous·ly /həˈren·də·sli/ *adv* • *These shoes were horrendously* (=extremely) **expensive***.*

hor·ren·dous·ness /həˈren·də·snəs/ *n* [U]

hor·ri·ble /£ˈhɒr·ɪ·bl̩, $ˈhɔːr-/ *adj* extremely and frighteningly bad, or very unpleasant or unkind • *a horrible accident/injury* • *Isn't the weather horrible today?* • *Mummy, Danny's being horrible* **to** *me!* • *I've got a horrible* **suspicion/feeling** *he's forgotten to take his medicine* (=I think he has forgotten, which would be bad).

hor·ri·bly /£ˈhɒr·ɪ·bli, $ˈhɔːr-/ *adv* • *His face was horribly scarred after the car crash.* • *Their plans went horribly* (=seriously) *wrong when the bomb went off too early.*

hor·rid /£ˈhɒr·ɪd, $ˈhɔːr-/ *adj infml* unpleasant or unkind; NASTY • *I was a horrid little child!* • *The medicine tasted horrid.*

hor·rid·ly /£ˈhɒr·ɪd·li, $ˈhɔːr-/ *adv infml*

hor·rid·ness /£ˈhɒr·ɪd·nəs, $ˈhɔːr-/ *n* [U] *infml*

hor·ri·fic /həˈrɪf·ɪk/ *adj* causing extreme shock and fear • *a horrific accident/murder/attack*

hor·ri·fi·cally /həˈrɪf·ɪ·kli/ *adv* • *The fight ended horrifically, with the killing of six people.*

hor·ri·fy *obj* /£ˈhɒr·ɪ·faɪ, $ˈhɔːr-/ *v* [T] to shock (someone) very greatly • *This news will horrify my parents.*

hor·ri·fied /£ˈhɒr·ɪ·faɪd, $ˈhɔːr-/ *adj* • *He looked horrified/gave me a horrified look and said it couldn't possibly be true.* • *We were horrified* **at/by** *the size of the bill.* • *I was horrified* **to** *hear of his death.* [+ *to* infinitive] • *I was horrified* **that** *they hadn't included you.* [+ *that* clause]

hor·ri·fy·ing /£ˈhɒr·ɪ·faɪ·ɪŋ, $ˈhɔːr-/ *adj* • *horrifying injuries/conditions/news*

hor·ri·fy·ing·ly /£ˈhɒr·ɪ·faɪ·ɪŋ·li, $ˈhɔːr-/ *adv* • *The prediction of 4 million unemployed now looks horrifyingly realistic.*

hor·ror /£'hɒr·əʳ, $'hɔːr·ɚ/ *n* an extremely strong feeling of fear and shock • *The crowd cried out* **in** *horror as the car burst into flames.* [U] • *She was filled with horror and panic when she saw the empty pill bottle.* [U] • *(Br infml)* If you call a child a horror, you mean that he or she behaves very badly: *Peter was a* **(real)** *little horror when he was four.* [C] • If you **have a horror of** something, you hate it very much, or you are very frightened of it: *Joanne has a horror of spiders.* • **Horror of horrors** (=How shocking), *our old church is to be turned into a shop!* • A **horror film** (*Am also* **horror movie**) is a film in which very frightening and esp. unnatural things happen, for example dead people come to life and people are murdered. • A **horror story** is a story in which very frightening and unnatural things happen, or a report of real events in which things go wrong: *Frequent flyers usually can tell a lot of airline horror stories about delayed and cancelled flights.* • *They watched,* **horror-struck/horror-stricken** (=full of horror) *as the lion walked towards the sleeping baby.*

hor·rors /£'hɒr·əz, $'hɔːr·ɚz/ *pl n* • *The population now faces the horrors of starvation/war/foreign occupation* (= all the unpleasant things connected with this event or situation). • *Nuclear war is one of the horrors that face the modern world.* • *(infml) It gives me/I get* **the horrors** (=I feel very worried and nervous) *every time I think of my oral exam!* • *"Little Shop of Horrors"* (title of film and musical, 1960)

hors d'oeuv·re /£ˌɔː'dɜːv, $ˌɔːr'dɜːrv/ *n* [C] *pl* **hors d'oeuvre** or **hors d'oeuvres** *Br and Aus* a small usually savoury dish eaten at the start of a meal, or *(Am)* small pieces of food eaten at a party

horse ANIMAL /£hɔːs, $hɔːrs/ *n* [C] a large animal with four legs which people ride on or use for carrying things or pulling vehicles • *to ride a horse* • *a horse and cart* • *a coach and horses* • *a horse-drawn vehicle* • *A female horse is a mare, a male horse is a stallion and a young horse is a foal.* • *Horses have hooves and a long flowing mane and tail.* • *He spends all his money on* **the horses** (=horse races where you try to win money by correctly guessing which horse will win). • If you hear something **(straight) from the horse's mouth**, you hear it from the person who has direct personal knowledge of the matter. • If you **change/swap horses in midstream**, you start to support something or someone different, or use a different method to achieve an aim, when you have already started doing something: *As you've started your English course, you should stick to it – it isn't wise to change horses in midstream.* • *(Am slang) You may think you're being funny, but everyone else thinks you're being a real* **horse's ass** (= stupid and annoying person). • *(esp. Am) Our pitching was fabulous but our hitting was* **horse manure** (=used to avoid saying HORSESHIT). • *(infml) Has he got enough* **horse sense** (=practical knowledge about the wisest thing to do) *to inform the police?* • *(Br and Aus saying)* 'It's (a case/question of) horses for courses' means that what is suitable for one person is not suitable for another. • *(saying)* 'You can lead/take a horse to water but you can't make him drink' means you can make it easy for someone to do something, but you cannot force them to do it. • *"A horse! a horse! my kingdom for a horse"* (Shakespeare, Richard III 5.4)

hors·ey, hors·y /£'hɔː·si, $'hɔːr-/ *adj* **horsier, horsiest** *infml* • *She's the horsey type* (=the type of person, esp. from the British upper classes, who is very interested in horses). • *(disapproving)* If you describe a woman's face as horsey, you mean she is quite ugly and looks like a horse.

horse WOODEN STRUCTURE /£hɔːs, $hɔːrs/, **vault·ing horse** *n* [C] a wooden structure which you jump over for exercise • PIC› **Sports**

horse DRUG /£hɔːs, $hɔːrs/ *n* [U] *slang* HEROIN

horse a·round/a·bout *v adv* [I] *infml* to behave in a silly and noisy way • *He horsed around a lot when he was at secondary school.*

horse·back /£'hɔːs·bæk, $'hɔːrs-/ *adj* [before n; not gradable] (riding) on a horse • *horseback riding* • *a horseback rider*

horse·back /£'hɔːs·bæk, $'hɔːrs-/ *n* • *Police* **on horseback** (=riding horses) *pushed the angry crowd back.*

horse·box *Br* /£'hɔːs·bɒks, $'hɔːrs·bɑːks/, *Am* **horse·car** /£'hɔːs·kɑːʳ, $'hɔːrs·kɑːr/, **horse trail·er**, *Aus* **horse float** *n* [C] a closed vehicle usually pulled by a car, used for transporting horses

horse chest·nut /£ˌhɔːs'tʃest·nʌt, $ˌhɔːrs-/, **chest·nut** *n* [C] (the shiny brown nut from) a large tree with pink or white flowers • See also CONKER. • PIC› **Nut, Tree**

horse·fly /£'hɔːs·flaɪ, $'hɔːrs-/ *n* [C] any of various large flying insects that bite horses, cattle and sometimes people

horse·hair /£'hɔːs·heəʳ, $'hɔːrs·her/ *n* [U] hairs from a horse's tail and MANE, used esp. in the past as a soft filling for furniture • *a horsehair sofa*

horse·man (*pl* **-men**), **horse·wo·man** (*pl* **-women**) /£'hɔːs·mən, $'hɔːrs-, -ˌwʊm·ən/ *n* [C] a person who rides a horse, esp. someone who rides well

horse·man·ship /£'hɔːs·mən·ʃɪp, $'hɔːrs-/ *n* [U] skill at riding horses

horse·play /£'hɔːs·pleɪ, $'hɔːrs-/ *n* [U] *slightly dated* rough noisy behaviour, esp. when people push each other as a joke

horse·pow·er /£'hɔːs·paʊəʳ, $'hɔːrs·paʊr/ (*abbreviation* **HP, hp**) *n pl* **horsepower** a unit for measuring the power of an engine • *a 10-horsepower engine* [C] • *(infml) This car could do with a bit more horsepower for getting up hills.* [U]

horse·rad·ish /£'hɔːsˌræd·ɪʃ, $'hɔːrs-/ *n* [U] a plant with large green leaves and a long white root with a strong sharp taste • *roast beef and horseradish sauce*

horse·shit /£'hɔːs·ʃɪt, $'hɔːrs-/ *n* [U] *esp. Am taboo slang* nonsense; BULLSHIT • *He described the film as middle-class bourgeois horseshit.* • *It was a horseshit excuse for not attending the wedding.*

horse·shoe /£'hɔːs·ʃuː, $'hɔːrs-/ *n* [C] a U-shaped metal object which is fixed to the bottom of a horse's HOOF (=foot) • *For many people the horseshoe is a symbol of good luck.*

horse·shoes /£'hɔːs·ʃuːz, $'hɔːrs-/ *n* [U] *Am* • Horseshoes is a game in which horseshoes are thrown at a wooden or metal rod in the ground.

horse·trad·ing /£'hɔːsˌtreɪ·dɪŋ, $'hɔːrs-/ *n* [U] *disapproving* unofficial discussion intended to reach an agreement • *There's been a lot of* **political** *horsetrading while the parties try to form a government.*

horse·trade /£'hɔːs·treɪd, $'hɔːrs-/ *v* [I] *disapproving* • *The Liberal Democrats are horsetrading with Labour* **over** *the school meals issue.*

horse·whip *obj* /£'hɔːs·wɪp, $'hɔːrs-/ *v* [T] **-pp-** to hit (someone) hard, esp. with a whip intended for horses, usually as a punishment for doing something immoral • *If you attempt to see my daughter again, sir, I shall horsewhip you.*

hor·ti·cul·ture /£'hɔː·tɪ·kʌl·tʃəʳ, $'hɔːr·t̬ə·kʌl·tʃɚ/ *n* [U] the study or activity of cultivating gardens

hor·ti·cul·tur·al /£ˌhɔː·tɪ'kʌl·tʃəʳr·əl, $ˌhɔːr·t̬ə'kʌl·tʃɚ·əl/ *adj* • *a horticultural show*

hor·ti·cul·tur·al·ist /£ˌhɔː·tɪ'kʌl·tʃəʳr·əl·ɪst, $ˌhɔːr·t̬ə'kʌl·tʃɚ-/, **hor·ti·cul·tur·ist** /£ˌhɔː·tɪ'kʌl·tʃəʳr·ɪst, $ˌhɔːr·t̬ə'kʌl·tʃɚ-/ *n* [C]

ho·san·na /£həʊ'zæn·ə, $hoʊ-/ *exclamation* a shout of praise to God

hose PIPE /£həʊz, $hoʊz/, *Br also* **hose·pipe** /£'həʊz·paɪp, $'hoʊz-/ *n* [C] a long esp. plastic pipe which can be bent, used to direct water onto fires, gardens etc. • *The severe drought has led to a hosepipe* **ban** *in eastern England.* • PIC› **Garden**

hose *obj* /£həʊz, $hoʊz/ *v* [T] • *After he'd fallen into the mud they had to hose him* **down** (=clean him with water from a hose).

hose CLOTHING /£həʊz, $hoʊz/, **ho·si·ery** /£'həʊ·ʒəʳr·i, $'hoʊ-/ *n* [U] *specialized* a general word for socks, TIGHTS or STOCKINGS • *The hosiery department is on the first floor of the shop.* • See also PANTYHOSE. • LP› **Shopping goods**

hose down /£həʊz, $hoʊz/ *v adv* [I] *Br slang* to rain heavily • **It** *was really hosing down.*

hos·pice /£'hɒs·pɪs, $'hɑː·spɪs/ *n* [C] a hospital for people who are dying, esp. from CANCER • *The report recommends government support to develop several housing options for people with AIDS, such as hospice care and rental subsidies.*

hos·pit·ab·le /£hɒs'pɪt·ə·bl̩, $hɑː'spɪt̬-/ *adj* friendly and welcoming to guests and visitors • *The villagers were very hospitable* **to/towards** *anyone who passed through.* • An hospitable **climate** or piece of land provides good conditions for living or growing: *It's difficult to think of a less hospitable environment than the surface of the Moon.*

hos·pit·ab·ly /£hɒs'pɪt·ə·bli, $hɑː'spɪt̬-/ *adv*

hos·pi·tal·i·ty /£ˌhɒs·pɪ'tæl·ə·ti, $ˌhɑː·spɪ'tæl·ə·t̬i/ *n* [U] • *The local people showed me great hospitality* (= welcomed me kindly, esp. into their homes). • Hospitality is also the food, drink and other comforts that an organization sometimes provides in order to keep its guests happy: *After the programme the director gave us drinks in the hospitality* **suite** (=set of rooms). ○ *The company's guests at Ascot are entertained in the* **corporate** *hospitality* **tent**. ○ *The hotel provides a hospitality* **coach** *to bring its guests from the airport.*

hos·pi·tal /£ˈhɒs·pɪ·tᵊl, $ˈhɑː·spɪ·t̬ᵊl/ *n* a place where people who are ill or injured are treated and taken care of by doctors and nurses • *a general/children's/maternity hospital* [C] • *hospital patients/staff* • *(Br and Aus) I've got to go* **(in)to** *hospital (Am* **to the** *hospital) for three weeks to have an operation.* [U] • *(Br and Aus) She spent a week* **in** *hospital (Am* **in the** *hospital) last year.* [U] • *He went to the hospital to see his mother.* [C]

hos·pi·tal·ize *obj, Br and Aus usually* **-ise** /£ˈhɒs·pɪ·tᵊl·aɪz, $ˈhɑː·spɪ·t̬ᵊl-/ *v* [T usually passive] • If someone is hospitalized, they are taken to stay in a hospital because they are ill.

hos·pi·tal·iz·a·tion, *Br and Aus usually* **-i·sa·tion** /£ˌhɒs·pɪ·tᵊl·aɪˈzeɪ·ʃᵊn, $ˌhɑː·spɪ·t̬ᵊl-/ *n* [U] • *The doctors advised immediate hospitalization.*

host [ENTERTAIN], *female also* **hos·tess** /£həʊst, $hoʊst/ *n* [C] someone who has guests • *Nick's the perfect host – he always looks after his guests very well.* • *We thanked our hosts for the lovely evening.* • *The city is twinned with Heidelberg and host* **families** *are needed for 40 visitors this summer.*

host [TELEVISION], *female also* **hos·tess** /£həʊst, $hoʊst/ *n* [C] a person who introduces guests and performers, esp. on television or radio; COMPERE • *Our host for tonight's show is Terry Wogan.*

host *obj* /£həʊst, $hoʊst/ *v* [T] • *to host a show/programme*

host [EVENT] /£həʊst, $hoʊst/ *n* [C] a place or organization that provides the space and other necessary things for a special event • *Japan is* **playing** *host* **to** *the next international conference. It's the host* **nation**.

host *obj* /£həʊst, $hoʊst/ *v* [T] • *Which country is hosting the next Olympic games?*

host [ANIMAL] /£həʊst, $hoʊst/ *n* [C] *specialized* a plant or animal that another plant or animal lives on as a PARASITE

host [LARGE NUMBER] /£həʊst, $hoʊst/ *n* [C usually sing] a large number • *There's a* **whole** *host* **of** *reasons why he didn't get the job.*

host [CHURCH] /£həʊst, $hoʊst/ *n* [U] **the host** *specialized* the holy bread eaten at **holy communion** (=a Christian religious ceremony)

hos·tage /£ˈhɒs·tɪdʒ, $ˈhɑː·stɪdʒ/ *n* [C] someone who is taken as a prisoner by an enemy in order to force the other people involved to do what the enemy wants • *I was* **taken/held** *(as a) hostage by the gunmen.* • *The terrorists have* **seized** *20 hostages and are threatening to kill one a day unless their demands are met.* • *The President* **gave/created** *a* **hostage to fortune** (=took a risk and said or did something that could cause trouble later) *when he said that taxes would never go up.* • *"He that hath wife and children, hath given hostages to fortune"* (Francis Bacon in his *Essays*, 1578) • LP› **Crimes and criminals**

hos·tel /£ˈhɒs·tᵊl, $ˈhɑː·stᵊl/ *n* [C] a large house where people can stay free or cheaply • *While I'm studying in London, I'm staying at a student hostel.* • *(Br)* A hostel (*Am* **shelter**) can be a building owned by a COUNCIL or other organization where people with no home can live for a short time: *a hostel for the homeless* ○ *a Salvation Army hostel* • Compare HOTEL.

hos·tel·ry /£ˈhɒs·tᵊl·ri, $ˈhɑː·stᵊl-/ *n* [C] *old use or humorous* a bar or PUB (=place for drinking alcohol)

hos·tess /£ˈhəʊ·stes, $ˈhoʊ·stɪs/ *n* [C] a woman who has guests • A hostess is also a woman who entertains customers, esp. men, at a NIGHTCLUB. Hostess can be used to avoid saying PROSTITUTE (=a woman who has sex for money).

hos·tile [UNFRIENDLY] /£ˈhɒs·taɪl, $ˈhɑː·stᵊl/ *adj* showing strong dislike; unfriendly • *a hostile attitude/glance/look/mood* • *a hostile crowd* • *The President had a hostile* **reception** *in Ohio this morning.* • *I'm not hostile* **to** (=I'm not against) *the idea of moving house.*

hos·til·i·ty /£hɒsˈtɪl·ɪ·ti, $hɑːˈstɪl·ə·t̬i/ *n* [U] • *They showed* **open** *hostility* **to/towards** *their new neighbours.*

hos·tile [DIFFICULT] /£ˈhɒs·taɪl, $ˈhɑː·stᵊl/ *adj* difficult or not suitable for living or growing • *hostile weather conditions* • *a hostile climate/environment*

hos·tile [ENEMY] /£ˈhɒs·taɪl, $ˈhɑː·stᵊl/ *adj* [before n; not gradable] connected with the enemy in a war • *hostile aircraft/ships/forces*

hos·til·i·ties /£hɒsˈtɪl·ɪ·tiz, $hɑːˈstɪl·ə·t̬iz/ *pl n fml* • *Hostilities* (=Fighting) **began/broke out/ended/ceased** *just after midnight.* • *Hostilities were* **suspended** (=fighting stopped temporarily) *during the talks.*

hot [VERY WARM] /£hɒt, $hɑːt/ *adj* **hotter, hottest** having a high temperature • *a hot sunny day* • *hot sun/weather* • *a hot meal* • *Something that is hot has a higher temperature than something that is warm.* • *It's too hot in here, can we turn down the heating?* • *After all that running she* **was/felt** *hot.* • *Bake the cake in a hot oven, about 220°C, for 30 minutes.* • *The food was* **piping** *hot* (=very hot). • *(infml) Dad gets* **(all) hot and bothered** (=confused and worried or angry) *whenever anyone parks in his parking space.* • If you are **in the hot seat**, you are the person who has to answer difficult questions or make difficult decisions. • *She sent me her article,* **hot off the press** (=immediately after it was printed). • If you are **hot under the collar**, you are confused or angry, or you are embarrassed by something: *He got* **(all)** *hot under the collar when they accused him of taking it without paying.* • If you are **in hot water** or you **get into hot water**, you are in or get into a difficult situation and are in danger of being punished: *Making that complaint could get you into hot water.* • If something **goes/sells like hot cakes**, people buy it quickly and eagerly: *The new video game's selling like hot cakes.* • *His promises turned out to be* **(so much/just) hot air** (=were not sincere). • A **hot-air balloon** is an aircraft consisting of a very large bag filled with heated air or other gas, with a BASKET (=container) hanging under it in which people can ride. PIC› **Sports** • A **hot-air gun** is an electrical tool which blows out hot air and is used to soften paint on surfaces so that it can be removed more easily. • If someone is **hot-blooded**, they show strong feelings very easily and quickly, esp. anger or love. • *(Am slang)* If something is described as **hot-button**, it causes strong feelings: *Abortion is a hot-button* **issue** *at the moment.* • A **hot-cross bun** is a round sweet bread-like cake with a cross marked on the top, which is eaten in Christian countries at EASTER. LP› **Holidays** PIC› **Bread and cakes** • A **hot dog** is a cooked SAUSAGE eaten in a long soft ROLL (=small loaf), often with fried onions: *a hot-dog stand/stall* • *(esp. Am and Aus infml)* A **hot dog**, or someone who **hot-dogs**, is also a person who makes fast skilful movements in particular sports, esp. SKIING, in order to make people notice them. • *(Am)* A **hot dog** is also a DACHSHUND (=small dog with a long body). • *(Am infml)* You say **"Hot dog!"** to show that you think something is very good. • If a woman has a **hot flush** (*Am usually* **hot flash**), she suddenly feels hot and uncomfortable, because of the effects of the MENOPAUSE (=time when she stops being able to have children). • *(Am)* A **hot foot** is when, as a joke, you put a MATCH (=a short stick which burns at one end) between the upper and lower part of someone's shoe and light it, then wait until it burns their foot: *They* **gave** *him a hot foot.* • *(Br infml esp. disapproving)* A **hot-gospeller** is a religious speaker who tries to make people who are listening to him or her very excited, by using an emotional way of speaking. • A **hot potato** is something that is difficult to deal with: *The abortion issue is a* **political** *hot potato in the United States.* • *(Am slang)* If something or someone is **hot shit** (*Br* **shit hot**), they are very good: *That guitarist's real hot shit!* • A **hot spot** is a place where war or other fighting is likely to happen: *The border is a major hot spot.* See also **hot spot** at HOT [EXCITING]. • A **hot tub** is a large, usually wooden, container full of hot water in which more than one person can sit: *We always reserved late afternoon for a long soak in the hotel's hot tub.* • A **hot-water bottle** is a rubber container which you fill with hot water and use to warm a bed or part of the body. PIC› **Bottles and flasks** • *(Br)* A **hot water cylinder** (*Am* **hot water tank**) is a metal container usually found in or near the bathroom, which holds and heats the water for a house: *If you cover your hot water cylinder with a good quality jacket, you can save a fortune on electricity bills.* PIC› **Bathroom** • *"Some Like It Hot"* (film title, 1959) • See also HEAT [TEMPERATURE]. • LP› **Measurements** (J)

hot [SPICY] /£hɒt, $hɑːt/ *adj* **hotter, hottest** (of food) causing a strong burning feeling in the mouth • *a hot curry* • *hot spicy food* • *Chilli, cayenne, mustard and pepper are all hot.* • (J)

hot [CLOSE] /£hɒt, $hɑːt/ *adj* **hotter, hottest** close • *They were* **hot on the trail/tracks/heels of** (=very close behind) *the thieves.* • *The gang drove off, with the police* **in hot pursuit** (=following closely behind). • (J)

hot·ly /£'hɒt·li, $'hɑːt·li/ *adv* • *He set off, hotly* **pursued** (= closely followed) *by his two friends.*

hot [ANGRY] /£hɒt, $hɑːt/ *adj* **hotter, hottest** (of a person's mood) easily made worse • *She's got a very hot temper* (= quickly gets angry). • *Tom's very hot-***tempered**. • (J)

hot·ly /£'hɒt·li, $'hɑːt·li/ *adv* • *She hotly* (= angrily) **denied** *having taken the money.*

hot [SKILFUL] /£hɒt, $hɑːt/ *adj* **hotter, hottest** *infml* (of a person) knowing a lot; skilful • *She's hot* **at** *maths.* • *My Spanish is* **not all that** *hot*/**not so** *hot* (= not very good). • If you are **hot stuff** at something, you do it very well: *Sally's hot stuff* **at** *(doing) crosswords.* See also **hot stuff** at HOT [SEXY]. • (J)

hot [DEMANDING] /£hɒt, $hɑːt/ *adj* [after v; always + *on*] **hotter, hottest** *infml* demanding that things should be done correctly • *You'd better dress smartly for the interview – the manager's hot* **on** *presentation.* • (J)

hot [DANGEROUS] /£hɒt, $hɑːt/ *adj* **hotter, hottest** (esp. of stolen goods) difficult to sell or dangerous to deal with, esp. because the police are still looking for them, or (of a situation) risky • *The dealer wasn't interested in the jewels because they were still hot.* • *As soon as the situation becomes too hot, he gets out.* • *The Mafia were making it/things too hot for them, so they left the country.* • If something is **too hot to handle**, it is too difficult to deal with or talk about: *For many politicians, abortion is an issue that's too hot to handle.* • (J)

hot [SEXY] /£hɒt, $hɑːt/ *adj* **hotter, hottest** *dated slang* sexually attractive • *She's a real hot* **chick**. • *Mike is a* **hot-blooded** (= having strong sexual feelings) *male.* • If a man says a woman is **hot stuff**, he means she is sexy. See also **hot stuff** at HOT [SKILFUL]. • If someone is **hot to trot** they desire sexual activity: *Kate was wearing her black see-through top and she looked hot to trot.* ○ *He used to buy her hot-to-trot* (= sexy) *underwear and little red Lycra numbers with plunging necklines.* • (J)

hots /£hɒts, $hɑːts/ *pl n* **the hots** *slang* • *He's* **had** *the hots* (= a strong feeling of sexual attraction) **for** *Sue ever since he met her.*

hot [EXCITING] /£hɒt, $hɑːt/ *adj* **hotter, hottest** exciting and energetic • *the hot new FM station* • *The band were really hot tonight.* • *The hottest* **news/gossip** *of the week is the royal marriage break-up.* • *This actor is Hollywood's hottest* **property** (= is very fashionable and many people would like to employ him). • If someone gives you a hot **tip** for a race, or tells you who the hot **favourite** is, they tell you who is very likely to win. • *(infml)* A **hot spot** is a place which is very popular and exciting: *The Manhattan Nightclub is one of the best hot spots in town.* See also **hot spot** at HOT [VERY WARM]. • (J)

hot up *(obj)*, **hot** *(obj)* **up** /£hɒt, $hɑːt/ *v adv* • *A few days before the elections, the* **pace** *began to hot up* (= to become faster and more exciting). [I] • If you hot up a car's engine, you change it so that the car will go faster. [M]

hot·bed /£'hɒt·bed, $'hɑːt-/ *n* [C usually sing] a place or situation where a lot of a particular activity, esp. an unwanted or unpleasant activity, is happening or might happen • *The city is a* **(real)** *hotbed* **of crime/unrest/terrorism**.

hotch·potch /£'hɒtʃ·pɒtʃ, $'hɑːtʃ·pɑːtʃ/, *Am usually* **hodge·podge** *n* [C] a confused mixture of different things • *New Age thinking seems to be a hotchpotch* **of** *old and new ideas.*

ho·tel /£həʊ'tel, $hoʊ-/ *n* [C] a building where you pay to have a room to sleep in, and where you can often eat meals • *hotel guests* • *a 4-star hotel* • *the hotel dining-room/lounge* • *the Clarendon Hotel* • *to manage/run a hotel* • *We stayed* **in/at** *a hotel on the sea-front.* • Compare HOSTEL.

ho·tel·i·er /£həʊ'tel·i·əʳ, $ˌhoʊ·tᵊl'jeɪ/ *n* [C] • A hotelier is a person who manages or owns a hotel.

hot·foot /£ˌhɒt'fʊt, $'hɑːt·fʊt, '-/ *adv infml* very quickly and without delay • *She'd come hotfoot from the palace with the latest news.*

hot·foot /£'hɒt·fʊt, $'hɑːt·fʊt, ˌ-'-/ *v infml* • *The thieves* **hotfooted it** (= ran very fast) **down** *the street*/**out of** *the house.*

hot·head /£'hɒt·hed, $'hɑːt-/ *n* [C] *disapproving* someone who does things or reacts to things quickly and without thinking carefully first

hot·head·ed /£ˌhɒt'hed·ɪd, $'hɑːtˌhed·ɪd/ *adj disapproving* • *She's a bit hotheaded and rash.*

hot·head·ed·ly /£ˌhɒt'hed·ɪd·li, $'hɑːtˌhed·ɪd·li/ *adv disapproving*

hot·head·ed·ness /£ˌhɒt'hed·ɪd·nəs, $'hɑːtˌhed·ɪd·nəs/ *n* [U] *disapproving*

hot·house /£'hɒt·haʊs, $'hɑːt-/ *n* [C] **hothouses** /£'hɒtˌhaʊ·zɪz, $'hɑːt-/ a usually large heated glass building in which plants are grown • *hothouse tomatoes* • *Cucumbers and tomatoes ripened in her hothouses.* • *(fig.) He was attracted by the hothouse* **atmosphere** *of Britain's top schools* (= in which children are forced to develop quickly). • *(Am)***Hothouse children** are children who are protected from experiencing the more unpleasant parts of life and society by their parents.

hot·line /£'hɒt·laɪn, $'hɑːt-/ *n* [C] a special direct telephone connection for emergencies • *A national telephone hotline has been* **set up** *for students suffering from stress.* • *A hot line links the two heads of state in Moscow and Washington.*

hot·plate /£'hɒt·pleɪt, $'hɑːt-/ *n* [C] a small movable esp. electric cooker, on which pans of food are heated • *(Br and Aus)* A hotplate is also a round flat metal surface on an electric cooker, on which pans of food are heated.

hot·pot /£'hɒt·pɒt, $'hɑːt·pɑːt/ *n* a mixture of meat and vegetables, usually including sliced potatoes, cooked slowly in a covered dish inside a cooker • *(a) Lancashire hotpot* [C/U]

hot·rod /£'hɒt·rɒd, $'hɑːt·rɑːd/ *n* [C] *dated slang* a car which is specially built or changed so that it will go very fast

hot·shot /£'hɒt·ʃɒt, $'hɑːt·ʃɑːt/ *n* [C] *esp. Am and Aus infml* someone who is skilful and successful at something • *Now he's a lecturer, he thinks he's a* **(real)** *hotshot!* • *She's* **(quite)** *a hotshot* **at** *chess.*

hot-wire *obj* /£'hɒt·waɪəʳ, $'hɑːt·waɪr/ *v* [T] *slang* to start (a car engine) without using the key, esp. in order to steal the car

hou·mous, hum·mus /'hʊm·əs/ *n* [U] a soft smooth savoury food made from crushed CHICKPEAS and lemon juice

hound [ANIMAL] /haʊnd/ *n* [C] a dog used for hunting, esp. a FOXHOUND • See also BLOODHOUND; GREYHOUND; NEWSHOUND.

hound *obj* [CHASE] /haʊnd/ *v* [T] to chase (someone) or refuse to leave them alone, esp. because you want to get something from them; HARASS • *The reporters/press wouldn't stop hounding me.* • If someone hounds you **out** (**of** a place or position), they force you to leave: *He was hounded out of office/his job by the constant attacks by the newspapers.*

hour /£aʊəʳ, $aʊr/ *n* [C] a period of 60 minutes • *The exam lasted an hour/three hours/half an hour/a quarter of an hour/an hour and a half.* • *There are 24 hours in a day.* • *How many hours' sleep do you need?* • 'Hour' or 'hours' can also mean a time or period of time when a particular thing happens: *What time's your lunch/dinner hour?* ○ *I work normal office/business hours.* • *I'll be back in an hour's/two hours'* **time** (= after one/two hours). • If you **keep regular/late/unusual** hours, you go to bed, get up or work at regular/late/unusual times. • *The village is an hour from Cambridge/an hour away* (= It takes an hour to travel there). • *He gets paid* **by the** *hour* (= gets a particular amount of money for each hour he works). • *The clock strikes* **the** *hour* (= It makes a noise at one o'clock, two o'clock, etc.). • *Trains leave* **every** *hour* **on the** *hour* (= at exactly one o'clock, two o'clock, etc.). • *Weather conditions in these mountains change* **(from) hour to hour** (= they are different every hour). • *Buses leave at ten minutes past/to* **the** *hour* (= at ten past/to one o'clock, two o'clock, etc.). • *(specialized) War was declared at eighteen hundred/18.00 hours* (= at six o'clock in the evening). • *At the* **agreed** *hour* (= At the time arranged in advance), *a car stopped outside the bank.* • *The doctor said we could call her* **at any hour of the day or night** (= at any time) *if we were worried.* • *What are you doing here* **at this** *hour* (= at this time)*?* • *(disapproving) Who could be phoning us at this* **ungodly** *hour* (= at this unreasonable time)*?* • *He works* **long** *hours* (= starts work early and finishes late). • *Granny spent* **long** *hours* (= a long time) *talking about her childhood.* • *I often do some of my own work* **after hours** (= after the usual times of work). • *(esp. Br)* If you drink in a bar, etc. **out of hours** (*Am and Aus* **after hours**), you drink alcohol at a time when it is not allowed by law: *The police are trying to stop out-of-hours drinking.* • *I waited for him* **for hours (and hours)** (= for a very long time). • *(esp. disapproving) They keep ringing me up* **at all hours (of the day and night)** (= continually during the day and the night). • *(esp. disapproving) He stays up drinking* **till all hours** (= very late). • *I sat by her bedside for* **hour after hour/hour upon hour** (= many hours without stopping). • *(literary) She helped me* **in** *my* **hour of need** (= when I urgently needed help). • *(literary)* If you think your **hour has come**, you think you are going to die: *I thought my hour had come when he pointed his gun at me.* • LP› **Periods of time, Time**

hour·ly /£ˈaʊə·li, $ˈaʊr-/ *adj* [not gradable] • *Take two tablets at hourly intervals* (= every hour). • *There's an hourly bus service* (= once every hour) *into town.*

hour·ly /£ˈaʊə·li, $ˈaʊr-/ *adv* [not gradable] • *Trains call here hourly* (= once every hour). • *(fig.) She changes her mind hourly* (= continuously). • An hourly-**paid** worker is paid according to how many hours he or she has worked. • *(dated) We are hourly* **expecting** *news* (= We think we will soon hear news) *from the climbers.*

hour·glass /£ˈaʊə·glɑːs, $ˈaʊr·glæs/ *n* [C] a glass container filled with sand that takes one hour to move from an upper to a lower part through a narrow opening in the middle, used esp. in the past to measure time • If a woman has an **hourglass figure**, she has a very small waist. • PIC› **Clocks and watches**

house HOME /haʊs/ *n* [C] *pl* **houses** /ˈhaʊ·zɪz/ a building which people, usually one family, live in • *a detached/semi-detached house* • *to buy/rent/let a house* • *house prices* • *She lives in a little house (Br and Aus)* **in**/ *(Am)* **on** *Cross Street.* • A house can also be a building where animals are kept: *the monkey/snake/lion house at the zoo* ○ *a hen house* • A house can also be a building or part of a building which is used for a special purpose: *the Sydney Opera House* ○ *Broadcasting House* • You can also use house to mean all the people living in a house: *Try not to wake* **the whole** *house when you come in!* • *(infml) It's a simple problem – there's no need to go* **all round the houses** (= use a long and indirect method) *to find a solution.* • *You should* **set/put** *your* **own house in order** (= solve your own problems) *before giving me advice!* • If you are **(kept/put/ placed) under house arrest**, you are legally forced to stay in your house as if it were a prison: *The opposition leader has just been put under house arrest.* • If a doctor or other health worker makes a **house call**, they come to your home, usually to give some form of treatment. • If you go **house-hunting**, you look for a house to live in: *I'm going house-hunting today.* • A **house husband** is a man who stays at home and cleans the house, takes care of the children, etc. while his wife goes out to work. • A **house martin** is a small bird that makes its nest under the edge of the roof of a house. • A **house of cards** is a structure built with playing cards, which can easily fall down: *The regime collapsed* **like** *a* **house** *of* **cards**. • *(Am)* A **house of correction** is a building where people who have committed crimes that are not serious are sent to improve their behaviour. • *(esp. literary or fml)* A **house of God** is a church. • If you say you wouldn't **give** something **house-room**, you mean that you don't want it in your home: *I wouldn't even give that old piano house-room!* • If you **house-sit**, or are a **house-sitter**, you stay in someone's house while they are away in order to keep it safe. • A **house sparrow** is a common small grey and brown bird. • If you do something **house-to-house** (also **door-to-door**), you go to every house in a particular area or road: *to do a house-to-house collection/survey* • *to make house-to-house enquiries* • *(esp. Br and Aus)* If a pet, esp. a dog, is **house-trained** (*Am usually* **housebroken**), it has been taught to go outside to urinate and excrete the contents of its bowels. • See also FARMHOUSE; ROADHOUSE. • LP› **Shopping goods** PIC› **Accommodation**

house *obj* /haʊz/ *v* [T] • *It will be difficult to house all the refugees* (= to give them somewhere to live). • *The jail houses* (= has enough space for) *over 300 prisoners.* • *The museum houses* (= provides space for) *the biggest collection of antique toys in Europe.* • *The electric and gas meters are housed in* (= are in) *this cupboard.*

house·ful /ˈhaʊs·fʊl/ *n* • *We've got a houseful* **(of** *visitors)* (= Our house has a large number of them).

hous·ing /ˈhaʊ·zɪŋ/ *n* [U] • *The government has promised to provide cheap housing* (= houses) *for poor people.* • *In this neighbourhood, there are a lot of families who live in (Br)* **council**/*(Am and Aus)* **public** *housing* (= houses or apartments provided by the government). • *(esp. Br) These flats belong to a* **housing association** (= a group of people who join together so that they can build or buy houses or apartments at low cost). • *(Br)* A **housing estate** (also **estate**, *Am* **housing development**, *Am also and Aus* **subdivision**) is an area containing a large number of houses or apartments built close together at the same time: They live **on** a housing estate. ○ *We don't like living* **in** *a housing development.* • *(Am)* A **housing project** (also **project**) is a group of houses or apartments, usually provided by the government for families who have low incomes. • PIC› **Accommodation**

house BUSINESS /haʊs/ *n* [C] *pl* **houses** /ˈhaʊ·zɪz/ a business or organization • *a publishing/fashion house* • *a curry house* (= restaurant) • *In a gambling casino, the odds always favour* **the house** (= the owners of the place). • If you have something **on the house**, it is given to you free by a business: *All the drinks were on the house.* • *(Br and Aus)* A **house journal** (*Am* **house organ**) is a newspaper produced by a company to tell workers what is happening in the company. • *"House of the Rising Sun"* (title of a song by The Animals, 1964)

house SCHOOL GROUP /haʊs/ *n* [C] *pl* **houses** /ˈhaʊ·zɪz/ *Br and Aus* any of a small number of groups which the children in a school are put in for sports and other competitions • *Which house are you in? I'm in Livingstone's/Livingstone House.* • *an inter-house football match*

house FAMILY /haʊs/ *n* [C] *pl* **houses** /ˈhaʊ·zɪz/ an important family, esp. a royal one • *The British Royal Family belong to the House of Windsor.* • *"A plague o' both your houses"* (Shakespeare, Romeo and Juliet 3.1)

house POLITICS /haʊs/ *n* [C] *pl* **houses** /ˈhaʊ·zɪz/ an organization which makes laws, or its meeting place • In Britain the **Houses of Parliament** are called the **House of Commons** (also the **lower house** or **the Commons**) and the **House of Lords** (also the **upper house** or **the Lords**). • **The** House can also mean the members of the organization which makes laws: *The House began sitting at 3 p.m./rose at 2 a.m.* • In the parliaments of the United States, Australia and New Zealand, the **lower** House is called the **House of Representatives** and the **upper** house is called the Senate. • A house can also be the group of people who suggest a subject for a DEBATE (= formal discussion): *The motion for tonight's debate is, "This house believes that capital punishment should be abolished."*

house THEATRE /haʊs/ *n* [C] *pl* **houses** /ˈhaʊ·zɪz/ the people watching a performance, esp. in a theatre • *The opera* **played to** *a* **full/packed/empty** *house.* • The **house lights** light the place where the public sit in a theatre, cinema etc.

house·boat /£ˈhaʊs·bəʊt, $-boʊt/ *n* [C] a boat which people use as their home, often kept in one place on a river or CANAL

house·bound /ˈhaʊs·baʊnd/ *adj* [not gradable] unable to leave your home, esp. because you are ill • *She's been housebound since the accident.*

house·break·er /£ˈhaʊsˌbreɪ·kəʳ, $-kɚ/ *n* [C] a person who illegally enters a house in order to steal something

house·break·ing /ˈhaʊsˌbreɪ·kɪŋ/ *n* [U]

house·brok·en /£ˈhaʊsˌbrəʊ·kᵊn, $-ˌbroʊ-/ *adj Am for* **house-trained**, see at HOUSE HOME

house·buy·er /£ˈhaʊsˌbaɪ·əʳ, $-ɚ/ *n* [C usually pl] a person who wishes to buy, or is buying a house or other form of place to live in • *Housebuyers are now much less inclined to believe what estate agents tell them about potential new homes.*

house·fly /ˈhaʊs·flaɪ/ *n* [C] a small common FLY (= type of insect) often found in houses • PIC› **Insects**

house·ful /ˈhaʊs·fʊl/ *n* See at HOUSE HOME

house·guest /ˈhaʊs·gest/ *n* [C] *esp. Am and Aus* a person who stays at someone else's house for one or more nights; a guest • *Josja and Renée spent the weekend as our houseguests before returning to Holland.*

house·hold /£ˈhaʊs·həʊld, $-hoʊld/ *n* [C + sing/pl v] a group of people, often a family, who live together • *household chores/tasks* • *household expenses* • *The whole household was/were at home that morning.* • *By the 1960s, most households had a TV.* • *He was a* **household name** (= was famous) *in the 1950s, but now no one remembers him.* • *"McDonalds" quickly became a* **household word** (= a word that everyone knows). • LP› **Shopping goods**

house·hold·er /£ˈhaʊsˌhəʊl·dəʳ, $-ˌhoʊl·dɚ/ *n* [C] • A householder is the person who owns or is in charge of a house: *The letter was addressed to "The Householder, 1 River Lane".*

house·keep·er /£ˈhaʊsˌkiː·pəʳ, $-pɚ/ *n* [C] a person, esp. a woman, whose job is to organize another person's house and deal with cooking, cleaning, etc. • *After his wife's death he decided to employ a housekeeper.*

house·keep·ing (mon·ey) /ˈhaʊsˌkiː·pɪŋ/ *n* [U] • *We allow £75 a week housekeeping* (= money for buying food and other things necessary for keeping a house), *and spend the rest on clothes and entertainment.*

house·maid /ˈhaʊs·meɪd/ *n* [C] *dated* a woman servant who cleans the house • **Housemaid's knee** is a painful knee usually caused by KNEELING (= having your knees on the ground) too much.

house·man (*pl* **-men**) /ˈhaʊs·mən, -mæn/, *Am* **in·tern**, *Aus* **res·i·dent** *n* [C] *Br* a male or female doctor who is still training, and who works in a hospital

house·mast·er *male, female* **house·mi·stress** /£ˈhaʊsˌmɑː·stəʳ, $-ˌmæs·tɚ, -ˌmɪs·trəs/ *n* [C] a teacher who is in charge of the children who live in one of several separate buildings in a school

house·mate /ˈhaʊs·meɪt/ *n* [C] someone you live with in a house but are not related to • *Helen is leaving next month so we're looking for a new housemate.*

house (mu·sic) /haʊs/ *n* [U] popular music with a fast regular beat, usually produced on electronic equipment • *House music first appeared in the late 1980s.*

house·plant /£ˈhaʊs·plɑːnt, $-plænt/, *Br also and Aus* **pot plant** *n* [C] a plant which is grown in a container inside a house or other building • PIC› **Room**

house·proud /ˈhaʊs·praʊd/ *adj esp. Br and Aus* very anxious about your house being completely clean and tidy, and spending a lot of time making it so • *She's so houseproud that she makes everyone take their shoes off before they come in.*

house·wares *Am* /£ˈhaʊs·weəz, $-werz/, *Br* **house·hold goods** *pl n* equipment, utensils, tools and machines used in a house, esp. in the kitchen • *I bumped into him in the housewares department while I was looking for a coffee-making machine.* • LP› **Shopping goods**

house·warm·ing (par·ty) /£ˈhaʊsˌwɔː·mɪŋ, $-ˌwɔːr-/ *n* [C] a party which you give when you move into a new house • *We're* **having** *a housewarming on Friday if you'd like to come.*

house·wife /ˈhaʊs·waɪf/ *n* [C] *pl* **housewives** /ˈhaʊs·waɪvz/ a woman whose work is inside the home, cleaning, cooking etc., and who usually does not have any other job • *Nowadays women don't necessarily give up their jobs and become housewives when they get married.* • *Good value for money is what* **the** *housewife* (= women in general, esp. those who take care of the house) *wants.*

house·wife·ly /ˈhaʊsˌwaɪf·li/ *adj* • *The shop sells several magazines devoted to cookery, sewing, knitting and other such housewifely concerns.*

housework /£ˈhaʊs·wɜːk, $-wɜːrk/ *n* [U] the work of keeping a house clean and tidy • *In our family, we share the housework between us.* • *I hate* **doing** *housework.* • Compare HOMEWORK.

hove /£həʊv, $hoʊv/ *v* [I] **hove in(to) sight/view** *literary* appeared • *After 30 minutes, a large ship hove into view.*

hov·el /£ˈhɒv·əl, $ˈhɑː·vəl/ *n* [C] a small home, which is dirty and in bad condition • *The house was little more than a hovel and totally uninhabitable.*

hov·er /£ˈhɒv·əʳ, $ˈhɑː·vɚ/ *v* [I] to stay in the air in one place, esp. (of birds and insects) by moving the wings quickly, or (of a person) to stand somewhere, esp. near another person, nervously waiting for their attention • *The hawk hovered in the sky, waiting to swoop down on the rabbit on the ground.* • *Swarms of mosquitoes hovered over the water.* • *I heard the noise of a helicopter hovering overhead.* • *(fig.) Inflation is hovering at* (= staying very close to with only small changes) *3%.* • *She hovered outside her boss's office door, unsure whether to knock or not.* • *I could sense him behind me, hovering and building up the courage to ask me a question.* • *(fig.) She's hovering* **between** *taking the job and turning it down* (= is uncertain whether to take the job or not). • *(fig.) They're hovering* **on the brink** *of* (= are close to) *accepting our offer.* • *(Br)* A **hover (mower)** is a LAWNMOWER which cuts grass with blades that spin round in a circle and which is held slightly above the ground by a current of air below it. • PIC› **Garden**

hov·er·craft /£ˈhɒv·ə·krɑːft, $ˈhɑː·vɚ·kræft/ *n* [C] *pl* **hovercrafts** or **hovercraft** a vehicle which flies over land or water by keeping close to the surface and producing a current of air under it to support it • PIC› **Ships and boats**

hov·er·port /£ˈhɒv·ə·pɔːt, $ˈhɑː·vɚ·pɔːrt/ *n* [C] a place where people get on or off HOVERCRAFT

how /haʊ/ *adv* [not gradable], *conjunction* in what way; by what methods • *How do we get to the town from here?* • *How did you hear about the concert?* • *How does this machine work?* • *How do you plan to spend your holiday?* • *Roz doesn't know how* **to** *ride a bicycle.* [+ to infinitive] • *It all depends on how you look at it.* • *I don't care about fashion, I dress how I please.* • *I was horrified to hear about how* (= the way) *she had been treated.* • *(disapproving) How* **can/could** *he be so stupid?* • *(disapproving) I don't know how anyone* **could** *be interested in such a boring book.* • *(infml)* **How come/so?** are used to express surprise: *So how come* (= why is it that) *you got an invitation and not me?* ○ *"I don't think I'll be able to go swimming tomorrow." "***How come/How so?** (= Why is that)*"* • *"I think we need to reconsider our position." "***How do you mean?** (= I don't understand, please explain)*."* • *(Br)* **How do you mean** is also used to express annoyance or anger: *How do you mean* (= explain what happened when) *you crashed the car!* • How is often used to mean in what condition, esp. of physical or emotional health: *How is your mother?* ○ *How are you feeling this morning?* ○ *I'm just going to see how Mrs Baker is.* • How is also used in questions which ask what an experience or event was like: *How was your flight?* ○ *So how was the party?* ○ *How did you* **find** *the lecture?* (= did you think it was good)*?* ○ *How* **did** *you* **like** *the concert* (= did you enjoy it)*?* • **How are you?** is used as a greeting: *"Hi, how are you?" "Fine, thanks, how are you?"* • **How are things?/How's everything?/How's it going/How's life?** are informal greetings. • **How do you do?** is a formal greeting: *"I'm Jack Stewart." "How do you do, I'm Angela Black."* • *(dated)* A **how do you do** is a difficult, worrying and unpleasant situation: *"I had a row with my sister and now she's refusing to talk to me." "Well, that's a* **fine** *how do you do!"* • *She didn't say how* **far** *it is* (= what the distance is) *to her house.* • *How* **long** *are you going to be* (= what amount of time are you going to spend) *in the bathroom?* • *Do you know how* **many** (= what number of) *people are coming?* • *How* **much** *does this cost* (= what is its price)*?* • *How* **old** *is his daughter* (= what age is she)*?* • *"Can you lift this case?" "It depends on how heavy it is."* • *Do you remember how* (= the fact that) *we used to see every new film as soon as it came out?* • How is sometimes used for emphasis: *(slightly fml) How* (= It is very) *nice to see you!* ○ *"She paid for everything." "How* (= that was very) *generous."* ○ *I was thinking how pretty she looked in her green dress* (= I thought she looked very attractive). ○ *I can't tell you how pleased I am* (= I am very pleased) *that you came.* • *(infml)* How is used for making suggestions: **How('s) about** *going*/**How would you like to go** (= Would you like to go) *for a drink after work?* ○ **How about** (= Could we consider) *trying to expand our European market?* • *(infml) Sales were up by 12% last month.* **How about that/how's that for** *a good result* (= that's an extremely good result)*?* • *We discovered that we'd both gone to the same school.* **How about that** (= Isn't that surprising)*!* • *Let me give you a cushion.* **How's that** (= Are you comfortable)*?* • *If you help me with the painting, I'll help you do the gardening.* **How's that for** (= Is that satisfactory as) *an offer?* • *(infml) "I'll meet you on the corner of Oxford Street at 2.30." "***How's that?** (= Please repeat what you said)*."* • *(infml) "I'll be glad when these road repairs are finished." "***And how** (= I completely agree)*!"* • **How-to** *books* (= books offering advice) *on dieting are often at the top of the bestseller lists.* • *"How do they know?"* (Dorothy Parker on the death of US President Calvin Coolidge, 1933) • *"I like New York in June, how about you?"* (in the song *How About You?* written by Ralph Freed, 1941) • *"How Are Things in Glocca Morra?"* (song from the show *Finnian's Rainbow* by E.Y.Harburg and Burton Lane, 1947) • LP› **Clauses, Measurements**

how /haʊ/ *n* • *When you learn yoga, it's important to understand* **the how(s) and the why(s) of** *what you're doing* (= the way to do it and the reasons for it).

how·dy /ˈhaʊ·di/ *exclamation Am infml for* HELLO

how·ev·er DEGREE /£ˌhaʊˈev·əʳ, $-ɚ/ *adv* [not gradable] despite whatever amount or degree • *However hungry I am, I never seem to be able to finish off a whole pizza.* • *However fast we drive, we're not going to get there in time.* • *If Emma likes something she'll buy it however much it costs.* • *I'll see you after the show and give you £20 for the tickets or however much they cost.*

how·ev·er WAY /£ˌhaʊˈev·əʳ, $-ɚ/ *conjunction, adv* [not gradable] in whatever way • *However you look at it, it's still* *a mess.* • *You can do it however you like, it really doesn't matter.* • However can be used to express surprise: *However did you manage to get him to agree to that?*

how·ev·er DESPITE /£ˌhaʊˈev·əʳ, $-ɚ/ *adv* [not gradable] despite this; NEVERTHELESS • *This is one possible solution to the problem. However, there are others.* • *There may, however, be other reasons that we don't know about.*

how·it·zer /£ˈhaʊ·ɪt·səʳ, $-sɚ/ *n* [C] a large gun which fires SHELLS (= very large bullets) high into the air so that they drop onto the place at which they are aimed

howl *(obj)* /haʊl/ *v* (esp. of a dog or a WOLF) to make a long, high crying sound • *In the silence of the night, a lone* **wolf** *howled.* [I] • *An injured dog lay in the middle of the road, howling* **with/in** *pain.* [I] • *Is there someone outside, or is it just the* **wind** *howling* (= blowing loudly) *(***through/in** *the trees)?* [I] • *Toby ran howling* (= crying loudly) *to his mother because he'd fallen and cut his knee.* [I] • *"Leave me alone or I'll get my daddy," howled* (= said with a loud crying sound) *a small child.* [+ clause] • *The opposition howled* **down** *the government's proposals* (= made a loud noise to prevent them being heard). [M] • *(fig.) Everyone howls* **(with laughter)** (= laughs a lot) *at his jokes and they're not even funny.* [I]

howl /haʊl/ *n* [C] • *He leaves his dog shut up in the house all day, and we can hear its howls.* • *She* **gave/let out** *a howl* **of** *pain.* • *(fig.) The plans to build a new supermarket have been greeted with howls* **of** *protest* (= angry complaints) *from local residents.*

howl·ing /ˈhaʊ·lɪŋ/ *adj* • *In the distance I heard a howling wolf.* • *(fig.) There's a howling* (= strong and noisy) **gale** *blowing outside.* • See also HOWLING.

how·ler /£ˈhaʊ·ləʳ, $-lɚ/ *n* [C] a foolish mistake, esp. one made by using words in the wrong way • *I* **made** *an awful howler the first time I introduced them – I thought she was the secretary but she was the Managing Director.*

howl·ing /ˈhaʊ·lɪŋ/ *adj* [before n] very great • *The party/play was a howling* **success**. • See also **howling** at HOWL.

how·so·ev·er /£ˌhaʊ·səʊˈev·əʳ, $-soʊˈev·ɚ/ *adv* [not gradable] *fml or literary for* HOWEVER DEGREE *or* HOWEVER WAY

hp POWER /ˌeɪtʃˈpiː/ *n* [C/U] *pl* **hp** *abbreviation for* HORSEPOWER

HP PAYMENT /ˌeɪtʃˈpiː/ *n* [U] *Br infml abbreviation for* **hire purchase**, see at HIRE • *We bought our television on HP.*

HQ /ˌeɪtʃˈkjuː/ *n* [C + sing./pl v] *abbreviation for* HEADQUARTERS • *We've just received instructions from HQ.*

hr *n* [C] *pl* **hrs** *abbreviation for* HOUR • *He ran the marathon in 2 hrs 48 mins.* • *The plane departs at 15.00 hrs.*

HRH /£ˌeɪtʃ·ɑːˈreɪtʃ, $-ɑːrˈeɪtʃ/ *n abbreviation for* His/Her Royal Highness (= title given to some members of a royal family) • *The new hospital was formally opened by HRH Prince Charles.* [before n] • *(infml) Is HRH going to be at the party?* [U]

HRT /£ˌeɪtʃ·ɑːˈtiː, $-ɑːr-/ *n* [U] *abbreviation for* **hormone replacement therapy**, see at HORMONE.

HSC /ˌeɪtʃ·esˈsiː/ *n* [C] *abbreviation for* Higher School Certificate (= in Australia, an exam taken in the last two years of school education)

ht *n* [U] *abbreviation for* HEIGHT • *Ht of bridge 1·8 m.*

hub /hʌb/ *n* [C] the central part of a wheel into which the SPOKES (= bars connecting the central part to the outer edge of the wheel) are fixed • *The hub* **of** *my bicycle wheel has rusted.* • The hub of something is the central or main part where there is most activity: *The airline's hub is in St Louis.* ○ *The computer department is* **at the hub of** *the company's operations.* ○ *The City of London is the hub* **of** *Britain's financial world.*

hub·bub /ˈhʌb·ʌb/ *n* [U] a loud noise, esp. caused by a lot of people all talking at the same time • *I could hardly hear myself speak above all the hubbub in the theatre bar.* • *(fig.) Once the hubbub* **of** (= excitement and activity caused by) *the election had* **died down**, *it was back to normal for the President.*

hub·by /ˈhʌb·i/ *n* [C] *infml for* husband • *She speaks fondly of Richard Moreland, hubby No.1, whom she still sees regularly.* • LP› **Relationships**

hub·cap /ˈhʌb·kæp/ *n* [C] the circular metal covering over the HUB (= central part) of the wheel of a car or other motor vehicle • PIC› **Car**

hu·bris /ˈhjuː·brɪs/ *n* [U] *fml* very great pride and belief in your own importance • *It was hubris that led them to believe that they could take over the business without any opposition.* • *He was punished for his hubris.*

huck·le·ber·ry /ˈhʌk·l̩ˌber·i/ *n* [C] a small round dark blue fruit, or the low N American bush on which it grows • *(Am slang)* A huckleberry is also a foolish person.

huck·ster /£ˈhʌk·stəʳ, $-stɚ/ *n* [C] *esp. Am often disapproving* a person who writes advertisements, esp. for radio and television, or who sells things or brings ideas or people to the public's attention in a noisy annoying way

hud·dle /ˈhʌd·l̩/ *v* [I always + adv/prep] to come close together in a group, or to hold your arms and legs close to your body, esp. because of cold or fear • *The frightened monkeys huddled in the back of their cage.* • *Everyone huddled* **round** *the fire to keep warm.* • *It was so cold that we huddled* **together** *for warmth.* • *You children should go out in the fresh air rather than huddling* **(up)** *against the radiator like that.* • *Sophie was so frightened by the noise of the fireworks that she huddled* **(up)** *in a corner of the room.*

hud·dle /ˈhʌd·l̩/ *n* [C] • *A small group of people stood* **in a** *huddle* (= close together) *at the bus stop.* • *The judges* **went into a huddle** (= got into a group in order to talk secretly) *to decide who was to be the winner.* • In American football, a huddle is a group formed by the members of a team before they separate and continue to play.

hud·dled /ˈhʌd·l̩d/ *adj* • *When they found the missing children they were huddled in a barn.* • *We stood huddled* **together** *for warmth.* • *"Give me your tired, your poor, your huddled masses yearning to breathe free"* (Emma Lazarus, in the poem *The New Colossus* which is cut into the base of the Statue of Liberty in New York, 1883)

hue COLOUR /hjuː/ *n* [C] (a degree of lightness, darkness, strength, etc. of) a colour • *In the Caribbean waters there are fish of every hue.* • *The hues used in printing are cyan, magenta, yellow and black.* • *(fig.) All hues* (= different types) **of** *political opinion were represented at the meeting.*

hue DISAPPROVAL /hjuː/ *n* [U] **hue and cry** a noisy expression of public anger or disapproval • *There has been a* **great** *hue and cry about the council's plans to close the school.*

huff BREATHE /hʌf/ *v* [I] **huff and puff** *infml* to breathe loudly, usually after physical exercise • *We were huffing and puffing by the time we'd climbed to the top of the hill.*

huff COMPLAIN /hʌf/ *v* [I] **huff and puff** *infml disapproving* to complain loudly and express disapproval • *They huffed and puffed about the price but eventually they paid up.* • *All this moral huffing and puffing in the press about politicians' private lives is just a waste of time.*

huff BAD MOOD /hʌf/ *n* [C] an angry and offended mood • *Ted's* **gone into/got into** *one of his huffs again.* • If you are **in a huff** you are angry and offended: *She's in a real huff because I forgot her birthday.* ○ *Julia criticized some aspect of his work and he* **left/went off in** *a huff.* ○ *They* **went off** *in a huff* (= left, offended) *because we didn't invite them to our party.*

huff *obj* /hʌf/ *v* [T] • *"Well if that's how you feel, I'll go," she huffed* (= said in an annoyed or offended way). [+ clause]

huf·fy (-ier, -iest) /ˈhʌf·i/, **huff·ish** /ˈhʌf·ɪʃ/ *adj* • *You have to be careful what you say to Ellen, she's very huffy* (= is easily offended). • *I'd keep out of Jim's way, if I were you, he's very huffy* (= in a bad mood) *today.* • *Don't* **get** *huffy* **with** *me, young man!*

huf·fi·ly /ˈhʌf·ɪ·li/ *adv* • *"You might at least have said thank you," she said huffily* (= in an annoyed or offended way).

hug *(obj)* /hʌg/ *v* **-gg-** to hold (someone or something) close to your body with your arms to show that you like or love them • *Children need to be hugged.* [T] • *Have you hugged your child today?* [T] • *They hugged (each other) when they met at the station.* [I/T] • *Emily hugged her teddy bear* **tightly** *to her chest.* [T] • *She sat on the floor hugging her* **knees** (= with her knees bent up against her chest and her arms around them). [T] • *(fig.) Whenever I travel in the city I make sure I hug my handbag* **tightly** (= keep it close to my body). [T] • *(fig.) I hugged the idea* **to myself** (= thought about it secretly and with pleasure) *all through dinner.* [T] • *(fig.) The road hugs* (= keeps close to) *the coast for several miles, then turns inland.* [T] • *(fig.) This type of car will hug* (= not slide on) *the road, even in the wettest conditions.* [T] • LP› **Each other**

hug /hʌg/ *n* [C] • *Come here and* **give** *me a* **big** *hug* (= put your arms round me and hold me close to your body with your arms). • *We always exchange hugs* **and kisses** *when we meet.*

hug·gab·le /ˈhʌg·ə·bl̩/ *adj infml* • *He's so huggable* (= he makes me want to hug him)*!*

huge /hjuːdʒ/ *adj* **-r, -st** extremely large in size or amount • *They live in a huge house.* • *The costs involved in building a spacecraft are huge.* • *A huge number of people attended.* • *I've got a huge spot on my chin!* • *His last three films have all been huge successes.* • *We are faced with a huge problem.*

huge·ly /ˈhjuːdʒ·li/ *adv* • *He gave her a hugely expensive diamond ring.* • *Their business has been hugely successful.* • *We're hugely grateful for all your help.* • LP› **Very, completely**

huh /hə/ *exclamation infml* used in a variety of situations, for example, to show that you have not heard or understood something, *(humorous)* to express disapproval, or *(esp. Am)* at the end of a question • *"So what do you want to do tonight?" "Huh? What did you say?"* • *Huh? These instructions don't make sense!* • *(humorous) Huh, I don't think much of that idea!* • *(esp. Am) You want to go see a movie, huh?*

hu·la hoop /ˈhuː·lə/ *n* [C] *trademark* a ring, usually made of plastic, which children play with by putting it around their waist and moving their body so that it spins

hulk SHIP /hʌlk/ *n* [C] the body of an old ship, car or very large piece of equipment, which is broken and no longer used • *Here and there the rusted hulk of an abandoned car dotted the landscape.* • *(Am)* A hulk is also a part which continues from an old set of ideas or beliefs which are no longer accepted: *The hulk of Communism will not quickly fade away.*

hulk AWKWARD /hʌlk/ *n* [C] a large, heavy awkward person or thing • *Henry's a real hulk, but he's good-natured.* • *The Incredible Hulk is a character in a comic who turns from a scientist into a two-metre tall monster.*

hulk·ing /ˈhʌl·kɪŋ/ *adj* [not gradable] • *We were stopped by two hulking* (=large and heavy) *security guards.* • *(esp. Br)* Hulking **great** means extremely big or heavy: *How do you expect me to lift that hulking great box?* ○ *I can't imagine why that hulking great building was allowed to be built.*

hull SHIP /hʌl/ *n* [C] the body or frame of a ship, most of which goes under the water • *The hull was badly damaged when the ship hit an iceberg.* • PIC› **Ships and boats**

hull *obj* COVERING /hʌl/, *Am also* **shuck** *v* [T] to remove the covering or the stem and leaves from (some fruits, vegetables and seeds) • *We sat in the garden hulling strawberries.* • *Some kinds of peas and beans have to be hulled before they can be eaten.*

hul·la·ba·loo /ˌhʌl·ə·bəˈluː/ *n* [C] *pl* **hullaballoos** *dated* a loud noise made by people who are angry or annoyed • *There's a crowd of people* **making** *a real hullabaloo outside the Houses of Parliament in protest about the planned hospital closures.* • *The minister resigned after all the hullabaloo* (=public expression of anger or annoyance) *about his affair with an actress.*

hul·lo /£həˈləʊ, $-ˈloʊ/ *exclamation, n* [C] *pl* **hullos** *Br for* HELLO

hum *(obj)* /hʌm/ *v* **-mm-** to make a continuous low sound • *Bees, mosquitoes and certain other insects and birds hum.* [I] • *I think there's something wrong with the television – it's humming.* [I] • *Debbie often hums* (=sings a tune with her lips closed) **(to herself)** *while she's listening to music.* [I] • *I've forgotten how that tune goes – could you hum it for me?* [T] • *What's that strange humming sound?* • *(fig.) The pub was really humming* **(with life/activity)** (=it was busy and full of activity) *last night.* [I] • *We (Br and Aus)* **hummed and hah-ed/hawed** *(Am* **hemmed and hawed***)* (=were uncertain and took a long time) *before deciding to buy the house.*

hum /hʌm/ *n* [C usually sing] • *Our house is on a main road, so we can hear the constant hum* (=continuous low noise) **of** *traffic.* • *There's an annoying hum on this radio.*

hu·man /ˈhjuː·mən/ *adj* of or typical of people • *The human* **body** *is composed of 80% water.* • *Early human* **remains** *were found in the Dordogne region of France.* • *Victory in the war was achieved at the cost of great human* **suffering**. • *This meat is not* **fit for** *human* **consumption** (=for people to eat). • *Jenny's really quite human* (=kind, friendly and careful of the feelings of others) *when you get to know her.* • *Of course I make mistakes, I'm* **only** *human* (=I am not perfect). • *The fault was due to human* **error** (=a person making a mistake). • The **human genome project** is an attempt to produce a map of all the genetic information in the human body. • *I like newspapers that have a lot of* **human interest** *stories* (=stories which are about people's experiences and feelings). • **Human nature** is the natural ways of behaving that most people share: *You can't change human nature.* ○ *It's* **only** *human (nature)* (=it is natural) *to want the best for your children.* • *Some people think that the existence of nuclear weapons is a threat to the future of* **the human race** (=people in general). • *Experts in the field of* **human relations** (=the study of the relationships between groups of workers in a place of work) *have been called in to advise the company about how to improve its productivity.* • *She's claiming that her detention by the police was a violation of her* **human rights** (=rights which it is generally considered all people should have). • When people are used as a **human shield**, they are forced to stay in a place where they would be hurt or killed if there was an attack: *The bank robbers used hostages as human shields to keep the police away.* ○ *Military bases were protected by captured enemy soldiers who were housed there as a human shield.* • If someone has **the human touch**, they are friendly and informal in a way that makes other people feel relaxed: *He is certainly an effective lawyer but colleagues say that he lacks the human touch.* • LP› **Sexist language**

hu·man (being) /ˈhjuː·mən/ *n* [C] • *The greatest damage being done to our planet today is that being done by humans* (=people). • *No human being should have to suffer what these people have suffered.*

hu·man·i·ty /£hjuːˈmæn·ə·ti, $-t̬i/ *n* [U] • *Adolf Hitler was guilty of enormous crimes against humanity* (=people in general). • *For more than five years, the hostages were denied their humanity* (=they were not treated with the respect that should be shown to people). • See also **humanity** at HUMANE; HUMANITIES.

hu·man·ize *obj, Br and Aus usually* **-ise** /ˈhjuː·mə·naɪz/ *v* [T] • *Steps are being taken to humanize the prison* (=to make it less unpleasant and more suitable for people).

hu·man·iz·a·tion, *Br and Aus usually* **-i·sa·tion** /ˌhjuː·mə·naɪˈzeɪ·ʃən/ *n* [U]

hu·man·ly /ˈhjuː·mən·li/ *adv* • *Rescuers are doing everything humanly* **possible** (=everything that a person is able to do) *to free the trapped people.*

hu·man·oid /ˈhjuː·mə·nɔɪd/ *adj, n* • Humanoids are machines or creatures with the appearance and qualities of people: *I've just read a science fiction story about humanoids from outer space.* [C] ○ *In the film "Star Wars" there are two humanoid robots called R2D2 and C3PO.*

hu·mane /hjuːˈmeɪn/ *adj* showing kindness, care and sympathy towards others, esp. those who are suffering • *I don't think it's humane to keep people alive with machines.* • *The new prison governor is much more humane than her predecessor.* • *The humane way of dealing with a suffering animal* (=the way that causes the least pain) *is to kill it quickly.*

hu·mane·ly /hjuːˈmeɪn·li/ *adv* • *I don't support the death penalty, but if people are to be executed, it should be done humanely.*

hu·man·i·ty /£hjuːˈmæn·ə·ti, $-t̬i/ *n* [U] • *If only he would* **show/display** *a little humanity* (=understanding and kindness towards other people) *for once.* • See also **humanity** at HUMAN.

hu·man·i·sm /ˈhjuː·mə·nɪ·zəm/ *n* [U] a belief system based on the principle that people's spiritual and emotional needs can be fulfilled without following a religion

hu·man·ist /ˈhjuː·mə·nɪst/ *n* [C] • *Sir Thomas More was a leading humanist* (=a person who believes in humanism) *of his time.*

hu·man·ist /ˈhjuː·mə·nɪst/ *adj* • *humanist beliefs/writers/ideas*

hu·man·is·tic /£ˌhjuː·məˈnɪs·tɪk, $-tɪk/ *adj* • *Jonathan has a humanistic view of the world* (=one which relates to humanism).

hu·man·i·ta·ri·an /£hjuːˌmæn·ɪˈteə·ri·ən, $-ˈter·i-/ *adj, n* (a person who is) involved in or connected with improving people's lives and reducing suffering • *The prisoner has been released for humanitarian reasons.* • *The United Nations is sending humanitarian* **aid** (=food and supplies to help people) *to the areas worst affected by the conflict.* • *The well-known humanitarian, Joseph Rowntree, was concerned with the welfare of his employees.* [C]

hu·man·i·ta·ri·an·i·sm /£hjuːˌmæn·ɪˈteə·ri·ə·nɪ·zəm, $-ˈter·i-/ *n* [U]

hu·man·i·ties /£hjuːˈmæn·ɪ·tiz, $-ə·t̬iz/ *pl n* the study of subjects like literature, language, history and PHILOSOPHY • *Susan has always been more interested in* **the** *humanities than the sciences.*

hu·man·kind /ˌhjuː·mənˈkaɪnd, ˈ---/ *n* [U] the whole of the human race, including both men and women • *Humankind owes him a great debt for all that he has done for world peace.*

hu·man·ly /'hjuː·mən·li/ *adv* See at HUMAN

hu·man·oid /'hjuː·mə·nɔɪd/ *adj, n* See at HUMAN

hum·ble /'hʌm·bl̩/ *adj* **-r, -st** of low rank or position; not important • *He's just a humble mechanic.* • *Even when she became rich and famous, she never forgot her humble background.* • *They are of humble* **birth**. • *Frank strikes me as a very humble person* (=he does not consider himself very important). • *We live in a humble* (=ordinary) *little village.* • *(humorous) Welcome to our humble* **abode** (=our home). • *(fml) Please accept our humble* **apologies** *for the error.* • *In my humble* **opinion** (=I want to emphasize that I think that) *we should never have bought the car in the first place.* • *"Be it ever so humble, there's no place like home"* (from the song *Home, Sweet Home* written by J.H.Payne, 1823) • *"Ever so 'umble"* (popular version of statements by Uriah Heep in Charles Dickens' *David Copperfield*, 1850)

hum·ble *obj* /'hʌm·bl̩/ *v* [T] • *He was humbled* (=made to feel less important than he had thought he was) *by the child's generosity.* • *Visiting the hospital and seeing so many sick people being so brave was a humbling* **experience**. • *The world champion was humbled* (= unexpectedly defeated) *by an unknown outsider in last night's race.*

hum·bly /'hʌm·bli/ *adv* • *"I'm truly sorry that I made such a terrible mistake," he said humbly* (=in a way that showed he did not feel important or proud). • *(dated) Her parents objected to her choice of husband because he was humbly* **born** (=his family had a low social position). • *They live very humbly* (=in a simple way).

hum·bug DISHONESTY /'hʌm·bʌg/ *n* [U] dishonest talk, writing or behaviour that is intended to deceive people • *The minister claimed that the government didn't know about the arms sale but that's just humbug.* • *"Bah ...Humbug!"* (Scrooge in Charles Dickens' novel *A Christmas Carol*, 1843)

hum·bug SWEET /'hʌm·bʌg/ *n* [C] *Br* a hard sweet made of boiled sugar and tasting of PEPPERMINT, usually with strips of two different colours on the outside • *mint humbugs*

hum·ding·er /£ˌhʌm'dɪŋ·əʳ, $-ɚ, 'ˌ-ˌ--/ *n* [C] *humorous or dated* something or someone that is noticeable because it is a very good example of its type • *That was a humdinger* **of** *a party.* • *The girl playing Cinderella in the pantomime was a* **real** *humdinger* (=was very attractive)*!* • *My brother and sister had a* **real** *humdinger* **of a row** *last night.*

hum·drum /'hʌm·drʌm/ *adj* lacking excitement, interest or new and different events; ordinary • *We lead such a humdrum* **life/existence**.

hu·mer·us /'hjuː·mə·rəs/ *n* [C] *pl* **humeri** /'hjuː·mə·raɪ/ *specialized* the long bone in the upper half of your arm, between your shoulder and your ELBOW (=joint)

hu·mid /'hjuː·mɪd/ *adj* (of air and weather conditions) containing extremely small drops of water in the air • *New York is very hot and humid in the summer.* • *It was a hot sunny day, but it was so humid that my clothes were sticking to me.*

hu·mid·i·fy *obj* /hjuː'mɪd·ɪ·faɪ/ *v* [T] • *If the air in a room is too dry, you can put a bowl of water near the radiator to humidify it* (=make the air wetter).

hu·mid·i·fi·er /£hjuː'mɪd·ɪ·faɪ·əʳ, $-ɚ/ *n* [C] • A humidifier is a machine which makes dry air in a room wetter.

hu·mid·i·ty /£hjuː'mɪd·ɪ·ti, $-ə·t̬i/ *n* [U] • *I don't mind hot weather, but I hate this high humidity* (=the air making me feel wet). • *The humidity is expected to be high today.*

hu·mil·i·ate *obj* /hjuː'mɪl·i·eɪt/ *v* [T] to make (someone) feel ashamed or lose their respect for themselves • *How could you humiliate me by questioning my judgment in front of everyone like that?* • *England were humiliated* (= completely defeated) *in last night's match.*

hu·mil·i·at·ed /£hjuː'mɪl·i·eɪ·tɪd, $-t̬ɪd/ *adj* • *I've never felt so humiliated* (=been made to feel so ashamed) *in my life.*

hu·mil·i·at·ing /£hjuː'mɪl·i·eɪ·tɪŋ, $-t̬ɪŋ/ *adj* • *Losing my job was the most humiliating thing that ever happened to me.* • *The government suffered a humiliating* **defeat** *in yesterday's debate.* • *Some people think it's humiliating* **to** *have to work for someone younger than themselves.* [+ to infinitive] • *Don't you think it's a bit humiliating for Robert* **that** *his girlfriend is now dating his brother?* [+ *that* clause]

hu·mil·i·a·tion /hjuːˌmɪl·i'eɪ·ʃᵊn/ *n* • *Being forced to resign was a great humiliation* **for** *the minister.* [C] • *After the humiliation* **of** *last week's defeat, the Mets were back on top in today's game.* [U]

hu·mil·i·ty /£hjuː'mɪl·ɪ·ti, $-ə·t̬i/ *n* [U] the quality of not being proud because you are aware of your faults • *Sister Mary is a person of great humility.* • *He doesn't have the humility to admit when he's wrong.* • *They might be very rich, but it wouldn't hurt them to show/display/ demonstrate a little humility.*

hum·ming·bird /£'hʌm·ɪŋ·bɜːd, $-bɜːrd/ *n* [C] a very small brightly coloured bird with a long thin beak whose wings move very fast and make a HUMMING noise

hum·mock /'hʌm·ək/ *n* [C] *literary* a very small hill or raised part of the ground • *a grassy hummock*

hum·mus /'hʊm·əs/ *n* [U] HOUMOUS

hu·mour AMUSEMENT *Br and Aus, Am and Aus* **hu·mor** /£'hjuː·məʳ, $-mɚ/ *n* [U] the ability to be amused by things, the way in which people see that some things are amusing, or the quality of being amusing • *He has a wonderful* **sense of** *humour* (=he is very able to see things as amusing). • *The British* **sense of** *humour is very different from the American* **sense of** *humour* (=the things which British people see as amusing are different from the things which Americans see as amusing). • *I've never known anyone so lacking in humour* (=the ability to see that some things are amusing) *as Marion.* • *The best man's speech at Jill and Peter's wedding was full of humour* (= was amusing). • *Fortunately, she saw the humour* (=the amusing side) **of** *the situation.* • *I didn't think the play was very funny – it was just schoolboy humour* (=it contained the types of jokes that boys at school find amusing). • (KOR) (PL)

hu·mor·ist /'hjuː·mə·rɪst/ *n* [C] • *"Lake Woebegon Days" is a book by the American humorist* (=a person who writes or tells amusing stories) *Garrison Keillor.*

hu·mor·ous /'hjuː·mə·rəs/ *adj* • *A rather humorous* (= amusing) *thing happened yesterday.* • *I think Woody Allen is very humorous.*

hu·mor·ous·ly /'hjuː·mə·rə·sli/ *adv* • *"It's all right, I've got another one," she said humorously* (=in a joking way) *when he apologized for treading on her foot.*

hu·mour·less *Br and Aus* /£'hjuː·mə·ləs, $-mɚ-/, *Am and Aus* **hu·mor·less** *adj* • *David is so humourless* (=he is not able to see that some things are amusing). • *She struggled through the dense, humourless* (=not amusing) *prose.*

hu·mour MOOD *Br and Aus, Am and Aus* **hu·mor** /£'hjuː·məʳ, $-mɚ/ *n* [U] the state of your feelings; mood • *You seem* **in** *(a) very good humour today.* • *We finally decided who was going to have what part in the play, but there was a certain amount of bad humour about it.* • *She's in* **no** *humour* (=is not willing) **to** *be argued with today.* [+ to infinitive] • (KOR) (PL)

hu·mour *obj Br and Aus, Am and Aus* **hu·mor** /£'hjuː·məʳ, $-mɚ/ *v* [T] • *Philip's in rather a bad mood today, you'd better humour him* (=agree to his wishes so that he does not complain).

-hu·moured *Br and Aus* /£-'hjuː·məd, ˌ--, $-mɚd/, *Am and Aus* **-hu·mored** *combining form* • *Despite the bitter memories, the election campaign has been remarkably peaceful, even* **good**-*humoured.*

hump LUMP /hʌmp/ *n* [C] a large round raised lump or part • *The car swerved when it hit a hump in the road.* • A hump is also a round raised part on a person's or animal's back: *Some types of camel have two humps and others have one.* ○ *The humps that old ladies sometimes have are caused by bone disease.* See also HUMPBACKED. • *It's been a lot of hard work but I think we're* **over the hump** (=past the most difficult part of an activity) *now.*

hump *obj* CARRY /hʌmp/ *v* [T always + adv/prep] *infml* to carry or lift (something heavy) with difficulty • *My back really aches after humping those heavy boxes around all day.*

hump *(obj)* HAVE SEX /hʌmp/ *v* [I/T] *taboo slang* to have sex (with)

hump ANGER /hʌmp/ *n* [U] **the hump** *Br and Aus infml* an annoyed and unhappy mood • *Cath's really* **got** *the hump* (=is offended) *since you told her she looked fat in those jeans!* • *Oh, you've really* **got** *the hump* (=you are annoyed) *tonight, haven't you!* • *They wouldn't let him into the bar and it* **gave** *him the right hump* (=made him annoyed)*!*

hump·backed /'hʌmp·bækt/ *adj* (of an animal) having a round raised part on its back • *A camel is an example of a humpbacked animal.*

hump·backed bridge /'hʌmp·bækt/, **hump·back bridge** *n* [C] a small steep road bridge • PIC **Bridge**

humph /hʌmpf/ *exclamation often humorous* a short deep sound made with the lips closed, expressing (pretended) annoyance or dissatisfaction • *Humph, I see you've got yourself some lunch and you haven't made any for the rest of us!* • *Don't invite me, then! Humph, see if I care!*

hu·mus /ˈhjuː·məs/ *n* [U] dark earth made of ORGANIC material such as decayed leaves and plants • *Soil which contains a lot of humus is more fertile than that which only has a little.*

Hun /hʌn/ *n* [C] a member of a group of people from Asia who attacked Europe in the 300s and 400s A.D. • *(dated)* Hun is also an offensive word for a German person.

hunch IDEA /hʌntʃ/ *n* [C] an idea which is based on feeling and for which there is no proof • *I* **had** *a hunch* **that** *you'd be here.* [+ *that* clause] • *Sometimes you have to be prepared to* **act on/follow/play** *a hunch.* • *Few people are willing to stake their reputation on a hunch.*

hunch *(obj)* BEND /hʌntʃ/ *v* to lean forward with your shoulders raised or to bend (your back and shoulders) into a rounded shape • *We hunched round the fire to keep warm.* [I] • *Stand up straight and don't hunch your back.* [T] • *She hunched* **(up)** *her shoulders and wrapped her coat around her to keep out the rain.* [T/M]

hunched /hʌntʃt/ *adj* • *You'll get a backache if you sit with hunched shoulders.* • *She sat like a frightened child, hunched* **(up)** *in a corner.*

hunch·back /ˈhʌntʃ·bæk/ *n* [C] *dated* (a person who has) a back with a large round lump on it, either because of illness or age • *In the film 'Jean de Florette', Jean is a/has a hunchback.* • *"The Hunchback of Notre-Dame"* (title of a book by Victor Hugo, 1831)

hunch·backed /ˈhʌntʃ·bækt/ *adj*

hun·dred /ˈhʌn·drəd/ *determiner, n, pronoun pl* **hundred** or **hundreds** (the number) 100 • *ninety-eight, ninety-nine, a/one hundred, a hundred and one* • *We've driven a/one hundred miles in the last two hours.* • *"How many children are there in the school?" "About three hundred."* • *That dress must have cost hundreds* **(of** *pounds).* • *(fig.) If I've told you once, I've told you a hundred times* (= very often) *not to do that!* • *(fig.) There were hundreds* (= a lot) **of** *people at the pool today.* • *(fig.) I agree with you a/one hundred* **per cent** (= completely). • *(fig.) I'm better than I was last week but I'm still not (feeling) a hundred* **per cent** (= I'm not completely well). • *"Letting a hundred flowers blossom and a hundred schools of thought contend"* (from a speech by Mao Zedong, 1957)

HUNDRED, THOUSAND, MILLION

Numbers like 103 or 100000 are usually said using 'a': *a hundred and three; a hundred thousand.* This is also true for larger units: *a thousand and one; a million dollars.*

These numbers can be read using 'one' for emphasis or in order to be exact:
Last year three hundred people came but this year we only saw one hundred.
He reached a speed of 143mph (one hundred . . .)

In American English there is often no 'and' after 'hundred': *(Am) six hundred twenty-seven.*

The plural form *hundreds* can be used to give an approximate number: *Hundreds of people disappear every year.* • *The number of wild rhinos is thought to be* **in the** *hundreds.*

hun·dredth /ˈhʌn·drətθ/ *pronoun, n, adj, adv* [not gradable] • *He is now ranked one (Br also* **a***) hundredth in world tennis.* • *She has knocked one/***a** *hundredth* **of** *a second off the world record.* • *1991 was the two hundredth anniversary of Mozart's death.* • *(fig.) This is the hundredth time I've told you* (= I've told you many times) *not to do that.*

hun·dred·weight /ˈhʌn·drəd·weɪt/ *(abbreviation* **cwt***) n* [C] *pl* **hundredweight** a measure of weight equal to 50·80 kilograms in Britain or 45·36 kilograms in the USA • *We ordered a hundredweight* **of** *coal.*

hung HANG /hʌŋ/ *past simple of* HANG

hung EQUAL /hʌŋ/ *adj* [not gradable] having an equal or nearly equal number of members with opposing opinions, so that no decisions can be made • *The general election in Britain was expected to result in a hung* **parliament**, *but in fact, the Conservatives had a small overall majority.* • *We have a hung* **jury**, *so a new trial will have to be held.*

hun·ger FOOD /£ˈhʌŋ·gəʳ, $-gɚ/ *n* [U] the uncomfortable or painful feeling in your stomach caused by the need for or lack of food • *In the middle of the meeting, her stomach rumbled with hunger.* • *I can't believe that that enormous meal wasn't enough to* **satisfy** *your hunger.* • *All over the world, people are dying of hunger* (= lack of food) *every day.* • *He works for an organization which tries to alleviate world hunger.* • *I often suffer from hunger* **pangs** (= have the feeling of needing something to eat) *in the middle of the afternoon.* • *The prisoners have gone* **on (a) hunger strike** (= are refusing to eat) *to protest about prison conditions.* • *Altogether there are ten* **hunger strikers** *in the prison.*

hun·gry /ˈhʌŋ·gri/ *adj* **-ier, -iest** • *The children are always hungry* (= want something to eat) *when they get home from school.* • *There are too many hungry people* (= people without enough food) *in the world.* • *Digging the garden is hungry* **work** (= causes the need for food). • *She often* **goes** *hungry herself* (= doesn't eat) *so that her children can have enough to eat.*

hun·gri·ly /ˈhʌŋ·grɪ·li/ *adv* • *They sat down and ate hungrily.*

hun·ger DESIRE /£ˈhʌŋ·gəʳ, $-gɚ/ *n* [U] a strong wish or desire • *Kate has a real hunger* **for** *adventure.* • *I can't understand why he seems to have no hunger* **for** *knowledge* (= does not seem interested in learning things).

hun·ger /£ˈhʌŋ·gəʳ, $-gɚ/ *v* [I] • *I hunger* **for** your touch. • *George has always hungered* **after** *power.* • *She hungered* (= wanted very much) **to** *see him again.* [+ *to* infinitive]

hun·gry /ˈhʌŋ·gri/ *adj* **-ier, -iest** • *Joanne is so hungry* **for** *success* (= wants it so much) *that she'll do anything to achieve it.*

-hun·gry /-ˌhʌŋ·gri/ *combining form* • *power-hungry* • *cash-hungry*

hun·gri·ly /ˈhʌŋ·grɪ·li/ *adv* • *He looked at her hungrily* (= showing desire).

hung-o·ver /£ˌhʌŋˈəʊ·vəʳ, $-ˈoʊ·vɚ/ *adj* [after v] feeling ill with a bad pain in the head and often wanting to vomit after having drunk too much alcohol • *That was a great party last night, but I'm (feeling) really hung-over this morning.* • See also HANGOVER ILLNESS.

hunk PIECE /hʌŋk/ *n* [C] a large thick piece, esp. of food • *a hunk* **of** *bread/cheese/meat*

hunk MAN /hʌŋk/ *n* [C] *infml approving* a large strong man, esp. one who is attractive • *Who was that gorgeous hunk you were with last night?* • *Joe is a real hunk* **of a man.**

hunk·y /ˈhʌŋ·ki/ *adj* **-ier, -iest** *infml usually approving* • *I like my men to have really hunky* **bodies.** • *He's so hunky.*

hunk·er down /£ˈhʌŋ·kəʳ, $-kɚ/ *v adv* [I] *Am* to sit down on your heels • *We hunkered down round the campfire, toasting marshmallows.* • *(fig.) The press have hunkered down for the night outside the palace, waiting for news of the royal birth.*

hunk·y do·ry /£ˈhʌŋ·kiˌdɔː·ri, $-ˌdɔːr·i/ *adj* [after v] *dated infml* (esp. of a situation) very satisfactory and pleasant • *You can't lose your temper with everyone like that one minute, and expect* **everything/things** *to be* **(all)** *hunky dory the next.*

hunt *(obj)* CHASE /hʌnt/ *v* to chase and catch and kill (an animal or bird) for food, sport or profit • *Some animals hunt at night.* [I] • *Cats like to hunt mice and birds.* [T] • *When lion cubs are young, the mother stays with them while the father hunts* **for** *food.* [I] • *The Kung San people of the Kalahari Desert live mainly by hunting and gathering.* [I] • *They like to hunt/go hunting* (= chase and kill animals for sport) *at weekends.* [I] • In Britain, when people hunt they chase and kill FOXES using dogs and riding on horses. [I] • *In the US, people often wear brightly coloured hats when they go hunting deer so that they can be seen.* [T] • *Elephants are dying out because they are being hunted for the ivory from their tusks.* [T]

hunt /hʌnt/ *n* [C] • *After a long hunt* (= chasing it for a long time), *the lion finally tracked down a deer.* • *We're going* **on** *a deer hunt/fox hunt/bear hunt.* • A hunt is also a group of people who meet regularly in order to chase and kill animals, esp. (in Britain) FOXES: *They are members of the local hunt.* • A **hunt saboteur** is a person who tries to stop a hunt, especially a FOX hunt, because they think it is cruel to animals.

hunt·ed /£ˈhʌn·tɪd, $-t̬ɪd/ *adj* • *(fig.) Carla always has such a hunted* **look/expression** (= looks frightened and anxious).

hunt·er /£ˈhʌn·tər, $-t̬ɚ/ *n* [C] • A hunter is a person or an animal that hunts animals for food or for sport *Animals in the cat family are hunters.* ○ *Hunters kill crocodiles and alligators so that their skins can be made into shoes and handbags.* • Hunter is sometimes used as a combining form: *a fox-hunter* • A hunter is also a type of horse, esp. one used in hunting animals.

hunt·ing /£ˈhʌn·tɪŋ, $-t̬ɪŋ/ *n* [U] • *hunting dogs* • *a hunting rifle* • *a hunting expedition* • *Do you think hunting* (= chasing and killing animals for sport) *should be banned?* • In Britain, hunting is the chasing and killing of FOXES for sport, using dogs and riding horses.

hunts·man (*pl* **-men**), **hunts·wo·man** (*pl* **-women**) /ˈhʌnts·mən, -ˌwʊm·ən/ *n* [C] • A huntsman or huntswoman is a person who chases and kills animals, esp. (in Britain) FOXES for sport, using dogs and riding on horses.

hunt (*obj*) [SEARCH] /hʌnt/ *v* to search (for something or someone); to try to find (something or someone) • *I've hunted all over the place, but I can't find that book.* [I] • *Police are hunting the terrorists who planted the bomb.* [T] • *All the people in the area turned out to hunt* **for** *the missing child.* [I] • *I've hunted* **high and low** (= looked everywhere) **for** *my gloves.* [I] • *Detectives have finally managed to hunt* **down** (= succeed in finding after much effort) *the killer.* [M] • *I'll try and hunt* **out** *those old photographs* (= search for them although I do not know where they are) *for you.* [M] • *He's studying his family history, so he spends all his time in the library, hunting* **up** *references* (= looking for them, although they are difficult to find). [M] • *They have spent months* **house-/job-***hunting* (= looking for a house/a job). • *This market is a wonderful* **hunting ground for** *people who like buying second-hand books* (= a lot can be found there). • *(infml humorous) Before I finally head off for* **the happy hunting ground (in the sky)** (= before I die), *I'd like to feel that I've done something with my life.*

hunt /hʌnt/ *n* [C] • *After a long hunt* (= looking for a long time), *we finally found a house we liked.* • *The hunt* **for** *the injured climber continued throughout the night.* • *Police are* **on the** *hunt* (= searching) **for** *the kidnappers.* • **The** *hunt* **is on** (= the search has started) **for** *a successor to Sir James Gordon.*

-hunt·er /£ˈhʌn·tər, $-t̬ɚ/ *combining form* • *a job-/house-/bargain-hunter* (= a person who is looking for a job/a house/something cheap to buy) • See also HEADHUNTER.

hurd·le /£ˈhɜː·dl̩, $ˈhɜːr-/ *n* [C] a frame or fence for jumping over in a race • *The runner who had been expected to win fell at the last hurdle.* • *We all know that he's a fast horse but what is less certain is how he will take the hurdles.* • *He* **cleared** *all the hurdles easily and raced to the finishing line.* • *(fig.) There are a lot of hurdles* (= difficulties) *to be* **overcome** *before the contract can be signed.* • [PIC] **Sports**

hurd·le (*obj*) /£ˈhɜː·dl̩, $ˈhɜːr-/ *v* • To hurdle is to run in a race in which there are hurdles to be jumped over, or to jump over something while running: *I started to hurdle while I was at college.* [I] • *He hurdled the gate and scrambled up the hill.* [T]

hurd·ler /£ˈhɜː·dlər, $ˈhɜːr·dlɚ/ *n* [C] • *She's even better as a 110 metre hurdler than she is at long jump.* • A **champion hurdler** is a horse which runs in and often wins races in which there are hurdles to be jumped over

hurd·les /£ˈhɜː·dl̩z, $ˈhɜːr-/ *pl n* • *The American won the 400 metres hurdles* (= the 400 metres race over hurdles).

hur·dy gurd·y /£ˈhɜː·diˌgɜː·di, $ˈhɜːr·diˌgɜːr·di/ *n* [C] a musical instrument which is played by turning a handle, causing a small wheel to be rubbed against a set of strings

hurl *obj* /£hɜːl, $hɜːrl/ *v* [T] to throw (something) violently • *In a fit of temper he hurled the book* **across** *the room.* • *Rebel youths hurled stones* **at** *the soldiers.* • *(fig.) I'm not going to stand here and listen while you hurl* (= shout violently) **abuse/insults at** *me like that!* • *(fig.) After his wife's death, he hurled him***self into** *his work* (= worked extremely hard and did nothing else). • *(fig.) It's embarrassing the way she's hurling her***self at** (= is clearly expressing strong sexual interest in) *him.*

hur·ly–burl·y /£ˈhɜː·liˌbɜː·li, $ˈhɜːr·liˌbɜːr-/ *n* [U] noisy activity • *We got fed-up with the hurly-burly* **of** *city life, so we moved to the country.* • *"When the hurly-burly's done, / When the battle's lost and won"* (Shakespeare, Macbeth 1.1)

hur·ray /həˈreɪ, hʊ-/, **hoo·ray**, **hur·rah** /həˈrɑː, hʊ-/ *exclamation* used to express excitement, pleasure or approval • *"It's Katie's party on Saturday." "Hurray!"* • *Hurray* **for** *Santa Claus!* • See also HIP [APPROVAL].

hur·ri·cane /£ˈhʌr·ɪ·kən, -keɪn, $ˈhɜːr-/ *n* [C] a violent wind which has a circular movement, esp. found in the W Atlantic Ocean • *The state of Florida was* **hit** *by a hurricane that did serious damage.* • *Hurricane force* (= Very strong) *winds are expected tonight.* • A **hurricane lamp** (also **storm lantern**) is a light fuelled by PARAFFIN which has a strong glass cover to protect the flame from wind.

hur·ry (*obj*) /£ˈhʌr·i, $ˈhɜːr-/ *v* to (cause to) move or act quickly • *We'll have to hurry or we'll be late.* [I] • *She hurried* **to** *answer the telephone.* [+ *to* infinitive] • *I hate to hurry you, but I have to leave in a few minutes.* [T] • *He was hurried* (= taken quickly) *to hospital with a suspected heart attack.* [T] • *Don't hurry your food* (= eat it too quickly). [T] • *When I do something I like to take my time and do it properly, rather than hurry* (= do it too quickly) *and make mistakes.* [I] • *I refuse to be hurried* **into** *a decision* (= to be forced to make a decision too quickly). [T] • *Hurry* **along** *now* (= move quickly). [I] • *After spending her lunch hour shopping, she hurried* **back** (= returned quickly) *to work.* [I] • *Having made the criticism, the minister hurried* **on** (= quickly continued speaking) **to** *say that it did not apply to all schools.* [I] • To hurry **(up)** or hurry something **up** means to act or do something more quickly than you had been doing it: *Hurry (up), or we'll miss the train.* [I] ○ *Could you hurry the children up, or their dinner will get cold.* [M] ○ *I'd like you to hurry up your report, please.* [M]

hur·ry /£ˈhʌr·i, $ˈhɜːr-/ *n* [U] • *We left* **in** *such a hurry* (= so quickly) *that we forgot our tickets.* • *"What's (all) the hurry (for)/Why (all) the hurry* (= Why are you acting or moving so quickly) *– we've got plenty of time."* • *"Can you wait a few minutes?" "Yes, I'm not* **in** *a hurry/I'm not in any hurry/I'm* **in** *no hurry* (= I can wait)*."* • *"I'll let you have this back next week." "That's all right, there's no* **(great)** *hurry/there isn't any* **(great)** *hurry* (= no need to do it quickly)*."* • *I made a mistake adding up these figures because I did it* **in a hurry** (= too quickly and without taking enough care). • *Are you* **in a** *hurry* (= anxious or eager) **to** *leave?* [+ *to* infinitive] • *I wouldn't go there again* **in a hurry** (= willingly). • *She's* **in no hurry/not in any hurry** (= she doesn't want) **to** *see him again after the way he treated her.* • *We won't forget your kindness* **in a hurry** (= quickly).

hur·ried /£ˈhʌr·id, $ˈhɜːr-/ *adj* • Something that is hurried is done too quickly: *We left early, after a hurried breakfast.* ○ *I'm sorry this is such a hurried note.* • *She always seems so hurried* (= she seems to do things quickly because she has such a lot to do).

hur·ried·ly /£ˈhʌr·id·li, $ˈhɜːr-/ *adv* • *They left hurriedly when they were asked for identification.* • *The party was a rather hurriedly arranged affair so we didn't have time to ask everyone.*

hurt (*obj*) /£hɜːt, $hɜːrt/ *v past* **hurt** to (cause to) feel physical or emotional pain or to cause an injury • *Tell me where it hurts.* [I] • *My head hurts.* [I] • *Ow, that hurts!* [I] • *She says that her ear hurts her.* [T] • *Emma hurt her back when she fell off her horse.* [T] • *Joe, be more gentle with the dog or you'll hurt him!* [T] • *Several people were* **seriously/badly** *hurt in the explosion.* [T] • *I didn't mean to hurt your* **feelings** (= cause you emotional pain). [T] • *He was* **very/deeply/extremely** *hurt by* (= suffered emotional pain because of) *her criticisms of him.* [T] • *(infml)* **It won't/wouldn't hurt you to** *do the ironing for once* (= You should do the ironing because you never usually do it). • To hurt also means to cause harm or difficulty: *A lot of businesses are being hurt by the current high interest rates.* [T] ○ *These allegations have* **seriously** *hurt her reputation.* [T] ○ *(infml) One more drink won't hurt* (= won't cause any harm). [I] ○ *(infml) Hard work* **never** *hurt anyone* (= did anyone any harm). [T] ○ *(infml) Come and sit down – it won't/wouldn't hurt* (= it will not cause any harm) **to** *leave cutting the lawn till tomorrow.* [+ *to* infinitive] ○ *(infml)* **It never hurts** (= It is a good idea) **to** *check the flight departure time before you go to the airport.* • *"If it isn't hurting, it isn't working"* (John Major on his economic policy, 1989) • [LP] **Feelings and pains**

hurt /£hɜːt, $hɜːrt/ *adj* • *Are you hurt* (= feeling pain or suffering from an injury)? • *We found a hurt dog lying in the road, and took it to the vet.* • *I feel very hurt by* (= am suffering emotional pain because of) *what you said.* • *"That was very unkind," he said in a hurt voice* (= a voice expressing emotional pain). • *She's suffering from hurt* (= damaged) *pride.*

hurt /£hɜːt, $hɜːrt/ *n* • Hurt is emotional pain: *She could not disguise the* **deep** *hurt she felt* [U] • *He had suffered many hurts, but this was by far the worst.* [C]

hurt·ful /£'hɜːt·fəl, $'hɜːrt-/ *adj* • Hurtful means causing emotional pain: *That was a very hurtful remark!* • *How can you be so hurtful?*

hurt·ful·ly /£'hɜːt·fəl·i, $'hɜːrt-/ *adv*

hurt·ful·ness /£'hɜːt·fəl·nəs, $'hɜːrt-/ *n* [U]

hurt·le /£'hɜː·tl̩, $'hɜːr·t̬l̩/ *v* [I always + adv/prep] to move very fast, esp. in what seems a dangerous way • *He had no brakes on his bicycle and hurtled down the hill, laughing.* • *The truck was hurtling along at breakneck speed.*

hus·band MAN /'hʌz·bənd/ *n* [C] the man to whom a woman is married • *She came to stay for a week without her husband.* • *She says she's looking for a rich husband* (= she wants to marry a wealthy man). • *She's on her third husband* (= she has been married three times). • *Although never married, they lived together* **as husband and wife** (= as if married) *for fifty years.* • *"My husband and I"* (Queen Elizabeth II in various speeches, 1953-) • LP› **Relationships** PIC› **Family tree**

hus·band *obj* SAVE /'hʌz·bənd/ *v* [T] *fml* to take care of (something) and save it carefully • *Their money has not been wisely husbanded.*

hus·band·ry /'hʌz·bən·dri/ *n* [U] *fml* • *The proper husbandry* (= care and management) *of the forests concerns everyone.* • *The tablecloth, mended many times, showed the family's good husbandry* (= taking care of their possessions).

hus·band·ry /'hʌz·bən·dri/ *n* [U] farming • *He gave a lecture on crop and animal husbandry.*

hush /hʌʃ/ *n* [U] a sudden calm silence • *There was a* **deathly** *hush after she made the announcement.* • *An* **expectant** *hush* **descended/fell** *on the waiting crowd* (= the people suddenly became silent). • *The speaker dropped his voice* **to a hush** (= began to speak very quietly). • *Let's have some hush, please!* (= Quiet, please!) • *(infml)* If something is **hush-hush**, it is kept secret from people: *I can't tell you anything about it – it's all hush-hush.* ○ *The police were involved in a hush-hush operation to break a drugs ring.* • *(infml)* **Hush money** is money that is given to someone to keep something they know secret: *She claimed that the minister had offered her hush money to keep their child a secret.*

hush /hʌʃ/ *exclamation* • *Hush! You'll wake the baby!* • *"Hush little baby don't say a word"* (traditional song) • *"Hush!, Hush! Whisper who dares!/Christopher Robin is saying his prayers"* (from the poem *Vespers* by A.A.Milne, 1924)

hushed /hʌʃt/ *adj* • *In the hushed, packed hall she stood up to speak.* • *People still speak in hushed* **tones** (= very quietly) *of the murders.*

hush up *obj*, **hush** *obj* **up** *v adv* [M] *disapproving* to try to prevent people from discovering (particular facts) • *The mayor tried to hush up the fact that he had been in prison.* • *The incident has been hushed up for twenty years.*

husk /hʌsk/ *n* [C] the dry outer covering of some seeds

husk·y VOICE /'hʌs·ki/ *adj* **-ier, -iest** (esp. of a person's voice) low and rough, often in an attractive way, or because of emotion or illness • *"Hello, honey," she said, in her sexy, husky voice.* • *Her voice was husky* **with** *emotion/fatigue/anger.* • *The throat infection made his voice sound husky.*

husk·y STRONG /'hʌs·ki/ *adj Am* big and strong • *Doctors said the husky teenager survived because none of the bullets punctured vital organs.*

husk·y DOG /'hʌs·ki/ *n* [C] a large, furry dog which is used for pulling SLEDGES over the snow

hus·sy /'hʌs·i, 'hʌz-/ *n* [C] *esp. humorous* a woman or girl who is sexually immoral • *"You asked him out? Oh, you* **brazen/shameless** *hussy, you!"*

hust·ings /'hʌs·tɪŋz/ *pl n* **the hustings** the political activities and speeches that happen before an election and are intended to win votes • *The President's appearance* **on/at** *the hustings might do more harm than good.* • *He was one of the great hustings performers.*

hus·tle *obj* PUSH /'hʌs·l̩/ *v* [T always + adv/prep] to make (someone) move quickly by pushing or pulling them along • *After giving his speech, Johnson was hustled out of the hall by bodyguards.* • Ⓙ

hus·tle PERSUADE /'hʌs·l̩/ *v infml* to try very hard, using a lot of different methods, to persuade people to give you something • *You've got to hustle* (= be good at persuading people) *if you want to get to the top.* [I] • *At 20, he managed to hustle his first recording deal* (= to get it by persuading people). [T] • Ⓙ

hus·tler /£'hʌs·lər, $-lɚ/ *n* [C] • *You've got to be a hustler* (= be good at getting what you want) *if you want to get ahead.* • *(esp. Am)* A hustler is also someone who tries to obtain money by dishonest methods, or a PROSTITUTE: *He was a pool hall hustler who tricked people into losing money.* ○ *The street was full of hustlers, drug addicts and pimps.*

hus·tle NOISE /'hʌs·l̩/ *n* [U] a lot of noise and activity • *They love the hustle* **and bustle** *of the marketplace.* • Ⓙ

hut /hʌt/ *n* [C] a small, simple building • *The people of the village live in neat mud huts with grass roofs.* • *We spent the night in a mountain hut, continuing our climb the next day.* • *There was a row of beach huts in front of the hotel.* • Ⓙ

hutch /hʌtʃ/ *n* [C] a box made of wood with a wire front where small animals such as rabbits are kept

hy·a·cinth /'haɪ·ə·sɪnθ/ *n* [C] a pleasant-smelling plant with a lot of small flowers that grow close together around one thick stem • *Plant hyacinth bulbs in a bowl of earth for winter flowers.*

hy·ae·na /haɪ'iː·nə/ *n* [C] a HYENA

hy·brid /'haɪ·brɪd/ *n* [C] a plant or animal that has been produced from two different types of plant or animal, esp. to get better characteristics, or anything that is a mixture of two very different things • *The garden strawberry is a large-fruited hybrid.* • *At school he took up the cello, a kind of hybrid between a violin and a double bass.* • *He is a rare hybrid – a respected academic who pleases the masses.*

Hyde /haɪd/ See JEKYLL AND HYDE

hy·dra /'haɪ·drə/ *n* [C] in ancient Greek stories, a creature with many heads that grew again when cut off, or, more generally, a difficult problem that keeps returning

hy·dran·gea /haɪ'dreɪn·dʒə/ *n* [C] a bush on which grow round groups of pink, white or blue flowers

hy·drant /'haɪ·drənt/ *n* [C] a vertical pipe, usually at the side of the road, that is connected to the main water system of a town and from which water can be obtained esp. for dealing with fires • *Children were playing in the water that gushed from an open fire hydrant.*

hy·drate /'haɪ·dreɪt/ *n* [C] *specialized* a chemical that contains water

hy·draul·ic /£haɪ'drɒl·ɪk, $-'drɑː·lɪk/ *adj* [not gradable] operated by or involving the pressure of water or some other liquid • *The fire officers used a hydraulic platform to get to the roof.*

hy·draul·ics /£haɪ'drɒl·ɪks, $-'drɑː·lɪks/ *pl n* • Hydraulics are a system of using water to produce power: *The hydraulics failed and the digger stopped.*

hy·dro– WATER /£ˌhaɪ·drəʊ-, $-droʊ-/ *combining form* connected with or using the power of water

hy·dro– GAS /£ˌhaɪ·drəʊ-, $-droʊ-/ *combining form* showing the presence of HYDROGEN

hy·dro·car·bon /£ˌhaɪ·drəʊ'kɑː·bən, $-droʊ'kɑːr-/ *n* [C] a chemical combination of HYDROGEN and carbon, such as in oil or PETROL • *We must cut cars' fuel consumption and hydrocarbon emissions.*

hy·dro·chlor·ic ac·id /£ˌhaɪd·rə'klɒr·ɪk, $-'klɔːr-/ *n* [U] an acid containing HYDROGEN and CHLORINE

hy·dro·el·ec·tric /£ˌhaɪ·drəʊ·ɪ'lek·trɪk, $-droʊ-/ *adj* [not gradable] relating to or producing electricity by the force of fast moving water such as rivers or WATERFALLS • *a hydroelectric power station* • PIC› **Energy**

hy·dro·el·ec·tri·ci·ty /£ˌhaɪ·drəʊ·ɪ·lek'trɪs·ɪ·ti, $-droʊ·ɪ·lek'trɪs·ə·t̬i/ *n* [U]

hy·dro·foil /£'haɪ·drəʊ·fɔɪl, $-droʊ-/ *n* [C] a large boat which is able to travel quickly above the surface of the water on wing-like structures • *You can travel by ferry, hovercraft or hydrofoil.*

hy·dro·gen /'haɪ·drɪ·dʒən/ *n* [U] the lightest gas with no colour, taste or smell, that combines with oxygen to form water • The **hydrogen bomb** (also **H-bomb**) is a nuclear bomb which explodes when the central parts of its hydrogen atoms join together.

hy·drol·y·sis /£haɪ'drɒl·ə·sɪs, $-'drɑː·lə-/ *n* [U] *specialized* a chemical reaction in which one substance reacts with water to produce another

hy·dro·pho·bi·a /ˌhaɪ·drəʊ'fəʊ·bi·ə, $-droʊ'foʊ-/ *n* [U] *specialized* strong fear of drinking and of water, often as a sign of RABIES, or *(dated)* the disease of RABIES itself

hy·dro·plane /£'haɪ·drəʊ·pleɪn, $-droʊ-/ *v* [I] *Am for* AQUAPLANE

hy·dro·pon·ics /£ˌhaɪ·drəʊ'pɒn·ɪks, $-droʊ'pɑː·nɪks/ *n* [U] the method of growing plants in water to which special chemicals are added, rather than growing them in earth • *Hydroponics is used in large commercial greenhouses.*

hy·dro·pow·er /£'haɪd·rəʊ·paʊər, $-roʊ·paʊr/ *n* [U] producing electricity by the force of fast moving water; HYDROELECTRIC power

hy·dro·the·ra·py /£ˌhaɪ·drəʊ'θer·ə·pi, $-droʊ-/ *n* [U] a method of treating people with particular diseases or injuries by making them exercise in water • *Hydrotherapy and swimming enable people to exercise without straining their bodies.* • *They recommended hydrotherapy treatment for arthritis.*

hy·e·na /haɪ'iː·nə/ *n* [C] a wild animal from Africa and Asia that looks like a dog, hunts in groups, and makes a sound similar to an unpleasant human laugh • PIC **Dogs**

hy·giene /'haɪ·dʒiːn/ *n* [U] the degree to which people keep themselves or their surroundings clean, esp. to prevent disease • *Poor standards of hygiene mean that the disease spreads fast.* • *He doesn't care much about* **personal** *hygiene* (= washing his body).

hy·gien·ic /£haɪ'dʒiː·nɪk, $-'dʒen-/ *adj* • *It isn't hygienic* (= clean) *to let the cat sit on the dining table.*

hy·gien·ist /haɪ'dʒiː·nɪst, $-'dʒen·ɪst/, **den·tal hy·gien·ist** *n* [C] a person who works with a DENTIST and cleans people's teeth

hy·ing /'haɪ·ɪŋ/ *pres part of* HIE

hy·men /'haɪ·mən/ *n* [C] a thin piece of skin that covers part of a girl's or woman's vagina and breaks esp. when she has sex for the first time

hymn /hɪm/ *n* [C] a song of praise that Christians sing to God • *The wedding service began with the hymn 'The Lord's My Shepherd'.* • *We shall now sing a hymn* **to** (= praising) *nature.* • CS RUS

hym·nal /'hɪm·nəl/ *n* [C] *fml or dated* • A hymnal is a book containing HYMNS.

hype /haɪp/ *n* [U] *infml* a way of making something or someone sound very important or exciting by attracting a lot of public attention • *Hollywood times its blockbuster films to come out at Christmas, then deluges television and radio with advertising hype.* • *It's difficult to ignore the hype surrounding the book.*

hype *obj* /haɪp/ *v* [T] *infml* • *Other books are being hyped by their publishers, but this one really deserves to be read.* • *People's fears of AIDS were hyped* **up** (= increased) *by the newspapers.* [M]

hyped up /haɪpt/ *adj infml* emotionally excited, nervous or anxious • *I was feeling very hyped up after the exam.* • *Don't get so hyped up* **about** *what he said – he didn't really mean it.* • *The players were all hyped up* **for** (= eager for) *the match.*

hy·per- TOO MUCH /£'haɪ·pər-, $-pə-/ *combining form* having too much of the stated quality • *hyper-ambitious* • *hyper-aware* • *hyper-expensive*

hy·per EXCITABLE /£'haɪ·pər, $-pə/ *adj infml* too excited and out of control • *Chocolate makes their youngest child hyper and bad-tempered.* • *When he's frustrated he goes completely hyper.* • See also HYPERACTIVE.

hy·per·ac·tive /£ˌhaɪ·pə'ræk·tɪv, $-pə'æk·t̬ɪv/ *adj* (esp. of children) always in a state of activity or excitement; unable to stay calm or quiet • *Some food additives can make children hyperactive.* • *Hyperactive children often have poor concentration and require very little sleep.* • See also HYPER EXCITABLE.

hy·per·bo·la /£haɪ'pɜː·bəl·ə, $-'pɜːr-/ *n* [C] *specialized* a widening curve in the shape which you get when you cut through a cone from a point up on one side down to the base on the other side

hy·per·bo·le /£haɪ'pɜː·bəl·i, $-'pɜːr-/ *n* [U] a way of speaking or writing that makes someone or something sound bigger, better, more, etc. than they are • *The blurb on the back of the book was full of the usual hyperbole – enthralling, fascinating and so on.*

hy·per·bol·ic /£ˌhaɪ·pə'bɒl·ɪk, $-pə'bɑː·lɪk/ *adj* [not gradable] • *Politicians are fond of hyperbolic phrases like 'terrorist outrages' and 'murderous deeds'.*

hy·per·crit·i·cal /£ˌhaɪ·pə'krɪt·ɪ·kəl, $-pə'krɪt̬-/ *adj* [not gradable] too eager to find mistakes in everything; extremely critical

hy·per·in·fla·tion /£ˌhaɪ·pə·rɪn'fleɪʃ·ən, $-pə·-ɪn-/ *n* [U] a condition where the price of everything in a national economy goes out of control and increases very quickly • *In countries where there is hyperinflation, the value of the paper money in your hand decreases by the day or even by the hour.*

hy·per·mark·et /£'haɪ·pəˌmɑː·kɪt, $-pəˌmɑːr-/ *n* [C] a very large shop, usually outside the centre of town • *We drove to the hypermarket on the outskirts of the town.*

hy·per·sen·si·tive /£ˌhaɪ·pə'sent·sɪ·tɪv, $-pə'sent·sə·t̬ɪv/ *adj* [not gradable] extremely influenced, changed or damaged by physical conditions or social situations • *Her damaged eye is hypersensitive* **to** *light.* • *He's hypersensitive* **about** *his height.*

hy·per·ten·sion /£ˌhaɪ·pə'ten·tʃən, $-pə-/ *n* [U] *specialized* a medical condition in which your blood pressure is extremely high • *We are conducting extensive research into treatments for hypertension and heart disease.*

hy·per·text /£'haɪ·pə·tekst, $-pə-/ *n* [U] *specialized* a way of joining words, pictures and sound within a computer program

hy·per·ven·ti·la·tion /£ˌhaɪ·pəˌven·tɪ'leɪ·ʃən, $-pəˌven·t̬əl'eɪ-/ *n* [U] *specialized* breathing too quickly and so causing too much oxygen to enter the blood • *Hyperventilation can be caused by fear or panic.*

hy·per·ven·ti·late /£ˌhaɪ·pə'ven·tɪ·leɪt, $-pə'ven·t̬əl·eɪt/ *v* [I] *specialized*

hy·phen /'haɪ·fən/ *n* [C] a short written or printed line that joins two words together, or shows that a word has been divided into two parts at the end of one line and the beginning of the next • *We put a hyphen between 'short' and 'sighted' to make the word 'short-sighted', which describes a person who cannot see things that are far away.* • Compare DASH LINE.

HYPHEN [-]

A hyphen is used to join part of a word at the end of one line with the other part which is continued on the next line. For example, *interest-* at the end of one line might be followed by *ing* at the beginning of the next line. A hyphen is also used to join together words to make a new combination. Hyphens can be used to form the following types of combinations:

- **with a preposition or adverb**
  The recent **build-up** *of soldiers is alarming.*
  The government plans a huge **sell-off** *of local airports.*
  Regular exercise gives a sense of health and **well-being**.
  This cassette player has a **built-in** *microphone.*
  Neither driver was injured in the **head-on** *collision.*
  The new theatre will be opened by a **well-known** *actor.*
- **with some combining forms** (shown underlined)
  He beat David Taylor 21-3 in a **one-sided** *game.*
  A **wide-eyed** *little boy looked up and asked for his autograph.*
  And this is is a photo of my **great-grandfather**.
- **with some prefixes** (especially in British usage)
  They bought a **pre-war** *house in the suburbs.*
  We are developing **non-nuclear** *sources of energy.*
  She is hoping to introduce more **anti-drug** *laws.*
  He's been working as a **self-employed** *builder.*
  There has been good **co-operation** *between parents and teachers.*
  I don't think you ever met Isabelle, my **ex-wife**.
- **some longer combinations**
  I'm no good at **do-it-yourself**: *I can't even paint a wall!*
  This new CD player uses **state-of-the-art** *digital technology.*
- **fractions and numbers**
  Nearly **two-thirds** *of the population.*
  twenty-three
  There were 6-8 (read as 'six to eight') *climbers in the team.*
- **with pairs of adjectives or nouns** (notice the line is longer)
  I need to get a decent **French–English** *dictionary.*
  They had a good **father–son** *relationship.*
  How much is a **London–Istanbul** *ticket?*

hy·phen·a·tion /ˌhaɪ·fᵊn'eɪʃ·ən/ *n* [U] • *the rules of hyphenation*

hy·phen·ate *obj* /'haɪ·fᵊn·eɪt/ *v* [T] • *Her surname, Taylor-Wood, is hyphenated.*

hyp·nos·is /£hɪp'nəʊ·sɪs, $-'noʊ-/ *n* [U] an artificially produced state of mind in which a person is more suggestible than at other times • **Under** *deep hypnosis she remembered the traumatic events of that night.*

hyp·no·tic /£hɪp'nɒt·ɪk, $-'nɑː·t̬ɪk/ *adj* • *She went into a hypnotic* **trance**. • *(fig.) The beat of the music was strangely hypnotic* (= made you feel as if you were being hypnotized).

hyp·no·tize *obj, Br and Aus usually* **-ise** /'hɪp·nə·taɪz/ *v* [T] • *She agreed to be hypnotized* (= put in the state of hypnosis) *to try to remember what had happened.* • *(fig.) I was hypnotized by his steely grey eyes* (= I felt as if I could not move).

hyp·no·ti·sm /£'hɪp·nə·tɪ·zᵊm, $-t̬ɪ-/ *n* [U] • *Some people try hypnotism to cure themselves of addictions.*

hyp·no·tist /£'hɪp·nə·tɪst, $-t̬ɪst/ *n* [C] • A hypnotist is a person who uses hypnosis as a form of treatment, or sometimes entertainment: *I went to a hypnotist to try to give up smoking.*

hyp·no·the·ra·py /£ˌhɪp·nəʊ'θer·ə·pi, $-noʊ-/ *n* [U] the use of HYPNOSIS to treat particular emotional problems

hyp·o·chon·dri·a /£ˌhaɪ·pəʊ'kɒn·dri·ə, $-poʊ'kɑːn-/ *n* [U] a state in which a person continually worries about their health without having any reason to do so • *She was worried that her doctor would accuse her of hypochondria.*

hyp·o·chon·dri·ac /£ˌhaɪ·pəʊ'kɒn·dri·æk, $-poʊ'kɑːn-/ *n, adj* • *She's a well-known hypochondriac, complaining of everything from a throbbing knee to a sore ear.* • *He has a certain hypochondriac tendency to exaggerate his illness.*

hyp·o·cri·sy /£hɪ'pɒk·rɪ·si, $-'pɑː·krə-/ *n* [U] the activity of pretending to believe or feel something that you do not • *She is annoyed by the hypocrisy of some governments which claim to support equal rights but never give women important government posts.*

hyp·o·crite /'hɪp·ə·krɪt/ *n* [C] • *He's a hypocrite* **to** *tell us not to smoke – he smokes himself!* [+ *to* infinitive]

hyp·o·crit·i·cal /£ˌhɪp·əʊ'krɪt·ɪ·kᵊl, $-ə'krɪt̬-/ *adj* • *Their accusations of corruption are hypocritical – they have been just as corrupt themselves.*

hyp·o·der·mic /£ˌhaɪ·pəʊ'dɜː·mɪk, $-poʊ'dɜːr-/ *adj* [not gradable] *specialized* (of medical tools) used to INJECT drugs under a person's skin • *a hypodermic needle* • *The HIV virus can be spread by sharing hypodermic syringes/hypodermics.*

hyp·o·gly·cae·mi·a, *esp. Am* **hyp·o·gly·ce·mi·a** /£ˌhaɪ·pəʊ·glaɪ'siː·mi·ə, $-poʊ-/ *n* [U] *specialized* a medical condition resulting from dangerously low levels of sugar in the blood • *The danger signs to look out for with hypoglycaemia include sweating, anxiety and cramps.* • *Rapid onset of hypoglycaemia can result in death.*

hyp·o·gly·caem·ic, *esp. Am* **hyp·o·gly·ce·mic** /£ˌhaɪ·pəʊ·glaɪ'siː·mɪk, $-poʊ-/ *adj* [not gradable] *specialized* • *As a diabetic she was accustomed to the occasional hypoglycaemic* **attack**.

hyp·ot·en·use /£haɪ'pɒt·ᵊn·juːz, $-'pɑː·t̬ə·nuːz/ *n* [C] *specialized* the longest side of any triangle which has one angle of 90°

hyp·o·ther·mi·a /£ˌhaɪ·pəʊ'θɜː·mi·ə, $-poʊ'θɜːr-/ *n* [U] a serious medical condition in which a person's body temperature falls below the usual level as a result of being in severe cold for a long time • *In this current cold spell, many old people are dying needlessly of hypothermia.*

hyp·oth·es·is /£haɪ'pɒθ·ə·sɪs, $-'pɑː·θə-/ *n* [C] *pl* **hypotheses** /£haɪ'pɒθ·ə·siːz, $-'pɑː·θə-/ an idea or explanation for something that is based on known facts but has not yet been proved • *Several hypotheses for global warming have been suggested.* • *Dr Elwood said the belief that milk could be harmful was based on the hypothesis* **that** *fat causes heart disease.* [+ *that* clause]

hy·po·the·size /£haɪ'pɒθ·ə·saɪz, $-'pɑː·θə-/ *v* [T] • *There's no point hypothesizing* **about** *how the world began, since we'll never know.*

hyp·o·thet·i·cal /£ˌhaɪ·pəʊ'θet·ɪ·kᵊl, $-poʊ'θet̬-/ *adj* • *This is only a hypothetical example* (= not one that really exists), *but it will help us to consider the problem.* • *When asked if there were any circumstances under which they would declare war, he dismissed such questions as* **purely** *hypothetical* (= it was not known whether a situation needing such a decision would happen).

hys·ter·ec·to·my /£ˌhɪs·tᵊr'ek·tə·mi, $-tə'rek·t̬ə-/ *n* [C] *medical* a medical operation to remove part or all of a woman's womb

hys·te·ri·a /£hɪ'stɪə·ri·ə, $-'stɪr·i-/ *n* [U] uncontrolled excitement, fear or anger • *One woman, close to hysteria, grabbed my arm.* • *Tabloid hysteria about the murders has increased public fears.* • Ⓙ

hys·te·ri·cal /hɪ'ster·ɪ·kᵊl/ *adj* • *Calm down, you're getting hysterical.* • *The police were accused of hysterical over-reaction.* • *The audience came close to hysterical laughter* (= laughing uncontrollably). • *(infml) I thought the play was hysterical* (= extremely amusing). • (PL) (RUS)

hys·te·ri·cally /hɪ'ster·ɪ·kli/ *adv* • *She started laughing/crying hysterically* (= without control).

hys·te·rics /hɪ'ster·ɪks/ *pl n* • If someone **has** hysterics or is **in** hysterics, they become uncontrollably angry, frightened or excited: *Convinced the plane was about to crash, many people were sobbing and* **in** *hysterics.* • *(infml) He's a brilliant comedian and has audiences everywhere* **in** *hysterics* (= laughing uncontrollably).

Hz *n* [C] *pl* **Hz** *specialized abbreviation for* HERTZ

I i

I [LETTER] (*pl* **I's**), **i** (*pl* **i's**) /aɪ/ *n* [C] the 9th letter of the English alphabet

I [NUMBER], **i** /aɪ/ *n* [C] the sign used in the Roman system for the number 1 and as part of the numbers 2 (ii), 3 (iii), 4 (iv), 6 (vi), 7 (vii), 8 (viii), and 9 (ix)

I [PERSON SPEAKING] /aɪ/ *pronoun* (used as the subject of a verb) the person speaking • *I can see the bus coming.* • *Am I to blame if he's late?* • *I want that. Please give it to me.* • *Well, I* **for one** (= I am certain that I) *won't stand for it.*

I·be·ri·an /£aɪ'bɪə·ri·ən, $-'bɪr·i-/ *adj* [not gradable] of Spain and Portugal • *the Iberian Peninsula*

ib·id /'ɪb·ɪd/ *adv* [not gradable] *specialized abbreviation for* ibidem (= Latin for 'in the same place'). Used in writing to refer to a book or article that has already been mentioned.

-i·bil·i·ty /£-ɪ'bɪl·ɪ·ti, $-ə·t̬i/ *combining form* See at ABILITY [QUALITY] • *accessibility* • *responsibility*

-i·ble /-ɪ·bl̩, -ə·bl̩/, **-a·ble** *combining form* See at -ABLE [CAN BE] and -ABLE [WORTH BEING] • *convertible* • *legible* • *accessible* • *permissible* • [LP] **Combining forms**

-ic /-ɪk/, **-i·cal** /-ɪ·kᵊl/ *combining form* used to form adjectives • [LP] **Stress in pronunciation**

ice [FROZEN WATER] /aɪs/ *n* water which has frozen and become solid, or pieces of this • *The pond was covered in thick ice all winter.* [U] • *Would you like ice in your orange juice?* [U] • *(Br)* An ice is also an ice cream, esp. one bought in a shop: *She sat eating a* **choc** *ice* (= ice cream covered with chocolate). [C] ○ *The shop sign said 'Drinks, Cakes, Ices!'* [C] • *(Am)* An ice is a SORBET: *a strawberry ice* [C] • If you **put** something **on ice**, you decide to not do anything with it for a while: *Since they are short of money they have put their plans to move house on ice for the moment.* • An **Ice age** is a **glacial epoch**. See at GLACIER. • Something that is **ice-blue** is a very pale blue colour. • *(Aus)* An **ice-box** is also an old-fashioned cupboard in which large blocks of ice were put in order to keep things cold. • An **ice-breaker** is a strong ship that can break a passage through ice. • *(esp. Am and Aus)* An **ice-breaker** is also something such as a game, joke or story that makes people feel comfortable in a social situation, business meeting, etc. • An **ice cap/ice sheet** is a thick layer of ice that covers an area of land: *Global warming is expected to melt part of the polar ice caps and raise sea temperatures and levels.* • If something is **ice-cold**, it is extremely cold: *The sea is ice-cold at this time of year.* • **Ice cream** is a very cold sweet food made from milk and cream, and an ice cream (*Br also* **ice**) is an amount of this that you buy wrapped in paper or in an **ice cream cone** (= a shaped biscuit container). • An **ice-cream soda** is a sweet dish made from ice cream, thick fruit juice and SODA (= fizzy water), usually served in a tall glass. • An **ice cube** is a small block of ice, such as one you put into a drink to

ITALIAN FALSE FRIENDS (I)

English	Italian	Meaning
actually *adv*	attualmente	at present, currently, nowadays
attack *v*	attaccare	to attach, fasten, do up
attend *v*	attendere	to wait for; to expect, anticipate
audience *n*	udienza	court hearing; sitting
bald *adj*	baldo	bold, daring; gallant
bank *n*	banco	bench; counter; school (of fish)
brace *n*	brace	embers; charcoal
brave *adj*	bravo	well-behaved; honest; expert
bust *n*	busta	envelope; case; packet; cover
calamity *n*	calamita	magnet
camp *v*	campare	to live; to get by; to highlight
card *n*	carta	paper; map; menu; document
carton *n*	cartone	cardboard; cartoon
cassette *n*	cassetta	box; case; box office takings
caution *n*	cauzione	guarantee; surety; bail
cave *n*	cava	pit; quarry, mine
cave *n*	cavo	cable, rope
cement *n*	cimento	risk, danger; test; trial; stress
cholera *n*	collera	anger, fury, rage
cold *adj*	caldo	hot; warm
companion *n*	compagnone	boon; merry fellow
concussion *n*	concussione	extortion; misappropriation
convent *n*	convento	monastery
crude *adj*	crudele	cruel, merciless; painful; distressing
cupid *n*	cupido (adj.)	greedy, grasping; lustful
curt *adj*	corto	short, brief
cushion *n*	cuscino	pillow
cute *adj*	cute (n.)	skin
decant *v*	decantare	to praise, extol
decor *n*	decoro	decorum; propriety; dignity
delude *v*	deludere	to disappoint
delusion *n*	delusione	disappointment
demand *n*	domanda	question; application; request
demand *v*	domandare	to ask, enquire, request,
demented *adj*	dimenticato	forgotten
dispensary *n*	dispensa	pantry; kitchen cupboard; issue
distress *n*	destrezza	skill; dexterity
due *n*	due	two; a few, a couple
edited *adj*	edito	published
egregious *adj*	egregio	excellent; eminent, distinguished
engrossed *adj*	ingrossato	augmented; swollen
equally *adv*	equamente	justly, fairly; equitably
equivocate *v*	equivocare	to mistake, misunderstand
erratic *adj*	errato	false; wrong, mistaken
eventual *adj*	eventuale	if any, possible, probable
exalted *adj*	esaltato	excited; fanatical, hot-headed
exigency *n*	esigenza	necessity, need; demand
extenuate *v*	estenuare	to exhaust, wear out, waste
faggot *n*	fagotto	bundle, sack; oaf; bassoon
fame *n*	fama	report, rumour; word
fame *n*	fame	hunger; starvation; (fig.) thirst
fare *n*	fare	manner, way
fare *v*	fare	to do, make
fatally *adv*	fatalmente	unfortunately
file *n*	filo	thread; wire; blade; scrap; ounce
finger *v*	fingere	to feign, pretend; to imagine
firm *n*	firma	signature, signing, celebrity
flipper *n*	flipper	pinball machine
franchise *n*	franchezza	frankness, sincerity
gent *n*	gente	people; guests; family; parents
grade *v*	gradire	to enjoy; to accept; to welcome
grade *n*	grado (adv.)	willingly, gladly
grape *n*	grappa	cramp; brace; eau-de-vie
grave *n*	grave	(physics) mass, body
impinge *v*	impinguare	to fatten, (disapproving) cram; to get rich
injure *v*	ingiuriare	to insult, abuse
intemperance *n*	intemperie	bad/inclement weather
invidious *adj*	invidioso	envious
island *n*	Islanda	Iceland
jest *n*	gesto	act; gesture, sign; pose; position
lad *n*	ladro/a	thief, robber, burglar
land *n*	landa	moor, heath
lecture *n*	lettura	reading; reading matter
letter(s) *n*	lettura	reading; lecture
librarian *n*	libraio	book-seller; bookshop
library *n*	libreria	bookshop; book-seller; bookcase
lino *n*	lino	flax; linen
location *n*	locazione	renting, leasing; lease; tenancy
luxury *n*	lussuria	lust
magazine *n*	magazzino	department store; warehouse
mansion *n*	mansione	duty, task; job; function
media *n*	media	average, mean; secondary school

English	Italian	Meaning
marmalade *n*	marmellata	jam
mimic *n*	mimica	mime, gesticulation
morbid *adj*	morbido	soft, delicate; loose-fitting; mellow
morose *adj*	moroso	defaulting; in arrears
motorist *n*	motorista	engineer
nature *n*	in natura	in kind (of payment)
neat *adj*	netto	clean; sharp; clear-cut; (fig.) pure
notice *n*	notizia	news; information, data; note
novelist *n*	novellista	short-story writer
occasionally *adv*	occasionalmente	by chance
occur *v*	occorrere	to need; to be necessary
orifice *n*	orefice	jeweller; goldsmith
ostensible *adj*	ostensibile	demonstrable, that can be shown
pallet *n*	paletta	spade, shovel; (rail.) signal
parent *n*	parente	relative, kin
part *n*	parte	direction; faction; (legal) party
pass an exam *v*	passare un esame	to take/sit an exam
pavement *n*	pavimento	floor
pensioner *n*	pensionante	boarder, lodger
petulant *adj*	petulante	cheeky, troublesome
pragmatics *n*	prammatica	customary way of doing things
prevent *v*	prevenire	to precede; to avoid, avert
private *n*	privato	individual (person)
proffer *v*	proferire	to utter, pronounce
prosecution *n*	prosecuzione	continuation; carrying on
public schools *n*	scuole pubbliche	state schools
radish *n*	radicchio	chicory
radish *n*	radice	root; (fig.) origin, source
receipt *n*	ricetta	prescription; recipe; remedy
reclaim *v*	reclamare	to complain; to demand
reclamation *n*	reclamo	complaint
recluse *n*	recluso	prisoner, convict
record *v*	ricordare	to remember; to mention; to look like
refer *v*	riferire	to tell, relate; to connect
refuse *n*	refuso	misprint, (infml) typo
regalia *n*	rigaglia	(pl.) cloth scraps; giblets
relevant *adj*	rilevante	considerable, large, important
replica *n*	replica	repetition, reply, objection
report *v*	riportare	to take back; to quote; (fig.) to have, get; to suffer
rest *n*	resto	change (money); remainder; ruins
retribution *n*	retribuzione	reward; payment, salary
ride *n*	ridere	laughter, laughing
riotous *adj*	riottoso	unruly; intractable; quarrelsome
romanesque *adj*	romanesco	Roman
scatter *v*	scaturire	to gush, well up; (fig.) to ensue
scope *n*	scopo	purpose, aim, target
sensed *adj*	sensato	sensible
sensible *adj*	sensibile	sensitive
serviceable *adj*	servizievole	obliging, helpful; amiable
set *n*	setta	sect; secret society
sign oneself *v*	segnarsi	(religion) to cross oneself
slip *n*	slip	briefs, panties; bathing trunks
smack *n*	smacco	let-down, disappointment
smack *v*	smaccare	to humiliate, shame
smoking *adj*	smoking	(n.) dinner jacket, tuxedo
spa *n*	S.p.A.	joint-stock company, P.L.C.
spank *v*	spanciare	to (do a) bellyflop; to bulge
sparse *adj*	sparso	scattered, spilled; loose, flowing
spell *v*	spelare	to remove the hair from
spell *v*	spellare	to skin; to scrape; (infml) to fleece
spill *v*	spillare	to draw (off); to squeeze (out)
spire *n*	spira	spiral, coil; (elec.) loop, turn
stall *n*	stalla	stable; cowshed; herd; pigsty
stile *n*	stile	stylus
straight *adj*	stretto	narrow; tight; squeezed; tied
strange *adj*	straniero	foreign, alien
stranger *n*	straniero	foreigner, alien; foreign country
stuffy *adj*	stufo	sick (and tired) of, fed up
sympathetic *adj*	simpatico	nice, pleasant
talon *n*	tallone	heel; foot; bottom
test *n*	testo	text; work; textbook
travel *v*	travagliare	to afflict, torment, trouble
traverse *n*	traverso	side; width; breadth
tremendous *adj*	tremendo	terrible, dreadful, awful
trespass *v*	trapassare	to pierce, transfix; to pass
trivial *adj*	triviale	vulgar, coarse; obscene, lewd
turbine *n*	turbine	whirlwind, swirl; (fig.) turmoil
ultimately *adv*	ultimamente	recently, lately
vamp *n*	vampa	blaze; heat wave; (fig.) ardour
viable *adj*	viabile	practicable (of a road, etc.)
voluntary *adj*	volonteroso	willing; eager, keen
zoom *n*	zoom	zoom lens; zoom shot

make it cold. • An **ice floe** is a large area of ice floating in the sea. • **Ice hockey** is a game like HOCKEY played by two teams on ice. • *(Br)* An **ice lolly**, *(Aus)* **ice block** (*Am trademark* **Popsicle**) is sweet esp. fruit-flavoured ice on a small stick. • An **ice pack** is a bag containing ice which is put on a part of a person's body to make it cool and reduce swelling. • An **ice pick** is a sharp tool for breaking large blocks of ice. • An **ice rink** is a level area of ice, usually inside a building, that is kept frozen for people to SKATE on. • An **ice skate** is a special shoe with a thin metal bar fixed to the bottom that you wear to move quickly on ice. To **ice-skate** is to move about on ice wearing these special shoes. • *(esp. Am)* **Ice water** is water that has been made extremely cold: *The prisoners were tortured by being immersed in ice water.* • See also ICEBERG; ICEMAKER; ICICLE. • PIC› **Axe, Blade, Cone, Pick, Skate, Winter sports**

iced /aɪst/ *adj* [not gradable] • An iced drink is one that has been made very cold, either by putting ice in it or by having been kept somewhere cold: *iced tea* ○ *iced water (Am* **ice water***)*

ic·y /ˈaɪ·si/ *adj* **-ier, -iest** • *Freezing fog and icy patches caused problems on the roads yesterday.* • *She opened the window and I was hit by an icy* (= extremely cold) **blast** *of air.* • See also ICY.

ice o·ver /aɪs/, **ice up** *v adv* [I] • If something ices over or ices up it becomes covered with ice: *The lake has iced over.* ○ *The car windscreen is iced up.* ○ *The lock had iced up and I couldn't get into the house.*

ice *obj* [COVER CAKES] /aɪs/, *esp. Am* **frost** *v* [T] to cover (a cake) with ICING (= a mixture of sugar and water or the colourless part of eggs) • *The children liked to help their mother to ice the cakes.* • *There was a plate of dainty iced cakes on the table.*

ic·ing /ˈaɪ·sɪŋ/, *esp. Am* **frost·ing** *n* [U] • Icing is a sweet mixture of sugar, water and the colourless part of eggs or other substances, used to cover cakes: *The cake had 'Happy Birthday' written on it in chocolate icing.* • If something is **the icing on the cake** it is *(disapproving)* an unnecessary thing that has been added to something that is already satisfactory, or *(approving)* an unexpected extra good thing when you have already had good luck: *Having a fancy book cover is expensive and unnecessary – icing on the cake.* ○ *He was delighted to have his story published – getting paid for it was the icing on the cake.* • *(Br and Aus)* **Icing sugar** (*Am* **confectioners' sugar**) is soft, powdery sugar used to make icing for cakes. • PIC› **Bread and cakes** (N)

ice *obj* [KILL] /aɪs/ *v* [T] *Am slang* to murder (someone)

ice·berg /£ˈaɪs·bɜːg, $-bɜːrg/ *n* [C] a very large mass of ice that floats in the sea

ice·mak·er /£ˈaɪsˌmeɪ·kəʳ, $-kɚ/ *n* [C] *esp. Am* a device that makes small pieces of ice to put in drinks, etc.

ic·i·cle /ˈaɪ·sɪ·kl̩/ *n* [C] a long pointed stick of ice formed when drops of water freeze • *Icicles hung from the roof.*

ick·y /ˈɪk·i/ *adj* **-ier, -iest** *infml* unpleasant • *What an icky colour that green is!*

ick /ɪk/ *exclamation Am* • *Then he kissed her! Ick!*

i·con [HOLY PAINTING], **i·kon** /£ˈaɪ·kɒn, $-kɑːn/ *n* [C] a painting, usually on wood, of Jesus Christ, or of a person considered holy by some Christians, esp. in eastern countries • (GR)

i·con [REPRESENTATION] /£ˈaɪ·kɒn, $-kɑːn/ *n* [C] a very famous person or thing considered as representing a set of beliefs or a way of life • *Elvis Presley, Marilyn Monroe and James Dean are still icons for many young people.* • *The skyscraper is an American icon.* • (GR)

i·con·ic /£aɪˈkɒn·ɪk, $-ˈkɑː·nɪk/ *adj* • *John Lennon gained iconic status following his death.*

i·con·o·graph·y /£ˌaɪ·kəˈnɒg·rə·fi, $-ˈnɑː·grə-/ *n* [U] • Iconography is a way of studying symbolic meanings: *religious/political iconography* ○ *The iconography* **of** *this picture is fascinating.* ○ *I am studying the iconography* **of** *Islamic texts, with special reference to the representation of women.*

i·con [COMPUTER SYMBOL] /£ˈaɪ·kɒn, $-kɑːn/ *n* [C] a symbol on a computer screen that you point to with a MOUSE (= movable control device) to give the computer an instruction • *The word processor uses icons, pull down menus, and a mouse.* • (GR)

i·con·o·clast /£aɪˈkɒn·ə·klæst, $-ˈkɑː·nə-/ *n* [C] *fml* a person who criticizes generally accepted beliefs and traditions • *Rogers, an iconoclast in architecture, is sometimes described as putting the insides of buildings on the outside.*

i·con·o·clas·tic /£aɪˌkɒn·əˈklæs·tɪk, $-kɑː·nə-/ *adj* • *Tom is an irreverent, iconoclastic figure who refuses to conform.*

i·con·o·cla·sm /£aɪˈkɒn·əˌklæz·ᵊm, $-ˈkɑː·nə-/ *n* [U] • *healthy/vulgar iconoclasm* • *Imrhan's iconoclasm led him to mount a series of verbal and physical attacks on the church, the family and the state in his long political career.*

-ics /-ɪks/ *combining form* used to form nouns which refer to an area of work or study • *the world of politics* • *the study of economics/physics/ethics*

ic·y /ˈaɪ·si/ *adj* showing controlled and intentionally unfriendly dislike • *He spoke with icy politeness.* • See also at ICE [FROZEN WATER].

ic·i·ly /ˈaɪ·sɪ·li/ *adv* • *The President icily dismissed the possibility of surrender.*

I.D. /ˌaɪˈdiː/ *n* [U] *infml* any official card or document with your name and photograph or other information on it that you use to prove who you are • *Have you got any I.D.? A passport, driving licence or cheque card will do.* • An **I.D. card** is an **identity card**, see at IDENTITY.

id /ɪd/ *n* [C] (in PSYCHOANALYSIS) the deepest part of the unconscious mind that represents the most basic natural human needs such as hunger, sex and anger and the wish for pleasure

i·de·a [SUGGESTION] /aɪˈdɪə/ *n* [C] a suggestion, thought or plan for doing something • *A trip to the seaside? What a great idea!* • *Sarah's bubbling with good ideas.* • *"Let's go swimming." "Good idea!"* • *I've got an idea* **for** *a new type of shoe* (= a plan of how it could be made). • *Jane had* **the** *idea* **of** *starting* (= planned to start) *her own business.* • *Jack liked the idea* **of** *having his own farm, but wasn't so sure he'd like the reality.* • *Watching that holiday program has* **given** *Mandy ideas* **of** (= made her consider) *going abroad.* • *She's full of* **bright** (= good) *ideas, but they never come to anything.* • *The new manager brought with him* **fresh/radical** *ideas about how the business should be run.* • *Of course Morris hated my idea* **to** *move his department upstairs.* [+ *to* infinitive] • **It's** *not a good idea* **to** *drive for hours without a rest.* [+ *to* infinitive] • *The idea* **that** *the problem will resolve itself is ridiculous.* [+ *that* clause] • Your idea **of** something is your opinion of it: *Playing card games is* **not** *my idea of* (= not what I consider to be) *fun.* • If you **put an idea into** someone's **head**, you make them think of things they had never thought about before and sometimes hope for things that might not be possible: *John first put the idea into my head.* ○ *Don't go putting ideas into his head. We can't afford a new car.* • If you **toy with** the idea of doing something you consider it, but not seriously: *I'm toying with the idea* **of** *buying a new car.* • You say **What an idea!** or *(dated)* **The idea of it!** to show how silly or surprising you think a suggestion that someone has made is: *He suggested I took my son into the ladies' toilet. The* **very** *idea of it!*

i·de·a [KNOWLEDGE] /aɪˈdɪə/ *n* [C] knowledge or understanding of something without being certain about it • *I've never seen the house but I* **have** *an idea* **of** *what it is like.* • *Some people have a very clear idea* **about** *what is right and wrong.* • *I don't understand the details but I've* **got a** *rough idea* **of** *what you want.* • *Can you* **give** *me an idea* **of** *the cost* (= can you tell me approximately how much the cost is)*?* • *Do you have/Have you any idea* **of** *what you're asking me to do* (= do you understand it)*?* • *Do you have/Have you any idea* **who** *she went with* (= can you make a guess although you are not certain)*?* [+ *wh*- word] • *I haven't* **the slightest/faintest** *idea* **where** *they've gone.* [+ *wh*- word] • *I've got a* **pretty good** *idea* **why** *they left early.* [+ *wh*- word] • *"Where's Serge?" "I've* **no** *idea* (= I do not know)*."* • You say **you have no idea** to someone when you want to describe how good or bad an experience is: *Flying a plane is wonderful, you have no idea.* ○ *You have no idea* **how** *embarrassed I feel.* [+ *wh*- word]

i·de·a [BELIEF] /aɪˈdɪə/ *n* [C] a belief or opinion • *They have some very unconventional ideas.* • *Leach puts forward the idea* **that** *it is impossible to spoil a child.* [+ *that* clause] • *Whatever gave you that idea* (= What has made you believe that)*?* • *She's not married – where did you get that idea* (= what made you believe that)*?* • *Is this your idea* **of a joke** (= Do you think that this is amusing)*?*

i·de·a [PURPOSE] /aɪˈdɪə/ *n* [U] a purpose or reason for doing something • *The idea* **of** *this game is to get rid of all your cards as soon as you can.* • *The* **whole** *idea* (= only purpose) **of** *advertising is to make people buy things.* • *The idea* **behind** *the new national lottery is to raise money for good causes.*

i·de·al PERFECT /aɪˈdɪəl/ *adj* [not gradable] without fault; perfect, or the best possible • *At first he seemed to be an ideal husband.* • *In an ideal world no one would go hungry.* • *Terence is the ideal person* (= exactly the right type of person) *to sell books.* • *The television also comes in a compact 36 cm screen size, ideal* **for** *bedroom or kitchen use.* • *An activity holiday is ideal* **for** *getting to know people* (= it is the best way of doing this).

i·de·al /aɪˈdɪəl/ *n* [U] • *My ideal* (= perfect situation) *is to live in a warm, sunny climate.* • *Couples forced to spend long periods apart should write to each other, the ideal* (= the best way of behaving) *being two long letters a week.*

i·de·al·ly /aɪˈdɪə·li/ *adv* [not gradable] • *Living in a town is OK. Ideally, I'd like to live in the country* (= I would like that to happen, even if it is not possible). • *In the film Kelly plays a part ideally suited* (= as well suited as it is possible to be) *to her personality.* • *As a couple they're ideally matched.*

id·e·al·ize *obj, Br and Aus usually* **-ise** /aɪˈdɪə·laɪz/ *v* [T] • To idealize someone or something is to think of or represent them as better than they are: *Why do parents idealize their school days?*

i·de·al·ized, *Br and Aus usually* **-ised** /aɪˈdɪə·laɪzd/ *adj* • *The film presents a very idealized view of 19th-century Ireland* (= making it seem more pleasant than it was).

i·de·al·iz·a·tion, *Br and Aus usually* **-i·sa·tion** /aɪˌdɪə·laɪˈzeɪ·ʃən/ *n* [U] • *the idealization of women/the past*

i·de·al PRINCIPLE /aɪˈdɪəl/ *n* [C] a principle or a way of behaving of a very high standard • *Gus and Sarah share the same high ideals.* • *He was an ardent defender of the Olympic ideals.*

i·de·al·i·sm /aɪˈdɪə·lɪ·zəm/ *n* [U] • Idealism is the belief that IDEALS can be achieved: *She never lost her youthful idealism and campaigned for just causes all her life.* ○ *Experienced teachers are well aware of the conflict between idealism and everyday life in the classroom.* • *(specialized)* In PHILOSOPHY idealism is the belief that objects do not exist in the world, but only exist in the mind of God or the people who see them. • Compare **realism** at REAL NOT IMAGINARY.

i·de·al·ist /aɪˈdɪə·lɪst/ *n* [C] • An idealist believes that the world can be made a better place: *He said I was just an idealist who didn't understand the real world.*

i·de·al·is·tic /ˌaɪ·dɪəˈlɪs·tɪk/ *adj* • *When he went to Vietnam he was an idealistic* (= with beliefs that things can be better) *young man, happy and great fun to be with.* • *The plan may sound idealistic* (= not based on reality), *but it works.*

i·deal·is·ti·cally /ˌaɪ·dɪəˈlɪs·tɪ·kli/ *adv*

i·den·ti·cal /£aɪˈden·tɪ·kəl, $-t̬ə-/ *adj* [not gradable] exactly the same, or very similar • *I've got three identical navy suits.* • *The interests of both parties may not be identical, but they do overlap considerably.* • *The tests are identical* **to** *those carried out last year.* • **Identical twins** are two children who come from the same egg in the mother and so are the same sex and look extremely similar.

i·den·ti·cal·ly /£aɪˈden·tɪ·kli, $-t̬ə-/ *adv* [not gradable] • *The two sisters were always dressed identically* (= in the same clothes).

i·den·ti·fy *(obj)* /£aɪˈden·tɪ·faɪ, $-t̬ə-/ *v* to recognize or be able to name, or to prove who (a person) is • *Even the smallest baby can identify its mother by her voice.* [T] • *The Marines stood and watched planes flashing by, trying to identify them.* [T] • *The police officer identified* **himself** (= gave his name or proved who he was) *and asked for our help.* [T] • *The two witnesses who saw the shootings were able to identify* **who** *had fired first.* [+ *wh-* word] • To identify a problem, need, fact, etc. is to recognize it and show that it exists: *The research will be used to identify training needs.* [T] • If you identify **with** someone, you feel that you are similar to them in some way or that you can understand them: *Many women of normal weight feel unable to identify with the super-thin models in glossy magazines.* [I] • If you identify someone **with** something or someone else, you think of them as being connected: *Many football fans are unfairly identified with violent behaviour.* [T]

i·den·ti·fi·ab·le /£aɪˈden·tɪ·faɪ·ə·bl̩, $aɪˌden·t̬əˈ-/ *adj* • *In her bright yellow coat, she was easily identifiable* (= you could see where she was) *in the crowd.*

i·den·ti·fi·ca·tion /£aɪˌden·tɪ·fɪˈkeɪ·ʃən, $-t̬ə-/ *n* [U] • *The identification of the murdered woman took place* (= someone looked at her body to find out who she was) *last week.* • *We were asked to show some identification (infml* **ID***)* (= prove who we were) before the security guards let us in.

i·den·ti·kit *Br and Aus* /£aɪˈden·tɪ·kɪt, $-t̬ə-/, *Am* **com·pos·ite sketch** *n* [C] *trademark* a picture of the face of someone whom the police want to question, usually because that person is thought to have been involved in a crime. The picture is made from a collection of drawings of noses, eyes, ears etc. and is based on the descriptions of WITNESSES to the crime. • *an identikit picture* • *Police have issued an identikit of the wanted man.* • *(fig. disapproving) British pubs are becoming more like identikit* (= similar to each other) *restaurants.*

i·den·ti·ty /£aɪˈden·tɪ·ti, $-t̬ə·t̬i/ *n* who a person is, or the qualities of a person or group which them different from others • *The man's identity was being kept secret while he was helping the police with information about the murder.* [C] • *She said that as a journalist she could not reveal the identity of her source.* [C] • *The informant was given a new identity* (= a different name and new official documents) *for protection.* [C] • *The newspaper photo apparently showed him in Rome but it was a case of* **mistaken** *identity* (= it was the wrong person). [U] • *In prison people often suffer from* **a loss of** *identity.* [U] • *She said that her job gave her* **a sense of** *identity.* [U] • An **identity card** is an official document or plastic card with your name, date of birth, photograph or other information on it which proves who you are. • An **identity crisis** is a feeling of being unsure about who or what you are: *The colonial powers suffered an identity crisis when they lost their colonies.* • *(Br)* During an **identity parade** (*Am* **lineup**) at a police station, someone who saw a crime being committed tries to recognize the person who committed it, by looking at a row of people which includes the person accused of the crime.

id·e·o·gram /ˈɪd·i·ə·græm/, **id·e·o·graph** /£ˈɪd·i·ə·grɑːf, $-græf/ *n* [C] a written sign or symbol used in some writing systems such as Chinese, which represents an idea or object

id·e·ol·o·gy /£ˌaɪ·diˈɒl·ə·dʒi, $-ˈɑː·lə-/ *n* a theory, or set of beliefs or principles, esp. one on which a political system, party or organization is based • *The United States was opposed to the country's socialist ideology.* [C] • *The people are caught between two opposing ideologies.* [C] • *She was against all ideology.* [U]

id·e·o·logue /£ˈaɪ·di·ə·lɒg, $-lɑːg/ *n* [C] • An ideologue is a person who believes very strongly in particular principles and tries to follow them carefully.

id·e·o·lo·gi·cal /£ˌaɪ·di·əˈlɒdʒ·ɪ·kəl, $-ˈlɑː·dʒɪ-/ *adj* • *Half the political group isn't speaking to the other half because of profound ideological disagreements* (= differences in fixed political beliefs). • *Some of the protesters were more radical and ideological* (= had stronger fixed political beliefs) *than the others.*

id·e·o·lo·gi·cally /£ˌaɪ·di·əˈlɒdʒ·ɪ·kli, $-ˈlɑː·dʒɪ-/ *adv* • *The government is ideologically opposed to spending more on the arts* (= this is in opposition to its political beliefs). • *Little separates the two women ideologically* (= they believe in similar things).

id·i·om /ˈɪd·i·əm/ *n* [C] a group of words in a fixed order having a particular meaning, different from the meanings of each word understood on its own • *To "have bitten off more than you can chew" is an idiom that means you have tried to do something which is too difficult for you.* • The idiom of a particular person, place, or style of music, art, building, etc. is their particular and typical style of expression: *They hoped their brave action would,* **in the** *Marxist idiom, "bring about a proletarian revolution."* ○ *The opera is very much* **in the modern** *idiom.* • LP **Words used together**

id·i·o·mat·ic /£ˌɪd·i·əˈmæt·ɪk, $-ˈmæt̬-/ *adj* • *She was born in Italy but her English is fluent and idiomatic* (= completely natural and correct in grammar and style). • *To "bite the bullet" is an idiomatic expression that means to accept something unpleasant without complaining.* • LP **Labels**

id·i·o·syn·cra·sy /ˌɪd·i·əˈsɪŋ·krə·si/ *n* [C often pl] a particular strange or unusual habit, way of behaving or feature that someone or something has • *It's an idiosyncrasy of hers that she always smells a book before opening it.* • *One of the idiosyncrasies of this printer is that you can't stop it once it has started to print.*

id·i·o·syn·crat·ic /£ˌɪd·i·ə·sɪŋˈkræt·ɪk, $-ˈkræt̬-/ *adj* • *The film, 5 hours long, is directed in his usual idiosyncratic style.*

id·i·ot /ˈɪd·i·ət/ *n* [C] a very foolish person, esp. someone who has done something very stupid • *Some idiot left the tap running in the bathroom and there's water everywhere.* • *You stupid idiot – that's a month's work you've lost!* [as form of address]

id·i·ot·ic /£ˌɪd·iˈɒt·ɪk, $-ˈɑː·t̬ɪk/ *adj* • *How idiotic of him to get so worried about nothing.* • *There's some idiotic idea of combining the two departments.* • (GR)

id·i·ot·i·cally /£ˌɪd·iˈɒt·ɪ·kli, $-ˈɑː·t̬ɪ-/ *adv*

id·i·o·cy /ˈɪd·i·ə·si/ *n* • *the idiocies of war* [C] • *The idiocy of Mr. Portillo's scheme is obvious.* [U]

i·dle /ˈaɪ·dl̩/ *adj* **-r, -st** (of people) unwilling to work or be involved in any activity, or (esp. of machines or people) doing nothing, not working or operating • *Half these factories are* **lying/standing** *idle.* • *Thousands of workers in the town are idle* (= have no job) *now that the car factories have closed.* • *It's crazy to have £7000 in the bank* **sitting** *idle* (= not being used). • *He's a stupid, idle, good-for-nothing boy!* • Idle can also mean without any particular purpose: *an idle glance* ○ *a question asked out of idle curiosity* • Idle also means not useful or not based on fact: *The government has denounced the rumours as "idle and pointless speculation".* ○ *It is idle to expect a fair trial in this country* (= You should not expect one because it would be very unlikely). ○ *It is an idle* (= not real) *threat/promise.*

i·dle *(obj)* /ˈaɪ·dl̩/ *v* • If an engine is idling (also *Br* **ticking over**) it is operating at a slow speed because it is not connected to the machine it powers and is not doing any work: *Let the engine idle for a minute.* [I] ○ *The* **idling speed** (= speed at which an engine idles) *can be adjusted by turning a screw.* • If you **idle away** time, you spend it doing very little, often because you are waiting for something to happen: *We idled away the hours until the attack, drinking and playing cards.* • (LP) **Driving**

i·dle·ness /ˈaɪ·dl̩·nəs/ *n* [U] • *long summer days of idleness relaxing by the river*

i·dly /ˈaɪd·li/ *adv* • *He glanced idly* (= without any particular purpose) *through the book.* • *I will not* **stand** *idly* **by** (= do nothing) *when they need my help.*

i·dol /ˈaɪ·dᵊl/ *n* [C] a person who is greatly loved, admired or respected, or an object or picture which is worshipped as a god • *The Hollywood film idols of the 1940s were glamorous figures, adored by millions.* • *The present head of the Anti-Terrorist Squad is the idol* **of** *the younger police officers.* • *The ancient people of this area worshipped a huge bronze idol in the shape of an elephant.*

i·dol·ize *obj, Br and Aus usually* **–ise** /ˈaɪ·dᵊl·aɪz/ *v* [T] • *The fans idolize Elvis* (= love and admire him greatly or too much) *and will hear no criticism of him.*

id·yll /ˈɪd·ᵊl/ *n* [C] a very happy, peaceful and simple situation or period of time, or a piece of music, literature, etc. that describes this • *Most of the village's inhabitants are retired city folk enjoying a rural/pastoral idyll.*

id·yl·lic /ɪˈdɪl·ɪk/ *adj* • *picturesque villages in the idyllic Yorkshire dales*

id·yl·li·cally /ɪˈdɪl·ɪ·kli/ *adv* • *idyllically happy*

i.e. /ˌaɪˈiː/ *abbreviation for* id est (= Latin for 'that is'). Used esp. in writing before a piece of information that makes the meaning of something clearer or shows its true meaning. • *The hotel is closed during low season, i.e. from October to March.* • *Parliament approved a 'reformed' (i.e. stricter) Official Secrets Act.*

if [IN THAT SITUATION] /ɪf/ *conjunction* used to say that a particular thing can or will happen only after something else happens or becomes true • *I'll pay you double if you get the work finished by Friday.* • *We'll have the party in the garden if the weather's good. If* **not** (= If the weather is not good), *it'll have to be inside.* • *If anyone rings/(fml)If anyone should ring for me, please tell them I'll be back in the office at 4 o'clock.* • *If the police hadn't arrived, I don't know what I would have done.* • *I wouldn't work for them* **(even)** *if they paid me a million dollars.* • *We'll deal with that problem if* **and when** *it arises.* • *If disturbed, the bird may abandon the nest, leaving the chicks to die.* • If is also used to mean although: *She's a lovely woman,* **even** *if she can be a bit tiring at times.* ○ *(literary) It was a hot, if windy day.* • If is also used to mean every time: *If water is heated to 100°C it turns to steam.* ○ *If I don't get enough sleep I get a terrible headache.* • If is also used to mean if it is true that: *I'm very sorry if I've offended you.* • If is used to say that when the first of two statements is accepted as true, then the second must also be accepted as true: *If the USA is the last superpower, it is also a nation plagued by injustice and poverty.* • *(infml) "John is the best runner in the club." "Nonsense! If John is our best runner,* **then** *I'm Carl Lewis* (= He's certainly not our best runner)*!"* • If is also used when you want to make a polite request or remark or to say sorry: *If you send me the cheque today, I would be very grateful.* ○ *Would you mind if I open/opened* (= Can I open) *the window?* ○ *It's a stupid idea, if you ask me* (= in my opinion). ○ *There are, if you don't mind me saying so, several problems with this idea of yours.* • If is also used to talk about the amount or degree of something: *The desert gets little, if* **any** *rain* (= almost none). ○ *Turn the music down? It needs to be louder, if* **anything** (= in fact). ○ *Such a mistake could cost us thousands, if* **not** (= or possibly) *millions of pounds.* • **If ever** *I saw a true artist, it was James Still* (= He was obviously a true artist). • *I think you should get a job,* **if only** (= even if the only reason is) *to stop yourself getting so bored at home.* • **If only** (= I wish) *I had some money!* • **If I were you** is used when you give someone advice: *If I were you I'd accept his apology, because it's pointless to carry on being angry.* • *"If you were the only girl in the world / And I were the only boy"* (from the song *If You Were the only Girl in the World* written by Clifford Grey, 1916) • (LP) **Conditionals**

if /ɪf/ *n* [C] • *There's a big if hanging over the project still* (= it is doubtful if it will happen). • *I want no (Br and Aus)* **ifs and buts**/*(Am)* **ifs, ands or buts** (= excuses or doubts) *– just pay the money now!*

if [WHETHER] /ɪf/ *conjunction* (used to introduce a clause, often in indirect speech) whether • *Mrs Kramer rang half an hour ago to ask if her cake was ready.* • *I don't care if you're ready or not, we've got to leave now!* • *I was wondering if you'd like to come to the cinema with me this evening?* • (LP) **Clauses**

if·fy /ˈɪf·i/ *adj* **-ier, -iest** *infml* uncertain, not completely healthy or not working correctly • *Sharon is feeling a bit iffy about driving the car, if it isn't insured for her.* • *The weather looks a bit iffy.* • *MacDonald's injured back is still iffy so she may not play in tomorrow's game.*

–if·y, –fy /-ɪ·faɪ/ *combining form* used to form verbs meaning to cause an increase in the stated quality; to become • *to simplify* (= make more simple) • *to intensify* (= make more intense) • *to beautify* (= make beautiful) • *The cement had solidified* (= become solid). • (LP) **Combining forms**

ig·loo /ˈɪg·luː/ *n* [C] *pl* **igloos** a circular house made of blocks of hard snow, esp. as built by the Inuit people of northern N America

ig·ne·ous /ˈɪg·ni·əs/ *adj* [not gradable] *specialized* (of rocks) formed from MAGMA (= very hot liquid rock that has cooled)

ig·nite *(obj)* /ɪgˈnaɪt/ *v fml* to (cause to) start burning or explode • *The fuel spontaneously ignites because of the high temperature and pressure.* [I] • *(fig.) The murder of the young black mother was the spark which ignited* (= caused to happen) *the explosion of rioting.* [T]

ig·ni·tion /ɪgˈnɪʃ·ᵊn/ *n* [U] • **The** ignition in an engine is the electrical system that causes the fuel to burn or explode in order to start the engine: *Switch/Turn the ignition on.* ○ *an ignition key* • *(fml)* Ignition is also the

---

SPELLING OF WORDS WITH -IE- AND -EI-

The general rule is: I before E except after C

For example *believe, quiet* (**with -ie-**) and *receive* and *ceiling* (**with -ei-**). But -ei- is used before -gn, -gh and -ght: *foreign, weigh, height, eight.*

Here are the commonest exceptions to the rule:

beige	neither
counterfeit	reign
eight	rein
either	seize
foreign	their
forfeit	veil
freight	vein
height	weigh
heir	weight
leisure	weir
neigh	weird
neighbour	

act or process of something starting to burn. • LP> Driving

ig·no·ble /£ɪɡˈnəʊ·bl̩, $-ˈnoʊ-/ *adj literary* (esp. of behaviour) that you should be ashamed of • *an ignoble action/idea* • *She is accused of playing an ignoble part in the plot.*

ig·no·bly /£ɪɡˈnəʊ·bli, $-ˈnoʊ-/ *adv literary*

ig·no·min·i·ous /ˌɪɡ·nəˈmɪn·i·əs/ *adj literary* (esp. of events or behaviour) embarrassing because so completely a failure • *an ignominious defeat/failure/retreat*

ig·no·min·i·ous·ly /ˌɪɡ·nəˈmɪn·i·ə·sli/ *adv literary*

ig·no·min·y /ˈɪɡ·nə·mɪ·ni/ *n* [U] *literary* • *The Workers Coalition experienced the ignominy of total defeat in the last election.*

ig·no·ra·mus /ˌɪɡ·nəˈreɪ·məs/ *n* [C] *fml or humorous* a person who does not know anything • *I'm a complete ignoramus where computers are concerned.*

ig·no·rant /£ˈɪɡ·nᵊr·ᵊnt, $-nɚ-/ *adj* having no knowledge or awareness of something, or of things in general • *Many teenagers are surprisingly ignorant* **about** *current politics.* • *Thousands of children leaving school are ignorant* **of** *even basic skills.* • *We remained* **blissfully** *ignorant* **of** *the troubles that lay ahead.* • *How can they be so damned ignorant and prejudiced?* • *"Where ignorant armies clash by night"* (Matthew Arnold in the poem *Dover Beach*, 1867)

ig·no·rance /£ˈɪɡ·nᵊr·ᵊnts, $-nɚ-/ *n* [U] • *Public ignorance* **about** *AIDS is still a cause for concern.* • *It's awful, the way these patients were left/kept* **in** *ignorance* **of** *what was actually wrong with them.* • *(saying)* 'Ignorance is bliss' means that you are often happiest if you do not know the true facts of a situation.

ig·nore *obj* /£ɪɡˈnɔːʳ, $-ˈnɔːr/ *v* [T] to intentionally not listen or give attention to • *They call me rude names, but I just try and ignore it and walk on.* • *Safety regulations are being ignored by company managers in the drive to increase profits.* • *How can the government ignore the wishes of the majority?* • *I smiled at her but she ignored me.* • Ⓔ Ⓕ Ⓟ

ig·ua·na /ɪˈɡwɑː·nə/ *n* [C] a large greyish green LIZARD (= type of animal) of tropical America • PIC> **Reptiles and amphibians**

i·kon /£ˈaɪ·kɒn, $-kɑːn/ *n* [C] an ICON

il– /ɪl-/ *combining form* See at IN- • LP> **Opposites**

ilk /ɪlk/ *n* [U] *literary esp. disapproving* a particular type • *game show hosts and others* **of that/of the same** *ilk* • *Her view is that the Rolling Stones and others* **of their** *ilk were a bad influence on the teenagers of the time.*

ill NOT WELL /ɪl/ *adj* **-er, -est** in bad health • *You're not looking well – are you ill?* • *I felt ill, so I went home.* • *He's been ill* **with** *meningitis.* • *Phyllis* **fell** *ill/was* **taken** *ill* (= became ill) *while on holiday.* • *A climber who fell 90 metres is* **critically** *ill* (= very badly hurt) *with severe brain injuries.* • *(fig.) I'm dreading moving to another country, it* **makes** *me ill* (= it is unpleasant) *just to think about it.* • LP> **Feelings and pains**

ill·ness /ˈɪl·nəs/ *n* • *She had five days off work due to illness* (= because she was ill). [U] • *He died at home after a long illness.* [C]

ill BAD /ɪl/ *adv* [not gradable] *fml or dated* badly • If you **speak/think** ill of someone, you talk or think about them in an unkind way: *Don't speak ill of the dead, Mary.* • If you say that something **bodes/augurs** ill, you think that it will have a bad effect, or that it will make future events unlikely to happen or succeed: *The victory of the conservative candidates in the election bodes ill for the chances of reform.* • If you can ill **afford** something, you can only pay for it/ give it/etc. with difficulty: *They lost £20 000 at a time when they could ill afford to pay it out.* • *(fml or humorous) It ill* **behoves** *you to* (= you should not/you have no right to) *criticize me, when you're in such a mess yourself.* • Someone or something that is **ill-advised** is unwise or foolish: *It was ill-advised of him to make such risky investments.* • *(esp. Br and Aus)* People or things that are **ill-assorted** are a strange combination because they are different from each other: *What an ill-assorted group of people!* • If you are **ill at ease**, you feel anxious and not relaxed: *Patrick felt ill at ease* **with** *his family, wondering whether or not to announce his news.* • Someone who is **ill-bred** is not polite: *They're a pair of inconsiderate, ill-bred youngsters, is all I can say!* • If something is **ill-conceived** it is badly planned or unwise: *The idea of opening a new cinema here was ill-conceived, as there were two here already, both usually half-empty.* • If you are **ill-disposed** towards someone or something, you do not support them or agree with them: *Most of the audience seemed ill-disposed towards the speaker.* • If someone or something is **ill-equipped** to do something, they do not have the ability, qualities or equipment necessary to do it well enough: young parents ill-equipped **to cope** with their own children without extra help. ○ *school-leavers ill-equipped* **for** *adult life* • Something or someone that experienced failure or bad luck can be described as **ill-fated**: *The ill-fated aircraft later crashed into the hillside.* • *(esp. humorous)* **Ill-gotten** means dishonestly obtained: *Convicted criminals should be made to give up their ill-gotten* **gains**. • Someone who is **ill-informed** knows less than they should about a particular subject. • Someone who is **ill-mannered** is not polite. • **Ill-starred** and **ill-omened** are more literary ways of saying **ill-fated**. • Someone who is **ill-tempered** is often bad-tempered. • If an occasion, such as a game, is **ill-tempered**, people get angry during it: *an ill-tempered game with three players being sent off* ○ *an ill-tempered debate* • If something is **ill-timed**, it is done or made at a wrong or unsuitable time: *The idea of an election is being criticized as ill-timed and unnecessary.* ○ *Her* **comments** *were extremely ill-timed* (= rude or not suitable). • If someone **ill-treats** someone, they treat them badly, esp. by using violence on them or not taking care of them: *The court heard how the child had been severely ill-treated by his parents.*

ill /ɪl/ *adj* [before n; not gradable] *fml or dated* • *It was just ill* (= bad) *fortune/luck that the burglar picked on her house.* • *Did you experience any ill effects from the treatment?* • *(saying)* 'It's an ill wind (that blows nobody any good)' means that even a very bad situation must have some good results. • If you **bear** someone **ill-will** or **feel ill-will for** them, you have feelings of anger and dislike towards them, usually because they have behaved in an unfriendly way towards you: *I bear you no ill-will, despite everything.*

ill /ɪl/ *n* [U] *fml or dated* • *Well, it's done now,* **for good or ill** (= whether the results are good or bad).

ills /ɪlz/ *pl n* • *There seems to be no cure for Britain's economic/social ills* (= problems).

il·le·gal /ɪˈliː·ɡᵊl/ *adj* (esp. of an activity or action) against the law; not allowed by law • *a campaign to stop the illegal sale of cigarettes to children under 16* • *Prostitution is illegal in some countries.* • **It** *is illegal* **to** *drive a car that it is not taxed and insured.* [+ *to* infinitive] • *Cocaine, LSD and heroin are all illegal* **drugs/substances**. • An illegal **immigrant** is a person who has entered a country in order to live there, without having any legal right to do so. • *"All the things I really like to do are either illegal, immoral, or fattening"* (believed to have been said by Alexander Woollcott, 1887-1943) • LP> **Crimes and criminals, Law**

il·le·gal·i·ty /£ˌɪl·iːˈɡæl·ɪ·ti, $-ə·t̬i/ *n* [C; U]

il·le·gal·ly /ɪˈliː·ɡᵊl·i/ *adv* • *They entered the country illegally.*

il·le·gi·ble /ɪˈledʒ·ə·bl̩/ *adj* (of writing or print) impossible or almost impossible to read, because very unclear or untidy • *This note from Grandpa is almost illegible.*

il·le·gi·bly /ɪˈledʒ·ə·bli/ *adv*

il·le·gi·ti·mate /£ˌɪl·ɪˈdʒɪt·ə·mət, $-ˈdʒɪt̬-/ *adj* [not gradable] born of parents not married to each other • *an illegitimate child* • *He's illegitimate.* • *(fml)* Illegitimate can also mean not legal or fair: *The rebels regard the official parliament as illegitimate.*

il·le·gi·ti·ma·cy /£ˌɪl·ɪˈdʒɪt·ə·mə·si, $-ˈdʒɪt̬-/ *n* [U] • *He was never worried by the fact of his illegitimacy.*

il·lib·e·ral /£ɪˈlɪb·ᵊr·ᵊl, $ˈ-ɚ-/ *adj fml* limiting freedom of expression, behaviour, etc., or *(Am)* unwilling to accept other or new ways of thinking or behaving • *an illiberal policy/law/government, restricting women's right to abortion* • *Neo-Nazis and other illiberal demonstrators demanded that the foreign workers leave the country.*

il·li·cit /ɪˈlɪs·ɪt/ *adj* (esp. of substances) illegal or disapproved of • *illicit drugs such as cocaine and cannabis* • *The police are trying to stop the illicit trade in stolen vehicles.* • *In the past, sex outside marriage was illicit sex.*

il·li·cit·ly /ɪˈlɪs·ɪt·li/ *adv*

il·lit·er·ate /£ɪˈlɪt·ᵊr·ət, $-ˈlɪt̬·ɚ-/ *adj* (of a person) not knowing how to read and write • *A surprising percentage of the population are illiterate.* • Someone who is **functionally** illiterate can only read and write a little. • *(fig. disapproving) They know nothing and they read nothing – they're completely illiterate* (= badly educated and not knowing or caring about serious subjects.) • Compare INNUMERATE.

il·lit·er·ate /£ɪˈlɪt·ᵊr·ət, $-ˈlɪt̬·ɚ-/ *n* [C] *esp. fig. disapproving* • *She had to teach a class of illiterates.*

il·lit·er·a·cy /£ɪˈlɪt·ər·ə·si, $-ˈlɪţ·ɚ-/ *n* [U] • *In the rural areas, illiteracy is widespread.*

ill·ness /ˈɪl·nəs/ *n* See at ILL NOT WELL

il·log·i·cal /£ɪˈlɒdʒ·ɪ·kəl, $-ˈlɑː·dʒɪ-/ *adj* not reasonable, wise or practical, usually because directed by the emotions rather than by careful thought • *It's so illogical of him to refuse to eat meat and yet to carry an alligator skin bag.* • *It is an illogical statement, because if one part is true, then the other must be false.*

il·log·i·cal·i·ty /£ɪˌlɒdʒ·ɪˈkæl·ɪ·ti, $-ˌlɑː·dʒɪˈkæl·ə·ţi/ *n* [U]

il·log·i·cal·ly /£ɪˈlɒdʒ·ɪ·kli, $-ˈlɑː·dʒɪ-/ *adv*

il·lum·in·ate *obj* /ɪˈluː·mɪ·neɪt/ *v* [T] *fml* to light (something) and make it brighter or *(fig.)* to explain and show more clearly (something difficult to understand) • *The streets were illuminated with strings of coloured lights.* • *(fig.) The results of the recent research will illuminate the mystery of the creation of the Universe.* • An illuminated book or other piece of writing is one decorated with added colour, gold paint and small pictures: *an illuminated manuscript*

il·lum·in·at·ing /£ɪˈluː·mɪ·neɪ·tɪŋ, $-ţɪŋ/ *adj fml* • *The book is full of illuminating* (= helping to explain) *detail on the causes of the war.*

il·lum·in·a·tion /ɪˌluː·mɪˈneɪ·ʃən/ *n* [U] *fml* • *The only illumination* (= light) *was from a skylight.*

il·lum·in·a·tions /ɪˌluː·mɪˈneɪ·ʃənz/ *pl n esp. Br* • Illuminations are (coloured) decorative lights outside which make a town look bright and exciting at night: *the Blackpool illuminations along the sea front*

il·lu·sion /ɪˈluː·ʒən/ *n* [C] an idea or belief which is not true or not what it seems to be • *The boss is* **(labouring) under the illusion that** (= wrongly believes that) *the project will be completed on time.* [+ *that* clause] • *We* **have no** *illusions* **about** (= understand and accept) *how difficult the job will be.* • *The committee have managed to create the illusion* **of** *activity, but they have actually achieved very little.* • *The calm on the streets is an illusion – people are very angry.* • *The magician tricks the audience with skilful* **optical** *illusions, making things appear and disappear.* • Ⓔ

il·lu·sion·ist /ɪˈluː·ʒən·ɪst/ *n* [C] • An illusionist is an entertainer who performs tricks where objects seem to appear and then disappear.

il·lu·so·ry /£ɪˈluː·sər·i, $-sɚ-/, **il·lu·sive** /ɪˈluː·sɪv/ *adj fml* • *Their hopes of a peaceful solution turned out to be illusory* (= imagined or false). • *We were drawn into the illusory* (= artificial) *world of the film.*

il·lu·strate *obj* /ˈɪl·ə·streɪt/ *v* [T] to show the meaning or truth of (something) more clearly, esp. by giving examples, or to add pictures to (something, esp. a book) • *The lecturer illustrated his point* **with** *a diagram on the blackboard.* • *This latest conflict further illustrates the weakness of the UN.* • *a beautifully illustrated book/old manuscript* • *a lecture illustrated* **with** *photographs and drawings* • *A recent survey illustrated* **that** *the divorce rate has rocketed as women's financial dependence on men has plummeted.* [+ *that* clause] • *The exhibition will illustrate* **how** *life evolved from water.* [+ *wh-* word]

il·lu·stra·tion /ˌɪl·əˈstreɪ·ʃən/ *n* • *This delay is a perfect illustration of why we need a new computer system.* [C] • *A couple of examples are included,* **by way of** *illustration* (= to show the meaning more clearly). [U] • *The book has lots of beautiful illustrations.* [C]

il·lu·stra·tive /£ˈɪl·ə·strə·tɪv, $ɪˈlʌs·trə·ţɪv/ *adj fml* • *Falling house prices are illustrative* **of** (= are examples that show) *the crisis facing the construction industry.*

il·lu·strat·or /£ˈɪl·ə·streɪ·tər, $-ţɚ/ *n* [C] • An illustrator is a person who draws pictures, esp. for books.

il·lu·stri·ous /ɪˈlʌs·tri·əs/ *adj fml* famous, or of a very high quality, ability, etc. • *She comes from an illustrious political family which includes two former Cabinet ministers.*

im– /ɪm-/ *combining form* See at IN- • LP **Opposites**

im·age MENTAL PICTURE /ˈɪm·ɪdʒ/ *n* a picture in the mind of what something or someone is like • *I had this image of London in my head which was totally different from how it really is.* [C] • Something or someone's image is the way they are thought of by other people: *The city/country/company is trying to improve its poor image.* [C] ○ *He has dropped his old bad-boy image and now portrays himself as something of an angel.* [C] ○ *Max is very image-conscious.* [U] • *(specialized)* An image is also a mental picture or idea which descriptive language makes in a reader's or listener's mind: *The poem is full of images of birth and new life.* [C]

im·ag·e·ry /£ˈɪm·ɪ·dʒər·i, $-dʒɚ-/ *n* [U] • *The imagery* (= words used to describe things) *in the poem is mostly to do with death.*

im·age PICTURE /ˈɪm·ɪdʒ/ *n* [C] any picture, esp. one formed by a mirror or a LENS (= specially shaped glass) • *She painted/photographed images of all the poorest parts of New York.* • *The image you see in the mirror seems to be back to front.* • *The gorilla ignored the moving images on the TV screen.* • *She's* **the (living) image of** (= She looks very similar to) *her mother.*

im·ag·ine *obj* /ɪˈmædʒ·ɪn/ *v* [T] to form or have a mental picture or idea of (something) • *Imagine Robert Redford when he was young – that's what John looks like.* • *Imagine* **(that)** *you're eating an ice cream – try and feel how cold it is.* [+ (*that*) clause] • *Can you imagine* **how** *feels to be blind?* [+ *wh-* word] • *When I imagine seeing him again I feel so happy.* [+ v-*ing*] • *She imagined herself sitting in her favourite armchair back home.* [+ obj + v-*ing*] • *I imagine* (= think) **(that)** *San Francisco must be a wonderful place to live.* [+ (*that*) clause] • *"Will they change it?" "I imagine* (= expect) **so.***"* • *They hadn't imagined* (= expected) **(that)** *it would be so difficult.* [+ (*that*) clause] • *I can't imagine* (= I really don't know) *what he wants from us.* • If you imagine something, you think that it exists, has happened or is true, although in fact it is not real or true: *"Did you hear a noise?" "No, you're imagining* **things***/No, you must have imagined it."* ○ *He seems to imagine* **(that)** *he's being followed by the FBI!* [+ (*that*) clause] • Imagine is used in phrases which emphasize a statement: *You* **can/can't** *imagine what a mess the house was in after the party* (= it was extremely untidy). • Imagine **(that)**! is used to express surprise, shock or anger: *She got married at 16! Imagine (that)!* ○ *Imagine leaving her husband and going off with a man 20 years younger than her!*

im·ag·in·ab·le /ɪˈmædʒ·ɪ·nə·bl/ *adj* • *The school offers courses in every imaginable subject (in every subject imaginable)* (= in all possible subjects). • *Using computer graphics, you can create anything imaginable* (= anything that you have a mental picture of).

im·ag·in·a·ry /£ɪˈmædʒ·ɪ·nər·i, $-ə·ner-/ *adj* • Something that is imaginary is not real, because it is created by and only exists in the mind: *The child pulled the trigger of an imaginary gun.* ○ *We must consider our real options, not imaginary ones.* ○ *imaginary fears*

im·ag·in·a·tion /ɪˌmædʒ·ɪˈneɪ·ʃən/ *n* • *What a wonderful/***fertile** *imagination* (= ability to form mental pictures or ideas) *he must have, to have written such spellbinding stories.* [C] • *So many boring new buildings reveal a complete lack of imagination on the part of their architects.* [U] • *The story of the hostages* **captured** *the nation's imagination* (= was very interesting and so people gave it a lot of attention). [C] • *The photos of Marilyn naked* **leave nothing to the** *imagination* (= show everything). [U] • *He couldn't* **by any stretch of the** *imagination be called a handsome man* (= He's certainly not handsome). [U] • *He thought he was being followed, but it was* **all in** *the/his imagination* (= not real • imaginary). [U] • A person's imagination is also their ability to deal with difficulties and think of solutions to problems: *Don't despair – it just needs a bit of imagination!* [U] • **Is it my imagination, or** have you lost weight? (= It seems to me that you have lost weight.)

im·ag·in·a·tive /£ɪˈmædʒ·ɪ·nə·tɪv, $-ţɪv/ *adj* • *(approving)* Something that is imaginative is new, original and clever: *an imaginative new approach/policy* ○ *The architects have made imaginative use of glass and transparent plastic.* • *(approving)* Someone who is imaginative is good at producing ideas or things that are unusual, clever or show skill in inventing: *an imaginative designer*

im·ag·in·a·tive·ly /£ɪˈmædʒ·ɪ·nə·tɪv·li, $-ţɪv-/ *adv* • *His name will always be associated with the building of the new cathedral, poised so imaginatively next to the ruins of the old.*

im·am /ɪˈmɑːm/ *n* [C] a leader in the Islamic religion

im·bal·ance /ˌɪmˈbæl·ənts/ *n* [C] a state in which two or more things are not equally or fairly balanced or spread • *There is an imbalance* **between** *the many opportunities open to men and the few open to women.*

im·be·cile /£ˈɪm·bə·siːl, $-sɪl/ *n* [C] a person who behaves in a stupid way • *What an imbecile that boy is!*

im·be·cil·ic /ˌɪm·bəˈsɪl·ɪk/, **im·be·cile** *adj* • *That was an imbecilic thing to do!* • *She looked at me with an imbecile grin.*

im·bed /ɪm'bed/ *v* **-dd-** *Am also for* EMBED

im·bibe *obj* /ɪm'baɪb/ *v* [T] *fml or humorous* to drink (esp. alcohol), or *(fig.)* to receive and accept (information, etc.)

im·brog·lio /£ɪm'brəʊ·li·əʊ, $-'broʊ·li·oʊ/ *n* [C] *pl* **imbroglios** *literary* an unwanted, difficult and confusing situation, full of trouble and problems • *The Soviet Union became anxious to withdraw its soldiers from the Afghan imbroglio.*

im·bue *obj* **with** *obj* /ɪm'bjuː/ *v prep* [T usually passive] *fml* to fill (someone or something) with (a feeling, idea, etc.) • *She imbued him with a sense of self-worth.*

IMF /ˌaɪ·em'ef/ *n* [U] **the IMF** *abbreviation for* International Monetary Fund (= a part of the United Nations which encourages international trade and gives financial help to poor countries)

im·i·tate *obj* /'ɪm·ɪ·teɪt/ *v* [T] to behave in a similar way to (someone or something), or to copy exactly (someone or something's speech, behaviour, etc.) • *Some of the younger pop bands try to imitate their musical heroes from the past.* • *John makes me laugh when he imitates a monkey/the way his grandmother speaks.* • *They produce artificial chemicals which exactly imitate particular natural ones.*

im·it·a·tion /ˌɪm·ɪ'teɪ·ʃᵊn/ *n* • **In** *imitation* **of** *the older girls, even the ten-year-olds have started wearing lipstick and make-up.* [U] • *She can* **do** *a wonderful imitation* **of** *a blackbird's song.* [C] • An imitation is also a copy: *The wine that is made and sold here is a* **pale** *imitation* **of** (= it is similar to but not as good as) *the real thing.* [C] ○ *His songs are just* **cheap** (= low quality) *imitations of Beatles tunes.* [C]

im·it·a·tion /ˌɪm·ɪ'teɪ·ʃᵊn/ *adj* [not gradable] • Something that is imitation has been made so that it looks like something else: *a cheap watch with an imitation leather strap* ○ *horrible imitation grass* ○ *It's not real silk – it's just imitation.*

im·i·ta·tive /£'ɪm·ɪ·tə·tɪv, $-teɪ·t̬ɪv/ *adj esp. disapproving* • *All these magazines are imitative* **of** (= copy) *each other.* • *He's an imitative artist, who does very little original stuff.*

im·i·tat·or /£'ɪm·ɪ·teɪ·tər, $-t̬ɚ/ *n* [C often pl] • *The difference between Ms McArthur and her countless imitators is the elegance of her writing.*

im·mac·u·late /ɪ'mæk·jʊ·lət/ *adj approving* (of clothes, appearance, etc.) perfectly clean or tidy or (esp. of an action or performance) perfect and without any mistakes • *dressed in an immaculate white suit* • *an immaculate garden lawn* • *He gave an immaculate performance as the aging hero.* • The **Immaculate Conception** is the Roman Catholic belief that Jesus Christ's mother Mary, or (more generally) Jesus Christ himself, were CONCEIVED (= created) without any SIN (= breaking religious law).

im·mac·u·late·ly /ɪ'mæk·jʊ·lət·li/ *adv* • *immaculately dressed* • *an immaculately sung version of 'After You've Gone'*

im·ma·te·ri·al /£ˌɪm·ə'tɪə·ri·əl, $-'tɪr·i-/ *adj* [not gradable] not important; not relating to the matter you are interested in • *Whether the book is well or badly written is immaterial – it is making an important point.*

im·ma·ture /£ˌɪm·ə'tʃʊər, $-'tʊr/ *adj disapproving* childish; unable to be or act as calmly and wisely as people expect you to, at the age you have reached • *Stop being so silly and immature, Derek!* • *She's rather immature for her age, don't you think?* • *She's politically immature* (= has had little experience of politics). • *(specialized)* If something is described as immature it can also mean that it is not yet completely grown or developed: *While the animals are still immature, they do not breed.*

im·ma·tu·ri·ty /£ˌɪm·ə'tʃʊə·rɪ·ti, $-'tʊr·ə·t̬i/ *n* [U] • *I think his selfishness is just immaturity – after all, he's only 17.* • *The problem was the immaturity* (= newness) *of the country's democratic system.*

im·mea·sur·ab·le /£ɪ'meʒ·ᵊr·ə·bl̩, $'-ɚ-/ *adj* [not gradable] so large or great that it cannot be measured or known exactly • *China is a market of immeasurable potential.* • *Her films had an immeasurable effect on a generation of Americans.*

im·mea·sur·ab·ly /£ɪ'meʒ·ᵊr·ə·bli, $'-ɚ-/ *adv* [not gradable] • *The damage from the 1956 hurricane was immeasurably greater.*

im·me·di·ate /ɪ'miː·di·ət/ *adj* happening or done without delay or very soon after something else • *We need to take immediate action.* • *Dioxin is a poison that takes immediate effect.* • Immediate also describes something or someone that is close to, or is a cause of or an effect of, something or someone else: *There are no good facilities in the immediate area.* ○ *What will you do in the immediate* **future** (= next)? ○ *She lives with her immediate* **family** – *husband, two children and her parents.* ○ *An immediate result/effect of the war has been a breakdown of law and order.* ○ *The immediate* (= direct) *cause of the accident was engine failure.* • Immediate also means in the present or as soon as possible: *We have no immediate plans.* ○ *MPs have demanded his immediate resignation.*

im·me·di·ate·ly /ɪ'miː·di·ət·li/ *adv, conjunction* • *We must leave immediately* (= now • without delay). • *Immediately* **after**/*(Br also) Immediately* (= As soon as) *she'd gone, the boys started to mess about.* • *Immediately (to* *the) north of the factory is the airport runway.* • *Milton Street is on the left, immediately* **after** *the bank* (= the first road after and very close to the bank). • *The people most immediately* (= directly or soonest) *affected by the drought are the farmers themselves.*

im·me·di·a·cy /ɪ'miː·di·ə·si/, **im·me·di·ate·ness** /ɪ'miː·di·ət·nəs/ *n* [U] • The immediacy of something is its quality of seeming real and important, so that you feel involved with it: *Pre-recorded TV programmes have so much less immediacy and warmth than live theatre.*

im·me·mor·i·al /£ˌɪm·ə'mɔː·ri·əl, $-'mɔːr·i-/ *adj* [not gradable] *literary* so old that its beginning cannot be remembered; existing or traditional for an extremely long time • *Her family had farmed that land* **since/from time** *immemorial.* • *(fml) She said it was the immemorial custom of the villagers to have a feast after the harvesting.*

im·mense /ɪ'ments/ *adj* [not gradable] extremely large in size or degree • *The square is dominated by an immense statue of the President.* • *They spent an immense amount of time getting the engine into perfect condition.* • *A healthy diet during pregnancy is of immense importance.*

im·men·sely /ɪ'ment·sli/ *adv* [not gradable] • *He's an immensely arrogant man.* • LP **Very, completely**

im·men·si·ty /£ɪ'ment·sə·ti, $-ṭi/ *n* [U] *fml* • *The immensity* (= great size) *of the task is daunting.*

im·men·si·ties /£ɪ'ment·sə·tiz, $-ṭiz/ *pl n* • *the immensities* (= immensity) **of space**

im·merse *obj* /£ɪ'mɜːs, $-'mɜːrs/ *v* [T] to involve completely in something, or *(fml)* to put (something or someone) completely under the surface of a liquid • *She got some books out of the library and immersed herself* **in** *Jewish history and culture.* • *(fml) The shells should be immersed in boiling water* **for** *two minutes.*

im·mer·sion /£ɪ'mɜː·ʃən, $-'mɜːr-/ *n* • *Her immersion* **in** *her studies was total.* [U] • *(fml) Repeated immersions* **in** *boiling water will soften the material.* [C] • An **immersion heater** is an electric heater used for heating liquid.

im·mi·grant /'ɪm·ɪ·grənt/, *Aus also* **mi·grant** /'maɪ·grənt/ *n* [C] a person who has come, esp. legally, into a foreign country in order to live there permanently • *New York has a huge number of immigrants/a large immigrant population.* **Illegal** *immigrants are sent back across the border if they are caught.*

im·mi·gra·tion /ˌɪm·ɪ'greɪ·ʃən/ *n* [U] • *There are strict limits on immigration* **(into** *the country).* • *Immigration rules/officers would not allow us to take fruit into the country.* • *After they've finished with you at immigration* **(control)** (= the process of checking that you can be allowed to enter the country) *you can go and get your luggage.*

im·mi·grate /'ɪm·ɪ·greɪt/ *v* [I] • *He immigrated with his parents, Louis and Anne, in 1895, at the age of five, and grew up in Patchogue, Long Island.*

im·mi·nent /'ɪm·ɪ·nənt/ *adj* (esp. of something unpleasant) likely to happen very soon • *facing imminent disaster* • *no imminent danger* • *A strike is imminent.* • *The Prime Minister denied reports that a general election is imminent.*

im·mi·nence /'ɪm·ɪ·nənts/ *n* [U] • *The imminence of an attack made us all nervous.*

im·mo·bile /£ɪ'məʊ·baɪl, $-'moʊ·bəl/ *adj* not moving or not able to move • *She sat immobile, wondering what to do next.*

im·mo·bil·i·ty /£ˌɪm·əʊ'bɪl·ə·ti, $-oʊ'bɪl·ə·ṭi/ *n* [U]

im·mo·bi·lize *obj, Br and Aus usually* **-ise** /£ɪ'məʊ·bəl·aɪz, $-'moʊ-/ *v* [T] • *My leg was immobilized in a plaster cast.* • *You can immobilize the car by removing the spark plugs.*

im·mo·bi·liz·a·tion, *Br and Aus usually* **-i·sa·tion** /£ɪˌməʊ·bəl·aɪ'zeɪ·ʃən, $-ˌmoʊ·bə·lɪ-/ *n* [U]

im·mo·bi·liz·er, *Br and Aus usually* **-iser** /£ɪ'məʊ·bəl·aɪ·zəʳ, $-zɚ/ *n* [C] • An immobilizer is a device fitted to esp. a car which stops it from moving so that it cannot be stolen: *Some immobilizers not only shut off the engine if someone attempts to steal the car, they also immobilize the doors so that the car-thief can't escape.*

im·mod·er·ate /£ɪ'mɒd·ər·ət, $-'mɑː·dɚ-/ *adj fml* more than what is usual or reasonable; extreme • *immoderate drinking* • *immoderate demands*

im·mod·er·ate·ly /£ɪ'mɒd·ər·ət·li, $-'mɑː·dɚ-/ *adv fml* • *He laughed immoderately at his own jokes.*

im·mod·est /£ɪ'mɒd·ɪst, $-'mɑː·dɪst/ *adj fml disapproving* showing too much self-confidence, or showing too much of the body • *He makes these immodest statements of his own brilliance.* • *a dress showing an immodest amount of leg*

im·mod·est·y /£ɪ'mɒd·ə·sti, $-'mɑː·də-/ *n* [U] *fml*

im·mo·late *obj* /'ɪm·ə·leɪt/ *v* [T] *fml* to kill (esp. yourself) or to destroy (something), usually by burning, esp. as an expression of anger

im·mo·la·tion /ˌɪm·ə'leɪ·ʃən/ *n* [U] *fml*

im·mor·al /£ɪ'mɒr·əl, $-'mɑːr-/ *adj* not within society's standards of acceptable, honest and moral behaviour; morally wrong • *Of course it's immoral to cheat someone out of their money.* • *It's an immoral tax because the poor will pay relatively more.* • If someone is living off **immoral earnings**, they are earning money from PROSTITUTION (= selling sex for money). • Compare AMORAL; MORAL.

im·mor·al·ly /£ɪ'mɒr·əl·i, $-'mɑːr-/ *adv*

im·mor·al·i·ty /£ˌɪm·ə'ræl·ə·ti, $-ɑː'ræl·ə·ṭi/ *n* [U] • *The beauty of the photographs does not excuse their immorality.*

im·mor·tal /£ɪ'mɔː·təl, $-'mɔːr·ṭəl/ *adj* [not gradable] living or lasting forever, or very special and famous and therefore likely to be remembered for a long time • *The Greek gods were immortal and so could not die.* • *The Catholic priest warned him he was endangering his immortal soul.*

im·mor·tal /£ɪ'mɔː·təl, $-'mɔːr·ṭəl/ *n* [C] • The Greek and Roman gods were called the immortals. • *She is one of the immortals among classical opera singers.*

im·mor·tal·i·ty /£ˌɪm·ɔː'tæl·ə·ti, $-ɔːr'tæl·ə·ṭi/ *n* [U] • *The Wright brothers achieved immortality with the first powered flight in 1903.*

im·mor·tal·ize *obj, Br and Aus usually* **-ise** /£ɪ'mɔː·təl·aɪz, $-'mɔːr·ṭəl-/ *v* [T usually passive] • If someone or something is immortalized, they become so famous that they are remembered for a long time after they are dead: *Marlene Dietrich was immortalized for millions of people through her roles* **in** *films like "The Blue Angel".*

immovable /ɪ'muː·və·bl/ *adj* [not gradable] (of an object) fixed and impossible to move, or (of an opinion or the person who holds it) firm and impossible to change • *The rock weighed over a ton and was completely immovable.* • *She has stated her immovable opposition to abortion.*

im·mune /ɪ'mjuːn/ *adj* protected against a particular disease by particular substances in the blood, or *(fig.)* unable to be influenced by something, esp. something bad • *He seems to be immune* **to** *colds – he just never gets them.* • *(fig.) The press had criticised her so often that in the end she had become immune* **(to** *it)* (= was not worried or annoyed by it). • *(fig.) Journalists, he insisted, must not be immune* (= be protected) **from** *prosecution.* • The **immune response** is the reaction within the body which is caused by the presence of ANTIGENS (= foreign substances), and results in the production of ANTIBODIES which can fight disease by killing the bacteria or viruses which cause it. • The **immune system** is the various cells and tissues in the body which make it able to protect itself against infection.

im·mun·i·ty /£ɪ'mjuː·nɪ·ti, $-ə·ṭi/ *n* [U] • *The vaccination gives you immunity* **against** *the disease for up to six months.* • *(fig.) He was told that he would be granted immunity* **from** *prosecution if he confessed the names of the other spies in the ring.* • *(fig.) His immunity* **to** *adverse criticism served him well as a politician.*

im·mun·ize *obj, Br and Aus usually* **-ise** /'ɪm·jʊ·naɪz/ *v* [T] • If a person or an animal is immunized they are given protection against a particular disease by introducing special substances into the body, esp. using an INJECTION: *Children are routinely immunized* **against** *polio.*

im·mun·iz·a·tion, *Br and Aus usually* **-i·sa·tion** /ˌɪm·jʊ·naɪ'zeɪ·ʃən/ *n* [U] • *The government have started a programme of child immunization to combat the disease.*

im·mun·o·de·fi·cien·cy /£ˌɪm·jʊ·nəʊ·dɪ'fɪʃ·ənt·si, $-noʊ-/ *n* [U] *specialized* • Immunodeficiency is the body's inability to produce enough ANTIBODIES to fight bacteria and viruses, often resulting in infection and disease: *People can have the human immunodeficiency virus (HIV) for many years without developing AIDS.*

im·mun·ol·o·gy /£ˌɪm·jə'nɒl·ə·dʒi, $-'nɑː·lə-/ *n* [U] *specialized* • Immunology is the study of immunity and its causes and effects.

im·mun·o·sup·pres·sion /£ˌɪm·jə·nəʊ·sə'preʃ·ən, $-noʊ-/ *n* [U] *specialized* • Immunosuppression is intentionally stopping the body's immune system from working, or making it less effective, usually by drugs, esp. in order to help the body accept an organ which has been taken from another person's body.

im·mured /£ɪ'mjʊəd, $-'mjʊrd/ *adj* [not gradable] *literary or fml* in prison or closed away and out of sight • *Immured in a dark airless cell, the hostages waited six months for their release*

im·mut·ab·le /£ɪ'mjuː·tə·bl̩, $-t̬ə-/ *adj* [not gradable] *fml or literary* not changing or unable to be changed • *an immutable law* • *Some people regard grammar as an immutable set of rules that must be obeyed.*

im·mut·ab·il·i·ty /£ɪˌmjuː·tə'bɪl·ɪ·ti, $-t̬ə'bɪl·ə·t̬i/ *n* [U] *fml or literary* • *The president stressed once more the immutability of his country's borders.*

imp /ɪmp/ *n* [C] a small evil spirit, or *(often humorous)* a badly behaved but playful child • *Come here, you little imp!*

im·pish /'ɪm·pɪʃ/ *adj* • Impish is usually used of adults who take or look like they take a child-like pleasure in being playful and making trouble: *Though seventy years old he still retains an impish grin.*

im·pish·ly /'ɪm·pɪʃ·li/ *adv* • *Her eyes twinkled impishly.*

im·pish·ness /'ɪm·pɪʃ·nəs/ *n* [U]

im·pact /'ɪm·pækt/ *n* [U] the force with which one thing hits another or with which two things hit each other, or *(fig.)* a powerful effect that something, esp. something new, has on a situation or person • *The impact of the crash had reduced the car to a third of its original length.* • *The bullet explodes* **on** *impact* (=at the moment when it hits something). • *(fig.) The anti-smoking campaign had* **had/made** *quite an impact* **on** *young people.* • *(fig.) The new proposals were intended to* **soften** *the impact of the reformed tax system.*

im·pact *(obj)* /ɪm'pækt/ *v esp. Am and Aus* • *Falling export rates have impacted* **(on)** (= influenced) *the country's economy quite considerably.* [T; I + *on*]

im·pact·ed /£ɪm'pæk·tɪd, $-t̬ɪd/ *adj* [not gradable] • An impacted tooth is unable to grow in the right way, usually because it is growing against another tooth below the GUM: *She's having problems with an impacted wisdom tooth.*

im·pair *obj* /£ɪm'peəʳ, $-'per/ *v* [T] to spoil or weaken (something) so that it is less effective • *Lack of sleep had impaired her concentration.* • *A recurring knee injury may have impaired his chances of winning the tournament.*

im·paired /£ɪm'peəd, $-'perd/ *adj* • *She suffers from impaired vision/hearing.*

im·pair·ment /£ɪm'peə·mənt, $-'per-/ *n* [U] • *Lack of oxygen at birth can result in mental impairment.*

im·pale *obj* /ɪm'peɪl/ *v* [T usually passive] to push a sharp object through (esp. the body of an animal or person), often to hold it in position • *The dead deer was impaled on a spear.*

im·pal·pab·le /ɪm'pæl·pə·bl̩/ *adj literary* difficult to feel or understand • *When I awoke, a few impalpable images and sensations were all I could remember of the dream.*

im·pan·el *obj* /ɪm'pæn·ᵊl/ *v* [T] to EMPANEL

im·part *obj* /£ɪm'pɑːt, $-'pɑːrt/ *v* [T] *fml or literary* to give or make known (information or a particular feeling or quality) to something or someone else • *I spoke to Don but he didn't have anything of note to impart.* • *I was rather quiet as I didn't feel I had much wisdom to impart on the subject.* • *The leafy green stage imparts a feeling of tranquility* **to** *the first act of the play.*

im·par·tial /£ɪm'pɑː·ʃᵊl, $-'pɑːr-/ *adj* not supporting any of the sides involved in an argument • *It was very interesting to have an impartial observer's account of the dispute.* • *Impartial news coverage is quite hard to find.*

im·par·tial·ly /£ɪm'pɑː·ʃᵊl·i, $-'pɑːr-/ *adv* • *She's too personally bound up in the situation to judge it impartially.*

im·par·ti·al·i·ty /£ɪmˌpɑː·ʃi'æl·ɪ·ti, $-ˌpɑːr·ʃi'æl·ə·t̬i/ *n* [U] • *Certain ministers are pressing for new rules on broadcasting impartiality.*

im·pass·ab·le /£ɪm'pɑː·sə·bl̩, $-'pæs·ə-/ *adj* [not gradable] (of roads and paths) unable to be travelled on because of bad weather conditions or things blocking the way • *Many roads were flooded and impassable following the storm.* • *(fig.) He considered the barrier between himself and his brother to be impassable.*

im·passe /£æm'pæs, $'ɪm·pæs/ *n* [U] a point at which further development is impossible because something is preventing it • *The dispute had* **reached**/*was* **at** *an impasse, as neither side would compromise.*

im·pas·sioned /ɪm'pæʃ·ᵊnd/ *adj* (esp. of speech) full of strongly felt and strongly expressed emotion • *Relatives of the dead have made an impassioned* **plea** *to have the bodies flown back to this country.*

im·pas·sive /ɪm'pæs·ɪv/ *adj* (of a face) not expressing any emotion, as if a situation is not having any effect on the person experiencing it • *A group of children were staring at the corpse, their faces strangely impassive.* • See also PASSIVE [BEHAVIOUR].

im·pas·sive·ly /ɪm'pæs·ɪv·li/ *adv* • *The defendant sat impassively in the dock while evidence was given against him.*

im·pas·siv·i·ty /£ˌɪm·pæs'ɪv·ɪ·ti, $-ə·t̬i/ *n* [U]

im·pa·tience /ɪm'peɪ·ʃᵊnts/ *n* [U] annoyance and dissatisfaction at faults or because something is slow, or anxious eagerness to do something • *There's a growing impatience among the electorate* **with** *the old two-party system.* • *"Well, I have shown you how to do this before," she said, unable to disguise her impatience.* • *He was already half an hour late which explains his impatience to leave.* [+ *to* infinitive]

im·pa·tient /ɪm'peɪ·ʃᵊnt/ *adj* • *He's a good teacher but inclined to be a bit impatient with slow learners.* • *You'd be hopeless looking after children – you're too impatient!* • *He's got a lot of exciting ideas for the project and I think he's impatient* **to** *get it all started.* [+ *to* infinitive] • *By Friday afternoon I'm usually quite impatient* **for** *the weekend to begin.*

im·pa·tient·ly /ɪm'peɪ·ʃᵊnt·li/ *adv* • *"Yes, you've already told me that story," she said, impatiently.*

im·peach *obj* /ɪm'piːtʃ/ *v* [T] (esp. in the US) to make a formal statement saying that (a public official) is guilty of a serious offence in connection with their job • *The governor was impeached for wrongful use of state money.*

im·peach·ab·le /ɪm'piː·tʃə·bl̩/ *adj* [not gradable] • *an impeachable offence*

im·peach·ment /ɪm'piːtʃ·mənt/ *n* [C/U]

im·pec·ca·ble /ɪm'pek·ə·bl̩/ *adj* [not gradable] perfect; not damaged by any faults or bad parts • *impeccable taste/manners/credentials* • *His clothes are always impeccable.* • *We've just witnessed an impeccable performance by one of America's finest athletes.*

im·pec·ca·bly /ɪm'pek·ə·bli/ *adv* [not gradable] • *As usual she was impeccably dressed – every detail was perfect.*

im·pe·cun·i·ous /ˌɪm·pə'kjuː·ni·əs/ *adj fml* poor; having very little money, esp. temporarily • *I first knew him as an impecunious* **student** *living in one small room.*

im·pede *obj* /ɪm'piːd/ *v* [T] *slightly fml* to slow down or cause problems for the advancement or completion of (something); get in the way of (something) • *Although he's shy it certainly hasn't impeded his career in any way.*

im·ped·i·ment /ɪm'ped·ɪ·mənt/ *n* [C] • *In a number of developing countries war has been an additional impediment to progress.*

im·ped·i·ment·a /ɪmˌped·ɪ'men·tə/ *pl n humorous or fml* • People sometimes refer to the inconvenient or unnecessary objects which they take with them when travelling as impedimenta: *We were weighed down with sleeping bags, gas cookers and pans – all the impedimenta of camping.*

im·pel *obj* /ɪm'pel/ *v* [T] **-ll-** to force (someone) to do something • *She was in such a mess I* **felt** *impelled* **to** (= felt I had to) *offer your services.* [+ obj + *to* infinitive] • *I wonder what it is that impels him* **to** *exercise all the while.* [+ obj + *to* infinitive] • *I don't know why she didn't reveal his name – perhaps she felt impelled* **by** *loyalty.*

im·pend·ing /ɪm'pen·dɪŋ/ *adj* [not gradable] (often of something unpleasant or unwanted) going to happen soon • *People out at sea had been warned of the impending storms.* • *There was a sense of impending* **doom** *in the air just before my grandmother came to stay with us.*

im·pen·e·tra·ble /ɪm'pen·ɪ·trə·bl̩/ *adj* impossible to enter or go through, or *(fig.)* impossible to understand • *The prison lies behind a high impenetrable wall.* • *Outside the house the fog was thick and impenetrable* (= impossible to see through because it was so thick). • *(fig.) The latest record contains some of their most impenetrable lyrics yet.*

im·pen·e·tra·bly /ɪm'pen·ɪ·trə·bli/ *adv*

im·pen·i·tent /£ɪm'pen·ɪ·tᵊnt, $-t̬ᵊnt/ *adj fml* not sorry or ashamed about something bad you have done; not PENITENT • *To this day she remains impenitent about her criminal past.*

im·pe·ra·tive [URGENT] /£ɪm'per·ə·tɪv, $-t̬ɪv/ *adj* extremely important or urgent; needing to be done or given attention immediately • *The president said it was imperative* **that** *the release of all hostages be secured.* [+ *that* clause] • *It's imperative* **to** *act now before the problem gets really serious.* [+ *to* infinitive]

im·pe·ra·tive /£ɪm'per·ə·tɪv, $-t̬ɪv/ *n* [C] • *Getting the unemployed back to work, said the minister, is a* **moral** *imperative.*

im·pe·ra·tive GRAMMAR /£ɪm'per·ə·tɪv, $-t̬ɪv/ *n specialized* the form of a verb which is usually used for giving orders • *In the phrase 'Leave him alone!', the verb 'leave' is an imperative/is in* **the** *imperative.* [C; U]

im·pe·ra·tive /£ɪm'per·ə·tɪv, $-t̬ɪv/ *adj* [not gradable] *specialized* • *the imperative form of the verb*

im·per·cep·ti·ble /£ˌɪm·pə'sep·tɪ·bl̩, $-pɚ'sep·t̬ə-/ *adj* unable to be noticed or felt because of being very slight • *As we grow old, the changes come upon us so slowly that they are almost imperceptible.*

im·per·cep·ti·bly /£ˌɪm·pə'sep·tɪ·bli, $-pɚ'sep·t̬ə-/ *adv* • *Gradually, almost imperceptibly, her condition had worsened.*

im·per·fect NOT PERFECT /£ɪm'pɜː·fekt, $-'pɜːr-/ *adj* containing faults or lacking something important • *There were some clothes marked imperfect which they were selling off cheaply.* • *We're living in an imperfect world.* • *I explained as well as I was able, given my own imperfect understanding of the situation.*

im·per·fect·ly /£ɪm'pɜː·fekt·li, $-'pɜːr-/ *adv* • *The way in which the brain functions is imperfectly* **understood**.

im·per·fec·tion /£ˌɪm·pə'fek·ʃən, $-pɚ-/ *n* • *After living with him for a year, she began to notice one or two little imperfections in his character.* [C] • *She won't tolerate imperfection in her own or anyone else's work.* [U]

im·per·fect GRAMMAR /£ɪm'pɜː·fekt, $-'pɜːr-/ *n* [U] **the imperfect** *specialized* (being) the tense of a verb which most commonly describes an action which has not been completed in the past, used, for example, to refer to an action which was happening when it was suddenly interrupted by another • *In the sentence 'He was hit by a car as he was crossing the road' the verb 'cross' is* **in** *the imperfect.* • The imperfect tense is also used descriptively, often to begin a story: *In the sentence 'It was a cold December night and the snow was falling heavily' the verb 'fall' is in the imperfect tense.* • LP **Tenses**

im·pe·ri·al EMPIRE /£ɪm'pɪə·ri·əl, $-'pɪr·i-/ *adj* [not gradable] of an empire or the person who rules it • *Imperial China* • *Britain's imperial past* • *a great imperial power* • *the Imperial palace* • *imperial grandeur* • *Since the end of the Roman empire Italy has had no imperial* **ambitions** *in Europe.*

im·pe·ri·al·i·sm /£ɪm'pɪə·ri·ə·lɪ·zəm, $-'pɪr·i-/ *n* [U] *often disapproving* • Imperialism is a system in which a country rules other countries, sometimes having used force to obtain power over them: *The main era of imperialism was the end of the nineteenth century when many European powers gained territories in Africa and Asia.* • Imperialism can also refer more generally to a country's efforts to have a lot of power and influence over other countries, esp. in political and economic matters: *In her speech she accused the United States of* **economic** *imperialism.* • *The government's measures to resist* **cultural** *imperialism include limiting the number of foreign television programmes.*

im·perialist /£ɪm'pɪə·ri·ə·lɪst, $-'pɪr·i-/, **im·perialis·tic** /£ɪmˌpɪə·ri·ə'lɪs·tɪk, $-ˌpɪr·i·ə'lɪs·t̬ɪk/ *adj often disapproving* • *The Russian Revolution happened at the end of a long and destructive imperialist war.*

im·perialist /£ɪm'pɪə·ri·ə·lɪst, $-'pɪr·i-/ *n* [C] *often disapproving*

im·pe·ri·al MEASUREMENT /£ɪm'pɪə·ri·əl, $-'pɪr-/ *adj* of a system of weights and measures used in Britain and in the US, esp. in the past • *In the imperial system length is measured in inches, feet and yards, weight in ounces and pounds and volume in pints and gallons.* • LP **Units**

im·per·il *obj* /ɪm'per·əl/ *v* [T] **-ll-** or *Am usually* **-l-** *slightly fml* to put (something or someone) at risk or in danger of being harmed or destroyed • *This latest attack has seriously imperilled any hope of peace between the two countries.*

im·pe·ri·ous /£ɪm'pɪə·ri·əs, $-'pɪr·i-/ *adj* unpleasantly proud and expecting obedience • *an imperious manner/look/voice/gesture* • *She sent them away with an imperious wave of the hand.*

im·pe·ri·ous·ly /£ɪm'pɪə·ri·ə·sli, $-'pɪr·i-/ *adv*

im·pe·ri·ous·ness /£ɪm'pɪə·ri·ə·snəs, $-'pɪr·i-/ *n* [U]

im·per·ish·ab·le /ɪm'per·ɪ·ʃə·bl̩/ *adj literary* lasting forever; never weakening with age • *She has a strangely imperishable beauty, and she remains as glamorous today as she was thirty years ago.*

im·per·man·ence /£ɪm'pɜː·mə·nənts, $-'pɜːr-/ *n* [U] the quality of not lasting forever or not lasting for a long time • *There's an air of impermanence about the house, as if they've either just moved in or are about to leave.*

im·per·man·ent /£ɪm'pɜː·mə·nənt, $-'pɜːr-/ *adj* • *A lot of modern buildings seem somehow impermanent, as if they aren't built to last more than ten years.*

im·per·me·ab·le /£ɪm'pɜː·mi·ə·bl̩, $-'pɜːr-/ *adj* not allowing liquid or gas to go through • *an impermeable membrane*

im·per·mis·sib·le /£ˌɪm·pə'mɪs·ə·bl̩, $-pɚ-/ *adj* [not gradable] *slightly fml* not allowed or permitted • *There are certain topics of conversation that are impermissible in polite society.*

im·per·son·al /£ɪm'pɜː·sən·əl, $-'pɜːr-/ *adj* lacking human warmth and interest • *Hospitals always seem such impersonal places – rows of identical beds in dull grey rooms.* • *She has a very cold and impersonal manner.*

im·per·son·ate *obj* /£ɪm'pɜː·sən·eɪt, $-'pɜːr-/ *v* [T] to intentionally copy (another person's) characteristics, such as their behaviour, speech, appearance or facial expressions, esp. in order to make people laugh, or to attempt to deceive someone by pretending that you are (another person) • *She's the woman who impersonates the Queen on TV.* • *He was fined for impersonating a police officer.*

im·per·son·a·tion /£ɪmˌpɜː·sən'eɪ·ʃən, $-ˌpɜːr-/ *n* • *He does a brilliant impersonation of Charles.* [C] • *Is impersonation of a police officer a criminal offence?* [U]

im·per·son·a·tor /£ɪm'pɜː·sən·eɪ·tər, $-'pɜːr·sən·eɪ·t̬ɚ/ *n* [C] • An impersonator is someone who copies another person's speech, behaviour and facial expressions: *There's a competition to find the best Elvis impersonator in Britain.*

im·per·tin·ent /£ɪm'pɜː·tɪ·nənt, $-'pɜːr·t̬ən·ənt/ *adj* (of people or remarks) rude and not respectful, esp. towards someone older or in a higher position than you • *I hope he didn't think me impertinent when I asked him about his private life.* • *The minister has dismissed the journalist's comments as impertinent nonsense.*

im·per·tin·ent·ly /£ɪm'pɜː·tɪ·nənt·li, $-'pɜːr·t̬ən·ənt-/ *adv*

im·per·tin·ence /£ɪm'pɜː·tɪ·nənts, $-'pɜːr·t̬ən·ənts/ *n* • *Boldness in someone so young is sometimes seen as impertinence.* [U] • *I think she regarded my enquiries as an impertinence.* [C]

im·per·turb·ab·le /£ˌɪm·pə'tɜː·bə·bl̩, $-pɚ'tɜːr-/ *adj fml* always remaining calm and controlled, even in difficult situations that would cause anxiety to others • *As a nurse she was ideal – calmly competent and imperturbable in a crisis.*

im·per·turb·ab·ly /£ˌɪm·pə'tɜː·bə·bli, $-pɚ'tɜːr-/ *adv fml*

im·per·vi·ous /£ɪm'pɜː·vi·əs, $-'pɜːr-/ *adj* not allowing liquid to go through, or *(fig.)* unable to be influenced by something • *How does glue bond with impervious substances like glass and metal?* • *(fig.) The President remains impervious* **to** *public opinion.* • *(fig.) He is impervious* **to** *criticism and rational argument.* • *(fig.) Sadly, she seems to be impervious* **to** *my charms.*

im·pe·ti·go /£ˌɪm·pə'taɪ·gəʊ, $-goʊ/ *n* [U] an infectious skin disease in which yellowish sores appear on the body • *Constant scratching can weaken the normal defences of the skin, leading to impetigo and other contagious skin diseases.*

im·pet·u·ous /ɪm'pet·ju·əs/ *adj* (of a person) tending to act on a sudden idea or wish, without considering the results of your actions, or (of words or an action) said or done suddenly, without considering the likely results • *He's so impetuous – why can't he think things over before he rushes into them?* • *The Prime Minister may now be regretting her impetuous promise to reduce unemployment by half.*

im·pet·u·ous·ly /ɪm'pet·ju·ə·sli/ *adv*

im·pet·u·ous·ness /ɪm'pet·ju·ə·snəs/, *fml* **im·pet·u·os·i·ty** /£ɪmˌpet·ju'ɒs·ə·ti, $-'ɑː·sə·t̬i/ *n* [U] • *Pat's impetuousness will get her into trouble one of these days.*

im·pe·tus /£'ɪm·pɪ·təs, $-pə·t̬əs/ *n* [U] something which encourages a particular activity or makes that activity more energetic or effective • *The recent publicity *surrounding homelessness has given* **(a) fresh** *impetus to the cause.*

im·pi·e·ty /£ɪmˈpaɪ·ə·ti, $-t̬i/, **im·pi·ous·ness** /ˈɪm·pi·ə·snəs/ *n* [U] a lack of respect, esp. for God or religion; lack of PIETY • *The church accused him of impiety and had all his writings burned.*

im·pi·ous /ˈɪm·pi·əs/ *adj*

im·pi·ous·ly /ˈɪm·pi·ə·sli/ *adv*

im·pinge on *obj* /ɪmˈpɪndʒ/, **im·pinge u·pon** *obj v prep* [T] to have an effect on (something), often causing problems by limiting it in some way • *The government's spending limits will seriously impinge on the education budget.* • Ⓘ

im·pish /ɪm·pɪʃ/ *adj* See at IMP

im·plac·ab·le /ɪmˈplæk·ə·bl̩/ *adj slightly fml* (of opinions or feelings) unable to be changed • *She has long been the president's most implacable enemy.* • *What is so depressing about this war is the implacable hatred that both sides feel for each other.*

im·plac·ab·ly /ɪmˈplæk·ə·bli/ *adv slightly fml* • *The minister implacably opposes the proposed tax laws.*

im·plant *obj* /£ɪmˈplɑːnt, $-ˈplænt/ *v* [T] to put (an organ, group of cells or device) into the body in a medical operation, or *(fig.)* to fix (ideas) in someone else's mind • *She's had a kidney valve implanted.* • *(fig.) He's managed to implant some very strange attitudes* **in** *his children.* • Compare TRANSPLANT.

im·plant /£ˈɪm·plɑːnt, $-plænt/ *n* [C] • *She's had silicone breast implants to increase the size of her bust.* • *He's a specialist in implant surgery, especially heart valve implants.* • Compare TRANSPLANT.

im·plaus·ib·le /£ɪmˈplɔː·zɪ·bl̩, $-ˈplɑː·zə-/ *adj* difficult to believe; not probable • *The whole plot of the film is ridiculously implausible.*

im·plaus·ib·ly /£ɪmˈplɔː·zɪ·bli, $-ˈplɑː·zə-/ *adv* • *The tall solid actress is cast rather implausibly as a ballet dancer.*

im·plaus·i·bil·i·ty /£ɪmˌplɔː·zɪˈbɪl·ɪ·ti, $-ˌplɑː·zəˈbɪl·ə·t̬i/ *n* [U]

im·ple·ment [TOOL] /ˈɪm·plɪ·mənt/ *n* [C] a tool which works by being moved by hand or by being pulled across a surface, but which is not powered directly by electricity or fuel • *gardening/farming/household implements* • *Ploughs and other agricultural implements were on display at the exhibition.* • *Shopkeepers should not be allowed to sell knives and other sharp implements to children.*

im·ple·ment *obj* [USE] /ˈɪm·plɪ·ment/ *v* [T] to put (a plan or system) into operation • *The changes to the national health system will be implemented next year.*

im·ple·men·ta·tion /ˌɪm·plɪ·menˈteɪ·ʃən/ *n* [U] • *The effective implementation of the policy will depend heavily on the police force.*

im·pli·cate *obj* /ˈɪm·plɪ·keɪt/ *v* [T] to show that (someone) is involved in a crime or partly responsible for something bad that has happened • *He claims that the evidence has been made up to implicate him* **in** *the robbery.* • *A lot of people were implicated* **in** *the scandal.*

im·pli·ca·tion /ˌɪm·plɪˈkeɪ·ʃən/ *n* [U] • *His implication of his co-workers in the fraud was crucial to the government's case.* • See also **implication** at IMPLY.

im·pli·cit [SUGGESTED] /ɪmˈplɪs·ɪt/ *adj* suggested but not communicated directly; not EXPLICIT • *He interpreted her condemnation of recent political developments as an implicit criticism of the government.* • *Implicit* **in** *the poem's closing lines are the poet's own religious doubts.*

im·pli·cit·ly /ɪmˈplɪs·ɪt·li/ *adv*

im·pli·cit [COMPLETE] /ɪmˈplɪs·ɪt/ *adj* (esp. of trust and belief) complete and without any doubts • *All her life she had implicit faith in socialism.*

im·pli·cit·ly /ɪmˈplɪs·ɪt·li/ *adv* • *He trusts her implicitly.*

im·plode /£ɪmˈpləʊd, $-ˈploʊd/ *v* [I] *specialized* to fall inward with force • *The vacuum inside the tube caused it to implode when the external air pressure was increased.* • *(fig.) Their economy is in danger of imploding because of massive foreign debts.* • Compare EXPLODE [BURST].

im·plo·sion /£ɪmˈpləʊ·ʒən, $-ˈploʊ-/ *n* [C/U] *specialized*

im·plore *obj* /£ɪmˈplɔːʳ, $-ˈplɔːr/ *v* [T] to ask (someone) to do or not do something in a determined, sincere and sometimes emotional way, or *(literary)* to ask for (something) in this way • *She implored her parents not* **to** *send her away to school.* [+ obj + *to* infinitive] • *I implored him not* **to** *have all that beautiful hair cut off.* [+ obj + *to* infinitive] • *(literary) She was not expecting him to implore her forgiveness, but she did expect an apology.*

im·plor·ing /£ɪmˈplɔː·rɪŋ, $-ˈplɔːr·ɪŋ/ *adj* • *He had an imploring look in his eyes as I opened the bar of chocolate.*

im·plor·ing·ly /£ɪmˈplɔː·rɪŋ·li, $-ˈplɔːr·ɪŋ·li/ *adv*

im·ply *obj* /ɪmˈplaɪ/ *v* [T] to communicate (an idea or feeling) without saying it directly, or *(fml)* to involve (something) or make it necessary • *He said he only had time for a couple of pints, implying* **that** *he normally drank more.* [+ that clause] • *I'm not implying anything about your cooking, but could we eat out tonight?* • *(fml) Socialism implies equality.*

im·plied /ɪmˈplaɪd/ *adj* [not gradable] • *Her threat to resign was implied rather than stated explicitly.* • *Behind his announcement lies an implied* **criticism** *of the way he has been treated.*

im·pli·ca·tion /ˌɪm·plɪˈkeɪ·ʃən/ *n* • *From what she said I thought the implication was* **that** *they were splitting up.* [U + *that* clause] • *She accused the party, and* **by** *implication, accused its leader too.* [U] • People often refer to the implications of a decision or an action meaning the effect that it will have on something else in the future: *I know that the company is cutting back its spending but I'm not sure what the implications are* **for** *our department.* [C] ○ *What are the implications* **of** *the new law?* [C] • See also **implication** at IMPLICATE.

im·po·lite /ˌɪm·pəlˈaɪt/ *adj* rude; not POLITE • *It is considered impolite to ask a person how much they earn.* • [LP] Labels

im·po·lite·ly /ˌɪm·pəlˈaɪt·li/ *adv*

im·po·lite·ness /ˌɪm·pəlˈaɪt·nəs/ *n* [U]

im·pol·i·tic /£ɪmˈpɒl·ɪ·tɪk, $-ˈpɑː·lə·t̬ɪk/ *adj fml* (of words or actions) unwise; not clearly considered and likely to cause offence or difficulties esp. in social situations • *Fiona was coming to the party so I thought it impolitic to ask her ex-husband.*

im·pon·der·ab·le /£ɪmˈpɒn·dər·ə·bl̩, $-ˈpɑːn-/ *adj* (esp. of effects and results) unable to be guessed or calculated because of being completely unknown • *The impact on the environment of this massive oil spillage is imponderable.*

im·pon·der·ab·le /£ɪmˈpɒn·dər·ə·bl̩, $-ˈpɑːn-/ *n* [C] • *Exactly how many refugees will be left after this long and bloody war is one of many imponderables.*

im·port *obj* [BRING IN] /£ɪmˈpɔːt, $ˈɪm·pɔːrt/ *v* [T] to buy or bring in (products) from another country, or to introduce (new goods, customs, or ideas) to one country from another • *We import a large number of cars* **from** *Japan.* • *She works for a company that imports leather goods from India.* • *The fashion for wearing baseball hats was imported directly* **from** *the States.* • *(specialized)* To import information into a program or computer is to copy it from another program or form of storage: *I want to be able to import information from the database into my word-processor.* • Compare EXPORT.

im·port /£ˈɪm·pɔːt, $-pɔːrt/ *n* [C often pl] • Imports are goods bought by one country from another: *The minister is pressing for tighter restrictions on the volume of foreign imports.*

im·port /£ˈɪm·pɔːt, $-pɔːrt/, **im·por·ta·tion** /£ˌɪm·pɔːˈteɪ·ʃən, $-pɔːr-/ *n* [U] • Import can also refer to the action of bringing goods or fashions into a country: *the import/importation of coffee from South America* • *the illegal importation of drugs into the country* • *the importation of foreign theatre*

im·port·er /£ɪmˈpɔː·təʳ, $-ˈpɔːr·t̬ɚ/ *n* [C] • *After the USA, Japan is the second biggest importer of oil.* • *He is an importer of African foodstuffs.*

im·port [IMPORTANCE] /£ˈɪm·pɔːt, $-pɔːrt/ *n* [U] *fml* the importance or meaning of something • *It is still too early to judge the political import of her speech.*

im·por·tant /£ɪmˈpɔː·tənt, $-ˈpɔːr·t̬ənt/ *adj* necessary or of great value • *I sometimes think his career is more important* **to** *him than I am.* • **It's** *important* **for** *children* **to** *learn to get on with each other.* [+ *to* infinitive] • *If you really don't want to go to Italy,* **it's** *important* **that** *you tell her before she books the tickets.* [+ *that* clause] • **The** *important* **thing** *is to keep the heat low or the sugar will burn.* • *He's not amazingly handsome, but he's really nice and that's more important.* • Important also means having great effect or influence: *Somebody who was obviously very important arrived in a chauffeur-driven car.* ○ *He was one of the most important writers of that period.*

im·por·tant·ly /£ɪmˈpɔː·tənt·li, $-ˈpɔːr·t̬ənt-/ *adv* • *She's quite good-looking, but more importantly for Jonathon, she's got a lot of money.*

im·por·tance /£ɪm'pɔː·tᵊnts, $-'pɔːr·t̬ᵊnts/ *n* [U] • *The health report stresses the importance of fresh food in a diet.* • *It's a matter of considerable importance to a lot of people.* • *She* **attaches** *a lot of importance* **to** *personal possessions.* • *"A Woman of No Importance"* (title of a play by Oscar Wilde, 1893) • Ⓟ

im·por·tu·nate /£ɪm'pɔː·tjʊ·nət, $-'pɔːr·tʃə·nɪt/ *adj fml* (of people) making repeated and forceful attempts to get what you want and unwilling to allow yourself to be beaten, or (of requests) repeated and forceful • *We had spent almost an entire evening without mentioning the war, until some importunate journalist insisted on asking what we all thought about it.* • *Importunate admirers had blocked the entrance to the hotel in their efforts to catch a glimpse of the film star.*

im·por·tune *obj* /£,ɪm·pə'tjuːn, $,ɪm·pɔːr'tuːn/ *v* [T] *fml* • To importune is to make repeated forceful requests for something, usually in a way that is annoying or inconvenient: *As a tourist you are importuned for money the moment you step outside your hotel.* • To importune someone can also mean to request sex with them in return for payment: *He was arrested for importuning a young boy outside the station.*

im·pose *obj* /£ɪm'pəʊz, $-'poʊz/ *v* [T] to establish (something) as a rule to be obeyed or to force people to accept (something) • *Very high taxes have recently been imposed* **on** *cigarettes.* • *Teachers are striking in protest at this year's government-imposed pay settlement.* • *Judges are imposing increasingly heavy fines for minor driving offences.* • *The council has imposed a ban* **on** *alcohol in the city parks.* • *Colonial settlers imposed their own culture and religion* **on** *the countries that they conquered.* • *We need to impose some kind of order* **on** *the way we do things in the office.*

im·pos·i·tion /,ɪm·pə'zɪʃ·ᵊn/ *n* [U] • *Several government ministers have demanded the imposition* **of** *the death penalty for the murder of police officers.* • *The imposition of* **martial law** *will not halt the disintegration of the country.* • *The imposition of* **sanctions** *is unlikely to have any significant effect until winter.*

im·pose on *obj v prep* [T] to force your presence on (someone) when it is not wanted, or to cause inconvenience to (someone) • *Are you sure it's all right for me to come tonight? I don't want to impose on you.* • *She's always imposing on people – asking favours and getting everyone to do things for her.*

im·pos·i·tion /,ɪm·pə'zɪʃ·ᵊn/ *n* [C] • *Would it be too much of an imposition to ask you to pick my parents up from the airport?*

im·pos·ing /£ɪm'pəʊ·zɪŋ, $-'poʊ-/ *adj* having an appearance which looks important or causes admiration • *Her weekends are spent in an imposing mansion by the sea.* • *He was a tall imposing figure on stage.*

im·pos·si·ble /£ɪm'pɒs·ɪ·bl̩, $-'pɑː·sə-/ *adj* [not gradable] unable to exist, happen or be achieved; not POSSIBLE [ACHIEVABLE] • *She ate three plates of spaghetti and a piece of cake? That's impossible. I don't believe it!* • *It seems to be impossible* **to** *find a decent tailor these days.* [+ *to* infinitive] • *It seems impossible* **that** *I could have walked by and not noticed her.* [+ *that* clause] • *He made it impossible for me to say no.* • A situation might be described as impossible if is extremely difficult and there does not seem to be a solution: *It's an impossible situation – she's got to leave him but she can't bear losing her children.* • A person might be described as impossible if they are extremely difficult to deal with or are behaving badly: *I had to leave the job because my boss was impossible.* ○ *My niece gets impossible when she's tired – you can't do anything to please her.*

im·pos·si·ble /£ɪm'pɒs·ɪ·bl̩, $-'pɑː·sə-/ *n* [U] • **The impossible** is something which cannot be expected to happen or exist: *She wants a man who is bright, attractive and funny as well, which is asking the impossible in my opinion.*

im·pos·si·bil·i·ty /£ɪm,pɒs·ɪ'bɪl·ɪ·ti, $-,pɑː·sə'bɪl·ə·t̬i/ *n* • *What you're asking from can't be done – it's an impossibility.* [C] • *He complained of the impossibility of finding a British actor who could play the part.* [U]

im·pos·si·bly /£ɪm'pɒs·ɪ·bli, $-'pɑː·sə-/ *adv* [not gradable] • *Working with him can be impossibly difficult sometimes.* • *Doctors are being forced to work impossibly long hours.* • *(fig.) She has an impossibly* (=extremely) *thin waist.*

im·post·er, im·pos·tor /£ɪm'pɒs·təʳ, $-'pɑː·stɚ/ *n* [C] a person who pretends to be someone else in order to deceive others • *He felt like an imposter among all those intelligent people, as if he had no right to be there.* • *She plays the impostor in that new adventure film.* • *"If you can meet with Triumph and Disaster/ And treat those two imposters just the same"* (from the poem *If* by Rudyard Kipling, 1910)

im·pos·ture /£ɪm'pɒs·tjəʳ, $-'pɑː·stjɚ/ *n* [C/U] *fml or literary* • Imposture is the act of pretending to be someone else in order to deceive others.

im·po·tent [LACKING POWER] /£'ɪm·pə·tᵊnt, $-t̬ᵊnt/ *adj* lacking the power or ability to change or improve a situation; powerless • *You feel so impotent when your child is ill and there's nothing you can do.* • Ⓕ

im·po·tence /£'ɪm·pə·tᵊnts, $-t̬ᵊnts/ *n* [U] • *political impotence* • *There's a deepening sense of impotence among the staff in our department.*

im·po·tent [SEXUAL PROBLEM] /£'ɪm·pə·tᵊnt, $-t̬ᵊnt/ *adj* [not gradable] (of a man) unable to have sex because the penis cannot harden or stay hard • Ⓕ

im·po·tence /£'ɪm·pə·tᵊnts, $-t̬ᵊnts/ *n* [U] • *Men sometimes suffer from impotence after a serious illness.*

im·pound *obj* /ɪm'paʊnd/ *v* [T] to take possession of (something) by legal right • *The film was so violent it was impounded by the censors.* • *The police are impounding homes, cars and personal property belonging to the drug dealers.*

im·pov·er·ished /£ɪm'pɒv·ᵊr·ɪʃt, $-'pɑː·vɚ-/ *adj* poor and without money to live on, or *(fig. fml)* weakened or made worse in quality • *She's going out with an impoverished young actor.* • *(fig. fml) The breakdown of the family unit, warned the speaker, would lead to an impoverished society.*

im·pov·er·ish *obj* /£ɪm'pɒv·ᵊr·ɪʃ, $-'pɑː·vɚ-/ *v* [T] • *Lack of fertilizer had impoverished the soil.*

im·pov·er·ish·ment /£ɪm'pɒv·ᵊr·ɪʃ·mənt, $-'pɑː·vɚ-/ *n* [U] • *Continual wars and internal conflict have led to the country's impoverishment.* • *(fml) She writes about the impoverishment of the spirit in the materialist modern society.*

im·prac·ti·cab·le /ɪm'præk·tɪ·kə·bl̩/ *adj* (esp. of a course of action or plan) impossible to do in a way that is effective; not PRACTICABLE • *The changes to the tax system proved impracticable as they were impossible to enforce.*

im·prac·ti·cal /ɪm'præk·tɪ·kᵊl/ *adj* (of people) not naturally able to be practical, (of arrangements) unlikely to happen so that they are effective, or (of things) causing problems when they are used • *A lot of men just pretend to be impractical around the house so that women do their work for them.* • *It's impractical to have so many people all trying to use this equipment at the same time.* • *Silk clothes are so impractical because you can't put them in the washing machine.*

im·pre·ca·tion /,ɪm·prə'keɪ·ʃᵊn/ *n* [C] *fml* a swear word • *The old woman walked along the street* **muttering** (= saying quietly) *imprecations.*

im·pre·cise /,ɪm·prɪ'saɪs/ *adj* not accurate or exact; not PRECISE • *The figures are imprecise because they're based on a prediction of next year's sales.*

im·pre·ci·sion /,ɪm·prɪ'sɪʒ·ᵊn/ *n* [U] • *Imprecision in the manufacture of components has been a major problem with this engineering project.*

im·preg·na·ble /ɪm'preg·nə·bl̩/ *adj* (of a building) so strong and well-made that it cannot be broken into or taken by force, or *(fig. esp. Br)* (of a person or team) powerful and not likely to be beaten • *You can fit your house with burglar alarms and double locks but your home will never be impregnable against determined thieves.* • *(fig. Br and Aus) Three championship titles in one year has put this top-class golfer in an impregnable position.*

im·preg·nate *obj* [ABSORB] /£'ɪm·preg·neɪt, $-'--/ *v* [T usually passive] *specialized* to cause (esp. a solid substance) to absorb esp. a liquid substance • *This cloth has been impregnated* **with** *special chemicals for cleaning computer screens.* • Ⓓ

im·preg·nate *obj* [MAKE PREGNANT] /£'ɪm·preg·neɪt, $-'--/ *v* [T often passive] *specialized* to make (a woman or animal) pregnant • *Once the female guinea-pig has been impregnated the male can be removed from the cage.* • Ⓓ

im·pre·sa·ri·o /£,ɪm·prə'sɑː·ri·əʊ, $-'sɑːr·i·oʊ/ *n* [C] *pl* **impresarios** a person who arranges public entertainments, such as theatre, musical and dance events • *He's become London's leading theatrical impresario.*

im·press *(obj)* /ɪm'pres/ *v* [often passive; not *be impressing*] to cause (someone) to admire or respect you because of something that you have done or said • *I remember when I* *was a child being very impressed* **with** *how many toys she had.* [T] • *I don't think his mother was very impressed* **by** *our behaviour in the restaurant.* [T] • *"How was his cooking?" "Oh, it was pretty good, I was quite impressed."* • *Actually, I was trying to impress you with my extensive knowledge of wine.* [T] • *You managed to get both items for under £50? I'm impressed!* [T] • **It** *never* **fails to** *impress me* **how** *elegant the people look in Paris.* [T + obj + *wh-* word] • *I'm afraid the new theatre* **fails to** *impress.* [I]

im·pres·sive /ɪm'pres·ɪv/ *adj* • Something which is impressive causes you to feel admiration, often because it looks special or important, or because you feel that it is an achievement: *There are some very impressive buildings in the town.* ○ *They've got a very impressive collection of modern paintings.* ○ *That was an impressive performance from such a young tennis player.* • Someone who is impressive causes you to feel admiration because they are in some way very skilled and good at what they do: *She's a very impressive public speaker.* ○ *I saw him act for the first time last night – he was quite impressive.*

im·pres·sive·ly /ɪm'pres·ɪv·li/ *adv* • *He has an impressively large collection of sporting trophies and medals.*

im·press on/u·pon *obj v prep* [T] to make (someone) understand or be aware of the importance or value of something • *He's always trying to impress on me how much easier life is if you're well-organized.* • *Trying to impress on my brother the importance of personal hygiene was never an easy task.*

im·pres·sion OPINION /ɪm'preʃ·ən/ *n* [C] an idea or opinion of what something is like • *I didn't get much of an impression of the place* (= I didn't see or experience it fully) *because we drove through it in the dark.* • *What was your impression of Charlotte's husband?* (= What did you think of him?) • *I don't tend to trust* **first** *impressions.* • *When I first met him I* **got/had** *the impression* **that** *he was a rather shy, nervous sort of a bloke.* [+ *that* clause] • *From what you said I was* **under/of the** *impression* (= I understood) **that** *you didn't get on too well.* [+ *that* clause] • *I was* **under the** *mistaken impression* **that** *they were married.* [+ *that* clause]

im·pres·sion EFFECT /ɪm'preʃ·ən/ *n* [C] the way that something seems, looks or feels to a particular person • *I had the impression that he was a young man, but he turned out to be much older.* • *It* **makes/gives/creates** *a very bad impression if you're late for an interview.* • *He likes to* **give** *the impression* **that** *he's terribly popular and has loads of friends.* [+ *that* clause] • *Plain, light walls and minimal decor in a room* **create** *the impression of space.* • If you **make an impression on** someone, you cause them to notice and admire you, often because you have an attractive characteristic: *I think he made quite an impression on the girls at the tennis club.* ○ *She made such a good impression at work that she was soon promoted.*

im·pres·sion·able /ɪm'preʃ·ən·ə·bl̩/ *adj often disapproving* • Someone, usually a young person, who is described as impressionable is very easily influenced by the people around them and what they are told, sometimes tending to copy other people's behaviour: *He is* **at that** *impressionable* **age** *when he's very easily led by other children at school.*

im·pres·sion·is·tic /ˌɪmˌpreʃ·ən'ɪs·tɪk, $-t̬ɪk/ *adj* • Something which is impressionistic gives a general view or representation of something instead of particular details or facts: *The new play at the Youth Theatre is an impressionistic view of life in the fifties.*

im·pres·sion COPY /ɪm'preʃ·ən/ *n* [C] an attempt at copying another person's manner and speech, etc. or sometimes an animal's behaviour, esp. in order to make people laugh • *She* **does** *a really good impression of the president.* • *My dad used to do an impression of a monkey when we were kids.*

im·pres·sion·ist /ɪm'preʃ·ən·ɪst/ *n* [C] • An impressionist is a person who copies other people's manner and speech in order to entertain other people and make them laugh.

im·pres·sion MARK /ɪm'preʃ·ən/ *n* [C] a mark made on the surface of something by pressing an object onto it • *She had slept with her head on a folded jacket and the buttons had* **left** *an impression on her cheek.*

im·pres·sion BOOKS /ɪm'preʃ·ən/, *Am and Aus also* **print·ing** *n* [C often sing] all the copies of a book that have been printed at the same time without any changes being made • *This is the second impression of the encyclopedia.*

im·pres·sion·i·sm /ɪm'preʃ·ən·ɪ·zəm/ *n* [U] a style of painting, originating in France in the 1860s, in which the artists, including Renoir and Pissarro, tried to represent the effects of light on what they were painting

im·pres·sion·ist /ɪm'preʃ·ən·ɪst/ *n* [C] • *The impressionists tended to paint bright, cheerful pictures.*

im·pres·sion·ist /ɪm'preʃ·ən·ɪst/ *adj* • *Impressionist paintings are very popular for the home, with their views of bright cornfields and sparkling water.*

im·pri·ma·tur /£ˌɪm·prɪ'meɪ·təʳ, $-t̬ɚ/ *n* [C] *fml* official permission to do something given by a person in a position of power • *Once we've got the imprimatur of the director we can go ahead with the project.*

im·print *obj* MARK /ɪm'prɪnt/ *v* [T usually passive] to mark a surface by pressing something hard into it, or *(fig.)* to fix (esp. an event) so firmly in the memory that it cannot be forgotten although you do not try to remember it • *(fig.) That look of pure grief would be imprinted* **on** *her mind forever.* • *(fig.) The whole embarrassing episode had imprinted itself* **indelibly** (= so that it wouldn't leave) *on my mind.*

im·print /'ɪm·prɪnt/ *n* [C usually sing] • *She had left the imprint of her stiletto heels all over the floor.* • *(fig.) War has left its imprint on the strained faces of the people of this country.*

im·print BOOK /'ɪm·prɪnt/ *n* [C] the name of a publisher as it appears on a particular set of books

im·pris·on *obj* /ɪm'prɪz·ən/ *v* [T often passive] to put (someone) in prison • *He was imprisoned in 1965* **for** *attempted murder.* • *(fig.) Unable to go out because of the deep snow, she felt imprisoned in her own house.* • LP **Crimes and criminals**

im·pris·on·ment /ɪm'prɪz·ən·mənt/ *n* [U] • *She's been sentenced to five years' imprisonment.*

im·prob·a·ble /£ɪm'prɒb·ə·bl̩, $-'prɑː·bə-/ *adj* not likely to be true or to happen; not PROBABLE • *"Perhaps we haven't seen her because she's working so hard." "Sounds improbable."* • **It's highly** *improbable* **that** *Norris will agree.* [+ *that* clause] • *He came up with an improbable-sounding excuse as to why they were late.* • *An improbable-looking* (= very strange) *animal with a massively long nose crept out of a hole.*

im·prob·ab·ly /£ɪm'prɒb·ə·bli, $-'prɑː·bə-/ *adv* • *Do you see that man over there with the improbably* (= unusually) *large biceps?*

im·prob·a·bil·i·ty /£ɪmˌprɒb·ə'bɪl·ɪ·ti, $ˌɪm·prɑː·bə'bɪl·ə·t̬i/ *n* [U]

im·promp·tu /£ɪm'prɒmp·tʃuː, $-tuː/ *adj* done or said without earlier planning or preparation • *Sara unexpectedly announced that she was pregnant so we had a little impromptu party.*

im·prop·er DISHONEST /£ɪm'prɒp·əʳ, $-'prɑː·pɚ/ *adj* dishonest and against a law or a rule; not PROPER SOCIALLY ACCEPTABLE • *The governor has denied making improper* **use** *of state money.*

im·prop·er·ly /£ɪm'prɒp·ə·li, $-'prɑː·pɚ-/ *adv* • *There have been complaints that he was elected improperly and not according to the constitution.*

im·pro·pri·e·ty /£ˌɪm·prə'praɪ·ə·ti, $-t̬i/ *n* [C; U]

im·prop·er WRONG /£ɪm'prɒp·əʳ, $-'prɑː·pɚ/ *adj slightly fml* unsuitable or not correct for such a use or occasion • *In the report doctors are accused of improper prescription of medicines.* • *I was worried it might be considered improper to wear such a short skirt to so formal an occasion.* • *(specialized)* An **improper fraction** is a FRACTION in which the number below the line is smaller than the number above it: *$\frac{3}{2}$ is an improper fraction.*

im·prop·er·ly /£ɪm'prɒp·ə·li, $-'prɑː·pɚ-/ *adv slightly fml* • *If handled improperly such chemicals can cause severe skin irritations.*

im·pro·pri·e·ty /£ˌɪm·prə'praɪ·ə·ti, $-t̬i/ *n* • *The investigation into the attorney-general's* **alleged** *improprieties should be complete next week.* [C] • *She has strenuously denied the allegations of* **financial** *impropriety.* [U]

im·prop·er RUDE /£ɪm'prɒp·əʳ, $-'prɑː·pɚ/ *adj* related to sex in a way that is rude or socially unacceptable • *I trust you're not making improper suggestions to my husband!*

im·pro·pri·e·ty /£ˌɪm·prə'praɪ·ə·ti, $-t̬i/ *n* [C/U] *slightly fml or humorous*

im·prove *(obj)* /ɪm'pruːv/ *v* to (cause something to) get better • *He did a lot to improve conditions for factory workers.* [T] • *The only way to improve my French was by living in France for a while.* [T] • *If the situation at home* *doesn't improve soon, I'll have to move out.* [I] • *Even more handsome at fifty than at twenty, his looks just improved with age.* [I] • *Her health has improved dramatically since she started on this new diet.* [I] • If you improve **on/upon** something, esp. something that has already been achieved, you succeed in doing better than it: *Last time she ran the race in twenty minutes, so she's hoping to improve on that.* [I]

im·prove·ment /ɪm'pruːv·mənt/ *n* • *The last year has seen a slight improvement* **in** *the economy.* [C] • *He works for a company who do home improvements.* [C] • *These white walls are a big improvement* **on** *that disgusting old wallpaper.* [C] • *Unless there's an improvement in the weather we won't be going out today.* [C] • *He's been having treatment for two months now without any improvement.* [U] • *On my school reports teachers always used to write* **'room for** *improvement'* (= could be better). [U]

im·prov·i·dent /£ɪm'prɒv·ɪ·dᵊnt, $-'prɑː·və-/ *adj slightly fml* not giving thought to the future, esp. relating to having enough money for the future • *He thought it improvident of me to spend so much on a jacket so early on in the college term.*

im·prov·i·dence /£ɪm'prɒv·ɪ·dᵊnts, $-'prɑː·və-/ *n* [U] *slightly fml*

im·pro·vise *(obj)* /'ɪm·prə·vaɪz/ *v* to invent (something such as a speech or a device) at the time when it is needed without already having planned it, or (of actors or musicians) to perform without fixed speech or music, making it up as it is performed • *I hadn't prepared a speech so I suddenly had to improvise.* [I] • *During certain scenes of the play there isn't any script and the actors just improvise the dialogue.* [T] • *We didn't have anything to sleep on so we had to improvise a mattress from a pile of blankets.* [T] • *The band improvised* **on** *'When the saints go marching in'.* • *We lay on the beach, sheltered by an improvised windbreak.*

im·pro·vis·a·tion /£,ɪm·prə·vaɪ'zeɪ·ʃᵊn, $ɪm,prɑː·vɪ'-/ *n* • *Jazz saxophonist Charlie Parker was a master of improvisation.* [U] • *As a pianist, she was noted for the improvisations which she would insert into middle of classical pieces.* [C]

im·pru·dent /ɪm'pruː·dᵊnt/ *adj slightly fml* unwise; failing to consider the likely results of your actions • *The report criticises the banks for being imprudent in their lending.*

im·pru·dence /ɪm'pruː·dᵊnts/ *n* [U] *slightly fml*

im·pu·dent /'ɪm·pjʊ·dᵊnt/ *adj* rude and not respectful, esp. towards someone who is older or in a more important position • *an impudent remark*

im·pu·dence /'ɪm·pjʊ·dᵊnts/ *n* [U]

im·pugn *obj* /ɪm'pjuːn/ *v* [T] *fml* to cause people to doubt or not to trust (someone's character, qualities or reputation) by criticizing them • *He could no longer work as a doctor because his reputation had been impugned.*

im·pulse DESIRE /'ɪm·pʌls/ *n* a sudden strong desire to do something • *I had this sudden impulse* **to** *shout out "Rubbish!" in the middle of her speech.* [C + *to* infinitive] • If you do something **on** (an) impulse, you do it because you suddenly want to, although you haven't planned to: *I just did it on an impulse – I don't know why.* [C] • *"I didn't know you were looking for some new shoes." "Oh, I wasn't – I just bought them on impulse."* [U] • *Chocolates are often on sale next to supermarket checkouts to encourage impulse* **buying**. • *"Some men just can't help acting on Impulse"* (advertisment for the perfume called Impulse, 1980s-)

im·pul·sive /ɪm'pʌl·sɪv/ *adj* • Someone who is impulsive does things suddenly without any planning and without considering the possible effects of what is done: *Don't be so impulsive – think before you act.* ○ *It was typical of his impulsive generosity that he should have given away half his fortune to charity.*

im·pul·sive·ly /ɪm'pʌl·sɪv·li/ *adv* • *She has a tendency to act impulsively which makes working with her rather unpredictable.* • *I tend to buy things impulsively when I've got a lot of cash on me.*

im·pulse SIGNAL /'ɪm·pʌls/ *n* [C] a short electrical, radio or light signal which carries information or instructions between the parts of a system • *The remote control works by sending infra-red impulses to a receiver in the video recorder.* • *Nerve impulses pass messages from the brain to other parts of the body.*

im·pulse REASON /'ɪm·pʌls/ *n* [C] *fml* a reason for doing something • *What is the main impulse* **behind** *her writing?*

im·pun·i·ty /£ɪm'pjuː·nɪ·ti, $-ə·ṭi/ *n* [U] freedom from punishment or unpleasant results of something that has been done • *The ability of the nationalists to carry out bomb attacks* **with** *impunity has shocked the French people.*

im·pure MIXED /£ɪm'pjʊəʳ, $-'pjʊr/ *adj* mixed with other substances and therefore lower in quality • *Impure drinking water is a major cause of disease in the poorer countries of the world.*

im·pur·i·ty /£ɪm'pjʊə·rɪ·ti, $-'pjʊr·ə·ṭi/ *n* • *Impurities are removed from the blood by your kidneys and then excreted in your urine.* [C] • *The impurity of the water is a serious health risk.* [U]

im·pure IMMORAL /£ɪm'pjʊəʳ, $-'pjʊr/ *adj literary or humorous* involving immoral sexual thoughts or behaviour • *She was accused of having impure thoughts about her young students.*

im·pur·i·ty /£ɪm'pjʊə·rɪ·ti, $-'pjʊr·ə·ṭi/ *n* [U]

im·pute *obj* **to** /ɪm'pjuːt/ *v prep* [T] *fml* to consider, often unfairly, (something, esp. something bad), as someone's reason for doing something. • *In his arrogance he would always impute stupidity to those who disagreed with him.* • *I hope you are not imputing to me any intention to mislead the public.*

im·put·a·tion /,ɪm·pjʊ'teɪ·ʃᵊn/ *n fml* • *I completely reject your imputation(s) of dishonesty.* [U/C]

in CONTAINED /ɪn/ *prep, adv* [not gradable] (caused to be) positioned inside something, or contained, surrounded or enclosed by something • *There's a bucket in the cupboard under the sink.* • *I wish you'd put the butter back in the fridge when you've finished with it.* • *"Where's Guy?" "He's in the bedroom."/"He's in bed."* • *Sorry I'm late – I got stuck in a traffic jam for half an hour.* • *Are you coming in for a swim?* • *The sea was freezing, but in she went without a second thought.* • *When did you get home? I never heard you come in.* • *Why are you never in* (= at home) *when I phone?* • *Could we go out tomorrow night instead? I'd rather have a quiet evening in tonight.* • *Is Daniel in* (= at work) *this week?* • *What time is Roz's flight due in?* • *We'll miss the train if you don't hurry up and get in the car.* • *I never know what's going on in her head* (= what she's thinking about). • *They live in a cottage in the middle of a wood.* • *You'll get run over if you stand in the road like that.* • *They've got some lovely old-fashioned toys on display in the window* (= in the space behind the window of the shop). • *He's incredibly vain – he's always looking at himself in the mirror* (= at the reflection of his face produced by the mirror). • *I've got a pain in my back.* • *I've got something in* (= on the surface of) *my eye.* • *He was shining the light straight in my eyes, so I couldn't see a thing.* • *A large antique vase stood in the far corner of the room.* • *He was shot in the head, but remarkably he survived.* • *They used to live in Paris, but now they live somewhere in Austria.* • *Jersey is an island in the English Channel.* • *We always stay in the same hotel whenever we go to Rome.* • *Have you ever been in prison* (= been a prisoner)*?* • *Have you ever been in a prison* (= visited a prison)*?* • *My daughter's (Br and Aus) in hospital/(Am) in the hospital having her tonsils out.* • *I used to be a receptionist in a hospital.* • *She's been* **in and out of** (= frequently staying and receiving treatment in) *hospitals ever since the accident.* • *(Am) Is Erika still in school* (= does she still go to school)*?* • If the ball is in during a game of tennis or a similar sport, it has not gone outside the edges of the area on which the game is played: *I won that point, I'm telling you! The ball was definitely in!* • *I have breakfast at 7.30 and lunch at 1 o'clock and sometimes a snack* **in between** (= between the two meals). • *He knows quite a lot of French, but he's at an* **in-between** *stage and not fluent yet.* • *(esp. Br)* If something is **in-built** (*Am and Aus usually* **built-in**) it has always been a part of something larger and cannot be separated from it: *These plans have some in-built problems which can't be resolved without revising the entire project.* • Something that is **in-flight** happens or is available during a flight: *The range of the military jets can be extended by in-flight refuelling.* ○ *We hope you will enjoy your in-flight* **entertainment** (= films shown during a flight). ○ *I always read the in-flight* **magazine**. • *(Am)* Something that is **in-home** is provided at someone's home: *In-home care for the disabled is relatively cheap to provide.* • Something that is done **in-house** is done within an organization or business and does not involve people from outside: *The restaurant makes all its ice-cream in-house.* ○ *New recruits spend six months on our in-house training scheme.* • An **in-joke** is a private joke which can only be understood by a limited group of people who have a special knowledge of something that is referred to in the joke: *Her speech was full of in-jokes about people in her department which I couldn't really appreciate.* • An **in-patient** is a person who goes into hospital to receive medical care, and stays there while they are being treated. • *(Am)* **In-state** means for or happening within a single STATE (=part of a large country): *In-state students pay less to attend the state university than out-of-state residents.* • **In-store** services can be used or obtained by the customer inside a large shop, or happen inside a large shop: *an in-store credit card service /an in-store survey of customer attitudes*

in /ɪn/ *n* • The **ins and outs** of something are the detailed or complicated facts that relate to it: *I know how to use computers, but I don't really understand* **the** *ins and outs of how they work.* ○ *It's vital that you understand* **the** *ins and outs of this investment scheme before you commit any money to it.*

in PART /ɪn/ *prep* forming a part of something • *Who's the woman in that painting?* • *He used to be the lead singer in a rock 'n' roll band.* • *I'd love to be an extra in a film.* • *There are too many spelling mistakes in this essay.* • *I've been waiting in this queue for ages.* • *Do you take milk in your coffee?* • *What do you look for in a relationship?* • *Good looks alone in a man aren't enough.* • *In Kim he's got a very good friend as well as a lover.* • *Some people see a future President in Menendez* (=think that he/she might become President). • *It's rare to find talent like hers in someone so young and inexperienced.*

in INVOLVED /ɪn/ *prep* involved or connected with, or on the subject of • *I never knew you were in publishing.* • *Adrian's doing a degree in philosophy at Leeds University.*

in WEARING /ɪn/ *prep* wearing • *Do you recognise that man (dressed) in the grey suit?* • *They were dressed from head to toe in black leather.* • *Pat can't resist men in uniform.* • *You look nice in green* (=green clothes). • *He's too shy to sunbathe in the nude* (=naked).

in EXPRESSED /ɪn/ *prep* expressed with or by something • *Cheques should be written in ink.* • *Most of her paintings are done in watercolour.* • *They spoke in Russian the whole time.* • *Only a few of their songs were recorded in stereo.* • *He always talks in a whisper, so it's sometimes difficult to hear what he's saying.* • **In all honesty/seriousness/truthfulness** (=Honestly/Seriously/Truthfully), *I do have some criticisms to make.*

in DURING /ɪn/ *prep* during part or all of a period of time • *We're going to Italy in April.* • *Some trees lose their leaves in (the) autumn.* • *I started working here in 1991.* • *What was it like to be a student in the late 60s?* • *You must remember that life in the nineteenth century was very different from what it is now.* • *I'll be very busy on Friday afternoon, but I could see you in the morning instead.* • *Bye, see you in the morning* (=tomorrow morning). • *Did you hear the thunder in the night?* • *She was a brilliant gymnast in her youth* (=when she was young). • *How many civilians died in the Vietnam War?* • *She hasn't heard from him in six months.* (=It is six months since the last time she heard from him.) • *This is the first cigarette that I've had in three years.* • *I haven't had a decent night's sleep in years/ages* (=for a long time).

in NO MORE THAN /ɪn/ *prep* needing or using no more time than • *Can you finish the job in two weeks?* • *She could get that essay done in a couple of hours if she really tried.* • *They completed the journey in record time* (=faster than ever done before).

in BEFORE THE END /ɪn/ *prep* before or at the end of (a period) • *Dinner will be ready in ten minutes.* • *We'll all be dead in a hundred years so there's no point worrying about it.* • *I'm just setting off so I should be with you in half an hour.*

in EXPERIENCING /ɪn/ *prep, adv* [not gradable] experiencing a situation or condition, or feeling an emotion • *We watched in horror as they pulled the bodies from the wreckage.* • *She inherited enough money to live in luxury for the rest of her life.* • *Many countries are thought to be developing chemical weapons in secret.* • *He left in a hurry half an hour ago and I've no idea where he is.* • *You are in great danger and should leave the country immediately.* • *Do you think I could have a word with you in private?* • *Have you ever been in love?* • *He's always in a bad temper on Monday mornings.* • *Your car's in very good condition, considering how old it is.* • *I am in no doubt whatsoever that you will be very successful.* • If you are **in for** something, you are about to experience something unpleasant: *The weather forecast says we're in for heavy rain this evening.* ○ *You'll be in for* **it** (=experiencing serious trouble) *if you don't do what she tells you.* See also GO FOR IT; **have it in for** at HAVE POSSESS. • If you are **in on** something, you are involved with it or you know about it: *He seems to be in on everything that happens at work.* ○ *She's trying to* **get** *in on* (=become involved with) a research project organised by the university. ○ *My children never want to* **let** *me in on* (=tell me about) *what they've been doing at school.* • *(Br)* Someone who is **well in there** is likely to experience something good because of a situation they are in: *She's well in there now that she's married her boss's son.* • Something which is **in-depth** is done carefully and in great detail, or discovers the real reasons which cause something: *an in-depth report/interview/analysis* • A painter, poet, etc. **in-residence** works with an organization, usually for a limited period: *People are surprised that we have an artist-in-residence at the factory, but it's been a very successful venture.* • Something that is **in-service** happens during your time at work: *Rather than send employees away on courses, the company relies on in-service* **training**.

in RESULT /ɪn/ *prep* used when referring to something done as a result of something else • *I bought him a book for Christmas, but he didn't give me anything in return.* • *I'd like to do something for you in exchange for everything you've done for me.* • *The changes are in response to demand from our customers.* • *He refused to say anything in reply to the journalists' questions.* • *In answer to a question on human rights, she declared that her country had a very good record on the issue.*

in ARRANGEMENT /ɪn/ *prep* used to show how something is arranged or divided • *Then we sat down in* (=forming) *a circle around the campfire and started telling each other ghost stories.* • *The desks were arranged in rows of ten.* • *Substantial discounts are often available to people travelling in large groups.* • *Sometimes customers buy books in twos and threes, but rarely in larger quantities than that.* • *The encyclopaedia is being published gradually in twenty parts.* • *The potatoes will bake more quickly if you slice them in two beforehand.* • *People are dying in their thousands from typhoid, cold and starvation.* • *The bill came to £25* **in all** (=with everything added together) *for two of us.* • *(Am and Aus)* An **in-line skate** is a ROLLERBLADE.

in COMPARING AMOUNTS /ɪn/ *prep* used to compare a part of an amount of something with the total amount of it • *The survey found that one in ten people/one person in ten had problems with reading.* • *Doctors say she has a one in three chance of surviving longer than a year.* • *(Br and Aus) The basic rate of income tax is 25 pence in (Am* **on***) the pound.* • You can say there's **nothing/not much/very little** in **it** to mean that two things that are being compared are the same or very similar: *One house has a bigger garden but the rooms are smaller so there's really not much in it.*

in CHARACTERISTIC /ɪn/ *prep* used to show which characteristic of a person or thing is being described • *She's deaf in her left ear.* • *The new version is worse in every respect – I much preferred the original.* • *What can you use to find out if two things are equal in weight?* • *He's about six foot in height and has long brown curly hair.*

in CAUSE /ɪn/ *prep* [+ *v-ing*] used to show when doing one thing is the cause of another thing happening • *In refusing* (=Because she refused) *to work abroad, she missed an excellent job opportunity.* • *The government has decided to ban tobacco advertising and in* **doing so** (=and because of this) *has made a great contribution to the nation's health.* • *(fml) This research is important* **in that** (=because) *it confirms the existence of a relationship between aggression and the use of alcohol.*

in FROM OUTSIDE /ɪn/ *adv* [not gradable] from outside, or towards the centre • *Could you bring the clothes in for me?* • *They were killed when the roof of their house caved in during a hurricane.* • *Cut the pastry into squares and turn in the corners of each square.* • *When does your essay have to be in?* • *(Br and Aus)* An **in-tray** (*Am* **in-box**) is a flat open container where letters and other documents are put when they arrive in a person's office and where they are kept until the person has time to deal with them: *Just put it in the in-tray on my desk and I'll look at it later.*

in COAST /ɪn/ *adv* [not gradable] towards the coast or beach • *The tide comes in very quickly here and you can easily be left stranded on the remoter parts of the beach.* • *We stood on the harbour for a while watching the ship come in.*

in COMPLETION /ɪn/ *adv* [not gradable] used to show when an activity makes something complete • *Just pencil in the answer until you're sure it's correct.* • *The text is finished, but the pictures will have to be pasted in later.* • *(Br) Would you mind filling in a questionnaire about what you watch on television?*

in SPORT /ɪn/ *adv* [after v], *adj* [not gradable] taking a turn to play • A player who is in during a game of cricket or a similar sport is trying to score points by hitting the ball, rather than trying to prevent members of the opposing team from scoring points: It started to rain just as our team was going in to bat. ○ *He was only in for half an hour, but he still managed to score fifty runs.* • *He's* **going in for** *a half marathon next month.* • *(fig.) She only has a majority of 50, so she might not* **get in** (= be elected) *again.* • *(fig.) I can't see the government being voted back in* (= being given power again) *at the next election.*

in FASHIONABLE /ɪn/ *adj infml* fashionable or popular • *High heels are in this season.* • *Music like that hasn't be in for ages.* • *The new jazz club seems to be the in place to go at the moment.* • If you are **in with** someone, you have a friendly relationship with them: *He's always trying to* **get** *in with the teachers.* • An **in-group** is a social group whose members are very loyal to each other and share a lot of interests and characteristics that people outside the group do not: *She tried hard to join the in-group at school, but they rejected her.*

in AGE/TEMPERATURE /ɪn/ *prep* used when referring approximately to someone's age or the weather temperature • *If you are in* **your** *forties you are between 40 and 49 years old.* • *Nowadays many women are in* **their** *late twenties or early thirties when they have their first child.* • *Temperatures tomorrow will be in* **the** *mid-twenties* (= about 25 degrees).

in– LACKING, *before l* **il–**, *before b, m or p* **im–**, *before r* **ir–** /ɪn-/ *combining form* used to add the meaning 'not', 'lacking', or 'the opposite of' to adjectives and to words formed from adjectives • *incomplete/incompletely* • *illegal/illegality/illegally* • *impossible/impossibility/impossibly* • *irregular/irregularity* • Compare DIS-; NON-; UN-. • LP Opposites

in·a·bil·i·ty /£ˌɪn·ə'bɪl·ɪ·ti, $-ti/ *n* [U + *to* infinitive] lack of ability to do something • *Your inability* **to** *use a computer could be a serious disadvantage when you are applying for jobs.* • *The apparent inability of senior management* **to** *decide exactly what it wants has hampered our progress.* • See also **disability** at DISABLED.

in ab·sent·i·a /ˌɪn·æb'sen·ti·ə/ *adv* [not gradable] while the person involved is not present • *An Italian court convicted him in absentia for his terrorist activities and sentenced him to life imprisonment.*

in·ac·ces·si·ble /ˌɪn·ək'ses·ɪ·bl̩/ *adj* very difficult to travel to or difficult to understand or appreciate • *The top of Mount Everest is one of the most inaccessible places in the world.* • *Some of the houses on the hillside are inaccessible* **to** *cars.* • *Why is opera so inaccessible* **to** *so many people?* • *I found his lecture completely inaccessible – I couldn't understand a word of it.*

in·ac·ces·si·bil·i·ty /£ˌɪn·əkˌses·ɪ'bɪl·ɪ·ti, $-ə·ti/ *n* [U] • *Most of the main Honduran forests are being cut down, but the Mosquitia region has been protected by its inaccessibility.*

in·ac·cu·rate /£ɪ'næk·jʊ·rət, $-jɚ·ət/ *adj* not completely correct or exact • *Your estimate of the cost of the project has turned out to be* **wildly** (= extremely) *inaccurate.* • *At present these weapons are too inaccurate for use near civilian populations.*

in·ac·cu·rate·ly /£ɪn'æk·jʊ·rət·li, $-jɚ·ət-/ *adv* [not gradable] • *We inaccurately reported that she had been convicted of fraud and we apologise for any distress this may have caused.*

in·ac·cu·ra·cy /£ɪn'æk·jʊ·rə·si, $-jɚ·ə-/ *n* • *The film is entertaining but full of historical inaccuracies.* [C] • *I've found one small inaccuracy in your calculations.* [C] • *The inaccuracy of the missiles greatly diminishes their effectiveness.* [U]

in·ac·tion /ɪn'æk·ʃən/ *n* [U] *fml* failure to do anything which might provide a solution to a problem • *After weeks of confusion and inaction the government is finally ready to push for a series of new measures.* • *The West's inaction* **on** *the famine puts millions of people at risk of starvation.*

in·ac·tive /ɪn'æk·tɪv/ *adj* doing nothing • *It's bad for your health to be physically inactive.* • *The property market remains largely inactive, but activity could be increased by a reduction in interest rates.*

in·ac·ti·vi·ty /£ˌɪn·æk'tɪv·ɪ·ti, $-ə·ti/ *n* [U] • *It's important to remember that inactivity is extremely hazardous to your health.*

in·ad·e·quate /ɪ'næd·ɪ·kwət/ *adj* too low in quality or too small in amount; not good enough • *This work is* **woefully** (= extremely) *inadequate – you'll have to do it again.* • *She has rejected the $2 million offer as totally inadequate.* • *She's a real expert on art, so I feel completely inadequate whenever I talk to her about it.*

in·ad·e·quate·ly /ɪ'næd·ɪ·kwət·li/ *adv* • *We cannot expect to be a world leader in technological development as long as our scientific research is inadequately funded.*

in·ade·qua·cy /ɪ'næd·ɪ·kwə·si/ *n* • *The inadequacies of the public transport system could be a hindrance to economic growth.* [C] • *Her brilliant performance could not overcome the inadequacy of the script.* [U] • *I always suffer from feelings of inadequacy when I'm with him.* [U]

in·ad·mis·si·ble /ˌɪn·əd'mɪs·ə·bl̩/ *adj* [not gradable] unable to be accepted in a law court • *Her confession was ruled inadmissible as evidence because it was given under pressure from the police.*

in·ad·ver·tent /£ˌɪn·əd'vɜː·tənt, $-'vɜːr·tənt/ *adj* done unintentionally • *All authors need to be wary of inadvertent plagiarism of other people's work.*

in·ad·ver·tent·ly /£ˌɪn·əd'vɜː·tənt·li, $-'vɜːr·tənt-/ *adv* • *I know he was only trying to help, but he was inadvertently adding to our problems by phoning us up all the time.*

in·ad·ver·tence /£ˌɪn·əd'vɜː·tənts, $-'vɜːr·tənts/ *n* [U]

in·ad·vis·ab·le /ˌɪn·əd'vaɪ·zə·bl̩/ *adj* unwise and likely to have unwanted results and therefore worth avoiding • *Skiing is inadvisable if you have a weak heart.* • *It is inadvisable* **to** *generalise from the results of a single experiment.* [+ *to* infinitive]

in·a·li·en·a·ble /ɪ'neɪ·li·ə·nə·bl̩/ *adj* [not gradable] *fml* unable to be removed • *The invasion breaches the inalienable* **right** *of every nation to self-determination.* • *He maintains that Taiwan has always been an inalienable part of China.*

in·am·o·ra·ta *female (pl* **inamoratas**), *male* **in·am·o·ra·to** *(pl* **inamoratos**) /£ɪˌnæm·ə'rɑː·tə, $-tə, £-təʊ, $-toʊ/ *n* [C] *literary* someone with whom a person is in love • *He's had a tattoo with the name of a former lover removed, to avoid hurting the feelings of his current inamorata.* • *Georgina's latest inamorato is a jazz musician.*

in·ane /ɪ'neɪn/ *adj* extremely silly or lacking real meaning or importance • *There are too many inane quiz shows and imported detective series on television these days.*

in·ane·ly /ɪ'neɪn·li/ *adv* • *He grinned inanely.*

in·an·i·ty /£ɪ'næn·ə·ti, $-ti/ *n* • *His speech was full of inanities that were meant to be funny.* [C] • *Considering she's supposed to be such an expert on the subject, I was amazed at the inanity of her comments.* [U]

in·an·i·mate /ɪ'næn·ɪ·mət/ *adj* possessing none of the characteristics of life that an animal or plant has • *Stones, cars and houses are inanimate.* • *He always looks at me as if I'm an inanimate object.* • *Is a robot animate or inanimate?*

in·ap·pli·ca·ble /ˌɪn·ə'plɪk·ə·bl̩/ *adj* [not gradable] not directed at, intended for or suitable for someone or something • *Why are pay rates that apply to permanent staff inapplicable* **to** *temporary employees?* • *These regulations are inapplicable* **to** *visitors from outside the European Community.*

in·ap·pro·pri·ate /£ˌɪn·ə'prəʊ·pri·ət, $-'proʊ-/ *adj* unsuitable • *His casual behaviour was wholly inappropriate* **for** *such a formal occasion.* • *I think it would be inappropriate* (**for** *you*) **to** *invite her to a party so soon after her husband's death.* [+ *to* infinitive]

in·ap·pro·pri·ate·ly /£ˌɪn·ə'prəʊ·pri·ət·li, $-'proʊ-/ *adv* • *He was rather inappropriately dressed for the occasion.*

in·ap·pro·pri·ate·ness /£ˌɪn·ə'prəʊ·pri·ət·nəs, $-'proʊ-/ *n* [U]

in·ar·ti·cu·late /£ˌɪn·ɑː'tɪk·jʊ·lət, $-ɑːr-/ *adj* unable to express feelings or ideas clearly, or expressed in a way that is difficult to understand • *When it comes to expressing their emotions, most men are hopelessly inarticulate.* • *His speech was inarticulate and it was obvious he had been drinking.*

in·ar·ti·cu·late·ly /£ˌɪn·ɑː'tɪk·jʊ·lət·li, $-ɑːr-/ *adv* • *I'm afraid I'm expressing myself rather inarticulately.*

in·ar·tic·u·la·cy /£ˌɪn·ɑː'tɪk·ʊ·lə·si, $-nɑːr-/, **in·ar·ti·cu·late·ness** /£ˌɪn·ɑː'tɪk·jʊ·lət·nəs, $-ɑːr/ *n* [U] • *The inarticulacy of most politicians makes me wonder how they ever managed to get themselves elected.*

in·as·much as /ɪ·nə'smʌtʃ/ *conjunction fml* used to express the degree to which a person or thing is the cause of something described in another part of the sentence • *Inasmuch as you are* (= Because of your position as) *their commanding officer, you are responsible for the behaviour of these men.* • *Louise is making the arrangements, inasmuch as anyone is* (= no one is really doing it, although Chris should be).

in·at·ten·tion /ˌɪn·əˈten·tʃᵊn/ *n* [U] failure to give attention • *Her disappointing exam results are entirely due to her inattention in class.*

in·at·ten·tive /£ˌɪn·əˈten·tɪv, $-t̬ɪv/ *adj* • *He has been wholly inattentive* **to** *the needs of his children.*

in·at·ten·tive·ly /£ˌɪn·əˈten·tɪv·li, $-t̬ɪv-/ *adv*

in·aud·i·ble /ɪˈnɔː·dɪ·bl̩, $-ˈnɑː-/ *adj* unable to be heard • *The noise of the machinery made her voice inaudible.* • *These very high frequency sounds are inaudible* **to** *the human ear.*

in·aud·i·bly /ɪˈnɔː·dɪ·bli, $-ˈnɑː-/ *adv* • *"I think I'm dying," he whispered almost inaudibly.*

in·aud·i·bil·i·ty /£ɪˌnɔː·dəˈbɪl·ɪ·ti, $-ˌnɑː·dəˈbɪl·ə·t̬i/ *n* [U]

in·au·gur·ate *obj* /ɪˈnɔː·gjʊ·reɪt, $-ˈnɑː-/ *v* [T] to put (something) into use or action or to put (a person) into an official position with a ceremony • *The European Community inaugurated the Single European Market on 1st January 1993.* • *American presidents are always inaugurated on January 20th.* • *(fig.) The change of government inaugurated* (= marked the beginning of) *a new era of economic prosperity.*

in·au·gur·a·tion /ɪˌnɔː·gjʊˈreɪ·ʃᵊn, $-ˌnɑː-/ *n* • *The inauguration of the new national library is due to take place in two years time.* [U] • *She is an experienced journalist who has covered six presidential inaugurations.* [C] • *How many people attended the inauguration ceremony?* • In the United States, **Inauguration Day** is the day when a person officially becomes President in a special ceremony and takes responsibility from the previous President.

in·au·gur·al /£ɪˈnɔː·gjʊ·rəl, $-ˈnɑː·gjɚ-/ *adj* [before n; not gradable] • *I'd like to welcome you all to this inaugural meeting of the society.* • *In her inaugural address to the nation, she spoke of the 70 million people of Irish descent living around world.*

in·au·spi·cious /ˌɪn·ɔːˈspɪʃ·əs, $-ɑːˈ-/ *adj fml* showing that success is not likely • *After an inauspicious start, Scotland went on to win the match by three goals to two.* • *Her cinematic debut was inauspicious and she decided to return to the theatre where she remained for the rest of her career.*

in·au·spi·cious·ly /ˌɪn·ɔːˈspɪʃ·ə·sli, $-ɑːˈ-/ *adv fml*

in·born /£ˈɪm·bɔːn, £ˌ-ˈ-, $ˈɪm·bɔːrn/ *adj* [not gradable] possessed as a mental or physical characteristic from birth • *Their research suggests that some people have an inborn tendency to develop certain kinds of tumour.* • *She has an apparently inborn talent for physics.*

in·bound /ˈɪn·baʊnd/ *adj* [not gradable] travelling towards a particular point • *Track repairs are being carried out in the area so expect delays to both inbound and outbound trains.*

in·bred ESTABLISHED /£ˌɪmˈbred, $ˈ-ˌ-/ *adj* [not gradable] firmly established in a person • *It's important for children to have an inbred sense of right and wrong.*

in·bred RELATED /£ˌɪmˈbred, $ˈ-ˌ-/ *adj* [not gradable] produced by breeding between closely related plants, animals or people • *In general, inbred animals tend to suffer from reduced fertility.*

in·breed·ing /£ˌɪmˈbriː·dɪŋ, $ˈ-ˌ-ˌ-/ *n* [U] • *Many generations of inbreeding have made this remote community susceptible to hereditary disorders such as dwarfism and mental retardation.*

Inc /ɪŋk/ *adj* [after n; not gradable] *abbreviation for* incorporated (= organized as a legal company or group of companies. Used in the US as part of the names of some companies.). • *Bishop Computer Services Inc.* • LP Letters

in·cal·cu·la·ble /ɪŋˈkæl·kjʊ·lə·bl̩/ *adj* extremely large and therefore unable to be calculated • *This letter is a unique document of incalculable value.* • *The ecological consequences of a nuclear war are incalculable.*

in·cal·cu·la·bly /ɪŋˈkæl·kjʊ·lə·bli/ *adv* • *The cost of such a disaster would be incalculably large.*

in cam·era /£ˌɪŋˈkæm·ᵊr·ə, $ˌɪnˈkæm·ɚ-/ *adv* [not gradable] (esp. of a law case) in private, without the presence of the public, newspaper reporters, etc. • *The trial was* **held** *in camera because the accused was only 14 years old.*

in·can·des·cent /ˌɪŋ·kænˈdes·ᵊnt/ *adj* producing a bright light after being heated to a high temperature • *Replacing a 60 watt incandescent light bulb with a 14 watt fluorescent tube can cut your lighting bill by up to 75 per cent.* • *We looked out across a river valley to the broad snow-white ridge of Mount Ararat, its peak incandescent against the blue sky.* • *(fig.) He was absolutely incandescent* **(with** *rage)* (= angry). angry). • *(fig.) Her beauty had an incandescent quality to it.*

in·can·des·cence /ˌɪŋ·kænˈdes·ᵊnts/ *n* [U]

in·can·ta·tion /ˌɪŋ·kænˈteɪ·ʃᵊn/ *n* [C/U] (the performance of) words believed to have a magical effect when spoken or sung • *A fire was lit and the shamans and elders chanted incantations over offerings of sweets, coca leaves and alcohol.* [C] • *In his early poems he makes use of repetition and incantation.* [U] • Compare SPELL MAGIC.

in·ca·pa·ble /ɪŋˈkeɪ·pə·bl̩/ *adj* unable to do something • *He seems incapable* **of** *walking past a music shop without going in and buying another CD.* • *She's incapable* **of** *(doing) such a dreadful thing.* • *She's a brilliant mathematician, but as a lecturer she's totally incapable.*

in·ca·pa·ci·tate *obj* /ˌɪŋ·kəˈpæs·ɪ·teɪt/ *v* [T] to remove the ability to do something from (someone) • *Rubber bullets are intended to incapacitate people rather than kill them.* • *Our objective is to incapacitate their military machine and ensure they will never again threaten the security of the region.* • *The accident left me incapacitated for seven months.*

in·ca·pac·i·tat·ing /£ˌɪŋ·kəˈpæs·ɪ·teɪ·tɪŋ, $-t̬ɪŋ/ *adj* • *Extreme shyness can be very incapacitating as it limits a person's ability to deal with people that they don't know.*

in·ca·pa·ci·ty /£ˌɪŋ·kəˈpæs·ə·ti, $-t̬i/ *n* [U] lack of ability to do something • *The incapacity of the police* **to** *limit the rise in crime cannot be attributed solely to a shortage of funds.* [+ *to* infinitive] • *The novel tells the tragic story of one man's incapacity* **for** *love.*

in·car·cer·ate *obj* /£ɪŋˈkɑː·sᵊr·eɪt, $-ˈkɑːr·sə·reɪt/ *v* [T] *fml* to put or keep (someone) in prison or a place used as a prison • *Thousands of dissidents have been interrogated or incarcerated in recent weeks.* • *(fig.) We were incarcerated* **in** (= were inside and unable to leave) *that broken elevator for four hours.*

in·car·cer·a·tion /£ɪŋˌkɑː·sᵊrˈeɪ·ʃᵊn, $-ˌkɑːr·səˈreɪ-/ *n* [U] • *The government has been heavily criticized by human-rights groups for its incarceration of political prisoners.* • *His incarceration lasted fifteen years.*

in·car·nate /£ɪŋˈkɑː·nət, $-ˈkɑːr-/ *adj* [after n; not gradable] in human form • *One survivor described his torturers as* **devils** *incarnate.*

in·car·na·tion /£ˌɪn·kɑːˈneɪ·ʃᵊn, $-kɑːr-/ *n* [U] • *He was* **the** *incarnation* **of** *evil* (= was extremely evil). • *She is* **the** *incarnation* **of** *everything I hate about politics.* • The incarnation of a god is its appearance as a human. • See also INCARNATION.

in·car·na·tion /£ˌɪŋ·kɑːˈneɪ·ʃᵊn, $-kɑːr-/ *n* [C] a particular (temporary) physical form or condition • *He discovered in a session with a hypnotist that he'd been a Roman warrior in a* **previous** *incarnation.* • *This film is the latest incarnation of a fairy tale that dates back to the Middle Ages.* • See also **incarnation** at INCARNATE; REINCARNATION.

in·cau·tious /ɪŋˈkɔː·ʃəs, $-ˈkɑː-/ *adj fml* lacking careful thought about the possible results • *Bill and Sandra haven't spoken to each other since he made an incautious* **remark** *about her husband's drinking problem.*

in·cau·tious·ly /ɪŋˈkɔː·ʃəs·li, $-ˈkɑː-/ *adv fml* • *Many people who borrowed money incautiously now face severe financial difficulties.*

in·cen·di·ar·y FIRE /£ɪnˈsen·di·ᵊr·i, $-er·i/ *adj* [before n; not gradable] designed to cause fires • *an incendiary bomb* • *He is accused of placing an incendiary device* (= bomb) *in a litter bin in central London.* • *(fig. esp. Am) He made us one of his incendiary* (= very hot-tasting) *curries.*

in·cen·di·ar·y CAUSING ANGER /£ɪnˈsen·di·ᵊr·i, $-er·i/ *adj* likely to cause violence or strong feelings of anger • *In an incendiary speech he called for a popular uprising against the government, whom he accused of dictatorship and oppression.*

in·cense SUBSTANCE /ˈɪn·sents/ *n* [U] a substance that is burnt to produce a sweet smell, esp. as part of a religious ceremony • *Incense was used in ancient Egypt, Greece and Rome, and has been used by Christians since the sixth century.*

in·cense *obj* ANGER /ɪnˈsents/ *v* [T] to cause (someone) to be extremely angry • *The editor said a lot of readers would be incensed by my article on illegal abortion.* • *The leniency of the judge's sentence on such a violent criminal has incensed public opinion.* • *I was so incensed by what he was saying that I just had to leave the room.*

in·censed /ɪnˈsentst/ *adj* [after v] • *The villagers are incensed* **at** *the decision to close the railway station.*

in·cen·tive /£ɪn'sen·tɪv, $-t̬ɪv/ *n* something which encourages a person to do something • *Tax incentives have been very effective in encouraging people to save or invest more of their income.* [C] • *Our bonus payments for improved productivity provide an incentive* **to** *work harder.* [C + *to* infinitive] • *There is little incentive* **for** *people* **to** *leave their cars at home when public transport remains so expensive.* [U + *to* infinitive]

in·cep·tion /ɪn'sep·ʃᵊn/ *n* [U] the establishment of an organization or official activity • **Since its** *inception in 1968, the company has been at the forefront of computer development.*

in·ces·sant /ɪn'ses·ᵊnt/ *adj* [not gradable] (esp. of something unpleasant) never stopping • *Having endured weeks of incessant bombardment, they surrendered as soon as they had the opportunity.*

in·ces·sant·ly /ɪn'ses·ᵊnt·li/ *adv* [not gradable] • *He'll talk incessantly about their new baby if you give him the chance.*

in·cest /'ɪn·sest/ *n* [U] sexual activity involving people who are closely related and not legally permitted to marry • *They oppose abortion even when pregnancy has resulted from rape or incest.*

in·ces·tu·ous /ɪn'ses·tju·əs/ *adj* • *The film is about Auteil's incestuous love for his sister.* • *(fig. disapproving) Journalists and politicians often have a rather incestuous* (= too close) **relationship** *with each other.*

in·ces·tu·ous·ly /ɪn'ses·tju·ə·sli/ *adv*

in·ces·tu·ous·ness /ɪn'ses·tju·ə·snəs/ *n* [U]

inch [MEASUREMENT] /ɪntʃ/ *n* [C] a unit used for measuring length, which is approximately equal to 2·54 centimetres, sometimes shown by the symbol ″ • *Twelve inches are equal to one foot.* • *He had a cut an inch long above his left eye.* • *The snow was six inches deep in some places.* • *I need a piece of wood measuring 2″ by 2″.* • *There was an inch or so of snow on the ground this morning, but it had melted by lunchtime.* • *I avoided the dog* **by inches** (= I very nearly hit the dog). • *Detectives are searching the area around the scene of the murder* **inch by inch** (= in a lot of small stages). • **Every** *inch* (= All) *of her bedroom wall is covered with photos of pop stars.* • *Caroline knows* **every** *inch of London* (= She knows London extremely well). • *She looked* **every** *inch* (= exactly like) *a vampire in her costume.* • *She's absolutely certain that she wants to do it, and she'll* **not budge/give/move an inch** (= her opinion won't change) *however hard you try to persuade her.* • *(saying)* 'Give someone an inch and they'll take a mile' means that if you allow someone a small amount of power or freedom to do something, they'll try to obtain a lot more than you intended. • LP **Symbols, Units**

inch *(obj)* [MOVE] /ɪntʃ/ *v* [always + adv/prep] to move very slowly or in a lot of short stages • *We got caught in a traffic jam and we were inching along for ages.* [I] • *Can you help me inch this bookcase into the corner?* [T] • *We are inching towards an agreement but there's a lot of negotiating still to be done.* [I] • *Share prices started the day lower than yesterday, but they inched higher throughout the afternoon.* [I]

in·cho·ate /£ɪŋ'kəʊ·eɪt, $-'koʊ-/ *adj fml or literary* only recently or partly formed; not completely developed or clear • *She had a child's inchoate awareness of language.* • *As a dancer he managed to communicate a sense of inchoate, half-animal emotion.*

in·ci·dence /'ɪnt·sɪ·dᵊnts/ *n* the rate at which something happens • *Protesters claim there is a link between the nuclear power station and the increased incidence* **of** *cancer in the area.* • *There is a higher incidence* **of** *left-handedness among boys than girls.*

in·ci·dent /'ɪnt·sɪ·dᵊnt/ *n* [C] an event which is either unpleasant or unusual • *The attack on defenceless civilians was an isolated incident which will not happen again.* • *A 23-year-old man was seriously injured in a shooting incident which occurred outside a pub on Saturday night.* • *Police fears of violence at the demonstration proved to be unfounded when it passed off* **without incident**.

in·ci·den·tal /£ˌɪnt·sɪ'den·tᵊl, $-t̬ᵊl/ *adj* happening in connection with something of greater importance • *Try not to be distracted by trivial incidental details.* • *There are always a lot of incidental* **expenses** *when you go on foreign trips.* • *The points you make are true, but they're incidental* **to** *the main problem.* • **Incidental music** is music that is played in the background during a film, broadcast or play to help the people who are watching or listening feel emotions that suit what is happening in the performance. • *"The incidental things apply, / As time goes by"* (from the song *As Time Goes By* written by Herman Hupfield, 1931)

in·ci·den·tals /£ɪn·sɪ'den·tᵊlz, $-t̬ᵊlz/ *pl n* • *Remember to take some foreign currency to cover incidentals like a taxi from the airport to your hotel.*

in·ci·den·tal·ly /£ˌɪnt·sɪ'den·tᵊl·i, $-t̬ᵊl-/ *adv* [not gradable] used before saying something that is not as important as the main subject of conversation, but is connected to it in some way • *We had a marvellous meal at that restaurant you recommended – incidentally, I must give you the number of a similar one I know of that you might like.* • Incidentally can also be used when mentioning a subject that has not been discussed before, often making it seem less important than it really is: *Incidentally, I wanted to have a word with you about your expenses claim.*

in·cin·er·ate *obj* /£ɪn'sɪn·ᵊr·eɪt, $-ə·reɪt/ *v* [T] to burn (something) completely • *The company is accused of incinerating hazardous waste without the required licence.* • *Tens of thousands of conscripts were either incinerated with the fuel bomb or buried alive in the sand.*

in·cin·er·a·tion /£ɪnˌsɪn·ᵊr'eɪ·ʃᵊn, $-ə'reɪ-/ *n* [U]

in·cin·er·a·tor /£ɪn'sɪn·ᵊr·eɪ·təʳ, $-ə·reɪ·t̬ɚ/ *n* [C] • An incinerator is a device for burning things which are no longer wanted: *A lack of incinerators has meant that many of the 22 000 cattle that have died from the disease have been buried.*

in·cip·i·ent /ɪn'sɪp·i·ᵊnt/ *adj fml or specialized* just beginning • *The disease is curable if it is treated at an incipient stage.* • *There are signs of incipient public frustration with his handling of the economy.*

in·cise *obj* /ɪn'saɪz/ *v* [T] *fml* to cut the surface of (something) carefully with a sharp tool • *The design is incised into a metal plate.*

in·ci·sion /ɪn'sɪʒ·ᵊn/ *n* [C] • *The new technique involves surgeons making small incisions* **in** *the skin into which tubes are inserted.*

in·ci·sive /ɪn'saɪ·sɪv/ *adj* expressing an idea or opinion clearly and persuasively • *Sometimes a few incisive comments from an outsider can give you a whole new perspective on what you're doing.*

in·ci·sive·ly /ɪn'saɪ·sɪv·li/ *adv*

in·ci·sive·ness /ɪn'saɪ·sɪv·nəs/ *n* [U]

in·cis·or /£ɪn'saɪ·zəʳ, $-zɚ/ *n* [C] one of the sharp teeth at the front of the mouth which cut food when you bite into it • Compare **canine (tooth)** at CANINE; MOLAR.

in·cite *obj* /ɪn'saɪt/ *v* [T] to encourage (someone) to do or feel (something unpleasant or violent) • *He was kept in solitary confinement because it was feared he might incite another riot.* • *She faces charges of inciting racial hatred by distributing anti-semitic leaflets.* • *She was expelled for inciting her classmates* **to** *rebel against their teachers.* [+ obj + *to* infinitive]

in·cite·ment /ɪn'saɪt·mənt/ *n* [U] • *They were each sentenced to one years imprisonment for incitement* **to** *commit grievous bodily harm.* [+ *to* infinitive]

in·civ·il·i·ty /£ˌɪn·sɪ'vɪl·ɪ·ti, $-ə·t̬i/ *n* [U] *fml* rudeness • *I know she has strong feelings about this matter, but that doesn't excuse her incivility.* • See also UNCIVIL.

incl *abbreviation for* **including** or **inclusive**, see at INCLUDE • *The cost of the washing machine is $449 incl delivery charges.* • *The charge for hiring a small family car is £35 per day incl.* • This abbreviation is used mainly in advertisements.

in·clem·ent /ɪŋ'klem·ᵊnt/ *adj fml* (of weather) unpleasant, esp. cold or stormy • *I regret that this afternoon's match has had to be cancelled due to inclement weather.*

in·cli·na·tion /ˌɪŋ·klɪ'neɪ·ʃᵊn/ *n* a preference or tendency; a feeling that makes a person want to do something • *My own inclination, if I were in your situation, would be* **to** *look for another job.* [C + *to* infinitive] • *The inclination* **of** *most politicians seems to be* **to** *ignore the drugs problem.* [U + *to* infinitive] • *I've no inclination* **to** *follow my mother into accountancy.* [U + *to* infinitive] • *We should be basing our decisions on solid facts rather than our inclinations and hunches.* [C]

in·cline /ɪŋ'klaɪn/ *v* [always + adv/prep] *fml* • *The poor relations between the two countries incline me* **to** *feel* (= make me tend to feel) *pessimistic about an early settlement.* [T + obj + *to* infinitive] • *The Prime Minister is believed to be inclining* **towards** *an April election.* [I] • *I incline* **to** *disagree with you* (= I more disagree than agree) *on that point.* [+ *to* infinitive]

in·clined /ɪŋ'klaɪnd/ *adj* [after v; + *to* infinitive] • *I'm inclined* **to** *agree with what you were saying in the meeting.* •

She's more inclined than most people **to** *help out when you ask her.*

in·cline *obj* /ɪŋˈklaɪn/ *v* [T] to move (something) so that it points towards the ground more than it did before • *When he is introduced to someone he just inclines his head and says nothing.*

in·cli·na·tion /ˌɪŋ·klɪˈneɪ·ʃᵊn/ *n* [C] • *She acknowledged my arrival with a solemn inclination of her head.*

in·clude *obj* /ɪŋˈkluːd/ *v* [T] to contain (something) as a part of something else, or to make (something) part of something else • *The bill includes tax and service.* • *Tax and service are included* **in** *the bill.* • *Your responsibilities will include making appointments on my behalf.* [+ v-ing] • *Do you think I'm included* **in** *the invitation?* • *You have eight fingers altogether, or ten if you include your thumbs.* • Compare EXCLUDE.

in·clud·ed /ɪŋˈkluː·dɪd/ *adj* [after n; not gradable] • *The trip cost a total of £250, insurance included.*

in·clud·ing /ɪŋˈkluː·dɪŋ/ *prep* • *Eight people, including four men, were injured in the explosion.*

in·clu·sion /ɪŋˈkluː·ʒᵊn/ *n* [U] • *She is being considered for inclusion in the England team.*

in·clu·sive /ɪŋˈkluː·sɪv/ *adj* [not gradable] • *All our prices are inclusive* **of** (= include) *Value Added Tax.* • *My rent is $700 a month inclusive* **(of** *bills).* • *You can hire a car at an* **(all-)***inclusive rate of £25 per day.* • *I'll be away from the 20th to the 31st of May inclusive.*

in·cog·ni·to /£ˌɪŋ·kɒgˈniː·təʊ, $-kɑːgˈniː·t̬oʊ/ *adv* [not gradable] avoiding being recognized by changing your name or appearance • *The prince often travels abroad incognito.*

in·co·her·ent /£ˌɪŋ·kəʊˈhɪə·rənt, $-koʊˈhɪr·ᵊnt/ *adj* expressing yourself unclearly, or expressed unclearly or in a way in which words or ideas are joined together badly • *He was confused and incoherent and I didn't get much sense out of him.* • *Her speech was incoherent and badly prepared.*

in·co·her·ent·ly /£ˌɪŋ·kəʊˈhɪə·rənt·li, $-koʊˈhɪr·ᵊnt-/ *adv*

in·co·her·ence /£ˌɪŋ·kəʊˈhɪə·rənts, $-koʊˈhɪr·ᵊnts/ *n* [U] • *The recession, he said, was a direct result of the incoherence of the government's economic policy.*

in·come /ˈɪŋ·kʌm/ *n* money that is earned from doing work, or received from investments • *Average incomes have risen by 4·5% over the past year.* [C] • *More help is needed for people on low incomes.* [C] • *A government has to borrow money when its expenditure exceeds its income.* [C] • *I haven't had much income from my stocks and shares this year.* [U] • In the United Kingdom, **income support** is money that is paid by the government to people who have no income or very low income: *Many single mothers are* **on** *income support.* • An **income tax** is a tax on a person's income which is usually higher for people with larger incomes. • LP› **Money**

in·com·ing ARRIVING /ˈɪŋˌkʌm·ɪŋ/ *adj* [before n; not gradable] arriving at, coming into, or entering a place • *This small device automatically identifies the number from which an incoming telephone call is made.* • *An incoming missile has been detected.* • *(Am) Incoming freshmen* (= students in the first year at college) *start a week before everyone else.*

in·com·ing ELECTED /ˈɪŋˌkʌm·ɪŋ/ *adj* [before n; not gradable] recently elected or chosen • *What are the biggest problems faced by the incoming president?* • *It is too late for the incoming government to reverse the policy of its predecessor.*

in·com·mu·ni·ca·do /£ˌɪŋ·kəˌmjuː·nɪˈkɑː·dəʊ, $-doʊ/ *adj* [after v], *adv* [not gradable] *esp. fml or humorous* not communicating with anyone else because you do not want to or you are not allowed to • *We wanted to invite you to the wedding, but you were incommunicado and we had no idea how to contact you.* • *He was* **held** *incommunicado for the first 48 hours after he was arrested.*

in·com·par·a·ble /£ɪŋˈkɒm·pᵊr·ə·bl̩, $-ˈkɑːm·pɚ-/ *adj* [not gradable] so good or great that nothing else could achieve the same standard • *It was an incomparable performance and fully deserved the gold medal.* • *He is a man of incomparable kindness and generosity.*

in·com·par·ab·ly /£ɪŋˈkɒm·pᵊr·ə·bli, $-ˈkɑːm·pɚ-/ *adv* [not gradable] • *His second novel was incomparably better than his first one.*

in·com·pat·i·ble /£ˌɪŋ·kəmˈpæt·ɪ·bl̩, $-ˈpæt̬·ə-/ *adj* not able to exist or work with another person or thing • *It was only when we started living together that we found out how incompatible we were.* • *Any new video system that is incompatible* **with** *existing ones has little chance of success.* • *Maintaining quality is incompatible* **with** *increasing output* (= you can't do both).

in·com·pat·i·bil·i·ty /£ˌɪŋ·kəmˌpæt·ɪˈbɪl·ɪ·ti, $-ˌpæt̬·əˈbɪl·ə·t̬i/ *n* [U] • *There's an incompatibility problem which prevents the two pieces of software being used together.* • *The disease is caused by blood group incompatibility between a mother and her child.* • *Charles decided to leave the firm because of his incompatibility* **with** *his workmates.*

in·com·pe·tence /£ɪŋˈkɒm·pɪ·tᵊnts, $-ˈkɑːm·pə·t̬ənts/ *n* [U] lack of ability or skill to do something successfully or as it should be done • *Local politicians have accused the government of incompetence in failing to restore public services after the earthquake.* • *Management have demonstrated an almost unbelievable incompetence in their handling of the dispute.*

in·com·pe·tent /£ɪŋˈkɒm·pɪ·tᵊnt, $-ˈkɑːm·pə·t̬ənt/ *adj* • *Brian's far too incompetent to be put in charge of the factory.*

in·com·pe·tent /£ɪŋˈkɒm·pɪ·tᵊnt, $-ˈkɑːm·pə·t̬ənt/ *n* [C] • *The country's being governed by a* **bunch of** *incompetents who have no idea what they're doing.*

in·com·pe·tent·ly /£ɪŋˈkɒm·pɪ·tᵊnt·li, $-ˈkɑːm·pə·t̬ənt-/ *adv* • *Companies that are incompetently managed are bound to go bankrupt eventually.*

in·com·plete /ˌɪŋ·kəmˈpliːt/ *adj* lacking some parts, or not finished • *Many of these decisions seem to have been based on incomplete or inaccurate information.* • *They've been building that office block for three years now, and it's still incomplete.*

in·com·plete·ly /ˌɪŋ·kəmˈpliːt·li/ *adv* • *The chemical properties of the substance are still incompletely understood.*

in·com·plete·ness /ˌɪŋ·kəmˈpliːt·nəs/ *n* [U]

in·com·pre·hens·i·ble /£ɪŋˌkɒm·prɪˈhent·sɪ·bl̩, $-kɑːm-/ *adj* impossible or extremely difficult to understand • *These accounts are utterly incomprehensible. Can you explain them to me?* • *It's incomprehensible* **to** *me why he would want to kill himself.* • *Her northern accent is incomprehensible* **to** *the majority of southerners.* • Ⓕ

in·com·pre·hens·i·bly /£ɪŋˌkɒm·prɪˈhent·sɪ·bli, $ˌɪŋ·kɑːm-/ *adv*

in·com·pre·hens·i·bil·i·ty /£ɪŋˌkɒm·prɪˌhent·sɪˈbɪl·ɪ·ti, $ˌɪn·kɑːm·prɪ·hent·səˈbɪl·ə·t̬i/ *n* [U] • *We were baffled by the incomprehensibility of the message.*

in·com·pre·hen·sion /£ɪŋˌkɒm·prɪˈhen·tʃᵊn, $ˌɪn·kɑːm-/ *n* [U] • Incomprehension is a person's failure or inability to understand something: *I came up against a wall of incomprehension when I tried to explain the harassment problem to my boss.*

in·con·ceiv·a·ble /ˌɪŋ·kənˈsiː·və·bl̩/ *adj* impossible to imagine or think of • *Another nuclear accident in the same place is* **virtually/almost** *inconceivable.* • *The idea that they might not win was inconceivable* **to** *them.* • **It** *is not inconceivable* **that** *she could be lying.* [+ that clause] • **It** *would be inconceivable* **for her** *to change her mind.* [+ to infinitive]

in·con·ceiv·a·bly /ˌɪŋ·kənˈsiː·və·bli/ *adv* • *The book has sold an inconceivably large number of copies.*

in·con·clus·ive /ˌɪŋ·kəŋˈkluː·sɪv/ *adj* not giving or having a result or decision • *The evidence is inconclusive.* • *The medical tests were inconclusive, and will need to be repeated.* • *Because the discussion was (so) inconclusive, we shall have to meet again.* • *I thought the film had a very inconclusive ending.*

in·con·clus·ive·ly /ˌɪŋ·kəŋˈkluː·sɪv·li/ *adv* • *The two days of talks have ended inconclusively.*

in·con·gru·ous /£ɪŋˈkɒŋ·gru·əs, $-ˈkɑːŋ-/ *adj* unusual or different from the surroundings or from what is generally happening • *The new computer looked incongruous in the dark book-filled library.* • *Do you think* **it** *incongruous* **that** *a woman should be the editor of a men's magazine?* [+ that clause]

in·con·gru·i·ty /£ˌɪŋ·kəŋˈgruː·ə·ti, $-kənˈgruː·ə·t̬i/ *n fml* • *He seemed unaware of the incongruity* (= strangeness) *of his appearance.* [U] • *The obvious friendship between the two leaders was another incongruity* (= strange thing) *in these already unusual negotiations.* [C]

in·con·se·quen·tial /£ɪŋˌkɒnt·sɪˈkwen·tʃᵊl, $-ˌkɑːnt-/ *adj* not important • *Most of what she said was pretty inconsequential.* • *The increase in the company's profits this year was inconsequential.* • *He has become an increasingly inconsequential figure on the political scene.* • Ⓓ ⒹⓀ Ⓢ

in·con·se·quen·tial·ly /£ɪŋˌkɒnt·sɪˈkwen·tʃᵊl·i, $-ˌkɑːnt-/ *adv*

in·con·sid·er·a·ble /£ˌɪŋ·kən'sɪd·ər·ə·bl̩, $'-ɚ-/ *adj* small enough to be of little importance; not worth considering • *Even after tax had been deducted, the money he had inherited turned out to be a* **not** *inconsiderable* (= a large) **sum/amount.**

in·con·sid·er·ate /£ˌɪn·kən'sɪd·ər·ət, $'-ɚ-/ *adj disapproving* not caring about other people or their feelings; selfish • *Our neighbours are very inconsiderate – they're always playing loud music late at night.* • *I didn't mean to be so inconsiderate* **to/towards** *you.* • **It** *was very inconsiderate* **of you** *to be so late.* [+ *to* infinitive] • *He made some very inconsiderate remarks about her appearance.*

in·con·sid·er·ate·ly /£ˌɪŋ·kən'sɪd·ər·ət·li, $'-ɚ-/ *adv*

in·con·sid·er·ate·ness /£ˌɪŋ·kən'sɪd·ər·ət·nəs, $'-ɚ-/ *n* [U]

in·con·sis·tent NOT AGREEING /ˌɪŋ·kən'sɪs·tənt/ *adj* (of a reason, idea, opinion etc.) not in agreement between parts of itself or with something else • *Her argument contains a lot of contradictions and is very inconsistent.* • *Statements about the robbery given by the two suspects are inconsistent.* • *These findings are inconsistent* **with** *those of previous studies.*

in·con·sis·ten·cy /ˌɪŋ·kən'sɪs·tənt·si/ *n* • *There are a few inconsistencies in what you've written.* [C] • *There was a lot of inconsistency in what he said.* [U]

in·con·sis·tent CHANGEABLE /ˌɪŋ·kən'sɪs·tənt/ *adj* changing in behaviour; not staying the same • *She's an inconsistent piano player – sometimes she's good and sometimes not.* • *The teacher said that Alex's schoolwork was very inconsistent.*

in·con·sis·ten·cy /ˌɪŋ·kən'sɪs·tənt·si/ *n* [U] • *An increasing number of voters are becoming dissatisfied with what they see as the government's inconsistency in its economic policy.*

in·con·sis·tent·ly /ˌɪŋ·kən'sɪs·tənt·li/ *adv* • *Rogers played well but inconsistently and this gave his opponent the vital chances needed to win.*

in·con·sol·a·ble /£ˌɪŋ·kən'səʊ·lə·bl̩, $-'soʊ-/ *adj* [not gradable] impossible to comfort because of great sadness or unhappiness • *They were inconsolable after the death of their young son.* • *He was in an inconsolable mood of despair.*

in·con·sol·a·bly /£ˌɪŋ·kən'səʊ·lə·bli, $-'soʊ-/ *adv* [not gradable] • *The child was crying inconsolably.*

in·con·spi·cu·ous /ˌɪŋ·kən'spɪk·ju·əs/ *adj* not easily or quickly noticed or seen; not attracting attention • *This type of bird is very inconspicuous because of its dull feathers.* • *Considering she's the head of our company, she's highly inconspicuous.* • *Whenever he goes to parties, he always stands in a corner and tries to look inconspicuous.*

in·con·spi·cu·ous·ly /ˌɪŋ·kən'spɪk·ju·ə·sli/ *adv* • *Security officers will be operating as inconspicuously as possible at the concert.*

in·con·stant /£ɪŋ'kɒnt·stənt, $-'kɑːnt-/ *adj esp. literary or fml* not staying the same, esp. in emotion, behaviour or choice of sexual partner • *an inconstant lover*

in·con·stan·cy /£ɪŋ'kɒnt·stənt·si, $-'kɑːnt-/ *n* [U] *esp. literary or fml*

in·con·tes·ta·ble /ˌɪŋ·kən'tes·tə·bl̩/ *adj* [not gradable] *fml* impossible to question because obviously true • *There is now incontestable evidence that the killings did take place.* • **It** *is incontestable* **that** *the war has had a seriously damaging effect on the region.*

in·con·tes·ta·bly /ˌɪŋ·kən'tes·tə·bli/ *adv* [not gradable] *fml*

in·con·ti·nent /£ɪŋ'kɒn·tɪ·nənt, $-'kɑːn·tə-/ *adj* unable to control the excretion of urine or the contents of the bowels • *Many of our elderly patients are incontinent.* • *As the illness progressed, she became* **doubly** *incontinent* (= unable to control the excretion both of urine and the contents of the bowels).

in·con·ti·nence /£ɪŋ'kɒn·tɪ·nənts, $-'kɑːn·tə-/ *n* [U] • *Incontinence is one of the symptoms of the illness.* • *It has now become necessary for him to use incontinence* **pads.**

in·con·tro·ver·ti·ble /£ˌɪŋˌkɒn·trə'vɜː·tɪ·bl̩, $-ˌkɑːn·trə'vɜːr·t̬ə-/ *adj* [not gradable] *fml* impossible to doubt because obviously true • *Despite what seemed like incontrovertible* **proof/evidence,** *Ms Hangar maintained she had not committed the fraud.* • **It** *is incontrovertible* **that** *they have made a mistake.* [+ *that* clause] • *Her logic is utterly incontrovertible.*

in·con·tro·ver·ti·bly /£ˌɪŋˌkɒn·trə'vɜː·tɪ·bli, $-ˌkɑːn·trə'vɜːr·t̬ə-/ *adv* [not gradable] *fml* • *Your assertion is incontrovertibly true.*

in·con·ven·i·ence /ˌɪŋ·kən'viː·ni·ənts/ *n* a state or an example of difficulties, problems or trouble, which often causes a delay or loss of comfort • *We apologize for any inconvenience caused by the late arrival of the train.* [U] • *You must also consider the inconvenience of being unable to use the kitchen for several weeks while it's being rebuilt.* [U] • *For most people a bee sting is a painful inconvenience, but for a few it is much more serious.* [C]

in·con·ven·i·ence *obj* /ˌɪŋ·kən'viː·ni·ənts/ *v* [T] • *The strike inconvenienced many people.*

in·con·ven·i·ent /ˌɪŋ·kən'viː·ni·ənt/ *adj* • *Lots of older people find the new post office opening times inconvenient.* • *It's a very inconvenient place to hold the meeting.* • **It** *will be very inconvenient* **for me** *to have to wait.* [+ *to* infinitive] • Ⓔ Ⓟ

in·con·ven·i·ent·ly /ˌɪŋ·kən'viː·ni·ənt·li/ *adv* • *The cinema is inconveniently situated on the outskirts of town.*

in·cor·por·ate *obj* /£ɪŋ'kɔː·pər·eɪt, $-'kɔːr·pɚ-/ *v* [T] to include (something) in something larger • *Suggestions from the survey have been incorporated* **into/in** *the final design.* • *This aircraft incorporates several new safety features in addition to the standard ones.*

in·cor·por·a·tion /£ɪŋˌkɔː·pər'eɪ·ʃən, $-ˌkɔːr·pə'reɪ-/ *n* [U] • *The incorporation* **of** *corrections is easy with a word processor.*

in·cor·po·re·al /£ˌɪŋ·kɔː'pɔː·ri·əl, $ˌɪn·kɔːr'pɔːr·i-/ *adj* [not gradable] *fml* not having a physical body; of spiritual form • *In the film, the house was visited by a strange incorporeal being.*

in·cor·rect /£ˌɪŋ·kər'ekt, $-kə'rekt/ *adj* not correct; not true; not as it should be • *This answer is incorrect, which means you lose a point.* • *The assumptions that were made about the rate of growth of the economy* **proved** *to be incorrect.* • *The doctor made an incorrect* **diagnosis.** • **It** *is incorrect* **that** *these drugs cause serious side effects.* [+ *that* clause] • **It** *would be incorrect* (= not acceptable) **for** *people* **to** *use first names at such a formal event.* [+ *to* infinitive]

in·cor·rect·ly /£ˌɪŋ·kər'ekt·li, $-kə'rekt-/ *adv* • *The sculpture was for many years incorrectly thought to be by Donatello.*

in·cor·ri·gi·ble /£ɪŋ'kɒr·ɪ·dʒə·bl̩, $-'kɔːr-/ *adj* [not gradable] *esp. humorous* (of people and their behaviour) bad but impossible to change or improve • *He's an incorrigible* **liar/rogue,** *but he has great charm.*

in·cor·ri·gi·bly /£ɪŋ'kɒr·ɪ·dʒə·bli, $-'kɔːr-/ *adv* [not gradable]

in·cor·rup·ti·ble /ˌɪŋ·kə'rʌp·tɪ·bl̩/ *adj* [not gradable] morally strong enough not to be persuaded into doing something wrong • *In the film, Cooper is the incorruptible FBI agent working against the drug dealers.* • If something is incorruptible, it will not decay or be destroyed: *Some people think the soul, unlike the body, is incorruptible.*

in·cor·rup·ti·bly /ˌɪŋ·kə'rʌp·tɪ·bli/ *adv* [not gradable]

in·cor·rup·ti·bil·i·ty /£ˌɪŋ·kəˌrʌp·tɪ'bɪl·ɪ·ti, $-ə·t̬i/ *n* [U]

in·crease *(obj)* /ɪŋ'kriːs/ *v* to become or make larger in amount or size • *Incidents of armed robbery have increased over the last few years.* [I] • *The cost of the project has increased* **dramatically/greatly/substantially** *since it began.* [I] • *The company's sales have increased three/five/ten***fold** *in the last year.* [I] • *Do you find that walking increases the swelling in your ankle?* [T] • *Gently increase the heat until the sauce begins to boil.* [T] • *The interest rate was increased this morning* **to** *14%.* [T] • *Increased/Increasing efforts are being made to end the dispute.* • Compare DECREASE.

in·crease /'ɪŋ·kriːs/ *n* • *The increase* **in** *the number of unemployed was larger than expected.* [C] • *To add 5% to the top speed, an increase* **of** *20% in power output is needed.* [C] • *He said that the proposed tax increases would not affect low-paid workers.* [C] • *Any increase* **in** *production would be helpful.* [U] • *Homelessness is* **on the increase** (= increasing) *in many cities.*

in·creas·ing·ly /ɪŋ'kriː·sɪŋ·li/ *adv* [not gradable] • *Their argument became increasingly bitter.* • *Increasingly there is pressure on the council to reverse its decision.*

in·cred·i·ble NOT BELIEVABLE /ɪŋ'kred·ɪ·bl̩/ *adj* impossible or very difficult to believe • *What incredible nonsense – not a word of it is true!* • *The latest missiles can be fired with incredible accuracy.* • *She's only 12 years old? I find that completely incredible.* • **It** *seems incredible* **that** *no-one foresaw the crisis.* [+ *that* clause] • *"The Incredible Hulk"* (television series based on earlier cartoon, 1978-)

in·cred·i·bly /ɪŋˈkred·ɪ·bli/ *adv* • *Incredibly, no one was hurt in the accident.* • *An incredibly* (= extremely) *loud bang followed the flash.*

in·cred·i·ble GOOD /ɪŋˈkred·ɪ·bl̩/ *adj infml* extremely good • *Yeah, it was an incredible performance.* • *What an incredible motorbike!*

in·cred·u·lous /ɪŋˈkred·jʊ·ləs/ *adj* not wanting or not able to believe, and usually showing this • *Only a few incredulous spectators watched Paterson, ranked 23rd in the world, beat the champion.* • *The scientists were incredulous when they heard that research funding was to stop.*

in·cred·u·li·ty /£ˌɪŋ·krəˈdjuː·lɪ·ti, $-ˈduː·lə·t̬i/ *n* [U] • *He felt a sense of incredulity, anger and pain at the accusation made against him.* • *This official reply was* **greeted** *with incredulity by the aid agencies.*

in·cred·u·lous·ly /ɪŋˈkred·jʊ·lə·sli/ *adv* • *We could do nothing but watch incredulously while the mob looted the shops.*

in·cre·ment /ˈɪŋ·krə·mənt/ *n* [C] one of a series of increases • *You will receive annual salary increments every September.* • *This Celsius scale is divided into one hundred equal increments between the freezing and boiling points of water.*

in·cre·men·tal /£ˌɪŋ·krəˈmen·tᵊl, $-t̬ᵊl/ *adj* [not gradable] • *Most research proceeds by small incremental* (= in a series of amounts) *advances.* • *Changes at the newspaper are more incremental* (= small) *than radical.*

in·cre·men·tal·ly /£ˌɪn·krəˈmen·tᵊl·i, $-t̬ᵊl-/ *adv* [not gradable]

in·crim·in·ate *obj* /ɪŋˈkrɪm·ɪ·neɪt/ *v* [T] to make (someone) seem guilty, esp. of a crime • *A secret report incriminating the company was leaked last week.* • *He refused to say anything on the grounds that he might incriminate him***self**.

in·crim·in·at·ing /£ɪŋˈkrɪm·ɪ·neɪ·tɪŋ, $-t̬ɪŋ/ *adj* • *incriminating remarks/statements*

in·crim·in·a·tion /ɪŋˌkrɪm·ɪˈneɪ·ʃᵊn/ *n* [U] • **Self-incrimination** is saying or doing things which demonstrate that you are guilty of a crime: *The defendant replied, "I refuse to answer that question on the grounds of possible self-incrimination".*

in·crus·ta·tion /ˌɪŋ·krʌsˈteɪ·ʃᵊn/, *Am and Aus also* **en·crus·ta·tion** *n* [C] a layer of material, such as dirt or a chemical, which forms on something, esp. slowly • *Incrustations of sulphur develop on the mud beside these hot springs.*

in·cu·bate *(obj)* EGG /ˈɪŋ·kjʊ·beɪt/ *v* to keep (esp. birds' eggs) warm until the young come out, or (of eggs) to develop to the stage at which the young come out • *The female bird incubates the eggs for about sixteen days while the male brings food.* [T] • *Penguin eggs incubate on the feet of the males.* [I] • *(fig.) She's always incubating* (= planning) *new sales promotions.* [T]

in·cu·ba·tion /ˌɪŋ·kjʊˈbeɪ·ʃᵊn/ *n* [U] • *The sex of reptiles is determined by the temperature during incubation of the eggs in which they are contained.* • *The incubation* **period** *varies depending on the time of year when the eggs were laid.* • *(fig.) After a long incubation* **period** (= period of planning), *plans for the new fire station were finally proposed.*

in·cu·bat·or /£ˈɪŋ·kjʊ·beɪ·təʳ, $-t̬ɚ/ *n* [C] • An incubator is a container having controlled air and temperature conditions in which a weak or PREMATURE baby (= one which was born too early) can be kept alive. • An incubator is also a device which keeps eggs at the correct temperature to enable the young birds to develop until they break out of the shell.

in·cu·bate *(obj)* DISEASE /ˈɪŋ·kjʊ·beɪt/ *v* (of harmful bacteria or viruses) to grow and reproduce, but not yet produce the effects of disease in a human or an animal, or (of the body of a person or animal) to have (bacteria or viruses) growing and reproducing inside, but not yet show the effects of disease • *While incubating, this type of virus is very resistant to pharmaceutical treatment.* [I] • *It only takes one dog incubating an infectious disease to start off an epidemic.* [T]

in·cu·ba·tion /ˌɪŋ·kjʊˈbeɪ·ʃᵊn/ *n* [U] • *In smallpox, there is an incubation* **period** *of 8-18 days between initial infection and first symptoms.*

in·cul·cate *obj* /ˈɪŋ·kʌl·keɪt/ *v* [T] *fml* to fix (ideas, beliefs, facts etc.) in someone's mind, esp. by repeating them often • *Our football coach has worked hard to inculcate a team spirit* **in/into** *the players.* • *She has huge natural ability as a singer – we just have to inculcate her* **with** *self-discipline.*

in·cul·ca·tion /ˌɪŋ·kʌlˈkeɪ·ʃᵊn/ *n* [U]

in·cum·bent PERSON /ɪŋˈkʌm·bᵊnt/ *adj* [before n; not gradable] officially having the named position • *The incumbent president faces problems which began many years before he took office.*

in·cum·bent /ɪŋˈkʌm·bᵊnt/ *n* [C] • *The present incumbent* **(of** *the post)* (= The person who has the position) *is due to retire next month.*

in·cum·benc·y /ɪŋˈkʌm·bᵊnt·si/ *n* [C] • *During her incumbency as* (= the period during which she was) *commissioner, several changes were introduced.*

in·cum·bent NECESSARY /ɪŋˈkʌm·bᵊnt/ *adj* [after v; always + *on/upon*; not gradable] *fml* necessary; which must be done • *She felt it incumbent* **upon/on** *her* **to** (= felt she had to) *raise the subject at their meeting.*

in·cur *obj* /£ɪŋˈkɜːʳ, $-ˈkɜːr/ *v* [T] **-rr-** (of a person, group, etc.) to experience (esp. something unpleasant) as a result of actions they have taken • *It's a long-term investment, so you might expect to incur light* **losses** *in the early years.* • *This production of the play has incurred* **the wrath/anger** *of both audiences and critics.* • *Please detail any* **costs/expenses** *incurred by you in attending the interview.*

in·cur·a·ble /£ɪŋˈkjʊə·rə·bl̩, $-ˈkjʊr·ə-/ *adj* [not gradable] not able to be healed or cured • *As yet the illness is incurable.* • *Parkinson's disease is a debilitating and incurable* **disease** *of the nervous system.* • *(fig.)She is an incurable* (= not able to be changed) *optimist/pessimist.*

in·cur·a·bly /£ɪŋˈkjʊə·rə·bli, $-ˈkjʊr·ə-/ *adv* [not gradable] • *It was a shock for her to learn that she was incurably ill.* • *(fig.) He's always so incurably* (= in a way that cannot be changed) *cheerful.*

in·cur·i·ous /£ɪŋˈkjʊə·ri·əs, $-ˈkjʊr·i-/ *adj fml* not interested in knowing what is happening; not wanting to discover anything new • *He's strangely incurious* **about** *what goes on around him.*

in·cur·sion /£ɪŋˈkɜː·ʒᵊn, $-ˈkɜːr-/ *n* [C] a sudden entrance into a place, esp. across a border • *Terrorist forces* **made** *several incursions* **into** *occupied areas during the fighting.* • *(fig.) Any such inquiry would be a serious incursion* **on/upon** *their private lives.*

in·debt·ed GRATEFUL /£ɪnˈdet·ɪd, $-ˈdet̬-/ *adj* [after v; always + *to*] grateful because of help given • *And, of course, I'm most indebted* **to** *my husband – without his support the book would never have been written.* • *We're indebted* **to** *you* **for** *your help.*

in·debt·ed·ness /£ɪnˈdet·ɪd·nəs, $-ˈdet̬-/ *n* [U]

in·debt·ed OWING /£ɪnˈdet·ɪd, $-ˈdet̬-/ *adj* owing money • *International agreements need to be reached about helping the world's most* **deeply** *indebted countries.* • *The company is* **heavily** *indebted.*

in·debt·ed·ness /£ɪnˈdet·ɪd·nəs, $-ˈdet̬-/ *n* [U] • *This country faces a future of indebtedness unless there is substantial investment in manufacturing industry.*

in·de·cent IMMORAL /ɪnˈdiː·sᵊnt/ *adj* morally offensive, esp. in a sexual way • *Scenes in the film showing a rape were felt by many viewers to be indecent.* • *She said that he had made an indecent suggestion/proposal to her.* • *In some parts of the world* **it** *is considered indecent* **for** *a woman* **to** *wear short skirts.* [+ *to* infinitive] • *(law)* An **indecent assault** is an attack on someone which usually involves sexual actions but not RAPE (= forced sex). • *(law)* **Indecent exposure** is when someone shows their sexual organs in public in a way which is intended to upset people.

in·de·cenc·y /ɪnˈdiː·sᵊnt·si/ *n* [U] • *Stevens has a history of indecency* (= sexual attacks) *against young boys.*

in·de·cent·ly /ɪnˈdiː·sᵊnt·li/ *adv* • *She was arrested for behaving indecently at a cricket match.*

in·de·cent NOT SUITABLE /ɪnˈdiː·sᵊnt/ *adj* not suitable or correct for a situation • *The premier left his residence with almost indecent* **haste** *following his resignation.* • *She's been paying him an indecent amount of attention lately.*

in·de·ci·pher·a·ble /£ˌɪn·dɪˈsaɪ·fᵊr·ə·bl̩, $-fɚ-/ *adj* [not gradable] not possible to read or understand the meaning of • *What atrocious handwriting – it's virtually indecipherable!*

in·de·ci·sion /ˌɪn·dɪˈsɪʒ·ᵊn/, **in·de·ci·sive·ness** /ˌɪn·dɪˈsaɪ·sɪv·nəs/ *n* [U] inability to make a choice • *Indecision is not what we expect in our managers.* • *A moment's indecision when you've got the ball and you could lose the game.* • *There is a great deal of indecision* **about/over** *how to tackle the problem.*

in·de·ci·sive /ˌɪn·dɪˈsaɪ·sɪv/ *adj* • *He is widely thought to be an indecisive leader.* • Indecisive is sometimes used to mean not having a clear meaning: *The initial results of the* *survey are indecisive – more data is needed to make any sense of them.*

in·de·ci·sive·ly /ˌɪn·dɪˈsaɪ·sɪv·li/ *adv*

in·dec·o·rous /£ɪnˈdek·ər·əs, $ˈ-ɚ-/ *adj fml* behaving badly or rudely

in·dec·o·rous·ly /£ɪnˈdek·ər·əs·li, $ˈ-ɚ-/ *adv fml*

in·deed CERTAINLY /ɪnˈdiːd/ *adv* [not gradable] (often used to emphasize something) really; truly • *Indeed, his caution is legendary.* • *Indeed, it could be the worst environmental disaster that Western Europe has known this century.* • *The limited evidence suggests that errors may indeed be occurring.* • *Collecting the money is indeed an unrewarding task.* • *We live in strange times indeed.* • *This is bad news indeed.* • *(esp. Br) Many people are* **very** *poor indeed.* • *(esp. Br) It was a* **very** *loud noise indeed.* • *(esp. Br) Thank you* **very** *much indeed.* • Indeed can also be used to express that something is correct: *"Is this your dog?" "It is indeed."/"Indeed it is."* ○ *Yes, I did indeed say that.* • Indeed is sometimes used to add some extra information which makes stronger something you have just said: *He was too proud, too arrogant indeed, to know when he had failed*

in·deed EXPRESSION /ɪnˈdiːd/ *exclamation* used to express surprise, annoyance, lack of belief or lack of interest • *"She said she won't come back until Monday." "Won't she, indeed!"* • *Twenty thousand pounds indeed! That's an extortionate price.* • *"When will we get a pay rise?" "When indeed?"*

in·de·fat·i·ga·ble /£ˌɪn·dɪˈfæt·ɪ·gə·bl̩, $-ˈfæţ-/ *adj fml* never becoming tired • *For many years Annie has been an indefatigable campaigner for human rights.* • *He has been indefatigable in his fight to clear his name.*

in·de·fat·i·ga·bly /£ˌɪn·dɪˈfæt·ɪ·gə·bli, $-ˈfæţ-/ *adv*

in·de·fen·si·ble /ˌɪn·dɪˈfent·sɪ·bl̩/ *adj* (of behaviour) too bad to be protected from criticism, or (of a place) not able to be protected against attack • *The war is* **morally** *indefensible.* • *His opinions/attitudes are completely indefensible.* • *A few troops are still shooting from what seems like an indefensible position.*

in·de·fen·si·bly /ˌɪn·dɪˈfent·sɪ·bli/ *adv*

in·de·fin·a·ble, *Am and Aus also* **un·de·fin·a·ble** /ˌɪn·dɪˈfaɪ·nə·bl̩, ˌʌn-/ *adj* impossible to clearly describe or explain • *Messiaen's music frequently has an indefinable, mystical quality.*

in·de·fin·a·bly, *Am and Aus also* **un·de·fin·a·bly** /ˌɪn·dɪˈfaɪ·nə·bli, ˌʌn/ *adv*

in·def·i·nite /ɪnˈdef·ɪ·nət/ *adj* not exact; not clear; without clear limits • *The project has been postponed for an indefinite* **period** *due to a lack of funds.* • *An indefinite* **number** *of people have already died in the epidemic.* • *(specialized)* **Indefinite article** is the grammatical name for the words "a" and "an" in English or words in other languages which have a similar use. Compare **definite article** at DEFINITE. • LP› **Articles**

in·def·i·nite·ly /ɪnˈdef·ɪ·nət·li/ *adv* • *Promised negotiations between the two sides involved in the conflict have been* **put off** *indefinitely.* • *The company is indefinitely* **suspending** *work on what was to be a $1 billion cereal plant.*

in·del·i·ble /ɪnˈdel·ɪ·bl̩/ *adj* [not gradable] (of dirty marks, ink etc.) impossible to remove by washing or in any other way • *indelible ink* • *The blood had left an indelible* **mark** *on her shirt.* • *(fig.) In his twenty years working for the company, Joe Pearson made an indelible* **mark** (=had a strong influence) *on it.* • *(fig.) I have an indelible* **memory** (=one that I will not forget) *of that meeting with Anastasia.* • *(fig.) The album is indelible evidence* (=that which cannot be removed) *that he remains the best blues singer of our time.*

in·del·i·bly /ɪnˈdel·ɪ·bli/ *adv* [not gradable] • *The children's names are indelibly written inside their school clothes.* • *(fig.) Every event of that terrible day has been logged indelibly* (=in a way that will not be forgotten) *in the child's memory.*

in·del·i·cate /ɪnˈdel·ɪ·kət/ *adj* (of something which is talked about, or behaviour) not suitable for a situation and likely to be offensive • *an indelicate comment* • *Would* **it** *be indelicate* **to** *mention the fee at this point?* [+ *to* infinitive]

in·del·i·ca·cy /ɪnˈdel·ɪ·kə·si/ *n* [U]

in·dem·ni·ty /£ɪnˈdem·nə·ti, $-ţi/ *n fml or specialized* protection against possible damage or loss, esp. a promise of payment, or the money paid if there is such damage or loss • *Since the early 1980s, this insurance company has specialized in indemnity.* [U] • *The indemnity for any loss will be paid as soon as our inspector has completed her enquiries.* [C]

in·dem·ni·fy *obj* /ɪnˈdem·nɪ·faɪ/ *v* [T] • *The insurance also indemnifies the house* **against** (=protects it by paying the cost of any damage done by) *flooding.* • *If there is a breakage you will be indemnified* (=paid for the damage) *within 28 days.*

in·dent *obj* SPACE /ɪnˈdent/ *v* [T] to make a space in the edge or on the surface of (something) • *The coastline has been indented by processes of erosion.* • *Each new paragraph should be indented.*

in·den·ta·tion /ˌɪn·denˈteɪ·ʃən/ *n* [C] • *Leave an indentation at the beginning of every new paragraph.* • *There was a small indentation on her head where she had been hit by a heavy object.*

in·dent REQUEST /ɪnˈdent/ *v* [I] *Br and Aus specialized* to make an official request for goods • *We indented* **for** *the engine spares last month.*

in·dent /ˈɪn·dent/ *n* [C] • *We* **made** *an indent* **for** *the engine spares last week.*

in·den·ture *obj* /£ɪnˈden·tʃər, $-tʃɚ/ *v* [T] (esp. in the past) to officially agree that (someone, often a young person) will work for someone else, esp. in order to learn a job • *He was indentured* **to** *a coach-builder.* • *The land was worked on by indentured labourers.* • *In the late seventeenth century, African slaves began to replace white indentured* **servants** *in the southern US.*

in·de·pend·ent NOT INFLUENCED /ˌɪn·dɪˈpen·dənt/ *adj* not influenced or controlled in any way by other people, events or things • *The family are calling for an independent enquiry into the cause of the deaths.* • *An independent research organization was chosen to carry out the ecological study.* • *An independent financial adviser can tell you which is the best investment plan.* • *The committee of enquiry is completely independent* **of** *the government.* • *They all made the same comment, quite independent* **of** *each other* (=without deciding together to do so). • *The guide book is written for the independent-***minded** *traveller* (=one who makes their own decisions without being influenced by other people). • *All the wheels have fully independent suspension* (=the movement of one wheel is not influenced by movements of the other wheels). • An Independent is a politician who does not agree or vote with any particular political party. • In grammar, an independent clause is a clause which forms part of a sentence but can also form a separate sentence.

in·de·pend·ent·ly /ˌɪn·dɪˈpen·dənt·li/ *adv* • *So often in science the same discovery seems to be made independently at more or less the same time in different places.* • *Each part of the organization operates independently* **of** *the others.*

in·de·pend·ent NOT RULED /ˌɪn·dɪˈpen·dənt/ *adj* [not gradable] (of a country) not governed or ruled by another country • *Belize became fully independent* **from** *Britain in 1981.* • *Tibet, once an independent country, is now part of China.*

in·de·pend·ence /ˌɪn·dɪˈpen·dənts/ *n* [U] • *The majority of the population now wants independence for their country.* • An **Independence Day** is the day on which a country celebrates its independence from foreign rule. • In the US, **Independence Day** is the official name for the **Fourth of July** holiday; see at FOUR. • LP› **Holidays**

in·de·pend·ent NOT HELPED /ˌɪn·dɪˈpen·dənt/ *adj* not taking help or money from other people • *Grandma's very independent, she always goes to the shops on her own.* • *Independent television companies receive most of their income from advertising.* • *Now that Jean's got a job she's* **financially** *independent.* • *He can afford to spend his time writing because he has* **independent means** (=income which is not earned). • An **independent school** is a school in Britain which does not receive money from the government.

in·de·pend·ence /ˌɪn·dɪˈpen·dənts/ *n* [U] • *I like the feeling of independence I get from travelling as part of my job.* • *It's important that parents should allow their children some independence.*

in·de·scrib·a·ble /ˌɪn·dɪˈskraɪ·bə·bl̩/ *adj* impossible to describe, esp. because extremely good or bad • *The pain was indescribable when the horse kicked me.* • *As we turned the corner, a scene of indescribable beauty appeared before us.* • *These people live in conditions that are almost indescribable.*

in·de·scrib·a·bly /ˌɪn·dɪˈskraɪ·bə·bli/ *adv* • *What an indescribably awful film!*

in·de·struc·ti·ble /ˌɪn·dɪˈstrʌk·tɪ·bl̩/ *adj* impossible to destroy or break • *These plastic cups are* **virtually** *indestructible in normal use.* • *This is a wonderfully indestructible toy.*

in·de·struc·ti·bil·i·ty /£ˌɪn·dɪˌstrʌk·tɪˈbɪl·ɪ·ti, $-ə·t̬i/ *n* [U]

in·de·ter·min·ate /£ˌɪn·dɪˈtɜː·mɪ·nət, $-ˈtɜːr-/ *adj* not measured, counted or clearly described • *Indeterminate numbers of workers have already been exposed to the danger.* • *One tactic would be to take an indeterminate stance in these talks.*

in·de·ter·min·a·cy /£ˌɪn·dɪˈtɜː·mɪ·nə·si, $-ˈtɜːr-/ *n* [U]

in·dex LIST /ˈɪn·deks/ *n* [C] an alphabetical list, such as one printed at the back of a book showing which page a subject, name, etc. is found on, or computer information ordered in a particular way • *The book has a very thorough index, so you can easily find any name you want.* • *If you want to find what page the circulation of the blood is described on, look it up* **in** *the index.* • *All the library's books are catalogued* **on** *a computer index.* • An index can also be a set of cards with information on them, arranged in alphabetical order: *He has all his friends' names and addresses* **on a card** *index.*

in·dex *obj* /ˈɪn·deks/ *v* [T] • *It'll take days to index* (= prepare an index for) *the report.* • *Our computer indexes several thousand new records every second.*

in·dex COMPARISON /ˈɪn·deks/ *n* [C] *pl* **indices** /ˈɪn·dɪ·siːz/ or **indexes** a system of numbers used for comparing values of things which vary against each other or against a fixed standard • *the FTSE 100 Index* • *the Dow Jones Index* • *a wage/price index* • *(fig.) Consumer spending is often thought to be a reliable index* **of** (= show the state of) *public confidence in the government's economic policies.* • The **index of leading economic indicators** is the US government's system for describing how active the national economy will be. • If pay, taxes, etc. are *(Br)* **index-linked**/*(Am and Aus)* **indexed**, they are varied to rise or fall with the general level of prices.

in·dex *obj* /ˈɪn·deks/ *v* [T] • *Living expenses will be indexed* **to/in line with** (= varied to allow for) *inflation from April.*

in·dex·a·tion /ˌɪn·dekˈseɪ·ʃən/ *n* [U] • *Indexation of pay rises* (= varying them to rise and fall according) **to** *productivity will give people an incentive to work harder.*

in·dex fin·ger *n* [C] the finger next to the thumb; the FOREFINGER

In·di·an /ˈɪn·di·ən/ *n* [C], *adj* [not gradable] (a) **Native American**; see at NATIVE. This is considered offensive by many people.

In·di·an club *n* [C] an object shaped like a bottle, used esp. by **jugglers** (= entertainers who throw objects into the air and catch them) • PIC **Club**

In·di·an ink *Br and Aus, Am and Aus* **In·di·a ink** *n* [U] a thick black ink used esp. for drawing

In·di·an sum·mer *n* [C] a period of calm warm weather which sometimes happens in the early autumn • An Indian summer is also a pleasant or successful time nearly at the end of a particular period, such as the end of someone's life: *It's good to see that old film star of the 1960s enjoying an Indian summer with her second highly acclaimed film this year.*

in·di·a rub·ber *n* [U] *dated for* RUBBER

in·di·cate *(obj)* SHOW /ˈɪn·dɪ·keɪt/ *v* to show, point or make clear in another way • *The label on the packet indicated all the ingredients in the biscuits.* • *Data obtained from exploratory investigations indicate large amounts of oil below the sea-bed in this area.* • *Please indicate* **which** *free gift you would like to receive.* [+ *wh*-word] • *Initial results indicate* **(that)** *the election result is going to be very close.* [+ (*that*) clause] • *She indicated* **to** *me* **(that)** *she didn't want me to say anything.* [+ (*that*) clause]

in·di·ca·tion /ˌɪn·dɪˈkeɪ·ʃən/ *n* • *There is little indication* **(that)** *the protesters will leave the building peacefully.* [U + (*that*) clause] • *An indication* **of** *willingness to discuss the problem would be very helpful.* [C]

in·dic·a·tive /£ɪnˈdɪk·ə·tɪv, $-t̬ɪv/ *adj* • *Resumption of the talks is indicative* **of** *an improving relationship between the countries.* • *There are indicative signs that the economy may be improving.*

in·di·cat·or /£ˈɪn·dɪ·keɪ·təʳ, $-t̬ɚ/ *n* [C] • *For many years, doctors believed that the condition of hair, skin and so on was an indicator* **of** *general health.* • *Commodity prices can be a useful indicator* **of** *inflation, he claimed.*

in·di·cate *(obj)* SIGNAL /ˈɪn·dɪ·keɪt/ *v* (of a device) to show (a value or a change), or (of a person driving a vehicle) to show (a change of direction) • *The gauge indicates a temperature below freezing point.* [T] • *He was indicating left but he turned right.* [I] • *Slow down as you approach the junction and indicate* **which** *way you're going to turn.* [+ *wh*-word] • *Indicate before you drive away in the car.* [I] • LP **Driving**

in·di·cat·or /£ˈɪn·dɪ·keɪ·təʳ, $-t̬ɚ/ *n* [C] • *If the red indicator light is illuminated then the pilot light has gone out.* • *(Br and Aus)* An indicator (*Am* **turn signal**) is a light on a road vehicle which flashes to show which way it is going to turn. • PIC **Car**

in·di·cate *obj* SUGGEST /ˈɪn·dɪ·keɪt/ *v* [T often passive] to suggest (something) as being suitable • *Antihistamine is indicated for this patient as a treatment for her allergies.* • *(infml humorous) I'm so hot and tired – I think a long cool drink is indicated!*

in·di·ca·tion /ˌɪn·dɪˈkeɪ·ʃən/ *n* [C] • *The indication from* (= suitable action suggested by) *the trade figures is to reduce stock by at least 30%.*

in·di·ces /ˈɪn·dɪ·siːz/ *pl of* INDEX COMPARISON

in·dict *obj* /ɪnˈdaɪt/ *v* [T] *law* (of *Br* a law court or *Am* a **grand jury**) to accuse (someone) officially of a crime • *(Br) He was indicted* **on** *drug* **charges** *at Snaresbrook Crown Court.* • *(Am) A federal grand jury has indicted two New York men* **on** *firearms* **charges.** • *(Am) Five people were indicted* **for** *making and selling $17 million in counterfeit US currency.* • To indict is also to criticize or blame: *The company was indicted* **for** *making excessive profits.* • LP **Crimes and criminals**

in·dict·a·ble /£ɪnˈdaɪ·tə·bl̩, $-t̬ə-/ *adj* [not gradable] *law* • *Robbery is an indictable* **offence**.

in·dict·ment /ɪnˈdaɪt·mənt/ *n* [C] *law* • *The charges on the indictment* (= formal statement of accusation) *include murder and attempted murder.* • An indictment is also a reason for giving blame: *The level of illiteracy in schoolchildren is seen as a* **damning** *indictment* **of** *education policy.*

in·dif·fer·ent NOT INTERESTED /£ɪnˈdɪf·ər·ənt, £-rənt, $ˈ-ɚ-/ *adj* [not gradable] (completely) lacking in interest or feeling; UNCONCERNED • *Why don't you vote – how can you be so indifferent* **(to** *what is going on)!* • *In the past governments have seemed virtually indifferent* **to** *conservation issues.* • *He found it very hard teaching a class full of indifferent teenagers.*

in·dif·fer·ence /£ɪnˈdɪf·ər·ənts, £-rənts, $ˈ-ɚ-/ *n* [U] • *Many native speakers of a language show indifference* **to/towards** *grammatical points.* • *His attitude to his work was one of bored indifference.* • *The accident happened as a result of years of indifference on the part of the safety regulators.* • *I can bear love or hate, but not indifference.*

in·dif·fer·ent·ly /£ɪnˈdɪf·ər·ənt·li, £-rənt-, $ˈ-ɚ-/ *adv* [not gradable]

in·dif·fer·ent NOT GOOD /£ɪnˈdɪf·ər·ənt, £-rənt, $ˈ-ɚ-/ *adj* [not gradable] not good, but not very bad • *We didn't like the restaurant much – the food was indifferent and the room was cold.* • *Barnes, usually so skilful, played an indifferent game last night.*

in·dif·fer·ent·ly /£ɪnˈdɪf·ər·ənt·li, £-rənt-, $ˈ-ɚ-/ *adv* [not gradable]

in·dig·en·ous /ɪnˈdɪdʒ·ɪ·nəs/ *adj* [not gradable] naturally existing in a place or country; NATIVE • *indigenous people* • *Are there any species of frog indigenous* **to** *the area?* • *The indigenous medical traditions in the area make extensive use of plants.*

in·di·gent /ˈɪn·dɪ·dʒənt/ *adj fml* very poor

in·di·gence /ˈɪn·dɪ·dʒənts/ *n* [U]

in·di·gest·i·ble /ˌɪn·dɪˈdʒes·tɪ·bl̩/ *adj* (of food) impossible to break down inside a living creature so it can be used in its body • *For dinner they gave me a really tough and indigestible piece of steak.* • *(fig.) The statistics are virtually indigestible* (= impossible to understand) *presented in this form.*

in·di·gest·i·bil·i·ty /£ˌɪn·dɪˌdʒes·tɪˈbɪl·ɪ·ti, $-ə·t̬i/ *n* [U]

in·di·ges·tion /ˌɪn·dɪˈdʒes·tʃən/ *n* [U] pain caused in the region of the stomach by the stomach not correctly breaking down food so that it can be used by the body • *Do you* **suffer from** *indigestion after you have eaten?* • *You'll give yourself indigestion if you swallow your dinner so quickly.* • See also HEARTBURN.

in·dig·nant /ɪnˈdɪg·nənt/ *adj* angry because of something which is wrong or not fair • *Faced with accusations of corruption, the indignant officials walked out of the meeting.* • *She wrote an indignant letter to the paper complaining about the council's action.* • *He became very indignant when it was suggested he had made a mistake.* • *Residents in the area are indignant* **about/at** *the high rents that are being charged.*

in·dig·nant·ly /ɪnˈdɪg·nənt·li/ *adv* • *"I said no such thing!" she cried indignantly.*

in·dig·na·tion /ˌɪn·dɪgˈneɪ·ʃᵊn/ *n* [U] • *They reacted with shock and indignation to the charge of cheating.*

in·dig·ni·ty /£ɪnˈdɪg·nɪ·ti, $-nə·t̬i/ *n* (something which causes) a loss of respect or self-respect • *They were subjected to various indignities and discomforts throughout the voyage, including having to get dressed and undressed in public.* [C] • *Clint* **suffered** *the indignity of being called "Puppy" in front of his girlfriend.* [U] • Ⓔ

in·di·go /£ˈɪn·dɪ·gəʊ, $-goʊ/ *adj* [not gradable], *n* [C/U] (having) a bluish purple colour

in·di·rect NOT OBVIOUS /ˌɪn·daɪˈrekt/ *adj* happening in addition to an intended result, often in a way that is complicated or not obvious • *Benefits from pure research are often indirect, and it is usually impossible to predict what they will be.* • *Further investment in road building will have indirect consequences, such as less freight being moved by rail.* • *Dating of fossils is often confirmed by indirect* **evidence** (=that with a different, but related, cause), *for example by dating the soil they were found in.* • Indirect can also mean avoiding clearly mentioning something: *He didn't really say exactly what the plans for the future were, but just made a few indirect remarks about the need for change.*

in·di·rect NOT STRAIGHT /ˌɪn·daɪˈrekt/ *adj* not following a straight line; not directly or simply connected • *You could go through the city, but there are hold-ups, so it'll be quickest to take an indirect route through the suburbs.* • *It's difficult to fly straight from the US to Africa – you usually have to take an indirect flight via Europe.* • An **indirect cost** is an amount of money spent by a business on things other than the products they make: *Property taxes and rent are indirect costs for almost all businesses.* • *(specialized)* An **indirect object** is the person or thing which receives the effect of the action of a verb with two objects: *In the sentence 'Give Val some cake', 'Val' is the indirect object.* See also OBJECT GRAMMAR. Compare **direct object** at DIRECT STRAIGHT. LP **Two objects** • *(specialized)* **Indirect speech** (*Br and Aus also* **reported speech**, *Am also* **indirect discourse**) is the act of reporting something that was said, but not using exactly the same words: *If someone says "Jane said (that) she couldn't help it" to report that Jane had said "I couldn't help it", they are using indirect speech.* Compare **direct speech** at DIRECT STRAIGHT. LP **Clauses** • **Indirect tax(ation)** is *(Br and Aus)* tax charged on goods and services rather than on the money that people earn, or *(Am)* tax charged on goods before they reach their final buyer. • LP **Two objects**

in·di·rect·ly /ˌɪn·daɪˈrekt·li/ *adv* • *She still controls the company indirectly through her son, who is the managing director.* • *Freedom of speech has been controlled, whether* **directly** or *indirectly* (= in some way), *by the secret police.*

in·dis·cer·ni·ble /£ˌɪn·dɪˈsɜː·nɪ·bl̩, $-ˈsɜːr-/ *adj* impossible to see, see clearly or understand • *an indiscernible change/shape/reason*

in·dis·ci·pline /ɪnˈdɪs··plɪn/ *n* [U] *fml* a lack of control or obedience • *The manager apologized for his team's indiscipline after three players were involved in a fight.*

in·dis·creet /ˌɪn·dɪˈskriːt/ *adj* not careful in saying or doing things, esp. in such a way that it upsets someone • *In an indiscreet moment the president let his genuine opinions be known.* • *They have been rather indiscreet* **about** *their affair.*

in·dis·creet·ly /ˌɪn·dɪˈskriːt·li/ *adv*

in·dis·cre·tion /ˌɪn·dɪˈskreʃ·ᵊn/ *n* • *Jones was censured for indiscretion in leaking a secret report to the press.* [U] • *They were just* **youthful** *indiscretions* (=acts of bad behaviour, esp. bad sexual behaviour) – *perhaps we should forgive them.* [C]

in·dis·crim·i·nate /ˌɪn·dɪˈskrɪm·ɪ·nət/ *adj* not showing (careful) thought or planning, esp. so that harm results • *The report concludes that the indiscriminate use of some fertilizers in the area would cause long-term problems.* • *Indiscriminate attacks by terrorists on civilians are still occurring* • *She's completely indiscriminate* **in** *the way she spends money.*

in·dis·crim·i·nate·ly /ˌɪn·dɪˈskrɪm·ɪ·nət·li/ *adv* • *They fired indiscriminately into the crowd.*

in·dis·pens·a·ble /ˌɪn·dɪˈspent·sə·bl̩/ *adj* too important not to have; necessary • *First published in 1927, the charts remain an indispensable resource for researchers.* • *She's good but not indispensable* (**for** *the team) – no player is.* • *This guidebook is indispensable* **for** *the traveller to southern Italy.*

in·dis·pen·sa·bil·i·ty /£ˌɪn·dɪˌspent·sɪˈbɪl·ɪ·ti, $-ə·t̬i/ *n* [U]

in·dis·posed ILL /£ˌɪn·dɪˈspəʊzd, $-ˈspoʊzd/ *adj* [not gradable] *fml* ill, esp. so as to be unable to do something • *Sheila Jones is indisposed, so the part of the Countess will be sung tonight by Della Drake.*

in·dis·pos·i·tion /ˌɪn·dɪ·spəˈzɪʃ·ᵊn/ *n fml* • *Because of Mr Booth's indisposition, Mr Carter will be attending the meeting instead.* [U] • *I was sorry to hear of the indispositions you're both suffering.* [C]

in·dis·posed NOT WILLING /£ˌɪn·dɪˈspəʊzd, $-ˈspoʊzd/ *adj* [after v; + *to* infinitive] *fml* not willing • *They have been very rude to her in the past, so it's not surprising she feels indisposed* **to** *help them now.*

in·dis·pos·i·tion /ɪnˌdɪs·pəˈzɪʃ·ᵊn/ *n* [U + *to* infinitive] *fml* • *Their indisposition* **to** *cooperate has made things very difficult.*

in·dis·pu·ta·ble /£ˌɪn·dɪˈspjuː·tə·bl̩, $-t̬ə-/ *adj* [not gradable] true; impossible to doubt • *This exhibition shows her to be an artist of indisputable skill.* • *One fact is indisputable – this must never be allowed to happen again.* • **It** *is indisputable* **that** *the scheme has some advantages.* [+ *that* clause]

in·dis·pu·ta·bly /£ˌɪn·dɪˈspjuː·tə·bli, $-t̬ə-/ *adv* [not gradable] • *Segovia is indisputably the finest guitar player of the twentieth century, she said.*

in·dis·sol·u·ble /£ˌɪn·dɪˈsɒl·jʊ·bl̩, $-ˈsɑːl·jə-/ *adj* [not gradable] impossible to take apart or bring to an end; existing for a very long time • *Going through the tragedy together forged an indissoluble bond of friendship between them which would last until they died.* • *The links between the two nations are indissoluble.*

in·dis·sol·u·bly /£ˌɪn·dɪˈsɒl·jʊ·bli, $-ˈsɑːl·jə-/ *adv* [not gradable]

in·dis·sol·u·bil·i·ty /£ˌɪn·dɪˌsɒl·jʊˈbɪl·ɪ·ti, $-ˌsɑːl·jəˈbɪl·ə·t̬i/ *n* [U]

in·dis·tinct /ˌɪn·dɪˈstɪŋkt/ *adj* not clear • *an indistinct shape/sound/recollection* • Compare DISTINCT DIFFERENT; DISTINCT NOTICEABLE.

in·dis·tinct·ly /ˌɪn·dɪˈstɪŋkt·li/ *adv*

in·dis·tin·guish·a·ble /ˌɪn·dɪˈstɪŋ·gwɪ·ʃə·bl̩/ *adj* [not gradable] impossible to judge as being different when compared to another similar thing • *The markings on this type of fish make it virtually indistinguishable* **from** *the sand it swims over.* • *These forgeries are so good that they are more or less indistinguishable* **from** *the originals.* • *Which of these indistinguishable candidates are you going to vote for?*

in·di·vid·u·al SEPARATE THING /ˌɪn·dɪˈvɪd·ju·əl/ *n, adj* [before n; not gradable] (existing as) a single person or thing, esp. when compared to the group, set etc. to which it belongs • *He will be remembered by us all as an individual who always tried to make people happy.* • *Every individual has certain rights which must never be taken away.* • *Like many creative individuals she can be very bad-tempered.* • *Each individual table is finished by hand.* • Ⓟ

in·di·vid·u·al·i·sm /ˌɪn·dɪˈvɪd·ju·ə·lɪ·zᵊm/ *n* [U] • Individualism is the idea that freedom of thought and action for each person is the most important quality of a society, rather than shared effort and responsibility.

in·di·vid·u·al·ly /ˌɪn·dɪˈvɪd·ju·ə·li/ *adv* [not gradable] • *All the athletes are strong individually, so they should also do well as a team.* • *The children will first sing individually and then together as a group.*

in·di·vid·u·al PARTICULAR /ˌɪn·dɪˈvɪd·ju·əl/ *adj* [not gradable] of, suitable for or particular to a single thing, esp. a person • *Here we look after children who have individual needs.* • *You can always tell if it's written by Marion because she has such an individual style.* • Ⓟ

in·di·vid·u·al /ˈɪn·dɪˌvɪd·ju·əl/ *n* [C] • An individual is a person who thinks or behaves in a different way from other people: *If nothing else, the school will turn her into an individual.*

in·di·vid·u·al·ly /ˌɪn·dɪˈvɪd·ju·ə·li/ *adv* [not gradable] • *She always thinks very individually* (= in a different and esp. original way) *and it shows in what she does.*

in·di·vid·u·al·i·sm /ˌɪn·dɪˈvɪd·ju·ə·lɪ·zᵊm/ *n* [U] • *Because of the individualism* (= quality of being different and esp. original) *of her work, I think we should accept this candidate.*

in·di·vid·u·al·ist /ˌɪn·dɪˈvɪd·ju·ə·lɪst/ *n* [C] • *Chagall was very much an individualist in his style of painting, although there were some imitators.*

in·di·vid·u·al·is·tic /£ˌɪn·dɪˌvɪd·ju·əˈlɪs·tɪk, $-t̬ɪk/ *adj* • *a highly individualistic performance* • *His hobbies are also individualistic – table tennis and jazz.*

in·di·vid·u·al·is·ti·cal·ly /£ˌɪn·dɪˌvɪd·ju·əˈlɪs·tɪ·kli, $-t̬ɪ-/ *adv*

in·di·vid·u·al·i·ty /£ˌɪn·dɪˌvɪd·juˈæl·ə·ti, $-t̬i/ *n* [U] • *It's a competent essay but it* **lacks** *individuality.*

in·di·vid·u·al·ized, *Br and Aus usually* **-ised** /ˌɪn·dɪˈvɪd·ju·ə·laɪzd/ *adj esp. Am* • *The hospital gives individualized care/attention/treatment* (= that suitable for a particular person) *to all its patients.*

in·di·vis·i·ble /ˌɪn·dɪˈvɪz·ɪ·bl̩/ *adj* [not gradable] not able to be separated into different parts • *These subatomic particles are thought to be indivisible into smaller particles.* • *Europe could become a unit as economically indivisible as America's united states.*

in·di·vis·i·bly /ˌɪn·dɪˈvɪz·ɪ·bli/ *adv* [not gradable]

in·di·vis·i·bil·i·ty /£ˌɪn·dɪˌvɪz·ɪˈbɪl·ɪ·ti, $-ə·t̬i/ *n*

Indo– /ˌɪn·dəʊ-/ *combining form* of or connected with India • *Indo-European languages* • *the Indo-Chinese border*

in·doc·trin·ate *obj* /£ɪnˈdɒk·trɪ·neɪt, $-ˈdɑːk-/ *v* [T] to repeat an idea or belief frequently to (someone) to persuade them to accept it • *Some parents were critical of attempts to indoctrinate children* **in** *green ideology.* • *They have been indoctrinated by television to believe that violence is normal.*

in·doc·trin·a·tion /£ɪnˌdɒk·trɪˈneɪ·ʃᵊn, $-ˌdɑːk-/ *n* [U] • *The 'news' report was a piece of blatant indoctrination designed to persuade people that nuclear power is safe.*

in·dol·ent /ˈɪn·dᵊl·ᵊnt/ *adj* without real interest or effort; LAZY • *an indolent wave of the hand* • *an indolent reply*

in·dol·ent·ly /ˈɪn·dᵊl·ᵊnt·li/ *adv*

in·dol·ence /ˈɪn·dᵊl·ᵊnts/ *n* [U] • *After a sudden burst of activity the team lapsed back into indolence.*

in·dom·i·ta·ble /£ɪnˈdɒm·ɪ·tə·bl̩, $-ˈdɑː·mə·t̬ə-/ *adj* (of a person) strong, brave, determined and difficult to defeat or make frightened • *The indomitable Mrs Furlong said she would continue to fight for justice.*

in·dom·i·ta·bly /£ɪnˈdɒm·ɪ·tə·bli, $-ˈdɑː·mə·t̬ə-/ *adv* • *He pursued this course of action indomitably for several years.*

in·door /£ˌɪnˈdɔːʳ, $-ˈdɔːr/ *adj* [before n; not gradable] happening, used or situated inside a building • *indoor sports/activities* • *indoor shoes* • *an indoor racetrack/swimming pool*

in·doors /£ˌɪnˈdɔːz, $-ˈdɔːrz/ *adv* [not gradable] • *Come indoors, it's cold outside.* • *Shall we have the party indoors or outdoors?*

in·du·bi·ta·ble /£ɪnˈdjuː·bɪ·tə·bl̩, $-ˈduː·bɪ·t̬ə-/ *adj* [not gradable] *fml* that cannot be doubted; certain

in·du·bi·ta·bly /£ɪnˈdjuː·bɪ·tə·bli, $-ˈduː·bɪ·t̬ə-/ *adv* [not gradable] *fml* • *He looked different but it was indubitably John.*

in·duce *obj* /£ɪnˈdjuːs, $-ˈduːs/ *v* [T] *fml* to persuade (someone) to do something, or to cause (something) to happen • *They induced her* **to** *take the job by promising editorial freedom.* [+ obj + *to* infinitive] • *Pills for seasickness often induce drowsiness.* • **Nothing could** *induce me* (= I definitely cannot be persuaded) **to** *climb a mountain/ride a bike.* [+ obj + *to* infinitive] • If doctors induce a pregnant woman/a baby, they cause the baby to be born before its natural time: *Twins are often induced.* ○ *I was induced because the baby was three weeks overdue.*

-in·duced /£-ɪn·djuːst, $-duːst/ *combining form* • -induced means caused by the stated person or activity: *a self-induced illness* ○ *work-induced stress*

in·duce·ment /£ɪnˈdjuːs·mᵊnt, $-ˈduːs-/ *n* [C] • *The gift was meant as an inducement* **to** *silence.* • *Will she need an inducement* **to** *keep the matter confidential?* [+ *to* infinitive] • *Have they offered you any* **financial** *inducements* (= money to persuade you to do something)?

in·duc·tion /ɪnˈdʌk·ʃᵊn/ *n* [U] *fml* • *sleep induction* • *mood induction* • *There are different views on the induction* **of labour** *in pregnant women.*

in·duct *obj* /ɪnˈdʌkt/ *v* [T often passive] *fml* to introduce someone formally or with a special ceremony to an organization or group, or to beliefs or ideas • *Li Xiannian was inducted* **into** *the Politburo and secretariat in 1956 and 1958.* • *He was inducted* **into** *the Grand Order of Water Rats, the celebrities' charity organization, at the Hilton Hotel.* • *He saw university as a community of scholars, where students were inducted by teachers* **into** *an appreciation of different philosophical approaches.*

in·duc·tion /ɪnˈdʌk·ʃᵊn/ *n* • *What is needed for all new teachers is a properly structured programme of induction and professional development.* [U] • *At the studio he'll get an induction* **to** *the Method System of acting and emerge like Brando, De Niro and Hoffman.* [C] • *Their induction* **into** *the church took place in June.* [C] • *Her induction* **as** *councillor took place at a ceremony in the town hall.* [C] • *an induction course* • *an induction ceremony*

in·duc·tion [ELECTRICITY] /ɪnˈdʌk·ʃᵊn/ *n* [U] *specialized* the giving of electrical power from one object to another without the objects touching • *electricity produced by induction* • *an induction coil/motor*

in·duc·tion [THINKING] /ɪnˈdʌk·ʃᵊn/ *n* [U] *specialized* the process of discovering a general principle from a set of facts

in·duc·tive /ɪnˈdʌk·tɪv/ *adj* [not gradable] *specialized* • *inductive reasoning*

in·duc·tive·ly /ɪnˈdʌk·tɪv·li/ *adv* [not gradable] *specialized*

in·dulge *(obj)* /ɪnˈdʌldʒ/ *v* to allow (yourself or someone else) to have esp. a lot of something enjoyable • *The soccer fans indulged their patriotism, waving flags and singing songs.* [T] • *With his friend's family he was able to indulge his* **passion** *for the outdoors, especially skiing.* [T] • *I love champagne but it's not often I can indulge* **myself**. [T] • *The children indulged me* **with** *breakfast in bed.* [T] • *This was a deliberate decision by the company to indulge* **in** *a little nostalgia.* [I] • *She was furious with her boss and indulged* **in** *rapturous* **fantasies of** *revenge.* [I]

in·dul·gence /ɪnˈdʌl·dʒənts/ *n* • *Chocolate is my only* **occasional** *indulgence/***self-***indulgence.* [C] • *All the pleasures and indulgences of the weekend are over, and I have to get down to some serious hard work.* [C] • *She regarded expensive lingerie as a* **gross** *and unjustifiable indulgence.* [C] • *His health suffered from* **over-***indulgence* **in** (= eating too much or too often) *rich food and drink.* [U] • *My inability to do needlework was treated with surprising indulgence by my teacher.* [U]

in·dul·gent /ɪnˈdʌl·dʒənt/ *adj* • *indulgent relatives* • *an indulgent smile/chuckle* • *He had been a strict father but was indulgent* **to/towards** *his grandchildren.*

in·dul·gent·ly /ɪnˈdʌl·dʒənt·li/ *adv*

in·du·stri·ous /ɪnˈdʌs·tri·əs/ *adj* having the characteristic of regularly working hard • *He is a very industrious worker.* • *Every assistant is expected to be competent and industrious.* • Ⓔ

in·du·stri·ous·ly /ɪnˈdʌs·tri·ə·sli/ *adv* • *Marco was working industriously at his desk.* • *The bird was pecking industriously at a bag of nuts outside the kitchen door.*

in·du·stri·ous·ness /ɪnˈdʌs·tri·ə·snəs/ *n* [U] • *We are grateful for her industriousness in setting up this conference.*

in·du·stry /ˈɪn·də·stri/ *n* [U] *fml* • Industry is the quality of regularly working hard. • See also INDUSTRY [PRODUCTION].

in·du·stry [PRODUCTION] /ˈɪn·də·stri/ *n* [U] the companies and activities involved in the process of producing goods for sale, esp. in a factory or special area • *local business and industry* • *trade and industry* • *industry and commerce* • *The city needs to attract more industry.* • *These companies spearheaded the redevelopment of large sections of Welsh industry.* • *The strike had seriously reduced coal deliveries to industry.* • See also **industry** at INDUSTRIOUS. • Ⓟ

in·du·stri·al /ɪnˈdʌs·tri·əl/ *adj* • Industrial means related to industry: *industrial output* ○ *industrial expansion* • *It's an industrial* **city/country/landscape/nation** (= one which has a lot of industry and many factories). • *He has an industrial* **background** (= has worked in industry). • **Industrial action** is acting in a way intended to force an employer to agree to something, esp. by stopping work. • **Industrial archaeology** is the study of the buildings and places related to early types of industry. • An **industrial disease** is an illness related to the work that someone does and **industrial medicine** is the study of this type of illness. • **Industrial espionage** is when one company steals secrets from another company with which it is competing.

• *(Br)* An **industrial estate** (*Am and Aus* **industrial park**) is a special area on the edge of a town for factories and businesses. • **Industrial relations** are the relationships between companies and their workers. • **The industrial revolution** is the period of time during which work began to be done more by machines in factories than by hand at home: *In Britain the Industrial Revolution took place between approximately 1750 and 1850.* ○ *We must save the world from the worst environmental disaster since the industrial revolution.* ○ *The industrial revolution virtually bypassed the town, which looked much as it had done since Napoleon's day.* • An **industrial tribunal** is a type of law court which decides on disagreements between companies and their workers.

in·du·stri·al /ɪn'dʌs·tri·əl/ *n* [C] • An industrial is a manufacturing company or the STOCK (=market value) of such a company: *He owns a series of industrials across the US and beyond.* ○ *Industrials were up at the close of trading.*

in·du·stri·al·ly /ɪn'dʌs·tri·ə·li/ *adv* • *an industrially advanced country* (=one with a lot of industry) • *The human growth hormone is the next in a long line of chemicals to be manufactured industrially* (=by industry in large amounts).

in·du·stri·al·i·sm /ɪn'dʌs·tri·ə·lɪ·zᵊm/ *n* [U] • Industrialism is the idea or state of having a country's economy, society or political system based on industry.

in·du·stri·al·ist /ɪn'dʌs·tri·ə·lɪst/ *n* [C] • An industrialist is an owner or an employee in a high position in industry: *Mr Anand is an industrialist with a reputation for independent thinking.* ○ *Charles Booth is the industrialist and social scientist who wrote the great studies of poverty at the turn of the century.*

in·du·stri·al·ize *(obj), Br and Aus usually* **-ise** /ɪn'dʌs·tri·ə·laɪz/ *v* • *It was the first country to industrialize* (= develop industry). [I]

in·du·stri·al·ized, *Br and Aus usually* **-ised** /ɪn'dʌs·tri·ə·laɪzd/ *adj* • *industrialized nations/countries*

in·du·stri·al·iz·a·tion, *Br and Aus usually* **-i·sa·tion** /ɪn,dʌs·tri·ə·laɪ'zeɪ·ʃᵊn/ *n* [U]

in·du·stry TYPE OF WORK /'ɪn·də·stri/ *n* [C] the people and activities involved in one type of business • *the gas/electricity industry* • *the holiday/tourist industry* • *the banking/pensions industry* • *manufacturing industries* • *The computer industry has been booming.* • *(disapproving)* If something is referred to as an industry, then a lot of it is produced or available and it makes a lot of money: *the pulp fiction industry* ○ *the heritage industry* • Ⓟ

in·du·stry·wide /,ɪn·də·stri'waɪd, '----/ *adj, adv* [not gradable] • *an industrywide practice*

in·e·bri·at·ed /£ɪ'niː·bri·eɪ·tɪd, $-t̬ɪd/ *adj fml* having drunk too much alcohol • *After the party they were totally inebriated.* • *In her inebriated state she was ready to agree to anything.*

in·e·bri·a·tion /ɪ,niː·bri'eɪ·ʃᵊn/ *n* [U] *fml* • *He was in an advanced state of inebriation.*

in·ed·i·ble /ɪ'ned·ɪ·bl̩/ *adj* not suitable as food • *The potato plant produces inedible fruits which look like green tomatoes.*

in·ed·i·bil·i·ty /ɪ,ned·ɪ'bɪl·ə·ti/ *n* [U] • *The artificial fruits looked so delicious it was hard to believe in their inedibility.*

in·ef·fa·ble /ɪ'nef·ə·bl̩/ *adj fml* causing too much emotion, esp. pleasure, to be described • *ineffable joy/beauty* • *ineffable delight*

in·ef·fec·tive /,ɪn·ɪ'fek·tɪv/ *adj* not producing the effects or results that are wanted; not effective • *They made an ineffective attempt to get the rules changed.* • *Ramos was an ineffective commander who promoted officers on the basis of loyalty rather than competence.* • *The triple-check system was an ineffective mechanism for getting things done quickly.*

in·ef·fec·tu·al /,ɪn·ɪ'fek·tju·ᵊl/ *adj fml* not skilled at achieving, or not able to produce, good results • *an ineffectual leader* • *Several of the teachers were ineffectual* **at** *maintaining discipline.* • *Thanks to the ineffectual efforts of prosecutors many trials were lost or abandoned.* • *The management produced an ineffectual response to the criticisms of safety procedures.* • *He was well-meaning but ineffectual.*

in·ef·fi·cient /,ɪn·ɪ'fɪʃ·ᵊnt/ *adj* not organized, skilled or able to work satisfactorily; not EFFICIENT • *Many of their industries are* **grossly** *inefficient.* • *He criticized the hopelessly inefficient telephone/tax/distribution* **system**. • *Existing methods of production are expensive and inefficient.* • *I'm hopelessly inefficient* **at** *mending things.*

in·ef·fi·cient·ly /,ɪn·ɪ'fɪʃ·ᵊnt·li/ *adv* • *The boiler is working inefficiently and wasting gas.* • *The setting of the play is a big, inefficiently run hotel.*

in·ef·fi·cien·cy /,ɪn·ɪ'fɪʃ·ᵊnt·si/ *n* [U] • *He complained that the inefficiency of the department was leading to poor sales.* • *They were accused of* **gross** *inefficiency in their handling of the case.*

in·e·las·tic /£,ɪn·ɪ'læs·tɪk, $-t̬ɪk/ *adj* not changing much, or not permitting much change • *For skilled occupations the supply of labour is typically fairly inelastic, because few workers are capable of doing the work.* • *The demand for services such as water, gas and electricity is relatively inelastic.*

in·el·e·gant /ɪ'nel·ɪ·gᵊnt/ *adj* not pleasing or attractive • *an inelegant posture* • *They ate their meal in cramped and inelegant surroundings.* • *They were 'gobsmacked' – if I might use that inelegant expression.*

in·el·i·gi·ble /ɪ'nel·ɪ·dʒə·bl̩/ *adj* [not gradable] not suitable according to particular rules • *Mr McCloughlin was* **declared** *ineligible* **for** *the competition because he worked for the company that ran it.* • *Many people would become ineligible* **to** *receive state aid because their earnings, although small, are above the new limit.* [+ *to* infinitive]

ineligibility /£ɪ,nel·ɪ·dʒə'bɪl·ɪ·ti, $-t̬i/ *n* [U]

in·ept /ɪ'nept/ *adj* not skilled or effective • *Someone had made an inept attempt to iron the shirts.* • *He was always rather inept* **at** *sport.* • *That was a rather inept* **comment/remark** *for a trained counsellor.* • *He was criticized for his inept* **handling** *of the situation.* • *The election comes amid charges of inept* **leadership** *and government mismanagement.* • *Dick was* **socially** *inept and uncomfortable in the presence of women.*

in·ep·ti·tude /£ɪ'nep·tɪ·tjuːd, $-t̬ɪ·tuːd/ *n* [U] • *political/social/economic ineptitude* • *The newspaper editorial correctly pointed out the government's ineptitude* **in** *dealing with the ozone crisis.*

in·e·qual·i·ty /£,ɪn·ɪ'kwɒl·ə·ti, $-'kwɑː·lə·t̬i/ *n* a lack of equality or fair treatment in the sharing of wealth or the opportunities for jobs, homes etc. between different groups in society • *The law has done little to prevent racial discrimination and inequality.* [U] • *Women thus knocked down another bastion of* **sexual** *inequality.* [U] • *There remain major inequalities of opportunity in the workplace.* [C]

in·e·qui·ta·ble /£ɪ'nek·wɪ·tə·bl̩, $-wə·t̬ə/ *adj fml* not fair; good for some and bad for others • *Hundreds of people demonstrated against the inequitable food distribution system.* • *Mr Levy shows that the inequitable distribution of wealth was roughly as great at the end of the second world war as it is now.* • *The current health care system is so inequitable, and the disparities between rich and poor are so great, that it is clearly unjust.*

in·e·quit·y /£ɪ'nek·wɪ·ti, $-t̬i/ *n fml* • *Five hundred guests were invited to take part in a demonstration of the inequities of food distribution worldwide.* [C] • *The government has produced a plan for student funding that has problems of inequity, as well as inadequate resources.* [U]

in·e·rad·i·ca·ble /,ɪn·ɪ'ræd·ɪ·kə·bl̩/ *adj* [not gradable] *fml* not able to be removed • *He left us with the ineradicable impression that we had been speaking to a future leader.*

in·ert NOT MOVING /£ɪ'nɜːt, $-'nɜːrt/ *adj* not moving or not able to move, or *(fig.)* not energetic or interesting • *The inert figure of a man could be seen in the front of the car.* • *(fig.) The narrative is inert and sloppy, as if the author had been writing half-asleep.*

in·ert CHEMICAL CHARACTERISTIC /£ɪ'nɜːt, $-nɜːrt/ *adj* *specialized* not reacting chemically with other substances • *Gold is inert to the action of some acids which can dissolve other metals.* • *Light bulb filaments break because they oxidize – replacing all the air with an inert* **gas** *would prevent this.*

in·er·tia /£ɪ'nɜː·ʃə, $-'nɜːr-/ *n* [U] lack of activity or interest; unwillingness to make an effort to do anything • *Companies still benefit from the inertia which leaves insurance policies with the same companies year after year.* • *The organization is stifled by bureaucratic inertia and a failure to change to meet the needs of modern society.* • An **inertia reel** safety/seat belt is one which allows you to move about but holds you firmly in position if it is suddenly pulled. • *(Br)* **Inertia selling** (*Am* **negative marketing**) is when, if you don't actively refuse something, a company behaves as though you have agreed to buy it.

in·es·ca·pa·ble /ˌɪn·ɪˈskeɪ·pə·bl̩/ *adj* [not gradable] that cannot be avoided • *The inescapable* **fact**, *however, is that one day the water is going to run out or become too expensive to pump up.* • *The inescapable* **truth** *is, some taxes will have to be raised.*

in·es·ca·pa·bly /ˌɪn·ɪˈskeɪ·pə·bli/ *adv* [not gradable] • *We are inescapably conditioned by our own historical situation.*

in·es·sen·tial /ˌɪn·ɪˈsen·tʃᵊl/ *adj* [not gradable], *n* (something which is) not necessary or needed; not ESSENTIAL • *The gift shop was a tourist trap, full of china ornaments and other inessential items.* • *Road conditions were hazardous and the police called for motorists to avoid inessential journeys.* • *Most people would disagree but I still regard telephones and televisions as inessentials!* [C usually pl]

in·es·tim·ab·le /ɪˈnes·tɪ·mə·bl̩/ *adj fml* extremely great; too great, or usually too good, to be described or expressed exactly • *Because the Mafia runs the world's drug-dealing businesses, its wealth is inestimable.* • *Rain forests support half the world's species, whose medical importance is of inestimable* **value**. • *The group has the inestimable advantage of being directly elected by the people.* • *The story of how he saved inestimable treasures from destruction in the fire was often re-told.* • *Support for the anti-war protests came from one politician who called the war an 'inestimable tragedy'.*

in·es·tim·ab·ly /ɪˈnes·tɪ·mə·bli/ *adv fml* • *Sight is inestimably important, as you soon realize if you've ever damaged an eye.*

in·ev·it·a·ble /£ɪˈnev·ɪ·tə·bl̩, $-t̬ə-/ *adj* [not gradable] certain to happen; unable to be avoided or prevented • *The accident was the inevitable* **consequence/result/outcome** *of carelessness.* • *Four successive dry winters had made water shortages inevitable.* • **It** *seems almost inevitable* **that** *they will discover the error when they check the account*. [+ *that* clause] • *We have no option but to accept* **the inevitable** (= something which is not wanted but cannot be prevented).

in·ev·it·a·bly /£ɪˈnev·ɪ·tə·bli, $-t̬ə-/ *adv* [not gradable] • *This decision will inevitably result in more crimes and more victims.*

in·ev·it·a·bil·i·ty /£ɪˌnev·ɪ·təˈbɪl·ɪ·ti, $-t̬əˈbɪl·ə·t̬i/ *n* [U] • *With sad inevitability, he has ended up in prison.* • *These historic facts gave a kind of inevitability to what happened in January.*

in·ex·act /ˌɪn·ɪgˈzækt/ *adj* uncertain or not known in detail; not exact • *Estimates of the numbers involved remain inexact.* • LP **Approximate numbers**

in·ex·cus·a·ble /ˌɪn·ɪkˈskjuː·zə·bl̩/ *adj* (of behaviour) too bad to be accepted • *They attacked the murder of civilians as inexcusable.* • *We thought* **it** *was inexcusable* **for** *him to leave so early.* • **It**'*s inexcusable* **that** *such young children were left in the house alone.* [+ *that* clause] • *A senior doctor said it was 'ethically inexcusable' not* **to** *have explained what the side effects of the drug might be.* [+ *to* infinitive]

in·ex·haust·i·ble /£ˌɪn·ɪgˈzɔː·stɪ·bl̩, $-ˈzɑː-/ *adj* unable to be completely used or come to an end because there is so much; very large or great • *Fossil fuels like oil and coal will run out one day, but wind and wave power are inexhaustible.* • *There seemed to be an inexhaustible supply of champagne to drink.*

in·ex·or·a·ble /£ɪˈnek·sᵊr·ə·bl̩, $-sɚ-/ *adj* [not gradable] *fml* continuing without any possibility of being stopped • *There was an inexorable rise in the price of oil after 1974.* • *Ageing can be thought of as a gradual, albeit inexorable, slide from summer into autumn and, with any luck, on to winter.*

in·ex·or·a·bly /£ɪˈnek·sᵊr·ə·bli, $-sɚ-/ *adv* [not gradable] *fml* • *The writer steers the reader, gently but inexorably, towards sympathy with the values of the the main character.*

in·ex·or·a·bil·i·ty /£ɪˌnek·sᵊr·əˈbɪl·ɪ·ti, $-sɚ·əˈbɪl·ə·t̬i/ *n* [U] *fml*

in·ex·ped·i·ent /ˌɪn·ɪkˈspiː·di·ənt/ *adj fml* not a good idea; not suitable or convenient • **It** *was inexpedient* **for him** *to be seen to approve of the decision.* [+ *to* infinitive]

in·ex·pen·sive /ˌɪn·ɪkˈspent·sɪv/ *adj* not costing a lot of money • *It's an attractive and inexpensive perfume.* • *The scheme is popular and inexpensive to administer.* • Inexpensive is often used to avoid saying 'cheap'. • LP **Expensive**

in·ex·pe·ri·ence /£ˌɪn·ɪkˈspɪə·ri·ənts, $-ˈspɪr·i-/ *n* [U] lack of knowledge in or lack of having practised a particular activity; lack of experience • *Her tolerance of my youthful inexperience won my undying gratitude and admiration.* • *The boxer's inexperience showed and he was stopped in the fifth round.* • *As a leader, he has been criticized for his inexperience* **in** *foreign affairs and refusal to accept good advice.*

in·ex·pe·ri·enced /£ˌɪn·ɪkˈspɪə·ri·əntst, $-ˈspɪr·i-/ *adj* • *They are inexperienced parents and need support.* • *Most of the assistants seem to be young and inexperienced.* • *She is rather inexperienced* **in** *international marketing.* • *People inexperienced* **with** *guns are buying them for protection.*

in·ex·pert /£ɪˈnek·spɜːt, $-spɜːrt/ *adj* lacking in skill • *She had made an inexpert attempt to ice the cake.* • **To the** *inexpert* **eye**, *nothing appeared to be wrong.*

in·ex·pert·ly /£ɪˈnek·spɜːt·li, $-spɜːrt-/ *adv* • *The report criticized the power plant for being inexpertly operated and maintained.*

in·ex·pli·ca·ble /ˌɪn·ɪkˈsplɪk·ə·bl̩/ *adj* that cannot be explained or understood • *The paper reported the inexplicable disappearance of two mothers.* • *I found his decision inexplicable.* • *They tried to* **explain** *the inexplicable* (= explain something very strange) *as an effect of the wind.*

in·ex·pli·ca·bly /ˌɪn·ɪkˈsplɪk·ə·bli/ *adv* • *The computer started behaving oddly, inexplicably posting money to the wrong accounts.* • *Inexplicably, the men were never questioned about where the explosives came from.*

in·ex·pres·si·ble /ˌɪn·ɪkˈspres·ɪ·bl̩/ *adj* [not gradable] (of a feeling) too strong to be described • *The news filled him with inexpressible delight/joy/horror/pain.* • *She painted as a means of expressing feelings that were inexpressible* **in words**.

in·ex·pres·si·bly /ˌɪn·ɪkˈspres·ɪ·bli/ *adv* [not gradable] • *The jokes were inexpressively awful.* • *Through the loudspeakers came the inexpressibly melancholy refrain which is always played at the end of their concerts.*

in·ex·pres·sive /ˌɪn·ɪkˈspres·ɪv/ *adj* showing no feelings • *Although the shock must have been great, her face remained inexpressive.* • *She stared for a while at his inexpressive back then left the room quietly.*

in·ex·tin·guish·a·ble /ˌɪn·ɪkˈstɪŋ·gwɪ·ʃə·bl̩, -wɪ-/ *adj* [not gradable] unable to be stopped from burning or existing • *The inextinguishable fire burns in the cemetery in memory of all those who were killed in the war.* • *The pain and suffering of those days is an inextinguishable memory.*

in ex·trem·is /ˌɪn·ɪkˈstriː·mɪs, -ekˈstreɪ-/ *adv* [not gradable] *fml* in the most difficult situation, or *(specialized)* about to die • *I'll only ask the bank for a loan in extremis.* • *(specialized) A person in extremis may lie with head back and mouth open, sometimes with the tongue lolling out.*

in·ex·tri·ca·ble /ˌɪn·ɪkˈstrɪk·ə·bl̩/ *adj* unable to be separated, freed or escaped from • *inextricable economic difficulties* • *He believed there were inextricable links between poverty, environmental degradation and military activity.* • *There were pages of information but the facts were virtually inextricable* **from** *irrelevant details.* • *Our knowledge of things is inextricable* **from** *the language we use.*

in·ex·tri·ca·bly /ˌɪn·ɪkˈstrɪk·ə·bli/ *adv* • *His name was inextricably* **linked** *with the environmental movement.*

in·fal·li·ble /ɪnˈfæl·ɪ·bl̩/ *adj* [not gradable] never wrong, failing or making a mistake • *Police forensic evidence was regarded at that time as virtually infallible.* • *Parking there is an infallible way of getting a fine.* • *His memory is not infallible.*

in·fal·li·bly /ɪnˈfæl·ɪ·bli/ *adv* [not gradable] • *They acted their parts infallibly.* • *The solid hydrogen will infallibly explode if it even warms up slightly.* • *Diesel cars start infallibly, run without stalling when cold, and demand far less gear-changing than most petrol models.* • Infallibly also means always: *He is infallibly cheerful despite his difficulties.* ○ *Whenever we sit down to eat someone infallibly phones.*

in·fal·li·bil·i·ty /£ɪnˌfæl·əˈbɪl·ɪ·ti, $-ə·t̬i/ *n* [U]

in·fa·mous /ˈɪn·fə·məs/ *adj* well known for something considered bad; NOTORIOUS • *The list included the infamous George Drake, a double murderer.* • *It was the worst snow since the infamous winter of 1947.* • *These lads seemed proud of their city's infamous reputation as the capital of bad manners.* • *He is infamous* **for** *saying that cheating 'has become absolutely necessary in professional cricket today'.*

in·fa·my /ˈɪn·fə·mi/ *n fml* • *Property developers earned their infamy in the years when the country felt like a huge building site.* [U] • An infamy is a bad and shocking act or event: *For those who had fought and the relatives of those who had died in the war, the final infamy was the pardoning of the draft-dodgers.* [C] ○ *The programme was a tough criticism of the hidden infamies of factory farming, with animals bred for minimum life and maximum profit.* [C]

in·fant YOUNG CHILD /ˈɪn·fənt/ *n* [C] a very young child • *In the first few weeks after birth, the infant is not able to see properly objects that are more than a few centimetres away.* • *The nurse came into the room carrying a* **newborn** *infant.* • *Infant* **mortality** *has decreased considerably in recent years.* • **Infant formula** is *Am and Aus for* **baby milk**. See at BABY. • LP› **Age**

in·fan·ti·cide /£ɪnˈfæn·tɪ·saɪd, $-t̬ə-/ *n* [U] *fml* • Infanticide is the crime of killing a child.

in·fan·tile /£ˈɪn·fən·taɪl, $-tᵊl/ *adj* • *(disapproving)* Infantile means typical of a child and therefore unsuitable for an adult: *infantile behaviour* ○ *an infantile comment*

in·fanc·y /ˈɪn·fənt·si/ *n* • *Her youngest child died* **in** *infancy* (= when very young). • *(fig.) The system is still* **in** *its infancy* (= very new). • *"Heaven lies about us in our infancy"* (William Wordsworth in the poem *Ode. Intimations of Immortality*, 1809)

in·fant SCHOOL /ˈɪn·fənt/ *adj Br and Aus* used to refer to the first stage of school, for children aged 4 to 7 years • *John has started infant* **school**. • *She trained as an infant teacher.* • *The report notes a worrying increase in exclusions of pupils from infant* **classes** *because of disruptive behaviour.* • *Current teaching practices seem to be implicated in the decline in infant reading standards.* • See also JUNIOR SCHOOL. • LP› **Schools and colleges**

in·fant /ˈɪn·fənt/ *n* [C] *Br* • *Jenny is a top-year infant* (= student at an infant school) *now.*

in·fants /ˈɪn·fənts/ *pl n Br* • **The Infants** refers to infant school: *Andrew's still* **in** *the Infants.*

in·fan·try /ˈɪn·fən·tri/ *n* [U + sing/pl v] **the infantry** the part of an army that fights on foot and not on horses or in vehicles • *Their son is in the infantry.* • *He joined the infantry/an infantry* **regiment**. • *The infantry is/are being sent into the battle zone.* • *They are infantry soldiers.* • *It's a* **light/heavy** *infantry unit.* • Compare CAVALRY.

in·fan·try·man (*pl* **-men**) /ˈɪn·fən·tri·mən, -mæn/, **foot sol·dier** *n* [C]

in·fat·u·at·ed /£ɪnˈfæt·ju·eɪ·tɪd, $-t̬ɪd/ *adj* having a strong but not usually lasting feeling of love or attraction for someone or something • *For the whole summer she was infatuated* **with** *her friend's brother.* • *The plot centres on a young Japanese rice farmer who* **becomes** *infatuated* **with** *his neighbour's daughter.* • *He said society was infatuated* **by** *the idols of consumerism and sex.*

in·fat·u·a·tion /ɪnˌfæt·juˈeɪ·ʃᵊn/ *n* • *It's just an infatuation. She'll get over it.* [C] • *Was he going to let infatuation banish commonsense?* [U]

in·feas·i·ble /ɪnˈfiː·zɪ·bl̩/ *adj* [not gradable] *Am for* UNFEASIBLE

in·fect *obj* /ɪnˈfekt/ *v* [T] to cause illness by the movement of an organism into a living thing • *The ward was full of children infected* **with** *TB.* • *All the tomato plants are infected with a virus.* • *(fig.) A computer virus may lurk unseen in a computer's memory, calling up and infecting each of the machine's data files in turn.* • *(fig.) When hysteria about AIDS first infected the media in the early Eighties, those identified as vulnerable were all at the margins of society.*

in·fect·ed /£ɪnˈfek·tɪd, $-t̬ɪd/ *adj* • *an infected wound* • *infected tissues* • *infected people* • *After the operation the wound became infected.*

in·fec·tion /ɪnˈfek·ʃᵊn/ *n* • *a serious infection* [C] • *The advertising campaign has raised awareness of the* **risk** *of infection.* [U]

in·fec·tious /ɪnˈfek·ʃəs/ *adj* • *an infectious disease/patient* • If something is infectious it has an effect on everyone and makes them want to take part: *an infectious laugh* ○ *infectious enthusiasm*

in·fe·lic·i·tous /£ˌɪn·fəˈlɪs·ɪ·təs, $-t̬əs/ *adj fml or humorous* not suitable; not fitting the occasion • *an infelicitous remark*

in·fe·lic·i·ty /£ˌɪn·fəˈlɪs·ɪ·ti, $-ə·t̬i/ *n* [C usually pl] *fml or humorous* • *The short piece was full of mistakes and verbal infelicities* (= unsuitable expressions).

in·fer /£ɪnˈfɜːʳ, $-ˈfɜːr/ *v* **-rr-** *fml* to obtain information indirectly • *What do you infer* **from** *her refusal?* • *Although she agreed with me I inferred* **from** *her expression* **that** *she was reluctant.* [+ *that* clause] • *We inferred* **from** *comments they had made to friends* **that** *they were unlikely to support us.* [+ *that* clause] • *We can/may infer* **from** *the absence of women in university history* **that** *higher education was denied them.* [+ *that* clause] • *If you see a man and a woman in a bar holding hands, it's* **reasonable** *to infer* **that** *they're having some sort of relationship.* [+ *that* clause]

in·fer·ence /£ˈɪn·fᵊr·ᵊnts, £ˈ-frənts, $-fɚ-/ *n fml* • *They were warned to expect a heavy air attack and* **by** *inference many casualties.* [U] • *His change of mind was recent and sudden, the inference being that someone had persuaded him.* [C] • *From her reply we* **drew** *the inference that she had already seen the document.* [C]

in·fe·ri·or /£ɪnˈfɪə·ri·əʳ, $-ˈfɪr·i·ɚ/ *adj* not good, or not as good as someone or something else, or *(specialized)* lower • *They had bought goods of inferior quality.* • *She cited other cases to document her claim that women and minority-group members frequently receive inferior health care.* • *They felt inferior* **to** *the others until the team's international success gave them some pride.* • *It was clear the group were regarded as* **intellectually/morally/socially** *inferior.* • *(specialized) The High Court was acting to ensure that the inferior court was acting within the limits of the powers which had been granted to it.* • Compare SUPERIOR BETTER.

in·fe·ri·o·ri·ty /£ɪnˌfɪə·riˈɒr·ə·ti, $-ˌfɪr·iˈɔːr·ə·t̬i/ *n* [U] • *We were surprised by the inferiority of the workmanship.* • *His treatment as a child had given him a strong* **sense of** *inferiority.* • If you have an **inferiority complex** about something you feel you are not good enough and it has an effect on the way you behave: *He has always had an inferiority complex* **about** *not having a qualification despite his years of experience.* • Compare **superiority** at SUPERIOR BETTER.

in·fer·nal /£ɪnˈfɜː·nəl, $-ˈfɜːr-/ *adj* having the qualities of HELL (= place to which bad people go after death) or *(dated)* very bad or unpleasant • *The room was lit with an infernal red light.* • *He described a journey through the infernal world.* • *(dated) We've been having infernal* **weather**. • *(dated) What an infernal* **noise**!

in·fer·no /£ɪnˈfɜː·nəʊ, $-ˈfɜːr·noʊ/ *n* [C] *pl* **infernos** /£ɪnˈfɜː·nəʊz, $-ˈfɜːr·noʊz/ a very large uncontrolled fire • *He saw a policeman pull a man out of the inferno of his blazing car.* • *It may take a year to put out the inferno, as hundreds of oil fires are burning.* • *The building was an inferno by the time the fire service arrived, with flames leaping high into the air.*

in·fer·tile /£ɪnˈfɜː·taɪl, $-ˈfɜːr·t̬ᵊl/ *adj* [not gradable] not able to produce young living things or good crops • *It has been estimated that one in eight* **couples** *is infertile.* • *Many infertile* **women** *undergo treatment in the hope that it will help them to conceive.* • *Harvests are poor in this infertile area.* • *Poor farmers have little option but to try to grow food on these very infertile* **soils**.

in·fer·tile /£ɪnˈfɜː·taɪl, $-ˈfɜːr·t̬ᵊl/ *pl n* • *There is a telephone helpline to give professional advice and support to* **the infertile** (= people who are infertile).

in·fer·til·i·ty /£ˌɪn·fəˈtɪl·ɪ·ti, $-fɚˈtɪl·ə·t̬i/ *n* [U] • *They noted an increase in* **male** *infertility.* • *She is a leading researcher in the* **treatment of** *infertility.* • An **infertility clinic** is a special building or part of a hospital where people go to get medical treatment or advice when they are unable to produce children.

in·fest *obj* /ɪnˈfest/ *v* [T] (of animals and insects which carry disease) to cause a problem by being present in large numbers • *The barns were infested* **with** *rats.* • *This type of fly infests herds where poverty makes control impossible.*

in·fes·ta·tion /ˌɪn·fesˈteɪ·ʃᵊn/ *n* • *a severe infestation* **of** *cockroaches/head lice* [C] • *Cases of human infestation* **with** *this parasite are relatively rare.* [U]

in·fi·del /£ˈɪn·fɪ·dᵊl, £-del, $-fə·del/ *n* [C] *old use disapproving* (used esp. between Christians and Muslims) a person who does not have the same religious beliefs • *infidel armies* • *He lived among infidels/***the** *infidel.*

in·fi·del·i·ty /£ˌɪn·fɪˈdel·ə·ti, $-fəˈdel·ə·t̬i/ *n* (an act of) having sex with someone who is not your husband, wife or regular sexual partner, or (an example of) not being loyal or FAITHFUL • *The papers were full of moral judgements on* **marital/sexual** *infidelity.* [U] • *The marriage broke up because of the wife's infidelity.* [U] • *She could not forgive his many infidelities.* [C]

in·field /ˈɪn·fiːld/ *n* [U] **the infield** (in baseball) the part of the playing field enclosed by the path around the BASES that is not covered with grass, or the players, other than the PITCHER and CATCHER, who regularly play on this part of the field • *If you keep the ball in the infield, the runners will have a hard time scoring.* • *Brooks Robinson, Ozzie Smith, Willie Randolph and Don Mattingly – now there's an infield!* • Compare OUTFIELD.

in·field·er /£'ɪnˌfiːl·dəʳ, $-dɚ/ *n* [C] • In baseball, an infielder is any of the four players who regularly play between the positions of **first base** and **third base**.

in·fight·ing /£'ɪnˌfaɪ·tɪŋ, $-t̬ɪŋ/ *n* [U] competition between people within a group, esp. to improve their own position or to get agreement for their ideas • *political infighting* • *Years of infighting* **among** *the leaders have destroyed the party.* • *More energy was spent on infighting* **within** *the group than on working for progress.*

in·fil·trate *obj* /'ɪn·fɪl·treɪt/ *v* [T] (to cause someone) slowly and gradually to become part of a group to get information, or to influence the way that group thinks or behaves • *A small and well organised conspiratorial group, they infiltrated key military units.* • *They infiltrated their own people* **into** *the security firm.* • *(fig.) At about this time the new ideas about 'corporate management' had begun to infiltrate local government.*

in·fil·tra·tion /ˌɪn·fɪl'treɪ·ʃᵊn/ *n* [U] • *Refugees were moved out of their villages by the government because of guerrilla infiltration.*

in·fil·tra·tor /£'ɪn·fɪl·treɪ·təʳ, $-t̬ɚ/ *n* [C] • *The infiltrator was identified and killed.*

in·fin·ite /'ɪn·fɪ·nət/ *adj* [not gradable] without limits; extremely large or great • *The universe is theoretically infinite.* • *Hamlet blamed his bad dreams for his inability to reign over infinite* **space**. • *With infinite* **patience**, *members of his staff were using magnifying glasses to examine the piles of banknotes for signs of forgery.* • *The health service produces infinite* **demand** *which will always outstrip supply.* • *He said the planes were taking infinite* **care** *to avoid flying over residential areas.* • *There is an infinite* **variety/number** (= a large range) *of bank accounts and loan packages available.* • *(disapproving) The authorities,* **in** *their* **infinite wisdom**, *decided to close the advice centre* (= they thought this was the best thing to do, but other people disagreed). • God is sometimes called **the Infinite**.

in·fin·ite·ly /'ɪn·fɪ·nət·li/ *adv* [not gradable] • *infinitely* (= extremely) *great* • *infinitely* (= much) *better*

in·fin·it·es·i·mal /ˌɪn·fɪ·nɪ'tes·ɪ·məl/ *adj fml* extremely small • *The amounts of radioactivity were infinitesimal and seemed to presented no danger.*

in·fin·it·es·i·mal·ly /ˌɪn·fɪ·nɪ'tes·ɪ·mə·li/ *adv fml* • *infinitesimally small*

infinitive /£ɪn'fɪn·ɪ·tɪv, $-ə·t̬ɪv/ *n* [C] *specialized* the form of a verb that usually follows 'to' • *In the sentences 'I had to go' and 'I must go', 'go' is an infinitive.* • *'Go' is the infinitive form.* • LP **-ing form of verbs**

in·fin·i·ty /£ɪn'fɪn·ɪ·ti, $-ə·t̬i/ *n* [U] a point which is so far away that it cannot be reached • *The numbers continue in this pattern to infinity.* • *(fig.) The mountain range stretched away into infinity.* • *She stared into infinity* (= looked into the distance without really seeing anything) *and did not reply.*

in·firm /£ɪn'fɜːm, $-'fɜːrm/ *adj fml* ill or needing care, esp. for long periods and often because of old age • *State-run residential facilities for those who become too elderly or infirm to remain independent are few.*

in·firm /£ɪn'fɜːm, $-'fɜːrm/ *pl n* • **The infirm** are people who are ill for long periods: *There are an estimated six million unpaid carers looking after the disabled, elderly or mentally infirm.* ○ *The severe cold had claimed many victims amongst the old and infirm.*

in·fir·mi·ty /£ɪn'fɜː·mə·ti, $-'fɜːr·mə·t̬i/ *n fml* • *an advanced state of infirmity* [U] • *(esp. humorous) She gave me a long account of her many infirmities* (= her illnesses/medical problems). [C]

in·fir·ma·ry /£ɪn'fɜː·mᵊr·i, $-'fɜːr·mɚ-/ *n* [C] *old use* (esp. in names) a hospital • *Leeds General Infirmary* • *the Royal Infirmary* • *(Am)* An infirmary (*Br* **sick/first-aid room**) is also a room in a school, college or university where students who are injured or feeling ill can go to a nurse for treatment: *I think you'd better take Ryan along to the infirmary.*

in·flame *obj* /ɪn'fleɪm/ *v* [T] to increase (strong feelings) • *Her answer inflamed him* **with** *anger/enthusiasm/desire.* • *Reducing the number of staff is certain to inflame the uneasy mood in the hospitals.* • *Film of burnt bodies and crying, hysterical relatives inflamed* **feelings/passions** *further.* • See also INFLAMMATORY.

in·flamed /ɪn'fleɪmd/ *adj* (of a part of the body) red, sore and larger than its usual size, esp. because of infection • *an inflamed eye/toe*

in·flam·ma·tion /ˌɪn·flə'meɪ·ʃᵊn/ *n* • *an inflammation of the eye/toe/ear* [C] • *a high temperature caused by inflammation* [U]

in·flam·ma·to·ry /£ɪn'flæm·ə·tri, $-tɔːr·i/ *adj specialized* • *The drugs are used in the treatment of inflammatory and allergic disorders.* • See also INFLAMMATORY.

in·flamm·a·ble /ɪn'flæm·ə·bl̩/, *Am or specialized* **flam·ma·ble** /'flæm·ə·bl̩/ *adj* burning very easily • *a highly inflammable liquid* • *(fig.) It was a highly inflammable situation* (= one which could easily lead to trouble). • Compare **non-flammable** at NON-.

in·flam·ma·to·ry /£ɪn'flæm·ə·tᵊr·i, £-tri, $-tɔːr-/ *adj* intentionally causing trouble, strong negative feelings, etc. • *The men were using inflammatory* **language**/*making inflammatory* **remarks** *about the other team's supporters.*

in·flate *(obj)* FILL WITH AIR /ɪn'fleɪt/ *v* to (cause to) increase in size by filling with air • *He inflated the rubber dinghy with a foot pump.* [T] • *The hot-air balloon slowly inflated and took off.* [I] • *The partially inflated boat began to sink.*

in·flat·a·ble /£ɪn'fleɪ·tə·bl̩, $-t̬ə-/ *adj* [not gradable], *n* • *inflatable pillows/mattresses* • An inflatable is a boat or something similar which must be filled with air in order to float on the water. [C]

in·flate *obj* MAKE LARGER /ɪn'fleɪt/ *v* [T] to make something larger or more important • *The numbers attending the rally were inflated by the press.* • *They inflated their part in the rescue the more they told the story.* • *He has an inflated idea of his own importance/opinion of himself* (= He thinks he is more important than he is). • *They* **artificially** *inflated the value of the house so they could 'reduce' it and make people think it was a bargain.* • An inflated price/income is one that is higher than people think is reasonable.

in·fla·tion /ɪn'fleɪ·ʃᵊn/ *n* [U] • Inflation is a general continuous increase in prices in a country: *There is high inflation and mounting frustration over price rises for food and utilities like heating and telephone calls.* ○ *The grant will be increased in line with the 3% inflation expected this autumn.* ○ *"I hope the new measures, will contribute to preventing the resurgence of house price inflation," he said.* • Compare **deflation** at DEFLATE REDUCE MONEY SUPPLY.

in·fla·tion·a·ry /£ɪn'fleɪ·ʃᵊn·ᵊr·i, $-er·i/ *adj* • Something inflationary causes price increases and inflation: *inflationary policies/pressures/trends* • An **inflationary spiral** is a situation in which prices increase, then people are paid more in their jobs, which then causes the price of goods and services to increase again, and so on.

in·flec·tion GRAMMAR, **in·flex·ion** /ɪn'flek·ʃᵊn/ *n* [C] a change in or addition to the form of a word which shows a change in the way it is used in sentences • *If you add the plural inflection '-s' to 'dog' you get 'dogs'.* • LP **Forms of words (spelling)**

in·flect·ed /ɪn'flek·tɪd/ *adj* • *'Finds' and 'found' are inflected forms of 'find'.* • *In this dictionary, we show any irregular inflected* **forms** *of a word, such as the plural or past tense.* • An **inflected language** is one which changes the form or ending of some words when the way in which they are used in sentences changes: *Latin, Polish and Finnish are all highly inflected languages.*

in·flec·tion SPEECH, **in·flex·ion** /ɪn'flek·ʃᵊn/ *n* the way in which the sound of your voice changes during speech, for example when you emphasize certain words • *She uses her remarkable voice to create a wide range of accents, mannerisms and inflections in her one-woman show.* [C] • *His voice was low and flat, with almost no inflection.* [U]

in·flex·i·ble /ɪn'flek·sɪ·bl̩/ *adj usually disapproving* (esp. of opinions and rules) fixed and unable or unwilling to change • *The prime minister has adopted an inflexible position.* • *This type of computer is too slow and inflexible to meet many business needs.* • *Must you be so inflexible?*

in·flex·i·bil·i·ty /£ɪnˌflek·sɪ'bɪl·ɪ·ti, $-ə·t̬i/ *n* [U] *esp. disapproving* • *Britain was accused of inflexibility* **in** *its refusal to co-operate.* • *The inflexibility of the working day makes some people choose to go freelance.*

in·flict *obj* /ɪn'flɪkt/ *v* [T] to force someone to experience (something very unpleasant) • *This weapon is capable of inflicting massive military and civilian casualties.* • *The suffering inflicted* **on** *these children is terrible to see.* • *His forearms were covered in slash marks which he had inflicted* on *himself in prison.* • *I wish he wouldn't keep inflicting his views* **on** *me!*

in·flic·tion /ɪn'flɪk·ʃᵊn/ *n* [U] • *The soldiers took sadistic pleasure in the infliction of suffering.*

in·flow /£'ɪn·fləʊ, $-floʊ/ *n* [U] the action of people or things arriving somewhere • *The government wanted an inflow* **of** *foreign investment.* • *Supplies of workers grew sharply in September because of the inflow* **of** *immigrants from Eastern Europe.*

in·flu·ence /'ɪn·flu·ənts/ *n* the power to have an effect on people or things, or a person or thing that is able to do this • *Violence on TV may turn out to be a potent influence* **on** *some young people.* [C] • *The Royal Family enjoys huge wealth and considerable influence.* [U] • *How far can we blame environmental or social influences for crime?* [C] • *Christopher hoped to use his influence to make them change their minds.* [U] • *Helen's a* **bad/good** *influence* **on** *him.* [C] • *Can't you* **exert** (=use) *your influence and persuade him to come tonight?* [U] • *Photography had* **an** *important influence* **on** *how the Impressionists painted.* [U] • If a person or thing is **under the** influence **of** someone or something, it is controlled or AFFECTED by them, esp. in a bad way: *The empress had* **fallen** *under the influence of evil advisers, and was becoming increasingly unpopular.* [U] • *(humorous) Sandy says some outrageous things when she's* **under the influence** (=drunk).

in·flu·ence *obj* /'ɪn·flu·ənts/ *v* [T] • *Which designer do you think has most influenced fashion* (=had an effect on it) *in the past five years?* • *She's very good at making friends and influencing people.* • *Media coverage is directly influencing* **how** *the public responds to the war.* [+ *wh-*word] • *What influenced you* **to** *choose a career in nursing?* [+ obj + *to* infinitive]

in·flu·en·tial /ˌɪn·flu'en·tʃᵊl/ *adj* • *She wanted to work for a bigger and more influential* (=powerful) *newspaper.* • *Johnson was influential* **in** *persuading* (=partly caused) *the producers to put money into the film.*

in·flu·en·za /ˌɪn·flu'en·zə/ *n* [U] *fml for* FLU

in·flux /'ɪn·flʌks/ *n* [U] the arrival of a large number (of people or things) • *The film will be made in the town of Muchty, which is bracing itself to cope with the expected influx* **of** *TV people and journalists.* • *Turkey is expecting an influx* **of** *refugees running into several thousands.*

info /£'ɪn·fəʊ, $-foʊ/ *n* [U] *infml for* INFORMATION

in·fo·mer·cial /£ɪn·fə'mɜːʃ·ᵊl, $-mɝːʃ/ *n* [C] an unusually long television advertisement, broadcast esp. at night • *An infomercial can last as long as half an hour and often resembles a quiz show.* • *Infomercials first appeared on night-time TV in America, but they are now also broadcast on British satellite and European TV.*

in·form *(obj)* /£ɪn'fɔːm, $-'fɔːrm/ *v* to tell (someone) about particular facts • *The name of the dead man will not be released until his relatives have been informed.* [T] • *Why wasn't I informed* **about** *this earlier?* [T] • *Walters was not properly informed* **of** *the reasons for her arrest.* [T] • *I informed my boss* **(that)** *I was going to be away next week.* [T + obj + (*that*) clause] • If you inform **(on/against** someone else) you give the police information, usually secretly, about that person, showing that he or she has done something wrong: *The terrorists said that anyone caught informing (on them) would be killed.* [I]

in·for·mant /£ɪn'fɔː·mənt, $-'fɔːr-/ *n* [C] • Your informant is someone who tells you something: *My informant in the agricultural world tells me that farming methods are changing.*

in·for·ma·tion /£ˌɪn·fə'meɪ·ʃᵊn, $-fɚ-/ *n* [U] • Information is knowledge about something, esp. facts and news: *Do you have any information* **about/on** *train times?* ○ *I read an interesting* **bit/piece** *of information in the newspaper.* ○ **For further** *information* (=if you want to know more), *please contact your local library.* ○ *We have reliable information* **that** *a terrorist attack is planned next month.* [+ *that* clause] • **Information retrieval** is the process of finding stored information on a computer. • **Information technology** (*abbreviation* **IT**) is the science and activity of storing and sending out information by using computers. • Ⓕ

in·for·ma·tion·al /£ɪn·fə'meɪ·ʃᵊn·ᵊl, $-fɚ-/ *adj* • *The survey suggested that a mere 20% of television programmes watched by children under the age of ten had any informational content.*

in·for·ma·tive /£ɪn'fɔː·mə·tɪv, $-'fɔːr·mə·t̬ɪv/ *adj* • Something that is informative provides a lot of useful information: *This is an interesting and highly informative book.*

in·formed /£ɪn'fɔːmd, $-'fɔːrmd/ *adj* • *The school promised to* **keep** *parents informed* (=to tell them about anything that happens). • *I don't know the answer but I can make an informed* **guess** (=a guess based on the knowledge that I do have). • *Elizabeth is remarkably* **well-***informed* (=she knows a lot about many different things).

in·form·er /£ɪn'fɔː·məʳ, $-'fɔːr·mɚ/ *n* [C] • An informer is a person who gives information in secret, esp. to the police: *Most police informers receive a reward for their information.*

in·for·mal /£ɪn'fɔː·məl, $-'fɔːr-/ *adj* (of situations) not formal or official or (of clothing, behaviour, speech) suitable when you are with friends and family but not for official occasions • *The two groups agreed to hold an informal meeting.* • *He's the ideal sort of teacher – direct, friendly and informal.* • *The famous 1969 TV documentary took an informal approach to the Royal Family.* • *Journalists often pick up information in informal situations such as in bars and clubs.* • *'Hi' is an informal way of greeting people.* • LP〉 **Labels**

in·for·mal·ly /£ɪn'fɔː·məl·i, $-'fɔːr-/ *adv* • *It's an outdoor party, so dress informally.* • *They've informally agreed to separate.*

in·for·mal·i·ty /£ˌɪn·fɔː'mæl·ə·ti, $-fɔːr'mæl·ə·t̬i/ *n* [U] • *Although she is at the top of the medical profession, she has an informality of approach that is very appealing.*

in·formed /£ɪn'fɔːmd, $-'fɔːrmd/ *adj* [not gradable] See at INFORM

in·form·er /£ɪn'fɔː·məʳ, $-'fɔːr·mɚ/ *n* [C] See at INFORM

in·fo·tain·ment /£ɪn·fəʊ'teɪn·mənt, $-foʊ-/ *n* [U] *esp. disapproving* (in television) the reporting of news and facts in an entertaining and amusing way rather than providing real information • *It wasn't a real documentary – it was more what you'd call infotainment.*

in·frac·tion /ɪn'fræk·ʃᵊn/ *n* [C] *fml* (an example of) the breaking of a rule or law • *Any attempt to influence the judges will be seen as an infraction* **of** *the rules.* • *The infractions involved security breaches in the methods used to screen passengers and baggage at London and Frankfurt airports.*

in·fra dig /ˌɪn·frə'dɪg/ *adj* [after v] *dated* below what you consider to be socially acceptable for you • *I get the impression that Diane and her friends consider it a bit infra dig to do your own housework.*

in·frared /ˌɪn·frə'red/ *adj* [not gradable] of RAYS of light which cannot be seen, but give out heat • *Their pilots are guided by an infrared optical system that shows images clearly even at night.*

in·fra·struc·ture /£'ɪn·frəˌstrʌk·tʃəʳ, $-tʃɚ/ *n* [C] the basic structure on which an organization or system is built and which makes it able to work • *The war has badly damaged the country's infrastructure, from electricity plants and generators to roads and bridges.*

in·fre·quent /ɪn'friː·kwənt/ *adj* not happening often; rare • *His letters became infrequent, then stopped completely.*

in·fre·quent·ly /ɪn'friː·kwənt·li/ *adv* • *I only see him very infrequently these days.*

in·fringe *obj* /ɪn'frɪndʒ/ *v* [T] *fml* to break (a rule, law etc.) • If you infringe a person's **rights** or their **freedom**, you prevent them from doing what they are legally allowed to do: *The prisoners complained that their rights were being infringed.*

in·fringe·ment /ɪn'frɪndʒ·mənt/ *n* • *She claimed that being forced to eat was an infringement* **of** *her human rights.* [C] • *Minor infringements* **of** *the law will not be punished.* [C] • *The ban on smoking is particularly subject to infringement.* [U]

in·fu·ri·ate *obj* /£ɪn'fjʊə·ri·eɪt, $-'fjʊr·i-/ *v* [T] to make (someone) extremely angry • *What infuriates me is the way that he never listens to what you say.*

in·fu·ri·at·ing /£ɪn'fjʊə·ri·eɪ·tɪŋ, $-'fjʊr·i·eɪ·t̬ɪŋ/ *adj* • *It's infuriating when people keep spelling your name wrong, isn't it?*

in·fuse *(obj)* /ɪn'fjuːz/ *v* to fill (someone or something) with (an emotion or quality) • *The pulling down of the Berlin Wall infused the world* **with** *optimism.* [T] • *The arrival of a group of friends on Saturday infused new life* **into** *the weekend.* [T] • If you infuse a drink or it infuses, you leave a substance such as tea leaves or herbs in hot water so that its flavour goes into the liquid: *Allow the mint tea to infuse for five minutes.* [I]

in·fu·sion /ɪn'fjuː·ʒᵊn/ *n* • *An infusion of $100 000* **into** *the company is required* (= This amount of money needs to be put into the company). [C] • *She drinks an infusion of herbs every day* (= a drink made by leaving herbs in hot water). [C] • *Their herb teas are made by infusion.* [U] • *The patient will need regular infusions of blood* (= blood given by means of INJECTION). [C]

-ing /-ɪŋ/ *combining form* used to form the present participle of regular verbs • *calling* • *asking* • LP› **-ed and -ing adjectives, -ing form of verbs, Stress in pronunciation**

in·gen·i·ous /ɪn'dʒiː·ni·əs/ *adj* (of a person) very clever and skilful, or (of a thing) cleverly made or planned and involving new ideas and methods • *Johnny is so ingenious – he can make the most remarkable sculptures from the most ordinary materials.* • *Glancy had to come up with ingenious* **ways** *to finance his own films because major studios were not interested.* • *These plants have* **devised** *ingenious* **ways** *of snatching nutrients from the air.*

in·gen·i·ous·ly /ɪn'dʒiː·ni·ə·sli/ *adv* • *The umbrella was ingeniously devised to fold up into your pocket.*

in·ge·nu·i·ty /£ˌɪn·dʒə'njuː·ɪ·ti, $-ə·t̬i/ *n* [U] • A person's ingenuity is their ability to think of clever new ways of doing something: *Drug smugglers constantly use their ingenuity to find new ways of getting drugs into a country.*

in·ge·nue /£'æ̃n·ʒeɪ·nuː, $'æn·ʒə-/ *n* [C] *fml* a young woman who lacks experience and is very trusting, esp. as played in films and plays • *She plays a charming ingenue who arrives in Paris hoping to be a dancer.*

in·gen·u·ous /ɪn'dʒen·ju·əs/ *adj fml* honest, sincere and trusting, sometimes in a way that seems foolish • *It was rather ingenuous of him to ask a stranger to look after his luggage.* • *Sally was so obviously sincere and ingenuous that everyone liked her.*

in·gen·u·ous·ly /ɪn'dʒen·ju·ə·sli/ *adv fml* • *Despite the evidence, she still ingenuously believes that her husband was never unfaithful to her.*

in·gest *obj* /ɪn'dʒest/ *v* [T] *specialized* to take (food or liquid) into the stomach • *The chemicals can be poisonous if ingested.*

in·ges·tion /ɪn'dʒes·tʃᵊn/ *n* [U] • *This poison can enter the body by inhalation, absorption through the skin, or ingestion.*

in·gle·nook /'ɪŋ·gl̩·nʊk/ *n* [C] a partly enclosed space by a large open fireplace built so that you can sit close to the fire • *This 18th-century cottage has exposed oak beams and an inglenook fireplace.* • PIC› **Fires and space heaters**

in·glo·ri·ous /£ɪŋ'glɔː·ri·əs, $-'glɔːr·i-/ *adj* not honourable or not to be proud of • *The government played an inglorious role in the conflict.* • *This country has a long, inglorious record of dealing harshly with political prisoners.* • *He left behind an inglorious political career to start his own business.*

in·got /'ɪŋ·gət/ *n* [C] a piece of metal, usually in the shape of a narrow brick • *Once cooled, iron ingots are taken to a foundry, melted down and poured into moulds.* • *The gold ingots will be transported in a high-security van.*

in·grained /ɪŋ'greɪnd/ *adj* (of dirt) fixed firmly, or *(fig.)* (of beliefs) so firmly held that they are not likely to change • *Over the months the oil had become ingrained* **in** *his skin.* • *His jeans were ingrained* **with** *dirt.* • *(fig.) Such ingrained prejudices cannot be corrected easily.* • *(fig.) The belief that you should own your house is* **deeply** *ingrained* **in** *British society.*

in·grate /'ɪŋ·greɪt/ *n* [C] *literary* a person who is not grateful • *All children are ingrates.* • *After all I've done for you, ingrate!* [as form of address]

in·gra·ti·ate *obj* /ɪŋ'greɪ·ʃiː·eɪt/ *v* [T] *disapproving* to try to make (yourself) liked by and approved of by other people • *He's always trying to ingratiate* **himself** *(***with** *people in authority).*

in·gra·ti·at·ing /£ɪŋ'greɪ·ʃiː·eɪ·tɪŋ, $-t̬ɪŋ/ *adj disapproving* • *I hate that ingratiating little smile she has.*

in·gra·ti·tude /£ɪŋ'græt·ɪ·tjuːd, $-græt̬·ə·tuːd/ *n* [U] lack of gratitude • *Tim's parents were rather hurt by his ingratitude.*

in·gre·di·ent /ɪŋ'griː·di·ənt/ *n* [C] a food that is used with other foods in the preparation of a particular dish • *The* **list of** *ingredients included 500g of sugar and 200ml of cream.* • *(fig.) Trust is an* **essential/vital** *ingredient in a successful marriage.*

in·grow·ing /£'ɪŋˌgrəʊ·ɪŋ, $-groʊ-/, *Am usually* **in·grown** /£'ɪŋ·grəʊn, $'ɪŋ·groʊn/ *adj* [not gradable] growing inwards into the flesh • *She's having an operation on an ingrowing* **toenail**.

in·hab·it *obj* /ɪn'hæb·ɪt/ *v* [T] to live in (a place) • *These remote islands are inhabited only by birds and animals.* • (E)(F)

in·hab·i·tant /ɪn'hæb·ɪ·tᵊnt/ *n* [C] • *The inhabitants of the village* (= the people who live there) *protested against the new road.*

in·hab·it·a·ble /£ɪn'hæb·ɪ·tə·bl̩, $-t̬ə-/ *adj* • *Are the islands inhabitable* (= able to be lived on)? • (E)(F)

in·hale *(obj)* /ɪn'heɪl/ *v* to breathe (something) in • *She flung open the window and inhaled deeply.* [I] • *A tiny drop of nerve gas, inhaled or absorbed through the skin or eyes, is enough to kill.* [T] • *The president said he had smoked but never inhaled* (= breathed in the smoke). [I] • Compare EXHALE.

in·ha·la·tion /ˌɪn·hə'leɪ·ʃᵊn/ *n* [U] • *Two workers were treated for* **smoke** *inhalation at The London Hospital.*

in·hal·er /£ɪn'heɪ·ləʳ, $-lɚ/ *n* [C] • An inhaler is a small device you use to breathe in particular medicines: *Shaun uses an inhaler to relieve his asthma.*

in·her·ent /£ɪn'her·ᵊnt, £-'hɪə·rənt, $-'hɪr·ᵊnt/ *adj* existing as a natural or basic part of something; not able to be removed or changed • *There are* **dangers/risks** *inherent* **in** *almost every sport.* • *She seems completely unaware of the contradictions inherent* **in** *her professed point of view.* • *I have an inherent distrust of lawyers.* • *This war has shown again the inherent instability of this region.*

in·her·ent·ly /ɪn'her·ᵊnt·li/ *adv* • *Military regimes are inherently unstable.* • *Any kind of automatic privilege seems inherently unfair.*

in·her·it *(obj)* /ɪn'her·ɪt/ *v* to receive (money, a house etc.) from someone after they have died, or to be born with (a physical or mental quality) that a parent, grandparent or other relative has • *Who will inherit the house when he dies?* [T] • *All her children will inherit equally.* [I] • *(fig.) When I took on the job of manager, I inherited certain financial problems* (= they existed before I arrived). [T] • *Rosie inherited her red hair* **from** *her mother.* [T] • *The child has an inherited disease which attacks the immune system.* [T]

in·her·it·ance /ɪn'her·ɪ·tᵊnts/ *n* • *The large inheritance* **from** *his aunt meant that he could buy his own boat.* [C] • *At twenty-one she* **came into** *her inheritance* (= it was given to her). [C] • *My collection was formed partly by inheritance and partly through my own purchases.* [U] • *A particular gene is responsible for the inheritance of eye colour.* [U] • **Inheritance tax** is a tax paid from money you have received from someone who has died.

in·her·it·or /£ɪn'her·ɪ·təʳ, $-t̬ɚ/ *n* [C] • An inheritor is a person who has been given something by someone who is dead or in the past: *We are the inheritors* **of** *Greek and Roman culture.*

in·hi·bit *obj* /ɪn'hɪb·ɪt/ *v* [T] to prevent (someone) from doing something or to slow down (a process or the growth of something) • *Some officers were inhibited* **(from** *speaking) by the presence of more senior officers.* • *Fear of failure is an inhibiting factor for many people* (= makes them unwilling to do something). • *This drug will inhibit the progress of the disease.*

in·hi·bit·ed /£ɪn'hɪb·ɪ·tɪd, $-t̬ɪd/ *adj* • *The presence of strangers made her feel inhibited* (= nervous and unable to behave naturally).

in·hi·bi·tion /ˌɪn·hɪ'bɪʃ·ᵊn/ *n* • *After a couple of drinks he* **loses** *his inhibition(s)* (= shy feelings) *and starts talking and laughing loudly.* [U/C]

in·hos·pi·ta·ble /£ˌɪn·hɒs'pɪt·ə·bl̩, £ˌɪn·hɑː'spɪt̬-/ *adj* not welcoming or generous to people who visit you • *I'll have to cook them a meal or they'll think I'm inhospitable.* • An inhospitable area is one which is not suitable for humans to live in: *They had to trek for miles through inhospitable countryside.*

in·hu·man /ɪn'hjuː·mən/ *adj* extremely cruel and completely without sympathy, or not human in an unusual or frightening way • *Prisoners of war were subjected to inhuman and degrading treatment.* • *The ruler of his country for twenty years, he was described as an inhuman monster.* • *Most people feel that there is something almost inhuman about perfection.*

in·hu·man·i·ty /£ˌɪn·hjʊ'mæn·ə·ti, $-ə·t̬i/ *n* [U] • *They were accused of inhumanity in their treatment of the hostages.* • *Man's inhumanity to man seems to have no limits.* • *"Man's inhumanity to man / Makes countless thousands mourn!"* (from the poem *Man was made to Mourn* by Robert Burns, 1786)

THE -ING FORM OF VERBS

The -ing form and the present participle

Most verbs have an *-ing* form. One important use of the *-ing* form is to form continuous (or progressive) tenses: *Harry was feeling happy.* When used in this way, it is called the present participle or *-ing* participle.

- **Intransitive verbs which can be followed by an *-ing* participle**
  *He came rush***ing** *over when I fell* (= He came when I fell, and he was rushing). • *We sat in the cafe chatt***ing** *until late* (= We sat in the cafe, and we were chatting until late). In the dictionary, verbs with this grammar pattern are labelled [+ v-*ing*]. They usually describe the movement or position of someone. For example:

  arrive, come, go, remain, run, sit, stand, stay

- **Transitive verbs with the object followed by an *-ing* participle**
  *I heard the children open***ing** *their presents* (= I heard the children, and they were opening their presents). *Some people smoke because they think it stops them putt***ing** *on weight.* • *Charlie's very shy but we got him play***ing** (= persuaded or caused him to play) *the guitar.* This pattern is labelled [+ obj + v-*ing*]. Verbs that can be used in this way include the following:

  catch, discover, find, hear, notice, observe, remember, see, watch • show, reveal • bring, leave, send • get, have, set, take • prevent, start, stop • excuse, pardon • imagine, fancy • bear, stand, take

  Do not confuse this with the more common pattern of verb + possessive determiner + v-*ing*, as for example *I appreciate your mak***ing** *the effort to come.* This is used in formal English and is possible with many verbs labelled [+ v-*ing*].

- ***-ing* forms used like adjectives**
  It is very common to use an *-ing* form of a verb like an adjective: *She is a growing girl.* • *The news was most worrying.* Usually adjectives like this are placed immediately after the verb in the dictionary and do not need a separate definition.

  -ing adjectives often express the idea of activity, or action in progress: *It's a really exciting film* (= a film which excites you). • *Pour hot fat over the roasting meat* (=the meat that is roasting). Compare them with *-ed* adjectives, which often express the idea of the result of activity, or completed action: *The children were highly excited* (= Something had excited the children). • *Sprinkle roasted nuts* (= nuts that have been roasted) *over the icecream.*

LP **-ed and -ing adjectives** at -ED

Other uses of the -ing form

The *-ing* form can also be used in ways that are noun-like. Compare the following pairs of sentences:

Fast cars are dangerous.	*Driving too fast is dangerous.*
The actors were terrible.	*The acting was terrible.*
I like trains.	*I like travelling by train.*
Thank you for the meal.	*Thank you for cooking us a meal.*
Do you mind my questions?	*Do you mind my asking something?*

Some grammar books call this use of the *-ing* form a gerund. It is not always possible to distinguish clearly between a gerund and a present participle, so the term '*-ing* form' is now often used to refer to both these grammar forms, as in this dictionary.

An *-ing* form of this type is frequently necessary after some verbs. The following groups are important:

- **Verbs which can be followed by an *-ing* form but not by an infinitive**
  Many verbs require an *-ing* form if they are followed by another verb. For example, we say *I enjoyed talking to you* and never 'I enjoyed to talk to you'. Notice that an infinitive can never be used after a preposition, so in the pattern verb + preposition + verb the second verb is always an *-ing* form: *I've banked on gett***ing** *a rise this year.* *I look forward to play***ing** *netball tomorrow.* Some other verbs like this are:

  appreciate, detest, dislike, enjoy, fancy, mind, miss, can't stand, be used to • imagine, mention, recollect, suggest • avoid, can't help, consider, risk • delay, finish • admit • forgive • involve • practise

- **Verbs which mean the same when followed by an *-ing* form or an infinitive**
  A few verbs can be followed by either an *-ing* form or by an infinitive with 'to', and mean the same (or nearly the same) in both these patterns. For example, *He started writ***ing** *on the tablecloth* means the same as *He started* **to** *write on the tablecloth.* Other examples are:

  can't bear, hate, like, love • begin, continue, start

  With another group of verbs the *-ing* form is used when there is no object, and the 'to' infinitive is used if an object is mentioned: *The College does not allow eat***ing** *in the library. / The College does not allow people* **to** *eat in the library.* Other verbs like this are:

  advise • allow, forbid, permit

- **Verbs which can be followed by an *-ing* form or by an infinitive, but with a change of meaning**
  Sometimes both [+ v-*ing*] and [+ *to* infinitive] patterns are possible, but they do not mean the same. In the dictionary, example sentences show the different uses and meanings of these patterns. For example: *Try putt***ing** *the aerial over there – it might work better. / Of course the exercises are difficult, but you must try* **to** *do them.* • *I remember see***ing** *the first man walk on the moon. / I must remember* **to** (= I must not forget to) *send my grandfather a birthday card.* Some other common verbs like this are:

  forget, get, go, help, mean, regret, remember, stop, try

• Adjectives and nouns followed by an *-ing* form

Some adjectives can be followed by an *-ing* form: *Tess was busy throw***ing** *clothes into her bags.* • **It** *isn't easy find***ing** *a cheap apartment in Tokyo.* These are labelled [+ v-*ing*]. They include the following:

busy • fortunate, good, great, happy, wonderful • difficult, easy, useless, pointless • careful

Some nouns are used in a similar way: *We had some difficulty find***ing** *the right address.* • **There***'s no point* (= purpose or usefulness) *look***ing** *for your old shoes – I threw them away.* Other examples:

difficulty, problem, trouble, job (= problem) • to give someone help/a hand • point • to have no right

When a preposition comes between the adjective or noun and the *-ing* form, no grammar code is given but 'ing' and the preposition are printed in **bold**: *He was fearful* **of** *committ***ing** *himself to a real relationship.* • *We were surprised* **at** *see***ing** *Anna there.*

in·hu·mane /ˌɪn·hjʊˈmeɪn/ *adj* completely without any feelings of sympathy or kindness towards others, not caring about the suffering of people or animals • *Is this type of weapon more inhumane than any other kind?* • *Conditions for prisoners with psychiatric illnesses were described as inhumane.* • *Many people believe factory farming is inhumane.*

in·im·i·cal /ɪˈnɪm·ɪ·kəl/ *adj fml* harmful; having a bad effect or not allowing • *Newspaper editors regard any restrictions on them as being inimical* **to** *free speech.* • *Excess of control is inimical* **to** *creative expression.*

in·im·i·ta·ble /£ɪˈnɪm·ɪ·tə·bḷ, $-t̬ə-/ *adj* very unusual or of very high quality and therefore impossible to copy • *"It took people a long time to realise I was half English," she says in her inimitable husky-accented voice.* • *He was describing, in his* **own** *inimitable* **style/way**, *how to write a best-selling novel.*

in·iq·ui·tous /£ɪˈnɪk·wɪ·təs, $-t̬əs/ *adj fml* very wrong and unfair • *It is an iniquitous* **system** *that allows a person to die because they have no money to pay for medicine.*

in·iq·ui·ty /£ɪˈnɪk·wə·ti, $-t̬i/ *n fml* • *They fought long and hard against the iniquities of apartheid.* [C] • *The writer reflects on human injustice and iniquity.* [U]

in·i·tial BEGINNING /ɪˈnɪʃ·əl/ *adj* [before n; not gradable] of or at the beginning • *My initial surprise was soon replaced by delight.* • *Initial reports say that seven people have died, though this has not yet been confirmed.*

in·i·tial·ly /ɪˈnɪʃ·əl·i/ *adv* [not gradable] • *Initially* (= at the beginning), *most people approved of the new scheme.* • *The damage was far more serious than initially believed.*

in·i·tial FIRST LETTER /ɪˈnɪʃ·əl/ *n* [C] the first letter of a name, esp. when used to represent a name • *Paul M. Reynolds refused to say what the initial "M" stood for.* • Your initials are the first letters of each of your names: *He wrote his initials, P.M.R., at the bottom of the page.*

in·i·tial *obj* /ɪˈnɪʃ·əl/ *v* [T] **-ll-** or *Am usually, Aus also* **-l-** • *I initialled the documents* (= wrote my initials on them) *to show I approved of them.*

in·i·ti·ate *obj* START /ɪˈnɪʃ·i·eɪt/ *v* [T] to cause (something) to begin • *Who initiated the violence?* • *Our church initiated a project to send relief aid overseas.*

in·i·ti·ate *obj* TEACH /ɪˈnɪʃ·i·eɪt/ *v* [T] to teach (someone) about an area of knowledge, or allow (someone) into a group by a special ceremony • *At the age of thirteen, Harry was initiated* **into** *the art of golf by his father.* • *Each culture has a special ritual to initiate boys* **into** *manhood.*

in·i·ti·ate /ɪˈnɪʃ·i·ət/ *n* [C] • An initiate is a person who has recently joined a group and has been taught its secrets.

in·i·ti·a·tion /ɪˌnɪʃ·iˈeɪ·ʃən/ *n* • *My initiation* **into** *skiing* (= the occasion when I was first taught about it) *was not a success.* [U] • An initiation or **initiation ceremony** is a process that a person takes part in to become a member of a group: *Soldiers were accused of bullying and brutal initiations.* [C]

in·i·tia·tive JUDGMENT /£ɪˈnɪʃ·ə·tɪv, $-t̬ɪv/ *n* [U] the ability to use your judgment to make decisions and do things without needing to be told what to do • *He doesn't have much initiative.* • *When she began the job she* **showed** *initiative and was promoted to manager after a year.* • *I shouldn't always have to tell you what to do,* **use** *your initiative* (= use your own judgment to decide what to do) *for once!* • If you do something **on** your **own** initiative, you plan it and decide to do it yourself without anyone telling you what to do.

in·i·tia·tive FIRST ACTION /£ɪˈnɪʃ·ə·tɪv, $-t̬ɪv/ *n* [C] the first action or movement, often intended to solve a problem • *The talks form part of the latest* **diplomatic** *initiative intended to bring stability to this troubled region.* • *The* **peace** *initiative was welcomed by both sides.* • If you **have/seize the** initiative, you have/take power and are able to control events: *One group has attempted to seize the initiative in the talks.* • If you **lose the** initiative, you no longer have the position of control or power that you had before: *He is losing the initiative militarily, politically and socially.* • If you **take the** initiative, you are the first person to do something: *They have attempted to take the initiative* **in** *dealing with the problem.*

in·ject *obj* /ɪnˈdʒekt/ *v* [T] to use a needle and SYRINGE (= small tube) to put (a liquid such as a medicine) into (a person's body) • *The army doctor injected the man* **with** *morphine and amputated his foot.* • *(esp. Br and Aus) Older people should be injected* **against** *flu in winter* (= be injected with a medicine to prevent this illness). • *(fig.) A large amount of money will have to be injected* **into** (= put into) *the company if it is to survive.* • *(fig.) A competition was set up to inject some friendly rivalry* **into** *the proceedings.*

in·jec·tion /ɪnˈdʒek·ʃən/ *n* • An injection is the putting of a liquid, esp. a medicine, into a person's body using a needle and a SYRINGE (= small tube): *Daily insulin injections are necessary for some diabetics.* [C] • *(esp. Br and Aus) At school we were* **given** *injections* **against** *the most common illnesses.* [C] • *This antihistamine is usually given* **by** *injection.* [U] • *(fig.) A cash injection* (= the addition) *of £10 million will be used to improve one of Britain's most squalid housing estates.* [C]

in·ju·di·cious /ˌɪn·dʒuːˈdɪʃ·əs/ *adj fml* unwise; showing bad judgment • *I decided that it would be injudicious to speak to them.*

in·junc·tion /ɪnˈdʒʌŋk·ʃən/ *n* [C] an official order given by a court of law, usually to stop someone from doing something • *The court has* **issued** *an injunction* **to** *prevent the airline from increasing its prices.* [+ to infinitive] • *She is* **seeking** *an injunction bann***ing** *the newspaper from publishing the photographs.* [+ v-*ing*]

in·jure *obj* /£ˈɪn·dʒəʳ, $-dʒɚ/ *v* [T] to hurt; cause physical harm to • *A bomb exploded in a quiet street, injuring several people, none seriously.* • *He claimed that working too hard was injuring his health.* • (I)

in·jured /£ˈɪn·dʒəd, $-dʒɚd/ *adj, pl n* • *She was told to stay in bed to rest her injured back.* • If your feelings are injured, they are hurt: *William spoke in tones of injured innocence.* • **The** *injured* (= the people who were hurt) *were taken to the Queen Elizabeth Hospital.*

in·jury /£ˈɪn·dʒər·i, $-dʒɚ-/ *n* • An injury is (an example of) physical harm or damage done to a living thing: *Brinkworth won't be playing in Saturday's match owing to a knee injury.* [C] ○ *Several train passengers* **received/sustained** *serious injuries in the crash.* [C] ○ *Injuries* **to** *the spine are common amongst these workers.* [C] ○ *Cyclists are advised to wear helmets to reduce the risk of head injury.* [U] ○ *They were lucky to* **escape** *(without) injury.* [U] ○ *(Br and Aus humorous) Don't even think about lifting me up, Ted, you might* **do yourself an injury** (= hurt yourself)! • *(Br and Aus)* **Injury time** is a period of time added to the end of a sports game because play was stopped during the game to take care of players who were hurt: *They scored the winning goal* **in** *injury time.* • LP **Feelings and pains**

in·ju·ri·ous /£ɪnˈdʒʊə·ri·əs, $-ˈdʒʊr·i-/ *adj fml* causing damage; harmful • *Too much alcohol is injurious* **to** *your health.*

in·jus·tice /ɪnˈdʒʌs·tɪs/ *n* (an example of) unfairness and lack of justice • *The sight of people suffering arouses a deep* **sense of** *injustice in her.* [U] • *They were aware of the injustices of the system.* [C] • *You* **do** *him* **an** *injustice* (= you are judging him too severely) *if you think he is unwilling to help.* • See also UNJUST.

ink /ɪŋk/ *n* coloured liquid used for writing, printing and drawing • *Please write* **in** *ink, not in pencil.* [U] • *The book is* *printed in three different coloured inks.* [C] • *I need to get a bottle of ink.* [U] • *(fig.) The ink was barely dry on the peace agreement* (= the agreement had only recently been signed) *when fighting broke out again.* [U] • *(specialized)* **Ink-jet** printing is a very fast and quiet method of printing in which the ink is directed electronically onto the paper. • PIC› **Writing instruments**

ink *obj* /ɪŋk/ *v* [T] • *The printing plates have to be inked before they will print on the paper.* • *She did a pencil drawing of the farmhouse and later inked it* **in** (= used ink to draw over the lines).

ink·y /ˈɪŋ·ki/ *adj* **-ier, -iest** • *His pen had been leaking and his fingers were inky* (= covered with ink). • *(fig.) It was night and the water looked cold and inky* (= very dark).

ink·ling /ˈɪŋ·klɪŋ/ *n* [U] an idea that something is true or likely to happen, although it is not certain • *I didn't* **have** *the slightest inkling* **that** *she was unhappy.* [+ *that* clause] • *Did you have any inkling* **that** *they were having an affair?* [+ *that* clause] • *He must have had some inkling* **of** *what was happening.*

ink·stand /ˈɪŋk·stænd/ *n* [C] a container for bottles of ink, pens and pencils, etc.

ink·well /ˈɪŋk·wel/ *n* [C] a container for ink, used in the past, which fits into a hole in a table

in·land /ˈɪn·lənd, -lænd, ˌ-ˈ-/ *adj* [before n], *adv* towards or in the middle of a country, away from the sea • *Seabirds often come inland to find food.* • *The Black Sea is a large inland sea.* • *We left the coast road and headed inland.* • In Britain and New Zealand, the **Inland Revenue** is the government office which collects the main taxes, such as income tax: *The Inland Revenue is investigating donations made to the fund.*

in–laws /£ˈɪn·lɔːz, $-lɑːz/ *pl n* the parents and other members of your husband's or wife's family • *He's spending Christmas with his in-laws.* • PIC› **Family tree**

in·lay /ˈɪn·leɪ/ *n* a decorative pattern put into the surface of an object, or a substance such as gold which is used to fill a hole in a tooth • *The walls of the palace are marble with silver inlay.* [U] • *The dentist replaced two porcelain inlays with gold ones.* [C]

in·laid /ɪnˈlaɪd/ *adj* [not gradable] • *He bought one of those wooden boxes that's inlaid* **with** *ivory.*

in·let CHANNEL /ˈɪn·let/ *n* [C] a narrow strip of water that goes from a sea or lake into the land or between island • *They found a sheltered inlet and anchored the boat.*

in·let MACHINE PART /ˈɪn·let/ *n* [C] *Br* the part of the machine through which liquid enters • *Remove the inlet from the washing machine and check that there are no obstructions.*

in lo·co pa·ren·tis /£ɪnˌləʊ·kəʊ·pəˈren·tɪs, $-ˌloʊ·koʊ·pəˈren·t̬ɪs/ *adj* [after v], *adv* [not gradable] *fml* having the responsibilities of a parent to a child that you are taking care of • *While children are in school, teachers are legally in loco parentis.*

in·mate /ˈɪn·meɪt/ *n* [C] a person who is kept in a prison, **mental hospital** etc. • *The report said that inmates were forced to live in dirty and unhealthy conditions.*

inn /ɪn/ *n* [C] a PUB where you can stay for the night, usually in the countryside • *We stayed at an inn.*

in·nards /£ˈɪn·ədz, $-ɚdz/ *pl n infml* the inner organs of a person or animal, or the inside parts of a machine

in·nate /ɪˈneɪt/ *adj* (of a quality) which you are born with, rather than something you learn • *Looking back over the many years, Cyril's most impressive quality, for me, was his innate goodness.* • *He manages to combine two strands of the British character which is an innate conservatism with flashes of eccentricity.*

in·nate·ly /ɪˈneɪt·li/ *adv* • *You see I don't believe that human beings are innately good.* • *No one is born innately unlovable.*

in·ner /£ˈɪn·əʳ, $-ɚ/ *adj* [before n; not gradable] inside or contained within something else, or (of thoughts or feelings) secret and of the spirit • *Leading off the main hall is a series of small inner rooms.* • *The group is working mainly in the inner* (= central) *London area.* • *Sarah seemed to have an inner strength that nothing could shake.* • *He struggled to hide his inner turmoil* (= his confused feelings). • *Dr Simpson was a member of the inner* **circle** (= the most powerful group) *of influential directors.* • *(humorous) Few people ever managed to penetrate the manager's inner* **sanctum** (= very private room). • An **inner city (area)** is the central part of a city where people live and where there are often problems because of a lack of jobs, bad houses and POVERTY: *The report stated that inner-city schools were overcrowded and lacking in certain basic facilities.* • The **inner man/woman** is a person's soul and deepest feelings: *A good biography should allow you to glimpse the inner man.* • An **inner tube** is a tube filled with air that fits inside a car or bicycle tyre.

in·ner·most /£ˈɪn·ə·məʊst, $-ɚ·moʊst/, *old use or literary* **in·most** /£ˈɪn·məʊst, £ˈɪm-, $ˈɪn·moʊst/ *adj* [before n; not gradable] most secret and hidden, or nearest to the centre • *This was the diary to which Gina committed all her innermost* **thoughts** *and* **secrets**. • *He was not one of the innermost* (= most powerful) *circle of presidential advisers.*

in·ning /ˈɪn·ɪŋ/ *n* [C] the period in a game of baseball in which each team BATS (= tries to hit the ball) • *The game wasn't decided until the bottom of* (= second half of) *the ninth inning.*

in·nings /ˈɪn·ɪŋz/ *n* [C] *pl* **innings** the period in a game of cricket in which a team or a player BATS (= tries to hit the ball) • *Chappell had* **played** *98 first-class innings for Somerset before making his Test debut.*

in·nit *Br not standard* /ˈɪn·ɪt/ *short form of* isn't it • *It's wrong, innit?*

inn·keep·er /£ˈɪŋˌkiː·pəʳ, $-pɚ/ *n* [C] *esp. old use* esp. in the past, a person who owns or looks after an INN (= a place where you can buy meals and stay at night)

in·no·cent /ˈɪn·ə·sᵊnt/ *adj* (of a person) not guilty of a particular crime, or having no knowledge of the unpleasant and evil things in life, or (of a thing) harmlessly intended • *He firmly believes that she is innocent* **of** *the crime.* • *The task of deciding whether a person is innocent or guilty falls on the jury.* • *She has such an innocent face that I find it hard to believe anything bad of her.* • *Innocent* (= harmless) *substances could be mistaken for illegal drugs.* • *It was an innocent remark, I didn't mean to hurt his feelings.* • An innocent person is someone who is not involved with any military group or war in a particular harmful situation: *Several innocent* **bystanders** *were injured in the explosion.* ○ *Thousands of innocent* **civilians** *were killed in the conflict.* ○ *When innocent children are murdered by terrorists there's a public outcry.* • Compare GUILTY. • LP› **Crimes and criminals**

in·no·cence /ˈɪn·ə·sᵊnts/ *n* [U] • *She* **pleaded** *her innocence* (= said she was not guilty), *but no one believed her.* • *He was led away,* **protesting** *his innocence* (= saying he was not guilty). • *She has a child-like innocence which I find very appealing.* • *I asked her* **in all** *innocence* (= without knowing that it would offend) *how old she was, and she got quite annoyed.*

in·no·cent /ˈɪn·ə·sᵊnt/ *n* [C] • An innocent is a person who has very little experience or knowledge of the world: *When it comes to money, she's a complete innocent.*

in·no·cent·ly /ˈɪn·ə·sᵊnt·li/ *adv* • *"Have I done something wrong?", she asked innocently* (= seeming to be without any fault). • *He said he had obtained the television innocently, not knowing it had been stolen.*

in·noc·u·ous /£ɪˈnɒk·ju·əs, $-ˈnɑː·kju-/ *adj* completely harmless • *Some mushrooms look innocuous but are in fact poisonous.* • *The innocuous-looking parcel turned out to be a bomb.*

in·noc·u·ous·ly /£ɪˈnɒk·ju·ə·sli, $-ˈnɑːk-/ *adv*

in·noc·u·ous·ness /£ɪˈnɒk·ju·ə·snəs, $-ˈnɑːk-/ *n* [U]

in·no·vate /ˈɪn·əʊ·veɪt/ *v* [I] to introduce changes and new ideas • *The fashion industry is always desperate to innovate.*

in·no·va·tive /£ˈɪn·ə·və·tɪv, $-veɪ·t̬ɪv/, **in·no·vat·o·ry** /£ˈɪn·əʊ·və·tᵊr·i, $ˈɪn·ə·və·tɔːr·i/ *adj* • *Innovative* (= different and new) *ideas are needed to make the business a success.* • *She was an imaginative and innovative manager* (= full of new ideas).

in·no·va·tion /ˌɪn·əʊˈveɪ·ʃᵊn/ *n* • *Too many rules tend to stifle innovation.* [U] • *Other innovations included a plan for paternity leave.* [C]

in·no·vat·or /£ˈɪn·əʊ·veɪ·təʳ, $-t̬ɚ/ *n* [C] • *He is a very skilful writer, but not an innovator* (= someone who introduces new ideas).

Inns of Court *pl n* **the Inns of Court** the four societies in London for students of law, one of which a BARRISTER must belong to

in·nu·en·do /£ˌɪn·juˈen·dəʊ, $-doʊ/ *n pl* **innuendoes** or **innuendos** (the making of) a remark or remarks that suggest something sexual or something unpleasant but do not refer to it directly • *There's always an element of* **sexual** *innuendo in our conversations.* [U] • *The newspaper innuendos about his private life eventually made him resign.* [C]

in·nu·mer·a·ble /£ɪ'njuː·mər·ə·bl̩, $ɪ'nuː·mɚ-/ *adj* [not gradable] far too many to be counted • *The whole project has been beset by innumerable problems.*

in·nu·mer·ate /£ɪ'njuː·mə·rət, $ɪ'nuː·mɚ·ət-/ *adj* unable to understand and use numbers in calculations; not NUMERATE • *Some children still leave school both illiterate and innumerate.* • Compare ILLITERATE.

in·nu·mer·a·cy /£ɪ'njuː·mᵊr·ə·si, $ɪ'nuː·mɚ-/ *n* [U]

in·oc·u·late *obj* /£ɪ'nɒk·jʊ·leɪt, $-'nɑː·kjə-/ *v* [T] to give a weak form of a disease to (a person or animal) usually by INJECTION (=putting it directly into the blood using a needle) as a protection against that disease • *During the war allied troops were inoculated* **against** *diseases, because of fears that biological weapons might be used.* • *All children are inoculated* **against** *polio.*

in·oc·u·la·tion /£ɪˌnɒk·jʊ'leɪ·ʃᵊn, $-ˌnɑː·kjə'-/ *n* [C/U]

in·of·fen·sive /ˌɪn·ə'fent·sɪv/ *adj* (esp. of a person or their behaviour) not causing any harm or offence • *He seemed like a quiet, inoffensive sort of a guy – someone you couldn't object to.* • *It wasn't decorated as I would have done it but most of the house was inoffensive enough.*

in·op·er·a·ble DISEASE /£ɪ'nɒp·ᵊr·ə·bl̩, $ˌɪn'ɑː·pɚ-/ *adj* [not gradable] (of an illness, esp. a diseased growth or CANCER) that doctors are unable to treat or remove by an operation • *Her own death came cruelly, as a result of an inoperable brain tumour.*

in·op·er·a·ble NOT WORKING /£ɪ'nɒp·ᵊr·ə·bl̩, $ˌɪn'ɑː·pɚ-/ *adj* that cannot be done or made to work • *The system is inoperable without a large power supply.*

in·op·er·a·tive /£ɪ'nɒp·ᵊr·ə·tɪv, $ɪ'nɑː·pɚ·ə·ţɪv/ *adj* [not gradable] *fml* (of a law, rule, etc.) not having effect or power, or (of a machine, system, etc.) not working or not able to work as usual • *The old regulations became inoperative when the new ones were issued.*

in·op·por·tune /£ɪ'nɒp·ə·tjuːn, $ɪ'nɑː·pɚ·tuːn/ *adj fml* happening or done at a time which is not suitable or convenient • *Anderson's illness comes at a particularly inopportune* **time** *as he is due to start a tour of Australia next week.* • *I made a rather inopportune remark about divorce, not knowing that Kelly and her husband had just separated.*

in·op·por·tune·ly /£ɪ'nɒp·ə·tjuːn·li, $ɪ'nɑː·pɚ·tuːn-/ *adv fml*

in·or·di·nate /£ɪ'nɔː·dɪ·nət, $ˌɪn'ɔːr-/ *adj fml* unreasonably or unusually large in size or degree • *Margot has always spent an inordinate* **amount** *of time on her appearance.* • *I don't think $100 is an inordinate sum of money to pay for a pair of shoes, do you?*

in·or·di·nate·ly /£ɪ'nɔː·dɪ·nət·li, $ˌɪn'ɔːr-/ *adv fml* • *She had an ugly little black dog of which she was inordinately fond.*

in·or·gan·ic /£ˌɪn·ɔː'gæn·ɪk, $-ɔːr'-/ *adj* [not gradable] *specialized* not being or consisting of living material, or (of chemical substances) containing no carbon or only small amounts of carbon • *Rocks and metals are inorganic substances.* • *Salt is an inorganic chemical, but sugar is an organic one.* • **Inorganic chemistry** is the scientific study of chemical substances which do not contain carbon. • Compare ORGANIC.

in·put /'ɪm·pʊt/ *n* something such as energy, money, or information that is put into a system, organization or machine so that it can operate • *I didn't have much input* **into** *the project* (=The help I gave or work I did on it was small). [U] • *The French and German inputs will be in the form of raw materials and expertise.* [C] • *The power input will come largely from hydroelectricity.* • *(specialized)* An input is also the part that carries information to a machine, or the place where this is connected: *The inputs for the CD-ROM are at the back of the computer.* [C]

in·put *obj* /'ɪm·pʊt/ *v* [T] **inputting**, *past* **inputted** or **input** • *We've got a couple of typists inputting data* **into** *the computer* (=adding information using a keyboard).

in·quest /'ɪŋ·kwest/ *n* [C] an official examination of facts in an attempt to discover the cause of something, esp. of a sudden or violent death • *An inquest is always* **held** *if murder is suspected.* • *(fig.) The boss intends to* **hold** *an inquest* **into** *the poor monthly sales figures.*

in·quire *(obj)* /£ɪŋ'kwaɪəʳ, $-'kwaɪr/ *v Br dated and Am for* ENQUIRE

in·qui·si·tion /ˌɪŋ·kwɪ'zɪʃ·ᵊn/ *n* [C] *fml disapproving* a period of detailed and unfriendly questioning • *The police* **subjected** *him* **to** *an inquisition that lasted 12 hours.* • **The Inquisition** (1232-1820) was the official organization within the Roman Catholic Church whose work was to discover and punish HERESY (=religious beliefs that are considered to be wrong). • **The Spanish Inquisition** was the Inquisition that lasted until the 19th century in Spain, and which was established to protect Roman Catholicism and punish those people whose religious beliefs were considered wrong.

in·qui·si·tor, In·qui·si·tor /£ɪŋ'kwɪz·ɪ·təʳ, $-ţɚ/ *n* [C] *fml* • *At the end of his visit to the US last week, the prime minister found himself arraigned before the inquisitors of the American media.*

in·qui·si·to·ri·al /£ɪŋˌkwɪz·ɪ'tɔː·ri·əl, $-'tɔːr·i-/ *adj fml* • *I am now convinced of the need to switch from the adversarial system of justice to the inquisitorial method favoured by the French.*

in·qui·si·tive /£ɪŋ'kwɪz·ɪ·tɪv, $-ţɪv/ *adj* (of a person or their behaviour) (too) eager to know a lot about people or things • *an inquisitive child* • *an inquisitive mind* • *She could see inquisitive faces looking out from the windows next door.* • *(disapproving) It annoys me the way she's so inquisitive about everything that I do.*

in·qui·si·tive·ly /£ɪŋ'kwɪz·ɪ·tɪv·li, $-ţɪv·li/ *adv* • *The mouse looked around the room inquisitively.*

in·qui·si·tive·ness /£ɪŋ'kwɪz·ɪ·tɪv·nəs, $-ţɪv-/ *n* [U]

in·quor·ate /£ˌɪŋ'kwɔː·reɪt, $-kwɔːr·eɪt/ *adj* [not gradable] *esp. Br specialized* (of a meeting) not having enough people present and so unable to make any official decisions

in·roads /£'ɪn·rəʊdz, $-roʊdz/ *pl n* **make inroads** to start to have a direct and noticeable effect (on something) • *We have not so far made any inroads with our campaign to ban traffic from the city centre.* • *The government is definitely making inroads* **into** (=starting to deal with effectively) *the problem of unemployment.* • *The cost of the court case made serious inroads* **into** (=reduced noticeably) *their savings.* • *The Green Party failed to make significant inroads* **on** (=reduce noticeably) *the Labour vote.*

ins *pl n abbreviation for* INCHES

in·sa·lu·bri·ous /ˌɪn·sə'luː·bri·əs/ *adj fml* unpleasant, dirty or likely to cause disease • *The restaurant kitchen had a most insalubrious appearance.*

in·sane /ɪn'seɪn/ *adj dated or infml* mentally ill, or *(fig.)* extremely unreasonable and extreme • *For the last ten years of his life he was* **clinically** *insane.* • *(infml) I sometimes think I'm* **going** *insane* (=I feel very confused). • *(fig.) In a fit of insane* **jealousy** *he tried to stab her with a knife.* • *(fig.) I think some of her ideas are totally insane.*

in·sane /ɪn'seɪn/ *pl n dated or infml* • **The insane** refers to mentally ill people: *He used to work in a special prison hospital for the* **criminally** *insane.*

in·sane·ly /ɪn'seɪn·li/ *adv* • *She gets insanely* (= unreasonably and extremely) **jealous** *if he so much as looks at another woman.*

in·san·i·ty /£ɪn'sæn·ə·ti, $-ţi/ *n* [U] • *He was found not guilty of murder by reason of insanity.* • *Since the killings last May Mr Popper had* **pleaded** *temporary insanity.* • *He suffered from periodic* **bouts of** *insanity.* • *(fig.) The match became more and more violent, almost to the point of insanity.*

in·san·i·ta·ry /£ɪn'sæn·ə·tri, $-ter·i/ *adj slightly fml* dirty or unhealthy and therefore likely to cause disease • *insanitary toilets* • *insanitary living conditions*

in·sa·tia·ble /ɪn'seɪ·ʃə·bl̩/ *adj* (esp. of a desire or need) too great to be satisfied • *Like so many politicians, he had an insatiable* **appetite/desire/hunger** *for power.* • *Nothing, it seemed, would satisfy his insatiable* **curiosity**. • *There seems to be an insatiable* **demand** *for new computer video games.*

in·scribe *obj* /ɪn'skraɪb/ *v* [T] *fml* to write (words) in a book or CARVE (=cut) them on an object • *The prize winners each receive a book with their names inscribed* **on** *the first page.* • *The wall of the church was inscribed* **with** *the names of the dead from the Great War.*

in·scrip·tion /ɪn'skrɪp·ʃᵊn/ *n* [C] • *The inscription in the book read 'To darling Molly. Christmas 1904.'* • *Centuries of wind and rain had worn away the inscriptions on the gravestones.*

in·scrut·a·ble /£ɪn'skruː·tɪ·bl̩, $-ţə-/ *adj* (esp. of a person or their expression) not showing emotions or thoughts and therefore very difficult to understand or get to know • *an inscrutable face/expression/smile/look*

in·scrut·a·bly /£ɪn'skruː·tɪ·bli, $-ţə-/ *adv* • *She smiled inscrutably.*

in·scrut·a·bil·i·ty /£ɪnˌskruː·tɪˈbɪl·ɪ·ti, $-t̬əˈbɪl·ə·t̬i/ *n* [U] • *He looked at me with a kind of oriental inscrutability – I wondered what he was thinking of me.*

in·seam /ˈɪn·siːm/ *n* [C] *Am for* **inside leg**, see at INSIDE INNER PART

in·sect /ˈɪn·sekt/ *n* [C] a type of very small air-breathing animal with six legs, a body divided into three parts and usually two pairs of wings, or, more generally, any similar very small animal • *Ants, beetles, butterflies and flies are all insects.* • *The three parts of an insect's body are the head, the thorax and the abdomen.* • *Spiders are not technically insects, but people often think of them as such.* • *I've got some sort of insect* **bite** *on my leg.*

in·sec·ti·cide /ɪnˈsek·tɪ·saɪd/ *n* [C/U] (a) chemical substance made and used for killing insects, esp. those which eat plants • Compare HERBICIDE; PESTICIDE.

in·sec·ti·vore /£ɪnˈsek·tɪ·vɔːʳ, $-vɔːr/ *n* [C] *specialized* an animal which eats insects

in·sec·ti·vor·ous /£ˌɪn·sekˈtɪv·ᵊr·əs, $ˈ-ə-/ *adj specialized*

in·se·cure NOT CONFIDENT /£ˌɪn·sɪˈkjʊəʳ, $-ˈkjʊr/ *adj* (of people) lacking confidence and doubtful about their own abilities and about whether other people really like them • *I wonder what it was about her upbringing that made her so insecure.* • *If you* **feel** *insecure within a relationship there has to be a reason.* • *He still* **feels** *insecure* **about** *his ability to do the job.*

in·se·cu·ri·ty /£ˌɪn·sɪˈkjʊə·rɪ·ti, $-ˈkjʊr·ə·t̬i/ *n* • *Her* **(sense of)** *insecurity made her desperate to get other people's approval.* [U] • *She had developed an outgoing personality to mask her* **deep** *insecurities.* [C]

in·se·cure NOT SAFE /£ˌɪn·sɪˈkjʊəʳ, $-ˈkjʊr/ *adj* (of objects or situations) not fixed or safe and therefore likely to move or change • *Are you sure that package won't fall off your bike – it looks a bit insecure to me.* • *The situation in the east is still insecure, because of the number of guns held by the villagers.* • *Nations which are not self-sufficient in energy will face an insecure future.* • *We've gone through a few financially insecure years.*

in·se·cure·ly /£ˌɪn·sɪˈkjʊə·li, $-kjʊr-/ *adv* • *The boxes were insecurely fastened to the decks and got washed away during the storm.*

in·se·cu·ri·ty /£ˌɪn·sɪˈkjʊə·rɪ·ti, $-ˈkjʊr·ə·t̬i/ *n* [U] • *Sadly, high levels of economic insecurity tend to breed racial hatred and intolerance.*

in·sem·i·nate *obj* /ɪnˈsem·ɪ·neɪt/ *v* [T] to put a male animal's sperm into (a female animal), either by the sexual act or by an artificial method

in·sem·i·na·tion /ɪnˌsem·ɪˈneɪ·ʃᵊn/ *n* [U] • *modern insemination techniques*

in·sen·si·ble /ɪnˈsent·sɪ·bl̩/ *adj* [not gradable] *fml* unconscious • *We found her lying on the floor, drunk and insensible.* • If you are insensible **to/of** something you do not care about it or are unwilling to react to it: *I think he's largely insensible to other people's distress.* ○ *I'm certainly not insensible to his charms.*

in·sen·si·bil·i·ty /£ɪnˌsent·sɪˈbɪl·ɪ·ti, $-ə·t̬i/ *n* [C/U] *fml*

in·sen·si·tive /£ɪnˈsent·sɪ·tɪv, $-sə·t̬ɪv/ *adj disapproving* (of a person or their behaviour) not aware of or showing sympathy for other people's feelings, or refusing to give importance to (something) • *It was a bit insensitive of Fiona to go on so much about fat people when she knows Mandy is desperate to lose weight.* • *I've never known anyone as insensitive as Gina.* • *He apologized for his insensitive remarks about the homeless.* • *The police have been criticized for being insensitive* **to** *complaints from the public.* • *(specialized)* Insensitive can also mean not showing the effect of something as a reaction to it, or unable to feel something: *The protective covering must be insensitive* **to** *light and heat.* ○ *His feet seem to be insensitive* **to** *pain.*

in·sen·si·tiv·i·ty /£ɪnˌsent·sɪˈtɪv·ɪ·ti, $-ə·t̬i/ *n* [U] *disapproving* • *Is it insensitivity or just plain rudeness?* • *His insensitivity* **towards** *the feelings of others is remarkable.*

in·sep·ar·a·ble /ɪnˈsep·rə·bl̩/ *adj* (of two or more people) such good friends that they spend most of their time together, or (of two or more things) so closely connected that they cannot be considered separately • *When we were kids Zoe and I were inseparable.* • *Unemployment and inner city decay are inseparable issues which must be tackled together.*

in·sep·ar·a·bly /ɪnˈsep·rə·bli/ *adv* • *Russian literature and politics were ever inseparably linked.*

in·sert *obj* /£ɪnˈsɜːt, $-ˈsɜːrt/ *v* [T] to put (something) inside something else, or to add (something, esp. words) to something else • *Insert the key* **in/into** *the lock.* • *The notice on the machine said 'Insert 2 x 20p'.* • *I've filled in the form, but you still need to insert* (= add) *your bank details and date of birth.* • Ⓓ

in·sert /£ˈɪn·sɜːt, $-sɜːrt/ *n* [C] • *These magazines have too many annoying inserts* (= extra loose pages) *advertising various products.* • *Most running shoes have inserts* (= added pieces) *designed to increase comfort.*

in·ser·tion /£ɪnˈsɜː·ʃᵊn, $-ˈsɜːr-/ *n* [U] • *Scientists hope that the insertion of normal genes into the diseased cells will provide a cure.*

in·set /ˈɪn·set/ *n* [C] *specialized* something positioned within a larger object • *The necklace is gold with gilt silver insets.* • *The map has an inset* (= small extra map) *in the top corner, that shows the city centre in more detail.*

in·set /ˌɪnˈset/ *adj* [not gradable] • *He bought her a gold necklace inset* **with** *rubies.*

in·shore /£ˌɪnˈʃɔːʳ, $-ˈʃɔːr/ *adj, adv* near or towards the coast • *an inshore fishing zone* • *an inshore lifeboat* • *The ships moved slowly inshore.*

in·side INNER PART /ˌɪnˈsaɪd/ *n* [U] the inner part, space or side of (something) • *What shall I use to clean the inside of the car?* • *They broke the coconut open to reveal the white inside.* • The inside of a part of the body such as the arm or leg is the part facing in towards the rest of the body: *She tested a little of the perfume on the inside of her wrist.* • If something is **inside out**, it has the usual inside part on the outside and the usual outside part on the inside: *She had her jumper on inside out.* ○ *(fig. infml) I've* **turned** *the house inside out* (= looked everywhere) *but I can't find the keys.* ○ *(fig. infml) He* **knows** *the system inside out* (= knows it completely and in detail). • *(Br and Aus)* The inside or an **inside lane** is the part of the road nearest the edge, used esp. by slower vehicles: *In Britain it is considered dangerous to overtake on the inside.* • *(Am)* The **inside lane** is the part of the road nearest the vehicles going in the opposite direction: *In America buses and trucks are often prohibited from the inside lane.* • The inside or an **inside lane** is also the part of a RACETRACK nearest the middle: *The runner in the inside lane has a shorter distance to run.* • If someone has or is on **the inside track** they have a good position within an organization, system or competition and are therefore likely to obtain increasing amounts of power, influence or special knowledge. • Compare OUTSIDE OUTER PART. • PIC› **Motorway**

in·side /ˌɪnˈsaɪd/ *adv* [not gradable], *prep, adj* [not gradable] • *What's inside the big box?* • *Customs officials finally broke open the box and found 20 kilos of heroin inside.* • *Could you take your shoes off before going inside (the house).* • *"Is Anna in the garden?" "No, she's inside* (= in the house)*."* • *Some of these older houses still don't have inside toilets* (= toilets in the house, rather than in a building in the garden). • *He put the documents carefully in his inside* **pocket** (= pocket on the inner side of a jacket or coat). • *(fig.) She couldn't cope with the grief she felt inside (herself).* • *(fig.) Who can tell what goes on inside his head?* • If you do something inside a particular time or limit, you do it using less than that amount of time or under the limit: *With the new train you can do the journey inside two hours.* ○ *(infml) He finished it inside* **of** *two hours.* • *(infml)* A person who is inside is in prison: *Her husband's inside* **for** *armed robbery.* • *(Br and Aus)* Your **inside leg** (*Am* **inseam**) is the measurement from the top of your inner leg to your ANKLE (= the joint which connects the foot to the leg).

in·sides /ˌɪnˈsaɪdz/ *pl n infml* • *I cleaned the insides (of the pot) with scouring powder.* • *(infml)* Your insides are your stomach and other digestive organs: *I don't know what's wrong with him but I think it's something to do with his insides.* ○ *The insides of the cow are used to make dog food.*

in·side SPECIAL KNOWLEDGE /ˈɪn·saɪd, ˌ-ˈ-/ *adj* [before n; not gradable] (of information) obtained by someone in a group, organization or company and therefore involving special or secret knowledge • *inside information/knowledge* • The inside **story** is the true story that is known only by people who are involved or close to those involved: *I'll call up Clare and get the inside story.* • *(infml)* If someone is **on the inside** they have a job or position in which they have special or secret information: *Who do we know on the inside who can help us?* • An **inside job** is a crime, esp. stealing, committed by someone in the place where they work and which they therefore have special knowledge of.

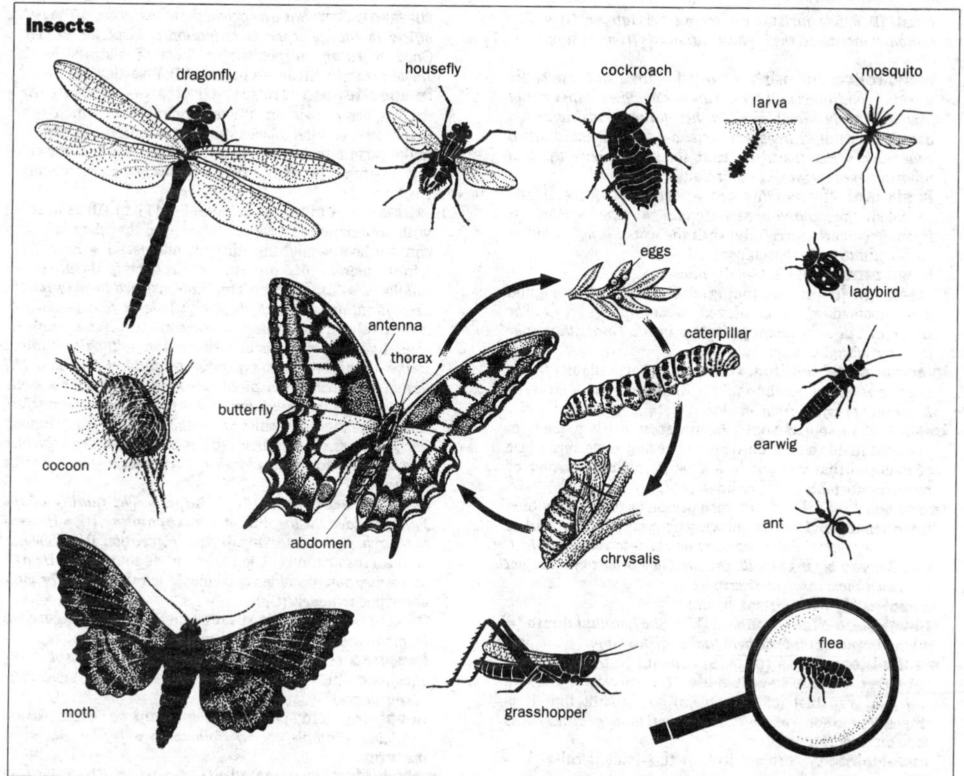

in·sid·er /£ɪnˈsaɪ·dəʳ, $-dɚ/ *n* [C] • An insider is someone who is an accepted member of a group and who therefore has special or secret knowledge or influence: *According to insiders, the committee is having difficulty making up its mind.* • **Insider trading/dealing** is the illegal buying and selling of company shares (=a financial part of the ownership of a company) by people who have special secret knowledge because they are involved with those companies.

in·sid·i·ous /ɪnˈsɪd·i·əs/ *adj* (of something unpleasant or dangerous) gradually and secretly causing harm • *Organized crime has an insidious influence on all who come into contact with it.* • *Alcohol-abuse is a more insidious problem than drug-abuse because alcohol is almost universal.* • *It's an insidious disease that attacks the central nervous system.*

in·sid·i·ous·ly /ɪnˈsɪd·i·ə·sli/ *adv* • *"Pornography", he said, "insidiously corrupts a society's attitude towards women".*

in·sight /ˈɪn·saɪt/ *n* (the ability to have) a clear, deep and sometimes sudden understanding of a complicated problem or situation • *Professor Becker* **provided** *me with*/**gave** *me many useful insights* **into** *the theory of money supply.* [C] • *It was an interesting read, full of* **fascinating/valuable** *insights* **into** *the most basic aspects of human relationships.* [C] • *Being with his family for a few days I* **gained** *one or two insights* **into** *the reason he behaves the way he does.* [C] • *He was a brilliant actor who brought deep psychological insight to his many roles.* [U]

in·sight·ful /ˈɪn·saɪt·fəl/ *adj approving* • *The reviewer describes it as "an intelligent, insightful book that reveals the truth behind the Presidency".*

in·sig·ni·a /ɪnˈsɪg·ni·ə/ *n* [C] an object or mark which officially shows either that a person or object belongs to a particular organization or country, or that a person has a particular rank • *a flag bearing the Communist insignia* • *the royal insignia of crown and sceptre*

in·sig·ni·fi·cant /ˌɪn·sɪgˈnɪf·ɪ·kənt/ *adj* not important or thought to be valuable, esp. because of smallness • *It seems to me a fairly insignificant sum of money to be arguing about.* • *He'll find a meaning in even the most insignificant of remarks.* • *The operation, said the surgeon, had a small, though not insignificant mortality rate.*

in·sig·ni·fi·cance /ˌɪn·sɪgˈnɪf·ɪ·kənts/ *n* [U] • *The traumas of my own upbringing* **pale/fade into** *insignificance* (=seem very unimportant) *when I hear stories about the way Peter's parents treated him.*

in·sig·ni·fi·cant·ly /ˌɪn·sɪgˈnɪf·ɪ·kənt·li/ *adv*

in·sin·cere /£ˌɪn·sɪnˈsɪəʳ, $-ˈsɪr/ *adj disapproving* not really feeling, believing or meaning something although pretending to; not sincere • *And all this praise just because the poor man has died – doesn't it strike you as a bit insincere?* • *I find her whole manner rather insincere.*

in·sin·cere·ly /£ˌɪn·sɪnˈsɪə·li, $-ˈsɪr-/ *adv* • *"Oh, I really love that jacket", he said insincerely.*

in·sin·cer·i·ty /£ˌɪn·sɪnˈser·ə·ti, $-ţi/ *n* [U]

in·sin·u·ate *obj* /ɪnˈsɪn·ju·eɪt/ *v* [T] to suggest, without being direct, that something unpleasant is true • *Are you insinuating* **(that)** *I'm losing my nerve?* [+ *(that)* clause] • *What are you insinuating, Daniel?* • *(fml disapproving)* If you **insinuate yourself into** something, you use clever, secret and often unpleasant methods to gradually become part of it: *Over the years she insinuated herself into the great man's life.* ○ *It's a computer virus that insinuates itself into a system via other software.*

in·sin·u·at·ing /£ɪnˈsɪn·ju·eɪ·tɪŋ, $-ţɪŋ/ *adj* • Insinuating means suggesting ideas without stating them directly: *She didn't reply – she merely smiled that insinuating smile.* ○ *Both songs are in danger of being banned for their sexy, insinuating lyrics.*

in·sin·u·a·tion /ɪnˌsɪn·juˈeɪ·ʃən/ *n* • *We resent these insinuations* **that** *we are not capable of leading the country.* [C + *that* clause] • *They use insinuation and lies to attack the opposition.* [U]

in·sip·id /ɪnˈsɪp·ɪd/ *adj disapproving* lacking a strong taste or character or lacking in interest or energy • *a pale insipid wine* • *insipid overcooked vegetables* • *Central control over content will only produce television that is insipid and uniform.* • *Why anyone buys music with such insipid lyrics is a mystery.*

in·sip·id·ly /ɪnˈsɪp·ɪd·li/ *adv*

in·sip·id·ness /ɪnˈsɪp·ɪd·nəs/, **in·sip·id·i·ty** /£ˌɪn·sɪˈpɪd·ɪ·ti, $-ə·ţi/ *n* [U]

in·sist *(obj)* /ɪnˈsɪst/ *v* to state or demand forcefully, esp. despite opposition • *Greg still insists* **(that)** *he did nothing wrong.* [+ *(that)* clause] • *Please go first – I* *insist!* [I] • *She insisted* **on seeing** *her lawyer.* [I] • *The company insists* **on** *the highest standards from its suppliers.* [I]

in·sis·tence /ɪn'sɪs·tᵊnts/ *n* [U] • *Insistence* **on** *better working conditions will get the unions nowhere if they're not prepared to be flexible.* • **At** *her father*'**s** *insistence* (= because her father insisted), *Amelia has been moved into a new class.* • *Her insistence* **that** *she should have the best room annoyed everyone.* [+ *that* clause]

in·sis·tent /ɪn'sɪs·tᵊnt/ *adj* • *insistent* (= forceful and repeated) *demands/appeals/signals* • *The teacher is insistent* (= states forcefully) **that** *the school is not to blame for the situation.* [+ *that* clause]

in·sis·tent·ly /ɪn'sɪs·tᵊnt·li/ *adv*

in si·tu /ˌɪn'sɪt·juː/ *adj* [not gradable] *fml* in the original place instead of being moved to another place • *The restorers will work on the paintings in situ rather than take them out of the museum.*

in·so·far as /£ˌɪn·sə'fɑːʳ, $-'fɑːr/ *adv* [not gradable] *fml* to the degree that • *Insofar as change has occurred, it has been because of pressure from outside.*

in·sole /£'ɪn·səʊl, $-soʊl/, **in·ner sole** *n* [C] a piece of material inside a shoe on which your foot rests, or a piece of material that you put in a shoe to make it warmer or more comfortable • PIC **Shoes**

in·sol·ent /'ɪnt·sᵊl·ənt/ *adj* (of a person or their behaviour) intentionally and rudely showing no respect • *At school he was the sort of child that teachers would describe as insolent.* • *As Moreau begins to talk, the shadowy brown eyes fix you with an almost insolent directness.*

in·sol·ent·ly /'ɪnt·sᵊl·ənt·li/ *adv*

in·sol·ence /'ɪnt·sᵊl·ənts/ *n* [U] • *She had that* **dumb** (= silent) *insolence that teachers find so disturbing.*

in·sol·u·ble DIFFICULT TO SOLVE /£ɪn'sɒl·jʊ·bl̩, $-'sɑːl·jə-/, *Am and Aus also* **in·solv·a·ble** /£ɪn'sɒl·və·bl̩, $-'sɑːl-/ *adj* [not gradable] (of a problem) so difficult that it is impossible to solve • *Traffic congestion in large cities seems to be an insoluble problem.*

in·sol·u·bil·i·ty /£ɪnˌsɒl·jʊ'bɪl·ɪ·ti, $-ˌsɑːl·jə'bɪl·ə·t̬i/ *n* [U]

in·sol·u·ble IMPOSSIBLE TO MIX /£ɪn'sɒl·jʊ·bl̩, $-'sɑːl·jə-/ *adj* (of a substance) impossible to dissolve • *These minerals are all insoluble in water.*

in·sol·u·bil·i·ty /£ɪnˌsɒl·jʊ'bɪl·ɪ·ti, $-ˌsɑːl·jə'bɪl·ə·t̬i/ *n* [U]

in·sol·vent /£ɪn'sɒl·vᵊnt, $-'sɑːl-/ *adj* [not gradable] *specialized* (esp. of a company) not having enough money to pay debts, buy goods, etc. • *They lost orders and were insolvent within weeks.*

in·sol·ven·cy /£ɪn'sɒl·vᵊnt·si, $-'sɑːl-/ *n* [U] • *The company simply couldn't sell its products in sufficient volume and was driven into insolvency.*

in·som·ni·a /£ɪn'sɒm·ni·ə, $-'sɑːm-/ *n* [U] inability to sleep, over a period of time • *She went to the doctor's because she was* **suffering from** *insomnia.*

in·som·ni·ac /£ɪn'sɒm·ni·æk, $-'sɑːm-/ *n* [C] • *My father's an insomniac so he's often very tired during the day.*

in·sou·ci·ance /ɪn'suː·si·ənts/ *n* [U] *literary* a light and happy way of acting without worry or guilt • *I admired his youthful insouciance.* • *We are angry at the insouciance with which Western newspapers are treating the prospect of war.*

in·sou·ci·ant /ɪn'suː·si·ənt/ *adj literary* • *"We'll try another way then" was his insouciant response.*

in·spect *obj* /ɪn'spekt/ *v* [T] to look at (something or someone) carefully in order to discover information, esp. about quality or correctness • *After the crash both drivers got out and inspected their cars for damage.* • *She held the bank note up to the light and inspected it* **carefully**. • *The boss inspected the work done so far and seemed quite pleased.* • If an official person inspects a place or a group of people, they visit it and look at it carefully in order to make certain it is in good condition and that rules are being obeyed: *An official from the Department of Health will be inspecting the restaurant this afternoon.* • When someone such as an important military officer or politician inspects a group of soldiers, they look at them as part of a ceremony: *The King inspected the troops.*

in·spec·tion /ɪn'spek·ʃᵊn/ *n* • *She arrived to* **carry out/make** *a health and safety inspection of the building.* [C] • *He had a suspicion the certificate was a forgery, but* **on closer** *inspection, it seemed okay.* [U]

in·spec·tor /£ɪn'spek·təʳ, $-t̬ɚ/ *n* [C] • *a tax inspector* • *a school inspector/inspector of schools* • An inspector is also a police officer of middle rank, above a SERGEANT and below a SUPERINTENDENT: *She was promoted to inspector.* ○ *The police officer in charge of the investigation is Inspector Brown.* ○ *Good morning, Inspector.* [as form of address] • *"An Inspector Calls"* (title of a play by J.B. Priestley, 1947)

in·spec·tor·ate /£ɪn'spek·tᵊr·ət, $-t̬ɚ-/ *n* [C] *esp. Br* • An inspectorate is an official organization which sends inspectors to visit places and organizations in order to make certain they are in good condition and that the rules are being obeyed: *the education/pollution/schools Inspectorate*

in·spire *obj* /£ɪn'spaɪəʳ, $-'spaɪr/ *v* [T] to fill (someone) with confidence and eagerness, esp. so that they feel they can achieve something difficult or special • *Even from within prison, his qualities of leadership inspired his followers.* • *Captain Scott's example inspired them* (**with** *the determination*) **to** *reach the South Pole on foot.* [+ obj + *to* infinitive] • If something or someone inspires something else, it causes, suggests or leads to it: *a politically inspired strike* ○ *a piece of music inspired by dolphin sounds* ○ *The design of the car has inspired many imitations.* • If someone or something inspires a particular feeling in someone else, they make them feel this: *She inspires great loyalty among her followers.* ○ *All these reports of crashes don't inspire much confidence* **in** *the planes.* ○ *They don't inspire me* **with** *confidence.*

in·spi·ra·tion /ˌɪn·spɪ·'reɪ·ʃᵊn/ *n* • *The quality of the light provided the inspiration* **for** *the painting.* [U] • *He went to church, perhaps seeking* **divine** *inspiration.* [U] • *She has been* **an** *inspiration* (= good example) **to** *us all.* [U] • *He* **had** *an inspiration* (= sudden good idea) – *why not apply for some government money?* [C]

in·spi·ra·tion·al /ˌɪn·spɪ'reɪ·ʃᵊn·əl/ *adj* • *He gave an inspirational reading of his own poems.*

in·spired /£ɪn'spaɪəd, $-'spaɪrd/ *adj* • *an inspired* (= excellent – much better than expected **guess**/*suggestion/performance*)

in·spir·ing /£ɪn'spaɪə·rɪŋ, $-'spaɪr·ɪŋ/ *adj* • *She was an inspiring example to her followers.* • *I find the story inspiring.*

in·sta·bil·i·ty /£ˌɪn·stə'bɪl·ɪ·ti, $-ə·t̬i/ *n* [U] a lack of strength, firmness and balance, likely to cause failure, damage or other negative effects • *political instability* • *Subsidence in such an old house can lead to instability in the foundations.* • *The instability of the pound continues.* • *His drinking and general poor behaviour shows instability of character.*

in·stall *obj* PUT IN, *Br also* **ins·tal** /£ɪn'stɔːl, $-'stɑːl/ *v* [T] **-ll-** to put (a large piece of equipment) in a place, esp. to put (a machine) in a place and connect it to the electricity/gas/water/etc. supply, so that it is ready for use • *The plumber is coming tomorrow to install the new washing machine.* • *The company will design, supply and install your new kitchen* (= fit all the machines and furniture ready for use). • *(Am and Aus) They're installing the* **carpets** *tomorrow.* • *(specialized)* If you install something such as a computer program, you put it into a computer so that the computer can use it.

in·stal·la·tion /ˌɪn·stə'leɪ·ʃᵊn/ *n* • *Do you have to pay extra for installation?* [U] • *The installation cost for the washing machine will be small.* • An installation is a nearly permanent place with people, buildings and equipment which have a particular, esp. military, purpose: *a nuclear installation* [C] ○ *The Americans still have several military bases and installations on the island.* [C] • *(specialized)* An installation is also a form of modern SCULPTURE where the artist uses sound, movement or space as well as objects in order to make an often temporary work of art. [C]

in·stall *obj* PLACE, *Am also* **ins·tal** /£ɪn'stɔːl, $-'stɑːl/ *v* [T] **-ll-** to place (someone) in an official position or to place (yourself) in a comfortable position where you wish to stay • *She has installed a couple of young Americans* **as** *her advisers.* • *When new bishops are installed there is a grand ceremony.* • *He seems to have installed* **himself** *in your spare room for good!*

in·stal·la·tion /ˌɪn·stə'leɪ·ʃᵊn/ *n* [U] • *The installation of the new archbishop will take place in January.*

ins·tal·ment, *Am usually* **in·stall·ment** /£ɪn'stɔːl·mənt, $-'stɑːl-/ *n* [C] one of a number of parts into which a story, plan or amount of money owed has been divided, so that each part happens or is paid at different times until the end or total is reached • *The novel has been serialized for radio* **in** *five instalments.* • *We agreed to* **pay for** *the car* **by** *instalments.* • **Installment plan** is *esp. Am for* **hire purchase**. See at HIRE. • LP **Money**

in·stance /ˈɪn·stənts/ *n* [C] a particular situation, event or fact, esp. an example of something that happens generally • *There have been several recent instances of planes taking off without adequate safety checks.* • *I don't usually side with the management, but* **in this** *instance* (= in this situation) *I agree with what they're saying.* • *In the coal industry,* **for instance** (= for example), *5000 jobs are being lost.* • ⓓ

in·stance *obj* /ˈɪn·stənts/ *v* [T] *fml* • *She argued the need for legal reform and instanced* (= gave as examples) *several recent cases with grossly unfair verdicts.*

in·stant /ˈɪn·stənt/ *n* [U] an extremely short moment of time • *His face appeared* **for** *an instant at the window.* • **In** *an instant the mood of the room changed.* • *The car drove off, and the* **next** *instant* (= after a very short pause) *there was a deafening explosion.* • *"Stop that noise* **this** *instant* (= now)!" • *The alarm bells started ringing and* **at** *the same instant all the lights went off.* • *I tried phoning her* **the** *instant* (= as soon as) *I got home.* • *He said he was telling the truth, but* **not for an** *instant* (= not at all) *did she believe him.*

in·stant /ˈɪn·stənt/ *adj* [not gradable] • Something that is instant happens immediately, without any delay: *The poison took instant effect.* ○ *This sort of account offers you instant* **access** *to your money.* ○ *If you want instant* **gratification**, *this is one dessert that you can put together in under ten minutes.* ○ *Contrary to expectations, the film was an instant* **success**. • An instant food or drink is one, usually in dried or powder form, that can be prepared very easily and quickly, by adding esp. hot water: *instant coffee/soup/mashed potato*

in·stant·ly /ˈɪn·stənt·li/ *adv* [not gradable] • *Both drivers were killed instantly* (= immediately). • *He's an instantly likable guy – so easy to talk to.*

in·stan·tan·e·ous /ˌɪn·stənˈteɪ·ni·əs/ *adj* [not gradable] happening immediately, without any delay • *an instantaneous response/reply/reaction*

in·stan·tan·e·ous·ly /ˌɪn·stənˈteɪ·ni·ə·sli/ *adv* [not gradable]

in·stead /ɪnˈsted/ *adv* [not gradable] rather than (something or someone); as an ALTERNATIVE • *There's no coffee – would you like a cup of tea instead?* • *You can have herbal tea instead* **of** *coffee, if you want.* • *Instead* **of** *throwing away your household rubbish, why not recycle it?*

in·step /ˈɪn·step/ *n* [C] the curved upper part of the foot between the toes and the heel, or the part of a shoe or sock which fits around this

in·sti·gate *obj* /ˈɪn·stɪ·geɪt/ *v* [T] *fml* to cause (an event or situation) to happen by making a set of actions or a formal process begin • *We are asking the government to instigate new laws on fighting dogs.* • *She is threatening to instigate criminal proceedings against her former employers.* • *The revolt in the North is believed to have been instigated by a disappointed ex-government official.*

in·sti·ga·tion /ˌɪn·stɪˈgeɪ·ʃən/ *n* [U] *fml* • *The inquiry was begun* **at the** *instigation* **of** *a local MP* (= a local MP asked for the inquiry).

in·sti·gat·or /£ˈɪn·stɪ·geɪ·təʳ, $-t̬ɚ/ *n* [C] • *The instigators of the riot have received 20-year prison sentences.*

in·stil *obj, Am usually* **in·still** /ɪnˈstɪl/ *v* [T] **-ll-** to put (a feeling, idea or principle) gradually into someone's mind, so that it has a strong influence on the way they live • *It is part of a teacher's job to instil self-***confidence in/into** *his or her students.*

in·stinct /ˈɪn·stɪŋkt/ *n* (an example of) the knowledge or ability which allows animals and people naturally to act in particular ways without having to think or be taught • *All his instincts told him to stay near the car and wait for help.* [C] • *Her* **first** *instinct was* **to** *shout and get angry with him.* [C + *to* infinitive] • **It is** *instinct* **that** *makes the female horse bend down and lick its newborn foal.* [U + *that* clause] • *Bob seems to* **have** *an instinct* **for** (= is naturally good at) *knowing which products will sell.* [U]

in·stinc·tive /ɪnˈstɪŋk·tɪv/ *adj* • Instinctive behaviour or reactions are not thought about, planned or developed by training: *One's instinctive reaction to defeat is to look for somebody to blame.* ○ *His reactions are spontaneous and instinctive rather than calculated.* ○ *I have an instinctive distrust of authority.*

in·stinc·tive·ly /ɪnˈstɪŋk·tɪv·li/ *adv* • *Instinctively, he flung up his hand to protect his eyes.* • *She's instinctively wary of people in authority.*

in·sti·tute ORGANIZATION /£ˈɪnt·stɪ·tjuːt, $-tuːt/ *n* [C] an organization which exists so that its members can do a particular, esp. educational or social, type of work, or the buildings which it uses • *The Massachusetts Institute of Technology is also known as MIT.*

in·sti·tute *obj* START /£ˈɪnt·stɪ·tjuːt, $-tuːt/ *v* [T] *fml* to start or cause (a system, rule, legal action, etc.) to exist • *The committee will institute a new appraisal system next year.* • *She is threatening to institute legal proceedings against the hospital.*

in·sti·tu·tion /£ˌɪnt·stɪˈtjuː·ʃən, $-ˈtuː-/ *n* [U] • *The institution of a Freedom of Information Act has had a significant effect.* • See also INSTITUTION BUILDING; INSTITUTION SYSTEM.

in·sti·tu·tion BUILDING /£ˌɪnt·stɪˈtjuː·ʃən, $-ˈtuː-/ *n* [C] *esp. disapproving* a building where large numbers of people, esp. the old, the mentally ill or children without parents live in order to be officially looked after • *He has a horror of ending his life* **in** *an institution.* • See also **institution** at INSTITUTE START.

in·sti·tu·tion·al /£ˌɪnt·stɪˈtjuː·ʃən·əl, $-ˈtuː-/ *adj* • *The hospital provides typically awful institutional food.* • See also **institutional** at INSTITUTION.

in·sti·tu·tion·al·ize *obj, Br and Aus usually* **-ise** /£ˌɪnt·stɪˈtjuː·ʃən·ə·laɪz, $-ˈtuː-/ *v* [T] • If you institutionalize someone, you send them to live in an institution, usually because they are mentally ill or because they are a child without any parents. • See also **institutionalize** at INSTITUTION.

in·sti·tu·tion·al·ized, *Br and Aus usually* **-ised** /£ˌɪnt·stɪˈtjuː·ʃən·ə·laɪzd, $-ˈtuː-/ *adj* • If someone **becomes** institutionalized, they gradually become less able to think and act independently, because they have lived for a long time under the rules of an institution: *We need to avoid long-stay patients in the hospital becoming institutionalized.*

in·sti·tu·tion SYSTEM /£ˌɪnt·stɪˈtjuː·ʃən, $-ˈtuː-/ *n* [C] a custom, system or organization that has existed for a long time and is accepted as an important part of a particular society • *The institution of marriage is still popular despite the high divorce rate.* • *Eastern European countries are eager to copy the financial institutions of the West.* • *Oxford and Cambridge universities are internationally respected institutions.* • *(infml) Mrs Daly is an institution – she's been with the company 40 years and knows absolutely everyone!* • *"Marriage is a great institution, but I'm not ready for an institution yet"* (believed to have been said by Mae West, 1892-1980) • See also **institution** at INSTITUTE START.

in·sti·tu·tion·al /£ˌɪnt·stɪˈtjuː·ʃən·əl, $-ˈtuː-/ *adj* • *The institutional framework of the country needs a massive overhaul.*

in·sti·tu·tion·al·ize *obj, Br and Aus usually* **-ise** /£ˌɪnt·stɪˈtjuː·ʃən·ə·laɪz, $-ˈtuː-/ *v* [T] • *What was once an informal event has now become institutionalized.* • *The harsh prison regime is just a form of institutionalized violence.* • *If the proposed changes to the way the arts festival is organized are introduced, they'll have the effect of institutionalizing it* (= make it part of society's accepted way of acting), *and we don't want that.* • See also **institutionalize** at INSTITUTION BUILDING.

in·struct *obj* ORDER /ɪnˈstrʌkt/ *v* [T] to order or tell (someone) to do something, esp. in a formal way • *The police have been instructed* **to** *patrol the building and surrounding area.* [+ obj + *to* infinitive] • *I've been instructed* **to** *take down the name of everyone present.* [+ obj + *to* infinitive] • *(Br and Aus)* To instruct a lawyer is to employ them to represent you in court. • When judges instruct a JURY, they tell it what the law means and how to use it.

in·struc·tion /ɪnˈstrʌk·ʃən/ *n* [C usually pl] • *He* **gave** *me strict instructions* **to** *get there by eight o'clock.* [+ *to* infinitive] • *I had instructions not* **to** *reveal any details.* [+ *to* infinitive] • *The police who broke into the house were only acting* **on/under** *instructions.*

in·struct *obj* TEACH /ɪnˈstrʌkt/ *v* [T] to teach (someone) how to do something • *I need someone to instruct me* **in** *how to use the computer.* • *He works in a sports centre instructing people* **in** *the use of the gym equipment.*

in·struc·tion /ɪnˈstrʌk·ʃən/ *n* [U] • *The company provides instruction* **on** *how to operate the computer.* • *The course gives you* **basic** *instruction* **in** *car maintenance and repairs.* • *Have you seen the instruction* **manual** *for the washing machine?*

in·struc·tions /ɪnˈstrʌk·ʃənz/, *Am and Aus also* **di·rec·tions** *pl n* • Instructions are advice and information about how to do or use something, often written in a small book or on the side of a container: *The* **cooking** *instructions say bake it for half an hour.* ○ *You obviously* *didn't read the instructions properly.* ○ *They need clear instructions* **on** *what to do in an emergency.*

in·struc·tive /£ɪn'strʌk·tɪv, $-t̬ɪv/ *adj approving* • Something which is instructive gives useful or interesting information.

in·struc·tor /£ɪn'strʌk·təʳ, $-t̬ɚ/ *n* [C] • An instructor is a person whose job is to teach people a practical skill: *an aerobics instructor* ○ *a driving/ski/swimming instructor* • *(Am)* An instructor is also a teacher of a college or university subject, who usually teaches a limited number of classes: *a history/science/sociology instructor*

in·stru·ment MUSIC /'ɪn·strə·mənt/, **mu·si·cal in·stru·ment** *n* [C] an object, such as a piano, guitar or drum, which is played to produce musical sounds • *Which instrument do you* **play**? • PIC **Musical instruments**

in·stru·men·tal /£ˌɪn·strə'men·təl, $-t̬əl/ *adj* [not gradable] • *Do you want the instrumental version or the one with vocals?*

in·stru·men·tal /£ˌɪn·strə'men·təl, $-t̬əl/ *n* [C] • *It's just an instrumental – there are no vocals at all.*

in·stru·men·tal·ist /£ˌɪn·strə'men·təl·ɪst, $-t̬əl-/ *n* [C] • An instrumentalist is a person who plays a musical instrument, esp. as a job: *He was one of the finest instrumentalists of his day.*

in·stru·men·ta·tion /ˌɪn·strə·men'teɪ·ʃən/ *n* [U] *specialized* • The instrumentation of a piece of music is the particular combination of musical instruments that are used to play it.

in·stru·ment TOOL /'ɪn·strə·mənt/ *n* [C] a tool or other device, esp. one that has no power, used for performing a particular piece of work, or *(fig. fml)* a way of achieving or causing something • *surgical instruments* • *instruments of torture* • *The man's injuries had obviously been caused by a blunt instrument.* • Instruments are also the various devices used for measuring speed, height, etc. that are found in vehicles, esp. aircraft: *the instrument panel* ○ *The lightning had damaged the plane's instruments, and they weren't giving any readings.* • *(fig. fml) He saw the theatre as an instrument* **of** *change – a way of forcing people to consider social and political issues.*

in·stru·men·tal /£ˌɪn·strə'men·təl, $-t̬əl/ *adj* [after v] *fml* • If someone or something is instrumental in a process, plan or system, they are one of the most important influences in causing it to happen: *She was instrumental* **in** *bringing about the prison reform act.*

in·stru·men·ta·tion /ˌɪn·strə·men'teɪ·ʃən/ *n* [U] *specialized* • If people refer to the instrumentation of a complicated machine they mean the set of instruments that are used in operating it.

in·sub·or·din·ate /£ˌɪn·sə'bɔː·dɪ·nət, $-'bɔːr-/ *adj disapproving* (of a person) not obedient; not willing to obey orders from people in authority, or (of actions and speech etc.) showing that you are not willing to obey orders • *The old school headteacher remembered him as an insubordinate child.*

in·sub·or·din·a·tion /£ˌɪn·səˌbɔː·dɪ'neɪ·ʃən, $-ˌbɔːr-/ *n* [U] *disapproving* • *The leader regarded such refusals to cooperate as insubordination.*

in·sub·stan·tial /ˌɪn·səb'stænt·ʃəl, £-'stɑːn-/ *adj* of little value or importance, or lacking strength, solidity or size • *It's a bad film, based on a hopelessly insubstantial plot.* • *Except for an insubstantial snack at lunch she had scarcely eaten.*

in·suf·fer·a·ble /£ɪn'sʌf·ər·ə·bl̩, $'-ɚ-/ *adj* annoying, unpleasant or uncomfortable, and therefore extremely difficult to bear • *She disliked the president, whom she once described as an 'insufferable bore'.* • *The metro is insufferable in this heat.*

in·suf·fer·a·bly /£ɪn'sʌf·ər·ə·bli, $'-ɚ-/ *adv* • *She's the most insufferably arrogant person I've met.*

in·suf·fi·cient /ˌɪn·sə'fɪʃ·ənt/ *adj* [not gradable] not large enough in amount or in number • *If there are insufficient numbers* **to** *fill the coach we'll have to cancel the trip.* [+ *to* infinitive] • *There was insufficient money* **to** *fund the tour.* [+ *to* infinitive]

in·suf·fi·cient·ly /ˌɪn·sə'fɪʃ·ənt·li/ *adv* [not gradable] • *I felt that the whole project was insufficiently researched.*

in·suf·fi·cien·cy /ˌɪn·sə'fɪʃ·ənt·si/ *n* [C/U]

in·su·lar /£'ɪn·sjʊ·ləʳ, $-lɚ/ *adj disapproving* interested only in your own country or group and not willing to accept different or foreign ideas • *Theirs is a very insular culture, protected as it is from outside influences.*

in·su·lar·i·ty /£ˌɪn·sjʊ'lær·ə·ti, $-t̬i/ *n* [U] *disapproving* • *The British tabloid press is often criticized for its insularity.*

in·su·late *obj* COVER /'ɪn·sjʊ·leɪt/ *v* [T] to cover and surround (something) with a material or substance in order to stop esp. heat, sound or electricity from escaping or entering • *You can insulate a house* **against** *heat loss by having the windows double-glazed.* • *(Br and Aus)* **Insulating tape**/*(Am)* **Friction tape** is a strip of sticky material which is put around a bare piece of electrical wire in order to stop someone or something from being harmed by the electricity.

in·su·la·tion /ˌɪn·sjʊ'leɪ·ʃən/ *n* [U] • *If houses had more effective (methods of) insulation it would cut down considerably on the energy needed to heat them.* • Insulation can also be the substance itself which prevents heat, sound or electricity from going through: *The animal's thick fur provides very good insulation against the arctic cold.* ○ *Glass fibre is often used as* **roof** *insulation.*

in·su·lat·or /£'ɪn·sjʊ·leɪ·təʳ, $-t̬ɚ/ *n* [C] • An insulator is a material or covering which electricity, heat or sound cannot go through: *Generally, plastics tend to be good insulators.*

in·su·late *obj* PROTECT /'ɪn·sjʊ·leɪt/ *v* [T] to protect (someone or something) from outside influences • *The rich and famous have a strange existence, insulated as they are* **from** *real life.* • *Until recently the country's economy has been insulated* **from** *recession by its reserves of raw materials.*

in·su·la·tion /ˌɪn·sjʊ'leɪ·ʃən/ *n* [U]

in·su·lin /£'ɪn·sjʊ·lɪn, $-sə-/ *n* [U] a HORMONE (=chemical substance) in the body which controls the amount of sugar in the blood and if not produced naturally or in large enough amounts in the body results in the disease DIABETES • *She has to have insulin injections for her diabetes.*

in·sult /'ɪn·sʌlt/ *n* [C] an offensive remark or action • *She* **made** *the usual insults about my appearance.* • *The steelworkers' leader rejected the 2% pay-rise saying it was an insult* **to** *the profession.* • *The instructions are so easy they are an insult* **to** *your* **intelligence** (=they seem to suggest you are not clever if you need to use them).

in·sult *obj* /ɪn'sʌlt, $'ɪn·sʌlt/ *v* [T] • *First he drank all my wine and then he insulted all my friends.* • *I feel a bit insulted that anyone would think me old enough to be her sister.* • *"I'd mistakenly assumed that he was your boyfriend." "Don't insult my taste!"*

in·sult·ing /£ɪn'sʌl·tɪŋ, $-t̬ɪŋ/ *adj* • *You can't offer such a low salary to someone who is so highly skilled – it's insulting.*

in·sult·ing·ly /£ɪn'sʌl·tɪŋ·li, $-t̬ɪŋ-/ *adv* • *The questions were insultingly easy.*

in·su·per·a·ble /£ɪn'sjuː·pər·ə·bl̩, $-'suː·pɚ-/ *adj fml* (esp. of a problem or a difficulty) so great or severe that it cannot be defeated or dealt with successfully • *The hospitals now face insuperable difficulties with too few staff and too little money.* • *She has battled against seemingly insuperable odds* (=against very great difficulties) *to win this race tonight.*

in·su·per·a·bly /£ɪn'sjuː·pər·ə·bli, $-'suː·pɚ-/ *adv fml*

in·sup·port·a·ble /£ˌɪn·sə'pɔː·tə·bl̩, $-'pɔːr·t̬ə-/ *adj fml* difficult or impossible to bear • *The war had put an insupportable financial burden on the country.*

in·sure *(obj)* /£ɪn'ʃɔːʳ, $-'ʃɔːr/ *v* [often passive] to protect yourself against risk by regularly paying a special company that in exchange will provide a fixed amount of money if in the future you are killed or injured or your home or possessions are damaged, destroyed or stolen • *This silver's very valuable – you should insure it.* [T] • *All our household goods are insured* **against** *accidental damage.* [T] • *I lost my camera on holiday and I wasn't insured* **for** *it.* [T] • *I'm not insured to drive his car.* [T + obj + *to* infinitive] • *As one of the world's highest paid models her face is insured* **for** *£5 million.* [T] • *We've always insured* **with** *the Acme Insurance Company.* [I always + adv/prep] • You can insure **against** something unpleasant or an event which would not be convenient by taking a particular action which will protect you against it: *We thought we'd insure against rain by putting a tent up where people could take shelter.* [I always + adv/prep]

in·sur·ance /£ɪn'ʃɔː·rənts, $-'ʃɔːr·ənts/ *n* [U] • *I'll need to* **take out** *extra car insurance for another driver.* • *The insurance doesn't* **cover** *you for* (=include) *household items.* • *We're* **claiming** *for the lost luggage* **on** *our insurance.* • *She's got private* **health** *insurance.* • *He sells* **life** *insurance.* • *She works for an insurance company.* • *If you have an* *accident in your car, the insurance* **(premium)** (= the money you pay to insure it) *goes up.* • An **insurance policy** is a written agreement between an insurance company and a person who wants insurance which states the rules of the agreement: *(fig.) There's one particular job I'm after but I'm applying for several others as an insurance policy* (= because I might not get the job I want). • Compare **assurance** at ASSURE [PROTECT].

in·sured /£ɪn'ʃɔːd, $-'ʃɔːrd/ *n* [U] *specialized* • **The** insured is the person, group of people or organization who is insured in a particular agreement.

in·sur·ers /£ɪn'ʃɔː·rəz, $-'ʃɔːr·ɚz/ *pl n* • Insurers are a company which provides insurance: *If you have a claim, write to your insurers.*

in·sur·er /£ɪn'ʃɔː·rəʳ, $-'ʃɔːr·ɚ/ *n* [C] • *Please contact your insurer if you have any inquiries.*

in·sur·gent /£ɪn'sɜː·dʒᵊnt, $-'sɜːr-/ *n* [C] a person who is fighting in a group against their own government, or the person who is in charge of the country • *All approaches to the capital are now under the control of the insurgents.* • *The small town is said to be in insurgent hands.* • *(Am)* An insurgent is also a person who takes action to show that they do not agree with some of the ideas and plans of the political party they support.

in·sur·gen·cy /£ɪn'sɜː·dʒᵊnt·si, $-'sɜːr-/ *n* [U] • *The government is reported to be concerned about the growing insurgency in the South.* • Compare COUNTERINSURGENCY.

in·sur·mount·a·ble /£ˌɪn·sə'maʊn·tə·bl̩, $-sɚ'maʊn·t̬ə-/ *adj* [not gradable] *fml* (esp. of a problem or a difficulty) so great that it cannot be dealt with successfully • *The government faces almost insurmountable difficulties in its attempt to unite its country's people.*

in·sur·rec·tion /£ˌɪn·sᵊr'ek·ʃᵊn, $-sɚ-/ *n* an organized attempt by a group of people to defeat the government or the person who is in power and take control of the country, usually by violence • *Guards were moving down from the North to crush the insurrection.* [C] • *Insurrection was seen as the only way of changing the government.* [U]

in·tact /ɪn'tækt/ *adj* complete and in the original state • *The church was destroyed in the bombing but the altar survived intact.* • *(fig.) It's difficult to emerge from such a scandal with your reputation still intact* (= not damaged).

in·take [BREATH] /'ɪn·teɪk/ *n* [C] an act of taking in esp. breath • *I heard a* **sharp** *intake* **of breath** *behind me.*

in·take [AMOUNT] /'ɪn·teɪk/ *n* [U] the amount of a particular substance which is eaten or drunk during a particular time • *It says on the packet that four slices of this bread contains one half of your recommended* **daily** *intake of fibre.*

in·take [NUMBER OF PEOPLE] /'ɪn·teɪk/ *n* [U] the number of people that are accepted at a particular time by an organization, esp. a college or university • *The teacher-training college has increased its intake of students by 50% this year.*

in·take [OPENING] /'ɪn·teɪk/ *n* [C] an opening through which air, liquid or gas is taken in • *The Tornado jet fighter-bomber has two* **air** *intakes, one at the base of each wing.*

in·tan·gible /ɪn'tæn·dʒɪ·bl̩/ *adj* not solid or able to be seen or felt, although real, and therefore difficult to explain exactly or show • *I don't know how to describe the feeling – it's more intangible than depression.* • *She has that intangible quality which you might call charisma.* • An **intangible asset** is something valuable which a company possesses which is not material, such as a good reputation.

in·tan·gible /ɪn'tæn·dʒɪ·bl̩/ *n* [C] • *Common sense and creativity are some of the intangibles we're looking for in an employee.*

in·tan·gi·bly /ɪn'tæn·dʒɪ·bli/ *adv*

in·te·ger /£'ɪn·tɪ·dʒəʳ, $-dʒɚ/ *n* [C] *specialized* a whole number and not a FRACTION • *The numbers -5, 0 and 3 are integers.*

in·te·gral /£'ɪn·tɪ·grəl, $-t̬ə-/ *adj* necessary and important as a part of, or contained within, a whole • *He's an integral* **part** *of the team and we can't do without him.* • *Bars and terrace cafés are integral* **to** *the social life of the city.* • *(specialized) One of the biggest problems is that the prison has no integral sanitation.*

in·te·grate *(obj)* /£'ɪn·tɪ·greɪt, $-t̬ə-/ *v* (of people) to mix with and join society or a group of people, often changing to suit their way of life, habits and customs, or (of systems and things) to be suitable for and combine with each other or with what already exists • *It's very difficult to integrate* **yourself into** *a society whose culture is so different from your own.* [T] • *He seems to find it difficult to integrate socially* [I] • *The aim, said the minister, was to integrate Britain both politically and economically* **into** *the European Community.* [T] • *The idea with young children is to integrate learning* **with** *play.* [T]

in·te·grat·ed /£'ɪn·tɪ·greɪ·tɪd, $-t̬ə·greɪ·t̬ɪd/ *adj* • *A more integrated transport system would discourage the use of private cars and develop public transport.* • *The town's modern architecture is very well integrated* **with** *the old.* • *(specialized)* An **integrated circuit** (abbreviation **IC**) is a very small electronic CIRCUIT which consists of a lot of small parts made on a piece of SEMICONDUCTING material.

in·te·gra·tion /£ˌɪn·tɪ'greɪ·ʃᵊn, $-t̬ə-/ *n* [U] • *There's a lot of integration in the schools because of the various racial communities that live in the area.* • *A good musical depends on the successful integration of acting* **with** *song and dance.*

in·te·grit·y [HONESTY] /£ɪn'teg·rə·ti, $-t̬i/ *n* [U] *approving* the quality of being honest and having strong moral principles that you refuse to change • *No one doubted that the president was a man of the highest integrity.* • People often refer to someone's **artistic/professional** integrity or their integrity **as** a writer, doctor, etc., meaning their high artistic standards or standards of doing their job and their determination not to lower them: *Keen to preserve his integrity as an actor, he refused several lucrative Hollywood offers.*

in·te·grit·y [UNITY] /£ɪn'teg·rə·ti, $-t̬i/ *n* [U] *specialized or fml* wholeness and unity • *A modern extension on the old building would ruin its architectural integrity.*

in·tel·lect /£'ɪn·tᵊl·ekt, $-t̬ə-/ *n* the ability to think intelligently and understand, or the ability to do these things to a high level • *Her writing appeals more to the intellect than the emotion.* [U] • *He is a man more noted for his intellect than his charm.* [U] • An intellect is also a highly educated person whose interests are studying and other activities that involve careful thinking: *Maria Gomez, historian, socialist and intellect, has died at the age of eighty-nine.* [C]

in·tel·lec·tu·al /£ˌɪn·tᵊl'ek·tju·əl, $-t̬ᵊl'ek·tʃu-/ *adj* • *He's quite bright but he's not what you would describe as intellectual.* • *Looking after a baby at home all day is nice but it doesn't provide much intellectual* **stimulation.** • *I like detective stories and romances – nothing too intellectual.* • **Intellectual property** is an original idea which can be used to earn money. The person or group who is recognized as having the idea can use the law to prevent other people from earning money by copying it. • *"An intellectual hatred is the worst, / So let her think opinions are accursed"* (W.B.Yeats in the poem *A Prayer for my Daughter*, 1920)

in·tel·lec·tu·al /£ˌɪn·tᵊl'ek·tju·əl, $-t̬ᵊl'ek·tʃu-/ *n* [C] • An intellectual is a highly educated person whose interests are studying and other activities that involve careful thinking and mental effort: *She was too much of an intellectual to find teaching young children rewarding.* ○ *He found himself in a room full of intellectuals discussing philosophy and politics.*

in·tel·lec·tu·al·ly /£ˌɪn·tᵊl'ek·tju·ə·li, $-t̬ᵊl'ek·tʃu-/ *adv* • *Intellectually speaking, the film is rather lacking.* • *She needs a job which is a little more demanding intellectually.*

in·tel·lec·tu·al·ize, *Br and Aus usually* **-ise** /£ˌɪn·tᵊl'ek·tju·ə·laɪz, $-t̬ᵊl'ek·tʃu-/ *v* [I] • If you intellectualize you consider a subject in an intellectual way, thinking about it and finding explanations for it, esp. in a way that is not necessary or does not consider the emotions: *She couldn't stand all that pointless intellectualizing about subjects that just didn't matter.*

in·tel·lec·tu·al·i·sm /£ˌɪn·tᵊl'ek·tju·ə·lɪ·zᵊm, $-t̬ᵊl'ek·tʃu-/ *n* [U] *usually disapproving* • *He had no time for intellectualism and would never analyse a film or book that he had read.*

in·tel·li·gence [CLEVERNESS] /ɪn'tel·ɪ·dʒᵊnts/ *n* [U] the ability to understand and learn and make judgments or have opinions that are based on reason • *an intelligence test* • *Boxers aren't really renowned for their intelligence.* • *Compared to monkeys, dogs have a fairly low intelligence.* • *It's the intelligence of her writing that impresses me.* • See also IQ.

in·tel·li·gent /ɪn'tel·ɪ·dʒᵊnt/ *adj* • *I didn't get the impression that he was very intelligent when we were at school.* • *Helen had a few intelligent things to say on the subject.* • *(humorous) "I've just locked myself out of my car." "That was intelligent of you!"* • (J) (RUS)

in·tel·li·gent·ly /ɪn'tel·ɪ·dʒᵊnt·li/ *adv*

in·tel·li·gence INFORMATION /ɪn'tel·ɪ·dʒənts/ *n* [U] a government department or other group of people who gather and deal with information about other countries or enemies, or the information that is gathered • *the Central Intelligence Agency* • *He worked for military intelligence during the war.* • *Intelligence say(s) that the enemy attack will probably start tomorrow.* [+ sing/pl v] • *They received intelligence (reports)* **that** *the factory was a target for the bombing.* [+ *that* clause] • *Intelligence sources, believed to be MI5, predicted the war six months before it happened.*

in·tel·li·gent·si·a /ɪn,tel·ɪ'dʒent·si·ə/ *n* [U + sing/pl v] **the intelligentsia** highly educated people in a society, esp. those interested in the arts and in politics • *She was born into the liberal intelligentsia – her mother was a doctor and her father a writer.*

in·tel·li·gi·ble /ɪn'tel·ɪ·dʒɪ·bḷ/ *adj* (of speech and writing) clear enough to be understood • *She was so upset that what she said was hardly intelligible.* • *The article is not really intelligible unless you already know a lot about genetics.*

in·tel·li·gi·bly /ɪn'tel·ɪ·dʒɪ·bli/ *adv*

in·tel·li·gi·bil·i·ty /£ɪn,tel·ɪ·dʒə'bɪl·ɪ·ti, $-ə·ţi/ *n* [U]

in·tem·per·ate /£ɪn'tem·pər·ət, $-pɚ-/ *adj fml* (of a person or their behaviour or speech) not controlled and too extreme or violent • *an intemperate outburst* • *The leader was accused of using intemperate language to stir up hatred and violence.* • *The governor said he would not be provoked into intemperate action.*

in·tem·per·ate·ly /£ɪn'tem·pər·ət·li, $-pɚ-/ *adv fml*

in·tem·per·ance /£ɪn'tem·pər·ənts, $-pɚ-/ *n* [U] *fml* • (I)

in·tend *(obj)* /ɪn'tend/ *v* to have as a plan or purpose • *We intend to go to Australia next year if all goes well.* [+ *to* infinitive] • *I had intended leaving the party before midnight but stayed rather later.* [+ v-*ing*] • *Somehow I gave the impression that I was interested in his son, which wasn't what I'd intended at all.* [T] • *I don't think she intended me* **to** *hear the remark.* [T + obj + *to* infinitive] • **It** *is intended* **that** *at least four thousand people take part in the scheme.* [+ *that* clause] • *The party is really intended* **for** *new students so they can meet each other.* [T] • *It was intended* (= meant) **as** *a compliment, honestly!* [T] • *I don't think there was any intended insult in the remark.* • *She intended it* **as** *a joke but a lot of people took her seriously.* [T] • *This sweet wine is intended* **to be** *drunk after a meal.* [T + obj + *to* infinitive] • (E)

in·tent /ɪn'tent/ *n* [U] *slightly fml* • *I ended up spending half the holiday working, which wasn't really my intent.* • *The attack was savage and there was no doubt that the intent was* **to** *kill.* [+ *to* infinitive] • *(law) She was charged with possessing weapons* **with** *intent* **to** *endanger life.* [+ *to* infinitive] • *(law) He was picked up by the police for* **loitering with** *intent* (= planning to do something illegal). • **To/For all intents and purposes** (= Almost or very nearly) *the project is completed.* • See also INTENT.

in·ten·tion /ɪn'ten·ʃən/ *n* • *It wasn't my intention* **to** *exclude her from the list – I just forgot her.* [C + *to* infinitive] • *I've no intention* **of** *changing my plans just to fit in with his.* [U] • *He's full of* **good** *intentions but he never does anything about them!* [C] • *"No one would have remembered the Good Samaritan if he'd had only good intentions. He had money as well"* (speech by Margaret Thatcher, 1986)

in·ten·tion·al /ɪn'ten·ʃən·əl/ *adj* • *Did you leave his name out by accident or was it intentional?*

in·ten·tion·al·ly /ɪn'ten·ʃən·əl·i/ *adv* • *I didn't ignore her intentionally – I just didn't recognize her.*

-in·ten·tioned /-ɪn'ten·ʃənd, -ˌ--/ *combining form* • *I'm sure he's* **well**-*intentioned – he wouldn't mean any harm.*

in·tend·ed /ɪn'ten·dɪd/ *n* [C usually sing] *dated or humorous* the person that you are going to marry • *I shall be there with my intended.*

in·tense /ɪn'tents/ *adj* extreme and forceful or (of a feeling) very strong • *intense cold/heat/hatred* • *an intense flavour/colour* • *What struck her was the intense competition between the two brothers.* • *He suddenly felt an intense pain in the lower part of his back.* • *At midday the light is at its most intense.* • A person might be described as intense if they have strong emotions and opinions which they talk about very seriously in a way that demands all of your attention: *You won't have much of a laugh with Andrew – he's rather intense.*

in·tense·ly /ɪn'tent·sli/ *adv* • *His strongest criticism is reserved for his father, whom he disliked intensely.* • *She was unimpressed by the actor, describing him as 'a vain man and intensely dull'.* • (LP) **Very, completely**

in·ten·si·ty /£ɪn'tent·sɪ·ti, $-sə·ţi/ *n* [U] • *His eyes blazed with a passion of such intensity that she was quite alarmed.* • *The explosion was of such intensity that it was heard five miles away.*

in·ten·si·fi·er /£ɪn'tent·sɪ·faɪ·ər, $-ɚ/, **in·ten·sive** /ɪn'tent·sɪv/ *n* [C] *specialized* • In English grammar, an intensifier is a word, esp. an adverb or adjective, which has little meaning itself but is used to add force to another adjective, verb or adverb: *In the phrases 'an extremely large man' and 'I strongly object', 'extremely' and 'strongly' are both intensifiers.* • (LP) **Very, completely**

in·ten·si·fy *(obj)* /ɪn'tent·sɪ·faɪ/ *v* • *It is reported that fighting around the capital has intensified in the last few hours.* [I] • *This button on the left of the computer allows you to intensify the colour.* [T]

in·ten·si·fi·ca·tion /ɪn,tent·sɪ·fɪ'keɪ·ʃən/ *n* [U]

in·ten·sive /ɪn'tent·sɪv/ *adj* • *Bombing, which was intensive* (= continuous and directed at a particular area) *in the city centre, has destroyed most of the major buildings.* • Intensive studying or training is intended to deal with a lot in a short period of time: *a month-long intensive course in teaching English* • In a hospital **intensive care** is continuous treatment provided for PATIENTS who are seriously ill or have just had an operation: *the intensive-care unit* ○ *She needed intensive care for three weeks.* • *(specialized)* **Intensive farming** uses methods which are intended to produce the largest amount of crops or meat possible from a particular area.

in·tent GIVING ATTENTION /ɪn'tent/ *adj* giving all your attention to something • *an intent stare* • *He was in the library, intent* **on** *his books.* • See also **intent** at INTEND.

in·tent·ly /ɪn'tent·li/ *adv* • *The child stared intently at her.*

in·tent DETERMINED /ɪn'tent/ *adj* [after v; always + *on*] determined to do something • *I've tried persuading her not to go but she's intent on it.* • *He seems intent on upsetting everyone in the room!* • See also **intent** at INTEND.

in·ter *obj* BURY /£ɪn'tɜːr, $-'tɜːr/ *v* [T] **-rr-** *fml* to put (a dead body) in the earth; to bury • *Many of the soldiers were interred* **in** *unmarked graves.*

in·ter·ment /£ɪn'tɜː·mənt, $-'tɜːr-/ *n* [C] *fml* • *His interment* (= burial) *was as he had requested, simple and without ceremony.*

in·ter- BETWEEN /£'ɪn·tər, $-ţɚ/ *combining form* between or among • *interactive* • *interconnect* • *intercontinental* • *interdepartmental* • *interfaith* • *intergovernmental* • Interdenominational means shared by different groups of the Christian church: *The Catholic and several Protestant churches held an inter-denominational church service.* • Compare INTRA-.

in·ter·act *(obj)* /£,ɪn·tə'rækt, $-ţɚ'ækt/ *v* to communicate with or react to (each other) • *Modern architects are designing buildings for the future which will interact* **with** *the user.* [T] • *It's interesting at parties to see how people interact socially.* [I]

in·ter·ac·tion /£,ɪn·tə'ræk·ʃən, $-ţɚ-/ *n* • *(specialized) elementary-particle interactions* [C] • *There's not enough interaction* **between** *the management and the workers.* [U] • *Language games are usually intended to encourage student interaction.* [U] • *The play follows the interactions of three very different characters who are shut up in a room together.* [C]

in·ter·ac·tive /£,ɪn·tə'ræk·tɪv, $-ţɚ'æk·ţɪv/ *adj* • A computer program which is interactive is designed to involve the user in the exchange of information while the computer is in operation: *The interactive help program teaches you how to use the computer by going through the steps yourself.* • *The concept is of an interactive museum where by pressing buttons, children can get the exhibits to work.*

in·ter·ac·tive·ly /£,ɪn·tə'ræk·tɪv·li, $-ţɚ'æk·ţɪv-/ *adv* • *The program lets you work through a text interactively, correcting as you go along.*

in·ter a·li·a /£,ɪn·tə'reɪ·li·ə, $-ţɚ'eɪ-/ *adv* [not gradable] *fml* among other things • *The agreement endorses, inter alia, the right to free and fair elections.*

in·ter·breed *(obj)* /£,ɪn·tə'briːd, $-ţɚ-/ *v past* **interbred** /£,ɪn·tə'bred, $-ţɚ-/ to breed or cause to breed with members of another breed or group • *The black crows had interbred* **with** *a lighter subspecies, producing birds with grey feathers.* [I] • *Farmers were interbreeding less hardy cattle* **with** *native breeds.* [T]

in·ter·breed·ing /£,ɪn·tə'briː·dɪŋ, $-ţɚ-/ *n* [U]

in·ter·cede /£ˌɪn·tə'siːd, $-t̬ɚ-/ *v* [I] to use your influence to persuade someone in authority to save someone else from punishment or to obtain forgiveness for this person • *Several religious leaders have interceded* **with** *the authorities on behalf of the condemned prisoner.*

in·ter·ces·sion /£ˌɪn·tə'seʃ·ᵊn, $-t̬ɚ-/ *n* • *Several political prisoners have been released through the intercession of Amnesty International.* [U] • Intercessions or **prayers of** intercession are prayers which ask God or a god to help or cure other people. [C/U]

in·ter·cept *obj* /£ˌɪn·tə'sept, $-t̬ɚ-/ *v* [T] to stop and catch (something or someone) that is travelling or being sent from one place to another so that it does not reach the second place • *The coastguard patrol's job is to intercept drugs from Latin America.* • *I managed to intercept him at the front door, giving Jane time to leave by the back.* • *De Silva's pass to Menendez was intercepted by Black, who then passed the ball back up the field.*

in·ter·cep·tion /£ˌɪn·tə'sep·ʃᵊn, $-t̬ɚ-/ *n* • *The information was obtained illegally by the interception of telephone calls and private mail.* [U] • *Cannabis interceptions account for 90% of drug seizures at customs.* [C]

in·ter·cep·tor /£ˌɪn·tə'sep·təʳ, $-t̬ɚ'sep·t̬ɚ/ *n* [C] • An interceptor is a fast aircraft which shoots down enemy aircraft.

in·ter·change EXCHANGE /£'ɪn·tə·tʃeɪndʒ, $-t̬ɚ-/ *n fml* an exchange, esp. of ideas or information, between different people or groups • *An international medical conference was established for the interchange of new ideas and approaches.* [U] • *There was an interchange of ideas after the lecture which was very informative.* [C]

in·ter·change *(obj)* /£ˌɪn·tə'tʃeɪndʒ, $-t̬ɚ-/ *v* [I/T]

in·ter·change ROAD /£'ɪn·tə·tʃeɪndʒ, $-t̬ɚ-/ *n* [C] *Br* a JUNCTION at which smaller roads meet a larger road, esp. a MOTORWAY • PIC **Motorway**

in·ter·chan·ge·a·ble /£ˌɪn·tə'tʃeɪn·dʒə·bl̩, $-t̬ɚ-/ *adj* able to be exchanged with each other without making any difference or without being noticed • *The terms 'drinking problem' and 'alcohol abuse' are often interchangeable.* • *The radio played the usual string of interchangeable disco hits.*

in·ter·chan·ge·a·bly /£ˌɪn·tə'tʃeɪn·dʒə·bli, $-t̬ɚ-/ *adv*

in·ter·ci·ty /£ˌɪn·tə'sɪt·i, $-t̬ɚ'sɪt̬-/ *adj* [before n; not gradable] *Br* (of a train) travelling fast between main cities • *The 3.15 intercity service between London and Coventry will depart from platform 9.*

in·ter·ci·ty /£ˌɪn·tə'sɪt·i, $-t̬ɚ'sɪt̬-/ *n* [C] *Br* • *If you get the intercity it's about an hour quicker than the normal train.*

in·ter·com /£'ɪn·tə·kɒm, $-t̬ɚ·kɑːm/ *n* [C] a device which people speak into when they want to communicate with, for example, someone who is inside a building or in a different room • *They live in a flat, and visitors have to ask* **through/via** *an intercom to be let in.*

in·ter·con·nect *(obj)* /£ˌɪn·tə·kə'nekt, $-t̬ɚ-/ *v* (of two or more things) to connect with or be related to each other • *The problems of poverty, homelessness and unemployment are all interconnected.* [T] • *Everything in the world interconnects somehow.* [I] • *A complex system of interconnecting tunnels joins the two buildings.*

in·ter·con·nec·tion /£ˌɪn·tə·kə'nek·ʃᵊn, $-t̬ɚ-/ *n* [C/U]

in·ter·con·ti·nen·tal /£ˌɪn·təˌkɒn·tɪ'nen·tᵊl, $-t̬ɚˌkɑːn·t̬ə'nen·t̬ᵊl/ *adj* [not gradable] between continents • *intercontinental flights*

in·ter·course SEX /£'ɪn·tə·kɔːs, $-t̬ɚ·kɔːrs/ *n* [U] the sexual activity in which the male's penis enters the female's vagina, or the sexual activity in which a male's penis enters another male's (or a female's) ANUS • *vaginal/anal intercourse* • *By 1991 24% of all HIV infections were as a result of* **sexual** *intercourse between men and women.* • *Our survey reveals that most couples* **have** *intercourse four times a week.*

in·ter·course CONVERSATION /£'ɪn·tə·kɔːs, $-t̬ɚ·kɔːrs/ *n* [U] *dated fml* conversation and social activity between people • *A certain level of manners is required for normal* **social** *intercourse.*

in·ter·de·pen·dent /£ˌɪn·tə·dɪ'pen·dᵊnt, $-t̬ɚ-/ *adj* dependent on each other • *All living things are interdependent.*

in·ter·de·pen·dence /£ˌɪn·tə·dɪ'pen·dənts, $-t̬ɚ-/ *n* [U] • *the economic interdependence of nations*

in·ter·dis·ci·plin·a·ry /£ˌɪn·tə'dɪs·ɪ·plɪ·nᵊr·i, $-t̬ɚ'dɪs·ə·plɪ·ner-/ *adj* [not gradable] (of courses studied at college or university) involving two or more different subjects • *interdisciplinary courses*

in·ter·est INVOLVEMENT /£'ɪn·tᵊr·est, $-t̬ɚ-/ *n* the feeling of having your attention held and your mind excited by something or of wanting to be involved with and to discover more about something • *He never seems to show much interest* **in** *his children.* [U] • *I've never had any interest* **in** *the royal family.* [U] • *Unfortunately, I lost interest half way through the film.* [U] • *She* **takes** *more of* **an** *interest in politics these days.* [U] • *(infml) Just* **out of** *interest* (= because I would like to know, and not for any more serious reason), *how old is your wife?* [U] • Your interests are the activities that you enjoy doing and the subjects that you like to spend time learning about: *On his form he lists his interests as cycling, the cinema and cooking.* [C] • Interest is also the power to hold your attention and excite your mind or to make you want to be involved or discover more about something: *Computers have never held any interest for me.* [U] ○ *"Did he have anything to say?" "Oh, nothing much of interest."* [U]

in·ter·est *obj* /£'ɪn·tᵊr·est, $-t̬ɚ-/ *v* [T] • *Sport has never really interested me.* • *Above all you need a job that interests you.* • Someone might ask if they can interest you **in** something when they are trying to persuade you to buy or when they are offering you something: *Can I interest you in our new range of kitchen fittings, madam?* ○ *Don't suppose I can interest you in a quick drink before lunch, can I?*

in·ter·est·ed /£'ɪn·tᵊr·es·tɪd, $-t̬ɚ·es·t̬ɪd/ *adj* • *I asked him if he wanted to come but he didn't seem very interested.* • *She's at that age where she's starting to get interested* **in** *boys.* • *He was trying to chat up this girl, but you could see from her face that she wasn't interested.* • *If you could send her that article some time, I think she'd be interested* **to** *see it.* [+ *to* infinitive] • *I'm interested* **to** *know why he left the job so suddenly.* [+ *to* infinitive] • *I was interested* **that** *they didn't get on together.* [+ *that* clause] • *"Really?" he said, with an interested look on his face.* • *Yes, I'd be very interested* **in** *knowing more about the services your firm offers.*

in·ter·est·ing /£'ɪn·tᵊr·es·tɪŋ, $-t̬ɚ·es·t̬ɪŋ/ *adj* • *She's quite an interesting woman.* • *There's an interesting looking TV documentary tonight on John F Kennedy.* • *She's got some very interesting things to say on the subject.* • *Tonight saw some interesting developments in Parliament.* • **It**'*s very interesting* **(that)** *you should say that.* [+ *(that)* clause] • **It** *is always interesting* **to** *hear other people's point of view.* [+ *to* infinitive] • *So, he's suddenly got a load of money from somewhere – very interesting!* • *Oh, I didn't know they were married – that's interesting.* • *(humorous)* Interesting is sometimes used to mean strange or different: *That's an interesting looking hat you're wearing, Neil!*

in·ter·est·ing·ly /£'ɪn·tᵊr·es·tɪŋ·li, $-t̬ɚ·es·t̬ɪŋ-/ *adv* • Interestingly is sometimes used to introduce a piece of information that the speaker finds strange and interesting: *Interestingly* **(enough)**, *he never actually said that he was innocent.*

in·ter·est ADVANTAGE /£'ɪn·tᵊr·est, $-t̬ɚ-/ *n* [C] an advantage; something that will provide you with something or help you in some way • *A union looks after the interests of its members* (= protects them and tries to get what is important or necessary for them). • *She had a* **vested** *interest in seeing the project fail* (= it will improve her situation if it fails). • *It's* **in** *his interest/***in** *his interests to keep in touch with a business contact.* • **In the** *interests* **of** (= In order to achieve) *safety, please do not smoke.* • *I don't want to drag you away from the party early but I'm only acting in your* **best** *interests* (= doing what is best for you). • *There are powerful business interests involved* (= important people from business who want to make something happen for their own advantage). • An **interest group** is a group or organization, esp. a small one, with particular aims and ideas: *There's too much lobbying of MPs by special interest groups.*

in·ter·est MONEY /£'ɪn·tᵊr·est, $-t̬ɚ-/ *n* [U] money which is charged by a financial organization such as a bank to people who have borrowed from them, or the profit which is made on money invested in a financial organization • *I got a loan from the bank at 10% interest per year.* • *Interest* **charges** *on an overdraft are high.* • *You should put the money in the building society where it will* **earn** *interest.* • Interest **rates** are the percentage at which interest is charged: *Interest* **rates** *have risen again.* • LP **Money**

in·ter·est LEGAL RIGHT /£'ɪn·tᵊr·est, $-t̬ɚ-/ *n* [C] an involvement or a legal right, usually relating to a business or possessions • *He is a multi-millionaire with business* *interests around the world.* • *(specialized) When they divorced she retained a legal interest in the property.*

in·ter·est·ed /£ɪn·tər·es·tɪd, $-t̬ɚ·es·t̬ɪd/ *adj* • *All interested* **parties** (= people who are involved with a matter or might get some benefit from it) *are advised to contact this office.*

in·ter·face /£ˈɪn·tə·feɪs, $-t̬ɚ-/ *n* a situation, way or area in which two things or groups can come together and have an effect on each other, or a connection between two electronic devices such as a computer and a printer • *We need more interface* **between** *management and the workforce.* [U] • *My computer has a network interface, which allows me to get to other computers.* [C] • *The new version of the program comes with a much better* **user** *interface* (= way of showing information to a user) *than the original.* [C]

in·ter·face *(obj)* /£ˈɪn·tə·feɪs, $-t̬ɚ-/ *v* • *The computers must be properly interfaced.* [T] • *What other equipment can you interface this laptop with?* [T] • *We've been told by the boss to interface on a regular basis and report our findings.* [I]

in·ter·fere /£ˌɪn·təˈfɪəʳ, $-t̬ɚˈfɪr/ *v* [I] to involve yourself in matters which are connected with other people when your involvement is neither wanted nor helpful • *I never try to stop them arguing in case they think I'm (Br) interfering* **between**/*(Am) interfering* **with** *them.* • *I'd never interfere (Br and Aus)* **between** *a husband and wife/ (Am)* **with** *a husband and wife.* • *Interfering* **in** *other people's relationships is always a mistake.* • If something or someone interferes **with** a situation or a process it spoils it or prevents its advancement: *She never had children because they would have interfered with her dancing career.* ○ *Even a low level of noise interferes with my concentration.* ○ *Someone has been interfering with my papers again* (= moving them around)*!* • *(Br)* To **interfere with** someone, esp. a child, is to touch or attack them sexually: *He was sent to prison for interfering with little boys.*

in·ter·fer·ence /£ˌɪn·təˈfɪə·rənts, $-t̬ɚˈfɪr·ənts/ *n* [U] • *She seems to regard any advice or help from me as interference.* • *The government's interference* **in** *the strike has been widely criticized.* • On a radio or television, interference is any sound, lines or colour etc. that comes from unwanted signals and prevents a clear sound or picture being received: *The radio's appalling in this car – there's so much interference I can't hear it properly.*

in·ter·fer·ing /£ˌɪn·təˈfɪə·rɪŋ, $-t̬ɚˈfɪr·ɪŋ/ *adj* [before n] *disapproving* • If someone is described as interfering they annoy other people by involving themselves in the matters of the other people when this is not wanted: *He's an interfering* **old busybody** *– it's none of his business!*

in·ter·fer·on /£ˌɪn·təˈfɪə·rɒn, $-t̬ɚˈfɪr·ɑːn/ *n* [C/U] *specialized* any of various PROTEINS in the body which are produced by cells as a reaction to infection by a virus

in·ter·ga·lac·tic /£ˌɪn·tə·gəˈlæk·tɪk, $-t̬ɚ-/ *adj* [before n; not gradable] between GALAXIES (= large groups of stars and other matter) • *intergalactic space*

in·ter·im /£ˈɪn·tər·ɪm, $-t̬ɚ-/ *adj* [before n; not gradable] temporary; intended for a short period only • *They're renting a flat as an interim measure until they are able to buy a house.* • *An interim* **government** *was set up for the period before the country's first free election.* • *The advisory committee has issued an interim* **report** *on the matter.*

in·ter·im /£ˈɪn·tər·ɪm, $-t̬ɚ-/ *n* [U] • *The new secretary starts in June, but* **in the** *interim* (= until then) *we're having to type our own letters.*

in·te·ri·or /£ɪnˈtɪə·ri·əʳ, $-ˈtɪr·i·ɚ/ *n* the inside part of something • *The estate agent had pictures of the house from the outside but none of its interior.* [C] • *The car's interior is very impressive – wonderful leather seats and a wooden dashboard.* [C] • The interior of a country or continent is the land which is furthest away from its outside or coast: *the African interior* [U] • In some countries **the** interior refers to the government department which deals with events and matters which are of importance to the country itself instead of events in other countries: *the Ministry of the Interior* [U] ○ *officials of the U.S. Interior Department* ○ *France's interior minister* • An **interior decorator** is a person whose job is either planning the decoration of the inside of a building such as a house or office or doing the decoration themselves. • **Interior design** is the art of planning the decoration of the inside of a building such as a house or office. A person who does this is called an **interior designer**. • Compare EXTERIOR.

in·te·ri·or /£ɪnˈtɪə·ri·əʳ, $-ˈtɪr·i·ɚ/ *adj* [before n; not gradable] • *The interior* (= inside) *walls have patches of damp on them.* • *The paintwork on the interior doors* (= those not in the outside wall of a building) *is in good condition.*

in·ter·ject *(obj)* /£ˌɪn·təˈdʒekt, $-t̬ɚ-/ *v fml* to interrupt, or to say (something) while another person is speaking • *He interjected several times during the conversation.* [I] • *"That's absolutely ridiculous!" Mary interjected, refusing to listen to the rest of his suggestions.* [+ clause]

in·ter·jec·tion /£ˌɪn·təˈdʒek·ʃən, $-t̬ɚ-/ *n* [C] *fml* • *Her controversial speech was punctuated with noisy interjections from the audience.* • In grammar an interjection is a word which is used to show a short sudden expression of emotion: *"Hey!" is an interjection.* • LP〉 **Exclamation mark**

in·ter·lace *obj* /£ˌɪn·təˈleɪs, $-t̬ɚ-/ *v* [T] to join (different parts) together to make a whole, esp. by crossing one thing over another or fitting one part into another • *In her latest book, she interlaces historical events* **with** *her own childhood memories.* • *The menu is mainly traditional French cooking, interlaced* **with** *some exotic dishes from further afield.* • *The nest was a framework of interlaced twigs plastered with mud or clay.*

in·ter·link *(obj)* /£ˌɪn·təˈlɪŋk, $-t̬ɚ-/ *v* to (cause to) join or connect together, with the parts joined often having an effect on each other • *In the battle against car crime, police forces across Europe are to interlink their databases on stolen cars.* [T] • *There was a building interlinking the farmhouse and cottage.* [T] • *Patterns of air pressure, surface winds and sea surface temperatures interlink.* [I] • *The disease is thought to be caused by a cluster of genes which interlink and work together in a complex way.* [I]

in·ter·linked /£ˌɪn·təˈlɪŋkt, $-t̬ɚ-/ *adj* • *The main point of his argument is that human rights are interlinked* **with** *the protection of the environment.* • *He claimed that unemployment, housing problems and crime are all interlinked.* • *A computer program which communicates with the user solely by providing choices from interlinked menus is said to be menu-driven.* • *The disease is thought to be caused by a cluster of interlinked genes, working together in a complex way.*

in·ter·link·ing /£ˌɪn·təˈlɪŋ·kɪŋ, $-t̬ɚ-/ *adj* [not gradable] • *There was an interlinking building between the farmhouse and cottage.*

in·ter·lock·ing /£ˌɪn·təˈlɒk·ɪŋ, $-t̬ɚˈlɑː·kɪŋ/ *adj* [not gradable] firmly joined together, esp. by one part fitting into another • *When paper is made, moisture is squeezed out of a wet mass leaving a web of dry, interlocking fibres.* • *The simplest and strongest framework is a system of interlocking triangles, similar to that we see supporting bridges and the roofs of houses.* • *The fish has strong jaws and sharp interlocking teeth.* • *The business is still dominated by a handful of powerful families and individuals, with interlocking interests.* • *The Olympic symbol of five interlocking rings was designed for the Games of 1920.*

in·ter·lock *(obj)* /£ˌɪn·təˈlɒk, $-t̬ɚˈlɑːk/ *v* • *She looked thoughtfully out of the window, with her fingers interlocked and pressed lightly against her mouth.* [T] • *The film interlocks an overview of American history* **with** *the life • stories of individual immigrant families.* [T] • *The decline of industry, the growth of low-paid, insecure employment and the rising population all interlock to trap young people in particular in a spiral of poverty and decline.* [I] • To interlock also means to connect in such a way that movement or change in one part causes movement or change in another: *In an increasingly interlocked world, we need to find global solutions to global problems.*

in·ter·lo·cu·tor /£ˌɪn·təˈlɒk·jʊ·təʳ, $-t̬ɚˈlɑː·kjə·t̬ɚ/ *n* [C] *fml* someone who is involved in a conversation • *In conversation he lacks any trace of self-importance, and defers constantly to the interlocutor.* • An interlocutor may also be involved in a conversation on behalf of someone else: *Abraham was able to act as interpreter and interlocutor for our group.* • *The intelligence agencies were instructed to identify potential interlocutors close to the terrorists.*

in·ter·lop·er /£ˈɪn·təˌləʊ·pəʳ, $-t̬ɚˌloʊ·pɚ/ *n* [C] *disapproving* someone who becomes involved in an activity or a social group without being asked, or enters a place without permission • *Some mothers angrily reported being made to feel like interlopers when they set foot in the school playground.* • *National borders will become blurred as more and more* **foreign** *interlopers move into their neighbours' most profitable businesses.* • *The security did not prevent an interloper getting on to the stage at the opening ceremony and making a speech in support of the* *local farmers. • Why these interlopers selected this farm is unclear, but their simple robbery was to go horribly wrong.*

in·ter·lude /£ˈɪn·tə·luːd, $-t̬ɚ-/ *n* [C] a brief period when a situation or activity is different from what comes before and after it • *To increase the audiences for their films, directors often add* **brief** *interludes of violence or sex that have very little to do with the story.* • *Except for a brief Christian interlude at the beginning of the 11th century, Istanbul has been a Muslim city for almost 1300 years.* • *A day in Versailles is a relaxing interlude during a hectic week in Paris.* • *The musical interludes don't really fit in with the rest of the play.*

in·ter·mar·riage /£ˌɪn·təˈmær·ɪdʒ, $-t̬ɚˈmer-/ *n* [U] marriage between people who are either from different social groups, races or religions, or are from the same family • *Have ethnic tensions in the area been reduced by intermarriage?* • *Intermarriage* **between** *close relatives is prohibited in most societies.*

in·ter·mar·ry /£ˌɪn·təˈmær·i, $-t̬ɚˈmer-/ *v* [I] • *Many of the immigrants have intermarried* **with** *the island's original inhabitants.* • *Brothers and sisters are not allowed to intermarry in case their children are born with genetic defects.*

in·ter·me·di·a·ry /£ˌɪn·təˈmiː·di·ə·ri, $-t̬ɚ-/ *n* [C] someone who carries messages between people who are unwilling or unable to meet personally • *The gunman refused to talk to the police directly, so they had to negotiate* **through** *an intermediary.* • *The former president has agreed to act as an intermediary* **between** *the government and guerrillas fighting for regional independence.* • *Insurance brokers are intermediaries* **between** *insurance companies and their customers.*

in·ter·me·di·ate /£ˌɪn·təˈmiː·di·ət, $-t̬ɚ-/ *adj* [not gradable] being between two other related things, levels or points • *Three levels of waste are produced: low, intermediate and high.* • *This novel is too difficult for intermediate students of English, but advanced ones should be able to cope with it.* • *Eventually we hope to be making profits of £100 000 a year, but our intermediate target is £60 000.* • *It is a vegetation zone intermediate* **between** *desert and savannah conditions, where rainfall is irregular and unpredictable.* • *(Am)* An **intermediate school** is a school for students who are 12 to 14 years old. It can also be a school for students who are 10 to 12 years old.

in·ter·ment /£ɪnˈtɜː·mənt, $-ˈtɜːr-/ *n* See at INTER

in·ter·mez·zo /£ˌɪn·təˈmet·səʊ, $-t̬ɚˈmet·soʊ/ *n* [C] *pl* **intermezzos** or **intermezzi** /£ˌɪn·təˈmet·si, $-t̬ɚ-/ a short piece of music written to be played on its own or as part of a longer piece

in·ter·min·a·ble /£ɪnˈtɜː·mɪ·nə·bl̩, $-ˈtɜːr-/ *adj* continuing for too long and seeming never to end • *The new government has promised an end to the food shortages and interminable queues for basic household items.* • Interminable also means annoying or uninteresting because continuing for too long: *After it ceased to be a hospital there followed the usual interminable saga of what to do with the building.* ○ *Our resident bore was stirred by the remark into one of his interminable stories of his youth.*

in·ter·min·a·bly /£ɪnˈtɜː·mɪ·nə·bli, $-ˈtɜːr-/ *adv* • *The managing director made an interminably long after-dinner speech.*

in·ter·min·gle /£ˌɪn·təˈmɪŋ·gl̩, $-t̬ɚˈ-/ *v* [I] to become mixed together • *The flavours of the ingredients intermingle to produce a very unusual taste.* • *Fact and fiction are intermingled throughout the book.* • *It is because ethnic and religious groups are so intermingled that re-drawing of borders seems impossible.* • *Their life stories are told through a collection of poems intermingled* **with** *song and dance.*

in·ter·mis·sion /£ˌɪn·təˈmɪʃ·ən, $-t̬ɚ-/ *n* [C] a brief period between the parts of a performance or *(Am also)* a period between parts of a game when the performers or players can rest and people watching can leave their seats • *(Am) After nearly defeating itself in the first half, the team did little wrong after the intermission and rallied to win 21-14.* • In Britain and Australia an intermission is esp. the brief period between two parts of a show in a cinema: *There will be two fifteen-minute intermissions during the show.*

in·ter·mit·tent /£ˌɪn·təˈmɪt·ənt, $-t̬ɚˈmɪt̬-/ *adj* not happening regularly or continuously; stopping and starting repeatedly or with long periods in between • *Tomorrow will be sunny in the south, but there will be intermittent rain in the north.* • *Although she made intermittent movie appearances, she will be best remembered for her role in the long-running TV comedy series.*

in·ter·mit·tent·ly /£ˌɪn·təˈmɪt·ənt·li, $-t̬ɚˈmɪt̬-/ *adv* • *There was a problem with the heating and hot water was only available intermittently.* • *We've discussed this problem intermittently, but so far we've failed to come up with a solution.*

in·tern *obj* PUNISH /£ɪnˈtɜːn, $-ˈtɜːrn/ *v* [T] to put in prison for political or military reasons • *The brothers were interned for the duration of the war because they were thought to pose a threat to national security.* • *Many academics and intellectuals were interned after the military coup.*

in·tern·ee /£ˌɪn·tɜːˈniː, $-tɜːr-/ *n* [C] • An internee is a person who has been put in prison for political or military reasons: *The Geneva Convention states that internees should not be treated in the same way as prisoners of war.*

in·tern·ment /£ɪnˈtɜːn·mənt, $-ˈtɜːrn-/ *n* [U] • *Security chiefs believe that the internment of 150 suspected terrorists would bring a rapid end to the violence.* • *These men had been held in internment* **camps** *during the war.*

in·tern STUDENT /£ˈɪn·tɜːn, $-tɜːrn/ *n* [C] *esp. Am* someone who is finishing their training for a skilled job esp. in medicine or teaching by obtaining practical experience of the work involved • *a hospital intern* • *Interns learn a lot from working alongside experienced teachers in the classroom.* • *She joined The Washington Post as a* **summer** *intern.*

in·tern /£ɪnˈtɜːn, $-ˈtɜːrn/ *v* [I] *Am* • *He is a Moscow attorney who will intern for six months with a San Francisco firm.*

in·tern·ship /£ɪnˈtɜːn·ʃɪp, $-ˈtɜːrn-/ *n* [C] *Am* • *He served his internship at Garfield Hospital.* • *Jane has a* **summer** *internship at a local TV station.*

in·ter·nal /£ɪnˈtɜː·nəl, $-ˈtɜːr-/ *adj* [not gradable] existing or happening inside a person, object, organization, place or country • *The bullet passed through his back and several internal* **organs** *and he died later in hospital.* • *The bank says it will conduct its own internal* **investigation** *into the disappearance of the money.* • *An internal (Am also* **inter-office)** **memo** *leaked to the press indicates that there had been concern about safety standards before the accident.* • *The removal of internal* **trade barriers** *in the European Union was expected to create between five and six million jobs.* • *The union's campaign against the factory closure has been hampered by its internal* **squabbles** *about the action it should take.* • *The international community is increasingly willing to intervene in the internal* **affairs** (=political activities within a country) *of countries where there is serious abuse of human rights.* • *The parent company has so far refused to involve itself in a dispute which it regards as being internal* **to** *its subsidiary.* • An **internal combustion engine** is an engine which produces energy by burning fuel within itself: *The internal combustion engine can run on almost anything that is flammable.* • *(Am)* **Internal medicine** is the part of medical science that is involved in the discovery of illnesses inside the body and the treatment of them without cutting the body open. • The **Internal Revenue Service** (*abbreviation* **IRS**) is the government department which collects most national taxes in the United States. • See also INTERIOR. Compare EXTERNAL.

in·ter·nal·ly /£ɪnˈtɜː·nəl·i, $-ˈtɜːr-/ *adv* [not gradable] • *This medicine is for external use only and should not be taken internally.* • *The latest nose reshaping techniques allow treatment to be carried out internally, thus avoiding any possibility of external marks.* • *It's cheaper to develop our software internally* (= in our own company) *than to pay another company to do it.*

in·ter·nal·ize *obj, Br and Aus usually* **-ise** /£ɪnˈtɜː·nəl·aɪz, $-ˈtɜːr-/ *v* [T] to accept or absorb (esp. a way of behaving or thinking) as your own, often from repeated experience, so that it becomes a natural and important part of your character • *He had not expected the people so readily to internalize the values of democracy and to develop a strong rejection of the values of a totalitarian system.* • *There is some evidence to suggest that children who are abused by their parents internalize violent behaviour through social learning and in turn are violent towards their children.* • To internalize is also to absorb feelings within yourself and not to express them to other people: *"I internalized a lot of the pressures at the New Yorker in those early years," he says.* ○ *Women tend to internalize all their anxiety and distress – men hit out.*

in·ter·nal·i·za·tion, *Br and Aus usually* **–i·sa·tion** /£ɪn ˌtɜː·nəl·aɪˈzeɪ·ʃən, $-ˌtɜːr-/ *n* [U] • *By internalization I mean ways in which people draw from their past and present experiences of the social world.*

in·ter·na·tion·al /£ˌɪn·təˈnæʃ·ən·əl, $-t̬ɚ-/ *adj* involving more than one country • *It is doubtful whether an international peace conference would resolve the conflict.* • *Thousands have already died of starvation and international relief organizations say a million others are threatened.* • *America's lead in international* **affairs** *at the time included the setting-up of the United Nations, NATO, the Bretton Woods monetary system and a network of alliances across the globe.* • *The province declared independence several years ago but remains unrecognized by* **the international community** (=other countries). • The **International Date Line** is an imaginary line between the most northern and southern points on the Earth which goes through the Pacific Ocean. The date on the west side of the line is one day earlier than the date on the east side of the line. • **International law** is the set of rules that most countries obey when dealing with other countries: *The use of chemical weapons is a violation of international law.* • The **International Monetary Fund** is the full name of the IMF: *Poland and the International Monetary Fund reached agreement on the terms for a $1 billion loan.* • The **International Phonetic Alphabet** is the full name of the IPA: *In this dictionary, pronunciations are shown in the International Phonetic Alphabet.*

in·ter·na·tion·al /£ˌɪn·təˈnæʃ·ən·əl, $-t̬ɚ-/ *n* [C] *Br* • An international is a sports event involving more than one country, or a person who competes in it: *Pakistan will play five one-day internationals* (=games of cricket lasting only one day) *in India this autumn.* ○ *The newspaper report alleged that six rugby internationals* (=players) *had taken drugs to improve their performance.*

in·ter·na·tion·al·ly /£ˌɪn·təˈnæʃ·ən·əl·i, $-t̬ɚ-/ *adv* [not gradable] • *Her internationally acclaimed novel has won several literary prizes.* • *The hospital's internationally renowned heart transplant unit is threatened with closure.* • *The new government has not been internationally recognized.* • *The results of the research will be available to other police forces both nationally and internationally.*

in·ter·na·tion·al·ize *obj*, *Br and Aus usually* **–ise** /£ˌɪn·təˈnæʃ·ən·əl·aɪz, $-t̬ɚ-/ *v* [T] • *They are trying to internationalize the civil war in the hope that diplomatic or military action from outside will bring a peaceful solution.* • *The hole in the ozone layer is a global problem and we need to internationalize the response to it.* • *Bob Marley internationalized reggae, making it known throughout the world.*

in·ter·na·tion·a·liz·a·tion, *Br and Aus usually* **–i·sa·tion** /£ˌɪn·təˌnæʃ·ən·əl·aɪˈzeɪ·ʃən, $-t̬ɚ-/ *n* [U] • *The internationalization of economic affairs has weakened the power of individual governments.*

in·ter·na·tion·al·i·sm /£ˌɪn·təˈnæʃ·ən·əl·ɪ·zəm, $-t̬ɚ-/ *n* [U] • Internationalism is the state of being international, or occurring in and between many countries: *the increasing internationalism of criminals* • Internationalism is also the belief that countries can benefit more by working together and trying to understand each other than by arguing and fighting wars with each other.

in·ter·na·tion·a·list /£ˌɪn·təˈnæʃ·ən·əl·ɪst, $-t̬ɚ-/ *n* [C] • An internationalist works for peaceful agreement between countries: *She was a true internationalist who devoted her whole life to the cause of peace through her work for the United Nations.*

In·ter·na·tion·a·le /£ˌɪn·təˌnæʃ·əˈnɑːl, $-t̬ɚ-/ *n* [U] **the Internationale** a song which is sung by people who believe in COMMUNISM (=the system that gives everyone the right to an equal share in the wealth of their country) • *The conference ended with everyone singing the Internationale.*

in·ter·ne·cine /£ˌɪn·təˈniː·saɪn, $-t̬ɚˈniː·sɪn/ *adj* [not gradable] *fml* involving military fighting or serious disagreement between members of the same group, religion or country • *The island has been torn by internecine* **strife/conflict**, *and the fighting between north and south has been only part of it.* • *The current internecine* **war/warfare** *in the vegetarian and vegan worlds shows no sign of ceasing.*

in·ter·nee /£ˌɪn·tɜːˈniː, $-tɜːr-/ *n* [C] See at INTERN [PUNISH]

in·ter·net /£ˈɪn·tə·net, $-t̬ɚ-/ *n* [U] **the Internet** the large system of many connected computers around the world which people use to communicate with each other • *I heard about the new development* **on** *the Internet.*

in·tern·ment /£ɪnˈtɜːn·mənt, $-ˈtɜːrn-/ *n* [U] See at INTERN [PUNISH]

in·tern·ship /£ɪnˈtɜːn·ʃɪp, $-ˈtɜːrn-, ˈ---/ *n* [C] See at INTERN [STUDENT]

in·ter·per·son·al /£ˌɪn·təˈpɜː·sən·əl, $-t̬ɚˈpɜːr-/ *adj* [not gradable] connected with relationships between people • *The successful applicant will have excellent interpersonal* **skills**. • *Harmonious interpersonal relationships are very important in creating a good working atmosphere.*

in·ter·plan·e·ta·ry /£ˌɪn·təˈplæn·ɪ·tri, $-ter·i/ *adj* [before n; not gradable] between planets • *Interplanetary travel is only possible for unmanned spacecraft.*

in·ter·play /£ˈɪn·tə·pleɪ, $-t̬ɚ-/ *n* [U] the effect that two or more things have on each other • *Permission to build the factory has been delayed by the complex interplay* **between** *industrial and environmental interests.* • *The interplay* **of** *economic forces makes it difficult to predict accurately the likely effect of the tax changes.*

Inter·pol /£ˈɪn·tə·pɒl, $-t̬ɚ·puːl/ *n* [not after *the*] an organization involving the police forces of more than 100 countries whose main activity is fighting international crime • *British police are cooperating with Interpol in their search for the child who is thought to have been smuggled into mainland Europe by her father.*

in·ter·po·late *(obj)* /£ɪnˈtɜː·pə·leɪt, $-ˈtɜːr-/ *v fml* to add (words) to a speech, text or a conversation • *It would help our readers to understand the technical terms if we interpolated some explanations* **into** *the text.* [T] • *(esp. literary) "That happened in Rome, not Paris!" Sam interpolated* (=interrupted). [+ clause]

in·ter·pol·a·tion /£ɪnˌtɜː·pəˈleɪ·ʃən, $-ˌtɜːr-/ *n* • *Dorothy Rose has edited this book, supplying a foreword and informed interpolations in the text.* [C] • *During a comic introductory chorus, he was supposed to step forward with the shouted interpolation, 'Oh, Mrs Gibson!'* [C] • *The writer did not sympathize with the interpolation* **of** *religion into affairs of state.* [U]

in·ter·pose *obj* [PUT BETWEEN] /£ˌɪn·təˈpəʊz, $-t̬ɚˈpoʊz/ *v* [T] *fml* to put (something) between two things, people or groups, esp. in order to stop them doing something • *Neighbouring countries should assemble an armed peace force that could be interposed between the warring factions.*

in·ter·pose [INTERRUPT] /£ˌɪn·təˈpəʊz, $-t̬ɚˈpoʊz/ *v fml, esp. literary* to interrupt; to speak while someone else is speaking • *"I can't agree with you, Mr Heathcliff," he interposed.* [+ clause]

in·ter·po·si·tion /£ˌɪn·tə·pəˈzɪʃ·ən, $-t̬ɚ-/ *n*

in·ter·pret *obj* [FIND MEANING] /£ɪnˈtɜː·prɪt, $-ˈtɜːr-/ *v* [T] to decide what the intended meaning of (something) is • *It's difficult to interpret these statistics without knowing how they were obtained.* • *A jury should not interpret the silence of a defendant* **as** *a sign of guilt.* • *Many people are interpreting the minister's statement* **as** *meaning that she intends to resign.* • (CS) (PL)

in·ter·pre·ta·tion /£ɪnˌtɜː·prɪˈteɪ·ʃən, $-ˌtɜːr-/ *n* • *The dispute is based on two widely differing interpretations of the law.* [C] • *What interpretation would you* **put on** *their refusal to attend the meeting?* [C] • *The rules are vague and* **open to** *interpretation* (=able to be understood in a different way). [U] • *It is difficult for many people to accept a* **literal** *interpretation of the Bible.* [C] • *His interpretation of the regulations is often too broad and flexible.* [U]

in·ter·pre·ta·tive /£ɪnˈtɜː·prɪ·tə·tɪv, $-ˈtɜːr·prə·t̬ə·t̬ɪv/, **in·ter·pre·tive** /£ɪnˈtɜː·prɪ·tɪv, $-ˈtɜːr·prə·t̬ɪv/ *adj fml* • *The book would be more useful if it was interpretative, but instead it presents a lot of facts and figures without explaining them.*

in·ter·pret *obj* [EXPRESS] /£ɪnˈtɜː·prɪt, $-ˈtɜːr-/ *v* [T] to express your own ideas about the intended meaning of (esp. a play or a piece of music) when performing it • *If Shakespeare's plays are to reach a large audience they need to be interpreted in a modern style.* • (CS) (PL)

in·ter·pret·er /£ɪnˈtɜː·prɪ·təʳ, $-ˈtɜːr·prɪ·t̬ɚ/ *n* [C] • *Firkusny, a native of Czechoslovakia, has long been acclaimed as a supreme interpreter of that country's music.* • *The Living History Foundation is a group of* **'historic** *interpreters' who dress up in period costumes at historic sites in Virginia, Maryland and the District.*

in·ter·pre·ta·tion /£ɪnˌtɜː·prɪˈteɪ·ʃən, $-ˌtɜːr·prɪˈt̬eɪ-/ *n* • *Their interpretations of Romeo and Juliet were two of the best performances I have ever seen.* [C] • *Interpretation is often as important as the text itself.* [U]

in·ter·pret *(obj)* BETWEEN LANGUAGES /£ɪn'tɜː·prɪt, $-'tɜːr-/ *v* to express (something that has just been said) in a different language so that people who do not speak each other's languages can understand each other • *The president's speech was interpreted rather inaccurately.* [T] • *The two leaders don't understand a word of each other's languages, so they have to have someone there to interpret.* [I] • Compare TRANSLATE. • (CS) (PL)

in·ter·pret·er /£ɪn'tɜː·prɪ·tər, $-'tɜːr·prɪ·t̬ɚ/ *n* [C] • *She works as an interpreter in Brussels.* • **Speaking through an** *interpreter, the president said the terms of the ceasefire were completely unacceptable.* • An interpreter is also a computer program that changes the instructions in another program one at a time into a form that can be easily understood by a computer. The computer performs each instruction as soon as it has been changed rather than waiting until all the instructions have been changed.

in·ter·ra·cial /£ˌɪn·tə'reɪ·ʃəl, $-t̬ɚ-/ *adj* [not gradable] involving different human races • *an interracial marriage/relationship* • *The government must act to stamp out interracial hatred and violence.*

in·ter·reg·num /£ˌɪn·tə'reg·nəm, $-t̬ɚ-/ *n* [C] *pl* **interregnums** or **interregna** /£ˌɪn·tə'reg·nə, $-t̬ɚ-/ *fml* a period when a country or organization lacks a leader • *After a brief interregnum, a new president was installed.* • *Following the ambassador's sudden death, there was an interregnum of several weeks before a successor was appointed.*

in·ter·re·late /£ˌɪn·tə·rɪ'leɪt, $-t̬ɚ-/ *v* [I] to be connected in such a way that each thing has an effect on or depends on the other • *Children need to be educated about the way that diet and health interrelate.*

in·ter·re·lat·ed /£ˌɪn·tə·rɪ'leɪ·tɪd, $-t̬ɚ·rɪ'leɪ·t̬ɪd/ *adj* [not gradable] • *interrelated problems/issues/activities* • *These events, although separate in time, are all interrelated and connected in various ways.* • *The problems of the environment are closely interrelated* **with** *our current way of life.*

in·ter·re·la·tion /£ˌɪn·tə·rɪ'leɪ·ʃən, $-t̬ɚ-/, **in·ter·re·la·tion·ship** /£ˌɪn·tə·rɪ'leɪ·ʃən·ʃɪp, $-t̬ɚ-/ *n* • *There is an indisputable interrelation* **between** *smoking and respiratory diseases.* [C] • *Population growth and economic development is a matter of complex interrelation.* [U]

in·ter·ro·gate *obj* /ɪn'ter·ə·geɪt/ *v* [T] to ask (someone) a lot of questions in a formal situation such as a police station or a law court, sometimes using extreme mental or physical pressure to obtain information • *The airport police who interrogated the girl concluded that she was innocent and hadn't known about the drugs.* • *Investigating officers would visit the claimant's home and interrogate neighbours to check that he or she was not concealing anything.* • *Thousands of dissidents have been interrogated or imprisoned in recent weeks.* • If you interrogate a computer, you obtain information from it: *The system uses an ordinary telephone for electronic mail, home banking and interrogating computer databases.*

in·ter·ro·ga·tion /ɪnˌter·ə'geɪ·ʃən/ *n* • *One by one the group were taken for interrogation.* [U] • *Many refugees have reported seeing mass executions and brutal interrogations.* [C] • *The Red Cross was only allowed to visit the prisoners after they had been transferred from the interrogation* **rooms.**

in·ter·ro·gat·or /£ɪn'ter·ə·geɪ·tər, $-t̬ɚ/ *n* [C] • *He never saw his interrogators because he was always blindfolded.*

in·ter·ro·ga·tive /£ˌɪn·tə'rɒg·ə·tɪv, $-t̬ə'rɑː·gə·t̬ɪv/ *n, adj* [not gradable] *specialized* (a word or the form of a sentence that is) used when asking a question • *an interrogative adverb* • *'Who' and 'why' are interrogatives.* [C] • *If you put a sentence into* **the** *interrogative, you turn it into a question.* [U]

in·ter·rupt *(obj)* /£ˌɪn·tə'rʌpt, $-t̬ə-/ *v* to stop (a person) from speaking for a short period by something you say or do, or to stop something from happening for a short period • *She tried to explain what had happened but he interrupted her several times.* [T] • *Her speech received an enthusiastic reception and was interrupted repeatedly by cheers and applause.* [T] • *I'd like to return to what I was saying before I was so* **rudely** *interrupted.* [T] • *I wish you'd stop interrupting.* [I] • *I had to interrupt my meal* (= stop it for a short period) *to answer the phone.* [T] • *We had to interrupt our trip* (= stop it) *when we heard John's mother was ill.* [T]

in·ter·rup·tion /£ˌɪn·tə'rʌp·ʃən, $-t̬ə-/ *n* • *We'd like to apologize for the brief interruption in transmission earlier this evening.* [C] • *Blocked arteries cause interruptions in the blood supply and damage to the heart.* [C] • *I wish it was possible to work without interruption in this office.* [U]

in·ter·schol·as·tic /£ˌɪn·tə·skɒ'læs·tɪk, $-t̬ɚ·skə-/ *adj* [before n; not gradable] *Am* involving two or more schools • *the Massachusetts Interscholastic Athletic Association*

in·ter·sect *(obj)* /£ˌɪn·tə'sekt, $-t̬ɚ-/ *v* to cross (esp. one straight line over another) • *Two diagonal lines drawn from opposite corners of a square intersect at its centre.* [I] • *The transport system is very efficient and the bus routes intersect conveniently* **with** *the railway network.* [I] • *The accident caused a traffic jam along a busy stretch of road where the expressway intersects the highway.* [T] • To intersect is also to divide an area into smaller parts by crossing it with straight lines: *The gardens are intersected by gravel paths.* [T]

in·ter·sec·tion /£'ɪn·təˌsek·ʃən, $-t̬ɚ-/ *n* • *The intersection of the lines on the graph marks the point where we start to make a profit.* [C] • *(esp. Am) Times Square in New York is formed by the intersection* **of** *Broadway with Seventh Avenue and 42nd Street.* [C] • *(esp. Am and Aus) She died of head injuries after she was hit by a car as she crossed a busy intersection* (= place where two roads join or cross each other). [C]

in·ter·sperse *obj* /£ˌɪn·tə'spɜːs, $-t̬ɚ'spɜːrs/ *v* [T] to mix one thing in with another in an irregular way • *The documentary intersperses the author's own experience of travel in the area* **with** *recent news pictures.* • *The arrival of great plates of food was interspersed* **with** *brief and witty speeches.* • *Next morning, interspersed* **among** *the music, the presenter read more letters and rhymes on the theme from listeners.* • *Interspersed* **between** *items for the orchestra or the trio were his solos, which he presented confidently.* • *A more thorough description of the method is needed at the beginning of the report rather than being interspersed* **throughout** *the text.*

in·ter·state /£ˌɪn·tə'steɪt, $'ɪn·t̬ɚ·steɪt/ *adj* [before n; not gradable] involving two or more of the STATES (= areas with their own government) into which some large countries are divided • *the interstate highway system* • *interstate banking legislation* • *interstate road transport costs*

in·ter·state /£ˌɪn·tə'steɪt, $'ɪn·t̬ɚ·steɪt/ *n* [C] • An interstate is a fast wide road which connects important cities in the United States.

in·ter·stel·lar /£ˌɪn·tə'stel·ər, $-t̬ɚ'stel·ɚ, £*also* '— *when attributive*/ adj [before n; not gradable] between the stars • *The edge of the solar system is where the sun's influence ends and cold interstellar* **space** *begins.*

in·ter·stice /£ɪn'tɜː·stɪs, $-'tɜːr-/ *n* [C usually pl] *fml* a very small crack or space • *The wall was old and crumbling with plants growing in the interstices* **between/in/of** *the bricks.*

in·ter·twine *(obj)* /£ˌɪn·tə'twaɪn, $-t̬ɚ-/ *v* to twist or be twisted together, or to be connected so as to be difficult to separate • *The town's prosperity is* **inextricably** *intertwined* **with** *the fortunes of the factory.* [T] • *The trees' branches intertwined to form a dark roof over the path.* [I] • *These bacteria have a tough outer shell made of intertwined sugar molecules.* [T] • *The film's storyline is built up from several intertwining plots.*

in·ter·val SPACE /£'ɪn·tə·vəl, $-t̬ɚ-/ *n* [C] a period between two events or times, or the space between two points • *We see each other at* **regular** *intervals – usually about once a month.* • *In the event of fire, the alarm will sound* **at** *15-second* **intervals/at intervals of** *15 seconds.* • *Will we have enough space for our coats if I put the hooks on the door* **at** *five-centimetre* **intervals?** • *There's often a long interval* **between** *an author completing a book and it appearing in the shops.* • *(Br)* An interval (*Am and Aus* **intermission**) is also a brief period between the parts of a performance or (**intermission**) a period between parts of the game when the performers or players can rest and the people watching can leave their seats: *There will be two twenty-minute intervals during the opera.* ○ *He scored his first goal of the match three minutes after the interval.*

in·ter·val MUSIC /£'ɪn·tə·vəl, $-t̬ɚ-/ *n* [C] the amount by which one note is higher or lower than another • *an interval of a 5th* (= the top note four notes higher than the bottom one)

in·ter·vene GET INVOLVED /£ˌɪn·tə'viːn, $-t̬ɚ-/ *v* [I] to become involved, intentionally, in a difficult situation in order to improve it or prevent it from getting worse • *At first we were just watching events rather than intervening to shape their course.* • *I didn't feel I could intervene* **in** *a family* *dispute.* • *The Central Bank intervened* **in** *the currency markets today to try to stabilize the exchange rate.* • *(disapproving) Several people thought it likely that the company was intervening* (= becoming involved in a way that is not wanted or helpful) **in** *French politics.* • *There is no possibility of this country intervening* **militarily**. • *The Minister intervened* **personally** *when she found out the museum was threatened with closure.* • *The management refused to investigate the matter, so the union intervened* **on** *my* **behalf**.

in·ter·ven·tion /£ˌɪn·təˈven·ʃᵊn, $-t̬ɚ-/ *n* • *Half the people questioned said they were opposed to* **military** *intervention (***in** *the civil war).* [U] • *Repeated interventions on the currency markets have failed to prevent the value of the currency falling.* [C]

in·ter·ven·tion·ist /£ˌɪn·təˈven·ʃᵊn·ɪst, $-t̬ɚ-/ *adj* [not gradable] • Individuals, esp. politicians, who are interventionist want to try to control the way in which events happen: *The new government has an interventionist economic policy and is determined to cut unemployment by 50%.* ○ *The President has decided to concentrate on domestic policy and take a less interventionist role in foreign affairs.*

in·ter·ven·tion·i·sm /£ˌɪn·təˈven·ʃᵊn·ɪ·zᵊm, $-t̬ɚ-/ *n* [U] • *Critics point to the lack of success of UN interventionism in recent years.*

in·ter·vene COME BETWEEN /£ˌɪn·təˈviːn, $-t̬ɚ-/ *v* [I] to happen between two times or between other events or activities • *Two decades intervened* **between** *the completion of the design and the opening of the theatre.* • *The minister abandoned her holiday plans when a surprise general election intervened.*

in·ter·ven·ing /£ˌɪn·təˈviː·nɪŋ, $-t̬ɚ-/ *adj* [before n; not gradable] • *It was a long time since my last visit to Berlin, and it had changed dramatically in the intervening* **period/years**.

in·ter·view *obj* /£ˈɪn·tə·vjuː, $-t̬ɚ-/ *v* [T] to ask (a person) a series of questions in a formal situation, usually in order to obtain information about them • *We've had 200 applicants for the job, but we only plan to interview about 20 of them.* • *Who's the most famous person you've ever interviewed on TV?* • *(Br)* The police often interview (*esp. Am* **question**) people who are thought to be involved in a crime: *Police are still interviewing a man in connection with the robberies.*

in·ter·view /£ˈɪn·tə·vjuː, $-t̬ɚ-/ *n* [C] • *He didn't* **even** *get an interview* **for** *the job, so he was very disappointed.* • *The opinion poll was based on telephone interviews* **with** *a representative sample of 1000 voters.* • **In** *a television interview last night she denied she had any intention of resigning.* • *He was very nervous before he* **had** *his job interview.* • *The last interview that she* **gave** *was recorded the day before she died.*

in·ter·view·ee /£ˌɪn·tə·vjuˈiː, $-t̬ɚ-/ *n* [C] • An interviewee is a person who is asked questions during an interview: *Practically every chat show interviewee has a new book or film to promote these days.* ○ *We try to make interviewees feel as relaxed as possible.*

in·ter·view·er /£ˈɪn·tə·vjuː·əʳ, $-t̬ɚ·vjuː·ɚ/ *n* [C] • An interviewer is the person who asks the questions during an interview: *I wish television interviewers would make politicians answer their questions properly.* ○ *He has told several interviewers that he has no intention of apologizing for his comments.*

in·ter·weave *obj* /£ˌɪn·təˈwiːv, $-t̬ɚ-/ *v* [T] *past simple* **interwove** /£ˌɪn·təˈwəʊv, $-t̬ɚˈwoʊv/, *past part* **interwoven** /£ˌɪn·təˈwəʊ·vᵊn, $-t̬ɚˈwoʊ-/ to weave together or combine (two or more things) so that they cannot be separated easily • *She has created an intriguing story by skillfully interweaving fictional and historical events.* • *Young children peer out from huts of cardboard, interwoven* **with** *tree branches and dried grass.*

in·tes·tate /ɪnˈtes·teɪt/ *adj* [after v; not gradable] *specialized* not having left instructions about who should be given your property when you die • *Many people* **die** *intestate because they thought they were too young to make a will.*

in·tes·tine /ɪnˈtes·tɪn/ *n* [C] (either of the two parts of) a long tube through which food travels from the stomach and out of the body while it is being digested • *Antibodies from the mother's milk line the baby's intestine and prevent infection.*

in·tes·tines /ɪnˈtes·tɪnz/ *pl n* • *He had something wrong with his intestines* (= intestine).

in·tes·ti·nal /ɪnˈtes·tɪ·nəl, ˌɪn·tesˈtaɪ-/ *adj* [not gradable] • *He died from a heart attack while recovering from intestinal surgery.* • *(Am)* **Intestinal fortitude** is bravery and determination: *The fact that he's still trying for the championship is a tribute to his intestinal fortitude.*

in·ti·mate PERSONAL /£ˈɪn·tɪ·mət, $-t̬ə-/ *adj* having, or being likely to cause, a very close friendship or personal or sexual relationship • *He had difficulty with intimate* **relationships** *and never married.* • *The restaurant has a very intimate* **atmosphere** *and is the perfect setting for a romantic dinner.* • *He's become very intimate* **with** *an actress.*

in·ti·mate /£ˈɪn·tɪ·mət, $-t̬ə-/ *n* [C] • *Intimates* (= Close friends) *of the star say that he has been upset by the personal attacks on him that have appeared in the press recently.*

in·ti·ma·cy /£ˈɪn·tɪ·mə·si, $-t̬ə-/ *n* • Intimacy is a close personal relationship: *Intimacy between teachers and students is not recommended.* [U] • Intimacies are things which are said or done only by people who have a close relationship with each other: *It was obvious from their witty intimacies that they had been good friends for many years.* [C usually pl]

in·ti·mate·ly /£ˈɪn·tɪ·mət·li, $-t̬ə/ *adv* • *Well, I know who she is although I'm not intimately* (= closely) **acquainted** *with her.* • *In an exclusive interview she will be talking intimately* (= giving personal information) *about her turbulent love life.*

in·ti·mate EXPERT /£ˈɪn·tɪ·mət, $-t̬ə-/ *adj* expert, detailed and obtained from a lot of studying or experience • *She has an intimate* **knowledge** *of Tuscany, where she has lived for twenty years.*

in·ti·mate·ly /£ˈɪn·tɪ·mət·li, $-t̬ə-/ *adv* • *She's been intimately* **involved** *in the project since it began, so she ought to know a lot about it.*

in·ti·mate *obj* SUGGEST /£ˈɪn·tɪ·meɪt, $-t̬ə-/ *v* [T] *fml* to make clear (what you think or want) without stating it directly • *She lit another cigarette and he intimated his disapproval by coughing loudly.* • *She has intimated* **that** *she will resign if she loses the vote.* [+ *that* clause]

in·ti·ma·tion /£ˌɪn·tɪˈmeɪ·ʃᵊn, $-t̬əˈ-/ *n fml* • *His suicide attempt was the first intimation* **of** *how depressed he was.* [C] • *I find your intimation* **that** *I have been been dishonest deeply offensive.* [C + *that* clause]

in·ti·ma·tions /£ˌɪn·tɪˈmeɪ·ʃᵊnz, $-t̬əˈ-/ *pl n* • *The appearance of bunches of violets in the shops provides intimations* (= an intimation) **of** *spring in the wettest and darkest weeks of the year.* • *Watching the children play he was seized with intimations* (= an intimation) **of** *his own* **mortality**. • *"Intimations of Immortality"* (title of a poem by William Wordsworth, 1807)

in·ti·mi·date *obj* /ɪnˈtɪm·ɪ·deɪt/ *v* [T] to frighten or threaten (someone), usually in order to persuade them to do something against their wishes • *They were intimidated* **into** *accepting a pay cut by the threat of losing their jobs.*

in·ti·mi·da·tion /ɪnˌtɪm·ɪˈdeɪ·ʃᵊn/ *n* [U] • *The campaign of violence and intimidation* **against** *them intensifies daily.* • *The police investigation into the murder has been hampered by* **the intimidation** *of key witnesses.*

in·ti·mi·dat·ing /£ɪnˈtɪm·ɪ·deɪ·tɪŋ, $-t̬ɪŋ/ *adj* • *an intimidating show of force* • *an intimidating array of weapons* • *an intimidating atmosphere* • *an intimidating person/figure* • *an intimidating manner* • *She can be very intimidating when she's angry.* • *(fig.) All this extra work is rather intimidating.*

into INSIDE /ˈɪn·tuː/ *prep* towards the inside or middle of something and about to be contained, surrounded or enclosed by it • *Would you put the jar back into the cupboard for me, please?* • *It's lovely and sunny outside. Shall we go into the garden?* • *Stop running around and get into bed!* • *I can't get into these trousers anymore. They're far too small for me.* • *Sometimes we have to work late into the evening.* • *The demonstrators* **burst** *into the building and took over the television station.* • *The Baltic states were* **incorporated** *into the Soviet Union in 1940.* • *Artificial blood was* **pumped** *into the man's heart during an operation to widen a coronary artery.* • *A con artist from a religious cult* **tricked** *him into giving away his life savings.* • *The Civil Aviation Authority intends to hold an* **inquiry** *into* (= about) *the accident.* • *These recently discovered letters give us an extraordinary* **insight** *into her private life.* • PIC> **Prepositions of movement**

into CHANGE /ˈɪn·tuː/ *prep* used to show when a person or thing is changing from one form or condition to another • *Peel the cucumber and chop it into small cubes.* • *There was a* *series of explosions and the van* **burst** *into flames* (= started to burn violently). • *They've* **transformed** *their house into a palace.* • *Her novels have been* **translated** *into nineteen languages.* • *We're planning to* **turn** *the smallest bedroom into an office.*

into [TOUCHING FORCEFULLY] /ˈɪn·tuː/ *prep* used to show movement which involves something touching something else with a lot of force but without moving inside it • *He's always walking into things when he hasn't got his glasses on.* • *You'll never guess who I* **bumped/ran** *into* (= met unexpectedly) *the other day!*

into [DIVISION] /ˈɪn·tuː/ *prep* used when referring to the division of one number by another number • *Five into ten is two with nothing left over.* • *Three into five won't go.* • *Does seven* **divide** *into nine?* • *Two* **goes** *into five two and a half times.* • [LP]> **Mathematics**

into [INTERESTED] /ˈɪn·tuː/ *prep* enthusiastic about or interested in • *What sort of music are you into?* • *I've never been able to get into classical music.* • *She's really into her new job.* • *I'd no idea Kate was into that sort of thing.* • *Rachel's really into her new boyfriend.*

in·tol·er·a·ble /£ɪnˈtɒl·ᵊr·ə·bl̩, $-ˈtɑː·lɚ-/ *adj* too bad to be acceptable or bearable • *The pain was so intolerable that I wished I was dead.* • *Three-quarters of the world's population live in conditions that people in the West would find intolerable.* • *The situation has become so intolerable that the peacekeepers may be forced to withdraw from the area.* • *Unemployment is approaching a politically intolerable level.*

in·tol·er·a·bly /£ɪnˈtɒl·ᵊr·ə·bli, $-ˈtɑː·lɚ-/ *adv* • *The murder rate is intolerably high in many American cities.*

in·tol·er·ant /£ɪnˈtɒl·ᵊr·ᵊnt, $-ˈtɑː·lɚ-/ *adj* disapproving of or refusing to accept ideas or ways of behaving that are different from your own • *He's too intolerant to work well with other people.* • *She can be very intolerant* **of** *students who don't understand what she's talking about.*

in·tol·er·ant·ly /£ɪnˈtɒl·ᵊr·ᵊnt·li, $-ˈtɑː·lɚ-/ *adv* • *Adults also need to be able to deal with the occasions when they themselves are treated intolerantly.*

in·tol·er·ance /£ɪnˈtɒl·ᵊr·ᵊnts, $-ˈtɑː·lɚ-/ *n* [U] • *Many communities are divided by racial and religious intolerance.* • *One side-effect of the drug is intolerance* **of** (= being unable to bear) *bright light.*

in·ton·a·tion /ˌɪn·təˈneɪ·ʃᵊn/ *n* the sound changes produced by the rise and fall of the voice when speaking, esp. when this has an effect on the meaning of what is said • *Stress and intonation are not easy to learn in a foreign language.* [U] • *The end of a sentence that is not a question is usually marked by falling intonation.* [U] • *It's difficult getting computers to talk with a natural intonation.* [C] • *She was a brilliant vocalist with perfect intonation.* [U] • In music intonation means the degree of accuracy of the notes that are played: *The violinist had good intonation, and a wonderful singing tone.*

in·tone *(obj)* /£ɪnˈtəʊn, $-ˈtoʊn/ *v fml* to say (something) slowly and seriously in a voice which does not rise or fall much • *The funeral was interrupted by a burst of gunfire as the priest intoned* **the liturgy** *for the latest victim of the fighting.* [T] • *"Let us pray," the priest intoned to his congregation.* [+ clause]

in to·to /£ɪnˈtəʊ·təʊ, $-ˈtoʊ·t̬oʊ/ *adv* [not gradable] *fml* as a total or whole • *The available information amounts to very little in toto.*

in·tox·i·cated /£ɪnˈtɒk·sɪ·keɪ·tɪd, $-ˈtɑːk·sɪ·keɪ·t̬ɪd/ *adj* excited, emotional or out of control, esp. because of drinking too much alcohol • *She was released on bail after being arrested and charged with driving while intoxicated.* • You can also be intoxicated because of an experience or an idea: *She was understandably intoxicated by her success in the national competition.* • Ⓔ

in·tox·i·cat·ing /£ɪnˈtɒk·sɪ·keɪ·tɪŋ, $-ˈtɑːk·sɪ·keɪ·t̬ɪŋ/ *adj* • If a drink is intoxicating it makes you drunk if you have too much: *intoxicating* **liquor** • An intoxicating experience or idea makes you feel excited and emotional: *an intoxicating thought*

in·tox·i·ca·tion /£ɪnˌtɒk·sɪˈkeɪ·ʃᵊn, $-ˌtɑːk-/ *n* [U] • *He used to claim that he had his best ideas after several days of intoxication* (= being drunk). • *The feeling of intoxication* (= excitement) *that followed her victory was cut short by her father's sudden death.* • Ⓔ

in·tox·i·cant /£ɪnˈtɒk·sɪ·kᵊnt, $-ˈtɑːk-/ *n* [C] *specialized* • An intoxicant is a substance such as alcohol that is used to produce feelings of pleasure or happiness in a person artificially.

in·tra- /ˈɪn·trə/ *combining form* used to form adjectives meaning 'within' (the stated place or group) • *intra-EU trade* • *intrafamily disputes* • Compare INTER- [BETWEEN].

in·trac·ta·ble /£ɪnˈtræk·tə·bl̩, $-t̬ə-/ *adj* very difficult and seeming to be impossible to control, manage or solve • *The war in the former Yugoslavia was the most intractable conflict in Europe since 1945.* • *Apparently intractable* **problems** *can sometimes be solved when a different person looks at them.*

in·trac·ta·bly /£ɪnˈtræk·tə·bli, $-t̬ə-/ *adv* • *an intractably violent relationship*

in·trac·ta·bil·i·ty /£ɪnˌtræk·təˈbɪl·ɪ·ti, $-t̬ə·bɪl·ə·t̬i/ *n* [U] • *The seeming intractability of the dispute will not deter us from trying to reach an agreement.*

in·tra·mur·al /£ˌɪn·trəˈmjʊə·rəl, $-ˈmjʊr·ᵊl/ *adj* [not gradable] happening within or involving the members of one school, college or university • *She won the intramural contest and went on to represent her university in the intercollegiate competition.*

in·tran·si·gent /ɪnˈtræn·zɪ·dʒᵊnt, £-ˈtrɑːn-/ *adj fml* refusing to be persuaded, esp. to change opinions that are strongly believed in • *A union spokeswoman said the negotiations had little chance of success while the management maintained such an intransigent position.*

in·tran·si·gent·ly /ɪnˈtræn·zɪ·dʒᵊnt·li, £-ˈtrɑːn- / *adv fml* • *Four-year-old Lydia, hitherto intransigently silent, suddenly started to chat to me.*

in·tran·si·gence /ɪnˈtræn·zɪ·dʒᵊnts, £-ˈtrɑːn- / *n* [U] *fml* • *The collapse of the talks is being blamed on the union's intransigence.*

in·tran·si·tive /£ɪnˈtræn·zɪ·tɪv, £ˈtrɑːn·zə-, $-t̬ɪv/ *adj* [not gradable] *specialized* (of a verb) having or needing no **direct object** (= noun or phrase which follows the verb) • *In the sentence 'I tried to persuade him, but he wouldn't play', 'persuade' is a transitive verb and 'play' is intransitive.* • *In this dictionary, verbs which are intransitive are marked* [I]. • Compare DITRANSITIVE; TRANSITIVE. • [LP]> **Verbs**

in·tran·si·tive /£ɪnˈtræn·zɪ·tɪv, £-ˈtrɑːn·zə-, $-t̬ɪv/ *n* [C] • *Intransitives do not take direct or indirect objects.*

in·tran·si·tive·ly /£ɪnˈtræn·zɪ·tɪv·li, £-ˈtrɑːn·zə-, $-t̬ɪv/ *adv* [not gradable]

in·tra·ve·nous /ˌɪn·trəˈviː·nəs/, **IV** *adj* [not gradable] into or connected to a VEIN (= one of the tubes that carry blood to the heart) • *He suffered serious brain damage in a car accident and has been kept alive by intravenous* **feeding**. • *The nurse set up an intravenous* **drip**. • *Users of intravenous* **drugs**/*Intravenous* **drug users** *are at particular risk of contracting the disease.*

in·tra·ve·nous·ly /ˌɪn·trəˈviː·nə·sli/ *adv* [not gradable] • *After an exhausting match he was given fluids intravenously to combat the effects of dehydration.*

in·trep·id /ɪnˈtrep·ɪd/ *adj* extremely brave and showing no fear of dangerous situations • *This new biography provides a fascinating account of the adventures of one of our most intrepid* **explorers**.

in·trep·id·ly /ɪnˈtrep·ɪd·li/ *adv* • *We drove intrepidly into the city centre, doing our best to follow the road signs.*

in·tri·cate /ˈɪn·trɪ·kət/ *adj* having a lot of small parts that are arranged in a complicated way and therefore sometimes difficult to understand, solve or produce • *The watch mechanism is extremely intricate and very difficult to repair.* • *The police officers who interrogated the suspects were involved in an intricate* **web** *of deceit.*

in·tri·cate·ly /ˈɪn·trɪ·kət·li/ *adv* • *The pendant bears an oblong sapphire and is intricately engraved.*

in·tri·ca·cy /ˈɪn·trɪ·kə·si/ *n* [U] • *Tapestries are very expensive to repair because of the intricacy* **of** *the work involved in making them.*

in·tri·ca·cies /ˈɪn·trɪ·kə·siz/ *pl n* • Intricacies are complicated details: *It was a really good movie, but I couldn't follow all the intricacies* **of** *the plot.* • *The intricacies* **of** *dealing on the stock market are an obstacle to wider share ownership.* [C]

in·trigue *obj* [INTEREST] /ɪnˈtriːɡ/ *v* [T] to interest (someone) a lot, esp. by being strange, unusual or mysterious • *Throughout history, people have been intrigued by the question of whether there is intelligent life elsewhere in the universe.* • *It always intrigues me how someone so intelligent could do such stupid things.*

in·trigu·ing /ɪnˈtriː·ɡɪŋ/ *adj* • *Going to work for one of our competitors is an intriguing possibility.* • *She found my idea so intriguing that she used it for her first book.* • **It's** *intriguing* **to** *speculate on what might have happened if the liberals had won the election.* [+ *to* infinitive]

in·trigu·ing·ly /ɪn'triː·gɪŋ·li/ *adv* • *Intriguingly, her lifestyle has remained very modest, in spite of her enormous wealth.*

in·trigue SECRET /'ɪn·triːg/ *n* (the making of) a secret plan to do esp. something that will harm another person • *The prize went to a tale of* **political** *intrigue by a young Czech novelist.* [U] • *His presidency will be remembered for the intrigues* **against** *his rivals that remain shrouded in a thick fog of secrecy, myth and rumour.* [C]

in·trin·sic /ɪn'trɪn·zɪk/ *adj* being an extremely important and basic characteristic of a person or thing • *It is immoral to treat animals as if they had no intrinsic* **value**. • *The face value of the coin is £1, but it's* **intrinsic** *value* (= the value of the metal) *is only a few pence.* • *According to the tourist brochures, tennis at Wimbledon and rowing at Henley are intrinsic parts of the traditional English summer.*

in·trin·si·cal·ly /ɪn'trɪn·zɪ·kli/ *adv* • *Jewellers will tell you that gold is intrinsically superior to other metals but the real difference is simply that it costs more.* • *There's nothing intrinsically wrong with your idea, I'm just not particularly keen on it.*

in·tro /£'ɪn·trəʊ, $-troʊ/ *n* [C] *pl* **intros** *infml* an **introduction**, see at INTRODUCE MAKE KNOWN, INTRODUCE BEGIN • *This song has a brilliant piano intro.* • *Would you mind doing the intros, Martha, while I pour some drinks?*

in·tro·duce *obj* MAKE KNOWN /£ˌɪn·trə'djuːs, $-'duːs/ *v* [T] to cause (someone or something) to be made known or experienced for the first time • *I'd like to introduce my younger son, Mark.* • *I'm so sorry. Haven't you two been introduced* **(to** *each other)?* • *When were you first introduced* **to** *sailing?* • *It was my older sister who introduced me* **to** *Fellini movies.* • LP **Meeting someone**

in·tro·duc·tion /ˌɪn·trə'dʌk·ʃᵊn/ *n* • *You'll have to* **do/make** *the introductions – I don't know everyone's name.* [C] • *My next guest* **needs no** *introduction, having become a household name when her first single went straight to number one in the charts.* [C] • *My introduction* **to** *smoking came at an age when most people start to think about giving up.* [C] • *Do you stock a recipe book called 'An Introduction* **to** *Indian Cuisine'?* [C] • *I've written him a* **letter of** *introduction to my aunt in New Zealand, so he'll have somewhere to stay in an emergency.* [U]

in·tro·duc·to·ry /£ˌɪn·trə'dʌk·tᵊr·i, $-tɚ-/ *adj* [not gradable] • *I'd like some information about your introductory course in word-processing.* • *Your report should include an introductory chapter that explains the objectives of your research.*

in·tro·duce *obj* PUT INTO USE /£ˌɪn·trə'djuːs, $-'duːs/ *v* [T] to put (something) into use, operation or a place for the first time • *The smaller 10 pence coin was introduced in 1992.* • *When we introduced this system, no one believed it would work.* • *Such unpopular legislation is unlikely to be introduced before the next election.* • *Exactly when the potato was introduced* **(in)to** *Europe is uncertain but it was probably around 1565.* • *You should try introducing a few jokes* **into** *your next speech.* • *(specialized) The tube which carries the laser is introduced* **into** *the abdomen through a small cut in the skin.*

in·tro·duc·tion /ˌɪn·trə'dʌk·ʃᵊn/ *n* [U] • *The introduction* **of** *new working practices has dramatically improved productivity.* • *They agreed that the introduction* **of** *the parking regulations should be postponed until the autumn.* • *Any introduction* **of** *a new product into the marketplace has to be carefully planned.* • *(specialized) The introduction* **of** *the tube into the artery is a very delicate procedure.* • *Within a few years of their introduction, compact discs were outselling vinyl records.*

in·tro·duc·to·ry /£ˌɪn·trə'dʌk·tᵊr·i, $-tɚ-/ *adj* [not gradable] • *The encyclopedia is published in seven volumes at an introductory* **price** *of £100.* • *Take advantage of our introductory* **offer** *and buy two for the price of one for a limited period only.*

in·tro·duce *obj* BEGIN /£ˌɪn·trə'djuːs, $-'duːs/ *v* [T] to represent the beginning of (something), or to show that (something) is about to begin • *The director will introduce the film personally at its world premiere.* • *This is the first official biography of her and it is introduced by her daughter.* • *The second movement of the symphony is introduced by a haunting oboe solo.*

in·tro·duc·tion /ˌɪn·trə'dʌk·ʃᵊn/ *n* [C] • *Useful background information about the book is given in the introduction.* • *The song's great, but the introduction's a bit too long.* • *The Chairman usually* **writes** *the introduction to the annual report.*

in·tro·duc·to·ry /£ˌɪn·trə'dʌk·tᵊr·i, $-tɚ-/ *adj* [not gradable] • *I'd like to make some introductory remarks before beginning the lecture properly.*

in·tro·spec·tion /ˌɪn·trə'spek·ʃᵊn/ *n* [U] examination and consideration of your own ideas, thoughts and feelings • *His defeat in the world championship led to a long period of gloomy introspection.*

in·tro·spec·tive /£ˌɪn·trə'spek·tɪv, $-tɪv/ *adj* • *She is famous for her introspective songs about failed relationships.*

in·tro·spec·tive·ly /ˌɪn·trə'spek·tɪv·li/ *adv*

in·tro·vert /£'ɪn·trə·vɜːt, $-vɜːrt/ *n* [C] someone who is shy, quiet and unable to talk to people and make friends easily • *He used to be very sociable, but he's been an introvert since his wife's death.* • Compare EXTROVERT.

in·tro·vert·ed /£ˌɪn·trə'vɜː·tɪd, $-'vɜːr·tɪd/ *adj* • *She's quite an introverted woman, so I don't think she'll like all this attention.*

in·tro·ver·sion /£ˌɪn·trə'vɜː·ʃᵊn, $-'vɜːr-/ *n* [U] • *The group was accused of introversion, turning their backs on society and its problems to develop their own interests.*

in·trude /ɪn'truːd/ *v* [I] to go into a place or situation in which you are not wanted or not expected to be • *I didn't realise your husband was here, Dr Jones – I hope I'm not intruding.* • *Newspaper editors are being urged not to intrude* **into** *the grief of the families of missing servicemen.* • *Inefficiency has intruded* **into** *every area of the company's activities.* • *It could soon be an offence to publish articles or photos which intrude* **(up)on** *personal relationships, finances or health.* • *Critics say that many of the regulations of the European Union intrude* **(up)on** *the national identities of member countries.*

in·trud·er /£ɪn'truː·dəʳ, $-dɚ/ *n* [C] • *I feel like an intruder when I visit their home.* • An intruder is often someone who enters a place without permission in order to commit a crime: *Intruders had entered the house through a back window.* ○ *I awoke to find a masked intruder in my bedroom.*

in·tru·sion /ɪn'truː·ʒᵊn/ *n* • *They complained about excessive government intrusion* **into** *their legitimate activities.* [U] • *Far from being a nuisance, his phone call was a* **welcome** *intrusion into an otherwise tedious morning.* [C]

in·tru·sive /ɪn'truː·sɪv/ *adj* • *The victims were subjected to intrusive questioning about their private lives.*

in·tu·i·tion /£ˌɪn·tjuː'ɪʃ·ᵊn, $-tuː-/ *n* [U] (knowledge obtained from) an ability to understand or know something immediately without needing to think about it, learn it or discover it by using reason • *The right side of the brain is concerned with imagination and intuition.* • *Often there's no clear evidence one way or the other and you just have to base your judgement on intuition.* • *I can't explain how I knew – I just had an intuition* **that** *you'd been involved in an accident.* [+ *that* clause] • *My own intuition is that we should continue to do what we're already doing.*

in·tu·i·tions /£ˌɪn·tjuː'ɪʃ·ᵊnz, $-tuː-/ *pl n* • *The natural mind is full of insights, intuitions* (= intuition)*, sympathies and affections that affect our response to situations.* • *I tried to rationalize the child's intuitions* (= intuition) *of doom and disaster – what had started her line of thought?* • *In many pleasant conversations, he shared his insights, knowledge and intuitions* (= intuition) *about the world of the theatre.*

in·tu·it *obj* /£ɪn'tjuː·ɪt, $ɪn'tuː-/ *v* [T] *fml* • *He intuited* **that** *I was worried about the situation.* [+ *that* clause]

in·tu·i·tive /£ɪn'tjuː·ɪ·tɪv, $-'tuː·ɪ·tɪv/ *adj* • *Men are often regarded as less intuitive than women.* • *It is difficult to emulate with a computer the intuitive* **leaps** *that a human brain can make.* • *Most people have an intuitive* **sense** *of right and wrong.* • *We tried doing it systematically, but in the end we adopted an intuitive* **approach**.

in·tu·i·tive·ly /£ɪn'tjuː·ɪ·tɪv·li, $-'tuː·ɪ·tɪv-/ *adv* • *I knew intuitively that something dreadful had happened to him.* • *Sometimes difficult problems can be solved by acting intuitively rather than thinking logically about it.* • *Why do we intuitively expect to find more advanced creatures in outer space?*

in·u·it /'ɪn·u·ɪt/ *n* [C] *pl* **Inuit** or **Inuits** a member of a group of people, also called Eskimos, who live in the icy northern areas of N America and Greenland • *Inuit make up most of the 50 000 population of Greenland.* • The Inuit of N America prefer the name Inuit to Eskimo.

in·un·date *obj* TOO MUCH /'ɪn·ʌn·deɪt/ *v* [T usually passive] to give (someone) so much work or so many things that they cannot deal with them all • *We have been* *inundated* **with** *requests for help.* • *Hospitals near to the scene of the disaster were inundated* **with** *casualties.* • *The newlyweds have been inundated* **with** (= have received very many) *good luck messages.*

in·un·da·tion /ˌɪn·ʌn'deɪ·ʃən/ *n* [U] • *No period has seen anything comparable to our own unending, daily inundation of the home by human violence on TV.*

in·un·date *obj* FLOOD /'ɪn·ʌn·deɪt/ *v* [T] *fml* to flood (an area) with water • *If the dam breaks it will inundate large parts of the town.*

in·un·da·tion /ˌɪn·ʌn'deɪ·ʃən/ *n* [U] *fml* • *The threat of inundation or flood is a feature of coastal life.* • *One of the most important of the island's defences is against erosion or inundation by the sea.*

in·ure *obj* **to** *obj* /£ɪn'jʊə, $-'jʊr/ *v prep* [T usually passive] *fml* to make (someone) familiar with and able to accept (something which is usually unpleasant) • *You'll just have to inure yourself to the criticism.* • *After spending some time on the island they became inured to the hardships.*

in·vade *(obj)* /ɪn'veɪd/ *v* to enter (a place) when not wanted, often by using force or in large numbers • *Concentrations of troops near the border look set to invade within the next few days.* [I] • *Antibodies seek out and bind with invading bacteria.* • *Hundreds of squatters have invaded waste land in the hope that they will be allowed to stay.* [T] • *(fig.) A crowd of rowdy youths invaded the peace of the evening with their singing and shouting.* [T] • *(fig.) Famous people often find their* **privacy** *is invaded by the press.* [T] • *(fig.) Maria looks set to invade* (= enter in a forceful and noticeable way) *the music scene with her style and image.* [T]

in·vad·er /£ɪn'veɪ·dəʳ, $-dɚ/ *n* [C] • *The jagged, inland mountains were once the hiding place for locals escaping the endless stream of* **foreign** *invaders.* • *Any new company is seen as an invader in an already competitive market.*

in·va·sion /ɪn'veɪ·ʒən/ *n* • *Who knew of the secret plans to mount an invasion* **of** *the north?* [C] • *Many refugees left the country after the invasion* **by** *hostile forces.* [C] • *The judge was clearly annoyed by the invasion* **of** *the defendant's* **privacy** *by the press.* [U] • *Invasion* **of** *local markets by foreign electronics manufacturers has been extensive.* [U] • *"Invasion of the Body Snatchers"* (film title, 1956)

in·va·sive /ɪn'veɪ·zɪv/ *adj* • *For three centuries, the local people traded with the invasive whites to get woollen blankets and beads.* • *Only 5% of ornamental grasses are invasive – all the rest are neat, clump-forming plants.* • *They treated the cancer with* **non-invasive** *methods/surgery* (= not cutting into the body).

in·val·id NOT CORRECT /ɪn'væl·ɪd/ *adj* [not gradable] not correctly thought out, or not correct in a legal way, and therefore not acceptable • *The line of reasoning is invalid in several places.* • *He claimed that the referendum, to be held tomorrow, is legally invalid.*

in·val·i·date *obj* /ɪn'væl·ɪ·deɪt/ *v* [T] • *Recognising the need to be financially successful does not invalidate* (= make wrong) *the argument for environmental protection.* • *Last year, the decision was invalidated* (= said to be wrong) *by a federal appeals court in St. Louis.*

in·val·i·da·tion /ɪnˌvæl·ɪ'deɪ·ʃən/ *n* [U] • *Premature disclosure of the test sites might lead to invalidation of the experiment.*

in·va·lid·i·ty /£ˌɪn·və'lɪd·ɪ·ti, $-ə·t̬i/ *n* [U] • *It is not evident that Brownsden has succeeded in averting logical invalidity in his argument.*

in·va·lid·ly /ɪn'væl·ɪd·li/ *adv* [not gradable]

in·val·id PERSON /'ɪn·və·lɪd/ *n* [C] *dated* someone who is ill, usually for a long time and often needing to be cared for by another person. Some people find this word offensive. • *He became an invalid as a result of a car accident.* • *She looked after her invalid mother for many years.*

in·va·lid·i·ty /£ˌɪn·və'lɪd·ɪ·ti, $-ə·t̬i/, *Am also* **in·va·lid·i·sm** /'ɪn·və·lɪ·dɪ·zəm/ *n* [U] • *After his accident, he had to leave his job and now the family's only income is his invalidity (Am* **disability***)* **benefit**.

in·val·id *obj* **out** *v adv* [T often passive] • To invalid out is to cause (someone) to leave a job, esp. a military one, because of illness: *She was invalided out* **of** *the service because of injuries she received when fighting a fire.*

in·val·u·a·ble /ɪn'væl·jʊ·bl̩/ *adj* [not gradable] extremely useful • *The new job should provide Jennings with invaluable experience.* • *Such data will prove invaluable to researchers studying fish populations.* • *We received invaluable help from many students in our research.* • If you want to say that something is so precious that its money value can not be calculated use the word PRICELESS. • LP Expensive

in·va·ri·a·ble /ɪn'veə·ri·ə·bl̩/ *adj* [not gradable] *fml* never changing; staying the same • *The menu is invariable but the food is always good.*

in·va·ri·a·bly /ɪn'veə·ri·ə·bli/ *adv* [not gradable] always • *The fuel used is almost invariably charcoal made from wood or coconut shells.* • *Invariably, strong periods in an economy give way to recession.*

in·va·sion /ɪn'veɪ·ʒən/ *n* See at INVADE

in·va·sive /ɪn'veɪ·sɪv/ *adj*

in·vec·tive /£ɪn'vek·tɪv, $-t̬ɪv/ *n* [U] *fml* unkind and unpleasant criticism or speech said with a lot of force • *He prefers to meet criticism with personal invective rather than with reasoned argument.* • *A* **stream of** *invective from some sectors of the press continues to assail the government.*

in·veigh a·gainst *obj* /ɪn'veɪ/ *v prep* [T] *fml* to strongly criticize (something or someone) • *There were politicians who inveighed against immigrants to get votes.*

in·vei·gle *obj* /ɪn'veɪ·gl̩, -'viː-/ *v* [T] *fml* to persuade (someone) to do something, esp. if they do not want to do it • *Her son tried to inveigle her* **into** *giving her the money for a car.* • *Eventually a nurse inveigled him* **into** *taking some of the medicine.*

in·vent *obj* /ɪn'vent/ *v* [T] to design and/or create something which has never been made before • *The first safety razor was invented by company founder King C. Gillette in 1903.* • *The fax is arguably the most useful machine to be invented since the telephone.* • *Over the past quarter century our advertising company has invented thousands of catchphrases.* • To invent is also to create a reason, excuse, story etc. which is not true, usually to deceive someone: *But I didn't invent the story – everything I told you is true.*

in·ven·tion /ɪn'vent·ʃən/ *n* • *Inventions such as the radio and the dishwasher brought communications and automation to the ordinary home.* [C] • *As far as cookery is concerned his* **(power of)** *invention* (= ability to do new things) *is quite surprising.* [U] • *Be careful what you believe – her* **powers of** *invention* (= ability to think of excuses etc.) *are well known.* [U] • *The whole report was just an invention* (= not true). [C]

in·ven·tive /£ɪn'ven·tɪv, $-t̬ɪv/ *adj approving* • *He is very inventive, always dreaming up new gadgets for the home.* • *Her inventive radio plays also show her inclination to explore a full range of media.* • *He was regarded as the most inventive poet of his generation.*

in·ven·tive·ly /£ɪn'ven·tɪv·li, $-t̬ɪv-/ *adv approving* • *The team responded inventively to the challenge of creating an environmentally friendly vehicle.* • *The office blocks now going up use space more inventively.*

in·ven·tive·ness /£ɪn'ven·tɪv·nəs, $-t̬ɪv-/ *n* [U] • *Our own inventiveness and patience will determine whether we succeed.*

in·ven·tor /£ɪn'ven·təʳ, $-t̬ɚ/ *n* [C] • *Television as we have it now is the product of many inventors, both amateur and professional.*

in·ven·tor·y /£'ɪn·vən·tri, $-tɔːr·i/ *n* [C] a detailed list of all the items in a place • *A set of twenty-four carved and gilded chairs appear on the inventory of the house for 1736.* • *(Am)* An inventory is also the amount of goods a shop has, or the value of them: *Our inventory of used cars is the best in town.* ○ *Manufacturers are keeping inventories low because of the poor economic situation.* • Inventory is also *Am for* **stocktaking**. See at STOCK SUPPLY.

in·vert *obj* /£ɪn'vɜːt, $-'vɜːrt/ *v* [T] *fml* to turn (something) upside down or change the order of two things • *Remove the cake from the oven and invert it onto a wire rack, lift off the pan, and let it cool completely.* • *Cover the bowl with an inverted plate.* • *In some languages, the word order in questions is inverted* (= the verb comes before the subject of the sentence). • *(Br)* An **inverted comma** is a **quotation mark**. See at QUOTE SAY. *(Br)* The phrase **(in) inverted commas** (also **quote unquote**) can be used in speech to show that the opposite of something is meant or the particular word or phrase used is not exactly suitable: *Sick prisoners in the camp were 'cared for', in inverted commas, by guards, not nurses.* • *(Br disapproving)* An **inverted snob** is a person who makes it known that they do not like things which suggest high social position but approve of things related to low social position. **Inverted snobbery** is the name for this type of behaviour.

in·verse /£ɪn'vɜːs, $-'vɜːrs/ *adj* [before n; not gradable] • *Their generosity was* **in** *inverse* **proportion/relation to**

their income (= the more money they had the less generous they were).

in·verse /£ɪn'vɜːs, $-'vɜːrs/ *n* [U] *fml* • **The inverse** is the opposite: *People complain of paying too much tax but they rarely complain of the inverse.* ○ *Dividing by two is the inverse* **of** *multiplying by two.*

in·verse·ly /£ɪn'vɜːsli, $-'vɜːr-/ *adv* [not gradable] • *Sometimes it seems that press coverage of an event is inversely* **proportional** *to its true importance* (= the more important the event the less attention paid to it).

in·ver·sion /£ɪn'vɜː·ʒᵊn, $-'vɜːr-/ *n* [U] • *Her account of the case was an inversion* **of** *the facts* (= said the opposite of what really happened).

in·ver·te·brate /£ɪn'vɜː·tɪ·brət, $-'vɜːr·t̬ə-/ *n* [C], *adj* [not gradable] *specialized* (an animal) having no BACKBONE (= row of bones down the middle of the back) • *Invertebrates, such as worms, are the main diet of these water birds.* • *invertebrate biology* • Compare VERTEBRATE.

in·vest *(obj)* /ɪn'vest/ *v* to put (money, effort, time etc.) into something to make a profit or get an advantage • *The company has invested millions of dollars* **in** *writing new programs.* [T] • *The institute will invest 5 million* **in** *the project.* [T] • *He refuses to invest* **in** *companies without a good social record.* [I] • *You have all invested significant amounts of time and energy* **in** *making this project the success that it is.* [T] • *(infml)* To invest **in** (esp. something you think is expensive) is to buy it: *I think it may be the time to invest in a new washing machine.* ○ *About 750 schools have invested in CD-ROM players and this number seems likely to triple over the next year.* • (P)

in·vest·ment /ɪn'vest·mənt/ *n* • *The company has made sizable investments in recent years to improve the plant's efficiency.* [C] • *Stocks are regarded as good long-term investments.* [C] • *New tax incentives will be introduced in the hope of stimulating future investment.* [U] • *The company ordered a report from their investment* **bankers.**

in·ves·tor /£ɪn'ves·tə^r, $-t̬ɚ/ *n* [C] • *A New York investor offered to acquire the company's shares for $13 each.* • **Small** *investors* (= people who invest only a small amount of money) *are hoping that the market will improve so that they can get back some of the interest lost last year.*

in·vest *obj* **with** *obj v prep* [T usually passive] to give authority, power, importance or special value • *(fml) Our government has invested the minister for trade with all the necessary powers to resolve the dispute.* • *(literary) In his poems everyday reality is invested with a sense of wonder and delight.*

in·ves·ti·gate *(obj)* /ɪn'ves·tɪ·geɪt/ *v* to examine (a crime, problem, statement, etc.) carefully, esp. to discover the truth • *Police are investigating allegations of corruption and bribery involving senior executives in the company.* [T] • *An individual could also petition the Commission to investigate an alleged breach of the directive.* [T] • *Food chemists have investigated the grain to see if it really does give the benefits claimed.* [T] • *Any merger proposal is bound to be investigated by the Monopolies Commission.* [T] • *We are of course investigating* **how** *an error like this could have occurred.* [+ *wh*- word]

in·ves·ti·ga·tion /ɪn,ves·tɪ'geɪ·ʃᵊn/ *n* • *An investigation has been under way for several days* **into** *the disappearance of a thirteen-year-old boy.* [C] • *The investigation concluded that there had not been an uncontrolled nuclear reaction at the site.* [C] • *Police said there would be a* **full/thorough** *investigation of the incident.* [C] • *Currently, the individuals who might have caused the accident are* **subject to/under** *investigation.* [U]

in·ves·ti·ga·tive /£ɪn'ves·tɪ·gə·tɪv, $-tɪv/, *fml* **in·ves·ti·gat·o·ry** /ɪn'ves·tɪ·gə·tri, £ɪn,ves·tɪ'geɪ·tə·ri, $-t̬ɚ-/ *adj* • *The investigative report showed that the shopkeeper had been victimized.* • *Children are encouraged to take an investigative approach to learning.* • *It is scandalous that three of the eight seats on the investigatory panel are occupied by members of the department being scrutinized.* • **Investigative journalism** is the activity of news reporters trying to discover information which is of public interest but which someone may be keeping hidden: *Conspiracy is a popular subject for investigative journalism.* ○ *He made his name as an* **investigative journalist.**

in·ves·ti·gat·or /$ɪn'ves·tɪ·geɪ·t̬ɚ, $-tə·geɪ·t̬ɚ/ *n* [C] • *Investigators have studied the possible effects of contamination from the oil spill.*

in·ves·ti·ture /£ɪn'ves·tɪ·tʃə^r, $-tʃɚ/ *n* [C] a ceremony in which someone is given an official rank, authority, power, etc. • *The investiture of the new president will take place this evening.* • *We were invited to the investiture ceremony.*

in·vet·er·ate /£ɪn'vet·ᵊr·ət, $-'vet̬·ɚ-/ *adj* [before n] *disapproving* (of behaviour) happening regularly or frequently esp. over a long period of time • *Every member of the family is an inveterate talker.* • *In international politics inveterate enemies can become allies almost overnight.*

in·vid·i·ous /ɪn'vɪd·i·əs/ *adj* likely to cause unhappiness or be unpleasant, esp. because unfair • *Such a difficult choice placed her in an invidious and unenviable* **position.** • *It is invidious to single out specific examples of failure and ignore the overall success of the project.* • (I)

in·vid·i·ous·ly /ɪn'vɪd·i·ə·sli/ *adv*

in·vid·i·ous·ness /ɪn'vɪd·i·ə·snəs/ *n* [U]

in·vig·i·late *(obj) Br and Aus* /ɪn'vɪdʒ·ɪ·leɪt/, *Am* **proc·tor** *v* to watch (people taking an exam) so that it is done fairly • *Miss Jekyll will be invigilating (your chemistry exam) today.* [T]

in·vig·i·lat·or *Br and Aus* /£ɪn'vɪdʒ·ɪ·leɪ·tə^r, $-t̬ɚ/, *Am* **proc·tor** *n* [C] • *How many invigilators will we need to supervise the whole room?*

in·vig·or·ate *obj* /£ɪn'vɪg·ᵊr·eɪt, $'-ɚ-/ *v* [T] to make (something) fresher and stronger • *We were invigorated by our walk.* • *While controlling social unrest they are also trying to invigorate the economy.*

in·vig·or·at·ing /£ɪn'vɪg·ə·reɪ·tɪŋ, $-t̬ɪŋ/ *adj* • *an invigorating swim/run* • *Her book raises many issues about biotechnology in an invigorating and highly readable way.*

in·vin·ci·ble /ɪn'vɪn·sɪ·bl̩/ *adj* impossible to defeat or prevent from doing what is intended • *When you're young you think you are invincible, you feel you can achieve anything.* • *Last year the company* **seemed/looked** *invincible but labour problems have recently had a devastating effect on its results.*

in·vin·ci·bil·i·ty /£ɪn,vɪn·sɪ'bɪl·ɪ·ti, $-ə·t̬i/ *n* [U] • *The myth of invincibility surrounding the champion was shattered by her failure to qualify.*

in·vin·ci·bly /ɪn'vɪn·sɪ·bli/ *adv*

in·vi·o·la·ble /ɪn'vaɪə·lə·bl̩/ *adj fml* which must not or can not be broken, damaged or doubted • *Surely everyone has an inviolable* **right** *to protection by a fair legal system.* • *Both communities regard their right to worship on the site as inviolable.*

in·vi·o·la·bil·i·ty /£ɪn,vaɪə·lə'bɪl·ɪ·ti, $-ə·t̬i/ *n* [U] *fml* • *One basic principle would be the inviolability of national borders.*

in·vi·o·late /ɪn'vaɪə·lət, -leɪt/ *adj* [after v; not gradable] *fml* • *For centuries the tomb lay inviolate* (= not harmed or damaged) *until, by chance, it was discovered by two miners.*

in·vis·i·ble /ɪn'vɪz·ɪ·bl̩/ *adj* [not gradable] impossible to see • *Most spiders weave webs that are almost invisible.* • *The Stealth fighter is an aircraft designed to be invisible* **to** *radar.* • *These bacteria live in a soft, almost invisible, film called plaque which coats the teeth.* • *Marks that are invisible* **to** *the eye are made visible using a new technique.* • *The scheme aims to boost the country's* **invisible exports** (= services supplied to foreign countries such as banking, rather than goods such as machines). • *It looked like a blank sheet of paper but there was a message on it in* **invisible ink** (= ink which can not be seen until it is treated with chemicals or heat). • *"The Invisible Man"* (book by H.G.Wells, 1897)

in·vis·i·bil·i·ty /£ɪn,vɪz·ə'bɪl·ɪ·ti, $-ə·t̬i/ *n* [U] • *The bits of gold in the sand were small* **to the point of** *invisibility* (= so small that they almost could not be seen). • *In her first novel, she examined the social invisibility of middle-aged women.*

in·vis·i·bly /ɪn'vɪz·ə·bli/ *adv* [not gradable]

in·vite *obj* ASK TO AN EVENT /ɪn'vaɪt/ *v* [T] to ask or request (someone) to go to an event • *All of you are invited* **to** *the party on Saturday.* • *Last week officials invited him* **for** *talks in Berlin.* • *Candidates who are successful in the written test will be invited* **for** *an interview.* • *Her family invited me* **to** *stay with them for a few weeks.* [+ obj + *to* infinitive] • *The charity performance will take place before an invited audience.*

in·vi·ta·tion /,ɪn·vɪ'teɪ·ʃᵊn/ *n* • *Kelly invited us to her wedding last week, and we* **received** *the written invitation yesterday.* [C] • *Thanks for the invitation* **to** *your birthday party.* [C] • *I'm happy to* **accept** *your invitation.* [C] • *Both performers have* **declined/***(infml)* **turned down** *invitations* **to** *perform in Cannes this month.* [C + *to* infinitive] • *Don't forget – you have a* **open/standing** (= permanent) *invitation* **to** *visit us in America whenever you want.* [C + *to* infinitive] • *The first day of the exhibition will be* **by** *invitation* **(only)** (=only those who have been invited can come). [U]

in·vi·ta·tion·al /ˌɪn·vɪˈteɪ·ʃᵊn·ᵊl/ *n* [C], *adj* [not gradable] *Am* • An invitational is a sports event that people can only go to if they have been invited: *an invitational basketball tournament* ○ *The stadium hosts an annual invitational between two football clubs.*

in·vite *obj* REQUEST FORMALLY /ɪnˈvaɪt/ *v* [T] to request (something), esp. formally or politely • *Offers in the region of £1 000 000 are invited* **for** *the property.* • *After the presentation the speaker invited questions which caused an animated discussion.* • *The newspaper invited readers* **to** *write in with their views.* [+obj + *to* infinitive]

in·vi·ta·tion /ˌɪn·vɪˈteɪ·ʃᵊn/ *n* • *This is a once in a lifetime invitation* **to** *invest in your dream home in the sun.* [C + *to* infinitive] • *He became a sponsor of the charity by invitation.* [U]

in·vite *obj* ENCOURAGE /ɪnˈvaɪt/ *v* [T] to act in a way which causes or encourages (something) to happen or (someone) to believe or feel something • *Behaving provocatively in class is just inviting* **trouble**. • *Such a badly presented exhibition invites* **criticism**. • *It's so easy to get credit – it's inviting people* **to** *get into debt.* [+ obj + *to* infinitive] • *The Gaia hypothesis invites us* **to** *view the planet as a living organism.* [+ obj + *to* infinitive]

in·vit·ing /£ɪnˈvaɪ·tɪŋ, $-t̬ɪŋ/ *adj* • If someone or something is inviting it encourages you to feel welcome or attracted: *Their kitchen was a cheerful, inviting room.* • *The restaurant staff could have been more inviting!* • Inviting can also mean attractive in a way that causes unpleasant results: *Companies saddled with high debt have become inviting targets for cash-rich competitors.*

in·vit·ing·ly /£ɪnˈvaɪ·tɪŋ·li, $-t̬ɪŋ-/ *adv* • *Each store offers a striking display of special-offer cans and packages invitingly spilling out of cardboard boxes.* • *He reached out and pressed an invitingly large red button.* • *It was invitingly easy to take the wallet out of the jacket on the back of the chair.*

in·vi·ta·tion /ˌɪn·vɪˈteɪ·ʃᵊn/ *n* [U] • *Officials believe that allowing government-backed loans would be an invitation* **to** *fraud.* • *Leaving your house unlocked is an* **open** *invitation* (=clear and strong suggestion) **to** *burglars.* [C]

in vi·tro /£ɪnˈviː·trəʊ, $-troʊ/ *adv, adj* [not gradable] (of biological processes or reactions) happening outside the body in artificial conditions, often in a **test tube** • *Scientists are studying these cells in vitro.* • *The theory is being tested in in vitro experiments.* • **In vitro fertilization** (*abbreviation* **IVF**) is the joining together of an egg and a sperm in artificial conditions, and then putting the resulting EMBRYO into the woman's womb in order to develop: *She gave birth to triplets following in vitro fertilization treatment.*

in·voice /ˈɪn·vɔɪs/ *v* [T], *n* [C] (to supply) a list of items provided or work done together with their cost, for payment at a later time • *Invoice me* **for** *the cost of the tools, will you?* • *Will you invoice me, or do I have to pay now?* • *All the parts have been taken from stock but they need to be invoiced before shipping.* • *Please will you* **make out** *the invoice for the tubing to my company?* • *Invoices must be* **submitted** *by the 24th of every month.*

in·voke *obj* /£ɪnˈvəʊk, $-ˈvoʊk/ *v* [T] *fml* to request or use (a power outside yourself, esp. a law or a god) to help when you want to improve a situation • *Police can invoke the law of trespass to regulate access to these places.* • *Mr. Pierce invoked the Fifth Amendment, which states that you do not have to be a witness against yourself, and refused to testify.* • *Invoking morality on this occasion would not be appropriate.* • *Their sacred dance is performed to invoke ancient gods.* • If something invokes a **memory** it makes you remember something: *The song invoked memories of that wonderful summer.*

in·vo·ca·tion /ˌɪn·vəˈkeɪ·ʃᵊn/ *n fml* • *On May Day young men sing invocations* **for** *good weather, good harvest and spiritual blessings.* [C] • *Invocation* **of** *obscure rules won't help you.* [U]

in·vol·un·tar·y /£ɪnˈvɒl·ən·tri, $-ˈvɑː·lən·ter·i/ *adj* [not gradable] not done by choice; done unwillingly, or without the decision or intention of the person involved • *A sharp tap on the leg beneath the knee usually causes an involuntary movement of the lower leg.* • *They argued that legalising voluntary euthanasia* (=letting people choose to die) *would eventually lead to involuntary euthanasia.* • *Facial expressions, body movements and posture provide involuntary clues to the emotional state of the person observed.* • *There may have to be some involuntary redundancies.*

in·vol·un·tar·i·ly /ɪnˈvɒl·ən·trəl·i, ɪnˌvɒl·ənˈter·ᵊl·i, $-ˈvɑː·lən·ter·ᵊl·i/ *adv* [not gradable] • *Arthur shivered involuntarily as he came out of the building.*

in·volve *obj* /£ɪnˈvɒlv, $-ˈvɑːlv/ *v* [T; not *be involving*] to include (someone or something) in something, or to make them take part in or feel part of it • *The second accident involved two cars and a lorry.* • *Do we need to involve someone from the computer department at this stage in our discussions?* • *The four men were all involved* **in** *organising and carrying out the murders.* [+ obj + v-*ing*] • *The new system involves little, if any, new technology.* • *The operation involves putting a small tube into your heart.* [+ v-*ing*] • *Research involving the use of biological warfare agents is supposed to be only for defensive purposes.* • *The President said a future government would be formed after a national conference involving all rebel groups.* • *Criminal law involves acts which are considered harmful to society as a whole, such as murder.* • *She's been involved* **with** *animal rights for many years.* • *It would be difficult not to involve the child's father* **in** *the arrangements.* • *She was so involved* **in** *the play that she cried in the final act.* • *They've been involved* (=having a relationship, possibly sexual) *for several years.*

in·volve·ment /£ɪnˈvɒlv·mənt, $-ˈvɑːlv-/ *n* • *After the complaint, their continued involvement* **in** *the competition is in some doubt.* [U] • *Brian's future involvement* **in** *the project is uncertain.* [U] • *Being on the committee is one involvement I could do without.* [C]

in·volved /£ɪnˈvɒlvd, $-ˈvɑːlvd/ *adj* complicated; not simple and therefore difficult to understand • *an involved reason/excuse/argument* • *The plot of the film was too involved – I couldn't understand it.*

in·vul·ne·ra·ble /£ɪnˈvʌl·nᵊr·ə·bl̩, $-nɚ-/ *adj* [not gradable] impossible to damage or hurt in any way • *The command bunker is virtually invulnerable even to a nuclear attack.*

in·vul·ne·ra·bil·i·ty /£ɪnˌvʌl·nᵊr·əˈbɪl·ɪ·ti, $-nɚ·əˈbɪl·ə·t̬i/ *n* [U]

–in–wait·ing /£ɪnˈweɪ·tɪŋ, $-t̬ɪŋ/ *combining form* (of a person) waiting or expecting to be given the authority, job or power named • *The press has identified several government ministers-in-waiting, saying that they are likely to be appointed in the autumn.*

in·ward /£ˈɪn·wəd, $-wɚd/ *adj* [not gradable] on or towards the inside • *The star would then fall in an inward spiral towards the middle of the galaxy.* • *Any large organisation is probably going to be* **inward-looking** *and support candidates who would keep the status quo.* • Inward may also refer to the mind or spirit: *His latest CD gives us a thoughtful and inward interpretation of the music.* • Compare OUTWARD.

in·ward·ly /£ˈɪn·wəd·li, $-wɚd-/ *adv* • *He was inwardly* (=in his mind) *relieved that the test was cancelled.* • *(dated saying)* 'Read, mark, learn and inwardly digest' means read carefully in order to understand.

in·ward /£ˈɪn·wəd, $-wɚd/, **in·wards** *adv* [not gradable] • *After the accident, her thoughts began to turn inward* (=to her own interests or problems). • *Fold the outside edges inward* (=towards the inside).

IOC /£ˌaɪ·əʊˈsiː, $-oʊ-/ *n* [U] **the IOC** *abbreviation for* International Olympic Committee

i·o·dine /ˈaɪ·ə·diːn, -daɪn/ *n* [U] an element found in small amounts in sea water and used to prevent infection

i·o·dized /ˈaɪ·ə·daɪzd/ *adj* • **Iodized salt** is salt with iodine added.

i·on ATOM /£ˈaɪ·ɒn, $-ɑːn/ *n* [C] *specialized* an atom or small group of atoms which has an electrical charge • See also IONOSPHERE.

i·on·ize *obj, Br and Aus usually* **–ise** /ˈaɪ·ə·naɪz/ *v* [I; T] *specialized*

i·on·ized, *Br and Aus usually* **–ised** /ˈaɪ·ə·naɪzd/ *adj specialized* • *Nebulae contain very large amounts of ionized gas.*

i·on·iz·a·tion, *Br and Aus usually* **–i·sa·tion** /ˌaɪ·ə·naɪˈzeɪ·ʃᵊn/ *n* [U] *specialized* • *Widespread ionization occurs readily in the Earth's upper atmosphere.*

i·on·iz·er, *Br and Aus usually* **–iser** /£ˈaɪ·əˌnaɪ·zə, $-zɚ/ *n* [C] • An ionizer is an electrical device which puts negatively charged ions into the air in a room, and this is believed to be good for health.

-i·on ACTION /-ᵊn/, **-a·tion** /-'eɪ·ʃᵊn/, **-i·tion** /-'ɪʃ·ᵊn/ *combining form* added to verbs to form nouns showing action or condition • In 'obsession' a noun has been formed from the verb 'obsess' by adding -ion. • In 'admiration' a noun has been formed from the verb 'admire' by removing the 'e' and adding -ation. • In 'repetition' a noun has been formed from the verb 'repeat' by changing the spelling and adding -ition. • LP> **Combining forms, Stress in pronunciation**

I·on·ic /£aɪ'ɒn·ɪk, $-'ɑː·nɪk/ *adj* (like) a style of ancient Greek building which has only a small amount of decoration • *an Ionic column* • Compare CORINTHIAN; DORIC. • PIC> **Column**

i·on·o·sphere /£,aɪ'ɒn·ə,sfɪːʳ, $-'ɑːn·ə,sfɪːr/ *n* [U] **the ionosphere** part of the Earth's ATMOSPHERE (= the gaseous layer surrounding the planet), from about 60 kilometres to about 1000 kilometres above the surface, in which there are many IONS. • Compare STRATOSPHERE.

i·on·os·pher·ic /,aɪ·ɒ·nə'sfer·ɪk/ *adj* [not gradable]

i·o·ta /£aɪ'əʊ·tə, $-'oʊ·t̬ə/ *n* [U often in negatives] an extremely small amount • *Our policies won't be changed* **one** *iota by the threats of terrorists.* • *I have seen* **not one** *iota* **of** *evidence to support the proposed restrictions.*

IOU /£,aɪ·əʊ'juː, $-oʊ'-/ *n* [C] *abbreviation for* I owe you (= a written promise to pay back money owed) • *We don't accept IOUs – no cash no goods!* • *(fig.) Later in the film the hero presents an IOU for his earlier help by asking to keep some of the jewels he found.*

IPA /,aɪ·piː'eɪ/ *n* [U] *abbreviation for* International Phonetic Alphabet (= a system of symbols for showing how words are spoken) • LP> **Pronunciation**

ipso fac·to /£,ɪp·səʊ'fæk·təʊ, $-soʊ'fæk·t̬oʊ/ *adv* [not gradable] *fml* by reasoning from previously known facts • *You admit you fired the gun and we now know that the shot killed the victim so you are, ipso facto, responsible for his death.*

IQ /,aɪ'kjuː/ *n abbreviation for* intelligence quotient (= a measure of someone's intelligence found from special standardized tests which are adjusted for age) • *A typical IQ is just on 100 with 1% or 2% of a group scoring 150 or above.* [C] • *Children with* **low/high** *IQs often have problems at school.* [C] • *IQ is just one measure of intelligence.* [U]

ir- /'ɪr-/ *combining form* See at IN- LACKING • LP> **Opposites**

IRA /£,aɪ·ɑː'reɪ, $-ɑːr'eɪ/ *n* [U] **the IRA** *abbreviation for* Irish Republican Army (= an illegal organization which wants N Ireland to be politically independent of the UK and united with the Republic of Ireland) • *From 1969 to 1994, the IRA used and supported the use of violence to achieve its goal.*

i·ras·ci·ble /ɪ'ræs·ə·bl̩/ *adj fml* (of a person) made angry easily • *She's becoming more and more irascible as she grows older.*

i·ras·ci·bil·i·ty /£ɪ,ræs·ə'bɪl·ɪ·ti, $-ə·t̬i/ *n* [U] *fml*

i·ras·ci·bly /ɪ'ræs·ə·bli/ *adv fml*

i·rate /aɪ'reɪt/ *adj* very angry • *When irate parents insist on action, police will usually give serious advice to a teenager.* • *We have received some irate phone calls from customers.*

ire /£aɪəʳ, $aɪr/ *n* [U] *fml or literary* anger • *Petty restrictions easily* **raised/aroused** *the ire of such a creative artist.*

i·ri·des·cent /,ɪr·ɪ'des·ᵊnt/ *adj* showing many bright colours which change with movement • *Her latest fashion collection features iridescent materials which make the models seem to be clothed in exotic butterfly wings.*

i·ri·des·cence /,ɪr·ɪ'des·ᵊnts/ *n* [U]

i·ri·di·um /ɪ'rɪd·i·əm/ *n* [U] a yellowish-white element which comes in the form of a metal • *Iridium is often combined with platinum to create a strong and highly corrosion-resistant alloy.*

i·ris FLOWER /'aɪ·rɪs/ *n* [C] a type of plant which grows esp. in wet places and which has flowers which are often blue, yellow or white and long narrow leaves

i·ris EYE /'aɪ·rɪs/ *n* [C] the coloured circular part of an eye surrounding the black PUPIL (= central part) • LP> **Eye and seeing**

I·rish A·mer·i·can /,aɪə·rɪʃ/ *n* [C] someone who lives in the US but whose family originally came from Ireland

I·rish cof·fee /,aɪə·rɪʃ/ *n* [U] hot coffee mixed with WHISKEY (= a strong alcoholic drink) and with thick cream on the top, which is usually served in a glass

I·rish stew /,aɪə·rɪʃ/ *n* [U] meat, often MUTTON (= meat from a sheep), cooked in water with onions, potatoes, etc.

irk *obj* /£ɜːk, $ɜːrk/ *v* [T] to annoy (someone) • *The negative reply to my complaint really irked me.* • *Officials say they are irked that the committee is insisting on such a short timetable.*

irk·some /£'ɜːk·səm, $'ɜːrk-/ *adj* • *The vibration can become irksome* (= annoying) *after a while.*

i·ron METAL /£aɪən, $aɪrn/ *n* [U] a common silver-coloured metal element which is magnetic. It is strong, used in making steel and found in very small amounts, in a chemically combined form, in blood. • *Iron rusts easily.* • *Liver is a particularly rich source of dietary iron.* • *(fig.) She has a reputation as being a woman of iron* (= great strength and determination) *in negotiations.* • Someone who **has/keeps many/several irons in the fire** is involved with many activities or jobs at the same time or makes certain that there are several possibilities: *She always kept several irons in the fire so if one relationship failed there was always another to fall back on.* • If something is done **with an iron hand/fist**, it is done firmly and often severely: *He controlled the finances with an iron fist.* • *(saying)* 'An iron hand/fist in a velvet glove' is used to describe someone who seems to be gentle but is in fact severe and firm. • The **Iron Age** is the period in early history starting about 1100 BC when iron was used for tools: *an Iron-Age settlement* Compare **Bronze Age** at BRONZE; **Stone Age** at STONE ROCK. • Something which is **iron-clad** is very certain and unlikely to be changed: *That is one of several iron-clad rules.* ○ *He responded by offering iron-clad pledges that he would pass a major anti-corruption package of political reform bills.* • From 1946-1989 the **Iron Curtain** was the name of the border between W Europe and the COMMUNIST countries of E Europe: *We no longer have to have an Iron-Curtain mentality.* • An **iron lung** is a machine with a large metal tube which pushes air in and out of someone's lungs to help them if they find it difficult to breathe because of an illness. • *(Am and Aus)* An **iron man** is a person of great physical strength and the ability to continue doing something difficult for a long time. • *(dated)* **Iron rations** means a basic amount of food for a person to live on: *The hotel food was dreadful, so for three days our iron rations were fruit, cheese and bread bought in the only shop in the village.* • *"An iron hand in a velvet glove"* (The Emperor Charles V quoted by Carlyle in his *Latter-Day Pamphlets*, 1850) • See also IRONS; IRONWORK; IRONWORKS.

i·ron /£aɪən, $aɪrn/ *adj* [not gradable] • *iron ore* • *iron deficiency* • *(fig.) I think you have to have an iron* (= very strong) **will** *to make some of these decisions.*

i·ron DEVICE /£aɪən, $aɪrn/ *n* [C] a device for making clothes smooth (esp. after they have been washed) which has a handle and a flat base, and is usually electrically heated • *a steam iron* • *a travel iron* • PIC> **Cleaning**

i·ron *(obj)* /£aɪən, $aɪrn/ *v* • *It takes about five minutes to iron a shirt properly.* [T] • *Cotton and silk iron* (= can be ironed) *well.* [I]

i·ron·ing /£'aɪə·nɪŋ, $'aɪr-/ *n* [U] • *Ironing is one job I really hate.* • *Put the ironing* (= clothes to be ironed) *in the basket.* • *I must* **do** *some/the ironing tonight.* • An **ironing board** is a narrow table, usually covered with cloth and having folding legs, on which clothes can be put flat to iron them. • PIC> **Cleaning**

i·ron GOLF /£aɪən, $aɪrn/ *n* [C] (in golf) a stick which has an iron or steel part at the end which hits the ball • *He'll probably use a 2 or 3 iron for the shot.* • PIC> **Sports**

i·ron out *obj*, **i·ron** *obj* **out** *v adv* [M] to remove problems or find solutions • *It merely remains to iron out the* **details** *of the plan.* • *We hope they can iron their* **differences** *out and get on with working together.*

i·ron·bark /£'aɪən·bɑːk, $'aɪrn·bɑːrk/ *n* [C] *Aus* a type of EUCALYPTUS tree which has deep lines on the stem

i·ron·mong·er *Br* /£'aɪən,mʌŋ·gəʳ, $'aɪrn,mʌŋ·gɚ/, *esp. Am and Aus* **hard·ware deal·er** *n* [C] someone who sells tools for the house and garden • *(Br)* An ironmonger's (*esp. Am and Aus* **hardware store**) is the name for the shop where tools are sold.

i·ron·mon·ger·y *Br* /£'aɪən,mʌŋ·gᵊr·i, $'aɪrn,mʌŋ·gɚ-/, *Am and Aus* **hard·ware** /£'hɑːd·weəʳ, $'hɑːrd·wer/ *n* [U] • *Ironmongery cluttered the front window of his shop.* • LP> **Shopping goods**

i·rons /£aɪənz, $aɪrnz/ *pl n* chain tied around someone to prevent them from escaping or moving • *It was common practice for the prisoners to be* **clapped in** *irons* (= tied with chains).

i·ron·work /£'aɪən·wɜːk, $'aɪrn·wɜːrk/ *n* [U] items made of iron such as gates, esp. if made in a decorated way

i·ron·works /£ˈaɪən·wɜːks, $ˈaɪrn·wɜːrks/ *n* [C usually + sing v] *pl* **ironworks** a factory where iron is produced or iron objects are made • *The ironworks is about two kilometres further along this road.*

i·rony FIGURATIVE SPEECH /£ˈaɪə·rə·ni, $ˈaɪ-/ *n* [U] a means of expression which suggests (humorously or angrily) a different meaning for the words used • *Her voice* **heavy with** *irony, Simone said, "We're so pleased you were able to stay so long."* (= Her voice made it obvious they were not pleased). • Compare SARCASM.

i·ron·ic /£aɪəˈrɒn·ɪk, $aɪˈrɑː·nɪk/, **i·ron·i·cal** /£aɪəˈrɒn·ɪ·kəl, $aɪˈrɑː·nɪ·kəl/ *adj* • *an ironic comment* • *an ironic reply.*

i·ron·i·cal·ly /£aɪəˈrɒn·ɪ·kli, $aɪˈrɑː·nɪ·kli/ *adv* • *"Our son is always so well dressed," he said ironically.* • *"I've put you down to work all day Saturday." "Well, thank you very much!" she replied ironically.*

i·rony WRONG RESULT /£ˈaɪə·rə·ni, $ˈaɪ-/ *n* [U] a situation in which something which was intended to have a particular result has the opposite or a very different result • *The irony* **(of it)** *is that the new tax system will burden those it was intended to help.* • *The boy who fell in the river survived but the man who jumped in to save him drowned – a tragic irony.*

i·ron·ic /£aɪəˈrɒn·ɪk, $aɪˈrɑː·nɪk/, **i·ron·i·cal** /£aɪəˈrɒn·ɪ·kəl, $aɪˈrɑː·nɪ·kəl/ *adj* • **It is ironic that** *although many items are now cheaper to make, fewer people can afford to buy them.* [+ *that* clause]

i·ron·i·cal·ly /£aɪəˈrɒn·ɪ·kli, $aɪˈrɑː·nɪ·kli/ *adv* • *Ironically, the widespread use of antibiotics seems to be causing a whole host of unexpected health problems.*

ir·ra·di·ate *obj* /ɪˈreɪ·di·eɪt/ *v* [T] *specialized* to treat with light or other types of RADIATION • *The cells are irradiated so that they cannot reproduce and are then injected back into the patient.* • *Many countries have had approval to irradiate a range of food products for human consumption.* • *The insects are artificially reared and irradiated to make them sterile.* • *The rule limited use of X-rays on women in order to avoid irradiating a very young embryo.* • *The research group looked at the molecule formed when the compound was irradiated* **with** *light.*

ir·ra·di·at·ed /£ɪˈreɪ·di·eɪ·tɪd, $-t̬ɪd/ *adj* • *irradiated fuel* • *irradiated food*

ir·ra·di·a·tion /ɪˌreɪ·diˈeɪ·ʃən/ *n* [U] • *Irradiation, exposing foods to gamma radiation, X-rays or high-energy electrons, does not cook food and so has the advantage of leaving it in a natural-looking state.* • *Irradiation is a natural part of life because radiation enters the Earth's atmosphere from space.*

ir·ra·tion·al /ɪˈræʃ·ən·əl/ *adj* not using reason or clear thinking • *It's totally irrational, but I'm frightened of mice.* • *The irrational consumer is one who fails to respond to a cheap price even when goods are identical in all other respects.* • *His parents were worried by his increasingly irrational behaviour.*

ir·ra·tion·al·i·ty /£ɪˌræʃ·ənˈæl·ə·ti, $-t̬i/ *n* [U] • *The irrationality of his decision took everyone by surprise.*

ir·ra·tion·al·ly /ɪˈræʃ·ən·əl·i/ *adv* • *People often behave irrationally when they are under stress.*

ir·rec·on·cil·a·ble /ˌɪr·ek·ənˈsaɪ·lə·bl̩/ *adj* [not gradable] impossible to find agreement between or with; impossible to deal with • *Over the years irreconcilable* **differences** *of opinion have developed between the sisters.* • *The talks have become irreconcilable with both sides refusing to compromise any further.*

ir·rec·on·cil·a·bly /ˌɪr·ek·ənˈsaɪ·lə·bli/ *adv* [not gradable] • *The couple are irreconcilably separated, and will probably divorce soon.*

ir·re·cov·er·a·ble /£ˌɪr·ɪˈkʌv·ər·ə·bl̩, $ˈ-ɚ-/ *adj* [not gradable] impossible to get back • *irrecoverable financial losses*

ir·re·cov·er·a·bly /ˌɪr·ɪˈkʌv·ər·ə·bli/ *adv* [not gradable] • *The computer went down and most of the data was irrecoverably* **lost**.

ir·re·deem·a·ble /ˌɪr·ɪˈdiː·mə·bl̩/ *adj* [not gradable] *fml* impossible to correct, improve or change • *Such stubbornness to refuse help is not courage but irredeemable stupidity.* • *There are irredeemable flaws in the logic of the argument.* • *He's an irredeemable optimist.*

ir·re·deem·a·bly /ˌɪr·ɪˈdiː·mə·bli/ *adv* [not gradable] *fml* • *The opportunity for a new approach seems to be irredeemably lost.*

ir·re·duc·i·ble /£ˌɪr·ɪˈdjuː·sə·bl̩, $-ˈduː-/ *adj* [not gradable] *fml* impossible to make smaller or simpler • *A few simple shapes are the irreducible forms from which all of the patterns are generated.*

ir·re·duc·i·bly /£ˌɪr·ɪˈdjuː·sə·bli, $-ˈduː-/ *adv* [not gradable] *fml*

ir·re·fut·a·ble /£ˌɪr·ɪˈfjuː·tə·bl̩, £ɪˈref·jʊ-, $-t̬ə-/ *adj* [not gradable] *fml* impossible to prove wrong • *an irrefutable* **argument** • *We have irrefutable* **evidence** *of the health risks posed by this type of fertilizer.*

ir·re·fut·a·bly /£ˌɪr·ɪˈfjuː·tə·bli, £ɪˈref·jʊ-, $-t̬ə-/ *adv* [not gradable] *fml*

ir·reg·u·lar SHAPE /£ɪˈreg·jʊ·ləʳ, $-lɚ/ *adj* not regular in shape or form; having parts of different shapes or sizes • *The design of the house has been dictated by the small size and irregular shape of the plot of land on which it is being built.* • *Because of the effects of weather the rock has an irregular surface.*

ir·reg·u·lar·i·ty /£ɪˌreg·jʊˈlær·ə·ti, $ɪˌreg·jəˈler·ə·t̬i/ *n* • *We can't use the lens in the camera if it has even a single irregularity.* [C] • *It is a slight irregularity in the motion of the Moon which makes it look as if it is wobbling.* [C] • *The pictures showed cracks and other irregularities in otherwise perfectly regular crystals.* [C] • *The uneven floor can be treated with a substance which fills in small holes and irregularities.* [C] • *The west of the island is famous for* **the** *irregularity* **of** *its coastline.* [U]

ir·reg·u·lar·ly /£ɪˈreg·jʊ·lə·li, $-lɚ-/ *adv* • *irregularly shaped*

ir·reg·u·lar TIME/SPACE /£ɪˈreg·jʊ·ləʳ, $-lɚ/ *adj* not happening at regular times or not with regular spaces in between • *She suffers from an irregular heartbeat but there are drugs which help.* • *Researchers blame the crisis on the irregular nature of the funding.* • *There were signs saying 'School Fair' and '20 June' at irregular intervals along the road.* • *(Am and Aus infml)* You can say you are irregular when you cannot empty your bowels as frequently as you would usually.

ir·reg·u·lar·i·ty /£ɪˌreg·jʊˈlær·ə·ti, $ɪˌreg·jəˈler·ə·t̬i/ *n* [U] • *After three years we had got used to the irregularity of her visits.*

ir·reg·u·lar·ly /£ɪˈreg·jʊ·lə·li, $-lɚ-/ *adv* • *An advertising supplement is issued irregularly with the newspaper.* • *The committee meets infrequently and irregularly.* • *The chairs were irregularly spaced round the room.*

ir·reg·u·lar RULE /£ɪˈreg·jʊ·ləʳ, $-lɚ/ *adj fml* (of behaviour or actions) not according to usual rules or what is expected • *Her rather irregular behaviour, although entertaining at first, soon became tiresome.* • *It's not possible to discover whether the irregular dealings between the contractor and the supplier were intentional.* • *Releasing the goods without an invoice is* **most** *irregular.* • In grammar an irregular verb, noun, adjective etc. does not obey the usual rules for words in the language.

ir·reg·u·lar·i·ty /£ɪˌreg·jʊˈlær·ə·ti, $ɪˌreg·jəˈler·ə·t̬i/ *n* • Irregularities are things which are not correct or acceptable: *The inspectors found several irregularities* **in** *the business accounts.* [C] ○ *The bank was fined for currency irregularities.* [C] ○ *Christopher was called back from a vacation in France after the irregularities were discovered and was suspended as branch manager.* [C] ○ *It was one among many minor electoral irregularities reported by opposition parties.* [C] ○ *"We detected what appeared to be an irregularity," said a lawyer for the laboratory.* [C] • **The** *irregularity* **of** (= The lack of rules for) *English spelling means that it is easy to make mistakes.* [U]

ir·reg·u·lar·ly /£ɪˈreg·jʊ·lə·li, $-lɚ-/ *adv* • *The verb acts irregularly.*

ir·reg·u·lar SOLDIER /£ɪˈreg·jʊ·ləʳ, $-lɚ/ *adj* [not gradable] (of a soldier) fighting for a country but not as a member of its official army • *They have recruited the services of an irregular force in this campaign.*

ir·reg·u·lar /£ɪˈreg·jʊ·ləʳ, $-lɚ/ *n* [C] • *They claimed that irregulars had destroyed the houses in the village*

ir·rel·e·vant /ɪˈrel·ɪ·vənt/ *adj* not related to what is being discussed or considered and therefore of no importance • *The charge that many are 'former communists' is true but irrelevant since it is their present views which matter.* • *Gender is irrelevant* **to** *how well men or women will do the job..* • *These documents are* **largely** *irrelevant* **to** *the present investigation.* • *Making a large profit is irrelevant* **to us** *– the important thing is to make the book available to the largest possible audience.* • **It's** *irrelevant* **what** *you say – nothing can change his attitude.* [+ *wh-* word]

ir·rel·e·vance /ɪˈrel·ɪ·vᵊnts/, *fml* **ir·rel·e·van·cy** /ɪˈrel·ɪ·vᵊnt·si/ *n* • *Sympathy is an irrelevance – we need practical help.* [C] • *The proposed reforms have forced people to think of the constitution as a working document, not a ceremonial irrelevance.* [C] • *Many of these problems may simply fade into irrelevance when the new rules come into action.* [U]

ir·rel·e·vant·ly /ɪˈrel·ɪ·vᵊnt·li/ *adv*

ir·re·li·gious /ˌɪr·ɪˈlɪdʒ·əs/ *adj fml often disapproving* having no interest in religion, or generally opposed to religion • *One assumes that they are not irreligious people, just that religion is not the first concern of their lives.*

ir·re·med·i·a·ble /ˌɪr·ɪˈmiː·di·ə·bl̩/ *adj* [not gradable] *fml* impossible to correct or cure • *The merits of this plan outweighed several obvious flaws in it, which were irremediable.*

ir·rep·a·ra·ble /ɪˈrep·rə·bl̩/ *adj* [not gradable] impossible to repair or make right again • *Unless the oil spill is contained, irreparable* **damage** *will be done to the coastline.*

ir·rep·a·ra·bly /ɪˈrep·rə·bli/ *adv* [not gradable] • *The ship has been* **irreparably damaged/damaged irreparably**.

ir·re·place·a·ble /ˌɪr·ɪˈpleɪ·sə·bl̩/ *adj* [not gradable] too special, unusual or valuable to replace with something else • *Most of the porcelain you see in the display cabinets is irreplaceable.* • *"There is no such thing as an irreplaceable player," the new team manager insisted.* • *No-one's irreplaceable!*

ir·re·pres·si·ble /ˌɪr·ɪˈpres·ə·bl̩/ *adj often approving* full of energy and enthusiasm; impossible to stop • *She's been irrepressible all morning – it must be the thought of going away next week.* • *Even the weather failed to dampen his irrepressible* **spirits**.

ir·re·pres·si·bly /ˌɪr·ɪˈpres·ə·bli/ *adv* • *The singer produced a miraculous, irrepressibly exuberant sound.*

ir·re·proach·a·ble /£ˌɪr·ɪˈprəʊ·tʃə·bl̩, $-ˈproʊ-/ *adj* [not gradable] *fml* without fault and therefore impossible to criticize • *The way she tackled the problem was irreproachable.*

ir·re·proach·a·bly /£ˌɪr·ɪˈprəʊ·tʃə·bli, $-ˈproʊ-/ *adv* [not gradable] *fml*

ir·re·sist·i·ble /ˌɪr·ɪˈzɪs·tə·bl̩/ *adj* impossible to refuse, oppose or avoid because too pleasant, attractive or strong • *an irresistible offer* • *She gave me one of those irresistible smiles and I just had to agree.* • *What happens when an irresistible force meets an immovable object?*

ir·re·sist·i·bly /ˌɪr·ɪˈzɪs·tə·bli/ *adv*

ir·res·o·lute /ɪˈrez·ᵊl·uːt/ *adj fml disapproving* not able or willing to take decisions or actions • *an irresolute reply*

ir·res·o·lu·tion /ɪˌrez·ᵊlˈuː·ʃᵊn/ *n* [U] *fml disapproving* • *Political irresolution and military doubts created a climate of inaction and strengthened the rebels' defiance.*

ir·res·o·lute·ly /£ɪˈrez·ᵊl·uːt·li/ *adv fml disapproving* • *"I still can't decide what to do," he muttered irresolutely.*

ir·re·spec·tive /£ˌɪr·ɪˈspek·tɪv, $-t̬ɪv/ *adv* [not gradable] without considering; not needing to allow for • *The legislation must be applied irrespective* **of** *someone's ethnic origins.* • *We must succeed irrespective* **of** *the number of casualties.* • *I told her it wasn't a pleasant thing to have to do, but she went ahead irrespective.*

ir·re·spon·si·ble /£ˌɪr·ɪˈspɒnt·sɪ·bl̩, $-ˈspɑːnt-/ *adj disapproving* not thinking carefully enough or not caring about what might result from actions taken • **It** *is irresponsible* **to** *suggest that even a 10% drop in ozone levels is not a serious problem.* [+ *to* infinitive] • **It** *would be irresponsible* **to** *ignore these warnings.* [+ *to* infinitive]

ir·re·spon·si·bil·i·ty /£ˌɪr·ɪˌspɒnt·səˈbɪl·ɪ·ti, $-ˌspɑːnt·səˈbɪl·ə·t̬i/ *n* [U] *disapproving* • *It was an act of gross irresponsibility to leave someone who wasn't properly trained in charge of the machine.*

ir·re·spon·si·bly /£ˌɪr·ɪˈspɒnt·sə·bli, $-ˈspɑːnt-/ *adv disapproving* • *They agreed that he had acted irresponsibly.*

ir·re·triev·a·ble /ˌɪr·ɪˈtriː·və·bl̩/ *adj* [not gradable] impossible to correct or return to an existing situation or condition • *I agree things look difficult, but the situation is far from irretrievable.* • *Once waste materials have become mixed, certain substances become virtually irretrievable.* • *The couple separated on the grounds of irretrievable* **breakdown** *(of their marriage).*

ir·re·triev·a·bly /ˌɪr·ɪˈtriː·və·bli/ *adv* [not gradable] • *The local ecosystem will be irretrievably damaged if the road is built.*

ir·rev·er·ent /£ɪˈrev·ᵊr·ᵊnt, $ˈ-ɚ-/ *adj* lacking the expected respect for official, important or holy things • *an irreverent comment approach/attitude* • *irreverent thoughts* • *irreverent humour* • *The programme takes an irreverent look at the medical profession.*

ir·rev·er·ence /£ɪˈrev·ᵊr·ᵊnts, $ˈ-ɚ-/ *n* [U] • *As a group, these five students achieved some notoriety for their irreverence and their practical jokes.* • *The comedy series has been given extra time this year because the irreverence and wit of the programme is so popular.*

ir·rev·er·ent·ly /£ɪˈrev·ᵊr·ᵊnt·li, $ˈ-ɚ-/ *adv*

ir·re·vers·i·ble /£ˌɪr·ɪˈvɜː·sɪ·bl̩ $-ˈvɜːr-/ *adj* [not gradable] not possible to change; impossible to return to a previous condition • *He listed some of the irreversible effects of ageing.* • *Technology has had an irreversible impact on society.*

ir·re·vers·i·bly /£ˌɪr·ɪˈvɜː·sə·bli, $-ˈvɜːr-/ *adv* [not gradable]

ir·rev·o·ca·ble /ɪˈrev·ə·kə·bl̩/ *adj* [not gradable] impossible to change • *The decision will not be irrevocable until everyone concerned has been consulted.*

ir·rev·o·ca·bly /ɪˈrev·ə·kə·bli/ *adv* [not gradable] • *Closing the factory would irrevocably alter the character of the local community.* • *They argued that only by joining the nations of Europe together irrevocably in political union would future conflicts be avoided.*

ir·ri·gate *obj* SUPPLY WATER /ˈɪr·ɪ·geɪt/ *v* [T] to supply (land) with water so that crops and plants will grow or grow stronger • *The report concerned plans to build reservoirs and pumping stations to irrigate land in the northeastern region.* • *Lush green fields which have been irrigated using water from the Nile suddenly give way to desert.*

ir·ri·ga·tion /ˌɪr·ɪˈgeɪ·ʃᵊn/ *n* [U] • *The main purposes of the dam were to provide irrigation and produce hydroelectric power.* • *Local irrigation* **projects** *could revitalise the area.*

ir·ri·gate *obj* WASH /ˈɪr·ɪ·geɪt/ *v* [T] *medical* to wash (an injured part of a person's body, esp. a cut) with a flow of liquid

ir·ri·tate *obj* MAKE ANGRY /ˈɪr·ɪ·teɪt/ *v* [T] to make angry or annoyed • *After a while the noise/her behaviour began to* **visibly** *irritate him.* • *I was* **intensely** *irritated by the way he spoke to me.* • Ⓓ

ir·ri·ta·ble /£ˈɪr·ɪ·tə·bl̩, $-t̬ə-/ *adj* • *Be careful what you say – he's rather irritable* (=easily made angry) *today.* • *"Don't disturb me again," she said in an irritable* (=angry) *voice.*

ir·ri·ta·bly /£ˈɪr·ɪ·tə·bli, $-t̬ə-/ *adv* • *"Don't bother me just now," he said irritably.*

ir·ri·ta·bil·i·ty /£ˌɪr·ɪ·təˈbɪl·ɪ·ti, $-t̬əˈbɪl·ə·t̬i/ *n* [U] • *If you take this drug over a long period, it can lead to memory loss, confusion, irritability and even depression.*

ir·ri·tant /£ˈɪr·ɪ·tᵊnt, $-t̬ənt/ *n* [C] • *The report is bound to add a new irritant* (=cause for trouble) *to inter-regional relations.*

ir·ri·tat·ing /£ˈɪr·ɪ·teɪ·tɪŋ, $-t̬ɪŋ/ *adj* • *We were continually delayed by small but irritating problems.*

ir·ri·tat·ing·ly /£ˈɪr·ɪ·teɪ·tɪŋ·li, $-t̬ɪŋ-/ *adv* • *I can't bear working with him – he's so irritatingly slow.*

ir·ri·ta·tion /ˌɪr·ɪˈteɪ·ʃᵊn/ *n* • *That kind of behaviour is sure to cause irritation.* [U] • *Traffic noise is just one of several* **minor** *irritations* (=small problems). [C]

ir·ri·tate *obj* MAKE SORE /ˈɪr·ɪ·teɪt/ *v* [T] to make sore or painful • *At first my contact lenses irritated my eyes.* • Ⓓ

ir·ri·tant /£ˈɪr·ɪ·tᵊnt, $-t̬ənt/ *n* [C] • *Pollen is an irritant* (=cause of pain), *causing red and sore eyes in sensitive people.*

ir·ri·ta·tion /ˌɪr·ɪˈteɪ·ʃᵊn/ *n* • *It is an antiseptic cream suitable for minor* **skin** *irritations.* [C] • *The rubbing of the strap against the skin had caused irritation.* [U]

is /ɪz/ *he/she/it form of* BE

ISBN /ˌaɪ·es·biːˈen/ *n* [C] International Standard Book Number (=a set of numbers used to IDENTIFY a particular book and show that it is different from other books)

-ise /-aɪz/ *combining form Br and Aus* See at -IZE • LP **American spelling**

-ish PLACE /-ɪʃ/ *combining form* used to form adjectives and nouns which say what country or area a person, thing or language comes from • *Spanish dancing* (=from Spain) • *Flemish lace* (=from Belgium) • *Are you English* (=from England)? • *I've always liked the Irish* (=people from Ireland). • *Do you speak Swedish* (=the language of Sweden)? • LP **Combining forms**

-ish LIKE /-ɪʃ/ *combining form esp. disapproving* used to form adjectives which say what a person, thing or action is like • *foolish* • *mannish* • *outlandish*

-ish QUITE /-ɪʃ/ *combining form* added to adjectives to give the meaning to some degree; partly; quite • *He had a sort of reddish beard.* • *She was oldish – about 60, I'd say.* • *"Is he young?" "(Young)-ish, 40 maybe."* • *We'll start at sevenish* (= about 7 o'clock). • LP> **Approximate numbers**

Is·lam /ˈɪz·lɑːm, -læm/ *n* [not after *the*] the Muslim religion, and the people and countries who believe in it • *Islam is the most common religion in the Arab world.* • *The tradition is common throughout Islam.*

Is·lamic /ɪzˈlæm·ɪk, -ˈlɑː·mɪk/ *adj* [not gradable] • *Islamic culture/beliefs/art/law*

is·land /ˈaɪ·lənd/ *n* [C] a piece of land completely surrounded by water • *a desert island* • *a Pacific island* • *an uninhabited island* • *They live* **on** *the large Japanese island of Hokkaido.* • *The map showed two small islands in the middle of the river.* • *She grew up in a small island community.* • An island is also a **traffic island**. See at TRAFFIC VEHICLES. • *"No man is an island, entire of it self"* (John Donne *Devotions*, 1624) • PIC> **Road** Ⓓ Ⓓⓚ Ⓕ Ⓘ Ⓝ Ⓝⓛ Ⓢ

is·land·er /£ˈaɪ·lən·dəʳ, $-dɚ/ *n* [C] • An islander is someone who lives on an island: *Scottish islanders*

isle /aɪl/ *n* [C] *literary or in place names* an ISLAND • *the Isle of Skye* • *the Scilly Isles* • *"this scepter'd isle ... this England"* (Shakespeare, Richard II 2.1)

-ism /-ɪ·zᵊm/ *combining form esp. disapproving* used to form nouns which describe social, political or religious beliefs or ways of behaving • *fanaticism* • *fogeyism* • *sexism* • *feminism* • *Buddhism* • LP> **Combining forms**

-ism /-ɪ·zᵊm/ *n* [C] • An -ism is an example of typical behaviour: *That expression was a real Taylor-ism* (= an example of behaving or speaking like someone called Taylor).

ism /ˈɪz·ᵊm/ *n* [C] *infml, esp. humorous* • An ism is a set of beliefs: *Thatcher is unique among her predecessors in having given the English language a brand new ism, created from her own name.*

-ist /-ɪst/ *combining form* • -ist is used to form adjectives and nouns which describe (a person with) a particular set of beliefs or way of behaving: *Marxist philosophy* • *a feminist* • *a sexist.* • Compare -ITE.

isn't /ˈɪz·ᵊnt/ *short form of* is not • *He isn't coming until tomorrow.* • *It's going to be quite easy to arrange, isn't it?*

i·so·bar /£ˈaɪ·səʊ·bɑːʳ, $-soʊ·bɑːr/ *n* [C] *specialized* a line drawn on a weather map joining all the places which have the same air pressure

i·so·late *obj* /ˈaɪ·sə·leɪt/ *v* [T] to separate (something from other things with which it is joined or mixed) or to keep separate from • *The police tried to isolate the protesters in a side street.* • *They tried to isolate the cause of the problem.* • *(specialized) Virus particles were eventually isolated* **from** *the tissue.* • *A high wall isolated the house* **from** *the rest of the village.*

i·so·lat·ed /£ˈaɪ·sə·leɪ·tɪd, $-t̬ɪd/ *adj* • *an isolated farm/village* (= not near other farms/villages) • *There were only a few isolated* (= not connected with each other, separate) *cases/examples of violent behaviour.*

i·so·la·tion /ˌaɪ·sᵊlˈeɪ·ʃᵊn/ *n* [U] • *I can't think about it* **in** *isolation – I need some examples of the problem.* • *The prisoner had been kept* **in** *isolation* (= alone without other people) *for three days.* • *After all the visitors had left, she experienced a feeling of complete isolation* (= loneliness).

i·so·la·tion·i·sm /ˌaɪ·sᵊlˈeɪ·ʃᵊn·ɪ·zᵊm/ *n* [U] *disapproving* • Isolationism is the political principle or practice of showing interest only in your own country and not being involved in international activities. • Compare **globalism** at GLOBE.

i·so·la·tion·ist /ˌaɪ·sᵊlˈeɪ·ʃᵊn·ɪst/ *adj* • *an isolationist policy/nation/attitude*

i·som·er /£ˈaɪ·sə·məʳ, $-soʊ·mɚ/ *n* [C] *specialized* any one of a group of chemical substances which all have the same number and type of atoms but the arrangement of the atoms is slightly different between each substance • *structural/geometrical/optical isomers*

i·sos·ce·les tri·an·gle /£aɪˈsɒs·ᵊl·iːz, $-ˈsɑː·sᵊl-/ *n* [C] a triangle with two sides of equal length • PIC> **Shapes**

i·so·therm /£ˈaɪ·səʊ·θɜːm, $-soʊ·θɜːrm/ *n* [C] *specialized* a line drawn on a weather map joining all the places which have the same temperature

isotonic /£aɪ·səʊˈtɒn·ɪk, $-ˈtɑː·nɪk/ *adj* (of food and esp. drinks) specially chemically balanced to fit the needs of the body • *Isotonic drinks are used to replace fluid and minerals which the body uses up during sporting activities.*

i·so·tope /£ˈaɪ·sə·təʊp, $-toʊp/ *n* [C] *specialized* a form of an atom which has a different atomic weight from other forms of the same atom but the same chemical structure • *a radioactive isotope of hydrogen*

Is·rae·lite /ˈɪz·rə·laɪt/ *n* [C] one of a race of people who lived in Israel in ancient times

is·sue SUBJECT /ˈɪʃ·uː, ˈɪs·juː/ *n* [C] a subject or problem which people are thinking and talking about • *environmental/scientific/ethical/personal/family issues* • *She has changed her mind on many issues, including nursery education.* • *The group had prepared a report on the issues* **of** *management and staff training.* • *As employers we need to be seen to be* **addressing** (= dealing with) *these issues sympathetically.* • *The* **burning** *issue* (= what we are discussing at present) *is whether we should buy a new car.* • *The* **main** (= most important) *issue is how many boxes we can produce each day.* • *Don't worry about who will do it – that's just a* **side** *issue* (= not the main problem). • *The need for more staff is not an issue/***at issue** (= there is no disagreement about it), *but finding suitable people has not been easy.* • If you say you won't **make an issue of** something, you mean you won't try to make it seem more important than it should be or argue about it: *I don't want to make an issue of your lateness, but I would like you to try to improve.* ○ *Of course I'll help you, there's no need to make an issue of it.* • *(fml)* If you **take issue with** someone you disagree strongly: *I took issue with him* **over** *his interpretation of the instructions.* ○ *They took issue with his interpretation.* • Ⓕ

is·sue *(obj)* PRODUCE /ˈɪʃ·uː, ˈɪs·juː/ *v* to produce or provide (something official) • *Local authorities will shortly issue street litter control notices.* [T] • *The office will be issuing permits on Tuesday and Thursday mornings.* [T] • *The school issued a statement about its plans* **to** *the press./The school issued the press* **with** *a statement about its plans.* [T] • *The staff newsletter is issued three times a year.* [T] • *(literary) A terrible scream issued* **from** (= came out of) *the room.* [always + prep] • Ⓕ

is·sue /ˈɪʃ·uː, ˈɪs·juː/ *n* [C] • An issue of a newspaper or a magazine is either a set published at the same time or a single one: *There's an article on motorbikes in the latest/next issue.* ○ *An old issue of 'Homes and Gardens' lay on the table.* • An issue of shares is when a company gives people the chance to buy part of it or gives extra shares to people who already own some: *a rights issue.* [C] • *(old use)* If someone dies **without issue**, they have no children.

is·su·ance /ˈɪʃ·u·ᵊnts, ˈɪs·ju-/ *n* [U] *fml* • *a stock issuance* • *The recent issuance* (= release) **of** *ten million dollars' worth of shares into the stock-market has caused a great deal of excitement in the big financial centres.* • *In Britain, the organisation responsible for the issuance* (= giving out) **of** *driving-licences is called the D.V.L.C..*

-ist /-ɪst/ *combining form* See at -ISM • LP> **Combining forms**

isth·mus /ˈɪsθ·məs, ˈɪs-/ *n* [C] a narrow piece of land with water on each side which joins two larger areas of land • *the Isthmus of Panama* • *the Isthmus of Suez* • *The north and south of the island are linked by a narrow isthmus.*

IT /ˌaɪˈtiː/ *n* [U] *abbreviation for* **information technology**, see at INFORMATION

it /ɪt/ *pronoun* (as subject or object) the thing, animal or situation which has already been mentioned • *"Where's my pen? It was on my desk a minute ago." "You left it by the phone."* • *Fear grows. It obsesses you. You can't ignore it.* • *The company was losing money and it had to make people redundant.* • *The argument was upsetting for us all – I don't want to talk about it.* • *Children who stay away from school do it for different reasons.*

its /ɪts/ *determiner* • *The dog hurt its paw.* • *The horse flicked its tail at the flies.* • *Her baby had something wrong with its hip joint.* • *The house has its own swimming pool.* • *The truck had all its tyres slashed by vandals.* • *The company increased its profits.* • *As a building material, brick has its own appeal.* • *I prefer the second option – its advantages are simplicity and cheapness.* • LP> **Determiners**

it·self /ɪtˈself/ *pronoun* • *The cat licked itself all over.* • *The government has got itself into trouble over this new tax.* • Itself can be used to put emphasis on a word: *The shop itself* (= only the shop and nothing else) *started 15 years ago but the mail order side of the business is new.* • *The dog managed to drag the box into the room* **by** *itself* (= without

IT

'It' is often used in a way that does not refer to a particular thing, person, etc. 'It' is used as the subject in:

- **sentences giving the time, the date, the weather and distances**
  It's three o'clock. • *It was Tuesday.* • *It's the fifth of March.* • *(Am) It's March fifth.* • *It rained all day.* • *It's 230 miles to New Orleans.*
  Notice the question forms: *What time/day/date is it?* • *What was it/the weather like?* • *How far is it to New Orleans?*
- **sentences with *appear, seem, look, sound, happen, occur to, take***
  It **appears that** *we have lost.* • *It* **looks** *unlikely* **that** *we shall get the order.* • *It* **sounds** *an absolutely awful situation.* • *It just* **happened that** *I was there when the visitor came.*
  It **occurred to** *me* **that** *you might be hungry, so I brought you a sandwich.*
  When I had a broken arm, it **took** *(me) an hour* **to** *get dressed in the morning.*
  Notice that 'appear', 'seem' and 'happen' often take 'there' as a subject: LP **There**.
- **sentences with an adjective, noun or verb followed by:**
  - *to*-infinitive *It isn't* **easy to** *find a cheap flat.* • *It's* **important to** *trust me.*
  - *-ing* form *It's* **no use** *knocking, she can't hear you.*
  - *that* clause *It's* **unlikely that** *she will arrive on time.* • *It's* **true** *I don't like Sarah.*
    It's **important that** *you should see a doctor.* • *It's* **a shame** *I can't come.*
  - *wh-* word *It's* **amazing wh***at people will do on TV for money.* • *It's* **interesting how** *often she talks to him.*
- **passive sentences with verbs of opinion and attitude** (This use is formal)
  It is **thought** (= People think) **that** *he tried to contact his family on Friday.*
  It was **considered** *necessary* **to** *increase the price of fares.*
  It is **said that** *she has left the country.*
  It is **hoped/feared (that)** *a new airport will be built near the town.*
- **sentences intended to emphasize something** Compare these sentences:
  Paul came here in September.
  It was Paul **who** *came here in September* (emphasizes Paul).
  It was in September **that** *Paul came here* (emphasizes September).

'It' is also used as the object in sentences in which 'it' has no meaning in itself but introduces a clause. This often happens with the verbs 'find', 'feel', 'think', 'consider', 'like' and 'hate'.
Compare these sentences: *I find my job difficult.*
I find having two jobs difficult.
*I find it difficult hav***ing** *two jobs.*
Other examples: *I found it impossible* **to** *get to sleep last night.* • *He thought it strange* **that** *she refused to talk to him.* • *I like it in the autumn* **when** *the weather is crisp and bright.*

help). • *The animal had been left in the house* **by** *itself* (= alone) *for a week.* • *The plan wasn't illegal* **in** *itself* (= there was nothing in the plan that was illegal) *but it would lead to some doubtful practices.* • *The committee* **kept** *the results of the survey* **to** *itself* (= did not tell anyone), *fearing a bad public reaction.* • LP **Reflexive pronouns and verbs**

i·tal·ics /ɪˈtæl·ɪks/ *pl n* a style of writing or printing in which the letters lean to the right • *This sentence is printed* **in** *italics.*

ITALICS

In printed text italics are used:

- **to emphasise something that is important.** (Underlining is used instead when text is written by hand or typed.)
  This emergency door must be kept clear *at all times.*
  She spent *over twenty years* of her life in prison.
- **for the titles of books, newspapers, television programmes, etc.** (quotation marks '. . .' can be used instead)
  Dickens' *Oliver Twist* • a new production of *Hamlet*
  in today's *Daily Times* • Bob Dylan's *Blood on the Tracks*
- **for foreign words which are not commonly used or which could be mistaken for English words** (quotation marks '. . .' can be used instead)
  Did you drink any *sake* when you were in Tokyo?
  They put on some music and danced the *lambada* all night.

i·tal·ic /ɪˈtæl·ɪk/ *adj* • *italic type/print/script*

i·tal·i·cize *obj, Br and Aus also* **–ise** /ɪˈtæl·ɪ·saɪz/ *v* [T] • *Words are sometimes italicized for emphasis or to make people take special notice of them.*

I·tal·o– /£ɪˈtæl·əʊ-, $-oʊ-/ *combining form* of or connected with Italy • *an Italo-German production* • *An Italophile is a person who greatly admires Italy and Italian people and culture.*

itch /ɪtʃ/ *v, n* (to have or cause) an uncomfortable feeling on the skin which makes you want to rub or SCRATCH it • *The mosquito bites itched so much I couldn't sleep.* [I] • *He was itching all over.* [I] • *I've got an itch on the back of my neck.* [C] • *(infml)* If you itch **for** something/itch **to** do something, you want to do it very much and as soon as possible: *He was itching to hear the results.* [+ *to* infinitive] ○ *I itched to tell her what I'd heard.* [+ *to* infinitive] ○ *By four o'clock I was itching for the meeting to end.* • *(infml) He had an itch* (= very much wanted) **to** *change things.* [C + *to* infinitive] • LP **Feelings and pains**

itch·ing /ˈɪtʃ·ɪŋ/ *n* [U] • *This cream will reduce the itching.*

itch·y /ˈɪtʃ·i/ *adj* **-ier, -iest** • *The sweater was itchy* (= made of rough material). • *The dust made me* **feel** *itchy all over.* • *(Br and Aus infml)* If you have **itchy feet** you want to travel or move on from what you have been doing: *After three years in the job she began to have itchy feet.* ○ *She's off to Australia next – she's always had itchy feet.* • *(Br dated disapproving)* Someone with an **itchy palm** likes to be paid for what they do for you.

–ite /aɪt/ *combining form* used for a person who supports particular beliefs, actions or ideas, esp. when added to the name of the person who is the origin of the ideas • *He's a Heathite/Thatcherite/Reaganite.* • Compare -IST.

i·tem /£ˈaɪ·təm, $-t̬əm/ *n* [C] something which is part of a list or group of things • *The restaurant has a long menu of about 50 items.* • *Tax is not payable on many essential items of family expenditure including domestic energy and water supplies, public transport and most foods.* • *A car can hardly be classed as a* **luxury item** (= not really necessary) *when* *public transport is so poor.* • *Several items* **of clothing** (= clothes) *lay on the floor.* • *The earthquake was the most important* **news item/item of news** (= piece of news) *this week.* • *Buyers from stores are given the opportunity to go through fashion collections* **item by item** (= one thing at a time) *and place orders.* • An item is also one of several subjects to be considered: *There are three items on the agenda.* ○ *Item one* (= the first of several things to be considered)*: a report on the car park project, Item two: future plans.* • *(infml)* If two people are said to be **an item**, they are having a close/romantic/sexual relationship: *I understand they're an item now.* ○ *Are you two an item, or just friends?*

i·tem·ize *obj, Br and Aus usually* **-ise** /£ˈaɪ·tə·maɪz, $-t̬ə-/ *v* [T] • *The parcels were all individually itemized* (= shown in a list)*, with information on destination and cost.* • *We asked for an itemized* **bill***, listing all our phone calls and how long they were.*

i·tin·er·ant /£aɪˈtɪn·ər·ənt, $ˈ-ɚ-/ *n, adj* (a person) travelling from one place to another, usually to work for a short period • *You can read the book as history, as politics or simply as the amusing tales of an itinerant journalist.* [before n] • *The farms relied heavily on itinerants during the harvest period.* [C]

i·tin·er·ar·y /£aɪˈtɪn·ər·ər·i, $-ə·rer-/ *n* [C] a detailed plan or route of a journey • *Travellers who are willing to fix their own itinerary are able to avoid the tourist crowds.* • *Several tour companies have changed their announced itineraries.*

-i·tion /-ɪ·ʃən/ *combining form* See at -ION [ACTION] • [LP] **Combining forms**

its /ɪts/ *determiner* See at IT

it·self /ɪtˈself/ *pronoun* See at IT

it·sy–bit·sy *Br and Am* (**-ier, -iest**) /ˌɪt·siˈbɪt·si/, *Am and Aus also* **it·ty–bit·ty** (**-ier, -iest**) /£ˌɪt·iˈbɪt·i, $ˌɪt̬·iˈbɪt̬·i/ *adj humorous* extremely small • *The baby had itsy-bitsy little hands and feet.* • *It's the itsy-bitsiest hat I've ever seen.* • *"Itsy bitsy teeny weeny, yellow polka dot bikini"* (title of a song written by Paul Vance and Lee Pockriss, 1960)

ITV /ˌaɪ·tiːˈviː/ *n* [U not after *the*] *abbreviation for* Independent Television (= a group of British television companies which earn most of their income from advertising) • *There's a good film on ITV tonight.* • Compare BBC.

-i·ty /£-ɪ·ti, $-ə·t̬i/ *combining form* added to adjectives to form nouns referring to a state or quality • [LP] **Combining forms, Stress in pronunciation**

IUD /ˌaɪ·juːˈdiː/ *n* [C] *abbreviation for* intra-uterine device (= a small object put by a doctor in the womb of a woman who wants to avoid becoming pregnant) • *An IUD is inserted into the uterus to prevent a woman from becoming pregnant.*

IV /aɪˈviː/ *adj* [not gradable] *abbreviation for* INTRAVENOUS • *IV drug users*

-ive /-ɪv/, **-a·tive** /£-ə·tɪv, $-t̬ɪv/, **-i·tive** /£-ɪ·tɪv, $-t̬ɪv/, **-tive** /£-tɪv, $-t̬ɪv/ *combining form* added to verbs to form adjectives meaning showing the ability to perform (to a great degree) the activity represented by the verb • In 'creative', the adjective has been formed from 'create' by adding '-ive'. • In 'imaginative', the adjective has been formed from 'imagine' by removing the 'e' and adding '-ative'. • In 'acquisitive', the adjective has been formed from 'acquire' by changing its ending and adding '-itive'. • In 'descriptive', the adjective has been formed from 'describe' by changing its ending and adding '-tive'.

IVF /aɪ·viːˈef/ *n* [U] *abbreviation for* **in vitro fertilization**, see at VITRO

i·vor·y /£ˈaɪ·vər·i, $-vɚ-/ *n* [U] the hard white substance from which the TUSKS (= long teeth growing outside the mouth) of some animals such as ELEPHANTS are made • *intricately carved ivory* • *a ban on ivory trading* • *ivory handles* • To live or be in an **ivory tower** is not to know about or to want to avoid the ordinary and unpleasant things that happen in people's lives: *You can tell from their comments about children that they are living in an ivory tower where no one ever shouts or argues.* ○ *Academics in their ivory towers don't seem to worry about how it will affect ordinary people.* ○ *He was criticized for taking an ivory-tower approach to the problem.*

i·vor·ies /£ˈaɪ·vər·iz, $-vɚ-/ *pl n* • *a collection of ivories* (= objects made from ivory) • *(infml humorous)* If you **tinkle/tickle the ivories**, you play the piano.

i·vy /ˈaɪ·vi/ *n* an evergreen plant which often grows up trees or buildings • *Ivy covered the broken walls.* [U] • *Scarcely any wild fruits remain, except the black berries of* **the ivy**. [U] • *Variegated ivies* (= types of ivy) *are a popular choice for covering fences.* [C] • The **Ivy League** is a group of established colleges in the northeastern US with a good reputation: *It's a good school, but it's just not part of the Ivy League.* ○ *an Ivy League education*

i·vied /ˈaɪ·vid/ *adj literary* • *There was a half-hidden door in the ivied wall.*

-i·za·tion, *Br and Aus usually* **-i·sa·tion** /-aɪˈzeɪ·ʃən/ *combining form* used to form nouns • *the modernization of the office* • [LP] **American spelling**

-ize, *Br and Aus usually* **-ise** /-aɪz/ *combining form* added to adjectives to form verbs meaning to cause to become • *to modernize* (= to make modern) • *to centralize* • [LP] **American spelling, Combining forms**

J j

J (*pl* **J's** or **Js**), **j** (*pl* **j's** or **js**) /dʒeɪ/ the 10th letter of the English alphabet

J–cloth, Jeye cloth /ˈdʒeɪ/ *n* [C] *trademark* a cloth used for cleaning, esp. in the home • *Where do you keep your J-cloths?*

jab *(obj)* /dʒæb/ *v* **-bb-** to push or hit (something) hard and quickly, esp. with a thin or sharp object • *She jabbed two sticks* **in(to)** *the ground and tied string between them.* [T] • *The doctor jabbed the needle* **in(to)** *my arm.* [T] • *Watch out! You nearly jabbed me* **in** *the eye with your umbrella!* [T] • *He was jabbing a finger* **at** (= in the direction of) *them and shouting.* [T] • *"There!" he jabbed* **(at)** *the paragraph with his pencil. "It says it there!"* [T; I + *at*] • In boxing to jab is to make quick hard straight hits with your closed hand: *Just keep jabbing and you'll soon have the other boxer in trouble.* [I] • To jab can also mean to kick hard and quickly: *He received the ball from the right near the penalty spot, then jabbed it wide of the goal.* [T]

jab /dʒæb/ *n* [C] • *She gave me a sharp jab* **in** *the ribs with her elbow to stop me from saying any more.* • *The boxer was floored by a punishing left jab.* • *(Br and Aus infml)* A jab is also an INJECTION: *a typhoid jab* ○ *a flu jab* ○ *daily insulin jabs* ○ *What jabs do I need for Egypt?*

jab·ber *(obj)* /£ˈdʒæb·ər, $-ɚ/ *v disapproving* to speak or say quickly in a way that is difficult to understand • *Nearby, another passenger was jabbering* **(away)** *into one of those portable phones.* [I] • *He jabbered* **(out)** *something about an accident further down the road.* [T]

jack [EQUIPMENT] /dʒæk/ *n* [C] a piece of equipment which can be opened slowly to allow heavy weights to be raised • *We lifted the car on two jacks.* • [PIC] **Jack**

jack up *obj*, **jack** *obj* **up** /dʒæk/ *v adv* [M] • *They jacked up the car to change the wheel.* • *(fig. infml) They jack up* (= raise) *the prices in the school holidays.* • [PIC] **Jack**

jack [CARD] /dʒæk/, **knave** *n* [C] a playing card with a picture of a man on it. It has a lower value than the cards showing a king or queen. • *the jack of clubs* • *She dealt out the ten, jack, queen and king of diamonds.* • *"From a Jack to a King"* (title of a song by Ned Miller, 1963) • [LP] **Cards**

jack [MAN] /dʒæk/ *n* [C] (esp. used in phrases) a person, esp. a man • *(used by or to children)* **Jack Frost** is cold and ice thought of as a man: *It feels as though Jack Frost is coming* (= The weather is getting very cold). • A **jack-in-the-box** is a children's toy consisting of a box with a model of a person inside it which jumps out and gives you a surprise when the top of the box is raised: *(fig.) She was up and down to the phone all morning like a jack-in-the-box.* • A **jack-of-all-trades** is someone who can do many different jobs: *A mother has to be a jack-of-all-trades – cook, nurse, teacher, sports coach and lots more!* • *(Am)* A **jack-o'-lantern** is a light made from a hollow PUMPKIN with holes cut into the sides like the eyes and mouth of a person's face, inside which there is a candle. • *(dated)* If something happens **before you can/could say Jack Robinson**, it happens very quickly: *I put the plate of food on the floor and before you could say Jack Robinson the dog had eaten it.* • *(Br infml)* A **Jack the Lad** is a young man who behaves in an

JAPANESE FALSE FRIENDS

accent *n*	アクセント	contrasting highlight
animation *n*	アニメ	cartoons, cartoon programmes
apart *adj*	アパート(n)	apartment house
at home *adj*	アットホーム	cozy, homely atmosphere
attack *n*	アタック	challenging a difficult goal
axle *n*	アクセル	car accelerator
beer *n*	ビール	lager
bike *n*	バイク	motorbike
bond *n*	ボンド	very strong adhesive
boss *n*	ボス	leader of gang of criminals
bust *n*	バスト	bust measurement
cape *n*	カッパ	plastic rain cape
checkpoint *n*	チェックポイント	something that needs checking
chorus *n*	コーラス	choral singing
cider *n*	サイダー	soda pop/lemonade
circle *n*	サークル	informal interest group among university students
claim *n*	クレーム	complaint
classic *n*	クラシック	western classical music
cock *n*	コック	tap for water or gas; a cook
common sense *n*	コモンセンス	knowledge of and compliance with social rules
compact *adj*	コンパクト	small
companion *n*	コンパニオン	attractive female guide at a large exhibition
concentric *adj*	コンセント	electric socket
corner *n*	コーナー	section of shop or magazine
country *n*	カントリー	country club; golf club
crank *n*	クランケ	patient
cunning *n*	カンニング	cheating in an exam
deck *n*	デッキ	plimsolls
denomination *n*	デノミ	currency devaluation
depart *v*	デパート(n)	department store
diagram *n*	ダイヤ	railroad timetable
drama *n*	ドラマ	television or radio play
echo *n*	エコー	the accoustics of a space
ego *n*	エゴ	selfishness
enamel *n*	エナメル	patent leather; nail varnish
episode *n*	エピソード	unknown, interesting past event in person's life
escape *n*	エスケープ	to be absent from school or work
evening *n*	イブニング	evening dress
fastener *n*	ファスナー	zip
feminist *n*	フェミニスト	ladies' man
float *n*	フロート	iced, flavoured soda containing a scoop of ice cream
form *n*	ホーム	railway platform
front *n*	フロント	hotel reception desk
fruit punch *n*	フルーツポンチ	non-alcoholic fruit punch
gang *n*	ギャング	group or individual involved in organized crime
glamorous *adj*	グラマー(n)	attractively buxom woman
gown *n*	ガウン	dressing gown
guarantee *n*	ギャラ	performance fee
gum *n*	ゴム	rubber
half *n*	ハーフ	Japanese person of mixed race
handle *n*	ハンドル	steering wheel; handlebars of bike
happening *n*	ハプニング	unexpected incident
hearing *n*	ヒアリング	listening comprehension test for foreign languages
heart *n*	ハート	good or warm feeling
heartfelt *adj*	ハートフル	with good or warm feeling
hip *n*	ヒップ	hip measurement; buttocks
hire *n*	ハイヤー	limousine car hired with driver
hot *adj*	ホット(n)	hot coffee
hustle *n*	ハッスル	complete determination
hut *n*	ヒュッテ	simple accomodation for mountain climbers
hysteria *n*	ヒステリー	bad temper
intelligent *adj*	インテリジェント	something which is computerised
jar *n*	ジャー	electric rice cooker
jeans *n*	ジーンズ	denim
jumper *n*	ジャンパー	jacket of thick, rough cloth
just *adj*	ジャスト	exact
just *adv*	ジャスト	exactly
lemon squash *n*	レモンスカッシュ	fresh lemon drink
lemonade *n*	レモネード	lemon juice and sugar
lip *n*	リップ	lipsalve
machine *n*	ミシン	sewing machine
magic *n*	マジック	marker pen

(JAP)

man to man *adj*	マンツーマン(n)	a one-to-one talk, regardless of sex
mania *n*	マニア	enthusiast
mansion *n*	マンション	large, luxury block of flats
marmot *n*	モルモット	guinea pig
maroon *adj*	マロン(n)	chestnuts
mask *n*	マスク	hygienic cotton face mask
master *n*	マスター	manager of small coffee shop, bar or night club
merit *n*	メリット	advantage
moody *adj*	ムーディ	good atmosphere
morning *n*	モーニング	morning coat
morning service *n*	モーニングサービス	set breakfast at coffee shop
mutton *n*	ムートン	sheepskin
naive *adj*	ナイーブ	sensitive
note *n*	ノート	notebook
one-piece *n*	ワンピース	dress
over *adv*	オーバー(n)	overcoat
pan *n*	パン	bread
part *n*	パート	part-time job
pension *n*	ペンション	small Western-style guesthouse
pest *n*	ペスト	bubonic plague
pierce *n*	ピアス	earings for pierced ears
pill *n*	ピル	contraceptive pill
pincers *n*	ピンセット	tweezers
pink *adj*	ピンク	pornographic, as "blue" in English
pitch *n*	ピッチ	pace
pot *n*	ポット	large domestic thermos flask
potage *n*	ポタージュ	cream of vegetable soup
print *n*	プリント	printed handout made by a teacher for use in class
pudding *n*	プリン	caramel custard
punk *n*	パンク	puncture
range *n*	レンジ	cooking-stove; microwave oven
reform *n*	リフォーム	alteration; repair
report *n*	レポート	written homework assignment
Roman *n*	ロマン	yearning for adventure
running *n*	ランニング	sleeveless undershirt, singlet
sabotage *v*	サボる	to be absent from school or work
sample *n*	サンプル	display models for dishes served in a restaurant
sash *n*	サッシ	aluminium window frame
scoop *n*	スクープ	trowel
seal *n*	シール	sticky label
sense *n*	センス	good taste, particularly in clothes
service *n*	サービス	gratis
sherbet *n*	シャーベット	sorbet
shirt *n*	シャツ	undershirt
short cut *n*	ショートカット	short haircut for women
shortcake *n*	ショートケーキ	slice of cake, especially strawberry/cream cake
sign *n*	サイン	autograph; signature
silver *adj*	シルバー	relating to old age
skin *n*	スキン	condom
slip *v*	スリップ	to skid
smart *adj*	スマート	slim
snack *n*	スナック	small drinking place
spats *n*	スパッツ	leggings
spout *n*	スポイト	dropper
spur *n*	シュプール	ski tracks
steam *n*	スチーム	attachment in a heater to emit steam to humidify the air
stock *n*	ストック	ski stick
stove *n*	ストーブ	room heater
style *n*	スタイル	someone's figure
super *adj*	スーパー(n)	supermarket
talent *n*	タレント	young media celebrity
text *n*	テキスト	textbook, expecially one for foreign language learning
theme *n*	テーマ	subject of research or a thesis
tobacco *n*	タバコ	a cigarette or cigarettes
trap *n*	タラップ	ramp or steps to plane or ship
truck *n*	トロッコ	trolley train
trump *n*	トランプ	playing cards or card game
veteran *n*	ベテラン	expert
vinyl *n*	ビニール	polythene bag; plastic sheet
waist *n*	ウエスト	waist measurement
wet *adj*	ウェット	tender-hearted; sentimental
yell *n*	エール	supportive cheers of spectators at sports game

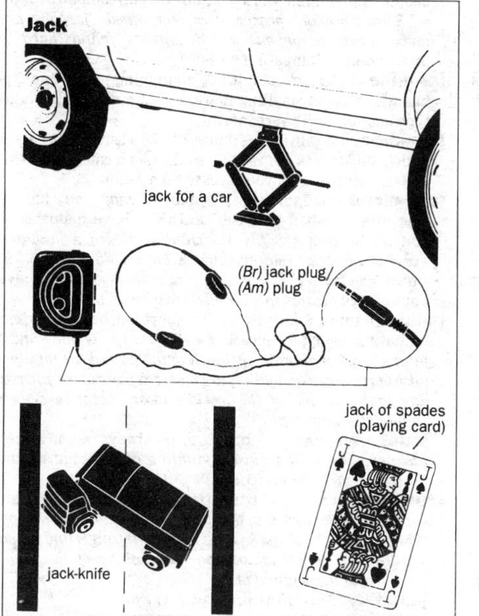

over-confident way which makes you notice him. • *(saying)* 'Jack-of-all-trades, master of none' means a person is able to do many things but is not really very skilled at any of them.

jack [BALL] /dʒæk/ *n* [C] a small ball towards which other balls are rolled or thrown in the games of BOWLS or BOULES

jack in *obj*, **jack** *obj* **in** /dʒæk/ *v adv* [M] *Br infml* to stop doing (esp. something you do not like) • *He jacked in his job after only two weeks.* • *I'm going to jack it in – I'm really tired.* • [PIC]› **Jack**

jack·al /ˈdʒæk·ᵊl/ *n* [C] a wild dog-like animal that lives in Africa and southern Asia and eats animals which have died or been killed by others, or *(fig. disapproving)* a person, country etc. that uses or takes advantage of what is left by others • [PIC]› **Dogs**

jack·a·roo /dʒæk·əˈruː/ *n* [C] *pl* **jackaroos** *Aus* a man who is learning to work on a sheep or cattle farm • Compare JILLAROO.

jack·ass /ˈdʒæk·æs/ *n* [C] *dated* a person who behaves foolishly • Jackass is also *dated Aus for* KOOKABURRA.

jack·boot /ˈdʒæk·buːt/ *n* [C] a long boot which covers the leg up to the knee, esp. as worn by the soldiers of Nazi Germany • If a country is **under the jackboot** it is suffering from a cruel government.

jack·boot·ed /£ˈdʒækˌbuː·tɪd, $-ţɪd/ *adj* • *The play's 'hero', leather-clad and jackbooted* (= wearing jackboots), *was brought brilliantly to life by Joe King.*

jack·daw /£ˈdʒæk·dɔː, $-dɑː/ *n* [C] a black and grey bird of the CROW family, which is thought of as liking to take bright objects back to its nest

jack·et /ˈdʒæk·ɪt/ *n* [C] a short coat • *a leather/denim/tweed/waxed/ski/army jacket* • *The keys are in my jacket pocket.* • A jacket is also the outer loose covering of a book (also **dust jacket**) or the inner covering of a record (also **(inner) sleeve**). • *(Br and Aus)* A **jacket potato** or a potato cooked **in its jacket** is baked whole without the skin being removed. • [PIC]› **Coats and jackets**

jack·ham·mer /£ˈdʒækˌhæm·əʳ, $-ɚ/ *n* [C] *Am and Aus for* a **pneumatic drill**, see at PNEUMATIC [AIR]

jack·knife /ˈdʒæk·naɪf/ *n* [C] a large knife with a blade which folds into the handle

jack–knife /ˈdʒæk·naɪf/ *v* [I] • If a truck which has two parts jack-knifes, the front part swings round to face the back: *The container lorry skidded on the icy road and then jack-knifed.* • [PIC]› **Jack**

jack plug *Br*, *Am* **plug** *n* [C] a metal pin that can be pushed into a SOCKET (= opening) called a **jack** to connect one part of an electrical device to another part, esp. HEADPHONES to a WALKMAN

jack·pot /£ˈdʒæk·pɒt, $-pɑːt/ *n* [C] the largest prize offered in a competition • *We* **won** *the jackpot.*

jack·rab·bit /ˈdʒækˌræb·ɪt/ *n* [C] a large type of N American rabbit

jacks /dʒæks/ *n* [U] *esp. Am* a children's game where you throw a ball into the air and try to pick up a number of small metal or plastic objects with the same hand before catching the ball again

Jac·o·be·an /ˌdʒæk·əˈbiː·ᵊn/ *adj* [not gradable] of the period 1603-1625 when James I was king of the British Isles • *Jacobean furniture* • *a Jacobean mansion*

Ja·cuz·zi, ja·cuz·zi /dʒəˈkuː·zi/ *n* [C] *trademark* a bath or pool of water into which warm water flows through small holes producing a pleasant bubbling effect

jade /dʒeɪd/ *n* [U] a precious green stone from which jewellery and small models are made, esp. in China, Japan and other Eastern countries • *pieces of jade* • *jade earrings* • *a jade brooch*

jad·ed /ˈdʒeɪ·dɪd/ *adj* lacking or losing interest because something has been experienced too many times • *Flying is exciting the first time you do it but you soon become jaded.* • *Perhaps some caviare can tempt your jaded* **palate**.

jag·ged /ˈdʒæg·ɪd/ *adj* rough and uneven, with sharp points • *a jagged cut/tear* • *jagged rocks* • *jagged writing* • *a jagged line* • *a jagged edge*

jaggedly /ˈdʒæg·ɪd·li/ *adv*

jaguar /£ˈdʒæg·ju·əʳ, $-juː·ɑːr/ *n* [C] a large wild cat which lives in Central and S America • [PIC]› **Cats**

jail, *Br dated* **ga·ol** /dʒeɪl/ *n* a place where criminals are kept as a punishment for their crime or while waiting for their trial • *The state of the country's jails was a cause for concern.* [C] • *I hope you realise you will* **go to** *jail* (= be kept in prison) *for a very long time.* [U] • *The financier was* **released from** *jail last week.* [U] • *They spent ten years* **in** *jail* **for** *fraud.* [U] • *The rules were simple – speeds above 120mph meant jail, below 120 meant a large cash fine.* [U] • *He is serving a 13-year jail* **sentence/term** *for smuggling explosives.* • *"Go directly to jail"* (Instruction on the 'Community Chest' card in the game *Monopoly*, 1931) • [LP]› **Crimes and criminals**

jail *obj*, *Br dated* **ga·ol** /dʒeɪl/ *v* [T] • *He was jailed* **for** *three years/***for** *life.*

jailer, *Br dated* **gaol·er** /£ˈdʒeɪ·ləʳ, $-lɚ/ *n* [C] • *The jailer* (= prison guard) *opened the cell door with a large key.*

jail·bird, *Br dated* **ga·ol·bird** /£ˈdʒeɪl·bɜːd, $-bɜːrd/ *n* [C] *infml* a person who has been in prison • *I recognized several old jailbirds among the photographs.*

jailbreak, *Br dated* **ga·ol·break** /ˈdʒeɪl·breɪk/ *n* [C] an escape from prison • *Three prisoners were involved in a dawn jailbreak today.*

jalopy /£dʒəˈlɒp·i, $-ˈlɑː·pi/ *n* [C] *infml humorous* an old car • *I've sold my old jalopy to my neighbour's son.*

jam [FOOD] /dʒæm/, *Am also* **jel·ly** *n* a sweet soft substance made by cooking fruit with sugar to preserve it. It is eaten on bread or cakes. • *strawberry/raspberry jam* [U] • *Has that recipe book got a 'Jams and jellies' section?* [C] • A **jam sandwich** is either two pieces of bread with jam between them or a type of cake made in two parts with jam spread between. • **Jam tomorrow** means something is promised which never happens because tomorrow never comes. If you want **jam today** you mean you want something immediately: *As children we were always being promised jam tomorrow, if only we would be patient.* ○ *The company has to satisfy its shareholders who want jam today.* • *"The rule is jam to-morrow and jam yesterday – but never jam today"* (from the book *Through the Looking Glass* by Lewis Carroll, 1872)

jammy /ˈdʒæm·i/ *adj* **-ier, -iest** • *She left jammy fingermarks on the tablecloth.* • See also JAMMY [EASY]; JAMMY [LUCKY].

jam *(obj)* [STICK] /dʒæm/ *v* **-mm-** to be unable to move; stick • *The door jammed behind me and I was locked out.* [I] • *He jammed the window open with a piece of wood.* [T + obj + adj] • *The motorway was jammed* **solid** (= the traffic could not move) *all morning.* [T + obj + adj] • To jam is also to stop radio signals from reaching the people who want to receive them: *Foreign radio broadcasts were regularly jammed.* [T]

jam /dʒæm/ *n* [C] • *We were* **stuck** *in a* **(traffic)** *jam* (= a line of vehicles unable to move) *for two hours.* • *(infml dated) I'm* **in** *(a bit of)* **a jam** (= a difficult situation) *– could you lend me some money till next week?*

jammed /dʒæmd/ *adj* • *This drawer is jammed.* • *The traffic was jammed* **(up)** *for miles.* • *"The Gatling's* (= type of gun) *jammed and the Colonel's dead"* (from the poem *Vitai Lampeda* by Sir Henry Newbolt, 1897)

jam MUSIC /dʒæm/ *v* [I] **-mm-** to play (esp. popular) music with other people informally without planning it or practising together • *We jammed together for a couple of hours.* • *(infml)* A **jam session** is an informal performance of music when the musicians who play have not planned it or practised together.

jam *obj* PUSH /dʒæm/ *v* [T always + adv/prep] **-mm-** to push or hit (something) hard or with difficulty into something else • *He jammed the boxes* **into** *the back of the car.* • *She jammed* **on** *the brakes when the lights turned red.* [M] • If something is **jam-packed**, it is full of people or things which are pushed closely together: *The streets were jam-packed* **with** *tourists.*

jam /dʒæm/ *n* [U] • *It's/There's a real jam* (= It is full of people) *in there – it took me ten minutes to get to the bar to order drinks.*

jam·boree /ˌdʒæm·bəˈriː/ *n* [C] a large organized event which many people go to, or a busy, noisy occasion or period • *The beer festival was a huge open-air jamboree with music, stalls, activities and everyone enjoying themselves.* • *The 4000 Scouts and Guides at the week-long international jamboree were from 20 countries.* • *(disapproving) The issue was ignored during the huge political jamboree of the Presidential elections.*

jammy LUCKY /ˈdʒæm·i/ *adj* **-ier, -iest** *infml* unfairly lucky • *He wasn't even trying to score – the ball just bounced off the jammy* **beggar's/bastard's** *head into the goal.* • *What a jammy shot!* • See also **jammy** at JAM FOOD.

jammy EASY /ˈdʒæm·i/ *adj* **-ier, -iest** *infml* very easy • *It was a jammy assignment – more of a holiday really.* • See also **jammy** at JAM FOOD.

jangle *(obj)* /ˈdʒæŋ·gl̩/ *v* to make a noise like metal hitting metal or *(fig.)* to cause unpleasant worried feelings • *He jangled his keys in his pocket.* [T] • *The wind-chimes jangled gently in the tree above us.* [I] • *(fig.) The constant whine of the equipment jangled his* **nerves**. [T]

jangled /ˈdʒæŋ·gl̩d/ *adj* • *jangled* **nerves**

jan·gling /ˈdʒæŋ·glɪŋ/ *n* [U] • *the jangling of sleigh bells* • *a loud jangling noise* • *The constant jangling of the telephones got on her nerves.*

janitor /£ˈdʒæn·ɪ·təʳ, $-t̬ɚ/ *n* [C] *Am and Scot Eng for* CARETAKER BUILDING WORKER

January /£ˈdʒæn·juə·ri, $-juː·er·i/ *(abbreviation* **Jan***)* *n* the first month of the year, after December and before February • *22(nd) January/January 22(nd)/22(nd) Jan/Jan 22(nd)* [U] • *Work starts again* **on** *the fifth of January/January the fifth/(esp. Am) January fifth* [U] • *The film came out* **last** *January/is coming out* **next** *January.* [U] • *We're going to America some time* **in/during** *January.* [U] • *It was one of the coldest Januaries ever recorded.* [C] • LP **Dates**

jape /dʒeɪp/ *n* [C] *dated or humorous* an activity done to cause amusement or to trick someone • *Most saw their extraordinary behaviour for what it was – a huge jape.* • *Pretending to jump from a hotel roof was another jape that went wrong when the parachute didn't open.* • *He had a love of schoolboy jokes and* **jolly** *japes.*

jar CONTAINER /£dʒɑːʳ, $dʒɑːr/ *n* [C] a glass or clay container, with a wide opening at the top and sometimes a fitted lid, which is usually used for storing food • *a jar of coffee/tomato sauce/pickles* • *a jam jar* • *Plastic pots are cheaper to transport than glass jars or metal cans.* • *I can't unscrew the lid of this jar.* • *(infml) We* **had** *a jar* (= a drink of beer) *or two at the pub after work.* • PIC **Bottles and flasks, Containers, Coverings** Ⓙ

jar·ful /£ˈdʒɑː·fʊl, $ˈdʒɑːr-/ *n* [C] • *The recipe uses a whole jarful/two jarfuls of jam.*

jar *(obj)* SHAKE /£dʒɑːʳ, $dʒɑːr/ *v* **-rr-** to shake or influence unpleasantly, or to cause unpleasant feelings • *The train stopped suddenly, jarring me against the door.* [T] • *A screech of brakes jarred the silence.* [T] • *The harsh colours jarred the eye* (= were unpleasant to look at). [T] • *His rather superior manner jars* **on** *me.* [I] • To jar **with** is to disagree with, or not to match or fit suitably: *This comment jars with the opinions we have heard expressed elsewhere.* [I] • Ⓙ

jar /£dʒɑːʳ, $dʒɑːr/ *n* [C] • *The tram started to move off* **with** *a jar* (= sudden unpleasant shake).

jar·ring /£ˈdʒɑː·rɪŋ, $ˈdʒɑːr·ɪŋ/ *adj* • Something which is jarring causes unpleasant feelings, esp. because it does not match or fit suitably with other things: *a jarring cry* ○ *jarring colours* ○ *jarring points of view* ○ *a jarring experience*

jar·gon /£ˈdʒɑː·gən, $ˈdʒɑːr-/ *n* [U] *disapproving* special words and phrases which are used by particular groups of people, esp. in their work • *military/legal/computer jargon* • *Some school prospectuses contained jargon and unexplained acronyms which parents found hard to understand.* • Compare TERMINOLOGY.

jas·mine /ˈdʒæz·mɪn/ *n* [C; U] a climbing plant. One type has white sweet-smelling flowers in summer and another type has yellow flowers in winter.

jaun·dice /£ˈdʒɔːn·dɪs, $ˈdʒɑːn-/ *n* [U] a serious disease in which substances not usually in the blood cause your skin and the white part of your eyes to turn yellow

jaun·diced /£ˈdʒɔːn·dɪst, $ˈdʒɑːn-/ *adj fml* judging everything as bad because bad things have happened to you in the past • *Sadly, the child developed a jaundiced* **view** *of personal relationships.* • *I'm afraid I look on all travel companies' claims with a rather jaundiced* **eye**, *having been disappointed by them so often in the past.*

jaunt /£dʒɔːnt, $dʒɑːnt/ *n* [C] a short journey, sometimes including a stay, for pleasure • *Half the fun of our Sunday jaunts to the mountains is lunch with Joe and his family.* • *(disapproving) The soldiers are on extra pay during their 10-day jaunt at one of the world's most expensive resorts, supposedly training.*

jaunt /£dʒɔːnt, $dʒɑːnt/ *v* [I always + adv/prep] *disapproving* • *He's always jaunting* **off** *(abroad/around the world) on business trips.*

jaun·ty /£ˈdʒɔːn·ti, $ˈdʒɑːn·t̬i/ *adj* **-ier, -iest** happy and confident • *He came into the room with a jaunty grin/step.* • *When he came back his hat was at a jaunty angle and he was smiling.* • *The TV adaptation has nothing of the jaunty freshness of the original play.*

jaun·ti·ly /£ˈdʒɔːn·tɪ·li, $ˈdʒɑːn·t̬ɪ-/ *adv*

jaun·ti·ness /£ˈdʒɔːn·tɪ·nəs, $ˈdʒɑːn·t̬ɪ-/ *n* [U]

jave·lin /ˈdʒæv·lɪn/ *n* [C] a long stick with a pointed end which is thrown in sports competitions • *They let him try* **throwing** *the javelin.* • *She was first in* **the** *javelin* (= the competition in which it is thrown). • *The world javelin champion is out of action after a shoulder operation.* • PIC **Sports**

jaw BODY PART /£dʒɔː, $dʒɑː/ *n* [C] the lower part of your face which moves when you open your mouth • *a broken jaw* • *a punch (Br and Aus)* **on**/*(Am)* **in** *the jaw* • *His jaw* **dropped (open)** (= He looked very surprised) *when I walked in.* • If you say someone has a **strong/square** jaw you mean that they look strong and determined. • The **upper** jaw and **lower** jaw are the bones inside the mouth which hold the teeth. • The **jaw bone** is the bone which forms the shape of the lower part of the face.

jaw·line /£ˈdʒɔː·laɪn, $ˈdʒɑː-/ *n* [C usually sing] • *He has a very strong/prominent jawline* (= line made by the bone at the bottom of your face).

jaws /£dʒɔːz, $dʒɑːz/ *pl n* • Jaws are a large mouth and teeth, esp. of a large or fierce animal, or *(fig.)* something which looks like this or is thought of as dangerous : *The lion opened its jaws and roared.* ○ *(fig.) His foot was caught in the jaws of the trap.* ○ *(fig.) We were rescued at the last minute, snatched from the jaws* **of death** (= we nearly died). ○ *(fig.) They still hoped to seize victory from the jaws* **of defeat** (= they were about to be defeated).

jaw TALK /£dʒɔː, $dʒɑː/ *v* [I] *infml disapproving* to talk for a long time • *They were still jawing when I went to bed.* • *He was jawing* **away to** *his girlfriend for hours on the phone.* • *"Jaw-jaw is better than war-war"* (speech by Harold Macmillan, 1958)

jaw /£dʒɔː, $dʒɑː/ *n* [U] • *I met Jane and we had a good jaw over lunch.*

jaw·bon·ing /£ˈdʒɔːˌbəʊ·nɪŋ, $ˈdʒɑːˌboʊ-/ *n* [U] *Am slang* speaking in public or using public pressure to persuade a person, country or organization to do something • *Congresswoman Weintrob accused the committee of excessive jawboning over the issue of trade talks with Europe.*

jaw·break·er SWEET /£ˈdʒɔːˌbreɪ·kəʳ, $ˈdʒɑːˌbreɪ·kɚ/ *n* [C] *Am and Aus* a large hard sweet

jaw·break·er TALK /£ˈdʒɔːˌbreɪ·kəʳ, $ˈdʒɑːˌbreɪ·kɚ/ *n* [C] *infml* a **tongue twister** or *(Aus)* a word which is difficult to pronounce

jay /dʒeɪ/ *n* [C] a noisy, brightly coloured bird

jay·walk /£ˈdʒeɪ·wɔːk, $-wɑːk/ *v* [I] to walk across a road slowly, without being careful about moving vehicles, and in the US at an illegal place or time

jay·walk·er /£ˈdʒeɪ·wɔː·kəʳ, $-wɑː·kɚ/ *n* [C] • *We nearly knocked down a couple of jaywalkers who walked out in front of the car.*

jazz MUSIC /dʒæz/ *n* [U] a type of modern music with a strong beat in which the players do not necessarily follow written musical notes for all or part of the piece • *Jazz originated among black musicians in the southern US.* • PIC› **Musical instruments**

jaz·zy /ˈdʒæz·i/ *adj* **-ier, -iest** • *He enjoyed the jazzy element in the third movement of the symphony.*

jazzed–up /ˌdʒæzdˈʌp/ *adj* • *It's a jazzed-up version of Swan Lake.*

jazz NONSENSE /dʒæz/ *n* [U] *Am slang disapproving* speech without real meaning; nonsense • *I asked where he'd been, but he just gave me* **a line of** *jazz.* • *(also Br and Aus) She told me about her family, her problems* **and all that jazz** (=and other similar things).

jazz *obj* /dʒæz/ *v* [T] *Am slang* • *Don't try to jazz me – tell me what really happened!*

jazz up *obj*, **jazz** *obj* **up** *v adv* [M] *infml* to make (something) more interesting, exciting or enjoyable • *Jazz the dress up* **with** *some bright accessories.* • *He jazzed up the food* **with** *a spicy sauce.*

jaz·zy /ˈdʒæz·i/ *adj* **-ier, -iest** *infml* very bright and colourful • *a jazzy tie/dress* • *jazzy wallpaper/curtains.* • *The range of ceramic jars uses a jazzy combination of spots, stripes and geometric patterns.*

JCB /ˌdʒeɪ·siːˈbiː/ *n* [C] *Br* a machine used for digging and moving earth

jeal·ous UNHAPPY /ˈdʒel·əs/ *adj* unhappy and angry because someone has something you want, or because you think they might take something, such as love, away from you • *Her colleagues are jealous* **of** *her success.* • *Tommy has become very jealous* **of** *his new baby sister because his parents spend so much time with her.* • *Anna* **feels** *jealous every time another woman looks at her boyfriend.* • *He accused his wife of having an affair with another man and stabbed her in a jealous rage.* • Compare **envious** at ENVY.

jeal·ous·ly /ˈdʒel·ə·sli/ *adv* • *She gazed jealously at her friend's new car.*

jeal·ous·y /ˈdʒel·ə·si/ *n* • Jealousy is a feeling of unhappiness and anger because someone has something that you want: *He broke his brother's new bike* **in a fit of** *jealousy.* [U] ○ *She was* **consumed by/eaten up with** (=full of) *jealousy when she heard that he had been given a promotion.* [U] ○ *Nationalist jealousies began to reappear once the neighboring states became independent.* [C] ○ *The team has performed very badly this season due to* **petty** *jealousies* (=feelings of jealousy about unimportant things) *among the players.* [C] • Compare ENVY.

jeal·ous CAREFUL /ˈdʒel·əs/ *adj* extremely careful in protecting someone or something • *Her parents used to keep a jealous* **watch** *over her when she was young.* • If you are jealous **of** a particular quality in your life, you try very carefully to keep it: *She is very jealous of her independence, and doesn't want to get married.* ○ *The president was very jealous of his personal power, and was suspicious of all of his advisors.*

jeal·ous·ly /ˈdʒel·ə·sli/ *adv* • *The company is jealously* (=extremely) *protective of the designs they produce.* • *The exact location of the hotel where the royal couple is staying is a jealously* (=carefully) **guarded** *secret.*

jeans /dʒiːnz/ *pl n* trousers made of DENIM (=a strong cotton cloth) which are worn informally • *Some businesses don't let you wear jeans to the office.* • *He put on a* **pair of** *black cotton jeans and a white T-shirt.* • *She loves expensive clothes and owns at least three pairs of* **designer** *jeans.* • *(Am)* **Blue** jeans are trousers which are made of blue DENIM: *He tried to look like a typical American, eating Big Macs and wearing blue jeans.* • PIC› **Clothes** Ⓙ

jeep /dʒiːp/ *n* [C] a strongly built small American vehicle with four wheels which is used esp. by the army to travel over rough ground • *The mountain road was blocked with jeeps and tanks.* • *Soldiers carrying machine guns patrolled the streets in* **armoured** *jeeps.*

jeep·ers (creep·ers) /£ˈdʒiː·pəz, $-pɚz/ *exclamation esp. Am dated or humorous* an expression of surprise • *Jeepers, just look at the time! I'm going to be late!*

jeer *(obj)* /£dʒɪəʳ, $dʒɪr/ *v* to laugh or shout insults at (someone) in order to show you feel no respect for them • *As the manager came into the room, he was jeered by a group of employees.* [T] • *The people at the back of the hall jeered* **at** *the speaker.* [I] • *"You're in trouble again!" she jeered, after he was told off by one of the teachers for fighting.* [+ clause]

jeer /£dʒɪəʳ, $dʒɪr/ *n* [C] • *The news that the performance was being cancelled was greeted by* **boos and** *jeers from the audience.*

jeer·ing /£ˈdʒɪə·rɪŋ, $ˈdʒɪr·ɪŋ/ *n* [U] • *There was loud jeering from the opposition parties when the prime minister stood up to speak.*

jeer·ing /£ˈdʒɪə·rɪŋ, $ˈdʒɪr·ɪŋ/ *adj* • *Her speech was disrupted by a jeering group of protesters at the front of the crowd.*

jeer·ing·ly /£ˈdʒɪə·rɪŋ·li, $ˈdʒɪr·ɪŋ-/ *adv* • *His friends began to laugh jeeringly when his car broke down and wouldn't start again.*

jeez /dʒiːz/ *exclamation Am slang* an expression of surprise or strong emotion • *"Jeez, what a day!" he said, when he finally got back from the office at 10pm.*

Je·ho·vah /£dʒɪˈhəʊ·və, $-ˈhoʊ-/ *n* [U; not after *the*] the name of God used in the Old Testament of the Bible • A **Jehovah's Witness** is a member of a religious organization which believes that everything written in the Bible is true and whose members refuse to obey any law which opposes their religious principles: *The car crash victim, who was a Jehovah's Witness, refused to have a blood transfusion because it went against her faith.*

je·june /dʒɪˈdʒuːn/ *adj fml disapproving* very simple or childish • *He made jejune generalizations about how all students were lazy and never did any work.*

Jek·yll and Hyde /ˌdʒek·l̩·ənd ˈhaɪd/ *n* [C], *adj* [not gradable] *fml disapproving* (like or being) a person with two very different sides to their personality, one good and the other evil • *He's become something of a Jekyll and Hyde since he started drinking.* • *The professor was a real Jekyll and Hyde* **figure** *– sometimes kind and charming, and at other times rude and obnoxious.* • *"The Strange Case of Dr Jekyll and Mr Hyde"* (book by Robert Louis Stevenson, 1886)

jell /dʒel/ *v* [I] to GEL

Jell–O, jel·lo /£ˈdʒel·əʊ, $-oʊ/ *n* [U] *Am trademark for* JELLY • PIC› **Bread and cakes**

jel·ly /ˈdʒel·i/ *n* a soft, slightly wet substance that shakes when it is moved • *Frogs' eggs are covered in a sort of transparent jelly.* [U] • *Meat jellies are made by boiling animal bones and are often used in meat pies and pâtés.* [C] • *(Br and Aus)* Jelly *(Am* **Jell-O***)* is a soft, coloured sweet food made from sugar, GELATINE and fruit flavours: *I've made a raspberry jelly for the children's tea.* [C] ○ *He had a hamburger and chips and then jelly and ice cream for dessert.* [U] • Jelly is also a smooth sweet food used for spreading on bread which is made by boiling fruit juice and sugar together: *Anne made some redcurrant jelly using fruit from her garden.* [U] ○ *He always has a peanut butter and jelly sandwich when he gets home from school.* [U] ○ *The shelves in the kitchen were filled with jars of preserved vegetables and fruit jellies.* [C] • Jelly is also an oily transparent substance which you put on something to stop it from rubbing or sticking: **Petroleum** *jelly is used as a lubricant, a softener for the skin and as an ingredient in some medicines.* [U] • *(fig. esp. Br) They've threatened to* **beat** *him* **to a** *jelly* (=hit him repeatedly and with great force) *if he doesn't give them back the money he owes.* [U] • If your legs **turn to** jelly, they suddenly feel weak because you are frightened or ill: *As she knocked on the director's door, her legs turned to jelly.* [U] • *(Br)* A **jelly baby** is a small soft fruit-flavoured sweet in the shape of a baby. • A **jelly bean** is a small sweet in the shape of a bean which is soft in the middle and covered with hard sugar. • **Jelly roll** is *Am for* SWISS ROLL. • PIC› **Bread and cakes**

jel·lied /ˈdʒel·id/ *adj* [not gradable] • If meat or fish is jellied, it is cooked and then served in its own juices which become firm when cold: *jellied beef* ○ *jellied eels*

jel·ly·fish /ˈdʒel·i·fɪʃ/ *n* [C] *pl* **jellyfish** or **jellyfishes** a sea animal with a soft oval almost transparent body • *Some jellyfish can give you a nasty sting.* • *(fig. esp. Am) Don't be such a jellyfish* (=weak cowardly person) *– go ahead and ask her to the dance.*

jem·my *Br and Aus* /ˈdʒem·i/, *Am* **jim·my** *n* [C] a short strong metal bar with a curved end which is used esp. by thieves to force open windows or doors • *Thieves have stolen over twenty cars in the area by forcing the doors open with a jemmy.*

jem·my *obj Br and Aus* /ˈdʒem·i/, *Am* **jim·my** *v* [T] • If you jemmy something, such as a window or lock, you force it open using a jemmy: *They live in a violent neighbourhood, and have had strong hinges fitted onto their front door to stop it from being jemmied* (=removed) *from the frame.* ○

The robbers jemmied **open** *the window, grabbed some expensive watches and then made their getaway.* [+ obj + adj]

je ne sa·is quoi /ˌʒə·nə·seɪˈkwɑː/ *n* [U] a pleasing quality which cannot be exactly named or described • *Although he's not particularly attractive, he has this je ne sais quoi which makes him very popular with women.* • *This dish seems to lack* **a certain** *je ne sais quoi – perhaps it needs a bit more spice.*

jeo·par·dize *obj, Br and Aus usually* **-ise** /£ˈdʒep·ə·daɪz, $ˈ-ɚ-/ *v* [T] to cause (a plan or system) to be in danger of being harmed or damaged • *She knew that by failing her exams she could jeopardize her whole future.* • *The disagreement over trade restrictions could seriously jeopardize relations between the two countries.* • *University teaching may be jeopardised if the government increases the number of students without providing additional funding.*

jeo·par·dy /£ˈdʒep·ə·di, $ˈ-ɚ-/ *n* [U] • If something is **in jeopardy**, it is in danger of being damaged or destroyed: *The lives of thousands of birds are in jeopardy as a result of the oil spillage.* ○ *Bad management has* **put** *the company's future in jeopardy.*

jerk *(obj)* MOVE /£dʒɜːk, $dʒɜːrk/ *v* [always + adv/prep] to (cause someone or something to) make a short sudden movement • *She pulled one of the strings and the puppet's arms jerked upwards.* [I] • *"Why has she come?" he asked, jerking his head towards the woman who had just entered the room.* [T] • *The car made a strange noise and then jerked* **to a halt**. [I] • *The policeman jerked the prisoner* **to his feet** *and marched him off.* [T] • *(fig.) The shock of losing his job jerked* (= forced) *him out of his settled lifestyle.* [T]

jerk /£dʒɜːk, $dʒɜːrk/ *n* [C] • *As the train set off, I became aware of every jerk and jolt it was making.* • *She pulled the bush out of the ground* **with** *a sharp jerk.* • *The alarm clock went off and he woke up* **with** *a jerk.* • **With** *a jerk of his thumb, he drew my attention to the notice that said 'No Smoking'.*

jerk·y /£ˈdʒɜː·ki, $ˈdʒɜːr-/ *adj* **-ier, -iest** • *The disease causes sudden jerky* **movements** *of the hands and legs.* • *(fig.) I enjoyed the concert, although the playing was rather jerky* (= uneven) *at times.*

jerk·i·ly /£ˈdʒɜː·kɪ·li, $ˈdʒɜːr-/ *adv* • *Even six months after the accident, he was still moving quite jerkily.*

jerk·i·ness /£ˈdʒɜː·kɪ·nəs, $ˈdʒɜːr-/ *n* [U] • *The latest model of the car has none of the jerkiness of previous ones.*

jerk PERSON /£dʒɜːk, $dʒɜːrk/, *Am also* **jerk–off** /£ˈdʒɜːk·ɒf, $ˈdʒɜːrk·ɑːf/ *n* [C] *slang* a stupid person, esp. a man • *You stupid jerk! You've just spilled beer all down my new shirt!* • *I (Br and Aus)* **felt such a**/*(Am)* **felt like such** *a jerk when I went to the wrong house for the party.*

jerk off *v adv* [I] *taboo slang* (of a man) to MASTURBATE (= give yourself sexual pleasure by rubbing your penis)

jerk·in /£ˈdʒɜː·kɪn, $ˈdʒɜːr-/ *n* [C] a jacket with no sleeves or collar • *Leather jerkins were commonly worn by men in the 16th and 17th centuries.*

jerk·wat·er /£ˈdʒɜːkˌwɔː·təʳ, $ˈdʒɜːrkˌwɑː·t̬ɚ/ *adj Am infml* (of a place) unimportant and a long way from other places • *I grew up in a jerkwater* **town** *in the middle of nowhere that had no movie theater, no recreation center, no nothing.* • Compare BACKWATER.

jerk·y /£ˈdʒɜː·ki, $ˈdʒɜːr-/ *n* [U] *Am* meat that has been cut into long thin strips and dried in the sun • **Beef** *jerky is popular with people who want to lose weight, because it provides lots of iron but does not contain much fat.*

jer·o·bo·am /£ˌdʒer·əˈbəʊ·əm, $-ˈboʊ-/ *n* [C] a very large wine bottle which contains four or six times the usual amount • *First prize in the competition is a holiday for two in Spain and second prize is a jeroboam of champagne.*

jer·ry–built /ˈdʒer·i·bɪlt/ *adj disapproving* built quickly and badly using cheap materials • *The houses were jerry-built – they're only two years old and they're already falling apart.* • *The urgent need for housing has meant that jerry-built apartments have sprung up all over the city.*

jer·rycan, jer·ri·can /ˈdʒer·i·kæn/ *n* [C] a large metal container with flat sides used for storing or carrying liquids such as fuel or water

jer·sey CLOTHING /£ˈdʒɜː·zi, $ˈdʒɜːr-/ *n* [C] a piece of woollen or cotton clothing with sleeves which is worn on the upper part of the body and which does not open at the front • *It's cold outside – you'll need to put on a jersey.* • A jersey is also a shirt which is worn by a member of a sports team: *The leader in a cycling race wears a yellow jersey.* ○ *After spending four months recovering from a knee injury, he was back in an England jersey* (= in the English team) *for the match against New Zealand.* • PIC **Clothes**

jer·sey CLOTH /£ˈdʒɜː·zi, $ˈdʒɜːr-/ *n* [U] soft thin cloth, usually made from wool, cotton or silk, which is used for making clothes • *Jersey is slightly elastic and can stretch to fit your body.* • *She was wearing a tight black jersey dress.*

Jer·sey COW /£ˈdʒɜː·zi, $ˈdʒɜːr-/ *n* [C] a type of pale brown cow which produces very creamy milk • *They kept pigs, chickens and a herd of Jerseys on their farm.*

Je·ru·sa·lem ar·ti·choke /ˌdʒəˈruː·sə·ləm/ *n* [C] a vegetable with a smoky taste which looks like a potato • *The chicken was served with courgettes and Jerusalem artichokes.* • *I've made some Jerusalem artichoke* **soup** *for lunch.*

jest /dʒest/ *n* [C] *fml* something which is said or done in order to amuse • *His proposal was no jest – he was completely sincere.* • If you say something **in jest**, you say it as a joke and do not mean it seriously: *She claims her remarks were only spoken in jest, and that they should never have been published.* ○ *Although his criticisms were made* **half** *in jest, there was also some truth in them.* • *(saying)* 'Many a true word is spoken in jest' means that humorous remarks often contain serious or truthful statements. • Ⓘ

jest /dʒest/ *v* [I] *fml* • *He wasn't jesting when he said he was going to get married next month.* • *She's very embarrassed about what she's done, so we really shouldn't jest* **about** *it.* • *"Don't jest* **with** *me, young man!" said the teacher, looking sternly at the boy.*

jest·er /£ˈdʒes·təʳ, $-tɚ/ *n* [C] • A jester was a man in the past whose job was to tell jokes and make people laugh: *In medieval times, kings and queens often employed* **court** *jesters.*

Jes·u·it /ˈdʒez·juː·ɪt/ *n* [C] a Roman Catholic priest who is a member of the Society of Jesus (= a religious group begun in 1540) • *The Jesuits are active in missionary and educational work.* • *He was educated at a school in Dublin that was run by Jesuits.* • *He spent three years training to be a Jesuit* **priest**.

Je·sus (Christ) /ˈdʒiː·zəs/, **Christ** /kraɪst/ *n* [U; not after *the*] (the title given to) the man who his religious followers believe is the son of God and on whose teachings and life Christianity is based • *In his teachings, Jesus emphasized the importance of love, humility and charity.* • *(slang)* Jesus/Jesus Christ/Christ is sometimes used as an expression of surprise, shock or annoyance, and this is considered offensive by some people: *Jesus, just look what a mess they've made!* ○ *Jesus Christ! She's gone without me!* • *"Jesus Christ, Superstar"* (title of a musical by Tim Rice and Andrew Lloyd Webber, 1971) • *"Jesus loves me! this I know, / For the Bible tells me so"* (Child's hymn by Anna Warner, 1820-1915)

jet STREAM /dʒet/ *n* [C] a thin stream of something, such as water or gas, which is forced out of a small hole • *The whale blew a jet* **of** *water into the air.* • *She held her finger to the bike wheel and felt the jet* **of** *air coming out of the puncture.* • *As the oil well caught fire, a jet* **of** *flames shot 50 metres into the air.* • A jet is also the small hole in a piece of equipment through which gas or another fuel is forced before it is burned: *The* **gas** *jet must be blocked, because the oven won't light.* • A **jet engine** is a very powerful engine. When fuel is burned inside the engine, hot air and gases are produced and then pushed out of the back of the engine at high speed and this forces the engine forwards: *Many commercial and military aircraft are powered by jet engines.* • **Jet propulsion** is a system by which aircraft engines are powered. When fuel is burned inside the engine, hot air and gases are produced and then pushed out of the back of the engine at high speed and this forces the engine forwards: *Rockets and jet aircraft both work by jet propulsion.* • *(trademark)* A **Jet Ski** is a small vehicle on which one or two people can ride on the water and which is moved forward by a fast stream of water being pushed out behind it: *Jet Skis have been banned from the lake because of the danger to swimmers.* ○ *The bay is patrolled by lifeguards* **riding** *jet skis.* ○ *We'd planned to learn how to* **jet-ski**, *but eventually we decided we'd rather just lie around on the beach.* • A **jet stream** is a narrow current of strong winds high above the Earth which move from west to east: *Jet streams can reach speeds of up to 500 kilometres per hour.*

jet AIRCRAFT /dʒet/ *n* [C] an aircraft with a **jet engine**, which is able to fly at extremely high speeds • *We took a jet to the big island, then a propeller plane to the outer island.* • *We flew to New York* **by** *jet.* • *He is very wealthy and owns a $600 000 house and a* **private** *jet.* • *The Boeing 737 is the world's best-selling jet* **airliner**. • *An advanced jet* **fighter** *is being developed which will fly at twice the speed of sound.* •

Jet lag is the feeling of tiredness and confusion which people experience after making a long journey in an aircraft to a place where the time is different from the place they left: *Every time I fly to the States, I* **get** *really bad jet lag.* ○ *Her flight from Melbourne arrived early in the morning and she* **suffered from** *severe jet lag all day.* ○ *I've just got back from Hong Kong so I'm* **feeling** *totally* **jet-lagged**. • *(infml)* The **jet set** are rich fashionable people who travel around the world enjoying themselves: *Since she got married to a Greek millionaire, she's become part of* **the** *jet set.* ○ *Marbella was once thought of as the jet-set paradise for the rich and famous.* ○ *He's a real* **jet-setter** *and owns houses throughout the world.* ○ *She spends the summer* **jet-setting** *around the fashionable European resorts.* • See also JETLINER.

jet /dʒet/ *v* [I always + adv/prep] **-tt-** *infml* • If you jet somewhere, you travel there in a jet aircraft: *The President is jetting* **in** *from Washington tonight.* ○ *I'm jetting* **off** *to New Zealand next week to see Harold and Jennifer.*

jet [STONE] /dʒet/ *n* [U] a hard black stone which shines when rubbed and which is used to make jewellery and other decorative objects • *Her parents gave her a pair of jet earrings for her birthday.* • If something is **jet-black**, it is very dark black: *He has a dark complexion and jet-black* **hair**.

jet·foil /ˈdʒet·fɔɪl/ *n* [C] a HYDROFOIL (=boat with a special structure that makes it able to travel across the surface of water) that is powered by water being sucked in from the sea and forced out at the back at great pressure • *Jetfoils, hydrofoils and catamarans all compete for business on the busy route from Hong Kong to Macau.* • *The company used to operate a jetfoil* **service** *across the English Channel.*

jet·lin·er /£ˈdʒetˌlaɪ·nəʳ, $-nɚ/ *n* [C] a JET (=powerful aircraft) which can carry a lot of passengers

jet·sam /ˈdʒet·səm/ *n* [U] **flotsam and jetsam**, see at FLOTSAM

jet·ti·son *obj* /£ˈdʒet·ɪ·sᵊn, $ˈdʒeţ-/ *v* [T] to throw away or get rid of (something or someone that is not wanted or needed) • *The company has been forced to jettison 200 employees due to financial problems.* • *The airline has jettisoned first class and introduced a new business class on its flights.* • *Sue Jones, who has been running the department for over 10 years, has been jettisoned* **in favour of** *a younger manager.* • If you jettison an idea or plan, you decide not to use it: *We've had to jettison our holiday plans because of David's accident.* ○ *Old ideas of teaching foreign languages have been jettisoned* **for** *new ideas based on recent research.* • If a ship or aircraft jettisons goods, fuel or equipment, it throws them out in order to make itself lighter: *The plane was forced to jettison its load of provisions and make an emergency landing when one of its engines suddenly failed.*

jet·ty /£ˈdʒet·i, $ˈdʒeţ-/ *n* [C] a wooden or stone structure which is built out into the water from the edge of the sea or a lake and which is used by people getting on and off boats • *Small boats were moored along the jetty.* • *As the boat neared the shore, she could see him standing on the wooden jetty, waving at her.*

jet·way /ˈdʒet·weɪ/ *n* [C] the raised enclosed passage through which passengers walk from the airport building to an aircraft • *Would passengers for Stansted please proceed straight down the jetway.*

Jew /dʒuː/ *n* [C] a member of the Hebrew people whose religion is Judaism • *Although my family is Jewish, we're not* **practising** (=religiously active) *Jews.* • *He is an* **orthodox** *Jew* (=He follows traditional religious teachings exactly) *and will only eat kosher food which has been prepared according to strict rules.* • A **Jew's harp** is a small musical instrument which is held between the teeth and played by hitting a metal strip with the finger: *A Jew's harp has only one basic note but you can produce lots of different notes by changing the shape of your mouth.*

Jew·ish /ˈdʒuː·ɪʃ/ *adj* [not gradable] • *Israel was founded as a Jewish state in 1948.* • *New York has one of the largest Jewish communities in the world.*

Jew·ish·ness /ˈdʒuː·ɪʃ·nəs/ *n* [U] • *The artist Chagall believed his Jewishness had a deep influence on his painting.*

Jew·ry /£ˈdʒʊə·ri, $ˈdʒuː-/ *n* [U] *fml* • Jewry is all the members of the Hebrew people whose religion is Judaism: *The Star of David, which is a six-pointed star, has become a symbol of Jewry and appears on the Israeli flag.* ○ *Between 1880 and 1924, one-third of East European Jewry emigrated to other countries as a result of persecution and poverty.*

jew·el /ˈdʒuː·ᵊl/ *n* [C] a precious stone which is used to decorate valuable objects • *a jewel-encrusted sword* • *She was wearing a large gold necklace* **set with** *jewels.* • *(specialized dated)* A jewel is also a small precious stone or a piece of specially cut glass which is used in the machinery of a watch: *It's a Swiss timepiece with a 17-jewel movement.* • If something is described as being a jewel, it is very beautiful or valuable: *The Playhouse is a jewel of a theatre which has recently been restored to its former glory.* ○ *Many visitors consider the Sistine Chapel to be* **the** *jewel* **of** *the Vatican.* • *(dated)* If you say that someone is a jewel, you mean that they are very kind: *My son's a* **real** *jewel – he always makes me a cup of tea when I get home from work.* • If something is described as being the **jewel in the crown** of something or someone, it is the best or most valuable thing that belongs to them: *The island of Tresco, with its beautiful tropical gardens, is the jewel in the crown of the Scilly Isles.* • *"The Jewel in the Crown"* (title of a book about India by Paul Scott, 1966)

jew·els /ˈdʒuː·ᵊlz/ *pl n* • Jewels are decorative objects worn on clothes or on the body which are made from valuable metals, such as gold and silver, and which usually contain precious stones: *The actress has decided to auction her jewels to raise money for a children's charity.* ○ *She keeps her diamond bracelet in a jewel* **case/box** *in her bedroom.*

jew·elled, *Am usually* **jew·eled** /ˈdʒuː·əld/ *adj* • *She wore a green velvet dress with jewelled buttons for the opening night of the play.* • *Some of the famous Fabergé jeweled eggs, fashioned from gold and precious stones, are currently on exhibition in Paris.*

jew·el·ler, *Am usually* **jew·el·er** /£ˈdʒuː·ə·ləʳ, $-lɚ/ *n* [C] • A jeweller is a person who sells and sometimes repairs jewellery and watches: *My watch is at the jeweller's being repaired.* ○ *Thieves stole £25 000 worth of gold jewellery in an armed raid on a jeweller's shop.*

jew·el·lery *Br and Aus, Am* **jew·el·ry** /ˈdʒuː·ᵊl·ri/ *n* [U] • Jewellery is decorative objects worn on clothes or on the body which are usually made from valuable metals, such as gold and silver, and which usually contain precious stones: *Tourists have been advised not to wear expensive jewellery in public places or they will become easy targets for thieves.* ○ *The singer was wearing a leather suit and heavy* **gold** *jewellery for the interview.* ○ *She opened her jewellery* **box** *and took out a pearl necklace and matching earrings.* • [LP]› **Shopping goods** [PIC]› **Jewellery**

jew·fish /ˈdʒuː·fɪʃ/ *n pl* **jewfish** or **jewfishes** a large fish which lives in warm or tropical seas • *She'd caught a couple of jewfish.* [C] • *Jewfish is often eaten in cutlets.* [U]

Jeye cloth /ˈdʒeɪ/ *n* [C] *trademark* a J-CLOTH (=a cloth used for cleaning things)

Jez·e·bel /ˈdʒez·ə·bel/ *n* [C] *disapproving* an immoral woman who deceives people in order to get what she wants • *The main character in the novel is Alexa, a scheming Jezebel who is involved in corrupt business deals.*

jib [BOAT] /dʒɪb/ *n* [C] *specialized* a small triangular sail on a boat, in front of the main sail • *When the wind had died down a little, we hoisted the jib and set sail for the shore.*

jib [LIFTING DEVICE] /dʒɪb/ *n* [C] *specialized* a long horizontal bar that sticks out from a CRANE (=a tall machine for lifting heavy objects) and from which the hook hangs • *The jib of a crane is made from a very strong thick piece of steel to stop it from bending under heavy weights.*

jib at *obj v prep* [T] **-bb-** *dated* to be unwilling to do or continue with (something) • *She didn't mind working hard, but she jibbed at the prospect of doing overtime.* • *Although the new tax is unpopular, the government has jibbed at abolishing it completely.* [+ v-ing] • If a horse jibs at something, it stops suddenly and will not continue: *His horse jibbed at the final fence in the competition and he lost five marks.*

jibe, *Am usually* **gibe** /dʒaɪb/ *n* [C] an insulting remark that is intended to make someone look stupid • *She's very sensitive about her weight, so why did you have to* **make** *such a cruel jibe* **about** *her being fat?* • *Unlike many other politicians, he refuses to indulge in* **cheap** *jibes at other people's expense.*

jibe, *Am usually* **gibe** /dʒaɪb/ *v* [I] • *She jibed* **at** *the way he ran his business in such an unprofessional manner.*

jibe with *obj, not standard* **jive with** *v prep* [T] *Am and Aus infml* to be the same as (something else) or agree with it • *Her account of the accident jibes with mine.* • *The recent report showing economic growth doesn't jibe with an earlier report that showed a fall in consumer spending.*

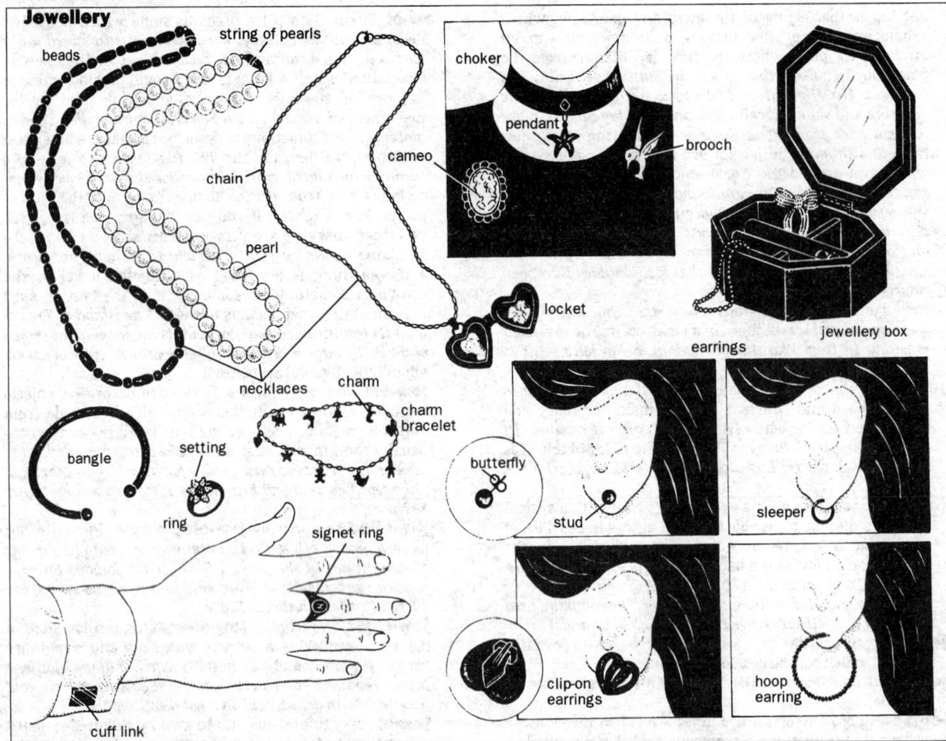

jif·fy /ˈdʒɪf·i/ *n* [U] *infml* a very short time • *I'm in the middle of a phone call right now, but I'll be with you* **in a** *jiffy.* • *I've just got to fetch some books from upstairs – I* **won't be a** *jiffy* (= I will be very quick).

Jif·fy bag /ˈdʒɪf·i/ *n* [C] *trademark* a thick light envelope in which things that need protecting are sent through the post

jig DANCE /dʒɪg/ *n* [C] an energetic traditional dance of Great Britain and Ireland, or the music that is played for such a dance • *At school we were taught how to do traditional folk dances such as jigs and reels.* • *The band started to* **play** *a jig and everyone got up to dance.* • *(fig.) When his team scored the winning goal, he* **danced** *a triumphant jig by the side of the pitch.*

jig *(obj)* MOVE /dʒɪg/ *v* [always + adv/prep] **-gg-** to (cause someone or something to) move quickly up and down or from side to side • *Stop jigging* **about**, *Billy, and just stand still for a moment!* [I] • *People in the audience were jigging* **up and down** *in time to the music.* [I] • *The baby laughed and smiled as she jigged it* **up and down** *on her knee.* [T]

jig DEVICE /dʒɪg/ *n* [C] *specialized* a device for holding a tool or some material, such as wood, firmly in position while you work with it

jig TRICK /dʒɪg/ *n* [U] **the jig is up** *Am infml* the secret or trick has been discovered • *Once they were seen holding hands, the jig was up – they couldn't pretend they were just friends any more.*

jig·ger CONTAINER /£ˈdʒɪg·əʳ, $-ɚ/ *n* [C] a small round metal container which is used for measuring strong alcoholic drinks • *(Am)* A jigger is also the amount of alcohol which this container holds: *a jigger of whiskey* ○ *A jigger is approximately equal to 1·5 oz or 45 ml.*

jig·ger *obj* CHANGE /£ˈdʒɪg·əʳ, $-ɚ/ *v* [T] *Am* to change (something), esp. unfairly or illegally • *The ruling party jiggered the election results to be sure they would stay in power.*

jig·gered SURPRISED /£ˈdʒɪg·əd, $-ɚd/ *adj* [after v; not gradable] *Br infml dated* surprised • *"Did you know that Ann's pregnant?" "Well,* **I'll be** *jiggered* (= I am surprised)*!"*

jig·gered TIRED /£ˈdʒɪg·əd, $-ɚd/ *adj* [not gradable] *Br and Aus infml dated* extremely tired • *"How did you feel after yesterday's match?" "Completely jiggered!"*

jig·ger·y–po·ke·ry /£ˌdʒɪg·ᵊr·iˈpəʊ·kᵊr·i, $-ɚ·iˈpoʊ·kɚ-/ *n* [U] *infml dated* secret or dishonest behaviour • *I think there's been some jiggery-pokery going on in the Finance Department.*

jig·gle *(obj)* /ˈdʒɪg·l̩/ *v* to (cause something to) move from side to side or up and down with quick short movements • *If the door won't open, try jiggling the key in the lock.* [T] • *He jiggled some loose coins* **about** *in his pocket while he waited his turn.* [T] • *His eyebrows jiggled* **up and down** *in amusement as she told him the story.* [I]

jig·gle /ˈdʒɪg·l̩/ *n* [C] • *If the radio doesn't work, just give it a quick jiggle.*

jig·saw (puz·zle) /£ˈdʒɪg·sɔː, $-sɑː/ *n* [C] a picture stuck onto wood or cardboard and cut into irregular pieces which must be joined together correctly to form the picture again • *We spent all evening* **doing** *a 1000-piece jigsaw.* • *(fig.) After the fall of Communism, the map of Eastern Europe started to look like a nationalistic jigsaw.* • *(fig.) The police are trying to* **piece together** *the jigsaw* (= solve the complicated problem) *of how the dead man spent his last hours.* • PIC› **Toy**

jig·saw /£ˈdʒɪg·sɔː, $-sɑː/ *n* [C] a tool with an electric motor and a thin steel blade which is used for cutting curves in flat materials, such as wood or metal • *A jigsaw can cut angles, corners and shapes quickly and precisely.*

ji·had /dʒɪˈhæd/ *n* a holy war which is fought by Muslims against people who are a threat to the Islamic religion or who oppose its teachings • *The end result of the holy jihad will be victory.* [C] • *Many people in the country have begun calling for armed jihad* **against** *the infidels.* [U] • A jihad can also be a spiritual fight against the evil in yourself. [C]

jil·lar·oo /ˌdʒɪl·əˈruː/ *n* [C] *pl* **jillaroos** *Aus* a woman who is learning to work on a sheep or cattle farm • Compare JACKAROO.

jilt *obj* /dʒɪlt/ *v* [T] to finish a close loving relationship with (someone) in a sudden and cruel way • *She was jilted two days before her wedding.* • *He was so unhappy after his girlfriend had jilted him* **for** *another man that he threatened to kill himself.*

jilt·ed /£ˈdʒɪl·tɪd, $-t̬ɪd/ *adj* [not gradable] • *Her jilted boyfriend has sworn revenge on her new husband.*

Jim Crow /£ˌdʒɪmˈkrəʊ, $-ˈkroʊ/ *n* [U; not after *the*] *Am dated disapproving* keeping black people apart from white people in public places, public vehicles and employment • *They moved to Alabama in the 1920s, the era of Jim Crow, and suffered from racist attacks because of the color of their skin.* • *As a child, my grandfather went to a jim crow* **school** (= a school for black children only). • Jim Crow **laws** were the laws made in the United States in the late 19th century to keep black people separate from white people: *Jim Crow* *laws were abolished in the 1960s as a result of the civil rights' movement.*

jim–dan·dy /ˌdʒɪmˈdæn·di/ *n* [C] *pl* **jim-dandies** *Am infml dated or humorous* something which is very pleasing or of excellent quality • *That new car you bought is a real jim-dandy.*

jim–dan·dy /ˌdʒɪmˈdæn·di/ *adj Am infml dated or humorous* • *He made a jim-dandy* **speech** *and persuaded everyone to vote for him.*

jim·jams [CLOTHING] /ˈdʒɪm·dʒæmz/ *pl n Br infml for* PYJAMAS (= shirt and trousers which are worn in bed) • *"Go and put your jimjams on, then I'll come and read you a bedtime story," she said to the children.*

jim·jams [SHAKING] /ˈdʒɪm·dʒæmz/ *pl n* **the jimjams** *infml* shaking of the body that happens when someone who drinks a large amount of alcohol stops drinking

jim·my /ˈdʒɪ·mi/ *n* [C], *v* [T] *Am for* JEMMY

jin·gle *(obj)* [RING] /ˈdʒɪŋ·gl̩/ *v* to (cause to) make a repeated gentle ringing sound • *He jingled the coins in his pocket, wondering what to buy.* [T] • *She waited for him by the car, jingling the keys in her hand.* [T] • *The ice cubes at the bottom of the glass jingled as she picked up her drink.* [I] • *"Jingle bells, jingle bells, jingle all the way"* (Christmas song written by J.S.Pierpont, 1957)

jin·gle /ˈdʒɪŋ·gl̩/ *n* [U] • *They could hear the jingle of bells as the sleigh came towards them.*

jin·gle [TUNE] /ˈdʒɪŋ·gl̩/ *n* [C] a short simple tune, often with words, which is very easy to remember and which is used to advertise a product on the radio or television • *I don't like listening to commercial radio because there are so many jingles.* • *She hummed an* **advertising** *jingle as she made herself a cup of coffee.*

jin·go·i·sm /£ˈdʒɪŋ·gəʊ·ɪ·zᵊm, $-goʊ-/ *n* [U] *disapproving* the extreme belief that your own country is always best, which is often shown in enthusiastic support for a war against another country • *Patriotism can turn into jingoism and intolerance very quickly.*

jin·go·ist /£ˈdʒɪŋ·gəʊ·ɪst, $-goʊ-/ *n* [C] *disapproving* • *He was a confirmed jingoist and would frequently speak about the dangers of Britain forming closer ties with the rest of Europe.*

jin·go·is·tic /£ˌdʒɪŋ·gəʊˈɪs·tɪk, $-goʊ-/ *adj disapproving* • *In wartime, newspapers tend to become jingoistic.* • *There were great celebrations and plenty of jingoistic flag-waving when the first troops returned from the war.*

jinx /dʒɪŋks/ *n* [U] bad luck, or a person or thing that is believed to bring bad luck • *There's* **a** *jinx* **on** *this computer – it's gone wrong three times this morning!* • *"Someone must have* **put** *a jinx* **on** *the team," said the coach, "because four of my players are injured and won't be able to play in the final."* • *He's sure the new play will be a great success and will* **break** *the jinx which has caused every new production in the theatre to be a disaster.*

jinxed /dʒɪŋkst/ *adj* • *I must be jinxed – whenever I touch a glass, it breaks.*

jit·ney /ˈdʒɪt·ni/ *n* [C] *Am* a small bus that follows a regular route

jit·ters /£ˈdʒɪt·əz, $ˈdʒɪţ·ɚz/ *pl n infml* a feeling of nervousness which you experience before something important happens • *I always* **get the** *jitters the morning before an exam.* • *By the second performance, some of* **the** *first-night jitters were over and the actors began to relax a bit more.* • *(fig.) The collapse of the company has caused jitters in the financial markets.* • If you **give** someone **the jitters**, you make them nervous or frightened: *Come away from that cliff edge! You're giving me the jitters!*

jit·ter·y /£ˈdʒɪt·ᵊr·i, $ˈdʒɪţ·ɚ-/ *adj* **-ier, -iest** *infml* • *Congress was in a jittery mood after the unexpected speech by the president.* • *He* **felt** *all jittery before the interview.* • *I* **get** *really jittery* (= shaky) *if I drink too much coffee.*

jiu·jit·su /ˌdʒuːˈdʒɪt·suː/ *n* [U] *Aus for* JU-JITSU

jive [DANCE] /dʒaɪv/ *n* [U] a fast dance which was very popular with young people in the 1940s and 1950s • *My father taught me how to do* **the** *jive.* • *He loved collecting old recordings of jazz and jive* **music**.

jive /dʒaɪv/ *v* [I] • *The band began playing some old Elvis Presley hits and they spent the evening jiving* **to** *their favourite songs.*

jive [TALK] /dʒaɪv/ *n* [U] *Am slang* talk which is meaningless or dishonest • *You can say what you like, but I'm not going to listen to any more of your jive.* • *Don't believe a word he says, it's all just* **a bunch of** (= a lot of) *jive!* • *"Jive Talkin'"* (title of song by the Bee Gees, 1975)

jive *obj* /dʒaɪv/ *v* [T] *Am slang* • If you jive someone, you try to make them believe something which is not true: *Quit jiving me and just tell me where you were!*

Jnr *Br and Aus* /£ˈdʒuː·ni·ər, $-ɚ/, *esp. Am* **Jr** *adj* [after n; not gradable] *abbreviation for* JUNIOR [YOUNGER]. Used after a man's name to refer to the younger of two people in the same family who have the same name.

job [EMPLOYMENT] /£dʒɒb, $dʒɑːb/ *n* [C] the regular work which a person does to earn money • *When she left college, she* **got** *a job* **as** *an editor in a publishing company.* • *My mother found it very difficult trying to bring up two children while* **doing** *a* **full-time** *job.* • *He has a* **part-time** *job working in a garage.* • *After 10 years as a freelance journalist, she finally got a* **steady** (= permanent) *job working for The Sydney Morning Herald.* • *Clive's got a* **temporary** *job working in a pub over the summer.* • *She's* **applied for** *a job* **with** *an insurance company.* • *The new supermarket will* **create** *50 new jobs in the area.* • *Are you going to* **give up** *your job when you have your baby?* • *(Br and Aus) The government is encouraging companies to provide new jobs for the unemployed with job* **creation schemes**. • *If the company is to increase its profits, there will have to be job* **cuts**. • *The closure of the factory will result in heavy job* **losses**. • *He's never managed to* **hold down** (= keep) *a* **regular** *job in his life.* • *I used to have a* **nine-to-five** *job* (= work regular hours) *in an office, but now I run my own business.* • *He lost his job as a security guard after falling asleep* **on the** *job* (= while at work). • *Her new employers have offered her* **on-the-job** *training* (= training while she is working). • *How long have you been* **out of** *a job* (= unemployed)? • *She decided to leave a* **top** (= high-ranking) *job in advertising to do charity work.* • *After a disastrous first month in office, many people are beginning to wonder if the new president is* **up to** (= able to do) *the job.* • *(Br and Aus infml disapproving)* **Jobs for the boys** is work which is given by someone in an important position to their friends or relatives: *The council has denied accusations of jobs for the boys, but it's well known that its supporters have been given important contracts.* • *(Br and Aus infml) It's* **more than** *my* **job's worth** *to lend you this key* (= I risk losing my job if I let you have it). • *(Am)* A **job action** is a temporary show of lack of satisfaction by a group of workers, often by doing their work more slowly, in order to make their demands noticeable. • *(Br)* A **job centre** is a government office where unemployed people can go for advice and information about jobs which are available. • A **job description** is a list of the responsibilities which you have and the duties which you are expected to perform in your work. • *(Br)* **Job evaluation** is the process of examining a job in relation to other jobs in an organization and of deciding how much the person who is doing the job should be paid. • **Job satisfaction** is the feeling of pleasure and achievement which you experience in your job when you know that your work is worth doing, or the degree to which your work fulfils your expectations and hopes: *Many people are more interested in job satisfaction than in earning large amounts of money.* • If you have **job security**, your job is likely to be permanent: *There is a lack of job security in professions such as acting and journalism in which people are only employed for short periods of time.* • [LP]> **Work**

job·less /£ˈdʒɒb·ləs, $ˈdʒɑːb·ləs/ *adj* [not gradable] • If you are jobless, you are unemployed: *He's been jobless for the past six months.*

job·less /£ˈdʒɒb·ləs, $ˈdʒɑːb·ləs/ *pl n esp. Br* • **The jobless** are unemployed people: *The council has been running training schemes for the jobless.* • *The jobless* **total** (= The number of people unemployed) *reached four million this week.*

job·less·ness /£ˈdʒɒb·lə·snəs, $ˈdʒɑːb·lə-/ *n* [U] • *Joblessness can cause poverty, depression and frustration.*

job [PIECE OF WORK] /£dʒɒb, $dʒɑːb/ *n* [C] a particular piece of work • *"How long will the work take you?" "I should get the job done by lunchtime."* • *A food processor makes the job of preparing food a lot easier.* • *He spent the afternoon doing jobs around the house, such as putting up shelves and repairing the broken pipe in the kitchen.* • *(infml) The living room badly needs a paint job* (= It needs to be painted), *but we just haven't got the time to do it at the moment.* • *(infml) Will you be able to carry all the shopping back home on your bike, or will it have to be a car job* (= will you need the car)? • *(infml)* If something **does the job**, it performs the piece of work you want to be done and achieves the result you want: *I don't have a box large enough to fit all your books in, but* *this bag should do the job.* • If you **do a** particular type of **job**, you do a piece of work in that particular way: *I didn't think Chris would be any good at fund raising for the society, but she seems to be doing a good job.* • If you **do/make a** particular type of **job of** something, you do that activity in that particular way: *The dry cleaner's did a good job of removing that oil stain from my shirt.* ○ *She did a splendid job of decorating the house for the party.* ○ *I'm not going to let him repair my bike again because he made a really bad job of it last time.* • The **job in hand**/*(Am also)* **job at hand** is the piece of work which you are doing at the present time: *Don't worry about what you have to do next week – just concentrate on the job in hand.* • If someone is described as being **just the man** or **woman for the job**, they are exactly suited to a particular piece of work: *We need someone who has experience in marketing and teaching, and I think Alex is just the woman for the job.*

job·bing /£ˈdʒɒb·ɪŋ, $ˈdʒɑː·bɪŋ/ *adj* [before n; not gradable] • A jobbing **actor/builder/gardener/journalist** does not work regularly for one person or organization but does small pieces of work for different people.

job DUTY /£dʒɒb, $dʒɑːb/ *n* [U] responsibility or duty • *She believed her job as a politician was* **to** *represent the views of her party and the people who voted for her.* [+ *to* infinitive] • *I know it's not my job* **to** *tell you how to run your life, but I do think you've made a mistake.* [+ *to* infinitive]

job PROBLEM /£dʒɒb, $dʒɑːb/ *n* [U] *infml* a problem or an activity which is difficult • **It** *was a real job getting the wheel off the bike.* [+ v-*ing*] • *We were only given an hour to do the exam, and I* **had a** *job finishing the paper.* [+ v-*ing*] • **What a job** (= How difficult) *it was, trying to persuade her to come with us!* [+ v-*ing*] • *"I'd like to speak to Ernest Brown." "You'll* **have a** *job – he's been dead five years!"*

job EXAMPLE /£dʒɒb, $dʒɑːb/ *n* [C] *infml* an example of a particular type • *"What sort of car are you interested in?" "I really like that red sports job in the showroom window."* • If you describe something as being **just the job**, it is exactly what you want or need: *I've been looking for a new stereo system for my car, and this one's just the job.*

job CRIME /£dʒɒb, $dʒɑːb/ *n* [C] *slang* a crime in which money or goods are stolen, or an action or activity which is dishonest or unpleasant • *He was put in prison for five years for* **doing** *a* **bank** *job.* • *The author has done a real* **demolition** *job* **on** (= She has written unpleasant things about) *the actor in her recent book about his life.* See also **hatchet job** at HATCHET. • *(Am) He really* **did** *a job* **on** *her, telling her that he would love her for ever and then moving to Fiji with someone else.*

job lot *n* [C] a collection of various objects which are bought or sold as a group • *I bought a job lot* **of** *children's books which were being sold off really cheaply.*

job·share /£ˈdʒɒb·ʃeəʳ, $ˈdʒɑːb·ʃer/ *v* [I] *Br* to divide the duties and the pay of one job between two or more people who work at different times during the day or week • *Sarah and her friend Liz are planning to jobshare – she'll work in the mornings and Liz will work in the afternoons.*

job·share /£ˈdʒɒb·ʃeəʳ, $ˈdʒɑːb·ʃer/ *n* [C] *Br* • *The City Council are encouraging jobshares in order to make it easier for parents of small children to work.*

job·shar·ing /£ˈdʒɒbˌʃeə·rɪŋ, $ˈdʒɑːbˌʃer·ɪŋ/ *n* [U] *Br* • *Jobsharing is becoming increasingly popular among people who want to study or spend more time with their families.*

Jock SCOTLAND /£dʒɒk, $dʒɑːk/ *n* [C] *Br slang* a man who comes from Scotland • *Jock is a name used by English people for Scotsmen and it is considered offensive by some people.* • *That pub's always full of Jocks.* • *When he first moved from Glasgow to Manchester, people made fun of his Scottish accent and called him Jock.*

jock SPORT /£dʒɒk, $dʒɑːk/ *n* [C] *Am infml disapproving* a person who is extremely enthusiastic about sport • *My class at college was full of real jocks whose only interests were football and baseball.* • *It's rare that a person is both a jock and an honors student.*

jock·ey SPORTSPERSON /£ˈdʒɒk·i, $ˈdʒɑː·ki/ *n* [C] a person whose job is riding horses in races • *At 1·5 metres, she was an ideal height to be a jockey.* • *He was champion jockey for ten consecutive years.*

jock·ey GET ADVANTAGE /£ˈdʒɒk·i, $ˈdʒɑː·ki/ *v* to attempt to obtain power or get into a more advantageous position than other people using any methods you can • *With the death of the president, opposition parties and the army have been jockeying* **for** *power.* [I always + prep] • *Jockeying* **for** *top jobs in the company has been fierce among many of the senior staff.* [I always + prep] • *As the singer came on stage, the photographers jockeyed* **for position** *at the front of the hall.* [I always + prep] • *The major oil companies were jockeying* **to** *appear the most environmentally concerned.* [+ *to* infinitive]

jock·ey *obj* **into** *obj v prep* [T] to persuade (someone) to do what you want, often by deceiving them in a clever way • *The bosses were eventually jockeyed into signing the union agreement.* [+ obj + v-*ing*]

jocks /£dʒɒks, $dʒɑːks/ *pl n Aus infml* a piece of underwear worn by men and boys which covers the area between the waist and the tops of the legs

jock·strap /£ˈdʒɒk·stræp, $ˈdʒɑːk-/, *fml* **ath·let·ic sup·port** *n* [C] a tight piece of clothing worn by men under their trousers or shorts to support and protect their sex organs when playing sport

jo·cose /£dʒəˈkəʊs, $dʒoʊˈkoʊs/ *adj fml or literary* amusing or playful • *His jocose manner was unsuitable for such a solemn occasion.*

jo·cose·ly /£dʒəˈkəʊ·sli, $dʒoʊˈkoʊ·sli/ *adv fml or literary*

joc·u·lar /£ˈdʒɒk·jʊ·ləʳ, $ˈdʒɑː·kjə·lɚ/ *adj slightly fml* amusing or intended to cause amusement • *She said she had called him an idiot in a jocular fashion and had not meant to offend him.* • *As we sat waiting for Carol, he made a jocular* **comment** *about her always arriving half an hour late.* • If a person is described as jocular, they are happy and like to make jokes: *Our next-door neighbour is a very cheerful, jocular man.* ○ *Michael was in a very jocular* **mood** *at the party, making jokes and telling funny stories.*

joc·u·lar·ly /£ˈdʒɒk·jʊ·lə·li, $ˈdʒɑː·kjə·lɚ-/ *adv slightly fml* • *The star player on the team, who is twice the size of everyone else, is jocularly known as 'Tiny Tim'.*

joc·u·lar·i·ty /£ˌdʒɒk·jʊˈlær·ə·ti, $ˌdʒɑː·kjəˈler·ə·t̬i/ *n* [U] *slightly fml* • *Her speech was dull and boring, despite an attempt at jocularity at the end.*

jodh·purs /£ˈdʒɒd·pəz, $ˈdʒɑːd·pɚz/ *pl n* trousers which are loose above the knees and tight below them and which are designed to be worn when riding a horse • *She's just bought herself a* **pair of** *jodhpurs even though she's only ever been riding once before.*

Joe Bloggs *Br* /£ˌdʒəʊˈblɒgz, $ˌdʒoʊˈblɑːgz/, *Am and Aus* **Joe Blow** /£ˌdʒəʊˈbləʊ, $ˌdʒoʊˈbloʊ/ *n* [U; not after *the*] *infml* an average or typical man • *This stereo system is the most expensive in the range and is not the sort of thing that Joe Bloggs would buy.*

Joe Pub·lic *Br infml* /£ˌdʒəʊˈpʌb·lɪk, $ˌdʒoʊ-/, *Am infml* **John Q Pub·lic** /£ˌdʒɒn·kjuːˈpʌb·lɪk, $ˌdʒɑːn-/ *n* [U; not after *the*] the general public • *The government's decision to tax gas and electricity has not been popular with Joe Public.*

jo·ey /£ˈdʒəʊ·i, $ˈdʒoʊ·i/ *n* [C] *Aus infml* a young KANGAROO (= a large Australian mammal which moves by jumping)

jog RUN /£dʒɒg, $dʒɑːg/ *v* [I] **-gg-** to run at a slow regular speed, esp. as a form of exercise • *"What do you do to keep fit?" "I jog and go swimming."* • *She jogs for twenty minutes every morning before breakfast.* • *He was walking at a very quick pace and I had to jog to keep up with him.* • *(infml)* If your work **jogs along**, it advances at a slow but regular speed: *"How's your research going?" "Oh, it's jogging along".* • If you move at a **jog-trot**, you run at a slow regular speed: *Bill's not a very fast runner and can't manage anything more than a jog-trot.*

jog /£dʒɒg, $dʒɑːg/ *n* [U] • *I haven't done much exercise all week, so I think I'll* **go for a** *jog this morning.*

jog·ger /£ˈdʒɒg·əʳ, $ˈdʒɑː·gɚ/ *n* [C] • *There was hardly anyone about when I went out early this morning – only a jogger and a man walking his dog.*

jog·ging /£ˈdʒɒg·ɪŋ, $ˈdʒɑː·gɪŋ/ *n* [U] • *My hobbies are jogging and playing tennis.* • *Regular jogging on hard surfaces such as roads or pavements can be bad for your knees.* • *When the president* **goes (out)** *jogging, he is surrounded by bodyguards.* • *When I went to see her in her office at 9.30a.m., she was still dressed in her jogging* **gear** (= clothing). • A **jogging suit** consists of a shirt and loose trousers, often made of cotton, which are worn informally or when going running.

jog *obj* PUSH /£dʒɒg, $dʒɑːg/ *v* [T] **-gg-** to push or knock (someone or something) slightly, esp. with the arm • *Don't jog me or I'll spill this drink!* • *As she came out of the shop, a man rushed past and jogged her* **elbow**, *making her drop her bag.* • If something **jogs** your **memory**, it makes you remember something: *The police showed him a photo to try to jog his memory about what had happened on the night of the robbery.*

jog /£dʒɒg, $dʒɑːg/ *n* [C usually sing] • *As he walked past the table, he accidentally* **gave** *the pile of books a jog with his arm, knocking several to the floor.* • *Hearing her voice will perhaps* **give** *your* **memory** *a jog* (= help you to remember).

jog MOVE FORWARD /£dʒɒg, $dʒɑːg/ *v* [I always + adv/prep] **-gg-** (of a vehicle) to move forward slowly and shakily • *The cart jogged* **down** *the rough track towards the farm.* • *We were getting more and more uncomfortable as we jogged* **along** *in the back of the truck.*

jog·gle *obj* /£'dʒɒg·l̩, $'dʒɑː·gl̩/ *v* [T] to shake or move (someone or something) up and down in a gentle way • *The baby will stop crying if you joggle her* **about** *a bit.*

john TOILET /£'dʒɒn, $'dʒɑːn/ *n* [C] *Am and Aus infml* a toilet • *I'm just* **going to** *the john – can you wait for me?* • LP **Phrases and customs**

john PERSON /£'dʒɒn, $'dʒɑːn/ *n* [C] *Am slang* a man who is the customer of a PROSTITUTE (= a woman who has sex for money)

John Bull /£ˌdʒɒn'bʊl, $ˌdʒɑːn-/ *n* [U; not after *the*] *dated infml* a character who represents a typical Englishman or the English people in general • *John Bull is traditionally depicted as a short fat man wearing a waistcoat with the British flag on it.* • *In political cartoons, national figures are often used to represent countries, such as John Bull for England or Uncle Sam for the United States.*

John Doe *male, female* **Jane Doe** /£ˌdʒɒn'dəʊ, $ˌdʒɑːn 'doʊ, ˌdʒeɪn-/ *n* [U; not after *the*] *Am law* a name used in a law court for a person whose real name is kept secret • *The pop group is bringing a law suit against John Doe Corporation, a record company which prefers to keep its identity secret.* • *(Am)* John Doe is also an average or typical man, and Jane Doe is an average or typical woman.

John Do·ry /£ˌdʒɒn'dɔː·ri, $ˌdʒɑːn'dɑːr·i/ *n* [C] *pl* **John Dory** or **John Dories** a thin edible fish which is valued as a food • *a shoal of John Dory* [C] • *The fish soup was made with sea bream, sea bass and John Dory.* [U]

John Han·cock /£ˌdʒɒn'hæŋ·kɒk, $ˌdʒɑːn'hæn·kɑːk/, **John Hen·ry** /£ˌdʒɒn'hen·ri, $ˌdʒɑːn-/ *n* [C] *Am slang* a person's signature • *Put your John Hancock at the bottom of the page.* • *A John Hancock is named after the man who was the first person to sign the American Declaration of Independence.*

john·ny /£'dʒɒn·i, $'dʒɑː·ni/ *n* [C] *Br slang* a CONDOM (= a cover for the penis during sex which prevents pregnancy or disease) • *He bought a packet of* **rubber** *johnnies from a slot machine in the pub.*

john·ny–come–late·ly /£ˌdʒɒn·i·kʌm'leit·li, $ˌdʒɑː·ni-/ *n* [C] *pl* **johnny-come-latelies** or **johnnies-come-lately** *disapproving* a person who starts a job or activity later than other people and who is thought to use the experience and knowledge of these people to try to obtain an advantage over them • *When he was given a managerial post, many of his colleagues were annoyed that this johnny-come-lately had been given such a swift promotion.*

joie de vi·vre /ˌʒwɑː·də'viː·vrə/ *n* [U] *fml* a feeling of great happiness and enjoyment of life • *He's lived in Spain for the past five years, and loves the warmth and joie de vivre of the Spanish people.* • *She's a very high-spirited person and is always* **full of** *joie de vivre.*

join *obj* CONNECT /dʒɔɪn/ *v* [T] to connect or fasten (things) together • *A long suspension bridge joins the two islands.* • *I joined my car battery* **to** *a friend's with jump leads.* • *Russia is joined* **to** *Eastern Europe by all sorts of economic ties.* • *If you join* **up** *the dots on the paper, you'll get a picture.* [M] • *Join the two pieces* **together** *using strong glue.* • *The curtains were slightly too short, so I had to join an extra strip of material* **on/onto** *the bottom.* • *(fml) During a marriage ceremony, it is customary for the priest to ask if there is any reason why the bride and groom should not be* **joined (together) in marriage/matrimony** (= married). • If two or more people **join hands**, they hold each other's hands, esp. in order to do something: *"Everyone join hands, and then form a circle," said the teacher.* • *(esp. Br)* If writing is **joined-up**, each letter in a word is connected to the next one: *My daughter is just starting to learn how to do joined-up* **writing** *at school.*

join /dʒɔɪn/ *n* [C] • A join is the place where two things meet or are fastened together: *You've papered this wall so well, I can't see the joins.*

join *(obj)* COME TOGETHER /dʒɔɪn/ *v* to come together with (someone) • *I don't have time for a drink now, but I'll join you later.* [T] • *"Do you mind if I join you?" he said, sitting down beside me.* [T] • *Why don't you ask your sister if she would like to join us* **for** *supper?* [T] • *She travelled to Rome by herself and was joined by her husband a few days later.* [T] • *We took the ferry across the Channel and then joined* (= got on) *the Paris train at Calais.* [T] • *I'm sure everyone will join me* **in** *wish***ing** *you a very happy retirement* (= everyone else will do this too). [T] • *She has joined members of other political parties* **in** *a call for more emergency aid for the war-torn country.* [T] • *The police have joined* **with** (= They have begun to work with) *the drugs squad* **in** *try***ing** *to catch major drug traffickers.* [I] • *The design company is planning to join* **up with** *a shoe manufacturer and create a new range of footwear.* [I] • If roads or rivers join, they meet at a particular point: *The A11 joins the M11 south of Cambridge.* [T] ○ *The River Neckar flows through Heidelberg and joins the Rhine at Mannheim.* [T] ○ *The River Murray and the River Darling join east of Adelaide.* [I]

join *(obj)* BECOME A MEMBER /dʒɔɪn/ *v* to become a member of (an organization) • *She's applied to join the Green Party.* [T] • *I felt so unfit after Christmas that I decided to join a gym.* [T] • *If you've come to buy tickets for tonight's performance, please join the (Br and Aus)* **queue**/*(Am)* **line** (= stand at the end of it). [T] • *It's a great club. Why don't you join?* [I] • *When I leave school at the end of this month, I'll probably have to* **join the ranks of** (= become one of) *the unemployed.* • *(infml)* If you say **join the club** in answer to something that someone has said, you mean you are in the same bad situation as they are: *"I've got no money till the end of this week." "Join the club!"* • *(Br and Aus)* If you **join up**, you become a member of one of the armed forces: *"Have you been in the army for a long time?" "I joined up as soon as I'd left school."*

join·er /£'dʒɔɪ·nəʳ, $-nɚ/ *n* [C] *infml* • A joiner is a person who likes to get involved in activities and become a member of organizations: *I don't think you'll persuade David to come along to tonight's meeting – he's not much of a joiner.* • See also JOINER.

join *(obj)* BECOME INVOLVED IN /dʒɔɪn/ *v* to become temporarily involved in (an activity) • *They're playing some good music, so let's go and join the dancing.* [T] • *We only need one more player for this game – can you persuade your sister to join* **in**? [I always + adv/prep] • *At the end of this verse, we'd like everyone to join* **in with** *the chorus.* [I always + adv/prep] • *(fml)* If armies **join battle**, they start to fight.

join·er /£'dʒɔɪ·nəʳ, $-nɚ/ *n* [C] a skilled worker who makes the wooden structures inside buildings, such as doors and window frames • *When we bought the house, we had to get a joiner to fit some new doors and a plumber to repair the pipes.* • See also **joiner** at JOIN BECOME A MEMBER.

join·er·y /£'dʒɔɪ·nᵊr·i, $-nɚ-/ *n* [U] • *She did a course in joinery* (= the work of a joiner) *and masonry at college.* • *He's doing all the joinery* **work** (= He is making the wooden structures) *in the new house by himself and has just put a skirting board in the living room.*

joint SHARED /dʒɔɪnt/ *adj* [not gradable] belonging to or shared between two or more people • *Do you and your husband have a joint bank account or separate accounts?* • *The police and social workers are conducting a joint investigation into teenage crime in the area.* • *The research project is the work of a joint French-Italian team.* • *The two Russian ice-skaters came joint second* (= They were both given second prize) *in the world championship.* • *In court, the parents were awarded joint* **custody** *of their son* (= the right to care for him was shared between them). • *(Br) Adrian has a joint* **honours** *(Aus* **double honours***) degree in English and philosophy* (= He studied both subjects to the same standard). • *The American and Japanese car companies have set up a joint* **venture** *to develop a new model of van for the American market.* • The **Joint Chiefs of Staff** are the leaders of the armed forces in the United States: *The Joint Chiefs of Staff act as the main military advisors to the US President.* • *(Am)* A **joint resolution** is a decision which is approved by both houses of the US Congress and becomes law when it is signed by the President: *The President yesterday formally signed the Joint Resolution of Congress granting him the authority to go to war.* • *(specialized)* A **joint-stock company** is a business which is owned by the group of people who have shares in the company: *The government is planning to transform most state-owned businesses into joint-stock companies which will be controlled by the employees.*

joint·ly /dʒɔɪnt·li/ *adv* [not gradable] • *Nelson Mandela and President De Klerk were jointly awarded the Nobel Prize for Peace in 1993.* • *The Middle East peace conference will be* *hosted jointly by the United States and Russia.* • *The Channel Tunnel was (Br) jointly* **funded***/(Aus)* **joint-funded** *by the French and the British.*

joint CONNECTION /dʒɔɪnt/ *n* [C] a place where two things are fixed together • *Repairs have involved replacing the joints between each 20-metre stretch of road.* • *The roof needs to be replaced because water has started to leak through the joints between the tiles.* • In the body, a joint is the place where two bones are connected: *The elbow is a joint in the arm.* ○ *There are three main types of joint which allow either some, slight or no movement of the bones.* ○ *As you become older, your joints get stiffer.* ○ *Sports shoes are now designed to help protect the knee and hip joints.* • If you **put out of joint** a part of your body such as your knee, shoulder or wrist, you force it suddenly out of its correct position: *I put my shoulder out of joint last weekend by lifting lots of heavy boxes.* • If you **put out of joint** something such as a plan, you prevent it from working correctly: *Our whole schedule was put out of joint by the designs arriving a week late.* • *"The time is out of joint; O cursed spite, / That ever I was born to set it right"* (Shakespeare, Hamlet 1.5)

joint·ed /£ˈdʒɔɪn·tɪd, $ˈdʒɔɪn·t̬ɪd/ *adj* [not gradable] • *A flute is made of wood or metal in three jointed sections.* • *He runs a business making well-crafted, properly jointed furniture out of solid wood.* • *Her favourite birthday present was a fully jointed teddy bear* (=with movable arms and legs) *given to her by her parents.* • *When I first started to walk again after the accident, I felt very* **stiff**-*jointed* (=the muscles in my legs hurt when I moved).

joint MEAT /dʒɔɪnt/ *n* [C] a large piece of meat which is cooked in one piece • *Joints are usually roasted in the oven.* • *I've bought a joint of beef for Sunday lunch.* • If you cut a chicken or rabbit into joints, you cut it into several quite large pieces: *Cook the four chicken joints in a pan with some mushrooms and garlic.*

joint *obj* /dʒɔɪnt/ *v* [T] • If you joint a chicken or rabbit, you cut it into large pieces ready for cooking: *For this recipe, you need a two-pound rabbit which has been jointed.*

joint PLACE /dʒɔɪnt/ *n* [C] *infml* a bar or restaurant which serves cheap food and drink • *They live in an area of town which is full of cheap bars and fast-food joints.* • *We had lunch at a* **hamburger** *joint and then went to see a movie.* • *(slang)* A joint is also a place where people go for some type of entertainment and which often has a bad reputation: *He owned several bars in the city and ran an illegal* **gambling** *joint.* ○ *We arrived at the club just before midnight and the joint was already* **jumping** (= busy). • *"The Joint is Jumpin'* (=full of activity)*"* (title of a song by Fats Waller, 1938) • *"Of all the gin joints in all the towns in all the world, she walks into mine"* (spoken by Humphrey Bogart in the film *Casablanca*, 1942)

joint DRUG /dʒɔɪnt/ *n* [C] *slang* a cigarette containing CANNABIS (=an illegal drug which produces a feeling of pleasant relaxation) • *Some people think that* **smoking** *joints is not as harmful as drinking alcohol.* • *They sat around drinking, laughing and* **rolling** *joints.*

joist /dʒɔɪst/ *n* [C] a long thick piece of wood, steel or concrete which is used in buildings to support a floor or ceiling • *The simplest way to construct a floor in your loft is to nail pieces of chipboard over the joists.*

jo·jo·ba /£həˈhəʊ·bə, $-ˈhoʊ-/ *n* [U] a large American plant with sharp leaves whose seeds contain a valuable oil which is used in beauty products • *Jojoba* **oil** *possesses excellent skin-softening properties.*

joke AMUSING /£dʒəʊk, $dʒoʊk/ *n* [C] something, such as an amusing story or trick, that is said or done in order to make people laugh • *Did I* **tell** *you the joke about the chicken crossing the road?* • *She spent the evening* **cracking** (=telling) *jokes and telling witty stories.* • *She tied his shoelaces together* **for a** *joke.* • *I hope Rob doesn't tell any* **dirty** *jokes* (=offensive jokes about sex) *at the party, because my grandmother's going to be there.* • *He tried to do a comedy routine for the end of term concert, but all his jokes* **fell flat** (=no one laughed at them). • *He doesn't have much of a sense of humour and rarely* **gets** (=understands) *jokes.* • *I tried explaining the joke to my German friends but I think it was* **lost on** *them* (=they did not understand it). • *They decided to* **play** *a joke* **on** *their father by hiding his reading glasses.* • If you say that someone **can't take** a joke, they get annoyed when someone says something amusing about them or plays a trick on them: *I thought Debbie would've laughed when she saw that photo of her on the noticeboard, but she just can't take a joke.* • If something **is getting/has gone beyond a** joke, it has become rather annoying or worrying: *Every time Russell borrows my bicycle he forgets to return it, and it's getting beyond a joke.* • If you **make a joke of** something, you laugh at it although it is serious or important: *He tried to make a joke of the fact that he hadn't been chosen for the college football team.* • *(infml)* If you say that something is **no joke**, you mean that it is not amusing or that it is very difficult: *Carrying that heavy suitcase up all those steps was no joke.* • *(infml)* If you say that **the joke is on** a particular person, you mean that they have tried to make someone else look foolish but have made themselves look foolish instead.

joke /£dʒəʊk, $dʒoʊk/ *v* • If you joke, you say amusing things: *They joked and laughed as they looked at the photos, remembering the times they'd spent together as children.* [I] ○ *The situation is much more serious than you think, so please don't joke* **about** *it.* [I] ○ *She did so much voluntary work that her friends used to joke* **that** *she earned her living in her spare time.* [+ *that* clause] ○ *"I didn't expect to be out so soon", he joked as he left the hospital, after spending nine months in there.* [+ clause] • If you think that someone is joking when they say something, you think that they do not really mean it: *Everyone thought he was joking when he said the project had to be finished by June, but in fact he was completely serious.* [I] ○ *She wasn't joking* (= She was serious) *when she said she was going to move out of the house by the end of the week.* [I] • If you say **(I'm) only joking**, you mean that you said something in a way which was not serious: *"Did you really mean it when you said you were going on holiday without me?" "Don't worry, I was only joking!"* • If you say **joking apart/aside**, you want to start speaking seriously about something after everyone has made jokes and laughed about it: *Joking apart, what do you really think of your new job?* • If you say **you're joking** in answer to something surprising that someone has said, you mean you have difficulty believing them: *"I've just been given a scholarship to study in the States." "You're joking! That's great news!"* • If you say **you must be joking/you've got to be joking** in answer to something that someone has said, you mean that you do not believe they said it seriously, or you think it is a ridiculous thing to say: *"Are you getting a new car this year?" "You must be joking! I can't afford to pay my bills, let alone buy a new car!"* ○ *You've got to be joking if you think I'm going to stand in the rain watching you play rugby!*

jok·er /£ˈdʒəʊ·kəʳ, $ˈdʒoʊ·kɚ/ *n* [C] • A joker is someone who likes telling amusing stories or doing stupid things in order to make people laugh: *He's always been a bit of a joker and can't resist playing tricks on people.* • See also JOKER; **joker** at JOKE RIDICULOUS.

jok·ey (**-ier**, **-iest**), **jok·y** (**-ier**, **-iest**) /£ˈdʒəʊ·ki, $ˈdʒoʊ-/ *adj infml* • *Her book is written in a lively jokey style which is fun to read.* • *His battered old car was covered in jokey stickers which said things like "My other car's a Porsche."*

jok·ing·ly /£ˈdʒəʊ·kɪŋ·li, $ˈdʒoʊ-/ *adv* • *The other players jokingly call him "The President", because he's the most forceful member of the team.* • *She suggested* **half**-*jokingly* (= in a way which was intended to be both amusing and slightly serious) *that they should sell the family car and all buy bikes instead.*

joke RIDICULOUS /£dʒəʊk, $dʒoʊk/ *n* [U] *infml* a person or thing that is ridiculous and that does not deserve respect • *Our new teacher's a bit of* **a** *joke – he can't control the class and he doesn't even know anything about his subject.* • *"Don't you use your bike any more?" "The brakes don't work and the seat's falling off. It's just* **a** *joke."* • *My parents expect me to take my driving test when I've only been learning for a month – it's* **a complete** *joke!* • *"Didn't Mike say he'd paint the kitchen this weekend?"* "**What a joke** (=How ridiculous)*! He's never picked up a paintbrush in his life!"* • If something such as a test is described as a joke, it is very easy: *The exam was* **a** *joke – everyone finished in less than an hour.*

jok·er /£ˈdʒəʊ·kəʳ, $ˈdʒoʊ·kɚ/ *n* [C] *infml* • A joker is a person who has done something which annoys you: *Some joker's been messing around with my motorbike.* ○ *There were a couple of jokers at the party who kept setting off the fire alarm.* • See also JOKER; **joker** at JOKE AMUSING.

jok·er /£ˈdʒəʊ·kəʳ, $ˈdʒoʊ·kɚ/ *n* [C] a special playing card which can be given any value and used in some card games instead of any other card • *The joker does not belong to any of the four suits in cards: hearts, diamonds, clubs or spades.* • If you say that someone or something is **the joker in the pack**, you mean that they are the person or thing that could change the situation in an unexpected way. • See also **joker** at JOKE [AMUSING], JOKE [RIDICULOUS].

jol·li·fi·ca·tions /£ˌdʒɒl·ɪ·fɪˈkeɪ·ʃənz, $ˌdʒɑː·lə·fə-/ *pl n infml* activities intended to be enjoyable and to celebrate something • *They have spent six months organising the carnival, and thousands of people are expected to join in with the jollifications.*

jol·li·fi·ca·tion /£ˌdʒɒl·ɪ·fɪˈkeɪ·ʃən, $ˌdʒɑː·lə·fə-/ *n* [U] *infml* • *Travel companies are now offering special winter breaks for people who are fed up with the tedious jollification* (= celebrations) *associated with Christmas.*

jol·ly [HAPPY] /£ˈdʒɒl·i, $ˈdʒɑː·li/ *adj* **-ier, -iest** (of a person) happy, or (of an event or place) enjoyable or attractive • *They loved going to see their grandfather, who was a good-natured jolly man.* • *Her next-door neighbour was a plump jolly woman who was always smiling and laughing.* • *We spent a very jolly evening together, chatting and listening to music.* • *Do you want to come out for a meal to celebrate Anne's birthday? I think it'll be quite a jolly night out.* • *I love the bright blue you've painted this room – it makes it look a lot jollier.* • *(humorous)* **Jolly hockey sticks** is an expression which refers to the traditional life of girls of the upper classes at private school. It is used to describe a particular type of woman who is very sociable and annoyingly enthusiastic about the people and things she is involved with: *"Are you coming to Fiona's party tonight?" "I don't think so. Her last party was full of her awful jolly-hockey-sticks type friends."* ○ *Her books about life in a girls' boarding school are written in a very jolly-hockey-sticks tone.* • **The Jolly Roger** is the black flag on a ship which belongs to PIRATES (= people who steal from other ships by force): *The Jolly Roger has a white skull and crossbones on it.* • Ⓕ

jol·li·ly /£ˈdʒɒl·ɪ·li, $ˈdʒɑː·lɪ-/ *adv* • *She was jollily dressed in a yellow flowery skirt and top.*

jol·li·ty /£ˈdʒɒl·ɪ·ti, $ˈdʒɑː·lə·ţi/ *n* [U] • *There was an atmosphere of great jollity at the party, as people met up with old friends and chatted and laughed together.*

jol·ly [VERY] /£ˈdʒɒl·i, $ˈdʒɑː·li/ *adv Br infml* very or extremely • *"Did you have a nice time in Scotland?" "Yes, it was jolly good fun."* • *That scarf you're wearing is jolly nice.* • *We had a lovely holiday in Stockholm, but it was jolly expensive.* • *Would you like to try a glass of this brandy? I've been told that it's jolly* **good stuff**. • *(dated)* If someone says jolly **good show**, they are expressing admiration for what someone has said or done: *"Did you hear that our team won at cricket?" "Oh, jolly good show."* • You would say **jolly good** if you wanted to express approval of something that someone has said or done, or if you wanted to show that you have heard or understood what someone has said: *"We should get there about 30 minutes early." "Oh, jolly good."* ○ *"I've left all the papers you need on your desk." "Jolly good."* • **Jolly well** is used to emphasize something you are saying, esp. when you are angry or annoyed: *I'm going to jolly well tell her what I think of her!* ○ *"Has John bought us some tickets for tonight's concert?" "I jolly well hope so!"* ○ *Sally's been in the bathroom for at least an hour. Just tell her to jolly well hurry up!* • Ⓕ

jol·ly *obj* [ENCOURAGE] /£ˈdʒɒl·i, $ˈdʒɑː·li/ *v* [T always + adv/prep] *infml* to encourage (someone) to do something by putting them in a good mood and using gentle persuasion • *I'll try to jolly my parents* **into** *letting me borrow the car this weekend.* • *She didn't really want to go to the party, so we had to jolly her* **along** *a bit.* • Ⓕ

jol·ly up *obj*, **jol·ly** *obj* **up** *v adv* [M] *infml* to make (something) brighter and more attractive • *I thought I'd jolly the room up* **with** *some colourful curtains.*

jolt *(obj)* /£dʒəult, $dʒoult/ *v* to (cause something or someone to) move suddenly and violently • *The train stopped unexpectedly and we were jolted forwards.* [T] • *I was jolted* **awake** *by a sudden intense pain in my chest.* [T + obj + adj] • *The truck jolted* **along** *the rough track through the field.* [I always + adv/prep] • *(fig.) Their relationship was badly jolted* (= weakened) *when she found out he had been seeing another woman.* [T] • *(fig.) The news that the company is being taken over by foreign investors has severely jolted* (= shocked) *the stock market.* [T] • *(fig.) The charity is using photos of starving children in their advertising campaign in an attempt to jolt the public* **conscience** (= make people feel guilty so they will act). [T] • If someone is **jolted into** or **out of** something, they are given a sudden shock which forces them to act: *The government is planning to cut unemployment benefit to jolt people into* **looking** *for work.* ○ *The shock of seeing some of his colleagues lose their jobs was enough to jolt him out of his lethargy.* ○ *She was jolted into* **action** *by the sudden realization that her exams began in less than a week.*

jolt /£dʒəult, $dʒoult/ *n* [C] • A jolt is a sudden violent movement: *As the plane touched the ground, there was a massive jolt and we were thrown forwards.* ○ *I woke up* **with a** *jolt as I thought I heard my bedroom door being pushed open.* ○ *There are fears that the slight jolts which Los Angeles has been experiencing recently may set off a full-scale earthquake.* ○ *(fig.) The announcement of an increase in profits for the company gave the stock market a slight jolt upwards.* • A jolt is also an unpleasant shock or surprise: *His self-confidence* **took** *a sudden jolt with the news that he had not been selected for the national team.* ○ *Government hopes for a quick recovery from recession received a sharp jolt with the announcement that unemployment had risen again this month.*

josh *(obj)* /£dʒɒʃ, $dʒɑːʃ/ *v infml* to joke, often with the intention of annoying (someone) in a playful way • *Don't worry! I was just joshing when I said I'd lost the car keys.* [I] • *The girls spent the morning joshing each other* **about** *their boyfriends and talking about what they were doing that evening.* [T] • *When his friends found out he'd bought a car, they joshed him* **for** *having abandoned his green ideals.* [T]

joss stick /£ˈdʒɒs, $ˈdʒɑːs/ *n* [C] a thin wooden stick covered with a substance which burns slowly and produces a pleasant smell that fills the air • *Joss sticks are made of sandalwood which is a very fragrant wood.*

jos·tle *(obj)* /£ˈdʒɒs·l̩, $ˈdʒɑː·sl̩/ *v* to knock or push roughly against (someone) in order to move past them or get more space when you are in a crowd of people • *As we came into the arena, we were jostled by fans pushing their way towards the stage.* [T] • *Photographers and camera crews jostled and shoved to get a better view of the royal couple as they drove past.* [I] • If two or more people **jostle for** something, they compete with each other in order to get what they want: *Outside the museum, souvenir stalls and food sellers jostled for space along the pavement.* ○ *Since the fall of the government, the two opposition parties have been jostling for* **position**. ○ *At the start of each academic year, banks jostle for new* **business** *among students.*

jos·tling /£ˈdʒɒs·lɪŋ, $ˈdʒɑː·slɪŋ/ *n* [U] • *There were scenes of angry jostling between the two teams when one of the players was accused of unfair play.* • *There has been plenty of jostling among the staff* **for** *the position of senior manager.*

jos·tling /£ˈdʒɒs·lɪŋ, $ˈdʒɑː·slɪŋ/ *adj* • *As we left the concert, we found ourselves in the middle of a crowd of jostling reporters, all trying to get an interview with the singer.* • *(fig.) The city, with its jostling* (= closely grouped) *mass of office buildings, shows a distinct lack of planning.*

jot *obj* [WRITE] /£dʒɒt, $dʒɑːt/ *v* [T] **-tt-** to make a quick short note of (something) • *Could you jot your address and phone number* **in** *my address book?* • *I always carry a pen and a notebook with me for jotting* **down** *my ideas.* [M]

jot·tings /£ˈdʒɒt·ɪŋz, $ˈdʒɑː·ţɪŋz/ *pl n* • Jottings are quickly written brief notes: *She* **made** *some jottings in the margin of the book she was reading.* ○ *His diaries contain both jottings of his own thoughts and notes of how he spent his time.*

jot·ter (pad) /£ˈdʒɒt·ər, $ˈdʒɑː·ţər/ *n* [C] *Br and Aus* • A jotter (pad) is a small book which is used for writing brief notes in: *He wrote a rough plan for his essay in a jotter before writing it up on his word processor.*

jot [SMALL AMOUNT] /£dʒɒt, $dʒɑːt/ *n* [U] *infml* a very small amount • *Don't listen to her! There's not* **a jot of** *truth* (= There is no truth) *in what she's saying.* • *None of the committee's proposals will matter* **a jot** (= They will not matter) *if the government isn't prepared to take notice of their report.* • *She doesn't* **give a jot** (= She does not care) *about her poor old father.* • *(dated) His performance should be judged on the overall result, and not on whether he achieves every* **jot and tittle** (= every detail) *of his original plan.*

joule /dʒuːl/ *n* [C] *specialized* a unit of energy or work done • *If you lift an apple from the floor onto a table, you have used about one joule of energy.* • *The symbol for joules is J.*

jour·nal [MAGAZINE] /£ˈdʒɜː·nəl, $ˈdʒɜːr-/ *n* [C] a serious magazine or newspaper which is published regularly, usually about a specialist subject • *Each club member will receive a journal four times a year which contains a mixture of news, reviews and articles.* • *He edits a quarterly journal on environmental issues.* • *She is features editor for the Wall Street Journal.* • *An article about the dangers of the new* *drug has recently been published in the British Medical Journal.* • *He continued to* **subscribe to** *the British journal 'The Economist' while he was living in the States.* • *She works for a* **trade** *journal for the car industry.* • Ⓕ Ⓟ

jour·nal RECORD /£ˈdʒɜː·nəl, $ˈdʒɜːr-/ *n* [C] a written record of what you have done each day; a DIARY • *Her journal is an important record of the life of a young woman growing up in rural England.* • *He* **kept** *a journal for over 50 years, in which he recorded his daily activities and observations about the city where he lived.* • *While travelling in South America, she kept a* **travel** *journal that was to provide valuable material for her first novel.* • Ⓕ Ⓟ

jour·nal·ese /£ˌdʒɜː·nəˈliːz, $ˌdʒɜːr-/ *n* [U] *disapproving* a style of language considered typical of newspapers, which is full of expressions that have been used so often that they have become almost meaningless • *There has been a lot of pressure on television reporters recently to move away from cliché-ridden journalese and back to standard English.*

jour·nal·i·sm /£ˈdʒɜː·nə·lɪ·zᵊm, $ˈdʒɜːr-/ *n* [U] the work of collecting, writing and publishing news stories and articles in newspapers and magazines or broadcasting them on the radio and television • *Journalism and advertising are popular career choices among arts graduates.* • *She plans to* **go into** *journalism when she leaves college.* • *In both the US and Britain,* **investigative** *journalism has played an important role in uncovering political scandals.* • *In 1989, he left the world of* **print** *journalism for a career in* **broadcast** *journalism.*

jour·nal·ist /£ˈdʒɜː·nə·lɪst, $ˈdʒɜːr-/ *n* [C] • A journalist is a person who writes news stories or articles for a newspaper or magazine, or who broadcasts on radio or television: *He's a* **freelance** *journalist who writes regular columns for The Times and the Daily Express.* ○ *The Watergate scandal was exposed by two* **investigative** *journalists working for the Washington Post.* ○ *She worked as a* **political** *journalist before becoming a politician.*

jour·nal·is·tic /£ˌdʒɜː·nəˈlɪs·tɪk, $ˌdʒɜːr-/ *adj* • *He left a job in banking to pursue a journalistic* **career**. • *There has a lot of debate recently about the decline of journalistic* **standards** *in the popular press.*

jour·ney /£ˈdʒɜː·ni, $ˈdʒɜːr-/ *n* [C] the act of travelling from one place to another, esp. in a vehicle • *It's a two-hour train journey* **from** *York* **to** *London.* • *The journey* **from** *home* **to** *the office takes about 15 minutes.* • *We* **broke** *our journey* (=stopped for a short time) *in Edinburgh before travelling on to Inverness the next day.* • *Have you had a* **good** *journey?* • *Can I borrow a book to read* **on** *the journey?* • *We crossed the Channel via Calais on the* **outward** *journey and Boulogne on the* **return** *journey.* • *Have a* **safe** *journey!* • *The journey* **time** *from London to New York is seven hours.* • *(fig.) As she looked through the old photograph albums, she was taken on a* **nostalgic** *journey back to her childhood.* • *(fig.) He views his life as a* **spiritual** *journey towards a greater understanding of his faith.* • *(fig.) Her voyage to India to find out about her family was also a journey* **of self-discovery**. • Ⓕ

jour·ney /£ˈdʒɜː·ni, $ˈdʒɜːr-/ *v* [I always + adv/prep] *esp. literary* • To journey somewhere is to travel there: *They journeyed into the desert on camels.* • *As we journeyed south, the landscape became drier and rockier.*

joust /dʒaʊst/ *v* [I] (in the past) to fight with a LANCE (=a long pointed weapon) while riding on a horse, esp. as a sport, or *(fig.)* to compete, esp. for power or control • *(fig.) Manchester United and Liverpool are jousting* **for** *position at the top of the football league.*

Jove /£dʒəʊv, $dʒoʊv/ *n* [U] **by Jove** *dated* used to express surprise or to emphasize a statement • *By Jove, I think he's won!*

jov·i·al /£ˈdʒəʊ·vi·əl, $ˈdʒoʊ-/ *adj* (of a person) friendly and in a good mood, or (of a situation) enjoyable because friendly and pleasant • *a jovial chap/fellow/person* • *a jovial time/evening/chat*

jov·i·al·i·ty /£ˌdʒəʊ·viˈæl·ə·ti, $ˌdʒoʊ·viˈæl·ə·t̬i/ *n* [U] • *They greeted us with great joviality* (=friendliness).

jov·i·al·ly /£ˈdʒəʊ·vi·ə·li, $ˈdʒoʊ-/ *adv*

jowls /dʒaʊlz/ *pl n* the loose skin and flesh under the JAW (=the lower part of the face) • *Certain kinds of dogs, such as bloodhounds, have* **heavy** *jowls* (=loose folds of skin and flesh on the lower parts of their faces).

jowl /dʒaʊl/ *n* [U] • A jowl is the same as jowls: *He has a* **heavy** *jowl.*

-jowled /dʒaʊld/ *combining form* • *a* **dark**-*jowled man* (=a man whose lower face is dark because of the hair growing under his skin).

jowl·y /ˈdʒaʊ·li/ *adj* • *She's become increasingly jowly* (=the skin and flesh on the lower part of her face has become looser) *as she's got older.*

joy /dʒɔɪ/ *n* great happiness • *They were* **filled with** *joy when their first child was born.* [U] • *Philip* **shouted for/with** *joy when he heard that he'd passed his exams.* [U] • *She* **wept for/with** *joy when she was told that her husband had been released from captivity.* [U] • *(Br infml)* Joy can mean success: *Did you* **have** *any joy* (=success in) *finding the book you wanted at the library?* [U + v-*ing*] • *(fig. Br infml) "I thought I might ask Josh to lend me some money." "You won't* **get** *much joy* **from** *him* (=You won't be successful)*."* [U] • A joy is a person or thing which causes happiness: *Listening to music is one of his greatest joys.* [C] ○ *Joyce's grandchildren are* **a great** *joy* **to** *her.* [C] ○ *Her singing is* **a** *joy* **to** *listen to.* [+ *to* infinitive] • *"The Joy of Sex"* (title of a book by Alex Comfort, 1972)

joy·ful /ˈdʒɔɪ·fᵊl/ *adj* • *Christmas is such a joyful time of year* (=one that contains or causes great happiness). • *I don't have very much to feel joyful* (=very happy) **about/over** *at the moment.*

joy·ful·ly /ˈdʒɔɪ·fᵊl·i/ *adv*

joy·ful·ness /ˈdʒɔɪ·fᵊl·nəs/ *n* [U]

joy·less /ˈdʒɔɪ·ləs/ *adj* • *Jane is trapped in a joyless* (=unhappy) *marriage.*

joy·less·ly /ˈdʒɔɪ·lə·sli/ *adv*

joy·less·ness /ˈdʒɔɪ·lə·snəs/ *n* [U]

joy·ous /ˈdʒɔɪ·əs/ *adj literary* • *a joyous* (=full of joy, happy) *hymn/event/voice*

joy·ous·ly /ˈdʒɔɪ·ə·sli/ *adv literary*

joy·ous·ness /ˈdʒɔɪ·ə·snəs/ *n* [U] *literary*

joy·ride /ˈdʒɔɪ·raɪd/ *n* [C] an act of driving around for enjoyment in a car, esp. one that you have stolen for that purpose • *We think the car was stolen for a joyride.*

joy·rid·er /£ˈdʒɔɪˌraɪ·dəʳ, $-dɚ/ *n* [C] *Br and Aus* • *He was knocked over by a car that was being driven by joyriders* (=people who have stolen a car in order to drive it for enjoyment). • LP **Crimes and criminals**

joy·rid·ing /ˈdʒɔɪˌraɪ·dɪŋ/ *n* [U] *Br and Aus* • Joyriding is driving around in a car you have stolen.

joy·stick /ˈdʒɔɪ·stɪk/ *n* [C] a vertical handle which can be moved sideways, backwards and forwards to control the direction or height of an aircraft or to control the operation of some machines • *These games can be operated either by using a keyboard or a joystick plugged into the home computer.*

JP /ˌdʒeɪˈpiː/ *n* [C] *abbreviation for* **Justice of the Peace**, see at JUSTICE JUDGE

Jr *esp. Am* /£ˈdʒuː·ni·əʳ, $-ɚ/, *Br and Aus* **Jnr** *adj* [after n; not gradable] *abbreviation for* JUNIOR YOUNGER. Used after a man's name to refer to the younger of two people in the same family who have the same name. • *Martin Luther King Jr*

ju·bi·lant /ˈdʒuː·bɪ·lənt/ *adj* feeling or expressing great happiness, esp. because of a success • *Jubilant cheers went up when the result of the election was announced.* • *The fans were jubilant* **at/about/over** *England's victory.*

ju·bi·lant·ly /ˈdʒuː·bɪ·lənt·li/ *adv*

ju·bi·la·tion /ˌdʒuː·bɪˈleɪ·ʃᵊn/ *n* [U] • *There was jubilation in the crowd as the winning goal was scored.*

ju·bi·lee /ˈdʒuː·bɪ·liː, ˌ--ˈ-/ *n* [C] (the celebration of) the day on which an important event happened many years ago • *Street parties were held all over the country to celebrate the Queen's jubilee.*

Ju·da·i·sm /ˈdʒuː·deɪ·ɪ·zᵊm/ *n* [U] the religion of the Jewish people • *Judaism is based on the Torah, which is the Old Testament of the Bible, and the Talmud.* • *The central belief of Judaism is that God is the creator of all things and the source of all righteousness.*

Ju·dae·o- *Br and Aus, Am* **Ju·de·o-** /£dʒuːˈdiː·əʊ-, $-oʊ-/ *combining form* • *Judaeo-*(=Jewish and)*Christian fellowship*

Ju·da·ic /dʒuːˈdeɪ·ɪk/ *adj* [not gradable]

Ju·das /ˈdʒuː·dəs/ *n* [C] a person who is not loyal to a friend and helps the friend's enemies • *He started waving his finger and calling me a Judas and said I was no longer his friend.* • In the Bible Judas was the friend of Jesus Christ who told his enemies how they could catch him.

jud·der *Br and Aus* /£ˈdʒʌd·əʳ, $-ɚ/, *Am* **shud·der** *v* [I] (esp. of a vehicle) to shake violently • *I don't like the way this plane is juddering – do you think it's all right?* • *The train juddered* **to a halt**.

jud·der *Br and Aus* /£ˈdʒʌd·əʳ, $-ɚ/, *Am* **shud·der** *n* [U] • *The car gave* **a** *sudden judder, then stopped dead.*

judge [PERSON] /dʒʌdʒ/ *n* [C] a person who is in charge of a trial in a court and decides how a person who is guilty of a crime should be punished, or who makes decisions on legal matters • *a British high-court judge* • *a US Supreme Court judge* • *Judge Hardy has been criticized for the severity of the sentence he passed.* • [LP] **Law**

judg·ment, judge·ment /ˈdʒʌdʒ·mənt/ *n* • *It is the judgment* (=decision) **of** *this court that you are guilty of murder.* [C] • *We are still waiting for the court to* **pass/ pronounce** *judgment* (=give a decision) **on** *the case.* [U] • *His death in the accident seemed like a judgment* (=punishment) **(from** *God/heaven)* **on** *him for his cruelty.* [C]

judge *(obj)* [DECIDE] /dʒʌdʒ/ *v* to form, give or have as an opinion, or to decide about (something or someone), esp. after thinking carefully • *So far, he seems to be handling the job well, but it's really too soon to judge.* [I] • *It's difficult to judge yet* **wh**ether *the new system is really an improvement.* [+ *wh-* word] • *I'd judge* **that** *it'll take us about five years to cover our costs.* [+ *that* clause] • *Everyone present judged the meeting* **(to** *have been) a success.* [+ obj + (*to be*) n/adj] • *She judged* **it** *better not to tell him what had happened.* [+ obj + n/adj] • *I'm hopeless at judging* **distance(s)** (=guessing how far it is between places). [T] • If you judge someone or something you decide whether it is good or bad: *What do you think gives you the right to judge people?* [T] ○ *They judged the system on how quickly it could respond to their queries.* [T] ○ *You shouldn't judge* **by/on** *appearances alone.* [I] ○ *Our salespeople are judged* **on/according to** *the number of cars they sell.* [T] • To judge is also to officially decide who will be the winner of a competition: *I've been asked to judge the fancy-dress competition.* [T] • The expressions **judging by/from** or **to judge by/from** are used to refer to the reasons you have for thinking something: *Judging by what he said, I think it's very unlikely that he'll be able to support your application.* • *(saying)* 'You can't judge a book by its cover' means you can't tell what something or someone is like by looking only at the outside appearance. • *"Judge not, that ye be not judged"* (Bible, Matthew 7.1)

judge /dʒʌdʒ/ *n* [C] • A judge is the person who officially decides who is the winner of a competition: *The judges all awarded the Russian skaters the highest marks.* ○ *The winner will be decided by a* **panel of** *judges.* • A judge is a person who has the knowledge to give an opinion about something or who is able to decide whether someone or something is good or bad: *I'm no judge* **of** *art.* ○ *She's such a bad judge* **of** *character.* ○ *I thought the performance was boring, but then I'm not a good judge.* ○ *"I really don't think you should have another drink." "I'll be/ Let me be the judge* **of** *that* (=I am able to make my own decision about that)."

judg·ment, judge·ment /ˈdʒʌdʒ·mənt/ *n* • Judgment is the ability to form valuable opinions and make good decisions: *Recent events have called into question the chairperson's judgment.* [U] ○ *He's a person of* **good/ sound/poor/weak** *judgment.* [U] ○ *She always demonstrates/displays/exhibits/shows excellent judgment.* [U] • *He always thinks he has the right to* **pass** *judgment* **(on** *others)* (=to say whether he thinks other people are good or bad). [U] • *I'm going to* **reserve** *judgment* **(on** *the decision)* (=not say whether I think it is good or bad) *for the time being.* [U] • **In** *my* **judgment** (=According to my opinion), *we should accept the lowest estimate.* • A judgment is a decision: *What do you think we should do about this problem – I'm finding it hard to* **come to/form/ make** *a judgment.* [C] ○ *I've come to the judgment* **that** *we should merge the two companies.* [C + *that* clause] • **The final/last Judgment** (also **the Day of Judgment** or **Judgment Day**) is believed to be the time when the world ends and all the dead people come back to life so that everyone can be judged by God for the way they lived their lives on Earth.

judg·men·tal /£dʒʌdʒˈmen·tᵊl, $-t̬ᵊl/ *adj disapproving* • *I always try not to be judgmental* (=not to form or express either a good or a bad opinion) **about** *people.*

judg·men·tal·ly /£dʒʌdʒˈmen·tᵊl·i, $-t̬ᵊl-/ *adv*

ju·di·ca·ture /£ˈdʒuː·dɪ·kə·tʃəʳ, $-tʃɚ/ *n* [U] *specialized* the giving of justice in a court of law • *The Scottish system of judicature is slightly different from the English one.*

ju·di·ci·a·ry /£dʒuːˈdɪʃ·ᵊr·i, $ˈ-ɚ-/ *n* [U + sing/pl v] the part of a country's government which is responsible for its legal system and which consists of all the judges in the country's courts of law • *a member of* **the** *judiciary* • *The judiciary is/are expected to publish its/their report next week.*

ju·di·cial /dʒuːˈdɪʃ·ᵊl/ *adj* [not gradable] • Judicial means involving a court of law: *Dickens' book "Bleak House" is about the failings of the English judicial system in Victorian times.* ○ *judicial* **enquiry/review**

ju·di·cial·ly /dʒuːˈdɪʃ·ᵊl·i/ *adv* [not gradable]

ju·di·cious /dʒuːˈdɪʃ·əs/ *adj* having or showing reason and good judgment in making decisions • *We should try and make judicious use of the resources available to us.*

judi·cious·ly /dʒuːˈdɪʃ·ə·sli/ *adv* • *"You may say that is what happened, but I wasn't there so I can't comment," he said judiciously.*

ju·do /£ˈdʒuː·dəʊ, $-doʊ/ *n* [U] a sport in which two people fight using their arms and legs and hands and feet, and try to throw each other to the ground • Judo fighters wear special loose white clothes with different coloured belts which indicate the level of their skill: *He's a* **black belt** (=has the highest level of skill) **in/at** *judo.*

jug [CONTAINER] *Br and Aus* /dʒʌg/, *Am usually* **pitch·er** *n* [C] a container for holding liquids which has a handle and a shaped opening at the top for pouring • *a glass/ earthenware jug* • *She put a jug* **of** *water on the table.* • A jug (also **jugful**) is the amount of liquid such a container will hold: *I spilt a jug/jugful* **of** *coffee on the kitchen floor.* • *(Am)* A jug is also a container for holding liquids which has a wide round base, straight sides and a narrow round opening at the top. • [PIC] **Jug**

jug·ful /ˈdʒʌg·fʊl/ *n* [C] • *There was a jugful of water on each table.*

jug [PRISON] /dʒʌg/ *n* [U] *dated slang* prison • *I always knew he'd end up* **in** *jug.*

jug·ger·naut [POWERFUL FORCE] /£ˈdʒʌg·ə·nɔːt, $-ɚ·nɑːt/ *n* [C] *disapproving* a large powerful force or organization that cannot be stopped • *It's often impossible for small companies to compete with the great juggernauts* **of** *industry.*

jug·ger·naut [VEHICLE] *Br* /£ˈdʒʌg·ə·nɔːt, $-ɚ·nɑːt/ *n* [C], *Am* **trac·tor–trail·er** /£ˌtræk·təˈtreɪ·ləʳ, $-t̬ɚˈtreɪ·lɚ/ *n*, *esp. Aus* **semi(–trail·er)** *n* a very large heavy truck • *The peace of the village has been shattered by juggernauts thundering through it.* • [PIC] **Vehicles**

jug·gle *(obj)* /ˈdʒʌg·l̩/ *v* to throw (several objects) into the air, catch them, and throw them up again, so that one or more stays in the air, usually in order to entertain people • *Steve can juggle* **with** *four balls, and is now learning to do it with five.* [I] • *We all watched in amazement as he juggled* *flaming torches.* [T] • *(fig.) Many women find it hard to juggle children and a career* (= to arrange their lives so that they have time for both). [T] • *(fig.) Many women today have to perform a* **juggling act** (= have to deal with their work and home duties). • *(fig.) It won't matter if we juggle the figures* (= change them so that they seem to be as we wish them) *– no one will know.* [T]

jug·gler /£ˈdʒʌg·ləʳ, $-lɚ/ *n* • *A juggler* (= person who throws objects into the air) *came to entertain the children at the party.*

jug·gling /ˈdʒʌg·lɪŋ, ˈdʒʌg·lɪŋ/ *n* [U] • *He was keen to learn the skill of juggling.* • *The shop sells juggling balls and clubs.* • *(fig.) To win new readers to the newspaper while keeping existing readers happy is a difficult juggling* **act**.

jug·u·lar (vein) /£ˈdʒʌg·jʊ·ləʳ, $-lɚ/ *n* [C] any of several large VEINS (= tubes which carry blood to the heart) in the neck • *(fig. infml) In a savage review of the book, the reviewer first criticized the author's arguments, then* **went for the** *jugular* (= made a fierce attack in order to cause as much damage as possible), *and accused him of getting his facts wrong.*

juice [LIQUID] /dʒuːs/ *n* [U] the liquid that comes from fruit or vegetables • *Squeezing lemon juice over peeled apples stops them going brown.* • *Please may I have some grapefruit juice* (= as a drink)*?* • *I dropped* **a carton of** *juice on the floor.* • [PIC›] **Containers**

juic·er /£ˈdʒuː·səʳ, $-sɚ/ *n* [C] *esp. Am* • A juicer is a machine for removing juice from fruit.

juices /ˈdʒuː·sɪz/ *pl n* • Juices are liquid in meat or in the body: *Fry the meat first to seal in the juices.* ○ *Ulcers can be caused by the* **digestive/gastric** *juices* (= the liquid in the stomach that helps the body to digest food) *being too acidic.* ○ *(fig. infml) This early in the morning it's hard to get the* **creative** *juices flowing* (= it is difficult to think of good ideas).

jui·cy /ˈdʒuː·si/ *adj* **-ier**, **-iest** • *a* **nice** *juicy orange/a* **nice** *juicy steak* (= containing a lot of liquid and therefore enjoyable to eat) • *(fig.) If sales continue like this, we should be showing a* **nice** *juicy* **profit** (= receiving a lot of money) *at the end of the year.* • *(fig.) Shakespeare's plays have few juicy* (= important and interesting) **parts/roles** *for women.* • Juicy can also mean interesting because immoral: *I've got some really juicy* **gossip** *for you.* ○ *Tell me all the juicy* **details**.

jui·ci·ness /ˈdʒuː·sɪ·nəs/ *n* [U]

juice [POWER] /dʒuːs/ *n* [U] *Am slang* power or influence • *I'll introduce you to my cousin, he's got all the juice* (= influence) *in this neighborhood.*

ju–jit·su, *esp. Am* **jiu-jit·su** /ˌdʒuːˈdʒɪt·suː/ *n* [U] a type of self-defence from Japan which does not involve weapons and which is done as a sport, and on which other similar sports such as JUDO and KARATE are based

juke·box /£ˈdʒuːk·bɒks, $-bɑːks/ *n* [C] a machine in bars etc. which plays recorded music when a coin is put into it • *Why don't you put a song* **on** *the jukebox* (= make it play a song)*?*

ju·lep /ˈdʒuː·lɪp/, **mint ju·lep** *n* [C] a drink originally from the US made from alcohol (usually WHISKEY), sugar, MINT (= a type of herb) leaves and ice

Ju·ly /dʒʊˈlaɪ/ (*abbreviation* **Jul**) *n* the seventh month of the year, after June and before August • *22(nd) July/July 22(nd)/22(nd) Jul/Jul 22(nd)* [U] • *Clea's birthday is* **on** *the eleventh of July/July the eleventh/(esp. Am) July eleventh.* [U] • *She left school* **last**/*is leaving school* **next** *July.* [U] • *The film festival is* **in/during** *July.* [U] • *This is one of the coolest Julys I can remember.* [C] • [LP›] **Dates**

jum·ble /ˈdʒʌm·bl̩/ *n* [U] an untidy and confused mixture (of things, feelings or ideas) • *Don't leave your clothes* **in a** *jumble like that.* • *He rummaged through the jumble* **of** *papers on his desk.* • *Visiting New York for the first time left me with a jumble* **of** *sensations.* • *Her ideas for the book are just a jumble at the moment, but she's sorting them out.* • *(Br)* Jumble is things you no longer want: *Do you have any jumble that we could have for our sale on Saturday?* [U] • *(Br)* A **jumble sale** (*Am* **rummage sale**) is a sale of a mixed collection of things that people no longer want in order to get money to help people or organizations who need it.

jum·ble *obj* /ˈdʒʌm·bl̩/ *v* [T] • To jumble things is to mix them together untidily: *Don't jumble your clothes like that – put them away carefully.* ○ *The events of the last few weeks are all jumbled* **(together/up)** *in my mind.*

jum·bo /£ˈdʒʌm·bəʊ, $-boʊ/ *adj* [before n] extremely large • *a jumbo bottle of soda* • *a jumbo-***sized** *packet* • *Washing powder works out cheaper if you buy the jumbo* **size**.

jum·bo (jet) /£ˈdʒʌm·bəʊ, $-boʊ/ *n* [C] *pl* **jumbos** or **jumbo jets** • *The Boeing 747 is a jumbo (jet)* (= a very large aircraft which can carry a lot of people). • [PIC›] **Aircraft**

jump *(obj)* [IN THE AIR] /dʒʌmp/ *v* to raise yourself off the ground and into the air using your legs and feet • *They watched the children running and jumping.* [I] • *Ballet dancers can jump very high* **(into** *the air).* [I] • *He killed himself by jumping* **out of** *a window.* [I] • *Our cat is always jumping* **up** *on/onto the furniture.* [I] • *The children are jumping* **up and down** *with excitement.* [I] • *(infml Br and Aus) Bill's* **jumping up and down** (= is annoyed) *because Mark didn't get his report finished in time.* • *(fig.) There's something wrong with the television – the picture keeps jumping.* [I] • *(fig. infml) The joint's really jumping* (= This place of entertainment is very active and crowded) *tonight.* [I] • To jump sometimes means to raise yourself off the ground in order to go over something: *Can you jump* **(over/across)** *this stream?* [T; I + prep] ○ *All the horses are finding it difficult to jump the last fence.* [T] • If a noise or action causes you to jump your body makes a sudden sharp movement because of surprise or fear: *The loud explosion* **made** *everyone jump.* [I] ○ *Oh, you* **made** *me jump – I didn't hear you come into the room.* ○ *I almost jumped* **out of my skin** *when I heard a loud crash downstairs.* • *Simon* **jumped for joy** (= was very happy) *when he got his exam results.* • *(infml) I told him to* **go (and) jump in the lake** (= go away). • *That's a very effective advertisement – it really* **jumps out at** *you* (= strongly attracts your attention). • *Let's take the question of the future of the existing workforce as a* **jumping-off point** (= a point from which to start) *for our negotiations.* • *The car battery was dead so we had to start the engine with (Br)* **jump leads**/*(Am)* **jumper cables**/*(Aus)* **jumper leads** (= two wires which carry electrical power from one car engine to another which does not have any power). • To **jump rope** is *Am for* SKIP. A **jump rope** is *Am for* a **skipping rope**. See at SKIP [JUMP]. • To **jump-start** a car is to start its engine by pushing the car, or by using jump leads. A **jump-start** is the act of starting a car in either of these ways. • [PIC›] **Playground**

jump /dʒʌmp/ *n* [C] • *The dancer's solo involved lots of jumps* (= acts of leaving the ground using the legs and feet) *and pirouettes.* • *Angela is* **making** *a* **parachute** *jump* (= leaving an aircraft while it is flying and landing with a PARACHUTE) *next week to raise money for charity.* • *Several horses fell at the last jump* (= fence or other thing to be jumped over).

jump·er /£ˈdʒʌm·pəʳ, $-pɚ/ *n* [C] • *That horse is a great little jumper.*

jump [DO QUICKLY] /dʒʌmp/ *v* [I always + adv/prep] to do an action suddenly or quickly • *He suddenly jumped* **from** *his seat/jumped* **to his feet**/*jumped* **up** *and left.* • *Come on, children, jump* **in/into** *the car.* • *She said the man jumped* **out of** *the shadows and attacked her.* • To **jump at** something is to accept it eagerly: *She jumped at the* **chance** *of a trip to Paris.* ○ *Everyone expected them to jump at the* **offer**. • *He really* **jumped down** *my* **throat** (= spoke suddenly and angrily to me) *when I suggested he'd made a mistake.* • To **jump in** is to interrupt when someone else is speaking: *I wish you'd stop jumping in and finishing my sentences for me all the time.* • *That's just like Julie – always* **jumping in with both feet** (= becoming involved in a situation too quickly without necessarily understanding what is happening). • To **jump on** someone is to show immediate disapproval of them or criticize them: *She jumps on her children instantly if they're disobedient.* ○ See also **jump on** at JUMP [ATTACK]. • *(fig.) Whenever anyone criticizes her husband, she jumps to his* **defence** (= quickly defends him). • *I told you to tidy this room – now* **jump to it** (= do it quickly)*!* • *They've only just met – isn't it* **jumping the gun** (= acting too soon or before the right time) *to be talking about marriage already?*

jump *(obj)* [POINT] /dʒʌmp/ *v* to move suddenly from one point to another, often missing out what comes between the points • *When you're programming a computer, you can't jump any stages, or it won't work properly.* [T] • *This novel is very hard to follow because it keeps jumping* **from** *one thing* **to** *another.* [I always + adv/prep] • *The film is about his adult life, but it keeps jumping* **(back) to** *when he was a child.* [I always + adv/prep] • If you **jump to a conclusion**, you judge a situation by its appearance instead of considering the matter in depth: *Don't jump to conclusions! Perhaps it was his daughter he was dancing with.* ○ *Just because you saw them having a drink together doesn't mean you can jump to the conclusion that they're having an affair.*

• *(Br and Aus infml disapproving) He thinks he's so important, but really he's just a* **jumped-up** *office boy* (= he thinks he's more important than he is, because he's risen to a higher position).

jump /dʒʌmp/ *n* [C] • *The way to be successful in business is always to be/stay/keep/remain* **one/a jump ahead** *(***of** *your competitors)* (= to do something before the people you are competing with do it). • *(infml)* To **get a jump on** someone or something is to do something before other people or *(Am)* before something happens: *They were determined to get a jump on their competitors.* ○ *(Am) I like to leave work early on Fridays so I can get a jump on the traffic.*

jump INCREASE /dʒʌmp/ *v* [I] to increase suddenly by a large amount • *House prices have jumped* **dramatically.** • *Student numbers are expected to jump* **from** *2000* **to** *around 4000 next year.* • *The cost of building the road has jumped* **by** *70%.*

jump *(obj)* ATTACK /dʒʌmp/ *v infml* to attack suddenly • *(esp. Am) They were just walking home when a bunch of guys jumped them.* [T] • *He jumped* **(on)** *her as she turned the corner.* [T; I + *on*] • See also **jump on** at JUMP DO QUICKLY.

jump *obj* MOVE ILLEGALLY /dʒʌmp/ *v* [T] to go away from or go past (something) wrongly or illegally • *The police video showed that she had jumped the* **(traffic) lights.** • *(Br and Aus) Don't jump* (= go to the front of) *the* **queue** *(Am* **cut in line***) – wait your turn.* • *Several sailors jumped* **ship** (= left without permission the ship on which they were working) *in New York.* • *I'd never have thought Hugh would jump* **bail** (= fail to appear for a court trial after being released until the trial in exchange for payment).

jump·er /£ˈdʒʌm·pəʳ, $-pɚ/ *n* [C] *Br and Aus* a woollen item of clothing which covers the upper part of the body and the arms, and which does not open at the front • *a woollen/woolly jumper* • *I'm knitting Myra a jumper for her birthday.* • *(Am and Aus)* A jumper is also a dress which does not cover the arms and which is usually worn over another item of clothing which does cover the arms. • PIC〉 **Clothes** Ⓙ Ⓚ

jump·suit /£ˈdʒʌmp·sjuːt, $-suːt/ *n* [C] a single item of clothing which covers both the upper body and the legs

jump·y /ˈdʒʌm·pi/ *adj* **-ier, -iest** *infml* nervous and anxious, esp. because of fear or guilt • *My mother gets very jumpy when she's alone in the house.* • *I'm rather jumpy* **about** *travelling on the metro late at night.* • *He was so jumpy in the interview that the police thought he was lying.*

junc·tion /ˈdʒʌŋk·ʃᵊn/ *n* [C] a place where things, esp. roads and railways, come together • *(esp. Br) When driving a car, you should always slow down as you approach a junction (Am and Aus usually* **intersection***).* • *(esp. Br) There's a service station at the junction (Am and Aus usually* **intersection***) of the motorway and the road to Leeds.* • *The bomb exploded at a busy railway junction.* • *The next stop is Clapham Junction.* • A **junction box** is a plastic or wooden box or other container in which electrical wires can be safely joined together.

junc·ture /£ˈdʒʌŋk·tʃəʳ, $-tʃɚ/ *n* [U] *fml* a particular point in time • **At** *this juncture, it is impossible to say whether she will make a full recovery from her illness.* • *We are* **at** *an important juncture in the negotiations.*

June /dʒuːn/ *(abbreviation* **Jun***) n* the sixth month of the year, after May and before July • *22(nd) June/June 22(nd)/ 22(nd) Jun/Jun 22(nd)* [U] • *He arrived* **on** *the fifth of June/ June the fifth/(esp. Am) June fifth* [U] • *I haven't seen her since* **last** *June/will be seeing her* **next** *June.* [U] • *I went to visit my father* **in/during** *June.* [U] • *It was one of the coolest and wettest Junes since 1900.* [C] • *"June is bustin' out all over"* (title of a song written by Oscar Hammerstein II, 1945) • LP〉 **Dates**

Jung·i·an /ˈjʊŋ·i·ən/ *adj* of or connected with the ideas of the Swiss PSYCHOANALYST Carl Gustav Jung • *In Jungian theory, there are certain archetypes of human personality.*

jun·gle /ˈdʒʌŋ·gl/ *n* a tropical forest in which trees and plants grow very closely together • *The Yanomami people live in the South American jungle.* [C] • *Either side of the river is dense, impenetrable jungle.* [U] • Jungle **warfare** is war fought in a tropical forest where it is difficult to see the enemy and they can attack unexpectedly. • A jungle is also an uncontrolled or confusing mass of things: *Our garden is a real jungle.* [C] ○ *Too many people fail to apply for the benefits to which they're entitled because of the jungle* **of regulations/laws** *surrounding them.* [C] ○ *It's a jungle out there* (= Life is difficult and you have to fight for what you want), *kid.* [C] • **Jungle gym** is *Am and Aus for* **climbing frame**. See at CLIMB RISE. • PIC〉 **Frame, Playground**

jun·i·or YOUNGER /£ˈdʒuː·ni·əʳ, $-njɚ/ *n, adj* [not gradable] (someone) younger • *My brother is my junior* **by** *three years./My brother is three years my junior* (= He is three years younger than me). • *(esp. Am)* Junior *(abbreviation* esp. *Am* **Jr** or *Br* **Jnr**) is used after a man's name to refer to the younger of two people in the same family who have the same name: *Sammy Davis, Jr* • *(esp. Am)* Junior is also used to refer to your son: *I've asked Mom to take care of Junior for us.* ○ *Come on, Junior, time for bed.* [as form of address] • Compare SENIOR OLDER.

jun·i·or LOW RANK /£ˈdʒuː·ni·əʳ, $-njɚ/ *n, adj* (someone) low or lower in rank • *Do you think I'm too junior to apply for this job?* • *I object to being told what to do by someone junior* **to** *me.* • *Junior doctors have protested about having to work long hours.* • *He's the junior partner in the business.* • *(Am)* A **junior college** is a college in the US where students study for two years: *Linda is at junior college.* • *The work was done by juniors on the staff* (= people with jobs at a low level), *but he took all the credit.* [C] • *Jill has just started work as an* **office** *junior.* [C] • Compare SENIOR HIGH RANK.

jun·i·or SCHOOL /£ˈdʒuː·ni·əʳ, $-njɚ/ *adj* used to refer to one of several stages of education • *(Br)* Junior refers to a stage of education in England and Wales for children aged 7 to 11 years: *My children go to (a) junior school.* ○ *a junior teacher* • *(Am)* A **junior high (school)** is a school in the US for children who are 12 to 15 years old: *I used to write for the school newspaper in junior high.* • *(Am) They met in their junior* **year** (= third of four years) *at college and married soon after they graduated.* • LP〉 **Schools and colleges**

jun·i·or /£ˈdʒuː·ni·əʳ, $-njɚ/ *n* [C] • *(Br) Debbie is a junior* (= student at a junior school) *now.* • *(Am)* A junior is a student in the third year of a course that lasts for four years at a school or college: *The juniors are performing a play at the end of the semester.*

jun·i·ors /£ˈdʒuː·ni·əz, $-njɚz/ *pl n Br* • **The Juniors** is junior school: *Lewis has just moved up to the Juniors.*

jun·i·per /£ˈdʒuː·nɪ·pəʳ, $-pɚ/ *n* [C/U] a small evergreen bush which has sharp leaves and small purple fruits which are used in medicine and in making GIN (= an alcoholic drink) • *juniper berries*

junk RUBBISH /dʒʌŋk/ *n* [U] things that are considered to be of no use or value, or of low quality • *We ought to clear out this cupboard – it's full of junk.* • *All he ever reads is junk* (= books, magazines etc. of low quality). • *I can't get the children to eat anything except junk/***junk food** (= food that is unhealthy but is quick and easy to eat). Compare **health food** at HEALTH. • *"Was there any mail today?" "No, just junk/***junk mail** (= post, usually advertising products or services, which is sent to people although they have not asked for it)*."* • *We furnished our house entirely from* **junk shops** (= shops which sell old unwanted furniture, etc. at low prices).

junk *obj* /dʒʌŋk/ *v* [T] *infml* • *I think the TV has finally packed up – why don't we junk it* (= get rid of it because it is of no value) *and get a new one?*

junk DRUG /dʒʌŋk/ *n* [U] *esp. Am slang* a dangerous drug, esp. HEROIN

junk·ie, junk·y /ˈdʒʌŋ·ki/ *n* [C] *slang* • *This place is a regular hang-out for drunks and junkies* (= people who regularly take and are dependent on drugs, esp. HEROIN.) • *(fig.) I'm a turning into a real coffee junkie* (= I have a need to drink a lot of coffee, more than is healthy).

junk SHIP /dʒʌŋk/ *n* [C] a Chinese ship with a flat bottom and square sails

junk·et /ˈdʒʌŋ·kɪt/ *n* [C] *disapproving* a journey or visit made for pleasure by an official or officials, which is paid for by someone else, often with public money • *David's* **gone** *off* **on** *another one of those junkets* **to** *Paris this weekend.*

junk·yard /£ˈdʒʌŋk·jɑːd, $-jɑːrd/ *n* [C] a place to which people take esp. large things, such as old furniture or machines, that they no longer want • *I found this television in a junkyard – it's amazing what people will throw away.*

jun·ta /ˈdʒʌn·tə, ˈhʊn-/ *n* [C + sing/pl v] a government, esp. a military one, that has taken power in a country by force and not by election • *The* **military** *junta has/have today broadcast an appeal for calm.*

Ju·pi·ter /£ˈdʒuː·pɪ·təʳ, $-t̬ɚ/ *n* [U not after *the*] the planet fifth in order of distance from the Sun, after Mars and before Saturn • *Jupiter is the largest planet.*

ju·ris·dic·tion /£ˌdʒʊə·rɪsˈdɪk·ʃᵊn, $ˌdʒʊr·ɪs-/ *n* [U] the authority of an official organization to make and deal with (esp. legal) decisions • *The court* **has** *no jurisdiction* **in/**

over *cases of this kind.* • *Issues of citizenship are* **beyond/ outside** *the jurisdiction* **of** *local government.* • *School admissions are not* **under/within** *our jurisdiction.*

ju·ris·pru·dence /£ˌdʒʊə·rɪˈspruː·dənts, $ˌdʒʊr·ɪ-/ *n* [U] *specialized* the study of law and the principles on which law is based

ju·rist /£ˈdʒʊə·rɪst, $ˈdʒʊr·ɪst/ *n* [C] *specialized* an expert in law, esp. a judge • decides whether a person is guilty in court.

ju·ry /£ˈdʒʊə·ri, $ˈdʒʊr·i/ *n* [C + sing/pl v] a group of people who have been chosen to listen to all the facts in a trial in a law court and to decide whether a person is guilty or not guilty, or whether a claim has been proved • *Several members of the jury wept as they heard how the child was killed.* • *The jury has/have been unable to return a verdict* (= reach a decision). • *Have you ever* **been/sat/served on** *a jury?* • *The jury is/are still* **out** (= still thinking about their decision). • *(fig.) As far as the safety of irradiated food is concerned, the jury's still out* (= the answer is not known). • *(Br) I won't be at work next week because I'm* **on/doing** *jury* **service** *(Am and Aus* **duty***)* (= acting as a member of a jury). • A jury is also a group of people chosen to decide the winner of a competition: *The jury chose an unexpected winner for the literary prize.* • A **jury box** is the place in a court where the jury sits. • LP› **Law**

ju·ror, ju·ry·man *(pl* **-men***)*, **ju·ry·wo·man** *(pl* **-women***)* /£ˈdʒʊə·rəʳ, $ˈdʒʊr·ɚ, -mən, -ˌwʊm·ən/ *n* [C] • A juror is a member of a jury: *Five of the jurors were women.*

just NOW /dʒʌst/ *adv* [not gradable] now or (almost) at the same time, or very soon, or very recently • *"Where are you, Jim?" "I'm just coming."* • *The children arrived at school just* **as** *the bell was ringing.* • *We're just* **about to** *leave* (= We will leave very soon). • *I'll just* (= very soon) *finish this, then we can go.* • *The doctor will be with you in just* **a minute/moment/second** (= very soon). • **Just a minute/ moment/second** (= Wait a short period of time) – *I've nearly finished.* • *(esp. Br)* **Just a minute/moment/ second** can also be used to interrupt someone to ask them to explain something, to calm them, or to express disagreement: *Just a minute – there's no need to be so rude.* • *He'd just* (= recently) *got into the bath when the phone rang.* • *I've just* **recently** *seen Tom.* • *It's just after/past/(Br also) gone* (= has recently become) *ten (o'clock).* • *She's just* **turned** (= has very recently become) *15.* • *Who was that at the door* **just now** (= a short time ago)? • (E)(J)(P)

just EXACTLY /dʒʌst/ *adv* [not gradable] exactly or equally • *This carpet would be just right for the dining room.* • *The twins look just like each other.* • *The trip cost us just $500.* • *She's just 15.* • *We always try to treat our children just the same (***as** *each other).* • *Things turned out just* **as** *I expected.* • *You've got just* **as** *many toys* **as** *your brother.* • *This device is just* **the thing** (= exactly what is needed) *for clearing blocked drains.* • *The staff committee was set up to deal with just* **this kind of/***just* **such a** *problem.* • *Thank you, it's just* **what** *I've always wanted.* [+ *wh-* word] • *Just* **where** *do you think you're going?* [+ *wh-* word] • *I'll help you later, but I can't do it just* **now/***just* **at the moment.** • *Just* **then**, *the lights went out.* • *They haven't made their minds up just* **yet.** • *(Br and Aus) It was just* **on** (= exactly) *six o'clock when they arrived.* • *(infml approving) That dress is just you/her* (= suits you/her very well). • *For the little extra it'll cost, we* **might** *just* **as well** (= with good reason) *stay for another night.* • *I* **might** *just* **as well** *not be* (= It would make no difference if I were not) *here for all the notice you take of me.* • *It's beginning to rain –* **(it's) just as well (that)** (= it's good that) *we brought our umbrellas.* • *It's* **just my luck** (= typical of the bad things that usually happen to me) *not to be able to get tickets for the concert.* • *"Just like that"* (catchphrase of comedian Tommy Cooper, 1921-1984) • *"Just So Stories"* (title of a children's book by Rudyard Kipling, 1902) • (E)(J)(P)

just ONLY /dʒʌst/ *adv* [not gradable] only; simply • *"Would you like another drink?" "OK, just one more."* • *I'm driving, so I'll just have orange juice, please.* • *It was just a joke.* • *His daughter's just a baby/just a few weeks old.* • *They said that they'd stolen the car just* **for fun/for kicks/for a laugh/ for the hell of it.** • *We'll just have to* (= The only thing we can do is) *wait and see what happens.* • *She lives just down the road* (= She only lives down the road/She lives near). • **Not** *just anybody* (= Only a special person) *could do this, you know.* • *He thinks that just* **because** *he's got so much money, he can do what he likes.* • *Don't just look at me like that – say something!* • Just can be used to make a statement or command stronger: *He just won't do as he's told.* ○ *It's just too expensive.* ○ *You'd better take an umbrella just* **in case** *it rains.* ○ *Well, just look at this!* • Just can also be used to reduce the force of a statement and to suggest that it is not very important: *Can I just borrow the scissors for a second?* ○ *I just wanted to ask you if you're free this afternoon.* • *I know I said I'd have the report finished by today, it's just* **that** (= I haven't done it because) *I've been so busy.* • *Their son went off and got married last week,* **just like that** (= suddenly and unexpectedly). • *(saying)* 'It's just one of those things' means it is simply something that happened and no one could expect it or prevent it. • (E)(J)(P)

just ALMOST /dʒʌst/ *adv* [not gradable] almost not or almost • *We arrived at the airport just in time to catch the plane.* • *This dress just/***only** *just/just* **about** *fits.* • *"Can you see the stage?" "Yes, just/***only** *just/just* **about.***"* • *She spoke so quietly I could just/***only** *just/just* **about** *hear her.* • if something is just **possible** there is a small possibility that it will happen: *It's just possible that we might be going away that weekend.* ○ *It might just* **possibly** *help if you were to go and see him and explain.* • If you say you can just hear/see/ feel/taste something, you mean that you can imagine how it sounds/looks/feels/tastes. If you can just see someone **as** something you can imagine them as that thing: *Her description of the mountains was so vivid, I could just see the snow.* ○ *I can just see her* **as** *a police officer.* • (E)(J)(P)

just VERY /dʒʌst/ *adv* [not gradable] very; completely • *You look just wonderful!* • *It's just dreadful what happened to her.* • *(infml) "This is expensive."* "**Isn't** *it* **just** (= I completely agree)?" • (E)(J)(P)

just FAIR /dʒʌst/ *adj* fair; morally correct • *The judge's sentence was perfectly just in the circumstances.* • *I don't really think he had just* **cause** *to complain.* • *Her success is just* **reward** *for all her hard work.* • *We should all work together to create a just* **society.** • *He* **got** *his* **just deserts** (= Unpleasant things happened to him, which he deserved because he had behaved badly). • *"God is just"* (Thomas Jefferson in *Notes on the State of Virginia*, 1781-5) • *"He maketh his sun to rise on the evil and on the good, and sendeth rain on the just and on the unjust"* (Bible, Matthew 5.45) • (E)(J)(P)

just /dʒʌst/ *pl n old use* • **The** just are the people who behave in a morally correct way.

jus·tice /ˈdʒʌs·tɪs/ *n* [U] • *There's no justice* (= fairness) *in the world when people can be made to suffer like that.* • *The winner has been disqualified for cheating, so justice has been* **done** (= a fair situation has been achieved). • *To* **do** *him justice* (= To be fair to him), *I think he would have protested if he'd been here.* • *This photograph doesn't really* **do justice to** *her beauty/***do** *her beauty* **justice** (= show how beautiful she really is). • *If you eat all those biscuits now, you won't be able to* **do justice to** *your dinner/***do** *your dinner* **justice** (= be able to enjoy it and eat it all). • *She didn't really* **do justice to** *herself/***do** *herself* **justice** (= behave in a way that showed her real qualities) *in the interview.*

just·ly /ˈdʒʌst·li/ *adv* • *The teacher acted justly in punishing all the children.* • *She has justly been called one of the greatest singers of her time.* • *He is justly proud of his daughter's achievements.*

just·ness /ˈdʒʌst·nəs/ *n* [U] • *I accept the justness* **of** *your criticism* (= I accept that your criticism is deserved).

jus·tice LAW /ˈdʒʌs·tɪs/ *n* [U] the putting of the law into action • *The system of justice in this country consists of a series of law courts at different levels.* • *They claim that they are victims of a* **miscarriage of** *justice* (= that the law has been carried out wrongly). • *The police are doing all they can to* **bring** *those responsible for the bombing* **to** *justice* (= to catch them and try them in a court of law). • *He has been accused of* **obstructing (the course of)** *justice* (= preventing the law being put into action). • (CS)

jus·tice JUDGE /ˈdʒʌs·tɪs/ *n* [C] a judge • *(Am) The President is expected to name a new Supreme Court justice within the next few days.* • *(Br and Aus) The judge, Mr Justice Ellis, severely reprimanded the offenders.* • *(Am, Aus also) The unanimous decision, written by Justice Ben Overton, upheld the lower court's ruling.* • A **Justice of the Peace** (abbrev. **JP**) is a person who is not a lawyer but who acts as a judge in local law courts and, in the US, can marry people. • (CS)

jus·ti·fy *obj* /ˈdʒʌs·tɪ·faɪ/ *v* [T] to give or to be a good reason for • *I can't really justify taking another day off work* [+ v-*ing*] • *I hope you're able to justify your***self/***your actions* (= give a good reason for what you have done). • *These recommendations will need to be justified* **to** *the committee* *before they can be implemented.* • *The results of the study have certainly justified the money that was spent on it.* • *Are you sure that these measures are justified?* • *I'm sure I'll be able to justify your faith in me* (= will be able to do what you expect me to do).

jus·ti·fi·a·ble /ˈdʒʌs·tɪ·faɪ·ə·bl̩, ˌ--ˈ---/ *adj* • *Her actions were quite justifiable* (= there was a good reason for them) *in the circumstances.* • *Could* **it** *ever be justifiable* **to** *use atomic weapons against towns and cities?* [+ *to* infinitive] • *(Am)* **Justifiable homicide** is an act of killing someone, esp. in self-defence, which is considered to be lawful.

jus·ti·fi·a·bly /ˈdʒʌs·tɪ·faɪ·ə·bli, ˌ--ˈ---/ *adv* • *He was justifiably proud of his achievements.*

jus·ti·fi·ca·tion /ˌdʒʌs·tɪ·fɪˈkeɪ·ʃən/ *n* [U] • *We expect you to provide a justification* **of/for** (= an acceptable explanation for) *your actions.* [C] • *It can be said,* **with** *some justification* (= There is good reason to say), *that she is one of the greatest actresses on the English stage today.* [U]

jus·ti·fied /ˈdʒʌs·tɪ·faɪd/ *adj* • *I accept that the criticism is completely justified* (= there is a good reason for it). • *I think you were quite justified* **in** (= had a good reason to) *complaining.*

jut /dʒʌt/ *v* **-tt-** to (cause to) stick out, esp. above or beyond the edge or surface of something • *The pier juts* **(out) into** *the sea.* [I always + adv/prep] • *You can only see the tips of icebergs jutting* **out of/from** *the water.* [I always + adv/prep] • *He jutted his* **chin/jaw** *defiantly.* [T]

jut·ting /£ˈdʒʌt·ɪŋ, $ˈdʒʌt̬-/ *adj* [before n] • *high jutting walls* • *jutting rocks* • *The photos showed the jutting rib and hip bones of a famine victim.*

jute /dʒuːt/ *n* [U] a substance which comes from a SE Asian plant and which is used for making rope and cloth

ju·ve·nile /£ˈdʒuː·vən·aɪl, $-nəl/ *adj esp. fml or law* of, by or for a young person who is not yet old enough to be considered an adult • *There has been a big increase in juvenile crime in the last few years.* • *Rates of juvenile* **delinquency** (= crimes committed by young people) *are on the increase.* • *Their car was broken into by a gang of juvenile* **delinquents** (= young people who commit crimes). • *Juvenile* **offenders** *should not be tried in adult courts.* • *(disapproving) Your behaviour is really juvenile* (= silly and like a child)*!* • LP **Age**

ju·ve·nile /£ˈdʒuː·vən·aɪl, $-nəl/ *n* [C] • *(fml or law) The attack is believed to have been carried out by juveniles* (= young people). • *Rachel is playing the juvenile* **lead** (= the main character who is a young person) *in the Christmas show.*

jux·ta·pose *obj* /£ˌdʒʌk·stəˈpəʊz, $-ˈpoʊz/ *v* [T] to put (things which are not similar) next to each other • *The exhibition juxtaposes Picasso's early drawings* **with** *some of his later works.*

jux·ta·po·si·tion /ˌdʒʌk·stə·pəˈzɪʃ·ən/ *n* [U] • *The juxtaposition* (= putting close together) **of** *cultures in New York makes it a varied and interesting city.* • *Placing the two designs* **in** *juxtaposition* **with** (= next to) *each other draws out the differences between them.*

K k

K LETTER (*pl* **K's** or **Ks**), **k** (*pl* **k's** or **ks**) /keɪ/ *n* [C] the 11th letter of the English alphabet • LP **Silent letters**

K COMPUTER /keɪ/ *n* [C] *pl* **K** *abbreviation for* KILOBYTE • *a computer with 256K* **of** *memory*

K MONEY *Br and Aus* (*pl* **K**) /keɪ/, *Am* **G** (*pl* **G**) *n* [C] *infml for* £1000 or $1000 • *His car cost him £20K/$20G.* • LP **Money**

K TEMPERATURE /keɪ/ *n* [after n] *abbreviation for* KELVIN • *273°K*

ka·bu·ki /kəˈbuː·ki/ *n* [U] a type of Japanese theatre in which only male actors perform in a traditional and artificial manner

kaf·tan /£ˈkæf·tæn, $-t̬æn/ *n* [C] a CAFTAN

ka·goul, ka·goule /kəˈguːl/ *n* [C] a CAGOULE

Ka·lash·ni·kov /£kəˈlæʃ·nɪ·kɒf, $-kɑːf/ *n* [C] a Russian-made RIFLE (= a type of gun) which can fire bullets continuously • *They believed that the weapons used last night were Kalashnikovs/Kalashnikov assault rifles.*

kale /keɪl/ *n* [U] a vegetable with green or purple tightly curled leaves; a type of CABBAGE

ka·lei·do·scope /£kəˈlaɪ·də·skəʊp, $-skoʊp/ *n* [C] a tube-like device you look through to see different patterns of light made by pieces of coloured glass and mirrors • *(fig.) The street bazaar was a kaleidoscope* (= a changing mixture or pattern) **of** *colours, smells and sounds.*

ka·lei·do·scop·ic /£kəˌlaɪ·dəˈskɒp·ɪk, $-ˈskɑː·pɪk/ *adj* • Kaleidoscopic means quickly changing from one thing to another: *The music was inspired by a kaleidoscopic view of a carnival procession in Lucca.* • *The biography traces his kaleidoscopic career: poor boy in Memphis, professor of law at Yale, rich Washington lawyer.* • *From the top of the skyscraper we could see the kaleidoscopic pattern of people and cars in the streets below.*

ka·lei·do·scop·i·cal·ly /£kəˌlaɪ·dəˈskɒp·ɪ·kli, $-ˈskɑː·pɪ-/ *adv* • *The light was changing colour kaleidoscopically with the different pitch of the musical sounds, bright reds and yellows in the high register, deep purple in the low.*

ka·mi·ka·ze /ˌkæm·ɪˈkɑː·zi/ *adj* [before n] of a sudden violent attack on an enemy, esp. one in which the person or people attacking know that they will be killed • *a kamikaze attack* • *Driving the explosive-laden car into the barracks was a kamikaze* **mission** *for the terrorists.* • *(fig.) Discussions were getting nowhere, so the protesters decided on kamikaze tactics/a kamikaze approach.* • In World War II, a kamikaze PILOT was one of a group of Japanese pilots who intentionally flew aircraft into enemy ships destroying both the aircraft and ship.

kan·ga·roo /£ˌkæŋ·gərˈuː, $-gəˈruː/ *n* [C] *pl* **kangaroos** or *specialized* **kangaroo** a large Australian mammal with a long stiff tail, short front legs and long powerful back legs on which it moves by jumping • *Female kangaroos carry their young in a pouch on their stomachs.* • A **kangaroo court** is an unofficial court of law set up by a group of people, esp. in a prison, **trade union** or other organization, to deal with a disagreement or with a member of the group who is considered to have broken the rules.

ka·o·lin /ˈkeɪə·lɪn/ *n* [U] a white clay which is used in making some medicines and in making PORCELAIN (= a hard substance from which cups, plates, decorative objects etc. are made) • *Kaolin* **and morphine** *is sometimes used as a medicine for diarrhoea.*

kap·ok /£ˈkeɪ·pɒk, $-pɑːk/ *n* [U] a soft white material that is used as the filling in soft toys and CUSHIONS (= cloth bags used on chairs) or for making a thick warm layer in clothes

kap·ut /kəˈpʊt/ *adj* [after v; not gradable] *infml* broken; not working correctly • *The radio's kaput.*

ka·ra·o·ke /£ˌkær·iˈəʊ·ki, $ˌker·iˈoʊ·ki/ *n* [U] a form of public entertainment, originally from Japan, in which people sing to a recording of the music of popular songs, sometimes reading the words on a screen • *"Karaoke is popular because anyone can join in," he explained.* • *a karaoke bar/club* • *a karaoke machine* • *Thursday night is karaoke* **night** *at our local pub.*

ka·rat /£ˈkær·ət, $ˈker-/ *n* [C] *Am for* CARAT

ka·ra·te /£kəˈrɑː·ti, $-t̬i/ *n* [U] a sport originally from Japan in which people fight using their arms, legs, hands and feet. The level of skill a person has is shown by what colour belt they wear. • *It's possible to break a piece of wood using a karate* **chop** (= a hit with the side of the hand).

kar·ma /£ˈkɑː·mə, $ˈkɑːr-/ *n* [U] (in the Buddhist and Hindu religions) the force produced by a person's actions in one of their lives which influences what happens to them in their future lives • *(fig. infml) There was* **good/bad** *karma* (= the general character or feeling among a group of people or in a place) *in the room that night.*

kay·ak /ˈkaɪ·æk/ *n* [C] a light narrow boat with a covering over the top, esp. used by the Inuit or for sport; a type of CANOE • PIC **Ships and boats**

kay·ak /ˈkaɪ·æk/ *v* [I] • *We're* **going** *kayaking* (= travelling by kayak) *on our trip to the US.*

ka·zoo /kəˈzuː/ *n* [C] *pl* **kazoos** a small musical instrument consisting of a plastic or metal tube with a small piece of paper inside which shakes when the player HUMS into it, making a high sound

KC /ˌkeɪˈsiː/ *n* [C] *abbreviation for* king's counsel (= a title given in Britain to a high-ranking lawyer while a king is ruling) • *They are being defended by one of the country's leading K.C.s.* • *Sir William Garner, KC* • Compare QC.

ke·bab /£kɪˈbæb, $-ˈbɑːb/, **shish ke·bab** *n* [C] a dish consisting of small pieces of meat and vegetables that have been put on a long thin stick or metal rod and cooked together. It comes from E Mediterranean countries such as Greece and Turkey. • *There are plenty of burger bars and kebab shops for late-night snacks.*

kedg·er·ee /£ˈkedʒ·ər·i, $ˈ-ə-/ *n* [U] a cooked dish esp. in Britain consisting of rice, fish and eggs mixed together • *Would you like kedgeree for breakfast?*

keel /kiːl/ *n* [C] the long piece of wood or steel along the bottom of a boat that forms part of its structure and helps to keep the boat balanced in the water • *We realized that the boat had lost its keel.* • PIC **Ships and boats**

keel o·ver *v adv* [I] to fall over suddenly • *The heat was too much for one woman who keeled over in a dead faint.*

keel·haul *obj* /£ˈkiːl·hɔːl, $-hɑːl/ *v* [T] *infml* to speak severely to or punish (someone) • *He was keelhauled for not following orders.*

keen EAGER /kiːn/ *adj* **-er, -est** very interested, eager or wanting (to do) something very much • *The new editor of the newspaper is very young and keen* (= works hard and is interested in everything). • *Joan wanted to go to a movie but I wasn't keen* (= I didn't want to go). • *She's a keen tennis player* • *She's keen* **on** *(playing) tennis.* • *(Br) My son's* **mad** *keen on cycling.* • *He's rather keen* **on** *a girl in his school* (= he is very attracted to her). • *We were very keen* **to** *start work.* [+ *to* infinitive] • *They were keen* **for** *their children* **to** *go to the best schools.* • *(Br dated infml)* Someone who is **as keen as mustard** is very eager and interested in everything.

keen·ness /ˈkiːn·nəs/ *n* [U] • *Personal qualities and keenness* (= interest in everything and willingness to work) *can be more important in finding a job than previous work experience.* • *The company's quick agreement to the unions' proposals showed their keenness* (= strong desire) **to** *avoid a strike.* [+ *to* infinitive]

keen EXTREME /kiːn/ *adj* **-er, -est** extreme, very strong or (of an ability) very good or clever • *The competition for almost every job is now very keen.* • *Many people are taking a keen* **interest** (= a very great interest) *in the result of the vote.* • *Even at the age of 95 he still had a keen mind* (= he was very clever and quick to understand). • *You must have a keen eye to be able to read those numbers at this distance!* • *(fig.) She has a keen* **eye for** (= She is very good at noticing) *the ridiculous side of life.*

keen·ly /ˈkiːn·li/ *adv* • *It was an injustice she felt keenly* (= very strongly). • *They are keenly* (= extremely) **aware** *that this will be their last chance to succeed.* • *He watched her face keenly* (= very closely) *for any sign of emotion.*

keen SHARP /kiːn/ *adj* **-er, -est** *literary* very sharp • *A kitchen knife needs a keen blade.* • *A keen north wind blew through the gaps around the door.*

keen CRY /kiːn/ *v, n literary* (to make) a loud, long, sad sound, esp. because someone has died • *The women sat around the coffin keening loudly.* [I]

keep *obj* POSSESS /kiːp/ *v* [T] *past* **kept** /kept/ to have or continue to have in your possession • *Do you want this photograph back or can I keep it?* • *I told him to keep the book for as long as he liked.* • *"Keep the change," she said to the taxi driver.* • *We keep the medicines in a locked cupboard* (= We store them there). • A person who keeps a shop owns and manages it: *My uncle kept a little tobacconists' in Gloucester.* • A person who keeps animals owns and takes care of them: *They keep a pig in their back garden.* • In some sports, such as football and HOCKEY, a player who keeps **goal** tries to prevent players from the other team scoring goals. • *(Am)* A person who keeps someone's children watches and cares for them while their parents are away: *Jody will keep the children while I shop.* • If you keep your **promise/word** or an **appointment**, you fulfil it or do what you have told someone that you would do: *I made a promise to you and I've kept it.* ○ *She phoned to say she couldn't keep her appointment.* • If you keep a **diary** or other written records, you make a regular record of events or other information so that you can refer to it later: *Anita kept a diary for twelve years.* ○ *Keep an account of how much you're spending.* • *Can you keep* **a secret** (= know about it without telling other people)? • *This watch keeps very good* **time** (= shows the correct time). • See also WELL-KEPT HIDDEN.

keep·er /£ˈkiː·pər, $-pə/ *n* [C] • A keeper is a person who takes care of animals or is in charge of valuable objects, a building, etc.: *a zoo keeper* ○ *the keeper of British Art at the Tate Gallery* ○ *a lighthouse-keeper* • Keeper is also *infml* for GOALKEEPER: *He fired three shots past the keeper.* • *"Am I my brother's keeper?"* (Cain in the Bible, Genesis 4.9)

keep·ing /ˈkiː·pɪŋ/ *n* [U] • If something is **in** your keeping, you are taking care of it: *I left my word processor in her keeping when I went abroad.* • *Don't worry about your son, he's* **in safe** *keeping with me* (= I am taking good care of him). • If something is **in keeping with** something else it is suitable and right for it: *His dark suit was in keeping with his position as bank manager.* ○ *In keeping with tradition, they always have turkey on Christmas Day.* ○ *Their behaviour was definitely* **not in keeping with** *the occasion.* • *The modern furniture was* **out of keeping with** (= was not suitable for) *the old house.*

keeps /kiːps/ *pl n infml* • *"Do you want it back?" "No it's yours,* **for keeps** (= forever)*".*

keep *(obj)* STAY /kiːp/ *v past* **kept** /kept/ to (cause to) stay in a particular place or condition • *I wish you'd keep quiet.* [L only + adj] • *Having a cold shower is the only way to keep cool in this weather.* [L only + adj] • *I like to keep busy.* [L only + adj] • *Keep left* (= Stay on the road that goes to the left) *when you come to the fork, then take the second on the right.* [L only + adj] • *"Shall I move this painting to the other wall?" "No, keep it here/keep it where it is."* [T] • *Can't you keep that dog of yours under control?* [T] • *Close the door to keep the room warm.* [T + obj + adj] • *The noise from their party kept me awake half the night.* [T + obj +adj] • *He kept his eyes fixed on me while I spoke.* [T + obj + v-*ed*] • To keep someone is to delay them or prevent them from doing something: *He's very late, what's keeping him?* [T] • *Sorry for keeping you* **waiting** (= for making you wait). [T + obj + v-*ing*] • *She kept me talking on the phone for half an hour.* [T + obj + v-*ing*] • *Am I keeping you* **from** *your work?* [T] • *Keep* **away/back** *– it might be dangerous.* [I always + adv/prep] • If you keep something **back** you do not use it all or tell it all at the same time: *When she told me about her illness, I was sure she was keeping something back/keeping back the truth.* [M] • To keep the size or number of something **down** is to control it and prevent it from increasing: *We need to work hard to keep our prices down.* [M] • If you keep a person or group of people **down**, you prevent them from having any power or freedom: *You can't keep a good woman down.* [T] • If you say that you can't keep food or liquid **down**, you mean that you vomit when you eat or drink: *On the day after her operation she couldn't keep anything down.* [T] • If you keep something **from** someone, you do not tell them about it: *I think he's keeping the extent of his illness from me.* [T] • If you **keep from** something, you do not do it: *I'm afraid I couldn't keep from smiling when she told me what she'd done.* • *(esp. Br dated)* If you ask someone **how** they are keeping, you are asking if they are well: *"How is your mother keeping?"* [I always +adv/prep] • *As a child Simon was often kept* **in** *after school* (= forced to stay in school as a punishment). [T] • *The hospital kept her* **in** *overnight for observation* (= asked her to stay so that they could decide what was wrong with her). [T] • *She likes to keep* **in with** *the fashionable crowd* (= to stay friendly with them because she hopes to get some advantage). [I always + adv/prep] • *There was a notice saying 'Keep* **off** *the grass'* (= don't walk on the area of grass). [I always + adv/prep] • *Wear a hat to keep the sun* **off** (= to prevent it from reaching your skin). [M] • *(esp. Br)* If you keep **off** a particular subject, you avoid talking about it. [I always + adv/prep] • A sign that says "Keep **Out**" is telling you not to enter a building or area of land. [I always + adv/prep] • *I prefer to keep* **out of** (= avoid becoming involved in) *arguments about money.* [I always + adv/prep] • *Keep this news* **to** *your***self** (= do not tell anyone else). [T] • *He's a very private person – he* **keeps** *himself* **to** *him***self** (= does not talk to other people very much). • If you **keep to** a place, you stay there: *Please keep to the left hand side of the stairs.* • If you **keep to** a subject or an agreement, you limit yourself to it: *For heaven's sake let's keep to the point or we'll never reach any decisions.* ○ *I've kept to my side of the agreement – it's you that's broken it.* • If you keep a family, country, etc. **together** you stop the individuals or groups from separating: *They tried to keep the family together for the sake of the children.* [T] • *I hope I'm not keeping you* **up** (= preventing you from going to bed). [T] • If someone or something keeps **up** (**with** someone or something else), they do whatever is necessary to stay level or equal with that person or thing: *He was walking so fast that I had to run to keep up (with him).* [I always + adv/prep] ○ *Wages are failing to keep up with inflation.* [I always + adv/prep] ○ *(fig.)*

I read the papers to keep up with (= to discover) *what's happening in the outside world.* [I always + adv/prep] • *(disapproving)* If you are trying to **keep up with the Joneses** you always want to own the same expensive possessions and do the same things as your friends or NEIGHBOURS because you are worried about seeming less important socially than they are. • *(infml)* If you tell someone to **keep** their **shirt on**/*(Br)* also **keep** their **hair on**, you are telling them to stop being so angry or upset: *Keep your hair on! Your car isn't badly damaged!* • *(Br and Aus)* **Keep-fit** (*Am and Aus* **physical fitness** or **fitness**) is the activity of keeping your body in good condition by doing physical exercises: *Do you go to keep-fit (classes)?* • See also WELL-KEPT [TIDY].

keep [CONTINUE DOING] /kiːp/ *v past* **kept** /kept/ to continue doing something without stopping, or to do it repeatedly • *He keeps* **(on)** *trying to distract me.* [+ v-*ing*] • *Keep* **(on)** *taking the tablets.* [+ v-*ing*] • *I keep* **(on)** *thinking I've seen her before somewhere.* [+ v-*ing*] • *Don't keep* **(on)** *asking silly questions!* [+ v-*ing*] • *I kept* **(on)** *hoping that he'd phone me.* [+ v-*ing*] • If you **keep at** something such as work, or if someone **keeps** you **at** it, you continue to do it although you want to stop: *I kept at* **it** *and finally finished at 3 o'clock in the morning.* ○ *She got bored with homework quickly, but we kept her at* **it** *or she'd have failed the exam.* • If you say that someone **keeps on (at** you**) about** something, you are complaining that they will not stop talking about it: *Don't keep on at me about the money, you know I'll pay you back.* ○ *(infml) "You still haven't cleaned the car, have you?" "All right, there's no need to keep on."* • To **keep** something **up** is to continue doing or having it: *You're doing well, keep* **it** *up!* ○ *When I stopped studying I was still keen to keep up my French.* • If you **keep up appearances** you pretend to be happier, less poor, etc. than you really are, because you do not want people to know how bad your situation is: *They were unhappily married but kept up appearances for the sake of their children.* • [LP] **Get: verbs meaning 'cause'**

keep [STAY FRESH] /kiːp/ *v* [I] *past* **kept** /kept/ (of food) to stay fresh and in good condition • *Milk keeps much longer in a fridge.* • *This cheese keeps well* (= stays fresh for a long time). • *This cheese has good keeping qualities.* • *(fig.) Whatever your news is, it will keep* (= you can tell me later). • *(fig.) "I must tell you something." "Can't it keep* (= Please tell me later), *I'm in a hurry!"*

keep *obj* [PROVIDE] /kiːp/ *v* [T] *past* **kept** /kept/ to provide food, rent, clothing and necessary things for (yourself or another person) • *She doesn't earn enough to keep herself.* • *He wanted to keep his family in comfort.*

keep /kiːp/ *n* [U] • A person's keep is the cost of providing food, heating and other necessary things for them: *He's old enough now to* **earn** *his keep and stop living off his parents.*

kept /kept/ *adj* [before n; not gradable] • *(usually humorous)* A **kept woman/man** is someone who does not work but is instead given money and a place to live by a person with whom she or he is having a sexual relationship.

keep [TOWER] /kiːp/ *n* [C] *specialized* the strong main tower of a castle • *The inhabitants of the castle lived in the keep.*

keep·net /'kiːp·net/ *n* [C] a cone-shaped net which is used by people who catch fish for sport to keep live fish at the edge of a river after they have been caught

keep·sake /'kiːp·seɪk/ *n* [C] a small present, usually not expensive, that is given to you by someone so that you will remember that person • *Her aunt gave her a little wooden elephant as a keepsake.*

keg /keg/ *n* [C] a small BARREL (= container with a circular top and bottom and curved sides) usually used for storing beer or other alcoholic drinks • In the US, a **keg party** is a party in which people drink beer which is poured from kegs rather than bottles or other containers.

kelp /kelp/ *n* [U] a type of large brown SEAWEED (= plant that grows in the sea), used in some foods and medicines

kel·vin /'kel·vɪn/ (*abbreviation* **K**) *n* [C/U] *specialized* a standard unit of temperature. One degree kelvin is equal to one degree CELSIUS.

ken /ken/ *n* [U] **beyond** *someone's* **ken** *dated* not in your area of knowledge; (something) about which you know nothing • *Financial matters are beyond my ken, I'm afraid.*

ken *(obj)* /ken/ *v* [not *be kenning*] **-nn-** *Scot Eng and N Eng* • To ken someone is to know them: *Do you ken that man over there?* • *"D'ye ken John Peel"* (song written by J.W.Graves, 1820)

ken·nel /'ken·ᵊl/, *Am usually* **dog·house** *n* [C] a small, usually wooden shelter for a dog to sleep in outside • *The dog sleeps in her kennel at night.* • Kennel is also *Am for* kennels.

ken·nels /'ken·ᵊlz/ *n* [C] *pl* **kennels** • A kennels is a place where people leave their dogs to be taken care of while they are away. Often dogs are bred and trained there too: *I planned to leave my dog in a kennels when I went on holiday.*

kept /kept/ *past simple and past participle of* KEEP

kerb *Br and Aus* /£kɜːb, $kɜːrb/, *Am* **curb** *n* [C] the edge of a raised path nearest the road • *There was a sudden bump as the car* **hit** *the kerb.* • *(Br)* **Kerb crawling** is the activity of driving slowly along a road close to the path at the side in order to ask PROSTITUTES for sex: *He was accused of kerb-crawling, though he claims he was only asking for directions.* • [PIC] **Road**

kerb·side *Br and Aus* /£'kɜːb·saɪd, $'kɜːrb-/, *Am* **curb·side** *n* [U], *adj* [before n] the area near the point at which a road and the raised path next to it join • *You're supposed to leave the bike at* **the** *kerbside for the next user.*

ker·chief /£kɜː'tʃiːf, $kɜːr-/ *n* [C] *old use* a square piece of cloth worn around the neck or on the head

ker·fuf·fle /£kə'fʌf·l̩, $kɚ-/ *n* [C usually sing] *Br infml* noise, excitement and argument • *Everyone rushed outside and in the kerfuffle her glasses were broken.* • *There was a great kerfuffle when he announced his decision to resign.*

ker·nel /£'kɜː·nᵊl, $'kɜːr-/ *n* [C] the edible part of a nut that is inside the shell • *The almond shells are cracked by machine and the kernels extracted.* • A kernel can also be the whole seed of the MAIZE plant: *corn kernels* • The kernel of something is the most important part of it, although it might not always be easy to find: *There is often a kernel* **of truth** *in what they say.* • [PIC] **Nut** (DK)

ker·o·sene /'ker·ə·siːn/, *Aus infml* **ke·ro** /£'ker·əʊ, $-oʊ/ *n* [U] *esp. Am and Aus for* PARAFFIN, esp. as used as fuel for aircraft with **jet engines**

ke·strel /'kes·trᵊl/ *n* [C] a type of small FALCON (= a meat-eating bird)

ketch·up /'ketʃ·ʌp/, **to·ma·to ketch·up**, *Am also* **cat·sup** *n* [U] a thick cold red sauce made from TOMATOES and eaten with food • *Do you want some tomato ketchup with your chips?*

ket·tle /£'ket·l̩, $'keţ-/ *n* [C] a covered metal or plastic container with a handle and a SPOUT (= pointed part for pouring), used for boiling water • *People often say "I'll put the kettle on" when they are going to make tea or coffee.* • *(infml) He knows all about computers but being able to explain them to others is a different* **kettle of fish** (= something very different). • *(infml dated) You've lost your car keys? Well, this is a* **pretty/fine kettle of fish** (= a very difficult and annoying situation)! • (NL)

ket·tle·drum /£'ket·l̩.drʌm, $'keţ-/ *n* [C] a very large drum with a round bottom which is played esp. in an ORCHESTRA • See also TIMPANI.

Kev·lar /£'kev·lɑːʳ, $-lɑːr/ *n* [U] *trademark specialized* a very strong artificial material that is not damaged by high temperatures • *Helmets and bullet-proof vests are often made out of Kevlar.*

key [METAL SHAPE] /kiː/ *n* [C] a piece of metal that has been cut into a special shape and is used for locking a door, starting a car engine, etc. • *Her bag contained door keys, pens and notebook, lipstick, mirror and credit cards.* • *I put the key in the lock and turned it slowly.* • A key or **keycard** is also an electronic device in the form of a small plastic card which is used to open a door, for example a hotel room door. • **Key money** is a payment demanded by the owner of a house, apartment or shop from the person who is going to rent it: *Tenants have to pay key money before they can take over their high-street shops.* • A **key ring** is a metal or plastic ring used for keeping your keys together. • [PIC] **Key, Locks and home security, Ring**

key [MOVABLE PART] /kiː/ *n* [C] any of the set of movable parts that you press with your fingers on a computer, TYPEWRITER or musical instrument, to produce letters, numbers, etc. or musical notes • *Just* **press** *a couple of keys to send a command to the printer.* • *This is an old typewriter so you have to* **hit** *the keys quite hard.* • *Her hands moved swiftly over the piano keys.* • [LP] **Switching on and off** [PIC] **Key**

key *obj* /kiː/ *v* [T] • If you key **(in)** information you put it into a computer using a keyboard: *I learned how to key* **(in)** *new data.* [T/M] ○ *Daniel's job is to key written texts* **into** *the computer.* • See also KEYBOARD.

key IMPORTANT /kiː/ *adj* [before n] very important and having a lot of influence on other people or things • *The rebel soldiers have occupied the television station and other key buildings.* • *She was a key figure in the international art world.* • *Female literacy is a key factor in birth control in the developing world.*

key WAY OF ACHIEVING /kiː/ *n* [U] **the key** the way of achieving or explaining a situation • *This chemical could be the key* **to** *unlocking the mysteries of Parkison's disease.* • *The key* **to** *the magazine's success was that it employed new exciting writers.* • *The key* **to** *confidence is liking yourself.*

key MUSICAL NOTES /kiː/ *n* [C] a set of musical notes based on one particular note • *Halfway through the song there is a change of key.* • *It starts in the key of C minor.* • A **key signature** is the symbols on a printed piece of music that show the key in which that music is to be played. • PIC› **Key**

key LIST /kiː/ *n* [C] a list of the symbols used in a map or book with explanations of what they mean • *The key is printed at the bottom of the diagram.* • *an answer key* (= a list of answers to exercises in a book)

key *obj* **to** *obj v prep* [T] to make (something) in such a way that it is suitable for (something or someone else) • *The books are keyed to the interests of very young children.*

key *obj* **up** *v adv* [T usually passive] to cause (someone) to be very excited or nervous, usually before an important event • *She always gets keyed up before she goes on stage.*

key·board /£ˈkiː·bɔːd, $-bɔːrd/ *n* [C] the set of keys on a computer or TYPEWRITER that you press in order to make it work, or the row of keys on a musical instrument such as a piano • *The new model of word processor has a smaller keyboard.* • *The new band features Steve Lodder on electronic keyboards, the great Claude Deppa on trumpet and newcomer Dave Adams on drums.* • PIC› **Musical instruments, Office**

key·board *(obj)* /£ˈkiː·bɔːd, $-bɔːrd/ *v* • *Could you keyboard this information, please* (= put it into a computer using a keyboard)*?* [T] • *We have 10 people keyboarding 24 hours a day.* [I]

key·board·er /£ˈkiːˌbɔː·dər, $-ˌbɔːr·dɚ/ *n* [C] • A keyboarder is someone whose job is to put information into a computer using a keyboard.

key·board·ist /£ˈkiːˌbɔː·dɪst, $-ˌbɔːr-/ *n* [C] • A keyboardist is a person who plays music on a musical instrument which has a keyboard.

key·hole /£ˈkiː·həʊl, $-hoʊl/ *n* [C] a hole in a lock that you put a key into • *She peeked through the keyhole to see if anyone was there.* • *(Br)* **Keyhole surgery** is a medical operation in which a very small hole is made in a person's body to reach the organ or tissue inside. • PIC› **Locks and home security**

key·note /£ˈkiː·nəʊt, $-noʊt/ *n* [C] the most important part or something that is emphasized most strongly • *This issue has become the keynote of the election campaign.* • *Governor Tom Kean is the convention's keynote* **speaker**. • *In a keynote* **address/speech**, *the President stressed his commitment to world peace.* • See also KEY IMPORTANT.

key·pad /ˈkiː·pæd/ *n* [C] a small set of keys with numbers on them that is part of a device for changing television stations, or the keys on a calculator, on the right side of a computer keyboard, etc. • *The keypad is useful for entering accounts and other numeric information.*

key·punch /ˈkiː·pʌntʃ/ *n* [C] *Am and Aus for* CARDPUNCH

keys·tone /£ˈkiː·stəʊn, $-stoʊn/ *n* [C] the middle stone in the top of an arch which has a special shape and holds all the other stones in position, or *(fig.)* the most important part of a plan, idea, etc. on which everything else depends • *The keystone* **of** *the entrance arch is decorated with the date it was built.* • *(fig.) Japan's co-operation was the keystone in developing the regional agreement.* • See also KEY IMPORTANT.

kg *n* [C] *pl* **kg** *or* **kgs** *abbreviation for* KILOGRAM • LP› **Units**

kha·ki /ˈkɑː·ki/ *n* [U] a type of cloth that is dark yellowish-brown in colour, often worn by soldiers • *Armed troops in khaki marched across the square.*

kha·ki /ˈkɑː·ki/ *adj* • A khaki colour is a dark yellowish-brown colour: *I bought a khaki raincoat.*

kHz *n* [C] *pl* **kHz** *abbreviation for* KILOHERTZ

kib·butz /kɪˈbʊts,/ *n* [C] *pl* **kibbutzim** /ˌkɪb·ʊtˈsiːm/ or **kibbutzes** a place in Israel where people have come to live and work on usually a farm or a factory etc. where all profits and duties are shared • *Naomi spent two years working* **on** *a kibbutz.*

ki·bosh /£ˈkaɪ·bɒʃ, $-bɑːʃ/ *n* [U] **put the kibosh on** *infml* to spoil or destroy (esp. a hope or plan) completely • *The rain certainly put the kibosh on our plans for a picnic.*

kick *(obj)* HIT /kɪk/ *v* to hit (someone or something) with the foot, or to move the feet and legs suddenly and violently • *I kicked the ball as hard as I could.* [T] • *He was accused of kicking a man* **in** *the face.* [T] • *He kicked her* **up** *the backside when she wasn't looking.* [T] • *Astley kicked his fourth goal in the final minute.* [T] • *She felt the baby kicking inside her.* [I] • If a gun kicks, it jumps back suddenly and with force when the gun is fired. [I] • *(Am)* If you kick **about** something you complain about it: *I wouldn't kick about the size of your pay raise if I were you.* [I] • *(Br infml)* If you kick **against** something you refuse to accept it and react strongly against it: *As a boy he always kicked against his father's authority.* [I] • *(infml)* If you kick an idea **around** you talk about it generally in a group. [M] • *When they realized it was locked, the youths just kicked the door* **in/ down** (= opened it by kicking it very hard). [M] • When a game of football kicks **off** it begins, with one player kicking the ball: *(fig.) The new TV series kicks off* (= begins) **with** *an investigation into private healthcare.* See also KICKOFF. [I] • *I sat in a comfortable armchair and kicked* **off** *my shoes* (= removed them by shaking my feet). [M] • *At the age of fifteen she was kicked* **out** *of school* (= forced to leave by the people in charge). [M] • *There's no point in* **kicking against the pricks** (= complaining about things that you cannot change). • *(Am slang) When the sergeant finds out what you guys have been doing, he's really going to* **kick (some) ass** (= punish the people who have done wrong). • *(slang)* To **kick the bucket**/*(Am)* **kick off** is to die: *When did old Albert kick the bucket then?* • If you **kick a/the habit** you give up something that you have done for a long time: *She used to be a heavy smoker but she kicked the habit last year.* • *(Br)* If you are **kicking** your **heels** you are forced to wait for something and have nothing to do while you wait. • *(Am* *and Aus)* If you **kick up** your **heels** you have an enjoyable time or are suddenly very pleased: *We really like to kick up our heels when friends come to visit, take them to dinner and a show and so on.* • *(Br) Our plans to buy a new car have had to be* **kicked into touch** (= moved to a later time). • *(dated)* If someone **kicks over the traces** they behave badly and show no respect for authority: *It was no wonder that soldiers who risked death every day tended to kick over the traces on their evenings off.* • *(infml)* If someone **kicks up a fuss/row** they show great annoyance about something, esp. when this does not seem necessary: *He kicked up a tremendous fuss about not being given the best table at the restaurant.* • If you say that someone has been **kicked upstairs** you mean that they have been moved to a job which although it seems better than the one they had, in fact has less power: *In Britain important politicians are given a peerage and kicked upstairs to the House of Lords.* • If you say you are **kicking** your**self**, you mean that you are very annoyed because you have done something stupid or missed a chance: *They must be kicking themselves for having sold their shares too early.* ○ *When I realized what I had done I could have kicked myself.* • To **kick-start** a motorcycle is to make its engine start by pressing with your foot a metal bar connected to the engine: *(fig.) The Marshall Plan helped to kick-start western Europe's economic recovery* (= to make it start working again). • *"To kick against the pricks"* (Bible, Acts 9.5)

kick /kɪk/ *n* [C] • A kick is the action of kicking something: *She aimed a kick at the cat when no-one was looking.* ○ *The match was won on penalty kicks.* • *She was dismissed from her job, which was a* **(real) kick in the teeth** (= a great and unexpected disappointment) *for her after all the work she'd done.* • *(infml)* If you say that someone **needs** a **kick up/in the arse/backside/pants** you think that they are behaving in a silly way and they should be told forcefully to improve their behaviour: *He hasn't got any real problems, he just needs a good kick up the backside.* • If you say that an alcoholic drink **has a** kick you mean that it is very strong when you were not expecting it to be: *Watch out for the fruit punch, it's got a* **real** *kick.*

kick [EXCITEMENT] /kɪk/ *n* [C] a strong feeling of excitement and pleasure • ***I get a** kick **out of** owning my own car.* • *He decided to steal something from the shop, just* **for** *kicks* (= because he thought it would be exciting). • *"I get a Kick out of You"* (title of a song written by Cole Porter, 1934)

kick [INTEREST] /kɪk/ *n* [C usually sing] a new interest, esp. one that does not last long • *He's* **on an** *exercise kick* (= He exercises a lot) *at the moment.*

kick a·bout, kick a·round *v adv* [I always + adv/prep] *infml* to be or lie in a place, not being used • *I think the suitcase is kicking about in the cupboard somewhere.*

kick·a·bout /'kɪk·ə·baʊt/ *n* [C usually sing] *Br slang* a very informal game of football • *Let's go in the back garden and have a kickabout.*

kick·back /'kɪk·bæk/ *n* [C] an amount of money that is paid or returned to someone illegally in exchange for secret help or for a job, a piece of business, etc. • *The organization was accused of trying to get big client orders by using kickbacks, gifts and free holidays.*

kick·off /£'kɪk·ɒf, $-ɑːf/ *n* the time when a game of football starts or begins again, for example following a goal • *Play was stopped ten minutes after the kickoff.* [C] • *We arrived at the ground only moments before kickoff.* [U] • See also **kick off** at KICK [HIT].

kid [CHILD] /kɪd/ *n* [C] *infml* a child or *(esp. Am and Aus)* young person • *I took the kids to the park.* • *The nursery was full of crying kids.* • *He's only 19, just a kid really.* • *(esp. Am)* Someone's kid **sister** or **brother** is their younger sister or brother. • You can call someone, usually someone younger than yourself, 'kid', esp. if you are giving them some advice: *Listen, kid, don't try to be funny.* [as form of address] • *(disapproving)* **Kids' stuff**/*(Am usually)* **kid stuff** is something which is too easy and suitable only for children, not adults: *She was bored by university lectures, saying it was just kids' stuff.* • [LP] **Age**

kid [ANIMAL] /kɪd/ *n* a young goat, or very soft leather made from the skin of a young goat • *Outside the farm we saw a goat with her kids.* [C] • *What are these gloves made from – is it kid?* [U] • If you **treat/deal with** someone **with kid gloves**, you are extremely polite and careful because you do not want to make that person angry or upset: *As an interviewer he refuses to handle his subjects with kid gloves.*

kid *(obj)* [JOKE] /kɪd/ *v* **-dd-** *infml* to say something as a joke, often making (someone) believe something that is not true • *Did he really call round or are you just kidding?* [I] • *You're kidding, aren't you? She didn't really say that?* [I] • *I'm just kidding you.* [T] • *"You've just missed her – she was here five minutes ago." "Oh, you're kidding"* (= I am disappointed/annoyed). [I] • If you kid your**self**, you believe something that is not true, usually because you want it to be true: *He says there's a good chance she'll come back to him but I think he's kidding himself.* [T] • *I think he's a lovely person.* **Just/Only kidding** (= I am not telling the truth). • *He's going to join the army,* **no kidding/I kid you not** (= I am telling the truth).

kid·die, kid·dy /'kɪd·i/ *n* [C] *infml* a young child • *I saw the couple next door taking their kiddie for a walk.* • *I've bought him a* **kiddy car** (= child's toy car) *for his birthday.*

kid·nap *obj* /'kɪd·næp/ *v* [T] **-pp-** or *Am also* **-p-** to take (a person) away illegally by force, usually in order to demand money in exchange for releasing them • *The wife of a businessman has been kidnapped from her home in Surrey.* • [LP] **Crimes and criminals**

kid·nap /'kɪd·næp/ *n* • Kidnap is the crime of taking someone away by force and demanding money in exchange for releasing them: *He was sentenced to 15 years in prison after admitting kidnap and fraud.* [U] ○ *Three further kidnaps were reported in the region.* [C]

kid·nap·per, *Am also* **kid·nap·er** /£'kɪd·næp·əʳ, $-ɚ/ *n* [C] • *The kidnappers threatened to kill the girl if the ransom was not paid.*

kid·ney /'kɪd·ni/ *n* either of a pair of small organs in the body which take away waste matter from the blood to produce urine • *Eighteen years ago Adrian suffered complete kidney failure.* • Kidneys are also these organs from an animal, used as food: *grilled kidneys* [C] ○ *steak and kidney pie* [U] • A **kidney machine** is a machine used to do the work of a human kidney for people whose kidneys have stopped working or have been removed. See also DIALYSIS. • A **kidney stone** is a mass of stone-like material that forms in the kidney and causes pain. • A **kidney bean** is a small dark-red edible bean which has a curved shape like a kidney. • [PIC] **Peas and beans**

kike /kaɪk/ *n* [C] *Am taboo* (a very offensive word for) a Jew

kill *(obj)* /kɪl/ *v* to cause (someone or something) to die • *Her parents were killed in a plane crash.* [T] • *She killed her husband after years of abuse.* [T] • *Just a tiny drop of this poison is enough to kill.* [I] • *Food must be heated to a high temperature to kill harmful bacteria.* [T] • *(fig.) My sister would kill me* (= be very angry with me) *if she heard me say that.* [T] • *(fig.) Lack of romance can kill* (= destroy) *a marriage.* [T] • *(fig.) The housing project was killed* (= stopped) *before building was even started.* [T] • *(fig.) The doctor gave her some tablets to kill* (= stop) *the pain.* [T] • *(fig. infml) I must sit down, my feet are killing me* (= causing me a lot of pain)*!* [T] • *(fig. infml) He didn't exactly kill* **himself** *trying* (= He did not try very hard) *to get the work finished.* [T] • *(fig. infml) It wouldn't kill you to apologize* (= it is not as difficult as it might seem). [T] • *(fig. infml) We were killing* **ourselves** *laughing* (= we laughed a lot). [T] • *(esp. Am)* If something or someone kills someone else it entertains them very much: *That comedian kills me.* [T] • If you kill something **off**, you destroy it completely, usually over a period of time: *Many people thought the disease had been killed off in the last century.* [M] • *(fig. esp. Am) The two of them killed* **(off)** (= drank all of) *a bottle in one evening.* [T] • *(Br)* If you say that something will **kill or cure**, you mean that it is an extreme thing to do which will either be very successful or fail completely: *A weekend away might kill or cure a troubled marriage.* • If you **kill** someone **with kindness** you are so good to them that you in fact do them harm. • *So Tom's coming home – we must* **kill the fatted calf** (= have a special celebration to greet someone who has been away for a long time). • If you **kill the goose that lays the golden egg** you destroy something that brings you good things. • If you **kill time** or kill an amount of time, you do something that keeps you busy while you are waiting for something else to happen: *The train was late so I killed an hour window-shopping.* • If you **kill two birds with one stone** you manage to achieve two things in a single action: *If I take grandma to the station on the way to picking up the kids from school, I can kill two birds with one stone.* • *"Thou shalt not kill: but need not strive / Officiously to keep alive"* (Arthur Hugh Clough in the poem *The Latest Decalogue*, 1862. The first words quote one of the Ten Commandments) • [LP] **Crimes and criminals**

kill /kɪl/ *n* [U] • A kill is an animal or bird which has been hunted and killed, or the action of killing: *The leopard* *seizes its kill and drags it into the bushes to eat.* • If you **move/go in for the kill** you prepare to destroy completely the arguments or ideas of someone you disagree with: *I asked her a couple of difficult questions and then moved/went in for the kill.* • If you are **in at the kill** you are present at the end of an unpleasant process.

kill·er /£'kɪl·əʳ, $-ɚ/ *n* [C] • *Police are still hoping to find the dead woman's killer* (= person who killed her). • *Heart disease is the number-one killer of* (= cause of deaths among) *American men.* • *This chemical is found in most weed killers* (= substances used to kill weeds). • *(infml)* If something is described as a **(real)** killer, it is especially difficult: *The test was a real killer.* • *(Am and infml Aus)* A **(real)** killer is also a person, story, show, etc. that is very entertaining or shows great skill: *a killer story* ○ *Dizzy was a killer on the trumpet.* • *(Am)* The killer can also be the most exciting or interesting part of a story or event: *It took her six weeks to get there, but* **the** *killer was that when she arrived she discovered that she'd gone to the wrong place.* • *I'm afraid Lawrence lacks the* **killer instinct** (= the desire to act for his own advantage even if it harms others). • A **killer whale** is a small black-and-white WHALE (= a mammal that lives in the sea) that eats large fish and other sea animals.

kill·ing /'kɪl·ɪŋ/ *n* [C] • A killing is when a person is murdered: *Quarrels between rival gangs have led to a series of brutal killings.* • *The deputy coroner, Paul Singleton, recorded a verdict of unlawful killing.* • *(infml)* If a person **makes a killing**, they earn a lot of money in a short time and with little effort: *She's been making a killing since she established her chain of health-food shops two years ago.*

kill·ing /'kɪl·ɪŋ/ *adj infml* • Killing means extremely tiring: *Our aerobics teacher put us through some killing stomach exercises last night.* • *(dated)* Killing also means extremely amusing: *She told us a killing story about her driving test.*

kill·joy /'kɪl·dʒɔɪ/ *n* [C] *disapproving* a person who does not like other people enjoying themselves • *He's doesn't like it when she dances, he's such a killjoy.* • *She asked us to turn the music down, the killjoy!*

kiln /kɪln/ *n* [C] a type of large OVEN (= box in which things can be heated to high temperatures) which is used for making bricks and clay objects hard after they have been shaped • *The clay pots are baked/***fired** *in kilns in the potter's studio.*

ki·lo /£'kiː·ləʊ, $-loʊ/ *n* [C] *pl* **kilos** a kilogram • *We bought two kilos (***of** *apples).* • *The chain is fixed to a 200 kilo block of concrete.*

ki·lo– /'kɪl·ə-/ *combining form* • Kilo- means 1000 times the stated unit: *kilogram/kilohertz*

ki·lo·byte /'kɪl·ə·baɪt/ (*abbreviation* **k**) *n* [C] *specialized* a unit of measurement of computer memory consisting of 1024 BYTES • *a 20-kilobyte word processing file*

ki·lo·gram /'kɪl·ə·græm/ (*abbreviation* **kg**) *n* [C] a unit of mass equal to 1000 grams, or 2·2 POUNDS • LP› **Units**

ki·lo·hertz /£'kɪl·ə·hɜːts, $-hɜːrts/ (*abbreviation* **kHz**) *n* [C] *pl* **kilohertz** a unit of measurement of radio waves which is equal to 1000 HERTZ • *Radio station frequencies are often given in terms of kilohertz.*

ki·lo·me·tre *Br and Aus, Am* **ki·lo·met·er** /£'kɪl·əˌmiː·təʳ, $kɪ'lɑː·mə·t̬ɚ/ (*abbreviation* **km**) *n* [C] a unit of measurement equal to 1000 metres • *We were only four kilometres outside the town.* • LP› **Units**

ki·lo·watt /£'kɪl·ə·wɒt, $-wɑːt/ (*abbreviation* **kW**) *n* [C] a unit of power equal to 1000 WATTS

kilt /kɪlt/ *n* [C] a skirt with many folds, made from TARTAN cloth and traditionally worn by Scottish men and boys, but also worn by women and girls

kil·ter /£'kɪl·təʳ, $-t̬ɚ/ *n* [U] **out of kilter** *infml* (in a state of) not working well • *Missing more than one night's sleep can throw your body out of kilter.* • *I'm having terrible trouble adding up these totals – I think my brain must be out of kilter!*

ki·mo·no /£kɪ'məʊ·nəʊ, $-'moʊ·noʊ/ *n* [C] *pl* **kimonos** a long loose piece of outer clothing with very wide sleeves, traditionally worn by the Japanese

kin /kɪn/ *pl n dated* family and relatives • *All of her immediate kin are dead.* • *The names of the three other soldiers killed have not yet been released, but* **next of** *kin* (= the closest relatives) *have been informed.*

kind GOOD /kaɪnd/ *adj* **-er, -est** generous, helpful and caring about other people's feelings • *She's a very kind and thoughtful person.* • *Caspar has gentle, kind eyes.* • *Thank you for giving me your seat, that was very kind* **of** *you.* • *Soft lighting is kind* **to** *your face* (= makes it look better). • *(fml) Would you be kind* **enough** *to/***so** *kind* **as** *to close the door?* (= please would you do this) • A **kind-hearted** person is one who cares a lot about other people and always wants to help them. Compare **hard-hearted** at HARD SEVERE. • *"Kind hearts are more than coronets, / And simple faith than Norman blood"* (from the poem *In Memoriam* by Alfred, Lord Tennyson, 1850) • Ⓓ

kind·ly /'kaɪnd·li/ *adv* • *"Please don't cry," he said kindly.* • *Stella has very kindly offered to help out with the food for the party.* • "Kindly" is used when asking someone to do something, usually if you are annoyed with them but still want to be polite: *Kindly put that book away!* ○ *You are kindly requested to leave the building.* • If you do **not take kindly to** something, you do not like it: *After years of being looked after by his mother, Bill did not take kindly to having to cook for himself.*

kind·ly /'kaɪnd·li/ *adj dated* • A kindly person or action is a kind one: *Lily is a kindly old woman so she offered to help out.*

kind·ness /'kaɪnd·nəs/ *n* • *The children never received love or kindness from their parents.* [U] • *I wanted to thank them for all their kindnesses.* [C] • *"I have always depended on the kindness of strangers"* (from the play *A Streetcar Named Desire* by Tennessee Williams, 1947)

kind TYPE /kaɪnd/ *n* [C] a group with similar characteristics, or a particular type • *I don't usually like that kind* **of** *film.* • *Today's vehicles use two kinds* **of** *fuel – petrol and diesel.* • *What kind* **of** *(a) job are you looking for?* • *He would never deceive me, he's not that kind (***of** *person).* • *I just don't have that kind* **of** *money* (= I haven't got so much money). • *The cupboard contained* **all** *kinds* **of** *strange things.* • *This car was the first* **of its kind** (= of others that are similar) *in the world.* • *Human beings have always been cruellest to their* **own** *kind* (= other human beings). • *"You said I was fat." "I didn't say anything* **of the kind** (= I said nothing like that)*!"* • *(infml)* You say **kind of** to mean that you are not certain about something or that it is only partly true: *It was kind of strange to see him again.* ○ *I kind of thought you might help me.* See also KINDA. • If something is **of a kind** it is not of a very good quality: *She has found happiness of a kind with him, but it's still not perfect.* • Ⓓ

kind PAYMENT /kaɪnd/ *n* [U] **in kind** (of payment) given in the form of goods or services and not money • *She wouldn't take any money but she said I could pay her in kind by lending her the car for the weekend.* • If you do something in kind, you do the same thing to someone that they have just done to you: *He swore at me so I answered in kind.* • Ⓓ

kin·da /'kaɪ·ndə/ *adv* [not gradable] *infml* used in writing to represent an informal way of saying "kind of" • *I kinda hoped we'd be able to meet up some time this week.* • *I was kinda sorry to see him go.*

kin·der·gar·ten /£'kɪn·dəˌgɑː·tᵊn, $-dɚˌgɑːr-/ *n esp. Am* the first year of **primary school** (= a school for children aged 5 to 11) • *There are two or three kindergartens in the area to choose from.* [C] • *In some rural schools there is still only one teacher to handle kindergarten through sixth grade.* [U] • Kindergarten is also *Br and Aus for* **nursery school**. [C/U] • LP› **Schools and colleges**

kin·dle *obj* /'kɪn·dl̩/ *v* [T] to cause (a fire) to start burning by lighting paper, wood etc. • *Tightly-rolled paper will help to kindle the fire.* • *(fig.) Her imagination was kindled* (= started to work) *by the exciting stories her grandmother told her.*

kin·dling /'kɪnd·lɪŋ/ *n* [U] • Kindling is small dry sticks or other materials used to start a fire: *Place the kindling at the base of the fire.*

kin·dred spi·rit /'kɪn·drəd/ *n* [C] a person who has the same opinions, feelings and interests as you • *We recognized each other as kindred spirits as soon as we met.*

ki·net·ic /£kɪ'net·ɪk, $-'net̬-/ *adj* [not gradable] *specialized* involving movement • Kinetic **art** is art, esp. SCULPTURE, that has parts in it that move. • Kinetic **energy** is the energy produced by something moving.

ki·net·ics /£kɪ'net·ɪks, $-'net̬-/ *n* [U] *specialized* • Kinetics is the scientific study of forces on things that are moving.

kin·folk /£'kɪn·fəʊk, $-foʊk/, **kin·folks** *pl n Am for* KINSFOLK

king /kɪŋ/ *n* [C] (the title of) a male ruler of a country, who holds this position because of his royal birth • *Prince Henry became king when his father died.* • *During the war, the King and Queen visited those areas of London worst affected by the bombing.* • The king of a group of animals, things or people is the largest, most important or best of that group:

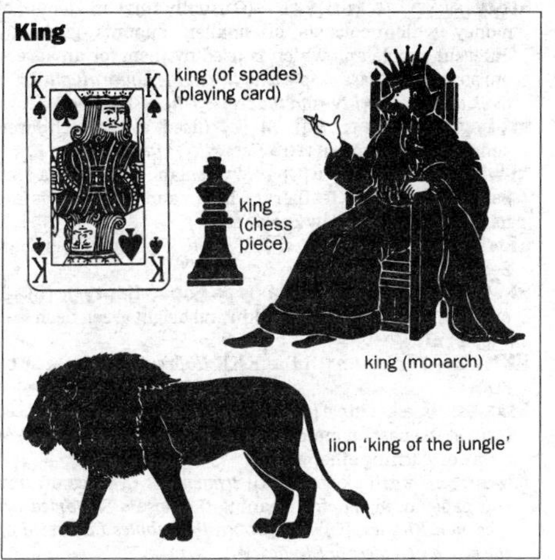

The lion is called the king of the jungle. ○ *In chess, the king is the most important piece.* ○ *Petrus is the king of wines.* ○ *Segovia was (the) king of the guitar* (= the best player of that instrument). • If something has king as part of its name, it means it is larger than the ordinary type: *king prawns* ○ *a king cobra* • A king is also a card with a picture of a king on it, used in games: *the king of hearts* • *Her diamond necklace must have cost* **a king's ransom** (= a lot of money). [C] • If something is **king-size** or **king-sized**, it is larger than the ordinary size: *a king-size bed* ○ *a king-size hamburger* • *"King of the Wild Frontier"* (from the song *The Ballad of Davy Crockett* written by Bill Hayes, 1956) • *"The Man who would be King"* (title of a story by Rudyard Kipling, 1888) • *"King of the Road"* (title of a song by Roger Miller, 1965) • LP **Cards** PIC **Games, King**

king·ship /ˈkɪŋ·ʃɪp/ *n* [U] *fml* • *the duties of kingship* (= being a king)

king·dom /ˈkɪŋ·dəm/ *n* [C] a country ruled by a king or queen • *She was queen of an ancient kingdom in northern Europe.* • *I'm a citizen of the United Kingdom of Great Britain and Northern Ireland.* • A kingdom is also an area which is controlled by a particular person or organization: *the kingdom of the oil-producers* ○ *the kingdom of God/Heaven* • A kingdom is also an area of activity: *the kingdom of the theatre* ○ *the kingdoms of the mind* • A kingdom is also one of the groups into which natural things can be divided, depending on their type: *the animal kingdom* ○ *the plant kingdom* ○ *the mineral kingdom* • *I don't want to have to wait* **till/until kingdom come** (= forever) *for you to make up your mind.* • *The bombs are capable of* **blowing/blasting** *a whole city* **to kingdom come** (= so that it is completely destroyed).

king·fish·er /£ˈkɪŋˌfɪʃ·əʳ, $-ɚ/ *n* [C] a brightly-coloured bird with a long pointed beak, which lives near rivers and lakes and eats fish

king·mak·er /£ˈkɪŋˌmeɪ·kəʳ, $-kɚ/ *n* [C] a person who has influence over people who will obtain powerful positions in politics or within an organization • *He never wanted to be prime minister himself – he was content with the role of kingmaker within the party.*

king·pin /ˈkɪŋ·pɪn/ *n* [C] the most important person within a particular organization • *a drug kingpin* • *He was for many years the kingpin* **of** *the Democratic organization in Chicago.* • *An accident of history has made the country a kingpin* **in** *the region.*

king·side /ˈkɪŋ·saɪd/ *n* [U], *adj* [not gradable] *specialized* (in the game of CHESS) (on) the side of the board on which your king is positioned at the start of the game • *Peters castled on the kingside.* • *Your kingside development/attack looks strong.*

kink /kɪŋk/ *n* [C] an unwanted twist or bend in a wire, rope, pipe, etc. that is usually straight • *There must be a kink* **in** *the pipe which is preventing the water from coming through.* • *She asked her hairdresser to make her hair straight and take out any kinks.* • *(Am and Aus)* A kink is also a sore muscle, esp. in the neck or back: *Carol had a kink in her neck when she woke up this morning.* • A kink can also be something that is wrong: *Pete is turning into an excellent tennis player, but he still needs to* **iron out** *a few kinks in his game.* • See also **kink** at KINKY.

kink·y /ˈkɪŋ·ki/ *adj* **-ier, -iest** *infml* unusual, strange and possibly exciting, esp. in ways involving unusual sexual acts • *kinky ideas/behaviour* • *a kinky black leather skirt*

kink /kɪŋk/ *n* [C] • *He does have some peculiar kinks* (= strange habits).

kins·folk /£ˈkɪnz·fəʊk, $-foʊk/, **kin**, *Am also* **kin·folk** /£ˈkɪn·fəʊk, $-foʊk/, **kin·folks** *pl n old use* members of the same family

kin·ship /ˈkɪn·ʃɪp/ *n* [U] the relationship between members of the same family, or a feeling of closeness or similarity between people or things • *Different ethnic groups have different systems of kinship.* • *As a former soldier, he said he felt a real sense of kinship* (= feeling of closeness) **with** *the young men in the current fighting.* • *There is a certain kinship* (= similarity) **between** *desire and violence.*

kins·man (*pl* **-men**), **kins·wo·man** (*pl* **-women**) /ˈkɪnz·mən, -wʊ·mən/ *n* [C] *old use* a member of the same family

ki·osk /£ˈkiː·ɒsk, $-ɑːsk/ *n* [C] a small building where things such as sweets, drinks or newspapers are sold through an open window • *I got a magazine and some cigarettes from a kiosk on the station platform.* • *(Br fml)* A **(telephone)** kiosk is a **telephone box**. See at TELEPHONE.

kip /kɪp/ *v* [I always + adv/prep] **-pp-** *Br and Aus infml* to sleep, esp. in a place which is not your home • *When they are on tour, the musicians tend to kip in the van.* • *You can have my bed and I'll kip* **(down)** *on the sofa.*

kip /kɪp/ *n* [U] *Br and Aus infml* • *I must* **get** *some kip* (= sleep) *– good night.* • *I* **had a** *quick kip after lunch.*

kip·per /£ˈkɪp·əʳ, $-ɚ/ *n* [C] a HERRING (= type of fish) that has been preserved by being treated with salt and then with smoke • *Kippers are sometimes eaten for breakfast.*

kir /£kɪəʳ, $kɪr/ *n* a drink consisting of a mixture of white wine and an alcoholic BLACKCURRANT drink • *I particularly like kir made with champagne.* [U] • *I'll have a kir* (= a glass of kir), *please.* [C]

kirk /£kɜːk, $kɜːrk/ *n* [C] *Scot Eng* a church • **The Kirk** is the name of the Church of Scotland.

kirsch /£kɪəʃ, $kɪrʃ/ *n* a strong alcoholic drink made from CHERRIES • *I added some kirsch to the trifle.* [U] • *Would you like a kirsch* (= a glass of kirsch)*?* [C]

kiss *(obj)* /kɪs/ *v* to touch with your lips, esp. as a greeting, or to press your mouth onto another person's mouth in a sexual way • *The three old friends embraced and kissed each other on both cheeks.* [T] • *There was a young couple on the sofa, kissing passionately.* [I] • *She kissed him full* **on** *the mouth.* [T] • *He kissed the children* **goodnight/goodbye** (= kissed them as a part of saying goodnight/goodbye). [+ two objects] • *(infml)* If you **kiss** something **goodbye/kiss goodbye to** something, you lose it and have to accept that you will not be able to have it: *If France lose this game, they can kiss their chances of winning the cup goodbye.* • *She gently kissed* **away** *his* **tears** (= stopped his tears by kissing him). [M] • *"Mummy, I hurt my knee" "Come here, darling, and let me kiss it* **better** (= make it feel better by kissing it)*".* [T + obj + adj] • *(fig. literary) The breeze/sun kissed* (= gently touched) *her bare shoulders.* [T] • If you **kiss-and-tell**, you make publicly known a past sexual relationship with a famous person, usually for money: *She gave a kiss-and-tell interview to one of the newspapers.* • *(slang)* To **kiss** someone's *(Br)* **arse/***(Am)* **ass** is to be too respectful and obedient towards them, in order to get some advantage: *She'll never be made manager, even though she's always kissing the boss's arse.* • *(esp. Am slang)* To **kiss ass** is to be too respectful and obedient towards someone in authority: *He's always kissing ass.* • *(slang)* You say **kiss my** *(Br)* **arse/***(Am)* **ass** to someone when you are angry with them and want to offend them: *When she demanded an apology or explanation from him, he just said, "(You can) kiss my arse!"* • *"Kiss me, Hardy"* (last words of Horatio Nelson, 1805) • *"Kissing with Confidence"* (title of a song by Will Powers, 1983) • *"I Wonder who's Kissing her Now"* (title of a song written by Frank Adams and Will M.Hough, 1909) • LP **Each other**

kiss /kɪs/ *n* [C] • **Give** *your granny a kiss and say goodnight.* • *She* **gave** *him a long lingering kiss* **on** *the lips.* • To **blow** someone **a kiss** or **blow a kiss at** someone is to kiss your hand and blow on it in the direction of someone: *He blew (her) a kiss as the train moved off.* • *(infml)* If you describe something as the **kiss of death**, you mean that it is certain to cause something else to fail: *Rain is the kiss of death* **for** *a barbecue.* • *(esp. Br infml)* The **kiss of life** is **artificial respiration**. See at ARTIFICIAL. • A *(Br)* **kiss curl** *(Am* **spit curl***)* is a curved piece of hair that hangs flat against the face on the CHEEK or FOREHEAD.

kis·ser /£ˈkɪs·əʳ, $-ɚ/ *n* [C] • *Oh, he's a wonderful kisser, my boyfriend!* • *(dated slang) She punched him right in the kisser* (= mouth).

kis·sa·gram, kis·so·gram /ˈkɪs·ə·græm/ *n* [C] a message delivered by someone who kisses the person who is receiving it, esp. one which other people have arranged to be sent as a surprise to that person on a day when they are celebrating something • *The office arranged a kissagram for the boss on his birthday, to try and embarrass him a bit.*

kit /kɪt/ *n* a set of things, such as tools or clothes, used for a particular purpose or activity • *I keep a tool/repair/first-aid kit in the back of my car.* [C] • *The fighter plane's crew all have* **survival** *kits in case they are shot down.* [C] • *Many women now use home pregnancy-***testing** *kits rather than going to their doctor if they think they are pregnant.* [C] • A kit is also a set of parts sold ready to be put together: *He wants a model tank kit for his birthday.* [C] ○ *We bought the bed in kit form.* • *(esp. Br)* Kit is also the particular clothing worn by a sports team, or the particular clothing and small pieces of equipment worn and used by people such as soldiers and sailors: *The hockey team has bought new kit – blue shorts and yellow shirts.* [U] ○ *The soldiers lined up for a kit inspection.* • *(esp. Br slang humorous)* Kit can also mean clothes: *Come on,* **get** *your kit* **off**. [U] • A **kit bag** is a long narrow bag used by soldiers, sailors, etc. for carrying their clothes and small pieces of equipment.

kit out *obj*, **kit** *obj* **out** /kɪt/. *v adv* [M often passive] *esp. Br* • *They went shopping to get kitted out* (= to buy the things they needed) **for** *the trip.*

kit·chen /ˈkɪtʃ·ᵊn/ *n* [C] a room where food is kept, prepared and cooked and where the dishes are washed • *The kitchen has an electric cooker, a fridge and a sink.* • *We often eat breakfast and lunch at the kitchen table.* • *We've got a new* **fitted** *kitchen* (= cupboards that look the same fixed to the walls and floor in the kitchen). • *(fig.)* A **kitchen cabinet** is a small unofficial group of people who give advice to a political leader. • A **kitchen garden** is a garden or part of a garden where fruit, vegetables and herbs are grown, not usually as a business. • *(Br)* **Kitchen paper/Kitchen roll/Kitchen towel** (*Am and Aus* **paper towel**) is soft, thick paper on a roll, from which square pieces are torn off and used in the kitchen or other places, esp. for removing liquid: *Drain the fried chicken on a piece of kitchen roll.* • *(Br and Aus)* **Kitchen-sink** is used to refer to plays, films, etc. which are about ordinary people's lives. • **Kitchen towel** is *Am for* **tea towel**. See at TEA.

kit·chen·ware /£ˈkɪtʃ·ᵊn·weəʳ, $-wer/ *n* [U] plates, bowls, knives, forks, spoons, etc. used in the kitchen • LP〉 **Shopping goods**

kite FLYING OBJECT /kaɪt/ *n* [C] an object consisting of a frame covered with plastic, paper or cloth that is flown in the air at the end of a long string, esp. for amusement • *On windy days the kids* **fly** *their kites in the park.* • *The traditional shape for a kite is flat with four straight sides, the lower two sides longer than the top two sides.* • **Kite-flying** is the act of trying to find out what people's opinion about something new will be by informally spreading news of it: *These rumours of a new political party are obviously a kite-flying exercise.* See also **go fly a kite** at FLY WAVE. • In Britain, the **Kite mark** is the mark on goods that have been officially said to be of high quality. • PIC〉 **Toy**

kite BIRD /kaɪt/ *n* [C] a large HAWK (= bird that kills and eats small birds and animals)

kith /kɪθ/ *pl n* **kith and kin** *esp. old use* people with whom you are connected esp. by family relationship • *How could he do such an awful thing to his own kith and kin?*

kitsch /kɪtʃ/ *n* [U] *disapproving* works of art or decorative objects that are ugly, silly or worthless • *Their house is full of awful kitsch – but kitsch is coming back into fashion now isn't it?*

kitsch·y /ˈkɪtʃ·i/ *adj* **-ier, -iest** *disapproving*

kit·ten /£ˈkɪt·ᵊn, $ˈkɪt̬-/ *n* [C] a very young cat • *Our cat has just had six kittens.* • If you say that someone is **having kittens** (*Am also* **having a cow**), you mean that they are very worried, upset or angry about something: *My mother nearly had kittens when I said I was going to buy a motorbike.*

kit·ten·ish /£ˈkɪt·ᵊn·ɪʃ, $ˈkɪt̬-/ *adj* • If you describe a woman as kittenish, you mean that she behaves in a playful way and is too friendly, esp. as a way of attracting sexual attention: *She's the most flirtatious, kittenish woman I've ever met.*

kit·ten·ish·ly /£ˈkɪt·ᵊn·ɪʃ·li, $ˈkɪt̬-/ *adv*

kit·ty MONEY /£ˈkɪ·ti, $-t̬i/ *n* [C usually sing] an amount of money which consists of smaller amounts given by different people and which is used by them for an agreed purpose • *The three people who live in the house all put £20 a week in/into the kitty, and that covers the cost of food.*

kit·ty CAT /£ˈkɪ·ti, $-t̬i/ *n* [C] (used esp. by children addressing) a cat or KITTEN • *Here kitty, kitty, kitty!*

ki·wi BIRD /ˈkiː·wiː/ *n* [C] a New Zealand bird, with a long beak and hair-like feathers, which cannot fly and is the national symbol of New Zealand

ki·wi PERSON /ˈkiː·wiː/ *n* [C] *infml* a person from New Zealand

ki·wi (fruit) /ˈkiː·wiː/, **Chi·nese goose·ber·ry** *n* [C] an oval fruit with brown hairy skin and bright green flesh • PIC〉 **Fruit**

KKK /ˌkeɪ·keɪˈkeɪ/ *n* [U] **the KKK** *abbreviation for* KU KLUX KLAN

klax·on /ˈklæk·sᵊn/ *n* [C] *trademark* a very loud horn used (esp. in the past on motor vehicles used in emergencies) as a way of warning other people

Klee·nex /ˈkliː·neks/ *n* [C/U] *trademark* (a piece of) thin soft paper used esp. for cleaning the nose • *She dried her eyes on a Kleenex.* [C] • *I wrapped the pebbles I collected on the beach in a piece of Kleenex.* [U]

klep·to·ma·ni·a /£ˌklep·təʊˈmeɪ·ni·ə, $-t̬oʊ-/ *n* [U] a very strong and uncontrollable desire to steal, esp. without any need or purpose, usually considered to be a type of mental illness

klep·to·ma·ni·ac /£ˌklep·təʊˈmeɪ·ni·æk, $-t̬oʊ-/ *n* [C]

klutz /klʌts, klʊts/ *n* [C] *esp. Am slang* a very foolish or stupid person, or a person who moves awkwardly • *He's such a klutz!*

km *n* [C] *pl* **km** *abbreviation for* KILOMETRE

knack /næk/ *n* [U] a skill or an ability to do something easily and well • *As a politician, she has to have the knack* **of** *inspiring confidence in her listeners.* • *Paul always had* **a** *knack* **for** *(writing) a good story.* • *I have* **an** *unfortunate knack* **for** *saying the wrong thing at the wrong time.* • *There's* **a** *knack* **to** *using this corkscrew.* • *Making pastry isn't really difficult – it's just* **a** *knack that you can soon pick up.*

knack·ered /£ˈnæk·əd, $-ɚd/ *adj* [after v] *Br and Aus slang* very tired • *I'm too knackered to go out this evening.*

knack·er·ing /£ˈnæk·ᵊr·ɪŋ, $ˈ-ɚ-/ *adj Br slang* • *What a knackering day it's been!*

knack·er's yard /£ˈnæk·əz·jɑːd, $-ɚz·jɑːrd/ *n* [C usually sing] a place where old or useless horses are killed • *(fig. infml) The state of the economy has led to many small businesses ending up in the knacker's yard* (= failing completely).

knap·sack /ˈnæp·sæk/ *n* [C] *Br dated or Am* a bag carried on the back or over the shoulder, usually quite small and made of cloth and leather, esp. used by walkers or climbers for carrying food and possessions

knave /neɪv/ *n* [C] *old use* a dishonest man • A knave is also a JACK CARD. • LP〉 **Cards**

knead *obj* /niːd/ *v* [T] to press (esp. mixture for making bread) firmly and repeatedly with the hands and fingers • *Knead the dough until the mixture is smooth and then place in baking tins.* • *If your muscles are stiff, knead them with your fingers for a minute.* • PIC〉 **Food preparation**

knee /niː/ *n* [C] the middle joint of the leg, which allows it to bend • *The baby was crawling around on its* **hands and** *knees.* • *He got/went* **down on** *his knees* (= got into a position where his knees were on the ground) *in front of the altar.* • *She took the child and sat it on her knee* (= on the part of the leg above the knee when sitting down). • The knee of a piece of clothing is the part that covers the knee: *She was wearing an old pair of trousers with rips at the knees.* • If you **bring/force** someone or something **to** their **knees**, you completely defeat or almost destroy them: *The coal miners' strike brought the economy to its knees.* • If you are **knee-deep** in something, it reaches your knees: *We walked through the wood, knee-deep* **in** *autumn leaves.* ○ *(fig.) I'm knee-deep* **in** (= have a lot of) *work.* • **Knee-high** means tall enough to reach your knees: *knee-high grass/boots* • *(infml humorous)* **Knee-high to a grasshopper** means very small or young: *My Dad has been taking me to hear jazz ever since I was knee-high to a grasshopper!* • *(disapproving)* A **knee-jerk** reaction/opinion is one made or held automatically, as a result of habit, rather than of serious thought: *Whenever the crime rate rises, the government's knee-jerk* **reaction** *is just to train more police.* • Something that is **knee-length** is long enough to reach

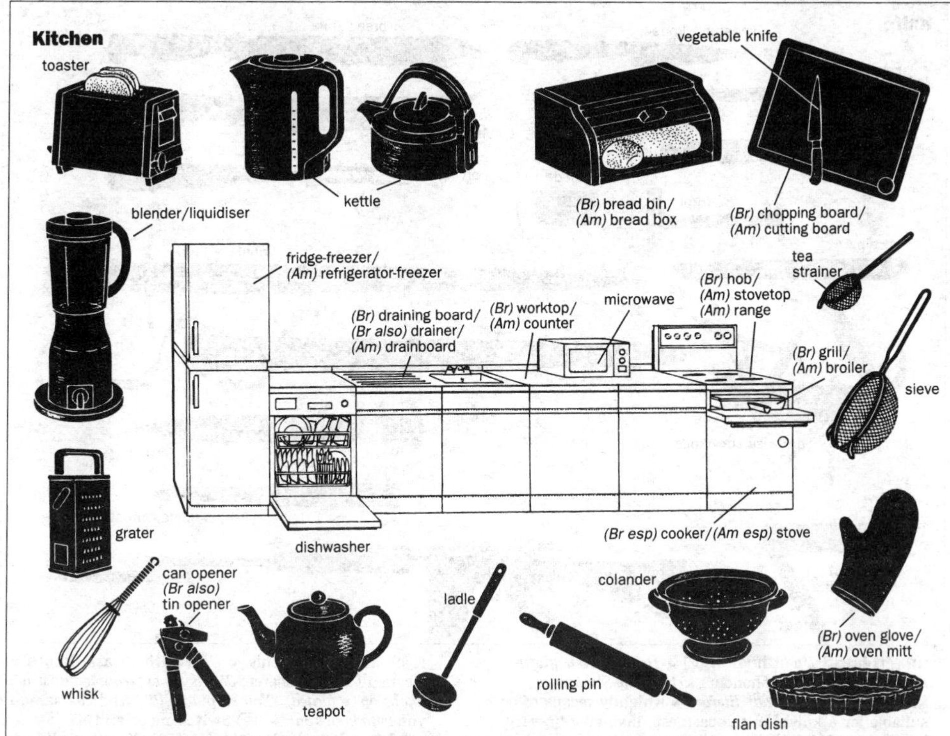

the knee: *knee-length socks* ○ *The skirt should be knee-length.* ● *(Br infml dated or humorous)* A **knees-up** is an energetic noisy party where people dance.

knee *obj* /niː/ *v* [T] ● *She kneed him* (= hit him with her knee) **in** *the groin.*

knee·cap /ˈniː·kæp/, *medical* **pa·tel·la** *n* [C] the bone at the front of the knee joint

knee·cap *obj* /ˈniː·kæp/ *v* [T] **-pp-** ● To kneecap someone is to injure, esp. by shooting, them in the knee as a punishment: *Kneecapping is a typical terrorist punishment for 'traitors'.*

kneel /niːl/ *v* [I] *past* **knelt** /nelt/ or *esp. Am* **kneeled** to go down into, or stay in, a position where one or both knees are on the ground ● *She knelt* **(down)** *and tried to see under the door.* ● *Kneeling in front of the altar, he prayed for an answer.*

knell /nel/ *n* **death knell**, see at DEATH

knew /£njuː, $nuː/ *past simple of* KNOW

knick·er·bock·er glo·ry /£ˌnɪk·əˌbɒk·əˈglɔː·ri, $ˌnɪk·ɚˌbɑː·kɚˈglɔːr·i/ *n* [C] *Br* a sweet food consisting of layers of **ice cream**, fruit, JELLY and cream, served in a tall glass

knick·er·bock·ers /£ˈnɪk·əˌbɒk·əz, $-ɚˌbɑː·kɚz/, *Am also* **knick·ers** *pl n* short loose trousers that fit tightly below the knee, worn esp. in the past or for ceremonies ● *The page boys at the wedding wore black velvet knickerbockers.*

knick·ers /£ˈnɪk·əz, $-ɚz/ *pl n Br* a piece of underwear worn by women and girls covering the area between the waist and the tops of the legs ● *a pair of black cotton knickers* ● *(Br and Aus infml humorous)* If you **get** your **knickers in a twist**, you become confused, worried or annoyed about something: *Now, before you get your knickers in a twist, let me explain the situation.* ● *(Br slang humorous)* People sometimes say 'knickers' to express their disagreement with something someone has said. ● Knickers is also *Am for* KNICKERBOCKERS.

knick–knack, **nick–nack** /ˈnɪk·næk/ *n* [C usually pl] *infml* a small decorative object, esp. in a house ● *The room was crowded with ornaments and useless knick-knacks.*

knife /naɪf/ *n* [C] *pl* **knives** /naɪvz/ a tool or weapon used for cutting, usually consisting of a metal blade and a handle ● *a fish/butter/steak knife* ● *We took plastic knives* **and forks** *on our picnic.* ● *He* **drew/pulled** *a knife and stabbed the soldier between the shoulder-blades.* ● *She was attacked by a gang* **wielding/brandishing** *knives.* ● *Two knives – a* **bread** *knife and a* **carving** *knife – believed to have been the murder weapons, were found close to the bodies.* ● To **put/stick the knife into** someone/To **put/stick the knife in** is to be unpleasant about someone or to try to harm them: *She's always putting the knife into her former colleagues.* ○ *That review of his latest book really put the knife in.* ● If you **get/have** your **knife into/in** someone, you try to upset or harm them because you disagree with or dislike them. ● *(Br and Aus infml)* If you say **the knives are out**, you mean that people are being unpleasant about someone, or trying to harm them: *The knives are out* **for** *the former president.* ● If you **twist/turn the knife (in the wound)**, you make someone who is annoyed, anxious or upset feel even worse: *Just to turn the knife a little, he told me he'd seen my old girlfriend with her new man.* ● If someone is **on a knife-edge**, they are in a difficult or worrying situation of which the result is uncertain: *The company is existing on a financial knife-edge.* ○ *At the moment the election seems* **balanced** *on a knife-edge.* ● *The game had a* **knife-edge** *conclusion* (= it was uncertain who was going to win). ● **Knife-edge** also means narrow and sharp: *We had to climb over a knife-edge mountain ridge.* ● *(dated)* If you are **under the knife**, you are having a medical operation in which a doctor cuts into your body: *He died under the knife.* ● See also PENKNIFE. ● PIC **Cutlery, Knife**

knife *obj* /naɪf/ *v* [T] ● *He was knifed* **in** *the back.*

knight /naɪt/ *n* [C] a man given a rank of honour by a British king or queen because of his special achievements, and who has the right to be called 'Sir', or (in the past) a man of high social position trained to fight as a soldier on a horse ● *He hopes to be made a knight for his work at the Bank of England.* ● *I've been reading a book about the adventures of King Arthur and his knights* **(in armour)**. ● In the game of CHESS, a knight is a piece in the shape of a horse's head that moves two squares in one direction and then one square at an angle of 90°. ● A **knight in shining armour** is someone who saves you from a difficult or dangerous situation: *She is hoping that one day a knight in shining armour will come and rescue her from her dull and boring life.* ● Compare DAME TITLE. ● PIC **Games**

knight *obj* /naɪt/ *v* [T] ● *He was knighted* (= given a rank of honour) *by the Queen* **for** *his work for the hospital service.*

knight–er·rant /ˌnaɪtˈer·ənt/ *n* [C] *pl* **knights-errant** /ˌnaɪtsˈer·ənt/ ● A knight-errant was in the past a knight who travelled about, helping people who were in trouble and performing brave acts.

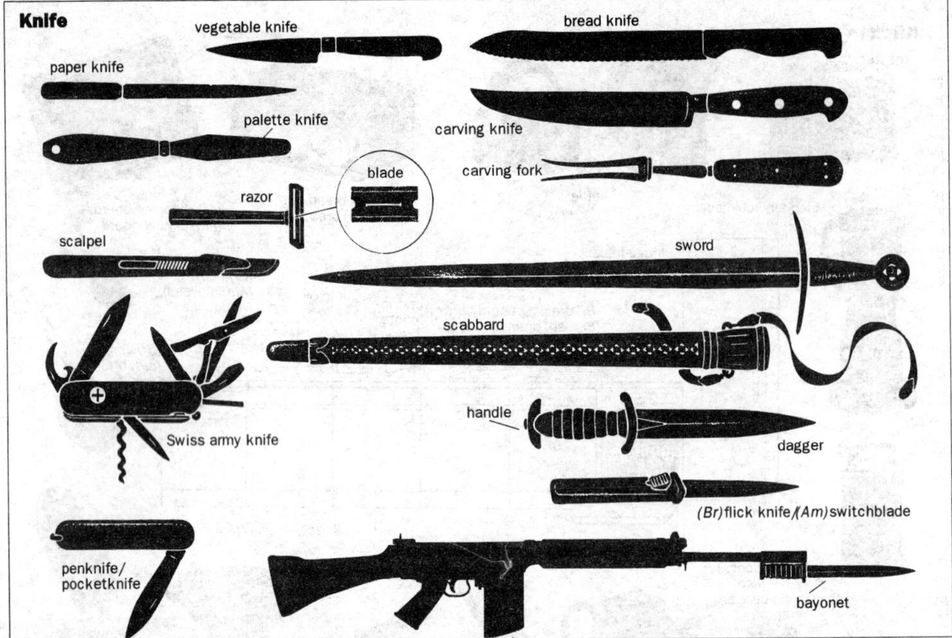

knight·hood /ˈnaɪt·hʊd/ *n* [C] • *He has been given a knighthood* (= a rank of honour), *so he's now Sir James.*

knight·ly /ˈnaɪt·li/ *adj literary* • Knightly means of or suitable for a knight in the past, esp. involving bravery, honour, etc.: *knightly virtue*

knit MAKE CLOTHES /nɪt/ *v past simple* **knitted** or **knit**, *past part* **knitted** or *Am also* **knit** to make (things such as clothes) by using two long needles to connect wool or another type of thread into joined rows • *He enjoys knitting.* [I] • *She knitted a scarf as a Christmas present for him.* [T] • *My granny knitted me some gloves/knitted some gloves* **for** *me.* [+ two objects] • *She was wearing a sweater knitted* **in** *cotton.* • *(esp. Br) She knitted* **(up)** *a woolly blanket.* [M] • *(esp. Br and Aus) This wool knits* **(up)** *very easily* (= it is easy to make things with). [I] • *(specialized)* To knit is also to do the most basic type of stitch, when knitting something: *Knit one, purl one.* [T] • See also KNITWEAR. • PIC> **Pins and needles**

knit·ted /£ˈnɪt·ɪd, $ˈnɪt̬-/, **knit** *adj* [not gradable] • *a knitted jumper* • *hand-knitted gloves* • *Is your hat knitted or crocheted?*

knit·ter /£ˈnɪt·əʳ, $ˈnɪt̬·ɚ/ *n* [C] • *Paula's a wonderful knitter* (= person who knits) – *she makes beautiful things.*

knit·ting /£ˈnɪt·ɪŋ, $ˈnɪt̬-/ *n* [U] • *She takes her knitting* (= the thing she is making with wool and the equipment to make it) *with her everywhere.* • *I'm hopeless at knitting* (= the act of making things with wool). • *You need size eight knitting* **needles** *to make this cardigan.* • PIC> **Handicraft**

knit *(obj)* JOIN /nɪt/ *v past simple* **knitted**, *past part* **knitted** or **knit** to join together • *The broken bone should begin to knit* **(together)** *in a few days.* [I] • *He is trying to knit the various opposition groups* **into** *an effective political party.* [T] • If you **knit** your **brows**, you FROWN (= move your EYEBROWS down and together) because you are thinking carefully, or because you are angry or worried: *He knitted his brows in concentration.*

–knit /nɪt/ *combining form* • *They are a very* **close(ly)/tight(ly)**-*knit family* (= the members of the family all support each other). • *The project is being run by a* **loose(ly)**-*knit* (= not closely connected) *group of people.*

knit·wear /£ˈnɪt·weəʳ, $-wer/ *n* [U] clothes made by connecting wool or another type of thread into joined rows • LP> **Shopping goods**

knob /£nɒb, $nɑːb/ *n* [C] a round handle or a small round device for controlling a machine or electrical equipment • *She tried to open the door, but the knob came off in her hands.* • *Turn/Twiddle the little knob* (= device) *to adjust the volume.* • A knob is also a round lump on the surface or end of something: *a brass knob on top of the bed-post* • A knob can also be a small amount of something solid, esp. butter: *Put a knob of butter in the frying pan.* • *(taboo slang)* Knob also means penis. • *(Br)* **With (brass) knobs on** means to a great degree: *Jon is an environmentalist with knobs on.* • *(dated) "You stupid fool!"* **"And the same to you** *with knobs on!"* • LP> **Switching on and off**

knob·bly (**-ier**, **-iest**) /£ˈnɒb·l̩.i, £ˈ-bli, $ˈnɑː·bli/, *Am* **knob·by** (**-ier**, **-iest**) /£ˈnɒb·i, $ˈnɑː·bi/ *adj* having lumps on the surface • *knobbly tyres* • *knobbly knees/elbows*

knock MAKE NOISE /£nɒk, $nɑːk/ *v* [I] to repeatedly hit (something), producing a noise • *Jane knocked* **on** *the window to attract his attention.* • *He knocked* **on/at** *the door and called out, "Is anyone at home?"* • 'Knock, knock!' is a way of describing the sound made when you hit a door. It is often used as the first line of a joke: *"Knock, knock!" "Who's there?" "Boo" "Boo who?" "There's no need to cry – it's only a joke."* • *The noise of a rope knocking* **against** *the side of the ship woke him up.* *(specialized)* If an engine is knocking, it is producing a repeated high sound either because the fuel is not burning correctly or because a small part is damaged and is therefore allowing another part to move in ways that it should not. • If something such as a pipe knocks, it makes a repeated high sound: *We must get the plumber in – the central heating is knocking again.* • If you say that someone's **knees** are knocking, you mean that they are so frightened that their legs are shaking. • *(infml)* If someone or something **is knocking on** a particular age or number, they have almost reached it: *She was knocking on 80 when she died.* • **Knock on wood** or **knock wood** is *Am and Aus for* **touch wood**. See at TOUCH USE FINGERS. • If someone is **knock-kneed**, their knees bend towards each other.

knock /£nɒk, $nɑːk/ *n* [C] • *There was a knock* **at/on** *the door.* • *People had come to fear* **the knock at/on the door** *in the middle of the night* (= the situation in which the police or soldiers came to take them from their homes).

knock·er /£ˈnɒk·əʳ, $ˈnɑː·kɚ/, **door·knock·er** *n* [C] • A knocker is a metal object fixed to a door which visitors use to hit the door in order to attract attention. • *(Aus infml)* They said they'd arrive at six and they were there right **on the knocker** (= at exactly that time).

knock *(obj)* HIT /£nɒk, $nɑːk/ *v* to hit, esp. forcefully, and cause to move or fall • *Please don't knock the table while I'm drawing.* [T] • *I'll knock a nail* **into** *the wall to hang the picture on.* [T] • *As she turned she knocked the pot* **off** *the table with her hand.* [T] • *A low branch knocked her* **off** *her horse.* [T] • *A mugger knocked her to the ground and stole her handbag.* [T] • *She was knocked* **down/over** (= hit so that she fell to the ground) *by a hit-and-run driver/a truck.* [M] • *(saying)* 'You could have knocked me down/over with a feather' means I was extremely surprised or shocked. • *Who knocked* **over** *this vase?* [M] • *Some thug knocked him* **unconscious/senseless**. [T + obj + adj] • *He fell off his bike and knocked two teeth* **out**. [T + obj + adj] • If you knock a hole **in** something, you make a hole in it by hitting it: *She took a hammer and knocked a hole in the wall.* [T] • If you knock two rooms **into each other/through**, you remove the wall between them so that they form one room. [T] • If you knock something **out** you remove it, esp. by hitting it: *We'll knock that window out.* [M] ○ *He knocked out his pipe* (= emptied it of old tobacco). [M] • If a person or team is knocked **out**, they are defeated and so play no more games in it: *The champion was unexpectedly knocked out* (**of** *the tournament) in the first round.* LP〉 **Sports** • To knock a quality **out of** someone or something is to cause them to lose it: *Failing her exams has knocked some of her arrogance out of her.* • To **knock** someone **about/around** is to treat them violently and hit them: *His father used to knock him about and even once broke his nose.* • If you say that you will **knock** someone's **block off**, you are threatening to hit them very hard, esp. on the head: *I'll knock his block off if he tries anything with me!* • If something **knocks the bottom out of** something else, it damages it, esp. by destroying its support: *The rise in mortgage rates really knocked the bottom out of the housing market.* • *(Am)* If you say to someone **knock 'em dead**, you are telling them to perform or play as well as they can: *Okay, son – get out on that stage and knock 'em dead!* • *(Br and Aus)* If something **knocks** you **sideways/knocks** you **back/knocks** you **for six**, it shocks or surprises you so much that you do not know what to say or do: *The news of his death knocked me for six.* • To **knock** someone **off** their **pedestal** is to cause them to be no longer treated with great respect or admiration: *This recent scandal has really knocked the President off his pedestal.* Compare **put** someone **on a pedestal** at PEDESTAL. • *(Br and Aus)* To **knock** something **on the head** is either to prevent it from happening or finally to finish it: *Now that the Government has knocked the proposed motorway on the head, local communities can relax.* ○ *The work's half finished – I need another couple of hours to knock it on the head.* • If you **knock sense into** someone, you forcefully teach them not to be foolish: *A couple of years in the army will knock some sense into him.* • *(Br)* If something or someone **knocks spots off** something or someone else, it is much better than them: *Geoff's new bike knocks spots off everyone else's.* • *(esp. Br)* When an event or situation has a **knock-on effect**, it indirectly causes other events or situations: *If one or two trains run late, it has a knock-on effect on the entire rail service.*

knock /£nɒk, $nɑːk/ *n* [C] • *He received a nasty knock* **on** *the head from a falling slate.* • *(fig.) Her confidence has* **taken/had** *a knock* (= been damaged) *with all this criticism.*

knock *obj* CRITICIZE /£nɒk, $nɑːk/ *v* [T] *Br and Aus infml* to criticize, esp. unfairly • *She knocks every suggestion I make.* • *Don't knock him – he's doing his best.*

knock·er /£ˈnɒk·əʳ, $ˈnɑː·kɚ/ *n* [C] *infml disapproving* • *Pay no attention to the knockers – I thought you did very well.*

knock a·round/a·bout *(obj) v adv, v prep infml* to be present or to travel in (a particular place or places), esp. without much purpose • *I think there's a spare pair of walking boots knocking about* (= somewhere). [I] • *She left her job and knocked around the Far East for a few years.* [T] • If a person knocks about/around **with** someone else, or if two or more people knock about/around **together**, they spend a lot of time together, or *(Br)* they have a (sexual) relationship: *She used to knock around with the local gangs when she was younger.* [I] ○ *(Br) Kevin and Cathy have been knocking around together for a few years, but I don't think they've thought about getting married or anything like that.* [I]

knock *obj* **back** *(obj)* COST *v adv* [T] *Br and Aus infml* to cost (someone) (a large amount of money) • *I bet that computer knocked you back a few thousand.* • *His new car must have really knocked him back.*

knock back *obj* DRINK, **knock** *obj* **back** *v adv* [M] *infml* to drink (esp. an alcoholic drink) quickly • *Knock that whisky back and let me get you another.*

knock down *obj* DESTROY, **knock** *obj* **down** *v adv* [M] to destroy and remove (a building, wall, etc.); to DEMOLISH • *The Council plans to knock the library down and replace it with a hotel complex.* • *(fig.) She easily knocked down every argument he put up.*

knock down *obj* REDUCE, **knock** *obj* **down** *v adv* [M] to reduce (a price), or to persuade (someone) to reduce the price of something they are selling • *The salesman knocked down the price* **to** *less than $100.* • *She wanted £200 but I knocked her down* **to** *£175.* • See also KNOCKDOWN.

knock down *obj* SELL, **knock** *obj* **down** *v adv* [M usually passive] to sell at an AUCTION (= public sale) • *The brass bed was knocked down* **to** *Mrs Kelly* **for** *£130.* • *The painting is expected to be knocked down* **at** *over £3 million.* • *At yesterday's large sale, the auctioneer knocked down 90 items an hour – one every 40 seconds.*

knock off *(obj)* STOP *v adv* [no passive], *v prep* to stop working or doing (something) • *The factory workers all knock off (work) at 3.00 p.m..* [I/T] • *The workers knock off* **for** *the afternoon at 3.00 p.m..* [I] • *Knocking-off* **time** *is 3.00 p.m.* • *(infml)* If you tell someone to **knock it off** you are telling them to stop doing something which annoys you: *Oh, knock it off Robert, and give me those balls.*

knock off *obj* REDUCE, **knock** *obj* **off** *(obj) v adv, v prep* (of a seller) to take (a particular amount) away from (a price) • *The manager knocked £5 off because the dress had a few buttons missing.* [M] • *The manager knocked £5 off the price.* [T]

knock off *obj* STEAL, **knock** *obj* **off** *v adv* [M] *slang* to steal (something) from (a place or person) • *He has a stack of computer equipment he's knocked off* **from** *various shops.* • *Terrorist groups are knocking off (Am also* **knocking over**) *banks to get money.*

knock off *obj* PRODUCE, **knock** *obj* **off** *v adv* [M] to produce (something) quickly and easily • *With a photocopier, you can knock off as many copies as you like.* • *She can knock off* (= write) *a novel in a couple of weeks.* • See also KNOCK OUT PRODUCE.

knock-off /£ˈnɒk·ɒf, $ˈnɑːk·ɑːf/ *n* [C] *Am infml* • A knockoff is a cheap copy of a product that has a trademark: *This isn't a real Versace dress, it's one of those knockoffs.*

knock off *obj* MURDER, **knock** *obj* **off** *v adv* [M] *slang* to murder (someone) • *She hired a hit-man to knock off her business rivals.*

knock off *obj* HAVE SEX, **knock** *obj* **off** *v adv* [M; no passive] *dated taboo slang* (esp. of a man) to have sex with (esp. a woman) • *I could hear George upstairs, knocking off some woman he'd found.*

knock out *obj* MAKE UNCONSCIOUS, **knock** *obj* **out** *v adv* [M] to hit (someone) so that they become unconscious, or (of a drug) to cause (someone) to go to sleep • *His fall from the ladder knocked him out.* • *She hit her head on the ceiling and knocked her***self** *out.* • *(fig.) If you carry on working like this, you'll knock your***self** *out* (= make yourself ill with tiredness). • *The sleeping tablets knocked him out* (= made him go to sleep) *for 18 hours.* • If something such as a piece of equipment is knocked out by something else, it is made useless, damaged or destroyed: *The surge in the power supply knocked out all the computers.* ○ *Enemy aircraft have knocked out 25 tanks.* • See also KNOCKOUT UNCONSCIOUS.

knock out *obj* PRODUCE, **knock** *obj* **out** *v adv* [M] *infml* to produce (something) esp. quickly without spending time thinking about the details of it • *The speechwriters will knock out a first draft which the President will then amend.* • See also KNOCK OFF PRODUCE.

knock out *obj* CAUSE ADMIRATION, **knock** *obj* **out** *v adv* [M usually passive] *dated slang* to cause enjoyment or admiration in (someone) • *We were all really knocked out by the film, especially by the photography.*

knock o·ver *obj*, **knock** *obj* **o·ver** *v adv Am for* KNOCK OFF STEAL

knock to·geth·er *obj*, **knock** *obj* **to·geth·er** *v adv* [M] to make (something) quickly and without much care • *I have some material from which I could knock together an article if you want me to.*

knock up PRACTISE *v adv* [I] (in games of tennis) to practise before beginning a game, by hitting the ball to each other • *The players have a couple of minutes to knock up before the match starts.*

knock–up /£ˈnɒk·ʌp, $ˈnɑːk-/ *n* [C usually sing] • *The players need time for a knock-up before the game.*

knock up *obj* WAKE UP, **knock** *obj* **up** *v adv* [M] *Br and Aus infml* to wake (someone) up, by knocking on the door of their house or bedroom • *I'm sorry to have to knock you up in the middle of the night.*

knock up *obj* MAKE PREGNANT, **knock** *obj* **up** *v adv* [M] *esp. Am slang* to make (a woman) pregnant • *What! You got knocked up again?*

knock·a·bout /£ˈnɒk·ə·baʊt, $ˈnɑːk-/ *adj* [before n; not gradable] (esp. of a theatre performance) causing laughter by very silly behaviour; SLAPSTICK

knock·down /£ˈnɒk·daʊn, $ˈnɑːk-/ *adj* [before n] (of a price) extremely cheap • *They're selling jeans for ridiculous knockdown* **prices.** • See also KNOCK DOWN REDUCE.

knock·ers /£ˈnɒk·əz, $ˈnɑː·kɚz/ *pl n slang* a woman's breasts. Some people consider this offensive

knock·out UNCONSCIOUS /ˈnɒk·aʊt/ *n* [C] (in boxing) the act of hitting the other fighter so that they fall to the ground and are unable to get up again within ten seconds • *He won the fight by a knockout in the tenth round.* • *(fig.) Already out of training, the latest illness has dealt her hopes of a gold medal a knockout* (= severe) **blow**. • *(dated infml)* **Knockout drops** are a drug, usually put secretly into your drink, that makes you sleep. • See also KNOCK OUT MAKE UNCONSCIOUS.

knock·out COMPETITION /ˈnɒk·aʊt/, *Am* **e·lim·i·na·tion tour·na·ment** *n* [C] a competition in which only the winners of each stage play in the next stage, until one competitor or team is the final winner • *The tournament is a straight knockout.* • *They won the knockout competition/cup/championship/match.* • LP **Sports**

knock·out ATTRACTIVE /ˈnɒk·aʊt/ *n* [C] *infml* a person or thing that looks, sounds, etc. extremely attractive • *Samantha was a knockout at the party.*

knock·out /ˈnɒk·aʊt/ *adj infml* • *That's a real knockout dress she's wearing.*

knoll /£nəʊl, $noʊl/ *n* [C] a small low hill with a rounded top • *A grassy knoll was visible through the trees.*

knot FASTENING /£nɒt, $nɑːt/ *n* [C] a fastening made by tying together the ends of a piece or pieces of string, rope, cloth, etc. • **Tie** *a knot* **in** *the rope to stop it from coming undone.* • *(fig.) My stomach was* **in** *knots* (= felt tight and uncomfortable) *from nervousness.* • See also GRANNY KNOT. • (T)

knot *(obj)* /£nɒt, $nɑːt/ *v* **-tt-** • *He chose a striped tie and knotted it carefully.* [T] • *A sailor caught the rope and knotted it* **around** (= fastened it to) *a post.* [T] • *(fig.) His muscles knotted* (= swelled) *with the strain.* [I]

knot·ted /£ˈnɒt·ɪd, $ˈnɑː·t̬ɪd/ *adj* • *Climbing up the knotted rope was the only way into the tree house.* • *(Br slang)* If you tell someone to **Get knotted!**, you are angrily telling them to stop doing or saying something that is annoying you.

knot GROUP /£nɒt, $nɑːt/ *n* [C] a small group of people standing close together • *Knots* **of** *anxious people stood waiting in the hall.* • (T)

knot WOOD /£nɒt, $nɑːt/ *n* [C] a small hard area on a tree or piece of wood where a branch was joined to the tree • (T)

knot·ty /£ˈnɒt·i, $ˈnɑː·t̬i/ *adj* **-ier, -iest** • *a knotty piece of wood* • See also KNOTTY.

knot MEASUREMENT /£nɒt, $nɑːt/ *n* [C] *specialized* a measure of the speed of ships, aircraft or movements of water and air. One knot is approximately 1·85 kilometres per hour • *The boat's top speed is about 20 knots.* • *There is a current of warm water flowing at about 2 knots.* • (T)

knot·ty /£ˈnɒt·i, $ˈnɑː·t̬i/ *adj* **-ier, -iest** *infml* (of a problem or difficulty) complicated and difficult to solve • *That's rather a knotty question.* • See also **knotty** at KNOT WOOD.

know *(obj)* HAVE INFORMATION /£nəʊ, $noʊ/ *v* [not *be knowing*] *past simple* **knew** /£njuː, $nuː/, *past part* **known** /£nəʊn, $noʊn/ to have (information) in the mind • *"What does it cost?" "Ask Kate. She's sure to know."* [I] • *"Where did he go?" "I wouldn't* (= do not) *know."* [I] • *Does anyone know the answer?* [T] • If someone **knows all the answers**, they think they know much more than other people: *I wouldn't trust Henry completely – he doesn't know all the answers* (= he is not as knowledgeable and powerful as he thinks he is). • *She knows the names of every kid in the school.* [T] • *To every question the police asked, she said, "I don't know anything* **about** *it."* [T] • *We don't know* **when** *he's arriving.* [+ *wh-* word] • *I knew* **(that)** *it was going to be a disaster, from the start.* [+ (*that*) clause] • *Even small amounts of these substances are known* **to** *cause skin problems.* [T + obj + *to* infinitive] • *(fml) The authorities know him* **to be** (= know that he is) *a cocaine dealer.* [T + obj + *to be* n/adj] • *Does the boss know* (= Is the boss aware) **(that)** *you are here?* [+ (*that*) clause] • *She knew* (= was aware) **(that)** *something was wrong.* [+ (*that*) clause] • *I don't know* (= understand) **what** *all the fuss is about.* [+ *wh-* word] • *I want to know* (= be told) **how** *much this will cost.* [+ *wh-* word] • If you ask someone if they know a piece of information, you are often really asking them to tell you it: *Do you know the time?* [T] ○ *Do you know* **where** *the Post Office is?* [+ *wh-* word] • To know is also to be certain: *"Are you going to go to university?" "I don't know – in some ways I'd prefer to get a job instead."* [I] ○ *I know* **(that)** *you will be pleased to hear the news.* [+ (*that*) clause] ○ *I don't know* **whether** *I should tell her or not.* [+ *wh-* word] ○ *The party is at Sarah's house* **as/so far as** *I know* (= I think but I am not certain). [I] • *(infml)* **Goodness/God/Heaven/Christ knows** are used to mean 'I don't know' or to emphasize a statement: *God* **only** *knows what'll happen next!* ○ *Take your shirt off – Heaven knows it's hot enough today!* • You say **How was I to know** to express your opinion that something you did wrong was not your fault because you did not have enough information to have acted differently: *OK, so I didn't bring my winter coat, but how was I to know it'd be snowing in June!* • You can use **I don't know** to express your lack of understanding and/or annoyance at something that someone has done: *"I don't know," he said, "however many notices I put up, people still park in my space."* • You can also use **I don't know** to add force to criticisms, expressions of surprise, etc.: *I don't know how you can eat that revolting stuff!* • **I don't know about** you, **but** means 'whatever you are going to do' or 'whatever you think': *I don't know about you, but I'm going out to the cinema.* • You say **I know** when you suddenly think of a good idea, an answer or a solution: *I know – let's go to the beach!* • You also say **I know** to show your agreement with something someone has just said: *"The weather's been so good." "I know, isn't it wonderful."* • *(approving)* If someone **knows all there is to know** about a subject or activity they are very good at it. • If someone **knows a thing or two**, they have practical skills and knowledge obtained from experience: *She knows a thing or two* **about** *living and teaching abroad.* • If you **know better** than someone else, you have, or think you have, better ideas than them because you have more experience and knowledge: *In this case, the doctor knows better* **(than** *you)!* • If someone **knows better**, they are wise enough to behave in a more responsible and acceptable way: *She's only six, but she's still* **old enough** *to know better* **than** *to run out into the traffic.* ○ *I'm surprised at you behaving so badly – you* **ought to/should** *know better.* ○ *Don't take any notice of what they say – they don't know* **any** *better!* • If someone **knows best**, they are, or think they are, the most suitable person to have responsibility and make important decisions: *It's dangerous to assume that the politicians always know best.* • To **know** your **own mind** is to be certain about what you believe or want. • If you **know** your **place**, you accept your position within society, an organization, your family, etc. and do not wish to improve it: *I just get on with my job and do as I'm told – I know my place.* • If you **know the score**, you understand and can act effectively in situations because of your experience and knowledge of life: *Jill knows the score – she won't say anything stupid.* • To **know what** you **are doing** is to be able to do something well and effectively because of your skills and knowledge obtained from experience: *I know what I'm doing, so will you please let me get on with it!* • If you **know what** you **are talking about**, you understand a subject because of your experience: *He doesn't know what he's talking about – he's never even been to Africa.* • If you **know what's what**, you understand and can act effectively in situations, because of your experience and knowledge of life. • If you **know which side** your **bread is buttered (on)**, you are careful not to act in ways that would lose you other people's approval, or lose you an advantage that you have: *I'm not going to criticize my boss and risk losing my job – I know which side my bread's buttered on.* • To **not know the first thing about** something is not to have any information at all about it: *I'm afraid I don't know the first thing about computers.* • If you do **not know what hit** you, something unpleasant suddenly and unexpectedly happens to you: *My dad always used to say to me, "You won't know what's hit you when you have to start earning your own living."* • If you do **not know where to put** your**self**, you experience a particular feeling so strongly that you do not know how to act: *I was so embarrassed by what he said about me that I didn't know where to put myself.* • To **not know whether to laugh or cry** is not to know how to react in a particular situation: *I've just had my exam results and I don't know whether to laugh or cry.* • To **not know which way to turn** is to not know what to do or who to ask for help: *When both her parents died, she didn't know which way to turn.* • If you answer a question by saying **not that I know of**, you mean that, judging from the information you have, the answer is no: *"Does the child have any trouble at school?" "Not that I know of."* • If you say **there's no knowing**, you mean it is impossible to be certain about something: *There's no knowing what she'll do if she finds out about this.* • *(esp. Am infml)* You say **(Well) what do you know!** when something surprising happens or when something that you almost expected happens: *I go to the front door, and what do you know, it's my brother who I haven't seen for 12 years.* ○ *Well, what do you know! The Raiders have lost again!* • *(infml)* **You know something** and **You know what** are used before an opinion or a piece of information: *You know what? I think it's time to go home.* • *(infml)* **You know** or **you know what I mean** are phrases without much meaning, which you use while you are trying to think of what to say next: *Well I just thought, you know, I'd better agree to it.* • *(infml)* **You know** is also used when trying to help someone remember something or when trying to explain something: *What's the name of that guy on TV – you know, the American one with the silly voice?* • *(infml)* **You know what I mean** is also used when you think that the person listening understands and so you do not need to say any more: *I think at 80 miles per hour in these conditions we could have a nasty accident, you know what I mean?* • *(infml)* You say **you never know** when you are not certain of how something will happen in the future, esp. when you do not want to give a direct answer to a question: *"So will Daddy bring me a present when he comes home from his trip?" "You never know, he might."* • *(infml disapproving)* A *(Br and Aus)* **know-all**/*(Am)* **know-it-all** is a person who thinks that they know much more than other people: *She's such an annoying know-all, she makes me feel really ignorant.* • *(infml)* **Know-how** is practical knowledge and ability: *The bigger companies have the money, but they don't always* **have** *the know-how* **to** *get the job done right.* ○ *I can operate a computer, but I don't* **have** *any technical know-how* **about** *them.* • *"Do they know it's Christmas?"* (title of a song written by Bob Geldof and Midge Ure to raise money for charity, 1984) • *"'I don't,' she added, 'know anything about music, really. But I know what I like'"* (from the comic novel *Zuleika Dobson* by Sir Max Beerbohm, 1911)

know /£nəʊ, $noʊ/ *n* [U] • If someone is **in the know**, they have information about something secret: *It must have been someone who is in the know* **about** *the project who told the press about it.*

know·a·ble /£'nəʊ·ə·bl̩, $'noʊ-/ *adj* • *Philosophers try to determine what is knowable* (= can be known) *and what is not.*

know·ing /£'nəʊ·ɪŋ, $'noʊ-/ *adj* • Knowing means showing that you know what someone is really thinking, even if they have not directly expressed it: *As soon as I mentioned her, Colin started giving me knowing* **looks**.

know·ing·ly /£'nəʊ·ɪŋ·li, $'noʊ-/ *adv* • *She smiled knowingly at him* (= in a way showing that she knew what he was really thinking). • *The shop assistant talked knowingly* (= gave lots of information) **about** *the technical details of the machine.* • If you do something knowingly, you do it with awareness, esp. of its likely effect: *They are accused of knowingly dealing in stolen goods.*

know *(obj)* BE FAMILIAR WITH /£nəʊ, $noʊ/ *v* [not *be knowing*; not as a command] *past simple* **knew** /£njuː, $nuː/, *past part* **known** /£nəʊn, $noʊn/ to be familiar with or have experience and understanding of • *I've known Daniel since we were at school together.* [T] • *She grew up in Paris so she knows it well.* [T] • *Do you know the words to this song?* [T] • *I know this part of London* **like the back of my hand** (= very well). [T] • *I've seen the film 'Casablanca' so many times that I know a lot of it* **by heart**. [T] • *I know her* **as** *a colleague, but not really* **as** *a friend.* [T + obj + *as* n] • *Knowing Sarah* (= from my experience of her in the past), *she'll have done a good job.* [T] • *(fml) I have known* (= experienced) *a lot of happiness in my life.* [T] • If you know **(about)** a subject, you are familiar with it and understand it: *Do you know* **about** *computers?* [I always + prep] ○ *She knows her subject* **inside out**/*(Br and Aus also)* **backwards** (= very well). [T] • If you know a language, you can speak and understand it: *Everyone in the class knows a bit of English.* [T] • *(esp. Br and Aus)* If you know **of** something or someone you have heard of or about them: *Do you know of a good doctor?* [I always + prep] • To know something or someone can be to recognize them: *That's Peter – I'd know him anywhere!* [T] ○ *I know a bargain when I see one.* [T] • If you know one thing **from** another thing or if you know **the difference between** two things, you recognize each by seeing the differences between them: *Would you know a deer from an elk?* [T] • If you know **how to** do something, you are able to do it because you have the necessary skill or knowledge: *Do you know how to print on this computer?* [+ *wh-* word] • To **know how to** do something is to be skilled at it: *He really knows how to sing!* • To **get to know** someone or something is to spend time with them so that they become familiar: *The first couple of meetings are for the doctor and patient to get to know each other.* ○ *I'll need a few weeks to get to know the system.* • If you **know** someone **by name**, you have heard the name of a person but have never seen or talked to them. • If you **know** someone **by sight**, their face is familiar to you, but they are not a friend of yours. • If something, esp. a feeling, **knows no bounds**, it is extreme: *Our happiness at hearing the results knew no bounds.* • To **know** your **stuff**/*(dated)* **know** your **onions** is to have good practical skills and knowledge in a particular activity or subject. • If you **know** your **way around**/**know the ropes**, you are familiar with a place or organization and can act effectively within it. • If you **know what** you are **talking about**, you are an authority or expert on something. • To **know what it is (like) to** be or do something is to be familiar with how it feels to be or do it: *She knows what it's like to go bankrupt – it happened to her 20 years ago.* • If you do **not know** someone **from Adam**, you have never met them before and do not recognize them or their name: *The police showed me a photo of the guy, but I had to admit I didn't know him from Adam.* • If someone **wouldn't know** something **if** they **fell over one**/**if one hit** them **in the face**, they would not recognize it even if it was obvious: *Anna wouldn't know a bargain* **even** *if she fell over one.* • *"Knowing Me, Knowing You"* (title of a song by Abba, 1977) • *"Know thyself"* (saying, written on the ancient temple of Apollo in Delphi)

known /£nəʊn, $noʊn/ *adj* [not gradable] • Something or someone that is known is familiar to or understood by people: *These people are known criminals.* ○ *There is no known reason for the accident to have happened.* ○ *It is a* **little** *known fact that he was married before.* ○ *He is known* **to** *the police because of his previous criminal record.* • If someone or something is **known as** a particular name, they are called by that name: *And this is Terry,* **otherwise** *known as 'Muscleman'.* ○ *These chocolate bars are known as something else in the US, but I can't remember what.* • If you **make known** something/**make** something **known**, you tell people about it so that it becomes publicly known: *Local residents have made known their objections to the proposed new road.* ○ *I made* **it** *known* **that** *I was not happy with what had been decided.* • If you **make** yourself **known (to** someone), you tell them who you are: *Just go to the hotel reception and make yourself known (to the receptionist).* • See also WELL-KNOWN.

know·ledge /£'nɒl·ɪdʒ, $'nɑː·lɪdʒ/ *n* [U] understanding of or information about a subject which has been obtained by experience or study, and which is either in a person's mind or possessed by people generally • *Her knowledge* **of** *English grammar is very extensive.* • *I* **have** *no knowledge* **of** *how a car works.* • *He has* **a** *limited knowledge* **of** *French.* • *Human knowledge* **of** *planets outside our own solar system is very limited.* • *The details of the scandal are now* **common** *knowledge* (= familiar to most people). • *She started to photograph the documents, safe* **in the** *knowledge* **that** (= knowing that) *she wouldn't be disturbed for at least an hour.* • *In this town there are only a couple of restaurants that* **to** *my knowledge* (= judging from my personal experience and information) *serve good food.* • Knowledge can also mean awareness: *The owner claims the boat was being used without her knowledge.* ○ *The Government* **deny all** *knowledge* **of** *the affair.* ○ *It has* **come**/**been brought** *to our knowledge* (= We have discovered) **that** *several computers have gone missing.* • *"Knowledge itself is power"* (Francis Bacon in *Religious Meditations*, 1597)

know·ledge·a·ble /£'nɒl·ɪ·dʒə·bl̩, $'nɑː·lɪ-/ *adj* • *She's a knowledgeable woman* (= She knows a lot). • *He's very knowledgeable* (= knows a lot) **about** *German literature.*

knowl·edge·a·bly /£'nɒl·ɪ·dʒə·bli, $'nɑː·lɪ-/ *adv* • *The minister spoke knowledgeably about the technical problems involved in building the tunnel.*

knuck·le /'nʌk·l̩/ *n* [C] one of the joints of the fingers, esp. between the hand and the fingers • *I accidentally scraped my knuckles on the wall.* • *The first rules were drawn up in 1743 when boxing was with* **bare** *knuckles.* • *He* **cracked** *his knuckles* (= pulled each of his fingers until the bones made a noise) *loudly.* • *(Br infml) The subject matter of the film is certainly* **near the knuckle** (= about sex in a way that some people would find unacceptable). • A **knuckle-duster** (also **brass knuckles**) is a metal weapon which is fitted over the knuckles and intended to increase the damage that is caused when hitting a person or *(fig. infml)* a large and noticeable ring. • PIC **Body**

KOREAN FALSE FRIENDS

agitating point *n*	아지트	underground headquarters
all back *adj*	올백 *(n)*	straight hair style
announcer *n*	아나운서	newsreader
apart *adj*	아파트 *(n)*	apartment
asphalt *n*	아스팔트	asphalted road
back *n*	백	supporter exerting covert influence
back mirror *n*	백미러	side mirror
back number *n*	백넘버	athlete's identification number
bond *n*	본드	strong adhesive
boy *n*	보이	waiter
carpet *n*	카페트	rug
checkpoint *n*	체크포인트	something that needs checking
cider *n*	사이다	soda pop
circle *n*	서클	informal interest group
classic *n*	클래식	western classical music
clover *n*	크로바	club (suit of playing cards)
combination *n*	콤비	unmatching pair, suit
concentric *adj*	콘센트	electrical outlet
concise *adj*	콘사이스 *(n)*	small dictionary, esp. English
cost down *v*	코스트 다운	cost reduction *(n)*
cunning *n*	컨닝	cheating in an exam
cup *n*	컵	a glass
driver *n*	도라이바	screwdriver
dry *adj*	드라이*(v)*	to perm straight hair or straighten curly hair
event *n*	이벤트	social occasion
eye shopping *n*	아이쇼핑	window-shopping
flash *n*	플래시,후래시	torch (Br.), flashlight (Am.)
form *n*	폼	affected manner
guarantee *n*	게런티	performance fee
handle *n*	핸들	steering wheel

(KOR)

happening *n*	해프닝	unexpected, interesting incident
humour *n*	유머	something amusing
jumper *n*	잠바	windbreaker
level up *v*	레벨업	upgrade, raise the level
name value *n*	네임밸류	social reputation
note *n*	노트	notebook; memorandum
office girl/lady *n*	오피스 걸/레이디	white collar working woman
old miss *n*	오피스 미스	unmarried woman past the conventional age for marrying
over *adv*	오바 *(n)*	overcoat
overhead *adj*	오바헤드 *(n)*	vomiting
prim *adj*	프림 *(n)*	nondairy coffee whitener
pro *n*	프로	TV or radio programme
pro *adj, n*	프로	percent
puncture *n*	펑크	cancellation
register *n*	레지	tearoom waitress
room saloon *n*	룸살롱	hostess bar
rotary *adj*	로타리*(n)*	traffic roundabout
rouge *n*	루즈	lipstick
second *adj*	세컨드 *(n)*	(kept) mistress
service *n*	서비스	gratis
sharp pencil *n*	샤프 펜슬	mechanical pencil
side brake *n*	사이드 브레이크	handbrake
sign *n*	사인	signature
super *adj*	수퍼 *(n)*	supermarket
T *n*	티	T-shirt
talent *n*	탈렌트	TV actor
training *n*	츄리닝	track suit
version up *v*	버전업	to introduce an upgraded version
villa *n*	빌라	upmarket town house (row house)
white shirt *n*	와이샤쓰	shirt

knuck·le down /ˌnʌk·l̩/ *v adv* [I] *infml* to start working or studying hard • *You're going to have to really knuckle down to catch up on all the work you've missed.* • *I can't seem to knuckle down* **to** *my studies these days – there are too many distractions.*

knuck·le un·der /ˌnʌk·l̩/ *v adv* [I] *infml* to accept someone's power over you; allow yourself to be beaten • *The boys were encouraged to knuckle under and get trained as chippies, mechanics or electricians.* • *The government, he declared, would never again knuckle under* **to** *the demands of trade unions.*

knuck·le·head /ˈnʌk·l̩.hed/ *n* [C] *esp. Am infml* a stupid person; IDIOT • *They're just a bunch of knuckleheads.*

KO *obj* /£ˌkeɪˈəʊ, $-ˈoʊ/ *v* [T] he/she/it **KO's**, **KO'ing**, *past* **KO'd** *infml* to KNOCK OUT (= make unconscious), esp. in boxing • *Amazing! We've just seen the world's number one boxer KO'd in the first round!* • *(fig.) That flu really KO'd me* (= made me very weak) *for a while.*

KO /£ˌkeɪˈəʊ, $-ˈoʊ/ *n* [C] *pl* **KOs** *infml* • *Smith won with a KO in the third round.* • See also KNOCKOUT [UNCONSCIOUS].

ko·a·la (bear) /£kəʊˈɑː·lə, $koʊ-/ *n* [C] an Australian animal which lives in trees and looks like a small bear with grey fur • *Koala bears eat eucalyptus leaves.*

kohl /£kəʊl, £kɒl, $koʊl/ *n* [U] a dark substance which people put around their eyes, esp. the edge of their EYELIDS, to make them more attractive • *Her eyes were outlined with kohl.* • *She used a kohl* **pencil**.

kook·a·bur·ra /ˈkʊk·əˌbʌr·ə/, *Aus dated* **laugh·ing jack·ass** *n* [C] a large Australian bird which lives in trees and makes a strange sound like laughter

kook·y /ˈkuː·ki/ *adj* **-ier**, **-iest** *infml esp. Am* (esp. of a person) strange in their appearance or behaviour, esp. in a way that is interesting • *She's got this kooky, high-pitched voice.*

kook /kuːk/ *n* [C] *Am infml* • *She's a real kook* (= strange person).

kook·i·ness /ˈkuː·kɪ·nəs/ *n* [U] *esp. Am infml*

Koo·ri, **Koo·rie** /ˈkʊə·ri/ *n* [C], *adj* [not gradable] an ABORIGINE

Ko·ran, **Qur'an** /£kɒrˈɑːn, $kəˈrɑːn/ *n* [U] **the Koran** the holy book of the Islamic religion • *the Holy Koran*

kor·ma /£ˈkɔː·mə, $ˈkɔːr-/ *n* [U] an Indian food which consists of meat, fish or vegetables in a creamy sauce • *vegetable/lamb korma*

kosh·er /£ˈkəʊ·ʃəʳ, $ˈkoʊ·ʃɚ/ *adj* (of food or places where food is sold etc.) prepared or kept in conditions that follow the rules of Jewish law, or *(fig. infml humorous)* lawful, able to be trusted and therefore good • *kosher food/meat* • *a kosher restaurant/butcher/shop* • *(fig.) Their business activities aren't quite kosher.*

kow·tow /ˌkaʊˈtaʊ/ *v* [I] *disapproving* to show too much respect to someone in authority, always obeying them and changing what you do in order to please them • *I want a promotion but I'm not prepared to kowtow* **to** *the boss for it.*

kph *abbreviation for* kilometres per hour

Krem·lin /ˈkrem·lɪn/ *n* [U] **the Kremlin** a group of buildings in Moscow which is now the centre of government of Russia, or the government itself. In the past the Kremlin also meant the government of the Soviet Union. • *When the delegation returned to Moscow, they went to the Kremlin for a meeting.* • *The Kremlin and the Senate are for once both saying the same thing.* • *He's an experienced Kremlin-watcher.*

Krish·na /ˈkrɪʃ·nə/ *n* [U not after *the*] one of the most important of the Hindu gods

Kris Krin·gle /ˌkrɪsˈkrɪŋ·gl̩/ *n* [U not after *the*] *Am for* **Father Christmas**, see at FATHER

kryp·ton /£ˈkrɪp·tɒn, $-tɑːn/ *n* [U] a gas which is used in particular types of lights and LASERS

ku·dos /£ˈkjuː·dɒs, $-dɑːs/ *n* [U] the fame and public admiration that a person receives as a result of a particular achievement or position in society • *Being an actor has a certain amount of kudos attached to it.*

Ku Klux Klan /ˌkuː·klʌksˈklæn/ (*abbreviation* **KKK**) *n* [U] **the Ku Klux Klan** a secret US organization of white PROTESTANT Americans, esp. in the south of the country, who oppose people of other races or religions • *You see photographs of the Ku Klux Klan wearing pointed white hoods which cover their faces.*

kum·quat, **cum·quat** /ˈkʌm·kwæt/ *n* [C] a small oval orange-like fruit, with a sweet skin which can be eaten • PIC› **Fruit**

kung fu /ˌkʌŋˈfuː/ *n* [U] a Chinese method of fighting which involves using your hands and feet and not using weapons

Kurd /£kɜːd, $kɜːrd/ *n* [C] a member of a NOMADIC (= moving from place to place) race who live mainly in E Turkey, W Iran and N Iraq

Kurd·ish /£ˈkɜː·dɪʃ, $ˈkɜːr-/ *adj* [not gradable] • *the Kurdish language* • *Kurdish people*

kW *n* [C] *pl* **kW** *abbreviation for* KILOWATT

K–Y jel·ly /ˌkeɪ·waɪ/ *n* [U] *trademark* a transparent cream-like substance that can be put on part of the body in order to make the skin less dry and which is used esp. during sexual activity

L l

L LETTER (*pl* **L's** or **Ls**), **l** (*pl* **l's** or **ls**) /el/ *n* [C] the 12th letter of the English alphabet • LP› **Silent letters**

L NUMBER, **l** /el/ *n* [C] the sign used in the Roman system for the number 50

L DIRECTION *adj, adv, n* [U] *abbreviation for* left • *Some damage noted to L eye.* • *Go l. at traffic lights.* • *Take next road on l.*

L LAKE *n abbreviation for* LAKE (used in writing before the name of a lake) • *L Ontario*

l LINE OF PRINTING *n* [C] *pl* **ll** *abbreviation for* LINE (used esp. before the number of a line on a printed page) • *l. 96*

l LITRE *n* [C] *pl* **l** *abbreviation for* LITRE • *a 25 l container*

L SIZE /el/ *adj* (esp. used on clothing to show its size) *abbreviation for* LARGE

laa·ger /£'lɑː·gəʳ, $-gɚ/ *n* [C] a place or situation in which people feel protected from unpleasant things happening in other places • *Public violence compels especially women and the old to* **retreat into** *a private laager because they find everything around them threatening.* • *As most people here are comfortably off they are adopting a laager* **mentality** *to defend what they've got.* • In S Africa in the past a laager was a CAMP (= area of land with temporary buildings) surrounded by vehicles.

lab SCIENCE /læb/ *n* [C] *infml* a LABORATORY • *a science/ hospital lab* • *He's a lab technician/assistant.*

Lab POLITICS /læb/ *adj abbreviation for* LABOUR (= political party) • *The debate in Parliament was initiated by Clare Short (Lab).* • *The results of the Bradford South election were as follows: Philip Duggan (Con) 881, Ann Stamford (Lab) 1200.*

la·bel SIGN /'leɪ·bᵊl/ *n* [C] a piece of paper or other material which is stuck on or joined to an object, telling you what the object is, how to use it, to whom it belongs or other information • *The label on the bottle says not to take more than six tablets a day.* • *Remember to put some address labels on the suitcases.* • *It was a new skirt and there weren't any washing instructions on the label.* • A label is also a name or a phrase which is used to describe the characteristics or qualities of people, activities or things: *'Middle-class' is the label generally applied to this magazine.* ○ *The only derogatory label for older men that comes to mind is 'an old woman'!* • LP› **Labels**

la·bel *obj* /'leɪ·bᵊl/ *v* [T] **-ll-** or *Am usually* **-l-** • *He was busy labelling* (= putting labels on) *all the bottles of wine that he'd made that year.* • *This jam is labelled 'apple and blackberry'.* [+ obj + n] • *The parcel was* **clearly** *labelled 'Fragile'.* [+ obj + adj] • *If you spend any time in prison you're labelled* (= considered or referred to by most people) **(as a)** *criminal for the rest of your life.* [+ obj + (as) n/adj]

la·bel COMPANY /'leɪ·bᵊl/ *n* [C] a company which produces goods for sale, the goods themselves, or the company's name or symbol • *Her favourite* **designer** *label* (= maker of expensive clothes) *is Armani.* • *He only wears* **designer** *labels.* • *The pasta is marketed* **under** *the supermarket's* **own** *label.* • *They tested several types of ice-cream including the store's* **own** *label.* • *Their own-label vegetarian products have been a huge success.* • *The group have just signed* (= arranged to record) **with** *a new* **record** *label.* • *Her new record is* **on** (= recorded by) *the Jiffy label.*

la·bi·a /'leɪ·bi·ə/ *pl n* folds on the outside of the female sex organs that are shaped like lips • *the inner/outer labia*

La·bor /£'leɪ·bəʳ, $-bɚ/ (*abbreviation* **ALP** /ˌeɪ·el'piː/) *n* [U not after *the*], *adj* [not gradable] (belonging to or supporting) the Labor Party, an Australian political party that believes in social equality and the rights of workers • See also LABOUR POLITICAL PARTY.

la·bor·a·tory /£lə'bɒr·ə·tri, $'læb·rə·tɔːr·i/, *infml* **lab** *n* [C] a room or building with scientific equipment for doing scientific tests or for teaching science, or a place where chemicals or medicines are produced • *the European Laboratory for Nuclear Physics* • *Laboratory tests suggest that the new drug may be used to treat cancer.* • *The study took place* **in/under** *laboratory conditions.*

la·bo·ri·ous /£lə'bɔː·ri·əs, $-'bɔːr·i-/ *adj* needing a lot of time and effort • *Checking the entire report for mistakes was a laborious business.*

la·bo·ri·ous·ly /£lə'bɔː·ri·ə·sli, $-'bɔːr·i-/ *adv* • *Dr Vercoe wrote out the list laboriously by hand.*

Laboratory

la·bo·ri·ous·ness /£lə'bɔː·ri·ə·snəs, $-'bɔːr·i-/ *n* [U]

la·bour WORK *Br and Aus, Am and Aus* **la·bor** /£'leɪ·bəʳ, $-bɚ/ *n* [U] practical work, esp. that which involves physical effort • *There's so much labour involved in redecorating a house.* • *The car parts themselves are not expensive, it's the labour that costs the money.* • *People doing jobs that involve* **manual** *labour* (= hard work using the hands) *use up a lot of energy.* • Labour also refers to the workers themselves, esp. those who do practical work with their hands: *skilled/unskilled labour* • A **labour camp** is a place in which people are kept as prisoners and forced to do hard physical work in bad conditions. • **Labour day** is, in some countries, a public holiday which celebrates the worker. LP› **Holidays** • The **labour force** is either all the people in a particular country who are of the right age to work or all the people who work for a particular company: *Fewer teenagers are leaving school and joining the labour force at 16.* ○ *The car manufacturers are planning to cut their labour force by half.* • Industries and methods which are **labour-intensive** need a lot of workers: *A lot of farming techniques have been abandoned because they were too labour-intensive.* • The **labour market** is the supply of people in a particular country or area who are able and willing to work: *More women are being encouraged into the labour market these days.* • A **labour of love** is a piece of hard work which you do because you enjoy it and not because you will receive money or praise for it, or because you need to do it: *He's always working on his car – but it's a labour of love.* • **Labour relations** are the relationships between employees and employers: *The firm prided itself on its good labour relations.* • A **labour-saving** device or method is one which saves a lot of effort and time: *A personal computer can be very labour-saving.* • *"Love's Labour's Lost"* (title of a play by William Shakespeare) • Ⓓ

la·bour (*obj*) *Br and Aus, Am and Aus* **la·bor** /£'leɪ·bəʳ, $-bɚ/ *v* • If you labour you do hard physical work: *She was exhausted – she'd been labouring in the garden for hours.* [I] ○ *He travelled around Europe labouring/doing labouring*

LABELS IN THE DICTIONARY

When a label is given before the definition of a word, the label applies to all uses of the word. For example, the grammatical word 'determiner' is always a specialized word. When an example is labelled, the label describes the use of the word or phrase in that particular situation. For example, in the sentence *I was impressed by her professional attitude* the speaker is praising someone, but in *He works as a professional photographer* no praise is intended. Therefore only the first use of *professional* would be marked *(approving)*.

Labels showing formality and informality

fml **Formal:** words and phrases used in a serious way, for example in business documents, serious newspapers and books, lectures, news broadcasts. Formal language is often used when people want to appear polite. Examples: *He is anxiously* **awaiting** (= waiting for) *the result of the medical tests.* • *Guests are requested to* **comply with** (= obey) *all the fire and safety rules.*

infml **Informal:** used with friends or family or people you know in relaxed situations. Informal words are more common in speech than in writing. *She works as an* **admin assistant** (= administrative assistant). • *She always stops for a* **cuppa** (= cup of tea) *at 11 o'clock.* It might be considered not polite to use very informal language in formal situations.

slang Informal language which might include words which are not polite. Slang is often used between members of a particular group when speaking together, and might stay in use only for a short time. *That's a load of* **bullshit** (= nonsense) • *(Br dated)* **The fuzz** (= The police) *have searched my flat four times this year.*

taboo Words which are likely to offend someone and are not used in formal situations. Certain words referring to sex or sexual organs, excretion and people's nationality or race can be particularly offensive. Strong swear words are also marked taboo.

Labels showing the speaker's feelings or opinion

approving Words usually used in a positive way, showing that the speaker has a good opinion of someone or something, or good feelings towards them: *Her designs were always* **original** *and imaginative.* • *This steak is beautifully* **tender** (= easy to cut).

disapproving Words usually used in a negative way, showing that the speaker has a bad opinion or feelings: *She seems to have a very* **clinical** (= emotionless) *attitude towards her children. She's a bit* **fussy** (= not easily satisfied) *about what she'll eat and what she won't.*

humorous Words or phrases which are often intended to make people laugh or smile. Some are informal or slang words: *With a* **pot** (= big stomach) *like this, do I look as though I get any exercise?* Often a dated or formal word is used humorously in an informal situation: *Let me take you to my humble* **abode** (= home).

Labels referring to the origin of a word, or to the situation in which the word is used

specialized Used especially by people with special knowledge about a particular area of work or subject of study. People who do not have this knowledge might not understand the words: *The river has been polluted with* **heavy metals** *such as chromium and mercury.* • *Beethoven's ninth symphony was a model for many* **Romantic** *composers.*

law Specialized words used by lawyers and when referring to legal subjects: *Mr Reynolds, the* **defendant**, *denied all the charges brought against him.*

medical Specialized words used by doctors and when referring to medical subjects: *Her cough is due to a slight* **bronchial** *infection and no medication is necessary.*

literary Words and phrases which are mainly used in literature, (for example in a novel or a play), or when writing in a literary way: *The valley was* **enshrouded** (= covered) *in thick mist.*

poetic Literary words usually found only in poetry: *The* **zephyr** (= light wind) *wafted a sweet perfume of flowers* **o'er** (= over) *the fields.*

saying Well known and wise statements: *A friend in need is a friend indeed* (= A friend who helps you when you really need help is a true friend).

trademark Names of particular products which cannot be legally used by any other producer: *I always take my* **Walkman** *when I go jogging.*

dated Words or phrases which sound old-fashioned, not modern: *My grandmother still calls the radio 'the* **wireless**'.

old use Used before the 20th century but now rare: *She suffered from* **melancholia** (= a condition of great sadness) *after the untimely death of her father.*

Labels referring to different varieties of English

The following labels are applied to words or phrases which are used especially by people in or from particular countries. When a word or a spelling is not labelled this means it is commonly used in all varieties of English. LP **Varieties of English** at VARIETY.

Am	American English
Aus	Australian English
Br	British English
Canadian Eng	Canadian English
Irish Eng	Irish English
Scot Eng	Scottish English
regional	Used mostly by people from particular areas of Britain or the US.

Other labels

abbreviation Short words or combinations of letters used instead of longer words or phrases: *Jan.* (= January), *UN* (= United Nations). Notice that some abbreviations are not spoken in the way they are written: *contd* (kənˈtɪn·juːd), *no.* (ˈnʌmbəʳ).

fig. **Figurative:** when a word or phrase is used figuratively, its basic meaning is applied to something in a way which gives a picture of what it is like: *A thick* **blanket** *of fog lay over the city.* • *She* **exploded** *with laughter when she saw my new shoes.*

female, male Some nouns have two or more forms, depending on the sex of the person or animal which is referred to. A form marked with one of these labels refers only to the sex shown, e.g. **lioness** *(female)*. The form which can refer to both females and males, e.g. **lion**, is not labelled. Other examples: **firefighter**, **fireman** *(male)*, **firewoman** *(female)*.

not standard Words or short forms used in very informal spoken English, and not considered correct by most speakers: "**Gimme** (= give me) *the key, will you?*" "*I* **ain't** (= have not) *got no key.*"

jobs to pay his way. ○ *Three hours after the explosion, rescue teams were still labouring* **to** *free those trapped.* [+ to infinitive] • To labour is also to do something slowly with great physical or mental effort: *He laboured up the hill, a child and two bags of shopping in his arms.* [I] ○ *She's been labouring over the same composition for days, poor thing.* [I] • If you labour (*Am* also **belabor**) a **point** you try too hard to express an idea, feeling or opinion, repeating it unnecessarily: *Look, there's no need to labour the point – I made a mistake – I admit it!* [T] • If you labour **under a delusion/illusion/misapprehension** you wrongly believe something to be true which is not in fact true: *At the time I was still labouring under the delusion that the project might be a success.* [I]

la·boured *Br and Aus, Am and Aus also* **la·bored** /£ˈleɪ·bəd, $-bɚd/ *adj* • An attempt at something can be described as laboured if it looks as if it is done with difficulty and not skilfully or with natural ability: *His writing was rather laboured, lacking the graceful ease of his conversation.* ○ *a laboured joke* ○ *Her breathing was heavy and laboured and she was sweating.*

la·bour·er *Br and Aus, Am and Aus also* **la·bor·er** /£ˈleɪ·bᵊr·əʳ, $-bɚ·ɚ/ *n* [C] • A labourer is a person who does unskilled physical work, esp. outside: *a farm labourer* • Ⓓ

la·bours *Br and Aus, Am and Aus also* **la·bors** /£ˈleɪ·bəz, $-bɚz/ *pl n literary or fml* • People can refer to their labours meaning all the effort and hard work that have been involved in doing a particular piece of work: *Are you tired after your labours?* ○ *West was paid very little for his labours.* ○ *Retirement is the time to enjoy* **the fruits of** *your labours.*

La·bour POLITICAL PARTY /£ˈleɪ·bəʳ, $-bɚ/ *adj* [not gradable], *n* [U] (belonging to or supporting) the Labour Party, the political party in Britain that believes in social equality, a more equal sharing out of wealth, and the rights of workers • *She's a member of the Labour Party.* • *Who is the Labour candidate for Coventry North?* • *They're mainly Labour (voters) in this area.* • *I'm hoping that Labour will get in at the next election.* [not after *the*] • *I voted Labour in the last election.* [not after *the*]

la·bour BIRTH *Br and Aus, Am and Aus* **la·bor** /£ˈleɪ·bəʳ, $-bɚ/ *n* [U] the last stage of pregnancy from the time when muscles of the womb start to push the baby out of the body until the baby appears • *labour pains* • *the labour ward* • *She* **went into** (=started) *labour at twelve o'clock last night.* • *I was* **in** *labour for twelve hours with my first baby.* • Ⓓ

Lab·ra·dor (re·triev·er) /£ˈlæb·rə·dɔːʳ, $-dɔːr/ *n* [C] a big golden or black dog with short hair • *Labradors are used as guide-dogs for blind people.* • PIC> **Dogs**

la·bur·num /£ləˈbɜː·nəm, $-ˈbɜːr-/ *n* [C; U] a small tree with groups of yellow flowers hanging down

lab·y·rinth /ˈlæb·ɪ·rɪnθ/ *n* [C] *literary* a confusing set of connecting passages or paths in which it is easy to get lost; MAZE • *Finally through a labyrinth of corridors she found his office.* • *(fig.) He was no stranger to the labyrinth* **of** *love.*

lab·y·rin·thine /ˌlæb·ɪˈrɪn·θaɪn/ *adj literary* • *Beneath the city lies a labyrinthine network of tunnels.* • Labyrinthine can also be used of something that has lots of parts and is therefore confusing: *It takes a fair amount of concentration to follow the film's labyrinthine plot.*

lace MATERIAL /leɪs/ *n* [U] a decorative cloth which is made by weaving thin thread in delicate patterns with holes in them • *There's a shop in the village that sells hand-made lace.* • *a lace blouse/collar/handkerchief/tablecloth* • *lace curtains*

la·cy /ˈleɪ·si/ *adj* **-ier, -iest** • *lacy knickers/underwear*

lace CORD /leɪs/ *n* [C usually plural] a cord or string which you use to fasten openings, esp. in shoes, by putting it through two lines of small holes and tying the ends together • *I'll just* **do up/tie** *(Br* **up**) *my laces.* • *Your* **(shoe)***laces are undone.*

lace *obj* /leɪs/ *v* [T] • You lace a shoe or boot by putting the lace through its holes: *It must take ages to lace boots with so many holes.* • If you lace **up** a shoe or boot you fasten it by pulling the two ends of its lace tightly and tying the ends together: *She can lace up her shoes and she's only five!*

lace–ups /ˈleɪs·ʌps/ *pl n* • Lace-ups are shoes or boots which are fastened using laces: *a pair of lace-ups* ○ *lace-up shoes*

lace ADD ALCOHOL /leɪs/ *v* [T often passive] to add alcohol or drugs to (food or drink), often secretly • *This coffee tastes as if it's been laced* **with** *brandy or something.* • *She had felt so strange that evening she even wondered if her drink had been laced* **with** *something.*

lac·er·ate *obj* /£ˈlæs·ᵊr·eɪt, $-ə·reɪt/ *v* [T] *fml or specialized* to cut or tear (something, esp. flesh) • *The man's face was severely lacerated in the accident.* • *(fig.) He reserved his most lacerating* (=severe) *criticism for the English, whom he detested.*

lac·er·a·tion /£ˌlæs·ᵊrˈeɪ·ʃᵊn, $-əˈreɪ-/ *n fml or specialized* • *The boy had received horrific injuries in the attack, including lacerations to both arms.* [C] • *The body showed signs of laceration and bruising.* [U]

lach·ry·mose /£ˈlæk·rɪ·məʊs, $-moʊs/ *adj literary* sad and/or tending to cry often and easily • *Julia Moreno plays the lachrymose heroine of the film.* • *He is better known for his lachrymose ballads than hard rock numbers.*

lack *obj* /læk/ *v* [T] to not have (something, esp. something necessary or wanted) or to not have enough of it • *What we lack in this house is space to store things.* • *I lack the energy that's required to look after children!* • Ⓓ

lack /læk/ *n* [U] • *Her only problem is lack* **of** *confidence.* • *Lack* **of** *sleep had made him irritable.* • *We aren't having a holiday because of* **a** *lack* **of funds** (=money). • *If he fails it won't be* **for/through** *lack* **of** *effort* (=he has certainly tried).

lack·ing /ˈlæk·ɪŋ/ *adj* [after v] • *We are lacking three members of staff due to illness.* • *Enthusiasm has been* **sadly** *lacking* (=noticeably absent) *these past months at work.* • *He's totally lacking* **in** *charm of any sort.*

lack·a·dai·si·cal /ˌlæk·əˈdeɪ·zɪ·kᵊl/ *adj* lacking enthusiasm and effort; LAZY • *The food was nice enough but the service was rather lackadaisical.*

lack·a·dai·si·cal·ly /ˌlæk·əˈdeɪ·zɪ·kli/ *adv*

lack·ey /ˈlæk·i/ *n* [C] *disapproving* a servant or someone who behaves like one by obeying someone else's orders without questioning them or by doing all their unpleasant work for them • *He treats us all like his lackeys, expecting us to be here whenever he wants us.* • *The opera singer arrived with her attendant lackeys.*

lack·lus·tre *Br and Aus, Am* **lack·lust·er** /£ˈlækˌlʌs·təʳ, £ˌ-ˈ--, $-tɚ/ *adj* lacking energy and effort • *Britain's number-one tennis player gave a disappointingly lacklustre performance.*

la·con·ic /£ləˈkɒn·ɪk, $-ˈkɑː·nɪk/ *adj fml* using very few words to express what you mean • *"No," was the laconic reply.* • *She had a laconic* **wit/sense of humour**.

la·con·i·cal·ly /£ləˈkɒn·ɪ·kli, $-ˈkɑː·nɪ-/ *adv fml*

lac·quer WOOD/METAL /£ˈlæk·əʳ, $-ɚ/ *n* [U] a shiny hard substance which is painted on wood or metal to create a protective surface

lac·quer *obj* /£ˈlæk·əʳ, $-ɚ/ *v* [T] • *She lacquered the table top.*

lac·quer HAIR /£ˈlæk·əʳ, $-ɚ/, **hair lac·quer, hair spray** *n* [U] a substance which is SPRAYED onto the hair in order to make the hair stay in a particular position • *Do you use lacquer on your curls?*

la·crosse /£ləˈkrɒs, $-ˈkrɑːs/ *n* [U] a game played by two teams in which the players each use a long stick with a net at the end to catch, carry and throw a small ball, and try to get the ball in the other team's goal

lac·tate /lækˈteɪt/ *v* [I] *specialized* (of a woman or female mammal) to produce milk

lac·ta·tion /lækˈteɪ·ʃᵊn/ *n* [U] *specialized*

lac·tic /ˈlæk·tɪk/ *adj* [not gradable] *specialized* of or relating to milk • **Lactic acid** is a clear acid found in milk which is old and sour and also produced in the muscles when a person has been exercising a lot.

lac·tose /£ˈlæk·təʊs, $-toʊs/ *n* [U] *specialized* a type of sugar which is found in milk • *Lactose is used in the manufacture of baby foods.*

la·cu·na /ləˈkjuː·nə/ *n* [C] *pl* **lacunas** or **lacunae** /ləˈkjuː·niː/ *fml* an absent part, esp. in a book or other piece of writing

la·cy /ˈleɪ·si/ *adj* See at LACE MATERIAL

lad /læd/ *n* [C] a boy or young man • *A group of young lads were standing outside the shop.* • *He's a nice lad.* • *The Prime Minister's a* **local** *lad* (=he was born and lived in this area). • *(dated) lads* **and lasses** • *Come on, lads, let's get this job finished, shall we!* [as form of address] • *(Br infml)* A young man who has sex with a lot of different women might be described as **a bit of a lad**. • LP> **Age, Titles and forms of address** Ⓘ

lad·dish /ˈlæd·ɪʃ/ *adj Br disapproving* • Behaviour that is laddish is typical of young men in social groups.

lad·dish·ness /ˈlæd·ɪʃ·nəs/ *n* [U] *Br disapproving*

lads /lædz/ *pl n Br and Aus infml* • Esp. a man might use **the lads** to refer to the group of men that he spends time with socially, esp. those with whom he drinks alcohol in PUBS or plays sport with: *I'm having a night out with the lads tonight.* ○ *You'll always find Ian in some bar with his mates – he's* **one of** *the lads all right* (= certainly a typical member of this group). ○ *The lads played some great football this afternoon.* • LP› **Titles and forms of address**

lad·der EQUIPMENT /£'læd·əʳ, $-ɚ/ *n* [C] a piece of equipment used for climbing up and down, which consists of two vertical bars or lengths of rope joined to each other by a set of horizontal steps • *You'll need a ladder to paint the ceiling.* • *She was* **up** *a ladder, cleaning the window.* • *(fig.) Only those who are further up the company ladder* (= have highly ranked jobs) *are given a car.* • PIC› **Emergency services**

lad·der HOLE *Br and Aus* /£'læd·əʳ, $-ɚ/, *esp. Am* **run** *n* [C] a long vertical hole in a STOCKING or a pair of TIGHTS • *I had to change my tights because they had a ladder in them.*

lad·der *(obj)* /£'læd·əʳ, $-ɚ/ *v Br* • *Damn! That's the second pair of tights I've laddered today!* [T] • *Those thin tights ladder easily.* [I]

lad·der (tour·na·ment) /£'læd·əʳ, $-ɚ/ *n* [C] *esp. Br and Aus* (in particular sports) a system in which all the players who play regularly are given a position in a list and can improve their position by beating other players in that list • *a squash ladder*

lad·die /'læd·i/ *n* [as form of address] *infml esp. Scot Eng for* LAD • *Hey, laddie, you're standing in my way.*

lad·en /'leɪ·dᵊn/ *adj* carrying or holding a lot of something • *He always comes back from France laden* **with** *presents for everyone.* • *The table, as always, was laden* **with** *food.* • **Heavily** *laden tank-transporters rumbled past.*

la–di–da, lah–di–dah /ˌlɑː·dɪ'dɑː/ *adj infml dated* (esp. of a woman's speech or manner) not sincere because the person is pretending to belong to a higher social class • *a la-di-da voice/manner* • *She's so la-di-da – I can't stand her!*

la·dies /'leɪ·diz/ *n* See at LADY WOMAN

lad·le /'leɪ·dḷ/ *n* [C] a big spoon with a long handle and a deep cup-shaped part, used esp. for serving soup • *a soup ladle* • PIC› **Cutlery, Kitchen**

lad·le *obj* /'leɪ·dḷ/ *v* [T] • If you ladle **(out)** soup or other liquid food you put it into individual bowls to give to people, using a ladle. [T/M] • *(infml)* To **ladle out** money or goods is to give (too) generously to a lot of people: *Doctors ladled out antibiotics to patients in those days.*

la dol·ce vi·ta /£læd,ɒl·tʃeɪ'viː·tə, £-ˌɑːl·tʃeɪ'viː·ṭə/ *n* [U] a comfortable, pleasant and easy way of life with a lot of money and the freedom to do what you want to do • *They were invited to spend a few weeks on the millionaire's yacht* **enjoying** *la dolce vita.*

la·dy WOMAN /'leɪ·di/ *n* [C] a woman • Lady is a way of referring to or addressing a woman which esp. older people consider polite: *She's a very attractive lady.* ○ *Would you mind your language – there are ladies present!* ○ *Say thank you to the lady, Joe, for letting you stroke her dog.* • *(saying humorous)* 'That's no lady (that's my wife)' is sometimes used as an answer to the polite use of lady: *"There's a lady on the phone for you." "That's no lady, that's my sister!"* • Ladies **and gentlemen** is used formally to introduce a speech to a group of people: *Good evening ladies and gentlemen, I'd like to welcome you all to the performance this evening.* • *(dated) Is the lady* **of the house** (= the most important or only woman who lives in the house) *in?* • *The* **cleaning** *lady* (= woman who cleans the house) *comes on Mondays.* • *(dated)* Lady is sometimes added to the names of particular jobs: *a lady doctor.* • *(dated)* A woman might be described as **a** lady if she has the gentleness of manner and politeness considered suitable for a woman: *Of course I remember Mrs Connor – she was a real lady.* • *(Am slang) Hey, lady, what's the rush?* [as form of address] • *(disapproving)* A **lady bountiful** is a woman who is well-known for her generosity: *Some of the poorer villagers were offended by the way she was always* **acting the** *lady bountiful.* • *(Aus)* A **lady's finger** (also **ladyfinger**) is a short type of BANANA, or a type of black GRAPE. • *(Br dated)* **Ladies' fingers** is another name for OKRA. • *(dated)* A **lady-killer** is a man who, knowing that he is sexually attractive to women, uses this quality to create sexual relationships with many women: *With his good looks and charm he usually played the lady-killer in Hollywood films.* • *(dated)* A **ladies' man** is a man who gives women a lot of attention and likes to be in their company: *John was always* **a bit of** *a ladies' man.* • *"Lady in Red"* (title of a song by Chris de Burgh, 1986) • LP› **Titles and forms of address**

la·dies /'leɪ·diz/ *n* [U] • A ladies is a public toilet for women: *Excuse me, could you tell me where* **the** *ladies is?* ○ *I'm just going to the ladies.* • *(esp. Br)* A ladies (*esp. Am* **ladies' room**) is also a women's toilet in a hotel, restaurant or other building. See also GENTS.

la·dy–in–wait·ing /£ˌleɪ·di·ɪn'weɪ·tɪŋ, $-ṭɪŋ/ *n* [C] *pl* **ladies-in-waiting** • A lady-in-waiting is a woman whose job is to act as an assistant to a queen or other woman of high social position: *The Princess was accompanied by her lady-in-waiting.*

la·dy·like /'leɪ·di·laɪk/ *adj dated* • Ladylike means graceful, controlled and behaving in a way that is socially acceptable for a woman: *Well, it might not be ladylike but I'm going to pull my skirt up to get over this fence.*

Lad·y TITLE /'leɪ·di/ *n* [U] (in Britain) the title given to a female who has the social rank of a PEER or to the wife of a peer or KNIGHT • *Before she married Charles her title was Lady Diana Spencer.* • *Sir Charles and Lady Finlater* • *"Close the curtains, Withers." "Yes,* **my** *Lady."* [as form of address] • *(Br infml disapproving)* A woman might be referred to as **Lady Muck** if she pretends to be of a high social class, considering herself to be better than other people. • Compare LORD TITLE.

la·dy·ship /'leɪ·di·ʃɪp/ *n* [C] *fml* • Ladyship is a respectful way of referring to or addressing a female who has the rank of a PEER or KNIGHT without using her title: *We are honoured to welcome* **your** *ladyship* (= you) *here tonight.* • **Her** *ladyship* (= She) *will shortly be speaking to us about the charity of which she is patron.* • *More cake,* **your** *Ladyship?* [as form of address] • Compare **lordship** at LORD TITLE.

la·dy·bird *Br and Aus* /£'leɪ·di·bɜːd, $-bɜːrd/, *Am* **la·dy·bug** /'leɪ·di·bʌg/ *n* [C] a small red BEETLE (= type of insect) which is round and has black spots • PIC› **Insects**

lag MOVE SLOWLY /læg/ *v* [I] **-gg-** to move or advance so slowly that you are behind other people or things • *He's lagging* **behind** *a bit – I think we'd better wait for him to catch us up.* • *As far as prison reform is concerned we lagged* **(way/well/one step) behind** *a lot of other countries for years.* • *Until they get the formula right they are going to be lagging, and their competitors are already years ahead of them.* • *Sales are lagging at the moment.*

lag /læg/ *n* • *There is often a lag* (= a period of time) *between becoming infected and the first signs of the illness.* [C] • *The project is suffering from (a) severe* **time** *lag* (= it is delayed). [C/U]

lag·gard /£'læg·əd, $-ɚd/ *n* [C] • *The newspaper article said the company had become a technological laggard* (= had not advanced as quickly as other companies), *leading to financial problems.*

lag *obj* COVER /læg/ *v* [T] **-gg-** to cover (something) with a thick layer of material in order to stop heat from escaping or to stop esp. water freezing; to INSULATE • *You are advised to lag your roof and hot water tank to reduce your heating bills.* • *The pipes froze because they weren't lagged.*

lag·ging /'læg·ɪŋ/ *n* [U] • Lagging is the thick layer of material which is used to cover pipes, water TANKS (= large containers) and other surfaces in order to stop the heat from escaping or esp. water freezing. *The Cold Weather Code advises you to ensure that you have thick lagging around pipes and tanks with no parts left uncovered.* ○ *The existing lagging is bulky and inefficient.*

lag *obj* PRISON /læg/ *v* [T] *Aus infml* to send (someone) to prison, or to ARREST (someone)

lag /læg/ *n* [C] *Br and Aus infml* • A lag is a prisoner or a person who has often been a prisoner in the past: *an* **old** *lag*

la·ger /£'lɑː·gəʳ, $-gɚ/ *n* a type of beer which is pale in colour and usually contains a lot of bubbles • *Two pints of lager and a packet of crisps, please.* [U] • *Did he want lager or bitter?* [U] • *Do you fancy a lager* (= a glass, bottle or CAN of lager)*?* [C] • *(Br infml)* **Lager louts** are groups of young men whose behaviour is noisy, offensive and often violent after drinking too much alcohol.

lag·ging /'læg·ɪŋ/ *n* See at LAG COVER

la·goon /lə'guːn/ *n* [C] an area of sea water separated from the sea by a REEF (= a line of rocks and sand) • *a tropical lagoon*

lah–di–dah /ˌlɑː·dɪ'dɑː/ *adj* LA-DI-DA

laid /leɪd/ *past simple and past participle of* LAY • *Have you laid the table?* • *She laid the baby down on its front.*

laid–back /ˌleɪd'bæk/ *adj infml* relaxed in manner and character; not tending to get anxious about other people's behaviour or things that need to be done • *I've never seen her worried or anxious in any way – she's so laid-back.* • *For an office it's fairly laid-back – you can choose your own hours and which days you want to work.* • *He's got a laid-back* **attitude** *to timetables and schedules.*

laid up *adj* [after v; not gradable] See at LAY

lain /leɪn/ *past participle of* LIE [POSITION] • *After I'd lain down for an hour my headache went.*

lair /£leəʳ, $ler/ *n* [C usually sing] a place where a wild animal lives, often underground and hidden, or a place where a person hides • *a fox's lair* • *the thieves' lair*

laird /£leəd, $lerd/ *n* [C] a Scottish man who owns a large area of land

lais·sez–faire /£ˌleɪ·seɪˈfeəʳ, $-ˈfer/, **lais·ser–faire** *n* [U] unwillingness to get involved in or influence other people's activities • If a government has a policy of laissez-faire it does not have many laws and rules which control the buying and selling of goods and services: *Insofar as they have an economic programme at all it seems to be all-out laissez-faire.* • *The problems began long before he became headteacher, but they worsened under his laissez-faire* **approach/attitude.**

la·i·ty /£ˈleɪ·ə·ti, $-t̬i/ *n* [U + sing/pl v] See at LAY [CHURCH]

lake /leɪk/ *n* [C] a large area of water that is not salty, surrounded by land and not connected to the sea except by rivers or streams • *We used to go boating on that lake.* • *Lake Windermere* • *(disapproving)* A milk/oil/wine etc. lake is the result of too much of a liquid product being produced, making it necessary to store it or waste it: *Overproduction caused butter mountains and wine lakes.*

la·ma /ˈlɑː·mə/ *n* [C] a title given to a Tibetan Buddhist spiritual teacher • See also DALAI LAMA.

La·ma·i·sm /ˈlɑː·mə·ɪ·zᵊm/ *n* [U] • Lamaism is a way of referring to Tibetan Buddhism.

lamb /læm/ *n* a young sheep, or the flesh of a young sheep eaten as meat • *She watched the lambs gambolling about in the fields.* [C] • *I chose lamb for the meat course.* [U] • *lamb chops* [U] • *roast lamb* [U] • If a person does something or goes somewhere **like a lamb to the slaughter** they do it without knowing what is going to happen and therefore act calmly and without fighting against the situation. • In the Christian religion, **The Lamb (of God)** is another name for Christ. • *"Mary had a little lamb"* (nursery rhyme by Sarah Josepha Hale, 1830) • See also MUTTON.

lamb /læm/ *v* [I] • When sheep lamb they give birth to lambs. • The **lambing season** is the time in the year when sheep give birth to lambs.

lam·ba·da /læmˈbɑː·də/ *n* [C] a dance, originally from Brazil, in which two people hold each other closely and move their hips at the same time

lam·baste *obj*, **lam·bast** *obj* /læmˈbæst/ *v* [T often passive] to criticize (someone or something) severely • *His first novel was well and truly lambasted by the critics.*

lam·bent /ˈlæm·bᵊnt/ *adj literary* shining softly • *a lambent glow* • *(fig.)* Lambent **wit** is clever and playful but not unkind.

lamb·skin /ˈlæm·skɪn/ *n* [U] leather made from the skin of a LAMB with the wool still joined to it

lamb·swool /ˈlæmz·wʊl/ *n* [U] the soft wool which is obtained from a young sheep, used esp. to make clothes • *a lambswool sweater/suit*

lame [UNABLE TO WALK] /leɪm/ *adj* **-r, -st** (esp. of animals) not able to walk correctly because of physical injury to or weakness in the legs or feet • *Infection in this part of the foot can make the horse* **(go)** *permanently lame.* • A **lame duck** is someone or something that is not effective at what they do: *His recovery strategy does not mean old-style intervention which just throws money at lame ducks.* ○ *A lame duck chief justice cannot make many changes in the judicial system.* • In American politics, a **lame duck** is a person who has had an elected position and who is not elected again: *We hope our governor will be a lame duck after election day.*

lame·ness /ˈleɪm·nəs/ *n* [U]

lame [NOT SATISFACTORY] /leɪm/ *adj* **-r, -st** (esp. of an excuse or argument) weak and not deserving to be believed; not satisfactory • *He didn't come to my party because he had a headache which, if you ask me, is a pretty lame* **excuse.**

lame·ly /ˈleɪm·li/ *adv* • *"I think I must have lost my ticket," she told the inspector lamely.*

la·mé /ˈlɑː·meɪ/ *n* [U] a type of cloth with threads of gold or silver in it • *a dress of gold lamé* • *silver lamé trousers*

la·ment *(obj)* /ləˈment/ *v* to express sadness and regret about • *The poem opens by lamenting* **(over)** *the death of a young man.* [T; I + prep] • *My grandmother, as usual, lamented the decline in moral standards in today's society.* [T] • *The* **late** *lamented* (= dead and remembered with affection) *Frank Giotto used to live here.*

la·ment /ləˈment/ *n* [C] • *The whole play can be interpreted as a lament* **for** *lost youth.* • A lament is also a song or a poem which expresses sadness about someone's death.

la·men·ta·tion /ˌlæm·enˈteɪ·ʃᵊn/ *n fml* • *For all the lamentations that schools do not teach the game, it is still played in some areas.* [C] • *Voices were raised* **in** *lamentation.* [U] • *Abruptly, the rejoicing of the chorus turns to lamentation.* [U]

la·ment·a·ble /£ləˈmen·tə·bl̩, £ˈlæm·ən-, $-t̬ə-/ *adj fml* deserving severe criticism; very bad • *the lamentable state of the economy* • *The school's handling of the situation had been, she said, "lamentable".*

la·men·ta·bly /£ləˈmen·tə·bli, $-t̬ə-/ *adv fml* • *The government, says the report, have carried out lamentably few of their promises.*

lam·i·nat·ed /£ˈlæm·ɪ·neɪ·tɪd, $-t̬ɪd/ *adj* [not gradable] consisting of several thin layers of wood, plastic, glass, etc. stuck together, or (of surfaces) covered with a thin protective layer of plastic • *Laminated wood has the advantage of being very strong.* • *The recipe cards are laminated so they can be wiped clean.*

lam·i·nate /ˈlæm·ɪ·nət/ *n* • Laminate is any material which is made by sticking several layers of the same material together: *self-adhesive laminate* [U] ○ *a manufacturer of carpet tiles and laminates* [C] ○ *a laminate finish*

lam·ing·ton /ˈlæm·ɪŋ·tən/ *n* [C; U] *Aus* a type of cake • *A lamington is a sponge cake covered with chocolate icing and coconut.*

lamp /læmp/ *n* [C] a device for giving light, esp. one that has a covering or is contained within something • *an electric/oil lamp* • *a gas lamp* • *a street lamp* • *Could you switch the table/bedside lamp on?* • *a pottery lamp base* • A lamp is also any of various devices that produce particular types of light: *an infrared lamp* • See also SUNLAMP. • [LP>] **Switching on and off** [PIC>] **Beds and bedroom, Lights**

lamp·light /ˈlæmp·laɪt/ *n* [U] *literary* • *We used to cook/read/sew* **by** *lamplight* (= the light produced by a lamp). • *She studied the pale skin of his face* **in the** *dim lamplight.*

lamp·stand /ˈlæmp·stænd/ *n* [C] • A lampstand is the heavy base of a lamp or light, which is often decorated.

lam·poon /læmˈpuːn/ *n* [C] a piece of writing, a poem or drawing, etc. which criticizes in an amusing way a famous person or a public organization, allowing their faults to be seen and making them seem stupid • *The magazine is famed for its merciless political lampoons.*

lam·poon *obj* /læmˈpuːn/ *v* [T] • *The relationship was mercilessly lampooned in all the papers.*

lamp·post /£ˈlæmp·pəʊst, $-poʊst/ *n* [C] a tall post which holds a light, esp. at the side of roads and in other public places • *I wasn't watching where I was going and walked into a lamppost.*

lam·prey /ˈlæm·pri/ *n* [C] a long snake-like fish which uses its sucking mouth to feed off the blood of other animals

lamp·shade /ˈlæmp·ʃeɪd/ *n* [C] a covering which is put over or around a light to reduce brightness or direct the light, and also to look attractive • *We bought matching silk lampshades.* • [PIC>] **Lights**

lance [WEAPON] /£lɑːnts, $lænts/ *n* [C] a long thin pole with a sharp point which soldiers used in the past as a weapon when riding horses • A soldier who is a **lance corporal** has the second lowest rank in the British, Australian or other army.

lanc·er /£ˈlɑːnt·səʳ, $ˈlænt·sɚ/ *n* [C] • A lancer is a soldier who belongs to the part of an army that used lances in the past: *the Queen's Royal Lancers* ○ *The lancers led the procession.*

lance *obj* [CUT] /£lɑːnts, $lænts/ *v* [T] to cut the skin with a sharp tool in order to release infected matter that has collected under it • *She had a* **boil** *lanced at the doctor's this morning.*

lan·cet /£ˈlɑːnt·sɪt, $ˈlænt-/ *n* [C] a small knife with two cutting edges and a sharp point that a doctor uses when cutting the skin

land [DRY SURFACE] /lænd/ *n* [U] the surface of the Earth that is not covered by water • *It is cheaper to drill for oil* **on** *land than at sea.* • *The treaty has led to a dramatic reduction in the number of land-***based** *missiles in Europe.* • *The military commanders won't deploy their land* **forces** *until they're satisfied that the air attacks have done their job.* •

Land also means a particular part of the dry surface of the Earth, sometimes used for a special purpose: *This sort of land is no good for growing potatoes.* ○ *I always prosecute people who trespass on my land.* ○ *We want to buy* **a plot of** *land to build a house.* ○ *Many modern agricultural practices result in tremendous environmental damage to farm land.* ○ *The field was sold as building land.* ○ *They found the bike on a piece of waste land.* • **The** land refers to farms, farming and the countryside: *Most of the families* **lived off** *the land* (=grew their own food etc.). ○ *My parents* **worked (on)** *the land all their lives.* ○ *After a few years living in a city, we wanted to get* **back to the** *land* (=go to live in the countryside instead.) • If you want to **find out** or **see how the land lies**, you want to wait until you have all the available information about a situation before you take any action. • *(Am)* If someone is **land-poor**, they own a lot of land but have little money. • A *(trademark)* **Land Rover** is a strong, powerful vehicle that is designed for travelling over rough or steep ground and is used esp. by people such as farmers who work in the countryside. • **Land tenure** is the rules and arrangements concerned with the ownership of land, esp. land that is used for farming. *Share-cropping is one system of land tenure.* • People who are involved in **land-use policy** or **planning** make decisions about the types of buildings or the uses particular pieces of land can have.

land·ed /ˈlæn·dɪd/ *adj* [before n; not gradable] • Landed families or **the** landed **gentry** are people who have owned a lot of land for many years: *She belongs to one of the oldest landed families in England.* ○ *At that time the courts were suspected of being sympathetic to the landed gentry.*

land·less /ˈlænd·ləs/ *adj* [not gradable] • People who are landless do not have any land for farming or they are prevented from owning the land that they farm by the economic system or by rich people who own a lot of land: *landless labourers/peasants*

lands /lændz/ *pl n fml* • *The family's extensive lands* (=area of ground that they own) *account for most of their wealth.*

land [COUNTRY] /lænd/ *n* [C] *usually literary* a country • *Not everyone enjoys the luxury of living in a land that is free and democratic.* • *The group want to promote their ideas in schools* **throughout** *the land.* • *(infml humorous) She went to bed very late last night, so I don't imagine she'll be in* **the land of the living** (=awake) *before lunchtime.* • A **land flowing with/land of milk and honey** is a country where living conditions are good and people have the opportunity to make a lot of money: *Many Mexicans regard the United States as a land of milk and honey.* • The **Land of the Midnight Sun** is the part of Norway, Sweden and Finland inside the Arctic Circle where the sun is in the sky very late at night in the summer. • *(infml dated) Jamie's in* **the land of nod** (=Jamie's sleeping), *so don't disturb him.* • The **Land of the Rising Sun** is a name for Japan. • *"Land of Hope and Glory, Mother of the Free"* (song *Land of Hope and Glory* written by A.C.Benson, 1902) • *"The Land that Time Forgot"* (title of a book by Edgar Rice Burroughs, 1924) • See also FATHERLAND; HOMELAND; MOTHERLAND. • [LP] **Nations and nationalities**

land *(obj)* [ARRIVE] /lænd/ *v* to (cause to) arrive at a place, esp. after moving down through the air • *I always feel nervous when the plane's* **coming in** *to land.* [I] • *You can land a plane on water in an emergency.* [T] • *The plates landed* **on** *the ground with a loud crash.* [I] • *The report first landed* **on** *my desk this morning.* [I] • *If his punch had landed/If he'd landed* **(with)** *his punch* (=If he had hit me), *I'd have been knocked out.* [I/T] • If you land **on** a particular square in a board game, you have put the object you play with on it according to the rules of the game. [I] • To land is also to arrive in a boat: *We landed at Port Said in the early evening.* [I] • To **land** someone **in/with** an unpleasant situation is to cause them to be involved in it: *Revealing confidential information to a rival company could land you in serious trouble with your boss.* ○ *The demonstration outside the embassy landed some of the protesters in jail overnight.* ○ *I hope you don't mind me landing you with the children at such short notice.* ○ *Alan's gone off on holiday and I've been landed with the job of sorting out his mistakes.* ○ *He really landed himself* **in deep/hot water** (=in a very difficult or unpleasant situation) *when he lied to the tax office about how much he'd earned.* • If you **land on** your **feet**, you return to a good situation after experiencing difficulties, esp. because of good luck rather than skill or hard work: *She was very upset when she lost her job, but she landed on her feet and found another one a week later.* • To **land up** is to arrive in a place at the end of a long journey: *When we accepted that lift in Paris, we never expected to land up in Athens.* To **land up** is also to come to be in an unpleasant situation at the end of a long series of events or actions: *If he carries on drinking like that, he'll land up jobless and penniless.* ○ *However hard I try, I always land up talking to really boring people at Sheila's parties.*

land·ing /ˈlæn·dɪŋ/ *n* [C] • *One person has died after the pilot of a light aircraft was forced to make a* **crash/emergency** *landing in a field.* • The **landing gear** (*Br also* **undercarriage**) of an aircraft with wings is the set of wheels and other parts which support it when it is on the ground and make it possible to take off and land. • A **landing strip** is a long flat area of ground that is used by aircraft with wings when taking off and landing.

land *obj* [UNLOAD] /lænd/ *v* [T] to unload (people or things) from a ship or aircraft onto the ground • *The fishermen's blockade is intended to prevent cheap foreign imports of fish being landed at the port.* • *The general's plan involved landing undercover troops behind enemy lines.* • **Landing craft** are small boats with flat bottoms that open at one end and are used to take soldiers and their equipment from a ship onto land that is controlled by enemy forces. • A **landing stage** is a flat structure, often wooden and floating, that acts as a bridge with the land when loading and unloading boats or ships.

land *obj* [ACHIEVE] /lænd/ *v* [T] to get or achieve (something desirable), esp. in a way which seems easy or unexpected • *The company's survival was secured when it landed a major contract to supply components to a Japanese computer manufacturer.* • *Elaine has just landed an editorial job with a top fashion magazine.* • To land is also to catch a fish with a hook on the end of a fishing rod and remove it from the water: *He landed a huge salmon.*

land·fall /£ˈlænd·fɔːl, $-fɑːl/ *n* (an arrival on) the first land that is reached or seen at the end of a journey across the sea or through the air • *Shannon Airport in Ireland was the first European landfall for airplanes flying from N America.* [C] • *The chances of* **making** *a safe landfall by helicopter in these conditions is only 30%.* [C] • *Twelve hours after landfall/after* **making** *landfall a hurricane has lost about half its power.* [U]

land·fill /ˈlænd·fɪl/ *n* getting rid of large amounts of rubbish by burying it, or a place where rubbish is buried • *The long-term effects of landfill are as hazardous as incineration.* [U] • *Nobody wants to live near a landfill.* [C] • *Ninety per cent of American rubbish is dumped in landfill* **sites.**

land·hold·ing /£ˈlænd,həʊl·dɪŋ, $-hoʊl-/ *n* [C] an area of land that someone owns or rents

land·hold·er /£ˈlænd,həʊl·dəʳ, $-,hoʊl·dɚ/ *n* [C]

land·ing /ˈlæn·dɪŋ/ *n* [C] an area of floor joining two sets of stairs, or an area of floor or a passage at the top of a set of stairs which leads to bedrooms and other rooms • *There's room for a small bookcase* **on** *the landing.*

land·locked /£ˈlænd·lɒkt, $-lɑːkt/ *adj* [not gradable] enclosed by the land of other countries and having no sea coast • *Zimbabwe is a landlocked country, so much of its trade depends on having access to ports in Mozambique.*

land·lord [OWNER], *also* **land·la·dy** /£ˈlænd·lɔːd, $-lɔːrd, -,leɪ·di/ *n* [C] a person or organization who owns a building or an area of land and is paid by other people for the use of it • *The landlord promised to redecorate the bedrooms before we moved in, but he still hasn't done it.* • *Housing associations are the biggest landlords in this area.* • *My landlady's threatening to evict me if I don't pay the rent by the end of the week.*

land·lord [BAR MANAGER] *Br, also* **land·la·dy** /£ˈlænd·lɔːd, $-lɔːrd, -,leɪ·di/, *esp. Aus* **pub·li·can** *n* [C] someone who is in charge of a PUB or bar

land·lub·ber /£ˈlænd,lʌb·əʳ, $-ɚ/ *n* [C] *dated* a person who does not have much knowledge or experience of ships and travelling by sea

land·mark [OBJECT] /£ˈlænd·mɑːk, $-mɑːrk/ *n* [C] a building or place that is easily recognized, esp. one which you can use to judge where you are • *I couldn't pick out any landmarks in the dark and got completely lost.* • *The Rock of Gibraltar is one of Europe's most* **famous** *landmarks.* • *The boat ride on the Moscow River past the Kremlin and other* **historic** *landmarks takes two hours.*

land·marked /£ˈlænd·mɑːkt, $-mɑːrkt/ *adj* • **Landmarked building** is *Am for* **listed building**. See at LIST [RECORD].

land·mark STAGE /£ˈlænd·mɑːk, $-mɑːrk/ *n* [C] an important stage in something's development • *The invention of the silicon chip is a landmark* **in the history of** *the computer.* • *In a landmark* **case/decision**, *the Governor has pardoned a woman convicted of killing her husband, who had physically abused her.*

land·mass /ˈlænd·mæs/ *n* [C] *specialized* a large area of land that is in one piece and not broken up by seas • *Millions of years ago all the southern continents formed a single landmass known as Gondwanaland.*

land·mine /ˈlænd·maɪn/, **mine** *n* [C] a bomb that is hidden in the ground and explodes when a person steps on it or a vehicle drives over it • *Two UN peacekeepers were killed when a massive landmine exploded yesterday.*

land·own·er /£ˈlænd·əʊ·nəʳ, $-oʊ·nɚ/ *n* [C] someone who owns land, often a lot of land • *Local people are protesting against farmers and landowners who block public footpaths.*

land·own·ing /£ˈlænd·əʊ·nɪŋ, $ˈ-oʊ-/ *adj* [before n; not gradable] • *She was born into a wealthy landowning* **family**.

land·scape COUNTRYSIDE /ˈlænd·skeɪp/ *n* [C] a large area of countryside, esp. in relation to its appearance • *a mountainous/rural/wooded landscape* • *The landscape is* **dotted** *with the tents of campers and hikers.* • *The landscape has been* **scarred** *by quarrying and coal mining.* • *They are planning to revitalise vast areas of the* **urban** *landscape* (= the town, its buildings and open spaces) *that business has ignored and deserted for decades.* • A landscape is also a view or picture of the countryside: *a watercolour landscape* ○ *J.M.W. Turner is one of Britain's best-known landscape* **painters**.

land·scape *obj* CHANGE APPEARANCE /ˈlænd·skeɪp/ *v* [T] to change the appearance of (an area of land, esp. next to a building or road) so that it looks more like natural countryside • *The slagheap was still an eyesore after it had been landscaped.* • *It'll take us several months to landscape the garden.* • **Landscape gardening/architecture** is the art of making gardens and parks and the area around buildings look more natural and attractive. Someone who does this is a **landscape gardener/architect** (*Am also* a **landscaper**).

land·scap·er /£ˈlænd,skeɪ·pəʳ, $-pɚ/ *n* [C] • *(Am)* A landscaper is a **landscape gardener**. See at LANDSCAPE CHANGE APPEARANCE.

land·slide FALLING EARTH /ˈlænd·slaɪd/, **land·slip** /ˈlænd·slɪp/ *n* [C] a mass of rock and earth moving suddenly and quickly down a steep slope • *Landslides can be caused by earthquakes and floods.*

land·slide VICTORY /ˈlænd·slaɪd/ *n* [C] the winning of an election with an extremely large number of votes • *The opinion polls are predicting a Liberal landslide in next week's election.* • *His popularity has fallen dramatically since he won a landslide* **victory** *last year.*

lane ROAD /leɪn/ *n* [C] a narrow road in the countryside or in a town • *It is very dangerous to drive fast along narrow country lanes.* • *I live at the end of Church Lane.*

lane STRIP /leɪn/ *n* [C] a specially marked strip of a road, sports track or swimming pool that is used to keep vehicles or competitors separate • *a bus/cycle lane* • *The northbound/southbound/etc. lane is closed because of an accident.* • *You'll need to change lanes if you want to turn off at the next junction.* • *There's bound to be delays when four lanes* **of** *traffic* (= cars in four lines) *merge into two.* • *I find driving in the* **fast** *lane rather stressful so I prefer to stay in the* **middle** *lane or the* **slow** *lane.* • *The British runners/swimmers are in lanes 4 and 6.* • A lane is also a route through the sea or the air which ships or aircraft regularly sail or fly along: *The English Channel is the busiest* **shipping** *lane in the world.* • PIC〉 **Motorway**

lan·guage /ˈlæŋ·gwɪdʒ/ *n* a system of communication consisting of a set of small parts and a set of rules which decide the ways in which these parts can be combined to produce messages that have meaning • *Human language consists of words that are usually spoken or written.* [U] • *"Do you* **speak** *any foreign languages?" "Well, I* **learnt** *three languages at school, but I don't speak any of them fluently."* [C] • *How old is the English language?* [C] • *I found her lecture quite difficult to follow because she used a lot of technical language.* [U] • *COBOL, C and BASIC are three of the most important computer programming languages* (= systems of writing instructions). [C] • *We come from similar backgrounds, so we* **speak/talk the same language** (= we have the same ideas and ways of expressing them), *and understand each other's problems.* • A **language laboratory** (*infml* **language lab**) is a room in a school, college or university in which students use sound recordings, television or computers to learn foreign languages. • LP〉 **Nations and nationalities**

lan·guid /ˈlæŋ·gwɪd/ *adj literary* lacking energy, effort or enthusiasm

lan·guid·ly /ˈlæŋ·gwɪd·li/ *adv literary* • *They lay down languidly on the riverbank and gazed up at the clouds.*

lan·guish /ˈlæŋ·gwɪʃ/ *v* [I] to exist in an unpleasant or unwanted situation, often for a long time • *After languishing* **in obscurity** *for many years, her early novels have recently been rediscovered.* • *He has been languishing* **in jail** *for the past twenty years.* • *The ruling party is languishing* **in** *third place in the opinion polls.* • *Despite the increased profits, the company's shares are still languishing well below last year's peak.*

lan·guor /£ˈlæŋ·gəʳ, $-gɚ/ *n* [U] *literary* pleasant mental or physical tiredness or lack of activity • *She enjoyed living in London, but she missed the languor of a siesta on a hot summer afternoon.*

lan·guor·ous /£ˈlæŋ·gə·rəs, $-gɚ·əs/ *adj literary* • *She was extremely photogenic, in all her various moods: joyous, playful, languorous, meditative.*

lan·guor·ous·ly /£ˈlæŋ·gə·rə·sli, $-gɚ·ə·sli/ *adv literary* • *She lazed languorously by the pool, waiting for Frankie to bring her another drink.*

lank /læŋk/ *adj* **-er, -est** (of hair) unattractively straight and lifeless • *His lank greasy hair looked like it hadn't been washed for a month.*

lank·y /ˈlæŋ·ki/ *adj* **-ier, -iest** tall and thin and tending to move awkwardly as a result • *It was comic to see him trying to get his lanky frame* (= body) *into that small car.*

lan·o·lin /ˈlæn·ə·lɪn/, **lan·o·line** *n* [U] a fatty substance that is obtained from wool and used for making skin creams

lan·tern /£ˈlæn·tən, $-tɚn/ *n* [C] a light enclosed in a container which has a handle for holding it or hanging it up, or the container itself • *The children were carrying coloured* **Chinese/paper** *lanterns.* • PIC〉 **Lights**

lap LEGS /læp/ *n* [C usually sing] the top surface of the upper part of the legs of a person who is sitting down • *Come and sit* **on** *my lap and I'll read you a story.* • *She has quite a high income but I wouldn't say she was living* **in the lap of luxury** (= very great comfort that only extremely rich people have enough money to pay for). • *(Br) The doctors have done everything possible for him, so his recovery now is* **in the lap of the gods** (= cannot be controlled and depends only on luck).

lap *obj* DRINK /læp/ *v* [T] **-pp-** to drink (a liquid) by taking it in small amounts into the mouth with a lot of short quick movements of the tongue • *The cat lapped* **(up)** *the water as if she hadn't had anything to drink for a month.* [T/M] • If a person laps **up** something they take it eagerly and enthusiastically: *He lapped* **up** *the praise as his colleagues congratulated him on his success.* [M] ○ *Shoppers have been lapping the bargains* **up** (= buying eagerly) *in the busiest January sales on record.* [M]

lap *(obj)* HIT GENTLY /læp/ *v* **-pp-** (of waves) to hit (something) gently, producing quiet sounds • *The water lapped* **against** *the side of the pool.* [I] • *The waves gently lapped the shore.* [T]

lap RACING /læp/ *n* [C] a complete journey around a race track that is repeated several times during a competition • *He recorded the fastest lap in last weekend's Hungarian Grand Prix.* • *After a strong start, she was passed by several runners* **in/on** *the final/last lap and finished ninth.* • *(fig.) It is still uncertain who will win the election as the candidates enter the final/last lap* (= part) *of the campaign.* • *(fig.)We're* **on** *the last lap* (= nearly finished) *now.* • *(Br)* A **lap of honour** (*Am* **victory lap**) is a journey around a track or sports field that is made by a winner of a race or a team that has won a game: *After they had* **done** *their lap of honour they were besieged by fans demanding their autographs.*

lap *(obj)* /læp/ *v* **-pp-** • If you lap someone in a race you go past someone who has been round the track one less time than you: *He finished last after being lapped twice by the leading runners.* [T] • To lap is also to make one complete journey around a track: *Senna lapped 1·2 seconds faster than Patrese.* [I]

lap·dog DOG /£ˈlæp·dɒg, $-dɑːg/ *n* [C] a small pet dog that is given too much attention by its owner

lap·dog PERSON /£ˈlæp·dɒg, $-dɑːg/ *n* [C] someone who is willing to do anything that a more important person tells them to do • *Opposition parties accuse the newspaper's editor of being a government lapdog.*

la·pel /lə'pel/ *n* [C] a strip of cloth which is part of the front of esp. a coat. It is joined to the collar and folded back onto the chest. • *His jacket had* **wide/narrow** *lapels.* • *A brooch/ flower was pinned to her lapel.* • *He grabbed me* **by the** *lapels and shook me.* • *All the conference delegates had a lapel* **badge** *with their name on.* • PIC〉 **Clothes**

lapse FAILURE /læps/ *n* [C] a temporary failure • *The management's decision to ignore the safety warnings demonstrates a remarkable lapse* **of** *judgment.* • *A key witness claimed that a lapse* **of memory** *prevented him from remembering exactly what had happened.* • *I called Dr Swift by her first name by mistake, but I don't think she minded my little lapse.*

lapse /læps/ *v* [I] • *Can you explain why the quality of your work has lapsed so much?*

lapse PERIOD /læps/ *n* [U] a period during which something that should happen does not happen • *Except for a lapse of a few weeks when she was taking her exams, she has written to us regularly ever since she left home.*

lapse END /læps/ *v* [I] to end legally or officially by not being continued or made effective for a longer period • *The President's emergency powers will lapse next week unless the parliament agrees to extend them.* • *We will be allowing our contract with you to lapse when it comes up for renewal on December 31st.* • *The association needs to win back former members who have allowed their subscriptions to lapse.*

lapsed /læpst/ *adj* [before n; not gradable] • Lapsed means no longer involved in an activity or organization: *a lapsed member of CND* ○ *a lapsed Catholic* • Lapsed also means no longer being continued or paid: *a lapsed subscription* ○ *lapsed membership*

lapse into *obj v prep* [T] • To lapse into something is to end one activity and change to a less active one: *No one could think of anything more to say, and the meeting lapsed into* **silence**.

lap·top (com·put·er) /£'læp·tɒp, $-tɑːp/, **note·book** *n* [C] a computer which is small enough to be carried around easily and is designed for use outside an office • *A laptop would be really useful for when I'm working on the train.* • Compare DESKTOP COMPUTER, NOTEBOOK, PALMTOP.

lap·wing /'læp·wɪŋ/, **pee·wit** /'piː·wɪt/, **pe·wit** *n* [C] a small dark bird with a white chest and raised feathers on its head

lar·ceny /£'lɑː·sᵊn·i, $'lɑːr-/ *n* stealing, esp. *(Am law)* the crime of taking something that does not belong to you, without getting illegally into a building to do so • *Burglaries have increased by 3%, but larcenies are down 4%.* [C] • *He was charged with larceny.* [U] • LP〉 **Crimes and criminals**

lar·cen·ous /£'lɑː·sᵊn·əs, $'lɑːr-/ *adj Am law* • *The banks were closed because of their larcenous misuse of depositors' money.*

larch /£lɑːtʃ, $lɑːrtʃ/ *n* [C] a tall tree which grows in cold northern countries and loses its needle-shaped leaves in winter

lard /£lɑːd, $lɑːrd/ *n* [U] a soft white creamy substance made from pig fat. It is used in cooking and when making some types of PERFUME (= a pleasant smelling liquid) and OINTMENT (= a type of cream used as a medicine). • (F) (P)

lard *obj* **with** *obj* /£lɑːd, $lɑːrd/ *v prep* [T] *slightly fml* to add (esp. something unnecessary) to (speech or writing) • *Her speech was larded with literary quotations.* • *Many television dramas are larded unnecessarily with swearing and violence.*

lar·der /£'lɑː·dəʳ, $'lɑːr·dɚ/ *n* [C] a cupboard or small room used, esp. in the past, for storing food in a person's home • *a well-stocked* (= full of food) *larder* • *The cat got into the larder and stole tomorrow's lunch.* • *(fig.) People are* **stocking up** *their larders* (= increasing their store of food) *in case of shortages.*

large /£lɑːdʒ, $lɑːrdʒ/ *adj* **-r, -st** bigger or greater than is usual, typical or average • *Who lives in that large house at the end of the road?* • *Are you planning to buy a larger car when the twins are born?* • *Which company is the world's largest computer manufacturer?* • *We didn't expect such a large number of people to attend the concert.* • *We've made good progress, but there's still a large amount of work to be done.* • *(humorous) She was the rather large* (= fat) *lady in the red dress.* • *There was a larger-***than-expected** *fall in unemployment last month.* • *Researchers have just completed the largest-***ever** *survey of criminal behaviour in the UK.* • *The population faces starvation this winter without large-***scale** *emergency food aid.* • *Rachel had told me she wasn't going to the party, but when I arrived she was there,* **(as) large as life** (= behaving in a way which made her presence obvious) *and the centre of attention.* • *Twelve prisoners are* **at large** (= free when they should not be) *following a series of escapes.* • *Abortion is an important issue which needs to be debated by society* **at large** (= by the whole of society together) *and not just by politicians.* • *There's a few small things that I don't like about my job, but* **by and large** (= when everything about my job is considered together) *it's very enjoyable.* • The characteristics of someone or something that is **larger than life** are much more obvious than usual: *She was always larger than life and well-known throughout the hospital.* • The **large intestine** is the lower part of the bowels in which water is removed from digested food before it is excreted as solid waste. • *"It's as large as life and twice as natural"* (Lewis Carroll in his book *Alice Through the Looking-Glass*, 1872) • (E) (F) (P)

lar·gish /£'lɑː·dʒɪʃ, $'lɑːr-/ *adj* [not gradable] • Something that is largish is not small but not very large: *Their new house is largish, but it's not as big as their old one.*

lar·ge·ly /£'lɑːdʒ·li, $'lɑːrdʒ-/ *adv* [not gradable] almost completely • *Until recently the civil war had been largely ignored by the outside world.* • *His mysterious and brutal murder went largely unreported by the press.* • (E)

lar·gesse, lar·gess /£lɑː'ʒes, $lɑːr-/ *n* [U] *fml* generosity of a very rich person, a large organization or a government, or something given because of this • *The national theatre will be the main* **beneficiary** *of the millionaire's largesse.* • *General elections are often preceded by government largesse in the form of tax cuts.*

lark BIRD /£lɑːk, $lɑːrk/, **sky·lark** *n* [C] a small bird which builds its nest on the ground and is well known for singing while it flies • *(esp. Br) I'm catching a train at six o'clock in the morning, so I'll have to* **be up with the lark** (= get out of bed very early).

lark ACTIVITY /£lɑːk, $lɑːrk/, *Br* **sky·lark** *n* [C] *infml* an activity, esp. done for amusement, which is slightly bad but is not intended to cause serious harm or damage • *(dated) We had a few larks at school, didn't we?* • *(dated) The kids hid their teacher's bike* **for a lark**. • *(dated) "Then we let all the air out of her tyres." "Oh, what a lark!"* • Sometimes lark is used to refer to an activity or a situation in a disapproving or doubtful way: *I don't really think I'm suited to this marriage lark* (= to marriage). ○ *I've had enough of this commuting lark* (= of travelling a long way to work every day). ○ *(Br) Sod this* **for a lark**! (= I've had enough of this!) – *I've been waiting for him for an hour and I'm going home.*

lark a·bout/a·round /£lɑːk, $lɑːrk/ *v adv* [I] *infml* • If you lark about or around you behave in a silly or playful way: *I was woken up by a couple of drunks larking around with a dustbin in the street.* ○ *We were just larking about – we didn't mean to do any damage.* • See also SKYLARK ACTIVITY.

lar·ri·kin /'lær·ə·kɪn/ *n* [C] *Aus* a young person who does things which are slightly bad but not intended to cause serious harm

lar·va /£'lɑː·və, $'lɑːr-/ *n* [C] *pl* **larvae** /£'lɑː·viː, $'lɑːr-/ a form of an insect or of some animals such as a FROG that has left its egg but is not yet completely developed • *The larvae of butterflies and moths are called caterpillars.* • *The transformation of a larva into an adult is called metamorphosis.* • PIC〉 **Insects**

lar·val /£'lɑː·vᵊl, $'lɑːr-/ *adj* [not gradable] • *The larval form of a fly is a maggot.*

lar·yn·gi·tis /£ˌlær·ɪn'dʒaɪ·tɪs, $-t̬ɪs/ *n* [U] a painful swelling of the LARYNX that is usually caused by an infection • *Some people temporarily lose their voice when they're suffering from laryngitis.*

lar·ynx (*pl* **larynxes**) /'lær·ɪŋks/, *infml* **voice box** *n* [C] a muscular hollow organ between the nose and the lungs which contains the tissue that moves very quickly to create the human voice and many animal sounds • *She lost the ability to speak when her larynx was removed because of cancer.* • *Men have deeper voices than women because their larynxes are larger.*

la·sa·gne, *Am usually and Aus also* **la·sa·gna** /£lə'zæn·jə, $-'zɑː·njə/ *n* [U] thin wide sheets of pasta, or savoury food consisting of layers of this combined with cheese and meat or vegetables • *Would you like vegetable or meat lasagne?*

las·civ·i·ous /lə'sɪv·i·əs/ *adj fml disapproving* expressing, creating or feeling a desire for sexual activity • *"Why don't* *you come and sit over here next to me, darling," he said, giving her a lascivious leer* (= smile).

las·ci·vi·ous·ly /lə'sɪv·i·ə·sli/ *adv fml disapproving*

las·ci·vi·ous·ness /lə'sɪv·i·ə·snəs/ *n* [U] *fml disapproving*

las·er /£'leɪ·zəʳ, $-zɚ/ *n* [C] (a device which produces) a powerful beam of light that is a single pure colour and consists of light waves moving in exactly the same way as each other • *Lasers are used for cutting hard substances such as metal and for performing delicate surgical operations.* • *Lasers are also used to read information from compact discs and bar codes.* • *Laser* **treatment** *involves the surgeon destroying the cancerous cells with a laser* **beam** *instead of cutting them out with a knife.* • *There were heavy civilian casualties when a laser-***guided** *bomb missed its target.* • A **laser disc** is a disc which stores information in a form that can be obtained using a laser: *Some movies are now available on laser disc as well as on video cassette.* • A **laser printer** is a computer printer which works by shining a laser beam at a tube covered with carbon powder. Powder that is hit by the laser loses its electrical charge and falls off the tube and the powder that is left forms the image to be printed. ○ *The quality and speed of* **laser printing** *are much greater than dot-matrix and bubble-jet systems.* • Ⓟ

lash *(obj)* [HIT] /læʃ/ *v* to hit with a lot of force • *The prisoners were regularly kicked and beaten, and sometimes lashed with electric cable.* [T] • *Twenty people died in the storms which lashed the British Isles at the weekend.* [T] • *The sound of the rain lashing* **against** *the windows was deafening.* [I] • *The salmon was lashing* **around** (= waving its tail violently) *with all its strength as she pulled it out of the water.* [I] • *(fig.) Wherever they perform they always manage to lash* (= excite) *their audience* **into** *a wild frenzy.* [T] • To lash is also to criticize severely: *The job of a restaurant critic is to lash bad restaurateurs and compliment goods ones.* [T] • If someone lashes **out** they suddenly attack someone or something physically or with words: *His attackers lashed out with kicks and punches as he lay on the ground.* [I] ○ *I was only teasing him about his spots and suddenly he lashed out* **(at** *me)* *and hit me in the face.* [I] ○ *Why's Tina in such a bad mood? She really lashed out* **(at** *me)* *when I was late for work.* [I] ○ *The speaker lashed out* **against** *the new regulations.* [I] • See also LASH OUT.

lash /læʃ/ *n* [C] • A lash is a thin strip of leather at the end of a whip, or a hit with this, esp. as a form of punishment: *He received 30 lashes for the crime.* ○ *The punishment for disobedience was* **the** *lash.* • Lash also refers to severe criticism: *The player felt the full lash* **of** *his manager's* **tongue** *for his poor performance.* ○ *The sales team came* **under the lash** (= were severely criticized) *for poor results.* • A lash is also a sudden violent movement of something that can bend: *With a powerful lash of its tail, the fish jumped out of the net and back into the river.* • See also WHIPLASH.

lash·ing /'læʃ·ɪŋ/ *n* [C usually sing] • *Our house takes quite a lashing from the sea and wind.* • *The captain gave him a verbal lashing* (= criticized him severely) *after his disappointing performance.*

lash *obj* [TIE] /læʃ/ *v* [T always + adv/prep] to tie together tightly and firmly • *There isn't enough room for your case inside the car, so I've lashed it* **to** *the roof rack.* • *These poles will be easier to carry if we lash them* **together** *with a rope.*

lash [HAIR] /læʃ/ *n* [C] an EYELASH • *Could you help me get this lash out of my eye?* • [LP]› **Eye and seeing**

lash out *(obj) v adv Br and Aus infml* to spend (a large amount of money) unnecessarily or wastefully • *He lashed out £5000* **for/on** *his daughter's wedding.* [T] • *I like to lash out* **on** *souvenirs when I'm on holiday.* [I] • *We usually live quite cheaply, but we do lash out occasionally.* [I]

lash·ings /'læʃ·ɪŋz/ *pl n Br dated or humorous* a lot of food or drink • *We would always take lashings* **of** *ginger beer with us when we went on a picnic.* • *"Was there much to eat at the party?" "Ooh yes! Lashings!"*

lass /læs/, **las·sie** /'læs·i/ *n* [C] *esp. Scot & N Eng* a girl or young woman • *Kath's a good lass – she always brings me my breakfast in bed.* • *I want our lass* (= daughter) *to have a proper education.* • *In those days we didn't have any tractors, so the lassies from the village would help us with the harvest.* • *Come on, lass, get a move on!* [as form of address]

las·si·tude /£'læs·ɪ·tjuːd, $-tuːd/ *n* [U] *fml or literary* physical or mental tiredness • *Shareholders are blaming the company's problems on the lassitude of the managing director.*

las·so /læs'uː/ *n* [C] *pl* **lassos** or *Am also* **lassoes** a rope which is shaped in a ring at one end, which can be tightened by pulling the other end • *Lassos are used particularly by cowboys to catch cattle and horses.*

las·so *obj* /læs'uː/ *v* [T] he/she/it **lassoes, lassoing,** *past* **lassoed** • If you lasso an animal you catch it by throwing the ring of a lasso over its head and then tightening it around its neck.

last [FINAL] /£lɑːst, $læst/ *adj, adv* [not gradable], *pronoun* (the person or thing) after everyone or everything else • *Why are you always* **the last?** • *I hate being* **the** *last one* **to** *arrive at a meeting.* [+ *to* infinitive] • *She's always* **the** *last* **to** *reply to my invitations.* [+ *to* infinitive] • *Our house is the last one on the left before the traffic lights.* • *The Mets will surely finish the season in last* **place** (= at the lowest rank of their division). • *(esp. Br and Aus) I'm almost finished – this is* **the last but one** *(Am usually* **the next to last***)* (= the one before the final one) *box to empty.* • *I know Johnson finished last in the race, but who was* **second to** *last* /*(Br and Aus also)* **second** *last* (= the one before the one at the end)? • *I don't know why he bothers to bet – his horses always come in last.* • **At** *the last* **moment** (= as late as possible) *he changed his mind.* • *He always leaves important decisions* **to** *the last (possible)* **moment** (= as late as possible). • *I've finished my essay* **at last** (= after too long a time)! • **At long last** (= After a very long period of waiting) *the government is starting to listen to our problems.* • *(fml) I think my policy is right, and I'll defend it* **to the last** (= until the end). • *(fml) She is patriotic* **to the last** (= and she always will be). • *He has calculated the costs* **down to the last** *penny* (= very accurately). • *The model of the village is accurate* **(down) to the last** *detail* (= including every detail). • *Both sides have declared themselves ready to fight* **to the last (man)** (= until every person is dead). • *I would like to thank my publisher, my editor and,* **last but not least** (= importantly, despite being mentioned after everyone else), *my husband without whose encouragement the book would never have been written.* • *He never even thanked me, so that's* **the last time** *I do him a favour* (= I'll never do it again). • A **last-ditch** or **last-gasp** effort or attempt is one which is made at the end of a series of failures to solve a problem, and is not expected to succeed: *In a last-ditch* **attempt** *to save his party from electoral defeat, he resigned from the leadership.* • Someone who has **the last laugh** finally benefits from an argument or disagreement, when it seemed that they would not: *They sacked her six months ago, but she* **had** *the last laugh when she went to work for their rivals for twice the pay.* • **The last minute** is the latest possible opportunity for doing something: *They only told me* **at** *the last minute that they couldn't come, so there wasn't time to invite anyone else.* ○ *When approaching a roundabout, do not* **leave it to** (= wait until) *the last minute to slow down.* ○ *All the major airlines are reporting a flood of* **last-minute** *cancellations following the latest terrorist attacks.* ○ *A* **last-minute** *reprieve is highly unlikely, and his execution next week seems inevitable.* • Your **last name** is your family name and the one that you use in formal situations or with people whom you do not know well: *She refused to give her last name because she wanted to keep her identity secret.* • In a British bar, **last orders** are the drinks that customers are allowed to buy just before the bar closes: *I'm sorry, madam, I* **called** *last orders twenty minutes ago.* ○ *Last orders, please!* • **The last post** is a tune that is played on a BUGLE at military funerals or when it is time for soldiers to go to bed. • **The last rites** are a religious ceremony that is performed for someone who is just about to die: *The chaplain is going to* **administer** *the last rites.* ○ *(fig.) Receivers are accountants who* **give** *the last rites to bankrupt companies.* • The **Last Supper** is the meal Christ ate with his friends the night before he died. • If you do something **last thing** you do it just before you go to bed at night: *I'll switch on the washing machine last thing so it'll be finished when I get up in the morning.* • Your **last will and testament** is your written instructions about what should happen to your possessions after your death. • The **last word** is the final remark in an argument or discussion: *I'm not going to give you a promotion and that's my last word* **on** *the matter.* ○ *She always has to* **have the** *last word* (= win the argument). ○ *Digital audio is* **the** *last word* (= is the best) **in** *sound reproduction.*

last·ly /£'lɑːst·li, $'læst-/, **last** *adv* [not gradable] • Lastly is used to show when something comes after all the other items in a list: *In accepting this award, I would like thank the producer, the director, the scriptwriter and, lastly, the film crew.* ○ *I'll tell you why we can't do it – firstly, we haven't got the expertise, second, we haven't got the money, and lastly, we haven't got the time.*

last NO MORE /£lɑːst, $læst/ *adj* [before n; not gradable], *n* [U], *pronoun* (being) the only one or part that is left • *Do you mind if I have the last chocolate?* • *Could I borrow some money for lunch? I'm down to my last 50p.* • *"Is this the last bag?" "No, there's still one more in the car."* • *I'm afraid Martha's eaten* **the last of** *the ice cream.* • *She was* **the last of** *the great educational reformers.* • *(infml)* If you **hear/see the last of** something unpleasant or difficult it does not cause you trouble again: *I paid them £100 for the damage and I hope that's the last I'll hear of it.* ○ *You haven't heard the last of this! – I'll see you in court.* ○ *He's a horrible man and I hope we've seen the last of him.* • *We'll never* **hear the last of it** (= They won't stop talking about it) *if they win that competition.* • *(infml)* Something that is **on its last legs** is in such bad condition that it will soon be unable to work as it should: *My bike's on its last legs, but it still gets me to work in the morning.* • *(infml)* A person who is **on their last legs** is very tired or near to death: *We'd been out walking all day and I was on my last legs when we reached the hotel.* ○ *It looks as though her grandfather's on his last legs.* • *British police are supposed to use guns only* **as a last resort** *(Br also* **in the last resort***)* (= if all other ways fail). • *"Last Tango in Paris"* (title of a film, 1972)

last MOST RECENT /£lɑːst, $læst/ *adj, adv* [not gradable], *pronoun* (being) the most recent or the one before the present one • *Did you hear the storm last night* (= during the previous night)? • *Did you see the news on TV* **last night** (= yesterday evening)? • *They got married last November.* • *When was the last time you had a cigarette?* • *When did you have a cigarette last.* ○ *When did you last have a cigarette?* • *I last had a cigarette six years ago.* • *She started working there last month.* • *She's been working there for the last month* (= for the four weeks until now). • *This month's weather has been even worse than last month's.* • *We had lunch together the week* **before last** (= during the week before this one). • *Where were you last Sunday?* • *(fml) Could you account for your whereabouts on Sunday last?* • *We went skiing in France last year and we're hoping to go again next year.* • *The/These last five years have been very difficult for him.* • **The** *last we heard of her, she was working as an English teacher in France.* • *He visited us a few months ago, but that's* **the** *last we've seen of him.* • *Her work is always improving. Each of her paintings is better than* **the** *last.* • LP **Calendar**

last UNSUITABLE /£lɑːst, $læst/ *adj* [before n; not gradable] the most unsuitable, unwanted or unlikely • *Travelling five hundred miles by car with two small children is* **the** *last* **thing** *I want to do.* • **The** *last* **thing** *I wanted was to make you unhappy.* • *He's* **the** *last* **person** *I want to see at the moment.* • *Chris is* **the** *last* **person** *I'd expect to be interested in physics.* • *They're* **the** *last* **people** *to trust with a job as important as this.*

last *(obj)* CONTINUE /£lɑːst, $læst/ *v* to continue to exist • *How long will the meeting last?* [I] • *The meeting lasted two hours.* [L only + n] • *The rain is expected to last all weekend.* [L only + n] • *The drought lasted* **for** *several months.* [I] • *They say the snow will last* **until** *the end of next week.* [I] • *I can't see the ceasefire lasting.* [I] • *I'm trying to make this box of chocolates last longer than the previous one.* [I] • *We only have enough supplies to last (us) a week* (= There will be nothing left after a week). [L (+ obj) + n] • *They haven't had an argument for two weeks, but it's* **too good** **to** *last* (= they'll have an argument soon). [I] • *I doubt their enthusiasm will last.* [I] • *He's working very efficiently at the moment, but it can't/won't last.* [I] • To last/*(Br also)* **last out** also means to continue to stay active or alive: *How long can they last* **(out)** *without food?* [I] ○ *Her previous secretary only lasted a month* (= left after this period). [L only + n] ○ *He won't last* **(out)** *the night* (= he will die tonight). [L only + n] ○ *Many of the refugees are too weak to last* **(out)** (= still be alive at the end of) *the winter.* [L only + n] • If you **won't last five minutes/won't last long** you will not be successful: *England's got no chance of winning the match against Scotland – they won't last five minutes.* ○ *I wouldn't last five minutes in the police force – it's far too tough for me.* ○ *You won't last long in your job if you carry on being so rude to the customers.* • To last is also to continue being good or suitable: *There's no point buying something that isn't going to last.* [I] • *The cheaper washing machines should last about five years.* [L only + n] • *This pen should last (you) a lifetime if you look after it.* [L (+ obj) + n]

last·ing /£ˈlɑː·stɪŋ, $ˈlæs·tɪŋ/ *adj* • Something that is lasting continues to exist for a long time or forever: *Few observers believe that the treaty will bring a lasting* **peace** *to the region.* ○ *Did any of your teachers make a lasting* **impression** *on you?* ○ *The strike has done lasting* **damage** *to the company's reputation.* ○ *The tablets make you feel better for a while but the effect isn't* **(long-)***lasting.*

lat /læt/ *n* [U] *abbreviation for* LATITUDE POSITION • *lat 20°N*

latch /lætʃ/ *n* [C] a device for keeping a door or gate closed without locking it that consists of a movable bar which fits into a hole and which is lifted by pushing down on another bar • *(Br)* Some locks have a button on the inside of a door which can prevent the door from being opened from the outside, and if a door with such a lock is **on the latch**, the button is in a position which allows the door to be opened: *Don't forget to* **leave** *the front door on the latch if you go to bed before I get back.* • PIC **Locks and home security**

latch *(obj)* /lætʃ/ *v* • *The cargo door opened in mid-flight because it had not been latched properly before takeoff.* [T] • *That gate won't latch shut.* [I]

latch on *v adv* [I] *Br infml* to begin to understand • *You'll have to explain what you want him to do slowly and clearly, otherwise he won't latch on.* • *It took me ages to latch on* **to** *what she was talking about.*

latch on·to *obj v prep* [T] *infml* to become connected to • *The antibodies work by latching onto proteins on the surfaces of the viruses and bacteria.* • *(fig.) She latched onto me as soon as she arrived and I had to spend the rest of the evening talking to her.* • *(fig.) Tom always takes a while to latch onto* (= become interested in) *new ideas.*

latch·key child /ˈlætʃ·kiː/ *n* [C usually pl] a child who has a key to his or her home and is often alone at home after school has finished for the day because his or her parents are out at work • *The survey found that latchkey children usually call their parents at work to tell them that they were safely home from school.*

late NEAR THE END /leɪt/ *adj, adv* **-r, -st** (happening or being) near the end of a period or in the recent past • *"Could we arrange a meeting for late tomorrow morning?" "How about 11 o'clock?"* • *This part of town gets quite dangerous later at night.* • *We talked late into the night.* • *Late last night* (= In the middle of the night) *he phoned me to ask for my advice.* • *Her controversial late-***night** *show has made her a household name.* • *Goodness! Is that the time? I'd no idea* **it** *was so late.* • *Is* **it** *too late* **to** *call Jean?* [+ to infinitive] • *Late summer is my favourite time of year.* • *He'll be home in late March.* • *You could get a cheaper flight if you were willing to go later in the season.* • *That sort of hairstyle went out of fashion in the late eighties.* • *I think he's in his late twenties, but he looks a lot older.* • *He's an expert on late nineteenth-century literature.* • *I prefer her earlier paintings to her later work.* • *What's the latest time that we can arrive?* • *As late* (= As recently) *as the 1980s they were still using horses on this farm.* • *We used to hear from him regularly, but he hasn't been in touch* **of late** (= recently). • *"It is Later than you Think"* (title of a poem by Robert Service, 1921) • See also LATEST. Compare EARLY. • Ⓟ

late·ly /ˈleɪt·li/ *adv* [not gradable] • Lately means recently: *Have you been doing anything interesting lately?* ○ *We lived in Manchester until lately.* ○ *The factory has been sold just lately to a small engineering firm.* ○ *(fml) Dr Averley, lately (also* **late***)* **of** (= until recently working at) *Newcastle General Hospital, will be joining us next month.*

late·ness /ˈleɪt·nəs/ *n* [U] *fml* • *Given the lateness* **of the hour***, she left writing the rest of the letters until the next day.*

late AFTER /leɪt/ *adj, adv* **-r, -st** (happening or arriving) after the planned, expected, usual or necessary time • *This train is always late.* • *You'll be late* **for** *your flight if you don't hurry up.* • *Sorry I'm late. I was held up in the traffic.* • *How come you got up so late this morning?* • *Summer started late* (= The weather became warm after the usual time) *that year.* • *It's too late to start complaining now.* • *We always have a late breakfast on Sunday mornings.* • *England's performance was not helped by the unexpected late changes to the team.* • *Some late* **news** (= news of something which happened after the news programme started) *has just come in – a bomb has exploded in central London.* • *Our ferry was two hours late because of the strike.* • *Pat's just phoned to say she's working late and won't be back till nine.* • *A spokeswoman for the charity described the aid for the refugees as* **too little, too late**. • Something that is **late in the day** happens much later than is necessary and would have been better done earlier: *It's rather late in the day to start studying – your exams are next week.* • *I'm just going into town for a couple of hours, so I'll see you later.* • *She said she'd prefer us to arrive* **no** *later* **than** (=not after) *nine o'clock.* • **Later on** is a slightly more informal way of saying later: *What are you doing later on this evening?* • *(infml)* **See you/Talk to you/Catch you** later (*Am also* Later) can mean goodbye: *"Bye, have a good weekend." "Thanks, see you later."* • *I have to get this finished by Friday* **at the latest** (=not after Friday). • *We should arrive by twelve* **at the very latest** (=certainly not after twelve). • *(Br)* A **late developer** (*Am and Aus* **late bloomer**) is someone who becomes good at something after people usually become good at it: *At school she was a late developer, and it wasn't until she went to university that her talents became apparent.* • See also LATECOMER. Compare EARLY. • Ⓟ

late·ness /ˈleɪt·nəs/ *n* [U] • *Complaints about lateness, cancellations and overcrowding on public transport are the highest on record.*

late [DEAD] /leɪt/ *adj* [before n; not gradable] no longer alive, esp. having recently died • *She gave her late husband's clothes to charity.* • [LP] **Relationships** Ⓟ

late·com·er /£ˈleɪtˌkʌm·əʳ, $-ɚ/ *n* [C] a person who arrives late • *We regret that latecomers cannot be admitted until a suitable break in the performance.*

la·tent /ˈleɪ·tᵊnt/ *adj* [not gradable] present but needing particular conditions to become active, obvious or completely developed • *Recent developments in the area have brought latent ethnic tension out into the open.* • *We're trying to bring out the latent artistic talents that many people possess without realising it.* • *A new treatment causes the disease to enter a latent phase during which all symptoms disappear, but the sufferer will never be fully cured.*

la·tenc·y /ˈleɪ·tᵊnt·si/ *n* [U] *fml*

lat·er·al /£ˈlæt·rᵊl, $ˈlæt̬·ɚ·ᵊl/ *adj* [not gradable] *specialized* relating to the sides of an object or to sideways movement • *Strong lateral forces are exerted on the driver of a racing car that is travelling round a bend.* • *Lateral shoots on a plant are ones which grow sideways from the main stem.* • **Lateral thinking** is a way of solving a problem by thinking about it imaginatively and originally and not using traditional or expected methods.

lat·er·al·ly /£ˈlæt·rᵊl·i, $ˈlæt̬·ɚ·ᵊl·i/ *adv specialized* • *To solve this puzzle you'll need to* **think** *about it laterally.*

lat·est /£ˈleɪ·tɪst, $-t̬ɪst/ *adj* [before n; not gradable], *n* [U] the newest or most recent or modern (thing in a series of things) • *Have you seen her latest movie?* • *This is just the latest of several crises to affect the department.* • *This machine is* **the latest in** *video recorder technology.* • *Have you heard* **the latest** (=the most recent news) **about** *Pam and Patrick – they're getting a divorce*

la·tex /ˈleɪ·teks/ *n* [U] a white liquid produced by many plants, esp. rubber trees, or a rubber-like substance made from this or from plastic, which is used in making clothes, paint, glue, etc. • *a latex mask* • *a pair of latex surgical gloves*

lath /£lɑːθ, $læθ/ *n* [C] a long thin flat strip of wood, used to make a structure to support PLASTER on walls or TILES on the roof of a building • *a lath* **and plaster** *wall*

lathe /leɪð/ *n* [C] a machine for changing the shape of a piece of wood, metal, etc. which works by turning the material while a sharp tool is pressed against it.

lath·er /£ˈlɑː·ðəʳ, $ˈlæð·ɚ/ *n* [U] a pale, usually white, mass of small bubbles produced esp. when soap is mixed with water • *Wet the hair, apply shampoo and massage into a rich lather.* • Lather is also small bubbles of SWEAT produced by physical effort: *The horse's neck was covered with lather.* • If someone is **in a lather** or gets **into a lather** they are (becoming) upset or excited and not able to think clearly: *Don't* **work yourself** *into a lather – she'll be here soon.* ○ *The fans, who had been waiting for several hours, were in a real lather.*

lath·er *(obj)* /£ˈlɑː·ðəʳ, $ˈlæð·ɚ/ *v* • *Most soaps won't lather in sea water.* [I] • *He stood under the shower lathering himself with the soap.* [T]

lath·er·y /£ˈlɑː·ðᵊr·i, $ˈlæð·ɚ-/ *adj* • *This shaving foam isn't very lathery.*

Lat·in /£ˈlæt·ɪn, $ˈlæt̬-/ *n* [U] the language used by ancient Romans and as the language of educated people in many European countries in the past

Lat·in /£ˈlæt·ɪn, $ˈlæt̬-/ *adj* [not gradable] • *a Latin poem* • Latin also refers to countries which use a language which developed from Latin: *Italy, Spain, Portugal, France, Mexico and Brazil are Latin countries.* ○ *She came from Spain, and had the fiery Latin temperament.* • A **Latin lover** is a dark, attractive and sexually experienced man.

Lat·in A·mer·i·can /£ˈlæt·ɪn, $ˈlæt̬-/ *n* [C], *adj* [not gradable] (a person) from South America, Central America or Mexico • Latin American (also **Latin**) is a type of BALLROOM dancing (=dancing in formal clothes) which is based on South American dances, or the music for this.

La·ti·no *male* (*pl* **Latinos**), *female* **La·ti·na** (*pl* **Latinas**) /£ˌlætˈiː·nəʊ, $-noʊ, -nə/ *n* [C] *esp. Am* a person who lives in the US and who comes from or whose family comes from Latin America

lat·i·tude [POSITION] /£ˈlæt·ɪ·tjuːd, $ˈlæt̬·ɪ·tuːd/ *n* the position north or south of the equator measured from 0° to 90° • *The village of Cranbrook in Kent, England, lies just south of latitude 51 degrees 10 minutes North.* [U] • *Generally for the Scandinavian resorts, the higher the latitude* (=the further north they are) *the more snow there is.* [U] • *The town is at a low latitude* (=in the south). [C] • Compare LONGITUDE.

lat·i·tudes /£ˈlæt·ɪ·tjuːdz, $ˈlæt̬·ɪ·tuːdz/ *pl n* • *At these latitudes* (=area near to a particular latitude) *the sun does not rise at all on winter days.*

lat·i·tud·in·al /£ˌlæt·ɪˈtjuː·dɪ·nəl, $ˌlæt̬·ɪˈtuː-/ *adj* [not gradable] *specialized* • *The navigational error was due to a latitudinal miscalculation.*

lat·i·tude [FREEDOM] /£ˈlæt·ɪ·tjuːd, $ˈlæt̬·ɪ·tuːd/ *n* [U] *fml* freedom to behave, act or think in the way you want to • *Courts can show a considerable* **degree of** *latitude when it comes to applying that particular law.* • *We give them latitude to generate their own ideas when choosing a career.*

la·trine /ləˈtriːn/ *n* [C] a toilet, esp. a simple one such as a hole in the ground, used in a military area or when CAMPING (=living in a tent for a short period)

lat·ter [END] /£ˈlæt·əʳ, $ˈlæt̬·ɚ/ *adj* [before n; not gradable] near or towards the end of something • *Building of the new library should begin in* **the latter part** *of next year.* • *In* **the** *latter* **stages** *of the fight he began to tire.* • **Latter-day** means a new form of a person or thing from the past: *They are the evil actions of a latter-day Caligula.*

lat·ter [SECOND] /£ˈlæt·əʳ, $ˈlæt̬·ɚ/ *n* [U + sing/pl v], *adj* [before n] **the latter** the second of two people, things or groups previously mentioned • *We have to decorate the kitchen and the hall – I'd rather do the latter (room) first.* • *There are plastic and wooden garden chairs but the latter are more expensive.* • *(not standard)* The latter is sometimes used to mean the last of more than two people, things or groups previously mentioned. • Compare FORMER [FIRST].

lat·ter·ly /£ˈlæt·ə·li, $ˈlæt̬·ɚ-/ *adv* [not gradable] *fml* recently • *Latterly, her concentration hasn't been so good when under pressure.*

lat·tice /£ˈlæt·ɪs, $ˈlæt̬-/, **lat·tice·work** /£ˈlæt·ɪs·wɜːk, $ˈlæt̬·ɪs·wɜːrk/ *n* [C] a structure made from strips of wood or other material which cross over each other with spaces between • *a lattice screen* • *a latticework basket* • A **lattice window** is a window made from small pieces of glass which are held in place by metal strips.

laud·a·ble /£ˈlɔː·də·bl̩, $ˈlɑː-/ *adj fml* (of actions and behaviour) deserving praise, even if there is little or no success • *The report is a laudable attempt to bring the problem to a wider audience.* • *Her concern for accurate recording is laudable.* • *The recycling programme is laudable, but does it save much money?*

laud·a·bly /£ˈlɔː·də·bli, $ˈlɑː-/ *adv*

laud·a·tory /£ˈlɔː·də·tri, $ˈlɑː-/ *adj fml* • *She was the subject of laudatory* (=expressing praise) *articles in several New York magazines.*

laud *obj* /£lɔːd, $lɑːd/ *v* [T] *fml* • *The German leadership had lauded* (=praised) *the Russian initiative.*

laugh /£lɑːf, $læf/ *v* [I] to make the typical sound of being happy or amused • *They all laughed when she fell over.* • *What a brilliant comedian – we couldn't stop laughing.* • *He laughed nervously when they asked him where he had been on that evening.* • *The joke made her laugh* **aloud/out loud**. • *All of the children were laughing* **at** *the clown, who was pretending to eat a book.* • If you laugh **at** someone or something you treat them as if they are not important or do not deserve serious attention: *If you don't say something better than that, people will just laugh* **at** *you.* ○ *Some of these stunt artists simply laugh* **at** *danger.* • *She's so amusing – she* **makes me laugh**. • *His threats* **make me laugh** (=I don't take them seriously). • *You'll pay?* **Don't make me laugh** (=I don't take your suggestion seriously)*!* • *It was so* *funny that we laughed* **till/until** *we* **cried.** • *(infml) We'll* **be laughing all the way to the bank** (=earning lots of money easily) *if this deal works out.* • *(Br infml)* If someone **is laughing** they do not need to be worried by a particular situation, esp. because they will get some benefit from it: *If the storm holds off until we get to the shelter we'll be laughing.* ○ *If the loan is approved you'll be laughing.* • *(infml)* To **laugh** your **head off** is to laugh loudly and strongly or *(fig.)* to suggest that you don't believe something: *What a ludicrous story – I laughed my head off.* • If you **laugh in** someone's **face** you show them an obvious lack of respect: *He suggested that they go on holiday together but she laughed in his face.* • *(Br infml)* When someone **laughs like a drain** they laugh very loudly. • *It would be easy to* **laugh off** *his criticism* (=pretend that it is less serious than it really is), *but he did make some valid points.* • If someone **laughs on the other side of** their **face**/*(Am also)* **laughs out of the other side of** their **mouth** they were pleased at first but now they are upset or disappointed, esp. because something does not happen as they planned: *She's pleased with her promotion but she'll be laughing on the other side of her face when she sees the extra work.* • *(dated) It was an excellent film – we* **laughed** *ourselves* **silly** (=laughed very much). • *The proposal for redevelopment of the area was* **laughed out of court** (=dismissed because it was too silly). • *They're very polite in his presence, but all the time they're* **laughing up** *their* **sleeves** (=are secretly amused) *at him.* • *It might seem funny to you but getting stuck up a tree was* **no laughing matter** (=was serious). • *(infml) Sorry I smiled but no one was hurt and besides* **you've got to laugh/you have to laugh** (=you must find the humour in a situation rather than worry about what might have happened). • **Laughing gas** is a type of gas which is used as an ANAESTHETIC (=substance which makes you unable to feel pain). • A **laughing stock** is someone or something which seems stupid or ridiculous, esp. by trying to be serious or important and not succeeding: *Another performance like that and this team will be* **the** *laughing stock* **of** *the league.* ○ *Stop fooling around – you're* **making** *yourself a laughing stock.* • *(saying)* 'He who laughs last laughs longest/*(Am usually)* best' means the person who has control of a situation in the end is most successful even if other people had seemed originally to have an advantage. • *"Laugh and the world laughs with you; / Weep, and you weep alone"* (in the poem *Solitude* by Ella Wheeler Wilcox, 1883)

laugh /£lɑːf, $læf/ *n* [C] • *She let out a small laugh when she heard the noise.* • *"That's wonderful," Mitch said with a laugh (in his voice).* • *Some of the comedians* **got**/*(Br and Aus also)* **raised** *a laugh or two but none of them was particularly funny.* • *(infml)* You can also use laugh to mean an enjoyable or amusing activity: *Wouldn't it be a great laugh to set light to the bottom of his newspaper while he's reading it!* ○ *The office picnic was a real laugh.* • *(infml)* If you do something **for a laugh/for laughs** you do it for amusement: *Don't get uptight – we only did it for a laugh.* ○ *He didn't need the money, he just took the job for laughs.* • *(esp. Br infml)* If someone is described as a laugh it means they are an amusing person to be with: *Invite Sharon – she's* **a good** *laugh*/**a bit of a** *laugh.*

laugh·a·ble /£'lɑː·fə·bl̩, $'læf·ə-/ *adj* • *Privately they thought the idea laughable* (=foolish and not deserving serious attention).

laugh·ing·ly /£'lɑː·fɪŋ·li, $'læf·ɪŋ-/ *adv* • *He laughingly* (=He laughed as he) *told us of the confusion caused by our mistake.* • *It is only one of the absurd rules in the system of law laughingly* (=unsuitably) *known as British justice.*

laugh·ter /£'lɑːf·tər, $'læf·tɚ/ *n* [U] • Laughter is the act or sound of laughing: *She simply* **roared with** *laughter.* ○ *As we approached the hall we could hear laughter.* • *(saying)* 'Laughter is the best medicine' means that trying to be happy is a good way to fight worries. • *"Laughter in the Dark"* (title of a book by Vladimir Nabokov, 1932)

launch *obj* SEND /£lɔːntʃ, $lɑːntʃ/ *v* [T] to send (something) out, such as a new ship into water or a ROCKET into space • *A spokesman for the dockyard said they hoped to launch the first submarine within two years.* • *Before launching the missile the pilot locks it onto the target.* • *In a real war the missiles would leave their bases for launch/launching* **sites** *in wooded areas of the countryside.* • *(fig. esp. Br) The defender launched* **himself** (=jumped with great force) **at** *the attacking player, bringing him to the ground.* • A **launch pad** (also **launching pad**) is a special area from which ROCKETS or MISSILES are launched: *The rocket blew up on the launch pad.* • PIC› **Pad**

launch /£lɔːntʃ, $lɑːntʃ/ *n* [C] • *The launch of the space shuttle was delayed for 24 hours because of bad weather.*

launch·er /£'lɔːn·tʃər, $'lɑːn·tʃɚ/ *n* [C] • *a mobile* **rocket** *launcher*

launch *(obj)* BEGIN /£lɔːntʃ, $lɑːntʃ/ *v* to begin (something such as a plan) or introduce (something new such as a product) • *Although a job-sharing scheme was launched a year ago very few people have shown any interest in it.* [T] • *Early last year the company researched the possibility of launching a new late-night show.* [T] • *A devastating attack was launched* **on** *the rebel stronghold, leaving many of them dead.* [T] • *He launched* **into** *a verbal attack on her handling of the finances.* [I always + adv/prep] • *(Br) After working for the company for several years she decided to launch* **out** *(by) herself/on her own and set up in business.* [I always + adv/prep]

launch /£lɔːntʃ, $lɑːntʃ/ *n* [C] • A launch (also **launch party**) is an event to celebrate or introduce something new: *Yes, the author will be at the launch of/at the launch party for her latest novel.*

launch BOAT /£lɔːntʃ, $lɑːntʃ/ *n* [C] a boat which has an engine and carries passengers for short distances, esp. on a lake or a river, or from the land to a larger boat

laun·der *obj* CLOTHES /£'lɔːn·dər, $'lɑːn·dɚ/ *v* [T] to wash, dry and IRON (=make smooth) (bed sheets, clothes, etc.) • *Tomorrow will you take the sheets to be laundered please.*

laun·dry /£'lɔːn·dri, $'lɑːn-/ *n* • Laundry is the dirty clothes and sheets which need to be, are being or have been washed: *When shall we* **do** (=wash) *the laundry?* [U] • A laundry is a business which washes clothes, sheets, etc. for customers. [C] • A **laundry basket** (*Am* also **hamper**) is a large container which dirty clothes are kept in until they are washed. • PIC› **Basket**

laun·der *obj* MONEY /£'lɔːn·dər, $'lɑːn·dɚ/ *v* [T] to move (money which has been obtained illegally) through banks and other businesses to make it seem to have been obtained legally • *Officials were accused of laundering the stolen funds overseas before returning them to the US.*

laun·der·ette *esp. Br,* **laun·drette** /£ˌlɔːn'dret, $ˌlɑːn-/, *trademark Am and Aus* **laun·dro·mat** /£'lɔːn·drə·mæt, $'lɑːn-/ *n* [C] a shop where you pay to use the machines there which will wash, and sometimes dry, clothes • *"My Beautiful Laundrette"* (film title, 1985)

lau·re·ate /£'lɒr·i·ət, $'lɑːr-/ *n* [C] a person who has been given a very high honour because of their ability in a subject of study • *a Nobel laureate*

laur·el /£'lɒr·əl, $'lɑːr-/ *n* [C/U] a small evergreen tree which has shiny leaves and small black fruit • A **laurel wreath** is a circle of leaves which, in the past, was worn on the head by an important person or the winner of a competition, or *(fig.)* an honour.

laur·els /£'lɒr·əlz, $'lɑːr-/ *pl n* praise for a person because of something which they have done, usually in sport, the arts or public life • *The actors are very good, but when all is considered the laurels must surely go to the director of the play.*

lav /læv/ *n* [C] *Br and Am infml for* LAVATORY (=toilet) • *the school lavs*

la·va /'lɑː·və/ *n* [U] hot liquid rock which comes out of the earth through a VOLCANO, or the solid rock formed when it cools • *molten lava* • *a lava flow*

lav·a·tory *esp. Br* /'læv·ə·tri/, *Br and Am infml* **lav** *n* [C] a toilet • LP› **Phrases and customs** PIC› **Bathroom** Ⓟ

lav·a·tor·i·al /£læv·ə'tɔː·ri·əl, $-tɔːr·i-/ *adj Br esp. disapproving* • **Lavatorial humour** refers to jokes about toilets and related subjects.

lav·end·er PLANT /£'læv·ɪn·dər, $-dɚ/ *n* [U] a plant which has grey-green needle-like leaves and small pale purple flowers with a strong smell, or its dried flowers and stems which are sometimes kept with sheets and clothes to make them smell pleasant • *The path was edged with lavender.* • *She put a lavender* **bag** (=small bag filled with dried lavender flowers) *in every drawer.*

lav·end·er COLOUR /£'læv·ɪn·dər, $-dɚ/ *adj* [not gradable], *n* [U] (of) a pale purple colour

lav·ish /'læv·ɪʃ/ *adj* more than enough, esp. if expensive; very generous • *lavish gifts/promises* • *lavish spending* • *lavish banquets* • *No doubt the evening will be a lavish affair, with the best food and wine and a professional band.* • *The lavish production makes the musical truly* memorable. • *Cost-effectiveness is so often the subject of lavish* **praise** *these days.*

lav·ish·ly /ˈlæv·ɪʃ·li/ *adv* • *The studio is lavishly equipped with cameras and audio equipment.*

lav·ish·ness /ˈlæv·ɪʃ·nəs/ *n* [U]

lav·ish *obj* **on** *obj* /ˈlæv·ɪʃ/ *v prep* [T] • When you lavish something on someone or something, you give them a lot, or too much, of it: *The attention she lavishes on her hair makes her feel better.* ○ *The British lavish time, effort and huge sums of money on pets.*

law RULE /£lɔː, $lɑː/ *n* a rule, usually made by a government, that is used to order the way in which a society behaves, or the whole system of such rules • *Don't forget there's a law about exporting certain antiques.* [C] • *The laws* **governing** *the possession of firearms are being reviewed.* [C] • *There's no law* **against** *being happy – not yet anyway.* [C] • *The age-discrimination law doesn't apply to elected officials.* [C] • *She's going to study law at university.* [U] • *The suit charges that New York's mandatory retirement age of 76* **violates** *federal law.* [U] • *(fml) This book gives the laws (=rules)* **of** *the game.* [C] • *Many doctors want to see a law* **banning/to** *ban all tobacco advertising.* [C + v-*ing*/C + *to* infinitive] • **The** law is the system of rules of a particular country: *What does the law say about having alcohol in the blood while driving?* [U] ○ *Of course robbery is* **against** *the law!* [U] ○ *You can't take that course of action and remain* **within** *the law.* [U] ○ *The judge ruled that the directors had knowingly* **broken** *the law.* [U] ○ *As president of the university she made it clear that she intended to* **obey** *the law.* [U] • *(infml)* **The** law is also the police: *The law was/were out in force at the demonstration.* [U + sing/pl v] • To be **a law unto** yourself is to behave in a way which is independent and does not follow the usual rules for a situation: *He never fills in the record forms – he's a law unto himself.* • When someone **goes to law** about something they ask a court to decide if it was done legally. • If someone **takes the law into** their **own hands** they take action against someone they think deserves to be punished: *He took the law into his own hands and shot the van driver who had killed his child.* • Someone who is **law-abiding** obeys the law: *Such actions against law-abiding* **citizens** *will not be tolerated.* • **Law and order** is a general expression for law being obeyed in a society, esp. when the police or army are used to make certain it is obeyed: *She warned that the president would be responsible for any* **breakdown of** *law and order.* • A **law-breaker** is a person who does not obey the law, esp. intentionally and often. • *(esp. Am)* **Law-enforcement** organizations or officials are those which make certain that the laws of an area are obeyed: *a law-enforcement agency* ○ *a law-enforcement officer* • A **law-maker** is someone, such as a politician, who is responsible for making and changing laws. • **The law of the jungle** is the idea that people who care only about themselves will be most likely to succeed in a society or organization: *We hope for a world where the rule of law, not the law of the jungle, governs the conduct of nations.* • *(saying)* 'There's one law for the rich and another for the poor'. • See also BYLAW; LAWSUIT; LAWYER. • LP **Crimes and criminals, Law**

law·ful /£ˈlɔː·fəl, $ˈlɑː-/ *adj fml* • *Judge Keenan concluded that the surveillance had been lawful* (=according to or acceptable to the law).

law·ful·ly /£ˈlɔː·fəl·i, $ˈlɑː-/ *adv fml* • *Such a policy could not lawfully be adopted.*

law·less /£ˈlɔː·ləs, $ˈlɑː-/ *adj* • *The film is set in a lawless* (=not controlled by law) *city sometime in the future.* • *We cannot tolerate such lawless* (=illegal) *behaviour.*

law·less·ly /£ˈlɔː·lə·sli, $ˈlɑː-/ *adv*

law·less·ness /£ˈlɔː·lə·snəs, $ˈlɑː-/ *n* [U] • *The widespread atmosphere of lawlessness has caused chaos and insecurity.*

law PRINCIPLE /£lɔː, $lɑː/ *n* [C] a general rule which states what always happens when the same conditions exist • *Newton's laws* **of** *motion* • *The* **first** *law* **of** (=the most important principle in) *politics is – if you're going to lie, don't get found out!* • The **law of averages** is the belief that if something happens often then it will also happen regularly: *If you toss a coin a hundred times, the law of averages suggests roughly fifty will come up heads and fifty tails.* • The **law of supply and demand** is the idea that the price of goods and services depends on how much of something is being sold and how many people want to buy it: *When there's a lot of unemployment, wages stay low – it's the law of supply and demand.* • See also MURPHY'S LAW; PARKINSON'S LAW.

lawn /£lɔːn, $lɑːn/ *n* an area of grass, esp. near to a house or in a park, which is cut regularly to keep it short • *At the back of the house were lawns which stretched down to the river.* [C] • *Put the chairs out* **on** *the lawn.* [C] • *Will you* **mow** *the lawn at the weekend?* [C] • *The house is surrounded by several acres of lawn.* [U] • **Lawn bowling** is *Am for* BOWLS. • **Lawn party** is *Am for* **garden party**. See at

PEOPLE IN A LAW COURT

the accused / the defendant — the person who is on trial in a criminal court of law. They are charged with committing (=accused of doing) a crime.

the Crown — the ruling authorities. In criminal courts the Crown accuses someone of having done something illegal.

Many cases in a court of law are not criminal ones, for example if you make a legal claim for money from someone who has failed to pay what they owe you. Most legal cases like this are called civil actions. In a civil law court **the plaintiff** is the person who makes a legal complaint about another person, **the defendant**.

(Br) **solicitor** — a lawyer who is trained to give advice about the law, and to prepare a law case before it is considered by the court. For serious or complex matters, solicitors often employ barristers to speak in court instead of them.

(Br) **barrister** — a lawyer who represents someone in court, particularly in the higher courts. They often give advice to solicitors on specialized or complex matters.

lawyer — In Britain lawyers can be either solicitors or barristers, who have different training and work. The US legal system does not have these two types of lawyer. US lawyers (also known as **attorneys**) prepare a case before trial and speak in all levels of court.

witness — a person who states what they know about a particular person, or about matters related to a legal case. This is called giving evidence.

jury — a group of twelve ordinary people, called **jurors**. In criminal trials, they consider all the evidence, decide what the facts are, and decide whether the accused person is guilty or not guilty.

judge — the person in charge of a criminal trial or court case who decides the answers to legal questions in the trial or tells the jury what the law is. In criminal cases if a person is found guilty, the judge decides what punishment should be given.

In some courts in England and Wales the people who act as judges are called **magistrates**. Magistrates are respected people who usually do not have any legal qualifications, and are not paid for their work. Serious legal matters are examined by legally trained judges in other types of courts.

GARDEN. • **Lawn tennis** is *fml or specialized for* TENNIS. • PIC〉 **Garden**

lawn•mow•er /£ˈlɔːnˌməʊ·əʳ, $ˈlɑːnˌmoʊ·ɚ/ *n* [C] a machine used for cutting grass. Some types have an engine or use electric power. • PIC〉 **Garden**

law•suit /£ˈlɔː·sjuːt, $ˈlɑː·suːt/, **suit** *n* [C] a problem taken to a court of law, by an ordinary person or an organization rather than the police, for a legal decision • *Two of the directors* **brought**/*(esp. Am)* **filed** *a lawsuit against their former employer.*

law•yer /£ˈlɔɪ·əʳ, $ˈlɑː·jɚ/, *Am also* **at•torn•ey** *n* [C] someone whose job is to give advice to people about the law and speak for them in court, esp. *(Br)* a SOLICITOR • *The General's lawyer welcomed the judge's ruling.* • *Jane Coker, lawyer for a number of those detained, said yesterday that she would be making applications for habeas corpus.* • LP〉 **Law**

lax /læks/ *adj* **-er, -est** lacking care, attention or control; not severe or strong enough • *He took a gun through baggage control to highlight the lax security.* • *The subcommittee contends that the authorities were lax* **in** *investigating most of the cases.*

lax•i•ty /£ˈlæk·sə·ti, $-t̬i/, **lax•ness** /ˈlæk·snəs/ *n* [U] • *When it comes to safety regulations, laxity costs lives.*

lax•ly /ˈlæk·sli/ *adv* • *The laws, both federal and state, tend to be laxly enforced.*

lax•a•tive /£ˈlæk·sə·tɪv, $-t̬ɪv/ *n* a substance that helps a person excrete the contents of their bowels • *If you're constipated, you should take a laxative.* [C] • *This medicine has a laxative* **effect**.

lay *obj* PUT DOWN /leɪ/ *v* [T] *past* **laid** /leɪd/ to put (something) in esp. a flat or horizontal position, usually carefully or for a particular purpose • *She laid the baby* **(down)** *in its cot.* • *I'll lay your coats* **on** *the bed upstairs.* • *Perhaps we should lay paper* **over** *the floor while we're decorating the room .* • *She laid* **aside** *her book and went to answer the phone.* [M] • *(fig.) He has temporarily laid* **aside** (= stopped doing) *some interesting projects to earn money by writing a film script.* [M] • *The dog laid its ears* **back** (= put them flat against its head) *and howled.* [M] • *He laid* **down** *his knife and fork, saying he couldn't possibly eat any more.* [M] • If someone **lays down** their weapons they stop fighting, esp. when they have been beaten: *Lay down your weapons and surrender – your situation is hopeless.* ○ *The soldiers from both sides laid down their* **arms** *and greeted each other once more as friends.* • To **lay down** your **life** is to die for something you believe in strongly: *Today we remember those who laid down their lives for their country.* See also **lay down** at LAY EXPRESS. • *Lay the rug* **flat** *on the ground.* • *The explosion* **laid** *trees* **flat** (= knocked them onto the ground) *for several hundred metres.* • *There will be some disruption for the next few weeks while contractors lay a new cable/sewer.* • *We're having a new carpet laid in the hall next week.* • *They've been laying bricks* (= making a wall with bricks) *for two weeks and the first floor is already finished.* • *The plan is to lay* (= build) **the foundation(s)** *for the new apartments in October.* • *(fig.) These discussions have laid* **the foundation(s)** (= started to prepare) *for a change of policy.* • *(fig.) The initial negotiations are seen as laying the basis* (= preparing) *for more detailed talks.* • *(fig.) Even the* **best** *laid* (= prepared) **plans** *go wrong sometimes.* • *Don't you dare* **lay a finger on** (= even slightly harm) *me.* • *If you* **lay a hand on** (= harm) *the child you'll be sorry.* • *I know I put my glasses somewhere, but I can't* **lay** *(my)* **hands on** (= find) *them.* • *(esp. Br and Aus)* If you **lay** something **at** someone's **door** you blame them for it: *You're the one who forgot to buy more bread, so don't try to lay it at my door.* • **Lay** someone **to rest** is used to avoid saying bury: *She was laid to rest next to her husband.* • *(fig.) I hope what he said has* **laid** *your fears* **to rest** (= removed them). • *(fig.) Isn't it time you* **laid the ghost of** *that experience* **to rest/laid that ghost** (= stopped being worried by it)*?* • **Laying on of hands** is a Christian ceremony in which someone puts their hands on someone else to give them spiritual help or support. • Compare LIE POSITION.

-lay•er /£-ˌleɪ·əʳ, $-ɚ/ *combining form* • *A bricklayer lays bricks.*

lay *obj* CAUSE /leɪ/ *v* [T + obj + adj] *past* **laid** /leɪd/ to cause to be in a particular condition • *Such an outspoken article lays her* **open** *to attack/criticism/ridicule* (= makes her likely to be attacked, etc.). • *The committee's report* **lays bare** (= makes known) *corruption on a massive scale.* • If an illness **lays** someone **low** it causes them to be unable to do what they usually do: *The kidney infection laid her low for a couple of months.* • *(dated)* To **lay** someone **low** is also to knock them to the ground: *The first punch laid him low.* • *The bomb* **laid waste** (= destroyed and flattened) *the whole of the city centre./The bomb* **laid** *the city centre* **to waste**.

lay NOT TRAINED /leɪ/ *adj* [before n; not gradable] not trained in or not having a detailed knowledge of a particular subject • *To the lay mind, symbolic logic can be very difficult.* • *From a lay viewpoint the questionnaire is virtually incomprehensible.* • See also LAYPERSON NOT TRAINED.

lay CHURCH /leɪ/ *adj* [before n; not gradable] having a position in an organization, esp. a religious one, that is not a full-time job and is not paid • *a lay preacher* • A **lay brother** or **lay sister** is someone who belongs to a religious group, esp. one living together in a MONASTERY or CONVENT, but is at a low level in it and usually does simple work for the organization, such as preparing food. • See also LAYPERSON CHURCH.

la•i•ty /£ˈleɪ·ə·ti, $-t̬i/ *n* [U + sing/pl v] • **The** laity are all the people who are involved with a church but are not priests.

lay *(obj)* PRODUCE EGGS /leɪ/ *v past* **laid** /leɪd/ (of an animal or bird) to produce (eggs) from out of its body • *Soon after it has laid its eggs the mayfly dies.* [T] • *Thousands of turtles drag themselves onto the beach and lay their eggs in the sand.* [T] • *The chickens just aren't laying – something must have frightened them.* [I]

lay•er /£ˈleɪ·əʳ, $-ɚ/ *n* [C] • *These hens are good layers* (= produce many eggs). • See also LAYER.

lay *obj* HAVE SEX /leɪ/ *v* [T often passive] *past* **laid** /leɪd/ *slightly taboo slang* to have sex with (someone) • *They go away on holiday hoping to* **get** *laid* (= to have sex).

lay /leɪ/ *n* [C] *slightly taboo slang* • *He was a surprisingly good lay* (= good to have sex with)*!* • *She's an easy lay* (= willing or easily persuaded to have sex) *– one drink and she's anybody's.*

lay *obj* RISK /leɪ/ *v* [T] *past* **laid** /leɪd/ to risk (something, usually money) on the result of an event; to BET • *He laid fifty pounds* **on** *the horse and it didn't even finish the race.* • *Minnie won't get the job – I'll lay money* **on** *it!* • *It'll never happen – I'll lay odds/my life/my shirt* **on** *it.* • *I'll lay you 3 to 1* **(that)** *John won't come.* [+ two objects + *(that)* clause] • To **lay** something **on the line** is to risk harm to it: *I'd be laying my career/life on the line by giving you that information.* See also **lay** something **on the line** at LAY EXPRESS.

lay *obj* EXPRESS /leɪ/ *v* [T] *past* **laid** /leɪd/ to express (a claim, legal statement, etc.) in a serious or official way • *She can't accept she made a mistake and now she's trying to lay* **the blame on** (= accuse) *her assistant.* • *Do you understand the seriousness of the* **charge** (= legal accusation) *which has been laid* **against** *you?* • *The company* **lays claim to** (= says it owns) *the designs.* • If you **lay down** a decision you announce it officially: *We laid new guidelines down recently for reporting accidents.* ○ *This is in line with the policy laid down by the management.* ○ **It's** *clearly laid down* **that** *no one is allowed in without a permit.* • *(infml)* When someone **lays down the law** they forcefully make known what they think should happen: *She's always laying down the law about keeping the house tidy.* • *(infml)* When someone **lays** something **on the line** they say very clearly that something is the case: *She laid it on the line – either we arrive at the proper time or we would no longer be allowed to attend.* See also **lay** something **on the line** at LAY RISK. • *(infml)* If someone **lays it on (a bit thick/with a trowel)** they make something, such as praise or a complaint, seem more important or serious than it really is: *He hurt his hand in the accident but he was laying it on a bit thick about how painful it was.* ○ *"It's very good indeed, really excellent," he said, laying on the praise with a trowel.*

lay LIE /leɪ/ *past simple of* LIE POSITION

lay a•side *obj*, **lay** *obj* **a•side** *v adv* [M] to keep for use in the future • *She lays aside a few dollars whenever possible so that one day she can buy a flute.* • *(fig.) Shall we lay an afternoon aside* (= keep an afternoon free) *for another meeting next week?* • See also **lay aside** at LAY PUT DOWN. .

lay down *obj*, **lay** *obj* **down** *v adv* [M] *specialized* to store (wine) for drinking in the future • *Should I lay this claret down, or can I drink it now?*

lay in *obj*, **lay** *obj* **in** *v adv* [M] to obtain and store • *We'd better lay in plenty of food in case we're cut off when it snows.*

lay into *obj v prep* [T] *infml* to attack (someone) physically or with words • *The interrogator then laid into his prisoner using a club.* • *You should have heard her laying into the kids for getting dirty!*

lay off *obj* NOT EMPLOY, **lay** *obj* **off** *v adv* [M] to stop employing (a worker), esp. if it might be possible to employ them again in the future • *Several hundred more employees will have to be laid off if the company does not get any new orders soon.* • LP> **Work**

laid off /£leɪd'ɒf, $-'ɑːf/ *adj* [after v; not gradable] • *He's been laid off for nearly three months now.*

lay–off /£'leɪ·ɒf, $-ɑːf/ *n* [C] • *Recent cuts in housing investment have led to large numbers of lay-offs in the building industry.*

lay off *(obj)* STOP *v adv, v prep infml* to stop using or dealing with (something or someone) • *You'd better lay off alcohol for a while.* [T] • *Why can't you lay off* (= stop worrying or hurting) *the kid for once!* [T] • *The doctor advised him to lay off smoking.* [+ v-ing] • *Here, lay off* (= stop what you are doing), *can't you! The noise is awful.* [I]

lay on *obj* PROVIDE, **lay** *obj* **on** *v adv* [M] to provide (a lot of something) • *They lay on free entertainment at the club every day, with things like video films and games.* • *They laid on a wonderful buffet after the wedding.*

lay *obj* **on** *obj* TELL *v prep* [T] *Am slang* to tell (someone) (something, esp. something they were not aware of) • *I hate to be the one to lay this on you, man, but your girlfriend has just moved in with another guy.*

lay out *obj* ARRANGE, **lay** *obj* **out** *v adv* [M] to arrange (the parts of a building, garden, town, pattern etc.) • *Most of Manhattan is laid out* **in/on** *a grid pattern with avenues going north-south and streets east-west.* • *We laid the pieces of the dress pattern out on the floor.*

lay·out /'leɪ·aʊt/ *n* [C] • *The layout of the house is more a series of spaces opening on to each other than distinct rooms.* • *Application forms vary greatly in layout and length.*

lay out *obj* DEAD BODY, **lay** *obj* **out** *v adv* [M] to prepare (a dead person's body) to be buried

lay out *obj* SPEND, **lay** *obj* **out** *v adv* [M] *infml* to spend (money), esp. if it seems like a large amount • *It's not every day you lay out £2000* **on** *a holiday.* • See also OUTLAY.

lay out *obj* HIT, **lay** *obj* **out** *v adv* [M] *infml* to knock unconscious • *She was wearing a helmet but the falling brick still laid her out.*

lay up *obj* STAY IN BED, **lay** *obj* **up** *v adv* [M usually passive] *infml* to force to stay in bed • *She's been laid up (in bed)* **with** *flu for a week.*

lay up *obj* CAUSE *v adv* [T] **lay up trouble(s)** to cause trouble in the future by your actions now • *She's laying up trouble* **for herself** *by ignoring her health problems now.*

lay·a·bout /'leɪ·əˌbaʊt/ *n* [C] *infml* a person who is unwilling to work

lay·a·way /'leɪ·ə·weɪ/ *n* [U] *Am for* **hire purchase**, see at HIRE

lay–by ROAD *Br* /'leɪ·baɪ/, *Am* **rest stop**, *Aus* **rest a·re·a** *n* [C] a place beside a road where a vehicle can stop without interrupting other traffic • *We pulled into a lay-by to look at the map.* • PIC> **Road**

lay–by PAYMENT /'leɪ·baɪ/ *n Aus* a system of paying for goods in small amounts and receiving the goods after the full amount has been paid, or goods bought in this way • *Could I* **buy/put** *the dress* **on** *lay-by?* [U] • *I've come to collect my lay-by.* [C]

lay·er /£'leɪ·əʳ, $-ɚ/ *n* [C] a level of material, such as a type of rock or gas, which is different from the material above or below it, or a thin sheet of a substance • *the ozone layer* • *A thick layer of clay lies over the sandstone underneath.* • *There was a thin layer* **of** *oil on the surface of the water.* • *A layer* **of** *skin peeled off her sunburnt back.* • *We stripped several layers* **of** *paint off the door.* • *You should be warm enough wearing all those layers* **of** *clothing!* • *(fig.) The study looked at ways to eliminate the present layers* **of** *bureaucracy.* • *(Am)* A **layer cake** is two or more soft cakes put on top of each other with ICING (= a sweet creamy mixture) between the cakes and covering the top and sides: *Carol wanted a simple chocolate layer cake with chocolate icing for her 40th birthday.* • PIC> **Bread and cakes**

lay·er *obj* /£'leɪ·əʳ, $-ɚ/ *v* [T] • *Layer the pasta* (= put it in layers) **with** *slices of tomato.*

lay·ered /£'leɪ·əd, $-ɚd/ *adj* [not gradable] • *The pastry should be folded and rolled out several times to make it* **many-/ multi-***layered.* • *(fig.) The issues are highly complex and* **many-/multi-***layered.*

lay·ette /leɪ'et/ *n* [C] *dated* a complete set of clothes, sheets, bed covers and the other items needed for a baby which has recently been born

lay·out /'leɪ·aʊt/ *n* [C] See at LAY OUT ARRANGE

lay·per·son NOT TRAINED (*pl* **lay people**), **lay·man** (*pl* **-men**), **lay·wo·man** (*pl* **-women**) /£'leɪˌpɜː·sən, $-ˌpɜːr-, -mən, -ˌwʊm·ən/ *n* [C] a person who is not trained in or does not have a detailed knowledge of a particular subject • *The book is supposed to be* **the** *layperson's guide to home repairs.* • *Specialists and lay people alike will be able to enjoy the programme.* • See also LAY NOT TRAINED.

lay·per·son CHURCH (*pl* **lay people**), **lay·man** (*pl* **-men**), **lay·wo·man** (*pl* **-women**) /£'leɪˌpɜː·sən, $-ˌpɜːr-, -mən, -ˌwʊm·ən/ *n* [C] a person who is part of a religious organization but who is not paid or specially trained • See also LAY CHURCH.

la·zy /'leɪ·zi/ *adj* **-ier, -iest** not willing to work; avoiding activity • *(disapproving) The managers complained that the workers were lazy and unreliable.* • *(disapproving) Get out of bed you lazy thing – you can't lie there all day!* • *(approving) We spent a lazy day on the beach sunbathing.* • *(approving) Prague is a place for lazy* (= slow and pleasant) *strolling, with its street life and culture and cafés.* • A **lazy Susan** is a circular piece of wood or plastic which is put on a table and can be turned around so that everyone can reach the food that is on it.

laze *(obj)* /leɪz/ *v* • *(approving) We spent the morning just lazing (in bed).* [I] • *(disapproving) You can't laze* **about/around** *for the rest of your life – sooner or later you'll have to get a job!* [I] • *(approving) We lazed* **away** *an afternoon by the river.* [M]

la·zi·ly /'leɪ·zɪ·li/ *adv* • *Palm trees swayed lazily in the soft breeze.*

laz·i·ness /'leɪ·zɪ·nəs/ *n* [U]

la·zy·bones /£'leɪ·zi·bəʊnz, $-boʊnz/ *n* [C] *pl* **lazybones** *infml disapproving* someone who is LAZY • *Hey lazybones, get up from the sofa and help me with the dishes!* [as form of address]

lb *n* [C] *pl* **lb** or **lbs** *abbreviation for* POUND AMOUNT • *a 3lb bag of flour* • *The baby weighed 8lbs 2oz when it was born.* • LP> **Units**

lbw /ˌel·biː'dʌb·l̩.juː/ *adj* [not gradable], *n* [C] *Br* leg before wicket; (in cricket) a way of dismissing the BATSMAN (= person who is trying to hit the ball) by hitting his legs with the ball • *Spiby was very upset when the lbw* **decision** *went against him.* • *Ambrose has more lbws to his name than any other bowler on the tour.*

LCD /ˌel·siː'diː/ *n* [C] *abbreviation for* **liquid-crystal display**, see at LIQUID SUBSTANCE

L–driv·er *n* [C] *Br* a learner driver (= a person who is learning to drive a car) • See also L-PLATE.

leach *obj* /liːtʃ/ *v* [T] *specialized* to remove (a substance) from a material, esp. from earth, by the process of water moving through the material, or to remove parts of (a material) using water • *Rain water leaches heavy metals* **out** *of the dump site and carries them into the local water.* • *The soil has been so heavily leached because of intensive farming that it is no longer fertile.* • *(fig.) Some Native Americans believed that being photographed could leach the spirit* **from** *the body.*

lead *(obj)* CONTROL /liːd/ *v past* **led** /led/ to control (a group of people); to be the person who makes the decisions or the most important person in a group • *I think we've chosen the right person to lead the expedition.* [T] • *She leads (the company) by doing her job well and expecting everyone else to do the same.* [I/T] • *I've asked Gemma to lead the discussion about new products.* [T] • *Who will be leading the inquiry into the accident?* [T] • *When you lead there are a lot of extra pressures – everyone depends on you.* [I] • *(infml)* If you **lead** someone **by the nose** you completely control what they do. • *(Br)* A **leading article** is an **editorial**. See at EDIT. • *(Aus)* A **leading hand** is the most experienced person in a factory etc. • A **leading lady/actress** or **leading man/actor** is the actor or actress who has the most important part in a play or a film. • *(infml)* If someone is a **leading light** of an organization they are very important in it.

lead /liːd/ *n* [C] • *Whoopi Goldberg will* **play** *the lead* (= be the main actor) *in the sequel.* • See also **leading lady/man** at LEAD CONTROL *v.*

lead·er /£'liː·dəʳ, $-dɚ/ *n* [C] • *The Russian leader wants to introduce further changes.* • *He's a natural leader – people* *are very happy to work for him.* • *She was elected as leader* **of** *the students.* • The leader (*Am and Aus usually* **concertmaster**) of an ORCHESTRA (= group of musicians) is the main VIOLIN player. • Leader is also *Am for* CONDUCTOR of an ORCHESTRA. • *(Br)* A leader is also an **editorial**. See at EDIT.

lead·er·ship /£ˈliː·də·ʃɪp, $-dɚ-/ *n* [U] • Leadership refers to the set of characteristics that make a good leader: *Strong and effective leadership might have made the team more successful.* ○ *The organization lacked leadership.* ○ *He did not have any leadership* **qualities**. • Leadership is also the position of being the leader: *The group flourished* **under** *her firm leadership.* ○ *R&M gained* **market** *leadership* (= sold more goods than other companies) *by selling products that were of superior quality.* • **The** leadership is the person or persons who lead: *The election for the leadership* **of** (= person who leads) *the council will take place on Tuesday.* ○ *The leadership* (= group of people in control) **of** *the expedition was/were very experienced.* [+ sing/pl v]

lead *(obj)* [SHOW WAY] /liːd/ *v past* **led** /led/ to show the way, esp. to people, animals, vehicles etc. that follow • *If you lead* **(on)** *in the jeep we'll follow behind on the horses.* [I] • *The local youth band will lead the parade this weekend.* [T] • *Our guide led us* **over/through** *the mountains.* [T] • *You've been there before – why don't you* **lead the way** (= show the way by going in front). • *(fig.) The company has been* **leading the way in** (= been the first to produce) *network applications for several years.* See also **lead the field/pack/world** at LEAD [IN FRONT]. • *Lead the discussion* **off**/*Lead* **off** *the discussion* (= Begin the discussion) **with** *a summary of statistics.* [M] • *(infml)* To **lead** someone **a (merry) chase/dance** is to cause them a lot of trouble, esp. by getting them to do a lot of things that are not necessary. • *(infml)* If you **lead** someone **up/down the garden path** you deceive them: *It seems as if we've been led up the garden path about the position of our hotel – it's miles from the beach!* • A **lead-in** is something that introduces something else, such as the words and music that are used to introduce a television programme. • *(saying humorous)* 'Lead on, Macduff' means you lead and I will follow.

lead /liːd/ *n* [C usually sing] • *We'll go through the dance routine again –* **follow** *my lead* (= do what I do). • *He gave us a strong lead.*

lead *(obj)* [DIRECTION] /liːd/ *v* [always + adv/prep] (esp. of roads, paths, doors, signs, information, etc.) to (allow or cause to) go in a particular direction or have a particular result • *About two kilometres down this road a track to the right leads* **(up) to** *the reservoir.* [I] • *A flight of narrow steps leads* **(up/down) to** *the kitchen.* [I] • *Behind the tapestry a concealed door led* **into** *a secret room.* [I] • *The French windows lead* **(out) onto** *a wide shady terrace.* [I] • *A narrow trail of blood led directly* **into** *the cave.* [I] • *It was very foggy but the sound of the bell led the boat* **to** *safety.* [T] • *Following the signs led us* **into** *a small square with a fountain.* [T] • *The new information led (the police)* **to** *a house near the harbour.* [I/T] • *Years of painstaking research have led* **to** *a new vaccine.* [I] • *Ignoring safety procedures led* **to** *a tragic accident.* [I] • *Indifference to pollution now will lead us* **into** *serious problems in the future.* [T] • To lead **up to** something is to prepare slowly or indirectly for it: *She led up to her request for a new bike by telling her parents how much money she was spending on bus fares.* [I] • A period of time which leads **up to** an event or activity comes before it: *We're going to be very busy in the week leading up to our holiday.* [I] • *(specialized)* The **lead time** for a new product is the time needed to design it before it can be made.

lead /liːd/ *n* [C] • A lead is a piece of information which allows a discovery to be made or a solution to be found: *A lead from an informer enabled the police to make several arrests.* ○ *Survey results gave the lead needed to find the virus's origin.*

lead *(obj)* [IN FRONT] /liːd/ *v past* **led** /led/ (esp. in sport or other competitions) to be in front, to be first or to be winning • *After thirty minutes the challengers were leading (their opponents)* **by** *two goals.* [I/T] • *With two laps to go Ngomo led* **by** *less than two seconds.* [I] • If you **lead the field/pack/world** you are better than other people or things: *The company's new software leads the field.* ○ *Their research group leads the world* **in** *nutrition research.* ○ See also **lead the way** at LEAD [SHOW WAY].

lead /liːd/ *n* [U] • *For the first time in the race Smith is* **in** *the lead.* • *With a final burst of speed she* **went/moved into** *the lead.* • *After last night's win Johnson has* **taken (over)** *the lead in the championship table.* • *By the end of the day's play Davies* **had/held** *a lead* **of** *three points.* • *Another mistake like that and Martin could* **lose** *his lead.* • *American companies hold about 70% of the world computing market and this lead will probably increase.*

lead·er /£ˈliː·dəʳ, $-dɚ/ *n* [C] • *Hill was the leader up to the 54th lap, when his car ran out of petrol.* • *They interviewed Dr. Jones, a leader in the field of microbiology.* • *"Leader of the Pack"* (title of a song by the Shangri Las, 1965)

lead·ing /ˈliː·dɪŋ/ *adj* [before n] • *She is a leading* **expert** *on the country's ecology.* • If something is **at the leading edge** or is **leading-edge** it is more advanced than other similar things: *leading-edge technology*

lead *obj* [INFLUENCE] /liːd/ *v* [T] *past* **led** /led/ *disapproving* to influence (someone) to think or do something in a particular way or cause them to do something bad • *Being under pressure can easily lead people* **(on) to** *make the wrong decisions.* [+ obj + *to* infinitive] • *But the brochure led me* **(on) to believe** *that the price included home delivery.* [+ obj + *to* infinitive] • *It's worrying that such a prominent politician is so* **easily** *led* **(on)** (= easily persuaded esp. to do something wrong). • *I'm sure it's someone at school who led Tom* **on/astray** (= caused him to behave badly). • To lead someone **on** is to persuade them to believe something which is not true: *He really believed her story about the holiday being cancelled but she was only leading him on.* • *All the time she'd been leading him on* (= pretending she liked him) *but she was only interested in his money.*

lead·ing /ˈliː·dɪŋ/ *adj* [before n] • A **leading question** is a question which, by the words used in it, suggests the answer that the questioner wants: *We know you asked leading questions at the interrogation because the prisoner stated facts he couldn't have known.*

lead [METAL] /led/ *n* [U] a very dense, soft, dark-grey, metallic element which is used on roofs and for protection against RADIATION. It is also poisonous. • *The lead pipes in many older houses have been replaced by copper ones.* • *Some types of paint on toys might cause* **lead-poisoning** (= an illness caused by lead) *in children.* • If something **goes down like a lead balloon**, it is not popular or successful: *Well, your suggestion that we work all weekend went down like a lead balloon.*

lead·ed /ˈled·ɪd/ *n* [U], *adj* [not gradable] • *Does the car take leaded (petrol)* (= fuel with small amounts of lead added to help it burn smoothly)*?* See also UNLEADED. • **Leaded lights** (also **leaded windows**) are windows made from small pieces of glass fixed together with lead strips. • PIC〉 **Window**

lead·ing /ˈled·ɪŋ/ *n* [U] • *(Br)* Leading is the lead used to cover (parts of) a roof. • Leading (*Br* also **leads**) is also the thin strips of lead which hold together the small pieces of glass in **leaded lights**.

leads /ledz/ *pl n* • *(Br)* Leads are the LEADING between pieces of glass in a window.

lead [PENCIL] /led/ *n* (the narrow strip of) coloured material, usually black and made of GRAPHITE, in the centre of a pencil • *Have you got a spare pencil Kate? Peter's broken the lead in his.* [C] • *Do you think* **pencil** *lead will wash out of this white shirt?* [U] • *(taboo slang)* To **have/put lead in** your **pencil** means to have/give an ERECTION (= have the penis temporarily larger and harder).

lead *obj* [LIVE] /liːd/ *v* [T] *past* **led** /led/ to live (a particular type of life) • *After retiring from the movies she led* **a quiet life** *on the Riviera.* • *We hardly lead* **a life of luxury** *but we're not poor either.*

lead [ANIMAL] *esp. Br and Aus* /liːd/, *esp. Am* **leash** *n* [C] a piece of rope, chain, etc. tied to an animal, esp. to a dog at its collar when taking it for a walk • *Please keep your dog* **on** *a lead when on the beach.* • *There aren't any sheep around so let the dog* **off** *the lead.* • *(often humorous)* If someone is **(let) off the lead/leash** they are (temporarily) free from a previous limit to their freedom, esp. in a relationship: *He's away on business so you're (let) off the lead for the evening – let's go to the club.* • PIC〉 **Dogs**

lead [ELECTRICAL] /liːd/, *Br also* **flex**, *Am and Aus also* **cord**, *Am also* **wire** *n* [C] a wire used to connect electrical equipment to a PLUG (= device through which it receives power from the electrical system) or to other pieces of equipment • *She tripped over the television lead.* • PIC〉 **Fires and space heaters, Lights**

lead·en /ˈled·ᵊn/ *adj disapproving* dark or *(fig.)* lacking excitement • *The sky looks leaden* (= full of dark clouds). •

(fig.) What a leaden expression – have you just had bad news? • *(fig.) That was a rather leaden attempt to answer the question.*

leaf PLANT /liːf/ *n pl* **leaves** /liːvz/ any of the flat, usually green parts of a plant which are joined at one end to the stem or branch • *a palm leaf* [C] • When a plant is **in** leaf or when it **comes into** leaf it has leaves on it: *The trees are in leaf early this year.* [U] ○ *The bushes are just coming into leaf.* [U] • **Leaf mould** is a type of FERTILIZER (= substance which makes plants grow well) made from leaves which fall from trees in the autumn. • PIC› **Leaf, Tree**

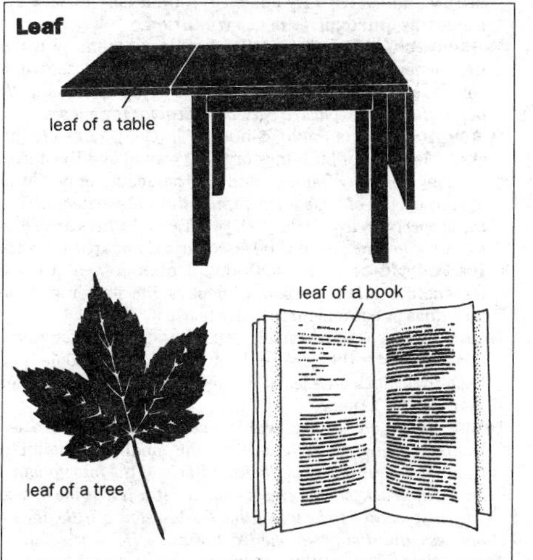

leaf·y /ˈliː·fi/ *adj* **-ier, -iest** • *leafy parks/avenues* (= pleasant because there are many plants and esp. trees)

-leaved /-liːvd/ *combining form* • *a large-leaved bush* (= a bush with large leaves)

leaf PAPER /liːf/ *n* [C] *pl* **leaves** /liːvz/ a thin flat object or layer of something • *A leaf* **of paper** *fell out of the book.* • *She turned the leaves* **of the book** (= pages) *slowly.* • *We had to put in/pull out the extra leaf* **of the table** (= extra part of the table that can be folded away when not wanted) *because there were eight of us for dinner.* • If you **take a leaf from/out of** someone's **book** you copy the way they behave because they are a good example to follow: *You'd do well to take a leaf out of John's book.* • PIC› **Leaf, Table**

leaf through *obj v prep* [T] • You leaf through a book or a magazine by turning the pages quickly and reading only a little of it: *The passengers were leafing through magazines in the airport shop.*

leaf·let /ˈliː·flət/ *n* [C] a piece of paper, or sometimes several pieces of paper folded or fixed together like a book, which gives you information or advertises something • *A leaflet about the new bus services came today.* • *They were handing out advertising leaflets outside the supermarket.* • *The leaflets about the concert were delivered with the local papers.*

leaf·let *(obj)* /ˈliː·flət/ *v* **-t-** or *Br also* **-tt-** • *They leafleted* (= gave leaflets to people in) *the area for two weeks before the event.* [T] • *First we leaflet, then we phone to arrange for representatives to visit.* [I] • *The campaign will include mass leafleting to build up huge anti-hunting support.*

league SPORT /liːg/ *n* [C] a group of players or teams playing a sport who take part in competitions between each other • *It's a better team than the one that* **won** *the league last year.* • *Liverpool were* **top of** *the Football League that year.* • *His first season in charge saw the team win the league* **championship**. • *He has played in only three league* **games/matches** *this season.* • *My team is at the bottom of the league (Br)* **table**/*(Am) (league)* **standings** (= the list of teams in the order of the points they have won). • League is also used in comparing the parts of any group: *He said Britain used to be second in the league of prosperous industrial nations and was now much lower.* ○ *His new film is highly watchable but* **not in the same** *league* **as** (= not as good as) *his first two epics.* ○ *This fraud is* **in a different** *league* **(altogether)** (= much worse than any others). ○ *This hotel is* **in a different** *league* **(altogether) from** (= much better than) *the one we stayed in last time.* ○ *Those cars were* **out of** *my league* (= too expensive or too fast). ○ *He said we were bottom of the league table for spending* (= we spent less than anyone else) *on research and development.* • LP› **Sports**

league ORGANIZATION /liːg/ *n* a group of people or countries who join together because they have the same interest • *the Arab League* [C] • *The UN's predecessor, the League of Nations, was a league of colonial powers and other countries.* [C] • **In** league means making secret plans to do something, esp. illegal or wrong: *The criminals had been in league* **with** *the owners of the company.* [U] ○ *I'm sure those two are in league.* [U]

leak *(obj)* /liːk/ *v* (of a liquid or gas) to escape from a hole or crack in a pipe or container or (of a container) to allow liquid or gas to escape • *Water was leaking* **from** *the pipe.* [I] • *Oil leaked* **out** *of the car.* [I] • *The car leaked oil all over the drive.* [T] • *The tin was leaking.* [I] • To leak is also to allow (secret information) to become generally known: *He leaked the names* **to** *the press.* [T] ○ *The news of the pay cuts leaked* **out** *quickly.* [I] • If something leaks **like a sieve** it cannot stop liquid from escaping: *That bucket leaks like a sieve.* [I]

leak /liːk/ *n* [C] • *There's water on the floor – we must have a leak somewhere.* • *If you suspect a* **gas** *leak, phone the emergency number.* • A leak is also the origin of secret information which becomes known more widely or the act of making it known: *There have been several* **security** *leaks recently.* ○ *They traced the leak to a secretary in the finance department.* • *(slang)* If you **take a leak**/*(Br and Aus also)* **have a leak** you urinate.

leak·age /ˈliː·kɪdʒ/ *n* • Leakage is the act of leaking or the leak itself: *The leakage was traced to an oil pipe in the cellar.* [C] ○ *A lot of water is wasted through leakage.* [U] • Leakage also refers to making known secret information: *The chairman was shocked that any leakage of the report should have taken place.* [U]

leak·y /ˈliː·ki/ *adj* **-ier, -iest** • *leaky pipes* • *a leaky valve*

lean *(obj)* SLOPE /liːn/ *v* [always + adv/prep] *past* **leant** /lent/ or *esp. Am* **leaned** /liːnd, lent/ to (cause to) slope in one direction; to be neither vertical nor horizontal; to INCLINE • *She leant the brush* **against** *the wall.* [T] • *The paintings were on the floor, leaning* **against** *the wall.* [I] • *As the police officer approached Mr Walsh he seemed to lean* **forward** *and swallow something.* [I] • *She stopped and leaned* **on** *her stick for a moment to recover.* [I] • *(infml) We will have to* **lean** *heavily* **on** (= depend on) *my parents* **for** *financial support in future.* • *(infml) He* **leant on** *me so hard* (= persuaded me strongly/threatened me) *I had to agree to do it.* • *The fence is leaning too much* **to the right.** [I] • *I sat down next to Bernard, who leaned* **over** *to me and said "You're late."* [I] • *"We* **lean over backwards** (= try very hard) *to spot people who are serious suicide risks," he said.* • A **lean-to** is a building joined to one of the sides of a larger building with which it shares one wall: *a cottage with a lean-to (garage).* • *(Am and Aus)* A **lean-to** is also a shelter or simple building with a roof that slopes in one direction, which is slept in when CAMPING. See also **lean** at LEANING.

lean NOT FAT /liːn/ *adj* **-er, -est** not having much fat and therefore healthy • *The new style of hamburger is based on lean* **meat** *with water replacing much of the fat.* • *Yesterday, he looked lean, fit and fresh – a likely winner.* • *He preferred plump to lean models for his paintings.* • *(fig.) He's got that lean* **and hungry** *look* (= looks as if he wants something very much). • A lean **season/time/year** is one when there is not enough of something, esp. money or food: *It is a particularly lean year for the science budget.* ○ *The poor consumer is finding that times are getting leaner.* • *(approving)* A lean **business/company** has only the smallest number of employees it needs to do its work: *Nowadays even efficient, lean, well-run industries are failing.*

lean·ing /ˈliː·nɪŋ/ *n* [C] a tendency to be interested in a subject, sport, way of life, etc. or to support a political party; INCLINATION • *He showed an early leaning* **for/towards** *sport of all kinds.* • *It will depend on the political leanings of the new committee members.* • *The group shows little sign now of their earlier musical leanings.* • *In those days it had been dangerous to be suspected of homosexual leanings.*

lean /liːn/ *v* [I always + adv/prep] *past* **leant** /lent/ or *esp. Am* **leaned** /liːnd, lent/ • *In the 1950s he leaned* **to** *the left/* **towards** *socialism.* • See also LEAN SLOPE.

leap *(obj)* /liːp/ *v past* **leapt** /lept/ or *esp. Am* **leaped** /lept, liːpt/ to make a large jump or sudden movement, usually from one place to another • *He tried to leap from an upstairs window.* [I] • *The reporter leapt forward holding out her* *microphone.* [I] • *The dog/man leapt* **(over)** *the gate into the field.* [T; I + prep] • *I saw him leap* **(up)** *from his chair and go to the window.* [I] • *The girl leapt* **to** *hold the door open.* [+ *to* infinitive] • *(fig.) He leapt* **to** *his friend's defence* (= quickly spoke to support his friend). [I] • If your **heart** leaps you have a sudden strong feeling of pleasure or fear: *My heart leapt as a dark shape slid across the path in front of me.* [I] • Things which leap **(up)** increase, improve or grow very quickly: *House prices will leap (up) in the spring.* [I] ○ *The children had leapt up* (= grown much taller) *since I last saw them.* [I] • If you **leap at** something you are very eager to do it: *When I offered her the job, she leapt at it.* • Something which **leaps (out) at** you is very noticeable: *As I turned the page his picture leapt out at me.* • If something **leaps to mind** you immediately think of it: *Your comments leapt to mind as I was trying to explain the problem to him.*

leap /liːp/ *n* [C] • *David* **took/made** *a brave leap at the ledge but missed and fell.* • *(fig.) The leaps* (= increases) **in** *pay at the universities have been very great this year.* • *(fig.) It takes quite a leap* **of the imagination** (= you have to try hard) *to believe that it's the same person.* • If someone or something gets better **by/in leaps and bounds**, they improve very quickly: *She has* **come on** *in leaps and bounds with her reading.* ○ *Her reading has improved by leaps and bounds this term.* • A **leap in the dark** is something you do without being certain what will happen as a result: *Booking the holiday was a leap in the dark – we got the address out of the paper.* • A **leap year** happens once every four years and has an extra day on 29 February: *Next year is a leap year.*

leap·frog /£ˈliːp·frɒg, $-frɑːg/ *n* [U] a children's game in which a number of children bend down and another child jumps over them one at a time • *a game of leapfrog* • PIC› **Playground**

leap·frog *obj* /£ˈliːp·frɒg, $-frɑːg/ *v* **-gg-** • If you leapfrog you improve your position by going past other people quickly or by missing out some stages: *The team has leapfrogged from third to first place.* [I always + adv/prep] ○ *She leapfrogged into the job past older colleagues.* [I always + adv/prep] ○ *They planned to leapfrog the main army convoy and surprise them from the north.* [T]

learn *(obj)* /£lɜːn, $lɜːrn/ *v past Br and Aus* **learnt** /£lɜːnt, $lɜːrnt/ or *esp. Am* **learned** to obtain knowledge of facts or of how to do things, or an understanding of ideas • *They're learning French at school.* [T] • *He's not very good yet, but he's learning.* [I] • *You soon learnt not* **to** *speak too loudly.* [+ *to* infinitive] • *They learnt* **what** *to do very quickly.* [+ *wh-* word] • *First you'll learn* **(how) to** *use this machine.* [+ *wh-* word/ + *to* infinitive] • *I later learnt* **that** *the message had never arrived.* [+ *that* clause] • *We were shocked when we learnt* **about/of** *his sudden death.* [I] • If you learn a poem, part of a play, etc. **(by heart)** you can say it from memory without reading it: *We were told to learn Portia's speech (by heart) for homework.* [T] • *I hope you'll learn* **by/from** *your* **mistakes** (= not do the same bad thing again). [I] • *He certainly* **learnt** *his* **lesson/ learnt the hard way** (= suffered a bad experience and will not do it again). • *She'll just have to* **learn to live with** *it* (= accept a new but unpleasant situation). • LP› **Memory** DK

learn·ed /£ˈlɜː·nɪd, $ˈlɜːr-/ *adj specialized* • Learned behaviour is a way of behaving that is not automatic but which has been copied from others: *I believe that the way boys respond to conflict by hitting out is learned behaviour which starts at an early age.*

learn·ed /£ˈlɜː·nɪd, $ˈlɜːr-/ *adj fml* • A learned person has studied for a long time and has a lot of knowledge: *a learned professor/judge* • A **learned journal** is a collection of writings regularly published for specialists in a particular subject.

learn·er /£ˈlɜː·nəʳ, $ˈlɜːr·nɚ/ *n* [C] • A learner is a person who is still learning something: *We keep these machines for learners.* ○ *He's a quick learner.* ○ *(esp. Br) I was following a learner* **(driver)** *all the way home.*

learn·ing /£ˈlɜː·nɪŋ, $ˈlɜːr-/ *n* [U] • Learning is the activity of obtaining knowledge: *This technique makes learning fun.* ○ *For the first month in her new job she was on a steep learning* **curve** (= she learnt a lot quickly). • Learning is also knowledge obtained by study: *His friends praised his generosity, wit and learning.* • If you say someone has **learning difficulties** you mean that they have low mental abilities, often because of accident or illness or since birth: *Some of the children have* **specific** *learning difficulties.* • *"A little learning is a dangerous thing"* (Alexander Pope in the poem *Essay on Criticism*, 1711)

lease *obj* /liːs/ *v* [T] to make a legal agreement by which money is paid in order to use (land, a building, a vehicle or a piece of equipment) for an agreed period of time • *The estate contains 300 new homes, about a third of which are leased* **to** *the council.* • *It was agreed they would lease the flat* **to** *him/lease him the flat.* [+ two objects] • *The company leases its cars* **from** *a local supplier.* • *The photocopier could be leased at a reasonable rate per month.* • *Mered Air owns three of its 37 aircraft, but the rest are leased.* • LP› **Borrow**

lease /liːs/ *n* [C] • *He has the flat* **on** *a long lease.* • *The lease* **runs out/expires** *in two years' time.*

lease·back /ˈliːs·bæk/ *n* [U] a legal agreement by which the owner of an item allows the person who sold it to continue to use it for payment • *They discussed the possibility of leaseback/a leaseback deal for the houses.*

lease·hold /£ˈliːs·həʊld, $-hoʊld/ *n* [C/U], *adj*, *adv* [not gradable] (esp. of buildings or land) owned and lived in or used by legal agreement and for payment, only for an agreed period of time • *His family* **held** *the leasehold/***had** *the property* **on** *leasehold.* [C/U] • *leasehold offices and shops* • *She bought the apartment leasehold.* • Compare FREEHOLD.

lease·hold·er /£ˈliːs·həʊl·dəʳ, $-hoʊl·dɚ/ *n* [C] • A leaseholder is the person who pays the owner of land, buildings or equipment in order to use it.

leash /liːʃ/ *n* [C] *esp. Am for* LEAD ANIMAL • A **leash law** is a law in many US cities and towns that says people must keep their dogs on a leash when they are away from their home. • PIC› **Dogs**

least /liːst/ *adv* [not gradable], *determiner*, *pronoun* less than anything or anyone else, the smallest amount or number • *This group is the least likely of the four to win.* • *Disaster struck when we least expected it.* • *It was the answer she least wanted to hear.* • *I like the blue one a little, the red one less, and the green one least of all.* • *He's the relative I like* **(the)** *least.* • *Which car costs* **(the)** *least?* • *No one believed her, least* **of all** (= especially not) *the police.* • *They refused to admit her,* **not** *least because* (= there were several reasons but this was an important one) *she hadn't got her membership card with her.* • **At (the very) least** means not less than or shows the lowest amount possible: *It will cost at least $100.* ○ *It will be £200 at the very least.* • **At least** is also used to reduce the effect of a statement: *I've met the President – at least, he shook my hand once.* See also LEASTWAYS. • **At least** is also used to emphasize that something is good in a bad situation: *The letter was very short, but at least she did write to me.* • **It is/was the least I can/could do** is a polite answer to someone who thanks you: *"Thanks for offering to deliver the parcel." "It's the least I can do."* • **Not in the least** is used to express strong feeling in negative sentences and means not in any way: *I don't like travelling in the least.* ○ *"Are you satisfied with it?" "Not in the least."* • **Not the least** is used for emphasis with nouns: *I haven't the least idea* (= I do not know) *who he was.* ○ *She hasn't the least interest* (= She has no interest) *in the project.* • **To say the least** is used to show that you could have said something stronger: *He wasn't happy with the decision, to say the least!* • *(saying)* 'Least said soonest mended' means a bad situation can be quickly forgotten if people do not keep talking about it.

least·ways /ˈliːst·weɪz/ *adv* [not gradable] used to reduce the effect of a statement • *He said he'd be back later – leastways, I think he did.* • See also **at least** at LEAST.

leath·er /£ˈleð·əʳ, $-ɚ/ *n* [U] animal skin treated in order to preserve it, and used to make shoes, bags, clothes, equipment, etc. • *The coat was made of black leather with a fur collar.* • *a leather coat/belt/handbag*

leath·er·ette /ˌleð·əˈret/ *n* [U] *trademark* • Leatherette is an artificial material which is made to look like leather.

leath·er·y /£ˈleð·ᵊr·i, $ˈ-ɚ-/ *adj* **-ier**, **-iest** • *leathery leaves* (= thick and feeling firm when you touch them, like leather) • *(disapproving) slices of leathery meat* (= too firm like leather and difficult to cut) • *His hands were hard and leathery.*

leath·er·neck /£ˈleð·ə·nek, $ˈ-ɚ-/ *n* [C] *Am slang* a soldier in the US Marine Corps

leave *(obj)* GO AWAY /liːv/ *v past* **left** /left/ to go away from (someone or something that stays in the same place), for a short time or permanently • *I'll be leaving at five o'clock tomorrow.* [I] • *He left the house by the back door.* [T] • *The girl left the group of people she was with and came over to speak to us.* [T] • *The bus leaves (the bus station) in five minutes.* [I/T] • *"I'm leaving on a jet plane/ Don't know* *when I'll be back again"* (from the song *Leavin' on a Jet Plane* by Peter, Paul and Mary, 1970)

leave *(obj)* NOT TAKE /liːv/ *v past* **left** /left/ to not take something with you when you go, or to allow or cause something to stay • *I'll leave my winter coat* **(behind)**, *I won't need it.* [T] • *Hey, you've left your keys* **(behind)** (= you've forgotten your keys). [T] • *(fig.) She's left that kind of student life* **behind**. [T] • *Hurry up or you'll get left* **behind** (= you will not be able to stay level with others). [T] • *There is some anxiety that we'll be left* **behind** (= we will not be able to stay at the same standard as others) *in the technology stakes.* [T] • *You'd better leave a note to say you'll be late.* [T] • *Can I leave a message* **for** *Sue* (= give a message which can later be given to Sue)*?* [T] • If something leaves something else, a part or effect of it stays after it has gone or been used: *The shoes left muddy marks on the floor.* [T] ○ *The incident left* **(behind)** *a feeling of resentment.* [T] ○ *If you take two, then that leaves me three/leaves three* **for** *me.* [+ two objects] ○ *I'll have three left* **over** *for next week.* ○ *If I give you £10 that won't leave me enough cash to pay the bill.* [+ two objects] ○ *I won't have enough cash left to pay the bill.* ○ *How much time does that leave us?* [+ two objects] ○ *How much time is left before the train goes?* ○ *We were left* **with** *five pieces that we couldn't fit into the jigsaw.* [T] ○ *Five from twelve leaves seven* (= Seven is the result of taking five from twelve). [T] • *I think the new arrangement has left me in a better position* (= I am in a better position after the new arrangement). [T] • *Far from improving things the new law has left many people worse off* (= they are now in a worse situation) *than before.* [T + obj + adj] • To leave a wife, husband or other close family member is to die while these family members are still alive: *He left a wife and two children.* [T] • If you leave something (in a particular condition) you do not touch it, move it or act to change it in any way and it stays in the same condition: *He left the photo on the table and stood looking down at it.* [T] ○ *Leave that chair where it is.* [T] ○ *The child left the food on the plate* (= didn't eat it). [T] ○ *The family were left* (= became and continued to be) *homeless.* [T + obj + adj] ○ *I'll have to go back – I think I've left the iron on.* [T + obj + adj] ○ *You can leave the window open.* [T + obj + adj] ○ *I told you to leave that paint alone – now you've spilt it!* [T + obj + adj] ○ *Leave me alone – take your hand off my arm.* [T + obj + adj] ○ *Leave your sister alone* (= do not annoy her) *– she's been teased about her boyfriend enough.* [T + obj + adj] ○ *He won't leave me alone – he's always phoning or coming to see me.* [T + obj + adj] ○ **Leave** *her* **be** (= Do not worry her/let her continue what she is doing). • If you leave something **off** a list you do not include it: *He left three people off (the list) by mistake.* [T/M] • If you leave **out** something you do not include it: *She left the almonds out of the cake.* [M] ○ *Here, don't leave me out – I'd like to come too!* [M] ○ *None of the other children play with her, and I think she feels rather left out* (= no one wants to be her friend). • *(Br slang) Hey,* **leave it out** (= stop doing that)*! That hurt.* • *(Br slang) "I tell you, there were two of them, with huge eyes and bright green skin!"* "**Leave it out** (= I don't believe you)." • If you leave something or someone do**ing** something they are still doing it when you go away: *I left the children watching television.* [T + obj + v-*ing*] ○ *He left the engine running.* [T + obj + v-*ing*] • If you leave (do**ing**) something, you wait before you do it: *I'll leave the rest of the work* **for** *tomorrow.* [T] ○ *I'll leave these letters* **till** *Monday* (= write them on Monday). [T] ○ *Don't leave it too late* (= wait too long). [T] ○ *They left booking their holiday* **till/to** *the last minute.* [+ v-*ing*] • If you leave money or possessions **to** someone, you say they should receive it or them when you die: *He left his nieces all his money./He left all his money* **to** *his nieces.* [+ two objects] • If something **leaves a bad/sour/unpleasant taste (in** your **mouth)** it leaves an unpleasant memory: *The disagreement left a sour taste.* • Something which **leaves a lot to be desired** is not as good as it could be: *The holiday left a lot to be desired.* • If something **leaves** you **cold** it does not make you feel interested or excited: *I know you love opera, but honestly it leaves me cold.* • If you are **left out in the cold** you feel you do not belong to a particular group of people and are not admired by them. • *(infml) Those staff* **left holding the** *(Br)* **baby/***(Am)* **bag** (= who had to deal unexpectedly with the problem) *were very junior and confused.* • If you **leave** someone **in the lurch**, you do not do what you had promised you would do: *He said he would help with the payments but then he left me in the lurch.* • If you **leave no stone unturned** you do everything you can to achieve a good result, esp. when looking for something: *He left no stone unturned in his search for his natural mother.* • If you **leave the door open to** something, you make it possible: *This will leave the door open to domestic companies to compete for international business.* • *He* **left** *the others* **standing/on the sidelines** (= was much better than the others). • *He seemed to be a responsible person, so I* **left** *him* **to** *his* **own devices** (= to make his own decisions about what to do). • Something which you **leave up in the air** is left without having been decided: *We talked about lunch but we left the date up in the air.* • To **leave well alone** is to allow something to stay as it is because doing more might make things worse: *It's going to get in a muddle if you carry on. I should just leave well alone if I were you.* • *(Br)* A **left-luggage office** (*Am and Aus* **baggage room** or *Am* **checkroom**) is a place at a station, airport, hotel, etc. where you can put your bags for a short time until you need them.

leave *(obj)* STOP /liːv/ *v past* **left** /left/ to stop doing something • *Many children leave school at sixteen instead of staying on for further education.* [T] • *She left* **home** (= stopped living with her parents) *at 18 to go and work in Africa.* [T] • *She's left her husband* (= stopped living with him) *and gone to live with another man.* [T] • *Could we leave that (subject)* (= stop discussing that subject) *for the moment and go on to the next item on the agenda?* [T] • *Leaving that* **aside** (= stopping discussion of that until later), *we still need to make a decision on the payments.* [M] • *He left work in June.* [T] • *I've had to leave* **(off)** *work because of my bad back.* [T] • *Is there any sign of the rain leaving* **off**? [I] • *"Sorry, I got interrupted." "That's all right, carry on from where you left* **off**." [I] • *(dated) Leave* **off** *teasing that dog. It'll bite you!* [+ v-*ing*] • *(dated) Hey,* **leave off** (= stop being annoying)*! I hate people touching my hair.* • **Leave go of/Leave hold of** (= Stop holding) *my arm.* • To **leave it at that** is to agree that there has been enough discussion, study, etc. and that it is time to stop: *It's getting late, so let's leave it at that for today and continue tomorrow.*

leav·er /£ˈliː·vər, $-vɚ/ *n* [C] • *school leavers*

leave *obj* GIVE RESPONSIBILITY /liːv/ *v* [T] *past* **left** /left/ to allow (someone) to make a choice or decision about (something), or to make (someone) responsible for something • *I left the decision* **(up) to** *her.* • *I left (it to) her* **to** *make the decision.* [+ obj + *to* infinitive] • *"Shall we go on Thursday or Friday?" "I don't mind. I'll leave it* **(up) to** *you."* • *I'll leave (it to) you* **to** *decide.* [+ obj + *to* infinitive] • *Don't leave (it to) me* **to** *explain it to him.* [+ obj + *to* infinitive] • *Leave it* **to** *me – I'll sort it out tomorrow.* • *I'll leave it* **to chance** (= wait and see what happens without planning). • *I leave choosing the wine to my husband.* [+ v-*ing*] • *You can leave the children* **with** *me on Thursday* (= they can stay with me on Thursday and I will be in charge of them). • *Leave it* (= the problem/matter) **with** *me, I'll see what I can do.*

leave PERMISSION /liːv/ *n* [U] *fml* permission or agreement • *He did it* **without** *(my) leave.* • *(dated) They started smoking* **without so much as a by your leave** (= without permission). • *Did you have/get leave* **to** *do that?* [+ *to* infinitive]

leave HOLIDAY /liːv/ *n* [U] time permitted away from work for holiday or illness • *How much* **annual/paid** *leave do you get?* • *She's* **(gone) on** *leave* (= holiday). • *I've asked if I can take a week's* **unpaid** *leave.* • *(Br and Aus) I've used up my leave* **entitlement** (= the amount of leave allowed) *for this year.* • *He asked for (a)* **leave of absence** (= permission to be away for a time). • LP› **Work**

leave GOODBYE /liːv/ *n* [U] **take leave** to say goodbye • *He decided the time had come to take his leave* **(of** *the family/town).* • *She didn't want to be involved in an emotional* **leave-taking** (= act of saying goodbye) *so she slipped out of the room quietly.* • *(fig. fml) Have you* **taken leave of** *your* **senses** (= lost your good judgment) *to do such a dangerous thing?*

-leaved /-liːvd/ *combining form* See at LEAF PLANT

leav·en *obj* /ˈlev·ən/ *v* [T usually passive] to add a substance to (bread and other things made with flour) to make it get bigger when it is cooked • *The dough is leavened* **with** *yeast.* • *(fig.) Even a speech on a serious subject should be leavened* **by/with** *a little humour.*

leav·ened /ˈlev·ənd/ *adj* [not gradable] • *Some people are not allowed to eat leavened bread at certain times of the year for religious reasons.*

leaves /liːvz/ *pl of* LEAF

lech·er·ous /£ˈletʃ·ər·əs, $ˈ-ɚ-/ *adj disapproving* (esp. of men) showing interest in people only for sexual reasons •

In the film he plays a lecherous soldier. • *He gave the girl/boy a lecherous look.*

lech af·ter *obj* /letʃ/ *v prep* [T] *infml disapproving* • *He's always leching after young girls/boys.*

lech·er /£ˈletʃ·əʳ, $-ɚ/, *infml* **lech**, **letch** *n* [C] *disapproving* • *If you believe his novels, all bankers are hypocrites and lechers* (= lecherous people).

lech·er·y /£ˈletʃ·ᵊr·i, $ˈ-ɚ-/ *n* [U] *disapproving*

lec·ith·in /ˈles·ɪ·θɪn/ *n* [U] a substance found in plant and animal tissue which is often used in food products to help the different parts mix together well

lec·tern /£ˈlek·tən, $-tɜːrn/ *n* [C] a piece of furniture with a sloping part on which a book or paper is put to be read from • *The speaker arranged her papers on the lectern.*

lec·ture /£ˈlek·tʃəʳ, $-tʃɚ/ *n* [C] a formal talk on a serious or specialist subject given to a group of people, esp. students • *Chemistry lectures were always boring to me.* • *The institute provides lectures* **on** *such matters as food photography and landscape gardening.* • A lecture is also a serious talk to advise or criticize someone: *She gave me a lecture* **on** *the importance of being tidy and well-organized.* • Compare SEMINAR. • LP **Schools and colleges** Ⓕ Ⓘ Ⓟ

lec·ture *(obj)* /£ˈlek·tʃəʳ, $-tʃɚ/ *v* • *She lectures* **in** *science.* [I] • *He lectured me* **on** *twentieth century poetry when I was a student.* [T] • *I can't see you now, I'm lecturing at ten.* [I] • *He lectured me* **on** *the need to keep clear records.* [T]

lec·tur·er /£ˈlek·tʃᵊr·əʳ, $-tʃɚ·ɚ/ *n* [C] • *The history department has five lecturers* (= specialist teachers) *and one professor.* • *The gardening club only pays its lecturers their travelling expenses.*

lec·ture·ship /£ˈlek·tʃə·ʃɪp, $-tʃɚ-/ *n* [C] • *She has a lectureship* (= the job of a college lecturer) **in** *economics at Durham University.*

led LEAD /led/ *past simple and past participle of* LEAD

–led PLANNED /-led/ *combining form* planned or controlled by a particular person or thing • *Part of the time is devoted to child-led activities* (= children decide what to do).

LED LIGHT /ˌel·iːˈdiː/ *n* [C] *specialized abbreviation for* light-emitting diode (= a device which produces a light esp. on electronic equipment) • An **LED display** is the letters or numbers shown in lights on a piece of electronic equipment.

ledge /ledʒ/ *n* [C] a narrow shelf which sticks out from a vertical surface • *The birds were nesting on ledges high up on the cliffs.*

ledg·er /£ˈledʒ·əʳ, $-ɚ/ *n* [C] a book in which items are regularly recorded, esp. business activities and money received or paid • *The client keeps full control of the sales ledger, sends out invoices and chases payment.*

lee /liː/ *n, adj* [before n; not gradable] (shelter) on the side away from the wind • *Most avalanche accidents occur on north- and east-facing lee slopes.* • *We sheltered* **in the lee of** *the coast/hill/wall.*

leech /liːtʃ/ *n* [C] a fat WORM which lives in wet places and fastens itself onto the bodies of humans and animals to take their blood • *He struggled through the swamp, tormented by mosquitoes and leeches.* • *Biologists have learned that leeches secrete an anticoagulant to keep blood from clotting as they suck it from their victims.* • *The kids* **clung** *to any passing person* **like** *leeches, demanding attention.* • *(disapproving)* A leech is also a person who gives attention to someone over a long period in order to get their money or support. • PIC **Worm**

leek /liːk/ *n* [C] a vegetable which looks like a white stick with long green leaves on top and which tastes a little like onion • PIC **Vegetables**

leer /£lɪəʳ, $lɪr/ *v* [I] (esp. of men) to look at someone in an unpleasant and sexually interested way • *He leered across the room* **at** *the girls.*

leer /£lɪəʳ, $lɪr/ *n* [C] • *He gave a hideous, drunken leer in her direction.*

leer·ing /£ˈlɪə·rɪŋ, $ˈlɪr·ɪŋ/ *adj* [before n] • *The song has leering lyrics and is full of smutty innuendo.* • *Along with one or two other drawbacks, the novel displays a leering attitude towards women.*

leer·y /£ˈlɪə·ri, $ˈlɪr·i/ *adj* [after v] **-ier, -iest** *infml* not very trusting of someone or something and tending to avoid them if possible; WARY • *I've always been a bit leery* **of** *authority figures.*

lees /liːz/ *pl n* **the lees** the substance which is left at the bottom of a container of liquid, esp. in a bottle of wine • *There's nothing left, only the lees.*

lee·ward /£ˈliː·wəd, $-wɚd/ *adj, adv* [not gradable] *specialized* (on the side of a hill, etc.) facing away from the wind • *We lit a fire on the leeward side of the hill, out of the wind.*

lee·way FREEDOM /ˈliː·weɪ/ *n* [U] freedom to act within particular limits • *We need some leeway if we are to act effectively.* • *The military men will be left some leeway* **to** *choose the exact time for attack.* [+ *to* infinitive]

lee·way PERIOD OF TIME /ˈliː·weɪ/ *n* [U] an amount or period of time, which might be additional or wasted • *The decision to* **give** *the company two years' leeway is a victory for the lawyers.* • *There is a lot of leeway to* **make up** *after the holiday period.*

left DIRECTION /left/ *adj, adv* [not gradable], *n* (on or towards) a position that is the opposite of 'right', for example in the word 'the', 't' is on the left of 'h' and 'th' is on the left of 'e' • *His left foot/eye/hand was heavily bandaged.* • *You are reading this sentence* **from** *left* **to** *right.* [U] • *After 2 kms* **turn (to the)** *left* (= turn into the road on the left side). [U] • *(Am) After the grocery store I* **made/took/** *(infml)* **hung** *a left* (= turned into the next road on the left side). [C] • *Take the first/second/third left* (= Turn into the first/second/third road on the left side). • *Walter Street is the second left* (= second road on the left side). • *My sister is third* **from (the)** *left in the back row of the choir.* [U] • *Our seats are near the front* **on/to the** *left of the central aisle.* [U] • *First I'll introduce the speakers sitting* **on** *my left.* [U] • **Left field** is the left part of the field in baseball, or *(fig. Am)* somewhere far from the main activity or belief. • *(Am)* If someone or something is **out in left field** they are completely wrong: *Some of my colleagues think I'm out in left field for promoting racial equality.* • **Left-hand** means on or to the left: *the left-hand side* ○ *a left-hand bend.* • A **left-hand drive** vehicle has the **steering wheel** on the left-hand side: *I'm not used to left-hand drive (cars).* • Someone who is **left-handed** or is a **left-hander** uses their left hand to write with and to do most things: *a left-handed bowler.* Something left-handed is designed to be used by such a person or is done with the left hand: *left-handed scissors* ○ *a left-handed stroke.* • *(infml)* A **left-hander** (also a **left**) is a hit with the left hand: *a powerful left-hander* ○ *a left to the chin.* [C] • A **left-handed** (also **back-handed)** compliment is a remark that seems to say something pleasant about a person but also could be an insult. • Compare RIGHT DIRECTION.

left POLITICS /left/ *n* [U], *adj* (political groups) believing wealth and power should be shared between all parts of society, or taking a **socialist** position or a position close to SOCIALISM • *This opinion is shared by all parties* **on the** *left.* • *(disapproving) He has won considerable admiration for coping with the* **loony** (= extreme) *left in his party.* • *The left* **wing** *of the party is/are demanding a vote.* • *Her views are fairly* **left-wing/left of centre** (= she supports the left). • *A well-known* **left-winger** (= supporter of the left), *he refused to pay his tax as a protest.* • Compare RIGHT POLITICS.

lef·tie /ˈlef·ti/, **left·y** *n* [C], *adj disapproving* • *The march involved not just local lefties and students but also elderly residents.* • *That's a typical leftie comment!*

left·ish /ˈlef·tɪʃ/ *adj* • *a leftish* (= having some sympathy with the left) *journal/newspaper* • *She has leftish views/opinions/attitudes.*

left·ist /ˈlef·tɪst/ *n* [C], *adj sometimes disapproving* • A leftist is a supporter of the political left: *Many leading leftists have condemned the central government for allowing the film to go ahead.* ○ *He cultivated Latin America's leftists and ultra-leftists.* ○ *leftist militants/newspapers* ○ *a leftist hero*

left·i·sm /ˈlef·tɪ·zᵊm/ *n* [U] *sometimes disapproving* • *There has been a swing from leftism to consensus.*

left·wards /£ˈleft·wədz, $-wɚdz/, *esp. Am* **left·ward** /£ˈleft·wəd, $-wɚd/ *adv* • *He accused the party leadership of moving leftwards.*

left LEAVE /left/ *past simple and past participle of* LEAVE

left·ov·er /£ˌleftˈəʊ·vəʳ, $ˌleftˈoʊ·vɚ/ *adj* [before n; not gradable] that still has not been used, eaten etc. when other parts have been • *The leftover wire was lying in the corner.* • *The children can use the leftover paper for scribbling.*

left·ov·ers /£ˈleftˌəʊ·vəz, $ˈleftˌoʊ·vɚz/ *pl n* • *This recipe can serve four easily, and the leftovers* (= food which has been prepared but not eaten) *are just as good eaten cold.* • *The notices warned me to keep off the ancient stonework – leftovers from 6000 years' worth of building one city on another.*

leg BODY PART /leg/ *n* one of the parts of the body of a human or animal that is used for standing or walking, or one of the thin vertical parts of an object on which it stands

• *He broke his leg skiing.* [C] • *The horse broke its front leg in the fall.* [C] • *The table/bed/chair has carved legs.* [C] • *I don't remember what it was that she was wearing but she was certainly showing a lot of leg* (= a large area of her legs could be seen). [U] • The leg of a piece of clothing is the part you put your leg in. [C] • *This leaves us* **without a leg to stand on**/*We have***n't** *got* **a leg to stand on** (= we have no good arguments to support our case). • *(Br slightly taboo slang)* For a man, to **get** his **leg over** is to have sex. • *(infml)* You **give** someone **a leg up** by helping them to climb over something, or *(fig. dated)* by helping them to improve their situation, esp. at work. • *(Am)* If you **have a leg up on** someone you have an advantage over them. • If someone **pulls** your **leg** they try to persuade you to believe something which is not true as a joke: *Is it really your car or are you pulling my leg?* ○ *He's a great* **leg-puller**. • In the game of cricket, **leg before wicket** (*abbreviation* **lbw**) means your time as the person trying to hit the ball is ended because the ball has hit your leg when it should not have. • *"Four legs good, two legs bad"* (George Orwell in the book *Animal Farm*, 1945) • PIC **Body, Chair, Table**

-leg·ged /-ˈleg·ɪd/ *combining form* • *a three-legged stool* • *a six-legged creature*

leg·gy /ˈleg·i/ *adj* **-ier, -iest** • *She was an elegant, leggy* (= having very long legs) *blonde.*

leg *obj* /leg/ *v* [T] **-gg-** *infml* • *They* **legged it** (= walked or ran fast to escape) *round the corner when they saw us coming.* • *I missed the bus so I had to* **leg it** (= walk) *home.*

leg STAGE /leg/ *n* [C] a part of a journey, competition or activity which has several stages • *He had tickets for the* **first** *leg* **of** *the UEFA Cup tie.* • *The* **last** *leg* **of** *the race was Paris to London.*

leg·a·cy /ˈleg·ə·si/ *n* [C] money, possessions etc. which you agree to give to another person when you die, or *(fig.)* something that is a part of your history or which stays from an earlier time • *An elderly cousin had* **left** *her a small legacy.* • *(fig.) The Greeks have a rich legacy of literature.* • *(fig.) The increase in consumer borrowing has created a legacy* **of** *instability and indebtedness.* • *(fig.) New technology, the main legacy* **of** *the Eighties, has been a mixed blessing.* • *(fig.) Oil slicks and black smoke were the environmental legacies* **of** *the war.*

le·gal /ˈliː·gəl/ *adj* connected with or allowed by the law • *legal advice* • *a legal obligation/requirement* • *legal status* • *your legal rights* • *legal action/proceedings* • *the legal profession* • *the legal system* • *financial and legal fees* • *a legal and ethical debate* • *her legal parents* • *my legal representatives* (= lawyers) • *a legal battle* • *Is abortion legal in your country?* • If you **make legal history**, the case you win in court or take to court is the first of its type and changes the way future cases will be dealt with. • **Legal aid** is a system of providing free advice about the law and practical help with legal matters for people who are too poor to pay for it: *Will we qualify for legal aid?* • **Legal tender** is the money which can be officially used in a country: *This coin/note is no longer legal tender.* • *"Legal, decent and honest"* (qualities demanded for advertisements by the Advertising Standards Authority, 1960s-)

le·gal·i·ty /£liːˈgæl·ə·ti, $-t̬i/ *n* [U] • The legality of something is the fact that it is allowed by the law: *Six journalists sought to challenge in court the legality* **of** *the ban on broadcasting.* ○ *The report is not clear on the legality* **of** *burying waste under the seabed.* ○ *Doubts about the legality* **of** *the present system of appointing judges were raised today.*

le·gal·i·ties /£liːˈgæl·ə·tiz, $-t̬iz/ *pl n* • Legalities are the things which are demanded by law: *I'm not sure about the legalities, but I suggest we go ahead with the plan and see what happens.* ○ *Never mind the legalities, these people need our help.*

le·gal·ize *obj*, *Br and Aus usually* **-ise** /ˈliː·gəl·aɪz/ *v* [T] • If you legalize something, you allow it by law: *He was posing as a wealthy Las Vegas gambler who wanted lawmakers to legalize casinos in Arizona.* ○ *The Irish government announced it was to legalize homosexuality.*

le·gal·iz·a·tion, *Br and Aus usually* **-i·sa·tion** /ˌliː·gəl·aɪˈzeɪ·ʃən/ *n* [U] • *the legalization of drugs*

le·gal·ly /ˈliː·gəl·i/ *adv* • *legally protected animals* • *drugs legally on sale in Britain* • *legally acquired assets* • *politically and legally sensitive material* • *The books had been obtained legally.*

le·gal·ese /ˌliː·gəlˈiːz/ *n* [U] *disapproving* formal language that is similar to the language in which legal documents are written and is difficult to understand

le·gal·is·tic /liː·gəlˈɪs·tɪk/ *adj disapproving* giving too much attention to rules and details • *The press coverage of the crisis has ranged from earnest legalistic debates to lurid innuendo.* • *The decision was based on a highly legalistic interpretation of the anti-defection law.*

le·gal·is·ti·cally /liː·gəlˈɪs·tɪ·kli/ *adv*

le·ga·tion /lɪˈgeɪ·ʃən/ *n* [C] *specialized* a group of officials who represent their government in a foreign country but who have less importance than an EMBASSY • *Britain has sent a legation to discuss trade and tariffs.* • A legation is also the building in which these officials work: *The marchers were demonstrating outside the legation.*

leg·end STORY /ˈledʒ·ənd/ *n* a very old story or set of stories from ancient times, or the stories, not always true, that people tell about a famous event or person • *The dance was based on several Hindu legends.* [C] • *She is writing a thesis on Irish legend and mythology.* [U] • *Many of the legends surrounding the artist's life have been disproved.* [C] • *Legend* **has it** (= People say) *that he always wore his boots in bed.* [U] • *This match will go into tennis legend* (= it will always be remembered). [U]

leg·en·da·ry /£ˈledʒ·ən·dri, $-der·i/ *adj* [not gradable] • *Was King Arthur a real or a legendary character?*

leg·end FAME /ˈledʒ·ənd/ *n* [C] someone or something very famous and admired, usually because of their ability in a particular area • *Louis Armstrong was a jazz legend.* • *She was a legend* **in** *her* **own lifetime** (= very famous while still alive). • *"She was a legend in her own lifetime, and she knew it"* (Lytton Strachey about Florence Nightingale in *Eminent Victorians*, 1918)

leg·en·da·ry /£ˈledʒ·ən·dri, $-der·i/ *adj* • *He became editor of the legendary* (= very famous and admired) *Irish journal 'The Bell.'* • *The British are legendary* **for** (= very famous for) *their incompetence with languages.*

leg·end EXPLANATION /ˈledʒ·ənd/ *n* [C] *fml* the words written on or next to a picture, map, coin, etc. that explain what it is about or what the symbols on it mean • *The legend on the diagram shows how the engine works.*

leg·gings /ˈleg·ɪŋz/ *pl n* a pair of very tight trousers made from a material that stretches easily, usually worn by women • PIC **Clothes**

leg·gy /ˈleg·i/ *adj* **-ier, -iest** See at LEG BODY PART

leg·i·ble /ˈledʒ·ɪ·bl̩/ *adj* (of writing or print) able to be read easily • *Her handwriting is so bad that it is barely legible.*

leg·i·bly /ˈledʒ·ɪ·bli/ *adv* • *Please write your name legibly on the board.*

le·gion SOLDIERS /ˈliː·dʒən/ *n* [C] a large group of soldiers who form one part of an army, esp. the ancient Roman army • *Caesar's legions marched through France and into Britain.*

le·gion MANY /ˈliː·dʒən/ *adj* [after v; not gradable] *fml* very large in number • *The difficulties surrounding the court case are legion.*

le·gions /ˈliː·dʒənz/ *pl n* • *The band's legions* **of** (= very many) *fans were disappointed when the concert was cancelled.*

Le·gion·naire's dis·ease /£liː·dʒənˈeəz, $-erz/ *n* [U] a serious and infectious disease of the lungs caused by bacteria in the air • *Four people have died following an outbreak of Legionnaire's disease in a hotel.*

leg·is·late /ˈledʒ·ɪ·sleɪt/ *v* [I] *fml* to make a law • *They promised to legislate* **against** *cigarette advertising.*

leg·is·la·tion /ˌledʒ·ɪˈsleɪ·ʃən/ *n* [U] • Legislation is a law or set of laws suggested by a government and made official by a parliament: *The government has promised to introduce legislation* **to** *limit fuel emissions from cars.* [+ to infinitive]

leg·is·la·tive /£ˈledʒ·ɪ·slə·tɪv, $-t̬ɪv/ *adj* [not gradable] *fml* • *The European Parliament will have greater legislative powers* (= ability to make laws). • The **legislative assembly** (*Am usually* **assembly**) is one of the two parts of the organization which makes laws in some American and Australian states, most Canadian provinces and some countries: *The lower house of the state parliaments of New South Wales, Victoria and Western Australia is called the legislative assembly.* • The **legislative council** is one of the two parts of the organization which makes laws in some Australian and Indian states: *The upper house of the state parliaments of New South Wales, South Australia, Tasmania, Victoria and Western Australia is called the legislative council.*

leg·is·lat·or /£ˈledʒ·ɪ·sleɪ·tər, $-t̬ɚ/ *n* [C] *fml* • A legislator is a member of a group of people who together have the power to make or change laws: *A Texas legislator has proposed stricter sentences for drug offenders.*

leg·is·la·ture /£'ledʒ·ɪ·slə·tʃʊəʳ, $-tʃɚ/ *n* [C + sing/pl v] *fml* • The legislature of a country or part of a country is the group of people who have the power to make and change laws: *South Carolina's legislature passed a law forbidding new houses to be built on its coast.*

legit /lə'dʒɪt/ *adj* [after v] *infml* LEGITIMATE • *I'm not getting involved in this fund-raising scheme if it isn't legit.*

le·git·i·mate /£lə'dʒɪt·ɪ·mət, $-'dʒɪţ-/ *adj* allowable according to law, or reasonable and acceptable • *He said that the restaurant bill was a legitimate business expense.* • *The army must give power back to the legitimate government.* • *This is a legitimate question* (= I have a right to ask it). • A legitimate **child/daughter/son** is one whose parents are legally married at the time of his or her birth: *Since she was his legitimate daughter, she would inherit a share of his fortune when he died.*

le·git·i·mate·ly /£lə'dʒɪt·ɪ·mət·li, $-'dʒɪţ-/ *adv* • *Most foreign visitors to Britain enter the country legitimately* (= obeying the law).

le·git·i·ma·cy /£lə'dʒɪt·ɪ·mə·si, $-'dʒɪţ-/ *n* [U] • *The government expressed serious doubts about the legitimacy of military action* (= about whether it is allowed by law).

le·git·i·mize *obj, Br and Aus usually* **-ise** /£lə'dʒɪt·ɪ·maɪz, $-'dʒɪţ-/, *Am* **le·git·i·mate** /£lə'dʒɪt·ɪ·meɪt, $-'dʒɪţ-/ *v* [T] *fml* • *They decided to legitimize* (= make legal) *their business relationship.* • *The government fears that talking to terrorists might legitimize* (= make acceptable) *their violent actions.*

leg·less /'leg·ləs/ *adj* [after v] *Br slang* extremely drunk • *He said he was going to get legless at the party.*

Le·go /£'leg·əʊ, $-oʊ/ *n* [U] *trademark* a toy for children consisting of small plastic bricks and other pieces such as wheels and windows, which can be joined together to make models of many different objects • *a Lego car/house* • PIC **Toy**

leg·room /'leg·ruːm/ *n* [U] the amount of space available for your legs when seated • *There isn't much legroom between the seats in this cinema.* • *The car has plenty of legroom for back-seat passengers.*

leg·ume /'leg·juːm/ *n* [C] *specialized* a plant that has its seeds in a POD (= a long thin case), such as the bean or PEA • *The soya bean, used to make tofu, is a very nutritious legume.*

le·gum·i·nous /ˌleg'juː·mɪ·nəs/ *adj specialized* • *Leguminous plants play a more important part in the diet of Mediterranean than North European countries.*

leg·warm·er /£'legˌwɔː·məʳ, $-ˌwɔːr·mɚ/ *n* [C] a woollen leg-covering that looks like a thick sock without feet • *a pair of legwarmers*

leg·work /£'leg·wɜːk, $-wɜːrk/ *n* [U] *infml* practical work that needs to be done • *Stephanie plans and writes the books herself, but she has an assistant who does the legwork, gathering background information and other facts.*

leis·ure /£'leʒ·əʳ, $-ɚ/ *n* [U] the time when you are not working or doing other duties • *Most people only have a limited amount of leisure* **(time)**. • *The town lacks leisure* **facilities** *such as a swimming pool or squash courts.* • Leisure **wear/clothes/garments** are clothes that are worn for relaxing in when you are not at work: *The company makes leisure clothing such as sweatshirts and tracksuits.* • *You can take the documents home and study them* **at (your) leisure** (= when you want to and when you have time to). • *(Br)* A **leisure centre** is a building containing a swimming pool and a large room or other places where you can play sports. • LP **Shopping goods**

leis·ure·ly /£'leʒ·ə·li, $'-ɚ-/ *adj* • A leisurely action is one that is done in a relaxed way, without hurrying: *We enjoyed a leisurely picnic lunch on the lawn.* • *Sue ran out of the room in tears, followed, at a more leisurely pace, by her husband.*

leit·mo·tiv /£'laɪt·məʊ·tiːf, $-moʊ·ţiːf/, **leit·mo·tif** *n* [C] *specialized or fml* a phrase or other feature that is repeated frequently in a work of art, literature or esp. music and that tells you something important about it • *Wagner used musical leitmotivs in his operas.* • *"Puzzle" and "mystery" are the leitmotifs running through the novel.*

lem·ming /'lem·ɪŋ/ *n* [C] an animal that looks like a large mouse and lives in cold northern areas • Lemmings MIGRATE (= move from one place to another) in large groups, and are often thought (wrongly) to jump off cliffs together, so groups of people who all do something foolish together without thinking for themselves can be called lemmings: *People rushed like lemmings to invest their money in the company that later went bankrupt.*

lem·on /'lem·ən/ *n* an oval fruit which has a thick yellow skin and sour juice • *For this recipe you need two lemons.* [C] • *Would you like* **a slice of** *lemon in your tea?* [U] • Lemon is also the juice of a lemon or a drink made from this juice: *He treated himself to some hot lemon and honey.* [U] ○ *a glass of lemon and lime* [U] • Something that is lemon is a pale yellow colour: *The kitchen walls are lemon and the floor is black and white.* [U] • *(Br and Aus slang)* A lemon is a very foolish person: *I felt such a lemon when I discovered I'd missed my appointment.* [C] • *(infml)* A lemon is something that does not work well, or at all: *Only one of his inventions turned out to be a lemon.* [C] • *(esp. Br)* **Lemon curd/cheese** (*Aus* **lemon butter**) is a thick sweet substance made from lemons that you can spread on bread or cakes. • **Lemon grass** is a tropical grass with a lemon-like flavour, used esp. in South East Asian cooking. • *(Am infml)* A **lemon law** is a law that lets people who buy large machines, esp. cars, get money from the seller if those machines don't work well. • A **lemon sole** is a flat fish that can be cooked and eaten. • *(Br and Aus)* **Lemon squash** is a sweet drink made from lemons. You add water to it before drinking it: *Would you like a lemon squash?* (J) • (D)

lem·on·ade /ˌlem·ə'neɪd/ *n* [U] *(Br and Aus)* a cold sweet bubbly drink or *(esp. Am)* a drink made with the juice of lemons, water and sugar • (J)

le·mur /£'liː·məʳ, $-mɚ/ *n* [C] a small monkey-like animal from Madagascar with thick fur and a long tail which lives in trees and is active at night

lend *(obj)* /lend/ *v past* **lent** /lent/ to give (something) to someone for a short period of time, expecting it to be given back • *She doesn't like lending her books.* [T] • *If you need a coat I can lend you one/lend one* **to** *you.* [+ two objects] • A bank or other organization that lends gives money to you and you agree that you will pay the money back in the future, usually with additional money added to the original amount: *The bank refuses to lend to students.* [I] ○ *The bank agreed to lend him $5000/lend $5000 to him.* [+ two objects] • If something lends a particular quality to something else, it adds that quality to it: *Vases of flowers all around the room lent the place a cheerful look/lent a cheerful look to the place.* [+ two objects] ○ *Photographs lent some credibility* **to** *his story.* [T] ○ *(fml) These events lend* **support** *to the view that the law is inadequate.* [T] • If you **lend an ear (to** someone or something) you listen carefully and patiently: *She's an expert on wines, so when she speaks it's worth lending an ear.* • *(fml)* If something **lends itself to** something else, it is suitable for that thing or can be considered in that way: *The computer lends itself to many different uses.* • If you **lend** your **name to** something, you give it your support: *Some of the world's top dancers have lent their names to the project.* • **Lending library** is *dated for* a public LIBRARY (= an organization with a collection, esp. of books, which anyone can borrow). • *(esp. Br and Aus)* A bank's **lending rate** (*Am usually, Aus also* **interest rate**) is the amount that it charges on money that it lends you: *Banks have raised their lending rates by 2%.* • Compare BORROW. • LP **Borrow**

lend·er /£'len·dəʳ, $-dɚ/ *n* [C] • A lender is often a large financial organization such as a bank: *the Council of Mortgage Lenders* ○ *The smaller local lenders charge high interest rates.* ○ *Most lenders refuse to lend money for apartments in buildings where more than half the units are rented.*

length DISTANCE /leŋkθ/ *n* the measurement of something from end to end or along its longest side • *Passengers will be charged according to the lengths of their vehicles.* [C] • *This elastic cord stretches to twice its normal length.* [C] • *The boat is ten metres* **in** *length* (= ten metres long). [U] • *She planted rose bushes* **(along) the** *length* **of the** *garden* (= the whole distance along it). [U] • A length of something such as string or pipe is a piece of it: *He used a short length of steel pipe as a weapon.* [C] • A length is a unit used in describing the distance by which a horse or boat wins a race. It is equal to the measurement from one end of the horse or boat to the other: *The Cambridge boat won by two lengths.* [C] • A length in a swimming pool is the distance from one end to the other: *She swims forty lengths a day.* [C] • If you travel **the length and breadth** of a place, you go to every part of it: *She travelled the length and breadth of Ireland looking for her missing brother.* • LP **Measurements, Units**

length·en *(obj)* /ˈleŋk·θən/ *v* • If you lengthen something you make it longer and if it lengthens it becomes longer: *I'll have to lengthen this skirt.* [T] ○ *The queue outside the shop was lengthening.* [I]

-length /-leŋkθ/ *combining form* • Something which is a particular -length is long enough to reach the stated place: *a knee-length skirt* ○ *shoulder-length hair* ○ *a floor-length evening dress*

length·ways /ˈleŋkθ·weɪz/, **length·wise** /ˈleŋkθ·waɪz/ *adv* [not gradable] • Lengthways means in the direction of the longest side: *Cut the beans in half lengthways.*

length [TIME] /leŋkθ/ *n* an amount of time • *He is unable to concentrate on his work for any length* **of time** (=for anything more than a short time). [C] • The length of a film, book, etc. is the amount of time it lasts or material it contains: *In an article of this length I cannot discuss all the issues involved.* [C] • If you do something **at length** you either do it for a long time, or *(fml)* you do it after a long period of time: *George went on at* **great** *length about his various illnesses.* ○ *(fml) At length the authorities allowed her to go home.* • If you say that someone would **go to great/any lengths** to do something, you mean that they would make a great deal of effort to achieve this thing: *Some people go to great lengths to make their homes attractive.*

length·en *(obj)* /ˈleŋk·θən/ *v* • If you lengthen something, or it lengthens, it takes longer to happen: *There is a plan to lengthen the three-year course to four years.* [T] ○ *The minutes lengthened into hours.* [I]

length·y /ˈleŋk·θi/ *adj* **-ier, -iest** • *Many airline passengers face lengthy* (=long) *delays because of overcrowded airports.*

-length /-leŋkθ/ *combining form* • *A full-length movie* (=one which has not been shortened) *lasts about two hours.* • See also DAYLENGTH.

le·ni·ent /ˈliː·ni·ənt/ *adj* not as severe or strong in punishment or judgment as would be expected • *They believe that judges are too lenient* **with** *terrorist suspects.* • *The referee took a surprisingly lenient* **view** *of the foul and did not even punish the player.* • *In view of the quantity of drugs involved, 16 years was the most lenient* **sentence** (=punishment) *the judge could impose.*

le·ni·ent·ly /ˈliː·ni·ənt·li/ *adv* • *He was dealt with much more leniently than we expected.*

len·i·enc·y /ˈliː·ni·ənt·si/ *n* [U] • *The defending lawyer asked for leniency on the grounds of her client's youth.*

Len·in·i·sm /ˈlen·ɪ·nɪ·zᵊm/ *n* [U] a theory based on the writings of V.I. Lenin, which states (among other things) that a small group of armed and highly trained REVOLUTIONARIES (=political soldiers) should lead the workers in the fight against the ruling class • *Leninism is often seen as the natural extension of* MARXISM.

Le·nin·ist /ˈlen·ɪ·nɪst/ *n* [C], *adj* [not gradable] • *There are still a number hard-line Leninists in Russia.* • *Do you remember the famous Leninist slogan, 'All power to the soviets!'?*

lens [GLASS] /lenz/ *n* [C] a thin piece of glass, plastic or other transparent material which usually has a curved surface and makes objects seem closer, larger, smaller, etc. Lenses are used in cameras, people's glasses and TELESCOPES. • *This type of camera has a zoom lens.* • *The lenses of my glasses steamed up in the sudden warmth of the room.* • Lens is also another word for **contact lens**. See at CONTACT [TOUCH].

lens [EYE] /lenz/ *n* [C] the part of the eye behind the PUPIL (=the black hole at the front of the eye) that helps you to see clearly by FOCUSING (=collecting) light onto the RETINA • *A laser beam is sometimes used on the surface of a damaged eye to reshape the lens.*

lent [LEND] /lent/ *past simple and past participle of* LEND

Lent [RELIGION] /lent/ *n* [U not after *the*] in the Christian religion, the 40 days before Easter, a period during which, for religious reasons, some people stop doing particular things that they enjoy • *The children have promised to* **give up** *sweets* **for** *Lent.* • [LP] **Holidays**

len·til /£ˈlen·tᵊl, $-t̬ᵊl/ *n* [C] a small round flat seed, cooked and eaten in soups and other dishes • *Lentils can be orange, green or brown.* • *The vegetable curry is served with rice and lentils.*

Le·o /£ˈliː·əʊ, $-oʊ/ *n* [not after *the*] *pl* **Leos** the fifth sign of the the ZODIAC, relating to the period 23 July to August 22, represented by a lion, or a person born during this period • *He was born* **under** *Leo* (=during this period). [U] • *We're both typical Leos.* [C]

le·o·nine /ˈliː·ə·naɪn/ *adj fml* (often of a person's head or hair) like a lion • *She tossed her leonine mane of hair indignantly.*

leop·ard /£ˈlep·əd, $-ɚd/ *n* [C] a large wild cat that has yellow fur with black spots on it and lives in Africa and S Asia • *(saying)* 'A leopard can't change its spots' means that a person's character, especially if it is bad, never really changes, even if that person might pretend it has: *He has promised not to tell lies any more, but a leopard can't change its spots.* • [PIC] **Cats**

le·o·tard /£ˈliː·ə·tɑːd, $-tɑːrd/ *n* [C] a tight piece of clothing that covers the top part of the body but not the legs, usually worn by women or women dancers, esp. when they are doing physical exercise

lep·re·chaun /£ˈlep·rɪ·kɔːn, $-kɑːn/ *n* [C] (in old Irish stories) a magical creature in the shape of a little old man who likes to cause trouble

lep·ro·sy /ˈlep·rə·si/ *n* [U] an infectious disease that damages a person's nerves and skin

lep·er /£ˈlep·əʳ, $-ɚ/ *n* [C] • A leper is a person who has leprosy, or *(fig.)* a person who is strongly disliked and avoided by other people because of something bad that he or she has done: *(fig.) She claimed that the rumours had made her a* **social** *leper.*

les·bi·an /ˈlez·bi·ən/, *infml* **les** /lez/ *n* [C] a woman who is sexually attracted only to other women • *They are trying to change stereotypes about gays and lesbians.*

les·bi·an /ˈlez·bi·ən/ *adj* [not gradable] • *She has joined a group for lesbian mothers.*

les·bi·an·i·sm /ˈlez·bi·ə·nɪ·zᵊm/ *n* [U] • Lesbianism is the condition of being a lesbian: *Queen Victoria refused to acknowledge the existence of lesbianism, which was never outlawed in Britain.*

le·sion /ˈliː·ʒᵊn/ *n* [C] *specialized* an injury to a person's body or to an organ inside their body, esp. to a particular part of a body or organ • *There were photographs showing lesions* **to** *backs and thighs.* • *Brain lesions can be caused by bacterial infections.*

less [SMALLER AMOUNT] /les/ *determiner, pronoun, adv* [not gradable] a smaller amount (of); not so much, or to a smaller degree • *Most of the women there were aged forty or less.* • *We must try to spend less money.* • *You should work more and talk less.* • *I eat less chocolate and fewer biscuits* **than** *I used to.* • *We had walked less* **than** *three kilometres when Robert said he wanted to rest.* • *Getting out of bed in summer is less difficult* **than** *in winter.* • *I think he was being* **less than** *honest* (=not at all honest) *with me.* • If something happens **less and less** it becomes gradually not so frequent or smaller in amount: *She phones me less and less.* ○ *His uncle is less and less able to look after himself.* • *(fml)* You say **much less** or **still less** to make a negative statement stronger: *At the age of fourteen I had never even been on a train, much less an aircraft.* • You say **no less than** to show your surprise at a large number: *There were no less than a thousand people there buying tickets.* • *(humorous)* You can use **no less** to show your surprise or admiration at the importance of someone or something: *Who should arrive at the party but the Prime Minister, no less!* • You can say **the less** to show that two things are connected in a particular way: **The more** *she hears about the place, the less she wants to go there.* ○ *The less* **said about** *this unpleasant business,* **the better**. • It is quite common for English speakers to use 'less' before countable nouns, meaning 'not so many': *The trees have produced less apples this year.* But this is traditionally considered bad English. The standard word for 'not so many' is 'fewer': *The trees have produced fewer apples this year.* The standard use of 'less' is before uncountable nouns, meaning 'not so much': *Give me less cream, please.* • [LP] **Quantity words**

les·sen *(obj)* /ˈles·ᵊn/ *v* • If something lessens or is lessened, it becomes less strong: *The rain eventually lessened to a soft mist.* [I] ○ *Eating properly can lessen the risk of heart disease.* [T]

les·ser /£ˈles·əʳ, $-ɚ/ *adj* [before n; not gradable] • Lesser is used to describe something that is not as great in size, amount or importance as something else: *A lesser* **man** (=a man who was not as strong or brave) *might have given up at that point.* ○ *The charge of murder was altered to the lesser* (=less serious) *charge of manslaughter.* ○ *Ethiopia and,* **to a** *lesser* **extent/degree**, *Kenya will be badly affected by the drought.* • If something is **the lesser of two evils** it is bad, but not as bad as something else: *He said that allowing a* *criminal to escape was the lesser of two evils when the alternative was imprisoning an innocent person.*

-less WITHOUT /-ləs, -lɪs/ *combining form* used to form adjectives meaning without (the thing mentioned) • *Something without meaning is meaningless.* • *He has no friends at all – he is friendless.* • LP› **Opposites, Stress in pronunciation**

less SUBTRACT /les/ *prep* before subtracting (an amount); MINUS SUBTRACTION • *The total is thirty pounds, less the five pounds deposit that you've paid.*

les·son /ˈles·ᵊn/ *n* [C] a period of time in which a person is taught about a subject or how to do something • *How can we make science lessons more interesting?* • *She has never* **taken** *acting lessons.* • A lesson can also be a useful piece of information learned through experience: *We can* **learn/draw** *important lessons* **from** *this disaster.* ○ *There is a lesson for all parents* **in** *this tragic case of child death.* ○ *She decided to* **teach** *the boy* **a lesson** (= to punish him for doing something so that he would not do it again). • LP› **Schools and colleges**

lest /lest/ *conjunction literary* in order to prevent any possibility that (something will happen) • *They were afraid to complain about the noise lest they annoyed the people next door.* • *Lest you think the film is too violent, I must assure you that it is not.*

let *obj* ALLOW /let/ *v* [T] **letting**, *past* **let** to allow (something to happen or someone to do something) by not doing anything to stop it from happening or by giving your permission • *Let me go home – I'm tired.* [+ obj + infinitive without *to*] • *She wanted to go but her parents wouldn't let her.* • *He decided to let his hair grow long.* [+ obj + infinitive without *to*] • *Let your shoes dry completely before putting them on.* [+ obj + infinitive without *to*] • *I'm letting you stay up late, just this once.* [+ obj + infinitive without *to*] • *Don't let it worry you.* [+ obj + infinitive without *to*] • *(fml)* You can use 'let me' as a polite way of saying something: *Let me first ask you how much money you would wish to invest.* • If you let someone or something **alone** or let them **be**, you stop touching them, criticizing them or doing something to them that is annoying. • When you **let** something that a person says **go/pass**, you do not give it any attention or say that the thing said is wrong: *I could have complained about the mistake but I just let it go.* ○ *When he made a racist remark I couldn't let it pass.* • If you **let yourself go**, you either behave much more freely than usual and enjoy yourself, or you stop caring about your appearance and look untidy: *The music got louder and I let myself go, dancing wildly.* ○ *Since he lost his job he's really let himself go.* • If you **let** your **hair down** you allow yourself to behave much more freely than usual and enjoy yourself: *Come on, it's a party so let your hair down!* • If you let someone **in** you allow them to enter a place: *She opened the door and let me in.* ○ *These shoes let in the rain* (= allow the rain to go in). [M] ○ *I had borrowed a key and so let myself* **into** *the house* (= opened the door and went in). • If you let someone **in on**/*(Br and Aus also)* **into** a secret you allow them to know something that you have not told anyone else: *Shall I let you into a little secret?* • *(dated slang)* If you **let it all hang out** you behave freely without being shy or feeling worried about what other people will think of you. • If you **let it/things lie** you take no action about something: *Instead of going to the police they let things lie for a couple of months.* • If you **let off** someone who expects to be punished, you do not punish them at all, or punish them less severely than they expected: *Instead of a prison sentence they were let off* **with** *a fine.* ○ *You won't be let off so* **lightly** (= you will be punished more severely) *the next time.* • If you let someone or something **out**, you allow them to leave a place: *I heard a voice from the cupboard shouting "Let me out!"* • *(Am) When does school* **let out** (= end) *for the summer?* • If you **let slip**/*(Br also)* **drop/fall** information or **let it slip**/*(Br also)* **drop**, you tell people about it (as if) unintentionally: *He let slip/let it slip that it was his birthday the next day.* • To **let slip** also means to say something that you did not intend to say: *Having spent ten minutes criticizing the film, he let slip that he had never actually seen it.*

let *obj* CAUSE /let/ *v* [T] **letting**, *past* **let** to cause to happen or be in a particular condition • *If he needs money, let him* (= make him) *earn it.* [+ obj + infinitive without *to*] • *(Br and Aus)* If you let **down** something filled with air, you cause the air to go out of it: *Some kids have let my bike tyres down.* [M] • If you let **down** a piece of clothing you make it longer: *My trousers shrunk in the wash so I let them down.* [M] • **Let go (of)** (= Stop holding) *my hand, you're hurting me!* • *Hold on tight and don't* **let go** (= don't stop holding it)*!* • If you **let** someone **have it** you attack them with words or physically: *Just wait till your parents hear how you've behaved, they'll really let you have it!* • *(Br)* If something has been let **into** a flat surface, it has been positioned in it so that it does not stick out: *A skylight had been let into the roof.* • If you **let** someone **know**, you tell them something: *Let us know* **when** *you get there.* ○ *Let me know if you need any help.* ○ *Thank you for coming to the interview – we'll let you know* (= tell you whether we are going to offer you a job). • To **let** something **be known** is to make certain that people are aware of it: *I let* **it** *be known* **that** *I was not happy about the decision that had been made.* • If you let **off** a gun, bomb, etc. you fire the gun or make the bomb explode: *Don't let off fireworks near the house.* [M] • *(infml)* If you **let off steam** you get rid of too much energy or strong feelings by behaving noisily: *The children ran around the garden shouting and letting off steam.* • If you let air, water, etc. **out** of something, you cause it to come out: *He let the air out of the balloon.* [M] • *(literary) She let* **out** *a scream* (= She made this noise). [M] • If you let **out** clothes you make them wider: *During pregnancy she still wore her normal clothes, though she did have some dresses let out.* [M] • To **let** (something) **rip** is to cause something to be as loud or fast as possible: *In their last number the band really let (it) rip.* ○ *The road was empty and they let (it) rip* (= drove fast). • If you **let rip/fly** you lose control, esp. showing anger forcefully: *Eventually she lost her temper and let rip.*

let *obj* SUGGEST /let/ *v* [T + obj + infinitive without *to*; not *be letting*; not in past tenses] used to express a suggestion which includes you and the other person or people, or a request or order • *(fml) Let us consider all the possibilities.* • *Let's go out to dinner, shall we?* • *Let's not argue/(Br also)* **Don't** *let's argue.* • **Let's face it** (= We should accept the truth), *you're never going to be a great artist.* • You say **let's see/let me see/let me think** when you want to think carefully about something or are trying to remember: *Next Saturday, let's see, that's when we're going to the theatre.* ○ *The last time I spoke to her was, now let me think, three weeks ago.* • You can use let to show that you accept what is going to happen although you do not like it: *Let him come and speak to me, I'm not scared of him.* ○ *Let it rain, it won't spoil our afternoon.* • You can say 'let me' as a threat: *Just let me hear you saying such a thing again and you'll be sorry!* ○ *Don't let me catch you in here again!* • *(specialized)* When making a plan or calculating a number, you use let to introduce the purpose of the argument: *Let a = 4, b = 5.* • *"Let's Call the Whole Thing Off"* (title of a song written by Ira Gershwin, 1937)

let CERTAINLY NOT /let/ *v* **let alone** used after a negative statement to emphasize how unlikely a situation is because something much more likely has never happened • *She can't afford to buy a bicycle, let alone a car.* • *Some people never even read a newspaper, let alone a book.*

let *obj* RENT *esp. Br and Aus* /let/, *esp. Am* **rent** *v* [T] **letting**, *past* **let** to allow (your house or land) to be lived in or used by someone else in exchange for a payment made regularly • *They are letting their house* **(out)** *for the summer.* [T/M] • *He's let his flat* **to** *a young couple.* • *She has a room* **to** *let in her house.* • *House* **to** *let.* • LP› **Borrow**

let /let/ *n* [C] *Br* • A let is the act of allowing someone to use your house, land, etc. in exchange for regular payments: *We signed for a five-year let* **on** *a cottage outside the town.*

let·ting /£ˈlet·ɪŋ, $ˈleṭ-/ *n* [C] *Br* • *The town offers several holiday lettings* (= buildings that can be rented).

let SPORT /let/ *n* [C] (in tennis or similar games) a situation in which the ball touches the net as it crosses it, so that you have to play the point again

let LAW /let/ *n* [U] **without let or hindrance** *specialized* without being prevented from doing something • *People will be able to travel from country to country without let or hindrance.*

let down *obj*, **let** *obj* **down** *v adv* [M] to cause (someone) disappointment, often by failing to do what you have promised • *You'll be there tomorrow – you won't let me down, will you?* • *When I was sent to prison, I really felt I had let my parents down.* • *(Br and Aus)* If you say that someone has **let the side down**, you mean that they have done something which is bad for the group of people they belong to: *I think Sid rather let the side down when he admitted we couldn't afford it.* • See also **let down** at LET CAUSE.

let·down /ˈlet·daʊn/ *n* [C usually sing] *infml* • *Well, that film was a bit of a letdown* (= disappointing because not as good as expected).

let on *v adv infml* to tell other people about (something that you know), esp. when it is a secret • *If he did know the truth, he didn't let on* **(about** *it).* [I] • *You mustn't let on* **who** *we saw last night.* [+ *wh*-word] • *I gather he let on* **that** *she's to be the new director.* [+ *that* clause]

let up *v adv* [I] (esp. of something unpleasant) to become less strong or stop • *When the rain lets up we'll go for a walk.* • *(fig.) You're much too strict, why don't you let up* **on** *him* (= be less severe towards him)*?*

let·up /£ˈlet·ʌp, $ˈlet̬-/ *n* [U] • *The airline authorities are not expecting a letup in delays* (= are not expecting delays to stop) *for the rest of the summer.*

le·thal /ˈliː·θəl/ *adj* able to cause or causing death; extremely dangerous • *Three minutes after the fire started, the house was full of lethal fumes.* • *In the car the police found guns, knives and other lethal* **weapons** (= weapons which can kill). • *A 59-year-old man was executed by lethal* **injection** (= by having a poisonous substance put into his body) *this morning.* • *(infml) When it comes to getting what she wants, Gillian is lethal* (= uses strong and determined methods).

le·thal·ly /ˈliː·θəl·i/ *adv*

leth·ar·gic /£ləˈθɑː·dʒɪk, $-ˈθɑːr-/ *adj* lacking in energy; feeling unwilling and unable to do anything • *Being depressed makes him lethargic and unable to get out of bed in the mornings.*

leth·ar·gy /£ˈleθ·ə·dʒi, $ˈ-ɚ-/ *n* [U] • *Sleep deprivation can cause stress, loss of appetite and lethargy.*

let·ter [MESSAGE] /£ˈlet·əʳ, $ˈlet̬·ɚ/ *n* [C] a written or printed message from one person to another, usually put in an envelope and sent by the postal service • *Many people phone rather than write letters.* • *I got a letter* **from** *the bank manager this morning.* • *If you have any complaints, please inform me* **by letter.** • A **letter bomb** is a small bomb that is placed in an envelope or parcel and sent to someone through the postal service. • **Letter carrier** is *Am for* POSTMAN. • A **letter of credit** is a letter from a bank allowing the person who has it to take a particular amount of money from a bank in another country: *Some foreign suppliers won't release goods until they receive cash payment or a letter of credit from the bank.* • A **letter-opener/paper knife** is a long thin knife that is sharp enough only to open letters. • *"I'm going to sit right down and write myself a letter / And make believe it comes from you"* (from a song written by Joe Young and Fred Ahlert, 1935) • (I)

let·ter [SYMBOL] /£ˈlet·əʳ, $ˈlet̬·ɚ/ *n* [C] any of the set of symbols used to write a language, representing a sound in the language • *In this game you have seven letters with which to make a word.* • *She wrote her name on the board in large letters.* • If you **keep to/follow the letter of the law** you obey the exact words of the law rather than its more general meaning: *The jury clearly thought that the spirit* (= the general meaning)*, not the letter, of the law was more important in this case.* • If you obey instructions or rules **to the letter** you do exactly what you have been told to do, giving great attention to every detail: *If you follow these instructions to the letter you will succeed in this task.* • **Letter-perfect** is *Am for* **word-perfect**. See at WORD.

let·ter·ing /£ˈlet·ər·ɪŋ, $ˈlet̬·ɚ-/ *n* [U] • *The perfume comes in a black box with gold lettering* (= letters).

let·ter·box *Br and Aus* /£ˈlet·ə·bɒks, $ˈlet̬·ɚ·bɑːks/, *Am* **mail slot** *n* [C] a rectangular hole in the door or in a wall near the entrance of a person's house, through which letters, etc. are delivered • *I tried to push the package through the letterbox.* • A letterbox (*Am and Aus also* **mailbox**) is also a box outside a person's house, into which letters, etc. are put when they are delivered. • Letterbox is another word for POSTBOX. • [PIC] **Doors**

let·ter·head /£ˈlet·ə·hed, $ˈlet̬·ɚ-/ *n* the top part of a piece of writing paper where the name and address of a person or business is printed • *The phone number wasn't on the letterhead.* [C] • *She prints brochures, letterheads and logos for local businesses.* [C] • Letterhead is also paper with a name and address printed at the top: *I'll need a few sheets of letterhead.* [U]

let·tuce /£ˈlet·ɪs, $ˈlet̬-/ *n* a plant with usually large green leaves, eaten raw in salads • *I planted a row of lettuces.* [C] • *I'd like a bacon, lettuce and tomato sandwich, please.* [U] • [PIC] **Vegetables**

let·up /£ˈlet·ʌp, $ˈlet̬-/ *n* [U] See at LET UP

leu·cot·o·my /£luːˈkɒt·ə·mi, $-ˈkɑː·t̬ə-/ *n* [C] *Br for* LOBOTOMY

leu·kae·mi·a, *esp. Am and Aus* **leu·ke·mi·a** /luːˈkiː·mi·ə/ *n* [U] a disease in which the body produces too many white blood cells, causing weakness and sometimes leading to death

lev·el [HORIZONTAL] /ˈlev·əl/ *adj* horizontal and/or flat, or having the same height, position, standard, etc. • *The swimming pool is located on the only level ground in the town.* • *The picture's not level – the left side is slightly higher.* • *She poured a bit more wine, until the amounts in our glasses were level* **(with** *each other).* • *The top of the tree is level* **with** *his bedroom window.* • *Teams A and B are (Br and Aus)* **on** *a* **level with/(Am) even with** *each other* (= both have the same number of victories). • *The unions are fighting to keep wages level (Am usually* **even)** **with** *inflation.* • *Chiappucci would have to win the next three stages in order to* **draw** *level* **with** (= reach the same position as) *Indurain in the Tour de France.* • A level **spoonful/cupful** contains enough liquid or substance to fill the spoon/cup but not enough to go above the edges. • *(esp. literary)* If you speak in a level voice or give someone a level look, you do it in a calm and controlled way: *In a level voice, he ordered the soldiers to aim and fire.* ○ *She gave him a level look that seemed to express her determination.* • *I'll* **do** *my* **level best** (= try as hard as I can) *to get you a ticket.* • *(Br and Aus) Both teams are* **(on) level pegging** (= in an equal position). • *If the tax systems are different in each European country, how can industries start on a* **level playing field** (= with the same advantages and disadvantages for everyone)*?* • *(Br and Aus)* A **level crossing** (*Am* **grade crossing**) is a place where a railway and a road cross each other, usually with gates that stop the road traffic while a train goes past. • If you describe someone as **level-headed**, you mean that they are calm and able to deal easily with difficult situations. • [PIC] **Road**

lev·el /ˈlev·əl/ *adv* • *Is the picture hanging level* **with** *the floor?*

lev·el /ˈlev·əl/ *n* • A level is a position, esp. of height: *The water level in the lake is much higher after heavy rain.* [C] • *Inflation is going to rise 2% from its present level.* [C] • *The big debate is whether more decisions should be taken at* **local** *or* **national** *level.* [U] • *Company policy is decided* **at** *the very highest level* (= by the top managers). [U] • *There is some danger of low level* (= a continuing small amount of) *radiation.* • A level is also a standard: *I played the cello, but never reached a very high level.* [C] ○ *The exam can be taken at three levels.* [C] ○ *We publish course books and a dictionary for intermediate level students/ students* **at** *intermediate level.* [U] ○ *I thought the level of discussion was rather low.* [C] • A level is also one of several STOREYS or floors at different heights in a large building: *The library has three levels, including an underground parking area, a reception area* **at ground** *level, and reading rooms above that.* [C] ○ *The exhibition is* **at/on** *level three of the building.* • *It's a children's story but adults can appreciate it* **at/on another/a deeper level** (= there is another meaning). • **On a more serious level** (= Changing the subject to discuss more serious things)*, could we turn now to the question of funding?* • *(Br) After the earthquake the only houses still standing were those built* **on the level** (= on flat ground). • If someone or something **finds** their **own level** they find and stay in the position which is suitable for them: *She's found her own level as an instructor overseas.* • Level is *esp. Am for* SPIRIT-LEVEL. • [PIC] **Building and construction**

lev·el *obj* /ˈlev·əl/ *v* [T] **-ll-** or *Am usually* **-l-** • If you level something **(off/out)** you make it smooth and flat: *We use a heavy roller to level the ground.* ○ *Builders came and levelled the shed* (= knocked it down and destroyed it completely). • If an aircraft **levels off/out**, it starts to travel horizontally rather than going up or down: *The jet levelled off at 10 000 feet.* • If something **levels off** it stops increasing or becoming less: *Unemployment rose to 10% and then levelled off.* • If two or more things **level out**, they become equal with each other: *The younger trees grow faster, but the rates level out within two years.* • (KOR)

lev·el·ler, *Am usually* **lev·el·er** /£ˈlev·əl·əʳ, $-ɚ/ *n* [U] *literary* • *Time/Poverty/Disease is* **a great leveller** (= has the same effect on everyone so that no one has an advantage).

LETTERS

Business letters and other formal letters

There are several modern styles of business letter. Notice that often these use no commas (,) in the address details, opening greeting or closing phrase. The abbreviations used are explained below.

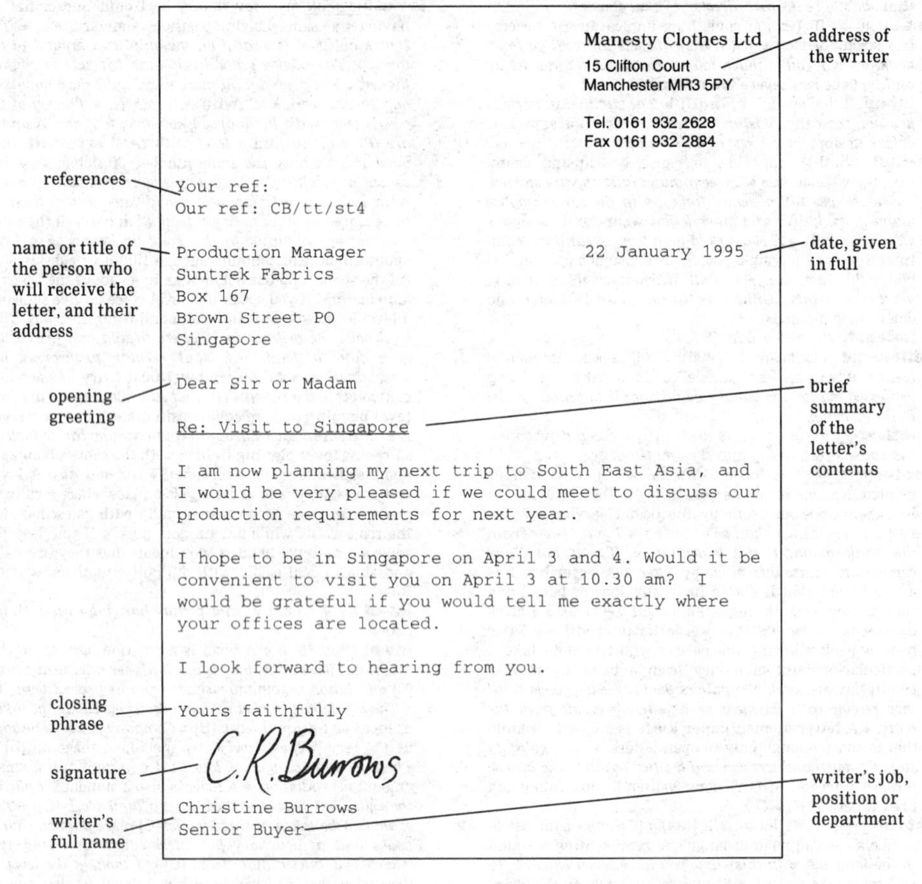

Manesty Clothes Ltd
15 Clifton Court
Manchester MR3 5PY

Tel. 0161 932 2628
Fax 0161 932 2884

Your ref:
Our ref: CB/tt/st4

Production Manager
Suntrek Fabrics
Box 167
Brown Street PO
Singapore

22 January 1995

Dear Sir or Madam

Re: Visit to Singapore

I am now planning my next trip to South East Asia, and I would be very pleased if we could meet to discuss our production requirements for next year.

I hope to be in Singapore on April 3 and 4. Would it be convenient to visit you on April 3 at 10.30 am? I would be grateful if you would tell me exactly where your offices are located.

I look forward to hearing from you.

Yours faithfully

C. R. Burrows

Christine Burrows
Senior Buyer

lev·el·ly /ˈlev·ᵊl·i/ *adv* [not gradable] • *He looked levelly* (=calmly and without excitement) *across at me.*

lev·el *obj* AIM /ˈlev·ᵊl/ *v* [T] **-ll-** or *Am usually* **-l-** to aim (esp. a weapon) at someone • *She picked up the gun and levelled it* **at** *me.* • *(fig.) Criticism has been levelled* **against/at** *senior figures in the industry.*

lev·el with *obj v prep* [T] *infml* to tell (someone) the truth about something; to not hide the truth • *I'll level with you – the salary's not particularly good, and there's little chance of promotion.*

lev·el /ˈlev·ᵊl/ *n* [U] • *(infml)* If a person or thing is **on the level** they are behaving honestly or speaking truthfully: *I think they're on the level* **about** *the price.* ○ *John's a friend and if he gave you a price, then it's on the level.* See also **on the level** at LEVEL HORIZONTAL.

le·ver /£ˈliː·vəʳ, $ˈlev·ɚ/ *n* [C] a bar or handle which moves around a fixed point, so that one end of it can be pushed or pulled in order to control the operation of a machine or move a heavy or stiff object • *a gear lever in a car* • *(Br) a brake lever (Am and Aus* **handbrake***) on a bicycle* • *She balanced an iron bar on a stone and used it as a lever to lift open the drain cover.* • *A door handle is a type of lever.* • *(fig.) The blackmailer used the threat of scandal as a lever to get money from his victims.* • A **lever arch file** is a type of large container used to hold paper, in which paper is held on two big curved pieces of metal which are opened or closed using a metal bar. • PIC **Bicycles, Stationery**

le·ver *obj* /£ˈliː·vəʳ, $ˈlev·ɚ/ *v* [T always + adv/prep] • *She levered* **up** *the drain cover.* [M] • *The old man levered himself* **(up) out of** *the armchair* (=used his arms to push himself out of it with a lot of effort).

le·ver·age /£ˈliː·vᵊr·ɪdʒ, $ˈlev·ɚ·ɪdʒ/ *n* [U] • Leverage is the action or advantage of using a lever: *With a longer handle you get more leverage.* • *(fig.) If the United Nations had more troops in the area, it would have greater leverage* (=power to influence people and get desired results).

le·ver·age /£ˈliː·vᵊr·ɪdʒ, $ˈlev·ɚ·ɪdʒ/ *n* [U] *specialized* the use of borrowed money to buy a company

le·ver·aged /£ˈliː·vᵊr·ɪdʒd, $ˈlev·ɚ·ɪdʒd/ *adj specialized* • A **leveraged buyout** is an attempt to buy a company using borrowed money: *The airline was bought in a leveraged buyout.*

le·vi·a·than, Le·vi·a·than /ləˈvaɪə·θᵊn/ *n* [C] *literary* something or someone that is extremely large and powerful • *For many years the US was an economic leviathan.*

Le·vi's /ˈliː·vaɪz/ *pl n trademark* JEANS

lev·i·tate *(obj)* /ˈlev·ɪ·teɪt/ *v* to (cause to) rise and float in the air without any physical support • *I often dream that I can levitate.* [I] • *He tried to levitate the table.* [T]

lev·i·ta·tion /ˌlev·ɪˈteɪ·ʃᵊn/ *n* [U]

lev·i·ty /£ˈlev·ɪ·ti, $-t̬i/ *n* [U] *literary* amusement or lack of seriousness, esp. during a serious occasion • *The only moment of levity during the conference came when one speaker sang at the end of her speech.*

lev·y /ˈlev·i/ *n* [C] an amount of money, such as a tax, that you have to pay to a government or organization • *They* **imposed** *a 5% levy* **on** *alcohol.*

• how to start and end a letter

opening and closing phrases	when you would use these phrases
Dear Sir or Madam Yours faithfully	you do not know the name, sex or title of the person you are writing to (for example when writing to a company)
Dear Mr Cox/Ms Cox/Mrs Cox/Miss Cox Yours sincerely / Yours truly	you know the name, sex and title, and you want to sound formal. LP on **Titles and forms of address** at TITLE
Dear John With best wishes / With kind regards	you know the person's first name and want to be less formal

• some common phrases used in business letters

The language of business letters might be formal or informal, depending on the relationship between the people involved. Below are examples of common phrases given in formal and informal styles. Writing can be made even more informal by using short forms like 'I've' (= I have).

formal style	informal style
Thank you for your letter of 22 January concerning...	Thank you for your letter about...
I am writing to inquire about...	I am writing to ask about...
I am writing to inform you that...	I am writing to say that...
I am pleased to inform you that...	I am pleased to say...
I regret to inform you that...	I am sorry to have to tell you that...
I hope this information has been of use.	I hope this has been useful.
Please give my regards to Peter Hogan.	Remember me to Peter. / Regards to Peter.
Thank you for your time/help.	Thanks for your time/for all you have done.
I look forward to hearing from you soon.	I hope to hear from you soon.

• abbreviations used in business letters and documents

There are very many abbreviations used in business documents, but the following are commonly found:

Tanner **& Co.**	Tanner and Company
*(esp Br)*NewTech **Ltd**	NewTech Limited (= a LIMITED company)
NewTech **plc**	(= a public LIMITED company)
*(Am)*NewTech **Inc.**	NewTech Incorporated (= a business CORPORATION)
*(Am)*NewTech **Corp.**	NewTech Corporation
*(Austr)*NewTech **Pty**	(= a PROPRIETARY LIMITED company)
Attn J K Long	attention of (= to be read by) J K Long
cc H Peters, N Vance	(= copies are being sent to the named people)
Tel. no.	telephone number
Re:	(= the letter is about the following matter)
asap	as soon as possible
pp	(put before your name if someone else signs the letter for you)

• informal and personal letters

When writing to someone you know well, you would use an informal style close to conversational English. Other features include:

- first names are used, shortened names like 'Bob' or 'Liz', and informal forms of address such as 'Mom' or 'Dad'
- the name and address of the person who receives the letter are not given
- a comma (,) is put at the end of the first lines of an address, after the opening greeting and after the closing phrase
- the date might be given in a short form (LP at DATE)
- informal greetings are used when writing to family, people you love or good friends: Dearest..., My dear..., Darling...
- informal closing phrases are used, for example: All the best, Best wishes, Love, Regards

lev·y *obj* /ˈlev·i/ *v* [T] • *They are going to have to levy some new* **taxes**.

lewd /luːd/ *adj* **-er, -est** *disapproving* (of behaviour, speech, dress, etc.) sexual in an obvious and usually socially unacceptable way • *He is being accused of making lewd and suggestive comments to a female employee.*

lewdly /ˈluːd·li/ *adv*

lewd·ness /ˈluːd·nəs/ *n* [U]

lex·i·cal /ˈlek·sɪ·kᵊl/ *adj* [not gradable] *specialized* relating to words • *The students were asked to make a lexical and grammatical analysis of the President's speech.*

lex·i·cog·ra·phy /£ˌlek·sɪˈkɒg·rə·fi, $-ˈkɑː·grə-/ *n* [U] *specialized* the activity or job of writing dictionaries

lex·i·co·gra·pher /£ˌlek·sɪˈkɒg·rə·fəʳ, $-ˈkɑː·grə·fɚ/ *n* [C] • *They're lexicographers, otherwise known as dictionary writers.*

lex·i·con /ˈlek·sɪ·kən/ *n* [C] *specialized* (a list of) all the words used in a particular language or subject, or a dictionary

lex·is /ˈlek·sɪs/ *n* [U] *specialized* all the words of a language • *The first section of the book covers the grammar and lexis of English.*

ley line /leɪ/ *n* [C] the imaginary line that is formed by some important places such as hills or very old churches in Britain, believed to be where there were very old paths

li·a·ble RESPONSIBLE /ˈlaɪ·ə·bl̩/ *adj* [after v; not gradable] *specialized* having (legal) responsibility for something or someone • *The law holds parents liable if a child does not attend school.* • *If we lose the case we may be liable* **for** (= have to pay) *the costs of the whole trial.* • *(Br and Aus law) If found guilty, she would be liable* **to** (= would have to pay) *a large fine.*

li·abil·i·ty /£ˌlaɪ·əˈbɪl·ɪ·ti, $-ə·t̬i/ *n* • *(specialized) Your employer's liability does not cover accidents that you have on your way to work.* [U] • *(specialized) He denies any liability* **for** *the costs of the court case.* [U] • *(infml)* If something or someone is a liability, they cause you a lot of trouble, often when they are supposed to be helping you: *The computer breaks down so often, I think it's more of a liability than a help.* [C] ○ *Her husband's a bit of a liability around the house – he's always breaking things.* [C] ○ *The girl's so rude and unpleasant – she's a* **social** *liability.* [C]

li·a·bil·i·ties /£ˌlaɪ·əˈbɪl·ɪ·tiz, $-ə·t̬iz/ *pl n* • *The business has liabilities* (= debts) *of £2 million.* • Compare ASSET.

li·a·ble [LIKELY] /ˈlaɪ·ə·bl̩/ *adj* [after v] very likely to happen • *Both children are liable* **to** (= often get) *asthma during cold weather.* • *The areas of town near the river are liable* **to** *flooding* (= are often flooded). • *There's been so little rain, the forest is liable* **to** *go up in flames at any moment.* [+ *to* infinitive] • *They're liable* **to** *sack you if you start complaining about your salary.* [+ *to* infinitive]

li·aise /liˈeɪz/ *v* [I] to work closely with more than one group in order to communicate information between them • *His job is to liaise* **with** *other similar organizations and to plan a joint campaign.*

li·ais·on /£liˈeɪ·zɒn, $-zɑːn/ *n* • *There is an unfortunate lack of liaison* **between** *the various government departments.* [U] • *The police have appointed a liaison* **officer** *to encourage liaison* **with** *the local community.* [U] • *(esp. Am) He's a liaison* (= a person who acts as a connection) *between the two groups.* [C] • A liaison is also a sexual relationship, esp. between two people not married to each other: *He's had many notorious liaisons, even with people in the same office.* [C]

li·ar /£ˈlaɪ·əʳ, $-ɚ/ *n* [C] a person who has just told a lie or who lies habitually • *He's such a liar – you can't trust a word he says.* • *You liar – I never touched it!* [as form of address]

lib [FREEDOM] /lɪb/ *n* [U] (esp. in the usually informal names of organizations which try to remove the disadvantages experienced by particular groups within society) *dated infml for* **liberation**, see at LIBERATE • *gay-lib groups/activists* • *Were you involved with* **women's** *lib in the 1970s?*

lib·ber /£ˈlɪb·əʳ, $-ɚ/ *n* [C] *infml* • *She was a former* **women's** *libber* (= a person who supports women's **liberation**).

Lib [POLITICS] /lɪb/ *n* [C], *adj abbreviation for* LIBERAL [POLITICS]; a member of the **Liberal Party** • *(Br infml)* A **Lib Dem** is a **Liberal Democrat**.

li·ba·tion /laɪˈbeɪ·ʃᵊn/ *n* [C] *fml* an amount of alcoholic drink poured out or drunk in honour of a god or a dead relative, or *(humorous)* a drink of alcohol • *At the opening ceremony of the festival, a libation will be* **poured/made** *to the ancient gods.* • *(humorous) Would you care for a libation?*

li·bel /ˈlaɪ·bᵊl/ *n* a piece of writing which contains bad and false things about a person • *He claims the statements in 'The Times' are pure libel.* [U] • *The whole story was a vicious libel* **(on** *my character***)**. [C] • *The papers were full of the libel* **case**. • *It's time they reformed the libel laws.* • Compare SLANDER. • [LP] **Crimes and criminals**

li·bel *obj* /ˈlaɪ·bᵊl/ *v* [T] **-ll-** or *Am usually* **-l-** • *She apparently libelled him in the 'New Yorker' by saying he had been in jail for dealing in drugs.*

li·bel·lous, *Am usually* **li·bel·ous** /ˈlaɪ·bᵊl·əs/ *adj* • *libellous accusations* • *accusations declared to be libellous*

lib·er·al [SOCIETY] /£ˈlɪb·ᵊr·ᵊl, £ˈ-rəl, $ˈ-ɚ-/ *adj* respecting and allowing many different types of beliefs or behaviour • *a liberal society/church/ideological position/person* • *(esp. Am)* The **liberal arts** are college or university subjects such as history, languages and literature but not sciences, mathematics or practical subjects: *a liberal arts course/degree* • Compare CONSERVATIVE [AGAINST CHANGE].

lib·er·al /£ˈlɪb·ᵊr·ᵊl, £ˈ-rəl, $ˈ-ɚ-/ *n* [C] • *He's a good old-fashioned liberal.*

lib·er·al·i·sm /£ˈlɪb·ᵊr·ᵊl·ɪ·zᵊm, £ˈ-rəl-, $ˈ-ɚ-/ *n* [U]

lib·er·al·ize *obj*, *Br and Aus usually* **–ise** /£ˈlɪb·ᵊr·ᵊl·aɪz, £ˈ-rəl-, $ˈ-ɚ-/ *v* [T] • *They have plans to liberalize* (= make less severe) *the prison system.*

lib·er·al·iz·a·tion, *Br and Aus usually* **–i·sa·tion** /£ˌlɪb·ᵊr·ᵊl·aɪˈzeɪ·ʃᵊn, £-rəl-, $ˌ-ɚ-/ *n* [U] *esp. Am* • *Today we shall be studying the democratization and liberalization* **of** *Eastern Asia.* • *Political reform and* **economic** *liberalization don't always go together.*

lib·er·al [POLITICS] /£ˈlɪb·ᵊr·ᵊl, £ˈ-rəl, $ˈ-ɚ-/ *adj* [not gradable] (of a political party or a country) believing in or allowing more personal freedom and a development towards a fairer sharing of wealth and power within society

Lib·er·al /£ˈlɪb·ᵊr·ᵊl, £ˈ-rəl, $ˈ-ɚ-/ *n* [C] • *She's a Liberal* (= a member or supporter of the Liberal Party). • In Britain, the **Liberal Democrats** are a political party that believes in more power for local government, more personal freedom and a gradual development towards a fairer sharing of wealth and power within society. • In Britain, the **Liberal Party** was a political party that joined with the **Social Democrats** to become the Liberal Democrats. See **Social Democrats** at SOCIETY [PEOPLE].

lib·er·al·i·sm, **Lib·er·al·i·sm** /£ˈlɪb·ᵊr·ᵊl·ɪ·zᵊm, £ˈ-rəl-, $ˈ-ɚ-/ *n* [U] • *They believe liberalism is the only sensible, moderate choice.*

lib·er·al [GENEROUS] /£ˈlɪb·ᵊr·ᵊl, £ˈ-rəl, $ˈ-ɚ-/ *adj fml* giving or given generously • *There was a liberal supply of cream to go with the cake.*

lib·er·al·ly /£ˈlɪb·ᵊr·ᵊl·i, £ˈ-rəl·i, $ˈ-ɚ-/ *adv fml* • *She gives liberally to local charities.*

lib·er·al·i·ty /£ˌlɪb·əˈræl·ə·ti, $-t̬i/ *n* [U] *fml*

lib·er·al [NOT EXACT] /£ˈlɪb·ᵊr·ᵊl, £ˈ-rəl, $ˈ-ɚ-/ *adj* not exact; without attention to or interest in detail • *a liberal interpretation of the law*

lib·er·ate *obj* /£ˈlɪb·ᵊr·eɪt, $-ɚ·eɪt/ *v* [T] to release (someone) from political or military control, social duties and limits, prison, etc. • *They said they sent troops in to liberate the people/the country* **from** *a dictator.* • *(fig. infml or humorous)* To liberate something is also to steal it: *She liberated those spoons from a restaurant last week.*

lib·er·at·ed /£ˈlɪb·ᵊr·eɪ·tɪd, $-ɚ·eɪ·t̬ɪd/ *adj* • *She's chosen career advancement instead of having children – does that make her a liberated woman?*

lib·er·a·tion /ˌlɪb·əˈreɪ·ʃᵊn/ *n* [U] • *Leaving school was such a liberation for me!* • Liberation is used to refer to activities connected with removing the disadvantages experienced by particular groups within society: *the women's liberation (infml* **lib***) movement* • *animal liberation organizations* • In the Roman Catholic countries of South America, **liberation theology** is a form of Catholic religious teaching which aims to improve people's social, political and economic situation. • See also LIB [FREEDOM].

lib·er·at·or /£ˈlɪb·ᵊr·eɪ·təʳ, $-ɚ·eɪ·t̬ɚ/ *n* [C] • *The people came out into the streets to welcome the liberators.*

lib·er·tar·i·an /£ˌlɪb·əˈteə·ri·ən, $-ɚˈter·i-/ *n, adj* (a person) believing that people should be free to think and behave as they want and should not have limits put on them by governments • **Civil** *libertarians are worried about what they see as government censorship.* [C] • *He holds very libertarian views.*

lib·er·tine /£ˈlɪb·ə·tiːn, $-ɚ-/ *n* [C] *fml disapproving* a person, usually a man, who lives immorally, having sexual but not loving relationships with many people

lib·ert·y [FREEDOM] /£ˈlɪb·ə·ti, $-ɚ·t̬i/ *n fml* the freedom to live as you wish or go where you want • *For most citizens, liberty means the right to choose their own religion, politics or place of work.* [U] • *Hundreds of political prisoners are to be* **given** *their liberty* (= released from prison). [U] • *Of the ten men who escaped this morning from Dartmoor Prison, only two are still* **at** *liberty* (= free or not yet caught). [U] • *(fml) Are you* **at liberty to** (= allowed to) *reveal any names?* • *"Give me liberty or give me death"* (speech by Patrick Henry, 1775) • *"Liberty, Equality, Fraternity"* (translation of the phrase used in the French Revolution, 1789)

lib·er·ties /£ˈlɪb·ə·tiz, $-ɚ·t̬iz/ *pl n fml* • *These laws will restrict our ancient rights and liberties.*

lib·ert·y [BAD BEHAVIOUR] /£ˈlɪb·ə·ti, $-ɚ·t̬i/ *n* [C] an example of speech or behaviour that upsets other people because it lacks respect or does not follow what is thought to be polite or acceptable • **What a** *liberty, to refuse the invitation on your behalf, without even asking you!* • *(fml) I* **took the liberty of** *borrowing your bicycle* (= I borrowed it without asking you) *last night, but I brought it back this morning.* • If you **take liberties (with)** someone, you are too friendly with them to be polite or acceptable: *She slapped his face for taking liberties.* • If you **take liberties (with)** something, you deal with it in ways that other people disagree with, esp. by changing it a lot: *Her translation takes liberties with the original text.*

li·bid·in·ous /lɪˈbɪd·ɪ·nəs/ *adj fml* having or showing strong sexual desires • *lewd and libidinous behaviour*

li•bid•o /£lɪˈbiː·dəʊ, $-doʊ/ *n* [C] *pl* **libidos** a person's sexual energy • *The pills claimed to be able to increase one's libido.*

Li•bra /ˈliː·brə/ *n* [not after *the*] the seventh sign of the ZODIAC, relating to the period 23 September to 22 October, represented by a pair of measuring SCALES, or a person born during this period • *People born* **under** *Libra* (= during this period) *are supposed to be well balanced.* [U] • *She's a Libra.* [C]

Li•bran /ˈliː·brən/ *n* [C] • *He's a Libran.*

li•bra•ry /ˈlaɪ·brər·i, ˈ-bri/ *n* [C] a building, room or organization which has a collection, esp. of books, for people to read or borrow usually without payment • *a public library* • *a record library* • *a library book* • *Only members of the university may borrow books from the university library.* • A library is also a collection or set of books, records or other items, all produced in the same style or about the same subject: *the Penguin Shakespeare Library* ○ *We have a small library* **of** *grammar books.* • Ⓔ Ⓕ Ⓘ Ⓟ

li•bra•ri•an /£laɪˈbreə·ri·ən, $-ˈbrer·i-/ *n* [C] • A librarian is a person who works in a library: *She asked the librarian to reserve the book for her.* • Ⓔ Ⓕ Ⓘ

li•bret•to /£lɪˈbret·əʊ, $-ˈbreṱ·oʊ/ *n* [C] *pl* **librettos** *specialized* the words that are sung or spoken in an opera or a musical

li•bret•tist /£lɪˈbret·ɪst, $-ˈbreṱ-/ *n* [C] *specialized* • A librettist is a person who writes the words for an opera or a musical.

lice /laɪs/ *pl of* LOUSE

li•cence *Br, Am* **li•cense** /ˈlaɪ·sᵊnts/ *n* an official document which gives you permission to own, do or use something, usually after you have paid money and/or taken a test • *a dog licence* [C] • *a (Br and Aus) driving licence/(Am) driver's license* [C] • *a gun licence* [C] • *a TV licence* [C] • *The police officer asked to see my licence.* [C] • *We've applied for a licence* **to** *stage boxing matches.* [C + *to* infinitive] • *If you want to fish in this river, you have to pay a licence fee.* • *(fml)* Licence is also permission or freedom to behave as you wish: *As parents, they didn't* **allow** *their children much licence.* [U] ○ *Each section of the company has been* **given** *more licence* **to** *work in its own way.* [U + *to* infinitive] • **Artistic** licence is the freedom that writers, artists, etc. have to change the facts of the real world and not do or show things in the usual way when they produce a work of art: *"That picture doesn't look like a tree at all!" "Oh, well – that's artistic licence."* [U] • A **licence to print money** is something that makes it possible for esp. a business to make a lot of money: *This new drug has turned out to be a licence to print money for the manufacturers.* • *It's a German product, made* **under licence** (= with special permission from the German maker) *in British factories.* • **License plate** is *Am for* **number plate**. See at NUMBER [SYMBOL]. • [PIC]› **Car**

li•cense *obj* /ˈlaɪ·sᵊnts/ *v* [T] • *Several companies have been licensed* **to** *sell these products.* [+ obj + *to* infinitive] • *This form should be returned to the vehicle licensing centre.* • In Britain **licensing laws** are the laws which control when and where alcoholic drinks can be sold.

li•censed /ˈlaɪ·sᵊntst/ *adj* [not gradable] • *a licensed pilot* • *a licensed* (= allowed to sell alcohol) *restaurant* • A **licensed practical nurse** is a NURSE in the US who has been trained to do practical NURSING (= looking after people who are ill) but who is not allowed to give medicines without permission. • *"Licensed to kill"* (from the James Bond films, 1960s-)

li•cen•see /ˌlaɪ·sᵊntˈsiː/ *n* [C] *fml* • A licensee is a person who has official permission to do something, esp. to sell alcoholic drinks.

li•cen•tious /laɪˈsen·tʃəs/ *adj fml disapproving* (esp. of a person or their behaviour) sexual in an uncontrolled and socially unacceptable way

li•cen•tious•ly /laɪˈsen·tʃə·sli/ *adv fml disapproving*

li•cen•tious•ness /laɪˈsen·tʃə·snəs/ *n* [U] *fml disapproving*

li•chen /ˈlaɪ·kən, ˈlɪtʃ·ən/ *n* a grey, green or yellow plant-like organism that grows esp. on rocks, walls and trees • *The tree trunks were covered with lichen.* [U] • *We found several different lichens on the rocks.* [C]

lick *(obj)* [MOVE TONGUE] /lɪk/ *v* to move the tongue across the surface of (something) as a way of eating it or making it wet or clean • *Before eating the cake he licked the chocolate icing off the top.* [T] • *The child finished the dessert and then licked the plate* (= licked off the last bits of food). [T] • *He licked the stamps and stuck them on the parcel.* [T] • *The cat licked and washed its paws.* [T] • *(fig.) Within a few seconds flames were licking* **(at)** (= lightly touching) *the curtains.* [T; I + prep] • To **lick** your **lips** is to move your tongue along your lips and/or to feel pleasure at the thought of something: *She took a bite of doughnut and licked her lips.* ○ *He licked his lips at the thought of all that money.* • To **lick** someone's **boots** or *(taboo slang)* **lick** someone's *(Br and Aus)* **arse**/*(Am)* **ass** is to be extremely obedient to them, usually in order to get some personal advantage: *He expects his workers to lick his boots.* See also **kiss** someone's **ass** at KISS. • To **lick** your **wounds** is to spend time getting back your strength or happiness after a defeat or bad experience: *After the election defeat he went home for a few weeks to lick his wounds.*

lick /lɪk/ *n* [C] • *Can I* **have** *a lick of your ice cream?* • A **lick and a promise** means *(Br dated infml)* a quick and careless cleaning or wash, or *(Am)* anything done quickly and carelessly.

lick *obj* [DEFEAT] /lɪk/ *v* [T] *esp. Am infml* to defeat easily in a competition, fight, etc. • *The Colchester girls' team licked all other teams.* • *(fig.) The puzzle has got us licked.* • *(fig.) The computer people seem to have licked* (= solved) *the problem.*

lick•ing /ˈlɪk·ɪŋ/ *n* [C] • *The home team were given a licking by the professionals.*

lick *obj* [HIT] /lɪk/ *v* [T] *infml dated* to hit (someone) repeatedly with your hands, a stick, etc., esp. as a punishment

lick•ing /ˈlɪk·ɪŋ/ *n* [C] *infml dated* • *Dad will* **give** *you a licking if he finds you messing with the car.*

lick [SPEED] /lɪk/ *n* [U] *Br infml* a fast speed • *The trains go by* **at** *a hell of* **a** *lick* (= very fast).

lick [SMALL AMOUNT] /lɪk/ *n* [C] *infml* a small amount or thin layer • *The living room could do with a lick* **of paint**. • *(specialized)* A lick is also a short musical PHRASE (= a group of musical notes which have a clear beginning and end within a piece of music): *Parker played a few licks and the audience suddenly quietened.*

lick•e•ty–split /£ˌlɪk·ə·tiˈsplɪt, $-ṱi-/ *adv dated infml* very quickly • *I want that job done lickety-split, okay?*

lic•o•rice /£ˈlɪk·ᵊr·ɪs, £-ɪʃ, $ˈ-ɚ-/ *n* [U] *esp. Am for* LIQUORICE

lid /lɪd/ *n* [C] a cover on a container, which can be lifted up or removed • *Can you get the lid off this jar* (= Can you open the jar)? • *Put a lid on the saucepan.* • A lid is also an EYELID: *She looked at him from under half-closed lids.* • *(infml)* If you **put/keep the lid on** something you keep it secret. • *(infml)* If you **take/blow the lid off** something you make it public: *These newspaper articles have taken the lid off government corruption.* • *(Br and Aus)* If something or someone **puts the lid on** something it destroys it by being the last in a series of misfortunes: *Well, James' resignation just about puts the lid on the project.* • *(esp. Am)* If you **put a lid on** something or someone, you stop it: *Would you please put a lid on all that chatter, I'm trying to work.* • [LP]› **Eye and seeing** [PIC]› **Bottles and flasks, Coverings**

li•do /£ˈliː·dəʊ, £ˈlaɪ-, $ˈliː·doʊ/ *n* [C] *pl* **lidos** *esp. Br dated* a public swimming pool which is outside, or part of a beach where people can swim, lie in the sun or do water sports

lie [POSITION] /laɪ/ *v* **lying**, *past simple* **lay** /leɪ/, *past part* **lain** /leɪn/ to be in or move into an esp. horizontal position on a surface • *The mechanic was lying on his back underneath my car.* [I always + adv/prep] • *The cat just loves to lie in front of the fire.* [I always + adv/prep] • *She lay* **back** *in the dentist's chair and tried to relax.* [I always + adv/prep] • *Lie still a moment, John.* [I always + adv/prep] • *He lies* **awake** *at night, worrying.* [L] • *He lay* **down** *on the bed and cried.* [I always + adv/prep] • *I usually lie* **down** (= rest/sleep) *for an hour after lunch.* [I always + adv/prep] • *Snow lay thickly over the fields.* [I always + adv/prep] • *(fig.) Worries about the wedding lay* **heavily** *on his mind.* [I always + adv/prep] • If something lies in a particular place, position or direction it is in that place, position or direction: *There's an old pair of shoes of yours lying at/in the bottom of the wardrobe.* [I always + adv/prep] ○ *Seattle lies on the route from Vancouver to San Francisco.* [I always + adv/prep] ○ *(Br) Cambridge United are lying third in the league/are lying bottom.* [L] ○ *The river lies 40 km to the south of us.* [I always + adv/prep] ○ *(fml) Here lies the body of Mary Taylor* (= This is where Mary Taylor is buried). [I always + adv/prep] ○ *(fig.) The hardest part of the competition still lies ahead of us.* [I always + adv/prep] • *There are several houses lying empty in the town.* [L] • *The book wouldn't lie flat.* [L] • *The town lay in ruins.* [I always + adv/prep] • *He says bandits are lying* **in wait** (= hiding in order to make a surprise attack) *further along the road.* [I always + adv/prep] • If something lies **behind** something else, it is the (hidden) cause of it: *Do you know what lies behind their decision?* [I always + adv/prep] • If a cause, a solution, your interest, etc. lies **in** something, it is the cause, the solution or the area in which you are interested: *The causes of the war lie in the greed and incompetence of politicians on both sides.* [I always + adv/prep] ○ *(fml) Where do your interests lie?* [I always + adv/prep] ○ *My real interest lies in developing a new sort of robot.* [I always + adv/prep] • If responsibility, blame, a decision, a choice, etc. lies **with** someone, they have responsibility, must make the decision, etc.: *Responsibility for the disaster must ultimately lie with the government.* [I always + adv/prep] ○ *The choice lies with you.* [I always + adv/prep] ○ *Where does the blame lie?* [I always + adv/prep] • If something lies **about/around**, it is in a place because it has been left there: *The box lay around in the kitchen for weeks before anyone noticed it.* [I always + adv/prep] ○ *Have you seen my hairbrush lying about anywhere?* [I always + adv/prep] • If someone **lies around/about** they spend time doing very little and not working: *They spent Sunday lying around the house, watching TV.* See also LAYABOUT. • *(infml dated)* To **lie doggo** is to keep still and hide so that you cannot be found. • *(esp. Am and Aus disapproving)* If you **lie down on the job** you fail to work as hard or as well as you should. • If you **lie in** you stay in bed later than usual in the morning: *It was a Sunday, so she could lie in till almost lunch time.* • When the dead body of a person **lies in state** it is arranged so that the public can see and honour it before it is buried. • If you **lie low** you hide so you will not be found: *He planned to escape and then lie low for at least a year.* ○ *(fig.) She decided it was best to lie low* (= try not to be noticed) *and not attract attention while the boss was still angry.* • *(specialized)* If a ship **lies off** the coast or another ship, it stays near it: *The American fleet are lying off the coast of Italy.* • *(esp. Br)* To **lie up** is to hide from police officers, soldiers, etc. who are looking for you: *The escaped prisoners lay up in a barn for a few weeks, until the search had died down.* • If you **take** something unpleasant **lying down** you accept it without complaining or fighting against it: *She refused to take such an insult lying down.* • *(esp. Br infml)* A **lie down** is a short rest, usually in bed: *I usually have a bit of a lie down after lunch.* • *(esp. Br infml)* A **lie-in** is time spent in bed after the usual time when you get up in the morning. • Compare LAY [PUT DOWN].

lie /laɪ/ *n* [U] • *(Br and Aus)* **The lie of the land** (*Am and Aus* **lay of the land**) is the shape or height of the land or *(fig.)* what a situation is like: *He climbed a tall tree to try and find out the lie of the land.* ○ *(fig.) She spoke to a few people to find out the lie of the land before making any suggestions.* See also **find out/see how the land lies** at LAND [DRY SURFACE].

lie *(obj)* [SPEAK FALSELY] /laɪ/ *v* **lying**, *past* **lied** to say something which is not true in order to deceive • *Both witnesses lied* **to** *the police* **about** *what happened in the accident.* [I] • *Don't trust her – she's lying.* [I] • *I used to lie* **about** *my age but nowadays I don't bother.* [I] • *She lied her way past the guards.* [T always + adv/prep] • *(fig.) They used to say "The camera never lies* (= never gives a false image)*".* [I] • *(infml)* If he told you that, he's **lying through** his **teeth** (= not telling the truth). • *"Father, I cannot tell a lie; I did it with my little hatchet"* (believed to have been said by George Washington as a child when accused of chopping down a cherry tree, 1732-1799) • *"If any question why we died, / Tell them, because our fathers lied"* (Rudyard Kipling in the poem *Common Form*, 1919) • See also LIAR.

lie /laɪ/ *n* [C] • *Don't* **tell** *me lies!* • *The report is* **a pack/tissue of lies** (= is not true in any way). • *The fact that the number of deaths from cancer has doubled surely* **gives the lie to** (= proves wrong) *official assurances of the safety of nuclear power.* • *(dated) Her name is Paula, no,* **I tell a lie** (= I'm wrong) *– it's Pauline.* • A **lie detector** (also *specialized* **polygraph**) is a piece of equipment used to try to discover if someone is telling lies.

lieu /ljuː, luː/ *n* [U] **in lieu (of)** *fml* instead (of) • *The paintings were left to the nation by the Duke of Norfolk in lieu of inheritance taxes.*

Lieut *n* [before n] *abbreviation for* LIEUTENANT • *Lieut. Taylor*

lieu·ten·ant /£lefˈten·ənt, $luː-/ *n* [C] (the title of) an officer in the armed forces, or a person who has a rank just below that of the person in charge

life /laɪf/ *n pl* **lives** /laɪvz/ the period between birth and death; the experience or state of being alive • *Life is too short to worry about money!* [U] • *He went a little bit mad towards the end of his life.* [C] • *Cats are supposed to have nine lives.* [C] • *Life at the top in any sport does involve a lot of sacrifice.* [U] • *He doesn't know what he really wants in/out of life.* [U] • *Spending six months in Russia changed my* **outlook on** *life.* [U] • *(fml) She departed this life* (= she died) *at the age of 95.* [U] • *He* **lost** *his life* (= died suddenly because of a violent event or an accident) *in the Great War.* [C] • *A simple mixture of glucose and water can* **save** *lives in many parts of the world.* [C] • *She's a life (Am usually* **lifetime***) member of Amnesty International* (= She will belong to it until she dies). • *He ran off with her life savings* (= all the money she had saved). • Life is also used to refer to particular types or parts of someone's experience: *He had a long and interesting* **working** *life* [C] ○ *They were investigating her* **private** *life* [C] ○ *We interviewed senior politicians, famous writers and others in* **public** *life.* [U] ○ *What's your* **sex** *life like?* [C] ○ *Drugs and violence are deeply rooted in American life.* [U] ○ *I left home at 16 to see life* (= have different experiences with a lot of people in lots of places). [U] ○ *Teaching has been her life* (= the most important and enjoyable thing in her life). [U] • The life of something such as a machine or organization is the period for which it works or lasts: *The newer batteries have a much longer life – up to 100 hours.* [C] ○ *The legislation won't be passed during the life of the present parliament.* [U] • Life is also the quality which makes people, animals and plants different from objects, substances and things which are dead: *The doctor frantically tried to discover some* **sign of** *life in the boy's mangled body.* [U] • Life is also energy or enthusiasm: *The show was so* **full of** *life.* [U] ○ *Put more life into your voice.* [U] • Life is also everything which is alive: *animal life* [U] ○ *plant life* [U] ○ *In the jungle there is an overwhelming abundance of life.* [U] • In phrases such as **the next/another** life or **a future/past/previous** life, people express their belief that after you die you are born again as a different person or as an animal: *She believes in reincarnation and she says we must have met before in a previous life.* [C] • *(specialized)* In art, if you work **from** life, you paint, draw, etc. real people or objects usually while they are in front of you rather than from memory: *They drew the cat from life.* [U] ○ *In life (drawing) classes a model is employed to pose for the students.* See also **still life** at STILL [NOT MOVING]. • *(infml)* Esp. in children's games, a life is one of the limited number of times that you can lose, but still continue playing: *Every time the little man gets hit you* **lose** *a life.* [C] • If you say that a work of art **brings** someone or something **to life** you mean that it shows them in a believable and interesting way: *The film really brought the story of the rebellion to life.* • If something or someone **comes to life** they stop being dead or *(fig.)* begin to show energy, activity, enthusiasm, etc.: *The story is about a statue that comes to life.* ○ *(fig.) The dancers only really came to life during the jazz numbers.* • If something is **for life** it is for the whole of your life: *I believe marriage is for life.* • *(infml) I can't* **for the life of** *me remember her name* (= I cannot remember it although I'm making a great effort to). • To **give/lay down** your **life for** someone/something is to die willingly while defending or supporting them/it: *They were ready to give their lives for their country.* • **"How's life?"** and **"How's life treating you?"** are informal greetings. • If you believe in **life after death** you believe that people continue to exist in some form after they die. • A **life and death** situation is a very serious and important or dangerous one: *These groups are in the middle of a life and death struggle for survival.* ○ *It's a life and death issue.* See **a matter of life and death** at MATTER [SITUATION]. • If you describe someone as the *(Br)* **life and soul of the party**/*(Am and Aus)* **life of the party** you mean that they are energetic and amusing and are at the centre of activity during social occasions. • *(humorous) The market for those dreadful compilation records you see advertised on TV is* **one/another of life's great mysteries** (= it's not clear why people want to buy them). • *"How do you feel about the divorce?" "Oh, it's all part of* **life's rich tapestry** (= it's part of the series of good and bad experiences that you cannot avoid in life)*."* • *She's decided to* **make/start a new life** (= change how she lives). • *(infml)* **The man/woman in** someone's **life** is the person they love or are married to or with whom they have a close and usually sexual relationship: *Who's the man in your life now then, eh?* • When a machine or vehicle coughs or roars **into life** it suddenly starts working: *The motorcycle thundered into life.* • *(dated infml)* If you say that someone is **leading/living**

the life of Riley, you mean that they are living an easy and comfortable life, without any need to work hard. • *(infml)* You say **Not on your life!** as a way of strongly refusing someone's suggestion or request: *"Shall we spend the holiday at home?" "Not on your life! I'm determined to go to Italy this year."* • *(fml)* If you **take** someone's **life**, you kill them. • *(fml)* To **take** your **(own) life** is to kill yourself. • *(infml)* To **take** your **life in** your **hands** is to do something that is very dangerous, esp. where you risk death: *Every time you go parachuting you are taking your life in your hands.* • You say **That's life** after something bad or unlucky has happened, to express your feeling that such events will sometimes happen and have to be accepted: *"We bought our house just before house prices slumped." "Oh, well, I suppose that's life, isn't it."* • If you say **This is the life** you mean that you are very much enjoying the situation you are in: *Relaxing by the swimming pool, he lifted his glass and said, "This is the life for me!"* • To scare, frighten, etc. **the life out of** someone is to scare them very much. • *(dated)* If a picture or description is someone **to the life** it is exactly like them: *That sketch is Joanna to the life.* • If you describe something as **life-affirming**, you mean that it makes you feel positive about life: *Such a warm, life-affirming film!* • A **life belt** or **life buoy** is a piece of equipment, usually a ring or belt filled with air or light material that floats which is designed to help someone float if they fall into water. PIC> **Emergency services** • The **life cycle** or **life history** of a living thing is the series of changes it goes through from the beginning of its life until death: *Perhaps the main event in the life cycle of a salmon is the return to its breeding grounds.* ○ *(fig.) The life cycle of new technologies gets shorter and shorter these days.* • The **life expectancy** of a living thing, esp. a human being, is the length of time that it is likely to live: *Life expectancy in Europe has increased greatly in the 20th century.* • A **life form** is any living thing: *They are searching for* **intelligent** *life forms in other solar systems.* • Something that is **life-giving** is necessary for life or gives energy: *life-giving fresh water* • A person's **life history** or **life story** is the series of events that they have lived through since their birth: *The woman sitting next to me started to tell me her whole life history!* See also **life (story)**. • **Life imprisonment** (also *infml* **life**) is the punishment of being put in prison for a very long time without an arranged time for release or *(Am)* until death: *The judge jailed him for life.* ○ *She got life imprisonment.* See also **life sentence**. • **Life insurance** (also *esp. Br* **life assurance**) is a system in which you make regular payments to an INSURANCE company in exchange for a fixed amount of money which will be paid to someone you have named, usually a member of your family, when you die. • A **life jacket** is a piece of equipment like a jacket without sleeves that is filled with air or light material and is designed to help someone float if they fall into water. PIC> **Emergency services** • In Britain, a **life peer** is a person who is given the honour of a title such as 'Lord' and a place in the House of Lords as a reward for the good things they have done for the country. This honour and position is called a **life peerage**. • **Life preserver** is *Am for* **life belt** or **life jacket**. • A **life raft** is a type of boat which is joined to a large ship and is used in emergencies, for example when the main ship is sinking, to take people to safety. • In **life-saving** classes you learn how to save someone's life when they have fallen into water: *My kids go to life-saving once a week.* • A **life-saver** is a person who is trained to save the life of someone who has fallen into water. • **Life-saver** is also *Aus for* LIFEGUARD. • A **life-saver** can also be something which helps you to feel better after an unpleasant experience: *Oh, yes please – a glass of whisky would be a life-saver.* • A **life science** is one of the sciences dealing with the structure and behaviour of living things including human beings, such as BOTANY, ZOOLOGY, BIOCHEMISTRY and ANTHROPOLOGY. • A **life-size(d)** work of art is the same size as the person or thing that it represents: *a life-size statue of the Prime Minister* • A **life sentence** (also *infml* **life**) is the punishment of being put in prison for a very long time without an arranged time for release, or *(Am)* until death: *As a murderer, he'll receive/get a life sentence.* See also **life imprisonment**; **lifer**. • A **life (story)** is a book, film, etc. that tells the story of a person's life: *He's written yet another life of Shakespeare.* • A **life-support system** is the equipment used to keep a person alive when they are very ill or when they are in a dangerous situation: *Since the crash he has been* **on** *a life-support system.* • A **life-support system** can also be the natural structures and systems that are necessary for living things, especially human beings, to be able to live: *The lack of rain is threatening all the region's life-support systems* (= the earth, trees and rivers). • A **life-threatening** disease is a very serious one that can cause death: *life-threatening diseases such as cancer* • A person's **life's work** (also **life work**) is the work that is most important to them and that they spend much of their time and energy doing: *The creation of a charity for the blind was her life's work.* • *"Life begins at Forty"* (title of a book by Walter B. Pitkin, 1932) • *"It's life, Jim, but not as we know it"* (phrase used in the television series *Star Trek*, 1966-) • *"Life is too short to stuff a mushroom"* (Shirley Conran in the book *Superwoman*, 1975) • See also AFTERLIFE; PRO-LIFE. NEXT; **real life** at REAL NOT IMAGINARY.

lif·er /£ˈlaɪ·fəʳ, $-fɚ/ *n* [C] • A lifer is someone who has been punished by being put in prison for a very long time, or *(Am)* until they die.

life·less /ˈlaɪ·fləs/ *adj* • *The lifeless* (= dead) *body of the little bird lay on the grass.* • *(fig.) The offices are still empty and lifeless* (= not in use). • *(fig.) a lifeless* (= lacking interest or energy) *performance/story/game*

life·like /ˈlaɪf·laɪk/ *adj* • If something is lifelike it appears real or very similar to reality: *a lifelike portrait of the queen* ○ *The mask was so lifelike it was quite frightening.*

life·blood /ˈlaɪf·blʌd/ *n* [U] the thing which is most important to the continuing success and existence of something else • *Tourism is the lifeblood of Hawaii's economy.*

life·boat /£ˈlaɪf·bəʊt, $-boʊt/ *n* [C] a large boat which is kept ready to take out to sea and save people who are in danger, or a smaller boat kept on a ship for people to leave in if the ship is not safe or might sink • PIC> **Ships and boats**

life·guard /£ˈlaɪf·gɑːd, $-gɑːrd/, *Aus* **life·sav·er** /£ˈlaɪf ˌseɪ·vəʳ, $-vɚ/ *n* [C] a person on a beach or at a swimming pool whose job is to make certain that the swimmers are safe and save them if they are in danger • *a tanned and muscular lifeguard*

life·line /ˈlaɪf·laɪn/ *n* [C] something, esp. a way of getting help, on which you depend to lead your life in a satisfactory way • *For many old people living on their own the telephone is their lifeline* **to** *the outside world.* • *The small local shop provides the lifeline for the community – the contact, the gossip, the help, the news.* • *Our school is on the brink of a financial precipice – either someone* **throws** *us a lifeline, or we'll disappear over the edge.* • A lifeline is also a rope which is thrown to someone who is in the water, esp. the sea, and is in danger.

life·long /£ˈlaɪf·lɒŋ, $-lɑːŋ/ *adj* [before n; not gradable] lasting for the whole of a person's life • *She was a lifelong member of the Labour party.* • *It's so hard to stop smoking when it's been a lifelong habit.*

lif·er /£ˈlaɪ·fəʳ, $-fɚ/ *n* See at LIFE

life·span /ˈlaɪf·spæn/ *n* [C] the length of time for which a person, animal or thing exists • *The* **average** *human lifespan in the developed countries has increased over the last hundred years.* • *In the experiment, small animals were found to have a shorter lifespan than larger ones.* • *The project's lifespan is estimated at about five years.*

life·style /ˈlaɪf·staɪl/ *n* [C] someone's way of living; the things that a person or particular group of people usually do • *He doesn't have a very healthy lifestyle – a lot of stress, a lot of food and no exercise.* • *It's a TV show that looks at the lifestyles of movie stars.* • *The group of women had pursued an* **alternative** *lifestyle, bringing up their children communally and sharing their resources.*

life·time /ˈlaɪf·taɪm/ *n* [C usually sing] the period of time during which someone lives or something exists • *She had devoted a lifetime/***half** *a lifetime to the peace campaign.* • *The lifetime* **of** *the car tyres on such poor roads is about three months.* • *We'll see a tremendous lot of technological changes* **during/in** *our lifetime.* • *There will not be an opportunity to see the comet again, even* **in the** *lifetime* **of** *the youngest of us.* • *Winners of the competition will receive the holiday* **of a** *lifetime* (= the best holiday they will ever have). • *We've only been here two days, but* **it seems like a** *lifetime.* • *The watch is high quality and should* **last a** *lifetime.* • *Enter our competition and this* **once-in-a-***lifetime experience could be yours!* • *Marriage is no longer always seen as a lifetime* **commitment**. • *She won a lifetime/lifetime's supply of toothpaste.*

lift *obj* RAISE /lɪft/ *v* [T] to move (something) from a lower to a higher position • *Could you help me lift this table,* *please?* • *I can't lift you* **(up)** *– you're a big boy now!* • *Could you lift your chair a bit – I've got my bag caught under it.* • *She lifted the cigarette* **(up) to** *her lips.* • *She lifted her face* **up** *to be kissed.* • *(fig.) He lifted his eyes* (=looked up) *from the paper and glared.* • *(fig.) Nothing – not even the prospect of dinner – could lift his heavy* **spirits** (=make him feel happier). • *(fig.) The article is informative enough, but it's a bit dull – we need something to lift it* (=make it more interesting and amusing). • *(specialized)* If you lift underground vegetables or plants, you dig them out of the ground: *They're lifting potatoes.* • If someone has a part of their body, esp. their face or breasts, lifted, they have an operation to make the skin tighter so that the face looks younger or the breasts are firmer. • If you lift your voice, you make it louder, esp. when performing: *You really have to lift your voice to reach the back of the theatre.*

lift /lɪft/ *n* • A lift is an act of lifting or raising something: *Give it one more lift and we'll have it at the top of the stairs.* [C] • *(infml) I want a bra that'll give me a bit of lift, d'you know what I mean?* [U] • *(infml) Flat heels are all right for the day but I like shoes with a bit of lift for the evening.* [U] • *(fig.) She'd been feeling a bit low but hearing that she'd got the job gave her a lift* (=made her happier). [U] • *(specialized)* Lift is also the force on the wing of a bird or aircraft that keeps it in the air as it moves forward: *The wing has been redesigned to give it more lift.* [U] • **Lift-off** is the time when a spacecraft or ROCKET leaves the ground: *We* **have** *lift-off.*

lift *(obj)* TAKE HOLD /lɪft/ *v* [always + adv/prep] to take hold of and raise in order to remove, carry or move to a different position • *(Br and Aus) He lifted the box carefully* **down** *from the shelf.* [T] • *The top of the stool lifts* **off** (=can be removed) *so you can store things in it.* [I] • *She lifted the baby* **out of** *her chair.* [T]

lift GO AWAY /lɪft/ *v* [I] (of MIST or fog) to go away until none is left • *The morning mist had lifted and the sun was starting to come through.*

lift *obj* END /lɪft/ *v* [T] to end (a rule or law) • *The restrictions on water usage have been lifted now that the river levels are normal.* • *At last they've lifted the ban on jeans at the club.*

lift *obj* STEAL /lɪft/ *v* [T] *infml* to steal (something) • *Those radios were so cheap I'm sure they'd been lifted.* • If you lift someone else's writing, music or idea, you use it, pretending that it is your own: *I used to lift whole passages from critics' essays when I was at college and nobody noticed.*

lift CARRYING DEVICE *Br and Aus* /lɪft/, *Am* **el·e·vat·or** *n* [C] a box-like device which moves up and down, carrying people or goods from one floor of a building to another or raising and lowering people underground in a MINE (=place where coal, gold etc. is dug up) • **Take** *the lift to the sixth floor.* • *I hate going in lifts – I always think they're going to get stuck.*

lift JOURNEY /lɪft/ *n* [C] a free journey in another person's vehicle, esp. a car • *I'll* **give** *you a lift* **to** *the station if you like.* • *He* **hitched/thumbed** *a lift* (=stood by the road and made a signal asking a car to stop and take him) **to** *Birmingham.*

lig·a·ment /ˈlɪg·ə·mənt/ *n* [C] any of the strong strips of tissue in the body that connect various bones together, that limit movements in joints and support muscles and other tissue • *She tore a ligament in her ankle while she was playing squash.*

lig·a·ture /£ˈlɪg·ə·tʃəʳ, $-tʃɚ/ *n* [C] *specialized* a thread or wire used for tying or tightening something • *Ligatures are used in surgery to stop the flow of a bleeding artery.*

light BRIGHTNESS /laɪt/ *n* the brightness which comes naturally from the sun, moon, fire, etc. and from electrical devices, that takes away darkness and allows things to be seen • *sunlight/firelight/moonlight/electric light* [U] • *The light was so bright that it was hurting my eyes.* [U] • *It's a north-facing room so it doesn't get much light* (=brightness from the sun). [U] • *The light is causing a reflection on my computer screen.* [U] • *I'm putting the plant near the window because it needs a lot of light.* [U] • *Is there enough light to take a photograph?* [U] • *As a painter he made great use of the effects of light and shadow.* [U] • *When I was camping I used to read* **by the** *light* **of** *a gas-lamp.* [U] • A light is also anything which provides light, such as a LAMP or an electric **light bulb**: *Could you put/switch/turn the light* **on/off**, *please.* [C] ○ *She could see the city lights in the distance.* [C] ○ *We need another light for the lounge.* [C] ○ *As the lights went down the audience grew quiet.* [C] ○ *My front bike light isn't working, it needs a new battery.* [C] PIC> **Bicycles** ○ *I think it would be a good idea to have an* **outside** *light in the porch.* [C] ○ *Rear/side lights are the lights at the back and on either side of a vehicle.* [C] PIC> **Car** • If you say that you can see the **light at the end of the tunnel**, you mean that there are signs of improvement in a situation which has been bad for a long time, or that a long and difficult piece of work is almost completed: *As the exams approached, she felt that at last she could see the light at the end of the tunnel.* • *(fig. humorous)* **The light of** your **life** is the person whom you love most. • If facts are **brought to light** or they **come to light**, they become known: *Fresh evidence has recently come to light which suggests that he didn't in fact commit the murder.* • Something or someone that **casts/sheds/throws light on** a situation provides an explanation for it or information which makes it easier to understand: *Hoping that he might be able to shed some light on the problem, I asked Mario to look at the engine.* • *(infml)* If you **go out like a light**, you fall into a complete sleep very quickly or become unconscious. • *He was concerned that the film had shown him* **in a bad light** (=made him seem to be a bad person). • *Ever since she'd learned of his castle in Scotland, Julia had started to see Henry* **in a** *different/new* **light** (=her opinion of him had changed). • **In the light of/** *(Am usually)* **In light of** (=Because of) *recent incidents, we are asking our customers to take particular care of their personal belongings.* • A **light bulb** (also **bulb**) is a rounded glass container containing a thin thread of metal which produces light when an electric current goes through it: *The light bulb in the bathroom has gone* (=stopped working) *– could you change it for me, please?* • **Light globe** (also **globe**) is *Aus for* **light bulb**. • A **light meter** is a device for measuring how much light there is, esp. to show how much light should be allowed to reach a film when taking a photograph. • At a school where children live or in the army, **lights-out** is the time in the evening when the lights are switched off in the room where people sleep: *No talking after lights-out!* • A **light-pen** (also **bar-code reader**) is a pen-shaped device which is used for reading **bar codes** (=the part on goods in shops etc. containing information such as the price). • A **light year** is the distance that light travels in one year (about 9 500 000 000 000 kilometres). • *(infml)* **Light years away** means an extremely long time in the past or future: *It all happened when I was at college which seems light years away.* ○ *When I was ten, being 50 seemed light years away.* • *"Lead kindly Light, amid the encircling gloom"* (from a hymn by Cardinal Newman, 1834) • LP> **Switching on and off** PIC> **Lights**

light *(obj)* /laɪt/ *v past* **lit** /lɪt/ or *Am also* **lighted** • *The room is lit from above.* [T] • *The stage had been lit with candles.* [T] • *Fireworks lit* **(up)** *the sky with their explosions of red and gold.* [T] • *(fig.) Rosie's whole face lit* **(up)** *with* (=showed) *pleasure and excitement when she saw the presents under the Christmas tree.* [I] • *(Br)* **Lighting-up time** is the time in the afternoon or evening when the law states that vehicles must have their lights switched on.

light /laɪt/ *adj* **-er, -est** • *The big windows make the room feel wonderfully light and airy.* • *It gets light very early these summer mornings.* • *I like it now that summer is coming and the evenings are getting lighter* (= getting dark later).

light·en /£ˈlaɪ·tᵊn, $-t̬ᵊn/ *v* [I] • *The sky had lightened and there were breaks in the clouds.*

light·ing /£ˈlaɪ·tɪŋ, $-t̬ɪŋ/ *n* • The lighting is the arrangement of lights used in a room, house, theatre, etc.: *The set was cleverly designed and well complemented by the lighting.* ○ *I must do something about the lighting in the living room.*

light FLAME /laɪt/ *n* [U] something which will produce a flame and cause burning, such as a MATCH or a cigarette LIGHTER • *"Have you got a light, please?" "No, sorry, I don't smoke."* • *(Br)* If something **sets** light **to** something, it causes it to start burning: *The lamp caught fire and set light to the curtains near it.*

light *(obj)* /laɪt/ *v past* **lit** /lɪt/ or **lighted** • *Something's wrong with the cooker – I can't get it to light.* [I] • *The fire won't light – perhaps the wood's too damp.* [I] • *He lit his fifth cigarette in half an hour.* [T] • To **light up** is to light a cigarette.

light·ed /£ˈlaɪ·tɪd, $-t̬ɪd/ *adj* [before n; not gradable] • *Someone dropped a lighted* **match** *on the floor.* • *A young boy holding a lighted* **candle** *led the procession.*

light·er /£ˈlaɪ·təʳ, $-t̬ɚ/ *n* [C] • A lighter is a small device for providing a flame for a cigarette or a cooker: *She found a silver lighter in the bottom of her bag.*

light NOT HEAVY /laɪt/ *adj* **-er, -est** weighing only a small amount; not heavy • *This suitcase is quite light – I was expecting it to be heavy.* • *He's a few pounds lighter than he used to be.* • *You are lightest first thing in the morning.* • *Whisk your egg-whites until they are light* (= have a large amount of air in them) *and fluffy.* • *How do you get your cakes so wonderfully light, Felicity?* • *You're* **(as) light as a feather** (= very light). • Clothes which are light are made of thin material which allows you to be cool: *a light summer dress* • A light meal is small and easy to digest: *I don't eat much for lunch – just a light snack.* • *She's very light* **on her feet** (= she moves gracefully). • *He has a very light* (= gentle) **touch**, *which is what is required in massage.* • *(fig.) He tends to lack the light* **touch** (= delicacy) *when it comes to dealing with people, and can easily upset them.* • *(fig.) The current team is rather light* **on** (= does not have much) *experience.* • A **light aircraft** is suitable for carrying small loads. • *(infml)* If you describe someone as **light-fingered** you mean that they have a habit of stealing things. • If you feel **light-headed** you feel weak and as if you are going to lose your balance: *She'd had a couple of glasses of champagne and was starting to feel light-headed.* • In boxing a **light heavyweight** is a person whose weight is between MIDDLEWEIGHT and HEAVYWEIGHT. • **Light industry** is the type of industry which makes small items and does not need to use large heavy machinery. • A **light railway** is a transport system for people, usually in a city.

light·en *obj* /£'laɪ·tᵊn, $-t̬ᵊn/ *v* [T] • *(fig.)* If something **lightens** your **burden/load**, it makes a difficult situation or responsibility easier to bear: *If two people share the flat it lightens the burden of rent and bills.* ○ *Getting a new assistant will lighten* (= reduce) *the workload considerably.*

light·ness /'laɪt·nəs/ *n* [U] • *This metal is valued for its comparative lightness.* • *He marvelled at the lightness* (= gracefulness) *of her step.*

light NOT SERIOUS /laɪt/ *adj* **-er, -est** entertaining and easily understood, but not serious and not intended to make you think • *I want some light* **reading** *for the summer holidays – a romance or something.* • *I prefer light opera to the more serious stuff.* • **Light-hearted** means happy and not serious: *It was a fairly light-hearted discussion.* ○ *This morning's radio play takes a light-hearted* (= amusing) *look at the world of acting.* ○ *It was with a* **light heart** (= happy and not worried) *that we set out that day.* • If you **make light of** a situation, esp. a problem, you behave as if it is not serious or important: *She made light of her disappointment.* ○ *It is easy enough to make light of other people's problems.*

light·en *(obj)* /£'laɪ·tᵊn, $-t̬ᵊn/ *v* • If your **mood** lightens or something lightens your mood, you become happier and less anxious: *After the phone call his mood had lightened.* [I] ○ *Being with friends had done nothing to lighten her mood.* [T] • *(Am and Aus)* If you **lighten up** you become less serious or less angry: *Lighten up, would you? – She broke it by accident.*

light·ly /'laɪt·li/ *adv* • If you say something lightly you say it without being very serious: *"Anyway, it won't affect me because I'm leaving," she said lightly.* • If something is **not** said or treated lightly, it is said or treated in a serious way, after great consideration: *Accusations like these from a top minister are not made lightly.* ○ *Threats from terrorists can never be* **taken** *lightly by the police.*

light NOT STRONG /laɪt/ *adj* **-er, -est** not great in strength or amount • *A light wind was blowing.* • *The traffic was quite light so we got through London quickly.* • *It's only light rain – you don't need an umbrella.* • *Did you want a light perfume, madam, something you can wear to the office?* • *I need a fresher, lighter* (= not thick) *make-up for the daytime.* • Alcoholic drinks described as light are not strong in flavour: *It's described on the label as 'light, fruity wine'.* • A light **beer** or **wine** is also one made with less alcohol and fewer CALORIES. See also LITE. • A light **eater/drinker/smoker** eats, etc. only a little. • A light **sleeper** is easily woken up by noise, etc.: *She's a very light sleeper – even the cat coming in at night wakes her.*

light·ly /'laɪt·li/ *adv* • *She patted him very lightly on the shoulder.* • *Dust the cake lightly with icing-sugar.* • *Very lightly, fold the eggs into the mixture with a metal spoon.* • *He sleeps lightly* (= wakes easily) *and always hears the baby if it cries.* • If food is lightly cooked, it is cooked for only a short time: *Lightly cooked vegetables retain their crispness.*

light PALE /laɪt/ *adj, adv* **-er, -est** (of colours) not deep or strong; pale • *The paint was a lovely shade of light green.* • *I like you best in that light brown suit.* • *He was wearing light-coloured clothes to show off his tan.*

light·en *obj* /£'laɪ·tᵊn, $-t̬ᵊn/ *v* [T] • *He must use something to lighten his hair – it can't be natural!*

light NOT SEVERE /laɪt/ *adj* **-er, -est** easy to bear or not severe and needing only a very small amount of effort • *The doctor told him to take a bit of light exercise, such as walking.* • *I can manage a bit of light housework but my back won't let me do anything strenuous.* • A light **sentence**

in prison is a short one: *She got off with a fairly light sentence because it was her first conviction.*

light·ly /ˈlaɪt·li/ *adv* • If you **get off** or are **let off** lightly you are punished less severely than might have been expected: *I think he got off/was let off quite lightly considering it's his third driving offence.*

light on/u·pon *obj v prep* [T] *fml or literary* to find or discover, esp. unexpectedly • *It was Simpson who lighted on the solution, when he was doing some experiments with rats.*

light·er /£ˈlaɪ·tər, $-t̬ɚ/ *n* See at LIGHT [FLAME]

light·house /ˈlaɪt·haʊs/ *n* [C] *pl* **lighthouses** /ˈlaɪtˌhaʊ·zɪz/ a tower or other tall structure by the sea with a flashing light at the top to warn ships of dangerous rocks or to show them the way into a port

light·ning /ˈlaɪt·nɪŋ/ *n* [U] a flash of bright light in the sky which is produced by electricity moving between clouds or from clouds to the ground • *thunder and lightning* • *There was a* **flash of** *lightning and then a loud peal of thunder.* • *That blackened tree was* **struck** *by lightning in a thunderstorm last week.* • *I'll be as* **quick as** *lightning* (= extremely quick). • *She changed her clothes* **with** *lightning* **speed** (= extremely quickly). • A *(Br)* **lightning conductor**/*(Am)* **lightning rod** is a strip of metal going from the highest point of a building to the ground which prevents the lightning from damaging the building by taking the electricity to the ground before it can reach a dangerous level. • *(Am)* Someone who is a **lightning rod** attracts criticism or anger that should really be directed at someone else: *Civil servants are often the lightning rods for criticism that should be directed at politicians.* • *(Br and Aus)* A **lightning strike** (*esp. Am* **wildcat strike**) is a sudden STRIKE (= stopping of work because of a disagreement) without the usual warning by the workers and often without the official support of the **trade unions**. • *(saying)* 'Lightning never strikes twice in the same place'.

light·weight /ˈlaɪt·weɪt/ *adj* weighing only a little or less than average, or *(fig. disapproving)* not showing deep understanding or knowledge of any subject • *I need a lightweight jacket for the summer evenings.* • *(fig. disapproving) She's the author of some fairly lightweight historical romances.* • Compare HEAVYWEIGHT.

light·weight /ˈlaɪt·weɪt/ *n* [C] • In some sports, including boxing, a lightweight is a person whose weight is between FEATHERWEIGHT and WELTERWEIGHT. • *(fig. disapproving)* A lightweight is a person whose work in a particular area of activity does not show a deep understanding or knowledge of that subject: *In certain circles he has been dismissed as a literary lightweight.*

like *(obj)* [ENJOY] /laɪk/ *v* [not usually *be liking*] to enjoy or approve of (something or someone) • *I like your new haircut.* [T] • *I like his accent – where's he from?* [T] • *"Do you like fish?" "Yes, I love it."* [T] • *I like it when a book is so good that you can't put it down.* [T] • *I quite like wine but I could live without it.* [T] • *He's very* **well-liked** (= popular) *at work.* • *I like lying in bed on Sunday morning.* [+ v-*ing*] • *I don't like upsetting people.* [+ v-*ing*] • *He likes* **to** *spend his evenings in front of the television.* [+ *to* infinitive] • *She doesn't like* **to** *ask him for money.* [+ *to* infinitive] • *She likes her men big.* [T + obj + adj] • *He likes his meat cooked until it's almost black.* [T + obj + v-*ed*] • *"***How do you like** (= How do you usually make, serve or drink) *your tea?" "Milk and one sugar, please."* • Like can be used when asking someone for an opinion: *"***How do you like** *my new shoes?" "They're wonderful!"* • If you say **I'd like to see** someone do something, you mean that you do not believe that they could do it: *He said women have an easier life than men, did he? – I'd like to see him bring up children and go to work at the same time.* • **How would** you **like** something means you would not like it: *I'm not surprised he shouted at you! – How would you like to have a big boy pull your hair and push you over?* • Like can be used to mean the opposite: *I like* (= am annoyed by) *the way he just assumes we'll listen to him when he doesn't take in a word anyone else says!* [T]

like·a·ble, *Am and Aus* **lik·a·ble** /ˈlaɪ·kə·bl̩/ *adj* • If someone is likeable they have qualities such as friendliness which cause people to like them: *He's a very likeable sort of bloke.*

likes /laɪks/ *pl n* • Your likes are the things that you enjoy: *The pop-star lists his likes as 'my new Porsche, my girlfriend and staying up all night'.* ○ *They can't expect me to accommodate all their silly little likes* **and dislikes**.

lik·ing /ˈlaɪ·kɪŋ/ *n* [U] • *She has a liking* **for** (= she likes) *expensive liqueurs.* • *I'm developing quite a liking* **for** (= I'm starting to like) *jazz.* • *(fml) Is the room* **to** *your liking, sir* (= are you satisfied with it)? • *The dessert was a bit sweet* **for** *my liking* (= I like it less sweet).

like *(obj)* [WANT] /laɪk/ *v* to want (something) • **Would/Should/'d** like is used to say that you want or desire something: *I think I'd like the soup for my starter.* [T] ○ *I'm sure we'd all like more money!* [T] ○ *I'd like* **to** *go to Moscow for my holidays.* [+ *to* infinitive] ○ *I would like* **to** *say a big thankyou to everyone who's helped to make our wedding such a special occasion!* [+ *to* infinitive] ○ *I should like* **to** *have another baby but my husband says no.* [+ *to* infinitive] • **Would/Should/'d** like can also be used in requests: *I'd like one of the round loaves, please.* [T] ○ *I would like* **to** *book a seat for tonight's performance.* [+ *to* infinitive] ○ *I'd like you* **to** *send this for me first class, please.* [T + obj + *to* infinitive] ○ *I would like the whole lot finished by the weekend.* [T + obj + v-*ed*] • **Would** like is also used in offering something or inviting someone: *Would you like a drink?* [T] ○ *Which sort of coffee would you like, madam?* [T] ○ *Would you like* **to** *join us for dinner tonight?* [T + *to* infinitive] ○ *Would you like me* **to** *take you in the car?* [T + obj + *to* infinitive] • *We can leave now* **if** *you* **like** (= if that is what you want). [I] • *I'm not sure if I have the confidence, the nerve* **if you like** (= if this phrase is suitable) *to apply for the job.* • See also FEEL LIKE.

like [SIMILAR TO] /laɪk/ *prep, conjunction* similar to; in the same way or manner as • *He* **looks** *like his brother/He's like his brother to look at.* • *Is Japanese food like Chinese?* • *She is very like her father in looks.* • *It's silly to buy a jumper when you've already got one that's* **just** *like it.* • *Her hair was so soft it was like silk.* • *You're acting like a complete idiot!* • *She sings like an angel!* • *You laugh just like your brother does.* • *Like I said* (= As I have already said), *I don't even wear perfume myself.* • *What***'s** *their new flat like/What* **was** *your holiday like/What* **does** *it taste like?* (= Describe their new flat/the holiday/the taste.) • *"I met Carla's new boyfriend." "What***'s** *he like?"* (= Describe his character/physical appearance.) • *"I met Carla's new boyfriend." "What* **does** *he* **look** *like?"* (= Describe his physical appearance.) • *Like most people* (= As most people would), *I'd prefer to have enough money not to work* • *It* **feels/seems** *like* (= as if it was) *ages since we last spoke and yet it was only last week.* • *What colour did you want – is it* **anything** *like this?* • *He's* **nothing** *like* **as/so** *fat as his father* (= his father is much fatter than him)! • *Instant coffee is all right but it's* **nothing** *like* **as/so** *good as the real thing* (= real coffee is much better). • *There's* **nothing** *like enough* (= not nearly enough) *food for fifty people.* • *There's* **nothing** *like a good cup of coffee* (= it's better than anything)! • *There are* **something** *like* (= approximately) *6 million people living in the capital.* • *She's working* **like crazy/mad** (= working extremely hard) *to get the job finished.*

like /laɪk/ *adj* [not gradable] • *(fml) Certainly on this point we are* **of like mind** (= we agree). • *The twins are* **as like as/like two peas in a pod** (= very similar to each other). • People who are described as **like-minded** share the same opinions, ideas or interests: *A dedicated football-fan herself, she started the magazine for like-minded women.*

like /laɪk/ *n* [U] • *(infml) There's a big sports hall for tennis and badminton* **and the/and such** *like* (= similar things). • *He was a very great actor – we won't see his like/(infml) see* **the** *like (also* **likes**) *of him again* (= there will not be anyone as good as him). • *(infml) First-class travel is not for* **the** *like (also* **likes**) *of us* (= people such as us).

-like /-laɪk/ *combining form* • *The paper criticized what it described as the animal-like behaviour of the football fans.* • *There was a large, ball-like structure on top of the building.*

lik·en *obj* **to** *(obj)* /ˈlaɪ·kᵊn/ *v prep* [T] • *She likened the experience to* (= said it was like) *sink***ing** *into a warm bath.* [+ v-*ing*] • *She's been likened to a young Elizabeth Taylor.*

like·ness /ˈlaɪk·nəs/ *n* [C] • *She* **bears** *a much stronger likeness* (= similarity) **to** *her mother than to her father.* • *There's a definite* **family** *likeness around the eyes.* • A painting or other representation of a person can be described as a **good** likeness if it looks very like them. • *(dated)* A likeness is also a painting or other representation of a person.

likes /laɪks/, **like** /laɪk/ *pl n infml often humorous* • *First-class travel is for posh people – it's not for* **the** *likes* **of** *us* (= people such as us).

like [TYPICAL OF] /laɪk/ *prep* typical or characteristic of; to be expected of • *That's just like Patricia to turn up half an hour late to her own party!* • *It's really not like Sara to be rude.* • *It's not like you to be so quiet – are you all right, my love?*

like [SUCH AS] /laɪk/ *prep* such as; for example • *She looks best in bright, vibrant colours, like red and pink.* • *I prefer clothes which are made out of natural materials like cotton and wool.*

like [AS IF] /laɪk/ *prep, conjunction* as if; in a way that suggests • *It* **looks** *like I'm going to be in the office until late tonight.* • *It* **sounds** *to me like you ought to change jobs.* • *It* **looks** *like rain* (=I think it is going to rain). • *You look like you've just got out of bed!* • *My head hurt so much it felt like someone was hammering on my skull.* • *(not standard) She acts like she's stupid!* • *(not standard) He spoke like he was foreign.*

like [PAUSE] /laɪk/ *adv* [not gradable] *infml* used in conversation as a pause or to emphasize an adjective • *We're just having a chat, like, and his girlfriend walks up to us and starts shouting for no reason.* • *If there's nothing you can do to change the situation, it's like – why bother?* • *He's, like, really friendly – someone you can talk to.*

like·ly /ˈlaɪ·kli/ *adj* expected to happen; probable • *What's the likely outcome of this whole business?* • *I suppose he might be at the party tonight, but it's not very likely.* • *It's quite likely* **(that)** *we'll be in Spain this time next year.* [+ (*that*) clause] • *Do remind me because I'm likely* **to** *forget.* [+ *to* infinitive] • **As likely as not** (=Probably) *she'll end up in court over this problem.* • *(infml) "He said he bought them all very cheaply from some bloke he knows." "(That's)* **a likely story** (=I don't believe that)*!"* • *(infml) "Do you want to join me on a ten-mile run?" "***Not** *likely* (=certainly not)*!"*

like /laɪk/ *adj* • *He'll come tomorrow* **(as) like as not** (=probably).

like·ly /ˈlaɪ·kli/ *adv* • *I'll* **most** *likely get there at about ten o'clock.* • *She'll* **very** *likely come on her own.*

like·li·hood /ˈlaɪ·kli·hʊd/ *n* [U] • *This latest dispute greatly increases the likelihood* (=probability) **of** *a strike.* • *"What's the likelihood* **of** *Italy winning?"* • *There is* **every** *likelihood* **that** (=It is very probable that) *more jobs will be lost later this year.* [+ *that* clause] • *There is* **little** *likelihood now* **that** *interest rates will come down further.* [+ *that* clause]

like·wise /ˈlaɪk·waɪz/ *adv* [not gradable] in the same way/manner; similarly • *Just water these plants twice a week, and likewise the ones in the bedroom.* • *Watch how she does it and then* **do** *likewise.* • *(infml) "I haven't got time to spend hours preparing one dish!" "Likewise* (=It's the same for me)*."*

li·lac [PLANT] /ˈlaɪ·lək/ *n* [C] a bush or small tree with sweet-smelling purple or white flowers • *The lilacs are in bloom.*

li·lac [COLOUR] /ˈlaɪ·lək/ *n* [U] a pale pinkish-purple colour • *The bridesmaids were all in lilac dresses.*

lil·li·pu·tian /ˌlɪl·ɪˈpjuː·ʃən/ *adj esp. humorous* extremely small • *Everything about the house seemed small, from its front door to its lilliputian furniture.*

li·lo *Br trademark* /£ˈlaɪ·ləʊ, $-loʊ/, *Am and Aus* **air mat·tress** *n* [C] *pl* **lilos** a type of plastic or rubber MATTRESS (=flat object for lying on) which you fill with air before using • *He stretched out on his lilo, feeling the gentle waves of the sea beneath him.* • *We can't offer you a bed, just a lilo on the floor.*

lilt /lɪlt/ *n* [U] a gentle and pleasant rising and falling sound in a person's voice • *He's got that lovely Irish lilt in his voice.*

lilt·ing /£ˈlɪl·tɪŋ, $-t̬ɪŋ/ *adj* • A lilting voice or tune gently rises and falls in a way that is pleasant to listen to.

li·ly /ˈlɪl·i/ *n* [C] any of various plants with a large, bell-shaped flower on a long stem • *(literary)* Someone who is described as **lily-livered** is cowardly. • A **lily of the valley** is a small plant with large oval leaves and small bell-shaped white flowers which smell sweet. • **Lily pads** are the large round-shaped leaves of the water lily which float on the surface of water. • **Lily-white** means pure white: *He marvelled at her lily-white hands.* • *(Am slang disapproving)* **Lily-white** can also mean CAUCASIAN: *a lily-white suburb* ○ *a lily-white taste in music* • *(fig.)* Someone who is described as **lily-white** has a faultless character: *It's ironic that he should criticize such conduct – he's not exactly lily-white himself* • PIC› **Flowers and plants, Pad**

li·ma bean /ˈlaɪ·mə, ˈliː-/, **but·ter bean** *n* [C] a large flat creamy-yellow or pale green bean • PIC› **Peas and beans**

limb /lɪm/ *n* [C] an arm or leg of a person or animal, or a large branch of a tree • *The accident victims mostly had injuries to their lower limbs* (=legs). • *He'd had an artificial limb fitted.* • *She lay down to rest her tired and aching limbs.* • *The cat had climbed onto an upper limb of the tree.* • If you are **out on a limb** you have an opinion which is different from most people's and unpopular: *It's not exactly* **going out on a limb** *to criticize the government at the moment.*

–limbed /lɪmd/ *combining form* • *a long-limbed athlete*

lim·ber /£ˈlɪm·bəʳ, $-bɚ/ *adj* **-er, -est** (of a person) able to bend and move easily and gracefully • *She had the lithe limber body of a dancer.*

lim·ber up /£ˈlɪm·bəʳ, $-bɚ/ *v adv* [I] to do gentle exercises to stretch the muscles, esp. in order to prepare the body for more active physical exercise • *He was just limbering up before his tennis match.*

lim·bo [UNCERTAINTY] /£ˈlɪm·bəʊ, $-boʊ/ *n* [U] a state of uncertainty about a situation that you cannot control and in which there is no advancement or improvement • *Until we've got official permission to go ahead with the plans we're* **in** *limbo.*

lim·bo [DANCE] /£ˈlɪm·bəʊ, $-boʊ/ *n* [C] *pl* **limbos** a dance from the West Indies in which the dancer bends backwards to go under a low bar which is made lower each time he or she goes under it

lime [FRUIT] /laɪm/ *n* a juicy round fruit which is sour like a lemon but smaller and green, or the small Asian tree on which this fruit grows • *lemons and limes* [C] • *A slice of lime in a drink makes a refreshing change from lemon.* [U] • Lime or **lime cordial/juice** is a drink which is not alcoholic, made from the juice of limes: *vodka and lime* [U] • **Lime-green** is a light bright greenish-yellow colour: *a lime-green swimming costume*

lime [CHEMICAL] /laɪm/, **quick·lime** /ˈkwɪk·laɪm/ *n* [U] a white powdery substance which is used esp. to spread on the land to improve the quality of earth so that crops grow better • Lime or **limescale** is material that collects inside water pipes, KETTLES, etc. in areas where the water is HARD (=contains a lot of natural chemicals). See also SCALE [COVERING].

lime *obj* /laɪm/ *v* [T] • To lime a piece of land is to spread lime on it.

li·my /ˈlaɪ·mi/ *adj* **-ier, -iest** • Limy ground has been covered with lime or contains it naturally: *Does limy soil make good farmland?*

lime (tree) /laɪm/, *Am usually* **lin·den** /ˈlɪn·dən/ *n* [C] a large tree with leaves shaped like a heart and pale yellow flowers • *an avenue of limes*

lime·light /ˈlaɪm·laɪt/ *n* [U] **the limelight** public attention and interest • *She's been* **in** *the limelight* (=receiving a lot of public attention and interest) *recently following the release of her controversial new film.* • *Leading politicians must get used to the limelight.*

lim·er·ick /£ˈlɪm·ᵊr·ɪk, $ˈ-ɚ-/ *n* [C] a humorous poem with five lines

lime·stone /£ˈlaɪm·stəʊn, $-stoʊn/ *n* [U] a white or light grey rock which is used as a building material and in the making of CEMENT

lime·y /ˈlaɪ·mi/ *n* [C] *Am and Aus dated slang* a British person

lim·it /ˈlɪm·ɪt/ *n* [U] the greatest amount, number or level of something that is either possible or allowed • *What's the limit* **on** *how many bottles of wine you can bring through customs?* • *I think we ought to* **put** *a strict limit* **on** *the amount of time we can spend on the project.* • *There's a limit* **to** *the number of times I can stop what I'm doing just so I can help him!* • *We* **set** *a* **(time)** *limit* **of** *thirty minutes for the test.* • *Finally, she had* **reached** *the limit* **of** *her patience.* • *(infml dated)* A limit is also the amount of something that is enough and not too much: *Three martini cocktails are my limit.* ○ *I won't have any more – I* **know** *my limit!* ○ *(disapproving) Some viewers thought the programme* **overstepped** (=went too far past) *the limit (of good taste).* • *(dated infml)* Something can be described as **the** limit if it is so annoying or inconvenient that it is impossible to bear: *And now you're cutting your toenails in bed! – That really is the limit!* • People refer to **the (legal)** limit meaning the largest amount of alcohol that is legally allowed to be present in the blood while a person is driving a vehicle: *She was prosecuted for driving* **above/over** *the limit.* ○ *The level of alcohol in his blood was well* **below** *the limit.*

lim·its /ˈlɪm·ɪts/ *pl n* • *I'd like to play squash, but I'm sixty and I* **know** *my limits* (=limit). • *My genius* **knows no** *limits* (=has no limit). • *The pay rise was in excess of* **(spending)** *limits* (=the limit on spending) **imposed/set** *by the government.* • *(esp. Am)* If a place is **off** limits, you are not allowed to go there: *The playing fields were off limits* **to** *the school-children during the winter months.* •

You can wear what you like – **within** *limits – though I don't suppose they'd welcome you in if you were wearing jeans.*

lim·it *obj* /ˈlɪm·ɪt/ *v* [T] • To limit something is to control it so that it is not greater than a particular amount, number or level: *I've been asked to limit my speech* **to** *ten minutes maximum.* ○ *Having so little money to spend on an apartment does limit you (in your choice).* ○ *Concerned about her weight, she'd limited* **herself to** *two meals a day.*

lim·i·ta·tion /ˌlɪm·ɪˈteɪ·ʃən/ *n* [U] • Limitation is the act of controlling and esp. reducing something: *the limitation of nuclear weapons*

lim·i·ta·tions /ˌlɪm·ɪˈteɪ·ʃənz/ *pl n disapproving* • If someone or something has limitations they are not as good as they could be: *Living in a flat is all right, but it* **has its** *limitations – for example, you don't have your own garden.* ○ *The problem with Luis is that he doesn't know his limitations – he just assumes he can do everything.* ○ *Despite her limitations as an actress, she was a great entertainer.*

lim·it·ed /£ˈlɪm·ɪ·tɪd, $-t̬ɪd/ *adj* • Limited means not much (of something) is available: *There was a very limited choice of sofas in the style that we wanted.* ○ *She's had very limited movement in her legs since the accident.* ○ *Guinea-pigs are animals of very limited intelligence.* ○ *I'd imagine that clothes made out of plastic have a rather limited appeal* (= are not very popular). ○ *I was quite lucky to get tickets because they're only doing the play for a limited season/run* (= a short period). • Limited also means kept within a particular size, range, time, etc.: *Places on the bus are limited* **to** *fifty – so book early!* ○ *The problem of stress is certainly not limited* **to** *people who work* (= it exists for others too). • A **limited edition** of a book or picture is one of a small set that were printed: *She's got some very valuable limited editions on her shelves.* • Limited is also used in the name of some companies. See LTD. • LP **Letters**

lim·it·ing /£ˈlɪm·ɪ·tɪŋ, $-t̬ɪŋ/ *adj* • Something which is limiting prevents you from having much choice: *If you don't eat meat or fish it can be very limiting when you go to a restaurant.*

lim·it·less /ˈlɪm·ɪt·ləs/ *adj* [not gradable] • *the limitless sky* • *The minister said that the days of limitless spending were over.*

li·mou·sine /£ˌlɪm·əˈziːn/, *infml* **li·mo** /£ˈlɪm·əʊ, $-oʊ/ *n* [C] a large luxurious car, often driven by a CHAUFFEUR (= a person employed to drive a car for someone else), or *(Am and Aus)* a small bus to take people to and from an airport

limp WALK /lɪmp/ *v* [I] to walk unevenly and slowly because of having an injured or painful leg or foot • *Three minutes into the match, Jackson limped off the pitch with a serious ankle injury.* • *(fig.) After limping along* (= growing slowly and irregularly) *for almost two years, the economy is starting to show signs of recovery.* • *(fig.) He didn't make a very good speech – it just limped along* (= developed slowly and unevenly) *and sent most of us to sleep.*

limp /lɪmp/ *n* [U] • *He has walked with* **a** *limp ever since he had polio as a child.* • *She has* **a** *slight limp which was caused by a riding accident.*

limp SOFT /lɪmp/ *adj* **-er, -est** soft and neither firm nor stiff • *His idea of a salad is half a tomato on a limp lettuce leaf.* • *When you meet my father remember to shake his hand firmly, because he doesn't trust people with a limp* **handshake.** • *(fig.) I felt completely limp* (= lacking energy) *after the race.* • *(fig.) The government does not want to be seen as having a limp* (= weak) **response** *to terrorism.* • If you say that a man has a **limp wrist** you mean that he lacks the characteristics which men are traditionally expected to possess, or that he is homosexual: *Jane's new boyfriend seems a little* **limp-wristed** *to me.* ○ *(fig.) The government's* **limp-wristed** (= weak and not effective) *policy on law and order is encouraging crime.*

limp·ly /ˈlɪm·pli/ *adv* • *(fig.) "I suppose you're right," he conceded limply* (= weakly).

limp·ness /ˈlɪmp·nəs/ *n* [U]

lim·pet /ˈlɪm·pɪt/ *n* [C] a small sea animal with a shell shaped like a pointed hat which fixes itself to rocks • *Thomas ran to greet her and clung to her like a limpet, begging her never to leave him again.* • A *(Br and Aus)* **limpet mine**/*(Am)* **limpet** is a type of bomb that is fixed to what it is intended to destroy with a magnet or glue and is very difficult to remove.

lim·pid /ˈlɪm·pɪd/ *adj literary* transparent, or *(fig.)* clearly expressed and easily understood • *This fertile territory is watered by numerous small rivers and limpid streams.* • *(fig.) Her book is limpid, incisive, highly readable and often very funny.*

lim·pid·ly /ˈlɪm·pɪd·li/ *adv*

li·my /ˈlaɪ·mi/ *adj* **-ier, -iest** See at LIME CHEMICAL

linch·pin, lynch·pin /ˈlɪntʃ·pɪn/ *n* [C] an important member of a group or part of a system, which holds together the other members or parts or makes it possible for them to operate as intended • *Woodford is the linchpin* **of** *the British athletics team.* • *The king is the linchpin* **of** *national unity.* • *The dollar is the linchpin* **of** *the system of international payments.* • *(Am) California was the linchpin* (= most important) *state in the last presidential election.*

linc·tus /ˈlɪŋk·təs/ *n* [U] *Br* a thick sweet liquid medicine that is used to treat coughs and sore throats

lin·den /ˈlɪn·dən/ *n* [C] *esp. Am* a LIME (TREE)

line LONG MARK /laɪn/ *n* [C] a long thin mark on the surface of something • *If you want to draw a straight line, use a ruler.* • *Cut along the dotted line.* • *How long is the line joining points X and Y?* • *She was very old and her face was covered with lines.* • *My legs felt all wobbly when I stood up and I couldn't walk* **in a straight** *line* (= walk without moving to the side while moving forward). • A **line drawing** is a pen or pencil drawing that consists only of lines: *There are no solid blocks of colour in line drawings, so dark areas are formed by lines that are thicker or closer together.* • A **line of sight** is the direction in which a person must look in order to see a particular object: *The cannon can be linked to the line of sight of the gunner so that it points in the same direction that he is looking in.* • PIC **Drawing and painting**

lined /laɪnd/ *adj* • *All essays should be written on lined paper or typed.* • *His face was heavily lined and wrinkled.*

line EDGE /laɪn/ *n* [C] a long thin and sometimes imaginary mark that forms the edge, border or limit of something • *That ball was definitely in! It was nowhere near the line!* • *Double white lines in the middle of a road mean you're not allowed to overtake.* • *(Am) He threw the ball on a line* (= straight and without it going high in the air) *to the catcher.* • *Only half the horses on the* **starting** *line reached the* **finishing** *line.* • *The police couldn't arrest him because he'd fled across the* **state** *line.* • *For many television viewers the* **dividing** *line between fact and fiction is becoming increasingly blurred.* • *Firefighters* **put** *their lives* **on the line** (= risk their lives) *every working day.* • *Would you really* **lay** *your job* **on the line** (= risk your job) *for something so unimportant?* • *The company's reputation is* **on the line** (= at risk) *and we desperately need this product to be a success.* • *Almost 3000 jobs have been lost recently, and a further 3000 of the remaining 29000 are* **on the line** (= at risk of being lost).

line SHAPE /laɪn/ *n* [C] the shape of something that has been designed or created • *They have a reputation for designing cars with elegant aerodynamic lines.*

line SUPPORT /laɪn/ *n* [C] a long strong thin piece of material, such as string, rope or wire, that is used to support something • *Could help me hang the washing out on the* **clothes** *line?* • *Can you feel the fish tugging on the line?* • *We threw him a line and tried to pull him in, but the sea was too strong.* • PIC **Line**

line ROW /laɪn/ *n* [C] a group of people or things arranged in a row • *He arranged the jars neatly in a line on the shelf.* • *When you've disarmed the prisoners, have them form a line against the wall.* • *I'm trying to hang this picture* **in line** (= level) **with** *the other ones, but it's not very easy when the walls aren't straight.* • **In line with** means similar to: *The company's results are in line with stock market expectations.* ○ *We're seeking a pay rise that's in line with* (= at the same level as) *inflation.* ○ *The salaries of temporary employees ought to be* **brought into** *line with* (= made similar to) *those of permanent staff.* ○ *We're trying very hard to* **keep** *our prices in line with* (= keep them similar to) *what our customers expect.* • *Jane was* **(stepping) out of line** (= behaving unsuitably) *when she told the chairman he was talking a load of rubbish.* • *Their predictions were hopelessly* **out of line with** (= different from) *the actual results.* • *(esp. Am)* A line is also a group of people standing one behind the other who are waiting for something: *There were long lines outside the theatre on the opening night.* ○ *Just* **get in** *line and wait your turn like everyone else.* ○ *To make* **waiting in** *line more bearable she carries around a folding chair that's small enough to fit in her handbag.* ○ *The snack bar on the corner is very busy and you often have to* **stand in** *line for a quarter of an hour to buy some lunch.* • A line is also a series of people or things that follow each

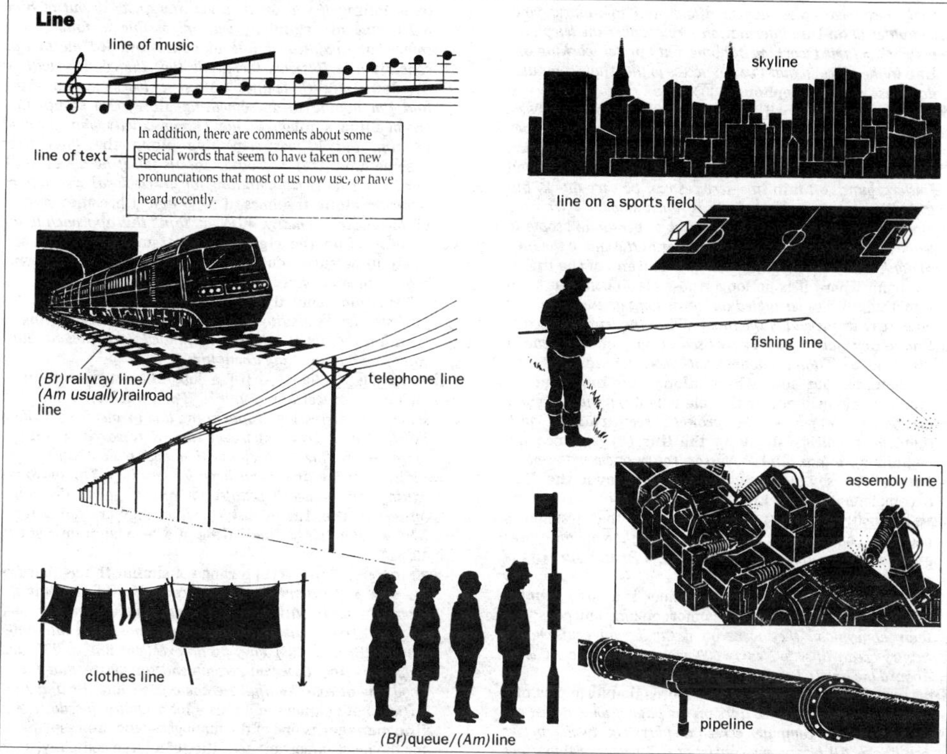

other in time: *She is the latest in a* **long line of** *controversial leaders of the council.* ○ *The flood is just the latest in a* **long** *line* **of** *disasters that have hit the country recently.* ○ *He comes from a* **long** *line* **of** *doctors.* (= A lot of his relatives were doctors before him.) ○ *I'm an only child and my parents want me to have children to prevent the* **family** *line dying out.* • *Prince Charles is first* **in line to** *the British throne* (= will become king after the present Queen). • Someone who is **in line to** do something has a very good chance of doing it: *Dr Doolittle is in line to succeed Professor Brainstawn as head of the English Department.* ○ *Kim Bailey is (the)* **next** *in line to replace Chris Finlay as managing director.* ○ *I want this company to be* **first** *in line to* (= be the best prepared to) *compete for new contracts when the economy recovers.* • Someone who is **in line for** something is likely to receive it: *Smith is in line for the captaincy of the England team next season.* ○ *I'll be in line for promotion if I get this work finished on time.* • PIC〉 **Line**

line *obj* /laɪn/ *v* [T] • *Thousands of people lined* (= stood along the sides of) *the* **streets** *to watch the presidential procession pass by.* • *None of the police officers who lined the* **route** *of the demonstration were injured.* • *I love driving along narrow country roads that are lined* **with** *trees.*

line up *(obj)*, **line** *(obj)* **up** *v adv* • When people or things line up or are lined up, they are arranged in a row: *Please line up* (= stand in a row) *behind everyone else and you'll be dealt with as soon as possible.* [I] ○ *A fight broke out behind me as we lined up to receive our food rations.* [I] ○ *The soldiers lined us up against a wall and I thought they were going to shoot us.* [M] ○ *Could you line those books up neatly on the shelf?* [M] ○ *Do you want me to line up this picture* (= make it level) *with the other ones, or should I hang it lower down?* [M] • To line up can also mean to prepare, organize or arrange: *Have you got anything exciting lined up* **for** *the weekend?* [T] ○ *I've lined up a meeting with them* **for** *tomorrow morning.* [M] ○ *We'll have to get a mortgage lined up before we can make an offer on a house.* [T] ○ *Have you got anyone lined up* **to** *do the catering at the Christmas party?* [T + obj + *to* infinitive] ○ *The unions have lined up* **behind** (= They are ready to support) *the management in the fight to save the factory from closure.* [I] ○ *He has little chance of defeating the forces that are lined up* **against** (= opposing) *him.* [T] • Someone who is **lined up** in a race is going to compete in it: *She will be lined up* **against** *the world champion in tomorrow's race.*

line *obj* COVER /laɪn/ *v* [T] to cover the surface of (an object) that is on the inside or is not usually seen • *The drawers were rather dirty so I lined them* **with** *some old wallpaper.* • *Sometimes curtains are lined* **with** *cheap cloth to protect them from the damaging effects of bright sunlight.* • *How much would it cost to have this jacket lined?* • *Full-length mirrors lined each wall of the bathroom.* • If you **line** your **pocket(s)** you earn money using dishonest or illegal methods: *Staff at the bank have been lining their pockets* **with** *money from investors' accounts.*

lin·er /£ 'laɪ·nəʳ, $-nɚ/ *n* [C] • A liner is a piece of material such as cloth or plastic that is put inside something to protect it and can be easily removed from it: *We put all the rubbish into a grey plastic* **dustbin** *liner.* • *(Am)* **Liner notes** are information about a performer or a performance that is supplied with a sound recording: *According to the liner notes, all the songs were recorded in her attic.*

lin·ing /'laɪ·nɪŋ/ *n* [C] • A lining is material that covers the inside surface of something: *She was arrested after being discovered with packets of cocaine sewn into the lining of her coat.*

line MILITARY /laɪn/ *n* [C] a row of defensive positions, particularly the ones closest to enemy positions • *France started building the Maginot Line in 1929 to defend its border with Germany.* • *They were taken prisoner while on a reconnaissance mission* **behind enemy** *lines.* • *(fig.) Using a condom is the first line of defence against catching AIDS and other sexually transmitted diseases.* • *(fig.) In a game of football, the goalkeeper is the last line of defence.*

line TELEPHONE /laɪn/ *n* [C] a connection to a telephone system • *I'm afraid your line's been disconnected because your last bill hasn't been paid.* • *The phone lines to the village were blown down in the hurricane.* • *The line's amazingly clear. You sound like you're speaking from next door, not the other side of the world.* • *As well as the cost of the calls, you have to pay for the line* **rental**, *which is £20 a quarter.* • *If you want to air your opinions live on the radio, the lines will be open* (= you can telephone) *from eight o'clock.* • *Would you stay* **on** *the line while I talk to the next caller?* • *I've got Chris Foster* **on** *the line for you. Do you want to take it now or call her back later?* • *(fml) Please* **hold the** *line* (= wait). *I'll see if she's available.* • *(fml) Dr Brown's line is busy at the moment. Can I take a message?* • When something **goes** or **comes on line** it becomes connected to a system: *The new power station is scheduled to come on line* *early next year.* ○ *A modem allows you to connect your computer to* **on-line** *information services over the telephone network.* • *I tried working at home, but I prefer working* **on-line** *in the office so that I've got access to the whole computer database.* • [LP] **Telephone** [PIC] **Line**

line [RAILWAY] /laɪn/ *n* [C] (the route followed by) a railway track • *Get off the line! There's a train coming!* • *They should reopen some of the lines that were closed in the sixties.* • *The Northern Line is the worst on the London Underground.* • **Main** *line services can be very quick, but travelling on the* **branch** *lines is much slower.* • *We need more investment in* **commuter** *lines to persuade people to leave their cars at home.* • *Your stop is at the end of the line, so don't worry about falling asleep.* • **The end of the line** is the point where it is no longer possible to continue with something: *We've struggled on for as long as we could, but now we're* **at** *the end of the line.* ○ *When the bank refused to lend us any more money we realised we'd* **reached** *the end of the line.* • *I don't know what went wrong with our relationship, but* **somewhere along the line** (= at an unknown moment during the relationship) *we just stopped loving each other.* • *The project's been plagued with financial problems* **all along the line** (= ever since the beginning). • *(esp. Am) Professor Tolley opposes the plan, but Dr Johnson agrees with us* **right down the line** (= completely). • [PIC] **Line**

line [COMPANY] /laɪn/ *n* [C] a company that transports people or goods • *Ferry tickets can be bought from the offices of the* **shipping** *lines on the quayside.* • *British Airways is one of the world's biggest* **air***lines.*

lin·er /£ˈlaɪ·nəʳ, $-nɚ/ *n* [C] • A liner is a large ship for carrying passengers in great comfort on long journeys: *For their honeymoon they went on a Caribbean cruise on a luxury ocean liner.* ○ *Nearly 600 passengers and crew were aboard the liner when it started to sink.*

line [WORDS] /laɪn/ *n* [C] a row of words that form part of a text • *We could get more lines on the page if we reduced the type size.* • *The computer screen displays eighty characters per line.* • *All her poems consist of five verses of four lines each.* • *(infml)* A line is a short informal letter: *Do try to* **drop** (= send) *us a line when you've got a spare moment.* • A line of music is a short series of musical notes. • *(Am specialized)* A **line item** is a single part of a financial statement, esp. one giving details of the accounts of a company or government: *The charge for each phone call will appear as a line item on a customer's monthly credit card statement.* ○ *The line-item* **veto** *allows the president to cancel part of a big congressional spending program without abandoning the entire measure.* • [PIC] **Line**

lines /laɪnz/ *pl n* [C] *Br* • Lines are a punishment for school students in which a sentence has to be written repeatedly: *The sentence that has to be copied out when a pupil is* **given** *some lines usually refers to the offence that has been committed.* ○ *She got 200 lines for swearing at her teacher. Imagine having to write "I must not swear at my teachers" 200 times!*

line [REMARK] /laɪn/ *n* [C] a remark that is intended to amuse, persuade or deceive • *His speech was full of memorable lines.* • *He keeps giving me that line* **about** *not being able to do any work because his computer isn't working properly.* • *Who was it who came up with that famous line about "lies, damned lies and statistics"?* • *"Do you come here often?" is such a boring (Br)* **chat-up** *line/ (Am)* **come-on** *line.* • *The best bits of the movie are the* **throwaway** *lines* (= clever or amusing remarks that are not an important part of the story) *between all the violence and explosions.* • The lines of an actor or actress are the words that they speak when performing in a film, play or television or radio programme: *She hasn't* **learned** *her lines yet, and we've got our first rehearsal tomorrow.* ○ *I'm terrified of* **forgetting** *my lines when I'm performing live.* ○ *I auditioned for the lead role, but I ended up with a tiny part and only one line* (= a single sentence). • *"Whose Line is it Anyway?"* (British television show title, 1980s-)

line [APPROACH TO SUBJECT] /laɪn/ *n* [C] a way of dealing with or thinking about something or someone • *The government's* **official** *line has always been to refuse to negotiate with terrorists.* • *The courts should* **take** *a tougher line with* (= punish more severely) *sex offenders.* • *Several Labour MPs disagree with their party's line* **on** *taxation.* • *What sort of line* (= method of arguing) *do you think we should* **take** *in the pay negotiations?* • *The police are confident that this new line* **of inquiry** *will lead them to the murderer.* • *You'll have to try a different line* **of questioning** *if you want to get any answers out of him.* • *His line* **of argument** *was impossible to follow.* • *A somewhat complicated line* **of reasoning** *led me to this conclusion.* • *It seems inevitable that the country will be* **divided along** *ethnic lines.* • *My sister works in publishing and I'm hoping to do something* **along the same** *lines* (= something similar). • *I don't know exactly what she said to him, but it was something* **along the** *lines* **that** (= something like) *he would lose his job if he didn't work harder.* • *They're campaigning for the electoral system to be reformed* **along the** *lines* **of** (= so that it becomes similar to) *the one in Germany.* • *Do you think this approach to the problem is* **on the right** *lines* (= a suitable method and likely to be successful)? • If you get **a** line **on** someone, esp. someone you do not yet know, you find out information about them: *Can you give me a line on the professor who's visiting us tomorrow?* ○ *I've been trying to get a line on this guy they've nominated for president, but I can't find out anything about him.*

line [INTEREST] /laɪn/ *n* [C] a job, interest or activity • *"What line* **of work** *are you in?" "I'm a teacher."* • *You meet some very interesting people in my line* **of** *business.* • *She's involved in a very important line* **of** *research.* • *Jazz is more* **in** *my line than classical music.* • *Football's never really been my line. I much prefer tennis.* • *The mayor is calling for the death penalty for anyone who kills police officers* **in the line of duty** (= when they are doing their job). • *"What's My Line?"* (title of a television quiz show, 1950s-)

line [GOODS] /laɪn/ *n* [C] a range of similar things that are for sale • *We don't have any beachwear in stock at the moment – we're still waiting for our summer lines to come in.* • *There are discounts on many items from our older lines.* • *(Br and Aus) They* **do** *an excellent line* **in** *TVs and videos.* • *(Am) Can you recommend anywhere that has a good line* **of** *coats?* • *(fig.) He has a good line (Br and Aus)* **in**/*(Am)* **of** (= knows and tells a lot of) *witty anecdotes.* • A **line manager** is one of the managers who are responsible for the most important activities of a large company, such as production: *You might have more chance of getting a job if you write directly to a line manager rather than the personnel director.*

lin·e·age /ˈlɪn·i·ɪdʒ/ *n fml* the members of a person's family who are directly related to that person and who lived a long time before him or her • *They're offering a service to trace people's lineages back at least 500 years.* [C] • *She's very proud of her ancient royal lineage.* [U]

lin·e·al /ˈlɪn·i·əl/ *adj* [not gradable] *fml* • *She claims lineal descent from* (= She claims to be directly related to) *Henry VIII.*

lin·e·al·ly /ˈlɪn·i·ə·li/ *adv* • *He claims to be lineally descended from the French royal family.*

lin·e·ar [LINES] /£ˈlɪn·i·əʳ, $-ɚ/ *adj* consisting of or to do with lines • *A linear diagram of the car might be more informative than a full-colour illustration.* • *(fig.) These mental exercises are designed to break linear thinking habits* (= habits of thought in which one idea follows directly from another one) *and encourage the creativity that is needed for innovation.* • *(fig.) For most people life is a linear affair which involves a steady progression from one stage to the next.* • *(fig.) Is there a linear* (= direct) **relationship** *between salaries and productivity? I mean if someone's pay is doubled, will they work twice as hard?*

lin·e·ar [LENGTH] /£ˈlɪn·i·əʳ, $-ɚ/ *adj* [before n; not gradable] relating to length, rather than area or volume • *The metre is a unit of linear* **measurement.** • *This carpet is sold in 3 metre rolls and costs £20 per linear metre.*

line·back·er /£ˈlaɪnˌbæk·əʳ, $-ɚ/ *n* [C] *Am* a defensive player in American football who stands behind the first line of defenders and tries to stop players from the other team from moving the ball along the field • *a middle/ outside linebacker*

lin·en /ˈlɪn·ɪn/ *n* [U] strong cloth that is woven from the fibres of the FLAX plant and lasts a long time, or sheets, cloths and clothing made from this or from a similar material such as cotton • *Linen is cooler than other fabrics and ideal for hot weather.* • *I've been wearing this linen jacket all summer.* • *I usually change my* **bed** *linen* (= sheets and covers for my bed) *once a week.* • *The food was excellent, but the* **table** *linen* (= TABLECLOTH and NAPKINS) *was rather dirty for such an expensive restaurant.* • *Should I put these sheets in the* **linen basket** (= container for clothes and sheets that need washing) *or straight into the washing machine?* • *"One does not wash one's dirty* *linen in public"* (believed to have been said by Napoleon, 1769-1821) • LP〉 **Shopping goods**

line·out /ˈlaɪn·aʊt/ *n* [C] *Br* a way of continuing a game of RUGBY after the ball has gone off the field in which the attacking players from both teams form two parallel lines at the edge of the field and jump to catch the ball when it is thrown between the two lines • *There's often a lot of pushing and shoving* **in the** *lineout.* • *Victory in the match will depend on our ability to win lineout* **ball** (=obtain control of the ball in lineouts).

lines·man /ˈlaɪnz·mən/ *n* [C] *pl* **-men** an official at a sporting event who is responsible for deciding when the ball has crossed the line that marks the edge of the playing area • *The linesman claimed the ball was out, but the umpire decided it was in.* • A linesman also helps the official in charge of a game to decide when a player has broken a rule: *The referee consulted the linesman before sending the captain off the field.*

line-up /ˈlaɪn·ʌp/ *n* [C] a group of people that has been brought together to form a team or take part in an event • *Following England's defeat against Wales, several important changes are expected in the lineup for Thursday's match against Scotland.* • *The band's revised lineup includes a new drummer and an extra keyboardist.* • *The lineup* (=set of performers) *for the Cambridge Folk Festival looks really interesting.* • *We've got a star-studded lineup of guests on tonight's show.* • Lineup is also *Am for* **identity parade**. See at IDENTITY. • *(Am)*A baseball team's lineup is usually the order in which the players BAT (=try to hit the ball): *The lineup for the series has Armetta batting third and Silverman fourth.*

ling·er /£ˈlɪŋ·gəʳ, $-gɚ/ *v* [I] to take a long time to leave or disappear • *After the play had finished, we lingered for a while in the bar hoping to catch sight of the actors.* • *The smell of the curry lingered in the kitchen for days after we'd eaten it.* • *It's impossible to forget such horrific events – they linger in the memory forever.* • *Although she died ten years ago, her influence still lingers* **(on).** • *I want my death to be quick and sudden. I don't want to be lingering* **on** *for ages with everyone waiting for me to die.* • *Why do TV cameras always seem to linger* **on** *the most attractive woman in the audience?* • *There's nothing I like more than lingering* **over** (=looking for a long time at) *the exotic fruit and vegetables in the market.*

lin·ger·er /£ˈlɪŋ·gᵊr·əʳ, $-gɚ·ɚ/ *n* [C] • *We have to wait around for the lingerers to leave before we can close the museum.*

ling·er·ing /£ˈlɪŋ·gᵊr·ɪŋ, $-gɚ·ɪŋ/ *adj* [before n] • *"I'm really going to miss you", she said, giving him a long lingering kiss.* • *A slight improvement in industrial production has helped chase away lingering fears that the economy is slipping into recession.* • *She's says she's stopped seeing him, but I still have lingering* **doubts**. • *They've recovered physically from the attack, but they're still suffering from the lingering psychological* **effects** *of their ordeal.* • *The defeat ends any lingering* **hopes** *she might have had of winning the championship.*

ling·er·ing·ly /£ˈlɪŋ·gᵊr·ɪŋ·li, $-gɚ·ɪŋ·li/ *adv*

ling·er·ie /£ˈlæːn·ʒᵊr·i, $ˌlɑːn·ʒəˈreɪ/ *n* [U] attractively designed women's clothing that is worn in bed or as underwear • *Lingerie is usually designed to be sexually exciting for the wearer and her partner.* • LP〉 **Shopping goods**

lin·go /£ˈlɪŋ·gəʊ, $-goʊ/ *n* [C] *pl* **lingoes** *infml* a foreign language or a type of language that contains a lot of unusual or technical expressions • *She hates travelling in countries where she doesn't speak the lingo.* • *In typical Hollywood lingo, he said "This is going to be big".*

lin·gua fran·ca /ˌlɪŋ·gwəˈfræŋ·kə/ *n* [C] a language which is used for communication between groups of people who speak different languages but which is not used between members of the same group • *Latin was the lingua franca of the Roman Empire.* • *(fig.) Movies are the lingua franca* (=way of communicating between different cultures) *of the 20th century.*

lin·guist /ˈlɪŋ·gwɪst/ *n* [C] someone who is learning a foreign language or can speak it very well, or someone who has a specialist knowledge of the structure and development of languages • *First-year linguists are expected to study at least two languages, one of which should be completely new to them.* • *Only the best linguists can become interpreters at the United Nations.* • *French linguists have calculated that every 166th word in the Le Monde newspaper is English.*

lin·guis·tic /lɪŋˈgwɪs·tɪk/ *adj* [not gradable] connected with language or the study of language • *Many peoples live together in Europe without clearly defined boundaries between ethnic, linguistic and religious communities.* • *I'm particularly interested in the linguistic development of young children.*

lin·guis·ti·cally /lɪŋˈgwɪs·tɪ·kli/ *adv* [not gradable]

lin·guis·tics /lɪŋˈgwɪs·tɪks/, **lin·guis·tic sci·ence** *n* [U] • Linguistics is the systematic study of the structure and development of language in general or of particular languages: *I specialised in French linguistics at university.*

lin·i·ment /ˈlɪn·ə·mənt/ *n* [U] an oily liquid, usually containing alcohol, that is rubbed into the skin to reduce pain or stiffness in a joint • *Rubbing this liniment into your knee should relieve the ache.*

lin·ing /ˈlaɪ·nɪŋ/ *n* See at LINE COVER

link CHAIN /lɪŋk/ *n* [C] one of the rings in a chain • *I'd like to have a few links removed from this necklace.*

link CONNECTION /lɪŋk/ *n* [C] a connection between two things • *The sanctions will involve a ban on all military, economic, cultural and sporting links.* • *There is a clear link* **between** *poverty and malnutrition.* • *The closure of the line resulted in the loss of a direct rail link* **between** *Cambridge and Oxford.* • *Britain* **severed** *diplomatic links* **with** *Argentina when the Falkland Islands were invaded.* • LP〉 **Linking verbs**

link *obj* /lɪŋk/ *v* [T] • *The explosions are not thought to be linked in any way.* • *The use of CFCs has been linked* **to** *the depletion of the ozone layer.* • *Government opponents maintain that the level of any new tax should be linked* **to** *an individual's ability to pay.* • *It is now possible to have a computer system that is spread all over the country and linked* **together** *over the telephone network.* • *The European Monetary System was designed to link* **together** *the currencies in the European Community.* [M] • *(specialized)* In grammar, a **linking verb** is a verb which links the properties of an object or person to that object or person: *In the sentences 'She was friendly', 'Suddenly he went quiet' and 'My bags weigh 45kg', the verbs are all linking verbs.*

link·age /ˈlɪŋ·kɪdʒ/ *n* • Linkage is the existence or establishment of connections between two things so that one thing happening or changing depends on the other thing happening or changing: *The President refused to accept any linkage* **between** *Iraqi withdrawal from Kuwait and Israeli withdrawal from the Golan Heights.* [U] • *I would be very concerned about offering unconditional economic support – there ought to be linkages* **with** *democratic reform.* [C]

link up *(obj)*, **link** *(obj)* **up** *v adv* to form a connection, esp. in order to work or operate together • *There's no point buying a computer that can't be linked up* **to** *the other machines in the office.* [T] • *The organization's aim is to link up people from all over the country who are suffering from the disease.* [T] • *After years of rivalry, the two companies have decided to link up for a multi-million pound research project.* [I] • *We offer advice to Polish companies who want to link up* **with** *Western businesses.* [I] • *Sometimes two or three separate traffic jams get longer and longer until they all link up.* [I]

link–up /ˈlɪŋk·ʌp/ *n* [C] • *Later in this bulletin we'll be talking in a live satellite link-up to the Prime Minister in Washington.* • *What can be done to promote business link-ups between companies in eastern and western Europe?*

links /lɪŋks/, **golf links** *n* [C + sing/pl v] *pl* **links** a large area of sandy and slightly hilly land beside the sea which is used for playing golf, or *(Am)* any area of land which is used for playing golf

lin·o·le·um /£lɪˈnəʊ·li·əm, $-ˈnoʊ-/, *Br also* **li·no** /£ˈlaɪ·nəʊ, $-noʊ/ *n* [U] a stiff smooth material that is used for covering floors • *Linoleum consists of canvas that has been covered with a mixture of powdered cork and linseed oil under high pressure while being heated.* • *The lino in the bathroom was old and cracked, so we replaced it with a carpet.* • ⓘ

lin·seed /ˈlɪn·siːd/ *n* [U] a type of FLAX plant grown for its seeds from which oil is made • **Linseed oil** is oil obtained from linseed which is used for making LINOLEUM, paint and ink, and for protecting wood: *Apply the linseed oil by rubbing along the grain of the wood with a lint-free cloth.* • PIC〉 **Cereals**

lint FIBRES /lɪnt/ *n* [U] cloth fibres loosely gathered together, or soft material made from such fibres and used for protecting injuries • *Dressings made from lint are very absorbent.*

LINKING VERBS

Linking verbs like 'be' and 'become' are used to say something about the subject of the sentence and are typically followed by an adjective or noun: *The meal* **was** *delicious.* • *He* **became** *a photographer.* • *You* **look** *great.* They do not have an object, because they refer to a state or process and not to an action or activity that is being done to an object. Linking verbs are marked [L] in this dictionary. There are three types of linking verb:

[L] : Followed by a noun or adjective or by a noun phrase or adjective-like phrase:

I **feel** *a complete fool.*	*I* **feel** *completely foolish.*
The house **looks** *a mess.*	*The house* **looks** *messy.*
It **seems** *a pity to leave early.*	*It* **seems** *unsatisfactory to leave early.*
Can we **stay/remain** *friends?*	*Can we* **stay/remain** *friendly with each other?*
It's **turned** *winter early this year.*	*It's* **turned** *cold early this year.*

[L only + adj] : Followed only by an adjective or adjective-like phrase:
I'm **getting** *cold.* • *The problem is* **growing** *worse.* • *Please* **keep** *quiet.* • *Hundreds of chairs in the hall* **stood** *empty.*

[L only + n] : Followed only by a noun or noun phrase:
It **costs** *$5.* • *Two coffees and a cake* **came to** *£4.50.* • *The packet* **weighed** *85 g.* • *Two nines* **equal** *eighteen.* • *The company* **consists of** *5 young women.* • *She will* **make** *a good doctor.*

Linking verbs are:

- **not used with most adverbs** Although you can say *She looks marvellous,* you cannot say 'She looks marvellously'. There are a few types of adverbs that can be used with linking verbs:
  Adverbs of frequency: *She always seems relaxed.* • *Tickets usually cost £5.50.*
  Adverbs showing attitude: *Unfortunately it's getting late.* • *Perhaps he was asleep.*
- **often used in phrases beginning with 'it' and 'there'**
  There seems *to be nobody at home.* • **It's getting** *late.* • **It sounds** *really dangerous.*
  LP It and There

lint LOOSE MATERIAL /lɪnt/ *n* [U] *esp. Am* FLUFF SOFT MASS • *I've got a bit of lint stuck in my belly button.*

lin·tel /£'lɪn·tᵊl, $-t̬ᵊl/ *n* [C] a long thin horizontal piece of stone or wood at the top of a door or window frame which supports the bricks above

li·on, *female also* **li·on·ess** /'laɪ·ən, ˌlaɪ·ə'nes/ *n* [C] a large strong African and Indian animal with four legs and light brown fur which eats meat and belongs to the cat family • *Lions live in small groups called prides in grassland and open woodland.* • *A mature male lion can be identified by the long dark mane of hair around its face and neck.* • *His face was scarred for life when he was* **mauled** *by a circus lion.* • *Lionesses usually have about four cubs in a litter but they can have as many as seven.* • *Stephanie was an amazing girl and had the courage of a lioness.* • A lion is someone who is important or successful and is very enthusiastic and energetic about what they are doing: *He is one of the* **young** *jazz lions* (= people who are starting to become important or successful) *on the New York music scene.* • A **lion's den** is a dangerous or threatening place: *It's your turn for the lion's den. Paul wants to see you in his office straightaway.* • *(literary)* Someone who is **lion-hearted** is very brave: *Our lion-hearted fighter pilots are the rulers of the skies.* • The **lion's share** of something is the largest part of it or most of it: *Reputable charities spend* **the lion's share of** *donations on aid and a tiny fraction on administration.* • *"The Lion, the Witch and the Wardrobe"* (title of a children's book by C.S.Lewis, 1950) • PIC Cats

li·on·ize *obj, Br and Aus usually* **-ise** /'laɪ·ə·naɪz/ *v* [T] to make (someone) famous, or to treat (someone) as if they were famous • *When his first book was published in Britain it was so well received that he came to London to be lionised.*

li·on·iz·a·tion, *Br and Aus usually* **-i·sa·tion** /ˌlaɪ·ə·naɪ'zeɪ·ʃᵊn/ *n* [U]

lip BODY PART /lɪp/ *n* [C] (the area around) one of the two narrow delicate pieces of flesh which form the top and bottom edges of the mouth and are darker than the surrounding skin • *Herpes causes blisters on the lips and gums.* • *She* **kissed** *me on the lips.* • *He* **pursed** *his lips in deep concentration.* • If you **give/pay lip service** to something, you say that you agree with it but you do nothing to support it: *She claims to be in favour of training, but so far she's only paid lip service to the idea.* • If you tell someone your **lips are sealed**, you are promising to keep secret something they have told you: *"You won't tell Dad I've started smoking again, will you?" "Don't worry. My lips are sealed."* • Something that is **on everyone's lips** is being talked about by a lot of people: *The question now on everyone's lips is "Will the Prime Minister resign?"* • **Lip gloss** is a type of make-up that is put on the lips to make them look shiny. Compare LIPSTICK. • To **lip-read** is to understand what someone is saying by watching the movements of their mouth: *I learned to lip-read when I started to go deaf.* ○ *Is* **lip-reading** *difficult?* ○ See also **read** someone's **lips** at READ. • **Lip salve** is a type of cream which is used to keep the lips soft or to help sore lips heal. • *(infml)* Food or drink that is **lip-smacking** tastes extremely pleasant: *Her new restaurant is famous for its lip-smacking steaks.* • Performers who **lip-synch** (*Am also* **lip-sync**) songs pretend to be singing them when in fact they are just moving their lips in time to the music: *A lot of singers lip-synch when they appear on television.* • Ⓙ

lip EDGE /lɪp/ *n* [C] a part of an edge of a container that is shaped to allow liquid to be poured easily from the container • *This jug would be worth a lot more if the lip wasn't cracked.* • Ⓙ

lip SPEECH /lɪp/ *n* [U] *infml* a style of speaking to someone in authority that is rude and likely to get the speaker into trouble • *If I have any more of your lip, Chris, I'll send you straight home to your parents.* • Ⓙ

lip·py /'lɪp·i/ *adj* **-ier, -iest** *infml esp. Am* • *That kid's so lippy. He should learn some respect.*

lip·id /'lɪp·ɪd/ *n* [C] *specialized* a substance such as a fat, oil or wax that dissolves in alcohol but not in water and is an important part of living cells • *Carbohydrates, proteins and lipids are the main constituents of plant and animal cells.*

lip·o·suc·tion /£'laɪp·əʊˌsʌk·ʃᵊn, $'laɪ·poʊ-/ *n* [U] an operation for improving someone's appearance in which fat is sucked out from under skin • *Stubborn areas of fat that refuse to respond to diet or exercise can be removed by liposuction.*

lip·stick /'lɪp·stɪk/ *n* waxy make-up which brightens or changes the colour of a person's lips, or a bar of this contained in a tube • *I don't usually* **wear** *lipstick.* [U] • *Bother! I've* **smudged** *my lipstick again.* [U] • *We've got a new range of lipsticks coming into stock next week.* [C] • PIC Cosmetics

li·que·fy *obj,* **li·qui·fy** /'lɪk·wɪ·faɪ/ *v* to (cause a gas or a solid to) change into a liquid form • *Gases liquefy under pressure.* [I] • *Candle wax becomes transparent when it is liquefied.* [T] • *(fig.) Assets have little value if they cannot be liquified* (= changed into money). [T]

li·queur /£lɪ'kjʊəʳ, $-'kjʊr/ *n* [C] a strong sweet alcoholic drink which is usually drunk in small amounts at the end of a meal • *Liqueurs are made by adding fruits, herbs or spices to spirits such as whisky and brandy.*

liq·uid SUBSTANCE /ˈlɪk·wɪd/ *n* a substance which is neither a gas nor a solid, flows easily and has the same shape as its container • *Mercury is a liquid at room temperature.* [C] • *Oxygen turns into liquid below minus 183°C.* [U] • *Remove two cups of liquid from the stew and place it in a small pan.* [U] • **Liquid courage** is *Am for* DUTCH COURAGE. • A **liquid-crystal display** (*abbreviation* **LCD**) is a screen for showing text or pictures which uses a liquid that darkens when an electric current flows across it: *Liquid crystal displays are used in calculators, portable computers and digital watches and clocks.* ○ *LCD technology will eventually make it possible to hang large-screen televisions on your living-room wall.* • *(trademark)* **Liquid Paper** is a white liquid for covering mistakes in a text or drawing so that they can be corrected. • (F)

liq·uid /ˈlɪk·wɪd/ *adj* • *The fuel used by space shuttles is a combination of liquid hydrogen and liquid oxygen.* • *Water is normally liquid between 0°C and 100°C.*

liq·uid·ize *obj, Br and Aus usually* **–ise** /ˈlɪk·wɪ·daɪz/ *v* [T] • If you liquidize food you change it into a thick liquid using a BLENDER (= machine with blades that turn very quickly): *Liquidise the remaining ingredients until they form a smooth paste.* • Compare LIQUEFY.

liq·uid·i·ser, –iz·er /£ˈlɪk·wɪ·daɪ·zəʳ, $-zɚ/ *n* [C] • Liquidiser is *Br and Aus for* BLENDER: *Chop the vegetables into small chunks before putting them in the liquidiser.* • PIC **Kitchen**

liq·uid MONEY /ˈlɪk·wɪd/ *adj* [not gradable] in the form of money, rather than investments or property, or able to be changed into money easily • *She has very few liquid* **assets** *as most of her wealth is tied up in stocks and shares.* • (F)

liq·uid·ate *obj* /ˈlɪk·wɪ·deɪt/ *v* [T] • *The firm has already paid half the fine, but it will have to liquidate additional assets* (= sell them to obtain money) *in order to pay the rest.* • See also LIQUIDATE CLOSE.

liq·uid·i·ty /£lɪˈkwɪd·ɪ·ti, $-ə·ţi/ *n* [U] • *She says she can afford to pay us, but she's got a liquidity problem and we'll have to wait until she's sold some of her shares.*

liq·uid·ate *(obj)* CLOSE /ˈlɪk·wɪ·deɪt/ *v* to cause a business to close, so that its ASSETS can be sold to pay its debts • *The company will have to be liquidated if it fails to secure new loans by the end of the month.* [T] • *Without government assistance the bank will have to liquidate.* [I] • See also **liquidate** at LIQUID MONEY.

liq·uid·a·tion /ˌlɪk·wɪˈdeɪ·ʃən/ *n* • *After three years of heavy losses the company* **went into** *liquidation with debts totalling £100 million.* [U] • *The rise in the jobless total is due to a dramatic increase in bankruptcies and liquidations.* [C]

liq·uid·a·tor /£ˈlɪk·wɪ·deɪ·təʳ, $-ţɚ/ *n* [C] • *The company's liquidators* (= people who are in charge of closing down the company) *have warned creditors that there is little chance of them receiving any of the money that is owed to them.*

liq·uid·ate *obj* KILL /ˈlɪk·wɪ·deɪt/ *v* [T] to kill or make powerless (someone who threatens a government or political organization) • *The dissident writer Georgi Markov was liquidated in London in 1978 with a poison-tipped umbrella.*

li·qui·fy *obj* /ˈlɪk·wɪ·faɪ/ *v* to LIQUEFY

li·quor /£ˈlɪk·əʳ, $-ɚ/ *n* [U] *Am and Aus* strong alcoholic drink • *Liquor includes drinks like whisky and gin, but not beer or wine, and it is produced by distillation rather than fermentation.* • *There's a liquor* **store** *around the block where you could get some vodka.* • *"The lips that touch liquor must never touch mine"* (title of a song written by George W. Young, c.1870)

li·quo·rice *Br and Aus, Am and Aus* **lic·o·rice** /£ˈlɪk·ər·ɪs, £-ɪʃ, $-ɚ-/ *n* [U] the dried root of a Mediterranean plant which is used in medicines and for flavouring food, particularly sweets • *When liquorice is eaten as a sweet it is usually in the form of a long thin soft black stick.*

lisp SPEECH /lɪsp/ *v* to pronounce 's' and 'z' sounds like 'th', so that 'sin' sounds like 'thin' and 'zen' sounds like 'then' • *I started to lisp when I lost my front teeth in an accident.* [I] • *"Pleathe thing me a thong," he lisped.* [+ clause]

lisp /lɪsp/ *n* [C] • *I was teased a lot at school because I* **spoke with a** *lisp.* • *It's not kind to laugh at people with lisps.*

LISP COMPUTERS /lɪsp/ *n* [U] a computer programming language designed for processing lists of textual information • *LISP is the standard research tool of artificial intelligence scientists in the United States.*

lis·som, lis·some /ˈlɪs·əm/ *adj literary* attractively thin and able to move quickly and gracefully

list RECORD /lɪst/ *n* [C] a record of short pieces of information, such as people's names, usually written or printed with a single item on each line and often ordered in a way that makes a particular item easy to find • *What's on your* **birthday** *list?* • *Damn! I've left the* **shopping** *list at home.* • *Should I* **make** *a list of the people I want to invite to my party?* • *I've* **made** *a list of places I'd like to visit while we're in Paris.* • *I've got* **a list as long as** *my* **arm** (= a very long list) *of the things we need to do before we go on holiday.* • The **list price** of a product is the price at which its maker suggests it should be sold: *If you shop around you should be able to find most models selling for around 10% less than the manufacturer's list prices.* • LP **Colon** (D)

list *obj* /lɪst/ *v* [T] • *I've listed some useful reading material on the handout.* • *(Br)* A **listed building** (*Am* **landmarked building**, *Aus* **heritage-listed building**) is a building of great historical or artistic value which has official protection to prevent it from being changed or destroyed. • A **listed company** is one whose shares can be traded on a country's main **stock market**: *It is one of the largest listed companies on the Hong Kong Stock Exchange.*

list·ings /ˈlɪs·tɪŋz/ *pl n* [C] • Listings are lists of information about entertainments and activities that are published in newspapers and magazines: *Some newspapers print television listings for the whole week.* ○ *If you want to find out what's happening in London, buy a listings* **magazine**.

list LEAN /lɪst/ *v* [I] (of a ship) to lean to one side, particularly as a result of damage • *The tanker is listing badly and liable to sink at any moment.* • (D)

list /lɪst/ *n* [U] • *The boat developed a list when its cargo slid to one side in a heavy storm.*

lis·ten /ˈlɪs·ən/ *v* [I] to give attention to a person or thing that you can hear • *You just don't listen, do you? I told you you'd burn yourself if you touched that pan, didn't I?* • *Mike's happy to talk about his problems to anyone who'll listen.* • *We listened in silence as the names of the dead were read out.* • *Listen, we really need to sort out our insurance claim this weekend.* • *He just lies on his bed all day listening* **to** *loud music.* • *Listen carefully* **to** *the conversation on the tape and then answer the questions which follow.* • *She listened politely* **to** *my complaint, but I don't think she'll do anything about it.* • *Did you listen* **to** *the news this morning?* • *Listen* **to this**! *You can win a holiday for two in the south of France just by answering three simple questions.* • *It's painful to listen* **to** *Lizzie trying to play the violin.* • If you listen **in on** a conversation you listen to it, esp. secretly, without saying anything: *I wish Dad would stop listening in on my phone conversations with my friends.* • If you listen **(out) for** something you make an effort to hear a noise that you are expecting: *I'm waiting for an important call so will you listen out for the phone while I'm in the garden?* ○ *We used to sit huddled in the air-raid shelter listening* **for** *the roar of the bombers overhead.* • LP **Sound**

lis·ten /ˈlɪs·ən/ *n* [U] • *Don't hog the headphones, Kate, let Daryl* **have a** *listen too.* • **Have a** *listen* **to** *this! I've never heard anything like it before.*

lis·ten·er /£ˈlɪs·ən·əʳ, £ˈ-nəʳ, $ˈlɪs·ən·ɚ/ *n* [C] • *We don't watch much television, but we're very keen radio listeners.* • *We've received a lot of complaints about the changes from regular listeners* **to** *the programme.* • Someone who is a **good** listener gives a lot of attention to you when you are talking about your problems or worries and is very understanding, sympathetic and supportive: *If you want to talk to someone about your divorce then Jonathan's a good listener.*

lis·te·ri·a /£lɪˈstɪə·ri·ə, $-ˈstɪr·i-/ *n* [U] a bacteria which causes food poisoning, found esp. in cheese and other products made from milk • *Food needs to be cooked at 70°C to be sure of killing harmful bacteria such as listeria and salmonella.*

lis·te·ri·o·sis /£lɪˌstɪə·riˈəʊ·sɪs, $-ˈoʊ-/ *n* [U] • Listeriosis is a serious type of food poisoning, caused by listeria, which is particularly harmful to babies before they are born.

list·less /ˈlɪst·ləs/ *adj* lacking energy and enthusiasm and unwilling to do anything needing effort • *The doctor's put him on a special diet, but he's still listless and lethargic.* • *(fig.) A report from leading businesses suggests that the economy will remain listless until the end of the year.*

list·less·ly /ˈlɪst·lə·sli/ *adv* • *He sat listlessly in front of the television, happy to watch anything that happened to be on.*

list·less·ness /ˈlɪst·lə·snəs/ *n* [U] • *The symptoms of potassium deficiency include weakness, listlessness and drowsiness.*

lit [LIGHT] /lɪt/ *past simple and past participle of* LIGHT [BRIGHTNESS] *or* LIGHT [FLAME] • *The* **dimly** *lit room was packed with emaciated children barely able to move.* • *"Cancer doesn't worry me," said Tom as he lit another cigarette.*

lit [LITERATURE] /lɪt/ *n* [U], *adj* [not gradable] *infml for* literature or literary • *Caroline studied English Lit at university.* • *How did you do in your lit paper?* • **Lit crit** is *infml for* **literary criticism**, see at LITERARY: *I find all this lit crit rather heavy-going.*

lit·a·ny /ˈlɪt·ən·i/ *n* [C] a long Christian prayer in which some parts are spoken by the priest and other parts are spoken by the worshippers • A litany is also a long list of unpleasant things, particularly things that are repeated: *The manufacturers are reported to have received* **a litany of** *complaints from dissatisfied customers.* ○ *There is* **a litany of** *medical problems facing the prison population.*

lite /laɪt/ *adj* [not gradable] containing less energy than similar types of food and therefore less likely to make you fat • *'Lite' is usually used by food manufacturers to make their products appeal to people who want to lose weight.*

lit·er /£ˈliː·təʳ, $-t̬ɚ/ *n* [C] *Am for* LITRE • *The car's 3·6 liter engine has been criticized for its lack of power during acceleration.* • [LP] **Units**

lit·er·a·cy /£ˈlɪt·ər·ə·si, $ˈlɪt̬·ɚ-/ *n* [U] the ability to read and write • *Research suggests that children who leave primary school without a firm grounding in literacy and numeracy never catch up.* • *Far more resources are needed to improve adult literacy.* • *(fig.)* **Computer** *literacy* (= Knowledge of how to use computers) *is becoming as essential as the ability to drive a car.* • *(fig.) According to a national survey of economic literacy, most Americans know little about economics.*

lit·er·ate /£ˈlɪt·ər·ət, $ˈlɪt̬·ɚ-/ *adj* • *Literacy in the country has increased, with the literate proportion of the population rising to 52·1% from 43·6% a decade ago.* • *(fig.) People who are* **computer** *literate have a better chance of finding a job.* • *(fig.) He was a brilliant inventor, but he needed a financially literate partner to help him develop his business.* • *Do the children of highly literate parents* (= intelligent parents who read a lot and have had a good education) *have an advantage at school?*

lit·er·al /£ˈlɪt·ər·əl, $ˈlɪt̬·ɚ-/ *adj* exactly the same as the original basic meaning of a word or expression • *The literal meaning of 'television' is 'seeing from a distance'.* • *You need to demonstrate to the examiners that you have more than a literal understanding of the text.* • *Her translation is too literal* (= done one word at a time and therefore unnatural), *resulting in heavy, colorless prose.* • *I can't accept literal interpretations of Bible stories like Adam and Eve.* • *Richard can be very literal-***minded** *sometimes. When I said I'd rather die than spend a weekend with Nancy, he thought I meant it.* • Compare FIGURATIVE [LANGUAGE].

lit·er·al·ly /£ˈlɪt·ər·əl·i, £ˈ-rə·li, $ˈlɪt̬·ɚ-/ *adv* • *You'll lose marks if you translate too literally.* • *You shouldn't take everything she says literally. She doesn't mean half the things she says.* • *20 million people are threatened by famine and the food aid required runs* **quite** *literally* (= completely truthfully) *into millions of tonnes.*

lit·er·al·ly /£ˈlɪt·ər·əl·i, £ˈ-rə·li, $ˈlɪt̬·ɚ·əl·i/ *adv* [not gradable] *infml* used for emphasizing an already forceful statement • *There were literally millions of tourists in the village over the weekend.* • *My boss'll literally murder me when she finds out what I've done.*

lit·er·ar·y /£ˈlɪt·ər·ər·i, $ˈlɪt̬·ə·rer-/ *adj* connected with literature • *Before becoming a full-time writer she was a university professor and a literary critic.* • *What does a literary editor do?* • *How many literary prizes has he won?* • *It's unusual to see so many literary words in a newspaper report.* • *Your style is rather too literary for a popular magazine like ours.* • *She's a very literary woman* (= She knows a lot about literature). • A **literary agent** is someone who deals with a writer's business matters. • **Literary criticism** is the formal study and discussion of works of literature which involves judging and explaining the importance and meaning of them.

lit·er·a·ti /£ˌlɪt·ərˈɑː·tiː, $ˌlɪt̬·əˈrɑː·t̬iː/ *pl n* people with a good education who know a lot about literature • *Her novels are popular with university literati, but they have failed to attract a wider audience.* • Compare GLITTERATI.

lit·er·a·ture [WRITING] /£ˈlɪt·ər·ɪ·tʃəʳ, $ˈlɪt̬·ɚ·ɪ·tʃɚ/ *n* [U] written artistic works, particularly those with a high and lasting artistic value • *Literature includes novels, short stories, plays and poetry.* • *'Wuthering Heights' is a classic of English literature.* • *I specialized in nineteenth-century literature at university.*

lit·er·a·ture [SPECIALIST TEXTS] /£ˈlɪt·ər·ɪ·tʃəʳ, $ˈlɪt̬·ɚ·ɪ·tʃɚ/ *n* [U] all the texts relating to a subject, particularly those written by specialists • *It's important to keep up-to-date with the literature in your field.* • *There is only a small literature* **on** *the author you have chosen to write about.* • *Scientific literature is usually incomprehensible to the lay reader.*

lit·er·a·ture [INFORMATION] /£ˈlɪt·ər·ɪ·tʃəʳ, $ˈlɪt̬·ɚ·ɪ·tʃɚ/ *n* [U] printed material published by a company which is intended to encourage people to buy that company's products or services • *Have you got any literature* **on/about** *these washing machines?* • *Could you send me your literature* **on/about** *car insurance policies, please?* • Literature can also be material that an organization publishes in order to persuade people to agree with its opinions: *The Republicans were quick to highlight the Democrats' proposed tax increases in their* **campaign** *literature.*

lithe /laɪð/ *adj* **-r, -st** young, healthy, attractive and able to move and bend gracefully • *He had the lithe, athletic body of a ballet dancer.*

lithe·ly /ˈlaɪð·li/ *adv*

lith·i·um /ˈlɪθ·i·əm/ *n* [U] the least dense metallic element • *Lithium is soft, has a silvery-white colour and is used in the manufacture of batteries, medicines and alloys.*

lith·o·graph /£ˈlɪθ·əʊ·grɑːf, $-oʊ·græf/ *n* [C] a picture printed using a stone or metal block on which an image has been drawn with a thick oily substance that attracts ink • *This lithograph is one of a limited edition of 500 that have been printed and signed by the artist.*

lith·o·graph·ic /£ˌlɪθ·əʊˈgræf·ɪk, $-oʊ-/ *adj* [not gradable] • *The lithographic printing plates that were used to produce the illustrations are also in the exhibition.*

li·thog·ra·phy /£lɪˈθɒg·rə·fi, $-ˈθɑː·grə-/ *n* [U] • *Lithography was invented in 1796.*

lit·i·gate *(obj)* /£ˈlɪt·ɪ·geɪt, $ˈlɪt̬-/ *v* to cause (an argument) to be discussed in a law court so that a judgment can be made which must be accepted by both sides • *Many discrimination claims against employers are too costly to litigate and almost impossible to win.* [T] • *The bank was awarded $300 000 toward its expenses of litigating the case.* [T] • *In spite of its denials, the company is wholly responsible for the accident, and we are prepared to litigate if necessary.* [I]

lit·i·ga·tion /£ˌlɪt·ɪˈgeɪ·ʃən, $ˌlɪt̬-/ *n* [U] • *The company has consistently denied responsibility, but it agreed to the settlement to avoid the expense of lengthy litigation.*

lit·i·gant /£ˈlɪt·ɪ·gənt, $ˈlɪt̬-/ *n* [C] • A litigant is a person who is fighting a legal case: *Communal waiting rooms force litigants to sit for hours with their opponents.*

lit·i·ga·tor /£ˈlɪt·ɪ·geɪ·təʳ, $ˈlɪt̬·ɪ·geɪ·t̬ɚ/ *n* [C] *Am* • A litigator is a lawyer who specializes in taking legal action against people and organizations: *She was a leading civil rights litigator before she went into politics.*

li·ti·gious /lɪˈtɪdʒ·əs/ *adj* tending to take arguments to a law court for a decision • *The United States is the most litigious society in the world.*

li·ti·gious·ness /lɪˈtɪdʒ·ə·snəs/ *n* [U] • *Her libel actions against several newspapers have won her a reputation for litigiousness.*

lit·mus /ˈlɪt·məs/ *n* [U] a powder which is turned red by acid • *The litmus* **paper** *will turn red in an acid and blue in an alkali.* • *You can discover the acidity of the solution with a litmus test.* • A **litmus test** is someone's decision or opinion about something which suggests what they think about a wider range of related things: *The President's policy on abortion is regarded as a litmus test of his views on women's rights.*

li·tre *Br and Aus, Am usually* **lit·er** /£ˈliː·təʳ, $-t̬ɚ/ (*abbreviation* **l**) *n* [C] a unit for measuring the volume of a liquid or a gas • *One litre is the same as 1000 millilitres or 1000 cubic centimetres.* • *The tax increase will add 4p to a litre of leaded petrol.* • *A driver with more than 0·8 of a gram of alcohol per litre of blood will fail the breathalyser.* • *Her new car's got a 6-litre engine and a top speed of 155 mph.* • [LP] **Units**

lit·ter RUBBISH /£ˈlɪt·əʳ, $ˈlɪţ·ɚ/ *n* [U] small pieces of rubbish that have been left lying on the ground in public places • *The streets around the stadium are always strewn with beer cans, cigarette packets and other litter after a match.* • *About 2% of fast-food packaging ends up as roadside litter.* • *(esp. Br and Aus) Don't drop that wrapper in the street – put it in a litter* **bin** (= container for waste in a public place). • A *(Br)* **litter lout**/*(Am and Aus)* **litter bug** is someone who drops rubbish on the ground in public places: *The increased fines for litter louts are part of a range of measures for cleaning up the environment.*

lit·ter *obj* /£ˈlɪt·əʳ, $ˈlɪţ·ɚ/ *v* [T] • *The park was littered* **with** *bottles and cans after the concert.* • *(fig.) Dirty clothes littered* (= were spread untidily over) *the floor of her bedroom.* • *(fig.) The newspaper has a reputation for being littered* **with** (= having a large number of) *spelling mistakes.* • *(fig.) He is one of the great figures in the north-east's history and the region is littered* **with** (= has a lot of) *bridges and buildings named after him.*

lit·ter SET /£ˈlɪt·əʳ, $ˈlɪţ·ɚ/ *n* [C + sing/pl v] a group of animals that are born at the same time and have the same mother • *Martha's cat's just had a litter of four kittens.*

lit·ter BED /£ˈlɪt·əʳ, $ˈlɪţ·ɚ/ *n* [U] dried grass or plant stems used by animals as a bed • *We sell most of our straw to the local stables who use it as litter for their horses.*

lit·ter TOILET /£ˈlɪt·əʳ, $ˈlɪţ·ɚ/ *n* [U] a substance that is put in a container to be used as a toilet by pets • *Don't forget to change the* **cat** *litter while we're away.*

lit·tle SMALL /£ˈlɪt·l̩, $ˈlɪţ-/ *adj* **-r, -st** small in size or amount • *Little drops of water rested on the leaves after the rain.* • *She lives in a little room at the top of our house.* • *A little old man came into the shop.* • *Two little eyes peered out from behind the bush.* • *He gave a little smile.* • *It'll take a little while to clear up the rest of the broken glass.* • If someone says **a little bird told me (so)**, they mean that they know who gave them the information being discussed but will not say who it was: *"How did you know he was leaving?" "Oh, let's just say a little bird told me so."* ○ *A little bird told me (that) you're getting married.* • A **little finger** (*Am, Aus and Scot Eng also* **pinkie** or **pinky**) is the smallest of the four fingers on a hand. • *(esp. Irish Eng)* The **little people/little folk** are small imaginary creatures, such as LEPRECHAUNS, which look quite like small humans. • A **little something** is a small drink or small amount of food: *I always like to have a little something around 11 o'clock in the morning.* See also **little something** at LITTLE UNIMPORTANT. • A **little toe** is the smallest of the five toes on a foot.

lit·tle /£ˈlɪt·l̩, $ˈlɪţ-/ *pronoun, n* • *"Help yourself to more wine." "I will have* **a** *little* (= a small amount of wine), *thank you."* • *I could only hear* **a** *little* **of** *what they were saying.* • *There's not much flour left but you're welcome to* **the/what** *little there is.* • *He's always trying to get away with doing as little as possible at work.* [U] • *Ms Perez is on the phone right now. Would you mind waiting* **a** *little* (= a short time)? [U] • **A little** means a small amount of: *This sauce needs a little salt.* ○ *With a little training she could do very well in the championships.* ○ *Can I give you a little advice?* • **A little** can also mean slightly: *She was a little worried by the noise.* ○ *We'll wait a little longer and then I'll phone them.* ○ *There's only a little further to go.* ○ *Would you like a little more to eat.* ○ *"Oh, all right then," he said, sighing a little.* ○ *Could you slow down? You're walking a little too fast for me.* • **Little by little** means slowly or gradually: *Little by little she came to understand the way the gorillas' society operated.* • *"A Little of what you Fancy does you Good"* (title of a song written by Fred W. Leigh and George Arthurs, 1915) • 'A little' is used with uncountable nouns. Compare FEW.

lit·tle YOUNG /£ˈlɪt·l̩, $ˈlɪţ-/ *adj* **-r, -st** young • *Here's a photograph of your mother when she was really little.* • *When you were both little you and your brother were always fighting.* • *My little* (= younger) **brother/sister** *is a real nuisance.* • *He isn't at work today because his little* **girl/boy** (= young daughter/son) *is ill.* • *The* **little ones** (= children) *can play in the garden while we get lunch ready.*

lit·tle NOT ENOUGH /£ˈlɪt·l̩, $ˈlɪţ-/ *determiner* **less** /les/ or **least** /liːst/ not much or enough • *It now seems there will be little chance of starting the aid flights within the next six weeks.* • *I see little use in continuing with this discussion if you won't listen to what I'm saying.* • *Her mother's comforting words had little effect on the crying child.* • *There seems little hope of a ceasefire, and even less hope of peace.* • *They have very little money.* • *When we went to Rome we had too little time to see all the things we wanted to see.* • 'Little' is used with uncountable nouns. Compare FEW. • LP **Quantity words**

lit·tle /£ˈlɪt·l̩, $ˈlɪţ-/ *pronoun, n* • *Unfortunately, little* **of** *the artist's work has survived.* • *He's not a very good teacher – I could* **understand** *(very) little of what he said.* • *He's not a very good teacher – I could* **make** (= understand) *(very) little of what he said.* [U] • *She's eating* **so** *little – I'm quite worried.* [U] • *The government has* **done** *little* **or nothing** *to help the poorest people in this country.* [U] • **The** *little we do know about the people who lived here suggests they had a very sophisticated society.* [U]

lit·tle /£ˈlɪt·l̩, $ˈlɪţ-/ *adv* [not gradable] • *For many years his theories were little understood.* • *It matters little to Carin what people think of her.* • *Their house was little cared for during the war.* • *I spent a lot of money having my hair cut, but it actually looks little different.* • *Jacks, a little-known* (= not famous or known to the general public) *outsider, is through to this year's final.* • *We little expected that we would win.* • *Little did he* **know/realize** *what lay in store for him.* • *I agreed to go to their party, little* **though** *I wanted to* (= even though I did not want to).

lit·tle EMPHASIZE /£ˈlɪt·l̩, $ˈlɪţ-/ *adj* [before n; not gradable] used to emphasize an opinion which is being given about something or someone, whatever their size • *What a nice/nasty little play.* • *The first hotel we stayed in was a strange little place.* • *My sister is a little monster.* • *He's a horrid little man.*

lit·tle UNIMPORTANT /£ˈlɪt·l̩, $ˈlɪţ-/ *adj* [before n; not gradable] not very important or serious • *I had a little problem with my car, but it's been fixed now.* • *Her speech caused a little stir at the time, but had no lasting impact.* • *It's often the little things that count the most.* • *Can I have a little word* (= a short discussion about something not very important) *with you?* • *He* **made little of** (= gave only small importance to) *the ordeal he'd been through.* • A **little fish** is someone who is not important. • A **little something** is a present that is not of great value: *I want to buy a little something to take to Val when I visit her in hospital.* See also **little something** at LITTLE SMALL.

li·tur·gy /£ˈlɪt·ə·dʒi, $ˈlɪţ·ɚ-/ *n* (a particular set of) the words, music and actions used in ceremonies in some religions, including Christianity • *Liturgies exist in a wide variety of forms, depending on the different religious communities in which they are used.* [C] • *There have been arguments within the Church about liturgy.* [U]

li·tur·gi·cal /£lɪˈtɜː·dʒɪ·kəl, $-ˈtɜːr-/ *adj* [not gradable]

liv·a·ble, live·a·ble /ˈlɪv·ə·bl̩/ *adj* acceptable or suitable to a way of life • *The aim is to create a more livable planet.* • *(infml) The apartment is livable/(Br also) livable* **in** *although it's far from perfect.* • *(infml) Yes, there is a lot of discomfort, but it's livable/(Br also) livable* **with** *for a while.* • *(Br infml humorous) Yes, a £5000 pay increase would be quite livable* **with**!

live HAVE LIFE /lɪv/ *v* [I] (to continue) to be alive or have life • *He was so badly injured in the accident that the doctors don't expect him to live.* • *Some lichens are thought to have been living* **for** *at least 9000 years.* • *Her granny lived* **to (be)** *the ripe old age of 94.* [+ to infinitive] • *Do you think he will live (long enough)* **to see** *his plans come to fruition?* • *Can the right to live ever be denied to any human?* • People sometimes say **you/we live and learn** when they hear or discover something which is surprising: *"Did you know that 98% of American households have a television?" "Well, you live and learn."* • To **live to fight another day** is to have another chance to fight in a competition: *We didn't win this time, but we live to fight another day.* • If you **live to tell the tale**, you successfully deal with a difficult situation or experience: *We had an absolutely awful journey, but we lived to tell the tale.* • *"Milton! thou shouldst be living at this hour"* (William Wordsworth in the poem *Sonnets Dedicated to Liberty*, 1807) • *"Live and let die"* (title of a book about James Bond by Ian Fleming, 1954)

live /laɪv/ *adj* [before n; not gradable] • *There was a tank of live lobsters in the restaurant.* • *We were walking along a path in the woods when suddenly we saw a* **real** *live grizzly bear.*

liv·ing /ˈlɪv·ɪŋ/ *adj* [not gradable] • *All living creatures that we know about contain carbon.* • *He is the most famous living Austrian architect.* • *Do you have any living grandparents?* • *Are any of your grandparents living?* • Living is also used in a particular few expressions to make them stronger: *You scared the living daylights out of me* (= frightened me very much). ○ *He's the living image of* (= looks exactly like) *his father.* • **A living death** is a period in which a person suffers a lot. • A **living will** is a written document in which a person says what type of medical treatment they would like to have if they become so ill that they are certain to die and lose the ability to communicate their wishes about their treatment: *I have made a living will, which states that I don't want to be kept alive artificially if I am in a coma and there is no chance of me waking up.* • If something has happened within **living memory**, it can be remembered by some people who are still alive: *Do you think that there is less chance of another World War while the last one is* **in/within** *living memory?*

liv·ing /'lɪv·ɪŋ/ *pl n* • **The living** are people who are still alive: *On this anniversary of the tragedy we remember the living as well as the dead.*

live HAVE A HOME /lɪv/ *v* [I always + adv/prep] (of a person or animal) to have as their home or as the place where they stay or return, esp. to sleep • *Where do you live?* • *We live* **in** *London now but we used to live* **in** *France.* • *Many people want to live* **in** *the country.* • *Few people these days still employ a housekeeper who lives* **in** (= lives in the house where they work). • *Some students live* **on** *the University campus.* • *(Br) Other students live* **out** *in rented accommodation in the town.* • *My brother lives* **(together) with** *four other people in a shared house.* [I] • *Few animals live above the snowline.* • *Our dog lives* **in** *a kennel in the garden.* • *(fig.) Where do the knives live* (= Where is the place they are usually kept) *in your kitchen?* • *You've only been here a week and already the room looks very* **lived in** (= comfortable and regularly used). • If two people **live together/live with** each other/*(esp. humorous)* **live in sin**, they share a house and have a sexual relationship but are not married: *Many young people nowadays live together before they get married.* LP> **Relationships** • *I think we could call him her* **live-in lover/boyfriend** (= someone who shares a house and has a sexual relationship with a partner without being married to them). • *We have a* **live-in** *nanny* (= one who lives in the house where she works) *who looks after the children.* • A **living room** (also *Br* **sitting room**, *Am* **lounge room**) is the room in a house or an apartment in which people sit or relax together but do not usually eat. • **Living room suite** is *Am for* **three-piece suite**. See at THREE. • PIC> **Room**

live STAY ALIVE /lɪv/ *v* [I] to stay alive, esp. by getting enough money to pay for food, a place in which to stay, clothing, etc., or by eating a particular food • *For several years she lived* **by** *begging.* • *She has an inheritance to live* **off** *(Am also live* **off of**) *so she doesn't need to get a job.* • *Many people live* **off** *the profits of cocaine production.* • *He only agreed to marry her so he could live* **off** *her (money).* • *His wage won't be enough to live* **on** *if we have another child.* • *The natives live* **on** (= stay alive by eating) *a diet of fruit and occasionally meat.*

liv·ing /'lɪv·ɪŋ/ *n* [C] • *What do you do for a living* (= What is your job)? • *She's not happy working at the hospital but at least it's a living* (= a way of earning money). • *You can make a good living* (= earn a lot of money) *in sales if you have the right attitude.* • *(dated)* In the Church of England, a living is the job, given to a priest, of being in charge of a particular area: *He was offered the living in Norwood, where he knew he would remain for the rest of his life.* • A **living wage** is enough money to buy the things that are necessary for staying alive such as food and clothes: *He does make a living wage but only by working 72 hours a week.* • See also LIVELIHOOD. • LP> **Work**

live *(obj)* SPEND LIFE /lɪv/ *v* [always + adv/prep] to spend (your life) (in a particular way) • *After a while you get used to living alone.* [I] • *He lived under a constant threat of his health problems returning.* [I] • *When you retire, you want to live life comfortably.* [T] • *So the prince and princess got married, and lived* **happily ever after**. [I] • *I always try to live* **by** *what I believe in.* [I] • *The US is living* **beyond** *its* **means** (= spending more than it earns). [I] • *She just lives* **for** (= Her main or only interest in life is) *parties and having a good time.* [I] • *He simply wants to live* **out** (= experience or do) *the rest of his days in peace.* [T] • *Winning the money allowed her to live* **out** (= do) *a lot of the things she'd only dreamed of doing before.* [M] • *He lived* **with/through** (= experienced) *terrible suffering because of back pain until the age of fifty.* [I] • *I'm sorry your tooth is hurting but you'll just have to live* **with** (= bear) *it until we get you to the dentist.* [I] • *The TV's broken – we'll just have to live* **without** (= not have) *it for a while.* [I] • *She certainly lived her life* **to the full** (= was always doing something interesting). [T] • If someone is **living a lie**, they behave in a way that hides something they think or know: *She doesn't know you're married? You must stop living a lie and tell her.* • When a person **lives and breathes** something, it is very important to them: *He lived and breathed music – he was a truly dedicated musician.* • If you say to someone **live and let live**, you mean that they should accept the way other people live and behave, esp. if they do things in a different way: *You can't criticize someone for not liking sport just because you do – you have to live and let live.* • When someone **lives like a king/lord**, they have a luxurious style of life. • To **live** your **own life** means to spend your life doing what you want usually because something is no longer stopping you from doing so: *Now that the children have left home I can live my own life again.* • Someone who **lives by/on** their **wits** makes money by deceiving people rather than by working honestly. • *"Live now, pay later"* (title of a film, 1962)

liv·ing /'lɪv·ɪŋ/ *n* [U] • *Our style of living is very different from that of a hundred years ago.* • *Declining living* **standards** *have eroded the president's popularity.* See also **standard of living** at STANDARD QUALITY. • *"Summer time and the living is easy / Fish are jumping, and the cotton is high"* (song from the opera *Porgy and Bess*, words by Du Bose Heyward and Ira Gershwin, 1935)

live AS IT HAPPENS /laɪv/ *adj* [not gradable] (of a performance) broadcast, recorded or seen while it is happening; real • *This evening there will be a live broadcast of the debate.* • *Don't you think live recordings have more atmosphere than studio recordings?*

live /laɪv/ *adv* [not gradable] • *I've got two tickets to see Genesis* **(perform)** *live.*

live CONTINUE /lɪv/ *v* [I] (of things which can not be alive) to exist or continue to exist • *His body may be dead but his kindness will live with us always.* • *The memory of those terrible days lives* **on** *with all who were at the camps.* • If something **lives (on) in the memory**, it has such an effect that it is remembered for a long time: *What a brilliant production – it will certainly live on in the memory of many people.* See also **living memory** at LIVE HAVE LIFE.

liv·ing /'lɪv·ɪŋ/ *adj* [not gradable] • *The pyramids are a living monument to the skill of their builders.* • *Zoroastrianism is a living religion, although not many people practise it.*

live ELECTRICITY /laɪv/ *adj* [not gradable] (of a wire) carrying or charged with electricity • *a live wire* • *Internal parts of the toaster may be live so disconnect it before working on it.* • If you say someone is a **live wire**, you mean they are very energetic and active.

live EXPLODE /laɪv/ *adj* [not gradable] able to explode • *live rounds of ammunition* • *On this exercise you will be firing live shells.*

live BURNING /laɪv/ *adj* [not gradable] (of a fire, coals or a MATCH) still burning or able to burn • *There are live coals in the fireplace.*

live INTERESTING LIFE /lɪv/ *v* [I] to have an interesting life • *I don't want to get a regular job yet – I want to live* **(a bit/a little)** *first!* • *When she was in her twenties she lived – I mean really lived – but now she's settled down.* • *If you haven't seen Venice, you haven't lived.* • If you **live it up** you have an exciting and very enjoyable time with parties, good food and drink: *He's alive and well and living it up in the Bahamas.*

live down *obj*, **live** *obj* **down** *v adv* [M] to stop feeling uncomfortable about (something embarrassing or bad that you have done) usually by waiting long enough for other people to forget it or by behaving well • *I'll never be able to live down addressing Admiral Keene by the wrong name.*

live up to *obj v adv prep* [T] to achieve (what is expected, esp. high standards) • *The concert was brilliant – it lived up to all our expectations.* • *It'll be difficult to live up to the standards set by our last captain.*

live·a·ble /'lɪv·ə·bl̩/ *adj* LIVABLE

live·li·hood /'laɪv·li·hud/ *n* (the way someone earns) the money people need to pay for food, a place to live, clothing, etc. • *Many ship workers could* **lose** *their livelihoods because of falling orders for new ships.* [C] • *They* **earn** *their livelihood from farming.* [U] • *For most of the people of the country, a home, clothes and a means of livelihood were pressing concerns.* [U] • See also LIVING at LIVE STAY ALIVE.

live·ly /'laɪv·li/ *adj* **-ier, -iest** having or showing a lot of energy and enthusiasm, or showing interesting and exciting thought • *The pensioners were a lively group who spent their afternoons dancing.* • *It can be hard work teaching a class of lively children.* • *The orchestra gave a* *lively performance.* • *They take a lively interest in their grandchildren.* • *There was some lively discussion at the meeting.* • *What we need for this job is someone with a lively and enquiring mind who will have lots of new ideas.* • *(fig.) That dress is a very lively* (= bright) *pink!*

live·li·ness /ˈlaɪv·lɪ·nəs/ *n* [U] • *Most inhabitants love the liveliness of the city.*

li·ven up *(obj)*, **li·ven** *(obj)* **up** /ˈlaɪ·vᵊn/ *v adv* • *A new coat of paint would liven the kitchen up* (= make it more interesting). [M] • *I'm going to liven up* (= make myself feel more energetic) *a bit* **by** *going for a run.* [I]

liv·er /£ˈlɪv·əʳ, $-ɚ/ *n* a large organ in the body which cleans the blood and produces BILE, or this organ from an animal used as meat • *Her liver is damaged, probably because of alcohol abuse.* [C] • *Juniper berries go well with liver.* [U] • **Liver sausage** *(Am and Aus usually* **liverwurst**) is a type of cooked SAUSAGE which contains liver and is usually eaten cold on bread.

liv·er·ish /£ˈlɪv·ᵊr·ɪʃ, $ˈ-ɚ-/ *adj dated or humorous* feeling ill, usually because of having drunk or eaten too much

Liv·er·pud·li·an /£ˌlɪv·əˈpʌd·li·ən, $-ɚˈ-/ *n* [C], *adj* [not gradable] (a person) from Liverpool, a city in NW England

liv·er·y /£ˈlɪv·ᵊr·i, $ˈ-ɚ-/ *n* a special uniform worn by servants or particular officials • *The leading horse is being ridden by a servant wearing his livery/wearing fine livery.* [C/U] • *(Br)* A company's livery is a special pattern or design which is put on their goods and possessions to show that they belong to the company: *We saw several of the vans* **in** *their familiar blue and yellow livery.* [U]

lives /laɪvz/ *pl of* LIFE

live·stock /£ˈlaɪv·stɒk, $-stɑːk/ *pl n* animals, such as cows and sheep, and birds, such as chickens, kept on a farm

liv·id [ANGRY] /ˈlɪv·ɪd/ *adj* extremely angry • *The rude letter from his bank made him livid.*

liv·id [COLOUR] /ˈlɪv·ɪd/ *adj* (esp. of marks on the skin) of an unpleasant purple or dark blue colour • *Her arm had livid bruises where it was hit when she fell.* • *He had a long livid scar across his cheek.*

liz·ard /£ˈlɪz·əd, $-ɚd/ *n* [C] a REPTILE (= type of animal) which is usually small and has a long body, four short legs, a long tail and strong skin

'll /ᵊl/ *short form of* will or shall • *I'll see you next week.* • *We'll be arriving on Friday evening.* • *Amy'll know, if you ask her.* • *What'll happen if I press this button?*

lla·ma /ˈlɑː·mə/ *n* [C] a S American animal which is similar to a horse but has a long neck and has long hair • *Llamas, which are related to camels, are used as pack animals and as a source of wool.*

LLB /ˌel·elˈbiː/, *Am also* **BL** /ˌbiːˈel/ *n* [C] *abbreviation for* Bachelor of Laws (= degree in law or a person having this degree) • [LP] **Schools and colleges**

lo /£ləʊ, $loʊ/ *exclamation old use* look; see • *(literary or humorous)* People say **lo and behold** to show that they are about to mention something interesting or surprising: *I was in Vienna sitting quietly in a café when, lo and behold, my cousin walked in.*

load [AMOUNT CARRIED] /£ləʊd, $loʊd/ *n* [C] the amount (of weight) carried, esp. by a vehicle, a structure such as a bridge, or an animal • *Delivery vans* **with** *heavy loads always drive slowly up this hill.* • *The maximum load* **for** *this elevator is eight persons.* • *One truck involved in the accident was* **carrying** *a load* **of** *soap.* • *With a* **full load of** *200 passengers, the boat can cruise at 35 km/h.* • *This bridge was built over 200 years ago and was not designed to* **take** *the load* **of** *modern traffic.* • *(specialized)* In an electrical system, a load is an electrical device which takes power, or the electrical power put into the system. • *(infml)* **A load of** means much or many: *I've got a load of work to get through before tomorrow.* ○ *A load of people who we weren't expecting turned up to the party.* • *(infml)* **A load of** can also be used to express your disapproval of something or a group of people: *The play was a load of* **(old)** *rubbish.* ○ *I never take any notice of what my teachers say – they're a load of idiots.* • *(slang)* **Get a load of** something means give attention to something because it is interesting: *Get a load of his new car!*

-load /£-ləʊd, $-loʊd/ *combining form* • -load means all the people or goods in the stated type of vehicle or container: *a shipload of goods/cargo* ○ *coachloads of football fans* ○ *a basketload of washing* ○ *a carload of shopping* ○ *Busloads* **of** *tourists pour into this place in the summer.* ○ *A planeload* **of** *volunteers arrived to help dig out survivors after the earthquake.* ○ *Truckloads of food and medical supplies arrived in the refugee camp.*

load *(obj)* /£ləʊd, $loʊd/ *v* • *How long will it take to load this sand* **(onto** *the lorry)?* [T] • *It's always interesting to watch the cranes loading at the docks.* [I] • *Let's load* **(up)** *the car and then we can go.* [T/M] • *Let me help – you're loaded* **down with** *shopping.* [T] • A *(Br)* **loading bay**/ *(Am)* **loading dock** is a space at the back of a shop where goods are delivered or taken away. • See also OVERLOAD.

loads /£ləʊdz, $loʊdz/ *pl n, adv infml* • *"Have you got many apples on your tree this year?" "Yes, there are loads* (= a lot)*."* • *This book is loads better than the last one he wrote.* • *You need* **loads of** (= much) *patience to look after children.* • *He's got a job on Wall Street – he must have* **loads of** *money.*

load [AMOUNT OF WORK] /£ləʊd, $loʊd/ *n* [C] the amount of work to be done by a person • *If we share the organization of the party, that will help spread the load a bit.* • *I've got so much work to do, and I can't see any way of* **lightening** *the load.* • *I've got a* **heavy/light** *teaching load this term.* • *(fig.) The death of her husband is a great load* (= difficult situation) *for her to cope with.* • See also CASELOAD; WORKLOAD.

load *obj* [PUT INTO] /£ləʊd, $loʊd/ *v* [T] to put (something which is operated by a piece of equipment) into (the piece of equipment) • *How do you load a cassette into this player?* • *Phil loaded a new* **program** *onto his computer.* • *Load the* **bullets** *into the rifle quietly.* • *I don't know how to load* (= put bullets into) *a* **gun**. • *Do not load the* **film** (= put it into the camera) *in bright light.* • *It's very easy to load* (= put film into) *my new* **camera** *– the motor winds the film on to the right place.*

load·ed /£ˈləʊ·dɪd, $ˈloʊ-/ *adj* • *It's dangerous to leave a loaded* **gun** (= one with bullets in it) *lying around.*

load·ed [NOT FAIR] /£ˈləʊ·dɪd, $ˈloʊ-/ *adj* not fair, esp. by being helpful to one person instead of another, or (of a question) having particularly chosen words which suggest the wanted answer • *It seems that the report is loaded in favour of the developers.* • *A survey should avoid asking loaded* **questions** *but that's quite difficult to do in practice.* See also **leading question** at LEAD [INFLUENCE].

load·ed [RICH] /£ˈləʊ·dɪd, $ˈloʊ-/ *adj* [after v] *infml* having a large amount of money • *He inherited the family business – he must be loaded!*

load·ed [DRUNK] /£ˈləʊ·dɪd, $ˈloʊ-/ *adj* [after v] *slang, esp. Am* drunk • *What a party – everyone was loaded!*

loaf [BREAD] /£ləʊf, $loʊf/ *n* [C] *pl* **loaves** /£ləʊvz, $loʊvz/ a mass of bread which is shaped and baked in a single piece and can be sliced for eating • *a wholemeal loaf* • *two loaves of white bread* • *a sliced loaf* • *Have a slice of* **fruit** *loaf* (= sweet bread containing RAISINS, SULTANAS, etc.). • *(saying)* 'Half a loaf is better than none'. • See also **use your loaf** at USE [PURPOSE]. • [PIC] **Bread and cakes**

loaf [AVOID WORK] /£ləʊf, $loʊf/ *v* [I] *infml* to avoid activity, esp. work • *Stop loafing* **(about/around)** *and get on with cleaning the windows!*

loaf·er /£ˈləʊ·fəʳ, $ˈloʊ·fɚ/ *n* [C] • *an idle loafer* • See also LOAFER.

loaf [FOOD] /£ləʊf, $loʊf/ *n* [usually used as a combining form] *pl* **loaves** /£ləʊvz, $loʊvz/ savoury food cut into small pieces then pressed together and cooked in a single solid piece • *Would you like some/a slice of meat loaf?* [U] • *I made a nut loaf.* [C]

loaf·er /£ˈləʊ·fəʳ, $ˈloʊ·fɚ/ *n* [C] *esp. Am trademark* a type of shoe with stitches around the top, and a wide strip across the top, which a person's foot slides into • See also **loafer** at LOAF [AVOID WORK].

loam /£ləʊm, $loʊm/ *n* [U] high-quality earth which is a mixture of sand, clay and decaying plant material

loam·y /£ˈləʊ·mi, $ˈloʊ·mi/ *adj* **-ier, -iest**

loan [SUM] /£ləʊn, $loʊn/ *n* [C] a sum of money which is borrowed, often from a bank, and has to be paid back, esp. together with an additional amount of money that you have to pay as a charge for borrowing • *She's trying to* **get** *a $50 000 loan to start her own business.* • *We could* **apply for/take out** *a loan to buy a car.* • *(infml disapproving)* A **loan shark** is a person who charges very large amounts of money for lending a sum to someone.

loan *obj* /£ləʊn, $loʊn/ *v* [T + two objects] • *I'd loan you the money if I could./I'd loan the money* **to** *you if I could.*

loan [BORROW] /£ləʊn, $loʊn/ *n* an act of borrowing or lending something • *All the library's loans are recorded on a computer.* [C] • *Thank you very much for the loan* **of** *your bike.* [U] • *This exhibit is* **on** *loan* (= being borrowed/lent) **from/to** *another museum.* [U]

loan *obj* /£ləʊn, $loʊn/ *v* [T] *esp. Am and Aus* • To loan something is to lend it: *This library loans books, CDs and videotapes.* • *Liza will loan you a suitcase/loan a suitcase* **to** *you.* [+ two objects] • LP **Borrow**

loan·word /£'ləʊn·wɜːd, $'loʊn·wɜːrd/ *n* [C] a word taken from one language and used in another

loath, **loth**, *Am also* **loathe** /£ləʊθ, £ləʊð, $loʊθ/ *adj* [after v; + *to* infinitive] unwilling; RELUCTANT • *She'd be loath* **to** *admit it but she doesn't really want to go away for the weekend.*

loathe *(obj)* /£ləʊð, $loʊð/ *v* to feel strong hate, dislike or disgust for (someone or something) • *From an early age the brothers have loathed each other.* [T] • *"Do you like fish?" "No, I loathe it."* [T] • *I loathe* **doing** *housework.* [+ v-*ing*]

loath·ing /£'ləʊ·ðɪŋ, $'loʊ·ðɪŋ/ *n* [U] • *Both fighters went into the ring with* **deep** *loathing in their eyes.* • *The girl clearly has* **a** *loathing* **for/of** *her mother.* • *He reacted to the idea of killing his rival with* **fear and** *loathing.*

loath·some /£'ləʊð·səm, $'loʊð-/ *adj* • *War is a loathsome business.* • *I think spiders are loathsome little creatures.*

loath·some·ly /£'ləʊð·səm·li, $'loʊð-/ *adv*

loath·some·ness /£'ləʊð·səm·nəs, $'loʊð-/ *n* [U]

loaves /£ləʊvz, $loʊvz/ *pl of* LOAF BREAD

lob *obj* /£lɒb, $lɑːb/ *v* [T] **-bb-** to kick, hit or throw (something, esp. a ball in a game) in a high curve • *He lobbed* (= kicked) *the ball* **over** *the goalkeeper and into the net.* • *Police started lobbing* (= throwing) *tear gas canisters* **into** *the crowd.*

lob /£lɒb, $lɑːb/ *n* [C] • *Jones hit a beautiful lob* (= high curving hit) *that arced over his opponent's head.*

lob·by ROOM /£'lɒb·i, $'lɑː·bi/ *n* [C] the (large) room into which the main entrance door opens in a hotel or other large building • *I'll meet you in the hotel lobby in ten minutes.*

lob·by *(obj)* PERSUADE /£'lɒb·i, $'lɑː·bi/ *v* to try to persuade (a politician, an official or an official group) that a particular thing should or should not happen, or that a law should be changed • *Small businesses have lobbied hard* **for/against** *changes in the tax laws.* [I] • *Local residents lobbied* **to** *have the factory shut down.* [+ *to* infinitive] • *They have been lobbying Congress* **to** *change the legislation concerning guns.* [T + obj + *to* infinitive]

lob·by /£'lɒb·i, $'lɑː·bi/ *n* [C] • *Representatives of the anti-abortion lobby* (= group) *will meet sympathetic MPs this afternoon.* • *The environmental lobby has been arguing for a reduction in the use of cars.* • In the British parliament, a lobby is a room where someone meets a member of parliament whom they have arranged to talk to. A lobby is also one of the two passages which members of parliament walk through as a way of voting. • A **lobby correspondent** is a reporter who spends a lot of time in the British parliament trying to discover news about recent and future political events.

lob·by·ist /£'lɒb·i·ɪst, $'lɑː·bi-/ *n* [C] • A lobbyist is someone who tries to persuade a politician or official group that a particular thing should be done or that a law should be changed: *Lobbyists for the tobacco industry have expressed concerns about the restriction of smoking in public places.*

lobe ORGAN /£ləʊb, $loʊb/ *n* [C] *specialized* any part of an organ which seems to be separate in some way from the rest, esp. one of the divisions of the brain • *a lobe of the liver* • *the frontal lobe of the brain*

lobed /£ləʊbd, $loʊbd/ *adj* [not gradable]

lobe EAR /£ləʊb, $loʊb/ *n* [C] an EARLOBE

lo·bot·o·my /£lə'bɒt·ə·mi, $-'bɑː·t̬ə-/, *Br also* **leu·cot·o·my** /£ljuː'kɒt·ə·mi, $luː'kɑː·t̬ə-/ *n* [C] *medical* a medical operation in which cuts are made in or near the front part of the brain, used in the past for the treatment of severe mental problems

lob·ster /£'lɒb·stəʳ, $'lɑːb·stɚ/ *n* an animal which lives in the sea and has a long jointed body with a hard outside, two large CLAWS and eight legs, or its flesh when used as food • *Lobsters are grey in colour when they're alive, but turn pink when they're cooked.* [C] • *We had lobster and salad for lunch.* [U] • A **lobster pot** is a special container used for catching lobsters which is usually made from long thin pieces of wood which are tied together to make a type of cage. • PIC **Crustaceans**

lo·cal AREA /£'ləʊ·kəl, $'loʊ-/ *adj* [not gradable] from, existing in, serving, or responsible for a small area, esp. of a country • *a local accent* • *local issues* • *local housing* • *a local newspaper/radio station* • *Most of the local population depend on fishing for their income.* • *Our children all go to the local school.* • *Many local shops will be forced to close if the big new supermarket is built.* • *We're going to talk to our local councillor about the new swimming pool.* • *I stopped and asked a man the way, but he wasn't local* **to** (= did not come from) *the area and he couldn't tell me.* • *(medical)* Local also means limited to a particular part of a body: *a local anaesthetic* ○ *local swelling* • *(Br)* A **local authority** is the group of people who govern an area, esp. a city: *There was a lengthy debate about whether local authorities are spending enough on the arts.* • **Local colour** is the special or unusual features of a place or a time, esp. as described or shown in a story, picture or film to make it seem more real. • *(Br)* A **local derby** (also **derby**) is a sporting competition, esp. a game of football, between two teams from the same city or area. • **Local government** is the control and organization of towns and small areas by people who are elected from them: *The group is dependent on local government grants.* • **Local time** is the official time in a country or an area: *The statement will be broadcast at 8 p.m. local time.* • CS D PL

lo·cal /£'ləʊ·kəl, $'loʊ-/ *n* [C] • A local is a person who lives in the particular small area (which you are talking about): *We were lost in the centre of Paris, and couldn't find any locals to give us directions.* ○ *The café was popular with both locals* (= people who live near it) *and visitors.*

lo·cal·ize *obj*, *Br and Aus usually* **-ise** /£'ləʊ·kəl·aɪz, $'loʊ-/ *v* [T] *fml or medical* • *Has the electrician been able to localize* (= find exactly) *the fault in the wiring?* • *Specially equipped aircraft were trying to localize the oil slick* (= keep it within a small area) *and prevent it from spreading.* • *We should be able to localize the swelling* (= stop it spreading) *with antibiotics.* • *Fortunately, the dispute/problem seems to be localized* (= limited to a small area).

lo·cal·ly /£'ləʊ·kəl·i, $'loʊ-/ *adv* [not gradable] • Locally means in the particular small area which you are talking about: *Only locally produced food* (= food produced in the same small area) *is cooked in our restaurant.* ○ *Both sisters were born and still live locally.* ○ *The shopkeeper said all his fruit and vegetables are grown locally.*

lo·cal BUILDING /£'ləʊ·kəl, $'loʊ-/ *n* [C] *Br* a PUB (= a building where alcohol can be bought and drunk) near to where a person lives, esp. if they often go there to drink • *We'll probably go round to our/the local at about nine.* • CS D PL

lo·cal VEHICLE /£'ləʊ·kəl, $'loʊ-/ *n* [C] *esp. Am* a train or bus which stops at all or most of the places on its route where passengers can get on or off • *the 12.24 local to Poughkeepsie* • CS D PL

lo·cal ORGANIZATION /£'ləʊ·kəl, $'loʊ-/ *n* [C] *Am* a division within an organization, esp. a national workers' organization, representing people from a particular area • *My shop steward suggested I ask the local to follow up on my grievance.* • *She's a member of union local 1103.* • CS D PL

lo·cale /lə'kɑːl/ *n* [C] *fml* an area or place, esp. one where something special happens, such as the action in a book or a film • *The Jazz Café is a perfect locale for this type of music.* • *The book's locale is a seaside town in the summer of 1958.*

lo·cal·i·ty /£lə'kæl·ə·ti, $loʊ'kæl·ə·t̬i/ *n* [C] a particular area • *There are several shops in the locality.* • *In 19th-century Britain, industries became concentrated in particular localities.*

lo·cate *(obj)* FIX PLACE /£ləʊ'keɪt, $loʊ-/ *v* [always + adv/prep] *slightly fml* to fix, put or establish (something such as a building) in a place • *Our office is located* **at** *the end of the road.* [T] • *The plan is to locate the new police station* **in** *the town centre.* [T] • *Many power stations are located* **on** *coastal land so that they are near to a good supply of water.* [T] • *(Am) The company hopes to locate* **in** *its new offices by June.* [I]

lo·cate *obj* FIND POSITION /£ləʊ'keɪt, $loʊ-/ *v* [T] *slightly fml* to find or discover the position of (something) • *Underwater archaeologists will try to locate the remains of the sunken ship.* • *I'm sorry but we can't locate your order form at the moment.*

lo·ca·tion /£ləʊ'keɪ·ʃən, $loʊ-/ *n* [U] *slightly fml* • *The latest navigational aids make the location of the airfield quite easy.*

lo·ca·tion POSITION /£ləʊ'keɪ·ʃən, $loʊ-/ *n* [C] *slightly fml* a place, esp. one where something special is or where something happens • *The hotel is* **in** *a location overlooking the lake.* • *We're trying to find a good location* **for** *our party.*

• *A map showing the location* **of** *the property will be sent to you.* • Ⓕ Ⓘ

lo·ca·tion [OUTSIDE] /£ləʊˈkeɪ·ʃᵊn, $loʊ-/ *n* a place away from a STUDIO where all or part of a film or a television show is recorded • *His latest movie was filmed in three different locations.* [C] • *The documentary was made* **on** *location in the Gobi desert.* [U] • Ⓕ Ⓘ

loch /£lɒk, $lɑːk/ *n* [C] *ScotEng* a LAKE • *Loch Lomond*

loci /£ˈləʊ·kaɪ, £-kiː, £ˈlɒk·aɪ, $ˈloʊ-/ *pl of* LOCUS

lock [FASTEN] /£lɒk, $lɑːk/ *v, n* (to fasten using) a device which prevents something such as a door being opened, esp. by turning a key • *Don't forget to lock all of the doors when you go out.* [T] • *The garage door won't lock now because Dad drove into it last week.* [I] • *Strong locks are fitted to all of our safes.* [C] • *Thieves got in by smashing the lock off the door.* [C] • *The key has snapped off in the lock of my desk drawer.* [C] • **Lock, stock and barrel** means all of something: *My wife's got a new job so we're moving our things lock, stock and barrel to the other side of the country.* • See also PADLOCK.

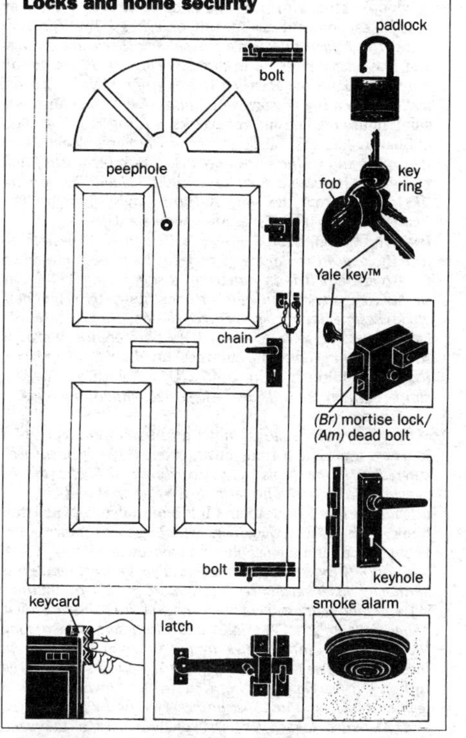

Locks and home security

lock·a·ble /£ˈlɒk·ə·bḷ, $lɑː·kə-/ *adj* [not gradable] • *All the suitcases on that shelf are lockable.*

lock *(obj)* [MAKE SAFE] /£lɒk, $lɑːk/ *v* [always + adv/prep] to make (something) safe by putting it in a special place and then fastening the entrance closed • *He locked the confidential documents* **in** *his filing cabinet.* [T] • *If you keep valuables in your house, lock them* **away/up** *somewhere safe.* [M] • *People who commit serious crimes should be locked* **away/up** (= put into prison) *for a long time.* [M] • *He's not only mad, he's also dangerous – he really should be locked* **away/up** (= kept in a hospital for people who are mentally ill). [M] • *After what she did, they should lock her* **up and throw away the key** (= put her in prison for the rest of her life). [T] • *The front door slammed behind our daughter and she was locked* **in** *(the house)* (= unable to get out) *for a couple of hours.* [T] • *The door slammed and our keys were inside, so we were locked* **out** (= unable to get in). [T] • *I've locked myself* **out of** (= made myself unable to get in) *the house twice in the last week.* [T] • *You really should lock your car* **up**, *or it'll get stolen.* [M] • *Sandra, will you lock* **up** *tonight when you go?* [I] • *(esp. Br)* A **lock-up** is a GARAGE (= a small building) where objects, esp. a car, can be safely kept. See also LOCKUP.

lock *n* [U] • If something is **under lock and key**, it is being kept safely: *Don't worry – your necklace is securely under lock and key at the bank.* • If a person, esp. a criminal, is **under lock and key**, they are being kept in a place from which they cannot escape, usually a prison.

lock [WATER] /£lɒk, $lɑːk/ *n* [C] a length of water with gates at each end where the level of water can be changed to allow boats to move between parts of a CANAL or river which are at different heights • A **lock keeper** is a person who is in control of a lock, esp. by opening or closing its gates. • PIC▷ **Canal**

lock [HOLD FIXED] /£lɒk, $lɑːk/ *n, v* (to be or hold something in) a fixed position where movement or escape are not possible • *The smaller wrestler held his opponent in a (full body) lock from which he couldn't escape.* [C] • *Sometimes, fighting stags become locked together* **by** *their antlers.* [T] • *This is the arena in which gladiators used to lock* **in** *mortal combat.* [I] • *(fig. Am) We were locked* (= unable to move) **in** *traffic for more than two hours when we came back to the city Sunday evening.* [T] • *(fig.) Both parties wish to avoid being locked* **in/into** (= unable to advance from) *discussions which will resolve nothing.* [T] • *A heat sensor in the nose of the missile locks* **on/onto** (= finds and then follows) *the hot exhaust outlet from a target aircraft.* [I] • *(Am infml)* A lock is something that is certain to happen: *She's a lock for promotion this year.* [C] • If two people **lock horns**, they begin to argue or fight: *The mayor and her deputy will probably lock horns* **over** *plans for the new road.*

lock [HAIR] /£lɒk, $lɑːk/ *n* [C] a small group of hairs, esp. a curl • *There is a lock of Napoleon's hair in the display cabinet.*

locks /£lɒks, $lɑːks/ *pl n poetic or dated* • Locks is another word for the hair on someone's head: *flowing golden locks*

lock [CAR] /£lɒk, $lɑːk/ *n* [U] *Br and Aus* the amount a road vehicle's front wheels can be turned from one side to the other by turning its **steering wheel** • *My car hasn't got enough lock for me to be able to turn it round in this small space.* • *Cars with* a *good lock are easier to park.*

lock·er /£ˈlɒk·əʳ, $ˈlɑː·kɚ/ *n* [C] a cupboard, often tall and made of metal, in which someone can lock their possessions, and leave them for a period of time • *We had several hours to wait for our train, so we left our luggage in a* **(luggage)** *locker, and went to look around the town.* • A **locker room** is a room with lockers where people can keep their personal things, esp. clothes, such as in a school, a **leisure centre** or a place of work. • **Locker-room** is used to refer to something said, thought or done that is rude or has a sexual meaning: *locker-room talk/mentality/jokes*

lock·et /£ˈlɒk·ɪt, $ˈlɑː·kɪt/ *n* [C] a small item of jewellery which opens to show a small picture or piece of hair, usually worn on a chain around a person's neck • PIC▷ **Jewellery**

lock·jaw /£ˈlɒk·dʒɔː, $ˈlɑːk·dʒɑː/ *n* [U] *infml for* TETANUS

lock·out /£ˈlɒk·aʊt, $ˈlɑːk-/ *n esp. disapproving* (an) action taken by an employer to stop workers going into their place of work until they agree to particular conditions given by the employer • *A series of lockouts ended with the workers returning to work on the employers' terms.* [C] • *The General Strike in Britain in 1926 was caused by the lockout* **of** *coalminers.* [U]

lock out *obj*, **lock** *obj* **out** *v adv* [M] *usually disapproving* • *Management has threatened to lock out the workforce if they do not accept the proposed changes in working methods.*

lock·smith /£ˈlɒk·smɪθ, $ˈlɑːk-/ *n* [C] a person who repairs and/or makes locks and supplies keys

lock·step /£ˈlɒk·step, $ˈlɑːk-/ *n* [U] *Am* a process that is not changeable and exactly follows a particular pattern • *After a long series of defeats, the team's new manager seems to have broken the lockstep, and they finally won a game last night.* • *The two currencies seem to be moving* **in** *lockstep* **with** (= in exactly the same way as) *each other.*

lock·up /£ˈlɒk·ʌp, $ˈlɑː·kʌp/ *n* [C] a (small) room, used as a prison, usually in a small town, in which criminals can be kept for a short time • *A couple of drunks were brought in and thrown in the lockup to sober up.* • See also **lock-up** at LOCK [MAKE SAFE].

lo·co [MENTALLY ILL] /£ˈləʊ·kəʊ, $ˈloʊ·koʊ/ *adj* [after v] *esp. Am slang for* MAD [MENTALLY ILL] or MAD [FOOLISH] • *He's* **gone** *completely loco over his new girlfriend.*

lo·co [ENGINE] /£ˈləʊ·kəʊ, $ˈloʊ·koʊ/ *n* [C] *pl* **locos** *infml for* LOCOMOTIVE

lo·co·mo·tion /£ˌləʊ·kəˈməʊ·ʃᵊn, $ˌloʊ·kəˈmoʊ-/ *n* [U] *specialized or fml* the ability to move; movement • *The muscles which control locomotion are of several different* *kinds.* • *A fish uses its fins for locomotion.* • *"Do the Locomotion"* (From the song *The Locomotion* written by Gerry Goffin and Carole King, 1962)

lo·co·mo·tive /£ˌləʊ·kəˈməʊ·tɪv, $ˌloʊ·kəˈmoʊ·t̬ɪv/ *adj* [not gradable] *specialized or fml* • *The motor applies locomotive force directly to the drive shaft.*

lo·co·mo·tive /£ˌləʊ·kəˈməʊ·tɪv, $ˌloʊ·kəˈmoʊ·t̬ɪv/, *infml* **lo·co** *n* [C] *fml* the engine of a train that pulls it along • *a diesel locomotive*

locum /£ˈləʊ·kəm, $ˈloʊ-/ *n* [C] *esp. Br and Aus* a person who does someone else's job for a period of time, esp. a medical worker such as a doctor • *Your doctor is on holiday – would you like to see her locum?*

locus /£ˈləʊ·kəs, £ˈlɒk·əs, $ˈloʊ·kəs/ *n* [C] *pl* **loci** /£ˈləʊ·kaɪ, £ˈlɒk·aɪ, £ˈləʊ·kiː, $ˈloʊ·kaɪ/ *fml* the place where something happens or the central area of interest in something being discussed • *The locus* **of** *decision making is sometimes far from the government's offices.*

locust /£ˈləʊ·kəst, $ˈloʊ-/ *n* [C] a large type of GRASSHOPPER (= a winged insect with long back legs), esp. found in hot areas. There are several different types of locust. • *a swarm of locusts* • *Locusts often destroy large areas of plants and crops.*

lode /£ləʊd, $loʊd/ *n* [C] metal in its natural form when found in a layer between other rock

lodes·tar /£ˈləʊd·stɑːʳ, $ˈloʊd·stɑːr/ *n* [C usually sing] a star, esp. the **Pole Star**, used to help find direction • *(fig.) The party manifesto is no longer the lodestar it used to be* (= no longer an example that people want to follow).

lodes·tone /£ˈləʊd·stəʊn, $ˈloʊd·stoʊn/ *n* [C/U] (a piece of) rock which contains a lot of iron and can therefore be used as a magnet, as happened esp. in the past in a compass

lodge [STAY] /£lɒdʒ, $lɑːdʒ/ *v* [I always + adv/prep] *fml* to stay somewhere, usually paying rent to do so and often for only a short time, such as a few days or weeks • *He lodges* **in** *London during the week but lives at home at the weekends.* • *You could lodge* **with** *Mrs. Higgins for a few weeks until you find somewhere to rent permanently.*

lodger /£ˈlɒdʒ·əʳ, $ˈlɑː·dʒɚ/, *Am also* **room·er** /£ˈruː·məʳ, $-mɚ/ *n* [C] • *She* **takes in** *lodgers to make a bit of extra money.*

lodg·ing /£ˈlɒdʒ·ɪŋ, $ˈlɑː·dʒɪŋ/ *n fml* • *The price includes* **board and** *lodging* (= a room to sleep in) *for the first night.* [U] • *It's getting late, we really should find a lodging* (= a place to stay) *before it gets dark.* [C] • A **lodging house** (*Am also* **rooming house**) is a house which has rooms that people can rent.

lodg·ings /£ˈlɒdʒ·ɪŋz, $ˈlɑː·dʒɪŋz/, *esp. Br infml* **digs** *pl n* • *Most athletes will* **stay** *in lodgings* (= a rented room or rooms) *near to the arena.*

lodge [SMALL BUILDING] /£lɒdʒ, $lɑːdʒ/ *n* [C] a small building, esp. one used by people who take part in sports held in the countryside or one on the land owned by a large house • *a ski/hunting lodge* • *Buildings of the estate include two lodges and a dairy.* • A lodge is also the name of the home of a BEAVER. • *(Am)* A lodge is a WIGWAM.

lodge *(obj)* [FIX] /£lɒdʒ, $lɑːdʒ/ *v* [always + adv/prep] to (cause to) become fixed (in a place or position) • *A fish bone which had lodged* **in** *her throat was successfully removed.* [I] • *Several bullets lodged* **in** *the wall.* [I] • *The explosion lodged a small piece of metal* **in** *his skull.* [T]

lodge *obj* [MAKE] /£lɒdʒ, $lɑːdʒ/ *v* [T] to formally make (a statement, esp. one which expresses a lack of approval), usually to an official • *The US lodged a formal* **protest** *against the arrest of the foreign reporters.* • *Lee's solicitor said last night that they would be lodging an* **appeal** *against the sentence.* • *If you are not satisfied with the treatment you've received, you should lodge an official* **complaint** (**with** *the appropriate department).*

lodge *obj* [STORE] /£lɒdʒ, $lɑːdʒ/ *v* [T always + adv/prep] *esp. Br and Aus fml* to put (something) in a safe place where it can be kept • *Her jewellery is lodged* **with** *the bank.* • *You should lodge a copy of the letter* **with** *your solicitor.*

lodge [GROUP] /£lɒdʒ, $lɑːdʒ/ *n* [C + sing/pl v] a local group of a larger organization • *Masonic Lodge No.227* • *The lodge is/are meeting tomorrow evening.*

lodge [ROOM] /£lɒdʒ, $lɑːdʒ/ *n* [C] *Br* the room used by a person who controls the entrance to a large building such as a hotel or college • *the porter's lodge*

loft [ROOF SPACE] /£lɒft, $lɑːft/ *n* [C] a space at the top of a building under the roof used for storage and usually entered by a LADDER (= set of movable steps), or sometimes made into a room • *We put all the camping gear up in the loft for the winter.* • *loft insulation* • *a loft ladder* • *The firm specializes in loft* **conversions** (= making lofts into rooms). • *(Am)* A loft can also be an upper floor or room: *Carol designed the loft we built in our apartment in New York.* • *(Am)* A loft can also be an apartment in a building that was previously used for industry: *Sue used to live in a* **converted** *loft in New York City.* • ⓓⓚ

loft *obj* [HIT] /£lɒft, $lɑːft/ *v* [T] to hit (a ball) high • *With a clever shot, the batsman lofted the ball over the fielder.* • ⓓⓚ

lofty /£ˈlɒf·ti, $ˈlɑːf·t̬i/ *adj* **-ier, -iest** *fml* high or *(fig.)* with (too) strong principles, standards and IDEALS • *a lofty ceiling/mountain/wall* • *lofty heights* • *a man of lofty stature* • • *(fig.) lofty sentiments/aims/ambition* • *(fig. disapproving) lofty indifference/isolation* • *(fig. disapproving) a lofty attitude/air/tone* • *(Br and Aus humorous)* **Lofty** is sometimes used as a NICKNAME (= informal name) for a tall person: *Over here, Lofty!* [as form of address]

lof·tily /£ˈlɒf·tɪ·li, $ˈlɑːf-/ *adv* • *(disapproving) She loftily dismissed all my suggestions.*

lof·ti·ness /£ˈlɒf·tɪ·nəs, $ˈlɑːf-/ *n* [U]

log [WOOD] /£lɒg, $lɑːg/ *n* [C] a thick piece of tree trunk or branch, esp. one cut for burning on a fire • *The logs were stacked in a neat pile.* • *We crossed small streams on logs and one larger river on a kind of bridge.* • *Those not on duty sit around the open log* **fire**. • *(infml) 'Did you sleep well?'* **'Like a log** (= very well), *thanks!'* • A **log cabin** is a small house made from tree trunks. • A **log jam** is a mass of floating logs that block a river or *(fig.)* any block: *There was a log jam* **in** *the system because a member of staff had been ill.* • *"It's been a hard day's night, I should be sleeping like a log"* (from the song *A Hard Day's Night* by The Beatles, 1964) • [PIC〉 **Fires and space heaters**

log *(obj)* /£lɒg, $lɑːg/ *v* **-gg-** • *The forest has been so heavily logged* (= so many of its trees have been cut down for wood) *that it is in danger of disappearing.* [T] • *The timber company continued to log* (= cut down trees for their wood) *despite having been ordered to stop.* [I]

log·ger /£ˈlɒg·əʳ, $ˈlɑː·gɚ/ *n* [C] • *Environmental groups say loggers* (= people who cut trees) *are destroying forests.*

log·ging /£ˈlɒg·ɪŋ, $ˈlɑː·gɪŋ/ *n* [U] • *The scars of logging can be seen on the hillsides.* • *logging companies* • *logging operations*

log [RECORD] /£lɒg, $lɑːg/ *n* [C] a full written record of a journey, a period of time, or an event • *The incident was entered on/in the ship's log.* • *According to the police log, he was arrested at 9.17 a.m. yesterday.* • *She produced Louisa's attendance log.* • *(Br)* A car's **log book** (also **registration book**) is the official document which records information about the car and the people who have owned it.

log *(obj)* /£lɒg, $lɑːg/ *v* **-gg-** • *The Police Complaints Authority has logged* (= recorded) *more than 90 complaints.* [T] • *Senior management were exempt from having their phone calls logged.* [T] • *Iowa and Minnesota were among the few major farm states to log* (= have) *a decline in income.* [T] • *The plane had logged (Br and Aus also logged* **up***) only a few hours' flying time* (= had flown for only a few hours) *when it lost one engine.* [T] • *(fig.) We logged (Br and Aus also logged* **up***)* (= travelled) *over a thousand kilometres touring about on holiday.* [T] • If you **log in/out** or someone **logs** you **in/out**, an official record is made that you have arrived or left a place: *She logged in* **to** *work late this morning.* ○ *He was logged out by the security guard at 4.30.* • When you **log in/on** to a computer system you start using it, esp. by giving a PASSWORD (= a word by which the system recognizes an approved user). When you **log off/out**, you finish using the system by following an approved set of instructions.

log [NUMBER] /£lɒg, $lɑːg/ *n* [C] *infml* a LOGARITHM

logan·berry /£ˈləʊ·gᵊnˌbᵊr·i, $ˈloʊ·gənˌber-/ *n* [C] a small red fruit, similar to a RASPBERRY, or the tall plant on which it grows • [PIC〉 **Berries**

logarithm /£ˈlɒg·ə·rɪ·ðᵊm, $ˈlɑː·gə-/, *infml* **log** *n* [C] the number which shows how many times a number, called the BASE, has to be multiplied by itself to produce another number. Adding or subtracting logarithms can replace multiplying or dividing large numbers. • *The logarithm of 1 000 000 in base 10 is 6.* • *Look up the log of 14·73 in your logarithm/log* **tables** (= book containing a list of logarithms).

logarith·mic /£ˌlɒg·ᵊrˈɪð·mɪk, $ˌlɑː·gəˈrɪð-/ *adj* [not gradable]

logarith·mi·cally /£ˌlɒg·ᵊrˈɪð·mɪ·kli, $ˌlɑː·gəˈrɪð-/ *adv* [not gradable]

log·ger·heads /£ˈlɒg·ə·hedz, $ˈlɑː·gɚ-/ *pl n* **at loggerheads** strongly disagreeing • *The two families have been at loggerheads for years.* • *The major cider makers are constantly at loggerheads* **with** *the farmers' union.* • *Jones and White are at loggerheads* **over** *the way the issue was handled.*

logic REASONABLE THINKING /£ˈlɒdʒ·ɪk, $ˈlɑː·dʒɪk/ *n* [U] a particular way of thinking, esp. one which is reasonable and based on good judgment • *If prices go up, wages will go up too – that's just logic.* • *You have to admit the logic* **of** *his argument.* • *There is logic* **in** *the argument which asks how the association can retain credibility if one of its members is breaking the rules.* • *There's no logic* **in** *the decision* (=it does not show good judgment) *to reduce staff when orders are the highest for years.* • *It's not always good commercial logic* (=wise judgment) *to raise prices.* • *He strongly defended the logic* (=wisdom) *of sanctions.* • *It* **defies** *logic to believe that he would do such an irresponsible thing.* • *Logic* **dictates** *neutrality in these circumstances.* • *He refused to accept* **the force of** *logic* (=be persuaded by reasonable argument), *now he will have to yield to* **the logic of force** (=physical power). • *The* **internal** *logic* (=logic within itself) *of the composition made the different parts work well together.* • *(Br)* A **logic device** (*Am and Aus* **logic circuit**) is a type of electronic switch: *Logic devices enable computers to make millions of calculations every second.*

log·i·cal /£ˈlɒdʒ·ɪ·kᵊl, $ˈlɑː·dʒɪ-/ *adj* • *Computers "think" in a much more logical way than human beings.* • *Spelling is much less important than the ability to construct a logical* **argument**. • *He reached this logical* **conclusion** *on the basis of the postmarks on the letters he had received* (=his decision was based on thinking about this information). • *It was the logical thing to do* (=the decision was a reasonable one when all the facts were considered). • (GR)

log·i·cally /£ˈlɒdʒ·ɪ·kli, $ˈlɑː·dʒɪ-/ *adv* • *The jury are supposed to weigh the evidence in a case logically and objectively.* • *His hypothesis, while unlikely, is neither logically nor physically impossible.* • *There must, logically, be an end to it* (=it is reasonable to think that there is), *but we haven't reached it yet.*

logic FORMAL THINKING /£ˈlɒdʒ·ɪk, $ˈlɑː·dʒɪk/ *n* [U] a formal scientific method of examining or thinking about ideas • *a treatise on formal logic* • *He always thinks in terms of cold, hard logic – he seems to have no human emotions at all.*

log·i·cian /£lɒdʒˈɪʃ·ᵊn, $loʊˈdʒɪ-/ *n* [C] • A logician studies or is skilled in logic.

log·is·tics /ləˈdʒɪs·tɪks/ *pl n* the careful organization of a complicated military or business activity so that it happens in a successful and effective way • *The resulting improvements in airline operating logistics might even bring airfares down.* • *(fig.) Carole was worrying about the logistics of transporting her huge collection of books.*

log·is·tic /ləˈdʒɪs·tɪk/, **log·is·ti·cal** /ləˈdʒɪs·tɪ·kᵊl/ *adj* • *logistic support/problems* • *The attack is being postponed for logistical reasons.*

log·is·ti·cally /ləˈdʒɪs·tɪ·kli/ *adv*

lo·go /£ˈləʊ·gəʊ, $ˈloʊ·goʊ/ *n* [C] *pl* **logos** a picture, pattern or way of writing its name that an organization uses as its symbol and puts on its products • *The idea of allowing players to wear the sponsor's logo may win approval.* • *Their distinctive logo is a caricature of the town's statue of Queen Victoria.*

lo·gy /£ˈləʊ·gi, $loʊ-/ *adj* [after v] **-ier, -iest** *Am infml* tired or lacking energy • *Everyone in the office seems a bit logy this afternoon.*

loin·cloth /£ˈlɔɪn·klɒθ, $-klɑːθ/ *n* [C] a piece of cloth worn by men that hangs down from around the waist, used esp. by poor people in hot countries

loins /lɔɪnz/ *pl n literary or dated* the part of the body which is above the legs and below the waist, esp. the sexual organs • *The patient lay naked with just a towel across his loins.* • *It is never pleasant to hear* **the fruit of** *your loins* (=your child/children) *described as hooligans.*

loin /lɔɪn/ *n* • Loin is (a piece of) meat from the back of an animal near the tail or from the top part of the back legs: *(a) loin of lamb* [C/U] • *loin steaks/chops* • See also SIRLOIN.

loit·er /£ˈlɔɪ·tər, $-t̬ɚ/ *v* [I] to move slowly, stand or wait, esp. in a public place without an obvious reason • *We loitered on the shore, reluctant to leave.* • *(disapproving) He loitered* **about** *the station, looking in the bookshop and watching the departure board.* • *(disapproving) It was a place where teenagers used to loiter* **about** *and cause trouble.*

loit·er·er /£ˈlɔɪ·tᵊr·ər, $-t̬ɚ·ɚ/ *n* [C]

loiter·ing /£ˈlɔɪ·tᵊr·ɪŋ, $-t̬ɚ-/ *n* [U] • *(law)* Loitering **with intent** is waiting in a place ready to do something illegal. • *(Am) The sign behind the bar read 'No Loitering'.*

Lo·li·ta /£lɒlˈiː·tə, £ləˈliː-, $loʊˈliː·t̬ə/ *n* [C] *literary* a name used esp. by men to describe a very young woman or girl who appears to have a strong sexual element to her character despite being very young • *He described her as a Lolita/Lolita figure.* • *His film contains a disturbing and highly unlikely scene in which dozens of young Lolitas throw themselves at the leading male character.*

loll /£lɒl, $lɑːl/ *v* [I always + adv/prep] to lie, sit or hang down in a relaxed informal or uncontrolled way • *The young lieutenant was lolling* **about/around** *with several dozen others in the armchairs of the hotel lobby.* • *The patient lay with her mouth open, the tongue lolling* **out**.

lol·li·pop /£ˈlɒl·i·pɒp, $ˈlɑː·li·pɑːp/ *n* [C] a hard sweet on a stick • *(Br and Aus)* A **lollipop man/lady** is a person who helps children to cross the road near a school by standing in the middle of the road and holding up a stick with a sign on it which means that the traffic must stop.

lol·lop /£ˈlɒl·əp, $ˈlɑː·ləp/ *v* [I always + adv/prep] *infml* (of a person or esp. a large animal) to move in an awkward, rolling way • *The old dog lolloped along behind its master.*

lol·ly SWEET /£ˈlɒl·i, $ˈlɑː·li/ *n* [C] *Br and Aus* an **ice lolly** (=sweet flavoured ice on a stick) or a LOLLIPOP • *(Aus)* A lolly is a wrapped sweet for sucking or chewing: *The children bought a bag of lollies.*

lol·ly MONEY /£ˈlɒl·i, $ˈlɑː·li/ *n* [U] *Br slang dated* money • *The footballers wanted to be paid for press interviews and chose Saturday's match to demand their lolly.*

lone /£ləʊn, $loʊn/ *adj* [before n; not gradable] without other similar ones; being the only one in a place or situation • *The body was discovered in the forest by a lone hunter.* • *Entering the competition as the lone outsider among established players does not worry him in the least.* • *He was a lone* **voice** (=the only person) *arguing against a reduction in resources.* • A **lone parent/mother/father** is one who has children but no partner living with them. • A **lone wolf** is a **loner.** • (LP) **One**

lon·er /£ˈləʊ·nər, $ˈloʊ·nɚ/ *n* [C] *usually disapproving* • A loner is a person who likes to do things on their own without other people: *Since he's been ill, he's become a bit of a loner.*

lone·ly /£ˈləʊn·li, $ˈloʊn-/ *adj* **-ier, -iest** (of people or their situation) unhappy because you are alone, or (of places) where there are not many people, buildings etc. • *Unable to leave their own homes, the women are lonely and isolated.* • *The results were a fitting reward for many lonely hours of study.* • *Many people forget how lonely the task of a judge is.* • *She* **felt** *lonely and miserable after they all left.* • *The streets are lonelier at night.* • *He lives in an isolated cottage in the lonely valley of Miterdale.* • A **lonely hearts club/column/advertisement** is for people who would like to make new friends or meet a sexual partner: *Her dad answered a lonely hearts ad and met a supermarket supervisor.* • *"Only the lonely, know why I cry"* (from the song *Only The Lonely* by Roy Orbinson, 1960) • Compare ALONE.

lone·li·ness /£ˈləʊn·li·nəs, $ˈloʊn-/ *n* [U] • *They met others looking after elderly or disabled relatives, who shared the same kind of loneliness and isolation.* • *"The Loneliness of the Long Distance Runner"* (title of a book by Alan Sillitoe, 1959)

lone·some /£ˈləʊn·səm, $ˈloʊn-/ *adj Am for* LONELY • *Foreign students are often lonesome at Christmas, when everyone else goes home.* • *That lonesome highway looked even more desolate when our car broke down.* • *At night I'd lie in bed listening to the lonesome whistle of the distant freight train.* • *"Are you Lonesome Tonight?"* (title of a song written by Roy Turk and Lou Handman, 1961)

lone·some /£ˈləʊn·səm, $ˈloʊn-/ *n* [U] *esp. Am* • If you are **by/on your lonesome** you are alone: *I was just sitting here all by my lonesome.*

long DISTANCE /£lɒŋ, $lɑːŋ/ *adj* **-er, -est** being a distance between two points which is more than average or usual • *The fashion was for long hair – both men and women wore their hair long.* • *Giraffes have long necks and long legs.* • *There was a long queue at the post office.* • *We're still a long way from the station.* • *It's a long book/report/letter/film* (=it has a lot of pages or information and takes a large amount of time to read/watch, but it can be any shape). • *"How long are these rods?" "They're twenty centimetres long."* • A four-sided thing which is described as long has a larger distance between one pair of its sides than between the other two sides: *I need a long envelope for this document.* • Long is used with adjectives ending in -'ed' formed from nouns: *a long-haired dog* (= a dog with long hair) ○ *a long-legged insect* (= an insect with long legs) ○ *a long-sleeved shirt* (= a shirt with long sleeves) • *There was a list of complaints* **as long as** *your* **arm** (= very long). • *You can't escape the* **long arm of the law** (= The police will catch you if you have done something illegal). • *He has got* **a long way to go** (= a lot of work to do or improvements to make) *before he can present the scheme to the public.* • *Information technology* **has come a long way** (= developed or improved a lot) *in the last twenty years.* • *The money the charity has received will* **go a long way towards** (= be very helpful) *providing essential food and medicine.* • *She is very intelligent and works hard, she'll* **go a long way** (= be successful). See also **go far** at FAR [DISTANCE]. • *We* **go back a long way** (= have known each other for a long time) – *we were at school together.* • *(infml) His second film wasn't as good as his first,* **not by a long chalk/shot** (= not at all). • **Long-distance** means travelling a long way or separated by a long distance: *a long-distance runner* ○ *long-distance lorry drivers* ○ *long-distance buses* ○ *a long-distance phone call* ○ *long-distance negotiations* • In mathematics, **long division** is a method of dividing esp. one large number by another, which makes it necessary to write down each stage of the work. • *I never get the chance to wear a* **long dress** (= a dress with a long skirt, worn in the evening at special parties, meals and dances) *these days.* • *I'd prefer a* **long drink** (= a large glass of cold liquid containing little or no alcohol). Compare a SHORT [DRINK]. • *He* **put on/pulled/made** *a* **long face** (= looked unhappy/disappointed) *when he heard there were no tickets left.* • **Long johns** are like long or short tight trousers which are worn under your outer clothes to keep you warm. • The **long jump** (*Am* also **broad jump**) is a sports event in which a person runs up to a mark and then jumps as far forward as they can. • *He's got a very* **long memory** (= remembers esp. bad things which happened a long time ago). • **Long-range** means for the future or across a long distance: *long-range forecasting/planning/implications* ○ *long-range missiles/bombers* • A **long shot** is something you try to do but which is unlikely to be successful: *It's a long shot, but you could try phoning him at home.* • A person who is **long-sighted** (*Am* also **far-sighted**) needs to wear glasses for reading or *(fig., esp. Am)* can make wise judgments about the results far in the future of an action taken now. Compare **short-sighted** at SHORT [DISTANCE]. [LP›] **Eye and seeing** • Someone's **long suit** is a special skill or strength they have: *She's great at writing poetry, but putting it to music is not her long suit.* • A **long-winded** speech, letter, article, etc. is too long. • *"Long-distance information, give me Memphis, Tennessee"* (from the song *Memphis Tennessee* by Chuck Berry, 1963) • See also LENGTH. • [LP›] **Measurements** Ⓟ

long·ish /£ˈlɒŋ·ɪʃ, $ˈlɑːŋ-/ *adj* [not gradable] • *She's got longish* (= quite long) *hair.*

long [TIME] /£lɒŋ, $lɑːŋ/ *adj* **-er, -est** being an amount of time which is more than average or usual • *In England in the summer the days are very long and it is light until about eleven at night on the longest day, which is around 21 June.* • *I've been hoping for this result for a long time.* • *It's a long time/while since I left that company.* • *It was a long time/while before I received a reply.* • *It was a fitting reward for long service.* • *There was a long argument and then a longer period of hostile silence.* • *"How long are the sessions?" "Each session is an hour long."* [after n] • *With all these problems it has been the longest day/month/year I can remember* (= it seemed to last for a large amount of time because of the difficulties). • **So long** is another way of saying goodbye: *So long, and do come again!* • **Before (very/too) long** or **Before much longer** means soon: *They'll be home before very long.* • **No longer/Not any longer** means in the past but not now: *We no longer travel as much as we used to.* ○ *We don't shop there any longer.* ○ *The cinema is no longer used.* ○ *She doesn't work here any longer.* • *(infml)* **The long and the short of** *it* (= Without giving details, the general situation) *is that they are willing to start the work in January.* • If you call someone **long in the tooth** you are saying that they are old: *He's a bit long in the tooth to be wearing jeans, don't you think?* • If something is **long-lasting** it stays fresh for a long time or lasts for a large period of time: *long-lasting beauty* ○ *his long-lasting popularity* • **Long-life** products have been made or treated in such a way that they last for a large period of time: *long-life milk* ○ *long-life light bulbs* • *She arrived at the premiere with her* **long-time** *companion* (= her companion for many years) *Peter Graham.* • *(Br and Aus)* The **long vacation** (*infml* **long vac**) is three months in the summer when college and university students do not have classes. • A **long weekend** is Saturday and Sunday with at least one additional day of holiday added, either Friday or Monday: *We took a long weekend in April.* ○ *We spent a long weekend with my parents.* • *(saying)* 'Long time no see' means I haven't seen you for a long period of time. • *"A Long Day's Journey into Night"* (title of a play by Eugene O'Neill, 1940) • [LP›] **Measurements** Ⓟ

long /£lɒŋ, $lɑːŋ/ *adv* **-er, -est** • Long is used to mean '(for) a long time,' esp. in questions and negative sentences: *"Have you been waiting* **(for)** *long?" "No, not* **(for)** *long, only a few minutes."* ○ *She went out into the garden but she didn't stay* **(for)** *long.* ○ *She sold it long* **before** *you were born.* ○ *Not long* **after** *the wedding he was sent to work abroad.* ○ *Get on with that letter now – it won't take long.* ○ *(fml) The authorities have long known that there were difficulties with this approach.* • *"How long have you been in England?" "I've been here* **(for)** *three weeks."* • *"How long are you in England (for)?* (= How long will your stay in England last?)*" "I'll be/I'm staying here for six months."* • *Don't rush – take as long as you like.* • *It all happened so long ago that I've forgotten what started it.* • *We've been walking all day long – I'm exhausted!* • *I've known her longer than you have.* • *I don't want to stay* **any** *longer – I want to go now.* • *Which product lasts longest?* • Long is used with the *-ed* and *-ing* forms of the verb to mean that the activity has been happening or happens for a long time: *a long-awaited letter* ○ *a* **long-drawn-out** (= too long) *reply* ○ *long-held opinions* ○ *long-serving employees* • **Long live** is shouted by a group of people or said or written by one person to show support for the person, country, activity or thing mentioned: *Long live the President!* ○ *Long live word processors! What would we do without them?* • *(dated or humorous)* If someone is **not long for this world** they are going to die soon. • A **long-lost** person (esp. a relative) or object is one that you haven't seen for a long time: *my long-lost cousin* ○ *the long-lost treasure* • Something **long-running** continues to happen for a long time: *a long-running musical* ○ *their long-running disagreement* • A **long-standing** activity or relationship has existed for a long time: *a long-standing friendship* ○ *a long-standing agreement* • A **long-suffering** person is patient despite being annoyed or insulted regularly over a period of time.

long·ish /£ˈlɒŋ·ɪʃ, $ˈlɑːŋ-/ *adj* [not gradable] • *It took a longish* (= quite long) *time to get the reply.*

long [WANT] /£lɒŋ, $lɑːŋ/ *v* [I] to want something very much • *They were longing* **for** *a drink.* • *They longed* **for** *the freedom to emigrate.* • *I'm longing* **to** *stop commuting every day.* [+ *to* infinitive] • Ⓟ

long·ing /£ˈlɒŋ·ɪŋ, $ˈlɑːŋ-/ *n* [C] • *I had forgotten how powerful this longing* (= strong desire) **for** *chocolate could be.* • *The story shows what happens when human longings confront an unforgiving system of laws and customs.*

long·ing·ly /£ˈlɒŋ·ɪŋ·li, $ˈlɑːŋ-/ *adv* • *He looked longingly at the cakes in the shop window.*

long [IF] /£lɒŋ, $lɑːŋ/ *adv* **as/so long as** if • *I can come as long as I can leave at 4.30 p.m.* • *We'll send it so long as you phone when it arrives.* • [LP›] **Conditionals** Ⓟ

long [MAP] /£lɒŋ, $lɑːŋ/ *n* [U] *abbreviation for* LONGITUDE • Ⓟ

lon·ge·vi·ty /£lɒnˈdʒev·ə·ti, £ˌlɒŋˈev-, $lɑːnˈdʒev·ə·t̬i/ *n* [U] living for a long time • *He* **attributed** *his longevity* **to** *two factors – taking exercise and not smoking.*

long·hand /£ˈlɒŋ·hænd, $ˈlɑːŋ-/ *n* [U] ordinary writing by hand (not using a shortened form or special symbols and not produced by machine) • *She wrote it all out* **in** *longhand before typing it.* • [PIC›] **Writing**

lon·gi·tude /£ˈlɒn·dʒɪ·tjuːd, £ˈlɒŋ·gɪ-, $ˈlɑːn·dʒə·tuːd/ (*abbreviation* **long**) *n* the position to the east or west of an imaginary line on the Earth's surface • *Local time is dependent on longitude, so how should you set your watch at the poles?* [U] • *Iceland is at a longitude west of the Greenwich meridian.* [C] • **Lines of** longitude are imaginary lines running north and south around the Earth. Degrees, minutes and seconds of longitude measure how far east or west you are: *Our current position is longitude 20 degrees east, latitude 30 degrees north.* [U] • Compare LATITUDE [POSITION].

lon·gi·tud·in·al /£ˌlɒn·dʒɪ'tjuː·dɪ·nᵊl, £ˌlɒŋ·gɪ'-, £ˌlɒŋ·ɪ-, $ˌlɑːn·dʒə'tuː-/ *adj* [not gradable]

long·shore·man /£'lɒŋ·ʃɔː·mən, $'lɑːŋ·ʃɔːr-/ *n* [C] *pl* **-men** *Am for* a **docker**, see at DOCK [ENCLOSED AREA]

lon·gueurs /£lɔ̃ːŋ'gɜːʳz, $-'gɜːrz/ *pl n literary* a boring period of time or part of something • *In the longueurs of the week-long official inquiry there were a few lighter moments.* • *The film does have its longueurs when nothing much is happening.*

long·ways /£'lɒŋ·weɪz, $'lɑːŋ-/, *Am also and Aus* **long·wise** /£'lɒŋ·waɪz, $'lɑːŋ-/ *adv* [not gradable] along the length • *Fold the paper longways.* • *The box will fit on the shelf if you put it longways.* • See also LENGTHWAYS.

loo /luː/ *n* [C] *pl* **loos** *Br and Aus infml* a toilet • *the downstairs loo* • *the ladies' loos* • *loo roll/cleaner* • [LP] **Phrases and customs**

loo·fah /'luː·fə/ *n* [C] a long rough object, part of a plant, which is used to rub the body when washing

look [SEE] /lʊk/ *v* [I] to direct your eyes in order to see • *Look! Here comes grandma.* • *They looked* **at** *the children playing to see if they recognized anyone.* • *Look* **at** *all this rubbish on the floor.* • *If you look out (of) the window you'll see her car.* • *Look over there – there's a rainbow!* • In a shop, you tell a SALESPERSON you are 'just looking' when they ask if they can help you but you do not plan to buy any particular item. • *They looked back down the road hoping to see a car.* • If you **look back** you remember what has happened in the past: *It's no good looking back – it's too late to change it now.* ○ *The broadcast looked back* **over** *her childhood in the Far East.* • If someone **never looked back** after doing something, they have continued to be successful: *She never looked back after that first exhibition.* • *He looked down on the town from the top of the tower.* • If you **look down on** or **look down** your **nose at** someone or something you act as if you think the person is not as important as you are or the thing is not good enough: *Graduates may look down on these people, but who is getting the jobs?* ○ *She's always looked down her nose at second-hand clothes.* See also **turn** your **nose up** at TURN UP [FOLD]. • *She looked* **up** *from her book and smiled at me.* • If you **look up to** someone you admire and respect them: *He'd always looked up to his uncle.* See also LOOK UP; **look** someone/something **up** at LOOK [SEARCH]. • If you **look daggers at** someone you look angrily at them. • If you **look in** you go in or visit for a short time: *I can't come to the whole party, but I may look in for a few minutes if I have time.* ○ *Carol likes to look in* **on** *Tyler at night to make sure she hasn't thrown her covers off.* ○ *She looked in* **on** *us on her way back to London.* ○ *I just looked in* **at** *the office to leave some documents.* • *Since I backed into her car I can't* **look** *her* **in the eye/face** (=I am ashamed to speak to her). • If you **look kindly on** something you like it and have a good opinion of it: *The critics looked kindly on her first novel.* • *A large crowd* **looked on** (=watched) *as the band played.* See also ONLOOKER. • When you **look on the bright side** you find good things in a bad situation: *Despite all his difficulties he always looks on the bright side* **of things**. ○ *Look on the bright side – no one was badly hurt.* • If you **look (straight) through** someone you look at them as if you cannot see them, either intentionally or because you are thinking about something else: *I said hello but she looked straight through me.* See also **look through** at LOOK [EXAMINE]. • If something is **not much to look at** it doesn't appear to be very good: *The house isn't much to look at but it's spacious and attractive inside.* • *(old use)* A **looking glass** is a mirror. • *(saying)* 'Never look a gift-horse in the mouth' means you should take anything that is offered to you for free, even if it is not exactly what you wanted. • *"I shall not look upon his like again"* (Shakespeare, Hamlet 1.2) • *"Always Look on the Bright Side of Life"* (song from the film *Monty Python's Life of Brian*, 1979) • *"Here's looking at you, kid"* (said by Humphrey Bogart in the film *Casablanca*, 1942) • See also LOOK OUT; **look out** at LOOK [SEARCH]. • [LP] **Eye and seeing**

look /lʊk/ *n* [C] • *His inspection was no more than a quick look into the room from the doorway.* • *The man gave an angry look in the direction of the police car.* • *Surprised looks passed between the couple.* • *She gave him a look* **of** *real dislike.* • **Take** *a* **good** *look* **at** *this picture and see if you recognize anyone.* • *(infml) "Have they arrived yet?" "I'll have a* **look-see** (=a look)." • *(saying)* 'If looks could kill...' is something you say when you see someone look very angrily at someone else.

-look·ing /'lʊk·ɪŋ/ *combining form* • *(fig.) She's a very inward-looking sort of person, always worrying about herself.* • *(fig.) Energy suppliers who are forward-looking* (=thinking about the future) *are experimenting with new ways of saving energy.*

look [SEARCH] /lʊk/ *v* [I] to try to find something • *Keep looking – it must be somewhere!* • *Look over there – I'm sure I left the book on that shelf.* • *I don't know much about it – you could try looking in the encyclopedia.* • *He looked down the list but couldn't find his name.* • *We're looking* **(around/round) for** *a new house.* • *I've been looking* **for** *that address all week.* • *I'll look* **(out) for** *a present for Jenny while I'm in town.* • If someone is **looking for trouble** they are acting in a way that will cause them trouble: *Parking outside the police station on double yellow lines is looking for trouble.* • *I'll* **look into** (=try to find out about) *the reasons for the decision.* • *(Br) I'll* **look out** (=find) *the recipe and send it to you.* ○ *I'll look it out.* See also LOOK OUT. • *(Br) She* **looked out** (=found) *some old clothes for the children to dress up in.* ○ *She looked them out.* • *If you don't know what the word means,* **look it up** (=look for it) *in a dictionary.* • **Look** *me* **up** (=come and see me) *when you're in Los Angeles.* • See also LOOK UP; **look up to** at LOOK [SEE].

look /lʊk/ *n* [U] • *I had another look* **for** *the watch but I still can't find it.*

look [SEEM] /lʊk/ *v* to show in appearance; to seem or appear to be from facts or information • *You look well/ill/happy/sad/tired/bored.* [L] • *The roads look very icy.* [L] • *These new designs really look good.* [L] • *The prospects of a successful outcome look good.* [L] • *That dress looks nice on you.* [L] • *You look nice in that dress.* [L] • *The future looks* **bleak**. [L] • *He has started to look his age* (=appear as old as he really is). [L] • **It** *looks very unlikely that we will be finished by January.* [L] • **It**'*s looking good* (=Things are going well). [L] • *He looked* **(like/to be)** *a friendly sort of person.* [L (+ *to be*); I always + adv/prep] • *The field looked* **(like)** *a possible site for the competition.* [L; I always + adv/prep] • *The twins look just* **like** (=are similar in appearance to) *their mother.* [I always + adv/prep] • *The container looks* **like** (=is similar to) *a small boat.* [I always + adv/prep] • *She looked* **as if/though** *she hadn't slept all night.* [I always + adv/prep] • **It** *looks* **like** *September for the wedding* (=We will probably have to have the wedding in September). [I always + adv/prep] • **It** *looks* **like** *rain.* [I always + adv/prep] • **It** *looks* **as if/though** *it might rain.* [I always + adv/prep] • *From the results,* **it** *looks* **as if/though** *we made the right choice.* [I always + adv/prep] • *(Br infml)* **Look alive/lively/sharp** means 'act quickly': *If you want me to give you a lift you'll have to look sharp – I'm going in ten minutes.* ○ *Look lively – we haven't got all day!* • If you make someone **look small**, you show they are wrong in a way that makes them appear foolish: *He denied the rumour, but the papers published the evidence and really made him look small.* • A **look-alike** is someone or something that is similar in appearance to someone or something else: *an Elvis Presley look-alike.* • [LP] **It**

look /lʊk/ *n* [C] • *They came in with flushed excited looks on their faces.* • *He had the look* **of** *an accountant or bank employee.* • *She loved the look* **and the feel of** *silk.* • *They liked the look of the hotel but it was too expensive.* • *I don't like the look of that fence* (=it appears to have something wrong with it). • **By the look(s) of things/it** (=Judging by the information we have now) *we won't be able to take our holiday till the autumn.*

look·er /£'lʊk·əʳ, $'lʊk·ɚ/ *n* [C] *infml* • A **good/nice looker** is an attractive person, esp. a woman.

looks /lʊks/ *pl n* • Looks are the appearance of someone or something, esp. when it is attractive: *Her looks improved as she grew older.* ○ *He put on weight and started to* **lose** *his looks.* ○ *Her fame and* **(good)** *looks did not lead to a Hollywood career.*

-look·ing /'lʊk·ɪŋ/ *combining form* • *good-looking* (=having an attractive appearance) • *odd-looking* • *healthy-looking* • *smart-looking*

look [EXAMINE] /lʊk/ *v* [I always + adv/prep] to examine or study, often quickly or informally • *Would you quickly look* **at/over/through** *these figures for me and see if there are any obvious mistakes?* See also **look (straight) through** at LOOK [SEE]. • *He looked* **over** *the proposals but didn't go through them in detail.* • *(fml) We need to look* **to** *our motives for wanting to do this.* • If you **look to** your **laurels** you have to look for ways of improving your position because you are competing with someone else: *The new girl is very good – you'll have to look to your laurels!* • 'Look' is often used when you are telling someone to be careful: *Look* **where** *you're going!* [+ *wh-* word] ○ *Look* **what** *you're doing.* [+ *wh-* word] ○ *Look* **how** *easy it is to confuse the two patterns.* [+ *wh*-word]

look /lʊk/ *n* [U] • **Take a** *look* **at** (= examine) *this – do you like it?* • **Have a** *close look* **at** *the figure in the background.* • *The article is a comic look* **at** (= considers in an amusing way) *young people's relationships with their families.* • *You need to* **take a long, hard look at** (= consider whether you are doing the correct thing with) *your finances.*

look [DIRECTION] /lʊk/ *v* [I always + adv/prep] to face a particular direction • *The garden looks north/south/east/west.* • *The viewpoint looks* **out over** *the countryside.* • *The windows look* **onto** *the lake.*

look [HOPE] /lʊk/ *v* [I always + adv/prep] to hope for, want or actively plan a course of action, or to hope someone will act in the way mentioned • If you look **ahead** you think and decide about the future: *We are trying to look ahead and see what our options are.* • *We want to look* **towards** *an early settlement of the dispute.* • *They're looking* **to** *have a meeting within a month.* [+ *to* infinitive] • *We're looking* **to** *Jim* **for** *guidance on this matter.* • *The school is looking* **to** *its new head* **to** *improve its image.*

look [EXPRESSION] /lʊk/ *exclamation* used to express anger or annoyance • *Look, I've already told you it's not possible.* • *Look* **here**, *that's not the way to do it.*

look af·ter *obj v prep* [T] to care for or be in charge of (someone or something) • *She wanted an evening job that would allow her to look after her son during the day.* • *The woman was helping her friend look after the shop.* • *The transport department looks after roads and railways.* • *Nice to see you, look after yourself, bye!* • *Don't worry about her – she can look after herself* (= she is independent and can make her own decisions). • *He's well known for looking after himself/***number one** (= he is selfish and only does what is good for himself). • *The organization certainly looks after* **its own** (= makes certain its own members are treated well, even if it doesn't treat other people so well).

look for·ward to *obj v adv prep* [T] to feel pleasure that (something) is going to happen • *I'm looking forward to my holiday.* • *She was looking forward to seeing the grandchildren again.* [+ v-*ing*] • *(fml, esp. in a business letter) I look forward to hearing from you* (= I expect an answer soon). [+ v-*ing*]

look on/u·pon *obj v prep* [T] to consider or think of (someone or something) as something else; to REGARD (someone or something) • *We looked on her* **as** *a daughter.* • *I've lived there so long I look on the town* **as** *my home.* • See also **look on** at LOOK [SEE].

look out *v adv* [I] to watch what is happening and be careful • *Look out, a car's coming!* • *The police warned shopkeepers to look out* **for** *forged notes.* • *She knows how to* **look out for number one** (= is selfish and only does what is good for herself). • See also **look out** at LOOK [SEARCH].

look·out /ˈlʊk·aʊt/ *n* [C] • *I had to* **keep a** *lookout* **for** *the house so that we did not drive past it.* • *Shoppers are always* **on the** *lookout* **for** (= watching to find) *something new.* • *(esp. Br infml) It's a* **bad/poor** *lookout* (= The future is not good) **for** *workers in these industries.* • A lookout is someone who watches esp. for danger: *The lookout was standing on the corner watching for police while the other man burgled the house.* • A lookout is also a place to look out from: *There's a lookout with a seat at the top of the cliff.* • *(Br infml)* **It's your own lookout** (= It's your own fault/problem) *if you aren't properly insured.*

look up *v adv* [I] to improve • *I hope things will start to look up in the New Year.* • See also **look** someone/something **up** at LOOK [SEARCH]; **look up to** at LOOK [SEE].

look–in /ˈlʊk·ɪn/ *n* [U] *Br and Aus infml* a chance to do something or to succeed • *There were so many children wanting a ride John didn't* **get** *a look-in.* • *The other team was very good – we didn't* **get** *a look-in.*

loom [APPEAR] /luːm/ *v* [I] to appear, esp. seeming very large and without being clearly seen or in a threatening way, or *(fig.)* (of something unpleasant) to be thought to be about to happen • *Suddenly, out of the blackness loomed a uniformed figure waving his rifle.* • *An expression of horror crossed their faces as I loomed into view.* • *We set off for the moors, which now loomed enticingly before us.* • *Here, too, the threat of unemployment has been looming* **on the horizon.** • If something **looms large** it becomes important and often causes worry: *The issue of pay will loom large at this Easter's teacher conferences.* ○ *How to pay the month's bills began to loom very large in their mind.*

loom [DEVICE] /luːm/ *n* [C] a piece of equipment on which thread is woven into cloth • [PIC] **Handicraft**

loon·y /ˈluː·ni/ *adj* **-ier**, **-iest** *infml* foolish or stupid • *He had lots of loony ideas about education.* • *(taboo slang humorous)* The **loony bin** is a hospital for people who are mentally ill. If you say someone should be in a/the loony bin you think they are stupid and have lost their good judgment.

loop /luːp/ *n* [C] the curved shape made when something long and thin, such as a piece of string or rope, bends until one part of it nearly touches or crosses another part of it • *a skirt with belt loops* • *a loop* **of** *string* • *the loop* **of** *the river* • *The tape is said to run in a continuous loop, a method of speeding up access time to data.* • *His writing was childish with large loops on the letters.* • In an electrical or other CIRCUIT (= a closed system) a loop is part of the system which leaves and comes back to the main structure: *These terminals are on a loop.* ○ *We could put in an extra loop for the upstairs rooms.* • A loop is also a type of IUD (= device for preventing pregnancy).

loop *(obj)* /luːp/ *v* • *Loop* (= make a loop with) *the rope over the bar.* [T] • *Turn left where the road loops* (= curves) *round the farm buildings.* [I always + adv/prep] • *We watched the little plane* **loop the loop** (= make the shape of a loop in the sky).

loop·y /ˈluː·pi/ *adj* **-ier**, **-iest** • *(infml)* Loopy means acting in a slightly strange or unusual way.

loop·hole /£ˈluːp·həʊl, $-hoʊl/ *n* [C] a chance to avoid doing something or to do something, esp. because of a mistake in the way rules or laws have been written • *Many of them were lawyers employed by those companies to* **find** *loopholes* **in** *environmental protection laws.* • *The police are anxious to* **close** *any loopholes to prevent copycat crimes.*

loop·y /ˈluː·pi/ *adj* **-ier**, **-iest** *infml* foolish, stupid • *He must have gone completely loopy to give up a good job like that.* • *I think I'm going a bit loopy, I'm sure I had my keys when we left the house.*

loose [NOT FIXED] /luːs/ *adj* **-r**, **-st** not firmly fixed in place • *There were some loose wires hanging out of the wall.* • *I'd better sew that loose button back on before it comes off.* • *The nails in the bridge had* **worked** *themselves* **loose.** • *The prisoners were so thin that their skin* **hung** *loose.* • Hair that is loose is not tied back: *Her hair was* **hanging** *loose about her shoulders.* • Loose items are those which are not fixed or held together or to anything else: *A few loose sheets of paper were lying around.* • If a dangerous person is loose in a place or **on the loose**, they are free to move around a place and harm people: *Police fear a serial killer might be loose in London.* ○ *Brewer escaped from prison last year and has been on the loose ever since.* • If you **let/set** an animal loose, you allow it to run around freely after it has been tied up: *She let her horse loose in the field.* • If you **let loose** something such as bullets or bombs, you release a lot of them all together: *The allies let loose an intensive artillery bombardment over the border.* ○ *(fig.) He let loose a shriek of delight* (= made it without trying to control it). • If you **let** a person loose **on** a place, you allow them to do what they want although you think they are likely to do something foolish: *A bunch of idiots was let loose on a nuclear power station.* • If you are **at a loose end**, you are bored because you have nothing to do. • *(Am infml)* If you **hang/stay loose**, you are calm and relaxed. • **Loose change** means the coins that you have in your pocket or PURSE: *Please donate your loose change to this worthwhile cause.* • **Loose covers** on a chair or SOFA are covers that you can remove for cleaning. • **Loose ends** are things that still need to be done or explained: *At the end of the film all the loose ends are neatly* **tied up.** • A **loose-leaf** book is one where the pages can easily be taken out and put back again.

loose·ly /ˈluː·sli/ *adv* • *His broken arm hung loosely from his shoulder.* • *The parcel had only been loosely wrapped, and the wrapping paper had come off.* • *The musical society I belong to is only loosely* **organized** (= is not controlled very closely, but contains people who share similar interests).

loos·en *(obj)* /ˈluː·sᵊn/ *v* • *Over the years, the screws holding the bed together had loosened* (= become less fixed). [I] • If you loosen your **grip on** something, or your **grip** loosens, you hold something less tightly: *Loosen your grip on the steering wheel, you're holding it too tightly.* [T] ○ *He held my hand very tightly at first but gradually his grip loosened.* [I] ○ *(fig.) The dictator's grip on the country has not loosened* (= he is still strongly in control). [I] • Something which loosens your **tongue** makes you speak more freely: *A couple of glasses of champagne had loosened my tongue* *and I said things that perhaps I shouldn't have.* [T] • If you loosen **up** (your muscles), you do stretching exercises to prepare your body for physical activity: *You might get a muscle injury if you don't loosen up properly before running.* [I] ○ *She did a few stretches to loosen up her muscles.* [M] • To loosen (someone) **up** is also to (cause them to) become more relaxed and less worried: *He seemed quite nervous at the beginning of the meeting, but he soon loosened up.* [I] ○ *A gin and tonic will loosen you up.* [M]

loose·ness /ˈluː·snəs/ *n* [U]

loose NOT TIGHT /luːs/ *adj* **-r, -st** (of clothes) not fitting closely to the body • *Wear comfortable, loose clothing to your exercise class.* • Loose can also mean not tightly controlled or not exact: *The film is a loose adaptation of Conrad's famous novel.* • *Just give me a loose translation of what the article is about.* • A **loose-fitting** item of clothing is one that is quite large and does not fit tightly.

loose·ly /ˈluː·sli/ *adv* • *The jacket hung loosely on his thin body.* • *Their hands were clasped loosely* (= not very tightly held together). • *This phrase can be loosely* (= not very accurately) *translated as 'Go away'.*

loos·en *obj* /ˈluː·sᵊn/ *v* [T] • *It was hot in the room and the men began to loosen their ties* (= make them fit less tightly).

loose·ness /ˈluː·snəs/ *n* [U]

loose IMMORAL /luːs/ *adj* **-r, -st** *dated disapproving, or humorous* lacking in morals; sexually free • *He had always thought of her as being a loose* **woman**. • *All those years of loose* **living** *are beginning to show an effect on him.*

loose *obj* EXPRESS FREELY /luːs/ *v* [T] *literary* to allow (a set of ideas or an emotion) to be freely expressed, esp. in an uncontrolled way • *The minister loosed an angry tirade against the leader of the opposition.*

loot *(obj)* /luːt/ *v* (usually of large numbers of people during a violent event) to steal from (shops and houses) • *During the riot shops were looted and cars damaged or set on fire.* [T] • *Discipline quickly broke down after the city fell, and the invading soldiers were found to be looting and sometimes killing.* [I]

loot·ing /£ˈluː·tɪŋ, $-t̬ɪŋ/ *n* [U] • Looting is the activity of stealing from shops during a violent event: *There were reports of* **widespread** *looting as football hooligans stampeded through the city centre.* ○ *Looting and vandalism caused thousands of dollars' worth of damage to businesses and public property.*

loot /luːt/ *n* [U] • Loot means money and valuable objects that have been stolen, esp. by an army from a defeated enemy: *Napoleon's army took priceless works of art from all over Europe as loot.* ○ *The men who robbed the camera store are trying to dispose of the loot by selling it in the street.* • *(infml humorous)* Loot can also be used to mean a lot of money or presents received: *The children always* **get** *lots of loot at Christmas.*

lop *obj* /£lɒp, $lɑːp/ *v* [T] **-pp-** to cut (esp. branches off a tree) with a single quick cutting action • *I'll need to lop* **off** *the lower branches of the tree.* [M] • *(fig.) The council has lopped thousands of pounds* **off/from** (= reduced by that amount in a single quick action) *its arts budget.*

lope /£ləʊp, $loʊp/ *v* [I] (of a person or animal) to run taking long relaxed steps • *The lion loped across the grass.*

lop·sid·ed /£ˌlɒpˈsaɪd·ɪd, $ˌlɑːp-/ *adj* with one side bigger, higher, etc. than the other; not equally balanced • *He has a charming, lopsided grin.*

lo·qua·cious /£ləʊˈkweɪ·ʃəs, $loʊˈkweɪ-/ *adj fml* talking a lot • *He is a loquacious character.* • *She was very loquacious* **about** *her experiences.*

lo·qua·cious·ly /£ləʊˈkweɪ·ʃə·sli, £lɒkˈweɪ-, $loʊˈkweɪ-/ *adv*

lord TITLE /£lɔːd, $lɔːrd/ *n* [C] the title used in front of the names of male PEERS (= people of high social rank) and officials of very high rank, or a male peer himself • *Lord Longford, second son of the fifth Earl of Longford* • *the Lord Chancellor* • *Lord Justice Bingham* • *They wanted their daughter to marry an English lord.* • In Britain, you address a judge or a PEER as 'my Lord'. • *(infml)* A lord can also be a man who has a lot of power in a particular area: *Several alleged drug lords are to be put on trial.* • *(esp. humorous)* Your lord **and master** is the person who has power over you. • *"The Lord of the Rings"* (title of a series of books by J.R.R.Tolkein, 1954) • Compare LADY TITLE.

Lords /£lɔːdz, $lɔːrdz/ *n* [U + sing/pl v] • **The Lords** is the **House of Lords**. See at HOUSE POLITICS: *The Government was defeated in the Lords when peers on all sides voted against the bill.* ○ *The Lords has/have rejected the Government's proposal.*

lord *obj* /£lɔːd, $lɔːrd/ *v* [T] *infml* • If you **lord it over** someone, you behave as if you are better than them and have the right to tell them what to do: *He likes to lord it over his little sister.*

lord·ly /£ˈlɔːd·li, $ˈlɔːrd-/ *adj* • A lordly person is someone who behaves as if they are better than other people: *Secretaries make executives feel lordly and important.*

lord·ship /£ˈlɔːd·ʃɪp, $ˈlɔːrd-/ *n* [C] *fml* • Lordship is a respectful way of referring to or addressing a male PEER without using his title: **His** *lordship will be out of the country until next week.* ○ *It is a great pleasure to welcome* **your** *lordship this evening.* ○ *I'm honoured to meet you,* **your** *lordship.* [as form of address] • Compare **ladyship** at LADY TITLE.

Lord GOD /£lɔːd, $lɔːrd/ *n* [U] (in the Christian religion) God or Jesus Christ • *the Lord God* • *the Lord Jesus Christ* • *Praise* **the** *Lord!* • *"***The** *Lord be with you." "And also with you."* • *Lord, hear our prayer.* [as form of address] • **Our** *Lord taught us that we should love one another.* • *(infml)* You can say '(Oh) Lord!' or 'Good Lord!' to express surprise, shock or worry: *Oh Lord! I've forgotten the tickets!* ○ *Lord knows how they can afford so many holidays.* • In the Christian religion, the **Lord's Prayer** (also **Our Father**) is the important prayer taught by Jesus Christ to his DISCIPLES (= followers). • The **Lord's Supper** is **Holy Communion**. See at HOLY GOOD.

lore /£lɔːʳ, $lɔːr/ *n* [U] traditional knowledge and stories about a subject • *Common lore often describes poison ivy as growing mainly in the woods.* • *It's been part of the lore* **of** *medicine over the years that lying on your right side will make heartburn worse.* • See also FOLKLORE.

lor·gnette /£lɔːˈnjet, $lɔːr-/ *n* [C] a very old-fashioned pair of glasses with a long handle that you hold in front of your eyes

lor·i·keet /£ˌlɒr·ɪˈkiːt, $ˌlɑː·rɪ-/ *n* [C] a small brightly coloured PARROT (= bird with a curved beak), found in Australia and SE Asia, which feeds esp. on the powder or sweet liquid produced by the flowers of bushes and trees

lor·ry *Br* /£ˈlɒr·i, $ˈlɔːr-/, *Am and Aus* **truck** /trʌk/ *n* [C] a large vehicle used for transporting goods • *The accident involved two cars and a lorry.* • *He works as a* **long-distance** *lorry* **driver**. • *Local residents are concerned about the number of* **heavy** *lorries that drive through their village.* • *The 38-***ton** *lorry was loaded with fish.* • *An* **articulated** *lorry has* **overturned**, *completely blocking the carriageway.* • LP **Driving**

lose *obj* NOT HAVE /luːz/ *v* [T] *past* **lost** /£lɒst, $lɑːst/ to no longer possess (something) because you do not know where it is or because it has been taken away from you • *I must have lost my train ticket on the journey.* • *At least 600 staff will lose their jobs if the firm closes.* LP **Work** • *He lost his leg in a car accident.* • If you lose a quality or ability, you do not have it any more: *The party has lost a lot of support recently.* ○ *She used to like tennis but lately she's lost interest in it.* ○ *When I saw how angry she was I lost courage and couldn't tell her.* • If you lose something such as blood, you have less of it: *He has decided that he needs to lose* **weight**. ○ *The child was losing a lot of* **blood** *so was rushed to hospital.* • If you lose time or an opportunity, you waste it: *They lost no time in telling me I was wrong.* • If a clock loses **time**, it goes more slowly than it should: *My watch loses twenty seconds an hour.* • A business that is losing **money** is spending more money than it is receiving: *Banks will lose millions of pounds because of new legislation.* • To lose **heart** is to give up hope or bravery: *Don't lose heart.* • To **lose** your **heart to** someone is to fall in love with them: *She lost her heart to the boy next door.* • A person who loses their **life** dies suddenly because of an accident or violent event: *Many people lost their lives in the floods.* • If you **have** something **to** lose in a particular situation, you may put yourself in a disadvantageous position because of what you do: *You might as well say yes, what have you got to lose?* ○ *Why don't you take the job? After all, you've got* **nothing** *to lose.* • If you **lose** your **head**, you lose control of yourself and do not stay calm: *Even though they were under threat, they didn't lose their heads.* • *(esp. humorous)* If you say that someone has **lost** their **marbles**, you mean that they are behaving strangely or foolishly or have become mentally ill. • To **lose your mind** is to become mentally ill, or to start behaving in a foolish or strange way: *You just spent all that money on a pair of shoes? Have you completely lost your mind?* • To **lose** your **rag** is to become very angry: *When I told my boss that I hadn't finished the work I was supposed* *to have done today, he really lost his rag* **(over/about it).** • *(infml)* If you **lose** your **shirt**, you lose a lot of money, esp. as a result of a BET: *He said he'd lost his shirt* **on** *that race.* • If you **lose sight of** something, esp. something important, you stop thinking about it: *We must not lose sight of the root of the problem.* • To **lose sleep over/about** something is to worry about it: *I wouldn't lose any sleep over what happened.* • If you **lose track (of** something), you do not know where it is, or you cannot remember it: *I'm not very good at keeping track of what I spend my money on.* ○ *What he was saying was so complicated that I lost track after the first couple of sentences.* ○ *I've lost track of the number of times he's asked me to lend him money* (= I cannot remember how many times he has asked because he has asked me so often). • *"To lose one parent, Mr Worthing, may be regarded as a misfortune; to lose both looks like carelessness."* (Lady Bracknell in the play *The Importance of being Earnest* by Oscar Wilde, 1895) • *"You've lost that loving feeling"* (song title, 1965)

lost /£lɒst, $lɑːst/ *adj* • To **be/get** lost is to not know where you are and how to get to a place: *I got lost in the London Underground.* • *Things tend to get lost* (= you do not know where they are) *mysteriously when you move house.* • *I'd be lost* (= would not know what to do) *without you.* • To be lost is also to give so much attention to what you are doing that you are not aware of anything else that is happening around you: *When Bernard listens to music he becomes completely lost* **to the world**. ○ *She was completely lost* **in** *her book.* ○ *Reading her work I was lost* **in** *admiration for what she had achieved.* • If something that you say is lost **on** another person, it has no effect or they do not understand it: *Financial discussions are lost on me, I'm afraid.* • You say **get lost** to someone when you want to tell them forcefully and quite rudely to go away: *You should have told him to get lost.* ○ *Oh go away, get lost!* • A **lost cause** is something that has no chance of succeeding: *She's always supporting some lost cause or other.* • **Lost property** means things that people have accidentally left in public places: *Have you asked at the (Br and Aus)* **lost property office**/*(Am)* **lost-and-found office** (= a place in a public building where lost things are stored)? • *"Not lost but gone before* (= dead)*"* (title of a poem by Caroline Norton, 1808-1877) • *"A lost generation"* (saying of Gertrude Stein, used to describe the generation who died in the First World War, 1874-1946)

loss /£lɒs, $lɑːs/ *n* • Loss is the fact of not having something any more: Many parents feel a sense of loss when *their children leave home.* [U] ○ *They never got over the loss of their son* (= his death). [U] • A loss is an act of losing something: *There will be substantial job losses if the factory closes down.* [C] ○ *He suffered a gradual loss of memory.* [C] • Loss **of life** is a number of people dying: *The plane crashed with serious loss of life.* [U] • In business, a loss is when you spend more money than you earn: *The company announced a pre-tax loss of three million pounds.* [C] • If you are **at a loss**, you do not know what to do: *I'm at a loss to know how I can help you.* • A **loss adjuster** is a person who works for an **insurance company** and decides how much money should be paid out in each case of something having been damaged or lost. • A **loss leader** is an article that is sold cheaply in order to attract the public and make them buy other, more expensive things. • *(saying)* 'One man's loss is another man's gain'.

lose *(obj)* BE DEFEATED /luːz/ *v past* **lost** /£lɒst, $lɑːst/ to fail to succeed in (a game, competition, etc.) • *If we lose this game, we're out of the championship.* [T] • *Cambridge United are likely to lose* **(to** *Arsenal).* [I] • *Everyone hates losing an argument.* [T] • To lose **out** is to suffer a disadvantage: *The new tax means that the vast majority of pensioners will lose out.* [I] • If you **lose the day**, you lose when you are competing: *In the end it was their weak defence which lost the day* **for** *the team.* • To **lose ground** is to become less popular or to be given less support: *Do you agree that left-wing politics are losing ground* (= becoming less popular) *among the working classes?* • LP **Sports**

los·er /£ˈluː·zəʳ, $-zɚ/ *n* [C] • A loser is a person who is defeated in a competition: *Even the loser of the tennis championship comes away with thousands of pounds.* • A **good** loser is a person who behaves well and does not show their disappointment when they are defeated. A **bad** loser is a person who complains when they are defeated. • *(infml)* A loser is also a person who is always unsuccessful at everything they do: *He's a* **born** *loser.* ○ *In the film she plays a romantic loser.* • The loser in a situation is the person who is at a disadvantage as a result of what has happened: *The latest price rises mean that the real loser, as usual, is the consumer.*

lot LARGE AMOUNT /£lɒt, $lɑːt/ *n* [U] a large amount or number (of something) • *We haven't got* **a** *lot, but we're happy.* • **A lot of** means many or much: *There were a lot of people at the meeting last night.* ○ *A lot of rain fell in Scotland last night.* ○ *They want to have a lot of children.* ○ *He does a lot of travelling in his job.* • **A lot** also means very much or very often: *Your sister looks a lot like you.* ○ *We go on walking holidays a lot.* ○ *I'm feeling a lot better today.* ○ *You can complain if you like, but a* **fat** *lot of good it'll do you* (= it will have no effect)*!* • **A lot** also means many: *Don't eat all those biscuits – there aren't a lot left.* • *(infml)* **The lot** is everything: *The thieves stole paintings, jewellery, the lot.* ○ *Have I got everything, is that the lot?* ○ *I'll sell you the* **whole** *lot for only £50.* • *(humorous saying)* 'There's a lot of it about' means that the stated thing is very common. • LP **Quantity words**

lots /£lɒts, $lɑːts/ *pl n, adv* • *Have a biscuit. There are lots* (= many). • *(infml) I'm feeling lots* (= very much) *better today.* • *They want to have* **lots of** (= many) *children.* • *There were* **lots of** (= many) *people at the meeting last night.*

lot GROUP /£lɒt, $lɑːt/ *n* [C] *Br and Aus* an amount or set of things, esp. when there are several of these amounts • *Another lot of visitors will be here this afternoon.* • *One lot of clothes will be thrown away, the other lot given to charity.* • *(Br infml)* A group of people can also be referred to as a lot: *You're an ignorant lot* (= group). ○ *Are you lot coming to lunch?* ○ *My lot* (= children and family generally) *won't eat tinned peas.*

lot SALE /£lɒt, $lɑːt/ *n* [C] (in an AUCTION) an object or set of objects that are being sold • *Lot number 134 is a fine old walnut bureau.* • See also JOB LOT.

lot LAND /£lɒt, $lɑːt/ *n* [C] *esp. Am and Aus* an area of land • *They're planning to build a house on a* **vacant** *lot on 35th Street.* • A lot is also a film STUDIO (= a building where films are made) and the land around it: *Film fans had gathered at the entrance of the Paramount lot.*

lot LIFE /£lɒt, $lɑːt/ *n* [U] the quality of life and the experiences that you have • *The society is trying to improve the lot* **of** *the lowest-paid workers.* • *I'm happy with my lot.*

lot CHANCE /£lɒt, $lɑːt/ *n* a way of choosing or deciding something by chance • If you **draw/cast** lots, you make a decision by having a set of objects such as pieces of paper or sticks that are all the same except for one. The person who chooses the different one is chosen. [C] • *The teams were chosen* **by** *lot* (= by this method). [U]

loth /£ləʊθ, £ləʊð, $loʊθ/ *adj* [after v; + *to* infinitive] LOATH

lo·tion /£ˈləʊ·ʃᵊn, $ˈloʊ-/ *n* a liquid that you put on your skin or hair in order to protect it, improve its condition or make it smell pleasant • *Don't forget to pack some* **suntan** *lotion.* [U] • *He's always borrowing his father's* **after-shave** *lotion.* [U] • *She has all these different lotions that she puts on her face and body.* [C]

lot·tery /£ˈlɒt·ᵊr·i, $ˈlɑː·t̬ɚ-/ *n* [C] a game, often organized by the state or a CHARITY in order to make money, in which people buy tickets with numbers on them. Several numbers are then chosen by chance and the people who have tickets with those numbers on them win prizes, esp. prizes of money. • *The national lottery will raise money for the arts.* • *(disapproving)* If you describe something as a lottery, you mean that it depends only on luck and it is not very fair: *Education in England is something of a lottery.*

lo·tus /£ˈləʊ·təs, $ˈloʊ·t̬əs/ *n* [C] a type of tropical **water lily** (= a plant with large flat leaves which float on the surface of lakes and pools) • A **lotus eater** is someone who has a very comfortable, lazy life and does not worry about anything. • A **lotus life** is a very comfortable, lazy life without any worries. • The **lotus position** is a way of sitting with your legs crossed and your feet resting on your THIGHS (= part of the leg above the knee), esp. used in YOGA (= a method of relaxation).

loud NOISY /laʊd/ *adj, adv* **-er, -est** consisting of or producing a large amount of sound • *I heard a loud bang and then saw black smoke.* • *There was loud applause when the play ended.* • *Could you speak a little louder, please?* • *That television is rather loud – could you turn it down?* • *This novel made me smile and occasionally laugh* **out** *loud.* • If something is **loud and clear**, it is very clear and easy to understand: *The message came through loud and clear: things would have to change.* • LP **Exclamation mark, Measurements, Sound**

loud·ly /ˈlaʊd·li/ *adv* • *Prisoners have complained loudly* (= in a forceful way) *about their living conditions.*

loud·ness /ˈlaʊd·nəs/ *n* [U] • *The human ear allows us to detect subtle differences in loudness* (= how loud something is) *and in pitch, and to locate the source of a sound.*

loud UNPLEASANT /laʊd/ *adj* **-er, -est** *disapproving* (of clothes) having unpleasantly bright colours or too strong patterns, or (of a person) demanding attention and talking and laughing loudly • *That tie's a bit loud to wear to a business meeting, isn't it?* • *The survey showed that men who wear gold medallions are often perceived as being loud and obnoxious.*

loud·hail·er /£ˌlaʊdˈheɪ·ləʳ, $-lɚ/ *n* [C] *Br and Aus for* MEGAPHONE

loud·mouth /ˈlaʊd·maʊθ/ *n* [C] *infml* a person who talks a lot, esp. in an offensive or stupid way • *He's such a loudmouth and know-all.*

loud·speak·er /£ˌlaʊdˈspiː·kəʳ, $ˈlaʊdˌspiː·kɚ/ *n* [C] a piece of equipment that changes electrical signals into sounds, esp. used in public places so that large numbers of people can hear someone speaking or music playing • *His words were relayed into the crowded square by loudspeaker.* • *Music blared from loudspeakers attached to cars.* • See also SPEAKER.

lough /£lɒk, $lɑːk/ *n* [C] (in Ireland) a lake, or a part of the sea that goes a long way into the land

lounge ROOM /laʊndʒ/ *n* [C] a comfortable room for sitting in, either in a person's house or in a hotel or bar • *All the family were sitting in the lounge watching television.* • *Several of the hotel guests were having a drink in the lounge before dinner.* • A **lounge bar** is a room in a PUB (= a building where alcoholic drinks can be bought and drunk) that is more comfortable than the other rooms in the pub and where the drinks are usually slightly more expensive than in the other rooms. • **Lounge room** is *Aus for* **living room**. See at LIVE HAVE A HOME. • A **lounge suit** is a man's SUIT (= a set of clothes) worn for work or on quite formal occasions during the day.

lounge RELAX /laʊndʒ/ *v* [I] to stand or sit in a very relaxed way • *Families lounged on the grass in the sunshine.* • *I wish you'd stop lounging* **around/about** (= doing nothing)*!*

loung·er /£ˈlaʊn·dʒəʳ, $-dʒɚ/ *n* [C] • A lounger is a comfortable chair on which people can sit or lie in order to relax, esp. outside in hot weather: *a sun lounger* • PIC **Chair**

louse /laʊs/ *n* [C] *pl* **lice** /laɪs/ a very small insect that lives on the bodies of people and animals • *Schoolchildren often become infected with head lice.*

lous·y /ˈlaʊ·zi/ *adj* **-ier, -iest** low in quality or quantity • *I thought that film was lousy.* • *The food at that restaurant is really lousy.* • *I had a lousy weekend.* • *All he offered me was a lousy £20!* • *I feel lousy* (= ill) *– I'm going home.*

louse up *obj*, **louse** *obj* **up** /laʊs/ *v adv* [M] *infml* • If you louse something **up**, you spoil it or cause it to fail: *This is a great opportunity, so don't louse it up.*

lout /laʊt/ *n* [C] *infml* a young man who behaves in a very rude, offensive and sometimes violent way • *Teenage louts roam the streets at night.*

lout·ish /£ˈlaʊ·tɪʃ, $-t̬ɪʃ/ *adj infml* • *I won't put up with such loutish behaviour.*

lout·ish·ness /£ˈlaʊ·tɪʃ·nəs, $-t̬ɪʃ-/ *n* [U] • Loutishness is rude, offensive behaviour.

louv·re *Br and Aus* /£ˈluː·vəʳ, £-vrə, $-vɚ/, *Am usually* **louv·er** *n* [C] a door or window with flat sloping pieces of wood, metal or glass across it to let light and air in while keeping rain out

louv·red /ˈluː·vrəd/ *adj* [not gradable] • *a louvred door/window*

love *obj* LIKE SOMEONE /lʌv/ *v* [T] to have strong feelings of affection for (another adult) and be romantically and sexually attracted to them, or to feel great affection and caring for (family and friends) • *"I love you and want to marry you, Emily," he said.* • *After forty years of marriage, they still love each other just as much as they always did.* • *As a child she had felt very loved and protected.* • Your **loved ones** are members of your family and the people that you care about: *They were overjoyed that their loved ones were out of danger.* • *(saying)* 'Love me, love my dog' means that if you really love someone, you will have to accept everything about them. • *"If you Love Somebody, Set them Free"* (title of a song by Sting, 1985) • *"I Love you Because"* (title of a song by Jim Reeves, 1964) • *"To love, honour and obey"* (from the marriage service in the Book of Common Prayer, 1662) • *"To love oneself is the beginning of a lifelong romance"* (Oscar Wilde in the play *An Ideal Husband,* 1895)

love /lʌv/ *n* [U] • Love means strong feelings of attraction towards and affection for another adult, or great affection for a friend or family member: *Our love will last forever.* ○ *Children need to be shown lots of love.* ○ *"I'm seeing Laura next week." "Oh, please* **give/send** *her my love"* (= Tell her I am thinking about her with affection). ○ *(infml) How's your love* **life** (= your romantic and/or sexual relationships) *these days?* • If you are **in** love (with someone), you feel strongly attracted to them and like them very much: *I'm in love for the first time and it's wonderful.* ○ *They're still madly in love* (**with** *each other).* • Your love is a person that you love and feel attracted to: *You are the love* **of my life** (= the person I feel greatest love for). • *(Br infml)* 'Love' is also used as a friendly form of address. It is not often used by a man talking to another man: *You look tired, love.* [as form of address] ○ *That'll be four pounds exactly, my love.* [as form of address] • *(infml)* You also write 'love/love from/all my love' before your name at the end of letters and on presents to friends and family. LP **Letters, Titles and forms of address** • If someone is love-**struck**, they are so in love with someone that it is difficult for them to behave as usual or even think of anything else except the person they love: *Look at me, I'm behaving like a love-struck teenager!* • If you cannot get something, or if someone will not do something, **for love (n)or money**, it is impossible to obtain it or to persuade them to do it: *You can't get hold of those tickets for love or money these days.* ○ *I'm not getting on that aeroplane for love nor money.* • If two people who have a close loving relationship **make love**, they have sex: *They made love for the first time that night.* • **Love-making** is sexual activity. • *(old use)* To **make love to** someone is to speak romantically and give a lot of attention to them, esp. in order to make them love you: *Mr Jackson, I do believe you are making love to me.* • If there is **no/little love lost between** two people, they do not like each other at all: *Ever since they had that quarrel there's been no love lost between them.* • A **love affair** is a sexual relationship between two people who are not married to each other: *Their secret love affair lasted seven years.* ○ *(fig.) Her love affair* **with** (= strong liking for) *ballet began when she was ten.* • *(dated)* A **love child** is a child whose parents are not married to each other. • *(humorous)* **Love handles** are the layer of fat around the middle of a person's body. • A **love letter** is a letter that you write to someone that you are having a romantic relationship with. • *"Love is a Many-Splendoured thing"* (title of a song written by Sammy Fain and Paul Francis Webster, 1955) • *"Love means never having to say you're sorry"* (Erich Segal in *Love Story*) • *"The love that dare not speak its name* (= homosexual love)*"* (from the poem *Two Loves* by Lord Alfred Douglas, 1896) • LP **Relationships**

lov·a·ble, love·a·ble /ˈlʌv·ə·bl̩/ *adj* • *She's a very lovable person/character.* • *He's a lovable old* **rogue** (= a man who behaves badly, but has such an attractive character that people still like him and forgive him despite his faults).

love·less /ˈlʌv·ləs/ *adj* • *She was trapped in a loveless marriage* (= one in which the husband and wife do not love each other). • *He said that he had had a loveless childhood* (= one in which he was not loved).

lov·er /£ˈlʌv·əʳ, $-ɚ/ *n* [C] • Your lover is a person with whom you are having a sexual relationship, but are not married to: *They were friends before they became lovers.* ○ *He was her* **live-in** *lover* (= they lived together having a sexual relationship) *for three years.* • Lovers can also mean two people who are in love with each other: *They will play the doomed young lovers, Romeo and Juliet.* • LP **Relationships**

lov·ing /ˈlʌv·ɪŋ/ *adj* • *He's a very loving child* (= one who shows his affection for people). • *You just need some loving* **care** (= that showing affection) *and you'll soon feel well again.*

lov·ing·ly /ˈlʌv·ɪŋ·li/ *adv* • *The furniture has been lovingly* (= with great pleasure and care) *restored.*

love *(obj)* LIKE SOMETHING /lʌv/ *v* to like (something) very much • *Most children love films about dinosaurs.* [T] • *I absolutely love chocolate ice cream.* [T] • *I would love a cup of tea if you're making one.* [T] • *He really loves his job.* [T] • *I love* **going** *for long walks.* [+ v-*ing*] • *She would* **dearly** *love* **to** *start her own business.* [+ *to* infinitive] • *I would love you* **to** *come to dinner some night.* [obj + *to* infinitive] • *(Am) I would love* **for** *you* **to** *come to dinner tonight.* [I] • *Love* **it or hate it**, *satellite TV is here to stay.* [T]

love /lʌv/ *n* • *I don't share my boyfriend's love* **of** (= strong liking for) *sport.* [U] • *She has a great love* **of** *music.* [U] • A love is also something that you like very much: *Music is one of her greatest loves.* [C]

lov·er /£ˈlʌv·əʳ, $-ɚ/ *n* [C] • *She's a great opera lover* (= she likes it very much). • *The remote island is a haven for nature lovers.*

love TENNIS /lʌv/ *n* [U] (in tennis) the state of having no points • *The score now stands at forty-love.* • LP› **Zero**

love·birds /£ˈlʌv·bɜːdz, $-bɜːrdz/ *pl n humorous* two people who are obviously very much in love with each other • *Look at those two lovebirds holding hands and gazing into each other's eyes.*

love·lorn /£ˈlʌv·lɔːn, $-lɔːrn/ *adj literary* sad because the person you love does not love you • *In the film she plays a lovelorn princess.*

love·ly /ˈlʌv·li/ *adj* **-ier, -iest** attractive and beautiful, or very pleasant and enjoyable • *What a lovely house!* • *You look absolutely lovely this evening, my darling.* • *Thank you for the lovely present.* • *We had a lovely time at the party.* • *"Oh What a Lovely War"* (title of a play by Joan Littlewood and Charles Clinton, 1963)

love·li·ness /ˈlʌv·lɪ·nəs/ *n* [U] • *She's not beautiful, but has a radiant loveliness.*

love·sick /ˈlʌv·sɪk/ *adj* sad because the person you love does not love you • *He was moping around like a lovesick teenager.*

lov·ing /ˈlʌv·ɪŋ/ *adj* See at LOVE LIKE SOMEONE

low DISTANCE /£ləʊ, $loʊ/ *adj, adv* **-er, -est** not measuring much from the base to the top, or close to the ground or the bottom of something • *There's a low wall around the house.* • *Don't bump your head on the low ceiling.* • *Vehicles above 2·5 metres high must take an alternative route in order to avoid the low bridge.* • *The picture is too low on the wall – can you put it higher up?* • *When we went skiing, I only went on the lower slopes.* • *The planes fly low across enemy territory.* • A dress that is **cut** low, has a low **neckline**, or is **low-cut** does not cover a woman's neck and the top part of her chest: *She was wearing a blouse cut low at the front/a* **low-cut** *blouse.* • **Low-lying** land is at or near the level of the sea: *People living in low-lying areas were evacuated because of the floods.* • A **low-rise** building is one with only one or two floors: *Tokyo is a city with a lot of low-rise buildings.* • **Low tide** or **low water** is the time when the sea has reached its lowest level: *At low tide you can paddle over to the island.* • A **low water mark** is a mark which shows the lowest point on a beach that is reached by the sea.

low·er *obj* /£ˈləʊ·əʳ, $ˈloʊ·ɚ/ *v* [T] • *The flag is lowered* (= moved into a position closer to the ground) *at the end of every day.* • *Heavily pregnant by now, she lowered* **herself** *carefully into the chair.* • *He lowered his eyes* (= looked down) *in embarrassment when he saw me.*

low SMALL IN AMOUNT /£ləʊ, $loʊ/ *adj* **-er, -est** small in size, number, value or amount, or of not good quality • **Temperatures** *are very low for the time of year.* • *The big supermarket offers the lowest* **prices** *in town.* • *These people are living on* **relatively** *low* **incomes**. • *The government is committed to keeping the inflation* **rate** *as low as possible.* • *There is a tremendous need for more low-***cost** *housing.* • *Low-energy light bulbs* (= those which use less energy) *are expensive to buy but repay the cost in lower electricity charges.* • *I'm on a low-***fat** *diet* (= one with very little fat). • *More people are now drinking low-***alcohol** *lager/beer* (= that with very little alcohol) *when they go out, so that they don't get drunk.* • *This chocolate is very low* **in** (= does not contain many) *calories.* • *The minister has been keeping a low* **profile** (= has not been seen much in public) *recently.* • *He said that he deplored television's tendency to be directed towards the lowest* **common denominator** (= things that are of interest or understood by most people in a group). • *There has been so little rain recently that the reservoirs are low* (= do not have much water in them). • If you **are/run/get** low (**on** something), you have very little of it left: *We're running low on milk, can you buy some more?* ○ *The radio batteries are running low.* • Low can also mean producing only a small amount of sound, heat or light: *They spoke in low voices so I would not hear what they were saying.* ○ *Turn the oven to a low heat.* ○ *Soft music was playing and the lights were low.* • Low can also mean of not good quality, esp. when referring to something that is not as good as it should be: **Standards** *in the recent tests were very low.* ○ *I have rather a low* **opinion** *of him.* ○ *She has very low self-***esteem** (= She does not have a very high opinion of herself). • In the Church of England, **low church** means not containing a lot of customary acts and ceremonies, or believing that church services should not contain a lot of customary acts and ceremonies: *a low church service* ○ *Our vicar is quite low church.* ○ Compare **high church** at HIGH ABOVE AVERAGE. • A **low-key** event is one that is quite quiet and without a great show of excitement: *The wedding will be a low-key affair, with fewer than thirty people.* • The **low season** is the period in the year when the fewest number of people visit a place and when the prices are at their lowest level: *Many hotels are closed during low season, from November to March.* ○ Compare **high season** at HIGH ABOVE AVERAGE. • Something that is **low-tech** does not use the most recent equipment or methods: *He prefers to use a low-tech fountain pen to write rather than a word-processor.* Compare HI-TECH. • *(specialized)* A **lowest common denominator** is the smallest number that can be exactly divided by all the bottom numbers in a group of FRACTIONS. • PIC› **Lights**

low /£ləʊ, $loʊ/ *adv* **-er, -est** • *The organization aims to help low-paid workers.* • *Share values dropped low on the stock market in trading yesterday.* • *Turn the oven on low.*

low /£ləʊ, $loʊ/ *n* [C] • *Things have been at a bit of a low* (= have not been good) *recently.* • An **all-time** or **record** low is a situation in which things are the worst they have ever been: *The dollar has hit an all-time low against the Japanese yen.*

low·er *obj* /£ˈləʊ·əʳ, $ˈloʊ·ɚ/ *v* [T] • *They're going to lower* (= make less) *the price of newspapers.* • *Interest rates have been lowered again.* • *Boil for 5 minutes, then lower the heat and simmer for half an hour.* • *Please lower your voice* (= speak more quietly). • To lower something is also to make it not as good as it was before: *We are against any lowering of standards.* ○ *His crude jokes lowered* **the tone of** *the evening* (= made it less respectable).

low NOT IMPORTANT /£ləʊ, $loʊ/ *adj* **-er, -est** not important because of being at or near the bottom of a range of things, esp. jobs or social positions • *Large numbers of women still work in jobs which only have a low status.* • *These measures have been taken to help improve the working conditions of the lower* **grades/levels** *of staff.* • *I want to put some new plants in the garden, but I've got so much else to do that it's quite a low* **priority** *at the moment.*

low·ly /£ˈləʊ·li, $ˈloʊ-/ *adj* **-ier, -iest** • Lowly means low in position and importance, or not respected: *His first job in the hotel was as a lowly porter.*

low NOT HONEST /£ləʊ, $loʊ/ *adj* **-er, -est** not honest or fair • *How low can you get?* • *That was a pretty low trick to play.* • **Low life** means people who exist by criminal activities or have a way of life most people disapprove of: *He started mixing with drug-dealers, pimps and other low life.* • *(infml)* A **low-down** person or action is a very dishonest and unfair one: *That was a pretty low-down thing to do.* See also LOWDOWN.

low·er *obj* /£ˈləʊ·əʳ, $ˈloʊ·ɚ/ *v* [T usually in negatives] • *I'd never have expected him to lower* **himself** (= behave dishonestly or immorally) *by stealing.* ○ *I wouldn't lower* **myself** (= behave in a way that is not honourable) **to** *respond to his insults if I were you.* [+ *to* infinitive]

low SOUND /£ləʊ, $loʊ/ *adj* (of a sound or voice) near or at the bottom of the range of sounds • *He has a very low voice.* • *Those low notes are played by the double bass.* • If a sound is **low-pitched**, it is at the bottom of the range of sounds: *He gave a low-pitched whistle.*

low SAD /£ləʊ, $loʊ/ *adj* **-er, -est** unhappy • *I was feeling low because I'd failed my driving test.* • *He seems in low* **spirits** *today, how can we cheer him up?* • *The meeting was a fairly* **low-spirited** (= not happy) *occasion.*

low COW NOISE /£ləʊ, $loʊ/ *v* [I] *literary* to make the deep, long sound of a cow; to MOO

low·brow /£ˈləʊ·braʊ, $ˈloʊ-/ *adj esp. disapproving* (of entertainment) not complicated or demanding much intelligence to be able to understand it • *She enjoys going to lowbrow action movies once in a while.* • Compare HIGHBROW; MIDDLEBROW.

low·brow /£ˈləʊ·braʊ, $ˈloʊ-/ *n* [C] *esp. disapproving* • *I don't take much account of what Jason thinks about books and films – he's a bit of a lowbrow.*

low·down /£ˈləʊ·daʊn, $ˈloʊ-/ *n* [U] **the lowdown** the most important facts and information (about something) • *So what's been happening while I've been away – who's going to* **give** *me the lowdown?* • *Our fashion editor* **gives** *you the lowdown* **on** *winter coats for this season.* • See also **low-down** at LOW NOT HONEST.

low·er /£ˈləʊ·əʳ, $ˈloʊ·ɚ/ *adj* [not gradable] positioned below one or more similar things, or of the bottom part of something • *Her lower lip trembled as if she was about to cry.* • *Our cabin on the ship was on one of the lower decks.* • *I've got a pain in my lower* (= the bottom part of my) *back, doctor.* • Letters that are printed or written in **lower case** are in the small form, not in capital letters: *Please change all capitals to lower-case letters.* Compare **upper case** at UPPER [HIGHER]. • **Lower class** means of the people who belong to the class that has the lowest position in society and the least money. The **lower classes** are these people considered as a group: *a lower class worker* ○ *lower class attitudes* ○ *The lower classes usually have the lowest paid jobs.* Compare **upper class** at UPPER [HIGHER]; **middle class** at MIDDLE • **working class** at WORK [ACTIVITY]. • The **lower house** is one of the two parts of a country's government that makes laws, usually the one with the most power. • [PIC]> **Writing**

low·er·ing /£ˈlaʊə·rɪŋ, $ˈlaʊɚ·ɪŋ/ *adj literary* (of the sky) very dark and looking as if it is about to rain • *The village fete took place under lowering skies.*

low·land /£ˈləʊ·lənd, $ˈloʊ-/ *n* [U] flat land that is at the same level as the sea • *Rice grows best in well-watered lowland.* • *These plants are mainly found in lowland areas/regions.*

low·lands /£ˈləʊ·ləndz, $ˈloʊ-/ *pl n* • *From the lowlands* (= areas of lowland) *of the south to the rugged peaks in the north, Derbyshire has something for everyone.*

lox /£lɒks, $lɑːks/, **smoked sal·mon** *n* [U] *Am* SALMON (= a type of fish) which has been preserved with smoke • *I'll have a bagel with lox and cream cheese.*

loy·al /ˈlɔɪ·əl/ *adj* firm and not changing in your friendship with or support for a person or an organization, or in your belief in your principles • *Jack has been a loyal worker in this company for almost 50 years.* • *When all her other friends deserted her, Steve remained loyal.* • *They believe passionately in being loyal* **to** *their country.* • *Even when threatened with death, she stayed loyal* **to** *her beliefs.*

loy·al·ist /ˈlɔɪ·ə·lɪst/ *n* [C] • A loyalist is a person who is firm in their support for the government or ruler in power: *Government loyalists rallied today to fight off a challenge from the opposition.* ○ *The rebel forces have been repeatedly attacked by loyalist troops.* • In N Ireland, a Loyalist is a person who believes that N Ireland should continue to be part of the UK.

loy·al·ly /ˈlɔɪ·ə·li/ *adv* • *All his life he loyally supported his local team.*

loy·al·ty /£ˈlɔɪ·əl·ti, $-t̬i/ *n* [U] • *His betrayal of his friends was a real test of his wife's loyalty* (= the firmness of her friendship or support for him). • *Her loyalty* **to** *the cause has never been in doubt.*

loyal·ties /£ˈlɔɪ·əl·tiz, $-t̬iz/ *pl n* • Your loyalties are your feelings of support or duty towards someone or something: *My loyalties* **to** *my family come before my loyalties* **to** *my work.* ○ *I'm having to cope with* **divided** *loyalties* (= feelings of support for two different and opposing people or things) – *whether to go to an important meeting at work or to my daughter's concert?*

loz·enge /£ˈlɒz·ɪndʒ, $ˈlɑː·zəndʒ/ *n* [C] a small flat sweet, which is either eaten for enjoyment or which contains medicine, and which dissolves when sucked in the mouth • *a fruit lozenge* • *a throat lozenge* • *a cough lozenge*

LP /ˌelˈpiː/ *n* [C] *abbreviation for* **long-playing record** (= a record which has a long piece of music or several different pieces of music on it) • *I wish I hadn't sold all my Beatles LPs.* • *Their third LP featured more complex orchestrations.*

L-plate /ˈel·pleɪt/ *n* [C] *Br and Aus* a square white sign with a red letter L on it, one of which is fixed to the back and one to the front of a vehicle driven by a person who is learning to drive • *(infml) I see you finally got the L-plates off* (= have passed your driving test). • See also L-DRIVER.

LPN /ˌel·piːˈen/ *n* [C] *Am abbreviation for* licensed practical nurse (= a person who is trained to provide medical care by following the instructions of a doctor or more highly trained nurse) • *LPNs are often supervised by registered nurses.*

LSD /ˌel·esˈdiː/, *slang* **ac·id** *n* [U] an illegal drug which causes people who use it to see the world differently from the way it really is or to see things that do not really exist • *In the seventies, people were always telling stories about someone who jumped out of the window under the influence of LSD, thinking they could fly.* • *They're* **on an LSD trip**/*They're* **tripping on** *LSD* (= They're experiencing the effects of LSD).

Lt /lefˈten·ənt/ *n* [before n] *abbreviation for* LIEUTENANT • *Lt Jeffries* ○ *Lt. Anderson*

Ltd /ˈlɪm·ɪ·tɪd/ *adj* [after n; not gradable] *Br and Aus abbreviation for* limited (liability) company (= a company whose owners are responsible only to a particular level for the money that it owes). Ltd often forms part of a company's name. • *Smith and Jones Ltd.* • [LP]> **Letters**

lu·au /ˈluː·aʊ/ *n Aus* a Hawaiian party or celebration

lu·bricant /ˈluː·brɪ·kənt/ *n* See at LUBRICATE

lu·bri·cate *obj* /ˈluː·brɪ·keɪt/ *v* [T] to use a substance such as oil or GREASE to make (esp. a machine) operate more easily, or to prevent (something) sticking or rubbing • *A car engine needs to be well lubricated with oil.* • *This door keeps sticking – I think the hinges need lubricating.* • *(fig.) Give him a few drinks – that'll lubricate his* **tongue** (= make him speak freely).

lu·bricant /ˈluː·brɪ·kənt/, *Am and Aus infml* **lube** /luːb/ *n* • *The engine won't work properly without lubricant* (= a substance such as oil which causes a machine to operate more easily). [U] • *When you give someone a massage, you can use oil or talcum powder as a lubricant* (= a substance which prevents rubbing or sticking). [C]

lu·bri·ca·tion /ˌluː·brɪˈkeɪ·ʃᵊn/, *Am and Aus infml* **lube** /luːb/ *n* [U] • *My bike chain needs some lubrication* (= needs to have a substance like oil put onto it to make it operate more easily). • *The car's lubrication system is faulty.* • *(Am)* If your car is given a **lube job** its moving parts are lubricated.

lu·bri·cat·or /£ˈluː·brɪ·keɪ·təʳ, $-t̬ɚ/ *n* [C] *specialized* • *Use silicone-based oil as a lubricator* (= a substance which makes a machine operate smoothly) *on the servo mechanism.*

lu·bri·cious /luːˈbrɪʃ·əs/ *adj fml* having or showing too great an interest in sex, esp. in an unpleasant way

lu·bri·cious·ly /luːˈbrɪʃ·ə·sli/ *adv fml*

lu·bri·cious·ness /luːˈbrɪʃ·ə·snəs/ *n* [U] *fml*

lu·cid /ˈluː·sɪd/ *adj* clearly expressed and easy to understand or (of a person) thinking or speaking clearly, esp. after not having been able to do so, for example because of illness • *She gave a clear and lucid account of her plans for the company's future.* • *He writes in a very lucid manner.* • *The drugs she's taking make her drowsy and confused, but there are times when she's quite lucid.* • *In one of his more lucid moments, he appeared to recognize his wife.*

lu·cid·i·ty /£luːˈsɪd·ɪ·ti, $-ə·t̬i/, **lu·cid·ness** /ˈluː·sɪd·nəs/ *n* [U] • *He writes with great lucidity* (= clearly). • *Most of the time she seems confused, but she does have occasional periods of lucidness* (= when she is thinking and speaking clearly).

lu·cid·ly /ˈluː·sɪd·li/ *adv* • *He explained it all very lucidly.* • *Today, for the first time in months, Bobby spoke to us quite lucidly.*

Lu·ci·fer /£ˈluː·sɪ·fəʳ, $-fɚ/ *n* [not after *the*] another name for Satan (= the originator of evil and the enemy of God) • *According to the Old Testament, Lucifer, in his pride, led the revolt of some of the angels against God, and was banished to Hell after their defeat. After this he was called Satan.* • *Jones was once described by a friend as being* **as proud as Lucifer** (= extremely proud or satisfied with himself).

Lu·cite /ˈluː·saɪt/ *n* [U] *Am trademark* a type of transparent plastic used to make paints and decorative objects such as picture frames

luck /lʌk/ *n* [U] the force that causes things, esp. good things, to happen to you by chance and not as a result of your own efforts or abilities • *It was just (a matter of) luck that she got that job.* • *He* **had** *the luck to be* (= By chance he was) *in the right place at the right time.* • *We thought we'd miss the train, but luck was* **on our side/with** *us* (= by chance something good happened), *and we just made it.* • *I* **couldn't believe** *my luck* (= what a good thing had happened by chance) *when I found my lost wallet.* • **It** *was a* **stroke of luck** (= something good that happened by chance) *that we found exactly the house we were looking for.* [+ *that* clause] • *She wears a charm that she thinks* **brings** *her* **(good)** *luck* (= makes good things happen). • *I hear your dad bought you a new car – some people* **have all the** *luck* (= good things happen to them by chance all the time). • *I didn't have much luck* (= success) *trying to find a birthday present for Sam.* • *Any luck* **with** (= Have you been successful in) *booking your flight?* • *He tried to get into teacher training college but with no luck* (= no success). • *We all wished Lisa* **(good/the best of)** *luck* **in/with** *her exams.* • *The team have had* **bad** *luck* (= bad things have happened to them) *throughout this series.* • You say **bad/hard/**

tough/ rotten luck to express sympathy with someone when something unlucky has happened to them: *"I broke my leg on the first day of my skiing holiday." "Oh, (what) rotten luck!"* • *Some people believe it's* **bad** *luck to* (= bad things will happen to you if you) *walk under a ladder.* • *We ran out of petrol on the way home, but* **as luck would have it** (= by chance), *we weren't far from a garage.* • *(esp. Br) It was* **bad luck on** *Alex that his bike was stolen.* • *He's been a bit* **down on** *his* **luck** *recently* (= Bad things, esp. having no money, have been happening to him). • *We have a horseshoe hanging on our wall* **for (good) luck** (= so that good things will happen to us by chance). • *I'll have two spoonsful of sugar, and one* **for luck** (= to bring good luck). • *"Do you have any bananas today?" "You're* **in luck/out of luck** (= What you want is available/not available)." • *(Br) My* **luck was in** (= something good happened to me by chance) *last night – I won every game in the darts match.* • *Sometimes it's just the* **luck of the draw** (= just chance) *whether you get picked for the team or not.* • *"You did amazingly well to get the ball in." "Oh, it was* **more by luck than judgment** (= It was by chance and not because of my skill)." • *(infml) "Can you get a day off work to come to the beach?"* "**No such luck** (= It is disappointing but I will not be able to)." • *(infml) I was rather hoping it would rain today and I wouldn't have to go on the walk but* **no such luck** (= it is disappointing that I did not get what I wanted). • *(infml)* **With (any/a bit of) luck** (= I hope that) *we should get to Newcastle by early evening.*

luck into *obj* /lʌk/ *v adv* [T] *Am infml* • If you luck into something you are successful or get something good by chance: *We lucked into tickets for the World Cup finals.*

luck out /lʌk/ *v adv Am infml* • *The Giants really lucked out* (= something good happened by chance) *in last night's game.*

luck·less /ˈlʌk·ləs/ *adj fml* • *A luckless junior clerk* (= one to whom bad things often happen by chance) *was blamed for the error.*

luck·y /ˈlʌk·i/ *adj* **-ier, -iest** • To be lucky is to have good things happen to you by chance: *She's one of those lucky people who always seems to get what she wants.* ○ *We'll be lucky if we get there by midnight at this rate.* ○ *You're lucky* **in** *having such a beautiful house.* ○ *They're lucky* **to** *be able to afford to go on a world cruise.* [+ *to* infinitive] ○ *He's lucky* **that** *he wasn't fired.* [+ *that* clause] ○ *(infml) "How did you manage to get that job?" "I don't know, I guess I just* **got** *lucky."* ○ *It sounds as if you had a lucky* **escape** (= by good chance you were able to avoid something dangerous or unpleasant that very nearly happened). ○ *Today is* **my** *lucky* **day**. ○ *She always wears a lucky* **charm** (= one that she thinks will cause good things to happen by chance) *on a chain round her neck.* ○ *(infml) "Guess what, I just won a new car in a competition!" "You lucky thing!"* • *(infml) Do you want to come to the party with us – you might* **get lucky** (= meet someone with whom you can have a sexual and/or romantic relationship with). • *(infml) "She's going to ask the boss for a salary increase." "She***'ll be lucky** (= She is not very likely to get what she wants)!" • *(Br infml) "Can you lend me £100?" "You***'ll be lucky** (= It is very unlikely that you will get what you're asking for)!" • *(Br and Aus)* A **lucky dip** is a game in which you pay to pick a wrapped object out of a container filled with wrapped objects of various different values, hoping to get something of higher value than the amount you have paid. • *(infml) "Did your husband give you those earrings?" "I* **should be so lucky** (= it is very unlikely that such a thing would happen)!"

luck·i·ly /ˈlʌk·əl·i/ *adv* • *Luckily, Steve didn't break any bones when he fell off his bike.*

lu·cra·tive /£ˈluː·krə·tɪv, $-t̬ɪv/ *adj* (esp. of a business, job or activity) producing a lot of money; making a large profit • *She has a lucrative business selling leather goods.* • *The merger proved to be very lucrative for both companies.*

lu·cra·tive·ly /£ˈluː·krə·tɪv·li, $-t̬ɪv-/ *adv*

lu·cra·tive·ness /£ˈluː·krə·tɪv·nəs, $-t̬ɪv-/ *n* [U]

lu·cre /£ˈluː·kəʳ, $-kɚ/ *n* [U] *dated disapproving or humorous* money or profit • *Nobody doubts the power of lucre.*

Lud·dite /ˈlʌd·aɪt/ *n* [C] *usually disapproving* a person who is opposed to the introduction of new working methods, esp. new machines • *You'll never get a Luddite like Geoff to use the new computer system.*

lu·di·crous /ˈluː·dɪ·krəs/ *adj* foolish or causing laughter because unreasonable or unsuitable; ridiculous • *Going out for a walk when it's pouring with rain is a ludicrous idea/suggestion.* • *You look absolutely ludicrous in those clothes!* • *It was ludicrous* **to** *think that they would agree to those proposals.* [+ *to* infinitive]

lu·di·crous·ly /ˈluː·dɪ·krə·sli/ *adv* • *It's a beautiful dress, but it's ludicrously* (= unreasonably) *expensive.*

lu·di·crous·ness /ˈluː·dɪ·krə·snəs/ *n* [U]

lug *obj* CARRY /lʌg/ *v* [T always + adv/prep] **-gg-** *infml* to carry or pull (something) with effort or difficulty because it is heavy • *I'm exhausted after lugging these suitcases all the way across London.* • *I don't want to lug these shopping bags* **(a)round/about** *with me all day.*

lug EAR /lʌg/ *n* [C] *Br and Aus* a LUGHOLE

lug PERSON /lʌg/ *n* [C] *Am slang* an awkward or stupid person • Lug can also be an affectionate term for a man: *Come over here and give me a kiss, you* **big** *lug.*

lug·gage /ˈlʌg·ɪdʒ/, *esp. Am* **bag·gage** *n* [U] the bags, cases, etc. which contain your possessions and that you take with you when you are travelling • *Never leave your luggage unattended.* • *I don't know why you have to take so much luggage with you.* • *All* **carry-on** *luggage* (= small bags and cases taken onto the part of an aircraft in which the passengers sit) *must be stored under your seat or in the overhead compartments.* • *Have you got any* **hand** *luggage* (= small bags and cases that you take onto the part of an aircraft, bus, etc. in which the passengers sit)? • *You can put those cases in the luggage* **compartment** (= the part of a bus, train, aircraft, etc. in which only large bags are transported). • A *(Br and Aus)* **luggage label**/*(Am)* **luggage tag** is a small piece of card or plastic with your name and address written on it, which you fasten to a bag or case to show that it belongs to you. • *(esp. Br)* A **luggage rack** is a shelf on a train or a bus on which you can put your bags and cases. • *We left our bags in the (Br and Aus)* **luggage van**/*(Aus also and Am)* **baggage car** (= the part of a train in which large bags are transported). • LP› **Shopping goods** PIC› **Luggage, Rack**

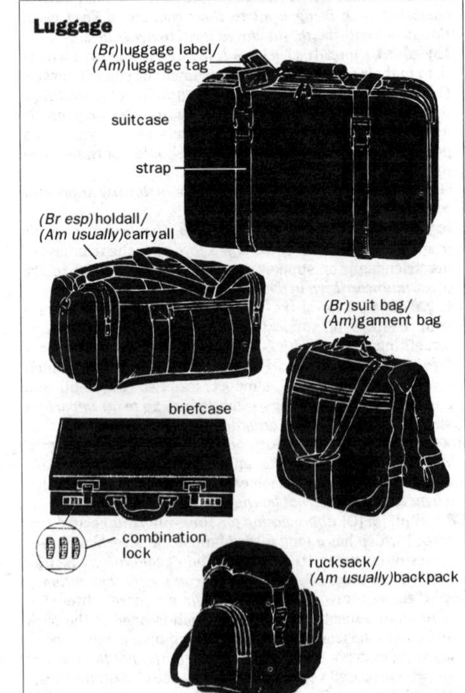

lug·hole /£ˈlʌg·həʊl, £-əʊl, $-hoʊl/, **lug** *n* [C] *Br slang humorous* an ear • *You'll get a clip round the lughole if you're not careful.* • *Pin back your lugholes* (= listen carefully) *and listen to this.*

lu·gu·bri·ous /luːˈguː·bri·əs/ *adj* sad, esp. in a slow or serious way • *He always has such a lugubrious look on his face.* • *She speaks in a slow, lugubrious manner.* • *This music is rather lugubrious.*

lu·gu·bri·ous·ly /luːˈguː·bri·ə·sli/ *adv*

lu·gu·bri·ous·ness /luːˈguː·bri·ə·snəs/ *n* [U]

luke·warm /£ˌluːkˈwɔːm, £ˈ-, $ˈluːk·wɔːrm/ *adj* [not gradable] (esp. of a liquid) only slightly warm; TEPID • *The* *baby's food needs to be heated until it's just lukewarm.* • *How can you bear to drink this lukewarm coffee?* • *(fig.) I asked Julia if she wanted to meet us for a drink, but she seemed rather lukewarm* (= not enthusiastic) **about** *the idea.* • *(fig.) Her proposals got a lukewarm* **response/reaction/ reception.**

lull *obj* /lʌl/ *v* [T] to cause to feel sleepy, calm or safe • *People who drive long distances need to be careful that the motion of the car doesn't lull them* **to sleep.** • *The minister's statement was designed to lull the public* **into** *believing that the situation is improving.* • *Their promises lulled us* **into a false sense of security** (= made us feel safe, when in fact we were not).

lull /lʌl/ *n* [C] • *We are currently experiencing a lull* (= period of quiet or reduced activity) **in** *consumer demand.* • *There has been no lull* **in** *the fighting for weeks.* • **The lull before the storm** is a time which seems quiet but which will very soon be followed by something unpleasant happening: *Everything seems all right now but this is just the lull before the storm.*

lull·a·by /ˈlʌl·ə·baɪ/ *n* [C] a quiet song which is sung to children to help them go to sleep • *Snuggle down now, and I'll sing you a lullaby.*

lu·lu /ˈluː·luː/ *n* [C] *Am and Aus slang* something which is extremely good or extremely bad • *It was a lulu* **of** *a party – we danced 'till three o'clock in the morning.* • *That black eye is a lulu.*

lum·ba·go /£lʌmˈbeɪ·gəʊ, $-goʊ/ *n* [U] general pain in the lower part of the back • *I've got dreadful lumbago.*

lum·bar /£ˈlʌm·bəʳ, $-bɚ/ *adj* [before n; not gradable] *medical* in or of the lower part of the back • *the lumbar region of the back* • *lumbar vertebrae*

lum·ber MOVE /£ˈlʌm·bəʳ, $-bɚ/ *v* [I always + adv/prep] to move slowly and awkwardly • *A line of tanks lumbered down the road.* • *In the distance, we could see a herd of elephants lumbering across the plain.*

lum·ber *obj* CAUSE DIFFICULTY /£ˈlʌm·bəʳ, $-bɚ/ *v* [T] *Br and Aus infml* to cause (someone) to do something difficult or not convenient that they do not want to do • *It's not fair – I'm always being lumbered* **with** *doing the laundry.* • *Wendy has lumbered me* **with** *sending out the invitations.* • *Jack asked who would stay behind to clear up, and as usual, I* **got** *lumbered.*

lum·ber WOOD /£ˈlʌm·bəʳ, $-bɚ/ *n* [U] *esp. Am and Aus* wood that has been prepared for building; TIMBER • *The lumber is transported by floating it down the river.*

lum·ber /£ˈlʌm·bəʳ, $-bɚ/ *v* [I] *Am* • A **lumber jacket** is a warm short coat, often coloured and with a pattern of squares on it. • PIC **Coats and jackets**

lum·ber·jack /£ˈlʌm·bə·dʒæk, $-bɚ/, **lum·ber·man** (*pl* **-men**) *n* [C] (esp. in the USA and Canada) a person whose job is to cut down trees which will be used for building etc. or to transport trees which have been cut down

lum·ber·man /£ˈlʌm·bə·mæn, $-bɚ-/ *n* [C] *pl* **-men** (esp. in the USA or Canada) a LUMBERJACK or a man whose business is the selling of wood

lum·ber·yard /£ˈlʌm·bə·jɑːd, $ˈlʌm·bɚ·jɑːrd/ *n* [C] an outside area where wood for building is stored and sold

lu·min·a·ry /£ˈluː·mɪ·nə·ri, $ˈluː·mə·ner·i/ *n* [C] a person who is famous and important in a particular area of activity • *Professor Morley is a well-known luminary* **in** *the field of cancer research.* • *The luminaries* **of** *stage and screen* (= famous actors) *assembled for last night's awards ceremony.*

lu·min·es·cent /ˌluː·mɪˈnes·ᵊnt/ *adj literary or specialized* producing a cool light • *a luminescent bulb* • *There was a strange luminescent glow in the sky.*

lu·min·es·cence /ˌluː·mɪˈnes·ᵊnts/ *n* [U] *literary or specialized*

lu·min·ous /ˈluː·mɪ·nəs/ *adj* producing or reflecting bright light (esp. in the dark) • *You should always wear luminous clothing when riding a bicycle at night.* • *The hands on my alarm clock are luminous, so that I can see what time it is in the dark.* • A luminous work, performance, etc. is clear, intelligent and shows deep or true understanding: *She gave a luminous performance of the Mozart piano concerto.*

lu·min·os·i·ty /£ˌluː·mɪˈnɒs·ə·tɪ, $-ˈnɑː·sə·t̬i/ *n* [U]

lu·min·ous·ly /ˈluː·mɪ·nə·sli/ *adv*

lum·mox /ˈlʌm·əks/ *n* [C] *infml* a stupid or awkward person • *Be careful, you* **great** *lummox, you trod on my foot!*

lump PIECE /lʌmp/ *n* [C] a mass or piece of something solid • *This sauce has got lumps in it – give it good stir to get rid of them.* • *Put a few more lumps* **of** *coal on the fire.* • *How many* **lumps of sugar/sugar lumps** (= small square-sided pieces of sugar) *would you like in your tea?* • *(fig.) I'll be getting the insurance money in two lumps* (= in two large amounts on two separate occasions). • A lump is also a hard swelling found in or on the body, esp. because of illness or injury: *She went to the doctor because she found a lump in her breast.* • **A lump in** your **throat** is a tight feeling in your throat because you are sad: *He* **had** *a lump in his throat as he said goodbye to his girlfriend at the airport.* ○ *The film* **brought** *a lump to my throat.* • *(Am dated infml) You know you shouldn't have skipped school like that, now you'll just have to* **take** *your* **lumps** (= suffer strong criticism or a beating as a result of having done something wrong). • *Alan received a* **lump sum (payment)** (= a payment in one large amount on one occasion) *from his employer when he was made redundant.*

lump *obj* /lʌmp/ *v* [T] • If you lump people or things (together) you combine them in a group or deal with them in the same way, often without thinking carefully about it: *All the children are lumped* **together** *in one class, regardless of their ability.* ○ *It's difficult for the teacher if new students are lumped* **with** *students who already have some experience.* ○ *You might as well lump all your expenses* **together** *and submit one claim.*

lump·y /ˈlʌm·pi/ *adj* **-ier, -iest** • *I'm sorry the custard is so lumpy* (= contains lumps). • *This lumpy old pillow is very uncomfortable.*

lump PERSON /lʌmp/ *n* [C] *infml* a heavy, awkward, stupid person • *Come on, you* **great** *lump, get up from in front of that television and do some work.* • *(humorous) What a* **(great/big/great big) heavy** *lump* (= How heavy) *you are!*

lum·pish /ˈlʌm·pɪʃ/ *adj* • *There was a group of lumpish* (= awkward and stupid) *adolescents hanging around outside the café.*

lump *obj* ACCEPT /lʌmp/ *v* [T] **lump it** *infml* to accept a situation or decision although you do not like it • *That's what we're going to do so you'll just* **have to (like it or)** *lump it.* • *The decision has been made, so if Tom doesn't like it, he* **can** *lump it.*

lum·pec·to·my /lʌmˈpek·tə·mi/ *n* [C] a medical operation to remove a lump from the breast

lum·pen /ˈlʌm·pən/ *adj infml* not clever and/or of low social class, or of low quality • *I can't bear her lumpen new boyfriend.* • *We stopped at an awful lumpen cafe where all they served was greasy food and lukewarm tea.*

lu·na·cy /ˈluː·nə·sɪ/ *n* [U] wild foolishness or dangerously unsuitable behaviour which is against reason • *It would be lunacy to try and climb the mountain in this weather.* • *"She said she was going to try and get him to change his mind." "But that's lunacy!"* • *It was* **sheer** *lunacy for him to think they would agree to his proposals.* • *It's the* **sheer** *lunacy of his comedy that appeals to such a wide range of people.* • *(dated, now taboo)* Lunacy is also mental illness.

lu·na·tic /£ˈluː·nə·tɪk, $-t̬ɪk/ *n* [C] • *Watch what you're doing, you lunatic* (= extremely foolish and careless person). • *You can't trust Ken – he's a complete lunatic.* • *He drives like a lunatic.* • *(dated, now taboo)* A lunatic is also a person who is mentally ill. • (F) (PL) (RUS)

lu·na·tic /£ˈluː·nə·tɪk, $-t̬ɪk/ *adj* • *That's a lunatic* (= extremely foolish and careless) *way to behave.* • *(disapproving or humorous) It's no longer just people* **on the lunatic fringe** (= people who have very strong opinions which are outside the usual range) *who are concerned about the growing use of nuclear power.* • *(dated, now taboo)* A **lunatic asylum** is a hospital for mentally ill people: *There are no longer any lunatic asylums in the UK.*

lu·nar /£ˈluː·nəʳ, $-nɚ/ *adj* [not gradable] of or relating to the moon • *lunar rocks* • *a lunar eclipse* • *the lunar surface* • *The first lunar* **module** (= part of a spacecraft in which people travelled to the moon) *is now on display at the Smithsonian Air and Space museum in Washington.* • A **lunar month** is the period of time (about 29·5 days) which the moon takes to go round the Earth. Compare **calendar month** at CALENDAR.

lunch /lʌntʃ/ *n* a meal that is eaten in the middle of the day • *What's for lunch?* [U] • *Let's have lunch in a pub today.* [U] • *I'm sorry, Ms Wilson isn't here at the moment, she's* **(gone) out to/gone to/gone for** *lunch.* [U] • *If we have an early lunch, we can start this afternoon's meeting earlier.* [C] • *The company is having/holding a lunch* (= a formal meal in the middle of the day to celebrate something) *next week in honour of Peter's retirement.* [C] • *The prize-giving will be followed by a* **buffet** *lunch* (= lunch which people collect for themselves and usually eat standing up). [C] • *I know a very* *good restaurant for* **business** *lunches* (=meals in the middle of the day at which business is discussed). [C] • *We're having a lunch* **party** *on Sunday – would you like to come?* • *This guy is really* **out to lunch** (=behaving in a strange or foolish way or CRAZY). • *I'm going shopping* **in/during** *my* **lunch hour/lunch break** (=the period in the middle of the day when people stop work to have lunch). • *(Am)*A **lunch room** (or *Br* **dining hall**) is the large room in a school where children can sit down to eat. • Compare DINNER.

lunch /lʌntʃ/ *v* [I] • *Are you lunching today?* • *I'm lunching* **with** *Giles.* • *We lunched* **on** *beer and sandwiches.*

lunch·box /£ˈlʌntʃ·bɒks, $-bɑːks/ *n* [C] a box, often made of plastic and often with a handle, in which food can be carried for eating in the middle of the day • *I'll have to buy Amy a new lunchbox for school.*

lunch·eon /ˈlʌnt·ʃən/ *n fml for* LUNCH • *Would you care to join us for luncheon?* [U] • *We're going to a charity luncheon next week.* [C] • **Luncheon meat** (*Am also* **lunch meat**) is a mixture of meat and CEREAL pressed into a block, which is usually sold in metal containers, and can be sliced and eaten cold: *We're having luncheon meat and salad today.* • *(Br) All our staff receive* **luncheon vouchers** *(Am and Aus* **meal tickets**) (=a type of ticket which people are given by their employer and which they can use instead of money for buying meals in some restaurants).

lunch·eon·ette /ˌlʌnt·ʃəˈnet/ *n* [C] *Am* a small restaurant serving simple, light meals

lunch·time /ˈlʌntʃ·taɪm/ *n* the time in the middle of the day when most people eat a meal • *They eat every lunchtime at the Market Cafe down the road.* [C] • *We spent an hour or so at the studio one lunchtime last week.* [C] • *Sunday lunchtimes are special in our family – everyone gets together for a big meal.* [C] • *It's a pleasant way to spend a lunchtime.* [C] • *What are you doing* **at** *lunchtime?* [U] • *He wants to get it all finished* **by** *lunchtime.* [U] • *You've got* **until** *lunchtime today to make up your mind..* [U] • *The decision was taken* **yesterday** *lunchtime.* [U] • *We went to listen to a lunchtime concert.*

lung /lʌŋ/ *n* [C] either of the two organs in the chest with which people and some animals breathe • *She breathed deeply to fill her lungs with the fresh sea air.* • *Smoking causes lung cancer.* • *(fig.) The Amazon rain forest is sometimes referred to as the lungs of the Earth* (=the trees in it produce oxygen that the Earth needs). • *(humorous) That baby* **has good lungs/a good pair of lungs/a healthy pair of lungs** (=can shout and cry very loudly).

lunge /lʌndʒ/ *v* [I always + adv/prep] to move forward suddenly and with force, esp. in order to attack someone • *She screamed as he lunged* **at/toward(s)** *her* **with** *a broken bottle.* • *They were just sitting having a drink, when suddenly he lunged* **at** *her* (=moved forward and took hold of her in a sexual way).

lunge /lʌndʒ/ *n* [C] • *A police officer was injured when the man he was arresting* **made** *a* **lunge at** *him.*

lu·pin, *Am usually* **lu·pine** /ˈluː·pɪn/ *n* [C] a garden plant which has a long pointed flower of various colours and is sometimes used to feed animals • PIC **Flowers and plants**

lurch /£lɜːtʃ, $lɜːrtʃ/ *v* [I] to move in an irregular way, esp. making sudden movements backwards or forwards or from side to side • *A crowd of drunken football supporters lurched down the street, singing and shouting.* • *The ship is lurching so much that it's making me feel sick.* • *The car lurched* **to a** *sudden* **halt** *at the traffic lights.* • *The train lurched* **forward** *and some of the people standing fell over.* • *(fig.) The government is weak and the country lurches* **from** *crisis* **to** *crisis* (=difficult and dangerous situations are happening continuously). • *(fig.) She seems to lurch* **from** *one bad relationship* **to** *another.* • *(fig.) None of us could understand the lecture because the speaker kept lurching* (=moving suddenly) **from** *one topic* **to** *another.* • *(fig.) They seemed to have lurched* **away from** *their earlier support for the government.*

lurch /£lɜːtʃ, $lɜːrtʃ/ *n* [C] • *The truck* **gave** *a sudden lurch as it was hit by a strong gust of wind.* • *(fig.) The party's lurch* (=sudden change) **to** *the left will lose it a lot of support.*

lure /£ljʊəʳ, $lʊr/ *n* the quality or power that something or someone has that makes them attractive • *They said that it was* **the** *lure* **of** *easy money that led them to commit the fraud.* [U] • *She was attracted to Hollywood by* **the** *lure* **of** *the silver screen.* [U] • A lure is an artificial insect or other small animal which is put on the end of a fishing line to attract fish: *Anglers use many different lures, depending on what kind of fish they want to catch.* [C]

lure *obj* /£ljʊəʳ, $lʊr/ *v* [T] • *It was the promise of free flights that lured* (=attracted) *them.* • *She was lured* **into** (=persuaded to take) *the job by the offer of a high salary.* • *Can I lure you* **away from** *what you're doing for a minute?* • *Cheese is often used to lure mice* **into** *traps.*

Lu·rex /£ˈluə·reks, $ˈlʊr·eks/ *n* [U] *trademark* (cloth made from) a type of thread that looks metallic • *She wore a black velvet skirt and a* **gold/silver** *Lurex top.*

lur·gy /£ˈlɜː·gi, $ˈlɜːr-/, **lurg** /£lɜːg, $lɜːrg/ *n Br and Aus infml humorous* an illness or disease, esp. one that is not serious • *He's got some awful kind of lurgy/lurg.* [U] • *I've got* **the (dreaded)** *lurgy.* [C]

lu·rid SHOCKING /£ˈljʊə·rɪd, $ˈlʊr·ɪd/ *adj disapproving* (esp. of a description) shocking because involving violence, sex or immoral activity • *The newspapers contained lurid accounts of the bombing.* • *This book is rather lurid.* • *She told me all the lurid* **details** *of her affair.*

lu·rid·ly /£ˈljʊə·rɪd·li, $ˈlʊr·ɪd-/ *adv* • *a luridly written description*

lu·rid·ness /£ˈljʊə·rɪd·nəs, $ˈlʊr·ɪd-/ *n* [U]

lu·rid COLOUR /£ˈljʊə·rɪd, $lʊr·ɪd/ *adj disapproving* too strong or extremely bright in colour • *Their living-room is decorated with lurid purple wallpaper.* • *That's a very lurid shade of lipstick she's wearing.*

lu·rid·ly /£ˈljʊə·rɪd·li, $ˈlʊr·ɪd-/ *adv*

lu·rid·ness /£ˈljʊə·rɪd·nəs, $ˈlʊr·ɪd-/ *n* [U]

lurk /£lɜːk, $lɜːrk/ *v* [I always + adv/prep] to wait or move in a secret way so that you cannot be seen, esp. because you are about to attack someone or do something wrong • *As I walked down the dark street, I thought I saw someone lurking* **in** *the shadows.* • *Why are you lurking* **about** *in the corridor?* • *They wondered what else lurked* **behind** *his official statement.* • *It seems that old prejudices are still lurking* **beneath** *the surface.* • *(fig.) The memory of the Wall Street crash still lurks* **in** (=has not completely gone away from) *the minds of bankers.* • *(fig.) There is* **danger** *lurking* (=existing where it cannot be seen) *around every corner.*

lurk·ing /£ˈlɜː·kɪŋ, $ˈlɜːr-/ *adj* [not gradable] • *The device is used to help spot lurking submarines.* • *(fig.) I have some lurking* **doubts** (=doubts which will not go completely away) *about whether Simon is really capable of doing this job.* • *(fig.) She said she had a lurking* **suspicion** (=she had a very slight feeling) *that he wasn't telling the truth.*

lus·cious /ˈlʌʃ·əs/ *adj* having a pleasant sweet taste and/or containing a lot of juice • *luscious tropical fruits* • *luscious figs* • *luscious cream cakes* • *(infml)* Someone or something that is luscious is also extremely attractive, pleasant or desirable: *Who was that luscious blonde you were with last night?* ○ *You look luscious tonight, my darling.* ○ *It was filmed against the backdrop of a luscious landscape of woods, streams and meadows.*

lus·cious·ly /ˈlʌʃ·ə·sli/ *adv*

lus·cious·ness /ˈlʌʃ·ə·snəs/ *n* [U]

lush PLANTS /lʌʃ/ *adj* **-er, -est** (of plants or an area of land) (with plants) growing thickly and strongly • *lush grass* ○ *lush tropical forest* ○ *lush green valleys*

lush·ly /ˈlʌʃ·li/ *adv*

lush·ness /ˈlʌʃ·nəs/ *n* [U]

lush LUXURIOUS /lʌʃ/ *adj* **-er, -est** (of places, furniture, decoration, etc.) expensive and luxurious • *lush furnishings* • *a lush carpet* • *a lush hotel*

lush·ly /ˈlʌʃ·li/ *adv*

lush·ness /ˈlʌʃ·nəs/ *n* [U]

lush DRINKER /lʌʃ/ *n* [C] *slang* a person who regularly drinks too much alcohol • *Bill has turned into a real lush.*

lust /lʌst/ *n* a very strong desire, either sexual or to get or possess something • *He looked at her with lust* (=strong sexual desire) *in his eyes.* [U] • *Her attraction to him is pure lust.* [U] • *All he's interested in is* **satisfying** *his lust.* [U] • *Her lust* (=strong desire) **for** *power has made her ruthless.* [U] • *It's wonderful to see the children's lust* **for** *life* (=how eager and enthusiastic they are about life). [U] • *He's driven by the twin lusts* **for** *money and success.* [C] • Ⓓ

lust af·ter/for *obj* /lʌst/ *v prep* [T] • *Jenny has been lusting after* (=feeling sexual desire for) *Dave for weeks.* • *Do you know how much I've lusted for you?* • *I've never really lusted after* (=had a strong desire for) *possessions very much.* • *He's always lusted for control of the organization – now he's got it.*

lust·ful /ˈlʌst·fəl/ *adj* • *I've been having lustful thoughts* (=thoughts expressing sexual desire) *about you.*

lust·ful·ly /ˈlʌst·fəl·i/ *adv* • *She stared lustfully at him.*

lust·ful·ness /ˈlʌst·fəl·nəs/ *n* [U]

lus·tre *esp. Br and Aus, Am usually* **lust·er** /£ˈlʌs·tər, $-t̬ɚ/ *n* [U] the brightness that a shiny surface has • *Restore the lost lustre to your car with new 'Carshine'.* • *He loved the curve of her cheek, the brightness of her eyes, the lustre* **of** *her hair.* • *Well-polished furniture often has* **a** *rich lustre.* • *(fig.) The dancing of the principal ballerina added lustre to* (= made splendid) *an otherwise unimpressive production of 'Giselle'.* [U]

lu·strous /ˈlʌs·trəs/ *adj* • *The TV advert says this conditioner will give you lustrous* (= shiny) *hair.*

lu·strous·ly /ˈlʌs·trə·sli/ *adv*

lust·y /ˈlʌs·ti/ *adj* **-ier, -iest** healthy; energetic; full of strength and power • *The playground is full of lusty children running around.* • *We could hear the lusty singing of the church choir.*

lus·ti·ly /ˈlʌs·tɪ·li/ *adv* • *The baby cried lustily* (= loudly) *the moment he was born.*

lus·ti·ness /ˈlʌs·tɪ·nəs/ *n* [U]

lute /luːt/ *n* [C] a musical instrument which has a body with a round back and a flat top, a long neck, and strings which are played with the fingers • *Lutes were popular from the 14th to the 18th centuries in the West, but are still common in the Middle East.*

Lu·ther·an /£ˈluː·θər·ən, $-θɚ-/ *adj* [not gradable] of or relating to a part of the Christian Protestant group that is based on the ideas of the German religious leader Martin Luther • *They are members of the Lutheran church.*

Lu·ther·an /£ˈluː·θər·ən, $-θɚ-/ *n* [C] • *Lutherans* (= members of the Christian group based on the ideas of Luther) *believe that people are accepted by God on the basis of faith alone.*

luv /lʌv/ *n Br and Aus not standard for* love • *Can I get you a drink, luv?* [as form of address] • Some people end informal letters by writing luv and their name: *That's all for now. Luv, Julie.* • LP **Titles and forms of address**

luv·vy /ˈlʌv·i/, **luv·vie** *n* [C] *humorous* an actor or actress who speaks and acts in a very artificial and noticeable way

lux /lʌks/ *n* [C] *pl* **lux** a measure of the amount of light produced by something

lux·u·ri·ant /£lʌgˈʒʊə·ri·ənt, $-ˈʒʊr·i-/ *adj* growing thickly and healthily • *Tall, luxuriant plants grew along the river bank.* • *This stretch of land was once covered with luxuriant forest, but is now bare.* • *Her luxuriant hair fell around her shoulders.* • *(fig.) We've bought a wonderfully luxuriant* (= thick) *carpet for our bedroom.* • *(fig.) Marcel Proust has a luxuriant* (= containing a lot of detail, not simple) *style of writing.*

lux·u·ri·ance /£lʌgˈʒʊə·ri·ənts, $-ˈʒʊr·i-/ *n* [U]

lux·u·ri·ant·ly /£lʌgˈʒʊə·ri·ənt·li, $-ˈʒʊr·i-/ *adv*

lux·u·ri·ate /£lʌgˈʒʊə·ri·eɪt, $-ˈʒʊr·i-/ *v* [I] to get great pleasure (from something), esp. because it provides physical comfort • *When I go on holiday, I just like to lie on a beach and luxuriate.* • *There's nothing better after a hard day's work than to luxuriate* **in** *a hot bath.*

lux·u·ry /£ˈlʌk·ʃər·i, $-ʃɚ-/ *n* great comfort, esp. as provided by expensive and beautiful things, or something which is pleasant to have but is not necessary • *We'll never have enough money to be able to live in luxury.* [U] • *It doesn't seem fair that some people live/lead lives of luxury, while others have nothing at all.* [U] • *When Jack retired, he and his wife went on a luxury cruise.* • *We stayed at a luxury hotel.* • *Champagne is a real luxury.* [C] • *I like to buy myself little luxuries from time to time.* [C] • *It would be a luxury to be able to have a day off work.* • *The government is expected to introduce a new tax on* **luxury goods/items** (= expensive items such as jewellery, PERFUME and works of art which are pleasant to have but are not necessary). • Ⓘ

lux·u·ri·ous /£lʌgˈʒʊə·ri·əs, $-ˈʒʊr·i-/ *adj* • *They live in a very luxurious house* (= one providing great comfort). • *We spent a luxurious weekend at a country hotel.* • *The cat gave a long, luxurious stretch* (= one expressing great pleasure and comfort). • Ⓟ

lux·u·ri·ous·ly /£lʌgˈʒʊə·ri·ə·sli, $-ˈʒʊr·i-/ *adv*

LW *n abbreviation for* **long wave**, see at WAVE [ENERGY]

-ly [ADVERB] /li/ *combining form* in the stated way or from the stated way of considering something, or at the stated regular period of time • *quickly* • *carefully* • *angrily* • *loudly* • *Personally* (= In my opinion), *I don't think animals should be killed for their fur.* • *This is an environmentally* (= in relation to the environment) *disastrous proposal.* • *Everyone in the office gets paid weekly/monthly* (= once a week/month). • LP **Combining forms, Stress in pronunciation**

-ly [ADJECTIVE] /li/ *combining form* like the stated person, or happening at the stated regular period of time • *fatherly advice* • *priestly duties* • *cowardly behaviour* • *a daily shower* • *a weekly meeting* • *a yearly check-up*

lyc·ée /ˈliː·seɪ/ *n* [C] a French school for older children, either in France or for French children living in other countries

ly·chee, li·tchi /ˈlaɪt·ʃiː/ *n* [C] a fruit with a rough brown shell and sweet white flesh around a large shiny brown seed, or the evergreen tree on which this fruit grows • *Lychees originally came from China.*

lych·gate /ˈlɪtʃ·geɪt/ *n* [C] a small gate with a small sloping roof over it which leads into the grounds of a church

Ly·cra /ˈlaɪ·krə/ *n* [U] *trademark* a stretchy material used esp. for making clothes which fit very tightly • *a Lycra swimsuit* • *Lycra leggings* • *These jeans have added Lycra for comfort and fit.*

ly·ing /ˈlaɪ·ɪŋ/ *present participle of* LIE

lymph /lɪmpf/ *n* [U] a colourless liquid which transports useful substances around the body, and carries waste matter, such as unwanted bacteria, from body tissue to prevent infection • *Lymph forms part of the body's defences against infection.* • **Lymph glands** or **lymph nodes** are small organs in the body which produce the white blood cells needed for the body to fight infection.

lym·phat·ic /lɪmpˈfæt·ɪk/ *adj* [not gradable] • *the lymphatic system*

lynch *obj* /lɪntʃ/ *v* [T] (esp. of a crowd of people) to kill by HANGING (= killing with a rope round the neck) (someone believed to be guilty of a crime) without a legal trial • *Fritz Lang's film, 'Fury', is about a mob who lynch a traveller whom they mistake for a murderer.* • *Following the arrest of the small child's suspected killer, a* **lynch mob** (= a group of people who want to kill someone who is thought to be guilty of a crime, without a legal trial) *has been out on the streets.* • **Lynch law** is the punishment of someone who is thought to be guilty of a crime, without a legal trial, by killing them.

lyn·ching /ˈlɪn·tʃɪŋ/ *n* • *The police believe that the attack was a lynching carried out by the Ku Klux Klan.* [C] • *He was a victim of lynching.* [U]

lynch·pin /ˈlɪntʃ·pɪn/ *n* [C] a LINCHPIN

lynx /lɪŋks/ *n* [C] *pl* **lynxes** or **lynx** a wild animal of the cat family which has brown hair, sometimes with dark spots on it, pointed ears and a short tail • PIC **Cats**

lyre /£laɪər, $laɪr/ *n* [C] an ancient musical instrument consisting of a U-shaped frame with strings fixed to it

lyre·bird /£ˈlaɪə·bɜːd, $ˈlaɪr·bɜːrd/ *n* [C] a long-legged Australian bird. The male has a tail which it can spread out into the shape of a LYRE (= a U-shaped musical instrument) • PIC **Birds**

ly·ric /ˈlɪr·ɪk/ *adj* [not gradable] (esp. of poetry and songs) expressing personal thoughts and feelings • *William Wordsworth wrote lyric poetry/was a lyric poet.* • *Her singing has a certain lyric quality.*

ly·ric /ˈlɪr·ɪk/ *n* [C] • A lyric is a short poem which expresses the feelings of the person who wrote it.

ly·ri·cal /ˈlɪr·ɪ·kl̩/ *adj* • *"The Rime of the Ancient Mariner" is a lyrical poem by Samuel Taylor Coleridge.* • *The book contains lyrical descriptions* (= descriptions expressing feelings) *of the author's childhood.* • *He's always* **waxing** *lyrical* (= speaking enthusiastically) *about the benefits of a daily 5-kilometre run.*

ly·ri·cal·ly /ˈlɪr·ɪ·kli/ *adv* • *This concerto should be played lyrically* (= like a song), *not crisply.* • *He wrote lyrically about the places he'd visited.*

ly·ri·ci·sm /ˈlɪr·ɪ·sɪ·zəm/ *n* [U] • *She is famous for the graceful lyricism of her dancing.* • *The harshness of the book's subject is softened by a certain lyricism in the writing.*

ly·ri·cist /ˈlɪr·ɪ·sɪst/ *n* [C] • *The lyricist* (= person who writes the words for songs), *Stephen Sondheim, wrote the songs for the musical 'West Side Story'.*

ly·rics /ˈlɪr·ɪks/ *pl n* • *Paul Simon writes the lyrics* (= words of a song, esp. a modern popular one) **for** *most of his own songs.*

M m

M [LETTER] (*pl* **M's** or **Ms**), **m** (*pl* **m's** or **ms**) /em/ *n* [C] the 13th letter of the English alphabet

M [NUMBER], **m** /em/ *n* [C] the sign used in the Roman system for the number 1000

M [ROAD] /em/ *n Br abbreviation for* MOTORWAY • *The M4 goes from London to Bristol.*

M [SIZE] /em/, **m**, **med** *adj* (esp. used on clothing to show its size) MEDIUM [VALUE]

m [AMOUNT], **M** *n* [C] *pl* **m** or **M** *abbreviation for* MILLION • *The new library cost £5m to build.*

m [LENGTH] *n* [C] *pl* **m** *abbreviation for* METRE [MEASUREMENT] • *Jeff is 1·8 m tall.* • *She's the women's 1500 m champion* (=the winner of a race run over that distance). • LP> **Units**

m [DISTANCE] *n* [C] *pl* **m** *abbreviation for* MILE • LP> **Units**

m [MALE] *adj abbreviation for* MALE (esp. on forms)

'm /ᵊm/ *short form of* am, used in spoken and in informal written English • *I'm sorry I'm late.*

ma [MOTHER] /mɑː/ *n* [C] *infml* a mother • *My old ma always used to say you can't spend what you ain't got.* • *I went to see my Ma and Pa yesterday.* • *How're you doing, Ma?* [as form of address] • Ma can be used when speaking, sometimes not politely, to an old woman: *Come along, Ma, you're holding everyone up.* [as form of address] • *(esp. Am)* Ma can also be used as a title for an old woman: *Ma Johnson always used to bake the best cookies.* • LP> **Titles and forms of address**

MA [DEGREE] /ˌemˈeɪ/ *n* [C] *abbreviation for* **Master of Arts**, see at MASTER [SKILLED PERSON] • *Julia Richards, MA.* • *My brother is/has an MA* **in** *linguistics.* • *She's studying for/doing an MA* **in** *French literature.* • LP> **Schools and colleges**

ma'am /mɑːm/ *short form of* [as form of address] MADAM • In some parts of the US, ma'am is used as a polite way of addressing a woman: *How can I help you, ma'am?* • In Britain, ma'am is used to address the Queen, or a woman of high rank, esp. in particular professions, such as the army or the police, or, esp. in the past, a woman of high social class. • LP> **Titles and forms of address**

mac [COAT], **mack** /mæk/ *n* [C] *esp. Br infml for* MACKINTOSH • *a* **plastic** *mac* • *It's raining – you'd better take your mac.*

mac [MAN] /mæk/ *n* [as form of address] *Am infml* used when speaking to a man whose name you do not know • *Hey, mac, will you watch where you're going?* • LP> **Titles and forms of address**

ma·ca·bre /məˈkɑː·brə/ *adj* causing shock, disgust and fear because connected with death, esp. strange or cruel death • *Even the police were horrified at the macabre nature of the killings.* • *The film 'Shoah' contains a macabre account of life in Auschwitz and other concentration camps.*

mac·a·ro·ni /£ˌmæk·ᵊrˈəʊ·ni, $-əˈroʊ-/ *n* [U] a type of pasta, in the shape of small tubes • *Macaroni is cooked in boiling water.* • *We had (Br)* **macaroni cheese**/*(Am)* **macaroni and cheese** (=a dish made from macaroni and cheese sauce) *for lunch.*

mac·a·roon /£ˌmæk·ᵊrˈuːn, $-əˈruːn/ *n* [C] a small light biscuit made from eggs and sugar and flavoured with ALMONDS or COCONUT

ma·caw /£məˈkɔː, $-ˈkɑː/ *n* [C] a brightly coloured, long-tailed bird of the PARROT family, found in Central and S America

mace [SPICE] /meɪs/ *n* [U] a spice made from the dried shell of NUTMEG (=a hard fruit) and used to flavour food

mace [ROD] /meɪs/ *n* [C] a decorated rod, which is carried by or put in front of particular public officials, as a symbol of authority • *In the British parliament the Speaker's mace is carried into the House of Commons at the beginning of the day's business.*

Mace [LIQUID] /meɪs/ *n* [U] *trademark* a chemical in a container which, when SPRAYED into a person's face, causes their eyes to sting and become full of tears • *Even though it's illegal in Britain, some women carry Mace with them at all times, in case they're attacked.*

mac·er·ate *(obj)* /ˈmæs·ə·reɪt/ *v* to (cause to) become soft by putting and leaving in liquid • *He served peaches macerated in wine for dessert.* [T] • *The body was so badly macerated that the police believe it had been in the river for weeks.* [T] • *Paper will macerate if it is left in water.* [I]

Mach /mɑːk/ *n* [U] the speed of esp. an aircraft related to the speed of sound • *An aircraft travelling at Mach 1 is travelling at the speed of sound – at Mach 2 it is travelling at twice the speed of sound.*

machete /£məˈʃet·i, $-ˈʃet̬-/ *n* [C] a large knife with a wide blade, used for cutting or as a weapon, esp. in tropical parts of the world • *The government troops were armed with guns, the rebels had only sticks and machetes.*

Mach·i·a·vel·li·an /ˌmæk·jəˈvel·i·ən/ *adj* using clever but often dishonest methods which deceive people so that you get what you want, esp. power or control • *Their use of Machiavellian tactics to win the election was widely condemned.* • *You'll have to be more Machiavellian if you want to get to the top.*

Mach·i·a·vel·li·an /ˌmæk·jəˈvel·i·ən/ *n* [C] • *The Machiavellians on the committee have managed to get the decision they wanted.*

mach·in·a·tions /ˌmæʃ·ɪˈneɪ·ʃᵊnz, ˌmæk-/ *pl n* complicated and secret plans to obtain power or control, or, sometimes, to do harm • *Despite a commitment to more open government, the public are still being kept in the dark about the inner machinations* **of** *the Cabinet.* • *Who knows what machinations lay behind this deal?*

ma·chine /məˈʃiːn/ *n* [C] a device with several moving parts which uses power to do a particular type of work • *We visited a factory in Hawaii where we saw machines for preparing pineapples to be put in cans.* • *Eggs are sorted into different sizes by a machine.* • *It would be nice to be shown some appreciation for all I do – I'm a person, not a machine.* • *(fig. disapproving) As far as my children are concerned, I'm just a meal-providing machine* (=I have no thoughts or feelings). • Machine is also often used when referring to devices used for a particular purpose: *If I'm not home when you call, leave a message on the machine (answering machine).* ○ *Don't forget to put the washing in the machine before you go out (washing machine).* ○ *I put 50p in the machine, but I didn't get anything out of it (drinks/vending machine)* • Machine is also used to mean computer: **machine-readable** *text* (=text that can be understood by a computer) ○ **machine code** (=a set of numbers that a computer can understand and which gives it instructions) ○ **machine translation** (=the process of changing text from one language into another language using a computer) • *(infml approving)* Machine is sometimes used to refer to a vehicle, esp. a motorcycle: *That's a* **mean** *machine* (=one attracting great admiration) *you've got there, Bill.* • A machine is also a group of people who control and organize something: *Churchill's* **war** *machine* ○ *The* **party** *machine has swung into action with its preparation for the election.* ○ *It's now up to the government's* **propaganda** *machine to restore the prime minister's image.* • A **machine gun** is an automatic gun which can fire a lot of bullets one after the other very quickly. To **machine-gun** someone is to shoot them with such a gun: *Snipers with machine guns are hiding out in high buildings above the city.* ○ *Several journalists were caught in machine-gun* **fire**. ○ *The raiders machine-gunned everyone in the bank before escaping in a van.* • *The car industry uses* **machine tools** (=tools which use power to cut and shape metal or other materials) *for cutting car body parts.* • *"A house is a machine for living in"* (Le Corbusier in *Towards an Architecture*, 1923) • LP> **Switching on and off** (J) (NL) (RUS)

ma·chine *(obj)* /məˈʃiːn/ *v* • *I've almost finished making the curtains – I just have to machine the hem* (=stitch it with a (sewing) machine). [T]

ma·chin·er·y /£məˈʃiː·nə·ri, $-nɚ·i/ *n* [U] • *People are sometimes frightened by all the machinery* (=machines) *that there is in hospitals.* • *Children should never play on farm machinery.* • *His hand was injured when he got it caught in the machinery* (=the moving parts of a machine). • *(fig.) The Foreign Office machinery* (=the method by which it works) *has been unsuccessful in securing the release of the hostages.*

ma·chin·ist /məˈʃiː·nɪst/ *n* [C] • *Ann works as a machinist* (=a person whose job it is to operate a machine) *in a clothing factory.* • (PL) (RUS)

mach·is·mo /£məˈkɪz·məʊ, $-moʊ/ *n* [U] *often disapproving* strong pride in behaving in a fierce and forceful way which is thought to be typically male •

Machismo plays an important part in life in some Mediterranean countries.

mach·o /£ˈmætʃ·əʊ, $ˈmɑː·tʃoʊ/ *adj infml, often disapproving* behaving or seeming to behave in a fierce and forceful way which is thought to be typical of a man • *He's too macho to admit he was hurt when his girlfriend left him.* • *I can't stand macho men.*

Mac·in·tosh /£ˈmæk·ɪn·tɒʃ, $-tɑːʃ/, *trademark* **Ap·ple Mac·in·tosh**, *infml* **Mac** /mæk/ *n* [C] *trademark* a type of computer, esp. a medium-sized one used for **word processing** or **desktop publishing** • *The design department uses Macintoshes rather than PCs.* • *I write my letters* **on** *the Mac.*

mack·er·el /ˈmæk·rəl/ *n pl* **mackerel** or **mackerels** an edible sea fish which has a green-blue skin • *Oily fish like mackerel is good for you.* [U] • *We had* **smoked** *mackerel for lunch.* [U] • *Mackerel are found in the N Atlantic.* [C]

mack·in·tosh /£ˈmæk·ɪn·tɒʃ, $-tɑːʃ/, *infml* **mac**, **mack** /mæk/ *n* [C] a waterproof coat

ma·cra·mé /məˈkrɑː·meɪ/ *n* [U] the art of weaving pieces of string together in knots to form a decorative pattern, or something made this way • *a piece of macramé* • *a macramé wall-hanging*

mac·ro– LARGE /£ˈmæk·rəʊ-, $-roʊ-/ *combining form* large; relating to the whole of something, rather than its parts • *macroscopic* (=large enough to be seen by the human eye) • Macroeconomics is the study of financial systems at a national level. • Compare MICRO- SMALL.

mac·ro COMPUTER /£ˈmæk·rəʊ, $-roʊ/ *n* [C] *pl* **macros** a single instruction given to a computer which produces a set of instructions for the computer to perform a particular piece of work • *I have set up a macro that enables me to type ® as just one keypress.*

mac·ro·bi·o·tic /£ˌmæk·rəʊ·baɪˈɒt·ɪk, $-roʊ·baɪˈɑː·t̬ɪk/ *adj* [not gradable] (of food) arranged into groups according to special principles, grown without chemicals and thought to help produce good health • *She will only eat macrobiotic food.* • *A macrobiotic diet consists mainly of whole grains and certain kinds of vegetables.*

mac·ro·co·sm /£ˈmæk·rəʊˌkɒz·ᵊm, $-roʊˌkɑː·zᵊm/ *n* any large organized system considered as a whole, rather than as a group of smaller systems • *Some sociologists view society as a macrocosm.* [C] • **The** macrocosm is the universe. [U] • Compare MICROCOSM.

mad MENTALLY ILL /mæd/ *adj* **madder** or **maddest** *esp. Br dated or infml* mentally ill, or unable to behave in a reasonable way; INSANE • *Aunt Ethel is certainly eccentric, but not mad.* • *Sometimes he felt as if he would* **go mad**, *lose his mind completely.* • *(Br infml)* **Mad cow disease** is another name for BSE. • *"Mad, bad and dangerous to know"* (Lady Caroline Lamb about the poet Byron, 1812) • *"Mad dogs and Englishmen go out in the mid-day sun"* (from the song *Mad Dogs and Englishmen* by Noel Coward, 1931) • Some people consider this use of 'mad' to be old-fashioned and offensive. • See also MADHOUSE; MADMAN.

mad·dened /ˈmæd·ᵊnd/ *adj literary* • *Maddened by grief, she refused to let go of his dead body.*

mad·ness /ˈmæd·nəs/ *n* [U] • *She felt as if she was sliding into madness* (=becoming mentally ill). • *"O! that way madness lies"* (Shakespeare, King Lear 3.4)

mad FOOLISH /mæd/ *adj* **madder**, **maddest** *esp. Br infml* extremely foolish or stupid; CRAZY • *You must be mad if you think such a plan could work.* • *Ben's got some mad scheme to cross the Atlantic in a canoe.* • *Some of the things Julie does are* **completely** *mad.* • *You're* **(stark) raving** *(Br also* **stark staring***) mad.* • *He's* **(as) mad as a hatter/(as) mad as a March hare**. • *"It's a mad, mad, mad, mad world"* (title of film, 1963) • See also MADCAP.

mad·ness /ˈmæd·nəs/ *n* [U] • *To begin a war would be absolute/***sheer** *madness.*

mad NOT CONTROLLED /mæd/ *adj* [before n; not gradable] (of activity) wild, fast or excited and not well controlled • *We made a mad* **dash** *for the train.* • *Before going on a business trip he gets into a mad* **panic**, *rushing round the house looking for things.* • *I can't stop to talk, I'm in a mad* **rush**.

mad·ly /ˈmæd·li/ *adv* • If you do something madly, you do it with great speed or in an uncontrolled way: *Just before the visitors arrived I rushed around madly tidying up.*

mad ANGRY /mæd/ *adj* **madder**, **maddest** *infml* very angry or annoyed • *(esp. Am) You'd better avoid him, he's mad as hell* **at/with** *you.* • *Bill's untidiness* **drives** *his girlfriend mad* (=makes her very angry).

mad·den *obj* /ˈmæd·ᵊn/ *v* [T] • *It maddens me to see how unfairly Jon has been treated.*

mad·den·ing /ˈmæd·ᵊn·ɪŋ/ *adj* • Something that is maddening is very annoying: *Her absent-mindedness can be maddening at times.*

mad·den·ing·ly /ˈmæd·ᵊn·ɪŋ·li/ *adv*

mad ENTHUSIASTIC /mæd/ *adj* **madder**, **maddest** *infml* very enthusiastic and interested • *Jane's mad* **about** *Italian food.* • *He's fashion mad, spends every penny on clothes.* • If you are mad **about** a person, you love or like them very much: *After twenty years of marriage they're still mad about each other.* • *(infml)* If you do something **like mad**, you do it very enthusiastically, quickly or a lot: *Since she decided to buy a car she's been saving like mad.* • *"Mad About the Boy (sometimes 'girl')"* (title of a Noel Coward song, 1932)

mad·ly /ˈmæd·li/ *adv* • *She said that she was madly* (=very much) **in love** *with him.* • *She won £5000 – I'm madly* (=very) *jealous.*

mad·am WOMAN /ˈmæd·əm/ *n* [U] a formal and polite way of speaking to a woman • *May I carry your cases for you, Madam?* [as form of address] • **Dear** Madam is the usual way of beginning a formal letter to a woman whose name you do not know. • *(infml dated disapproving)* If you call a young girl a madam, you mean that she behaves like an older person and expects others to obey her: *She's turning into* **a proper little** *madam.* • LP› **Titles and forms of address**

mad·am SEX /ˈmæd·ᵊm/ *n* [C] a woman who is in charge of a group of PROSTITUTES (=women who are paid to have sex) who all live or work in the same house

madcap /ˈmæd·kæp/ *adj* [before n] *dated* very foolish and (of a plan) not likely to succeed • *The madcap antics of the clowns made us laugh.* • *He has a madcap* **scheme** *to turn his house into a museum.*

made /meɪd/ *past simple and past participle of* MAKE • *He was wearing a suit made* **from** *pure silk.* • *On the bottom of the watch it said 'Swiss-made'.* • *The house was made* **of** *wood with an iron roof.* • *(infml)* If you **have (got) it made**, you are certain to be successful and rich: *He believed that if he married a rich woman he would have it made.* • If a piece of clothing is **made-to-measure** it is specially made to fit you exactly, rather than bought in a shop. • If you or your face is **made-up**, you are wearing make-up: *Sophie was heavily made-up, with dark red lipstick and green eye-shadow.* See MAKE-UP. • A story or report that is **made-up** has been invented and is not true: *She said she didn't like made-up stories.* See MAKE UP INVENT. • Do not confuse 'made of' and 'made from'. 'Made of X' implies that the X is still (visibly) present, so 'wine is made *from* grapes' not '*of* grapes'.

madhouse /ˈmæd·haʊs/ *n* [C] *pl* **madhouses** /ˈmæd ˌhaʊ·zɪz/ *infml (disapproving)* any place where there is a complete lack of order and control, or *(dated or literary)* a **mental hospital** • *(disapproving) With four small children running around, the place is a madhouse.* • *(disapproving) Several planes were cancelled, there were passengers and baggage everywhere – the airport lounge was like a madhouse.* • *(disapproving) He called government policy* **'the economics of the** *madhouse'.*

madman (*pl* **-men**), **madwoman** (*pl* **-women**) /ˈmæd·mən, -mæn, -ˌwʊm·ən/ *n* [C] *(disapproving)* someone who behaves in a very strange and uncontrolled way, or *(dated)* someone who is mentally ill • *(disapproving) He's a madman – I told him it wasn't safe to climb up that cliff.* • *(disapproving) He ran like a madman through the streets, shouting her name.* • *(disapproving) He* **drives** *like a madman* (=too fast).

Ma·don·na /£məˈdɒn·ə, $-ˈdɑː·nə/ *n* the mother of Jesus Christ, or a picture or statue that represents her • *a picture of* **the** *Madonna* [U] • *The painting depicts a Madonna and child.* [C]

madrigal /ˈmæd·rɪ·gᵊl/ *n* [C] a song written, esp. in the past, to be performed by several singers, each singing different notes

maelstrom /£ˈmeɪl·strɒm, $-strɑːm/ *n* [C] an area of water which moves with a very strong circular movement and sucks in anything that goes past, or *(fig.)* a situation in which there is great confusion, violence and destruction • *(fig.) The country is gradually being sucked into the maelstrom* **of** *civil war.*

maestro /£ˈmaɪ·strəʊ, $-stroʊ/ *n* [C] *pl* **maestros** or **maestri** /ˈmaɪ·stri/ a man who is very skilled at playing or CONDUCTING (=directing the performance of) music • *(humorous)* You can say "Music, maestro, (please)!" when you wish someone to start playing an instrument.

ma·fi·a /£ˈmæf·i·ə, £ˈmɑː·fi-/ *n* a criminal organization which began in Sicily and is active in Italy and the US • *The film was about* **the Mafia.** [U] • *This little village in Sicily is a Mafia stronghold.* • A mafia is also any close group of people who are involved in similar activities and who help and protect each other, sometimes to the disadvantage of others: *She calls her sister's friends the Cambridge mafia – they are all in computing and find work for each other.* [C]

ma·fi·o·so /£ˌmæf·iˈəʊ·səʊ, $ˌmɑː·fiˈoʊ·soʊ/ *n* [C] *pl* **mafiosi** /£ˌmæf·iˈəʊ·siː, $ˌmɑː·fiˈoʊ·siː/ • *Over one hundred mafiosi* (=members of the Mafia) *have been extradited to the United States in the last month, where they are expected to stand trial for a series of drug-related crimes.*

mag·a·zine BOOK /ˌmæg·əˈziːn/, *infml* **mag** /mæg/ *n* [C] a type of thin book with large pages and a paper cover which contains articles and photographs and is published every week or month • *She has written articles for several women's magazines.* • *He stood in the supermarket checkout queue, idly inspecting the magazine* **rack.** • *The shop sells blue movies and* **dirty** (=sexually exciting) *magazines.* • Ⓘ Ⓟ (RUS) Ⓢ

mag·a·zine GUN PART /ˌmæg·əˈziːn/ *n* [C] a part of a gun in which CARTRIDGES (=tubes containing an explosive substance) are stored, or a building in which explosives, weapons and supplies are kept • Ⓘ Ⓟ (RUS) Ⓢ

magenta /məˈdʒen·tə/ *adj* [not gradable] of a dark purplish red colour

maggot /ˈmæg·ət/ *n* [C] a creature like a very small WORM which later develops into a FLY (=a small insect with two wings) and is found in decaying meat and other foods

ma·gi /ˈmeɪ·dʒaɪ/ *pl n* **the Magi** in the Bible, the three men, thought to be kings or ASTRONOMERS, who followed a star to visit the baby Jesus Christ with presents. They are also called the Three Kings or the Three Wise Men.

mag·ic IMAGINARY POWER /ˈmædʒ·ɪk/ *n* [U], *adj* [not gradable] (of) the use of special powers to make things happen which would usually be impossible, such as in stories for children • *The group are known for their belief in witchcraft and magic.* • *The witch put a magic* **spell** *on the prince and turned him into a frog.* • *McKenna insists that there is nothing magic about hypnotism.* • **As if by** *magic/* **Like** *magic, the car changes into a boat when it hits the water.* • Magic is also (the skill of) performing tricks to entertain people, such as making things appear and disappear and pretending to cut someone in half: *He's a comedian who also does magic.* ○ *I'll show you a magic* **trick.** • Magic also means happening in an unusual or unexpected way, esp. easily or quickly: *The speakers stressed they had no magic* **solution** *for the refugees' plight.* ○ *The trainer said, "There's no magic* **formula** *– just lots of hard work."* • In stories, a **magic carpet** is a special CARPET that you can sit on as it flies through the air. • A **magic wand** is a small stick used by people who perform tricks for entertainment, or *(fig.)* is any quick and easy solution: *He warned that he had no magic wand to make everything all right.* • A **magic word** is a word said by someone performing a trick to help it work successfully: *I'll just say the magic word and the rabbit will disappear – Abracadabra!* ○ *(fig.) Like most mothers, she always asks her small children "What is the magic word?" when they haven't said 'please' or 'thank you'.* • Ⓙ

mag·i·cal /ˈmædʒ·ɪ·kəl/ *adj* • Something that is magical is produced by or uses magic: *Diamonds were once thought to have magical* **powers.**

mag·i·cal·ly /ˈmædʒ·ɪ·kli/ *adv*

magician /məˈdʒɪʃ·ən/ *n* [C] • A magician is a person who has magic powers in stories, or who performs tricks as entertainment: *Merlin was the magician in the stories of King Arthur and the Knights of the Round Table.* ○ *There'll be a magician and a hypnotist at the party.*

mag·ic SPECIAL QUALITY /ˈmædʒ·ɪk/ *n* [U], *adj* (having) a special exciting quality that makes something very different from ordinary things • *Although the film was made fifty years ago, it has lost none of its magic.* • *Can you ever forget the magic* **moment** *of your first kiss?* • *The magic of Alexander's name still lingers in mountain valleys where men swear they are descended from his soldiers.* • *The visitor suddenly catches a magic glimpse of the pyramids between tall buildings.* • Ⓙ

mag·ic /ˈmædʒ·ɪk/ *exclamation* • *(Br dated infml)* If you describe something as magic, you mean that it is very good and you like it very much: *"You're having a party? Magic!"*

mag·i·cal /ˈmædʒ·ɪ·kəl/ *adj* • *We walked home hand in hand through the magical moonlight.*

mag·i·cal·ly /ˈmædʒ·ɪ·kli/ *adv*

ma·gis·ter·i·al /£ˌmædʒ·ɪˈstɪə·ri·əl, $-ˈstɪr·i-/ *adj fml* having or seeming to have complete authority • *She has a magisterial way of dismissing her opponents.* • *The book has been praised as a magisterial study of Irish history.*

mag·i·strate /ˈmædʒ·ɪ·streɪt, -strət/ *n* [C] a person who acts as a judge in a law court dealing with crimes which are not serious • *He is to* **appear before** *the magistrates today.* • *In this decade, many more women were appointed to the magistrates'* **bench** (=became magistrates). • *Greenway appeared at Bow Street Magistrates'* **Court** *to face seven charges of accepting bribes.* • LP› **Law**

mag·i·stra·cy /ˈmædʒ·ɪ·strə·si/ *n* [U] *specialized* • A magistracy is the position of being a magistrate. • The magistracy means magistrates considered as a group.

mag·ma /ˈmæg·mə/ *n* [U] hot liquid rock found just below the surface of the earth

mag·na·nim·ous /mægˈnæn·ɪ·məs/ *adj fml* very generous and honourable, esp. towards an enemy • *Arsenal's manager was magnanimous in victory, and praised the losing team.*

mag·na·nim·ous·ly /mægˈnæn·ɪ·mə·sli/ *adv fml* • *"The best man won," George said magnanimously, conceding victory.*

mag·na·nim·i·ty /£ˌmæg·nəˈnɪm·ɪ·ti, $-ə·t̬i/ *n* [U] *fml* • *The soldiers have promised to treat the hostages that they capture with magnanimity* (=generosity and kindness).

mag·nate /ˈmæg·nət/ *n* [C] a person who is very rich and successful in business or industry • *He was once a well-known* **shipping** *magnate.*

mag·ne·sia /mægˈniː·ʒə/ *n* [U] a white substance used in stomach medicines

mag·ne·si·um /mægˈniː·zi·əm/ *n* [U] a silver-white metal element that burns very brightly and is used in making FIREWORKS (=explosions producing coloured patterns for entertainment) • *There was a blinding flash in the sky like a magnesium flare.*

mag·net /ˈmæg·nət/ *n* [C] an object that is able both to attract iron and steel objects and also push them away • *The physics teacher showed them the pattern that iron filings make when they were sprinkled over some paper covering a magnet.* • *The fridge door is covered with colourful* **refrigerator** *(Br and Aus usually* **fridge**) *magnets* (=decorative magnets which are placed on steel doors). • *(fig.) The United States has always acted as a magnet* **for/to** (=has strongly attracted towards itself) *people seeking fame and fortune.*

mag·net·ic /£mægˈnet·ɪk, $-ˈnet̬-/ *adj* • *An iron bar can be made magnetic* (=able to attract iron and steel objects) *by wrapping wire around it and passing an electric current through the wire.* • You can describe a person as magnetic if they have a character or appearance that attracts a lot of people to them: *He is the most magnetic male dancer in the Royal Ballet.* • A **magnetic field** is an area around a magnet or something magnetic, in which its power to attract objects to itself can be felt: *Bees navigate with the help of magnetic fields.* • A **magnetic head** is the same as a HEAD DEVICE. • **Magnetic north/south** is the direction towards north or south which the pointer of a COMPASS (=a device for finding direction) shows. • The Earth's **magnetic poles** are the two points, near the North and South POLES (=points at the most northern and southern parts of the earth), which the pointer of a COMPASS (=an instrument for finding direction) shows as north and south. • **Magnetic resonance imaging** *(abbreviation* **MRI**) is a medical method which doctors use to look at the inside of a person's body: *Magnetic resonance imaging provides a better picture than traditional X-rays of the body's internal organs and tissues.* • **Magnetic tape** is a plastic strip covered with a magnetic substance on which sound, images or computer information can be recorded.

mag·net·i·sm /£ˈmæg·nə·tɪ·zəm, $-t̬ɪ-/ *n* [U] • Magnetism is the power that some objects have to attract others towards them or force them away: *An electric current produces magnetism in a conductor.* ○ *(fig.) The sheer magnetism* (=ability to attract people's complete attention) *of her singing performance cannot be matched.*

mag·net·ize *obj, Br and Aus usually* **-ise** /ˈmæg·nə·taɪz/ *v* [T] • If you magnetize an object you cause it to become magnetic: *Each worker has to carry a magnetized plastic entry card.* • *(fig.) I was magnetized by his beautiful voice* (=it attracted my attention completely).

mag·ni·fi·cent /mægˈnɪf·ɪ·sənt/ *adj* very good, beautiful or to be admired • *They live in a magnificent Tudor house in* *the country.* • *This book is a magnificent piece of writing.* • *You look magnificent in that outfit.* • *"The Magnificent Seven"* (film title, 1960)

mag·ni·fi·cent·ly /mæg'nɪf·ɪ·sᵊnt·li/ *adv* • *It is a magnificently theatrical performance.* • *She seems to be coping magnificently in a difficult situation.*

mag·ni·fi·cence /mæg'nɪf·ɪ·sᵊnts/ *n* [U] • *I am always impressed by the splendour and magnificence of the pyramids/the Taj Mahal/Hampton Court.*

mag·ni·fy *obj* /'mæg·nɪ·faɪ/ *v* [T] to make (something) look larger than it is, esp. by looking at it through a specially cut piece of glass • *Although your skin looks smooth, when magnified it is full of bumps and holes.* • *(disapproving)* If you magnify a problem, you make it bigger and more important than it really is: *The hot summer magnified the racial tensions in the community.* • A **magnifying glass** is a piece of curved glass which makes objects look larger than they are: *He uses a magnifying glass to read the tiny print.*

mag·ni·fi·ca·tion /ˌmæg·nɪ·fɪ'keɪ·ʃᵊn/ *n* [U] • Magnification is the process of making something look bigger than it is, for example by using a magnifying glass: *Magnification of the leaf allows us to see it in detail.* • *These binoculars have x10 magnification* (= they magnify 10 times).

mag·ni·tude /£'mæg·nɪ·tjuːd, $-tuːd/ *n* [U] the large size or importance (of something) • *They don't seem to grasp the magnitude of the problem.*

mag·no·li·a /£mæg'nəʊ·li·ə, $-'noʊ-/ *n* [C] a type of tree with large, usually white or pink flowers

mag·num [WINE] /'mæg·nəm/ *n* [C] 1·5 litres of wine, or a bottle containing this • *She won a magnum* **of champagne**.

mag·num [GUN] /'mæg·nəm/ *n* [C] *trademark* a type of gun with bullets which are fired with more power than is usual for a gun of that size • *a ·357 magnum*

mag·num o·pus /£ˌmæg·nəm'əʊ·pəs, $-'oʊ-/ *n* [U] *fml* the most important piece of work done by a writer or artist • *Picasso's Guernica is considered by many to be his magnum opus.*

mag·pie /'mæg·paɪ/ *n* [C] a bird with black and white feathers and a long tail • *Magpies are attracted to small shiny objects which they carry away to their nests.* • A person who is described as a magpie likes to collect or use many different types of objects, styles, ideas, etc.: *He's a magpie of a singer, borrowing from Elvis, punk rock and classical music.*

ma·ha·ra·ja /ˌmɑː·hə'rɑː·dʒə/, **ma·ha·ra·jah** *n* [C] in the past, the male ruler of an Indian STATE (= part of a country which partly governs itself)

ma·ha·ra·ni /ˌmɑː·hə'rɑː·ni/ *n* [C] a female MAHARAJA or the wife of a MAHARAJA

mah–jong /£ˌmɑː'dʒɒŋ, $-'dʒɑːŋ/, **mah–jongg** *n* [U] a Chinese game in which players pick up and put down small painted pieces of wood or other material until they have the combination they want in order to win

ma·hog·an·y /£mə'hɒg·ᵊn·i, $-'hɑː·gᵊn-/ *n* [U] a dark red-brown wood used to make furniture • *She sat behind a handsome mahogany desk.*

maid [SERVANT] /meɪd/ *n* [C] a woman who works as a servant in a hotel or in someone's home • *In the beach resort, the apartments and villas have daily maid* **service** (= a woman cleans, tidies beds, etc. every day). • *In California many illegal immigrants work as maids, nannies and gardeners.*

maid [GIRL] /meɪd/ *n* [C] *literary or old use* a girl or young woman who is not married, or has not had sex • *Who is that pretty maid?* • *(esp. Am)* A **maid of honour** is the most important BRIDESMAID at a marriage ceremony.

maid·en [WOMAN] /'meɪ·dᵊn/ *n* [C] *literary* a girl or young woman • *In the story, the prince woos and wins the* **fair** (= beautiful) *maiden.* • A woman's **maiden name** is the family name she has before she gets married: *It is becoming more common for a British woman to keep her maiden name after getting married.* • A **maiden aunt** is an aunt who is not married and is no longer young. • *"Marrying left your maiden name disused"* (Philip Larkin in the poem *Maiden Name*, 1955)

maid·en [FIRST] /'meɪ·dᵊn/ *adj* [before n; not gradable] of or about the first of its type • *The Titanic sank on her maiden* **voyage**. • In Britain, a **maiden speech** is the first formal speech made by a Member of Parliament in the House of Commons or by a member of the House of Lords.

maid·en (o·ver) /'meɪ·dᵊn/ *n* [C] (in cricket) an OVER (= series of six throws) in which no RUNS (= points) are scored • *Warne finished the morning session with two wickets and seven maidens from the 15 overs he bowled, at a cost of only eleven runs.*

maid·en·head /'meɪ·dᵊn·hed/ *n* [C] *old use or literary* a HYMEN

mail [POST] /meɪl/, *esp. Br* **post** *n* [U] the letters and parcels which are transported and delivered by post, or the postal system itself • *She spent the morning reading and answering her mail.* • *All of our customers will be contacted* **by mail**. • *The book came* **in** *yesterday's mail.* • *Some strange things get sent* **through the** *mail.* • Mail is also used in the name of some newspapers: *the Daily Mail* • **Mail carrier** (also **letter carrier**) is *Am for* POSTMAN. • **Mail order** is a way of buying goods in which you choose what you want, usually from a CATALOGUE (= a special book showing what goods are available), and it is sent to you: *I often buy clothes* **by** *mail order.* ○ *They run a successful mail order firm.* • **Mail slot** is *Am for* LETTERBOX. • [PIC] **Doors** Ⓣ

mail *obj esp. Am* /meɪl/, *esp. Br* **post** *v* [T] • *She mailed it* (= sent it by the postal system) *last week but it still hasn't arrived.* • *I promised to mail him the article/mail the article* **to** *him.* [+ two objects] • A **mailing list** is a list of names and addresses kept by an organization so that it can send information and advertisements to the people on the list: *I asked to be put on their mailing list.*

mail [COVERING] /meɪl/ *n* [U] See **chain mail** at CHAIN [RINGS] • Ⓣ

mail·bag /'meɪl·bæg/ *n* [C] a large strong bag used by the post office for transporting and carrying letters and parcels • A person's or organization's mailbag (*Br* **postbag**) is all the letters they receive at one time or on one subject: *Since the controversial programme was broadcast, the BBC's mailbag has been bulging.*

mail·box /£'meɪl·bɒks, $-bɑːks/ *n* [C] (in the US) a box outside a person's house where letters are delivered, or a POSTBOX

Mail·gram /'meɪl·græm/ *n* [C] *Am trademark for* TELEMESSAGE

mail·man (*pl* **-men**) /'meɪl·mən/ *n* [C] *Am for* POSTMAN

mail·shot *esp. Br* /£'meɪl·ʃɒt, $-ʃɑːt/, *Am and Aus usually* **mass mail·ing** *n* [C] the posting of advertising or similar material to a lot of people at one time

maim *(obj)* /meɪm/ *v* to injure (a person) so severely that a part of their body will no longer work as it should • *Many children have been maimed for life by these bombs.* [T] • *They accused their enemies of killing, maiming and laying waste.* [I]

main [MOST IMPORTANT] /meɪn/ *adj* [before n; not gradable] larger, more important or more influential than others of the same type • *The main reason I don't like him is that he is boring.* • *The main* **thing** *is that you shouldn't worry.* • In grammar, main can also be used to refer to a clause which forms part of a sentence but can also form a separate sentence. • The **main course** is the largest or most important part of a meal in which there are different parts served separately: *It was a three-course meal, with stuffed tomatoes as a starter and salmon as the main course.* • *(Am and Aus infml)* The **main drag** is the largest or most important road in a town: *There's a great little restaurant just off the main drag in Maplewood.* • A **main line** is an important railway route between large towns or cities: *the main line between Belfast and Dublin* ○ *Three main-line railway stations were closed because of bomb threats.* • A **main road** is a large road which goes from one town to another: *Stick to the main roads and you won't get lost.* ○ *They live on the main road out of town.* • **Main street** is *Am for* **high street**. • The **main verb** in a clause is the verb that carries the meaning, esp. as compared with any auxiliary verbs that go with it: *In 'I should have been studying', 'studying' is the main verb.*

main [PIPE] /meɪn/ *n* [C] a large pipe which carries water or gas, or a wire carrying electricity, from one place to another, to which a house can be connected • *a* **gas** *main* • *The severe cold caused a* **water** *main to burst and flood the street.*

mains /meɪnz/ *pl n Br* • The mains is the system of pipes or wires which carry water or electricity into a house, or the pipes which carry SEWAGE (= waste water and human waste) away from a house: *The house isn't* **on** *the mains.* ○ *They bought a house with no mains supply.* ○ *They have been lacking mains electricity for three weeks now.* • The mains is also the place at which outside pipes or wires carrying water, electricity, etc. connect with the system inside a house or building: *Switch off the electricity at the mains before starting work.*

main·frame /ˈmeɪn·freɪm/ *n* [C] *specialized* a very large powerful computer with a lot of memory which many people can use at the same time

main·land /ˈmeɪn·lænd/ *n* [U] the main part of a country or continent, not including the islands around it • *He lives on an island off Scotland, but travels to* **the** *mainland once a month.* • *She is planning to hitch-hike through mainland Europe.*

main·line *(obj)* /ˈmeɪn·laɪn/ *v infml* to INJECT (=use a needle to put) (drugs) directly into the blood • *Several of her friends were mainlining heroin.* [T] • *Even young children were smoking crack or mainlining.* [I]

main·ly /ˈmeɪn·li/ *adv* [not gradable] usually or to a large degree • *I mainly go to bed around midnight.* • *The group is made up of mainly young people.* • *They argued that the tax will mainly benefit the rich.*

main /meɪn/ *n* [U] • If something is true **in the main** it is usually or mostly true: *Her friends are lawyers in the main.*

main·spring /ˈmeɪn·sprɪŋ/ *n* [C] the most important reason for something; the thing that makes something else happen • *Greed was* **the** *mainspring* **of** *his success.*

main·stay /ˈmeɪn·steɪ/ *n* [C] the most important part of something, providing support for everything else • *Although she is an actress,* **the** *mainstay* **of** *her income comes from cleaning other people's houses.* • *The white blouse will be* **the** *mainstay* **of** *your wardrobe this summer.* • *The BBC World Service was our mainstay while we were travelling abroad.* • *We need to restore the aviation industry* **as a** *mainstay of our economy.*

main·stream /ˈmeɪn·striːm/ *n* [U] **the mainstream** the way of life or set of beliefs accepted by most people • *The new law should allow more disabled people to enter the mainstream* **of** *American life.*

main·stream /ˈmeɪn·striːm/ *adj* • *This is the director's first mainstream Hollywood film.*

main·tain *obj* CONTINUE TO HAVE /meɪnˈteɪn/ *v* [T] to continue to have; keep in existence, or not allow to become less • *Despite living in different countries, the two families have maintained close links.* • *The film has maintained its position as the critics' favourite for another year.* • *(Am infml) It's not easy to maintain your* **cool** *when there's a riot going on.*

main·ten·ance /ˈmeɪn·tɪ·nənts/ *n* [U] • *the maintenance of living standards* • See also **maintenance** at MAINTAIN PRESERVE, MAINTAIN PROVIDE.

main·tain *obj* PRESERVE /meɪnˈteɪn/ *v* [T] to keep (a road, machine, building, etc.) in good condition • *A large country house costs a lot to maintain.* • *The roads around the town have been very poorly maintained.*

main·ten·ance /ˈmeɪn·tɪ·nənts/ *n* [U] • *Old houses need a lot of maintenance.* • *There are thorough maintenance checks on each plane before take-off.* • *The magazine offers tips on cutting your house maintenance costs.* • See also **maintenance** at MAINTAIN CONTINUE TO HAVE, MAINTAIN PROVIDE.

main·tain *obj* PROVIDE /meɪnˈteɪn/ *v* [T] to provide (someone) with food and whatever is necessary for them to live on • *They barely earn enough to maintain themselves and their four children.*

main·ten·ance /ˈmeɪn·tɪ·nənts/ *n* [U] • Maintenance is the money that a person must pay by law in order to support someone: *He refused to pay maintenance for his three children.* • *(Br and Aus)* A **maintenance order** is an order made by a court of law that a person must pay maintenance. • See also **maintenance** at MAINTAIN CONTINUE TO HAVE, MAINTAIN PRESERVE.

main·tain *(obj)* EXPRESS /meɪnˈteɪn/ *v* to express firmly your belief that something is true • *Throughout his prison sentence Dunn has always maintained his innocence.* [T] • *He maintained* **that** *he had never seen the woman before.* [+ *that* clause] • *The manufacturers of the drug still maintain the substance is safe.* [+ *(that)* clause]

mais·on·ette /ˌmeɪ·zəˈnet/ *n* [C] *Br* a small apartment on two levels which is part of a larger building but has its own entrance

mai·tre d' (ho·tel) /£ˌmet·rəˈdiː, $ˌmeɪ·t̬ər-/ *n* [C] *fml* the person in charge of a restaurant or of the people who bring food to your table in a restaurant

maize /meɪz/, *Am and Aus usually* **corn**, *Am also* **In·di·an corn** *n* [U] a tall plant grown in many parts of the world for its yellow seeds which are eaten as a basic food (also **sweetcorn**), made into flour or fed to animals • *Tortilla bread is traditionally made from maize/maize flour.* • PIC **Cereals**

maj·es·tic /məˈdʒes·tɪk/ *adj* beautiful, powerful or causing great admiration and respect • *The majestic Montana scenery will leave you breathless.*

maj·es·ti·cal·ly /məˈdʒes·tɪ·kli/ *adv* • *The white cliffs rise majestically from the sea.*

maj·es·ty /ˈmædʒ·ə·sti/ *n* [U] • If something has majesty, it causes admiration and respect for its beauty: *This music has majesty, power and passion.* ○ *The photograph captures the sunset* **in all** *its majesty* (= shows its great beauty). • See also MAJESTY.

Maj·es·ty /ˈmædʒ·ə·sti/ *n* [C] the title used to speak to or about a king or queen • *I was invited to tea with* **Her** *Majesty the Queen.* • **their** *Majesties, the King and Queen of Spain* • *The performance begins at 8.30,* **(Your)** *Majesty.* [as form of address] • See also **majesty** at MAJESTIC.

ma·jor IMPORTANT /£ˈmeɪ·dʒər, $-dʒɚ/ *adj* [before n; not gradable] more important, bigger or more serious than others of the same type • *All of her major plays have been translated into English.* • *Sugar is a major cause of tooth decay.* • *There are two problems with this situation, one major, one minor.* • *Citrus fruits are a major source of vitamin C.* • *There has been a major change in attitudes recently.* • *The United States is a major influence in the United Nations.* • Compare MINOR UNIMPORTANT.

ma·jor OFFICER /£ˈmeɪ·dʒər, $-dʒɚ/ *n* [C] an officer of middle rank in the British, US and many other armed forces such as the US Air Force • *Her father was a major in the Scots Guards.* • *I met Major Jones last year.* • *Thank you, Major Jones.* [as form of address] • Major is the rank between captain and lieutenant-colonel. • A **major-general** is an officer of high rank in the British Army, US Army and many other armed forces such as the US Air Force. Major-general is the rank between brigadier(-general) and lieutenant-general.

ma·jor SPECIAL SUBJECT /£ˈmeɪ·dʒər, $-dʒɚ/ *n* [C] *Am and Aus* the most important subject that a college or university student is studying, or the student himself or herself • *What is your major, English or French?* • *She was a philosophy major at an Ivy League college.*

ma·jor in *obj v prep* [T] *Am and Aus* • *She majored in philosophy at Harvard.*

ma·jor MUSIC /£ˈmeɪ·dʒər, $-dʒɚ/ *adj specialized* (of music) based on a SCALE (= range of eight notes) in which there is a whole TONE (= difference between two notes) between the second and third notes and a half tone between the third and fourth notes • *the key of C major* • *a concerto in A major* [after n] • Compare MINOR MUSIC. • PIC **Music**

ma·jor·do·mo /£ˌmeɪ·dʒəˈdəʊ·məʊ, $-dʒɚˈdoʊ·moʊ/ *n* [C] *pl* **majordomos** *(fml or dated)* the most important servant in a house, in charge of the other servants, or *(Am)* a person whose job is to make arrangements or organize things for other people • *(Am) Can you ask the majordomo in the hotel to get tickets for the tennis match?*

ma·jor·ette /£ˌmeɪ·dʒərˈet, $-dʒəˈret/, **drum ma·jor·ette** *n* [C] a young woman or girl who wears a uniform and makes a pattern of movements with a BATON (= stick) by spinning it and throwing it into the air, as part of a group of girls who do this or as the leader of a musical group

ma·jo·ri·ty NUMBER /£məˈdʒɒr·ə·ti, $-ˈdʒɑːr·ə·t̬i/ *n* the larger number or part of something • *The majority* **of** *the employees have university degrees.* [U] • *A large majority* **of** *people approve of the death sentence.* [U] • *In Britain women are* **in the/a** *majority* (= there are more of them than men). [U] • In an election, a majority is the difference in the number of votes between the winning person or group and the one that comes second: *The Socialists won by a* **narrow/large** *majority.* [C] • **Majority rule** is the system of giving the largest group in a particular place or area the power to make decisions for everyone: *Government by majority rule can be a threat to minority rights.* • Compare MINORITY.

ma·jo·ri·ty AGE /£məˈdʒɒr·ə·ti, $-ˈdʒɑːr·ə·t̬i/ *n* [U] *specialized* the age when you legally become an adult • *the* **age of** *majority* • *She will inherit her father's estate when she* **reaches** *her majority.*

make *obj* PRODUCE /meɪk/ *v* [T] *past* **made** /meɪd/ to produce (something), esp. using a particular substance or material • *He used the chicken bones to make soup.* • *She makes all her own clothes because she doesn't have money to buy them.* • *He made us some coffee./He made some coffee* **for** *us.* [+ two objects] • *The pot is made* **to** (= produced in such a way that it will) *withstand high temperatures.* • *Do you know a company which makes filing cabinets?* • *The label on* *the box said 'Made in Taiwan'.* • *Butter is made* **out of/from** *milk* (=Milk is used to produce something else – butter.) • *The earrings are made* **of** *gold* (=are gold). • *Her new trainer promises to make an olympic athlete* **of** *her.* • *The recycled paper will be made* **into** *cardboard boxes* (=changed into cardboard and used to produce boxes). • *They've made the attic* **into** (=changed it into) *a spare room.* • To make a film or television programme is to DIRECT it (=decide and control how it is performed), PRODUCE it (=control its organization and money) or act in it: *John Huston made some great films.* ○ *The film was made by Goldcrest Productions.* ○ *Why did Garbo make no films after 1941?* • If you **make a day/night/evening/weekend of it**, you decide to lengthen an activity or combine a series of activities so that they last for the whole of that particular period of time: *Let's make a evening of it and catch the last train home.* • If you **make do** you use something, even if it might not be enough or what you wanted: *Can you make do* **with** *a fiver for now and I'll give you the rest tomorrow?* • *The boss has the power to* **make or break** (=cause success or complete failure for) *your career.* • *I try to* **make time** (=be certain there is some time when I am not busy) *to read a story to my children.* • *The 1500 metres race next week will be a chance for her to show* **what** *she's* **(really) made of** (=how strong, brave, clever, etc. she really is). • If you say that someone is **made of money** you mean that they are very rich.

make /meɪk/ *n* [C] • A make is a type of product or the name of the company which made it: *The newer makes of computer are much more user-friendly.* ○ *The shop sells well-known makes like Sony and Panasonic.* • *(disapproving)* If you are **on the make** you are trying very hard to obtain more money and power.

mak·er /£ˈmeɪ·kəʳ, $-kɚ/ *n* [C] • *Bloggs Brothers is the largest maker of fast-food products in the UK.* • *The makers of the film will want to see a decent return on their investment.* • *(esp. Br) That's a nice bike – what's the name of the maker* (=the firm that produced it)*?* • People sometimes refer to God as their Maker. • See also BOOKMAKER; HOLIDAYMAKER; HOMEMAKER; ICEMAKER; KINGMAKER; MATCHMAKER; NOISEMAKER; PACEMAKER [RUNNER]; PACEMAKER [DEVICE]; PEACEMAKER; TROUBLEMAKER.

–mak·er /£-ˌmeɪ·kəʳ, $-kɚ/ *combining form* • A -maker is a person or machine which makes the stated thing: *a film-maker* ○ *a dressmaker* ○ *a watchmaker* ○ *car-makers* ○ *policy-makers* ○ *a coffee/tea-maker* ○ *an ice-maker*

mak·ers /£ˈmeɪ·kəz, $-kɚz/ *pl n esp. Br* • *That's a nice bike – what's the name of the makers* (=the company that produced it)*?*

mak·ing /ˈmeɪ·kɪŋ/ *n* [U] • *The making of the cake will take a good hour.* • Making is often used as a combining form: *dressmaking /furniture-making* • If a bad situation is **of** your **own making** it is completely your fault: *The problems she has with that child are of her own making.* • *By the time he was 12 he was obviously a chef* **in the making** (=he seemed likely to become a chef). • *The book was several years* **in the making** (=took several years to produce). • If something is **the making of** someone it develops in them good qualities and characteristics which would otherwise not have developed: *Five years in the army – that'll be the making of him!* • See also **makings** at MAKE [BE OR BECOME].

make *obj* [CAUSE] /meɪk/ *v* [T] *past* **made** /meɪd/ to cause (something) • *The cats have made a terrible mess in the kitchen.* • *The bullet made a hole right through his chest.* • *Don't make any noise.* • *The wind is making my eyes water.* [+ obj + infinitive without *to*] • *What made you change your mind?* [+ obj + infinitive without *to*] • *Just seeing Woody Allen's face is enough to make me laugh.* [+ obj + infinitive without *to*] • *The photograph makes me look about 80!* [+ obj + infinitive without *to*] • *He makes himself look ridiculous in that suit.* [+ obj + infinitive without *to*] • [LP] **Get: verbs meaning 'cause'**

make *obj* [CAUSE TO BE] /meɪk/ *v* [T] *past* **made** /meɪd/ to cause to be, to become or to appear as • *It's the good weather that makes Spain such a popular tourist destination.* [+ obj + n] • *She had to shout to make herself heard above the sound of the music.* [+ obj + v-*ed*] • *I can make myself understood in French* (=I can speak it well enough for French people to understand me). [+ obj + v-*ed*] • *They went up to the Ambassador and made themselves known (to her)* (=told her who they were). [+ obj + v-*ed*] • *The company accounts have not yet been made public.* [+ obj + adj] • *The book's advertised as "navigation made* **easy**.*"* [+ obj + adj] • *The President has made Lloyd Bentsen his Secretary of the Treasury* (=given him this job). [+ obj + n] • *I'll have a steak – no, make* **that** (=change it to) *chicken.* [+ obj + n] • If you **make certain/sure** of something you find out whether it is really so or you do something so that it will happen: *I'll just make certain I've turned the oven off.* ○ *Make sure* **(that)** *we have enough drink for the party.* ○ *Make sure you're* (=You should be) *home by midnight.* ○ *Jones made sure of his place in the side with three fine goals.* ○ *I think I locked the door but I'll go back and check* **just** *to make sure.* • [LP] **Get: verbs meaning 'cause'**

make *obj* [PERFORM] /meɪk/ *v* [T] *past* **made** /meɪd/ to perform (an action) • *I must make a call to* (=telephone) *my office.* • *Somebody has made a donation of* (=given) *£1 million to Oxfam.* • *I need to make a trip to the shops.* • *On foot they could only make* (=travel) *about 20 miles a day.* • *We must make a* **decision** (=decide) *by tomorrow.* • *You're not making any* **effort** *– try harder.* • *(Br and Aus) The builders made* **an** *excellent* **job of** (=did good work on) *the house.* • *Someone has made* **a mistake/an error**. • *The teacher's comment was, "Jane is making good* **progress** *in science."* • *She has made a* **request** *for a new car* (=she has requested one). • *We made an* **offer** *of £150 000 for the house.* • *She made a short* **speech**. • *Shall we make* **a start** *on* (=Shall we start) *the work?* • *Can I make a* **suggestion** (=suggest something)*?* • *We made good* **time** (=It took us a short time) *getting across town.* • *There's a drunk at the door making* **trouble** (=being annoying and refusing to go away). • If you make **way/space/room** for something or someone you move, or move other things, so that there is space for them. • *(fml) Just as we* **made to** (=were about to) *leave the captain called us back.* • *He* **made as if to** *speak* (=He seemed to be about to speak). • *(Am not standard) She* **made like** *she was about to leave* (=seemed to be about to leave), *but then stayed for hours.* • *(Am not standard) Stop* **making like** (=behaving as if) *you know everything, okay?* • [LP] **Do: verbs meaning 'perform'**

make *obj* [FORCE] /meɪk/ *v* [T] *past* **made** /meɪd/ to force (someone or something) to do something • *The vet put something down the dog's throat to make it vomit.* [+ obj + infinitive without *to*] • *The prisoners are made* **to** *dig holes and fill them in again.* [passive + obj + *to* infinitive]

make [BE OR BECOME] /meɪk/ *v* [L only + n] *past* **made** /meɪd/ to be or become (something), esp. by having the necessary characteristics • *I don't think he will ever make a (good) lawyer.* • *He's a competent enough officer, but I doubt he'll ever make* (=become a) *general.* • *It's a story that would make a great film.* • *She decided the back room would make a good study.* • *Champagne and caviar make a wonderful combination.* • *The story makes fascinating reading.* • If people or things make a particular pattern they are arranged in that way: *Let's make a circle.* ○ *Those seven bright stars make the shape of a saucepan.*

mak·ings /ˈmeɪ·kɪŋz/ *pl n* • *She* **has the** *makings* **of** (=has the character and skills needed to become) *a great violinist.* • *I think the plan* **has all the** *makings* **of** (=is likely to be) *a disaster.* • See also **making** at MAKE [PRODUCE].

make [TOTAL] /meɪk/ *v past* **made** /meɪd/ to produce (a total) when added together • *12 and 12 make 24.* [L only + n] • *Today's earthquake makes five since the beginning of the year.* [L only + n] • *I've got 29 different teapots in my collection – if I buy this one that'll make it 30.* [T + obj + n]

make *obj* [CALCULATE] /meɪk/ *v* [T + obj + n] *past* **made** /meɪd/ to calculate as • *How much do you make the total?* • *I make the answer* **(to be)** *105·6.* • *What do you make the time?/What time do you make it?* (=What time do you think or know that it is?)

make *obj* [EARN] /meɪk/ *v* [T] *past* **made** /meɪd/ to earn or get • *She makes $100 000 a year as a doctor.* • *How do you make* **a living** *as a painter?* • *The company has made huge profits/losses.* • *He's very good at making new friends.* • *The government has made itself too many enemies.* [+ two objects]

make *obj* [ARRIVE] /meɪk/ *v* [T] *past* **made** /meɪd/ *infml* to arrive at or reach, esp. successfully • *She made* **(it to)** *the airport just in time to catch her plane.* • *He made* **it to** *the bed and then collapsed.* • *Could you make a meeting at 8 am?/Could you make 8 am for the meeting?* • *She's very ambitious but, I don't think she'll ever really* **make it (to the top)** (=be very successful). • If you **make the grade** you are proved good enough for a job or team or are successful at something.

make *obj* [PERFECT] /meɪk/ *v* [T] *past* **made** /meɪd/ *infml* to cause to be perfect • *Those little bows round the neck*

really *make the dress!* • *"Go ahead, make my day"* (Clint Eastwood in the film *Dirty Harry*, 1971)

make *obj* [HAVE SEX] /meɪk/ *v* [T] *past* **made** /meɪd/ *Am and Aus slang* to have sex with • *He tried to make her after the party last night.* • To have sex with someone can also be described as **making it with** them. • See also MAKE OUT [HAVE SEX].

make /meɪk/ *n* [U] *Am slang* • If you **put the make on** someone you try to have sex with them.

make a·way with *obj v adv prep* [T] *dated* to kill (a person, esp. yourself), or to steal • See also DO AWAY WITH.

make for *obj* [GO TOWARDS] *v prep* [T no passive] to go in the direction of (a place) • *When you leave London, make for Birmingham.* • See also MAKE TOWARDS.

make for *obj* [MAKE POSSIBLE] *v prep* [T no passive] to result in or make possible • *Having faster computers would make for a more efficient system.*

make *obj* **of** *obj* [UNDERSTAND] *v prep* [T; often in negatives and questions] to find meaning in, understand or have an opinion about (something or someone) • *Can you make anything of this information?* • *What do you make of the new boss?* • *I don't know what to make of it, and even the police seem baffled*

make *obj* **of** [GIVE IMPORTANCE] *v prep* [T] to give a particular importance to (something) • *These ambitious people make too much of the benefits of an executive job* (=make it seem too important). • If you make **much** of someone, you treat them very well, praise them, etc.: *His mother used to make much of him when he went home for holidays.* • *(infml)* If you say **Do you want to make something of it?** to someone with whom you are arguing, you are threatening them and offering to fight them.

make off *v adv* [I] *infml* to leave quickly, esp. in order to escape • *The burglars made off as soon as the police arrived.*

make off with *obj v adv prep* [T] *infml* to steal (something) • *Somebody broke into the shop and made off with several TVs and videos.*

make out [SUCCEED] *v adv* [I always + adv/prep] *infml* to continue or succeed in life or in business • *How is Frances making out in her new job* (=How successfully is she dealing with her new job)? • *The business made out better than expected in 1992 and profits were slightly up.*

make *(obj)* **out** [CLAIM] *v adv infml* to claim, usually falsely, that something is true • *He made himself out* **to be** *a millionaire.* [T + obj + *to* infinitive] • *The British weather is not always as bad as it is made out* **(to be)**. [T + obj + *to* infinitive] • *He made out* **that** *he had been living in Paris all year.* [+ *that* clause] • *(Br and Aus)* To **make out a case**/ *(Am and Aus)* **make a case** for something is to argue that it is the best thing to do, giving your reasons: *We will only publish a new edition if you can make out a convincing case for it.*

make out *(obj)* [UNDERSTAND], **make** *(obj)* **out** *v adv* [usually in negatives and questions] to see, hear or understand (something or someone) with difficulty • *The numbers are too small – I can't make them out at all.* [M] • *I can't make out your writing.* [M] • *She's a strange person – I can't make her out at all.* [M] • *Nobody can make out* **why** *you should have been attacked.* [+ *wh-* word]

make out *obj* [WRITE], **make** *obj* **out** *v adv* [M] to write all the necessary information on (an official form, document, etc.) • *I made a cheque out* **for** *£20* **to** *'Henry's Supermarket'.*

make out [HAVE SEX] *v adv* [I] *esp. Am infml* to kiss and touch in a sexual way, or to succeed in having sex with someone • *Boys at that age are only interested in making out* **with** *a girl, any girl.* • See also MAKE [HAVE SEX].

make o·ver *obj* [GIVE], **make** *obj* **o·ver** *v adv* [M] *specialized* to give (money, land, etc.) to someone so that they legally own it • *Just before her death, she had made over $100 000* **to** *her new husband.*

make o·ver *obj* [CHANGE], **make** *obj* **o·ver** *v adv* [M] *esp. Am* to change or make again • *It's an old church that has been made over* **into** *homes.* • *The builders laid the wrong floor tiles, so they'll have to make the floor over* (=do it again).

make–o·ver /£ˈmeɪkˌəʊ·vəʳ, $-ˌoʊ·vɚ/ *n* [C] • If you have a make-over, a trained person gives your appearance a new style: *Her make-over consisted mainly of a new hairstyle and a different face powder.*

make to·wards *obj v prep* [T] *esp. Br* to go in the direction of • *He made towards the door, but stopped and turned to face me.* • See also MAKE FOR [GO TOWARDS].

make up *obj* [INVENT], **make** *obj* **up** *v adv* [M] to invent (an excuse, a story, etc.), often in order to deceive • *I was trying to make up a good excuse for being so late.* • *The child wanted him to make a story up about dragons and knights on horseback.* • If you make a story, an excuse, a tune, etc. up **as you go along**, you invent it without having thought before about how it will end. • See also **make up** at MAKE-UP.

make up *obj* [PREPARE], **make** *obj* **up** *v adv* [M] to prepare or arrange (something) by putting different things together • *Could you make up a list of all the things that need to be done?* • *He asked the man behind the counter to make up a box with a mixed selection of chocolates.* • *The maid will make up your room* (=make it tidy) *later.* • To make up **a bed** or make **a bed** up for someone is to put sheets, covers, etc. on a bed so that the person has a place to sleep in your home. See also MAKE [PERFORM]. • *(specialized)* To make up a page, book or newspaper is to arrange text, pictures, etc. in the form in which they will be printed.

make up *obj* [PRODUCE], **make** *obj* **up** *v adv* [M] *specialized* to produce (something) using cloth • *We could use the velvet material to make up some curtains.* • See also **make up** at MAKE-UP.

make up *obj* [COMPLETE], **make** *obj* **up** *v adv* [M] to make (something, esp. an amount) complete • *I have £20 000 and I need £25 000 – my parents have promised to make up* **the difference**. • *She owes £300, which she has to make up* (=pay back) *by March.* • *We're hoping to make up* **time** *on the return journey by not stopping at night.* • *(Am and Aus) You'll have to make up the work you've missed while you were away.* • *(Br) We'll invite Geoff and Sarah to the party to make* **the numbers** *up* **to** *ten.* • *(Br and Aus)* To make up a fire is to put more wood or coal, etc. on it: *Make up the fire – it's getting cold in here.* • See also **make up** at MAKE-UP.

make up [BECOME FRIENDS] *v adv* [I] to forgive and become friends again with a person after an argument or disagreement • *They* **kissed and** *made up, as usual, and so everyone relaxed.* • *We often quarrel but we always* **make it up** *(***with** *each other) soon after.* • See also **make up** at MAKE-UP.

make up *obj* [FORM] *v prep* [T] (of a number of people or things) to form as a whole • *Road accident victims make up almost a quarter of the hospital's patients.* • *The book is made up of a number of different articles.*

make–up /ˈmeɪk·ʌp/ *n* [C usually sing] • The make-up of something or someone is the combination of things that form it: *They argue that the membership of the Council does not reflect the racial make-up of the city.* ○ *Organizational ability is not one of the most obvious parts of his make-up* (=character). • See also **make up** at MAKE-UP.

make up *obj* [DECIDE], **make** *obj* **up** *v adv* [M] **make up** *your* **mind** to decide • *You have five minutes to make up your mind.* • *I can't make up my mind* **which** *I want.* • *At the age of 6 she made up her mind* **to** *become a judge.* • *He made up his mind* **(that)** *he'd visit Paul the next day.* • See also **make up** at MAKE-UP.

make up for *(obj) v adv prep* to take the place of (something lost or damaged); to COMPENSATE for (something bad) with something good • *No amount of money can make up for the death of a child.* [T] • *This year's good harvest will make up for last year's bad one.* [T] • *He bought me dinner to make up for* **being** *so late the day before.* [+ v-*ing*] • *I went to university at the age of 45 and worked and played very hard,* **making up for lost time** (=using and enjoying the experience as much as possible because it hadn't happened sooner).

make *obj* **up to** *obj* [GIVE] *v adv prep* [T] **make it up to** to give something to or do something for (esp. someone for whom you have caused trouble) • *You've been so helpful! How can I make it up to you?* • *I'm sorry we can't take you with us but I promise I'll make it up to you somehow.*

make up to *obj* [PRAISE] *v adv prep* [T] *Br and Aus disapproving* to praise and be too friendly to (someone) in order to get advantages • *Have you seen the disgusting way she makes up to the boss?*

make with *obj v prep* [T] *Am dated slang* to give, bring or do • *He pointed a gun and said "Make with the money bags, baby!"*

make–be·lieve /ˈmeɪk·bɪˌliːv/ *n* [U] believing in things that you want to believe because they are easy or exciting, but which are not real • *The ideal of a perfectly fair society is just make-believe.* • *He lives in a world of make-believe/a make-believe world.*

make·shift /ˈmeɪk·ʃɪft/ *adj* temporary and of low quality, but used because of a sudden need • *Thousands of refugees are living in makeshift camps.*

make·shift /ˈmeɪk·ʃɪft/ *n* [C] • *Can you use these tables as a makeshift, until we get you something better?*

make–up /ˈmeɪk·ʌp/ *n* [U] coloured substances used on your face to improve or change your appearance • *I put on a little eye make-up.* • *She wears ridiculously thick make-up.* • LP〉 **Shopping goods**

make up *(obj)*, **make** *(obj)* **up** *v adv* • *She takes ages to make (her face) up in the mornings* (= to put make-up on her face). [I/M] • *For the film, he was made up* **as** *an Indian.* [M] • See also MAKE OVER CHANGE.

make·weight /ˈmeɪk·weɪt/ *n* [C] something or someone, esp. without much value of its own, that is added so that there is the correct amount or number • *The tape has two Beethoven symphonies, plus a few overtures as makeweights.* • *She may be the youngest member of the team, but she's no makeweight* (= she is as good as the others).

mal– /mæl-/ *combining form esp. fml or specialized* badly or wrongly • *The disease rubella can cause pregnant women to have malformed* (= wrongly formed and shaped) *babies.* • LP〉 **Opposites**

ma·la·chite /ˈmæl·ə·kaɪt/ *n* [U] a green stone used in jewellery and decoration

mal·ad·just·ed /ˌmæl·əˈdʒʌs·tɪd/ *adj* (esp. of a child) having been raised in a way that does not prepare someone well for the demands of life, which often leads to problems with behaviour in the future • *She is head of a residential school for disturbed and maladjusted children.*

mal·ad·just·ment /ˌmæl·əˈdʒʌst·mənt/ *n* [U] • *His anti-social behaviour is a sign of maladjustment and inadequate parenting.*

mal·ad·min·is·tra·tion /ˌmæl·əd,mɪn·ɪˈstreɪ·ʃᵊn/ *n* [U] *fml* lack of care, judgment or honesty from people in authority • *Thousands of refugees are dying because of the incompetence and maladministration of local officials.*

mal·a·droit /ˌmæl·əˈdrɔɪt/ *adj fml* awkward in movement or unskilled in behaviour or action • *Her lack of self-confidence does make her rather maladroit in social situations.*

mal·a·droit·ly /ˌmæl·əˈdrɔɪt·li/ *adv*

mal·a·droit·ness /ˌmæl·əˈdrɔɪt·nəs/ *n* [U]

mal·a·dy /ˈmæl·ə·di/ *n* [C] *fml dated* a disease or *(fig.)* a problem within a system or organization • *All the rose bushes seem to be suffering from the same mysterious malady.* • *One of the Council's major maladies is the lack of optimism and enthusiasm amongst senior officials.*

mal·aise /mælˈeɪz/ *n* [U] a general feeling of bad health or lack of energy, or an uncomfortable feeling that something is wrong (esp. with society) and a lack of ability to change the situation • *She wrote about the depression and malaise* (= lack of energy and interest) *felt by women trapped in their suburban homes.* • *They claim it is* **a symptom of** *a* **deeper** *and more* **general** *malaise in society.* • *They spoke of the feeling of moral and* **spiritual** *malaise, the lack of will to do anything.* • *They were discussing the roots of the current* **economic** *malaise.*

malapropi·sm /£ˈmæl·ə·prɒp·ɪ·zᵊm, $-prɑː·pɪ-/ *n* [C] the wrong use of one word instead of another word because they sound similar to each other, and which is amusing as a result • *In the sentence, "The price of food in Japan is gastronomical", the word 'gastronomical' is a malapropism, because it should be 'astronomical'.*

ma·la·r·ia /£məˈleə·ri·ə, $-ˈler·i-/ *n* [U] a disease that you can get from the bite of a particular type of MOSQUITO (= small flying insect) and which causes periods of fever and feeling very cold and shaking. It is common in many hotter parts of the world.

ma·lar·key /£məˈlɑː·ki, $-ˈlɑːr-/ *n* [U] *slang disapproving, slightly dated* meaningless or silly (or sometimes slightly dishonest) activity or talk • *I like watching American football, but I can't be bothered with all those ridiculous cheerleaders, and the marching bands and all that malarkey.*

mal·con·tent /ˈmæl·kən·tent/ *n* [C] *fml disapproving* a person who is not satisfied with the way things are, esp. one who complains a lot and is unreasonable and difficult to deal with • *The usual malcontents turned up to the meeting and made trouble.*

male SEX /meɪl/ *adj* [not gradable] of men or boys; (typical) of the sex that FERTILIZEs eggs (= adds cells to them that make them produce new life), and does not produce young or eggs itself • *male students* • *a male giraffe* • *Coal-mining is very much a male-dominated industry.* • *What percentage of the adult male population is unemployed?* • *The male parts of the flower are the stamens and the anthers.* • **Male bonding** is the forming of close friendships between men: *Physical contact in rugby and soccer helps with male bonding.* • *(disapproving)* A **male chauvinist** is a man who believes that women are naturally less important, less clever, etc. than men and so does not treat them equally with men: *He's a* **male chauvinist pig** *(abbrev.* **mcp**) *– he doesn't see why he should have to help look after the kids.* ○ *It's a bad example of* **male chauvinism**. • *(esp. humorous)* The **male menopause** is a state of mind experienced by some men about 40 or 50 years old in which they start to worry that they are not successful enough, and to want suddenly to find a new job or a new partner. • **Male organ** is used to avoid saying penis. • See also MASCULINE MALE. Compare FEMALE SEX. • LP〉 **Sexist language**

male /meɪl/ *n* [C] • *Among the bodies are two unidentified British males.* • *Among these fish, the males are much less aggressive.* • *As a* **mere** *male, I wouldn't dare comment on that.*

male·ness /ˈmeɪl·nəs/ *n* [U] • *The birds make their maleness clear with a peculiar sort of dance.*

male CONNECTING PART /meɪl/ *adj* [not gradable] *specialized* (of a piece of equipment) having a part which sticks out and can be fitted into a hollow part in another piece of equipment • *a male plug* • Compare FEMALE CONNECTING PART.

mal·e·fac·tor /£ˈmæl·ɪ·fæk·təʳ, $-t̬ɚ/ *n* [C] *literary or very fml* a person who does bad or illegal things • *The malefactors will be prosecuted.*

mal·ev·o·lent /məˈlev·ᵊl·ənt/ *adj literary* causing or wanting to cause harm or evil • *The central character is a malevolent witch out for revenge.* • *I could feel his malevolent gaze as I walked away and wondered what he would do next.*

mal·ev·o·lent·ly /məˈlev·ᵊl·ənt·li/ *adv literary*

mal·ev·o·lence /məˈlev·ᵊl·ənts/ *n* [U] *literary* • *It was an act of great malevolence.*

mal·fea·sance /mælˈfiː·zᵊnts/ *n law* (an example of) dishonest and illegal behaviour, esp. by a person in authority • *Several cases of malpractice and malfeasance in the financial world are currently being investigated.* [U]

mal·for·ma·tion /£ˌmæl·fəˈmeɪ·ʃᵊn, $-fɚ-/ *n* the condition of being wrongly formed, or a part of something, esp. a part of the body, that is wrongly formed • *Exposure to radiation can lead to malformation of the embryo.* [U] • *She was born critically ill with a severe malformation of the heart.* [C]

mal·formed /£ˌmælˈfɔːmd, $-fɔːrmd/ *adj* • *The newspapers carried photographs of malnourished children with swollen empty stomachs and malformed limbs.*

mal·func·tion /ˌmælˈfʌŋk·ʃᵊn/ *v* [I] *slightly fml* (of a machine or piece of equipment) to fail to work correctly

mal·func·tion /ˌmælˈfʌŋk·ʃᵊn/ *n* [C] • *Shortly before the crash the pilot had reported a malfunction of the aircraft's navigation system.*

mal·ice /ˈmæl·ɪs/ *n* [U] the wish to harm other people • *Killing her dog was an act of sheer malice.* • *Don't be alarmed – I* **bear** *you no malice* (= do not want to harm you). • *(specialized)* To illegally harm someone **with malice aforethought** is to have thought about it and planned it before acting.

mal·i·cious /məˈlɪʃ·əs/ *adj* • *malicious gossip* • *a malicious look in his eyes* • *Our advisers can help you if you are receiving malicious (telephone) calls.* • *(law) He was charged with malicious* **wounding**.

mal·i·cious·ly /məˈlɪʃ·ə·sli/ *adv*

ma·lign /məˈlaɪn/ *adj fml* causing or intending to cause harm or evil • *Foreign domination had a malign* **influence** *on local politics.* • *She described pornography as 'a malign industry'.* • *Malign spirits and demons persuade the characters to betray each other.*

ma·lig·ni·ty /£məˈlɪg·nə·ti, $-t̬i/ *n* [U] *fml*

ma·lign *obj* /məˈlaɪn/ *v* [T] • If you malign someone, you say false and unpleasant things about them or unfairly criticize them: *They have been maligned in the gossip columns of several newspapers.* ○ **Much-***maligned for their bad taste, the band are nevertheless great performers.*

ma·lig·nant /məˈlɪg·nənt/ *adj medical* (of a disease or TUMOUR (= diseased growth)) likely to get uncontrollably worse and lead to death • *The process by which malignant cancer cells multiply isn't fully understood.* • *Is the tumour malignant or benign?* • *(fig.) I wouldn't trust him – he's a malignant little bastard* (= likes harming people). • Compare BENIGN.

ma·lig·nant·ly /məˈlɪg·nənt·li/ *adv medical*

ma·lig·nan·cy /məˈlɪg·nənt·si/ *n medical* • *The malignancy of these tumours makes them difficult to treat.* [U] • *(fig.) The central character's malignancy* (=desire to cause harm) *was shocking in its evil intensity.* [U] • *Tests revealed a malignancy* (=diseased growth) *that had to be removed.* [C]

ma·lin·ger /£məˈlɪŋ·gəʳ, $-gɚ/ *v* [I] *disapproving* to pretend to be ill in order to avoid having to work • *People recovering from injuries are often unfairly thought to be malingering by employers and doctors.*

ma·lin·ger·er /£məˈlɪŋ·gəʳ·əʳ, $-gɚ·ɚ/ *n* [C] *disapproving* • *There are too many malingerers in this company!*

mall /£mɔːl, $mɑːl/, **shop·ping mall** *n* [C] a large usually enclosed shopping area where cars are not allowed • *There are plans to build a new mall in the middle of town.*

mal·lard /£ˈmæl·ɑːd, $-ɑːrd/ *n* [C] *pl* **mallard** or **mallards** a wild DUCK (=type of water bird) that is common in Europe and N America • *The male mallard has a green head and reddish-brown chest.*

mal·le·a·ble /ˈmæl·i·ə·bl̩/ *adj* (of a substance) easily changed into a new shape or *(fig.)* (esp. of people) easily influenced, trained or controlled • *Lead and tin are malleable metals.* • *He had an actor's typically malleable features.* • *(fig.) Europe saw its colonies as sources of raw materials and a malleable labour force.*

mal·le·a·bil·i·ty /£ˌmæl·i·əˈbɪl·ɪ·ti, $-ə·t̬i/ *n* [U]

mal·lee /ˈmæl·i/ *n* [C] a tree of the EUCALYPTUS group which does not grow tall and is found in desert areas of Australia

mal·let /ˈmæl·ɪt/ *n* [C] a tool like a hammer with a large flattened end made of wood or rubber, or a wooden hammer with a long handle used in sports such as CROQUET and POLO • See also HAMMER [TOOL]. • [PIC] **Tools**

mal·nou·rished /£ˌmælˈnʌr·ɪʃt, $-ˈnɜːr-/ *adj* weak and in bad health because of a lack of food or because of a lack of the types of food necessary for good health • *The TV showed tragic pictures of malnourished and sickly babies, too weak even to cry.*

mal·nu·tri·tion /£ˌmæl·njuːˈtrɪ·ʃᵊn, $-nuː-/ *n* [U] physical weakness and bad health caused by a lack of food, or by a lack of the types of food necessary for good health • *Many thousands of refugees have already died from malnutrition.*

mal·o·dor·ous /£ˌmælˈəʊ·dᵊr·əs, $-ˈoʊ·dɚ-/ *adj fml* having an unpleasant smell or *(literary disapproving)* unpleasant or offensive • *The town is built on a malodorous swamp.* • *(literary disapproving) The film seemed to be an excuse to make money out of his own malodorous fantasies about sex, rape and murder.*

mal·prac·tice /ˌmælˈpræk·tɪs/ *n specialized* (a) failure to act correctly or legally when doing your job, esp. causing injury or loss • *They are accused of medical/financial/electoral/business malpractice.* [U]

malt /£mɒlt, $mɑːlt/ *n* [U] grain, usually BARLEY, that has been left in water until it starts to grow and is then dried. It is used in the making of alcoholic drinks such as beer and WHISKY • **Malt extract** is a sweet dark sticky substance made from malt and used in food. • **Malt whisky** (also **malt**) is whisky made using malt rather than ordinary grain: *a fine Highland malt* • **Malted milk** (also **malted**) is a drink made from milk and malt.

malt *obj* /£mɒlt, $mɑːlt/ *v* [T]

Mal·tese /ˌmɒlˈtiːz/ *adj* [not gradable] of the people or language of Malta • A **Maltese cross** is a cross with four equal parts that get wider further from the centre.

mal·treat *obj* /ˌmælˈtriːt/ *v* [T usually passive] *fml* to treat cruelly or violently • *His behaviour patterns suggested he had been badly maltreated as a child.*

mal·treat·ment /ˌmælˈtriːt·mənt/ *n* [U] • *They complained about the physical and psychological maltreatment of prisoners.*

mam /mæm/ *n* [C] *Br regional* (used esp. by or to children) a mother • *Mam! Can we go swimming?* [as form of address]

ma·ma /£məˈmɑː, $ˈmɑː·mə/ *n* [C] *Am infml, Br old use* (used esp. by or to children) a mother • *Where's Jimmy, mama?* [as form of address] • *(Am slang)* A mama is also a woman, esp. an attractive one: *There's a good-looking mama sitting at the bar.* • **Mama's boy** is *Am for* **mummy's boy**. See at MUMMY [MOTHER]. • [LP] **Titles and forms of address**

mam·ba /ˈmæm·bə/ *n* [C] a very poisonous snake that lives mainly in caves or trees in parts of Africa

mam·mal /ˈmæm·ᵊl/ *n* [C] any animal in which the female gives birth to babies, not eggs, and feeds them on milk from her own body • *Humans, dogs, elephants and dolphins are all mammals, but birds, fish and crocodiles are not.*

mam·ma·li·an /məˈmeɪ·li·ən/ *adj* [not gradable] *specialized* • *mammalian evolution* • *mammalian species*

mam·ma·ry /£ˈmæm·ᵊr·i, $ˈ-ɚ-/ *adj* [not gradable] *specialized* of the breasts or milk organs • Mammals have **mammary glands** which produce milk to feed their young.

mam·mog·ra·phy /£məˈmɒg·rə·fi, $-ˈmɑː·grə-/ *n* [U] the use of X-RAY photographs of the breasts to help discover possible CANCERS (=diseased growths)

mam·mo·gram /ˈmæm·ə·græm/, **mam·mo·graph** /£ˈmæm·ə·grɑːf, $-græf/ *n* [C] • A mammogram is an X-ray photograph of the breasts.

Mam·mon /ˈmæm·ən/ *n* [U] *disapproving* the force which makes people try to become as rich as possible and the belief that this is the most important thing in life • *The debate about new gambling laws is a confrontation between the forces of God and Mammon.*

mam·moth /ˈmæm·əθ/ *adj* extremely large • *Cleaning up the city-wide mess is going to be a mammoth* **task**. • *It's a mammoth* **undertaking** *– are you sure you have the resources to cope?*

mam·moth /ˈmæm·əθ/ *n* [C] • A mammoth was a type of large hairy ELEPHANT with TUSKS (=very long teeth that stick out of the mouth), and which no longer exists.

mam·my /ˈmæm·i/ *n* [C] *esp. Irish or Am* (used esp. by or to children) a mother • *(Am dated taboo)* A mammy is a black woman whose job is to look after white children. • [LP] **Titles and forms of address**

man [MALE] /mæn/ *n* [C] *pl* **men** /men/ an adult male human being • *a polite young man* • *Women live longer than men, on average.* • *He is now the men's 400 metres champion.* • *John can solve anything – the man's a genius.* • A man is also a general male employee, esp. without particular rank or title: *The gas company said they would send some men to fix the heating system.* ○ *The man* **from** *the BBC wrote some positive things about the film.* ○ *The expedition was made up of 100 officers and men* (=low-ranking soldiers). ○ *Our man* (=The male employee of this company) *in Washington sent us the news by fax yesterday.* ○ *(old use) My man* (=male servant) *will show you to the door.* • A marketing/media/etc. man is a man typical of or involved in marketing/media/etc. • *(infml)* A woman's husband or male partner is sometimes called her man: *Have you met her new man yet?* • *(infml)* Man is sometimes used when addressing an adult male human being, esp. when the speaker is annoyed: *Give me that, man – it's mine!* [as form of address] • *(infml dated)* Man is sometimes used as an exclamation, esp. when the speaker is expressing a strong emotion: *Man, we had a good time – we drank all through the night!* • **The** man is *Am slang for* the police or others in authority. • To **make a man (out) of** a young man or boy is to cause him to act like an adult and take responsibility: *A few years in the army will make a man of you.* • *(dated humorous) From 1910 to 1970 he worked in that factory,* **man and boy** (=all his life). • *(dated)* If a man and a woman are **man and wife** (*usually* **husband and wife**) they are married to each other: *They became man and wife on 26 April 1904.* • The **man in the moon** is the human face that you can imagine you see when you look at the moon. The word is used esp. in children's stories. • If you describe a man as **a man's man** you mean that he enjoys men's activities and being with other men: *I've seen him down the pub with the rugby team – he's a real man's man.* • If you talk to someone **(as) man to man**, or if you have a **man-to-man** talk with them, you talk seriously and honestly together as equals: *Can we talk man to man about this, rather than as father to son?* (J) • *(humorous)* A **man-eater** is a woman who uses men to have a series of sexual relationships without really loving them. See also **man-eater** at MAN [PERSON]. • A **man Friday** is a male helper who is loyal and can be trusted. • *(esp. humorous)* A **man of God/man of the cloth** is a priest. • *(fml)* A **man of letters** is a man, usually a writer, who knows a lot about literature. • **Man-sized** means big: *some man-sized tissues* ○ *a man-sized effort* • *(Am)* The **men's room** (*Br and Aus* **the gents**) is a toilet for men in a public building: *Could you tell me where the men's room is, please?* Compare **ladies' room** at LADY [WOMAN]. • *"The Man with the Golden Gun"* (title of a James Bond story by Ian Fleming, 1974) • *"A Man for All Seasons"* (Description of Sir Thomas More by Robert Whittington Vulgaria, 1521 used by Robert Bolt as title for his play & film about More) • *"A man's a man for a'* (=all) *that"* (from a poem by Robert Burns, 1759-1796) • *"Our Man in Havana"* (title of a book by

Graham Greene, 1958) • *"It's a man's world, but it wouldn't be nothing without a woman or a girl"* (from the song *It's a man's, man's, man's world* by James Brown, 1966) • LP **Age, Sexist language** Ⓓ

man·hood /ˈmæn·hʊd/ *n* [U] • *The story is seen through the eyes of a boy on the verge of manhood.* • *A celebration is held for the boy at the age when he is considered to have reached manhood.* • Manhood can also refer to possession of the qualities that are considered typical of a man: *Tall, square-jawed and handsome, this young actor is Hollywood's ideal of manhood.* • *(poetic)* Manhood can also be used to mean men, esp. all the men of a particular country: *The flower* (=best) *of the nation's manhood was killed in the war.* • *(esp. humorous)* A man's manhood can also be his sexuality, or *(humorous)* his sexual organs: *Why do you think he needs to have so many women around him – is it just a way of* **proving** *his manhood?* ○ *(humorous) He had a little accident and got his manhood trapped in his zip.*

man·ly /ˈmæn·li/ *adj* **-ier, -iest** *approving* • Manly means having the qualities which people think a man should have: *He has such a manly figure/voice/laugh.* ○ *My mother used to tell me it wasn't manly for little boys to cry.*

man·li·ness /ˈmæn·lɪ·nəs/ *n* [U] • *He claims that it is in the field of battle that the values of manliness and courage are put to the test.*

man·nish /ˈmæn·ɪʃ/ *adj esp. disapproving* • If you describe a woman as mannish you mean that her appearance or behaviour are too much like a man's: *her mannish voice* ○ *Ever since that bus driver called her 'sir', she wondered if short hair made her look a bit mannish.*

man·nish·ly /ˈmæn·ɪʃ·li/ *adv esp. disapproving*

man·nish·ness /ˈmæn·ɪʃ·nəs/ *n* [U] *esp. disapproving*

man PERSON /mæn/ *n pl* **men** /men/ the human race, or any member or group of it • *Man* (=The human race) *is rapidly destroying the Earth.* [U] • *This poison is one of the most dangerous substances* **known to** *man* (=the human race). [U] • *Men* (=Members of the human race) *are still far more intelligent than the cleverest robot.* [C] • *All men are* (=Each member of the human race is) *equal in the sight of the law.* [C] • *For medieval man* (=all medieval people considered together as a group) *syphilis was as terrifying as AIDS is to us today.* [U] • *Try to imagine what life must have been like for Neolithic man* (=all the people who lived in the Neolithic period) *10 000 years ago.* [U] • If a group of people do something **as one man** they do it together at exactly the same time: *As one man, the delegates made for the exit.* • *There were 400 people at the meeting and they all,* **to a man** (=every one of them), *voted in favour.* • Dogs are sometimes called **man's best friend**. • *The murder is just another example of* **man's inhumanity to man** (=how cruel people can be to each other). • A **man-eater** is an animal that can kill and eat a person: *That tiger's a man-eater!* ○ *There was a news report of a* **man-eating** *tiger.* ○ See also **man-eater** at MAN MALE. • *(esp. Br)* A **man of straw** is someone who has a weak character: *He was accused by his opponents of being a man of straw and lacking in decisiveness.* • A **man of straw** is also a **straw man**. See at STRAW DRIED STEMS. • If something is **man-made**, it is artificial rather than natural: *man-made fibres* ○ *It's a man-made lake.* • *"Man is a tool-using animal"* (Thomas Carlyle in his book *Sartor Resatus*, 1834) • *"Though every prospect pleases,/ and only man is vile"* (from a hymn by Reginald Heber, 1783-1826) • Some people find this use of man offensive because it does not seem to give women equal importance with men. They prefer to use other words such as humanity, humankind and people. • LP **Sexist language** Ⓓ

-man /-mæn, -mən/ *combining form* **-men** /-men/ • *an Irishman* • *a policeman* • *businessmen* • *a five-man team* • *a two-man helicopter* • Some people find this use offensive because it does not seem to give women equal importance with men. They prefer to use other words such as a police officer, business executives, a five-person team etc. • LP **Sexist language**

man *obj* /mæn/ *v* [T] **-nn-** • To man something such as a machine or vehicle is to be present in order to operate it: *Man the pumps!* ○ *The phones are manned 24 hours a day by young female volunteers.* ○ *Barricades were erected against the advancing government troops and they were manned throughout the night.* • *See Language Portrait on Using Language that is not Sexist.* • Some people find this use offensive because it does not seem to give women equal importance with men. They prefer to use other words such as, operate, crew, staff, etc. • See also OVERMANNED; UNDERMANNED; UNMANNED.

man OBJECT /mæn/ *n* [C] *pl* **men** /men/ any of the objects that are moved or played with in games such as CHESS • Ⓓ

man·a·cles /ˈmæn·ə·kl̩z/ *pl n* two metal rings joined by a chain, used to prevent a prisoner from escaping by fastening the legs or arms

man·a·cle *obj* /ˈmæn·ə·kl̩/ *v* [T] • *They had manacled her legs* **together**. • *His arm was manacled* **to** *a ring on the wall.*

man·age *(obj)* SUCCEED /ˈmæn·ɪdʒ/ *v* to succeed in doing (something, esp. something difficult) ○ *How do you expect a sick man to manage a ten mile walk?* [T] • *The bakery was shut so I didn't manage* **to** *get any bread.* [+ to infinitive] • *The car's brakes failed and the driver* **(only just)** *managed* **to** *avoid ploughing into a group of children at the bottom of the hill.* [+ to infinitive] • *A small dog had* **(somehow)** *managed* **to** *survive the fire.* [+ to infinitive] • *I can't manage (all this work) on my own, you know.* [I/T] • *Don't worry about us – we'll manage* (=be able to deal with all difficulties)*!* [I] • *Can you manage dinner on Saturday* (=Will you be able to come to dinner or will you be busy)*?* [T] • *(esp. Br) I'm afraid I can't manage the time* (=I'm too busy) *to see you at the moment.* [T] • To manage is also to succeed in living on a small amount of money: *After she lost her job, they had to manage* **on** *his salary.* [I]

man·age·a·ble /ˈmæn·ɪ·dʒə·bl̩/ *adj* • If something is manageable it is easy or possible to deal with it: *The work has been divided into smaller, more manageable sections.* ○ *Government targets for increased productivity are described as "tough but manageable."*

man·age *obj* CONTROL /ˈmæn·ɪdʒ/ *v* [T] to be responsible for controlling or organizing (someone or something, esp. the working of a business) • *It's a co-operative, so the workers manage the business themselves.* • *Has she had any experience of managing large projects?* • *A director needs to be good at managing people.* • *His job involved managing large investment funds.* • *When you have a job as well as children to look after, you have to learn how to manage* (=organize) *your time.* [T] • *Some people think television manages* (=controls) *the news instead of just reporting it.* • *(disapproving) She's a bit of a managing sort of person* (=She tries too hard to control other people, even against their wishes). • *(Br and Aus)* A **managing director** (abbreviation **MD**) of a company is the person in charge of the way it operates: *There's a board of five directors, but she is the Managing Director.* • See also MISMANAGE.

man·age·ment /ˈmæn·ɪdʒ·mənt/ *n* • Management is the control and organization of something: *The company has suffered from several years of bad management.* [U] ○ *There is a need for stricter financial management.* [U] ○ *She was sent on a management training scheme.* [U] ○ *Her management of a difficult situation was impressive.* [U] • The management of a company is/are the group of people responsible for controlling and organizing it: *Management has/have offered staff a 3% pay increase.* [C + sing/pl v]

man·ag·er /£ˈmæn·ɪ·dʒəʳ, $-dʒɚ/ *n* [C] • *a bank manager* • *a station manager* • *the production manager* • *If you have a complaint, could you speak to the manager?* • The manager of a sports team is the person whose job is to organize and sometimes train it. • The manager of a singer, actor, etc. is a person whose job is to arrange the business part of their work. • LP **Sports**

man·ag·er·ess /£ˌmæn·ɪ·dʒəʳˈes, $-dʒə·res/ *n* [C] • A manageress is a woman who controls or organizes esp. a shop or a restaurant. • A female manager is often called a manager, rather than a manageress.

man·a·ge·ri·al /£ˌmæn·əˈdʒɪə·ri·əl, $-ˈdʒɪr·i-/ *adj* [not gradable] • *managerial responsibilities/decisions/skills*

ma·ña·na /mænˈjɑː·nə/ *adv* some time in the future; later • *Mañana means tomorrow in Spanish, but it can also mean next week, next month or even next year.* • *'When will you do it?' 'Mañana!'*

Man·cun·i·an /mæŋˈkjuː·ni·ən/ *n* [C], *adj* [not gradable] (a person) of or from Manchester, a city in N England

man·da·rin OFFICIAL /£ˈmæn·dəʳ·ɪn, $-dɚ-/ *n* [C] *esp. disapproving* a person who has a very important job in the government, and who is sometimes considered to be too powerful • *It often seems that true power lies with the Civil Service mandarins, rather than MPs and cabinet ministers.*

Man·da·rin LANGUAGE /£ˈmæn·dəʳ·ɪn, $-dɚ-/ *n* [U] *infml* the standard language of China • *She speaks Mandarin/ Mandarin Chinese.*

man·da·rin (or·ange) /£ˈmæn·dəʳ·ɪn, $-dɚ-/ *n* [C] a small sweet type of orange but with a thinner, looser skin

man·date /ˈmæn·deɪt/ *n* [C usually sing] the authority given to an elected group of people, such as a government, to perform an action or govern a country • *There is concern that the latest wave of bombing has exceeded the United Nations mandate.* • *At the forthcoming elections, the government will be seeking a fresh mandate* **from** *the people.* • *The president secured the Congressional mandate* **to** *go to war by three votes.* [+ *to* infinitive] • *(specialized)* A mandate is also the name of an area of land which has been given to a country by the UN (= an international organization of most of the world's countries) esp. following or as part of a peace agreement. • (PL)

man·date *obj* /ˈmæn·deɪt/ *v* [T] • If you mandate something, you give official permission for it to happen: *The UN rush to mandate war totally ruled out any alternatives.* • If someone is mandated to do something, they are ordered to do it: *Our delegates have been mandated* **to** *vote against the proposal at the conference.* [+ *to* infinitive]

man·da·to·ry /£ˈmæn·də·tri, $-tɔːr·i/ *adj* [not gradable] *fml* which must be done, or which is demanded by law • *The minister is calling for mandatory prison sentences for people who assault police officers.* • *Athletes must undergo a mandatory drugs test before competing in the championship.* • *In 1991, the British government made it mandatory to wear rear seat belts in cars.*

man·do·lin, man·do·line /ˌmæn·dəlˈɪn/ *n* [C] a musical instrument with four pairs of metal strings and a rounded back • *She plays the mandolin in a folk band.*

man·drake /ˈmæn·dreɪk/ *n* [C] a plant with purplish flowers and a root which is divided into two parts • *The root of the mandrake was once thought to have magic powers and it was used to make drugs.*

man·drill /ˈmæn·drɪl/ *n* [C] a large West African monkey which has a red and blue face and a very short tail • *Mandrills live on the ground in small family groups.*

mane /meɪn/ *n* [C] the long thick hair that grows along the top of a horse's neck or around the face and neck of a lion • *It's only the male lion that has the wonderful golden mane.* • A mane is also thick long hair on a person's head: *The painting depicts a beautiful young man with a flowing mane of red hair.*

ma·neu·ver /£məˈnuː·vər, $-vɚ/ *n* [C], *v* [I/T] *Am for* MANOEUVRE

man·ful·ly /ˈmæn·fəl·i/ *adv* with determination and bravery, despite great difficulties • *The actors struggled manfully with some of the worst lines of dialogue ever written.*

man·ga·nese /ˈmæŋ·gə·niːz/ *n* [U] a grey-white metallic element, used esp. in the process of making steel

mange /meɪndʒ/ *n* [U] an infectious disease in hairy animals, such as dogs and cats, which makes hair fall out and causes areas of rough skin

man·gy /ˈmeɪn·dʒi/ *adj* **-ier, -iest** • *a thin mangy dog* • *When we first found the cat, its fur was all mangy, but now it's shiny and healthy.* • *(infml)* If an object is mangy, it is old and dirty and has been used a lot: *We need to get rid of that mangy old carpet in the bedroom.*

man·ger /£ˈmeɪn·dʒər, $-dʒɚ/ *n* [C] *old use* an open box from which cattle and horses feed • *Mangers were usually found in stables and barns.* • *According to Christian tradition, Jesus was born in a stable and a manger was used as his bed.* • *"Away in a manger, no crib for a bed/ The little Lord Jesus lay down his sweet head"* (traditional Christmas song)

mange·tout *Br* /ˌmɑ̃ːnʒˈtuː/, *Am and Aus* **snow peas**, *Am also* **su·gar peas** *pl n* the sweet PODS (= containers) of a particular type of PEA which are picked and eaten before the peas inside them grow • *The chicken is served with potatoes, carrots and mangetout.* • PIC **Peas and beans**

man·gle *obj* DESTROY /ˈmæŋ·gl/ *v* [T usually passive] to destroy (something) by twisting it with force or tearing it into pieces so that its original form is completely changed • *My new jumper got mangled in the washing machine.* • *Doctors managed to reattach the finger of a man whose hand had been mangled by an electric saw.* • *All that remains of yesterday's car crash is a pile of mangled metal.* • If you mangle a speech or a piece of written work, you make so many mistakes that you completely spoil it: *As he read the poem out loud, he mangled the rhythm so badly that it scarcely made any sense.*

man·gle MACHINE /ˈmæŋ·gl/, **wring·er** *n* [C] a machine used, esp. in the past, for pressing water out of clothes by putting the clothes between two heavy rollers which are turned by hand

man·go /£ˈmæŋ·gəʊ, $-goʊ/ *n* [C] *pl* **mangoes** or **mangos** an oval tropical fruit with a smooth skin, juicy orange-yellow flesh and a large hard seed in the middle • *Mangoes are used in a lot of south east Asian dishes.* • *Mango* **chutney** *is often eaten with curry.* • *They lived on a street lined with mango* **trees**.

man·grove /£ˈmæŋ·grəʊv, $-groʊv/ *n* [C] a tropical tree, found near water, whose twisted roots grow partly above ground • *Mangrove* **swamps** *are common along river banks in tropical and subtropical areas.*

man·gy /ˈmeɪn·dʒi/ *adj* **-ier, -iest** See at MANGE

man·han·dle *obj* HANDLE ROUGHLY /ˌmænˈhæn·dl̩/ *v* [T] to handle (someone) roughly and with force, often when removing them or taking them somewhere • *There were complaints that the police had manhandled some of the demonstrators.*

man·han·dle *obj* MOVE /ˌmænˈhæn·dl̩/ *v* [T] to move (something) using the physical strength of the body • *Several pieces of heavy equipment had to be manhandled into the lorry.*

man·hat·tan /£mænˈhæt·ən, $-ˈhæţ-/ *n* [C] a type of alcoholic COCKTAIL (= a mixed drink) • *A manhattan contains whisky and vermouth.*

man·hole /£ˈmæn·həʊl, $-hoʊl/ *n* [C] a covered opening in a road which a worker can enter in order to reach underground pipes, wires or DRAINS which need to be examined or repaired • *a manhole cover*

man·hood /ˈmæn·hʊd/ *n* [U] See at MAN MALE

man·hour /£ˈmæn·aʊər, $-aʊr/, **work·ing hour** *n* [C] the amount of work done by one person in one hour • *Just think how many manhours we could save if we computerized the system.*

man·hunt /ˈmæn·hʌnt/ *n* [C] an organized search for a person, esp. a criminal • *The police have* **launched** *a manhunt after the body of a six-year-old boy was found last night.*

ma·ni·a STRONG INTEREST /ˈmeɪ·ni·ə/ *n disapproving* a very strong interest in something which fills a person's mind or uses up all their time • *He was surprised by his wife's sudden mania* **for** *exercise and wondered whom she was trying to impress.* [C] • *The article describes the* **religious** *mania which is sweeping the US.* [U] • (J)

–ma·ni·a /-ˈmeɪ·ni·ə/ *combining form* • *Beatle-mania swept Britain in the 1960s* (= The Beatles were extremely popular then). • See also KLEPTOMANIA; **nymphomania** at NYMPHOMANIAC; PYROMANIA.

ma·ni·ac /ˈmeɪ·ni·æk/ *n* [C] • *(infml)* A maniac is a person who has a very strong interest in a particular activity: *My brother's always been a football maniac.* • If a person works or exercises **like a maniac**, they work extremely hard, directing all their attention to it: *She exercises like a maniac, and she'll injure herself badly if she's not careful.*

ma·ni·a·cal /məˈnaɪə·kəl/ *adj* • *He could hear the sound of maniacal* (= extremely active) *cleaning coming from the kitchen.*

ma·ni·a MENTAL ILLNESS /ˈmeɪ·ni·ə/ *n* a state in which someone directs all their attention to one particular thing, or *(specialized)* a state of extreme physical and mental activity, often characterized by a loss of judgment and periods of EUPHORIA • *Van Gogh suffered from acute persecution mania.* [U] • *She's always cleaning – it's like a mania with her!* [C] • *(specialized) Mania is one component in several affective disorders, such as depression.* [U] • (J)

ma·ni·ac /ˈmeɪ·ni·æk/ *n* [C] • A maniac is a person who behaves in an uncontrolled way, not caring about risks or danger: *Some maniac was running down the street waving a massive metal bar.* • *(infml) I won't get in the car with Richard – he drives* **like a** *maniac!*

ma·ni·a·cal /məˈnaɪə·kəl/ *adj* • *The disease causes delusions and maniacal behaviour.* • If a cry or laugh is described as maniacal, it is loud and wild: *As she saw him coming towards her, she let out a wild maniacal scream.* ○ *He suddenly exploded into maniacal* **laughter** *and then stopped again just as suddenly.*

man·ic /ˈmæn·ɪk/ *adj* very excited or anxious in a way that causes you to be very physically active • *He's a bit manic – I wish he'd calm down.* • *There's some manic* (= extremely energetic) *dancing going on in the next room.* • A **manic depressive** is a person whose mental state varies between extreme excitement and deep sadness with hopelessness. The illness is known as **manic depression** (or *specialized* **bipolar depression**): *She's a manic depressive.* ○ *He* **suffers from** *manic depression.*

man·i·cure /£ˈmæn·ɪ·kjʊəʳ, $-kjʊr/ *n* [C] a treatment for the hands which involves softening the skin and making the nails look better by cutting, smoothing and possibly painting them • *Have you ever had a manicure?* • *She spends $30 a week having a manicure and a facial treatment.* • A **manicure set** is a set of small tools which are used for cutting and smoothing the nails: *A manicure set usually contains a pair of scissors, a nail file and some emery boards.* • Compare PEDICURE.

man·i·cure *obj* /£ˈmæn·ɪ·kjʊəʳ, $-kjʊr/ *v* [T] • *She takes great care of her hands and nails which she manicures daily.*

man·i·cured /£ˈmæn·ɪ·kjʊəd, $-kjʊrd/ *adj* [not gradable] • *He has a neat haircut and* **well-***manicured hands.* • If something, such as a garden, is manicured, it is well cared for and looks very tidy: *The hotel is surrounded by perfectly manicured gardens.* ○ *Visitors admire the palace's beautifully manicured* **lawns.**

man·i·cur·ist /£ˈmæn·ɪ·kjʊə·rɪst, $-kjʊ·rɪst/ *n* [C] • A manicurist is a person whose job it is to give people manicures.

man·i·fest *obj* /ˈmæn·ɪ·fest/ *v* [T] *fml* to show (something) clearly, through signs or actions • *I showed it to him, but he manifested no interest* **in** *it.* • *The workers chose to manifest their dissatisfaction* **in** *a series of strikes.* • *The illness first manifested* **itself in/as** *severe stomach pains.* • *Lack of confidence in the company manifested* **itself in** *a fall in the share price.* • (F) (RUS)

man·i·fest /ˈmæn·ɪ·fest/ *adj fml* • Manifest means easily noticed or obvious: *There was manifest relief among the workers yesterday at the decision not to close the factory.* ○ *Her manifest lack of interest in the project has provoked severe criticism.*

man·i·fest·ly /ˈmæn·ɪ·fest·li/ *adv fml* • *He claims that he is completely devoted to his children and yet it is manifestly* (= clearly) *not the case.* • *The government has manifestly failed to raise educational standards, despite its commitment to do so.*

man·i·fes·ta·tion /ˌmæn·ɪ·fesˈteɪ·ʃən/ *n fml* • *She claimed that the rise in unemployment was just a further manifestation* (= example) **of** *the government's incompetence.* [C] • *Unlike acid rain or deforestation, global warming has no visible manifestation* (= it cannot be seen). [U] • (CS) (E) (PL)

man·i·fest·o /£ˌmæn·ɪˈfes·təʊ, $-toʊ/ *n* [C] *pl* **manifestos** or **manifestoes** a written statement of the beliefs, aims and POLICIES (= a set of ideas or plans) of a group of people, esp. a political party • *In their election manifesto, the Liberal Democrats proposed increasing taxes to pay for improvements in education.* • *The ecology organization has just published its manifesto for growing and protecting trees.* • *Many of the European modern art movements, such as Surrealism and Futurism, had their own manifestos.*

man·i·fold [MANY] /£ˈmæn·ɪ·fəʊld, $-foʊld/ *adj literary* many and of several different types • *Despite her manifold faults, she was a strong leader.* • *Our problems are manifold: too few staff, too little money and poor management.*

man·i·fold [PIPE] /£ˈmæn·ɪ·fəʊld, $-foʊld/ *n* [C] *specialized* a pipe or enclosed space in a machine which has several openings, allowing liquids and gases to enter and leave • *The exhaust manifold in a car carries the exhaust gases away from the cylinders.*

man·i·kin [MODEL], **man·ni·kin**, *Am also* **man·ne·quin** /ˈmæn·ə·kɪn/ *n* [C] a model of the human body, used esp. for teaching medical or art students

man·i·kin [MAN], **man·ni·kin** /ˈmæn·ə·kɪn/ *n* [C] *dated* a very short man • *Manikins often appear in children's stories.*

ma·ni·la, ma·nil·la /məˈnɪl·ə/ *adj* [not gradable] made of strong brown paper • *manila envelopes*

man·i·oc /£ˈmæn·i·ɒk, $-ɑːk/ *n* [U] CASSAVA

ma·ni·pu·late *obj* [INFLUENCE] /məˈnɪp·jʊ·leɪt/ *v* [T] *esp. disapproving* to control (something or someone) to your advantage, often unfairly or dishonestly • *Her remarkable success as a rock star is partly due to her ability to manipulate the media.* • *The opposition leader accused government ministers of manipulating the statistics to suit themselves.*

ma·ni·pu·la·tive /£məˈnɪp·jʊ·lə·tɪv, $-t̬ɪv/ *adj esp. disapproving* • If someone is manipulative, they try to control people to their advantage: *Even as a child she was manipulative and knew how to get her own way.*

ma·ni·pu·la·tion /məˌnɪp·jʊˈleɪ·ʃən/ *n esp. disapproving* • *They have been accused of fraud and stock market manipulations.* [C] • *There's been so much* **media** *manipulation of the facts that nobody knows the truth of the matter.* [U] • *The opposition party claims the president returned to power through* **political** *manipulation.* [U]

ma·ni·pu·lat·or /£məˈnɪp·jʊ·leɪ·təʳ, $-t̬ɚ/ *n* [C] *esp. disapproving* • *He is a ruthless, scheming manipulator.*

ma·ni·pu·late *obj* [CONTROL] /məˈnɪp·jʊ·leɪt/ *v* [T] to control (something) using the hands • *The wheelchair is designed so that it is easy to manipulate.* • To manipulate a part of the body is to treat it, using the hands to push back bones into the correct position and put pressure on muscles: *The doctor manipulated the base of my spine and the pain disappeared completely.*

ma·ni·pu·la·tion /məˌnɪp·jʊˈleɪ·ʃən/ *n* • *Osteopathy involves massage and manipulation of the bones and joints.* [U] • *The course of treatment for my back pain consisted of massage and regular manipulations.* [C]

man·kind /mæŋˈkaɪnd/, **hu·man·kind** *n* [U] the whole of the human race, including both men and women • *Mankind has always been obsessed by power.* • *One of the great achievements of the 20th century has been the scientific investigation of mankind's distant past.* • *"That's one small step for a man, one giant leap for mankind"* (Neil Armstrong on stepping on to the moon, 1969) • *"The proper study of Mankind is Man"* (Alexander Pope in the poem *Essay on Man*, 1733) • Compare WOMANKIND. • [LP] **Sexist language**

man·ky /ˈmæŋ·ki/ *adj* **-ier, -iest** *Br infml* (of an object) unpleasantly dirty, esp. because of being old or having been used a lot • *Here, use my tissue – I'm afraid it's a bit manky.* • *We had to put new carpets in the whole house when we moved in, as the old ones were really manky.*

man·ly /ˈmæn·li/ *adj* **-ier, -iest** See at MAN [MALE]

man·li·ness /ˈmæn·lɪ·nəs/ *n* [U]

man·na /ˈmæn·ə/ *n* [U] (in the Old Testament of the Bible) a food which dropped from heaven and prevented Moses and his people from dying of hunger in the desert • If food or drink is described as manna, it is beneficial and has a very pleasant taste: *Hot lemon juice and honey is manna for people with sore throats.* • **Manna from heaven** is completely unexpected help, esp. money: *The large anonymous donation was manna from heaven for the church hall fund.*

man·ne·quin /ˈmæn·ə·kɪn/ *n* [C] a large model of a human being, used esp. to show clothes in the window of a shop • *He is responsible for dressing the mannequins and arranging goods in the shop window.* • Mannequin is also *dated* for MODEL (= a person who wears clothes for photographs and fashion shows). • Mannequin is also *Am* for MANIKIN.

man·ner [WAY] /£ˈmæn·əʳ, $-ɚ/ *n* [U] the way in which something is done • *She stared at me* **in** *an accusing manner.* • *He was elected* **in** *the normal manner.* • *It was the manner* **of** *her death that stuck in the public's mind.* • *Her latest film is a suspense thriller very much* **in the manner of** (= in the style of) *Hitchcock.* • If you do something **as (if) to the manner born,** you do it very well and very naturally as if it is usual and easy for you: *You needn't have worried – you played the part of hostess as if to the manner born.* • **In a manner of speaking** is sometimes added to a statement to show that it is only partly true: *She is his daughter in a manner of speaking, because although he's not her real father, he did bring her up.* • *(Br dated)* **Not by any manner of means** is used to mean not at all: *I'm not satisfied with your explanation of where you were last night – not by any manner of means!*

man·ner [BEHAVIOUR] /£ˈmæn·əʳ, $-ɚ/ *n* [U] the usual way in which you behave towards other people, or the way you behave on a particular occasion • *She has a rather cold, unfriendly manner.* • *His gentleness of manner conceals a steely determination.* • *As soon as the salesman realized that we weren't going to buy anything, his whole manner changed.*

man·ner [TYPE] /£ˈmæn·əʳ, $-ɚ/ *n* [U] *fml* a type • *Very little is known about the new candidate – what manner* **of** *man is he?* • *There are* **all manner of** (= a lot of different types of) *architectural styles in the capital.*

man·nered /£ˈmæn·əd, $-ɚd/ *adj disapproving* (of a style of speaking or behaving) artificial, or intended to achieve a particular effect • *His performance as Hamlet was criticized for being very mannered.*

man·ner·i·sm [BEHAVIOUR] /£ˈmæn·ər·ɪ·zəm, $ˈ-ɚ-/ *n* [C] something that a person does repeatedly with their face, hands or voice, esp. something which they are not aware of

• *He's got some very strange mannerisms.* • *She has this irritating mannerism of sweeping her hair back with her hand.* • *We've spent so much time together that we've picked up each other's mannerisms.*

Man·ner·i·sm ART /£'mæn·ᵊr·ɪ·zᵊm, $'-ɚ-/ *n* [U] a style of 16th century art, common in Italy, France and Spain, which did not follow traditional rules of painting and tried to represent an image of beauty that was perfect rather than natural • *Mannerism is characterized by a distortion of proportions and perspective.* • *Mannerism is also used to describe a style in architecture which is typified by Michaelangelo's later works.*

Man·ner·ist /£'mæn·ᵊr·ɪst, $'-ɚ-/ *n* [C] • *Leading Mannerists include Parmigiano and Giulio Romano, whose pictures are painted in deep, rich colours.*

man·ners /£'mæn·əz, $-ɚz/ *pl n* polite ways of treating other people and behaving in public • *I've been trying to teach my six-year-old niece manners, but it really is hopeless.* • *It's* **bad** *manners to eat with your mouth open.* • *It's considered* **good** *manners in some societies to leave a little food on your plate.* • *(dated) You ought to teach that boy to* **mind** *his manners* (= to be polite).

–man·nered /£-'mæn·əd, $-ɚd, -‚--/ *combining form* • *an* **ill/bad**-*mannered boy* • *He was a* **mild**-*mannered* (= gentle and calm) *young man.* • *I noticed how* **well**-*mannered her children were.*

man·ni·kin /'mæn·ɪ·kɪn/ *n* [C] a MANIKIN

man·nish /'mæn·ɪʃ/ *adj* See at MAN MALE

ma·noeu·vre MILITARY OPERATION *Br and Aus, Am* **ma·neu·ver** /£mə'nuː·vəʳ, $-vɚ/ *n* [C usually pl] a planned and controlled movement or operation, esp. by the armed forces for training purposes and in war • *military/naval manoeuvres* • *In a well-rehearsed manoeuvre, the army swept into the city.* • *One of the manoeuvres that you have to perform in a driving test is reversing round a corner.* • *We saw the army* **on** (= doing) *manoeuvres in the mountains.*

ma·noeu·vre *(obj) Br and Aus, Am* **ma·neu·ver** /£mə'nuː·vəʳ, $-vɚ/ *v* • To manoeuvre something is to turn and direct it: *Loaded supermarket trolleys are often difficult to manoeuvre.* [T] ○ *This car manoeuvres well at high speed.* [I]

ma·noeu·vra·ble *Br and Aus, Am* **ma·neu·ver·a·ble** /mə'nuː·vrə·bl̩/ *adj* • Something which is manoeuvrable is easy to direct: *The new missile is faster and more manoeuvrable than previous models.*

ma·noeu·vra·bil·i·ty *Br and Aus, Am* **ma·neu·ver·a·bil·i·ty** /£mə‚nuː·vrə'bɪl·ɪ·ti, $-ə·ţi/ *n* [U] • *Power-assisted steering improves a car's manoeuvrability.*

ma·noeu·vring *Br and Aus, Am* **man·eu·ver·ing** /£mə'nuː·vᵊr·ɪŋ, $-vɚ-/ *n* [U] • *With some careful manoeuvring, I was able to get the car into the narrow space.*

ma·noeu·vre CLEVER ACTION *Br and Aus, Am* **ma·neu·ver** /£mə'nuː·vəʳ, $-vɚ/ *n* [C] a cleverly planned action which is intended to obtain an advantage • *A series of impressive manoeuvres by the chairman had secured a lucrative contract for the company.* • If you have **room/scope for manoeuvre**, you have the opportunity to change your plans or choose between different ways of acting: *The law in this area is very strict and doesn't allow us much room for manoeuvre.*

ma·noeu·vre *obj Br and Aus, Am* **ma·neu·ver** /£mə'nuː·vəʳ, $-vɚ/ *v* [T] • If you manoeuvre someone, you try to make them act in a particular way: *The other directors are trying to manoeuvre her* **into** *resigning.*

ma·noeu·vring *Br and Aus, Am* **man·eu·ver·ing** /£mə'nuː·vᵊr·ɪŋ, $-vɚ-/ *n* • *The directors managed to secure a good deal for the company with a bit of subtle manoeuvring.* [U] • *He claimed he knew nothing about the political manoeuvrings which had got him into power.* [C]

man·om·et·er /£mæn'ɒm·ɪ·təʳ, $mə'nɑː·mə·ţɚ/ *n* [C] a device for measuring the pressure of gases and liquids

man·or /£'mæn·əʳ, $-ɚ/ *n* [C usually sing] *Br slang* the area in which a person works or which they are responsible for • *A policeman needs to know about all the criminals* **on** (= in) *his manor.*

man·or (house) /£'mæn·əʳ, $-ɚ/ *n* [C] a large old house in the country with land belonging to it • *She sold Rudfin Manor for over £2 million.* • *They own a 400-year-old manor house in Surrey.*

man·pow·er /£'mæm·paʊəʳ, $-paʊr/, **staff** *n* [U] the supply of people who are able to work • *The industry has suffered from a lack of manpower.* • *The project has been constrained by a lack of resources and skilled manpower.* • *After years of manpower shortages in the social services, the government has decided to increase the number of training places.* • LP **Sexist language**

man·qué /mɑ̃ː'keɪ/ *adj* [after n; not gradable] *fml* (of a person) not having had the opportunity to do a particular job despite having the ability to do it • *an artist/poet/writer manqué* • *My brother did some wonderful sketches when he was on holiday – I think he's a bit of an artist manqué.* • If a person is described as manqué in a particular job, they are unsuccessful at it because of lack of skill: *An actress manqué, she was constantly trying to restart her career by being photographed with famous actors.*

man·ser·vant /£'mæn‚sɜː·vᵊnt, $-‚sɜːr-/ *n* [C] *old use* a male servant with responsibility for the personal needs of his employer, such as preparing his food and clothes

man·sion /'mæn·tʃᵊn/ *n* [C] a very large expensive house • *The street is lined with enormous mansions where the rich and famous live.* • Ⓘ Ⓙ

Man·sions /'mæn·tʃᵊnz/ *pl n Br* used in the name of some buildings that contain apartments • *Her new address is 12 Warwickshire Mansions.*

man·slaugh·ter /£'mæn‚slɔː·təʳ, $-‚slɑː·ţɚ/ *n* [U] *law* the crime of killing a person by someone who did not intend to do it or who cannot be responsible for their actions • *She was sentenced to five years imprisonment for manslaughter.* • *He denies murder but admits manslaughter on the grounds of diminished responsibility.* • Compare MURDER; SUICIDE. • LP **Crimes and criminals**

man·tel·piece, man·tle·piece /£'mæn·tᵊl·piːs, $-ţᵊl-/ *n* [C] a shelf above a fireplace, usually part of a frame which surrounds the fireplace • *She's got photographs of all her grandchildren on the mantelpiece.* • PIC **Fires and space heaters**

man·tis /£'mæn·tɪs, $-ţɪs/, **pray·ing man·tis** *n* [C] a large green insect that holds its front legs in a way that makes it look as if it is praying when it is waiting to catch another insect

man·tle RESPONSIBILITY /£'mæn·tl̩, $-ţl̩/ *n* [U] *fml* the responsibilities of an important position or job, esp. as given from the person who had the job to the person who replaces them • *She unsuccessfully attempted to* **assume** *the mantle of presidency.* • *It is widely believed that he will* **inherit** *his father's political mantle.* • *She has been asked to* **take on** *the mantle of managing director in the New York office.*

man·tle LAYER /£'mæn·tl̩, $-ţl̩/ *n* [C] a layer of something which covers a surface • *(literary) A thick mantle* **of** *snow lay on the ground.* • *(literary) We watched the building vanish under a mantle* **of** *thick grey smoke as the fire swiftly moved through it.* • *(fig. literary) She looked out towards the shore which was* **cloaked in** *a mantle of peace* (= quiet and calm). • *(specialized) The Earth's mantle is a layer of rock beneath the earth's crust and is 3000 km thick.* • *(specialized) The planet Jupiter has a gaseous atmosphere and a mantle* **of** *liquid hydrogen and helium.* • *(old use)* A mantle was a piece of clothing without sleeves which was worn over other clothes: *She wore a white silk dress under a mantle of black silk.* ○ *In the 18th century, female popular dress consisted of a skirt, bodice, petticoat, mantle and apron.*

man·tra /'mæn·trə/ *n* [C] (esp. in Hinduism and Buddhism) a word or sound which is believed to possess a special spiritual power • *A personal mantra is sometimes repeated as an aid to meditation or prayer.* • A mantra is also a word or phrase which is often repeated and which sometimes expresses a belief: *The crowds chanted that familiar football mantra: "Here we go, here we go, here we go..."*

ma·nu·al BY HAND /'mæn·ju·əl/ *adj* done with the hands • *She tried to cure the pain in my knee by putting manual pressure on the joint.* • *The latest post office machines can sort letters at 30000 items an hour, which is much faster than manual sorting.* • If a machine is manual, it is operated with the hands rather than by electricity or a motor: *I've replaced my old manual typewriter with an electric one.* • Manual **labour/work** is work which involves physical work rather than mental work: *Tourism is one of the few industries with a big demand for unskilled manual labour.* ○ *Computer-controlled robots are taking over manual jobs in many industries.* ○ *750 manual* **workers** *will lose their jobs as a result of company cutbacks.* • A person's **manual dexterity** is their ability to perform a difficult action with the hands skilfully and quickly so that it looks easy. • If a car has **manual transmission**, the GEARS (= devices that control the power in the engine) are changed by the driver:

The latest model is equipped with five-speed manual transmission. Compare **automatic transmission** at AUTOMATIC [INDEPENDENT].

ma·nu·al·ly /ˈmæn·ju·ə·li/ *adv* • *Some of the machines are not automated and have to be operated manually.*

ma·nu·al [BOOK] /ˈmæn·ju·əl/ *n* [C] a book which gives you practical instructions on how to do something or how to use something, such as a machine • *He learned how to mend a leaking pipe by reading a DIY manual.* • *The computer comes with a 600-page* **instruction** *manual.*

man·u·fac·ture *obj* [PRODUCE] /£ˌmæn·jʊˈfæk·tʃəʳ, $-tʃə/ *v* [T] to produce (goods) in large numbers, esp. in a factory using machines • *He works for a company that manufactures car parts.* • *The report notes a rapid decline in manufactured* **goods.** • *The number of people employed in manufacturing* **industries** *has dropped over the last five years.* • (NL) (RUS)

man·u·fac·ture /£ˌmæn·jʊˈfæk·tʃəʳ, $-tʃə/ *n* [U] • *Oil is used in the manufacture of a number of fabrics.* • *The amount of recycled glass used in manufacture doubled in five years.*

man·u·fac·tur·er /£ˌmæn·jʊˈfæk·tʃəʳr·əʳ, $-tʃə·ə/ *n* [C] • *Germany is a major manufacturer of motorcars.*

man·u·fac·tur·ers /£ˌmæn·jʊˈfæk·tʃəʳr·əz, $-tʃə·əz/ *pl n* • *Our kettle was leaking, so we had to send it back to* **the** *manufacturers* (= the company that made it).

man·u·fac·ture *obj* [INVENT] /£ˌmæn·jʊˈfæk·tʃəʳ, $-tʃə/ *v* [T] to invent (an excuse, reason, story etc.) in order to deceive someone • *He didn't want to go to the party so he manufactured an excuse about being ill.* • *She insisted that every scandalous detail of the story had been manufactured.* • (NL) (RUS)

ma·nure /£məˈnjʊəʳ, $-ˈnʊr/ *n* [U] excrement from animals, esp. horses, which is spread on the land in order to make plants grow well • *Primroses need to be grown in rich damp soil with plenty of manure or compost worked into it.*

man·u·script /ˈmæn·jʊ·skrɪpt/ (*abbreviation* **ms**) *n* [C] the original copy of a book or article before it is printed • *He sent the 400-page manuscript to his publisher two months late.* • *I read the book* **in** *manuscript before any changes were made.* • A manuscript is also an old document or book written by hand in the times before printing was invented: *It is thought that the manuscript is the work of a monk and dates from the twelfth century.*

Manx /mæŋks/ *adj* [not gradable] of the Isle of Man, the people who live there or their language • *The Manx language became extinct at the beginning of the 20th century.* • A **Manx cat** is a type of cat with no tail.

ma·ny /ˈmen·i/ *determiner, pronoun* a large number (of); a lot (of) • *Many people would disagree with your ideas.* • *Rachel was at the party with her many admirers.* • **How** *many students are there in each class?* • **Not** *many people have heard of him.* • *There are***n't** *very many weekends between now and Christmas.* • *The demand for the new type of CD player has been so great that the shop has***n't** *many (of them) left.* • *I've met him* **so** *many times and I still can't remember his name!* • *I don't want to invite* **too** *many people because it's quite a small flat.* • *There are* **too** *many people chasing too few jobs.* • *If there are only five of us going to the concert, then I've booked one too many seats* (= one more than the necessary number). • *If there were* **as** *many women as there are men in parliament, the situation would be very different.* • **As** *many* **as** (= The surprisingly large number of) *6000 people may have been infected with the disease.* • *There are already twelve bottles of wine, so if I buy* **as many again** (= another twelve bottles) *we'll have enough.* • *A* **good/great** *many* (= A large number of the) *people who voted for her in the last election will not be doing so this time.* • *She'd had five children* **in as many** (= in the same number of) *years and decided it was enough.* • *I've told you* **many a time** (= many times) *not to ride your bike on the pavement.* • *(humorous)* **Many's the** *hour I've spent* (= I have spent many hours) *by the telephone just waiting in case he should call.* • *(humorous)* **Many's the** *man who's* (= Many men have) *come out of her office trembling.* • If someone says something **in so many words**, they say it directly and clearly, using exactly the words described: *I told him in so many words that I thought he'd failed completely.* ○ *"Did he say he was unhappy with his job?" "Well,* **not** *in so many words, but that was the impression I got."* • *It was her birthday so I wished her* **many happy returns (of the day)** (= happy birthday). • *(infml)* If you have had **one too many**, you have drunk too much alcohol. • **Many-sided** means having many sides or a lot of different features or characteristics: *a many-sided object* ○ *A many-sided character, he wrote poetry and was a keen cricketer and cook.* • *(saying)* 'There's many a slip between/twixt cup and lip' means that you cannot be certain about what the result of something will be before it happens. • 'Many' is used with countable nouns. Compare MUCH. • (LP) **Measurements, Quantity words**

Mao·ism /ˈmaʊ·ɪ·zᵊm/ *n* [U] the type of Communism introduced in China by Mao Zedong • *Maoism was based on Marxism-Leninism, but the focus of the revolutionary struggle were the peasants rather than the urban workers.*

Mao·ist /ˈmaʊ·ɪst/ *n* [C], *adj* [not gradable] • *A well-known Maoist, he was made a Congress deputy in the recent elections.* • *They have committed themselves to fighting Maoist tendencies in economics and politics.* • *Sending students to the countryside to learn from the peasants was a Maoist practice which caused many young people great hardship.*

Mao·ri /ˈmaʊ·ri/ *n* [C] (a member of) the original people of New Zealand and the Cook Islands • *The Maoris arrived in New Zealand from Polynesia over 1000 years before the Europeans.*

Mao·ri /ˈmaʊ·ri/ *adj* [not gradable] • *The Maori language is now officially encouraged.* • *Before a rugby match, the New Zealand team perform a Maori war dance.*

map /mæp/ *n* [C] a drawing of (part of) the earth's surface showing the shape and position of different countries, political borders, natural features such as rivers and mountains, and artificial features such as roads and buildings • *a map of the world* • *a map of Paris* • *a road map* • *We need a large-scale map showing all the footpaths that we can walk along.* • *I'm hopeless at map* **reading** (= understanding maps). • A map can also give you a particular type of information about a certain area: *He bought a map showing the population distribution of Scotland.* • A map can also show the position of stars in the sky or the features on the surface of planets: *a celestial map* ○ *a map of Mars* • A map is also a very simple plan which shows a direction of travel between one place and another: *I'll draw you a quick map if you're worried about finding the hotel.* • If someone or something **puts** an unknown place or person **on the map**, it makes them important and famous: *The governor has managed to put this sleepy southern state in America on the map.* • If a place is blown/wiped/etc **off the map**, it is destroyed completely: *A nuclear bomb could* **wipe** *the whole country* **off** *the map.* • *"Roll up that map [of Europe]: it will not be wanted these ten years"* (William Pitt the Younger after hearing news of the Battle of Austerlitz, 1805) • (D) (S)

map *obj* /mæp/ *v* [T] **-pp-** • To map an area of land is to represent it in the form of a map: *Archeologists have managed to map an ancient Roman city using radar and aerial photography.* ○ *Parts of the mountainous region in the north of the country have still not been mapped.* • To **map out** the future or a plan of action is to plan it in detail: *The government has issued a new document mapping out its policies on education.* ○ *His future is all mapped out ahead of him – two years at college, three years' training and then a job promised at the end of it.*

ma·ple /ˈmeɪ·pl̩/ *n* a type of large tree which grows in northern areas of the world, or the wood of this tree • *Maples are particularly beautiful in the autumn when their leaves are red and purple.* [C] • *My new desk is made from pale maple.* [U] • *The Canadian flag has a maple* **leaf** *on it.* • *Acid rain has killed many of the maple* **trees** *of central and eastern Canada.* • **Maple syrup** is a sticky sugary liquid produced from the maple tree which is eaten with or used in making food: *pancakes with maple syrup* ○ *It takes about 40 gallons of sap from the maple to produce one gallon of maple syrup.*

mar *obj* /£mɑːʳ, $mɑːr/ *v* [T] **-rr-** *slightly fml* to spoil (something), making it less perfect or less enjoyable • *The text is marred by careless errors.* • *It was a really nice day, marred only by a little argument in the car on the way home.* • *I hope the fact that Louise isn't coming won't mar your enjoyment of the evening.* • *It was a beautiful and moving film, marred only by the fact that it bore no resemblance to what actually happened.*

ma·ra·cas /məˈræk·əz/ *pl n* a musical instrument consisting of two hollow containers filled with stones which are shaken to provide the rhythm for some types of music

mar·as·chino /£ˌmær·əˈskiː·nəʊ, £-ˈʃiː-, $-noʊ/ *n* [U] a slightly bitter LIQUEUR (=strong sweet alcoholic drink) made from a particular type of CHERRY (=small soft red or black fruit) • **Maraschino cherries** are preserved in maraschino or a similar drink and used to decorate drinks and food.

mar·a·thon /£ˈmær·ə·θən, $-θɑːn/ *n* [C] a running race of slightly over 26 miles (42·195 kilometres) • *the London/New York marathon* • *She did/ran her first marathon in just under three hours.* • A marathon is also an activity which takes a long time and makes you very tired: *The election broadcast, a nine-hour marathon, lasts until seven o'clock in the morning.*

mar·a·thon /£ˈmær·ə·θən, $-θɑːn/ *adj* [before n] • *a marathon runner* • *I had a marathon* (=extremely long) *session marking 55 exam papers yesterday.*

ma·raud·ing /£məˈrɔː·dɪŋ, $-ˈrɑː-/ *adj* [before n; not gradable] going from one place to another killing or using violence, stealing and destroying • *Witnesses reported gangs of marauding soldiers breaking into people's houses and setting fire to them.*

ma·raud·er /£məˈrɔː·dəʳ, $-ˈrɑː·dɚ/ *n* [C] • A marauder is a person or animal that goes from one place to another looking for something to kill or steal: *The marauders burst into the camp, shooting into houses, hurling stones and smashing car windows.*

marb·le ROCK /£ˈmɑː·bl̩, $ˈmɑːr-/ *n* [U] a type of very hard rock which has a pattern of lines going through it, feels cold and becomes smooth and shiny when cut and POLISHED • *a marble floor/statue* • *Marble is often used in sculpture and to decorate parts of buildings.* • *The table has curved brass legs and a marble top.* • *The entrance hall, with its deep carpets and pillars made of thick white marble, is extremely grand.*

marb·led /£ˈmɑː·bl̩d, $ˈmɑːr-/ *adj* [not gradable] • If something is marbled, it is decorated with a delicate pattern consisting of irregular lines and areas of colour: *The church has an ornate black and white marbled interior and striped pillars.* ○ *The plant has oval green leaves marbled* **with** *brownish-purple.* ○ *The steak was just how he liked – pink, juicy and marbled* **with** *fat.*

marb·le GLASS BALL /£ˈmɑː·bl̩, $ˈmɑːr-/ *n* [C] a small ball usually made of coloured or transparent glass which is used esp. in children's games • PIC› **Toy**

marb·les /£ˈmɑː·bl̩z, $ˈmɑːr-/ *n* [U] • Marbles is a children's game in which small round glass balls are rolled along the floor: *Do you want to play a game of marbles?*

mar·ca·site /£ˈmɑː·kə·saɪt, $ˈmɑːr-/ *n* [U] a MINERAL that can be cut and POLISHED to look like precious stones and is used to make cheap jewellery

March MONTH /£mɑːtʃ, $mɑːrtʃ/ (*abbreviation* **Mar**) *n* the third month of the year, after February and before April • *26(th) March/March 26(th)/26(th) Mar/Mar 26(th)* [U] • *My birthday is* **on** *the eleventh of March/March the eleventh/(esp. Am) March eleventh.* [U] • *He retired* **last** *March/is retiring* **next** *March.* [U] • *The meeting will be one day* **in/during** *March.* [U] • *It has been one of the windiest Marches for several years.* [C] • LP› **Dates**

march *(obj)* WALK /£mɑːtʃ, $mɑːrtʃ/ *v* to walk with regular steps keeping the body stiff, esp. in a formal group of people who are all walking in the same way • *The band marched through the streets.* [I] • *The soldiers marched 90 miles in three days.* [T] • *She could hear the approach of marching soldiers.* • *"Right turn, then* **quick march** (=start marching)," *ordered the captain.* • If you march somewhere, you walk there quickly and in a determined way, often because you are angry: *She marched into my office demanding to know why I hadn't written my report.* [I] • *(infml)* If you give someone their **marching orders** (*Am usually* **walking papers**), you dismiss them from their job, or *(Br)* you say that your relationship with them is finished: *He* **got** *his marching orders when they found out that he'd been working for another company as well.* ○ *(Br) He* **gave** *her her marching orders after she was unfaithful to him.*

march /£mɑːtʃ, $mɑːrtʃ/ *n* • *It had been a long march and the soldiers were weary and their feet sore.* [C] • *The border was within a day's march* (=could be reached by marching for a day). [U] • *The troops are* **on the march** (=have started marching). • *(fig.) It is impossible to stop the forward march* (=advance) *of progress/time.* [U] • A **march-past** is a march of the armed forces past an officer of high rank or a king or queen.

march *obj* FORCE /£mɑːtʃ, $mɑːrtʃ/ *v* [T always + adv/prep] to force (someone) to go somewhere by taking hold of them and leading them there • *Without saying a word, she took hold of my arm and marched me* **off** *to the headmaster's office.* • *The police marched a gang of youths* **out of** *the building.* • See also FROGMARCH.

march MUSIC /£mɑːtʃ, $mɑːrtʃ/ *n* [C] a piece of music with a strong regular rhythm which is written for marching to • *a funeral march* • *Mendelssohn's Wedding March is a popular piece of music that is often played as newly married couples leave the church.*

march PUBLIC EVENT /£mɑːtʃ, $mɑːrtʃ/ *n* [C] an event in which a large number of people walk through a public place to express their ideas, esp. their support for something or their disagreement with or disapproval of something • *She's going on a/taking part in a march on Saturday in protest over the closure of the hospital.*

march /£mɑːtʃ, $mɑːrtʃ/ *v* [I] • *Over four thousand people marched through London today to protest against the proposed new law.*

mar·cher /£ˈmɑː·tʃəʳ, $ˈmɑːr·tʃɚ/ *n* [C] • *The marchers* (=people marching) *stopped outside the American embassy, chanting slogans and waving banners.*

Mar·di Gras /£ˌmɑː·diˈgrɑː, $ˌmɑːr-/ *n* [C usually sing] (in some Christian countries) a celebration before the beginning of Lent, in which there is a lot of public enjoyment, including dressing in special clothes, dancing, eating and drinking, often in the road, or any large public event of this type • *Mardi Gras is a big celebration in New Orleans.* • *The Mardi Gras in Sydney, Australia is a celebration of the gay and lesbian community, and the procession attracts thousands of people every year.* • Mardi Gras is another name for Shrove Tuesday. • LP› **Holidays**

mare /£meəʳ, $mer/ *n* [C] an adult female horse • *A female horse is called a mare when it is over four years old.* • Compare STALLION.

mar·ga·rine /£ˌmɑː·dʒəˈriːn, $ˈmɑːr·dʒɚ-/, *Br infml* **marge** /£mɑːdʒ, $mɑːrdʒ/ *n* [U] a pale yellow food used for cooking and spreading on bread, which is similar to butter but softer and usually made from vegetable fat • *soya/sunflower/vegetable margarine*

mar·ga·ri·ta /£ˌmɑː·gəˈriː·tə, $-gəˈriː·t̬ə/ *n* [C] a type of alcoholic COCKTAIL (=a mixed drink) • *A margarita is made with tequila, an orange liqueur and lime or lemon juice.* • *Margaritas are usually served in glasses with salt round the rim.*

mar·gin OUTER PART /£ˈmɑː·dʒɪn, $ˈmɑːr-/ *n* [C] the outer edge of an area • *The plant tends to grow in the lighter margins of woodland areas.* • On a page, a margin is the empty space to the side of the text, sometimes separated from the rest of the page by a vertical line: *If I have any comments to make, I'll write them* **in** *the margin.* • *He spent the 1980s* **on the margins of** (=slightly involved in) *British politics.*

mar·gin·al /£ˈmɑː·dʒɪ·nəl, $ˈmɑːr-/ *adj* • A writer, poet, musician, etc. can be described as marginal if their work is different to most of the work in any particular period. • **Marginal land** is land which is found on the edge of cultivated areas and is often difficult to grow crops in: *The government is planning to transform large areas of marginal land into land suitable for crop growing.*

mar·gin DIFFERENCE /£ˈmɑː·dʒɪn, $ˈmɑːr-/ *n* [C] the amount by which one thing is different from another • *The Senate approved the use of military force by a margin of 52 votes to 47.* • *The poll shows that the government is leading by the* **narrowest** *of margins.* • *The August deadline for the project leaves us with no margin* **for** *error* (=no additional time if things do not happen as planned). • A **margin of error** is an additional amount of something, such as time or money, which you allow because there might be a mistake in your calculations: *When archaeologists date objects that are thousands of years old, they allow a margin of error of several hundred years.* ○ *The government estimates that its borrowing requirement this year could reach £150 billion, subject to a* **wide** *margin of error.* • In business, a **(profit) margin** is the difference between the amount of money that a company receives and the amount which it spends: *Many small companies operate on very* **narrow** *margins.*

mar·gin·al SMALL /£ˈmɑː·dʒɪ·nəl, $ˈmɑːr-/ *adj* very small in amount or effect • *The report suggests that there has only been a marginal improvement in women's pay over the past few years.* • Something which is of marginal **interest** is of interest to only a few people: *The TV channel* *aims to show programmes about subjects of marginal interest which will appeal to a limited audience.*

mar·gin·al·ly /£ˈmɑː·dʒɪ·nə·li, $ˈmɑːr-/ *adv* • *His performance this year was only marginally* (= slightly) *better than last year's.*

mar·gin·al·ize *obj, Br and Aus usually* **-ise** /£ˈmɑː·dʒɪ·nə·laɪz, $ˈmɑːr-/ *v* [T] • Something or someone that is marginalized is treated as unimportant: *Now that English has taken over as the main language, the country's native language has been marginalized.*

mar·gin·al·iz·a·tion, *Br and Aus usually* **-i·sa·tion** /£ˌmɑː·dʒɪ·nə·laɪˈzeɪ·ʃᵊn, $ˌmɑːr·dʒɪ·nə·lɪ-/ *n* [U] • *The marginalization* **of** *certain groups within the community may lead to social unrest.*

mar·gin·al POLITICS /£ˈmɑː·dʒɪ·nəl, $ˈmɑːr-/ *n* [C], *adj Br and Aus* (a political area or parliamentary position) which can be won by only a small number of votes because support for the main political parties is equally divided among the people voting • *Labour lost two of the key marginals in London.* • *The minister's own seat is a Tory marginal.* • *The marginal Tory* **constituency** *was held by 2 200 votes in 1992.* • *This is the most marginal* **seat** *in the country which the Liberal Democrats won by only seven votes.*

ma·ri·gold /£ˈmær·ɪ·gəʊld, $-goʊld/ *n* [C] a plant with bright yellow or orange flowers

ma·ri·jua·na, ma·ri·hua·na /ˌmær·ɪˈwɑː·nə/ *n* [U] a drug made from the dried leaves and flowers of a particular type of the HEMP plant, which produces a feeling of pleasant relaxation if smoked or eaten • *It is illegal to grow or use marijuana in many countries.* • *Regular smoking of marijuana can cause short-term memory loss and long-term health problems.*

ma·ri·na /məˈriː·nə/ *n* [C] a small port that is used for pleasure rather than trade, often with hotels, restaurants and bars • *The docklands were derelict for many years before they were converted into a marina.*

ma·ri·nade /ˌmær·ɪˈneɪd/ *n* [C] a mixture containing usually oil, wine or vinegar, herbs and spices, which you pour over fish or meat before it is cooked, in order to add flavour to it or make it easier to chew • *Pour the marinade over the beef and leave it to soak for 24 hours.*

ma·ri·nate *obj* /ˈmær·ɪ·neɪt/ *v* [T] • *Marinate the chicken in* (= leave it to absorb the) *white wine for a couple of hours before frying.*

ma·rine SEA /məˈriːn/ *adj* [before n; not gradable] of or related to the sea or sea transport • *The oil slick seriously threatens marine* **life** *around the islands.* • *Marine* **biologists** *are concerned about the effects of untreated sewage that is flowing into coastal waters.* • *Whales, dolphins and porpoises are marine mammals.* • *One plane, a marine F18, was lost in the raid.* • *The Central harbour area will be closed to all marine traffic from 3.45 pm to 4.30 pm.* • See also MARITIME. • Ⓝ

ma·rine SOLDIER /məˈriːn/ *n* [C] a soldier who works closely with the navy and is trained for military operations on land which begin from the sea • *Marines were the first to land on the beach.* • The **Marine Corps** is a part of the United States military forces that consists of soldiers who operate on land and at sea. • Ⓝ

Mar·ines /məˈriːnz/ *pl n* • **The Marines** is a part of a country's military forces which takes part in operations on land which begin from the sea: *He's in the Royal Marines.* ○ *They should send in the Marines.* • *(saying) 'Tell it/that to the Marines' means 'I don't believe it'.*

ma·rin·er /£ˈmær·ɪ·nəʳ, $-nɚ/ *n* [C] *literary or old use* a sailor • *Many a mariner lost his life on these rocks.*

mar·i·on·ette /ˌmær·i·əˈnet/, **pup·pet** *n* [C] a small model of a person or animal with movable parts of the body that are controlled with strings • *The show ingeniously combined actors and marionettes.*

mar·i·tal /£ˈmær·ɪ·tᵊl, $-ţᵊl/ *adj* [not gradable] *fml* connected with marriage • *The book is about a couple who have lived in marital* **bliss** *for twenty years but have no child.* • *The programme discussed the main causes of marital* **breakdown**. • *He won the election in spite of allegations of marital* **infidelity** *from rival candidates.* • *Their marital* **problems** *started soon after they had their first child.* • A **marital aid** is something which people can use to improve their sexual relationships with their partners: *Our catalogue contains a wide range of marital aids, including sex toys, erotic books and educational videos.* • **Marital status** refers to whether or not you are married: *Could I ask you about your marital status? Are you single, married or divorced?*

ma·ri·time /ˈmær·ɪ·taɪm/ *adj* [not gradable] *fml* connected with human activity at sea • *The blockade of the ports has eliminated maritime trade, but some supplies are still getting through over land.* • *Amalfi and Venice were important maritime powers.* • *Make sure you visit the maritime museum if you're interested in anything to do with ships or seafaring.* • Maritime also means near the sea or coast: *The temperature change in winter is less in maritime areas.*

mar·jor·am /£ˈmɑː·dʒᵊr·əm, $ˈmɑːr·dʒɚ-/ *n* [U] a sweet Mediterranean herb used to flavour food • *Sprinkle some marjoram and olive oil over the salad before serving.* • PIC〉 **Herbs and spices**

mark DIFFERENT AREA /£mɑːk, $mɑːrk/ *n* [C] a small area on the surface of something which is damaged, dirty or different in some way • *There were dirty marks on her trousers where she had wiped her hands.* • *His fingers had left marks on the table's polished surface.* • *I'm afraid the acid will leave a permanent/indelible mark on your car.* • *She had a red mark on her arm where she had burnt herself.* • A mark is also a typical feature or one which allows you to recognize someone or something: *Did your attacker have any identifying/distinguishing marks such as a scar or a birthmark?* ○ *You can tell which puppy is which from the marks (also* **markings***) on their fur.* ○ *Judging from the green marks (also* **markings***) on their backs, these sheep belong to the farmer up the road.* • *(fig.) Ten years away from home at boarding school have certainly* **left** *their* **mark on** (= had a permanent unpleasant effect on) *him.* • *(fig.) Daniel didn't work here for very long, but he definitely* **made** *his* **mark on** (= was successfully involved with) *the place.* • Ⓟⓛ

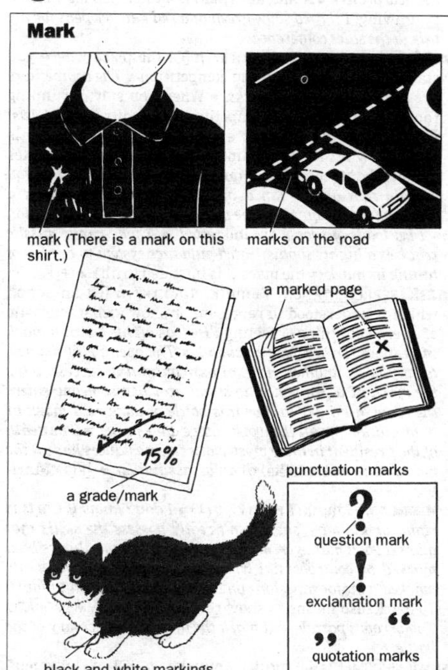

mark *(obj)* /£mɑːk, $mɑːrk/ *v* • *Make sure you don't mark the paintwork while you're moving the furniture around.* [T] • *The man's body was marked with blows from a blunt weapon.* [T] • *A dark carpet won't mark as easily as a light one.* [I] • PIC〉 **Mark**

mark·ing /£ˈmɑː·kɪŋ, $ˈmɑːr-/ *n* [C] • Markings are marks which make it possible to recognize something: *There are a couple of fish with blue markings, and a few more with gold stripes down the side.* ○ *A police spokeswoman said there were several ways for car thieves to alter identification markings on stolen cars.* ○ *The army said the relief flight would be too dangerous as none of its helicopters had Red Cross markings.* • Markings are also marks: *I have had little success in removing these paint markings.* • PIC〉 **Mark**

mark [SYMBOL] /£mɑːk, $mɑːrk/ *n* [C] a symbol which is used for giving information • *I've put a mark on the map where I think we should go for a picnic.* • *What do those marks in the middle of the road mean?* • A mark is also a written or printed symbol: *a question mark* ○ *an exclamation mark* ○ *punctuation marks* • [LP]> **Symbols** [PIC]> **Mark** (PL)

mark *obj* /£mɑːk, $mɑːrk/ *v* [T] • *I've marked the route around the one-way system on the town plan.* • *I'd like everyone to mark their progress on the chart every week.* • *This X marks the spot where the treasure is buried.* • If you mark **off** something that is on a list, you record that you have dealt with it: *I've already sent Paul an invitation, but I forgot to mark him off (on the list).* • If you mark **(off)**/*(Br also)* mark **(out)** something or someone you show in some way that it is separate or different: *The police marked out the area where the body was found.* [T/M] ○ *The digging will seem easier if you divide up the garden by marking out small sections with your spade.* [T/M] ○ *The piles of tattered and stained blankets marked out the living space of each family group.* [T/M] • *I can't speak a word of French so I'm (Br)* **marked out as**/*(Am)* **marked as** (= it is obvious that I'm) *a foreigner as soon as I arrive in France.* • *Having children often prevents women who've been (Br)* **marked out as**/*(Am)* **marked as** (= noticed as likely to be) *high-fliers from reaching their potential.*

mark·er /£ˈmɑː·kəʳ, $ˈmɑːr·kɚ/ *n* [C] • *I've put in some markers where I planted the seeds.* • *She reached the 500-metre marker in record time, but she fell back in the second half of the race.* • *(fig.) The Prime Minister's speech was a marker of a change in* (= showed clearly an intention to change) *government policy.* • *(fig.) He* **put down** *a marker for* (= showed clearly his intention was) *April as the start of the new project.* • A **marker (pen)** is a thick pen for writing or drawing: *I'll need some green and red marker pens for my talk at the sales conference.*

mark [PLACE] /£mɑːk, $mɑːrk/ *n* [C] the place where you stand to start esp. a running competition • *The competitors are moving onto their marks.* • When you start a running race, you call out to the competitors "**On your** *(Br and Aus)* **marks**/*(Am)* **mark ... get set ... go!**" • Someone who is quick/slow **off the mark** understands something or takes action about something quickly or slowly: *Could you explain that again? I'm a bit slow off the mark today.* ○ *You'll have to be quick off the mark* **with** *that job application – I bet loads of people are interested.* • *A long-range missile requires a highly sophisticated guidance system to be sure of hitting its mark* (= the place it is intended to hit). • (PL)

mark [REPRESENTATION] /£mɑːk, $mɑːrk/ *n* [C] an action which is understood to represent or show a characteristic of a person or thing or feeling • *He took off his hat as a mark* **of respect** *for her dead husband.* • *The opening of the new factory is yet another mark* **of** *our continuing success.* • *It's the mark* **of** *a gentleman to stand up when someone enters the room.* • *I'd like to give this bottle of wine as a mark* **of** *appreciation for all the work you've done for us.* • *The death of the President in these mysterious circumstances has all the marks (also* **hallmarks**) **of** *an assassination.* • [PIC]> **Mark** (PL)

mark *obj* /£mɑːk, $mɑːrk/ *v* [T] • *I don't know if Chris is right for the job – she doesn't really possess the skills that mark a good manager.* • *The band's songs have always been marked by controversial lyrics.* • *The signing of the treaty marked a major milestone on the road to European union.* • To mark also means to show respect for or COMMEMORATE: *Tomorrow's parade will mark the fiftieth anniversary of the battle.*

mark [JUDGMENT] /£mɑːk, $mɑːrk/ *n* [C] a judgment, expressed as a number or letter, about the quality of a piece of work done at school, college or university • *"What mark did you get in the biology exam?" "I got 90%/an A."* • *You could've got a higher mark if you'd worked harder.* • *Georgina's had very good marks in/for English throughout the year.* • *(Br and Aus) You scored* **full** *marks in the test – ten out of ten – Well done!* • *There are* **no marks for guessing** (= It is obvious) *who said we had to tidy up our rooms!* • (PL)

mark *obj* /£mɑːk, $mɑːrk/ *v* [T] • To mark is to correct mistakes in and give points to a piece of work: *Will you mark my test before the end of term?* • *(Br) You'll be marked* **down** (= given a lower mark) *for poor spelling and punctuation.* • See also MARK DOWN.

mark [LEVEL] /£mɑːk, $mɑːrk/ *n* [U] the intended or desired level • *Sales have already passed the million mark.* • *This work simply isn't* **up to the** *mark – it's certainly not as good as your usual standard.* • *I wasn't feeling* **up to the** *mark* (= as well as usual) *when I wrote that article.* • (PL)

mark [MACHINE] /£mɑːk, $mɑːrk/ (*abbreviation* **Mk**) *n* [C] (used before a number) a variation of a machine, particularly one that is an improvement on the original machine • *The car has enjoyed modest success since its launch, but the Mark 2 version is expected to be far more popular.* • *Marks II and III sold far more than the Mark I model.* • *(fig. Br infml) I am enclosing a list of my proposals, Mark 2* (= after making changes), *for you to consider before our next meeting.* • (PL)

mark *obj* [SPORT] *Br and Aus* /£mɑːk, $mɑːrk/, *Am* **cov·er** *v* [T] to prevent (a member of the opposing team) from taking control of the ball by staying close to them all the time • *Mike, I want you to mark Jones and make sure he doesn't get anywhere near the ball.* • (PL)

mark *obj* [MARCH] /£mɑːk, $mɑːrk/ *v* [T] **mark time** to march in one place without moving forward • *As the parade turned left, the soldiers on the left marked time while the others moved forward.* • *(fig.) She's just marking time until she goes off to university.* • (PL)

mark *obj* [NOTICE] /£mɑːk, $mɑːrk/ *v* [T] **mark my words** notice or pay attention to what I'm saying because future events will show I'm right • *He'll cause trouble – (you) mark my words!* • (PL)

mark down *obj* [REDUCE], **mark** *obj* **down** *v adv* [M] to reduce the price of (something), esp. in order to encourage people to buy it • *Low consumer demand has forced us to mark down a wide range of goods, sometimes* **by** *as much as 30%.* • *Shares in the electricity companies were marked down following the announcement of the new energy tax.* • See also **mark down** at MARK [JUDGMENT].

mark·down /£ˈmɑːk·daʊn, $ˈmɑːrk-/ *n* [C] • *Did they have any silk shirts among the markdowns?* • *The markdown racks are bulging as stores try to boost revenues.* • *We're offering a 10% markdown on selected items.* • *The company's shares suffered a markdown to 69p on the news that the chairman had resigned.*

mark down *obj* [RECORD], **mark** *obj* **down** *v adv* [M] to make a brief record of (information) • *Well, if you're not sure about the answer, I'll mark you down* **as** *a don't know.* • *(fig.) From what she was saying, I had her marked down* **as** (= I thought she was) *a radical feminist, but she's not very political.*

mark up *obj*, **mark** *obj* **up** *v adv* [M] to increase the price of (something) • *They buy paintings at auctions, mark them up and then resell them at a vast profit to collectors.* • *In the days of hyperinflation we would rush to the market as soon as we were paid and buy our weekly groceries before they were marked up.* • *Shares in retail businesses were marked up on the news that consumer spending rose last month.*

mark·up /£ˈmɑːk·ʌp, $ˈmɑːrk-/ *n* [C] • *She buys the shirts at £15 each and sells them in her shop for £30, which is a 100% markup* (= increase in price). • *Our markup on these shoes needs to be at least five bucks for it to be worth our while to keep them in stock.*

marked /£mɑːkt, $mɑːrkt/ *adj* (esp. of a change in behaviour or situation) very obvious or noticeable • *There was a marked improvement in my health when I gave up smoking.* • *Unemployment has fallen again, although the change is less marked than last month.* • *The president spoke with passion for an hour,* **in** *marked* **contrast** *to his subdued address to the parliament yesterday.* • A **marked man/woman** is someone who is at risk of unpleasant action being taken against them: *He became a marked man when he started spying for the Americans instead of the Soviets, so his murder was no great surprise.* ○ *She's been a marked woman ever since she criticized her boss's extravagant lifestyle.*

mark·ed·ly /£ˈmɑː·kɪd·li, $ˈmɑːr-/ *adv* • *Eye-witness accounts of the fighting differ markedly from police reports of what happened.* • *Her interests are markedly different from my own.*

mar·ket [PLACE] /£ˈmɑː·kɪt, $ˈmɑːr-/ *n* [C] a place or event at which people gather in order to buy and sell things • *Fruit and vegetables are much cheaper from/in/on the market than in the supermarket.* • *She runs a stall in/on the open-air market as well as her shop on the high street.* • *The indoor flower market is a big tourist attraction.* • *Did you get those candles at the craft market?* • *The town's always busy on market* **day**. • *(Br and Aus)* A **market garden** (*Am* **truck farm**) is a small farm where fruit and vegetables are grown for selling to the public: *Farmers and* **market**

gardeners *(Am* **truck farmers***) have been badly affected by the drought.* ○ *I got fed up with advertising and went into* **market gardening** *(Am* **truck farming***).* • A **market town** is a small town, esp. in the countryside, which has a regular market and acts as a business centre for surrounding farms and villages: *Steve runs a dental practice in a quiet market town in Northumberland.* • See also MARKETPLACE.

mar·ket [BUYING AND SELLING] /£ˈmɑː·kɪt, $ˈmɑːr-/ *n* [C] the people who might want to buy something, or a part of the world where something is sold • *Are you sure there's a market* **for** *something so unusual?* • *We estimate the potential market* **for** *the new phones to be around one million people in this country alone.* • *The domestic market is still depressed, but demand abroad is picking up.* • *The newly liberalized markets of this region are seen as a golden opportunity by foreign businesses.* • *They've increased their* **share of** *the market by 10% over the past year.* • In a **buyer's** market, people want to buy less of something than the amount which is available, resulting in lower prices. In a **seller's** market, people want to buy more than is available. • A market is also the business or trade in a particular product, including financial products: *the coffee market* ○ *the economic market* ○ *the commodities market* ○ *the stock market* ○ *the job market* ○ *the housing market* • *Thanks for the offer, but I'm not* **in the market for** (= interested in buying) *another car at the moment.* • **On the market** means available for sale: *We* **put** *our house on the market as soon as house prices started to rise.* ○ *This is one of the best televisions on the market.* ○ *The pictures would sell for half a million on the* **open** *market* (= if offered for sale without a fixed price). • **Market forces** are the forces that decide price levels in an economy or trading system whose activities are not influenced or limited by government: *The action of market forces means that the cost of something rises if demand for it rises and the amount available remains constant.* • A **market price** is a price which is likely to be paid for something: *They're asking £60 000 for their flat, but the market price is nearer £55 000.* • **Market research** is the collection and examination of information about things that people buy or might buy and their feelings about things that they have bought: *Companies employ* **market researchers** *when they want to find out how to increase sales of their products or how to make a new product successful.*

mar·ket·eer /£ˌmɑː·kɪˈtɪəʳ, $ˌmɑːr·kəˈtɪr/ *n* [C] • A marketeer is someone who works in or supports a particular market system: *Under the old regime* **black** *marketeers would buy almost anything from Western tourists and resell it at an enormous profit.* ○ **Free** *marketeers are vehemently opposed to the new safety regulations which they say will increase employers' costs.*

mar·ket *obj* [MAKE AVAILABLE] /£ˈmɑː·kɪt, $ˈmɑːr-/ *v* [T] to make (goods) available to buyers, esp. in a planned way which encourages people to buy more of them, for example by advertising • *The product would have sold more if it had been marketed better.*

mar·ket·ing /£ˈmɑː·kɪ·tɪŋ, $ˈmɑːr·kɪ·t̬ɪŋ/ *n* [U] • *She's hoping for a career in marketing, advertising or public relations.* • *Our marketing people have come up with a great idea for the launch of the new model.*

mar·ket·a·ble /£ˈmɑː·kɪ·tə·bl̩, $ˈmɑːr·kɪ·t̬ə-/ *adj* • *This is a highly marketable* (= easily sold) *product.*

mar·ket·a·bil·i·ty /£ˌmɑː·kɪ·təˈbɪl·ɪ·ti, $ˌmɑːr·kɪ·t̬əˈbɪl·ə·t̬i/ *n* [U] • *How do you expect us to sell something that has such low marketability* (= attractiveness to buyers).

mar·ket·er /£ˈmɑː·kɪ·təʳ, $ˈmɑːr·kɪ·t̬ɚ/ *n* [C] • *Marketers were trying to convince men that such products were not just for women.*

mar·ket [SHOP] /£ˈmɑː·kɪt, $ˈmɑːr-/ *v* [I] *Am* to shop, esp. for food and things used in the house • *Dad's* **gone** *marketing but he'll be back in an hour.*

mar·ket /£ˈmɑː·kɪt, $ˈmɑːr-/ *n* [C] *Am* • *We have to shop across town now that the market* (= shop) *has burned down.* • See also HYPERMARKET; SUPERMARKET.

mar·ket·ing /£ˈmɑː·kɪ·tɪŋ, $ˈmɑːr·kɪ·t̬ɪŋ/ *n* [U] *Am* • *We like to get the marketing done on Thursdays so we can have the weekend free.*

mar·ket·place /£ˈmɑː·kɪt·pleɪs, $ˈmɑːr-/ *n* [C] a small outside area in a town where a market takes place • *I'll meet you in the marketplace next to the fountain.* • Marketplace is also a set of trading conditions or the business environment: *To remain competitive the company has to be able to adapt to the changing marketplace.* ○ *It's essential that we maintain our position in the marketplace* (= keep our share of business activity).

marks·man (*pl* **-men**), **marks·wo·man** (*pl* **-women**) /£ˈmɑːks·mən, $ˈmɑːrks-, -ˌwʊm·ən/ *n* [C] someone who can shoot esp. a gun very accurately • **Police** *marksmen were called to the scene, but after a five-hour siege the gunman gave himself up without any shots being fired.* • *She was the first British markswoman to win a medal in the Olympic Games.*

marks·man·ship /£ˈmɑːks·mən·ʃɪp, $ˈmɑːrks-/ *n* [U] • *Their marksmanship* (= skill in shooting) *is remarkable when you consider that in this competition they ski between targets and have a time limit.*

mark·up /£ˈmɑːk·ʌp, $ˈmɑːrk-/ *n* [C] See at MARK UP

mar·ma·lade /£ˈmɑː·mə·leɪd, $ˈmɑːr-/ *n* [U] a soft substance with a sweet but slightly bitter taste, made by cooking fruit such as oranges with sugar to preserve it. It is eaten on bread, esp. at the first meal of the day. • *Marmalade is a type of jam which can be made from any type of citrus fruit.* • *I think I'll just have some* **toast and** *marmalade for breakfast.* • *Could you get me a jar of* **thick-cut/thin-cut** (= containing thick/thin strips of the skin of the fruit) *marmalade, please?*

mar·ma·lade /£ˈmɑː·mə·leɪd, $ˈmɑːr-/ *adj* [not gradable] *Br* • A marmalade cat has fur which is dark orange with small strips of yellow or brown. • (CS) (D) (DK) (GR) (I) (PL) (RUS)

mar·mo·set /£ˈmɑː·mə·set, $ˈmɑːr-/ *n* [C] a very small monkey from the tropical forests of South and Central America which has large eyes, thick fur, a long hairy tail and long curved and pointed nails

ma·rooned /məˈruːn/ *adj* left in a place from which you cannot escape • *What would you miss most if you found yourself marooned on a desert island?* • *The police are advising motorists marooned by the blizzards to stay in their cars until the rescue services can reach them.* • *Marooned in the dank cellar, I wondered how long it would be before I was missed.* • *Marooned passengers were taken to hotels for the night.*

ma·roon *obj* /məˈruːn/ *v* [T usually passive]

ma·roon /məˈruːn/ *n* [U], *adj* [not gradable] (being) a dark reddish purple colour • *Maroon is a popular colour for clothing and furnishings.* • (J)

mar·que /£mɑːk, $mɑːrk/ *n* [C] a name of a range of cars, which is sometimes different from the name of the company that produces them • *The car market has boomed over the past year, and sales of luxury marques like Porsche and BMW are rising.* • *Jaguar is a world-famous British marque which is now owned by Ford.*

mar·quee [TENT] /£mɑːˈkiː, $mɑːr-/ *n* [C] *Br and Aus* a large tent used esp. for eating and drinking in at events held mainly outside that involve a lot of people • *We're planning to hold the wedding reception in a marquee in the garden.* • *Delays at the airport are so bad that marquees have been erected to provide 1000 extra seats.*

mar·quee [ROOF] /£mɑːˈkiː, $mɑːr-/ *n* [C] *Am* a roof-like structure which sticks out over the entrance to a public building, esp. a theatre, and on which there is usually a sign • *Peter was excited when he saw his band's name up on the marquee.* • If someone has marquee **value** or is a marquee **name**, **player** or **performer** their name is thought to attract people to the show, film, sporting event, etc. they are taking part in: *The studio chiefs wanted a marquee name in the lead role, not some unknown.*

mar·que·try /£ˈmɑː·kɪ·tri, $ˈmɑːr-/ *n* [U] a decorative pattern on a piece of furniture which consists of thin sheets of very shiny wood of different colours fixed on the surface of the furniture • *Her lecture will include a slide-show of historic pieces of furniture decorated with marquetry.*

mar·quis, mar·quess /£ˈmɑː·kwɪs, $ˈmɑːr-/ *n* [C] (the title of) a person of a high social rank, who in the UK is less important than a DUKE and more important than an EARL • **The** *Marquis* **of** *Blandford is the son and heir of the Duke of Marlborough.* • *The rules that govern boxing were introduced by* **the** *Marquess* **of** *Queensberry in 1867.*

mar·riage /£ˈmær·ɪdʒ, $ˈmer-/ *n* a legally accepted relationship between a woman and a man in which they live as husband and wife, or the official ceremony which results in this • *Sally's parents have had a long and happy marriage.* [C] • *Almost one in ten divorces occur within the first two years of marriage.* [U] • *She went to live abroad after the break-up of her marriage/after her marriage broke up.* [C] • *She has two daughters by her first marriage.* [C] •

The couple had had an **arranged** *marriage* (= they had not chosen their husband/wife themselves). • *Their marriage* (= marriage ceremony) *took place in a church/registry office.* [C] • *I can't find my marriage* **certificate** (= document that shows two people are legally married). • *(fig.) The marriage of the two charities has not resulted in the benefits that had been predicted.* • *(esp. humorous)* If two people have **a marriage made in heaven**, they are very well suited to each other and their marriage is likely to be very happy and successful. • *(Br)* A **marriage bureau** *(Am, Br also* **dating agency**) is an organization which people who want to get married belong to so that they can be introduced to each other. • A **marriage of convenience** is a marriage in which the partners have married, not because they love each other, but in order to obtain some benefit, such as the right to live in the other partner's country: *His marriage of convenience to an American he hardly knew enabled him to get the green card which allows foreigners to work in the US.* ○ *(fig.) They never liked each other and their business partnership was only a marriage of convenience.* • *(Br and Aus)* **Marriage guidance**/*(Am and Aus also)* **Marriage counseling** is advice that is given by a trained person to people who are trying to find solutions to problems with their marriage: *If we hadn't gone to see the marriage guidance* **counsellor** *we'd probably have got divorced.* • *"Let me not to the marriage of true minds / Admit impediment"* (Shakespeare, Sonnet 116) • See also MARITAL; MARRY. • LP› **Relationships**

mar·riage·a·ble /£ˈmær·ɪ·dʒə·bl, $ˈmer-/ *adj* • *Chris goes to lots of parties hoping to meet someone marriageable* (= suitable to marry).

mar·row TISSUE /£ˈmær·əʊ, $-oʊ/, **bone mar·row** *n* [U] soft fatty tissue in the centre of a bone which is involved in the formation of new red blood cells and the destruction of old ones • *The charity has so far raised $2·5 million to finance* **bone** *marrow transplants for children.* • *We were frightened/thrilled* **to the marrow** (= extremely frightened/thrilled). • A **marrow bone** is a bone that contains a lot of edible marrow and is used in cooking, esp. to flavour soups.

mar·row VEGETABLE *Br and Aus* /£ˈmær·əʊ, $-oʊ/, *esp. Am* **squash**, **veg·e·ta·ble mar·row** *n n* a long round vegetable with a thick green or yellow skin, white flesh and a lot of seeds at its centre • *The gardener won a prize with his giant* **vegetable** *marrows.* [C] • *We had stuffed marrow for dinner.* [U] • PIC› **Vegetables**

mar·row·fat (pea) /£ˈmær·əʊ·fæt, $ˈ-oʊ-/ *n* [C] a large type of PEA (= seed eaten as a vegetable)

mar·ry *(obj)* /£ˈmær·i, $ˈmer-/ *v* to become the legally accepted husband or wife of (someone) in an official or religious ceremony • *Men tend to marry later than women.* [I] • *Paul married Lucy four years ago.* [T] • *Carol recently gave birth to a daughter, but she has no plans to marry at present.* [I] • To marry is also to perform the ceremony of marriage as a priest or official: *Who married them?* [T] ○ *The couple were married by the Archbishop of Canterbury*. [T] • *He married* **into** (= married someone from) *a wealthy farming family.* • *My father's trying to marry me* **(off) to** (= make me marry) *his accountant's daughter.* [T/M] • *(fig.) We need to marry* **(up)** (= match) *the names on your list with those on my list and see what the overlap is.* [T/M] • *Her parents said she* **married beneath** *her* (= married someone who was not good enough for her). • *(old use)* If someone has **married beneath** his/her **station** they have married someone with a lower social position. • *He always said he wanted to* **marry money** (= marry someone rich). • *I'm surprised she's accepted his proposal – I didn't think she was* **the marrying kind** (= likely to marry). • *(saying)* 'Marry in haste, repent at leisure' means that you will regret it if you get married without knowing the person well. • See also MARRIAGE. • LP› **Relationships**

mar·ried /£ˈmær·id, $ˈmer-/ *adj* [not gradable] • *How long have you been married* **to** *Nicky?* • *We've been* **happily** *married (for) five years.* • *Please state whether you are single, cohabiting, married, separated, divorced or widowed.* • *PC Smith was married with two children.* • *When are you* **getting** *married?* • *Chris and Pat* **got** *married last summer.* • *Jamie's decided to* **get** *married* **to** *Martha.* • *Tax allowances for married* **couples** *are to be increased in line with inflation.* • *So how are you enjoying married* **life**? • *Have you heard the rumours about her having an affair with a married* **man**? • *The survey reveals that two-thirds of married* **women** *earn less than their husbands.* • *(fig.) Rachel seems to be married* **to** (= very involved with) *her new job at the moment, so we hardly ever see her.* • A woman's **married name** is the family name of her husband: *She used to be Rachel Elliot – I think her married name is Cartwright.*

Mars /£mɑːz, $mɑːrz/ *n* [U not after *the*] the planet fourth in order of distance from the Sun, after the Earth and before Jupiter • *Mars is sometimes called the Red Planet because of its distinctive colour.* • *Despite much speculation, scientists have failed to find any sign of* **life on** *Mars.*

Mar·tian /£ˈmɑː·ʃən, $ˈmɑːr-/ *adj* [not gradable] • *A Martian year lasts for 687 Earth days.*

Mar·tian /£ˈmɑː·ʃən, $ˈmɑːr-/ *n* [C] • A Martian is a creature who lives on Mars: *Although science fiction writers have tried to convince us otherwise, there are no Martians.* ○ *Just because I'm so tall I get stared at as if I were a Martian* (= someone who looks strange and not like other people).

marsh /£mɑːʃ, $mɑːrʃ/ *n* ground, esp. near a lake, river or the sea, that tends to flood and is always wet • *At the mouth of the river is a large area of marsh.* [U] • *This marsh supports a wide range of plants which need wet conditions.* [C] • *Rain was falling fairly steadily and most of the ground had become a marsh.* [C] • **Marsh gas** is a gas produced in marshes by decaying plants that are covered by water: *Marsh gas consists mainly of methane.*

mar·shes /£ˈmɑː·ʃɪz, $ˈmɑːr-/ *pl n* • Marshes are a large area of marsh: *At low tide in the estuary, cows graze on the marshes.*

mar·shy /£ˈmɑː·ʃi, $ˈmɑːr-/ *adj* **-ier, -iest** • *This area was very marshy before the drainage system was installed.*

mar·shal *obj* ORGANIZE /£ˈmɑː·ʃəl, $ˈmɑːr-/ *v* [T] **-ll-** or *Am usually* **-l-** to gather or organize (people or things), esp. in order to achieve a particular aim • *The fighting in the city followed reports of the rebels marshalling their* **forces** *in the countryside.* • *The company is marshalling its* **forces/resources** *for a long court case.* • *Unfortunately, the book fails to marshal the facts into a coherent argument.* • *It is doubtful whether the President can marshal sufficient votes to prevent a defeat.* • *The company has marshalled an armada of 1000 boats and a squadron of 70 aircraft to help clear up the oil.* • *The rebels have little chance of marshalling as much firepower as the government troops.*

mar·shal OFFICIAL /£ˈmɑː·ʃəl, $ˈmɑːr-/ *n* [C] an official who is involved in the organization of a public event • *Marshals struggled in vain to prevent spectators rushing onto the racetrack.* • *(Am) The parade's* **grand** *marshal* (= the person leading it) *carried an elaborately carved staff.*

mar·shal LAW /£ˈmɑː·ʃəl, $ˈmɑːr-/ *n* [C] *Am* a government official who is responsible for putting the decisions of a law court into action • *US marshals specialize in finding fugitives and escapees.* • *Irene works as a deputy marshal, serving subpoenas, evicting lax tenants and serving as a bailiff in courts.*

mar·shal OFFICER /£ˈmɑː·ʃəl, $ˈmɑːr-/ *n* [C] a title used for important officers in the armed forces of some countries, or *(Am)* a title used for police or fire officers in some parts of the United States • *He's a* **field** *marshal/***air vice** *marshal.* • **Marshal of the Royal Air Force** is the highest rank in the British Air Force. • *(Am) The deputy state fire marshal led the arson investigation.* • *(Am) Marshal Dillon was the only law enforcement the territory had.*

marsh·land /£ˈmɑːʃ·lænd, $ˈmɑːrʃ-/ *n* an area of MARSH (= wet land) • *An area of marshland has been drained in order to build a shopping complex on it.* [U] • *The marshlands on the north and east edge of town are to be turned into nature reserves.* [C]

marsh·mal·low /£ˈmɑːʃˌmæl·əʊ, $ˈmɑːrʃˌmel·oʊ/ *n* [C] a soft sweet pink or white food • *Why don't we toast some marshmallows over the fire?* • *My American friend gave us brownies with marshmallow sauce for dessert.* • *(fig. Am) The situation called for someone tough and decisive, and I was just a complete marshmallow* (= someone who is cowardly, easily frightened, or unable to make decisions).

mar·shy /£ˈmɑː·ʃi, $ˈmɑːr-/ *adj* See at MARSH

mar·su·pi·al /£mɑːˈsuː·pi·əl, $mɑːr-/ *n* [C] a type of mammal from Australasia or South or Central America which is not completely developed when it is born and is carried around in a pocket on the mother's body where it is fed and protected until it is completely developed • *The book had pictures of marsupials, including koalas, wombats, possums and kangaroos.*

mart /£mɑːt, $mɑːrt/ *n* [C] *esp. Am and Irish Eng* a market or shopping centre • *Remember to get some bananas at the mart.* • *The freeway loops around clusters of discount marts.*

mar·tial /£'mɑː·ʃəl, $'mɑːr-/ *adj* [not gradable] relating to soldiers, war or life in the armed forces • *a country with a strong martial tradition* • **Martial arts** are the traditional skills of fighting or defending yourself which originated in Asian countries such as Japan and China and are now popular sports in western countries: *Kung fu, kendo and karate are martial arts.* ○ *The basic principles of martial arts are discipline, respect, confidence and self-defence.* • **Martial law** is government by the leaders of a country's own army or of a foreign army that has taken control of the country: *Intellectuals and economists played an important role in the resistance movement while the country was* **under** *martial law.* ○ *Martial law was* **imposed** *the same evening, and light infantry units with automatic weapons and shotguns were everywhere the next day.*

mar·tin /£'mɑː·tɪn, $'mɑːr·t̬ən/ *n* [C] a bird belonging to the SWALLOW family but with a shorter tail than related birds • *They live in a traditional country cottage, with wisteria climbing up the walls and martins nesting under the eaves.*

mar·ti·net /£ˌmɑː·tɪ'net, $ˌmɑːr·t̬ɪ-/ *n* [C] *fml* someone who demands that rules and orders should always be obeyed, even when it is unnecessary or unreasonable to do so • *He was a ruthless critic of his students' work, a stickler for accuracy and a martinet where grammar and spelling were concerned.*

Mar·ti·ni [WINE] /£mɑː'tiː·ni, $mɑːr-/ *n* [U] *trademark* an Italian wine containing herbs and other flavourings; a VERMOUTH • *Shall I take this bottle of Martini to Martha's party?* [U] • *I'd love a dry martini and lemonade.* [C]

mar·ti·ni [STRONG ALCOHOL] /£mɑː'tiː·ni, $mɑːr-/ *n* [C] *esp. Am* a COCKTAIL (= strong alcoholic drink) which combines GIN and VERMOUTH • *Would you like your martini shaken or stirred?* • *Mr Rawson prefers a very* **dry** *martini* (= one with very little vermouth).

mar·tyr /£'mɑː·təʳ, $'mɑːr·t̬ɚ/ *n* [C] a person who suffers greatly or is killed because of their political or religious beliefs, and is often admired because of it • *The problem with taking tougher action against the terrorists is that you risk making martyrs of them.* • *My wish is that the martyrs who died for the liberty of our country did not die for nothing.* • *The demonstrators carried placards dedicated to the first martyrs of the anti-Communist revolution.* • *Who was the first Christian martyr?* • *(fig.) After a year of experimenting with his diet, he developed a digestive disorder and died, a true martyr* **to** *science.* • *(fig.) My father's a martyr* **to** (= has suffered greatly and for a long time from) *arthritis.* • *(fig.) Georgina hardly ever does the washing-up and on the rare occasions that she does she makes such a martyr* **of herself** (= pretends to be suffering in order to obtain sympathy) *that it drives me mad.*

mar·tyr *obj* /£'mɑː·təʳ, $'mɑːr·t̬ɚ/ *v* [T usually passive] • *Hundreds of students are reported to have been martyred* (= killed) *for their political beliefs.*

mar·tyred /£'mɑː·təd, $'mɑːr·t̬ɚd/ *adj* • *a martyred saint* • *a martyred civil rights activist* • *Dietrich Bonhoeffer, the martyred German theologian, was remembered with a concert on Wednesday night at the Washington National Cathedral.* • If you look or sound martyred you show something has upset or annoyed you: *"I'm sure you're right – I'll enjoy it when I've got used to it," Mrs. Prisk said with a martyred* **smile**. ○ *She listened to him with a martyred* **expression** *on her face, trying to compose a suitable reply.*

mar·tyr·dom /£'mɑː·tə·dəm, $'mɑːr·t̬ɚ-/ *n* [U] • *These people are prepared to fight to the death for their beliefs – they're ready to* **suffer** *martyrdom* (= become martyrs).

mar·vel /£'mɑː·vəl, $'mɑːr-/ *v* **-ll-** or *Am usually* **-l-** to show or experience great surprise or admiration • *About 600 000 people stop here every year to marvel* **at** *the panoramic views.* [I] • *I never cease to marvel* **at** *the continued confusion in the public mind between nuclear power and nuclear weapons.* [always + **at**] • *I often marvel* **that** *humans can treat each other so badly.* [+ *that* clause] • *"Just look at that waterfall! Isn't it amazing?" she marvelled.* [+ clause]

mar·vel /£'mɑː·vəl, $'mɑːr-/ *n* [C] • A marvel is a thing or person that is very surprising or causes a lot of admiration: *This miniature TV is the latest technological marvel from Japan.* • **It's a marvel (to me) how** *they've managed to build the tunnel so quickly.* • *The people who travel in aircraft now take the marvel* **of** *flight for granted.* • *I'll try and get it finished for you by Friday – but don't expect marvels!*

mar·vel·lous, *Am usually* **mar·vel·ous** /£'mɑː·vəl·əs, $'mɑːr-/ *adj* extremely good • *This marvellous invention will help a great number of disabled people.* • *It took me ages to get it right, but it was a marvellous feeling when I did.* • *I've felt marvellous since I gave up smoking.* • *Jill is a marvellous person to work with.* • *I've got some marvellous news for you – you're going to be promoted.* • *We've achieved some marvellous results with this drug, but it won't be suitable for all patients.*

mar·vel·lous·ly, *Am usually* **mar·vel·ous·ly** /£'mɑː·vəl·ə·sli, $'mɑːr-/ *adv* • *We've had a few arguments over the years, but in general we get on marvellously.* • *They gave us a marvellously warm welcome.*

Marx·i·sm /£'mɑːk·sɪ·zəm, $'mɑːrk-/ *n* [U] a social, political and economic theory which is based on the writings of Karl Marx • *Marxism states that change in society is brought about by the interaction of different economic and social classes, that people's actions are based on their economic circumstances, and that Communism will replace Capitalism following social revolution and the victory of the working class.* • *Widespread protests against military rule and economic mismanagement forced him to abandon Marxism and introduce multi-party politics.* • **Marxism-Leninism** is the variation of Marxism that was developed by Lenin before the political changes in Russia in 1917: *According to Marxism-Leninism, imperialism is the final stage of a decaying capitalist society.* ○ *Marxism-Leninism was imposed upon the countries of Eastern Europe by the Soviet Union after the second world war.*

Marx·ist /£'mɑːk·sɪst, $'mɑːrk-/ *n* [C], *adj* [not gradable] • *He's been a Marxist since he was 16.* • *The government appealed for Western help in its battle against Marxist guerrillas.* • *The state had one of the last* **hard-line** *Marxist regimes.* • *They might have changed the name of their party, but they're still* **Marxist-Leninists** *at heart.* • *The businessman was murdered by a* **Marxist-Leninist** *group.*

mar·zi·pan /£'mɑː·zɪ·pæn, $'mɑːr-/, **al·mond paste** *n* [U] a soft sweet yellow or white substance that is used for decorating cakes and making sweets • *If you want to make your own marzipan you'll need sugar, egg whites or yolks and ground almonds.*

masc *adj* [not gradable] *abbreviation for* MASCULINE [GRAMMAR] • *"What's a male duck called?" "Well, my dictionary says 'duck – masc. drake'."*

mas·ca·ra /£mæs'kɑː·rə, $-'kɑːr·ə/ *n* a thick dark liquid make-up that is used for colouring EYELASHES and making them appear thicker or longer • *She always wears mascara, even when she's running.* [U] • *I rubbed my eyes and* **smudged** *my mascara.* [U] • *She'd been crying and her mascara had* **run**. [U] • *Have you got a black mascara* (= container of mascara) *I could borrow?* [C] • [PIC] **Cosmetics** Ⓔ Ⓟ

mas·ca·raed /£mæs'kɑː·rəd, $-'kɑːr·əd/ *adj* • *long mascaraed lashes*

mas·cot /£'mæs·kɒt, $-kɑːt/ *n* [C] a person, animal or object which is believed to bring good luck • *That teddy bear has been his* **lucky** *mascot in every exam he's ever taken.* • *Paul's a member of the local softball team and his daughter Tyler is their mascot.* • *Rome's mascot is a wolf, and Berlin's is a bear.* • *The Democratic Party adopted the donkey as its mascot in the 1870s.*

mas·cu·line [MALE] /'mæs·kjʊ·lɪn/ *adj* having characteristics that are traditionally thought to be typical of or suitable for men or boys • *I don't think Hugh'll like this flowery wallpaper – he'll probably want something more masculine.* • *By attacking conventions such as the wearing of a suit, shirt and tie, these designers have undermined the dull tradition of masculine dress.* • *Some research suggests that women with masculine sounding names like 'Sam' and 'Chris' are more successful in the business world.* • *People would be much better balanced if we could bring out the masculine side of women and the feminine side of men.* • Compare FEMININE [FEMALE]. • [LP] **Sexist language**

mas·cu·lin·i·ty /£ˌmæs·kjʊ'lɪn·ɪ·ti, $-ə·t̬i/ *n* [U] • *I would say that maleness is purely biological, whereas masculinity is based largely on upbringing and social conditioning.* • *Football is a bastion of masculinity all across Europe.*

mas·cu·line [GRAMMAR] /'mæs·kjʊ·lɪn/ (*abbreviation* **masc**) *adj* [not gradable] (in some languages) belonging to the group of nouns which are not FEMININE or NEUTER • *The French word for 'sun' is masculine – 'le soleil', but the German word is feminine – 'die Sonne'.* • In English there are masculine and feminine forms of some nouns, for example actor and actress, but the feminine forms are now being used less often.

mash *obj* /mæʃ/ *v* [T] to crush (food), esp. after cooking, so that it forms a soft mass • *You can mash the ingredients to give the soup a chunky consistency, or blend them in a liquidiser for a smoother texture.* [T] • *Mash the potatoes and then mix in the butter, onions and herbs.* [T] • *Mash* **(together)** *the garlic and salt into a thick paste.* [T/M] • *He always mashes* **(up)** *his peas before he eats them.* [T/M] • *(fig. esp. Am) He mashed his car* **up** (= damaged it) *trying to back into his garage.* [M] • *(fig. esp. Am) His face was badly mashed* **up** (= damaged) *in the accident.* [M] • PIC› **Food preparation**

mashed /mæʃt/ *adj* • *Do you want baked or mashed* **potato** *with your sausages?* • *Some of her sculptures are made of* **mashed-up** (= wet and crushed) *newspaper.* • *(esp. Am) Hurricane David tore through Dominica leaving people dead and homeless, and crops mashed up* (= damaged).

mash /mæʃ/ *n* [U] *Br infml* • *He loves potatoes and happily eats mash* (= mashed potatoes) *by the plateful.*

mash·er /£ˈmæʃ·əʳ, $-ɚ/ *n* [C] • *We need a* **(potato)** *masher* (= tool for mashing potatoes and other vegetables).

mask COVER /£mɑːsk, $mæsk/ *n* [C] a covering for the eyes, nose, mouth or the whole face which is worn to prevent people discovering who is wearing it, or for amusement or protection • *The police have been unable to identify the robbers as they were wearing masks throughout the raid.* • *Who was that person at the party who was wearing a Marilyn Monroe mask?* • *A leading scientist has warned that protective suits and gas masks will not guard troops against prolonged chemical and biological warfare.* • *(fig.) In spite of the threat of war, the city seems determined to put on a* **mask** **of** *normality* (= to appear as if nothing was wrong). • PIC› **Water sports** Ⓙ Ⓢ

masked /£mɑːskt, $mæskt/ *adj* [not gradable] • *Suddenly two masked gunmen burst into the shop and demanded all the cash in the till.* • *Last year's* **masked ball** (= a formal dance where masks are worn) *raised £5000 for the physically handicapped.*

mask *obj* HIDE /£mɑːsk, $mæsk/ *v* [T] to prevent (something) being seen or noticed • *They've masked the flavour of the meat by using too much spice.* • *His spots have got so bad that he's started masking them* **with** *make-up.* • *She accused the government of masking the true unemployment figures by manipulating the statistics.* • **Masking tape** is a strip of sticky material that is put around the edge of something that is being painted in order to protect the surfaces that you do not intend to paint: *Don't forget to put some masking tape on the windows before you paint the frames.* • Ⓙ Ⓢ

mas·o·chi·sm /ˈmæs·ə·kɪ·zᵊm/ *n* [U] the obtaining of esp. sexual pleasure from the pain or suffering caused by being hurt or controlled by another person, or *(infml)* acceptance of or happiness in a situation which is very unpleasant • *He described masochism as involving activities such as being insulted, tied up and whipped.* • *(infml) I reckon you need to be into masochism to enjoy running in marathons.* • Compare SADISM.

mas·o·chist /ˈmæs·ə·kɪst/ *n* [C] • *(infml) You'd have to be a masochist to enjoy practising for four hours every day!*

mas·o·chis·tic /ˌmæs·əˈkɪs·tɪk/ *adj* • *A lot of people have masochistic fantasies that they never actually put into practice.* • *(infml) She seems to get some kind of masochistic pleasure from driving through London in the rush hour.*

Ma·son SOCIETY MEMBER /ˈmeɪ·sᵊn/ *n* [C] a FREEMASON (= member of a secret society) • *Masons identify themselves to each other with a special handshake.*

Ma·son·ic /£məˈsɒn·ɪk, $-ˈsɑː·nɪk/ *adj* [not gradable] • *Do you know how to do a Masonic* **handshake**? • *He left money to several Masonic* **Lodges** *when he died.*

Ma·son·ry /ˈmeɪ·sᵊn·ri/ *n* [U] • Masonry is another word for **Freemasonry**, see at FREEMASON.

ma·son SKILLED WORKER /ˈmeɪ·sᵊn/ *n* [C] a STONEMASON (= person who cuts stone) or *(Am)* a BRICKLAYER • *Her interest in sculpture developed from her father's work as a mason.*

Ma·son–Dix·on Line /ˌmeɪ·sᵊnˈdɪk·sᵊn/ *n* [U] the border between Maryland and Pennsylvania in the US, traditionally considered to mark the division between the north and south • *The former slave states south of* **the** *Mason-Dixon Line have always been looked down on by northerners.*

ma·son·ry /ˈmeɪ·sᵊn·ri/ *n* [U] the bricks and pieces of stone that are used to make a building • *Firefighters battled through thick smoke to search the building, but the collapsing roof and falling masonry forced them back.* • *The walls were solid masonry that an earthquake couldn't have touched.* • *An old masonry* **wall** *collapsed, sending a large amount of debris crashing down onto the courtyard.* • *All our staff have qualifications in plumbing, joinery and masonry* (= the skill of building with brick and stone).

masque /£mɑːsk, $mæsk/ *n* [C] *literary* a theatrical entertainment including poetry, singing and dancing which was performed in England in the 16th and 17th centuries, esp. at a royal COURT (= official home of a king or queen), for people from the higher social classes • *Masques were often performed at banquets and the performers would wear masks and try to involve the audience in the performance.*

masq·uer·ade /£ˌmæs·kᵊrˈeɪd, $-kəˈreɪd/ *n* [C] an action that is intended to prevent the truth about something esp. unpleasant or not desirable from becoming known • *In an elaborate masquerade, he tried to make the murder look like suicide.* • *Many people hid their poverty behind* **a** *masquerade* **of** *a well-dressed appearance.*

masq·uer·ade /£ˌmæs·kᵊrˈeɪd, $-kəˈreɪd/ *v* [I] • To masquerade **as** something is to pretend or appear to be that thing: *Hooligans masquerading as football fans have once again caused disturbances.* ○ *In this business there are a lot of unqualified people masquerading as experts.* ○ *During World War II, they masqueraded as Nazis in order to conceal their real work as Resistance workers smuggling vast numbers of Jews to safety.* ○ *The reports contain a lot of political propaganda masquerading as fact.*

mass LARGE AMOUNT /mæs/ *n* [U] a large amount of something that has no particular shape or arrangement • *The explosion reduced the church to* **a mass of** *rubble.* • *He pulled* **a mass of** *notes from his pocket and asked if he could pay for the car in cash.* • *The forest is* **a mass of** *colour* (= full of colour) *in autumn.* • **The mass of** (= Most of) *the people support the government's reforms.* • *(esp. disapproving)* If you say that someone or something is **a mass of contradictions** you mean that they or it is strange and surprising because the combination of characteristics they or it have are not usually found together. • Ⓓ

mas·ses /ˈmæs·ɪz/ *pl n* [C] *infml* • Masses means a lot: *I've got masses* **to** *do at the weekend.* [+ *to* infinitive] ○ *There's masses* **of** *people in town today.* ○ *"Was there a lot of traffic on the way in to town?" "Oh yes, masses."*

mass INVOLVING MANY /mæs/ *adj* [before n; not gradable] having an effect on or involving a large number of people or forming a large amount • *Their weapons of mass destruction certainly include nuclear and chemical weapons and may also include biological ones.* • *France has the fastest mass transit rail system in the world.* • *The mass exodus of East Germans to the West led to the erection of the Berlin Wall in 1961.* • *She was a notorious female mass murderer.* • *Nearly six million people are affected by the drought and civil war, and there is a real danger of mass starvation.* • *Opposition groups plan to stage mass demonstrations all over the country.* • **Mass mailing** is *Am for* MAILSHOT. • Something that is designed for the **mass market** is intended to be bought by as many people as possible, and not just by people with a lot of money or a special interest: *Advances in microchip technology have made these cameras smaller and cheaper and affordable to the mass market.* ○ *It will be several years before costs come down sufficiently to make this a* **mass-market** *product.* • The **mass media** consists of the newspapers, magazines, and television and radio companies that reach large numbers of people and can influence what they do or think: **The** *mass media has become one of the main instruments of political change.* ○ *We are concerned about the negative image of blacks that is portrayed in* **the** *mass media.* ○ *The Department of Health is to launch a mass-media campaign against smoking.* • If you **mass-produce** something, you make a lot of it in a factory where production consists of many simple stages each of which is performed repeatedly by a person or machine: *Hand-made products tend to cost more than mass-produced ones, but they're often better made.* ○ *Detroit is the birthplace of the* **mass production** *of motor cars.* • Ⓓ

mass /mæs/ *v* [I] • To mass is to come together in large numbers: *100 000 troops have massed along the border in preparation for an invasion.* ○ *The crowd massed around the entrance to the exhibition.* ○ *Windows were smashed at a police station after up to 60 youths massed outside.*

massed /mæst/ *adj* • *Every day massed ranks of tourists passed slowly through the rooms of the palace.* • *The lake with its massed flamingos (a heart-stopping sight even* *television cannot make banal) is a comfortable drive away from the hotel.* • *Down the slope came the massed bands of the three Indian armed services.*

mas·ses /ˈmæs·ɪz/ *pl n* [C] • **The masses** are the ordinary people who form the largest group in a society: *She is popular with the aristocracy but she has not yet won the support of the masses.*

mass [MATTER] /mæs/ *n* [C] *specialized* the amount of matter in any solid object or in any volume of liquid or gas • *The acceleration of a body equals the force exerted on it divided by its mass.* • *1 litre of water has a mass of 1 kilogram.* • (D)

Mass [CEREMONY] /mæs/ *n* the Christian religious ceremony based on Christ's last meal with his friends, or music written for the parts of this ceremony that are sung • *a Catholic mass* [C] • *I haven't been to Mass for ages.* [U] • *Johann Sebastian Bach finished his Mass in B Minor in 1738.* [C] • See also **Holy Communion** at HOLY [GOOD].

mas·sa·cre /£ˈmæs·ə·kəʳ, $-kɚ/ *n* [C] an act of killing a lot of people violently or cruelly, esp. without good reason • *The victims of the massacre were mainly the very young and the very old.* • *(fig.) The changes to the team come after their 7-2 massacre* (= defeat) *against Scotland last week.*

mas·sa·cre *obj* /£ˈmæs·ə·kəʳ, $-kɚ/ *v* [T] • *His troops have regularly massacred unarmed civilians and prisoners since he took power in 1986.* • *The civilians were massacred by soldiers in retaliation for killings of members of the security forces.* • *(fig.) England was massacred* (= beaten) *5-0 by France in the semi-final.* • *(fig.) Opinion polls suggest that the ruling left-wing coalition will be massacred* (= beaten) *in the forthcoming elections.*

mas·sage *obj* /£ˈmæs·ɑːdʒ, $məˈsɑːdʒ/ *v* [T] to rub, press or hit (someone's body) with regular repeated movements, esp. in order to relax them or to reduce stiffness or pain in their joints or muscles • *I've got a dreadful ache in my neck. Would you mind massaging it for me?* • *Spread the cream evenly over your arms and legs and massage it into the skin.* • *(fig.) Some television companies have been massaging their viewing figures* (= making them seem better than they really are) *in order to attract more advertising revenue.*

mas·sage /£ˈmæs·ɑːdʒ, $məˈsɑːdʒ/ *n* [C] • *Osteopathy involves massage and manipulation of bones and joints and this stimulates the body to heal itself.* [U] • *Would a massage do anything for your backache?* [C] • *She gave me a wonderfully relaxing massage.* [C] • *I've booked a foot massage and pedicure for Friday.* [C] • A **massage parlour** is a place where you can pay someone to give you a massage. • A **massage parlour** can also sometimes be a place where a person can pay to have sex.

mas·seur *male, female* **mas·seuse** /£mæsˈɜːʳ, $-ˈsɜːr, £-ˈsɜːz, $-ˈsɜːrz/ *n* [C] a person whose job it is to give MASSAGES to people

mas·sif /mæsˈiːf/ *n* [C] *fml or specialized* a group or area of mountains • *The mountain is over 2000m tall and is the highest of the four summits along the eastern rim of the massif.*

mas·sive /ˈmæs·ɪv/ *adj* very large in size, amount or number • *The road is made of massive concrete slabs laid end to end.* • *A massive iceberg is floating off the coast of Argentina.* • *She died after taking a massive overdose of drugs.* • *Without a massive increase in investment, the company will collapse.* • *I've got a massive amount of work to do.* • *If the drought continues, deaths will occur on a massive scale.* • *(infml) A massive* **great** (= very large) *truck has just parked outside the house.* • (F)

mas·sive·ly /ˈmæs·ɪv·li/ *adv* • *The film is a massively* (= very) *ambitious project.*

mas·sive·ness /ˈmæs·ɪv·nəs/ *n* [U] • *The building is huge and solid, and capable of withstanding earthquakes by its sheer massiveness* (= large size).

mast /£mɑːst, $mæst/ *n* [C] a tall pole made from wood or metal • A mast is a wooden or metal pole used on a boat or ship to support the sail: *The ship had five sails set from its two masts.* ○ *During the storm, the crew of the vessel clung to the mast to stop themselves from being washed overboard.* • A mast is also wooden or metal pole which is used to raise a flag on: *There was a strong wind and the flags were fluttering from the top of their masts.* • A mast is also a metal pole used to support an AERIAL for radio or television signals: *A tall television mast was added to the top of the Empire State Building in 1951.* • See also **half-mast** at HALF.

mas·tec·to·my /mæsˈtek·tə·mi/ *n* [C] the removal of a woman's breast by a medical operation • *She underwent a mastectomy after contracting breast cancer.* • A **partial** mastectomy is when part of the breast is removed, and a **double** mastectomy is when both breasts are removed.

mas·ter [CONTROL], *female dated also* **mis·tress** /£ˈmɑː·stəʳ, $ˈmæs·tɚ/ *n* [C] a person who controls something or someone, or the most important or influential person or thing in a situation or organization • *The slave looked at his master with hatred in his eyes.* • *"Do not send me away, master," pleaded the slave.* [as form of address] • *With careful training, a dog will obey its master completely.* • *As a manager, she had a reputation for trying to be the unquestioned master of all those around her.* • *The Master of St. John's College will be launching the appeal.* • *Party members will often say whatever their* **political** *masters* (= leaders) *want them to say.* • *(Br dated)* A master/mistress is also a male or female school teacher: *Mr Wells was my Latin master at school.* ○ See also **headmaster** at HEAD [LEADER]. • If someone is their **own master**, they are independent and are able to make their own decisions: *I decided to become self-employed because I like being my own master.* • The **master bedroom** is the largest bedroom in a house: *The master bedroom has an ensuite bathroom.* • A **master key** is a key which can be used to open any of several different locks. • A **Master of Ceremonies** (*abbreviation* **MC**) is a person who makes certain that official events happen correctly, for example by introducing speakers at the right time. • A **master plan** is an organized set of decisions made by one person or a team of people about how to do something in the future: *Once the master plan is put into operation, we should begin to see a return on our investment.* • A **master race** is a group or race of people which considers itself to be better than all others. • A **master switch** is a switch that can be used to turn on or off all the lights or machines in a building. • *"I am the master of my fate / I am the captain of my soul"* (from the poem *Invictus* by W.E.Henley, 1888) • *"His Master's Voice"* (name of record company (now HMV)) • *"No man can serve two masters ... Ye cannot serve God and Mammon* (= wealth)*"* (Bible, Matthew 6.24) • (J)

mas·ter *obj* /£ˈmɑː·stəʳ, $ˈmæs·tɚ/ *v* [T] • If you master a situation, you learn how to deal with it: *She travels by air when possible in an attempt to master her fear of flying.*

mas·ter·ful /£ˈmɑː·stə·fəl, $ˈmæs·tɚ-/ *adj* • If someone is masterful, they are able to control people and situations: *Once she became a prosecutor, she quickly established herself as a masterful trial lawyer.* ○ *He has a deep, masterful voice.*

mas·ter·y /£ˈmɑː·stər·i, $ˈmæs·tɚ-/ *n* [U] • Mastery is complete control of something: *The two countries struggled for mastery of the Baltic coastal region.*

mas·ter [SKILLED PERSON] /£ˈmɑː·stəʳ, $ˈmæs·tɚ/ *n* [C] a person who is very skilled in a particular job or activity • *The terrorist was a master* **of** *disguise, and could easily cross the border unnoticed.* • *John Le Carré is widely acknowledged as the master* **of** *the spy novel* • *He is a master craftsman.* • *She is a master chef.* • A master is also a famous and very skilled painter: *This painting is clearly the work of a master, either Turner or Constable.* ○ See also **old master** at OLD [EXISTED MANY YEARS]. • A **Master of Arts** (*abbreviation* **MA**) is a second level college or university degree in a subject such as literature, language, history or social science, or a person who has this degree. • A **master class** is a class taught by someone who has an expert knowledge or skill in a particular area, esp. in music. • A **Master's degree** (*infml* **Master's**) is a second level college or university degree: *An MA and a MSc are both Master's degrees.* • A **Master of Philosophy** (*abbreviation* **MPhil**) is a second level college or university degree in any subject, or a person who has this degree: *An MPhil is below the level of a PhD.* ○ *She spent two years studying for a Master of Philosophy degree* **in** *management studies.* • A **Master of Science** (*abbreviation* **MSc**) is a second level college or university degree in a scientific subject, or a person who has this degree. • [LP] **Schools and colleges** (J)

mas·ter *obj* /£ˈmɑː·stəʳ, $ˈmæs·tɚ/ *v* [T] • If you master an activity, you become skilled at it: *Have you mastered skiing yet?* ○ *She quickly mastered* **the art of** (= became skilled at) *interviewing people.*

mas·ter·ful /£ˈmɑː·stə·fəl, $ˈmæs·tɚ-/ *adj* • If an action is masterful, it is very skilful: *Since the final months of her presidential campaign, she has displayed a masterful grasp of political tactics.*

mas·ter·ful·ly /£'mɑː·stə·fᵊl·i, $'mæs·tɚ-/ *adv* • *He masterfully handled the whole situation using diplomacy and tact.*

mas·ter·ly /£'mɑː·stə·li, $'mæs·tɚ-/ *adj* • If something is masterly, it is done extremely well: *She gave a masterly performance as Kate in 'The Taming of the Shrew'.*

mas·ter·y /£'mɑː·stᵊr·i, $'mæs·tɚ-/ *n* [U] • If someone has a mastery of something, they are extremely skilled at it: *She has a complete mastery of the violin.*

mas·ter COPY /£'mɑː·stəʳ, $'mæs·tɚ/ *n* [C] an original copy of something, such as a recording or film, from which copies can be made • *I have sent her a copy of the recording and have kept the master.* • *You should keep the master* **copy** *in a safe place.* • Ⓙ

mas·ter·mind *obj* /£'mɑː·stə·maɪnd, $'mæs·tɚ-/ *v* [T] to plan in detail (a difficult activity) and make certain that it happens successfully • *Who is going to mastermind the move to the new building?* • *He is said to have masterminded three bank robberies.*

mas·ter·mind /£'mɑː·stə·maɪnd, $'mæs·tɚ-/ *n* [C] • *The mastermind* **behind** (= The person who planned) *the escape has never been identified.*

mas·ter·piece /£'mɑː·stə·piːs, $'mæs·tɚ-/, **mas·ter·work** /£'mɑː·stə·wɜːk, $'mæs·tɚ·wɜːrk/ *n* [C] a work of art such as a painting, film or book which is done or made with great skill, esp. a person's greatest work • *'The Last Supper' is widely regarded as Leonardo da Vinci's masterpiece.* • *Have you ever seen the film 'Paths of Glory', Stanley Kubrick's masterpiece?* • A masterpiece is also a very good example of something: *Calling a seven-hour wait 'a slight delay' was a masterpiece* **of** *understatement.* • See also CHEF D'OEUVRE.

Mast·er's /£'mɑː·stəz, $'mæs·tɚz/ *n* [C] *pl* **Master's** *infml for* **Master's degree**, see at MASTER SKILLED PERSON • *She has a Master's* **in** *biotechnology.*

mas·ter·stroke /£'mɑː·stə·strəʊk, $'mæs·tɚ·stroʊk/ *n* [C] something which is very clever and produces success • *The director's masterstroke lay in choosing a very ordinary subject for his film and showing its extraordinary side.*

mas·ter·y /£'mɑː·stᵊr·i, $'mæs·tɚ-/ *n* [U] See at MASTER CONTROL, MASTER SKILLED PERSON

mast·head /£'mɑːst·hed, $'mæst-/ *n* [C] the title of a newspaper or magazine which is printed at the top of the front page • *After 28 years, the Glasgow Herald has dropped the prefix 'Glasgow' from its masthead to become simply the Herald.*

mas·ti·cate *(obj)* /'mæs·tɪ·keɪt/ *v fml* to chew (food) • *She slowly masticated an apple.* [T] • *The judges masticated, deliberated and eventually decided on a winner.* [I]

mas·ti·ca·tion /ˌmæs·tɪ'keɪ·ʃᵊn/ *n* [U] *fml*

mas·tiff /'mæs·tɪf/ *n* [C] a large strong short-haired dog • *Mastiffs and alsatians make very good guard dogs.*

mas·ti·tis /£mæs'taɪ·tɪs, $-t̬ɪs/ *n* [U] *medical* soreness and usually swelling of the breast or the UDDER (= the part of a cow which produces milk) • *Mastitis causes red and painful areas on the breast and a temperature, and usually has to be treated with antibiotics.*

mas·tur·bate *(obj)* /£'mæs·tə·beɪt, $-tɚ-/ *v* [I/T] to rub the sex organs of (yourself or your sexual partner) in order to give sexual pleasure

mas·tur·ba·tion /£ˌmæs·tə'beɪ·ʃᵊn, $-tɚ-/ *n* [U] • *mutual masturbation* • *He teaches people about the psychological benefits of masturbation.*

mas·tur·bat·o·ry /£ˌmæs·tə'beɪ·tᵊr·i, $-t̬ɚ'beɪ·tɔːr·i/ *adj* • *masturbatory fantasies*

mat FLOOR /mæt/ *n* [C] a small piece of strong material which covers and protects part of a floor • *She used to leave the key for the front door under the mat by the door.* • *He stood on the* **bath** *mat* (= the mat on the floor near the bath) *as he dried himself.* • See also DOORMAT.

mat TABLE /mæt/ *n* [C] a small piece of cloth, cardboard or plastic which is put on a surface such as a table to protect it • *She put the* **place** *mats and cutlery out on the table.* • *Pubs usually have* **beer** *mats to put the glasses on and protect the tables.* • PIC **Cutlery**

mat LAYER /mæt/ *n* [C] a thick layer of something, such as grass or hair, which has been twisted together untidily • *The top few buttons on his shirt were open, revealing a mat* **of** *dark hair on his chest.*

mat·ted /£'mæt·ɪd, $'mæt̬-/ *adj* • If something is matted, it is twisted into a firm, untidy mass: *Her hair was matted* **with** *mud and rain.*

mat·a·dor /£'mæt·ə·dɔːʳ, $'mæt̬·ə·dɔːr/ *n* [C] a person who fights and kills BULLS (= the male form of cattle) at a BULLFIGHT • *A matador often wears a cloak with a red lining to attract the bull.* • Compare PICADOR; TOREADOR.

match COMPETITION /mætʃ/ *n* [C] a sports competition or event in which two people or teams compete against each other • *a football/cricket/tennis match* • *We won/lost the match.* • *Liverpool have a match* **with** (= against) *Blackburn next week.* • A match is also a very angry, loud argument: *They were involved in a shouting/slanging match.* • If someone is described as the **man/woman of the match**, they score the most points or are the best player in the match. • A **match point** is a situation in a game such as tennis when the player who is winning will win the match if they get the next point: *Steffi Graf is now at/on match point.* ○ *He* **had** *two match points but lost them both.* • *"Match of the Day"* (title of a television sports programme) • LP **Sports**

match *obj* **a·gainst** *obj v prep* [T] • If one team or player is matched against another team or player, they are made to compete against each other: *Germany has been matched against Holland in the semi-final.*

match STICK /mætʃ/ *n* [C] a short thin stick made of wood or cardboard, which is covered with a special chemical at one end which burns when rubbed firmly against a rough or specially prepared surface • *Do you have any matches?* • *I'd like a* **box** *of matches, please.* • *You should always* **strike** *a match away from you.* • If you **put a match to** something, you make it burn: *She put a match to the bonfire, and it went up in flames in a matter of seconds.* • See also MATCHSTICK, **safety match** at SAFETY. • PIC **Containers**

Match

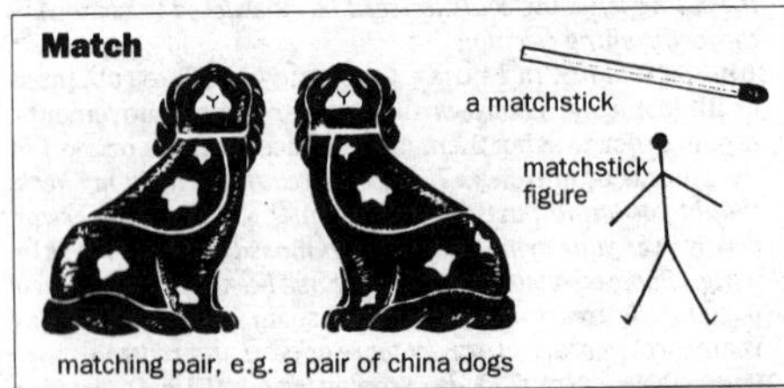

match SUITABLE /mætʃ/ *n* [U] a person or thing which is similar to someone or something else • If one colour or design is a match for another, it is similar to it and they look good together: *This new tablecloth is* **a good match for** *the carpet.* ○ *We found some paint which is* **a perfect** *match* **for** *the curtains we already have.* • *(dated)* If two people make a good match, they are likely to have a successful relationship: *I think they would be* **a** *good match* **for** *each other.* • *(dated)* If a person is a good match, they are considered a suitable marriage partner: *Your son makes* **a** *very good match.*

match *(obj)* /mætʃ/ *v* • If two colours or designs match, they are similar and look good together: *Do you think these two colours match?* [I] ○ *Does this shirt match these trousers?* [T] • If you match **up** a design or material, you look for something that would look good with it and be similar to it: *I'm trying to match up this wallpaper* **with** *some suitable curtain material.* [M] • If you match or match **up** one thing with another, you find a similarity or connection between them: *Can you match up these famous people* **with** *the countries where they come from?* [M] • If two things match **up**, they are similar and are designed to work together: *If the teeth on the cogs don't match up properly* (= If they are not in the correct place), *the mechanism will jam.* [I] • If two things or people are **well**-matched, they are similar and suitable for each other: *They're such a well-matched couple – they've been so happy since their wedding.* • If two things or people are **ill**-matched, they are not suitable for each other.

match EQUAL /mætʃ/ *n* [U] a person or thing which is equal to another person or thing in strength, speed or quality • *The four best runners are* **a** *good match* **for** *each other – it's going to be a close race.* • If something is **no match for** another thing, it is not as good as it: *The Ferrari was fast but was no match for the Lotus on the straights.* • If someone **meets** their **match**, they compete against someone whom they cannot beat: *It would seem that the defending champion has met her match in the new challenger.*

match *(obj)* /mætʃ/ *v* • *It would be difficult to match the service* (= give better service than) *this airline gives its customers.* [T] • *(Br)* If something matches **up with/to** something else, it is as good as it: *There was so much hype* *beforehand that it would have been difficult for the film to match up with our expectations of it.* [T] • If two things are **well-matched**, they are equal. • If two things are **ill-matched**, they are not equal: *The teams were ill-matched, and Hamburg won easily.*

match·less /ˈmætʃ·ləs/ *adj* [not gradable] • If something is matchless, it is of a very high standard or quality and nothing is as good as it: *The museum has concentrated on building a matchless art-history library with a computerized catalogue of the world's art stock.*

match·less·ly /ˈmætʃ·lə·sli/ *adv* [not gradable]

match·box /£ˈmætʃ·bɒks, $-bɑːks/ *n* [C] a small box containing MATCHES (= short wooden sticks), which usually has one or two sides covered with sand or special chemicals which a match can be rubbed against to make it burn

match·mak·er /£ˈmætʃˌmeɪ·kəʳ, $-kɚ/ *n* [C] a person who introduces one person to another in an attempt to make them form a relationship • *In some societies, matchmakers are paid by families to find suitable husbands or wives for their children.*

match·mak·ing /ˈmætʃˌmeɪ·kɪŋ/ *n* [U] • *Caroline tried to do a bit of matchmaking by introducing Paul to Lucy.*

match·play /ˈmætʃ·pleɪ/ *n* [U] a type of golf competition between two, three or four players where your score is calculated by how many holes you win rather than how many hits you take to complete the 18 holes • *He said that he wouldn't be playing in the Ryder Cup because he wasn't interested in matchplay.* • *She won three world matchplay championships in the 1980s.*

match·stick /ˈmætʃ·stɪk/ *n* [C] the short wooden stick of a MATCH (= a stick which burns when rubbed firmly against a surface) • *He likes making models out of matchsticks.* • A **matchstick figure** is a **stick figure** (= a simple picture of a person, in which the head is drawn as a circle, and the body, arms and legs are drawn as lines). • PIC› **Match**

match·wood /ˈmætʃ·wʊd/ *n* [U] the very small pieces of wood that are left after something wooden has been destroyed • *Many houses were reduced to matchwood by the hurricane.*

mate FRIEND /meɪt/ *n* [C] *Br and Aus infml* a friend or a person whom you work with • *We've been mates since our school days.* • *I usually play football with some of my mates from the office on Saturdays.* • *She's my* **best mate**. • *Feel like a drink, mate?* [as form of address] • See **running mate** at RUN. • LP› **Titles and forms of address**

mat·ey /£ˈmeɪ·ti, $-t̬i/ *adj, n* [C] **matier, matiest** *Br and Aus infml* • If two people are matey, they are friendly: *They've been very matey since they started working together.* • Matey is also used as an informal form of address: *"Here's the tenner I owe you." "Thanks, matey."*

mat·ey·ness /£ˈmeɪ·tɪ·nəs, $-t̬ɪ-/ *n* [U] *Br and Aus infml* • *I hate her false mateyness (= friendliness) and the way she pretends to be interested in what you're doing.*

mate *(obj)* REPRODUCE /meɪt/ *v* to (make a male and female animal) come together in order to have sex and produce young • *Male stags stay at the breeding site for the whole season, whereas females mate and leave as quickly as possible.* [I] • *Scientists have been conducting an experiment in which mice are mated* **with** *rats.* [T]

mate /meɪt/ *n* [C] • A mate is an animal's sexual partner: *Swans keep the same mate throughout their life.*

mate HELPER /meɪt/ *n* [C] a person who is employed to help a skilled worker • *He was apprenticed as a carpenter's/plumber's mate at the age of sixteen.*

mate SHIP /meɪt/ *n* [C] a type of officer on a trading ship rather than a military ship • *He had worked as a ship's mate for ten years.*

mate GAME /meɪt/ *n* [C], *v* [T] CHECKMATE

-mate SHARING /-meɪt/ *combining form* living or working in the same place • *flat mate* • *team-mate* • *workmate*

mat·er /£ˈmeɪ·təʳ, $-t̬ɚ/ *n* [C] *Br dated or humorous* your mother • *I'm going home next weekend to see my Mater and Pater.*

ma·te·ri·al PHYSICAL SUBSTANCE /£məˈtɪə·ri·əl, $-ˈtɪr·i-/ *n* [C] a physical substance which things can be made from • *Stone is often used as a building material.* • *Modern technology has produced a whole new range of synthetic materials for engineers to use.* • *Crude oil is used as the* **raw** (= basic) *material for making petrol, plastics and detergents.*

ma·te·ri·al /£məˈtɪə·ri·əl, $-ˈtɪr·i-/ *adj* [not gradable] • Material means relating to physical objects rather than emotions or the spiritual world: *You shouldn't ignore the material needs of your body – we all need to eat and drink.* ○ *This insurance policy also covers material* (= physical) *damage to your house.* ○ *Her high salary has brought many material* **benefits** *– a big house, a fast car, and meals at expensive restaurants.*

ma·te·ri·al·ly /£məˈtɪə·ri·ə·li, $-ˈtɪr·i-/ *adv* • *Many women were worried that divorce would leave them worse off materially* (= leave them with less money and possessions). • *He came from a home that was materially comfortable* (= that had a lot of possessions) *but was emotionally deprived.* • See also **materially** at MATERIAL IMPORTANT.

ma·te·ri·al·ize, *Br and Aus usually* **-ise** /£məˈtɪə·ri·ə·laɪz, $-ˈtɪr·i-/ *v* [I] • If an object materializes, it appears suddenly: *Suddenly a lorry appeared in front of her – it seemed to materialize out of nowhere.* ○ *(infml) I was thinking you'd never materialize* (= arrive), *you're two hours late!* • If an idea or hope materializes, it becomes real: *Her hopes of becoming a painter never materialized.*

ma·te·ri·al·iz·a·tion, *Br and Aus usually* **-i·sa·tion** /£məˌtɪə·ri·əl·aɪˈzeɪ·ʃən, $-ˌtɪr·i-/ *n* [C/U]

ma·te·ri·al CLOTH /£məˈtɪə·ri·əl, $-ˈtɪr·i-/ *n* cloth which can be used to make things such as clothes • *How many metres of material will you need to make a skirt?* [U] • *Which material do you prefer for the curtains – the red or the blue?* [C] • LP› **Shopping goods**

ma·te·ri·al EQUIPMENT /£məˈtɪə·ri·əl, $-ˈtɪr·i-/ *n* equipment that you need for a particular activity • *"Do we need any writing materials?" "Only a pen and a pencil."* [C] • *Remember to bring your painting materials when you come.* [C] • *(specialized)* In the game of CHESS, material is another word for the pieces: *I lost a lot of material in that last set of moves.* [U]

ma·te·ri·al INFORMATION /£məˈtɪə·ri·əl, $-ˈtɪr·i-/ *n* information used when writing something such as a book, or information produced in various forms to help people or to advertise products • *I'm in the process of collecting material for an article that I'm writing.* [U] • *The textbook comes with a pack of teaching materials.* [C] • *All sorts of publicity materials are being used in the campaign – videos, posters and leaflets.* [C]

ma·te·ri·al IMPORTANT /£məˈtɪə·ri·əl, $-ˈtɪr·i-/ *adj fml* important or having an important effect • *The new legislation could have very definite material implications for the proposed building.* • *If you have any information that is material* **to** *the investigation, you should state it now.*

ma·te·ri·al·ly /£məˈtɪə·ri·ə·li, $-ˈtɪr·i-/ *adv fml* • *She claims that even if mistakes had been made in the counting, they could not have materially affected* (= had an important effect on) *the results.* • See also **materially** at MATERIAL PHYSICAL SUBSTANCE.

ma·te·ri·al·i·sm MONEY /£məˈtɪə·ri·ə·lɪ·zəm, $-ˈtɪr·i-/ *n* [U] the belief that having money and possessions is the most important thing in life • *She claims that we have become a self-centred society, preoccupied with materialism and out of touch with each other.* • *Individualism and materialism are commonly cited as having a harmful effect on family life.*

ma·te·ri·al·ist /£məˈtɪə·ri·ə·lɪst, $-ˈtɪr·i-/ *n* [C] • *He's become such a materialist since he got his new job.*

ma·te·ri·al·is·tic /£məˌtɪə·ri·əˈlɪs·tɪk, $-ˌtɪr·i-/ *adj* • *People seemed to become much more materialistic during the 1980s.*

ma·te·ri·al·i·sm PHYSICAL /£məˈtɪə·ri·ə·lɪ·zəm, $-ˈtɪr·i-/ *n* [U] *specialized* the system of belief that states only physical matter exists and the spiritual world does not

ma·te·ri·al·ist /£məˈtɪə·ri·ə·lɪst, $-ˈtɪr·i-/ *n* [C] *specialized* • *He described himself as a materialist who saw death as nothing more than eternal sleep.*

ma·te·ri·al·ist /£məˈtɪə·ri·ə·lɪst, $-ˈtɪr·i-/ *adj specialized*

ma·te·ri·al·ize, *Br and Aus usually* **-ise** /£məˈtɪə·ri·ə·laɪz, $-ˈtɪr·i-/ *v* [I] See at MATERIAL PHYSICAL SUBSTANCE

ma·ter·nal /£məˈtɜː·nəl, $-ˈtɜːr-/ *adj* behaving or feeling in a way that a mother does towards her child, or related to a mother's side of a family • *His boyish nature appealed to her maternal instincts.* • *She is very maternal* **towards** *her staff.* • *In some societies, wealth is inherited through the maternal side of a family.* • *Her maternal grandmother* (= mother's mother) *is still alive.* • Compare PATERNAL.

ma·ter·nal·ly /£məˈtɜː·nəl·i, $-ˈtɜːr-/ *adv*

ma·ter·ni·ty /£məˈtɜː·nə·ti, $-ˈtɜːr·nə·t̬i/ *n* [U] • Maternity means the state of being a mother: *She's looking very well – maternity must suit her.* • Maternity clothes are clothes which are designed for pregnant women: *a maternity dress* • **Maternity leave** is a period in which a woman is legally allowed to be absent from work in the weeks before and after she gives birth. • A **maternity ward** is the part of a hospital in which women give birth and where they are taken care of after giving birth.

mat·ey /£'meɪ·ti, $-t̬i/ *n* [C], *adj infml* See at MATE [FRIEND]

math·e·mat·ics /£ˌmæθ'mæt·ɪks, $-'mæt̬-/, *Br and Aus infml* **maths** /mæθs/, *Am infml* **math** /mæθ/ *n* [U] the study of numbers, shapes and space using reason and usually a special system of symbols and rules for organizing them • See also ALGEBRA; ARITHMETIC; GEOMETRY. • [LP] **Mathematics**

ma·the·ma·ti·cal /£ˌmæθ·'mæt·ɪ·kᵊl, $-'mæt̬-/ *adj* [not gradable] • *a mathematical formula* • *In accountancy, it often helps to have a mathematical* **mind** (= to be good at solving problems involving numbers).

math·e·ma·ti·cal·ly /£ˌmæθ·'mæt·ɪ·kli, $-'mæt̬-/ *adv* [not gradable] • *It's often easy to state a problem in words but difficult to express it mathematically.*

math·e·ma·ti·cian /ˌmæθ·mə'tɪʃ·ᵊn/ *n* [C] • *Leonhard Euler is a famous Swiss mathematician.*

mat·i·née /£'mæt·ɪ·neɪ, $ˌmæt̬·ᵊn'eɪ/ *n* [C] a film shown or a play performed during the day, esp. the afternoon • *The play will be performed at 7p.m. all this week with a matinée at 2p.m. on Saturday.* • *(dated)* A **matinée idol** is a male actor, esp. in films of the 1930s and 1940s, who is thought to be very attractive by women: *He had the classic good looks of a matinée idol.*

mat·ins /£'mæt·ɪnz, $'mæt̬-/ *pl n* the morning ceremony in some Christian churches

ma·tri·arch /£'meɪ·tri·ɑːk, $-ɑːrk/ *n* [C] an old and powerful woman in a family, or the female leader of a society in which power passes from mother to daughter • *She saw herself as an elderly matriarch around whom younger people gathered to benefit from the fruits of her experience.* • Compare **patriarch** at PATRIARCHY.

ma·tri·ar·chal /£ˌmeɪ·tri'ɑː·kᵊl, $-'ɑːr-/ *adj* • *a matriarchal society* • Compare **patriarchal** at PATRIARCHY.

ma·tri·ar·chy /£'meɪ·tri·ɑː·ki, $-ɑːr-/ *n* [C/U] • A matriarchy is a type of society in which women have most of the authority and power, or a society in which property belongs to women and is given to children by women rather than men. • Compare PATRIARCHY.

ma·tri·cide /'mæt·rɪ·saɪd, 'meɪ·trɪ-/ *n* [U] a crime in which a person kills their mother • Compare PARRICIDE; PATRICIDE.

ma·tric·u·late /mə'trɪk·jʊ·leɪt/ *v* [I] to be formally admitted to study at a university or college • *She matriculated in 1988 and graduated in 1991.*

ma·tric·u·la·tion /məˌtrɪk·jʊ'leɪ·ʃᵊn/ *n* [C/U]

mat·ri·mo·ny /'mæt·rɪ·mə·ni/ *n* [U] *fml* the state of being married

mat·ri·mo·n·i·al /£ˌmæt·rɪ'məʊ·ni·əl, $-'moʊ-/ *adj* [not gradable] *fml* • Matrimonial means related to marriage or people who are married: *She left the matrimonial home following an argument with her husband.* ○ *He and his wife have been experiencing matrimonial difficulties* (= They have been arguing and fighting).

ma·trix [DEVELOPMENT] /'meɪ·trɪks/ *n* [C] *pl* **matrices** or **matrixes** *fml* the set of conditions which provides a background in which something grows or develops • *Europe is remaking itself politically within the matrix of the European Community.*

ma·trix [MATHEMATICS] /'meɪ·trɪks/ *n* [C] *pl* **matrices** /'meɪ·trɪ·siːz/ or **matrixes** /'meɪ·trɪk·sɪz/ *specialized* (in mathematics) a group of numbers or other symbols arranged in a rectangle which can be used together as a single unit to solve particular mathematical problems

ma·tron [SCHOOL] /'meɪ·trᵊn/ *n* [C] a woman who is responsible for children's health and general care in a school

ma·tron [HOSPITAL] /'meɪ·trᵊn/ *n* [C] *Br and Aus dated for* **senior nursing officer**, see at SENIOR [HIGH RANK]

ma·tron [PRISON] /'meɪ·trᵊn/ *n* [C] *esp. Am* a woman who is in charge of female prisoners and sometimes children in a prison

ma·tron·ly /'meɪ·trᵊn·li/ *adj esp. humorous* (of a woman) middle-aged, rather fat, and behaving in a serious way • *None of the women he interviewed were suitable for the job – they were either too glamorous or too matronly.*

ma·tron /'meɪ·trᵊn/ *n* [C] *esp. humorous*

matt (**-er, -est**) /mæt/, *Am usually* **matte** (**-r, -st**) *adj* (of a surface, colour or paint) not shiny • *The bookcase comes in white or matt black.* • *The paint is available in matt or gloss finish.* • Compare EMULSION; GLOSS [COVERING].

mat·ted /£'mæt·ɪd, $'mæt̬-/ *adj* See at MAT [LAYER]

mat·ter [SITUATION] /£'mæt·əʳ, $'mæt̬·ɚ/ *n* [C] a situation or subject which is being dealt with or considered • *Could I talk to you? It's a personal matter.* • *Divorce is always a traumatic matter.* • *Solving this equation will not be a trivial matter* (= will not be easy). • *The matter* (= problem) *was soon resolved.* • *Will you phone me back – it's a matter* **of** *great importance.* • *I told the shop about the fault, but they said it was a matter* **for** (= the responsibility of) *the manufacturer.* • *The matter is now* **closed** (= You must not talk about the subject any more). • *I've said I'm sorry, so why don't you* **let the** *matter* **drop** (= stop talking about the subject)? • *Talking about the world's problems is one thing, but solving them is* **another** *matter* **altogether** (= is completely different). • If something is a matter **of** doing something, it is quite easy and only involves doing the thing mentioned: *Cooking a goat isn't difficult – it's just a matter of following the recipe.* • **For that matter** is used to show that a statement is true in another situation or can also refer to another person: *I'm going to bed early, and so for that matter should you* (= you should also). • The **matter in hand** (*Am usually* **matter at hand**) is the subject or situation being considered: *Do these figures have any bearing on the matter in hand?* • If something is done **as a matter of course**, it is a usual part of the way in which things are done and is not special: *We observe the safety precautions as a matter of course.* • If something is a **matter of life and/or death**, it is extremely serious: *Don't worry about missing your bus – it's not a matter of life and death.* • If something is a **matter of opinion**, it is not a fact but is a personal preference: *Both performances were excellent, it's simply a matter of opinion to say which one was the best.* • If something is a **matter of record**, it is generally known to be true: *It is a matter of record that both sides committed atrocities during the war.* • *Being arrested by the police is* **no laughing matter** (= It is very serious).

mat·ters /£'mæt·əz, $'mæt̬·ɚz/ *pl n* • Matters refers to the situation being dealt with or discussed: *My financial matters are in a bit of a mess.* ○ *Her resignation is not going to* **help** *matters* (= make the situation better). • If something **makes matters worse**, it makes a bad or difficult situation even more unpleasant or difficult: *Three of their players are ill, and to make matters worse, their leading goal scorer has broken his ankle.* • If someone **takes matters into** their **own hands**, they decide to take responsibility for a situation themselves and act in a way which they think is suitable, often without thinking in a clear way before doing it: *When the police failed to catch her son's murderer, she decided to take matters into her own hands.*

mat·ter [BE IMPORTANT] /£'mæt·əʳ, $'mæt̬·ɚ/ *v* [not *be mattering*] to be important • *Both teams played as if the match really mattered, even though it was unimportant.* [I] • *We've missed the 8.30 train, but what matters now is that we don't miss the next one.* [I] • *"What did you say?" "Oh,* **it** *doesn't matter."* [I] • **It** *doesn't matter* **if** *you turn left or right – both roads lead to the park.* [+ *wh*- word] • **It** *doesn't matter* **wh***at you wear – just as long as you come.* [+ *wh*- word] • **It** *didn't matter* **that** *our best player was injured after 10 minutes – we still won.* [+ *that* clause] • *I know John doesn't think this project is important, but it really matters* **to** *me.* [I] • If you say **no matter** when something happens, you mean that it is not important: *"Whoops! I've spilt my drink." "No matter – here's another one."* • **No matter** is also used in expressions such as 'no matter what', to show that something must happen or be done whatever the situation is: *We have to get to the airport on time, no matter* **what**. [+ *wh*- word] ○ *We have to get the car fixed, no matter* **how** *much it costs.* [+ *wh*- word]

mat·ter [PROBLEM] /£'mæt·əʳ, $'mæt̬·ɚ/ *n* [U] **the matter** the reason for pain or worry • *Is anything the matter?* • *What's the matter? Why are you crying?* • *Your ankle looks swollen – what's the matter* **with** *it?* • *I don't know what the matter is* **with** *the car, but it won't start.* • If you say **what is the matter with** doing something, you means that you do not think there is anything wrong in doing it: *What is the matter with asking for a pay rise?*

mat·ter [SUBSTANCE] /£'mæt·əʳ, $'mæt̬·ɚ/ *n* [U] physical substance in the universe • *We believe that there is about ten times as much matter in the universe as astronomers have observed.*

mat·ter [TYPE] /£'mæt·əʳ, $'mæt̬·ɚ/ *n* [U] substance of the stated type • *advertising/printed matter* • *They sort their*

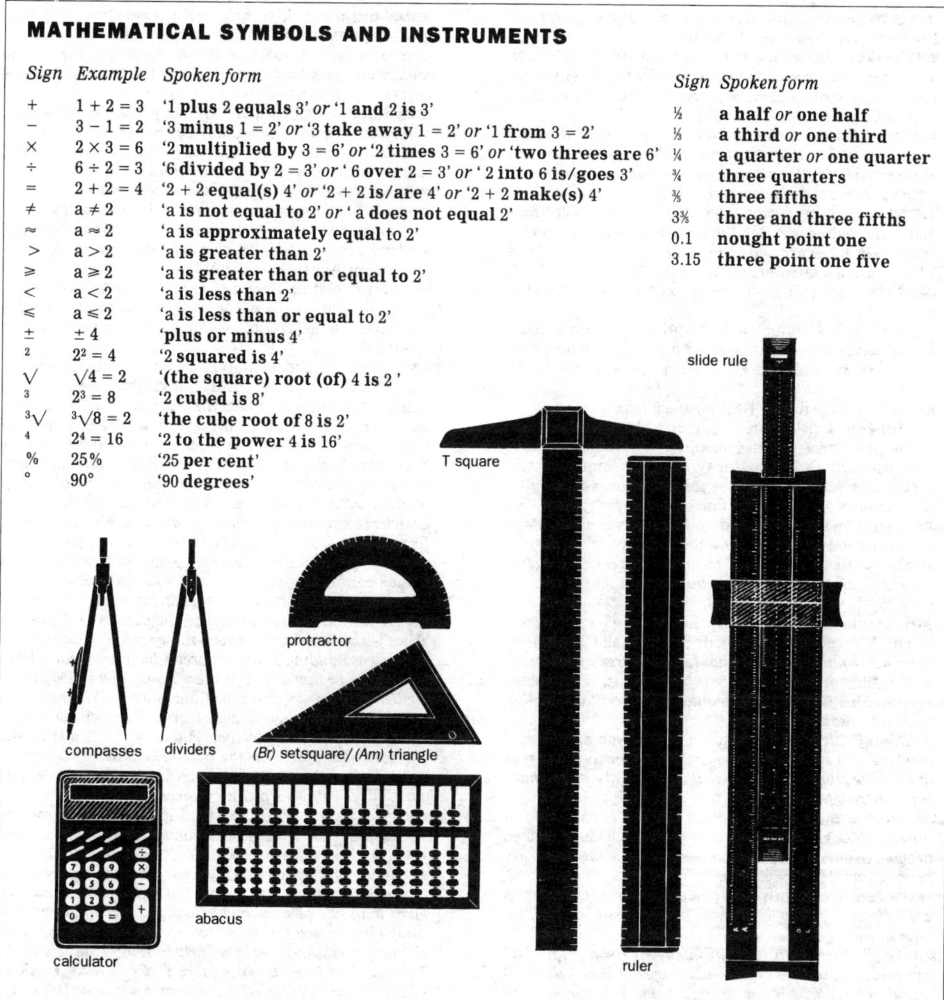

MATHEMATICAL SYMBOLS AND INSTRUMENTS

Sign	Example	Spoken form
+	$1 + 2 = 3$	'**1 plus 2 equals 3**' *or* '**1 and 2 is 3**'
−	$3 - 1 = 2$	'**3 minus 1 = 2**' *or* '**3 take away 1 = 2**' *or* '**1 from 3 = 2**'
×	$2 \times 3 = 6$	'**2 multiplied by 3 = 6**' *or* '**2 times 3 = 6**' *or* '**two threes are 6**'
÷	$6 \div 2 = 3$	'**6 divided by 2 = 3**' *or* '**6 over 2 = 3**' *or* '**2 into 6 is/goes 3**'
=	$2 + 2 = 4$	'**2 + 2 equal(s) 4**' *or* '**2 + 2 is/are 4**' *or* '**2 + 2 make(s) 4**'
≠	$a \neq 2$	'**a is not equal to 2**' *or* '**a does not equal 2**'
≈	$a \approx 2$	'**a is approximately equal** to 2'
>	$a > 2$	'**a is greater than 2**'
⩾	$a \geqslant 2$	'**a is greater than or equal to 2**'
<	$a < 2$	'**a is less than 2**'
⩽	$a \leqslant 2$	'**a is less than or equal** to 2'
±	± 4	'**plus or minus 4**'
^{2}	$2^2 = 4$	'**2 squared is 4**'
√	$\sqrt{4} = 2$	'**(the square) root (of) 4 is 2**'
^{3}	$2^3 = 8$	'**2 cubed is 8**'
∛	$\sqrt[3]{8} = 2$	'**the cube root of 8 is 2**'
^{4}	$2^4 = 16$	'**2 to the power 4 is 16**'
%	25%	'**25 per cent**'
°	90°	'**90 degrees**'

Sign	Spoken form
½	**a half** *or* **one half**
⅓	**a third** *or* **one third**
¼	**a quarter** *or* **one quarter**
¾	**three quarters**
⅗	**three fifths**
3⅗	**three and three fifths**
0.1	**nought point one**
3.15	**three point one five**

rubbish into four categories – paper, metal, plastics and vegetable matter. • *You should take plenty of* **reading** *matter* (=books) *away with you on your trip.* • *Do you find the* **subject** *matter of the book* (=the subject that the book deals with) *interesting?*

mat·ter SMALL AMOUNT /£ˈmæt·əʳ, $ˈmæt̬·ɚ/ *n* [U] used in expressions describing how small an amount or period of time is • *In a* **matter** *of seconds, the building was in flames.* • *The interview was over in a matter of minutes.* • *She complained he had short-changed her, but it was only a matter of a few pence.*

mat·ter-of-fact /£ˌmæt·ə·rəʊˈfækt, $ˌmæt̬·ɚ·əv-/ *adj* not showing feelings or emotion, esp. in a situation when emotion would be expected • *He spoke in a very matter-of-fact way about the accident.* • See also **as a matter of fact** at MATTER SITUATION.

mat·ter-of-fact·ly /£ˌmæt·ə·rəʊˈfækt·li, $ˌmæt̬·ɚ·əv-/ *adv* • *She tried to announce the news as matter-of-factly as possible.*

mat·ter-of-fact·ness /£ˌmæt·ə·rəʊˈfækt·nəs, $ˌmæt̬·ɚ·əv-/ *n* [U] • *It was the matter-of-factness of his reply that surprised me.*

mat·ting /£ˈmæt·ɪŋ, $ˈmæt̬-/ *n* [U] strong rough material, often woven, which is used to cover floors • *straw/coconut matting*

mat·tress /ˈmæt·rəs/ *n* [C] the part of a bed, made of a strong cloth cover filled with firm material, which makes the bed comfortable to lie on • *There is no bed in her room and she sleeps on a mattress on the floor.* • PIC **Beds and bedroom**

ma·ture GROW PHYSICALLY /£məˈtjʊəʳ, $-ˈtʊr/ *v* [I] to become completely grown physically • *Humans mature after a much longer time than most other animals.*

ma·ture /£məˈtjʊəʳ, $-tjʊr/ *adj* [not gradable] • Mature means fully grown physically: *Mature males of the species have brightly coloured tail feathers.* ○ *The garden has a lot of beautiful mature oak trees.* • A *(Br)* **mature student**/*(Aus)* **mature-age student** (*Am* **older student**) is a student at a college or university who is older than the usual age: *In Britain, mature students are over 25 years old, and in Australia, they are over 22 years old.*

ma·tur·i·ty /£məˈtjʊə·rɪ·ti, $-ˈtʊr·ə·t̬i/ *n* [U] • Maturity is the state of being completely grown physically: *How long does it take for the chicks to grow to maturity?* • CS

ma·tu·ra·tion /ˌmæt·jʊˈreɪ·ʃᵊn/ *n* [U] • Maturation is the process of becoming completely grown physically: *The process of physical maturation normally occurs more quickly in girls than in boys.*

ma·ture *(obj)* DEVELOP MENTALLY /£məˈtjʊəʳ, $-ˈtʊr/ *v esp. approving* to (cause someone to) become more developed mentally and emotionally and behave in a responsible way • *He matured a lot while he was at college.* [I] • *Girls are said to mature faster than boys.* [I] • *Hardship often matures young people.* [T] • If something matures, it reaches an advanced or developed state: *It took several years for her ideas to mature.* [I]

ma·ture /£məˈtjʊəʳ, $-ˈtjʊr/ *adj esp. approving* • If someone is mature, they behave in a responsible way and are more completely developed mentally and emotionally than other people of their age: *He is very mature for his age.* • *(fml)* A mature decision is one which is made after a lot of careful thought: *Upon mature reflection, we find the accused guilty.*

ma·ture·ly /£mə'tjʊə·li, $-'tʊr-/ *adv esp. approving* • *She behaves very maturely for her age.*

ma·tur·i·ty /£mə'tjʊə·rɪ·ti, $-'tʊr·ə·t̬i/ *n* [U] *esp. approving* • *At times, she seems to have maturity beyond her years.* • *Her writing came to maturity* (= reached its most developed form) *in the 1960s.* • Ⓒⓢ

ma·tu·ra·tion /£ˌmæt·jʊə'reɪ·ʃən, $-jʊ-/ *n* [U] *esp. approving* • *The time he spent in Paris represented the maturation* (= development) *of his ideas and his move away from a position of dependence on others.*

ma·ture *(obj)* FOOD /£mə'tjʊəʳ, $-'tʊr/ *v* to make (food and wine) old enough for the flavour to have developed completely • *The wine has been matured in oak vats.* [T] • *The cheese is left to mature for two years.* [I]

ma·ture /£mə'tjʊəʳ, $-'tjʊr/ *adj* • *Do you prefer mild or mature cheddar?*

ma·ture FINANCE /£mə'tjʊəʳ, $-'tʊr/ *v* [I] *specialized* (of an INSURANCE agreement or some types of investment) to become ready to be paid • *The policy matures after fifteen years.*

ma·ture /£mə'tjʊəʳ, $-'tʊr/ *adj specialized*

ma·tur·i·ty /£mə'tjʊə·rɪ·ti, $-'tjʊr·ə·t̬i/ *n* [U] *specialized* • *The investment* **reaches** *maturity* (= becomes mature) *after ten years.* • The maturity of an investment is the period after which it should be paid: *The bonds have a five-year maturity and do not pay interest for the first year.* • Ⓒⓢ

maud·lin /£'mɔːd·lɪn, $'mɑːd-/ *adj* feeling sad about life in general or your own life, esp. after you have drunk a lot of alcohol • *He never drank during the week, but when Saturday night arrived, he drank until he was quite maudlin.*

maul *obj* /£mɔːl, $mɑːl/ *v* [T usually passive] (of an animal) to attack (a person or animal) severely and hurt them badly • *The family's pet dog mauled their three-year-old son.* • If a film or performance is mauled, it is criticized severely: *His first film was mauled by the critics for being too sentimental.*

maul·ing /£'mɔː·lɪŋ, $'mɑː-/ *n* [C] • If you are given a mauling, you are criticized severely: *She* **received** *the type of mauling from her political allies which she might have expected from her opponents.*

mau·so·le·um /£ˌmɔː·zə'liː·əm, $ˌmɑː-/ *n* [C] an important-looking building in which the bodies of dead people are buried • *The bodies of rich or famous people are usually buried in a mausoleum.*

mauve /£məʊv, $moʊv/ *adj* [not gradable], *n* [U] (having) a pale purple colour • *She wore a mauve silk shirt and a pink skirt.*

mav·en /'meɪ·vən/ *n* [C] *Am infml* a person with good knowledge or understanding of a subject • *He's a baseball maven who knows Hank Aaron's home run statistics by heart.*

mav·er·ick /£'mæv·ər·ɪk, $'-ɚ-/ *n* [C] a person who thinks and acts in an independent way, often behaving differently from the expected or usual way • *She is widely regarded as a political maverick.* • *He was considered as something of a maverick in the publishing world.*

maw /£mɔː, $mɑː/ *n* [C] *fml* the mouth of a fierce animal • *The bear opened wide its maw, baring its teeth.* • *(fig. literary) She fears that the matter will simply be swallowed up by the maw of bureaucracy and that a decision will never be made.*

mawk·ish /£'mɔː·kɪʃ, $'mɑː-/ *adj* showing emotion or love in an awkward or foolish way • *The first half of the film is convincing, but it lapses into mawkish sentimentality at the end.*

mawk·ish·ly /£'mɔː·kɪʃ·li, $'mɑː-/ *adv*

mawk·ish·ness /£'mɔː·kɪʃ·nəs, $'mɑː-/ *n* [U] • *She disliked the air of sentimentality and mawkishness of the novel.*

max /mæks/ *adj, n* [C] *abbreviation for* MAXIMUM • Max is often used after an amount: *"How much will the trip cost?" "£40 max."*

max·im /'mæk·sɪm/ *n* [C] a brief statement of a general truth, principle or rule for behaviour • *He often preaches the maxim of 'use it or lose it'.* • *A Silicon Valley company is about to test the maxim that smaller is always better for computers.*

max·i·mum /'mæk·sɪ·məm/ (*abbreviation* **max**) *adj* [not gradable] being the largest amount or number allowed or possible • *The bomb was designed to cause the maximum amount of harm to the maximum number of people.* • *If you turn the stereo up to maximum volume, the neighbours will complain.* • Compare MINIMUM.

max·i·mum /'mæk·sɪ·məm/ *n* [C] *pl* **maxima** /'mæk·sɪ·mə/ or **maximums** • *The temperature will reach a maximum of 27°C today.* • If you do something **to the maximum** (*infml* **max**), you do it to the greatest possible degree. • Compare MINIMUM.

max·i·mal /'mæk·sɪ·məl/ *adj* [not gradable] *fml* • *Even when the brain has attained its maximal size and structure, signals from the body and the environment are still constantly changing it.* • Compare **minimal** at MINIMUM.

max·i·mize *obj, Br and Aus usually* **-ise** /'mæk·sɪ·maɪz/ *v* [T] • To maximize something is to make it as great in amount, size or importance as possible: *To maximize our walking time, we should be ready to start at dawn.* • Compare **minimize** at MINIMUM.

max·i·miz·a·tion, *Br and Aus usually* **-i·sa·tion** /ˌmæk·sɪ·maɪ'zeɪ·ʃən/ *n* [U] • *The company is striving for the maximization of profits.* • Compare **minimization** at MINIMUM.

may POSSIBILITY /meɪ/ *v aux* [+ infinitive without *to*; not *be maying*] he/she/it **may**, *past simple* **might** used to express possibility • *I may see you at the party later.* • *The cause of the accident may never be discovered.* • *"Are you going to Neil's party?" "I haven't decided yet, I suppose I may."* • *There may be side effects from the new drug.* • *In the future, it may be possible to fly across the Atlantic in about thirty minutes.* • *The explosion may have been caused by a faulty electrical connection.* • *We'd better not interfere – she mayn't like it.* • *From the noise the crowd is making, I think our team may* **have** *won* (= it is possible that we have won, but I am not certain). • *(fml) We should try to calm down so that we may begin to discuss the situation rationally.* • You can say **be that as it may** to change the subject being talked about without deciding on something which was just being discussed: *Building a new children's home will cost a lot of money, but be that as it may there is an urgent need for the facility.* • If you say that something **may well** happen, you mean that it is likely to happen: *You may well get lost, so take a map.* ○ *She may well not want to* (= It is likely that she will not want to) *go on the trip – she hates travelling.* ○ Compare **might well** at MIGHT. • Compare MIGHT POSSIBILITY. • LP **Auxiliary verbs**

may PERMISSION /meɪ/ *v aux* [+ infinitive without *to*; not *be maying*] he/she/it **may**, *past simple* **might** *slightly fml* used to ask or give permission • *Yes, you may go swimming, but be home by four.* • *A reader may borrow up to six books at any one time.* • *Passengers may not carry more than one piece of hand luggage onto the aircraft.* • *"May I help myself to some more food?" "Yes, you may."* • *Hi, my name's Tiffany. How may I help you?* • *If I may continue, I should like to show some more slides.* • **May I ask** is sometimes used in questions to show disapproval by being more polite than is expected: *What, may I ask, was the point of repeating the tests?* • This use of 'may' is slightly more formal and less common than CAN. • Compare MIGHT PERMISSION.

may INTRODUCE /meɪ/ *v aux* [+ infinitive without *to*; not *be maying*] he/she/it **may**, *past simple* **might** used to introduce a statement which is very different from the statement you really want to make, in order to compare the two thoughts or ideas • *There may be some evidence to suggest she's guilty,* **but** *it's hardly conclusive.* • *You may feel all the training is a waste of time,* **but** *later you'll be grateful you did it.* • *I may be overreacting to the letter,* **but** *I still think we should let the police see it.* • **Although** *it is of no direct consequence to our discussions, it may be worth noting that tomorrow is the fifth anniversary of the society's foundation.*

may WISH /meɪ/ *v aux* [+ infinitive without *to*; not *be maying*] he/she/it **may** *fml* used to introduce a wish or a hope • *Long may the peace continue.* • *Long may she reign.* • *May the rest of your married life be as happy as the first ten years have been.*

may TREE /meɪ/ *n* [U] the flowers of the HAWTHORN tree • *may blossom*

May MONTH /meɪ/ *n* the fifth month of the year, after April and before June • *30(th) May/May 30(th)* [U] • *My mother's birthday is* **on** *the seventh of May/May the seventh/(esp. Am) May seventh.* [U] • *We moved house* **last** *May/are moving house* **next** *May.* [U] • *They're getting married* **in/during** *May.* [U] • *This is predicted to be one of the sunniest Mays for many years.* [C] • **May Day** is the first day of May which is a holiday in many countries. It traditionally celebrates spring but now it is often used to honour workers. Compare MAYDAY. • LP **Dates, Holidays**

may·be /ˈmeɪ·bi, ˌ-ˈ-/ *adv* [not gradable] used to show that something is possible or that something might be true • *Maybe they'll come tomorrow.* • *Maybe you were right after all.* • *Maybe he's right or maybe he's wrong in his beliefs, but either way you have to admire him for what he's achieved.* • Maybe is also used to show that a number or amount is approximate: *Soldiers found maybe as many as fifty refugees hiding in the basement.* • Maybe can be used to politely suggest or ask for something: *Maybe we should start again.* • Maybe can also be used to avoid giving a clear or certain answer to a question: *"Will you or will you not be appealing against the judgment?" "Maybe."* • Maybe can also be used to mean that something is a possible explanation why something else happened: *"Why were you chosen for the team and not me?" "Maybe it's because I've been to more practice sessions than you."*

may·be /ˈmeɪ·bi, ˌ-ˈ-/ *n* [C] *infml* • A maybe is an answer to a question when you do not want to say either yes or no: *"Have you had any replies to your party invitations?" "So far we've had a yes, a no, and a couple of maybes."* ○ *"I can't say I'll be there for sure, but it's a* **definite** *maybe* (= it is quite likely that I will be there)*."*

may·day /ˈmeɪ·deɪ/ *n* [C] a radio signal sent from a ship or an aircraft when it needs help • *Mayday is an internationally recognized distress call.* • Compare **May Day** at MAY [MONTH].

may·fly /ˈmeɪ·flaɪ/ *n* [C] an insect which lives near water and only lives for a very short time as an adult

may·hem /ˈmeɪ·hem/ *n* [U] a situation in which there is little or no order or control • *We only left the children's party unattended for a few minutes, but it was mayhem when we returned.*

ma·yon·naise /ˌmeɪ·əˈneɪz, ˈ---/, *infml* **ma·yo** /£ˈmeɪ·əʊ, $-oʊ/ *n* [U] a thick creamy sauce made from oil, vinegar and the yellow part of eggs, which is usually eaten cold • *Would you like some mayonnaise with your salad?*

mayor /£meəʳ, $mer/ *n* [C] the person who is elected each year to be the leader of the governing group in a town or city

mayor·ess /£ˌmeəˈres, $ˈmer·ɪs/ *n* [C] • A mayoress is either the wife of a mayor or a female mayor. • A **lady** mayoress is the wife of a mayor.

mayor·al /£ˈmeə·rəl, $ˈmeɪ·ɔːr·əl/ *adj* [not gradable] • *mayoral duties*

mayor·al·ty /£ˈmeə·rəl·ti, $ˈmeɪ·ɔːr·əl-/ *n* [U] *Am* • A mayoralty is the office of being a mayor or the period of time for which it lasts.

may·pole /£ˈmeɪ·pəʊl, $-poʊl/ *n* [C] a tall pole with long RIBBONS (= narrow strips of cloth) fixed to the top of it, the ends of which people hold as they dance around the pole on the first of May

may've *infml* /ˈmeɪ·əv/ *short form of* MAY have • *"Did you see Jim last night?" "I may've done – I can't remember."*

maze /meɪz/ *n* [C] a complicated group of paths or passages, esp. one made with tall thick bushes at the sides of the paths which people try to find their way through for amusement • *The children completely exhausted themselves in the afternoon getting lost in the maze.* • *The old part of the town was a maze of narrow passages between whitewashed buildings.* • A maze is also a complicated set of rules, ideas or subjects which you find difficult to deal with or understand: *It's almost impossible to get through the maze of bureaucracy.*

MB *Br and Aus* /ˌemˈbiː/, *Am* **BM** *n* [C] *abbreviation for* Bachelor of Medicine (= a degree in medicine, or a person who has this degree) • [LP] **Schools and colleges**

MBA /ˌem·biːˈeɪ/ *n* [C] *abbreviation for* Master of Business Administration (= a high qualification in business from a college or university)

MC /ˌemˈsiː/ *n* [C] *abbreviation for* **Master of Ceremonies**, see at MASTER [CONTROL] • MC is also the title given to someone who is the main singer in a RAP (= a type of popular music) group: *The group roared in approval when MC Hammer came on stage.*

Mc·Car·thy·i·sm /£məˈkɑː·θi·ɪ·zəm, $-ˈkɑːr-/ *n* [U] the act of accusing someone of something that is considered unacceptable by many people, esp. when you have no proof • *McCarthyism is named after the American politician Joseph McCarthy, who in the 1950s accused many Americans of being Communists.* • *She was a victim of McCarthyism.*

Mc·Carth·y·ite /£məˈkɑː·θi·aɪt, $-ˈkɑːr-/, **Mc·Car·thy·ist** /$məˈkɑː·θi·ɪst, $-ˈkɑːr-/ *n* [C], *adj* • *He led a McCarthyite* **witch-hunt** *against homosexuals.*

Mc·Coy /məˈkɔɪ/ *n* [U] **the real McCoy**, see at REAL [NOT FALSE]

MCP /ˌem·siːˈpiː/ *n* [C] *infml abbreviation for* **male chauvinist pig**, see at MALE [SEX]

MD [DOCTOR] /ˌemˈdi/ *n* [C] *Am and Aus abbreviation for* Doctor of Medicine (= a degree which someone must have to work as a doctor) • *Steven Tay, MD*

MD [MANAGER] /ˌemˈdi/ *n* [C] *Br and Aus abbreviation for* **Managing Director**, see at MANAGE [CONTROL] • *You should talk to the MD about your proposal.*

me [PERSON] /miː, mɪ/ *pronoun* used, usually after a verb or preposition, to refer to the person speaking or writing • *Please will you pass me that book.* • *Please pass that book to me.* • *It wasn't me who offered to go, it was him.* • *"Me Tarzan, you Jane"* (the actor Johnny Weismuller of the *Tarzan* adventure films, 1932) • See also I [PERSON SPEAKING].

ME [ILLNESS] /ˌemˈiː/, **chron·ic fa·tigue syn·drome** *n* [U] *abbreviation for* MYALGIC ENCEPHALOMYELITIS (= an illness, sometimes lasting for several years, in which a person's muscles hurt and they are generally very tired) • *She suffers from ME.* • *Doctors still do not know what causes ME.*

mead /miːd/ *n* [U] an alcoholic drink made from HONEY (= a sweet substance produced by bees), drunk esp. in the past

mead·ow /£ˈmed·əʊ, $-oʊ/ *n* a field with grass and often wild flowers in it • *There was a path through the meadow to the village.* [C] • *This area used to be meadow (also* **meadowland***) but it was ploughed up during the war.* [U] • Meadow is used in the names of many wild flowers, insects and birds: *a meadow cranesbill* (= a type of flower) ○ *a meadow brown* (= a type of insect) ○ *a meadow pipit* (= a type of bird) • *"The sheep's in the meadow, the cow's in the corn"* (from the nursery rhyme *Little Boy Blue*)

mea·gre, *Am usually* **mea·ger** /£ˈmiː·gəʳ, $-gɚ/ *adj* very small in amount or number; only just as much or not as much as is needed or thought to be suitable • *He had to use his own meagre earnings to continue his research and often found himself in extreme poverty.* • *Stealing of the soldiers' meagre rations by officers was common.* • *When pressed, he contributed a meagre £5.* • *The crowd should be larger than the meagre 13 000 who watched the last match.*

meal [FOOD] /mɪəl/ *n* [C] an occasion when food is eaten, or the food which is eaten on such an occasion • *The first meal of the day is breakfast, the only meal when the family eat together.* • *After the meal there were several speeches.* • *We're going out for a meal on my birthday.* • *He cooked us all a meal on Sunday.* • *We only eat one* **cooked/hot** *meal a day.* • *They felt sleepy after such a* **heavy** (= large) *meal.* • *We had a* **light** (= small) *meal at midday – bread, cheese, some fruit and a drink.* • *(Br disapproving)* If you **make a meal (out) of** something, you do more or give more attention than is needed: *The press will make a meal of this story.* ○ *I want the room to look good for the party but there's no need to make a meal out of it.* • **Meal ticket** is *Am and Aus for* **luncheon voucher**. See at LUNCHEON. • A **meal ticket** is also someone or something which provides you with the money that you need in order to pay for food, somewhere to live, clothes, etc.: *I don't enjoy the job but it's my meal ticket for the moment.* ○ *Jim? He's her latest meal ticket.* • **Meals on wheels** are hot meals taken to the homes of old and/or ill people, either for free or for a small payment.

meal [POWDER] /mɪəl/ *n* [U] a substance which has been crushed to make a rough powder, esp. plant seeds crushed to make flour or for animal food • *In previous centuries, local farmers used to bring their corn to this mill, where it was ground into meal.* • Meal is often used as a combining form: *cornmeal* ○ *oatmeal* ○ *soya meal* ○ *bone meal*

meal·y /ˈmɪə·li/ *adj* **-ier, -iest** • Mealy means dry and powdery: *I don't like these mealy potatoes.* ○ *This type of apple doesn't get mealy inside – it has a long shelf-life.* • *(disapproving)* **Mealy-mouthed** means expressing something unpleasant in a way that is not direct: *mealy-mouthed excuses* ○ *a mealy-mouthed spokesperson*

meal·time /ˈmɪəl·taɪm/ *n* [C usually pl] a time at which a meal is eaten • *The only time the family all get together is at mealtimes* (= when we are eating our meals). • *We were taught to have regular mealtimes* (= to eat meals at the same times every day). • *The staff restaurant is only open at* **set** *mealtimes* (= at the agreed times when complete meals are served).

mean *(obj)* [EXPRESS] /miːn/ *v* [not *be meaning*] *past* **meant** /ment/ to express or represent (an idea, thought, fact, etc.) • *"What does 'rough' mean?" "It means 'not smooth or uneven'."* [T] • *As the well-known line from the film put it,*

*"Love means never hav***ing** *to say you're sorry".* [+ v-*ing*] • *These figures mean* **that** *almost 7% of the working population is unemployed.* [+ *that* clause] • *What do you mean* (= are you referring to) **by** *that remark?* • *"Did you have a good holiday?" "It depends what you mean* **by** (= what you are referring to when you say) *holiday – I was painting the house!"* • *You have to hold the bar down while you lock it – (do you/you) see what I mean* (= do you understand what I am trying to say)? • *She's an odd sort of person -(do you/you) know what I mean* (= do you understand what I am trying to say)? • Mean can also be used to add emphasis to what you are saying: *No means no.* [T] ○ *I want you home by midnight. And I mean midnight.* [T] • People sometimes say **I mean** when they are explaining something in a different way to make it more exact or easier to understand: *She was very talented – as a performer, not as a musician, I mean.* ○ *These people live a very sheltered life – I mean completely cut off from the outside world.* • **I mean (to say)** is used to introduce something, or to answer something, in a disapproving way: *I mean, I think he could have asked me before he borrowed my bike!* ○ *He said you were stupid? Well, I mean to say!* • **What do you mean** is used to show that you are annoyed or that you disagree: *What do you mean, it was my fault?* ○ *What do you mean* **by** *arriving so late?* • When people say **you mean** before or after a question, they are asking for additional explanation of something: *"Do you remember Jane Carter?" "The woman we met in Scotland, you mean?"* • *"'When I use a word' Humpty Dumpty said in a rather scornful tone, 'it means just what I choose it to mean, – neither more nor less'"* (Lewis Carroll in his book *Through the Looking-Glass*, 1872)

mean·ing /ˈmiː·nɪŋ/ *n* • The meaning of something is what it expresses or represents: *The word 'flight' has two different meanings : a plane journey, and the act of running away.* [C] ○ *People have to discover or learn acceptable meanings* **for** *the symbols of their language when they are children.* [C] ○ *The author was talking on television about the real meaning* **of** *the play.* [C] ○ *The* **full** *meaning* **of** *his enquiry didn't become clear till later.* [U] ○ *It wasn't obvious at first glance, but his paintings had (a)* **hidden** *meaning.* [C/U] ○ *(esp. humorous) "This place," said Mr. Reed looking at the palace, "gives the phrase 'detached housing' (a)* **new** *meaning* (= adds to or changes the meaning you knew)." [C/U] • *(esp. humorous)* **If you take my meaning** is used to suggest that what you are saying can be understood in an additional way: *When he started dancing on the table I'm sure he wasn't altogether sober, if you take my meaning* (= he was drunk). • Ⓓ Ⓓⓚ

mean·ing·less /ˈmiː·nɪŋ·ləs/ *adj* • *The leaflet was full of meaningless* (= not expressing anything) *information.*

mean *(obj)* HAVE RESULT /miːn/ *v* [not *be meaning*] *past* **meant** /ment/ to have as a result • *Lower costs mean lower prices.* [T] • *Advances in microelectronics mean* **that** *the technology is already available.* [+ *that* clause] • *If we want to catch the 7.30 train, that will mean leav***ing** *the house at 6.00.* [+ v-*ing*]

mean *obj* HAVE IMPORTANCE /miːn/ *v* [T; not *be meaning*] *past* **meant** /ment/ to have the importance or value of • *Experts say there isn't another state in the country where tests mean as much as they do in South Carolina.* • *Who can tell what that agreement might mean* **for** *a country so dependent on trade?* • *Does that name mean anything* **to** *you?* • *It wasn't a valuable picture but it meant a lot* **to** *me.* • *Possessions mean nothing* **to** *him.* • *"Lonesome would mean nothing to me at all"* (from the song *Tomorrow is a long time* by Bob Dylan, 1971) • *"It don't mean a thing/ If it ain't got that swing"* (title of a song by Duke Ellington, 1932)

mean·ing /ˈmiː·nɪŋ/ *n* [U] • Meaning is importance or value: *The birth of her first grandchild gave new meaning to her life.* ○ *Education had no great meaning* **for** *him until much later in his life.*

mean·ing·ful /ˈmiː·nɪŋ·fᵊl/ *adj* • *He does not try to prove points one way or the other, but he does ask meaningful* (= important and serious) *and relevant questions.* • *She seems to find it difficult to form meaningful relationships.* • *Having the opportunity to be productive would make retirement more meaningful* (= give it greater value) **for** *many pensioners.*

mean·ing·ful·ly /ˈmiː·nɪŋ·fᵊl·i/ *adv* • *He didn't participate very meaningfully in the discussion.*

mean·ing·ful·ness /ˈmiː·nɪŋ·fᵊl·nəs/ *n* [U] • *They has a long argument about the meaningfulness* **of** *existence.*

mean·ing·less /ˈmiː·nɪŋ·ləs/ *adj* • *It was a meaningless gesture.*

mean·ing·less·ly /ˈmiː·nɪŋ·lə·sli/ *adv*

mean·ing·less·ness /ˈmiː·nɪŋ·lə·snəs/ *n* [U]

mean *(obj)* INTEND /miːn/ *v past* **meant** /ment/ to say or do (something) intentionally; to intend • *Did she mean it when she said she had burnt the letters?* [T] • *Do you think they really meant Sunday? Weddings are usually on Saturdays.* [T] • *I'm sorry if I offended you – I didn't mean* **any harm**. [T] • *He didn't mean* **to** *upset her.* [+ *to* infinitive] • *I've been meaning* **to** *phone you for a week or two.* [+ *to* infinitive] • *I've been writing the wrong name when I didn't mean* **to**. [+ *to* infinitive] • *(Br and Aus) They didn't mean her* **to** *read the letter.* [T + obj + *to* infinitive] • *(Am) They didn't mean* **for** *her* **to** *read the letter.* [I] • *The painting looks like a child digging in the sand. What's it meant* **to** *be?* [T + obj + *to* infinitive] • **It** *isn't meant* **to** *be difficult.* [T + obj + *to* infinitive] • *You're meant* **to** (= It is expected that you will) *fill in a tax form every year.* [T + obj + *to* infinitive] • *The books with large print are meant* **for** (= intended to be used by) *our partially sighted readers.* [T] • *(fig.) "Don't Cathy and Max make a lovely couple?" "Yes, they were obviously meant* **for each other** (= they suit each other well as partners)." [T] • People sometimes say **I mean** in order to correct something that they have just said: *I'll see you on Sunday then – I mean Saturday.* • *(infml)* If you **mean business** you seriously plan to take action: *As the changes that she's made in the first week show, the new prime minister means business.* • Someone who **means mischief** does something which they know will cause harm to someone else. • If you **mean well** you do what you think will be helpful, although you might unintentionally cause problems by doing it: *The food was rather burnt, but the children had meant well and wanted to help.* ○ See also WELL-MEANING.

mean·ing /ˈmiː·nɪŋ/ *n* [U] • *(disapproving) What's the meaning of this?*

mean·ing·ful /ˈmiː·nɪŋ·fᵊl/ *adj* • Meaningful means intended to provide some information to a particular person or people, but not to everyone: *He raised one eyebrow in a meaningful way.* ○ *When he started to talk about the house, she gave him a meaningful* **look** *and he went quiet.*

mean NOT GENEROUS /miːn/ *adj* **-er, -est** not willing to give or use (something) freely; STINGY • *He was too mean to put any money in the charity collection.* • *She has a mean and selfish outlook.* • *My landlord's very mean* **with** *the heating – it's only on for two hours each day.*

mean·ly /ˈmiːn·li/ *adv*

mean·ness /ˈmiːn·nəs/ *n* [U] • *Scrooge is a character in Charles Dickens' book 'A Christmas Carol' who is famous for his meanness.*

mean NOT KIND /miːn/ *adj* **-er, -est** unkind or unpleasant • *I felt a bit mean when I said I wouldn't go with her to the hospital.* • *Dad, they're being mean* **to** *me, they won't let me play with them.* • *A mean-***looking** *youth came out of a door on the left.* • *To many of its residents, the city has become a meaner and tougher place in which to live.* • *"Down these mean streets a man must go who is not himself mean"* (Raymond Chandler in *The Simple Art of Murder*, 1944)

mean·ie, mean·y /ˈmiː·ni/ *n* [C] *infml* • *My dad's a meanie – he won't let me go to the disco.* • *Don't be such a meanie!* • *Meanie! Give Tom his ball back.* [as form of address]

mean BAD /miːn/ *adj* **-er, -est** in bad condition or of low standard or quality • *The house had a mean and dirty appearance.* • *They came from the mean* **streets** (= an area of a city or town which is dirty, in bad condition, and often dangerous) *of Chicago.* • *He's* **no mean** (= a very good) *cook.* • *Getting the job finished so quickly was* **no mean** (= a very good) **achievement/feat**.

mean GOOD /miːn/ *adj* [before n] **-er, -est** *esp. Am slang* very good • *He's got a mean new car.* • *She plays a mean piano* (= She plays very well).

mean VALUE /miːn/ *n* [C] the value which is obtained by adding a number of values together and dividing the total by the number of values that there were, or *(fig.)* a middle way; the AVERAGE AMOUNT • **The** *mean* **of** *5, 4, 10 and 15 is 8·5.* • *They compared* **the** *means* **of** *the different groups.* • *(fig.) We need to find* **a** *mean* **between** *exam questions which are too difficult and those which are too easy.*

mean /miːn/ *adj* [not gradable] • *a mean value* • *The east of England has low mean rainfall.*

me·an·der /£miˈæn·dəʳ, $-dɚ/ *v* [I always + adv/prep] (esp. of a river or stream) to follow a route which is not straight or direct • *The stream meanders in a leisurely way* **through**

the valley. • *We spent the afternoon meandering* **around** *the streets of the old town.* • *(fig.) The film meanders* **along** (=has no clear order) *with no particular story line.*

me·an·der /£mi'æn·dəʳ, $-dɚ/ *n* [C] • A meander is a curve of a river or stream: *The U-shaped area of land was almost completely enclosed by a meander* **of** *the Thames.* • *(fig.) The TV series continues its haphazard meander* (=journey which has no particular direction) *around the globe – this week it will be in Portugal.*

me·an·der·ing /£mi'æn·dᵊr·ɪŋ, $-dɚ-/ *adj* • *It is an area of marshy depressions and meandering rivers.* • *(fig.) The minister gave a long meandering* (=not direct) *speech.*

me·an·der·ings /£mi'æn·dᵊr·ɪŋz, $-dɚ-/ *pl n* • Meanderings are talk which continues for a longer time than is necessary and which is often not interesting: *No-one wanted to listen to his long meanderings.*

means [METHOD] /miːnz/ *pl n* a method or way (of doing something) • *We must use* **all/every** *means* **at** *our* **disposal.** • *The poll showed 32% of people approving* **every** *means* **short of** *the use of force.* • *She tried to explain* **by** *means* **of** *sign language.* • *We are being continually deluged with messages by radio, television, cellular phone and every other means* **of** *communication.* • *There are more than enough weapons in the world to provide the means* **of** *our own destruction.* • *The new-found means* **of** *fighting viruses could prove very successful.* • *There is no means* **of** *tracing the debt at all.* • *The family* **had** *no means* **of** *support* (=way of getting the money it needed to pay for food, somewhere to live, clothes, etc.) • *I worked on a voluntary basis first of all as* **a means to an end** (=as a way of achieving something else, for example a permanent job). • *(fml)* **By all means** is a polite way of giving permission: *"May I borrow this book?" "By all means."* • *(fml)* **By no means** or **not by any means** means 'emphatically not': *It is by no means certain that we will be able to move to our new office in June.* ○ *This isn't the last we'll hear of it by any means* (=We will certainly hear more about it).

means [MONEY] /miːnz/ *pl n* money, for example from an income, that allows you to buy things • *He* **has** *the means* **to** *be able to buy half the houses in the street if he wanted to.* [+ to infinitive] • *(dated or fml) She has* **private** *means* (=income received without working for it). • If you live **beyond** your **means** you spend more money than you receive as income. If you live **within** your **means**, you do not spend more money than you receive as income. • *They described him as a man* **of means** (=a rich man). • A **means test** measures how much income a person has in order to decide whether they should receive money, esp. from the government, for a particular purpose.

mean·time /'miːn·taɪm/ *n* [U] **in the meantime/ meanwhile** until something expected happens, or while something else is happening • *Rick wants to be an actor, but in the meantime he's working as a waiter.* • *The new hospital will be built next year, but doctors are having to work in the meantime in seriously overcrowded conditions in the old one.*

mean·while /'miːn·waɪl/, **mean·time** *adv* [not gradable] until something expected happens, or while something else is happening • *It's going to take several days for my car to be repaired, so meanwhile I'm borrowing one.* • *Carl is starting college in September. Meanwhile, he's travelling around Europe.* • *If I do the shopping, could you clean the house meanwhile?*

mean·y /'miː·ni/ *n* [C] a **meanie**, see at MEAN [NOT KIND]

meas·les /'miː·z̩lz/ *n* [U] an infectious disease, esp. of children, which produces small red spots all over the body • *(The) measles is much less common in Britain now than it used to be.*

meas·ly /'miːz·li/ *adj, adv* **-ier, -iest** *infml* too small in size or amount; not generous • *a measly sum of money* • *two measly chocolates* • *a measly little present* • *A recent survey revealed that a woman's average take-home pay is a measly 66% of a man's.* • *Don't be so measly!*

meas·li·ness /'miːz·lɪ·nəs/ *n* [U]

meas·ure *(obj)* [SIZE] /£'meʒ·əʳ, $-ɚ/ *v* to discover the exact size, amount, etc. of (something), or to be of a particular size • *"Will the table fit in here?" "I don't know – I'll measure it."* [T] • *The children's tasks in the lesson included measuring the volume of a cup.* [T] • *This machine measures your heart rate.* [T] • *There is no way of measuring the damage done to morale.* [T] • *She was measuring* **(off)** *metre lengths of string.* [T/M] • *He measured* **(out)** *the flour into the bowl.* [T/M] • *She measured the shoe* **against** (=compared the size of the shoe with the size of) *the footprint, but it was smaller.* [T] • *Yield, measured* **as** *weight of fruit per plant, was lower in dry years.* [T] • *Delays measured* **in** *weeks are frustrating.* [T] • *The tiled kitchen, measuring/which measures* (=is of the size) *5 metres by 3 metres, has a small dining area.* [L only + n] • *"What does the window measure?"* (=What is the size of the window?) *"1 metre by 1·5 metres."* [L only + n] • *(infml)* If something or someone doesn't **measure up (to** something) they are not as good as was expected or needed: *Production targets are set for each branch, and branch managers who don't measure up don't last.* ○ *According to the lab's records, one batch proved to be acceptable, but the other didn't measure up.* • A *(Br)* **measuring jug**/*(Am and Aus)* **measuring cup** is a container used for measuring liquids which has lines marked on the side of it showing how much it contains. • A **measuring cylinder** is a glass cylinder which has lines marked on the side of it showing how much it contains, used esp. by scientists: *Pour exactly 100 ml of sulphuric acid into a measuring cylinder.* • [LP]〉 **Measurements** [PIC]〉 **Jug, Laboratory**

meas·ure /£'meʒ·əʳ, $-ɚ/ *n* • A measure is a way of measuring: *What is the most efficient measure* **of** *progress?* [C] ○ *We have no accurate measure* **of** *the damage being done.* [C] • A measure is also a way of showing: *It is a measure* **of** *the singer's popularity that all the tickets for her concert were sold the first day they went on sale.* [C] • A measure is also an exact amount: *One unit is equal to half a pint of beer or a standard measure of spirits.* [C] • Measure can also mean amount: *There was* **a** *large measure* **of** *agreement between us about what we should do next.* ○ *There was* **a** *measure* **of** *truth in what he said.* ○ *His success was* **in** *some measure due to his being in the right place at the right time.* [U] • Measure is *Am for* BAR [MUSIC]. [C] • If you **get/take the measure of** someone you find out what they are like: *"We have now got the measure of the opposing team," said Mike.* • [PIC]〉 **Bar**

meas·ur·a·ble /£'meʒ·ᵊr·ə·bl̩, $'-ɚ-/ *adj* [not gradable] • Measurable means able to be measured, or large enough to be noticed: *The service produces clear, measurable benefits to people's health.* ○ *They mentioned the measurable improvements in the quality of colour prints.*

meas·ur·a·bly /£'meʒ·ᵊr·ə·bli, $'-ɚ-/ *adv* [not gradable] • *Her new haircut makes her look measurably* (=a lot) *younger.*

meas·ure·ment /£'meʒ·ə·mənt, $'-ɚ-/ *n* • Measurement is the act of measuring: *The test is based on the measurement of blood levels.* [U] ○ *The machine makes thousands of measurements every day.* [C] • A measurement is the length, height, width, etc. of something, which you discover by measuring it: *The measurements* **of** *several of the drawings were identical.* [C] ○ *What is your inside leg measurement?* [C] • Your **measurements** are the sizes of various parts of your body, esp. your chest, waist and hips, which you refer to when you want to buy clothes: *What are your measurements?* ○ *Ask the sales assistant to* **take** *your measurements* (=measure you). • *The company has won a new a contract to make electronic measurement equipment.*

meas·ure [METHOD] /£'meʒ·əʳ, $-ɚ/ *n* [C often pl] a way to achieve something; a method • *The new jobs are the result of special measures by the government.* • **In** *a further cost-cutting measure, the number of shows is to be reduced by two each week.* • *What further measures can we* **take** *to avoid shoplifting?* • *These measures were* **designed** *to improve car safety.* • *(Br) The government's change of policy has been described as a* **panic** *measure, designed to win support.* • *Emergency measures* **to** *help the refugees are badly need.* [+ to infinitive]

meas·ured [CONTROLLED] /£'meʒ·əd, $-ɚd/ *adj* [not gradable] careful and controlled, and not fast • *He examined the reasons for the measured gain in income.* • *She walked down the hall with measured steps.*

meas·ured [CALM] /£'meʒ·əd, $-ɚd/ *adj* thought about seriously; calm, without unnecessary excitement or noise • *Her response to the furore over her new book was calm and measured.* • *Instead of screaming, shouting and humiliating his players to get them to play well, the manager's tone is more measured now.*

meat [FOOD] /miːt/ *n* [U] the flesh of an animal when it is used for food • *cooked meat* • *raw meat* • *red meat* • *meat pies* • *meat products* • *meat scraps* • *the meat counter* (=the place where meat is sold in a big shop) • *Vegetarians don't eat meat.* • *Cut the meat from the bones.* • *Is there any meat left?* • *When cooking mince or other meat dishes, spoon or pour off any extra fat.* • *She complained that the hospital had treated her like a* **piece of** *meat* (=without showing any

ASKING ABOUT SIZE AND OTHER MEASUREMENTS

Informal questions using some common adjectives – **How big** *is your house?* – can be asked in a more formal way by using the noun form – **What is the size** *of your house?* or – **What size** *is your house?* You will often find formal questions like these in documents. In the following table, informal questions are given on the left and more formal questions on the right:

- **Asking about size**

How deep/wide *is the river?*	**What is the depth/width** *of the river?*
How long *is this bus?*	**What is the length** *of the bus?*
How high/tall *is that building?*	**What height** *is the building?*
How tall *are you?*	**What is your height?**
How big *is your room?*	**What is the size** *of your room?*
How much space/room *does it take?*	**What is its area? What area** *does it occupy?* **What is its volume?**
How much *does it hold?*	**What is its capacity?**

- **Asking about other measurements**

How far *is London from here*	**What distance** *is London from here?*
How much *do you* **weigh**?	**What is your weight?**
How heavy *are your bags?*	**What is the weight** *of your bags?*
How high *was the plane flying?*	**What was the** *plane's* **altitude**?
How fast *did you go?*	*(At)* **what speed** *were you travelling?*
How old *are you?*	**What is your age?**
How long *did you stay in the US?*	**What was the duration** *of your stay in the US?*
How hot/cold *is it outside?*	**What is the** *outside* **temperature**?
How loud *do you want the music?*	**What volume** *would you like the music?*

- **Asking about number and money**

How many *did you order?*	**What number/quantity** *did you order?*
How often *do you get headaches?*	**What is the frequency** *of your headaches?*
How much *money do you need?*	**What amount** *of money do you require?*
How much *does she earn?*	**What is her salary?/What salary** *is she on?*
How much *is it?*	**What price** *is it?*
How much *did the new road cost?*	**What was the cost** *of the new road?*

- **Giving information using units of measurement** Units of measurement can go before the noun they describe: *a six pound fish; a two gallon container; his 4000 mile journey.* (Notice that the noun for the unit is singular.) The following forms are also commonly used. With these forms the unit is usually plural.

It's 5 feet **deep; wide/across; long; high/tall.** I'm 6 feet **tall.**
My room is 4 metres **by** 3 metres (= 4 metres long and 3 metres wide).
(area:) This carpet **covers** 20 square feet. Our office **takes up/occupies** 6000 square feet.
(volume:) This car has 25 cubic feet **of** cargo space.
A microwave oven with 1.0 cubic foot **capacity**. This bottle **holds** half a litre.
London is 50 miles **away**. It's 50 miles **to** London. We're 50 miles **from** London.
I weigh 70 kilos. My bags **weigh** 25 kilos.
The plane was flying **at** 4000 feet. It was travelling **at** 600 miles per hour.
She's 20 years **old.**
We were in the US **for** 6 months.
It's 30 **(degrees)** outside today. The **temperature** is 30 **degrees.**
He has a **temperature of** 40 **(degrees).**

LP **Units of measurement** at UNIT

care for her feelings, wishes, etc.). • *(Br)* A meal is sometimes described as **meat and two veg**, which is hot cooked meat with two different types of vegetables. • *The atmosphere in the theatre will* **be meat and drink to** *him* (=he will like it very much). • *(Am)* If something is described as **meat-and-potatoes** it is more basic or important than other things: *For many unions, the meat-and-potatoes issue is no longer pay increases but job security.* • A **meat loaf** is meat cut into extremely small pieces, mixed with other things, cooked in a container and then cut into slices to be eaten. • *(saying)* 'One man's meat is another man's poison' means that not everyone likes the same things.

meat·y /£'miː·ti, $-ţi/ *adj* **-ier, -iest** • *The burger was meaty* (=full of or tasting of a lot of meat). • *(fig.) We bought some lovely meaty* (=large and strong-tasting) *tomatoes from the local market.*

meat INTEREST /miːt/ *n* [U] important, valuable or interesting ideas or information • *I think there was a lot more intellectual meat in the degree courses in those days, you know.*

meat·y /£'miː·ti, $-ţi/ *adj* **-ier, -iest** • *a meaty book/letter/report* • *She has written some wonderfully meaty parts for actresses.*

meat·i·ness /£'miː·tɪ·nəs, $-ţɪ-/ *n* [U]

meat·ball /£'miːt·bɔːl, $-bɑːl/ *n* [C] a small ball made of meat which is cut into small pieces that are then pressed together and cooked • *meatballs in tomato sauce* • *spaghetti and meatballs*

mec·ca /'mek·əʳ/ *n* [C usually sing] a place to which many people are attracted • *Many young people look on Miami as a kind of Mecca.* • *The scheme would transform the park into a tourist mecca.* • *These procedures reduce the need for patients to travel to the medical meccas.* • *The shop is a mecca* **for** *good-quality, reasonably priced clothes.* • *This is a town that at one time was a mecca* **of** *tiny businesses.* • Mecca, in Saudi Arabia, is the holy city of Islam.

me·chan·i·cal MACHINES /mə'kæn·ɪ·kᵊl/ *adj* [not gradable] of machines or their parts • *The company still produces mechanical parts for locomotives.* • *The plane appeared to have crashed because of a mechanical problem.* • *The car wasn't known for its mechanical reliability.* • *The museum has a good range of mechanical toys.* • *Connected to tubes and devices, he gave the impression of a man supported entirely by mechanical means.* • *I don't have a very mechanical mind* (=I do not understand how machines work). • **Mechanical engineering** is the study of the design and production of machines.

me·cha·nic /mə'kæn·ɪk/ *n* [C] • A mechanic is someone who repairs or works with machines, esp. as a job: *The car/garage/motor mechanic phoned to say your car was ready for collection.* • NL

me·chan·i·cally /mə'kæn·ɪ·kli/ *adv* • *Even lettuce, strawberries and grapes can now be picked mechanically*

(= by a machine). • *I'm not very mechanically minded* (= do not understand how machines work).

me·chan·i·cal WITHOUT THOUGHT /mə'kæn·ɪ·kᵊl/, **me·chan·is·tic** *adj* without thinking about what you are doing, esp. because you do it often • *The children were being taught to read in a mechanical way.*

me·chan·i·cally /mə'kæn·ɪ·kli/, **me·chan·is·ti·cally** *adv* • *"Thank you," replied the ticket collector mechanically as he took each ticket.*

me·chan·ics STUDY /mə'kæn·ɪks/ *n* [U] the study of the effect of physical forces on objects and their movement, or *(infml)* the way machines work • *(infml) My car is always breaking down, but I don't know enough about mechanics to be able to fix it myself.*

me·chan·ics WORKINGS /mə'kæn·ɪks/ *n* [U] **the mechanics** *infml* the way something works or happens • *He knows a lot about the mechanics* **of** *running a school.* • *We need to look at the mechanics* **of** *taking a survey of this type.*

me·chan·i·sm MACHINE PART /'mek·ə·nɪ·zᵊm/ *n* [C] a part of a machine, or a set of parts that work together • *These automatic cameras have a special focusing mechanism.* • *They are developing a new turning mechanism for the device.* • *There is supposed to be a* **fail-safe** *mechanism* (= device which stops something going wrong) *which makes it impossible for two trains to be on the same track.*

me·chan·i·sm SYSTEM /'mek·ə·nɪ·zᵊm/ *n* [C] a way of doing something, esp. one which is planned or part of a system • *The mechanism* **for** *collecting taxes needs revising.* • *Comedy can serve as a mechanism* **for** *releasing tension.* • A mechanism is also a part of your behaviour which helps you deal with a difficult situation: *She's actually rather insecure, and her rudeness is just a* **defence** *mechanism.*

me·chan·is·tic /ˌmek·ə'nɪs·tɪk/ *adj* thinking of living things as if they were machines • *According to mechanistic views of behaviour, human action can be explained in terms of cause and effect.* • *He argued that we live in a highly mechanistic world in which the importance of culture is often overlooked.*

me·chan·ize *obj, Br and Aus usually* **-ise** /'mek·ə·naɪz/ *v* [T] to use a machine to do something that used to be done by hand • *Farming has been mechanized, reducing the need for labour.* • *One family with mechanized equipment could farm crops formerly requiring 20 families.* • *He said that children growing up in a highly urbanized and mechanized society have little understanding of nature.*

me·chan·iz·a·tion, *Br and Aus usually* **-i·sa·tion** /ˌmek·ə·naɪ'zeɪ·ʃᵊn/ *n* [U]

med MEDICAL /med/ *adj abbreviation for* MEDICAL • *She's a student in med school.*

med·al /'med·ᵊl/ *n* [C] a small metal disc, with words and/or a picture on it, which is given as a reward for a brave action, for winning in a competition, or to remember a special event • *He was* **awarded** *a medal* **for** *bravery.* • *She* **won** *three Olympic gold medals.* • *The children were all given a Coronation medal when Elizabeth was crowned queen.*

me·dal·list *Br and Aus, Am and Aus* **med·al·ist** /'med·ᵊl·ɪst/ *n* [C] • A medallist is a person who has won a medal in sport: *She's a bronze medallist* **in** *judo.*

me·dal·lion /mə'dæl·jən/ *n* [C] a metal disc which is worn for decoration on a chain or string around the neck • *(Br humorous disapproving)* A **medallion man** is a man who tries to look younger than he is by wearing jewellery and tight clothes, and who often has his shirt open at the front to show his hairy chest.

med·dle /'med·l̩/ *v* [I] to try to change or have an influence on things which are not your responsibility • *My sister is having problems, and I'd like to help her, but I don't want her to think that I'm meddling.* • *This experience should have taught them what happens when you meddle* **with** *things you don't understand.* • *It's time foreign officials stopped meddling* **in** *the region.* • *I don't like people meddling* **in** *my* **affairs** (= trying to tell me what I should do).

med·dler /£'med·l̩.əʳ, $-ɚ/ *n* [C] • *She's a real meddler.*

med·dling /'med·l̩.ɪŋ, '-lɪŋ/ *n* [U] • *The family criticized their relatives for meddling.* • *His meddling produced some unexpected results.*

med·dle·some /'med·l̩.səm/ *adj* • *Teachers were discussing the parents they regarded as meddlesome* (= tending to meddle). • *We have very meddlesome neighbours, who always want to know what we're doing.*

me·di·a NEWSPAPERS /'miː·di·ə/ *n* [U + sing/pl v] **the media** newspapers, magazines, radio and television considered as a group • *the local/national media* • *the news media* • *media attention/coverage/hype/reports* • *media executives/stars* • *"The press blew it all out of proportion," said the actor, who is no longer speaking to the media about the film.* • *The media suggest/suggests that the schools are full of drugs and weapons.* • *The company has been the victim of several attacks* **in** *the media.* • *The bombing received widespread coverage* **in** *the* **mass** *media* (= newspapers and television which are read or seen by many people). • A **media event** is an activity planned to attract the attention of the media. • See also MEDIUM METHOD; MULTIMEDIA. • Ⓘ Ⓟ

me·di·a MEDIUM /'miː·di·ə/ *pl of* MEDIUM METHOD

med·i·aev·al /ˌmed·i'iː·vᵊl/ *adj* [not gradable] MEDIEVAL

me·di·an /'miː·di·ən/ *adj* [not gradable], *n* [C] *specialized* (of) the value which is the middle one in a set of values arranged in order of size • *Median household income fell last year.* • *In this hospital, the median wait for treatment is 198 days.* • *The median age* **of** *a set of children aged 6, 9, 10, 15 and 16 is 10.* • **Median strip** is *Am and Aus for* **central reservation**. See at CENTRAL NEAR THE MIDDLE. • PIC **Motorway**

me·di·ate *(obj)* /'miː·di·eɪt/ *v* to arrange (an agreement) by talking to two separate people or groups involved in a disagreement, or to arrange (a connection between two things, people or groups) • *The teachers and parents couldn't agree and she had to mediate* **between** *them.* [I] • *The two envoys have succeeded in mediating an end to the war.* [T] • *Feinberg is a Washington lawyer who has mediated dozens of complex out-of-court* **settlements.** [T] • *She arrived here knowing no English, with her contact with the outside world mediated* **through** *her husband.* [T]

me·di·a·tion /ˌmiː·di'eɪ·ʃᵊn/ *n* [U] • *Last-minute attempts at mediation failed.* • *The dispute is now being handled by a conciliation and mediation service.*

me·di·at·or /£'miː·di·eɪ·təʳ, $-t̬ɚ/ *n* [C] • *They had ideal qualifications for being mediators* **between** *the two sides involved in the conflict.*

med·ic /'med·ɪk/ *n* [C] *infml* a medical student or doctor, or *(Am)* any person who does medical work, esp. in the military medical CORPS (= specially trained part of the army)

Med·ic·aid /'med·ɪ·keɪd/ *n* [U] a government service in the US which allows poor people to receive medical treatment both in and out of hospitals • *Medicaid is funded jointly by federal, state and local governments.* • Compare MEDICARE.

med·i·cal /'med·ɪ·kᵊl/ *adj* [not gradable] of, for, or offering the treatment of illness and injuries • *medical advice* • *medical books* • *a medical charity* • *medical language* • *medical products* • *a medical team* • *medical workers*

med·i·cal /'med·ɪ·kᵊl/, *Am also* **phys·i·cal** *n* [C] • During a medical a doctor examines you to see if you are healthy: *The insurance company wanted me to have a medical.*

med·i·cally /'med·ɪ·kli/ *adv* [not gradable] • *Although she still felt unable to work, the doctor who examined her said she was medically* **fit** (= she had no illness or injury).

Med·i·care /£'med·ɪ·keəʳ, $-ker/ *n* [U] (in the US) a government service which allows people aged 65 and over to receive medical treatment both in and out of hospitals, or (in Australia) a government service which allows all people to receive medical treatment • Compare MEDICAID.

med·i·cat·ed /£'med·ɪ·keɪ·tɪd, $-t̬ɪd/ *adj* [not gradable] containing a medical substance • *medicated lotion/shampoo/tissues*

med·i·ca·tion /ˌmed·ɪ'keɪ·ʃᵊn/ *n* a medicine, or a set of medicines or drugs used to improve a particular condition or illness • *Five of the children were treated with a similar medication.* [C] • *In the study, patients were taken off their usual medications.* [C] • *He is currently* **on/taking** *medication* **for** *his heart.* [U]

med·i·cine TREATMENT /'med·ɪ·sən/ *n* [U] (the study of the) treatment for illness or injury • *paediatric/preventative medicine* • *orthodox/Western medicine* • *a career in medicine* • *The continuing search for drugs to combat viral infections presents modern medicine with one of its greatest challenges.* • *He plans to register as a mature student in law or medicine.* • *She is a doctor, but is unable to* **practise** *medicine* (= work as a doctor) *in her own country.*

med·i·cine SUBSTANCE /'med·ɪ·sən/ *n* a substance which is drunk or swallowed as a treatment for illness or injury • *One of my medicines tastes of strawberries.* [C] • *She knows quite a lot about herbal medicines.* [C] • **Take** *two spoonfuls*

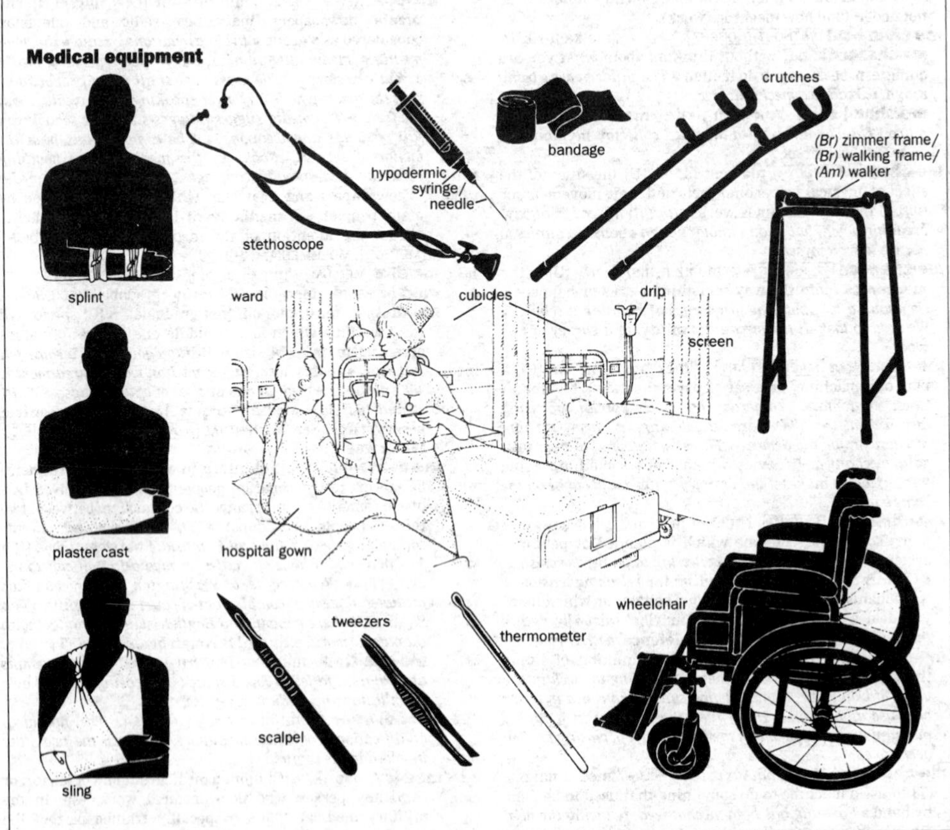

of cough medicine [U] • *An international appeal for food and medicine has been launched for the people left homeless by the floods.* [U] • If you give someone **a dose/taste of** their **own medicine** you treat them as badly they were treating to you: *The bully got/needs/was given a dose of his own medicine.*

med·ic·in·al /mə'dɪs·ɪ·nəl/ *adj* • *The spring water has medicinal properties* (= it is like a medicine).

med·ic·in·al·ly /mə'dɪs·ɪ·nə·li/ *adv* • *The leaves of this plant are used medicinally* (= as medicine).

med·i·co /£'med·ɪ·kəʊ, $-koʊ/ *n* [C] *pl* **medicos** *dated infml* a doctor

med·i·ev·al, **med·i·aev·al** /ˌmed·i'iː·vəl/ *adj* [not gradable] of or from **the Middle Ages** (= the period from about 1000 AD to 1500 AD, or from about 600 AD to 1500 AD) • *a medieval building/painting/town*

me·di·o·cre /£ˌmiː·di'əʊ·kər, $-'oʊ·kɚ/ *adj* not very good; not good enough • *The film's plot is predictable, the dialogue is second-rate, and the acting is mediocre.* • *What had been a good little business became a mediocre large activity.* • *The middle range wines are generally less exciting, but they are rarely mediocre.* • *If I was so mediocre, how come I was making several hundred thousand dollars a year in salary and bonus?*

me·di·o·cri·ty /£ˌmiː·di'ɒk·rə·ti, $-'ɑː·krə·ţi/ *n* • *A goal just before half-time rescued the match from mediocrity.* [U] • *These people are just mediocrities* (= people who do not have much skill or ability at anything). [C]

med·i·tate /'med·ɪ·teɪt/ *v* [I] to think seriously (about something), esp. for a long time • *They decided to meditate* **on/upon** *the matter for an additional week or so.* • If you meditate, you give your attention to one thing, and do not think about anything else, usually as a religious activity or as way of calming or relaxing your mind: *He meditated for 20 minutes every day.*

med·i·ta·tion /ˌmed·ɪ'teɪ·ʃən/ *n* • Meditation is serious thought or study, or the product of this activity: *I left him deep in meditation.* [U] ○ *What is the outcome of your meditations? Do you think it's a good idea?* [C] ○ *The film was 'Cezanne', a 50-minute meditation* **on** *the painter and his work.* [C] ○ *The book is a meditation* **on** *the morality of art.* [C] • Meditation is also the act of giving your attention to only one thing, either as a religious activity or as a way of becoming calm and relaxed: *prayer and meditation* [U] ○ *She practises meditation.* [U]

med·i·ta·tive /£'med·ɪ·tə·tɪv, $-ţɪv/ *adj* • *As she grew older, the author became more meditative, and this is reflected in her later books.*

Med·i·ter·ran·e·an /£ˌmed·ɪ·tər'eɪ·ni·ən, $-tə'reɪ-/ *n* [U] **the Mediterranean** *(infml* **the Med***)* the sea surrounded by southern Europe, northern Africa and the Middle East, or the countries beside it • *We enjoyed swimming in the warm waters of the Mediterranean.* • *They lived in the Mediterranean for many years.*

Med·i·ter·ran·e·an /£ˌmed·ɪ·tər'eɪ·ni·ən, $-tə'reɪ-/ *adj* [not gradable] • *We greatly enjoyed our two weeks in the Mediterranean sun.* • *Our waiter was a young man of dazzling Mediterranean good looks.* • *He came from the Mediterranean island republic of Malta.*

med·i·um VALUE /'miː·di·əm/ *adj* [not gradable] being in the middle between an upper and lower amount, size, degree or value; average • *a girl of medium height* • *a journey of medium length* • *a medium-sized book* • *medium blue* • Medium is also used to refer to a way of cooking meat so that it is no longer red in the middle: *Would you like your* **steak** *rare, medium, or well-done?*

med·i·um METHOD /'miː·di·əm/ *n* [C] *pl* **mediums** or **media** /'miː·di·ə/ a method or way of expressing something • *the broadcasting/print medium* • *the medium* **of** *television/the press* • *They told the story* **through** *the medium* **of** *dance.* • *The variety of the artist's work* **in** *these different mediums is quite astounding.* • *"The medium is the message"* (Marshall McLuhan in the book *Understanding Media*, 1964)

med·i·um SPIRITUALIST /'miː·di·əm/ *n* [C] a person who says that they can receive messages from people who are dead

med·ley /'med·li/ *n* [C] a mixture of different items, esp. tunes put together to form a longer piece of music • *He* played a medley **of** popular tunes for them to sing. • The menu described the dessert as a medley **of** exotic fruits topped with ice-cream and nuts. • A medley (relay) is a swimming competition in which each of four swimmers in a team uses a different method of swimming.

meek /miːk/ *adj* **-er, -est** quiet, gentle and (too) willing to do what other people want you to; not giving your own opinions in a strong or noticeable way • *The law still seems to regard women as meek and submissive and men as strong breadwinners.* • *When the report was published, various environmental groups criticized it for being too meek.* • *"Blessed are the meek: for they shall inherit the earth"* (Bible, Matthew 5.5)

meek·ly /ˈmiː·kli/ *adv*

meek·ness /ˈmiːk·nəs/ *n* [U]

meet *(obj)* BECOME FAMILIAR WITH /miːt/ *v past* **met** /met/ to become familiar with (someone) for the first time • *They met at work.* [I] • *"Have we met before?" "Yes, we met at your sister's last summer."* [I] • *I met her in Hawaii.* [T] • *Would you like to meet a film star?* [T] • *Come and meet* (= Let me introduce you to) *my friend Laura.* [T]

meet *(obj)* COME TOGETHER /miːt/ *v past* **met** /met/ to come together (esp. with another person) • To meet (someone) can be to come together intentionally: *We agreed to meet on Tuesday to discuss the next stage of the project.* [I] ○ *They meet (each other) for lunch once a month.* [I/T] ○ *The children's club meets every Thursday afternoon.* [I] ○ *They suggested we meet (infml* **up***) at Margaret's.* [I] ○ *She had met (infml* **up with***) the child in the street.* [T] ○ *They're meeting (esp. Am and Aus* **with***) their advisers to work out a new plan.* [T; I + with] • To meet someone is also to come together with them unintentionally: *The doctor met one of her patients in the supermarket.* [T] ○ *We met a runaway horse trotting down the middle of the road.* [T] • *Will you meet me at the airport* (= be there when the aircraft arrives)*?* [T] • *A bus meets every train* (= is at the station when the train arrives). [T] • *The teams have met* (= come together to compete) *twice this season.* [I] • If you **meet** someone **halfway**, you change your plans a little to satisfy them: *I can't agree to wait a week but I'll meet you halfway and say three days.* • *(esp. humorous)* **Meet** your **maker** is used to avoid saying die. • If you **meet** your **match**, you come together with someone who is better or stronger than you are, or *(fig.)* who is not frightened of you: *He was a good player but he met his match* **in** *Peter.* ○ *(fig.) The child was a real bully, but she met her match in Alice.* • If you **meet** your **Waterloo**, something happens which has a seriously damaging effect on you and which you are unable to deal with. • A **meeting point** is the area in a large public place, such as an airport or station, where people can arrange in advance to come together with someone else: *Their parents put the children on the plane in London, and their grandparents collected them at the meeting point at the other end of their flight.* • *"Ill met by moonlight, proud Titania"* (Shakespeare, A Midsummer Night's Dream 2.1) • LP **Each other**

meet /miːt/ *n* [C] • A meet is a sports event: *the first meet of the new season* • *(Br)* A meet is also an occasion when people go FOXHUNTING.

meet·ing /£ˈmiː·tɪŋ, $-t̬ɪŋ/ *n* [C] • A meeting is an occasion when people come together intentionally or unintentionally: *We have* **called** *a meeting of all members for Friday.* ○ *Her last meeting with him before he died was by chance at Euston station.* ○ *A* **chance** (= unintentional) *meeting with a publisher had helped his career.* • A meeting is also a sports competition: *This will be the first time that she will have competed in an international meeting.* • A meeting can also be a group of people who have met for a particular purpose: *The meeting wants to look at the proposal again.* • A **meeting of minds** is a situation when two or more people have the same opinions about something. • **Meeting house** is the name used by Quakers (= a Christian group, also called Friends) for their place of worship: *The Friends' Meeting House* ○ *an eighteenth-century Quaker meeting house*

meet *(obj)* TOUCH /miːt/ *v past* **met** /met/ (esp. of objects) to touch or join • *The curtains don't meet (each other) in the middle of the window.* [I/T] • *Turn left where the lane meets the main road.* [T] • *Their* **eyes** *met* (= they looked at each other) *across the table.* [I] • *She* **met** *his* **eye** (= they looked at each other) *across the room.* • *I couldn't* **meet** *his* **eye** (= I was too ashamed to look at him directly because I had done something wrong or was trying to hide something). • *(saying)* 'There is more in/to this than meets the eye' means that there are facts which are not known about the situation: *He was late again today – I think there's more to this than meets the eye.*

meet *obj* FULFIL /miːt/ *v* [T] *past* **met** /met/ to fulfil, satisfy, or achieve • *The workers'* **demands** *for higher pay were not met by the management.* • *We haven't yet been able to find a house that meets our* **needs/requirements**. • *They will only agree to sign the contract if certain* **conditions** *are met.* • *He has failed to meet his* **obligations**. • *Do you think we will be able to meet our* **deadline/target***?* • Meet can also mean pay: *The company has agreed to meet all our expenses.*

meet *obj* EXPERIENCE /miːt/ *v* [T] *past* **met** /met/ to experience (something) • *I've never met that kind of problem/system before.* • *She usually succeeds in meeting* (= dealing with) *any challenge that is put before her.* • *He met his death* (= he died) *in the icy waters of the South Atlantic.* • If you **meet with** something, you experience something which is usually unpleasant: *I heard she'd met with an accident.* ○ *They'd never met with such poor service before.* ○ *If you meet with any difficulties, just let me know.* ○ *The announcement was met with loud applause* (= People clapped at the announcement).

meg·a BIG /ˈme·gə/ *adj, exclamation infml* very good or very big • *These are the mega issues/trends of the moment.* • *The airline was described as a mega carrier.* • *"Did you enjoy the concert?" "Yeah, it was mega!"* • *"Shall we go out for pizza tonight?" "Yeah, mega!"*

meg·a– /ˈmeg·ə-, ˌ--/ *combining form infml* • *He's megarich* (= extremely rich). • *They're earning megabucks* (= a lot of money).

meg·a– NUMBER /ˈmeg·ə-, ˌ--/ *combining form* 1 000 000 times the stated unit • *a megawatt* • *a megabyte*

meg·a·byte /ˈmeg·ə·baɪt/ (*abbreviation* **M**) *n* [C] *specialized* a unit used in measuring the amount of information a computer can store, which has the value 1 048 576 BYTES

meg·a·hertz /£ˈmeg·ə·hɜːts, $-hɜːrts/ (*abbreviation* **MHz**) *n* [C] *pl* **megahertz** a unit for measuring how many million times something happens every second, esp. in electronics

meg·a·lith /ˈmeg·ə·lɪθ/ *n* [C] a large stone, sometimes forming part of a group or circle, which is thought to have been important to people in the distant past for social or religious reasons

meg·a·lith·ic /ˌmeg·əˈlɪθ·ɪk/ *adj* [not gradable] • *megalithic monuments/remains* • *megalithic times* (= the period when the stones were important)

meg·a·lo·ma·ni·a /ˌmeg·əl·əˈmeɪ·ni·ə/ *n* [U] the belief that you are very much more important and powerful than you really are • *She has a bad case of megalomania, and always wants to take charge of everything she gets involved in.* • *It was his megalomania that convinced the president he could invade.*

meg·a·lo·man·i·ac /ˌmeg·əl·əˈmeɪ·ni·æk/ *n* [C] • *They soon realised he was a megalomaniac.*

meg·a·lo·man·i·ac /ˌmeg·əl·əˈmeɪ·ni·æk/, **meg·a·lo·man·i·a·cal** /£ˌmeg·ə·ləʊ·məˈnaɪ·ə·kəl, $-loʊ-/ *adj* [before n] • *a megalomaniac dictator* • *megalomaniac ambitions*

meg·a·phone /£ˈmeg·ə·fəʊn, $-foʊn/, *Br and Aus also* **loud-hail·er**, *Am also* **bull·horn** *n* [C] a cone-shaped device which makes your voice louder when you speak into it, so that people can hear you although they are not near to you

meg·a·star /£ˈmeg·ə·stɑːʳ, $-stɑːr/ *n* [C] a very famous person, esp. a film actor or popular musician • *the Australian housewife and megastar, Dame Edna Everage.*

meg·a·store /£ˈmeg·ə·stɔːʳ, $-stɔːr/, **su·per·store** *n* [C] a very large shop • *a furniture megastore* • *out-of-town megastores*

meg·a·ton /ˈmeg·ə·tʌn/ *n* [C] a unit which has the same value as the force produced by 1 000 000 TONS of TNT (= an explosive), and which is used for measuring explosive power • *Nuclear explosions are measured in megatons.*

meg·a·watt /£ˈmeg·ə·wɒt, $-wɑːt/ *n* [C] a unit of electricity which has the value of 1 000 000 WATTS

mel·an·chol·y /£ˈmel·əŋ·kɒl·i, $-kɑː·li/ *adj, n* (expressing) unhappiness or sadness, esp. that which is felt for a long period of time and without any obvious reason • *a melancholy piece of music* • *melancholy autumn days* • *Her mood was melancholy.* • *He is an actor who is famous for roles full of sentimental melancholy.* [U]

MEETING SOMEONE

ATTRACTING SOMEONE'S ATTENTION

you know them
(infml) Kevin, . . .
(fml) Mrs Patten, . . .
(fml) Excuse me Mr McDermott, . . .

you don't know them
Excuse me, . . .
(fml Br) Excuse me Sir, . . . (not fml in Am)
(Am infml) Say, . . .

impolite, angry or to give a warning
Hey!

GREETING SOMEONE

you know them (all can be followed by a name)
(infml) Hi. • All right? • Okay?
(fml) Hello, Miss Reeves.
Hello, Michael. • Hello, how are you?
Morning • Afternoon • Evening.
(more fml) Good morning/afternoon/evening.
(Australian English infml) G'day.

you don't know them
(infml) Hi.
Hello.
(Good) morning/afternoon/evening.
(fml) How do you do? (esp. when being introduced)

REPLYING TO A GREETING

A short greeting is often repeated in response: "*Hi, Dave.*" "*Hi, Angela.*" If a longer greeting was used, it is usual to reply with a different phrase: "*Hello, how are you?*" "*Morning, Ann.*"

INTRODUCTIONS

When meeting someone you don't know, you might want them to know your name and who you are.

introducing yourself
I'm Lauren Clark.
I'm Bill Harding, your new neighbour.
(infml) I'm Glen.
(esp. on the telephone) *My name's Angela Peters*

introducing someone else
I'd like you to meet Eric Sturton.
This is my friend Rachel.
This is Mr. Franks from Boston.
Do you know Bill Durant?
Have you met Mr Jacobs?
Angela, Terry. (Introduces Terry to Angela)

replying
Nice/pleased to meet you.
(fml)A pleasure to meet you.

ASKING HOW SOMEONE IS

A speaker often asks the other person how they are and is usually given a short reply. *Thank you* can be used instead of *thanks* but is more formal.

How are you?	
How are things?	*Okay, thanks.*
How's everything?	*Fine, thanks.*
Are you okay?	*Can't complain.*
Everything okay?	*Not so bad, thanks.*
All right?	

The first speaker might then be asked *And you?* or *And how are you?*

OFFERING

It is very common for a guest to be offered tea or coffee.

offering
Would you like some tea/a coffee?
Coffee/tea?
Can I get you anything?

accepting
Yes, please.
That'd be great, thanks.
I'd like a coffee/a cup of tea, please.

refusing
Nothing for me, thanks.
No thanks.
I'm okay, thanks.

LEAVING

Before saying goodbye, it is polite to show that you are about to leave. You might also thank the other person.

I'm afraid I really must go.
Well, I've got to go now.
I think I'd better be off.
Nice to have met you.

Thank you for lunch/the coffee.	*Not at all.*
Thanks a lot/very much.	*Don't mention it.*
Thanks for having me.	*My pleasure.*
Thanks for a great time.	*You're welcome.*

Goodbye • Good night • See you next week.
(infml) Bye • Cheerio • See you • So long
(esp. Am) Have a nice day.

mel·an·cho·li·a /£ˌmel·əŋˈkəʊ·li·ə, $-ˈkoʊ-/ *n* [U] *fml old use* • Melancholia is the condition of feeling unhappy or sad, esp. for no obvious reason.

mel·an·chol·ic /£ˌmel·əŋˈkɒl·ɪk, $-ˈkɑː·lɪk/ *adj esp. fml or literary* • *a melancholic expression* • *melancholic songs*

mé·lange /melˈɑ̃ːʒ/ *n* [C usually sing] *fml* a mixture; a group of different things or people • *The area is a mélange* of *shops, offices and homes.* • *Her book presents an interesting mélange* of *ideas from different philosophies.* • *The dessert was described as a mélange* of *summer fruits in a light syrup.*

mel·a·no·ma /£ˌmel·əˈnəʊ·mə, $-ˈnoʊ-/ *n* [C] *specialized* a coloured growth on the skin, which can be harmful if it increases in size • *There is a worldwide increase in the number of* **malignant** (= harmful) *melanomas, particularly in places where people are exposed to the sun for long periods.*

mel·ee /ˈmel·eɪ/ *n* [C usually sing] a large noisy uncontrolled crowd, in which people are moving in different directions and sometimes fighting with each other • *We lost sight of each other* **in** *the melee.* • *She dropped her bag* **in** *the melee* **of** *people trying to get tickets.*

mel·li·flu·ous /melˈɪf·lu·əs/ *adj fml* sounding pleasant and flowing • *a deep mellifluous voice* • *the mellifluous sound of the cello*

mel·low SMOOTH /£ˈmel·əʊ, $-oʊ/ *adj* **-er, -est** pleasingly smooth, soft or developed; not too sharp, bright, new or rough • *mellow flavours* • *mellow sounds* • *mellow evening sunlight* • *a mellow stone facade*

mel·low /£ˈmel·əʊ, $-oʊ/ *v* [I] • *The new walls and flowerbeds are starting to mellow.* • *The mellowed brickwork blends well with the surroundings.*

mel·low RELAXED /£ˈmel·əʊ, $-oʊ/ *adj* **-er, -est** (of a person or their mood) relaxed; pleasant; not severe • *After a few drinks, he became very mellow.* • *I'm going to wait till Dad's in a more mellow mood before I ask him if I can borrow some money.* • *"Mellow Yellow"* (title of a song by Donovan, 1967)

mel·low *(obj)* /£ˈmel·əʊ, $-oʊ/ *v* • *She used to be very impatient, but she has mellowed over time/the years.* [I] • *She used to be very impatient, but time/the years have mellowed her.* [T] • *He hasn't mellowed* (= made less strong) *his views on soft drugs – he's as opposed to legalization as he ever was.* [T] • *(Am) Oh don't be so tough on yourself, Bill – mellow* **out** (= become more relaxed and less severe). [I]

mel·o·dra·ma /£ˈmel·əˌdrɑː·mə, $-ˌdræm·ə/ *n* a play or style of acting in which the characters show strong emotions and behave in a more noticeable way than real people usually do • *I think you'd call the play a melodrama – it's full of unrequited love, unhappy deaths and unrelenting* *parents.* [C] • *The film is pure melodrama.* [U] • *(esp. Br) The car's hardly damaged – there's no need to* **make** *a melodrama* **out of** *it* (= make the situation more important than it is). [C]

mel·o·dra·mat·ic /£ˌmel·ə·drəˈmæt·ɪk, $-ˈmæt̬-/ *adj* • Melodramatic means very noticeable or with too much emotion: *He gave a melodramatic wave.* ○ *The audience was not persuaded by his melodramatic speech.*

mel·o·dra·mat·i·cal·ly /£ˌmel·ə·drəˈmæt·ɪ·kli, $-ˈmæt̬-/ *adv* • *"Life is not worth living," she declared melodramatically.*

mel·o·dy /ˈmel·ə·di/ *n* a tune, often forming part of a larger piece of music • *He played a few well-known melodies.* [C] • *The slow movement builds up round a simple surging melody.* [C] • *Ellington was a composer concerned not only with melody, but with harmony, rhythm and instrumentation too.* [U]

me·lod·ic /£məˈlɒd·ɪk, $-ˈlɑː·dɪk/ *adj* • *(specialized)* Melodic is used to describe music in which tunes are the most important feature.

me·lo·di·ous /£məˈləʊ·di·əs, $-ˈloʊ-/ *adj fml* • A melodious sound is pleasant to listen to: *the melodious sound of a harp*

mel·on /ˈmel·ən/ *n* [C] a large round fruit with yellow or green skin which grows on climbing plants and which has a sweet taste • See also WATERMELON.

melt *(obj)* /melt/ *v* to (cause to) turn from something solid into something soft or liquid • *The spring sun usually melts the snow by mid March.* [T] • *It was so hot the butter started to melt.* [I] • *(fig.) He only has to look at her, and she melts* (= her feelings soften). [I] • *The ice on the lake melted* **(away)** (= became completely liquid) *overnight.* [I] • If strong feelings melt **(away)**, they slowly go away or disappear: *Her anger/embarrassment/reserve melted away when she read the letter.* [I] • *(fig.) As the police sirens were heard the crowd started to melt* **away** (= slowly go away). [I] • If someone or something melts **(away) into** something else, they mix in so well with it that they disappear and you cannot see them: *The security men just melted (away) into the background until they were needed.* [I] • If you melt something, esp. a metal object, **down**, you heat it until it turns to liquid because you want the metal rather than the object: *They melted down the gold rings and bracelets.* [M] • If solid food melts **in** the/your **mouth** it is soft and pleasant and easy to eat: *The meat was beautifully cooked – it just melted in your mouth.* [I] • If someone's **heart** melts, they start to have kinder feelings: *He had been going to refuse but his heart melted when he saw the children's faces.* [I]

melt·ed /£ˈmel·tɪd, $-t̬ɪd/ *adj* [not gradable] • *melted butter/chocolate*

melt·ing /£ˈmel·tɪŋ, $-t̬ɪŋ/ *adj* [not gradable] • A melting **look** or **voice** is one which can persuade you to do something that you had decided not to do. • **Melting point** is the temperature at which a substance melts. • A **melting pot** is a place where many different people and ideas exist together often mixing and producing something quite new: *a cultural melting pot* ○ *New Orleans is one of the great melting pots of America.* • Ideas or plans which are **in** or are put **into** the **melting pot** are not fixed or decided and are likely to be changed: *The financial problems have thrown long-term international plans into the melting pot.* • *"America is God's Crucible, the great Melting-Pot where all the races of Europe are melting and reforming!"* (Israel Zangwill in the play *The Melting Pot*, 1908)

melt·down /ˈmelt·daʊn/ *n* a dangerous situation in a nuclear power station when the material used for power becomes very hot and is likely to explode • *A pool of molten fuel would form on the floor of the reactor during a meltdown.* [C] • *An accident at the power station last month brought the system close to meltdown.* [U] • *(fig. infml) The last few months have seen the progressive meltdown* (= failure) **of** *the country's political system.* [U]

mem·ber PERSON /£ˈmem·bəʳ, $-bɚ/ *n* [C] a person, animal or thing which is part of a group • *a member of my family* • *a member of the older generation* • *male and female members of the group* • *The lion is a member* **of** *the cat family.* • *Representatives of the member states will be meeting next week.* • A member is also a person who joins a group to take part in a particular activity: *a new club member* ○ *Car parking facilities are for members only.* ○ *Michael is a member* **of** *the Royal Society for the Protection of Birds.* • **A Member of Parliament** (*abbreviation* **MP**) is a person who has been elected to the parliament of a country. • *"Please accept my resignation. I don't want to belong to any club that will accept me as a member"* (Groucho Marx, 1895-1953)

mem·ber·ship /£ˈmem·bə·ʃɪp, $-bɚ-/ *n* • Membership is the state of belonging to an organization: *You have to* **apply for** *membership (Br)* **of**/*(Am)* **in** *the sports club.* [U] ○ *I've* **taken out** *a year's membership* (= paid to become a member for one year). [U] ○ *After the scandal he* **resigned** *all his memberships* (= stopped being a member of all the groups to which he belonged). [C] ○ *When you join the club, you have to pay a membership fee and you will be given a membership card.* • *Annual membership* (= the amount you have to pay to join a particular organization) *is £25.* [U] • *The society has* **a** *very large membership* (= number of members). • A membership is all the people who belong to an organization: *Our membership is/are divided on the issue.* [C + sing/pl v]

mem·ber BODY PART /£ˈmem·bəʳ, $-bɚ/ *n* [C] *fml* a leg or arm; a LIMB • A member is also a PENIS: *the* **male** *member*

mem·brane /ˈmem·breɪn/ *n* a thin piece of skin that covers or connects parts of a person's or animal's body • *The cornea is the transparent membrane that covers the front of the eye.* [C] • *The eardrum is membrane that stretches across the end of the ear canal.* [U] • A membrane is also the outer covering of a cell: *An animal or plant cell consists of a nucleus and cytoplasm enclosed within a cell membrane.* [C]

me·men·to /£memˈen·təʊ, $-toʊ/ *n* [C] *pl* **mementos** or **mementoes** an object that you keep to make you remember a person or a special event • *Please keep this brooch as a memento* **of** *our friendship.*

me·mo /£ˈmem·əʊ, $-oʊ/, *fml* **mem·o·ran·dum** *n* [C] *pl* **memos** a message or other information in writing sent by one person or department to another in the same business organization • *Kevin prefers to send memos to his colleagues rather than talk to them.*

mem·oirs /£ˈmem·wɑːz, $-wɑːrz/ *pl n, Am also* **mem·oir** *n* [C] a written record of a usually famous person's own life and experiences • *She plans to write her memoirs.* • *Waugh's first volume of memoirs dealt with his childhood and youth.*

mem·oir /£ˈmem·wɑːʳ, $-wɑːr/ *n* [C] • A memoir is a book or other piece of writing based on the writer's personal knowledge of famous people, places or events: *She has written a memoir of her encounters with W.H. Auden over the years.* • Memoir is also *Am for* MEMOIRS.

mem·o·ra·bil·i·a /ˌmem·ᵊr·əˈbɪl·i·ə/ *pl n* objects that are collected because they are connected with a person or event which is thought to be very interesting • *The War Museum is crammed with military memorabilia.*

mem·o·ra·ble /ˈmem·ᵊr·ə·bl̩/ *adj* likely to be remembered or worth remembering • *The show has instantly memorable tunes.* • *I haven't seen them since that memorable evening when the boat capsized.*

mem·o·ra·bly /ˈmem·ᵊr·ə·bli/ *adv* • *The book includes a range of memorably amusing and eccentric characters.* • *In her long acting career she played a large number of leading roles, most memorably Lady Bracknell in 'The Importance of Being Earnest'.*

mem·o·ran·dum DOCUMENT /ˌmem·əˈræn·dəm/ *n* [C] *pl* **memoranda** /ˌmem·əˈræn·də/ or **memorandums** *specialized* a short written report prepared specially for a person or group of people which contains information about a particular matter • *The defence lawyers prepared a 15-page memorandum for the judge.* • *(law)* A memorandum is also an informal legal agreement: *The three countries have signed a memorandum in which they agree to work together.* ○ *The company has signed a memorandum* **of understanding** *with a group of investors to sell its steel operations.*

mem·o·ran·dum MESSAGE /ˌmem·əˈræn·dəm/ *n* [C] *pl* **memoranda** /ˌmem·əˈræn·də/ or **memorandums** *fml* a MEMO

me·mor·i·al /£məˈmɔː·ri·əl, $-ˈmɔːr·i-/ *n* [C] an object, often large and made of stone, which has been built to honour a famous person or event • *The statue was erected as a memorial* **to** *all the people who died in the war.* • *Thousands of people go to visit the Vietnam Veterans Memorial in Washington every year.* • A memorial event is a way of remembering a person or people who have died: *Hundreds of friends and former students came to Professor Conner's memorial* **service**.

mem·or·ize *obj, Br and Aus usually* **-ise** /ˈmem·ə·raɪz/ *v* [T] to learn (something) so that you will remember it exactly • *She has memorized all her friends' phone numbers.*

• *When I was at school, we were required to memorize a poem every week.* • LP› **Memory**

mem·o·ry ABILITY TO REMEMBER /£ˈmem·ᵊr·i, $ˈ-ɚ-/ *n* the ability to remember information, experiences and people • *After the accident he suffered from* **loss of** *memory/ memory* **loss**. [U] • *I've got a very good/bad memory.* [C] • *She has* **an** *excellent memory* **for** *names* (= She can remember names easily). [C] • *(specialized)* A computer's memory is the part of a computer in which information or programs are stored either permanently or temporarily: *A computer memory needs eight bits called a byte to represent a single alphabetical character.* [C] ○ *Two basic types of internal memory are used in digital computers: Read-Only Memory (ROM) and Random-Access Memory (RAM).* [C] • If you say something such as a poem, or sing a song **from memory**, you speak or sing without looking at any words or music: *He can recite whole chunks of books from memory.* • If you do something **in memory of** someone who has died, you do it as a way of remembering that person: *A service was held in memory of those who had died from AIDS.* • If you have a **memory like an elephant**, you are able to remember things easily. • If you **take a stroll/trip/walk down memory lane**, you remember happy times in the past: *They took a nostalgic stroll down memory lane.* • If something has happened **within** your **memory**, it has happened in a time that you are able to remember: *Women gained the vote within her grandmother's memory.* • *(specialized)* The **memory span** of a person is the number of items they can remember after having been shown a set of objects only once. • LP› **Memory**

mem·o·ry EVENT REMEMBERED /£ˈmem·ᵊr·i, $ˈ-ɚ-/ *n* [C] something that you remember from the past • *She had vivid memories* **of** *her last trip to London when she got lost five times.* • *That tune really* **brings back** *memories* (= makes me remember past events). • *School is just a* **dim/distant** *memory for me now* (= something I cannot remember very well).

men /men/ *pl of* MAN MALE

men·ace /ˈmen·ɪs/ *n* something that is likely to cause serious harm • *They believe that bikes are a menace* **to** *pedestrians.* [C] • *Dogs running loose are a* **public** *menace* (= They could cause harm to people). [C] • *Jane spoke with a hint of menace* (= in a slightly threatening way). [U] • *He was accused of unlawfully demanding money* **with menaces** (= using threats). • If you say that a person is a menace, you mean that they are very annoying: *That child is a menace! He's just spilled paint all over the carpet!* [C]

men·ace *obj* /ˈmen·ɪs/ *v* [T] *slightly fml* • If someone or something menaces a person or thing, they threaten seriously to harm it: *The last hurricane to menace the US coast was three years ago.*

men·ac·ing /ˈmen·ɪ·sɪŋ/ *adj* • *He picked up the knife in a menacing way.*

men·ac·ing·ly /ˈmen·ɪ·sɪŋ·li/ *adv* • *She walked towards him menacingly* (= as if going to harm him).

me·nage, mé·nage /ˈmen·ɑːʒ/ *n* [C + sing/pl v] *fml* a group of people living together in the same house • *The menage consisted of four adults, three children and assorted pets.* • A **ménage à trois** is an arrangement in which three people live together, one of whom is having a sexual relationship with both of the others: *She shocked the village by living with two brothers in a ménage à trois.*

me·nag·er·ie /£məˈnædʒ·ᵊr·i, $ˈ-ɚ-/ *n* [C] a collection of wild animals which are kept privately or to show to the public • *The singer Michael Jackson has a private menagerie of zebras, llamas and giraffes.*

mend *obj* REPAIR /mend/ *v* [T] to repair (something that is broken or damaged) • *Could you mend this hole that I've torn in my shirt?* • *I've left my watch at the jeweller's to be mended.* • *They called in the plumber to mend the burst pipe.* • *The country's president is seeking to mend relations with the United States.* • To **mend fences** is to try to be friendly again after a period of dislike, arguments or disagreement: *They finally decided to mend fences with their neighbours after years of disagreement.* ○ *Politicians often spend so much time mending political fences in the capital that they ignore what is happening in the rest of the country.* • If someone **mends** their **ways**, they begin to behave well after behaving badly: *He's very untidy by nature but has promised to mend his ways.* • In American English it is more usual to 'mend' things that are torn, such as clothes or sheets, and to 'repair' things that are broken, such as watches or furniture.

mend /mend/ *n* [C] • A mend is a place in a piece of clothing where a repair has been made: *Their shirts are always full of mends.*

mend·ing /ˈmen·dɪŋ/ *n* [U] • Mending is clothes that need to be mended: *I have a pile of mending to do.* ○ *I always take a small mending* **kit** *with me when I travel.*

mend *(obj)* BECOME WELL /mend/ *v* to become well again after an illness or injury • *Will his broken heart ever mend?* [I] • *Bones tend to mend themselves after they are broken.* [T]

mend /mend/ *n* [C] • *(infml)* If you are **on the mend**, you are getting better after an illness or injury: *Sarah has been ill with flu but now she's on the mend.*

men·da·cious /menˈdeɪ·ʃəs/ *adj fml* not truthful • *Some of these statements are misleading and some downright mendacious.*

men·da·ci·ty /£menˈdæs·ə·ti, $-t̬i/ *n* [U] *fml* • *Politicians are often accused of mendacity* (= telling lies).

men·di·cant /ˈmen·dɪ·kᵊnt/ *n* [C], *adj* [not gradable] *fml* (of) a person who asks people they do not know for money; a BEGGAR • *High unemployment has caused the number of homeless people and mendicants to rise in the city.* • Mendicant is also used to refer to a member of a religious group established in the Middle Ages, whose members were not allowed to own property and who lived by asking people to give them food and money: *The Franciscans were a mendicant* **order**. ○ *Mendicant* **friars** *were often involved in missionary work.*

men·folk /£ˈmen·fəʊk, $-foʊk/ *pl n* the men in a family or society • *The villagers still follow the old tradition of women and children sitting on one side and their menfolk on the other.*

men·i·al /ˈmiː·ni·əl/ *adj disapproving* (of work) boring, tiring and given a low social value • *In my last job I did menial work like washing dishes and cleaning floors.* • *He was given the menial* **job** *of operating the office photocopying machine.* • *Many nurses find themselves given menial* **tasks**, *such as making beds and washing patients, which make little use of their skills.*

men·in·gi·tis /£ˌmen·ɪnˈdʒaɪ·tɪs, $-t̬ɪs/ *n* [U] a disease caused by infection in which the outer part of the brain becomes swollen • *Meningitis can be a very serious disease.* • *Features of meningitis include fever, headache and vomiting.*

men·o·pause /£ˈmen·ə·pɔːz, £ˈmiː·nə-, $-pɑːz/, *infml* **the change (of life)** *n* [U] the time in a woman's life when she gradually stops MENSTRUATING (= having a monthly flow of blood) • *Modern scientific techniques have made it possible for a woman past menopause to have a baby.* • *Hormone Replacement Therapy has been developed to counteract the effects of the menopause.* • *(esp. Br) Most women have* **the** *menopause between the ages of 40 and 50.*

men·o·paus·al /£ˌmen·əˈpɔː·zᵊl, £ˌmiː·nəˈ-, $-pɑː-/ *adj* [not gradable] • *Not everyone agrees that hormone use is good for menopausal women.* • *This is still a lot of controversy over whether medical technology should help* **post-***menopausal women to get pregnant.*

men·stru·ate /ˈment·stru·eɪt/ *v* [I] *slightly fml* to have a monthly flow of blood from the womb; have a PERIOD • *She lost so much weight that she stopped menstruating.*

men·stru·al /ˈmen·strəl/ *adj* [not gradable] *slightly fml* • *Female athletes often notice changes in their menstrual* **cycles**. • **Menstrual period** (also **menstrual cycle**) is *fml for* PERIOD. • See also PREMENSTRUAL.

men·stru·a·tion /ˌmen·struˈeɪ·ʃᵊn/ *n* [U] *slightly fml* • *The onset of menstruation seems to get earlier with each generation.*

mens·wear /£ˈmenz·weəʳ, $-wer/ *n* [U] clothing for men • *It's hard to find interesting menswear in the major stores.* • Menswear is also the part of a large shop where you find men's clothing: *"Menswear is on the second floor, sir."* • LP› **Shopping goods**

–ment /-mənt/ *combining form* used to form nouns which refer to an action or process or its result • *strong government* • *successful management* • *a great achievement* • *a bitter disappointment* • LP› **Combining forms, Stress in pronunciation**

men·tal /£ˈmen·tᵊl, $-t̬ᵊl/ *adj* [not gradable] of or about the mind, or involving the process of thinking • *He's planning to take a holiday for mental relaxation.* • *His physical and mental* **health** *had got worse.* • *Many people suffer from some form of mental* **illness** *during their lives.* • *She had a mental* **picture** (= a picture in her mind) *of how the house would look when they finished decorating it.* • *(infml)* Mental can be used to describe someone who acts in a

MEMORY

You might remember someone or something

- **because you have tried to remember it:**
  Can you **remember** *wh*ere *we first met Frank?*
  I'm sorry, I just can't **recall** *your name.*
  Joan can't **remember** *seeing Dr Davies, just two days ago.*
  Try to (fml) **call to mind** *what you were doing on June 27th.*
  Notice that you remember to do something **before** it happens: *Did you* **remember to** *lock the door when you left?* ('recall' cannot be used)
- **because something now reminds you of it:**
  Lisa **reminds** *me* **of** *her mother: they look so similar.*
  Remind *me* **to** *pay the electricity bill tomorrow.*
  Remind *me* **about** *phoning Ms Gregson next week.*
  Will you **remind** *me* **that** *Arnold's coming to dinner on Monday?*
  I'll put the date of the meetings in my diary, **as a reminder** (= to remind me).
- **because you learned it or memorized it in the past:**
  Many musicians can **memorize** *a new piece of music in just a few hours.*
  Please try to **memorize** *the PIN numbers of your credit cards.*
  I **learned** *Latin at school and I can still remember a few words.*
  Walter sat at the piano and played some dance music **from memory**.
- **because you have seen or heard it before and now recognize it:**
  My car was stolen, but a few days later I **recognized** *it in a car park.*
  As soon as I heard his voice on the phone, I **recognized** *him.*
- **or because a memory simply comes into your mind**
  Gill had a painful **memory of** *a very nasty car accident.*
  Alice cried as she **recalled/remembered** *saying goodbye to her mother.*
  Suddenly he **recalled/remembered that** *he had met Fraser before.*

You may not remember something

- **because you have forgotten it:**
  Oh no, the door's locked and I've **forgotten** *my key!*
  Sorry, I **forgot that** *you're busy on Tuesday.*
  I promised to phone him, but **it went right out of my mind**.
  My memory's awful – I'm so **forgetful** *these days.*
  Dr Faber was old and terribly **absent-minded**.
- **because the thing did not really happen:**
  I don't **remember** *that happening at all.*
  (fml) I **have no memory of** *speaking to Mr Tyson in August.*
  McGregor said he (fml) **had no recollection of** *hitting the police officer.*

foolish or stupid way: *Laura's planning to cycle from Brighton to Edinburgh – she must be mental!* • A person's **mental age** is a measurement of their ability to think when compared to the average person's ability at that age: *Although Andrew is twenty-five, he has a mental age of six.* • **Mental arithmetic** is calculations that you do in your mind, without writing down any numbers: *I always use a calculator when I add things up because I've never been any good at mental arithmetic.* • If you have a **mental block** about something, you cannot understand it or do it because something in your mind prevents you: *He's got a mental block* **about** *names – he just can't remember them.* • **Mental cruelty** is behaviour that causes extreme unhappiness to another person but which does not involve physical violence: *She divorced her husband on the grounds of mental cruelty.* • **Mental handicap** is *dated for* **learning disabilities**. See at LEARN. • A **mental hospital** is *dated or infml for* **psychiatric hospital**. See at PSYCHIATRY. • If you make a **mental note** of something, you make certain you will remember it in the future: *I made a mental note of her address.* • Compare PHYSICAL [BODY].

men·tal·ly /£ˈmen·tᵊl·i, $-ţᵊl-/ *adv* [not gradable] • *It's going to be a tough competition but I'm mentally prepared for it* (= I am in the necessary mood to attempt it). • *(dated) He works with physically and mentally* **handicapped** *people.* • *The government has a policy of letting the mentally* **ill** *be cared for in the community.* • *(dated)* If you say that someone is **mentally defective**, you mean that their brain has been damaged from an accident, illness or since birth and that they have low mental abilities.

men·tal·i·ty /£menˈtæl·ə·ti, $-ţi/ *n* [U] • A person's mentality is their particular way of thinking about things, especially when it is fixed: *He hopes that closer links between Britain and the rest of Europe will change the British mentality towards foreigners.* ○ *Using the term 'non-white' promotes an 'us and them' mentality.* ○ *The rise in crime has led to many people developing a* **siege** *mentality, in which they see everyone as a threat and are scared to go out alone.*

men·thol /£ˈmen·θᵊl, $-θɑːl/ *n* [U] a solid white natural substance that smells and tastes like MINT (= a plant with a fresh strong smell) • *Menthol can help to clear your nose when you have a cold.* • *Menthol is used as a flavouring in sweets, cigarettes and liqueurs.*

men·tho·lat·ed /£ˈmen·θᵊl·eɪ·tɪd, $-ţɪd/ *adj* [not gradable] • If something is mentholated, it contains menthol as a flavouring: *Patricia smokes mentholated cigarettes.*

men·tion *(obj)* /ˈmen·tʃᵊn/ *v* to speak about (something) briefly or without giving much detail or using many words • *I have time only to mention some of the week's most important events.* [T] • *He casually mentioned* **that** *he was leaving his job.* [+ *that* clause] • *My wife mentioned seeing you the other day.* [+ v-*ing*] • *Did she happen to mention whether she would be coming?* [+ *wh-* word] • If you mention something or someone, you refer to it or them: *I promised never to mention the incident again.* [T] ○ *Did she mention me in her letter?* [T] • You use **not to mention** when you want to emphasize something that you are adding to a list to make what you are saying stronger: *He is one of the most intelligent, not to mention handsome, people I know.* • You say **don't mention it** to someone after they have thanked you: *"Thanks for your help." "Not at all, don't mention it."*

men·tion /ˈmen·tʃᵊn/ *n* [C] • *The story didn't even get a mention in the newspaper* (= It was not written about at all). • *When I ordered the catalogue, there was no mention* **of** *any payment.* • *Even the mention* **of** *her name makes him blush.* • When a person gets a mention, they are honoured for having done something, such as their job, particularly well: *At the awards ceremony, Chris Scott* **received** *a special mention for her reporting of the conflict.*

men·tor /£ˈmen·tɔːʳ, $-tɔːr/ *n* [C] *fml* a person who gives another person help and advice over a period of time and often also teaches them how to do their job • *The older writer was her mentor and friend, encouraging her to write.* • Compare PROTEGE.

me·nu /ˈmen·juː/ *n* [C] a list of the food that you can eat in a restaurant • *The waiter brought two menus and a wine list.* • *What's on the menu today?* • *Can I see the dessert menu, please?* • *(specialized)* A menu is also a list of choices that can be made to appear on a computer screen: *Select the 'Print' menu and then choose the number of copies you want.* • *(specialized)* A computer that is **menu-driven** is operated by making choices from different menus rather than by giving separate instructions on a keyboard.

me·ow /ˌmiːˈaʊ/ *n* [C], *v* [I] *Am for* MIAOW

MEP /ˌem·iːˈpiː/ *n* [C] *abbreviation for* Member of the European Parliament (= a person who represents an area of a European country in the European Parliament) • *He was elected as the MEP for South East Wales in the recent elections.* • *She is an active MEP who campaigns for women's rights.*

Meph·is·to·phe·les /£ˌmef·ɪˈstɒf·əl·iːz, $-ˈstɑː·fə·liːz/ *n* [not after *the*] the DEVIL (= the main evil spirit and enemy of God in the Christian religion) • *In the legend of Faust, Faust sells his soul to Mephistopheles.*

mer·can·tile /£ˈmɜː·kən·taɪl, $ˈmɜːr-/ *adj* [not gradable] *fml* of trade or business • *The 18th century saw a rise in the mercantile class all over Europe.* • *Valencia is the capital of a prosperous region in Spain which has a long mercantile tradition.*

mer·cen·ar·y SOLDIER /£ˈmɜː·sən·ri, $ˈmɜːr-/ *n* [C] a person who fights for any country or group that pays them • *Many mercenaries are ex-soldiers who seek the excitement of a real war.*

mer·cen·ar·y WANTING MONEY /£ˈmɜː·sən·ri, $ˈmɜːr-/ *adj disapproving* interested only in the amount of money that can be obtained from a situation • *He has a mercenary scheme to marry a wealthy widow.*

mer·chan·dise /£ˈmɜː·tʃən·daɪs, $ˈmɜːr-/ *n* [U] *fml* goods that are bought and sold • *Shoppers complained about poor quality merchandise and high prices.* • *Japan exported $97 billion in merchandise to the US in 1992.*

mer·chan·dise *obj* /£ˈmɜː·tʃən·daɪs, $ˈmɜːr-/ *v* [T] *specialized or Am* • If you merchandise goods, you encourage the sale of them by advertising them or by making certain that they are noticed: *She had to merchandise a product line that was overpriced and unavailable in most of the country.*

mer·chan·dis·ing /£ˈmɜː·tʃən·daɪ·zɪŋ, $ˈmɜːr-/ *n* [U] • Merchandising is (the selling of) products connected with a popular film, singer, event, etc.: *The company has bought merchandising rights to the latest Disney film.* ○ *The film's merchandising includes toys, books and T-shirts.*

mer·chant /£ˈmɜː·tʃənt, $ˈmɜːr-/ *n* [C] a person whose job it is to buy and sell products in large amounts, esp. by trading with other countries • *The main canals in Amsterdam are lined with houses built by wealthy merchants in the 17th and 18th centuries.* • *They worked illegally as* **arms** *merchants.* • *The booklet lists restaurants, baker's shops and* **wine** *merchants which remain open in August.* • *(slang disapproving)* A merchant is also someone who is involved in or enjoys something which is unpleasant or annoying to others: *My next door neighbour's a real gossip merchant* (= She enjoys talking about people's private lives). ○ *The film is being ruthlessly promoted by Hollywood's hype merchants* (= people who try to get as much public attention as they can for the film). ○ *Police have set up hidden cameras on main roads to catch speed merchants* (= people who like to drive too fast). • A **merchant bank** is a bank which is involved with companies rather than with people. • *(infml)* Companies which make weapons are sometimes called **merchants of death**. • *(infml)* A **merchant of doom/gloom** is a person who tends to see the negative side of a situation: *With exports rising and unemployment falling, the merchants of gloom are having to revise their opinions of the economy.* • The **merchant navy** or **merchant shipping** (*esp. Am* **merchant marine**) means a country's ships that are involved with trade, not fighting. • A **merchant seaman** is a sailor who works on a trading ship.

mer·cu·ri·al /£mɜːˈkjʊə·ri·əl, £-ˈkjɔː-, $mɜːrˈkjʊr·i-/ *adj literary* changing suddenly and often • *She is entertaining but unpredictable, with mercurial mood swings.* • *The area's mercurial weather causes many would-be visitors to stay away.*

mer·cu·ry METAL /£ˈmɜː·kjʊ·ri, $ˈmɜːr-/, *old use* **quick·sil·ver** *n* [U] a heavy silver-coloured metal which is liquid at ordinary temperatures • *Mercury is used in batteries, pesticides and thermometers.* • *(dated infml)* **The mercury** means the temperature: *With the mercury climbing to 40 degrees, beaches and pools will be crowded this afternoon.*

Mer·cu·ry PLANET /£ˈmɜː·kjʊ·ri, $ˈmɜːr-/ *n* [U not after *the*] the planet closest in distance to the Sun, before Venus

mer·cy KINDNESS /£ˈmɜː·si, $ˈmɜːr-/ *n* [U] kindness and forgiveness shown towards someone whom you have the power to treat severely or punish • *People who are caught drinking and driving can expect little mercy from the courts.* • *The current civil war is a conflict that knows no mercy.* • *She appealed to the president to* **have mercy on** *her husband.* • *The prisoners* **pleaded for** *mercy.* • *The gunmen* **showed** *no mercy in killing innocent men and women.* • *He* **threw himself upon the** *mercy of the queen* (= He asked her for mercy). • If you are **at the mercy of** someone or something, that person or thing has complete power over you: *Poor people are increasingly at the mercy of money-lenders.* • A **mercy killing** is the act of killing a person who is severely ill and who is going to die, in order to prevent them from suffering more pain. It is another word for EUTHANASIA.

mer·ci·ful /£ˈmɜː·sɪ·fəl, $ˈmɜːr-/ *adj approving* • If someone is merciful, they show kindness and forgiveness to people who are in their power: *"God is merciful," said the priest.*

mer·ci·ful·ly /£ˈmɜː·sɪ·fəl·i, $ˈmɜːr-/ *adv approving* • *As a first-time offender, the judge treated him mercifully and did not give him a prison sentence.*

mer·ci·less /£ˈmɜː·sɪ·ləs, $ˈmɜːr-/ *adj disapproving* • *As a journalist, Tom is merciless towards hypocrites* (= he shows them no kindness).

mer·ci·less·ly /£ˈmɜː·sɪ·lə·sli, $ˈmɜːr-/ *adv disapproving* • *Louis was teased mercilessly* (= very unkindly) *by his schoolmates.*

mer·cy LUCK /£ˈmɜː·si, $ˈmɜːr-/ *n* [U] an event or situation which is considered to be good or lucky because it is not as bad as it had been or could have been • *It is a mercy that no-one was killed in the car crash.* • *After months of suffering, his death was a mercy.* • If something such as a flight is described as a mercy, it brings help to people who are suffering: *A mercy* **flight** *bringing 68 seriously wounded refugees from Bosnia arrived in Britain last night.* ○ *The trucks were on a mercy* **mission** *taking badly needed aid to the war zone when they were hit by mortar shells.*

mer·ci·ful /£ˈmɜː·sɪ·fəl, $ˈmɜːr-/ *adj approving* • *After such a long illness, her death came as a merciful* **release** (= it brought an end to her pain).

mer·ci·ful·ly /£ˈmɜː·sɪ·fəl·i, $ˈmɜːr-/ *adv approving* • *She accidentally knocked over her mother's favourite vase, but mercifully* (= luckily) *it did not break.* • *The bomb exploded after the shops had closed and so there were mercifully few casualties.*

mere /£mɪəʳ, $mɪr/ *adj* [not gradable] no more important than; nothing more than • *The damage to the car was a mere scratch.* • *The plane crashed mere minutes after take-off.*

mere·ly /£ˈmɪə·li, $ˈmɪr-/ *adv* [not gradable] • *I wasn't complaining, I merely* (= only) *said that I was tired.* • *He is not merely* (= not just) *a good artist, but a great one.*

mer·est /£ˈmɪə·rɪst, $ˈmɪr·ɪst/ *adj* [not gradable] • You say **the merest** to emphasize the surprising or strong effect of a very small action or event: *The baby sleeps so badly that the merest noise wakes her up.* ○ *The merest* **mention** *of seafood makes Guy feel sick.* ○ *The merest* **suggestion** *that the car crash was partly his fault sent him into an angry rage.* • **The merest** also means the smallest: *I managed to escape the fighting* **by the merest chance**.

me·re·tri·cious /ˌmer·ɪˈtrɪʃ·əs/ *adj fml* seeming attractive but really false or of little value • *He claims that a lot of journalism is meretricious and superficial.*

merge *(obj)* /£mɜːdʒ, $mɜːrdʒ/ *v* to (cause to) combine or join together • *They decided to merge the two companies into one.* [T] • *The country's two biggest banks are planning to merge in order to fight off competition from abroad.* [I] • *The Liberals and the Social Democrats merged in 1987 to form the Liberal Democrats.* [I] • *Pink, blue and orange colours merged in the evening sky.* [I] • *After a while the narrow track merges* **with** *a wider path.* [I] • Merge is also *Am for* **filter in**. [I] • PIC〉 **Driving**

merg·er /£ˈmɜː·dʒəʳ, $ˈmɜːr·dʒɚ/ *n* [C] • A merger is when two or more companies join together: *Their company gives advice about mergers and takeovers.* ○ *The merger of the two companies would create the world's biggest accounting firm.* ○ *The German tyre company is holding merger* **talks** *with its Italian rival.*

me·ri·di·an /məˈrɪd·i·ən/ *n* [C] an imaginary line from the North Pole to the South Pole, drawn on maps to help to show the position of a place • *The prime meridian of longitude is in Greenwich, South London.* • *In the United States, the Plains is the area between the Rocky Mountains and the 98th meridian.*

me·ringue /məˈræŋ/ *n* a very light sweet cake made by baking a mixture of sugar and the colourless parts of eggs • *A large meringue with a soft centre which is served with cream and fruit on top is called a pavlova.* [C] • *Some sweet cakes are covered with a soft layer of meringue.* [U]

me·ri·no /£məˈriː·nəʊ, $-noʊ/ *n* [C] a breed of sheep which produces soft good-quality wool • *A flock of merinos were grazing on the grass behind their house.* • *Australia is the largest producer of merino* **wool**.

mer·it /ˈmer·ɪt/ *n* the quality of being good and deserving praise • *This film is entertaining but has little artistic merit.* [U] • *One of her great merits as a teacher is her ability to listen.* [C] • *Professor Barr's book has the merit of being both very readable and beautifully produced.* [C] • The merits of something are its advantages compared to something else: *We discussed the merits of drinking herbal tea instead of coffee.* [C] • If something is judged **on its (own) merits**, it is judged on the qualities it possesses and not by people's opinions of it: *The committee say they will consider the applicants' cases on their own merits and not in comparison with other cases.* ○ *He believes that a film should be a success or failure on its own merits and not because of the number of awards it wins.* • Ⓙ Ⓢ

mer·it *obj* /ˈmer·ɪt/ *v* [T; not *be meriting*] *fml* • If something merits a particular treatment, it deserves or is considered important enough to be treated in that way: *This plan merits careful attention.* ○ *The accident merited only a small paragraph in the local paper.*

mer·it·o·ri·ous /£ˌmer·ɪˈtɔː·ri·əs, $-ˈtɔːr·i-/ *adj fml* • If something is meritorious, it deserves great praise: *Six employees were given awards for meritorious service.*

mer·i·toc·ra·cy /£ˌmer·ɪˈtɒk·rə·si, $-ˈtɑː·krə-/ *n* a social system or society in which people have power because of their abilities, not because of their wealth or social position • *The prime minister claims he wants to create a classless meritocracy in Britain.* [C] • *A lot more women need to be promoted to top company positions before business can claim to be a genuine meritocracy.* [C] • *There is much more opportunity and meritocracy in the company I work for at present than in my previous company.* [U]

mer·maid /£ˈmɜː·meɪd, $ˈmɜːr-/ *n* [C] (in stories) a creature with the upper body of a woman and the tail of a fish • *Hans Christian Andersen wrote a famous children's story about a little mermaid.* • PIC **Imaginary creatures**

mer·ry HAPPY /ˈmer·i/ *adj* **-ier, -iest** happy or showing enjoyment • *(dated) Ethel is a merry* **soul** (=person), *always smiling and laughing.* • *(dated) From the other room, we could hear the merry sound of laughter and glasses clinking.* • *According to English legend, Robin Hood and his band of merry* **men** *lived in Sherwood Forest and robbed from the rich to give to the poor.* • You say **Merry Christmas** to people at Christmas time: *The shop assistant* **wished** *me a merry Christmas.* LP **Holidays** • A **merry-go-round** (*Br and Aus also* **roundabout**, *Am also* **carousel**) is a machine which turns round and has wooden or plastic animals or vehicles on which children ride: *The girls wanted the merry-go-round to go faster.* ○ *(fig.) The merry-go-round* (=very busy activity) *of parties at this time of year can be exhausting.* • *"Old King Cole was a merry old soul"* (from a nursery rhyme)

mer·ri·ly /ˈmer·ɪ·li/ *adv* • *(dated) Ellen tried not to laugh, but her eyes sparkled merrily* (=showed her enjoyment). • *(infml)* If you do something merrily, you do it without thinking about the result of what you are doing or about the problems it might cause: *He seems completely oblivious to the problems he's caused and just merrily continues along his way.* ○ *The factory has been merrily pumping chemical waste into the river for the past ten years and no one has done anything to stop them.*

mer·ry–mak·ing /ˈmer·iˌmeɪ·kɪŋ/ *n* [U] *literary* • Merry-making means the activities of celebrating and having an enjoyable time: *The eating, drinking and merry-making went on late into the night.*

mer·ri·ment /ˈmer·ɪ·mənt/ *n* [U] • Merriment means laughter or the activity of people having an enjoyable time together: *His unusual name has long been a source of merriment for his friends.* ○ *Sounds of merriment from the party could be heard in the street.*

mer·ry DRUNK /ˈmer·i/ *adj* **-ier, -iest** *Br infml* used to avoid saying slightly drunk • *Joan got a bit merry last night!*

mes·ca·lin /ˈmes·kəl·ɪn/, **mes·ca·line** /ˈmes·kəl·iːn/ *n* [U] a drug obtained from a CACTUS plant which causes HALLUCINATIONS (=seeing things that are not there) • *Hallucinogens, such as LSD and mescalin, were widely used during the 1960s.*

mesh NET /meʃ/ *n* [U] (a piece of) material with spaces in it like net which is made from wire, plastic or thread • *Push the strawberries through a sieve with fine mesh.* [U] • *There was a wire mesh over the shop window to prevent vandalism.* [C]

mesh *(obj)* JOIN /meʃ/ *v* (of two or more things) to fit together or be suitable for each other • *The car's gears aren't meshing properly.* [I] • *The members of the team just didn't mesh* (**with** *each other*). [I]

mes·mer·ize *obj, Br and Aus usually* **-ise** /ˈmez·mə·raɪz/ *v* [T] to have (someone's) attention completely so that they cannot think of anything else • *The audience was completely mesmerized by her singing voice.* • Mesmerize is also *dated for* HYPNOTIZE.

mes·mer·iz·ing, *Br and Aus usually* **-is·ing** /ˈmez·mə·raɪ·zɪŋ/ *adj* • *Elsie is tall with mesmerizing blue eyes.*

mes·mer·ic /mezˈmer·ɪk/ *adj* • *He has a gently mesmeric guitar style.* • *She gave a mesmeric performance in the film as a woman dying from cancer.*

mess UNTIDINESS /mes/ *n* a state of untidiness, dirtiness or lack of organization • *The sweets she had left in the back of the car had melted into a huge sticky mess.* [C] • *Can you* **clear up** *that mess you made in the kitchen?* [U] • *I always* **make a** *mess when I try to cook anything.* [U] • *You look* **a** *mess – you can't go out like that!* [U] • *The room was* **a** *mess* **of** *clothes and paper which had been scattered all over the floor.* [U] • *My brother's house is always* **in a** *mess.* [U] • If you describe a situation as **a** mess, you mean it is full of problems and difficulties: *She said that her life was a mess.* [U] ○ *The company has called in a team of accountants to* **sort out** *the mess.* [U] ○ *I've* **got** *myself* **into** *a* **bit of** *a mess by telling a lie.* [U] ○ *She was constantly trying to get her brother out of the messes he had* **gotten** *himself* **into**. [C] ○ *The company's finances are* **in a** *mess.* [U] • A person can be **a** mess if their life is full of problems and difficulties they cannot deal with: *She's a real mess – twice divorced, hooked on drugs and now living on the streets!* [U] • An animal's mess is its excrement: *Fido has left another mess on the carpet.* [C] ○ *The council will fine owners who do not clear up their dog's mess in public places.* [C] • If you **make a mess of** something, you do it badly or spoil it: *I've made a real mess of my exams.* ○ *She despairs of the way that human society has made such a mess of the Earth.* • *(infml)* A **mess-up** is a something which has been done badly: *He made a real mess-up of the sales figures.*

mess *(obj)* /mes/ *v infml* • If you mess something, you make it untidy: *(Am) Don't you dare mess my hair!* [T] ○ *Who's messed* **up** *the bookshelf?* [M] • *Next door's dog has messed* (=left its excrement) *on our steps again!* [I] • If you **mess about/around**, you do things without any particular purpose or plan: *She spent the day with her friends just messing about.* ○ *He spends his weekends messing around in his boat on the Thames.* ○ *My brother likes messing about* **with** *computers.* • *(disapproving)* To **mess about/around** is also to do something stupid or annoying: *Stop messing about and listen to me!* ○ *Don't mess around* **with** *sharp knives!* • *(esp. Am)* If a man or woman who is married **messes about/around with** someone, they have a sexual relationship with someone who is not their wife or husband: *She found out that her husband was messing around with his secretary.* • If you **mess** someone **about/around**, you treat them badly: *I'm tired of being messed around by my bank.* ○ *Don't mess me about!* • If you mess **up** something, you spoil or damage it: *I feel I've messed up my chances of becoming a great singer.* [M] ○ *You'll mess up your insides if you don't eat properly.* [M] ○ *He says that his divorce has really messed his life up.* [M] • If you **mess up**, you do something badly or make a mistake: *You've really messed up this time.* • *(Am slang)* To **mess** someone **up** is to hit someone so that they are badly injured. • *(esp. Am)* To **mess with** something is to use or treat it without enough care: *He was messing with his bike and then he couldn't fit the parts back together.* • To **mess with** something dangerous is also to become involved with it: *You shouldn't mess with drugs.* • If you **mess with** someone, you treat them badly: *I've warned you already, don't mess with me!* • *(Br)* You say **no messing** as a way of emphasizing that you want something to be done: *I want you both in bed by 9 o'clock, no messing!* • *"Believe me, my young friend, there is nothing – absolutely nothing – half so much worth doing as simply messing about in boats"* (from Kenneth Graham's *The Wind in the Willows*, 1908)

messed–up /ˌmest'ʌp/ *adj slang* • If someone is **messed-up**, they are unhappy and emotionally confused: *She was really messed-up as a teenager.* ○ *In spite of his messed-up parents, he's a really nice, caring person.*

mess·y /'mes·i/ *adj* **-ier, -iest** • *I hate a messy* (= untidy) *kitchen.* • *The journey took two days and he felt really dirty and messy when he arrived.* • An activity which is messy causes dirt and untidiness: *Eating a ripe peach can be messy.* ○ *Vicky cooks really well but she's rather messy.* • A messy situation is one which is confused and unpleasant: *A war will be a long and messy business.* ○ *They had a bitter, messy divorce.*

mes·si·ly /'mes·ɪ·li/ *adv*

mess ROOM /mes/, *Am also* **mess hall** *n* [C] a room or building in which members of the armed forces have their meals or spend their free time • *During the war, the church hall was used as a mess for air force crews.* • *He found the group captain in the mess hall, having breakfast with the ground crew.* • *They used to spend their evenings in the* **officers'** *mess, drinking and playing cards.*

mes·sage INFORMATION /'mes·ɪdʒ/ *n* [C] a short piece of information that you give to a person when you cannot speak to them directly • *If I'm not there when you phone, leave a message.* • *Did you get the message* **that** *she can't come?* [+ *that* clause] • *James sent a message* **to** *meet him at the hotel.* [+ *to* infinitive] • *"This message will self-destruct in thirty seconds"* (from the opening of the television series *Mission Impossible*, 1966-)

mes·seng·er /£'mes·ɪn·dʒəʳ, $-dʒɚ/ *n* [C] • A messenger is someone who takes a message or documents from one person to another: *In Roman mythology, Mercury was the messenger of the gods.* ○ *The documents were delivered to the president by special messenger while he was on vacation.* ○ *(disapproving) I'm not your messenger* **boy**, *do your own errands.* • *(saying)* 'Don't shoot the messenger (who brings bad news)' means do not be angry with someone because they tell you something bad.

mes·sage IDEA /'mes·ɪdʒ/ *n* [C] the most important idea in a book, film or play • *The film's message is that rich and poor are alike.* • *(infml)* If someone **gets the message**, they understand what you mean: *Even when I started yawning, he didn't get the message but just kept talking.* • If you **get the message across** to someone, you make them understand: *We need to get the message across* **that** *too much sun is dangerous.* [+ *that* clause]

mes·si·ah /mə'saɪ·ə/ *n* [C usually sing] a leader who is believed to have the power to solve the world's problems • *An ordinary priest, he was hailed by thousands as the new messiah.* • In the Christian religion, the Messiah is Jesus Christ. • In the Jewish religion, the Messiah is the king of the Jews who is still to come.

mes·si·an·ic /ˌmes·i'æn·ɪk/ *adj* [not gradable] *fml* • *He announced the imminent arrival of a messianic* **leader**. • A messianic religious group is one which has the belief that a leader will or has come who has the power to change the world and bring peace: *a messianic cult/movement/sect* • A messianic speech or style is one which is very persuasive and full of emotion: *She talks about her work with a messianic zeal.*

Messrs *fml* /£'mes·əz, $-ɚz/ *pl of* MR (= title used before a man's name), esp. used before the names of two or more people in the title of a company • *Messrs Wood and Laurence, solicitors*

met MEET /met/ *past simple and past participle of* MEET

met WEATHER /met/ *adj* [before n] *esp. Br infml for* **meteorological**, see at METEOROLOGY

met·a·bol·i·sm /mə'tæb·əl·ɪ·zəm/ *n* [C] *specialized* all the chemical processes in your body, esp. those that cause food to be used for energy and growth • *Exercise is supposed to speed up your metabolism.* • *He says he's got a fast metabolism, so he can eat a lot without putting on weight.*

met·a·bol·ic /£ˌmet·ə'bɒl·ɪk, $ˌmeţ·ə'bɑː·lɪk/ *adj* [not gradable] *specialized* • *The athletes had taken pills to stimulate their metabolic* **rate** (= the speed at which their bodies used energy).

met·a·fic·tion /£'met·əˌfɪk·ʃən, $'meţ-/ *n* [U] *specialized* writing about imaginary characters and events in which the process of writing is discussed or described

met·a·fic·tion·al /£ˌmet·ə'fɪk·ʃən·əl, $ˌmeţ-/ *adj* [not gradable] *specialized* • *The novel contains several complex metafictional elements.*

met·al /£'met·əl, $'meţ-/ *n* a chemical element, such as iron or gold, or a mixture of such elements, such as steel, which electricity and heat can travel through and which is generally hard and strong • *Metals are used for making machinery and tools.* [C] • *Metal, paper and glass can be recycled.* [U] • *Steel is a* **ferrous** *metal* (= It contains iron) *and some types of it rust when exposed to air.* [C] • *Iron, copper, tin and lead are all* **heavy** (= dense) *metals and are commonly used in engineering.* [C] • **Molten** *metal* (= Metal in a liquid state) *is shaped by pouring it into a mould of the required shape and leaving it to cool.* [U] • *Silver, gold and platinum are* **precious** *metals.* [C] • *The wooden beam is reinforced with a metal plate.* • A **metal detector** is a machine that you move over the ground or an object to discover if there is metal there: *Many people use metal detectors in fields and on beaches in the hope of finding buried treasure.* ○ *Metal detectors are used in airports to check that people are not carrying weapons.* • **Metal fatigue** is a weakness which develops in metal structures which are used repeatedly: *Metal fatigue was blamed for the plane crash, which was caused by one of the engines disintegrating.*

met·al·lic /mə'tæl·ɪk/ *adj* • If a sound, appearance or taste is metallic, it is like metal: *The explosion had a dull, metallic sound.* ○ *The paintings are full of bright blues and metallic golds.* ○ *Beer from a can often has a metallic taste.* • *(specialized)* Metallic also means consisting of, or partly consisting of, metal: *Brass is a metallic alloy of copper and zinc.*

met·a·lan·guage /£'met·əˌlæŋ·gwɪdʒ, $'meţ-/ *n* [C] *specialized* a specialized form of language or a set of symbols which is used when discussing or describing the structure of a language • *A metalanguage usually contains specialist terminology to make it possible to refer to linguistic structures accurately.*

met·alled /£'met·əld, $'meţ-/ *adj* [not gradable] *Br* (of a road) covered with small stones to make a level surface • *The metalled road became a muddy track.*

met·al·lur·gy /£met'æl·ə·dʒi, $'meţ·əl·ɜːr-/ *n* [U] the scientific study of the structures and uses of metals • *She has a doctorate in metallurgy from the University of Utah.* • *One of the most important aspects of modern metallurgy is the study of the changes undergone by metals during fabrication and treatment.*

met·al·lur·gi·cal /£ˌmet·əl'ɜː·dʒɪ·kəl, $ˌmeţ·əl'ɜːr-/ *adj* [not gradable] • *a metallurgical process* • *the metallurgical industry*

met·al·lur·gist /£met'æl·ə·dʒɪst, $'meţ·əl·ɜːr-/ *n* [C] • A metallurgist is a person who studies or knows about metals.

met·al·work /£'met·əl·wɜːk, $'meţ·əl·wɜːrk/ *n* [U] the activity of making metal objects • *Her favourite subject at school is metalwork.* • Metalwork is also the metal part of something: *Rust has damaged the metalwork of the bicycle.*

met·a·mor·phose /£ˌmet·ə'mɔː·fəʊz, $ˌmeţ·ə'mɔːr·foʊz, —'-/ *v* [I] *fml* to change into a completely different form or type • *The awkward boy I knew had metamorphosed* **into** *a tall, handsome man.*

met·a·mor·phos·is /£ˌmet·ə'mɔː·fə·sɪs, $ˌmeţ·ə'mɔːr-/ *n pl* **metamorphoses** /£ˌmet·ə'mɔː·fə·siːz, $ˌmeţ·ə'mɔːr-/ • A metamorphosis is a complete change: *Under the new editor, the magazine has undergone a metamorphosis.* [C] • *(specialized)* Metamorphosis is the process by which the young form of insects and some animals, such as FROGS, develops into the adult form: *In the transformation of a tadpole into a frog, metamorphosis happens gradually.* [U]

met·a·phor /£'met·ə·fɔːʳ, $'meţ·ə·fɔːr/ *n* an expression which describes a person or object in a literary way by referring to something that is considered to possess similar characteristics to the person or object you are trying to describe • *'The mind is an ocean' and 'the city is a jungle' are both metaphors.* [C] • *The sporting term 'being on the inside track' is used in business as a metaphor to mean* *'having an advantage'.* [C] • *Metaphor and simile are the most commonly used figures of speech in everyday language.* [U] • To be a metaphor **for** something is to be a symbol which represents that thing: *In the film, the city is a metaphor for confusion and loneliness.* [C] ○ *The author uses disease as a metaphor for the corruption in society.* [C]

met·a·phor·i·cal /£ˌmet·əˈfɒr·ɪ·kəl, $ˌmeţ·əˈfɑːr-/, **met·a·phor·ic** /£ˌmet·əˈfɒr·ɪk, $ˌmeţ·əˈfɑːr-/ *adj* • Language which is metaphorical contains a lot of metaphors: *Her second novel is written in a very metaphorical style.* • If something is metaphorical, it does not really exist but is symbolic and shows some truth about its subject: *There is a metaphorical ocean* (= a large area of disagreement) *between the two opposing groups.* ○ *By threatening to sack them if they refused to work overtime, he held a metaphoric gun to their head* (= he used a threat to force them to work). ○ *The mediator was able to build a metaphorical bridge between the two sides* (= bring them closer to agreement) *using negotiation and compromise.* ○ *There is a danger that America's metaphoric 'war on drugs' may turn into a bloody reality.*

met·a·phor·i·cally /£ˌmet·əˈfɒr·ɪ·kli, $ˌmeţ·əˈfɑːr-/ *adv* • *The phrase 'born again' is used metaphorically* (= as a metaphor) *to mean that someone has suddenly become very religious.* • *The thunder storm dampened our enjoyment of the picnic, literally and metaphorically.* • *By leaving school without any qualifications, she has, metaphorically* **speaking**, *shot herself in the foot* (= harmed her chances of success).

met·a·phys·ics /£ˌmet·əˈfɪz·ɪks, $ˌmeţ-/ *n* [U] the part of PHILOSOPHY that is about understanding existence and knowledge

met·a·phys·i·cal /£ˌmet·əˈfɪz·ɪ·kəl, $ˌmeţ-/ *adj* • *Most teenagers ask themselves metaphysical questions* (= questions about what exists) *such as "What is love?" and "What is death?"*

mete out *obj*, **mete** *obj* **out** /miːt/ *v adv* [M] *fml* to give or order (a punishment or similar esp. unpleasant behaviour) • *Victorian schoolteachers regularly meted out physical punishment to their pupils.*

met·e·or /£ˈmiː·ti·ɔːʳ, $-ţi·ɔːr/, **shoot·ing star**, *infml* **fall·ing star** *n* [C] *specialized* a piece of rock or other matter in space that produces a bright light as it travels close to Earth • *We saw a meteor streak across the night sky.*

met·e·or·ic /£ˌmiː·tiˈɒr·ɪk, $-ţiˈɑːr-/ *adj* [not gradable] • *The sudden flash of light in the night sky was caused by a meteoric fireball.* • If something, such as a rise, is meteoric, it is very fast and easily noticed: *The group had a meteoric* **rise** *to fame in the 70s, but are now almost forgotten.* ○ *Her parliamentary* **career** *has been meteoric.*

met·e·or·ite /£ˈmiː·ti·ər·aɪt, $-ţi·ə·raɪt/ *n* [C] a piece of rock or other matter from space that has landed on Earth • *Some people believe that dinosaurs were destroyed because of the effects of a gigantic meteorite.*

met·e·or·ol·o·gy /£ˌmiː·ti·ərˈɒl·ə·dʒi, $-ţi·əˈrɑː·lə-/ *n* [U] the scientific study of the processes that cause particular weather conditions • *Meteorology is used to forecast the weather.*

met·e·or·ol·og·i·cal /£ˌmiː·ti·ər·əˈlɒdʒ·ɪ·kəl, $-ţi·ə·əˈlɑː·dʒɪ-/, *infml* **met** *adj* [not gradable] • *Accurate meteorological records* (= reports of weather conditions) *began 100 years ago.* • In Britain, the **Meteorological Office** (also **Met Office**) is the government department that studies weather conditions and says what is expected to happen with the weather: *The Met Office has forecast heavy snow tonight.*

met·e·or·ol·o·gist /£ˌmiː·ti·ərˈɒl·ə·dʒɪst, $-ţi·əˈrɑːl-/ *n* [C] • *Meteorologists gathered for a conference in Brighton to discuss rainfall trends across Europe.*

met·er DEVICE /£ˈmiː·təʳ, $-ţɚ/ *n* [C] a device that measures the amount of something that is used • *The* **electricity** *meter is in the cupboard under the stairs.* • *If you park in the centre of town, you'll need some change for the* **parking** *meter.* • *The man from the gas board came to* **read** *the meter* (= see how much gas had been used). • In a TAXI, a meter is the device that measures the distance or the amount of time spent travelling and shows how much you have to pay: *I asked the taxi driver to switch on the meter.* • PIC〉 **Meters and gauges**

met·er *obj* /£ˈmiː·təʳ, $-ţɚ/ *v* [T] • To meter something such as gas, electricity or water is to measure how much of it is used: *Britain's water companies are planning to meter water consumption.*

met·er DISTANCE /£ˈmiː·təʳ, $-ţɚ/ *n* [C] *Am for* METRE

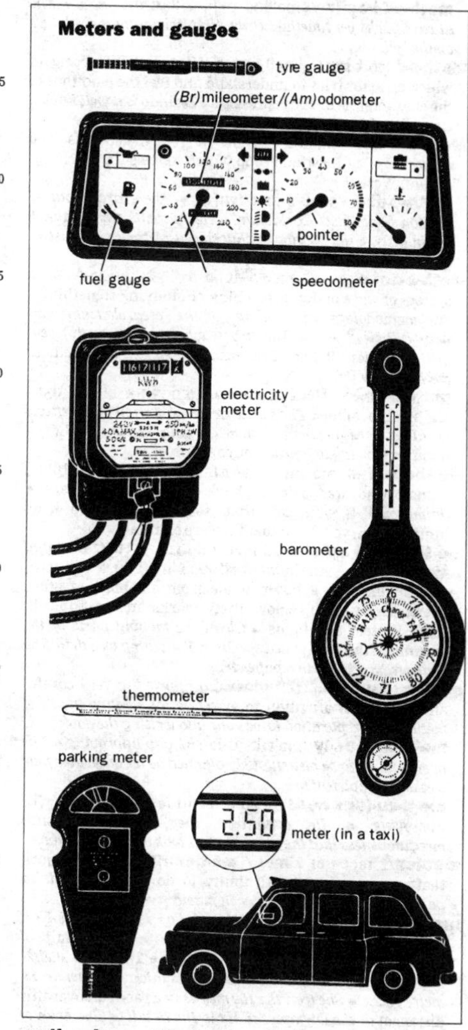

Meters and gauges

meth·a·done /£ˈmeθ·ə·dəʊn, $-doʊn/ *n* [U] a drug which is often used instead of HEROIN • *Methadone is often given to heroin addicts as a way of helping them to overcome their addiction problem.*

me·thane /ˈmiː·θeɪn/ *n* [U] a colourless gas without a smell which is often used as a fuel • *Natural gas is composed of methane, ethane, propane and butane.* • *A major contributor to the destruction of the ozone layer is the methane produced by cows.*

meth·a·nol /£ˈmeθ·ə·nɒl, $-nɑːl/ *n* [U] a poisonous chemical substance which is the simplest type of alcohol

me·thinks /mɪˈθɪŋks/ *v old use or humorous for* I think • *There's more to this than meets the eye, methinks.*

meth·od /ˈmeθ·əd/ *n* a particular way of doing something • *Travelling by train is still one of the safest methods of transport.* [C] • *The new teaching methods encourage children to think for themselves.* [C] • Method is also an ordered way of doing something: *You'll need method to sort out this mess.* [U] • If you describe someone as having **method in** their **madness** (*Am usually* **a method to** their **madness**), you mean that although that person seems to be behaving strangely, they have a good reason for what they are doing. • *"You know my methods. Apply them"* (The detective Sherlock Holmes to Dr Watson in the story *The Sign of Four* by Sir Arthur Conan Doyle, 1890)

meth·od·i·cal /£məˈθɒd·ɪ·kəl, $-ˈθɑː·dɪ-/ *adj* • If someone is methodical, they do things in a very ordered, careful way: *Tom is a very methodical person and writes lists for everything.*

meth·od·i·cally /£mə'θɒd·ɪ·kli, $-'θɑː·dɪ-/ *adv* • *She always packs very methodically, first arranging her clothes on the bed.*

meth·od (act·ing) /'meθ·əd/ *n* [U] a style of acting in which an actor tries to understand and feel the emotions of the character he or she represents • *Brando is a well-known exponent of* **the** *Method.* • *a method actor*

Meth·o·di·sm /'meθ·ə·dɪ·zᵊm/ *n* [U] the beliefs and activities of a Christian group which follows the teachings of John Wesley

Meth·o·dist /'meθ·ə·dɪst/ *n* [C] • *There are about 25 million Methodists worldwide.* • *Her parents were staunch Methodists.* • *the Methodist church* • *a Methodist minister/preacher*

meth·o·dol·o·gy /£ˌmeθ·ə'dɒl·ə·dʒi, $-'dɑː·lə-/ *n* a system of ways of doing, teaching or studying something • *The methodology and findings of the research team have been criticized.* [C] • *The two teachers use very different methodologies.* [C] • *I've never been much good at methodology.* [U]

meth·o·do·log·i·cal /£ˌmeθ·ə·dᵊl'ɒdʒ·ɪ·kᵊl, $-'ɑː·dʒɪ-/ *adj* [not gradable] • *The scientific investigation of the effects of alternative medicine, such as acupuncture, raises a number of methodological* **issues/problems**.

Me·thu·se·lah /mə'θuː·zᵊl·ə/ *n* [not after *the*] (in the Bible) a man who was said to have lived for 969 years • *(humorous)* If you say that someone is **as old as Methuselah**, you mean that they are extremely old.

me·thy·lated spi·rits /£'meθ·ɪ·leɪ·tɪd, $-t̬ɪd/, *Br infml* **meths** /meθs/, *Aus infml* **meth·o** /£'meθ·əʊ, $-oʊ/ *n* [U] *esp. Br and Aus* a liquid made from alcohol and other chemicals, used to remove dirty marks and as a fuel in small heaters and lights • *Clean the moving parts of the machine using methylated spirits.* • *The tramp was drinking meths from a bottle in a paper bag.*

me·ti·cu·lous /mə'tɪk·jʊ·ləs/ *adj approving* very careful and with great attention to every detail • *Many hours of meticulous preparation have gone into writing the book.*

me·ti·cu·lous·ly /mə'tɪk·jʊ·lə·sli/ *adv approving* • *The project needs to be meticulously planned as we only have four weeks to complete it in.*

me·ti·cu·lous·ness /mə'tɪk·jʊ·lə·snəs/ *n* [U] *approving* • *He organized the event with such meticulousness that the preparations took over six months.*

met·ier /£'met·ɪ·eɪ, $'met̬-/, **mé·tier** *n* [C] the type of work that you have a natural ability to do well • *Rose tried painting but found her metier in music.*

met·re MEASUREMENT *esp. Br and Aus* /£'miː·tər, $-t̬ɚ/, *Am usually* **met·er**, *abbreviation* **m** *n* [C] a unit of measurement equal to 100 centimetres • *The bomb shelter has concrete walls that are three metres thick.* • *He owns a 15-metre yacht.* • *She won the 100 metres* (= a race run over this distance) *at the Olympics.* • *He is 1m 75 tall.* • *The price of water has risen from 41p to 48p per* **cubic** *metre* (= a unit of volume equal to 1000 litres). • *The carpet costs £15·95 per* **square** *metre* (= a unit of area). • LP **Units**

met·re POETRY *esp. Br and Aus* /£'miː·tər, $-t̬ɚ/, *Am usually* **met·er** *n specialized* the regular arrangement of syllables in poetry according to the number and type of beats in a line • *When you read a poem out loud, you become more conscious of the stresses and metre.* [U] • *He composes poems in a classical style, in strict metre and with internal rhymes.* [U] • *Many church hymns have a firm, regular metre.* [C]

met·ric /'met·rɪk/ *adj* [not gradable] a system of measurement that uses metres, centimetres, litres etc. • *The recipe is given in both metric and imperial measures.* • *Most high-tech industry has been metric* (= uses the metric system of measurement) *for decades.* • A **metric ton** is equal to 1000 kilograms. • LP **Units**

met·ri·ca·tion /ˌmet·rɪ'keɪ·ʃᵊn/ *n* [U] • Metrication is the process of changing from the old system of measuring things in IMPERIAL units to measuring them using metric units.

metro /£'met·rəʊ, $-roʊ/ *n* [U] an underground electric railway system in some cities, esp. in France • *Let's* **go** *by Metro.* • *Shall we* **take** *the metro, or go by bus?*

metronome /£'met·rə·nəʊm, $-noʊm/ *n* [C] a device that produces a regular sound to help musicians play a piece of music at a particular speed

metropolis /£mə'trɒp·ᵊl·ɪs, $-'trɑː·pᵊl-/ *n* [C] *fml* a very large city, esp. the most important city in a large area or country • *Singapore has been rebuilt as a metropolis of skyscrapers, shopping areas and hotels.*

metropolitan /£ˌmet·rə'pɒl·ɪ·tᵊn, $-'pɑː·lɪ-/ *adj* • *the Metropolitan Museum of Art in New York* • *the Metropolitan Police* (= the London police force) • *Aged 25, he left his home town, drawn to the metropolitan glamour and excitement of Paris.*

mettle /£'met·l̩, $'met̬-/ *n* [U] *fml* ability and determination, esp. when competing or doing something difficult • *The German athletes* **showed/proved** *their mettle in the final round.* • *The real* **test** *of her political mettle will come in the May elections.* • *Both players were* **on** *their* **mettle** (= playing as well as they could) *in the final round.*

mew /mjuː/ *v* [I], *n* [C] (to make) the soft crying sound of a cat • Compare MIAOW; PURR.

mews /mjuːz/ *n* [C] *pl* **mews** *esp. Br* a building which was used in the past for keeping horses and is now used as a house, or the short narrow road where these buildings are found • *They bought a* **converted** *mews.* • *They live in a tiny mews house.* • *The shop is at number 6 Gloucester Mews.*

Mex·i·can stand off /'mek·sɪ·kᵊn/ *n* [C] *Aus* a situation in which people on opposite sides threaten each other but neither tries to come to an agreement

Mex·i·can wave *Br* /'mek·sɪ·kᵊn/, *Am* **the Wave** *n* [C] a movement made by a large group of people, esp. while watching a sports game, standing up and lifting up their arms and then sitting down, one after another, so producing a wave-like effect

mezzanine /'met·sə·niːn, 'mez·ə-/ *n* [C] a small additional floor between esp. the bottom floor of a building and the next floor up • *You can look down from the mezzanine into the ground floor lobby.* • *The shoe department is on the mezzanine floor.* • *(Am)* In a theatre, sports STADIUM, etc., the mezzanine is the front few rows of seats of the level, or all of the level, above ground.

mezzo so·pran·o /£'met·səʊ, $-soʊ/ *n* [C; U] *pl* **mezzo sopranos** (a woman with) a voice lower than a SOPRANO but higher than a CONTRALTO • *She sings mezzo.* [U] • *A leading mezzo soprano was given the part.* [C]

mg *n* [C] *pl* **mg** *abbreviation for* MILLIGRAM

MHz *n* [C] *pl* **MHz** *abbreviation for* MEGAHERTZ

MI5 /ˌem·aɪ'faɪv/ *n* [U not after *the*] the official British organization that is responsible for protecting military and political secrets

MI6 /ˌem·aɪ'sɪks/ *n* [U not after *the*] the official British organization that is responsible for discovering foreign military and political secrets

mi·aow, *Am usually* **me·ow** /ˌmiː'aʊ/ *v* [I], *n* [C] (to make) the high crying sound of a cat • *A cat was miaowing pitifully outside the door.* • Compare MEW; PURR.

miasma /mi'æz·mə/ *n* [C] *literary* an unpleasant fog which has a bad smell • *A miasma* **of** *pollution hung in the air above Mexico City.* • *Evil hangs over the city like a miasma.* • A miasma is also a very unpleasant general feeling or character of a situation or place: *After he lost his job, he seemed to sink into a miasma* **of** *poverty and despair.*

mic /maɪk/ *n Am infml for* MICROPHONE

mica /'maɪ·kə/ *n* [U] a natural glass-like substance that can be easily broken into thin layers and is not damaged by heat. It is used esp. in electrical equipment.

mice /maɪs/ *pl of* MOUSE

mick, **Mick** /mɪk/ *n* [C] *slang* an offensive word used to describe a person from Ireland or a Roman Catholic • *Hey, you stupid Mick!* • *He married into a mick family.*

mickey /'mɪk·i/ *n* [U] **take the mickey/mick** *Br and Aus infml* to make people laugh at someone, usually by copying what the person does in an amusing or unkind way • *She's always taking the mick – she's got no respect for the managers at all.* • *As soon as he left the room, the others started to take the mickey* **out of** *his mannerisms and way of speaking.*

mickey (finn) /ˌmɪk·i'fɪn/ *n* [C] *slang* a drug added to a drink, esp. an alcoholic drink, in order to make the person who drinks it unconscious • *He must have* **slipped** *the guard a mickey finn.*

Mickey Mouse /ˌmɪk·i'maʊs/ *adj* [before n] *infml disapproving* (of an organization, place, machine or course of study) small and simple; not to be taken seriously • *He works for some Mickey Mouse outfit in Oklahoma.* • *This is a real Mickey Mouse computer compared to the one I've got at work.*

mi·cro– SMALL /£ˌmaɪ·krəʊ, $-kroʊ/ *combining form* very small • *a microorganism* • *a microclimate* • *microbiology* • Micro is often used instead of very small: *The company has a 20% share in the market for mini or* *micro cars.* ○ *The skirt she was wearing was a micro mini.* • Compare MACRO- [LARGE].

mi·cro [COMPUTER] /£ˈmaɪ·krəʊ, $-kroʊ/ *n* [C] *pl* **micros** *infml for* MICROCOMPUTER

mi·cro– [MEASUREMENT] /£ˌmaɪ·krəʊ-, $-kroʊ-/ *combining form* 1 000 000th of the stated unit • *a micrometre* • *a microgram*

microbe /£ˈmaɪ·krəʊb, $-kroʊb/ *n* [C] a very small living thing, esp. one which causes disease, and which is too small to see without a MICROSCOPE • *This toilet cleaner gets rid of germs and microbes.*

mi·cro·bi·ol·o·gy /£ˌmaɪ·krəʊ·baɪˈɒl·ə·dʒi, $-kroʊ·baɪˈɑː·lə-/ *n* [U] the study of very small living things, such as bacteria

microbiological /£ˌmaɪ·krəʊˌbaɪ·əˈlɒdʒ·ɪ·kᵊl, $-kroʊˌbaɪ·əˈlɑː·dʒɪ-/ *adj* [not gradable] • *microbiological research*

microbiologist /£ˌmaɪ·krəʊ·baɪˈɒl·ə·dʒɪst, $-kroʊ·baɪˈɑː·lə-/ *n* [C]

mi·cro·chip /£ˈmaɪ·krəʊ·tʃɪp, $-kroʊ-/ *n* [C] a CHIP [COMPUTER PART]

microcircuit /£ˈmaɪ·krəʊˌsɜː·kɪt, $-kroʊˌsɜːr-/ *n* an **integrated circuit**, see at INTEGRATE

mi·cro·com·put·er /£ˈmaɪ·krəʊ·kəmˌpjuː·təʳ, $-kroʊ·kəmˌpjuː·t̬ɚ/, *infml* **mi·cro** *n* [C] a small computer containing a MICROPROCESSOR (=part which controls operations) • Most microcomputers are also **personal computers**. See at PERSON.

mi·cro·co·sm /£ˈmaɪ·krəʊˌkɒz·ᵊm, $-kroʊˌkɑː·zᵊm/ *n* a small place, society or situation which has the same characteristics as something much larger • *The audience was selected to create a microcosm* **of** *American society.* [C] • *The worldwide problems we are facing are illustrated* **in** *microcosm by the situation in our own country.* [U] • Compare MACROCOSM.

microeconomics /£ˌmaɪ·krəʊ·iː·kəˈnɒm·ɪks, $-kroʊ·iː·kəˈnɑː·mɪks/ *n* [U] the part of economics in which small parts of an economy are studied, for example particular goods, businesses, etc.

microelectronics /£ˌmaɪ·krəʊˌɪl·ekˈtrɒn·ɪks, $-kroʊ·ɪˌlekˈtrɑː·nɪks/ *n* [U] the part of electronics dealing with very small electronic parts

microfiche /£ˈmaɪ·krəʊ·fiːʃ, $-kroʊ-/, **fiche** /fiːʃ/ *n* a small rectangular sheet of film on which information is photographed in a reduced size • *Insert the microfiche this way up.* [C] • *The information is now available* **on** *microfiche.* [U] • A **microfiche (reader)** is a machine which shows information from a microfiche on a screen, made larger so that it can be read: *Does the library have a microfiche reader?*

microfilm /£ˈmaɪ·krəʊ·fɪlm, $-kroʊ-/ *n* (a length of) film which is used for photographing information in a reduced size • *The microfilm was smuggled out in a hollowed-out book.* [C] • *We can look up the article* **on** *microfilm.* [U] • A **microfilm reader** is a machine which shows information from microfilm on a screen, made larger so that it can be read.

microfilm *obj* /£ˈmaɪ·krəʊ·fɪlm, $-kroʊ-/ *v* [T] • *The paper records were microfilmed to save storage space.*

mi·cro·gram /£ˈmaɪ·krəʊ·græm, $-kroʊ-/ *n* [C] 0·000 001 of a gram • *The report claims that some people in England and Wales are consuming about 300 micrograms of lead per day from drinking water.*

mic·ro·light /£ˈmaɪ·krəʊ·laɪt, $-kroʊ-/, **mic·ro·lite** *n* [C] an extremely light and small aircraft, with a very small engine, that can carry only one or two people • [PIC] **Aircraft**

micrometer /£maɪˈkrɒm·ɪ·təʳ, $ˈkrɑː·mɪ·t̬ɚ/ *n* [C] a device used for making very exact measurements or for measuring very small things

micrometre *Br*, *Am* **micrometer** /£ˈmaɪ·krəʊˌmiː·təʳ, $-kroʊˌmiː·tɚ/, *dated* **micron** /£ˈmaɪ·krɒn, $-krɑːn/ *n* [C] 0·000 001 of a metre

mi·cro·or·gan·i·sm /£ˌmaɪ·krəʊˈɔː·gᵊn·ɪ·zᵊm, $-kroʊˈɔːr-/ *n* [C] a living thing which on its own is too small to see without a MICROSCOPE

mi·cro·phone /£ˈmaɪ·krə·fəʊn, $-foʊn/, *infml* **mike**, *Am infml also* **mic** *n* [C] a device that records sound or increases the loudness of sounds by changing the sound waves into electrical waves • *The interviewer asked her to* **speak into/use** *the microphone.* • *Without a microphone, the speakers could not be heard by at least half the audience.*

mi·cro·pro·ces·sor /£ˌmaɪ·krəʊˈprəʊ·ses·əʳ, $-kroʊˈprɑː·ses·ɚ/ *n* [C] a part of a computer that controls its main operations

mi·cro·scope /£ˈmaɪ·krə·skəʊp, $-skoʊp/ *n* [C] a device that uses LENSES (=pieces of curved glass) to make very small objects look larger, esp. so that they can be scientifically examined and studied • *They are looking at the blood samples* **under** *the microscope.* • *(fig.) The latest investigation will* **put** *the company's financial accounts* **under** *the microscope* (=examine them carefully and in detail). • [PIC] **Laboratory**

microscopic /£ˌmaɪ·krəˈskɒp·ɪk, $-ˈskɑː·pɪk/ *adj* • Something that is microscopic is *(infml)* extremely small or *(specialized)* so small that it can only be seen with a microscope: *(infml) Oh, the helpings you get in the office canteen are microscopic!* ○ *(specialized) We looked at microscopic algae in the lab.*

microscopically /£ˌmaɪ·krəˈskɒp·ɪ·kli, $-ˈskɑː·pɪ-/ *adv infml or specialized* • *(infml) It's a microscopically* (=extremely) *small house.*

mi·cro·scop·y /£maɪˈkrɒs·kə·pi, $-ˈkrɑː·skə-/ *n* [U] *specialized* • Microscopy is the use, design and production of microscopes: *Microscopy is an invaluable technique for studying the structure of cells.*

microsecond /£ˈmaɪ·krəʊˌsek·ᵊnd, $-kroʊ-/ *n* [C] 0·000 001 of a second

mi·cro·sur·ger·y /£ˌmaɪ·krəʊˈsɜː·dʒᵊr·i, $-kroʊˈsɜːr·dʒɚ-/ *n* [U] operations on very small areas of a body, for example nerve fibres or the small tubes that carry blood • *Two of her fingers had been cut off in the machine but fortunately the surgeons were able to reattach them using microsurgery.*

microwave (ov·en) /£ˈmaɪ·krəʊ·weɪv, $-kroʊ-/ *n* [C] a machine that cooks food very quickly • **Put** *the fish* **in** *the microwave and it'll only take 5 minutes.* • A microwave is also a very short ELECTROMAGNETIC wave that is used to cook food or to send information by radio or RADAR. • [PIC] **Kitchen**

microwave *obj* /£ˈmaɪ·krəʊ·weɪv, $-kroʊ-/ *v* [T] • *Shall I microwave something for dinner?*

microwaveable, *Am and Aus* **microwavable** /£ˈmaɪ·krəʊ·weɪ·və·bl̩, $-kroʊ-/ *adj* [not gradable] • *packets of microwaveable frozen chips*

mid [AMONG] /mɪd/ *prep poetic* among; in the middle of

mid– [MIDDLE] /mɪd-/ *combining form* the middle of • *mid-March to mid-April* • *mid-afternoon* • *(Am)the Mideast* [LP] **World regions** • *He's in his mid-thirties.* • *He stopped (in) mid-sentence.* • A **mid-life crisis** is feelings of unhappiness, anxiety and disappointment that some people experience at about 40 years old and that can sometimes lead them to make important changes in their life.

midair /£mɪdˈeəʳ, $mɪdˈer/ *n* [U] a point in the air, not on the ground • *She caught the ball* **in** *midair.* • *a midair collision between two helicopters*

mid·day /ˌmɪdˈdeɪ/ *n* [U] 12 o'clock in the middle of the day; NOON • *I just have a sandwich* **at** *midday/for my midday meal.*

mid·dle /ˈmɪd·l̩/ *n* [C usually sing] the central point, position or part • *This is my class photo – I'm the one* **in the** *middle.* • **The** *middle* **of** *the road is not a good place to stop.* • *Like many Indian women, she has a red dot* **in the** *middle* **of** *her forehead.* • *The noise woke us up* **in the** *middle* **of** *the night.* • *Someone did ring the doorbell, but I was* **in the middle of** (=busy with) *bathing the baby.* • *(infml disapproving)* If you describe a place as **(in) the middle of nowhere** you mean that it is very far from towns and cities and does not have many people living there or many services: *He wanted me to live with him in some tiny village in the middle of nowhere.* • *(infml)* Your middle is your waist: *Those trousers look a bit tight around your middle.* • If you **divide/split** something **down the middle** or if something **splits/divides down the middle** you divide it or it divides into two equal parts: *Let's split the cost right down the middle.* ○ *The family is split down the middle on this issue.* • (D)

mid·dle /ˈmɪd·l̩/ *adj* [before n; not gradable] • *In the sequence a, b, c, d, e the middle letter is c, because there are an equal number of letters on each side of it.* • *Jane sits at the middle desk, between the other two.* • *It's a* **middle-sized** (=average-sized) *sheepdog.* • *The measures will assist low and middle* **income** *families.* • *The scheme was discussed at a meeting of about 30 junior and middle-***ranking** *ministers.* • The middle child in a family is the one who has the same number of older brothers and sisters as younger brothers and sisters: *She's the middle child of three.* • A language which is described as Middle comes from a stage in its development between its origin and its present form: *14th century Middle English* ○ *Middle French* • To **follow/steer/take** a/the middle **course/path/way** is to act in a way that is not extreme and that you consider will cause least harm: *Most parents try to steer a middle course between imposing very strict discipline and letting their kids run wild.* ○ *I'd rather take the middle way and not do anything too extreme.* • **Middle age** is the period of your life, usually considered to be from about 40 to 60 years old, when you are no longer young, but are not yet old: *(humorous) You know you've reached middle age when you start to worry about mortgages and pensions.* ○ *They're a* **middle-aged** *couple, with grown-up children.* ○ *(disapproving) What a conventional, middle-aged* (= too careful and not showing the enthusiasm, energy or style of someone young) *attitude he has to life!* LP **Age** Ⓓ Ⓓ︎K Ⓝ • **Middle-age spread** is a humorous name for the fatness, esp. around the waist, that some people get as they grow older. • **The Middle Ages** were a period in European history, esp. between about 1000 AD and 1500 AD, when the power of kings, people of high rank and the Christian Church was strong. Some people consider that the Middle Ages began in about 600 AD. • **Middle America/England** is the part of American/English society that is neither rich nor poor and does not have extreme political or religious opinions. • **Middle America** is also Mexico, Central America, Panama and the West Indies, or it is the MIDWEST in the US. LP **World regions** • *(specialized)* **Middle C** is the musical note C near to the middle of the piano's range. • The **middle class** or **middle classes** are the people in a society who are not of high social rank or extremely rich but are not poor. They expect to be able to have a good job and/or a college education: *It's an agricultural country without a large middle class.* ○ *The upper middle class tend to go into business or the professions, becoming, for example, lawyers, doctors or accountants.* ○ *White Plains is a largely middle-class suburb of New York.* ○ Compare **lower class** at LOWER; **upper class** at UPPER HIGHER • **working class** at WORK ACTIVITY. • In running, a **middle-distance** race is run over a medium distance, esp. 800 or 1500 metres: *a middle-distance event* ○ *a middle-distance runner* • The **middle distance** is the part of a picture or a view that is neither very near nor very far away: *From the top of the hill we could see the ocean far away and in the middle distance the village.* Compare BACKGROUND; foreground. • The **middle ear** is the central part of the ear, behind the EARDRUM, through which sound travels. • The **Middle East** (*Am also* **Mideast**) is the area from the eastern Mediterranean to Iran. It includes Syria, Jordan, Israel, Lebanon, Saudi Arabia, Iran and Iraq. It sometimes also includes Egypt: *He's from somewhere in* **the** *Middle East.* ○ **Middle Eastern** *capitals include Baghdad and Tel Aviv.* Compare **Far East** at FAR DISTANCE. LP **World regions** • Your **middle finger** is your longest finger. • In an argument, the **middle ground** is a position between two opposite opinions: *The UN peace envoy has failed to find any middle ground between the government and the opposition parties.* • **Middle management** is the people within a company who are in charge of departments or groups but who are below those who are in control of the company as a whole: *There are very few women above middle management.* ○ *She's a* **middle manager**. • A **middle name** is the name some people have between their first name and their last name: *Henry George James Smythe has two middle names – George and James.* ○ *(fig. infml) Can he tell a joke? – Funny is his middle name* (= He is very amusing). • A person, organization, opinion or type of entertainment that is **middle-of-the-road** is not extreme and is acceptable to or liked by most people: *They adopted a sensible, middle-of-the-road policy on defence spending.* ○ *(disapproving) They criticised boring, predictable middle-of-the-road TV broadcasts that are screened because they are safe and unlikely to offend.* • In some parts of the UK and the US, and in some other countries, a **middle school** is a school for children between the ages of about 9 and 14. • The **Middle West** is the MIDWEST.

mid·dle·brow /ˈmɪd·l̩.braʊ/ *adj esp. disapproving* (of music, literature, art or film) of good quality, interesting and often popular, but not needing very much thought to understand • Compare HIGHBROW; LOWBROW.

mid·dle·brow /ˈmɪd·l̩.braʊ/ *n* [C] *esp. disapproving* • A **middlebrow** is a person who enjoys middlebrow music, literature, art or films. • Compare HIGHBROW.

mid·dle·man /ˈmɪd·l̩.mæn/ *n* [C] *pl* **-men** a person who buys goods from a producer and makes a profit by selling them to a shop or a user • *One way to lower the price would be to* **cut out** *the middleman and buy directly from the factory.*

mid·dle·weight /ˈmɪd·l̩.weɪt/ *n* [C] a boxer whose weight is between **light heavyweight** and WELTERWEIGHT

mid·dling /ˈmɪd·l̩.ɪŋ, -lɪŋ/ *adj* [not gradable] *infml* medium or average; neither very good nor very bad • *a middling attitude* • *a fat man of about middling height* • *It was a* **disappointingly** *middling performance of 'Anthony and Cleopatra'* • *The TV adaptation of his book is* **fair to** *middling – I've certainly seen better.*

mid·dy /ˈmɪd·i/ *n* [C] *Aus* a beer glass of medium size, which contains 285 ml

mid·field /ˈmɪd·fiːld/ *n* the central area of a sports field, or a central structure of a sports team • *Simon's a defender, but I always play* **in** *midfield.* [U] • *Arsenal's defence were strong, but their midfield fell apart in the first five minutes of the match.* [C]

mid·field·er /£ˌmɪdˈfiːl·dəʳ, $-dɚ/ *n* [C] • *Inter Milan have signed two new midfielders for the start of the season.*

midge /mɪdʒ/ *n* [C] a small fly which flies in groups, and sometimes bites

midg·et /ˈmɪdʒ·ɪt/ *adj* [before n; not gradable] very small; much smaller than usual • *a midget submarine* • *a midget car* • *(Am)* Midget sports are organized competitions for children: *Tyler wasn't interested in signing up for midget football.*

midg·et /ˈmɪdʒ·ɪt/ *n* [C] • A midget is a very small person.

MIDI sys·tem /ˈmɪd·i/ *n* [C] a piece of high-quality electronic equipment for playing music that usually includes a **CD player**, a **cassette player** etc. and is larger than a **mini-system**

mid·lands /ˈmɪd·ləndz/ *n* [U] **The Midlands** the central part of England, including the cities of Birmingham, Coventry, Nottingham and Derby • *There is a lot of manufacturing industry in the Midlands.*

mid·lands /ˈmɪd·ləndz/, **mid·land** /ˈmɪd·lənd/ *adj* [not gradable] • *You can tell he comes from Birmingham – he's got a real midlands accent.*

mid·morn·ing /£ˌmɪdˈmɔː·nɪŋ, $ˈmɔːr-/ *adj* [before n], *adv* [not gradable] in the middle of the morning • *a midmorning coffee break*

mid·night /ˈmɪd·naɪt/ *n* [U] 12 o'clock in the middle of the night • *There's a great film on TV* **at** *midnight.* • *The midnight film tonight is 'Death in Venice'.* • *(Br) The children raided the fridge for a* **midnight feast** (= secret late night meal). • The **midnight sun** is the sun when seen in the middle of the night in summer in the ARCTIC or ANTARCTIC (= the parts of the world furthest to the north and the south). • LP **Time**

mid·point /ˈmɪd·pɔɪnt/ *n* [C usually sing] a point half the distance along something, esp. a line, or a point in the middle of a period of time • *The driveway is 20 m long, so the midpoint must be at 10m.* • *At the midpoint of the football season the team started to lose games.*

mid·riff /ˈmɪd·rɪf/, *Am also* **mid·sec·tion** /ˈmɪd·sek·ʃən/ *n* [C] the part of the human body between the chest and the waist • *She wore a short T-shirt that revealed her midriff.*

mid·ship·man /ˈmɪdˌʃɪp·mən/ *n* [C] *pl* **-men** (the rank of) a person training to become an officer in a navy

mid·sized /ˈmɪd·saɪzd/, **mid–size** /ˈmɪd·saɪz/ *adj* [not gradable] *esp. Am* (esp. of organizations or vehicles) neither large nor small • *a midsized family car* • *She owns two or three midsized companies in Oregon.*

midst /mɪdst, mɪtst/ *n* [U] in the middle of or surrounded by • *In the midst of the endless coniferous forest stood a single group of oak trees.* • *She caught sight of Johnny in their midst* (= among them), *laughing and talking.* • *(fig.) I'm afraid I'm too busy – I'm in the midst of* (= busy with) *writing up a report.* • *"In the midst of life we are in death"* (Book of Common Prayer, burial service, 1662)

midst /mɪdst, mɪtst/ *prep literary* • *The summit of the mountain appeared midst* (= among) *the clouds.*

mid·stream /ˌmɪdˈstriːm/ *n* [U] the middle of a river where the water flows fastest • *They slowly paddled the boat into midstream.* • *(fig.) She interrupted him* **in** *midstream* (= while he was still speaking) *to ask a question.*

mid·sum·mer /£ˌmɪdˈsʌm·əʳ, $-ɚ/ *n* [U] the middle of summer, or the particular day of the year on which it is light for the longest length of time (21 June in northern parts of the world, 22 December in southern parts of the world) • *Midsummer is usually a good time for a holiday.* • *It's midsummer sometime this week, isn't it?* • **Midsummer('s) Day** *is 24 June.*

mid·term /£ˈmɪd·tɜːm, $-tɜːrm/ *n* [U] the middle of the period when a government is in office • *The governing party usually does badly in midterm (by-elections).* • Midterm is also *Am for* **half term**. See at HALF.

mid·way MIDDLE /ˌmɪdˈweɪ/ *adv* [not gradable] in the middle between two places or in the middle of a process or period of time • *Leeds is midway* **between** *London and Edinburgh.* • *She stopped working midway through her pregnancy.*

mid·way AMUSEMENT /ˈmɪdˌweɪ/ *n* [C] *Am* a part of a FUNFAIR, CIRCUS etc. where there are games of skill and other amusements • *Some people go to the state fair to see the livestock, but I prefer the midway.*

mid·week /ˌmɪdˈwiːk/ *n* [U] the middle of the week • *By midweek the situation had become worrying.* • *Midweek prices are $10 cheaper.* • *The magazine comes out midweek.*

Mid·west /ˌmɪdˈwest/, **Mid·dle West**, **Mid·dle A·mer·i·ca** *n* [U] **the Midwest** a central and northern part of the US which includes Ohio, Indiana, Michigan, Illinois, Wisconsin, Iowa, Minnesota, Nebraska, Missouri and Kansas • *A tornado has destroyed grain crops across much of the Midwest.*

mid·wife /ˈmɪd·waɪf/ *n* [C] *pl* **midwives** /ˈmɪd·waɪvz/ a person, usually a woman, who is trained to help women when they are giving birth to children

mid·wif·er·y /£mɪdˈwɪf·ər·i, $ˈ-ɚ-/ *n* [U] • *At nursing college she specialized in midwifery.*

mid·winter /£ˌmɪdˈwɪn·tər, $-t̬ɚ/ *n* [U] the middle of the winter, or the particular day of the year on which it is light for the shortest period of time (22 December in northern parts of the world, 21 June in southern parts of the world) • *Temperatures can drop well below freezing in midwinter.* • *They celebrate midwinter by lighting candles.*

mien /miːn/ *n* [C] *literary* a person's appearance, esp. the typical expression on their face • *His aristocratic mien and smart clothes singled him out.*

miffed /mɪft/ *adj infml* annoyed, esp. at someone's behaviour towards you • *She hadn't phoned for a week and I was getting quite miffed.*

might MAY /maɪt/ *past simple of* MAY (esp. when reporting what someone has said, thought, asked etc.) • *I brought him some sandwiches because I thought he might be hungry.* • *Very politely the little boy asked if he might have another piece of cake* (= he said "May I have another piece of cake, please?".

might POSSIBILITY /maɪt/ *v aux* [+ infinitive without *to*; not *be mighting*] he/she/it **might** used to express the possibility that something will happen or be done, or is true, although not very likely; MAY POSSIBILITY • *I might come and visit you in America next year, if I can save enough money.* • *Don't go any closer – it might be dangerous/it mightn't be safe.* • *He's very fast and in this race he might* **even** *finish in the top three.* • *Ask your father – he might* **just** *have £10* (= there is a slight possibility that he has £10). • *Driving so fast, he might* **have** *had a nasty accident* (= it could have happened but it did not). • *Don't blame him – it might* **have** *been* (= there is a possibility that it was) *an accident.* • *The rain might* **have** *stopped* (= it is possible that it has stopped) *by now.* • *(esp. humorous or disapproving) And who might you be* (= Who are you)? • *There's no point now in regretting the* **might-have-beens** (= positive things that could have been achieved, but were not achieved in fact). • Traditionally, there is a difference between *might have* and *may have*. *Might have* means that there was a possibility in the past but it no longer exists: *You shouldn't have gone back into the burning building – you might have been badly burnt* (= but luckily you weren't). *May have* means that the possibility still exists: *I last saw him going back into that burning building – he may have been badly hurt* (= we don't know yet whether he has been or not). *However, it is now quite common to use might have for situations that are still not certain: The rain might have stopped by now.* • LP **Auxiliary verbs**

might PERMISSION /maɪt/ *v aux* [+ infinitive without *to*; not *be mighting*] he/she/it **might** *Br fml* used as a more polite form of *may* when asking for permission • *Might I ask a question?* • *I wonder if I might have a quick look at your newspaper?* • Might I **ask/inquire/know** etc. is sometimes used in questions to show disapproval by being more polite than is expected: *And what are you doing in there, might I ask?*

might SUGGESTION /maɪt/ *v aux* [+ infinitive without *to*; not *be mighting*] he/she/it **might** used to make a suggestion or suggest a possibility in a polite way • *You might like to try a little more basil in the sauce next time.* • *I thought you might like to join me for dinner.*

might SHOULD /maɪt/ *v aux* [+ infinitive without *to*; not *be mighting*] he/she/it **might** used to suggest, esp. angrily, what someone should do to be pleasant, correct, polite etc. • *You might at least try to look like you're enjoying yourself!* • *That woman was so rude – she might* **have** *apologized!* • *"I've asked the boss to dinner tonight." "Well, you might* **have** *told me (before/sooner)!"* • *I* **might have known** *he'd still be in bed at noon* (= I should have known, because it is typical of him).

might INTRODUCE /maɪt/ *v aux* [+ infinitive without *to*; not *be mighting*] he/she/it **might** MAY INTRODUCE • *Leeds might be an excellent team,* **but** *today they played appallingly.* • *Paris might be a wonderful city,* **but** *it's not somewhere I'd like to live.*

might POWER /maɪt/ *n* [U] power, strength or force • *Pizarro defeated the might of the Inca Empire with only a few hundred men.* • *She struggled* **with all** *her might to free herself from under the car.* • *They shouted* **with might and main** (= as hard as they could) *but nobody came to rescue them.*

might·y /£ˈmaɪ·ti, $-t̬i/ *adj, adv* **-ier, -iest** • *It was possible to hear the mighty* (= very large and powerful) *missiles falling on the city.* • *In the next game they will face the mighty* (= very successful and famous) *Redskins.* • *Through the fields flows the mighty* (= extremely large and important) *River Po.* • *(esp. Am infml) The company are offering to raise salaries by 12% – now that's a mighty* (= very) *generous deal.*

might·i·ly /£ˈmaɪ·tɪ·li, $-t̬ɪ-/ *adv literary* • *He spent ten years struggling mightily* (= with great effort) *with the bureaucracy.*

might·n't /ˈmaɪ·tənt/ *short form of* might not • *It mightn't be such a bad thing if we postponed the meeting till next week.*

might've /£ˈmaɪ·təv, $-t̬əv/ *short form of* might have • *Do you think she might've taken it with her?*

mi·graine /£ˈmiː·greɪn, $ˈmaɪ-/ *n* (a) severe continuous pain in the head, often with vomiting and difficulty in seeing • *Do you suffer from migraine?* [U] • *Considering the amount of stress she's under, it's not surprising she gets migraines/a migraine so often.* [C] • *I've been getting more migraine headaches since working on the computer.*

mi·grate /maɪˈgreɪt/ *v* [I] to move from one place to another • *Cancer-causing agents could migrate* **from** *your plastic container* **into** *your food while it's in the microwave.* • *(fig.) Trade is migrating* **from** *local shops* **to** *the larger out-of-town stores.* • When an animal migrates it travels to a different place, esp. when the season changes: *These animals migrate annually in search of food.* ○ *In September these birds migrate 2000 miles south* **to** *a warmer climate.* ○ *Young salmon migrate long distances but return to their place of birth to breed.* ○ *Migrating* **birds** *flying over the area are shot in large numbers.* • If people migrate they travel in large numbers to a new place to live temporarily: *Mexican farmworkers migrate* **into** *the US each year to find work at harvest time.*

mi·grant /ˈmaɪ·grənt/ *n* [C] • *The birds that gather along the North African coast are winter migrants from Scandinavia.* • *The cities are full of migrants looking for work.* • *Migrant* **workers** *are cheap to employ.*

mi·gra·tion /maɪˈgreɪ·ʃən/ *n* • *Fish migrations are usually back* **to** *their breeding grounds.* [C] • *Mass migration of poverty-struck farmers* **into** *the cities has brought yet more problems for the authorities.* [U] • Compare **immigration** at IMMIGRANT; **emigration** at EMIGRATE.

mi·gra·tor·y /£ˈmaɪ·grə·tri, £maɪˈgreɪ·tər·i, $-tɔːr-/ *adj* [not gradable] • Migratory means having the characteristic of migrating regularly: *migratory birds* ○ *the migratory patterns of fish*

mike /maɪk/, *Am also* **mic** *n* [C] *infml for* MICROPHONE

mild SLIGHT /maɪld/ *adj* **-er, -est** not violent, severe or extreme; slight • *She can't accept even mild criticism of her work.* • *With mild surprise we realized we were almost home already.* • *He has suffered a mild heart attack – nothing too serious.* • If food or the flavour of food is described as mild, it is not very strong: *He doesn't like a hot spicy curry – he prefers a mild one.* ○ *The sauce has a* *mild flavour.* • Mild weather is not very cold or not as cold as usual: *We've had a mild winter this year.*

mild /maɪld/ *n* [U] • In the UK, mild is a dark-coloured beer that does not have a very strong or bitter taste: *Can I get you a* **pint** *of mild?* • Compare BITTER [TASTE].

mild·ly /ˈmaɪld·li/ *adv* • *We were mildly surprised to see him again so soon.*

mild·ness /ˈmaɪld·nəs/ *n* [U] • *a cheese of unacceptable mildness*

mild [GENTLE] /maɪld/ *adj* **-er, -est** gentle and calm • *a shy, mild sort of guy* • *a* **mild-mannered** *philosophy professor*

mild·ly /ˈmaɪld·li/ *adv* • *"I think you've made a mistake," he said mildly.*

mild·ness /ˈmaɪld·nəs/ *n* [U] • *mildness of manner*

mil·dew /£ˈmɪl·dju:, $-du:/ *n* [U] a soft usually white, green or black area caused by a FUNGUS that sometimes grows on things such as plants, food, paper or buildings, usually if the conditions are warm and wet • *The walls have mildew on them where the rain has been getting in.*

mil·dewed /£ˈmɪl·dju:d, $-du:d/ *adj* • *mildewed rose bushes*

mile /maɪl/ *n* [C] a unit of distance equal to 1760 YARDS or 1·6 kilometres • *a ten-mile drive* • *The nearest town is ten miles away/a ten-mile drive away.* • *The speed limit is 30 miles* **an/per** *hour.* • Miles is also used to mean a very long way: *From the hilltop we could see for miles and miles in every direction.* ○ *In my weakened state, even the telephone on the table seemed miles away.* • *(esp. Br)* If you are **miles away** you are not aware of what is happening around you because you are thinking about something else. • *British restaurant food is better* **by miles** (= much better) *than it used to be 20 years ago.* • **Miles from anywhere/nowhere** means a long distance from other houses or a town: *They live miles from nowhere in the the middle of the countryside.* • *No Gerry, that's* **miles too** (= much too) *expensive!* • If you **can see/tell** something **a mile off** you notice it easily and quickly: *I can always tell an American a mile off.* • If something **stands/sticks out a mile** it is very obvious or easy to see: *His lack of experience sticks out a mile.* ○ *A concrete skyscraper in a small village would stick out a mile.* • [LP] Units

mile·age, *Am and Aus also* **mi·lage** /ˈmaɪ·lɪdʒ/ *n* [U] • Mileage is the distance that a vehicle has travelled or the distance that it can travel using a particular amount of fuel: *'What's the mileage on your car?' 'Oh, about 40 000'.* ○ *Smaller cars have better mileage and so cost less to run.* • Mileage (also **mileage allowance**) is also the amount of money that you are paid or that you must pay for each mile you travel: *If I use my own car for company business, I get a mileage allowance of 40p per mile.* ○ *It cost £30 a day to rent the car, but you got* **unlimited** *mileage* (= no charge for the miles travelled). • *(fig. infml) There's no mileage* **in** (= advantage to be had from) *complaining to the Director – she'll just ignore you.*

mile·o·met·er *Br and Aus, Br also* **mi·lo·met·er** /£maɪˈlɒm·ɪ·təʳ, $-ˈlɑ:·mɪ·t̬ɚ/, *Am or specialized* **od·o·met·er** *n* [C] a device in a vehicle that measures and shows the distance it travels • [PIC] **Meters and gauges**

mile·stone /£ˈmaɪl·stəʊn, $-stoʊn/, **mile·post** /£ˈmaɪl·pəʊst, $-poʊst/ *n* [C] a stone or post at the side of the road on which is marked the distance to various places, esp. to the nearest large town, or *(fig.)* an important event in the development or history of something or in someone's life • *(fig.) At the time, the shooting seemed like a fateful milestone on the road to war.* • *(fig.) He felt that moving out from his parents' home was a real milestone in his life.*

mi·lieu /£mɪˈljɜ:, $mi:lˈjɜ:/ *n* [C] *pl* **milieus** or **milieux** /£mɪˈljɜ:, $mi:lˈjɜ:/ the people, physical and social conditions and events which provide a background in which someone acts or lives • *It is a study of the social and cultural milieu in which Michelangelo lived and worked.*

mil·it·ant /ˈmɪl·ɪ·tᵊnt/ *adj* active, determined and often willing to use force • *The group has taken a militant position on the abortion issue and is refusing to compromise.* • *Militant union extremists are threatening to bring down the government.*

mil·it·ant /ˈmɪl·ɪ·tᵊnt/ *n* [C] • *Militants within the party are demanding radical reforms.*

mil·it·ant·ly /ˈmɪl·ɪ·tᵊnt·li/ *adv*

mil·it·anc·y /ˈmɪl·ɪ·tᵊnt·si/ *n* [U] • *The group has always been characterised by an uncompromising militancy.* • *He's a mild-mannered man not known for his militancy.*

mil·it·ar·y /ˈmɪl·ɪ·tri, $-ter·i/ *adj* [not gradable] relating to or belonging to the armed forces • *military spending* • *foreign military intervention* • *military targets* • *military forces* • *military uniform* • *(fig.) The business is run with an almost military* (= with very careful) *attention to detail and discipline.* • A **military academy** is a place where soldiers are trained to become officers. • A **military academy** is also a private school in the US that expects obedience to rules, has uniforms and is generally run like the armed forces. • A **military band** is a group of musicians within the armed forces who play esp. marching and military music: *Military bands usually play brass, woodwind and percussion instruments.* • **Military honours** are ceremonies performed by soldiers to honour a king, queen or other important person or to honour someone important who has died: *The Colonel was buried with* **full** *military honours.* • The **Military Police** are the police force within the armed forces: *He joined the Military Police.* ○ *Two off-duty soldiers were stopped and questioned by a* **military policeman** *(abbreviation* **MP**). • *All young people between 17 and 19 have to do* **military service** (= be trained in the armed forces) *for a year.* • *(esp. Am)* The **military-industrial complex** is the armed forces and the industries that supply them, esp. considered as a strong influence on government decisions and actions: *He imagines there is a right-wing conspiracy organized by the CIA and the military-industrial complex to maneuver the country into another war.*

mil·i·tar·i·ly /ˌmɪl·ɪˈter·ɪ·li/ *adv* [not gradable] • *The vote was against intervening militarily.*

mil·it·ar·y /ˈmɪl·ɪ·tri, $-ter·i/ *pl n* • *The US* **military** (= armed forces) *are opposing the cuts in spending.*

mil·it·ar·i·sm /£ˈmɪl·ɪ·tᵊr·ɪ·zᵊm, $-t̬ɚ-/ *n* [U] *disapproving* • Militarism is the belief that it is necessary to have strong armed forces and that they should be used in order to win political or economic advantages.

mil·it·ar·ist /£ˈmɪl·ɪ·tᵊr·ɪst, $-t̬ə·rɪst/ *n* [C] *disapproving* • *The militarists* (= people who want more powerful armed forces) *are demanding that the army be expanded.*

mil·it·ar·is·tic /£ˌmɪl·ɪ·tᵊrˈɪs·tɪk, $-t̬əˈrɪs-/ *adj disapproving* • *a militaristic policy/government*

mil·it·ar·ize *obj, Br and Aus usually* **-ise** /£ˈmɪl·ɪ·tᵊr·aɪz, $-t̬ə·raɪz/ *v* [T] • A militarized area, country or organization has a large strong army and other armed forces and many weapons: *North Korea is said to be the world's most heavily militarized country, with over 1 million men in the armed forces.*

mil·it·ate a·gainst *obj* /ˈmɪl·ɪ·teɪt/ *v prep* [T] *fml* (of a situation, event etc.) to make (something) less likely to happen or succeed • *The complexity and costliness of the judicial system militate against justice for the individual.*

mi·li·tia /mɪˈlɪʃ·ə/ *n* [C + sing/pl v] a military force which only operates for some of the time and whose members often have other jobs, used either instead of or to support the official army • *A UN force has been sent in to stop fighting in the city between three rival militias.* • *The government has* **called out** *the militia to help cope with the rioting.*

mi·li·tia·man (*pl* **-men**), **mi·li·tia·wo·man** (*pl* **-women**) /mɪˈlɪʃ·ə·mən, -mæn, -ˌwʊm·ən/ *n* [C]

milk /mɪlk/ *n* [U] the white liquid produced by female mammals as food for their young • *a glass/carton of milk* • *skimmed milk* (= milk with most of the fat removed) • *pasteurized milk* (= milk that has been treated to reduce the risk of disease) • *dried milk* (= milk with the water removed) • *a milk bottle* • *The milk produced by cows, goats and sheep is drunk by humans or made into butter or cheese.* • **Breast/Mother's** *milk is the best nourishment for a baby.* • The white liquid obtained from some plants and trees is also called milk: *coconut milk* • *She's* **full of the milk of human kindness** (= care for the sufferings of others). • *(esp. Aus)* A **milk bar** is a shop which sells milk products, bread and sweets. • **Milk chocolate** is sweet chocolate which contains milk: *biscuits coated with thick milk chocolate* ○ *She brought in a box of sweets, but she had already eaten all the milk chocolates* (= all the ones made with milk chocolate). Compare **plain chocolate** at PLAIN [WITH NOTHING ADDED]. • *(Br)* A **milk float** is a vehicle, often electric-powered, used to deliver milk to people's houses in the UK. • **Milk of magnesia** is a white liquid medicine containing MAGNESIUM, taken to cure slight illness in the stomach. • *(Br infml)* The **milk round** is the series of visits made at a particular time of the year by large companies to colleges to discuss giving jobs to students after they have finished their education. • A **milk run** is a journey that is made often, esp. one that includes many stops: *It was her usual milk run from work to home, with stops at the supermarket, the dry cleaner's and the bank.* • A **milk shake** is a drink made of milk and usually ice cream and fruit, chocolate or some other flavouring, mixed together very fast until it is full of bubbles. • A **milk tooth** is a **baby tooth**. See at BABY. • *(Am)* A **milk truck** is a vehicle used to deliver milk in the US. • *"Yet do I fear thy nature; / It is too full o' the milk of human kindness"* (Shakespeare, Macbeth 1.3) • PIC> **Bottles and flasks, Containers, Vehicles**

milk *(obj)* /mɪlk/ *v* • *Milking a cow by hand is a skilled process.* [T] • *Some goats seem to milk* (=produce milk) *better than others.* [I] • *(fig. disapproving)* To milk something or someone is to get as much money, information, etc. out of them as possible, often in a selfish or dishonest way: *The newspapers milked the story dry.* [T + obj + adj] ○ *Two dishonest directors were found to have milked the company* **of** *several million pounds.* [T] • A **milking machine** is a machine used to take milk from many cows at the same time.

milk·y /ˈmɪl·ki/ *adj* **-ier**, **-iest** • *a cup of milky coffee* (=made with a lot of milk) • *the milky white* (=milk-coloured) *river water* • The **Milky Way** is the paler strip across the sky which you can see at night. It forms part of the GALAXY (=star system) which includes the Earth: *There could be 10 million civilizations in Earth's very own Milky Way!*

milk·man (*pl* **-men**) /ˈmɪlk·mən/ *n* [C] the person who delivers milk (and sometimes eggs, bread, fruit-juice etc.) to your house in the early morning • *Britain is one of the few countries in the world where milk is delivered daily to the doorstep by milkmen.*

mill /mɪl/ *n* [C] a building where grain is crushed into flour • *The mill is still used to grind flour.* • A mill is also a small machine for crushing things into powder: *a pepper mill* ○ *a coffee mill* • A mill is also a factory where a particular substance is produced: *a cotton mill* ○ *a steel mill* ○ *a paper mill* • If you **put** someone **through the mill** you cause them to have a difficult and unpleasant experience, esp. by asking them a lot of difficult questions: *I had the interview this morning – they really put me through the mill.* • *"The mills of God grind slowly, yet they grind exceeding small"* (Freidrich von Logau *Sinngedichte*, 1653) • See also WATERMILL; WINDMILL. • PIC> **Mill**

mill *obj* /mɪl/ *v* [T] • *The grain is still milled locally.* • *(specialized)* To mill metal is to shape it by removing parts from it using a special machine.

mil·ler /£ˈmɪl·əʳ, $-ɚ/ *n* [C] • A miller is a person, esp. in the past, who owned or was in charge of a mill.

mill a·bout/a·round *v adv* [I] (of a group of people) to move about esp. in a confused way within a particular place or area • *The crowd milled hopefully about the exit, waiting for the stars to appear.* • *There were people milling around everywhere.*

mil·len·ni·um /mɪˈlen·i·əm/ *n* [C] *pl* **millennia** /mɪˈlen·i·ə/ or **millenniums** a period of 1000 years • *Big celebrations are planned for the arrival of the next millennium.* • *The corpse had lain preserved in the soil for almost two millennia.* • Compare CENTURY. • LP> **Periods of time**

mil·len·ni·al /mɪˈlen·i·əl/ *adj* [not gradable]

mil·le·pede /ˈmɪl·ɪ·piːd/ *n* [C] a MILLIPEDE

mil·let /ˈmɪl·ɪt/ *n* [U] a grass-like plant, or the small edible seeds from this plant • PIC> **Cereals**

mil·li– /ˈmɪl·ɪ-/ *combining form* 0·001 of the stated unit • *milliamp* • *millijoule*

mil·li·bar /£ˈmɪl·ɪ·bɑːʳ, $-bɑːr/ (*abbreviation* **mb**, *infml* **bar**) *n* [C] a unit of air pressure • *An anticyclone of 1030 millibars is over the British Isles.*

mil·li·gram, *Br also* **mil·li·gramme** /ˈmɪl·ɪ·græm/ (*abbreviation* **mg**) *n* [C] a unit of mass which is equal to 0·001 grams

mil·li·lit·re *Br and Aus, Am* **mil·li·lit·er** /£ˈmɪl·ɪˌliː·təʳ $-t̬ɚ/ (*abbreviation* **ml**) *n* [C] a unit of volume which is equal to 0·001 litres. It is the same as a **cubic centimetre**.

mil·li·met·re *Br and Aus, Am* **mil·li·met·er** /£ˈmɪl·ɪˌmiː·təʳ, $-t̬ɚ/ (*abbreviation* **mm**) *n* [C] a unit of length which is equal to 0·001 metres

mil·lin·er /£ˈmɪl·ɪ·nəʳ, $-nɚ/ *n* [C] a person who makes or sells women's hats

mil·lin·er·y /£ˈmɪl·ɪ·nᵊr·i, $-ner-/ *n* [U] • Millinery is the hats and other goods that are sold by a milliner.

mil·li·on /ˈmɪl·jən, -i·ən/ *determiner* [C], *n*, *pronoun pl* **million** or **millions** (the number) 1 000 000 • *She got eight million dollars for appearing in that film.* • *How much do you reckon their house cost – two million?* • *(infml) He told a few jokes that I've heard a million* (=a lot of) *times.* • *(infml) I've got millions* **of** (=a lot of) *letters to write.* • *(infml) "I've done what you asked."* "**Thanks a million** (=Thankyou very much)!" • *(infml esp. humorous)* If you **look/feel like a million dollars** (*Am also* **bucks**) you look or feel extremely good, often because you are experiencing something luxurious: *"You look a million dollars in that dress, honey!"* • *(infml) My wife's a woman* **in a million** (=a very special woman). • *(infml) You're* **one in a million** (=very special)*!* • *Don't worry – there's a* **one-in-a-million** (=extremely slight) *chance of anything going wrong.* • LP> **Hundred**

mil·li·on·aire, *female also* **mil·li·on·air·ess** /£ˌmɪl·jəˈneəʳ, $-ˈner, £-ˈneə·res, $-ˈner·es/ *n* [C] • A millionaire is a person who has at least 1 000 000 in any country's money or who owns land, buildings, possessions etc. worth this amount: *The harbour was full of millionaires' yachts.* ○ *You want me to buy you a new car – do you think I'm a millionaire or something?*

mil·li·onth /ˈmɪl·jəntθ, -i·əntθ/ *determiner*, *n* [C], *pronoun* • *Coventry City football club counted their millionth supporter through the gates last Saturday.* • *(infml) They're showing the film 'High Noon' tonight for the millionth time* (=having already shown it a lot of times). • *Miraculously, the whole process only takes a millionth* (=one of a million equal parts) **of** *a second.*

mil·li·pede, **mil·le·pede** /ˈmɪl·ɪ·piːd/ *n* [C] a small creature with a long cylindrical body consisting of many parts, each one with two pairs of legs • *Millipedes eat plants and generally move slowly.*

mil·li·sec·ond /ˈmɪl·ɪˌsek·ənd/ (*abbreviation* **ms**, **msec**) *n* [C] a unit of time which is equal to 0·001 seconds • *(fig. infml) You can be there and back in milliseconds* (=a very short time).

mill·pond /£ˈmɪl·pɒnd, $-pɑːnd/ *n* [C] a pool of water which provides the power to make the wheel of a MILL turn round, or *(fig.)* any area of water which is very calm and not moving • *(fig.) The sea that day was* **(like)** *a millpond.* • PIC> **Mill**

mill·stone /£ˈmɪl·stəʊn, $-stoʊn/ *n* [C] one of a pair of large circular flat stones used, esp. in the past, to crush grain in order to make flour, or *(fig.)* a responsibility that is difficult to bear and causes you trouble • *(fig.) The mortgage on his house had become* **(like)** *a* **millstone around** *his* **neck**, *leaving him very little money for anything else.* • PIC> **Mill**

mi·lo·met·er /£maɪˈlɒm·ɪ·təʳ, $-ˈlɑː·mɪ·t̬ɚ/ *n* [C] *Br* a MILEOMETER

mime /maɪm/ *n* the use of bodily movements without speech to communicate emotions and actions or to tell a story • *Two of the play's scenes were enacted entirely in mime.* [U] • *Charades is a game in which you have to convey the title of a famous film or book through mime.* [U] • A mime is also a short play without speech. [C] • A **mime artist** is a person who performs mime in a theatre, film etc.: *Marcel Marceau was a famous mime artist.*

mime *(obj)* /maɪm/ *v* • *The whole of the banquet scene is mimed.* [T] • *Most of the bands that appear on the show just mime* **to** *a recording of their songs* (=pretend to sing/play their music). [I] • *He was miming something at me across the pub but I couldn't understand what he was trying to say.* [T]

mim·et·ic /£mɪˈmet·ɪk, $-ˈmet̬-/ *adj* [not gradable] *specialized* using MIME (=bodily movements without speech) • *Much of the play's action is performed without speech, so the actors have to rely on their mimetic skills.*

mim·et·i·cal·ly /£mɪˈmet·ɪ·kli, $-met̬-/ *adv* [not gradable] *specialized*

mim·ic *obj* /ˈmɪm·ɪk/ *v* [T] **mimicking**, *past* **mimicked** to copy the way in which a particular person usually speaks and moves etc., or the noise that an animal makes, esp. in order to amuse people • *She was mimicking the various people in our office.* • Ⓓ Ⓘ

mim·ic /ˈmɪm·ɪk/ *n* [C] • A mimic is a person who can copy the sounds or movements of people or animals: *She's a brilliant mimic – she can copy anyone.* ○ *I'm not much of a mimic.*

mim·ic·ry /ˈmɪm·ɪ·kri/ *n* [U] • *I've never had much of a talent for mimicry* (=copying people or animals).

min SMALLEST /mɪn/ *n* [C], *adj* [before n] *abbreviation for* MINIMUM • *Min stay – three days.*

min TIME /mɪn/ *n* [C] *abbreviation for* minute • *Cooking time required: 30-35 mins*

min·ar·et /ˌmɪn·əˈret/ *n* [C] a tall thin tower on or near a MOSQUE from which a man calls Muslims to pray

mince *obj* CUT /mɪnts/ *v* [T] to cut (food, esp. meat) into very small pieces, sometimes using a special machine (a mincer) • *Mince two pounds of chicken finely.*

mince *esp. Br and Aus* /mɪnts/, *Am usually, Aus also* **ground beef** *n* [U] • Mince is meat, esp. BEEF (= meat from cattle), which has been cut up into very small pieces. • Mince is also *Am for* MINCEMEAT.

minced /mɪntst/, *Am usually* **ground** *adj* [not gradable] • *minced meat/beef/lamb/(Am) onions*

min·cer *Br and Aus* /£ˈmɪnt·səʳ, $-sɚ/, *Am usually* **meat grind·er** *n* [C] • A mincer is a machine for cutting food, esp. meat, into small bits.

mince WALK /mɪnts/ *v* [I] to walk in an artificial way, with small delicate steps • *He minced across the room in a pair of tight pink trousers.*

minc·ing /ˈmɪnt·sɪŋ/ *adj* • *He's got a rather mincing walk.* • *She took short mincing steps.*

mince *obj* SPEAK /mɪnts/ *v* [T usually in negatives] **mince words** to say things carefully and not in a direct way, esp. in order not to upset people • *The report does* **not** *mince words, describing the situation as 'ludicrous'.* • *They are mincing* **no** *words in their criticism of the organizers of the event.* • **Never** *a woman to mince (her) words, she describes the former minister as "self-centred and arrogant – a total pig".*

minc·ing /ˈmɪnt·sɪŋ/ *adj* • *She found herself irritated by the interviewer's mincing* (= too delicate and not direct enough) *way of asking questions.*

mince·meat /ˈmɪnts·miːt/, *Am also* **mince** *n* [U] a sweet, spicy mixture of small pieces of apple, CURRANTS and other fruit which is eaten, esp. at Christmas, inside pastry cases • *(infml)* If you **make mincemeat of** someone you defeat them very easily, either with words or through physically fighting them: *A decent lawyer would have made mincemeat of them in court.*

mince pie *n* [C] a covered pastry case filled with MINCEMEAT

mind THOUGHTS /maɪnd/ *n* [C] the ability to think, feel emotions and be aware of things, or the way in which a person thinks • *Her mind was so full of what had happened the night before that she could think of little else.* • *Of course I'm telling the truth – you've got such a suspicious mind!* • *I don't think I have a very logical mind.* • *My mind had begun to* **wander** *and I couldn't concentrate on what she was saying.* • *I just said the first thing that* **came into** *my mind.* • *For some reason the words that he said* **stuck in** *my mind.* • *I saw some horrific pictures on the news last night and I can't* **get** *them* **out of** *my mind* (= can't stop thinking about them). • *I'm not quite* **clear in** *my mind about what I'm doing.* • If your mind **goes/is a (complete) blank** you temporarily lose the ability to remember something: *There's that awful moment just before an exam when your mind goes blank.* • If your mind is **on** something, you are thinking about it or giving attention to it: *I couldn't concentrate on my work – my mind was on my mother's illness.* ○ *My mind wasn't on what he was saying so I'm afraid I missed half of it.* • *She's got a lot* **on** *her mind at the moment* (= has many esp. worrying things to think about). • You can refer to a person, esp. a very clever person, as a particular type of mind: *She was one of the most brilliant minds of the last century.* • If someone tells you that a problem you have is **all in the mind** they mean that it doesn't really exist and that you have imagined it: *You're not fat at all – it's all in the mind!* • *I find it hard to* **get** *my* **mind round** (= understand) *such complex issues.* • *(infml) I'd* **go out of** *my* **mind** (= I would feel extremely annoyed and unhappy because bored) *if I had to do her job all day!* • If you **go over** an event that has happened **in your mind** or **turn it over in** your **mind**, you think about it repeatedly: *She would go over the accident again and again in her mind, wishing that she could somehow have prevented it.* • *(esp. humorous)* A machine or other object can be said to **have a mind of its own** if it seems to be controlling the way it behaves or moves, independently of the person using it: *Susan's computer has a mind of its own – it keeps on making data disappear.* • If you receive a piece of information that stops you from worrying about something you might say that it is **a load/weight off** your **mind**: *I'm so relieved that I don't have to do the after-dinner speech – it's such a weight off my mind!* • *She was* **out of** *her* **mind with** *grief* (= extremely unhappy). • *(infml) You must be* **out of** *your* **mind** (= extremely stupid) *paying £200 for one night in a hotel!* • *(infml) I was bored/drunk/stoned* **out of my mind** (= extremely bored/drunk). • If you **put** someone or something **out of** your **mind** you force yourself not to think about them: *It's over, put it out of your mind.* • *If you'd just* **set/put** *your* **mind to** *it* (= direct all your thoughts and attention to it), *I'm sure you could do it.* • Someone or something that **sets/puts** your **mind at rest/ease** stops you from worrying about a particular thing: *I'm so glad you didn't think he was offended by my remarks – it's put my mind at rest.* • *(esp. law)* If someone is **of sound/unsound mind**, they are SANE/INSANE (= not mentally ill/mentally ill). • *He's in a much more positive* **state/frame of mind** (= He's happier) *these days.* • If something **takes** your **mind off** a problem or a pain, it stops you from worrying or thinking about it, often by forcing you to think about other things: *The good thing about running is that it takes my mind off any problems I've got.* ○ *He says that having visitors takes his mind off the pain.* • *(slang)* An experience which is **mind-blowing** fills you with great surprise and is difficult to believe: *It's not a very original film but its special effects are pretty mind-blowing.* • *(infml)* If something is **mind-boggling** or **mind-bending** it is extremely surprising and often difficult to understand or imagine: *That was the film for which she was paid the mind-boggling sum of ten million pounds.* • If a drug is described as **mind-expanding** (also **mind-altering**) it means that it has a strong influence on the mental state, causing feelings of extreme happiness and causing people to consider or understand things in a different way: *mind-expanding drugs such as LSD* • People sometimes say **in** their **mind's eye** meaning in their memory for the appearance of things: *In my mind's eye she remains a little girl of six although she's actually a grown woman.* • If something is **mind-numbing** or **mind-numbingly** boring it is extremely boring: *As a secretary you're given the most mind-numbing of tasks to do.* • **Mind over matter** is the power of the mind to control and influence the body and the physical world generally: *My grandfather firmly believed that he had cured his own cancer through mind over matter.* • *(esp. humorous)* A **mind reader** is a person who knows another person's thoughts without being told them: *If you weren't happy with the situation you should have told me – I'm not a mind reader, you know!* • A person's **mind-set** is their way of thinking and their opinions: *I don't think their relationship will ever work – they're* **of a** *different mind-set.* • *"Hamlet: 'My father – methinks I see my father.' Horatio: 'Where, my lord?' Hamlet: 'In my mind's eye, Horatio.'"* (Shakespeare, Hamlet 1.2)

–mind·ed /-ˈmaɪn·dɪd/ *combining form* • *She's very strong/independent-minded* (=She has a very strong/independent character). • *I don't imagine that he's very politically-minded* (=interested in politics). • *It's an important centre for growing truffles – for the food-minded among you* (=for those who enjoy good food). • See also BROADMINDED.

mind·less /ˈmaɪnd·ləs/ *adj disapproving* • *It's just another film with a load of mindless* (=stupid and meaningless) **violence**. • *Most pop songs have fairly mindless lyrics.* • *I'm afraid it's fairly mindless work* (=not needing any mental effort) *– opening mail and keying data into a computer.*

mindlessly /ˈmaɪnd·lə·sli/ *adv disapproving* • *A group of children started mindlessly hurling stones at passing vehicles.*

mind·less·ness /ˈmaɪnd·lə·snəs/ *n* [U] *disapproving*

mind [MEMORY] /maɪnd/ *n* [U] memory • *I can see his face now but I can't* **call/bring** *his name* **to mind** (=can't remember his name). • If something **puts** you **in mind of** something else it causes you to remember it: *The mention of skiing holidays put me in mind of a travelogue that I saw last week.*

mind [INTENTION] /maɪnd/ *n* [C usually sing] an intention or plan • *Did you* **have** *anything* **in** *mind* (=Were you considering anything) *for Helen's present?* • *I've* **half a mind to/a good mind to** (=It's possible that I will) *go without him if he's going to be such a bore!* • *I haven't* **made up** *my* **mind/made** *my* **mind up** (=made a decision) *where to go yet.* • *My* **mind is made up** (=I have decided) *– I'm leaving!*

mind [OPINION] /maɪnd/ *n* [C usually sing] an opinion • *We're* **of the same/of one mind** (=have the same opinion) *on most political issues.* • *He's got pink walls and a green carpet, which* **to my mind** (=in my opinion) *looks all wrong.*

mind *(obj)* [BE CAREFUL] /maɪnd/ *v esp. Br* to be careful (of); give attention (to) • *The announcement warned Underground passengers to mind the gap.* • *Mind that box – the bottom isn't very strong.* [T] • *Mind* **(that)** *you don't bang your head on the shelf when you stand up.* [+ *(that)* clause] • *Mind the plates don't fall off when you move it!* [+ *(that)* clause] • *Mind* **where** *you're going with that sharp pole – you might kill someone!* [+ *wh-* word] • *Mind* (=Make certain) **(that)** *you take enough money with you.* [+ *(that)* clause] • *(dated) Mind your language* (=Don't use swear words), *young lady!* [T] • People sometimes say 'mind!' or *(Br)* 'mind **out**!' when they want you to move or they want to warn you of danger: *Mind out* (=Move out of the way)*! We're coming through with the stretcher.* [I] • *'Here, mind* (=be more careful)*!' he said when she trod on his foot.* [I] ○ *Mind out* **for** (=Be careful of) *falling rocks when you're on this part of the trail.* [I] • *(Br infml)* People sometimes say **mind how you go** when they say goodbye to someone, meaning 'take care'. • If someone who is present in the same room as you says **don't mind me** they are asking you not to pay any attention to them because they do not want to interrupt what you are doing: *Don't mind me – I'm just sorting out some files here.* • If you say that you have to **mind** your **p's and q's** in a particular situation it means that you have to make an effort to be polite: *I have to mind my p's and q's when I'm with my grandmother.*

mind·ful /ˈmaɪnd·fᵊl/ *adj fml* • If you are mindful of something, you are careful about it or careful not to forget about it: *Mindful* **of** *the poor road conditions, she reduced her speed to 30 mph.* ○ **Ever** *mindful* **of** *her comfort, he had warmed her slippers by the fire.* ○ *Politicians are increasingly mindful* **that** *young voters are turning away from traditional parties.* [+ *that* clause]

mind *obj* [TAKE CARE OF] /maɪnd/ *v* [T] to take care of (someone or something) • *She asked me if I'd mind the children for an hour while she went shopping.* • *My sister has offered to mind the cat while we're away.* • *Could you mind my bag for a moment while I go to the toilet?* • *(infml esp. humorous)* If someone tells you to **mind** your **own business** (abbreviation **MYOB**) they are telling you not to be so interested in other people's private matters: *"Where have you been?" "Mind your own business!"*

mind·er /£ˈmaɪn·dəʳ, $-dɚ/ *n* [C] • A minder is someone who protects another person, esp. a famous person, from danger and unwanted public attention, or who controls what another person says and does: *The actress employed a minder after receiving a number of death threats.* ○ *The President arrived surrounded by his minders.* ○ *His public-relations minder refused to allow him to answer any of the journalists' questions.*

mind *(obj)* [OPPOSE] /maɪnd/ *v* [not *be minding*] (often used in requests and negative sentences) to find annoying or offensive or to oppose • *I don't mind hav***ing** *a dog in the house so long as it's clean and it doesn't smell.* [+ v-*ing*] • *I don't mind his coming home late but I do mind* **being** *woken up by the noise of him crashing around!* [+ v-*ing*] • *(infml) I wouldn't mind* (=I would like) *something to eat, actually.* [T] • *Would you mind turn***ing** (=Please would you turn) *your radio down a little please?* [+ v-*ing*] • *Do you mind* **if** (=Can) *I put the television on?* [+ *wh-* word] • *Do you mind me smok***ing** (=Does my smoking trouble you)*?* [T + obj + v-*ing*] • *I don't mind* **wh***at you wear so long as it's not that awful pink shirt.* [+ *wh-* word] • *If you don't mind, I won't be joining you at the party tonight – I'm just so tired.* [I] • *I'd prefer to stay in tonight, if you don't mind.* [I] • *If you don't mind me say***ing** *so* (=I hope it won't offend you if I say) *I think the curry could be a little hotter next time.* [T + obj + v-*ing*] • *(esp. Br) "Would you like tea or coffee?" "I don't mind – either."* [I] • *(esp. Br) "Shall we go out or stay in?" "I don't mind – it's up to you."* [I] • *"There's plenty more cake if you'd like another piece."* "**I don't mind if I do** (=I'd like some)." • *(esp. dated)* The phrase **do you mind?** is sometimes used to express sudden annoyance with someone for something that they have done or said: *Do you mind? That's my seat you're sitting on!* ○ *Do you mind? There are ladies present who I'm sure don't want to hear that sort of language!*

mind (you) /ˌmaɪndˈjuː/ *adv* [not gradable] although or despite this • *He's very untidy about the house – mind you, I'm not much better.* • *She's fairly rude to her father – mind you, he deserves it most of the time.* • *I know I'm lazy – I did go swimming yesterday, mind.*

mine [BELONGING TO ME] /maɪn/ *pronoun* the one(s) belonging to or connected with me • *"Whose bag is this?" "It's mine."* • *Your skin is lighter than mine.* • *She's an old friend* **of** *mine.* • *"A poor thing, but mine own (Originally 'An ill-favoured thing, sir, but mine own)"* (Shakespeare, As You Like It 5.4)

mine /maɪn/ *determiner old use* • Mine was used in the past instead of 'my' before nouns that begin with a vowel or *h*: *mine eyes* ○ *mine host*

mine [HOLE] /maɪn/ *n* [C] a hole or system of holes in the ground made for the removal of coal, metal, salt etc. by digging • *a coal mine/tin mine/salt mine/diamond mine/gold mine* • *My grandfather used to work* **in/***(Br)* **down** *the mines.* • *He died after falling down a mine* **shaft** (=passage leading down to a mine). • Someone who has a lot of knowledge and is willing to give this knowledge to other people can be called a **mine of information**: *She's a mine of information about the countryside.*

mine *(obj)* /maɪn/ *v* • *They're mining* **for** *salt.* [I] • *Some of the hills are mined* **for** *tin.* [T] • *They mine* (=dig up) *a lot of copper around these parts.* [T] • *(fig.) Polidori, the right-wing politician, is* **mining a rich seam of** (=taking advantage of the high level of) *fear and prejudice.*

min·er /£'maɪ·nər, $-nɚ/ *n* [C] • A miner is a person who works in a mine: *a coal miner*

min·ing /'maɪ·nɪŋ/ *n* [U] • Mining is the industry or activity of removing coal, metal, salt, etc. from the ground by digging: *coal/diamond/salt mining*

mine BOMB /maɪn/ *n* [C] a type of bomb put below the earth or in the sea which explodes when vehicles, ships or people go over it • *He was killed when his tank ran over a mine.* • *The US forces were clearing the surrounding area of mines.* • A **mine detector** is a device which is used to discover whether there are mines in a particular area. • See also LANDMINE.

mine *obj* /maɪn/ *v* [T] • If an area of land or sea is mined it has had this type of bomb hidden in it: *The desert had been heavily mined.*

mine·field /'maɪn·fiːld/ *n* [C] an area of land or water which contains MINES (=bombs), or *(fig.)* a situation or subject which is very complicated and full of hidden problems and dangers • *Much land is still unusable because of the cost and danger of* **clearing** *minefields.* • *(fig.) The judge said that the case had uncovered a legal minefield.* • *(fig.) The report is an attempt to steer a course through a minefield* **of** *ethical problems.*

min·er·al /'mɪn·ər·əl/ *n* [C] a chemical substance such as a rock which is formed naturally in the ground, or any substance which is MINED (=removed from the ground) • **Mineral oil** is an oil obtained from PETROLEUM. • **Mineral water** (*Am also* **bottled water**) is natural water from underground containing dissolved minerals which are believed to be good for your health, and which is usually sold in bottles: *carbonated mineral water* ○ *Many people drink mineral water because they do not want to drink tap water.*

min·er·al·o·gy /ˌmɪn·ə'ræl·ə·dʒi/ *n* [U] • Mineralogy is the study of minerals.

min·er·als /'mɪn·ər·əlz/ *pl n Br dated* cold sweet fizzy drinks without alcohol • *On sale in the shop were sweets, cigarettes and minerals.*

min·e·stron·e (soup) /£ˌmɪn·ɪ'strəʊ·ni, $-'stroʊ-/ *n* [U] a type of Italian soup containing a mixture of vegetables and pasta

mine·sweep·er /£'maɪnˌswiː·pər, $-pɚ/, *infml* **mine·hunt·er** /£'maɪnˌhʌn·tər, $-tɚ/ *n* [C] a ship that is used to discover if MINES (=bombs) are present and to remove them from the sea

ming·le *(obj)* MIX /'mɪŋ·gl̩/ *v* to mix (with); combine • *Any excitement you have at starting a new job is always mingled* **with** *a certain amount of fear.* [T] • *This soup recipe mingles the flavours of orange and ginger very successfully.* [T] • *The two flavours mingle well.* [I]

ming·le BE WITH /'mɪŋ·gl̩/ *v* [I] to be with or among other people, esp. talking to them • *Darling, you've been talking to Roger all evening when you really ought to be mingling* **with** *the other guests.* • *One of the aims of language games is to get students to mingle* **together** *and talk.*

min·gy /'mɪn·dʒi/ *adj* **-ier, -iest** *infml* (of a person) not generous and unwilling to give money, or (of something) smaller than expected • *I only gave five dollars towards his present – do you think that was a bit mingy?* • *The problem with that restaurant is that they give you such mingy (little) portions of food.*

min·i– SMALL /'mɪn·i-/ *combining form* small or less important than others of the same type • *There's a mini-library in each classroom as well as the central library.* • *We took the kids to play mini-golf.* • A **mini-series** is a programme divided into several different parts which is broadcast on television over a short period of time. • A **mini-system** is a very small set of electronic equipment used to play recorded sound and which usually includes a **CD player** and a **cassette player** but not a **record player**.

min·i SKIRT /'mɪn·i/ *n* [C] a MINISKIRT

Min·i CAR /'mɪn·i/ *n* [C] *trademark* a type of small British car very popular in the 1960's • PIC› **Mini**

min·ia·ture /£'mɪn·ɪ·tʃər, $-tʃɚ/ *adj* [before n; not gradable] extremely small • *She was buying miniature furniture for her niece's dolls' house.* • *He looks just like a miniature version of his father.*

min·ia·ture /£'mɪn·ɪ·tʃər, $-tʃɚ/ *n* • *They've got a model village that you can visit, with all the buildings and roads* **in** *miniature.* [U] • A miniature is a very small painting, usually of a person. [C] • A miniature is also any object that is made very much smaller than usual, for example a very small bottle of alcoholic drink or a small model of something much larger: *She got out of her pocket a*

Mini

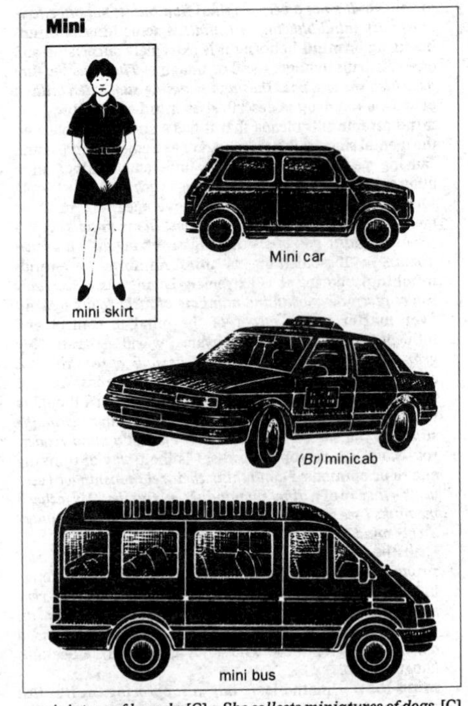

miniature of brandy. [C] ○ *She collects miniatures of dogs.* [C] • *"And every day is a life in miniature"* (from the Eugene O'Neill play *Marco Millions*, 1928)

min·ia·tur·iz·a·tion, *Br and Aus usually* **-i·sa·tion** /£ˌmɪn·ɪ·tʃər·aɪ'zeɪ·ʃən, $-tʃɚ-/ *n* [U] • *It's done by using a miniaturization process/a process of miniaturization.* • *The silicone chip is a classic example of the benefits of miniaturization.*

min·ia·tur·ized, *Br and Aus usually* **-ised** /£'mɪn·ɪ·tʃər·aɪzd, $-tʃɚ-/ *adj* [not gradable] • *Our latest computer is, in fact, simply a miniaturized version of the previous model, with the advantage that it can be fitted into a briefcase.*

min·i·bus /'mɪn·ɪ·bʌs/ *n* [C] a small bus in which there are seats for about ten people • *We used the school minibus to take us to basketball matches.* • PIC› **Mini**

min·i·cab /'mɪn·ɪ·kæb/ *n* [C] *Br* a TAXI which can only be called by telephone or from a special office • *Shall I phone for a minicab?* • PIC› **Mini**

min·i·cam /'mɪn·ɪ·kæm/ *n* [C] *esp. Am* a small **video camera** used esp. by television news reporters

min·i·com·put·er /£'mɪn·ɪ·kəmˌpjuː·tər, $-t̬ɚ/ *n* [C] a computer of medium power which is used esp. by businesses

Min·i Disc *n* [C] *trademark* a very small plastic disc on which high-quality sound, esp. music, is recorded

min·im *Br and Aus* /'mɪn·ɪm/, *Am usually* **half note** *n* [C] *specialized* a musical note with a time value equal to half a SEMIBREVE

min·i·mum /'mɪn·ɪ·məm/ (*abbreviation* **min**) *n* [C] *pl* **minimums** or *specialized* **minima** /'mɪn·ɪ·mə/ the smallest amount or number allowed or possible • *Wage increases are being* **kept to** *a minimum in many companies because of the recession.* • *She hoped that her fiftieth birthday would pass with the minimum* **of** *fuss.* • *Being a lazy child, he did the* **bare** *minimum of work at school.* • *We need a minimum* **of** *ten people to play this game.* • *(specialized) They plotted the temperature minima for the whole month.* • Compare MAXIMUM.

min·i·mum /'mɪn·ɪ·məm/ (*abbreviation* **min**) *adj* [not gradable] • *The preparatory certificate is the minimum qualification required to teach English in most language schools.* • *Eighteen is the minimum age for entering most nightclubs.* • *She reckons that you should do three exercise classes a week minimum to get any of the benefits.* • A **minimum wage** is the smallest amount of money that an employer is allowed to pay someone who works for them, as permitted by law or by special agreement. • Compare MAXIMUM.

min·i·mal /ˈmɪn·ɪ·məl/ *adj* [not gradable] • *Fortunately there were no injuries and damage to the factory was minimal* (=very slight). • *According to the clothes show, the look for the autumn is plain fabrics, simple lines and minimal* (=very little) *jewellery.* • Compare **maximal** at MAXIMUM.

min·i·mal·i·sm /ˈmɪn·ɪ·mə·lɪ·zᵊm/ *n* [U] • In art, design and theatre, minimalism is a theory or style which involves using the smallest range of materials, colours etc. possible and only the most simple shapes or designs: *The minimalism of Samuel Beckett's plays can be extraordinarily powerful.*

min·i·mal·ist /ˈmɪn·ɪ·mə·lɪst/ *adj* [not gradable], *n* • Minimalist is used to refer to an artist, designer etc. who bases their work on the theory or style of minimalism: *The set for the ballet is minimalist – three white walls and a chair.* ○ *The painter, Ad Reinhardt, was a minimalist.* [C] • If you have minimalist ideas or a minimalist way of dealing with a situation you take as little action as possible and do not become too involved in any particular situation: *The party's traditional minimalist* **approach** *to economic policy is now moving towards one of more state intervention.*

min·i·mal·ly /ˈmɪn·ɪ·mə·li/ *adv* [not gradable] • *The factory was only minimally* (=slightly) *damaged by the fire.*

min·i·mize *obj, Br and Aus usually* **-ise** /ˈmɪn·ɪ·maɪz/ *v* [T] • To minimize something is to reduce to the least possible level or amount: *We do all that we can to minimize the risk of infection.* ○ *Environmentalists are doing everything within their power to minimize the impact of the oil spill.* • To minimize something is also to make it seem less important or smaller than it really is: *She accused the government of minimizing the suffering of thousands of people.* ○ *The important thing in an interview is to make the most of your strengths and minimize your weaknesses.* • Compare **maximize** at MAXIMUM.

min·i·miz·a·tion /ˌmɪn·ɪ·maɪˈzeɪ·ʃᵊn/ *n* [U] • Compare **maximization** at MAXIMUM.

min·ing /ˈmaɪ·nɪŋ/ *n* [U] See at MINE [HOLE]

min·ion /ˈmɪn·jən/ *n* [C] *often disapproving* a person who only exists in order to do what another person orders them to do • *Hovering around the rock star are her minions, putting each blond curl and black eyelash in place.*

min·i·pill /ˈmɪn·ɪ·pɪl/ *n* a type of pill containing only PROGESTERONE which women can take every day to prevent them from becoming pregnant when they have sex

min·i·scule /ˈmɪn·ɪ·skjuːl/ *adj* MINUSCULE

min·i·skirt /£ˈmɪn·ɪˌskɜːt, $-skɜːrt/, **min·i** *n* [C] a very short skirt, often tight • [PIC] **Clothes, Mini**

min·is·ter [POLITICIAN] /£ˈmɪn·ɪ·stəʳ, $-stɚ/ *n* [C] a member of the government in Britain and many other countries who is in charge of, or has an important position in a particular department • *the foreign/health minister* • *the Minister of Education* • Compare SECRETARY [GOVERNMENT]. • (P)

min·i·ste·ri·al /£ˌmɪn·ɪˈstɪə·ri·əl, $-ˈstɪr·i-/ *adj* [not gradable] • *ministerial responsibilities*

min·i·stry /ˈmɪn·ɪ·stri/ *n* [C] • A ministry is a department of the government led by a minister: *the Ministry of Defence/Agriculture/Finance*

min·is·ter [COUNTRY'S REPRESENTATIVE] /£ˈmɪn·ɪ·stəʳ, $-stɚ/ *n* [C] *specialized* a person below the rank of AMBASSADOR whose job is to represent his or her country in a foreign country • *the Belgian minister in Madrid* • (P)

min·is·ter [PRIEST] /£ˈmɪn·ɪ·stəʳ, $-stɚ/ *n* [C] a priest in particular parts of the Christian church • *The Reverend Phillip Foster was inducted as minister of the local Baptist church in 1992.* • (P)

min·i·stry /ˈmɪn·ɪ·stri/ *n* [U] • *He exercised a preaching and teaching ministry in that town for over 40 years.* • **The ministry** is the name for the priesthood in some parts of the Christian Church: *In 1985 he decided to* **go into/leave** *the ministry.*

min·is·ter to *obj v prep* [T] *literary* to give help to or care for (people, esp. ill people) • *The priest ministers to his flock* (=cares for the people who go to his church). • *(humorous) I spent the most part of the morning ministering to my sick husband.* • *(Br humorous)* A woman who takes care of people who are ill is sometimes referred to as a **ministering angel.** • *"When pain and anguish wring the brow/ A ministering angel thou!"* (Sir Walter Scott *Marmion*, 1808)

min·i·stra·tions /ˌmɪn·ɪˈstreɪ·ʃᵊnz/ *pl n literary* • *(humorous) I'm afraid that plant seems to be dying in spite of my loving ministrations* (=attention).

mink /mɪŋk/ *n* [U] the fur of a small brown animal from Europe, N America and Asia which can be made into expensive clothes • *a mink* **coat**

min·now /£ˈmɪn·əʊ, $-oʊ/ *n* [C] a very small fish found in lakes and rivers or *(fig.)* an unimportant organization or person with little influence or power • *The minnows of the second division meet the big fish in tonight's football cup finals.*

mi·nor [UNIMPORTANT] /£ˈmaɪ·nəʳ, $-nɚ/ *adj* having little importance, influence or effect, esp. when compared with other things of the same type • *An appendectomy is a fairly minor operation – I don't think there's any need to worry.* • *He was a minor poet of the sixteenth century – you probably won't have heard of him.* • *She'd had one or two minor parts in films but nothing really interesting.* • *It's only a minor problem – I'll soon put it right.* • *He always resented the fact that he'd been to a minor university and not one of the famous ones.* • *The increase in crime has been in* **relatively** *minor offences such as traffic violations and petty theft.* • *She suffered minor* **injuries** *in the accident – a few cuts and bruises.* • *It was a comparatively minor* **adjustment** *but it was still quite expensive.* • *These restrictions have proved only a minor* **inconvenience** *to companies trading in the area.* • *No casualties were reported in the explosion, which caused only minor* **damage.** • *The trials of the new machine have gone well, with only minor* **modifications** *necessary for the production version.* • Compare MAJOR [IMPORTANT].

mi·nor [YOUNG PERSON] /£ˈmaɪ·nəʳ, $-nɚ/ *n* [C] a person who is below the age at which he or she legally becomes an adult • *Six years ago he was accused of having sex with a minor.*

mi·nor [MUSIC] /£ˈmaɪ·nəʳ, $-nɚ/ *adj* [not gradable] (of music) written using a SCALE (=range of eight notes) in which there is typically a half TONE (=difference between two notes) between the second and third and usually between the fifth and sixth notes and a whole tone between each of the others • *Music written in a minor* **key** *often sounds sad or moody.* • *She played a piano concerto* **in** *D minor.* [after n] • Compare MAJOR. • [PIC] **Music**

mi·no·ri·ty /£maɪˈnɒr·ɪ·ti, $ˈnɑːr·ə·ţi/ *n* a smaller number or part • *It's a privileged minority* **of** *people who can afford two homes.* • *It's only a tiny minority* **of** *people who are causing the violence.* • *There were a few children with single parents at my school but they were very much* **in the/a** *minority* (=there were not many). • *There's a section in the book store that caters for minority* **interests** (=subjects that interest only a few people). • A minority (or **minority group**) is also any small group in society that is different from the rest with reference to their race, religion or political beliefs: *ethnic/religious minorities* [C] • If you say you are **in a minority of one** you mean you are the only person who has your opinion, idea, etc. • Compare MAJORITY [NUMBER].

min·ster /£ˈmɪn·stəʳ, $-stɚ/ *n* (esp. in Britain) used in the name of a large or important church • *York Minster*

min·strel /ˈmɪnt·strəl/ *n* [C] (between the 11th and 15th centuries) a travelling musician and singer • *a wandering minstrel* • *(Am)* Minstrel is also used as a word for a singer. • A **minstrel show** was, in the past, a type of show in which white performers made themselves look like black people.

mint [PLANT] /mɪnt/ *n* a herb whose leaves have a strong fresh smell and taste and are used for giving flavour to food • *sprigs of mint* [U] ○ *mint tea* ○ *mint-flavoured chewing gum* ○ *mint-choc-chip ice cream* (=mint-flavoured ice cream with very small bits of chocolate in) • A mint is also a sweet which has this strong fresh flavour: *a packet of mints* [U] ○ *chocolate mints* [C] • *(esp. Am)* A **mint julep** is an alcoholic COCKTAIL (=mixed drink) containing WHISKY, crushed ice, sugar and pieces of mint. • *(esp. Br and Aus)* **Mint sauce**/*(Am usually)* **mint jelly** is a sauce made of vinegar, sugar and mint cut into very small pieces, which is often served with LAMB (=meat from young sheep). • [PIC] **Herbs and spices**

mint [COIN FACTORY] /mɪnt/ *n* [C] a place where the new coins of a country are made • *In Britain the mint is called the Royal Mint.* • *(fig. infml)* A mint is also an extremely large amount of money: *If his books sell in the States he'll* **make** *a mint.*

mint /mɪnt/ *adj* [before n; not gradable] • Mint stamps, coins etc. are ones which have not been used: *He bought the complete set of mint stamps and hoped to collect used ones later.* ○ *A collector would pay $500 for a mint copy.* • If something is **in mint condition** it is perfect, as if new: *CD player for sale, brand new and in mint condition – £150.*

mint *obj* /mɪnt/ *v* [T] • To mint a coin is to make it. • To mint a new phrase or word is to invent it.

mi·nus SUBTRACTION /ˈmaɪ·nəs/ *prep* reduced by (the stated number) • *What is 57 minus 39?* • *Eleven minus six equals five is written in figures as 11 – 6 = 5.* • *That will be £1500 minus the deposit of £150 that you have already paid.* • *(infml) We're minus a chair for Ian – could you get one from the other room?* • Compare PLUS ADDITION. • LP〉 **Mathematics**

mi·nus /ˈmaɪ·nəs/ *n* [C] *pl* **minuses** • A minus or a **minus sign** is the sign – which is put between two numbers to show that the second number is to be subtracted from the first, or in front of one number to show that it has a value of less than 0. • See also MINUS DISADVANTAGE.

mi·nus /ˈmaɪ·nəs/ *adj* [not gradable] • Minus a number is that number or amount less than zero: *Minus 9 is nine less than zero.* • *My bank balance isn't too good at the moment – it's definitely in minus figures* (=I owe money). • If the temperature is minus three/five/six it is three/five/six degrees Celsius below the temperature at which water freezes, or three/five/six degrees Fahrenheit below zero: *Temperatures could fall to minus eight tonight.* • If a piece of written work is given a mark such as B minus (B-) by a teacher it is of a standard which is slightly below the B mark: *I'm improving! I got B plus for last week's composition and A minus for this.* • See also NEGATIVE BELOW ZERO.

mi·nus DISADVANTAGE /ˈmaɪ·nəs/ *n* [C] *pl* **minuses** a disadvantage or a bad feature • *Having to travel such a long way to work is a definite minus.* • See also MINUS SUBTRACTION.

mi·nus /ˈmaɪ·nəs/ *adj* • *One of the minus* (=disadvantageous) *points of working at home is that you lack the social contact with other people.*

min·us·cule, **min·i·scule** /ˈmɪn·ɪ·skjuːl/ *adj* extremely small • *For his first course all he got was two minuscule pieces of toast thinly spread with pâté.*

min·ute TIME /ˈmɪn·ɪt/ (*abbreviation* **min**) *n* [C] any of the 60 parts which an hour is divided into; 60 seconds • *It takes me twenty minutes to get to work.* • *Give me five minutes and I'll be ready.* • *It's only a twenty minute bus ride to town.* • *The train leaves at three minutes to eight, so we'd better get there a few minutes before.* • *Chopin's 'Minute Waltz' lasts about one minute.* • **The minute (that)** (= As soon as) *I saw him I knew something was wrong.* • *I'm not suggesting* **for a minute** (=I certainly do not believe) *that she meant to cause a lot of trouble.* • *It doesn't have to be done* **this minute** (=now), *but if you've got a free moment at some point this week you could finish it then.* • Something which is described as **up-to-the-minute** is modern or contains all the most recent information: *up-to-the-minute fashion/news* • Minute is also used in spoken English to mean a very short time: **Wait a** *minute – I'll just get my bag.* ○ **Just a** *minute – I'll be with you when I've finished this.* ○ *If you can* **hang on** *a minute, I'll join you.* ○ *I* **won't be a** *minute* (=I will be ready soon). ○ *When you've* **got a** *minute, I'd like a brief word with you.* • A **minute hand** on a clock or watch is the part which points to the minutes, and is usually longer than the **hour hand**. • A **minute steak** is a thin slice of STEAK (= a type of meat esp. from cattle) that can be cooked very quickly. • *"In the future everybody will be famous for 15 minutes"* (saying by Andy Warhol, 1960s) • LP〉 **Periods of time, Time** PIC〉 **Clocks and watches**

min·ute SMALL /£maɪˈnjuːt, $-ˈnuːt/ *adj* extremely small • *I bought some minute knives and forks to go in my niece's doll's house.* • *I've never seen a man with such tiny hands – they're minute!* • *The documentary showed an eye operation* **in minute detail** (= all the details of it).

min·ute·ly /£maɪˈnjuːt·li, $-ˈnuːt-/ *adv* • *The papers have minutely examined* (= examined every detail of) *all the events surrounding the royal scandal.*

min·ute DEGREE PART /ˈmɪn·ɪt/ *n* [C] any of the 60 parts that the degrees of any angle are divided into

min·ute MESSAGE /ˈmɪn·ɪt/ *n* [C] *fml, esp. Br* an official message from one person to another in an organization, giving permission for or suggesting a particular action; a MEMO • *I've just received a minute from Jeremy authorizing the purchase of six more computers.*

min·utes /ˈmɪn·ɪts/ *pl n* the written record of what was said at a meeting • *Could you* **take/do** (=write) **the** *minutes, Daniel?* • *The minutes of the last meeting were* **approved** *unanimously* (= everyone agreed that they were correct).

min·ute *obj* /ˈmɪn·ɪt/ *v* [T] • *The chairman is minuted* (= recorded in the minutes) *as having said that profits had fallen to an all-time low.*

mi·nu·ti·ae /mɪˈnuː·ʃi·aɪ/ *pl n* **the minutiae** small and often unimportant details • *The committee went over the minutiae of the report for what seemed like hours.* • *So often the roots of comedy are based in the minutiae of everyday life.*

minx /mɪŋks/ *n* [C] *usually humorous, slightly dated* a girl or young woman who knows how to control other people, esp. men, to her advantage

mir·a·cle /ˈmɪr·ɪ·kl̩/ *n* [C] an unusual and mysterious event that is thought to have been caused by a god, or any very surprising and unexpected event • *When you look at the state of his car it's a miracle* **(that)** *he wasn't killed!* [+ *(that)* clause] • *The Prime Minister said that he could not promise a miracle* **cure** *for the economy.* • *(infml) You've* **performed/worked** *a miracle on this kitchen – I've never seen it so clean!* • *(literary) He looked at his baby's hands – they were a miracle* **of** *smallness* (= extremely small). • *Every time a baby is born,* **the miracle of life** *is renewed.*

mi·rac·u·lous /mɪˈræk·jʊ·ləs/ *adj* • *He read yet another ad for a diet that promised miraculous weight-loss.* • *Well, you've made a miraculous* (= extremely surprising) *recovery since last night!*

mi·rac·u·lous·ly /mɪˈræk·jʊ·lə·sli/ *adv*

mi·rage /mɪˈrɑːʒ/ *n* [C] an image, produced by very hot air, of something which seems to be far away but does not really exist • *A common mirage is a sheet of water that seems to appear on a road in hot weather.* • A mirage is also a hope or desire that has no chance of being achieved: *Electoral victory is just a distant mirage on the political horizon.*

mire /£maɪəʳ, $maɪr/ *n* [C usually sing] an area of deep wet sticky earth, or *(fig.)* an unpleasant situation that is difficult to get out of • *Conservationists are demanding government action to save the one remaining ancient mire in the region.* • *(fig.) The banks are* **deep in the** *mire, industry is gloomy and unemployment is continuing to rise.* • *(fig.) The civil war is a mire which Western leaders are understandably reluctant to be drawn into.*

mi·ry /£ˈmaɪə·ri, $ˈmaɪ-/ *adj* **-ier, -iest**

mir·ror GLASS /£ˈmɪr·əʳ, $-ɚ/ *n* [C] a piece of glass with a shiny metallic back which reflects light, producing an image of whatever is in front of it • *I'm afraid I've just broken the bathroom mirror.* • *Our cat loves looking at her reflection* **in** *the mirror.* • Something that is a **mirror image** of something else is exactly the same as it, except that the left and right sides of the original have changed position with each other: *The children's bedrooms are mirror images of each other.* ○ *(fig.) The current economic situation is a mirror image of* (= very similar to) *the situation in France a few years ago.* • PIC〉 **Beds and bedroom**

mir·ror *obj* REPRESENT /£ˈmɪr·əʳ, $-ɚ/ *v* [T] to represent (something) truthfully, or to be very similar to (something) • *Our newspaper aims to mirror the opinions of ordinary people.* • *Her on-screen romances seem to mirror her experiences in her private life.*

mir·ror /£ˈmɪr·əʳ, $-ɚ/ *n* [C] • *The movie is a mirror* **of** *daily life in wartime Britain.* • *The newspaper has always tried to be a mirror* **of** *public opinion.*

mirth /£mɜːθ, $mɜːrθ/ *n* [U] *esp. literary or fml* laughter, amusement or happiness • *Her impersonations of our teachers were a source of considerable mirth.*

mirth·less /£ˈmɜːθ·ləs, $ˈmɜːrθ-/ *adj esp. literary or fml* • *I was determined that my own children should not experience anything like the mirthless childhood that I had endured.* • *"It's looks as though we're going to lose the match," he said with a mirthless laugh.*

mis- /mɪs-/ *combining form* added to the beginning of a verb or word formed from a verb to show that the action referred to by the verb has been done wrongly or badly • *I never said that! You must have misheard me.* • *This sort of glue can be very dangerous if you misuse it.* • *His misbehaviour eventually led to him being expelled from school.* • LP〉 **Opposites**

mis·ad·dress *obj* /ˌmɪs·əˈdres/ *v* [T] to put the wrong address on (a letter or parcel) • *We have now corrected the error in our computer records which resulted in our letters to you being misaddressed.*

mis·ad·ven·ture /£ˌmɪs·ədˈven·tʃəʳ, $-tʃɚ/ *n literary or fml* an unlucky event or bad luck • *Too many drivers behave as though any misadventures that occur are the fault* *of the car, rather than the driver.* [C] • *(Br law) The coroner said he had taken a drugs overdose and she recorded a verdict of* **(death by)** *misadventure.* [U]

mis·a·lign *obj* /ˌmɪs·əˈlaɪn/ *v* [T] to arrange (parts of a system) badly, with the result that they do not work well together • *You can avoid excessive wear on your tyres by checking that the wheels are not misaligned.*

mis·a·lign·ment /ˌmɪs·əˈlaɪn·mənt/ *n* [U] • *The misalignment of the dollar* **against** *other currencies in the early 1980s led to the United States' massive trade deficit.*

mis·an·thrope /£ˈmɪs·ᵊn·θrəʊp, £ˈmɪz- £-θrɒp, $-θroʊp/, **mis·an·throp·ist** /mɪˈsæn·θrə·pɪst/ *n* [C] someone who dislikes other people and avoids involvement with society • *Shakespeare's 'Timon of Athens' is a play about a neurotic philanthropist who turns into an embittered misanthrope.*

mis·an·throp·ic /£ˌmɪs·ᵊnˈθrɒp·ɪk, $-ˈθrɑː·pɪk/ *adj*

mis·an·throp·y /mɪˈsæn·θrə·pi/ *n* [U]

mis·ap·ply *obj* /ˌmɪs·əˈplaɪ/ *v* [T] to use (something) badly, wrongly or in a way that was not intended • *The charity has wasted millions of pounds and it will be impossible to recover all the misapplied money.*

mis·ap·pli·ca·tion /ˌmɪs·æp·lɪˈkeɪ·ʃᵊn/ *n* • *The inquiry has found evidence of serious mismanagement and misapplication* **of** *funds over the past five years.* [U] • *The scientific community is increasingly worried by misapplications* **of** *technological developments.* [C]

mis·ap·pre·hen·sion /ˌmɪs·æp·rɪˈhen·tʃᵊn/ *n* [C] a failure to understand something, or an understanding or belief about something that is not correct • *Most industrialists* **labour under** *a misapprehension* (= wrongly believe) **that** *unrestrained economic growth can be achieved without damaging the environment.* [+ *that* clause] • *He slowly spelled out each word to ensure there were no mistakes or misapprehensions.*

mis·ap·pro·pri·ate *obj* /£ˌmɪs·əˈprəʊ·pri·eɪt, $-ˈproʊ-/ *v* [T] to steal (something that you have been trusted to take care of) and use it for your own benefit • *Solicitors who misappropriate clients' funds risk being sent to prison.* • *He is accused of misappropriating $30 000 to pay for personal taxes, gambling debts and travel expenses.*

mis·ap·pro·pri·a·tion /£ˌmɪs·əˌprəʊ·priˈeɪ·ʃᵊn, $-ˌproʊ-/ *n* [U] • *He was charged with forgery, embezzlement and misappropriation* **of** *union funds.*

mis·be·got·ten BADLY PLANNED /£ˌmɪs·bɪˈgɒt·ᵊn, $-ˈgɑː·t̬ᵊn/ *adj* badly or foolishly planned or designed • *Increased car use was the inevitable result of the council's misbegotten decision to ban buses from the middle of the town.*

mis·be·got·ten NOT RESPECTED /£ˌmɪs·bɪˈgɒt·ᵊn, $-ˈgɑː·t̬ᵊn/ *adj* [before n] not deserving to be respected or thought valuable • *Her misbegotten father spent most of his adult life in prison.*

mis·be·have /ˌmɪs·bɪˈheɪv/ *v* [I] to behave badly • *What sort of punishments were you given for misbehaving at school?* • *There is a huge temptation to misbehave* (= be dishonest) *on the financial markets when there is money to be made.* • *(fig.) If computer circuits are allowed to overheat they will misbehave* (= fail to operate as intended).

mis·be·hav·i·our *Br and Aus, Am and Aus* **mis·be·hav·i·or** /£ˌmɪs·bɪˈheɪ·vjəʳ, $-vjɚ/ *n* [U] • *The school expelled him for persistent misbehaviour.*

mis·cal·cu·late *(obj)* /mɪˈskæl·kjʊ·leɪt/ *v* to calculate (an amount) wrongly • *We had a lot of food left over from the party because I'd miscalculated* **how much** *people would eat.* [+ *wh-* word] • *(fig.) The management has miscalculated* (= judged badly) *the union's determination to win this dispute.* [T] • *(fig.) He miscalculated badly when he underestimated the response of the international community to the invasion.* [I]

mis·cal·cu·la·tion /ˌmɪs·kæl·kjʊˈleɪ·ʃᵊn/ *n* [C] • *The project went over budget because of a miscalculation at the planning stage.* • *(fig.) The conspirators' plot to overthrow the President failed because they* **made** *two fatal miscalculations.*

mis·car·riage /£ˈmɪsˌkær·ɪdʒ, $-ˌker-/ *n* an early unintentional end to a pregnancy which results in the death of the developing baby because it is unable to live outside its mother's body • *The chemical is suspected of causing genetic damage, birth defects and miscarriages.* [C] • *The amniocentesis test for identifying handicapped babies before they are born carries a high risk of miscarriage.* [U] • Compare **abortion** at ABORT; STILLBIRTH.

mis·car·ry /£ˌmɪsˈkær·i, $-ˈker-/ *v* [I] • *The embryo was implanted successfully, but she miscarried eight weeks into the pregnancy.*

mis·car·riage of jus·tice *n* [C] a wrong decision in a law court that someone is guilty of a crime that they have not committed • *Many people oppose the death penalty because of the possibility of miscarriages of justice.*

mis·cast *obj* /£ˌmɪsˈkɑːst, $-ˈkæst/ *v* [T usually passive] *past* **miscast** to choose (actors and actresses) that are unsuitable for the characters in (a film or play) • *The film was hopelessly miscast.* • *He was miscast in a role that required someone who could sing and dance, when he could do neither.* • *(fig.) She was a good health minister, but she is miscast* **as** *the employment minister* (= she is not suitable for that job).

mis·cel·la·ne·ous /ˌmɪs·ᵊlˈeɪ·ni·əs/ *adj* [not gradable] consisting of a mixture of various things which are not usually connected with each other • *The increase in inflation is due to higher prices for food and miscellaneous household items.* • *My daughter's bedroom is full of guitars, amplifiers, keyboards and miscellaneous gadgetry.*

mis·cel·la·ny /mɪˈsel·ə·ni/ *n* [C] • A miscellany is a mixture of different things: *The museum houses a fascinating miscellany of nautical treasures.* • Sometimes a miscellany is a book containing a collection of pieces of writing either by different writers or by one writer on different subjects: *She's just finished editing "A Miscellany of English Cookery".*

mis·chance /£mɪsˈtʃɑːnts, $-ˈtʃænts/ *n fml* bad luck or an unlucky event • *It was sheer mischance that the stone struck her in the eye.* [U] • *They proceeded on their journey without any mischance.* [C]

mis·chief /ˈmɪs·tʃɪf/ *n* behaviour, esp. of a child, which is slightly bad but is not intended to cause serious harm or damage • *He needs a hobby to keep him busy and stop him from* **getting into** *mischief.* [U] • *Perhaps a new bike would* **keep** *him* **out of** *mischief.* [U] • *I hope you haven't been* **up to** *any mischief while I was away.* [U] • *Helen's great fun at parties – she's* **full of** *mischief and always playing tricks on people.* [U] • *(dated) Just sit quietly, Chrissy, and don't be such a mischief* (= a child who behaves badly). [C] • Sometimes mischief is used to avoid referring to something worse, such as damage: *Those vandals were* **up to** *some mischief at the factory again last night.* [U] ○ *Missiles like these can* **do** *a lot of mischief.* [U] ○ *(Br infml) You'll* **do** *yourself* **a mischief** (= hurt yourself) *if you're not careful with that knife.* • *(dated)* If you **make mischief** you say something which causes other people to be upset or annoyed with each other: *My children often try to make mischief* **between** *me and my new husband.* ○ *In spite of the arms reductions, the potential for some serious* **mischief-making** *remains.*

mis·chiev·ous /ˈmɪs·tʃɪ·vəs/ *adj* • *She has a mischievous sense of humour.* • *He is currently writing a book based on the mischievous antics of his ten-year-old daughter.* • *He has long blond hair and mischievous blue eyes* (= eyes that suggest he will behave in a playfully bad way). • *I think these rumours are mischievous* (= intended to cause harm).

mis·chiev·ous·ly /ˈmɪs·tʃɪ·və·sli/ *adv*

mis·chiev·ous·ness /ˈmɪs·tʃɪ·və·snəs/ *n* [U]

mis·com·mun·i·ca·tion /ˌmɪs·kə·mjuː·nɪˈkeɪ·ʃᵊn/ *n* [U] failure to communicate ideas or intentions successfully • *A spokeswoman blamed the confusion on miscommunication* **between** *the company and its customers.*

mis·con·ceived /ˌmɪs·kənˈsiːvd/ *adj* based on a failure to understand a situation and therefore unsuitable or unlikely to succeed • *The plan to build the road through the forest is wholly misconceived.*

mis·con·cep·tion /ˌmɪs·kənˈsep·ʃᵊn/ *n* [C] • A misconception is an idea which is wrong that has been based on a failure to understand a situation: *We hope our work will help to change* **popular** *misconceptions* **about** *disabled people.* • *I'd like to clear up the* **common** *misconception* **that** *American society is based on money.* [+ *that* clause]

mis·con·duct BEHAVIOUR /£mɪˈskɒn·dʌkt, $-ˈskɑːn-/ *n* [U] wrong or immoral behaviour of someone in a position of authority or responsibility • *The psychiatrist was found guilty of* **professional** *misconduct after she persuaded a patient to give money to a non-existent charity.* • *A former priest has denied* **allegations of** *sexual misconduct with his children's babysitter.*

mis·con·duct *obj* MANAGE /ˌmɪs·kənˈdʌkt/ *v* [T] to manage (the activities of an organization) badly • *The aid programme has been misconducted, resulting in large quantities of food failing to reach the famine victims.*

mis·con·duct /£mɪˈskɒn·dʌkt, $-ˈskɑːn-/ *n* [U] • *Two directors have resigned following accusations of misconduct of the company's financial affairs.*

mis·con·strue *obj* /ˌmɪs·kənˈstruː/ *v* [T] *fml* to form a false understanding of the meaning or intention of (something that someone does or says) • *I think you've misconstrued what I was trying to say.* • *Their caution was misconstrued* **as** *cowardice.*

mis·con·struc·tion /ˌmɪs·kənˈstrʌk·ʃᵊn/ *n* [U] *fml* • *A lot of his speech was* **open to** *misconstruction* (= risked being not understood or wrongly understood).

mis·count *(obj)* /ˌmɪsˈkaʊnt/ *v* to reach a total, when counting, which is not correct • *I thought we had enough plates for the party, but perhaps I miscounted.* [I] • *The shop assistant was very apologetic when I told him he'd miscounted my change.* [T]

mis·count /ˈmɪsˌkaʊnt/ *n* [C] • *A miscount of the votes delayed the announcement of the result by a few hours.*

mis·cre·ant /ˈmɪs·kri·ənt/ *n* [C] *fml* someone who behaves badly or does not obey rules • *The penalties for dropping litter are too low to discourage miscreants.* • *Tougher fines are to be imposed on miscreant employers who ignore health and safety regulations.*

mis·deed /mɪsˈdiːd/ *n* [C] *fml* an act that is criminal or bad • *It's not fair to blame them for their parents' misdeeds.* • *Since her release from prison she's been making up for her past misdeeds by doing a lot of voluntary work.*

mis·de·mean·our *Br and Aus, Am and Aus* **mis·de·mean·or** /£ˌmɪs·dɪˈmiː·nəʳ, $-nɚ/ *n* [C] (in the US or in the past in Britain) a crime considered to be one of the less serious types of crime • *Possession of small amounts of cannabis is a misdemeanour, whereas large-scale dealing in heroin is a felony* (= serious crime). • A misdemeanour is also an action which is slightly bad or breaks a rule but is not a crime: *Sarah was really drunk last night, but she paid for her misdemeanours this morning with a dreadful hangover.*

mis·di·rect *obj* /ˌmɪs·daɪˈrekt/ *v* [T] to send (a person or thing) to the wrong place or in the wrong direction • *It appears that your luggage has been misdirected* **to** *a different airport.* • *The report accuses the charity of wasting money and misdirecting large quantities of aid.* • *(fig.) The public's admiration for the president is misdirected as he has done nothing to deserve it.*

mis·di·rec·tion /ˌmɪs·daɪˈrek·ʃᵊn/ *n* [U] • *The misdirection* **of** *financial resources has resulted in a great deal of unnecessary expense.*

mi·ser /£ˈmaɪ·zəʳ, $-zɚ/ *n* [C] someone who has a great desire to possess money and hates to spend it, sometimes living in very unpleasant conditions because of this • *He had a reputation in the village for being a wealthy miser who would never pay for anything if he could possibly avoid it.*

mi·ser·ly /£ˈmaɪ·zᵊl·i, $-zɚ·li/ *adj* • *It's very miserly of her to refuse to give any money to the church appeal when she could so easily afford it.*

mi·ser·li·ness /£ˈmaɪ·zᵊl·ɪ·nəs, $-zɚ·lɪ-/ *n* [U]

mis·e·ra·ble [UNHAPPY] /£ˈmɪz·ᵊr·ə·bl̩, $ˈ-ɚ-/ *adj* very unhappy, or causing unhappiness by being unpleasant • *She's been so miserable since her dog died.* • *What a miserable existence! How could anyone live in such dreadful conditions?* • *We could* **make life** *very miserable for you if you refuse to cooperate.* • *The forecast is for more miserable weather over the weekend.* • *It's far too* **cold and** *miserable to go out for a walk.* • Ⓔ

mis·e·ra·bly /£ˈmɪz·ᵊr·ə·bli, $ˈ-ɚ-/ *adv* • *"I'm so unhappy," sobbed Chris, miserably.* • *It's been miserably wet* (= raining a lot) *all week.*

mis·er·y /£ˈmɪz·ᵊr·i, $ˈ-ɚ-/ *n* • *We have witnessed the most appalling scenes of* **human** *misery.* [U] • *Drought has* **brought** *misery and death to the area for the fifth successive year.* [U] • *Ten years of marriage to him have made her life a misery.* [C] • *Every day, millions of people have to endure the miseries of travelling to work on crowded commuter trains.* [C] • A misery is also someone who is often very unhappy and is always complaining about things: *He's been such a misery since his girlfriend went abroad without him.* [C] • If you **put** an animal **out of** its **misery**, you kill it because it is in great pain and so that it does not have to suffer any more: *We asked the vet to put our cat out of her misery after she was run over by a bus.* ○ *(fig.) We try to put our students out of their misery* (= stop them worrying) *and give them their exam results as early as possible.* • Ⓔ

mis·e·ra·ble [LOW VALUE] /£ˈmɪz·ᵊr·ə·bl̩, $ˈ-ɚ-/ *adj* [before n] having little value by being very low in quality or existing in a very small amount • *I thought the vase would be worth a fortune, but she only offered me a miserable £20 for it.* • *Some miserable little bastard has gone and vandalised my car again.* • Ⓔ

mis·e·ra·bly /£ˈmɪz·ᵊr·ə·bli, $ˈ-ɚ-/ *adv* • *The weather forecasters* **failed** *miserably* (= completely failed) *to warn us about the storm.* • *Over half the country's population is miserably* **poor**.

mis·fire /£mɪsˈfaɪəʳ, $-ˈfaɪr/ *v* [I] to fail to fire, explode, or burn as intended or expected • *He tried to shoot me, but his gun misfired and I managed to escape.* • *Two of the missiles misfired because of computer problems.* • When an engine misfires the fuel inside it starts to burn at the wrong moment: *That loud bang is caused by the engine misfiring.* • *(fig.) The coroner said that the boy's death resulted from a practical joke that had misfired* (= that had not happened as intended).

mis·fit /ˈmɪs·fɪt/ *n* [C] someone who is not suited to a situation or is not accepted socially by other people because his or her behaviour is unusual or strange • *I didn't really know anyone at the party, so I felt a bit of a misfit.* • *At college I became a* **social** *misfit because I didn't like going out in the evenings.* • *"The Misfits"* (title of a film starring Marilyn Monroe, 1961)

mis·for·tune /£mɪsˈfɔː·tʃuːn, $-ˈfɔːr·tʃən/ *n* bad luck, or an unlucky event • *He's the most unpleasant man that I've ever had the misfortune* **of** *meeting.* [U] • *That was the worst film I've ever had the misfortune* **to** *see.* [+ to infinitive] • *She's suffered a good deal of misfortune over the years.* [U] • *It's not fair to take advantage of other people's misfortunes.* [C]

mis·giv·ing /mɪsˈgɪv·ɪŋ/ *n* a feeling of doubt, uncertainty or worry about a future event • *Many teachers have expressed serious misgivings* **about** *the new exams.* [C] • *My only misgiving is that we might not have enough time to do the job properly.* [C] • *The plan seemed to be utterly impractical and I was* **filled with** *misgiving about it.* [U]

mis·gov·ern *obj* /£mɪsˈgʌv·ᵊn, $-ɚn/ *v* [T] to govern (a country) badly

mis·gov·ern·ment /£mɪsˈgʌv·ᵊm·mənt, $-ɚn·mənt/ *n* [U] • *A decade of misgovernment has bankrupted the country.*

mis·guid·ed /ˌmɪsˈgaɪ·dɪd/ *adj* unreasonable or unsuitable because of being based on a bad judgment of a situation or on information or beliefs that are wrong • *He was shot as he made a well-intentioned but misguided attempt to stop the robbers single-handed.* • *The company is blaming its disappointing performance on a misguided business plan.*

mis·guid·ed·ly /ˌmɪsˈgaɪ·dɪd·li/ *adv*

mis·hand·le *obj* /mɪsˈhæn·dl̩/ *v* [T] to deal with (something) without the necessary care or skill • *This equipment is fragile and easily damaged if it is mishandled.* • *The police have been accused of mishandling the investigation.*

mis·hand·ling /mɪsˈhæn·dlɪŋ/ *n* [U] • *Who do you blame for the mishandling* **of** *the economy?*

mis·hap /ˈmɪs·hæp/ *n* bad luck, or an unlucky event or accident • *The parade was very well organised and passed without mishap.* [U] • *Her brother's brain damage was caused by a mishap in the operating theatre.* [C] • **A series of** *mishaps led to the nuclear power plant blowing up.* [C]

mis·hear *(obj)* /£mɪsˈhɪəʳ, $-ˈhɪr/ *v past* **misheard** /£mɪsˈhɜːd, $-ˈhɜːrd/ to fail to hear (someone or what someone says) correctly or as intended by the speaker and to think that something different was said • *I'm sure I never said that! You must have misheard (me).* [T]

mish·mash /ˈmɪʃ·mæʃ/ *n* [U] a badly organized mixture • *The new housing development is* **a** *mishmash* **of** *architectural styles.* • *Their proposals are just* **a** *mishmash* **of** *ideas at the moment.*

mis·in·form *obj* /£ˌmɪs·ɪnˈfɔːm, $-ˈfɔːrm/ *v* [T] to tell (someone) information that is not correct • *The report accuses tobacco companies of misinforming smokers* **about** *the dangers of cigarettes.* • *I was told she would come to the meeting, but I was obviously misinformed.*

mis·in·for·ma·tion /£ˌmɪs·ɪn·fəˈmeɪ·ʃᵊn, $-fɚ-/ *n* [U] • *There's a lot of misinformation* **about** *AIDS that needs to be corrected.* • *The President's election campaign was based on misinformation* (= information intended to deceive) **about** *the rival candidates.*

mis·in·ter·pret *obj* /£ˌmɪs·ɪnˈtɜː·prɪt, $-ˈtɜːr-/ *v* [T] to form an understanding that is not correct of (something that is said or done) • *My speech has been misinterpreted by* *the press.* • *When we re-examined the regulations we realised that we had misinterpreted them.*

mis·in·ter·pre·ta·tion /£ˌmɪs·ɪnˌtɜː·prɪˈteɪ·ʃən, $-ˌtɜːr-/ *n* • *The minister's statement is unclear and* **open to** *misinterpretation* (=could easily be misinterpreted). [U] • *The jury's decision to convict the defendant was based on a misinterpretation* **of** *the evidence.* [C]

mis·judge *obj* /mɪsˈdʒʌdʒ/ *v* [T] to form an opinion or idea about (a person or thing) which is unfair or not correct • *I thought he wasn't going to support me, but I misjudged him.* • *She lost the race after she badly misjudged the ability of the other competitors.* • *Chris totally misjudged the situation and behaved quite inappropriately.*

mis·judg·ment, **mis·judge·ment** /mɪsˈdʒʌdʒ·mənt/ *n* • *Her misjudgment* **of** *the public's concern about environmental issues lost her the election.* [U] • *Their decision to sell the house was a disastrous misjudgement.* [C]

mis·lay *obj* /ˌmɪsˈleɪ/ *v* [T] *past* **mislaid** /ˌmɪsˈleɪd/ to lose (something) temporarily by forgetting where you have put it • *Could I borrow a pen? I seem to have mislaid mine.* • *He's terribly disorganised and always mislaying things.*

mis·lead *obj* /ˌmɪsˈliːd/ *v* [T] *past* **misled** /ˌmɪsˈled/ to cause (someone) to believe something that is not true, or to cause (someone) to behave in an unsuitable way • *He has admitted concealing the man's body and misleading the police* **about** *his movements on the night of the murder.* • *Clearer food labelling is needed to prevent consumers being misled* **into** *eating things that are bad for them.* • *I was misled by my elder brother* **into** *a life of drinking and gambling.*

mis·lead·ing /ˌmɪsˈliː·dɪŋ/ *adj* • *misleading information/statements* • *The town's new shopping centre gives a misleading* **impression** *of prosperity, when unemployment there is at its highest-ever level.*

mis·lead·ing·ly /ˌmɪsˈliː·dɪŋ·li/ *adv*

mis·man·age *obj* /ˌmɪsˈmæn·ɪdʒ/ *v* [T] to organize or control (something) badly • *The restaurant went bankrupt after being hopelessly mismanaged by a former rock musician with no business experience.*

mis·man·age·ment /ˌmɪsˈmæn·ɪdʒ·mənt/ *n* [U] • *Mismanagement* **of** *the economy/Economic mismanagement has plunged the country into recession.* • *The charity has refused to comment on the allegations of fraud and mismanagement.*

mis·match *obj* /ˌmɪsˈmætʃ/ *v* [T] to put together (people or things) that are unsuitable for each other • *I always thought Chris and Monique were mismatched, so I wasn't surprised when they got divorced.* • *We'll have to redecorate the bedroom because the carpet and wallpaper are hopelessly mismatched.*

mis·match /ˈmɪs·mætʃ/ *n* [C] • *There is a mismatch* **between** *the capacity of the airport and the large number of people wanting to fly from it.*

mis·nom·er /£ˌmɪsˈnəʊ·mər, $-ˈnoʊ·mɚ/ *n* [C] a name that does not suit what it refers to, or a use of such a name • *It was scruffiest place I've ever stayed in, so 'Hotel Royal' was* **a bit of a** *misnomer.* • *It's* **something of a** *misnomer to refer to these inexperienced boys as soldiers.*

mis·o·gyn·ist /£mɪˈsɒdʒ·ɪ·nɪst, $-ˈsɑː·dʒɪ-/ *n* [C] someone, usually a man, who hates women or believes that men are much better than women

mis·o·gyn·ist /£mɪˈsɒdʒ·ɪ·nɪst, $-ˈsɑː·dʒɪ-/, **mis·o·gyn·is·tic** /£mɪˌsɒdʒ·ɪˈnɪs·tɪk, $-ˌsɑː·dʒɪˈ-/ *adj* • *She left the Church because of its misogynist teachings on women and their position in society.*

mis·o·gyn·y /£mɪˈsɒdʒ·ɪ·ni, $-ˈsɑː·dʒɪ-/ *n* [U] • *The club's refusal to allow women to become members is sheer misogyny.*

mis·place *obj* /ˌmɪsˈpleɪs/ *v* [T] to lose (something) temporarily by forgetting where you have put it • *She used to misplace her keys so often that her secretary had to carry spare ones for her.*

mis·placed /ˌmɪsˈpleɪst/ *adj* wrongly or unwisely directed towards someone or something • *I'm afraid your confidence in my abilities is misplaced.* • *His misplaced loyalty to the government resulted in his imprisonment after the revolution.*

mis·print /ˈmɪs·prɪnt/ *n* [C] a mistake, such as a word that is spelled wrong, in a printed text • *We can't publish the newsletter like this – it's full of misprints.*

mis·pro·nounce *obj* /ˌmɪs·prəˈnaʊnts/ *v* [T] to pronounce (a word or sound) wrongly • *French learners of English often mispronounce "ch"* **as** *"sh".*

mis·pro·nun·ci·a·tion /ˌmɪs·prəˌnʌnt·siˈeɪ·ʃən/ *n* • *Mispronunciation can be a serious obstacle to making yourself understood in a foreign language.* [U] • *Music lovers have criticized the radio station for its presenters' frequent mispronunciations of composers' names.* [C]

mis·quote *obj* /£ˌmɪsˈkwəʊt, $-ˈkwoʊt/ *v* [T] to repeat (something someone has said) in a way that is not accurate • *Her promise was deliberately misquoted by her opponents who then used it against her.* • *I never said that at all – I was misquoted by the press.*

mis·quot·a·tion /£ˌmɪs·kwəʊˈteɪ·ʃən, $-kwoʊ-/ *n* • *That was a deliberate misquotation of what I said.* [C] • *It's important to avoid misquotation of other people's work in your essay.* [U]

mis·read *obj* /mɪsˈriːd/ *v* [T] *past* **misread** /mɪsˈred/ to make a mistake when reading (something), or *(fig.)* to form a wrong understanding or judgment of (something) • *I was given the wrong tablets when the chemist misread my prescription.* • *(fig.) I thought he fancied me, but I'd misread the signals and he was only interested in me as a friend.*

mis·read·ing /mɪsˈriː·dɪŋ/ *n* [C] • *(fig.) His misreading* **of** *the situation could have serious consequences.*

mis·re·port *obj* /£ˌmɪs·rɪˈpɔːt, $-ˈpɔːrt/ *v* [T] to make known information that is not completely true or correct • *The magazine misreported its sales figures in order to boost advertising revenue.*

mis·represent *obj* /ˌmɪs·rep·rɪˈzent/ *v* [T] to describe falsely (an idea, opinion or situation) or the opinions of (someone), often in order to obtain an advantage • *She accused her opponents of deliberately misrepresenting her* **as** *an extremist.* • *I've grown used to my* **views** *being misrepresented in the press.* • *A company spokeswoman said the union's report misrepresented the conditions that the miners were working in.*

mis·rep·re·sen·ta·tion /ˌmɪs·rep·rɪ·zenˈteɪ·ʃən/ *n* • *The documentary was a misrepresentation* **of** *the truth and bore little resemblance to actual events.* [C] • *Your opinions will be liable to misrepresentation by the media if you don't clarify exactly what you think.* [U]

mis·rule /ˌmɪsˈruːl/ *n* [U] bad government that lacks justice or fairness • *She blames her country's economic collapse on forty years of communist misrule.*

Miss [TITLE] /mɪs/ *n* a title or form of address for a girl or a woman who has never been married • *Dr White will see you now, Miss Green.* • *Would you sign at the bottom of the page please, Miss.* • Some women, esp. famous ones, continue to use 'Miss' and their original family name after they have married. • 'Ms' is sometimes used instead of 'Miss' or 'Mrs' by women who do not want other people to know whether or not they are married. • A woman who has won a beauty competition is often given the title 'Miss' and the name of the place that she represents: *Has Miss UK ever won the Miss World contest?* • *(dated)* 'Miss' is also a form of address for a girl or young woman who does not appear to be married: *Excuse me, Miss, could you tell me the way to the station?* • *(esp. Br)* 'Miss' is sometimes used by children to address teachers who are women: *Can I go to the toilet, Miss?* • *(Br dated)* A miss is a girl or young woman whose behaviour is rude or not respectful: *Pat's daughter is a right little miss! She's always being cheeky and refusing to do as she's told.* [C] • [LP] **Sexist language**, **Titles and forms of address** (KOR)

miss *(obj)* [NOT HIT] /mɪs/ *v* to fail to hit or to avoid hitting (something) • *The bullet missed his heart by a couple of centimetres.* [T] • *I swerved to avoid the other car and only just missed a tree.* [T] • *He threw a stone at me, but fortunately he/it missed.* [I]

miss /mɪs/ *n* [C] • *Well done! You scored eight hits and only two misses.*

miss *obj* [NOT DO] /mɪs/ *v* [T] to fail to do or experience (something that is often planned or expected) • *I missed the start of the exam because my bus was late.* • *Often I miss* (=do not eat) *breakfast and have an early lunch instead.* • *You'll miss* (=be too late to catch) *your train if you don't hurry up.* • *I was sorry I missed* (=did not see) *you at Pat's party – I must have arrived after you left.* • *I hate missing* (=not seeing) *the beginning of a film.* • *I've missed* (=not had) *my period and I think I might be pregnant.* • *You'll fall* *behind in your studies if you keep missing* (=not going to) *school.* • *She missed* (=did not take advantage of) *the chance of promotion when she turned down the job of assistant manager.* • *Her latest movie is* **too good to** *miss* (=It certainly should be seen). • *What you say is true, but you've missed* **the point of** (=not understood what is important about) *my argument.* • *"I didn't manage to see that programme." "Don't worry, you didn't miss much* (=it was not worth seeing)*."* • *You don't miss much, do you? Nobody else noticed that mistake.* • *My office is first on the right with a bright red door. You* **can't** *miss* **it** (=It is very easy to find). • *You should leave early if you want to miss* (=avoid) *the rush hour.* • *I'm trying to find an excuse for missing* (=not going to) *the office party.* • *I* **narrowly** *missed* (=I only just avoided) *being run over by a bus this morning.* [+ v-*ing*] • To **miss the boat** is to lose an opportunity to do something by being slow to act: *There were still some tickets available last week, but he missed the boat by waiting till today to try to buy some.* • Something that **misses the mark** fails to achieve what it is intended to achieve: *Her speech missed the mark and failed to generate the public support she had been hoping for.* • If you **miss a trick** you fail to notice and take advantage of a good opportunity: *She missed a trick when she decided not to go on that business trip to China.* ○ *Jonathan* **never** *misses a trick! If there's a bargain to be had at the market, he'll find it.*

miss /mɪs/ *n Br and Aus infml* • If you **give** something **a miss**, you avoid it: *We usually go to France for our summer holiday, but we've decided to give it a miss this year.* ○ *The restaurant's very good for fish, but I'd give their vegetarian options a miss.*

miss *obj* REGRET /mɪs/ *v* [T] to be unhappy or regret that (a person or thing) is not present • *He really missed his girlfriend when she went away.* • *Her death was sudden and she will be sadly missed by all who knew her.* • *My new car's very reliable, but I still miss my old one, in spite of all its faults.* • *What did you miss most about England when you were living France?* • *I haven't missed smoking like I'd expected to.* [+ v-*ing*]

miss *obj* NOTICE /mɪs/ *v* [T] to notice that (something) is lost or absent • *He didn't miss his wallet until the waiter brought the bill.*

miss·ing /ˈmɪs·ɪŋ/ *adj* [not gradable] • People or things that are missing cannot be found because they are not where they should be: *Her father has been missing since September 1992.* ○ *The burglars are in prison now but the jewellery's still missing.* ○ *When did you realise the money was missing* **from** *your account?* • *(Br and Aus) A girl who* **went** *missing during a family outing to Mount Snowdon has been found dead on the mountainside.* • *If your bike was stolen last week, why haven't you* **reported** *it missing until now?* • A soldier or military vehicle that is missing has not returned from fighting in a war but is not known with total certainty to be dead or destroyed: *He was* **listed as** *missing* **in action.** • The **missing link** is an animal which no longer exists or might never have existed and is thought to explain how humans developed from animals similar to monkeys: *Experts believe the skeleton could be* **the** *missing link between apes and humans.* • A **missing link** is also anything that is necessary to complete a series or solve a problem: *Those documents provided the missing link, and the police were able to make an arrest soon after they discovered them.* • A **missing person** is someone who has disappeared and is no longer in communication with their family and friends: *Have you reported your son's disappearance to the missing persons bureau?*

miss out *obj* NOT INCLUDE, **miss** *obj* **out** *v adv* [M] *Br* to fail to include (someone or something that should be included) • *You've missed out your address on the form.* • *Oh I'm sorry, Tina, I've missed you out. What would you like to drink?*

miss out NOT USE *v adv* [I] to fail to use an opportunity to enjoy or benefit from something • *(Br) Of course I'm coming to the party! I'd hate to miss out.* • *Britain is missing out* **on** *the full benefits of the Channel Tunnel by failing to build a high-speed rail link to the rest of the country.*

mis·shapen /mɪsˈʃeɪ·pᵊn, mɪʃ-/ *adj* having an unusual shape or a shape which is not natural • *The drug was banned after it was found to be causing some babies to be born with misshapen limbs.*

mis·sile /£ˈmɪs·aɪl, $-ᵊl/ *n* [C] a flying weapon which has its own engine so that it can travel a long distance before exploding at the place that it has been aimed at • *The ceasefire was broken when missile* **attacks** *on the capital resumed at dawn this morning.* • *Satellite photographs have provided conclusive proof of the existence of the missile* **sites.** • *Our primary objective is to destroy the enemy's missile* **launchers.** • *(fml)* A missile can also be any object that is thrown with the intention of causing injury or damage: *Several police officers were injured by the stones, bottles and other missiles that were thrown by the rioters.*

mis·sion JOB /ˈmɪʃ·ᵊn/ *n* [C] an important job, esp. a military one, that someone is sent somewhere to do • *Your mission is to isolate the enemy by destroying all the bridges across the river.* • *Mission* **accomplished**, *sir! We've put all the bridges out of action.* • *More than 2600 sorties were flown yesterday, about half of them on* **combat** *missions.* • *This latest* **peace** *mission seems doomed to failure.* • *She met the leaders of the warring factions while on a* **fact-finding** *mission to the region last month.* • *A* **rescue** *mission to save a girl who had fallen down a well ended happily last night.* • **Mission control** is the place on Earth from which a journey into space is controlled: *A technical problem resulted in the astronauts losing radio contact with mission control for a few tense minutes.* • Someone's mission can also be any work that they believe it is their duty to do: *I see my mission in life as being to educate the rich about the suffering of the poor.* ○ *She's a woman* **with a** *mission and she's absolutely determined to finish the project.* • *"On a mission from God"* (phrase from *The Blues Brothers* film, 1980) • *"Mission Impossible"* (title of a television series, 1966-72)

mis·sion PEOPLE /ˈmɪʃ·ᵊn/ *n* [C] a group of people whose job is to increase what is known about their country, organization or religion in another country or area, or the place where such people are based • *More funds are needed to establish* **trade** *missions in eastern Europe.* • *When I was 21 I joined a Catholic mission and went to teach in India.* • *The Methodist mission is situated in one of the poorest parts of the city.*

mis·sion·ary /£ˈmɪʃ·ᵊn·ri, $-er·i/ *n* [C] • Missionaries are people who have been sent to a foreign country to teach their religion to the people who live there: *He did missionary work for the Presbyterian Church in Alaska.* • *(fig.) Paul manages to inspire us with a missionary* **zeal** (=very great enthusiasm) *for our work.* • The **missionary position** is a position for having sex in which a woman lies on her back and her partner is above and facing her.

mis·sive /ˈmɪs·ɪv/ *n* [C] an official, formal or long letter, or *(humorous)* a letter • *She gave details of her objections to the plans in a ten-page missive to the council.* • *(humorous) Thank you so much for your last letter. We always look forward to receiving your long missives about what you've been up to.*

mis·spell *obj* /mɪsˈspel/ *v* [T] *past* **misspelled** or *Br* **misspelt** /mɪsˈspelt/ to fail to spell (a word) correctly

mis·spell·ing /mɪsˈspel·ɪŋ/ *n* • *This essay is full of misspellings.* [C] • *You'll lose marks for misspelling.* [U]

mis·spend *obj* /mɪsˈspend/ *v* [T] *past* **misspent** /mɪsˈspent/ to use (time or money) in a manner that is wasteful or unwise • *A lot of my time at college was misspent in jazz clubs.* • *Being a good pool player is usually a sign of a misspent* **youth.**

mis·state *obj* /mɪsˈsteɪt/ *v* [T] *fml esp. Am* to express (a fact that is not correct) • *Yesterday's obituary of Randall M. Klose misstated the date of his death.*

mis·state·ment /mɪsˈsteɪt·mənt/ *n* [C; U] *fml esp. Am*

mis·sus /ˈmɪs·ɪs/ *n* [U] *infml* a man's wife, or the wife of a man who is being spoken to or referred to • *Me and* **the** *missus* (=my wife) *are going to our daughter's for Christmas.* • *I was sorry to hear about your missus, Mike. Is she feeling any better?* • *Have you met Jack's new missus?* • LP **Relationships**

mist /mɪst/ *n* thin fog produced by very small drops of water gathering in the air just above an area of ground or water • *The mountain villages seem to be permanently* **shrouded in** *mist.* [U] • *The early-morning mist had lifted by breakfast time, giving us a magnificent view over the lake.* [U] • *Wisps of grey hair were drifting around his head like a light sea mist.* [C] • *(fig.) The precise details of what happened have been lost in the mists* **of time** (=forgotten because they happened so long ago). • A mist is also a thin layer of liquid on the surface of something which makes it difficult to see: *(Br) There's always a mist (Am* **fog**, *Am and Aus* **steam**) *on the windows when I've had a shower.* [U] ○ *(Br) The bathroom mirror was covered with faces that Martha had drawn in the mist (Am* **fog**, *Am and Aus* **steam**). [U] ○ *He looked at me sadly through a mist* **of tears**

and gave me a final hug before getting on the train. [C] • Ⓟ

mist *(obj)* /mɪst/ *v* • If something that you can see through mists **up** or mists **over**, it becomes covered with a thin layer of liquid so that it is more difficult to see through it: *(Br) Open the bathroom window when you have a shower to stop the mirror misting (Am* **fogging**, *Am and Aus* **steaming**) *over.* [I] ○ *His eyes misted over as he thought back to his wedding day.* [I] ○ *(Br) Turning on the heater should stop the windscreen misting (Am and Aus usually* **fogging**) *up.* [I] ○ *(Br) The steam from the kettle misted (Am* **fogged**, *Am and Aus* **steamed**) *up her glasses.* [T] ○ *"Why did they have to kill him?" she said, her eyes misting with tears.* [I]

mist·y /ˈmɪs·ti/ *adj* **-ier, -iest** • *The morning will start off misty, but by ten o'clock we should be enjoying bright sunshine.* • *Thursday night's concert was her first for twenty years, so there were plenty of misty* **eyes** *among the audience.* • *He goes all* **misty-eyed** *whenever he hears that song.*

mis·ti·ly /ˈmɪs·tɪ·li/ *adv*

mis·ti·ness /ˈmɪs·tɪ·nəs/ *n* [U]

mis·take *obj* NOT RECOGNIZE /mɪˈsteɪk/ *v* [T] *past simple* **mistook** /mɪˈstʊk/, *past part* **mistaken** /mɪˈsteɪ·kᵊn/ to be wrong about or to fail to recognize (something or someone) • *You can't mistake their house – it's got a bright yellow front door.* • *There's* **no mistaking** (=It is easy to recognize) *a painting by Picasso.* • *There was* **no mistaking** *her relief that she hadn't got cancer.* • *I often mistake her* **for** (=think wrongly that she is) *her mother on the phone.* • *(fml) I mistook your signature and thought the letter was from someone else.*

mis·tak·en /mɪˈsteɪ·kᵊn/ *adj* • *If you think you can carry on drinking so much without damaging your health, then you're mistaken* (=wrong). • *I'm afraid I was mistaken* **about** *how much it would cost.* • *The negotiations have continued in the mistaken* **belief** *that an agreement can be reached without military intervention.* • *Throughout his trial he claimed that the charges against him were based on* **a case of** *mistaken* **identity**. • **Unless I'm very much** *mistaken, you still owe me fifteen pounds.*

mis·tak·en·ly /mɪˈsteɪ·kᵊn·li/ *adv* • *She mistakenly* **believed** *that she could get away with not paying her taxes.*

mis·tak·a·ble, *Br also* **mis·take·a·ble** /mɪˈsteɪ·kə·bl̩/ *adj* [not gradable] • *She's* **easily** *mistakeable* **for** *a man when she wears that suit and hat.*

mis·take WRONG ACTION /mɪˈsteɪk/ *n* [C] an action, decision or judgment which produces an unwanted or unintentional result • *We all* **make** *mistakes, so I'm not blaming you for the accident.* • *We must try to* **learn from** *our mistakes.* • *Marrying Pat was the* **biggest** *mistake I ever made.* • *I'm afraid we've made a* **terrible** *mistake and amputated the wrong leg.* • **It** *would be a* **fatal** *mistake* **to** *ignore my advice.* [+ to infinitive] • *How can we avoid* **repeating** *past mistakes/the mistakes of the past?* • *This essay is full of silly* **spelling** *mistakes and there's not enough time to* **correct** *them.* • *I've discovered a few mistakes* **in** *your calculations.* • *Why am I under arrest? There must be* **some** *mistake.* • *I've paid this bill twice* **by mistake** (=accidentally). • *(esp. Br) He's a strange bloke* **and no mistake** (=He certainly is very strange). • **Make no mistake about it** (=It is completely certain), *this decision is going to cause a lot of problems for you.*

Mis·ter /£ˈmɪs·təʳ, $-tɚ/ *n* the complete form of the title MR, or an informal and often rude form of address for a man • *Mister George Brown has been invited to the dinner.* • *Excuse me, Mister, could you spare some change for a cup of tea.* • *Listen to me, Mister, I don't wanna see you in this bar ever again.* • *Paul's* **Mister Big** (=the most important person) *in our department, so it's important to make a good impression on him.* • LP **Titles and forms of address**

mis·time *obj* /mɪˈstaɪm/ *v* [T] to do (something) at the wrong moment with the result that it is unsuccessful or has an unwanted effect • *She mistimed her stroke and the ball went into the net.*

mis·tle·toe /£ˈmɪs·l̩.təʊ, $-toʊ/ *n* [U] an evergreen plant with small white fruits and pale yellow flowers which grows on trees rather than in earth • *In Britain and the US, mistletoe is used as a Christmas decoration and is hung up so that people can stand underneath it and kiss each other.* • *Did you see what Chris and Pat were doing* **under** *the mistletoe at the office party?*

mi·stral /mɪˈstrɑːl/ *n* [U] **the mistral** a strong cold dry wind that blows south through France to the Mediterranean, usually in winter

mis·treat *obj* /mɪˈstriːt/ *v* [T] to treat (a person or animal) badly, cruelly or unfairly • *We were extremely relieved to hear that he hadn't been mistreated by the kidnappers.* • *Both parents have denied charges of mistreating their children.* • *I think people who mistreat their pets should be banned from keeping them.*

mis·treat·ment /mɪˈstriːt·mənt/ *n* [U] • *She stabbed her husband to death after suffering twenty years of mistreatment from him.*

mis·tress RESPONSIBLE WOMAN /ˈmɪs·trəs/ *n* [C] *dated* a woman who is in a position of responsibility or control • *I'll inform* **the** *mistress* **of** *the house of your arrival, madam.* • *She intends to remain* **the** *mistress* **of** (=in charge of) *her own life when she gets married.* • *(Br)* A mistress is also a female school teacher: *You've got a very good report from your German mistress.* • The mistress of a dog is the woman or girl who owns it.

mis·tress SEXUAL PARTNER /ˈmɪs·trəs/ *n* [C] a woman who is having a sexual relationship with a married man • *The wife of an army major was charged with murdering her husband's mistress last night.*

mis·tri·al /ˈmɪs·traɪəl/ *n* [C] a trial during which a mistake has been made, causing the judgment to have no legal value, or *(Am)* a trial in which no decision can be reached about whether a person is guilty or not

mis·trust *obj* /mɪˈstrʌst/ *v* [T] to have doubts about the honesty or abilities of (someone) • *I've always mistrusted politicians.*

mis·trust /mɪˈstrʌst/ *n* • *The British seem to have* **a** *deep mistrust* **of** *being linked physically to the European mainland.* • *Although the dispute ended two years ago there is still considerable mistrust* **between** *the management and the workforce.* [U]

mis·trust·ful /mɪˈstrʌst·fᵊl/ *adj* • *Voters are bound to be mistrustful* **of** *a government that has broken so many promises.*

mis·trust·ful·ly /mɪˈstrʌst·fᵊl·i/ *adv*

mist·y /£ˈmɪs·ti, $-t̬i/ *adj* See at MIST

mis·un·der·stand *(obj)* /£ˌmɪs·ʌn·dəˈstænd, $-dɚ-/ *v past* **misunderstood** /£ˌmɪs·ʌn·dəˈstʊd, $-dɚ-/ to think you have understood (someone or something) when you have not • *To suggest that these transport problems can be solved by building more roads is to misunderstand the* **nature** *of the problem.* [T] • *I told him to meet me here half an hour ago, but perhaps he misunderstood and thought I meant a different restaurant.* [I]

mis·un·der·stand·ing /£ˌmɪs·ʌn·dəˈstæn·dɪŋ, $-dɚ-/ *n* • *His ridiculous comments were obviously based on a complete misunderstanding* **of** *the situation.* [C] • *There must be some misunderstanding. I never asked for these chairs to be delivered.* [C] • *The inventor of Esperanto hoped that his artificial language would help reduce misunderstanding between nations.* [U] • Sometimes a misunderstanding is a disagreement, argument or fight: *"How did you get your black eye?" "Oh, I had a little misunderstanding* **with** *someone at a football match."* [C]

mis·use *obj* /ˌmɪsˈjuːz/ *v* [T] to use (something) in an unsuitable way or in a way that was not intended • *She's been accused of misusing company funds to pay for personal expenses.*

mis·use /ˌmɪsˈjuːs/ *n* • *This new computer system is completely unnecessary and a misuse* **of** *taxpayers' money.* [C] • *Young people ought to be taught about the dangers of alcohol misuse.* [U]

mite ANIMAL /maɪt/ *n* [C] a very small animal similar to a SPIDER • *a red spider mite*

mite CHILD /maɪt/ *n* [C] *infml esp. Br* a young child, esp. one deserving sympathy because they are ill or hungry • *Poor little mite, he looks so tired.*

mite SMALL AMOUNT /maɪt/ *n* [U] a (very) small amount • *(dated) "Would you like some more dessert?" "No thank you, I couldn't eat another mite."* • *The suggestion that they had taken the money made them* **a mite** (=slightly) *resentful.* • *I think you're being* **a mite** *stingy by offering them £350. £370 would be fairer.*

mit·i·gate *obj* /£ˈmɪt·ɪ·geɪt, $ˈmɪt̬-/ *v* [T] *fml* to make (something) less harmful, unpleasant or bad • *It is unclear how to mitigate* **the effects** *of tourism on the island.* • *Being polite now is not going to mitigate his earlier rudeness.*

mit·i·gat·ing /£ˈmɪt·ɪ·geɪ·tɪŋ, $ˈmɪt̬·ɪ·geɪ·t̬ɪŋ/ *adj* [not gradable] *fml* • *Are there any mitigating* **circumstances**/*reasons which might help explain her appalling behaviour?* • *(law) Duress can be a mitigating* **circumstance** (=reason for considering a crime to be less serious) *for crimes which are subject to the death penalty.* • Compare UNMITIGATED.

mit·i·ga·tion /£ˌmɪt·ɪˈgeɪ·ʃᵊn, $ˌmɪţ-/ *n* [U] *fml* • *The bad weather could be used* **in** *mitigation* **of** *the team's poor performance.*

mi·to·sis /£maɪˈtəʊ·sɪs, $-ˈtoʊ-/ *n* [U] the process by which a cell divides to become two similar cells

mi·tre /£ˈmaɪ·təʳ, $-ţɚ/, *Am also* **mit·er** *n* [C] a tall pointed hat worn by BISHOPS (= priests of high rank in the Christian church) on ceremonial occasions • *a bishop's mitre*

mi·tre (joint) /£ˈmaɪ·təʳ, $-ţɚ/, *Am also* **mit·er (joint)** *n* [C] a joint, esp. one made by two pieces of wood which have both been cut at an angle of 45 degrees at the joining ends

mitt /mɪt/ *n* [C] a special type of GLOVE for protecting a person's hand from extreme conditions • *a catcher's mitt* (= a mitt used by one of the defending players in a baseball game) • A mitt (also **mitten**) is also a type of glove with no covering on the ends of the fingers and the thumb. • *(slang)* Mitts are also a person's hands: *Get your filthy mitts off my sandwich!*

mit·ten /£ˈmɪt·ᵊn, $ˈmɪţ-/ *n* [C] a type of GLOVE, either with a single part for all the fingers and a separate part for the thumb, or (also **mitt**) with no covering on the ends of the fingers and the thumb • *sheepskin mittens* • *woollen mitt(en)s* • Compare GLOVE.

mix *(obj)* COMBINE /mɪks/ *v* to (cause different things to) combine, esp. so that the result cannot easily be separated into its parts • *Oil doesn't mix* **with** *water. Even if you shake them together they separate into two layers.* [I] • *Oil and water can't be mixed.* [T] • *Chemical analysis showed that radioactive material was mixed* **in** *(with) the effluent.* [T] • *Mix the eggs* **in with/into** *the flour.* [T] • *Gently mix* **up/together** *the flour, sugar and raisins in a bowl.* [T] • *Would you mix* (= make) *me a cocktail?/Would you mix a cocktail* **for** *me?* [+ two objects] • *Some people are happy to mix business* **with/and** *pleasure, but I'm not one of them.* [T] • If you **mix** your **metaphors** you combine two or more METAPHORS, esp. producing a silly or an amusing result: *Mixing his metaphors, he described the problem by saying "We've opened up a can of worms here, and now we have to get the genie back in the bottle".*

mix /mɪks/ *n* • *The mix* (= combination) **of** *racial groups in this city makes it a fascinating place.* [C] • *There was an* **odd** *mix of people at Patrick's party.* [U] • *"She's studying physics and philosophy." "That's an interesting mix."* [C] • *We use* **a** *mix* **of** *teaching methods which we vary according to the needs of our students.* [U] • Sometimes a mix is something which is sold in the form of a powder and to which a liquid, such as water, can be added later: *a cake mix* [C] ○ *a bag of cement mix* [U]

mixed /mɪkst/ *adj* • *There has been a mixed* **reaction** *to the changes* (= some people like them, but others do not). • Mixed also means for both sexes: *Our children go to a mixed* **school**. ○ *(dated) Some of his jokes were very rude – they weren't suitable for mixed* **company** (= a group where both males and females are present). • Mixed can also mean combining people of a different religion or race: *a mixed marriage/relationship* ○ *There is often a lot of prejudice against people of mixed* **race**. • **Mixed-ability** teaching is where children of different abilities are taught together: *mixed-ability teaching/classes* • A **mixed bag** is a range of different things or people: *There's a real mixed bag* **of** *people on the course.* ○ *We received a mixed bag* (= some good and some bad) *of entries to the competition.* • *Getting into the team is a* **mixed blessing** (= has advantages and disadvantages). *It's good to have the place, but I'll have to spend a lot of time training.* • If you play a game of **mixed doubles**, you play a game, such as tennis, with each team consisting of one female and one male player. • *(Am)* A **mixed drink** is an alcoholic drink made by mixing at least two liquids, one of them containing alcohol: *Gin and tonic is a mixed drink.* • A **mixed economy** is an economic system in which some industries are controlled privately and some by the government. • **Mixed farming** is a method of farming in which crops are grown and animals are kept on the same farm. • *We have* **mixed feelings** (= both good and bad emotions) *about the move. There will be new opportunities, but problems also.* • A **mixed grill** is a meal in which several types of meat are served together which have been cooked under a very hot part of a cooker. • A **mixed metaphor** is when two or more METAPHORS are combined, esp. to produce a silly or an amusing effect: *"The new job has allowed her to spread her wings and really blossom" is a mixed metaphor.*

mix·er /£ˈmɪk·səʳ, $-sɚ/ *n* [C] • A mixer is a machine which mixes things: *a cement mixer* ○ *To speed matters up, you can prepare the dough in a (food) mixer.* • A mixer is also a drink which does not contain alcohol and which can be mixed with an alcoholic drink, esp. a SPIRIT (= strong alcoholic drink): *We have tonic or orange juice if anyone wants mixers with their vodka.* • *(Br)* A **mixer tap**/*(Am)* **faucet** is a device for controlling the flow of water in which hot and cold water come out of the same pipe, but the flow of each is controlled separately so that the temperature of the water coming out can be adjusted. • PIC› **Bathroom, Building and construction** ⓒⓢ

mix·ture /£ˈmɪks·tʃəʳ, $-tʃɚ/ *n* • *The mixture* (= combination) **of** *flour, water and yeast is then left in a warm place for four hours.* [C] • *Gases produced in the reaction can form an explosive mixture.* [C] • *Her house is furnished in a curious mixture* **of** *old and modern styles.* [C] • *Their latest CD is a mixture* **of** *new and old songs.* [C] • *Mixture* (= The process of mixing) *occurs within five minutes of the liquids coming into contact.* [U] • *(medical)* A mixture is a type of medicine which has to be shaken before being used: *cough mixture* [U]

mix SOCIALIZE /mɪks/ *v* [I] (of a person) to be with or communicate well with other people • *I suppose you mix* **with** *a wide variety of people in your job.* • *She mixes very well – perhaps that's why she's so popular.* • *(infml esp. Br)* If someone **mixes it** they behave in a very confident way when the people around them are unpleasant or difficult to deal with: *She's just what we need for a negotiator – she doesn't mind mixing it* **with** *the worst of them.*

mix·er /£ˈmɪk·səʳ, $-sɚ/ *n* [C] • *You'll get to know lots of people at college if you're a* **good** *mixer –* **bad** *mixers have a difficult time.* • *(Am)* A mixer can also be a party or dance which has been organized so that people in a group can get to know each other: *The school always holds a mixer on the second week of the term.*

mix *obj* RECORD MUSIC /mɪks/ *v* [T] *specialized* to control (the amounts of various sounds which are combined on a recording) • *She finished recording her new album last year, but she's still in the process of mixing it.*

mix /mɪks/ *n* [C] • *A new mix of their hit single is due to be released early next month.*

mix up *obj* CONFUSE, **mix** *obj* **up** *v adv* [M] to confuse (someone), or to mistake (someone or something) for someone or something else • *The noise and the heat mixed us up and we got lost.* • *It's easy to mix up the mayor and his deputy – neither of them have much charisma.*

mix up *obj* WRONG ORDER, **mix** *obj* **up** *v adv* [M] to put (objects) into the wrong order • *Don't mix up the bottles – you'll have to repeat the experiment if you do.* • *(Am)* If two people **mix it up** they fight: *He's usually pretty peaceful, but he and that other guy really mixed it up at the bar last night.*

mix–up /ˈmɪks·ʌp/ *n* [C] *slightly infml* • *There was a mix-up at the office and we all received the wrong forms.* • *I'm afraid there's been* **a bit of a** *mix-up* (= some confusion) **with** *your reservation, madam. Would you mind waiting ten minutes for a table?*

mixed up *adj* [after v; not gradable] *usually disapproving* connected with a bad or unpleasant person or thing • *Was she really mixed up* **with** *that terrorist group?* • *If you want my advice, don't get mixed up* **with** *him. You'll regret it if you do.* • *I knew a couple of people who were mixed up* **in** *that corruption scandal.*

mixed–up /ˌmɪkstˈʌp/ *adj* upset, worried and confused, esp. because of personal problems • *It's not surprising he's such a mixed-up* **kid** *when he has parents as irresponsible as that.*

miz·zle /ˈmɪz·l̩/ *n* [U] *esp. Am* rain made of many very small drops • See also DRIZZLE.

miz·zle /ˈmɪz·l̩/ *v* [I] *esp. Am* • *It's been mizzling most of the morning.*

miz·zly /ˈmɪz·li/ *adj* **-ier, -iest** *esp. Am*

Mk *n* [before n] *abbreviation for* MARK MACHINE (= the model number of a car or machine) • *She was driving a bright yellow Mk XI Lotus two-seater.*

ml /mɪl/ *n* [C] *pl* **ml** or **mls** *abbreviation for* MILLILITRE • *A 7 ml bottle of the perfume costs £39.*

mm *n* [C] *pl* **mm** *abbreviation for* MILLIMETRE • *a 6mm (diameter) drill*

mne·mon·ic /£nɪˈmɒn·ɪk, $-ˈmɑː·nɪk/ *n* [C], *adj* [not gradable] (something such as a very short poem or a special word) used to help a person remember something • *'Roy G Biv' is a mnemonic for the colours of the spectrum and the order in which they appear: red, orange, yellow, green, blue, indigo, violet.*

mo MONEY /£ˌemˈəʊ, $-ˈoʊ/ *n* [C] *esp. Am abbreviation for* **money order**, see at MONEY

mo MOMENT /£məʊ, $moʊ/ *n* [U] *infml* (used mainly in spoken English) a short period of time; a moment • *"Come on! We're going to be late." "Hang on* **a** *mo! I just get my wallet."* • *I'll be with you in* **half** *a mo* (= very soon). • See also BIG MO.

moan *(obj)* SOUND /£məʊn, $moʊn/ *v, n* (to make) a long low sound of pain, suffering or other strong emotion • *He moaned* **with** *pain before losing consciousness.* [I] • *Moaning* **in** *grief at the death of her husband she could not be consoled.* [I] • *"Let me die," he moaned.* [+ clause] • *We could hear moans from someone trapped under the rubble.* [C] • *Their moans* **of** *ecstasy could be heard in the corridor.* [C]

moan *(obj)* COMPLAIN /£məʊn, $moʊn/ *v, n infml disapproving* (to make) a complaint made in an unhappy voice, esp. about something which does not seem important to other people • *Thelma is always moaning* **(about** *something), which is stupid because she has a very pleasant life.* [I] • *"I don't like potatoes," he moaned.* [+ clause] • *She moans* **(that)** *she's too hot, so you open the window and then she complains that it's too cold.* [+ *(that)* clause] • *Apart from a slight moan about the service our meal was most enjoyable.* [C] • *(Br infml)* A **moaning minnie** is someone who annoys other people by complaining all the time: *I wish you'd just stop being such a moaning minnie!*

moan·er /£ˈməʊ·nəʳ, $ˈmoʊ·nɚ/ *n* [C] • *Foreigners often think that the British are a nation of moaners.*

moat /£məʊt, $moʊt/ *n* [C] a long wide channel which is dug all the way around a safe place, such as a castle or hill, and is usually filled with water, making the place more difficult to attack

moat·ed /£ˈməʊ·tɪd, $ˈmoʊ·t̬ɪd/ *adj* [not gradable] • A moated **castle** is one that has a moat around it.

mob GROUP /£mɒb, $mɑːb/ *n* [C + sing/pl v] *infml* a large group of people involved in similar activities, which are often violent or lacking in order • *a lynch mob* • *The usual mob were/was hanging out at the bar.* • A mob is also a group or organization of criminals. • *He's the second New York mob leader to be convicted this month.* • See also MOBSTER.

mob CROWD /£mɒb, $mɑːb/ *n* [C + sing/pl v] *usually disapproving* a large angry crowd, esp. one which could easily become violent • *The* **angry** *mob outside the jail was/were ready to riot.* • *Almost fifty people were killed in three days of mob* **violence**. • *Diplomats are forecasting mob* **rule** *for the country if the president is not restored to power.*

mob *obj* GATHER /£mɒb, $mɑːb/ *v* [T] **-bb-** to gather around (someone) in a crowd to express admiration, interest or anger • *They were mobbed* **by** *fans when they arrived at the theatre.* • *Reporters mobbed the minister as he left the building.* • *(Am) I don't want to go to the Old Town tonight – it's always mobbed* (= there are always a lot of people there) *on Fridays.*

mo·bile /£ˈməʊ·baɪl, $ˈmoʊ·bᵊl/ *adj* able to move freely or be easily moved • *You've broken your ankle but you'll be fully mobile* (= able to walk as usual) *within a couple of months.* • A **mobile home** is a movable building, often on wheels, which people live in and which usually stays in one place, but it can be moved using a vehicle or sometimes its own engine. • *(Br and Aus)* A **mobile library** (*Am* **bookmobile**) is a large road vehicle which travels around, esp. in the countryside, carrying books for people to borrow. • A **mobile phone** (also **mobile telephone**) is a telephone which is connected to the telephone system by radio, rather than by a wire, and can therefore be used anywhere where its signals can be received. • PIC〉 **Accommodation, Office**

mo·bile /£ˈməʊ·baɪl, $ˈmoʊ·bᵊl/ *n* [C] • A mobile is a decoration or work of art in which many of its parts move freely often because each one is hung by a thread and therefore moved by the air.

mo·bil·i·ty /£məʊˈbɪl·ɪ·ti, $moʊˈbɪl·ə·t̬i/ *n* [U] *slightly fml* • *Mobility of the arm will gradually improve after we remove the plaster.* • *(fig. esp. Br) For children from poorer families, the main hope of* **social** *mobility (Am and Aus usually* **upward mobility**) (= the ability to change social class) *is through education.*

mo·bil·ize *obj* ORGANIZE, *Br and Aus usually* **-ise** /£ˈməʊ·bɪ·laɪz, $ˈmoʊ-/ *v* [T] to organize or prepare (something such as a group of people) for a purpose • *Representatives for all the main candidates are trying to mobilize voter support for the election.*

mo·bil·iz·a·tion, *Br and Aus usually* **-i·sa·tion** /£ˌməʊ·bɪ·laɪˈzeɪ·ʃᵊn, $ˌmoʊ·bɪ·lɪ-/ *n* [U]

mo·bil·ize *(obj)* MILITARY, *Br and Aus usually* **-ise** /£ˈməʊ·bɪ·laɪz, $ˈmoʊ-/ *v* to (cause something such as an army to) prepare to fight, esp. in a war • *The government has mobilized several of the army's top combat units.* [T] • *Troops have been mobilising for the past three weeks.* [I]

mo·bil·iz·a·tion, *Br and Aus usually* **-i·sa·tion** /£ˌməʊ·bɪ·laɪˈzeɪ·ʃᵊn, $ˌmoʊ·bɪ·lɪ-/ *n* [U]

Mö·bi·us strip /ˌmɜː·bi·əs, £ˌməʊ-, $ˌmoʊ-/ *n* [C] *specialized* an object with only one surface which is made by twisting a long strip of material once and then joining its two ends

mob·ster /£ˈmɒb·stəʳ, $ˈmɑːb·stɚ/ *n* [C] *esp. Am for* GANGSTER

moc·ca·sin /£ˈmɒk·ə·sɪn, $ˈmɑː·kə-/ *n* [C] a shoe which the wearer's foot slides into and which is made from soft leather with stitches around the top at the front • PIC〉 **Shoes**

moch·a /£ˈmɒk·ə, $ˈmoʊ·kə/ *n* [U] a type of coffee of good quality, or a flavouring which tastes of this

mock *(obj)* LAUGH AT /£mɒk, $mɑːk/ *v slightly fml* to laugh at (someone), esp. by copying them in an amusing but unkind way • *It was cruel the way he mocked her hopes of marriage and happiness.* [T] • *Don't mock* **(at)** *him just because he keeps falling off his bike.* [I/T] • *She made fun of him by mocking his limp.* [T] • *(fig.) A cruel wind mocked the boat's attempts to reach the shore by pushing it further and further out to sea.* [T]

mock·er·y /£ˈmɒk·ᵊr·i, $ˈmɑː·kɚ-/ *n* [U] • Mockery is unkind critical remarks or actions: *She agreed with him, but there was mockery in her eyes.* • *Bill's mockery of his dad's twitch was a bit cruel, but it made us laugh.* • A mockery is also something which is a failure and therefore insulting to the people it has an effect on: *The trial was* **a** *mockery – the judge had decided the verdict before it began.* ○ *The renewed fighting has* **made a mockery of** *the peace agreement* (= made it look stupid).

mock·ing /£ˈmɒk·ɪŋ, $ˈmɑː·kɪŋ/ *adj* • *a mocking voice* • *mocking humour/laughter*

mock·ing·ly /£ˈmɒk·ɪŋ·li, $ˈmɑː·kɪŋ-/ *adv*

mock ARTIFICIAL /£mɒk, $mɑːk/ *adj* [before n; not gradable] artificial, but similar to the original • *She's a vegetarian, so she wants a jacket that's made of mock leather.* • *"Might be true," said Harry with a look of mock* (= pretended) *horror on his face.* • *The film set is made from mock façades with no real buildings behind them.* • *(Am)* A **mock turtleneck** is a TURTLENECK. • PIC〉 **Clothes**

mock– /£mɒk-, $mɑːk-/ *combining form* • A mock-Tudor house is a modern house which is intended to look as if it was built during the Tudor period. • *In a long gallery, gilded Italian mock-baroque armchairs, settees, and tables are stored.*

mock EXAM *Br* /£mɒk, $mɑːk/, *Aus* **trial** *n* [C] an exam taken at school for practice before a real exam • *You will have your mocks during the first two weeks of March.* • *In Australia, trials take place in July.*

mock·ing·bird /£ˈmɒk·ɪŋ·bɜːd, $ˈmɑː·kɪŋ·bɜːrd/ *n* [C] any of the types of North American or Australian birds which copy the sounds made by other birds

mock–up /£ˈmɒk·ʌp, $ˈmɑːk-/ *n* [C] a full-size model of something large that has not yet been built which shows how it will look or operate • *She showed us a mock-up of what the car will look like when it goes into production.* • Mock-ups are also used when the real thing is not needed: *Mock-up aircraft are used when staff are being trained to deal with emergencies.*

mock up *obj*, **mock** *obj* **up** *v adv* [M] • *They mocked up the new car in clay.*

Mod /£mɒd, $mɑːd/ *n* [C] *Br* a member of a group of young people formed in the 1960s who wore stylish clothes and rode SCOOTERS (= small motorcycles) • *In the 1960s Mods used to get in fights with rockers, but in the late 70s and early 80s skinheads were the enemy.*

MoD /£ˌem·əʊˈdiː, $ˌ-oʊˈ-/ *n* [U] **the MoD** *Br abbreviation for* Ministry of Defence (= the British government department that deals with military defence and war)

mod·al /£ˈməʊ·dᵊl, $ˈmoʊ-/, **mod·al verb**, **mod·al aux·il·ia·ry** *n* [C] *specialized* a verb used with another verb to express an idea such as possibility that is not expressed by the main verb of a sentence • *The modal verbs in English are 'can', 'could', 'may', 'might', 'must', 'ought',* *'shall', 'should', 'will' and 'would'.* • *The first verb in the following sentence is a modal: We must pay the gas bill.* • LP> **Auxiliary verbs**

mod con /£ˌmɒd'kɒn, $ˌmɑːd'kɑːn/ *n* [C usually pl] *Br and Aus infml slightly dated* a modern convenience; something, such as a washing machine, which makes the ordinary regular jobs in a home easier • *The kitchen of this delightful cottage is fully equipped with all mod cons including a dishwasher.*

mode WAY /£məʊd, $moʊd/ *n* [C] *slightly fml* a way of operating, living or behaving • *Each department in the company has its own mode of operation and none of them are compatible.* • *You'll have to change your mode of life now that you have a baby.* • *Railways are the most important mode of transport for the economy.* • Ⓓ

mode FASHION /£məʊd, $moʊd/ *n* [U] *slightly fml* a fashion or style, esp. a present one in clothing • *Miniskirts were* **all the** *mode in the 60s.* • *Platform shoes were* **in** *mode in the 70s and again in the 90s.* • See also A LA MODE MODERN. • Ⓓ

mod·ish /£'məʊ·dɪʃ, $'moʊ-/ *adj slightly fml* • *She was wearing an extravagantly modish outfit at the party.*

mod·ish·ly /£'məʊ·dɪʃ·li, $'moʊ-/ *adv slightly fml*

mod·el REPRESENTATION /£'mɒd·əl, $'mɑː·dəl/ *n* [C] a representation of something, either as a physical object which is usually smaller than the real object, or as a simple description of the object which might be used in calculations • *a plastic model aircraft* • *By looking at this model you can get a better idea of how the bridge will look.* • *to construct a statistical/theoretical/mathematical model* • *No model* **of** *the economy can predict when the next recession will be.* • *Computer models have been used to predict long-term climatic changes.*

mod·el *obj* /£'mɒd·əl, $'mɑː·dəl/ *v* [T] *Am also and Br* **-ll-** • *to model animals out of clay* • *to model clay into animal shapes* • *The whole car can be modelled on a computer before a single component is made.*

mod·el COPY /£'mɒd·əl, $'mɑː·dəl/ *n* [C] something which a copy can be based on, esp. because it is an extremely good example of its type • *The educational system was a model for those of many other countries.* • *She gave a model* (=extremely good) *presentation to the directors.* • *The council plans to build a model town on the site* (=a town which is so good that it will be copied by others). • *Some groups want to set up an Islamic state* **on the** *Iranian model.* • *She really is a model* (=perfect) *student. She studies for three hours every night and hands in all her homework on time.* • *Even Chris,* **the very** *model* **of** *calmness* (=someone who is usually extremely calm), *was angered by having to work such long hours.* • *Sports stars are* **role** *models for thousands of youngsters.* • *"I am the very model of a modern Major-General"* (First line of song from the operetta *The Pirates of Penzance* by W.S.Gilbert and A.S.Sullivan, 1880)

mod·el *obj* /£'mɒd·əl, $'mɑː·dəl/ *v* [T] *Am also and Br* **-ll-** • *The building's roof is supposedly modelled* **on** *the great pyramid.* • *She models herself* **on** *Madonna.*

mod·el PERSON /£'mɒd·əl, $'mɑː·dəl/, *dated* **man·ne·quin** *n* [C] a person who wears clothes so that they can be photographed or shown to possible buyers, or a person who is employed to be photographed or painted • *a fashion/nude model* • *I'm going out with a male model at the moment.* • *I worked as an artist's model for a while when I was a student.* • See also SUPERMODEL.

mod·el *(obj)* /£'mɒd·əl, $'mɑː·dəl/ *v Am also and Br* **-ll-** • *Tatjana is modelling another Quant design.* [T] • *Martin's such a hunk – he could easily get a job modelling!* [I]

mod·el MACHINE /£'mɒd·əl, $'mɑː·dəl/ *n* [C] a particular type of machine, esp. a car, which is slightly different to machines of the same type • *a luxury/new model* • *the latest model* • *Spare parts are hard to get – they stopped making this model in 1967!*

mo·dem /£'məʊ·dem, $'moʊ·dəm/ *n* [C] *specialized* an electronic device which allows one computer to send information to another through standard telephone wires and therefore over long distances

mod·er·ate MEDIUM-SIZED /£'mɒd·ər·ət, $'mɑː·dɚ-/ *adj* neither small nor large but between the two; clearly within the limits of a range of possibilities • *moderate growth/inflation* • *I'm a moderate drinker – I have about four pints of beer a week.* • *The cabin is of moderate size – just right for a small family.* • *It's a moderate price for a car of its type.* • *Imposing sanctions is a moderate action when you consider that the alternative is military intervention.*

mod·er·ate·ly /£'mɒd·ər·ət·li, $'mɑː·dɚ-/ *adv* • *There's very little moderately* **priced** *housing in this area.*

mod·er·a·tion /£ˌmɒd·ər'eɪ·ʃən, $ˌmɑː·də'reɪ-/ *n* [U] • *All parties will have to show great moderation during these very difficult negotiations.* • *There is still no clear evidence* **of** *moderation in wage settlements.* • *Some people believe in eating whatever they want as long as it's* **in** *moderation.* • *(saying)* 'Moderation in all things' means do not have or do too much or too little of anything.

mod·er·a·tor /£'mɒd·ər·eɪ·tər, $'mɑː·də·reɪ·t̬ɚ/ *n* [C] • *(fml)* A moderator (*Am and Aus usually* **mediator**) is someone who tries to help other people come to an agreement: *An independent moderator should be appointed to oversee the negotiations.* • *(Am)* A moderator is also someone who makes certain that a formal discussion happens without difficulties and follows the rules: *He challenged the president to a series of TV debates. Just the two of them, with no moderator.* • *(Br specialized)* A moderator can also be someone who makes certain that all the examiners marking a student's work use the same standards: *The final marks awarded for coursework will depend upon the moderator.*

mod·er·ate OPINIONS /£'mɒd·ər·ət, $'mɑː·dɚ-/ *n, adj* (relating to) a person whose opinions, esp. their political ones, are not extreme and are therefore acceptable to a large number of people • *He is well-known as a moderate in the party.* [C] • *The party leader is an extreme left-winger, but her deputy is more moderate in her views.*

mod·er·ate SLIGHT /£'mɒd·ər·ət, $'mɑː·dɚ-/ *adj* slight or limited; not as great as desired • *There has been a moderate improvement in her health since she began the treatment.* • *We have had moderate success in changing people's attitudes.*

mod·er·ate·ly /£'mɒd·ər·ət·li, $'mɑː·dɚ-/ *adv* • *The company remains moderately profitable, but it is not making as much money as it should.*

mod·er·ate *(obj)* REDUCE /£'mɒd·ər·eɪt, $'mɑː·də·reɪt/ *v* to (cause to) become less in size, strength, or force; to reduce (something) • *There have been repeated calls for the president to moderate his stance on contraception.* [T] • *Weather conditions have moderated, making a rescue attempt possible.* [I]

mod·er·a·tion /£ˌmɒd·ər'eɪ·ʃən, $ˌmɑː·də'reɪ-/ *n* [U] *slightly fml* • *We can't sail until there is some moderation in the storm.*

mod·ern MOST RECENT /£'mɒd·ən, $'mɑː·dɚn/ *adj* (designed and made) using the most recent ideas and methods • *modern technology/architecture/medicine/art* • *We're in the very modern-looking building opposite the station.* • *(approving) Her attitudes are very modern, considering her age.* • **Modern dance** is a style of dance usually performed in a theatre, which is very expressive and does not have many rules for the dancer's movements. • **Modern jazz** is a type of jazz music which began in the 1940s and is of an advanced level musically.

mod·ern·i·sm /£'mɒd·ən·ɪ·zəm, $'mɑː·dɚ·nɪ-/ *n* [U] *specialized* • Modernism is the ideas and methods of modern art, esp. in the simple design of buildings in the 1940s, 50s and 60s which were made from modern materials: *Modernism seeks to find new forms of expression and rejects traditional or accepted ideas.*

mod·ern·ist /£'mɒd·ən·ɪst, $'mɑː·dɚ·nɪst/ *adj, n specialized* • *Modernist architecture tries to conquer nature instead of working with it.* • *The design of the new library has been acclaimed by Modernists.* [C]

mod·ern·ist·ic /£ˌmɒd·ən'ɪs·tɪk, $ˌmɑː·dɚ'nɪs-/ *adj* • If something is modernistic it has been designed in way that is obviously modern: *The new airport has a very modernistic appearance.*

mod·ern·i·ty /£mɒd'ɜː·nə·ti, $mɑː'dɜːr·nə·t̬i/ *n* [U] • Modernity is the condition that results from being modern: *There is a tense contrast between tradition and modernity on the streets of the city.* ○ *She tends to be very old-fashioned, but she has finally given in to modernity and bought herself a personal computer.*

mod·ern·ize *(obj), Br and Aus usually* **-ise** /£'mɒd·ən·aɪz, $'mɑː·dɚ·naɪz/ *v* • *Wouldn't you like to modernize the kitchen – you don't even have space for a washing machine!* [T] • *There has been a lot of opposition to modernizing working practices in our office.* [T] • *If they want to increase output from the factory, they'll have to modernize.* [I]

mod·ern·iz·a·tion, *Br and Aus usually* **-i·sa·tion** /£ˌmɒd·ən·aɪ'zeɪ·ʃən, $ˌmɑː·dɚ·naɪ-/ *n* [U] • *The* *modernization of the 100-year-old sewage and water systems will cost millions of pounds.*

mod·ern PRESENT /£'mɒd·ᵊn, $'mɑː·dɚn/ *adj* [not gradable] of the present or recent times, esp. the period of history from the beginning or the end of the **Middle Ages** (= the period from 600 AD or 1000 AD to 1500 AD) • *The great source of terror in early modern Europe was bubonic plague.* • *The collapse of communism in Eastern Europe was one of the great events of modern* **times.** • *What do you think is the role of religion in the modern* **world?** • *(esp. Br)* **Modern languages** are languages that are spoken at the present time, esp. European languages such as French, German and Spanish: *He's going to study modern languages at university.*

mod·est NOT LARGE /£'mɒd·ɪst, $'mɑː·dɪst/ *adj* not large in size or amount, or not expensive • *They live in a fairly modest house, considering their wealth.* • *There has been a modest improvement/recovery in housing conditions for the poor.* • *The party made modest gains in the elections, but nothing like the huge gains that were predicted.*

mod·est·ly /£'mɒd·ɪst·li, $'mɑː·dɪst-/ *adv* • *At just £9, the training video is very modestly priced.*

mod·est QUIETLY SUCCESSFUL /£'mɒd·ɪst, $'mɑː·dɪst/ *adj usually approving* tending not to talk about or make obvious your own abilities and achievements • *He's very modest* **about** *the success of his research in genetics.*

mod·est·ly /£'mɒd·ɪst·li, $'mɑː·dɪst-/ *adv usually approving* • *"I'd never have won the prize without the help of my two assistants," she said modestly.*

mod·est·y /£'mɒd·ɪ·sti, $'mɑː·dɪ-/ *n* [U] *usually approving* • *She does a lot of work for charities, but (her) modesty* **forbids** *her from talking about it.* • *Quite frankly, and* **in all modesty** (= without wanting to seem too important), *we'd probably have lost the game if I hadn't been playing.*

mod·est CLOTHES/BEHAVIOUR /£'mɒd·ɪst, $'mɑː·dɪst/ *adj dated* (esp. of a woman's clothes or behaviour) intended to avoid attracting sexual interest • *a modest walk/manner*

mod·est·ly /£'mɒd·ɪst·li, $'mɑː·dɪst-/ *adv dated* • *Visitors are requested to dress modestly in this church.*

mod·est·y /£'mɒd·ɪ·sti, $'mɑː·dɪ-/ *n* [U] *dated*

mod·i·cum /£'mɒd·ɪ·kəm, $'mɑː·dɪ-/ *n* [U; usually in negatives and questions] *fml or literary* a small amount, esp. of something good such as truth or honesty • *There's not even* **a** *modicum* **of** *truth in her statement.* • *Anyone with* **a** *modicum* **of** *common sense could have seen that the plan wouldn't work.*

mod·i·fy *obj* CHANGE /£'mɒd·ɪ·faɪ, $'mɑː·dɪ-/ *v* [T] to change (something such as a plan, opinion, law or way of behaviour), esp. slightly, usually to improve it or make it more acceptable • *Instead of simply punishing them, the system encourages offenders to modify their behaviour.* • *The proposals were unpopular and were only accepted in a modified form.* • **Modified American plan** (abbreviation **MAP**) is *Am for* **half board**. See at HALF.

mod·i·fi·ca·tion /£,mɒd·ɪ·fɪ'keɪ·ʃᵊn, $,mɑː·dɪ-/ *n* • *Modification of the engine to run on lead-free fuel is fairly simple.* [U] • *A couple of modifications and the speech will be perfect.* [C]

mod·i·fy *obj* LIMIT /£'mɒd·ɪ·faɪ, $'mɑː·dɪ-/ *v* [T] *specialized* (of a word or phrase) to limit or add to the meaning of (another word or phrase that it is put with) • *In the sentence 'She ran quickly', the adverb 'quickly' modifies the verb 'ran'.*

mod·i·fi·ca·tion /£,mɒd·ɪ·fɪ'keɪ·ʃᵊn, $,mɑː·dɪ-/ *n* [U] *specialized*

mod·i·fier /£'mɒd·ɪ·faɪ·əʳ, $'mɑː·dɪ·faɪ·ɚ/ *n* [C] *specialized* • *In 'safety barrier', the noun 'safety' is being used as a modifier.*

mod·ish /£'məʊ·dɪʃ, $'moʊ-/ *adj* See at MODE FASHION

mod·u·late *obj* VOICE /£'mɒd·jʊ·leɪt, $'mɑː·dʒə-/ *v* [T] to vary (a voice) for example in strength or quality to achieve an effect or express an emotion • *His gentle introductory tone modulates into a football coach's pre-game pep talk.*

mod·u·la·tion /£,mɒd·jʊ'leɪ·ʃᵊn, $,mɑː·dʒə-/ *n* [C; U]

mod·u·late *obj* CHANGE /£'mɒd·jʊ·leɪt, $'mɑː·dʒə-/ *v* [T] *fml* to change (something such as an action or a process) to make it more suitable for its situation • *An elected committee will meet monthly to modulate the council's energy policy.*

mod·u·la·tion /£,mɒd·jʊ'leɪ·ʃᵊn, $,mɑː·dʒə-/ *n* [C; U] *fml*

mod·u·late *obj* BROADCASTING /£'mɒd·jʊ·leɪt, $'mɑː·dʒə-/ *v* [T] *specialized* to mix (an electrical signal which represents sounds or pictures) with a radio signal so that it can be broadcast

mod·u·la·tion /£,mɒd·jʊ'leɪ·ʃᵊn, $,mɑː·dʒə-/ *n* [C/U] *specialized* • *frequency/amplitude modulation* • See also AM RADIO; FM.

mod·ule /£'mɒd·juːl, $'mɑː·dʒuːl/ *n* [C] one of a set of separate parts which, when combined, form a complete whole • *The emergency building is transported in individual modules, such as bedrooms and a kitchen, which are put together on site.* • *The full computer program is made of several modules* (= small programs) *which should be individually tested before being integrated.* • A module is also one of the units which together make a complete course taught esp. at a college or university. • A module can also be a part of a spacecraft which can operate independently of the other parts, esp. when separate from them: *a lunar landing module*

mod·u·lar /£'mɒd·jʊ·ləʳ, $'mɑː·dʒə·lɚ/ *adj* [not gradable] • *Many colleges and universities now offer modular degree courses.*

mo·dus op·e·ran·di /£,məʊ·dəs,ɒp·ə'ræn·diː, $,moʊ·dəs ,ɑː·pə-/ *n* [U] *specialized* a particular way of doing something • *The modus operandi of one writer rarely has anything in common with that of another.*

mo·dus vi·ven·di /£,məʊ·dəs·vɪ'ven·diː, $,moʊ-/ *n* [U] *fml* an arrangement allowing people or groups of people who have different opinions or beliefs to work or live together • *Our two countries must put aside the memory of war and seek a modus vivendi.*

mog·gy /£'mɒg·i, $'mɑː·gi/, **mog·gie** *n* [C] *Br and Aus infml* a cat, esp. one which is ordinary or has an untidy appearance • *What's your moggie called?*

mo·gul PERSON /£'məʊ·gᵊl, $'moʊ-/ *n* [C] an important person who has great wealth or power • *movie/media/industry moguls*

mo·gul SNOW /£'məʊ·gᵊl, $'moʊ-/ *n* [C] *specialized* a small pile of hard snow on a slope where people SKI

mo·hair /£'məʊ·heəʳ, $'moʊ·her/ *n* [U] (a soft cloth made from) the silky outer hair of ANGORA goats • *mohair suits*

Mo·ham·med·an /£məʊ'hæm·ɪ·dᵊn, $moʊ-/ *n* [C] a Muslim. This word was previously often used in English, but Muslims consider it offensive because it suggests that they worship Mohammed rather than Allah.

Mo·hi·can *Br* /£məʊ'hiː·kᵊn, $moʊ-/, *Am* **Mo·hawk** /£'məʊ·hɔːk, $'moʊ·hɑːk/ *n* [C] a sometimes brightly coloured hairstyle, often worn by PUNKS, in which the hair is removed from the sides of the head and the strip around the centre is made to point out from the head

moi /mwɑː/ *pronoun humorous* (used to express often false surprise about something you have been accused of) me • *"You made a complete idiot of yourself at Pete's party." "Who? Moi?"*

moist /mɔɪst/ *adj* slightly wet • *As he walked through the forest, he could feel the warm moist air on his face.* • *Keep the soil in the pot moist, but not too wet.* • *(approving) This cake is lovely and moist!* • See also DAMP.

moist·en *(obj)* /'mɔɪ·sᵊn/ *v* • *Moisten the cloth* (= Make it slightly wet) *before using it to clean glass.* [T] • *She didn't cry during the sad part, but her eyes moistened.* [I]

moist·ness /'mɔɪst·nəs/ *n* [U]

mois·ture /£'mɔɪs·tʃəʳ, $-tʃɚ/ *n* [U] a liquid such as water in the form of very small drops, either in the air, or on a surface, esp. a cold one • *All the cooking's caused so much moisture that it's misting up the windows.*

mois·tur·ize *(obj), Br and Aus usually* **-ise** /£'mɔɪs·tʃᵊr·aɪz, $-tʃɚ-/ *v* • *It's a good idea to moisturize (your skin) before you apply make-up.* [T] • *I always put moisturizing* **lotion/cream** *on my hands after washing.*

mois·tur·iz·er, *Br and Aus usually* **-iser** /£'mɔɪs·tʃᵊr·aɪ·zəʳ, $-tʃɚ·aɪ·zɚ/ *n* [C; U] • Moisturizer is a thick liquid usually white or pale in colour which a person puts on their skin to stop it from being too dry.

mol·ar /£'məʊ·ləʳ, $'moʊ·lɚ/ *n* [C] any one of the large teeth at the back of the mouth in humans and some other animals used for crushing and chewing food • Compare **canine (tooth)** at CANINE; INCISOR.

mol·as·ses /mə'læs·ɪz/ *n* [U] a thick dark brown liquid made from sugar plants which is used in cooking

mold /£məʊld, $moʊld/ *n, v Am for* MOULD

mold·er /£'məʊl·də, $'moʊl·dɚ/ *v* [I] *Am for* MOULDER

mole ANIMAL /£məʊl, $moʊl/ *n* [C] a small mammal which is nearly blind, has dark fur and lives in passages that it digs under the ground • PIC› **Wild animals in Britain**

mole SPOT /£məʊl, $moʊl/ *n* [C] a small dark spot or lump on a person's skin which stays for a long time, often for the whole of their life • *Some types of mole are a sign of skin cancer.* • Compare FRECKLE.

mole PERSON /£məʊl, $moʊl/ *n* [C] *infml* a person who works for an organization such as a government department and secretly gives information to people who are opposed to or interested in the organization • *A mole inside the Department of Transport leaked secret proposals to the press.* • Compare SPY SECRET PERSON.

mol·e·cule /£'mɒl·ɪ·kjuːl, $'mɑː·lɪ-/ *n* [C] *specialized* the simplest unit of a chemical substance, usually a group of two or more atoms • *a hydrocarbon/protein/water molecule*

mo·lec·u·lar /£mə'lek·jʊ·lər, $-lɚ/ *adj* [not gradable] • **Molecular biology** is the study of the structure and action of important molecules which are found in living things.

mole·hill /£'məʊl·hɪl, $'moʊl-/ *n* [C] a small pile of earth pushed up to the surface of the ground by the digging of a MOLE (= a mammal that lives underground)

mole·skin /£'məʊl·skɪn, $'moʊl-/ *n* [U] a strong cotton cloth which is slightly furry on one side • *moleskin trousers*

mo·lest *obj* FORCE SEXUALLY /mə'lest/ *v* [T] to touch, force or attack (someone, esp. a child or a woman) in a sexual way against their wishes • *The girl had been molested frequently by her stepfather from the age of eight until she was twelve.* • *The man had previously been arrested several times for molesting young boys.* • Ⓔ Ⓟ

mo·les·ta·tion /£,mɒl·es'teɪ·ʃən, $,mɑː·les-/ *n* [U] • *sexual molestation*

mo·les·ter /£mə'les·tər, $-tɚ/ *n* [C] • *a* **child** *molester*

mo·lest *obj* TROUBLE /mə'lest/ *v* [T] *fml* to trouble or annoy (a person or an animal) sometimes by using violence, esp. to prevent them from doing something • *At the time of the pull-out, United Nations premises had been looted and personnel were being molested.* • Ⓔ Ⓟ

mo·les·ta·tion /£,mɒl·es'teɪ·ʃən, $,mɑː·les-/ *n* [U]

moll /£mɒl, $mɑːl/ *n* [C] *Am and Aus slang* a female companion of a GANGSTER • *(Aus)* A moll is also a female companion of a member of a group of people who ride motorcycles or SURF (= ride on waves using special boards) together.

mol·li·fy *obj* /£'mɒl·ɪ·faɪ, $'mɑː·lɪ-/ *v* [T] to make (someone) less angry or upset; to make (something) less severe or more acceptable • *You won't be able to mollify her with flowers.* • *A shorter working week has been proposed to mollify the effects of the new working arrangements.*

mol·lusc /£'mɒl·əsk, $'mɑː·ləsk/, *Am also* **mol·lusk** *n* [C] any member of the group of animals which have soft bodies, no BACKBONE and are often covered with a shell. Many molluscs live in water. • *Oysters are molluscs, as are snails and cuttlefish.*

mol·ly·cod·dle *obj* /£'mɒl·i,kɒd·l̩, $'mɑː·li,kɑː·dl̩/ *v* [T] *infml usually disapproving* to give (someone) too much care or protection • *You're not helping the children by mollycoddling them – they have to grow up at some stage.*

Mol·o·tov cock·tail /£,mɒl·ə·tɒf, $,mɑː·lə·tɑːf/ *n* [C] *dated* a type of **petrol bomb**, see at PETROL

molt /£məʊlt, $moʊlt/ *n*, *v Am for* MOULT

molt·en /£'məʊl·tən, $'moʊl-/ *adj* [not gradable] (esp. of metal or rock) in a liquid state, esp. because of great heat • *molten glass/lava/lead*

mol·yb·den·um /£mɒl'ɪb·dɪ·nəm, $mɑː'lɪb-/ *n* [U] a very hard silver-coloured metallic element which is often mixed with other metals and esp. used to make steel stronger

mom /£mɒm, $mɑːm/ *n* [C] *Am for* MUM MOTHER • *I miss my Mom and Dad a lot.* • *I was only 5 years old when Mom and Pop got divorced.* • *We're expecting most of the moms and dads to come to the show.* • *Aw, mom, why can't I go?* [as form of address] • LP› **Titles and forms of address**

mo·ment SHORT TIME /£'məʊ·mənt, $'moʊ-/ *n* [C] a very short period of time • *Can you wait a moment?* • *I'll be ready* **in** *just* **a** *moment.* • *A car drew up outside and a few moments later the doorbell rang.* • *You've missed them – they only left* **a** *moment* **ago.** • *I'm expecting her to come* **at any** *moment* (= very soon). • *This will only take/won't take a moment* (= it will be quick). • *Have you* **got** *a moment* (= Are you busy or have you got time to speak to me)? • *She did*n't *believe the story* **for a moment** (= she strongly refused to believe it). • *The plans are being changed* **from one moment to the next** (= frequently). • *Help arrived – and* **not a moment too soon** (= it was nearly too late). • LP› **Periods of time**

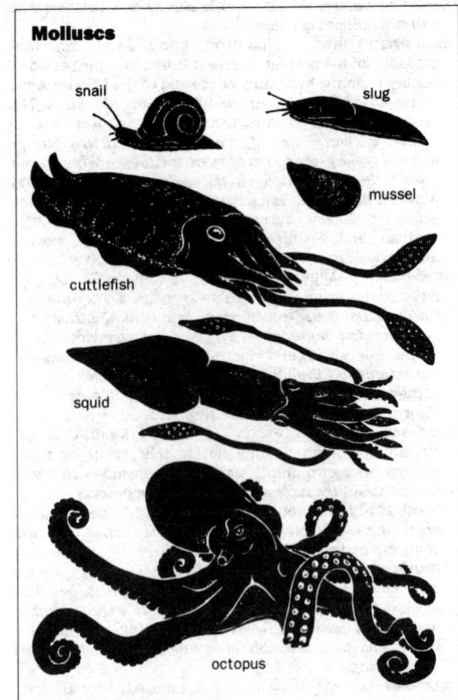

mo·men·tary /£'məʊ·mən·tri, $'moʊ-/ *adj* [not gradable] • *a momentary hesitation* • *a momentary lapse of memory* • *the momentary sound of a shot*

mo·men·ta·ri·ly /£,məʊ·mən'ter·ɪ·li, $'moʊ-/ *adv* [not gradable] • *She was momentarily* (= for a short time) *confused by the road signs but soon found the right way.* • *(Am)* Momentarily also means very soon: *I'll be ready to leave momentarily, I just have to put my shoes on.*

mo·ment OCCASION /£'məʊ·mənt, $'moʊ-/ *n* [C] a particular time or occasion • *When would be* **the** *best moment to tell the family?* • *Don't leave it to/till* **the last** *moment* (= the latest time possible). • *If you want a private conversation with her you'll have to* **choose** *your moment* (= find a suitable time). • *I can't find the address* **at/for the moment** (= now) *but I'll get it for you later.* • *He held up the poster just at* **the (exact/precise)** *moment when the TV cameras were on him.* • If you **have** your **moments** there are occasions when you do well in some way that is unusual for you: *I'm not a very good cook, but I have my moments.* ○ *The film had its moments but was generally pretty dull.* • **The** *moment* **(that)** (= As soon as) *I get the money I'll send the ticket.* • A **moment of truth** is an occasion when something important happens which tests someone and which will have an effect on the future: *The interview was my moment of truth – I realised I would be making a mistake if I accepted the job.*

mo·ment IMPORTANT /£'məʊ·mənt, $'moʊ-/ *n* [U] **of (great) moment** *fml* very important • *a decision of great moment* • See also MOMENTOUS.

mo·men·tous /£mə'men·təs, $-t̬əs/ *adj* important because of effects on future events • *Christopher Columbus's momentous discovery* • *the momentous news of the President's death* • *Whether or not to move overseas was a momentous* **decision** *for the family.*

mo·men·tous·ly /£mə'men·tə·sli, $-t̬ə-/ *adv*

mo·men·tous·ness /£mə'men·tə·snəs, $-t̬ə-/ *n* [U]

mo·men·tum /£mə'men·təm, $-t̬əm/ *n* [U] the force that keeps an object moving or an event developing after a start has been made • *Once you push it, it keeps going* **under** *its own momentum.* • *The spacecraft will fly round the Earth to* **gain** *momentum for its trip to Jupiter.* • *The play* **loses** *momentum by its half-way stage.* • *Several attempts to arrange a protest march failed to* **gather** *momentum.* • *The firm has been growing rapidly, but you can't* **keep** *that kind of momentum* **up** *forever.* • *In an attempt to* **give** *new momentum to their plans, the committee set a date for starting detailed discussions.* • *The* gathering *momentum* **towards** *central control of the economy is worrying.*

mom·ma /£ˈmɒm·ə, $ˈmɑː·mə/ *n* [C] *Am infml for* MOTHER [PARENT]

mom·my /£ˈmɒm·i, $ˈmɑː·mi/ *n* [C] *Am infml for* MUMMY [MOTHER] • [LP]> **Titles and forms of address**

Mon *n abbreviation for* Monday

mon·arch /£ˈmɒn·ək, $ˈmɑː·nɚk/ *n* [C] a king or queen • *The country is ruled by a* **hereditary** *monarch.* • *Britain's head of state is a* **constitutional** *monarch* (=only has very limited ruling powers). • *"I am monarch of all I survey"* (*Verses Supposed to be Written by Alexander Selkirk* by William Cowper, 1782)

mon·ar·chic /£məˈnɑː·kɪk, $ˈnɑːr-/, **mon·ar·chi·cal** /£məˈnɑː·kɪ·kəl, $ˈnɑːr-/ *adj* [not gradable] *fml* • *a monarchic system*

mon·ar·chist /£ˈmɒn·ə·kɪst, $ˈmɑː·nɚ-/ *n* [C] • A monarchist is a person who supports the system of having a king or queen.

mon·ar·chy /£ˈmɒn·ə·ki, $ˈmɑː·nɚ-/ *n* • A monarchy is a country which has a king or queen: *European monarchies* • *a modern monarchy* [C] • Monarchy is also the system of having a king or queen: *Is monarchy relevant in the modern world?* [U]

mon·as·ter·y /£ˈmɒn·ə·stri, $ˈmɑː·nə·ster·i/ *n* [C] a large building or group of buildings in which MONKS (=religious men) live and worship • Compare CONVENT; **nunnery** at NUN.

mon·as·tic /məˈnæs·tɪk/ *adj* of or connected with MONASTERIES or MONKS • If someone leads a monastic **life** they live quietly and simply without a lot of money or unnecessary things.

mon·as·ti·ci·sm /məˈnæs·tɪ·sɪ·zəm/ *n* [U] • *the origins of European monasticism* (=system of living in MONASTERIES).

Mon·day /ˈmʌn·deɪ/ (*abbreviation* **Mon**) *n* the day of the week after Sunday and before Tuesday • *It's Monday tomorrow.* [U] • *I start my new job* **on** *Monday.* [U] • *(Br infml and Am) They'll be arriving Monday.* [U] • *We visited them* **last** *Monday.* [U] • *It's my birthday* **next** *Monday.* [U] • *Term doesn't start* **this** *Monday* (=the first one from now), *it starts (on) Monday* **week** (=the second one from now). [C] • *Don't you hate going back to school* **on** *Mondays?* [C] • *The baby was born on* **a** *Monday.* [C] • *She went home on* **the** *Monday* (=on the Monday of that particular week). [C] • *(infml)* A **Monday morning feeling** (*Aus* **Mondayitis**) is the way people feel after the weekend when they do not want to go to work or school. • *(Am)* A **Monday-morning quarterback** is someone who says how an event or problem should have been dealt with by others after it has already been dealt with. • *"I don't like Mondays"* (title of a song by The Boomtown Rats, 1979) • [LP]> **Calendar**

mon·e·tar·i·sm /£ˈmʌn·ɪ·tər·ɪ·zəm, $-t̬ɚ·ɪ-/ *n* [U] a system of controlling a country's economy by limiting how much money is in use at a particular time

mon·e·tar·ist /£ˈmʌn·ɪ·tər·ɪst, $-t̬ɚ-/ *n* [C] • *a convinced monetarist* • *monetarist policies*

mon·ey /ˈmʌn·i/ *n* [U] the coins or notes which are used to buy things, or the amount of these that one person has • *"How much money have you got on* (=with) *you?" "£10 in notes and a few coins."* • *Could you lend me some money until tomorrow?* • *The children were told to keep their money in a purse with their name on it.* • *Savers were advised to invest their money in a high-interest bank account.* • *I wanted to buy it but it* **cost** *too much money* (=was too expensive). • *Don't waste your money on toys that will only last a few days.* • *We spent so much money redecorating the house that we didn't have any left over for a holiday.* • *You can't pay in English money. You'll have to* **change** *some money* (=buy some foreign money) *at the bank.* • *How much money do you* **earn** (=What are you paid to do your job)? • **Good** money usually means an amount of money that you think is a lot: *I paid good money for it.* ○ *She spent good money on it.* ○ *They earn good money in that company.* • Someone who **has** money is rich: *Her family has money so she's never needed to be as careful as the rest of us.* • If you say that there is money **in** something, it means that the activity will produce a profit: *There's money in sport these days.* ○ *Is there any money in car hire?* ○ *There's money in it for you.* • *He enjoyed acting but he wasn't* **making** (=earning) *much money.* • *Her investments haven't* **made** (=produced as profit) *much money this year.* • *They* **made** *their money* (=became rich) *in the fashion business.* • *He tried to persuade me to* **put** *money* **into** *the company* (=invest in the company). • If you **put** money **on** something, you BET on it (=risk a sum of money in the hope of winning more): *He put £10 on the horse.* ○ *I'd put money on Chris being* (=I feel certain that Chris will be) *the next director.* • *We need to* **raise** (=collect) *money for a new school pool from the parents.* • *Try to* **save** (=keep) *some money for your holiday.* • *We're* **saving** (=not spending as much) *money by using volunteers.* • *Don't* **spend** *all your money at once.* • *I didn't like the job, but* **the** *money* (=amount of pay) *was good.* • *Money is* **tight/short** (=We haven't got much money) *at the moment.* • *I had some very expensive dental treatment recently – but it was money* **well spent** *– it'll save me problems in the future.* • **For my money** means 'in my opinion': *For my money, Sunday is the best day to travel because the roads are quiet.* • To **get/have** your **money's worth** is to receive good value from something you have paid for: *I was determined to get my money's worth out of Eurodisney – we were there when the gates opened and we stayed till it closed.* ○ *She's had her money's worth out of that dress – she's been wearing it for years.* • *If we win this competition we'll be* **in the money** (=have a lot of money). • *He can afford it – he's* **made of money** (=very rich). • *One way to get rich is to* **marry money** (=marry a rich person). • *(Br)* **Money for jam/old rope** means you are paid for doing something very easy: *Babysitting is money for jam if the children don't wake up.* • *I had no idea what his job was but he certainly seemed to have* **money to burn** (=have a lot of money). • If you **put** your **money where** your **mouth is** you show by your actions and not just your words that you support or believe in something. • Someone or something that is **money-grubbing** has money as their main interest and does anything they can to get lots of it. • The **money market** is the system in which banks and other similar organizations buy and sell money from each other. • A **money-maker** or a **money-spinner** is something which produces a lot of money: *The book has turned out to be a real money-spinner.* • Someone who is **money-minded** is interested in money or is good at using their money: *I've never been very money-minded – I leave all my business affairs to my financial adviser.* ○ *(disapproving) He's very money-minded – he's always asking what you paid for things.* • *(esp. Am and Aus)* A **money order** is a piece of paper from a bank or post office that can be used to send money to someone else: *You can pay your bills with cash, money orders or personal cheques.* • The **money supply** is all the money which is in use in a country. • *(saying)* 'Money talks' means that people or organizations that are wealthy are more powerful than those that are not, and therefore can get what they want. • *(saying)* 'Money doesn't grow on trees' means that you haven't got an unlimited amount of money because the money you have to spend depends on what you earn: *"Mum, I'd like a new bike." "I'll have to think about it – money doesn't grow on trees, you know!"* • *(saying)* 'You pays your money and takes your choice' means that there are different things you could do but you have to decide for yourself which is best. • *"Money makes the world go round"* (song from the film *Cabaret*, 1972) • *"We're in the Money"* (title of a song written by Al Dubin and Harry Warren, 1933) • *"The love of money is the root of all evil"* (Bible, I Timothy 6.10) • *"Take the Money and Run"* (title of a film by Woody Allen, 1968) • *"Money doesn't talk, it swears"* (from the song *It's Alright, Ma* by Bob Dylan, 1965) • *"Money for Nothing"* (title of a song by Dire Straits, 1985) • *"Money's too tight to mention"* (title of a song by Simply Red, 1985) • [LP]> **Money, Nations and nationalities** Ⓕ

mon·eyed /ˈmʌn·id/ *adj fml* • If you are moneyed you are rich: *a moneyed family*

mon·e·tary /ˈmʌn·ɪ·tri/ *adj* [not gradable] • *monetary policy* • *monetary control* • The monetary **system** of a country is the system used by a country to provide money and to control the exchange of money: *the International Monetary System* ○ *The new government introduced widespread changes in the monetary system.* • *The monetary* **unit** *of the United States, Australia and Canada is the dollar.*

mon·ey·bags /ˈmʌn·i·bægz/ *n* [C] *pl* **moneybags** *infml humorous and or disapproving* a rich person

mon·ey·box /£ˈmʌn·ɪ·bɒks, $-bɑːks/ *n* [C] *esp. Br* a closed container in which money is kept, esp. one with a long thin hole in the top through which coins can be pushed • *The child's moneybox was shaped like a house.*

mon·ey·lend·er /£ˈmʌn·iˌlen·dər, $-dɚ/ *n* [C] *esp. disapproving* a person or organization whose job is to lend

MONEY

cash dispenser
cheque book
(Br) cheque/ (Am) check
sorting code
credit card or banker's card/ (Br) cheque card
card number
cashier
account name
account number
cheque number
counterfoil/ (esp. Am) stub

- **informal words for money**
  - **British**: *a quid* (= a pound), *a fiver* (= a five pound note), *a tenner* (= a ten pound note), *a grand* (= a thousand pounds). 'Quid' and 'grand' are used as units (notice they do not take 's' in the plural): *That'll cost you 25 quid.* • *They're going to spend a hundred grand on a new boat.* Amounts in pence are spoken informally as 'p': '65p' can be spoken as 'sixty-five pence' or 'sixty-five p'. The 1p coin is called a penny (*pl.* pennies).
  - **American**: *a penny* (= a one cent coin), *a nickel* (= a five cent coin), *a dime* (= a ten cent coin), *a quarter* (= a 25 cent coin), *a buck* (a dollar), *a fiver* (= five dollars), *a grand* (= a thousand dollars). 'Buck' and 'grand' are used as units: *The tickets are 80 bucks each.* Notice that a piece of paper money is a bill: *a five dollar bill.*

- **Words and phrases for ways of paying**

Would you rather pay **in cash, by cheque** *or* **by credit card?**
You can pay **in** *either British or American* **currency** *at this shop.*
I paid for my shopping with a five pound note. The bill came to £1.50, so I had £3.50 **change**.
I'm buying a stereo **on** *(Br)* **hire purchase**/*(Am)* **the installment plan**. *I pay a £50* **deposit** *then six monthly* **instalments** *of £12.50.*

- **Using a bank account**

You only need £1 to open a (Br) **current account**/*(Am)* **checking account** *with this bank.*
I'd like to **pay** *this cheque* **into** *my account and* **take out** *£50 in cash.*
You can **withdraw** (= take out) *or* **deposit** (= pay in) *money at any time using the machines outside the bank.*
Could you tell me the **balance of** (= amount of money in) *these two accounts?*
With a **deposit account,** *you can invest your savings and earn* **interest** *on your money.*
Please **transfer** *$100 from my account in New York to my account here.*
I pay my electricity bill by (esp. Br) **standing order/banker's order**. *Money is automatically* **debited** (= taken out) *from my account every three months.*

- **The money you earn**

A **salary** is usually paid monthly in Britain, especially for work that requires a college education; it is often paid directly into the worker's bank account: *Warren* **is on/gets/earns** *a salary of around £20,000 a year.*
A **wage** is usually paid weekly, especially for work that needs physical skills or strength: *We're hoping for a wage increase next year.* • *Women working from home often receive very low* **wages**/*a very low wage.*
Your **income** is the total amount of money you have coming in. Your **pay** is what you receive for your work.

money to people in return for payment • *Families with money problems often fall into the hands of the moneylenders and get further into debt.*

-mon·ger /£-ˈmʌŋ·gəʳ, $-gɚ/ *combining form esp. disapproving* a person who encourages a particular activity, esp. one which causes trouble • *a rumour-monger* • *war-mongers* • *a well-known scandal-monger* • *doom-mongers* • See also IRONMONGER; FISHMONGER.

-mon·ger·ing /£-ˈmʌŋ·gə·rɪŋ, $-gɚ·ɪŋ/ *combining form* • *war-mongering attitudes* • *They accused him of rumour-mongering/scandal-mongering.*

mon·gol /£ˈmɒŋ·gəl, $ˈmɑːŋ-/, *Am also* **mon·go·loid** /£ˈmɒŋ·gə·lɔɪd, $ˈmɑːŋ-/ *n* [C] *taboo dated* a person who has DOWN'S SYNDROME

mon·go·li·sm /£ˈmɒŋ·gəl·ɪ·zəm, $ˈmɑːŋ/ *n* [U] *taboo dated* • Mongolism is DOWN'S SYNDROME.

mon·goose /£ˈmɒŋ·guːs, $ˈmɑːŋ-/ *n* [C] *pl* **mongooses** a small animal with a long tail. It kills snakes, other small animals and birds for food and eats birds' eggs.

mon·grel /ˈmʌŋ·grəl/, *Am and Aus infml also* **mutt** *n* [C] *esp. disapproving* a dog whose parents belonged to different breeds • *They bought a mongrel/a mongrel puppy.* • *That stupid mutt's been digging up the flowerbed again.*

mon·ik·er /£ˈmɒn·ɪ·kəʳ, $ˈmɑː·nɪ·kɚ/, **mon·ick·er** *n* [C] *slang* a name or NICKNAME • *Joe's bride must be in love with him to accept her new moniker of Mrs Jessica Jessington.*

mon·i·tor SCREEN /£ˈmɒn·ɪ·təʳ, $ˈmɑː·nɪ·t̬ɚ/ *n* [C] a device with a screen on which words or pictures can be shown • *The room contained a lot of equipment including several TV monitors.* • *The plane arrivals are shown* **on** *large monitors in different parts of the air terminal.* • *The travel agent checked the name* **on** *her monitor.* • *My computer has a colour monitor* (= it shows things in different colours).

mon·i·tor *obj* WATCH /£ˈmɒn·ɪ·təʳ, $ˈmɑː·nɪ·t̬ɚ/ *v* [T] to watch (something) carefully for a period of time in order to discover something about it • *A national agency to monitor education standards was proposed yesterday.* • *The new findings suggest that women ought to monitor their cholesterol levels.*

mon·i·tor /£ˈmɒn·ɪ·təʳ, $ˈmɑː·nɪ·t̬ɚ/ *n* [C] • A monitor is a person who has the job of watching or noticing particular things: *United Nations monitors were not allowed to enter the area.* • A monitor is also a machine which regularly tests something: *The research has spin-offs on the development of radiation monitors.* • In school, a monitor is a child who has special jobs to do: *The library monitors help in the library.*

monk /mʌŋk/ *n* [C] a man who is one of a group of men who, because of their religious beliefs, do not marry and usually live together in a MONASTERY, esp. to pray, worship and study

mon·key ANIMAL /ˈmʌŋ·ki/ *n* [C] an animal that usually has a long tail and climbs trees. Monkeys are PRIMATES (= the group of animals which are most like humans). • *Cutting down the forests has taken away the monkeys' natural habitat.* • *(Br slang)* If you **don't/couldn't give a monkey's** about something you are not interested in or worried about it: *"Mary won't like it." "I couldn't give a monkey's."* • *(dated) Well,* **I'll be a monkey's uncle** (= I'm very surprised)! • If you **make a monkey out of** someone, you make them appear foolish.

monk·ey CHILD /ˈmʌŋ·ki/ *n* [C] *infml* someone, esp. a child, who behaves badly or annoyingly • *They ate all the cakes, the* **little** *monkeys.* • *Stop making that noise, you* **little** *monkey.* [as form of address] • **Monkey business** is behaviour which is dishonest or not acceptable in some way: *The teacher suspected that there had been some monkey business going on in the class.*

monk·ey /ˈmʌŋ·ki/ *v* [I always + adv/prep] *infml* • If you monkey **about/around** you do things in a playful, not serious way, without taking a lot of care and esp. doing things that are wrong: *The children were bored and started monkeying about, throwing things at each other.* ○ *Who's been monkeying around* **with** *my tools?* • *(Am)* To monkey is also to copy or MIMIC what someone else does.

monk·ey MONEY /ˈmʌŋ·ki/ *n* [C] *Br slang* £500

monk·ey–puz·zle (tree) /ˈmʌŋ·kiˌpʌz·l̩/ *n* [C] a type of large evergreen tree. It has stiff branches which spread out at the side and very dark green sharp leaves • PIC **Tree**

monk·ey suit *n* [C] *slang* a man's formal SUIT (= jacket and trousers) worn in the evening

monk·ey wrench *n* [C] *esp. Am for* a tool which can be adjusted to tighten or unfasten any size of NUT and BOLT (= metal fasteners which screw together)

mon·o SOUND /£ˈmɒn·əʊ, $ˈmɑː·noʊ/ *n* [U] recorded or broadcast sound that seems to come from a single direction • *The recording was available in mono or stereo.*

mon·o /£ˈmɒn·əʊ, $ˈmɑː·noʊ/, *fml* **mon·o·phon·ic** *adj* [not gradable] • *She had an old mono record player.* • Compare STEREO; QUADRAPHONIC.

mon·o DISEASE /£ˈmɒn·əʊ, $ˈmɑː·noʊ/ *n* [U] *Am infml for* MONONUCLEOSIS • Mononucleosis is *esp. Am for* **glandular fever**. See at GLAND.

mon·o– SINGLE /£ˈmɒn·əʊ-, $ˈmɑː·noʊ-/ *combining form* one; single • *monolingual* • *a monorail*

mon·o·chrome /£ˈmɒn·ə·krəʊm, $ˈmɑː·nə·kroʊm/ *adj* [not gradable] using only black, white and grey, or using only one colour • *monochrome display monitors for computers* • *Fashion designers have been emphasizing the monochrome look with clothing done entirely in black and white.* • *Kodak is distributing a video on how to develop its monochrome film.* • *The park at this time of year is usually a rather depressing monochrome brown.* • *(fig. Br disapproving)* Monochrome is sometimes used to mean not interesting or exciting: *a monochrome, dreary existence* ○ *I hate those monochrome discussions which end with everyone agreeing – they're so boring.*

mon·o·chro·mat·ic /£mɒn·əʊ·krəˈmæt·ɪk, $mɑː·noʊ·krəˈmæt̬-/ *adj* [not gradable] • *a monochromatic picture* • *The light from a laser is monochromatic* (= all one colour).

mon·o·cle /£ˈmɒn·ə·kl̩, $ˈmɑː·nə-/ *n* [C] a round piece of glass worn, esp. in the past, in front of one eye in order to help you to see more clearly

mon·og·a·my /£məˈnɒg·ə·mi, $məˈnɑː·gə-/ *n* [U] the social system which allows a person to be married to only one person at a time • Monogamy is also used to refer to the state of having only one permanent sexual partner at a time: *Although they're not married, they've lived in a state of monogamy for years.* • Compare BIGAMY; POLYGAMY.

mon·og·am·ous /£məˈnɒg·ə·məs, $məˈnɑː·gə-/ *adj* • *monogamous relationships* • *monogamous species/primates* • *We're more monogamous than we used to be, but both of us has the occasional fling.*

mon·o·gram /£ˈmɒn·ə·græm, $ˈmɑː·nə-/ *n* [C] a symbol, usually formed from the first letters of a person's names joined together, which is sewn or marked on clothes or other possessions • *handkerchiefs/towels with a monogram in the corner*

mon·o·grammed /£ˈmɒn·ə·græmd, $ˈmɑː·nə-/ *adj* [not gradable] • *monogrammed envelopes* • *a monogrammed case*

mon·o·graph /£ˈmɒn·ə·grɑːf, £-græf, $ˈmɑː·nə·græf/ *n* [C] a long article or a short book, esp. on a subject that the writer has spent a lot of time studying • *He has just published a monograph* **on** *Beethoven's symphonies.*

mon·o·lin·gual /£ˌmɒn·əʊˈlɪŋ·gwəl, $ˌmɑː·noʊ-/ *adj* [not gradable] speaking or using only one language • *Are there still any monolingual Welsh speakers?* • Compare BILINGUAL; MULTILINGUAL.

mon·o·lith /£ˈmɒn·ə·lɪθ, $ˈmɑː·nə-/ *n* [C] a large column or block of stone standing by itself which is thought to have been important to people in the distant past, for social or religious reasons

mon·o·lith·ic /£ˌmɒn·əˈlɪθ·ɪk, $ˌmɑː·nə-/ *adj disapproving* too large, too regular or without interesting differences, and unwilling or unable to be changed • *monolithic state-run organizations*

mon·o·logue /£ˈmɒn·əl·ɒg, $ˈmɑː·nə·lɑːg/ *n* [C] a long speech by one person • *(disapproving) He subjected me to a monologue* **on** *his last stay in hospital.* • A monologue is also a short play for one actor: *During his monologue the actor has to make the bed and tidy the room.*

mon·o·nu·cle·o·sis /£ˌmɒn·əʊˌnjuː·kliˈəʊ·sɪs, $ˌmɑː·noʊˌnuː·kliˈoʊ-/, *infml* **mon·o** *n* [U] *esp. Am for* **glandular fever**, see at GLAND

mon·o·phon·ic /£ˌmɒn·əʊˈfɒn·ɪk, $ˌmɑː·noʊˈfɑː·nɪk/ *adj* [not gradable] *fml for* MONO SOUND

mon·o·plane /£ˈmɒn·ə·pleɪn, $ˈmɑː·nə-/ *n* [C] an aircraft with a single pair of wings • Compare BIPLANE.

mon·op·o·ly /£məˈnɒp·əl·i, $-ˈnɑː·pəl-/ *n* [C] (an organization or group which has) a power of control which is not shared by other people or groups, esp. in business to make and sell goods or provide a service • *The government is determined to protect its tobacco monopoly.* • *The airline's 15-year domestic monopoly is over.* • *The huge monopoly both generates electricity and distributes it.* • *The drafting of a new constitution cannot be* **a** *monopoly* **of** *the white minority regime* (= other people should do it too). • *He does not* **have a/the** *monopoly* **on** (= He is not the only one who has) *good looks.* • *monopoly industries* • *high monopoly prices* • *(trademark)* Monopoly is a game which is played on a board and the players pretend to buy land and buildings in order to make money. The money used in the game is not real and **monopoly money** means money with no value.

mon·o·pol·is·tic /£məˌnɒp·əlˈɪs·tɪk, $-ˌnɑː·pəˈlɪs-/ *adj usually disapproving* • *Huge monopolistic state firms fixed prices at whatever level they liked.*

mon·op·o·lize *obj, Br and Aus usually* **–ise** /£məˈnɒp·əl·aɪz, $-ˈnɑː·pə·laɪz/ *v* [T] • In business, to monopolize something is to control it completely and to prevent other people having any effect on what happens: *The company had monopolized the photography market for so many decades that they didn't worry about competition from other companies.* • If someone monopolizes a person or **the conversation** they talk a lot or stop other people being involved: *She monopolized the visitors and we didn't have time to meet them.*

mon·op·o·liz·ation, *Br, Australian usually* **–i·sa·tion** /£məˌnɒp·əl·aɪˈzeɪ·ʃən, $-ˌnɑː·pəl-/ *n* [U]

mon·o·rail /£ˈmɒn·ə·reɪl, $ˈmɑː·nə-/ *n* [C] a railway system which has a single RAIL, often above ground level, or the train which travels along it

mon·o·so·di·um glu·ta·mate /£ˌmɒn·əˌsəʊ·di·əmˈgluː·tə·meɪt, $ˌmɑː·nəˌsoʊ·di·əmˈgluː·t̬ə-/ *(abbreviation* **MSG**) *n* [U] a chemical which is sometimes added to food, esp. food sold in containers, to improve the taste

mon·o·syl·lab·ic /£ˌmɒn·əʊ·sɪˈlæb·ɪk, $ˌmɑː·noʊ-/ *adj* containing only one syllable • *The child could only say monosyllabic words like 'yes' and 'no'.* • *(disapproving)* If someone is monosyllabic they do not say very much and often appear to be rude and not helpful: *A normally monosyllabic man, he surprised us with a passionate speech.* ○ *a monosyllabic reply*

mon·o·syl·lab·ic·al·ly /£ˌmɒn·əʊ·sɪˈlæb·ɪ·kli, $ˌmɑː·noʊ-/ *adv* • *(disapproving) He replied monosyllabically* (= with few words).

mon·o·syll·a·ble /£ˈmɒn·əʊˌsɪl·ə·bl̩, $ˈmɑː·noʊ-/ *n* [C] • *'Jump', 'buy' and 'heat' are monosyllables.*

mon·o·the·i·sm /£ˌmɒn·əʊˈθiː·ɪ·zəm, $ˌmɑː·noʊ/ *n* [U] the belief that there is only one god

mon·o·the·is·tic /£ˌmɒn·əʊ·θiːˈɪs·tɪk, $ˌmɑː·noʊ-/ *adj* [not gradable] • *The three monotheistic religions with the most followers are Christianity, Judaism and Islam.*

mon·o·to·nous /£məˈnɒt·ən·əs, $-ˈnɑː·t̬ən-/ *adj* staying the same and not changing and therefore boring • *a monotonous job* • *monotonous work* • *monotonous music* • *The hypnotist told him in monotonous tones/a monotonous voice that he was becoming more relaxed and sleepy.*

mon·o·to·ny /£məˈnɒt·ən·i, $-ˈnɑː·t̬ən-/, **mon·o·to·nous·ness** /£məˈnɒt·ən·ə·snəs, $-ˈnɑː·t̬ən-/ *n* [U] • *Monotony is a reason for some road accidents.* • *The routine was the same every day, with only a visit from the children on Wednesday to* **break** *the monotony.*

mon·o·tone /£ˈmɒn·ə·təʊn, $ˈmɑː·nə·toʊn/ *n* [U] • A monotone is a sound which stays on the same note without going higher or lower: *He spoke in a boring monotone.*

mon·sig·nor /£ˌmɒnˈsiː·njər, $ˌmɑːnˈsiː·njɚ/ *(abbreviation* **Msgr**) *n* [U] a title used with the name of a Roman Catholic priest of high rank • *I believe Monsignor*

Healey has agreed to speak. • *This way please, monsignor.* [as form of address]

mon·soon /£mɒn'suːn, $mɑːn-/ *n* [C] the season of heavy rain during the summer in hot Asian countries • *The failure of* the *monsoon would destroy harvests on which 1000 million people rely.* • *We got used to monsoons when we lived in India.* • *They are hoping desperately that the monsoon season is not late.* • *(fig.) It was a real monsoon* (=very heavy rain) *– we all got soaked.*

mon·soons /£mɒn'suːnz, $mɑːn-/ *pl n* • *The monsoons are* (=The monsoon is) *late this year.*

mon·ster CREATURE /£'mɒnt·stəʳ, $'mɑːnt·stɚ/ *n* [C] any imaginary frightening creature, esp. one which is large and strange • *a sea monster* • *prehistoric monsters* • *the Loch Ness monster* • *The story was about a monster who wanted children to like him.*

mon·strous /£'mɒnt·strəs, $'mɑːnt-/ *adj* • *The illustrations show monstrous beasts with bodies like bears and heads like tigers.*

mon·ster PERSON /£'mɒnt·stəʳ, $'mɑːnt·stɚ/ *n* [C] a cruel and frightening person • *Only a monster could beat a child so severely.*

mon·ster LARGE /£'mɒnt·stəʳ, $'mɑːnt·stɚ/ *n* [C] *infml* something which is very big, or too big • *You should have seen the onions he grew for the competition – they were monsters!*

mon·ster /£'mɒnt·stəʳ, $'mɑːnt·stɚ/ *adj* [before n; not gradable] *infml* • *a monster sandwich* • *a monster housing development* • *monster discounts*

mon·stros·i·ty /£mɒn'strɒs·ə·ti, $mɑːn'strɑː·sə·ţi/ *n* [C] something which is very ugly and usually large • *The new office building is a real monstrosity.* • *Who hung that monstrosity on the wall?* • *Among other monstrosities in the room was a large glass case full of stuffed animals.*

mon·strous /£'mɒnt·strəs, $'mɑːnt-/ *adj* very bad • *monstrous cruelty* • *monstrous behaviour* • *After the accident she was faced with monstrous bills for repairs.* • *But that's monstrous! You shouldn't have to pay!* • *"The Monstrous Regiment of Women"* (title of a pamphlet by the preacher John Knox, 1558)

mon·strous·ly /£'mɒnt·strə·sli, $'mɑːnt-/ *adv* • *monstrously unfair* • *monstrously wicked*

mon·tage /£'mɒn·tɑːʒ, $'mɑːn-/ *n* [C] a piece of work produced by combining smaller parts • *The ads feature a montage* **of** *images – people surfing, playing football and basketball.*

month /mʌntθ/ *n* [C] a period of about four weeks, esp. one of the twelve periods into which a year is divided • *I'll be away for a month from mid-June to mid-July.* • *February is the shortest month and has an extra day every four years.* • *He rented the house for the whole month of September.* • *The puppy is two months old.* • *It is a two-month-old puppy* • *The project will be finished* **in the next few months** (=quite soon). • *They haven't been in contact with me* **for** *months* (=a long time). • *She has two months' holiday every year.* • **A month of Sundays** is a very long time or never: *We'd never get that piano out in a month of Sundays because the doorway's too narrow.* • A thing or person **of the Month** is one that has been chosen as the best in a particular month: *Book/Man/Recipe of the Month* • *"April is the cruellest month"* (from the poem *The Waste Land* by T.S.Eliot, 1922) • LP **Calendar, Dates, Periods of time**

month·ly /'mʌnt·θli/ *adj, adv* [not gradable] • *a monthly report* • *monthly payments* • *Most of these people are paid monthly.*

month·ly /'mʌnt·θli/ *n* [C] • A monthly is a magazine which is published once a month: *The newsagent sells all the computer monthlies.*

mon·u·ment /£'mɒn·jʊ·mənt, $'mɑːn-/ *n* [C] an object, esp. large and made of stone, built to remember and show respect to a person or group of people, or a special place made for this purpose • *The splendid National Monument was erected in memory of the country's founders.* • *In the square in front of the hotel stands a monument* **to** *all the people killed in the war.* • *(fig.) The annual arts festival is a monument* **to** (=is a result of) *her vision and hard work.* • An **ancient** or **historic** monument is an old building or place which is an important part of a country's history: *Parts of the Berlin wall are being allowed to stand as historic monuments.*

mon·u·men·tal /£ˌmɒn·jʊ'men·tᵊl, $ˌmɑːn·jʊ'men·ţᵊl/ *adj* very big • *a monumental task* • *a monumental waste of time* • *Building the Channel Tunnel was a monumental feat of earth-moving.*

mon·u·men·tal·ly /£ˌmɒn·jʊ'men·tᵊl·i, $ˌmɑːn·jʊ'men·ţᵊl-/ *adv* • *monumentally dull/tiresome*

moo /muː/ *n* [C] *pl* **moos** (esp. in children's books) a written representation of the noise that a cow makes • *"Moo, moo," said the cow, agreeing with the other animals.*

moo /muː/ *v* [I] **moos, mooing**, *past* **mooed** • *The cow mooed.*

mooch MOVE /muːtʃ/ *v* [I always + adv/prep] *infml* to walk slowly and carelessly as if without a purpose, or to act in a relaxed way doing nothing important • *I was mooching through Soho, gazing in shop windows.* • *The girl mooched across to the shelves and started to look through the magazines.* • *(disapproving) Stop mooching* **(about/around)** *in your room and do something useful!*

mooch /muːtʃ/ *n* [U] *infml* • *I'm going for* a *mooch round the shops* (=to look at what is there, not to buy a particular thing).

mooch *(obj)* OBTAIN /muːtʃ/ *v Am slang* to obtain (something) without paying or working for it, or to borrow (something) without intending to return it • *You're old enough to get a job and stop mooching* **off** *your family.* [I] • *She's not above mooching a drink or a meal, even when she can afford to buy them.* [T] • *He mooched a ten* **off** *me, and I knew right then I'd never see it again.* [T]

mood /muːd/ *n* [C] the way you feel at a particular time • *She's* **in a** *good/bad* **mood** *today.* • *Suddenly her mood changed and she began to take notice and ask questions* (=she was not interested before). • *The good food and drink had put him in a talkative mood* (=made him want to talk a lot). • *I'll do it tomorrow – I'm in a lazy mood today.* • *The mood* **of** *the crowd turned* (=The crowd became) *aggressive.* • *You won't get a sensible answer – she's* **in one of** *her* **moods** (=feeling angry, difficult or not helpful in a way that is typical of her). • *"Do you want to go to the cinema?" "No, I'm not* **in the mood** (=I don't want to do that)*."* • *(fml) The official was* **in no mood to** (=was unlikely to decide to) *agree to these proposals.*

moody /'muː·di/ *adj* **-ier, -iest** • A moody person has the habit of changing quickly from being happy to being unhappy and not wanting to talk or take part in activities, often for no clear reason. The way they look or act can also be described as moody: *a moody teenager* ○ *a moody expression.* • Ⓙ

mood·i·ly /'muː·dɪ·li/ *adv* • *He stared moodily at the photos.*

mood·i·ness /'muː·dɪ·nəs/ *n* [U]

moon PLANET /muːn/ *n* the object, similar to a planet, which moves in the sky around the Earth once every 28 days and which can often be seen clearly at night when it shines with the light coming from the sun • **The** *moon* **rises** (=appears in the sky) *at 6.30 p.m. tonight.* [U] • The **phases of** the moon are the stages that the moon goes through during a month, from **crescent** or **new** moon to **half** moon and then **full** moon. When more of the moon can be seen every night it is **waxing** and when less can be seen every night it is **waning.** [U] • *There's no moon* (=You cannot see the moon) *tonight.* [U] • A moon is also a similar object that moves around another planet: *Jupiter has at least sixteen moons.* [C] • *(dated)* Something which happened **many moons ago** happened a long time ago. • If you are **over the moon** you are very pleased: *She was over the moon* **about/with** *her new bike.*

moonless /'muːn·ləs/ *adj* [not gradable] • *a dark moonless night*

moon LACK PURPOSE /muːn/ *v* [I always + adv/prep] *disapproving* to move or spend time in a way which shows a lack of care and interest and no clear purpose • *She was mooning* **about/around** *the house all weekend.* • *He's been mooning* **over** (=looking foolishly at) *those holiday photos all afternoon.*

moon·beam /'muːm·biːm/ *n* [C] a beam or line of light which comes from the moon

Moonie /'muː·ni/ *n* [C] a member of the Unification Church, a religious group whose members must obey its rules and teachings completely • *He has joined the Moonies.*

moon·ing /'muː·nɪŋ/ *n* [U] *slang* showing your naked bottom

moon·light LIGHT /'muːn·laɪt/ *n* [U] the pale light of the moon, sometimes thought of as connected with love and pleasant things and at other times as cold and hard • *Moonlight bathed the garden where the young lovers sat.* • *The taxi crossed the bridge with the river glittering coldly in the moonlight.* • *The world, he clearly feels, is not* **all moonlight and roses** (=pleasant and happy things). • *(Br* *infml)* To **do a moonlight flit** is to leave secretly, esp. to avoid paying for something: *The shop was shut up and the owners had clearly done a moonlight flit.* • *"Moonlight Becomes You"* (title of a song written by Johnny Burke and Jimmy Van Heusen, 1942)

moon·lit /ˈmuːn·lɪt/ *adj* [before n; not gradable] • *a bright moonlit night* • *a moonlit room*

moon·light WORK /ˈmuːn·laɪt/ *v* [I] *past* **moonlighted** to work at an additional job, esp. without telling your main employer • *A qualified teacher, he moonlighted* **as** *a cabbie in the evenings to pay the rent.* • *She had been moonlighting* **as** *a weekend waitress for several months.*

moon·light·ing /£ˈmuːn·laɪ·tɪŋ, $-t̬ɪŋ/ *n* [U] • *We know a lot of moonlighting takes place but it's hard to trace.*

moon·shine ALCOHOL /ˈmuːn·ʃaɪn/ *n* [U] *infml* alcoholic drink made illegally

moon·shine SPEECH /ˈmuːn·ʃaɪn/ *n* [U] *infml* nonsense; foolish talk

moor COUNTRYSIDE /£mɔːʳ, £mʊəʳ, $mʊr/ *n* [C] an open area of hilly countryside covered with rough grass and other short plants like HEATHER • *mountains, lakes and moors* • *Bodmin Moor* • *the Yorkshire moors* • *I scanned the bleak moor for sheep grazing.*

moor *(obj)* TIE /£mɔːʳ, £mʊəʳ, $mʊr/ *v* to cause (esp. a boat) to stay in the same position on the sea or a lake or river by tying it to something on the land or at the bottom of the sea • *We moored further up the river.* [I] • *We moored the boat* **to** *a large tree root.* [T] • *Several tankers were moored in the estuary/off the coast.* [T] • *The oil rig was towed out to sea and moored.* [T]

mooring /£ˈmɔː·rɪŋ, £ˈmʊə-, $ˈmʊr·ɪŋ/ *n* [C] • *We rented a mooring* (= a place to tie a boat).

moor·ings /£ˈmɔː·rɪŋz, £ˈmʊə-, $ˈmʊr·ɪŋz/ *pl n* • Moorings are the ropes or chains which keep esp. a boat from moving away from a particular place: *They had been sleeping in the boat when friends untied its moorings.*

moorhen /£ˈmɔː·hen, £ˈmʊə-, $ˈmʊr-/ *n* [C] a small black bird which lives near water

Moorish /£ˈmʊə·rɪʃ, $ˈmʊr·ɪʃ/ *adj* [not gradable] of the Muslim people who were the rulers of Spain from 711 to 1492 • *the Moorish conquest* • *the Moorish city of Granada* • *Moorish architecture*

moorland /£ˈmɔː·lənd, £ˈmʊə-, $ˈmʊr-/ *n* an area of MOOR (= high open countryside with grass and small bushes) • *heather moorland* • *moorland scenery/birds* [U] • *The path led across deserted moorlands.* [C]

moose /muːs/ *n* [C] *pl* **moose** a type of large deer with large flat horns found in N America and N Europe

moot *obj* /muːt/ *v* [T usually passive] *fml* to suggest or introduce (an idea/matter) for discussion • *a much/long mooted proposal* • *The idea was first mooted as long ago as the 1840s.* • *His name was mooted as a possible successor.* • **It** *was mooted* **that** *golf should be included in the Olympics.* [+ *that* clause]

moot /muːt/ *adj* [not gradable] • A **moot point** is a subject about which different people have different opinions: *It's* **a** *moot point* **whether** *God exists outside our own thought processes.*

mop /£mɒp, $mɑːp/ *n* [C] a stick with soft material fixed at one end, esp. used for washing floors or dishes • *a floor mop* • *a dish mop* • PIC **Cleaning**

mop *obj* /£mɒp, $mɑːp/ *v* [T] **-pp-** • *He mopped the bathroom floor* (= washed it with a mop). • If you mop your **brow/forehead/face** you use a cloth to remove SWEAT (= liquid produced because you are hot): *He mopped his forehead* **with** *a large handkerchief.* • If you mop something **up** you use a cloth or a mop to remove liquid or *(fig.)* you make things tidy or arrange them in a better way: *Get a cloth to mop up the milk from the floor.* ○ *I'll mop it up.* ○ *(fig. infml) There was a lot of mopping-up to do after the earthquake.* ○ *(fig. infml) We had quite a mopping-up operation after the party.* • *(infml)* **Mop up** also means to finish or use something completely: *There are only three parcels left to wrap – we'll soon mop it up.* ○ *The repair bill mopped up all my spare cash.*

mope /£məʊp, $moʊp/ *v* [I] *disapproving* to be unhappy and unwilling to think or act positively, esp. because of a disappointment • *There's no point in sitting at home and moping – get out there and find yourself another job!* • To **mope about/around** is to move about without any particular purpose and without any energy or enthusiasm, because you are unhappy and/or disappointed: *He was driving me mad, moping about the house all day.*

moped /£ˈməʊ·ped, $ˈmoʊ-/ *n* [C] a small motorcycle which sometimes also has PEDALS like a bicycle which can be used when starting it or travelling up a hill • PIC **Bicycles**

mo·poke /£ˈməʊ·pəʊk, $ˈmoʊ·poʊk/ *n* [C] a type of Australian and New Zealand OWL whose call sounds like its name • *(Aus infml)* A mopoke is also someone who is stupid or looks very unhappy.

mop·pet /£ˈmɒp·ɪt, $ˈmɑː·pɪt/ *n* [C] *infml* an affectionate word for a small child, esp. a girl • *a curly-haired moppet*

mor·al /£ˈmɒr·əl, $ˈmɔːr-/ *adj* relating to the standards of good or bad behaviour, fairness, honesty, etc. which each person believes in, rather than to laws or other standards • *It's her moral* **obligation** *to tell the police what she knows.* • *It is not part of a novelist's job to make moral judgments.* • *She was the only politician to condemn the proposed law on moral grounds* (= for moral reasons). • *The Democrats are attempting to* **capture the** *moral* **high ground** (= are trying to appear more honest and good than the other political parties). • A moral person behaves in ways considered by most people to be correct and honest: *She is an extremely moral woman.* ○ *Oh, stop being so moral!* • *Those who campaign against the death penalty believe they are on a moral* **crusade**. • *Is TV responsible for weakening people's moral* **fibre** (= ability to behave well and honestly and work hard)? • If you win a moral **victory**, you are defeated in an argument, but you show that really you were right. • The **moral majority** are those people in a society, esp. the US in the 20th century, who support severe and old-fashioned Christian standards of behaviour. • *Not being a member of staff, he could not intervene directly, but he did give the strikers his* **moral support** (= approval and encouragement). • Compare AMORAL; IMMORAL.

mor·al /£ˈmɒr·əl, $ˈmɔːr-/ *n* [C] • The moral of a story, event or experience is the message which you understand from it about how you should or should not behave: *The moral* **of/to** *the story is that honesty is always the best policy.*

mor·al·ist /£ˈmɒr·əl·ɪst, $ˈmɔːr-/ *n* [C] *often disapproving* • A moralist is a person who tries to force or teach other people to behave in ways he or she considers to be most correct and honest: *He was a* **stern** *moralist.*

mor·al·is·tic /£ˌmɒr·əlˈɪs·tɪk, $ˌmɔːr-/ *adj disapproving* • Someone or something that is moralistic judges people by fixed and possibly unfair standards of right and wrong and tries to force or teach them to behave according to these standards: *The priest was a humourless and moralistic man.* ○ *Drug addicts need sympathetic, not moralistic, treatment.*

mor·al·i·ty /£məˈræl·ə·ti, $mɔːˈræl·ə·t̬i/ *n* • Morality is a personal or social set of standards for good or bad behaviour and character, or the quality of being right, honest or acceptable: *They argued for a new morality based on self-sacrifice and honesty.* [C] ○ *I have to question the morality of forcing poor people to pay for their medical treatment.* [U] ○ *I think it's rather old-fashioned to cast doubt on a couple's morality just because they're living together without being married.* [U] • *"We know of no spectacle so ridiculous as the British public in one of its periodical fits of morality."* (Lord Macaulay *Essays*, 1843)

mor·al·ize, *Br and Aus usually* **-ise** /£ˈmɒr·əl·aɪz, $ˈmɔːr-/ *v* [I] *often disapproving* • To moralize is to express judgments on right and wrong: *A good teacher manages to educate without moralizing.* ○ *He has an infuriating habit of moralizing* **on/about** *subjects he knows nothing about.*

mor·al·ly /£ˈmɒr·əl·i, $ˈmɔːr-/ *adv* • *Morally you're right, but in practice I don't think it would work.* • *For a teacher to hit a child is not just morally wrong but also illegal.* • *Any war would be morally repugnant.* • *They think they're morally superior to the rest of us.* • *The company is morally bound to pay its employees a decent wage.* • If you act morally, you act in a way that you or people in general consider to be right, honest or acceptable: *She gives the impression of acting morally although her job is to exploit workers.*

mor·als /£ˈmɒr·əlz, $ˈmɔːr-/ *pl n* • Morals are standards for good or bad character and behaviour: *public/private morals* • *(dated disapproving) a person of* **loose** *morals* (= whose character and behaviour, esp. in relation to sex, are unacceptable)

mor·ale /məˈrɑːl/ *n* [U] the amount of confidence felt by a person or group of people, esp. when in a dangerous or difficult situation • *Morale was high/good/low/bad amongst the strikers.* • *A couple of victories would* **raise/boost** *the team's morale enormously.*

mor·ass /məˈræs/ *n* [C usually sing] *slightly literary* an area of soft wet ground in which it is easy to get stuck, or *(fig.)* something that is extremely complicated and difficult to deal with and makes any advance almost impossible • *The farmer's tractor had turned the lane into a morass* **of** *mud which was difficult to walk through.* • *(fig.) The morass* **of** *rules and regulations is delaying the start of the project.* • *(fig.) The country is caught in a morass* **of** *debt.*

mor·a·to·ri·um /£ˌmɒr·əˈtɔː·ri·əm, $ˌmɔːr·əˈtɔːr·i-/ *n* [C] *pl* **moratoriums** or **moratoria** /£ˌmɒr·əˈtɔː·ri·ə, $ˌmɔːr·əˈtɔːr·i-/ *fml* a stopping of an activity for an agreed amount of time • *a five-year worldwide moratorium* **on** *whaling/nuclear weapons testing*

mor·bid /£ˈmɔː·bɪd, $ˈmɔːr-/ *adj disapproving* too interested in unpleasant subjects, esp. death • *a morbid* **curiosity** *about torture and murder* • *The poet demonstrates his morbid devotion to his dead wife by sleeping next to her grave.* • Ⓘ

mor·bid·ly /£ˈmɔː·bɪd·li, $ˈmɔːr-/ *adv disapproving* • *She seemed morbidly obsessed with the idea of her own death.*

mor·bid·i·ty /£ˌmɔːˈbɪd·ɪ·ti, $ˌmɔːrˈbɪd·ə·t̬i/ *n* [U] *disapproving*

mor·dant /£ˈmɔː·dᵊnt, $ˈmɔːr-/ *adj fml* (esp. of humour) cruel; criticizing in an amusing way • *mordant* **wit/humour** • *a mordant remark*

mor·dant·ly /£ˈmɔː·dᵊnt·li, $ˈmɔːr-/ *adv fml*

more /£mɔːʳ, $mɔːr/ *determiner, pronoun, adv* [not gradable] a larger or extra number or amount (of) • *She kept on asking if I wanted more (food).* • *The doctors can't cope with* **any more** *patients.* • *Why are there no more seats left?* • *Add some more cream to the sauce.* • *You need to listen more, and talk less!* • *More people live in the capital* **than** *in the whole of the rest of the country.* • *We spent more time* (=longer) *on the last job* **than** *usual.* • *The noise was more* **than** *I could bear.* • *Disneyworld was a hundred times more fun* **than** *I'd expected.* • *Their beliefs are more Christian* **than** *Buddhist* (=have a larger number of Christian characteristics than Buddhist ones). • More is used to form the comparative of many adjectives and adverbs: *Let's find a more sensible way of doing it.* ○ *You couldn't be more wrong.* ○ *He finds physics* **far/much** *more difficult* **than** *other science subjects.* ○ *Play that last section more passionately.* • More is also used to emphasize the largeness of something: *More* **than** *20 000 demonstrators crowded into the square.* ○ *Each diamond was worth £10 000* **or** *more.* • *(fml)* If you say that you **couldn't agree/disagree** more, or you **couldn't like/dislike** something more, you mean that you agree/disagree completely, or like/dislike something completely: *I couldn't agree with you more, Professor.* • **No/Not** more is used to emphasize the smallness of something: *There's about 20 kilos here, not more.* ○ *It's no more* **than** *an inch long.* • *Can you play the song through once/twice more* (=once/twice again), *please?* • *Several publishers rejected her book, but that just made her* **all the** *more determined* (=increased her determination). • *He won the race,* **and what's more** (=additionally and more importantly), *he broke the world record.* • *I don't do yoga* **any more** (=I no longer do it). • *It gets* **more and more** (=increasingly) *difficult to understand what is going on.* • *(Br infml disapproving)* If you say **(the) more fool you** to someone, you are saying that you think that what they have done or might do is foolish: *"I'm going to resign and try to find a better job." "More fool you."* • *(infml)* People say **that's more like it** to show that they think something or someone has improved: *For this exercise don't bend your legs too far – that's more like it!* • *She's* **more of a** *poet* **than a** *musician.* (=She spends more time being or is better suited to being a poet than a musician.) • **More often than not** (=On most occasions), *the computer comes up with the wrong answer.* • *The project was* **more or less** (=mostly) *a success.* • *It's 500 kilos,* **more or less** (=approximately). • *He* **more or less** (=very nearly) *admitted he'd done it.* • **More than** is also used to mean very: *It's more than* **likely** *that there's oil here under the ground.* ○ *(fml) I was more than a little* (=I was very) *curious about the whole business.* ○ *(fml) We will be more than glad/happy/willing to help you in any way we can.* • **The more** *he insisted he was innocent,* **the less** *they seemed to believe him.* • **The more** *he drank,* **the more** *violent he became.* • *Please bring as much food as you can –* **the more the better** (=the more food you bring, the better it will be). • *Do come to the picnic –* **the more the merrier** (=it will be more enjoyable if more people are there). • *"Please, Sir. I want some more"* (from the musical film *Oliver* based on Charles Dicken's *Oliver Twist,* 1968) • LP› **Comparing and grading, Quantity words**

more·ish /£ˈmɔː·rɪʃ, $ˈmɔːr·ɪʃ/ *adj Br and Aus infml approving* (of food) having a very pleasant taste and making you want to eat more • *These peanuts are very moreish, aren't they?*

more·ov·er /£ˌmɔːˈrəʊ·vəʳ, $ˌmɔːrˈoʊ·vɚ/ *adv* [not gradable] *fml* (used to add information) also and more importantly • *It was a good car, and it was, moreover, a fair price they were asking for it.*

mo·res /£ˈmɔː·reɪz, $ˈmɔːr·eɪz/ *pl n fml* the traditional customs and ways of behaving that are typical of a particular (part of) society • *social mores* • *middle-class mores* • *the mores and culture of the Japanese*

morgue /£mɔːg, $mɔːrg/ *n* [C] *esp. Am and Aus for* MORTUARY (=place where dead bodies are kept) • *(fig. disapproving) I'm fed up with this place – it's a morgue* (=too quiet and boring).

mor·i·bund /£ˈmɒr·ɪ·bʌnd, $ˈmɔːr-/ *adj fml disapproving* (esp. of an organization or business) not active or successful • *How can the Trade Department be revived from its present moribund state?* • *The city centre is usually moribund in the evening, so the council is trying to encourage more cafés and bars to open there.*

Mor·mon /£ˈmɔː·mən, $ˈmɔːr-/ *n* [C] a member of a religious group called the Church of Jesus Christ of Latter-Day Saints, which originated in the US in 1830

morn /£mɔːn, $mɔːrn/ *n* [C] *poetic* a morning • *Yonder breaks a new and glorious morn.*

morn·ing /£ˈmɔː·nɪŋ, $ˈmɔːr-/ *n* the part of the day from the time when the sun rises until the middle of the day or **lunch time** • *a beautiful/sunny/wet morning* [C] • *I work three mornings a week at the bookshop.* [C] • *She only works* **in the** *mornings.* [C] • *What's our schedule for* **this** *morning?* [U] • *I'd like an appointment for* **tomorrow** *morning, please.* [U] • *I'll see you* **on** *Saturday morning.* [U] • *He's been angry* **all** *morning.* [U] • *We work all day, morning* **till night**. [U] • *I had too much to drink at Sarah's party, and I felt terrible* **the** *morning* **after**. [U] • *If possible, I'd like an early-morning or mid-morning flight* (=a flight which leaves in the early morning or in the middle of the morning). • Morning is also the half of the day between twelve o'clock at night and twelve o'clock in the middle of the day: *The murder took place at four* **in the** *morning, when it was still dark.* [U] • *She said she would see you* **in the morning** (=the next morning). • *Our neighbour's baby cries* **morning, noon and night** (=all the time). • The **morning-after pill** is a pill containing a drug which prevents a woman from getting pregnant if it is taken less than 78 hours after she has had sex. • **Morning dress** (also a **morning suit**) is a very formal set of clothes worn by some men on occasions such as marriage ceremonies, including a long black or grey coat, STRIPED trousers, and a **top hat**: *The bridegroom was wearing morning dress/a morning suit.* • **Morning sickness** is the feeling of wanting to vomit experienced soon after waking by some women during the first months of pregnancy. • The **morning star** is a planet, esp. Venus, which can be seen shining brightly in the east just before or as the sun rises. • *"It's morning in America again"* (Ronald Reagan, 1980s) • LP› **Time** Ⓙ

morn·ings /£ˈmɔː·nɪŋz, $ˈmɔːr-/ *adv esp. Am* • *Mornings* (=Every morning) *we go running in the park.*

mor·on /£ˈmɔː·rɒn, $ˈmɔːr·ɑːn/ *n* [C] *infml disapproving* a very stupid person • *Some moron smashed into the back of my car yesterday.* • *You moron! Can't you do anything right?* [as form of address]

mor·on·ic /£məˈrɒn·ɪk, $mɔːˈrɑː·nɪk/ *adj infml disapproving* • *her moronic assistant* • *a moronic grin* • *He came up with some really moronic ideas about how to solve the problem.*

mo·rose /£məˈrəʊs, $-ˈroʊs/ *adj* unhappy and/or annoyed and unwilling to speak, smile or be pleasant to people; SULLEN • *a morose expression* • *Why are you so morose these days – what's depressing you?* • Ⓔ Ⓘ

mo·rose·ly /£məˈrəʊ·sli, $-ˈroʊ-/ *adv* • *He spent the evening morosely watching the usual rubbish on TV.*

mo·rose·ness /£məˈrəʊ·snəs, $-ˈroʊ-/ *n* [U]

mor·pheme /£ˈmɔː·fiːm, $ˈmɔːr-/ *n* [C] *specialized* the smallest bit of language that has its own meaning, either a word or a part of a word • *'Work' is a morpheme.* • *'Worker' contains two morphemes – 'work' and '-er'.*

mor·phine /£ˈmɔː·fiːn, $ˈmɔːr-/ *n* [U] a drug made from OPIUM, used to stop people from feeling pain or to make people feel calmer • *She begged me for another shot of morphine to kill the pain.* • *His foot was gangrenous, so an army doctor injected him with morphine and sawed off his leg below the knee to save his life.*

mor·phol·o·gy /£mɔːˈfɒl·ə·dʒi, $mɔːrˈfɑː·lə-/ *n* [U] *specialized* the scientific study of the structure and form of either animals and plants or words and phrases.

mor·pho·log·i·cal /£ˌmɔː·fəˈlɒdʒ·ɪ·kəl, $ˌmɔːr·fəˈlɑː·dʒɪ-/ *adj* [not gradable] *specialized*

mor·ris danc·ing /£ˈmɒr·ɪs, $ˈmɔːr-/ *n* [U] a type of traditional English dancing in which a group of people, esp. men, dance together, wearing special clothes decorated with little bells

mor·ris dance /£ˈmɒr·ɪs, $ˈmɔːr-/ *n* [C]

mor·ris dan·cer /£ˈmɒr·ɪs, $ˈmɔːr-/ *n* [C]

mor·row /£ˈmɒr·əʊ, $ˈmɑːr·oʊ/ *n* [U] *old use* the next day, or TOMORROW • *They arranged to meet* **on the** *morrow.* • *We must wait until* **the** *morrow.*

Morse (code) /£mɔːs, $mɔːrs/ *n* [U] a system used internationally for sending messages, in which letters and numbers are represented by short and long marks, sounds or flashes of light • *The ship's radio officer tapped out a message* **in** *Morse code.* • *Dot dot dot, dash dash dash, dot dot dot is Morse code for SOS.*

mor·sel /£ˈmɔː·səl, $ˈmɔːr-/ *n* [C] a very small piece of food, or *(fig.)* a very small piece or amount • *a morsel* **of** *cheese* • *The prisoners ate every last morsel.* • *(fig.) There's a morsel* **of** *good economic news this morning – the inflation rate has fallen slightly.*

mor·tal /£ˈmɔː·təl, $ˈmɔːr·t̬əl/ *adj* [not gradable] *slightly literary* (of living things, esp. people) unable to continue living forever; having to die • *Gods live forever, but humans are mortal beings and must die.* • A mortal **blow/injury** is one that causes death: *(fig.) New computing technology dealt a mortal blow to the power of the old printing unions.* Compare LETHAL. • Mortal **combat** is a fight in which two enemies try to kill each other: *(fig.) Management and the union seem to be locked in mortal combat.* • A mortal **enemy/danger/threat** is a very serious and dangerous one: *To sheep farmers in the area, the wolf is a mortal enemy.* ○ *The police delay exposed her to mortal danger.* • *He was in mortal* (= very great) **fear/terror** *of what might happen.* • In the Roman Catholic religion a **mortal sin** is an action that is so bad that you will be punished forever after your death, if you do not ask for forgiveness from God. • Compare IMMORTAL.

mor·tal /£ˈmɔː·təl, $ˈmɔːr·t̬əl/ *n* [C] *literary, often humorous* • A mortal is an ordinary person, rather than a god or a special, important or powerful person: *The police officers guarding the door let in the celebrities, but they prevented us* **ordinary/lesser** *mortals from going inside.* ○ *I never expected that someone as famous as her would stop and talk to a* **mere** *mortal like myself.* • *"Lord, what fools these mortals be!"* (Shakespeare, Midsummer Night's Dream 3.2)

mor·tal·i·ty /£mɔːˈtæl·ə·ti, $mɔːrˈtæl·ə·t̬i/ *n* [U] *fml* • *A sense of her own mortality* (= the fact that she, like all living creatures, would die) *overcame her.* • Mortality is also the number of deaths within a particular society and within a particular period of time: *A clean water supply played a large part in reducing mortality/the mortality* **rate**. ○ **Infant** *mortality/The* **infant**-*mortality* **rate** *is much higher in the poorest areas of the city.* • Compare **immortality** at IMMORTAL.

mor·tal·ly /£ˈmɔː·təl·i, $ˈmɔːr·t̬əl-/ *adv* • *mortally wounded* (= injured so badly that death is likely) • *(fig.) Apparently the criticisms mortally* (= very much) **offended** *him.*

mor·tar MIXTURE /£ˈmɔː·təʳ, $ˈmɔːr·t̬ɚ/ *n* [U] a mixture of sand, water and CEMENT or LIME that is used to fix bricks or stones to each other when building walls

mor·tar GUN /£ˈmɔː·təʳ, $ˈmɔːr·t̬ɚ/ *n* [C] a large gun with a short wide BARREL which fires bombs and other explosive weapons at low speed over short distances and very high into the air, or an explosive device fired from such a gun • *Our mortars were completely ineffective against their artillery.* • *More than 100 mortars hit the village during the night, damaging a church and other buildings.* • *Terrorists have mounted three mortar* **attacks** *on the police station over the past year.*

mor·tar BOWL /£ˈmɔː·təʳ, $ˈmɔːr·t̬ɚ/ *n* [C] a hard strong bowl in which substances are crushed into a powder by hitting or rubbing them with a PESTLE • *Use a* **pestle and** *mortar to crush the spices.*

mor·tar·board /£ˈmɔː·tə·bɔːd, $ˈmɔːr·t̬ɚ·bɔːrd/, *Aus* **trench·er** *n* [C] a black hat with a square flat top, worn on formal occasions by some teachers and students at college or university, and in the past by some school teachers

mort·gage /£ˈmɔː·gɪdʒ, $ˈmɔːr-/ *n* [C] an agreement which allows you to borrow money from a bank or similar organization, esp. in order to buy a house or apartment, or the amount of money itself • *If you fail to repay the mortgage, the bank will repossess your house.* • *They* **took out** *a £40 000 mortgage* (= They borrowed £40 000) *to buy the house.*

mort·gage *obj* /£ˈmɔː·gɪdʒ, $ˈmɔːr-/ *v* [T] • To mortgage something, esp. land or a building, is to make an agreement with a bank or similar organization in which you borrow money from it and it becomes the owner of the land or building and can take possession of it if you fail to pay back the money: *The house was mortgaged* **up to the hilt** (= The full value of the house had been borrowed).

mort·ga·gee /£ˌmɔː·gɪˈdʒiː, $ˌmɔːr-/ *n* [C] *specialized* • A mortgagee is a bank or similar organization which gives mortgages to people, esp. so that they can buy a house or apartment.

mor·ti·cian /£mɔːˈtɪʃ·ən, $mɔːr-/ *n* [C] *Am for* UNDERTAKER (= person who buries dead bodies)

mor·ti·fy *obj* /£ˈmɔː·tɪ·faɪ, £-tə-, $ˈmɔːr·t̬ə-/ *v* [T usually passive] to cause (someone) to feel extremely ashamed • *She remembered how mortified she'd been as a child, having to wear her sister's old dress to school.* • *The interview turned out to be a mortifying experience.*

mor·ti·fi·ca·tion /£ˌmɔː·tɪ·fɪˈkeɪ·ʃən, $ˌmɔːr·t̬ə-/ *n* [U] • **To the** *mortification* **of** *the show's organizers, the top performers withdrew just before due to start.* • **Mortification of the flesh** is punishment of yourself, esp. by hitting your body with a whip: *(fig. humorous) I don't really want to spend the weekend working, but as they say, a little mortification of the flesh is good for the soul.*

mor·tise, **mor·tice** /£ˈmɔː·tɪs, $ˈmɔːr·t̬ɪs/ *n* [C] *specialized* a rectangular hole in a piece of wood, stone, etc. into which another piece is fixed, so that they form a joint • *The structure was made in the traditional manner, using mortice and tenon joints secured with oak pegs.* • *(Br)* A **mortise lock** (*Am* **dead bolt**, *Aus* **deadlock**) is a lock that is enclosed within the edge of a door, so that it cannot be seen or removed when the door is closed: *After the robbery, the police advised me to have a mortice lock fitted on the back door.* • PIC **Locks and home security**

mor·tu·a·ry *Br* /£ˈmɔː·tjʊ·ri, $ˈmɔːr·tʃu·er·i/, *esp. Am and Aus* **morgue** *n* [C] a building, or a room in a hospital, where dead bodies are kept so that they can be examined before the funeral • *(Am)* A mortuary is also a **funeral parlour**. See at FUNERAL.

mo·sa·ic /£məʊˈzeɪ·ɪk, $moʊ-/ *n* [C] a pattern or picture made using many small pieces of coloured stone or glass • *a beautiful 10th century mosaic* • *a mosaic ceiling* • *(fig.) The country is now a cultural and social mosaic* (= complicated mixture of different parts) *due to the influx of several different ethnic groups.*

mos·ey /£ˈməʊ·zi, $ˈmoʊ-/ *v* [I always + adv/prep] *esp. Am infml* to walk or go slowly, usually without a special purpose • *I'll just mosey* **on down** *to the beach for a while.*

Mos·lem /ˈmʊz·lɪm, $ˈmɑː·zlɪm/ *n, adj* [not gradable] MUSLIM

mosque /£mɒsk, $mɑːsk/ *n* [C] a building for Islamic religious activities and worship

mos·qui·to /£mɒsˈkiː·təʊ, $-t̬oʊ/, *Br and Aus infml* **moz·zie** /£ˈmɒz·i, $ˈmɑː·zi/, **mos·sie**, *Aus also and Am infml* **skeet·er** /£ˈskiː·təʳ, $-t̬ɚ/ *n* [C] *pl* **mosquitoes** or **mosquitos** a small flying insect that bites people and animals, and sucks their blood • *Some types of the anopheles mosquito transmit malaria to humans.* • A **mosquito net** is a net that hangs over and around a bed to keep mosquitoes away from someone who is sleeping. • PIC **Insects**

moss /£mɒs, $mɑːs/ *n* [U] a very small green or yellow plant that grows esp. in wet earth or on rocks, walls and tree trunks • *The rocks near the river were covered with moss.*

mos·sy /£ˈmɒs·i, $ˈmɑː·si/ *adj* **-ier, -iest** • *a mossy tree/rock/lawn*

most /£məʊst, $moʊst/ *determiner, pronoun, adv* [not gradable] the biggest number or amount (of); more than anything or anyone else • *What's* **the** *most you've ever won at cards?* • *Which of you earns* **the** *most money?* • *She said she would share the food equally, but as usual John got* **the** *most.* • **The** *most they can expect is a 4% pay increase* (= 4%

is the largest possible pay increase they can expect). • *He wanted to do* **the** *most good he could with the £200, so he gave it to charity.* • *It's a lovely day – we must* **make the most of** *it* (= take full advantage of it for as long as it continues). • *The kids loved the fair, but they enjoyed the bumper cars most* **of all**. • Most is used to form the superlative of many adjectives and adverbs: *Joanne is* **the** *most intelligent person I know.* ○ *The department needs three more computers in order to work most effectively* (= to work as effectively as possible). • Most also means almost all: *I don't eat meat, but I like most types of fish.* ○ *Most sausages contain pork.* ○ *In this school, most* **of** *the children are from the Chinese community.* • *(fml)* Most also means very: *It was a most beautiful morning.* ○ *He argued his case most persuasively.* • *(esp. Am infml)* Most also means almost: *You'll find her in the bar most* **every** *evening about six o'clock.* • LP› **Comparing and grading, Quantity words**

–most /£-məust, $-moust/ *combining form* • *John O'Groats is the northernmost part of the British mainland* (= the part that is farther to the north than any other part). • *Thoughts of dinner were uppermost* (= more important and clearer than other thoughts) *in his mind.*

most·ly /£'məust·li, $'moust-/ *adv* [not gradable] • *In the smaller villages, it's mostly* (= usually) *very quiet at nights.* • *The story seemed to be mostly true* (= most of it seemed true). • *They're mostly* (= Most of them are) *teenagers, I think.*

MOT /£ˌem·əu'tiː, $-ou'-/ *n* [C] a test which all British road vehicles more than three years old have to pass each year in order to prove that they are safe to drive • *The car will fail its MOT if we don't get the brakes fixed.* • *an MOT certificate*

MOT *obj* /£ˌem·əu'ti, $-ou-/ *v* [T often passive] **MOTing**, *past* **MOT'd** • *I want to get the car MOT'd before we drive to France.*

mote /£məut, $mout/ *n* [C] *literary* something, esp. a bit of dust, that is so small it is almost impossible to see • *Sulphur dioxide dissolves in the motes* **of** *dust and water droplets that make up smog, producing sulphuric acid.*

mo·tel /£məu'tel, $mou-/, *Am also* **mo·tor court, mo·tor lodge** *n* [C] a hotel by the side of a road, usually with spaces for cars next to each room • Ⓣ

moth /£mɒθ, $mɑːθ/ *n* [C] an winged insect similar to a BUTTERFLY that flies esp. at night and is attracted to light • *A moth was fluttering around the candle flame.* • *Some types of moths eat holes in clothes.* • If you say that clothing or furniture is **moth-eaten**, you mean that it looks old and has holes in it. • PIC› **Insects**

moth·ball *obj* /£'mɒθ·bɔːl, $'mɑːθ·bɑːl/ *v* [T usually passive] to stop work on an idea, plan or job, but leaving it in such a way that you can start on it again at some point in the future • *It's a good idea Ms Jones, but I'm afraid we're going to have to mothball it until next year at the earliest.* • *The six coal pits were mothballed in the hope that they could they could be reopened in a time of better economic conditions.*

moth·er PARENT /£'mʌð·əʳ, $-ɚ/ *n* [C] a female parent • *My mother was 21 when she had* (= gave birth to) *me.* • *All the mothers* **and fathers** *had been invited to the end-of-term concert.* • *Hello, can I speak to your mother, please?* • *(fml or dated) May I borrow your car, Mother?* [as form of address] • *The little kittens and their mother were all curled up asleep in the same basket.* • *While they were at sea they got caught in* **the mother of all** *storms* (= an extremely severe storm). • *Didn't you learn to cook* **at your mother's knee** (= when you were very young)? • Your **mother country** (also **fatherland**) is the country where you were born or which you feel is your original home: *Even though she has not lived in Spain for 50 years, she still calls it her mother country.* • A **mother figure** is a woman who you feel you can ask for help, support or advice: *She never saw much of her own mother as a child, and in later life Susan was very much a mother figure to her.* • **Mother Nature** is another word for nature, used esp. humorously and when considering it as a force that controls the weather and all living things: *It is better to try to work with, rather than against, Mother Nature.* • **Mother-of-pearl** is a smooth hard substance forming a layer inside the shells of some sea animals. It is white but also seems to shine with many different colours. It is used to make buttons and for decoration. • **Mother's Day** (also *Br fml* **Mothering Sunday**) is a day each year when people give a present to their mother or do something special for her as a way of expressing their love and gratitude: *Did you remember to send Mum a Mother's Day card?* • A **mother-to-be** is a woman who is pregnant: *Stylish and practical clothes for the mother-to-be/for mothers-to-be can be hard to find.* • A person's **mother tongue** is the first language that they learned when they were a baby, rather than a language learned at school or as an adult: *All children are now allowed to take exams in their mother tongue.* • *"Mother Knows Best"* (title of a story by Edna Ferber, 1927) • *"England is the mother of Parliaments"* (from a speech by John Bright, 1865) • LP› **Holidays, Relationships, Titles and forms of address** PIC› **Family tree**

moth·er *obj* /£'mʌð·əʳ, $-ɚ/ *v* [T] *often disapproving* • To mother a person is to treat them with (too) much kindness and affection and to try to protect them from anything dangerous or difficult: *Stop mothering her – she's 40 years old and can take care of herself perfectly well.*

moth·er·hood /£'mʌð·ə·hud, $'-ɚ-/ *n* [U] • *Brian's really keen to start a family, but his wife doesn't feel ready for motherhood* (= the experience of having and taking care of a baby). • *Many women now try to combine motherhood with their careers.*

moth·er–in–law /£'mʌð·ə·rɪn·lɔː, $-ɚ·ɪn·lɑː/ *n* [C] *pl* **mothers-in-law** or *Br also* **mother-in-laws** • Someone's mother-in-law is the mother of the person they have married. • PIC› **Family tree**

moth·er·ly /£'mʌð·əl·i, $-ɚ·li/ *adj usually approving* • If you describe a woman as motherly, you mean that she treats other people with a lot of kindness and affection and tries to make certain they are happy: *A nice, motherly old woman runs the hostel, and I'm sure she'd make you a packed lunch if you asked her.*

Moth·er RELIGIOUS WOMAN /£'mʌð·əʳ, $-ɚ/ *n* [U] the title of a woman who is in charge of, or who has a high rank within, a CONVENT (= group of Christian women living together) • *Mother Theresa* • *a mother* **superior** • *Good morning, Mother.* [as form of address]

moth·er·board /£'mʌð·ə·bɔːd, $-ɚ·bɔːrd/ *n* [C] *specialized* a **printed circuit board** that contains the **central processing unit** of a computer and makes it possible for the other parts of a computer to communicate with each other

moth·er·fuck·er /£'mʌð·əˌfʌk·əʳ, $-ɚˌfʌk·ɚ/, *Am also* **moth·er** *n* [C] *esp. Am taboo slang* an extremely insulting name for a stupid, unpleasant or unpopular person, esp. one who has done something which has made you angry • *If that motherfucker touches my car again, I'll break his fingers!* • *(fig.) That was a motherfucker of an exam.* (= It was extremely difficult.) • Motherfucker can also be a person or thing which is admired: *He was a sweet old motherfucker, and I miss him a lot.*

moth·er·land /£'mʌð·ə·lænd, $'-ɚ-/ *n* [U] FATHERLAND

moth·proof /£'mɒθ·pruːf, $'mɑːθ-/ *adj* [not gradable] (esp. of clothes) chemically treated in order to keep MOTHS away

mo·tif /£məu'tiːf, $mou-/ *n* [C] a pattern or design • *We chose some curtains with a flower motif.* • A motif is also an idea that is used many times in a piece of writing or music: *The motif of betrayal and loss is crucial in all these stories.* • PIC› **Patterns** Ⓓ

mo·tile /£'məu·taɪl, $'mou·t̬əl/ *adj specialized* (esp. of plants, organisms and very small forms of life) able to move by itself • *highly motile bacteria*

mo·til·i·ty /£məu'tɪl·ə·ti, $mou'tɪl·ə·t̬i/ *n* [U] *specialized* • *These cells have low motility.*

mo·tion MOVEMENT /£'məu·ʃən, $'mou-/ *n* the act or process of moving, or a particular action or movement • *the motion of the Earth around the sun* [U] • *The violent motion of the ship upset her stomach.* [U] • *He rocked the cradle with a gentle backwards and forwards motion.* [C] • *They showed the goal again* **in slow** *motion* (= at a slower speed so that the action could be more clearly seen). [U] • *A single motion* **of** *her head was enough to tell me she was unhappy.* [C] • *(Br dated, Aus specialized)* People sometimes use motion or motions as a polite way of referring to the process of excretion of solid waste: *The nurse asked if her motions were regular.* [C] • *(infml disapproving)* To **go through the motions** is to do something without caring very much about it or having much interest in it: *He says he's been investigating my complaint and that he's very sympathetic, but I feel he's just going through the motions.* • To **put/set** a machine or process **in motion** is to start it: *Once the printing processes have been put in motion, they're not so easy to stop.* ○ *We wrote to the passport office to set the official process in motion.* ○ *A telephone call would set* **the wheels** *in motion* (= cause action to start), *wouldn't it?* • **Motion**

picture is *Am fml for* MOVIE. • **Motion sickness** is another word for **travel sickness**. See at TRAVEL. • Ⓢ

mo·tion·less /£ˈməʊ·ʃᵊn·ləs, $ˈmoʊ-/ *adj* [not gradable] • *The horse lay motionless* (=without moving) *on the ground, as if it was dead.* • *The trees were reflected in the motionless water of the lake.*

mo·tion *(obj)* SIGNAL /£ˈməʊ·ʃᵊn, $ˈmoʊ-/ *v* [always + adv/prep] to make a signal to (someone), usually with your hand or head • *I saw him motion* **to** *the man at the door, who quietly left.* [I] • *Her attendants all gathered round her, but she motioned them away.* [T] • *He motioned me* **to** *sit down.* [T + obj + *to* infinitive] • Ⓢ

mo·tion SUGGESTION /£ˈməʊ·ʃᵊn, $ˈmoʊ-/ *n* [C] a formal suggestion made, discussed and voted on at a meeting • *Someone* **proposed** *a motion* **to** *increase the membership fee to £500 a year.* [+ *to* infinitive] • *The motion was accepted/passed/rejected/defeated.* • Ⓢ

mo·tive REASON /£ˈməʊ·tɪv, $ˈmoʊ·t̬ɪv/ *n* [C] a reason for doing something • *I don't think she could have killed him – she has no motive.* • *Does he have a motive* **for** *lying about where he was?* • *What is the motive* **behind** (=the reason for) *the bombing?* • *I think you should* **examine/question** *their motives* **in** *offering to lend you the money.* • *The* **profit** *motive* (=desire to make a profit) *is very strong.* • *She denies that she has has an* **ulterior** (=secret) *motive, such as gaining publicity for her new book, for making the donation.*

mo·ti·vate *obj* /£ˈməʊ·tɪ·veɪt, $ˈmoʊ·t̬ɪ-/ *v* [T] • *What motivates Derek* (=gives him the reason for doing what he does) *is pure greed.* • *They are motivated by a desire to help people.* • *We are looking for someone who will be able to motivate the staff* **to** *work hard.* [+ obj + *to* infinitive]

mo·ti·vat·ed /£ˈməʊ·tɪ·veɪ·tɪd, $ˈmoʊ·t̬ɪ·veɪ·t̬ɪd/ *adj* [not gradable] • *The closure of the school was a financially motivated act* (=money was the reason for it). • *Our staff are hard-working and* **highly** *motivated* (=enthusiastic).

mo·ti·va·tion /£ˌməʊ·tɪˈveɪ·ʃᵊn, $ˌmoʊ·t̬ɪ-/ *n* • *The motivation* (=reason) **for** *the decision is the desire to improve our service to our customers.* [C] • *One of the motivations* (=reasons) **behind** *the job losses was the need to cut costs.* [C] • *Joe's teacher says that he lacks motivation* (=that he sees no reason to work hard). [U] • *Pat's problem is that she has no motivation* (=she is not willing to make the effort necessary) **to** *succeed.* [U + *to* infinitive]

mo·tive·less /£ˈməʊ·tɪv·ləs, $ˈmoʊ·t̬ɪv-/ *adj* [not gradable] • *It was an apparently motiveless murder.*

mo·tive MOVEMENT /£ˈməʊ·tɪv, $ˈmoʊ·t̬ɪv/ *adj* [before n] *specialized* (of power or force) causing movement or action • *Water provides the motive* **power** *that operates the mill.* • *(fig.) The desire to provide for his family is a strong motive* **force** *for him* (=is an important reason why he acts as he does).

mot juste /£ˌməʊˈʒuːst, $ˌmoʊ-/ *n* [C usually sing] *pl* **mots justes** /£ˌməʊˈʒuːst, $ˌmoʊ-/ the word or phrase that is exactly right in a particular situation • *I can't think of* **the** *mot juste to describe how I'm feeling.*

mot·ley /£ˈmɒt·li, $ˈmɑːt-/ *adj* [before n] **motlier, motliest** *usually disapproving* consisting of many different types, therefore seeming quite unusual, and typically of low quality • *There's a motley* **collection** *of old furniture in the house we're renting at the moment.* • *The people who turned up to the meeting were a motley* **crew** (=a group consisting of many different types of people). • *The museum has been converted into offices and is now inhabited by a motley* **assortment** *of architects, designers and artists.*

mo·to·cross /£ˈməʊ·tə·krɒs, $ˈmoʊ·t̬ə·krɑːs/, **scram·bling** *n* [U] the sport of racing over rough ground on specially strengthened motorcycles • *Motocross circuits include natural obstacles such as streams and hills.*

mo·tor DEVICE /£ˈməʊ·təʳ, $ˈmoʊ·t̬ɚ/ *n* [C] a device that changes electricity or fuel into movement and makes a machine work or *(esp. Am)* a vehicle move • *The pump is powered by a small* **electric** *motor.* • *The washing machine needs a new motor.* • *(esp. Am) I've had a new motor put in my car.* • *This boat has an* **(outboard)** *motor* (=engine) *fitted to it.* • A **motor mower** is a powered machine for cutting grass. • In British and Australian English, 'motor' is used mainly for devices powered by electricity. In American English, it is also commonly used for devices powered by PETROL, steam, etc. • LP **Switching on and off**

mo·tor CAR /£ˈməʊ·təʳ, $ˈmoʊ·t̬ɚ/ *adj* [before n; not gradable] *esp. Br and Aus* connected with cars or other vehicles which have engines and use roads • *(Br) This has been a difficult year for the motor* **industry/trade** (=businesses which make and sell cars). • *(Br) They were involved in a motor* **accident** (=an accident involving cars). • *(Br) Everyone who owns a car must have motor* **insurance**. • **Motor car** is *fml for* CAR: *The motor car is responsible for much of the pollution in our cities today.* • *(Br)* A **motor caravan** (*esp. Am* **motor home**) is a large vehicle which contains kitchen equipment, tables, seats, beds, etc., and is used for holidays instead of staying in hotels, or sometimes for living in: *They've bought a motor caravan to go touring around Europe.* • **Motor lodge** is *Am for* MOTEL. • **Motor racing** is the sport of racing extremely fast and powerful cars around roads which have usually been specially designed for this purpose: *He's a former world motor racing* **champion**. • A **motor scooter** **(scooter)** is a very light motorcycle, with small wheels, a covered engine, usually at the back, and a wide curved covering at the front which protects the legs of the person riding it. • *(fml or law) The council has forbidden* **motor vehicles** (=vehicles which have engines) *from entering the city centre.* • LP **Driving**

mo·tor /£ˈməʊ·tə, $ˈmoʊ·t̬ɚ/ *n* [C] *esp. Br infml* • Sometimes a motor is a car: *Do you know anyone who's looking for a second-hand motor?*

mo·tor /£ˈməʊ·təʳ, $ˈmoʊ·t̬ɚ/ *v* [I] • *I was just motoring* (=driving) **along**, *minding my own business, when suddenly I was stopped by the police.* • *(infml) Those guys are really motoring* (=driving fast). • *(fig. infml) It took a while for the painters to get started on our house, but now they're really motoring* (=doing it quickly).

mo·tor·ing /£ˈməʊ·tᵊr·ɪŋ, $ˈmoʊ·t̬ɚ-/ *adj* [before n; not gradable] *esp. Br* • *The company makes a contribution towards my motoring* **costs**. • *It was the first time he'd been convicted of a motoring* **offence** (=of breaking a law relating to driving a car.). • *If you're a member of a motoring* **organization** (=an organization for people who drive cars or other vehicles), *they'll come and help you if you break down.* • *Driving conditions are hazardous, and the police and motoring* **organizations** *are warning motorists not to drive unless their journey is essential.*

mo·tor·ist /£ˈməʊ·tᵊr·ɪst, $ˈmoʊ·t̬ɚ-/ *n* [C] • *The steep rise in the tax on fuel will make the government very unpopular with motorists* (=people who drive cars and other vehicles). • Ⓘ

mo·tor·ized, *Br and Aus usually* **-ised** /£ˈməʊ·tᵊr·aɪzd, $ˈmoʊ·t̬ə·raɪzd/ *adj* [not gradable] • A motorized vehicle is one that has been specially fitted with an engine or a motor: *a motorized wheelchair* • Soldiers who are motorized are provided with wheeled vehicles which have engines: *motorized infantry* • *a motorized regiment*

mo·tor MUSCULAR /£ˈməʊ·tə, $ˈmoʊ·t̬ɚ/ *adj* [before n; not gradable] *medical* relating to muscles that produce movement, or the nerves and parts of the brain that control these muscles • *Ben's parents are worried because he seems to have poor motor* **control** (=is not able to control his muscles easily). • *She's suffering from a disease which impairs her motor* **functions** (=her ability to move).

mo·tor·bike /£ˈməʊ·tə·baɪk, $ˈmoʊ·t̬ɚ-/ *n* [C] *infml for* MOTORCYCLE • *She jumped on her motorbike and raced off down the road.* • *He was seriously injured in a motorbike* **accident** *a couple of years ago.* • *(Am)* A motorbike is often a small light motorcycle. • PIC **Bicycles**

mo·tor·boat /£ˈməʊ·tə·bəʊt, $ˈmoʊ·t̬ɚ·boʊt/ *n* [C] a usually small and often fast boat which is powered by an engine

mo·tor·cade /£ˈməʊ·tə·keɪd, $ˈmoʊ·t̬ɚ-/, *Am also* **au·to·cade** /£ˈɔː·təʊ·keɪd, $ˈɑː·t̬oʊ-/ *n* [C] a series of cars and other motor vehicles which moves slowly along a road during an official ceremony and carries someone important • *President Kennedy was shot as his motorcade drove through the streets of Dallas.*

mo·tor·cy·cle /£ˈməʊ·təˌsaɪ·kl̩, $ˈmoʊ·t̬ɚ-/, *infml* **mo·tor·bike** *n* [C] a two-wheeled vehicle which is similar to a bicycle, but is much bigger and heavier, has a seat for two people, and is powered by an engine • *He was assassinated by two terrorists* **riding** *a motorcycle.* • PIC **Bicycles**

mo·tor·cy·clist /£ˈməʊ·təˌsaɪ·klɪst, $ˈmoʊ·t̬ɚ-/ *n* [C] • *The law requires all motorcyclists* (=people riding on motorcycles) *to wear crash helmets.*

mo·tor·man /£ˈməʊ·tə·mən, $ˈmoʊ·t̬ɚ·mæn/ *n* [C] *pl* **-men** a driver of an underground train

mo·tor·mouth /£ˈməʊ·tə·maʊθ, $ˈmoʊ·t̬ə-/ *n* [C] *esp. Am slang disapproving* a person who talks quickly and continuously, often without considering what they are saying • *She's a real motormouth.* • *He's known as a motormouth disc jockey – he plays very little music and talks a lot.*

mo·tor·way *Br* /£'məʊ·tə·weɪ, $'moʊ·t̬ɚ-/, *Am* **in·ter·state**, *Am and Aus* **free·way** *n* [C] a wide road built for fast moving traffic travelling long distances, with a limited number of points at which drivers can enter and leave it • *In Britain, motorways usually have three lanes in each direction.* • *Because of the bad weather, motorway (driving) conditions are expected to be hazardous tonight.* • PIC〉 **Motorway**

Mo·town /£'məʊ·taʊn, $'moʊ-/ *n* [not after *the*] *trademark* (an American record company, based in Detroit, and started by black people, which produces) popular music which is quite like **rhythm and blues** (=popular music of the 1950s and 1960s) • *a new album on the Motown label* • *Motown was particularly popular in the 1960s and 1970s.*

mot·tled /£'mɒt·l̩d, $'mɑː·t̬l̩d/ *adj* marked with areas of different colours which do not form a regular pattern • *a mottled jacket* • *mottled skin*

mot·to /£'mɒt·əʊ, $'mɑː·t̬oʊ/ *n* [C] *pl* **mottos** or **mottoes** a short sentence or phrase that expresses a principle of good or correct behaviour • *His family motto is 'God helps those who help themselves.'* • *The motto* **of** *the Royal Air Force is 'Per ardua ad astra'* (=Through difficulty to the stars).

mould GROWTH *Br and Aus, Am usually* **mold** /£məʊld, $moʊld/ *n* [U] a soft green or grey growth which develops on old food or on objects that have been left for too long in warm wet air • *There's mould all over this bread.* • *When we stripped the wallpaper off the wall, we discovered mould growing underneath it.*

mould·y *Br and Aus* (**-ier**, **-iest**), *Am usually* **mold·y** (**-ier**, **-iest**) /£'məʊl·di, $'moʊl-/ *adj* • *This cheese has (Br and Aus)* **gone/(Am) gotten** *mouldy.* • *There's a very mouldy smell in the fridge.* • *(fig. esp. Am) the moldy* (=old-fashioned) *traditions of a dying culture*

mould SHAPE *Br and Aus, Am usually* **mold** /£məʊld, $moʊld/ *n* [C] a hollow container with a particular shape into which soft or liquid substances are poured, so that when the substance hardens it takes the shape of the container • *When the jelly is set, turn the mould upside down to tip it out onto a plate.* • *We made these figures by pouring plaster into animal-shaped plastic moulds.* • *(fig.) We're looking for people of a particular mould* (=type) *to join our team of sales representatives.* • *(fig.) Both their children are* **out of** *the same mould* (=are very similar). • *(fig.) He's* **cast in** *a very different mould* (=is a different type of person) *from his brother.* • *(fig.) She doesn't* **fit (into)** *the mould* **of** (=is not like) *a typical police officer.*

mould *(obj) Br and Aus, Am usually* **mold** /£məʊld, $moʊld/ *v* • *Iron has to be heated to a very high temperature before it can be moulded* (=shaped into a particular form). [T] • *This plastic is going to be moulded* **into** *plates.* [T] • *The children moulded little pots* **out of/ from/in** (=made them by shaping) *clay.* [T] • *(fig.) Firm discipline helps mould* (=influence the development of) *a child's character.* [T] • *(fig.) I hate the way you're always trying to mould* (=change) *me* **into** *something you want me to be.* [T] • *(fig.) He was wearing an extremely tight costume which moulded* **to/round** *the contours of* (=fitted closely round the shape of) *his body.* [I always + adv/prep]

mould·ed *Br and Aus, Am usually* **mold·ed** /£'məʊl·dɪd, $'moʊl-/ *adj* [not gradable] • *a chair made of moulded plastic* (=plastic formed into a particular shape)

mould·ing *Br and Aus, Am usually* **mold·ing** /£'məʊl·dɪŋ, $'moʊl-/ *n* • A moulding is a piece of wood, plastic, stone, etc. which has been made into a particular shape to decorate the top or bottom of a wall, or a door, window or piece of furniture: *Large Victorian houses often have high ceilings with attractive mouldings.* [C] • *A piece of moulding has broken off the picture frame.* [U]

mould·er *Br and Aus, Am* **mold·er** /£'məʊl·dəʳ, $'moʊl·dɚ/ *v* [I] to decay slowly; to ROT • *I found these apples mouldering in the cupboard.* • *(fig.) That old bike has been mouldering* **away** (=has been left without being used or cared for) *in the shed for ages – we should get rid of it.*

mould·y /£'məʊl·di, $'moʊl-/ *adj* [before n] **-ier**, **-iest** *Br dated slang* of little value; unpleasant • *All he gave me was a mouldy 50p.* • *It's time you got rid of that mouldy* **old** *coat.*

moult *Br and Aus, Am usually* **molt** /£məʊlt, $moʊlt/ *v* [I] (of a bird or animal) to lose feathers, skin or hair as a natural process at a particular time of year so that new feathers, skin or hair can grow • *Our parrot/dog is moulting again.*

mound /maʊnd/ *n* [C] a pile of earth, stones etc. • *A small mound showed where the grave had been dug.* • *Archaeologists are investigating whether the small hill is really a* **burial** *mound* (=a place where people were buried in ancient times). • *(fig.) Will you really be able to eat that mound* (=large pile) **of** *potatoes?* • In baseball, the mound is the raised area from which the PITCHER throws the ball.

mount *(obj)* GET ON /maʊnt/ *v* to (cause someone to) get on (a horse, bicycle etc.) in order to ride • *She mounted her horse and rode off.* [T] • *When I say so, I want you all to mount.* [I]

mount /maʊnt/ *n* [C] • *Snowy is an excellent mount for a child* (=an excellent horse for a child to ride).

mount·ed /£'maʊn·tɪd, $-t̬ɪd/ *adj* [not gradable] • **Mounted police** (=Police officers riding horses) *ensured that the demonstration was peaceful.* • *The children were all mounted* (=seated) **on** *their ponies, ready for the ride.*

mount *obj* GO UP /maʊnt/ *v* [T] to go up or onto • *The funeral procession slowly mounted the steps of the cathedral.* • *He mounted the platform and began to speak to the assembled crowd.* • *Be careful not to mount the pavement/kerb/sidewalk when you're parking the car.* • *(fml) Queen Elizabeth II mounted* **the throne** (=became queen) *in 1952.*

mount INCREASE /maʊnt/ *v* [I] to increase, rise, or get bigger • *The children's excitement is mounting* (=increasing) *as Christmas gets nearer.* • *The death toll from the plane crash is expected to mount* (=rise) **to** *over 100.* • *It isn't a good idea to let bills mount* **up** (=become added together to make a greater amount).

mount·ing /£'maʊn·tɪŋ, $-t̬ɪŋ/ *adj* [not gradable] • *Sally waited for her examination results with mounting* (=gradually growing) *anxiety.* • *We're faced with mounting debts.*

mount *obj* ORGANIZE /maʊnt/ *v* [T] to prepare and produce; to organize • *Local residents have mounted a* **campaign** *against the building of a new supermarket.* • *The union is mounting a* **challenge** *to the management.* • *Soldiers last night mounted an* **attack** *on rebel troops.* • *The library is mounting a* **display/an exhibition** *of old photographs of the city.*

mount *obj* FIX /maʊnt/ *v* [T] to fix (something) on a wall, in a frame etc., so that it can be viewed easily • *The children's work has been mounted* **on** *cards and put up on the walls of the classroom.* • *I'm going to mount these photographs* **in** *a frame.* • *The specimen can be mounted* **on** *a glass slide and examined under a microscope.*

mount /maʊnt/ *n* [C] • *I'm looking for something I can use as a mount* **for** *this picture* (=something on which this picture can be fixed).

mount *obj* GUARD /maʊnt/ *v* [T] to place (someone) on guard • *Sentries are mounted outside the palace at all times.* • To **mount guard** (*esp. Br* **over** someone or something) is to guard them: *Armed security officers are employed to mount guard (over the president).*

Mount MOUNTAIN /maʊnt/ (*abbreviation* **Mt**) *n* [U] used as part of the name of a mountain, usually before the name • *Mount Everest* • *Mount McKinley* • *Mount Etna* • *Mt Fuji is the highest mountain in Japan.*

moun·tain /'maʊn·tɪn, $-tᵊn/ *n* [C] a raised part of the Earth's surface, larger than a hill, the top of which might be covered in snow • *The Matterhorn is one of the biggest mountains in Europe.* • *Some people find that the mountain air makes them dizzy.* • *He was the first climber to reach the mountain's* **summit/peak**. • *The Rockies are a mountain* **chain/range** *in the western USA.* • *At this time of year, the mountain* **roads/paths** *are blocked by snow.* • *I'd love to go mountain-***climbing**. • *We're going to the mountains* (=an area where there are mountains) *for our holiday.* • Mountains is also used as part of a name for a group of mountains: *the Blue Ridge Mountains of Virginia* • *(fig.) I've got a mountain/mountains* (=a lot) **of** *work to do.* • *(fig.) You'll never eat that mountain* (=large amount) **of** *food.* • *(Br)* A mountain is also a large amount of food which is kept in storage instead of being sold, so that prices for it do not fall: *Something should be done about the grain mountains and wine lakes of the EU.* • *I think you're* **making a mountain out of a molehill** (=making something unimportant seem important). • A **mountain bike** is a bicycle with thick tyres, straight HANDLEBARS and usually a lot of GEARS, originally made for riding on hills

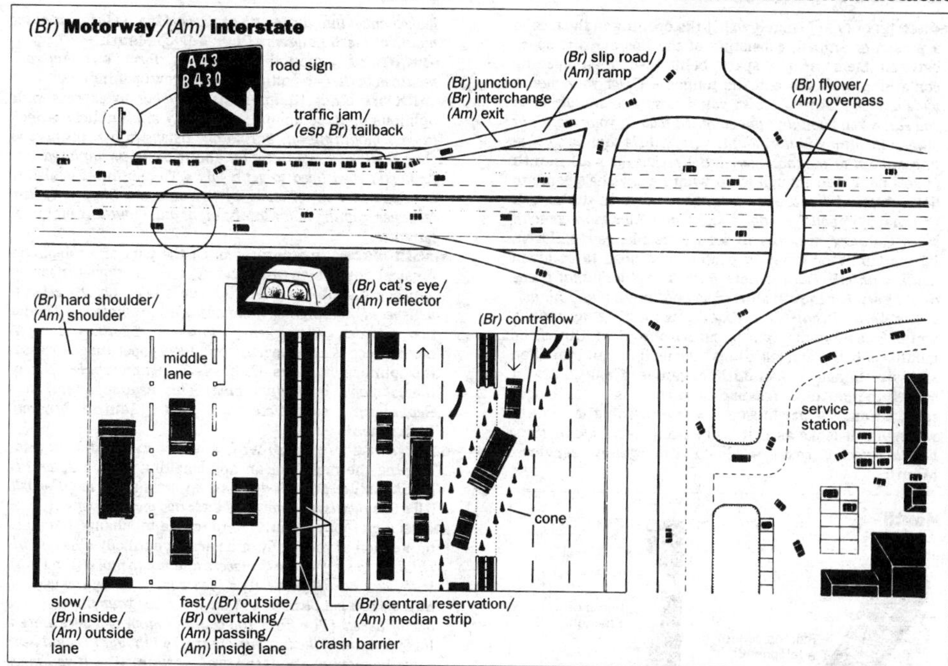

or rough ground, but now often used on roads. • A **mountain lion** is a COUGAR. • PIC> **Bicycles**

moun·tain·eer /£ˌmaʊn·tɪˈnɪəʳ, $-tᵊnˈɪr/ *n* [C] • *Sir Edmund Hillary and Tenzing Norgay were the first mountaineers* (= people who climb mountains as a sport or a job) *to reach the top of Everest.*

moun·tain·eer·ing /£ˌmaʊn·tɪˈnɪə·rɪŋ, $-tᵊnˈɪr·ɪŋ/ *n* [U] • *Frank is very interested in mountaineering* (= the sport or job of climbing mountains).

moun·tain·ous /£ˈmaʊn·tɪ·nəs, $-tᵊn·əs/ *adj* • *The countryside round here is very mountainous* (= contains a lot of mountains). • *(fig.) The ship sank in mountainous* **seas/waves** (= very high waves).

moun·tain·side /ˈmaʊn·tɪnˌsaɪd, $-tᵊn-/ *n* [C usually sing] the side or slope of a mountain • *Can you see those goats high up* **on** *the mountainside?*

moun·tain·top /£ˌmaʊn·tɪnˈtɒp, $-tᵊnˈtɑːp/ *n* [C] the top of a mountain • *The mountaintops are covered with snow.* • See also PEAK MOUNTAIN TOP; SUMMIT HIGHEST POINT.

Moun·tie /£ˈmaʊn·ti, $-ṭi/ *n* [C] *infml* a member of the Royal Canadian Mounted Police, a Canadian police force which often does its work riding on horses

mourn *(obj)* /£mɔːn, $mɔːrn/ *v* to feel or express great sadness, esp. because of someone's death • *Queen Victoria mourned Prince Albert/Prince Albert's death for 40 years.* [T] • *When someone we know dies, we need to take the time to mourn.* [I] • *She is mourning* **for** *her brother.* [I] • *Are we mourning the* **passing of** *a decade* (= feeling sad because it has come to an end and will not return), *or celebrating the beginning of a new one?* [T] • *They're mourning* **for/over** *their lost opportunities.* [I]

mourn·er /£ˈmɔː·nəʳ, $ˈmɔːr·nɚ/ *n* [C] • *The mourners* (= people present at a funeral) *walked behind the coffin in the funeral procession.* • *The dead man's wife and children were among the mourners.*

mourn·ful /£ˈmɔːn·fᵊl, $ˈmɔːrn-/ *adj* • *What are you looking so mournful* (= sad) *about?* • *She looked at him with mournful eyes.* • *This music is rather mournful* (= sounds rather sad). • *We heard the mournful cry of a wolf.*

mourn·ful·ly /£ˈmɔːn·fᵊl·i, $ˈmɔːrn-/ *adv*

mourn·ful·ness /£ˈmɔːn·fᵊl·nəs, $ˈmɔːrn-/ *n* [U]

mourn·ing /£ˈmɔː·nɪŋ, $ˈmɔːr-/ *n* [U] • *Shops will be closed today as a sign of mourning for the king* (= as an expression of sadness about his death). • Mourning is also the usually black clothes that are worn in some countries as an expression of sadness about someone's death: *She is* **in/has gone into** *mourning* **for** *her father* (= She is wearing/has started to wear mourning). ○ *He is in* **deep** *mourning* (= wearing only black clothes). • *(fig.) The film industry is* **in** *mourning* **for** (= is feeling and expressing sadness about the death of) *one of its greatest actors.* • Mourning is also a loud crying that people in some countries make when someone dies: *The mourning could be heard all day and all night.*

mouse ANIMAL /maʊs/ *n* [C] *pl* **mice** /maɪs/ a small mammal with short usually brown, grey or white hair, a pointed face, and a long tail • *a house mouse* • *a field mouse* • *a harvest mouse* • *My brother has a pet mouse.* • *Some people believe it's wrong for scientists to use mice for experiments.* • *(fig. esp. disapproving or humorous) He's such a mouse* (= a shy, quiet, nervous person), *he never dares complain about anything.* • *"Of Mice and Men"* (title of a book by John Steinbeck, 1937) • *"The Mouse that Roared* (= something small that acted fiercely)*"* (title of a film, 1959) • *"If you build a better mousetrap the world will beat a path to your door"* (believed to have been said by Ralph Waldo Emerson, 1803-82)

mous·er /£ˈmaʊ·səʳ, $-sɚ/ *n* [C] • A mouser is a cat that catches mice: *She's a good mouser.*

mous·y, mous·ey /ˈmaʊ·si/ *adj* **mousier, mousiest** *disapproving* • *I'm fed up with having such mousy* (= plain pale brown) **hair** – *I'm going to dye it blonde.* • *(fig.) I wasn't able to see the manager – just her mousy* (= nervous, quiet and shy) *little assistant.*

mouse DEVICE /maʊs/ *n* [C] *pl* **mice** /maɪs/ a small device with a ball which is moved by hand across a special flat surface, and which controls the movement of the CURSOR (= pointer) on a computer screen by copying on the screen the movements of the ball • *Move the cursor to the top of the screen with the mouse and click onto the grey box.*

mouse·trap /ˈmaʊs·træp/ *n* [C] a small device that is used in houses and other buildings for catching and killing mice

mous·sa·ka /muːˈsɑː·kə/ *n* [U] a dish, originally from Greece, consisting of thinly cut meat, TOMATO and AUBERGINE (= a large purple vegetable) cooked together in a cheese sauce

mousse /muːs/ *n* a light food which is made from eggs mixed together with cream and other things, such as fruit, chocolate, fish or meat, and is served cold • *chocolate mousse* • *lemon mousse* • *salmon mousse* [U] • *I'm going to make a mousse to bring to the party.* [C] • Mousse is also a light creamy substance which is put on the hair or skin to improve its appearance or condition: *styling mousse* • *conditioning mousse* • *moisturizing mousse* [U]

mous·tache, *Am usually* **mus·tache** /£mʊˈstɑːʃ, $ˈmʌs·tæʃ/ *n* [C] hair which a man grows above his upper lip • *Groucho Marx had a thick black moustache.* • *The last time I saw him he was* **sporting** (= wearing) *a moustache.* • PIC> **Hair**

mouth BODY PART /maʊθ/ *n* [C] the opening in the face of a person or animal, consisting of the lips and the space between them, or the space behind such an opening containing the teeth and the tongue • *Open your mouth wide and say "Ah".* • *I wish you'd close your mouth when you eat.* • *You shouldn't put so much food in your mouth at once.* • *He hit me in the mouth.* • *(infml) He says he's going to complain to the manager, but I reckon he's* **all mouth** (= he's not brave enough to do what he says he's going to do). • *(infml) What are you looking so* **down in the mouth** (= unhappy) *about?* • *I don't know how they manage with seven* **(hungry) mouths to feed** (= people, esp. children, in one family or group of people, who need to be given food). • *(infml) The burglars told the old lady that if she didn't* **keep** *her* **mouth shut** (= say nothing), *they'd hit her.* • *The smell of that bacon cooking is* **making** *my* **mouth water** (= making me want to eat it). • *(saying)* 'Out of the mouths of babes and sucklings' means that children often say wise things. • A **mouth organ** is a HARMONICA. • **Mouth-to-mouth (resuscitation)** is **artificial respiration**. See at ARTIFICIAL. • If something is **mouth-watering**, it looks as if it will taste good: *Look at those mouth-watering cakes.* • PIC› **Emergency services, Mouth**

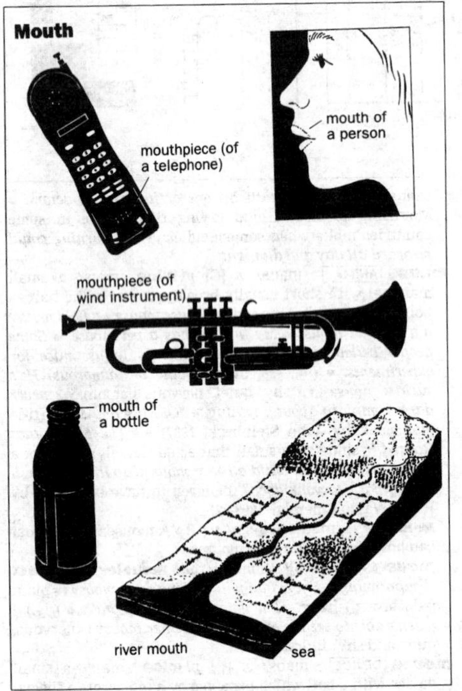

mouth *obj* /maʊð/ *v* [T] • *It looks to me as if the singers are only mouthing the words* (= forming them with their lips without making any sound). • *"Can we go?" mouthed Mary.* [+ clause] • *I don't want to stand here listening to you mouthing* (= saying in a way that is not sincere) *excuses – I want you to correct the mistake you made.* • See also BADMOUTH.

-mouthed /-maʊðd/ *combining form* • *loud-mouthed teenagers* (= those who talk very loudly, esp. to attract attention) • *a foul-mouthed drunk* (= one who swears) • *We stared* **open-***mouthed as the elephant walked slowly down Fairview Close.*

mouth·ful /ˈmaʊθ·fʊl/ *n* [C] • A mouthful is the amount of food or drink which fills your mouth, or which you put into your mouth at one time: *He only ate a few mouthfuls, then he said he couldn't eat any more.* ○ *"Would you like some more chicken?" "Yes, I'll have another mouthful* (= a small amount), *please."* • *(fig. infml humorous) Dinosaur names like 'ichthyosaurus' are* **a bit of a/quite** *a mouthful* (= difficult to pronounce) *for a small child.*

mouth OPENING /maʊθ/ *n* [C usually sing] the opening of a container, such as a bottle, or the opening of a hole or cave, or the place where a river flows into the sea • *This stopper is too big to fit into the mouth* **of** *the bottle/jar.* • *We looked down into the mouth* **of** *the volcano.* • *Quebec is at the mouth* **of** *the St Lawrence River.* • PIC› **Mouth**

-mouthed /-maʊðd/ *combining form* • *a narrow-mouthed bottle* (= a bottle with a narrow opening)

mouth off *v adv* [I] *infml disapproving* to express your opinions or to complain, esp. loudly and publicly • *She's always mouthing off, but no one listens to her anymore.* • *Greg is always mouthing off* **about** *being unemployed, but he hasn't even tried to get a job.* • To mouth off is also to speak rudely or offensively to someone: *She's a typical teenager, coming home late at night and mouthing off* **to** *her parents.*

mouth·piece /ˈmaʊθ·piːs/ *n* [C] the part of a telephone, musical instrument or other device that goes near or between the lips • *"Shall I say you're not here?" she whispered, holding her hand over the mouthpiece.* • *To play the recorder, blow gently into the mouthpiece.* • A mouthpiece is also a person or a newspaper that expresses the opinions of others: *He has become a mouthpiece* **for/of** *the company.* ○ *(disapproving) This newspaper is just a Republican mouthpiece.* • PIC› **Mouth, Musical instruments**

mouth·wash /£ˈmaʊθ·wɒʃ, $-wɑːʃ/ *n* a liquid used for keeping the mouth clean and smelling fresh • *After I've brushed my teeth, I always rinse my mouth with mouthwash.* [U] • *Our dentist recommends these two mouthwashes.* [C]

move *(obj)* BODY /muːv/ *v* to (cause to) change the place or position of your body or a part of your body • *He told his children to stay where they were and not to move.* [I] • *I'm so stiff I can hardly move.* [I] • *Please move out of the way, so that we can get past.* [I] • *"Can you move your fingers?" the doctor asked.* [T] • *(fig.) You couldn't move* (= There were a lot of people) *in the bar last night.* [I] • *I thought I could hear someone moving* **about/around** *upstairs.* [I] • *If you move* **along/over/up** (= go further to the side, back or front) *a bit, Tess can sit next to me.* [I] • *Police officers at the scene of the accident were asking passers-by to move* **along/on** (= to go to a different place). [I] • *(infml) Come on, it's time we were moving* (= going to a different place). [I] • *I think we should* **get** *moving* (= start to leave). [I] • *Let's stay here tonight, then move* **on** (= continue our journey) *tomorrow morning.* [I] • *(fig.) If you want to move* **ahead** (= advance) *in your career, you'll have to start working a bit harder.* [I] • *(fig.) They only move* **among/with** *the best people* (= spend their time with people they think are important). [I] • *(fig.) She moves* **in/among** (= spends her time with) *a very small circle of people.* [I] • *(infml) Come on, Phil,* **move it** (= hurry). • *The defendant stood without* **moving a muscle** (= not moving at all) *as the judge passed sentence.* [usually in negatives]

move /muːv/ *n* [U] • *She held the gun to his head and said, "One move* (= act of moving), *and you're dead!"* • *I hate the way my boss watches my* **every** *move* (= everything I do) *all the time.* • *(infml) Come on, you two,* **get a move on** (= hurry)! • *(infml) I think it's time we* **made a move**/*were* **on the move** (= started to leave). • *(infml) I've been* **on the move** (= very physically active) *all day – I'm really tired.* • *(infml) We're going to be* **on the move** (= travelling around) *all next week, but we'll call you when we get to Edinburgh.*

move·ment /ˈmuːv·mənt/ *n* • *When people shiver, their uncontrolled muscular movements produce heat and so keep them warm.* [C] • *For a long time after the accident, he had no movement* **in** (= was unable to move) *his legs.* [U]

mov·er /£ˈmuː·vəʳ, $-vɚ/ *n* [C] • *Paul's a wonderful mover on the dance-floor* (= He dances very well).

move *(obj)* POSITION /muːv/ *v* to (cause to) change position or place • *Will you help me move this table?* [T] • *I asked you not to move my shoes – now I can't find them.* [T] • *The lid on this jar is so tight that I can't move it.* [T] • *I'm trying to get this screw out of the wall, but it won't move.* [I] • *We've moved the furniture* **(a)round** *in our bedroom to create more space.* [T] • *The baby's so ill that she's been moved* **to** *Great Ormond Street Hospital.* [T] • *A small group of protesters outside the embassy were moved* **along/on** (= told to go to a different place) *by the police.* [M] • *Sophie has moved* **(up)** *into* (= become more advanced and been put into) *a higher ballet class.* [I] • *She has been moved* **(up)** *into a different class.* [T] • *Tom wasn't coping very well at school, so he's moved* **down** *a grade* (= been put into a lower class). [I] • *He's been moved* **down** *into a lower class.* [T] • *You should never open the door while the car is moving* (= going along the road). [I] • *(fig.) Nigel's new car can really move* (= go fast). [I] • *(fig.) It took a long time for the building work on our house to start, but things are really moving* **(ahead)**

(= advancing well) *now.* [I] • *(fig.) OK, everybody, let's* **get (things)** *moving* (= start an activity, or do it more quickly). [I] • *Their car was just moving* **off/away** (= leaving) *as we arrived.* [I] • *(fig.) The last time I saw Toby he was just a baby – time moves* **(on)** (= time passes) *so quickly!* [I] • *(fig.) That film was really boring – it moved* (= the story developed) *so slowly.* [I] • *Can we move* (= change the time of) *the meeting* **from** *Tuesday* **to** *Wednesday?* [T] • In a **board game**, if a PIECE or a person moves, or if a player moves a piece, the position of a piece changes: *In chess, the pieces can only move* **in** *certain directions.* [I] ○ *Whose turn is it to move next?* [I] ○ *Would you move my piece for me? I can't reach from here.* [T] • *Share prices moved* (= changed their value) **(up/down)** *slowly yesterday.* [I] • *(fig.) This new shampoo is moving* (= being sold) *really fast.* [I] • *(fig.) No one wants to buy these toys – we just can't move* (= sell) *them.* [T] • *If Brian wants something, Jackie will* **move heaven and earth/move mountains** (= do everything possible) *to get it for him.* • *(Br and Aus infml) We'd almost signed the contract when the other guys* **moved the goalposts** (= changed the conditions of the agreement) *and said they wanted more money.*

move /muːv/ *n* [C] • In some **board games**, a move is a change of the position of one of the PIECES used to play the game, or a change of position that is permitted by the rules, or a player's turn to move their piece: *That move has given Keith the advantage.* ○ *It takes a long time to learn all the moves in chess.* ○ *It's your move.*

mov·a·ble, move·a·ble /ˈmuː·və·bl̩/ *adj* [not gradable] • If something is movable it is designed to be moved easily: *We have movable screens dividing our office into working areas.* • *Easter is a* **movable feast** (= the day on which it happens changes from year to year).

move·ment /ˈmuːv·mənt/ *n* • *There has been little movement in the dollar* (= It has not changed in value very much) *today.* [U] • A movement is one of the main parts of a piece of CLASSICAL music and is separated from the other parts with pauses: *Beethoven's fifth symphony has four movements.* [C] • The movement of a clock or watch is the part which turns the narrow pointers that show the time: *This watch has a fine Swiss movement.* [C]

mov·er /£ˈmuː·vəʳ, $-vɚ/ *n* [C] • *(fig.) These skirts have been one of our best movers* (= our best selling items) *this spring.*

mov·ing /ˈmuː·vɪŋ/ *adj* [before n; not gradable] • *The fewer moving* **parts** (= parts that change their position) *that a machine has, the fewer there are to go wrong.* • *There's a moving walkway* (= path which carries people along) *from the airport terminal to the gate.*

move OPINION /muːv/ *v* to (cause to) change an opinion or the way in which you live or work • *That's my final decision, and I'm not going to move* **on** *it.* [I] • *He's made up his mind, and nothing you can say will move him.* [T] • *More and more people are moving* **towards** *buying products that don't harm the environment.* [I] • *Would you say that public opinion is moving* **towards** *accepting that some women should be able to have babies on their own?* [I] • *A lot of young people are moving* **away from** *eating* (= stopping eating) *meat.* [I] • *It's time this company moved* **into** (= started to take advantage of the benefits of) *the computer age.* [I]

move·ment /ˈmuːv·mənt/ *n* • *There has been a movement* (= change in the way people think and feel) **towards** *more women going back to work while their children are still small.* [C] • *Recently there has been some movement* **away from** *traditional methods of teaching.* [U]

move *(obj)* DIFFERENT PLACE /muːv/ *v* to (cause someone to) go and live or work in a different place • *We're moving/* *(Br and Aus also)* **moving house** (= going with all our possessions to live in a different place) *next week.* [I] • *I've decided to move* **(from** *the town)* **to** *the country.* [I] • *They've bought a new house, but it'll need a lot of work before they can move* **into** *it/move* **in**. [I] • *I have to move* **around** *a lot* (= frequently change the place where I live and work) *in my job.* [I] • *It's not good for children to be moved* **around** *a lot while they're at school.* [T] • *She's been head of this school for 20 years, and it's time she moved* **aside/over** *to make room for a younger person* (= gave up her job so that a younger person can have it). [I] • *The people next door have moved* **away** (= gone to live somewhere else). [I] • *After living in Australia for many years, they're now moving* **back** *to* (= returning to live in) *England.* [I] • *My sister just moved* **in on** *us* (= came to live with us, esp. without being invited) *last weekend.* [I] • *I hear Paula has moved* **in with** (= gone to live with) *Steve.* [I] • *Her landlord has given her a week to move* **out** (= take her possessions and go to live somewhere else). [I] • *He's moved his mother* **out of** *her house and* **into** *a home for elderly people.* [T] • *A lot of businesses are moving* **out of** *London because it's so expensive there.* [I] • *He's moving* (= changing his job) **from** *the publicity department* **to** *the sales department.* [I] • *My boss wants to move me* **into** (= give me) *a different job.* [T] • *These nomadic people don't stay in one place for long – they soon move* **on**. [I] • *(fig.) Can we move* **(on)** (= change) **to** *the next item for discussion, please?* [I] • *(fig.) I think it's time we moved* **off** (= stopped discussing) *this subject.* [I] • *(esp. humorous) I hear you've* **moved on to higher things**/*(Am usually)* **moved on to better things** (= got a better or more important job).

move /muːv/ *n* [C] • *When is the move going to be* (= When are you going to live in a different place)? • *We've had four moves* (= changed the place where we live four times) *in three years.* • *I've only been working here for eighteen months, so I don't feel like another move just yet.*

mov·er *Am* /£ˈmuː·vəʳ, $-vɚ/, *Br* **re·mov·er**, *Aus* **re·mov·al·ist** /rɪˈmuː·vəl·ɪst/ *n* [C] • A mover is someone who helps people move their possessions to a different place to live or work.

mov·ing /ˈmuː·vɪŋ/ *n* [U] • *I hate moving* (= going to a different place to live or work). • *Any moving expenses* (= costs caused by going to live in a different place) *will be paid by the company.*

move *obj* FEELINGS /muːv/ *v* [T] to cause (someone) to have strong feelings, such as sadness, sympathy, happiness or admiration • *Their kindness really moved me.* • *She said that she was* **deeply** *moved by all the letters of sympathy she had received.* • *It was such a sad film that it moved him* **to tears** (= made him cry).

moved /muːvd/ *adj* • *When she told me about her daughter's death, I was too moved* (= upset) *even to speak.*

mov·ing /ˈmuː·vɪŋ/ *adj* • *That was a very moving story* (= It caused very strong emotions). • *I find some of Brahms's music* **deeply** *moving.*

mov·ing·ly /ˈmuː·vɪŋ·li/ *adv* • *He spoke movingly about his experiences working with handicapped children.*

move *(obj)* ACT /muːv/ *v* to (cause someone to) take action • *I can't imagine what could have moved him* **to** *say such a thing.* [T + obj + *to* infinitive] • *I think the council ought to move* **to** *repair this road straightaway.* [+ *to* infinitive] • *If we don't move quickly* **on** *this deal, we'll lose it.* [I always + prep]

move /muːv/ *n* [C] • *What do you think our next move should be* (= What do you think we should do next)? • *Buying those shares when we did was a* **good/smart/clever** *move* (= act intended to achieve something). • *This move* (= step in a plan of action) **towards** *improving childcare facilities has been widely welcomed.* • *When the teacher asked who wanted to try the experiment first, none of the students* **made** *a move* (= took any action). • *The council is* **making** *a move* (= taking action) **to** *ban traffic in some parts of the city.* [+ *to* infinitive] • *Neither side seems prepared to* **make the first move** *towards* (= be the first to take action in) *reaching a peace agreement.*

move·ment /ˈmuːv·mənt/ *n* [C] • A movement is a group of people with a particular set of aims: *The suffragette movement campaigned for votes for women in Britain and the US.* ○ *The 1980s saw the decline of the trade-union movement in Britain.* ○ *He is involved with a movement* **to** *stop animals being killed for their fur.* [+ *to* infinitive]

move·ments /ˈmuːv·mənts/ *pl n* • *(Br and Aus) What are your movements* (= all of your activities) *today?* • *Clare's been behaving rather strangely at work, so I'm keeping an eye on her movements* (= watching what she's doing).

mov·er and shak·er /£ˈmuː·vəʳ, $-vɚ/ *n* [C] *pl* **movers and shakers** • A **mover and shaker** is someone with a lot of power and influence who introduces changes and makes things happen quickly: *The new managing director of the company is a real mover and shaker.*

mov·ing /ˈmuː·vɪŋ/ *adj* [before n; not gradable] • *Local parents were the moving* **force/spirit** *behind the safety improvements at the playground* (= They were the people who made them happen).

move *(obj)* SUGGEST /muːv/ *v* to suggest (something), esp. formally at a meeting or in a court of law • *A vote was just about to be taken when someone stood up and said that they wished to move an amendment.* [T] • *I should like to move* **that** *the proposal be accepted.* [+ *that* clause] • *Your Honour,* *we wish to move* **for** *dismissal of the charges.* [I always + prep]

mov·er /£ˈmuː·vəʳ, $-vɚ/ *n* [C] • A mover is a person who formally makes a suggestion during a formal meeting or discussion: *Who is the mover* **of** *this motion?*

move *(obj)* EXCRETE /muːv/ *v fml or medical* to excrete the contents of (the bowels) • *The doctor asked him if he'd moved his bowels.* [T] • *"Have your bowels moved* (=Have you excreted their contents) *today?" asked the nurse.* [I]

move·ment /ˈmuːv·mənt/ *n* [C] *fml or medical* • A movement is an act of emptying the bowels: *When did you last* **have a (bowel)** *movement?*

move in *(obj)*, **move** *(obj)* **in** *v adv* to (cause someone to) take control or attack • *When a company goes out of business, officials usually move in to take control of it.* [I] • *Government officials have moved in to settle the dispute.* [I] • *The decision has been made to move UN troops in to try and stop the fighting.* [M]

move in on *obj v adv prep* [T] to come close to (something or someone) in order to take control of or attack it or them • *There are reports that the police are moving in on the terrorists.* • *Government troops are moving in on the rebel stronghold.*

mov·ers /£ˈmuː·vəz, $-vɚz/ *pl n Am for* **removers**, see at REMOVE

mov·ie /ˈmuː·vi/ *n* [C] *esp. Am and Aus for* a cinema film • *My favourite movie is 'Casablanca'.* • *Steven Spielberg is one of the most successful movie* **directors** *of all time.* • *Greta Garbo was one of the great movie* **stars** *of the 1930s.* • **Movie theater** is *Am for* CINEMA: *There's a season of Bergman films on at our local movie theater.*

mov·ies /ˈmuː·viz/ *pl n esp. Am and Aus* • *What's on/showing at* **the** *movies* (=the cinema) *this week?* • *I haven't been to* **the** *movies* (=seen a film at a cinema) *for ages.*

mov·ie·go·er *esp. Am and Aus* /£ˈmuː·viˌgəʊ·əʳ, $-ˌgoʊ·ɚ/, *esp. Br* **film·go·er**, **ci·ne·ma·go·er** *n* [C] a person who often goes to the cinema • *There has been an enthusiastic response from moviegoers to Woody Allen's latest film.*

mov·ie·go·ing *esp. Am and Aus* /£ˈmuː·viˌgəʊ·ɪŋ, $-ˌgoʊ-/, *esp. Br* **film·go·ing**, **ci·ne·ma·go·ing** *n* [U], *adj* [before n] • *We want to make moviegoing more affordable for poor families.* • *The cinemagoing public is fed up with unnecessary violence.*

mow *(obj)* /£məʊ, $moʊ/ *v past simple* **mowed**, *past part* **mown** /£məʊn, $moʊn/ or **mowed** to cut (plants, such as grass or wheat, which have long thin stems and grow close together) • *You can't mow the grass/lawn if it's wet.* [T] • *We'll start mowing tomorrow.* [I] • *I love the smell of* **new-mown** *hay.* • If people are **mown down** they are killed or seriously injured in a violent event, often in large numbers: *Three people were mown down last night when a drunken driver lost control of his car.* ○ *The gunman had mown fifteen children down before he was shot by a police markswoman.*

mow·er /£ˈməʊ·əʳ, $ˈmoʊ·ɚ/ *n* [C] • A mower is a machine for cutting esp. grass: *an electric mower* • *a motor mower.* See also LAWNMOWER.

moz·za·rel·la /£ˌmɒt·səˈrel·ə, $ˌmɑːt-/ *n* [U] a slightly soft Italian cheese, which becomes threadlike when it melts and is often used on PIZZA

MP /ˌemˈpiː/ *n* [C] *abbreviation for* **Member of Parliament**, see at MEMBER PERSON • *Tony Blair MP* • *Who is the MP* **for** *Hertfordshire South?* • *I'm going to write to my MP and protest about the plans to close the hospital.* • *MPs will vote tonight on the government's education bill.*

mpg /ˌem·piːˈdʒiː/ *abbreviation for* miles per gallon (=the number of miles a vehicle travels using one GALLON of fuel) • *My car* **does** *about 40 mpg.* • *How many mpg do you* **get** *from your car?*

mph /ˌem·piːˈeɪtʃ/ *abbreviation for* miles per hour (=the number of miles a vehicle travels in one hour; its speed) • *The speed limit in towns in Britain is usually 30 mph.* • *My car won't* **do/go** *more than 70 mph.* • *She was caught driving* **at** *120 mph.*

MPhil /ˌemˈfɪl/ *n* [C] *Br abbreviation for* **Master of Philosophy**, see at MASTER SKILLED PERSON • *Alison Wells, MPhil* • *He has/is doing an MPhil* **in** *psychology.* • *She's studying for an MPhil* **in** *linguistics.* • LP› **Schools and colleges**

Mr /£ˈmɪs·təʳ, $-t̬ɚ/ *n* [U] a title used before the family name or full name of a man who has no other title, or when addressing a man who holds a particular official position • *Mr Jones/Mr David Jones* • *Good afternoon, Mr Dawson.* [as form of address] • *We're looking for a Mr* (=a man called) *George Smith.* • *I'm afraid I can't agree with what's just been said, Mr Chairman.* Compare MADAM. • *It's an honour to have you here today, Mr President.* Compare MADAM. • *I'm retiring at the end of the year, and the dentist who will be taking my place is Mr Steven Brown.* • Mr is also used when expressing the idea that a man is typical of or represents a quality, activity or place: *She's still hoping to meet Mr Right* (=the perfect man). ○ *He's been called Mr Television* (=He is said to represent what is thought to be typical about television). ○ *He thinks he's Mr Big* (=that he is very important). • If someone says **no more Mr Nice Guy**, it means that they are going to stop thinking about the wishes and feelings of other people: *OK, it's no more Mr Nice Guy – I'm fed up with being messed around.* • Compare MISS TITLE; MRS; MS. See also MESSRS. • LP› **Titles and forms of address**

Mrs /ˈmɪs·ɪs/ *n* [U] a title used before the family name or full name of a married woman who has no other title • *Mrs Wood/Mrs Jean Wood* • *Hello, Mrs Taylor, how are you today?* [as form of address] • *This is Dr Wilson, and Mrs Bullon, the surgeon who will perform your operation.* • Mrs is also used when expressing the idea that a married woman is typical of or represents a quality, activity or place: *Mrs Average* (=a woman who is typical of an ordinary woman) • Compare MADAM; MISS TITLE; MR; MS. • LP› **Titles and forms of address**

ms DOCUMENT /ˌemˈes/ *n* [C] *pl* **mss** *abbreviation for* MANUSCRIPT

Ms TITLE /məz/ *n* [U] a title used before the family name or the full name of a woman, whether she is married or not • *Ms Hill/Ms Paula Hill* • *What can I do for you, Ms Wood?* [as form of address] • Ms is also used when expressing the idea that a woman is typical of or represents a quality, activity or place: *She's Ms Independent* (=very independent). ○ *For many people, she was Ms Rock 'n' Roll* (=she represented what was thought to be typical of popular music). • Compare MISS TITLE; MR; MRS. • LP› **Sexist language, Titles and forms of address**

MS ILLNESS /ˌemˈes/ *n* [U] *abbreviation for* **multiple sclerosis**, see at MULTIPLE MANY

MSc /ˌem·esˈsiː/, *Am also* **MS** /ˌemˈes/ *n* [C] *abbreviation for* **Master of Science**, see at MASTER SKILLED PERSON • *Lyn Walker MSc* • *He has/is doing/is studying for an MSc* **in** *biochemistry.* • LP› **Schools and colleges**

MS-DOS /£ˌem·esˈdɒs, $-ˈdɑːs/ *n* [not after *the*] *trademark* a set of programs for controlling the storage and organization of information on the magnetic discs of personal computers and for controlling access to that information

msec *n* [C] *abbreviation for* MILLISECOND

MSG /ˌem·esˈdʒiː/ *n* [U] *abbreviation for* MONOSODIUM GLUTAMATE

Msgr *n* [before n] *abbreviation for* MONSIGNOR

Mt *n* [C/U] *abbreviation for* MOUNT or MOUNTAIN • *Mt Everest* • *the Rocky Mts*

much AMOUNT /mʌtʃ/ *determiner, pronoun, adv* **more** /£mɔːʳ, $mɔːr/, **most** /£məʊst, $moʊst/ a large amount (of); to or by a large amount • *I don't earn much money, but I enjoy my job.* • *You haven't said much, Joan – what do you think?* • *I don't think there's much to be gained by catching an earlier train.* • *The children never eat* **(very)** *much, but they seem quite healthy.* • *"Is there any wine left?"* **"Not** *much."* • *There's* **not/nothing** *much to do around here.* • **How** *much* (=What amount of) *sugar do you take in your coffee?* • *How much are these shoes?/How much do these shoes cost?* • *He wants to buy a new car, but he doesn't want to spend* **too** *much on it.* • *Mark isn't coming to the cinema because he's got* **too** *much work to do.* • *I think you've drunk* **much too much** (=a larger amount than is safe for you) *to drive.* • *"Is this piece of cake OK for you?" "No, it's* **a bit** *much* (=a larger amount than I want). *Can I have a smaller piece, please?"* • *I don't have* **as** *much time* **as** (=I have less time than) *I would like for visiting my friends.* • *I've said* **as** *much* **as** *I'm prepared to say* (=I'm not willing to say anything more) *at this point.* • *Because of the rain, we weren't able to spend much* **of the** *day on the beach.* • *Have you* **seen/heard** *much* **of** *Polly* (=often seen or heard about her) *recently?* • *Joyce isn't much* **of a one for** *opera* (=does not like it). • *I don't much like the sound of that cough/I don't like the sound of that cough much – you should see a doctor.* • *It doesn't matter* **(very)** *much to me whether we go out or not.* • *Thank you for the invitation to your party – we should* **very** *much like to come.* • *We enjoyed the concert* **very/so** *much.* • *Thank you* **very/so** *much for the lovely *present.* • *One day I hope I'll be able to do* **as much** (= the same amount) *for you* **as** *you've done for me.* • *Things around here are much* **as** *always/usual/ever* (= have not changed a lot). • *The two schools are much* **the same** (= very similar). • *"How are you feeling today, Mrs White?" "Much* **the same** (= in the same condition), *doctor."* • *Much* **to** *our surprise,* (= We were very surprised that) *they accepted our offer.* • *I'm* **not** *much* **good at** *knitting* (= do not do it very well). • *She doesn't go out much* (= very often) *since her husband died.* • *Whether a person's intelligence is something they are born with or something they acquire is a much* (= often) *discussed question.* • *Brian's become a much* (= greatly) *changed person since his car accident.* • *"Are you feeling better now?" "Yes, thank you – much* (= a lot) *better."* • *I've been feeling much healthier* (= a lot more healthy) *since I became a vegetarian.* • *The repairs to our car cost much* **more than** *we were expecting.* • *You'll be much* **more comfortable** *if you come and sit over here.* • *I'm* **very** *much aware of the problems.* • *She's much* **the** *best person for the job* (= She is certainly better than everyone else). • *She says she* **would** *much* **rather** *have her baby at home than in hospital.* • *(infml)* You can also use much at the end of a negative sentence to suggest the opposite of what you have just said: *I can see you don't like cream cakes – much!* • If you say that you thought/expected/said **as much**, it means that something you thought/expected/said would happen has happened: *"I'm afraid I haven't got the money to pay you back yet." "That doesn't surprise me – I expected as much."* • *Go on, lend me the money – you know I'd do* **as much** (= the same) *for you.* • *He* **as much as** (= almost) *admitted that it was his fault.* • *My fare was nearly £10, and it was almost* **as much again** (= the same amount) *for the children.* • *I felt so ill this morning, it was* **as much as** *I* **could do** (= I was almost unable) *to get out of bed.* • *She is* **as much a** *friend to me* **as a** *mother* (= although she is my mother, she is also a friend). • **Much as** (= Although) *I would like to help you, I'm afraid I'm simply too busy at the moment.* • *Tony can barely boil an egg,* **much less** (= and certainly not) *cook dinner.* • *I don't feel angry* **so much as** *sad* (= I feel more sad than angry). • *They're* **not so much** *friends* **as** *lovers* (= They're more lovers than friends). • *By the time you've paid* **so much** (= a particular amount) *for the ferry and* **so much** *for the train fare, it would be cheaper to go by plane.* • *The car's broken down again.* **So much for** (= Because of that, it's no longer possible to have) *our trip to the seaside.* • If someone says that they will say **this much** or **that much** (for someone or something), they want to say something good or positive about someone or something considered to be bad or poor: *I'll say this much for Kay, she always agrees to help whenever we ask her.* ○ *That old car was reliable, I'll say that much.* • *The party was* **too much/a bit much/a bit too much** *for the children* (= they have not been able to deal with it successfully) – *they're all exhausted.* • *I think it's* **too much/a bit much/a bit too much** (= unreasonable) *for you to expect me to do all the cleaning.* • 'Much' is used with uncountable nouns. Compare MANY. • LP **Measurements, Quantity words, Very, completely**

much·ness /'mʌtʃ·nəs/ *n* [U] *infml* • *The songs you hear on the radio these days all sound* **much of a muchness** (= very similar) *to me.*

much GOOD /mʌtʃ/ *pronoun, adv* [usually in negatives; not gradable] (something) of good quality • *He's* **not** *much* **to look at**, *but he has a wonderful personality.* • *I've never been much* **of a** *dancer* (= good at dancing, or interested in doing it). • *There's* **not/nothing** *much on TV tonight.*

muck /mʌk/ *n* [U] animal excrement, esp. used as FERTILIZER to make plants grow well, or *(infml)* dirt or waste matter • *There were piles of* **dog/dog's** *muck all over the path.* • *When the farmers* **spread** *muck on their fields you can smell it for miles.* • *I use stable muck as a mulch for my roses.* • *There was a large muck* **heap** *in the corner of the yard.* • *(infml) You're treading muck into the carpet with your dirty shoes!* • *(infml) There's greasy muck all over the front of the bike.* • *(infml) Nuclear power's biggest problem is toxic muck.* • *The immigrants were* **treated like** *muck* (= treated as if they were not important). • Muck also means something of very bad quality, for example a book, a TV show or food: *You're not watching that muck again are you?* ○ *I'm not eating that muck!* • *(disapproving)* **Muck-raking** is the activity, esp. of newspapers and reporters, of trying to find out unpleasant information about people or organizations in order to make it public: *There was so much muck-raking about his family life and previous business activities that he decided not to stand for election.* ○ *A muck-raking documentary exposed her past relationships with famous people.* ○ *At the very least these so-called* **muck-rakers** *have exposed the dark side of society, such as worsening corruption and political favours.* • *(Br saying)* 'Where there's muck there's brass' means that a lot of money can be made by someone from a business activity which other people find dirty or unpleasant.

muck·y /'mʌk·i/ *adj* **-ier, -iest** *infml* • *The child's feet were mucky* (= dirty) *and covered with cuts.* • *(Br infml)* Mucky also means PORNOGRAPHIC: *a mucky book/film/magazine*

muck out *(obj)* /mʌk/ *v adv* • To muck out is to clean a horse's STABLE (= building) by removing the excrement and old straw: *We muck out early every morning.* [I] • *Whose turn is it to muck the* **stable** *out?* [M]

muck *(obj)* **a·bout/a·round** /mʌk/ *v adv esp. Br infml* to behave in a silly way, or to treat (a person) in a careless way • *Stop mucking about* (**with** *those ornaments), you'll break something!* [I] • *I'm fed up with them mucking me about and cancelling our arrangements.* [T]

muck in /mʌk/ *v adv* [I] *Br infml* to share the work that needs to be done • *All my friends mucked in* **and helped** *when I moved house.*

muck up *obj*, **muck** *obj* **up** /mʌk/ *v adv* [M] *infml* to spoil (something) completely, or to do (something) badly • *I wanted to make a good impression at the interview but I mucked it up.* • *I mucked up the whole exam!*

muck /mʌk/ *n* [U] *infml* • *I've* **made** *a muck* **of** *it – I'll have to do it again.*

muck–up /'mʌk·ʌp/ *n* [C] *infml* • *We had a couple of muck-ups last week – appointments missed and so on.* • *They* **made** *a muck-up of our order – it won't be ready till next week now.*

mu·cous mem·brane /'mjuː·kəs/ *n* [C] *specialized* the thin skin that covers the inner surface of parts of the body such as the nose and mouth and produces MUCUS (= thick liquid) to protect them

mu·cus /'mjuː·kəs/ *n* [U] a thick liquid produced by the tissue inside your nose and other parts of the body

mud /mʌd/ *n* [U] earth that has become wet and sticky • *The heavy rain caused a landslide of mud and stones.* • *The vehicles got bogged down* **in the** *heavy mud.* • *Her bicycle was* **caked with** (= covered with dry) *mud.* • *The soldiers* **squelched** (= moved noisily) *through the mud.* • *The pigs were* **wallowing** (= lying) *in the mud.* • *Modern houses have replaced the one-room mud* **huts** *with grass roofs that had been home to generations of peasants.* • *These mud* **flats** (= level ground near the sea) *are a site of special scientific interest.* • If you **hurl/throw/sling mud** at someone you say insulting or unfair things about them, esp. to try to damage their reputation: *Although no hint of the scandal has stuck to him, there are still people willing to throw mud in his direction.* ○ *Business relationships suffered from the* **mud-slinging**, *muck-raking and bad blood of the takeover war.* • *The court cleared him of fraud – but* **mud sticks** (= a bad reputation is hard to lose). • A **mud pie** is a small round shape made of mud by children playing. • **Mud wrestling** is a sport in which one woman fights with another woman in mud by holding her and trying to make her fall, while men watch. • *"Mud! Mud! Glorious mud! / Nothing quite like it for cooling the blood."* (from the song *The Hippopotamus* by Michael Flanders and Donald Swann, 1952)

mud·dy /'mʌd·i/ *adj* **-ier, -iest** • *I peered into the muddy water of the pond.* • *Don't wear those muddy boots inside!* • Muddy colours are dark and not bright: *The sitting-room has been painted in muddy browns and greens.*

mud·dy *obj* /'mʌd·i/ *v* [T] • *Industrial activity has muddied the river, like so many of the other once clear chalk streams of the area.* • *(fig.) The party has not only muddied its message* (= made it complicated and confused) *but has also cluttered its political programme with gimmicks.* • *(fig.) She's the sort of journalist who likes to ask awkward questions and muddy* **the waters** (= make the situation more confused, complicated and difficult).

mud·dle /'mʌd·l̩/ *n* [U] an untidy and confused state • *The documents were all* **in a** *muddle.* • *I hate all this muddle – I'll have to tidy it up.* • *Whenever I go abroad I get* **in a** *muddle* **about/over** (= become confused about) *the money.* • A **muddle-headed** person is someone who does not think clearly or in an organized way.

mud·dle *(obj)* /'mʌd·l̩/ *v* • To muddle **(up)** something is to make it untidy and lacking in order: *I've arranged the books alphabetically so don't muddle them up.* [T/M] •

Grandfather was muddled **about** *the children's names.* • If you muddle **along** you continue doing something with no clear purpose or plan: *Decide what you want in life, don't just muddle along.* [I] • If you muddle **through**, you manage to do something although you are not organized and do not know how to do it: *I'm afraid I can't help you – you'll just have to muddle through on your own.* [I]

mud·flap *Br and Aus* /ˈmʌd·flæp/, *Am* **splash guard** *n* [C] one of the pieces of rubber which are fixed to a vehicle behind the wheels to prevent dirt and small objects from being thrown up • PIC› Car

mud·guard /£ˈmʌd·gɑːd, $-gɑːrd/, *Am usually* **fend·er** *n* [C] a piece of metal or plastic which partly covers the wheels of a bicycle and prevents dirt from getting on your legs • PIC› Bicycles

mud·pack /ˈmʌd·pæk/ *n* [C] a special substance that you put on your face and leave for a short time to improve your skin

mues·li /ˈmjuːzli/ *n* [U] a mixture of raw grains, dried fruit and nuts that is eaten with milk as part of the first meal of the day • *Would you like muesli or porridge for breakfast?* • Compare GRANOLA.

mu·ez·zin /muːˈez·ɪn/ *n* [C] a man who calls Muslims to prayer from the tower of a MOSQUE

muff [CLOTHING] /mʌf/ *n* [C] a short tube of fur or warm cloth, into which esp. women in the past put their hands in cold weather in order to keep them warm

muff *obj* [SPOIL] /mʌf/ *v* [T] *infml* to spoil (an opportunity) or do (something) badly • *It was a golden opportunity to impress them and I muffed* **it**. • *She muffed her* **lines/words** *in her first stage appearance.*

muf·fin [BREAD] *Br and Aus* /ˈmʌf·ɪn/, *Am* **Eng·lish muf·fin** *n* [C] a small round flat type of bread, usually sliced in two and eaten hot with butter

muf·fin [CAKE] *Am and Aus* /ˈmʌf·ɪn/, *Br* **A·mer·i·can muf·fin** *n* [C] a small sweet cake that often has fruit inside it • *blueberry muffins*

muf·fle *obj* [MAKE QUIET] /ˈmʌf·l̩/ *v* [T] to make (a sound) quieter and less clear • *The house's windows are double-glazed to muffle the noise of aircraft.* • *(fig.) The report concluded that business pressure on the government had muffled* (= made less strong or clear) *the impact of the legislation.*

muf·fled /ˈmʌf·l̩d/ *adj* • *I could hear muffled* **voices** *next door but couldn't make out any words.* • *The muffled* **roar** *of the traffic could be heard in the distance.*

muf·fler /£ˈmʌf·ləʳ, $-lɚ/ *n* [C] *Am and Aus* • A muffler is a SILENCER.

muf·fle *(obj)* [KEEP WARM] /ˈmʌf·l̩/ *v* to wear (esp. thick warm clothes) in order to keep warm • *I muffled* **myself (up) against** *the night air and left.* [T] • *His mother made him muffle him***self up** *before he could go out to play in the snow.* [T] • *Make sure you muffle* **up** *well – it's very cold.* [I] • *Muffled* **in** *gloves, thick coats and scarves, the protesters stood outside the building all day.*

muf·fler /£ˈmʌf·ləʳ, $-lɚ/ *n* [C] *dated* • A muffler is a thick SCARF.

muf·ti /ˈmʌf·ti/ *n* [U] *dated* ordinary clothes worn by people who usually wear uniforms, esp. soldiers • *The admiral arrived* **in** *mufti.*

mug [CONTAINER] /mʌg/ *n* [C] a container with a handle on one side used esp. for hot drinks such as tea or coffee. It is usually bigger than a cup and used without a SAUCER. • *The shop sells coffee pots and mugs with bright designs.* • *I made myself a large mug* **of** *cocoa* (= enough to fill a mug) *and went to bed.* • *(esp. Am)* A **beer** mug is a heavy glass with a handle and usually with patterns cut into its side, out of which you drink beer.

mug [STUPID PERSON] /mʌg/ *n* [C] *esp. Br infml* a person who is stupid and easily deceived • *He's such a mug, he believes everything she tells him.* • If you describe an activity as a **mug's game**, you mean that it will not bring money or satisfaction to the person who does it: *"Working in an office is a mug's game," she said.*

mug [FACE] /mʌg/ *n* [C] *infml* someone's face • *I don't want to see your* **ugly** *mug around here again.* • *(slang)* A **mug shot** is a photograph taken by the police of a person who has been charged with a crime: *A poster with mug shots of wanted men was on the wall.*

mug *obj* [ATTACK] /mʌg/ *v* [T] **-gg-** to attack (a person) in a public place and steal their money • *The old man was mugged in broad daylight.* • LP› **Crimes and criminals**

mug·ging /ˈmʌg·ɪŋ/ *n* • A mugging is an act of attacking someone and stealing their money: *Many tourists are victims of muggings and petty theft.* [C] ○ *Police are concerned that mugging is on the increase.* [U]

mug·ger /£ˈmʌg·əʳ, $-ɚ/ *n* [C] • A mugger is a person who attacks people in order to steal their money.

mug up *v adv Br infml* to study (a subject) quickly before taking an exam • *I've got to mug up my History before tomorrow's exam.* [M] • *He hardly came to any classes – he just mugged it all up the night before.* [M] • *The audience received a summary of the plot with their tickets, so they had time to mug up* **on** *the action in advance.* [I]

mug·gins /ˈmʌg·ɪnz/ *n* [U] *Br humorous* a stupid person, often used to describe yourself when you have done something silly or when you feel you are being treated unfairly • *I suppose muggins* **(here)** *will have to look after the cat when they go on holiday* (= I will have to do it but I don't want to).

mug·gy /ˈmʌg·i/ *adj* **-ier, -iest** (of weather) unpleasantly warm and HUMID

mul·ber·ry /£ˈmʌl·bᵊr·i, $-ber-/ *n* [C] a small soft purple fruit, or the tree that has these fruit • *Silkworms are fed mulberry leaves after they have hatched.*

mulch /mʌltʃ/ *n* a covering, esp. made out of a mixture of decaying leaves, grass or plant material, which is used to keep water in the earth near plants and/or to protect them from WEEDS (= unwanted plants) • *Don't apply mulch until the soil has warmed up.* [U] • *A bark mulch will keep down the weeds.* [C]

mulch *obj* /mʌltʃ/ *v* [T] • *Mulch* (= Put mulch) *around the base of the shrubs.*

mule [CARRIER] /mjuːl/ *n* [C] an animal whose mother is a horse and whose father is a DONKEY which is used for transporting loads, or *(fig.)* a person who agrees to carry illegal drugs into another country in return for payment by the person selling the drugs • *He strapped the heavy sacks onto the mule.* • *In those days all the goods were transported across the mountains by mule* **train** (= a group of mules). • *It's no use arguing with her, she's* **as stubborn as** *a mule* (= very stubborn). • *(fig.) These very poor women who are used as mules by drug barons often get long prison sentences.*

mul·ish /ˈmjuː·lɪʃ/ *adj* • A mulish person is one who is very determined and refuses to change their plans for anyone else.

mule [SHOE] /mjuːl/ *n* [C] a woman's shoe or SLIPPER that has no back • *She wore tight trousers and high-heeled mules.*

mul·ga /ˈmʌl·gə/ *n* [C/U] *Aus* a type of tree found in dry regions, or its wood • **The mulga** is also *Aus for* **the bush**: *(infml) They live* **up** (= in) *the mulga.* See at BUSH [AREA OF LAND].

mull *obj* /mʌl/ *v* [T] to heat (wine or beer) with added sugar and spices • *We had mulled wine at the party.*

mull o·ver *obj*, **mull** *obj* **o·ver** *v adv* [M] to think carefully about (something) for a long time • *I need a few days to mull things over before I decide.*

mul·lah /ˈmʊl·ə/ *n* [C] an Islamic religious teacher or leader

mul·let /ˈmʌl·ɪt/ *n* [C] a small sea fish that can be cooked and eaten • *grey mullet* • *red mullet*

mul·li·ga·tawn·y /£ˌmʌl·ɪ·gəˈtɔː·ni, $-ˈtɑː-/ *n* [U] a very spicy soup that has CURRY powder in it

mul·li·oned /ˈmʌl·i·ənd/ *adj* [not gradable] (of windows) having vertical esp. stone divisions between the glass parts

mul·ti– /£ˌmʌl·ti-, $-t̬i-/ *combining form* having many • *a multi-layered skirt* (= a skirt with many layers of material) • *a multi-millionaire* (= a person with many million pounds or dollars) • *a multi-vitamin tablet* (= a pill which contains several vitamins) • *The dictatorship was overthrown and replaced by a multi-party democracy.* • **Multi-cultural** means including people who have different customs and beliefs: *a multicultural society* • **Multi-dimensional** means with many different features: *Crime is a multi-dimensional problem.* • **Multi-disciplinary** means involving different subjects of study in one activity:*The multi-disciplinary team includes teachers, educational psychologist, parents and school doctor.* ○ *We have adopted a multi-disciplinary approach to tackle this problem.* • **Multi-faceted** means having many different parts: *It's a multi-faceted business, offering a range of services.* • **Multi-racial** means involving people of several different races: *a multi-racial school* ○ *South Africa's first multi-racial elections took place in 1994.* • *(Br and Aus)* **Multi-storey** *(Am* **multistory)** means having several floors: *a multi-storey apartment block* ○ *(Br) a multi-storey car park* • *(Br)* A **multi-storey** is a multi-storey car park: *I left the car in the multi-storey.* • **Multi-tasking** is the ability of a computer to operate several programs at one time: *The machine allows multi-tasking without the need to buy extra hardware.* ○ *This software doesn't offer multi-tasking capability, but it does have easy-to-use graphics.*

mul·ti·fa·ri·ous /£ˌmʌl·tɪˈfeə·ri·əs, $-t̬ɪˈfer·i-/ *adj fml* very many in number and of many different types • *The newspaper report detailed the fraudster's multifarious business activities.*

mul·ti·gym /£ˈmʌl·ti·dʒɪm, $-t̬i-/ *n* [C] *Br* a machine on which you can do several different exercises, or a room in which several different exercise machines can be used

mul·ti·lat·er·al /£ˌmʌl·tiˈlæt·ər·əl, $-t̬iˈlæt̬·ɚ-/ *adj* [not gradable] involving more than two groups or countries • *Seven countries are taking part in the multilateral talks.* • *The project is funded by the World Bank and other multilateral agencies.* • Compare BILATERAL; UNILATERAL.

mul·ti·lin·gual /£ˌmʌl·tiˈlɪŋ·gwəl, $-t̬ɪ-/ *adj* [not gradable] (of people or groups) able to use more than two languages for communication, or (of a thing) written or spoken in several different languages • *The individuals and groups in any multilingual democracy need to have their language rights defined.* • *They have developed a multilingual European on-line database.* • Compare BILINGUAL; MONOLINGUAL.

mul·ti·med·i·a /£ˌmʌl·tiˈmiː·di·ə, $-t̬i-/ *n* [U] the use of a combination of moving and still pictures, sound, music and words, esp. in computers or entertainment • *There are other exhibits which provide hands-on experience of multimedia.* • *Software technology is going multimedia, carrying pictures, video and sound.* • *The company is working on a multimedia computer system including text, video and graphics.* • *As part of the celebrations they staged a big, open-air multimedia* **event**, *with music, videos, poetry readings, dance and improvisations.*

mul·ti·mil·li·on·aire /£ˌmʌl·tiˌmɪl·jəˈneəʳ, $-t̬iˌmɪl·jəˈner/ *n* [C] a person who has money and property worth several MILLION POUNDS or DOLLARS • *At 25 she inherited a fortune and became a multimillionaire.*

mul·ti·na·tion·al /£ˌmʌl·tiˈnæʃ·ən·əl, $-t̬i-/ *adj* [not gradable] involving several different countries, or (of a business) working in several different countries • *The UN has sent a multinational peace-keeping force.* • *They have established a multinational fund to help students who want to study abroad.* • *He works for one of the major multinational food companies.*

mul·ti·na·tion·al /£ˌmʌl·tiˈnæʃ·ən·əl, $-t̬i-/ *n* [C] • A multinational is a multinational company: *They claimed that multinationals increased employment in their host countries.* [C]

mul·ti·ple MANY /£ˈmʌl·tɪ·pl̩, $-t̬ɪ-/ *adj* [not gradable] very many of the same type, or of different types • *The youth died of multiple* (= many) *injuries/gunshot wounds.* • *We made multiple* (= many) *copies of the report.* • *These children have multiple* (= many different) *handicaps.* • *What the person does next is the result of the multiple* (= many different) *influences to which they have been exposed.* • A **multiple birth** is when more than two babies are born to the same woman on one occasion: *Multiple births – of triplets, quadruplets and quintuplets – are becoming more common because of fertility drugs.* • A **multiple-choice** exam or question is one in which you are given a list of different answers to a question and you have to choose the right one. • **Multiple sclerosis** is a disease in which the covering of the nerves gradually becomes destroyed, sometimes damaging a person's speech and sight and ability to move.

mul·ti·ple /£ˈmʌl·tɪ·pl̩, $-t̬ɪ-/ *n* [C] • A multiple is a large company which has shops in many towns: *All the multiples sell two grades of olive oil – extra virgin and pure.* ○ *The analyst said that High St. multiples appear to be holding on until next year before deciding to expand.*

mul·ti·ple NUMBER /£ˈmʌl·tɪ·pl̩, $-t̬ɪ-/ *n* [C] a number that can be divided by a smaller number an exact number of times, and which is the result of multiplying the number you have with another whole number • *18 is a multiple* **of** *3, because 18 = 3 x 6.* • *Try counting them* **in multiples** (= groups) **of** *five.*

mul·ti·plex /£ˈmʌl·tɪ·pleks, $-t̬ɪ-/ *n* [C] a very large cinema that has a lot of separate cinemas inside it • *A new ten-screen multiplex has recently opened in the town.*

mul·ti·plic·i·ty /£ˌmʌl·tɪˈplɪs·ɪ·ti, $-t̬əˈplɪs·ə·t̬i/ *n* [U] *fml* a large number or wide range (of something) • *There is a multiplicity* **of** *fashion magazines to choose from.*

mul·ti·ply *(obj)* /£ˈmʌl·tɪ·plaɪ, $-t̬ɪ-/ *v* to increase greatly in number, or (in mathematics) to add (a number) to itself a particular number of times • *In warm weather these germs multiply rapidly.* [I] • *If you multiply seven* **by** *15 you get 105.* [T] • Compare DIVIDE CALCULATE; SUBTRACT. • LP Mathematics

mul·ti·pli·ca·tion /£ˌmʌl·tɪ·plɪˈkeɪ·ʃən, $-t̬ɪ-/ *n* [U] • *Emma's learning multiplication* (= how to multiply numbers) *and division this year in school.* • A **multiplication table** is a list that shows the results of multiplying one number by a set of other numbers, usually from one to twelve. Children sometimes learn these lists at school: *Do schools still teach the children their multiplication tables?*

mul·ti·tude /£ˈmʌl·tɪ·tjuːd, $-t̬ə·tuːd/ *n* [U] a large number (of something) • *The city has* **a** *multitude* **of** *problems, from AIDS to drugs and murder.* • *A multitude* **of** *people crowded round the entrance to the hotel.* • *(literary) He hesitated before going forward to address* **the** *multitude* (= the crowd). • **A multitude of sins** is a bad situation: *A growing economy* **covers** *a multitude of sins for the government.* ○ *Make-up can* **hide** *a multitude of sins!*

mul·ti·tudes /£ˈmʌl·tɪ·tjuːdz, $-t̬ə·tuːdz/ *pl n* • Multitudes are large numbers, esp. of people: *A civilization that kills multitudes in mass warfare can hardly be called advanced.* • *They have been kicked out of their homes, as has happened to multitudes* **of** (= a multitude of) *others who fail to accept the aggressors' decree.* • *(literary) The minister preached to* **the** *multitudes* (= the multitude) *from the front porch.*

mum MOTHER *Br and Aus* /£mʌm, $mɑːm/, *Am* **mom** *n* [C] *infml* mother • *"Happy birthday, Mum."* [as form of address] • *Ask your mum if you can come to the party.* • *All the mums* **and dads** *are invited to the school play.* • LP **Titles and forms of address**

mum·sy /ˈmʌm·zi/ *adj* **-ier, -iest** *Br infml esp. disapproving* • A mumsy woman is one with an old-fashioned appearance: *As she became more successful, she changed her mumsy hairstyle for something more glamorous.*

mum SECRET /mʌm/ *adj* [not gradable] *infml* silent in order not to tell anyone what you know • *Don't tell your friends unless you're sure they'll* **keep** *mum.* • *(saying)* 'Mum's the word' is used to tell someone, or to agree, that something must be kept a secret: *"Don't tell a soul about this." "OK, mum's the word!"*

mum·ble *(obj)* /ˈmʌm·bl̩/ *v* to speak or say (something) unclearly and quietly so that the words are difficult to understand • *The old woman mumbled* **something** *that I couldn't hear.* [T] • *I do wish you'd stop mumbling!* [I] • *"I'm sorry," he mumbled.* [+ clause]

mum·bo jum·bo /£ˌmʌm·bəʊˈdʒʌm·bəʊ, $-boʊˈdʒʌm·boʊ/ *n* [U] *infml* words or activities that are unnecessarily complicated or mysterious and seem meaningless • *You don't believe in horoscopes and all that mumbo jumbo, do you?*

mum·my MOTHER *Br and Aus* /£ˈmʌm·i, $ˈmɑː·mi/, *Am* **mom·my** *n* [C] *infml* (used by or to children) mother • *I want to go home, Mummy.* [as form of address] • *Could I speak to your mummy, Billy?* • *(disapproving)* A **mummy's boy** (*Am* **mama's boy**) is a boy or man who appears to do whatever his mother tells him to. • LP **Titles and forms of address**

mum·my BODY /ˈmʌm·i/ *n* [C] (esp. in ancient Egypt) a dead body that has been preserved from decay by being treated with special substances before being wrapped in cloth • *Several ancient Egyptian mummies are on display in the museum.*

mum·mi·fy *obj* /ˈmʌm·ɪ·faɪ/ *v* [T] • To mummify a dead body is to preserve it as a mummy.

mumps /mʌmps/ *n* [U] an infectious disease that causes painful swellings in the neck and slight fever • *At 15 months a child is injected with a vaccine against mumps and rubella.* • *He's got* **the** *mumps.*

mum·sy /ˈmʌm·zi/ *adj* See at MUM MOTHER

munch *(obj)* /mʌntʃ/ *v* to eat (esp. something hard) noisily and without trying to be quiet • *He was munching an apple.* [T] • *We watched her munch (her way)* **through** *two packets of peanuts.* [I] • *They sat munching their* **sandwiches** *during the lecture.* [T]

munch·ies /ˈmʌn·t̬ʃiz/ *pl n esp. Am infml* • Munchies are small light things to eat: *Have you any munchies – any peanuts or crackers?* • **The** munchies are slight feelings of hunger: *I've got the munchies.*

mun·dane /mʌn'deɪn/ *adj* not interesting in any way; very ordinary • *Mundane matters such as eating and drinking do not interest her.*

mung bean /'mʌŋ/ *n* [C] a seed which is often eaten as a BEANSPROUT when it has produced a small shoot, or the plant on which it grows

mu·ni·ci·pal /mjuː'nɪs·ɪ·pᵊl/ *adj* [not gradable] of or belonging to a town or city • *municipal authorities* • *municipal tennis courts* • *municipal elections*

mu·ni·ci·pal·i·ty /£mjuː,nɪs·ɪ'pæl·ə·ti, $-t̬i/ *n* [C] • A municipality is a city or town with its own local government, or this local government itself: *The municipality provides services such as electricity, water and rubbish collection.*

mu·ni·fi·cent /mjuː'nɪf·ɪ·sᵊnt/ *adj fml* very generous with money • *A former student has donated a munificent sum of money to the college.*

mu·ni·fi·cence /mjuː'nɪf·ɪ·sᵊnts/ *n* [U] • *I thanked them for their munificence* (= generosity with money).

mu·ni·tions /mjuː'nɪʃ·ᵊnz/ *pl n* military weapons such as guns and bombs • *The army used precision-guided munitions to blow up enemy targets.* • *a munitions depot* • *a munitions factory*

mu·ral /£'mjʊə·rəl, $'mjʊr·ᵊl/ *n* [C] a large picture that has been painted on the wall of a room or building • *One of the walls enclosing the park is decorated with a huge mural showing Hollywood stars.*

mur·der /£'mɜː·dəʳ, $'mɜːr·dɚ/ *n* the crime of intentionally killing a person • *Two sisters have been charged with attempted murder.* [U] • *There were three murders in the town last year.* [C] • *The man was* **charged with** (= accused of) *murder.* • *The three were* **convicted** (= proved guilty) **of** *murder.* • *The* **cold-blooded** *murder of the teenager shocked the country.* [C] • *(infml)* **It's murder** (= It's extremely difficult) *finding a parking space in town.* • *She bought/watched the latest murder* **mystery** (= book, film or play about a murder and how it is solved). • *The police are still hunting for the murder* **weapon** (= the weapon used to commit the murder). • **Mass murder** means killing a lot of people: *The regime solved the problem of dissent with a programme of mass murder.* • *(Br and Aus infml)* If you **scream/shout blue murder** (*Am infml* **scream bloody murder**) you show your annoyance about something and make a lot of noise: *He'll scream blue murder if he doesn't get his way.* • *"Murder most foul"* (Shakespeare, Hamlet 1.5) • *"Murder on the Orient Express"* (title of a book by Agatha Christie, 1934) • Compare MANSLAUGHTER; SUICIDE. • LP **Crimes and criminals**

mur·der *obj* /£'mɜː·dəʳ, $'mɜːr·dɚ/ *v* [T] • To murder is to commit the crime of intentionally killing a person: *They murdered the priest at the altar of the cathedral.* ○ *Her husband was murdered by gunmen as she watched.* ○ *(fig. infml) If he's late again I'll murder him* (= I will be very angry with him)*!*

mur·der·er, *female dated also* **mur·der·ess** /£'mɜː·dᵊr·əʳ, $'mɜːr·dɚ·ɚ, -əs, -es/ *n* [C] • A murderer is someone who illegally and intentionally kills another person: *A* **convicted** *murderer was executed in North Carolina yesterday.* • *The news report said the police had caught the* **mass** *murderer* (= person who has killed a large number of people illegally).

mur·der·ous /£'mɜː·dᵊr·əs, $'mɜːr·dɚ-/ *adj* • *He was a murderous gangster* (= someone who killed a lot of people illegally). • *She gave me a look of murderous hatred* (= as if she wanted to kill me because she hated me). • *(infml)* Murderous also means extremely unpleasant: *Summers in Washington bring murderous heat and humidity.* ○ *The traffic was murderous in town today.*

murk /£mɜːk, $mɜːrk/ *n* [U] darkness or thick cloud, preventing you from seeing clearly • *It was foggy and the sun shone feebly through the murk.*

murk·y /£'mɜː·ki, $'mɜːr-/ *adj* **-ier, -iest** • *The river was brown and murky* (= dark and dirty) *after the storm.* • *(fig.) I don't want to get into the murky* **waters** (= complicated area) *of family arguments.* • *(fig.) He became involved in the murky* (= secret and unpleasant) *world of international drug-dealing.*

mur·mur *(obj)* /£'mɜː·məʳ, $'mɜːr·mɚ/ *v* to speak or say very quietly • *"I love you", she murmured.* [+ clause] • *He was murmuring* **to himself** *in a corner.* [I] • If you murmur **about** something that you disagree with, you complain about it but not in a public way: *They were murmuring about the boss's nephew getting the job.* [I] • *(humorous) He murmured* **sweet nothings** (= romantic talk) *in her ear.* [T]

mur·mur /£'mɜː·məʳ, $'mɜːr·mɚ/ *n* [C] • *A murmur* **of** *agreement came from the crowd.* • *After the report was published, there were murmurs* **of discontent** (= complaints by people to each other but not publicly) *round the office.* • *For once the children went to bed* **without a murmur** (= without even a small complaint). • *(fig.) The murmur* (= soft continuous sound) *of the waves on the beach lulled me to sleep.*

Mur·phy's law /£'mɜː·fiz, $mɜːr-/, **Sod's law** /£sɒdz, $sɑːdz/ *n* [U] *humorous* the tendency of things to go wrong • *I believe in Murphy's law – what can go wrong, will!* • *The bus is always late but today when I was late it came on time – that's Murphy's law I suppose!*

mus·cle /'mʌs·l̩/ *n* one of many tissues in the body that can tighten and relax to produce movement • *neck muscles* [C] • *facial muscles* [C] • **bulging/rippling** (= large and clear to see) *muscles* [C] • *Russell* **pulled/strained/tore** *a back muscle early in the game.* [C] • *He* **flexed/tensed** *his muscles* (= tightened, esp. his arm muscles, to make them look large and strong) *so that everyone could admire them.* [C] • *(fig.) This is the first sign of the new regime* **flexing** *its muscles* (= showing its power). [C] • *(fig.) In response to criticism, Mr. Owen insists that the commission's statement wasn't just* **muscle-flexing** (= a show of power). • *These exercises build muscle and increase stamina.* [U] • *The bacteria produce a toxin which induces convulsions and muscle* **spasms** (= sudden uncontrollable tightening movements). • *These daily exercises are designed to improve muscle* **tone** (= produce strong firm muscles). • Muscle is also the power to do difficult things or to make people behave in a certain way: *This magazine has considerable financial muscle and can afford to pay top journalists.* [U] ○ *The company lacks the marketing muscle to compete with drug giants.* [U] • A **muscle-bound** person is one who has very large hard muscles as a result of doing too much physical exercise.

mus·cle in /'mʌs·l̩/ *v adv* [I] *infml* • If you muscle in, you force your way into a situation and make certain you are included although you are not wanted: *He's always muscling in where he's not wanted.* ○ *Mark muscled in* **on** *our meeting, with the excuse that Mike had asked him to be there.*

mus·cu·lar /£'mʌs·kjʊ·ləʳ, $-lɚ/ *adj* • *The pains women have during labour are due to the muscular* (= muscle) **contractions** *connected with giving birth.* • Muscular also means having well-developed muscles: *muscular arms/legs* ○ *He wished he was more muscular and didn't have such a flat chest.* ○ *(fig.) It was a muscular* (= powerful), *hard-hitting documentary.* • **Muscular dystrophy** is a serious disease in which a person's muscles gradually weaken until walking is no longer possible.

mus·cu·la·ture /£'mʌs·kjʊ·lə·tʃəʳ, $-tʃɚ/ *n* [U] • *He took off his shirt and exposed his impressive musculature* (= well-developed muscles). • *By looking at the bones of this animal, we can discover quite a lot about the kind of musculature* (= structure and position of the muscles) *it had when it was alive.*

mus·cly /'mʌs·li/ *adj* **-ier, -iest** *infml* • *She's got big muscly* (= muscular) *legs* (= legs with well-developed muscles).

mus·cle·man /'mʌs·l̩.mæn/ *n* [C] *pl* **-men** a man who has very large muscles as a result of doing special exercises to improve them

Mus·co·vite /'mʌs·kə·vaɪt/ *n* [C] a person from Moscow

muse THINK /mjuːz/ *v* [I] *fml* to think about something carefully and for a long time • *I began to muse* **about/on** *the possibility of starting my own business.*

muse IMAGINARY FORCE /mjuːz/ *n* [C] *esp. literary* an imaginary force that gives someone ideas and helps them to write, paint or make music • *The muse has left me – I haven't written any poetry for months!* • *Juliet was not only the painter's best model but also his muse* (= the person who causes him to have the most ideas for his work). • In ancient Greek stories, the Muses were imaginary women who were believed to give encouragement in different areas of literature, art and music.

mu·se·um /mjuː'ziː·əm/ *n* [C] a building where objects of historical, scientific or artistic interest are kept • *a museum of modern art* • *the Imperial War Museum* • *He's a museum* **curator** (= someone who helps to look after a museum or is in charge of some of the objects in a museum). • *(humorous)* A **museum piece** is something that is very old-fashioned and should no longer be used: *That old car is a museum piece – you should get a new one.*

mush /mʌʃ/ *n* [U] *infml esp. disapproving* any thick soft substance, such as food that has been cooked for too long • *If you overcook the potatoes they'll* **turn to** *mush.* • *(fig.) I panicked and my brain* **turned to** *mush* (=stopped being able to think). • If you describe something such as a book or film as mush, you mean that it is unpleasantly emotional: *The film was just romantic mush.*

mush·y /ˈmʌʃ·i/ *adj* **-ier, -iest** *infml* • *Cook the lentils until they are mushy.* • *(disapproving) The meat was mushy and tasteless.* • *(disapproving) I hate those mushy* (=unpleasantly emotional) *love stories.* • *(Br)* **Mushy peas** is a food that is made from dried MARROWFAT PEAS (=a type of large pea).

mush·room /£ˈmʌʃ·ruːm, $-rʊm/ *n* [C] a fast-growing FUNGUS with a round top and short stem. There are many different types of mushroom, some of which can be eaten. • *wild/cultivated mushrooms* • *button* (=very small) *mushrooms* • *dried/grilled/stuffed/sliced mushrooms* • *cream of mushroom soup* • *For this recipe choose mushrooms with large* **caps** (=top parts). • *Unfortunately some poisonous mushrooms look like* **edible** *mushrooms.* • A **mushroom cloud** is a very large cloud of dust that rises into the air in the shape of a large mushroom after esp. a nuclear explosion: *The mushroom cloud over Hiroshima is a horrific image of war.* • Compare TOADSTOOL. • PIC **Vegetables**

mush·room /£ˈmʌʃ·ruːm, $-rʊm/ *v* [I] • If something mushrooms, it grows very quickly: *The number of computers in schools has mushroomed in recent years.*

mu·sic /ˈmjuː·zɪk/ *n* [U] a pattern of sounds made by musical instruments or singing or a combination of both, intended to give pleasure to people listening to it • *classical/pop/dance/rock 'n' roll music* • *What kind of music do you like?* • *The band plays all sorts of music, from country to jazz.* • *They play good music* (=recordings of music) *on Radio One.* • *I spent the afternoon listening to music and writing letters.* • *Who composed this music?* • *Shall I* **put on** *some music* (=play a recording)*?* • Music is also the art or study of music: *I studied music at college.* ○ *Music lessons are so expensive these days!* • Music can also mean the written system of symbols representing musical notes: *Can you read music?* ○ *Put the music in the music* **case**/*on the music* **stand**. • *(specialized)* In some cases, music can be used in its plural form, musics, to mean type of music: *He is an expert on Eastern musics.* • To **make** music is to play it: *It's a wonderful thing to get together with a few friends and make music.* ○ *A lot of* **music-making** *goes on in schools these days.* • If you say that something is **music to** your **ears**, you mean that you are very pleased to hear it: *The rattle of the letterbox was music to my ears – the letter had arrived at last.* • **Music box** is *Am for* **musical box**. • *(Br dated)* **Music centre** is *Br dated for* **music system**. • A **music hall** (*Am also* **vaudeville theater**) was a theatre, in the past, that presented shows which included music, dancing and jokes, or it was this type of show: *He likes telling old music hall jokes that start with "I say, I say, I say".* • A **music system** is a piece of equipment for playing recorded sound that consists of a **record player**, a **tape recorder**, a radio and sometimes a **CD player**. • **Music theatre** is a type of theatre involving acting and music, performed by a small number of people. • *"If music be the food of love, play on"* (Shakespeare, Twelfth Night 1.1)

mu·si·cal /ˈmjuː·zɪ·kəl/ *adj* • *Mozart's musical compositions include symphonies and operas.* • *A guitarist supplied the musical accompaniment.* • *The shop sells musical instruments, sheet music, tapes and CDs.* • If you are musical you have a skill in or great liking for music: *The family all play instruments – they're all very musical.* • *Sylvie has a very musical* (=sounding like music) *speaking voice.* • A **musical box** (*Am* **music box**) is a decorative box with a device inside it that plays a tune when you open the lid. • **Musical chairs** is a game in which children walk around a group of chairs while music plays. When the music stops they have to sit quickly on a chair, but since one chair is removed, one child has to leave the game each time: *(fig.) It's a game of musical chairs* (=a situation in which people change jobs often) *as editors move from one newspaper to another.*

mu·si·cal /ˈmjuː·zɪ·kəl/ *n* [C] • A musical is a play or film in which part of the story is sung to music: *'West Side Story' is her favourite musical.*

mu·si·cal·i·ty /£mjuː·zɪˈkæl·ə·ti, $-t̬i/ *n* [U] • Musicality is skill and good judgment in playing music:

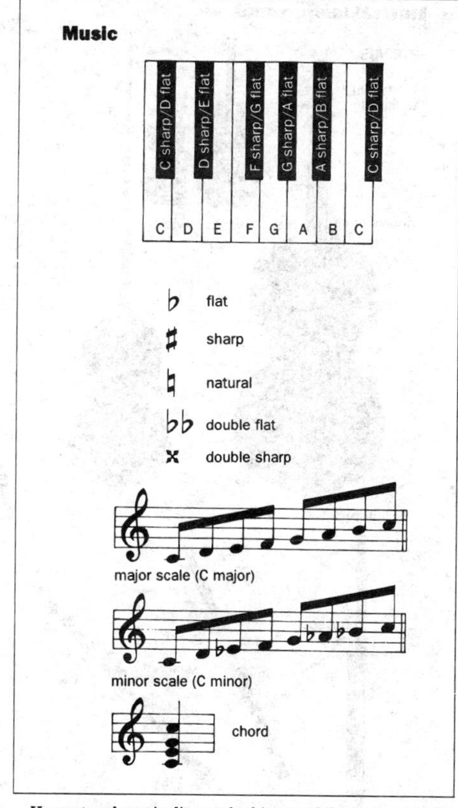

Her natural musicality made this one of the most enjoyable concerts of the year.

mu·si·cal·ly /ˈmjuː·zɪ·kli/ *adv* • *It's a school for musically* **gifted** *children* (=those who are very good at playing a musical instrument or singing). • *Musically speaking* (=referring to the music they produce), *this band has a lot of talent.*

mu·si·cian /mjuːˈzɪʃ·ən/ *n* [C] • A musician is someone who is skilled in playing music, usually as their job: *The concert features dancers, singers and musicians of all nationalities.*

mu·si·cian·ship /mjuːˈzɪʃ·ən·ʃɪp/ *n* [U] • A person's musicianship is their skill in playing a musical instrument or singing: *The sheer musicianship of this young woman is breathtaking.*

mu·si·col·o·gy /£ˌmjuː·zɪˈkɒl·ə·dʒi, $-ˈkɑː·lə-/ *n* [U] • Musicology is the study of the history, theory and science of music.

mu·si·col·o·gist /£ˌmjuː·zɪˈkɒl·ə·dʒɪst, $-ˈkɑː·lə-/ *n* [C] • *Andrew is a respected musicologist.*

musk /mʌsk/ *n* [U] a substance with a strong sweet smell, used in making PERFUMES • *Sabrina always wears musk.* • *Musk is produced naturally by the musk deer and is used to attract other deer sexually.*

musk·y /ˈmʌs·ki/ *adj* **-ier, -iest** • *Her skin had a warm musky odour.*

mus·ket /ˈmʌs·kɪt/ *n* [C] a gun with a long BARREL, used in the past • *The musket was replaced by the rifle in the 19th century.*

Mus·lim /ˈmʊz·lɪm/, **Mos·lem**, **Mu·ham·mad·an** /məˈhæm·ə·dən/, **Mo·ham·med·an** *n* [C] a person who follows the religion of Islam • *At the age of thirty Sam became a Muslim.*

Mus·lim /ˈmʊz·lɪm/ *adj* [not gradable]

mus·lin /ˈmʌz·lɪn/ *n* [U] a very thin cotton material • *A 19th-century painting of a girl in a muslin dress hung on the wall.* • *The soured milk is strained through muslin to leave a soft ball of cheese ready to be shaped.*

muss *obj* /mʌs/ *v* [T] *esp. Am* to make untidy • *The wind is mussing my hair.*

muss /mʌs/ *n* [U] *Am* • *This room is all a muss* (=in an untidy state).

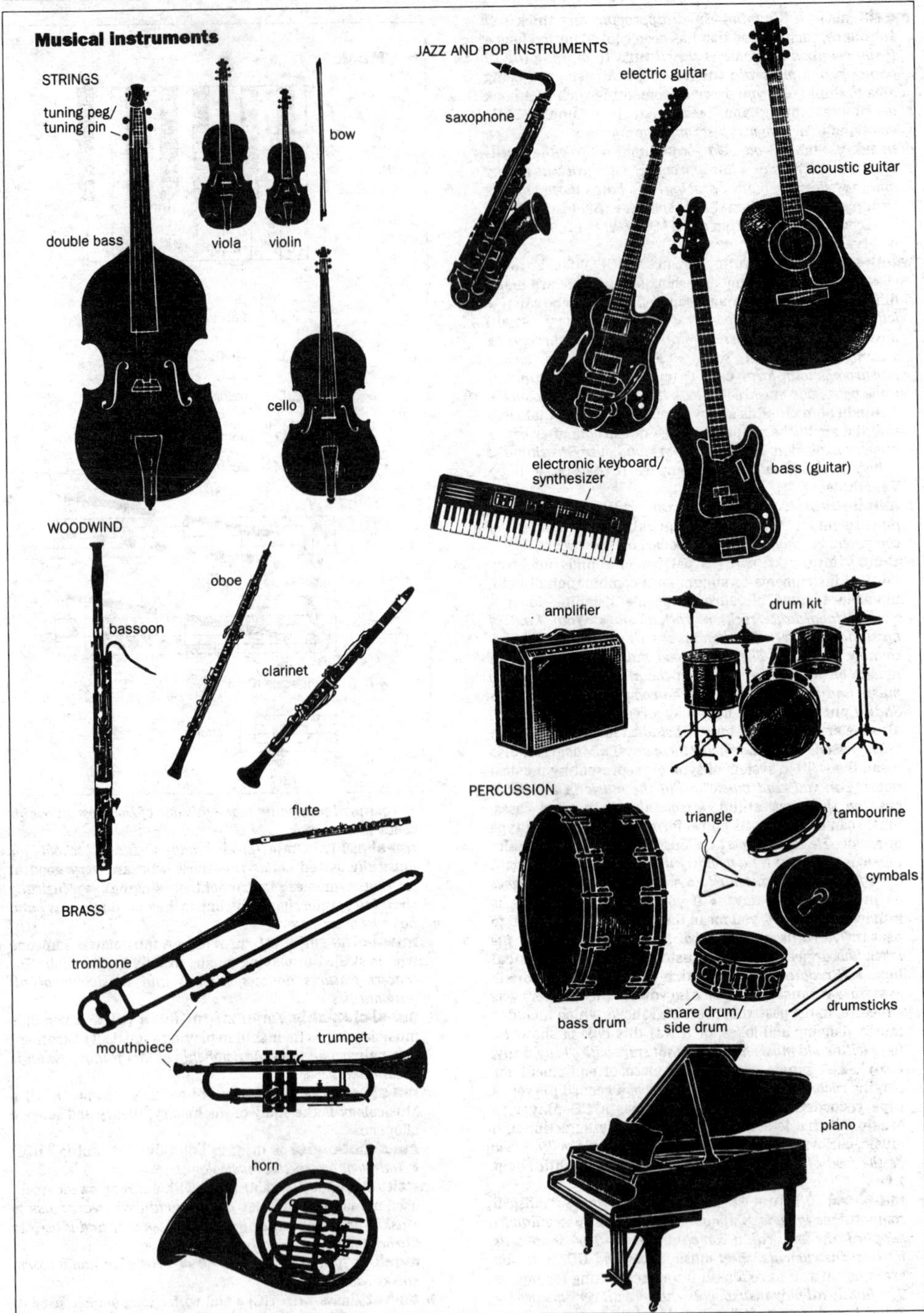

mus·sel /'mʌs·əl/ *n* [C] a small edible sea animal that lives inside a dark-coloured shell with two parts that close tightly together • *Mussels are found on rocks near the sea, and can be cooked and eaten.* • PIC〉 **Mollusc**

must NECESSARY /mʌst/ *v aux* [+ infinitive without *to*; not *be musting*] he/she/it **must** used to show that it is necessary or very important that something happens in the present or future • *You must take these pills every day.* • *This letter must not be shown to anyone else.* • *Luggage must not be left unattended* (= it is against the rules). • *"Must you leave so soon?" "Yes, I must."* • *"Can you let me come in?" "No, I mustn't."* • *"Must I sign this?" "No, you needn't."* • If you say that you must do something, you might mean that you have a firm intention to do something in the future: *I must phone my sister.* ○ *I mustn't bite my nails.* ○ *We mustn't argue any more.* • Must is sometimes used for emphasis: *I must* **admit** *I didn't know what to do.* ○ *You're looking very well,* **I must say**. • If you tell someone else that they must do something pleasant, you are emphasizing that you think it is a good idea for them to do that: *You must come and stay with us for the weekend.* ○ *We must meet for lunch soon.* • When talking about things that were necessary in the past, it is usual to use *had to*: *I must go tomorrow. I had to go yesterday.* When describing what someone said in the past, *must* or *had to* can be used as the past form: *He told me that I must sit down* means *He said "You must sit down"*. • LP〉 **Auxiliary verbs**

must /mʌst/ *n* [C] *infml* • If something is a must, it is necessary: *If you live in the country a car is a must.*

must- /mʌst-/ *combining form infml esp. Am* • Sometimes 'must-' is used with other verbs to show that the stated action is good to do: *This film is a must-see.* • *As far as she was concerned, a sports car was a must-have.*

must PROBABLY /mʌst/ *v aux* [+ infinitive without *to* not *be musting*] he/she/it **must** used to show that something is very likely, probable or certain to be true • *Harry's been driving all day – he must be tired.* • *You're having a baby! You must be very happy.* • *There's no food left – we must have eaten it all.* • *When you got lost in the forest you must have been very frightened.* • *£300 for that load of junk? You must be joking* (= I certainly do not think you are being serious)*!* • *"You must know Frank." "No, I don't."* • *"It must* **have** *been fun." "No, it wasn't."* • *"That must be Jackie over there." "No, it can't be."* • *"He must have told her." "No, surely he can't have done."*

mus·tache /£mʊ'stɑːʃ, $'mʌs·tæʃ/ *n* [C] *Am for* MOUSTACHE

mus·tach·i·o /£mə'stæʃ·i·əʊ, $-oʊ/ *n* [C] *pl* **mustachios** a large MOUSTACHE with curly ends

mus·tach·i·oed /£mə'stæʃ·i·əʊd, $-oʊd/ *adj* [not gradable] • *The mustachioed gentleman introduced himself as Martin.*

mus·tard /£'mʌs·təd, $-tɚd/ *n* [U] a yellow or brown thick liquid that tastes spicy and is eaten in small amounts, esp. with meat • *Mustard is made from the seeds of the mustard plant.* • **Mustard gas** is a very poisonous gas, used as a weapon, that burns the skin, damages organs inside the body and can kill.

mus·ter *obj* PRODUCE /£'mʌs·təʳ, $-tɚ/ *v* [T] to produce or encourage (esp. an emotion or support) • *She managed to muster* **(up)** *(the/enough)* **courage** *to ask him to the cinema.* • *For this venture to be really successful we must start by mustering the* **enthusiasm** *of parents, teachers and pupils.* • *The team will need all the* **strength** *they can muster to win this game.* • *He mounted a series of successful exhibitions, but was unable to muster the necessary financial* **support**. • *Opponents are unlikely to be able to muster enough* **votes** *to override the veto.*

mus·ter GATHER /£'mʌs·təʳ, $-tɚ/ *v* (esp. of soldiers) to (cause to) gather together, esp. in preparation for fighting • *The twelfth division mustered on the hill.* [I] • *The general mustered his* **troops**. [T] • *(fig.) The Welsh National Opera has mustered* **its forces** (= made great preparations and efforts to) *to mount its second production of Tristan in only 14 years.*

mus·ter /£'mʌs·təʳ, $-tɚ/ *n* [C] • A muster of soldiers is a group of soldiers. • A **muster point/muster station** is the place where everyone in a place or on a boat has to meet when there is an emergency.

must·n't /'mʌs·ᵊnt/ *short form of* must not • *You mustn't worry too much about this.*

must·y /'mʌs·ti/ *adj* **-ier, -iest** smelling unpleasantly old and slightly wet • *musty old books* • *a musty smell* • *a musty room*

mu·tate /mjuː'teɪt/ *v.* [I] to develop new physical characteristics because of a permanent change in the GENES. These changes can happen naturally or can be produced by the use of chemicals or RADIATION. • *These bacteria have mutated* **into** *forms that are resistant to certain drugs.* • *(fig.) Jon has mutated* **from** *an awkward teenager* **into** *a sophisticated young man.*

mu·ta·tion /mjuː'teɪ·ʃᵊn/ *n* • Mutation is the way in which GENES change and produce permanent differences: *It is well-known that radiation can cause mutation.* [U] • A mutation is a permanent change in an organism, or the changed organism itself: *Environmental pressures encourage genes with certain mutations to persist and others to die out.* [C] ○ *Some people with red-cell mutations such as thalassaemia and sickle cell anaemia inherit an immunity to malaria.* [C] ○ *As for the pink form of the plant, the original mutation was found in England and its cuttings have spread across the world.* [C]

mu·tant /£'mjuː·tᵊnt, $-t̬ᵊnt/ *n* [C] • A mutant is an organism that is different from others of its type because of a permanent change in its GENES: *These mutants lacked a vital block of genetic instructions giving them immunity to the disease.* ○ *The sweet lime is possibly a natural mutant* **of** *lemon.* ○ *This mutant* **gene** *is thought to cause cancer.* ○ *(fig. humorous) I'm convinced he's a mutant – he's not a bit like the rest of our family!* • *(disapproving)* Mutants are sometimes thought of as unpleasant and frightening: *The result of these experiments will be a nightmarish world filled with two-headed monsters and other mutants.*

mute /mjuːt/ *adj* [not gradable] (of a person) unable or unwilling to speak, or (of an activity) silent • *Because of his strange home life, when the boy started school he was almost mute and totally withdrawn.* • *The president has* **remained** *mute about plans to curtail the number of immigrants.* • *I gazed at her in mute* (= silent) *admiration.* ○ *He frowned in mute* (= silent) *disapproval.* • A **mute swan** is the largest type of SWAN and it makes no cries when flying.

mute /mjuːt/ *n* [C] • A mute on a musical instrument is a button on it or an object that can be fixed to it in order to make it quieter. • *(dated)* A mute is also a person who is not able to speak.

mute *obj* /mjuːt/ *v* [T] • If you mute a noise, you do something to make it less loud: *Double glazing muted the noise of the traffic.*

mut·ed /£'mjuː·tɪd, $-t̬ɪd/ *adj* • Muted means not loud or *(fig.)* not very enthusiastic: *There was polite, muted applause when I finished speaking.* ○ *(fig.) The idea received a muted response.* • Muted colours are not bright: *She prefers wearing muted blues and greens rather than bright primary colours.*

mu·ti·late *obj* /£'mjuː·tɪ·leɪt, $-t̬ᵊl·eɪt/ *v* [T] to damage severely, esp. by violently removing a part • *Self-hatred apparently drove her to mutilate her own face.* • *The dead bodies had been mutilated beyond recognition.* • *A madman had mutilated the painting with a knife.* • *(fig.) They have mutilated* (= spoilt) *a beautiful film by making these changes.*

mu·til·a·tion /£ˌmjuː·tɪ'leɪ·ʃᵊn, $-t̬ᵊl'eɪ-/ *n* [C; U] • *He admitted the murder and mutilation of between 12 and 16 young men.* [U] • *Newspaper accounts described the events as a 'race riot', with lynchings, shootings and mutilations.* [C]

mu·ti·ny /£'mjuː·tɪ·ni, $-t̬ɪ-/ *n* (a) refusal to obey orders and/or a violent attempt to take control from people in authority, esp. in a military situation or on a ship • *Conditions on the ship were often very bad, and crews were* **on the point of** *mutiny.* [U] • *There were rumours of mutiny* **among** *the troops.* [U] • *Deepening disillusionment bordering on* **open** (= not secret) *mutiny is stirring in the militia.* [U] • *Soldiers and police killed 250-300 prisoners while crushing mutinies in three jails.* [C] • *As the president of the university, he has successfully battled against student sit-ins and faculty mutinies.* [C]

mu·ti·ny /£'mjuː·tɪ·ni, $-t̬ɪ-/ *v* [I] • *The crew mutinied and murdered the ship's captain.* • *The troops mutinied* **against** *their officers.*

mu·ti·neer /£ˌmjuː·tɪ'nɪəʳ, $-t̬ɪ'nɪr/ *n* [C] • *The mutineers* (= people taking part in a mutiny) *who tried to take over the ship were all hanged.*

mu·ti·nous /£'mjuː·tɪ·nəs, $-t̬ɪ-/ *adj* • *The mutinous sailors took control of the ship.* • *The chairman of the company is trying to persuade mutinous* (= not satisfied) *shareholders to give him renewed support.*

mutt PERSON /mʌt/ *n* [C] *infml esp. Am* a person who behaves in a silly or careless way • *Come on you mutts, play harder!* [as form of address]

mutt DOG /mʌt/ *n* [C] *esp. Am and Aus* a MONGREL

mut·ter *(obj)* /£'mʌt·əʳ, $'mʌt̬·ɚ/ *v* to speak quietly and in a low voice that is not easy to hear, often when you are anxious or complaining about something • *He was pacing back and forth muttering* **(away) to himself**. [I] • *He muttered something* **under** *his* **breath** *to the person next to him, but I only heard the word 'unexpected'.* [T] • *When the shop burned down, some people muttered* **(darkly) about** (= suggested it might be the result of) *arson, but nothing was proved.* [I] • *She was muttering* (= making) **threats** *against her neighbour's noisy dog.* [T] • *"Looks like it could use a coat of paint," muttered someone as we approached the hotel.* [+ clause]

mut·ter /£'mʌt·əʳ, $'mʌt̬·ɚ/ *n* [C] • *There were mutters* (= complaints) **that** *other developments might receive more of the money available.* [+ *that* clause]

mut·ter·ings /£'mʌt·ə·rɪŋz, $'mʌt̬·ɚ-/ *pl n* • *There are mutterings* **of discontent** *among the staff* (= some of them are starting to complain).

mut·ton /£'mʌt·ᵊn, $'mʌt̬-/ *n* [U] the meat from an adult sheep eaten as food • *a shoulder of mutton* • *mutton stew* • *You rarely see mutton sold in shops these days – sheep meat of any kind is usually called lamb.* • *(Br infml disapproving)* If you describe a person, usually a woman, as **mutton dressed (up) as lamb**, you mean that they are trying in a too obvious way to look younger than they are, in order to seem sexually attractive: *Do you think this dress is too young-looking for me? – I don't want to look like mutton dressed as lamb.* • Ⓙ

mut·ton·chops /£'mʌt·ᵊn·tʃɒps, $'mʌt̬·ᵊn·tʃɑːps/, **mut·ton·chop whisk·ers** *pl n* long hair growing down each side of the face, worn by men esp. in the 19th century

mu·tu·al /'mjuː·tʃu·əl/ *adj* [not gradable] (of two or more people or groups) feeling the same emotion, or doing the same thing to or for each other • *Their relationship fast degenerated into mutual* **recrimination(s)**. • *Despite differences in background and outlook, their partnership was based on mutual* **respect, trust** *and* **understanding**. • *Both countries are acting* **to their mutual advantage**. • *The agreement was terminated* **by** *mutual* **consent**. • A **mutual friend** is a person who is the friend of two people but in separate situations, so that the two people might not know each other: *Lynn and Phil* **met through** *a mutual friend.* • **Mutual fund** is *Am for* **unit trust**. See at UNIT [SEPARATE PART]. • *(saying)* 'The feeling's mutual' is sometimes said after one person has expressed dislike for another: *He said, "I hate your guts" and I just said, "Well, the feeling's mutual!".* • [LP〉 **Each other**

mu·tu·al·ly /'mjuː·tʃu·ə·li/ *adv* [not gradable] • *It will be a mutually* **beneficial** *project.* • *Being rich and being a Socialist are not mutually* **exclusive** (= they can exist together at the same time).

mu·zak /'mjuː·zæk/ *n* [U] *trademark* recorded music that is played quietly and continuously in public places such as airports, shops, etc., esp. to make people feel relaxed • *I hate those restaurants/supermarkets where they play muzak.* • See also **canned music** at CAN [CONTAINER]; **piped music** at PIPE [TUBE].

muz·zle [ANIMAL] /'mʌz·l̩/ *n* [C] the mouth and nose of an animal, esp. a dog, or a covering put over this in order to prevent the animal from biting • [PIC〉 **Dogs, Muzzle**

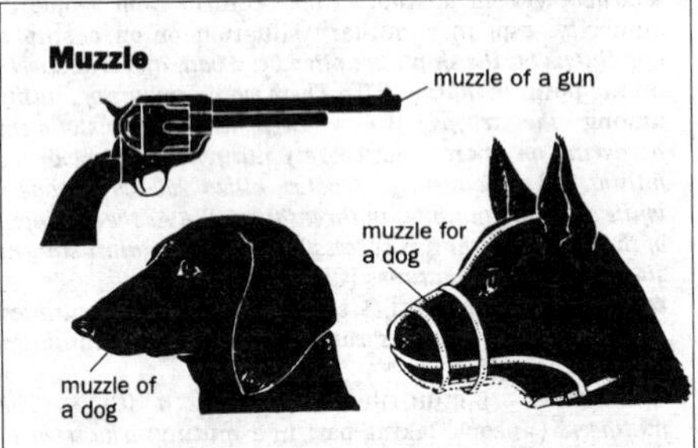

muz·zle *obj* /'mʌz·l̩/ *v* [T] • *Dangerous dogs should be muzzled.* • *(fig.) The new Secrecy Act will muzzle the media and the opposition* (= prevent them from expressing independent opinions).

muz·zle [GUN] /'mʌz·l̩/ *n* [C] the end of a gun BARREL (= the cylindrical part of a gun), where the bullets come out • [PIC〉 **Muzzle**

muz·zy /'mʌz·i/ *adj* **-ier, -iest** (of a person) confused and unable to think clearly because of tiredness, illness, alcohol or drugs, or (of a situation, plans, language, etc.) not clear or well-explained • *Feeling muzzy from the blow on his head, he got up very slowly.* • *Until a week ago, the group's objectives were slightly muzzy.*

muz·zi·ly /'mʌz·ɪ·li/ *adv*

muz·zi·ness /'mʌz·ɪ·nəs/ *n* [U]

MW *n abbreviation for* **medium wave**, see at WAVE [ENERGY]

my [OF ME] /maɪ/ *determiner* of or belonging to me (= the speaker or writer) • *my parents* • *my feet* • *my name* • *my jacket* • *It wasn't my fault, I promise.* • *She was rather surprised at my* **asking** (= that I asked) *for the book to be returned.* • My **own** is used to emphasize belonging to or connected with me and no one else: *I want my own car very soon.* ○ *It was my own decision.* ○ *(humorous) This cake is* **all** *my own* **work** (= I made it without help). • My is sometimes used in front of a noun as a way of expressing love or as a polite or humorous form of address: *My darling!* ○ *Do you want any help, my dear?* • See also I; ME; MINE. • [LP〉 **Determiners**

my·self /maɪ'self/ *pronoun* • Myself is the reflexive pronoun of I: *I've bought myself a new coat.* ○ *I caught sight of myself in the mirror.* ○ *Yes, I thought to myself, it's time to take a holiday.* • Myself is sometimes used to emphasize 'I' as the subject of a sentence: *I myself like a sandwich rather than a full meal at lunchtime.* ○ *I don't like a heavy meal at lunchtime myself.* • *I had to do the whole job* **by** *myself* (= with no help from other people). • *I live* **by** *myself* (= alone) *in a small flat in Islington.* • *I never get an hour* **to** *myself* (= for my own use). • *(dated) I'm well (enough)* **in myself** *despite the problems with the leg* (= I am happy despite a physical illness or problem). • Myself is sometimes used instead of I or me: *My husband and myself were delighted with the gift.* ○ *They very kindly invited my sister and myself to the inauguration.* • [LP〉 **Reflexive pronouns and verbs**

my [EXPRESSION] /maɪ/ *exclamation* used to express surprise or pleasure • *My, my! What a strange haircut!* • *My, this food is wonderful.* • *My, oh, my, what a busy day!*

my·nah (bird), **my·na (bird)** /'maɪ·nə/, *Aus* **In·di·an my·nah** *n* [C] a black or dark brown bird from Asia, some types of which can copy human speech

my·o·pi·a *fml* /£maɪ'əʊ·pi·ə, $-'oʊ-/, **short–sight·ed·ness** /£ˌʃɔːt'saɪ·tɪd·nəs, $ˌʃɔːrt'saɪ·t̬ɪd-/ *n* [U] inability to see distant things clearly

my·o·pic *fml* /£maɪ'ɒp·ɪk, $-'ɑː·pɪk/, **short–sight·ed** /£ˌʃɔːt'saɪ·tɪd, $ˌʃɔːrt'saɪ·t̬ɪd/ *adj* • *(fig. disapproving) Their myopic* (= not considering the future) *refusal to act now will undoubtedly cause problems in the future.* • [LP〉 **Eye and seeing**

myr·i·ad /'mɪr·i·əd/ *n* [C] a very large number of (something) • *And now myriads* **of** *bars and hotels are opening up along the coast.* • *There are* **a** *myriad different varieties of insect life.*

myr·i·ad /'mɪr·i·əd/ *adj* • *They offered no solution for all our myriad problems.*

myrrh /£mɜːʳ, $mɜːr/ *n* [U] a sticky brown substance with a strong smell which is used in making PERFUME and INCENSE

myr·tle /£'mɜː·tl̩, $'mɜːr·t̬l̩/ *n* [C] a small tree with shiny green leaves, pleasant-smelling white flowers and blue-black fruit

my·self /maɪ'self/ *pronoun* See at MY [OF ME]

mys·te·ry /£'mɪs·tᵊr·i, $-tə-, '-tri/ *n* something strange or unknown which has not yet been explained or understood • *How the massive stones were brought here from hundreds of miles away* **is/remains** *a mystery.* [C] • *The mystery was* **solved** *when the police discovered the murder weapon.* [C] • *His disappearance remains* **one of the** *great* **unsolved** *mysteries of recent times.* [C] • *The behaviour of the animals in this situation is a mystery that scientists are finding difficult to* **unravel** (= solve). [C] • *He never abandoned the idea that he might* **solve** *the mystery* **of** *his friends' disappearance.* [C] • *The book tries to explain some of the mysteries* **of** *creation/life.* [C] • *An element of mystery always adds excitement to a story.* [U] • *The visitor had* **an air of** *mystery.* [U] • *The details of the scandal remain* **cloaked/shrouded/wrapped in** *mystery.* [U] • *Apparently he didn't have another job to go to and mystery* **surrounds** *his reasons for leaving.* [U] • *Her visit to France* **is (something of) a mystery** *(to us)* (= we do not understand why she went). • **It's a** *complete* **mystery (***to* **me) that/why** (= I do not understand why) *she married him at all!* • A mystery is also a book, film or play, esp. about a crime or a murder, with a surprise ending which explains all the strange events that have happened: *I really enjoy* **murder** *mysteries.* [C] ○ *My favourite authors are all mystery* **writers**. • A **mystery guest** or a **mystery voice** is a person you cannot see or recognize immediately: *Each week the TV show has a mystery guest.* ○ *Listeners phoned in to try to guess who was the mystery voice.* • A **mystery tour** is a short journey, esp. with a group of other people in a bus, to visit places which are kept secret from you until you get there. • *"Magical Mystery Tour"* (title of a song and a film by The Beatles, 1967)

mys·te·ri·ous /£mɪ'stɪə·ri·əs, $-'stɪr·i-/ *adj* • *She's an actress whose inner life has remained mysterious, despite the many interviews she has given.* • *He died in mysterious* **circumstances**, *and there is still a possibility that it was murder.* • *"God moves in a mysterious way/ His wonders to perform"* (from a hymn by William Cowper, 1779)

mys·te·ri·ous·ly /£mɪ'stɪə·ri·ə·sli, $-'stɪr·i-/ *adv* • *"Perhaps, and perhaps not," she said mysteriously.* • *Mysteriously, the light came on, although no one was near the switch.*

mys·ti·cism /'mɪs·tɪ·sɪ·zᵊm/ *n* [U] the belief that there is hidden meaning in life or that each human being can unite with God

mys·tic /ˈmɪs·tɪk/ *n* [C] • *They are religious mystics who spend a lot of time praying and meditating.*

mys·ti·cal /ˈmɪs·tɪ·kᵊl/, **mys·tic** /£ˈmɪs·tɪk, $-t̬ɪk/ *adj* • *a mystical religion*

mys·ti·fy *obj* /ˈmɪs·tɪ·faɪ/ *v* [T] to confuse (someone) by being or doing something very strange or impossible to explain • *Most Americans seem totally mystified by cricket.* • *He mystified us all by pouring his drink out of the window.*

mys·ti·fi·ca·tion /ˌmɪs·tɪ·fɪˈkeɪ·ʃᵊn/ *n* [U] • *And then, to the audience's mystification, the band suddenly stopped playing.* • *The government's statement seems to be a deliberate exercise in mystification* (= is intentionally difficult to understand).

mys·ti·fy·ing /ˈmɪs·tɪ·faɪ·ɪŋ/ *adj* • *After ten years her mystifying disappearance was still unexplained.*

mys·ti·fy·ing·ly /ˈmɪs·tɪ·faɪ·ɪŋ·li/ *adv*

mys·tique /mɪˈstiːk/ *n* [U] *fml* a quality of being special in a mysterious and attractive way • *There's great mystique* **attached to/surrounding** *the life of a movie star.* • *These days air travel has* **lost** *its mystique.* • *Too much publicity will destroy the mystique of the monarchy.* • *The noises and puffs of steam are all part of the mystique of producing a small cup of expresso coffee.*

myth /mɪθ/ *n* an ancient story or set of stories, esp. explaining in a literary way the early history of a group of people or about natural events and facts • *The children enjoyed the stories about the gods and goddesses of Greek and Roman myth.* [U] • *Most societies have their own creation myths.* [C] • *(disapproving)* A myth is also a commonly believed but false idea: *Statistics* **disprove/ explode** *the myth* **that** *women are worse drivers than men.* [C + *that* clause]

myth·i·cal /ˈmɪθ·ɪ·kᵊl/ *adj* • Mythical means existing only in stories: *the mythical island of Atlantis* ○ *the mythical hero, Robin Hood* ○ *dragons and other mythical creatures* • Mythical also means imaginary or not real: *Start living life here and now instead of waiting for that mythical day when you'll be slim.* ○ *The town is 90 miles north of the mythical line from the Severn to the Wash that supposedly divides Britain into north and south.* ○ *The play is set in an all-female legislative assembly in a mythical province where only women held office and no man had the vote.*

myth·o·log·i·cal /£ˌmɪθ·ᵊlˈɒdʒ·ɪ·kᵊl, $-əˈlɑː·dʒɪ-/ *adj* [not gradable] • Something or someone that is mythological is mentioned in myths: *a mythological hero such as Achilles*

myth·ol·o·gy /£mɪˈθɒl·ə·dʒi, $-ˈθɑː·lə-/ *n* [U] • Mythology is myths in general: *She's fascinated by the stories of* **classical** *mythology* (= ancient Greek and Roman myths). • *(fig.) It's just a piece of* **popular** *mythology* (= a common belief that is probably not true) *that people always get sacked when they are away on holiday.*

myth·ol·o·gize *(obj), Br and Aus usually* **-ise** /£mɪˈθɒl·ə·dʒaɪz, $mɪˈθɑː·lə-/ *v Am* • To mythologize is to create a false picture of a situation: *People tend to mythologize* **(about)** *their schooldays/the past.* [T; I + *about*]

myx·o·ma·to·sis /£ˌmɪk·sə·məˈtəʊ·sɪs, $-ˈtoʊ-/ *n* [U] an infectious disease of rabbits that causes them to become blind and usually kills them

N n

N LETTER (*pl* **N's** or **Ns**), **n** (*pl* **n's** or **ns**) /en/ *n* [C] the 14th letter of the English alphabet • *I think his name begins with an N.* • In mathematics, *n* is used to mean a number whose value is not known or not stated: *If 3n = 12, what is the value of n?* • *(fig. infml) There are n* (= very many different) *possibilities here – take your pick.* • Compare NTH. • LP **Silent letters**

n NOUN /en/ *abbreviation for* NOUN

N NORTH, *Br also* **Nth**, *Am also* **No** *n* [U], *adj abbreviation for* NORTH or NORTHERN

'n' /-ᵊn-/ *conjunction abbreviation for* AND • *fish 'n' chips* • *rock 'n' roll*

n/a, NA *adj abbreviation for* not applicable (= not connected or related) • *Most of the questions on the tax form weren't relevant to me, so I just put n/a in all the spaces.*

nab *obj* /næb/ *v* [T] **-bb-** *infml* to take (something) suddenly, or to catch or ARREST (a criminal) • *Someone nabbed my apple when I wasn't looking!* • *Could you nab me a seat* (= get a seat for me and stop anyone else from sitting in it) *if you get to the theatre before me?* [+ two objects] • *Undercover police officers nabbed* (= caught) *the men as they were taking possession of a consignment of heroin.*

nabe /neɪb/ *n* [C usually sing] *Am slang for* NEIGHBOURHOOD • *Most weekends I just hang out in the nabe.*

nab·ob /£ˈneɪ·bɒb, $-bɑːb/ *n* [C] *dated* a rich or powerful person • *He is a president who goes out and talks to the ordinary people, not just the nabobs.*

nach·os /£ˈnætʃ·əʊz, $ˈnɑː·tʃoʊz/ *pl n* small pieces of thin dry bread made from MAIZE flour and eaten with melted cheese and a spicy sauce that usually contains beans

na·cho /£ˈnætʃ·əʊ, $ˈnɑː·tʃoʊ/ *adj* • *nacho chips*

na·dir /£ˈneɪ·dɪəʳ, $-dɚ/ *n* [C usually sing] *fml* worst moment; moment of least hope and least achievement • *The defeat was* **the** *nadir* **of** *her career.* • Compare ZENITH.

nae /neɪ/ *adv* [not gradable] *Br regional or Scottish for* NO NOT

naff /næf/ *adj* **-er, -est** *Br slang* not stylish or fashionable, and therefore worthless • *He was wearing incredibly naff trousers in an awful bright colour.* • *The way she sings is so naff, don't you think?*

naff off /næf/ *v adv* [I usually in commands] *Br slang* to go away • *The reporters were shouting questions at her until finally she just said, "Oh, naff off, the lot of you!"*

nag *(obj)* CRITICIZE /næg/ *v* **-gg-** to criticize or complain repeatedly and annoyingly, often as a way of trying to persuade (someone) to do something • *My mum's always nagging me* **to** *get my hair cut.* [T + obj + *to* infinitive] • *The way he keeps on nagging* **about** *the smallest things really gets on my nerves.* [I] • If something such as a worry, doubt or question is nagging (at) you, it is continuously and annoyingly in your mind: *Several worries were nagging* **(at)** *her.* [T; I + *at*]

nag·ging /næg/ *adj* • *a nagging* (= complaining and criticizing) *voice* • *nagging* (= continuous) *doubts/pain*

nag·ging /ˈnæg·ɪŋ/ *n* [U] • *I can't stand her nagging* (= complaining and criticizing) *any more.*

nag HORSE /næg/ *n* [C] a horse, esp. one that is too old to be useful

nah /næ, nɜː/ *adv* [not gradable] *slang for* NO NEGATIVE ANSWER

nail METAL /neɪl/ *n* [C] a small thin piece of metal with one pointed end and one flat end which you hit into something with a hammer, esp. in order to fasten or join it to something else • *a three-inch nail* • *She tore her skirt on a nail sticking out of the chair.* • **Hammer** *a nail into the wall and we'll hang the mirror from it.* • If you say that a fact or event **is a nail in** someone's or something's **coffin** (*also* **drives a nail into** someone's **coffin**) you mean that it makes that person's or thing's failure more likely: *Each successive revelation of incompetence is* **another** *nail in the chairman's coffin.* ○ *The report drove* **the final** *nail into the company's coffin.* • If someone is **(as) hard/tough as nails,** they are very strong and in good physical condition and/or they act without worrying about the pain or danger they might cause to themselves or others. • PIC **Nail, Tools**

nail *obj* /neɪl/ *v* [T] • *She had nailed a wooden cross* **to** *the door.* • *A notice had been nailed* **up** *on the wall.* • *The lid of the coffin had been nailed* **down**. • *(infml)* If you **nail** someone **down**, you force them to give you a firm answer, price, etc.: *They nailed him down* **to** *a specific time and place.* • *(infml)* If you **nail down** an agreement, etc. you agree to the details of it: *After an all-night meeting, we finally nailed down a deal.* • *(slang)* To nail someone is to catch them, esp. when they are doing something wrong, or to make it clear that they are guilty: *The police had been trying to nail those guys for months.* ○ *Newspapers do their best to nail politicians involved in illegal deals.* • If you **nail** your **colours to the mast** you make it obvious what your opinions or plans are. • *(dated infml)* To **nail a lie** is to prove that it really is a lie.

nail BODY PART /neɪl/ *n* [C] a thin hard area that covers the upper side of the end of each finger and each toe • *beautifully manicured nails* • *She was* **biting/cutting/ painting** *her nails.* • *He's a* **nail-biter** (= he regularly bites

NORWEGIAN FALSE FRIENDS (N)

English	Norwegian	Meaning
anger *n*	anger	repentance, self-reproach, remorse
backbone *n*	bakbein	hind leg
bane *n*	bane	underground, tube, railway
behold *v*	beholde	to keep, retain
beholder *n*	beholder	container; recepticle, vessel
blank *adj*	blank	shiny, bright; clear; plain; (colloq)broke
casserole *n*	kasserol(e)	saucepan
characteristic *n*	karakteristikk	study/sketch/portrait of a person; characterization
classic *adj*	klassisk	classical
closet *n*	klosett	lavatory, w.c.
concept *n*	konsept	rough draft, outline; senses
concurrence *n*	konkurranse	competition
conjunctive *adj*	konjunktiv	subjunctive mood (grammar)
control *v*	kontrollere	to supervise; to inspect, check
corn *n*	korn	grain, granule
craft *n*	kraft	power, electricity
dam *n*	dam	pool, pond; draughts (game)
damp *adj*	damp	steam, vapour, fumes; (fig.) energy, steam
delicate *adj*	delikat	delicious, tasty
delicatessen *n*	delikatessen	table delicacies
feast *n*	fest	party; celebration; fun
fiend *n*	fiende	enemy, foe
flask *n*	flaske	bottle, phial
flick *v*	flikke	to mend, darn, patch
flick *n*	flik	corner, flap (of paper/material)
floor *n*	flor	cow barn; barn floor; bloom; flowering; profusion; crepe (for mourning)
floor *n*	flore	ice floe, layer
formula *n*	formular	form
genial *adj*	genial	brilliant, ingenious
geniality *n*	genialitet	genius, brilliance
gift *n*	gift	poison
grin *n*	grin	grimace, sneer; (constant) complaining; fretting; nagging, whining, petty criticism
hold out *v*	holde ut	to stand, bear, tolerate
icing *n*	ising	cold shiver
island *n*	Island	Iceland
marine *n*	marine	navy; seascape
middle-aged *adj*	middelalderlig	medieval; old-fashioned
novel *n*	novelle	short story
receipt *n*	resept	prescription; conception, idea
rubric *n*	rubrikk	space, blank; article; paragraph
rug *n*	rug	rye
scab *n*	skabb	itch; dandelion
sky *n*	sky	cloud
sympathetic *adj*	sympatisk	likeable, pleasant; attractive
technique *n*	teknikk	technology, engineering
Thursday *n*	Tirsdag	Tuesday
trivial *adj*	triviell	trite, hackneyed
truck *n*	truck	(fork)lift
under *prep*	under	close to, near, right up to; at the time of, during; in the process of, while; amidst, in the midst of; to the accompaniment of
vest *n*	vest	waistcoat

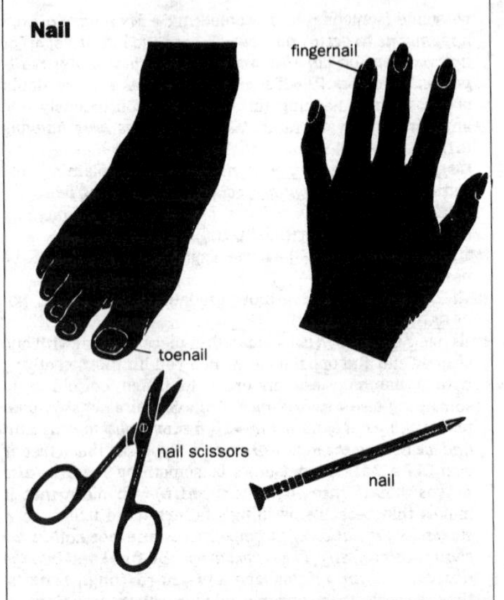

his nails). • *(fig.) We spent two* **nail-biting** (=anxious) *hours waiting for the results.* • A **nail brush** is a small stiff brush used for cleaning your nails and your hands. • A **nail file** is a small strip of metal or paper with a rough surface used for making the edges of your nails smooth and curved. • **Nail enamel/nail polish** (*Br and Aus usually* **nail varnish**) is a liquid, usually red or pink, which is painted on nails as a decoration. • **Nail scissors** are a small pair of curved SCISSORS used to cut your nails. • See also FINGERNAIL; TOENAIL. • PIC **Brush, Cosmetics, File, Nail**

na·ive, na·ïve /naɪˈiːv/ *adj esp. disapproving* (too) willing to believe that someone is telling the truth, that people's intentions in general are good or that life is simple and fair. People are often naive because they are young and/or have not had much experience of life. • *Young, naive and trusting as I was, I believed every lying word he said.* • *They make the naive assumption that because it's popular it must be good.* • *We had a naive belief that with democracy and freedom would come prosperity.* • *The plan exposed their naive idealism.* • **It** *was naive* **of** *you* **to** *think Lawson would listen to your suggestions.* [+ *to* infinitive] • Ⓙ

nai·ve·ly, na·ïve·ly /naɪˈiːv·li/ *adv* • *David naively believed the boss would support him.*

na·ive·ty, na·ïve·té /£naɪˈiː·vɪ·ti, $-və·t̬i/ *n* [U] • Naivety is trust based on lack of experience: *(disapproving) He demonstrated a worrying naivety about political issues.* • *(approving) I think her naivety is charming – she's so unspoilt and fresh.*

na·ked /ˈneɪ·kɪd/ *adj* not covered by clothes • *a naked man* • *a naked foot* • *naked bodies* • *There were pictures of the actress naked and clothed.* • *He was naked* **to the** *waist* (= not wearing clothes above his waist). • *The children were* **half-***naked* (= partly naked)/**stark** *(Am also* **buck/butt***) naked* (= completely naked). • *They* **stripped** *naked* (= took off their clothes) *and ran into the sea.* • Something that is naked is lacking its usual covering: *a naked flame/(light) bulb* (= one with nothing surrounding or covering it) ○ *a naked hillside* (= one without trees or plants) ○ *(fig.) He displayed naked* (= obvious and not hidden) **aggression/ambition**. • *These stars are too small to be seen with* **the naked eye** (= can only be seen using a special device). • *"The Naked Ape* (= the human being)*"* (title of a book by Desmond Morris, 1967)

na·ked·ly /ˈneɪ·kɪd·li/ *adv* • *(fig.) His vulnerability was nakedly on display* (= it was obvious and not at all hidden).

na·ked·ness /ˈneɪ·kɪd·nəs/ *n* [U] • *Adam and Eve tried to hide their nakedness with fig leaves.*

nam·by–pam·by /ˌnæm·biˈpæm·bi/ *adj infml disapproving* weak, foolish or silly • *I hate these awful namby-pamby poems.* • *He regarded vegetarians as namby-pamby animal-lovers.* • *He thought the boys were namby-pamby and decided to toughen them up.*

name /neɪm/ *n* [C] what a person or thing is called; the particular word(s) regularly connected with a person or thing so that you can recognize, refer to or address them • *Hello – my name's Philip.* • *Her* **full** (= complete) *name is Anna Maria Theresa Crutchley.* • *What is the name of that mountain in the distance?* • *Solanum tuberosum is the Latin name for the potato.* • *The students were listed* **by** *name and by country of origin.* • If you say that something or someone has a **(good)** name, you mean that they have a good reputation, but if they have a **bad** name, they have a bad reputation: *Sony* **has** *a name* **for** *producing high-quality electrical equipment.* ○ *She went to court to* **clear** *her name* (= prove that the bad things said about her were not true). ○ *Their actions* **gave** *British football a bad name in Europe at that time.* ○ *He has* **made** *a name* **for** *himself* (= developed a reputation) *as a talented journalist.* • A name is also someone who is famous or has a good reputation: *She's now a* **(big/important)** *name in the world of media consultancy.* • *(fml) I've got to talk to a professor* **by the name of** (= called) *Bin Said.* • To **call** someone **names/a name** is to say or shout rude words at them or describe them in an unpleasant way: *She came from school crying because some of the other kids had been calling her names.* ○ *Then the teacher arrived and said that the* **name-calling** *had got to stop.* • *In the business world he* **goes by the name of** (= uses the false name of) *J. Walter Fortune.* • *She is vice-president* **in all but name** (= in fact but without the title). • *It has been an island* **in name only** (= It has been called an island although it is not an island) *since the sea level dropped in 1992.* • If something such as a document, ticket or object is **in the name of** someone or is **in** someone's **name** it belongs to them: *I've come to collect my tickets – I reserved them by phone yesterday in the name of Tremin.* ○ *The house is in my wife's name.* • If something is done or said **in** someone's or something's **name** or **in the name of** a particular idea, belief, religion or group of people, it is done or said by someone who uses that idea, belief, religion or group of people as the reason and cause for their action: *The group decided to undertake a civil disobedience campaign in the name of freedom and justice.* ○ *In old movies the police shouted "Open up in the name of* (= by the right of) *the law" before they broke the door down.* ○ *As members of the union we have the right to know what action the union is taking in our name.* • **In God's/heaven's name** or **In the name of God/heaven** can be used to add force to something which is said, although some people might find the use of 'God' offensive: *What in God's name caused that outburst?* ○ *Why in the name of God didn't you tell me sooner?* • If you say that a particular name is **a name to conjure with** you mean that it is a very important name or a name that has a lot of meaning for you, or is an interesting and unusual name which gives you an image of something pleasant or exciting: *In those days Churchill was still a name to conjure with.* ○ *The House of the Blue Lagoon – now there's a name to conjure with!* • *(infml)* If you say your **name** is **mud** you mean that you will be criticized or your reputation will be spoiled: *The company knew that if this project failed their name would be mud* **with** *their bankers.* ○ *My* **name** *was* **mud** *when I accidentally lost the tickets.* • *(infml) People say that in politics* **the name of the game** (= the most important activity) *is making the right friends.* • To **take** someone's **name in vain** is to refer to them when they are not present, esp. in an unkind way: *I said "Susan wants us to go home early today" and just then she walked in and said "Who's taking my name in vain?"* • If you have nothing or very little **to** your **name** you own very little or have no money: *He had arrived in America without a cent to his name.* • *Her detective stories were written* **under the name of** (= using the false name of) *Kramer.* • *(disapproving)* **Name-dropping** is the habit of often mentioning famous people's names and pretending you know the people, in order to make yourself seem more important and special: *What a* **name-dropper** *that guy is!* ○ *Jane* **name-drops** *in the most annoying way.* • *"The man with no name"* (a character in a series of Western films starring Clint Eastwood, 1964-) • *"The Name of the Rose"* (title of a book by Umberto Eco, 1981) • *"What's in a name? That which we call a rose / By any other name would smell as sweet"* (Shakespeare, Romeo and Juliet 2.2) • [LP] **Capital letters** (KOR)

name *obj* /neɪm/ *v* [T] • *Paul was named* **after/***(Am also)* **for** (= given the same name as) *his grandad.* • *On independence, they named the new country Ghana.* [+ obj + n] • *The lead actor was a guy named Allwork.* [+ obj + n] • To name something or someone is also to say what their name is: *In the first question you had to name three types of monkey.* ○ *He couldn't name his attacker.* ○ *The police apparently have caught someone who is willing to* **name names** (= tell them the names of the people involved in something secret or illegal). • To name someone or something is also to choose them: *Just name the time and I'll be there on the dot.* ○ *Name your conditions/terms/price.* ○ *Ms Martinez has been named* **(as)** (= she will be) *the new Democratic candidate.* [+ obj + *(as)* n] ○ *Gin, vodka, whisky, beer –* **you name it** (= whatever you choose), *I've got it.* • *When are you going to* **name the day** (= decide on which day you are getting married)*?*

name·less /ˈneɪm·ləs/ *adj* [not gradable] • Something that is nameless does not have a name or has a name that you do not know: *the nameless author of a medieval text* • If someone **is/remains** nameless their name is not given publicly: *Those responsible for the delay have already been punished and shall be nameless.* ○ *The journalist insisted that his source of information should remain nameless.* ○ *One boy, who shall remain nameless, has been late every day this week.*

name·ly /ˈneɪm·li/ *adv* [not gradable] which is or are • *The minister would only repeat the official government position, namely that it can do nothing at the moment.* • Namely is also used when you want to give more detail or be more exact about something you have just said: *Switzerland is surrounded by four large neighbours, namely* (= that is) *France, Germany, Austria and Italy.*

name·plate /ˈneɪm·pleɪt/ *n* [C] a piece of metal or other material usually fastened on or near the door of a building or room with the name on it of the person who lives or works there • *There was a brass nameplate outside the door saying Dr A. Hepdey.*

name·sake /ˈneɪm·seɪk/ *n* [C] a person or thing having the same name as another person or thing • *The player's performance would not have disgraced his more famous namesake in the national team.* • *The Endeavour is a new ship, built to replace its namesake which was taken out of service last year.*

na·na, **nan·na** /ˈnæn·ə/ *n* [C] *Br infml or Am regional for* GRANDMOTHER • *She enjoys visiting her nana.* • *Will you read me a story, Nana?* [as form of address]

nan (bread), **naan (bread)** /nɑːn/ *n* [C; U] a flat Indian bread

nanc·y (boy) *Br* /ˈnænt·si/, *Am* **nance** /nænts/ *n* [C] *dated slang* a homosexual. Many people consider this word offensive.

nan·ny [GRANDMOTHER] /ˈnæn·i/, **nan** /næn/ *n* [C] *infml for* GRANDMOTHER • *She stays with her nanny on Fridays.* • *Can I come with you, Nanny?* [as form of address]

nan·ny [CARER] /ˈnæn·i/ *n* [C] a woman whose job is to take care of a particular family's children • *As their parents were away so much of the time, the children were really brought up by their nanny.* • *(dated) Nanny Smith*

nan·ny (goat) /ˈnæn·i/ *n* [C] a female goat

nan·o·me·tre *Br and Aus* /£nænˈɒm·ə·təʳ, $-ˈɑː·mə·tɚ/, *Am* **nan·o·me·ter** *n* [C] 0·000 000 001 metre

nan·o·sec·ond /£ˈnæn·əʊˌsek·ənd, $-oʊ-/ *n* [C] 0·000 000 001 second

nap [SLEEP] /næp/ *n* [C] a short sleep, esp. during the day • *Grandpa usually* **has/takes a** *little nap after lunch.* • (S)

nap /næp/ *v* [I] **-pp-** • *He likes to nap for an hour when he gets home from work.*

nap [CLOTH] /næp/ *n* [U] the surface of a piece of cloth such as VELVET or leather such as SUEDE, consisting of short threads which have been brushed in one direction • (S)

na·palm /ˈneɪ·pɑːm/ *n* [U] a substance containing PETROL which burns fiercely and is used in bombs, esp. to destroy areas of plants so that enemy soldiers cannot hide

nape /neɪp/ *n* [C usually sing] the back of the neck • *She kissed* **the** *nape* **of** *his* **neck.** • [PIC] **Body**

nap·kin /ˈnæp·kɪn/ *n* [C] a small square piece of cloth or paper used while you are eating for protecting your clothes or to clean your mouth or fingers; a SERVIETTE • *Each place setting had a napkin folded into the shape of a water lily.* • A **napkin ring** is a small ring which holds a particular person's cloth napkin between meals when they are not using it. • [PIC] **Cutlery**

nappy [CLOTHING] *Br and Aus* /ˈnæp·i/, *Am* **dia·per** *n* [C] a square of thick soft cloth or a piece of clothing made of thick soft paper which is fastened around a baby's bottom and between its legs to absorb its urine and excrement • *Most parents prefer to use* **disposable** *nappies if they can.* • *I knew him when he was* **(still) in nappies** (= a baby). • *(Br and Aus)* **Nappy rash** (*Am* **diaper rash**) is an area of skin around a baby's bottom that has become rough and painful because it has been rubbed by a wet nappy.

nappy [CURLED] /ˈnæp·i/ *adj* **-ier, -iest** *Am* (of hair) tightly curled and twisted

nar·cis·si·sm /£ˈnɑː·sɪ·sɪ·zəm, $ˈnɑːr·sə-/ *n* [U] too much interest in and admiration for your own physical appearance and/or your own abilities • *Actors must need a certain amount of narcissism to get up on a stage and perform in front of an audience.*

nar·cis·sist /£ˈnɑː·sɪ·sɪst, $ˈnɑːr·sə-/ *n* [C] • *What a narcissist* (= a person with great admiration for himself) *he must be – all these mirrors everywhere.*

nar·cis·sis·tic /£ˌnɑː·sɪˈsɪs·tɪk, $ˌnɑːr·sə-/ *adj* • *a narcissistic personality*

nar·cis·sus /£nɑːˈsɪs·əs, $nɑːr-/ *n* [C] *pl* **narcissuses** or **narcissi** /£nɑːˈsɪs·aɪ, $nɑːr-/ or **narcissus** a yellow, white or orange flower, similar to a DAFFODIL

nar·co·lep·sy /£ˈnɑː·kəʊ·lep·si, $ˈnɑːr·kə-/ *n* [U] a disease or medical condition which makes you sleep a lot
nar·co·lep·tic /£ˌnɑː·kəʊˈlep·tɪk, $ˌnɑːr·kəˈ-/ *n* [C], *adj*

nar·cotic /£nɑːˈkɒt·ɪk, $nɑːrˈkɑːt̬-/ *n* [C] *(esp. Am)* an illegal drug such as HEROIN or COCAINE, or *(medical)* a drug which makes you sleepy and stops you from feeling pain • *(esp. Am) He faces three years in jail for selling narcotics.* • *(medical) Morphine is a narcotic.* • See also NARK POLICE OFFICER. • LP> **Crimes and criminals**
nar·cotic /£nɑːˈkɒt·ɪk, $nɑːrˈkɑːt̬-/ *adj* • *narcotic drugs* • *a narcotic effect*

nark *obj* ANNOY /£nɑːk, $nɑːrk/ *v* [T usually passive] *Br and Aus slang* to annoy (someone) • *His behaviour really narked me.* • *I was/got really narked* **with** *Johnny about the damage to the house.*
nark /£nɑːk, $nɑːrk/ *n* [C] *Aus* • A nark is a person who complains and spoils other people's enjoyment.
nark·y /£ˈnɑː·ki, $ˈnɑːr-/ *adj* **-ier, -iest** *Br slang* • *What a narky* (= bad-tempered) *bastard he is!*

nark CRIMINAL /£nɑːk, $nɑːrk/ *n* [C] *Br dated slang* a person, esp. a criminal, who gives the police information about other criminals • *a* **coppers'** *nark*

nark POLICE OFFICER /£nɑːk, $nɑːrk/, **narc** *n* [C] *Am slang* a police officer whose job is to catch people who produce, sell or use illegal drugs

nar·rate *obj* /£nəˈreɪt $ˈnær·eɪt/ *v* [T] to tell (a story), often by reading aloud from a text, or to describe (events) as they happen • *The documentary is narrated by a well-known actor.* • *One by one the witnesses narrated the sequence of events which led up to the disaster.*
nar·ra·tion /£nəˈreɪ·ʃᵊn, $nærˈeɪ-/ *n* [U] • *Judi Dench did the narration for the documentary* (= she spoke the explanation of the pictures being shown).
nar·ra·tive /£ˈnær·ə·tɪv, $-t̬ɪv/ *n fml* • *It is an almost incredible narrative* (= story) *of wartime adventure.* [C] • *The professor criticized her essay for having too little argument and too much narrative* (= description of events). [U]
nar·rator /£nəˈreɪ·təʳ, $ˈnær·eɪ·t̬ɚ/ *n* [C] • The character who tells you what is happening in a book or film is the narrator: *Annie, the novel's narrator, is a young girl who looks on while the adults around her argue and fight.*

nar·row /£ˈnær·əʊ, $-oʊ/ *adj* **-er, -est** having a small distance from one side to the other esp. in comparison with its length; not wide • *a narrow bridge/passage/gap/room/bed/face* • *The little village has very narrow* **streets**. • *(esp. disapproving)* Narrow also means limited to a small area of interest or thought: *Prices today stayed within a narrow range.* ○ *Such a narrow concept of religion would exclude Buddhism.* ○ *They are unable to see beyond the narrow world of the theatre.* ○ *It was regarded as a very narrow interpretation of the law.* ○ See also **narrow-minded** below. • If you achieve a narrow result, the result could easily have been different because the amount by which you failed or succeeded was very small: *The election was won by the very narrow* **margin** *of only 185 votes.* ○ *The opposition had a narrow* **defeat**. ○ *We got out in time but it was a narrow* **escape** (= we almost did not get out). ○ *We won a narrow* **victory**. • **Narrow boat** is another word for **canal boat**. See at CANAL. Compare BARGE BOAT. • A **narrow-gauge** railway is one with metal tracks that are closer together than the standard British and American distance of 56·5 INCHES. • *(disapproving)* **Narrow-minded** means refusing to try to understand or accept ideas or ways of behaving that are different from their own: *narrow-minded opinions/views* ○ *a narrow-minded person* ○ *The article made free use of stereotypes about the military as being narrow-minded, authoritarian and bigoted.* ○ *They displayed the typical* **narrow-mindedness** *of a small community.* Compare BROADMINDED. • A **narrow squeak** is a success that was almost a failure: *We caught the ferry but it was a narrow squeak.* • Compare BROAD WIDE. • PIC> **Canal**
nar·row *(obj)* /£ˈnær·əʊ, $-oʊ/ *v* • *The road narrows* (= becomes less wide) *after the bridge.* [I] • *He narrowed* (= almost closed) *his* **eyes** *in suspicion.* [T] • *(fig.) The gap between the main contenders for the presidency narrows* (= becomes smaller) *every day.* [I] • *They have narrowed* (= limited) *the focus of the investigation, to concentrate on younger adults.* [T] • To narrow **down** something, such as a list, is to make it smaller and clearer by taking out the least important: *We narrowed the list of candidates down* **from** *ten* **to** *three.* [M]
nar·row·ly /£ˈnær·əʊ·li, $-oʊ-/ *adv* • *She narrowly* (= just) *missed winning an Oscar.* • *(fml) The officer looked at him narrowly* (= carefully) *through half-closed eyes.*
nar·row·ness /£ˈnær·əʊ·nəs, $-oʊ-/ *n* [U] • *The narrowness of the opening prevents people wheeling their bikes through it.*
nar·rows /£ˈnær·əʊz, $-oʊz/ *pl n* • Narrows are a narrow strip of sea: *There is a deep-water channel through the narrows.*

NASA /ˈnæs·ə/ *n* [U not after *the*] *abbreviation for* National Aeronautics and Space Administration (= the US government organization that plans and controls US space travel and the scientific study of space for the US)

nas·al /ˈneɪ·zᵊl/ *adj* of the nose • *nasal passages* • *nasal congestion* • *the nasal cavity* • *a nasal spray* • *(usually disapproving)* If a person's voice is nasal it has a particular sound because air is going through their nose when they speak: *a nasal accent* ○ *She spoke in nasal tones.*
na·sal·ly /ˈneɪ·zᵊl·i/ *adv*

nas·cent /ˈnæs·ᵊnt/ *adj fml* small because only recently formed or started, but likely to grow larger quickly • *a nascent political party* • *a nascent problem* • *a nascent emotion*

na·si gor·eng /£ˌnɑː·zi·gəˈreŋ, $ˌnæz·i-/ *n* [U] an Indonesian rice dish with colourful bits of meat and vegetables added

nas·tur·tium /£nəˈstɜː·ʃᵊm, $-ˈstɜːr-/ *n* [C] a plant with yellow, red or orange flowers and round leaves

nas·ty /£ˈnɑː·sti, $ˈnæs·ti/ *adj* **-ier, -iest** very unpleasant to see, hear, smell, taste, touch or experience • *There's a nasty smell – has someone left the gas on?* • *In an emergency you could get out through a window, but it would be a nasty* (= long and difficult) *drop.* • *He had a nasty* (= bad) *cut above the eye.* • *He shouted a nasty* (= rude) *word at her.* • *The car has a nasty* (= bad) **habit** *of breaking down just when I really need it.* • *What a nasty* **mind** (= a rude or unkind way of thinking) *you have.* • *Unless some action is taken now, the Government could be in for a nasty* **shock/surprise**. • *It's not very good wine – rather* **cheap and** *nasty in fact.* • *The situation could* **turn** (= become) *nasty* (= unpleasant, esp. violent) *at any moment.* • A nasty person is someone who is rude or unpleasant to other people: *The landlord of the pub was really nasty* **to** *John last night.* • If you **have a nasty feeling** about something, you think that it is likely to happen or to be true: *She'd always had a nasty feeling about Geoff, and now events had proved her right to have been suspicious.* ○ *I've got a nasty feeling* **that** *I forgot to tell Joe I couldn't come.* • If you describe someone as **a nasty piece of work** you mean that they are very unpleasant. • *"The life of man, solitary, poor, nasty, brutish and short"* (Thomas Hobbes in his book *Leviathan*, 1651) • *"Something nasty in the woodshed"* (Stella Gibbons in the book *Cold Comfort Farm*, 1932)
nas·ti·ly /£ˈnɑː·stɪ·li, $ˈnæs·tɪ-/ *adv* • *He laughed nastily* (= unkindly) *and walked away.*
nas·ti·ness /£ˈnɑː·stɪ·nəs, $ˈnæs·tɪ-/ *n* [U]

na·tion /ˈneɪ·ʃᵊn/ *n* [C] a country, esp. when thought of as a large group of people living in one area with their own government, language, traditions, etc. • *All the nations of the world will be represented at the conference.* • *The Germans, as a nation, are often thought to be well organized.* • *Practically the whole nation watched the ceremony on television.* • A nation is also a large group of people of the same race who share the same language, traditions and history, but who might not all live in one area: *the Jewish nation* • A **nation state** is an independent country, esp. when thought of as consisting of a single large group of people all sharing the same language, traditions and history. • *"Nation shall speak peace unto nation"* (motto of the BBC) • LP> **Nations and nationalities, World regions**
na·tion·al /ˈnæʃ·ᵊn·ᵊl, ˈnæʃ·nəl/ *adj* [not gradable] • National means relating to or typical of a whole country and its people, rather to part of that country or to other countries: *Britain has more than ten national newspapers.* ○ *The company's national headquarters is in Rome.* ○ *The children were wearing traditional national* **costume/dress**. ○ *Exuberance is regarded as their most endearing national* **characteristic**. ○ *The government's view is that raising taxes now would not be in the national* **interest** (= would not be good for the country). • A **national anthem** is a country's official song which is played and/or sung on public occasions. • In Britain, the **national curriculum** is the set of subjects that all children have to study at school

from age 5 to 16. • A country's **national debt** (*Am also* **public debt**) is the total amount of money that is owed by its government. • In Britain, the **National Front** (*abbreviation* **NF**) is a small political party that believes that only white British people have the right to live in Britain. • *(Br and Aus)* A **national grid** is a system of special wires that take electricity from **power stations** (=places where electricity is made) to all parts of a country. • In Britain, the **National Health (Service)** (*abbreviation* **NHS**) is a system which provides free or cheap medical treatment for everyone, the cost of which is paid from taxes: *a National Health dentist/doctor/hospital* ○ *You'll be able to get treatment* **on** (=paid for by) *the National Health.* • In Britain, **national insurance** is a system of taxation in which the government collects money from companies and workers and makes payments to people who are too old or ill to work or who have no job: *Every month income tax and national insurance* **(contributions)** *are automatically deducted from my pay.* • A **national park** is an area of a country that is protected by the government because of its natural beauty or because it has a special history: *Each year the Snowdonia National Park receives hundreds of thousands of visitors.* • *(Br and Aus)* **National service** (*Am* **selective service** or **draft**) is the system in which young people, esp. men, have to spend a few years being trained in the armed forces: *In some countries they all* **do** *two years' national service after leaving school.* ○ *In Britain, national service was abolished in 1962.* • *(Am)* **National service** is a system in which young people spend a period of time doing useful work for their country, such as repairing old houses, putting out forest fires or teaching children. • **National socialism** is another word for **Nazism**. See at NAZI. • In Britain, the **National Trust** is an organization which owns and takes care of many beautiful and old buildings and beautiful areas of countryside.

na·tion·al /ˈnæʃ·ən·əl, ˈnæʃ·nəl/ *n* [C usually pl] • A national is any person legally recognized as living in and belonging to the country in which they were born or the country they chose to move to, or someone who lives in another country but is legally considered still to belong to the country where they were born: *Thirty people, including six UK nationals, were killed in yesterday's plane crash in the Himalayas.* ○ *All* **foreign** *nationals were advised to leave the country following the outbreak of civil war.*

na·tion·al·i·ty /£ˌnæʃ·ənˈæl·ə·ti, £ˌnæʃˈnæl-, $-ţi/ *n* • *He's applied for British nationality* (=he wants to be officially British). [U] • *What nationality are you* (=Which country do you officially belong to)? [C] • A nationality is also a group of people of the same race, religion, traditions, etc. but not always from a politically independent country: *At the International School they have pupils of 46 different nationalities.* [C]

na·tion·al·ly /ˈnæʃ·ən·əl·i, ˈnæʃ·nə·li/ *adv* • *The party has support regionally* (=in some local areas), *but nationally it's not very important.* • *The group has 3000 members nationally and at least 100 000 internationally.*

na·tion·al·i·sm /ˈnæʃ·ən·əl·ɪ·zəm, ˈnæʃ·nə·lɪ-/ *n* [U] • Nationalism is the desire for and the attempt to achieve political independence for your country or nation: *resurgent nationalism* ○ *Nineteenth-century Italian nationalism culminated in Garibaldi's triumphant creation of an Italian nation state.* • Nationalism is also a great or too great love of your own country: *The book documents the rise of the political right with its accompanying strands of nationalism and racism.*

na·tion·al·ist /ˈnæʃ·ən·əl·ɪst, ˈnæʃ·nə·lɪst/ *n, adj* • Nationalists want political independence for their country: *Scottish/Welsh nationalists* [C] • *a nationalist movement*

na·tion·al·is·tic /ˌnæʃ·ən·əlˈɪs·tɪk, ˌnæʃ·nəˈlɪs·ţɪk/ *adj esp. disapproving* • *They tend to judge things from a very nationalistic viewpoint* (=believing that their own country is more important than others).

na·tion·al·ize *obj, Br and Aus usually* **-ise** /ˈnæʃ·ən·əl·aɪz, ˈnæʃ·nə·laɪz/ *v* [T] (of a government) take control of (a business or industry) • *A socialist government would immediately nationalize the coal and steel industries and the railways.*

na·tion·al·iz·a·tion, *Br and Aus usually* **-i·sa·tion** /ˌnæʃ·ən·əl·aɪˈzeɪ·ʃən, ˌnæʃ·nə·laɪ-/ *n* [U] • *Nationalization of agriculture is on the government's agenda.*

na·tion·wide /ˌneɪ·ʃənˈwaɪd/ *adj* [not gradable] existing or happening in all parts of a particular country • *a nationwide network/chain of shops* • *a nationwide survey/referendum* • *nationwide indignation*

na·tion·wide /ˌneɪ·ʃənˈwaɪd/ *adv* [not gradable] • *Schools nationwide report increasing numbers of pupils staying on at school after they are 16.* • *The company plans to* **go** *nationwide very shortly, with new branches in every major city.*

na·tive /£ˈneɪ·tɪv, $-ţɪv/ *adj* [not gradable] relating to the country or place where you were born, or (of plants and animals) growing naturally in a place, rather than brought from somewhere else • *She returned to live and work in her native Japan.* • *After stepping off the plane she knelt down to kiss her native soil.* • *Henderson Island in the Pacific has more than 55 species of native flowering plants.* See also INDIGENOUS. • *French is his native* **language/tongue.** • *The horse is not native* **to** *America – it was introduced by the Spanish.* • A native ability or characteristic is one that a person or thing has naturally and is part of their basic character: *His native stupidity will never be affected or changed by further education.* See also INNATE. • A **Native American** is a member of one of the races who were living in N America before the Europeans arrived: *There are over 1·5 million Native Americans in the United States today.* ○ *Films that deal more sensitively with Native American history are replacing the clichés of 'Red Indians' and 'Cowboys.'* • A **native speaker** is someone who has spoken a particular language since they were a baby, rather than having learnt it as a child or adult: *All the teachers are native speakers of English.* ○ *Native-speaker dictionaries are quite different from those intended for the foreign learner of English.*

na·tive /£ˈneɪ·tɪv, $-ţɪv/ *n* [C] • *The missing man is believed to be a native* **of** *Monaco* (=person born in Monaco). • *(humorous) He asked me in the pub if I was a native, so I confessed I was from Coventry, not a local girl.* • Native is also used of a person who lives in a simple and traditional way in a country considered to be less developed than the speaker's own country. This usage is increasingly considered offensive: *a native village* ○ *native customs and traditions* ○ *In this small African city, the white European workers didn't mix with 'the natives,' as they called the local people.* • *(infml disapproving or humorous)* If a person who is in a foreign country **goes native**, they begin to live and/or dress like the people who live there: *The first guy they sent out to do a deal with the local people went native, took a wife and never came back.*

na·tiv·i·ty /£nəˈtɪv·ɪ·ti, $-ə·ţi/ *n* [U] **the nativity** the birth of Jesus Christ, which is celebrated by Christians at Christmas • A **nativity play** is a play which tells the story of Jesus Christ's birth, usually performed by children at Christmas time.

NATO, Nato /£ˈneɪ·təʊ, $-ţoʊ/ *n* [U not after *the*] *abbreviation for* North Atlantic Treaty Organization (=an international military organization consisting of the US, Canada, Britain and 13 other European countries, formed in 1949 to improve the defence of Western Europe) • *The president's speech came at the opening session of the two-day NATO summit in Rome.*

nat·ter /£ˈnæt·əʳ, $ˈnæţ·ɚ/ *v* [I] *infml* to talk continuously for a long time without any particular purpose • *Once he starts nattering you just can't stop him.* • *My mother and her friends natter* **away** *on the phone all evening.*

nat·ter /£ˈnæt·əʳ, $ˈnæţ·ɚ/ *n* [C] *infml* • *We* **had** *a long natter over coffee.*

nat·ty /£ˈnæt·i, $ˈnæţ-/ *adj* **-ier, -iest** *infml dated* stylish and tidy in every detail • *That's a natty little sports car you've got there!* • *He's always been a natty* **dresser.**

nat·ti·ly /£ˈnæt·ɪ·li, $ˈnæţ-/ *adv infml dated* • *You're very nattily dressed today!*

na·tur·al [EXPECTED] /£ˈnætʃ·ər·əl, $ˈ-ɚ-/ *adj* to be expected; usual • *Of course you're upset about your dog's death – that's only natural.* • **It's** *natural* **that** *you should feel upset when you first leave home – that's an entirely natural reaction.* [+ *that* clause] • **It's** *quite natural* **to** *experience a few doubts just before you get married.* [+ *to* infinitive] • See also **natural** at NATURE [LIFE].

na·tur·al·ly /£ˈnætʃ·ər·əl·i, $ˈ-ɚ-/ *adv* • *Naturally* (=As is to be expected) *we want to see as few job losses in the industry as possible.* • *"You will try to be tactful when you explain to her why she hasn't been invited, won't you?" "Naturally* (=Yes, obviously)."

na·tur·al [MUSIC] /£ˈnætʃ·ər·əl, $ˈ-ɚ-/ *adj* [after n; not gradable] (of a musical note) not SHARP or FLAT • *E natural* • See also **natural** at NATURE [LIFE]. • [PIC] **Music**

NATIONS AND NATIONALITIES

The following list includes all countries recognised as members by the United Nations. The language(s) given are the official languages. See the notes below for an explanation of the ADJECTIVE and PERSON columns.

COUNTRY	ADJECTIVE	PERSON	MONEY	LANGUAGE(S)
Afghanistan	Afghan	Afghan, Afghani	afghani	Pushtu, Dari (Persian)
Albania	Albanian		lek	Albanian
Algeria	Algerian		Algerian dinar	Arabic
Andorra	Andorran		peseta and franc	Catalan
Angola	Angolan		new kwanza	Portuguese
Antigua & Barbuda	Antiguan		E. Caribbean dollar	English
Argentina	Argentine, Argentinian		Argentinian peso	Spanish
Armenia	Armenian		manat	Armenian
Australia	Australian		Austr. dollar	English
Austria	Austrian		Schilling	German
Azerbaijan	Azerbaijani		manat	Azeri
Bahamas	Bahamian		Bahamian dollar	English
Bahrain	Bahrain		Bahrain dinar	Arabic
Bangladesh	Bangladesh Bangladeshi	Bangladeshi	taka	Bengali
Barbados	Barbadian		Barbados dollar	English
Belarus (Belorussia)	Belorussian		Belorussian rouble	Belorussian
Belgium	Belgian		Belgian franc	Flemish/Dutch, French, German
Belize	Belizean		Belize dollar	English
Benin	Beninese		CFA franc	French
Bhutan	Bhutanese		ngultrum	Dzongkha
Bolivia	Bolivian		boliviano	Quechua, Ayamara, Spanish
Bosnia and Herzegovina	Bosnian		dinar	Serbo-Croat
Botswana	Motswana *(pl)* Batswana		pula	English
Brazil	Brazilian		real	Portuguese
Brunei	Bruneian		Brunei dollar	Malay
Bulgaria	Bulgarian		lev	Bulgarian
Burkina Faso	Burkinabe		CFA franc	French
Burundi	Burundi	Burundian	Burundi franc	French, Kirundi
Cambodia	Cambodian		riel	Khmer
Cameroon	Cameroonian		CFA franc	French, English
Canada	Canadian		Canadian dollar	English, French
Cape Verde	Cape Verdean		CV escudo	Portuguese
Central African Republic	Central African		CFA franc	French
Chad	Chadian		CFA franc	Arabic, French
Chile	Chilean		Chilean peso	Spanish
China	Chinese		renminbi yuan	Chinese (Mandarin, Putonghua), Cantonese (Yue)
Colombia	Colombian		Colombian peso	Spanish
Comoros	Comoran		CFA franc	Arabic, French
Congo	Congolese Congo	Congolese	CFA franc	French
Costa Rica	Costa Rican		CR colón	Spanish
Côte d'Ivoire (Ivory Coast)	Ivorian		CFA franc	French
Croatia	Croatian	Croat	dinar	Serbo-Croat
Cuba	Cuban		Cuban peso	Spanish
Cyprus	Cypriot		Cyprus pound	Greek, Turkish
Czech Republic	Czech		koruna	Czech
Denmark	Danish	Dane	Danish krone	Danish
Djibouti	Djiboutian		Djibouti franc	Arabic
Dominica	Dominican		E Caribbean dollar	English
Dominican Republic	Dominican		Dominican peso	Spanish
Ecuador	Ecuadorian		sucre	Spanish
Egypt	Egyptian		Egyptian pound	Arabic
El Salvador	Salvadoran		colón	Spanish
Equatorial Guinea	Equatorial Guinean		CFA franc	Spanish
Eritrea	Eritrean		birr	Amharic
Estonia	Estonian		kroon	Estonian
Ethiopia	Ethiopian		Ethiopian birr	Amharic
Fiji	Fijian		Fiji dollar	English
Finland	Finnish	Finn	markka	Finnish, Swedish
France	French	French(wo)man	French franc	French
Gabon	Gabonese		CFA franc	French
Gambia, the Gambia	Gambian		dalasi	English
Georgia	Georgian		rouble	Georgian
Germany	German		Deutsche Mark	German
Ghana	Ghanaian		cedi	English

COUNTRY	ADJECTIVE	PERSON	MONEY	LANGUAGE(S)
Greece	Greek		drachma	Greek
Grenada	Grenadan		E Caribbean dollar	English
Guatemala	Guatemalan		quetzal	Spanish
Guinea	Guinean		Guinean franc	French
Guinea-Bissau	Guinea-Bissauan		G-B peso	Portuguese
Guyana	Guyanese		Guyana dollar	English
Haiti	Haitian		gourde	French
Honduras	Honduran		lempira	Spanish
Hungary	Hungarian		forint	Hungarian (Magyar)
Iceland	Icelandic	Icelander	króna	Icelandic
India	Indian		Indian rupee	Hindi, English
Indonesia	Indonesian		Indon. rupiah	Indonesian
Iran	Iranian		Iranian rial	Farsi
Iraq	Iraqi		Iraqi dinar	Arabic
Ireland	Irish	Irish(wo)man	Irish pound / punt	English, Irish Gaelic
(Eire or the Irish Republic) Notice that Northern Ireland is part of the United Kingdom				
Israel	Israeli		new Israeli shekel	Hebrew, Arabic
Italy	Italian		lira (*pl* lire)	Italian
Jamaica	Jamaican		Jamaican dollar	English
Japan	Japanese		yen	Japanese
Jordan	Jordanian		Jordanian dinar	Arabic
Kazakhstan	Kazakhstani		rouble	Kazakh
Kenya	Kenyan		Kenyan shilling	Swahili, English
South/North Korea	South/North Korean		won	Korean
Kuwait	Kuwaiti		Kuwaiti dinar	Arabic
Kyrgyz Republic	Kyrgystanian		rouble	Kyrgyz
Laos	Lao, Laotian	Lao	kip	Lao
Latvia	Latvian		Latvian rouble	Latvian
Lebanon	Lebanese		Lebanese pound	Arabic
Lesotho	Mosotho, *(pl)* Basotho		loti (*pl* maloti)	English, Sesotho
Liberia	Liberian		Liberian dollar	English
Libya	Libyan		Libyan dinar	Arabic
Liechtenstein	Liechtenstein	Liechtensteiner	Swiss franc	German
Lithuania	Lithuanian		rouble	Lithuanian
Luxembourg	Luxembourg	Luxembourger	Luxembourg franc	French, German, Letzeburgish
Macedonia (the former Yugoslav Republic of Macedonia)	Macedonian		dinar	Macedonian
Madagascar	Malagasy		Madag. franc	Malagasy
Malawi	Malawian		kwacha	English, Chichewa
Malaysia	Malaysian		M. dollar (ringgit)	Malay
Maldives	Maldivian		rufiyaa	Dhivehi
Mali	Malian		CFA franc	French
Marshall Islands	Marshallese		US dollar	Marshallese
Mauritania	Mauritanian		ouguiyja	Arabic
Mauritius	Mauritian		M. rupee	English
Mexico	Mexican		Mexican peso	Spanish
Micronesia	Micronesian		US dollar	English
Moldova	Moldovan		rouble	Moldovan
Monaco	Monacan, Monegasque		French franc	French
Mongolia	Mongolian	Mongol	tugrik	Khalka Mongol
Morocco	Moroccan		M. dirham	Arabic
Mozambique	Mozambican		metical	Portuguese
Myanmar (Burma)	Burmese		kyat	Burmese
Namibia	Namibian		S African rand	English
Nepal	Nepalese		Nepalese rupee	Nepali
the Netherlands (Holland)	Dutch	Dutch(wo)man	guilder	Dutch
New Zealand	New Zealand	New Zealander	NZ dollar	English, Maori
Nicaragua	Nicaraguan		new córdoba	Spanish
Niger	Nigerien		CFA franc	French
Nigeria	Nigerian		naira	English
Norway	Norwegian		N. krone	Norwegian
Oman	Omani		Omani rial	Arabic
Pakistan	Pakistani		Pakistan rupee	Urdu, English
Panama	Panamanian		balboa	Spanish
Papua New Guinea	Papua New Guinean		kina	English, Motu
Paraguay	Paraguayan		guarani	Spanish
Peru	Peruvian		new sol	Spanish, Quechua
the Philippines	Philippine	Filipino	Philippine peso	Pilipino (Tagalog), English
Poland	Polish	Pole	zloty	Polish
Portugal	Portuguese		escudo	Portuguese
Qatar	Qatari		Qatari ryal	Arabic
Romania (also Roumania, Rumania)	Romanian		leu (*pl* lei)	Romanian

COUNTRY	ADJECTIVE	PERSON	MONEY	LANGUAGE(S)
Russia (Russian Federation)	Russian		rouble	Russian
Rwanda	Rwandan		Rwanda franc	French, Kinyarwanda
Saint Kitts & Nevis	Kittsian, Nevisian		E Caribbean dollar	English
Saint Lucia	Saint Lucian		E Caribbean dollar	English
Saint Vincent & the Grenadines			E Caribbean dollar	English
Samoa	Samoan		tala	Samoan, English
San Marino	Sanmarinese		Italian lira	Italian
São Tomé & Príncipe	São Toméan		dobra	Portuguese
Saudi Arabia	Saudi, Saudi Arabian		SA riyal	Arabic
Senegal	Senegalese		CFA franc	French
Seychelles	Seychelles	Seychellois	Seychelles rupee	Creole
Sierra Leone	Sierra Leonean		leone	English
Singapore	Singaporean		S. dollar (ringgit)	English, Malay, Chinese, Tamil
the Slovak Republic	Slovak		Slovak crown	Slovak
Slovenia	Slovene, Slovenian		tolar	Slovene, Serbo-Croat
the Solomon Islands	Solomon Islander		SI dollar	English
Somalia	Somali, Somalian		Somali shilling	Somali, Arabic
South Africa	South African		rand	English, Afrikaans
Spain	Spanish	Spaniard	peseta	Spanish
Sri Lanka (Ceylon)	Sri Lankan (Ceylonese)		Sri L. rupee	Sinhala, Tamil
the Sudan	Sudanese		Sudanese pound	Arabic
Suriname	Surinamese	Surinamer	S. guilder/florin	Dutch
Swaziland	Swazi		lilangeni	English, Siswati
Sweden	Swedish	Swede	Swedish krona	Swedish
Switzerland	Swiss		Swiss franc	German, French, Italian, Romansch
Syria	Syrian		Syrian pound	Arabic
Taiwan	Taiwanese	Taiwanese	new Taiwan dollar	Mandarin Chinese
Tajikistan	Tajikistani		rouble	Tajik
Tanzania	Tanzanian		Tanz. shilling	Swahili, English
Thailand	Thai		baht	Thai
Togo	Togolese		CFA franc	French
Trinidad & Tobago	Trinidadian, Tobagonian		T. & T. dollar	English
Tunisia	Tunisian		Tunisian dinar	Arabic
Turkey	Turkish	Turk	Turkish lira	Turkish
Turkmenistan	Turkmenistani		manat	Turkmenian
Uganda	Ugandan		Ugandan shilling	English
Ukraine	Ukrainian		hryvna	Ukrainain
United Arab Emirates	Emirian		UAE dirham	Arabic
the United Kingdom	British	Briton	pound sterling	English
the United States	American, US	American	US dollar	English
Uruguay	Uruguayan		new U peso	Spanish
Uzbekistan	Uzbekistani		rouble	Uzbek
Vanuatu	Vanuatuan		vatu	English, French, Bislama
Venezuela	Venezuelan		bolivar	Spanish
Vietnam	Vietnamese		dông	Vietnamese
Yemen	Yemeni		Yemeni riyal	Arabic
Yugoslavia	Yugoslavian	Yugoslav	Yug. dinar	Serbo-Croat
Zaïre	Zaïrean		zaïre	French
Zambia	Zambian		kwacha	English
Zimbabwe	Zimbabwean		Zimb. dollar	English

Notes

- For most countries, the ADJECTIVE in column two is also used as a noun to refer to people from that country. You can use it to talk about a particular group of people: *I was chatting to a couple of* **Australians** *on the train*, or to all the people in general belonging to a country: **Tanzanians** *gained their independence in 1961.* Sometimes there is a special noun for people from a country (see column three, PERSON): *"Have you ever met any* **Finns***?" "Yes, I shared a house with a Finnish student once."*
- Nouns ending in *-ese, -ish, -s* or *-ch* do not change in the plural *Three* **Chinese** *and two* **Swiss** *came to the meeting.* • *The* **Dutch** *are generous people.*
- The United Kingdom is made up of Great Britain and Northern Ireland. Great Britain is made up of England, Scotland and Wales, so that Scottish and Welsh people are also British, but not English. LP **World regions** at WORLD for other geographical areas.
- The Soviet Union or USSR no longer exists, though some of its republics belong to the CIS (Commonwealth of Independent States).

na·tur·al·ize *obj, Br and Aus usually* **-ise** /£ˈnætʃ·ᵊr·ᵊl·aɪz, $-ɚ·rə·laɪz/ *v* [T often passive] to make (someone) a legal CITIZEN of a country that they were not born in • *She has lived in the States for a long time, and recently she was naturalized.*

na·tur·al·ized, *Br and Aus usually* **-ised** /£ˈnætʃ·ᵊr·ᵊl·aɪzd, $-ɚ·rə·laɪzd/ *adj* [not gradable] • *He's a naturalized Australian citizen.*

na·tur·al·iz·a·tion, *Br and Aus usually* **-i·sa·tion** /£ˌnætʃ·ᵊr·ᵊl·aɪˈzeɪ·ʃᵊn, $-ɚ·rə·lɪ-/ *n* [U]

na·ture LIFE /£ˈneɪ·tʃəʳ, $-tʃɚ/ *n* [U not after *the*] all the animals, plants, rocks, etc. in the world and all the features, forces and processes that happen or exist independently of people, such as the weather, the sea, mountains, reproduction and growth • *Even as a child he loved nature, and enjoyed being in the countryside surrounded by animals.* • *This new technique of artificially growing cells copies what actually happens* **in nature**. • *She's very interested in nature articles/books/programmes.* • Nature is often used to refer to the force that is responsible for physical life and is sometimes spoken of as a person: *Feeling tired-out is Nature's* **way** *of telling you to* *rest.* • To go/get **back to nature** is to live a more simple life using fewer artificial or processed products: *They moved out of the city and went to live on a farm so that they could* **get** *back to nature.* ○ *Some of our friends laugh at our back-to-nature lifestyle, but we enjoy it.* • *He could be kept alive artificially, but I think it would be kinder to* **allow nature to/let nature take its course** (=allow him to die). • A **nature reserve** is an area of land which is protected in order to keep safe the animals and plants that live there, often because they are rare. • *(Aus)* A **nature strip** is a strip of grass, and often trees and other plants, which separates a path used by walkers from the part of a road used by vehicles. • A **nature trail** is a path through an area of the countryside which is intended to attract the walker's attention to interesting plants, animals and other features. • *"Nature red in tooth and claw"* (Alfred, Lord Tennyson in the poem *In Memoriam*, 1850) • ⓘ

na·tur·al /£ˈnætʃ·ər·əl, $ˈ-ɚ-/ *adj* • Natural means not involving anything made by people: *That's the wool in its natural state before it's spun and dyed.* ○ *People say that breast-feeding is better than bottle-feeding because it's more natural.* ○ **It's** *not natural* **for a woman** *to be so thin!* [+ *to* infinitive] • *He died from natural* **causes** (=because he was old or ill and not because he was killed in an accident or killed himself) • *Floods and earthquakes are natural* **disasters** (=are caused by nature and not by people.) • A natural ability or characteristic is one that you were born with: *He has a natural talent for sports.* ○ *She's a natural leader.* ○ *You shouldn't wear so much make-up – it spoils your natural beauty.* ○ *She's a natural blonde* (=her hair is not artificially made a lighter colour). • A person's natural mother and father are the parents who caused them to be born, although they might not be their legal parents or the parents who raised them. See Language Portrait **Relationships** at RELATE. • If food or drink is described as natural, it is generally because it is pure and has no chemical substances added to it and is therefore thought to be healthy: *natural mineral water* ○ *Our products are prepared using only the finest natural ingredients.* • **Natural childbirth** is a method of giving birth in which special preparation and breathing exercises are used to make the birth easier, instead of drugs. • **Natural gas** is gas, found underground, which is used as a fuel. • **Natural history** is the study of plants, animals, rocks, etc.: *We went to see the dinosaur skeletons in the Natural History Museum.* • **Natural language** is language which has developed in the usual way as a method of communicating between people: *Computers are increasingly being used for natural language* **processing**. • **Natural resources** are materials such as coal and wood which exist or are produced in nature and can be used by people: *It's a country which is very rich in natural resources.* • **Natural science** (also **natural sciences**) is biology, physics and chemistry considered together as a subject. • **Natural selection** is the process which results in the continued existence of only the types of animals and plants which are best able to produce young or new plants in the conditions in which they live. • *(Br)* **Natural wastage** (also **wastage**, *Am and Aus* **attrition**) is a reduction in the number of people who work for an organization which is achieved by not replacing those people who leave. • See also NATURAL [EXPECTED], NATURAL [MUSIC].

na·tur·al /£ˈnætʃ·ər·əl, $ˈ-ɚ-/ *n* [C] *infml* • If a person is a natural, they were born with the right characteristics or abilities for doing something: *She won't have any troubles learning to ride a horse – you can see she's a natural.*

Nat·ur·a·li·sm /£ˈnætʃ·ər·əl·ɪ·zəm, $-ɚ·rə·lɪ-/ *n* [U] • In art and literature, Naturalism is the style of showing people and experiences as they really are, instead of suggesting that they are better than they really are or representing them in a fixed style: *Strindberg, Ibsen and Chekhov are a few of the dramatists who were influenced by Naturalism.*

na·tur·al·ist /£ˈnætʃ·ər·əl·ɪst, $ˈ-ɚ-/ *n* [C] • A naturalist is a person who studies and knows a lot about plants and animals. • A Naturalist is also a person who writes, paints, etc. in the style of Naturalism.

na·tur·al·is·tic /£ˌnætʃ·ər·əlˈɪs·tɪk, $-ɚ·rəˈlɪs·t̬ɪk/, **na·tur·al·ist** /£ˈnætʃ·ər·əl·ɪst, $-ɚ·rə·lɪst/ *adj* • *The aquarium will be rebuilt to display freshwater and marine life in more naturalistic* (=similar to what exists in nature) *settings.* • *He is a Naturalistic dramatist/painter/writer.*

na·tur·al·ly /£ˈnætʃ·ər·əl·i, $ˈ-ɚ-/ *adv* • *A healthy body will be able to fight off the illness naturally* (=without involving anything made by people) *without the use of medicine.* • *I didn't try to lose weight – it just happened naturally after I'd had my baby.* • *He's naturally funny* (=He was born with this characteristic) *– he doesn't even have to try.* • *You don't have to be naturally talented to play a musical instrument – it's something you can learn.* • If a particular skill **comes** naturally (**to** you) you are able to do it easily, without much effort or learning: *Dancing seemed to come naturally to her.* ○ *I've had to concentrate very hard on learning to drive – it didn't come naturally to me.*

na·tur·al·ness /£ˈnætʃ·ər·əl·nəs, $ˈ-ɚ-/ *n* [U] • *The film tries to compare the naturalness and simplicity of childhood with the artifice and complexity of adult life.*

na·ture [TYPE] /£ˈneɪ·tʃər, $-tʃɚ/ *n* the type or main characteristic (of something) • *I have a problem of a rather delicate nature that I'd like to discuss with you in private.* [C] • *The severity of the punishment depends very much on the nature* **of** *the crime.* [C] • *It's the nature* **of** *linen* **to** *crumple easily.* [C + *to* infinitive] • *Motor-racing is* **by** *nature a dangerous sport.* [U] • *There are problems in every relationship – it's* **in the nature of things** (=it is usual and to be expected). • If you say that something is **the nature of the beast**, you mean that that is what it is like or what it involves: *Owning a car involves a lot of expense – that's the nature of the beast.* • ⓘ

na·ture [CHARACTER] /£ˈneɪ·tʃər, $-tʃɚ/ *n* the character (of a person) • *As a child she had a lovely sunny nature – everyone loved her.* [C] • **It's** *not really* **in her nature** *to be aggressive.* [C + *to* infinitive] • *He is* **by** *nature inclined to be rather lazy.* [U] • *She's very cheerful* **in** *nature.* [U] • ⓘ

-na·tured /£-neɪ·tʃəd, $-tʃɚd/ *combining form* • *He's such a good-natured/sweet-natured little boy.*

na·tur·ist /£ˈneɪ·tʃər·ɪst, $-tʃɚ-/ *n* [C] *fml* a NUDIST (=a person who sometimes wears no clothes because they think that this is healthy) • *Naturists believe that being naked encourages acceptance of and respect for the human body*

na·tur·i·sm /£ˈneɪ·tʃər·ɪ·zəm, $-tʃɚ-/ *n* [U]

naught [NOTHING] /£nɔːt, $nɑːt/, **nought** *n* [U] *old use or literary* nothing • *All our efforts were* **for** *naught.* • *There was naught* **to** *comfort them in what she said.* [+ *to* infinitive] • *His promises* **counted** *for naught.* • *All their plans* **came to** *naught* (=did not achieve anything).

naught [ZERO] /£nɔːt, $nɑːt/ *n* [U] *Am and Aus for* NOUGHT [ZERO]

naught·y [BADLY BEHAVED] /£ˈnɔː·ti, $ˈnɑː·t̬i/ *adj* **-ier, -iest** (esp. of children) behaving badly and not being obedient, or (of behaviour) bad • Naughty is usually used when talking to children: *You're a very naughty girl, pulling the head off your sister's doll!* ○ *Now that's naughty* (=bad) *– you mustn't throw food on the floor!* • *Our boss treats us all like naughty schoolchildren.* • Naughty can be used humorously to describe adults or their actions: *"I'm afraid I borrowed your book without asking." "Yes, that was very naughty of you – I needed it at the weekend!"* • *"Naughty but nice"* (advertisement for cream cakes, 1980s)

naught·i·ly /£ˈnɔː·tɪ·li, $ˈnɑː·t̬ɪ-/ *adv*

naught·i·ness /£ˈnɔː·tɪ·nəs, $ˈnɑː·t̬ɪ-/ *n* [U]

naught·y [SEXUAL] /£ˈnɔː·ti, $ˈnɑː·t̬i/ *adj* **-ier, -iest** *infml humorous* involving or suggesting sex; sexual • *The film was shown on television but they'd cut out all the naughty scenes/(Br) bits.* • *He always buys her naughty underwear for her birthday.*

naught·i·ly /£ˈnɔː·tɪ·li, $ˈnɑː·t̬ɪ-/ *adv infml usually humorous*

naught·i·ness /£ˈnɔː·tɪ·nəs, $ˈnɑː·t̬ɪ-/ *n* [U] *infml usually humorous*

nau·se·a /£ˈnɔː·zi·ə, £-ʒə, $ˈnɑː-/ *n* [U] a feeling of illness in the stomach, often making you feel as if you are going to vomit • *If I miss breakfast, I always suffer from nausea in the middle of the morning.* • [LP] **Feelings and pains**

nau·se·ate *obj* /£ˈnɔː·zi·eɪt, $ˈnɑː-/ *v* [T often passive] *fml* • *He is nauseated* (=made to feel ill) *by the smell of meat cooking.*

nau·se·at·ing /£ˈnɔː·zi·eɪ·tɪŋ, $ˈnɑː·zi·eɪ·t̬ɪŋ/ *adj* • Something which is nauseating makes you feel as if you are going to vomit: *There was a nauseating smell of blood/rotting food.* • *(fig.) Her strongest criticism was reserved for the prime minister whom she accused of 'nauseating* (=extremely unpleasant) *hypocrisy'.* • *(fig. esp. humorous) She's good at everything she does – it's quite nauseating* (=other people don't like it, esp. because they wish that they had the same qualities)*!*

nau·se·at·ing·ly /£ˈnɔː·zi·eɪ·tɪŋ·li, $ˈnɑː·zi·eɪ·t̬ɪŋ-/ *adv* • *(fig. esp. humorous) I detest the sort of ads that use nauseatingly* (= in a way that I do not like) *cute children and animals.*

nau·se·ous /£ˈnɔː·zi·əs, £-ʒəs, $ˈnɑː·ʃəs/ *adj* • If you feel nauseous, you feel as if you might vomit: *After only half an hour on the boat she began to feel slightly nauseous.* • *(fig.) Wearing a nauseous* (= extremely unattractive) *combination of green and yellow, the bride's mother stood up to make a speech.*

nau·se·ous·ly /£ˈnɔː·zi·ə·sli, £-ʒə·sli, $ˈnɑː·ʃə-/ *adv*

nau·se·ous·ness /£ˈnɔː·zi·ə·snəs, £-ʒə·snəs, $ˈnɑː·ʃə·snəs/ *n* [U]

nau·ti·cal /£ˈnɔː·tɪ·kᵊl, $ˈnɑː·t̬i-/ *adj* [not gradable] relating to ships, sailing or sailors • *You're looking very nautical in your navy blue sweater.* • A **nautical mile** (also **sea mile**) is a unit of distance used at sea which is equal to 1852 metres. Compare MILE. • Ⓖⓡ

nau·ti·cal·ly /£ˈnɔː·tɪ·kli, $ˈnɑː·t̬i-/ *adv* [not gradable]

na·val /ˈneɪ·vᵊl/ *adj* [not gradable] See at NAVY

nave /neɪv/ *n* [C] the long central part of a church, often with AISLES (= long passages) on both sides

na·vel /ˈneɪ·vᵊl/, *infml* **bel·ly but·ton, tum·my but·ton** *n* [C] the small round part in the middle of the stomach which is left after the UMBILICAL CORD (= long tube of flesh joining the baby to its mother) has been cut at birth • *We can't afford to spend all this time* **contemplating/gazing at/staring at** *our* **navels** (= thinking deeply about ourselves and our intentions) – *we need to take action.*

nav·i·ga·ble /ˈnæv·ɪ·gə·bl̩/ *adj* (of an area of water) deep, wide or safe enough for a boat to go through • *That stretch of river is too shallow to be navigable.*

nav·i·ga·bil·i·ty /£ˌnæv·ɪ·gəˈbɪl·ɪ·ti, $-ə·t̬i/ *n* [U]

nav·i·gate *(obj)* /ˈnæv·ɪ·geɪt/ *v* to direct the way that (a ship, aircraft, etc.) will travel, or to find a direction across, along or over (an area of water or land) • *Sailors have special equipment to help them navigate.* [I] • *Radio signals are used for navigating both ships and aircraft.* [T] • *We couldn't navigate* (= find a direction along) *such a wide river in our small boat.* [T] • *Some birds can navigate* (= find a direction across) *distances of 1000 miles or more and return to the place they had started from the next year.* [T] • A passenger in a car navigates by telling the driver the direction in which they must drive, usually using a map to plan the way. [I]

nav·i·ga·tion /ˌnæv·ɪˈgeɪ·ʃᵊn/ *n* [U] • *In the past, navigation depended largely on the position of the stars.* • *Very severe storms had caused difficulties in the navigation of the plane.* • Ⓔ

nav·i·ga·tion·al /ˌnæv·ɪˈgeɪ·ʃᵊn·ᵊl/ *adj* [not gradable] • *navigational errors*

nav·i·gat·or /£ˈnæv·ɪ·geɪ·təʳ, $-t̬ɚ/ *n* [C] • A navigator is a person in a vehicle who decides on the direction in which the vehicle travels.

nav·vy /ˈnæv·i/ *n* [C] *Br infml dated* a man who is employed to do unskilled physical work, usually building or making roads

na·vy /ˈneɪ·vi/ *n* [C + sing/pl v] the part of a country's armed forces which is trained to operate at sea • *My brother is in* **the** *Navy.* • *There are plans to reduce* **the** *navy by a quarter.* • **The** *Navy has/have announced that one of its/their bases is to be closed.*

na·val /ˈneɪ·vᵊl/ *adj* [not gradable] • Naval means belonging to a country's navy, or relating to military ships: *a naval officer* • *naval forces* • *a naval* (= relating to military ships) *museum/battle*

na·vy (blue) /ˈneɪ·vi/ *adj* [not gradable], *n* dark blue • *He was wearing a navy sweater.* • *He was wearing a sweater of a dark navy blue.* [C] • *I prefer navy to black.* [U]

nay [EVEN MORE] /neɪ/ *adv* [not gradable] *fml* even more; greater than that • Nay is used to introduce a second, and more extreme descriptive phrase in a sentence when the first phrase was not strong enough: *It is my pleasure, nay (my) privilege, to introduce to you on the show tonight one of the greatest entertainers in show-business.*

nay [NO] /neɪ/ *adv* [not gradable] *old use or regional* no • *Nay lass, don't cry.*

Na·zi /ˈnɑːt·si/ *n* [C] a member of the FASCIST National Socialist (Workers') Party which, led by Adolf Hitler, controlled Germany from 1933 to 1945, or someone now who has the same political beliefs, esp. that their own race is better than others

Na·zi /ˈnɑːt·si/ *adj* [not gradable] • *a Nazi officer* • *Nazi Germany*

Na·zi·sm, Na·zi·i·sm /ˈnɑːt·sɪ·zᵊm/ *n* [U]

NB /ˌenˈbiː/ *exclamation abbreviation for* nota bene (= Latin for 'notice especially'). It is written before something important to make the reader take notice of it. • *NB Any applications received after the closing date will not be accepted.*

NC-17 /ˌen·siˌsev·ənˈtiːn/ *n* [C], *adj* [not gradable] *Am* (a film) containing clearly shown sexual acts and/or a great deal of violence which is not considered suitable for children under the age of 17 • *Dad wouldn't let us go to the film because it was an NC-17.* • *The producers were unwilling to make cuts that were needed to avoid an NC-17 rating.* • Compare G [FILM], PG, U [FILM], X [FILM].

NCO /£ˌen·siːˈəʊ, $-ˈoʊ/ *n* [C] *pl* **NCOs** *abbreviation for* non-commissioned officer (= a member of the military forces who has achieved the rank of officer (usually CORPORAL or SERGEANT) by rising from the lower ranks rather than by receiving a COMMISSION) • See also **commissioned officer** at COMMISSION [MILITARY].

NE *n* [U], *adj* [not gradable] *abbreviation for* NORTHEAST or NORTHEASTERN

NEA /ˌen·iːˈeɪ/ *n* [U] **the NEA** *abbreviation for* the National Education Association (= a large organization of American teachers) • *The headquarters of the NEA is in Washington DC.*

ne·an·der·thal /£niːˈæn·dəˈtɑːl, $-dɚ-/ *adj* of a type of PRIMITIVE people who lived in Europe and Asia in the past, or *(fig.)* (of people or beliefs) very old-fashioned and strongly against social and political change • *(fig.) He criticized what he described as the 'neanderthal tendencies' of the right wing of the party.* • **Neanderthal man** was a type of PRIMITIVE people who lived mainly in Europe and Asia 250 000 to 30 000 years ago.

near (-er, -est) /£nɪəʳ, $nɪr/, **near to** *prep* close to; not far away in distance, time or relationship from • *Is there a train station near here?* • *Don't come too near me – you might catch my cold.* • *We live quite near* **(to)** *a school.* • *He asked her to come and sit nearer* **(to)** *him.* • *Which bus stop is nearest* **(to)** *your house?* • *I shan't be home till some time near midnight.* • *I was near* **(to)** *tears* (= almost cried) *at one point during the film.* • *He came near* **to** *punching him* (= almost punched him)*!* • **Nothing/Not anything near** means a long way from (something) in relationship: *What he said was nothing near the truth.* • **Nowhere/Not anywhere near** means a long way from (something) in distance, time or relationship: *The house was nowhere near the sea.* ○ *It's nowhere near time for us to leave yet.* ○ *I'm nowhere near finishing the book – I'm only half-way through it.* [+ v-ing]

near /£nɪəʳ, $nɪr/ *adv* [after v] **-er, -est** • *I wish we lived nearer – we'd see much more of each other.* • *I was standing just near enough to hear what they were saying.* • *As the wedding* **drew/got** *nearer, she started to feel nervous.* • *I like to have my books* **near at hand** (= where I can reach them) *when I'm working.* • *(infml) They're the same age or* **near enough** (= almost the same age). • *A student grant is* **nowhere/not anywhere near** (= is certainly not) *enough to live on.* • *He's* **nowhere/not anywhere near** *as/so tall as his sister* (= his sister is much taller than him).

near /£nɪəʳ, $nɪr/ *adj* [before n] **-er, -est** • *"Do you know Jane Harris?" "Yes, she's a near neighbour of mine."* • *I think it's unlikely that we'll move in the near* **future** *but perhaps after a couple of years.* • *I couldn't get any cream cheese so I bought the nearest equivalent that I could find.* • *In the absence of a monarchy, the president is the nearest* (= most similar) **thing** *they have* **to** *a king or queen.* • Your near relatives are those who are closely related to you, such as your parents, brothers or sisters. • *(Br and Aus)* The near part of a vehicle or road is the NEARSIDE one (= the one on the left): *The near front tyre has blown.* • *(humorous)* Your **nearest and dearest** are your family, esp. those that you live with or are very involved with. • A **near miss** or **near thing** is a situation in which an accident almost happened and was only just avoided: *That was a near miss – we must have come within an inch of that lorry!* • A **near miss** is also a bomb or shot which comes close to the place that it is intended to hit but does not hit it exactly, or *(fig.)* an attempt to do something which fails although it almost succeeds. • A **near thing** is also a situation in which the winner of a competition only just succeeds in winning: *The result of the match will be a very near thing.* • *I can't tell you exactly how many people are coming, but* **to the nearest** *ten there'll probably be about sixty.* • *(esp. Am)* Someone who is **near-sighted** can only see objects clearly which are close to them. • LP› **Eye and seeing**

near– /£nɪəʳ-, $nɪr-/ *combining form* • Near- combines with adjectives and nouns to mean almost: *We had a near-disaster this morning in the car!* ○ *She was near-hysterical by the time I arrived there.* • A **near-death experience** is an experience described by some people who have been extremely ill and close to death, in which the person feels as if they have left their body and are watching themselves from above.

near *(obj)* /£nɪəʳ, $nɪr/ *v* • *As the big day nears* (= gets closer) *I'm starting to wonder if it's all been a bit of a mistake.* [I] • *One or two students are now nearing* (= approaching) *the stage when they're good enough to take the exam.* [T] • *I'm pleased to say the project is nearing completion* (= almost finished). [T]

near·ness /£'nɪə·nəs, $'nɪr-/ *n* [U] • *One of the reasons I bought my house was its nearness* **to** *the office where I work.*

near·by /£ˌnɪə'baɪ, $ˌnɪr-/ *adv, adj* close; not far away in distance • *If there's a cafe nearby we could stop for a snack.* • *I noticed a policeman standing nearby.* • *We stopped at some nearby shops to pick up some food.*

near·ly /£'nɪə·li, $'nɪr-/ *adv* [not gradable] almost or not completely • *I've nearly finished that book you lent me.* • *She's nearly as tall as her father now.* • *It was so funny – we nearly died laughing.* • *I nearly asked her where her husband was, but then I remembered that he had left her.* • *I was so annoyed that I nearly said something, but I managed to stop myself.* • *There's* **not nearly** *enough* (= There is much too little) *food for all these people!* • *The problem* **isn't nearly** *as bad as it used to be* (= it was much worse before).

near·side /£'nɪə·saɪd, $'nɪr-/, **near** (**-er, -est**) *adj* [before n; not gradable] *Br and Aus* on the left side of esp. a vehicle or road • *Most of the damage was done to the front nearside wing of the car.* • *A car pulled out from the nearside lane without signalling.*

neat [TIDY] /niːt/ *adj* **-er, -est** tidy and ordered; with everything in its place • *You've got such neat handwriting.* • *They did a very neat job stitching up your knee – there's hardly a scar there.* • *She likes everything neat* **and tidy**. • (I)

neat·en *obj* /£'niː·tᵊn, $-t̬ᵊn/ *v* [T] • *She sewed carefully over the edges of the seams of the skirt she was making, in order to neaten them.* • *I think I'll just ask the hairdresser to neaten* **(up)** *the ends of my hair.* [T/M]

neat·ly /'niːt·li/ *adv* • *His clothes are all neatly folded in their drawers.*

neat·ness /'niːt·nəs/ *n* [U] • *When writing your homework, remember that neatness counts.*

neat [NOTHING ADDED] /niːt/ *adj* [not gradable] (of a strong alcoholic drink) without anything, such as water or ice or another drink, added to it • *I'll have a neat gin, please.* • *She likes her whisky neat.* • (I)

neat [GOOD] /niːt/ *adj* **-er, -est** *esp. Am and Aus slang* good • *"How did the party go?" "Oh, it was real neat – we had a good time."* • *That's a neat bike you've got there, Joey.* • (I)

'neath /niːθ/ *prep poetic* BENEATH • *'Neath stars and sun we wandered*

neb·u·la /'neb·jʊ·lə/ *n* [C] *pl* **nebulae** /'neb·jʊ·liː/ or **nebulas** *specialized* a cloud of gas or dust in space, appearing either bright or dark

neb·u·lar /£'neb·jʊ·ləʳ, $-lə/ *adj specialized*

neb·u·lous /'neb·jʊ·ləs/ *adj* (esp. of ideas) unclear and lacking form; VAGUE • *She has a few nebulous ideas about what she might like to do in the future but nothing firm.*

neb·u·lous·ness /'neb·jʊ·lə·snəs/ *n* [U]

ne·ces·sa·ry /'nes·ə·ser·i/ *adj* needed in order to achieve a particular result • *He lacks the necessary skills for the job.* • *I don't have much time so I won't be staying any longer than necessary.* • *Just do what's necessary and then leave.* • **If** *necessary, we can always change the dates of our trip.* • *Is* **it** *necessary* **for all of us** *to be present at the meeting this afternoon?* [+ *to* infinitive] • *We don't want to take any more luggage with us than is* **strictly** *necessary.* • Necessary can be used in negatives and questions to show that you disapprove of something and do not think it should be used or done: *I really don't think that sort of language is necessary on television.* ○ *Was* **it** *really necessary* **for you** *to say that?* [+ *to* infinitive] • A **necessary evil** is something which you do not like doing but which you know must be done: *I think he regards work as a necessary evil.* • (D)

ne·ces·sa·ries /'nes·ə·ser·iz/ *pl n* • Necessaries are the items that are needed, esp. for a particular purpose: *He packed drinks, a map and a compass – all the necessaries for a day's walking in the countryside.*

ne·ces·sa·ri·ly /'nes·ə·ser·ɪl·i/ *adv* [not gradable] • Necessarily is often used in negatives to mean 'in every case' or 'therefore': *The fact that something is cheap doesn't necessarily mean it's of low quality.* ○ *You may love someone without necessarily wanting to marry them.* ○ *"Does the verb 'to near' take an object in English?" "Not necessarily."* • *"It ain't necessarily so"* (song from the opera *Porgy and Bess* music by George Gershwin, words by Du Bose Heyward and Ira Gershwin, 1935)

ne·ces·si·tate *(obj)* /nə'ses·ɪ·teɪt/ *v fml* to cause (something) to be needed; to make (something) necessary • *Reduction in government spending will necessitate further cuts in public services.* [T] • *An important meeting necessitates my* **being** *in London on Friday.* [+ v-*ing*]

ne·ces·si·ty /£nə'ses·ɪ·ti, $-ə·t̬i/ *n* the need for something • *You can come early and help if you want to, but there's no necessity.* [U] • *Is there any necessity* **for** *me* **to** *be in the office tomorrow?* [U +*to* infinitive] • *The report stresses the necessity* **of eating** *plenty of fresh fruit and vegetables.* [U] • *With a personal fortune of six million pounds she certainly doesn't work* **out of** *necessity* (= because she needs to). [U] • *There's no necessity* **to** *pay in advance.* [U + *to* infinitive] • *We'll employ extra staff to help out as and when the necessity* **arises** (= when we need to). [U] • A necessity or **bare** necessity is something that you need, esp. in order to live: *They lack the money even for basic food and heating – the necessities of life.* [C] • *(saying)* 'Necessity is the mother of invention' means that if it is very important to you that you do something, you will find a way of doing it, even if it is very difficult. • See also **necessaries** at NECESSARY.

neck [BODY PART] /nek/ *n* [C] the part of the body which joins the head to the shoulders • *He had the thickest neck that she had ever seen.* • The neck of a piece of clothing is the part of it which goes around a person's neck: *a sweater with a* **round** *neck* ○ *He wasn't wearing a tie and his shirt was open at the neck.* • A neck is also a part of an object which is at the top of the object and has a shape like that of a person's neck: *the neck* **of** *a bottle/guitar* • *(infml)* If you **get it in the neck** you are punished or severely criticized for something that you have done: *Poor old Bob got it in the neck* **for** *being late this morning.* • If two people who are competing against each other are **neck and neck** they are level with each other and have an equal chance of winning: *They were neck and neck until the last hundred metres when Pritchard suddenly sprinted ahead of Sanchez.* • *(infml)* If you are **up to** your **neck in** a situation you are very involved in it: *She's up to her neck in debt/problems/work.* ○ *Right now I'm up to my neck in* **it** (= I have a lot of work to do). • *(infml)* A **neck of the woods** is a part of a particular area: *I'm surprised to see you in this neck of the woods – what are you doing here?* ○ *There's someone over there from your neck of the woods* (= the place where you live or were born). • See also BOTTLENECK; HALTERNECK; LEATHERNECK; REDNECK; ROUGHNECK; TURTLENECK. • PIC› **Neck**

-necked /-nekt/ *combining form* • -necked refers to the type of neck someone or something has, or to the style of a piece of clothing around the neck or the way that it is worn: *a stocky, stiff-necked little man* ○ *a round-necked jumper* ○ *an open-necked shirt*

neck KISS /nek/ *v* [I] *infml dated* to kiss and hold a person in a sexual way • *It was one of those parties where couples were necking in corners.*

neck·band /ˈnek·bænd/ *n* [C] a narrow strip which goes round the neck of an item of clothing • *I can't get this sweater over my head – the neckband's too tight.*

neck·er·chief /£ˈnek·ə·tʃiːf, $ˈ-ɚ-/ *n* [C] *pl* **neckerchiefs** or **neckerchieves** /£ˈnek·ə·tʃiːvz, $ˈ-ɚ-/ *old use* a piece of square cloth which is folded and worn around the neck

neck·lace JEWELLERY /ˈnek·ləs/ *n* [C] a piece of jewellery worn around the neck, such as a chain or a string of decorative stones, BEADS, etc. • *a gold/silver/pearl necklace* • PIC **Jewellery**

neck·lace *obj* MURDER /ˈnek·ləs/ *v* [T] to kill (someone) by putting a burning rubber tyre around their neck • *One man was shot and a second was necklaced with a burning tyre.*

neck·lac·ing /ˈnek·lə·sɪŋ/ *n* [C] • *There have been four necklacings in the Soweto area since the beginning of the year.*

neck·line /ˈnek·laɪn/ *n* [C] the shape made by the edge of a dress or shirt at the front of the neck or on the chest • *She wore a dress with a* **low/plunging** *neckline* (= one showing part of her breasts).

neck·tie /ˈnek·taɪ/ *n* [C] *esp. Am for* TIE FASTEN

nec·ro·manc·y /£ˈnek·rəʊ·mænt·si, $-rə-/ *n* [U] the act of communicating with the dead in order to discover what is going to happen in the future, or **black magic** (= magic involving evil spirits used for bad purposes)

nec·ro·phil·i·a /£ˌnek·rəʊˈfɪl·i·ə, $-rə-/, **nec·ro·phil·i·sm** /£nekˈrɒf·ɪ·lɪ·zᵊm, $nekˈrɑː·fə-/ *n* [U] sexual attraction to or sexual activity with dead bodies

nec·ro·phil·i·ac /£ˌnek·rəʊˈfɪl·i·æk, $-rə-/ *n, adj* • A necrophiliac is a person who is sexually attracted to or has sex with dead bodies. [C] • *He is said to have necrophiliac* (= showing sexual attraction to dead bodies) *tendencies.*

ne·crop·o·lis /£nekˈrɒp·ᵊl·ɪs, $nekˈrɑː-/ *n* [C] an ancient CEMETERY (= piece of ground where people are buried)

nec·tar /£ˈnek·təʳ, $-tɚ/ *n* [U] a sweet liquid produced by flowers and collected by bees and other insects, or (in ancient Greek and Roman stories) the drink of the gods • *The bee turns nectar into honey.* • *This wine tastes like nectar* (= tastes excellent).

nec·tar·ine /£ˈnek·tᵊr·iːn, £-ɪn, $ˌnek·tɚ-/ *n* [C] a type of PEACH (= type of fruit) with a smooth skin

née /neɪ/ *adj* [after n; not gradable] used after a woman's married name to introduce the family name by which she was known before she married • *to Ian and Elaine Gibson (née Gillett) a son, James*

need *(obj)* MUST HAVE /niːd/ *v* [not usually *be needing*] to have to have (something) or to want (something) very much • *Children need a good balanced diet.* [T] • *I need some new winter shoes.* [T] • *Do we need anything from the shops?* [T] • *You need a lot of stamina to run that sort of distance.* [T] • *To make pastry, you need flour, fat and water.* [T] • *Will I be needed in the office tomorrow?* [T] • *I need you* (= want you very much). [T] • *I need* (= very much want) *you* **to** *advise me on what to wear tomorrow night.* [T + obj + *to* infinitive] • *I* **badly** *need* (= strongly want) *a rest from all this.* [T] • *(infml)* If you say that you **don't** need something, it can mean that you do not want it because it is causing you trouble: *I don't need all this hassle.* [T] • If you say that someone or something needs something else, you can mean that they should have it, or would benefit from having it: *What you need, my son, is a nice hot bowl of soup.* [T] ○ *This room needs brighten***ing** *up a bit.* [+ v-*ing*] ○ *She needs her hair wash***ed***/(Br) wash***ing**. [+ obj + v-*ed*/+ v-*ing*] • Be needing is usually used only with a future tense, often in the negative: *You won't be needing your raincoat today – it isn't going to rain.* [T] • *(humorous)* **I need** *all this extra work* **like (I need) a hole in the head** (= I do not want it at all). • *(esp. humorous)* **Who needs** something means that the thing referred to is not necessary or useful, or causes trouble: *Men! Who needs them?* • *"All you need is love"* (title of song by The Beatles, 1967)

need /niːd/ *n* [U] • Need is the state of having to have something that you do not have, esp. something that you must have so that you can have a satisfactory life: *There's* **a** *growing need* **for** *cheap rented accommodation in the larger cities.* ○ *As winter approaches, there's* **a** *desperate need* **for** *shelter and food in the refugee camps.* ○ *You can go in front of me – your need is* **greater** *than mine.* ○ *They're* **in** *need* **of** *help.* • Need is also a feeling or state of strongly wanting something: *He seems to have* **a** *desperate need* **to** *be loved by everyone.* [+ *to* infinitive] ○ *We* **have** *no need* **of** *your sympathy.* ○ *I don't know about you but I'm* **in** *need* **of** *a drink.* • *You look as if you're* **in** *need* **of** (= should have) *a bath!* • People who are **in** need do not have enough money or need some type of help: *You just hope that the money goes to those who are most in need.* • Need is also the state of being necessary: *If I leave the paper by the machine you can help yourself to it as the need* **arises**. ○ **If** *need/needs* **be**, *we can take a second car to fit everyone in.* ○ *There's no need* (= it is not necessary) **to** *go to the shops – there's plenty of food in the fridge.* [*to* infinitive] ○ *I don't think there's any need* **for** *all of us* **to** *attend the meeting.* [+ *to* infinitive] • *Having seen how much he ate at lunch, I don't think there's any need* (= reason) **to** *worry about his health!* [+ *to* infinitive] • *I understand why she was angry but* **there was no need to** *be so rude to him* (= it was wrong for her to be rude). • **There's no need to** (= Don't) *shout, for goodness' sake! Just calm down.* • *"Thy need (originally 'necessity') is greater than mine"* (Sir Philip Sydney giving his water bottle to a dying soldier at the battle of Zutphen, shortly before he died himself)

need·ed /ˈniː·dɪd/ *adj* [not gradable] • *After six hours work in the garden we sat down for a* **much**-*needed rest* (= one which we felt we had to have). • *Most people like to feel needed* (= wanted).

needs /niːdz/ *pl n* • Your needs are the things that you must have in order to have a satisfactory life: *Housing, enough money to live on and education are* **basic** *needs.* ○ *They don't have enough food to* **meet** *their needs.*

need·y /ˈniː·di/ *adj* **-ier, -iest** • *The proceeds from the sale go to help needy* (= poor) *people in the area.*

need·y /ˈniː·di/ *pl n* • **The needy** are poor people: *Let us pray for those who are not so fortunate as ourselves – the sick, the old and the needy.*

need MUST DO /niːd/ *v* [not *be needing*] he/she/it **needs** or **need** to have (to) • *He needs* **to** *lose a bit of weight.* [+ *to* infinitive] • *Before we make a decision, we need* **to** *consider our options.* [+ *to* infinitive] • *I need* **to** *do some shopping on my way home from work.* [+ *to* infinitive] • *We need* **to** *find a solution to the problem of pollution in our cities.* [+ *to* infinitive] • *I don't think we need ask him.* [+ infinitive without *to*] • *Nothing need be done about this till next week.* [+ infinitive without *to*] • *(slightly fml) "Need we take your mother?" "No, we needn't/I don't think we need."* [+ infinitive without *to*] • *We needn't go till about ten o'clock.* [+ infinitive without *to*] • If you say that someone or something needn't do something, you can also mean that there is no reason for them to do it: *You needn't worry – I'm not going to mention it to anyone.* [+ infinitive without *to*] ○ *It's a wonderful way of getting to see Italy, and it needn't cost very much.* [+ infinitive without *to*] • If you say that someone **didn't** need **to** do something, it means either that they did it although they did not have to, or that they did not do it because they did not have to: *I didn't need* **to** *buy any extra material.* [+ *to* infinitive] • *(esp. Br)* If you tell someone they needn't **have** done something you mean that it was not necessary for them to have done it, although they did do it: *You needn't have washed all those dishes, you know – I'd have done them myself when I got home.* [+ infinitive without *to*] ○ *You needn't have worried about the dinner – it was absolutely delicious!* [+ infinitive without *to*] • *The accident need never* (= should not) **have** *happened.* [+ infinitive without *to*] • Needn't can also be used in a threatening way to mean 'shouldn't': *He needn't think I'm going to clean up after him all the while!* [+ infinitive without *to*] ○ *You needn't laugh! It'll be your turn next!* [+ infinitive without *to*] • *"Did he upset a lot of people at the meeting?"* **"Need you ask** (= Yes, as expected)!**"** • **I need hardly say** (= It is obvious) *what a pleasure it is to see you.* • **Need I say** (= Obviously), *I'm extremely sorry to hear the news about your father.* • *Tom was doing the cooking –* **need I say more?** (= you know what to expect after I have told you that). • When followed by 'to' + infinitive, the he/she/it form of 'need' is 'needs'. When it is used on its own or followed by an infinitive without 'to', the he/she/it form is 'need'. In questions and negative sentences, you can follow 'need' with either 'to' + infinitive, or with an infinitive without 'to'. But in ordinary positive sentences, it can only be followed by 'to' + infinitive. To form the negative of 'need', you can say either 'need not/needn't go' or 'do not/ don't need to go'. When describing what someone said in the past, 'need' can be used as a past form: *He told me I needn't be afraid* means *He said "You needn't be afraid"*. • LP> **Auxiliary verbs**

need·less /ˈniːd·ləs/ *adj* [not gradable] • If something is needless, it is completely unnecessary: *All that needless worrying over what I'd say to him at the party, and he wasn't even there!* • **Needless to say** means 'as you would expect', and introduces or is added to a remark giving information which is expected and not at all surprising: *Needless to say, because of the accident he had, he'll be off work for a while.*

need·less·ly /ˈniːd·lə·sli/ *adv* [not gradable] • *She'd worried quite needlessly about whether there would be enough food for everyone – there was plenty.*

needs /niːdz/ *adv* [not gradable] • *I don't want to work all weekend, but* **needs must** (= it is necessary, so I will). • *(fml or old use) Well, if there's no choice in the matter I suppose I* **needs must/must needs** (= must) *attend.*

need·le SEWING TOOL /ˈniː·dl̩/ *n* [C] a thin metal pin, used in sewing, which is pointed at one end and has a hole called an EYE at the other end for thread, or a longer stick, without a hole, which is used with another stick of the same type to KNIT • *a needle and cotton/***thread** • *Here, your eyes are better than mine – could you* **thread** (= put thread through) *this needle for me?* • *What size* **knitting** *needles did you use for that sweater?* • If you say that trying to find something is like looking for **a needle in a haystack**, you mean that it is impossible or extremely difficult to find, esp. because the area you have to search is too large. • See also NEEDLEWORK. • PIC> **Handicraft, Pins and needles**

need·le MEDICAL TOOL /ˈniː·dl̩/, **hyp·o·der·mic need·le** *n* [C] the long hollow pointed part of a HYPODERMIC which goes under the skin when giving an INJECTION (= putting a drug into the body through the skin) • *Each needle is sterile and is disposed of after use to prevent the spread of infection.* • *I used to be terrified of* **the** *needle/(Am and Aus infml)* **getting needles** (= being INJECTED) *when I was a kid.* • A **needle bank** is a place where people who use (esp. illegal) drugs can go to exchange their old, dirty or used needles for new clean ones. • PIC> **Pins and needles**

need·le POINTER /ˈniː·dl̩/ *n* [C] on a compass or measuring device, the thin moving part which points in a particular direction or points to a particular measurement • *The needle on a compass always points to magnetic north.* • PIC> **Pins and needles**

need·le LEAF /ˈniː·dl̩/ *n* [C] a long thin stiff leaf of a FIR tree • *We want a Christmas tree that won't drop its needles all over the carpet.* • *Pine needles covered the ground under the trees.* • PIC> **Pins and needles**

need·le MUSIC /ˈniː·dl̩/, **sty·lus** *n* [C] *infml* the part of a **record player** (= a machine on which records are played) which touches the record as it turns round and which is made of a hard material, such as a DIAMOND • *It sounds like the needle on your record player needs to be replaced.*

need·le *obj* ANNOY /ˈniː·dl̩/ *v* [T] *infml* to annoy (someone), esp. by repeated criticism • *As always, after he had been with his mother for a couple of days, she had begun to needle him.*

need·le·point /ˈniː·dl̩·pɔɪnt/ *n* [U] making a picture by sewing onto a tightly stretched piece of cloth using only one type of stitch • *Needlepoint is something of a dying art.*

need·less /ˈniːd·ləs/ *adj* [not gradable] See at NEED MUST DO

nee·dle·work /£ˈniː·dl̩·wɜːk, $-wɜːrk/ *n* [U] sewing, esp. decorative sewing, done by hand with needle and thread • LP> **Shopping goods**

needn't /ˈniː·dᵊnt/ *short form of* need not • *You needn't come until later.*

need·y /ˈniː·di/ *pl n, adj* **-ier, -iest** See at NEED MUST HAVE

ne'er /£neəʳ, $ner/ *adv* [not gradable] *poetic* never • *Ne'er the night passes without my dreaming of you.*

ne'er–do–well /£ˈneə·duː·wel, $ˈner-/ *n* [C] *dated* a worthless person

ne·fa·ri·ous /£nəˈfeə·ri·əs, $-ˈfer·i-/ *adj fml* (esp. of activities) evil; immoral • *The company seems to have been involved in some nefarious practices/***activities.** • *It was revealed that investors' savings had been diverted for nefarious purposes.*

ne·fa·ri·ous·ly /£nəˈfeə·ri·ə·sli, $-ˈfer·i-/ *adv fml*

ne·fa·ri·ous·ness /£nəˈfeə·ri·ə·snəs, $-ˈfer·i-/ *n* [U] *fml*

ne·gate *obj* /nɪˈgeɪt/ *v* [T] *slightly fml* to cause (something) to have no effect and therefore to be useless • *The increase in our profits this year has been negated by the rising costs of running the business.*

ne·ga·tion /nɪˈgeɪ·ʃᵊn/ *n* [U] *slightly fml*

neg·a·tive NO /£ˈneg·ə·tɪv, $-t̬ɪv/ *adj* expressing 'no' • *We received a negative answer to our request.* • A negative sentence or phrase is one which contains a word such as 'not', 'no', 'never' or 'nothing': *'I've never seen him in my life' is a negative sentence.* ○ *'Don't' and 'do not' are negative forms of 'do'.* • LP> **Opposites**

neg·a·tive /£ˈneg·ə·tɪv, $-t̬ɪv/ *n* • *I didn't hear your answer, Edward – was that a negative?* [C] • *I'm afraid the reply was* **in the** *negative* (= was 'no'). [U] • Compare **affirmative** at AFFIRM.

neg·a·tive·ly /£ˈneg·ə·tɪv·li, $-t̬ɪv-/ *adv*

neg·a·tive WITHOUT HOPE /£ˈneg·ə·tɪv, $-t̬ɪv/ *adj* tending to consider only the bad side of a situation; not hopeful • *She's got such a negative attitude that it's depressing to be with her.* • *You're so negative about everything!* • *The fact that he's having difficulty breathing is a negative* (= not good) *sign.* • Compare POSITIVE HOPEFUL.

neg·a·tive·ly /£ˈneg·ə·tɪv·li, $-t̬ɪv-/ *adv*

neg·a·tiv·i·sm /£ˈneg·ə·tɪ·vɪ·zᵊm, $-t̬ɪ-/, **neg·a·tiv·i·ty** /£ˌneg·əˈtɪv·ɪ·ti, $-ə·t̬i/ *n* [U] • *There's a real attitude of negativism among the team at the moment.*

neg·a·tive ELECTRICITY /£ˈneg·ə·tɪv, $-t̬ɪv/ *adj* [not gradable] of the type of electrical charge which is carried by ELECTRONS • *The* **negative pole** *(also* **cathode**) *of a* BATTERY *is the part which releases* ELECTRONS. • Compare POSITIVE ELECTRICITY.

neg·a·tive PHOTOGRAPH /£ˈneg·ə·tɪv, $-t̬ɪv/, *infml* **neg** /neg/ *n* [C] a piece of film from which a photograph can be produced, and in which light and dark areas appear the opposite way round to the way in which they appear in the photograph • *black-and-white/colour negatives* • *I've borrowed the negatives* **of** *her wedding photos so I can get some pictures printed.*

neg·a·tive TEST RESULTS /£ˈneg·ə·tɪv, $-t̬ɪv/ *adj* [not gradable] (of a medical test) showing that the patient does not have the disease or condition for which he or she has been tested • *a negative pregnancy test* • *They did an HIV test on him but fortunately the results were negative.* • Compare POSITIVE TEST RESULTS.

neg·a·tive BELOW ZERO /£ˈneg·ə·tɪv, $-t̬ɪv/ *adj* [not gradable] (of a number or amount) less than zero • *-1 is a negative number.* • Compare POSITIVE ABOVE ZERO.

ne·glect *(obj)* /nɪˈglekt/ *v* to give not enough care or attention to (people or things that are your responsibility) • *He neglects that poor dog – he never takes him for walks or gives him any attention.* [T] • *I'm afraid I've rather neglected the house this week so it's a bit of a mess.* [T] • If you neglect **to** do something, you don't do it, usually because you forget: *I'd neglected to tell him that I wouldn't be home that night and he hadn't slept for worrying.* [+ *to* infinitive]

ne·glect /nɪˈglekt/ *n* [U] • *Both parents were found guilty of neglect and their child was taken away from them.* • *Over the years the church has fallen into a state of neglect.*

ne·glect·ed /£nɪˈglek·tɪd, $-t̬ɪd/ *adj* • *She was distressed at how neglected the children looked – their clothes were dirty and their hair unwashed.*

ne·glect·ful /nɪˈglekt·fᵊl/ *adj* • *I'm sure my boss thinks I've been neglectful* **of** *my duties recently.*

neg·li·gée /£ˈneg·lɪ·ʒeɪ, $ˌ--ˈ-/, **neg·li·gee** *n* [C] a decorative piece of clothing for a woman which is typically worn over a NIGHTDRESS (= a dress worn in bed) and is made of light material

neg·li·gent /ˈneg·lɪ·dʒᵊnt/ *adj* not being careful enough or giving enough attention to people or things that are your responsibility • *The judge said that the teacher had been negligent* **in** *allowing the children to swim in dangerous water.*

neg·li·gent·ly /ˈneg·lɪ·dʒᵊnt·li/ *adv*

neg·li·gence /ˈneg·lɪ·dʒᵊnts/ *n* [U] • *My mother accuses me of negligence unless I phone her every day.* • *(law) The doctor's failure to diagnose the illness was described to the court as 'an instance of* **gross** (= extreme) *negligence.'*

neg·li·gi·ble /ˈneg·lɪ·dʒə·bl̩/ *adj* too slight or small in amount to be of importance • *The difference in experience between the two players is negligible.* • *I have a negligible knowledge of German.*

neg·li·gi·bly /ˈneg·lɪ·dʒə·bli/ *adv*

ne·go·ti·ate *(obj)* DISCUSS /£nəˈgəʊ·ʃi·eɪt, £-si-, $-ˈgoʊ-/ *v* to have formal discussions with someone in order to reach an agreement with them • *The strike was caused by the management's refusal to negotiate* **with** *the unions.* [I] • *I'm negotiating* **for** *a new contract at the moment.* [I] • *I've managed to negotiate* (= obtain by discussion) *a five per cent pay increase* **with** *my boss.* [T]

ne·go·tia·ble /£nəˈgəʊ·ʃə·bl̩, $-ˈgoʊ·ʃi·ə-/ *adj* • *Everything is negotiable* (= can still be discussed) *at this stage – I'm ruling nothing out.*

ne·go·ti·at·or /£nɪˈgəʊ·ʃi·eɪ·təʳ, £-si-, $-ˈgoʊ·ʃi·eɪ·t̬ɚ/ *n* [C] • *Some very skilful negotiators will be needed to settle this dispute.*

ne·go·ti·a·tion /£nə,gəʊ·ʃiˈeɪ·ʃᵊn, £-si-, $-,goʊ-/ *n* • *The agreement was reached after a series of difficult negotiations.* [C] • *Negotiation* **for** *the pay increase is likely to take several weeks.* [U] • *The exact details of the agreement are still* **under** *negotiation.* [U]

ne·go·ti·ate *obj* TRAVEL /£nəˈgəʊ·ʃi·eɪt, £-si-, $-ˈgoʊ-/ *v* [T] to manage to travel along a (difficult route) • *The only way to negotiate the path is on foot.* • *(fig.) The company's had some tricky problems to negotiate* (= deal with) *in its first year in business.*

ne·go·ti·a·ble /£nəˈgəʊ·ʃə·bl̩, $-ˈgoʊ·ʃi·ə-/ *adj* • *Many of the mountain roads are not negotiable* (= able to be travelled along) *by motor vehicles in the winter.*

ne·go·ti·ate *obj* EXCHANGE /£nəˈgəʊ·ʃi·eɪt, £-si-, $-ˈgoʊ-/ *v* [T] *specialized* to obtain or give a sum of money in exchange for (a financial document of the same value)

ne·go·ti·a·ble /£nəˈgəʊ·ʃə·bl̩, $-ˈgoʊ·ʃi·ə-/ *adj* [not gradable] *specialized* • *A cheque that is not negotiable cannot be exchanged for cash and must be paid into a bank account.*

Ne·gro, ne·gro /£ˈniː·grəʊ, $-groʊ/ *n* [C] *pl* **Negroes** *dated* someone with black or dark brown skin and typically tightly curled black hair who lives in Africa or whose family originally came from Africa • 'Negro' is now considered offensive by many people and words such as 'Black' and 'African-American' are used instead.

ne·groid /ˈniː·grɔɪd/ *adj specialized* • *People from North African countries have an Arabic rather than a Negroid appearance.*

neigh /neɪ/ *n* [C] a long loud high call that is produced by a horse when it is excited or frightened

neigh /neɪ/ *v* [I] • *When he laughs he sounds like a horse neighing.*

neigh·bour *Br and Aus, Am and Aus* **neigh·bor** /£ˈneɪ·bəʳ, $-bɚ/ *n* [C] someone who lives very near to you • *Some of* **the** *neighbours have complained about the noise from our party.* • *Have you met Pat, my* **next-door** *neighbour?* • *(fig.) The relationship between Scotland and its southern neighbour* (= England) *has not always been peaceful.*

neigh·bour·hood *Br and Aus, Am and Aus* **neigh·bor·hood** /£ˈneɪ·bə·hʊd, $-bɚ-/ *n* [C] • A neighbourhood is the area of a town that surrounds someone's home, or the people who live in this area: *This part of the town is quite poor. The wealthy neighbourhood is near the river.* ○ *She's well-known in the neighbourhood for her charity work.* • *I wouldn't like to live* **in the** *neighbourhood* **of** (= in the area around) *an airport.* • *(fig.) We're hoping to get something* **in the neighbourhood of** (= approximately) *£70 000 for our house.* • **Neighbourhood watch** is a way of reducing crime by organizing the people who live in an area to watch each other's property and tell the police about possible criminals: *Burglaries in our area have fallen by 50% since the neighbourhood watch* **scheme** *was introduced.*

neigh·bour·ing *Br and Aus, Am and Aus* **neigh·bor·ing** /£ˈneɪ·bᵊr·ɪŋ, $-bɚ-/ *adj* [before n; not gradable] • Neighbouring places are next to or near each other: *She married a man from the neighbouring village.* ○ *There are increasing fears that neighbouring* **countries/states** *might be drawn into the civil war.*

neigh·bour·ly *Br and Aus, Am and Aus* **neigh·bor·ly** /£ˈneɪ·bᵊl·i, $-bɚ·li/ *adj* • Someone living near you who is neighbourly is friendly or helpful: *It was very neighbourly* **of** *you to do her shopping for her.*

neigh·bour·li·ness *Br and Aus, Am and Aus* **neigh·bor·li·ness** /£ˈneɪ·bᵊl·ɪ·nəs, $-bɚ·lɪ-/ *n* [U] • *The lack of* **good** *neighbourliness has led to a breakdown in the traditional life of the community.*

nei·ther /£ˈnaɪ·ðəʳ, £ˈniː-, $-ðɚ/ *determiner, pronoun, conjunction, adv* [not gradable] not one and not the other of two things or people • *We've got two TVs, but neither works properly.* • *We've got a difficult decision to make, because neither option is very pleasant.* • *I asked two people to help me start my car, but neither* **of** *them knew what to do.* • *Neither one* **of** *us is particularly interested in gardening.* • *"Which one would you choose?" "Neither. They're both terrible."* • *If she doesn't agree to the plan, neither will Tom* (= Tom also will not). • *Chris wasn't at the meeting and neither was her assistant.* • *(infml) "I don't feel like going out this evening." "Me neither."* • *On two occasions she was accused of stealing money from the company, but* **in** *neither* **case** *was there any evidence to support the claims.* • You can use **neither...nor** when you want to say that two or more things are not true: *Neither my mother nor my father went to university.* ○ *Vegans eat neither meat, nor fish, nor animal products.* ○ *My doctor told me I should neither smoke nor drink.* ○ *She neither knows nor cares what has happened to her ex-husband.* ○ *They speak neither French nor German, but a curious mixture of the two.* • Something that is **neither one thing nor the other** is a mixture of things and not clearly one particular thing: *The colour of my eyes is neither one thing nor the other – it's just a strange grey-blue mixture.* • Something that is **neither here nor there** is not important: *It's essential that she has this medicine, and the cost is neither here nor there.* • LP **Determiners, Two**

nel·ly /ˈnel·i/ *n* [U] **not on your nelly** *Br dated humorous* there is no possibility of that • *"Perhaps you could take Simon to the party." "Not on your nelly!"*

nem·e·sis /ˈnem·ə·sɪs/ *n* [C] *pl* **nemeses** /ˈnem·ə·siːz/ *literary* (a cause of) punishment or defeat that is deserved and cannot be avoided • *The tax increases proved to be the President's political nemesis at the following election.* • Someone's nemesis is the person who opposes them: *Walters will face his great rival and nemesis in Friday's match.* • *In Greek mythology, Nemesis was the goddess of retribution and vengeance.*

ne·o- /£,niː·əʊ-, $-oʊ-/ *combining form* new or recent, or in a modern form • *Neo-***fascist** *groups are an increasing threat to ethnic minorities across Europe.* • *More than 13 000 people joined the demonstration against the recent wave of neo-***Nazi** *attacks on foreign workers.* • *Italian neo-***realist** *cinema focussed on working-class subjects, using amateur actors and filming on location, rather than in the studio.*

ne·o·clas·si·cal /£,niː·əʊˈklæs·ɪ·kᵊl, $-oʊ-/ *adj* [not gradable] *specialized* made in a style which is based on the art and building designs of ancient Rome and Greece • *Beautiful neoclassical buildings, squares and monuments can be found all over central Liverpool.*

ne·o·clas·si·ci·sm /£,niː·əʊˈklæs·ɪ·sɪ·zᵊm, $-oʊ-/ *n* [U] • *Neoclassicism originated in Rome in the 18th century, partly as a reaction against the 'excesses' of Baroque and Rococo.*

ne·o·co·lon·i·al·i·sm /£,niː·əʊ·kəˈləʊ·ni·ᵊl·ɪ·zᵊm, $-oʊ·kəˈloʊ-/ *n* [U] political control by an economically powerful country of a poorer country that should be independent and free to govern itself

ne·o·co·lon·i·al·ist /£,niː·əʊ·kəˈləʊ·ni·ᵊl·ɪst, $-oʊ·kəˈloʊ-/ *adj* [not gradable]

ne·o·lith·ic /£,niː·əʊˈlɪθ·ɪk, $-oʊ-/ *adj* [not gradable] belonging to the period when humans used tools and weapons made of stone and had just developed farming • *This area has been used as a burial ground since neolithic times.* • *The Neolithic* **Period** *is sometimes called the New Stone Age.* • Compare PALAEOLITHIC.

ne·ol·og·i·sm /£niˈɒl·ə·dʒɪ·zᵊm, $-ˈɑː·lə-/ *n* (the creation or use of) a new word or expression • *An up-to-date dictionary ought to include the latest neologisms.* [C] • *Technological developments are often the cause of neologism.* [U]

ne·on /£ˈniː·ɒn, $-ɑːn/ *n* [U] a rare colourless gas which has no smell, does not react with other chemicals, and shines red when an electric current goes through it • *Neon* **lights** *and* **signs** *consist of glass tubes filled with neon, and are often used for advertising because the tubes can be bent into unusual shapes.*

ne·o·na·tal /£,niː·əʊˈneɪ·tᵊl, $-oʊˈneɪ·t̬ᵊl/ *adj* [before n; not gradable] of or for babies that were born recently • *Their baby is still in the hospital's neonatal unit but the doctors expect him to make a complete recovery.*

ne·o·phyte /£ˈniː·əʊ·faɪt, $-oʊ-/ *n* [C] *fml* someone who has recently become involved in an activity and is still learning about it • *Unfortunately the manual is written by people who seem to have forgotten that most of their readers are neophytes.*

neph·ew /ˈnef·juː, £ˈnev-/ *n* [C] a son of your sister or brother or a son of the sister or brother of your husband or wife • *I've got no children of my own, but I do have a niece and a nephew.* • Compare NIECE. • PIC› **Family tree**

nep·o·tism /'nep·ə·tɪ·zᵊm/ *n* [U] *disapproving* the use of a powerful or influential position in an organization or government to obtain good jobs or unfair advantages for members of your own family • *The government was dismissed following revelations about corruption, nepotism and political incompetence.*

nep·o·tis·tic /ˌnep·ə'tɪs·tɪk/ *adj disapproving* • *The company was criticized recently for its nepotistic recruitment policy.*

Nep·tune /£'nep·tjuːn, $-tuːn/ *n* [U not after *the*] the planet eighth in order of distance from the Sun, after Uranus and before Pluto • *Neptune was discovered in 1846.*

nerd, *Aus also* **nurd** /£nɜːd, $nɜːrd/ *n* [C] *infml* a person, esp. a man, who is unattractive and awkward or embarrassing socially • *People who work with computers are often dismissed as spotty nerds.*

nerd·y (**-ier**, **-iest**), *Aus also* **nurd·y** (**-ier**, **-iest**) /£'nɜː·di, $'nɜːr-/ *adj infml* • *I switched to contact lenses because I felt so nerdy wearing glasses.*

nerve FIBRES /£nɜːv, $nɜːrv/ *n* [C] a group of long thin fibres that carry information or instructions between the brain and other parts of the body • *The visual cortex is the part of the brain where nerve* **impulses** *from the eye are analysed.* • *She was paralysed when nerve* **fibres** *were accidentally cut during an operation.* • A **nerve cell** is a NEURON. • A large organization's **nerve centre**/*(Am)* **nerve center** is the place where it is controlled or managed: *The nerve center of the Customs Service's squadron of anti-drug patrol planes is in Oklahoma City.* • *The warheads contained conventional high explosive, and not* **nerve gas** (= gas that stops the nerves from working correctly) *as had been feared.*

nerv·ous /£'nɜː·vəs, $'nɜːr-/ *adj* • *He suffers from a nervous* **disorder** (= disease of the nerves) *and is confined to a wheelchair.* • *She has a nervous* **twitch** *which makes her blink a lot.* • An animal's **nervous system** consists of its brain and all the nerves in its body which together make movement and feeling possible by sending messages around the body. • (CS) (F) (PL) (RUS)

nerve BRAVERY /£nɜːv, $nɜːrv/ *n* [U] bravery or confidence necessary to do something difficult, unpleasant or rude • *It takes a lot of nerve to be a bomb disposal expert.* • *I went parachuting once but I* **lost** *my nerve just before the jump and stayed in the plane.* • *I didn't have* **the** *nerve* **to** *tell him what I really thought of his suggestion.* [+ *to* infinitive] • *She's late for work every day, but she still has* **the** *nerve* **to** *lecture me about punctuality.* [+ *to* infinitive] • *That man has such a nerve! He's always blaming me for things that are his fault.* • *She drove the car into a tree and then told me it was my fault for not concentrating,* **of all the** *nerve!* • Something that is **nerve-racking** or **nerve-wracking** is difficult to do and causes a lot of worry for the person involved in it: *My wedding was the most nerve-racking thing I've ever experienced.*

nerve *obj* /£nɜːv, $nɜːrv/ *v* [T] *Br* • *She had known him for several months before she eventually nerved her***self (up)** (= became brave enough) **to** *invite him to her house.* [+ obj + *to* infinitive]

nerves /£nɜːvz, $nɜːrvz/ *pl n* • *You need to have nerves* **of steel** (= to be very brave) *to be a fighter pilot.*

nerv·y /£'nɜː·vi, $'nɜːr-/ *adj* **-ier**, **-iest** *Am* • *That nervy* (= rude) *teenager pushed in front of the younger children.* • *You have to be nervy* (= brave) *to take a rescue ship out in a stormy sea.*

nerves /£nɜːvz, $nɜːrvz/ *pl n* [C] worry or anxiety about something that is going to happen • *I never suffer from nerves when I'm speaking in public.* • *She was* **a bundle of** *nerves* (= very nervous) *before the audition.* • *I always have a cigarette to* **calm/steady** *my nerves* (= make me less nervous) *before I go on stage.* • If you **get on** someone's **nerves** you annoy them a lot: *We really got on each other's nerves when we were living together.* ○ *Please stop making that noise! It really gets on my nerves.*

nerve·less /£'nɜːv·ləs, $'nɜːrv-/ *adj* • Someone who is nerveless is calm and confident about something difficult that they are doing: *He didn't quite fit the stereotype of the nerveless, ice-cool racing driver.*

nerve·less·ly /£'nɜːv·lə·sli, $'nɜːrv-/ *adv*

nerv·ous /£'nɜː·vəs, $'nɜːr-/ *adj* • *Do you feel nervous* (= worried or slightly frightened) *during exams?* • *He's a quiet, nervous man who doesn't like meeting new people.* • *She doesn't know her uncle very well and she's always been nervous* **of** *him.* • *I was very nervous* **about** *driving again after the accident.* • *One of the flight attendant's jobs is to smile and reassure nervous passengers that all is well, even if it isn't.* • *I was a bit nervous beforehand but once the match had begun I felt brilliant.* • *The dollar rose strongly on the foreign exchange markets as nervous investors sought a safe haven for their cash.* • *We would like to warn viewers* **of a nervous disposition** (= who are easily upset) *that the following programme contains scenes which they may find disturbing.* • A **nervous breakdown** is a period of mental illness, usually without a physical cause, which results in anxiety, difficulty in sleeping and thinking clearly, a lack of confidence and hope, and a feeling of great sadness: *He was forced to give up his job after suffering a nervous breakdown.* • (CS) (F) (PL) (RUS)

nerv·ous·ly /£'nɜː·və·sli, $'nɜːr-/ *adv* • *He looked nervously over his shoulder, making sure no one else was listening.*

nerv·ous·ness /£'nɜː·və·snəs, $'nɜːr-/ *n* [U] • *There is growing nervousness* **about** *the possibility of a war in the region.*

nerv·y /£'nɜː·vi, $'nɜːr-/ *adj* **-ier**, **-iest** *Br* • *I'm always nervy* (= worried) *before an exam.*

-ness /-nəs/ *combining form* added to adjectives to form nouns which refer to a quality or a condition • *happiness* (= the quality of being happy) • *sadness* • *nervousness* • *selfishness* • *In 'kindness' a noun has been formed from the adjective 'kind'.* • *the causes of homelessness* (= the condition of people who do not have a home) • LP› **Combining forms, Stress in pronunciation**

nest HOME /nest/ *n* [C] the structure where animals such as birds, insects and mice give birth or leave their eggs to develop • *Cuckoos are famous for laying their eggs in the nests of other birds.* • *The alligators build their nests out of grass near the water's edge.* • *(fig.) We're really looking forward to getting married and turning the cottage into a cosy nest* (= comfortable home). • Sometimes a nest is a place where something unpleasant or unwanted has developed: *The diplomats have been sent home because their embassy has become a nest* **of** *spies and espionage.* • A **nest egg** is a sum of money that has been saved or kept for a special purpose: *Regular investment of small amounts of money is an excellent way of building a nest egg.* • See also NESTLING.

nest /nest/ *v* [I] • *We've got some swallows nesting in our roof at the moment.* • *Stone farm buildings are ideal nesting* **sites** *for barn owls.* • A **nesting box** (also **nest box** *Am* **birdhouse**) is a box for birds to nest in.

nest SET /nest/ *n* [C] a set of things that are similar but different in size and have been designed to fit inside each other • *I'd like a nest* **of** *tables for the living room.* • PIC› **Table**

nest·ing /£'nes·tɪŋ, $-t̬ɪŋ/ *adj* [not gradable] • *Moscow's street vendors do a roaring trade in nesting* **dolls** *painted with the faces of Soviet and Russian leaders.*

nest·le /'nes·l̩/ *v* [always + adv/prep] to be or put in a warm, comfortable, protected or sheltered position • *I love nestling* **down** *in bed with a cup of hot chocolate.* [I] • *Lake Gyogy nestles* **among** *the volcanic hills of western Hungary.* [I] • *Bregenz is a pretty Austrian town that nestles* **between** *the Alps and Lake Constance.* [I] • *He nestled his head on her lap and gazed up into her eyes.* [T]

nest·ling /'nes·l̩ɪŋ, 'nest·lɪŋ/ *n* [C] a young bird which has not yet learned to fly and still lives in the nest built by its parents

net MATERIAL /net/ *n* material made of threads of rope, string, wire or plastic that are woven loosely so that there are spaces between them, allowing gas, liquid or small objects to go through, or an object made with this material which is used to limit the movement of something • *The living-room windows have net* **curtains** *which let in sunlight but stop passers-by looking in from the street.* [U] • *Dolphins often get tangled in the nets that are used to catch tuna fish.* [C] • *(fig.) The terrorists have once again slipped through the police net* (= avoided being caught by the police). [C] • *You ought to put a net over your strawberry plants to stop the birds eating the fruit.* [C] • A net is also a rectangular piece of material made from string which is used to separate the two sides in various sports: *If the ball touches the net during a service in a game of tennis, you have to serve again.* [C] • A net is also the area surrounded by a piece of material made from string into which a ball or PUCK is put in order to score points in various sports: *He headed the ball down, and it finished up in the back of the net*

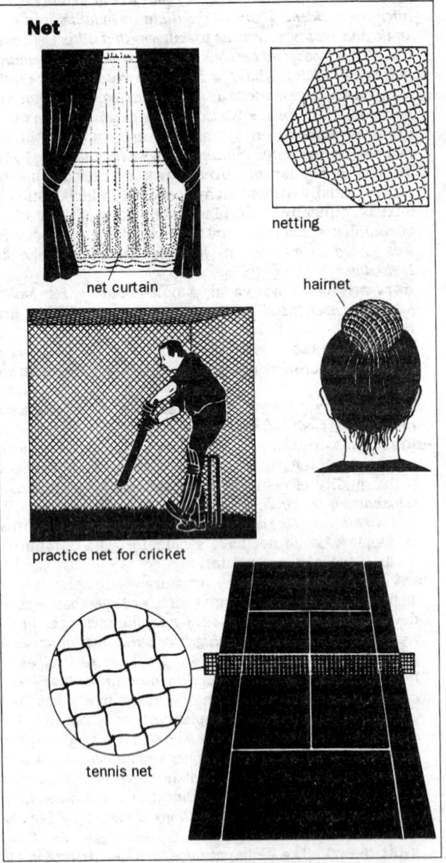

– *another goal for England.* [C] • See also HAIRNET. • PIC› **Net** DK

net *obj* /net/ *v* [T] **-tt-** • *How many fish did you net* (= catch) *this afternoon?* • *He secured a dramatic victory for England by netting* (= kicking into the net) *the ball half a minute before the end of the game.* • *(fig.) Mark's netted himself* (= managed to obtain) *a top job with an advertising company.* [+ two objects] • *(fig.) She netted* (= earned) *£10 million* **(for** *herself) from the sale of her company.* • *(fig.) She netted herself a fortune when she sold her company.* [+ two objects]

net·ting /£ˈnet·ɪŋ, $ˈnet̬-/ *n* [U] • Netting is any material in the form of a net: *Two skiers were injured by safety netting that was too close to the course.* • PIC› **Net**

net LEFT OVER, *Br also* **nett** /net/ *adj* [before or after n; not gradable] left when there is nothing else to be subtracted • *I earn £15 000 gross, but my net* **income** (= income that is left after tax has been paid) *is about £12 000.* • *The savings account pays interest at 8%, or 6% net to basic-rate taxpayers.* • *The net* **weight** *of something excludes the weight of the material that it is packed in.* • *This bar of chocolate* **weighs** *100 grams net.* • *(fig.) The net* **result** (= result after everything has been considered) *of the changes will be increased fares and reduced services for most rail travellers.* • Compare GROSS TOTAL. • DK

net·ball /£ˈnet·bɔːl, $-bɑːl/ *n* [U] *Br* a sport played by two teams of seven players, usually women or girls, in which goals are obtained by throwing a ball through a net hanging from a ring at the top of a pole • *She was captain of the school netball team.* • LP› **Sports**

neth·er /£ˈneð·əʳ, $-ɚ/ *adj* [before n; not gradable] *literary or humorous* in a lower position • *The boiler room is somewhere down in the building's nether* **regions**. • *(fig.) The secret service decided that his terrorist talents could be useful, so he spent ten years in the nether* (= hidden) **world** *of military intelligence.*

net·tle PLANT /£ˈnet·l̩, $ˈnet̬-/ *n* [C] a wild plant with heart-shaped leaves that are covered in hairs which sting • *Watch out for those* **stinging** *nettles!* • **Nettle rash** is a condition in which slightly raised red or white areas appear on the skin, making you want to rub it: *Nettle rash is an allergic reaction that can be caused by things other than nettles.* • PIC› **Flowers and plants**

net·tle *obj* ANNOY /£ˈnet·l̩, $ˈnet̬-/ *v* [T] to make (someone) annoyed or slightly angry • *She looked up at me sharply, clearly nettled by the interruption.*

net·work /£ˈnet·wɜːk, $-wɜːrk/ *n* [C] a large system consisting of many similar parts that are connected together to allow movement or communication between or along the parts or between the parts and a control centre • *The World Athletics Championships will be broadcast on 100* **television** *networks worldwide.* • **Cable** *networks can distribute phone calls and computer data as well as television and radio programmes.* • *Throughout the crisis, uncensored news reports were distributed around the country on private* **computer** *networks.* • *Massive investment is needed to modernise the country's* **telephone** *network.* • *(Br) Almost every week traffic restrictions are imposed on another section of the* **motorway** *network.* • *The French* **rail(way)** *network is the most advanced in Europe.* • *We could reduce our costs by developing a more efficient* **distribution** *network.* • *The country's* **extensive** *network* **of** *secret agents has kept the government informed of its opponents' activities.*

net·work *(obj)* /£ˈnet·wɜːk, $-wɜːrk/ *v* • *The series was originally broadcast only in the London area, but it was so popular that it was networked* (= broadcast on a television network) *nationwide.* [T] • *Our computer system consists of about twenty personal computers networked* (= connected by a network) **to** *a powerful file-server.* [T] • *The system allows documents to be shared simultaneously with networked colleagues, regardless of their location.* [T] • *(fig.) If you want to get on in this business you'll need to spend a lot of time networking* (= meeting people who might be useful to know) *and building up contacts.* [I] • *(fig.) I don't really enjoy these conferences, but they're a good opportunity to do some networking.*

neu·ral /£ˈnjʊə·rəl, $ˈnʊr·əl/ *adj* [before n; not gradable] involving a nerve or the system of nerves that includes the brain • *Some people suffered severe neural damage as a result of the vaccination.* • A **neural network** is a computer system that is designed to copy the way in which the human brain operates: *Neural networks can learn solutions to difficult problems.*

neu·ral·gi·a /£njʊəˈræl·dʒə, $nʊrˈæl-/ *n* [U] a condition caused by a nerve that is damaged or not working correctly, in which severe brief pains are felt suddenly along the nerve • *I've got neuralgia and can't turn my neck to the left.*

neu·ral·gic /£njʊəˈræl·dʒɪk, $nʊrˈæl-/ *adj* [not gradable]

neur(o)– /£ˈnʊə·rəʊ, $-roʊ/ *combining form* relating to nerves • *Advances in neuroscience are providing a better understanding of how the brain works.* • *A neurotransmitter is a chemical that nerve cells use to communicate with each other and with muscles.*

neu·rol·o·gy /£njʊəˈrɒl·ə·dʒi, $nʊrˈɑː·lə-/ *n* [U] the study of the structure and diseases of the brain and all the nerves in the body which together make movement and feeling possible by sending messages around the body

neu·ro·log·i·cal /£ˌnjʊə·rəˈlɒdʒ·ɪ·kəl, $ˌnʊr·əˈlɑː·dʒɪ-/ *adj* [not gradable] • *Alzheimer's disease is a neurological* **disorder** *that sometimes affects older people.*

neu·rol·o·gist /£njʊəˈrɒl·ə·dʒɪst, $nʊrˈɑː·lə-/ *n* [C] • *Neurologists regard the brain as a network of billions of interconnecting nerve cells.*

neu·ron /£ˈnjʊə·rɒn, $ˈnʊr·ɑːn/, **neu·rone** /£ˈnjʊə·rəʊn, $ˈnʊr·oʊn/, **nerve cell** *n* [C] a cell that carries information between the brain and other parts of the body • *A single human neuron can be several feet long and stretch from the brain all the way down the spine to a leg.*

neu·ros·is /£njʊəˈrəʊ·sɪs, $nʊrˈoʊ-/ *n pl* **neuroses** /£njʊəˈrəʊ·siːz, $nʊrˈoʊ-/ a mental state resulting in high levels of anxiety, unreasonable fears and behaviour and, often, a need to repeat actions unnecessarily • *If you want my opinion, I think she's suffering from some form of neurosis.* [U] • *She's obsessively clean – it's almost become a neurosis with her.* [C]

neu·ro·tic /£njʊəˈrɒt·ɪk, $nʊrˈɑː·t̬ɪk/ *adj* • *In 'Play It Again, Sam', Woody Allen plays a neurotic film critic.* • *She's neurotic* (= extremely worried) **about** *her weight – she weighs herself three times a day.*

neu·ro·tic /£njʊəˈrɒt·ɪk, $nʊrˈɑː·t̬ɪk/ *n* [C] • *Neurotics often lack self-confidence.*

neu·ro·ti·cally /£njʊəˈrɒt·ɪ·kli, $nʊrˈɑː·t̬ɪ-/ *adv* [not gradable] • *Martin Smith started behaving neurotically soon after he lost his job and his wife left him both in the same week.*

neu·ro·sur·geon /£ˈnjʊə·rəʊˌsɜː·dʒən, $ˈnʊr·oʊˌsɜːr-/ *n* [C] a doctor who performs operations involving the brain or nerves

neu·ro·sur·ger·y /£ˈnjʊə·rəʊˌsɜː·dʒər·i, $ˈnʊr·oʊˌsɜːr·dʒɚ-/ *n* [U]

neu·ter GRAMMAR /£ˈnjuː·tər, $ˈnuː·t̬ɚ/ *adj* [not gradable] *specialized* relating to a group of nouns in a particular language which have the same grammatical behaviour and which do not usually include words that refer to females or males • *The German word for 'book', 'das Buch', is neuter.*

neu·ter *obj* REMOVE SEX ORGANS /£ˈnjuː·tər, $ˈnuː·t̬ɚ/ *v* [T] to remove part of (an animal's) sexual organs, so that it cannot reproduce • *The owners of dangerous dogs are legally obliged to have them neutered.* • *(fig.) The primary objective of any Western offensive would be to neuter* (=make powerless) *their war machine.*

neu·tral NO OPINION /£ˈnjuː·trəl, $ˈnuː-/ *adj* not saying or doing anything that would encourage or help any of the groups involved in an argument or war • *My daughter often tries to get me to take her side in her arguments with her mother, but I always* **remain** *neutral.* • *Both sides have agreed to attend a peace conference on the condition that it is held in a neutral* **country**. • *I'd rather meet on neutral* **ground/territory** (=somewhere that neither of us is connected to) *rather than in his apartment.* • *Many newspapers claim to be* **politically** *neutral, but few actually are.*

neu·tral /£ˈnjuː·trəl, $ˈnuː-/ *n* [C] • *Sweden and Switzerland were neutrals during the war.* • *I don't want to get involved in this argument – I'm a neutral on this.*

neu·tral·i·ty /£njuːˈtræl·ə·ti, $nuːˈtræl·ə·t̬i/ *n* [U] • *It is unlikely that Sweden will ever abandon its traditional neutrality and join a military alliance.* • *The Queen has maintained political neutrality throughout her reign.*

neu·tral NOT NOTICEABLE /£ˈnjuː·trəl, $ˈnuː-/ *adj* having features or characteristics that are not easily noticed • *Huw wants to paint the living room walls dark red but I'd rather a more neutral* **colour** *like cream.* • *The neutral flavour of this wine is the perfect complement to beef dishes with rich sauces.* • In chemistry, a substance that is neutral is neither an acid nor an ALKALI: *Pure water is neutral and has a pH of 7.* • In physics, something that is neutral has no electrical charge: *Atoms consist of positively-charged protons, negatively-charged electrons and neutral particles called neutrons.*

neu·tral·ize *obj, Br and Aus usually* **-ise** /£ˈnjuː·trə·laɪz, $ˈnuː-/ *v* [T] • *To neutralize* (=make less strong) *the strong taste of goat meat, she washes it in water and vinegar.* • *Acidity in soil can be neutralized* (=the acidity removed) *by spreading lime on it.*

neu·tral·iz·a·tion, *Br and Aus usually* **-i·sa·tion** /£ˌnjuː·trə·laɪˈzeɪ·ʃən, $ˌnuː-/ *n* [U]

neu·tral VEHICLE /£ˈnjuː·trəl, $ˈnuː-/ *n* [U] the position of the GEARS (=the parts of a vehicle that carry power from the engine to the wheels) when they are not connected to the engine • *In Britain, you're supposed to put your car* **into** *neutral whenever you stop at a junction.* • *(fig.) After two years* **in** *neutral, the economy is finally moving forward again.* • LP **Driving**

neu·tral·ize *obj, Br and Aus usually* **-ise** /£ˈnjuː·trə·laɪz, $ˈnuː-/ *v* [T] to remove the ability of (something) to have an effect • *The aerial bombardments have neutralized the threat of artillery attacks on allied ground forces.* • *The increase in indirect taxation is intended to neutralize the reduction in income tax.* • *The Democrats need to neutralize the Republican claim that they have no coherent foreign policy.*

neu·tral·iz·a·tion, *Br also* **-i·sa·tion** /£ˌnjuː·trə·laɪˈzeɪ·ʃən, $ˌnuː-/ *n* [U]

neu·tron /£ˈnjuː·trɒn, $ˈnuː·trɑːn/ *n* [C] a part of an atom that has no electrical charge • *The nucleus of an atom consists of neutrons and protons.* • A **neutron bomb** is a nuclear weapon for use across short distances which is designed to kill people rather than destroy buildings or vehicles: *Neutron bombs release lethal radiation instead of exploding with a lot of heat and wind.* • Compare ELECTRON; PROTON.

nev·er /£ˈnev·ər, $-ɚ/ *adv* [not gradable] not at any time or not on any occasion • *I've never been to Australia.* • *He was never seen alive again.* • *"Do you know a guy called Anthony Edwards?" "Never heard of him."* • *I've never heard anything like this before in my life.* • *I'd never been so angry in all my life* (=I was extremely angry). • *Let us never forget those who gave their lives for their country.* • *I never forget a face.* • *"I hope you're not planning to borrow my car tonight." "The thought had never even crossed my mind."* • *He's never quite forgiven me for what I said about his father.* • *There will never be another Charlie Chaplin.* • *Wars never* (=not in any conditions) *solve anything.* • *I thought she'd never stop* (=would not stop). • *He threatened to shoot, but I never thought* (=did not think) *he would go through with it.* • *"You told me you liked Julia." "I never said* (=certainly did not say) *that!"* • *I never realised* (=I didn't know that) *you knew my brother.* • *(Br) "He's never 61!* (=It's difficult to believe he's 61!) *He looks so young."* • *(not standard) "You stole my drink!" "No, I never* (=I didn't)." • *I'd never had so much money* **before**. • *(fml) Never* **before** *had I had so much money.* • *I never want to see you* **ever** *again.* • *I never* **ever** *want to see you again.* • *Ideally, you would have been eating a healthy diet even before you became pregnant, but it's never* **too late** *to start.* • *Satellite technology offers the opportunity,* **as never before** (=in a way that has not been possible until now), *for continuous television coverage of major international events.* • **Never fear!** (=Don't worry!) *Guy's here! I'll have that leak fixed in a few moments.* • *"I hope you're not planning to get drunk at the party."* "**Never fear!** (=There's no chance of that happening.) *I always feel terrible when I drink too much."* • *"I'm afraid I've lost that wallet you gave me." "Well,* **never mind** (=don't worry about it), *I can easily buy you another one."* • **Never mind** (=Don't give any attention to) *the price, just look at the quality.* • *Midsummer House is one of the best restaurants in the country,* **never mind** (=and not just one of the best in) *Cambridge.* • *He's going on holiday for the third time this year,* **never mind that** (=despite the fact that) *he has hardly any money left.* • *"Sophie's brother's been married seven times."* "**Well, I never (did)!** (=I'm extremely surprised to discover that!)" • *"He promised to pay me back last week, but he didn't." "Dear me, that* **will never do** (=is completely unacceptable)*!"* • Something that is **never-ending** never ends or seems as if it will never end: *Writing a dictionary is never-ending.* • *(Br infml)* If you buy something **on the never-never**, you use a system of payment in which part of the cost is paid immediately and then small regular payments are made until the debt is reduced to nothing: *I don't like buying things on the never-never because they charge you such a lot in interest.* • **Never-never land** is an imaginary place where everything is pleasant or perfect in a way that is impossible to achieve in reality: *She seems to be completely out of touch with the real world and living in her own never-never land.* • *(saying)* 'Never the twain shall meet' means that two things or people are completely different or not suitable to be with each other or unable to agree. • *"You'll Never Walk Alone"* (title of a song written by Oscar Hammerstein II, 1945) • *"Never Never Land"* (a place where children never grow up, in J.M.Barrie's children's book *Peter Pan*, 1904) • *"You've never had it so good"* (from a speech by Harold Macmillan, 1957) • *"Never on Sunday"* (title of a film, 1959)

nev·er·the·less /£ˌnev·ə·ðəˈles, $ˌ-ɚ-/, *slightly fml* **none·the·less** *adv* [not gradable] despite what has just been said or referred to • *I disagreed with everything she said,* **but** *she's a very good speaker nevertheless.* • *"We really can't afford to buy any new equipment at present." "Nevertheless, we need to invest to keep up with our competitors."*

new RECENTLY CREATED /£njuː, $nuː/ *adj* **-er, -est** recently created or having started to exist recently • *a new car* • *Have you seen Steven Spielberg's new movie?* • *What's new in the fashion world?* • *She's very creative and always coming up with new ideas.* • *What have they decided to call their new baby?* • *The association is trying to attract new members by offering discounts on subscriptions for the first year.* • *We have to invest in new* **technology** *if we are to remain competitive.* • **New potatoes** are potatoes that are taken out of the ground earlier than the others in the crop. • See also BRAND-NEW.

new /£njuː, $nuː/ *n* [U] • *Out with the old and in with* **the new** (=new things).

new– /£njuː-, $nuː-/ *combining form* • *The government's new-***found** (=recently found) *enthusiasm for green issues has been welcomed by environmentalists.*

new·ish /£'njuː·ɪʃ, $'nuː·ɪʃ/ *adj* [not gradable] *infml* • Something that is newish is slightly new: *Two generations ago, most people would carry on working till they died, so retirement is a newish idea.*

new·ly /£'njuː·li, $'nuː·li/ *adv* [before v-*ed* or adj; not gradable] • *The newly* (=recently) *formed residents' association has made an official complaint to the police about the incident.* • *Iceland was the first country to establish diplomatic ties with the newly independent Baltic states.* • *Newly-discovered documents cast doubt on the guilt of the two men.* • *"Getting married is the best thing I've ever done," beamed the newly-***wed** *Chris.* See also NEWLYWED.

new·ness /£'njuː·nəs, $'nuː-/ *n* [U]

new DIFFERENT /£njuː, $nuː/ *adj* [before n] **-er, -est** different to one that existed earlier • *Have you met the new secretary?* • *After being unemployed for 18 months, she has given up hope of ever finding a new job.* • *Have you seen Ann's new house* (=the house that Ann has just started living in)*?* • *That holiday did me the world of good – I've been feeling like a new* (=greatly improved) *woman since I came back.* • *The voters have given the National Party a mandate to eradicate apartheid and negotiate a new* **deal** *for the whole of South Africa.* • *He belongs to a new generation of terrorists who are even more ruthless than their predecessors.* • *They've just launched a new generation of computers that are much more powerful than earlier models.* • **New Age** is a way of life and thinking which developed in the late 1980s and includes a wide range of beliefs and activities that are not accepted by most people and are based on ideas that existed before modern scientific and economic developments: *Astrology and alternative medicine are part of the New Age movement.* ○ *Martin's really into New Age* **music**. ○ *Many* **New Agers** *are vegetarians and environmentalists.* • **New blood** is people with a lot of energy or fresh ideas who are brought into an organization in order to improve it: *Let's hope the new blood in the team will improve our chances of victory against Italy in next week's match.* • A **new broom** is someone who has just started to work for an organization and intends to make a lot of changes: *The new broom was supposed to improve the way the department is managed, but things have been worse than ever since she arrived.* • *(saying)* 'A new broom sweeps clean' means that when someone new takes control of an organization they will make many changes. • *(esp. Br)* **New girls/New boys** are children who have recently started going to a school or people who have recently become involved with an activity or organization: *There will be a tea party for the new girls and their parents at four o'clock.* ○ *Mark Kennedy is the new boy in the government.* • If someone or something has/gets/is given a *(Br and Aus)* **new lease of life**/*(Am)* **new lease on life** they become more energetic and active than before or the period of use is increased: *His grandchildren have* **given** *him a new lease of life.* ○ *The project suddenly* **got** *a new lease of life when the developers agreed to provide some more funding.* • *(esp. Br)* A **New Man** is a man who believes that women and men are equal and should be free to do the same things, and that people should not be treated differently because of their sex: *I want a New Man for a partner who'll insist on doing at least half of the household chores.* • A **new moon** is the Moon when it is shaped like a CRESCENT or a time when the Moon is shaped like this. • **The New Right** is a group of people who believe that government should be separated from a country's economy and that traditional morality is very important. • **The New Testament** is the second of the two main parts of the Bible: *The New Testament describes the life and work of Jesus Christ and the early development of Christianity.* ○ *Most of his paintings are of New Testament scenes such as the Resurrection.* Compare **Old Testament** at OLD FROM THE PAST. • A **new town** is a British town which did not develop gradually but was established and planned by the government: *Milton Keynes is a new town which was founded in 1967.* • A **new wave** is a fashion in something such as art, music, cinema or politics, which is intentionally different from traditional ideas about such things: *Godard and Truffaut were two of the most important film directors involved in the French New Wave of the 1960s.* • If there is a **new wave** of something it is happening again or being repeated after a pause: *The company shed 2000 employees last year and a new wave* **of** *job losses is expected this year.* • **The New World** is North, Central and South America: *Early European settlers used to refer to America as the New World.* • **The new world order** is a political situation in which the countries of the world are no longer divided because of their support for either the United States or the Soviet Union and instead work together to solve international problems: *The new world order was expected to come into existence after the collapse of Communism in eastern Europe and the end of the Cold War.* • **New Year** is the beginning of the year which is about to begin or has just begun: *We'll have to wait until* **the** *New Year before we can make any definite plans.* ○ *I'm spending New Year* (=the first days of the new year) *in Scotland with my parents.* ○ *To Angi, with best wishes for Christmas and a* **Happy** *New Year.* ○ *The chairman warned of the need for further redundancies in a bleak New Year's message to employees.* • **New Year's Day** (*Am also* **New Year's**) is the first day of the year and is a public holiday in many countries: *Kate was born on New Year's Day in 1969.* • **New Year's Eve** is the last day of the year: *Are you going to Diane and John's New Year's Eve party?* See also HOGMANAY. • A **New Year's Resolution** is a promise that you make to yourself to start doing something good or stop doing something bad on the first day of the year: *"Have you* **made** *any New Year's resolutions?" "Yes, I'm going to eat more healthily and give up smoking."*

new NOT FAMILIAR /£njuː, $nuː/ *adj* [after v] **-er, -est** not yet familiar or experienced • *She's new* **to** *the job so you can't expect her to know how to do everything already.* • *Our next-door neighbours are new* **to** *the area, having only moved in a few weeks ago.* • *Camille says she's heard of him, but the name's new* **to** *me.* • *Excuse me, I'm new around here. Would you mind showing me how the photocopier works?*

new NOT USED /£njuː, $nuː/ *adj* **-er, -est** not previously used or owned • *They sell second-hand CDs as well as new ones.* • *Used car sales have risen because of the increased cost of new cars.* • *Did you buy your bike new or second-hand?* • *This television was* **brand** (=completely) *new a month ago, and it's already broken.*

new RECENTLY DISCOVERED /£njuː, $nuː/ *adj* **-er, -est** recently discovered or made known • *This new cancer treatment offers hope to many sufferers.* • *How often is a new solar system discovered?* • *A retrial can only take place when new evidence has emerged.* • *(infml) "Sian and Richard are getting married." "Really! that's* **a new one on me**" (=I did not know this information).

new·born /£'njuː·bɔːn, $'nuː·bɔːrn/ *adj* [before n; not gradable] recently born • *Breast-feeding is extremely beneficial to the health of newborn* **babies**. • *(fig.) The West has a responsibility to nurture the newborn democracies of the world.* • LP ▷ **Age**

new·com·er /£'njuːˌkʌm·əʳ, $'nuːˌkʌm·ɚ/ *n* [C] someone who has recently arrived in a place or recently become involved in an activity • *We've lived here for 20 years, but we're* **relative** *newcomers* **to** *the village. There's one 99-year-old who's been here all her life!* • *The newcomer* **on the** *radio* **scene** *is a commercial station that is devoted to classical music.*

new·fang·led /£njuː'fæŋ·gl̩d, $nuː-/ *adj* [not gradable] recently made for the first time, but not necessarily an improvement on what existed before • *I really don't understand these newfangled computer games that my children are always playing.*

new·ly·wed /£'njuː·li·wed, $'nuː-/ *n* [C usually pl] someone who has recently got married • *The hotel has a special discount rate for newlyweds.* • *"The wedding day was just the happiest day of my life," beamed newlywed Chris Opalinski.*

news /£njuːz, $nuːz/ *n* [U] information or reports about recent events, or a television or radio programme consisting of such reports • *That's the best* **(piece of)** *news I've heard for a long time!* • *We've had no news* **of** *them since they left for Australia.* • *Have you heard the news* **about** *Tina and Tom? They're getting divorced.* • *Do write and tell us all your news.* • *Is there any news, Doctor? Is she going to be alright?* • *The news* **that** *Madge had resigned took everyone by surprise.* [+ *that* clause] • *I like to watch the early evening news when I get home from work.* • *Was there anything interesting* **on** *the news this evening?* • *Shares in the company rose 7p to 90p* **on the** *news* **of** *the increased profits* (=when this became generally known). • *They've been* **in** *the news* (=reported about) *a lot recently because of their marital problems.* • *Our news* **desk** (=place where news is collected) *is staffed twenty-four hours a day.* • *She* **made** *news* (=was publicly reported) *last year when she broke the world record for the 100 metres.* • *I'm afraid I've got some* **bad** *news for you, madam. Your husband's been *seriously injured in a road accident.* • *We've got some* **good** *news for you. We're getting married.* • If you **break** the news to someone, you tell them about something bad which has just happened and which has an effect on them: *I was absolutely devastated when the doctor broke the news to me about my illness.* • *Where were you when the news of the assassination* **broke** (= became known)*?* • *"I hear you and Phil are going to Paris for the weekend." "Really? That's news* **to** *me* (= I didn't know about that)*."* • *(fig.) He's* **bad** *news* **for** (= has a bad effect on) *the company. He should never have been given the job.* • *(fig.) Madeleine says Kate's new boyfriend is very* **good** *news* (= is a good person and suitable for her). • *I've* **got news for him** (= He'll be unpleasantly surprised), *if he thinks he can carry on living here free of charge.* • A **news agency** is an organization which supplies reports to newspapers, magazines and broadcasters. • A **news conference** is a meeting in which someone makes a statement to reporters or answers questions from them: *As soon as the allegations were published, she* **called** *a news conference to give her side of the story.* • *(saying)* 'No news is good news' means that you would have been told if anything bad had happened: *We haven't heard anything from the hospital today, but I suppose no news is good news.* • *"All the news that's fit to print"* (motto of the *New York Times*, 1858-1935) • *"Have I Got News for You"* (title of television quiz show, 1990s)

news·y /£ˈnjuː·zi, $ˈnuː-/ *adj* **-ier, -iest** • Something that is newsy contains a lot of news that is personal or not very serious: *I really look forward to getting a letter from Georgina – they're always so newsy.* ○ *The paper hopes to attract more readers by adopting a newsier style.*

news·ag·ent *Br and Aus* /£ˈnjuːzˌeɪ·dʒᵊnt, $ˈnuːz-/, *Am* **news deal·er** *n* [C] a shop whose main business is selling newspapers and magazines, or a person who manages such a shop • *Let's look for a newsagent. They'll probably have a map of the town.* • *Do you want anything from the newsagent's apart from a paper?* • *A newsagent has been seriously injured in an armed raid in which £2000 was stolen.*

news·cast·er /£ˈnjuːzˌkɑː·stəʳ, $ˈnuːzˌkæs·t̬ɚ/, *Br and Aus also* **news·read·er** *n* [C] someone who reads the reports on a television or radio news programme

news·cast /£ˈnjuːz·kɑːst, $ˈnuːz·kæst/ *n* [C] *esp. Am* • A newscast is a radio or television programme that consists of news reports.

news·flash /£ˈnjuːz·flæʃ, $ˈnuːz-/ *n* [C] a brief news report on radio or television, giving the most recent information about an important or unexpected event

news·hound /£ˈnjuːz·haʊnd, $ˈnuːz-/ *n* [C] a reporter who puts a lot of effort into discovering new stories, often working in difficult or dangerous situations

news·let·ter /£ˈnjuːzˌlet·əʳ, $ˈnuːzˌlet̬·ɚ/ *n* [C] a printed document containing information about the recent activities of an organization which is sent regularly to the organization's members • *Our* **monthly** *newsletter will keep you up to date with all the latest developments.*

news·pap·er /£ˈnjuːzˌpeɪ·pəʳ, $ˈnuːzˌpeɪ·pɚ/ *n* (an organization which makes and publishes) a regularly printed document consisting of news reports, articles, photographs and advertisements that are printed on large sheets of paper which are folded together but not permanently joined • *Which newspaper do you read regularly?* [C] • *In the UK, a* **daily** *newspaper is usually one which is published every day except Sunday.* [C] • *He wants to work for a newspaper when he leaves school.* [C] • *You ought to wrap that mirror up in newspaper* (= old newspapers) *before you put it in the car.* [U]

new·speak /£ˈnjuː·spiːk, $ˈnuː-/ *n* [U] language used by politicians and government officials which is intentionally difficult to understand or which does not mean what it seems to mean and is therefore likely to deceive people

news·print /£ˈnjuːz·prɪnt, $ˈnuːz-/ *n* [U] cheap paper that newspapers are printed on • *Increasing amounts of newsprint are made by recycling old newspapers.* • *A huge amount of newsprint has been devoted to the question of who the prince will marry.*

news·read·er /£ˈnjuːzˌriː·dəʳ, $ˈnuːzˌriː·dɚ/ *n* [C] *Br and Aus for* NEWSCASTER

news·reel /£ˈnjuːz·riːl, $ˈnuːz-/ *n* [C] a short film that consists of news reports and has usually been made to be shown in a cinema • *The movie contains some recently discovered newsreel* **footage** *of the war.*

news·room /£ˈnjuːz·rʊm, $ˈnuːz·ruːm/ *n* [C] an office at a television or radio station or a newspaper where news is gathered and reports are prepared for broadcasting or publishing

news·stand /£ˈnjuːz·stænd, $ˈnuːz-/ *n* [C] a movable table or temporary structure used as a small shop for selling newspapers and magazines outside in public places • *You can buy foreign newspapers at a newsstand in front of the station.*

news·ven·dor /£ˈnjuːzˌven·dəʳ, $ˈnuːzˌven·dɚ/ *n* [C] someone who sells newspapers

news·wor·thy /£ˈnjuːzˌwɜː·ði, $ˈnuːzˌwɜːr-/ *adj* interesting enough to be described in a news report • *Nothing newsworthy ever happens around here. It's so boring.*

news·y /£ˈnjuː·zi, $ˈnuː-/ *adj* See at NEWS

newt /£njuːt, $nuːt/ *n* [C] a small animal which has a long thin body and tail, short weak legs and cold wet skin • *Newts are amphibians and live mainly on land, but breed in water.* • PIC› **Reptiles and amphibians**

next /nekst/ *adj* [not gradable], *pronoun* being the first one after the present one or after the one just mentioned, or being the first after the present moment • *Who works in the office next* **to** *yours?* • *Go straight on at the traffic lights and then take the next turning on the right.* • *They've only just recovered from their last party and they're already planning the next one.* • *The opinion poll found that law and order is the most important political issue for voters and education is the next most important.* • *I originally wanted to work in television but I ended up in radio which is the next* **best thing**. • *Who do you think will be the next president?* • *Nothing really changes around here. One day is pretty much like* **the** *next.* • *I gave her a cigarette and the next moment she was gone.* • *I'm so busy I can hardly remember what I'm supposed to be doing* **from one moment to the** *next.* • *I'll be on holiday for the next couple of days.* • *"What do you think she'll say the next time that happens?" "Maybe there won't be a next time."* • *You'll have to wait until your next birthday for a new bike.* • *(The) next time you want to borrow something, please ask me first.* • *Can we arrange a meeting for the week after next?* • *What do you think you'll be doing this time next year?* • *We had a dreadful argument in the restaurant, but he phoned me* **the** *next* **day** (= the day after) *to apologise.* • *Who's next, please?* • *Excuse me, it's my turn to be served – I was next.* • *We've arranged ourselves a mortgage, so* **the** *next* **step** (= what we need to do next) *is to find a house to buy.* • *She is widely regarded in the company as the next managing director* **but one** (= the person who will follow the person who follows the present one). • *"So he's decided to get married at last.* **Whatever** *next!" "Children, I expect."* • *I enjoy winning awards* **as much as the next** *person* (= as much as anyone would enjoy it), *but other things are more important to me.* • If you live **next door** to someone, no one else's home is between your home and their home: *A Russian couple have just moved in next door.* ○ *Who lives next door* **to** *you?* ○ *There was a lot of noise coming from next door last night.* ○ *Margot and Mike are our* **next-door** *neighbours.* ○ *(fig.) Would you want to live next door* (= very close) *to a nuclear power station?* ○ *(fig. Br) If you're asked to resign from your job it's* **next door to** (= nearly the same as) *being fired.* • Your **next of kin** are your closest relatives and the people who will take responsibility for things such as funeral arrangements when you die: *The names of the three soldiers who were killed have not yet been released, but their next of kin have been informed.* • LP› **Calendar**

next /nekst/ *adv* [not gradable] • *So what happened next?* • *What would you like next?* • *First, fry the garlic. Next, add the ginger.* • *When are you next going to London?* • Two people or things that are next **to** each other are very close to each other and have nothing between them: *I prefer to sit next to the window when I'm on a plane.* ○ *There was a really strange man sitting next to me on the train.* ○ *(fig.) Cheese is my favourite food, and next to cheese I like chocolate* (= Cheese is the only food that I like more than chocolate). • Sometimes **next to** means almost: *They pay me next to* **nothing** (= very little) *but I really enjoy the work.* ○ *I bought this vase for next to* **nothing** (= at a very low price) *at an antiques market.* ○ *It's next to* **impossible** (= extremely difficult) *to find somewhere cheap to live in the city centre.* ○ *There was very little traffic and it took next to* **no time** (= very little time) *to get home.* • *(esp. Am) He injured himself in a climbing accident on the* **next-to-last** *day* (= the day before the last day) *of his vacation.*

nex·us /ˈnek·səs/ *n* [C usually sing] an important connection between the parts of a system or a group of things • *Times Square is the nexus of the New York subway.*

NF /ˌen'ef/ *n* [U] *abbreviation for* **National Front**, see at NATION

NHS /ˌen·eɪtʃ'es/ *n abbreviation for* **National Health Service**, see at NATION • *NHS hospitals* • *Many forms of cosmetic surgery are not* **available on** (=paid for by) **the** *NHS.*

nib /nɪb/ *n* [C] the pointed part of some types of pen through which ink flows onto paper when writing or drawing • *Fountain pens and cartridge pens have nibs, but ballpoints don't.* • PIC› **Writing instruments**

nib·ble *(obj)* /'nɪb·l̩/ *v* to eat (something) by taking a lot of small bites • *We ought to have some peanuts to nibble while the party warms up.* [T] • *I don't really feel like having a proper meal, but I wouldn't mind something to nibble* **(on/at)**. [T; I + prep] • *A mouse has nibbled through the cables that link our computers together.* [I] • *Jenny's hamster's nibbled a hole* **in** *the sofa.* [T] • *She nibbled* (=bit gently and repeatedly) *his ear.* [T] • *(fig.) Even when inflation is low, it nibbles* **away at** (=slowly reduces) *people's savings, reducing their value considerably over several years.* [I] • *(fig.) Investors started to nibble* **at** (=buy small amounts of) *the company's shares after the new contract was announced.* [I]

nib·ble /'nɪb·l̩/ *n* [C] • *Just* **take** *a nibble to see if you like the taste.* • *(fig.) Our house has been on the market for six months, but we haven't had a single nibble* (=but no one has shown any interest in buying it).

nib·bles /'nɪb·l̩z/ *pl n Br infml* • Nibbles are small amounts of food that are eaten between or before meals, often with alcoholic drinks: *I've asked Kimberley and Johnny to drop round for some wine and nibbles before we go on to the party.*

nibs /nɪbz/ *n* [U] **his nibs** *dated infml* a man who is in a position of authority or who thinks he is more important than he really is • *Did his nibs say when he would be back in the office?* • *His nibs always travels first class.*

nice PLEASANT /naɪs/ *adj* **-r, -st** pleasant, enjoyable or satisfactory • *Did you have a nice holiday?* • *I hope you have a nice time.* • *Have a nice day!* • *This milk doesn't smell very nice.* • *It's* **far** *nicer here than anywhere else I've lived.* • *If you must turn down the invitation, try to do it in the nicest possible way.* • *I'm pleased that you rang, Huw – it's been nice talking to you.* [+ v-ing] • **It** *was nice* **to** *see you last week.* [+ *to* infinitive] • *Wasn't* **it** *nice* **of** *them* **to** *invite us?* [+ *to* infinitive] • **It**'*s nice* **that** *you're staying here after all.* [+ *that* clause] • *Isn't Gill's husband nice-***looking** (=attractive)? • *This orange is* **nice and** (=pleasantly) *juicy.* • If you say that something is **nice work if you can get it**, you mean that it is an easy way of earning money which you would like to do if you could: *She was paid one million dollars to appear on television for five minutes – that's nice work if you can get it!* • *(infml) I never expected the café to make much money, but it's turned out to be a* **nice little earner** (=profitable activity).

nice·ly /'naɪ·sli/ *adv* • *Those trousers fit you nicely.* • *You've painted the woodwork very nicely.* • *Bake the mixture for 35 to 40 minutes until the cake is nicely browned.* • *They* **did** *very nicely* (=made a large profit) *from the sale of their company.* • *The prince said the princess and their baby were both* **doing** *nicely* (=healthy) *and would soon be back at home.* • **That'll do nicely** (=That is satisfactory), *thank you.* • *"That'll do nicely"* (used in advertisements for American Express)

nice KIND /naɪs/ *adj* **-r, -st** kind or friendly • *Jane's new boyfriend is a really nice guy.* • *I wish you'd be nice* **to** *your brother.* • **It** *was very nice* **of** *her* **to** *drive you home.* [+ *to* infinitive] • *Nice boys* (=boys who behave well) *don't say nasty things like that.* • *(infml) That's a nice* (=unkind) *thing to say to your poor old mother!* • *"Nice guys finish last"* (comment by Leo Durocher, 1946)

nice·ly /'naɪ·sli/ *adv* • *I don't know why you dislike her so much – she's always treated me very nicely.* • *You can only have another biscuit if you ask nicely* (=politely).

nice SLIGHTLY DIFFERENT /naɪs/ *adj* [before n] **-r, -st** based on very slight differences and needing a lot of careful and detailed thought • *I wasn't convinced by the minister's nice* **distinction** *between a lie and an untruth.*

ni·ce·ty /£'naɪ·sə·ti, $-t̬i/ *n* • *I'm afraid I don't understand the nicety of your argument.* [U] • Niceties are details or small differences which are only obvious after careful consideration: *Our divorce settlement was delayed by a year because our lawyers spent a lot of time arguing about* **legal** *niceties.* [C] • *We don't bother with all the* **social** *niceties here.* [C]

niche POSITION /£niːʃ, $nɪtʃ/ *n* [C] a job or position which is very suitable for someone, esp. one that they like • *Lloyd has* **carved/made** *a niche for himself as a professional tennis player.* • A niche is also an area or position which is exactly suitable for a small group of the same type: *an ecological niche* • A **niche market** is a small area of trade within the economy, often involving specialized products: *Lotus make luxury cars for a small but significant niche market.*

niche HOLLOW /£niːʃ, $nɪtʃ/ *n* [C] a hollow in a wall, esp. one made to put a statue in so that it can be seen

nick CUT /nɪk/ *n, v* (to make) a small cut in a surface or an edge • *Apart from a few nicks in the varnish the guitar is in very good condition.* [C] • *Paintwork on the corner of a stairway tends to get nicked and scratched as people pass by.* [T] • If something happens **in the nick of time** it happens at the last possible moment: *She lashed out at the boy who ducked back just in the nick of time.*

nick *obj* STEAL /nɪk/ *v* [T] *Br and Aus infml* to steal (something) • *We don't know exactly how many bikes are nicked each day in the city.*

nick *obj* CATCH /nɪk/ *v* [T] *Br slang* (of the police) to catch (someone) committing a crime • *The sooner we nick these thugs the better.* • *They nicked him* **for** *driving at seventy in a fifty speed limit area.*

nick PRISON *Br slang* /nɪk/ *n* [U] **the nick** *(Am slang* **the slammer***)* prison • *My hubby's been in the nick for twelve years and he's got eight to go.*

nick CONDITION /nɪk/ *n* [U] *Br and Aus slang* a stated condition, esp. of health • *He's* **in** *good nick for a man of his age.* • *The car really is* **in** *excellent nick.*

nick *obj* CHARGE /nɪk/ *v* [T] *Am infml* to charge (someone) money, esp. too much; to cheat (someone) • *$50 for a meal like that – we were nicked!* • *If your bank account balance falls below the minimum, you'll be nicked for a $5 service charge.*

nick·el METAL /'nɪk·l̩/ *n* [U] a silvery white metallic element • *a nickel alloy* • *Nickel is useful because of its high corrosion resistance.* • If something is **nickel-plated** its surface is covered with nickel which is usually done by putting an electric current through the object while it is held in a liquid containing nickel.

nick·el COIN /'nɪk·l̩/ *n* [C] a US or Canadian coin worth five CENTS • *(Am)* If something is **nickel-and-dime** it is unimportant, esp. because it does not involve much money: *a nickel-and-dime dispute* • *(Am)* To **nickel-and-dime** something is to damage or weaken it either by taking away many small amounts of money or by giving too much attention to details: *It may be a small fee, but added together small fees will nickel-and-dime me* **to death.** • LP› **Money**

nick–nack /'nɪk·næk/ *n* [C] a KNICK-KNACK

nick·name /'nɪk·neɪm/ *n* [C] an informal name for someone (or sometimes something), used esp. by their friends or family, usually based on their name or a characteristic that they have • *We always use the nickname Beth for our daughter Elizabeth.* • *Principi's knowledge of the department's myriad regulations has earned him the nickname 'Mr. Inside'.*

nick·name *obj* /'nɪk·neɪm/ *v* [T + obj + n] • *The campsite has been nicknamed 'tent city' by visiting reporters.*

nic·o·tine /£'nɪk·ə·tiːn, $-t̬iːn/ *n* [U] a poisonous chemical found in tobacco which often makes people who breathe it in habitually want more of it • A **nicotine patch** is a small piece of material with nicotine on it which is thought to help a person stop smoking if it is stuck on their skin.

niece /niːs/ *n* [C] a daughter of someone's brother or sister, or a daughter of someone's husband's or wife's brother or sister • Compare NEPHEW. • PIC› **Family tree**

niff /nɪf/ *n* [C usually sing] *Br infml* an unpleasant smell • *a nasty niff*

nif·fy /'nɪf·i/ *adj* **-ier, -iest** *Br infml*

nif·ty /'nɪf·ti/ *adj* **-ier, -iest** *infml* good, pleasing or effective • *a nifty addition* • *a nifty piece of work*

nig·gard·ly /£'nɪg·əd·li, $-ɚd-/ *adj disapproving* slight in amount, quality or effort • *a niggardly donation/attempt*

nig·ger /£'nɪg·əʳ, $-ɚ/ *n* [C] *taboo slang* a black person. This is a very offensive word when used to or about a black person by a white person.

nig·gle *(obj)* WORRY /'nɪg·l̩/ *v* to worry (someone) slightly, usually for a long time • *I just can't remember his name – it's been niggling (me) for a couple of weeks.* [I/T]

nig·gle /ˈnɪg·l̩/ *n* [C] • *Don't you feel even a slight niggle* (= a small doubt which causes worry) *about the morality of your experiments?*

nig·gling /ˈnɪg·l̩.ɪŋ, ˈ-lɪŋ/ *adj* [before n] • *a niggling doubt/fear*

nig·gle *(obj)* CRITICIZE /ˈnɪg·l̩/ *v* to criticize (someone) about small details or give too much attention to details • *Make sure the document is perfect – she'll niggle endlessly to find mistakes.* [I] • *The accounts department has been niggling me for ten cents which I owe them.* [T]

nig·gle /ˈnɪg·l̩/ *n* [C] • *I do have a few minor niggles* (= criticisms) *about the book but generally it's very good.*

nig·gling /ˈnɪg·l̩.ɪŋ, ˈ-lɪŋ/ *adj* [before n] • *Repairing watches can be a niggling job* (= one which needs a lot of attention to detail) *but that's part of the challenge.*

nigh /naɪ/ *adv* [not gradable], *prep old use* near • *She must have written nigh* **on** (= nearly but not quite) *550 books.* • **The time is** *nigh* (= It is nearly the time) *for us to make a decision.*

night DARK PERIOD /naɪt/ *n* the part of every 24 hour period when it is dark because there is very little light from the sun • *It often gets cold* **at** *night in the desert.* [U] • *Last night was certainly a night to remember.* [C] • *Bats and owls generally hunt* **at** *night.* [U] • *You can* **spend** *the night here if you want – we have a spare bed.* [C] • *We'll be travelling on the night ferry.* • **Night after night** means every night: *The howling of wild animals kept him awake night after night.* • *Bright lights illuminate the tunnel* **night and day** (= all the time) *so that digging never needs to stop.* See also **day and night** at DAY. • **Night blindness** is the inability to see when the general amount of light is very slight. • A **night shift** is a group of workers who work for a period during the night, or the period for which they work: *People who work (on the) night shift are paid more but it's still very unpopular.* • A **night table/night stand** is *Am for* **bedside table**. See at BEDSIDE. • **Night-time** is the time in every 24 hour period when it is dark. • A **night watchman** is a person who guards a building at night. • *"Night and day, you are the one"* (from the song *Night and Day* written by Cole Porter, 1932) • See also NIGHTS; NOCTURNAL.

night·ly /ˈnaɪt·li/ *adj, adv* [not gradable] • *Nightly bombardment of the city looks set to continue.* • *He longed nightly to be with her again.*

night EVENING /naɪt/ *n* the period of time between the late afternoon and going to bed; the evening • *Shall we go dancing on Saturday night?* [C] • *It's no wonder you're tired – you've been out every night this week.* [C] • *She's a singer in a bar* **by** *night and a secretary* **by** *day.* [U] • *He phoned us late last night.* [C] • *I saw Naomi at the club* **the other** *night* (= on a recent night). [C] • **Night after night** means every evening: *She went to the cinema night after night, always to see 'The Sound of Music'.* • *(infml)* **Night-night** is used esp. by or to children and is another way of saying **good night**, see at GOOD GREETING. • A **night on the town** is an evening when you go out of the place where you live to enjoy many entertainments such as dancing, eating in a restaurant and drinking in a bar: *We'll be graduating soon, let's* **have/go for** *a night on the town to celebrate.* • A **night out** is an enjoyable evening spent at a restaurant, theatre, etc. rather than staying at home: *Let's* **have** *a night out together on Saturday – we could go dancing.* • *(infml)* A **night owl** is a person who prefers to be awake and active at night. • **Night school** is a series of classes held (often in a school) in the evening, esp. for adults who work during the day. • LP› **Time**

night·ly /ˈnaɪt·li/ *adj, adv* [not gradable]

night SPECIAL EVENT /naɪt/ *n* [C] the evening on which a special event happens • *When's the* **last** *night of the play you're in?* • *The* **first/opening** *night of her new film was a great success.*

night·cap DRINK /ˈnaɪt·kæp/ *n* [C] a drink, often alcoholic, which someone has just before they go to bed

night·cap HAT /ˈnaɪt·kæp/ *n* [C] a type of hat made from soft cloth and worn in bed, esp. in the past

night·clothes /£ˈnaɪt·kləʊðz, $-kloʊðz/ *pl n* clothes which are worn in bed

night·club /ˈnaɪt·klʌb/, *infml* **night·spot** *n* [C] a place which is open until late at night where people can go to drink and dance and often see some type of entertainment • PIC› **Club**

night·club·bing /ˈnaɪtˌklʌb·ɪŋ/ *n* [U] *dated* • *Does she still go out nightclubbing every night?* • See also CLUBBING.

night·dress /ˈnaɪt·dres/, *infml* **night·ie** /£ˈnaɪ·ti, $-t̬i/, *Am also* **night·gown** /ˈnaɪt·gaʊn/ *n* [C] a comfortable piece of clothing like a loose dress worn by a woman or a girl in bed • PIC› **Beds and bedroom**

night·fall /£ˈnaɪt·fɔːl, $-fɑːl/ *n* [U] the time in every day when it becomes dark; DUSK

night·in·gale /£ˈnaɪ·tɪŋ·geɪl, $-t̬ɪŋ-/ *n* [C] a small brown bird found in Europe. The male has a beautiful song which is heard esp. during the night • *"A Nightingale Sang in Berkeley Square"* (title of a song written by Eric Maschwitz, 1940)

night·life /ˈnaɪt·laɪf/ *n* [U] entertainment and social activities which happen in the evening in bars and NIGHTCLUBS • *There isn't much nightlife at the resort – you'll have to go into the main town for that.*

night·light /ˈnaɪt·laɪt/ *n* [C] a light that is not bright which can be left on through the night, esp. for a child

night·long /£ˌnaɪtˈlɒŋ, $-ˈlɑːŋ/ *adj, adv* [not gradable] *literary* through the night

night·mare /£ˈnaɪt·meəʳ, $-mer/ *n* [C] a very upsetting or frightening dream, or *(fig.)* an extremely unpleasant event or experience • *a terrifying nightmare* • *(fig.) The* **worst** *nightmare for many people would be to be trapped in a car at an accident.* • *(fig.) An earthquake under a major city would be a nightmare* **(scenario)**. • *(fig.) The whole journey was a nightmare – we lost our luggage and we arrived two days late.* • *"Nightmare on Elm Street"* (horror film title, 1984)

night·mar·ish /£ˈnaɪt·meə·rɪʃ, $-mer·ɪʃ/ *adj*

night·mar·ish·ly /£ˈnaɪt·meə·rɪʃ·li, $-mer·ɪʃ-/ *adv*

nights /naɪts/ *adv* [not gradable] at night, esp. every night • *Because she's a nurse she has to* **work** *nights one week in every three.* • *(Am) I like to go out nights and sleep during the day.*

night·shirt /£ˈnaɪt·ʃɜːt, $-ʃɜːrt/ *n* [C] a comfortable piece of clothing like a long loose shirt worn esp. in the past by a man or a boy and sometimes by a woman or a girl in bed

night·spot /£ˈnaɪt·spɒt, $-spɑːt/ *n* [C] a NIGHTCLUB

night·stick /ˈnaɪt·stɪk/ *n* [C] *Am for* TRUNCHEON

night·wear /£ˈnaɪt·weəʳ, $-wer/ *n* [U] clothes worn in bed or while preparing to go to bed

ni·hil·i·sm /£ˈnɪh·ɪ·lɪ·zᵊm, $ˈnaɪ·ə·lɪ-/ *n* [U] a belief that all political and religious organizations are bad, or a system of thought which says that there are no principles or beliefs which have any meaning or can be true

ni·hil·ist /£ˈnɪh·ɪ·lɪst, $ˈnaɪ·ə-/ *n* [C]

ni·hil·is·tic /£ˌnɪh·ɪˈlɪs·tɪk, $ˌnaɪ·ə-/ *adj*

Nik·kei (in·dex) /£ˈnɪk·eɪ, $ˈniː·keɪ, nɪˈkeɪ/ *n* [U] a list which gives the price of shares in the most important Japanese companies • Compare DOW JONES (INDUSTRIAL); FTSE100 (INDEX).

nil /nɪl/ *n* [U] nothing • *She claims that operating risks are virtually nil for this type of nuclear power station.* • *(Br) The challengers lost the game seven-nil* (= zero) *to the champions.* • LP› **Zero**

nim·ble /ˈnɪm·bl̩/ *adj* **-r, -st** *usually approving* quick and exact either in movement or thoughts; AGILE • *Even at the age of fifty-four her nimble feet show what a great dancer she still is.* • *His nimble mind calculated the answer before I could key the numbers into my computer.*

nim·bly /ˈnɪm·bli/ *adv*

nim·ble·ness /ˈnɪm·bl̩·nəs/ *n* [U]

nim·bus /ˈnɪm·bəs/ *n* [U] dark-grey cloud which often produces rain or snow • Compare CIRRUS; CUMULUS.

NIM·BY /ˈnɪm·bi/ *n* [C] *abbreviation for* not in my back yard (= a person who does not want something unpleasant to be built or done near where they live) • *If everyone was a NIMBY, nothing would ever get built.* • *A spokesperson for the chemicals company said that local NIMBY attitudes were arresting development of the site.*

nin·com·poop /ˈnɪŋ·kəm·puːp/ *n* [C] *infml* a foolish or stupid person

nine /naɪn/ *determiner, pronoun, n* (the number) 9 • *eight, nine, ten* • *a nine-month prison sentence* • *Nine cities have shown an interest in hosting the next Olympic games.* • *She'd just had a birthday and was wearing a badge with a nine on it.* [C] • *(infml)* If someone is **done/dressed (up) to the nines** they are wearing very stylish and fashionable clothes often as a way of trying to influence someone: *She had washed her hair and dressed herself up to the nines by the time we arrived.* • *(dated)* A **nine days' wonder** is something which causes excitement or interest for a short time but is then quickly forgotten. • If something happens **nine times out of ten** it almost always happens: *Nine times out of ten if parents fuss too much they simply alienate their children.* ○ See also **ninety-nine times out of a hundred** at NINETY. • If someone says that they work **nine to five** they start work at nine o'clock in the morning and finish at five, which are the hours worked in many offices from Monday to Friday: *a nine-to-five routine*

ninth /naɪntθ/ *determiner, pronoun, adj, adv* [not gradable], *n* • *The ninth letter of the alphabet is I.* • *The school term ends on the ninth (of July).* • *She currently is/ranks ninth in the world.* • *A ninth* (=one of nine equal parts) *of 27 is 3.* [C]

999 /ˌnaɪn·naɪn'naɪn/ *n* [U] the number used in Britain when telephoning for the emergency services • *a hoax 999 call* • *There's been an accident – dial 999 and ask for an ambulance.*

911 /ˌnaɪn·wʌn'wʌn/ *n* [U] the number used in the US when telephoning for the emergency services • *Using my portable phone, I called 911 to summon emergency medical help.*

nine·pins *Br* /'naɪm·pɪnz/ *pl n* **going down/falling like ninepins** falling, breaking or being damaged, esp. in large numbers • *Trees were going down like ninepins in the strong wind.*

nine·teen /ˌnaɪn'tiːn/ *determiner, pronoun, n* (the number) 19 • *eighteen, nineteen, twenty* • *A group of students were trapped in the cave for nineteen hours.* • *Simson, aged nineteen, was convicted on two charges of burglary.* • *I'm looking for a birthday card with a nineteen on it.* [C]

nine·teenth /ˌnaɪn'tiːntθ, '--/ *determiner, pronoun, adj, adv* [not gradable], *n* • *She's an expert in nineteenth century industrial history.* • *"Which century was the cathedral built in?" "The nineteenth."* • *At the end of the first round, he was (lying) nineteenth.* • *(infml)* In golf, the **nineteenth hole** is a bar where people go to socialize after they have finished a game.

nine·ty /£'naɪn·ti, $-ṭi/ *determiner, pronoun, n* (the number) 90 • *eighty, ninety, a hundred* • *Ninety percent of the people surveyed said they were often tired.* • *We've got about ninety (people) coming to the party.* • If something happens **ninety-nine times out of a hundred** it is almost certain to happen. ○ See also **nine times out of ten** at NINE.

nine·ties /£'naɪn·tiz, $-ṭiz/ *pl n* • **The** nineties is the range of temperature between 90° and 99°. • **The** nineties is also the period of years between 90 and 99 in any century: *Queen Victoria's diamond jubilee was in the nineties* (=between 1890 and 1899). • A person's nineties are the period in which they are aged between 90 and 99: *She was well* **into** *her nineties when she died.*

nine·ti·eth /£'naɪn·ti·əθ, $-ṭi-/ *determiner, pronoun, adj, adv* [not gradable], *n* • *Tomorrow is Aunt Elma's ninetieth (birthday).* • *The team is/is lying ninetieth in the competition so far.* • A ninetieth is one of ninety equal parts of something. [C]

nin·ja /'nɪn·dʒə/ *n* [C] (esp. in the past) a Japanese fighter who moves and acts without being seen and usually carries a short sword

nin·ny /'nɪn·i/ *n* [C] *infml dated* a foolish person

ninth /naintθ/ *pronoun, n, adj, adv* See at NINE

nip [GO QUICKLY] /nɪp/ *v* [I always + adv/prep] **-pp-** *Br and Aus infml* to go somewhere quickly or be somewhere for only a short time • *Can you nip* **out/round** *to the shop for me?* • *Nip* **across** *to the neighbour's house and see if she's alright.* • *Shall we nip* **in** *to the bar for a bite to eat before the show?* • *(slightly dated) With the wind behind them they were nipping* **along** (=travelling quickly) *on their bikes.*

nip·py /'nɪp·i/ *adj* **-ier, -iest** *Br and Aus infml* • *It's a very nippy* (=can change speed and direction easily) *little car.*

nip *(obj)* [PRESS QUICKLY] /nɪp/ *v* **-pp-** to press (something) quickly and quite hard between two, often sharp, objects such as teeth or the nails on fingers • *It's alright sleeping in the loft – as long as the rats don't nip you!* [T] • *He dropped the crate which nipped his hand but he wasn't injured.* [T] • *This type of turtle will often nip* **at** *people who try to feed it.* [I] • If you **nip** something **in the bud** you stop it before it has an opportunity to become established: *Many serious illnesses can be nipped in the bud if they are detected early enough.*

nip /nɪp/ *n* [C] • *I gave my thumb quite a nip when the pliers slipped.* • **Nip and tuck** is *Am for* **neck and neck**. See at NECK [BODY PART]. • *(Am infml)* **Nip and tuck** is also another way of saying **plastic surgery** (=a medical operation to repair or change a person's appearance): *You could tell from the magazine photo that he'd had a little nip and tuck to make himself look younger.* • *(Am infml)* **A nip here and a tuck there** means a series of small reductions: *The department made a nip here and a tuck there but they were still way over budget.*

nip [COLD] /nɪp/ *n* [U] **a nip in the air** *infml* quite cold • *You can tell it's still spring – there's a real nip in the air in the mornings.*

nip·py /'nɪp·i/ *adj* **-ier, -iest** *infml* • When the weather is nippy it is quite cold: *It's a bit nippy today – you might need a coat.*

nip [DRINK] /nɪp/ *n* [C] *Br infml* a small amount of strong alcoholic drink • *a nip of gin*

Nip [PERSON] /nɪp/ *n* [C] *taboo slang* (a very offensive word for) a Japanese person

nip·per /£'nɪp·əʳ, $-ɚ/ *n* [C] *infml* a small child

nip·ple /'nɪp·l̩/ *n* [C] the dark part of the skin which sticks out from the breast of a mammal and through which milk is supplied to the young • *(Am)* A nipple is also a TEAT.

nir·va·na /£nɪə'vɑː·nə, $nɚ-/ *n* [U] (in Buddhism) a high spiritual state of freedom from all suffering which is achieved by removing all personal desires, or *(fig.)* a state of perfection • *(fig.) In her speech the candidate promised a nirvana of better jobs, less crime, and more education.*

Nis·sen hut /'nɪs·ən/ *n* [C] a building shaped like a tube cut along the middle made from CORRUGATED iron sheets

nit [PERSON] /nɪt/ *n* [C] *Br and Aus infml disapproving* a NITWIT

nit [EGG] /nɪt/ *n* [C] the egg of an insect, esp. a LOUSE, which is sometimes found sticking to people's or animal's hair

nit·pick·ing /'nɪtˌpɪk·ɪŋ/ *adj, n infml disapproving* (showing) too much interest in unimportant details, esp. as a way of criticizing • *a nitpicking attitude* • *If you spent less time nitpicking you'd get more work done.* [U]

nit·pick /'nɪt·pɪk/ *v* [I] • *Must you nitpick* (=find fault with details) *all the time?*

nit·pick·er /£'nɪtˌpɪk·əʳ, $-ɚ/ *n* [C]

ni·trate /'naɪ·treɪt/ *n* a chemical which includes NITROGEN and oxygen, often used as a FERTILIZER (=a substance which helps plants to grow) • *potassium/sodium nitrate* • *If too much nitrate is used on an area it can contaminate local water supplies.* [U] • *Nitrogen is converted into nitrates in the soil which plants can then use.* [C]

ni·tric ac·id /'naɪ·trɪk/ *n* [U] a very acidic transparent colourless liquid which is used in making many chemicals, esp. FERTILIZERS and explosives

ni·tro·gen /'naɪ·trə·dʒən/ *n* [U] a gaseous element having neither colour nor taste which forms about 78% of the Earth's ATMOSPHERE and is a part of all things which live

ni·tro·glyc·er·ine /£ˌnaɪ·trəʊ'glɪs·ᵊr·iːn, $-troʊ'glɪs·ɚ-/, *Am also* **ni·tro·glyc·er·in** *n* [U] a very powerful liquid explosive

nit·ty-grit·ty /£ˌnɪt·i'grɪt·i, $ˌnɪṭ·i'grɪṭ-/ *n* [U] **the nitty-gritty** *infml* the basic facts of a situation • *Let's* **get down to** *the nitty-gritty – when can you finish the building and how much will it cost?*

nit·wit /'nɪt·wɪt/, **nit** *n* [C] *infml disapproving* a foolish or stupid person • *You're such a nitwit – you're bound to fall off your bike if you ride it on ice.* • *Get down from that tree right now, nitwit!* [as form of address]

nix *obj* /nɪks/ *v* [T] *Am infml* to stop, forbid or refuse to accept (something) • *The film studio nixed her plans to make a sequel.*

nix /nɪks/ *n* [U], *adv* [not gradable] *Am infml* • *All that effort for nix* (=nothing). • *I suppose mom will say nix to us going* (=say we cannot go) *to the movies.*

no [NOT ANY] /£nəʊ, $noʊ/ *determiner* not any; not one; not a • *There's no butter left.* • *No trees grow near the top of the mountain.* • *That's my kind of holiday – no telephone, no TV and no worries.* • *Not surprisingly no life forms were detected on the planet.* • *There's no chance* (=no possibility) *of us getting there by eight.* • *She no* **longer** *goes* (=does not continue to go) *to music lessons.* • *There is no* **doubt** *in my mind that he is the person I saw with the gun.* • In signs and official notices, 'no' is used to show that something is not allowed: *No smoking/fishing* • *This waiting is the worst part – the audition itself will flash by* **in no time** (=very quickly). • *(infml) We're so pleased you came, you cheered us up* **no end** (=a lot). • *(infml) They tried for hours to persuade her to come down from the roof, but it was* **no go** (=impossible or hopeless). • *(infml) "Will you be able to repair the light?" "Yeah,* **no problem/sweat** (=without any serious difficulties)." • *(infml)* If someone says **there's no knowing/telling/saying** they mean it is not possible to know what will happen: *She's very unpredictable so there's no knowing how she'll react to the news.* • *(Am infml)* **No-account** means (a person who is) of little use. • In cricket and some other games a **no-ball** is when the ball is BOWLED (=thrown) in a way which is not allowed by the rules. • *(Br*

DUTCH FALSE FRIENDS (NL)

English	Dutch	Meaning
acre *n*	akker	field
agenda *n*	agenda	diary
allure *n*	allures	airs; ways
arrest *n*	arrest	decision; judgement
automatic *adj*	automatiek (n)	cafeteria, self-service snack bar
bastard *n*	bastaard	mongrel, hybrid
beholder *n*	behoeder	protector, defender
benzene *n*	benzine	petrol; gasoline
billet *n*	biljet	ticket; handbill
blank *adj*	blank	white; fair
blind *adj*	blind	hidden; fake; sham
blind *adj*	blind (adv)	blindly
blink *v*	blinken	to shine, gleam, glimmer
bond *n*	bond	union, federation; association
brief *n*	brief	letter, epistle
brutal *adj*	brutaal	impudent, rude; daring, bold
brutality *n*	brutaliteit	sauce, cheek, effrontery
camp *n*	kamp	fight, struggle, contest, battle
can *n*	kan	jug; pot; tankard; mug
candidate *n*	kandidaat	university graduate
carton *n*	karton	cardboard; cardboard box; cartoon
censure *n*	censuur	censorship
central *adj*	centrale (n)	power station; telephone exchange, agency
chef *n*	chef	chief; leader; boss
christen *v*	christen (n)	christian
classic *adj*	klassiek	classical
cling *v*	klingelen	to jingle, tinkle
college *n*	college	lecture; course of lectures
comedy *n*	komedie	farce; fuss, to-do
competition *n*	competitie	sports league
concept *n*	concept	rough draft, outline, plan
conjunctive *adj*	conjunctief	subjunctive mood (grammar)
consequence *n*	consequentie	consistency; sense
conserve *n*	konserve	tinned goods, preserves
consumption *n*	consumptie	catering; food and drink
control *v*	controleren	to supervise; to inspect, check
cord *n*	koord	rope
costume *n*	kostuum	suit
crane *n*	kraan	tap, cock, faucet
crummy *adj*	kruimelig	crumbly, floury, mealy
dame *n*	dame	lady; dance/dinner partner
dancing *n*	dancing	dance hall
deception *n*	deceptie	disappointment; disenchantment
delicatessen *n*	delicatessen	table delicacies
dilettante *n*	dilettante	amateur
discussion *n*	discussie	argument, debate
douche *n*	douche	shower
drift *n*	drift	drove, flock; passion
dwell *v*	dwalen	to roam, wander
entree *n*	entree	entrance, entry
fabricate *v*	fabriceren	to manufacture
fail *v*	falen	to make a mistake; to be lacking
fantasy *n*	fantasie	imagination; fancy, whim
feast *n*	feest	party
fierce *adj*	fier	proud
flirt *n*	flirt	flirtation
foyer *n*	foyer	lobby
glance *v*	glanzen	to gleam, shine, to polish, brighten
glance *n*	glans	shine, gloss, lustre; glory; glamour
gracious *adj*	gracieus	graceful
grade *n*	graad	degree, eg temperature, rank
gratification *n*	gratificatie	bonus; gratuity
grief *n*	grief	grievance, wrong
gymnasium *n*	gymnasium	grammar school
hard *adj*	hard	loud; harsh
haven *n*	haven	harbour; port; dock
island *n*	IJsland	Iceland
kettle *n*	ketel	cauldron, boiler
machine *n*	machine	engine
manufacture *n*	manufacturen	drapery; linen
mechanic *n*	mechanisch	mechanical
pertinent *adj*	pertinent	categorical; positive
place *n*	plaats	farm; seat; scene; room
pocketbook *n*	pocketboek	paperback
price *n*	prijs	prize, award
prize *v*	prijzen	to praise; to price
rayon *n*	rayon	radius; bookshelf; department of shop; area; territory
sauce *n*	saus	flavouring; distemper paint; rain
scenario *n*	scenario	script
shield *n*	schild	carapace, shell
ship *n*	schip	barge; boat; nave
sluice *n*	sluis	canal lock
snore *v*	snorren	to drone, whir, buzz, purr, whiz
sympathetic *adj*	sympathiek	likeable, pleasant; attractive
tempo *n*	tempo	movement of a symphony, etc
uproar *n*	oproer	revolt, rebellion, mutiny, sedition
warehouse *n*	warenhuis	department store, emporium

and Aus) A **no-claim bonus** (also **no-claims bonus**) is an amount subtracted from the money paid to an **insurance company**, esp. for motor vehicles, because no claims have been made for a particular period. • If something is described as **no-frills** it is basic and without any unnecessary detail: *a no-frills performance* ○ *It's a no-frills shop supplying only basic goods at affordable prices.* • *(Br and Aus)* A **no-hoper** is someone or something which will fail: He's a no-hoper, he'll never achieve anything. • **No one** (also **nobody**) means not one person: *At first I thought there was no one in the room.* ○ *"Who was that on the phone?" "No one you would know."* ○ *I'd like to go to the concert but no one* **else** (= no other person) *wants to come.* ○ *No-one told me she left yesterday.* ○ *They were told that no one should leave their bags unattended.* • **No trump** or **no trumps** in a game of BRIDGE means that the four groups of cards have equal value. • LP **Quantity words**

no NEGATIVE ANSWER /£nəʊ, $noʊ/ *adv* [not gradable] used to give negative answers • *"Did you go to the shops?" "No, I forgot."* • *"Would you like some more cake?" "No thank you, I couldn't eat any more."* • *"Were there any survivors?" "No."* • *(infml)* **No way** is a way of emphasizing no: *"Did you pay the bill?" "No way, not until they deliver the computers."* See also **no way** at NO NOT.

no /£nəʊ, $noʊ/ *n* [C] *pl* **noes** • *The continued fighting answers an emphatic no to the calls for a cease-fire.* • A no is also a voter or a vote against a question which is being discussed: *14 ayes to 169 noes – the noes have it.* Compare AYE. • *(infml or humorous)* A **no-no** is something which is thought to be unsuitable or unacceptable: *Total nudity is still a definite no-no on most of Europe's beaches.*

no NOT /£nəʊ, $noʊ/ *adv* [not gradable] not; not any • *The exam is no more difficult than the tests you've been doing in class.* • *It's no colder today than it was yesterday but it's no warmer either.* • *She has no small influence* (= a large influence) *on the decisions he makes.* • *The issues are of no great interest* (= only a little interest) *to me.* • *(fml) Whether you like it* **or no** (= or not) *you'll have to get used to doing your exercises every day.* • *(law)* A **no-fault** agreement is one where blame does not have to be proved before action can be taken, esp. paying money: *a no-fault divorce* • *a no-fault compensation scheme* • A **no-fly zone** is an area where aircraft from one country are not allowed to fly in an attempt to protect either the people living in that area or soldiers from another country in that area: *Aircraft from several countries will enforce the no-fly zone to protect UN forces on the ground.* • *(Am infml)* If something is (a) **no-go** it doesn't happen: *The launch was no-go due to the weather.* • *(infml)* A **no-go area/zone** is an area, esp. in a town, where it is very dangerous to go usually because a group of people who have weapons prevent the police, army and other people from entering: *Armed guerillas have made the old city a no-go area.* • *(Am slang disapproving)* A person described as **no-good** does nothing useful or helpful and is therefore considered to be of little value: *a no-good* **son of a bitch** • Something which is **no-holds-barred** has no limits or controls: *The report gives a no-holds-barred view of the politics.* • *(Am slang)* When a set of conditions are described as **no-lose** it means that whatever happens there will be a happy and successful result: *For him this is a no-lose campaign – he will become either vice president-elect or a much stronger presidential contender for the next election.* • A **no-man's-land** is an area or strip of land which no one owns or controls such as a strip of land between two countries' borders, esp. in a war: *(fig.) Many poor people are caught in a no-man's-land – unable to get work because they have no home and unable to find a home because they have no work.* • **No-nonsense** means practical and interested in doing only what is necessary to achieve what is intended: *a no-nonsense manner/leader* • When something is described as **no-questions-asked** it means it is done without people asking about it: *a no-questions-asked appointment* • A **no-**

show is a person who is expected but does not arrive: *a no-show passenger* • If you say **no way** about something you mean that it is impossible to make it happen: *There's no way we'll get there this afternoon.* See also **no way** at NO NEGATIVE ANSWER. • *(infml)* When a set of conditions are described as **no-win** it means that whatever happens there will be an unhappy and unsuccessful result: *Nursing auxiliaries are in a no-win* **situation** *because they are low-paid but at the same time not taken seriously by their superiors.* • LP **Opposites**

no NUMBER *n* [before n] *pl* **nos** *abbreviation for* number • *He'll race wearing no. 7 today.* • *Do you know the people who live at No.17?* • *The answers to nos 13-20 are on page 21.* • *Apartment Nos. 4 to 72 inclusive will be without electricity this afternoon.* • The abbreviation **No. 10** is often written for **Number Ten**, see at NUMBER SYMBOL. • LP **Letters**

No·ah's ark /£ˌnəʊ·əz, $ˌnoʊ-/ *n* [U not after *the*] See at ARK

nob /£nɒb, $nɑːb/ *n* [C] *esp. Br infml humorous or disapproving* a rich person whose family has been important for a long time

nob·ble *obj* CAUSE TO FAIL /£ˈnɒb·l̩, $ˈnɑː-/ *v* [T] *Br and Aus slang* to make (something) fail, esp. to make (a horse in a race) fail by giving it drugs • *The knee injury has almost certainly nobbled his chance of a place in the final.*

nob·ble *obj* CATCH ATTENTION /£ˈnɒb·l̩, $ˈnɑː-/ *v* [T] *Br and Aus slang* to intentionally catch the attention of someone so that you can talk to them • *He nobbled her in the corridor to sign the invoice.*

No·bel prize /£ˈnəʊ·bel, $ˈnoʊ-/ *n* [C] any of the six international prizes which are given each year to people who make important discoveries or advances in chemistry, physics, medicine, literature, peace and economics

no·ble MORAL /£ˈnəʊ·bl̩, $ˈnoʊ-/ *adj* **-r, -st** moral in an honest, brave and not selfish way • *It was a noble attempt to bring peace to the conflict.* • *His followers believe they are fighting for a noble cause.* • Ⓓ

no·bil·i·ty /£nəʊˈbɪl·ɪ·ti, $noʊˈbɪl·ə·t̬i/, **no·ble·ness** /£ˈnəʊ·bl̩·nəs, $ˈnoʊ-/ *n* [U] • *There is nobility in her writing, an honest caring for the well-being of others.*

no·bly /£ˈnəʊ·bli, $ˈnoʊ-/ *adv*

no·ble HIGH RANK /£ˈnəʊ·bl̩, $ˈnoʊ-/ *adj* [not gradable] belonging to a high social rank, esp. by birth • *a noble family* • Ⓓ

no·ble /£ˈnəʊ·bl̩, $ˈnoʊ-/ *n* [C] • *Although he was a noble he worked in a factory and never used his title.*

no·bil·i·ty /£nəʊˈbɪl·ɪ·ti, $noʊˈbɪl·ə·t̬i/ *n* [U + sing/pl v] • *Many of her essays on* **the** *nobility* (= nobles considered as a group) *were highly critical.*

no·ble ADMIRABLE /£ˈnəʊ·bl̩, $ˈnoʊ-/ *adj* **-r, -st** admirable in appearance or quality • *a noble profile* • *The new building has a noble facade which is not overbearing.* • Ⓓ

no·bil·i·ty /£nəʊˈbɪl·ɪ·ti, $noʊˈbɪl·ə·t̬i/, **no·ble·ness** /£ˈnəʊ·bl̩·nəs, $ˈnoʊ-/ *n* [U]

no·ble·man (*pl* **-men**), **no·ble·wo·man** (*pl* **-women**) /£ˈnəʊ·bl̩·mən, $ˈnoʊ-, -ˌwʊm·ən/ *n* [C] a member of **the nobility**, see at NOBLE HIGH RANK

no·blesse o·blige /£nəʊˌbles·əʊˈbliːʒ, $noʊˌbles·oʊ-/ *n* [U] the belief that someone with power and influence should use their position to help other people

no·bod·y /£ˈnəʊ·bə·di, £-bɒd·i, $ˈnoʊ·bɑː·di/ *pronoun, n* [C] **no one**, see at NO NOT ANY • *Is there nobody here who can answer my question?* • *We walked all afternoon and saw nobody (else).* • A nobody is also someone who is completely unimportant: *Most people at the party were nobodies trying to be noticed by the press.* • LP **Quantity words**

noc·tur·nal /£nɒkˈtɜː·nəl, $nɑːkˈtɜːr-/ *adj* [not gradable] *fml or specialized* of, happening in or active during the night • *nocturnal light* • *nocturnal wanderings* • *Most bats and owls are nocturnal.* • Compare DIURNAL.

noc·tur·nal·ly /£nɒkˈtɜː·nə·li, $nɑːkˈtɜːr-/ *adv* [not gradable]

noc·turne /£ˈnɒk·tɜːn, $ˈnɑːk·tɜːrn/ *n* [C] a gentle piece of CLASSICAL music • *Frédéric Chopin and John Field both composed sets of nocturnes.*

nod *(obj)* MOVE HEAD /£nɒd, $nɑːd/ *v* **-dd-** to move (the head) down and then up, sometimes repeatedly, esp. to show agreement, approval or greeting, or to show (something) by doing this • *She nodded to greet us when we walked in.* [I] • *His teacher nodded (her head)* **in** *pleasure as soon as the recital ended.* [I/T] • *Many people in the audience nodded* **(in)** *agreement as the proposal was made.* [I/T]

nod /£nɒd, $nɑːd/ *n* [C usually sing] • *Each* **gave** *the other a quiet nod of recognition across the crowded room.* • *(Br infml)* If a suggestion is approved **on the nod** it is accepted without discussion: *The new proposal* **went through** *on the nod.* • A **nodding acquaintance** is a slight knowledge of a person or a subject: *I know him as a nodding acquaintance but nothing more.* ○ *She has only a nodding acquaintance* **with** *the issues involved.* • *(infml saying)* 'A nod's as good as a wink (to a blind horse/man)' means that only a slight sign is needed to make something clear because a situation is already understood well.

nod SLEEP /£nɒd, $nɑːd/ *v* [I] **-dd-** *infml* to begin sleeping or be almost sleeping, esp. not intentionally • *After our busy day we both sat and nodded in front of the TV.* • *What a boring play – loads of people were nodding* **off** *toward the end!*

nod·dle /£ˈnɒd·l̩, $ˈnɑː·dl̩/, *Am usually* **nood·le** *n* [C] *dated slang* the head of a person or their ability to think • *Did that hit you on the noddle?* • *Use your noddle – clear the shelves before you paint the cupboard!*

node LUMP /£nəʊd, $noʊd/ *n* [C] *specialized* a lump or swelling on or in a living object • *a lymph node*

node JOIN /£nəʊd, $noʊd/ *n* [C] *specialized* a place where things join, for example lines, or where a leaf and stem join on a plant • *You might expect towns to develop at nodes where major roads cross.*

nod·al /£ˈnəʊ·dəl, $ˈnoʊ-/ *adj* [not gradable] *specialized* • *a nodal point*

nod·ule /£ˈnɒd·juːl, $ˈnɑː·djuːl/ *n* [C] a small lump or swelling • *Repeated rubbing sometimes causes fibrous tissue which can build up into nodules.* • *Mining companies have been studying manganese nodules on the floor of the deep oceans.*

no·du·lar /£ˈnɒd·jʊ·ləʳ, $ˈnɑː·djə·lɚ/ *adj* [not gradable]

No·el /£nəʊˈel, $noʊ-/, **No·ël** *n* [U not after *the*] (esp. in songs and written greetings) Christmas • LP **Holidays**

noes /£nəʊz, $noʊz/ *pl of* NO NEGATIVE ANSWER

nog·gin AMOUNT OF DRINK /£ˈnɒg·ɪn, $ˈnɑː·gɪn/ *n* [C] *dated* a small amount of alcoholic drink, usually a quarter of a PINT

nog·gin HEAD /£ˈnɒg·ɪn, $ˈnɑː·gɪn/ *n* [C] *esp. Am infml* the head or mind of a person • **Use** *your noggin – think before you decide what to do!*

Noh /£nəʊ, $noʊ/, **No** *n* [U] a type of traditional Japanese theatre which uses music and dance and is based on ancient or religious stories

no·how /£ˈnəʊ·haʊ, $ˈnoʊ-/ *adv* [not gradable] *esp. Am not standard* not in any way • *Nohow will we get there today.*

noise SOUND /nɔɪz/ *n* (a) sound, esp. when it is unwanted, unpleasant or loud • *The main street was packed with bars and discos and the noise was deafening.* [U] • *There was a loud noise, and he woke with a start.* [C] • *Trees along the sides of roads can reduce traffic noise.* [U] • *High noise levels may be even more damaging to children than to adults.* • *(infml)* If someone **makes a noise about** something they talk about it a lot or complain about it: *She's been making a lot of noise about moving to a new house.* • *(infml)* If a person **makes noises** they show what they think or feel without explaining it clearly or directly: *She made very positive noises at the interview about me getting the job.* • *(infml)* **Make noises** also means to complain or make trouble: *I don't like to make noises but this soup is cold – I'm going to send it back.* • If someone **makes (all) the right/proper/correct noises** they show enthusiasm for something but sometimes not sincerely: *He made all the right noises about my audition but I couldn't tell if he was genuinely impressed.* • **Noise pollution** is noise, such as that from traffic, which upsets people where they live or work and is considered to be unhealthy for them: *Complaints about alarms ringing prompted a new law to ease environmental noise pollution.* • LP **Sound**

nois·y /ˈnɔɪ·zi/ *adj* **-ier, -iest** • *A noisy crowd of fans had gathered at the airport to meet the singer's plane.*

nois·i·ly /ˈnɔɪ·zɪ·li/ *adv*

nois·i·ness /ˈnɔɪ·zɪ·nəs/ *n* [U]

noise·less /ˈnɔɪz·ləs/ *adj* [not gradable] • *Above them an eagle circled in noiseless* (= silent) *flight.*

noise·less·ly /ˈnɔɪz·lə·sli/ *adv* [not gradable]

noise SIGNAL /nɔɪz/ *n* [U] *specialized* any unwanted change in a signal, esp. in a signal produced by an electronic device • *Using a single chip instead of a transistor array reduces (the) noise on the output signal by 90%.*

nois·y /ˈnɔɪ·zi/ *adj* **-ier, -iest** *specialized* • *a noisy signal/component*

noise·mak·er /£ˈnɔɪzˌmeɪ·kəʳ, $-kɚ/ *n* [C] *Am* a device which can be used to make noise, esp. a HORN or RATTLE for use at a party

noi·some /ˈnɔɪ·səm/ *adj literary* very unpleasant; offensive • *a noisome stench*

no·mad /£ˈnəʊ·mæd, $ˈnoʊ-/ *n* [C] a member of a group of people who move from one place to another rather than living in one place all of the time • *Nomads travel these arid regions with their camel herds.*

no·mad·ic /£nəʊˈmæd·ɪk, $noʊ-/ *adj* • *nomadic tribes* • *a nomadic existence*

nom de plume /£ˌnɒm·dəˈpluːm, $ˌnɑːm-/ *n* [C] *pl* **noms de plume** /£ˌnɒm·dəˈpluːm, $ˌnɑːm-/ a **pen name**, see at PEN [WRITING DEVICE]

no·men·cla·ture /£nəʊˈmeŋ·klə·tʃəʳ, $ˈnoʊ·men·kleɪ·tʃɚ/ *n specialized* a system for naming things, esp. in a particular area of science • *(the) nomenclature of organic chemicals* [C/U]

nom·in·al [NOT IN REALITY] /£ˈnɒm·ɪ·nəl, $ˈnɑː·mə-/ *adj* in name or thought but not reality • *She's the nominal head of our college – the real work is done by her deputy.*

nom·in·al·ly /£ˈnɒm·ɪ·nə·li, $ˈnɑː·mə-/ *adv* • *The province is nominally independent.*

nom·in·al [SMALL] /£ˈnɒm·ɪ·nəl, $ˈnɑː·mə-/ *adj* (of a sum of money) very small compared to an expected price or value • *a nominal sum/charge* • *There will only be a nominal admission fee for the concert.*

nom·in·ate *obj* [SUGGEST] /£ˈnɒm·ɪ·neɪt, $ˈnɑː·mə-/ *v* [T] to officially suggest (someone) for an election, job, position or honour • *He's been nominated by the Green Party as their candidate in the next election.* • *Would you like to nominate anyone* **for/as** *director?* • If a film, song, programme, etc. is nominated for a prize, it is officially stated that it will be included in a competition for the prize.

nom·in·a·tion /£ˌnɒm·ɪˈneɪ·ʃən, $ˌnɑː·mə-/ *n* • *There have been two nominations* (= official suggestions of suitable people) *for the new job.* [C] • *The president is decided by nomination* **from** *within the committee.* [U]

nom·in·ee /£ˌnɒm·ɪˈniː, $ˌnɑː·mə-/ *n* [C] • *All nominees* (= people who have been suggested as suitable) *will be considered.*

nom·in·ate *obj* [EMPLOY] /£ˈnɒm·ɪ·neɪt, $ˈnɑː·mə-/ *v* [T] to officially give (someone) a position or job • *She has been nominated* **as** *the delegation's official interpreter.*

nom·in·a·tion /£ˌnɒm·ɪˈneɪ·ʃən, $ˌnɑː·mə-/ *n* • *The nomination* **of** (= act of officially giving a job to) *Judge Watkins as head of the inquiry was a surprise.* [C] • *Nomination* **to** *a post in the intelligence services is usually kept secret.* [U]

nom·in·ee /£ˌnɒm·ɪˈniː, $ˌnɑː·mə-/ *n* [C] • *The nominee* (= person officially given a position or job) *vice-president of the company is very young.*

non– /£nɒn-, $nɑːn/ *combining form* used to add the meaning 'not' or 'the opposite of' to adjectives and nouns • *non-sexist* • *non-racist* • If a drug is **non-addictive**, it does not make a person who takes it want to habitually take more of it. • **Non-aggression** is the attempt to avoid fighting, esp. between two countries: *a non-aggression pact* • If a drink is **non-alcoholic**, it does not contain alcohol: *non-alcoholic beer* • If a country is **non-aligned**, it does not support or depend on any powerful country or group of countries: *At the UN, India and other non-aligned countries stepped up the pressure for a cease-fire.* • **Non-alignment** is the condition or principle of being non-aligned. • A **non-believer** is a person who has no religious beliefs. • If powder or liquid which is used for washing clothes is **non-bio** or **non-biological**, it does not contain ENZYMES (= special chemicals) to help make the clothes clean. • A **non-combatant** is a person, esp. in the armed forces, who does not fight in a war, for example a priest or a doctor. • If a person has a financial agreement with the company they work for which is **non-contributory**, it is completely paid for by their employer: *a non-contributory insurance policy* ○ *a non-contributory pension plan* • Paint which is **non-drip** is specially made so that it does not produce unwanted drops when it is being used. • *(infml)* If an occasion is a **non-event**, it is disappointing and not interesting, esp. if it was expected to be exciting and important: *The party turned out to be a bit of a non-event – hardly anybody turned up.* • If something is **non-existent**, it does not exist or is not present in a particular place: *Government funding of alternative health care is virtually non-existent.* ○ *Many species of bee are almost non-existent in this area now.* • Writing that is **non-fiction** is about real events and facts rather than stories which have been invented. Compare FICTION. • Something which is **non-flammable** (also **non-inflammable**) will not burn or is very difficult to make burn. • A person or thing that is **non-judgmental** does not judge or express opinions: *a non-judgmental book/counsellor* • Something which is **non-negotiable** cannot be changed by discussion: *The terms of this agreement are non-negotiable.* • **Non-payment** is a failure to pay money which is owed: *Two inspectors called to interview them about non-payment of employees' taxes.* • An organization which is **non-profit(-making)**/*(esp. Am)* **nonprofit** does not make a profit, esp. intentionally: *Charities are non-profit-making organizations and can get considerable tax relief.* • **Non-proliferation** is the limitation of the spread and/or amount of something, esp. nuclear or chemical weapons: *a non-proliferation treaty* • **Non-racist** means without being influenced by a person's racial group: *We've always tried to be a non-sexist and non-racist employer.* • Someone or something which is **non-resident** does not live or stay in the stated place: *Non-resident holidaymakers increase the town's population in the summer to almost twice its usual size.* • If something is **non-returnable**, it cannot be returned: *a non-returnable deposit* • A **non-returnable bottle** is a bottle which, when empty, cannot be taken back to a shop so that it can be used again. • A **non-smoker** is a person who does not smoke. • A **non-smoking** (also **no-smoking**) area, building or vehicle is one in which people are not allowed to smoke: *a non-smoking flight/restaurant* • If something is **non-standard**, it is not what would usually be fitted or accepted: *Fitting of non-standard parts will invalidate the guarantee.* • When talking about language, a **non-standard** word, phrase or way of saying something is one which is not generally thought of as correct by educated speakers of the language. • If something is **non-slip**, it is designed to prevent sliding, esp. by being made of sticky material or by having cuts in its surface which makes it easier to hold: *a non-slip surface/grip* • *(infml)* A **non-starter** is a person or an idea or a plan which has no chance of success: *The proposal was a non-starter from the beginning because there was no possibility of funding.* • A cooking pan which is **non-stick** has a special surface which prevents food from sticking to it while the food is being cooked: *a non-stick frying pan* • **Non-stop** means without stopping or without interruptions: *a non-stop flight* ○ *It felt like we travelled non-stop for the entire week.* • *(Br and Aus dated)* Behaviour or ways of speaking which are **non-U** would not be considered acceptable by people of high social class. • Something which is **non-verbal** does not use spoken language: *Body language is a potent form of non-verbal communication.* • **Non-violence** is the avoidance of fighting and physical force, esp. when trying to make political change: *The Dalai Lama has always counselled non-violence.* ○ *Gandhi was one of this century's greatest exponents of* **non-violent** *protest.* • **Non-white** means (a person who is) not white. This is usually considered offensive. • Compare DIS-; IN-; UN-. • [LP] **Opposites**

non·ag·en·a·ri·an /£ˌnɒn·ə·dʒəˈneə·ri·ən, $ˌnɑː·nə·dʒəˈner·i-/ *n* [C], *adj* [not gradable] (a person who is) between 90 and 99 years old

nonce word /£ˈnɒnts·wɜːd, $ˈnɑːnts·wɜːrd/ *n* [C] a word invented for a particular occasion or situation

non·cha·lant /£ˈnɒn·tʃəl·ənt, $ˌnɑːn·ʃəˈlɑːnt/ *adj* behaving in a calm manner, often in a way which suggests lack of interest or care • *Unlike many of the runners who were obviously nervous the champion seemed almost nonchalant before the race.*

non·cha·lance /£ˈnɒn·tʃəl·ənts, $ˌnɑːn·ʃəˈlɑːnts/ *n* [U]

non·cha·lant·ly /£ˈnɒn·tʃəl·ənt·li, $ˌnɑːn·ʃəˈlɑːnt-/ *adv*

non·com·mit·tal /£ˌnɒŋ·kəˈmɪt·əl, $ˌnɑːŋ·kəˈmɪt̬-/ *adj* not expressing an opinion or decision • *The ambassador was typically noncommittal when asked whether further sanctions would be introduced.*

non·com·mit·tal·ly /£ˌnɒŋ·kəˈmɪt·əl·i, $ˌnɑːŋ·kəˈmɪt̬-/ *adv*

non com·pos men·tis /£ˌnɒŋˌkɒm·pəsˈmen·tɪs, $ˌnɑːŋˌkɑːm·poʊsˈmen-/ *adj* [after v; not gradable] *law* (of a person) unable to think clearly, esp. because of mental illness, and therefore not responsible

non·con·form·ist /£ˌnɒŋ·kənˈfɔː·mɪst, $ˌnɑːŋ·kənˈfɔːr-/ *adj, n* [C] (of or being) a person who lives and thinks in a way which is different from that of other people • *nonconformist behaviour* • The word Nonconformist also means (a member) of a Christian group which is Protestant but does not belong to the Church of England: *a Nonconformist minister*

non·con·form·i·ty /£ˌnɒŋ·kən'fɔː·mə·ti, $ˌnɑːŋ·kən'fɔːr·mə·t̬i/, **non·con·form·i·sm** /£ˌnɒŋ·kən'fɔː·mɪ·zᵊm, $ˌnɑːŋ·kən'fɔːr-/ *n* [U] • *Her clothes were an immediate signal of her nonconformity.*

non·de·script /£'nɒn·dɪ·skrɪpt, $'nɑːn-/ *adj* having no interesting or exciting features or qualities; very ordinary • *The meteorological bureau is in a nondescript building on the outskirts of town.* • *A nondescript man wearing a suit approached us.*

none /nʌn/ *pronoun* not one (of a group of people or things), or not any • *None* **of** *my children has/have blonde hair.* [+ sing/pl v] • *None* **of** *the houses has/have a large garden.* [+ sing/pl v] • *He was clever but he had none* **of** *his parents' charisma.* • *The four goals showed that the team had* **lost** *none* **of** *their old abilities.* • *"I'd like some more cheese." "I'm sorry there's none left".* • *"Have you any idea how much this cost?" "None* **at all**/*None* **whatsoever**.*"* • *He has every right to be there and I have none* **at all**/*none* **whatsoever**. • *She went to the shop to get some oranges but they had none.* • *(fml) None* **but** (= Only) *a dedicated scientist would want to read such a detailed report.* • *(fml)* If someone says they will **have none of** something they mean they will not accept, agree with or support it: *She tried to persuade him to retire, but he would have none of* **it**. • *(fml)* You can say **none other (than)** someone or something when you want to show that they are an unexpected choice or example: *The first speech was given by none other than Clint Eastwood.*

none /nʌn/ *adv* [not gradable] • **None the** means not, not any or in no way: *It was finished quickly but it's none the worse for that.* • If you are **none the wiser** you do not understand after something has been explained to you: *I read the instruction book, but I'm still none the wiser.* • *(fml)* **None too** means not very: *He seemed none too* **happy**/**pleased** *at the prospect of meeting the family.* ○ *The assistant on duty was none too helpful.*

non·en·ti·ty /£nɒn'en·tɪ·ti, $nɑː'nen·t̬ə·t̬i/ *n* *disapproving* a person without strong character, ideas or influence, or a state of being unknown because these characteristics are lacking • *The film is full of decorative nonentities.* [C] • *She was once a political nonentity but has since won a formidable reputation as a determined campaigner.* [C] • *The collection of essays is saved from nonentity by the stature of the contributors.* [U]

none·the·less /ˌnʌn·ðə'les/ *adv* [not gradable] NEVERTHELESS • *There are serious problems in our country, nonetheless, we feel this is a good time to return.*

non·in·ter·ven·tion /£ˌnɒn·ɪn·tə'ven·tʃᵊn, $ˌnɑː·nɪn·tɚ-/ *n* [U] refusal to take part, esp. in a disagreement between countries or within a country • *a policy of nonintervention*

non·plussed /£ˌnɒm'plʌst, $ˌnɑːm-/ *adj* surprised, confused and not certain how to react • *I was, to say the least, nonplussed by his reply.* • *Almost half of the detectives were nonplussed if a suspect refused to answer questions.*

non·sense /£'nɒn·sᵊnts, $'nɑːn·sents/ *n* an idea, something said or written, or behaviour which is foolish or ridiculous • *He said that the report was nonsense and nothing but a waste of paper.* [U] • *Those accusations are* **(absolute/complete/mere/utter)** *nonsense.* [U] • *"It won't be ready for another week." "Nonsense!/Don't* **talk** *nonsense! I was promised it would be ready today."* [U] • *She's been very ill so don't upset her with your nonsense about her returning to work!* [U] • **It's** *nonsense* **to** *say that he's too old for the job.* [U + *to* infinitive] • **It** *is a nonsense* **to** *suggest that four murders taking place in the same area within a month are not related.* [C + *to* infinitive] • *What's all this nonsense* (= foolish or bad behaviour)*?* [U] • Nonsense is also language which cannot be understood because it does not mean anything: *The translation of the instructions was so poor they were just nonsense.* [U] • *(Br and Aus)* To **make (a) nonsense of** something is to make it appear ridiculous or wrong or to spoil it: *His repeated lack of promotion makes nonsense of the theory that if you work hard you'll be successful.* ○ *The players made such a nonsense* **(of it)** (= played so badly) *that they lost the game.* • If someone **won't stand any nonsense**/*(Br also)* **stands no nonsense**, they will not accept bad or foolish behaviour: *The new teacher won't stand any nonsense.* • **Nonsense verse/rhymes/poems** are poems which use words a writer has invented to express unusual or amusing ideas: *'Brillig' is a made-up word used in a piece of nonsense verse by Lewis Carroll.* • **Nonsense words/syllables** seem like words or parts of words but do not exist in the language: *The child repeated the nonsense syllables 'boo di doo doo'.*

nonsensical /£nɒn'sent·sɪ·kḷ, $nɑːn-/ *adj* • *It's nonsensical to blame all the world's troubles on one man.* • *Their methods of assessment produce nonsensical results.* • *Don't be nonsensical! No one would agree to that suggestion.*

non se·qui·tur /£ˌnɒn'sek·wɪ·tər, $ˌnɑːn'sek·wɪ·t̬ɚ/ *n* [C] a statement which does not correctly follow from the meaning of the previous statement

non·un·i·on /£ˌnɒn'juː·ni·ᵊn, $ˌnɑːn-/ *adj* (of a company or organization) not employing workers who belong to a union, or (of a person) not belonging to a union • *nonunion employers* • *For the past five years, unions haven't managed to win wage increases as large as those granted to nonunion workers.*

nood·le [HEAD] /'nuː·dḷ/ *n* [C] *Am infml for* NODDLE

nood·le [MAKE MUSIC] /'nuː·dḷ/ *v* [I] *Am infml* to play a musical instrument without giving it full or serious attention • *I just sat at the piano noodling.*

noodles /'nuː·dḷz/ *pl n* a food in the form of long thin strips made from flour, water and sometimes eggs which are cooked in boiling liquid and then eaten with other foods • *The company makes frozen noodles and pre-cooked pasta.* • *Foods such as instant noodles are popular as snacks.* • *(infml)* Noodles is also *Am for* pasta.

nook /nʊk/ *n* [C] *literary* a small space which is hidden or partly sheltered • *He sat in a nook between the fire and the corner of the room.* • *Every* **nook and cranny** (= Every single place, even the smallest) *of the house was stuffed with souvenirs of their trips to other countries.*

nook·y, **nook·ie** /'nʊk·i/ *n* [U] *slang* sex • *Lying on a sunbed always puts Helen in the mood for a bit of nooky.*

noon /nuːn/ *n* [U] (approximately) twelve o'clock in the middle of the day; MIDDAY • *We used to ski before noon then take a long lunch.* • *By noon, we had had ten phone calls.* • *The radio station broadcast throughout the entire night and did not go off the air until noon the next day.* • [LP] **Time**

noose /nuːs/ *n* [C] one end of a rope tied to form a circle which can be tightened round something such as a person's neck to HANG (= kill) them • *They put the man on the back of a horse, ran a rope over the branch of a stout tree, looped the noose around his neck and jerked the horse away.* • *He hanged himself in his cell with a noose of sheets tied to the bars.* • *(fig.) The noose* (= problem) *of poverty was* **tightening** *daily.* • *He felt the company* **had a noose around** *its* **neck** (= had big problems).

nope /£nəʊp, $noʊp/ *adv* [not gradable] *slang* (esp. used in spoken answers) no • *"Are you going out tonight?" "Nope."*

no·place /£'nəʊ·pleɪs, $'noʊ-/ *adv* [not gradable] *Am infml for* NOWHERE • *Soon there would be noplace for them to go for help.*

nor /£nɔːr, $nɔːr/ *conjunction* used before the second or last of a set of negative possibilities, usually after 'neither' • *We can neither change nor improve it.* • *Neither the train nor the bus will get us there on time.* • *Strangely, neither Betty nor Bob nor Juan saw what had happened.* • *She will not leave, nor will she allow him to continue treating her badly.* • *(esp. Br)* Nor is also used to mean neither: *"I've never been to Iceland." "Nor have I."* ○ *I can't be at the meeting and nor can Andrew.*

Nordic /£'nɔː·dɪk, $'nɔːr-/ *adj* [not gradable] of the people of Scandinavia • *He was a classic Nordic type – tall with blond hair and blue eyes.*

normal /£'nɔː·məl, $'nɔːr-/ *adj* ordinary or usual; the same as would be expected • *Lively behaviour is normal for a four-year-old child.* • **It's** *not normal* **to** *refuse to eat.* [+ *to* infinitive] • *Until she won the prize she'd led a normal life.* • *It was a normal working day.* • *They were selling the goods at half the normal cost.* • **It** *is normal practice to consult the patient's doctor.* • *The temperature was* **above/below** *normal for the time of year.* • *Things are* **back to** *normal now that we've paid off all our debts.*

norm /£nɔːm, $nɔːrm/ *n* [C] • A norm is an accepted standard or a way of behaving or doing things that most people agree with: *Europe's varied cultural, political and ethical norms* ○ *Most large Parisian tourist developments are designed to reflect specifically French norms and values.* ○ *The play is a sympathetic comment on individuals who stray from the norms of the society in which they live.* ○ *One child per family is becoming* **the** *norm in some countries.*

nor·mal·i·ty /£nɔː'mæl·ə·ti, $nɔːr'mæl·ə·t̬i/, *Am also* **nor·mal·cy** /£'nɔː·məl·si, $'nɔːr-/ *n* [U] • Normality is the state of being normal: *In children these symptoms might be regarded as being within the range of normality.* ○ *Now that* *the civil war is over relative normality has now returned to the south of the country.* ○ *Long-term patients need help to return to normality.*

nor·mal·ize *(obj), Br and Aus usually* **-ise** /£'nɔː·mə·laɪz, $'nɔːr-/ *v* ● To normalize is to return to the normal or usual situation: *There is a lot of evidence that the new drug normalizes blood pressure.* [T] ○ *Relations between the two countries are gradually normalizing again.* [I] ● *(specialized)* To normalize **data** is to compare a small set of information with a set which represents the norm: *Research psychologists normalize the results of their studies by comparing their subjects' behaviour with that of the general public.* [T]

normally /£'nɔː·mə·li, $'nɔːr-/ *adv* ● If you normally do something you usually or regularly do it: *She doesn't normally stop working to have lunch.* ○ *Normally, I plan one or two days ahead.* ● If something happens normally it happens in the usual or expected way: *Is the phone working normally again?* ○ *He has only one lung functioning normally.* ○ *The photo showed a normally developed plant and a diseased one.*

Norm·an /£'nɔː·mən, $'nɔːr-/ *adj* [not gradable] of the people from northern France, esp. those who INVADED (= used force to enter) England in 1066 and became its rulers, or of buildings which were made during their rule ● *The cathedral is one of the glories of Norman architecture.* ● The **Norman Conquest** was the defeat of England by Norman soldiers in the 11th century.

Norm·an /£'nɔː·mən, $'nɔːr-/ *n* [C] ● *The Anglo-Saxons were defeated by the Normans.*

Norse /£nɔːs, $nɔːrs/ *adj* [not gradable] of the people who lived in Scandinavia in the past, esp. the Vikings ● *The museum has several fine Norse crosses.*

Norse·man /£'nɔːs·mən, $'nɔːrs-/ *n* [C] *pl* **-men**

north /£nɔːθ, $nɔːrθ/ *(abbreviation* **N**, *Br also* **Nth**, *esp. Am* **No**) *n* [U] the direction which goes towards the part of the Earth above the equator, opposite to the south, or the part of an area or country which is in this direction ● *The points of the compass are North, South, East and West.* ● *The countryside is more mountainous* **in the** *north* **(of** *the country).* ● *Cambridge* **is/lies to the** *north* **of** *London.* ● *The studio has a north-***facing** *window.* ● **The North** can be used to refer to the rich industrial countries of the world, most of which are above the equator. ● **The North** can also mean the northeastern STATES of the US: *The North defeated the South in the American Civil War.* ● If someone refers to the **North-South divide** they mean the difference in wealth between the rich countries which are in the North and the poor countries in the South. ● In Britain, the **North-South divide** refers to the difference in conditions, esp. economic, between the poorer north and the richer south of the country. ● [LP] **Directions**

north /£nɔːθ, $nɔːrθ/ *(abbreviation* **N**, *Br also* **Nth**, *esp. Am* **No**) *adj, adv* [not gradable] ● *North America* ● *North Africa* ● *the north coast of Iceland* ● *You have to travel north from Italy to get to Switzerland.* ● *Go* **due** (= directly) *north for two miles.* ● *The lake is* **due** (= directly) *north of the village.* ● *The garden* **faces** *north and doesn't get much sun in winter.* ● *(infml) They live* **up** *north* (= in the north of the country or region). ● A north **wind** is a wind coming from the north. ● The **North Pole** is the point on the Earth's surface which is furthest north. ● The **North Star** is a bright star which can be seen in the northern part of the sky almost exactly above the North Pole.

north·bound /£'nɔːθ·baʊnd, $'nɔːrθ-/ *adj* [not gradable] ● Northbound means going or leading towards the north: *Northbound traffic is heavy this evening.* ○ *Two northbound buses were cancelled.* ○ *A 20-mile jam built up on the northbound lanes near Birmingham.* ○ *(Br) Traffic is flowing normally on the M6 northbound.*

north·er·ly /£'nɔː·ðəl·i, $'nɔːr·ðər·li/ *adj* ● *For three days they walked in a northerly direction* (= towards the north) *across the desert.* ● *There are plans to build a hotel on the most northerly* (= nearest the north) *point of the island.* ● *Strong northerly* **winds** (= winds from the north) *are forecast for later today.*

north·ern /£'nɔː·ðən, $'nɔːr·ðərn/ *(abbreviation* **N**, *esp. Am* **No**) *adj* [not gradable] ● *northern Europe* ● *the Northern Hemisphere* ● *northern locations* ● **The Northern Lights** is another name for the AURORA BOREALIS.

north·ern·er /£'nɔː·ðən·əʳ, $'nɔːr·ðər·nər/ *n* [C] ● A northerner is a person who comes from the north of a country.

north·ern·most /£'nɔː·ðən·məʊst, $'nɔːr·ðərn·moʊst/ *adj* ● *Cape Columbia is the northernmost* (= furthest towards the north) *point of Canada.*

north·ward /£'nɔːθ·wəd, $'nɔːrθ·wərd/ *adj* [not gradable] ● *She cycled off in a northward* (= towards the north) *direction.*

north·wards /£'nɔːθ·wədz, $'nɔːrθ·wərdz/, **north·ward** *adv* [not gradable] ● *The dust from the volcano spread northwards* (= towards the north). ● *Migrant workers follow the harvest northwards.* ● *The plane turned northwards.*

north·east /£ˌnɔːθ'iːst, $ˌnɔːrθ-/ *(abbreviation* **NE**) *n* [U] the direction which is between north and east ● *Northeast is that way, towards the village.* ● *She works in* **the** *Northeast* **(of** *the country).* ● *The wind is* **in/***coming from* **the** *northeast.* ● [LP] **Directions**

north·east /£'nɔːθ·iːst, $'nɔːrθ-/ *adj, adv* [not gradable] ● *They're forecasting a cold northeast* **wind** (= wind coming from the northeast). ● *Go northeast for about five miles.* ● *The town* **is/lies** *roughly northeast* **of** *here.*

north·east·er·ly /£nɔː'θiː·stə·li, $nɔːr'θiː·stər-/ *adj* ● *a northeasterly direction* (= towards the northeast) ● A northeasterly **wind** is a wind which comes from the northeast.

north·east·ern /£nɔː'θiː·stən, $nɔːr'θiː·stərn/ *(abbreviation* **NE**) *adj* [not gradable] ● *the Northeastern states* ● *northeastern China* ● *the northeastern region*

north·east·ward /£nɔː'θiːs·twəd, $nɔːr'θiːs·twərd/ *adj* [not gradable] ● *They were last seen driving in a northeastward* (= towards the northeast) *direction.*

north·east·wards /£ˌnɔːθ'iːs·twədz, $ˌnɔːrθ'iːs·twərdz/, **north·east·ward** /£ˌnɔːθ'iːs·twəd, $ˌnɔːrθ'iːs·twərd/ *adv* [not gradable] ● *We travelled northeastwards* (= towards the northeast) *for about 250 kilometres.*

north·west /£nɔːθ'west, $nɔːrθ-/ *(abbreviation* **NW**) *n* [U] the direction which is between north and west ● *the northwest* **of** *Australia* ● *The wind is coming from* **the** *northwest.* ● [LP] **Directions**

north·west /£'nɔːθ·west, $'nɔːrθ-/ *adj, adv* [not gradable] ● *Proceeds from the sale of the company's northwest division are expected to total about $100 million.* ● *Turn northwest.* ● *The town* **is/lies** *about 100 miles northwest* **of** *Las Vegas.*

north·west·er·ly /£nɔːθ'wes·təl·i, $nɔːrθ'wes·tər·li/ *adj, n* [C] ● *a northwesterly direction* (= towards the northwest)

north·wes·tern /£nɔːθ'wes·tən, $nɔːrθ'wes·tərn/ *(abbreviation* **NW**) *adj* [not gradable] ● *northwestern Mexico* ● *the northwestern area*

north·west·ward /£nɔːθ'wes·twəd, $nɔːrθ'wes·twərd/ *adj* [not gradable] ● *in a northwestward* (= towards the northwest) *direction*

north·west·wards /£ˌnɔːθ'wes·twədz, $ˌnɔːrθ'wes·twərdz/, **north·west·ward** *adv* [not gradable] ● *The road went northwestwards* (= towards the northwest) *over the hills.*

nos. *pl of* NO.

nose [BODY PART] /£nəʊz, $noʊz/, *slang* **snout** *n* [C] the part of the face that sticks out above the mouth through which you breathe and smell ● *a small/large/long nose* ● *I think I've got a cold – I've got a* **runny** *nose* (= a lot of liquid coming out of the nose) *and a sore throat.* ● *I need to* **blow** *my nose* (= breathe out suddenly and strongly through my nose into a HANDKERCHIEF to empty it). ● *(specialized)* When describing wine, nose means smell: *a wine praised for its smoky nose.* ● *(esp. Br and Aus infml)* If you **get up** someone's **nose** you annoy them in some way: *People who drive like that really get up my nose.* ○ *He's been getting up my nose lately, asking a lot of silly questions.* ● *(infml)* If you **have a (good) nose for** something, you are good at finding things of the stated type: *She's got a good nose for a bargain!* ○ *That reporter has a nose for a good story.* ● *(infml)* To **keep** your **nose clean** means to avoid getting into trouble: *He cares only about keeping the department's nose clean and won't take any risky decisions.* ○ *I don't accept the company's explanation, but I've decided to pay my bill and keep my nose clean.* ● *(infml)* If you tell someone to **keep** their **nose out of** your activities, you mean that they are too interested in them or want to influence them in a way you do not like: *I've already decided how to do it so you can just keep your nose out of* **it**. ○ *He can't keep his nose out of other people's affairs.* ● *(infml)* If you **keep/put** your **nose to the grindstone**, you work very hard for a long time: *She kept her nose to the grindstone all year and got the exam results*

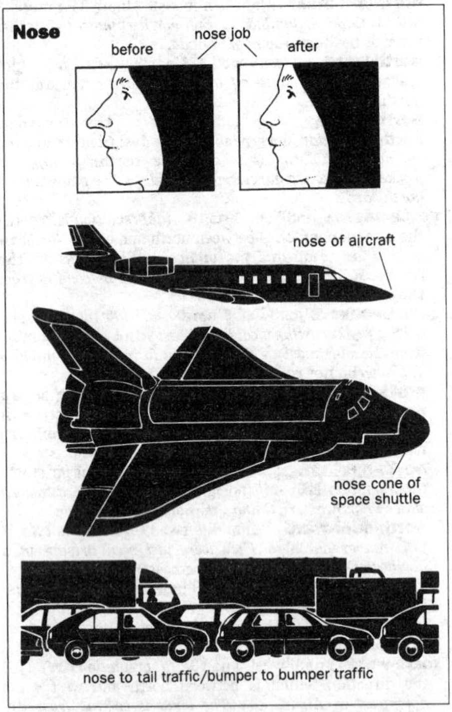

Nose

nose job

before

after

nose of aircraft

nose cone of space shuttle

nose to tail traffic/bumper to bumper traffic

she wanted. • *She walked past me with her* **nose in the air** (=looking as if she thought she was better than other people). • *She's always got her* **nose in a book** (=She is always reading). • *(infml)* If you **poke/stick** your **nose into** something you try to discover things which are not really related to you: *I wish he'd stop poking his nose into my personal life!* • *(infml)* If you **put** someone's **nose out of joint** you offend them or upset them, esp. by getting something that they were wanting for themselves: *John's nose was put out of joint when Jane was promoted and he wasn't.* • Something which happens **(from) under** your **nose**/*(Am also)* **right out from under your nose** happens in an obvious way but you do not notice or cannot prevent it: *He's a scoundrel – he's won contracts under my nose by bribing people.* ○ *A shoplifter had stolen the shoes from under the assistant's nose.* • If something is **(right) under** someone's **nose**, it is where they can clearly see it: *I spent ages looking for the book and it was right under my nose all the time.* ○ *She shoved the letter under her boss's nose* (=made certain he saw it). • *(infml)* If someone has a **nose job** they have an operation to change the shape of their nose. • See also NOSY; NASAL. • PIC〉 **Nose**

-nosed /£-nəʊzd, $-noʊzd/ *combining form* • *a sharp-nosed man* • *children red-nosed with the cold* • See also **-nosed** at NOSE FRONT.

nose FRONT /£nəʊz, $noʊz/ *n* [C] the front of a vehicle, esp. an aircraft • *The symbol was painted on each side of the plane's nose.* • **Nose to tail** means one closely behind the other: *The cars were parked nose to tail down the street.* • A **nose cone** is the front part of a spacecraft, aircraft or MISSILE (=flying weapon). • A **nose wheel** is the wheel at the front of an aircraft. • PIC〉 **Nose**

nose /£nəʊz, $noʊz/ *v* [I always + adv/prep] • *The car nosed* (=moved forward slowly and carefully) **out** *of the side street, its driver peering anxiously around.* • *He carefully nosed his lorry* **into** *the small gap.* • See also **nose out** at NOSE SEARCH.

-nosed /£-nəʊzd, $-noʊzd/ *combining form* • *a blunt-nosed missile* • See also **-nosed** at NOSE BODY PART.

nose SEARCH /£nəʊz, $noʊz/ *v* [I always + adv/prep] *infml* to look around or search in order to discover something, esp. something that other people do not want you to find • *"We'll easily be able to spot any burglars if they come nosing* **about/round**,*" he said.* • *I watched the police nosing* **into** *drawers and looking through papers.*

nose out *obj*, **nose** *obj* **out** *v adv* [M] *infml* • To nose something out is to discover it by searching carefully: *He soon nosed out the details of the accident by chatting innocently to people and making some phone calls.* • See also **nose out** at NOSE FRONT.

nose·bag /£'nəʊz·bæg, $'noʊz-/, *Am* **feed·bag** *n* [C] a bag for holding food which is hung around a horse's head

nose·bleed /£'nəʊz·bli:d, $'noʊz-/ *n* [C] a condition in which blood comes out of a person's nose

nose·dive /£'nəʊz·daɪv, $'noʊz-/ *n* [C] a fast and sudden fall to the ground with the front pointing down • *The plane roared overhead and went into a nosedive.* • A nosedive is also a sudden fast fall in prices, value, etc.: *There was alarm in the markets when the dollar* **took** *a nosedive.*

nose·dive /£'nəʊz·daɪv, $'noʊz-/ *v* [I] • *Spectators in the crowd watched in horror as the plane nosedived.* • *House prices nosedived without warning.*

nosh /£nɒʃ, $nɑ:ʃ/ *n* [U] *Br and Aus slang* food or a meal • *They serve good nosh in the cafeteria.* [U] • *You take your own nosh with you on the bus.* [U] • *We just had time for a* **quick** *nosh* (=meal) *then we had to leave.* [C] • *(Am)* A nosh is a small amount of food eaten between meals or as a meal: *I'll just have a little nosh at lunchtime, perhaps a hot dog.* [U] • A **nosh-up** is a big, enjoyable meal: *We had some good nosh-ups on holiday.*

nosh /£nɒʃ, $nɑ:ʃ/ *v* [I] *Br and Aus slang* • *Let's find somewhere to nosh – I'm starving.* • *(Am) We noshed on a burger before the match.*

nos·tal·gia /£nɒs'tæl·dʒə, $nɑ:'stæl-/ *n* [U] a feeling of pleasure and sometimes slight sadness at the same time as you think about things that happened in the past • *Some people feel nostalgia* **for** *their schooldays.* • *He'd last heard the tune in his childhood and hearing it again* **filled** *him* **with** *nostalgia.* • *A* **wave of** *nostalgia has hit the village as the school is preparing to close down.* • (GR)

nos·tal·gic /£nɒs'tæl·dʒɪk, $nɑ:'stæl-/ *adj* • *The film provided an evening of nostalgic viewing.* • *They had a nostalgic longing for India where they had spent their childhood.*

nos·tal·gi·cally /£nɒs'tæl·dʒɪ·kli, $nɑ:'stæl-/ *adv* • *We spent the evening looking nostalgically at old photos.*

nos·tril /£'nɒs·trᵊl, $'nɑ:·strᵊl/ *n* [C] either of the two openings in the nose through which air moves • *The horses came to a halt, steam streaming from their nostrils.* • *As he left the meadow the sweet smell of wild flowers was still in his nostrils.*

nos·y, **nos·ey** /£'nəʊ·zi, $'noʊ-/ *adj* **nosier**, **nosiest** *disapproving* too interested in what other people are doing and wanting to discover too much about them • *She was complaining about her nosy parents.* • *(infml)* A **nosy parker** is a person who is nosy. • (S)

nos·i·ly /£'nəʊ·zɪ·li, $'noʊ-/ *adv* • *"Who was that on the phone?" she asked nosily.*

nos·i·ness /£'nəʊ·zɪ·nəs, $'noʊ-/ *n* [U]

not /£nɒt, $nɑ:t/ *adv* [not gradable] used to make a word or group of words negative, or to make them mean the opposite of what they did before • *not happy/big/clean/interested* • *Not all the children like swimming.* • *"Who's taken my pen?" "Not me!"* • *Not a single person* (=There was no single person who) *would help me.* • *It's a girl, not a boy.* • *He's not bad-looking* (=He quite attractive). • *It's not uncommon* (=It is quite common) *for people to get lost in this building.* • Not is often shortened to **n't** when it follows a verb, except when it is being emphasized: *She isn't/She's not/She is not willing to come.* ○ *We have not/haven't seen her for a long time.* ○ *He cannot/can't ride a bike.* ○ *She doesn't like apples.* ○ *We won't have time to visit her.* • Not can be used to express a negative in place of part of a sentence: *"Is he coming with us?" "I hope not."* ○ *"Are you staying late?" "I'd rather not."* ○ *She isn't sure whether she is leaving next week* **or not**. • *There was not* **much** *we could do to help by the time we arrived.* • *She* **not only** *took me home* **but also** *came the next day to see if I had recovered.* • *(infml)* Not is sometimes used on its own at the end of a statement to show that you did not mean what you have said. It is often intended to be amusing when used in this way: *That was the best meal I've ever had – not!* ○ *I'm really pleased to get more responsibility with no raise in pay...not.* • **Not at all** is a polite answer or is used to say no strongly: *"Thanks for helping." "Not at all."* ○ *"Did you ask him to come here?" "Not at all, I know nothing about it."* • *She wouldn't tell me how much it cost,* **not that** *I was* (=I was not) *really interested.* • **Not that** *I* (=I do not) *mind but why didn't you phone yesterday?* • *The food at the restaurant was* **not up to much** (=not very good) *"Not the Nine O'Clock News"* (television comedy show, 1970s) • LP› **Clauses, Opposites, Short forms**

not·a·ble /£ˈnəʊ·tə·bl̩, $ˈnoʊ·t̬ə-/ *adj* important and deserving attention, or important and very good • *The Botanical Garden has built up a notable collection of rare plants.* • *Getting both sides to agree was a notable achievement.* • *All of her books are lively and interesting, with two notable* **exceptions.** • *It is an attractive building, notable in particular* **for** *its garden setting.*

not·a·ble /£ˈnəʊ·tə·bl̩, $ˈnoʊ·t̬ə-/ *n* [C] • A notable is an important or famous person: *All the local notables were there.* ○ *Other notables among his pupils were the kings of Saudi Arabia and Thailand.*

not·a·bly /£ˈnəʊ·tə·bli, $ˈnoʊ·t̬ə-/ *adv* • Notably means particularly or most importantly: *The new law affects the confidentiality enjoyed by many professions – notably lawyers, doctors and journalists.* ○ *They have begun attracting investors, most notably big Japanese financial houses.* • Notably can also mean to an important degree in a way which can or should be noticed: *The newspapers are notably biased.*

not·a·ry (pub·lic) /£ˈnəʊ·tᵊr·i, $ˈnoʊ·t̬ɚ-/ *n* [C] *law* an official who has the legal authority to say that documents are correctly signed or truthful or to make an OATH (= promise) official • *The translation of her birth certificate had to be sworn to before a notary.*

no·ta·tion /£nəʊˈteɪ·ʃᵊn, $noʊ-/ *n* a system of written symbols used esp. in mathematics or to represent musical notes • *The system of notation that was perfected for and by classical music doesn't always work for jazz.* [U] • *Working separately both mathematicians developed similar notations.* [C]

notch *obj* CUT /£nɒtʃ, $nɑːtʃ/ *v* [T], *n* [C] (to make) a V-shaped cut in a hard surface • *He notched the edge of the table with his knife.* • *The stick has two notches, one at each end.* • *(Am)* A notch is a narrow valley: *The interstate highway is only two lanes wide where it passes through the notch.* ○ *Franconia Notch*

notched /£nɒtʃt, $nɑːtʃt/ *adj* [not gradable] • *a notched measuring rod*

notch POSITION /£nɒtʃ, $nɑːtʃ/ *n* [C] an imaginary point or position in a system of comparing values, where a higher position is better and a lower position is worse • *Among current players, she is rated a notch* **above** (= is better than) *the rest.* • *We felt the food was a notch below* (= was not as good as) *its usual standard.*

notch *obj* RECORD /£nɒtʃ, $nɑːtʃ/ *v* [T] *infml* to achieve or keep a record of something good • *The police force has notched more than 130 arrests since June.* • *Usually, the first two months of the year are when TV stations notch* **up** *the biggest audience.* • *She has recently notched* **up** *her third win at a major tennis tournament.*

note WRITING /£nəʊt, $noʊt/ *n* [C] a short piece of writing • *He left a note to say he would be home late.* • *There was a note pinned to the door saying when the shop would open again.* • If you **make/take** a note you write something down or you carefully remember it: *Make a note on the calendar that he's coming on Tuesday.* ○ *I'll just take a note* **of** *your name and address.* ○ *She made a* **mental** *note* **of** (= she carefully remembered) *the title.* ○ *Make a note* **to** *phone again next week.* • A note is sometimes added to a longer piece of writing to give more information: *The book has notes at the bottom of each page to explain the old-fashioned language.* ○ *For a further explanation see Note 3.* ○ See also FOOTNOTE. • PIC› **Note** Ⓙ Ⓚ

notes /£nəʊts, $noʊts/ *pl n* • Notes are written information: *The wind blew my notes all over the room.* ○ *The journalist* **took** *notes throughout the interview.*

note SOUND /£nəʊt, $noʊt/ *n* [C] a single sound at a particular level esp. in music, singing, etc., or a written symbol which represents this sound • *high/low notes* • *She played a few loud notes on the piano.* • *The T-shirt had a few notes of music printed on the front.* • *The noise suddenly* **changed** *its note/(Br also)* **changed** *note and rose to a whine.* • Note can be used in describing an emotion or the way something is expressed: *There was* **a** *note* **of** *caution in her letter.* ○ *Her voice took on an angry note.* ○ *His speech* **struck** *just the right note* **of** *encouragement and praise.* ○ *The meeting ended on an optimistic note.* • PIC› **Note** Ⓙ Ⓚ

note MONEY *esp. Br and Aus* /£nəʊt, $noʊt/, *Am usually* **bill** *n* [C] a piece of paper money • *a £20 note* • *a wad of notes* • LP› **Money** Ⓙ Ⓚ

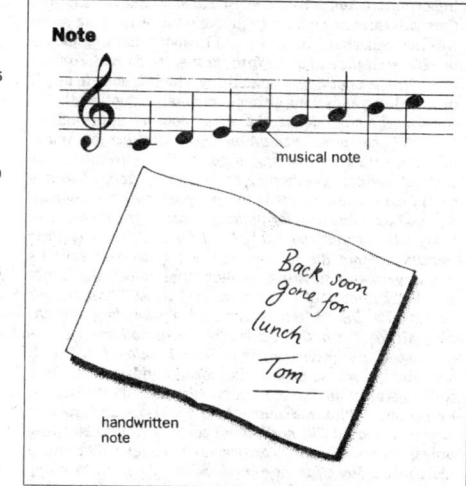

Note

musical note

handwritten note

note *(obj)* NOTICE /£nəʊt, $noʊt/ *v slightly fml* to take notice of, give attention to or make a record of (something) • *They noted the consumers' growing demand for quicker service.* [T] • *He said the weather was beyond our control, noting* **that** *last summer was one of the hottest on record.* [+ *that* clause] • *Please note* **(that)** *we will be closed on Saturday.* [+ *(that)* clause] • *The committee noted* **that** *'the proposed development would not give rise to a public health hazard'.* [+ *that* clause] • *Note* **how** *easy it is to release the catch quickly.* [+ *wh*- word] • Ⓙ Ⓚ

note /£nəʊt, $noʊt/ *n* [U] • To **take note of** something is to give it attention, esp. because it is important: *You should take note of what she tells you because she knows their strategy well.*

note IMPORTANCE /£nəʊt, $noʊt/ *n* [U] **of note** *fml* of importance or having fame • *a historian of note* • *There was nothing of note in the report, just lots of familiar statistics.* • Ⓙ Ⓚ

not·ed /£ˈnəʊ·tɪd, $ˈnoʊ·t̬ɪd/ *adj* • *a noted example of modern architecture* • *a noted campaigner for women's rights* • *The school was noted* **for** *its progressive policies.* • *She isn't usually noted* **for** *her patience* (= She is not a patient person).

note·book /£ˈnəʊt·bʊk, $ˈnoʊt-/ *n* [C] a book of plain or lined paper for writing on • *She went from picture to picture, jotting things down in a little notebook.* • A **notebook (computer)** (also **laptop computer**) is a small computer which can be easily carried.

note·let /£ˈnəʊt·lət, $ˈnoʊt-/ *n* [C] *Br* a small folded sheet of paper or card, usually with a picture on the front, on which you write a short letter • *notelets with pictures of flowers* • *I had a notelet from her thanking me for their wedding present.*

note·pad /£ˈnəʊt·pæd, $ˈnoʊt-/ *n* [C] a set of sheets of plain or lined paper, joined at the top edge, for writing on • *a* **ruled** *notepad* (= a notepad with lines) • A **notepad (computer)** is a small computer which you enter DATA (= information) into using a special pen. • PIC› **Stationery**

note·pap·er /£ˈnəʊtˌpeɪ·pəʳ, $ˈnoʊtˌpeɪ·pɚ/ *n* [U] plain paper for writing letters on • *three sheets/pieces of notepaper* • *matching notepaper and envelopes* • *headed notepaper*

note·wor·thy /£ˈnəʊtˌwɜː·ði, $ˈnoʊtˌwɜːr-/ *adj slightly fml* deserving attention because important or interesting • *Their investigation produced a number of noteworthy conclusions.* • *The performance was excellent even though no noteworthy actors were in the cast.* • .

noth·ing /ˈnʌθ·ɪŋ/ *pronoun* not anything • *There's nothing in the drawer – I took everything out.* • *I wasn't sure what had happened so I said nothing to either of them.* • *Nothing I could say would cheer her up.* • *He wouldn't listen so there was nothing I could do.* • *There was nothing new in the report.* • *She said nothing interesting.* • *There's nothing* **else** (= no other thing) *we can do to help.* • *He's nothing* **if not** (= He is very) *charming.* • *There's nothing* **much** (= not very much) *to do in our village.* • *(fml) The story was nothing* **but** (= only) *lies.* • *Money* **is/means** *nothing* (= it is not important) **to** *him.* • *We were fascinated by what we saw and time* **was/meant** *nothing* (= the amount of time we spent was not important) **to** *us.* • *(Am)* In sports nothing means no points: *At the end of the fifth inning, the score is Yankees three, Red Sox nothing.* • Something which is done in an **all or nothing** way is done either completely or not at all: *The Government has rejected the all or nothing* **approach** *in favour of a compromise solution.* ○ *She will either love you or hate you – it's all or nothing.* • **For nothing** means free or without paying: *I got the picture for nothing from a friend.* • **(All) for nothing** means without a good result: *He queued for two hours and (all) for nothing – there were no seats left.* ○ *My wish is that those who died for the liberty of their country did not die for nothing.* • *(infml)* You say **it's nothing/it was nothing** to show that something is not especially important: *"You seem very upset." "No, no, it's nothing, I'm OK."* ○ *"It was very kind of you to look after the baby all day." "Oh, that's all right, it was nothing* (= it was not especially generous or kind), *I enjoyed it."* • If something or someone is/looks/sounds/tastes **like nothing (else) on earth**, it seems very strange, unusual or unpleasant: *With the outrageous make-up and strange clothes he looked like nothing on earth.* • *(infml)* **Nothing doing** means no, esp. in answer to a request: *We asked if she'd take a day off work to help us, but she said, "Nothing doing".* • *There's* **nothing for it but to** (= There is no other possible thing to do except) *get some extra help.* • *I heard the rumour that she's leaving but apparently* **there's nothing in it** (= it is not true). • **Nothing less than** is used to emphasize how important or desirable something is: *Their dream was nothing less than a revolutionary project to bring computers and ordinary people together.* • *He dismissed Bryan as* **nothing more than** (= only) *an amateur.* • You say **nothing of the sort/kind** to emphasize a negative statement: *I told him nothing of the sort* (= I did not tell him anything like that). • *In the summer she sleeps with* **nothing on** (= wearing no clothes). • **Nothing on** also means having no arrangements for a stated period: *I've just looked in her diary and she* **has** *nothing on on/for Tuesday afternoon.* • *The play was* **nothing special** (= not very good). • *It's* **nothing to do with** *me* (= I am not involved). • *We* **have/are nothing to do with** (= We are not involved with) *the firm which has the offices next door.* • *In the evening he likes to read books and articles which* **have/are nothing to do with** (= are not related to) *his work.* • *Windsurfing is easy – there's* **nothing to it** (= there is no difficulty in doing it). • *"Workers of the World unite, you have nothing to lose but your chains"* (from the *Communist Manifesto* by Karl Marx and Friedrich Engels, 1848) • *"You ain't heard nothing yet! (Sometimes 'You ain't seen nothing yet')"* (words spoken by Al Jolson in the first talking film *The Jazz Singer*, 1927) • *"Nothing, like something, happens anywhere"* (Philip Larkin in the poem *I Remember, I Remember*, 1954) • [LP] **Quantity words, Zero**

noth·ing /ˈnʌθ·ɪŋ/ *adj* [not gradable] *infml* • *People who do that sort of thing are just nothing.*

noth·ing /ˈnʌθ·ɪŋ/ *n* [C] *infml* • *He's a nothing, a low-down, useless nobody.*

noth·ing /ˈnʌθ·ɪŋ/ *adv* [not gradable] • *(esp. Br) He had two letters of refusal but,* **nothing daunted** (= not discouraged), *he tried again.* • *The party was* **nothing short of** (= it was) *a disaster.*

noth·ing·ness /ˈnʌθ·ɪŋ·nəs/ *n* [U] • Nothingness is a state where nothing is present, or where nothing is present that is important or gives meaning to life: *As she got older it was the fear of nothingness in her life that disturbed her most.* ○ *He felt an overwhelming sense of hopelessness, silence, nothingness.*

no·tice *(obj)* [SEE] /£ˈnəʊ·tɪs, $ˈnoʊ·t̬ɪs/ *v* [not be noticing] to become aware of, esp. by looking; to see • *I noticed a crack in the ceiling.* [T] • *Mary waved at the man but he didn't seem to notice.* [I] • *We noticed a car stop outside the house.* [+ obj + infinitive without *to*] • *We noticed a car stopping outside the house.* [+ obj + v-*ing*] • *He noticed* **(that)** *the woman was staring at him.* [+ (*that*) clause] • *Did you notice* **how** *she did that?* [+ *wh-* word] • *She was first noticed* (= Her skill was first recognized) *by the critics at the age of 12, and went on to become a world-famous violinist.* [T] • Ⓓ Ⓔ Ⓘ

no·tice /£ˈnəʊ·tɪs, $ˈnoʊ·t̬ɪs/ *n* [U] • *What Nico has to say deserves some notice* (= attention). • *The mistake on my bank statement* **escaped** *my notice* (= I did not see it or become aware of it). • *It has* **come to/been brought to** *my notice* (= I have been told) *that you have been late for work every day this week.* • If you **take notice (of** something), you give attention to it: *I asked him to drive more slowly but he didn't take any notice.* ○ *Don't take any notice of/Take no notice of what your mother says – she's just in a bad mood.* ○ *The news made everyone* **sit up and** (= suddenly) *take notice.*

no·tice·a·ble /£ˈnəʊ·tɪ·sə·bl̩, $ˈnoʊ·t̬ɪ-/ *adj* • Something that is noticeable is easy to see or recognize: *There has been a noticeable improvement in Tim's cooking.* ○ *It's noticeable* **that** *the weather is getting colder.* [+ *that* clause]

no·tice·a·bly /£ˈnəʊ·tɪ·sə·bli, $ˈnoʊ·t̬ɪ-/ *adv* • *After her illness, Fiona had become noticeably thinner* (= so much thinner that it was easily recognized).

no·tice [INFORMATION] /£ˈnəʊ·tɪs, $ˈnoʊ·t̬ɪs/ *n* (a board, piece of paper, etc. containing) information or instructions • *There was a large notice on the wall saying 'No Parking'.* [C] • *I saw a notice in the paper announcing their marriage.* [C] • Notice is information or a warning given in advance about something that is going to happen in the future: *The next time you visit, can you* **give** *me more notice?* [U] ○ *I can't cancel my arrangements* **at** *such* **short** *notice.* [U] ○ *The emergency services are ready to spring into action* **at a moment's** *notice.* [U] ○ *The building is closed* **until further** *notice* (= until another official announcement is made). [U] • If you **give/hand in** your notice, you tell your employer that you intend to leave your job after a particular period of time: *I've decided to hand in my notice.* [U] • If your employer **gives** you notice, he or she asks you to leave your job, usually after a particular period of time: *My boss has given me a month's notice.* [U] • *(Br and Aus)* A **notice board** (*Am* **bulletin board**) is a board on a wall on which notices can be fixed: *I've put the list of players up on the notice board.* • [LP] **Work** [PIC] **Office** Ⓓ Ⓔ Ⓘ

no·tic·es /£ˈnəʊ·tɪ·sɪz, $ˈnoʊ·t̬ɪ-/ *pl n* • A play's, film's, book's, etc. notices are the REVIEWS (= printed statements of opinion) of it in the newspapers: *The musical has received wonderful notices.*

no·ti·fy *obj* /£ˈnəʊ·tɪ·faɪ, $ˈnoʊ·t̬ə-/ *v* [T] to tell (someone) officially about something • *The school is required to notify parents if their children fail to come to school.* • *Has everyone been notified* **of** *the decision?* • *We notified the police* **that** *the bicycle had been stolen.* [+ obj + *that* clause]

no·ti·fi·a·ble /£ˈnəʊ·tɪ·faɪ·ə·bl̩, $ˈnoʊ·t̬ə-/ *adj* • A notifiable **disease** or **offence** is one that must be reported to the authorities: *If the animals have died from a notifiable disease their bodies must be burnt.*

no·ti·fi·ca·tion /£ˌnəʊ·tɪ·fɪˈkeɪ·ʃᵊn, $ˌnoʊ·t̬ə-/ *n* • *You must give the bank (a) written notification if you wish to close your account.* [C/U]

no·tion /£ˈnəʊ·ʃᵊn, $ˈnoʊ-/ *n* (a) belief or idea • *The programme makers reject the notion* **that** *seeing violence on television has a harmful effect on children.* [C + *that* clause] • *I have only a* **vague** *notion* **of** *what she does for a living.* [C] • *Have you any notion* **how** *much it costs to keep a dog?* [U + *wh-* word] • *However did you get such a notion* (= silly idea)? [C] • *(dated)* If you **have/take** a notion **to** do something, you suddenly want to do it: *I had a notion to write them a letter.* [U + *to* infinitive]

no·tion·al /£ˈnəʊ·ʃᵊn·ᵊl, $ˈnoʊ-/ *adj fml* • Something that is notional exists only as an idea, not in reality: *Almost everyone will have to pay a higher tax bill than the notional amount suggested by the Government.*

no·to·ri·ous /£nəʊˈtɔː·ri·əs, $noʊˈtɔːr·i-/ *adj* famous for something bad • *This prison holds some of Britain's most notorious criminals.* • *The company is notorious* **for** *paying its bills late.* • Compare **celebrated** at CELEBRATE [PRAISE]. • Ⓔ Ⓟ

no·to·ri·ous·ly /£nəʊˈtɔː·ri·ə·sli, $noʊˈtɔːr·i-/ *adv* • *The crime of rape is notoriously* (= famous as being) *difficult to prove.*

no·to·ri·e·ty /£ˌnəʊ·tᵊrˈaɪ·ə·ti, $ˌnoʊ·t̬əˈraɪ·ə·t̬i/ *n* [U] • Notoriety is the state of being famous for something bad: *He* **achieved/acquired/gained** *notoriety* **for** *murdering eleven women in the north of England.*

not·with·stand·ing /£ˌnɒt·wɪðˈstæn·dɪŋ, $ˌnɑːt-/ *prep, adv fml* despite (the fact or thing mentioned) • *Notwithstanding some members' objections, I think we must go ahead with the plan.* • *A large fire in the grate notwithstanding, the room was cold.*

nou·gat /£ˈnuː·gɑː, £ˈnʌg·ət, $ˈnuː·gət/ *n* [U] a hard chewy white or pink sweet food, usually containing nuts

nought [ZERO] *esp. Br* /£nɔːt, $nɑːt/, *Am usually* **naught** *n* [C] the number 0; zero • *He said it was only worth £10, but I reckon you could add a couple of noughts to that* (= it is really worth £1000). • *(Br and Aus)* **Noughts and crosses** (*Am* **tick-tack-toe**) is a game played on a piece of paper in which two players write either O or X in a pattern of nine squares. The first player who places three noughts or crosses in a straight line wins the game. • LP> **Zero** PIC> **Games**

nought NOTHING /£nɔːt, $nɑːt/ *n* [U] NAUGHT NOTHING

noun /naʊn/ *n* [C] (in grammar) a word that refers to a person, place, thing, event, substance or quality • *'Doctor', 'tree', 'party', 'coal' and 'beauty' are all nouns.* • A **noun phrase** is a group of words in a sentence which together behave as a noun: *In the sentences 'We took the night train' and 'Do you know the man sitting in the corner', 'the night train' and 'the man sitting in the corner' are noun phrases.* • LP> **Plurals, Stress in pronunciation**

nour·ish *obj* /£ˈnʌr·ɪʃ, $ˈnɜːr-/ *v* [T] to provide (people or animals) with food in order to make them grow and keep them healthy • *Children need plenty of good fresh food to nourish them.* • *After an illness, nourish yourself* **on/with** *healthy soups.* • *The children look happy and well nourished.* • *This cream is supposed to help nourish* (= keep healthy) *your skin.* • *(fml)* If you nourish a feeling, belief or plan, you think about it a lot and encourage it: *Lisa has long nourished the hope of becoming a famous writer.*

nour·ish·ing /£ˈnʌr·ɪ·ʃɪŋ, $ˈnɜːr-/ *adj* • A nourishing drink or food is one that makes you healthy and strong: *Sweets aren't very nourishing.*

nour·ish·ment /£ˈnʌr·ɪʃ·mənt, $ˈnɜːr-/ *n* [U] • *A young baby obtains all the nourishment* (= food to make it healthy) *it needs from its mother's milk.*

nous /naʊs/ *n* [U] *Br and Aus infml* good judgment and practical ability; SENSE GOOD JUDGMENT • *Anyone with a bit of nous would have known what to do.* • *She had the business nous to buy property just before prices went up.*

nou·veau riche /£ˌnuː·vəʊˈriːʃ, $-voʊ-/ *adj disapproving* typical of or being a person from a low social class who has recently become very rich and likes to show how rich they are by living in a big house, driving an expensive car, spending a lot of money, etc. • *Don't you think having lions on pillars at the side of your gate is rather nouveau riche?* • **The nouveau riche** are nouveau riche people.

nou·velle cui·sine /ˌnuː·vel·kwɪˈziːn/ *n* [U] a style of cooking in which food is lightly cooked, usually using little fat and often in unusual combinations, and served in attractive patterns on the plate in small amounts • *Jim prefers traditional cooking to nouvelle cuisine because he likes to eat a lot.*

nov·el BOOK /£ˈnɒv·əl, $ˈnɑː·vəl/ *n* [C] a long printed story about imaginary characters and events • *I'm taking a few novels to read on holiday.* • *Have you read any of Jane Austen's novels?* • *His latest novel is selling really well.* • *It is said that first novels are often* **autobiographical**. • *She writes* **historical/detective/spy** *novels.* • See also NOVELLA. • (CS) (D) (DK) (N) (PL) (RUS) (S)

nov·el·ist /£ˈnɒv·əl·ɪst, $ˈnɑː·və-/ *n* [C] • A novelist is a person who writes novels: *She's a successful novelist and biographer.* • (D)

nov·el NEW /£ˈnɒv·əl, $ˈnɑː·vəl/ *adj* new and original; not like anything seen before • *Keeping a sheep in the garden is a novel way of keeping the grass short!* • *That's a very novel idea/suggestion.* • *We need to find a novel approach to our advertising.* • (CS) (D) (DK) (N) (PL) (RUS) (S)

nov·el·ty /£ˈnɒv·əl·ti, $ˈnɑː·vəl·t̬i/ *n* • *The novelty* (= quality of being new or unusual) *of the toys soon* **wore off** *and the children became bored with them.* [U] • *Television in Britain in the 1950s had a novelty* **value**. [U] • If something is a novelty, it has not been experienced before and so is interesting: *Tourists are still a novelty on this remote island.* [C] • A novelty is also a cheap unusual object such as a small toy, often given as a present: *A Christmas cracker usually contains a paper hat, a joke and a novelty.* [C] ○ *The shop sells novelty hats like plastic policeman's helmets and cowboy hats.*

nov·el·ette /£ˌnɒv·əlˈet, $ˌnɑː·vəl-/ *n* [C] a short NOVEL, which is not usually very serious and is often about romance

no·vel·la /£nəʊˈvel·ə, $noʊ-/ *n* [C] *pl* **novellas** or **novelle** a short NOVEL

No·vem·ber /£nəʊˈvem·bəʳ, $noʊˈvem·bɚ/ (*abbreviation* **Nov**) *n* the eleventh month of the year, after October and before December • *5(th) November/November 5(th)/5(th) Nov/Nov 5(th)* [U] • *Guy Fawkes' Night is* **on** *the fifth of November/November the fifth/(esp. Am) November fifth.* [U] • *The factory opened* **last** *November/is opening* **next** *November.* [U] • *He's starting his new job* **in/during** *November.* [U] • *It was one of the coldest Novembers in living memory.* [C] • LP> **Dates**

nov·ice /£ˈnɒv·ɪs, $ˈnɑː·vɪs/ *n* [C] a person who is not experienced in a job or situation • *I've never driven a car before – I'm a complete novice.* • *Although she was a political novice, she was elected to parliament.* • *This is quite a difficult plant for novice gardeners to grow.* • A novice is also a person who is still training to be a NUN or a MONK.

No·vo·caine /£ˈnəʊ·və·keɪn, $ˈnoʊ-/ *n* [U] *trademark* a drug given to people to stop them feeling pain, esp. during an operation on their teeth

now AT PRESENT /naʊ/ *adv* [not gradable] at the present time, not in the past or future; immediately • *She used to be a teacher, but now she works in publishing.* • *Where do you live now?* • *I may eat something later, but I'm not hungry now.* • *Many people now own a video recorder.* • *I don't want to wait until tomorrow, I want it now!* • Now can be used to express how long something has been happening, from when it began to the present time: *She's been a vegetarian for ten years now.* ○ *I haven't heard from Gail for a couple of months now.* • If you say that something will happen **any day/minute/moment/second** now or **any time** now, you mean that it will happen very soon: *Our guests will be arriving any moment now and the house is still a mess.* • **Just** now means either a very short time ago, or at the present time: *I saw her drive past just now.* ○ *John's in the bath just now, can he call you back?* • In stories or reports of past events, now is used to describe a new situation or event: *It was getting dark now and we were tired.* • Now can also be used to refer to a result of something that has just been said or done: *Oh yes, now I know who you mean.* • If you do something **(every) now and then/(every) now and again**, you do it sometimes but not very often: *I still see her for lunch now and then, but not as often as I used to.* • You can say **now for** when you are introducing a new subject: *And now for what we're going to do tomorrow.* • *(saying)* '(It's) now or never' means that you must do something immediately, esp. because you will not get another chance. • *(saying)* 'Now you're/we're talking' means that that is a much better suggestion or offer. • LP> **Periods of time**

now /naʊ/ *n* [U] • Now is the present moment or time: *Now isn't a good time to speak to him.* ○ *I thought you'd have finished* **by** *now.* ○ *You should have mentioned it before* **now**. ○ *That's all* **for** *now* (= until a future point in time). ○ **As from/of** *now*/**From** *now* **on** (= From this moment and always in the future) *the gates will be locked at midnight.*

now (that) /naʊ/ *conjunction* • You use now (that) to give an explanation of a new situation: *Now (that) I've got my own car I don't get as much exercise as I used to.* ○ *She's enjoying the job more now (that) she's got more responsibility.*

now IN SPEECH /naʊ/ *adv* [not gradable] used in statements and questions to introduce or give emphasis to what you are saying • *Now, where did I put my hat?* • *There was a knock at the door. Now Jan knew her mother had promised to visit, so she assumed it was her.* • *Now what have I told you about remembering to say thank you?* • *Hurry, now, or you'll miss the bus!* • *Well, now, what's been going on?* • *I'm afraid I can't go today. Now* (= But), *if you'd asked me yesterday I would have said yes.* • You say **now, now** to someone when you want to make them feel better or give them a gentle warning: *Now, now, don't cry.* ○ *Now, now, children, stop fighting!* • You say **now then** to attract attention to what you are going to ask or suggest: *Now then, what's all this fuss about?*

NOW ac·count /£ˌen·əʊˈdʌb·l̩·juː, $-oʊˈ-/ *n* [C] *Am* a negotiable order of withdrawal account (= a bank account which you can take money out of at any time and which also earns a profit)

now·a·days /ˈnaʊ·ə·deɪz/ *adv* [not gradable] at the present time, in comparison to the past • *Who remembers those films nowadays?* • *Nowadays, I bake my own bread rather than buy it.* • LP> **Periods of time**

no·where /£ˈnəʊ·weəʳ, $ˈnoʊ·wer/ *adv* [not gradable] in, at or to no place; not anywhere • *These young people have nowhere (else) to go.* • *Nowhere does the article mention the names of the people involved.* • *Nowhere is the help needed more than in the inner cities.* • If someone or something appears **from/out of** nowhere, they appear very suddenly and unexpectedly: *A car appeared (as if) from nowhere and the driver beckoned him to get in.* ○ *The team has come from nowhere* (= from a very bad position) *to win football's* *biggest prize.* • Someone or something that is **going/getting/heading** nowhere is not having any success or achieving anything: *I'm trying to persuade her to come but I'm getting nowhere.* ○ *The company was heading nowhere until the new boss arrived.* ○ *That sort of bad manners will get you nowhere* (=will not make it possible for you to succeed). • Nowhere can also mean not in a successful or a winning position: *The horse I bet on finished nowhere.*

nowt /naʊt/ *pronoun* [U] *Br regional* nothing • *That's got nowt to do with it!* • *(saying)* 'There's nowt so queer as folk' means people sometimes behave in a very strange way. • Compare OWT.

no·xious /£ˈnɒk·ʃəs, $ˈnɑːk-/ *adj fml* (esp. of a gas or substance) poisonous; very harmful • *The people in the house had died from inhaling noxious smoke/fumes.* • *It has been alleged that the factory is dumping noxious chemicals in the river.* • *He was smoking a noxious cigarette.* • *I think this government has some noxious* (=harmful and unpleasant) *policies.*

noz·zle /£ˈnɒz·l̩, $ˈnɑː·zl̩/ *n* [C] a narrow piece fixed to the end of a tube so that the liquid or air that comes out can be directed in a particular way • *Attach the nozzle to the garden hose before turning on the water.*

nr *prep* (when used as part of an address) *abbreviation for* NEAR • *Bray, nr Dublin*

–n't /-ᵊnt/ *combining form, short form of* NOT • *didn't* • *shouldn't* • *mustn't* • *can't*

nth /enθ/ *adj* [before n; not gradable] *infml* (used when you do not know how many things there are) being the most recent in a long series • *I glanced at my watch for the nth time that morning.* • **To the nth degree** means as much or as far as possible: *We were questioned to the nth degree.* ○ *She takes vegetarianism to the nth degree.* • Compare N [LETTER].

nu·ance /£ˈnjuː·ɑːnts, $ˈnuː-/ *n* [C] a very slight difference in appearance, meaning, sound, etc. • *The painter has managed to capture every nuance* **of** *the woman's expression.* • *Kate can imitate the* **subtle** *nuances* **of** *a person's voice.* • *Example sentences in this dictionary help convey the nuances* **of** *meaning of a word.*

nub /nʌb/ *n* [U] the most important or basic part of something • *The book never really gets to the nub* **of** *the matter.* • *What do you think is the nub* **of** *the problem?*

nu·bile /£ˈnjuː·baɪl, $ˈnuː-/ *adj humorous* (of a woman) young and sexually attractive • *Rich old men often like to be surrounded by nubile young women.*

nu·cle·ar /£ˈnjuː·klɪəʳ, $ˈnuː·klɪr/ *adj* [not gradable] being or using the power produced when the NUCLEUS (=central part) of an atom is divided or joined to another nucleus • *nuclear energy/power* • *a nuclear power plant* • *a nuclear reactor* • *the nuclear industry* • *No one has yet solved the problem of how to get rid of nuclear* **waste** (=unwanted, dangerously RADIOACTIVE material made when producing nuclear power). • Nuclear is also used to refer to (the use of) weapons which use the power produced when the NUCLEUS of an atom is divided or joined to another nucleus: *nuclear weapons* • *a nuclear war* • *a nuclear attack* • *nuclear disarmament* ○ *There must be a possibility that a conventional war could* **go** *nuclear.* ○ *How many nations have a nuclear* **capability** (=have nuclear weapons)*?* ○ *Would the human race survive a nuclear* **holocaust** (=a war with nuclear weapons that destroys almost everything)*?* • A **nuclear-free** area is one in which nuclear weapons and nuclear energy are not allowed: *The city has declared itself a nuclear-free* **zone**. • A **nuclear winter** is a period that scientists believe would follow a large nuclear explosion, when there would be very little light or heat and nothing would grow in the world. • See also **nuclear** at NUCLEUS. • [PIC] **Energy**

nu·cle·ar fam·i·ly *n* [C] a family consisting of two parents and their children, but not including aunts, uncles, grandparents etc. • Compare **extended family** at EXTEND [REACH].

nu·cle·ic ac·id /£njuːˈkleɪ·ɪk, $nuː-/ *n specialized* a type of acid that exists in all living cells • *DNA and RNA are both nucleic acids.* [C] • *DNA and RNA are both types of nucleic acid.* [U]

nu·cle·us /£ˈnjuː·kli·əs, $ˈnuː-/ *n* [C] *pl* **nuclei** /£ˈnjuː·kli·aɪ, $ˈnuː-/ or **nucleuses** *specialized* the central part of an atom, usually made up of PROTONS and NEUTRONS, or the part of a cell that controls its growth • *DNA is stored in the nucleus of a cell.* • People or things that form **the** nucleus **of** something else are the most important part of it: *The three new players will form the nucleus of a revised and stronger team.*

nu·cle·ar /£ˈnjuː·klɪəʳ, $ˈnuː·klɪr/ *adj specialized* • Nuclear means relating to a nucleus: *nuclear physics* ○ *nuclear fission* (=the dividing of a nucleus) ○ *nuclear fusion* (=the joining of two nuclei) • See also NUCLEAR.

nude /£njuːd, $nuːd/ *adj* [not gradable] not wearing any clothes; naked • *As a young actress she had posed nude for a magazine.* • *Nude sunbathing is only allowed on certain beaches.*

nude /£njuːd, $nuːd/ *n* • A nude is a picture or other piece of art showing a person who is not wearing any clothes: *In his collection he had several superb nudes.* [C] • If you are **in the nude** you are not wearing any clothes: *The children were running around the garden in the nude.*

nu·di·sm /£ˈnjuː·dɪ·zᵊm, $ˈnuː-/ *n* [U] • Nudism is the activity of sometimes wearing no clothes because you believe that wearing no clothes is healthy.

nu·dist /£ˈnjuː·dɪst, $ˈnuː-/ *n* [C] • *The whole family are committed nudists* (=people who sometimes do not wear clothes because they believe that not wearing clothes is healthy). • *There are several nudist beaches on the island.*

nu·di·ty /£ˈnjuː·dɪ·ti, $ˈnuː·də·t̬i/ *n* [U] • Nudity is the state of wearing no clothes: *The film was criticized for its excessive violence and nudity.*

nudge *(obj)* /nʌdʒ/ *v* to push (someone or something) gently • *He nudged the cat off the sofa so that he could sit down.* [T] • *The children were giggling and nudging each other* (=pushing each other gently with their ELBOWS to attract each other's attention). [T] • *(fig.) Many men in their fifties are being nudged* (=gently persuaded) *into early retirement.* [T] • *(fig.) He must be nudging* (=approaching the age of) *40 now.* [T] • *(fig.) Oil prices continue to nudge* (=move slowly) *higher.* [I always + adv/prep] • *(Br and Aus infml)* People say **nudge nudge (wink wink)** when they want to suggest that there is a sexual meaning in something that has just been said.

nudge /nʌdʒ/ *n* [C] • *I gave him a nudge to wake him up.*

nu·ga·tor·y /£ˈnjuː·gə·tᵊr·i, $ˈnuː·gə·tɔːr-/ *adj fml* of little value; worthless • *a nugatory amount*

nug·get /ˈnʌg·ɪt/ *n* [C] a small roughly shaped lump, esp. of gold • *You can still find gold nuggets in the Alaskan rivers.* • A chicken or fish nugget is a small piece of it that has been covered in BREADCRUMBS and fried: *She won't eat anything except chicken nuggets and chips.* • *(esp. humorous)* A nugget is also something that a person has said or written that is very wise, informative or true: *The book contains nuggets like "All you need is love".* ○ *Have you got any other astonishing nuggets* **of** *wisdom/information for us?*

nuis·ance /£ˈnjuː·sᵊnts, $ˈnuː-/ *n* something or someone that annoys you or causes trouble for you • *These mosquitoes are a nuisance.* [C] • *I've forgotten my umbrella –* **what a** *nuisance!* [U] • *Local residents claimed that the noise from the concert was causing a* **public** *nuisance.* [C] • **It**'*s a nuisance* **that** *I've got to work on Saturday.* [U + *that* clause] • **It**'*s such a nuisance hav***ing** *to rewrite those letters.* [U + v-*ing*] • *I hate to be a nuisance, but could I ask for your help?* [C] • *Those kids are* **real** *nuisances.* [C] • If you **make a nuisance of yourself**, you cause trouble or annoyance to other people.

nuke *obj* /£njuːk, $nuːk/ *v* [T] *slang* to bomb with nuclear weapons • *The two countries were threatening to nuke each other.* • *(esp. Am and Aus)* To nuke food is to cook it in a MICROWAVE OVEN: *If your coffee has gone cold you can put it in the microwave and nuke it for a minute.*

nuke /£njuːk, $nuːk/ *n* [C] *slang* • A nuke is a nuclear weapon: *'No nukes here!' the banner read.*

null and void *adj* [after v; not gradable] *law* having no legal force • *The change in the law makes the previous agreement null and void.*

nul·li·fy *obj* /ˈnʌl·ɪ·faɪ/ *v* [T] to make (an agreement) have no legal force, or to cause (something) to have no value or effect • *The state death penalty law was nullified in 1977.* • *The referee nullified the goal, ruling that a player's hand had touched the ball.* • *All my hard work was nullified when I lost my notes.*

numb /nʌm/ *adj* **-er, -est** (of a part of the body) unable to feel anything, usually for a short time • *I had been lying awkwardly and my leg had* **gone** *numb.* • *My fingers were so cold that they* **felt** *numb.* • If you are numb (**with** shock, fear, etc.), you are not able to feel any emotions or think clearly because you are so shocked or frightened: *When she first heard the news she was numb with disbelief.* ○ *Ever* *since his girlfriend left him he has* **felt** *numb.* • LP› **Feelings and pains**

numb *obj* /nʌm/ *v* [T] • *The extreme cold numbed her face and hands* (=caused them to lose feeling.) • *The children are still numbed by* (=they cannot feel any emotion because of) *their father's death.*

numb·ly /ˈnʌm·li/ *adv*

numb·ness /ˈnʌm·nəs/ *n* [U] • *Numbness* (=lack of feeling) *in the fingers is one of the first signs of frostbite.*

num·ber SYMBOL /£ˈnʌm·bəʳ, $-bɚ/ *n* [C] (a sign or symbol representing) a unit which forms part of the system of counting and calculating • *One, six, fifteen, sixty-two and one hundred are all numbers.* • *"What's your favourite number?" "Seven."* • *I never was much good at/with numbers* (=adding, subtracting, etc.). • A number (*abbreviation* **no**) can also be one of a series of the symbols used in counting, which is used to mark a particular example of something: *They used to live at number 34 Orchard Street.* ○ *Please write your credit card number on this form.* ○ *What's our flight number?* ○ *The prisoners were all known by number.* • A number is also a telephone number: *I gave him my number and he promised to call me.* • If you do something *(Br and Aus)* **by numbers**/*(Am)* **by the numbers**, you do it according to a plan that has been decided previously, without using your own imagination and ideas: *This is story-writing/painting by numbers – there's nothing original here.* • *(slang)* If you **have** someone's **number**, you know a lot about them and so you have an advantage over that person: *Don't worry, I've got his number, he doesn't fool me.* • *(infml)* If someone's **number is up**, they are going to die: *When the plane started to shake, Colin thought his number was up.* • **Number-crunching** is mathematical work performed either by people or computers which is often quite simple but takes a long time: *It's really not very interesting work, just a lot of number-crunching.* ○ *I'm only a* **number-cruncher** *in the accounts department.* • *(infml)* **Number one** (*esp. Am also* **numero uno**) means yourself and no one else: *Frank is completely selfish – he only cares about number one.* ○ *I'm going to* **look out for** *number one* (=take care of myself only). • A person or organization that is **number one** is the most important one: *She's still the world number one in tennis.* • *(Br and Aus)* A **number plate** (*Am* **license plate**) is the sign on the front and the back of a motor vehicle that shows its **registration number**. • In the US, a **numbers game** or **the numbers** is an illegal way of risking paying money in order to guess about the appearance of particular combinations of numbers, such as in a newspaper. • In Britain, **Number Ten** (*abbreviation* **No 10**) is used to refer to the Prime Minister or to the people who work for or represent the Prime Minister. It is short for 'Number Ten, Downing Street,' in London, where the Prime Minister lives and meets with government officials and other people: *Number Ten announced tonight that the election will be on April 6.* • *"I'm not a number – I'm a free man!"* (phrase from the television series *The Prisoner*, 1967-) • Ⓣ

num·ber *obj* /£ˈnʌm·bəʳ, $-bɚ/ *v* [T] • To number something is to give it a number in a series and usually write this number on it: *All the folders have been carefully numbered and filed away.* ○ *Number the pages* **from** *one* **to** *ten.*

num·ber AMOUNT /£ˈnʌm·bəʳ, $-bɚ/ *n* [U + sing/pl v] an amount or total • *The number* **of** *people killed in road accidents fell last month.* • *There has been* **an** *increasing number* **of** *cases of the disease.* • *A small number* **of** *children are educated at home.* • *(slightly fml)* **A** *small number* **of** *children is educated at home.* • **A** *large number* **of** (=Many) *invitations have been sent.* • *(slightly fml)* **A** *large number* **of** *invitations has been sent.* • *Letters of complaint were surprisingly few* **in** *number* (=there were not many of them). • **A** number **of** things is several of them: *I decided not to go for a number of reasons.* • **Any** number **of** things is a lot of them: *There are any number of kinds of pasta on sale in that shop.* • If people or things are **beyond/without** number, there are too many of them to be counted: *An earthquake in the city could result in deaths beyond number.* • One or more **of** a group's number is a member of that group: *One of our number on the trip fell ill.* • LP› **Approximate numbers, Measurements** Ⓣ

num·ber *(obj)* /£ˈnʌm·bəʳ, $-bɚ/ *v* • If people or things number a particular amount, there are this many of them: *After the hurricane the homeless numbered over 200 000.* [L only + n] • *(fml)* If someone or something is numbered **among** a group, they belong to that group: *At one time the club numbered an archbishop* **among** *its members.* [T always + prep]

num·ber·less /£ˈnʌm·bᵊl·əs, $-bɚ·ləs/ *adj* [not gradable] *esp. literary* • Numberless means too many to be counted: *the numberless stars in the night sky*

num·bers /£ˈnʌm·bəz, $-bɚz/ *pl n* • *Small numbers of* (=A small number of) *children are educated at home.* • *Large numbers* **of** (=A large number of) *invitations have been sent.* • *These magazines are produced* **in** *vast numbers.* • *The crowd managed to force its way in* **by (sheer) force/weight of** *numbers* (=because there were so many of them). • *(saying)* 'There's safety in numbers' means the more people there are in a group, the less likely you are to be harmed.

num·ber PARTICULAR THING /£ˈnʌm·bəʳ, $-bɚ/ *n* [C] a particular example of something • A number of a magazine is a particular copy of it: *Have you got last week's number* **of** *the New Yorker?* ○ *He's got all the* **back** *numbers* **of** *the magazine.* KOR • *(infml)* A number is also a piece of clothing, especially a dress, that you admire: *She was wearing a stylish Dior number.* • *(Am slang)* A number can also be a person with a particular characteristic: *He's quite a sexy number, don't you think?* • In music, a number is a short tune or song: *Sing one of those romantic numbers.* • *(esp. Am slang)* A number can also be something that is often said: *He tried his usual number about how his wife didn't understand him, but she didn't fall for it.* • *(Am slang)* If you **do a number on** someone, you hurt, defeat or embarrass them: *She really did a number on her old boyfriend, making him beg her to come back and then turning him down.* • Ⓣ

numb·skull /ˈnʌm·skʌl/ *n* [C] a NUMSKULL

nu·mer·al /£ˈnjuː·mə·rəl, $ˈnuː-/ *n* [C] a symbol that represents a number

nu·mer·ate /£ˈnjuː·mə·rət, $ˈnuː-/ *adj specialized* able to add, subtract, etc. • *He was 10 and still only just numerate.*

nu·mer·a·cy /£ˈnjuː·mə·rə·si, $ˈnuː-/ *n* [U] • *The Minister claimed that the latest statistics on the* **literacy and** *numeracy* (=ability to do basic mathematics) *of eleven to sixteen-year-olds did not reflect a decline in the standard of education in the country.*

nu·mer·at·or /£ˈnjuː·mə·reɪ·təʳ, $ˈnuː·mə·reɪ·t̬ɚ/ *n* [C] the number above the line in a FRACTION (=a division of a whole number) • *In the fraction ¾, 3 is the numerator.* • Compare DENOMINATOR.

nu·mer·i·cal /£njuːˈmer·ɪ·kl̩, $nuː-/ *adj* [not gradable] involving or expressed in numbers • *a numerical calculation* • *numerical skill/ability* • *All those applying for the job are given a numerical and a verbal reasoning test.* • *We do not yet have any numerical information about casualties.* • *Keep your files in numerical* **order**. • *The UN forces have a numerical superiority over the rebels* (=There are more of the UN forces).

nu·mer·i·cal·ly /£njuːˈmer·ɪ·kli, $nuː-/ *adv* [not gradable] • *numerically superior*

nu·mer·ous /£ˈnjuː·mə·rəs, $ˈnuː-/ *adj* [not gradable] many • *We have discussed these plans on numerous occasions.* • *She is the author of three books and numerous articles.* • *Shops of this type, once rare, are now numerous* (=there are many of them).

nu·mis·matics /£ˌnjuː·mɪzˈmæt·ɪks, $ˌnuː·mɪzˈmæt̬·ɪks/ *n* [U] the study or collecting of coins, bank notes and MEDALS (=small metal discs given as prizes or honours)

num·skull, numb·skull /ˈnʌm·skʌl/ *n* [C] *dated* a very stupid or silly person • *You've spilt my coffee, you numskull!* [as form of address]

nun /nʌn/ *n* [C] a member of a female religious group which lives in a CONVENT • *As a child she went to a convent school run by Catholic nuns.*

nun·nery /£ˈnʌn·ᵊr·i, $ˈ-ɚ-/ *n* [C] *dated or literary* • A nunnery is a CONVENT. • Compare MONASTERY.

nup·tial /ˈnʌp·tʃᵊl/ *adj* [not gradable] *fml or literary* of a marriage or the state of being married • *nuptial rites* • *nuptial vows/promises* • *the nuptial bed*

nup·tials /ˈnʌp·tʃᵊlz/ *pl n fml or humorous* • A person's nuptials are their marriage and marriage celebrations: *Their nuptials will take place in France.*

nurse PERSON /£nɜːs, $nɜːrs/ *n* [C] (the title given to) a person whose job is to care for people who are ill or injured, esp. in a hospital • *A doctor and a nurse will attend the injured.* • *He worked as a nurse in a psychiatric hospital.* • *Nurse Millard will be with you shortly.* • *Nurse, come quickly! Mr Hicks has fallen out of bed!* [as form of address] • A nurse is also a woman employed to take care of a young child or children: *As children they were looked after by various nurses and nannies.*

nurse *obj* /£nɜːs, $nɜːrs/ *v* [T] • If you nurse someone or an animal, you care for them while they are ill: *He gave up his job so that he could nurse his mother at home in her last months.* ○ *They found an injured cat and carefully nursed it* **back to health** (=cared for it until it was well again). • If you nurse something such as a plant, you spend a lot of time taking care of it: *These young trees were carefully nursed by the head gardener.* ○ *The project will have to be nursed through its first few months.* • If you nurse an illness or injury, you rest until it gets better: *Robert's in bed nursing a back injury.* • To nurse a child is to hold it lovingly in your arms as a way of comforting it: *He nursed the crying child on his lap.* • If you nurse a desire or an emotion, you feel it for a long time: *She has long nursed a passion for Japanese art.* • To nurse a drink is to hold it for a long time without drinking it: *Mark was sitting in the corner of the pub nursing an almost empty pint glass.*

nurs·ing /£'nɜː·sɪŋ, $'nɜːr-/ *n* [U] • Nursing is the job of being a nurse: *She studied nursing at Garfield Hospital.* • **Nursing aid** is *Aus for* **auxiliary nurse**. See at AUXILIARY. • A **nursing home** is a private hospital where ill and very old people can stay and be cared for.

nurse *obj* [FEED] /£nɜːs, $nɜːrs/ *v* [T] (of a woman) to feed (a baby) with milk from your own breast

nurs·ing /£'nɜː·sɪŋ, $'nɜːr-/ *adj* [before n; not gradable] • A nursing **mother** is a woman who is feeding her baby with her own breast milk: *Pregnant and nursing mothers are advised to eat plenty of leafy green vegetables.*

nurse·maid /£'nɜːs·meɪd, $'nɜːrs-/ *n* [C] a woman who takes care of someone else's young children • *I'm not going to be a nursemaid to you – make your own bed!*

nur·ser·y [FOR CHILDREN] /£'nɜː·sᵊr·i, $'nɜːr·sɚ-/ *n* [C] a place where young children and babies are taken care of while their parents are at work, or a room in a house where small children sleep and play • *Their two children have been going to a nursery since they were small babies.* • *We're turning one bedroom into a nursery and painting it in bright colours.* • Nursery **education** is the teaching of children who are between the ages of two or three to five years old. • *(Br)* A **nursery nurse** is a person who has been trained to take care of young children. • A **nursery school** (*Am and Aus also* **preschool**) is a school for children between the ages of two and five. • A **nursery rhyme** is a short poem or song for young children: *Most nursery rhymes are very old and known by most of the people in the particular country in which they are found.* • *(Br)* **Nursery slopes** (*Am and Aus* **beginners' slopes**) are gentle slopes on a mountain used by people learning to SKI. • [LP] **Schools and colleges**

nur·ser·y [FOR PLANTS] /£'nɜː·sᵊr·i, $'nɜːr·sɚ-/ *n* [C] a place where plants and trees are grown • *Your local nursery or garden centre should be able to provide you with a good range of hardy geraniums.*

nur·ture *obj* /£'nɜː·tʃəʳ, $'nɜːr·tʃɚ/ *v* [T] *fml* to take care of, feed and protect (esp. a young child or plant) and help it to develop • *She wants to stay at home and nurture her children, not go out to work.* • *I visited their carefully nurtured gardens of bananas, mangoes and papayas.* • If you nurture a plan or a person, you help it or them to develop and be successful: *As a record company director, his job is to nurture young* **talent**. ○ *The group wants to nurture democracy in former Communist countries.* • If you nurture an emotion, you feel it for a long time: *Winifred nurtured ambitions for her daughter to be a surgeon.*

nur·ture /£'nɜː·tʃəʳ, $'nɜːr·tʃɚ/ *n* [U] • Nurture is the way in which children are treated as they are growing, esp. as compared with the characteristics they are born with: *Do you believe that* **nature or** *nurture has the strongest influence on how children develop?*

nut [FOOD] /nʌt/ *n* [C] the dry fruit of particular trees which grows in a very hard shell. Many types of nut can be eaten. • *I bought a bag of mixed nuts: Brazil nuts, almonds, hazelnuts and cashews.* • *She sprinkled some roasted chopped nuts on top of the ice cream.* • A person who is a **tough**/*(Br also)* **hard** nut is one who is very unpleasant and difficult to deal with: *As a teenager, Jack was a real hard nut, always getting into fights.* • If you describe a problem or a person as **a hard/tough nut to crack**, you mean the problem is very difficult to solve or the person is very difficult to understand. • [PIC] **Nut**

nut·ty /£'nʌt·i, $'nʌt̬-/ *adj* **-ier, -iest** • *This wine has a pleasant nutty taste.*

nut·ti·ness /£'nʌt·ɪ·nəs, $'nʌt̬-/ *n* [U]

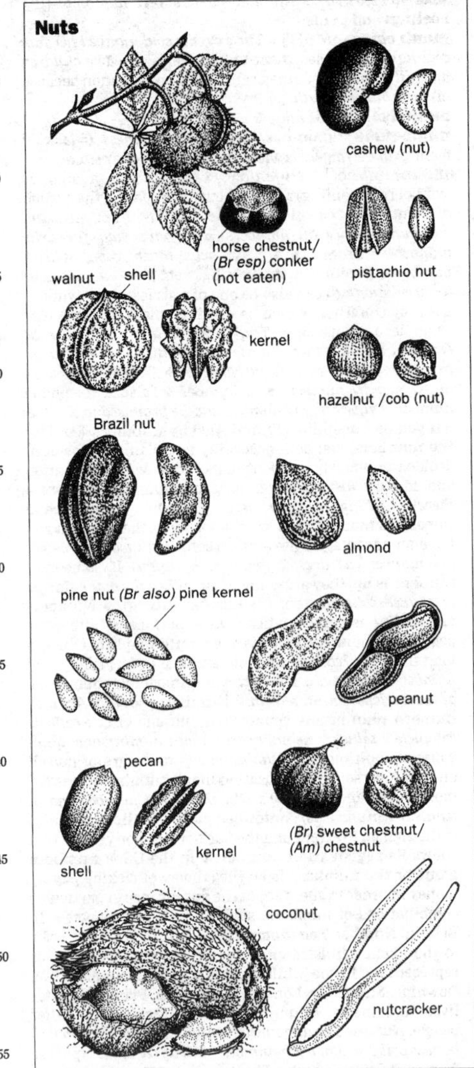

nut [METAL OBJECT] /nʌt/ *n* [C] a small piece of metal with a hole in it that a BOLT (=a screw-like object) can be screwed into • *Nuts and bolts are used to hold pieces of machinery together.* • The **nuts and bolts** of something are the practical facts of that thing rather than theoretical ideas about it: *When it came to the nuts and bolts of running a business, he was clearly unable to cope.* • [PIC] **Bolt, Tools**

nut [PERSON] /nʌt/ *n* [C] *infml* a person who is mentally ill or who behaves in a very foolish or stupid or strange way • *What kind of nut would leave a car on a railway track?* • A nut is also a person who is extremely enthusiastic about a particular activity or thing: *Ian's a tennis nut – he plays every day.*

nuts /nʌts/ *adj* [after v] *infml* • A person who is nuts behaves in a foolish or stupid or strange way: *You must be nuts* **to** *go climbing mountains in winter.* [+ *to* infinitive] • If you **go** nuts, you become extremely angry: *My sister will go nuts when she finds out I've wrecked her car.* • If you are nuts **about/over** a thing, activity or person, you are very enthusiastic about them: *Sophie's nuts about dinosaurs.* ○ *I'm nuts over Kevin Costner.*

nut·ty /£'nʌt·i, $'nʌt̬-/ *adj* **-ier, -iest** *infml* • *She's got some nutty* (=foolish or strange) *idea about setting up a school for cats.* • *He's really nutty* (=enthusiastic) **about** *that girl – it must be love.* • *That guy is* **(as) nutty as a fruitcake** (=behaves in a very foolish or stupid or strange way, or is mentally ill).

nut·ter /£'nʌt·əʳ, $'nʌţ·ɚ/ *n* [C] *Br and Aus infml* • A nutter is a person who behaves in a very foolish or stupid or strange way: *Only a* **complete** *nutter would go out in this storm.*

nut HEAD /nʌt/ *n* [C] *infml* a person's head • *a bang on the nut* • *Come on,* **use** *your nut* (= think clearly)*! You do it like this.* • *(Br and Aus)* If you **do** your **nut**, you become extremely angry: *My Mum'll do her nut when she finds out I failed all my exams.* • Someone who is **off** their **nut** is behaving in a foolish or stupid way: *You can't do that! Are you off your nut?*

nut MONEY /nʌt/ *n* [U] *Am infml* the amount of money necessary to operate a business or pay for expenses • *With two houses, three cars and child-support payments, he just couldn't meet his nut, even with a second job.*

nut·case /'nʌt·keɪs/ *n* [C] *infml disapproving* someone who is mentally ill or who behaves in an extremely silly way • *That Johnny's a real nutcase – he ought to be locked up.*

nut·crack·er /£'nʌtˌkræk·əʳ, $-ɚ/ *n* [C] a tool for breaking the shell of a nut, so that you can remove and eat the softer part inside • PIC **Nut**

nut·crack·ers /£'nʌtˌkræk·əz, $-ɚz/ *pl n Br* • *Use* **(a pair of)** *nutcrackers* (= a nutcracker) *to open the walnuts.*

nut·house /'nʌt·haʊs/ *n* [C] *pl* **nuthouses** /'nʌtˌhaʊ·zɪz/ *slang* a **psychiatric hospital**, see at PSYCHIATRY

nut·meg /'nʌt·meg/ *n* the hard fruit of a tropical tree, or a brown powder made from this and used as a spice to give a special taste to food • **Grate** *some nutmeg on top of the pudding.* [U] • *There were five nutmegs left in the jar.* [C] • PIC **Herbs and spices**

Nu·tra·Sweet /£'njuː·trə·swiːt, $'nuː-/ *n* [U] *trademark* ASPARTAME

nu·tri·ent /£'njuː·tri·ᵊnt, $'nuː-/ *n* [C] *specialized* any substance which plants or animals need in order to live and grow • *It's good soil – full of nutrients.* • *The plants are showing signs of nutrient deficiency.*

nu·tri·tion /£njuː'trɪʃ·ᵊn, $nuː-/ *n* [U] *specialized* the process of taking in and using food, or the scientific study of this • *Good nutrition* (= Eating healthy food) *is essential if patients are to make a quick recovery.* • *Improvements in nutrition have been mostly to do with persuading people to eat less fatty food and more raw vegetables.* • *She's a professor of nutrition at Columbia University.*

nu·tri·tion·al /£njuː'trɪʃ·ᵊn·ᵊl, $nuː-/, **nu·tri·tive** /£'njuː·trə·tɪv, $'nuː·trə·ţɪv/ *adj specialized* • *Chemical sweeteners, like preservatives and colourings, have no nutritional* **value**.

nu·tri·tious /£njuː'trɪʃ·əs, $nuː-/ *adj* • *a nutritious diet* • *Raw spinach is especially nutritious* (= contains many of the substances needed for life and growth).

nu·tri·tion·ist /£njuː'trɪʃ·ᵊn·ɪst, $nuː-/ *n* [C] *specialized* • *The doctor advised him to see a nutritionist about his diet.*

nuts BODY PART /nʌts/ *pl n esp. Am slightly taboo slang for* TESTICLES

nuts FOOLISH /nʌts/ *adj* See at NUT PERSON

nut·shell /'nʌt·ʃel/ *n* [U] **(to put** *something***) in a nutshell** (to say something) using as few words as possible • *Well, to put it in a nutshell, we're going to have to start again.* • *"Is he coming with us?" "In a nutshell, no."*

nut·ti·ness /£'nʌt·ɪ·nəs, $'nʌţ-/ *n* [U] See at NUT FOOD

nut·ty /£'nʌt·i, $'nʌţ·i/ *adj* **-ier, -iest** See at NUT FOOD and NUT PERSON

nuz·zle *(obj)* /'nʌz·l̩/ *v* to touch, rub or press gently and/or affectionately, esp. with the head or nose, usually with small repeated movements • *When I'm feeling depressed my dog comes and nuzzles my foot to try and cheer me up.* [T] • *The kittens like to nuzzle* **up against/up to** *their mother.* [I always + adv/prep] • *When six o'clock came, she nuzzled closer* (= pressed herself more closely against the other person) *and said "Don't go just yet."* [I always + adv/prep]

NVQ /ˌen·viː'kjuː/ *n* [C] *abbreviation for* National Vocational Qualification (= a British standard achieved in different subjects related to the work you do)

NW *n* [U], *adj* [not gradable] *abbreviation for* NORTHWEST or NORTHWESTERN

NY /ˌen'waɪ/, **NYC** /ˌen·waɪ'siː/ *n* [U not after *the*] *abbreviation for* New York (City)

ny·lon /£'naɪ·lɒn, $-lɑːn/ *n* [U] an artificial substance used esp. to make clothes, ropes and brushes • *The shirts are 100% nylon.* • *Nylon ropes are extremely strong.*

ny·lons /£'naɪ·lɒnz, $-lɑːnz/ *pl n dated* • Nylons are women's nylon STOCKINGS or TIGHTS: *The American soldiers used to give presents of nylons, cigarettes and chocolate.*

nymph /nɪmpf/ *n* [C] (in ancient traditional stories, esp. of the Greeks and Romans) a goddess or spirit in the form of a young woman, living in a tree, river, mountain, etc.

nym·phet /£nɪmp'fet, $'nɪmp·fət/ *n* [C] *infml* a girl about 10 to 14 years old considered to be sexually attractive

nym·pho·ma·ni·ac /£ˌnɪmp·fəʊ'meɪ·ni·æk, $-foʊ-/, *infml*

nym·pho /£'nɪmp·fəʊ, $-foʊ/ *n* [C] *disapproving* a woman who likes to have sex very often, esp. with lots of different men • *Do you know that Mandy's slept with half the rugby club – she's a complete nymphomaniac!*

nym·pho·ma·ni·a /£ˌnɪmp·fəʊ'meɪ·ni·ə, $-foʊ-/ *n* [U] • *The lawyer tried to argue that nymphomania is a medical condition.*

NZ *n* [U not after *the*] *abbreviation for* New Zealand

O o

O LETTER *(pl* **O's** or **Os**), **o** *(pl* **o's** or **os**) /£əʊ, $oʊ/ *n* [C] the 15th letter of the English alphabet • O is used in speech to mean zero, and is sometimes written as 'oh': *My phone number is three, one, o, five, one, double o* (= 3105100). ○ *The date 1705 can be pronounced seventeen o five.* • An **O level** is a public examination in a particular subject that was taken in the past in British schools by children aged 15 or 16, or the qualification obtained: *I failed my History O level.* [C] ○ *She's got 10 O levels.* [C] ○ *O levels were replaced by GCSEs in 1988.* [C] ○ Compare **A level** at A. • LP **Zero**

O EMOTION /£əʊ, $oʊ/ *exclamation old use or poetic* used when addressing someone or something, or when expressing strong emotion • *O Zeus! Hear my prayer.* • Compare OH.

o' /ə/ *prep* used in writing to represent *of* when its *f* is not pronounced • *a bottle o' beer* • *a bag o' chips* • O' is also part of many last names: *Jeanne O'Connor* ○ *John O'Groats is often considered to be the most northerly point of Britain.*

oaf /£əʊf, $oʊf/ *n* [C] *infml disapproving* a stupid, rude or awkward person, esp. a man • *She was in the restaurant with her husband – an oaf who spent all his time talking into a portable phone.* • *You clumsy oaf! You've broken it!* [as form of address]

oaf·ish /£'əʊ·fɪʃ, $'oʊ-/ *adj infml disapproving* • *oafish behaviour* • *an oafish young man*

oaf·ish·ness /£'əʊ·fɪʃ·nəs, $'oʊ-/ *n* [U] *infml disapproving*

oak /£əʊk, $oʊk/ *n* a large tree common esp. in northern countries, or the hard wood of this tree • *a mighty oak* [C] • *an oak table/cupboard* • *oak panelling* • *King Charles II hid from his enemies in an oak (tree).* [C] • *The timbers of those old sailing ships were mainly oak.* [U] • *(saying)* 'Tall/Great oaks from little acorns grow' means that plans or organizations which start off very simple or small can sometimes develop into something which is extremely powerful and successful. • PIC **Tree**

oak·y /£'əʊ·ki, $'oʊ-/ *adj* **-ier, -iest** • An oaky wine is one which has a slightly woody flavour, esp. because it has been left to develop in a container made of oak: *Kate said she and Adrian had a deliciously oaky red wine with their dinner.*

OAP /£ˌəʊ·eɪ'piː, $ˌoʊ-/ *n* [C] *Br abbreviation for* **old age pensioner**, see at OLD EXISTED MANY YEARS • *OAPs get cheaper bus and train tickets.* • LP **Age**

oar /£ɔːʳ, $ɔːr/ *n* [C] a long pole with a wide flat part at one end which is used for ROWING a boat. The flat part is pushed against the water so that the boat moves along. • *a pair of oars* • *She dipped her oars into the water and pulled.* • *(infml disapproving)* To **put/stick** your **oar in** is to say or do something which annoys other people because they have not asked you to join their conversation or activity: *No-one asked him to help – he's always sticking his oar in.* • Compare PADDLE POLE. • PIC **Water sports**

oars·man *(pl* **-men**), **oars·wo·man** *(pl* **-women**) /£'ɔːz·mən, $'ɔːrz-, -ˌwʊm·ən/ *n* [C] • An oarsman or oarswoman is a person who ROWS a boat, esp. in competitions.

oar·lock /£'ɔː·lɒk, $'ɔːr·lɑːk/ *n* [C] *Am for* ROWLOCK

o·a·sis /£əʊ'eɪ·sɪs, $oʊ-/ *n* [C] *pl* **oases** /£əʊ'eɪ·siːz, $oʊ-/ a place in a desert where there is water and therefore plants and trees and sometimes a village or town • *(fig.) The city is an oasis* (= a place much better than its surroundings) **of** *peace and sanity amid the chaos of the rest of the country.*

oat·cake /£'əʊt·keɪk, $'oʊt-/ *n* [C] a thin savoury biscuit made from OATS, esp. common in Scotland

oath PROMISE /£əʊθ, $oʊθ/ *n* [C] a promise, esp. that you will tell the truth in a law court • *In the Middle Ages, knights* **took** *an oath* **of** *allegiance/loyalty to their lord.* • *The witness placed her hand on the Bible and* **took the** *oath* (= promised to tell the truth). • *Witnesses are, of course,* **under**/*(Br also)* **on** *oath* (= have promised) *to tell the truth.*

oath SWEAR WORD /£əʊθ, $oʊθ/ *n* [C] *dated* a swear word, esp. one which uses a name for God

oat·meal /£'əʊt·miːl, $'oʊt-/ *n* [U] a type of flour made from OATS • *oatmeal porridge* • Oatmeal is also *Am for* PORRIDGE.

oats /£əʊts, $oʊts/ *pl n* a grass-like plant, the seeds of which are used to make flour or are fed to animals • *a field of oats* • *Oats are a good source of carbohydrate.* • *The biscuits contain oats.* • PIC **Cereals**

OB /£ˌəʊ'biː, $ˌoʊ-/ *n* [C] *Am infml for* **obstetrician**, see at OBSTETRICS

ob·du·rate /£'ɒb·djʊ·rət, $'ɑːb·dʊr·ɪt/ *adj fml disapproving* extremely determined to act in a particular way and not to change at all, despite argument or persuasion; STUBBORN • *The President remains obdurate* **on** *the question of cutting taxes.* • *(fig.) Several obdurate* (= very difficult to deal with) *facts/differences remain, preventing a compromise solution.*

o·be·di·ent /£əʊ'biː·di·ənt, $oʊ-/ *adj* doing or willing to do what you have been asked or ordered to do by someone in authority • *Students are expected to be quiet and obedient in the classroom.* • *The army is quite unlikely to be obedient* **to** *the new president.* • See also OBEY.

o·be·di·ent·ly /£əʊ'biː·di·ənt·li, $oʊ-/ *adv* • *I pulled on the reins and the horse obediently slowed down.*

o·be·di·ence /£əʊ'biː·di·ənts, $oʊ-/ *n* [U] • *They demand unquestioning obedience from every follower.* • *Obedience* **to** *a strict moral code is central to such societies.*

o·bei·sance /£əʊ'beɪ·sᵊnts, $oʊ-/ *n fml* obedience and respect, or something you do which expresses this • *He attacks the newspapers for their uncritical obeisance* **to** *the rich and the powerful.* [U] • *The noblemen came forward one by one and* **made** *their obeisances* (= bent at the waist) **to** *the Queen.* [C]

ob·e·lisk /£'ɒb·ᵊl·ɪsk, $'ɑː·bᵊl-/ *n* [C] a tall stone column, usually with four decorated, sloping sides and a pointed top, made in honour of an important person or event

o·bese /£əʊ'biːs, $oʊ-/ *adj* extremely and unhealthily fat • *Obese people are more at risk from diabetes and heart disease.*

o·bes·i·ty /£əʊ'biː·sɪ·ti, $oʊ'biː·sə·t̬i/ *n* [U] • *A diet that is high in fat can lead to obesity.*

o·bey *(obj)* /£əʊ'beɪ, $oʊ-/ *v* to act according to (what you have been asked or ordered to do by someone in authority), or to act according to (what you are expected to do in relation to a rule, law, etc.) • *The soldiers refused to obey* **(orders)**. [I/T] • *They are countries which don't obey the* **rules** *of international law.* [T] • *Falling objects obey the* **law** *of gravity.* [T] • *(fig.) After 19 miles she dropped out of the race because her legs just wouldn't obey her any longer* (= she could no longer run). [T] • See also OBEDIENT.

ob·fus·cate *obj* /£'ɒb·fʌs·keɪt, $'ɑːb·fə·skeɪt/ *v* [T] *fml* to make (something) less clear and harder to understand, esp. intentionally • *Then she was criticized for using arguments that obfuscated the main issue.*

ob·fus·ca·tion /£ˌɒb·fʌs'keɪ·ʃᵊn, $ˌɑːb·fə'skeɪ-/ *n* [U] *fml* • *In writing popular science books, technical obfuscation is to be avoided at all costs.*

OB–GYN /£ˌɒb'gaɪn, $ˌɑːb-/ *n* [C] *Am infml abbreviation for* obstetrician gynecologist (= a medical specialist who deals with pregnancy, the birth of children and women's diseases)

o·bit·u·a·ry /£əʊ'bɪtʃ·ʊə·ri, $oʊ'bɪtʃ·u·er·i/, *infml* **o·bit** /£'ɒb·ɪt, £'əʊ·bɪt, $'oʊ-/ *n* [C] a report, esp. in a newspaper, which gives the news of someone's death and details about their life

ob·ject THING /£'ɒb·dʒɪkt, $'ɑːb-/ *n* [C] an esp. solid thing that can be seen or felt, but that is not usually a living animal, plant or person • *a material/physical object* • *a glass/ metal object* • *The bag was full of precious objects of different kinds.* • *Look, there's a strange object in the sky!* • *The boss saw his employees as objects, never as human beings.* • *(specialized)* In computing, if something is **object-oriented**, it is based on groups of information and their effects on each other, rather than on a series of instructions: *C++ is a common object-oriented* **programming** *language.* • See also UFO.

ob·jec·ti·fi·ca·tion /£ɒbˌdʒek·tɪ·fɪ'keɪ·ʃᵊn, $ɑːbˌdʒek·t̬ɪ-/ *n* [U] *specialized* • Objectification is treating people like tools or toys, as if they had no feelings, opinions or rights of their own: *Pornography is often cited as an example of the objectification of women by men.*

ob·ject PURPOSE /£'ɒb·dʒɪkt, $'ɑːb-/ *n* [C usually sing] a purpose, desired result, or reason for doing something • **The** *object* **of** *their expedition was to discover the source of the River Nile.* • *In the session that follows, the* **the object of the exercise** (= the desired result of what is being done) *is that you should all improve your interpersonal skills.* • See also OBJECTIVE AIM.

ob·ject CAUSE /£'ɒb·dʒɪkt, $'ɑːb-/ *n* [C usually sing] *slightly fml* someone or something which causes particular feelings or actions to be directed towards them • *He became an object* **of** *ridicule among the other workers.* • If you say that something, such as money, is **no object** you mean that it should not be considered as a problem, because you have a lot of it: *For a millionaire like him, money is no object.* • *(approving)* An **object lesson** is an action or story from which you can learn how or how not to act, or which clearly shows the facts of an esp. bad situation: *The disaster was an object lesson* **in** *how not to run a ship.*

ob·ject GRAMMAR, *abbreviation* **obj** /£'ɒb·dʒɪkt, $'ɑːb-/ *n* [C] *specialized* a noun, pronoun or noun phrase that represents the person or thing that the action of a verb is done to, or that is involved in the result of an action • *In the sentence 'I like ice cream', 'ice cream' is the object of the verb 'like'.* • An object is also a word that follows a preposition. • Compare SUBJECT GRAMMAR. • LP **Two objects, Verbs**

ob·ject OPPOSE /əb'dʒekt/ *v* to feel or express opposition to or dislike of something or someone • *Would anyone object if we started the meeting now?* [I] • *They want to demolish his house, and naturally he objects!* [I] • *He objects* **to** *the label 'magician' which people often give him.* [I] • *No-one objected when the boss said it was time to go home.* • *Our offer was £3 million, but they objected* **that** (= opposed it because) *they had paid £4 million for the property in the first place.* [+ *that* clause]

ob·jec·tion /əb'dʒek·ʃᵊn/ *n* [C] • *Her objection* **to/against** *the plan is based on incorrect facts.* • *A couple of people* **raised/voiced** *objections.* • *The only objection (we* **have**) *is* **that** *it may cost us more than you think.* [+ *that* clause]

ob·jec·tion·a·ble /əb'dʒek·ʃᵊn·ə·bl̩/ *adj fml* • If you describe someone or something as objectionable, you dislike or oppose them because they seem very unpleasant or wrong to you: *an objectionable smell* ○ *Didn't you* **find** *the violence in that film really objectionable?*

ob·jec·tor /£əb'dʒek·təʳ, $-t̬ɚ/ *n* [C] • *200 objectors were present at the inquiry into the M77 motorway.*

ob·jec·tive AIM /£əb'dʒek·tɪv, $-t̬ɪv/ *n* [C] something which you plan to do or achieve • *Her* **main/prime** *objective now is simply to stay in power.* • *Is the European sales force* **achieving/attaining/meeting** *its financial objectives?* • *The military objectives are simple – to capture and hold the city.* • See also OBJECT PURPOSE.

ob·jec·tive FAIR OR REAL /£əb'dʒek·tɪv, $-t̬ɪv/ *adj* not influenced by personal beliefs or feelings; based on real facts • *How can you make an objective assessment of her if she's your own daughter?* • *It's an admirably objective and impartial report.* • *Science is usually concerned only with objective* **facts** *that can be proved or disproved.* • Compare SUBJECTIVE.

ob·jec·tive·ly /£əb'dʒek·tɪv·li, $-t̬ɪv-/ *adv* • *Judges are supposed to weigh the evidence in each case logically and objectively.* • *Are the laws of physics objectively true?*

ob·jec·tiv·i·ty /£ˌɒb·dʒek'tɪv·ɪ·ti, $ˌɑːb·dʒek'tɪv·ə·t̬i/ *n* [U] • *Perhaps objectivity in a critic is impossible because every work of art will strike different critics in different ways.*

ob·jet d'art /£ˌɒb·ʒeɪ'dɑːʳ, $ˌɑːb·ʒeɪ'dɑːr/ *n* [C] *pl* **objets d'art** /£ˌɒb·ʒeɪ'dɑːʳ, $ˌɑːb·ʒeɪ'dɑːr/ an esp. small object considered to have some worth or value as art

o·blige *obj* FORCE /ə'blaɪdʒ/, *esp. Am or fml* **ob·li·gate** /£'ɒb·lɪ·geɪt, $'ɑː·blɪ-/ *v* [T + obj + *to* infinitive] to force (someone) to do something, or to make it necessary for (someone) to do something; to COMPEL • *The law obliges companies* **to** *pay decent wages to their employees.*

ob·li·ga·tion /£ˌɒb·lɪ'geɪ·ʃᵊn, $ˌɑː·blə-/ *n* • *If you have not signed a contract, you are* **under** *no obligation* **to** (= it is not necessary to) *pay them any money.* [U + *to* infinitive] • *You have a* **legal** *obligation* **to** (= The law says you must) *ensure your child receives a proper education.* [C + *to* infinitive] • *I haven't got time to do his work for him – I've got too many obligations* (= things I must do) *as it is.* [C] • (DK) (RUS) (S)

ob·lig·a·to·ry /£ə'blɪg·ə·tᵊr·i, $-tɔːr-/ *adj* [not gradable] • *The medical examination before you start work is obligatory.* • **It** *is obligatory* **to** (= You must) *go through a password routine before you can get into the computer database.* [+ *to* infinitive] • Obligatory can also mean expected because it usually happens: *Then the secret service agents turned up – all in the obligatory raincoat and hat.*

ob·liged /ə'blaɪdʒd/, *esp. Am or fml* **ob·li·gat·ed** *adj* [after v; + *to* infinitive] • *Doctors are, after all, legally obliged/obligated* **to** *take certain precautions.* • *She feels obliged* **to** *be nice to Jack because he's her boss.*

o·blige *(obj)* [HELP] /ə'blaɪdʒ/ *v* to please or help (someone), esp. by doing something they have asked you to do • *We only really went to the party to oblige some old friends – they had asked us to be there.* [T] • *We needed a guide and he was only too* **happy to** *oblige.* [I] • *(slightly fml)* **I'd be obliged if** *you would* (= Please) *complete and return the form as soon as possible.* • *(fml) Could you oblige me* **with** (= give me) *a pen and a piece of paper, please?* [T] • *(dated) "Here's the information." "Oh,* **much obliged** *(***to you***)* (= thank you)*."*

o·blig·ing /ə'blaɪ·dʒɪŋ/ *adj approving* • Someone who is obliging is willing or eager to help: *He found an obliging doctor who gave him the drugs he needed.*

o·blig·ing·ly /ə'blaɪ·dʒɪŋ·li/ *adv*

o·blique [INDIRECT] /£əʊ'bliːk, $oʊ-/ *adj* **-r, -st** (esp. of a person's remarks) indirect, so that the real meaning is not immediately clear • *In her speech she made several oblique* **references** *to the current financial situation.* • *He gave her an oblique* **glance** *which she interpreted as a warning.*

o·blique·ly /£əʊ'bliː·kli, $oʊ-/ *adv*

o·blique [DIAGONAL] /£əʊ'bliːk, $oʊ-/ *adj* **-r, -st** having a sloping direction, angle or position • *In through the window came the last few oblique rays of evening sunshine.* • *(specialized)* An oblique angle is one that has either more or less than 90°: *Any angle which is not at right angles is oblique.*

o·blique·ly /£əʊ'bliː·kli, $oʊ-/ *adv*

o·blique (stroke) /£əʊ'bliːk, $oʊ-/ *n* [C] *Br and Aus* • An oblique (also **slash** or *specialized* **solidus**) is a sloping line often used for separating numbers or words: *Fractions can be written with oblique strokes, for example 2/3.* • *Every student must hand in her/his* (= her or his) *completed application form by the end of the week.* • [LP]› **Slash**

o·blit·e·rate *obj* /£ə'blɪt·ᵊr·eɪt, $-'blɪt̬·ə·reɪt/ *v* [T] to remove all sign of (something) either by destroying it or by covering it so that it cannot be seen • *The missile strike was devastating – the target was totally obliterated.* • *Centuries of wind and rain had obliterated the words carved on the gravestones.* • *All of a sudden the view was obliterated by the fog.* • *(fig.) Perhaps she gets drunk to obliterate* (= forget) *painful memories.*

o·blit·e·ra·tion /£əˌblɪt·ᵊr'eɪ·ʃᵊn, $-ˌblɪt̬·ə'reɪ-/ *n* [U]

o·bliv·ion [UNCONSCIOUSNESS] /ə'blɪv·i·ən/ *n* [U] the state of being unconscious • *He sought oblivion in a bottle of whisky.*

o·bliv·ion [NO MEMORY] /ə'blɪv·i·ən/ *n* [U] the state of being completely forgotten • *He was another minor poet, perhaps unfairly* **consigned to** *oblivion.* • *She made one startlingly good last recording and then* **fell/sank into** *oblivion.* • *(fig.) The planes bombed the city* **into** *oblivion* (= completely destroyed it).

o·bliv·i·ous /ə'blɪv·i·əs/ *adj* not aware of something, esp. what is happening around you • *Absorbed in her work, she was totally oblivious* **of/to** *her surroundings.* • *The government seems oblivious* **of/to** *the likely effects of the new legislation.* • *The camera moved over the faces of the oblivious workers.*

o·bliv·i·ous·ly /ə'blɪv·i·ə·sli/ *adv*

o·bliv·i·ous·ness /ə'blɪv·i·ə·snəs/ *n* [U] • *It's her total obliviousness* **to** *what's going on around her that amazes me.*

ob·long /£'ɒb·lɒŋ, $'ɑː·blɑːŋ/ *n* [C] an object or shape that is longer than it is wide, esp. a four-sided flat shape with four angles of 90° and opposite sides of equal length; a rectangle • [PIC]› **Shapes**

ob·long /£'ɒb·lɒŋ, $'ɑː·blɑːŋ/ *adj* [not gradable] • *an oblong box*

ob·nox·ious /£əb'nɒk·ʃəs, $-'nɑːk-/ *adj disapproving* (esp. of a person or their behaviour) unpleasant and rude • *Some of his colleagues will say that he's loud and obnoxious and that everyone hates him.* • *Newspaper editors don't print the really obnoxious letters that they receive.* • *When she's in a bad mood she's obnoxious* **to** *everyone.*

ob·nox·ious·ly /£əb'nɒk·ʃə·sli, $-'nɑːk-/ *adv disapproving* • *an obnoxiously unpleasant police officer* • *(humorous) Why are you so obnoxiously cheerful today?*

ob·nox·ious·ness /£əb'nɒk·ʃə·snəs, $-'nɑːk-/ *n* [U] *disapproving*

o·boe /£'əʊ·bəʊ, $'oʊ·boʊ/ *n* [C] a tube-shaped musical instrument of the WOODWIND group with two REEDS at the top through which you blow, and holes and keys which allow you to play different notes • [PIC]› **Musical instruments**

o·bo·ist /£'əʊ·bəʊ·ɪst, $'oʊ·boʊ-/ *n* [C] • An oboist is a person who plays the oboe.

ob·scene /əb'siːn/ *adj* offensive, rude or shocking, usually because too obviously related to or showing sex • *In the raid police found several boxes of obscene videotapes.* • *He was jailed for making obscene* **phone calls** (= ones in which unwanted sexual suggestions were made to the listener). • *The play was banned because of the obscene* **language** *it contained.* • *Someone had sprayed obscene graffiti on the wall outside school.* • *In a country where the average wage is less than $50 a month* **it's** *obscene* **that** *the President should earn $500 000 a year.* [+ *that* clause]

ob·scene·ly /əb'siːn·li/ *adv* • *Talking obscenely like that will make him very unpopular.* • *That guy was just obscenely fat.*

ob·scen·i·ty /£əb'sen·ɪ·ti, $-ə·t̬i/ *n* • *obscenity laws* • *The people who made that film could be prosecuted for obscenity.* [U] • *He was taken away by the police, shouting and screaming obscenities* (= offensive words and sentences). [C] • *Such deliberate destruction of the environment is an obscenity* (= an offensive and shocking situation or event). [C]

ob·scure [UNKNOWN] /£əb'skjʊəʳ, $-'skjʊr/ *adj* **-r, -st** not known to many people • *an obscure provincial town* ○ *an obscure island in the Pacific* ○ *an obscure 12th-century mystic* • (CS) (D)

ob·scur·i·ty /£əb'skjʊə·rɪ·ti, $-'skjʊr·ə·t̬i/ *n* [U] • *He was briefly famous in his twenties but then* **sank into** *obscurity.*

ob·scure [UNCLEAR] /£əb'skjʊəʳ, $-'skjʊr/ *adj* **-r, -st** unclear and difficult to understand or see • *Official policy has changed, for reasons that remain obscure.* • *They talk in an obscure jargon that's almost impossible to understand.* • (CS) (D)

ob·scure *obj* /£əb'skjʊəʳ, $-'skjʊr/ *v* [T] • *Two new skyscrapers had sprung up, obscuring* (= hiding) *the view from her window.* • *Managers deliberately obscured the real situation* **from** *federal investigators* (= made it difficult for them to discover and understand it).

ob·scur·i·ty /£əb'skjʊə·rɪ·ti, $-'skjʊr·ə·t̬i/ *n* [U] • *The obscurity of the language means that few people are able to understand the new legislation.*

ob·se·qui·ous /əb'siː·kwi·əs/ *adj fml disapproving* too eager to praise or obey someone • *She is almost embarrassingly obsequious to anyone in authority.* • (P)

ob·serve *obj* [WATCH] /£əb'zɜːv, $-'zɜːrv/ *v* to watch carefully (the way something happens or someone does something), esp. in order to learn more about it • *The role of scientists is to observe and describe the world, not to try to control it.* [T] • *Now, observe the way the motor causes the little wheels to move up and down.* [T] • *He spent a year in the jungle, observing* **how** *deforestation is affecting local tribes.* [+ *wh-* word]

ob·ser·va·tion /£ˌɒb·zə'veɪ·ʃᵊn, $ˌɑːb·zɚ-/ *n* [U] • *Observation* **of** *the bear's habitat has revealed a lot about its activities.* • *She was admitted to hospital* **for** *observation* (= so that doctors could watch her and see if anything was wrong with her) *after complaining of chest pains.* • *The police have him* **under** *observation* (= He is being watched and followed by the police). • An **observation post** is a place or building from which you can watch someone, esp. an enemy.

ob·ser·va·to·ry /£əbˈzɜː·və·tri, $-ˈzɜːr·və·tɔːr·i/ *n* [C] • An observatory is a building from which scientists can watch the planets, the stars, the weather, etc.

ob·serv·er /£əbˈzɜː·vəʳ, $-ˈzɜːr·vɚ/ *n* [C] • An observer is a person who watches what happens but has no active part in it: *Observers of the political situation/Political observers say it's going to be a closely fought election.* ○ *The conference was attended by 200 delegates and also by observers from another 30 countries.* ○ *UN observers are monitoring the ceasefire.*

ob·serve *obj* NOTICE /£əbˈzɜːv, $-ˈzɜːrv/ *v fml* to notice or see • *Jack observed a look of anxiety on his brother's face.* [T] • *The guards failed to observe* **who** *delivered the package.* [+ *wh-* word] • *In all these films one observes* **that** *directors are taking a new interest in Native American culture.* [+ *that* clause] • *A teacher observed her climb***ing** *over the gate.* [+ obj + v-*ing*] • *A teacher observed her climb over the gate.* [+ obj + infinitive without *to*]

ob·serv·a·ble /£əbˈzɜː·və·bl̩, $-ˈzɜːr-/ *adj* [not gradable] • *There's no observable connection between the two events.*

ob·serv·a·bly /£əbˈzɜː·və·bli, $-ˈzɜːr-/ *adv* [not gradable] • *The river is observably dirtier than it was last year.*

ob·ser·vant /£əbˈzɜː·vᵊnt, $-ˈzɜːr-/ *adj approving* • *"Isn't that a new dress?" "Aren't you observant* (= good at noticing things)*?"*

ob·ser·va·tion /£ˌɒb·zəˈveɪ·ʃᵊn, $ˌɑːb·zɚ-/ *n* [U] • *She has remarkable* **powers of** *observation* (= is very good at noticing things).

ob·serve *obj* SAY /£əbˈzɜːv, $-ˈzɜːrv/ *v fml* to make a remark about something • *"I've always found German cars very reliable," he observed.* [+ clause] • *She observed* **that** *it would soon be time to stop for lunch.* [+ *that* clause]

ob·ser·va·tion /£ˌɒb·zəˈveɪ·ʃᵊn, $ˌɑːb·zɚ-/ *n* [C] *fml* • *The book is full of interesting observations* (= ideas expressed) **on/about** *the nature of musical composition.* • *May I* **make** *an observation* (= remark)*?*

ob·serve *obj* OBEY /£əbˈzɜːv, $-ˈzɜːrv/ *v* [T] *fml* to obey (a law, rule or custom) • *The judge has warned the local council that it must observe the law.* • *Do you observe* (= celebrate in the traditional way) *Passover?*

ob·ser·vance /£əbˈzɜː·vᵊnts, $-ˈzɜːr-/ *n fml* • *Religious observances* (= following a religious rule) *such as fasting can be hard to follow.* [C] • *We expect all players to show complete observance* **of** (= obedience to) *the rules of the game.* [U]

ob·sessed /əbˈsest/ *adj* unable to stop thinking about something; too interested in or very worried about something • *The government seems obsessed* **by** *the need for secrecy.* • *Why are people so obsessed* **with** *money?* • *They're both obsessed* **with** *the fear of getting AIDS.*

ob·sess *obj* /əbˈses/ *v* [T] • *The idea of finding her real mother seemed to obsess her* (= she could not stop thinking about it and trying to do it).

ob·ses·sion /əbˈseʃ·ᵊn/ *n* • *Her obsession is to become the first ever woman chess grandmaster.* [C] • *The problems began when his love for her turned to obsession.* [U] • *He has an obsession* **with** *looking good.* [C] • *(specialized)* In PSYCHOLOGY, an obsession is characterized by continuous and unreasonable thoughts or desires, which the obsessed person often finds very upsetting.

ob·ses·sive /əbˈses·ɪv/, **ob·ses·sion·al** /əbˈseʃ·ᵊn·ᵊl/ *adj* • *obsessive secrecy* • *She has an obsessive need to have everything perfect.* • *My partner is obsessive* **about** *punctuality.* • *His obsessive* **behaviour** *is characterized by the need to check everything 10 or 20 times.*

ob·ses·sively /əbˈses·ɪv·li/, **ob·ses·sion·al·ly** /əbˈseʃ·ᵊn·ᵊl·i/ *adv* • *She diets and exercises obsessively.*

ob·ses·sive /əbˈses·ɪv/ *n* [C] • *It's hard to get obsessives* (= people who are obsessed with something) *to take life less seriously.*

ob·sid·i·an /£ɒbˈsɪd·i·ən, $ɑːb-/ *n* [U] a type of almost black glass-like rock

ob·so·lete /£ˌɒb·sᵊlˈiːt, $ˌɑːb-/ *adj* [not gradable] not in use any more, because something newer and better or more fashionable has replaced it • *Gas lamps became obsolete when electric lighting became possible.*

ob·so·les·cence /£ˌɒb·səˈles·ᵊnts, $ˌɑːb-/ *n* [U] • **Built-in/Planned obsolescence** is intentionally designing and making a product so that it will not last for a long time.

ob·so·les·cent /£ˌɒb·səˈles·ᵊnt, $ˌɑːb-/ *adj* [not gradable] • *The amateur movie gauges of 8 mm, Super-8 and 9·5 mm are obsolescent.*

ob·sta·cle /£ˈɒb·stɪ·kl̩, $ˈɑːb-/ *n* [C] something that blocks you so that movement, going forward or action are prevented or made more difficult • *an insurmountable/insuperable obstacle* • *The worst obstacles that we had to negotiate were tree trunks that had fallen across the road.* • *This decision has removed the last obstacle* **to** *the hostages' release.* • *Their refusal to compromise is a major obstacle* **in the way of** (= something preventing) *further peace talks.* • *Eventually they* **overcame** *all the obstacles and their firm was very successful.* • An **obstacle course** is a race in which runners have to climb over, under or through a series of obstacles or *(fig.)* something which is difficult to do: *(fig.) Any attempt to get the money back is going to have to pass through the obstacle course* **of** *the British legal system.* • PIC〉 **Outdoor games for children**

ob·stet·rics /£ɒbˈstet·rɪks, $ɑːb-/ *n* [U] *specialized* the area of medicine which deals with pregnancy and the birth of babies • *She is qualified in obstetrics and gynaecology.*

ob·stet·ric /£ɒbˈstet·rɪk, $ɑːb-/ *adj* [not gradable] *specialized* • *an obstetric nurse*

ob·ste·tri·cian /£ˌɒb·stəˈtrɪʃ·ᵊn, $ˌɑːb-/, *Am infml* **OB** *n* [C] *specialized* • An obstetrician is a doctor with special training in how to care for pregnant women and help in the birth of babies.

ob·sti·nate /£ˈɒb·stɪ·nət, $ˈɑːb·stə-/ *adj* unreasonably determined, esp. to act in a particular way and not to change at all, despite argument or persuasion; STUBBORN • *The bank is being obstinate* **about** *my overdraft – they're refusing to let me have more than £500 this time.* • *He has an obstinate belief in his own ability.* • An obstinate problem, situation or thing is one that is difficult to deal with, remove or defeat: *obstinate weeds* ○ *There is some obstinate dry rot in the floor of our house.* ○ *Invading troops met with obstinate resistance by guerilla forces.*

ob·sti·nate·ly /£ˈɒb·stɪ·nət·li, $ˈɑːb·stə-/ *adv* • *My Grandma obstinately insists on doing her own shopping and cleaning, despite being in her 80s.*

ob·sti·na·cy /£ˈɒb·stɪ·nə·si, $ˈɑːb·stə-/ *n* [U]

ob·strep·er·ous /£əbˈstrep·ᵊr·əs, $ɑːbˈstrep·ɚ·əs/ *adj fml* too eager to have an argument; difficult to deal with and noisy • *obstreperous customers* ○ *We saw an obstreperous drunk outside the pub arguing with a policewoman.*

ob·strep·er·ous·ness /£əbˈstrep·ᵊr·ə·snəs, $ɑːbˈstrep·ɚ·ə-/ *n* [U] *fml*

ob·struct *obj* /əbˈstrʌkt/ *v* [T] to block (a road, passage, entrance, etc.) so that nothing can go along it, or to prevent (something) from correctly happening by putting difficulties in its way • *After the earthquake many roads were obstructed by collapsed buildings.* • *Her view of the stage was obstructed by a pillar.* • *He got ten years in prison for withholding evidence and obstructing the course of justice.* • *Conservatives have been obstructing reform for years.* • If you obstruct a vehicle or a person, you prevent them from moving in the direction they are trying to go: *An accident is obstructing traffic on the M11.*

ob·struc·tion /əbˈstrʌk·ʃᵊn/ *n* • *There's some sort of obstruction* (= blockage) *on the railway tracks.* [C] • *They were charged with obstruction of the police/of justice* (= preventing the police/law courts from doing their jobs). [U] • *The referee said it was obstruction* (= that one player had got in the way of another and so prevented them from moving freely). [U] • PL

ob·struc·tion·ism /əbˈstrʌk·ʃᵊn·ɪ·zᵊm/ *n* [U] *disapproving* • *The government's obstructionism* (= action of purposely preventing something) *has delayed discussion of the proposals from being talked about until next year.*

ob·struc·tion·ist /əbˈstrʌk·ʃᵊn·ɪst/ *adj disapproving* • *obstructionist policies/tactics*

ob·struc·tive /£əbˈstrʌk·tɪv, $-t̬ɪv/ *adj disapproving* • *We'd have made a decision by now if Jean had not been so obstructive* (= purposely made things difficult).

ob·struc·tive·ly /£əbˈstrʌk·tɪv·li, $-t̬ɪv-/ *adv disapproving*

ob·struc·tive·ness /£əbˈstrʌk·tɪv·nəs, $-t̬ɪv-/ *n* [U] *disapproving*

ob·tain *obj* GET /əbˈteɪn/ *v* [T] to get (something), esp. by asking for it, buying it, working for it or producing it from something else • *You must first obtain permission* **from** *your council.* • *First editions of these books are now almost impossible to obtain.* • *In the second experiment they* *obtained a very clear result.* • *Sugar is obtained* **by** *crushing and processing sugar cane.*

ob·tain·a·ble /əbˈteɪ·nə·bl̩/ *adj* [not gradable] • *That particular drug is not obtainable* (= cannot be obtained) *any more in this country.*

ob·tain EXIST /əbˈteɪn/ *v* [I] *fml* (esp. of a situation) to exist • *Conditions of extreme poverty now obtain in many parts of the country.*

ob·trude /əbˈtruːd/ *v* [I] *fml* (esp. of something unwanted) to make or become too noticeable, esp. by interrupting • *It's a pity that she mars the account of what happened by obtruding her own views too much.* [T] • *I don't want to obtrude* **upon** *her grief.* [I]

ob·tru·sive /əbˈtruː·sɪv/ *adj* (esp. of something unwanted and/or unpleasant) too noticeable, so that you cannot avoid being aware of it • *Bright green wallpaper would be too obtrusive, wouldn't it?* • *The soldiers were in civilian clothes, to make their presence less obtrusive.*

ob·tru·sive·ly /əbˈtruː·sɪv·li/ *adv*

ob·tru·sive·ness /əbˈtruː·sɪv·nəs/ *n* [U]

ob·tuse ANGLE /£əbˈtjuːs, $ɑːbˈtuːs/ *adj* (of an angle) more than 90° and less than 180° • Compare ACUTE ANGLE.

ob·tuse STUPID /£əbˈtjuːs, $-ˈtuːs/ *adj fml* stupid and slow to understand, or unwilling to try to understand • *Surely the answer's obvious – or are you being deliberately obtuse?*

ob·tuse·ly /£əbˈtjuː·sli, $ɑːbˈtuː-/ *adv fml*

ob·tuse·ness /£əbˈtjuː·snəs, $ɑːbˈtuː-/ *n* [U] *fml*

ob·verse /£ˈɒb·vɜːs, $ɑːbˈvɜːrs/ *n* [U] *fml* the other side of something; opposite • *False humility and its obverse, arrogance, are equally unpleasant.* • *Of course,* **the** *obverse* **of** *the theory may also be true.* • *(specialized)* **The** obverse **of** a coin or MEDAL is its front side, which has the main picture on it.

obviate *obj* /£ˈɒb·vi·eɪt, $ˈɑːb-/ *v* [T] *fml* to remove (a difficulty), esp. so that action to deal with it becomes unnecessary • *A peaceful solution would obviate* **the need** *to send a UN military force.*

ob·vi·ous /£ˈɒb·vi·əs, $ˈɑːb-/ *adj* clear; easy to see, recognize or understand • *The company representative will be obvious – she'll be wearing a red uniform.* • *Speaking in obvious distress, he described his ordeal in prison.* • *They do have a small child, and so* **for** *obvious* **reasons** *they need to find work as soon as possible.* • *I know you don't like Helen, but there's no need to* **make** *it so obvious* **(to** *everyone).* • *We all know the problems, so there's no need to* **state** *the obvious* (= to say what everyone already knows). • **It** *is becoming obvious* **(that)** *the school will have to close.* [+ (*that*) clause] • **It**'*s obvious* **wh***at they want.* [+ *wh-* word] • *There is no obvious* **solution**. • *(disapproving) The play has an obvious* (= too familiar and not imaginative) *story line of the 'boy-meets-girl' variety.*

ob·vi·ous·ly /£ˈɒb·vi·ə·sli, $ˈɑːb-/ *adv* • *He was in tears and obviously very upset.* • *Obviously the school cannot function without teachers.* • *"We'll need some more food if they're staying." "Obviously."*

oc·ca·sion PARTICULAR TIME /əˈkeɪ·ʒᵊn/ *n* [C] a particular time, esp. when something happens or has happened, or a special or formal event • *Occasions when I have the time to spend a day with my kids are quite rare.* • *Sara's party was quite an occasion – there were hundreds of people there.* • *I saw Bob Dylan play in 1968 and* **on** *that occasion he was simply brilliant.* • *At the wedding he sang a song specially written* **for** *the occasion.* • *She promised she would make a speech if the occasion seemed to* **demand** *it.* • *The coronation of a new king is a* **historic** *occasion.* • *Congratulations on* **the** *occasion* **of** *your wedding anniversary.* • *Of course a funeral is not* **the** *occasion* (= suitable time) **for** *a light-hearted song and dance.* • *(fml)* An occasion is also an opportunity or reason for doing something or for something to happen: *The 200th anniversary of Mozart's death was the occasion* **for** *hundreds of special films, books and concerts.* ○ *An occasion may* **arise** *when you can use your knowledge of French.* ○ *The bride* **took/used** *the occasion to make a short speech.* • *A good teacher has authority but rarely* **has occasion to** (= needs to) *use it.* • **There's no occasion to** (= You should not) *be so rude.* • **On occasion** means sometimes but not often: *He has, on occasion, made small mistakes.* • (PL) (RUS)

oc·ca·sion *obj* CAUSE /əˈkeɪ·ʒᵊn/ *v* [T] *fml* to cause (something) • *Her refusal occasioned a lot of trouble.* • *The case occasioned the authorities a lot of worry/The authorities were occasioned a lot of worry* **by** *the case.* [+ two objects] • (PL) (RUS)

oc·ca·sion·al /əˈkeɪ·ʒᵊn·ᵊl, -ˈkeɪʒ·nəl/ *adj* [not gradable] not happening often or regularly • *He makes occasional appearances for the local football team.* • *My father has the occasional cigar after dinner.*

oc·ca·sion·al·ly /əˈkeɪ·ʒᵊn·ᵊl·i, -ˈkeɪʒ·nəl-/ *adv* [not gradable] • *I'm in London occasionally – about once a month.* • (I)

Oc·ci·dent /£ˈɒk·sɪ·dᵊnt, $ˈɑːk·sə-/ *n* [U] **the Occident** *fml or poetic* the western part of the world, esp. the countries of Europe and America • Compare ORIENT.

oc·ci·den·tal /£ˌɒk·sɪˈden·tᵊl, $ˌɑːk·səˈden·t̬ᵊl/ *adj* [not gradable] *fml or poetic* • *occidental cultures* ○ *Occidental music* • Compare **oriental** at ORIENT.

oc·cult /£ˈɒk·ʌlt, £-ˈ-, $ˈɑː·kʌlt/ *adj* [not gradable] relating to magical powers and activities, such as those of WITCHCRAFT and ASTROLOGY • *She claims to have occult* **powers**, *given to her by some mysterious spirit.*

oc·cult /£ˈɒk·ʌlt, £-ˈ-, $ˈɑː·kʌlt/ *n* [U] • *She became interested in* **the** *occult and magic when she was in her twenties.*

oc·cu·pa·tion /£ˌɒk·jʊˈpeɪ·ʃᵊn, $ˌɑː·kjə-/ *n* [C] *slightly fml* a person's job • *In the space marked 'occupation' she wrote 'police officer'.* • An occupation is also a regular activity: *It seems to me his favourite occupation is eating!* • (RUS)

oc·cu·pa·tion·al /£ˌɒk·jʊˈpeɪ·ʃᵊn·ᵊl, $ˌɑː·kjə-/ *adj* [not gradable] • An **occupational disease** is a disease that you can get if you are doing a particular job: *Silicosis is an occupational disease among certain types of miners.* • An **occupational hazard** is something dangerous or unpleasant that you risk if you do a particular job or activity: *Death or serious injury are accepted occupational hazards for mountain climbers.* • *(specialized)* **Occupational therapy** is a way of treating mentally or physically ill people by getting them to do useful activities.

oc·cu·py *obj* FILL /£ˈɒk·jʊ·paɪ, $ˈɑː·kjʊ-/ *v* [T usually passive] to fill, use or exist in (a place or a time) • *The Vice President occupies an important position within the corporation.* • *The bathroom's occupied – I think John's in there.* • *The rest of the time was occupied* **with** *writing a report.* • *The house hasn't been occupied* (= lived in) **by** *anyone for a few months.* • *(fml) A large picture of the battle of Waterloo occupied the space above the fireplace.* • To occupy someone is also to keep them busy and/or interested: *On long car journeys I occupy* **myself** *with solving maths puzzles.* ○ *All the new toys kept the kids occupied for hours.*

oc·cu·pan·cy /£ˈɒk·jʊ·pᵊnt·si, $ˈɑː·kjə-/ *n* [U] *fml* • *The family's occupancy of the apartment lasted only six months.*

oc·cu·pant /£ˈɒk·jʊ·pᵊnt, $ˈɑː·kjə-/ *n* [C] *fml* • An occupant of a building is a person who lives there: *All the occupants of the building are unhappy about the increased charges.* • An occupant of a car, room, seat, place or position is a person who is in it: *One of the occupants of the car was slightly injured.* ○ *There have been many distinguished occupants of the position of artistic director.*

oc·cu·pi·er /£ˈɒk·jʊ·paɪ·əʳ, $ˈɑː·kjə·paɪ·ɚ/ *n* [C] • *The envelope was simply addressed to 'The Occupier'* (= person living in the building).

oc·cu·py *obj* TAKE CONTROL /£ˈɒk·jʊ·paɪ, $ˈɑː·kjuː-/ *v* [T] (of an army or group of people) to move into and take control and/or possession of (a place) • *Troops quickly occupied the city.* • *Protesting students occupied the university office for two weeks.* • *The occupying forces behaved with appalling brutality.*

oc·cu·pa·tion /£ˌɒk·jʊˈpeɪ·ʃᵊn, $ˌɑː·kjə-/ *n* [U] • *The occupation of the TV station was achieved without any bloodshed.* • *The Italian occupation* **of** *Ethiopia lasted less than ten years.*

oc·cu·pied /£ˈɒk·jʊ·paɪd, $ˈɑː·kjʊ-/ *adj* [not gradable] • *She spent two years in occupied Paris* (= Paris under foreign control) *during the war.*

oc·cu·pi·er /£ˈɒk·jʊ·paɪ·əʳ, $ˈɑː·kjə·paɪ·ɚ/ *n* [C] • *The occupiers were driven out after fierce street fighting.*

oc·cur HAPPEN /£əˈkɜːʳ, $-ˈkɜːr/ *v* [I] **-rr-** (esp. of accidents and other unexpected events) to happen; TAKE PLACE • *An accident involving over ten vehicles has occurred in the east-bound lane.* • *If any of these symptoms occur while you are taking the medicine, consult your doctor immediately.* • (I)

oc·cur·rence /£əˈkʌr·ᵊnts, $-ˈkɜːr-/ *n* [C] • *Street-fights are an* **everyday** *occurrence in this area of the city.*

oc·cur EXIST /£əˈkɜːʳ, $-ˈkɜːr/ *v* [I] **-rr-** to exist or be present • *Violence of some sort seems to occur in every society.* • (I)

oc·cur·rence /£ə'kʌr·ənts, $-'kɜːr-/ *n* [U] • *The study compares the occurrence* (=existing amount) *of heart disease in various countries.*

oc·cur to *obj v prep* [T] (of a thought or idea) to come into (someone's) mind • *The thought occurred to me this morning* **that** *it's Natalie's birthday tomorrow and we haven't got her a present.* [+ obj + *that* clause] • *Just jot down anything that occurs to you.* • *I don't believe he would do that – the thought would never occur to him.* • **It** *never even occurred to us* **that** *he hadn't been invited.* [+ obj + *that* clause] • *Does* **it** *never occur to you* **that** *I might like to be on my own occasionally?* [+ obj + *that* clause] • **It** *never occurred to his parents* **to** *ask where he'd been.* [+ obj + *to* infinitive] • LP **It**

o·cean /£'əʊ·ʃən, $'oʊ-/ *n* a very large area of sea • *These mysterious creatures live at the bottom of* **the ocean**. [U] • The word 'Ocean' is also used in the name of each of the world's five main areas of sea: *the Atlantic/Pacific/Indian/Arctic/Antarctic Ocean* [C] • *(dated)* **Oceans of** means a lot of: *Don't worry – we've got oceans of time.*

o·ce·an·ic /£ˌəʊ·ʃi'æn·ɪk, $ˌoʊ-/ *adj* [not gradable] • Oceanic means of or relating to the sea.

o·cean·go·ing /£'əʊ·ʃənˌgəʊ·ɪŋ, $'oʊ·ʃənˌgoʊ-/, **sea·go·ing** /£'siːˌgəʊ·ɪŋ, $-ˌgoʊ-/ *adj* [not gradable] (of a ship, boat, etc.) designed for travelling across large areas of sea • *an oceangoing vessel*

o·ce·an·og·ra·phy /£ˌəʊ·ʃə'nɒg·rə·fi, $ˌoʊ·ʃə'nɑː·grə-/ *n* [U] the scientific study of the sea

o·chre, *Am also* **o·cher** /£'əʊ·kər, $'oʊ·kɚ/ *n* [U] a yellowish orange colour, or a substance obtained from the earth which is used for giving this colour to paints

ock·er, **ok·ker** /£'ɒk·ər, $'ɑː·kɚ/ *n* [C] *Aus* a type of Australian who is not well educated and does not behave in a polite way

o'clock /£ə'klɒk, $-'klɑːk/ *adv* [not gradable] used after a number from one to twelve to say the time when it is exactly that hour • *"Have you got the time?" "It's two o'clock."* • *I got a phone-call from him at four o'clock in the morning.* • *It's almost ten o'clock, the news will be on soon.* • LP **Time**

OCR /£ˌəʊ·siː'ɑːr, $ˌoʊ·siː'ɑːr/ *n* [U] *abbreviation for* **optical character recognition**, see at OPTICAL

oc·ta·gon /£'ɒk·tə·gən, $'ɑːk·tə·gɑːn/ *n* [C] a flat eight-sided shape • PIC **Shapes**

oc·ta·gon·al /£ɒk'tæg·ən·əl, $ɑːk-/ *adj* [not gradable] • *an octagonal* (=eight-sided) *tower*

oc·tane (num·ber) /£'ɒk·teɪn, $'ɑːk-/ *n* [C] a number showing the quality of PETROL (=a type of fuel) in representing how well and with how much power it can make an engine work • *The Super Plus unleaded is around 110 octane.*

-oc·tane /£-'ɒk·teɪn, $-'ɑːk-/ *combining form* • *Racing cars use a* **high-***octane* (=powerful) *fuel.*

oc·tave /£'ɒk·tɪv, $'ɑːk-/ *n* [C] *specialized* the space between two musical notes which are eight musical notes apart • *She's got an amazing vocal range of three and a half octaves.* • *Electric keyboards tend to have about three or four octaves.*

oc·tet /£ɒk'tet, $ɑːk-/ *n* [C + sing/pl v] a group of eight singers or musicians performing together, or a piece of music written for eight singers or musicians

Oc·to·ber /£ɒk'təʊ·bər, $ɑːk'toʊ·bɚ/ (*abbreviation* **Oct**) *n* the tenth month of the year, after September and before November • *22(nd) October/October 22(nd)/22(nd) Oct/Oct 22(nd)* [U] • *We're leaving for Italy* **on** *October the ninth/the ninth of October/(esp. Am) October ninth.* [U] • *Sara's birthday is some time* **in/during** *October.* [U] • *We went to Vermont* **last** *October/We're going to Vermont* **next** *October to see the autumn foliage.* [U] • *It has been one of the rainiest Octobers for several years.* [C] • LP **Dates**

oc·to·ge·na·ri·an /£ˌɒk·təʊ·dʒə'neə·ri·ən, $ˌɑːk·toʊ·dʒɪ'ner·i-/ *n* [C] a person who is between 80 and 89 years old

oc·to·pus /£'ɒk·tə·pəs, $'ɑːk·tə·pəs/ *n* [C] *pl* **octopuses** or **octopi** /£'ɒk·tə·paɪ, $'ɑːk-/ a sea creature with a soft oval body and eight TENTACLES (= arms) • *Octopuses are found at the bottom of the sea.* • PIC **Mollusc**

oc·u·lar /£'ɒk·jʊ·lər, $'ɑː·kjə·lɚ/ *adj* [not gradable] *specialized* of or related to the eyes or sight

oc·u·list /£'ɒk·jʊ·lɪst, $'ɑː·kjə-/ *n* [C] *dated for* **ophthalmologist**, see at OPHTHALMOLOGY

OD /£ˌəʊ'diː, $ˌoʊ-/ *v* [I] **OD'ing**, *past* **OD'd** or **ODed** *slang* to take an OVERDOSE (=too much) of a drug • *She OD'd* **on** *heroin and died.* • *(fig.) Casey sometimes OD's* **on** *video games, and then he gets wild and uncontrollable.*

OD /£ˌəʊ'diː, $ˌoʊ-/ *n* [C] *pl* **OD's** *esp. Am slang*

odd STRANGE /£ɒd, $ɑːd/ *adj* **-er, -est** strange or unexpected • *Her father was an odd man.* • *That was an odd thing to say – what do you think he meant?* • *Separately the skirt and jacket are fine, but they look a bit odd together.* • *That's odd* (=surprising) *– I'm sure I put my keys in this drawer and yet they're not here.* • **It's** *odd* **that** *no-one has seen Brian for days.* [+ *that* clause] • **It** *must be odd* **to** *live on the 43rd floor.* [+ *to* infinitive]

odd·i·ty /£'ɒd·ɪ·ti, $'ɑː·də·t̬i/ *n* [C] • An oddity is someone or something that is strange and unusual: *Even today a man who stays at home to look after the children is regarded as something of an oddity.* ○ *She's an oddity, my mother – I still don't feel I know her even after thirty years.*

odd·ly /£'ɒd·li, $'ɑːd-/ *adv* • *Didn't you think she was behaving rather oddly at the party yesterday?* • **Oddly enough** (=This is strange/surprising), *she didn't mention anything about the fact that she was getting married.*

odd·ness /£'ɒd·nəs, $'ɑːd-/ *n* [U]

odd SEPARATED /£ɒd, $ɑːd/ *adj* [before n; not gradable] (of something that should be in a pair or set) separated from its pair or set • *He's got a whole drawer full of odd socks.* • *I'd got a few odd* (=I had various) *balls of wool left over from various sweaters that I'd knitted.* • The **odd one out/odd man out** is a person or thing that is different from or kept apart from others that form a group or set: *Guess which number of the following sequence is the odd one out.* ○ *She was always the odd one out at school – she didn't really mix with the other children.*

odd NUMBERS /£ɒd, $ɑːd/ *adj* [not gradable] (of numbers) not able to be divided exactly by two • *3, 5, 7 are all odd numbers.* • *The houses on this side of the street have all got odd numbers and on the other side they've got even numbers.*

odd NOT OFTEN /£ɒd, $ɑːd/ *adj* [before n; not gradable] not happening often • *She does* **the** *odd teaching* **job** *but nothing permanent.* • *You get* **the** *odd person who's rude to you but they're generally quite helpful.* • An **odd-job man/odd-jobber** is a man who is paid to do a variety of jobs, esp. in the house or garden.

-odd APPROXIMATELY /£ɒd, $ɑːd/ *combining form infml* used after a number, esp. a number that can be divided by ten, to show that the exact number is not known • *How many people do you think were there last night – 50-odd* (= about 50)*?* • *"How old d'you reckon he is?" "Oh, I'd say about forty-odd – maybe forty-five."* • *This firm owns 200-odd acres of the best land.* • LP **Approximate numbers**

odd·ball /£'ɒd·bɔːl, $'ɑːd·bɑːl/ *n* [C] *infml* a person whose behaviour is unusual and strange • *His oldest sister is something of an oddball – I've never really understood her.*

odd·ball /£'ɒd·bɔːl, $'ɑːd·bɑːl/ *adj* [before n] *infml* • *The oddball superstar's habits include watching TV with his chimpanzee.*

odd·ment /£'ɒd·mənt, $'ɑːd-/ *n* [C often pl] a part of something which is left, esp. when the rest has been used • *It's a good way of using up any oddments* **of** *cloth that are left over from clothes that you've made.*

odds PROBABILITY /£ɒdz, $ɑːdz/ *pl n* the probability that a particular thing will or will not happen • *Judging by how ill she looked yesterday, I think the odds* **are** *she won't be coming in today.* • *If you drive a car all your life, the odds* **are** *that you'll have an accident at some point.* • *There are heavy odds* **against** *people succeeding in such a bad economic climate.* • *What are the odds* **on** *him being* (=Do you think he will be) *late again?* • If you say that you would **give long** odds **on/against** something happening, you mean that you believe/do not believe it will happen: *I'd give long odds against that marriage lasting more than a couple of years!* • If something **lengthens/shortens** (*Am usually* **increases/decreases**) the odds **on** something that might happen, it makes it less/more likely to happen: *If you want to live to a ripe old age, giving up smoking does tend to shorten the odds.* • The odds are also the probability expressed as a number when making a BET: *The odds* **against** *my horse winning* (=that it will not win)*/***on** *my horse winning* (=that it will win) *are a hundred to one.* ○ *The odds* **that** *the US entrant will win the race are ten to one.* [+ *that* clause] • **Against all (the) odds** (=Very unexpectedly), *he managed to walk again after the accident.* • **Odds-on** means very probable: *It's odds-on she'll be late and I've rushed for no reason!* ○ *The odds-on* **favourite** *to win in the 3.30 race is Killjoy.*

odds DISAGREEMENT /£ɒdz, $ɑːdz/ *pl n* **at odds** in disagreement • *The firm's two senior partners are at odds, which doesn't help matters.* • *He's been at odds* **with** *his brother ever since I've known him.* • *Her version of the events of that night are quite dramatically at odds* **with** (=very different from) *his.*

odds DIFFERENCE /£ɒdz, $ɑːdz/ *pl n esp. Br and Aus infml* noticeable difference • *I don't mind whether you come or not – it* **makes** *no odds* (=it isn't important) **to** *me.* • *Does it* **make** *any odds whether you use butter or oil in this recipe?* [+ *wh-* word]

odds MORE THAN /£ɒdz, $ɑːdz/ *pl n* **over the odds** *Br and Aus infml* (esp. of money) more than is expected or agreed, or more than something is worth • *If my calculations are right, I got paid a bit over the odds for that job.*

odds and ends, *Br and Aus slang* **odds and sods** *pl n infml* various items of different types, usually small and unimportant or of little value • *I've taken most of the big things to the new house, but there are a few odds and ends left to collect.*

ode /£əʊd, $oʊd/ *n* [C] a poem expressing the writer's thoughts and feelings about a particular person or subject, usually addressed to that person or subject • *'Ode* **to** *a Nightingale' and 'Ode* **on** *a Grecian Urn' are poems by Keats.*

o·di·ous /£ˈəʊ·di·əs, $ˈoʊ-/ *adj fml* extremely unpleasant; causing and deserving hate • *an odious crime* • *an odious little man* • *Henry Bavington plays the part of Mr Grimes, the odious headmaster.*

o·di·um /£ˈəʊ·di·əm, $ˈoʊ-/ *n* [U] *fml* • Odium is hate and strong disapproval: *It seemed strange to see the country's former president held up to such public odium.*

od·o·met·er /£əʊˈdɒm·ɪ·təʳ, $oʊˈdɑː·mə·t̬ɚ/ *n* [C] *Am for or Br and Aus specialized for* MILEOMETER • PIC› **Meters and gauges**

o·dour *Br and Aus, Am and Aus* **o·dor** /£ˈəʊ·dəʳ, $ˈoʊ·dɚ/ *n slightly fml* a particular smell • *Inside the room there was the unmistakable odour* **of** *sweaty feet.* [C] • *Suddenly, he smelt the sweet odour* **of** *her perfume.* [C] • *Odour* (=Smells generally) *can become a problem if the ventilation in a room is inadequate.* [U] • *(fig. literary) The odour* **of** *hypocrisy hung about everything she said.* [C] • LP› **Smells**

o·dour·less *Br and Aus, Am and Aus* **o·dor·less** /£ˈəʊ·də·ləs, $ˈoʊ·dɚ-/ *adj* [not gradable] *fml* • *an odourless gas*

od·ys·sey /£ˈɒd·ɪ·si, $ˈɑː·dɪ-/ *n* [C usually sing] *literary* a long journey containing a lot of exciting or dangerous events • *The film follows one man's odyssey to find the mother from whom he was separated at birth.* • *(fig.) She describes her first novel as 'a sort of spiritual odyssey in search of Jesus'.*

Oe·di·pus com·plex /ˈiː·dɪ·pəs-/ *n* [C] (in Freudian PSYCHOANALYSIS) a child's sexual desire for a parent of the opposite sex, esp. that of a boy for his mother

Oe·dip·al /ˈiː·dɪ·pᵊl/ *adj* • *Freud argued that all people go through an Oedipal* **phase** *of sexual development.* • *(infml) He's very Oedipal* (=too emotionally involved with his mother).

oe·no·phile /ˈiː·nə·faɪl/ *n* [C] *fml* a person who loves wine and knows a lot about it

o'er /£əʊəʳ, $ɔːr/ *prep poetic short form of* over • *O'er land and sea they sped.*

oe·so·phag·us, *esp. Am* **e·so·pha·gus** /£ɪˈsɒf·ə·gəs, $ɪˈsɑː·fə-/, **gul·let** *n* [C] **oesophaguses** *medical* the tube in the body which takes food from the mouth to the stomach

oe·stro·gen, *esp. Am* **es·tro·gen** /£ˈiː·strəʊ·dʒᵊn, $ˈes·trə-/ *n* [U] a female HORMONE (=a chemical substance produced in the body) that causes development and change in the reproductive organs • *Oestrogen is secreted mainly by the ovaries and placenta.*

oeuv·re /ˈɜː·vrə/ *n* [C usually sing] *literary* the complete works of a writer, painter or other artist • *His oeuvre is now considered one of the greatest achievements in the history of ballet.*

of POSSESSION /£ɒv, $ɑːv/ *prep* used to show possession, belonging or origin • *a friend of mine* • *the president of the United States* • *a man of God* • *employees of the company* • *people of this island* • *the colour of his hair* • *the language of this country* • *a habit of mine* • *that revolting dog of hers* • *the cruelty of children* • *the love of a good woman* • *the complete plays of* (=written by) *Federico Garcia Lorca*

of AMOUNT /£ɒv, $ɑːv/ *prep* used after words or phrases expressing amount, number or particular unit • *a kilo of apples* • *loads of food* • *hundreds of people* • *most of them* • *none of them* • *both of us* • *a third of all people* • *a speck of dust* • *a drop of rain* • LP› **Quantity words**

of CONTAINING /£ɒv, $ɑːv/ *prep* containing • *a bag of sweets* • *a bottle of beer* • *a book of short stories* • *sacks of rubbish* • *a class of idiots*

of POSITION /£ɒv, $ɑːv/ *prep* used in expressions showing position • *the top of his head* • *the back of your dress* • *on the corner of the street* • *the front of the queue* • *I've never been north of Edinburgh.* • *Leeds is (to the) north of London.*

of TYPICAL /£ɒv, $ɑːv/ *prep* typical or characteristic of • *She moves with the grace of a dancer.* • *She has the face of an angel.* • *That man's got the brain of a donkey!*

of DAYS /£ɒv, $ɑːv/ *prep* used to describe a particular day • *the eleventh of March* • *the first of the month*

of TIME /£ɒv, $ɑːv/ *prep Am* used in saying what the time is • *It's ten (minutes) of five* (=ten minutes before five o'clock). • LP› **Time**

of DURING /£ɒv, $ɑːv/ *prep dated* during • *I like to relax with my gramophone of an evening.*

of USED AFTER ADJECTIVES /£ɒv, $ɑːv/ *prep* used to connect particular adjectives with nouns • *fond of swimming* • *sick of his excuses* • *frightened of spiders*

of JUDGMENT /£ɒv, $ɑːv/ *prep* used after an adjective when judging someone's behaviour • *You told her she was looking fat – that was a bit unkind of you!* • *How thoughtful of you* **to** *remember my birthday.*

of RELATING TO /£ɒv, $ɑːv/ *prep* about; relating to • *Speaking of Elizabeth, here she is.* • *One of the advantages of travelling by train is being able to read.* • *There's a chapter on the use of herbs for medicinal purposes.* • *Let us consider the events of the last five months.* • *Of her childhood we know very little.* • *And what of* (=Tell me about) *young Adrian? How is he?*

of MADE OF /£ɒv, $ɑːv/ *prep* made or consisting of; having • *dresses of lace and silk* • *plates of gold and silver* • *a rod of iron* • *a crown of thorns* • *a land of ice and snow* • *a woman of great charm and beauty* • *a subject of very little interest*

of SEPARATE FROM /£ɒv, $ɑːv/ *prep* used in expressions showing distance from something in place or time • *We live within a mile of the city centre.* • *She came within two seconds of beating the world record.*

of LOSS /£ɒv, $ɑːv/ *prep* used in expressions showing loss • *They were robbed of all their savings.* • *I feel I've been deprived of your company these past few weeks.* • *At last I've managed to cure him of that nasty little habit.*

of THAT IS/ARE /£ɒv, $ɑːv/ *prep* that is/are • *the problem of homelessness* • *a rise of 2% in inflation* • *the skill of negotiating* • *the difficulty of bringing up twins* • *the pain of separation* • *At the age of six she could read a newspaper.* • *This complete idiot of a man drove straight out in front of me without even looking!*

of COMPARING /£ɒv, $ɑːv/ *prep* used when comparing related things • *Best of all I liked the green one.* • *Worst of all was the food!* • *He's the best looking of the three brothers.* • *I think that of all his films it's my favourite.* • Phrases such as **of all people/things/places** are used to express the idea that these particular people/things/places are unlikely or surprising: *I can't understand why you live in Iceland, of all places.* ○ *Jane, of all people is the last one I'd expect to see at the club.*

of DONE TO /£ɒv, $ɑːv/ *prep* done to • *the massacre of hundreds of innocent people* • *the oppression of a nation* • *the destruction of the rain forest* • *the coronation of the queen*

of FELT BY /£ɒv, $ɑːv/ *prep* felt or experienced by • *the suffering of millions* • *the anguish of the murdered child's parents*

of THROUGH /£ɒv, $ɑːv/ *prep* through; having as the cause • *He died of cancer.* • *I didn't have to go there – I did it of my own free will.* • *I want to know how it happened because it certainly didn't happen of itself.*

off NOT OPERATING /£ɒf, $ɑːf/ *adj* [after v], *adv* [not gradable] (esp. of machines, electrical devices, lights, etc.) not operating because they are not switched on • *Make sure the computers are all off before you go home.* • **Turn/Switch** *the light/engine/television off.* • *I can't find the off switch.* • LP› **Switching on and off**

off NOT LIKING /£ɒf, $ɑːf/ *prep* not liking or taking (something or someone) • *He's been off his food ever since he had the stomach upset.* • *I used to love wine but I've* **gone** *off it* (=stopped liking it) *recently.* • *She's well enough to be off the medicine now.* • *The doctor says he can come off the tablets so long as he feels all right.* • *She* **went** *off* (=stopped liking) *him when she found out he was a car salesman.*

off [AWAY FROM] /£ɒf, $ɑːf/ *adv, adj* [not gradable], *prep* away from a place or position, esp. the present place or position • *He drove off at the most incredible speed.* • *Keep the dog on the lead or he'll just run off.* • *Someone's run off with* (= taken) *my pen.* • *I won't be long – I'm just (going/nipping/running) off to the shops.* • *If we can get off* (= leave) *early tomorrow morning we'll avoid most of the traffic.* • *(fig.) I didn't get off to a very good start* (= I started badly) *this morning – I'd been at work five minutes and my computer stopped working!* • *I'm off now – see you tomorrow.* • *She's off* **to** *Canada next week.* • *Don't feel you have to get up just to see us off* (= say goodbye and watch us leave). • *There was a 'keep off the grass' sign.* • *The ship went a long way off* (= away from the intended) **course** *during the storm.* • *(esp. Br infml) You're* **(way) off beam** *there* (= (very) wrong). • If something is **off-centre**, it is nearly but not quite in a central position. • *You're singing* **off key** (= singing the wrong note). • *(Br)* An **off-licence** (*Am and Aus* **liquor store** or *Am* **package store**) is a shop that sells mainly alcoholic drinks to be taken away and drunk at home. • If an area of land is **off-limits**, it is forbidden that you enter it. • A computer which is **off-line** is not connected to or directly controlled by a central system. • *(esp. Br)* **Off-piste** SKIING is done on snow away from the areas that have been specially prepared: *When you get a little more advanced you can ski off-piste.* • If a situation is **off-putting**, it is slightly unpleasant or worrying so that you are discouraged from getting involved in it in any way: *What I found off-putting was the amount of work that you were expected to do.* ○ *He's slightly aggressive, which a lot of people find a bit off-putting when they first meet him.* • *(Br)* In a bar, **off-sales** are sales of alcoholic drinks which are still in a bottle or other container, so that you can take them away and drink them at home. • [PIC] **Prepositions of movement**

off /£ɒf, $ɑːf/ *n* [U] *Br* • **The off** is the act of leaving: *Are we* **ready for** *the off, then?*

off [REMOVED] /£ɒf, $ɑːf/ *adv* [not gradable], *prep* used with actions in which something is removed or removes itself from another thing • *I'm hot – I think I'll take my jacket off.* • *Oh, one of my buttons has come off.* • *She's had all that lovely long blonde hair cut off!* • *I can't get the lid off this jar.* • *Has anyone taken a book off my desk?* • *She jumped off a cliff.* • *He fell off his bike coming round a corner.* • *Could you cut me a small piece off that big white cheese?* • *Take your feet off that seat, young man!* • *I don't like taking money off you* (= asking you for money)*!* • *I hope she knows where to get off* (= leave) *the bus/train.* • *Get off me* (= Stop touching me)*!* • *(not standard) I got the knife off of him before he ran away.* • If someone says **off with** something, they are ordering someone to remove something: *Off with his head!* ○ *Off with your jacket!* • *"Off with his head!"* (the White Queen in *Alice Through the Looking Glass* by Lewis Carroll, 1872)

off [NEAR TO] /£ɒf, $ɑːf/ *prep* near to • *He lives just off the main road.* • *It's an island off the east coast of Spain.*

off [BAD] /£ɒf, $ɑːf/ *adj* [after v; not gradable] (of food and drink) no longer fresh or good to eat because of being too old • *How long have you had this milk – it smells off.* • *I'd better eat the cheese before it* **goes** *off.*

off [NOT AT WORK] /£ɒf, $ɑːf/ *adv, adj* [not gradable] not at work; at home or on holiday • *I'm going to* **take/have** *some time off to work on my house.* • *She had six weeks off because of sickness last year.* • *He's off at the moment – I think he's ill again.* • When a police officer or other person who works special hours is **off-duty**, he or she is not at work: *He looks completely different when he's off-duty and in his normal clothes.* • If someone is **taken/caught off-guard**, they are not prepared for something unexpected that happens and are therefore surprised or confused: *He hadn't realized that they were filming and they caught him off-guard.*

off [COMPLETELY] /£ɒf, $ɑːf/ *adv* [not gradable] in such a way as to be completely absent, esp. because of having been used or killed • *It says on the bottle that it kills off all known germs.* • *Unfortunately, in building on land like this we kill off a lot of wild life.* • *It'll take some time before she manages to pay off all her debts.* • *The good thing about exercise is that it burns off calories.* • *(infml) Between us we managed to finish off* (= finish) *eight bottles of wine.*

off [BELOW USUAL LEVEL] /£ɒf, $ɑːf/ *adv* [before n], *adj* [not gradable] below the usual standard or rate • *She used to have a lovely voice but I think it's* **gone** *off recently* (= is not as good as it was). • *I'm having an off* **day** *today – I just can't seem to do anything right!* • If you are feeling **off-colour**, you are slightly ill: *I'm not really ill – I've just been feeling a bit off-colour recently.* • **Off-colour** can also refer to remarks or jokes about sex that are slightly shocking. • If you use the telephone or another service when it is **off-peak**, you do so at a time when fewer people are using the service and it will usually be cheaper: *I usually wait until it's off-peak to make long-distance calls.* • **Off-season** refers to a period of the year when there is less activity in business: *We tend to go skiing during the off-season because it's cheaper.* • **Off-white** is white with a little grey or yellow in it: *The walls were painted off-white.*

off [DISTANT] /£ɒf, $ɑːf/ *adv* [not gradable], *prep* distant (from) in time or space • *The exams are so far off that I'm not even thinking about them yet.* • *How far off finishing the project are we* (= How much more is there to do)*?* • *We've been working on the flat for six months now but we're still a long way off finishing.* • *We're not far off* (= We are quite near) *London now.*

off [STOPPED] /£ɒf, $ɑːf/ *adj* [after v], *adv* [not gradable] (of an arranged event) stopped or given up in advance • *The wedding's off – she's decided she's too young to settle down.* • *The football has been called off this afternoon because of snow.* • *His hockey match was rained off* (= stopped because of rain). • *(infml) It's all off* (= The relationship is finished) *between Philippa and Mike.*

off [LESS MONEY] /£ɒf, $ɑːf/ *adv* [not gradable], *prep* (of money) subtracted from the original price • *You can get some money off if you pay cash.* • *There's 40% off this week on all winter coats.* • *The manager of the shop gave me ten pounds off the sweater because a button was missing.* • *There was $40 or $50 off most jackets in the shop.*

off [SEPARATED] /£ɒf, $ɑːf/ *adv* [not gradable] in such a way as to be separated • *The police have shut off all streets leading to the city.* • *The area in the park where the kids play is fenced off for safety reasons.*

off [GET RID OF] /£ɒf, $ɑːf/ *adv* [not gradable] in such a way as to get rid of something • *We went out for a while to walk off some of our dinner.* • *He's gone to sleep off a headache after rather too much wine.* • *There's no point in getting upset about such remarks – you've just got to laugh them off.*

off [PROVIDED FOR] /£ɒf, $ɑːf/ *adj* [not gradable] having a particular amount or number, esp. of money • *(Br and Aus) How are you off* **for** *money* (= Have you got enough/How much have you got)*?* • *Andrew must be so* **well-off** (= rich) *by now.* • *I think they're fairly* **badly-off** (= poor) *now that David has lost his job.* • *I'm quite* **well off for** (= have a lot of) *sweaters having just received three for my birthday.*

off [NO LONGER SERVED] /£ɒf, $ɑːf/ *adj* [after v; not gradable] (of food in a restaurant) not being served because there is none left • *I'm sorry, sir, the salmon is off.*

off [RUDE] /£ɒf, $ɑːf/ *adj* [after v; not gradable] *esp. Br infml* not caring about other people's feelings; rude • *He didn't even ring her up on her birthday – I thought that was* **a bit** *off.*

off *obj* [KILL] /£ɒf, $ɑːf/ *v* [T] *Am slang* to kill (someone) • *They offed him and dumped his body in the swamp.*

of·fal /£ˈɒf·əl, $ˈɑː·fəl/, *esp. Am* **va·ri·e·ty meat** *n* [U] the organs inside an animal, such as the brain, the heart and the LIVER, which are eaten as food

off·beat /£ˌɒfˈbiːt, $ˌɑːfˈbiːt/ *adj* unusual and strange and therefore surprising or noticeable • *an offbeat sense of humour* • *Her taste in clothes remained offbeat, even into her eighties.*

of·fence [CRIME], *Am usually* **of·fense** /əˈfents/ *n* [C] *law* an illegal act; a crime • *a serious/minor offence* • *a criminal/drink-driving offence* • *Driving without a licence is an offence.* • *It's the third time that he's been* **convicted of** *a drug offence.* • [LP] **Crimes and criminals**

of·fend /əˈfend/ *v* [I] *law* • To offend is to commit a crime: *Obviously if a police officer offends it's a fairly serious matter.*

of·fend·er /£əˈfen·dər, $-dɚ/ *n* [C] *law* • An offender is a person who is guilty of a crime: *first-time offenders* • *sex offenders* ○ *It's an institution to which young offenders are sent instead of prison.* • An **offender profile** is *specialized for* **psychological profile**. See at PSYCHOLOGY.

of·fence [UPSET FEELINGS], *Am usually* **of·fense** /əˈfents/ *n* [U] upset and hurt feelings or feelings of annoyance, often because someone has been rude or shown a lack of respect • *I really didn't mean (to* **cause/give***) any offence* (= did not intend to upset anyone) *– I was just stating my opinion.* • *Do you think he* **took** *offence* (= was upset) *at what I said about his hair?* • *(infml) If you don't mind I'd rather go on my own –* **no** *offence (intended), but I think it would be better.*

of·fend *(obj)* /ə'fend/ *v* • *I think she was a bit offended* **that** *she hadn't been invited to the party.* [T + obj + *that* clause] • *I won't describe the wonderful meat dishes that we had in France, because it might offend the vegetarians among us.* [T] • *He looked a bit offended when you called him middle-aged.* [T] • *If the sight of a few dirty dishes offends you then I think you've got problems!* [T] • *(fml)* If someone or something offends **against** a rule or principle, it goes against or breaks it: *Do you suppose it would be offending against good taste to wear a patterned tie with my striped shirt?* [I]

of·fen·sive /ə'fent·sɪv/ *adj* • Offensive means causing offence: *It said at the start of the broadcast that the interview contained language that some viewers might find offensive.* ○ *He told some really offensive racist and sexist jokes.* • Offensive can be used more generally to mean unpleasant: *Care is taken to remove any smells that might be offensive.*

of·fen·sive·ly /ə'fent·sɪv·li/ *adv*

of·fen·sive·ness /ə'fent·sɪv·nəs/ *n* [U]

of·fend·ing /ə'fen·dɪŋ/ *adj* [before n] *often humorous* unwanted, often because unpleasant and causing problems or inconvenience • *"There's a hair in my soup!" "Well, pass it over here and I'll remove the offending* **article**.*"*

of·fen·sive /ə'fent·sɪv/ *n* [C] a planned military attack • *They* **launched** *the land offensive in the middle of the night.* • If a side **takes the** offensive, it attacks first. • *UN troops have gone* **on the** *offensive* (= started to attack).

of·fen·sive /ə'fent·sɪv/ *adj* • *Since the other side had taken offensive action* (= attacked), *we had no choice but to defend ourselves.* • *It's against the law to carry knives – they're classed as offensive* **weapons**.

of·fer *(obj)* AGREE TO GIVE /£'ɒf·əʳ, $'ɑː·fɚ/ *v* to ask (someone) if they would like to have (something) or if they would like you to do something • *I feel really bad that I didn't offer them any food/offer any food* **to** *them.* [+ two objects] • *They're offering the first three runners money prizes/They're offering money prizes* **to** *the first three runners.* [+ two objects] • *She was offered a job in Paris/A job in Paris was offered* **to** *her.* [+ two objects] • *Can I offer you* (= Would you like) *a drink?* [+ two objects] • *"Would you sell me that painting?" "What are you offering* (= What will you pay) **for** *it?"* [T] • *My father has very kindly offered* **to** *take us to the airport.* [+ *to* infinitive] • *"I'll do the cooking for the party," he offered.* [+ clause] • *"I'll do that for you." "No thanks." "Well, don't say I didn't offer."* [I] • To offer **(up)** a prayer or a SACRIFICE is to give one to a god: *Dear Lord, we offer up our prayers...* [M] • Ⓕ Ⓢ

of·fer /£'ɒf·əʳ, $'ɑː·fɚ/ *n* [C] • *"If you like I can do some shopping for you." "That's a very kind offer."* • *I must say the offer* **of** *a weekend in Barcelona quite tempts me.* • *(infml) One day I'll* **take** *you* **up on** (= accept) *that offer.* • If you **make** or **put in** an offer **for** something, such as a house, you state that you will buy it at a particular price: *They were asking one hundred and eighty thousand for the place, so I put in an offer of one hundred and seventy.* • *(Br and Aus)* If goods in a shop are **on (special) offer**, they are being sold at a lower price than usual. • *(Br)* If a house is **under offer**, someone has already suggested a particular price at which they would be willing to buy it. • *"He's a businessman ... I'll make him an offer he can't refuse"* (in Mario Puzo's *The Godfather*, 1961)

of·fer·ing /£'ɒf·ᵊr·ɪŋ, $'ɑː·fɚ-/ *n* [C often pl] • An offering is something that is offered: *a religious/sacrificial offering*

of·fer *obj* PROVIDE /£'ɒf·əʳ, $'ɑː·fɚ/ *v* [T] to provide or supply (something) • *It's an organization that offers free legal advice to people on low incomes.* • *It says in the guide that this area of the countryside offers some of the best walks in England.* • *We are now offering you the chance to buy the complete set of pans at half price.* [+ two objects] • *Did he offer any explanation for his strange behaviour?* • *It doesn't* **have much to** *offer as a town – its shops are fairly poor and there's only one cinema.* • *"I have nothing to offer but blood, toil, tears and sweat (Sometimes 'blood, sweat and tears')"* (speech by Winston Churchill, 1940) • Ⓕ Ⓢ

off·hand NOT INTERESTED /£ˌɒf'hænd, $ˌɑːf-/, *Br infml* **off·ish** *adj* not friendly, and showing lack of interest in other people in a way that seems slightly rude • *I hope I didn't appear offhand* **with** *her – it's just that I was in such a hurry.*

off·hand·ed·ly /£ˌɒf'hæn·dɪd·li, $ˌɑːf-/ *adv*

off·hand·ed·ness /£ˌɒf'hæn·dɪd·nəs, $ˌɑːf-/ *n* [U]

off·hand INFORMAL /£ˌɒf'hænd, $ˌɑːf-/ *adj* not formal; relaxed • *He has a very offhand approach to office management.* • *It was the sort of offhand remark that could be thought of as racist.*

off·hand IMMEDIATELY /£ˌɒf'hænd, $ˌɑːf-/ *adv* without looking for information and without thinking carefully; immediately • *I can't quote the exact statistics for you offhand, but they're there for you to see in the report.*

of·fice WORK ROOM /£'ɒf·ɪs, $'ɑː·fɪs/ *n* [C] a room or part of a building in which people work, esp. sitting at tables with computers, telephones etc., usually as a part of a business or other organization • *the director's office* • *an office chair* • *office equipment* • *office clothes* (= clothes suitable for the office) • *I didn't leave the office until eight o'clock last night.* • *The sandwich bars are mainly used by office* **workers**. • An office can also be a part of a company: *They've got offices in Paris, London and Madrid.* • Office (also **doctor's office**) is *Am for* SURGERY ADVICE. • An *(Br and Aus)* **office block**/*(Am)* **office tower**/*(Am)* **office building** is a large building in which there are several offices. • *(Br and Aus)* **Office hours** are the hours during the day when people who work in offices are usually at work: *I'll have to do it* **outside/out of** (= before or after) *office hours.* • *(Br)* An **office junior** is a young person, often one who has recently left school, who works in an office doing mainly unskilled jobs. • PIC〉 **Office** (KOR)

Of·fice GOVERNMENT DEPARTMENT /£'ɒf·ɪs, $'ɑː·fɪs/ *n* [C] (in Britain) a department of the national government, or an official government organization • *the Home Office* • *the Foreign Office* • *the Office of Fair Trading* • *the Office of Data Protection*

of·fice RESPONSIBILITY /£'ɒf·ɪs, $'ɑː·fɪs/ *n* a position of authority and responsibility in a government or other organization • *the office of vice-president* • *As chairman of the association, he* **held** *office for over twenty years.* [U] • *The socialist party have been* **in** *office* (= governing)/**out of** *office* (= not governing) *for almost ten years.* [U] • *She's held various offices during her time as a minister.* [C]

of·fi·cer /£'ɒf·ɪ·səʳ, $'ɑː·fɪ·sɚ/ *n* [C] • An officer is a person in the armed forces who has a position of authority: *a senior officer* • *a naval officer* • *a top-ranking officer* • An officer is also a person who has a position of authority in an organization, esp. a government organization: *a careers/customs/personnel officer* • A member of the police force might also be addressed as 'officer': *"Were you aware of the speed you were driving at, madam?" "No, officer."* [as form of address] ○ *(Am) Officer Clarke will show you where to go, sir.*

of·fi·cial /ə'fɪʃ·ᵊl/ *n* [C] • An official is a person who has a position of responsibility in an organization: *a government/trade-union/council official*

of·fi·cial /ə'fɪʃ·ᵊl/ *adj* • Official means relating to a position of responsibility: *He visited China in his official capacity as America's trade representative.* ○ *Number Ten Downing Street is the British prime minister's official residence.* • Official also means agreed to or arranged by people in positions of authority: *The official photos of the Prime Minister's tour of India are in the magazine.* ○ *The queen will attend the official opening of the theatre in June.* ○ *There is to be an official inquiry into the incident.* • If a piece of information is official, it has been announced publicly with authority: *Their engagement is now official.* ○ *Inflation has fallen below 2%, and that's official.* • *(Br)* An **official receiver** is a person who is instructed by the government to deal with the income and property of a company or a person after they have gone BANKRUPT (= are unable to pay their debts). • *(Br)* An **official secret** is a piece of information which is known only by the government and its employees: *She was accused of leaking* (= telling) *official secrets to the newspapers.* • The **Official Secrets Act** is a law in Britain that forbids government workers to make known particular information which could be used against the government: *They had stolen sensitive military documents and were charged under the Official Secrets Act.* ○ *She had to* **sign** *the Official Secrets Act when she started her new job.*

of·fi·cial·dom /ə'fɪʃ·ᵊl·dəm/ *n* [U] *disapproving* • Officialdom is used to refer to those people who have a position of authority, esp. in government, usually when they are preventing you from doing what you want to do or are slow or not effective.

of·fi·cial·ese /əˌfɪʃ·ᵊl'iːz/ *n* [U] *Am* • Officialese is the language often used in government documents which is formal and often difficult to understand.

of·fi·cial·ly /ə'fɪʃ·ᵊl·i/ *adv* • *The royal engagement was announced officially* (= with authority) *this morning.*

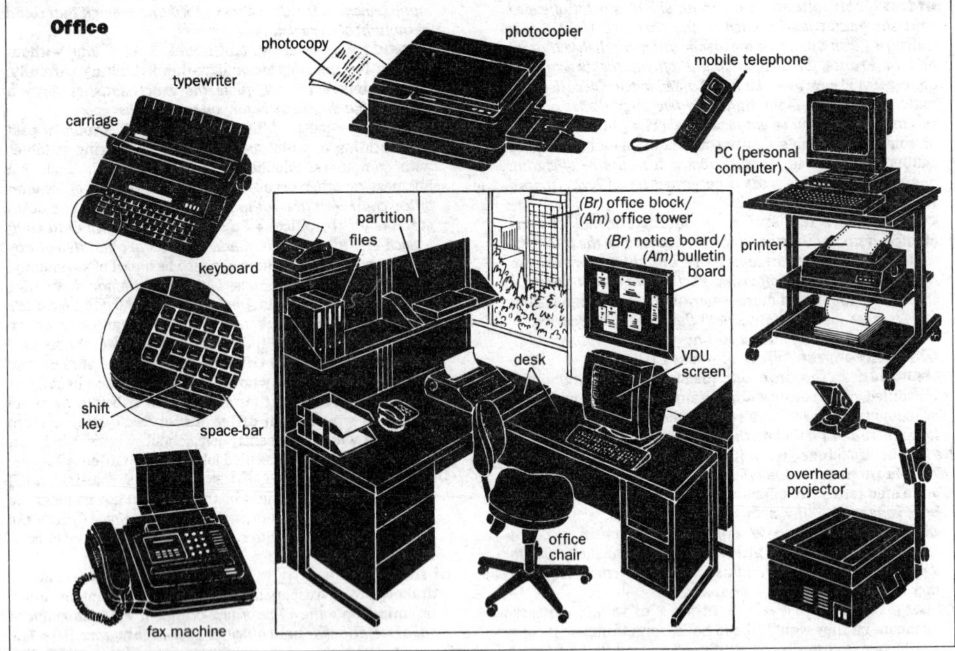

of·fi·ci·ate /ə'fɪʃ·i·eɪt/ *v* [I] *fml* • To officiate at a ceremony or other public event is to be in charge of or lead it: *A priest officiated* **at** *the wedding.* ○ *The same referee had officiated* **at** *both matches.*

of·fi·cious /ə'fɪʃ·əs/ *adj disapproving* too eager to tell people what to do and having too high an opinion of your own importance • *He's an officious little man and widely disliked in the company.*

of·fi·cious·ly /ə'fɪʃ·ə·sli/ *adv disapproving*

of·fi·cious·ness /ə'fɪʃ·ə·snəs/ *n* [U] *disapproving*

of·fing /£'ɒf·ɪŋ, $'ɑː·fɪŋ/ *n* [U] **in the offing** likely to happen soon • *With an election in the offing, the prime minister is keen to maintain his popularity.*

of·fish /£'ɒf·ɪʃ, $'ɑː·fɪʃ/ *adj Br* OFFHAND NOT INTERESTED; *(Am)* STANDOFFISH

off·load *obj* /£,ɒf'ləud, $,ɑːf'loud/ *v* [T] to get rid of something that you do not want by giving it to someone else • *I've managed to offload some of our old furniture* **onto** *a friend who's just moved into a new place.*

off·set *obj* /£,ɒf'set, $,ɑːf-/ *v* [T] **offsetting**, *past* **offset** to balance (one influence) against an opposing influence, so that there is no great difference as a result • *The extra cost of travelling to work is offset* **by** *the lower price of houses here.* • *(Br and Aus) He keeps his petrol receipts because petrol is one of the expenses that he can offset* **against** *tax* (= can show to the government as being a business cost, and so not pay tax on it).

off·shoot /£'ɒf·ʃuːt, $'ɑːf-/ *n* [C] something which has developed from something larger which already existed • *It's an offshoot* **of** *a much larger company based in Sydney.* • *The Gulf is a shallow offshoot* **of** *the Indian Ocean.*

off·shore AT SEA /£,ɒf'ʃɔːʳ, $,ɑːf'ʃɔːr/ *adj, adv* away from or at a distance from the coast • *offshore engineering* • *an offshore breeze* • *The wind was blowing offshore.*

off·shore IN A DIFFERENT COUNTRY /£,ɒf'ʃɔːʳ, $,ɑːf'ʃɔːr/ *adj* [not gradable] (of companies and banks) based in a different country with advantageous banking and tax rules • *offshore banking/funds*

off·side NOT ALLOWED /£,ɒf'saɪd, $,ɑːf-/ *adj, adv* (in particular sports, esp. football and HOCKEY) in a position which is not allowed by the rules of the game, often in front of the ball • *Coventry had a goal disallowed for (being) offside.*

off·side RIGHT SIDE /£'ɒf·saɪd, $'ɑːf-/ *adj* [before n; not gradable], *n esp. Br* (esp. of a part of a vehicle or road) on the right side • *The offside rear wheel needs replacing.* • *He got out of the car on* **the** *offside because the nearside door was broken.* [U]

off·spring /£'ɒf·sprɪŋ, $'ɑːf-/ *n* [C] *pl* **offspring** the young of an animal or *(humorous)* a person's children • *In the case of the guinea pig, the number of offspring varies between two and five.* • *(humorous) Tom's sister came round on Saturday with her numerous offspring.*

off·stage /£,ɒf'steɪdʒ, $,ɑːf-/ *adv, adj* [not gradable] happening behind or at the side of the stage, so that people who are watching cannot see • *He never actually appears in the second half of the play – you just hear his voice offstage.* • *He spoke the lines as he walked offstage* (= was leaving the stage). • *The main characters are offstage* (= do not appear on the stage) *for most of the second act.* • Offstage can also be used to refer to a performer when they are not performing: *Though best known for the funny and outspoken roles that she plays on screen, offstage she is shy and rather serious.*

oft /£ɒft, $ɑːft/ *adv* [not gradable] *old use or fml* often • *(fml) The only comfort he could offer was that oft-***repeated** *cliché, 'Time heals'.*

of·ten /£'ɒf·tᵊn, $'ɑːf·t̬ᵊn/ *adv* frequently; many times • *I often wonder what he's really thinking.* • *How often do you wash your hair?* • *I don't often drink spirits.* • *It's not often that you meet someone who you're instantly attracted to.* • *I see my parents about once a month, but not as often as I'd like to.* • *Christmas is often mild and wet in this country.* • **As often as not** (= Most times) *when I make the effort to visit her, I wonder why I've even bothered.* • LP **Measurements**

o·gle *(obj)* /£'əu·gl̩, $'ou-/ *v* to look at (someone) with obvious sexual interest • *He's revolting – he ogles* **(at)** *every woman who walks past him.* [I] • *Stop ogling, Roz – for goodness sake show a little restraint!* [I]

o·gre /£'əu·gəʳ, $'ou·gɚ/ *n* [C] a large frightening character in children's stories who eats children, or *(infml)* a fierce and frightening person • *(infml) The headmaster at my junior school was a real ogre.*

oh EMOTION /£əu, $ou/ *exclamation* used to express a variety of emotions, such as surprise, disappointment and pleasure, often as a reaction to something someone has said • *"He's been married three times." "Oh, really? I didn't know that!"* • *"I'm afraid I can't come to the party." "Oh, that's a shame."* • *"Oh, you're so kind! Thank you very much."* • *"I'm sorry I forgot to ring you." "Oh, don't worry, honestly it doesn't matter."* • Oh is also used to introduce an idea that you have just thought of, or something that you have just remembered: *Oh, I've just thought of a problem.* ○ *Oh, and don't forget to lock the back door.* • Oh is also used with other expressions of disappointment, sadness, anger, annoyance, etc.: *oh dear* ○ *oh hell* ○ *oh damn*

oh NUMBER, **o** /£əu, $ou/ *n* [C] sometimes used in writing for the number zero • *My phone number is five, double oh, seven, six, six.* • LP **Zero**

ohm /£əʊm, $oʊm/ *n* [C] *specialized* the standard unit of electrical RESISTANCE

-o·hol·ic /£-əʊˈhɒl·ɪk, $-əˈhɑː·lɪk/ *combining form* -AHOLIC

OHP /£ˌəʊ·eɪtʃˈpiː, $ˌoʊ-/ *n* [C] *abbreviation for* **overhead projector**, see at OVERHEAD

oik /ɔɪk/ *n* [C] *Br slang disapproving* a man from a low social class whose rough behaviour and speech is offensive and shows lack of education and respect for other people • *In his latest film he plays a racist oik from the East End of London.*

oil /ɔɪl/ *n* any of several types of smooth thick sticky liquid, most of which burn easily and do not dissolve in water. They are obtained from animals and plants and from under the ground. • Oil is used as a fuel and also for making the parts in a machine move easily without sticking: *diesel/lubricating oil* [U] • Some types of oil are used in cooking and as a food: *cooking/olive/corn/vegetable/sunflower oil* [U] • Other types of oil are used to improve the appearance or quality of the skin or hair: *a bath/hair oil* [C/U] • Oil is another name for PETROLEUM, the black oil obtained from below the surface of the Earth from which PETROL comes: *drilling for oil* [U] • *Those two brothers of yours mix* **like oil and water** (= are not friendly with each other). • If a heating system is **oil-fired**, it uses REFINED oil (= that from which unwanted substances have been removed) as a fuel. • **Oil paint** is a thick type of paint with an oil base, used for painting pictures. See also **oils**. • An **oil painting** is a picture painted with oil paints: *(fig. Br and Aus usually humorous) He's* **no oil painting** (= He is not attractive)*!* • An **oil slick** is a layer of oil that is floating over a large area of the surface of the sea, usually because an accident has caused it to escape from a ship or container: *Oil slicks are generally an ecological disaster.* • An **oil tanker** is a ship which carries a large amount of oil. • An **oil well** is a hole made in the ground for the removal of oil. • See also WELL-OILED.

oil *obj* /ɔɪl/ *v* [T] • If you oil something, such as a machine, you put oil on it, often to make it work more easily without sticking: *I think I'll oil the hinge of that door to stop it from creaking.* • *(infml)* If you **oil the wheels**, you make it easier to complete what is being done, solve a problem, etc.

oil·y /ˈɔɪ·li/ *adj* **-ier, -iest** • An oily substance consists of or is similar to oil: *an oily liquid* • Oily also means covered in oil or containing a lot of oil: *an oily rag* • *oily fish* ○ *Black olives are too oily for me.* ○ *I've got an oily skin* (= it produces a lot of oil). • A person who is oily is so friendly and polite that it is unpleasant.

oils /ɔɪlz/ *pl n* • Oils are thick paints with an oil base, used for painting pictures: *Do you paint in oils or watercolours?*

oil·can /ˈɔɪl·kæn/ *n* [C] a container for oil, esp. one with a long thin tube for putting oil on machinery

oil·field /ˈɔɪl·fiːəld/ *n* [C] an area underground where there is a large amount of oil • *the North Sea/Saudi Arabian oilfields*

oil·man /ˈɔɪl·mən/ *n* [C] *pl* **-men** a man who owns or operates **oil wells** or who buys and sells oil • *He started off his career as a Texas oilman.*

oil·rig /ˈɔɪl·rɪg/ *n* [C] a large structure with equipment for removing oil from under the ground, esp. under the sea

oil·seed /ˈɔɪl·siːd/ *n* [U] any of a variety of seeds from cultivated crops which provide oil • *oilseed rape* • PIC› **Cereals**

oil·skin /ˈɔɪl·skɪn/ *n* cotton cloth which has a thin layer of oil on it to make it waterproof, or a piece of protective clothing made out of this cloth • *a hat made of oilskin* [U] • *The fishermen were all wearing oilskins* (= clothing made of this cloth). [C]

oink /ɔɪŋk/ *n* [C] *infml* (esp. in children's books) a written representation of the noise that a pig makes • *'Oink oink,' went the pig, 'moo moo' went the cow.*

oink /ɔɪŋk/ *v* [I] *infml*

oint·ment /ˈɔɪnt·mənt/ *n* a thick oily substance, usually containing medicine, which is put on the skin where it is sore or where there is an injury, in order to cure it • *eye ointment* [U] • *The hospital gave him some ointment to stop the cut from becoming infected.* [U]

o·kay AGREED, **OK** /£ˌəʊˈkeɪ, $ˌoʊ-, ˈ--/ *adj* [after v; not gradable], *exclamation infml* agreed or acceptable; ALL RIGHT AGREED • *Is it okay if I bring a friend to the party?* • *If it's okay* **by/with** *you, I'll leave the shopping till tomorrow.* • *"I'll take the car if you're not going to use it." "Okay."* • *I'll see you at six-thirty, okay?* • *"If you lend me ten pounds I promise I'll pay you back tomorrow." "OK, no problem."* • *I mean, OK* (= I accept that)*, I wasn't exactly polite to him, but I don't think I was that rude!*

o·kay *obj* (**okaying**, *past* **okayed**), **OK** (**OKing**, *past* **OKed**) /£ˌəʊˈkeɪ, $ˌoʊ-, ˈ--/ *v* [T] *infml* • *Have the committee okayed* (= agreed to) *your proposal?*

o·kay, OK /£ˌəʊˈkeɪ, $ˌoʊ-/ *n* [U] *infml* • **The okay** is permission: *He's* **got** *the okay to go ahead with his building project.*

o·kay SATISFACTORY, **OK** /£ˌəʊˈkeɪ, $ˌoʊ-, ˈ--/ *adj* [not gradable] *infml* in a satisfactory state or of a satisfactory quality; ALL RIGHT SATISFACTORY • *How's Paula? Is she okay after her fall yesterday?* • *Are you OK? You look a bit pale.* • *"Is everything OK with you?" "Yes, fine."* • *I'll just check that the car's okay – that was a bit of a bang!* • *Yeah, he's an okay bloke – I really quite like him.* • Okay is sometimes used to mean not bad but certainly not good: *"Did you have a good meal last night?" "It was okay, but I've had better."* ○ *Her voice is OK, but it's nothing special.* • LP› **Meeting someone**

o·kay, OK /£ˌəʊˈkeɪ, $ˌoʊ-/ *adv* [not gradable] *infml* • *Everything was going OK until the printer stopped working.* • *Did you sleep okay in that old bed?* • *I just phoned to make sure that you got there okay.*

o·kay EXPRESSION, **OK** /£əʊˈkeɪ, $oʊ-, ˈ--/ *exclamation infml* used as a way of showing that you are going to take action or start something new • *Okay, let's go.* • *Okay then, if you're ready we'll start.* • *(not standard)* Okay is sometimes used in the middle of a sentence as a way of pausing: *We saw these guys, okay, so we went up to them and started talking.*

oke·y–doke /£ˈəʊ·ki·dəʊk, $ˈoʊ·ki·doʊk/, **oke·y–doke·y** /£ˈəʊ·kiˌdəʊ·ki, $ˈoʊ·kiˌdoʊ-/ *exclamation infml for* OKAY AGREED

ok·ker /£ˈɒk·əʳ, $ˈɑː·kəʳ/ *n* [C] an OCKER

ok·ra /£ˈəʊ·krə, $ˈoʊ-/, *Br dated also* **la·dy's fin·gers**, *Am also* **gum·bo** *n* [U] a small thin green vegetable, that can be used to thicken soups and other dishes • PIC› **Vegetables**

old EXISTED MANY YEARS /£əʊld, $oʊld/ *adj* **-er, -est** having lived or existed for many years • *An old man and his dog walked slowly along the street.* • *I must be getting old – those few steps have left me quite out of breath.* • *"I was shocked by how old he looked." "Well, he isn't a young man any more, you know."* • *Now come on, you're old enough to tie your own shoelaces, Carlo.* • *Isn't he a bit old* **to** *be playing with toy soldiers?* [+ to infinitive] • *They've got a beautiful old farm house somewhere out in the country.* • *I prefer old furniture to new stuff.* • *He was driving a battered old car.* • *We're collecting old clothes for charity.* • *That's an old joke – I've heard it about a thousand times.* • *I think this cheese is a bit old* (= has existed for a long period of time) *judging by the smell of it.* • *He's* **as old as the hills** (= very old). • *(humorous)* The **oldest profession (in the world)** is PROSTITUTION (= the job of having sex for money). • **Old age** is the period in a person's life when he or she is old: *She got very depressed in (her) old age.* ○ *Loneliness is one of the major problems of old age.* • *(Br and Aus)* An **old age pension** (also **retirement pension, state pension,** *Am* **social security**) is the money that is paid regularly by the state to people who have reached an age when they can no longer work. • *(Br and Aus)* An **old age pensioner** (*abbreviation* **OAP**, *Am* **retiree**) is a person who regularly receives money from the state because they have reached an age when they are considered too old to work. • *(esp. Br infml)* An **old boy** is an old man or *(dated)* a way that some men address male friends that they have know for many years: *There was a poor old boy tottering across the road with a walking stick.* ○ *(dated) Come on, old boy, drink up.* [as form of address] • *(infml)* An **old buffer** is a foolish old man. • *(esp. Br infml)* An **old girl** is an old woman: *The poor old girl can't get out much these days.* • *(Am and Aus)* **Old growth** is trees that have been growing for a very long time: *New legislation will protect vast areas of old growth in the Pacific Northwest from the logging companies.* • Someone who is an **old hand** is very experienced and skilled in a particular area of activity: *We should be able to trust Silva to negotiate a good deal for us – he's an old hand* **at** *the game.* • *(disapproving)* Something which is **old hat** is not modern and is not considered exciting: *He may be old hat among the trendy younger generation, but his shows draw more viewers than any other comedian.* • *(slang)* People sometimes refer to their mothers, or men to their wives, as their **old lady**: *I haven't seen your old lady for months, Bill – what've you done with her?* • *(dated esp. disapproving)* An **old maid** is a **middle-aged** (= over 40) or old woman who is not married and has never had a sexual relationship. • *(slang)* People sometimes refer to their fathers, or women to their husbands, as their **old man**: *Thought I'd take* **the** *old man out for a drink tonight.* ○ *My old man says he's going to buy me a new washing-machine.* • An **old master** is a painting by a famous European artist of the past, esp. from the 13th to the 17th century. • **Old money** is used to refer to rich people whose families have been rich for a long time: *Much of big business is still controlled by old money.* ○ *She's from an old-money family who didn't think much of her choice of husband.* See also **old money** at OLD [FROM THE PAST]. • *(humorous dated)* **Old Nick** is another name for the Devil. • An **old people's home** is a place where old people can live together and be cared for when they are too weak or ill to take care of themselves. • *(infml)* An **old-timer** is an old man, or someone who has been or worked in a place for a long time. • An **old wives' tale** is a piece of advice or a theory, often related to matters of health, that was believed in the past but which we now know to be wrong. • *(disapproving)* If you describe a man as an **old woman**, you mean that he gets anxious over unimportant matters and details: *You know what an old woman Dave is – he nearly had a fit because he got a few specks of mud on his shoes!* • *"Old soldiers never die / They simply fade away"* (song written by J.Foley, 1920) • *"Ol' man river ...he keeps on rollin' along"* (from the song *Ol' Man River* by Oscar Hammerstein II, 1927) • See also ELDERLY. • [LP]> **Age**

old /£əʊld, $oʊld/ *pl n* • *A lot of services have been cut that particularly affect* **the old** (= old people).

ol·dish /£'əʊl·dɪʃ, $'oʊl-/ *adj* [not gradable] • A person or thing that is oldish is quite old: *I wouldn't say her parents are old – oldish, perhaps, but not old.*

old [OF AGE] /£əʊld, $oʊld/ *adj* **-er, -est** having a particular age • *How old is your father?* • *Rosie's six years old now.* [after n] • *It's not very dignified behaviour for a 54-year-old man.* [after n] • *He's a couple of years older than me.* [after n] • [LP]> **Measurements**

old [FROM THE PAST] /£əʊld, $oʊld/ *adj* [before n] **-er, -est** from a period in the past; FORMER [EARLIER] • *I saw my old English teacher last time I went home.* • *He's bought me a smart new camera to replace my old one.* • *That dreadful grey building is/was my old school.* • *You don't mind me keeping letters from my old boyfriend, do you?* • *In my old job I wasn't paid for days that I had to take off sick.* • A language which is described as Old comes from an early stage in its development: *Old French* • *Old English* • *(Br and Aus)* An **old boy/girl** of a particular school is a man/woman who went to school there as a child: *She is one of the school's most famous old girls.* ○ *We're having an old-boy reunion next Saturday.* • *(Br and Aus)* The **old-boy network** is the system by which men who went to the same school, esp. an expensive school, use their influence to help each other, esp. in their work, all through their adult lives: *He only got that job because he's part of the old-boy network.* • *(Am)* An **old-boy network** is also a group of men who have known each other for a long time and who are important and have influence, esp. in politics and business. • The **old country** is the country that a person or a person's family originally came from: *I think I'll stay in Australia for the rest of my life – I've no plans to go back to* **the** *old country.* • *(esp. disapproving)* Something that is **old-fashioned** is not modern, and belongs to or is typical of a time in the past: *old-fashioned clothes/ideas/words* • *(esp. disapproving)* If a person is **old-fashioned** they behave or think in a way that is not modern and is more typical of a time in the past: *She's a bit old-fashioned in her outlook.* • An **old flame** is a person that you loved or had a sexual relationship with in the past. • The **old guard** of an organization or society are those people who oppose change and whose beliefs and ideas belong to a period in the past: *Radical reform was, of course, opposed by the old guard.* • **Old money** is a type of money that is no longer used: *The equivalent of twenty-five pence* **in** *old money is five shillings.* See also **old money** at OLD [EXISTED MANY YEARS]. • If someone is described as **of the old school**, their ideas are traditional and old-fashioned. • The **old school tie** is used to refer to the system by which people, esp. men, who went to the same **public school** (= expensive school) use their influence to help each other, esp. in their work, through all their adult lives. • **The Old Testament** is one of the two main parts of the Christian Bible. It records the history of the Jewish people before the birth of Christ. Compare **New Testament** at NEW [DIFFERENT]. • *(esp. Am)* **Old-time** things are things from a long time ago: *old-time dancing* ○ *The church organ is similar to the ones used in old-time movie theaters.* ○ *The bar only opened recently but it has a real old-time atmosphere.* • If you do something **for old times' sake**, you do it in order to remember a happy time that you had in the past: *We should all meet up again – just for old times' sake.* • *(approving)* **Old-world** means belonging to or typical of a period in the past: *Much of the town centre retains its old-world* **charm**, *with buildings dating from Shakespeare's day.* ○ *He greeted us with old-world courtesy.* ○ Compare OLDE WORLDE. • The **Old World** is Asia, Africa and Europe.

old /£əʊld, $oʊld/ *n* [U] *literary* • *In days/stories* **of old** (= from the past), *a wizard lived in these hills.* • *(esp. Br) I know him* **of old** (= have known him for a very long time).

old [VERY FAMILIAR] /£əʊld, $oʊld/ *adj* [before n] **-er, -est** (esp. of a friend) known for a long time • *She's one of my oldest friends – we met at school.* • *(infml)* Old can also be used before someone's name when you are referring to or addressing them, as a way of showing that you know them well and like them: *There's old Sara working away in the corner.* ○ *I hear* **poor** *old Frank's lost his job.*

ol·den /£'əʊl·dᵊn, $'oʊl-/ *adj* [before n; not gradable] *old use or literary* from a long time ago • *We didn't have things like televisions and computers* **in the** *olden* **days**. • **In** *olden* **times**, *people didn't travel as much as they do nowadays.*

olde world·e /£ˌəʊl·di'wɜːl·di, $ˌoʊl·di'wɜːrl-/ *adj Br and Aus infml* old in a very noticeable or artificial way; (as if) preserved from the past • *The village is very pretty, but it's a bit too olde worlde and more of a museum than a thriving community.*

ol·die [SONG] /£'əʊl·di, $'oʊl-/ *n* [C] *infml* an old popular song • *Join me after the news for an hour of* **golden** *oldies from the sixties.*

ol·die [PERSON] /£'əʊl·di, $'oʊl-/ *n* [C] *infml* an old person • *His new movie is aimed at a young audience, but it could prove popular with the oldies as well.*

o·le·ag·i·nous /£ˌəʊ·li'ædʒ·ɪ·nəs, $ˌoʊ-/ *adj fml* extremely polite, kind or helpful in a false way that is intended to benefit yourself • *In his latest film, he plays an oleaginous advertising executive who is prepared to do almost anything to further his career.*

o·le·an·der /£ˌəʊ·li'æn·dəʳ, $ˌoʊ·li'æn·dɚ/ *n* [C/U] an evergreen Mediterranean tree or bush with strong leaves and white, red or pink flowers • *The council has decided to uproot poisonous oleander shrubs from city parks.*

ol·fac·to·ry /£ɒl'fæk·tᵊr·i, $ɑːl'fæk·ter·i/ *adj* [before n; not gradable] *specialized* connected with the ability to smell • *Damage to the olfactory nerves can result in the loss of the sense of smell.*

ol·ig·ar·chy /£'ɒl·ɪ·gɑː·ki, $'ɑː·lɪ·gɑːr-/ *n* (government by) a small group of powerful people • *Do you think oligarchy is preferable to dictatorship?* [U] • *The oligarchy* (= group of people) *that controls the region is/are well-known for their radical views.* [C + sing/pl v]

ol·ive /£'ɒl·ɪv, $'ɑː·lɪv/ *n* [C] a small bitter oval fruit used in cooking and medicine, or an evergreen Mediterranean tree on which this fruit grows • *Olives turn from green to black as they ripen.* • *We had a wonderful view of the olive* **groves** *from our hotel.* • An **olive branch** is something that is said or done to express a desire for an end to a disagreement, argument or war: *After winning the leadership election she* **held out** *an olive branch to the other candidates by offering them senior positions in the party.* • *(Am)* **Olive drab** is a greyish green colour that is often used for military uniforms. • **Olive green** is the colour of olives that are not ripe. • **Olive oil** is a yellow or green oil obtained by pressing ripe olives: *Mix olive oil and vinegar to make a salad dressing.* ○ *The best type of olive oil is* **extra virgin**, *which is also the greenest.*

-ol·o·gy [SCIENTIFIC STUDY] /£-'ɒl·ə·dʒi, $-'ɑː·lə·dʒi/ *combining form* the scientific study of a particular subject • *geology* • *climatology*

-ol·og·i·cal /£-ə'lɒdʒ·ɪ·kᵊl, $-'lɑː·dʒɪ-/ *combining form* • *biological* • *technological*

-ol·o·gist /£-'ɒl·ə·dʒɪst, $-'ɑː·lə-/ *combining form* • *archaeologist*

ol·o·gy [SUBJECT] /£'ɒl·ə·dʒi, $'ɑː·lə-/ *n* [C] *infml* a subject that is studied at school, college or university and is thought to need an unusually large amount of specialist knowledge • *"What's his new girlfriend studying?" "Oh, some ology or other. Pharmacology, I think."*

Ol·ym·pi·ad /£əʊ'lɪm·pi·æd, $oʊ-/ *n* [C] an occasion on which the Olympic Games are held • *The XXV Olympiad* *was held in Barcelona in 1992.* • *She has competed in three Olympiads.*

Ol·ym·pi·an /£əʊˈlɪm·pi·ən, $oʊ-/ *adj* [not gradable] *literary* having the qualities of a god • *She has maintained an Olympian* **detachment** *from* (= avoided being involved with and worried by) *the everyday business of the office.* • *It will be an Olympian* **feat** (= a very great achievement) *if they finish building the tunnel before the end of the year.* • See also **Olympian** at OLYMPICS.

Ol·ym·pics /əˈlɪm·pɪks/, **Ol·ym·pic Games** *pl n* a set of international sporting competitions that take place once every four years • *The Olympic Games are held in a different country on each occasion.* • *The 1992* **Summer** *Olympics were held in Barcelona and the* **Winter** *Olympics were held in Albertville.* • *He won a gold medal at the Helsinki Olympics in 1952.*

Ol·ym·pic /£əʊˈlɪm·pɪk, $oʊ-/ *adj* [before n; not gradable] • *The Olympics are governed by the International Olympic Committee.* • *Her swimming coach is an Olympic gold* **medallist**. • *Tessa Sanderson is a former Olympic javelin* **champion**.

Ol·ym·pi·an /£əʊˈlɪm·pi·ən, $oʊ-/ *n* [C] *esp. Am* • An Olympian is a competitor in the Olympic Games: *A three-time Olympian is someone who has competed in three sets of Olympic Games.* • See also OLYMPIAN.

om·buds·man /£ˈɒm·bʊdz·mən, $ˈɑːm·bədz-/ *n* [C] *pl* **-men** someone who works for a government or large organization and deals with the complaints made against it • *Complaints to the Banking Ombudsman grew by 50 per cent last year.* • *The ombudsman's* **report** *condemns the time taken by some insurance companies to settle the claims of their customers.*

ome·lette, *Am also* **ome·let** /£ˈɒm·lət, $ˈɑː·mə·lət/ *n* [C] a savoury dish made by mixing together the yellow and transparent parts of an egg and frying it, usually with small pieces of other food • *"Do you fancy a mushroom omelette for lunch?" "I'd prefer a plain one, actually."* • *(saying)* 'You can't make an omelette without breaking (a few) eggs' means that it is hard to achieve something successfully without someone being hurt or upset.

o·men /£ˈəʊ·mən, $ˈoʊ-/ *n* [C] something that is considered to be a sign of how a future event will take place • *England's victory over France is a* **good** *omen* **for** *next week's match against Germany.* • *There is no famine at present, but the omens* **for** *the winter are not good and many people will face starvation.* • *The delay at the airport was a* **bad** *omen* **for** *our holiday.* • *Many people believe that a broken mirror is an omen* **of** *bad luck.*

om·i·nous /£ˈɒm·ɪ·nəs, $ˈɑː·mə-/ *adj* • Something that is ominous suggests that something unpleasant is likely to happen: *The by-election result has ominous* **implications** *for the government.* ○ *The company's disappointing sales figures are an ominous* **sign** *of worse things to come.* ○ *There was an ominous* **silence** *when I asked whether my contract was going to be renewed.* ○ *The engine had been making an ominous* **sound** *all the way from London, so I wasn't surprised when the car broke down.*

om·i·nous·ly /£ˈɒm·ɪ·nə·sli, $ˈɑː·mə-/ *adv* • *I went into the kitchen and found him lying ominously still on the floor.*

o·mit *(obj)* /£əʊˈmɪt, $oʊ-/ *v* **-tt-** to fail to include or do (something) • *I would be very cross if I were omitted* **from** *the list of contributors to the report.* [T] • *The Princess's tour conveniently omitted the most deprived areas of the city.* [T] • *She omitted* **to** *mention she was going to Yorkshire next week.* [+ *to* infinitive]

o·mis·sion /£əʊˈmɪʃ·ən, $oʊ-/ *n* • *Measures to control child employment are a* **glaring** *omission* **from** *new legislation to protect children.* [C] • *There are some serious errors and omissions in the book.* [C] • *Many of the fans believe that the omission* **of** *Heacock* **from** *the team cost England the match.* [U]

om·ni- /£ˈɒm·ni-, $ˈɑːm·ni-/ *combining form* everywhere or everything • *An omnidirectional microphone picks up sounds coming from every direction.*

om·ni·bus BOOK OR PROGRAMME /£ˈɒm·nɪ·bəs, $ˈɑːm-/ *n* [C] a book or *(Br)* programme consisting of two or more parts that have already been published or broadcast separately • *Martha gave me a Virginia Woolf omnibus for my birthday.* • *(Br) Do the viewing figures for a soap opera include the omnibus* **edition** *as well as the original broadcasts?* • Compare ANTHOLOGY.

om·ni·bus TRANSPORT /£ˈɒm·nɪ·bəs, $ˈɑːm-/ *n* [C] *old use* a bus • *a horse-drawn omnibus* • *(Br dated)* The **man/woman on the Clapham omnibus** is an imaginary person whose opinions or ideas are considered to be typical of those of ordinary British people: *He can't win the election without the support of the man and woman on the Clapham omnibus.*

om·nip·o·tent /£ɒmˈnɪp·ə·tənt, $ɑːmˈnɪp·ə·t̬ənt/ *adj* [not gradable] having enough power to be able to do anything that is desired • *He is behaving more like an omnipotent dictator than a president who could be voted out of office.* • *Until his illness, I'd always thought of my father as omnipotent.*

om·nip·o·tence /£ɒmˈnɪp·ə·tənts, $ɑːmˈnɪp·ə·t̬ənts/ *n* [U]

om·ni·pres·ent /£ˌɒm·nɪˈprez·ənt, $ˌɑːm-/ *adj* [not gradable] *slightly fml* present or having an effect everywhere at the same time • *She's been omnipresent in the media since the song went to number one in the charts.*

om·ni·pres·ence /£ˌɒm·nɪˈprez·ənts, $ˌɑːm-/ *n* [U] • *The omnipresence of the secret police made it impossible to do anything without the authorities finding out.*

om·ni·sci·ent /£ɒmˈnɪs·i·ənt, $ɑːmˈnɪʃ·ənt/ *adj* having or seeming to have unlimited knowledge • *Medical knowledge has expanded so much over the past century that it's impossible for doctors to be omniscient.*

om·ni·sci·ence /£ɒmˈnɪs·i·ənts, $ɑːmˈnɪʃ·ənts/ *n* [U]

om·niv·o·rous /£ɒmˈnɪv·ər·əs, $ɑːmˈnɪv·ɚ-/ *adj* [not gradable] naturally able to eat both plants and meat • *Pigs are omnivorous animals.* • *(fig.) Georgina's an omnivorous* **reader** (= reads a lot of different types of literature).

om·ni·vore /£ˈɒm·nɪ·vɔːʳ, $ˈɑːm·nɪ·vɔːr/ *n* [C] • *Surely it's better to be an omnivore and eat a variety of plants and animals in case there's a shortage of one particular type of food.* • Compare CARNIVORE, HERBIVORE.

on ABOVE /£ɒn, $ɑːn/ *prep* used to show that something is in a position above something else and touching it, or that something is moving into such a position • *There are too many books on my desk.* • *Ow, you're standing on my foot!* • *I think your suitcase is on top of the wardrobe.* • *They live in that old farmhouse on the hill.* • *Put your cup on the saucer, not on the table.* • *I was so drunk that I fell over as I was getting on my bike.*

on CONNECTED /£ɒn, $ɑːn/ *prep* covering the surface of, being held by, or connected to • *If you aren't the murderer then how did you get that blood on your shirt?* • *You shouldn't run around without any shoes on your feet.* • *Which finger are you supposed to wear your wedding ring on?* • *I've never been able to stand on my head.* • *We could hang this picture on the wall next to the door.* • *Could you help me put the washing on the line.* • *Dogs should be kept on their leads at all times.* • *(Br and Aus) We've just moved house and we're not on the phone* (= not connected to the telephone service) *yet.* • *Don't disturb Martha. She's on* (= using) *the phone.* • *Some people's voices are hard to recognise on the phone.* • *What's* **on** *your* **mind**? (= What are you worrying about?) • **On-board** things are things that are carried by a vehicle and form part of it: *In the future, cars equipped with on-board* **computers** *will be able to detect and avoid traffic jams automatically.* • Something that is **on-line** is connected to a system: *Working on-line is sometimes slower than when the computer is not connected to the network.* ○ *If your computer is equipped with a modem you can use an on-line information service to keep up to date with developments.* ○ *The new power station is expected to be on-line by the end of next year.* • Something that is **on-screen** appears on a television or computer screen: *Her on-screen husband is also her partner in real life.*

on /£ɒn, $ɑːn/ *adv, adj* [after v; not gradable] • *It's very cold outside, so put a jumper on.* • *They like wandering about the house with nothing on.* • *Can you remember what he had on?* • *I tried on a few jackets, but none of them really suited me.* • *Surgeons have managed to sew the man's ear back on after it was bitten off in a fight.* • *I wish you wouldn't screw the lid on so tightly.* • *Make sure the top's on properly.*

on WRITING /£ɒn, $ɑːn/ *prep* used to show where something has been written, printed or drawn • *Who drew that silly picture on the blackboard?* • *Which page is that curry recipe on?* • *His initials were engraved on the back of his watch.* • *What's on the menu* (= What food is available) *tonight?*

on RECORDING/PERFORMANCE /£ɒn, $ɑːn/ *prep* used to show the form in which something is recorded or performed • *"Is this recording available on cassette?" "No, I'm afraid you can only buy it on CD."* • *How much data can you store on a floppy disk?* • *When's the movie coming out on video?* • *I was really embarrassed the first time I saw myself* *on film.* • *I enjoy my television work, but I prefer acting on stage.* • *What's on television tonight?* • *I wish there was more jazz on the radio.*

on PERFORMING /£ɒn, $ɑːn/ *adv, adj* [after v; not gradable] performing • *Hurry up with the make-up – I'm on in ten minutes.* • *The audience cheered as the band went on* (= went onto the stage). • *(Am) The band was really on* (= performed very well) *tonight.* • *(fig. Am) Living in a foreign country requires you to be on* (= aware of the surroundings and often being watched) *for most of the time.*

on PAIN /£ɒn, $ɑːn/ *prep* used to show what causes pain or injury as a result of being touched • *I hit my head on the shelf as I was standing up.* • *You'll cut yourself on that knife if you're not careful.* • *I stung myself on some nettles as I was sitting down.*

on TO /£ɒn, $ɑːn/ *prep* to or towards • *Our house is the first on the left after the post office.* • *The attack on the village lasted all the night.* • *Her dog suddenly turned on me and chased me down the street.* • *I wish you wouldn't creep up on me like that.*

on RELATING /£ɒn, $ɑːn/ *prep* relating to • *Did you see that documentary on volcanoes last night?* • *Susannah's thesis is on Italian women's literature.* • *There will be a parliamentary debate on the crisis tomorrow, but MPs will not be voting on it.* • *The minister has refused to comment on the allegations.* • *Criticism has no effect on him.* • *Have the police got anything on you* (= have they got any information about you which can be used against you)*?* • *My new bike* **has nothing/does not have anything on** (= is not nearly as good as) *the one that was stolen.* • **On-the-job** activities are things that happen while someone is working: *I had no formal qualifications when I started working here so I was given on-the-job* **training**. ○ *She didn't receive any compensation because her employer wasn't insured for on-the-job injuries.*

on MONEY /£ɒn, $ɑːn/ *prep* used to show something for which a payment is made • *Jonathan refuses to spend more than twenty pounds on a pair of shoes.* • *I've wasted a lot of money on this car.* • *I never bet more than a fiver on a horse.* • *We made a big profit on that deal.* • *How much interest are you paying on the loan?*

on NECESSARY /£ɒn, $ɑːn/ *prep* used to show a person or thing that is necessary for something to happen or that is the origin of something • *We're relying on you to find a solution to this problem.* • *Whether I buy a new house depends on me getting a pay increase.* • *Most children remain dependent on their parents while at university.* • *His new movie is based on a traditional fairy story.*

on NEXT TO /£ɒn, $ɑːn/ *prep* next to or along the side of • *Cambridge is on the River Cam.* • *Ann's new house is on the river.* • *Our house is on Sturton Street.* • *Strasbourg is on the border of France and Germany.* • *My parents live in Southend-on-Sea.* • *(fig.) His suggestion borders on the* (= is almost) *ridiculous.*

on TIME /£ɒn, $ɑːn/ *prep* used to show when something happens • *Many shops don't open on Sundays.* • *What are you doing on Friday?* • *I'm free on Saturday morning.* • *My birthday's on the 30th of May.* • *(slightly fml) Would you mind telling me what you were doing on the afternoon of Friday the 13th of March?* • *Trains to London leave on* **the hour** (= at exactly one o'clock, two o'clock etc.) *every hour.* • *On a clear day you can see the mountains from here.* • *She was dead on arrival* (= dead when she arrived) *at the hospital.* • *Please hand in your keys at reception on your departure from* (= when you leave) *the hotel.* • LP **Calendar**

on AFTER /£ɒn, $ɑːn/ *prep* happening after and usually because of • *Acting on information given to them anonymously, the police arrested him.* • *He inherited a quarter of a million pounds on his mother's death.* • *On receiving their letter I decided to make a donation to help their campaign.* • *On my arrival in Montpellier I found a job as an English teacher.* • *On their return they discovered that their house had been burgled.*

on TRAVEL /£ɒn, $ɑːn/ *prep* used for showing some methods of travelling • *I love travelling on buses.* • *She said she'd be arriving on the five-thirty train.* • *We went to France on the ferry.* • *We could go by car, but it's so difficult to park that it'd be quicker on foot.* • *They watched two figures on horseback move slowly across the horizon.*

on /£ɒn, $ɑːn/ *adv, adj* [after v; not gradable] • *The train suddenly started moving as I was getting on.* • *When you fall off a horse you should get back on immediately, otherwise you'll lose confidence.* • *Her horse galloped off as soon as she was on.*

on FOOD/ FUEL/ DRUG /£ɒn, $ɑːn/ *prep* used to show something which is used as food, fuel or a drug • *What do mice live on?* • *Does this radio run on batteries?* • *He behaves as though he's on drugs most of the time.* • *My doctor's put me on antibiotics to reduce the swelling in my knee.* • *I've been on the pill ever since I started having sex regularly.*

on FINANCIAL SUPPORT /£ɒn, $ɑːn/ *prep* used to show what is providing financial support or an income • *I've only got £50 a week to live on at the moment.* • *She's been living on welfare since her husband left her.* • *He retired on a generous pension from the company.* • *People on average salaries will be hit hardest by the tax increases.* • *(Br and Aus) She's on* (= earning) *£15 000 a year.*

on PROCESS /£ɒn, $ɑːn/ *prep* used to show that a condition or process is being experienced • *He was playing with matches and set his bed on fire.* • *When does your new range of televisions go on sale?* • *Their flights to Paris are on special offer at the moment.* • *Martin's on holiday this week.* • *I'll be away on a training course next week.* • *I often feel carsick when I'm on a long journey.* • *Crime is on the increase* (= is increasing) *again.* • *I'd been* **on the go** (= extremely busy) *all day, so I went to bed as soon as I got home.* • *(Br)* **On the go** also means in the process of being produced: *Did you know that she's got a new book on the go* (= being written).

on INVOLVEMENT /£ɒn, $ɑːn/ *prep* used to show when someone is involved or taking part in something • *I'm working on a new book.* • *She's out on a job for me, but she'll be back soon.* • *In the last lesson we were on the causes of the First World War, weren't we?* • *"Where had we got up to?" "We were on page 42."*

on MEMBER /£ɒn, $ɑːn/ *prep* used to show when someone is a member of a group or organization • *Have you ever served on a jury?* • *Why aren't there any women on the committee?* • *How many people are on your staff?* • *She's got herself a job as a researcher on a women's magazine.* • *I've worked on a farm all my life.* • *In a game of cricket there are eleven players on each side.* • *Whose side are you on in this argument?*

on AGAIN /£ɒn, $ɑːn/ *prep* used to show when something is repeated one or more times • *The government suffered defeat on defeat in the local elections.* • *Wave on wave of refugees has crossed the border to escape the fighting.*

on COMPARISON /£ɒn, $ɑːn/ *prep* used when making a comparison • *£950 is my final offer, and I can't improve on it.* • *The productivity figures are down on last week's.*

on POSSESSION /£ɒn, $ɑːn/ *prep* [before pronoun] used to show when someone has something with them in their pocket or in a bag that they are carrying • *Have you got a spare cigarette on you?* • *I thought I had my driving licence on me, but I must have left it at home.*

on PAYMENT /£ɒn, $ɑːn/ *prep infml* used to show who is paying for something • *This meal is on me. You deserve a treat.* • *You'll have to wait longer for your operation if you want it done on the National Health Service.*

on FAULTY /£ɒn, $ɑːn/ *prep* used to show who suffers when something does not operate as it should • *She was really worried when the phone went dead on her.* • *Their car broke down on them in the middle of the motorway.*

on TOOL /£ɒn, $ɑːn/ *prep* used when referring to a tool, instrument or system that is used to do something • *I do all my household accounts on computer.* • *Chris is on drums and Pat's on bass guitar.* • *Can you play that tune on the piano as well as the guitar?* • *We work on flexitime so I can take Friday off if I work longer hours the rest of the week.*

on NOT STOPPING /£ɒn, $ɑːn/ *adj* [after v], *adv* [not gradable] continuing or not stopping • *If her phone's engaged, keep on trying.* • *Stop talking and get on with your work.* • *Although the tax was abolished a few years ago, it has lived on in a modified form.* • *If Elise would just* **hang on** (= wait) *a little longer she'd certainly get the promotion.* • *The noise just went on* **and on** (= continued for a long time) *and I thought it would never stop.* • *We talked on* **and on** (= for a long time) *into the night.* • *(Br and Aus)* Someone who is **on about** something is talking about it, particularly for too long or in a boring way: *I never understand what she's on about.* • If you are *(Br and Aus)* **on at** someone (*Am* **on someone's case**), you speak to them in a complaining way and/or try to persuade them to do something: *My parents are always on at us* **about** *having a baby.* ○ *Sam's been on at me* **to** *give him a job.*

on MOVING FORWARD /£ɒn, $ɑːn/ *adj, adv* [after v; not gradable] in a way which results in forward movement • *You cycle on and I'll meet you there.* • *Just move on, please, and let the ambulance through.* • *We've lived here for five years and we feel it's time to move on.* • *When you've finished reading it would you pass it on to Paul?* • *(fig.) I'd never have managed this if my parents hadn't urged me on.* • *They never spoke to each other* **from that day** *on* (= after that day). • *It took longer to pack than I'd expected and it was* **well** *on* (= quite late) *in the morning when we eventually set off.* • *What are you doing* **later** *on?*

on POSITION /£ɒn, $ɑːn/ *adv* [not gradable] used when talking about the position of one thing compared with the position of another • *It's amazing nobody was injured because the two buses collided* **head** *on* (= the front parts of the buses hit each other). • *(Br and Aus) The bike hit our car* **side** *on* (= hit the side of the car rather than the front or back). • *(Br and Aus) It would be easier to get the bookcase through the doorway if we turned it* **sideways** *on* (= turned it so that one of its sides is at the front). • *(Br and Aus) It might fit better if you put it* **this way** *on* (= in this position).

on OPERATING /£ɒn, $ɑːn/ *adv, adj* [not gradable] used to show when something is operating or starting to operate • *Could you switch on the radio?* • *Would you turn the TV on?* • *This tap's jammed and I can't turn it on.* • *When you go out, leave the bedroom light on to scare off the burglars.* • *Is the central heating on? The house seems very cold.* • *Where's the on switch?* • LP **Switching on and off**

on HAPPENING /£ɒn, $ɑːn/ *adv, adj* [not gradable] happening or planned • *I'm busy tomorrow, but I've got nothing on the day after.* • *I've got a lot on at the moment and I can't spare any time for a holiday.* • *Is the party still on* **for** *tomorrow?* • *Food had to be rationed when the war was on.* • *Are there any good films on* (= being shown) *at the cinema this week?* • On can be used as is a way of expressing agreement to something happening: *"I'll give you fifty quid for your bike." "You're on!"* • *(esp. Br and Aus)* Something that is **not on** is unacceptable or not desirable and should not happen: *My boss expects me to stay late at the office and take work home with me as well. It's just not on!* • If something happens **on and off** or **off and on**, it does not happen all the time, and the periods between the times when it happens are of different lengths: *I've had toothache on and off for a couple of months.*

on POINTS /£ɒn, $ɑːn/ *prep Br and Aus* used to show the amount of points a person or team has in a competition • *Clive's team is on five points while Joan's is on seven.*

once ONE TIME /wʌnts/ *adv* [not gradable] one single time • *I went to France once, but I didn't like it very much.* • *We have lunch together once a month.* • **At once** means at the same time: *Don't all shout* **at once**. ○ *I can't do it* **all** *at once but I'll have it finished by the end of the week.* • **(Just) for once** (= On this occasion, even if on no other occasion), *I wish you'd listen to what I'm telling you.* • **For once** (= It is not usual, but this time), *Clare offered to buy me a drink.* • *Would you mind driving me to work* **just this once** (= on this particular occasion and not on any other)? • *An opportunity as good as this arises* **once in a lifetime** (= very rarely). • *Our trip to Australia is going to be a* **once-in-a-lifetime** *experience.* • **Once again** (= Again and as has happened in the past) *racist attacks are increasing across Europe.* • Something that is done **once and for all** is done completely and as a final solution to a problem: *Our intention is to destroy their offensive capability once and for all.* ○ *I'm fed up with discussing this and I wish we could just settle this argument once and for all.* ○ *We need to find a* **once-and-for-all** *solution to the debt problem of developing countries.* • **(Every) once in a while** (= Sometimes) *a film is made which seems destined to win every award there is.* • *We see each other* **(every) once in a while**, *but not as often as we used to.* • *I'd like to go to Egypt* **once more** (= one more time) *before I die.* • *I'm pleased that Daniel's working with us* **once more** (= again and as he did in the past). • The expression **once or twice** means a few times: *I've only had a cigarette once or twice in my whole life.* ○ *She goes swimming once or twice a month.* • **Once upon a time** means a long time ago, and is often used at the beginning of stories for children: *Once upon a time a farmer planted a little seed in his garden, and after a while it sprouted and became a vine.* • **Once upon a time** can also be used in a slightly literary way when referring to something that happened in the past, particularly when expressing regret that it no longer happens: *Once upon a time* (= There was a time when) *everyone knew the difference between right and wrong, but nowadays nobody seems to care.* • *I've only played rugby* **the once** (= on a single occasion), *and I never want to play it again.* • *(infml)* A **once-over** is a brief and not very detailed examination of something: *I* **gave** *the bike a once-over in the shop and I didn't realize the lights weren't working until I got it home.* ○ *The security guards* **gave** *me* **the** *once-over, but they didn't ask me for any identification.* • *(infml)* A **once-over** is also a brief act of cleaning or preparing something: *Would you mind* **giving** *the living-room carpet a once-over* **with** *the vacuum cleaner?* ○ *It's worth* **giving** *the wood a once-over* **with** *a sander before you varnish it.* • LP **One**

once PAST /wʌnts/ *adv* [not gradable] in the past, but not now • *I lived in France once, but now I'm living in Italy.* • *Computers are much cheaper nowadays than they once were/than they were once/(fml) than once they were.* • *A few kilometres from the crowded beaches of Spain's Mediterranean coast, many once-***thriving** *villages stand deserted and in ruins.*

once AS SOON AS /wʌnts/ *conjunction* as soon as, or from the moment when • *Once you've been to Iceland you'll understand why I like it so much.* • *The journey there was terrible, but once we'd arrived we had a wonderful time.* • *Remember that you won't be able to cancel the contract once you've signed.* • *Do you want me to phone him* **at once** (= immediately) *or should I wait until later?* • *He seemed to be perfectly all right, and then* **all at once** (= suddenly) *he started coughing violently and fell to the floor.* • *(saying)* 'Once bitten, twice shy' means that if something you did had a bad result in the past, you are often unwilling to take a similar risk again.

oncogene /£'ɒŋ·kəʊ·dʒiːn, $'ɑːn·kə-/ *n* [C] a GENE that is present in every cell and causes a healthy cell to become CANCEROUS (= causing diseased cell growth) under particular conditions

on·col·o·gy /£ɒŋ'kɒl·ə·dʒi, $ɑːn'kɑː·lə-/ *n* [U] the study and treatment of unusual growths in the body • *Oncology is an important part of the search for a cure for cancer.*

on·col·o·gist /£ɒŋ'kɒl·ə·dʒɪst, $ɑːn'kɑː·lə-/ *n* [C]

on·com·ing /£'ɒŋ,kʌm·ɪŋ, $'ɑːn-/ *adj* [before n; not gradable] moving towards you or approaching • *The car veered onto the wrong side of the road and collided with an oncoming truck.* • *There seemed to be no way of averting the oncoming crisis.*

one NUMBER /wʌn/ *n, determiner, pronoun* (the number) 1 • *One is the smallest whole number.* [U] • *Three ones are three.* [C] • *We have two daughters and one son.* • *She'll be one-year old tomorrow.* • *The number 1 111 101 in words is one million, one hundred and eleven thousand, one hundred and one.* • *Americans drive one third of the 400 million cars on the planet.* • *They bought two terraced houses next door to each other and turned them into one.* • *Four parcels came this morning, but only one was for Mark.* • *(Br and Aus infml dated) "When he told me I couldn't have the job, I told him I never really wanted it in the first place." "Ooh, you are* **a one** (= someone who shows a lack of respect or is rude in an amusing way)*."* • *(literary) The news of his resignation came as a surprise to* **one and all** (= everyone). • *(fml) We have discussed the matter fully and are* **as one** (= in complete agreement) *on our decision.* • *(fml) We disagree on most things, but on this question we are* **at one** (= we completely agree) **with** *each other.* • *They rest of you may disagree, but I,* **for one** (= even if you do not), *think we should proceed with the plan.* • *He thinks it's really cool to drink a pint of beer down* **in one** (= all at the same time). • *With this model you get a radio, CD player and cassette deck* **(all) in one** (= combined in a single thing). • *(infml) I threatened to* **land/sock** *him* **one** (= hit him) **(on** *the jaw) if he insulted me again.* • Things that happen **one after another/one after the other** happen one at a time in a series: *I can happily eat chocolates one after the other until the box is finished.* ○ *One politician after another has promised to support our campaign, but none of them has done anything yet.* • *I've only had* **one or two** (= a few) *cigarettes in my whole life.* • *We expected a flood of applications for the job, but we're only receiving them* **in ones and twos** (= in small amounts). • **A hundred/thousand/million and one** means very many: *I can't stand around chatting – I've got a hundred and one things to do this morning.* ○ *There's a thousand and one ways of persuading people to give you money.* • To be **one of** a group of people or things is to be a member of that group: *The money was here this morning so one of you must have taken it.* ○ *One of our daughters has just got married.* ○ *Paula's had*

WORDS WITH THE MEANING 'ONE'

counting one thing or person

Pete started his **first** *job last week.*
He was the **first** *to arrive.*
I don't have a **single** *free moment today.*
Maths is the **only** *subject I really like.*
Larry was the **only one** *to write to me.*
He was the **sole/only** *survivor of the crash.*
Lou is an **only** *child.*

counting one event

I've (only) been to Scotland **once**.
She phones her sister **once a week**.
Is this your **first** *time on a plane?*
I **first** *visited Peking in 1990.*
The **one/only** *time I went on a boat, I was sick.*

other adjectives and adverbs

Do you have a **single** *room with shower?*
How much is a (Br) **single**/*(Am)* **one-way** *ticket?*
Garry's still **single**: *I don't think he'll ever marry.*
Only half of all **lone** *mothers* (= mothers without a partner) *have a job.*
To play against a world champion is a **unique** *opportunity.*
I don't like living **alone**: *I feel very* **lonely**.
Four prisoners were put in **solitary** *confinement.*
He used to take long **solitary** *walks in the hills.*

verbs

Europe may soon be politically **unified**.
All the workers **united** *to try to save the company.*

Notice that **firstly** does not mean 'first in time', and is only used in lists: *Firstly . . . Secondly . . . Thirdly.*

another *one of her crazy ideas.* ○ *PolyGram is one of* **the (world's) largest** *record companies.* ○ *Luxembourg is one of* **the (world's) smallest** *countries.* ○ *Dr McKusick is one of* **the (world's) leading experts** *on human genetics.* ○ *Shirley Williams was one of* **the founders** *of the Social Democratic Party.* ○ *Finding a cure for cancer is one of* **the biggest challenges** *facing medical researchers.* ○ *Our organization is just one of* **many** *charities that are providing famine relief in the region.* ○ *We've known Albert for thirty years and he's become one of* **the family** (= he's become very close to us and is like a member of the family). • If you are **one up on** someone, you have an advantage that they do not have: *He's always trying to* **get** *one up on his brother.* • *(esp. Am and Aus)* A **one-armed bandit** is an old-fashioned type of **slot machine**. See at SLOT [LONG HOLE]. • Something that is **one-dimensional** has either height or width or length, but not two or all of these: *A line is one-dimensional, a square is two-dimensional, and a cube is three-dimensional.* • Something that is **one-dimensional** is boring or lacks variety: *The characters in his novels tend to be rather one-dimensional.* • If you do something **one-handed**, you use just one hand to do it: *He's injured his left arm and can only type one-handed.* • A **one-hit wonder** is performer of popular music who makes one successful recording but then no others. • A **one-horse race** is a race or competition which only one of the competitors has a real chance of winning: *This election has been a one-horse race right from the start.* • *(esp. Am and Aus)* A **one-horse town** is a town that is small and unimportant: *Santa Cruz was a one-horse town 20 years ago, but the drugs trade has helped turn it into a boom town.* • A **one-liner** is a joke or a clever and amusing remark or answer which is usually one sentence long: *The best bits of the film are the* **witty** *one-liners.* • A **one-man band** is a musician who performs alone, usually outside, carrying and playing several instruments at the same time: *(fig.) The organization seems to have become a one-man band with just one person making all the decisions.* • A **one-night stand** is a musical or theatrical performance that happens once in a particular place: *Steve and Andy are doing a one-night stand in Durham followed by a couple of nights in Newcastle.* • A **one-night stand** is also a sexual relationship which begins and ends on the same night or evening: *I'd rather have a long-term relationship than a series of one-night stands.* • A *(Br and Aus)* **one-off**/*(Am)* **one-shot** is something that happens or is made or done only once: *The Prime Minister described his party's defeat in the by-election as a one-off which would not be repeated in the general election.* ○ *They gave him a one-shot payment to compensate for the extra hours that he had to work.* • *(Am)* In sports, if something is done **one-on-one**, it means that each player from one team is matched to a single player from the other team: *The Knicks can shift from a zone defence to one-on-one at the drop of a hat.* See also **one-to-one** in this entry. • A **one-parent family** (also **single-parent family**) is a family which includes either a mother or a father but not both: *The increased number of divorces and children born outside marriage has led to the rise in one-parent families.* [LP]› **Relationships** • A **one-person/one-man/one-woman** play or show is a performance or show of artistic works by just one person: *This is the first time her one-woman show has been on television.* ○ *(fig.) For many years his business was a one-man show and he worked entirely on his own.* • A *(Br and Aus)* **one-piece**/*(Am usually)* **one-piece swimsuit** is an item of women's clothing that is worn when swimming or on a beach and consists of a single piece of material rather than a separate top and bottom: *Their range of swimwear includes one-pieces and bikinis.* • If something is **one-sided**, it is not balanced, and one side has a big advantage over the other: *They blamed their defeat on the media's one-sided* **reporting** *of the election campaign.* ○ *His presentation of the evidence was one-sided and told only part of the story.* ○ *She alienated many members of the audience with the* **one-sidedness** *of her speech.* • *(esp. Am)* A **one-size-fits-all** piece of clothing is designed to fit a person of any size: *We only stock one-size-fits-all T-shirts.* ○ *(fig.) This is a one-size-fits-all solution which will satisfy no-one completely.* • A **one-star** hotel or restaurant is one which is not especially good but has achieved the lowest acceptable standard in an official quality test: *We used to stay in one-star* **hotels**, *but now we feel it's worth paying a bit extra for a two-star.* • **One-stop** activities involve stopping at a single place: *One-stop* **shopping** *for hardware and software has made buying a computer system as easy as buying a television.* ○ *We offer our customers one-stop banking services and investment advice.* • *She is a television presenter and* **one-time** (= was once but is no longer a) *journalist.* • Something that is in a **one-to-one** relationship with another thing strongly influences the way that the other thing changes: *Is there a one-to-one* **relationship** *between pay levels and productivity?* • A **one-to-one**/*(Am also)* **one-on-one** activity involves just two people working together: *These children have special educational needs and require one-to-one attention.* See also **one-on-one** in this entry. • Someone who has a **one-track mind** tends to think about one particular thing and nothing else: *People say I've got a one-track mind, but I am interested in things apart from sex.* ○ *She has a one-track mind and is only bothered about making money these days.* • *(Am)* If someone or something receives a **one-two punch**, two difficult things happen to them in a short time: *An earthquake and riots in the same week was a real one-two punch for the local community.* • **One-upmanship** or **one-upping** is an activity or skill which results in someone getting an advantage over someone else, or doing something better than them: *I'm fed up with Pat's oneupmanship and the way she always buys something slightly better than I've just bought.* • **One-way** describes something that travels or allows travel in only one direction: *She got a warning from the police for driving the wrong way down a one-way* **street**. ○ *(esp. Am) The one-way* **fare** *(Br and Aus usually A* **single**) *to Cambridge is £14·50.* ○ *(esp. Am) How much is a one-way* **(ticket)** *(Br and Aus usually a* **single**) *to New York?* ○ *(fig.) Rejection of the peace deal would be a one-way ticket to disaster.* ○ *(fig.) He didn't say much and it was a bit of a one-way conversation.* • *"One for the money, two for the show, three to get ready, now go, man, go."* (from the song *Blue Suede Shoes* sung by Elvis Presley and others, 1956) • [LP]› **One** [PIC]› **Road**

one [FUTURE TIME] /wʌn/ *determiner* at a time in the future which is not yet decided • *Why don't we meet for lunch one day next week?* • *I'd like to go to Berlin again* **one day** (= at some time in the future). • *I'd like to go skiing one Christmas.* • *We must have a drink together one evening.*

one [PARTICULAR OCCASION] /wʌn/ *determiner* used to refer to a particular occasion while avoiding stating the exact moment • *We first met each other one day in the park.* • *One night we stayed up talking till dawn.* • *He was attacked as he was walking home from work late one afternoon.* • *One moment he says he loves me, the next moment he's asking for a divorce.* • *She never seems to know what she's doing from one minute to the next.*

one [UNKNOWN PERSON] /wʌn/ *determiner fml* used before the name of someone who is not known • *There's one Caroline Howlett on the phone for you. Would you like me to take a message?* • *Her solicitor is one John Wintersgill.*

one [SINGLE] /wʌn/ *determiner, pronoun* not two or more • *Do you think five of us will manage to squeeze into* **the** *one car?* • *There's too much data to fit onto just* **the** *one disk. We'll need at least two.* • *Don't gobble them up all at once. Eat them one* **at a time** (= separately). • *I think we should paint the bedroom* **all** *one* (= in a single) *colour.* • **One by one** (= Separately and gradually) *the old buildings in the city have been demolished and replaced with modern tower blocks.*

one [ONLY] /wʌn/ *determiner* used when saying there is no other person or thing • *He's* **the** *one person you can rely on in an emergency.* • *This is* **the** *one type of computer that is easy to use for people who aren't experts.* • *This may be your one* **and only** (= only ever) *opportunity to meet her.* • *My final guest on tonight's show needs no introduction. Please welcome* **the** *one* **and only** *Michael Jordan* (= there is no other such person)*!*

one [COMPARISON] /wʌn/ *determiner, pronoun* used when making comparisons between similar things • *Paint one side, leave it to dry, and then paint the other.* • *He can't tell one wine from another, so don't give him any of the expensive stuff.* • *We can't afford to employ two secretaries. One or other of them will have to leave.* • *There is no evidence one way or the other about the effectiveness of the drug.* • *They look very similar and it's often difficult to distinguish one from the other until you actually taste them.* • *You may have one or the other, but not both.* • *Crime and freedom are inseparable. You can't have one without the other.* • *Everyone at the party was related in one way or another* (= in some way that is not stated). • *These bills have to be paid one way or another* (= in any way that is possible). • *We have to make a decision one way or another about what needs to be done.*

one [EMPHASIS] /wʌn/ *determiner esp. Am* used to emphasize an adjective • *His mother is one* (= a very) *generous woman.* • *That's one* (= a very) *big ice-cream you've got there.* • *It was one hell of a* (= a very great) *shock to find out I'd lost my job.*

one [PARTICULAR THING/PERSON] /wʌn/ *pronoun* used to refer to a particular thing or person within a group or range of things or people that are possible or available • *I've got a few books on Chinese food. You can borrow one if you like.* • *Which one would you like?* • *Would you make a copy for everybody in the office and a few extra ones for the visitors.* • *Could I have those ones, please?* • *"Which cake would you like?" "The one at the front."* • *I'd rather eat French croissants than English ones.* • *There were lots of people standing watching, and not one of them offered to help.* • *I've received no replies to my job applications – not a single one* (= none). • *Chris is the one* (= the person) *with curly brown hair.* • *Viv was running around* **like** *one* (= a person) *possessed before the presentation.* • One can also be used to mean the type of person: *You're not usually one* **who** *complains about the service in a restaurant.* ○ *He's always been one* **that** *enjoys good food.* ○ *I've always been active and never really been one* **to** *sit around doing nothing.* [+ *to* infinitive] ○ *He's never one* **to** *say no to* (= He never refuses) *a curry.* [+ *to* infinitive] • *(infml)* If you are **(a)** one **for** something you like it or do it a lot: *She was never a one for playing hockey.* [+ *v-ing*] ○ *He's a* **great** *one for telling other people what to do.* [+ *v-ing*] ○ *I'm* **not much of** *a one for chocolate* (= I do not like it very much). • *"What's the capital of Zaire?" "Oh, that's a difficult one* (= question)*."* • *That's a* **good** *one* (= That is a very amusing joke). • *Have you heard* **the one about** (= the joke about) *the Italian, the American and the Australian?* • **One another** means EACH OTHER. • If someone or something is **one of a kind** there is no other person or thing like them: *In the world of ballet she was certainly one of a kind as a dancer.* Compare **two of a kind** at TWO.

one [ANY PERSON] /wʌn/ *pronoun fml* any person, but not a particular person • *One has an obligation to one's friends.* • *One ought to make the effort to vote.* • *What ought one to do when a beggar asks one for money?* • *Disasters such as this make one ask oneself what one can possibly do to help.* • If you use 'one' with this meaning, it will seem that you are formal or old-fashioned or that you think you are very important, so 'you' is usually used instead.

one [I OR ME] /wʌn/ *pronoun fml* the person speaking or writing • *One* (= I) *tried to warn him but he simply refused to listen.* • *Of course, one would be delighted to dine with the Queen.* • If you use 'one' with this meaning, it will seem that you are very formal or that you think you are very important, so 'I' is usually used instead.

on·er·ous /£ˈəʊ·nᵊr·əs, £ˈɒn·ᵊr-, $ˈɑː·nɚ-/ *adj fml* difficult to do or needing a lot of effort • *The* **task** *of finding a peaceful solution is almost too onerous to bear.* • *We intend to remove the onerous rules and regulations that are discouraging foreign investment in our country.*

on·er·ous·ness /£ˈəʊ·nᵊr·ə·snəs, £ˈɒn·ᵊr-, $ˈɑː·nɚ-/ *n* [U] *fml*

one·self [SAME PERSON] /ˌwʌnˈself/ *pronoun fml* used to refer to the object of a verb or preposition which is the same person as a subject represented by ONE [ANY PERSON] or ONE [I OR ME] • *The best way to avoid becoming a victim of violence is to acquire the ability to defend oneself.* • *Anger is never greater than when there is nobody to blame but oneself.* • *One hopes that one's children will be more successful than oneself.* • *It can be very lonely living* **(all) by** *oneself* (= alone). • *One ought to be able to carry out simple repairs on one's car* **by** *oneself* (= without help). • *It's lovely to have the house* **(all) to** *oneself* (= with no other person present) *for a while.* • 'Oneself' is generally considered formal or old-fashioned, so 'yourself' is usually used instead. • LP› **Reflexive pronouns and verbs**

one·self [EMPHASIS] /ˌwʌnˈself/ *pronoun fml* used to emphasize a subject that is represented by ONE [ANY PERSON] or ONE [I OR ME] • *One has little idea of what one can achieve oneself until one attempts to do it.* • 'Oneself' is generally considered formal or old-fashioned, so 'yourself' is usually used instead.

one·self [USUAL CONDITION] /ˌwʌnˈself/ *pronoun fml* in a person's usual mental or physical condition • *Often a cup of tea and a rest is all that is needed when one isn't feeling oneself.* • 'Oneself' is generally considered formal or old-fashioned, so 'yourself' is usually used instead.

on·go·ing /£ˈɒŋˌgəʊ·ɪŋ, £ˌ-ˈ--, $ˈɑːnˌgoʊ-/ *adj* [not gradable] continuing to exist or develop, or happening at the present moment • *The development of this drug is an ongoing project which is expected to be complete at the end of next year.* • *No agreement has yet been reached and the negotiations are still ongoing.*

on·ion /ˈʌn·jən/ *n* a round white vegetable which is made up of several layers surrounding each other, and which has a strong smell and flavour • *Onions have such a strong flavour that they are usually cooked before they are eaten.* [C] • *I always cry when I'm chopping onions.* [C] • *Heat the oil in the pan and fry the onion and garlic for about two minutes.* [U] • *Do you like French onion soup?* • PIC› **Vegetables**

on·look·er /£ˈɒnˌlʊk·əʳ, $ˈɑːnˌlʊk·ɚ/ *n* [C] someone who watches something that is happening in a public place but is not involved in it • *A crowd of curious onlookers soon gathered to see what was happening.* • *(fig.) I don't want to be just an onlooker – I want to be directly involved in the project.*

on·ly [SINGLE OR FEW] /£ˈəʊn·li, $ˈoʊn-/ *adj* [before n; not gradable] used to show that there is a single one or very few of something, or that there are no others • *I was the only person on the train.* • *The only people still working at the factory are the maintenance staff.* • *The only problem with your suggestion is that we haven't enough time to carry it out.* • *Is this really the only way to do it? Are you sure there's no alternative?* • *The only thing I can suggest is that you consult your lawyer about it.* • *The only thing that matters is that the baby is healthy.* • *It was the only thing I could do under the circumstances.* • *Rita was the only person to complain.* • *Chris really is the only person* (= the one person who is suitable) *for the job.* • An **only child** is one who has no sisters or brothers: *I was an only child so I got a lot of attention from my parents.* ○ *As the birth rate falls, increasing numbers of children are only children.* • LP› **One**

on·ly [LIMIT] /£ˈəʊn·li, $ˈoʊn-/ *adv* [not gradable] used to show that something is limited to the people, things, amount or activity stated • *Andy and Steve are both very musical, but only Steve plays the piano. Andy plays the* *guitar.* • *Steve only plays the piano/(fml) plays only the piano, and no other instruments.* • *Steve only plays the piano, he doesn't write music for it.* • *At present these televisions are only available in Japan/(slightly fml) are available only in Japan.* • *Only Mary and Mark bothered to turn up for the meeting.* • *This club is for members only.* • *Their food is made only from organically grown vegetables.* • *Only a qualified electrician should attempt to do this.* • *Only an idiot would do something as dangerous as that.* • *These shoes only cost £20.* • *I'm not badly injured – it's only a scratch.* • *I didn't mean what I said. I was only joking.* • *I was only trying to help.* • *He can't be dead – I only spoke to him this morning.* • *The party can't be finishing already. I only arrived half an hour ago.* • *She spoke to me only* (= no more than) *a few minutes ago on the telephone.* • *It's only four o'clock and* (= It is surprising that it is no later than four o'clock because) *it's already getting dark.* • *"Who's there?" "Hello, it's only me* (= it is not someone you should worry about). *I've locked myself out."* • *It's only* **natural** (= It is not unreasonable) *that you should be concerned about your baby's health, but there's absolutely nothing to worry about.* • Only can be used to express regret about something that cannot happen when explaining why it cannot happen: *I'd love to go to Australia. I only* **wish** *I could afford to.* • Only can be used when saying that something unpleasant will happen as a result of an action or a failure to act: *You may as well paint it properly now, because you'll only have to paint it again later if you don't.* • *(infml)* Only can also also be used to show that you think someone has done something foolish: *She's only locked herself out of her flat again!* • *Daryl's* **not** *only extremely intelligent – he's* **also** *very good-looking.* • *If this project fails it will affect* **not** *only our department,* **but also** *the whole organization.* • *This washing machine was* **not** *only expensive, it's unreliable* **as well.** • If you say you **have only (got) to** do something, you mean that it is all you need to do in order to achieve something else: *If you want any help, you have only to ask.* ○ *You've only got to look at her face to see that she's not well.* • **If only** is used when you want to say how doing something simple would make it possible to avoid something unpleasant: *If only she would listen to what I was saying we might be able to sort out this problem.* ○ *If he'd only bothered to get some insurance before his house burnt down, he wouldn't be in such a mess now.* • You can use **only just** to refer to something that happens almost immediately after something else: *Pam's annoyed because she's only just arrived and people are already leaving.* ○ *We'd only just set off when the car broke down.* • **Only just** can also mean almost not: *He has only just enough money to pay the rent.* ○ *There was only just enough food to go round.* ○ *After spending an hour in a traffic jam, we arrived in time for our flight, but only just* (= but we almost did not).

on·ly [BUT] /£ˈəʊn·li, $ˈoʊn-/ *conjunction* used to show what is the single or main reason why something mentioned in the first part of the sentence cannot be performed or is not completely true • *I'd invite Frances to the party, only* (= but I will not because) *I don't want her husband to come with her.* • *I'd phone him myself, only* (= but I cannot because) *I've got to go out.* • *I'd be happy to do it for you, only* (= but) *don't expect it to be done before next week.* • *This fabric is similar to wool, only* (= except that it is) *cheaper.* • *The liquid looked like water, only* (= but) *it wasn't water.* • You can use **only if** to say that you will not do one thing if another thing does not happen: *She'll go only if Pete goes/She'll only go if Pete goes/(slightly fml) Only if Pete goes will she go.* • **Only to** is used to show that something is surprising or unexpected when something done earlier is considered: *He spent ages negotiating for a pay increase, only to resign from his job soon after he'd received it.*

ono *Br and Aus abbreviation for* or near(est) offer • If you want to sell one of your possessions and you put an advertisement for it in a newspaper or shop window or on a notice board, you can use ono to say that you would be willing to accept a payment that is almost as high as the price you are charging: *One-year-old personal computer for sale with original box and manuals – £700 ono.*

on·o·mat·o·poe·ia /£ˌɒn·əʊˌmæt·əˈpiː·ə, $ˌɑː·noʊˌmæt̬·oʊ-/ *n* [U] the creation and use of words which include sounds that are similar to the noises that the words refer to

on·o·mat·o·poe·ic /£ˌɒn·əʊˌmæt·əˈpiː·ɪk, $ˌɑː·noʊˌmæt̬·oʊ-/ *adj* • *"Pop", "boom" and "squelch" are onomatopoeic words.*

on·set /£ˈɒn·set, $ˈɑːn-/ *n* [U] the moment at which something that is usually unpleasant begins • *There are usually several years between exposure to the virus and the onset of* **illness.** • *The new treatment can* **delay** *the onset* **of** *the* **disease** *by several years.* • *The negotiators have given up hope of signing a peace settlement before* **the** *onset of* **winter.**

on·shore /£ˌɒnˈʃɔːʳ, $ˈɑːn·ʃɔːr/ *adj, adv* [not gradable] moving towards land from the sea, or on land rather than at sea • *The ship was blown onto rocks by onshore winds.* • *Norway has large reserves of oil offshore while those of the Netherlands are onshore.* • Compare OFFSHORE [AT SEA].

on·side /£ˌɒnˈsaɪd, $ˈɑːn·saɪd/ *adj, adv* [not gradable] (in football and some other sports) in a position where you are allowed to kick, throw or receive the ball or PUCK • *In football, a player is onside if there is a member of the opposing team between the player and the opposing team's goal when a member of the player's own team kicks the ball.* • Compare OFFSIDE [NOT ALLOWED].

on·slaught /£ˈɒn·slɔːt, $ˈɑːn·slɑːt/ *n* [C] a very powerful attack • *It is unlikely that his forces could withstand an allied onslaught for very long.* • *Scotland's onslaught* **on** *Wales in the second half of the match earned them a 4-1 victory.* • *The President* **faces** *an onslaught of* **criticism** *for his handling of the crisis.*

on·stage /£ˌɒnˈsteɪdʒ, $ˈɑːn-/ *adv, adj* [not gradable] onto or on a stage for a performance • *The audience cheered as the band walked onstage for another encore.* • *The documentary gives a fascinating account of life onstage and backstage.* • *He's famous for his onstage destruction of his guitars.*

on·to, on to /£ˈɒn·tu, $ˈɑːn·tu/ *prep* into a position on or towards • *Should I put this vase back onto the shelf?* • *Don't walk in the middle of the road. Get back onto the path.* • *For longer journeys the sheep are loaded onto trucks.* • *I've been having problems loading this software onto my computer.* • *Imir's been voted onto the union committee.* • *Hold onto* (= Keep holding) *my hand and you'll be perfectly safe.* • *Do you mind if I hold onto* (= keep) *this book for a while longer?* • If you are onto something, you start talking about it: *How did we* **get** *onto this subject?* ○ *Can we* **move** *onto the next item on the agenda?* ○ *I'd now like to* **come** *onto my next point.* • *(Br and Aus)* If you are onto someone, you talk to them, esp. to ask them to do something or to complain: *Did you remember to* **get** *onto the plumber about the shower?* ○ *Have you been onto the council about the street lights yet?* ○ *Dad was on to me again yesterday about doing my homework.* • To be onto something or someone is also to be in a situation which benefits you or to know about someone who can benefit you: *How did you manage to* **get** *onto this deal?* ○ *You're onto* **a good thing** *with this buy-one-get-one-free offer at the shop.* ○ *David* **put** *me onto* (= told me about) *this great new restaurant.* ○ *Can you* **put** *me onto a good dentist?* • To be onto someone can also be to know about something bad that they have done: *The teacher's onto you and it won't be long before he finds out what you've done.* ○ *Who* **put** *the police onto* (= told the police about) *her?* • PIC> **Prepositions of movement**

o·nus /£ˈəʊ·nəs, $ˈoʊ-/ *n* [U] **the onus** *fml* a responsibility or duty to do something • **The** *onus is* **on** *the landlord* **to** *ensure that the property is habitable.* [+ *to* infinitive] • *We are trying to shift* **the** *onus* **for** *passenger safety onto the government.* • *A defendant is innocent until proven guilty, and* **the** *onus* **of proof** *rests with the prosecution.* • **The** *onus* **lies with** *the customer* **to** *check every detail before signing any contract.* [+ *to* infinitive]

on·ward /£ˈɒn·wəd, $ˈɑːn·wɚd/ *adj* [before n; not gradable] moving forward to a later time or a more distant place • *There's nothing you can do to halt the onward* **march** *of time.* • *(esp. Br and Aus) Onward* **trains** *from Calais and Boulogne go to Paris Gare du Nord.* • *(esp. Br and Aus) If you are continuing on an onward* **flight,** *your bags will be transferred automatically.* • *Her publishing career started as an editorial assistant on a women's magazine and it was* **onward and upward** (= gradual successful development) *from there.*

on·wards /£ˈɒn·wədz, $ˈɑːn·wɚdz/, *esp. Am* **on·ward** *adv* [not gradable] • **From** *its foundation onwards the company has been involved with charitable activities.* • **From** *her first novel onwards she has highlighted social injustices in her work.* • *She gave up smoking on her 25th birthday and* **from** *that day onwards she hasn't touched a cigarette.* • *Many of the passengers flying into regional airports are travelling onwards to other destinations.*

on·yx /£'ɒn·ɪks, $'ɑː·nɪks/ *n* [U] a valuable stone with white and grey strips that is used in jewellery and decorations • *an onyx brooch*

ood·les /'uː·dl̩z/ *pl n infml* a very large amount (of something pleasant) • *"How much cream would you like on your strawberries?" "Oodles, please!"* • *She inherited oodles* **of** *money from her uncle.*

ooh /uː/ *exclamation* an expression of surprise, pleasure, approval, disapproval, or pain • *Ooh, you never told me you were getting married!* • *Ooh, he's good-looking, isn't he?* • *Ooh, that's a dreadful thing to say about your dad.* • *Ooh, that really hurts!* • *"Ooh you are awful – but I like you!"* (phrase used by Dick Emery, 1970s)

ooh /uː/ *n* [C usually pl] • *There was a chorus of oohs* **and aahs** *from her fellow MPs as she launched a vehement attack on the Prime Minister.*

ooh /uː/ *v* [I] • *The crowed oohed when the skier lost his footing and tumbled down the slope.* • *Thousands of spectators oohed* **and aahed** (= expressed admiration) *as the pilots performed amazing stunts in their planes.*

oomph /ʊmpf, uːmpf/ *n* [U] *infml* power, forcefulness or energetic activity • *Her new car has a lot more oomph than her old one.* • *The government seems to be running out of oomph.* • *It's important to have someone with a bit of oomph in charge of the department.*

oops /uːps, ʊps/, **whoops** *exclamation infml* an expression of surprise or regret about a mistake or slight accident • *Oops! I've typed two 'L's by mistake.* • *A couple of teenagers get together one night and, oops, another girl's pregnant.* • When someone, esp. a child, falls over, you might say to them **oops-a-daisy** (also **ups-a-daisy**). • LP> **Phrases and customs**

ooze *(obj)* /uːz/ *v* to flow slowly out of something through a small opening, or to slowly produce (a thick sticky liquid) • **Blood** *was still oozing* **from** *the cut on his wrist.* [I always + adv/prep] • *He felt slightly ill as he looked at the grease oozing* **from** *his dinner.* [I always + adv/prep] • *Little green patches of moss grew on the rock where water had oozed* **out**. [I always + adv/prep] • *She removed the bandage to reveal a red swollen wound oozing pus.* [T] • *The waiter brought her a massive pizza that oozed cheese.* [T] • *(fig.) She oozes talent* **from** *every pore.* [T] • *(fig.) Peter's someone who oozes charm and charisma.* [T]

ooze /uːz/ *n* [U] • Ooze is a thick brown liquid that is found at the bottom of a river or lake and is a mixture of earth and water: *Many millions of years ago, our ancestors climbed out of the primeval ooze onto dry land.*

oo·zy /'uː·zi/ *adj* **-ier, -iest** • *Her pizza was covered with oozy cheese.*

op OPERATION /£ɒp, $ɑːp/ *n* [C] *esp. Br and Aus infml* a medical operation • *How long did you take to recover from your op?*

Op MUSIC *n* [before n] *abbreviation for* OPUS • *Her most recent recording includes Dvorak's Piano Concerto in G Minor, Op. 33.*

op OPPORTUNITY /£ɒp, $ɑːp/ *n* [C] *Am* an opportunity • *a photo op* (= a chance for esp. a politician to be photographed looking good or doing good things) • *There were plenty of snack ops* (= places to eat) *at the street fair.* • *Hong Kong is the mother of all shop ops* (= places to shop).

o·pal /£'əʊ·pᵊl, $'oʊ-/ *n* a precious stone whose colour changes when the position of the person looking at it changes • *A giant black opal worth £3 million has been found in Western Australia.* [C] • *The pendant is made of opal and the chain is silver.* [U]

o·pal·es·cent /£,əʊ·pᵊl'es·ᵊnt, $,oʊ-/ *adj* • Something that is opalescent reflects light and changes colour like an opal: *the opalescent scales of a fish*

o·pal·es·cence /£,əʊ·pᵊl'es·ᵊnts, $,oʊ-/ *n* [U]

o·paque /£əʊ'peɪk, $oʊ-/ *adj* preventing light from travelling through, and therefore not transparent or TRANSLUCENT • *Candle wax is opaque when it is solid, but it becomes transparent when it melts.* • *(fig.) Her explanation of the problem was rather opaque* (= difficult to understand).

o·paque·ly /£əʊ'peɪ·kli, $oʊ-/ *adv* • *(fig.) The book is opaquely written and requires a lot of specialist knowledge to be understood.*

o·pac·i·ty /£əʊ'pæs·ə·ti, $oʊ'pæs·ə·t̬i/ *n* [U] • Opacity is the state of being opaque, or the degree to which something is opaque.

op art /£'ɒp·ɑːt, $'ɑːp·ɑːrt/ *n* [U] a type of modern art which uses patterns that do not exist naturally in order to create images which appear to move or to be something that they are not • *Stripes, spots and abstract spiral and wavy patterns are used in op art to produce optical illusions.*

op cit /£,ɒp'sɪt, $,ɑːp-/ *adv* [not gradable] *fml* used by writers to avoid repeating the details of a book or article that has already been referred to • *Jackson (op cit, page 53) calls this phenomenon 'the principle of minimal effort'.*

OPEC /£'əʊ·pek, $'oʊ-/ *n* [not after *the*] *abbreviation for* Organization of Petroleum-Exporting Countries (= a group of countries which all produce oil and act together to sell it)

op–ed /£,ɒp'ed, $,ɑːp-/ *adj* [not gradable] *Am* (of a piece of writing in a newspaper which is usually printed opposite to the page on which the **editorial** is printed) expressing personal opinions • *an op-ed article/column/page* • *In her op-ed* **piece**, *she wrote that the proposed changes to the health service would have disastrous results.*

o·pen NOT CLOSED /£'əʊ·pᵊn, $'oʊ-/ *adj* not closed or fastened • *An open suitcase lay on her bed.* • *Her desk was covered with open books.* • *Don't leave the packet open, or the cornflakes will go soft.* • *Police officers tried to* **push** *the door open.* • *When we got there the window was* **wide** (= completely) *open.* • *He had several nasty open* **wounds** (= those which had not begun to heal). • If you welcome or receive someone or something **with open arms**, you do it in a very sincere and enthusiastic way: *Refugees will be* **welcomed** *here with open arms.* • If you do something **with** your **eyes open**, you do it knowing what the likely results of your action will be. • A problem or legal matter which is **open-and-shut** is easy to prove or answer: *Our lawyer thinks that we have an open-and-shut* **case**. • **Open-door** means allowing people and goods to come freely into a place or country: *an open-door policy* ○ *open-door regulations* ○ *an open-door system* • **Open-eyed** means with your eyes completely open, esp. because you find it difficult to believe what you are seeing or feeling: *open-eyed amazement* ○ *He stared open-eyed at all the food on the table.* • **Open-heart surgery** is a medical operation in which the body is cut open and the heart is repaired, while the body's blood is kept flowing by a machine. • **Open-mouthed** means with your mouth wide open, esp. because you are surprised or shocked: *open-mouthed horror* ○ *They stared open-mouthed at the extent of the damage.* • An **open-necked** shirt or BLOUSE is one which is not fastened at the neck of the person who is wearing it. • .

o·pen *(obj)* /£'əʊ·pᵊn, $'oʊ-/ *v* • *It's very hot in here, would you open a window please?* [T] • *Don't open a new bottle just for me.* [T] • *She was so excited she could hardly open the letter.* [T] • *Just open your mouth a little wider – this won't hurt a bit.* [T] • *You can open your eyes now – here's your present.* [T] • *The flowers open* **(out)** *in the morning but close again in the afternoon.* [I] • *The door opens easily now the hinges have been oiled.* [I] • *From the kitchen there is a door which opens* **(out) into/onto** *the garden.* [I] • *I was so embarrassed that I wished the earth/floor/ground would open* **(up)** *and swallow me.* [I] • *(infml) "Open* **up** (= Open the door) *– it's the police!" shouted the police officer, banging on the door.* [I] • *(fig.) There are hopes that the new rules will open* **doors/the door** (= lead) **to** *a whole host of new opportunities.* [T] • *(infml) The doctor said that the only way they could find out what's wrong with my chest is to open me* **up** (= do a medical operation) *and see.* [M] • If you **open** someone's **eyes**, you show them something, esp. something surprising or shocking, which they had not known about or understood before: *She opened my eyes* **to** *how foolish I'd been.* • If something **opens the floodgates**, it allows action to be taken that has not previously been allowed, or feelings to be expressed that have previously been controlled: *Officials are worried that allowing these refugees into the country will open the floodgates* **to** *thousands more.* • *She's very understanding – you feel you can really* **open** *your* **heart** *to her* (= tell her all your worries and secret thoughts). • *(infml) Don't look at me – I never* **opened** *my* **mouth** (= did not say anything). • If something is an **open sesame**, it is a very successful way of getting a desired result: *A science degree can be an open sesame* **to** *almost any job in almost any field.* • LP> **Switching on and off**

o·pe·ner /£'əʊ·pᵊn·əʳ, $'oʊ·pᵊn·ɚ/ *n* [C] • An opener is a device for opening closed containers. Opener is often used as a combining form: *a bottle opener* ○ *a can/tin opener* • PIC> **Kitchen**

o·pen·ing /£'əʊ·pᵊn·ɪŋ, $'oʊp·nɪŋ/ *n* [C] • *There's an opening* (= hole) *high up* **in** *the wall – you'll find a key hidden in it.* • *The children crawled through an opening* (= space) **in** *the fence.*

o·pen READY /£ˈəʊ·pᵊn, $ˈoʊ-/ *adj* [after v; not gradable] ready to be used or provide a service • *The supermarket is open till 8.00 p.m.* • *The road is open now, but it is often blocked by snow in the winter.* • If a building, place or event is **declared** open, someone, usually someone important, officially states that it is ready to be used or to operate: *The new hospital was declared open by the mayor.*

o·pen *(obj)* /£ˈəʊ·pᵊn, $ˈoʊ-/ *v* • *The café opens* (= becomes ready to provide a service) *at ten o'clock.* [I] • *He opens* **(up)** *his café* (= makes it ready to provide a service) *at ten o'clock.* [T/M] • If someone, usually someone important, opens a building or place or event, they officially state that it is ready to be used or to start operating: *The new hospital will be* **(officially)** *opened by the mayor on Tuesday.* [T]

o·pen·ing /£ˈəʊ·pᵊn·ɪŋ, $ˈoʊp·nɪŋ/ *n* [U] • *The* **official** *opening* **of** *the new school will take place next month.* • *(Br)* The **opening hours** of a business, such as bar, restaurant, shop or bank, are the times when it is open for people to use it. • *(Br)* The **opening time** of a bar or PUB is the time at which it opens.

o·pen NOT DECIDED /£ˈəʊ·pᵊn, $ˈoʊ-/ *adj* not decided or certain • *We can leave our offer open for another week, but we must have your decision by then.* • *I want to keep my* **options** *open and not make a decision yet.* • *Whether we move to Oxford or not is still an open* **question**. • An activity or situation which is **open-ended** is intentionally left without a clear decision or end: *Firm action would be more helpful to the country's homeless people than open-ended promises.* • *We should keep an* **open mind** (= not form any opinions) *until all of the evidence is available.* • If a person is **open-minded**, they are willing to listen to other people and consider new ideas, suggestions and opinions: *She is a designer who clearly has an* **open-mindedness** *about fashion.* • *(Br law)* An **open verdict** is a legal decision which records a death but does not state its cause: *Because of lack of evidence, the inquest* **returned** *an open verdict* **on** *his death.*

o·pen NOT SECRET /£ˈəʊ·pᵊn, $ˈoʊ-/ *adj* not secret • *There has been open hostility between them ever since they had that argument last summer.* • A person who is open is honest and not secretive: *He is quite open about his weaknesses.* ○ *I wish you'd be more open* **with** *me, and tell me what you're feeling.* ○ *She has an honest, open face/nature.* • *(esp. Am)* **Open adoption** is an arrangement by which a child legally goes to live with a person or people who are not the parents who caused him or her to be born, but still continues to communicate with these parents. • If a person is an **open book**, it is easy to tell what they are thinking and feeling. If something is an open book, it is easy to understand: *Sarah is an open book, so you'll know right away if she doesn't like the present you've bought her.* ○ *I've never been able to understand computers, but they're an open book* **to** *Andrew.* • Someone who is **open-hearted** is kind, caring and honest. • An **open letter** is a letter intended to be read by a lot of people, not just the person it is addressed to: *An open letter to the prime minister, signed by several MPs, appeared in today's papers.* • If a fact or situation is an **open secret**, it should be a secret but in reality many people know about it: *It's an open secret around the office that they're having an affair.*

o·pen up *v adv* [I] • *The child won't open up* (= speak honestly) *(to anyone)* **about** *what happened to her.*

o·pen /£ˈəʊ·pᵊn, $ˈoʊ-/ *n* [U] • If something is **in the open**, people are aware of it: *I hope this meeting will provide us all with the opportunity of* **getting** *our feelings* **out into** *the open.*

o·pen·ly /£ˈəʊ·pᵊn·li, $ˈoʊ-/ *adv* • *They were openly contemptuous of my suggestions.* • *We discussed our reservations about the contract quite openly.*

o·pen·ness /£ˈəʊ·pᵊn·nəs, $ˈoʊ-/ *n* [U] • *If these discussions are to succeed, we'll need openness from/on both sides.*

o·pen *(obj)* BEGIN /£ˈəʊ·pᵊn, $ˈoʊ-/ *v* to (cause to) begin • *I would like to open my talk by giving a brief background to the subject.* [T] • *I'm going to open an account with another bank, because my present one doesn't provide a very good service.* [T] • *The company plans to open* **(up)** *an office in Madrid.* [T/M] • *The Olympic Games open tomorrow.* [I] • *A new radio station is due to open* **(up)** *next month.* [I] • *The film opens* (= will be shown for the first time) *in New York and Los Angeles next week.* [I] • *Do not* **open** *fire* (= begin shooting) *until you hear the command.* [T]

o·pen·ing /£ˈəʊ·pᵊn·ɪŋ, $ˈoʊp·nɪŋ/ *adj* [not gradable] • *She spoke so quietly at first that the audience could barely hear her opening words.* • The **opening night** of a play, film, etc. is the first night it is performed or shown: *The ballet's opening night was a huge success.*

o·pen·ing /£ˈəʊ·pᵊn·ɪŋ, $ˈoʊp·nɪŋ/ *n* [C] • *The opening* (= beginning) *of the novel is by far the best part.* • An opening is also the beginning of a game of CHESS: *If you want to get anywhere in chess, you have to study the various openings.*

o·pe·ners /£ˈəʊ·pᵊn·əz, $ˈoʊ·pᵊn·ɚz/ *pl n infml* • *Just* **for** *openers* (= to begin with), *let's look at how much the whole thing will cost.*

o·pen NOT ENCLOSED /£ˈəʊ·pᵊn, $ˈoʊ-/ *adj* not enclosed or covered • *From the garden there was a marvellous view over open countryside.* • *It isn't a very good idea to camp in the middle of an open field* (= one which is not covered with trees, bushes, etc.), *where there isn't any shelter.* • *The survivors were adrift in an open boat* (= one without a roof) *on the open sea* (= that far from land). • **The open air** is anywhere which is not inside a building, esp. the countryside or a park or garden: *I work in an office all week, so I like to get out* **in** *the open air at weekends.* ○ *We went to an open-air concert/market.* • **Open-cut** is *Am and Aus for* OPENCAST. • An **open fire**/*(Am usually)* **open fireplace** is a space in a wall of a building in which wood or coal is burnt, and which has a CHIMNEY inside the wall to take the smoke away, or a fire which burns in such a space: *We roasted chestnuts on the open fire.* • **Open-pit** is *Am for* OPENCAST. • A room or building which is **open-plan** intentionally has few or no walls inside, so it is not divided into smaller rooms: *an open-plan office* • *(Br)* An **open prison** (*Am and Aus* **minimum-security prison**) is a prison where prisoners are not locked inside because they are trusted not to escape. • An **open sandwich** is a single slice of bread with various types of food, such as cold fish or meat, on the top.

o·pen /£ˈəʊ·pᵊn, $ˈoʊ-/ *n* [U] • **The open** is somewhere outside, rather than in a building: *It's good to be* **(out) in** *the open after being cooped up in an office all day.*

o·pen out/up *obj*, **o·pen** *obj* **out/up** *v adv* [M] • *We're going to open up our kitchen* (= make it larger or less enclosed) *by knocking down a couple of walls.* • *If we remove the bushes, that will help open the garden out* (= make it less covered) *a bit.*

o·pen AVAILABLE /£ˈəʊ·pᵊn, $ˈoʊ-/ *adj* [after v; not gradable] available; not limited • *Are there any vacancies open in the marketing department at the moment?* • *Don't get depressed because you failed, there are still several possibilities open* **to** *you.* • *The competition is open* **to** *anyone over the age of sixteen.* • *No, this library is not open* **to** *the general public.* • *Their whole attitude to these negotiations is open* **to** *criticism* (= can be criticized). • *I think his sincerity is open* **to** *doubt* (= can be doubted). • *I'd like to think I'm open* **to** (= willing to consider) *any reasonable suggestion.* • *An accident would* **lay** *the whole issue of safety open* (= cause it to be considered). • In Britain, the **Open University** is a college especially established to educate older people who did not get a degree when they were young. Students study by special television and radio programmes and they usually send their work to their teachers by post. • *(Am)* **Open admissions/open enrollment** is a system which allows students to go to a college without having any special qualifications for it. • In the US, **open classroom** is a system for educating young children in which classes and activities are informal and changed to suit each child. • An *(Br and Aus)* **open day**/*(Am)* **open house** is a day when an organization such as a school, college or factory allows members of the public to go in and see what happens there. • **Open-handed** means generous: *open-handed assistance* • **Open house** is a situation in which people welcome visitors at any time: *We* **keep** *open house, so come and see us any time.* ○ *The club chairman* **declared** *open house for supporters to drop in for a chat.* • *(Am)* An **open house** is also a time when a house or apartment that is being sold can be looked at by the public. • An **open market** is a trading situation in a country which allows companies from another country to do business freely there: *open-market economics* • An **open marriage** is a marriage in which both partners independently follow their own social interests and are free to have sexual relationships with other people. • The **open season** is the period in the year when it is legal to hunt particular animals, or *(fig.)* a situation which allows a particular group of people to be unfairly treated: *(fig.) To pass this legislation would be to* **declare** *open season* **on** *homosexuals.* Compare **closed**

season at CLOSE [END]. • *"In England justice is open to all – like the Ritz Hotel"* (believed to have been said by Sir James Matthew, 1830-1908)

o·pen *obj* /£ˈəʊ·pᵊn, $ˈoʊ-/ *v* [T] • To open **(up)** something is to make it available: *This research opens (up) the possibility of being able to find a cure for the disease.* [T/M] ○ *The country is planning to open (up) its economy* **to** *foreign investment.* [T/M] • If you open **up** something, you make it less limited: *Guide dogs can help open up the lives of blind people.* ○ *The government has announced plans to open up access to higher education.*

o·pen·ing /£ˈəʊ·pᵊn·ɪŋ, $ˈoʊp·nɪŋ/ *n* [C] • *Good openings* (=possibilities for doing advantageous things) *exist* **for** *investors in the current financial conditions.* • *I hear you're looking for an opening* (=a job) **in** *international sales.*

o·pen·cast *Br* /£ˈəʊ·pᵊŋ·kɑːst, $ˈoʊ·pᵊn·kæst/, *Am and Aus* **o·pen–cut** /£ˈəʊ·pᵊŋ·kʌt, $ˈoʊ·pᵊn-/, *Am* **o·pen–pit** /£ˈəʊ·pᵊm·pɪt, $ˈoʊ·pᵊn-/ *adj* [not gradable] being or involving rocks, esp. coal, taken from the surface of the ground rather than from passages dug under it • *opencast coal* • *opencast mining*

op·e·ra /£ˈɒp·ᵊr·ə, £ˈɒp·rə, $ˈɑː·pɚ·ə/ *n* (an example of) formal plays in which all or most of the words are sung to music • *What's your favourite opera?* [C] • *I don't like opera very much.* [U] • *He goes to* **the** *opera* (=to see an opera) *whenever he can.* [U] • *Maria Callas was a famous opera singer.* • **Opera glasses** are small BINOCULARS which can be used in large theatres by people sitting far from the stage, so that they can see the performers more clearly. • An **opera house** is a theatre which is specially designed for operas to be performed in: *The Royal Opera House, Covent Garden* • Compare OPERETTA.

op·e·ra·tic /£ˌɒp·ᵊrˈæt·ɪk, $ˌɑː·pəˈræt̬-/ *adj* [not gradable] • *an operatic tenor* • *(fig.) She waved us away with an operatic* (=very full of emotion) *gesture.*

o·pe·rat·i·cal·ly /£ˌɒp·ᵊrˈæt·ɪ·kli, $ˌɑː·pəˈræt̬-/ *adv* [not gradable]

op·e·rate *(obj)* [WORK] /£ˈɒp·ᵊr·eɪt, $ˈɑː·pə·reɪt/ *v* to (cause to) work, be in action or have an effect • *He took the machine to pieces to try and find out how it operated.* [I] • *How do you operate the remote control unit?* [T] • *If there's an electrical failure, it's possible to operate the lift manually.* [T] • *Changes are being introduced to make the department operate more efficiently.* [I] • *Does the company operate a pension scheme?* [T] • *For several years she operated a dating agency from her basement flat.* [T] • *Specially equipped troops are operating (undercover activities) in the hills.* [I/T] • *We have representatives operating* **in** *most countries.* [I] • *Exchange rates are currently operating to the advantage of exporters.* [I] • *Destructive forces are clearly operating* **on/within** *the community.* [I] • An **operating system** is a special program that controls the way a computer system works, esp. how its memory is used and the timing of other programs. • [LP] **Switching on and off**

op·e·ra·tion /£ˌɒp·ᵊrˈeɪ·ʃᵊn, $ˌɑː·pəˈreɪ-/ *n* • *I understand the operation* **of** *computers* (=the way in which they work) *in a general way, but not in detail.* [U] • *There are several reactors of the type* **in** *operation* (=working) *at the moment.* [U] • *We expect the new scheme for assessing claims to* **come into** *operation* (=start working) *early next year.* [U] • *Repairing a watch is a very delicate operation* (=act of doing something). [C] • *Less profitable business operations* (=organizations) *will have difficulty in finding financial support.* [C] • An operation is also an activity which is planned to achieve something: *He has been in charge of several* **covert/undercover (military)** *operations.* [C] ○ *Following the earthquake, a large-scale* **rescue** *operation was* **launched.** [C] ○ *A huge* **security** *operation was* **mounted** *during the president's state visit.* [C] ○ *The operation* **to** *fly in supplies will begin as soon as possible.* [C + *to* infinitive] • *(specialized)* An operation is a mathematical process, such as addition or multiplication, in which one set of numbers is produced from another. [C]

op·e·ra·tion·al /£ˌɒp·ᵊrˈeɪ·ʃᵊn·ᵊl, $ˌɑː·pəˈreɪ-/ *adj* [not gradable] • *There are operational* (=connected with the way something works) *advantages in putting sales and admin in the same building.* • *Repairs have already begun and we expect the factory to be* **fully** *operational* (=working correctly and completely) *again with six months.* • *(Br specialized)* **Operational research** *(esp. Am and Aus* **operations research**, *abbreviation* **OR**) is the systematic study of how best to solve problems in business and industry.

op·e·ra·tion·al·ly /£ˌɒp·ᵊrˈeɪ·ʃᵊn·ᵊl·i, $ˌɑː·pəˈreɪ-/ *adv* [not gradable]

op·e·ra·tive /£ˈɒp·ᵊr·ə·tɪv, $ˈɑː·pɚ·ə·t̬ɪv/ *adj* • *Our computerized stock-control system is now operative* (= working). • *Financial reasons for not banning the pesticides still remain operative* (=in existence). • An **operative word** is a word which someone wants to emphasize, either because it is very suitable or because it has two meanings, as in a joke: *Inside the house there were more statues – 'more' being the operative word, I've never seen so many in one place.*

op·e·ra·tive /£ˈɒp·ᵊr·ə·tɪv, $ˈɑː·pɚ·ə·t̬ɪv/ *n* [C] • *(fml or specialized)* An operative is a worker, esp. one who is skilled in working with their hands. • *(esp. Am)* An operative is also a person who works secretly for an organization: *a CIA operative*

op·e·ra·ble /£ˈɒp·ᵊr·ə·bl̩, $ˈɑː·pɚ·ə-/ *adj* • *Everything's operable* (=can be made to work) *from a new, simpler control unit.* • *There will be a delay before the modified machines are operable* (=able to work).

op·e·rat·or /£ˈɒp·ᵊr·eɪ·təʳ, $ˈɑː·pə·reɪ·t̬ɚ/ *n* [C] • An operator is a person who makes something work or be in action: *a computer/lathe/machine operator* ○ *a nightclub operator* ○ *a tour operator* (=a company which organizes holidays) • An operator is also a person who works on a telephone SWITCHBOARD: *Dial 100 for the operator if you have any difficulties making a call.* • *(esp. disapproving)* An operator is also a person who deals with people or problems in the particular stated way, esp. for their own advantage: *a smooth operator* ○ *He has shown himself to be a canny operator in wage negotiations.* • [LP] **Telephone**

op·e·rate [MEDICAL PROCESS] /£ˈɒp·ᵊr·eɪt, $ˈɑː·pə·reɪt/ *v* [I] to cut a body open for medical reasons in order to repair, remove or replace a diseased or damaged part • *We will have to operate in order to remove the growth.* • *He was badly injured in the crash and they're operating* **on** *him now.* • An **operating table** is a special table on which a person is operated on. • *(Br and Aus)* An **operating theatre** (also **theatre**, *Am* **operating room**, *abbreviation* **OR**) is a special, usually very clean, room in a hospital in which people are operated on.

op·e·ra·tion /£ˌɒp·ᵊrˈeɪ·ʃᵊn, $ˌɑː·pəˈreɪ-/, *Br infml* **op** *n* [C] • *a major/minor/routine operation* • *an abdominal/cataract/transplant operation* • *He's got to* **have/undergo** *an operation* **for** *a hernia/an operation* **on** *his wrist.* • *We will know in a couple of days if the operation* **to** *restore her sight was* **successful.** [+ *to* infinitive]

op·e·ra·ble /£ˈɒp·ᵊr·ə·bl̩, $ˈɑː·pɚ·ə-/ *adj* • *In about half of diagnosed cases, the condition is operable.*

o·pe·ret·ta /£ˌɒp·ᵊrˈet·ə, $ˌɑː·pəˈret̬-/ *n* (an example of) amusing plays in which many or all of the words are sung to music and which might include some dancing • *a Gilbert and Sullivan operetta* [C] • *Operetta is usually less serious and more light-hearted than opera.* [U]

oph·thal·mol·o·gy /£ˌɒf·θælˈmɒl·ə·dʒi, $ˌɑːf·θælˈmɑː·lə-/ *n* [U] *medical* the scientific study of eyes and their diseases • Compare OPTOMETRY.

oph·thal·mol·o·gist /£ˌɒf·θælˈmɒl·ə·dʒɪst, $ˌɑːf·θælˈmɑː·lə-/, *dated* **oc·u·list** *n* [C] *medical* • An ophthalmologist is a doctor who treats eye diseases. • Compare **optician** at OPTICAL; **optometrist** at OPTOMETRY.

oph·thal·mic /£ɒfˈθæl·mɪk, $ɑːf-/ *adj* [not gradable] *medical* • *(Br)* An **ophthalmic optician** is an OPTICIAN.

o·pi·ate /£ˈəʊ·pi·ət, $ˈoʊ-/ *n* [C] a drug which contains OPIUM, esp. one which causes sleep

o·pine /£əʊˈpaɪn, $oʊ-/ *v fml* to give an opinion • *She likes to opine* **about/on** *what she reads in the newspapers.* [I] • *Power grows from the barrel of a gun, opined Mao Tse-tung.* [+ clause] • *Ernest Rutherford opined* **that** *his work on radioactive substances would be of little or no practical use.* [+ *that* clause]

o·pin·i·on /əˈpɪn·jən/ *n* (one of) the ideas that a person or a group of people have about something or someone, which are based mainly on their feelings and beliefs • *Many people* **have** *strong opinions* **about/on** *capital punishment.* [C] • *Would you care to* **express/give/state** *an opinion* **about/on** *my proposed course of action?* [C] • *There is a large range of opinion* **about/on** *the issue of abortion.* [U] • *It would seem that* **public** *opinion is not behind the government.* [U] • *My husband and I agree about most things, but we have an ongoing* **difference of** *opinion about politics.* [U] • *Ranking artists for greatness is just* **a matter of** *opinion* (=something which can not be proved). [U] • *Who,* **in** *your opinion,* (=Who do you think) *is the best* *football player in the world today?* [U] • **It's** *my* **considered** *opinion* (= I think) **that** *you have made a mistake.* [U + *that* clause] • *(fml) After two years of working in a kitchen, he was firmly* **of the** *opinion* (= he thought) **that** *there must be easier ways to earn a living.* [U + *that* clause] • An opinion is also a judgment about someone or something: *Her opinion* **of** *Adam changed after he'd been so helpful at the wedding.* [C] ○ *She* **has** *a* **good/high** *opinion* **of** *his abilities* (= thinks he is good) *as an actor.* [C] ○ *I* **have** *a rather* **bad/low/poor** *opinion* **of** *my sister's boyfriend* (= I think he has little worth). [C] ○ *He has a very* **high** *opinion* **of** *himself* (= thinks he is very able, although other people might not agree). [C] • An opinion is also a judgment made by an expert: *My doctor has referred me to a specialist for a* **second** *opinion on the results of my blood test.* [C] • In an **opinion poll**, people are asked what they think about a particular subject.

o·pin·ion·at·ed /£əˈpɪn·jə·neɪ·tɪd, $-t̬ɪd/ *adj disapproving* • If a person is opinionated, they are certain about what they think and believe, and they express their ideas strongly and often: *She thought he was opinionated and selfish, but also extremely clever.*

o·pi·um /£ˈəʊ·pi·əm, $ˈoʊ-/ *n* [U] a drug made from POPPY plants and used to control pain or help people sleep. It can make a person who takes it want more of it and is sometimes used by people to give them temporarily pleasant effects. • *The use of opium for non-medical purposes is illegal in many countries.* • *He's an opium addict.* • *"Religion ... is the opium of the people"* (Karl Marx in *A Contribution to the Critique of Hegel's Philosophy of Right*, 1843-4)

o·pos·sum /£əˈpɒs·əm, $-ˈpɑː·səm/ *n* [C] a POSSUM

op·pon·ent /£əˈpəʊ·nənt, $-ˈpoʊ-/ *n* [C] a person who disagrees with something and speaks against it or tries to change it, or the person being competed against in a sports event • *Leading opponents* **of** *the proposed cuts in defence spending will meet later today.* Compare PROPONENT. • *In the second game her opponent hurt her leg and had to retire.* • See also OPPOSE. • LP **Sports**

op·por·tune /£ˈɒp·ə·tjuːn, $ˌɑː·pɚˈtuːn/ *adj fml* happening at a time which is likely to give success or which is convenient • *This would seem to be an opportune* **moment** *for reviving our development plan.* • *Would* **it** *be opportune* **to** *discuss the contract now?* [+ *to* infinitive]

op·por·tun·ist /£ˌɒp·əˈtjuː·nɪst, $ˌɑː·pɚˈtuː-/ *n* [C] *usually disapproving* a person who takes advantage of every chance they have for success, without thinking about the effects of their actions on other people • *He said that if you want to be successful in business, you have to be an opportunist.*

op·por·tun·i·sm /£ˌɒp·əˈtjuː·nɪ·zᵊm, $ˌɑː·pɚˈtuː-/ *n* [U] *usually disapproving* • *The president's decision to call an election while he was at the height of his popularity seemed like blatant opportunism.*

op·por·tun·ist /£ˌɒp·əˈtjuː·nɪst, $ˌɑː·pɚˈtuː-/ *adj disapproving* • *In her speech she came across as an opportunist politician who wanted to win votes.*

op·por·tun·is·tic /£ˌɒp·ə·tjuːˈnɪs·tɪk, $ˌɑː·pɚ·tuːˈnɪs·t̬ɪk/ *adj esp. disapproving* • *an opportunistic crime* • An **opportunistic infection** is an infection caused by bacteria or a virus which is harmless to a healthy person but harms a person whose body's natural defence against infection is damaged.

op·por·tun·is·ti·cal·ly /£ˌɒp·ə·tjuːˈnɪs·tɪ·kli, $ˌɑː·pɚ·tuːˈnɪs·t̬ɪ-/ *adv*

op·por·tun·i·ty /£ˌɒp·əˈtjuː·nə·ti, $ˌɑː·pɚˈtuː·nə·t̬i/ *n* an occasion or situation which makes it possible to do something that you want to do or have to do, or the possibility of doing something • *If I* **have** *an opportunity today, I'll take your books back to the library for you.* [C] • *There are far more opportunities now* **for** *school-leavers than there were fifty years ago.* [C] • *I've been offered the opportunity* **of** *working in India for a year, but I'm not sure whether to* **take** *it or not.* [C] • *When he was given the opportunity* **of** *going to college, he* **grabbed/seized** *it* **with both hands**. [C] • *The exhibition is a* **unique** *opportunity* **to** *see her later work.* [C + *to* infinitive] • *An ankle injury meant she* **missed** *the opportunity* **to** *run in the qualifying heat.* [C + *to* infinitive] • *(fml) Please contact us* **at the earliest** *opportunity* (= as soon as possible). [C] • *He goes fishing* **at every** *opportunity* (= as often as possible). [C] • Opportunity is the possibility of doing something that you want or have to do: *I used to enjoy going to the theatre, but I don't get much opportunity now.* [U] ○ *A four-hour train journey offered* **ample** *opportunity* **for** *reflection.* [U] ○ *Critical acclaim of her first play opened up* **a world of** *opportunity for her* (= made it possible for her to do a lot of advantageous things). [U] • *(Aus)* An **opportunity shop** (*infml* **op-shop**) is a shop which is run by an organization that makes money to help people who are ill or hungry or who have nowhere to live, and which sells clothes and goods that have been previously owned. • *"Opportunity Knocks"* (title of a television show, 1957-1977)

op·pose *(obj)* /£əˈpəʊz, $-ˈpoʊz/ *v* to disagree with (something or someone), often by speaking or fighting against them • *The proposed new examination system has been vigorously opposed by teachers.* [T] • *Most of the local residents opposed the closing of their hospital.* [T] • *The panel opposed bringing back old-fashioned laws and restrictions.* [+ v-*ing*] • See also OPPONENT.

op·posed /£əˈpəʊzd, $-ˈpoʊzd/ *adj* [after v] • *She's opposed* **to** *religious education in schools* (= She thinks it is a bad thing).

op·pos·ing /£əˈpəʊ·zɪŋ, $-ˈpoʊ-/ *adj* [before n; not gradable] • *Opposing* **factions** *on the committee are refusing to compromise.*

op·po·si·tion /£ˌɒp·əˈzɪʃ·ᵊn, $ˌɑː·pə-/ *n* • *At the meeting there was a lot of opposition* **to** *the proposed changes.* [U] • *There will be considerable/vociferous opposition* **to** *increasing the budget.* [U] • *The unions are* **in** *opposition* **to** *the government over the issue of privatization.* [U] • In some political systems, the Opposition is the elected politicians who belong to the largest party which does not form the government: *the Leader of the Opposition* • *the Opposition spokesperson on defence* ○ *The Opposition has/have condemned the Government's proposed tax increases.* [C + sing/pl v] • The opposition is also the team or person being played against in a sports competition: *The opposition has/have some good players, and it's going to be a difficult match for us to win.* [C + sing/pl v]

op·po·site DIFFERENT /£ˈɒp·ə·zɪt, $ˈɑː·pə-/ *adj* [not gradable] completely different • *If you want to go to the station, you should be walking in the opposite direction.* • *You'd never know they're sisters – they're completely opposite* **to** *each other in every way.* • *She put her arm around him to help him relax, but it had exactly the opposite effect* (= it made him anxious). • Someone's **opposite number** is a person who has a very similar job or rank to them but in a different organization or company: *The Foreign Secretary has suggested to his Japanese opposite number that they should meet early next week.* • If a man refers to **the opposite sex**, he means women, and if a woman refers to the opposite sex, she means men: *Which sporting figure of the opposite sex do you most admire and why?* • LP **Opposites**

op·po·site /£ˈɒp·ə·zɪt, $ˈɑː·pə-/ *n* • *My father is a very calm person, but my mother is just* **the** *opposite.* [U] • *She's turned out to be* **the** *exact* **opposite of** *what everyone expected.* [U] • **The** *opposite* **of** *'fast' is 'slow'.* [U] • *Do you think it's true that opposites* (= people or things that are completely different in character) *attract?* [C]

op·posed /£əˈpəʊzd, $-ˈpoʊzd/ *adj* • *Two opposed* (= completely different so not both able to be right) *interpretations of the facts have been presented.* • *His view of the situation is* **diametrically** (= very strongly) *opposed* **to** *mine.* • *I'd prefer to go on holiday in May,* **as opposed to** (= rather than) *September.*

op·po·site FACING /£ˈɒp·ə·zɪt, £-sɪt, $ˈɑː·pə-/ *adj* [not gradable] being in a position on the other side; facing • *My brother and I live on opposite sides of London.* • *The map on the opposite page shows where these birds commonly breed.* • *They sat at opposite ends of the table* (**to/from** *each other*), *refusing to talk to each other.* • Opposite also means facing the speaker or stated person or thing: *No, this isn't where you buy tickets – you need to go to the counter opposite.* ○ *Who owns that shop opposite* (= on the other side of the road)*?*

op·po·site /£ˈɒp·ə·zɪt, £-sɪt, $ˈɑː·pə-/ *prep* • *We're in the building opposite* (= facing) *the government offices.* • *They sat opposite each other.* • *Put a tick opposite* (= next to) *the answer that you think is correct.* • If a person in a film or play **acts/plays/stars** opposite someone else, they take a part in the film or play with that person, esp. as their partner: *Katharine Hepburn played opposite Henry Fonda in many films.*

op·po·site /£ˈɒp·ə·zɪt, £-sɪt, $ˈɑː·pə-/ *adv* [not gradable] • *She asked the man sitting opposite* (= facing her) *if he minded if she opened the window.* • *The people who live opposite* (= on the other side of the road) *are always making a lot of noise.*

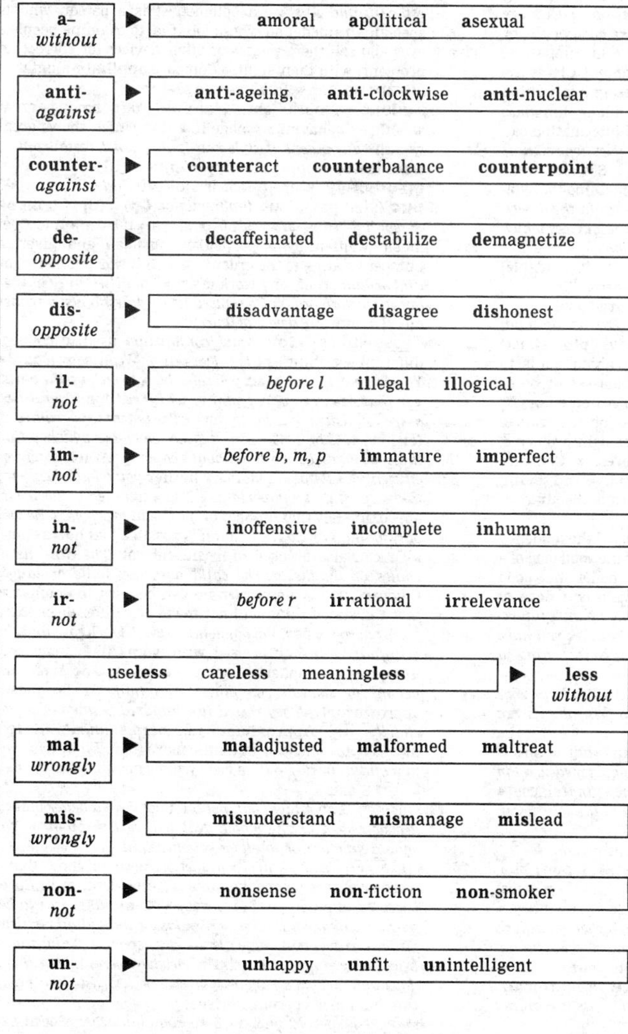

OPPOSITE AND NEGATIVE MEANINGS

A number of combining forms are added to words to give opposite or negative meanings. For example, the opposite of 'comfortable' is '**un**comfortable', and **mis**behaviour is bad behaviour. These combining forms are usually added to the beginning of a word, for example 'anti-', 'counter-' or 'non-'. The word ending '-less' is also used in this way.

a- *without* ▶ **a**moral **a**political **a**sexual

anti- *against* ▶ **anti**-ageing, **anti**-clockwise **anti**-nuclear

counter- *against* ▶ **counter**act **counter**balance **counter**point

de- *opposite* ▶ **de**caffeinated **de**stabilize **de**magnetize

dis- *opposite* ▶ **dis**advantage **dis**agree **dis**honest

il- *not* ▶ *before l* **il**legal **il**logical

im- *not* ▶ *before b, m, p* **im**mature **im**perfect

in- *not* ▶ **in**offensive **in**complete **in**human

ir- *not* ▶ *before r* **ir**rational **ir**relevance

use**less** care**less** meaning**less** ▶ **less** *without*

mal *wrongly* ▶ **mal**adjusted **mal**formed **mal**treat

mis- *wrongly* ▶ **mis**understand **mis**manage **mis**lead

non- *not* ▶ **non**sense **non**-fiction **non**-smoker

un- *not* ▶ **un**happy **un**fit **un**intelligent

op·press *obj* RULE /əˈpres/ *v* [T] to govern (people) in an unfair and cruel way and prevent them from having opportunities and freedom • *For years now, the people have been oppressed by a ruthless dictator.*
op·pres·sion /əˈpreʃ·ən/ *n* [U] • *Every human being has the right to freedom from oppression.* • *War, famine and oppression have forced people in the region to flee from their homes.* • *She said that the oppression of women would not be ended simply by changing the law.*
op·pres·sive /əˈpres·ɪv/ *adj* • *an oppressive military regime* • *oppressive taxes*
op·pres·sive·ly /əˈpres·ɪv·li/ *adv*
op·pres·sive·ness /əˈpres·ɪv·nəs/ *n* [U]
op·pres·sor /£əˈpres·əʳ, $-ɚ/ *n* [C] • *Sisters, we must rise up and defeat our oppressors.*

op·press *obj* MAKE UNCOMFORTABLE /əˈpres/ *v* [T] to make (a person) feel uncomfortable or anxious, and sometimes ill • *Strange dreams and nightmares oppressed him.*
op·pres·sion /əˈpreʃ·ən/ *n* [U] • *Several people had experienced the same feeling of oppression when they slept in that room.*
op·pres·sive /əˈpres·ɪv/ *adj* • *She felt an oppressive sense of guilt.* • Air and weather conditions that are oppressive are very hot and wet, and cause people to feel uncomfortable: *The atmosphere was oppressive, as if there were about to be a thunderstorm.* ○ *We were unable to sleep because of the oppressive heat.*
op·pres·sive·ly /əˈpres·ɪv·li/ *adv* • *It was oppressively* (= uncomfortably) *hot in the bus.*
op·pres·sive·ness /əˈpres·ɪv·nəs/ *n* [U]

op·pro·bri·um /£əˈprəʊ·bri·əm, $-ˈproʊ-/ *n* [U] *fml* dislike and/or blame, esp. as felt by everyone for one person • *You acted quite correctly, and no opprobrium attaches to you for what you did.* • *International opprobrium has been* **heaped on** *the country following its attack on its neighbours.*

op–shop /£ˈɒp·ʃɒp, $ˈɑːp·ʃɑːp/ *n* [C] *Aus infml for* **opportunity shop**, see at OPPORTUNITY

opt /£ɒpt, $ɑːpt/ *v* to make a choice, esp. for one thing or possibility in preference to any others • *There are several things on the menu I'd like to try, but I think I'll opt* **for** *the salmon.* [I] • *When he left school, he opted* **to** *go to college and study for a degree, rather than getting a job straight away.* [+ to infinitive] • *Within any society, there will usually be people who decide to opt* **out** (= choose to not live the way most people do). [I] • *The government has been encouraging individuals to opt* **out of** (= not take part in) *the state* *pension scheme.* [I] • An **opt-out** is an act of not continuing to do something, esp. (in Britain) an act of removing something from the control of local government: *Since the opt-out, the hospital has been responsible for its own budgeting.* ○ *There are several opt-out schools in the area.*

op·ti·cal /£'ɒp·tɪ·kᵊl, $'ɑːp-/ *adj* [not gradable] connected with the eyes or sight, or connected with or using light • *an optical effect* • *an optical microscope/telescope* • *CDs are optical* (=using light) *storage media, unlike hard or floppy disks which are magnetic storage media.* • In computing, **optical character recognition** (*abbreviation* **OCR**) is the process by which an electronic device recognizes written letters or numbers. • An **optical fibre** is a long thin glass rod through which very large amounts of information can be sent in the form of light: *Many TV and telephone signals are now distributed through optical fibres.* See also **fibre optic** at FIBRE. • An **optical illusion** is something that you think you see, but which is not really there: *In the desert, the heat can sometimes cause people to see palm trees which aren't really there, but are just optical illusions.*

op·tic /£'ɒp·tɪk, $'ɑːp-/ *adj* [before n; not gradable] *medical* • Optic refers to the eyes: *the optic nerve*

op·ti·cal·ly /£'ɒp·tɪ·kli, $'ɑːp-/ *adv* [not gradable]

op·ti·cian /£ɒp'tɪʃ·ᵊn, $ɑːp-/ *n* [C] • *(Br)* An optician (also **ophthalmic optician**, *esp. Am and Aus* **optometrist**) is someone who is specially trained, and whose job it is, to examine a person's eyes and sell them glasses or other things to correct sight problems. • *(Am)* An optician (*Br* **dispensing optician**) is a person whose job it is to sell people glasses and other things to correct sight problems, but who does not examine people's eyes. • Compare **ophthalmologist** at OPTHALMOLOGY. • [LP]> **Eye and seeing**

op·tics /£'ɒp·tɪks, $'ɑːp-/ *n* [U] • Optics is the study of light.

op·ti·mi·sm /£'ɒp·tɪ·mɪ·zᵊm, $'ɑːp·tə-/ *n* [U] the tendency to be hopeful and to emphasize or think of the good part of a situation rather than the bad part; the belief that good things will happen in the future • *There was a* **note of** *optimism in his voice as he spoke about the company's future.* • *Judging from your examination results, I think you have cause/grounds for* **cautious** *optimism about getting a university place.* • Compare PESSIMISM.

op·ti·mist /£'ɒp·tɪ·mɪst, $'ɑːp·tə-/ *n* [C] • *You have to be a* **born/natural** *optimist to be able to do this job and not despair.*

op·ti·mis·tic /£,ɒp·tɪ'mɪs·tɪk, $,ɑːp·tə-/ *adj* • *She is optimistic* **about** *her chances of winning a gold medal.* • *I'm optimistic* **that** *we can finish the job on time.* [+ *that* clause] • **It**'s *a bit optimistic* **to** *think that we can do the journey in under five hours.* [+ *to* infinitive]

op·ti·mis·ti·cally /£,ɒp·tɪ'mɪs·tɪ·kli, $,ɑːp·tə-/ *adv*

op·ti·mum /£'ɒp·tɪ·məm, $'ɑːp-/, **op·ti·mal** /£'ɒp·tɪ·məl, $'ɑːp-/ *adj* [before n; not gradable] best or most advantageous; most likely to bring success or advantage • *The balloonists are waiting for optimum weather conditions before taking off.* • *A mixture of selected funds is an optimum* **choice** *for future security and return on investment.*

op·ti·mize *obj, Br and Aus usually* **-ise** /£'ɒp·tɪ·maɪz, $'ɑːp·tə-/ *v* [T] • *Further research into the belts is required to optimize passenger safety.*

op·tion /£'ɒp·ʃᵊn, $'ɑːp-/ *n* one thing which can be chosen from a set of possibilities, or the freedom to make a choice • *One option would be to cancel the trip altogether.* [C] • *Leaving on Thursday would be another option.* [C] • *There are many/several/various options* **open** *to someone who is willing to work hard.* [C] • *When I left school I wanted to travel, but I had no money so I had no option* (=freedom to choose) **but to** *work.* [U + *to* infinitive] • *This type of bank account gives you the option* **to** *withdraw up to £500 without prior arrangement.* [U + *to* infinitive] • *They didn't leave him much option – either he paid or they'd beat him up.* [U] • *(specialized)* An option is also the right to buy something in the future: *a share option* [C] ○ *The publishers decided not to take up their option* **on** *the paperback version.* [C] • If someone **keeps/leaves** their options **open** they wait before making a choice: *I don't have to decide which subjects I'm going to study until next term, so I'll keep my options open till then and think about it over the summer.* [C]

op·tion·al /£'ɒp·ʃᵊn·ᵊl, $'ɑːp-/ *adj* [not gradable] • If something is optional, you can choose whether to do it, pay it, buy it, etc.: *English, maths and science are compulsory for all students, but art and music are optional.* ○ *The charge for going into the museum is optional.* ○ *The computer comes with a number of optional accessories.*

op·to·me·try /£ɒp'tɒm·ə·tri, $ɑːp'tɑː·mə-/ *n* [U] *esp. Am and Aus* the science or activity of testing people's sight and providing people with glasses or **contact lenses** (=small transparent circles worn on the surface of the eyes) to correct problems with their sight • Compare OPHTHALMOLOGY.

op·to·me·trist /£ɒp'tɒm·ə·trɪst, $ɑːp'tɑː·mə-/ *n* [C] *esp. Am and Aus* • An optometrist is a person who is specially trained, and whose job it is, to examine people's eyes and sell them glasses or other devices for correcting problems with their sight. • Compare **ophthalmologist** at OPHTHALMOLOGY. • [LP]> **Eye and seeing**

op·u·lent /£'ɒp·jʊ·lənt, $'ɑː·pjʊ-/ *adj* having great wealth, or behaving or made in a way which shows great wealth • *an opulent lifestyle* • *an opulent hotel/restaurant*

op·u·lence /£'ɒp·jʊ·ləns, $'ɑː·pjʊ-/ *n* [U]

op·u·lent·ly /£'ɒp·jʊ·lənt·li, $'ɑː·pjʊ-/ *adv*

o·pus /£'əʊ·pəs, $'oʊ-/ (*abbreviation* **Op**) *n* [C] *pl* **opuses** or *specialized* **opera** /£'ɒp·ᵊr·ə, $'ɑː·pɚ·ə/ a piece of music written by a particular musician and given a number relating to the order in which it was published, or *(fml or humorous)* any work of art • *Carl Nielsen's Opus 43 quintet* • *(humorous) He showed us his latest opus, a rather awful painting of a vase of flowers.*

or [POSSIBILITIES] /£ɔːʳ, $ɔːr/ *conjunction* used to connect different possibilities • *Is it Tuesday or Wednesday today?* • *You can pay now or when you come back to pick up the paint.* • *In that size we have red, pink or white/red or pink or white.* • *Are you listening to me or* **not**? • *The patent was granted in* **(either)** *1962 or 1963 – I can't quite remember which.* • *Can these changes be made without reducing* **either** *safety or efficiency?* • *It doesn't matter* **whether** *you win or lose – it's taking part that's important.* • *There were ten or twelve* (= approximately that number of) *people in the room.* • *He was only joking – or was he* (= but it is possible that he was not)? • Or can also be used to mean and not: *The child never smiles or laughs.* ○ *The child does not smile or laugh.* Compare NOR. • *(infml)* **Or no** can be used to emphasize that the stated thing will not make any difference: *Extra pay or no extra pay, I'm not going to work late again tonight.* • *(infml)* **Or other** is used with words like 'some' and 'someone' to emphasize lack of certainty: *The keys must belong to someone or other.* • *(infml)* **Or so** means approximately: *They raised two hundred pounds or so for charity.* [LP]> **Approximate numbers** • *(infml)* **Or two** means approximately or a little more than: *I'll be with you in a minute or two.* ○ *It's a good year or two since we last met.* • [LP]> **Slash**

or [IF NOT] /£ɔːʳ, $ɔːr/ *conjunction* if not • *We'd better make a decision soon or the whole deal will fall through.* • *You should eat more, or you'll make yourself ill.*

or [EXPLAIN] /£ɔːʳ, $ɔːr/ *conjunction* used to show that a word or phrase means the same as, or explains or limits or corrects, another word or phrase • *Rosalind, or Roz to her friends, took the initiative.* • *Photons, or individual particles of light, travel over huge distances in space.* • *Things have been going quite well recently. Or they were, up until two days ago.* • *Tom's resigned, or so I've heard* (=I've heard this, but I'm not certain it's true).

-or [PERFORMER] /£-əʳ, £-ɔːʳ, $-ɚ/ *combining form* See at -ER [PERFORMER] • [LP]> **Combining forms**

or·a·cle /£'ɒr·ə·kl̩, $'ɔːr-/ *n* [C] a place in ancient Greece where a person, esp. a female priest, gave people wise but often mysterious advice from a god, or the person giving this advice • *the oracle at Delphi* • *(fig.) I've come to* **consult** *the oracle* (=someone who knows a lot about a particular subject or gives wise advice), *Joe – how early in the year can I put these plants out of doors?*

or·ac·u·lar /£ɒr'æk·jʊ·ləʳ, $ɔːr'æk·juː·lɚ/ *adj fml* • *an oracular* (=mysterious and difficult to understand, or wise) *statement*

o·ral [SPOKEN] /£'ɔː·rəl, $'ɔːr·əl/ *adj* [not gradable] spoken; not written • *an oral agreement/exam* • **Oral history** is information about an historical event or period which is told to you by people who experienced it. • **Oral tradition** is a way of preserving a group's beliefs, customs and history by parents telling their children about them, and the children telling their children and so on.

o·ral /£'ɔː·rəl, $'ɔːr·əl/ *n* [C] • *When do you have your Spanish oral* (=exam in spoken Spanish)?

o·ral·ly /£'ɔː·rə·li, $'ɔːr·ə-/ *adv* [not gradable]

o·ral [MOUTH] /£'ɔː·rəl, $'ɔːr·əl/ *adj* [not gradable] *esp. medical* of, taken by, or done to the mouth • *oral hygiene* • *oral contraceptives* • *oral surgery* • **Oral sex** is the activity of using the tongue, lips and mouth to give pleasure to someone's sexual organs.

o·ral·ly /£'ɔː·rə·li, $'ɔːr·ə-/ *adv* [not gradable] • *This medicine is to be taken orally.*

or·ange COLOUR /£'ɒr·ɪndʒ, $'ɔːr-/ *adj* [not gradable], *n* (of) a colour between red and yellow • *The setting sun filled the sky with a deep orange glow.* • *Her blouse is a very bright orange.* [C] • *They'd decorated the room in brown and orange.* [U]

oran·ge·ness /£'ɒr·ɪnʒ·nəs, $'ɔːr-/ *n* [U]

or·ange FRUIT /£'ɒr·ɪndʒ, $'ɔːr-/ *n* a round juicy sweet but sharp-tasting fruit which has orange-coloured skin and orange-coloured flesh in the form of SEGMENTS (= parts like slices), and which grows on trees in hot countries • *oranges and lemons* [C] • *a piece of orange* [U] • *a glass of orange juice* • *orange blossom* • *orange groves* • *(Br)* **Orange squash** (*Am* **orangeade**) is a drink that tastes of oranges, to which you add water before you drink it. • *"Oranges are not the only fruit"* (title of a book by Jeanette Winterson, 1985)

or·ange·ade *Br* /£,ɒr·ɪndʒ'eɪd, $,ɔːr-/, *Am* **or·ange so·da** *n* [U] a usually fizzy sweet drink, which tastes of oranges • *a can of orangeade* • Orangeade is *Am for* **orange squash**. See at ORANGE FRUIT.

o·rang–u·tan /£ɔː'ræŋ·u·tæŋ, -,--'-, $ɔːr'æŋ-/ *n* [C] a large APE (= animal like a monkey) with reddish brown hair and long arms which lives in the forests of Sumatra and Borneo • PIC〉 **Apes and monkeys**

o·ra·tion /£ɔː'reɪ·ʃən, £ɒr'eɪ-, $ɔːr'eɪ-/ *n* [C] a formal public speech about a serious subject • *a funeral oration*

or·a·to·ri·o /£,ɒr·ə'tɔː·ri·əʊ, $,ɔːr·ə'tɔːr·i·oʊ/ *n* [C] *pl* **oratorios** a large formal musical work for singers and players of instruments which tells a story, usually on a religious subject, without acting • *a Handel oratorio* • Compare CANTATA.

oratory /£'ɒr·ə·tər·i, $'ɔːr·ə·tɔːr-/ *n* [U] *fml* the activity of giving skilful and effective speeches in public • *She has a reputation for powerful oratory.* • *The oratory was spellbinding, but it remains to be seen whether it will move Congress to action.*

or·a·tor /£'ɒr·ə·tər, $'ɔːr·ə·t̬ɚ/ *n* [C] • *He is very skilled as an orator.*

or·a·to·ri·cal /£,ɒr·ə'tɒr·ɪ·kəl, $,ɔːr·ə'tɔːr-/ *adj fml* • *oratorical skill*

orb /£ɔːb, $ɔːrb/ *n* [C] *poetic* something spherical • *the glowing orb of the sun*

or·bit /£'ɔː·bɪt, $'ɔːr-/ *n* the curved path through which objects in space move around a planet or star which has GRAVITY (= a pulling force) • *a stable orbit* [C] • *Most planetary orbits are not circles but ellipses.* [C] • *Once in space, the spacecraft went* **into** *orbit* **around** *the Earth.* [U] • *The spacecraft is now* **in** *orbit* **round/around** *Venus.* [U] • *(fig.) Taxation falls within the orbit* (= area of power or influence) *of a different department.* [C] • *(fig. infml) Prices have gone* **into** *orbit* (= become very high) *this year.* [U] • *(fig. infml) When I told him what I'd done, he really went* **into** *orbit* (= became very angry). [U]

or·bit *(obj)* /£'ɔː·bɪt, $'ɔːr-/ *v* • *On this mission the Shuttle will orbit (the Earth) at a height of several hundred miles.* [I/T]

or·bi·tal /£'ɔː·bɪ·təl, $'ɔːr·bɪ·t̬əl/ *adj* [not gradable] • *an orbital space station* • *(Br)* An **orbital road** is one which takes traffic around a city rather than through it.

or·chard /£'ɔː·tʃəd, $'ɔːr·tʃɚd/ *n* [C] an area of land where fruit trees (but not orange trees or other CITRUS trees) are grown • *an apple orchard* • *a cherry orchard*

or·che·stra /£'ɔː·kɪ·strə, $'ɔːr-/ *n* [C + sing/pl v] a usually large group of musicians who together play many different instruments • *the City of Birmingham Symphony Orchestra* • *the New York Philharmonic Orchestra* • *The school orchestra is/are practising in the hall at the moment.* • Orchestra is *Am for* STALLS THEATRE: *We've got seats in* **the orchestra** *for tonight's concert.* • An **orchestra pit** is the area of a theatre in which musicians play their instruments, and which is in front of, or under the front of, the stage.

or·che·stral /£ɔː'kes·trəl, $ɔːr-/ *adj* [not gradable] • *an orchestral arrangement*

or·che·strate *obj* /£'ɔː·kɪ·streɪt, $'ɔːr-/ *v* [T] • If a piece of music is orchestrated, it is arranged or written to be played by an orchestra. • See also ORCHESTRATE.

or·che·stra·tion /£,ɔː·kɪ'streɪ·ʃən, $,ɔːr-/ *n* [C/U]

or·che·strate *obj* /£'ɔː·kɪ·streɪt, $'ɔːr-/ *v* [T] to arrange (something) carefully, and sometimes unfairly, so as to achieve a desired result • *Their victory was largely a result of their* **brilliantly** *orchestrated election campaign.* • *No matter how bad the product which is being sold,* **carefully** *orchestrated marketing can produce reasonable sales.* • See also **orchestrate** at ORCHESTRA.

or·che·stra·tion /£,ɔː·kɪ'streɪ·ʃən, $,ɔːr-/ *n* [U]

or·chid /£'ɔː·kɪd, $'ɔːr-/ *n* [C] a plant with unusually shaped and beautifully coloured flowers, or one of its flowers • *Many of Britain's wild orchids are endangered species.* • PIC〉 **Flowers and plants**

or·dain *obj* CHURCH /£ɔː'deɪn, $ɔːr-/ *v* [T often passive] to make (someone) officially a Christian priest, in a religious ceremony • *He was ordained* **(as)** *a priest in Oxford cathedral in 1987.* • *She has become an ordained minister.*

or·din·a·tion /£,ɔː·dɪ'neɪ·ʃən, $,ɔːr-/ *n* • *Some people were opposed to the ordination* (= the act of officially making a priest) **of** *women when it was first introduced into the Church of England.* [U] • *The ordination* (= a religious ceremony at which someone is officially made a priest) *took place in Bristol cathedral.* [C] • (CS) (RUS)

or·dain *(obj)* ORDER /£ɔː'deɪn, $ɔːr-/ *v fml or humorous* (of God or someone in authority) to order (something to happen) • *There is strong support here for the tough economic reforms ordained in the federal capital, Prague.* [T] • *(humorous) The council, in its wisdom, has ordained* **that** *all the local libraries will close on Mondays.* [+ *that* clause]

or·deal /£ɔː'dɪəl, $ɔːr-/ *n* [C] a severe experience which is very painful, difficult or tiring • *The hostages' ordeal came to an end when soldiers stormed the building.*

or·der INSTRUCTION /£'ɔː·dər, $'ɔːr·dɚ/ *n* [C] something you are told to do by someone else and which you must do • *Clean up this room immediately – and that's an order!* • *When he* **gave** *the order, the candidates opened their exam papers and started to write.* • *At 8 a.m. we* **received** *the order* **to** *attack.* [+ *to* infinitive] • *(Br)* **At**/*(Am, Aus usually)* **On** *an order from their leader, the group picked up their bags and got on the bus.* • *The road was closed all day* **by order of** *the police* (= The police gave instructions that it should be closed). • An order is also an instruction telling someone what they can or cannot do, or a written instruction to a bank to pay money to a particular person: *She obtained a* **court** *order to stop her ex-husband from coming near her house.* • Compare REQUEST. • LP〉 **Exclamation mark** (RUS)

or·ders /£'ɔː·dəz, $'ɔːr·dɚz/ *pl n* • *What are your orders* (= What have you been told you must do)? • *She* **gave** *orders* (= an order) **that** *she wasn't to be disturbed.* [+ *that* clause] • *My orders are* **to** *search everyone's bag as they come in.* [+ *to* infinitive] • *We* **have/are under** *orders* (= We have been told) *not* **to** *allow anyone into the building.* [+ *to* infinitive] • *I was only* **obeying** *orders.* • **Orders are orders** (= We must do what we have been told to do), *I suppose.*

or·der *obj* /£'ɔː·dər, $'ɔːr·dɚ/ *v* [T] • If a person in authority orders someone to do something, or orders something to be done, they tell someone to do it: *The management has ordered a cutback in spending.* ○ *"Wait over there," she ordered.* [+ clause] ○ *The captain ordered* **that** *all his officers should attend the parade.* [+ *that* clause] ○ *They ordered him* **to** *leave the room.* [+ obj + *to* infinitive] ○ *All the squatters have been ordered* **out** (= told to leave). • To be ordered **about/around** is to be told to do things in an unpleasant and forceful way by someone who has no real power to tell you what to do: *When he was a child, his brother always used to order him about.*

or·der *(obj)* REQUEST /£'ɔː·dər, $'ɔːr·dɚ/ *v* to ask for (something) to be made, supplied or delivered, esp. in a restaurant or shop • *Are you ready to order, or would you like to look at the menu for a little longer?* [I] • *I ordered some pasta and a mixed salad.* [T] • *The customer says she ordered the books six weeks ago and she still hasn't received them.* [T] • *There are no shirts left in this size but we could order one* **for** *you/order you one.* [+ two objects] • (RUS)

or·der /£'ɔː·dər, $'ɔːr·dɚ/ *n* [C] • An order is a request to make, supply or deliver food or goods: *Can I* **take** *your order now or would you like to have a drink first?* ○ *I would like to* **place** (= make) *an order for a large pine table.* • An order is also the object which has been requested: *The shop phoned to say your order has come in.* • If something is **on** order, you have asked for it to be obtained but have not yet received it: *The equipment has been on order for several weeks.* • If something is done or made **to** order, it is done or made especially for the person who requested it: *We only make wedding cakes to order.* • An **order book** is a book in which a company or shop keeps a record of customers' orders. • An **order form** is a printed form which a customer uses to request goods or a service: *You can book your holiday by* **filling out** *the order form provided.*

or·der [ARRANGEMENT] /£'ɔː·də^r, $'ɔːr·dɚ/ *n* [U] the way in which people or things are arranged in relation to one another or according to a particular characteristic • **In** *what order do you want to interview the candidates?* • *The children lined up* **in** *order* **of** *age/height.* • *List your choices* **in** *order* **of** *preference.* • *I can't find the file I need because they're all* **out of** *order* (= they are no longer arranged in the correct way). See also **out of order** at ORDER [CORRECT BEHAVIOUR], ORDER [USABLE]. • *Put the names in* **alphabetical** *order.* • *He wrote down the events in* **chronological** *order* (= according to when they happened). • *They read out the winners in* **reverse** *order – third, second and then first.* • *(esp. Br) Here's the* **running** *order for the concert* (= the order in which each item will happen). See also **running order** at ORDER [USABLE]. • *As they went into the church, each wedding guest was handed an order* **of service** (= a piece of paper listing the order in which each item in the marriage ceremony would happen). • *(fml)* In parliament or in formal meetings, **the order of the day** is the list of matters to be discussed on a particular day. • *(infml)* If something is **the order of the day**, it is the most important matter or commonest activity among a group of people, or it is the only choice available: *For countries undergoing a recession, large cuts in government spending seem to be the order of the day.* ○ *He claims that if there is a further cut in spending, poor quality TV programmes will become the order of the day* (= they will be the only programmes that are available). • In parliament, an **order paper** is a list which shows the order in which matters will be discussed on a particular day. • *"Stand not upon the order of your going* (= leave in any order you like)*"* (Shakespeare, Macbeth 3.4) • (RUS)

or·der *obj* /£'ɔː·də^r, $'ɔːr·dɚ/ *v* [T] • *I've ordered* (= arranged) *the application forms* **into** *three groups.* • *Just give me a moment to order my* **thoughts** (= plan what I want to say), *and then I'll explain the system to you.*

or·der [TIDINESS] /£'ɔː·də^r, $'ɔːr·dɚ/ *n* [U] the condition in which everything is arranged in its correct place • *The room was so untidy that she spent the whole day trying to reestablish some sort of order.* • If you **leave/put** things **in** order, you make them tidy: *I want to leave my desk in order before I go away.* ○ *Make sure you leave the room in* **good** *order* (= tidy) *before you go.* ○ *Before you go into hospital, you must put your* **affairs** *in order* (= make special arrangements for your personal and business matters). • (RUS)

or·dered /£'ɔː·dəd, $'ɔːr·dɚd/ *adj* • *a well ordered* (= tidy) *room*

or·der·ly /£'ɔː·d^{ə}l·i, $'ɔːr·dɚ·li/ *adj* • Orderly means well arranged or organized: *She put the letters in three orderly piles.* ○ *There must be an orderly transition of power to the new government.* ○ *People formed an orderly queue as they waited to be served.* ○ *During the bomb scare, the customers were asked to proceed* **in an** *orderly* **fashion** *out of the shop.* • See also ORDERLY.

or·der [PURPOSE] /£'ɔː·də^r, $'ɔːr·dɚ/ *n* [U] **in order to/in order for/in order that** with the aim or purpose of (achieving something) • *He came home early in order to see the children before they went to bed.* • *I agreed to her suggestion in order* **not** *to upset her.* • *In order for us to assess what is needed, everyone will have to keep a diary of what they do for a week.* • *(fml) Parents offered to help in order that the children could have an after-school club every day.* • (RUS)

or·der [CORRECT BEHAVIOUR] /£'ɔː·də^r, $'ɔːr·dɚ/ *n* [U] a situation in which rules are obeyed and people do what they are expected to do • *The children were so excited at the party that their parents found it hard to* **keep** *order.* • *The teacher found it hard to* **keep** *her class* **in** *order.* See also **in order** at ORDER [USABLE]. • *After some heated discussion, the chair* **called** *the meeting* **to** *order* (= told everyone to stop talking so that the meeting could continue). • *As the demonstration began to turn violent, the police were called in to* **restore** *order.* • *His behaviour in the meeting was (well)* **out of** *order* (= not suitable for the situation). See also **out of order** at ORDER [ARRANGEMENT], ORDER [USABLE]. • *(Br and Aus) Is it* **in** *order* (= allowed) *for me to park my car outside the building?* • *(fml)* In parliament or a formal meeting, the expression **Order! Order!** is used to get people's attention and make them stop talking so that the meeting or discussion can start or continue. • (RUS)

or·der [USABLE] /£'ɔː·də^r, $'ɔːr·dɚ/ *n* [U] the state of working correctly or of being suitable for use • *TV for sale* **in (good) working** *order.* • *This old motorbike is still* **in** *perfect* **running** *order* (= working well). See also **running order** at ORDER [ARRANGEMENT]. • *Are your immigration papers* **in** *order* (= legally correct)*?* See also **in order** at ORDER [CORRECT BEHAVIOUR]. • *The coffee machine is* **out of** *order* (= not working). See also **out of order** at ORDER [ARRANGEMENT], ORDER [CORRECT BEHAVIOUR]. • (RUS)

or·der [SYSTEM] /£'ɔː·də^r, $'ɔːr·dɚ/ *n* [C] a social or political system • *the old order* • *a new economic order* • *The collapse of Communism at the end of the 1980s encouraged hopes of a* **new world** *order.* • (RUS)

or·der [GROUP OF PEOPLE] /£'ɔː·də^r, $'ɔːr·dɚ/ *n* [C + sing/pl v] a group of people who join together for esp. religious reasons and live according to particular rules • *religious/holy orders* • *monks of the Cistercian/Franciscan Order* • *the Masonic order* • An order is also a group which people are made members of as a reward for services they have done for their country: *He was made a knight of the Order of the Garter.* ○ *The Order of Merit is an order of distinguished men and women which has 24 members.* • *(fml)* An order is also a group or class in society: *In Britain, a duke is a nobleman of the highest order.* ○ *The propaganda campaign had a greater effect upon the middle and upper classes than upon the* **lower** *orders.* • (RUS)

or·der [TYPE] /£'ɔː·də^r, $'ɔːr·dɚ/ *n* [U] the type or size of something • *These were problems of a completely different order from anything we had faced before.* • *(fml) No democracy can run without political skills* **of the highest** *order* (= great political skills)*, such as foresight, boldness and patience.* • **Of the order of/***(Br also)* **In the order of** means approximately: *There were of the order of 2 000 people at the festival.* ○ *"How much is the project going to cost?" "Something in the order of £500."* • The **order of magnitude** of something, esp. a number, is its approximate size: *The estimate for the building work is* **of** *the order of magnitude we were expecting.* ○ *The country's debt this year will be* **of** *the same order of magnitude as it was last year.* ○ *No one knows, even to the nearest order of magnitude, how many species exist on the Earth.* • (RUS)

or·der [BIOLOGY] /£'ɔː·də^r, $'ɔːr·dɚ/ *n* [C] *specialized* (used in the CLASSIFICATION of plants and animals) a group of related plants or animals • *An order is below a class and above a family.* • (RUS)

or·der·ly [HOSPITAL WORKER] /£'ɔː·d^{ə}l·i, $'ɔːr·dɚ·li/ *n* [C] a hospital worker who does jobs for which no training is necessary, such as helping the nurses or carrying heavy things • *He has a part-time job as a* **hospital** *orderly.* • See also **orderly** at ORDER [TIDINESS].

or·der·ly [SOLDIER] /£'ɔː·d^{ə}l·i, $'ɔːr·dɚ·li/ *n* [C] a soldier who acts as an officer's servant • See also **orderly** at ORDER [TIDINESS].

or·di·nal (num·ber) /£'ɔː·dɪ·nəl, $'ɔːr·d^{ə}n·^{ə}l/ *n* [C] a number like 1st, 2nd, 3rd, 4th, which shows the position of something in a list of items • *Ordinal numbers are used in these sentences: 'She was fifth in the race' and 'They celebrated the 200th anniversary of the university's foundation'.* • Compare CARDINAL (NUMBER).

or·di·nance /£'ɔː·dɪ·nənts, $'ɔːr·d^{ə}n·^{ə}nts/ *n* [C] *fml* a law or rule made by a government or authority • *City Ordinance 126 forbids car parking in this area.*

or·di·na·ry /£'ɔː·dɪ·nə·ri, $'ɔːr·d^{ə}n·er·/ *adj* not different, special or unexpected in any way; usual • *They live in a perfectly ordinary, undistinguished neighbourhood.* • *Readers of the magazine said they wanted more stories about ordinary people and less stories about the rich and famous.* • *We're very ordinary people really – there's nothing special about us.* • *Her last concert appearance in Britain was* **no** *ordinary* (= a very special) *performance.* • *For the police, the incident seemed* **nothing out of the** *ordinary/did not seem* **out of the** *ordinary* (= it was not unusual). • *(Br) If we hadn't seen the TV programme, we would have carried on giving money to the charity* **in the ordinary way** (= as we usually did). • *(Br)* **Ordinary level** is *fml for* O LEVEL (= a British school examination). • (CS) (D) (E) (P) (PL)

or·di·nar·i·ly /£'ɔː·dɪ·nə·rə·li, £ˌɔː·d^{ə}n'er·ɪ·, $'ɔːr·d^{ə}n·er·/ *adv* • Ordinarily means usually: *Solicitors in England are lawyers who ordinarily do not appear in court.* ○ *Ordinarily, we send a reminder about a month before payment is required.*

or·di·na·ri·ness /£'ɔː·dɪ·nə·rɪ·nəs, $ˌɔːr·d^{ə}n'er·/ *n* [U] • *She expected him to act like a star, but she was surprised at his very ordinariness* (= how ordinary he was).

or·din·a·tion /£ˌɔː·dɪˈneɪ·ʃᵊn, $ˌɔːr·dᵊnˈeɪ-/ *n* [U] See at ORDAIN [CHURCH]

ord·nance /£ˈɔːd·nənts, $ˈɔːrd-/ *n* [U] **the Ordnance Survey** *(abbreviation* **OS***)* the government organization which makes detailed official maps of Britain and Northern Ireland

ore /£ɔːʳ, $ɔːr/ *n* a MINERAL or a combination of such chemical substances, which are formed naturally in the ground and from which metal can be obtained • *iron/copper ore* [U] • *an ore mine/producer* [U] • *6000 tons of ore can be processed at the site each day.* [U] • *Metal ores are often found mixed with rock, dirt and clay and are rarely pure enough to be processed straight away.* [C] • *The main* **iron** *ores are oxides, which are combinations of iron with oxygen.* [C]

o·re·gan·o /£ˌɒr·ɪˈgɑː·nəʊ, $ɔːˈreg·ə·noʊ/ *n* [U] a herb whose dried leaves are used in cooking to add flavour, and which is especially common in Italian cooking

or·gan [BODY PART] /£ˈɔː·gən, $ˈɔːr-/ *n* [C] a part of the body of an animal or plant which performs a particular job • *The ear is an* **external** *organ.* • *The heart, lungs and kidneys are* **internal** *organs.* • *A plant's male and female* **reproductive** *organs are contained in the flower.* • *A recent survey showed that nearly three-quarters of us are prepared to be organ* **donors***, but only a quarter of us have donor cards.* • *Organ* **transplants** *are among the most expensive operations in medicine.* • *She was in a critical condition after the heart transplant operation when her body* **rejected** *the organ.* • *(fml)* A newspaper or broadcasting organization which is used to give information or influence the way people think can be described as an organ **of** the organization which produces it: *The newspaper Pravda was known as the organ of the Communist Party in the Soviet Union.*

or·gan·ic /£ɔːˈgæn·ɪk, $ɔːr-/ *adj* [not gradable] *fml* • An organic disease or illness is one which produces a physical change in the structure of an organ or part of the body: *The doctor told her that her chest pains were caused by stress rather than by an organic disease.* • See also ORGANIC.

or·gan [INSTRUMENT] /£ˈɔː·gən, $ˈɔːr-/ *n* [C] a musical instrument with a keyboard in which sound is produced by air being forced through pipes of different sizes and lengths when you press the keys with your hands or feet, or in which sound is produced electronically • *She plays the organ in her local church.* • *The largest* **church** *organs have three manual keyboards.* • **Electronic** *organs are much smaller and cheaper than* **pipe** *organs.* • *He collects recordings of Bach's organ music.* • *(dated)* An **organ grinder** is a person who earns money by playing a type of organ that is operated by turning a handle in public places.

or·gan·ist /£ˈɔː·gᵊn·ɪst, $ˈɔːr-/ *n* [C] • An organist is a person who plays an organ, esp. in a church or as a job: *He is the organist of Canterbury Cathedral.*

or·gan·ic [LIVING] /£ɔːˈgæn·ɪk, $ɔːr-/ *adj* [not gradable] being or consisting of living plants and animals • *The display case contained organic remains found in the tomb – seeds, dried fruit, and small pieces of leather and bone.* • *A quarter of the contents of an average family's dustbin is organic* **matter**. • *(specialized)* Chemical substances which are organic contain carbon: *Organic chemicals are used in the manufacture of plastics, fibres, solvents and paints.* ○ *Oxygen occurs widely in organic and inorganic* **compounds**. • **Organic chemistry** is the scientific study of chemical substances which contain carbon, including artificial substances such as plastics. • See also **organic** at ORGAN [BODY PART]. Compare INORGANIC.

or·gan·ic [NO CHEMICALS] /£ɔːˈgæn·ɪk, $ɔːr-/ *adj* not using artificial chemicals in the production of plants and animals for food • *Our local supermarket stocks a limited range of organic fruit and vegetables.* • *He claims that many people are discouraged from buying organic foods because of their high price.* • *The Government is offering grants to help farmers adopt organic farming methods.* • See also **organic** at ORGAN [BODY PART].

or·gan·i·cally /£ɔːˈgæn·ɪ·kli, $ɔːr-/ *adv* • *The wine is made from organically grown grapes.*

or·gan·i·sm /£ˈɔː·gᵊn·ɪ·zᵊm, $ˈɔːr-/ *n* [C] a single living plant, animal, bacterium or virus • *Reproduction is one of the essential properties of a living organism.* • *The illness is caused by a common organism which is carried by most people.* • *Amoebae and bacteria are* **single-celled** *organisms.* • See also MICROORGANISM.

or·gan·iz·a·tion, *Br and Aus usually* **-i·sa·tion** /£ˌɔː·gᵊn·aɪˈzeɪ·ʃᵊn, $ˌɔːr-/ *n* [C] a group of people who work together in a structured way for a shared purpose • *the World Health Organization* • *the Organization of African Unity* • *Several women's organizations contributed information for the book.* • *The article was about the major international aid organizations.* • See also **organization** at ORGANIZE [ARRANGE], ORGANIZE [MAKE A SYSTEM].

or·gan·ize *obj* [ARRANGE], *Br and Aus usually* **-ise** /£ˈɔː·gᵊn·aɪz, $ˈɔːr-/ *v* [T] to make arrangements for (something) to happen • *The group organizes theatre trips once a month.* • *They organized a meeting between the teachers and students.* • *(Br) She had organized a car* **to** *meet me at the airport.* [+ obj + *to* infinitive] • *(Br and Aus slang)* If you say that someone **couldn't organize a piss-up in a brewery**, you mean that they are unable to organize the simplest things.

or·gan·iz·a·tion, *Br and Aus usually* **-i·sa·tion** /£ˌɔː·gᵊn·aɪˈzeɪ·ʃᵊn, $ˌɔːr-/ *n* [U] • *We did all the organization* **for** *the wedding ourselves.* • *He didn't want to be involved in the organization* **of** *the conference, although he was willing to attend and speak.* • See also ORGANIZATION.

or·gan·ized, *Br and Aus usually* **-ised** /£ˈɔː·gᵊn·aɪzd, $ˈɔːr-/ *adj* • *I don't like going on organized tours.*

or·gan·iz·er, *Br and Aus usually* **-iser** /£ˈɔː·gᵊn·aɪ·zəʳ, $ˈɔːr·gᵊn·aɪ·zɚ/ *n* [C] • *She has been the organizer of the summer course for the past five years.* • *There aren't enough seats for all the guests – I must tell the organizers.*

or·gan·ize *obj* [MAKE A SYSTEM], *Br and Aus usually* **-ise** /£ˈɔː·gᵊn·aɪz, $ˈɔːr-/ *v* [T] to do or arrange (something) according to a particular system • *The books were organized on the shelves according to their size.* • *She had organized her study so that she could reach everything from her wheelchair.* • *"Will you tell us about your new project?" "Yes, of course. Just give me a moment to organize my thoughts* (= to think about what I will say).*"* • *(infml) My mother is always trying to organize me* (= make me do things in the way she likes).

or·gan·iz·a·tion, *Br and Aus usually* **-i·sa·tion** /£ˌɔː·gᵊn·aɪˈzeɪ·ʃᵊn, $ˌɔːr-/ *n* [U] • *We have introduced a new system of organization for processing orders.* • See also ORGANIZATION.

or·gan·iz·a·tion·al, *Br and Aus usually* **-i·sa·tion·al** /£ˌɔː·gᵊn·aɪˈzeɪ·ʃᵊn·ᵊl, $ˌɔːr-/ *adj* [before n; not gradable] • *We were impressed by his organizational* **ability**. • *She is looking for a personal assistant with good organizational* **skills**.

or·gan·ized, *Br and Aus usually* **-ised** /£ˈɔː·gᵊn·aɪzd, $ˈɔːr-/ *adj* • *The letters had been placed in organized piles, one for each letter of the alphabet.* • If someone is organized, they plan things carefully and keep things in a tidy way: *She's not a very organized person and she always arrives late at meetings.* • **Organized crime** is criminal organizations which plan and commit crime, or the crimes which are committed by such organizations: *There is speculation that the murders may be linked to organized crime.* ○ *The company is alleged to have ties with a leading figure in organized crime.*

or·gan·iz·er, *Br and Aus usually* **-iser** /£ˈɔː·gᵊn·aɪ·zəʳ, $ˈɔːr·gᵊn·aɪ·zɚ/ *n* [C] • *We need someone who is a* **good** *organizer.*

or·ga·sm /£ˈɔː·gæz·ᵊm, $ˈɔːr-/ *n* the moment of greatest pleasure and excitement in sexual activity • *to have an orgasm* [C] • *a multiple orgasm* [C] • *to achieve/reach orgasm* [U] • *The survey revealed that two out of five women* **fake** *orgasm during intercourse.* [U]

or·ga·sm /£ˈɔː·gæz·ᵊm, $ˈɔːr-/ *v* [I] • *She orgasmed three times in half an hour.*

or·gas·mic /£ɔːˈgæz·mɪk, $ɔːr-/ *adj* • *In her book, she wrote that all women were capable of achieving orgasmic fulfilment.* • *(infml)* An orgasmic activity or experience is one which gives feelings of great pleasure or excitement: *During their market research, they found that many people described eating the ice-cream as an orgasmic experience.*

or·gy /£ˈɔː·dʒi, $ˈɔːr-/ *n* [C] an occasion when a group of people behave in a wild uncontrolled way, esp. involving sexual activity • *There was evidence that they had taken part in sex orgies.* • *People were drinking a lot and the party soon turned into an orgy.* • *(disapproving)* An orgy **of** something is too much of it: *The protest demonstration degenerated into an orgy of looting and shooting.* ○ *When she got her first salary cheque, she indulged in an orgy of spending.*

or·gi·as·tic /£ˌɔː·dʒiˈæs·tɪk, $ˌɔːr-/ *adj fml* • An orgiastic activity is one which involves wild, uncontrolled behaviour and feelings of great pleasure and excitement: *They worked themselves up with singing and dancing to an orgiastic* **frenzy**.

O·ri·ent /£ˈɔː·ri·ənt, $ˈɔːr·i-/ *n* [U] **the Orient** *fml or dated* the countries in the east and south-east of Asia • *She had lived in the Orient as a child.* • *He believes that the West has created unfair myths of the Orient.* • Compare OCCIDENT. • [LP]› **Nations and nationalities**

o·ri·en·tal /£ˌɔː·riˈen·tᵊl, $ˌɔːr·iˈen·t̬ᵊl/ *adj* [not gradable] • *oriental cuisine/fruits/plants* • *He is passionate about oriental art.* • *She is studying Japanese at the School of Oriental Studies.* • *He creates clothes with both Oriental and Western influences.* • Compare **occidental** at OCCIDENT.

o·ri·en·tal·ist /£ˌɔː·riˈen·tᵊl·ɪst, $ˌɔːr·iˈen·t̬ᵊl-/ *n* [C] • An orientalist is a person who studies the languages and culture of countries in the east and south-east of Asia.

o·ri·en·tate *obj* [FIND DIRECTION] /£ˈɔː·ri·ən·teɪt, $ˈɔːr·i-/, *esp. Am* **o·ri·ent** /£ˈɔː·ri·ənt, $ˈɔːr·i-/ *v* [T] to discover the position of (yourself) in relation to your surroundings • *As she came out of the station, she paused to orientate* **herself**. • *If you get lost while you are out walking, try to use the sun to orientate* **yourself**. • *When we first went to Paris, we went on a sight-seeing tour to orientate* **ourselves in** *an unfamiliar city.*

o·ri·en·ta·tion /£ˌɔː·ri·enˈteɪ·ʃᵊn, $ˌɔːr·i-/ *n* [U] *fml or specialized* • *The building has an east-west orientation* (= It is built on a line between east and west). • *When the liquid crystal molecules are activated, they may adopt a random orientation* (= arrangement).

o·ri·en·teer·ing /£ˌɔː·ri·ənˈtɪə·rɪŋ, $ˌɔːr·i·enˈtɪr·ɪŋ/ *n* [U] • Orienteering is a sport in which you have to find your way to somewhere on foot as quickly as possible by using a map and a compass: *He loved outdoor activities such as orienteering, sailing and hill-walking.*

o·ri·en·tate *obj* [AIM] /£ˈɔː·ri·ən·teɪt, $ˈɔːr·i-/, *esp. Am* **o·ri·ent** /£ˈɔː·ri·ənt, $ˈɔːr·i-/ *v* [T always + adv/prep] to aim (something) at someone or something, or make (something) suitable for a particular group of people • *The World Bank is taking steps to orientate its lending* **to** *reducing poverty.* • *It is essential that the public sector orientates itself more* **towards** *the consumer.* • *The industry is* **heavily** *orientated* **towards** *export markets.*

o·ri·en·ta·tion /£ˌɔː·ri·enˈteɪ·ʃᵊn, $ˌɔːr·i-/ *n* [U] • The orientation of someone or something is the particular interests, activities or aims that they have: *The orientation of the course is very much towards psychology, so I don't think you would find it useful.* ○ *The job is open to everyone, irrespective of* **political** *orientation.* ○ *He considered it an invasion of privacy to be asked about his* **sexual** *orientation* (= the sex of the people whom he was sexually attracted to).

–o·ri·en·tat·ed /£-ˌɔː·ri·enˈteɪ·tɪd, $-ˌɔːr·i·enˈteɪ·t̬ɪd/, *esp. Am* **–o·ri·ent·ed** /£-ˌɔː·ri·en·tɪd, $-ˌɔːr·i·en·t̬ɪd/ *combining form* • Orientated shows the direction in which something is aimed: *The Department of Education wants colleges to put more emphasis on practical,* **career**-*orientated teaching.* • *She wants to turn the company into a* **profit**-*orientated organization.*

or·i·fice /£ˈɒr·ɪ·fɪs, $ˈɔːr·ə-/ *n* [C] *fml* an opening or hole, esp. one in the body such as the mouth • *Blood flowed from his facial orifices* (= nose and mouth). • *A flood of water gushed out of an orifice in the wall.* • (!)

or·i·ga·mi /£ˌɒr·ɪˈɡɑː·mi, $ˌɔːr-/ *n* [U] the art of making objects for decoration by folding sheets of paper into shapes • *Origami originated in Japan where it is still widely practised.* • *She was given a present of some origami paper and a booklet to show her how to fold it into birds and figures.*

or·i·gin /£ˈɒr·ɪ·dʒɪn, $ˈɔːr·ə-/ *n* the beginning or cause of something • *This project has an interesting origin.* [C] • *It's a book about the origin* **of** *the universe.* [C] • *Her unhappy childhood was the origin* **of** *her problems later in life.* [C] • *Can anyone tell me the origin* **of** *this saying* (= where it came from)? [C] • A person's origin is where they were born: *He is of North African origin.* [U] ○ *What is your country of origin?* [U] • An object's origin is where it was made: *The furniture was American and French in origin.* [U]

or·i·gins /£ˈɒr·ɪ·dʒɪnz, $ˈɔːr·ə-/ *pl n* • *The story has obscure origins* (= No one knows how it started). • *The president's family was* **of** *humble origins* (= They were poor people without a good position in society).

or·ig·in·al /əˈrɪdʒ·ɪ·nəl/ *n* [C] • Something which is the original is the first one made and is not a copy: *Can you let me have the original of your report – I can't read this photocopy.* • An original is also a piece of work by a famous artist or designer and not a copy by someone else: *The original is in the museum in Naples.* ○ *If the painting is an original, it will be very valuable, but I think it may be a fake.* • If you read something **in the original**, you read it in the language in which it was first written: *Is your English good enough to read Shakespeare in the original, or do you use a translation?*

or·ig·in·al /əˈrɪdʒ·ɪ·nəl/ *adj* [before n; not gradable] • Original is used to describe something which existed from the beginning of a process or which is the first or earliest form of something: *Her original plan was to stay for a month, but she had to leave after two weeks.* ○ *The proposed route of the railway line has been changed twice since the original announcement.* ○ *The gardens have recently been restored to their original glory.* • An original piece of work, such as a painting or drawing, is produced by the artist or writer and is not a copy: *The original manuscript is in Paris – this is just a facsimile.* ○ *Is this an original Rembrandt* (= Was it painted by him)? • In the Christian religion, **original sin** is the idea that all human beings are born with a tendency to be evil. • See also ORIGINAL.

or·ig·in·al·ly /əˈrɪdʒ·ɪ·nə·li/ *adv* [not gradable] • *Originally* (= First of all) *it was a bedroom, but we turned it into a study.* • *They now live in Canada, but originally they came from Australia.*

or·ig·in·ate *(obj)* /əˈrɪdʒ·ɪ·neɪt/ *v* • If something originates in a particular place or at a particular time, it comes from there or begins there: *The news story originated* **in** *Paris.* [I] ○ *Although the technology originated* **in** *the UK, it has been developed on a large scale in the US.* [I] ○ *School uniform is thought to have originated in the 1840s and 50s.* [I] ○ *The game is thought to have originated* **among** *the native peoples of Alaska.* [I] • If you originate something, you start it or cause it to happen: *Who originated the saying 'Small is beautiful'?* [T]

or·ig·in·at·or /£əˈrɪdʒ·ɪ·neɪ·təʳ, $-t̬ɚ/ *n* [C] • The originator of something is the person who first thinks of it and causes it to happen: *He is best known as the originator of a long-running TV series.*

or·ig·in·al /əˈrɪdʒ·ɪ·nəl/ *adj esp. approving* not the same as anything or anyone else and therefore special and interesting • *His essay was full of original ideas.* • *This is your most original work so far.* • *Their suggestions were original and challenging.* • *She's a* **highly** (= very) *original young designer.* • See also **original** at ORIGIN. • (RUS)

or·ig·in·al·i·ty /£əˌrɪdʒ·ɪˈnæl·ə·ti, $-t̬i/ *n* [U] *esp. approving* • *The judges will be looking for originality as well as for style and content.* • *We were impressed by the originality* **of** *the children's work.*

or·na·ment /£ˈɔː·nə·mənt, $ˈɔːr-/ *n* an object which is beautiful rather than useful • *She has a large display case full of glass ornaments in her living room.* [C] • *The shop stocks a wide range of garden ornaments, such as statues and fountains.* [C] • *(fml)* Ornament is also decoration which is added to increase the beauty of something: *The building relies on clever design rather than on ornament for its impressive effect.* [U] ○ *Holly is widely cultivated* **for** *ornament, especially at Christmas time.* [U] • [PIC]› **Room**

or·na·ment *obj* /£ˈɔː·nə·ment, $ˈɔːr-/ *v* [T] *slightly fml* • *She ornamented her letters* **with** *little drawings in the margin.* • *The* **highly** (= very) *ornamented staircase in the hall dates from the 16th century.*

or·na·men·tal /£ˌɔː·nəˈmen·tᵊl, $ˌɔːr·nəˈmen·t̬ᵊl/ *adj* • *There was a bowl of ornamental china fruit in the middle of the table.* • *Jade is often used in ornamental carvings.* • *The handles on each side of the box are purely ornamental* (= They are for decoration only). • *The ornamental* **garden** *at Sissinghurst in Kent was created by Vita Sackville-West.*

or·na·men·ta·tion /£ˌɔː·nə·menˈteɪ·ʃᵊn, $ˌɔːr-/ *n* [U] *slightly fml* • *The plain silver tray with no ornamentation was valued at $220.* • *She buys gold jewellery not only for ornamentation but also as an investment.*

or·nate /£ɔːˈneɪt, $ɔːr-/ *adj* having a lot of decoration • *The church, with its gold dome and ornate interior, is breathtaking.* • *The room's ornate ceiling and wood panelling was destroyed in the fire.* • *Victorian architecture was once criticized as being heavy and* **over**-*ornate.* • *(esp. disapproving)* Language which is ornate contains too many complicated words or phrases: *Some students are put off studying his work because of the ornate language of the poetry.*

or·nate·ly /£ɔːˈneɪt·li, $ɔːr-/ *adv* • *The City Museum has a collection of ornately decorated porcelain.* • *In the countryside, the wooden houses are ornately carved in traditional patterns.*

or·ne·ry /£ˈɔː·nə·ri, $ˈɔːr-/ *adj Am* tending to get angry and argue with people • *He had been in an ornery mood all day, rowing with his wife and his boss.*

or·ni·thol·o·gy /£ˌɔː·nɪˈθɒl·ə·dʒi, $ˌɔːr·nəˈθɑː·lə-/ *n* [U] *specialized* the study of birds • *His main interests are botany and ornithology.*

or·ni·tho·log·i·cal /£ˌɔː·nɪ·θəˈlɒdʒ·ɪ·kəl, $ˌɔːr·nə·θəˈlɑː·dʒɪ-/ *adj* [before n; not gradable] *specialized* • *She is a member of the local ornithological society.*

or·ni·thol·o·gist /£ˌɔː·nɪˈθɒl·ə·dʒɪst, $ˌɔːr·nəˈθɑː·lə-/ *n* [C] *specialized* • *The children belong to a club for young ornithologists.*

or·phan /£ˈɔː·fən, $ˈɔːr-/ *n* [C] a child whose parents are dead • *The civil war is making orphans of many children.* • LP **Relationships**

or·phan *obj* /£ˈɔː·fən, $ˈɔːr-/ *v* [T usually passive] • *She was orphaned at the age of 14 and was brought up by her older sister.* • *He was orphaned* **as a baby** (= His parents died when he was a baby). • *He and his wife took in two children who had been orphaned by the war* (= whose parents had been killed in the war). • *The charity provides homes for orphaned and abandoned children.*

or·phan·age /£ˈɔː·fən·ɪdʒ, $ˈɔːr-/ *n* [C] • An orphanage is a home for children whose parents are dead or unable to care for them: *He had grown up in an orphanage because his mother could not take care of him.* ○ *She and her two sisters were brought up in an orphanage.*

or·tho·don·tics /£ˌɔː·θəʊˈdɒn·tɪks, $ˌɔːr·θoʊˈdɑːn·t̬ɪks/ *n* [U] *specialized* the skill and activity of correcting the position of teeth and dealing with and preventing problems of the teeth • *Orthodontics includes the treatment of tooth decay and dealing with facial abnormalities caused by the incorrect position of the teeth.*

or·tho·don·tic /£ˌɔː·θəʊˈdɒn·tɪk, $ˌɔːr·θoʊˈdɑːn·t̬ɪk/ *adj* [before n; not gradable] *specialized* • *Modern orthodontic techniques can have a dramatic effect on children's long-term dental health and facial appearance.* • *She needs orthodontic* **treatment** *to have her teeth straightened.*

or·tho·don·tist /£ˌɔː·θəʊˈdɒn·tɪst, $ˌɔːr·θoʊˈdɑːn·t̬ɪst/ *n* [C] *specialized* • *I have an appointment to see the orthodontist at 3 o'clock this afternoon.*

or·tho·dox /£ˈɔː·θə·dɒks, $ˈɔːr·θə·dɑːks/ *adj* (of beliefs, ideas or activities) following generally accepted beliefs or standards • *orthodox treatment/methods* • *orthodox views/opinions* • *We would prefer a more orthodox approach/solution to the problem.* • In religion, people who are orthodox have more traditional beliefs than other people in the same religious group: *orthodox Christians/Jews/Muslims* • The Orthodox Church is one part of the Christian Church, with many members in Greece and eastern Europe: *a Greek Orthodox bishop* ○ *Russian Orthodox Christians* • **Orthodox medicine** uses drugs and operations to cure illness: *She is a cancer sufferer who has rejected orthodox medicine and turned instead to acupuncture and other forms of alternative medicine.* • Compare HETERODOX.

or·tho·dox·y /£ˈɔː·θə·dɒk·si, $ˈɔːr·θə·dɑːk-/ *n* • Orthodoxy is the generally accepted beliefs of society at a particular time: *She was a playwright who challenged the political and social orthodoxies of her time.* [C] ○ *The current economic orthodoxy is of a free market and unregulated trade.* [C] • Orthodoxy is also the traditional beliefs of a religious group or political party: *She is a strict defender of Catholic orthodoxy.* [U] ○ *He claims that there is no such thing as a single Christian orthodoxy and that people choose what they will and will not believe.* [C] • Orthodoxy is also the degree to which someone believes in traditional religious or political ideas: *His orthodoxy began to be seriously questioned by his priest.* [U]

or·thog·ra·phy /£ɔːˈθɒg·rə·fi, $ɔːrˈθɑː·grə-/ *n* [U] *specialized* the accepted way of spelling and writing words • *English orthography is difficult for both native speakers and foreign learners.*

or·tho·graph·ic /£ˌɔː·θəʊˈgræf·ɪk, $ˌɔːr·θə-/ *adj* [before n; not gradable] • *orthographic conventions* • *The two languages employ different orthographic* **systems**.

or·tho·graph·i·cally /£ˌɔː·θəʊˈgræf·ɪ·kli, $ˌɔːr·θə-/ *adv* [not gradable] • *orthographically correct*

or·tho·paed·ics /£ˌɔː·θəˈpiː·dɪks, $ˌɔːr·θə-/, *esp. Am* **or·tho·ped·ics** *pl n specialized* the medical study and skill of treating bones which have not grown correctly or which have been damaged • *She is a consultant in orthopaedics at St Bartholomew's Hospital in London.*

or·tho·pae·dic, *esp. Am* **or·tho·pe·dic** /£ˌɔː·θəʊˈpiː·dɪk, $ˌɔːr·θə-/ *adj* [before n; not gradable] *specialized* • *an orthopaedic surgeon/specialist/hospital* • An orthopaedic device is one which helps people who have an injury involving their bones: *an orthopaedic mattress*

OS /£ˌəʊˈes, $ˌoʊ-/ *n* [U] *abbreviation for* **Ordnance Survey**, see at ORDNANCE

Os·car /£ˈɒs·kər, $ˈɑː·skɚ/ *n* [C] *trademark* one of a set of American prizes given each year to the best film, the best actor or actress in any film and to other people involved in the production of films • *The movie won an Oscar for best costumes in this year's awards.* • *The Oscar* **ceremony** *takes place in March.* • *The role gained her an Oscar* **nomination** *in 1988.*

os·cil·late /£ˈɒs·ɪ·leɪt, $ˈɑː·səl·eɪt/ *v* [I] to move repeatedly from one position to another • *The needle on the dial oscillated* **between** *'full' and 'empty'.* • *(fml)* If you oscillate between feelings or opinions, you change repeatedly from one to the other: *Their emotions were oscillating* **between** *desperation and hope.* ○ *He oscillated* **between** *disgust at their behaviour and sympathy for the terrible situation which had caused it.* • *(specialized)* A wave or an electric current which oscillates changes regularly in strength or direction.

os·cil·la·tion /£ˌɒs·ɪˈleɪ·ʃən, $ˌɑː·səlˈeɪ-/ *n* • *(fml) Throughout the novel, the protagonist demonstrates a continual oscillation between guilt and a sense of victimization.* [C] • *(specialized) The experiment showed that the oscillation of waves occurred in a fixed direction.* [U]

os·cil·lo·scope /£əˈsɪl·ə·skəʊp, $-skoʊp/ *n* [C] a device which represents a changing amount on a screen in the form of a wavy line • *The oscilloscope showed his weakening heartbeat.*

os·mo·sis /£ɒzˈməʊ·sɪs, $ɑːzˈmoʊ-/ *n* [U] *specialized* the process in plants and animals by which a liquid moves gradually from one part of the body or the plant to another through a MEMBRANE (= tissue that covers or connects animal or plant cells) • *Fluid flows back into the tiny blood vessels* **by** *osmosis.* • Osmosis is also the way in which ideas and information gradually spread between people: *The children were never taught the songs, they just listened to other children singing them and learned them* **by** *osmosis.* ○ *Reading is not picked up* **by a process of** *osmosis, but needs to be taught.*

os·mot·ic /£ɒzˈmɒt·ɪk, $ɑːzˈmɑː·t̬ɪk/ *adj* [before n; not gradable] *specialized* • *an osmotic process* • **Osmotic pressure** is the amount of pressure needed to stop the flow of a liquid through a MEMBRANE (= tissue that covers or connects animal or plant cells).

os·prey /£ˈɒs·preɪ, $ˈɑː·spri/ *n* [C] a large fish-eating bird with black and white feathers

os·si·fy *(obj)* /£ˈɒs·ɪ·faɪ, $ˈɑː·sə-/ *v fml disapproving* (of habits or ideas) to (cause to) become fixed and unable to change • *Years of easy success had ossified the company's thinking.* [T] • *This is a broadcast for anyone whose musical preferences ossified a decade before the Beatles.* [I] • *(specialized)* If tissue ossifies, it hardens and changes into bone: *A child's cartilage starts to ossify at a very young age.* [I]

os·si·fi·ca·tion /£ˌɒs·ɪ·fɪˈkeɪ·ʃən, $ˌɑː·sə-/ *n* [U] *fml* • *(disapproving) The company has employed no new staff for years and this has led to an ossification of practices.* • *(specialized) It is a rare type of bone, formed directly from soft tissue and not by the ossification of cartilage.*

os·si·fied /£ˈɒs·ɪ·faɪd, $ˈɑː·sə-/ *adj fml disapproving* • *The new prime minister has promised economic reform to replace the ossified policies of the former ruling party.*

os·ten·si·ble /£ɒsˈten*t*·sɪ·bl̩, $ɑːˈsten*t*-/ *adj* [before n; not gradable] *fml* appearing or claiming to be one thing when it is really something else • *Their ostensible goal was to clean up government corruption, but their real aim was to unseat the government.* • *Many black people training to become lawyers still encounter prejudice, despite the ostensible commitment by official legal bodies to equal opportunities.* • Ⓔ Ⓘ

os·ten·si·bly /£ɒsˈten*t*·sɪ·bli, $ɑːˈsten*t*-/ *adv* [not gradable] *fml* • *He has spent the past three months in Florida, ostensibly for medical treatment, but in actual fact to avoid prosecution.* • *Her novel is ostensibly about a girl growing up in post-war Brooklyn, but it offers more than just a memoir of the period.*

os·ten·ta·tion /£ˌɒs·tenˈteɪ·ʃən, $ˌɑː·stən-/ *n* [U] *disapproving* a show of wealth, possessions or power in order to cause admiration in other people • *Her wealth,* *lifestyle and personal ostentation were a source of criticism throughout her career.* • *He was widely respected in the business world for both his business skills and lack of ostentation.*

os·ten·ta·tious /£ˌɒs·tenˈteɪ·ʃəs, $ˌɑː·stən-/ *adj disapproving* • *They criticized the ostentatious lifestyle of their leaders.* • Ostentatious also means behaving in a way to make people notice you: *an ostentatious gesture/manner*

os·ten·ta·tious·ly /£ˌɒs·tenˈteɪ·ʃə·sli, $ˌɑː·stən-/ *adv disapproving* • *The room was ostentatiously decorated, with a white marble staircase and gold fittings.* • If you do something ostentatiously, you do it in an obvious way, making certain that everyone can see or notice what you are doing: *He took his heavy gold watch from his wrist and laid it ostentatiously on the table in front of him.*

os·te·o·ar·thri·tis /£ˌɒs·ti·əʊ·ɑːˈθraɪ·tɪs, $ˌɑː·sti·oʊ·ɑːr ˈθraɪ·t̬ɪs/ *n* [U] a disease which causes pain and stiffness in the joints • *By middle age, osteoarthritis is the most common cause of knee problems.*

os·te·o·path /£ˈɒs·ti·əʊ·pæθ, $ˈɑː·sti·oʊ-/ *n* [C] a person who is trained to treat injuries to bones and muscles using pressure and movement • *The osteopath carefully manipulated my damaged shoulder.*

os·te·o·path·y /£ˌɒs·tiˈɒp·ə·θi, $ˌɑː·stiˈɑː·pə-/ *n* [U] • Osteopathy is the treatment of injuries to bones and muscles using pressure and movement: *Osteopathy aims to stimulate the body to heal itself.*

os·te·o·po·ro·sis /£ˌɒs·ti·əʊ·pəˈrəʊ·sɪs, $ˌɑː·sti·oʊ·pəˈroʊ-/ *n* [U] a disease which causes the bones to weaken and become easily breakable • *Osteoporosis afflicts many older women because of the loss of calcium and estrogen that commonly occurs in women after menopause.*

o·stra·cize *obj, Br and Aus usually* **-ise** /£ˈɒs·trə·saɪz, $ˈɑː·strə-/ *v* [T] to avoid (someone) intentionally or to prevent them from taking part in the activities of a group because you dislike them or disapprove of something they have done • *His colleagues ostracized him after he criticized the company in public.* • *For centuries, lepers were ostracized by society and banished to remote colonies.*

o·stra·ci·sm /£ˈɒs·trə·sɪ·zᵊm, $ˈɑː·strə-/ *n* [U] • *AIDS victims often experience social ostracism and discrimination in jobs and housing.* • *The country faces diplomatic ostracism if it refuses to join the political negotiations.*

os·trich /£ˈɒs·trɪtʃ, $ˈɑː·strɪtʃ/ *n* [C] a very large flightless bird from Africa, which is sometimes bred on farms • *ostrich eggs* • *an ostrich ranch* (=farm) • *The ostrich is the fastest animal on two legs.* • *She wore a hat trimmed with ostrich* **feathers**. • If someone is described as an ostrich or as **ostrich-like**, they are unwilling to accept the truth about something unpleasant which is obvious to everyone else: *A firm supporter of nuclear power, he has been ostrich-like about the high incidence of cancer near nuclear sites.*

oth·er PART OF A SET /£ˈʌð·əʳ, $-ɚ/ *pronoun pl* **others** the second of two things or people, or the item or person that is left in a group or set of things • *Hold the racquet in one hand and the ball in* **the** *other.* • *Some people prefer a vegetarian diet, while others prefer a meat-based diet.* • *She gave me one book last week and promised to bring* **the** *others on Wednesday.* • *I visited two of the families and Paul went to see* **the** *others.* • See also EACH OTHER.

oth·er /£ˈʌð·əʳ, $-ɚ/ *determiner* • *Where's* **the** *other key for this cupboard?* • *I've found one earring – do you know where* **the** *other* **one** *is?* • *What did* **the** *other members of the group think about the proposal?* • The other **end/side** means the opposite end or side: *Put the chair at the other end of the desk.* ○ *We heard a noise on the other side of the door.* ○ *A door opened at the other end of the corridor.* ○ *The man was waiting on the other side of the street.* • LP **Determiners**

oth·er ADDITIONAL /£ˈʌð·əʳ, $-ɚ/ *determiner* additional to the item or person already mentioned • *The product has many other time-saving features.* • *What other leisure facilities does the town have?* • *There is no other work available at the moment.* • *There is only one other person who could help us.* • *There is one other point I would like to discuss with you.* • *The police have questioned several other families.* • *Are there any other people we should speak to?* • You can use other at the end of a list to show that there are more things, without being exact about what they are: *The plan has been opposed by schools, businesses and other local organizations.* • See also ANOTHER ADDITIONAL.

oth·ers /£ˈʌð·əz, $-ɚz/ *pl pronoun* • *I only know about this book but there might be others* (=other books). • *This is broken – can you find any others?* • Others also refers to people in general, not including yourself: *You shouldn't expect others to do your work for you.*

oth·er DIFFERENT /£ˈʌð·əʳ, $-ɚ/ *determiner* different from the item or person already mentioned • *I'm going to have to take this TV apart – there's no other way of mending it.* • *He likes travelling abroad and learning about other people's customs and traditions.* • *Ask me some other time, when I'm not so busy.* • *He was economical with the truth –* **in other words** (=to explain it in a simpler way), *he was lying.* • *(fml)* After a noun, **other than** means different from or except: *Holidays other than those in this brochure do not have free places for children.* ○ *The form cannot be signed by anyone other than yourself.* • In a negative sentence, **other than** means except: *We missed the last bus so there was no choice other than* **to** *walk home.* [+ *to* infinitive] • *(infml)* You use **or other** after words such as some, someone, something or somewhere, when you cannot or do not want to be exact about the information you are giving: *The event was going to be held in some park or other.* ○ *We'll find someone or other to help us.* ○ *I'm determined to find out somehow or other.* • You say **the** other **day/evening/week** to refer to a time in the recent past without saying exactly when it was: *I saw him just the other day.* ○ *We visited them only the other week.* ○ *She phoned me the other night to say she could come.* • See also ANOTHER DIFFERENT.

o·ther·ness /£ˈʌð·ə·nəs, $ˈ-ɚ-/ *n* [U] *fml or specialized* • Otherness is the quality of being different in appearance or character from what is familiar, expected or generally accepted: *In the film, he is able to depict the sense of otherness and alienation that many people feel when they are growing up.* ○ *Female writers often share a concern with otherness – of being different and distinct from the literary mainstream.*

oth·er·wise /£ˈʌð·ə·waɪz, $ˈ-ɚ-/ *adv* [not gradable] differently, or in another way • *The police believe he is the thief, but all the evidence suggests otherwise* (=that he is not). • *I'll assume you want to come out on Saturday, unless you let me know otherwise* (=that you do not want to come). • *Under the Bill of Rights, a person is presumed innocent until proved otherwise* (=guilty). • *People who spoke out against the regime were executed, jailed or otherwise persecuted.* • *Marion Morrison, otherwise* **known as** *the film star John Wayne, was born in 1907.* • *(fml) I can't meet you on Tuesday – I'm otherwise* **engaged/occupied** (=doing something else). • Otherwise is also used to refer to the general condition of something after you have given an exception to this general condition: *The bike needs a new saddle,* **but** *otherwise* (=except for this) *it's in good condition.* ○ *The orchestra uses modern instruments, but otherwise they remain faithful to the Renaissance style.* ○ *The poor sound quality ruined an otherwise splendid film.* ○ *The peace talks offer the first glimmer of hope in an otherwise hopeless situation.* • **Or otherwise** is used to refer to the opposite of the word which comes before it: *Hand in your exam papers, finished or otherwise* (=not finished). ○ *The success or otherwise* (=failure) *of the project will not become apparent until it is almost complete.* ○ *It is not clear whether any action, military or otherwise, will be taken to prevent the demonstration.*

oth·er·wise /£ˈʌð·ə·waɪz, $ˈ-ɚ-/ *conjunction* • Otherwise is used after an order or suggestion to show what the result will be if you do not follow that order or suggestion: *You'd better phone home, otherwise your parents will start to worry.* ○ *Write her address down, otherwise you'll forget it.* ○ *Put the milk back in the fridge, otherwise it will go off.*

oth·er·wise /£ˈʌð·ə·waɪz, $ˈ-ɚ-/ *adj* [after v; not gradable] *fml or dated* • Otherwise is used to show that something is completely different from what you think it is or from what was previously stated: *He might have told you he was a qualified electrician, but the truth is quite otherwise.*

oth·er·world·ly /£ˌʌð·əˈwɜːld·li, $-ɚˈwɜːrld-/ *adj* more closely connected to spiritual things than to the ordinary things of life • *The hero in the novel is given magical powers and otherworldly attributes.* • *The children in the picture look delicate and otherworldly, as though they had never run or shouted.*

OTT /£ˌəʊ·tiːˈtiː, $ˌoʊ-/ *adj Br abbreviation for* **over the top**, see at TOP HIGHEST PART

ot·ter /£ˈɒt·əʳ, $ˈɑː·t̬ɚ/ *n* [C] a four-legged mammal with brown fur which swims well and eats fish

ouch /aʊtʃ/ *exclamation* used to express sudden physical pain or in answer to something unkind • *Ouch, you're* *hurting me!* • *"You're too fat." "Ouch, that was a bit unkind."*

PRONUNCIATION OF WORDS WITH *-OUGH-*

The combination of letters 'ough' is included in a number of words, and is pronounced in several different ways.

Words ending with 'ought' are usually pronounced /£ɔːt/ or /$ɑːt/. For example:

bought, brought, fought, nought, ought, sought, thought

Other ways of pronouncing 'ough', with the most common examples, are:

/£əʊ/	although, dough, though
/$oʊ/	although, borough, dough, thorough, though
/ʌf/	enough, rough, tough
/uː/	through
/aʊ/	bough, drought, plough
/£ə/	borough, thorough
/ɒf/	cough, trough
/əp/	hiccough

Notice that 'borough' and 'thorough' are pronounced differently by British and American speakers.

ought DUTY /£ɔːt, $ɑːt/ *v aux* [+ *to* infinitive; not *be oughting*] he/she/it **ought** used to show when it is necessary, desirable or advisable to perform the activity referred to by the following verb • *We ought* **to** *tidy up before we go home.* • *She ought* **to** *tell him not to be so rude.* • *The government ought* **to** *be doing more to help the homeless.* • *We ought not/oughtn't* **to have** *agreed without knowing what it would cost.* • *"We ought* **to** *be getting ready now." "Yes, I suppose we ought* **(to)**." • When describing what someone said in the past, ought can be used as a past form: *She said I oughtn't to worry* means *She said "You oughtn't to worry".* • LP **Auxiliary verbs**

ought PROBABLE /£ɔːt, $ɑːt/ *v aux* [not *be oughting*; + *to* infinitive] he/she/it **ought** used to express something that you expect will happen • *He ought* **to** *be home by seven o'clock.* • *The curtains ought* **to** *be ready for you on Monday.* • *They ought* **to have** *arrived at lunchtime but the flight was delayed.* • *If you show the receipt, there ought not* **to** *be any difficulty getting your money back.* • *There oughtn't* **to** *be a queue for tickets at this time in the evening.*

ought·n't /£'ɔː·tᵊnt, $'ɑː-/ *short form of* ought not • *He oughtn't to do that.*

oui·ja board /'wiː·dʒə/ *n* [C] a board marked with letters of the alphabet and numbers, which people use in the belief that it will help them receive messages from people who are dead

ounce /aʊnts/ (*abbreviation* **oz**) *n* [C] a unit of weight equal to approximately 28 grams • *There are 16 ounces in one pound.* • *The price of gold has risen by $1·25 an ounce.* • *a 12-oz pack of bacon* • *(infml)* An ounce is also a very small amount: *She can eat as much as she wants and she never puts on an ounce* (= her weight does not increase). ○ *If he's got an ounce of common sense, he'll realise that this project is bound to fail.* • LP **Units**

our /£aʊəʳ, £ɑːʳ, $aʊɚ/ *determiner* of or belonging to us • *We bought our house several years ago.* • *He walked off and left us on our own.* • *A new swimming pool has just been built in our town.* • *It was a photo of one of our well-known national politicians.* • *Drugs are one of the greatest threats in our society.* • **Our Father** is *infml for* **Lord's Prayer**. See at LORD GOD. • In some parts of the Christian religion, **Our Lady** is a name for Mary, the mother of Jesus, and **Our Lord** is a name for Jesus (or God). • LP **Determiners**

ours /£aʊəz, £ɑːz, $aʊɚz/ *pronoun* • *Which table is ours?* • *He's a cousin of ours.* • *That's their problem – not ours.* • *I think these seats are ours – those are yours.* • *Ours is the red car, parked over there.* • *Ours is a multicultural community.*

our·selves /£ˌaʊə'selvz, £ˌɑː-, $ˌaʊɚ-/ *pronoun* • *We promised ourselves a good holiday this year.* • *Will we be able to do it ourselves or will we need help?* • *We told ourselves it would be easy.* • *It's a big garden, but we do all the gardening* **(by)** *ourselves* (= without help). • *We think we will have to go* **by** *ourselves* (= without other people) *as everyone else is busy.* • *The hotel was very quiet so we* **had** *the swimming pool all* **to** *ourselves* (= we did not have to share it with other people). • *We enjoyed* **having** *the house* **to** *ourselves* (= not having to share it with other people) *again after our visitors had left.* • *(fml)* Ourselves can be used to emphasize the subject: *We ourselves realize that there are flaws in the scheme.* • LP **Reflexive pronouns and verbs**

oust *obj* /aʊst/ *v* [T] to force (someone) to leave a job or a position, often taking their job or position yourself • *The troops quickly ousted the invaders.* • *He was ousted* **as** *chairman after 30 years.* • *Maria ousted Bill* **from** *the committee last June and now she's busy changing everything.* • *The team knew that they were capable of ousting the cupholders* **from** *the competition.*

oust·er /£'aʊ·stəʳ, $-stɚ/ *n* [U] *Am* • *Public opinion remains overwhelmingly in favor of the president's ouster* (= Most people think he should be forced to leave his job).

out MOVE OUTSIDE /aʊt/ *adv* [not gradable] used to show movement to a place or position that is not inside a building or an enclosed area • *Are you going out today?* • *She opened the window and stuck her head out.* • *The bag burst and the apples fell out.* • *Get out!* • *Out you go* (= Go out)! • *Can you find your own way out?* • *My secretary will* **see** *you out* (= go with you to the door). • *Turn the trousers* **inside** *out* (= put the inside on the outside). • Out can also be used to refer to when an object is removed from a place where it is stored: *He opened the drawer and took out a pair of socks.* ○ *She got out her photograph album and showed me her holiday photos.* • *(infml)* If you say **out with it** to someone, you want them to tell you something which they do not want you to know: *Did he say anything about me? Come on, out with it!* • *(Br and Aus)* An **out-tray** (*Am* **out-box**) is a flat open container where letters and other documents that have already been dealt with are put so that they can be sent to someone else.

out of, *infml* **out** *prep* • *I jumped out of bed and ran downstairs.* • *My daughter's just come out of hospital.* • *The car drove out of the car park.* • *He leaned out of the window.* • *She got the boxes out of the cupboard.* • *Can you get some more ice-cream out of the freezer?* • *(infml) He ran out the back door.* • *(infml) She threw all my clothes out the window.* • PIC **Prepositions of movement**

out OUTSIDE /aʊt/ *adv* [not gradable] outside a building or room • *The children like to sleep in a tent out in the garden in the summer.* • *Your guide is waiting out at the front of the hotel.* • *It's bitterly cold out today.* • *Would you like to wait out here, and the doctor will come and fetch you in a minute?* • *Danger!* **Keep** *out* (= Do not enter)! • *"Will you be living in college next year?" "No, I've decided to* **live** *out* (= in a house not owned by the college)." • If someone is **out and about** after an illness, they are able to do the things they usually do: *The doctor says she's making a good recovery and she should be out and about in a few days' time.*

out ABSENT /aʊt/ *adj* [after v; not gradable] absent for a short time from the place where you live or work • *I came round to see you this morning, but you were out.* • *My colleague is out until lunchtime – can I take a message?* • *Someone phoned for you while you were out.* • Out is also used to show that someone is away from the main office of the company or organization they work for to do a particular job: *The thieves were spotted by a postman out on his rounds* (= as he was delivering the post). ○ *The police were out in force* (= There were a lot of police) *at the football match.* • In a LIBRARY (= a place from which books can be borrowed), if a book is out, it has been borrowed by someone: *I tried to find a copy of Wuthering Heights in the college library, but both copies were out.*

out /aʊt/ *adv* [not gradable] • Out is used to refer to when someone goes away from home for a social activity: *Are you going out tonight?* ○ *Our kitchen is being redecorated, so we will have to eat out* (= eat in restaurants) *for the next few weeks.* ○ *He's asked me out* (= to go with him) *to the cinema next week.*

out DISAPPEAR /aʊt/ *adv* [not gradable] to the point where something is removed or disappears • *I spilt paint on my skirt and now I can't get the stain out.* • *This oil stain won't come out of shirt.* • *Cross out any words that are not on the list.* • *Never use water to put out fires in electrical equipment.*

• *Our time/money/patience ran out.* • *Cut out* (= Stop) *all the arguing and make some decisions.* • If you are **out of** something, no more of it is available: *We're nearly out of petrol.* ○ *The shop was out of milk.* ○ *I'm running out of patience.* ○ *I'm sorry, you're out of time – you'll have to finish there.* • *"Out, damned spot!"* (Shakespeare, Lady Macbeth in Macbeth 5.1)

out /aʊt/ *adj* [after v; not gradable] • If a light or fire is out, it is no longer shining or burning: *When we got home, all the lights were out.* ○ *Is that fire properly out?*

out MOVE AWAY /aʊt/ *adv* [not gradable] starting at a central point and then moving away from it • *One of the children handed out the books to the rest of the class.* • *We sent out letters to everyone last week giving our new address.* • *The police spread out across the street.*

out VERY /aʊt/ *adv* [not gradable] used to make the meaning of a word stronger • *Your room needs a good clean out.* • *We walked all day and were tired out/(esp. Am) all played out* (= very tired) *by the time we got home.* • Out is also used to show that a problem or difficulty has been solved or has ended: *She didn't want to become involved in their dispute and so left them to fight it out between them* (= solve their problems themselves). ○ *Can you sort out your differences* (= stop disagreeing with each other) *and start working together like adults?* • **Out and away** is used with superlatives to mean by a great amount: *She is out and away the best student I have ever taught.* • **Out-and-out** is used to emphasize an esp. unpleasant quality of a person or thing: *That's an out-and-out lie!* ○ *The whole project was an out-and-out disaster.* ○ *He's an out-and-out* (= extreme) *nationalist.*

out LOUD /aʊt/ *adv* [not gradable] used with verbs describing sounds to emphasize the loudness of the sound • *She called out, "Where are you going?"* • *He cried out in pain as he hit his head.* • *Charlie Chaplin films always make me laugh out loud.*

out FAR AWAY /aʊt/ *adj* [after v], *adv* [not gradable] a long distance away (from land, a town or your own country) • *The fishing boats were out at sea for three days.* • *They live out in the countryside, miles from anywhere.* • *He lived out in Zambia for seven years.* • *(esp. Am) The weather's better out* **west** (= a long distance away in the west of the country). • Out is also used to emphasize the distance that someone or something is from a town or city: *Does she live in York? No, she lives out in a village, ten miles away.* ○ *Our cottage is 25 miles out of town, in the middle of the countryside.* • *(infml)* **Out here** is used to describe a town or place which you think is a long distance from a main town: *There's not much to do out here, except lie in the sun.*

out AVAILABLE /aʊt/ *adj* [after v], *adv* [not gradable] (of a book, magazine, film or musical recording) available to the public • *Is Jeffrey Archer's new novel out yet?* • *The new Spielberg movie* **comes** *out in August.*

out MADE PUBLIC /aʊt/ *adj* [after v], *adv* [not gradable] *infml* (of information) no longer kept secret • *You can't hide your gambling any longer – the secret's out.* • *Once the news gets out that he's been given a pay increase, everyone will want one.* • If a person, esp. a homosexual, is out, they have stopped keeping their sexual preferences a secret: *She's been out for three years.* ○ *Don't let his sister know he's gay, because he hasn't* **come** *out* **to** *his family yet.*

out *obj* /aʊt/ *v* [T usually passive] • If a famous person is outed, their homosexuality is made public when they want to keep it secret: *Hardly a week went by without a judge or a politician being outed.*

out·ing /£ˈaʊ·tɪŋ, $-t̬ɪŋ/ *n* • *Over the past few months, she has lived in fear of outing* (= of her homosexuality being made public). [U] • *There have been several outings of well-known film stars recently.* [C] • See also OUTING.

out OPEN /aʊt/ *adv, adj* [after v; not gradable] open or flat • *(Br) She opened out the map on the table.* • *(Br) Can you open out the sofa bed for me?* • *(Br and Aus) The flowers opened out in the heat of the room.* • If flowers are out, their petals are open: *The roses will be out in June.*

out APPEAR /aʊt/ *adj* [after v], *adv* [not gradable] able to be seen • *The stars are out tonight.* • *The rain stopped and the sun came out* (= appeared).

out UNCONSCIOUS /aʊt/ *adv, adj* [after v; not gradable] unconscious or sleeping • *She was knocked out* (= made unconscious) *by a sharp blow to the head.* • *He passes out* (= loses consciousness) *at the sight of blood.* • *I was hit on the head, and I must have been out* **cold** (= completely unconscious) *for about ten minutes.* • *She took a couple of pills and went out* **like a light** (= lost consciousness immediately). • *(infml) By 2 a.m. Sally and Kate were still dancing, but Guy was out* **for the count** (= sleeping).

out FINISHED /aʊt/ *adj* [after v; not gradable] used to show that a period of time is finished • *I think I can finish this project before the month's out.* • *Their business was so successful that they managed to pay back the bank loan before the year was out.*

out DEFEATED /aʊt/ *adj* [after v], *adv* [not gradable] (in sport) no longer able to play, or (in politics) no longer able to govern • In a sport such as cricket or baseball, if a player or team is out, their turn has finished and they can no longer play: *Two of the best players on the team were out after ten minutes.* ○ *New Zealand were all out* **for** *246* (= The team finished with a score of 246). • If a political party is out, they have been defeated and are no longer able to govern: *The Social Democrats were out after 15 years in power.* ○ *The ruling party may be voted out at the next election.*

out BALL /aʊt/ *adj* [after v; not gradable] (of a ball in a sport such as tennis) landing beyond one of the lines which mark the area where the game is played • *He thought the ball had bounced on the line, but the umpire said it was out.* • *My first serve was out, but my second serve was just in.*

out COAST /aʊt/ *adv, adj* [after v; not gradable] away from the coast or beach • *We watched the boats going out to sea.* • *Is the tide coming in or going out?* • *You can only walk along that stretch of the beach when the* **tide** *is out.*

out NOT ACCEPTABLE /aʊt/ *adj* [after v; not gradable] *infml* not acceptable or not possible • *Smoking is definitely out among my friends.* • *The option of taking on more staff is out at present.*

out NOT FASHIONABLE /aʊt/ *adj* [after v], *adv* [not gradable] *infml* no longer fashionable or popular • *Every month the magazine lists what's out and what's in* (= fashionable). • *The little black dress has never quite* **gone** *out* (= It is still fashionable). • *Trousers like that* **went** *out* (= stopped being fashionable) *in the 70s.* • *That hairstyle* **went out with the ark** (= is very old-fashioned).

out NOT ACCURATE /aʊt/ *adj* [after v; not gradable] *infml* not accurate • *Our estimates were only out by a few dollars.* • *You were 25cm out/out by 25cm in your measurements.* • *You're not hitting the ball because your timing's completely out.* • *Those sales figures were* **way** *out* (= completely wrong). • *(Am) I'm out $25 on this trip* (= It cost me $25 more than expected).

out EXISTING /aʊt/ *adv* [not gradable] *infml* (used with superlatives) available or in existence • *This is the best automatic camera out.* • *I think he's the greatest footballer out.*

out INTEND /aʊt/ *adj* [after v; not gradable] **out for/to** *infml* doing or intending to do something for an often selfish or unpleasant reason • *He doesn't really care about you – he's just out for a good time.* • *She doesn't usually help the charity – she's only out for the publicity.* • *They've been out* **to** *get me ever since I told the police about them.* [+ *to* infinitive] • *He's always been out* **to** *cause trouble between us.* [+ *to* infinitive]

out of NO LONGER IN *prep* no longer in the place or condition described by the following noun • *Mr James is out of the country until July 4th.* • *Professor Aitchison is out of* **town** *this week.* • *The dogs became excited and out of* **control** (= uncontrolled). • *Tight jeans are out of* **fashion** (= not fashionable) *at the moment.* • *The patient is now out of* **danger**. • *This photo is out of* **focus**. • *The coffee machine is out of* **order** (= does not work). • *The apple was just out of* **reach** (= could not be reached). • *The girl was out of* **sight** (= could not be seen). • *Both she and her husband are out of* **work** (= no longer have jobs).

out of MADE FROM *prep* used to show what something is made from • *The dress was made out of velvet.* • *The statue was carved out of a single block of stone.* • *Coral is formed out of the skeletons of hundreds of tiny sea creatures.* • Out of is also used to refer to the origin of something: *She dresses like a character out of a 19th century novel.* ○ *He copied his essay straight out of a textbook.* ○ *I paid for the computer out of* (= using some of) *my savings.*

out of BECAUSE OF *prep* used to show the reason why someone does something • *I gave him the job out of necessity – none of the other candidates were suitable.* • *She gave the charity a lot of money out of pity for the children.* • *You might like to come and see what we're doing out of interest* (= because I think you might be interested).

out of FROM AMONG *prep* from among (an amount or number) • *Nine out of ten people said they would like to try* *the new product.* • *No one got 20 out of 20* (= all the answers correct) *for the test, but several people got 17 out of 20.*

out of [NOT INVOLVED] *prep* no longer involved in • *He missed two practice sessions and now he's out of the team.* • *It was a disastrous project and I'm glad to be out of it.* • *Since I bought my car, I've got out of the habit of cycling to work.* • *(infml)* If you are **out of it (all)**, you are in a dreamy state as a result of taking alcohol or drugs. • *(infml)* If you feel **out of it (all)**, you feel unhappy because you are not included in what is happening: *I didn't know anyone at the party and I felt really out of it.* • *(infml)* If someone is **out of** their **mind/head**, they are extremely foolish: *He must be out of his mind to have spent that much money on an old car!*

out [EXCUSE] /aʊt/ *n* [C usually sing] *infml* an excuse or reason for avoiding an unpleasant situation • *We must arrange things so we have an out if we need it.*

out– [NOT CENTRAL] /aʊt-/ *combining form* used to add the meaning 'not central' to nouns and adjectives • *outlying areas* (= areas far away from the centre of towns and cities) • *the outskirts of town* (= the areas that form the edge of the town) • *the Australian outback* (= the areas of Australia that are far away from towns and cities)

out– [FURTHER] /aʊt-/ *combining form* used to add the meaning 'going beyond' or 'being better than' to verbs • *She doesn't drink or smoke and I'm sure she'll outlive* (= live longer than) *us all.* • *Children outgrow* (= become too big for) *their clothes very quickly.* • *The Redskins were outplayed* (= defeated) *by the Minnesota Vikings.*

out– [AWAY FROM] /aʊt-/ *combining form* used to add the meaning 'out of' or 'away from' to nouns and adjectives • *She turned away from their outstretched hands* (= hands held out towards her). • *The huge outflow* (= removal) *of capital from the poorer countries has done nothing to help their economic recovery.*

out·back /ˈaʊt·bæk/ *n* [U] **the outback** the areas of Australia that are far away from towns and cities, esp. the desert areas in central Australia

out·bid *obj* /ˌaʊtˈbɪd/ *v* [T] **outbidding**, *past simple* **outbid**, *past part* **outbid** or **outbidden** to offer to pay a higher price for something than (someone else), esp. at an AUCTION (= public sale) • *During the 1980s boom, residential property became too expensive for overseas buyers who were always outbid by the UK buyer.* • *The retail group outbid all three competitors* **for** *space in the shopping centre.*

out·board (mo·tor) /£ˈaʊt·bɔːd, $-bɔːrd/ *n* [C] a motor with a PROPELLER (= device with blades that turn round) that is designed to be fixed to the back of a small boat • An outboard is also a boat with an outboard motor.

out·bound /ˈaʊt·baʊnd/ *adj* [not gradable] travelling away from a particular point • *There has been an increase in outbound* **traffic**, *leaving London airport for the Mediterranean resorts.*

out·break /ˈaʊt·breɪk/ *n* [C] a sudden beginning of something, esp. of a disease or something else dangerous or unpleasant • *an outbreak* **of** *cholera/food poisoning/rioting/war* • *Last weekend saw further thundery outbreaks as the low pressure areas drifted over the country.* • *He left the country three days before the outbreak* **of hostilities**. • See also **break out** at BREAK [NOTICE].

out·build·ing /ˈaʊtˌbɪl·dɪŋ/ *n* [C] a usually small building near to and on the same piece of land as a larger building • *The stables and other outbuildings were sold together with the main house.*

out·burst /£ˈaʊt·bɜːst, $-bɜːrst/ *n* [C] a sudden, violent expression of feeling, esp. anger • *Her comments provoked an uncharacteristic outburst* **of** *anger from the Secretary.* • *In an astonishing outburst* **against** *the proposed road widening, Councillor Weymerth accused the minister of trying to destroy the community.* • *Reiss reported a case study of a 22-year old man who had a history of occasional violent outbursts.*

out·cast /£ˈaʊt·kɑːst, $-kæst/ *n* [C] a person who has no place in their society or in a particular group, because the society or group refuses to accept them • *She has spent her life trying to help gypsies, beggars and other* **social** *outcasts.* • *She doesn't like to talk about her years as a political outcast, after the Party expelled her in 1982.* • *HIV-infected children, he said, were outcasts – rejected by schools and hospitals alike.* • *It's one of those outcast nations, hated and feared by its neighbours for its willingness to use terrorism.* • See also **cast out** at CAST.

out·class *obj* /£ˌaʊtˈklɑːs, $-ˈklæs/ *v* [T] to be much better than (someone) • *Jack is such a gifted player, he just outclasses the rest of the team.* • *The latest 500 cc road bike easily outclasses all the competition.*

out·come /ˈaʊt·kʌm/ *n* [C usually sing] a result or effect of an action, situation, etc. • *It's too early to predict the outcome* **of** *the meeting.* • *In the end, ten votes determined the outcome* **of** *the election.* • *What do you think the* **likely** *outcome will be?*

out·crop /£ˈaʊt·krɒp, $-krɑːp/ *n* [C] a large rock or group of rocks that sticks out of the ground or that can be seen at the surface of the ground

out·cry /ˈaʊt·kraɪ/ *n* [C] a strong expression of anger and disapproval about something, made by a group of people or by the public • *The government's proposal to release two of the terrorists from prison has provoked a* **public** *outcry.* • *The outcry* **over** *such practices has led to reform.*

out·dat·ed /£ˌaʊtˈdeɪ·tɪd, $-t̬ɪd/ *adj* old-fashioned and therefore not as good or as fashionable as something modern • *outdated weapons/technology/ideas* • *Nowadays this technique is rather outdated.* • See also **out of date** at DATE.

out·dis·tance *obj* /ˌaʊtˈdɪs·tᵊnts/ *v* [T] to be faster in a race than (other competitors), or (more generally) to be much better than (someone) • *A runner like him can outdistance any European with no trouble.* • *The company outdistance their nearest business competitors* **by** *a long way.*

out·do *obj* /ˌaʊtˈduː/ *v* [T] he/she/it **outdoes** /ˌaʊtˈdʌz/, *past simple* **outdid** /ˌaʊtˈdɪd/, *past part* **outdone** /ˌaʊtˈdʌn/ to do or be better than (someone else) • *He pulled a muscle in his arm trying to outdo everybody else in the weight training room.* • *Pat was wearing an outrageous backless purple dress, so* **not to be outdone** (= trying to be more extreme), *I put on my new gold and black trouser suit.*

out·door /£ˌaʊtˈdɔːʳ, $-ˈdɔːr/ *adj* [before n; not gradable] existing, happening or done outside, rather than inside a building • *an outdoor swimming pool* • *an outdoor festival* • *outdoor clothes* • *outdoor hockey* • An outdoor person is one who likes outdoor activities, such as walking and climbing: *He's very much an outdoor person.* ○ *Sara's not really the outdoor type.*

Outside games for children

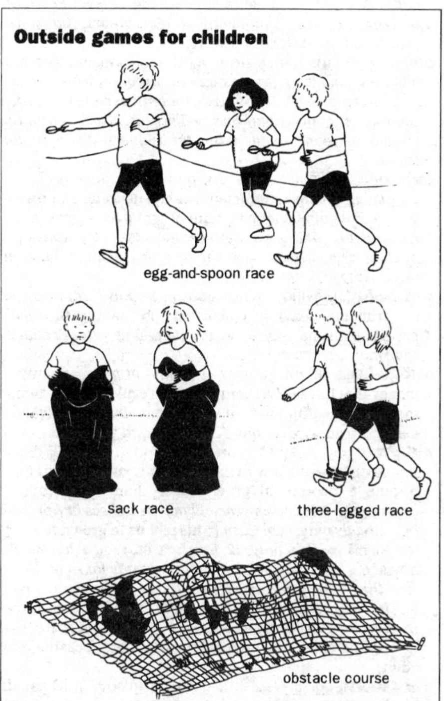

out·doors /£ˌaʊtˈdɔːz, $-ˈdɔːrz/ *adv* [not gradable], *n* • *If the weather's good, we'll eat outdoors* (= outside, rather than in a building). • *Every year he takes a month off work to go trekking in* **the great** *outdoors* (= in the countryside, far away from towns). • See also **out of doors** at DOOR.

out·er /£ˈaʊ·təʳ, $-t̬ɚ/ *adj* [before n; not gradable] at a greater distance from the centre • *outer London* • *the outer* *suburbs • the outer lane of the motorway • an outer layer •* **Outer space** is the part of space that is very far away from Earth.

out·er·most /£ˈaʊ·tə·məʊst, $-t̬ɚ·moʊst/ *adj* [before n; not gradable] • *The outermost* (= outer) *layers are peeled back. • These spacecraft may send back data about the outermost reaches* (= the area furthest away) *of the Solar System until well into the 21st century.*

out·field /ˈaʊt·fiːld/ *n* [U] **the outfield** the part of a cricket or baseball field that is the longest distance away from the player with the BAT (= wooden stick for hitting) • *He could play second base or third base and* **in the outfield.** • Compare INFIELD.

out·field·er /£ˈaʊtˌfiːl·dəʳ, $-dɚ/ *n* [C] • *Born in Cairo, he became a star infielder and outfielder for the Brooklyn Dodgers.*

out·fight *obj* /ˌaʊtˈfaɪt/ *v* [T] *past* **outfought** /ˌaʊtˈfɔːt, $-fɑːt/ to fight better than (someone) • *The former heavyweight champion was outwitted and generally outfought.*

out·fit CLOTHES /ˈaʊt·fɪt/ *n* [C] a set of clothes worn for a particular occasion or activity • *I've got a cowboy outfit you could borrow if you're going to a fancy dress party. • Have you bought your wedding outfit yet? • Kate was wearing a beautiful black velvet outfit she'd just bought.* • See also **fit out** at FIT.

out·fit·ters /£ˈaʊtˌfɪt·əz, $-ˌfɪt̬·ɚz/ *pl n dated* • An outfitters is a shop that sells a particular type of clothes, esp. men's clothes or uniform: *a gentlemen's outfitters • schools' outfitters*

out·fit GROUP /ˈaʊt·fɪt/ *n* [C + sing/pl v] *infml* an organization, company, team, military unit, etc. • *He has recently set up his own research outfit, which has as yet no name. • She's the director of some public-relations outfit in London. • They're a decent outfit – they have several good players.*

outflank *obj* /ˌaʊtˈflæŋk/ *v* [T] to move forward past (an enemy position) in order to attack it from the side or from the back • *The choice is between a direct frontal attack and an outflanking movement to the west. • (fig.) In an attempt to outflank* (= get an advantage over) *the Labour Party, the government has announced a £3 billion investment programme in the Health Service.*

out·flow /£ˈaʊt·fləʊ, $-floʊ/ *n* [C] a movement away from a place • *I'm trying to measure the outflow of water/sewage from that pipe. • On March 12th, the central bank announced controls on* **capital** *outflows. • There is also a continuing outflow* **of** *young people* **from** *the island to the mainland towns.*

out·go·ing FRIENDLY /£ˌaʊtˈgəʊ·ɪŋ, $ˈaʊt·goʊ-/ *adj approving* (of a person) friendly and energetic and finding it easy and enjoyable to be with others • *Sales reps need to be outgoing and dynamic, because they are constantly meeting new customers. • She has an engaging, outgoing personality.*

out·go·ing LEAVING /£ˈaʊtˌgəʊ·ɪŋ, $-ˌgoʊ-/ *adj* [before n; not gradable] leaving a place or job, having finished a period of time there • *the outgoing Vice-President/chairman/governor*

out·go·ings /£ˈaʊtˌgəʊ·ɪŋz, $-ˌgoʊ-/ *pl n Br* amounts of money that have to be spent, usually regularly, for example to pay for heating or rent • *Our outgoings are higher in winter, because we use more electricity and gas.*

out·grow *obj* /£ˌaʊtˈgrəʊ, $-ˈgroʊ/ *v* [T] *past simple* **outgrew** /ˌaʊtˈgruː/, *past part* **outgrown** /£ˌaʊtˈgrəʊn, $-ˈgroʊn/ to grow bigger than or too big for (something) • *My seven-year-old had new shoes in April and he's already outgrown them* (= his feet have grown too large for them). • *He's only 12 but he's outgrown his mother already. • The company, which has already taken on 75 new staff this year, is beginning to outgrow* (= become too large for) *its office space. • (fig.) He outgrew his adolescent interest in war and guns when he left home to go to university* (= as he became older, his interests changed and became more adult).

out·growth RESULT /£ˈaʊt·grəʊθ, $-groʊθ/ *n* [C usually sing] a result of or further development of something • *The innovations in social policy during this period are sometimes seen as the outgrowth of ideas developed in the nineteenth century. • Racism and anti-Semitism were not just an outgrowth of Nazism but its basis.*

out·growth GROWTH /£ˈaʊt·grəʊθ, $-groʊθ/ *n* [C] *specialized* a growth on the outside of an animal or plant • *Antlers are the bony outgrowths on the heads of deer.*

out·gun *obj* /ˌaʊtˈgʌn/ *v* [T usually passive] **-nn-** to win a war or fight by having more weapons than the other side, or to beat someone (or another team) at any sport or activity • *Despite being heavily outgunned, the rebel forces seem to have held on to the South side of the city. • Arsenal were outgunned in all departments in their 3-0 defeat at the hands of Norwich City last night.*

out·house /ˈaʊt·haʊs/ *n* [C] *pl* **outhouses** /ˈaʊtˌhaʊ·zɪz/ a small building joined to or separate from a larger one, or *(Am)* a toilet in an OUTBUILDING

out·ing /£ˈaʊ·tɪŋ, $-t̬ɪŋ/ *n* [C] an esp. short journey, usually one made for pleasure or education by a group of people • *We don't* **go on** *many outings these days. • Rosie's going on a* **class/school** *outing* **to** *the Museum of Modern Art. • We used to take Zoe with us on most of our* **family** *outings.* • See also **outing** at OUT MADE PUBLIC.

out·land·ish /ˌaʊtˈlæn·dɪʃ/ *adj disapproving* strange and unusual and difficult to accept or like • *an outlandish hairstyle/outfit • Looking even further into the future, he said he expected designers to experiment with even more outlandish ideas.*

out·land·ish·ly /ˌaʊtˈlæn·dɪʃ·li/ *adv disapproving* • *I imagined him living in some outlandishly designed house.*

out·land·ish·ness /ˌaʊtˈlæn·dɪʃ·nəs/ *n* [U] *disapproving*

out·last *obj* /£ˌaʊtˈlɑːst, $-ˈlæst/ *v* [T] to live or exist or stay energetic and determined longer than (someone or something) • *The business they set up outlasted them all. • The Orioles outlasted the Yankees, finally winning 10 to 9.*

out·law /£ˈaʊt·lɔː, $-lɑː/ *n* [C] (esp. in the past) a person who has broken the law and who lives separately from the other parts of society because they want to escape legal punishment • *According to English legend, Robin Hood was an outlaw who lived in the forest and stole from the rich to give to the poor. • They belong to an outlaw terrorist group.*

out·law *obj* /£ˈaʊt·lɔː, $-lɑː/ *v* [T] • To outlaw something is to make it illegal and unacceptable: *The European Convention of Human Rights outlaws discrimination between the sexes.* ○ *Last week the government warned that it would consider legislation to outlaw smoking in public places.* ○ *An outlawed political group has no choice but to go underground.*

out·lay /ˈaʊt·leɪ/ *n* [C] an amount of money spent for a particular purpose, esp. as a first investment in something • *For an* **initial** *outlay* **of** *£2000 to buy the equipment, you should be earning up to £500 a month if the product sells well.*

out·lay *obj* /ˌaʊtˈleɪ/ *v* [T] *past* **outlaid** /ˌaʊtˈleɪd/ *esp. Am* • *When starting a business like this you can expect to outlay several thousand dollars* **on** *computers and office furnishings.* • See also **lay out** at LAY.

out·let WAY OUT /ˈaʊt·let/ *n* [C] a way, esp. a pipe or hole, for liquid or gas to go out, or *(fig.)* a way in which emotion or energy can be expressed or made use of • *a waste water outlet • an outlet pipe • (fig.) Her work* **provided** *no outlet* **for** *her energies and talents. • (fig.) Writing poetry was his only form of emotional outlet.* • PIC› **Bathroom**

out·let SHOP /ˈaʊt·let/ *n* [C] a shop that is one of many owned by a particular company and that sells the goods which the company has produced • *a fast-food outlet • a retail outlet • The bigger breweries own hundreds or thousands of pubs that are outlets* **for** *their own beers.*

out·let ELECTRICITY /ˈaʊt·let/ *n* [C] *Am for* **power point**, see at POWER

out·line /ˈaʊt·laɪn/ *n* [C] the main shape of something, without any details • *She drew the outline* **of** *the boat and then coloured it in. • It was a quick outline sketch. • The mountain was visible only* **in outline** *as the light faded. • (fig.) If you read the minutes of the meeting, they'll give you a* **broad** *outline* (= general idea of the main items) **of** *what was discussed.* • An outline is also a piece of writing that tells the main points of a story without any details: *Some writers prefer to do an outline first and then flesh out the plot and characters.* • PIC› **Drawing and painting**

out·line *obj* /ˈaʊt·laɪn/ *v* [T] • *The area we're interested in is outlined* **in** *red on the map. • (fig.) At the interview she outlined* (= described the main parts of) *what I would be doing.*

out·live *obj* /ˌaʊtˈlɪv/ *v* [T] to live or exist longer than (someone or something) • *He outlived all of his brothers. • I certainly hope I won't outlive any of my children. • Eventually we decided that the system had* **outlived its usefulness** (= was no longer useful or necessary).

out·look FUTURE SITUATION /ˈaʊt·lʊk/ *n* [C usually sing] the likely future situation • *The outlook should improve* *next year, as the economy emerges from the recession.* • *Overall the outlook* **for** *the company seems fairly rosy.* • *Management seem optimistic about the outlook* **for** *next year.* • *In the long term the* **economic** *outlook is bleak.* • *In summary, the outlook* **for** *today is cloudy and dry at first with showers later.*

out·look OPINION /ˈaʊt·lʊk/ *n* [C usually sing] a person's way of understanding and thinking about something • *He has a fairly positive outlook* **on life**.

out·look VIEW /ˈaʊt·lʊk/ *n* [C] *fml* a view • *From the top of the tower, the outlook over the city was breathtaking.*

out·ly·ing /ˈaʊtˌlaɪ·ɪŋ/ *adj* [before n] far away from esp. the main towns and cities • *Many of the pupils travel in by bus from outlying areas.*

out·ma·noeu·vre *obj Br and Aus, Am* **out·ma·neu·ver** /£ˌaʊt·məˈnuː·vəʳ, $-vɚ/ *v* [T] to cleverly obtain an advantage over (esp. a competitor) • *In the negotiations, he outmanoeuvred his rivals by offering a higher price at the last moment.*

out·mod·ed /£ˌaʊtˈməʊ·dɪd, $-ˈmoʊ-/ *adj disapproving* old-fashioned; no longer modern, useful or necessary • *The concept of monarchy is decidedly outmoded.* • *Outmoded working practices are being phased out.*

out·num·ber *obj* /£ˌaʊtˈnʌm·bəʳ, $-bɚ/ *v* [T] to be greater in number than • *In our office the females outnumber the males 3 to 1.* • *In the long run successes do outnumber failures.*

out·pace *obj* /ˌaʊtˈpeɪs/ *v* [T] to go, run or drive more quickly than other people esp. in a sporting competition • *Ovett managed to outpace the rest of the field in a brilliant display of 1500m running.* • *(fig.) This company seems to have completely outpaced its rivals in the market.*

out·per·form *obj* /£ˌaʊt·pəˈfɔːm, $-pɚˈfɔːrm/ *v* [T] to do well in a particular job or activity compared to others of a similar type • *The Peugeot engine has consistently outperformed its rivals this season.*

out·play *obj* /ˌaʊtˈpleɪ/ *v* [T] to play a game more cleverly and successfully than (another person or team) • *The French chess players were completely outplayed by the Russian team.*

out·post /£ˈaʊt·pəʊst, $-poʊst/ *n* [C] a place, esp. a small group of buildings or a town, which maintains the authority or business interests of a distant government or company • *a police/military/colonial outpost* • *The Hong Kong office is one of several outposts recently established by the company.* • *Berlin was a capitalist outpost in the middle of communist East Germany.* • *(fig.) Free jazz has been described as the* **last** *outpost* **of** (= the only and last existing example of) *modernism.*

out·pour·ing STRONG FEELING /£ˈaʊtˌpɔː·rɪŋ, $-ˌpɔːr·ɪŋ/ *n* [C] an uncontrollable expression of strong feeling • *His death at the age of 35 has occasioned an outpouring* **of** *grief in South Africa where he was seen as a future leader.* • *The outpouring* **of** *public emotion after the court's decision yesterday took a lot of people by surprise.* • *After a few pages you realise that these writings are the outpourings* **of** *a deeply troubled man.*

out·pour·ing LARGE NUMBER /£ˈaʊtˌpɔː·rɪŋ, $-ˌpɔːr·ɪŋ/ *n* [C] a very large number of things produced at the same time • *The last year has seen an outpouring* **of** *books on the subject of alternative energy sources.*

out·put /ˈaʊt·pʊt/ *n* an amount of something produced by a person, machine, factory, country, etc. • *In the decade to 1990 Britain expanded* **manufacturing** *output by 14% while Ireland achieved 86%.* [U] • **Industrial** *output continues to fall with production down more than 6% as at the end of July.* [U] • *In 1981, nuclear power produced nearly 40% of the country's* **total** *output.* [U] • *Radio Two plans to double its daily news output from next month.* [C] • *Much of her output as a writer* (= What she wrote) *was first published in magazines.* [U] • *An assessment of the Welfare System would involve careful study of its inputs and outputs.* [C]

out·rage *obj* /ˈaʊt·reɪdʒ/ *v* [T often passive] (esp. of an unfair action or statement) to cause (someone) to feel very angry, shocked or upset • *A crowd of people gathered, outraged* **at/by** *the way the police officers were hitting the two men.* • *A proposed 5% pay cut has outraged staff at the warehouse.* • *Many outraged viewers wrote to the BBC to complain about the programme's bad language and nude scenes.* • *His description of abortion as "a terrible offence against God and humanity" produced an outraged response from the audience.*

out·rage /ˌaʊtˈreɪdʒ/ *n* • Outrage is a feeling of anger and shock: *The sadistic murder of a two-year-old boy in Liverpool last week* **provoked** *public outrage.* [U] ○ *Many politicians and members of the public* **expressed** *outrage at the verdict.* [U] • *Racist attacks have caused* **moral** *outrage.* [U] ○ **Public** *outrage forced the government to stop the road building, and the forest was saved.* [U] ○ *The* **sense of** *moral outrage* **at** *the unfairness of the tax was very strong.* [U] • An outrage is also a shocking, morally unacceptable and usually violent action: *The bomb, which killed 15 people, was the worst of a series of terrorist outrages.* [C] • **It's** *an outrage* (= it is shocking and morally unacceptable) *that so much public money should have been wasted in this way.* [C + *that* clause]

out·rag·eous /ˌaʊtˈreɪ·dʒəs/ *adj* • Outrageous means shocking and morally unacceptable: *For some reason, there is something absolutely outrageous about a naked man on television.* ○ *The judge criticized the "outrageous greed" of some of the lawyers and doctors involved in the case.* ○ **It** *is outrageous* **that** *these buildings remain empty while thousands of people have no homes.* [+ *that* clause] ○ *The prices those late-night shops charge are just outrageous* (= much too high). • Outrageous also means shocking because unusual and strange: *Patrick is an outrageous character.* ○ *I should imagine it'll be a fairly sober party so don't wear anything too outrageous.*

out·rag·eous·ly /ˌaʊtˈreɪ·dʒə·sli/ *adv* • *They charge outrageously high prices.* • *It's described as 'an outrageously funny comedy'* (= one that is amusing in a shocking way).

out·ran /ˌaʊtˈræn/ *past simple of* OUTRUN

out·rank *obj* /ˌaʊtˈræŋk/ *v* [T] to have a higher rank than (someone) • *As a Chief Superintendent, she outranked all the other police officers in the room.*

ou·tré /ˈuː·treɪ/ *adj fml* unusual, strange and shocking, esp. in an amusing way • *In the sixties he wrote an outré comedy about Hitler's childhood.* • *I don't think I shall buy the hat – it's absolutely splendid but a little outré for my sober tastes.*

out·reach /ˈaʊt·riːtʃ/ *adj* [before n; not gradable] relating to efforts to bring government and a range of social services to people where they live or spend time • *an outreach worker* • *AIDS outreach programs bring medical care, condoms and counselling to prostitutes on the streets.*

out·rid·er /£ˈaʊtˌraɪ·dəʳ, $-dɚ/ *n* [C] a person, esp. a police officer, who rides on a motorcycle next to or in front of an official vehicle • *The Mayor went by in a black limousine, complete with motorcycle outriders sounding their horns to clear a path through the traffic.*

out·right /ˌaʊtˈraɪt/ *adv* [not gradable] completely, clearly, directly or immediately • *The union have* **rejected** *both proposals outright.* • *The driver and all three passengers were* **killed** *outright.* • *Most people said they thought that cigarette advertising should be* **banned** *outright.*

out·right /ˈaʊt·raɪt/ *adj* [before n; not gradable] • *This is a region in which outsiders are regarded with suspicion bordering on outright* **hostility**. • *His outright* **condemnation** *of the BBC's new soap opera surprised a lot of people.* • *A regional election in Spain's Basque country failed to produce an outright* **winner**. • *Neither side found it possible to win an outright military* **victory**. • *They demand the outright and immediate* **abolition** *of the tax on children's clothes.*

out·run *obj* /ˌaʊtˈrʌn/ *v* [T] **outrunning**, *past simple* **outran** /ˌaʊtˈræn/, *past part* **outrun** to run faster than (someone) or *(fig.)* to increase faster than or go beyond (something) • *The thieves easily outran the policewoman who was chasing them.* • *(fig.) In the future, demand for metals like tungsten will outrun supply.* • *(fig.) Her campaign costs during the election disastrously outran her income.*

outs /aʊts/ *pl n* **on the outs** *Am infml* unfriendly • *Sometimes Lizzie and Tyler are best of friends, but they're really on the outs today.*

out·sell *obj* /ˌaʊtˈsel/ *v* [T] *past* **outsold** /£ˌaʊtˈsəʊld, $-ˈsoʊld/ (of a product) to be sold in greater numbers than (another product) • *CDs soon began to outsell records.* • *Rock music massively outsells jazz and rap.*

out·set /ˈaʊt·set/ *n* [U] **the outset** the beginning • **At** *the outset of the play there is a lot of confused violence.* • *Employees knew* **from** *the outset that their jobs would finish this year.*

out·shine *obj* /£ˌaʊtˈʃaɪn/ *v* [T] *past* **outshone** /£ˌaʊtˈʃɒn, $-ˈʃɑːn/ to be much more skilful and successful than (someone) • *Ben Palmer easily outshone his rivals by winning the 200 metres freestyle at the European Junior Championships yesterday.*

out·side OUTER PART /ˌaʊtˈsaɪd, ˈ--/ *n* [U] the outer part or side of something • *Although the outside of a passion fruit looks strange, the flesh inside is delicious.* • *The outside of the house needs painting.* • *Somehow the house looks larger when looked at from the outside.* • *Perhaps the company needs to get help from outside* (= from people who work for other organizations). • *(Br)* **The outside** or an **outside lane** is the part of the road nearest the vehicles going in the opposite direction, used esp. by faster vehicles: *She cruised by at 160 kilometres per hour* **on the** *outside*/**in** *the outside lane.* • *(Am)* The **outside lane** is the part of the road nearest the edge, esp. used by slower vehicles. • **The outside** or the **outside lane** is also the part of a RACETRACK that is furthest from the centre: *The runner* **in** *the outside lane has a longer distance to run.* • *The job will take about ten days* **at the outside** (= not more than ten days, and probably less). • Compare INSIDE INNER PART. • PIC› **Motorway**

out·side /ˌaʊtˈsaɪd/ *adv* [not gradable], *prep*, *adj* [not gradable] • *Since it's such a nice day shall we eat/sit/go outside* (= not in the building, but not very far away from it). • *It was a lovely day outside, although no sunlight actually reached into the office.* • *She sat for two hours on the floor outside his room* (= not inside the room, but close to the door). • *One could hear the demonstrators screaming and shouting outside the courtroom.* • *(fig.) An over-protected childhood, then school and university, meant that at the age of 22 she had no idea about the* **world** *outside/ the outside* **world** (= the way of life for most people). • Outside is also used to mean not in a particular place: *Nobody outside this room must ever know what we have discussed.* ○ *Outside Japan* (= In other countries) *almost no research is being done.* • Outside is also used to mean beyond or not within or part of something: *I'm afraid that would be outside my job description.* • Outside also means coming from another place or organization: *The company badly needs outside support.* ○ *We've had to call in an outside adviser/expert.* • *(esp. Am)* **Outside of** means not within or except for: *There's a lot of really good theatre and opera outside of London these days.* ○ *Outside of us three, no one knows anything about the problem, yet.* • An outside **call** or outside **line** is a telephone call or connection going outside the place where you are: *You're not allowed to make outside calls on office phones, unless it's to do with work.* ○ *I'm trying to get an outside line but they're all busy.* • Outside can also mean the most that would be allowed: *The outside limit/figure would be £350.* • *(Br and Aus) an* **outside broadcast** *(Am* **remote broadcast***)* (= a broadcast not made within the television or radio building)

out·sid·er /£ˌaʊtˈsaɪ·dəʳ, $-dɚ/ *n* [C] • An outsider is a person who is not involved with a particular group of people or organization or who does not live in a particular place: *Outsiders have a glamorized idea of what it is like to work for the BBC.* ○ *Few outsiders have ever visited the tribes who live in the remote Indian state of Aranachal Pradesh.* ○ *It was one of those cutting jokes insiders make about outsiders.* • An outsider is also a person who is not liked or accepted as a member of a particular group, organization or society and who feels different from those people who are accepted as members: *As a child he was very much an outsider, never participating in the games other children played.* ○ *They moved to the area from London three years ago, but they still feel like outsiders.*

out·side SLIGHT /ˌaʊtˈsaɪd/ *adj* [before n] slight • *There's still an outside* **chance/possibility** *that Scotland will get through into the World Cup.*

out·sid·er /£ˌaʊtˈsaɪ·dəʳ, $-dɚ/ *n* [C] • *The race was won by a* **rank** *outsider* (= a person or animal with only a slight chance of winning).

out·size /ˈaʊt·saɪz/ *adj* [before n] (esp. of clothing) much larger than usual • *They sell outsize clothes for very tall or very large people.* • *We looked in the window of the shop called Les Olivades, which has nice outsize white coffee cups.* • *(fig.) She's one of the last surviving outsize personalities in journalism.*

out·sized /ˈaʊt·saɪzd/ *adj* • *He has a liking for baggy suits and outsized sunglasses.*

out·skirts /£ˈaʊt·skɜːts, $-skɜːrts/ *pl n* the areas that form the edge of a town or city • *The factory is* **in/on** *the outskirts* **of** *New Delhi.*

out·smart *obj* /£ˌaʊtˈsmɑːt, $-ˈsmɑːrt/ *v* [T] to OUTWIT

out·sold /£ˌaʊtˈsəʊld, $-ˈsoʊld/ *past simple and past participle of* OUTSELL

out·spok·en /£ˌaʊtˈspəʊ·kᵊn, $-ˈspoʊ-/ *adj* (of a person) expressing strong opinions very directly without worrying if other people are offended • *Mr Masack is an outspoken* **critic** *of the present government.* • *Davis has earned a reputation as an outspoken* **opponent** *of any kind of nuclear waste dumping at sea.* • *In recent years, he has been an outspoken* **supporter** *of radical reform.* • *He has outspoken views on the subject of nuclear power.* • *She can be quite outspoken and some people find it rather off-putting.*

out·spread /ˌaʊtˈspred/ *adj* spread as widely as possible • *The statue was of a bronze angel with outspread* **wings.** • *She was lying on the floor with arms outspread.*

out·stand·ing EXCELLENT /ˌaʊtˈstæn·dɪŋ/ *adj* excellent; clearly very much better than what is usual • *an outstanding performance/writer/novel* • *He had three outstanding years as a centre forward at Liverpool.* • Outstanding also means very special and important in a particular way: *The prize is awarded for 'an outstanding contribution to broadcasting'.* ○ *It's an area of outstanding* **natural beauty.**

out·stand·ing·ly /ˌaʊtˈstæn·dɪŋ·li/ *adv* • *He was an outstandingly* **successful** *mayor from 1981 to 1984.* • *The whole team performed outstandingly well.*

out·stand·ing NOT FINISHED /ˌaʊtˈstæn·dɪŋ/ *adj* not yet done, solved or paid • *The company's total* **debt** *outstanding at the end of August was $450 million.* • *They are Latin America's second biggest creditors with $30 billion in outstanding* **loans.** • *If there are any problems still outstanding, we must deal with them now.*

out·stay *obj* /ˌaʊtˈsteɪ/ *v* [T] **outstay** *your* **welcome** to continue to stay in a place although other people want you to leave • *I think I'll leave when I said I would – I don't wish to outstay my welcome.*

out·stretched /ˌaʊtˈstretʃt/ *adj* stretched as far as possible or held out in front • *He came running up to her, his* **arms** *outstretched.* • *She put some pesos into the little girl's outstretched* **hand.** • *Sit with your legs outstretched in front of you.*

out·strip *obj* /ˌaʊtˈstrɪp/ *v* [T] **-pp-** to be or become greater in amount, degree or success than (something or someone) • *The demand for firewood now far outstrips* **supply.** • *Export growth should far outstrip import growth.*

outta, out·a /£ˈaʊ·tə, $-t̬ə/ *prep esp. Am infml* out of • *We'd better get outta here, man!* • *I'm outta here* (= I'm leaving).

out–take /ˈaʊt·teɪk/ *n* [C] a short part of a film or television programme or music recording that was removed and not included, usually because it contains mistakes • *They showed a video of amusing out-takes from various films.*

out·vote *obj* /£ˌaʊtˈvəʊt, $-ˈvoʊt/ *v* [T often passive] to defeat (someone) by winning a greater number of votes • *The Democrats were outvoted, as usual.* • *I suggested we should go for a pizza, but I was outvoted* (= most people did not want to) *so we went for a curry.*

out·ward /£ˈaʊt·wəd, $-wɚd/ *adj* [before n; not gradable] relating to how people, situations or things seem to be, rather than how they are inside • *He is an odd mixture of outward confidence and inner doubt.* • *The book details the outward circumstances of her life but fails to reveal anything of her inner self.* • *The outward appearance of the building has not changed at all in 200 years.* • *We now have the chance to build an outward-***looking** *Europe that lives up to its global responsibilities.* • *If he is suffering he certainly shows no outward sign of it.* • **To all** *outward* **appearances** *everything was fine, but under the surface the marriage was very shaky.* • Compare INWARD.

outwardly /£ˈaʊt·wəd·li, $-wɚd-/ *adv* • *Outwardly, he seemed happy enough.*

out·wards /£ˈaʊt·wədz, $-wɚdz/, *esp. Am* **out·ward** *adv* [not gradable] going or pointing away from a particular place or towards the outside • *The door opens outwards.* • *New suburbs are pushing outwards into previously wooded areas.* • *At the port she managed to get a passage on an* **outward-bound** *ship.* • *It's much healthier to direct your emotions outwards than to bottle them up inside you.*

out·ward /£ˈaʊt·wəd, $-wɚd/ *adj* [before n; not gradable] • *The outward flight/journey took eight hours, but the return journey took only six hours.*

out·weigh *obj* /ˌaʊtˈweɪ/ *v* [T] to be likely to be more important than or have an effect on (something else) • *For me the advantages of living in a town outweigh the* **disadvantages/drawbacks.** • *We know these chemicals* *are dangerous, but their benefits far outweigh any risk to the environment.*

out·wit *obj* (**-tt-**) /ˌaʊtˈwɪt/, **out·smart** *v* [T] to obtain an advantage over (someone) by acting more cleverly and often by using a trick • *In the story the clever little fox outwits the hunters and escapes from the trap they set.*

out·worn /£ˌaʊtˈwɔːn, $-ˈwɔːrn/ *adj* [not gradable] (esp. of an idea or phrase) old-fashioned and used too often in the past, so no longer useful or important • *He used that outworn metaphor of society as a jungle where only the fittest survive.*

ou·zo /£ˈuː·zəʊ, $-zoʊ/ *n pl* **ouzos** an ANISEED flavoured Greek alcoholic drink which is often drunk with water • *Ouzo is colourless but turns milky white when water is added.* [U] • *She ordered a couple of ouzos* (= glasses of ouzo). [C]

o·va /£ˈəʊ·və, $ˈoʊ-/ *pl of* OVUM

o·val /£ˈəʊ·vᵊl, $ˈoʊ-/ *adj, n* (shaped like) a circle that is flattened either at one place or at two opposite places, so that it is like either an egg or an ELLIPSE • *an oval mirror* • *an oval face* • *Her eyes were large ovals.* [C] • The **Oval Office** is the office of the US President, in Washington: *The lies and cover-ups eventually worked their way to the Oval Office.* ○ *(fig.) It now seems unlikely that the Democratic nominee will reach the Oval office* (= become President). • PIC› **Shapes**

o·va·ry /£ˈəʊ·vᵊr·i, $ˈoʊ-/ *n* [C] either of the pair of organs in a woman's body which produce eggs, or the part of any female animal or plant that produces eggs or seeds

o·va·ri·an /£əʊˈveə·ri·ən, $oʊˈver·i-/ *adj* [not gradable] • *ovarian cancer* • *an ovarian cyst*

o·va·tion /£əʊˈveɪ·ʃᵊn, $oʊ-/ *n* [C] loud and long clapping that expresses a crowd of people's great enjoyment and/or approval of something • *She was given a* **standing** *ovation* (= the crowd stood up while they clapped, to show respect) *at the end of her speech.* • *The Royal ballet* **received** *a thunderous/ecstatic ovation when they danced here two months ago.*

ov·en /ˈʌv·ᵊn/ *n* [C] an enclosed space with a door, usually part of a piece of equipment which is used to cook food or heat other substances • *a conventional/gas/fan-assisted/microwave oven* • *Put the turkey* **in** *the oven now at about 200°C and take it out at one o'clock.* • *Calcutta in summer is* **like an** *oven* (= extremely and uncomfortably hot). • *(Br)* **Oven gloves** /*(Am and Aus)* **oven mitts** are thick cloth coverings for the hands which you can use for taking hot things out of an oven. • If food is **oven-ready** it is sold already prepared for cooking: *an oven-ready chicken* • PIC› **Kitchen** Ⓓ

ov·en·a·ble /ˈʌv·ᵊn·ə·bl̩/ *adj* [not gradable] • Ovenable means able to be cooked or used in an oven: *a packet of ovenable chips* ○ *an ovenable tray*

ov·en·proof /ˈʌv·ᵊm·pruːf/ *adj* [not gradable] • *Is this dish definitely ovenproof* (= can it be used in an oven without being damaged)*?*

ov·en·ware /£ˈʌv·ᵊn·weəʳ, $-wer/ *n* [U] dishes and other food containers in which food can be cooked • *You'll find ovenware on the next floor, madam, in the kitchen department.* • LP› **Shopping goods**

o·ver HIGHER POSITION /£ˈəʊ·vəʳ, $ˈoʊ·vɚ/ *prep* in, to or at a position above or higher than (something else), sometimes so that one thing covers the other; above • *The sign over the door said "Private. No entry".* • *He's so tall that he towers over the rest of us.* • *She wears a plastic cap over her hair when she goes swimming in order to keep it dry.* • *You can't wear a blue jacket over that shirt – it'll look awful.* • *He spread a plastic sheet over the motorbike, covering it completely.* • *His jacket was hanging over the back of his chair.* • *I put my hands over my eyes/ears because I couldn't bear to watch/listen.* • *She jumped over the gate and ran off.* • *Helicopters dropped leaflets over the city.* • *Place the test tube over the flame.* • *If you're going to pour that out, do it over the sink.* • *He poured some water over the fire.* • *Would you mind watching over* (= watching carefully and taking care of) *the sausages under the grill for a minute?* • *I couldn't hear what she was saying over the noise of the planes taking off* (= the aircraft were louder than her voice). • When doing calculations you might say that one number is over another number, meaning that the first number is divided by the second: *40 over 7 is roughly 7.* • Compare UNDER LOWER POSITION. • LP› **Mathematics** Ⓙ Ⓚ Ⓣ

o·ver /£ˈəʊ·vəʳ, $ˈoʊ·vɚ/ *adv* [not gradable] • *A man came to paint over* (= cover with paint) *the cracks in the wall.*

o·ver- /£ˌəʊ·vəʳ-, $ˌoʊ·vɚ-/ *combining form* • *She was knocked off her bicycle by an overhanging branch.* • *Of course the overland route is much slower than going by air.*

o·ver ACROSS /£ˈəʊ·vəʳ, $ˈoʊ·vɚ/ *prep* across from one side to the other, esp. by going up and then down • *She leaned over the table to get the bottle.* • *Hannibal made a famous march over the Alps with elephants.* • *The road goes through a tunnel rather than over the top of the hill.* • *The pilot flew over the mountains to give us a good view.* • *She used to have long chats with her neighbour over the garden wall.* • *From the top of the tower you could see for miles over the city.* • *Drive over the bridge and then turn left.* • *The magician passed his hand over the hat and a rabbit jumped out.* • *Tanks travel over the most difficult ground.* • Over also means on the other side of: *The story continues over the page.* ○ *The village is just over the next hill.* • If something is **all** over a place, it is everywhere in that place: *Soon the news was all over town.* ○ *(fig.) She was all over him, kissing him and stroking him – it was quite embarrassing.* • *"Over the hills and far away"* (title of a song by John Gay, based on a traditional song, 1728) • PIC› **Prepositions of movement** Ⓙ Ⓚ Ⓣ

o·ver /£ˈəʊ·vəʳ, $ˈoʊ·vɚ/ *adv* [not gradable] • *She leaned over and kissed me.* • *A fighter plane flew over.* • *Why don't you come over* (= come to my house) *for dinner on Thursday?* • *Now we're going over to* (= there will be a broadcast from) *Wembley for commentary on the Cup Final.* • *I've got a friend over from Canada this week* (= A friend came from Canada and is staying with me). • *Come over* **here** (= to this place from where you are) *– it's warmer.* • *Who's that man over* **there** (= in that place)*?* • Over also describes the way an object moves or is moved so that a different part of it is facing up: *She turned another page over.* ○ *The dog rolled over onto its back.* ○ *The children rolled over* **and over** (= turned over many times) *down the gentle slope.* ○ *Now that I've had a chance to think over your proposal* (= to consider it carefully)*, I'm not so sure it's a good idea.* ○ *Let's not decide immediately – we ought to talk it over first.* • If two people or things **change/swap** over, they exchange positions: *Would you mind swapping those plates over?* • If someone or something **changes/moves** over **to** something else, they exchange an old position or situation for a new one: *Changing over to cable television means you have a wider range of TV channels.* ○ *She changed over to marketing from being an editor.* • If you **hand/pass** someone or something over you give them to someone else: *He handed over £500 in cash.* ○ *The prisoners of war were handed over to the Russians.* ○ *Pass it over here when you've finished and I'll have a look.* • If you say "over" when you are talking to someone by radio, you mean that you have finished speaking and will wait for their answer: *"This is flight 595X. Do you read me? Over."* • You say "over **and out**" when you are talking to someone by radio in order to end the conversation: *"Thank you control tower. Over and out."* • *I've done all I can – it's over* **to you** (= it's your turn to take action) *now.*

o·ver MORE THAN /£ˈəʊ·vəʳ, $ˈoʊ·vɚ/ *prep* more than • *Most of the carpets cost/are over £100.* • *Children over* **(the age of)** *12* (= older than 12) *must have full-price air tickets.* • *To get an A grade in this exam you need to get over 80%.* • *So many people seem to value money over anything else, such as quality of life.* • If someone or something goes over a particular limit or point, it increases beyond it: *I've gone over my overdraft limit.* ○ *They are already $25 million over budget.* • *Mothers with young children receive an extra allowance* **over and above** (= in addition to) *the usual welfare payments.* • Ⓙ Ⓚ Ⓣ

o·ver /£ˈəʊ·vəʳ, $ˈoʊ·vɚ/ *adv* [not gradable] • *People who are 65 years old and over can get half-price tickets.*

o·ver- /£ˌəʊ·vəʳ-, $ˌoʊ·vɚ-/ *combining form* • *a club for the over-50s*

o·ver- TOO MUCH /£ˌəʊ·vəʳ-, $ˌoʊ·vɚ-/ *combining form* too much or more than usual • *The children got rather over-excited* (= too excited). • *It looks rather like an oversized orange.* • *The kid is an over-achiever* (= works and succeeds more than is usual). • *(disapproving) I'm all in favour of praising people's efforts, but I think telling her it was the best piece of work you'd ever seen was rather* **over-egging the pudding** (= saying or doing more than is necessary). • *"Overpaid, overfed, oversexed and over here"* (Tommy Trinder describing American troops in Britain during World War II, reported in *The Sunday Times*, 4 January 1976)

o·ver DOWN /£ˈəʊ·vəʳ, $ˈoʊ·vɚ/ *adv* [not gradable] from a higher to a lower position; down • *The little boy fell over and started to cry.* • *He was run/knocked over by a taxi.* • (J) (KOR) (T) .

o·ver /£ˈəʊ·vəʳ, $ˈoʊ·vɚ/ *prep* • *She tripped over the rug.* • If someone or something goes over something steep that has an edge, it falls off it: *Harold jumped out of the car just before it went over the cliff.*

o·ver USING /£ˈəʊ·vəʳ, $ˈoʊ·vɚ/ *prep* using • *They spoke over the phone.* • *He talked to the crowd over a portable sound system.* • *We heard the news over the radio.* • (J) (KOR) (T)

o·ver OTHER SIDE /£ˈəʊ·vəʳ, $ˈoʊ·vɚ/ *prep* on the other side of • *There's a pub over the road we could go to.* • *I'm just going over the road to feed Brenda's cat.* • (J) (KOR) (T)

o·ver DURING /£ˈəʊ·vəʳ, $ˈoʊ·vɚ/ *prep* during (something), or while doing (something) • *Many changes happened over the six months she was in charge of the company.* • *Over the years he became more and more depressed about life.* • *We lost £2 million over a six-month period.* • *It's fascinating to watch how a baby changes and develops over* **time** (= as time passes). • *I was in Seattle over the summer.* • *Shall we discuss it over lunch/over a drink?* • *They took/spent an hour over lunch* (= Their meal lasted an hour). • (J) (KOR) (T)

o·ver CONTROL /£ˈəʊ·vəʳ, $ˈoʊ·vɚ/ *prep* (used when describing who or what is more powerful) in control of or instructing (someone or something) • *A good teacher has an easy authority over a class.* • *She's a sales manager but she has a regional sales director over* (= with a higher rank than) *her.* • *Her husband always did have a lot of influence over her.* • *The victory over the French at Waterloo was Wellington's greatest triumph.* • *As Treasurer, she has control over how much money is spent and on what.* • (J) (KOR)

o·ver CONNECTED WITH /£ˈəʊ·vəʳ, $ˈoʊ·vɚ/ *prep* (used esp. to refer to something or someone that is a cause of interest, worry, discussion, etc.) connected with or about • *There's no point in arguing over something that's as unimportant as that.* • *She was reading a newspaper and puzzling over* (= trying to understand) *the political cartoon.* • *The legal battle was over who should have custody of the child.* • (J) (KOR) (T)

o·ver EXTRA /£ˈəʊ·vəʳ, $ˈoʊ·vɚ/ *adv* [not gradable] extra; not used • *I have some American dollars* **left** *over from the last time I was there.* • *(Br) When all the guests had gone, we realized there was lots of food over.* • (J) (KOR) (T)

o·ver FINISHED /£ˈəʊ·vəʳ, $ˈoʊ·vɚ/ *adj* [after v; not gradable] (esp. of an event) completed • *I'll be glad when the competition is over.* • *The game was over by 5 o'clock.* • *I used to have a thriving business and a happy marriage, but that's* **all** *over now.* • *The boss wants to* **get** *most of the research* **over with** (= finish most of it) *by January.* • *Her way of dealing with unpleasant tasks is to get it* **over and done with** (= completely finished) *as quickly as possible.* • (J) (KOR) (T)

o·ver AGAIN /£ˈəʊ·vəʳ, $ˈoʊ·vɚ/ *adv* [not gradable] again or repeatedly • *(Am) You've ruined it – now I'll have to* **do** *it over!* • If you do something or if something happens **over and over (again)**, you do it or it happens many times. • (J) (KOR) (T)

o·ver FEELING BETTER /£ˈəʊ·vəʳ, $ˈoʊ·vɚ/ *prep* feeling better, either physically or mentally, after (something) • *Is he over the flu yet?* • *His girlfriend of six years finished with him last year and I don't think he's over her yet.* • *It takes you a while to* **get** *over an illness like that.* • *He's not fully recovered but he's certainly over* **the worst** (= he has experienced the worst stage of the illness and is now improving). • (J) (KOR) (T)

o·ver CRICKET /£ˈəʊ·vəʳ, $ˈoʊ·vɚ/ *n* [C] (in cricket) a set of six BOWLS (= throws) from the same end of the field • *After each over the fielders change positions, and the next over is bowled from the other end.* • (J) (KOR) (T)

o·ver·act *(obj)* /£ˌəʊ·vəˈrækt, $ˌoʊ·vɚˈækt/ *v* *disapproving* to make your voice and movements express emotions too strongly when acting in a play • *The problem with Emilio is that he overacts.* [I] • *Don't you think she was overacting the despair?* [T]

o·ver·age /£ˌəʊ·vəˈreɪdʒ, $ˌoʊ·vɚˈeɪdʒ/ *adj* [not gradable] older than a particular age and therefore no longer allowed to do or have particular things • *She lost her place on the youth team when the manager discovered she was overage.*

o·ver·all /£ˌəʊ·vəˈrɔːl, $ˌoʊ·vɚˈɑːl/ *adj* [before n], *adv* [not gradable] in general rather than in particular, or including all the people or things in a particular group or situation • *The overall situation is good, despite a few minor problems.* • *There have been lots of negative news stories, the overall effect of which has been to make the President appear uncertain and weak.* • *She is the overall commander of three divisions of troops.* • *The overall winner, after ten games, will receive $250 000.* • *There were a couple of lectures that I thought were a bit dull but overall it was a really good week.*

o·ver·alls *Br* /£ˈəʊ·vəʳr·ɔːlz, $ˈoʊ·vɚ·ɑːlz/, *Am* **cov·er·all** /£ˈkʌv·əʳr·ɔːl, $-ɚ·ɑːl/ *pl n* a piece of clothing that covers both the upper and lower parts of the body and is worn esp. over other clothes to protect them • *She put on some overalls, got out the paint, and started on the living room ceiling.* • Overalls is also *Am for* DUNGAREES.

o·ver·arch·ing /£ˌəʊ·vəˈrɑː·tʃɪŋ, $ˌoʊ·vɚˈɑːr-/ *adj* [before n] *fml* most important, because reaching into or including all other areas • *The company has abandoned the idea of a grand overarching strategy in favour of a series of smaller investment programmes.* • *The overarching theme of the election campaign was the improvement of basic standards of education and health care.*

o·ver·arm /£ˈəʊ·və·rɑːm, $ˈoʊ·vɚ·ɑːrm/ *adj, adv* (esp. of a throw) made with the arm moving above the shoulder • *an overarm throw/serve* • *Bowl it overarm.*

o·ver·ate /£ˌəʊ·vəˈret, £-reɪt, $ˌoʊ·vɚˈeɪt/ *past simple of* OVEREAT

o·ver·awe *obj* /£ˌəʊ·vəˈrɔː, $ˌoʊ·vɚˈɑː/ *v* [T usually passive] to cause (someone) to feel a mixture of extreme respect and fear • *Some of the players were totally overawed by playing their first game at the national stadium.*

o·ver·bal·ance /£ˌəʊ·vəˈbæl·ənts, $ˌoʊ-/ *v* [I] to lose balance and therefore fall over or nearly fall over • *Halfway along the wall he overbalanced and fell.*

o·ver·bear·ing /£ˌəʊ·vəˈbeə·rɪŋ, $ˌoʊ·vɚˈber·ɪŋ/ *adj* *disapproving* too confident and too determined to tell other people what to do, in a way that is unpleasant and not easy to like • *Milligan's childhood was marked by an overbearing mother and a distant father.* • *She has a rather overbearing manner which some people find off-putting.*

o·ver·bid *(obj)* /£ˌəʊ·vəˈbɪd, $ˌoʊ·vɚ-/ *v* **overbidding**, *past* **overbid** to offer more money than (someone) in an attempt to buy something, or to offer too much money in an attempt to buy something • *They were overbid by a Japanese firm.* [T] • *The Commission felt the company were overbidding and gave the franchise to their competitors instead.* [I]

o·ver·blown /£ˌəʊ·vəˈbləʊn, $ˌoʊ·vɚˈbloʊn/ *adj* *disapproving* much larger, more complicated or more obviously artistic than necessary • *Compared to the rather overblown film version of the book, this is a very subtle stage adaptation.* • *Sir Neville's conducting is precise and delicate, never overblown.*

o·ver·board /£ˈəʊ·və·bɔːd, £ˌ--ˈ-, $ˈoʊ·vɚ·bɔːrd/ *adv* [not gradable] over the side of a boat or ship and into the water • *Someone had* **fallen** *overboard.* • *Don't drop rubbish overboard.* • *(infml esp. disapproving)* To **go overboard** is to be very enthusiastic or extreme about something or to do something with a lot of energy: *He had a right to be annoyed, but he went overboard and started shouting and hitting the desk.* ○ *In the past ten years, Japanese people have gone overboard for squid, consuming half a million tonnes annually.* • *(infml)* To **chuck/throw/toss** someone or something **overboard** is to stop employing or using them: *He has a habit of chucking assistants overboard once they've mastered the job.* ○ *She threw $2 million of energy shares overboard and bought computer technology shares instead.*

o·ver·book *(obj)* /£ˌəʊ·vəˈbʊk, $ˌoʊ·vɚ-/ *v* to sell more tickets or places for (an aircraft, holiday, etc.) than are available • *The hotel was overbooked.* [T] • *At the airport they told me there was no seat for me, because the airline had overbooked.* [I]

o·ver·bur·den *obj* /£ˌəʊ·vəˈbɜː·dən, $ˌoʊ·vɚˈbɜːr-/ *v* [T usually passive] to make (someone or something) work too hard or carry, contain or deal with too much • *The United Nations, the primary peace-keeper, is overburdened* **with** *operations around the world which it cannot afford.* • *This means 5000 new children will be attending the district's already overburdened school system.*

o·ver·cast /£ˈəʊ·və·kɑːst, £ˌ--ˈ-, $ˈoʊ·vɚ·kæst/ *adj* cloudy and therefore not bright and sunny • *The sky/weather was overcast.* • *It was one of those depressing, overcast winter mornings.*

o·ver·charge *(obj)* /£ˌəʊ·vəˈtʃɑːdʒ, $ˌoʊ·vɚˈtʃɑːrdʒ/ *v* to charge (someone) either more than the real price or more than the value of the product or service • *The shop overcharged me (*by *£10).* [T] • *They overcharged her £45.* [+

two objects] • *It's a fairly good restaurant but they really overcharge.* [I]

o·ver·coat /£ˈəʊ·və·kəʊt, $ˈoʊ·vɚ·koʊt/ *n* [C] a long thick coat worn in cold weather • PIC **Coats and jackets**

o·ver·come *(obj)* DEAL WITH /£ˌəʊ·vəˈkʌm, $ˌoʊ·vɚ-/ *v* *past simple* **overcame** /£ˌəʊ·vəˈkeɪm, $ˌoʊ·vɚ-/, *past part* **overcome** to defeat or succeed in controlling or dealing with (something) • *Support from his family and his own survivor instincts have helped him overcome* **obstacles** *before.* [T] • *We certainly hope that the programme will overcome its* **difficulties/problems** *and fulfil its aims.* [T] • *Eventually she managed to overcome her shyness in class.* [T] • *It's taken me a while but at last I've managed to overcome my fear of public speaking.* [T] • *She had to overcome strong resistance from within her own political party.* [T] • *The band overcame a last minute attack of nervousness and went on stage.* [T] • *Twenty thousand demonstrators sang "We shall overcome" as they marched through Washington today.* [I]

o·ver·come *obj* UNABLE TO ACT /£ˌəʊ·vəˈkʌm, $ˌoʊ·vɚ-/ *v* [T usually passive] *past simple* **overcame** /£ˌəʊ·vəˈkeɪm, $ˌoʊ·vɚ-/, *past part* **overcome** to prevent (someone) from being able to act or think in the usual way • *Many inhabitants were overcome* **by** *fumes from the burning factory and had to be carried out of their houses.* • *Overcome* **with/by** *emotion, she found herself unable to speak for a few minutes.* • *There have been times when I've been so overcome* **with** *grief and rage that I've doubted my sanity.*

o·ver·com·pen·sate /£ˌəʊ·vəˈkɒm·pən·seɪt, $ˌoʊ·vɚˈkɑːm-/ *v* [I] to act in a way that is intended to produce a usual or correct state from one that is not usual, but that in fact produces a new difficulty or lack of balance • *Realizing that the car was sliding to the left, he overcompensated* **by** *violently turning the steering wheel to the right, and sent the car crashing into a wall.* • *Chris is one of those small men who overcompensate* **for** *their lack of height* **with** *a larger than life personality.*

o·ver·cook *obj* /£ˌəʊ·vəˈkʊk, $ˌoʊ·vɚ-/ *v* [T] to cook (food) for longer than necessary, reducing its quality as a result • *Fry the chicken for three to four minutes on each side, being careful not to overcook it.* • *When our trout eventually arrived, it was overcooked.*

o·ver·crowd·ed /£ˌəʊ·vəˈkraʊ·dɪd, $ˌoʊ·vɚ-/ *adj* containing too many people or things • *overcrowded cities/prisons/schools* • *The world market for telecommunications is already overcrowded* **with** *businesses.*

o·ver·crowd·ing /£ˌəʊ·vəˈkraʊ·dɪŋ, $ˌoʊ·vɚ-/ *n* [U] • *Investment in the railway network would reduce overcrowding on the roads.*

o·ver·crowd *obj* /£ˌəʊ·vəˈkraʊd, $ˌoʊ·vɚ-/ *v* [T]

o·ver·de·vel·oped /£ˌəʊ·və·dɪˈvel·əpt, $ˌoʊ·vɚ-/ *adj* having developed too much • *I don't like body builders who are so overdeveloped you can see the veins in their bulging muscles.* • *The desire for power was enormously overdeveloped in Jonathan.*

o·ver·do *obj* /£ˌəʊ·vəˈduː, $ˌoʊ·vɚ-/ *v* [T] he/she/it **overdoes** /£ˌəʊ·vəˈdʌz, $ˌoʊ·vɚ-/, *past simple* **overdid** /£ˌəʊ·vəˈdɪd, $ˌoʊ·vɚ-/, *past part* **overdone** /£ˌəʊ·vəˈdʌn, $ˌoʊ·vɚ-/ to do, use or say (something) in a way that is too extreme • *After a heart attack you have to be careful not to overdo* **it/things** (= you have to work and live calmly). • *The secret of avoiding a hangover is of course just not to overdo* **it**/*overdo the drink the night before* (= not to drink too much). • *Rumours of mass starvation have been overdone – the situation is in fact not that bad.*

o·ver·done /£ˌəʊ·vəˈdʌn, $ˌoʊ·vɚ-/ *adj* (esp. of meat) cooked too long • *The roast lamb was dry and overdone.*

o·ver·dose /£ˈəʊ·və·dəʊs, $ˈoʊ·vɚ·doʊs/, *infml* **OD** *n* [C] a too large amount of a drug that a person or animal has taken or been given intentionally or by accident • *When he was 17 he* **took** *an overdose* **of** *sleeping pills and nearly died.* • *Jimi Hendrix died of a* **drug(s)** *overdose.* • *(fig. humorous) I think Liz's main problem is an overdose* **of** (= too much) *romantic fiction.*

o·ver·dose /£ˈəʊ·və·dəʊs, $ˈoʊ·vɚ·doʊs, ˌ--ˈ-/, *infml* **OD** *v* [I] • *She overdosed* **on** *aspirin and died.* • *(fig. humorous) I think I've just overdosed* **on** *cheesecake* (= eaten too much of it)*!*

o·ver·draft /£ˈəʊ·və·drɑːft, $ˈoʊ·vɚ·dræft/ *n* [C] an amount of money that a customer with a bank account is temporarily allowed to owe to the bank, or the agreement which allows this • *She used most of the money to* **pay off** *her overdraft.* • *Most banks offer overdrafts/overdraft* **facilities** *to students, to help them when they run short of money.*

o·ver·drawn /£ˌəʊ·vəˈdrɔːn, $ˌoʊ·vɚˈdrɑːn/ *adj* (of a person) having taken more money out of their bank account than the account contained, or (of a bank account) having had more money taken from it than was originally in it • *They were overdrawn* **by** *£150, so they couldn't write any cheques.* • *The account was overdrawn.*

o·ver·draw *obj* /£ˌəʊ·vəˈdrɔː, $ˌoʊ·vɚˈdrɑː/ *v* [T] *past simple* **overdrew** /£ˌəʊ·vəˈdruː, $ˌoʊ·vɚ-/, *past part* **overdrawn** • *Which bank charges the lowest interest rates if you overdraw?* [I] • *If you overdraw your account without making arrangements to do so you get charged a very high interest rate.* [T]

o·ver·dressed /£ˌəʊ·vəˈdrest, $ˌoʊ·vɚ-/ *adj* wearing clothes that are too formal or splendid for a particular occasion • *Everyone else was wearing jeans so I felt a bit overdressed in my best suit.*

o·ver·drive /£ˈəʊ·və·draɪv, $ˈoʊ·vɚ-/ *n* [U] a state of great activity, effort or hard work • *The official propaganda machine* **went into** *overdrive yesterday in an attempt to show that the government is still firmly in power.* • *The whole cast of the show were* **in** *overdrive, rehearsing for the first performance the next day.*

o·ver·due /£ˌəʊ·vəˈdjuː, $ˌoʊ·vɚˈduː/ *adj* not done or happening when expected or when needed; late • *She was an hour overdue at the first checkpoint, with suspected engine trouble.* • *The mother/The baby is two weeks overdue* (= The baby was expected to be born two weeks ago). • *Changes to the tax system are* **long** *overdue.* • *She feels she's overdue* **for** *promotion.*

o·ver·eag·er /£ˌəʊ·vəˈriː·gəʳ, $ˌoʊ·vɚˈiː·gɚ/ *adj* too eager • *Banks, he said, had been overeager to give loans to people and should now take their share of the responsibility for their customers' debts.*

o·ver·eat /£ˌəʊ·vəˈriːt, $ˌoʊ·vɚˈiːt/ *v* [I] *past simple* **overate**, *past part* **overeaten** /£ˌəʊ·vəˈriː·tᵊn, $ˌoʊ·vɚˈiː·t̬ᵊn/ to eat more food than your body needs, esp. so that you feel uncomfortably full • *If I overeat it slows my whole body down.*

o·ver·eat·ing /£ˌəʊ·vəˈriː·tɪŋ, $ˌoʊ·vɚˈiː·t̬ɪŋ/ *n* [U] • *Overeating is surely the main cause of obesity.*

o·ver·es·tim·ate *(obj)* /£ˌəʊ·vəˈres·tɪ·meɪt, $ˌoʊ·vɚˈes-/ *v* to think that (something) is or will be greater, more extreme or more important than it really is • *The Sales Director overestimated the demand and the company was consequently left with 20 000 unsold copies.* [T] • *The perceived risks of nuclear power, she said, had been grossly overestimated.* [T] • *They were forced to the conclusion that they had overestimated him/his abilities.* [T] • *I'm afraid when it came to the catering I rather overestimated and there was a lot of food left over.* [I]

o·ver·es·tim·ate /£ˌəʊ·vəˈres·tɪ·mət, $ˌoʊ·vɚˈes-/ *n* [C] • *An overestimate* **of** *the likely degree of error upset the calculations.*

o·ver·ex·pose *obj* /£ˌəʊ·və·rɪkˈspəʊz, $ˌoʊ·vɚ·ɪkˈspoʊz/ *v* [T] to give too much light to (a piece of photographic film) when taking a photograph • *Unfortunately the light was too bright and my photos were all overexposed.*

o·ver·flow *(obj)* /£ˌəʊ·vəˈfləʊ, $ˌoʊ·vɚˈfloʊ/ *v* (of a liquid) to flow over the edges of (a container, etc.) because the amount of liquid is too great to be held • *The milk overflowed when I poured it into the jug.* [I] • *Oh no, the washing machine is overflowing* (= water is coming out of it) *all over the kitchen floor.* [I] • *Because of heavy rain, there is a danger that the river will overflow its banks.* [T] • *Someone has filled the bath* **(full) to overflowing** (= so full that water is almost coming out of it.) • People overflow or a place overflows when there are too many people to fit into the place and some have to go outside: *The pub was so full that people were overflowing* **into/onto** *the street.* [I] ○ *So many journalists came to the press conference that they overflowed the small room.* [T] ○ *Cinemas are overflowing* (= more people are trying to get into them than there is space for) *as children and their parents flock to see the latest Disney film.* [I] ○ *The train was* **(full to)** *overflowing* (= so full that there was not space for any more passengers). • *His room is overflowing* **with** (= contains a lot of) *books.* [I] • *(fig.) Suddenly, her anger overflowed* (= she expressed it suddenly and strongly). [I] • *(fig.) He's one of those people who's always overflowing* **with** (= has a lot of) *good ideas.* [I] • *(fig.) They were* **(full to)** *overflowing* **with** *emotion at the birth of their baby.* [I]

o·ver·flow /£'əʊ·və·fləʊ, $'oʊ·vɚ·floʊ/ *n* [C] • *There seems to be an overflow* **from** (= water is flowing out of) *the water tank.* • *Put a bucket under the hole in the drainpipe to catch any overflow* (= any water which flows out of it). • *It looks as if the overflow/***overflow pipe** (= a pipe for carrying away extra water that is not needed) **from** *the sink is blocked.* • *The city hospital is full enough already, without having to cope with the overflow* **of** *patients* **from** *other hospitals* (= those which other hospitals cannot take because they do not have enough space).

o·ver·grown COVERED /£,əʊ·və'grəʊn, $,oʊ·vɚ'groʊn/ *adj* covered with plants that are growing thickly and in an uncontrolled way • *The house next door is empty and the garden is badly overgrown.* • *It's a shame that those fields have been allowed to become so overgrown* **with** *weeds.*

o·ver·grown TOO LARGE /£,əʊ·və'grəʊn, $,oʊ·vɚ'groʊn/ *adj disapproving* grown too large and esp. still behaving like a child while really an adult • *Jim is just an overgrown* **schoolboy**.

o·ver·hand /£'əʊ·və·hænd, $'oʊ·vɚ-/ *adj, adv* [not gradable] *Am for* OVERARM

o·ver·hang *obj* /£,əʊ·və'hæŋ, $,oʊ·vɚ-/ *v* [T] *past* **overhung** (of something at a high level) to stick out further than something at a lower level and therefore not to have any support from below, or to hang over • *The balcony overhangs the patio, offering a cool shady place to sit underneath.* • *Two large trees overhang the cottage.* • *The entrance to the cave is overhung* **with** *trailing plants* (= Plants hang over the entrance). • *(fig.) Overhanging* (= Having an effect on) *the controversy is the question how much the government knew about the arms deal.*

o·ver·hang /£'əʊ·və·hæŋ, $'oʊ·vɚ-/ *n* [C] • *Don't go too near the edge of the cliff, because of the overhang* (= the part of it that sticks out further than what is below it and which therefore is not supported from below). • *We need to reduce the overhang* **of** *the shelf* (= the amount by which it sticks out further than what is below it).

o·ver·hang·ing /£'əʊ·və,hæŋ·ɪŋ, $'oʊ·vɚ-, ,--'--/ *adj* • *We sheltered under the overhanging branches of a tree.* • *House martins often nest under the overhanging* **eaves** *of houses.*

o·ver·haul *obj* /£'əʊ·və·hɔːl, $'oʊ·vɚ·hɑːl/ *v* [T] to examine in a detailed way and if necessary repair (esp. a machine, vehicle, etc.), or make improvements to (esp. a system, idea, etc.) • *All the used cars we sell are completely overhauled first.* • *The government's plans to overhaul the health service have been widely criticized.*

o·ver·haul /£'əʊ·və·hɔːl, $'oʊ·vɚ·hɑːl/ *n* [C] • *I have to take my motorbike in for an overhaul.* • *There have been so many overhauls* **of** *the school curriculum recently, that teachers no longer know what they're expected to teach.*

o·ver·head /£'əʊ·və·hed, $'oʊ·vɚ-/ *adj, adv* [not gradable] at a level higher than a person's head; in the air or the sky above the place where you are • *The sign said 'Danger – overhead cables'.* • *I think this room would be better lit if it had overhead lighting* (= lights in the ceiling), *as well as table lamps.* • *A flock of geese flew overhead.* • An **overhead (projector)** (*abbreviation* **OHP**) is a device which makes images on a flat transparent sheet larger and shows them on a white screen or wall. An overhead is also the transparent sheet with the image on used on such a device: *Could you make sure we have an overhead (projector) for the meeting tomorrow?* ○ *I'm preparing some overheads* (= transparent sheets) *for my presentation at the sales conference next week.* • PIC› **Office** (KOR)

o·ver·heads *Br and Aus* /£'əʊ·və·hedz, $'oʊ·vɚ-/ *pl n* the regular and necessary costs, such as rent, heating and lighting a building or having a telephone, that are involved in operating a business and which do not increase with levels of production • *We're looking at ways of reducing our overheads.* • *If we cut our prices any further, we won't even cover our overheads.*

o·ver·head /£'əʊ·və·hed, $'oʊ·vɚ-/ *n* [U] *Am* • Overhead means the same as overheads: *Many businesses are moving out of New York because the overhead there is so high.*

o·ver·head /£'əʊ·və·hed, $'oʊ·vɚ-/ *adj* [before n; not gradable] • *One way of increasing profit margins is to cut overhead costs.*

o·ver·hear *(obj)* /£,əʊ·və'hɪəʳ, $,oʊ·vɚ'hɪr/ *v* *past* **overheard** /£,əʊ·və'hɜːd, $,oʊ·vɚ'hɜːrd/ to hear (what other people are saying) unintentionally and without their knowledge • *I overheard a very funny conversation on the bus this morning.* [T] • *Gwen didn't know that Bob had overheard her on the telephone.* [T] • *He overheard his daughter telling her teddy not to be so naughty.* [T + obj + v-ing] • *We were so embarrassed when we overheard them say that they didn't like the meal we'd cooked for them.* [T + obj + infinitive without *to*] • *I'm sorry, I couldn't help overhearing.* [I] • (D)

o·ver·heat *(obj)* /£,əʊ·və'hiːt, $,oʊ·vɚ-/ *v* to (cause to) become hotter than necessary or desirable • *I think the engine is overheating.* [I] • *It isn't healthy to overheat your house.* [T] • If an **economy** overheats, it grows very quickly, so that prices, etc. increase quickly. [I] • *(fig.) Things got a bit overheated* (= strong feelings were expressed) *at the meeting.*

o·ver·hung /£,əʊ·və'hʌŋ, $,oʊ·vɚ-/ *past simple and past participle of* OVERHANG

o·ver·in·dulge *(obj)* /£,əʊ·və·rɪn'dʌldʒ, $,oʊ·vɚ·ɪn-/ *v* to allow (yourself or someone else) to have too much of something that is wanted, esp. food or drink • *I wish I hadn't overindulged so much* (= had so much to eat and drink) *last night.* [I] • *Occasionally, she overindulges* **in** *chocolates.* [I] • *It's not good for children to be overindulged* (= always given what they want). [T]

o·ver·in·dul·gence /£,əʊ·və·rɪn'dʌldʒ·ᵊnts, $,oʊ·vɚ·ɪn-/ *n* [U] • *For many Americans, Thanksgiving is a time of overindulgence* (= eating and drinking too much).

o·ver·joyed /£,əʊ·və'dʒɔɪd, $,oʊ·vɚ-/ *adj* [after v] extremely pleased and happy • *They were overjoyed when their son told them he was getting married.* • *We're overjoyed* **at** *your news.* • *Helen was overjoyed* **to** *hear that she had got the job.* [+ *to* infinitive] • *I'm overjoyed* **that** *you're coming to visit me.* [+ *that* clause]

o·ver·kill /£'əʊ·və·kɪl, $'oʊ·vɚ-/ *n* [U] *disapproving* a greater amount or much more than is needed to achieve what is wanted • *The drastic measures that the government has taken recently to control the economy have been regarded by some people as overkill.* • *All these car advertisements on the television seem to me to be overkill.*

o·ver·land /£'əʊ·və·lænd, $'oʊ·vɚ-/ *adj, adv* [not gradable] (of travel) across the land in a vehicle, on foot or on a horse; not by sea or air • *We plan to make an overland trip across Australia.* • *Is your route going to be overland all the way from France to Greece, or will you drive as far as Italy and then take a ferry?* • *It took them a week to drive overland from Los Angeles to New York.*

o·ver·lap *(obj)* /£,əʊ·və'læp, $,oʊ·vɚ-/ *v* **-pp-** to cover (something) partly by going over its edge; to cover part of the same space • *The fence is made of panels which overlap.* [I] • *When you put up wallpaper, should you overlap the edges or put them next to each other?* [T] • *(fig.) The areas of responsibility of the two departments overlap* **(to some extent)** (= are partly the same). [I] • *(fig.) My musical tastes don't overlap* **with** *my brother's at all.* [I] • *(fig.) The night staff's shift slightly overlaps that of the day staff.* [T]

o·ver·lap /£'əʊ·və·læp, $'oʊ·vɚ-/ *n* • *There needs to be an overlap* **of** *several centimetres between the roof tiles* (= they need to cover each other by that amount), *in order to keep the rain out.* [C] • *(fig.) Although the two books have very similar titles, there's actually no overlap* **between** *them* (= they are about different subjects). [U] • *(fig.) There are some overlaps* **between** *the products of the two companies* (= they produce some of the same things). [C]

o·ver·lap·ping /£'əʊ·və,læp·ɪŋ, $'oʊ·vɚ-, ,--'--/ *adj* • *The overlapping slates of the roofs in the mountain village resembled fish scales.* • *The bird's body is streamlined with a smooth covering of short overlapping feathers.* • *The wooden box has overlapping slats that keep the rain out but allow in air and some light.* • *(fig.) There are three existing and overlapping schemes of social protection, which need to be reviewed.* • *(fig.) The word has two separate but overlapping meanings.*

o·ver·lay *obj* /£,əʊ·və'leɪ, $,oʊ·vɚ-/ *v* [T often passive] *past* **overlaid** /£,əʊ·və'leɪd, $,oʊ·vɚ-/ to cover (with a layer of something) • *The design is made by using thin pieces of polished wood to overlay a flat surface.* • *The foundation of the house is built from rubble overlaid* **with** *concrete.* • *(fig.) Her new novel is overlaid* **with** *political concerns.*

o·ver·lay /£'əʊ·və·leɪ, $'oʊ·vɚ-/ *n* [C] • *The wood frame has a gold overlay* (= thin covering of gold).

o·ver·leaf /£,əʊ·və'liːf, $,oʊ·vɚ-/ *adv* [not gradable] on the other side of the page • *See overleaf for a list of abbreviations.*

o·ver·load *obj* /£,əʊ·və'ləʊd, $,oʊ·vɚ'loʊd/ *v* [T] *past part* **overloaded** or *Br also* **overladen** /£,əʊ·və'leɪ·dᵊn,

$ˌoʊ· vɚ-/ to put too large a load in or on (something) • *Don't overload the washing machine, or it won't work properly.* • *If more goods were transported by rail, the country's roads would be less overloaded* **with** *heavy vehicles.* • *The boat that sank was grossly overloaded.* • *(fig.) The market is already overloaded* **with** *car magazines* (= there are a lot of them on the market) – *why would anyone want to produce another one?* • *(fig.) I can't come out tonight – I'm overloaded* **with** *work* (= have a lot of work to do). • If you overload an electrical system, you put too much electricity through it: *Using too many pieces of electrical equipment at once isn't a good idea because it will overload the* **circuit**.

o·ver·load /£ˈəʊ·və·ləʊd, $ˈoʊ·vɚ·loʊd/ *n* • *One of the problems of our society today is that we all suffer from* **information** *overload* (= being given too much information). [U] • *There was an overload on the electrical circuit and the fuse blew.* [C]

o·ver·long /£ˌəʊ·vəˈlɒŋ, $ˌoʊ·vɚˈlɑːŋ/ *adj, adv* [not gradable] too long • *I enjoyed the film, but I thought it was overlong.* • *Do you think this skirt is overlong?* • *(fml) We've been kept waiting overlong for the results of the tests.*

o·ver·look *obj* VIEW /£ˌəʊ·vəˈlʊk, $ˌoʊ·vɚ-/ *v* [T] to provide a view of, esp. from above • *Our hotel room overlooked the harbour.* • *Her bedroom has large windows overlooking a lake.* • *The house is surrounded by trees, so it's not overlooked at all* (= it cannot be seen from any other buildings).

o·ver·look *Am* /£ˈəʊ·və·lʊk, $ˈoʊ·vɚ-/, *Br* **view·point** *n* [C] • An overlook is a VIEWPOINT: *There are lots of* **scenic** *overlooks along the road from New York to Montreal.*

o·ver·look *obj* NOT NOTICE /£ˌəʊ·vəˈlʊk, $ˌoʊ·vɚ-/ *v* [T] not to notice, or to forgive or pretend not to notice • *The plight of the children who are caught up in the conflict is being overlooked.* • *When planning your holiday, make sure not to overlook* (= forget) *your travel insurance.* • *No one will be overlooked* (= Everyone will be considered) *in the selection of the team.* • *We'll overlook* (= forgive/pretend not to notice) *your bad behaviour this time, but don't do it again.*

o·ver·lord /£ˈəʊ·və·lɔːd, $ˈoʊ·vɚ·lɔːrd/ *n* [C] (in the past) someone who owned land on which other people worked and who had power over them, or (more generally) a person who is in a position of power • *This policy dates from the days when Kissinger was the overlord at the State Department.*

o·ver·ly /£ˈəʊ·vəl·i, $ˈoʊ·vɚ·li/ *adv* [before adj; not gradable] too; very • *I'm not overly happy at the decision.* • *Earlier sales forecasts seem to have been overly optimistic.* • *His films have been criticized for being overly violent.*

o·ver·manned /£ˌəʊ·vəˈmænd, $ˌoʊ·vɚ-/ *adj* See at OVERSTAFFED

o·ver·much /£ˌəʊ·vəˈmʌtʃ, $ˌoʊ·vɚ-/ *adv, adj* [not gradable] (esp. in negatives) too much or very much • *The doctor said that she didn't think he suffered overmuch before he died.* • *I don't have overmuch confidence in Tim's ability to do the job.*

o·ver·night /£ˌəʊ·vəˈnaɪt, $ˌoʊ·vɚ-/ *adj, adv* [not gradable] for or during the night • *We're making an overnight stop in Paris on our way to the Dordogne.* • *You can stay overnight if you want to.* • *He became ill overnight and had to see a doctor.* • *Don't forget to pack an overnight bag* (= a bag for things that you need when you stay away from home for a night). • *(fig.) The book was an overnight* (= sudden and unexpected) *success.* • *(fig.) She* **became** *a star overnight* (= suddenly and unexpectedly) *when she stepped in to play the leading role.*

o·ver·pack·aged /£ˌəʊ·vəˈpæk·ɪdʒd, $ˌoʊ·vɚ-/ *adj* (esp. of goods) being wrapped in more material than is needed or is desirable • *Some people refuse to buy goods that are overpackaged, because they feel that it is harmful to the environment.*

o·ver·pass /£ˈəʊ·və·pɑːs, $ˈoʊ·vɚ·pæs/ *n* [C] *Am for* FLYOVER BRIDGE • PIC **Motorway**

o·ver·pay *obj* /£ˌəʊ·vəˈpeɪ, $ˌoʊ·vɚ-/ *v* [T] *past* **overpaid** /£ˌəʊ·vəˈpeɪd, $ˌoʊ·vɚ-/ to pay a larger amount than is necessary or correct, esp. to pay (someone) too much when they do not deserve it • *The scheme offers home buyers the option to overpay their mortgage by amounts of £50 to £500 a month.* • *There were claims that the men had been overpaid for the job* (= have been paid more than they should have been).

o·ver·paid /£ˌəʊ·vəˈpeɪd, $ˌoʊ·vɚ-/ *adj* • *You can claim back the overpaid tax by filling in this form.* • *The bureaucrats, widely regarded as under-worked and overpaid* (= paid more than they deserve), *did not get much public sympathy for their pay claim.* • *I think company directors are often grossly overpaid.*

o·ver·play *obj* /£ˌəʊ·vəˈpleɪ, $ˌoʊ·vɚ-/ *v* [T] to make (something) seem more important than it really is • *I think she's overplaying the significance of his remarks.* • *The findings of the research committee have really been overplayed in the media.* • *They've* **overplayed** *their* **hand** (= promised to do something that they are not able to do) *by saying that they'd have the order ready by Friday.*

o·ver·pop·u·lated /£ˌəʊ·vəˈpɒp·jʊ·leɪ·tɪd, $ˌoʊ·vɚˈpɑː·pjə·leɪ·t̬ɪd/ *adj* (of a country, city, etc.) having too many people for the amount of food, materials and space available there • *As a result of the streams of people coming from the surrounding countryside looking for work, it has become a seriously overpopulated city.*

o·ver·pop·u·la·tion /£ˌəʊ·vəˌpɒp·jʊˈleɪ·ʃən, $ˌoʊ·vɚˌpɑː·pjə-/ *n* [U] • *Overpopulation is one of the country's most pressing social problems.*

o·ver·pow·er *obj* /£ˌəʊ·vəˈpaʊəʳ, $ˌoʊ·vɚˈpaʊɚ/ *v* [T] to defeat (someone) by having greater strength or power, or (esp. of a smell or emotion) to be so strong as to make (someone) feel weak or ill • *She was completely overpowered by the two men who attacked her.* • *The* **smell** *of gas/***heat** *overpowered me as I went into the house.* • *They were overpowered by grief when their son died.* • *The story is about a brother and sister overpowered by desire for each other after growing up apart.*

o·ver·pow·er·ing /£ˌəʊ·vəˈpaʊə·rɪŋ, $ˌoʊ·vɚˈpaʊɚ·ɪŋ/ *adj* • *Firefighters were driven back by the overpowering* (= too strong) **heat** *of the flames.* • *There's an overpowering* **smell** *of garlic in the kitchen.* • *He's suffering from overpowering feelings of guilt.*

o·ver·priced /£ˌəʊ·vəˈpraɪst, $ˌoʊ·vɚ-/ *adj* too expensive • *These shoes are very nice, but they're terribly overpriced.*

o·ver·pro·duce *(obj)* /£ˌəʊ·və·prəˈdjuːs, $ˌoʊ·vɚ·proʊˈduːs/ *v* to produce more (of something) than is needed, or to produce too much • *The farmers have been accused of failing to stick to their quotas, and overproducing.* [I] • *Car prices have shown no signs of falling, despite the fact that cars have been overproduced this year.* [T] • A play, film, song, etc. which is overproduced is prepared and provided for the public in a way that is more complicated than it needs to be.

o·ver·pro·duc·tion /£ˌəʊ·və·prəˈdʌk·ʃən, $ˌoʊ·vɚ-/ *n* • *There has been an overproduction* **of** *oil this month, which has led to a fall in prices.* [C] • *The company is in a bad financial position because of overproduction and distribution problems.* [U]

o·ver·pro·tec·tive /£ˌəʊ·və·prəˈtek·tɪv, $ˌoʊ·vɚ·prəˈtek·t̬ɪv/ *adj* wishing to protect (esp. a child) too much • *The children of overprotective parents are sometimes rather nervous.* • *He's very overprotective* **of/towards** *his daughter.*

o·ver·qua·li·fied /£ˌəʊ·vəˈkwɒl·ɪ·faɪd, $ˌoʊ·vɚˈkwɑː·lɪ-/ *adj* having more knowledge, skill and/or experience than is needed (for a particular job) • *The problem with employing overqualified people is that they often don't stay in the job for long.* • *They didn't give me the job because they said I was overqualified* **(for it)**.

o·ver·ran /£ˌəʊ·vəˈræn, $ˌoʊ·vɚ-/ *past simple and past participle of* OVERRUN

o·ver·rate *obj* /£ˌəʊ·vəˈreɪt, $ˌoʊ·vɚ-/ *v* [T] to have too good an opinion of (something); to value (something) too highly • *I think you're overrating my abilities if you think I can do that job.*

o·ver·rat·ed /£ˌəʊ·vəˈreɪ·tɪd, $ˌoʊ·vɚˈreɪ·t̬ɪd, ˈ--ˌ--/ *adj* • *In my opinion, she's a hugely overrated singer.* • *The writer Kingsley Amis has said that Keats is overrated as a poet.* • *"What do you consider the most overrated* **virtue***?" "A stiff upper lip* (= strong control of your feelings)."

o·ver·reach *obj* /£ˌəʊ·vəˈriːtʃ, $ˌoʊ·vɚ-/ *v* [T] to fail by trying to achieve more than you can • *You won't recover after your operation if you overreach your***self** *and try to do too much too soon.* • *I think he was overreaching him***self** *in taking on that job, which he really knew nothing about.*

o·ver·re·act /£ˌəʊ·və·riˈækt, $ˌoʊ·vɚ-/ *v* [I] to react in an angry or frightened way or to react too strongly • *She really overreacted when I said I thought she'd made a mistake.* • *You must learn not to overreact* **to** *criticism.* • *The markets have overreacted* **to** *the decision to raise interest rates.*

o·ver·re·ac·tion /£ˌəʊ·və·riˈæk·ʃən, $ˌoʊ·vɚ-/ *n* • *I realize now that my response was an overreaction.* [C] •

When you're dealing with a child who's done something wrong, be careful to avoid overreaction. [U]

o·ver·ride *obj* NOT ACCEPT /£ˌəʊ·vəˈraɪd, $ˌoʊ·vɚ-/ *v* [T] *past simple* **overrode** /£ˌəʊ·vəˈrəʊd, $ˌoʊ·vɚˈroʊd/, *past part* **overridden** /£ˌəʊ·vəˈrɪd·ᵊn, $ˌoʊ·vɚ-/ to refuse to accept (a suggestion, idea, way of doing something, etc.) because you have the authority to do so • *A US Presidential veto of a bill can be overridden if two-thirds of the members of Congress vote in favour of the bill.* • *Every time I make a suggestion at work, my boss overrides me/it.* • To override an automatic machine is to operate it by hand, usually because it is not working correctly or because it is not safe to allow it to operate automatically: *The factory is equipped with computer-controlled machinery, but the computer can be overridden if necessary.*

o·ver·ride /£ˌəʊ·vəˈraɪd, $ˌoʊ·vɚ-/ *n* [C] • *Our heating system is controlled automatically, but we can alter it by using the override/the override* **switch/facility** (=device that stops automatic control) *if we need to.* • In American politics, an override is the refusal of an elected group of people to accept a decision made by an elected leader: *The vote fell short of the majority needed for an override* **of** *the Governor's veto.*

o·ver·ride *obj* MORE IMPORTANT /£ˌəʊ·vəˈraɪd, $ˌoʊ·vɚ-/ *v* [T] *past simple* **overrode** /£ˌəʊ·vəˈrəʊd, $ˌoʊ·vɚˈroʊd/, *past part* **overridden** /£ˌəʊ·vəˈrɪd·ᵊn, $ˌoʊ·vɚ-/ to be more important than • *Parents' concern for their children's future often overrides all their other concerns.* • *For David, making money overrides everything else.*

o·ver·rid·ing /£ˌəʊ·vəˈraɪ·dɪŋ, $ˌoʊ·vɚ-/ *adj* [before n; not gradable] • *The overriding* (=most important) **aim** *of every school should be to enable each student to achieve their full potential.* • *The government's overriding* **concern** *is to reduce inflation.*

o·ver·ride TRAVEL /£ˌəʊ·vəˈraɪd, $ˌoʊ·vɚ-/ *v* [I] to travel on public transport further than your ticket allows you to • *There is a £20 penalty for passengers who travel without a ticket or override.*

o·ver·rid·ing /£ˌəʊ·vəˈraɪ·dɪŋ, $ˌoʊ·vɚ-, ˈ--ˌ--/ *n* [U] • *There is a penalty for overriding.*

o·ver·ripe /£ˌəʊ·vᵊrˈaɪp, $ˌoʊ·vɚˈraɪp/ *adj* too ripe; starting to decay • *These pears are overripe.* • *You can use overripe bananas to make banana bread.*

o·ver·rule *obj* /£ˌəʊ·vᵊrˈuːl, $ˌoʊ·vɚˈruːl/ *v* [T] to decide against (a decision that has already been made, or a suggestion, idea, etc.) because you have the official authority to do so • *In tennis, the umpire can overrule the line judge if they think that a ball has been incorrectly called in or out.* • *The school governors have overruled the head teacher/the head teacher's proposals.* • *"Objection overruled," said the judge.*

o·ver·run *obj* FILL /£ˌəʊ·vəˈrʌn, $ˌoʊ·vɚ-/ *v* [T] **overrunning**, *past simple* **overran** /£ˌəʊ·vəˈræn, $ˌoʊ·vɚ-/, *past part* **overrun** to fill (a place) quickly and in large numbers • *Rebel soldiers overran the embassy last night.* • *The meeting was overrun by protesters.* • *Our kitchen is overrun* **with** *cockroaches.* • *In the last year, the domestic market has been overrun* **with** *foreign goods.*

o·ver·run *(obj)* GO BEYOND /£ˌəʊ·vəˈrʌn, $ˌoʊ·vɚ-/ *v* **overrunning**, *past simple* **overran** /£ˌəʊ·vəˈræn, $ˌoʊ·vɚ-/, *past part* **overrun** to continue beyond (an intended limit, esp. a finishing time or a cost) • *I missed the last bus because my evening class overran.* [I] • *We've overrun our time, so I think we should stop now.* [T] • *The doctor is overrunning* (=her arranged meetings are continuing beyond their planned finishing times) **by** *about half an hour, but she'll see you as soon as she can.* [I] • *Our costs on this project are likely to overrun* **by** *several million dollars.* [I] • *We've overrun* **on** *costs.* [I] • *It looks as if we're going to overrun our budget.* [T]

o·ver·run /£ˌəʊ·vᵊrˈʌn, $ˌoʊ·vɚˈrʌn/ *n* [C] • *They're predicting an overrun* **of** *15%* (=that they will spend that amount beyond what they intended) **on** *that project.* • *Because of* **cost** *overruns on contracts, the company recorded a loss this year.*

o·ver·seas /£ˌəʊ·vəˈsiːz, $ˌoʊ·vɚ-, ˈ--ˌ-/ *adj, adv* [not gradable] in, from or to countries that are across the sea • *We are trying to build up overseas markets for our cars.* • *There are a lot of overseas students in Cambridge.* • *My brother is a student overseas.* • *If you are living overseas, you may not have to pay tax in your own country.* • *Many more people go/travel overseas for their holidays now than used to be the case.*

o·ver·see *obj* /£ˌəʊ·vəˈsiː, $ˌoʊ·vɚ-/ *v* [T] *past simple* **oversaw** /£ˌəʊ·vəˈsɔː, $ˌoʊ·vɚˈsɑː/, *past part* **overseen** /£ˌəʊ·vəˈsiːn, $ˌoʊ·vɚ-/ to watch or organize (a job or an activity) to make certain that it is being done correctly • *As marketing manager, her job is to oversee all the company's advertising.* • *The clean-up of the oil that has been spilt has been overseen by environmental experts.* • *The role of the UN force is to oversee the transport of aid to the parts of the country that need it most.* • *Specialized committees oversaw many aspects of the city's administration.* • Ⓓ

o·ver·se·er /£ˈəʊ·vəˌsiː·əʳ, $ˈoʊ·vɚˌsiː·ɚ/ *n* [C] *esp. old use* • An overseer is a person whose job it is to make certain that employees were working or that an activity is being done correctly.

o·ver·sell *obj* /£ˌəʊ·vəˈsel, $ˌoʊ·vɚ-/ *v* [T] *esp. Am* to sell more than is available • *The flight had been oversold.*

o·ver·sexed /£ˌəʊ·vəˈsekst, $ˌoʊ·vɚ-/ *adj esp. disapproving* having an unusually strong interest or involvement in sex • *In the film 'The Witches of Eastwick' Jack Nicholson plays a rich, oversexed man who is really the devil.*

o·ver·shad·ow *obj* /£ˌəʊ·vəˈʃæd·əʊ, $ˌoʊ·vɚˈʃæd·oʊ/ *v* [T] to be much taller than a building which is close and therefore to block off the sun from it, or to cause to seem less important or to be less happy • *Grand Central Station in New York is overshadowed by the PanAm building.* • *Karen has always been overshadowed by her elder sister.* • *The news that his father had been hurt in an accident overshadowed his first day in his new job.*

o·ver·shoes /£ˈəʊ·və·ʃuːz, $ˈoʊ·vɚ-/, *Am usually* **rub·bers**, *dated* **ga·losh·es** *pl n* waterproof shoes, usually made of rubber, for wearing over an ordinary shoe when it rains or snows

o·ver·shoot *obj* /£ˌəʊ·vəˈʃuːt, $ˌoʊ·vɚ-/ *v* [T] *past* **overshot** /£ˌəʊ·vəˈʃɒt, $ˌoʊ·vɚˈʃɑːt/ to go beyond the end of or past (something), without intending to • *The plane overshot the runway and finished up in the water.* • *Many civilians were injured when the rocket overshot its target and hit an apartment building.*

o·ver·sight /£ˈəʊ·və·saɪt, $ˈoʊ·vɚ-/ *n* (a mistake made because of) a failure to notice something • *Due to an oversight by my bank, there was less money in my account than there should have been.* [C] • *It was simply oversight on our part that you weren't invited.* [U] • Ⓓ

o·ver·sim·pli·fy *(obj)* /£ˌəʊ·vəˈsɪm·plɪ·faɪ, $ˌoʊ·vɚˈsɪm·plə-/ *v* to describe or explain (something) in such a simple way that it is no longer right or true • *That television documentary on industrial pollution grossly oversimplified the problem.* [T] • *It's hard to explain what happens in the play without oversimplifying.* [I]

o·ver·sim·pli·fi·ca·tion /£ˌəʊ·vəˌsɪm·plɪ·fɪˈkeɪ·ʃᵊn, $ˌoʊ·vɚˌsɪm·plə-/ *n* • *The report contained too many oversimplifications to be really useful.* [C] • *There's too much oversimplification in this language course.* [U]

o·ver·size /£ˌəʊ·vəˈsaɪz, $ˌoʊ·vɚ-/, **o·ver·sized** /£ˌəʊ·vəˈsaɪzd, $ˌoʊ·vɚ-/ *adj esp. Am* bigger than usual; too big • *My daughter loves to wear oversize clothes.* • *You'll need an oversize suitcase to take all those things with you.* • *The President has announced plans to cut the country's oversized defence force.* • *He has an oversized ego* (=His opinion of himself is too high).

o·ver·sleep /£ˌəʊ·vəˈsliːp, $ˌoʊ·vɚ-/ *v* [I] *past* **overslept** /£ˌəʊ·vəˈslept, $ˌoʊ·vɚ-/ to sleep for longer than you intended to and so wake up late • *I missed the train this morning because I overslept again.*

o·ver·sold /£ˌəʊ·vəˈsəʊld, $ˌoʊ·vɚˈsoʊld/ *past simple and past participle of* OVERSELL

o·ver·spend *(obj)* /£ˌəʊ·vəˈspend, $ˌoʊ·vɚ-/ *v past* **overspent** /£ˌəʊ·vəˈspent, $ˌoʊ·vɚ-/ to (cause to) spend more (money) than you should • *The council seems likely to overspend this year.* [I] • *The hospital refused to give her the expensive treatment she needed because it had already overspent* **(on)** *its drugs* **budget**. [T; I + on] • *We've overspent* **(on)** *our* **budget** *for decorating the house.* [T; I + on] • *The school is overspent* **on** *its book* **budget**. • *Steps are being taken to curb local government overspending.*

o·ver·spend /£ˈəʊ·və·spend, $ˈoʊ·vɚ-/ *n* [C] *Br* • *We're expecting to have a £5 million* **(budget)** *overspend this year.*

o·ver·spill /£ˈəʊ·və·spɪl, $ˈoʊ·vɚ-/ *n* [U] *Br* people who move out of a city because there are too many people living in it and into other towns or villages near the city • *Harlow New Town was designed to accommodate the* *overspill* **from** *London/the London overspill.* • *They live on an overspill housing estate.*

o·ver·staffed /£ˌəʊ·vəˈstɑːft, $ˌoʊ·vɚˈstæft/, **o·ver·manned** *adj* having more employees than are needed • *The department has been accused of being inefficient and hugely overstaffed.*

o·ver·state *obj* /£ˌəʊ·vəˈsteɪt, $ˌoʊ·vɚ-/ *v* [T] to describe or explain (something) in a way that makes it seem more important or serious than it really is • *The impact of the new legislation has been greatly overstated.* • *To say that all young people are involved with drugs is to overstate the problem.* • *The shareholders seem to think that the executive board is overstating the* **case** *for a merger.*

o·ver·state·ment /£ˌəʊ·vəˈsteɪt·mənt, £ˈ-ˌ--, $ˌoʊ·vɚ-/ *n* • *Few people were convinced by his overstatement* **of** *the advantages of the scheme.* [U] • *It would be an overstatement* (= a claim that is too positive or strong) *to say that Lewis deserved to win the race.* [C]

o·ver·stay *obj* /£ˌəʊ·vəˈsteɪ, $ˌoʊ·vɚ-/ *v* [T] to stay beyond the end of (the period of time you intended to stay in a place) • *People who overstay their visas are being treated more severely than in the past.*

o·ver·step *obj* /£ˌəʊ·vəˈstep, $ˌoʊ·vɚ-/ *v* [T] **-pp-** to go beyond (what is considered acceptable or correct) • *The bad language in that play overstepped the* **limits/boundaries** *of what ought to be allowed on television.* • *I think you're overstepping your authority.* • *You've* **overstepped the mark** (= behaved in an extremely unacceptable way) *this time, Simpson – you're fired!*

o·ver·stock *(obj)* /£ˌəʊ·vəˈstɒk, $ˌoʊ·vɚˈstɑːk/ *v* to (cause to) have more goods or supplies than are needed • *Many shops have overstocked* **with** *summer clothes that they can't sell because the weather has been so bad this year.* [I] • *The shop is overstocked (***with** *shoes that have gone out of fashion).* [T]

o·ver·stock /£ˈəʊ·və·stɒk, $ˈoʊ·vɚ·stɑːk/ *n* [U] • *We're trying to sell off our overstock* (= goods of which we have more than we need) **of** *last year's diaries.*

o·ver·stocks /£ˈəʊ·və·stɒks, $ˈoʊ·vɚ·stɑːks/ *pl n* • *We're trying to sell off our overstocks* (= overstock) **of** *last year's diaries.*

over·sub·scribed /£ˌəʊ·və·səbˈskraɪbd, $ˌoʊ·vɚ-/ *adj* [not gradable] having too many people attempt to buy more (esp. shares in a company or tickets for a show) than are available • *The $400 million oil company share issue was three times oversubscribed.* • *The Royal Philharmonic's concert season is expected to be hugely oversubscribed.*

o·ver·sup·ply /£ˌəʊ·və·səˈplaɪ, $ˌoʊ·vɚ-/ *n* a greater supply (of something) than is needed • *The coffee market is suffering from oversupply.* [U] • *We have an oversupply* **of** *unsold cars in the garage showroom.* [C]

o·vert /£əʊˈvɜːt, £ˈ--, $oʊˈvɜːrt/ *adj* done or shown publicly or in an obvious way; not secret • *There are no overt signs that Alex has been seriously harmed by his experiences.* • *The overt aim of the proposal is to improve productivity, but the unions are worried that the result of it will be a cut in jobs.* • *Many women at work have to deal with overt sexism.* • Compare COVERT.

o·vert·ly /£əʊˈvɜːt·li, £ˈ---, $oʊˈvɜːrt-/ *adv* • *He has started overtly criticizing his son-in-law.*

o·ver·take *(obj)* GO PAST /£ˌəʊ·vəˈteɪk, $ˌoʊ·vɚ-/ *v past simple* **overtook**, *past part* **overtaken** /£ˌəʊ·vəˈteɪ·kᵊn, $ˌoʊ·vɚ-/ to go beyond (something) by being a greater amount or degree, or *(Br and Aus)* to come from behind (another vehicle or a person) and move in front of it (*Am* **pass**) • *After only two years in the American market, our US sales have now overtaken our sales in Europe.* [T] • *We'd planned to hold a meeting to discuss the company's financial position, but* **events** *have overtaken us* (= things have changed), *and it won't now be necessary.* [T] • *(Br and Aus) Always check in your rear view mirror before you overtake.* [I] • *(Br and Aus) It's dangerous to overtake another car on a bend.* [T] • *(Br and Aus)* The **overtaking lane** (*Am* passing lane) on a MOTORWAY is the one used for overtaking that is nearest the centre of the road. • PIC **Driving**

o·ver·take *obj* HAPPEN /£ˌəʊ·vəˈteɪk, $ˌoʊ·vɚ-/ *v* [T often passive] *past simple* **overtook**, *past part* **overtaken** /£ˌəʊ·vəˈteɪ·kᵊn, $ˌoʊ·vɚ-/ to happen to (a person or a place) suddenly and unexpectedly • *The family was overtaken by tragedy several years ago, and they still haven't recovered.* • *She was overtaken by grief when her husband died.* • PIC **Motorway**

o·ver·tax *obj* MONEY /£ˌəʊ·vəˈtæks, $ˌoʊ·vɚ-/ *v* [T] to demand too much tax from (someone) or to put too much tax on (goods) • *It looks as if I've been overtaxed* (= have paid more tax than I should have done) *this month.* • *I think it's wrong to overtax* (= demand a lot of tax from) *people on low incomes.* • *Food, books and children's clothing should not be overtaxed* (= have a high tax put on them).

o·ver·tax *obj* DIFFICULTY /£ˌəʊ·vəˈtæks, $ˌoʊ·vɚ-/ *v* [T] to cause to be troubled, anxious or tired; to cause difficulty to or for • *This problem is really overtaxing me.* • *Remember you've been ill, and don't overtax your***self** (= make yourself tired by doing too much).

o·ver·throw *obj* DEFEAT /£ˌəʊ·vəˈθrəʊ, $ˌoʊ·vɚˈθroʊ/ *v* [T] *past simple* **overthrew** /£ˌəʊ·vəˈθruː, $ˌoʊ·vɚ-/, *past part* **overthrown** /£ˌəʊ·vəˈθrəʊn, $ˌoʊ·vɚˈθroʊn/ to remove from power, using force; to defeat • *Allende's government in Chile was overthrown by the armed forces in 1973.* • *A state of emergency had been in force since the coup which overthrew the dictator.*

o·ver·throw /£ˈəʊ·və·θrəʊ, $ˈoʊ·vɚ·θroʊ/ *n* [C] • *After the overthrow* **of** *the monarchy* (= after it was removed from power) *in 1649, Britain was for a time ruled by Parliament.*

o·ver·throw *(obj)* THROW /£ˈəʊ·və·θrəʊ, $ˈoʊ·vɚ·θroʊ, ˌ-ˈ-ˈ-/ *v Am and Aus* to throw a ball beyond the person or object you intended to throw to • *Joe Montana overthrew that pass, missing his wide receiver altogether.* [T] • *Be careful not to overthrow.* [I]

o·ver·throw /£ˈəʊ·və·θrəʊ, $ˈoʊ·vɚ·θroʊ/ *n* [C] • *(Am) That was Winfield's second overthrow of third base this game.* • In cricket, an overthrow is a score made when the ball is accidentally thrown beyond the person to whom it was intended to be thrown.

o·ver·time /£ˈəʊ·və·taɪm, $ˈoʊ·vɚ-/ *n* [U], *adv* [not gradable] (time spent working) beyond the usual time needed or expected in a job • *How much overtime did you* **do** *last week?* • *He gets paid 50% more for overtime.* • *Everyone is* **on** *overtime* (= being paid extra for working beyond the usual time) *this weekend.* • *(Br and Aus) The workers are on an overtime ban* (= are refusing to work beyond the usual time) *as a protest.* • *They're* **doing/working** *overtime to get the job finished on time.* • If you earn, get paid, or are paid overtime, you are given extra payment for working beyond the usual time: *I earn overtime for working after 6.00 p.m.* • Overtime is also *Am for* **extra time**. See at EXTRA MORE.

o·ver·tire *obj* /£ˌəʊ·vəˈtaɪəʳ, $ˌoʊ·vɚˈtaɪr/ *v* [T] to cause (esp. someone who is not well) to be very tired • *After your operation, you must be careful not to overtire your***self**.

o·ver·tired /£ˌəʊ·vəˈtaɪəd, $ˌoʊ·vɚˈtaɪrd/ *adj* [not gradable] • *Children often become tearful when they're overtired.*

o·vert·ly /£əʊˈvɜːt·li, £ˈ---, $oʊˈvɜːrt-/ *adv* See at OVERT

o·ver·tone /£ˈəʊ·və·təʊn, $ˈoʊ·vɚ·toʊn/ *n* [C] something that is suggested, but is not clearly stated • *Although the concert was supposed to be an event to raise money for charity, it* **had** *strong political overtones.* • *Feminists have criticized the TV broadcast for* **carrying** *sexist overtones.* • *There was an overtone* **of** *despair in what he said.*

o·ver·took /£ˌəʊ·vəˈtʊk, $ˌoʊ·vɚ-/ *past simple of* OVERTAKE

o·ver·ture MUSIC /£ˈəʊ·və·tjʊəʳ, $ˈoʊ·vɚ·tʃɚ/ *n* [C] a piece of music which is an introduction to a longer piece, esp. an opera • *the overture* **to** *"The Magic Flute"*

o·ver·ture APPROACH /£ˈəʊ·və·tjʊəʳ, $ˈoʊ·vɚ·tʃɚ/ *n* [C] an approach made (to someone) in order to offer something • *She seemed to be* **making** *overtures* **of** *friendship.* • *Neither side in the conflict seems willing to* **make** *an overture* **of** *peace/a peace overture* **to** *the other.* • *We've received an overture* **from** *another company who want to buy us out.* • *Overtures by the management* **to** *settle the dispute have so far met with little success.* [+ *to* infinitive] • *(infml, esp. humorous) So he's been* **making** *overtures* (= showing a sexual interest), *has he?*

o·ver·turn *(obj)* /£ˌəʊ·vəˈtɜːn, $ˌoʊ·vɚˈtɜːrn/ *v* to (cause) to turn over • *The car skidded off the road, hit a tree and overturned.* [I] • *It seems as if the boat was overturned by an unusually large wave.* [T] • *The burglars overturned all the furniture in the house.* [T] • *(fig.) The Court of Appeal overturned the earlier decision* (= said that it had been wrong). [T] • In a British election, if someone's **majority** is overturned, they are defeated: *The Labour candidate unexpectedly overturned the long-standing Tory majority.* [T]

o·ver·use *obj* /£ˌəʊ·vəˈjuːz, $ˌoʊ·vɚ-/ *v* [T] to use too often or too much • *Some pieces of music are very overused in television advertisements.* • *We all tend to overuse certain expressions.*

o·ver·use /£ˌəʊ·və'juːz, $ˌoʊ·vɚ-/ *n* [U] • *He condemned the overuse of agricultural chemicals.* • *The overuse and misuse of X-rays may be causing between 100 and 250 deaths each year.*

o·ver·val·ue *obj* /£ˌəʊ·və'væl·juː, $ˌoʊ·vɚ-/ *v* [T often passive] to put too high a value on • *The company is overvalued on the stock market.*

o·ver·view /£'əʊ·və·vjuː, $'oʊ·vɚ-/ *n* [C] a short description of something which provides general information about it, but no details • *I'll just* **give** *you an overview* **of** *what the job involves.*

o·ver·ween·ing /£ˌəʊ·və'wiː·nɪŋ, $ˌoʊ·vɚ-/ *adj* [before n] *fml disapproving* very great, or showing too much confidence in yourself • *His overweening pride/arrogance/vanity made him very unpopular.* • *She is driven by overweening ambition.*

o·ver·ween·ing·ly /£ˌəʊ·və'wiː·nɪŋ·li, $ˌoʊ·vɚ-/ *adv*

o·ver·weight /£ˌəʊ·və'weɪt, '---, $ˌoʊ·vɚ-/ *adj* (of people) too heavy or fat, or (of objects) heavier than is allowed • *He's become very overweight.* • *Overweight people sometimes join clubs to help them lose weight.* • *I'm only a few kilos overweight/I'm only overweight* **by** *a few kilos, but I just can't seem to lose them.* • *If your luggage is overweight, you have to pay extra.*

o·ver·whelm *obj* /£ˌəʊ·və'welm, $ˌoʊ·vɚ-/ *v* [T] to make powerless by using force, or to cause to feel sudden strong emotion • *Government troops have overwhelmed the rebels.* • *Her attacker overwhelmed her by squeezing her throat.* • *They were overwhelmed* **with/by** *grief when their baby died.* • *I was quite overwhelmed by all the flowers and letters of support I received.* • *Since I've been on a diet, I've been overwhelmed by a desire to eat.* • If water overwhelms a place it covers it suddenly and completely: *The whole valley will be overwhelmed if the dam bursts.*

o·ver·whelm·ing /£ˌəʊ·və'wel·mɪŋ, $ˌoʊ·vɚ-/ *adj* • Overwhelming means difficult to fight against: *She felt an overwhelming urge/desire/need to tell someone about what had happened.* • Overwhelming also means very great or very large: *She said how much she appreciated the overwhelming generosity of the public in responding to the appeal.* ○ *An overwhelming* **majority** *have voted in favour of the proposal.*

o·ver·whelm·ing·ly /£ˌəʊ·və'wel·mɪŋ·li, $ˌoʊ·vɚ-/ *adv* • *The team were overwhelmingly* (= strongly or completely) *defeated in yesterday's game.*

o·ver·work *(obj)* /£ˌəʊ·və'wɜːk, $ˌoʊ·vɚ'wɜːrk/ *v* to (cause to) work too hard • *Certain illnesses can be caused by overworking.* [I] • *He looks exhausted, they're overworking him.* [T] • *I'm overworked and underpaid.* • *(fig.) That article was full of overworked expressions* (= those that have been used so much that they have lost their value).

o·ver·work /£'əʊ·və·wɜːk, $'oʊ·vɚ·wɜːrk/ *n* [U] • *He was made ill by overwork* (= working too hard).

o·ver·write *(obj)* /£ˌəʊ·vᵊr'aɪt, $ˌoʊ·vɚ'raɪt/ *v past simple* **overwrote** /£ˌəʊ·vᵊr'əʊt, $ˌoʊ·vɚ'roʊt/, *past part* **overwritten** /£ˌəʊ·vᵊr'ɪt·ᵊn, $ˌoʊ·vɚ'rɪt̬-/ to write (something) in a way which is not clear and simple or is more detailed than it needs to be • *All the critics have said that his new book is massively overwritten.* [T] • *She's one of those authors who has a tendency to overwrite.* [I] • If you overwrite a letter, word, etc. when using a computer, you replace the letters that are on the screen by TYPING on top of them. [T]

o·ver·wrought /£ˌəʊ·vᵊr'ɔːt, $ˌoʊ·vɚ'rɑːt/ *adj* in a state of being upset, nervous and anxious • *She was so tired and overwrought that she burst into tears.* • *He was in an overwrought* **state/condition** *for weeks after the accident.*

ov·u·late /£'ɒv·jʊ·leɪt, $'ɑː·vjuː-/ *v* [I] (of a woman or female animal) to produce an OVUM (= a reproductive cell from which a baby can be formed) or several OVA • *Some women take drugs to help them ovulate, so that they can have a baby.*

ov·u·la·tion /£ˌɒv·jʊ'leɪ·ʃᵊn, $ˌɑː·vjuː-/ *n* [U] • *A woman can only become pregnant at or around the time of ovulation* (= the period when OVA are produced).

o·vum /£'əʊ·vəm, $'oʊ-/ *n* [C] *pl* **ova** *specialized* a reproductive cell produced by a woman or female animal • *If two ova are fertilized at the same time, the mother will have twins.*

ow /aʊ/ *exclamation* (used to express sudden pain) • *Ow, stop it, you're hurting me!* • See also OUCH.

owe *obj* HAVE DEBTS /£əʊ, $oʊ/ *v* [T not *be owing*] to need to pay or give (something) to (someone) because they have lent money to you, or in exchange for something they have done for you • *The police believe that he may have killed himself because he owed so much money.* • *My boss owes me* **for** *the extra work I did last weekend.* • *I owe Janet £10./I owe £10* **to** *Janet.* [+ two objects] • *You owe me a beer.* [+ two objects] • *(fml) We owe you our thanks, doctor/We owe our thanks* **to** *you, doctor.* [+ two objects] • *I think you owe* (= should give) *me an explanation.* [+ two objects] • *(infml) Thanks for the help, Bill – I won't forget that I* **owe you one** (= that I should do something for you because you have done something for me). • *(infml)* To **owe** someone **a living** is to have a duty to take care of them, whether they deserve it or not: *He seems to think* **the world** *owes him a living.* ○ *No-one owes you a living.* • If you **owe it to yourself** (to do something) you feel it is necessary to do something which will be good for you although it might hurt others: *You owe it to yourself to ask the children to leave home now they are both over thirty.* • See also IOU. • LP **Borrow**

ow·ing /£'əʊ·ɪŋ, $'oʊ-/ *adj* [after v; not gradable] • *We have several hundred pounds owing* **on** (= we still have to pay that amount for) *our car.* • *I've got $50 owing* **to** *me* **for** *a job I did last month.*

owe *obj* AS A RESULT /£əʊ, $oʊ/ *v* [T not *be owing*] to have (success, happiness, a job, etc.) only because of what someone has given you or done for you or because of your own efforts • *I owe my success* **to** *my education.* • *He owes his life* **to** *the staff at the hospital.* • *She owes her present position* **to** *having worked very hard.* • To owe someone can also mean to be grateful to them: *I owe my parents an enormous amount./I owe an enormous amount* **to** *my parents.* [+ two objects]

ow·ing to *prep* • *The concert has been cancelled owing to* (= because of) *lack of support.*

owl /aʊl/ *n* [C] a bird with a flat face, large eyes, a hook-shaped beak and strong curved nails, which hunts small mammals at night • *An owl kills its prey with its talons, and swallows it whole.* • *Owls are often considered to be wise.* • PIC **Birds**

owl·ish /'aʊ·lɪʃ/ *adj* • A person who is owlish, or who has an owlish face, has a round face, usually wears glasses, and looks serious: *He was an owlish figure, sitting in the corner of the library.*

owl·ish·ly /'aʊ·lɪʃ·li/ *adv* • *He peered owlishly over his glasses.*

own BELONGING /£əʊn, $oʊn/ *determiner, pronoun* belonging to or for, or kept by, a particular person or thing • *I'd like to have my* **(very)** *own car* (= to have a car that belongs just to me, and which I don't have to share or borrow). • *She makes all her own bread* (= makes her bread herself). • *I'm going to be out tonight, so you'll have to get your own dinner* (= prepare it yourself). • *Was that your own idea* (= Did you think of it by yourself or did someone suggest it to you)? • *These paintings are* **all** *my own work* (= I did them by myself, without help from anyone). • *You'll have to make up your own mind* (= decide by yourself) *what you want to do.* • *My own opinion* (= The opinion I have) *of the matter is that it's better not to say anything about it.* • *I don't think Clare will be able to help you – she has her own problems to deal with.* • *Each neighbourhood in New York has its own characteristics.* • *I'd never have believed it if I hadn't* **seen it with** *my own* **eyes/heard it with** *my own* **ears.** • *"Is that your mum's car?" "No, it's my own* (= it belongs to me)." • *It's time he left home and found a house* **of** *his own.* • *My daughter now has a daughter* **of** *her own.* • *She has reasons* **of** *her own for not wanting to say where she was last night.* • *James Joyce wrote in a style that was* **all** *his own* (= that was not like that of anyone else). • *Now that he's retired, his time is his own* (= he can spend his time in any way that he wants to). • *We like to take care of our own* (= take care of people who are members of our family, or who work for us). • *Eileen really* **comes into** *her* **own** (= shows her true qualities and value) *in a crisis.* • If you **do** something **in your own time** you do it at the speed at which you want to work: *Don't rush to finish those notes today – just do them in your own time.* • **In your own time** also means when you are not officially working: *I'll have to look at/do these reports in my own time – I'm too busy at work.* • *I'm studying English* **for its own sake** (= because it is interesting and enjoyable, not because I need to or have to).* • *(infml) I'll* **get** *my* **own back (on** *you) one day* (= I will do something harmful to you because you did something harmful to me). • If you say that someone **is** their **own man/woman/person**, it means that they are in control of their lives, and do not allow other people to tell them what to do: *Nobody tells me how to live my life – I'm my own man.*

• *Edith Piaf* **made** *the song "Je ne regrette rien"* **(all)** *her* **own** (= She was famous for singing it and people thought of it as belonging to her). • *I like living* **(all) on** *my* **own** (= alone). • *I did my buttons up* **(all) on** *my* **own** (= without help from anyone else), *Mummy.* • *(Br infml) As an entertainer, she's* **on** *her* **own** (= she is unusually good). • If you say to someone **on your own head be it** you are saying that they will have to take full responsibility for what they plan to do. • *It's hard to believe that he could treat his* **own flesh and blood** (= family) *so badly.* • *I always buy (Br)* **own brand/label** *(Am* **store brand/label**, *Aus* **generic brand/label**) *goods* (= goods in a shop marked with the name of the shop rather than that of the company which has produced them) *if I can.* • An **own goal** is a point scored unintentionally by a player for the opposing team, or *(fig.)* an act which unintentionally helps someone else and is harmful to yourself: *One spectacular own goal was when the research department suggested that a drug made by a rival company caused cancer – and were later proved wrong.* • *"A woman must have money and a room of her own if she is to write fiction"* (Virginia Woolf in the book *A Room of One's Own*, 1929)

own *obj* /£əʊn, $oʊn/ *v* [T not *be owning*] • *We own our house* (= It legally belongs to us). • *I've never owned* (= possessed) *a suit in my life.* • *(infml disapproving) He walked into the office on his first day* **as if**/*(Am and Aus)* **like he owned the place** (= in an unpleasantly confident way).

-owned /£-əʊnd, $-oʊnd/ *combining form* • *state-owned industry* (= industry controlled by the government) • *a family-owned business* (= a business belonging to a family)

own·er /£ˈəʊ·nəʳ, $ˈoʊ·nɚ/ *n* [C] • *Are you the owner* **of** *this car* (= Does it belong to you), *sir?* • *We're now the* **proud** *owners* **of** (= We now possess) *a new television.* • *Most of the people around here are* **owner-occupiers** (= the houses they live in belong to them). • *This street contains few* **owner-occupied** *houses* (= houses that belong to the people who live in them).

own·er·ship /£ˈəʊ·nə·ʃɪp, $ˈoʊ·nɚ-/ *n* [U] • *Do you have any proof of ownership* **of** *this car* (= proof that it belongs to you)? • *(Br and Aus) The debate continues about whether these industries should be* **in/under** *public or private ownership.* • *Rates of home ownership have remained relatively constant.*

own ADMIT /£əʊn, $oʊn/ *v* [not *be owning*] *fml* to admit • *I own* **(that)** *I was not very happy with the decision.* [+ *(that)* clause] • *He owned* **(that)** *the mistake was his fault.* [+ *(that)* clause] • *Many teachers would own* **to** *a sense of relief at the end of term.* [I] • *They owned* **to** *failing to pay their taxes.* [I]

own up *v adv* [I] • *Which of you children broke the window – come on, own up* (= admit that it was your fault)? • *They have owned up* **to** *the crime.* • *No one has owned up* **to** *stealing the money.*

owt /aʊt/ *pronoun Br regional for* ANYTHING • *I haven't heard owt about it.* • *Is there owt to drink?* • Compare NOWT.

ox /£ɒks, $ɑːks/, **bul·lock** *n* [C] *pl* **oxen** /£ˈɒk·sᵊn, $ɑːk-/ an adult male of the cattle family, which has had its sexual organs removed and which was used in the past for pulling loads on farms, or, more generally, an adult member of the cattle family which is kept on a farm

Ox·bridge /£ˈɒks·brɪdʒ, $ˈɑːks-/ *n* [not after *the*] the colleges of Oxford and/or Cambridge, considered as a unit separate from other colleges in Britain • *Many members of the British government went to Oxbridge* (= a college at either Oxford or Cambridge).

Ox·bridge /£ˈɒks·brɪdʒ, $ˈɑːks-/ *adj* [not gradable] • *She's an Oxbridge student* (= a student from Oxford or Cambridge). • *He's very Oxbridge in his manner* (= behaves as if he went to a college in Oxford or Cambridge). • Compare REDBRICK.

Ox·fam /£ˈɒks·fæm, $ˈɑːks-/ *n* [U not after *the*] *abbreviation for* Oxford Committee for Famine Relief (= a British organization which collects money to help people in countries where there are difficult local situations) • *Oxfam is sending aid to the regions worst affected by the civil war.* • *I bought this rug in an Oxfam shop.*

ox·ide /£ˈɒk·saɪd, $ˈɑːk-/ *n* a chemical combination of oxygen and one other element • *iron oxide* [U] • *an oxide* **of** *copper* [C]

ox·i·dize *(obj), Br and Aus usually* **-ise** /£ˈɒk·sɪ·daɪz, $ˈɑːk-/ *v* • If a substance oxidizes it combines with oxygen to form another substance: *Iron becomes rusty when it oxidizes.* [I] • To oxidize a substance is to combine it with oxygen: *Aldehydes are readily oxidized to carboxylic acids and reduced to alcohols.* [T] ○ *The open bottle of wine left from the night before had become oxidized and unpleasant to drink.*

ox·i·diz·a·tion, *Br and Aus usually* **-i·sa·tion** /£ˌɒk·sɪ·daɪˈzeɪ·ʃᵊn, £-dɪ-, $ˌɑːk·sɪ·dɪ-/, *Am* **ox·i·da·tion** /£ˌɒk·sɪˈdeɪ·ʃᵊn, $ˌɑːk-/ *n* [U]

ox·tail /£ˈɒk·steɪl, $ˈɑːk-/ *n* (the) tail of an OX which is used as meat or for making soup • *I bought an oxtail to make some soup.* [C] • *The butcher didn't have any oxtail today.* [U] • *We had oxtail* **soup** *for lunch.* [U]

ox·y·a·ce·tyl·ene /£ˌɒk·si·əˈset·ᵊl·iːn, $ˌɑːk·si·əˈset̬-/ *n* [U] *specialized* a mixture of oxygen and ACETYLENE (= a gas) that produces a hot bright flame, and that can be used for cutting metal • *He welded the pieces of metal together using oxyacetylene.* • *They cut a hole in the metal door with an oxyacetylene lamp/torch.*

ox·y·gen /£ˈɒk·sɪ·dʒən, $ˈɑːk-/ *n* [U] a colourless gas that forms a large part of the air on Earth and which is needed by most living things in order for them to live • *The air has less oxygen in it at high altitudes than it does at low altitudes.* • *If people are deprived of oxygen, they either suffer brain damage or die.* • **Oxygen masks** are pieces of equipment which can be put over a person's nose and mouth to supply oxygen. They can be used by passengers on an aircraft to help them breathe in an emergency, or by ill people who are having difficulty breathing. • An **oxygen tent** is a clear covering put over the head and upper body of an ill person to provide oxygen to help them breathe. • PIC〉 **Emergency services**

ox·y·gen·ate *obj* /£ˈɒk·sɪ·dʒə·neɪt, $ˈɑːk-/ *v* [T] • *Fish tanks often have a pump which oxygenates* (= adds oxygen to) *the water.*

oy·ster /£ˈɔɪ·stəʳ, $-stɚ/ *n* [C] a large flat SHELLFISH (= small fish that lives inside a shell with two parts), some types of which can be eaten either raw or cooked, and other types of which produce PEARLS (= small round white precious stones) • *She squeezed lemon on to her eleventh oyster and sucked it up from the shell.* • *Eating oysters is said to make men function better sexually.* • An **oyster bed** is an area at the bottom of the sea where oysters are bred either for food or to produce PEARLS.

oz MEASUREMENT *n* [C] *pl* **oz** *abbreviation for* OUNCE • *Add 8 oz* **of** *flour.* • LP〉 **Units**

Oz COUNTRY /£ɒz, $ɑːz/ *n Aus infml, Br slang for* Australia

Oz·zie *Aus infml, Br slang,* **Aus·sie** /£ˈɒz·i, $ˈɑː·zi/ *n, adj* [not gradable] • An Ozzie is an Australian. [C] • *Do you like Ozzie beer?*

o·zone /£ˈəʊ·zəʊn, $ˈoʊ·zoʊn/ *n* [U] a form of oxygen • *(infml)* Ozone is also used to refer to air that is clean and pleasant to breathe, esp. near the sea: *A few breaths of that ozone will soon clear your lungs.* • The **ozone layer** is a layer of air high above the Earth, which contains a lot of ozone, and which prevents harmful ULTRAVIOLET light from the sun from reaching the Earth: *Scientists are worried about the hole in the ozone layer which appeared over Antarctica in the 1980s.* ○ *Some kinds of aerosol spray produce gases that are harmful to the ozone layer.* • **Ozone-friendly** products do not produce gases which are harmful to the ozone layer while they are being made or used: *ozone-friendly packaging* • *an ozone-friendly refrigerator*

P p

P [LETTER] (*pl* **P's** or **Ps**), **p** (*pl* **p's** or **ps**) /piː/ *n* [C] the 16th letter of the English alphabet • [LP] **Silent letters**

p [MONEY] /piː/ *n* [C] *pl* **p** *Br abbreviation for* PENNY or PENCE • *Could you lend me 50p?* • *This packet of crisps costs 25p.* • *I need a 1p/5p/20p* **coin/piece.** • [LP] **Money**

p [PAGE] /piː/ *n* [C] *pl* **pp** *abbreviation for* PAGE [PAPER] • *See p. 27.* • *The references are on pp. 256-264.*

P [SIGN] /piː/ *n* [U] *abbreviation for* PARKING, esp. used on road signs

pa [FATHER] /pɑː/ *n* [C] *dated infml for* father • *I borrowed the money from Pa.* • *Don't worry, Pa, we'll be careful.* [as form of address] • *My pa always expected us to be well-behaved when we were children.* • Compare MA [MOTHER]. • [LP] **Titles and forms of address**

pa [YEARLY] /ˌpiːˈeɪ/ *adv* [not gradable] *abbreviation for* **per annum**, see at PER • *a salary of £20 000 p.a.*

PA [WORK] /ˌpiːˈeɪ/ *n* [C] *Br and Aus abbreviation for* personal assistant (= a person who is employed to help a person in a higher position to do their work, esp. that involving writing letters, arranging meetings, making telephone calls) etc. • *I'll get my PA to make the arrangements.* • *He works as a PA* **to** *the managing director.*

PA [ANNOUNCEMENTS] /ˌpiːˈeɪ/ *n* [C] *abbreviation for* public address (system) (= a device for making announcements to people in public places, such as stations, airports, etc.) • *It said on* **the** *PA that the flight would be delayed several hours.* • *A message came through for me* **on/over** *the PA system.*

pace [SPEED] /peɪs/ *n* [U] the speed at which someone or something moves, or with which something happens or changes • *If you're going to walk a long way, it's better to start out* **at** *a fairly slow pace.* • *When she thought she heard someone following her, she* **quickened** *her pace.* • *The train* **gathered** *pace* (= increased speed) *as it went down the hill.* • *Michael always* **sets** *the pace* (= decides the speed) *when we go out for a walk, and the rest of us have to keep up with him.* • *For many years this company has* **set** *the pace* (= has been the most successful company and others have tried to copy it) *in the communications industry.* • *Could you slow down a bit – I can't* **keep** *pace* **with** (= walk or run as fast as) *you.* • *We must make sure that we* **keep** *pace* **with** (= make changes in reaction to) *new developments in computer technology.* • To **force** the pace in a race is to make other people in the race go fast, by going fast yourself: *The record-holder really forced the pace in the 1500 m.* • *These changes seem to me to be happening* **at** *too fast a pace.* • *Schoolchildren should be allowed to work* **at** *their* **own** *pace* (= at the speed at which they want to work). • *I don't like the pace* (= the speed of activity) **of** *modern life.* • *They moved out of the city because they couldn't* **stand** *the pace* (= didn't like the hurried activity) **(of** *life there).* • *This recording of "Cosi fan tutte" has been criticized for its lack of pace* (= being too slow). • A **pace bowler** or **pace man** in cricket is a player who BOWLS the ball fast. • See also PACEMAKER.

pace *obj* /peɪs/ *v* [T] • *We have a lot to do today, so pace* **yourself** (= do not act too quickly), *or you'll get very tired.* • To pace someone who is training for a race or running in a race is to establish a speed for them, for example by running with them.

pa·cy, pa·cey /ˈpeɪ·si/ *adj* **pacier, paciest** *Br* • *a pacy novel/story/film* (= one containing a lot of or fast action)

pace [STEP] /peɪs/ *n* [C] a single step, or the distance you move when you take a single step • *Take two paces forwards/backwards.* • *They walked a few paces in silence.* • *The runner collapsed just a few paces from the finish.* • *(infml) I can spot a winner* **at** *twenty* **paces** (= easily). • If you **put** someone **through** their **paces**, you make them show their qualities and abilities: *All the candidates were put through their paces during the television debate.* ○ *I'm going to take my new car out and put it through its paces.*

pace *(obj)* /peɪs/ *v* • To pace a room or other place is to walk first in one direction and then in the opposite direction across it taking regular steps, esp. because you are anxious: *He paced the room nervously, waiting for the results of the tests.* [T] • To pace **(off/out)** a space is to measure it by taking steps of equal size across it and counting them: *You can get a rough idea of the area of the floor by pacing it* **(out)**. [T/M] • To pace **up and down** is to walk first in one direction and then in the opposite direction in an anxious way: *By the time I arrived at the station, my father was already pacing up and down.* [I] ○ *I hate to see animals pacing up and down in their cages.* [I]

pace·maker [RUNNER] /£ˈpeɪsˌmeɪ·kəʳ, $-kɚ/, **pace–set·ter** /£ˈpeɪsˌset·əʳ, $-ˌset̬·ɚ/ *n* [C] a person or animal which establishes the speed in a race, or a person or organization which is an example for others by being successful • *The leading woman in the marathon is running with a group of men who are acting as pacemakers for her.* • *They are the pacemakers in computer design.*

pace·ma·ker [DEVICE] /£ˈpeɪsˌmeɪ·kəʳ, $-kɚ/ *n* [C] a small device which is put inside someone's body, next to their heart, in order to make the heart beat regularly if it can not do so without one

pac·i·fy *obj* [CALM] /ˈpæs·ɪ·faɪ/ *v* [T] to cause (esp. someone who is angry or upset) to be calm and satisfied • *He pacified his crying child by cuddling her.* • *My boss was furious with me for being late, but I pacified her by saying I'd make up the time tomorrow.* • *It was difficult for the police to pacify the angry crowd.*

pa·ci·fi·ca·tion /ˌpæs·ɪ·fɪˈkeɪ·ʃᵊn/ *n* [U]

pac·i·fi·er /£ˈpæs·ɪ·faɪ·əʳ, $-ɚ/ *n* [C] • A pacifier is a person who makes other people calm when they are angry or upset: *She's a great pacifier* (= is good at making other people calm). • Pacifier is also *Am for* DUMMY [RUBBER OBJECT].

pac·i·fy *obj* [PEACE] /ˈpæs·ɪ·faɪ/ *v* [T] to bring peace to or end war in (a place) • *A UN force has been sent in to try and pacify the area worst affected by the civil war.* • *Attempts to pacify the country have so far failed.*

pa·ci·fic /pəˈsɪf·ɪk/ *adj* • *The new government appears to have more pacific views* (= to desire peace more) *than the previous one.* • *The rebels' pacific gestures* (= acts intended to achieve peace) *have met with little response from the army.*

pa·ci·fi·cal·ly /pəˈsɪf·ɪ·kli/ *adv*

pa·ci·fi·ca·tion /ˌpæs·ɪ·fɪˈkeɪ·ʃᵊn/ *n* [U] • *The pacification* **of** (= The achievement of peace in) *the area is expected to take a long time.*

pac·i·fi·er /£ˈpæs·ɪ·faɪ·əʳ, $-ɚ/ *n* [C] • *I don't believe in the old view that men are fighters and women are pacifiers* (= people who try and achieve peace).

pac·i·fi·sm /ˈpæs·ɪ·fɪ·zᵊm/ *n* [U] • Pacifism is the belief that war is wrong, and therefore that to fight in a war is wrong: *After the explosion of the atomic bombs at Hiroshima and Nagasaki, Japan became committed to pacifism.*

pac·i·fist /ˈpæs·ɪ·fɪst/ *n* [C] • *His experiences in the war turned him into a committed pacifist* (= someone who believes that war is wrong and refuses to fight in a war). • *The pacifist movement is gaining increasing support among young people.*

pack *(obj)* [PUT INTO] /pæk/ *v* to put (something) into (a bag, box, etc.) • *I'm leaving for my business trip early in the morning, so I'm going to pack* (= put clothes and other possessions into a bag or bags) *tonight.* [I] • *She packed a small* **suitcase (with** *the things she needed for the weekend).* [T] • *He just packed his* **bags** *and walked out on his wife and children.* [T] • *I haven't packed my clothes* (= put them into a bag etc.) *yet.* [T] • *Could you pack me a spare pair of shoes, please/pack a spare pair of shoes* **for** *me, please?* [+ two objects] • *These books need to be packed* **in/into** *a box.* [T] • *Would you like me to help you pack your shopping?* [T] • *Ian has a job packing jars in a factory.* [T] • *Come on, children, it's time to pack* **away** *your toys* (= put them into the place in which they are kept). [M] • *They've packed their house* **up** (= put the contents of their house into boxes etc.) *for six months, and gone abroad.* [M] • *I love this silk dress, but it doesn't pack very well* (= is not suitable to be put into a bag because that makes lines appear on it). [I] • *All this food will never pack* (= fit) **into** *that small basket.* [I] • *(fig.) I don't know how you manage to pack so much work* **into** (= do so much work in) *one day.* [T] • To pack a protective material **round** something is to cover it with that material before it is put into a bag or box etc. so that it will not break or be damaged when it is stored or transported: *She packed tissue paper round the shoes to protect them.* [T] • *"Pack up your troubles in your old kit-bag, / And smile, smile, smile"* (from a song written by George Asaf, 1915)

PORTUGUESE FALSE FRIENDS (P)

English	Portuguese	Meaning
abate *v*	abater	to pull down, demolish; to slaughter; to reduce prices
addition *n*	adição	restaurant bill
admire *v*	admirar	to be surprised
advance *v*	avançar	to jut out; to speak with indolence; (fig) to steal
adventure *n*	aventura	hazard, risk; love affair
amorous *adj*	amoroso	affectionate; pleasing; gentle
anticipate *v*	antecipar	to bring forward; to be early
apartment *n*	apartamento	separation
appreciate *v*	apreciar	to evaluate, estimate, appraise
argument *n*	argumento	story, plot; outline, summary; point of view
assist *v*	assistir	to be present, attend
assistant *n*	assistente	person present; audience; midwife
baby *n*	bébé	doll
base *n*	base	basis
batter *v*	bater	to strike, hit, knock, thump, bump, bang, whip; to fight; to beat, defeat
bizarre *adj*	bizarro/a	tall and handsome; brave
brave *adj*	bravo	wild, untamed; mad; furious
cabaret *n*	cabaret	night club
cafe *n*	café	coffee
calm *adj*	calmo	warm; hot, sultry
camp *v*	campear	to campaign; to prevail; to dominate
candid *adj*	cândido	naive; innocent; pure white
cargo *n*	cargo	charge,duty; office; responsibilty
casualty *n*	casualidade	fortuity, chance
cement *n*	cimento	foundations, basis
chef *n*	chefe	chief; leader; boss
cholera *n*	cólera	anger, fury, rage
circulation *n*	circulação	traffic
commodity *n*	comodidade	comfort; convenience
compartment *n*	compartimento	room
complete *adj*	completo	full up, full, no vacancies
comprehensive *adj*	compreensivo	understanding
compromise *n*	compromisso	commitment; appointment, date
concourse *n*	concurso	contest, competition; tender
condescending *adj*	condescendente	compliant, acquiescent
confer *v*	conferir	to check, count, verify; to grant
confused *adj*	confuso	embarrassed
control *v*	controlar	to supervise; to inspect, check,
convenient *adj*	conveniente	fitting, appropriate; desirable,
courier *n*	correio	post office; mail, post; postman
creature *n*	criatura	man; person
crisis *n*	crise	fit; economic depression
decide *v*	decidir	to convince, persuade,
decorate *v*	decorar	to memorize; to recite
defend *v*	defender	to resist; to shield; to prohibit,
delight *n*	delito	crime; offence, misdemeanour
demand *n*	demanda	law suit; plea; court action,
deposit *n*	deposito	depot, warehouse, storehouse
destination *n*	destinação	fate
deter *v*	deter	to detain; to restrain; to linger
disgrace *n*	desgraça	misfortune, calamity; adversity
disgust *n*	desgosto	grief
disgusting *adj*	desgostoso	sad, sorrowful; discontented
distracted *adj*	distraido	absentminded; thoughtless
door *n*	dor	pain, ache; suffering, sorrow, grief
editor *n*	editor	publisher
effective *adj*	efetivo	real, actual; positive; in office, in power
empathy *n*	empáfia	conceit; conceited person
enjoy *v*	enjoar	to nauseate, disgust; to feel sick
envy *v*	enviar	to send, dispatch, ship
eventual *adj*	eventual	fortuitious; casual; contingent
exit *n*	êxito	issue; result; success, hit
experience *n*	experiência	experiment, trial, test,
experiment *v*	experimentar	to experience; to taste; to try on
explore *v*	explorar	to exploit, use to one's own ends
extreme *adj*	estreme	unmixed, undiluted, pure
fast *adj*	fasto	happy; fortunate
fat *n*	fato	fact; event, occurrence; deed, act
fatality *n*	fatalidade	calamity, disaster
fatigue *v*	fatigar	to annoy, harass, bother
firm *n*	firma	signature
form *n*	forma	way; means, method; format
full *adj*	fula	furious
gentle *adj*	gentil	courteous, kind; gracious; thoughtful; genteel, refined
gracious *adj*	gracioso	graceful; cute; witty; facetious
grand *adj*	grande	large; wide; long; tall; grown-up
gymnasium *n*	ginásio	lower secondary school
history *n*	história	story, tale, fable; fib
ignore *v*	ignorar	to be ignorant, be unaware of
importance *n*	importância	sum of money; cost
inconvenient *adj*	inconveniente	improper; inappropriate; inopportune
individual *adj*	individuo	undivided
industry *n*	industria	skill, cleverness
invest *v*	investir	to attack, storm
journal *n*	jornal	newspaper
just *adj*	justo/a	exact, accurate; tight
lard *n*	lardo	fat or bacon (in strips)
large *adj*	largo	broad; spacious; square, plaza
laser *n*	lazer	leisure
late *adj*	lato	broad, wide; ample
lavatory *n*	lavatório	wash basin; washstand
library *n*	livraria	bookshop
long *adj*	longe	far, remote, distant
luxurious *adj*	luxurioso	lustful
magazine *n*	magazine	department store
mascara *n*	máscara	mask, disguise; masked person
media *n*	média	average, mean, median; large cup of milky coffee
minister *n*	ministro	magistrate, judge
mist *n*	misto	mixture, compound
molest *v*	molestar	to disturb, to harrass, to trouble
notorious *adj*	notório	well-known; public
obsequious *adj*	obsequioso	courteous, kind, obliging
ordinary *adj*	ordinário	bad, of poor quality; vulgar
parent *n*	parente	relative, kin
part *v*	partir	to break; to leave
particular *adj*	particular	private, personal
patio *n*	patio	playground; courtyard, inner court
pavement *n*	pavimento	storey (of a building); floor
pork *n*	porco	pig; filthy person; the Devil
precision *n*	precisão	need, necessity
presents *n*	presentes	persons present, those present; members of an audience
prevent *v*	prevenir	to anticipate; to warn, inform
private *n*	privado/a	WC; confidant, private friend
professor *n*	professor	teacher, master
propriety *n*	propriedade	property, possessions; attribute
prove *v*	provar	to test; to experience; to taste; to try on
prove *v*	prover	to provide; to bestow
real *adj*	real	royal
receipt *n*	receita	recipe; prescription; income
recipe *n*	recipe	doctor's prescription
repair *v*	reparar	to notice, observe
request *v*	requestar	to woo, make love to
rest *v*	restar	to remain, be left over/behind
retire *v*	retirar	to take/draw/pull back; to retract (something said); to withdraw
reunite *v*	reunir	to connect; to gather, collect; to assemble; to embody; to add, annex
rumour *n*	rumor	noise, rumbling, murmur
sack *n*	sacao	bag
scope *n*	escopo	purpose, aim; end; object, intention
sensible *adj*	sensível	tenderhearted; sensitive; touchy; sentient; impressionable
sin *n*	sina	fate; doom; destiny; curse, spell
single *adj*	singelo/a	simple, naive, guileless; sincere
sort *n*	sorte	fate, destiny; mode; manner
stranger *n*	estrangeiro	foreigner, alien; foreign lands
success *n*	sucesso	event; result; prosperity
sympathetic *adj*	simpático	likeable, pleasant; attractive
term *n*	termo	end, finish; limit; boundary
tremendous *adj*	tremendo	terrible, dreadful, awful
ultimately adv	ultimamente	lately, recently, not long ago
urge *v*	urgir	to be urgent, be pressing
use *v*	usar	to wear; to use up, wear out
vague *adj*	vago	vacant; unoccupied; disengaged; vagrant; fickle
valour *n*	valor	value; price; merit; excellence; (music) duration; (pl.) securities, valuables
vest *n*	veste	garment, (pl.) clothing, regalia

pack /pæk/ *n* [C] • A pack is a bag in which you put your possessions and which you usually carry on your back when you are travelling. A pack can also be a collection of your possessions wrapped together and carried on your back: *We'd been walking for about ten miles, when we stopped and took our sandwiches out of our packs.* See also BACKPACK. ○ *The soldiers had to carry their heavy packs for miles across rough ground.* • *In some parts of the world,* **pack animals** (= animals such as horses which are used for carrying things on their backs) *are used to transport things from one place to another.*

packed /pækt/ *adj* [after v; not gradable] • If someone says they are packed, it means that they have put their things into a bag, box, etc.: *Are you packed yet?* ○ *I'm all packed and ready to go.* • *(Br)* A **packed lunch** (*Am* **box lunch**, *Aus* **cut lunch**) is a light meal put in a container, usually to take with you somewhere to be eaten later: *My children usually take a packed lunch to school.*

pack·er /£ˈpæk·əʳ, $-ɚ/ *n* [C] • A packer is a person, company or machine which puts goods into boxes or food into containers: *She works as a packer in a warehouse.* • A packer is also a person who is employed to put the possessions of someone who is moving to a new house into boxes: *The packers are coming at 8.30 am.*

pack·ing /ˈpæk·ɪŋ/ *n* [U] • *Do you need any help with the packing* (= the act of putting things into bags, cases or boxes)? • *He always does his own packing.* • *We need some packing* (= protective material) *to put round these plates.* • *I don't think we've got enough (Br and Aus)* **packing cases**/ *(Am usually)* **packing crates** (= large strong boxes for putting things in to be sent somewhere) *for all the kitchen equipment.* • See **postage and packing** at POST.

pack *(obj)* FILL /pæk/ *v* [always + adv/prep] to come together in large numbers or to fill (a space) • *Thousands of visitors are packing* **into** *the Garden Show every hour.* [I] • *People are packing* **in** *to see the exhibition.* [I] • *The people on the bus were packed* **(together) like sardines** (= there were many of them very close together) . [T] • *The stadium was packed* **with** *local fans.* [T] • *This book is packed* **with** *useful information.* [T] • *Graham's proposal was approved only because he packed the meeting* **with** *his supporters* (= he made certain that a lot of people who supported him were at the meeting so that he would achieve what he wanted). [T] • If an entertainment of some type packs people **in** or **packs them in**, it attracts a large number of people to see it: *Spielberg's new film is really packing in the crowds.* [M] ○ *The latest computer exhibition is really packing them in.*

packed /pækt/ *adj* • *The train was so packed* (= full of people) *that I couldn't find a seat.* • *The musical "Cats" has been playing to a packed theatre/house* (= the theatre has been full of people) *for years.* • *(Br infml) The bar was* **packed out** (= full of people) *last night.*

-packed /-pækt/ *combining form* • *a fun-packed day* (= a day in which a lot of amusing and entertaining things happen) • *an action-packed film* (= a film containing a lot of action) • *a thrill-packed adventure story* (= one containing a lot of excitement)

pack *(obj)* MASS /pæk/ *v* [always + adv/prep] to (cause to) form into a solid mass • *The wind has packed the snow against the side of the road.* [T] • *The snow has packed* **down** *tightly, making the streets dangerous to walk on.* [I] • **Pack ice** is a mass of ice floating in the sea that has been formed by smaller pieces of ice being forced together: *Pack ice can be very dangerous to ships.*

pack /pæk/ *n* [C] • A pack is a thick mass of a substance, often like clay, which is used as a beauty treatment for the face. • A pack is also a thick mass of cloth, etc. which can be used dry or wet to treat an injury, such as to stop bleeding or swelling: *Hold this ice pack to your head to stop the bruising.* See also COMPRESS.

pack GROUP /pæk/ *n* [C] a group, set or collection (of something) • A pack **of** animals, esp. those of the dog family, is a group which lives and/or hunts together: *Wolves hunt in packs.* ○ *I think it's wrong to hunt foxes with a pack* **of** *hounds.* • A pack is also a group of fighting machines, such as aircraft or SUBMARINES, which fight together. • In RUGBY football, a pack is a group of players who try and get the ball for their team. • A pack is also an organized group of children who are BROWNIES or CUBS : *the 2nd Kempston Brownie Guide pack.* ○ *My uncle was the leader of my Cub pack.* • A pack (*esp. Am* **deck**) **of** (playing) cards is a complete set: *Mary took a pack of cards from the drawer and we all sat down to play.* LP **Cards** • *(esp. disapproving)* Pack is also used to refer to a group of people who do things together but not in an organized way, and who might be involved in activities which are not legal or acceptable: *a pack* **of** *kids* • *a biker pack* • *a pack* **of** *thieves.* ○ See also GANG.

pack CONTAINER /pæk/ *n* [C] *esp. Am for* PACKET • *a pack* **of** *cigarettes/gum*

-pack /-pæk/ *combining form* • -pack is used in combination with an amount to show that that many of a particular type of goods have been wrapped and are being sold together: *a six-pack* **of** *beer* (= six containers of beer wrapped and sold together •) *a twin-pack* **of** *soap* (= two pieces of soap wrapped and sold together) • *a multi-pack* **of** *toilet paper* (= several rolls of toilet paper wrapped and sold together)

pack *obj* CARRY /pæk/ *v* [T] *Am slang* to carry with you, esp. as part of your usual equipment • *to pack a* **gun** • *Press reports referred to the bank robber as a 'pistol-packing mama'.*

pack *obj* FORCE /pæk/ *v* [T] to have the force of (power, weapons, etc.) • *This gun packs* (= has) *a lot of firepower.* • *Each missile packs several warheads.* • *You'll never be a boxer if you don't learn to pack a hard/strong/powerful* **punch** (= hit forcefully). • To **pack a punch** is also to use forceful language, esp. in an effective way: *The minister's speech packed quite a punch.* • If an alcoholic drink **packs a punch**, it is very strong.

pack in *obj*, **pack** *obj* **in** *v adv* [M] *infml* to stop doing (something) • *Dick has packed in his job, and gone off round the world.* • *Sometimes I wish I could just pack* **it (all)** *in* (= stop doing what I'm doing). • *"Is Emma still seeing Joe?" "No, she's packed him in* (= has ended her relationship with him)*."* • If you tell someone to **pack it in**, it means you want them to stop doing something that you think is not acceptable: *That's enough of that fighting – now pack it in!*

pack off *obj*, **pack** *obj* **off** *v adv* [M] *infml* to send (someone) somewhere else • *We've packed the kids off for the weekend.* • *I usually get the family packed off* **to** *school by 8.30 am.*

pack up *(obj)*, **pack** *(obj)* **up** *v adv infml* to stop doing something or *(Br)* (of a machine) to stop working in the expected way • *Everyone packs up early on Fridays.* [I] • *She packed up her job, and went off to Australia.* [M] • *It's time you packed up smoking.* [+ v-ing] • *(Br) My camera has packed up.* [I] • Ⓢ

pack·age /ˈpæk·ɪdʒ/ *n* [C] an object or group of objects that have been wrapped up together in paper or cardboard; a small parcel • *The postman has just delivered a package for you.* • A package is also a related group of objects when they are offered together as a single unit: *The computer comes with a software package.* ○ *The Government has approved a £30 million* **rescue** *package for* (= money intended to help) *the threatened industry.* ○ *The* **aid** *package for the earthquake-hit area will include emergency food and medical supplies.* • Package is also *Am for* PACKET: *She bought a package* **of** *cookies (Br and Aus a packet of biscuits).* • A **package deal** is a set of arrangements that must be accepted together and not separately. • *(Am)* **Package goods** are alcoholic drinks that are bought in an **off-licence** (= a shop where alcoholic drink is sold). • **Package store** is *Am for* **off-licence**. See at OFF AWAY FROM. • A **package tour**/*(Br also)* **package holiday**/*(Aus also)* **holiday package** is a holiday at a fixed price in which the travel company arranges your travel, hotels and sometimes meals for you: *We went on a cheap package holiday to Spain and stayed in a big hotel by the sea.* • PIC **Bread and cakes**

pack·age *obj* /ˈpæk·ɪdʒ/ *v* [T] • To package goods is to put them into boxes or containers to be sold: *Their products are always attractively packaged.* ○ *The new toiletries range is packaged* **in** *recycled glass containers. (fig.) As a young film star, she was packaged* **as** (= her appearance and actions were controlled by others so that she appeared to the public to be) *a sex symbol.*

pack·ag·ing /ˈpæk·ɪ·dʒɪŋ/ *n* [U] • Packaging is the materials in which objects are wrapped before being sold: *We hope to make all our packaging biodegradable or able to be recycled.* ○ *There's far too much packaging on food bought in supermarkets.*

packed /pækt/ *adj* See at PACK PUT INTO, PACK FILL

pack·er /£ˈpæk·əʳ, $-ɚ/ *n* [C] See at PACK PUT INTO

pack·et /ˈpæk·ɪt/, *Am also* **pack·age** *n* [C] a small paper or cardboard container in which a number of small objects are sold • *a (Br and Aus) packet/(Am) box of cereal* • *a (Br and Aus) packet/(Am) pack of chewing gum* • *(Br and Aus) a* *packet of crisps (Am and Aus bag of chips)* • *How many seeds are there in a packet?* • *(Br and Aus) He opened a packet* **of** *biscuits (Am package of cookies) and took one out.* • *(Br and Aus) She smokes a packet (Am pack)* **of** *cigarettes* (= the contents of a packet) *a day.* • *(infml)* **A packet** is also a large amount of money: *That house must have cost a packet!* ○ *Someone's making a packet out of this business.* • *(Br taboo slang)* A packet is also a man's sex organs. • Compare PARCEL. • PIC› **Bread and cakes, Containers** Ⓓ

pack·ing /ˈpæk·ɪŋ/ *n* [U] See at PACK [PUT INTO]

pact /pækt/ *n* [C] a formal agreement between two people or groups of people • *The United States and Canada have* **signed** *a free-trade pact.* • *The Liberal Democrats may* **form** *a pact* **with** *Labour* **to** *try to beat the Conservatives in the next election.* [+ *to* infinitive]

pa·cy /ˈpeɪ·si/ *adj* **-ier, -iest** See at PACE [SPEED]

pad [MATERIAL] /pæd/ *n* [C] a piece of soft thick cloth or rubber which is used to protect a part of the body, give shape to something or clean something • *He wears knee and shoulder pads and a helmet when he goes skateboarding.* • *Footballers often wear* **shin** *pads to protect their legs.* • *In the 1980s,* **shoulder** *pads were very fashionable in women's clothes.* • *She wiped her eye make-up off with a cotton wool pad.*

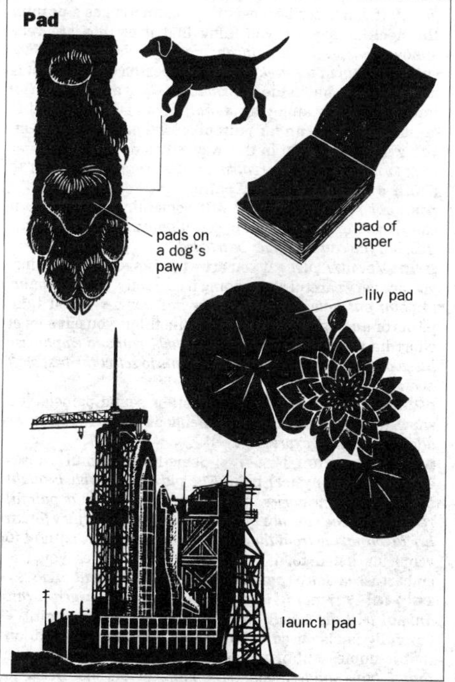

pad *obj* /pæd/ *v* [T] **-dd-** • If you pad something, you put pieces of soft thick cloth in it to make it soft, give it a different shape or protect what is inside: *These walking boots are padded with shock-resistant foam.* • If you pad **(out)** a speech or piece of writing, you add unnecessary words or information to make it longer and often to hide the fact that you are not saying anything very important: *His speech was padded out* **with** *repetition and clichés.*

pad·ded /ˈpæd·ɪd/ *adj* • *It's a short jacket with padded shoulders.* • *Do you wear a padded* **bra** (= one with extra layers of material in it to make the breasts seem bigger)*?* • A **padded cell** is a room in a mental hospital that has very soft walls to stop a seriously mentally ill person from hurting themselves.

pad·ding /ˈpæd·ɪŋ/ *n* [U] • Padding means the pieces of material used to protect something or give it shape: *When he plays cricket he wears a helmet and thick padding.* • Padding is also unnecessary words or information added to a speech or piece of writing: *It could have been an interesting essay, but there was too much padding.*

pad [PAPER] /pæd/ *n* [C] a number of pieces of paper that have been fastened together along one side, which is used for writing or drawing on • *I have a pad and pencil for taking notes.* • *I always keep a pad of paper by the phone for writing down messages on.* • See also NOTEPAD. • PIC› **Pad**

pad [FLAT SURFACE] /pæd/ *n* [C] a hard flat area of ground where HELICOPTERS (= a type of aircraft) can take off and land, or from which ROCKETS (= a space vehicle powered by burning fuel) are sent • *The hotel has its own helicopter pad.* • *Missiles have been launched from their pads deep in enemy territory.* • A pad is also one of the large flat leaves of a **water lily**. • PIC› **Pad**

pad [FOOT] /pæd/ *n* [C] the soft fleshy part at the bottom of a cat or dog's PAW (= foot) • PIC› **Pad**

pad [HOUSE] /pæd/ *n* [C] *slang* a person's house or apartment • *She's got a nice pad in Camden.*

pad·dle [POLE] /ˈpæd·l̩/ *n* [C] a short pole with a wide flat part at one end or both ends, used for moving a small boat or CANOE through the water • *You hold the paddle with both hands and push it through the water on both sides of the canoe.* • A paddle is also one of a set of flat blades fixed to a type of wheel (a **paddle wheel**) that turns in the water to push a boat along or operate a piece of machinery. • A **paddle steamer** (*Am* **side-wheeler**) is a large boat that uses steam and a paddle wheel to move through the water. • A **paddle wheel** is a type of wheel with small flat blades fixed around the edge which makes a boat more through the water or which operates a piece of machinery. • PIC› **Ships and boats**

pad·dle *(obj)* /ˈpæd·l̩/ *v* • *We took turns to paddle the little boat.* [T] • *Although I was paddling like mad, the canoe didn't seem to be moving.* [I] • If you paddle while you are swimming, you move your feet or hands up and down slowly: *We put on our snorkels and paddled along through the clear water.* [I] • *(infml)* If you describe a person as **paddling** their **own canoe**, you mean that they are independent and do not need help from anyone else.

pad·dle [WALK] *Br and Aus* /ˈpæd·l̩/, *Am* **wade** *v* [I] to walk with bare feet through water only a few centimetres deep, often at the edge of the sea • *We rolled up our trousers and paddled along the seashore.* • *(Br and Aus)* A **paddling pool** (*Aus also* **toddlers pool**, *Am* **wading pool**) is an artificial pool only a few centimetres deep that small children can play in. • PIC› **Playground**

pad·dle *Br and Aus* /ˈpæd·l̩/, *Am* **wade** *n* [C usually sing] • *Shall we go for a paddle* (= a walk at the edge of the sea)*?*

pad·dock /ˈpæd·ək/ *n* [C] a small field where animals, esp. horses, are kept, or *(Aus)* a field of any size which is used for farming • *They keep horses in a paddock behind their house.* • *(specialized)* A paddock is also an enclosed area where horses are shown to the public before a race. • PIC› **Farming**

Pad·dy [PERSON] /ˈpæd·i/ *n* [C] *infml* an Irish person. This word is considered offensive by most people.

pad·dy [ANGRY] /ˈpæd·i/ *n* [C] *Br infml dated* a very angry state • *She got* **in** *a paddy when I suggested she'd made a mistake.* • *There's no need to get* **into** *a paddy.* • *I'd keep away from Dad this morning – he's* **in** *one of his paddies.*

pad·dy (field) /ˈpæd·i/ *n* [C] a field planted with rice growing in water • *Farmers often use water buffalo to help them in the paddy fields.*

pad·dy wag·on /ˈpæd·iˌwæg·ən/ *n* [C] *Am and Aus infml* a police vehicle with an enclosed back to carry prisoners in

pad·lock /£ˈpæd·lɒk, $-lɑːk/ *n* [C] a lock with a movable U-shaped bar fixed to a metal block, used to fasten two things or two parts of an object together. The bar is pushed into the block, and released with a key. • *You should buy a good padlock and always lock your bike to something secure, like a railing.* • PIC› **Locks and home security**

pad·lock *obj* /£ˈpæd·lɒk, $-lɑːk/ *v* [T] • *The box was securely padlocked* (= fastened with a padlock).

pad·re /£ˈpɑː·dreɪ, $-dri/ *n* [C] a Christian priest, esp. in the armed forces • *The service will be conducted by the RAF padre.* • *Good morning, Padre.* [as form of address]

pae·an /ˈpiː·ən/ *n* [C] *literary* a song, film or piece of writing that praises someone or something very enthusiastically • *The song is a paean* **to** *solitude and independence.*

pae·der·ast /£ˈped·ər·æst, £ˈpiː·dər, $ˈpiː·dɚ-/ *n* [C] *Br and Aus dated for* PEDERAST

pae·di·a·tri·cian *Br and Aus, Am and Aus* **pe·di·a·tri·cian** /ˌpiː·di·əˈtrɪʃ·ən/ *n* [C] a doctor who has special training in medical care for children

pae·di·at·ric *Br and Aus, Am and Aus* **pe·di·at·ric** /ˌpiː·diˈæt·rɪk/ *adj* [not gradable] • *paediatric medicine* • *a paediatric hospital*

pae·di·at·rics *Br and Aus* /ˌpiː·diː'æt·rɪks/, *Am and Aus* **pe·di·at·rics** *n* [U] • *She specializes in paediatrics.*

pae·do·phile, *esp. Am* **pe·do·phile** /£'piː·dəʊ·faɪl, $'ped·oʊ-/ *n* [C] a person, esp. a man, who is sexually interested in children • A **paedophile ring** is a group of people who take part in illegal sexual activity involving children.

pae·do·phil·i·a, *esp. Am* **pe·do·phil·ia** /£ˌpiː·dəʊ'fɪl·i·ə, $ˌped·oʊ'fiː·li-/ *n* [U]

pa·el·la /£paɪ'el·ə, $pɑː'jel-/ *n* a Spanish dish consisting of rice mixed with vegetables, fish and chicken • *Have you ever eaten paella?* [U] • *I've made a seafood paella for lunch.* [C]

pa·gan /'peɪ·gən/ *adj* belonging to a religion which worshipped many gods and which existed before the main world religions • *The Easter egg has both pagan and Christian origins.* • *Some altars to pagan gods still remain.* • *The pagan festival of Eostre was converted into the Christian festival of Easter, celebrating Christ's Resurrection.*

pa·gan /'peɪ·gən/ *n* [C] • A pagan is a person who has pagan beliefs: *Pagans thought that eclipses happened when a powerful witch hid the moon in a cave.* • A pagan is also a person who has no religious beliefs.

pa·gan·ism /'peɪ·gən·ɪ·zəm/ *n* [U]

page PAPER /peɪdʒ/ (*abbreviation* **p**) *n* [C] a side of one of the pieces of paper in a book, newspaper or magazine, usually with a number printed on it • *For details on how to enter the competition, see page 134.* • *The article appeared on the* **front** *page of the Guardian.* • *When I buy a newspaper, I always turn to the sports pages first.* • *(fig. literary) The signing of the peace treaty will be seen as a glorious page* (= important event) **in** *our country's history.* • A page is also one of the sheets of paper in a book, newspaper or magazine: *Some pages have been torn out of this book.* ○ *She sat idly flicking through the pages of a magazine.* • *(Br and Aus)* A **page three** girl is a young woman who is photographed with naked breasts for some popular newspapers. • *(dated infml)* A book that is a **page-turner** is one that is so exciting that you have to read it quickly: *Her latest novel is a real page-turner – I couldn't put it down.*

pag·i·na·tion /£ˌpædʒ·ɪ'neɪ·ʃən, $-ən'eɪ-/ *n* [U] *specialized* • The pagination of a book is the way in which its pages have been numbered.

page *obj* CALL /peɪdʒ/ *v* [T] to call (a person) using a LOUDSPEAKER (= an electric device for making sounds louder) in a public place, or using a small device electronic carried by that person, in order to give them a message • *He was paged at the airport over the public-address system and told to return home immediately.* • *As a young doctor, she was often paged in the middle of the night and asked to attend emergencies.*

pa·ger /£'peɪ·dʒər, $-dʒɚ/, *Am usually, Aus also* **beep·er** *n* [C] • A pager is a small device that you carry or wear, which makes a noise to tell you that someone wants you to telephone them: *Most doctors carry pagers with them so that they can quickly respond to emergencies.*

page BOY /peɪdʒ/ *n* [C] (in the past) a boy who worked as a servant for a KNIGHT and who was learning to become a knight • Compare PAGEBOY.

page·ant /'pædʒ·ənt/ *n* [C] a show, usually performed outside, that consists of people wearing traditional clothing and acting out historical events • *Our youngest son is taking part in the school pageant.* • A pageant is also any colourful and splendid show or ceremony: *She has competed in three* **beauty** *pageants* (= a competition in which women are judged for their physical attractiveness).

page·an·try /'pædʒ·ən·tri/ *n* [U] • Pageantry is splendid, colourful and very expensive ceremonies: *She loved the pageantry and tradition of the Royal Family.*

page·boy /'peɪdʒ·bɔɪ/ *n* [C] a young boy who is one of the people to go with the BRIDE (= the woman who is getting married) into the church • *The little pageboys were dressed in kilts and the bridesmaids in pink dresses.* • If you have your hair in a pageboy **(hairstyle)**, your hair is cut so that it is straight and the same length all around your head. • Compare PAGE BOY.

pa·go·da /£pə'gəʊ·də, $-'goʊ-/ *n* [C] a tall building used for religious worship in China and SE Asia. Each level has its own curved and decorated roof, usually with the largest roof nearest the ground.

paid PAY /peɪd/ *past simple and past participle of* PAY

paid GIVEN MONEY /peɪd/ *adj* being given money for something • *Are you looking for paid work* (= work for which you are given money) *or voluntary work?* • Paid is also used in combinations to refer to the amount of money which someone is given for their work: *The benefit scheme aims to help* **low-paid** *workers.* ○ *He has a* **well-paid** *job in the City.* • Paid leave/holiday is when your employers continue paying you money when you are not working: *I've got four weeks paid leave starting from next week.* • If someone is a **paid-up** member of an organization, they have paid the money necessary to be a member of that organization: *She's a paid-up member of the Labour party.* • A **paid-up** member of a group is also an enthusiastic member of that group.

pail /peɪl/ *n* [C] *esp. Am* a BUCKET • *Fill the pail with sand.* • *It took several pails of water* (= the amount a pail contains) *to put out the fire.*

pain /peɪn/ *n* (a feeling of) physical suffering caused by injury or illness, or emotional suffering • *The symptoms of the disease include abdominal pain and vomiting.* [U] • *Are you* **in** (= suffering from) *pain?* [U] • *These tablets should help to* **ease** *the pain.* [U] • *I felt a sharp pain* **in** *my foot and realized I had stepped on some glass.* [C] • *He's been suffering various* **aches and** *pains for years.* [C] • *The prisoners were subjected to unnecessary pain* **and suffering**. [U] • *They were shattered by their daughter's death – the pain of their loss will be with them for many years.* [U] • *The parents are still in great pain* **over** *the death of their child.* [U] • *It's a film about the pains* **and pleasures** *of parenthood.* [C] • *(infml)* If you describe a person or a situation as **a pain in the neck** or **a pain**, you think that it or they are very annoying: *It's such a pain having to go shopping.* ○ *That child is a pain in the neck.* • *(slang)* A person or thing that is **a pain in the backside**/*(Br and Aus also)* **arse**/*(Am also)* **butt/ass** is very annoying. • *(fml)* If you are instructed to do something **on/under pain of** a particular punishment, you will be punished in this way if you do not do it: *They were ordered never to return to their country on pain of* **death**. • LP> **Feelings and pains**

pain *obj* /peɪn/ *v* [T] *fml* • If something pains you, it causes you to feel sad and upset: *It pains me to have to say this, but you can no longer be trusted.*

pains /peɪnz/ *pl n* • If you are **at pains** to do something, you are very careful about doing it correctly: *She is at pains to point out how much work she has done.* • If you **take pains** or **go to great pains** to do something, you put a lot of effort into doing it: *The President took pains to emphasize his good health.* ○ *I went to great pains to select the best staff available.*

pained /peɪnd/ *adj* • If you look or sound pained, you show that you are upset or offended: *When I refused he adopted a pained expression.*

pain·ful /'peɪn·fəl/ *adj* • Something painful causes emotional or physical pain: *The old photograph brought back painful memories.* ○ *The latest murder is a painful reminder of the violence in the city.* ○ *A painful injury forced her to withdraw from the game.* • If something is painful to watch or listen to, it is so bad that it makes you feel embarrassed: *It was painful to listen to his pathetic excuses.*

pain·ful·ly /'peɪn·fəl·i/ *adv* • *Without surgery, this animal will die slowly and painfully* (= suffering pain). • Painfully is also used to emphasize a quality or situation that is unpleasant or not desirable: *I am painfully aware that I have made mistakes.* • Painfully is also used to describe an action which is done slowly and with great effort: *The old lady made her way painfully slowly towards the door.*

pain·less /'peɪn·ləs/ *adj* • Something painless causes no physical pain: *The laser treatment of eye injuries is simple and painless.* • Painless also refers to something that causes no problems: *Opponents of the war do not believe that it will be short and relatively painless.* ○ *There is no painless solution to this problem* (= Every way of solving the problem will upset someone).

pain·less·ly /'peɪn·lə·sli/ *adv* • *The laser beam heals the eye painlessly.*

pain·kil·ler /£'peɪŋˌkɪl·ər, $-ɚ/ *n* [C] a pill or other medicine used to reduce or remove physical pain • *If you've got a headache, there are some painkillers in the bathroom cabinet which might help.*

pain·kill·ing /'peɪŋˌkɪl·ɪŋ/ *adj* [not gradable] • *This tiny capsule contains two types of effective painkilling* **ingredients**.

pains·tak·ing /'peɪnzˌteɪ·kɪŋ/ *adj* extremely careful and correct, and using a lot of effort • *It took months of painstaking research to write the book.* • *He was described by his colleagues as a painstaking journalist.*

pains·tak·ing·ly /ˈpeɪnzˌteɪ·kɪŋ·li/ *adv* • *She painstakingly explained* (=She took a lot of care in explaining) *how the machine worked.*

paint /peɪnt/ *n* a coloured liquid that is put on a surface such as a wall to decorate it • *I need to buy a tin of white paint.* [U] • *Use a brush or roller to put the paint on the walls.* [U] • *The paint* (=layer of dry paint) *has been stripped from the doors.* [U] • *We used a* **gloss** *paint for the woodwork and a* **matt** *paint for the walls.* [C] • *There were so many paints* (=types of paint) *to choose from that I couldn't decide which to buy.* [C] • A **paint box** is a box containing paints for making pictures. • **Paint-stripper** is a liquid used to remove old paint from wooden surfaces: *We used paint-stripper to strip the doors and skirting boards.* ○ *This wine tastes like paint-stripper* (=It has a strong chemical taste)*!* • PIC› **Brush, Containers, Drawing and painting**

paint *(obj)* /peɪnt/ *v* • When you paint a surface, you cover it with paint: *The hall was painted yellow.* [T + obj + adj] ○ *He always listens to the radio while he paints.* [I] ○ *I'll need to paint* **over** (=cover with another layer of paint) *these dirty marks on the wall.* [M] • When you paint a picture, you make it using paints: *All these pictures were painted by local artists.* [T] ○ *She started to paint at the age of twenty.* [I] ○ *I enjoy painting my children* (=painting pictures of them). [T] • If someone paints their nails or face, they put make-up on that part of their body: *She painted her nails a bright red.* [T + obj + n] ○ *The woman behind the bar had a heavily painted face.* • If you **paint a picture** of something, you describe it in a very clear way: *The article paints a gloomy picture of the future.* • When you **paint a rosy/grim picture** of something, you mention only the good/bad things about it: *He painted a rosy picture of family life.* • If you **paint the town (red)**, you go out and enjoy yourself, often drinking a lot of alcohol, usually in order to celebrate something. • *"Paint your Wagon"* (title of a musical written by Alan Jay Lerner and Frederick Lowe, 1951)

paints /peɪnts/ *pl n* • Paints are tubes of paint or blocks of dried paint used for making pictures: *Brushes and paints will be provided by the art teacher.*

paint·er /£ˈpeɪn·təʳ, $-t̬ɚ/ *n* [C] • A painter is either a person who paints pictures, or someone whose job it is to paint parts of buildings, such as walls or doors: *Which painter do you prefer, Picasso or Braque?* ○ *George is a painter* **and decorator** *by trade.*

paint·ing /£ˈpeɪn·tɪŋ, $-t̬ɪŋ/ *n* • A painting is a picture made using paint: *The walls are covered in framed oil paintings and watercolours.* [C] ○ *It's an exhibition of 19th-century French painting* (=paintings produced by painters of this time). [U] • Painting is also the skill or activity of making a picture or putting paint on a wall: *We were taught painting and drawing at art college.* [U] ○ *When we bought the house, we had to do a lot of painting and redecoration.* [U]

paint·ball /£ˈpeɪnt·bɔːl, $-bɑːl/ *n* [U] a game in which people dress up in military clothing, go out into the countryside and attempt to shoot each other with guns that fire paint rather than bullets • *Do you want a game of paintball this weekend?*

paint·brush /ˈpeɪnt·brʌʃ/ *n* [C] a brush used for putting paint on a surface or on a picture • PIC› **Brush, Drawing and painting**

paint·work /£ˈpeɪnt·wɜːk, $-wɜːrk/ *n* [U] the covering of paint on a surface • *The car's paintwork has been scratched.*

pair /£peəʳ, $per/ *n* [C] two things of the same appearance and size that are intended to be used together, or something that consists of two parts joined together • *a pair* **of** *shoes/gloves* • *a pair* **of** *scissors/glasses* • *I can't find a matching pair of socks.* • *He packed two pairs of trousers and four shirts.* • *I'd like you to do this exercise* **in pairs** (=in groups of two). • Two people who are a pair have a relationship or are doing something together: *They seem a very happy pair.* ○ *What have you pair been up to?* • A pair of animals is two animals that produce young and stay together. *(specialized)* A pair of horses is two horses that pull a vehicle together: *a carriage and pair* • LP› **Two** PIC› **Match**

pair *(obj)* /£peəʳ, $per/ *v* • When two people pair **off** or are paired off, they form a group of two, esp. to begin a loving relationship: *All my friends seem to be pairing off and getting married.* [I] ○ *I managed to pair my best friend Sue off* **with** *Mike.* [M] • If you pair **up** with another person, you join together temporarily in order to do something: *Everyone should pair up for the next dance.* [I]

pais·ley /ˈpeɪz·li/ *adj* [before n; not gradable] having a pattern of curved coloured petal shapes, usually on cloth • *He wore a paisley tie with a checked shirt which looked very strange together.* • PIC› **Patterns**

PAIR

HANDS	**LEGS**	**FEET**
gloves*	briefs	boots*
handcuffs	jeans	sandals*
tools like:	knickers	shoes*
forceps	pants	slippers*
pliers	shorts	socks*
scissors	stockings*	trainers*
secateurs	tights	
shears	trousers	
tweezers	trunks	

EYES	**EARS**
binoculars	earrings*
glasses	headphones
(infml) shades (= sunglasses)	
spectacles	
(infml) specs	

* *these words can be used in the singular to refer to a single item.*

pa·ja·mas /£pɪˈdʒɑː·məz, $-ˈdʒæm·əz/ *pl n Am for* PYJAMAS • PIC› **Beds and bedroom**

Pak·i /ˈpæk·i/ *n* [C] *taboo disapproving* a person from Pakistan. This word is considered offensive.

pal /pæl/ *n* [C] *infml* a friend • *You're my* **best** *pal.* • *It's my* **old** *pal Pete!* • Pal is sometimes used when talking to a man who is annoying you: *Look, pal, you're asking for trouble.*

pal /pæl/ *v* **-ll-** *infml* • *(Am)* If you **pal around** with someone, you do things together as friends. • *(Br and Aus dated)* If you **pal up** with someone you become friends with them: *I've palled up* **with** *some people from work and we're going on holiday together.*

pal·ly /ˈpæl·i/ *adj infml* • If you are pally with someone, you are friendly with them: *They've become very pally* (**with** *each other*). ○ *Suddenly she started acting very pally* **towards** *me.*

pal·ace /ˈpæl·ɪs/ *n* [C] a large house that is the official home of a king, queen or other person of high rank • *Demonstrators gathered in front of the presidential palace.* • *The Queen has agreed to open Buckingham Palace to the public.* • The Palace is used when referring to the people who live in a palace: *The Palace has issued a statement criticizing the newspaper report.* • A **palace coup** or **palace revolution** is a situation in which a leader is removed from power by the people who have worked with him or her until then, but who now take control themselves: *A palace coup led by General Rodriguez has toppled the dictator.* • *(dated)* Palace is sometimes used in the names of large buildings, such as cinemas or places where people go dancing: *An old movie palace is being restored.*

pa·la·tial /pəˈleɪ·ʃəl/ *adj* • A palatial house is one that is very large and splendid: *The magazine showed lavish pictures of their palatial country residence.*

pa·lae·o·lith·ic, pa·le·o·lith·ic /£ˌpæl·i·əʊˈlɪθ·ɪk, $ˌpeɪ·li·oʊ-/ *adj* [not gradable] belonging to the period when humans used tools and weapons made of stone • *The museum has palaeolithic tools made 200 000 years ago.* • *The Palaeolithic* **Period** *is sometimes called the Old Stone Age.* • Compare NEOLITHIC.

pa·lae·on·tol·o·gy, pa·le·on·tol·o·gy /£ˌpæl·i·ɒnˈtɒl·ə·dʒi, $ˌpeɪ·li·ɑːnˈtɑː·lə-/ *n* [U] the study of FOSSILS (=preserved bones or shells) as a way of getting information about the history of animals and plants and the structure of rocks

pa·lae·on·tol·o·gist, pa·le·on·tol·og·ist /£ˌpæl·i·ɒnˈtɒl·ə·dʒɪst, $ˌpeɪ·li·ɑːnˈtɑː·lə-/ *n* [C]

pal·a·mi·no /£ˌpæl·əˈmiː·nəʊ, $-noʊ/ *n* [C] *pl* **palaminos** PALOMINO

pal·ate /ˈpæl·ət/ *n* [C] the top part of the inside of your mouth • *The disease causes ulcers to appear on the tongue and palate and leads to lack of appetite.* • *This is an elegant wine with blackcurrant flavours on the palate* (=you can taste these when you drink it). • A person's palate is their ability to taste and judge good food and wine: *These are* *wines to suit the most* **discriminating** *of palates.* ○ *For less adventurous palates* (= For people who like simpler food), *the restaurant also serves burgers and roast chicken.*

pal·at·a·ble /£'pæl·ə·tə·bl̩, $-t̬ə-/ *adj* • Food or drink that is palatable can be eaten or drunk: *The meal was barely palatable – in fact, I thought it was disgusting.* • Something that is palatable is acceptable: *I'm afraid the members won't find all these changes very palatable.*

pa·la·ti·al /pə'leɪ·ʃᵊl/ *adj* See at PALACE

pa·la·ver /£pə'lɑː·vəʳ, $-'læv·ɚ/ *n* [U] *infml* unnecessary inconvenience and trouble • *I'll have to write these letters by hand and deliver them – what a palaver!* • *Do you remember all the fuss and palaver when Guy thought he had lost his passport?*

pale /peɪl/ *adj* **-r, -st** (of a person's face) having less colour than usual, or (of a colour or light) not bright or strong • *You're looking pale – do you feel ill?* • *Becky was looking sickly pale.* • *She has a naturally pale complexion and dark hair.* • *If you have pale skin, you must be careful not to lie in the sun for too long.* • *She wore a pale blue hat.* • **Pale ale** is a type of beer that does not contain much alcohol and is often sold in bottles. • If something is a **pale imitation** of something else, it is not as good as that thing: *Modern luxury ships are a pale imitation of the glamour and style of the early ocean liners.*

pale /peɪl/ *v* [I] • If a person's face pales, it loses its usual colour: *His face paled and he looked as if he might faint.* • If something **pales in comparison with** or **pales beside** something else, it seems less good, important or attractive when it is compared to that other thing: *It's an interesting book, but it pales in comparison with Webster's treatment of the subject.* • If something **pales into insignificance**, it seems completely unimportant when compared to something else: *Everything else that happened in my life pales into insignificance beside that one event.*

pale·ness /'peɪl·nəs/ *n* [U]

pa·lish /'peɪ·lɪʃ/ *adj* [not gradable] • *The sky was a palish* (= quite pale) *blue.*

pale·face /'peɪl·feɪs/ *n* [C] *disapproving* (said to have been used by Native Americans) a white person

pa·le·on·tol·o·gy /£,pæl·i·ən'tɒl·ə·dʒi, $-'tɑː·lə-/ *n* [U] PALAEONTOLOGY

pal·ette /'pæl·ət/ *n* [C] a thin board on which a person painting a picture mixes their paints before putting them on to the picture. It usually has rounded edges and a hole through which you put your thumb in order to hold it while you paint. • *She mixes her colours on the canvas rather than on the palette.* • *(specialized)* A palette is also the range of colours that an artist usually paints with: *Matisse's palette typically consists of bright blues, greens and oranges.* • A **palette knife** is a knife with a wide thin blade, a rounded end and no sharp edge, used to mix paints together and also to spread soft substances when cooking. • PIC **Drawing and painting, Knife**

pal·in·drome /£'pæl·ɪn·drəʊm, $-droʊm/ *n* [C] a word or group of words that is the same whether you read it from the beginning or backwards • *"Refer" and "level" are palindromes.* • *"Straw? No, too stupid a fad. I put soot on warts" is also a palindrome.*

pa·ling /'peɪ·lɪŋ/ *n* [C], *Br and Aus usually* **pa·lings** *pl n* a fence made from long thin pieces of wood • *He has just put up a paling around the house.*

pal·is·ade /£,pæl·ɪ'seɪd, $'—/ *n* [C] a strong fence made out of wooden or iron poles that is used to protect people or a place from being attacked

pal·is·ades /£,pæl·ɪ'seɪdz, $'—/ *pl n Am* a line of cliffs by the sea or a river • *From the Palisades in New Jersey you get a spectacular view of the New York skyline.*

pall BECOME BORING /£pɔːl, $pɑːl/ *v* [I] to become less interesting or enjoyable • *The pleasure of not having to work quickly palled.*

pall CLOUD /£pɔːl, $pɑːl/ *n* [C] a thick dark cloud of smoke • *A poisonous pall of smog hung over the town.* • *Palls of smoke obscured our view.* • *(fig.) The bad news* **cast** *a* **pall over** *the evening* (= caused a feeling of sadness).

pall CLOTH /£pɔːl, $pɑːl/ *n* [C] a cloth used to cover a COFFIN (= a box that holds a dead body) at a funeral, or *(Am)* the coffin itself at a funeral

pall·bear·er /£'pɔːl,beə·rəʳ, $'pɑːl,ber·ɚ/ *n* [C] a person who helps to carry a COFFIN (= a box that holds a dead body) at a funeral or who walks beside the people carrying it

pal·let /'pæl·ɪt/ *n* [C] a flat wooden structure onto which heavy goods are loaded so that they can be moved using a **fork-lift truck** (= a small vehicle with two strong bars of metal on the front which is used for lifting heavy goods) • ⓘ

pal·li·a·tive /£'pæl·i·ə·tɪv, $-t̬ɪv/ *adj* [not gradable], *n* [C] *specialized* (being) a drug or medical treatment that reduces pain without curing the illness itself • *The hospital offers palliative chemotherapy for advanced cases of cancer.* • *The doctor prescribed her a palliative that eased the pain, but prolonged the illness.* • *(fml)* A palliative is also something that makes a problem seem less serious but does not solve the problem or make it disappear: *We want long-term solutions, not short-term palliatives.* ○ *When she was depressed, she turned to food as a palliative.*

pal·lid /'pæl·ɪd/ *adj* very pale, in a way that looks unattractive and unhealthy • *Next to his tanned face, hers seemed pallid and unhealthy.* • If something is pallid, it lacks enthusiasm or excitement: *This is a pallid production of what should be a great ballet.*

pal·lor /£'pæl·əʳ, $-ɚ/ *n* [U] • Pallor is the state of being very pale: *The* **deathly** *pallor of her skin was frightening.*

pal·ly /'pæl·i/ *adj* See at PAL

palm /pɑːm/ *n* [C] the inside part of your hand from your wrist to the base of your fingers • *Your fingers bend towards your palm.* • *She was so nervous that her palms were all cold and sweaty.* • *This tiny mini-disc fits into* **the** *palm* **of** *your* **hand**. • When someone **reads** your palm, they look at the lines on the inside of your hand and tell you what these lines say about your character and your future. • If you have someone **in the palm of** your **hand** or have them **eating out of the palm of** your **hand**, you have complete control over them and can make them do anything you want them to: *He's got his boss eating out of the palm of his hand.* • PIC **Body**

palm *obj* /pɑːm/ *v* [T] • If you palm something, you make it seem to disappear by hiding it in the palm of your hand as part of a trick, or you steal it by picking it up in a way that will not be noticed: *I suspected that he had palmed a playing card.*

palm off *obj*, **palm** *obj* **off** *v adv* [M] to persuade someone to accept (something) because you do not want it and it has no value • *She tried to palm her old car off* **on** *me.* • *The dealer tried to palm the painting off* **as** *a genuine Picasso, but I knew it was a fake.* • If you palm someone off **with** something, you tell them something or give them something in order to make them go away: *You're not going to palm me off with that excuse.* ○ *They tried to palm her off with a cheap bottle of wine instead of paying her for the work.*

palm (tree) /pɑːm/ *n* [C] a tree that grows in hot countries and has a tall trunk without branches, with a mass of long pointed leaves at the top • *date palms* • *palm fronds* • *Coconuts grow on some types of palm.* • *The island has long golden beaches fringed by palm trees.* • **Palm oil** is an oil obtained from the nuts of some types of palm, used in some foods and to make soap. • **Palm Sunday** is the Sunday before Easter in the Christian year. • PIC **Tree**

pal·mist /'pɑː·mɪst/ *n* [C] a person who looks at the lines on the inside of your hand and tells you what these lines say about your character and your future

pal·mist·ry /'pɑː·mɪ·stri/ *n* [U] • Palmistry is the skill and activity of looking at the lines on the inside of people's hands and claiming to be able to see signs about their character and future.

palm·top /£'pɑːm·tɒp, $-tɑːp/ *n* [C] a type of computer which is small enough to be able to fit in your hand • *There are several palmtops available on the market.* • *Some people say that the palmtop will replace the laptop computer, but others think that the palmtop is too small and fiddly to use.*

pal·o·mi·no /£,pæl·ə'miː·nəʊ, $-noʊ/, **pal·a·mi·no** *n* [C] *pl* **palominos** a horse that is golden in colour with a white MANE (= neck hair) and tail

pal·pa·ble /'pæl·pə·bl̩/ *adj* so obvious that it can easily be seen or known, or (of a feeling) so strong that it seems as if it can be touched or physically felt • *The letters of protest have already had a palpable effect.* • *Her relief and happiness was palpable.* • *There was a palpable tension between the two groups.* • *The sense of excitement among the crowd was almost palpable.*

pal·pa·bly /'pæl·pə·bli/ *adv* • *The system was palpably* (= very obviously) *unfair.*

pal·pi·tate /£'pæl·pɪ·teɪt, $-pə-/ *v* [I] (of the heart) to beat very fast and irregularly • *My heart was palpitating* **with** *joy.*

pal·pi·ta·tions /£,pæl·pɪ'teɪ·ʃᵊnz, $-pə-/ *pl n* • *He ended up in hospital with heart palpitations* (= irregular beating of the heart). • *(humorous)* If someone has palpitations, they are very shocked: *My mother will have palpitations when she sees the new wallpaper.*

pal·try /£ˈpɔːl·tri, $ˈpɑːl-/ *adj* **-ier, -iest** (of a sum of money) very small and of little or no value • *Student grants these days are paltry, and many students have to take out loans.* • *The company offered Jeremy a paltry* **sum** *which he refused.* • Paltry also means low in quality: *The content of the programme is paltry and TV viewers have complained.*

pam·pas /ˈpæm·pəs/ *n* [U + sing/pl v] the large flat areas of grassy land in parts of S America • *The Argentinian pampas is among the most fertile lands in the world.* • **Pampas grass** is tall grass with silver-coloured flowers.

pam·per *obj* /£ˈpæm·pəʳ, $-pɚ/ *v* [T] to treat (a person or animal) with too much kindness and attention and give them too many things • *She pampers her dog* **with** *the finest fillet steak and cashmere blankets.* • *Why not pamper yourself* (= treat yourself well) **with** *a hot bath scented with oils?*

pam·pered /£ˈpæm·pəd, $-pɚd/ *adj* • *He was a pampered rich kid who was driven to school in a limousine.*

pam·phlet /ˈpæm·flət/ *n* [C] a thin book with only a few pages which gives information or an opinion about something • *I picked up a free pamphlet on places to visit in the region.* • *He was written a pamphlet denouncing the government's education bill.* • (CS) (E) (RUS)

pan CONTAINER /pæn/ *n* [C] a metal container that is round and often has a long handle and a lid, used for cooking things on top of a cooker, or *(esp. Am)* a metal container used for cooking things inside the cooker • *Heat the milk in a small pan.* • *This dishwasher even washes* **pots and pans** (= different types of pan). • To **pan-fry** food is to cook it in a very small amount of oil or fat: *We had pan-fried lobster for dinner.* • A **pan scourer** is a **scourer**. See at SCOUR CLEAN. • See also SAUCEPAN. • (J)

pan *obj* /pæn/ *v* [T] **-nn-** *esp. Am* • To pan food is to cook it in a pan.

pan TOILET /pæn/ *n* [C] *Br* the bowl-shaped part of a toilet • *(slang)* If something **goes down the pan**, it is lost or destroyed because it is no longer valued: *We don't want to see our business go down the pan.* • PIC> **Pan** (J)

pan MOVE SLOWLY /pæn/ *v* [I] **-nn-** (of a film camera) to move slowly from one side to another or up and down • *In the first scene, the camera pans slowly* **across** *the room.* • (J)

pan *obj* CRITICIZE /pæn/ *v* [T] **-nn-** *infml* to criticize (something) severely • *The critics panned the film version of the novel.* • (J)

pan– INCLUDING /pæn-/ *combining form* including or relating to all the places or people in a particular group • *a pan-American conference* • *a pan-European summit* • *the Pan-African Congress*

pan out *v adv* [I] *infml* to develop or be successful • *We'll have to see how things pan out.* • *Their attempt to start a new business didn't pan out.*

pan·a·ce·a /ˌpæn·əˈsiː·ə/ *n* [C] *esp. disapproving* something that will solve all problems or cure all illnesses • *So many politicians are desperate to find a quick panacea.* • *Technology is not a panacea* **for** *all our problems.* • *She warned that the drug is not a panacea and only kills some of the bacteria.*

pa·nache /pəˈnæʃ/ *n* [U] a stylish, original and very confident way of doing things • *The solo passages were played with great panache.*

pan·a·ma (hat) /ˈpæn·ə·mɑː/ *n* [C] a pale-coloured hat, worn esp. by men, that is woven from dried plant leaves • *In summer all the men wear panamas.*

pan·a·tel·la /ˌpæn·əˈtel·ə/ *n* [C] a long thin CIGAR (= a stick of rolled tobacco leaves that is smoked)

pan·cake /ˈpæŋ·keɪk/, **crepe** *n* [C] a thin flat usually round cake made from a mixture of flour, milk and egg that is fried on both sides • *Do you want a sweet pancake or a savoury one?* • *In America, pancakes are smaller and thicker than in Britain and are usually eaten for breakfast.* • **Pancake Day** is *esp. Br infml for* SHROVE TUESDAY (= the day before Lent starts, when pancakes are traditionally eaten). • A **pancake landing** is when an aircraft lands without using its wheels by dropping onto the ground from a low height, because it has a problem and cannot continue to fly. • LP> **Holidays**

pan·cre·as /ˈpæŋ·kri·əs/ *n* [C] an organ in the body that produces INSULIN (= a chemical substance that controls the amount of sugar in the blood) and substances which help to digest food so that it can be used by the body

pan·cre·a·tic /£ˌpæŋ·kriˈæt·ɪk, $-ˈæt̬-/ *adj* [not gradable] • *pancreatic cancer*

pan·da /ˈpæn·də/, **gi·ant pan·da** *n* [C] *pl* **pandas** or **panda** a large black and white mammal similar to a bear, that lives in forests in China and eats BAMBOO (= stems of a tropical grass)

pan·de·mic /pænˈdem·ɪk/ *adj specialized* (of a disease) existing in almost all of an area or in almost all of a group of people, animals or plants • *In some parts of the world malaria is still pandemic.* • *(fig.) a pandemic sense of hopelessness*

pan·de·mic /pænˈdem·ɪk/ *n* [C] *specialized* • *a pandemic* **of** *influenza* • *an influenza pandemic* • *(fig.) a pandemic* **of** *corruption*

pan·de·mo·ni·um /£ˌpæn·dəˈməʊ·ni·əm, $-ˈmoʊ-/ *n* [U] a state of extremely noisy confusion, produced among a group of people who have been very shocked and made esp. angry or frightened by something • *Pandemonium reigned in the hall as the unbelievable election results were read out.* • *(fig.) the pandemonium* (= loud noise) *of the school playground*

pan·der to *obj* /£ˈpæn·də, $-dɚ/ *v prep* [T] *disapproving* to do or provide exactly what someone wants, esp. when it is not acceptable, reasonable or approved of, usually in order to get some personal advantage • *It's not good the way she panders to his every whim.* • *Political leaders almost inevitably pander to big business.*

Pan·do·ra's box /£ˌpænˈdɔː·rəz-, $-ˈdɔːr·əz/ *n* [U] **Pandora's box** something that creates many new and unexpected problems • *Abolishing the regulations on financial dealing was like* **opening (up)** (= causing) *Pandora's box – it was chaos.*

P&P /ˌpiː·ᵊndˈpiː/ *n* [U] *Br abbreviation for* **postage and packing** (= the cost of wrapping something and sending it by post) • *The books cost £12·50 plus P&P.*

pane /peɪn/ *n* [C] a flat piece of glass, used in a window or door • *Have you noticed that one of the (window) panes is cracked?* • PIC> **Window**

pan·e·gyr·ic /ˌpæn·əˈdʒɪr·ɪk/ *n* [C] *fml* a speech or piece of writing that praises someone greatly and does not mention anything bad about them • *She delivered a panegyric* **on** *the President-elect.*

pan·el TEAM /ˈpæn·ᵊl/ *n* [C + sing/pl v] a small group of people chosen to give advice, make a decision, or publicly discuss their opinions as entertainment • *The competition will be judged by a panel* **of** *experts.* • *It's a radio show, where the panel get asked their opinion on the week's news and arts events.* • (RUS)

pan·el·list, *Am usually, Aus also* **pan·el·ist** /ˈpæn·ᵊl·ɪst/ *n* [C] • *Panellists on the Arts Review Board serve for a maximum of three years.* • *On tonight's Super Quiz we have panellists from all over Europe.*

pan·el PART /ˈpæn·ᵊl/ *n* [C] an esp. flat rectangular part, or piece of wood, metal, cloth, etc., that fits into or onto something larger • *a beautiful old door with oak panels* •

The car's left side panel had to be replaced after the crash. • *White silk panels were inset into the sides of the dress.* • *At the bottom of each page is a panel with grammatical information.* • (RUS)

pan·el *obj* /ˈpæn·ᵊl/ *v* [T] **-ll-** or *Am usually* **-l-** • *The walls of the dining hall were panelled* **in** *oak.* • *a panelled room/wall/door*

pan·ell·ing, *Am usually* **pan·el·ing** /ˈpæn·ᵊl·ɪŋ/ *n* [U] • *The house has many original features including oak doors and panelling.*

pan·el CONTROL BOARD /ˈpæn·ᵊl/ *n* [C] a board or surface which has controls and other devices on it for operating esp. an aircraft or a large machine • *There were dials and switches and flashing lights all over the* **control/instrument** *panel.* • (RUS)

pan·et·tone /£ˌpæn·əˈtəʊ·ni, $-ɪˈtoʊ-/ *n* [C/U] an Italian Christmas cake containing dried fruit and nuts

pang /pæŋ/ *n* [C] a sudden sharp feeling, esp. of painful emotion • *Thinking about her spending the day with another man gave him a sharp pang* **of** *jealousy.* • *Not eating for a week was hard, but the* **hunger** *pangs had to be ignored and endured.*

pan·hand·le AREA /ˈpænˌhæn·dl̩/ *n* [C] *Am* a long thin piece of land joined to a larger area • *the Alaskan panhandle in the US*

pan·hand·le *(obj)* ASK /ˈpænˌhæn·dl̩/ *v Am infml* to ask for money, esp. in a public place; to BEG • *We watched several people panhandling.* [I] • *She panhandled nickels and dimes from business executives on their way to lunch.* [T]

pan·ic /ˈpæn·ɪk/ *n* (a) sudden very strong feeling of anxiety and/or fear that prevents reasonable thought and action • *Panic* **spread** *through the crowd as the bullets started to fly.* [U] • *He* **got in(to)** *a panic that he would forget his lines on stage.* [C] • *(Am slang)* If something or someone is **a panic**, they are extremely amusing: *Zero Mostel was hysterically funny in some of his films, a real panic.* [C] • A **panic attack** is a sudden period of deep anxiety: *I've never been in an aeroplane since I had that panic attack when we flew to Spain.* • A **panic button** is a device, usually a button, that is used to call for help by someone in a dangerous situation: *The receptionist hit/pressed/pushed the panic button on her desk when the gunman came into the building.* ○ *(fig. esp. Am and Aus infml) As soon as the shares dropped below 40 cents, stockbrokers all over the country hit/pressed/pushed the panic button* (= reacted in an extreme way). • **Panic buying** is when many people suddenly try to buy as much food, fuel, etc. as they can because they are frightened about something bad such as a war that is going to happen soon: *Panic buying of basic foodstuffs set in this morning as the government announced a 300% increase in prices.* • **Panic selling** is when many people suddenly start to sell company shares that they own, because their value is being reduced: *There has been a* **wave** *of panic selling of US securities by people rushing to put their money into a stronger currency.* • *(Br) Two weeks before an exam it's always* **panic stations** (= an anxious time when something must be done quickly) *as I realise how much I still have to do.* • *The streets were full of* **panic-stricken** (= very frightened and anxious) *people running in every direction, trying to escape the soldiers and the tanks.*

pan·ic *(obj)* /ˈpæn·ɪk/ *v* **panicking**, *past* **panicked** • *Don't panic! Everything will be okay.* [I] • *The boss always panics* **over/about** *the budget every month.* [I] • *Rumours of war panicked many investors* **into** *selling their shares* (= caused them to do it quickly and without careful thought). [T]

pa·ni·cky /ˈpæn·ɪ·ki/ *adj infml* • *a panicky feeling/expression/action* • *Is he the panicky type?*

pan·ni·er /£ˈpæn·i·əʳ, $ˈ-jɚ/ *n* [C] a bag or similar container, esp. one of a pair that hang on either side of a bicycle, motorcycle, or animal such as a horse or DONKEY • PIC› **Bicycles**

pan·o·ply /ˈpæn·ə·pli/ *n* [U] *fml* a wide range or collection of different things • *There is a whole panoply* **of** *remedies and drugs available to the modern doctor.* • *200 million people watched on television as the couple were married with the full panoply* **of** *royal ceremony – trumpeters and bishops and lords and ladies in their splendid clothes.*

pan·o·ram·a /£ˌpæn·ᵊrˈɑː·mə, $-əˈræm·ə/ *n* [C] a view of a wide area • *From the hotel roof you can enjoy a panorama of the whole city.* • *(fig.) The investigation revealed a panorama of corruption and illegal dealings.*

pan·o·ram·ic /£ˌpæn·ᵊrˈæm·ɪk, $-əˈræm-/ *adj* • *a wonderful panoramic* **view** *of the countryside*

pan·pipes /ˈpæm·paɪps/ *pl n* a musical instrument made of short tubes of different lengths joined together, which you play by blowing across the open ends

pan·sy PLANT /ˈpæn·zi/ *n* [C] a small garden plant with flowers of many different colours which have rounded petals • PIC› **Flowers and plants**

pan·sy PERSON /ˈpæn·zi/ *n* [C] *dated* a man who behaves in a way that is considered to be more typical of a woman. Some people find this word offensive.

pant *(obj)* /pænt/ *v* to breathe quickly and loudly through your mouth usually because you have been doing something very energetic • *We ran up the hill and arrived at the top panting and covered in sweat.* [I] • *A young girl ran up to us. "They're coming. They're coming now," she panted* (= said while panting). [T] • *"As pants the hart for cooling streams / When heated in the chase"* (*New Versions of the Psalms* by Nahum Tate, 1652-1715)

pan·the·i·sm /ˈpænt·θi·ɪ·zᵊm/ *n* [U] belief in many or all gods, or the belief that God exists in and is the same as all things, animals and people within the universe

pan·the·ist /ˈpænt·θi·ɪst/ *n* [C], *adj* [not gradable]

pan·the·is·tic /ˌpænt·θiˈɪs·tɪk/, **pan·the·ist** /ˈpænt·θi·ɪst/ *adj* [not gradable]

pan·the·on /£ˈpænt·θi·ən, $-ɑːn/ *n* [C usually sing] *fml* a small group of people who are the most famous, important and admired in their particular area of activity • *Don't you agree that Malcolm X definitely has a place in* **the pantheon of** *black civil rights heroes?*

pan·ther /£ˈpænt·θəʳ, $-θɚ/ *n* [C] *pl* **panthers** or **panther** a black LEOPARD (= large wild cat) or *(Am also)* a COUGAR • PIC› **Cats**

pan·ties /£ˈpæn·tiz, $-t̬iz/, *Br also* **pants** *pl n* a short piece of underwear worn below the waist by women and girls; KNICKERS • (E)

pant·ing /£ˈpæn·tɪŋ, $-t̬ɪŋ/ *adj* very eager to do something • *There was the usual crowd of photographers waiting for her – all panting* **to** *get that perfect photo.* [+ to infinitive] • *The newspapers are panting* **for/after** *details of the scandal.*

pan·to·mime /£ˈpæn·tə·maɪm, $-t̬ə-/, *infml* **pan·to** (*pl* **pantos**) /£ˈpæn·təʊ, $-t̬oʊ/ *n* (in Britain) an amusing musical play based on traditional children's stories, performed esp. at Christmas • Pantomime is also used to mean MIME (= showing meaning with movement rather than speech): *It's an evening of music, drama and pantomime.* [U] ○ *She did a pantomime of putting a key in the lock and finally the guy understood that she wanted her room key.* [C] • *(Br)* A **pantomime horse** is two people pretending humorously to be a horse by dressing in special clothes and standing one behind the other so that the front person appears as the horse's front half and the person behind forms the back part. • (CS) (DK) (PL) (RUS)

pan·try /ˈpæn·tri/ *n* [C] a small room or large cupboard in a house where food is kept; LARDER

pants /pænts/ *pl n Br* a short piece of underwear worn below the waist; UNDERPANTS; KNICKERS • *a pair of pants* • *The boy was so scared he* **wet his pants** (= urinated in his clothes). • *(taboo slang) She* **pissed/shit** *her* **pants** (= felt suddenly very frightened) *when all the lights went out.* • Pants are *Am for* TROUSERS. • To scare, frighten, bore, etc. **the pants off** someone is to scare, frighten, bore, etc. them very much: *The way you drive* **scares** *the pants off me!*

pant·suit /£ˈpænt·sjuːt, $-suːt/ *n* [C] *Am for* **trouser suit**, see at TROUSERS

pan·ty·hose /£ˈpæn·ti·həʊz, $-t̬i·hoʊz/ *pl n Am and Aus for* TIGHTS

pan·ty lin·er /£ˈpæn·ti, $-t̬i/ *n* [C] a small length of absorbent material which can be stuck to the inside of a woman's underwear esp. during her PERIOD (= monthly flow of blood from the womb)

pap FOOD /pæp/ *n* [U] *esp. disapproving* soft, almost liquid, food suitable for babies or people who are ill

pap WORTHLESS ENTERTAINMENT /pæp/ *n* [U] *infml disapproving* entertainment or information such as television programmes, books, etc. that are considered to be worthless because they do not contain anything original or interesting • *The romantic fiction you buy at airports is just pap.*

pap·py /ˈpæp·i/ *adj infml disapproving* • *It's just another pappy novel.*

pap·a /£pəˈpɑː, $ˈpɑː·pə/ *n* [C] *Br fml dated or Am infml* father • *"Why is the sky blue, Papa?" she asked.* [as form of address] • LP› **Titles and forms of address**

pa·pa·cy /ˈpeɪ·pə·si/ *n* [U] the position or authority of the POPE (= leader of the Roman Catholic Church), or the length of time that a particular person is pope

pa·pal /ˈpeɪ·pᵊl/ *adj* [not gradable] • *a papal messenger/announcement/election*

pap·a·raz·zi /£ˌpæp·ᵊrˈæt·si, $ˌpɑː·pɑːˈrɑːt·si/ *pl n* the photographers who follow famous people everywhere they go in order to take photographs of them for newspapers and magazines

pa·pa·ya /pəˈpaɪ·ə/, **paw·paw** *n* [C] a large oval fruit with a yellowish skin and sweet orange flesh, or the tropical tree on which this grows • PIC> **Fruit**

pa·per /£ˈpeɪ·pəʳ, $-ɚ/ *n* a thin flat material made from crushed wood and/or cloth used esp. for writing, printing or drawing on • *a* **piece/sheet of** *paper* • *a packet of* **writing** *paper* (= for writing letters to other people) [U] • *Dictionaries are usually printed on thin paper.* [U] • *a paper bag* • *a paper towel* • *This card is printed on* **recycled** *paper* (= paper made from used paper). [U] • A paper is also a newspaper: *a daily/weekly/local/national paper* [C] ○ *The news was on the front page of all the papers.* [C] • *(Br and Aus)* A paper is also a set of printed questions that is used as (part of) an exam: *Candidates must answer two questions from each paper.* [C] ○ *The geography paper is not till next week.* [C] • A paper is also a piece of writing on a particular subject written by an expert in that subject and usually published in a book or JOURNAL (= serious magazine) or read aloud to other people: *He's* **giving** *a paper* **on** *thermodynamics at a conference at Manchester University.* [C] • Paper is also *Am for* ESSAY: *Ms Jones thought my history paper was terrific.* [C] • Paper is also short for WALLPAPER (= paper used for covering the inside walls of a room) : *I think (a) pretty flower-pattern paper might look nice in the children's bedroom.* [C/U] • *Get the idea* **down on** *paper* (= write it) *before you forget it.* [U] • *She works* **on** *paper* (= writes things on paper) *because she hates computers.* [U] • *The design looks good* **on paper** (= as an idea) *but would a real machine actually work?* • **On paper** (= from his accounts) *he's very rich, but he never has any money!* • *Several candidates looked good* **on paper** (= had good qualifications) *but failed the interview.* • A **paper clip** is a small piece of bent wire used for holding pieces of paper together. • A **paper knife** (also *esp. Am* **letter opener**) is a type of knife used esp. to open envelopes. • **Paper money** is money in paper form, rather than coins. • A **paper profit** is one that is shown in financial records but which has not yet been made by the company, esp. because they are waiting for payments they are owed: *The company made a paper profit last year, but they still got rid of six staff.* • A *(Br)* **paper round**/*(Am)* **paper route** is a job, usually done by children, delivering newspapers to people's homes. • A **paper shop** is a shop which sells newspapers: *I'm just popping down to the paper shop, I won't be long.* • If something is **paper thin** it is very thin: *paper thin layers of pastry* • *paper thin walls* • *(disapproving)* A **paper tiger** is something, such as an enemy or foreign country, that seems very strong and very dangerous, but is really weak and harmless: *The Soviet Union was suddenly revealed as a paper tiger.* • *He was easy to find, he left a* **paper trail** (= documents that showed a record of his activities) *a mile wide.* • *"All reactionaries are paper tigers"* (Mao Tse-Tung, 1946) • PIC> **Bags, Knife, Stationery**

pa·per *obj* /£ˈpeɪ·pəʳ, $-ɚ/ *v* [T] • To paper a wall is to cover it with WALLPAPER. • If you paper **over** a disagreement or difficulty or **paper over the cracks** you hide the unpleasant facts and try to make people believe that there is no problem: *He tried to paper over the country's deep-seated problems.* ○ *They have papered over many of the disagreements between the two countries.* ○ *They asked for real justice, no papering over the cracks so that important people were not embarrassed.*

pa·pers /£ˈpeɪ·pəz, $-pɚz/ *pl n* • Papers are official documents, esp. ones that show who you are: *The border guards stopped me and asked to see my papers.*

pa·pe·ry /£ˈpeɪ·pᵊr·i, $-pɚ·i/ *adj* • Something which is papery is thin and dry like paper: *The skin on his hands was wrinkled and papery.*

pa·per·back /£ˈpeɪ·pə·bæk, $-pɚ-/ *n* [C] a book with a cover made of thin card • *I'll buy some paperbacks at the airport.* • *She'd much rather buy hardbacks than paperbacks.* • *It will be published* **in paperback** (= as a paperback) *in March.* • Compare HARDBACK; SOFTBACK.

pa·per·bark /£ˈpeɪ·pə·bɑːk, $-pɚ·bɑːrk/ *n* [C] *Aus* a MELALEUCA (= type of tree)

pa·per·weight /£ˈpeɪ·pə·weɪt, $-pɚ-/ *n* [C] a small heavy object which is put on top of pieces of paper to keep them in position

pa·per·work /£ˈpeɪ·pə·wɜːk, $-pɚ·wɜːrk/ *n* [U] the part of a job which involves writing letters and reports and keeping records and is usually considered to be less interesting or important

pa·pier-mâch·é /£ˌpæp·i·eɪˈmæʃ·eɪ, $ˌ---ˈ-/ *n* [U] pieces of paper mixed with glue or with flour and water and used to make decorative objects or models • *a papier-mâché mask* • *a tray made out of papier-mâché and painted gold and black*

pap·ist /ˈpeɪ·pɪst/ *n* [C], *adj* [not gradable] *disapproving* (a) Roman Catholic

pa·poose /£pəˈpuːs, $pæpˈuːs/ *n* [C] *dated* a **Native American** baby or small child

pap·py /ˈpæp·i/ *adj* See at PAP WORTHLESS ENTERTAINMENT

pap·ri·ka /ˈpæp·rɪ·kə, pəˈpriː-/ *n* [U] a red powder used as a spice to give a slightly hot flavour to food, esp. in meat dishes • *Paprika is an essential ingredient in that Hungarian speciality, goulash.*

Pap smear /pæp/ *n* [C] *Am and Aus for* a **smear test**, see at SMEAR SPREAD

pa·py·rus /£pəˈpaɪə·rəs, $-ˈpaɪ-/ *n pl* **papyruses** or **papyri** /£pəˈpaɪə·raɪ, $-ˈpaɪ-/ a tall grass-like plant that grows in or near water, esp. in North Africa, or a type of or piece of paper made from this plant, esp. in the ancient past by Egyptians • *an ancient papyrus with a list of names on it* [C] • *At the pyramids tourists can buy pictures of ancient Egyptian gods* **on** *papyrus.* [U]

par EQUAL /£pɑːʳ, $pɑːr/ *n* [U] **on a par (with)** equal to or similar to • *In my opinion none of the new jazz trumpeters are on a par with* (= as good as) *the great figures of the 1960s.* • *In the eyes of the law these two offences are on a par with* (= as bad as) *each other.* • You describe something as **par excellence** when it is the best example of its type: *Bombay is a film town par excellence with studios that turn out hundreds of films a year in several different languages.*

par STANDARD /£pɑːʳ, $pɑːr/ *n* [U] the usual standard or condition • If you feel or are **below/under par**, you feel ill, so that your work is not as good as usual: *Are you feeling a bit under par?* • If something is **not up to par**, it is not as good as usual: *I'm afraid this week's essay was not up to par.* • If you say that something bad is **par for the course**, you mean that it is what you expected, from your past experience of it: *The school budget is going to be cut again this year, but then that's par for the course.* • In golf, par is the expected number of times a good player should have to hit the ball in order to get it into a hole or into all the holes: *The leaders all went round the course in less than 278, which is 10* **below/under** *par.* ○ *The further* **under** *par your golf score gets, the better you're playing.* • *(specialized)* Par **(value)** is the original value of a share of ownership in a business: *They make money by buying shares* **at** *or* **below** *par and selling them* **above** *par.*

par·a- BEYOND /£ˌpær·ə-, $ˌper·ə-/ *combining form* beyond • *Parapsychology is the study of abilities that go beyond what is natural and normal.*

par·a- SIMILAR /£ˌpær·ə-, $ˌper·ə-/ *combining form* similar to, or helping to do a similar job • *The soldiers are also paramedics – trained to act as doctors and nurses in an emergency.*

par·a SOLDIER /£ˈpær·ə, $ˈper·ə/ *n* [C] *esp. Br infml for* PARATROOPER

par·a TEXT /£ˈpær·ə, $ˈper·ə/ *n* [C] *abbreviation for* PARAGRAPH • *Paras 5 and 6 will have to be rewritten.*

par·a·ble /£ˈpær·ə·bl̩, $ˈper-/ *n* [C] a short simple story which teaches or explains an esp. moral or religious idea • *Jesus told many parables to his followers, such as the parable of the Good Samaritan.*

pa·rab·o·la /pəˈræb·ᵊl·ə/ *n* [C] *specialized* a type of curve such as that made by an object that is thrown up in the air and falls to the ground in a different place

par·ab·o·lic /£ˌpær·əˈbɒl·ɪk, $ˌper·əˈbɑː·lɪk/ *adj* [not gradable] • *a parabolic trajectory*

par·a·cet·a·mol *Br and Aus* /£ˌpær·əˈsiː·tə·mɒl, $ˌper·əˈsiː·t̬ə·mɑːl/, *Am* **a·ce·ta·mi·no·phen** /£əˌsiː·təʊˈmɪn·ə·fen, $-t̬oʊ-/ *n* a drug used to reduce pain • *If you've got a headache, why don't you* **take** *a/some paracetamol?* [C/U]

par·a·chute /£ˈpær·ə·ʃuːt, $ˈper-/ *n* [C] a large usually circular piece of special cloth fastened to someone or something that is dropped from an aircraft, in order to make them fall slowly and safely to the ground • PIC> Sports

par·a·chute *(obj)* /£'pær·ə·ʃuːt, $'per-/ *v* • *The plan is to parachute into the town.* [I] • *I parachuted once, to raise money for charity.* [I] • *Thousands of soldiers had already been parachuted behind enemy lines.* [T always + adv/prep]

par·a·chut·ist /£'pær·əˌʃuː·tɪst, $'per·əˌʃuː·t̬ɪst/ *n* [C] • A parachutist is someone who jumps out of an aircraft wearing a parachute on their back, esp. as a sport or a military job.

pa·rade /pə'reɪd/ *n* [C] a large number of people walking or in vehicles, all going in the same direction, usually as part of a public celebration of something • *After the 10-2 win, the crowd marched through town in a* **victory** *parade, carrying the players on their shoulders.* • A parade is also an occasion when soldiers march and practise military movements in front of important officials or as part of a public celebration or ceremony: *Did you see the soldiers* **on parade** (= taking part in a parade) *on TV last night?* • *(fig.) For three hours a committee of state senators listened to a parade* (= series) *of local residents giving their opinions.* • *(Br)* A parade is also a row of shops. • *(Br and Aus)* Parade is also used in the names of roads: *It's a small road off Park Parade.* • A **parade ground** is a large flat area where soldiers march and practise military movements.

pa·rade *(obj)* /pə'reɪd/ *v* • *The Saint Patrick's Day marchers paraded up Fifth Avenue, past the cathedral.* [I] • *In ancient Rome, captured generals were paraded through the streets in chairs.* [T] • *On Sunday afternoons the middle classes parade* (= walk about esp. in order to be seen and admired) *up and down the sea front in their best clothes.* [I] • *(fig.) The children came into the living room to parade their new clothes* (= show them in order to be admired). [T] • *(fig.) It's sickening the way he parades his wealth, his car and his expensive clothes* (= shows them in an obvious way in order to be admired). [T] • *(fig.) Publicly the government parades* (= tries to show in an obvious way) *its deep concern over unemployment, but in reality it does nothing to improve the situation.* [T]

par·a·digm /£'pær·ə·daɪm, $'per-/ *n* [C] *fml* a model of something, or a very clear and typical example of something • *Feldman's interview reads like a verbal exercise, almost setting itself up as a paradigm of the perfect interview.* • *Some of these educators are hoping to produce a change in the current cultural paradigm.* • *The scandal could stand as a paradigm for much of American political life.*

par·a·dig·mat·ic /£ˌpær·ə·dɪg'mæt·ɪk, $ˌper·ə·dɪg'mæt̬-/ *adj fml*

par·a·dise /£'pær·ə·daɪs, $'per-/ *n* [U] a place or condition of great happiness where everything is exactly as you would like it to be • *By comparison with their famine-struck villages, the city seemed like paradise.* • *His idea of paradise is to spend the day lying on the beach.* • *(infml) This place is a shopper's/children's/pickpocket's/etc. paradise* (= is the best place for them because the conditions are exactly right for them). • Paradise is another word for heaven: *They believe they would all go to Paradise after they died.* • Paradise is another word for the **garden of Eden** (= the place where Adam and Eve lived, in the Bible story).

par·a·dox /£'pær·ə·dɒks, $'per·ə·dɑːks/ *n* a situation, fact or statement which seems impossible and/or difficult to understand because it contains two opposite facts or characteristics • **It** *is a paradox* **that** *the French eat so much rich food and yet have a relatively low rate of heart disease.* [C + *that* clause] • *The statement "I am a liar" is a paradox because if the statement is true, it must be false and if it is false, it must be true.* [C] • *Her stories are full of mystery and paradox.* [U]

pa·ra·dox·i·cal /£ˌpær·ə'dɒk·sɪ·kəl, $ˌper·ə'dɑːk-/ *adj* • *It seems paradoxical to me, but if you drink a cup of hot tea it does seem to cool you down.*

par·a·dox·i·cal·ly /£ˌpær·ə'dɒk·sɪ·kli, $ˌper·ə'dɑːk-/ *adv* • *The harsh discipline of army life paradoxically produced a sense of liberation in me, because the army made all my decisions for me.*

par·af·fin *esp. Br* /£'pær·ə·fɪn, $'per-/, *Am and Aus usually* **ker·o·sene** *n* [U] a clear liquid with a strong smell made from coal or PETROL and used as a fuel esp. in heaters and lights • **Paraffin (wax)** is a white wax made from PETROL or coal used esp. to make candles.

par·a·glid·ing /£'pær·əˌglaɪ·dɪŋ, $'per-/ *n* [U] the sport of jumping out of an aircraft with a special PARACHUTE that allows you to travel a long horizontal distance before you land

par·a·gon /£'pær·ə·gən, $'per·ə·gɑːn/ *n* [C] a person or thing that is perfect or has an unusually large amount of a particular good characteristic • *The author seems to view the British system as a paragon* **of** *democracy.* • *I'm afraid Frederick is no paragon* **of** *discretion.*

par·a·graph /£'pær·ə·grɑːf, $'per·ə·græf/ (*abbreviation* **par·a**) *n* [C] a short part of a text, consisting of one or more sentences and beginning on a new line. It usually deals with a single event, description, idea, etc. • *You'll find the reference in book 2, paragraph 4, line 56.* • *The news rated only a few paragraphs in the local newspaper.* • CS PL RUS

par·a·keet /£ˌpær·ə'kiːt, £'---, $'per·ə·kiːt/ *n* [C] a small PARROT (= type of tropical bird) with a long tail

par·al·lel POSITION /£'pær·ə·lel, $'per-/ *adj* [not gradable] (of two or more straight lines) the same distance apart along all their length • *Draw a pair of parallel lines.* • *Hills Road is parallel* **to** *Mill Road.* • *The two opposite edges of this page are parallel* **to/with** *each other.* • In GYMNASTICS **parallel bars** are two horizontal bars which people exercising or competing use to swing themselves up in the air. • *(specialized)* If two or more parts of an electrical system are **in parallel**, they are arranged in a way that means they both receive the same amount of electricity. • *(specialized)* In computing, **parallel processing** is when a computer does two or more pieces of work at the same time. • PIC> **Sports**

par·al·lel /£'pær·ə·lel, $'per-/ *n* [C] • A parallel (also **parallel line**) is a line that is always at the same distance from another line. • *(esp. Am)* A parallel is an imaginary line around the Earth always at the same distance from the equator: *The Americans have declared the area south of/below the 32nd Parallel a no-fly zone for all military aircraft.*

par·al·lel /£'pær·ə·lel, $'per-/ *adv* [not gradable] • *Shoals of fish were swimming parallel* **with** *the boat.* • *It's a quiet street* **running** (= positioned) *parallel* **to** *the main road.*

par·al·lel SIMILARITY /£'pær·ə·lel, $'per-/ *n* [C] something very similar to something else, or a similarity between two things • *The executives involved in the dispute deny any parallel* **with** *the events of last year.* • *I'm trying to see if there are any obvious parallels* **between** *the two cases.* • *It would be easy to* **draw** *a parallel* **between** *the town's history and that of its football club* (= to make a comparison in order to show their similarity). • *These beautiful African churches have* **no parallel** *in Europe* (= There are none similar in Europe). • *It was a result* **without parallel** *in the history of the game* (= It was the best/worst ever result).

par·al·lel /£'pær·ə·lel, $'per-/ *adj* • A parallel event or situation is one that is happening at the same time as and/or is similar to another one: *a parallel example* • *a parallel contest* ○ *Parallel experiments are being conducted in Rome, Paris and London.*

par·al·lel *obj* /£'pær·ə·lel, $'per-/ *v* [T] • If something parallels something else it happens at the same time or is similar or equal to it: *She claimed that increases in "greenhouse gases" such as carbon dioxide and methane are paralleling the growth in car ownership.* ○ *The events of the last ten days in some ways parallel* (= are similar to) *those before the 1978 election.* ○ *His success is not paralleled anywhere else in the publishing industry.* • Compare UNPARALLELLED.

par·al·le·lo·gram /£ˌpær·ə'lel·ə·græm, $ˌper-/ *n* [C] *specialized* a flat shape which has four sides. The two sets of opposite sides are parallel and of equal length to each other. • PIC> **Shapes**

par·a·lyse *obj Br and Aus, Am* **par·a·lyze** /£'pær·əl·aɪz, $'per-/ *v* [T] to cause (a person or animal) to lose the ability to move or feel, or to cause (a person, animal, organization or place) to be unable to act, think or work correctly • *The effect of the drug is to paralyse the nerves so that there is no feeling or movement in the legs.* • *The huge volume of commuter traffic paralyses the city's roads every morning and evening.*

par·a·lysed *Br and Aus, Am* **par·a·lyzed** /£'pær·əl·aɪzd, $'per-/ *adj* • *He has been almost totally paralysed and in a wheelchair since the car crash two years ago.* • *The government seems paralysed* **by/with** *indecision.*

pa·ral·y·sis /pə'ræl·ə·sɪs/ *n pl* **paralyses** /pə'ræl·ə·siːz/ • *Doctors believe a drug overdose caused paralysis* **of** *the central nervous system.* [U] • *Some nervous disorders can produce paralyses.* [C]

par·a·lyt·ic /£ˌpær·əˈlɪt·ɪk, $ˌper·əˈlɪt̬-/ *adj infml* • *We went out to the pub and got paralytic* (=so drunk that we were almost unable to walk, think, talk, etc.).

par·a·med·ic /£ˌpær·əˈmed·ɪk, $ˌper·əˈmed-/ *n* [C] a person who is trained to do medical work, but who is not a doctor or nurse • *Most ambulance crews now contain at least one paramedic.* • PIC› **Emergency services**

pa·ra·me·ter /£pəˈræm·ɪ·təʳ, $-ə·t̬ɚ/ *n* [C usually pl] a set of facts or a fixed limit which establishes or limits how something can or must happen or be done • *The furniture designers are creative, but try to keep within the parameters of a given style or period.* • *The central office sets/establishes the parameters which guide policy at the local level.*

par·a·mil·i·ta·ry /£ˌpær·əˈmɪl·ɪ·tri, $ˌper·əˈmɪl·ə·ter·i/ *adj* [not gradable] similar to an army, but not official and often not legal • *Terrorist paramilitary organizations have been responsible for over 35 killings in the region over the past year.* • Paramilitary can also mean connected with and helping the official armed forces: *In some countries, police and fire officers have paramilitary training.*

par·a·mil·i·ta·ry /£ˌpær·əˈmɪl·ɪ·tri, $ˌper·əˈmɪl·ə·ter·i/ *n* [C] • *The radio and TV stations are guarded by well-armed paramilitaries.*

par·a·mount /£ˈpær·ə·maʊnt, $ˈper-/ *adj* [not gradable] *fml* more important than anything else • *There are many priorities, but reducing the budget deficit is paramount/is* **of** *paramount* **importance**.

par·a·mour /£ˈpær·ə·mɔːʳ, $ˈper·ə·mʊr/ *n* [C] *old use or literary* a lover

par·a·noi·a /£ˌpær·əˈnɔɪ·ə, $ˌper-/ *n* an extreme and unreasonable feeling that other people are going to harm you or that they have a bad opinion of you • *There's a lot of paranoia* **about** *crime at the moment.* [U] • *I promise you it's not just paranoia – someone has been following me.* [U] • *I'm fed up of all your stupid paranoias.* [C] • *(specialized)* Someone who has paranoia has unreasonable false beliefs as a part of another mental illness, for example SCHIZOPHRENIA. [U]

par·a·noid /£ˈpær·ən·ɔɪd, $ˈper·ə·nɔɪd/ *adj* • *He started feeling paranoid and was convinced other people were tricking him and lying to him.* • *Neighbouring countries are paranoid* (=extremely worried) **about** *the possibility of a disastrous explosion at one of these old-fashioned nuclear reactors.* • *They have a paranoid theory that it's all a big conspiracy.* • *(specialized) He was diagnosed as a paranoid* **schizophrenic** *and confined in a psychiatric hospital.* • *(saying)* 'Just because I'm paranoid it doesn't mean that they're not out to get me'.

par·a·nor·mal /£ˌpær·əˈnɔː·məl, $ˌper·əˈnɔːr-/ *adj* impossible to explain by known natural forces or by science • *paranormal powers/events/forces* • *This book is about people who claim to have paranormal abilities such as ESP and mind-reading.*

par·a·nor·mal /£ˌpær·əˈnɔː·məl, $ˌper·əˈnɔːr-/ *n* [U] • When people refer to **the paranormal** they mean all the things that are impossible to explain by known natural forces or by science: *investigations into the paranormal* ○ *a book on that fascinating subject – the paranormal*

par·a·pente /£ˈpær·ə·pɒnt, $ˈper-/ *n* [U] *Aus* the sport of jumping off a cliff or hill with a sheet-like PARACHUTE to control the direction and speed of landing

par·a·pet /£ˈpær·ə·pet, $ˈper-/ *n* [C] a low wall along the edge of a roof, bridge, etc. • *We sat down on the parapet and looked down over the city.* • PIC› **Bridge** (CS) (PL)

par·a·pher·na·li·a /£ˌpær·ə·fəˈneɪ·li·ə, $ˌper·ə·fɚˈneɪl·jə/ *n* [U] *esp. disapproving* a collection of esp. small objects, esp. those needed for or connected with a particular activity • *The wig is the most ridiculous part of the judicial paraphernalia that surrounds British judges and the courts.* • *Bags of cocaine and all sorts of drug paraphernalia were seized at the airport.*

pa·ra·phrase *obj* /£ˈpær·ə·freɪz, $ˈper-/ *v* [T] to repeat (something written or spoken) using different words, often in a humorous form or in a simpler and shorter form that makes the original meaning clearer • *Well, to paraphrase Marx, television has become the opium of the masses.*

pa·ra·phrase /£ˈpær·ə·freɪz, $ˈper-/ *n* [C] • *She gave us a quick paraphrase* **of** *what had been said.*

par·a·ple·gia /£ˌpær·əˈpliː·dʒə, $ˌper-/ *n* [U] *specialized* loss of the ability to move or feel in the legs and lower part of the body, usually because of a severe injury to the SPINE (=bones in the back)

par·a·ple·gic /£ˌpær·əˈpliː·dʒɪk, $ˌper-/ *adj* [not gradable], *n specialized* • *Is he paraplegic?* • *She does a lot of work with paraplegics.* [C]

par·a·psy·chol·o·gy /£ˌpær·ə·saɪˈkɒl·ə·dʒi, $ˌper·ə·saɪˈkɑː·lə-/ *n* [U] the study of mental abilities, such as knowing the future or TELEPATHY, which seem to go against or be beyond the known laws of nature and science

Par·a·quat /£ˈpær·ə·kwɒt, $ˈper·ə·kwɑːt/ *n* [U] *trademark* a very strong liquid poison used to kill unwanted plants

par·as·cend·ing /£ˈpær·əˌsen·dɪŋ, $ˈper-/ *n* [U] a sport in which you wear a PARACHUTE and you are connected by a long rope to a car or boat which pulls you up into the air as it moves forward on the ground or on water

par·a·site /£ˈpær·ə·saɪt, $ˈper-/ *n* [C] an animal or plant that lives on or in another animal or plant of a different type and feeds from it • *The older drugs didn't deal effectively with the malaria parasite.* • *(fig.) Financial speculators are parasites* **upon** *the national economy* (=They are useless people supported by other people's work).

par·a·si·tic /£ˌpær·əˈsɪt·ɪk, $ˌper·əˈsɪt̬-/, **par·a·si·ti·cal** /£ˌpær·əˈsɪt·ɪ·kəl, $ˌper·əˈsɪt̬-/ *adj* • *a parasitic disease* (=a disease caused by a parasite) • *parasitic bacteria* (=bacteria that are parasites)

par·a·sit·i·sm /ˈpær·ə·saɪ·tɪ·zəm/ *n* [U]

par·a·sol /£ˈpær·ə·sɒl, $ˈper·ə·sɑːl/ *n* [C] a type of SUNSHADE (=round cloth-covered frame on a stick) carried esp. by women in the past, to give protection from the sun • *Cynthia looked elegant with her long white dress and parasol.* • *My drink was decorated with a little paper parasol.* • (PL)

par·a·thy·roid (gland) /£ˌpær·əˈθaɪə·rɔɪd, $ˌper·əˈθaɪ-/ *n* [C] any of four GLANDS (=small organs in the body) that control the amount of two chemicals CALCIUM and PHOSPHORUS in the body

par·a·troops /£ˈpær·ə·truːps, $ˈper-/, *Br infml* **par·as** *pl n* (a military unit of) soldiers trained to be dropped from an aircraft with a PARACHUTE

par·a·troo·per /£ˈpær·əˌtruː·pəʳ, $ˈper·əˌtruː·pɚ/, *Br infml* **par·a** *n* [C] • *Paratroopers were dropped behind enemy lines to capture key points on the roads into the city.*

par·boil *obj* /£ˈpɑː·bɔɪl, $ˈpɑːr-/ *v* [T] to boil (food) for a short time until it is partly cooked

par·cel /£ˈpɑː·səl, $ˈpɑːr-/, *esp. Am and Aus* **pack·age** *n* [C] an object or collection of objects wrapped in paper, esp. so that it can be sent by post • *a parcel of books tied with string* • *a food parcel* • *Because it was her birthday she got several parcels and lots of cards.* • *(specialized or Am)* A parcel of land is an area of it. • *(Br)* A **parcel bomb** is a bomb wrapped up as a parcel and sent by post. • **Parcel post** is the system in which parcels are sent by post: *The cheapest way to send it would be by parcel post.* • Compare PACKET. • (CS)

par·cel *obj* /£ˈpɑː·səl, $ˈpɑːr-/ *v* [T] **-ll-** or *Am usually* **-l-** • If you parcel something **up** or *(Am)* parcel it, you wrap it up as a parcel: *Parcel up the tins and we'll send them off tomorrow.* [M]

par·cel out *obj v prep* [T] • *The bigger farms were parcelled out* (=divided into parts and given to different people) *after the revolution in 1973.* • *She parcelled out the gifts to the other children.*

parched /£pɑːtʃt, $pɑːrtʃt/ *adj* (esp. of earth or crops) dried out because of too much heat and not enough rain • *parched earth/fields/corn* • *That summer there was a drought and the countryside was parched and brown.* • *(fig. infml) I must get a drink – I'm absolutely parched* (=extremely thirsty)!

parch·ment /£ˈpɑːtʃ·mənt, $ˈpɑːrtʃ-/ *n* the dried pale yellowish skin of some animals which was used in the past for writing on, a high quality paper made to look like this, or a document written on either of these materials • *ancient parchment* [U] • *He'd been ill for a long time, and his skin was like parchment paper.* [U] • *A framed parchment* (=document) *hung on the wall.* [C]

pard·ner /£ˈpɑːd·nəʳ, $ˈpɑːrd·nɚ/ *n* [C] *Am infml* used as a form of address, usually between men • **Howdy** *pardner, how you doin'?*

par·don *obj* /£ˈpɑː·dən, $ˈpɑːr-/ *v* [T] to forgive (someone) for (something) • *Pardon my ignorance, but what exactly is ergonomics?* • *Pardon me interrupting, but there's a client to see you.* [+ obj + v-*ing*] • *George wasn't at our last meeting, so I think we can pardon him his lack of knowledge about what we decided then/pardon him* **for** *his lack of knowledge about* *what we decided then.* [+ two objects] • If someone who has committed a crime is pardoned, they are officially forgiven and their punishment is stopped: *Large numbers of political prisoners have been pardoned and released by the new president.* • People sometimes say **if you'll pardon the expression** before or after using language which other people might consider shocking: *The man doesn't know his arse from his elbow, if you'll pardon the expression.*

par·don /£ˈpɑː·dᵊn, $ˈpɑːr-/ *n* [C] • *He had actively sought a pardon* (= official forgiveness) *from the president.*

par·don /£ˈpɑː·dᵊn, $ˈpɑːr-/ *exclamation* • You say pardon (*Am also* **pardon me**) or (*fml*) **I beg your pardon** when you have not heard what someone has said to you and you want them to repeat it. • You might also say pardon (*Am also* **pardon me**, **excuse me**) or (*fml or humorous*) **I beg your pardon** to someone who has said something that offends you: *"Women tend to make fairly useless drivers, anyway." "I beg your pardon!"* • You might say **pardon (me)/excuse me** or (*fml*) **I beg your pardon** if you have done something that is generally considered rude, such as allowing air to come noisily out of your mouth. • **Pardon me** or **I beg your pardon** (*Am usually* **excuse me**) is also sometimes used as a way of saying sorry for accidentally behaving in a slightly rude way, esp. accidentally pushing someone. • (*infml*) *"If you're going to get in my way, James, could you just leave the kitchen!" "Oh,* **pardon me (for breathing/existing/living)** (= There's no need to be so unfriendly towards me)*!".* • LP› **Phrases and customs**

par·don·a·ble /£ˈpɑː·dᵊn·ə·bl̩, $ˈpɑːr-/ *adj* • *Calling his wife Anna instead of Annie was a pardonable mistake* (= one that could be forgiven) *when I'd only just met her.*

par·don·a·bly /£ˈpɑː·dᵊn·ə·bli, $ˈpɑːr-/ *adv*

pare *obj* /£peəʳ, $per/ *v* [T] to cut away (the outer layer) from (something, esp. a fruit or a vegetable), or (*fig.*) to reduce (something), esp. by a large amount • *He was busy paring apples in the kitchen.* • *Pare* **off** *any bits of pear skin that don't look very nice.* [M] • *Have you got some sharp scissors that I can pare* (= make shorter) *my nails with?* • (*fig.*) *Because of the current economic recession a lot of companies have pared their staff* **(down)**. [T/M] • (*fig.*) *The three-hour play has been pared* **(down)** *to two hours.* [T/M] • If something has been **pared (down) to the bone** it has been reduced to a level at which only what is necessary is left: *Expenses have been pared down to the bone for some months now.*

pa·ring /£ˈpeə·rɪŋ, $ˈper·ɪŋ/ *n* [C often pl.] • A paring is a thin piece that has been cut away from something: *We feed most of our vegetable parings to the guinea pigs.* ○ *I keep finding his nail parings all over the floor.* • A **paring knife** is a small knife which is used to cut away a thin outer layer of something.

pa·rent /£ˈpeə·rənt, $ˈper·ᵊnt/ *n* [C] a mother or father of a person or an animal • *The teacher had asked to see the boy's parents.* • *I'm going to meet his parents for the first time this weekend.* • *If both parents have blue eyes, their children will have blue eyes.* • A **parent company** is a company which controls other smaller companies. • A **parent-teacher association** (*abbreviation* **PTA**), (*esp. Am*) **parent-teacher organization** (*abbreviation* **PTO**), (*Aus*) **Parents and Citizens** (*abbreviation* **P and C**), is an organization to which the parents of children at a school and the teachers at the school can belong, and which tries to help the school, esp. by arranging activities that raise money for it. • LP› **Relationships** PIC› **Family tree** Ⓔ Ⓘ Ⓟ

pa·rent·age /£ˈpeə·rən·tɪdʒ, $ˈper·ᵊn·t̬ɪdʒ/ *n* [U] • When you refer to a person's parentage, you mean the fact of who their parents are: *The novel starts when a child of unknown parentage is left at the house of the local priest.* ○ *She is of mixed Australian and Japanese parentage.*

pa·ren·tal /£pəˈren·tᵊl, $-t̬ᵊl/ *adj* [not gradable] • *A great number of young people in further education are supported financially by parental contributions.* • *The government repeatedly stressed its support for parental* **choice** *in the selection of a child's school.*

pa·rent·hood /£ˈpeə·rənt·hʊd, $ˈper·ᵊnt-/ *n* [U] • *The prospect of parenthood* (= being a parent) *filled her with horror.*

pa·rent·ing /£ˈpeə·rən·tɪŋ, $ˈper·ᵊn·t̬ɪŋ/ *n* [U] • Parenting is the raising of children and all the responsibilities and activities that are involved in it: *She's been reading books and articles on good parenting for the last nine months.* ○ *The ability to listen is one of the chief parenting* **skills**.

pa·ren·the·sis MARK *esp. Am and Aus, Br specialized or fml* /pəˈrent·θə·sɪs/, *Br usually* **(round) brack·et** *n* [C usually pl] either of two marks () put round a word, sentence, etc. in a piece of writing to show that what is inside them should be considered as separate from the main part • *Men's tennis ranking, with last year's ranking* **in** *parentheses: 1 (1) Edwards, 2 (6) O'Neill, 3 (9) Jachim...* • LP› **Brackets**

pa·ren·the·sis ADDITIONAL PHRASE /pəˈrent·θə·sɪs/ *n* [C] *pl* **parentheses** /pəˈrent·θə·siːz/ a remark which is added to a sentence, often to provide an explanation or additional information, and which is separated from the main part of the sentence by commas, BRACKETS or DASHES • *The sentence 'Her youngest sister – the one who lives in Australia – is coming over next summer' contains a parenthesis.* • If, while you are talking, you say something **in** parenthesis, you say it as an addition and then continue with the main part of the sentence: *Of his origins he said very little, merely mentioning in parenthesis that his background was poor.*

par·en·thet·i·cal /£ˌpær·ᵊnˈθet·ɪ·kᵊl, $ˌper·ᵊnˈθet̬-/, **par·en·thet·ic** /£ˌpær·ᵊnˈθet·ɪk, $ˌper·ᵊnˈθet̬-/ *adj* [not gradable] *fml* • A parenthetical remark is one which is said in addition to the main part of what you are saying: *She said nothing about her brother, except for one parenthetical remark that they were not the best of friends.*

par·en·thet·i·cal·ly /£ˌpær·ᵊnˈθet·ɪ·kli, $ˌper·ᵊnˈθet̬-/ *adv* [not gradable] *fml* • *He referred only parenthetically to his illness so I didn't enquire further.*

par ex·cel·lence /£ˌpɑːˈrek·sᵊl·ɑ̃ːnts, $ˌpɑːrˌek·səˈlɑːnts/ *adj* [after n; not gradable] being the most excellent or the most typical example of its type • *This is undoubtedly the cooking chocolate par excellence.* • *The wedding ring is the symbol par excellence of eternal love.*

pa·ri·ah /pəˈraɪə/ *n* [C] a person who is not accepted by a social group, esp. because he or she is not liked, respected or trusted • *Mr Brown claims that ever since the allegations he has been treated as a pariah in the local community.* • (*fig.*) *The National Party's policy of racial segregation had made the country an international pariah* (= caused other countries to disapprove of it).

pa·ring /£ˈpeə·rɪŋ, $ˈper·ɪŋ/ *n* [C often pl.] See at PARE

par·ish /£ˈpær·ɪʃ, $ˈper-/ *n* [C] (in some Christian groups) an area cared for by one priest and which has its own church, or (in England) the smallest unit of local government • *the parish church/magazine/priest/register* • *Traditionally women went back to the church of the parish in which they were born to get married.* • In England, a **parish clerk** is an official whose duties are connected with a church. • In England, a **parish council** is a group of people who are elected to make decisions for their parish. • See also PAROCHIAL OF A CHURCH

pa·rish·ion·er /£pəˈrɪʃ·ᵊn·əʳ, $-ɚ/ *n* [C] • A parishioner is a member of a particular parish under the care of a priest, esp. one who frequently goes to its church.

par·i·ty /£ˈpær·ə·ti, $ˈper·ə·t̬i/ *n* [U] equality, esp. of pay or position • *What nurses would like to see is pay parity* **with** *fellow nurses in other major European countries.* • (*specialized*) *The banks are clearly hoping that the pound will maintain its current parity* **with** *the German mark* (= that the two units will stay level in value).

park AREA OF LAND /£pɑːk, $pɑːrk/ *n* [C] a large enclosed area of land with grass and trees, which is specially arranged so that people can walk in it for pleasure or children can play in it • *Central Park* • *Hyde Park* • *I jog round the local park.* • *She sat on the park bench watching the kids play on the swings and slides.* • (*Br*) A park is also an area of land around a large house in the countryside: *The park around Wickham Abbey is open to the public in the summer.* • (*Br*) A **park keeper** is a person who is in charge of and takes care of a public park.

park (*obj*) STOP /£pɑːk, $pɑːrk/ *v* to put (a vehicle) in a place where it can stay for a period of time, usually while you leave it, or (*fig. infml*) to put (yourself or something) in a particular place for a long time, often causing annoyance to others • *Where have you parked?* [I] • *Just park your car in the street.* [T] • (*fig. infml*) *He parked* **himself** *in front of the TV and stayed there all afternoon.* [T] • (*fig. infml*) *She's parked an enormous pile of papers on my desk and I haven't a clue what to do with them.* [T] • PIC› **Driving**

parked /£pɑːkt, $pɑːrkt/ *adj* [not gradable] • *That badly parked red car on the other side of the street is mine.* • *I'm parked* (= My car is parked) *just at the end of the road.*

park·ing /£ˈpɑː·kɪŋ, $ˈpɑːr-/ *n* [U] • *His car was towed away for illegal parking* (= leaving a vehicle in a place for a period of time). • *Please do not park your car outside the marked parking* **bays.** • *Parking* **fines** *are given for parking* **offences/violations.** • *You can't leave your car here unless you have a parking* **permit.** • *It took me ages to find a parking* **place/space.** • *Is there any parking* (= space in which you can leave your vehicle) *in the village itself?* • **Parking brake** is *Am for* HANDBRAKE. • **Parking light** is *Am and Aus also for* SIDELIGHT. • *(Am and Aus)* A **parking lot** is an outside **car park**. See at CAR. • A **parking meter** is a device at the side of the road that you put money into so that you can leave your vehicle there for a particular amount of time. • A **parking ticket** is a notice which might be put on your vehicle when you leave the vehicle in a place where it is not allowed to be, and which tells you that you must pay a particular amount of money as punishment: *I* **got** *another parking ticket this morning!* • PIC› **Car, Meters and gauges** ⓖⓡ

par·ka /£'pɑː·kə, $'pɑːr-/ *n* [C] a knee-length, often waterproof, coat with a fur-edged HOOD (= covering for the head), or *(Am also)* an ANORAK • PIC› **Coats and jackets**

Par·kin·son's (dis·ease) /£'pɑː·kɪn·sᵊnz, $'pɑːr-/ *n* [U] a disease of the nervous system which causes the muscles to become stiff and the body to shake, and which gradually gets worse as a person gets older

Par·kin·son's law /£'pɑː·kɪn·sᵊnz, $'pɑːr-/ *n* [U not after *the*] *humorous* the idea that any piece of work will increase to fill as much time as you have to do it in • *An extension of Parkinson's law applies to computers and their related equipment: they expand to fill the room available.*

park·land /£'pɑːk·lænd, $'pɑːrk-/ *n* [U] an area of land (available to be) used as a park • *The college is surrounded by 70 acres of parkland.*

park·way /£'pɑːk·weɪ, $'pɑːrk-/ *n* [C] *Am and Aus* a wide, usually divided, road with an area of grass and trees on both sides and in the middle

par·ky /£'pɑː·ki, $'pɑːr-/ *adj* **-ier, -iest** *Br infml* (of the weather) quite cold, although not very cold • *It's a bit parky today, love – you'll want your coat!*

par·lance /£'pɑː·lənts, $'pɑːr-/ *n* [U] *fml* a group of words or style of speaking used by a particular group of people • *The 1960s first saw the widespread use of the oral contraceptive or, as it is known in* **common** *parlance, 'the pill'.* • *It may take months before the government adopt or, in business parlance, 'take on board' the ideas suggested in the report.*

par·lay *obj* /£'pɑː·li, $'pɑːr·leɪ/ *v* [T] *esp. Am* to use or develop (money, skills, etc.) in a way that makes them more profitable or successful • *They parlayed a small inheritance* **into** *a vast fortune.* • *Computer technology skills are the easiest to parlay* **into** *jobs.*

par·ley /£'pɑː·li, $'pɑːr-/ *n* [C] *dated or humorous* a discussion between two (groups of) people, esp. one that is intended to end an argument

par·ley /£'pɑː·li, $'pɑːr-/ *v* [I] • *(dated) After some serious parleying, both sides agreed to settle their differences.* • *(humorous) Let's go and parley* **with** *the locals to find out where the best restaurants are near here.*

par·lia·ment /£'pɑː·lɪ·mənt, $'pɑːr·lə-/ *n* in some countries, the group of (usually) elected politicians or other people who make the laws for their country • *On Tuesday the country's parliament voted to establish its own army.* [C] • *In Britain, Parliament consists of the House of Commons, the House of Lords and the king or queen, although people often mean only the House of Commons when they refer to Parliament.* [U not after *the*] • *She believes that the right to hunt is a question that can only be resolved* **in** *Parliament* (= by a decision made by Parliament). [U not after *the*] • *Television cameras are now being allowed into the chambers whilst Parliament is* **in session** (= while Parliament is working). [U not after *the*] • Parliament also refers to a particular period of time during which a parliament is operating, between either holidays or elections: *By the end of the next parliament the aim is to ensure that all three services are privatized.* [C]

par·lia·men·ta·ri·an /£,pɑː·lɪ·men'teə·ri·ən, $,pɑːr·lə·men'ter·i-/ *n* [C] • A parliamentarian is a member of a parliament, esp. one who is respected for his or her experience and skill: *The question was raised by a senior parliamentarian, whose opinion is widely respected even amongst the opposition.* • *(Am)* A parliamentarian is also someone who is an expert on the rules and methods used by a group that makes laws or decisions: *She was a parliamentarian for a local service organization for many years.*

par·lia·men·ta·ry /£,pɑː·lɪ'men·tᵊr·i, $,pɑːr·lə'men·t̬ɚ-/ *adj* [not gradable] • *a parliamentary candidate/debate/election/session* • *parliamentary procedures/rules*

par·lour SHOP *Br and Aus, Am and Aus* **par·lor** /£'pɑː·ləʳ, $'pɑːr·lɚ/ *n* [C] a shop which provides a stated type of personal service or sells a stated product • *a beauty parlour* • *an ice-cream/pizza parlour*

par·lour ROOM *Br and Aus, Am and Aus* **par·lor** /£'pɑː·ləʳ, $'pɑːr·lɚ/ *n* [C] (esp. in the past) a room in a private house used for relaxing, esp. one which was kept tidy for the entertaining of guests • *the front parlour* • *an Edwardian parlour* • A **parlour game** is a game played inside a house, usually involving words or acting.

par·lous /£'pɑː·ləs, $'pɑːr-/ *adj fml or humorous* very bad, dangerous or uncertain • *I'd like to buy a new car, but my finances are in such a parlous* **state** *that I can't afford to.* • *Relations between the two countries have been in a parlous condition for some time.*

Par·me·san (cheese) /£,pɑː·mɪ'zæn, £'---, $'pɑːr·mə·zɑːn/ *n* [U] a hard dry Italian cheese used esp. in cooking and for scattering on particular types of Italian food, such as pasta

pa·ro·chi·al OF A CHURCH /£pə'rəʊ·ki·əl, $-'roʊ-/ *adj* [not gradable] connected with a PARISH (= an area which has its own church or priest) • *parochial boundaries* • *a parochial church council* • *The local priest has been accused of failing in his parochial duties.* • *(Am)* A **parochial school** is a school which is controlled by a religious organization, and which usually receives no money from the government.

pa·ro·chi·al LIMITED /£pə'rəʊ·ki·əl, $-'roʊ-/ *adj disapproving* showing interest only in a narrow range of matters, esp. those which directly influence yourself, your town or your country • *There's something parochial about her writing, as if she'd never travelled further than the next town.* • *Although it's just the local paper it somehow manages not to be too parochial in its outlook.*

pa·ro·chi·al·ly /£pə'rəʊ·ki·ə·li, $-'roʊ-/ *adv disapproving*

pa·ro·chi·al·i·sm /£pə'rəʊ·ki·ə·lɪ·zᵊm, $-'roʊ-/ *n* [U] *disapproving* • *He said that it was time the country abandoned its political parochialism.*

par·o·dy /£'pær·ə·di, $'per-/ *n* writing, music, art, something said, etc. which intentionally copies the style of someone famous or copies a particular situation, making the features or qualities of the original more noticeable in a way that is humorous • *He was an eighteenth-century poet and essayist who wrote parodies* **of** *other people's works.* [C] • *Her later writing so lacked subtlety that it almost read like a parody* **of** *her earlier work.* [C] • *There's a strong element of parody in the latest series, set in the office of a TV production company.* [U] • *There is a hint of* **self-***parody in his later paintings.* [U] • *(disapproving)* Something can be described as a parody if it so obviously fails to achieve the effect that was intended that it is ridiculous: *"It was a parody* **of** *a trial," said one observer.* [C] ○ *The film was so ridiculous it was almost a parody* **of itself.** [C] • Compare TRAVESTY.

par·o·dist /£'pær·ə·dɪst, $'per-/ *n* [C] • A parodist is a person who writes parodies.

par·o·dy *obj* /£'pær·ə·di, $'per-/ *v* [T] • *One of the papers is running a competition in which you've got to parody* (= write something in the style of) *a well-known author.*

pa·role /£pə'rəʊl, $-'roʊl/ *n* [U] the releasing of a prisoner either temporarily or before his or her period in prison is finished, with the agreement that he or she behaves well • *a life sentence* **without** *parole* • *The crime was committed while the prisoner was* **out on** *parole.* • *He has* **applied for** *parole after serving seven years of a 23-year sentence.* • *She hopes to be* **eligible for** *parole in 3 years.* • *He's been* **released on** *parole.*

pa·role *obj* /£pə'rəʊl, $-'roʊl/ *v* [T usually passive]

par·ox·y·sm /£'pær·ɒk·sɪ·zᵊm, $'per·ək-/ *n* [C] a sudden and powerful expression of strong feeling, esp. one that you cannot control • *In a sudden paroxysm* **of** *jealousy he threw her clothes out of the window.* • *These proposals have sent/thrown many people* **into** *paroxysms* **of** *rage.* • *She went* **into** *paroxysms* **of** *delight/joy when she heard that she had won first prize.*

par·quet /£'pɑː·keɪ, $pɑːr'keɪ/ *n* [U] floor covering that consists of small rectangular blocks of wood arranged in a pattern • *The vacuum cleaner can be used on both carpet and parquet.* • *We've laid a new parquet* **floor.** • See also WOODBLOCK.

par·ri·cide /£ˈpær·ɪ·saɪd, $ˈper·ə-/ *n law* the crime of murdering a close relative, esp. a parent, or a person who has committed this crime • *We don't know what it was that drove her to parricide.* [U] • *There have been two unusual parricides in recent months.* [C] • *In ancient Greek stories, Oedipus was a parricide* (= a person who killed one of his parents). [C] • Compare MATRICIDE; PATRICIDE.

par·rot /£ˈpær·ət, $ˈper-/ *n* [C] a bird with a curved beak and usually colourful feathers which is found mainly in tropical areas. There are many types of parrot, some of which can be trained to copy the human voice. • *She's got a pet parrot that she's taught to say rude words.* • *She repeats everything that you say – it's like having a parrot in the room.* • *(Br)* If you learn or repeat a piece of text **parrot-fashion** you learn or repeat the exact words, usually without understanding them: *I used to be able to recite the whole poem parrot-fashion.* • *"This parrot is no more! It has ceased to be! It's expired and gone to meet its maker! This is a late parrot!"* (from the television show *Monty Python's Flying Circus*, 1969) • PIC› **Birds**

par·rot *obj* /£ˈpær·ət, $ˈper-/ *v* [T] *disapproving* • To parrot what someone else says is to repeat it exactly, without understanding it or thinking about its meaning: *You have to be careful about what you say to young children, because they have a tendency to parrot it.* ○ *She doesn't have an original thought in her head – she just parrots anything that Sara says.*

par·ry *obj* /£ˈpær·i, $ˈper-/ *v* [T] to defend yourself from (a weapon or an attack) by pushing the weapon away or by putting something between your body and the weapon • *He went to strike her face but she parried his hand with her arm.* • *(fig.)* If you parry a difficult question or some criticism, you manage cleverly to avoid dealing with it: *Predictably the president parried enquiries about the arms scandal.*

par·ry /£ˈpær·i, $ˈper-/ *n* [C]

Par·see, Par·si /£ˌpɑːˈsiː, $ˈpɑːr·siː/ *n* [C], *adj* [not gradable] (a member) of a religious group found mainly in W India, whose religion, ZOROASTRIANISM, started in Persia (ancient Iran)

par·si·mo·ni·ous /£ˌpɑː·sɪˈməʊ·ni·əs, $ˌpɑːr·səˈmoʊ-/ *adj fml disapproving* not generous; unwilling to spend money or give something • *She's too parsimonious to heat the house properly.* • *My dad's always a bit parsimonious* **with** *the gin!* • *(fig.) I think that politicians are often rather parsimonious* **with** *the* (= do not tell the complete) *truth.*

par·si·mo·ni·ous·ly /£ˌpɑː·sɪˈməʊ·ni·ə·sli, $ˌpɑːr·səˈmoʊ-/ *adv fml disapproving*

par·si·mo·ny /£ˈpɑː·sɪ·mə·ni, $ˈpɑːr·sə·moʊ-/, **par·si·mo·ni·ous·ness** /£ˌpɑː·sɪˈməʊ·ni·ə·snəs, $ˌpɑːr·səˈmoʊ-/ *n* [U] *fml disapproving* • *For reasons of parsimony she'd used half the recommended number of eggs in the recipe.*

pars·ley /£ˈpɑː·sli, $ˈpɑːr-/ *n* [U] a herb with curly or flat leaves, used to add flavour to food and also to make it look attractive • *Sprinkle a little parsley on the soup as garnish.* • *I've made parsley sauce to go with the fish.* • PIC› **Herbs and spices**

pars·nip /£ˈpɑː·snɪp, $ˈpɑːr-/ *n* a long cream-coloured root of a plant, eaten as a vegetable • *parsnip and apple soup* [U] • *boiled/roasted parsnips* [C] • PIC› **Vegetables**

par·son /£ˈpɑː·sᵊn, $ˈpɑːr-/ *n* [C] *dated or humorous* any Christian priest • *the village parson* • *Parson James Woodforde*

par·son·age /£ˈpɑː·sᵊn·ɪdʒ, $ˈpɑːr-/ *n* [C] *dated* • A parsonage is a house that was built for a parson.

part SOME /£pɑːt, $pɑːrt/ *n* [U] some but not all of a thing • *Part* **of** *my steak isn't cooked properly.* • *Part* **of** *this form seems to be missing.* • *Part* **of** *what I like about skiing is that element of danger.* • *You have to take a few disappointments – it's all part* **of** *growing up.* • *I think part* **of** *her problem is that she doesn't listen to a word that anyone says.* • *When you've had a dog for several years, it just becomes part* **of** (= like a member of) *the family.* • *The deadline for applications is being extended,* **in part** (= to some degree) *because of pressure from the employer.* • *How quickly we can finish the project depends* **in (a) large part** (= to an important degree) *on when we get the payments through.* • *We spent the day* **for the most part** (= mainly) *looking round the museum.* • If you say that something is **part and parcel of** an experience you mean that it is a necessary feature of it which cannot be avoided: *Being recognized in the street is part and parcel of being a famous actress.* • Something or someone that is **part of the furniture** is so familiar that you no longer notice them. • If you work **part-time** or do **part-time** work, you work for only some of the day or the week: *a part-time job* • *part-time staff* ○ *Some women prefer to work part-time while their children are small.* ○ *We have several* **part-timers** (= people who work only a part of the day or week) *working in our office.* Compare **full-time** at FULL COMPLETE. • *"It's all part of life's rich pageant (sometimes '... rich tapestry')"* (Arthur Marshall, 1937) • LP› **Work** Ⓘ Ⓙ Ⓟ

part /£pɑːt, $pɑːrt/ *adj* [before n; not gradable] • *He's (a) part* **owner** *of a racehorse* (= he shares the ownership of it with other people). • *(esp. Br) I might offer them my old camera* **in/as part exchange** (= as a part of the payment) *for a new one.*

part /£pɑːt, $pɑːrt/ *adv* [not gradable] • *He's part African – his father was born in Somalia.* • *She's a puzzling mixture – part school-girl and part middle-aged matron.* • *The exam is part spoken and part written.*

part·ly /£ˈpɑːt·li, $ˈpɑːrt-/ *adv* [not gradable] • *His attractiveness is partly due to his self-confidence.* • *The house is partly owned by her father.* • *I left the door partly open for the breeze.*

part SEPARATE PIECE /£pɑːt, $pɑːrt/ *n* [C] a different or separate piece of something; a piece which combines with other pieces to form the whole of something • *One of the exam questions was to label all the different parts* **of** *the digestive system.* • *The lower part* **of** *her spine was crushed in the accident.* • *Parts* **of** *the film were good, but overall I didn't enjoy it very much.* • *The film was good* **in parts**, *but overall I didn't enjoy it very much.* • *I think there's always a part* **of** *you that doubts what you're doing.* • *This region has only recently become a* **constituent** *part of the republic.* • *Fresh fruit and vegetables form an* **essential/important/integral** *part* **of** *a healthy diet.* • *Falling in love is the* **easy** *part, but staying in love is the* **hard** *part.* • *There'll be snow in parts* (= particular areas) **of** *the Midlands tonight.* • A part is one of the pieces that together form a machine or some type of equipment: *He works for a company that makes navy submarine parts.* • A part can also be a division of something: *Divide the butter and sugar mixture into two equal parts.* • A part is also a single broadcast of a series of television or radio programmes or a division of a story: *'The life and times of Winston Churchill', a television series in eight parts.* ○ *Next week we publish part three of 'The Diana Diaries'.* • A part is also one of two or more equal, or almost equal, measures of something: *Mix one part* **of** *the medicine with three parts water.* • A part in a film, play or dance is one of its characters, or the words, actions or movements that are said or done by that character: *He's got a small part in an Arthur Miller play.* ○ *She* **plays** *the part of the sexy blonde mistress.* ○ *Ben is busy learning his part* (= words and actions) *for the school play.* ○ *(fig.) If you're going to be a high-powered businesswoman, you've got to* **dress/look the part** (= wear something that is suitable for that type of person). • *I spent* **the best/better part of** (= almost) *a day cleaning that kitchen!* • A part is also the music that a particular musician plays in a group: *The tune is* **in** *the violin part at this point.* ○ *a set of part songs* (= songs to be sung by several singers) • A **part of speech** (also **word class**) is any of the grammatical groups into which words are divided depending on their use: *'Verb', 'noun' and 'adjective' are examples of parts of speech.* • Ⓘ Ⓙ Ⓟ

parts /£pɑːts, $pɑːrts/ *pl n infml* • People sometimes refer to **these** or **those** parts meaning an area of the country: *I'm not used to seeing you around these parts.* ○ *We don't see many foreigners* **in** *these parts.*

part *(obj)* SEPARATE /£pɑːt, $pɑːrt/ *v* to (cause to) separate • *The curtains parted, revealing a darkened stage.* [I] • *He sustained severe knife-wounds whilst trying to part two men who were fighting in a night-club.* [T] • *To be parted* **from** *him even for two days made her sad.* [T] • If you part your hair, you arrange it so that it falls on either side of your head by separating it with a line down the middle or on one side. [T] • *(fml)* If two people part, they leave each other, often at the end of a relationship: *I'm afraid we parted on rather bad terms.* [I] • If two people **part company**, they finish their relationship: *The world's number one tennis player and his coach parted company earlier this month.* • If you **part with** something you give it away: *I've never had much success getting him to part with his cash.* ○ *I was going to give away her old baby clothes, but I couldn't bring myself to part with them.* • LP› **Each other** Ⓘ Ⓙ Ⓟ

part·ed /£ˈpɑː·tɪd, $ˈpɑːr·t̬ɪd/ *adj* [not gradable] • *On his wall he has a poster of Marilyn Monroe, her lips forever parted in anticipation.*

part·ing /£ˈpɑː·tɪŋ, $ˈpɑːr·t̬ɪŋ/ *n* • *She said that they'd had an amicable parting.* [C] • *The pain of parting had gradually lessened over the years.* [U] • *(Br and Aus)* A parting (*Am and Aus* **part**) is a line on someone's head from either side of which the hair is brushed in opposite directions: *I've got a* **centre/side** *parting.* [C] • A **parting of the ways** is the moment at which two people who have been working together, or involved in an activity together, have to separate: *The parting of the ways came after a series of disagreements between the singer and his song-writer.* • *"Parting is such sweet sorrow"* (Shakespeare, Romeo and Juliet 2.1) • [PIC]> **Hair**

part·ing /£ˈpɑː·tɪŋ, $ˈpɑːr·t̬ɪŋ/ *adj* [before n; not gradable] • *His parting words to me were "And don't come back till you're in a better mood!"* • A **parting shot** is a remark which you do not make until you are leaving, so that it has a stronger effect: *"And the dress that you bought me doesn't fit either!" was her parting shot.*

part [INVOLVEMENT] /£pɑːt, $pɑːrt/ *n* [U] involvement in or responsibility for an activity or action • *He admitted his part* **in** *the robbery.* • **I want no part in/of** (= I do not want to become involved in) *your crazy schemes!* • **For my** *part* (= To me), *it doesn't matter whether he comes or not.* • *(fml) It was a mistake* **on** *Julia's* **part/on the** *part* **of** *Julia* (= she was responsible for it). • If you **take** someone's **part**, you support them: *For once my brother took my part* **in** *the argument.* • Ⓘ Ⓙ Ⓟ

part [HAIR] /£pɑːt, $pɑːrt/ *n* [C] *Am and Aus for* **parting**, see at PART [SEPARATE] • [PIC]> **Hair** Ⓘ Ⓙ Ⓟ

par·take [EAT/DRINK] /£pɑːˈteɪk, $pɑːr-/ *v* [I] *past simple* **partook** /£pɑːˈtʊk, $pɑːr-/, *past part* **partaken** /£pɑːˈteɪ·kᵊn, $pɑːr-/ *fml, esp. humorous* to eat or drink • *Would you care to partake* **of** *a little wine with us?*

par·take [TAKE PART] /£pɑːˈteɪk, $pɑːr-/ *v* [I] *past simple* **partook** /£pɑːˈtʊk, $pɑːr-/, *past part* **partaken** /£pɑːˈteɪ·kᵊn, $pɑːr-/ *fml* to become involved with or take part in something • *Only very reluctantly did she finally agree to partake* **in** *the festivities.*

par·the·no·gen·e·sis /£ˌpɑː·θə·nəʊˈdʒen·ɪ·sɪs, $ˌpɑːr·θə·noʊˈdʒen·ə-/ *n* [U] *specialized* a type of reproduction in which the young develop from eggs which have not been FERTILIZED (= united with the male sexual cells)

par·tial [NOT COMPLETE] /£ˈpɑː·ʃᵊl, $ˈpɑːr-/ *adj* [not gradable] not complete • *He made a partial* **recovery** *but he was never able to walk properly after the accident.* • *The general has ordered a partial* **withdrawal** *of troops from the area.*

par·tial·ly /£ˈpɑː·ʃᵊl·i, $ˈpɑːr-/ *adv* [not gradable] • *You buy the bread partially cooked and then pop it in the oven for ten minutes.* • *Last year's drop in export sales was partially offset by a growth in the domestic market.* • People who are **partially sighted** are not completely blind but are able to see very little: *These books with large print are designed for partially sighted people.*

par·tial [UNFAIR] /£ˈpɑː·ʃᵊl, $ˈpɑːr-/ *adj* influenced by your personal preference for or approval of something so that you do not judge fairly • *The reporting in the papers is entirely partial and makes no attempt to be objective.*

par·ti·al·i·ty /£ˌpɑː·ʃiˈæl·ə·ti, $ˌpɑːr·ʃiˈæl·ə·t̬i/ *n* [U] • *The judges have been heavily criticized for their partiality in the whole affair.*

par·tial [LIKING] /£ˈpɑː·ʃᵊl, $ˈpɑːr-/ *adj* [after v; always + *to*] having a liking for something • *I'm rather partial* **to** *the odd cigar after dinner.*

par·ti·al·i·ty /£ˌpɑː·ʃiˈæl·ə·ti, $ˌpɑːr·ʃiˈæl·ə·t̬i/ *n* [U] • *He has a partiality* **for** *expensive suits.*

par·tic·i·pate /£pɑːˈtɪs·ɪ·peɪt, $pɑːrˈtɪs·ə-/ *v* [I] to take part in or become involved in an activity • *Did you participate* **in** *any of the activities that were on offer at the hotel?* • *She never participates* **in** *any of our discussions, does she?*

par·ti·ci·pa·tion /£pɑːˌtɪs·ɪˈpeɪ·ʃᵊn, $pɑːrˌtɪs·ə-/ *n* [U] • *The whole idea behind the show is that it's meant to encourage* **audience** *participation.*

par·ti·ci·pant /£pɑːˈtɪs·ɪ·pᵊnt, $pɑːrˈtɪs·ə-/ *n* [C] • A participant is a person who takes part in or becomes involved in a particular activity: *All participants finishing the race will receive a medal.*

par·ti·ci·pa·to·ry /£pɑːˈtɪs·ɪ·pə·tᵊr·i, £ˌpɑː·tɪ·sɪˈpeɪ-, $pɑːrˈtɪs·ə·pəˌtɔːr-/ *adj* • *Participatory sports are becoming more popular.*

par·ti·ci·ple /£ˈpɑːˈtɪs·ɪ·pl̩, $ˈpɑːr·tɪ·sɪ-/ *n* [C] (in grammar) a form of a verb which does not show the verb's tense or subject and which is used to form some tenses and as an adjective • *In the sentences 'He's sleeping' and 'I've already eaten' the words 'sleeping' and 'eaten' are both participles.* • *In the phrases 'buttered scones' and 'broken heart', the words 'buttered' and 'broken' are both participles acting as adjectives.* • [LP]> **-ed and -ing adjectives, -ing form of verbs**

par·ti·cle [SMALL PIECE] /£ˈpɑː·tɪ·kl̩, $ˈpɑːr·t̬ə-/ *n* [C] an extremely small piece of matter • *Dust particles must have got into the motor, which is why it isn't working properly.* • *(fig.) She wouldn't give me even the slightest particle* (= the smallest amount) *of information about what she'd been doing.* • A **particle accelerator** is a machine which makes extremely small pieces of matter travel at very high speeds, so that scientists can study the way they behave.

par·ti·cle [GRAMMAR] /£ˈpɑː·tɪ·kl̩, $ˈpɑːr·t̬ə-/ *n* [C] in grammar, a word or a part of a word which has a grammatical purpose but often has little or no meaning • *In the sentence 'I tidied up the room', the adverb 'up' is a particle.*

par·tic·u·lar [SPECIAL] /£pəˈtɪk·jʊ·ləʳ, $pəˈtɪk·jə·lɚ/ *adj* [before n; not gradable] special or single; this and not any other • *Do you have any particular preference where we sit?* • *When you said we should eat out, did you have a particular restaurant in mind?* • *"Why did you ask?" "Oh, no particular reason, just making conversation."* • Ⓔ Ⓟ

par·tic·u·lar /£pəˈtɪk·jʊ·ləʳ, $pɚˈtɪk·jə·lɚ/ *n* • *(fml)* A particular is a single part or detail of something: *His latest book is a bestseller, and yet in every particular it is exactly the same as his last.* [C] • *(fml)* If you are considering **the** particular, you are considering single examples rather than general matters or ideas: *The report focuses on the particular rather than the general and so doesn't draw any overall conclusions.* [U] • *"What did she have to say?" "Oh, nothing* **in particular** (= nothing special or important)." • *What* **in particular** (= special details) *did you like about the last apartment that we saw?*

par·tic·u·lar·ly /£pəˈtɪk·jʊ·lə·li, $pɚˈtɪk·jə·lɚ·li/ *adv* • *We're particularly* (= especially) *interested to hear from people who speak two or more European languages.* • *The new tax law will affect everyone, but particularly those on a low income.* • *Apparently it's been a particularly good year for strawberries.* • *He's not particularly handsome but he's a pleasure to be with.* • *I didn't particularly want to go, but I had to.* • Ⓔ

par·tic·u·lar·i·ty /£pəˌtɪk·jʊˈlær·ə·ti, $pɚˌtɪk·jəˈler·ə·t̬i/ *n* [U] *fml* • Particularity is the quality of being exact or very detailed: *It was the particularity of his criticisms that struck her.*

par·tic·u·lar·i·ties /£pəˌtɪk·jʊˈlær·ə·tiz, $pɚˌtɪk·jəˈler·ə·t̬iz/ *pl n fml* • Particularities are details: *The particularities* **of** *the case have not been revealed.*

par·tic·u·lars /£pəˈtɪk·jʊ·ləz, $pɚˈtɪk·jə·lɚz/ *pl n* • Particulars are details or information about a person or an event, esp. when officially recorded: *There's a form for you to note down all your particulars.* ○ *If I could just* **take down** *your particulars, madam* (= name, address and other details about you).

par·tic·u·lar [NOT EASILY SATISFIED] /£pəˈtɪk·jʊ·ləʳ, $pɚˈtɪk·jə·lɚ/ *adj* [after v] not easily satisfied; demanding that close attention should be given to every detail; FUSSY • *My mother-in-law is very particular* **about** *the kitchen – everything has to be perfectly clean and in its place.* • *She's very particular* **about** *what she eats* (= will not eat every type of food). • *"Would you like tea or coffee?" "Either – I'm not particular."* • Ⓔ Ⓟ

par·ti·san [UNFAIR], **par·ti·zan** /£ˌpɑː·tɪˈzæn, $ˈpɑːr·t̬ɪ·zən/ *adj* loyally supporting a person, principle or political party, often without considering or judging the matter very carefully • *The government report stresses very firmly that teachers must not take a partisan line in history lessons.* • *The audience was very partisan, and refused to listen to the points she was making in her speech.* • See also BIPARTISAN. • Ⓡⓤⓢ

par·ti·san, par·ti·zan /£ˈpɑː·tɪ·zæn, $ˈpɑːr·t̬ɪ·zən/ *n* [C] • *Now even the strongest partisans are complaining about the quality of candidates for party leadership.*

par·ti·san·ship, par·ti·zan·ship /£ˌpɑː·tɪˈzæn·ʃɪp, £ˈ– –, $ˈpɑːr·t̬ɪ·zən-/ *n* [U] • *There was a certain partisanship about the way that votes were cast.*

par·ti·san [SOLDIER], **par·ti·zan** /£ˈpɑː·tɪ·zæn, $ˈpɑːr·t̬ɪ·zən/ *n* [C] (in a country which has been defeated) a member of a secret armed force whose aim is to fight against the enemy which is controlling the country • (RUS)

par·ti·tion DIVIDING STRUCTURE /£pɑːˈtɪʃ·ᵊn, $pɑːr-/ *n* [C] a vertical structure like a thin wall which separates one part of a room or building from another • *It's an open-plan office but there are partitions* **between** *desks, so you do have some privacy.* • *The partitions* **between** *the toilets were very thin.* • PIC› **Office**

par·ti·tion *obj* /£pɑːˈtɪʃ·ᵊn, $pɑːr-/ *v* [T] • *Why don't you partition that large room* **into** *a lounge and a dining-room?* • *If we partition the kitchen* **off**, *it will make it seem as if we've got two separate rooms.* [M]

par·ti·tion NATIONAL DIVISION /£pɑːˈtɪʃ·ᵊn, $pɑːr-/ *n* [U] the dividing of a country into separate countries or areas of government • *The partition* **of** *India occurred in 1948.* • *It remains to be seen whether the country stays in one piece or is driven to civil war and partition.*

par·ti·tion *obj* /£pɑːˈtɪʃ·ᵊn, $pɑːr-/ *v* [T] • *Ireland was partitioned in 1921.*

part·ly /£ˈpɑːt·li, $ˈpɑːrt-/ *adv* See at PART SOME

part·ner /£ˈpɑːt·nəʳ, $ˈpɑːrt·nɚ/ *n* [C] a person you are closely involved with in some way • A partner in a company is one of the owners: *He's a partner* **in** *an insurance company/a law firm.* • Your partner can also be the person you are married to or living with as if you were married to them, or the person you are having a sexual relationship with: *I think I'd want to consult my partner on a decision as important as that.* ○ *Thirty per cent of the women questioned in the survey said they'd had more than eight* **sexual** *partners.* • A partner is also one of a pair of dancers or one of a pair who are playing a sport or a game together, esp. when the pair are playing as a team: *I can't go to the dance if I haven't got a partner.* ○ *Sarah is my new jogging partner.* • LP› **Relationships** (T)

part·ner *obj* /£ˈpɑːt·nəʳ, $ˈpɑːrt·nɚ/ *v* [T often passive] • If you partner someone in a sport, a game or a dance, you act as their partner: *Will you partner me in the tennis doubles on Saturday?*

part·ner·ship /£ˈpɑːt·nə·ʃɪp, $ˈpɑːrt·nɚ-/ *n* • Partnership is the state of being a partner: *She's* **gone into** *partnership* **with** *an ex-colleague of hers to start manufacturing mugs.* [U] ○ *Not since Nureyev's partnership* **with** *Fonteyn have we seen such chemistry between two dancers.* [C] • A partnership is also a company which is owned by two or more people: *the John Lewis Partnership* [C]

par·took /£pɑːˈtʊk, $pɑːr-/ *past simple of* PARTAKE

par·tridge /£ˈpɑː·trɪdʒ, $ˈpɑːr-/ *n* [C] *pl* **partridge** or **partridges** a short-tailed bird with a round body • *Partridges are shot for sport and food.* • *"A partridge in a pear tree"* (from the traditional Christmas song *The Twelve Days of Christmas*)

par·tu·ri·tion /£ˌpɑː·tjʊəˈrɪʃ·ᵊn, $ˌpɑːr·tuːˈrɪʃ-/ *n* [U] *specialized* the act of giving birth; CHILDBIRTH

par·ty CELEBRATION /£ˈpɑː·ti, $ˈpɑːr·t̬i/ *n* [C] a social event where a group of people meet to talk, eat, drink, dance etc., often in order to celebrate a special occasion • *a birthday party* • *an engagement party* • *a farewell party* • *an all-night party* • *Peter always* **has/gives/throws** *really wild parties.* • *Have you been invited to Georgina's 21st birthday party?* • *"Are you going to Alison's* **dinner** *party* (= a small often formal party where a meal is eaten) *on Tuesday night?" "No, I wasn't* **invited** *(to it)."* • *We had a (Br and Aus)* **fancy-dress/***(Am)* **costume** *party* (= a party where people wear clothes that make them look like someone or something else) *and four people came as pirates.* • A **party animal** is someone who enjoys parties and party activities very much and goes to as many as possible: *Sarah's a real party animal – she likes to dance all night.* • *(Br humorous)* Someone's **party piece** is a short performance or an action done in public, esp. one showing an unusual or amusing skill: *Arthur shocked everyone with his usual party piece – taking out his false teeth.* • *(humorous)* A **party pooper** is someone who spoils other people's enjoyment by disapproving of or not taking part in a particular activity. • A **party popper** is a small explosive device, held in the hand, which makes a loud noise and scatters strips of coloured paper when you pull the string at the top of it. • *"It's my party and I'll cry if I want to"* (From the song *It's My Party* written by Weiner, Gold and Gluck, 1963) • *"The Party's Over"* (title of a song written by Betty Comden and Adolph Green, 1956) • (D) (RUS)

par·ty /£ˈpɑː·ti, $ˈpɑːr·t̬i/ *v* [I] • If you party, you enjoy yourself by drinking and dancing, esp. at a party: *Let's party!* ○ *Yesterday they partied from noon to midnight at the street festival in Sydney.*

par·ty·ing /£ˈpɑː·ti·ɪŋ, $ˈpɑːr·t̬i-/ *n* [U] • *After all that partying* (= enjoying myself at a party) *last night, I'm rather tired this morning.*

par·ty POLITICAL GROUP /£ˈpɑː·ti, $ˈpɑːr·t̬i/ *n* [C + sing/pl v] an organization of people with particular political beliefs which competes in elections to try to win positions in local or national government • *the Democratic Party* • *the Green party* • *the Conservative party* • *The Labour party has/have just elected a new leader.* • *In Britain, the party* **in power** *has the right to choose the date of the next general election.* • *Mr Odinga left the government in 1966 and formed an* **opposition** *party which was banned three years later.* • *(Br) Nominations for the committee must be in by August 29th, the day before the party* **conference** *(Am* **convention***) starts.* • *Harold Wilson succeeded Hugh Gaitskell as party* **leader** *in 1963.* • *The party* **leadership** *is determined to keep a tight control over the publicity machine.* • *They contacted party* **members** *from across the nation to ask for their support.* • *(Br and Aus)* A **party political broadcast** (*Am* **paid political broadcast**) is a short television programme in which a politician talks about their party's ideas and plans in order to try to win more support. • **The party faithful** are people who have been loyal members or supporters of a party for a long time: *This policy may appeal to the party faithful, but will it gain the support of uncommitted voters?* • *They are likely once again to* **follow/toe the party line** (= obey official party opinion) *tonight.* See also **party line** at PARTY INVOLVEMENT. • When people talk about **party politics** they mean political activity and discussion within or relating to political parties rather than the whole country: *In the British system of government, the Queen is supposed to be* **above** (= not be involved with) *party politics.* • (D) (RUS)

par·ty VISITING GROUP /£ˈpɑː·ti, $ˈpɑːr·t̬i/ *n* [C + sing/pl v] a group of people who are involved in an activity together, esp. a visit • *A party* **of** *Britons is/are threatening to sue their tour operator because their hotel was infested with cockroaches.* • *There were at least three* **coach** *parties in the cathedral.* • *The* **royal** *party included Princess Mary and two future kings, Edward VIII and George VI, in sailor suits.* • *Most museums give a discount to* **school** *parties.* • (D) (RUS)

par·ty INVOLVEMENT /£ˈpɑː·ti, $ˈpɑːr·t̬i/ *n* [C] one of the people or groups of people involved in an official argument, arrangement or similar situation • *The UN called on all parties* **in** *the conflict to take a positive stance towards the new peace initiative.* • *It's often difficult to establish who the* **guilty** *party is following a road accident.* • To **be (a) party to** something, esp. something bad, is to be involved in it: *Despite all the evidence to the contrary, Jones denied having been a party to the crime.* • A **party line** is a telephone connection which is shared by two or more customers with separate telephones. See also **party line** at PARTY POLITICAL GROUP. • A **party wall** is a wall which divides two buildings that are joined together and belongs to both of them. • (D) (RUS)

par·ve·nu /£ˈpɑː·və·nuː, $ˈpɑːr-/ *n* [C] *fml disapproving* someone or something that has suddenly become successful but is not respected or thought to deserve success • *He is still seen as a parvenu in the aristocratic world of the Jockey Club.* • *For the second time in as many months, one of the top jobs at a fashion magazine has been snatched by a parvenu outsider.*

pas–de–deux /ˌpæ·dəˈdɜː/ *n* [C] *pl* **pas-de-deux** a dance for two people in BALLET

pass *(obj)* GO PAST /£pɑːs, $pæs/ *v* to go past (something or someone) or move in relation to it • *If you pass a supermarket can you get me some milk?* [T] • *A Rolls Royce passed us on the outside lane doing 110 mph.* [T] • *I spent the whole afternoon by the lake and not one car passed while I was there.* [I] • *I was just passing* (= going past the place where you are) *so I thought I'd drop in for a chat.* [I] • *A momentary look of anxiety passed* **across** *his face.* [I] • *The Queen passed* **among** *the crowd, stopping occasionally to shake a hand or exchange a few words with someone.* [I] • *She sat looking out of the train window at the countryside passing* **by**. [I] • *Do you ever feel that life is* **passing** *you* **by** (= you are missing important opportunities and experiences)? • *No one seeing the plight of these refugees could* **pass by on the other side** (= fail to give help). • *A vegetarian diet tends to be low in saturated fat and high in fibre, which helps prevent fats passing* **into** *the bloodstream.* [I] • *Let's now pass* **on to** *the next item on the agenda.* [I] • *A* *cloud passed* **over** *the sun.* [I] • *There was a brief moment of calm as the eye of the storm passed* **overhead**. [I] • *(fig.) Don't worry, his depression is only a temporary side-effect of the accident – it'll soon pass* (= finish). [I] • *(fig.) Don't buy goods which have passed their sell-by date* (= have not been sold before the correct date). [T] • *It* **passes (all) belief** (= It is difficult to believe) *that he could have been so selfish.* • LP> **Each other**

pass /£pɑːs, $pæs/ *n* [C] • A pass is a way to get between or over mountains: *The soldiers were trapped for two weeks until the* **mountain** *passes were free of snow.*

pass·a·ble /£ˈpɑː·sə·bl̩, $ˈpæs·ə-/ *adj* • *Because of the heavy snow, roads were passable* (= possible to travel on) *only with care in parts of Northern England.*

pass·er–by (*pl* **passers-by**) /£ˌpɑː·səˈbaɪ, $ˌpæs·ɚ-/ *n* [C] • A passer-by is someone who is going past a particular place, esp. when something unusual happens: *The would-be assassins opened fire, killing a policeman and a passer-by.* ○ *The assailant was captured and badly beaten by passers-by before being taken away by police.*

pass·ing /£ˈpɑː·sɪŋ, $ˈpæs·ɪŋ/ *adj* [before n; not gradable] • *A passing motorist stopped and gave her a lift to the nearby town.* • *A gunman in a passing car shot and wounded a pedestrian.* • *The elephants and giraffes got only a passing* **glance** *from* (= were not looked at for long by) *the teenagers heading from the car park to the games arcade.* • **Passing lane** is *Am for* **overtaking lane**. See at OVERTAKE GO PAST. • *(fig.) He bears more than a passing* (= slight) **resemblance** *to the young Marlon Brando.* • *(fig.) The matter is only of passing* (= temporary) *scientific interest.* • In tennis, if you make a **passing shot** you successfully hit the ball past the other player: *Time after time she charged to the net, leaving the Spaniard with time and room to make her passing shots.* • PIC> **Driving, Motorway**

pass·ing /£ˈpɑː·sɪŋ, $ˈpæs·ɪŋ/ *n* [U] • If something is said **in passing** it is said while talking about something else and is not the main subject of a conversation: *When asked if he had told the police about the incident, Mr Banks said he had* **mentioned** *it in passing to a detective.*

pass *(obj)* GIVE /£pɑːs, $pæs/ *v* to give (something) to (someone) • *Could you pass the salt please?* [T] • *I asked if I could see the letter, so she passed it* **to** *me reluctantly.* [T] • *Gerald passed me the note./Gerald passed the note to me.* [+ two objects] • *His is a family trade, passed* **(down) from** *generation* **to** *generation.* [T] • *Genes are the instructions by which parents' characteristics are passed* **on to** *their children.* [T] • *It's possible to pass* **on** *the virus* **to** *others through physical contact.* [M] • *If he provided us with any information, no one passed it* **on to** *me.* [M] • *Could you do me a favour and pass these sandwiches* **round/around/** *(Am also)* **out** (= offer them to all the people present)*?* [M] • In several sports, if you pass the ball, you kick, throw or hit it to someone in your team: *After making a solo run he passed the ball* **to** *Rosenthal, who ran into a tangle of defenders.* [T] ○ *He's a good football player but he's too selfish with the ball – he should pass more.* [I] • If you pass money, you give someone FORGED (= illegally made) money without telling them: *I saw someone get caught trying to pass forged £20 notes in the supermarket.* [T] ○ *I haven't trusted him since he passed me a forged fiver.* [+ two objects] • If you **pass the buck** you give a difficult problem to someone else to deal with, although it should really be your responsibility: *The Government has simply passed the buck* **to** *local authorities without offering any support.* • To **pass the hat (round)** is to try to collect money by asking people or organizations.

pass /£pɑːs, $pæs/ *n* [C] • In a team sport, a pass is a movement of the ball from one player to another member of the same team: *Jackie Mudie intercepted Alf Ramsey's pass* **to** *Ted Ditchburn and scored the winning goal.*

pass *(obj)* SUCCEED /£pɑːs, $pæs/ *v* to be successful in (an exam) • *Aspiring diplomats have to pass an examination to enter the diplomatic corps.* [T] • *The examination is so hard that fewer than 2% of all applicants pass.* [I] • *After failing his driving test five times, he finally passed last Tuesday.* [I] • *(fig.) If speaking the language is proof of Welshness then, in common with many of my compatriots, I do not pass the test.* [T] • To **pass muster** is to reach an acceptable standard: *New teams won't be admitted to the league if their stadiums don't pass muster.* • (F) (I)

pass /£pɑːs, $pæs/ *n* [C] • *(Br)* A pass is a successful result in an exam: *More school-leavers than ever are expected to have A-Level passes when results are announced on Thursday.* ○ *Jonathon Hill achieved grade A passes at A-level.* • *(Am)* A pass is a mark given to show that a student has successfully completed a course or an exam that they will not be given a GRADE (= numbered mark) for: *I got a pass in my World Lit course.* • *(Br)* A **pass degree** is a degree given to university or college students who have passed their exams, but not well enough to get an HONOURS degree. • *(Aus)* A **pass degree** is also a degree course which is designed to be completed in three years instead of the usual four. • *(esp. Am)* If an exam or course is **pass-fail**, no mark is given for it, and the only thing the students are told about their performance is whether or not they have passed. • *(Br and Aus)* The **pass mark** (*Am* **passing mark**) is the number of points that must be achieved in order to be successful in an exam: *The pass mark is usually around 50.* • The **pass rate** is the percentage of people who were successful in a particular exam: *Ulster children returned an 83 per cent A-level pass rate compared with 78 per cent in the rest of the United Kingdom.*

pass·a·ble /£ˈpɑː·sə·bl̩, $ˈpæs·ə-/ *adj* • Something which is passable is satisfactory but not excellent: *She had spent three months studying politics in the Soviet Union and could speak passable Russian.*

pass·a·bly /£ˈpɑː·sə·bli, $ˈpæs·ə-/ *adv* • *I'm not particularly musical but I play the piano passably.*

pass *(obj)* TIME /£pɑːs, $pæs/ *v* (of time) to go past • *Time seems to pass* **(by)** *so slowly when you're in school.* [I] • *The missing child's parents became more and more distraught as the hours passed.* [I] • *I was a bit worried about the party, but the evening passed without any great disasters.* [I] • If you pass time, you do something to stop yourself being bored during that period: *It was a long train journey, but they managed to pass three hours playing cards.* [T] ○ *The visitors pass their days swimming, windsurfing and playing volleyball.* [T] ○ *I'm not very good at drawing, but it helps to pass the time.* [T] • If you **pass the time of day** with someone, you have a short conversation with them: *I just wanted to pass the time of day* **with** *her, but she completely ignored me.*

pass·ing /£ˈpɑː·sɪŋ, $ˈpæs·ɪŋ/ *adj* [before n; not gradable] • *The situation seems to become more hopeless* **with each/every** *passing day.*

pass·ing /£ˈpɑː·sɪŋ, $ˈpæs·ɪŋ/ *n* [U] • *My parents seem to have mellowed* **with the** *passing* **of** *the years.*

pass *obj* APPROVE /£pɑːs, $pæs/ *v* [T] (of an official group of people) to give approval to (something) esp. by voting to make it law • *As early as the 1600s, the American colonies passed laws banning the sale of alcohol to Native Americans.* • *In 1984, the New York city council shocked private men's clubs by passing a law to open them to women.* • *The restaurant was serving meat that had not been passed* **as** *fit for human consumption.* • *He was passed* **fit** *for military service.* [+ obj + adj]

pass *obj* JUDGE /£pɑːs, $pæs/ *v* [T] to express (a judgment or opinion) • *Most countries were waiting to see how the new régime behaved before passing* **comment**. • *He's equally guilty, so he's in no position to pass* **judgment (on** *the rest of us).* • *I heard she'd been passing* (= making) **remarks** *about me behind my back.* • *A British judge is supposed to reflect society's values when passing* **sentence** (= stating what someone's official punishment will be).

pass *obj* EXCRETE /£pɑːs, $pæs/ *v* [T] *fml* to excrete (something) • If you pass **blood** it means there is blood in your urine or excrement: *If you pass blood you should go and see your doctor.* • People say **pass water** to avoid saying urinate.

pass NOT PLAY /£pɑːs, $pæs/ *v* [I] to choose not to play in a part of a card game or not to answer a question in a QUIZ • *Emilie must be having bad luck with her cards – she's passing* **on** *almost every hand.* • *Our second contestant scored 33 points and passed* **on** *four questions.* • *"Where did the Great Fire of London start?" "Pass* (= I don't know)*."*

pass CHANGE /£pɑːs, $pæs/ *v* [I always + adv/prep] to change (from one state to another) • *Wax passes* **from** *solid* **to** *liquid when you heat it.*

pass DOCUMENT /£pɑːs, $pæs/ *n* [C] an official document or ticket which shows that you have the right to go somewhere or use a particular form of transport • *Nowadays, many people use documents that carry photographs, such as* **bus** *passes and season tickets, as proof of identification.* • *A three-day festival pass is $15 for adults and $8 for kids.* • *(esp. Am)* A pass is also a document which allows a student to leave a class for a specific reason: *She had a pass to the library.*

pass SEXUAL ACTION /£pɑːs, $pæs/ *n* [C] an attempt to speak to or touch someone in a way that shows you are sexually attracted to them • *Steve got a little carried away and* **made** *a pass* **at** *me, even though his wife was there.*

pass BAD SITUATION /£pɑːs, $pæs/ *n* [U] a difficult or unpleasant condition • *If I'd been aware things had* **reached** *such* **a** *pass, I'd have told the police.* • *It's* **come to a pretty** *pass* (=It's a bad situation) *when you can't even have a few quiet drinks with some friends.*

pass as *obj*, **pass for** *obj v prep* [T] (of someone or something) to be accepted as being (something that they are not) • *I really want to go and see the film, but I don't think I'd pass as/for 18.* • *Do you think this jacket and trousers will pass as/for a suit? They're almost the same colour.*

pass a·way, **pass on** *v adv* [I] (used to avoid saying) to die • *She's terribly upset because her father passed away/passed on last week.*

pass·ing /£ˈpɑː·sɪŋ, $ˈpæs·ɪŋ/ *n* [U] • *Walter's death, at the age of 80, marked not simply the passing of a much loved and widely known member of the community, but also the end of an era.*

pass off HAPPEN *Br and Aus, Am* **come off** *v adv* [I always + adv/prep] to happen • *The pop festival passed off peacefully, despite the fears of local residents.*

pass off *obj* PRETEND, **pass** *obj* **off** *v adv* [M] to pretend that (someone or something) is someone or something that they are not • *Robertson is Scottish, but he could quite easily pass himself off* **as** *a Dubliner.* • *The dealer was trying to pass off fakes* **as** *valuable antiques.* • *It's hard to believe anyone would try to pass this nonsense off* **as** *literature.*

pass out BECOME UNCONSCIOUS *v adv* [I] to become unconscious; FAINT LOSE CONSCIOUSNESS • *When I opened the office door, I was hit on the head and passed out.* • *Residents walked past a dying man thinking that he had passed out after a party, police said.*

pass out LEAVE COLLEGE *v adv* [I] *Br and Aus* to leave a military college at the end of a course • *The new officers passed out* **from** *Britannia Royal Naval College on Thursday 1 August.* • *His parents attended the passing-out ceremony.*

pass o·ver *obj*, **pass** *obj* **o·ver** *v adv* [M] to ignore or to not give attention to (someone or something) • *I was very disappointed with the lecture – the lecturer seemed to pass over the most important points.* • *The woman alleges that her employers passed her over* **for promotion** *because she was pregnant.*

pass up *obj*, **pass** *obj* **up** *v adv* [M] to fail to take advantage of (an opportunity) • *I can't believe she passed up that chance to go to South America.* • *He's never one to pass up a free meal.* • *This might be the only chance you get, so don't pass it up.*

pas·sage CONNECTING WAY /ˈpæs·ɪdʒ/, **pas·sage·way** /ˈpæs·ɪdʒ·weɪ/ *n* [C] a usually long and narrow part of a building with rooms on one or both sides, or an enclosed path which connects places • *A narrow passage led directly through the house into the garden behind.* • *The bathroom's on the right at the end of the passage.* • *I was woken up by the sound of footsteps in the passageway.* • *We always leave the light on in the passage at night.* • A passage can also be a hollow part of the body through which something goes: *the nasal passages* • *the anal passage*

pas·sage PART /ˈpæs·ɪdʒ/ *n* [C] a short piece of writing or music which is part of a larger piece of work • *Several passages* **from** *the book were printed in a national newspaper before it was published.* • *The exam consisted of fifteen questions based on a passage taken from Jane Austen's 'Pride and Prejudice'.* • *It's a beautiful piece of music, but the fast passage at the end is too difficult for me to play.*

pas·sage TRAVEL /ˈpæs·ɪdʒ/ *n* travel, esp. as a way of escape • *The gunman then took a hostage and demanded a plane and* **safe** *passage* **to** *an unspecified destination.* [U] • *(slightly dated)* A passage is a journey, esp. over the sea: *Oliver had booked a passage* **to** *Rio de Janeiro.* [C] • If you **work** your passage, you do work on a ship during your journey instead of paying for a ticket: *(fig.) After several scandals, Johnson will have to work his passage back into the affections of the Canadian public* (=he will have to work hard to earn their affection).

pas·sage MOVEMENT /ˈpæs·ɪdʒ/ *n* [U] an act of moving through somewhere • *France had an easy passage* **through** *the championship, with several weak opponents.* • *Many meteorites explode during their passage* **through** *the atmosphere, and fall in showers.* • *The new law will prohibit the passage of troops and planes* **across** *the country's territory.*

pas·sage TIME /ˈpæs·ɪdʒ/ *n* [U] the action of time going past • *The passage* **of time** *is a concept seemingly grasped only by humans.* • **With** *the passage* **of time** (=After a period of time), *the memory will fade.*

pas·sage LAW /ˈpæs·ɪdʒ/ *n* [U] the official approval of esp. a new law • *He again urged passage* **of** *a constitutional amendment outlawing abortion.*

pass·book /£ˈpɑːs·bʊk, $ˈpæs-/ *n* [C] a small book that is used to officially record how much money is in a customer's account at a bank or **building society**

pas·sé /£pɑːˈseɪ, $pæsˈeɪ/ *adj disapproving* no longer fashionable • *In this age of computer art, drawing is often considered passé.* • *Australian wines were quite popular for a while, but now they're rather passé.*

pas·seng·er /£ˈpæs·ᵊn·dʒəʳ, $-dʒɚ/ *n* [C] a person who is travelling in a vehicle but is not driving it, flying it or working on it • *airline/rail/car passengers* • *London Tube and bus passengers will have to pay an average 9·7 per cent more on fares next year.* • *The manufacturers have just released details of their new passenger* **aircraft/jet** (=one for carrying people rather than for fighting or for carrying goods). • *Traffic frightens me so much that I find it difficult even to sit in the passenger* **seat** (=front seat next to the driver) *of a car.* • *The two passenger* **trains** (=ones carrying people rather than goods) *involved in the accident had both come from south-west London.*

pas·sion FEELING /ˈpæʃ·ᵊn/ *n* a very powerful feeling, for example of sexual attraction, love, hate, anger or other emotion • *Why is passion such a rare quality in the English?* [U] • *Many couples whose sexual relationship may have lapsed for years find their passion suddenly reignited.* [U] • *Football* **arouses** *a good deal of passion among its supporters.* [U] • A passion **for** something or someone is a great liking for them: *She has a* **consuming** *passion for romantic fiction.* [C] ○ *At school, his early interest in music developed into an* **abiding** *passion.* [C] ○ *He studied economics and sociology at Heidelberg in the 1920s, but politics and philosophy were his* **lifelong** *passions.* [C]

pas·sions /ˈpæʃ·ᵊnz/ *pl n* • Passions are very powerful feelings: *Touch a man's property and his passions are immediately aroused.* ○ *Three newspapers which had allegedly* **inflamed** *racial passions* (=caused more hate between racial groups) *were banned.* • If you say **passions are running high** you mean that people are feeling strong emotions about a particular subject at a particular time: *Passions run very high at election time.*

pas·sion·ate /£ˈpæʃ·ᵊn·ət, $-ə·nɪt/ *adj* • *The Italians are said to be the most passionate* (=full of emotion) *people in Europe.* • *The couple were caught in a passionate* **embrace** (=holding each other in a sexual way) *in a cupboard at the office party.* • *The child's mother made a passionate* (=filled with emotion) **plea** *for help.* • *Joe is passionate* **about** *baseball* (=he likes it very much).

pas·sion·ate·ly /£ˈpæʃ·ᵊn·ət·li, $-ə·nɪt-/ *adv* • *I felt so embarrassed when I walked into the room and found them kissing passionately.* • *She spoke passionately about her love of opera.* • *Ann has always believed passionately in a woman's right to choose.*

pas·sion·less /ˈpæʃ·ᵊn·ləs/ *adj disapproving* • Passionless means without any passion: *They had a passionless marriage.* ○ *This music is passionless.*

Pas·sion RELIGION /ˈpæʃ·ᵊn/ *n* [U] **the Passion** the suffering and death of Jesus Christ • A **passion play** is a play that tells the story of the suffering and death of Jesus Christ: *The passion play at Oberammergau in Germany has been performed every ten years since 1634.*

pas·sion·flo·wer /£ˈpæʃ·ᵊnˌflaʊ·əʳ, $-ɚ/ *n* [C] a climbing plant with large colourful flowers and edible oval purple or yellow fruit called **passion fruit** • PIC **Fruit**

pas·sive BEHAVIOUR /ˈpæs·ɪv/ *adj* (of a person or animal, or their behaviour) not acting to influence or change a situation; allowing other people to be in control • *(disapproving) I think Mark is too passive – he lets his girlfriend walk all over him.* • *For 2000 years, men have played an active part in leading worship and writing theology, while women have been confined to more passive* **roles**. • If you use **passive resistance** you show your opposition to something in a peaceful way rather than acting violently: *The Mahatma instigated several campaigns of passive resistance against the British government in India.* • When people talk about **passive smoking** they mean the unwanted breathing in of other people's cigarette smoke, esp. by people who do not smoke: *Doctors say passive smoking has caused his lung cancer.* • See also IMPASSIVE. Compare ACTIVE.

pas·sive·ly /ˈpæs·ɪv·li/ *adv* • *He never takes the initiative and tends to* **wait** *passively for his boss to tell him what to do.* • *You should try to negotiate a better contract instead of passively* **accepting** *whatever she offers you.*

pas·si·vi·ty /£pæsˈɪv·ɪ·ti, $-ə·t̬i/ *n* [U] • *He likes to give an impression of helpless passivity so that people will feel sorry for him.* • *Thirty years of political passivity have suddenly erupted into a dynamic surge of hopes, emotions, ideas and a feeling of genuine power.* • *It can be hard to understand the passivity of people who allow their partners to hit them.*

pas·sive GRAMMAR /ˈpæs·ɪv/ *n* [U] **the passive** *specialized* a way of structuring a sentence so that the grammatical subject is the person or thing which experiences the effect of an action, rather than the person or thing which causes the effect • *When changed into the passive, 'The dog chased the cat' becomes 'The cat was chased by the dog'.* • *In English, the passive is formed with the verb 'to be' and a past participle.* • Compare ACTIVE.

pas·si·vize *obj, Br and Aus usually* **-ise** /ˈpæs·ɪ·vaɪz/ *v* [T] *specialized* • If you passivize a verb or sentence you change it into the passive.

pas·si·vi·za·tion, *Br and Aus usually* **-i·sa·tion** /£ˌpæs·ɪ·vaɪˈzeɪ·ʃən, $-ɪ·vɪ-/ *n* [U] *specialized* • Passivization is the process of changing a verb or sentence into the passive.

pass·key /£ˈpɑːs·kiː, $ˈpæs-/ *n* [C] a key which can open either one important door or several doors and is only given to a limited number of people • *Still keeping the officer as a hostage, they used his passkey to get through the perimeter wall and into the yard.*

Pass·over /£ˈpɑːsˌəʊ·vəʳ, $ˈpæsˌoʊ·vɚ/ *n* [U not after *the*] a Jewish celebration in March or April every year to remember the escape of the Jews from Egypt • *During the eight days of Passover no leavened food such as bread or pasta is allowed.*

pass·port /£ˈpɑːs·pɔːt, $ˈpæs·pɔːrt/ *n* [C] an official document or small book containing some personal information and usually a photograph which is given to people by their own government to allow them to travel to foreign countries and to prove who they are • *Many refugees have arrived at the border without passports and with only the clothes they are wearing.* • *As an American working in France, I was disgusted that my new-born daughter was not granted a French passport.* • *He was a German, but travelling* **on** *a Swiss passport.* • *Where trains cross the frontier, customs and passport* **control** (=the examining of travellers' passports) *are handled on board.* • *You'll need to provide a passport* **photo** *for your membership card.* • *(fig.) Can beauty alone be a passport* **to** (=a certain way of getting) **success**, *or is some touch of genius required?* • *(fig.) Some careers officers fear that students opt too readily for business studies simply because it sounds like a passport* **to** (=an easy way to obtain) *a good job.*

pass·word /£ˈpɑːs·wɜːd, $ˈpæs·wɜːrd/ *n* [C] a secret word or combination of letters or numbers which is used for communicating with another person or with a computer to prove who you are • *I can't let you in unless you* **give** *the password.* • *You can't gain access to the computer system without* **entering** *your password.*

past TIME BEFORE /£pɑːst, $pæst/ *n* [U] **the past** the period before and until, but not including, the present time • *Evolution can successfully explain the past, but it can never predict the future.* • **In** *the past, scientists had to rely on cutting up dead brains to find out about living ones.* • *By winning the 1500 metres, he joins some of the great names* **of** *the past, including Coe, Ovett, Cram and Aouita.* • If someone is said to have a past, it means that what they did in their life before now is kept secret and was probably considered immoral in some way: *He's a man* **with** *a past.* • *"The past is a foreign country: they do things differently there."* (beginning of L.P.Hartley's book *The Go-Between*, 1953) • LP **Periods of time**

past /£pɑːst, $pæst/ *adj* [not gradable] • *Violent crime rose by 4 per cent, well below the rate of the past three years.* • *In fact, the average temperature worldwide has risen by about one degree Fahrenheit* **in** *the past 100 years.* • *I walk at least an hour a day on Hampstead Heath, and have been doing so* **for** *the past 30 years.* • *He was the fifth climber to die on these mountains* **over** *the past two days.* • *The country's imports of rainforest timber have fallen dramatically* **over** *the past year.* • *In* **centuries/years** *past* (=Many centuries/years ago) *even visiting the next village was considered a long journey.* • *I know from past* (=previous) **experience** *that you can't judge someone by their appearance.* • *The Prime Minister's family have been instructed not to discuss his past* **life** (=what he has done until now) *with the press.* • *I'm feeling much better now that the cold weather is past* (=finished). • A **past master** is a person who is very skilled in a particular activity: *Joe is a past master* **at** *getting invitations to parties.*

past GRAMMAR /£pɑːst, $pæst/ *n* [U], *adj* [before n; not gradable] (of) the form of a verb used to describe actions, events or states that happened or existed before the present time • *The past of 'change' is 'changed'.* • *'Must' doesn't have a past form.* • The **past continuous** (or **past progressive**) is the grammatical tense used to describe an action which someone was doing at a particular time. It is made with *was* or *were* and the *-ing* form of a verb: *'I was cooking' is an example of the past continuous.* • The **past participle** of a verb is the form, usually made by adding *-ed*, which is used in some grammatical structures such as the passive or PERFECT tenses: *The past participle of 'cook' is 'cooked'.* • The **past perfect** (or **pluperfect**) is the grammatical tense used to describe an action that had already finished when another action happened. It is made with *had* and a past participle: *'I had just cooked' is an example of the past perfect, and 'I had just been cooking' is an example of the* **past perfect continuous**. • The **past simple** (or **simple past**) is the form of a verb used to describe an action which happened before the present time and is no longer happening. It is usually made by adding *-ed*: *The past simple of 'cook' is 'cooked'.* • **Past tense** is used generally to describe grammatical structures that describe actions which have now finished. It is used by some people to refer to the **past simple**: *I think her husband must be dead – she always talks about him in* **the** *past tense.* • LP **Tenses, Varieties of English**

past BEYOND /£pɑːst, $pæst/ *prep, adv* [not gradable] in or to a position that is beyond a particular point • *I live on Station Road, just past the post office.* • *Jane finds it impossible to walk past cake shops without stopping.* • *Three boys went past us on mountain bikes.* • *Excuse me, has the number 37 bus gone past yet?* • *Was that Peter who just jogged past in those bright pink shorts?* • You use past to say what the time is when it is a particular number of minutes after an hour: *It's* **5/10/a quarter/20/25/half** *past three.* ○ *I've got to leave at twenty past or I'll miss that train.* • *She's past the age where she needs a babysitter.* • *Do what you want, I'm past* **caring** (=I don't care any longer). • *(infml)* Describing someone as being **past it** is a slightly rude or humorous way of saying that they are no longer able to do esp. physical activity because they are too old. • *(infml)* If you say you **wouldn't put it past** someone to do esp. something bad, it means that you would not be surprised if they did it: *I wouldn't put it past Helena to pass secrets to our competitors.* • LP **Time**

pas·ta /ˈpæs·tə, ˈpɑː·stə/ *n* [U] a food made from flour, water and sometimes egg which is cooked and usually served with a sauce. It is made in various shapes which have different names. • *Spaghetti, lasagne, vermicelli, ravioli and canneloni are types of pasta.* • (CS) (PL) (RUS)

paste STICKY SUBSTANCE /peɪst/ *n* [U] a thick soft sticky substance made either by mixing a liquid with a powder esp. to make a type of glue, or by crushing and mixing things such as fish, fruit or vegetables for food • *flour-and-water paste* • *wallpaper paste* • *tomato paste* • *anchovy paste* • *beef paste sandwiches* • *When I put wallpaper up I get paste all over my hands and clothes.* • *Mix the garlic and the salt together to obtain a paste.*

paste *obj* /peɪst/ *v* [T always + adv/prep] • To paste something is to stick it to something, esp. with paste: *When I was fat, I would cut pictures out and paste my own head* **onto** *the slim body to inspire myself.* • *You can make your own distorting mirror by pasting a sheet of kitchen foil* **to** *a piece of thin cardboard.* • *(specialized)* A **paste-up** is a piece of paper onto which text, pictures, etc. have been arranged and fixed during the designing of a magazine, book, etc.: *a paste-up* **artist** ○ *Printing plates are made by photographing the paste-ups.*

paste HARD MATERIAL /peɪst/ *n* [U] *specialized* a hard type of glass used to make artificial jewels • *Are these real diamonds or paste?*

paste·board /£ˈpeɪst·bɔːd, $-bɔːrd/ *n* [U] a type of thick cardboard made from sheets of paper that have been glued together

pas·tel MATERIAL /£'pæs·tᵊl, $pæs'tel/ *n* [C] (a picture made using) a colouring material which can be powdery or waxy and is usually in the shape of a small stick • *Do you prefer working in paints or pastels?* • *The show includes eighty-five paintings, pastels and sculptures by artists including Cézanne, van Gogh, Monet, Renoir and Sisley.*

pas·tel COLOUR /£'pæs·tᵊl, $pæs'tel/ *n* [C], *adj* (a colour that is) pale and soft • *The dancers are dressed in soft purples, light blues, and pastel greens.* • *Their house is decorated in pastel* **shades** (= colours). • *I think pastels are going out of fashion at last.*

pas·teur·ize *obj*, *Br and Aus usually* **–ise** /£'pæs·tʃᵊr·aɪz, £'pɑːs-, $'pæs·tʃə·raɪz/ *v* [T usually passive] to heat (esp. milk) at a controlled temperature for a fixed amount of time in order to kill bacteria • *pasteurized milk* ○ *pasteurized cheese* ○ *pasteurised beer* • *Yogurts contain live bacteria unless pasteurised for a second time after fermentation.*

pas·teur·iz·a·tion, *Br and Aus usually* **–i·sa·tion** /£,pæs·tʃᵊr·aɪ'zeɪ·ʃᵊn, £,pɑːs-, $,pæs·tʃɚ·ɪ-/ *n* [U] • *The introduction of pasteurization, which kills micro-organisms by heat, has been a major factor in making milk safer to drink.*

pas·tiche /£pæs'tiːʃ, £'--, $pɑː'stiːʃ/ *n* (the style of) a piece of art, music, literature, etc. which intentionally copies someone else's work or consists of parts taken from other places • *The film is a skilful, witty pastiche* **of** *'Jaws'.* [C] • *His latest building, a northern art gallery, is a dizzy pastiche* **of** *at least ten architectural styles.* [C] • *Writing pastiche is not only an amusing way of finding an author's stylistic tricks, it's practical and creative.* [U]

pas·tille /'pæs·tᵊl/ *n* [C] a type of small round sweet that can be sucked or chewed • *a fruit pastille* • *a throat pastille* (= a sweet for people with a cough or a sore throat)

pas·time /£'pɑːs·taɪm, $'pæs-/ *n* [C] an activity which is done for enjoyment; a hobby • *Watching football in England has never been a traditional family pastime.* • *(fig.) Suing people, especially doctors, is a great* **national** *pastime* (= is a very common activity) *in America.* • *If do-it-yourself is the nation's most* **popular** *pastime, then watching-someone-else-do-it comes a close second.*

past·ing /'peɪ·stɪŋ/ *n* [C usually sing] *infml* a severe beating, or a severe defeat in a game or competition • *John* **gets** *a pasting from his dad if he swears.* • *The England team is going to* **get** *a pasting in the next round.* • *(fig.) Shares in oil* **took** *a real pasting* (= fell a lot in value) *last week.*

pas·tis /pæs'tiːs/ *n* an alcoholic drink which is flavoured with ANISEED • *Pastis is now promoted as something to dilute – with water, tonic, or even orange juice.* [U] • *He looked like a real Frenchman, smoking Gitanes and drinking a pastis.* [C]

pas·tor /£'pɑː·stəʳ, $'pæs·tɚ/ *n* [C] a leader of a Christian group or church, esp. one which is Protestant • *The church's new pastor, the Rev. Gary Hollingsworth, will lead the congregation in two services and two Bible study sessions.*

pas·to·ral /£'pɑː·stᵊr·ᵊl, $'pæs·tɚ-/ *adj* • *a priest's pastoral duties* • *The Archbishop of New York probably has more AIDS victims under his pastoral* **care** (= help and care given to members of a religious group by their leader) *than any bishop in the world.* • *Many schools have established for their pupils excellent systems of* **pastoral care** (= help and care relating to problems the students have in their life rather than in school work).

pas·to·ral /£'pɑː·stᵊr·ᵊl, $'pæs·tɚ-/ *adj* (of a piece of art, writing or music) having or representing the pleasant, traditional features of countryside • *The painting showed a typical idyllic pastoral scene of shepherds watching over their grazing sheep.* • Pastoral farming is farming which involves keeping sheep, cattle, etc.

pas·tram·i /£pæs'trɑː·mi, $pə-/ *n* [U] spicy smoked BEEF (= meat from a cow) usually cut in thin slices and eaten cold on bread • *From pastrami on rye to baguette and camembert, this week's Food Programme examines the worldwide rise of the sandwich.*

pa·stry /'peɪ·stri/ *n* a food made from a mixture of flour, fat and water which is rolled flat and wrapped round or put over or under other foods and baked • *shortcrust/puff/filo/choux/flaky pastry* [U] • *Ann makes delicious pastry – you should try her apple pie.* [U] • *Use a pastry* **brush** *to glaze the pie with milk.* • A pastry is a type of sweet cake made of special pastry and usually containing something such as fruit or nuts: *We were offered a selection of cakes and pastries with our tea.* [C] • See also DANISH PASTRY. • PIC **Bread and cakes, Brush, Food preparation**

pas·ture /£'pɑː·s·tʃəʳ, $'pæs·tʃɚ/ *n* an area of land covered in grass or similar plants suitable for animals such as cows and sheep to eat • *The sheep were grazing on the lush green pastures.* [C] • *Some fields are planted with wheat, corn and sunflower for several years, and then returned to pasture for the cattle.* [U] • *(fig.) A lot of military officers, scientists and engineers who used to work for the government have left for* **greener** *pastures* (= better paid jobs) *in the private sector.* [C] • *(fig. Br) He has been director of the Festival for seven years, but he's off to* **pastures new** *(Am* **new pastures***)* (= is going somewhere else) *as soon as this year's Festival ends.* • *(fig. infml) After thirty years of working at the same company he was* **put out to** *pasture like an old work-horse* (= his employers got rid of him). [U] • *"Tomorrow to fresh Woods and Pastures new"* (John Milton in the poem *Lycidas*, 1638)

pa·sty FOOD /'pæs·ti/ *n* [C] a small case of pastry with a savoury filling such as meat, vegetables or cheese • *a cheese-and-onion pasty*

pa·sty APPEARANCE /'peɪ·sti/ *adj* **-ier**, **-iest** *disapproving* (of someone's face) very pale and unhealthy looking • *He's a rather unattractive man with long greasy hair and pasty skin.* • *Who's that* **pasty-faced** *girl over there?*

pat *obj* TOUCH /pæt/ *v* [T] **-tt-** to touch (someone or something) gently and usually repeatedly with the hand flat • *He patted my head/patted me* **on** *the head affectionately.* • *I bent down to pat the little puppy.* • *Pat the vegetables* **dry** (= Dry them by patting) *with a paper towel to remove excess moisture.* [+ obj + adj] • *My teacher* **patted** *me* **on the back** (= praised me) *for getting top marks in my English essay.*

pat /pæt/ *n* [C] • *I* **gave** *the little boy a pat* **on** *the head.* • *Mark got a* **pat on the back** *from* (= was praised by) *the boss for his excellent work.*

pat PIECE /pæt/ *n* [C] a small flat piece, esp. of butter • *Top the grilled fish with a pat of herb butter.*

pat WITHOUT THOUGHT /pæt/ *adj*, *adv* [not gradable] *usually disapproving* (esp. of an answer) having been already prepared and therefore said without thinking • *a pat answer/response* • *(Br and Aus)* If someone has or knows something **off pat** *(Am* **down pat***)* they know it so well that they can say or do it without having to try or think: *Salesmen* **have** *all their persuasive arguments off pat.*

patch AREA /pætʃ/ *n* [C] a small area which is different in some way from the area that surrounds it • *Our dog is called Patch because he's got a black patch on his back.* • *The hotel walls were covered in damp patches.* • *Be careful when you drive home – the weather report said there'd be* **fog** *patches.* • *There were lots of* **icy** *patches on the road this morning.* • *Mr and Mrs Green have got a* **vegetable** *patch* (= area for growing vegetables) *at the back of their garden.* • *This story is good* **in** *patches* (= some parts are good), *but I wouldn't really recommend it.* • *(infml)* If someone or something is **going through a bad/difficult/rough/sticky patch** they are experiencing a temporarily difficult situation: *Andy's going through a bit of a rough patch at the moment.* • *(infml)* A patch can also be a local area within which someone works: *He's been working as a policeman on the same patch for twenty years.* ○ *The prostitute was attacked by two other women for trying to work their patch.* • *(Br and Aus infml)* If you say something **isn't a patch on** something else you are emphasizing the fact that it is not as good as it: *This new washing machine isn't a patch on our old one.*

patch·y /'pætʃ·i/ *adj* **-ier**, **-iest** • *The varnish is a bit patchy on this table.* • *SE England will start with some patchy rain* (= rain in some areas)*/patchy cloud* (= cloud in some parts of the sky) *at first.* • *(fig.) Matthew found the service offered by estate agents extremely patchy* (= sometimes good and sometimes bad).

patch·i·ly /'pætʃ·ɪ·li/ *adv* • *The film was only patchily* (= in some parts) *entertaining.*

patch·i·ness /'pætʃ·ɪ·nəs/ *n* [U] • *The show's patchiness* (= The fact that only some parts of it are good) *has resulted in bad reviews.*

patch PIECE OF MATERIAL /pætʃ/ *n* [C] a small piece of material fixed over something to cover it • *I'll have to sew a patch onto these jeans – they're ripped at the knee.* • *He was wearing an old cardigan with leather patches on the elbows.* • Patch is another word for **eye-patch**: *Jo had an infection in her eye and had to wear a patch over it, which made her look like a pirate.* • A patch is also a small piece of material which can be stuck to the skin, from which particular substances can be absorbed into the body: *Some people wear* **nicotine** *patches to help them give up smoking.* ○ *I use a patch to stop me getting motion sickness.*

patch *obj* /pætʃ/ *v* [T] ● *I need some matching material to patch my jeans.* ● *My grandmother, too poor to buy a blanket, would patch* **together** (= sew small pieces together to make) *a quilt with old scraps of cloth.* [M] ● *(fig.) The two countries are trying to patch* **together** *a treaty* (= make one from the points they agree about) *on agricultural trade.* [M] ● *The whole town needed patching* **up** (= repairing) *after the explosion.* [M] ● *(fig.) Jackie and Bill are still trying to patch* **up** *their marriage.* [M]

patch *obj* CONNECT /pætʃ/ *v* [T always + adv/prep] *specialized* to connect (electronic or telephone equipment) to a system ● *The call was patched* **through** *to my phone.* [M] ● *I couldn't patch my computer* **into** *the network.*

patch·work /£ˈpætʃ·wɜːk, $-wɜːrk/ *n* [U] (the activity of making) cloth which is made by sewing together a lot of smaller usually square pieces of cloth with different patterns and colours ● *a patchwork quilt* ● *a patchwork jacket* ● *The old lady sat in the corner doing patchwork.* ● *(fig.) We looked out of the aircraft window down onto the patchwork of fields below.* ● *(fig.) Ipswich is a curious patchwork* (= mixture) *of the old and the new, a market town of pedestrianised streets and historic buildings alongside modern offices.* ● PIC› **Beds and bedroom**

pate /peɪt/ *n* [C] *dated or humorous* the top of a person's head ● *He always wears a hat in the sun to cover his* **bald** *pate.*

pâ·té /£ˈpæ·teɪ, $-ˈ-/ *n* a thick smooth soft savoury mixture made from meat, fish or vegetables ● *liver/salmon/vegetarian pâté* [U] ● *To enhance the flavour of a pâté, it should be served at room temperature with a complementary wine.* [C] ● *The delicate goose-liver pâté, pâté de foie gras, was invented by Jean Pierre Clause in Strasbourg, France around 1778.* [U]

pa·tel·la /pəˈtel·ə/ *n* [C] *pl* **patellae** /pəˈtel·iː/ *medical for* KNEECAP

pa·tent LEGAL RIGHT /£ˈpeɪ·tᵊnt, $ˈpæt·ᵊnt/ *n* [C] (a document given to someone to show) the official legal right to make or sell an invention for a particular number of years ● *In 1880 Alexander Graham Bell was granted a patent* **on** *an apparatus for signalling and communicating called a Photophone.* ● *Earlier this year, the company* **took out/filed** *a patent* **on** *a genetically engineered tomato that remains firm longer than untreated tomatoes.* ● Ⓓ

pa·tent /£ˈpeɪ·tᵊnt, $-t̬ᵊnt/ *adj* [before n; not gradable] ● *a patent screwdriver* ● A **patent medicine** is a medicine, usually not very powerful, which you can buy from a shop without the written permission of a doctor.

pa·tent *obj* /£ˈpeɪ·tᵊnt, $ˈpæt-/ *v* [T] ● *If you don't patent your invention, other people may make all the profit out of it.*

pa·ten·tee /£ˌpeɪ·tᵊnˈtiː, $ˌpæt̬·ᵊnˈtiː/ *n* [C] *specialized* ● A patentee is the person or organization that owns the legal right to make or sell something.

pa·tent SHINY /£ˈpeɪ·tᵊnt, $ˈpæt·ᵊnt/ *adj* (esp. of leather) having a very shiny surface ● *black patent leather shoes* ● *a red patent handbag* ● Ⓓ

pa·tent OBVIOUS /£ˈpeɪ·tᵊnt, $-t̬ᵊnt/ *adj* [before n] *fml* (esp. of bad characteristics) clear or obvious ● *a patent lie* ● *a patent disregard of the law* ● *"No," he replied, with patent distaste.* ● Ⓓ

pa·tent·ly /£ˈpeɪ·tᵊnt·li, $-t̬ᵊnt-/ *adv* ● *It's patently* **obvious** (= very obvious) *that he doesn't care.*

pa·ter /£ˈpeɪ·təʳ, £ˈpɑː-, $ˈpɑː·t̬ɚ/ *n* [C] *Br dated or humorous* your father ● *I'm spending Christmas with Mater and Pater.*

pa·ter·nal /£pəˈtɜː·nəl, $-ˈtɜːr-/ *adj* of or like a father ● *He's very paternal* (= showing the affectionate feelings of a father) *– it's lovely to see him with the baby.* ● *My paternal grandparents* (= My father's parents) *were Irish.* ● Compare MATERNAL.

pa·ter·nal·ly /£pəˈtɜː·nə·li, $-ˈtɜːr-/ *adv* ● *"It's OK," he says, patting me paternally.*

pa·ter·ni·ty /£pəˈtɜː·nɪ·ti, $-ˈtɜːr·nə·t̬i/ *n* [U] ● *Increasingly, the unmarried father of a child in Europe registers his paternity* (= the fact of being the father) *at the baby's birth.* ● *(fig.) There are a lot of arguments about the paternity* (= origin) *of this idea.* ● *Does your firm give paternity* **leave** (= time a man is allowed away from work when his wife or partner is having a child)*?* ● *He has recently lost a paternity* **suit** (= legal case in which a woman claims a particular man is the father of her child). ● *He had to take a paternity* **test** *to prove he wasn't the child's father.*

pa·ter·nal·ism /£pəˈtɜː·nə·lɪ·zᵊm, $-ˈtɜːr-/ *n* [U] *usually disapproving* an attitude of people in authority which results in them making decisions for other people which are often beneficial but which prevent those people from taking responsibility for their own lives ● *The company's paternalism extends to medical, dental and hairdressing facilities for its employees.* ● *The decision to restrict reproductive rights marks a return to the days of paternalism, when the state told women how to run their lives.*

pa·ter·nal·ist /£pəˈtɜː·nə·lɪst, $-ˈtɜːr-/ *n* [C] *usually disapproving* ● *He was a paternalist who believed that people should be compulsorily vaccinated against life-threatening diseases.*

pa·ter·nal·is·tic /£pəˌtɜː·nəˈlɪs·tɪk, $-ˌtɜːr·nəˈlɪs·t̬ɪk/ *adj esp. disapproving* ● *In a paternalistic gesture, the general has arranged for his troops to be covered by life insurance.*

path TRACK /£pɑːθ, $pæθ/ *n* [C] a route or track between one place and another, or the direction in which something is moving ● *a garden path* ● *a concrete path* ● *a* **well-trodden** *path* ● *This is the path* **to** *the cliffs.* ● *Many paths are overgrown but you can still see the way to go.* ● *It will be several days before snowploughs* **clear** *a path* **(through)** *to the village.* ● *They* **followed** *the path until they came to a gate.* ● *Carry on* **along** *this path until you come to a shop, then turn left.* ● *A fierce fire is still raging through the forest, burning everything in its path* (= as it moves forward). ● *The Weather Service issues warnings to people in the path* **of** *a hurricane* (= in the area in which it is moving) *so they have time to prepare or get out of the way.* ● *The charged particles move in spiral paths.* ● *(fig.) His path through life* (= The way he decided to live his life) *was never easy.* ● *(slightly fml) It was a pleasure meeting you – I hope our* **paths cross** (= we meet) *again in the future.* ● See also FOOTPATH; PATHWAY. ● PIC› **Accommodation**

path·less /£ˈpɑːθ·ləs, $ˈpæθ-/ *adj* [not gradable] *literary* ● *He was lost for days in the vast pathless desert.*

path ACTIONS /£pɑːθ, $pæθ/ *n* [C] a set of actions, esp. which lead to a goal or result ● *The path* **to** *success is fraught with difficulties.*

pa·thet·ic SAD /£pəˈθet·ɪk, $-ˈθet̬-/ *adj* causing feelings of sadness, sympathy or sometimes lack of respect, esp. because a person or an animal is suffering ● *The refugees were a pathetic* **sight** *– starving, frightened and cold.* ● *After the accident he became a pathetic* **figure**, *a shadow of his former self.* ● See also PATHOS. ● Ⓒⓢ Ⓓ Ⓟⓛ Ⓡⓤⓢ

pa·thet·i·cal·ly /£pəˈθet·ɪ·kli, $-ˈθet̬-/ *adv* ● *Other former captives spoke of pathetically inadequate food rations.* ● *I left the dog whimpering pathetically in the corner.*

pa·thet·ic UNSUCCESSFUL /£pəˈθet·ɪk, $-ˈθet̬-/ *adj disapproving* causing a lack of respect, often because unsuccessful or lacking ability, effort or bravery ● *And that was my own rather pathetic attempt to paint the view from the bedroom window.* ● *"I can't come – I've got to go home and feed my cat." "Oh, come on, that's a pathetic excuse!"* ● *It's a bit pathetic when a thirty-five year old man can't stand up to his own mother.* ● *As for the main actor's performance, it was absolutely pathetic!* ● *Are you telling me you're frightened to speak to her? Don't be so pathetic!* ● Ⓒⓢ Ⓓ Ⓟⓛ Ⓡⓤⓢ

pa·thet·i·cal·ly /£pəˈθet·ɪ·kli, $-ˈθet̬-/ *adv disapproving* ● *My parents' advice on the subject was pathetically inadequate.* ● *I thought they had pathetically little to say for themselves.* ● *He seems pathetically grateful for every little bit of help that's offered him.*

path·o·gen /ˈpæθ·ə·dʒən/ *n* [C] any small life form, such as a bacterium or a virus, which can cause disease ● *a dangerous pathogen*

path·o·gen·ic /ˌpæθ·əˈdʒen·ɪk/ *adj*

path·o·log·i·cal /£ˌpæθ·əˈlɒdʒ·ɪ·kᵊl, $-ˈlɑː·dʒɪ-/ *adj infml* (of a person) unable to control part of their behaviour; unreasonable ● *I've got a pathological fear of heights* ● *Anthony's a pathological* **liar**. ● *His dislike of people who showed off about their achievements and acquaintances was almost pathological.* ● *His extreme cynicism suggests a pathological condition.*

path·o·log·i·cal·ly /£ˌpæθ·əˈlɒdʒ·ɪ·kli, $-ˈlɑː·dʒɪ-/ *adv* ● *Computer companies are pathologically secretive, because success can hang on the progress of a single product.*

pa·thol·o·gy /£pəˈθɒl·ə·dʒi, $-ˈθɑː·lə-/ *n* [U] the scientific study of disease

pa·thol·og·ist /£pəˈθɒl·ə·dʒɪst, $-ˈθɑː·lə-/ *n* [C] • A pathologist is an expert in the study of diseases, esp. one who examines a dead person's body, often by cutting it open, to discover how they died.

path·o·log·i·cal /£ˌpæθ·əˈlɒdʒ·ɪ·kəl, $-ˈlɑː·dʒɪ-/ *adj* [not gradable] • *a pathological condition/complaint*

path·o·log·i·cal·ly /£ˌpæθ·əˈlɒdʒ·ɪ·kli, $-ˈlɑː·dʒɪ-/ *adv* [not gradable] • *It is feared that the fish in these polluted waters are becoming pathologically contaminated.*

pa·thos /£ˈpeɪ·θɒs, $-θɑːs/ *n* [U] *literary* the power of a situation, piece of writing, work of art or person to cause feelings of sadness, esp. because of sympathy • *There's a pathos in his performance which he never lets slide into sentimentality.* • Compare BATHOS. • Ⓓ Ⓖⓡ

path·way /£ˈpɑːθ·weɪ, $ˈpæθ-/ *n* [C] *slightly fml* a track which a person can walk along, or *(fig.)* a set of actions you take in life; a PATH • *New pedestrian pathways are being built alongside the road.* • *(fig.) Working your way up through a company is a difficult pathway.* • In biology, a pathway is a set of connected chemical reactions.

pa·tience /ˈpeɪ·ʃənts/ *n* [U] the ability to wait, or continue doing something despite difficulties, or suffer without complaining or becoming annoyed • *Patience – they'll be here soon.* • *You have to have such a lot of patience when you're dealing with kids.* • *In the end I* **lost** *my patience and shouted at her.* • *As a therapist he had* **infinite** *patience.* • *He's a good teacher but he doesn't have much patience* **with** *the slower pupils.* • *Making small scale models* **takes/requires** *a great deal of patience.* • *Their youngest son was beginning to* **try** *my patience* (= annoy me). • *(dated)* Someone who has **the patience of Job** has limitless patience and continues to do what they think they should do despite all difficulties. • If someone has **the patience of a saint**, they are always calm and nothing seems to upset them: *It's not surprising she left – the noise and smell in the flat would have* **tried** (= been difficult to deal with for someone who has) *the patience of a saint.* • *(Br and Aus)* Patience (*esp. Am* **solitaire**) is a game played with cards by one person.

pa·tient /ˈpeɪ·ʃənt/ *adj* • *Dinner will be ready in half an hour – just be patient!* • *Be patient* **with** *her – she's very old and can't do anything quickly.*

pa·tient·ly /ˈpeɪ·ʃənt·li/ *adv* • *There was a queue of people* **waiting** *patiently for the bus to arrive.*

pa·tient /ˈpeɪ·ʃənt/ *n* [C] a person who is receiving medical care, or who is cared for by a particular doctor or DENTIST when necessary • *I'm a patient of Dr Stephens, please could I make an appointment to see her?* • An **in**-patient is a person who goes into hospital to receive medical care, and stays there while they are being treated. • An **out**-patient is a person who stays at home while they receive medical care, but comes to the hospital at particular times, for example once a month, to see a doctor, nurse or other health worker.

pat·i·na /£ˈpæt·ɪ·nə, $-ən·ə/ *n* [U] a thin surface layer which develops on something because of use, age or chemical action • *His tomb was covered with* **a** *yellow patina* **of** *lichen.* • *(fig. fml) Beware their patina of civility, it's only an act.* • *(specialized)* Patina (also **verdigris**) is a blue-green layer that forms on COPPER or BRASS.

pat·i·o /£ˈpæt·i·əʊ, $ˈpæt̬·i·oʊ/ *n* [C] *pl* **patios** an area next to a house with a solid floor but no roof which is used, esp. for eating, in good weather • *In the summer Jim and I have breakfast out* **on** *the patio.* • *We need some new patio furniture.* • *I'd better go back – I can't remember if I locked the patio* **door**. • PIC **Doors, Garden** Ⓔ Ⓟ

pa·tis·se·rie /£pəˈtiː·sər·i, $-ˈt̬iː·sɚ·i/ *n pl* **patisseries** (a shop selling) cakes made in the French style • *We ate cakes in a patisserie off the Boulevard St Michel.* [C] • *Delia came home with a box of the most delicious patisserie.* [U]

pat·ois /ˈpæt·wɑː/ *n* [C/U] *pl* **patois** the form of a language spoken by people in a particular area which is different from the standard language of the country • *the local patois*

pa·tri·arch /£ˈpeɪ·tri·ɑːk, $-ɑːrk/ *n* [C] a BISHOP (= high-ranking priest) in particular Eastern Christian churches

pa·tri·ar·chy /£ˈpeɪ·tri·ɑː·ki, $-ɑːr-/ *n* (an example of a) society in which the oldest male is the leader of the family or, more generally, (an example of a) society controlled by men in which men use their power to their own advantage • *Their society always was and remains to this day a patriarchy.* [C] • *Patriarchy has not disappeared – it has merely changed form.* [U] • *She rails against patriarchy and hierarchy.* [U] • Compare **matriarchy** at MATRIARCH.

pa·tri·arch /£ˈpeɪ·tri·ɑːk, $-ɑːrk/ *n* [C] • *As well as having many privileges, the patriarch of each family unit has many responsibilities.* • Compare MATRIARCH.

pa·tri·ar·chal /£ˌpeɪ·triˈɑː·kəl, $-ˈɑːr-/ *adj* • *patriarchal structure* • *a patriarchal society* • Compare **matriarchal** at MATRIARCH.

pa·tri·cian /pəˈtrɪʃ·ən/ *n* [C], *adj slightly fml* (of or like) a person of high social rank • *He speaks English with a marked patrician accent.* • *He was born into a patrician New England family and privately educated.*

pat·ri·cide /£ˈpæt·rɪ·saɪd, $ˈpæt·rə-/ *n* [U] the crime of killing your own father • Compare MATRICIDE; PARRICIDE.

pat·ri·li·ne·al /£ˌpæt·rɪˈlɪn·i·əl, $ˌpæt·rə-/ *adj* [not gradable] *fml* establishing family membership by considering only male relatives

pa·tri·ot /£ˈpæt·ri·ət, $ˈpeɪ·tri·ɑːt/ *n* [C] a person who loves their country and, if necessary, will fight for it

pa·tri·ot·ic /£ˌpæt·riˈɒt·ɪk, $ˌpeɪ·triˈɑː·t̬ɪk/ *adj* • *patriotic fervour/pride* • *That was an era when many Americans felt it was their patriotic* **duty** *to buy bonds to support the war effort.* • *A folk group led the singing of patriotic* **songs**.

pa·tri·ot·i·cal·ly /£ˌpæt·riˈɒt·ɪ·kli, $ˌpeɪ·triˈɑː·t̬ɪ·kli/ *adv*

pa·tri·ot·ism /£ˈpæt·ri·ə·tɪ·zəm, £ˈpeɪ·tri-, $-t̬ɪ-/ *n* [U] • *A wave of euphoric patriotism seems to have swept the nation.* • *"Patriotism is the last refuge of the scoundrel"* (Samuel Johnson in *Boswell's Life of Johnson*, 1775)

pa·trol *(obj)* /£pəˈtrəʊl, $-ˈtroʊl/ *v* **-ll-** (esp. of soldiers or the police) to go around (an area or a building), usually regularly, to see if there is any trouble or danger • *The whole town is patrolled by police because of the possibility of riots.* [T] • *A security guard with a dog patrols the building site at night.* [T] • *Coastguards found a deserted boat while patrolling (along) the coast.* [T; I + prep]

pa·trol /£pəˈtrəʊl, $-ˈtroʊl/ *n* • *a patrol boat* • *a highway patrol* • *Three reconnaissance aircraft are permanently* **on** *patrol.* [U] • *The soldiers came under fire while* **on** *a routine patrol.* [C] • A patrol is also a small group of soldiers or military ships, aircraft or vehicles, esp. one which patrols an area or has been formed for a particular purpose: *Our forward patrol has/have spotted the enemy.* [C + sing/pl v] • A **patrol car** is a car used by the police when patrolling roads. • *(Am and Aus)* A **patrol officer** (*male* **patrolman**) is a police officer who wears a uniform and patrols a particular area. • *(Am and Aus)* A **patrol wagon** (also **paddy wagon**) is a road vehicle used for transporting prisoners. • PIC **Emergency services**

pa·trol·man /£pəˈtrəʊl·mən, £-mæn, $-ˈtroʊl-/ *n* [C] *pl* **-men** *Br* a person who works for an organization of car owners and drives to any of its members to help them if their car stops working

pa·tron SUPPORTER /ˈpeɪ·trən/ *n* [C] a person or group that supports an activity or organization, esp. by giving money, or an important person who allows their name to be used to support a particular organization • *What people sometimes forget about King George IV is that he was a patron* **of the arts**. • *The Princess Royal is a well-known patron* **of** *several charities.* • A **patron saint** is a Christian SAINT who is believed to give special help to a particular place, activity, person or type of object: *St. John Bosco is the patron saint* **of** *Turin.* • Ⓓ

pa·tron·age /£ˈpæt·rə·nɪdʒ, $ˈpeɪ·trə-/ *n* [U] • *This concert was made possible by the kind patronage of Smith Industries.* • *The Conservative Party* **enjoys** *the patronage of much of the business community.*

pa·tron CUSTOMER /ˈpeɪ·trən/ *n* [C] *fml* a person who uses a particular shop, restaurant, hotel, etc., esp. regularly; a customer • *Will patrons kindly note that this shop will be closed on 17th July.* • Ⓓ

pa·tron·age /£ˈpæt·rə·nɪdʒ, $ˈpeɪ·trə-/ *n* [U] *fml* • *We would like to thank all of our customers for their patronage in the past.*

pa·tron·ize *obj, Br and Aus usually* **-ise** /£ˈpæt·rə·naɪz, $ˈpeɪ·trə-/ *v* [T] *fml* • *We always patronize Beaumont's – the food is so good there.*

pa·tron·age /£ˈpæt·rə·nɪdʒ, $ˈpeɪ·trə-/ *n* [U] *esp. disapproving* the power of a person to give someone an important job or position • *Patronage itself is a potent force if used politically.*

pa·tron·ize *obj, Br and Aus usually* **-ise** /£ˈpæt·rə·naɪz, $ˈpeɪ·trə-/ *v* [T] *disapproving* to speak to or behave towards (someone) as if they are stupid or unimportant • *Stop patronising me – I understand the play as well as you do.* • *She was always patronizing the locals who were all very intelligent and hard-working.*

pa·tron·iz·ing, *Br and Aus usually* **-is·ing** /ˈpæt·rə·naɪ·zɪŋ/ *adj* • *It's that patronizing tone of hers that I can't bear.* • *He's sometimes very patronizing.*

pat·sy /ˈpæt·si/ *n* [C] *Am and Aus slang* a person whom it is easy to cheat or make suffer • *Listen, no one makes a patsy out of me, so don't give me any more of your eyewash!*

pat·ter [SPEECH] /£ˈpæt·əʳ, $ˈpæţ·ɚ/ *n* [U] continuous and sometimes amusing speech or talk, often learned in advance, esp. used by someone trying to sell things or by an entertainer • *He should succeed – he dresses well and his* **sales** *patter is slick and convincing.*

pat·ter [SOUND] /£ˈpæt·əʳ, $ˈpæţ·ɚ/ *v* [I always + adv/prep], *n* (to make, esp. by moving) a series of quick quiet soft sounds • *I heard the rain patter* **against/on** *the window.* • *We could hear mice pattering* **about/around** *looking for food.* • *I find* **the** *patter* **of** *rain on the roof soothing.* [U] • *(esp. humorous)* If a person refers to **the patter(ing) of tiny feet** they are talking about a baby which someone might have, is going to have or has recently had: *Two years after they were married their house was blessed by the patter of tiny feet* (= a baby). ○ *Are you telling me we're going to be hearing the patter of tiny feet?*

pat·tern [WAY] /£ˈpæt·ən, $ˈpæţ·ɚn/ *n* [C] a recognizable way in which something is done, organized or happens • *The pattern of family life has been changing over recent years.* • *A pattern is beginning to emerge from our analysis of the accident data.* • *In this type of mental illness, the usual pattern is bouts of depression alternating with elation.* • *Many* **behaviour(al)** *patterns have been identified in the chimp colony.*

pat·tern [ARRANGEMENT] /£ˈpæt·ən, $ˈpæţ·ɚn/ *n* [C] any regularly repeated arrangement, esp. a design made from repeated lines, shapes or colours on a surface • *Look, the frost has made a beautiful pattern on the window.* • *I've never really cared for* **floral** *patterns.* • *Patterns have been found carved on the tomb wall but no one knows what they mean.*

pat·terned /£ˈpæt·ənd, $ˈpæţ·ɚnd/ *adj* • *patterned textiles/wallpaper*

pat·tern [EXAMPLE] /£ˈpæt·ən, $ˈpæţ·ɚn/ *n* [C usually sing] something which is used as an example, esp. to copy • *The design is so good it's sure to* **set the** *pattern for many others.*

pat·tern *obj* /£ˈpæt·ən, $ˈpæţ·ɚn/ *v* [T] • *She patterns herself* **on** *her big sister.* • *The new course is patterned closely* **after** *a similar program offered by USC.*

pat·tern [DRAWING] /£ˈpæt·ən, $ˈpæţ·ɚn/ *n* [C] a drawing or shape used to show how to make something • *a knitting pattern* • *a dress pattern* • *Cut out all of the pieces from the paper pattern and pin them on the cloth.*

pat·tern [PIECE] /£ˈpæt·ən, $ˈpæţ·ɚn/ *n* [C] a small piece of cloth or paper taken from a usual-sized piece and used to show what it looks like; a SAMPLE [SMALL AMOUNT] • *a pattern book*

pat·ty /£ˈpæt·i, $ˈpæţ-/ *n* [C] a piece of food made into a disc shape which is then cooked • *minced meat patties/sweet corn patties*

pau·ci·ty /£ˈpɔː·sɪ·ti, $ˈpɑː·sə·ţi/ *n* [U] *fml* an amount which is not enough; a lack • *There is a paucity* **of** *information on the ingredients of many cosmetics.*

paunch /£pɔːntʃ, $pɑːntʃ/ *n* [C] a fat stomach, esp. on a man • *You're getting a bit of a paunch – a little exercise might help.*

paunch·y /£ˈpɔːn·tʃi, $ˈpɑːn-/ *adj* **-ier, -iest** • *"What's he look like?" "Oh, middle-aged, paunchy and balding."*

paunch·i·ness /£ˈpɔːn·tʃɪ·nəs, $ˈpɑːn-/ *n* [U]

pau·per /£ˈpɔː·pəʳ, $ˈpɑː·pɚ/ *n* [C] a very poor person

pause /£pɔːz, $pɑːz/ *n* [C] a short period in which something such as a sound or an activity is stopped before starting again • *There will be a brief pause* **in** *the proceedings while the piano is moved into place.* • *After a long, awkward pause someone asked a question.* • *She spoke for three quarters of an a hour without so much as a pause.* • *There followed a* **pregnant** (= filled with meaning) *pause in which both knew what the other was thinking but neither knew what to say.* • *(fml)* If something **gives** someone **pause** it makes them stop and think about what they were doing or intending to do. • [LP]›**Dots**

pause /£pɔːz, $pɑːz/ *v* [I] • *He paused and thought for a moment.* • *She paused to get her breath back and then carried on jogging.*

pave *obj* /peɪv/ *v* [T usually passive] to cover (an area of ground or a path) with a hard flat surface of, for example, pieces of stone, concrete or bricks • *The area from the shops to the beach is paved* **with** *bricks set in patterns.* • If someone uses the expression **paved with gold** about a city, they mean that it is easy to make money there: *Unemployed youngsters still come to London in their hundreds thinking that* **the streets are** *paved with gold.* • If something **paves the way for/to** something else, it makes the other thing possible: *Scientists hope that data from the probe will pave the way for a more detailed exploration of Mars.* • *"They paved paradise / And put up a parking lot"* (from the song *Big Yellow Taxi* by Joni Mitchell, 1970)

pav·ing /ˈpeɪ·vɪŋ/ *n* [U] • Paving is either a paved area, or material used to pave an area. • *(esp. Br)* A **paving stone** is a flat piece of stone which is usually either rectangular or square, many of which are put down together to pave a path or an area.

pave·ment *Br* /ˈpeɪv·mənt/, *Am* **side·walk**, *Br specialized* **foot·way**, *Aus* **foot·path** *n* [C] the path with a hard surface beside one or both sides of a road used esp. for walking on • *Keep to the pavement, Rosie, there's a good girl.* • *(Am and Aus)* A pavement is also the surface of a road if it has been specially put there, esp. if made from concrete or TARMAC. • *(Br)* A pavement artist (*Am* **sidewalk artist**) is a person who draws pictures on a pavement using coloured CHALKS, esp. so that people who walk past will give small amounts of money. • [PIC]›**Road** Ⓘ Ⓟ

pa·vil·ion [BUILDING] /pəˈvɪl·jən/ *n* [C] *Br* a building beside a sports field, esp. one where cricket is played, used by the players and sometimes by people watching the game • *a cricket pavilion* • *(Am)* A pavilion is also one of a group of related buildings: *the West Pavilion of Central General Hospital* • *(Am)* A pavilion is also a large building in which sports or entertainment take place: *The show will have its premiere at the Dorothy Chandler Pavilion in Los Angeles.*

pa·vil·ion [TEMPORARY STRUCTURE] /pəˈvɪl·jən/ *n* [C] a temporary structure, such as a large tent, esp. used at public events or for shows

pav·lo·va /£pævˈləʊ·və, $pɑːvˈloʊ-/ *n* a sweet cold dish consisting of a MERINGUE (= the transparent part of an egg cooked slowly with sugar) with a layer of fruit and cream on top • *Could I have your recipe for pavlova, Ann?* [U] • *She's made a pavlova.* [C]

paw /£pɔː, $pɑː/ *n* [C] the foot of an animal such as a cat, dog or bear which has CLAWS or nails • *Shem lifted his paw* *and put it on my knee.* • *I found paw prints in the kitchen.* • *(infml humorous)* A paw is also a human hand: *Take your filthy paws off my nice clean washing!* • Compare HOOF. • PIC> **Dogs**

paw *(obj)* /£pɔː, $pɑː/ *v* • *When their dog heard them it began pawing* **(at)** *the ground in excitement.* [I/T] • *You don't want to be near a bull if it's pawing and snorting.* [I] • *(infml)* To paw someone is to feel or touch them roughly with the hands, esp. in an unpleasant sexual way: *If you start pawing me again I'll kick you where it hurts.* [T]

pawn *obj* MONEY /£pɔːn, $pɑːn/ *v* [T] to leave (a possession) with a PAWNBROKER, for which they give money but which they can also sell if the money is not paid back within a particular time • *Of all items pawned, jewellery is the most common.* • A **pawn shop** (also **pawnbroker's**) is a shop where a pawnbroker operates their business.

pawn /£pɔːn, $pɑːn/ *n* [U] • *Her wedding ring is* **in** *pawn – that's how she could afford to make the journey.*

pawn GAME PIECE /£pɔːn, $pɑːn/ *n* [C] any one of the eight least valuable pieces which are all the same and which both players have at the beginning of a game of CHESS • *(fig.) The refugees are pawns* (= people without power) **in** *an international political dispute.* • PIC> **Games**

pawn·brok·er /£ˈpɔːnˌbrəʊ·kəʳ, $ˈpɑːnˌbroʊ·kɚ/ *n* [C] a person who lends money in exchange for items which they can sell if the person leaving them does not pay an agreed amount of money in an agreed time

paw·paw /£ˈpɔː·pɔː, $ˈpɑː·pɑː/ *n* [C] a PAPAYA • *(Am)* A pawpaw (also **papaw**) is also a type of apple. • PIC> **Fruit**

Pax /pæks/ *n* [U] a period of peace which has been forced on a large area, such as an empire or even the whole world, by the most powerful nation of that time • *Pax Romana* (= the peace forced by Rome on its empire) • *The Vice-President promised that there would be no attempt to impose a Pax* **Americana** *on the region.*

pay BUY /peɪ/ *v past* **paid** /peɪd/ to give (money) to (someone) usually for something which you want to buy, for services provided or because it is owed • *How much did you pay* **for** *the tickets?* [T] • *I pay my taxes.* [T] • *If you go to the bank, will you pay these cheques* **in** *(Am usually* **deposit** *these checks) for me?* [M] • *Will you pay these cheques* **into** *(Am usually* **deposit** *these checks* **in**) *my account for me?* [T] • *Can you lend me a fiver? I'll pay you/it* **back** *tomorrow.* [T] • *I'll pay you the fiver* **back** *tomorrow.* [+ two objects] • *I paid the driver* **(with)** *cash.* [+ two objects] • *Would you prefer to pay* **with/by** *cash, cheque or credit card?* [I] • *After a lot of haggling, we paid her $60 (for the table).* [+ two objects] • *I think we'll need to pay a builder* **to** *take this wall down.* [T + obj + *to* infinitive] • *Did Linda pay you* **for** *looking after her cats while she was away?* [T] • *(fig.) He swore he'd pay her* **back** (= make her suffer) *for all she'd done to him.* [T] • *(fig.) We all pay* **for** (= receive the bad results of) *our mistakes in some way at some time.* [I] • *We should be able to pay* **off** *the debt within two years.* [M] • *He wouldn't give evidence, I think someone paid him* **off** (= paid him not to talk about something which he knows is illegal). [M] • *(fig.) It'll be interesting to see if the investment pays* **off** (= is successful). [I] • *Things are looking bad, we might have to pay* **off** (= pay for the last time and then dismiss) *more workers.* [M] • *I paid* **(out)** *a lot of money to get the washing machine fixed and it still doesn't work!* [T/M] • *If you don't pay (Br also pay* **over**) *the money by Tuesday, my boss is going to want to know why.* [T/M] • *Every paying adult who goes on the trip can take a child with them absolutely free!* • *Eventually they paid* **up**, *but only after receiving several reminders.* [I] • *After its recent losses, the company intends to pay reduced* **dividends** *next month.* [T] • *(fig.) The extra training that he did is really paying* **dividends** (= showing itself to be worth the effort). [T] • To **pay** your **dues** is to do something that you do not enjoy in order to have something that you want, or because you feel it is your duty: *I've raised three children and I feel I've paid my dues. It's someone else's turn to take charge of the kids now.* • If something **pays for itself**, it works so well that it saves the same amount of money, usually over a period of time, that it cost: *The advertising should pay for itself by increasing sales.* • When someone or something **pays the price**, they experience the bad result of their actions: *If you abuse your body now, you'll pay the price when you're older.* • If a person **pays the ultimate price**, they die because of something they have done, esp. having taken an action for moral reasons: *If our soldiers have to pay the ultimate price for defending their country, then so be it.* • *(infml)* If a person **pays through the nose** for something, they pay a lot of money, usually too much, for it: *We paid through the nose to get the car fixed and it still doesn't go properly.* • *(Am)* If someone **pays top dollar** for something, they pay a lot of money for it: *He wants to develop the whole block and doesn't mind paying top dollar to get hold of the remaining properties.* • If someone **pays** their **way**, they pay for the things which they use or have rather than letting someone else pay. • *(Am)* **Pay-per-view** is a system for **cable television** in which viewers only pay for particular programmes which they watch. • A **pay phone** is a public telephone which is made to operate by putting coins into it. • *(saying)* 'He who pays the piper calls the tune' means that the person who provides the money can choose what is done with it. • *(infml saying)* 'You pays your money and you takes your choice/chance' means a person can choose whatever thing or action they prefer because all the choices are as good as each other. • LP> **Borrow, Money, Two objects**

pay·a·ble /ˈpeɪ·ə·bl̩/ *adj* [after v; not gradable] • *Interest payments are payable* (= to be paid) *monthly.* • *The price of the car is payable in 12 monthly instalments.* • If a CHEQUE is payable **to** someone or an organization then the money will be paid to them because their name is written on it: *Please make your cheque payable to WWF.*

pay·ee /peɪˈiː/ *n* [C] *specialized* • A payee is a person who money is or should be paid to.

pay·er /£ˈpeɪ·əʳ, $peɪ·ɚ/ *n* [C] • *They're good/bad payers* (= They usually pay on time/late). • Payer is often used as a combining form: *a fee/licence/mortgage/tax payer*

pay·ment /ˈpeɪ·mənt/ *n* • A payment is an amount of money paid: *a lump-sum payment* [C] ○ *Usually we ask for payment on receipt of the goods.* [U] ○ *We need a deposit of £165 followed by twelve monthly payments of £60.* [C] ○ *The charity can also make a one-off payment for special cases.* [C] ○ *When is the first payment* **due?** [C] • *(fig.) Verbal abuse was hardly the payment* (= reward) *I expected* **for** *my troubles.* [U] • A **back** payment is either a sum of money received by an employee because of a pay rise at an earlier time, or money given to a customer when a company has charged them too much. [C/U]

pay WORK /peɪ/ *v past* **paid** /peɪd/ to give (money) to (someone) for work which they have done • *The company pays £220 a week* **for** *people to act as couriers.* [T] • *We offer an annual salary of $26 600 which is paid monthly.* [T] • *Accountancy may be boring but at least it pays* **well.** [I] • *Most of these women are very* **poorly** *paid and work in terrible conditions.* [T] • LP> **Money**

pay /peɪ/ *n* [U] • *Can you lend me a tenner until I get my pay?* • *(Br and Aus) Any pay* **rise** *(Am usually* **raise**) *must be in line with inflation.* • *It's a nice job but the pay is appalling.* • If someone is **in the pay of** someone, esp. an enemy, that person is (secretly) working for them. • *(Br and Aus)* A **pay claim** is a demand for an increase in pay: *As expected, management said the workers' pay claim was too high.* • *(Br and Aus)* A **pay packet** (*Am* **pay envelope**) is an envelope containing a person's pay which they usually receive at the end of each week. • *(Br and Aus)* A **pay packet** (*Am* **paycheck**) is also the amount of money a person earns: *It's easy to go on expensive holidays when you have a pay packet the size of hers.*

pay *(obj)* PROFIT /peɪ/ *v past* **paid** /peɪd/ to give a profit, advantage or benefit (to) • *If the business doesn't pay soon we'll have to close it down.* [I] • *It never pays* **to** *take risks where human safety is concerned.* [I] • *Hard training now will pay (you) richly when it comes to the actual competition.* [I/T] • *(Am)* **Pay dirt** is something valuable or useful which is found after searching or effort: *If a salesperson does not quickly* **hit** *pay dirt with a customer they will usually move straight on to someone else.*

pay *obj* GIVE /peɪ/ *v* [T] *past* **paid** /peɪd/ to give or do (something) • *Please pay* **attention**, *I've got something important to say.* • *The commander paid* **tribute to** *the courage of his troops.* • *Their album pays* **homage to** *music masters Benny Goodman and Lionel Hampton.* • *It's always nice to be paid* **a compliment**. • *A crowd of mourners gathered to pay* **their respects to** *the dead man.* • *You should pay* **heed** (= listen) **(to** *what she's saying).* • *If you leave your address, I'll* **pay a call on** (= visit) *you when I'm in the area.* ○ *I'll pay you* **a call** *when I'm in the area.* [+ two objects] • *(Br and Aus)* If someone or something **puts paid to** something else they finish or destroy it: *A knee injury has put paid to her chances of getting into the final.* • LP> **Do: verbs meaning 'perform'**

pay out *obj*, **pay** *obj* **out** *v adv* [M] to release a piece of rope or CABLE in a controlled way

pay·back /ˈpeɪ·bæk/ *n* [U] *esp. Am* the advantage received from something, esp. the profit from a financial investment • *The payback for reorganization should be increased productivity.* • *(Am infml)* If a person says **payback's a bitch** they mean that something bad has happened as a result of something else: *For years he was having love affairs behind his wife's back and now she's asking for 90% of his income in alimony – man, payback's a bitch.* • A **payback period** is the amount of time it takes to get back the sum of money originally invested in something.

pay·check /ˈpeɪ·tʃek/ *n* [C] *Am for* **pay packet**, see at PAY [WORK]

pay·day /ˈpeɪ·deɪ/ *n* [U] the day on which a worker receives their pay

PAYE /ˌpiː·eɪ·waɪˈiː/ *n* [U] *Br and Aus abbreviation for* Pay As You Earn (= a system for collecting income tax in which a person's tax is subtracted and sent to the government by their employer before they are paid)

pay·load /£ˈpeɪ·ləʊd, $-loʊd/ *n* [C] the amount of goods or people which a vehicle, such as an aircraft, can carry, or the explosive which a MISSILE carries, or the equipment carried in a spacecraft

pay·mas·ter /£ˈpeɪˌmɑː·stəʳ, $-ˌmæs·t̬ɚ/ *n* [C] a person or an organization that pays for something to happen and therefore has or expects to have some control over it • *The government accused the opposition parties of being controlled by trade union paymasters.*

pay·ment /ˈpeɪ·mənt/ *n* See at PAY [BUY]

pay·off [PAYMENT] /£ˈpeɪ·ɒf, $-ɑːf/ *n* [C] money paid to someone, esp. so that they do not cause trouble or so that they will do what you want them to • *It has been alleged that the minister received a secret payoff from an arms dealer.* • See also **pay off** at PAY [BUY].

pay·off [RESULT] /£ˈpeɪ·ɒf, $-ɑːf/ *n* [C] *infml* the result of a set of actions, or an explanation at the end of something • *The payoff for years of research is a microscope which performs better than all of its competitors.* • See also **pay off** at PAY [BUY].

pay·o·la /£peɪˈəʊ·lə, $-ˈoʊ-/ *n* [C/U] *infml esp. Am dated* (the activity of making) a secret payment to someone for doing an illegal business action

pay·out /ˈpeɪ·aʊt/ *n* [C] a large sum of money which is paid to someone • *There is a maximum payout of £2500 if any newly-purchased items are lost or damaged while in transit home.* • See also **pay out** at PAY [BUY].

pay·roll /£ˈpeɪ·rəʊl, $-roʊl/ *n* [C] a list of the people employed by a company showing how much each one earns, or the total amount of money paid to the people employed by a particular company • *a payroll tax* • *McDermot Software is growing fast, adding another 100 employees to its payroll over the last year.* • *With debts of $4 million and a monthly payroll of $1·2 million the venture is clearly heading for trouble.* • *They must be the hardest working people* **on** *the council's* **payroll** (= employed by them).

pay·slip /ˈpeɪ·slɪp/ *n* [C] a piece of paper given to someone who is employed to show how much money they have earned and how much tax has been subtracted

PBS /ˌpiː·biːˈes/ *n* [U] *abbreviation for* Public Broadcasting Service (= a US organization broadcasting generally educational television programmes which is paid for by the people who watch it rather than from advertising)

PC [COMPUTER], **pc** /ˌpiːˈsiː/ *n* [C] *abbreviation for* **personal computer**, see at PERSON • *The price of PCs has been tumbling recently.* • [PIC]> **Office**

PC [POLICE] /ˌpiːˈsiː/ *n* [C] *Br abbreviation for* **police constable**, see at POLICE • *PC Owens* • See also WPC.

PC [CORRECT] /ˌpiːˈsiː/ *adj abbreviation for* **politically correct**, see at POLITICS • [LP]> **Sexist language**

pc *abbreviation for* PER CENT • *an increase of 22 pc*

PCB /ˌpiː·siːˈbiː/ *n* [C/U] *abbreviation for* polychlorinated biphenyl (= one of several chemicals which is used in industry and is harmful in the environment, esp. to humans and animals because it stays in their body tissue)

pcm /ˌpiː·siːˈem/ *Br abbreviation for* **per calendar month**, see at PER • *Fully furnished house to let, £650 p.c.m., quiet location.*

PDQ /ˌpiː·diːˈkjuː/, **pdq** *adv* [not gradable] *abbreviation for* pretty damn (*Am also* darn) quick (= very quickly or soon) • *If the theatre is to be saved someone will have to do something and PDQ.*

PE /ˌpiːˈiː/ *n* [U] *abbreviation for* **physical education**, see at PHYSICAL [BODY]

pea /piː/ *n* [C] a round green seed, several of which grow in a POD (= outer covering), eaten as a vegetable, or the plant which the pods grow on • *frozen/dried peas* • *pea soup* • A person who is **pea-brained**, or a **pea-brain**, appears to be extremely stupid. • **Pea green** is a bright yellowish green colour. • *(Br dated infml)* A **pea-souper** (*Am and Aus* **pea soup**) is a very dense fog which looks slightly yellow. • [PIC]> **Peas and beans**

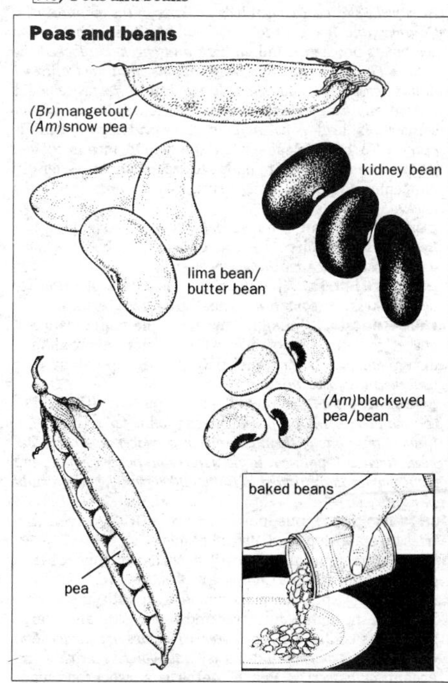

peace [NO VIOLENCE] /piːs/ *n* [U] (a period of) freedom from war and violence, esp. when people live and work together happily without disagreements • *peace talks/proposals* • *a peace conference/initiative* • *peace campaigners* • *Now that the war is over may there be* **a lasting** *peace between our nations.* • *Peace lasted in Europe for just over 20 years after 1918 before war broke out again.* • *After years of civil war most of the population long for peace.* • *She's very good at* **keeping** *(the) peace within the family.* • *The police act on the public's behalf to* **keep the** *peace.* • *Most spiritual leaders regard peace to be something we should all work for.* • *Stop fighting you two – shake hands and* **make** *(your) peace (with each other)!* • In the US **the Peace Corps** is an organization which sends people to work as VOLUNTEERS (= people who work without being paid) in poor countries. Compare VSO. • A **peace dividend** is money which is saved by a country when it is no longer needed to make or buy weapons because the threat of war has grown less. • **Peace-loving** means liking peace and trying to live and act in a way which will bring it: *a peace-loving people/nation* • A **peace offering** is something suggested, said or given by a person to show that they want to be friendly, esp. to someone they have argued with. • A **peace pipe** is a decorated tobacco PIPE used by Native Americans at ceremonial events, esp. as a sign of peace. • A **peace sign** is a sign made with the hand by holding it with the PALM forward and the first two fingers in the shape of a V, used to express peace or victory. See also **V-sign** at V [LETTER]. • *"Give Peace a Chance"* (song by John Lennon and the Plastic Ono Band, 1969) • *"I believe it is peace for our time ... peace with honour"* (Neville Chamberlain in a speech after the Munich Agreement with Hitler, 1938)

peace·ful /ˈpiːs·fᵊl/ *adj* • *a peaceful solution* • *peaceful demonstrators* • *She said that she hoped there would be a time when the members of all the different ethnic groups in the area could live together in peaceful co-existence.*

peace·ful·ly /ˈpiːs·fᵊl·i/ *adv*

peace·ful·ness /ˈpiːs·fᵊl·nəs/ *n* [U] • *Right up to August 1914 the optimists were still affirming the 'natural* *decline of warfare', the basic peacefulness of western civilization.*

peace·ab·le /'piː·sə·bl̩/ *adj* • *The members of this group believe only in peaceable, non-violent protest.* • Peaceable also means avoiding arguments: *a peaceable person*

peace·a·bly /'piː·sə·bli/ *adv* • *The crowd sang hymns, cheered the speakers, and then dispersed peaceably.*

peace [CALM] /piːs/ *n* [U] calm and quiet; lack of interruption or annoyance from worry, problems, noise or unwanted actions • *You'll need peace* **and quiet** *to study.* • *He says he's* **at** *peace when he's walking in the mountains.* • *Go away and* **leave** *us to finish our dinner* **in** *peace.* • *For everyone's peace* **of mind** *go back and check you locked the door.* • *There'll be* **no** *peace until she gets what she wants.* • *I didn't agree with what she said but I* **held** *my peace* (= did not say anything). • **At peace** is a gentle way of saying that someone is dead: *Now she is at peace and her suffering is over.* • To be **at peace with the world** means to feel peaceful because you are happy to accept what is generally happening to you. • *"There is no peace... unto* (= for) *the wicked"* (Bible, Isaiah 48.22)

peace·ful /'piːs·fəl/ *adj* • *a peaceful afternoon/place*

peace·ful·ly /'piːs·fəl·i/ *adv* • *He was back in her arms and she could once again sleep peacefully.*

peace·ful·ness /'piːs·fəl·nəs/ *n* [U] • *A kind of peacefulness overcame him as he stared up at the stars.*

peace·keep·ing /'piːs,kiː·pɪŋ/ *n* [U] the maintenance of peace, esp. the use of armed forces not involved in a disagreement to prevent fighting in an area • *a peacekeeping force/mission*

peace·keep·er /£'piːs,kiː·pəʳ, $-pɚ/ *n* [C] • *The commander of the proposed international force could find himself with one of the nastiest jobs a peacekeeper has ever been given.* • *If political leaders agreed a peace formula but some warlords continued to fight, 40 000 peacekeepers would be required.*

peace·mak·er /£'piːs,meɪ·kəʳ, $-kɚ/ *n* [C] a person who tries to establish peace between people

peace·time /'piːs·taɪm/ *n* [U] a period of time when a country is not at war • Compare WARTIME.

peach [FRUIT] /piːtʃ/ *n* [C] a round fruit with juicy sweet yellow flesh, slightly furry red and yellow skin and a large seed in its centre • *a peach tree* • *Peaches are grown and exported from warm countries.* • *Would you like peaches* **and cream** *for dessert?* • **Peach Melba** is a sweet food made from half a peach, **ice cream** and pressed RASPBERRIES. • [PIC] **Fruit**

peach [COLOUR] /piːtʃ/ *adj* [not gradable], *n* (of) a pale pinkish orange colour

peach [EXCELLENT] /piːtʃ/ *n infml* someone or something which is excellent or very pleasing • *She's* **a real** *peach.* • *We had a marvellous time at the ball, it was* **a** *peach* **of an** *evening.*

peach·y /'piː·tʃi/ *adj* **-ier, -iest** *infml* • *We had a bit of a disagreement but now everything is just peachy* (= very good and pleasant) *between us.*

pea·cock *male, female* **pea·hen** /£'piː·kɒk, $-kɑːk, -hen/ *n* [C] a large bird, the male of which has very long tail feathers which it can spread out to show bright colours and eye-like patterns • *peacock feathers* • *The peahen is less eye-catching then the peacock and has brown feathers.* • *(dated disapproving)* If a man is described as a peacock he is very proud of his appearance and gives a lot of attention to his clothes and the way he dresses. • **Peacock blue** is a bright slightly greenish blue colour. • [PIC] **Birds**

pea·hen /'piː·hen/ *n* [C] a female PEACOCK

peak [HIGHEST POINT] /piːk/ *n* [C], *v* [I] (to reach) the highest, strongest or best point, value or level of skill • *Holiday flights* **reach** *a peak during August.* • *Beat the egg whites until they are stiff enough to form firm peaks.* • *We saw a victory by an athlete* **at** *the very peak of her fitness and career.* • *Official figures show that unemployment peaked in November and then fell slowly over the next two months.*

peak /piːk/ *adj* [before n; not gradable] • *Traffic congestion is really bad at peak* (= the most busy) **periods.** • *The peak* (= biggest) *demand for gas supplies is during the winter.* • *To get peak* (= the best) *performance the car has to be properly tuned.* • *It is most expensive to advertise at peak viewing times* (= those with the most people watching). • *Don't go there in the peak* (= busiest) **season** – *it'll be hot and crowded.*

peak [MOUNTAIN TOP] /piːk/ *n* [C] the pointed top of a mountain, or the mountain itself • *It is one of the most difficult peaks to climb in the whole range.*

peak [HAT PART] *esp. Br* /piːk/, *Am usually* **vi·sor** *n* [C] the flat curved part of a CAP which goes above the eyes of the person who is wearing it • [PIC] **Hats**

peaked /piːkt/ *adj* • *a peaked cap* • [PIC] **Hats**

peak·y *esp. Br* (**-ier, -iest**) /'piː·ki/, *Am usually* **peaked** /piːkt/ *adj infml* slightly ill, often looking pale • *You look* **a bit** *peaky, love, are you all right?* • *I'm feeling* **a bit** *peaky – I think I may be getting a cold.*

peal [RING] /piːl/ *v* [I] (of bells) to ring with a loud sound • *After their wedding the bells pealed* **out** *from the tower.*

peal /piːl/ *n* [C] • *When we heard the peal of (the) bells we knew a truce had been declared.*

peal [LOUD SOUND] /piːl/ *n* [C] a long loud sound or series of sounds, esp. of laughter or thunder • *Her idea was met with peals* **of laughter.** • *A loud peal* **of thunder** *woke him from restless sleep.*

pea·nut /'piː·nʌt/, *also Br specialized* **ground·nut** *n* [C] a small seed which grows from a plant and ripens under the ground in a shell. They are often eaten with salt, esp. when cooked • *peanut/groundnut oil* • *salted/dry-roast(ed) peanuts* • **Peanut brittle** is hard TOFFEE (= a type of sweet made from butter and sugar) which contains peanuts. • **Peanut butter** is a soft pale brown substance made from crushed peanuts which is often eaten spread on bread: *a peanut butter sandwich* ○ *(esp. Am) The kids were eating peanut butter* **and jelly** *sandwiches.* • [PIC] **Nut**

pea·nuts /'piː·nʌts/ *n* [U] *infml* something so small it is not worth considering, esp. a sum of money • *They* **pay** *people peanuts in that organization.*

pear /£peəʳ, $per/ *n* [C] a sweet juicy fruit with a green skin which has a round base and is slightly pointed towards the stem • *a pear tree* • **Pear-shaped** means shaped like a pear: *a pear-shaped physique* • [PIC] **Fruit**

pearl /£pɜːl, $pɜːrl/ *n* (the substance which forms) a small round object, usually white, that forms around a grain of sand inside the shell of esp. an OYSTER (= a sea animal with a large flat shell), which is valuable because it is rare, and which is used to make jewellery • *earrings of diamond and pearl* [U] • *a string/rope/necklace of pearls* [C] • *a pearl necklace/brooch* • *(fig.) There were pearls* (= drops) **of** *dew on the shiny leaves.* [C] • **Cultured** pearls are those made by putting very small hard objects into OYSTER shells and allowing pearls to form round them. • Pearl also means the creamy white shiny colour of pearl or a pale colour: *a pearl silk wedding dress* • *pearl grey gloves* • Pearl is also **mother of pearl**: *a pearl-handled knife* ○ *pearl buttons* ○ See at MOTHER [PARENT]. • *(Br)* A **pearl of great price** is something which has great value but not always financial value: *Patience is a pearl of great price.* • A **pearl diver** is a person who swims deep down into the sea to find shells containing pearls. • [PIC] **Jewellery**

pearls /£pɜːlz, $pɜːrlz/ *pl n* • Pearls are jewellery made from pearls: *Do you think my pearls would go with this dress?* ○ *He gave her pearls for her birthday.*

pearl·y /£'pɜː·li, $'pɜːr-/ *adj* **-ier, -iest** • *pearly white teeth* • *(humorous)* **The pearly gates** are the imaginary entrance to heaven: *I'll meet you at the pearly gates* (= when we die) *and we'll compare notes.* • A **pearly king** and **pearly queen** are a particular man and woman from London who have the right to dress in special black clothes covered with pearl buttons, in order to collect money for CHARITY (= help given free to those who need it).

peas·ant /'pez·ənt/ *n* [C] a person who owns or rents a small piece of land and grows crops, keeps animals, etc. on it, esp. one who has a low income, very little education and a low social position. This is usually used of someone who lived in the past or of someone in a poor country. • *Tons of internationally donated food was distributed to the starving peasants.* • *In Mexico, hillside peasants use bullocks and horses to plough their fields and to carry the harvested crops.* • *On each page are little pictures of medieval peasants carrying out everyday tasks.* • *Most of the produce sold in the market is grown by peasant farmers.* • *Peasant women with scarves around their heads were working in the fields.* • Peasant is also used to refer to things considered typical of peasants: *peasant food* ○ *peasant art* ○ *peasant traditions* • *(infml disapproving)* A peasant is a person who is not well educated or is rude and does not behave well: *Joe's a real peasant.* ○ *You peasant!* [as form of address]

peas·ant·ry /'pez·ən·tri/ *n* [U] • *They gave land to the peasantry* (= esp. in the past, all the people who were peasants).

pea·shoot·er /£'piː,ʃuː·təʳ, $-t̬ɚ/ *n* [C] a long thin tube through which small objects, esp. dried PEAS, can be blown in order to hit something, or *(Am)* a small weapon, esp. a gun, which is not very effective

peat /piːt/ *n* [U] a dark brown earth-like substance which was formed by plants dying and becoming buried. It is sometimes added to ordinary garden earth to improve it and is sometimes used as fuel. • *I mixed some peat into the soil before I put the plants into the garden.* • *People in this area* **cut** *peat and burn it on their fires.* • A **peat bog** is an area of land from which peat is taken.

peat·y /£ˈpiː·ti, $-t̬i/ *adj* **-ier, -iest** • *a dark peaty brown* • *a strong peaty smell* • *peaty soil*

peb·ble /ˈpeb·l̩/ *n* [C] a small smooth round stone, esp. one found on a beach or in a river • *We hurt our feet walking across the pebbles on the beach.* • *This part of the coast has pebble beaches.*

peb·bled /ˈpeb·l̩d/, **peb·bly** /ˈpeb·li/ *adj* • *a pebbled beach* • *a pebbly path*

pe·can /£pɪˈkæn, $pɪˈkɑːn/ *n* [C] a type of nut which is long with an uneven surface and which has a smooth reddish shell • *chopped pecans* • *pecan pie* • PIC› **Nut**

pec·ca·dil·lo /£ˌpek·əˈdɪl·əʊ, $-oʊ/ *n* [C] *pl* **peccadillos** or **peccadilloes** a small fault or a not very bad action • *a youthful peccadillo* • *The president's sexual peccadillos were widely known about.* • *He dismissed what had happened as a mere peccadillo.*

peck *(obj)* /pek/ *v* (of a bird) to bite, hit or pick up (something small) with the beak • *The parrot pecked my finger through the bars of the cage – it really hurt!* [T] • *The birds learn to peck holes* (= form them by hitting with their beaks) *in the foil milk bottle tops by watching others do it.* [T] • *The geese were pecking around* (= biting at the ground) *for food.* [I] • *The chickens pecked* **at** (= picked up with their beaks) *the seeds which covered the ground.* [I] • *(fig.) The rescuers peck* **(away) at** *the rubble* (= pick it up and remove it), *searching for more of the 250 people thought to have died here.* [I] • *(fig.) The children just pecked* **at** (= only ate small quantities of) *their food, eating hardly anything.* [I] • To peck someone is also to give them a quick kiss, esp. on the side of the face: *He pecked his aunt* **on** *the cheek.* [T] • A **pecking order** is an informal social system in which some people or groups know they are more or less important than others: *There's a clearly established pecking order in this office.* ○ *He started as a clerk but gradually rose in the pecking order.*

peck /pek/ *n* [C] • *The hen moved the chicks along with pecks* (= bites with its beak) *and flaps of her wings.* • *She gave him a light peck* (= kiss) *of farewell.*

peck·er [PENIS] /£ˈpek·əʳ, $-ɚ/ *n* [C] *taboo slang for* PENIS

peck·er [STAY HAPPY] /£ˈpek·əʳ, $-ɚ/ *n* [C] **keep** *your* **pecker up** *Br infml dated to try to stay happy when things are difficult*

peck·ish /ˈpek·ɪʃ/ *adj Br and Aus* slightly hungry • *By ten o'clock I was feeling rather peckish, even though I'd had a large breakfast.*

pec·tin /ˈpek·tɪn/ *n* [U] a chemical found in some fruits which helps to make liquid firm when making JAM

pec·to·ral /£ˈpek·tᵊr·ᵊl, $-tɔːr-/ *adj* [not gradable] *specialized* of the chest • *He flexed his pectoral* **muscles**. • *Flying fish leap out of the water and glide, using their pectoral* **fins**.

pec·to·rals /£ˈpek·tᵊr·ᵊlz, $-tɔːr-/, *infml* **pecs** /peks/ *pl n specialized* • *He had well-developed pectorals* (= chest muscles) *and muscular arms.*

pe·cu·li·ar [STRANGE] /£pɪˈkjuː·li·əʳ, $-kjuːl·jɚ/ *adj* unusual and strange, sometimes in an unpleasant way • *She has the most peculiar ideas.* • *What a peculiar smell!* • **It** *'s peculiar* **that** *they didn't tell us they were going away.* [+ *that* clause] • *(Br) The video on road accidents made me* **feel** *rather peculiar* (= ill).

pe·cu·li·ar·ly /£pɪˈkjuː·li·ə·li, $-ˈkjuːl·jɚ-/ *adv* • *He looked at me most peculiarly.* • *The streets were peculiarly quiet for the time of day.* • See also PECULIARLY.

pe·cu·li·ar·i·ty /£pɪˌkjuː·liˈær·ə·ti, $-ˈer·ə·t̬i/ *n* • *You couldn't help but be aware of the peculiarity* **of** *the situation.* [U] • *Well, we all have our little peculiarities* (= strange habits), *don't we?* [C]

pe·cu·li·ar [BELONGING TO] /£pɪˈkjuː·li·əʳ, $-ˈkjuːl·jɚ/ *adj* [not gradable] belonging to, relating to or found in only particular people or things • *He gets on with things in his own peculiar way/manner/fashion.* • *They noted that special manner of walking which was peculiar* **to** *her alone.* • *I was longing to get home – a desire peculiar* **to** *all people who travel unwillingly.* • *This type of building is peculiar* **to** *the south of the country.*

pe·cu·li·ar·ly /£pɪˈkjuː·li·ə·li, $-ˈkjuːl·jɚ-/ *adv* [not gradable] • *He spent his entire life involved in the peculiarly American business of making Hollywood movies.* • See also PECULIARLY.

pe·cu·li·ar·i·ty /£pɪˌkjuː·liˈær·ə·ti, £-ˈer·ə·t̬i/ *n* [C] • A peculiarity is something which is typical of one person, group or thing: *This technique is applicable to a wide variety of crops, but some modifications may be necessary to accommodate the peculiarities* **of** *each type.* ○ *Over the centuries the isolated villages developed their own peculiarities.*

pe·cu·li·ar·ly /£pɪˈkjuː·li·ə·li, $-ˈkjuːl·jɚ-/ *adv* [not gradable] very or especially • *It's peculiarly painful where I burnt my hand.* • *She's a peculiarly attractive woman.* • See also **peculiarly** at PECULIAR [STRANGE]; PECULIAR [BELONGING TO].

pe·cu·nia·ry /£pɪˈkjuː·njᵊr·i, $-ni·er-/ *adj* [not gradable] *fml* relating to money • *pecuniary interest/loss/benefit* • *a pecuniary matter*

ped·a·gogue /£ˈped·ə·gɒg, $-gɑːg/ *n* [C] *(disapproving)* a teacher who gives too much attention to formal rules and is not interesting, or *(old use)* a teacher

ped·a·go·gy /£ˈped·ə·gɒdʒ·i, $-gɑː·dʒi/ *n* [U] *specialized* • Pedagogy is the study of the methods and activities of teaching.

ped·a·gog·ic /£ˌped·əˈgɒdʒ·ɪk, $-ˈgɑː·dʒɪk/, **ped·a·gog·i·cal** /£ˌped·əˈgɒdʒ·ɪ·kᵊl, $ˈgɑː·dʒɪ-/ *adj specialized*

ped·a·gog·i·cal·ly /£ˌped·əˈgɒdʒ·ɪ·kli, $-ˈgɑː·dʒɪ-/ *adv specialized* • *The minister's reforms are pedagogically questionable* (= not based on good teaching theory).

ped·al /ˈped·ᵊl/ *n* [C] a small part of a machine or object which is pushed down with the foot to operate or move (part of) the machine or object • *Tap lightly on the* **brake** *pedal to keep the car from skidding.* • *He put his foot down on the* **accelerator** *pedal, and sped off.* • *This sewing machine is operated by a* **foot** *pedal.* • *The pedals on a piano are the parts that you hold down with your feet to make the notes sound different.* • *He stood up on the pedals of his bike to get extra power as he cycled up the hill.* • Pedal is also used with other words to refer to an object or machine which is moved or operated by a pedal or pedals: *When he was little he wanted a pedal* **bike**, *and now he wants a motorbike.* ○ *We hired a pedal* **boat** *(Br and Aus also* **pedalo**) *and went out on the lake for an hour.* ○ *The children's favourite toy is their pedal* **car**. ○ *She emptied the ashtray into the pedal* **bin** (= one in which the lid can be opened by pressing a pedal). • LP› **Driving** PIC› **Bicycles, Toy**

ped·al *(obj)* /ˈped·ᵊl/ *v* **-ll-** or *Am usually* **-l-** • *In the cities many people now pedal around on bicycles instead of polluting the environment by using cars.* [I] • *He struggled to pedal his bicycle up the hill.* [T] • *We were pedalling like mad* (= very fast) *against the wind, but didn't seem to be getting anywhere.* [I] • See also BACKPEDAL.

ped·a·lo /£ˈped·ᵊl·əʊ, $-oʊ/ *n* [C] *pl* **pedalos** *Br and Aus* a small boat which is moved by pushing pedals with the feet • *Pedalo hire – £5 an hour.*

ped·ant /ˈped·ᵊnt/ *n* [C] *disapproving* a person who is too interested in formal rules and small unimportant details

pe·dan·tic /£pəˈdæn·tɪk, $pedˈæn-/ *adj disapproving* • *They were being unnecessarily pedantic* (= giving too much attention to formal rules or small details) *by insisting that Berry himself, and not his wife, should have made the announcement.*

pe·dan·ti·cal·ly /£pəˈdæn·tɪ·kli, $pedˈæn-/ *adv*

ped·ant·ry /ˈped·ᵊn·tri/ *n* [U] • *There was a hint of pedantry in his elegant style of speaking.*

ped·dle *obj* /ˈped·l̩/ *v* [T] *esp. disapproving* to sell (things), esp. by taking them to different places • *These products are generally peddled (from) door to door.* • *He travels around, peddling his* **wares**. • *The company has become a machine for making money that peddles everything from vacations to car insurance.* • *He was arrested for peddling drugs/pornographic magazines.* • If you peddle stories or information, you spread them by telling different people: *The organization has peddled the myth that they are supporting the local population.*

ped·dler /£ˈped·ləʳ, $-lɚ/, *esp. Br and Aus* **ped·lar** *n* [C] • A peddler was, esp. in the past, a person who travelled to different places to sell small goods, esp. by going from house to house. • *(disapproving)* A peddler **of** ideas is someone who gives them to other people: *a peddler of New Age philosophies* • *(Br and Aus)* A **(drug)** peddler is someone who sells illegal drugs to people.

ped·e·rast, *Br and Aus dated* **pae·der·ast** /£ˈped·ᵊr·æst, £ˈpiː·dᵊr-, $ˈped·ə·ræst/ *n* [C] *disapproving esp. Am for* a man who has illegal sex with a young boy

pe·des·tal /ˈped·ə·stᵊl/ *n* [C] a long thin column which supports a statue, or a tall column-like structure on which something rests • *In the riot, the statues were toppled from their pedestals.* • *A flower arrangement in a large basket stood on a (flower) pedestal* (=one which supports an arrangement of flowers) *in the corner of the room.* • *We have a pedestal washbasin* (= an open container for water which rests on a column-like structure) *in our bathroom.* • If you **put** someone **on a pedestal**, you treat them with great respect and admiration: *As a child, she had put her father on a pedestal.* Compare **knock** someone **off** their **pedestal** at KNOCK [HIT]. • [PIC]› **Sculpture**

pe·des·tri·an [WALKER] /pəˈdes·tri·ən/ *n* [C] a person who is walking, esp. in an area where vehicles go • *A few pedestrians carrying their evening shopping sheltered from the rain in doorways.* • *The death rate for pedestrians hit by cars is unacceptably high.* • *Pedestrians should take extra care on narrow country roads.* • *No pedestrians* (=People walking are not allowed in this area). • *Make sure you used the pedestrian entrance/bridge/tunnel/underpass.* • A **pedestrian crossing** (*Am* also **crosswalk**) is a marked place in a road where traffic must stop to allow people to walk across. Compare **pelican crossing** at PELICAN; **zebra crossing** at ZEBRA. • A *(esp. Br)* **pedestrian precinct**/*(Am and Aus usually)* **pedestrian mall** is an area with shops where vehicles are not allowed. • [PIC]› **Road**

pe·des·tri·an·ize *obj, Br and Aus usually* **-ise** /pəˈdes·tri·ə·naɪz/ *v* [T] • *They are pedestrianizing the town square* (= turning it into an area where vehicles are not allowed). • *Vehicles are only allowed in the pedestrianized area early in the morning and late at night.*

pe·des·tri·an [UNINTERESTING] /pəˈdes·tri·ən/ *adj fml* not interesting; showing very little imagination • *Her books, with few exceptions, are workmanlike but pedestrian.* • *His speech was long and pedestrian.* • *He works in a very pedestrian way, showing no imagination at all.*

pe·di·a·tri·cian /ˌpiː·di·əˈtrɪʃ·ᵊn/ *n* [C] *esp. Am for* PAEDIATRICIAN

pe·di·at·ric /ˌpiː·diˈæt·rɪk/ *adj* [not gradable] *esp. Am*

ped·i·cure /£ˈped·ɪ·kjʊəʳ, $-kjʊr/ *n* [C] a beauty treatment for the feet which involves cutting and sometimes painting the nails, and softening or MASSAGING (= rubbing) the skin • *She treated herself to a pedicure.* • Compare MANICURE.

ped·i·gree /ˈped·ɪ·griː/ *n* [C] (a record of) the set of animals, including the parents and older relations, involved in the history of a particular animal, esp. one in which all the animals are known and are of high quality • *The breeder showed us the dog's pedigree.* • *The champion bulls had impressive pedigrees.* • *He breeds pedigree poodles/cattle.* • A pedigree is also a person's family history, education and experience, or the history of an idea or activity: *His voice and manner suggested an aristocratic pedigree.* ○ *Taylor's athletic pedigree is impressive and stretches back to the time he played for his school soccer team.* ○ *Isolationism has a long and respectable pedigree in American history.*

ped·i·ment /ˈped·ɪ·mənt/ *n* [C] *specialized* a triangular part at the top of the front of a building which supports the roof and which is often decorated

ped·lar /£ˈped·ləʳ, $-lɚ/ *n* [C] See at PEDDLE

pe·dom·et·er /£pɪˈdɒm·ɪ·təʳ, £pedˈɒm-, $pɪˈdɑː·mə·t̬ɚ/ *n* [C] a device which measures how far someone has walked by counting the number of times the feet are raised and put down again

pe·do·phile /£ˈpiː·dəʊ·faɪl, $ˈped·oʊ-/ *n* [C] *esp. Am for* PAEDOPHILE

pe·do·phil·ia /ˌpiː·dəˈfɪl·i·ə/ *n* [U] *esp. Am*

pee *(obj)* /piː/ *v infml for* URINATE • *The child peed in his pants/on the carpet.* [I] • *The child peed* (= urinated in) *his pants.* [T] • *The child peed himself* (= urinated in his clothes). [T] • *(fig. Br infml) It was peeing* **down**/*peeing* **with rain** (= raining a lot). [I]

pee /piː/ *n infml* • *I must go for/must have a pee* (= urinate). [C] • *There was pee* (= urine) *all over the floor.* [U]

peek /piːk/ *v* [I] to look, esp. for a short time or while trying to avoid being seen • *Close your eyes. Don't peek. I've got a surprise for you.* • *She couldn't resist peeking inside the box that had been left on the table.* • *There are two ways of preventing people from peeking unauthorized into computer files.* • *The children peeked over the wall to see where the ball had gone.* • *The film peeks behind the scenes of a multinational corporation.* • *At 12 o'clock someone peeked* **in** *to say that lunch was nearly ready.* • *Peeking* **(out)** *from behind the car, I suddenly spotted the person I was looking for.* • If something peeks **(out)**, it sticks out a little bit and can be partly seen: *I could just see her petticoat peeking* **(out) from** *under her skirt.* ○ *Each jacket had a neatly folded white handkerchief peeking* **out of** *the breast pocket.* • **Peek-a-boo** (*Br also* **peep-bo**) is a game played with very young children in which you hide your face, esp. with your hands, and then suddenly take your hands away saying 'peek-a-boo': *Babies usually love to* **play** *peek-a-boo.*

peek /piːk/ *n* [C usually sing] • *He* **took** *a peek through the keyhole.* • *As we were passing, we* **took** *a peek into some surprisingly good tourist shops.*

peel *obj* [REMOVE SKIN] /piːl/ *v* [T] to remove the skin of fruit and vegetables • *Peel, core and chop the apples.* • *Be careful not to peel* **away** *too much of the potato.* • *"Beulah, peel me a grape"* (Mae West in the film *I'm No Angel*, 1933) • [PIC]› **Food preparation**

peel /piːl/ *n* [U] • The peel of fruit and vegetables is the skin, esp. after it has been removed: *apple peel* ○ *potato peel* ○ *The dessert was decorated with strips of lemon peel.* ○ *What shall I do with the peel?* • Compare RIND. • [PIC]› **Fruit**

peel·er /£ˈpiː·ləʳ, $-lɚ/ *n* [C] • A peeler is a utensil for removing the skin of fruit and vegetables: *a vegetable/potato peeler*

peel·ings /ˈpiː·lɪŋz/ *pl n* • Peelings are the unwanted pieces of fruit or vegetable skin which have been taken off: *potato/apple peelings* ○ *Put the vegetable peelings on the compost heap.*

peel *(obj)* [REMOVE COVERING] /piːl/ *v* to remove (a covering) slowly and carefully, or (of a covering) to come off • *We peeled the wallpaper off the walls.* [T always + adv/prep] • *We peeled* **away/off** *three layers of wallpaper.* [M] • *Peel* **away/off** *the backing strip and press the label down firmly.* [M] • *We watched while they peeled the protective wrappings* **away from/off** *the statue.* [T always + adv/prep] • *The posters were peeling* **off** (= gradually coming away from) *the damp walls.* [I] • *The wallpaper is starting to peel* (= to come away from the wall) *at the edges.* [I] • If you peel, or part of your body or your skin peels, parts of the top layer of your skin comes off because you are burnt from being in the sun: *My back is peeling.* [I] • If a person, animal or vehicle **peel away/off**, it moves away from a group: *A figure peeled off to the left.* ○ *One motorbike peeled away* **from** *the formation and circled round behind the rest.* [I]

peep [LOOK] /piːp/ *v, n* (to have) a quick and often secret look • *We peeped at the children through a hole in the fence.* [I] • *I saw her peeping through the curtains/into the room.* [I] • **Take/Have a** *peep* (= Look quickly) **at** *what it says in this letter.* [C] • *The documentary allowed* **a** *fascinating peep* **at/into** *how television broadcasts are made.* [C] • *(Br)* **Peep-bo** is **peek-a-boo**. See at PEEK. • *(disapproving)* A **peeping Tom** is a man who tries to secretly watch women when they are taking off their clothes or wearing no clothes: *The police said they had had reports of a peeping Tom.* ○ *She is suing a peeping tom photographer over the photographs he took of her swimming in the nude.*

peep [APPEAR] /piːp/ *v* [I always + adv/prep] to appear slowly and not be completely seen • *A few early flowers had peeped up through the snow.* • *It rained all morning and the sun didn't begin to peep* **out** *from behind the clouds till midday.* • *The cat's tail was peeping* **out** *from under the bed.*

peep [SOMETHING SAID] /piːp/ *n* [U] *infml* a statement, answer or complaint • *No one has* **raised a** *peep about this dreadful behaviour.* • *They didn't* **give a** *peep when I told them that we couldn't continue.* • *One more peep* **out of** *you and there'll be no television tomorrow.* • *Not (so much as)* **a** *peep has been* **heard** (=We have not had any form of communication) **from** *any of the people we wrote to.* • *There hasn't been* **a** *peep* **out of** (= any form of communication from) *my sister for a couple of weeks.*

peep [NOISE] /piːp/ *v, n* (esp. of young birds) to make a weak high noise, or the weak high noise made by young birds • *Tiny ducklings were peeping in the nest.* [I] • *We heard the chicks making tiny peeps.* [C]

peep·hole /£ˈpiːp·həʊl, $-hoʊl/, *Br and Aus* **spy·hole**, *Am and Aus* **eye·hole** *n* [C] a small hole in a door or a wall through which you can look esp. without being seen • *I have a security peephole in my front door that allows me a 360-degree view.* • *There's a small peephole in the door, through which the guards can see into the cell.* • [PIC]› **Locks and home security**

peep·show /£'piːp·ʃəʊ, $-ʃoʊ/ *n* [C] a sexually exciting picture or film, watched on a machine through a small hole

peer LOOK /£pɪəʳ, $pɪr/ *v* [I always + adv/prep] to look carefully or with difficulty • *When no one answered the door, she peered through the window to see if anyone was there.* • *The driver was peering into the distance trying to read the road sign.* • *He peered over my shoulder at the computer screen and asked about the figures.* • *The judge peered over his glasses at the jury.*

peer PERSON, *female also* **peer·ess** /£pɪəʳ, $pɪr, £'pɪə·res, $'pɪr·es/ *n* [C] (in Britain) a person who has a high social position and any of a range of titles, including BARON, EARL and DUKE, or a **life peer**, who is a member of the **House of Lords** • *a hereditary peer* • *a Conservative peer* • *Peers voted by 125 to 103 on Thursday to amend the Disability Allowances Bill.* • *Peers were told yesterday that there are no plans to sell off Britain's 2000 miles of canal.* • A **peer of the realm** is a member of the **House of Lords** (= the part of the British parliament which is not elected) who is not a **life peer**.

peer·age /£'pɪə·rɪdʒ, $'pɪr·ɪdʒ/ *n* • The peerage is those people who are peers, either because of the families of which they are members or because they are **life peers**: *a member of the peerage* [U] • A peerage is also the position of being a peer: *He renounced his peerage.* [C] ○ *She was given a peerage* (= the position of being a **life peer**). [C] • The peerage is also the state of being a **life peer**: *He was* **elevated to** *the peerage after distinguished service in industry.* [U] • A peerage is also a book containing information about peers who are not **life peers** and their family history: *Burke's Peerage* [C] ○ *Debrett's Peerage* [C]

peer EQUAL /£pɪəʳ, $pɪr/ *n* [C] a person who is the same age or has the same social position or the same abilities as other people in a group • *Do you think it's true that teenage girls are less self-confident than their male peers?* • *He wasn't a great scholar, but as a teacher he had few peers* (= people who were of the same ability as he was). • *These children scored significantly lower on intelligence tests than others in their* **peer group** (= the group of people of about the same age and of the same social position). • **Peer pressure**/*(Br also)* **Peer group pressure** is the strong influence of a group of esp. children or young people on members of that group to behave as everyone else does, even if that behaviour is not good: *There is tremendous peer pressure to wear fashionable clothes.* ○ *She denied that peer group pressure had led her to start taking drugs.*

peer·less /£'pɪə·ləs, $'pɪr-/ *adj* [not gradable] *fml* • Something which is peerless is better than any other: *peerless beauty/ability*

peeved /piːvd/ *adj infml* annoyed • *He was peeved because we didn't ask him what he thought about the idea.* • *They were peeved* **that** *the trip was reduced from the usual three weeks to 10 days.* [+ *that* clause] • *She was peeved* **to** *discover that they had gone without her.* [+ *to* infinitive]

peeve *obj* /piːv/ *v* [T] • *What peeved her most was his thoughtlessness.* • **It** *peeves me* **that** *she didn't bother to phone.* [+ obj + *that* clause]

peev·ish /'piː·vɪʃ/ *adj* • *a peevish* (= easily annoyed), *bad-tempered person*

pee·vish·ly /'piː·vɪʃ·li/ *adv* • *"I thought you might have helped," she replied peevishly.*

pee·wee /'piː·wiː/ *n* [C] *Am infml* someone or something very small • *Hey, peewee, come here a minute.* [as form of address] • *The six-year-old is on a peewee league baseball team.*

peg HOOK /peg/ *n* [C] a small stick or hook which sticks out from a surface and from which objects, esp. clothes, can hang • *He took off his coat/hat and hung it* **on** *the peg.* • *These metal pegs can be used for hanging small pots and pans* **on**. • *(fig.) They decided to use the anniversary as the peg* **for**/*a peg* **on which to hang** (= a reason for or a way of achieving) *a TV documentary.* • *(infml)* If you **bring/take** someone **down a peg (or two)**, you act in a way that shows them that they are not as important as they thought they were: *He* **needs/wants** *taking down a peg or two.* • *(Br)* If you buy clothes **off the peg** (*Aus* **off the hook**, *Am* **off the rack**), you do not have them made specially for you: *an off-the-peg suit* ○ *It's cheaper to buy off the peg.* ○ Compare **made-to-measure** at MADE.

peg FIXING DEVICE /peg/ *n* [C] a device which is used to fix something into a particular place • *(Br and Aus) There aren't enough pegs (also* **clothes pegs**, *Am* **clothes pins**) *to hang all this washing on the line.* • *Hammer the pegs (also* **tent pegs**) *firmly into the ground.* • *(infml dated)* A **peg-leg**

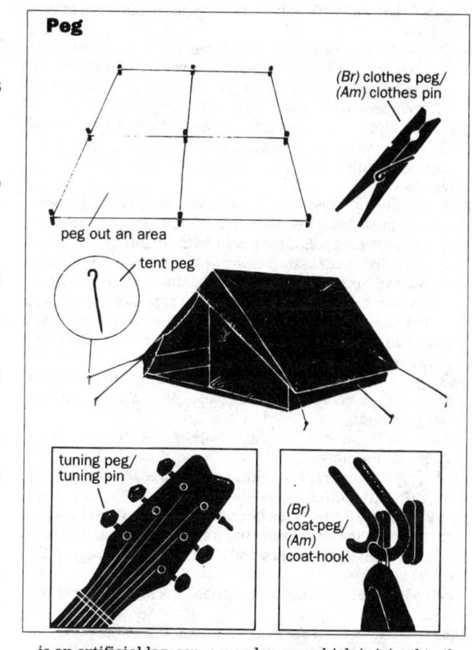

is an artificial leg, esp. a wooden one which is joined to the natural leg at the knee. • PIC> **Peg**

peg *(obj)* /peg/ *v* **-gg-** • *Make sure the tarpaulin is securely pegged* **down**/*pegged at the edges* (= fixed with pegs so that it does not move). [T] • *I'll peg* **out** *the clothes* (= use pegs to fix wet clothes to a length of rope or string outside a building) *before I go to work.* [M] • If you **peg out** an area, you mark the edges of it by hitting short sticks into the ground. [M] • *(Br and Aus infml)* If someone **pegs out**, they die. If something **pegs out**, it stops working: *Did you know that the old man next door finally pegged out?* ○ *The car finally pegged out about 20 miles from home.* • Peg can also mean to arrange something so that it stays at a particular level: *Britain has pledged to peg carbon dioxide emissions at current levels.* [T] ○ *The agreement works because member nations haven't tried to peg prices.* [T] • PIC> **Peg**

peg BASEBALL /peg/ *n* [C] *Am infml* (in baseball) a low fast throw • *Boggs made a solid peg to get the runner out at second.*

peg *obj* /peg/ *v* [T] **-gg-** *Am infml* • *Mattingly pegged* (= threw) *the ball to Stanley.*

pe·jor·a·tive /£pɪ'dʒɒr·ə·tɪv, $-'dʒɔːr·ə·t̬ɪv/ *adj fml* (of a word, speech, etc.) disapproving or suggesting that something is not good or is of no importance • *Do you think 'Brit' is a pejorative* **term**? • *Something terrible must have happened for the word 'home' to have come to have such a pejorative connotation for him.* • LP> **Labels**

pek·i·nese, **pek·in·gese** /ˌpɪ·kɪ'niːz/, **peke** /piːk/ *n* [C] *pl* **pekinese** or *Br* **pekineses** a small dog with long, silky hair and a wide flat nose

pel·i·can /'pel·ɪ·kᵊn/ *n* [C] a large bird which catches fish and carries them in the lower part of its beak, which is like a bag • *Pelicans generally nest within 20 minutes' flying time of a steady food supply.* • *Three breeding colonies of endangered brown pelicans were established in Virginia this year.* • *(Br)* A **pelican crossing** is a marked place in the road in Britain where traffic must stop for people to cross when a red light shows. The word pelican is based on the words PEdestrian LIght-CONtrolled crossing. Compare **pedestrian crossing** at PEDESTRIAN WALKER; **zebra crossing** at ZEBRA. • PIC> **Birds**

pel·let /'pel·ət/ *n* [C] a small hard ball or tube-shaped piece of any substance • *iron/lead/wax/plastic/paper pellets* • *food pellets* • *slug pellets* (= small pieces of a substance designed to kill those creatures) • The excrement of particular animals is called pellets: *rabbit/sheep pellets* • Metal pellets are shot from some types of gun: *airgun pellets* • *shotgun pellets* • *a pellet* **gun**

pel·let·ed /£'pel·ə·tɪd, $-t̬ɪd/ *adj* [not gradable] • *pelleted animal feed* • *pelleted chicken manure* • *pelleted* *seeds* (= covered with a special substance to make them into pellets)

pell-mell /ˌpel'mel/ *adv, adj dated* (in a way which is) very fast and not organized • *At the sound of the alarm bell, the customers ran pell-mell for the doors.* • *There has been a pell-mell dash to buy shares in the new company.*

pel·met /'pel·mət/, *Am usually* **val·ance** *n* [C] a narrow strip of wood or cloth which is fixed above a window or door and which hides the top of the curtains. • PIC› **Window**

pelt *obj* THROW /pelt/ *v* [T] to throw a number of things quickly at (someone or something) • *The largest meteorite shower on record pelted the Earth* **with** *an estimated 100 000 stones.* • *We saw rioters pelting police* **with** *bricks, rocks, bottles and cans.* • *Women pelted the singer* **with** *roses and blew him kisses.* • To pelt someone **with** questions is to ask a lot of them very quickly: *The children pelted their teacher with questions.* • **Pelting (down)** means raining heavily: **It's** *pelting down* **(with rain).**

pelt RUN /pelt/ *v* [I always + adv/prep] *infml* to run fast • *The children pelted down the bank, over the bridge and along the path.*

pelt /pelt/ *n* [U] **at full pelt** *Br* • See at FULL GREATEST POSSIBLE.

pelt SKIN /pelt/ *n* [C] the skin and fur of a dead animal, or the skin with the fur removed

pel·vis /'pel·vɪs/ *n* [C] the bones which form a bowl-shaped structure in the area below the waist at the top of the legs, and to which the leg bones and SPINE (= row of bones in the back) are joined

pel·vic /'pel·vɪk/ *adj* [not gradable] • *the pelvic region/area*

pen WRITING DEVICE /pen/ *n* [C] a long thin object used for writing or drawing with ink • *a fountain/ballpoint/rollerball/felt-tip pen* • *Don't write* **in** (= using a) *pen, or you won't be able to rub out any mistakes you make.* • If you **put/set pen to paper** you start to write: *It's time you put pen to paper and replied to that letter from your mother.* • A **pen pal**/*(Br and Aus also)* **pen friend** is someone you exchange letters with as a hobby but whom you usually have not met: *I've got a pen pal in Australia.* • A **pen name** is a name chosen by a writer to use instead of using their real name when publishing books. • *(Br and Aus)* A **pen pusher** (*Am* **pencil pusher**) is a person who has an uninteresting office job. • A *(Br)* **pen lid**/*(Am)* **pen cap** is a cover which goes over the top of a pen to stop the ink from escaping. • *(saying)* 'The pen is mightier than the sword' means that writers and thinkers have a stronger effect on the world, with regard to changing opinions and making things happen, than do military leaders. • PIC› **Writing instruments**

pen *obj* /pen/ *v* [T] **-nn-** *fml* • If you pen something, you write it: *She penned a note of thanks to her hostess.*

pen ENCLOSED SPACE /pen/ *n* [C] a small area surrounded by a fence in which esp. animals are kept • *a sheep/pig pen* • Pen is also *Am slang for* PENITENTIARY. • See also PLAYPEN.

pen *obj* /pen/ *v* [T] **-nn-** • *The sheep were penned behind the barn.* • *The men had been penned into a small room.*

pe·nal PUNISHING /'piː·nəl/ *adj* [before n] of or connected with punishment given by law • *penal consequences/sanctions* • *Many people believe that execution has no place in the penal* **system** *of a civilized society.* • *He had been in and out of penal institutions* (= prison) *from the age of 16.* • *In the past, attempts to commit murder were punishable by penal servitude* (= hard physical work in prison) *for life.* • A **penal code** is the system of legal punishment of a country. • A **penal colony/penal settlement** is a type of prison, which is often in a place far away from other people. • **Penal reform** is the attempt to improve the system of legal punishment.

pe·nal·ize *obj, Br and Aus usually* **-ise** /'piː·nə·laɪz/ *v* [T] • *The laws penalize* (= punish) *local councils that do not follow central government directives.* • To penalize someone can also be to punish them for breaking a rule: *The referee penalized Dave for a bad tackle and the other team scored a penalty goal.* • To penalize someone is also cause them to lose marks in a test or examination because they have done something in a way that is not correct: *Candidates will be penalized* **for** *bad spelling.*

pen·al·ty /£'pen·əl·ti, $-t̬i/ *n* • A penalty is a punishment, or the usual punishment, for doing something that is against a law: *Those suspected of activities for which the penalty is less than two years' imprisonment will be tried in ordinary civilian courts.* [C] ○ *The law carries a penalty* **of** *up to three years in prison.* [C] ○ *They asked for the* **maximum** *penalty* **for** *hoax calls to be increased to one year.* [C] ○ *The sign next to the lifebelt said 'Penalty* **for** *improper use £50'.* [C] • *The protesters were told to clear the area around the building,* **on** *penalty* **of** (= the punishment would be) *arrest if they did not.* [U] • A penalty is also a type of punishment, often involving paying money, that is given to you if you break an agreement or do not follow rules: *Currently, ticket holders* **pay** *a penalty equal to 25% of the ticket price when they change their flight plans.* [C] ○ *There was a penalty* **clause** *which said you had to pay half the cost if you cancelled your booking.* ○ *Will this change eliminate the higher premium penalty that people must pay if they join the insurance scheme later in life?* [C] • In sport, a penalty is an advantage given to a team/player when the other team/player breaks a rule: *The referee* **awarded** (= gave) *a penalty/a* **penalty kick**. [C] ○ *Hysen handled the ball and* **conceded** *the penalty that gave Manchester United the lead.* [C] ○ *The goalkeeper raced from goal and beyond the* **penalty area/penalty box** (= in football, the area marked with white lines in front of the goal) *to clear the ball away.* ○ *The game was decided by a* **penalty shoot-out** (= in football, a way of deciding who will win a game in which both teams finished with the same number of goals, by each team taking turns to have a set number of kicks at the goal.) ○ *Bruce scored his 11th goal of the season from the* **penalty spot** (= in football, the place marked with a white spot from which a penalty kick is taken). • In **ice hockey**, a **penalty box** is an area where players must sit when they are given a penalty.

pe·nal CAUSING DISADVANTAGE /'piː·nəl/ *adj Br* having a harmful effect; causing disadvantage • *They complained about the penal and counter-productive tax rates.* • *Employees regarded the childcare charges as penal.*

pe·nal·ize *obj, Br and Aus usually* **-ise** /'piː·nə·laɪz/ *v* [T] • *They thought it was unfair that some people who served on juries were penalized* (= put in a disadvantageous situtation) *by not being paid by their employer.* • *The scheme should ensure that borrowers are not penalized by sudden rises in mortgage rates.*

pen·al·ty /£'pen·əl·ti, $-t̬i/ *n* [C] • *Loss of privacy is one of the penalties* (= disadvantages) **of** *success.* • *She has* **paid** *a heavy penalty* (= suffered serious disadvantages) **for** *speaking the truth.*

pen·ance /'pen·ənts/ *n* an act which shows that you regret something that you have done, sometimes for religious reasons • *As a penance, she said she would buy them all a box of chocolates.* [C] • *They are* **doing** *penance* **for** *their sins.* [U]

pence /pents/ *pl of* PENNY (= a unit of monetary value) • See also SIXPENCE; TUPPENCE.

pen·chant /£'pɑ̃ːŋ·ʃɑ̃ːŋ, $'pen·tʃənt/ *n* [C usually sing] a liking for, an enjoyment of, or a habit of doing something, esp. something that other people might not like • *a penchant* **for** *detail/perfection/melodrama/skiing/exotic clothes* • *The article clearly showed his penchant* **for** *sneering at his critics.* • *Her penchant* **for** *disappearing for days at a time worries her family.*

pen·cil /'pent·səl/ *n* [C] a long thin usually wooden object for writing or drawing, with a sharp black or other coloured point, made from a type of carbon, at one end • *a box of coloured pencils* • *a notebook/notepad and pencil* • *pens and pencils* • *She got a pencil* **and paper**, *and wrote down the address.* • *He sat with his pencil* **poised**, *ready to take notes.* • *The pencil's* **blunt** *– you'd better* **sharpen** *it* (= make its point sharp). • *Write your comments in the margin of the report* **in** (= using) *(blue) pencil.* • *Both diamonds and pencil* **lead**, *or graphite, are made of pure carbon.* • Pencil is used to refer to things that are used for pencils: *a pencil box/case* ○ *a pencil sharpener* • Pencil can also be used to refer to something that has been drawn with a pencil: *pencil sketches/drawings* ○ *Cut on or just inside the pencil* **line** (= line drawn to show you where to cut). • Some types of make-up come in the form of a pencil: *an eyebrow pencil* ○ *a lip pencil* • A pencil **of light** is a thin beam of light: *A pencil of light showed as the door opened slightly.* • To **put/set pencil to paper** is to write: *Everyone should put pencil to paper and complain about the proposal.* • *(Am infml)* A **pencil pusher** is a **pen pusher**; see at PEN WRITING DEVICE. • If something is **pencil-thin**, it is very thin: *a pencil-thin fashion model* • PIC› **Writing instruments** Ⓓⓚ Ⓚⓞⓡ

pen·cil *obj* /'pent·səl/ *v* [T] **-ll-** or *Am usually* **-l-** • *She pencilled* (= wrote in pencil) *some comments on the top of the* *page.* • If you **pencil in** something/**pencil** something **in**, you record it in writing but understand that it might need to be changed later: *We'll pencil in the dates for the next two meetings and confirm them later.* ○ *They pencilled her name in on the preliminary list of speakers.*

pen·cilled, *Am also* **pen·ciled** /ˈpent·sᵊld/ *adj* [not gradable] • *pencilled comments/notes*

pen·dant /ˈpen·dᵊnt/ *n* [C] a piece of jewellery which is worn round the neck, consisting of a long chain with an object hanging from it, or the object itself • *She was wearing a crystal pendant.* • *He designed a portable radio to be worn like a pendant.* • *It was a beautiful necklace with a diamond pendant.* • See also PENDENT. • PIC **Jewellery**

pen·dent /ˈpen·dᵊnt/, **pen·dant** *adj fml* hanging from or over something • *pendent branches* • *a pendent lampshade* • See also PENDANT.

pend·ing /ˈpen·dɪŋ/ *adj* [not gradable] about to happen or waiting to happen • *There were whispers that a deal was pending.* • *The pending releases of the prisoners are meant to create a climate for negotiation.* • *The lawsuit is still pending in the state court.*

pend·ing /ˈpen·dɪŋ/ *prep* • You use pending to show that one thing must wait until another thing happens: *None of the four people killed was identified pending (the) notification of relatives.* ○ *Flights were suspended pending (an) investigation of the crash.*

pen·dul·ous /£ˈpen·djʊ·ləs, $-dʒə·ləs/ *adj fml* hanging down loosely • *pendulous blossoms*

pen·dul·um /£ˈpen·djʊ·ləm, $-dʒə·ləm/ *n* [C] a device consisting of a weight on a stick or thread which moves from one side to the other, esp. one which forms a part of some types of clocks, or *(fig.)* a change esp. from one opinion to an opposite one • *The pendulum in the grandfather clock* **swung** *back and forth.* • *He made pendulums of string and small weights and established the relationship between length of string and time of swing.* • *The spaceship's jets were fired periodically to dampen a side-to-side pendulum* **motion** *that had developed.* • *(fig.) As so often in education,* **the** *pendulum has* **swung back** *to the other extreme and testing is popular again.* • *(fig.)* **The** *pendulum* **of** *society's concern will* **swing** *again toward caring.* • PIC **Clocks and watches**

pen·e·trate *(obj)* MOVE /ˈpen·ɪ·treɪt/ *v* to move into or through (something) • *Amazingly, the bullet did not penetrate his brain, although its impact gave him a severe concussion.* [T] • *When an X-ray beam penetrates the body, part is absorbed and part passes through.* [T] • *In a normal winter, the frost penetrates deeply enough to kill off insect eggs in the soil.* [I] • *The organization had been penetrated by a spy.* [T] • *The company has been successful in penetrating overseas markets this year.* [T] • *The plane penetrated the enemy's air defences.* [T] • *(fig.) Our eyes couldn't penetrate* (= see through) *the dark/***the gloom** *of the inner cave.* [T]

pen·e·tra·tion /ˌpen·ɪˈtreɪ·ʃᵊn/ *n* [U] • *Sunscreens can help reduce the penetration of ultraviolet rays into the skin.* • *The company is trying to increase its penetration of the market.* • Penetration is also the act of a man putting his penis into his sexual partner's vagina or RECTUM during sexual activity.

pen·e·tra·tive /£ˈpen·ɪ·trə·tɪv, $-treɪ·t̬ɪv/ *adj* • *a penetrative attack* • *penetrative sex*

pen·e·trate *(obj)* UNDERSTAND /ˈpen·ɪ·treɪt/ *v* to study or INVESTIGATE (something) in order to understand, or to be understood • *It's hard to penetrate her mind.* [T] • *He penetrates deeper into the artist's life in the second volume of his autobiography.* [I] • *(infml) I'm sure she told me the details but they didn't penetrate* (= I did not remember/understand). [I]

pen·e·tra·tion /ˌpen·ɪˈtreɪ·ʃᵊn/ *n* [U] *fml* • Someone's penetration is their ability to understand quickly and easily.

pen·e·trat·ing /£ˈpen·ɪ·treɪ·tɪŋ, $-t̬ɪŋ/ *adj* • *She gave him a penetrating* **glance/look** (= one which showed that she was able to understand his thoughts). • A penetrating mind is one which understands things quickly and easily. • See also PENETRATING.

pen·e·tra·tive /£ˈpen·ɪ·trə·tɪv, $-treɪ·t̬ɪv/ *adj* • *a penetrative remark* (= a remark which shows understanding)

pen·e·trat·ing /£ˈpen·ɪ·treɪ·tɪŋ, $-t̬ɪŋ/ *adj* very loud • *I heard a penetrating scream.* • *He has a very penetrating voice.* • See also **penetrating** at PENETRATE UNDERSTAND.

pen·guin /ˈpeŋ·gwɪn/ *n* [C] a black and white sea bird which cannot fly but uses its small wings to help it swim. There are different types of penguin, many of which are found in the Antarctic. • PIC **Birds**

pen·i·cil·lin /ˌpen·əˈsɪl·ɪn/ *n* [U] *specialized* a type of medicine which kills bacteria; a type of ANTIBIOTIC

pe·nile /ˈpiː·naɪl/ *adj* [not gradable] of the penis

pe·nin·sula /£pəˈnɪnt·sjʊ·lə, $-sə-/ *n* [C] a long piece of land which sticks out from a larger area of land into the sea or into a lake • *the Korean/Arabian/Florida Peninsula* • *The sea is expected to break through the narrowest point of the peninsula any year now.*

pe·nis /ˈpiː·nɪs/ *n* [C] the part of a male's body which is used for urinating and in sexual activity

pen·i·tent /ˈpen·ɪ·tᵊnt/ *adj fml* regretting something you have done because you feel it was wrong • *"I'm sorry," she said with a penitent smile.* • *It was hard to be angry with him when he looked so penitent.*

pen·i·tence /ˈpen·ɪ·tᵊnts/ *n* [U] • *He expressed his penitence for what he had done.*

pen·i·tent /ˈpen·ɪ·tᵊnt/ *n* [C] *fml* • A penitent is a person who is performing a formal religious act to show regret for something they have done wrong.

pen·i·tent·ly /ˈpen·ɪ·tᵊnt·li/ *adv fml*

pen·i·ten·ti·a·ry /£ˌpen·ɪˈten·tʃᵊr·i, £-əˈ-, $-tʃə·riː/ *n* [C] *Am* a PRISON

pen·knife /ˈpen·naɪf/, **pock·et·knife** *n* [C] a small knife which folds into a case and is usually carried in a pocket • PIC **Knife**

pen·light /ˈpen·laɪt/ *n* [C] *Am* a small TORCH (= light that can be carried) about the size and shape of a pen

pen·nant /ˈpen·ᵊnt/ *n* [C] a triangular-shaped flag, several of which can be used in a line for decoration or to send a message • *The team pennant has an eagle emblem on it.* • *There was a pennant fluttering at the top of the mast.* • In baseball, the pennant is the flag which is the symbol showing that a team has that year won in the group of teams in which it plays: *the American League pennant race* • *the National League pennant winners* ○ *Divisional winners meet in the final to decide the pennant.*

pen·ny /ˈpen·i/ *n* [C] *pl* **pence** or **p** or **pennies** the smallest unit of money in Britain of which there are 100 in a POUND, or a small coin worth this much • *(Br)* You use 'pence' or, more informally, 'p' when you are speaking of the unit of money and 'pennies' when you are speaking of the coins themselves: *Could you lend me 50 pence/50p please?* ○ *I found a ten/twenty/fifty pence* **piece** (= a coin of this value) *in the phone booth.* ○ *I keep pennies and other small coins in a jar.* • In the US and Canada, a penny is a CENT or a coin of this value. • In Britain before 1971, a penny or **old** penny was a large coin. There were twelve pennies in a SHILLING. • In many phrases, penny is used when speaking of the smallest amount of money possible: *Buy a TV now and it won't cost you a penny for 3 months.* ○ *It was an expensive meal but worth every penny.* • *(Br infml)* If you say that **the penny (has) dropped**, you mean that you or someone else suddenly understands or becomes aware of something that you or they did not know about before: *She looked confused for a moment, then suddenly the penny dropped and she burst out laughing.* ○ *It took a long time for the penny to drop.* • You say **a penny for your thoughts** or **a penny for them** when you want to know what another person is thinking, usually because they have been quiet for a while. • If someone **doesn't have a penny to** their **name** or **doesn't have two pennies to rub together**, they are very poor. • If someone is described as **penny-wise and pound-foolish**, they are thought to be too careful about very small amounts of money and not able to consider larger, more important matters. • *(Br infml)* If you describe something as **two/ten a penny** (*Am* **a dime a dozen**), you mean that there is a lot of that thing and so it is not special or worth very much: *Antique toy cars are ten a penny nowadays.* • *(Am)* If something is described as **penny-ante** it is unimportant or not worth doing: *He wanted us to get involved in some penny-ante deals.* • A **penny-farthing** is a type of bicycle used in the past which had a very large front wheel and a small back wheel. • **Penny-pinching** is avoiding spending even the smallest amounts of money: *Local residents have accused the council of penny-pinching.* ○ *I became tired of his penny-pinching friends.* • A **penny whistle** is a small cheap musical instrument shaped like a tube with holes along one side and a part for your mouth at one end that you blow into. • *(Br saying)* 'In for a penny, in for a pound' means that since you have started something or are involved in it, you should complete the work although it has become more difficult or complicated than you had expected. • *(Br saying)* 'Take care of/Look after the pennies and the pounds will take care of/look after themselves' means that if you do not waste small amounts of money, you will succeed in saving large amounts of money in the future. • *"Pennies from Heaven"* (title of a song written by Johnny Burke, 1936) • LP› **Money**

-pen·ny /-pə·ni/ *combining form Br* • The combining use -penny is used with numbers to show how many pence something costs, esp. in the past: *a fourpenny ice-cream*

pen·ni·less /ˈpen·i·ləs/ *adj* • If you are penniless, you have no money: *She fell in love with a penniless artist.*

pen·ny·worth /£ˈpen·i·wəθ, £ˈpen·əθ, $ˈpen·i·wɚθ/, *Br* **penn'orth** /£ˈpen·əθ, $-ɚθ/ *n* [U] *dated* • A pennyworth or penn'orth of something is as much as can be bought for a penny: *I'd like a pennyworth of humbugs, please.* • *(fig.) It won't make a pennyworth of difference* (= It will make no difference) *to me.*

pen·sion /ˈpent·ʃən/ *n* [C] a sum of money paid regularly by the government or a private company to a person who does not work any more because they are too old or they have become ill • *They find it hard to live on their state pension.* • *He won't be able to* **draw** (= receive) *his pension until he's 65.* • A **pension plan**/*(Br and Aus also)* **pension scheme** is a financial plan that allows you to receive money after you or your employer have paid money into it for a number of years. • A **pension fund** is a supply of money which many people pay into, esp. employees of a company, and which is invested in order to provide them with a pension when they are older. • (CS) (J) (PL)

pen·sion *obj* /ˈpent·ʃən/ *v* [T] • If someone is pensioned **off**, they are made to leave their job and are given a pension: *Workers in the company are being pensioned off at 50.*

pen·sion·able /ˈpent·ʃən·ə·bl̩/ *adj* [not gradable] *Br* • *She is* **of** *pensionable* **age** (= is old enough to claim a pension). • A pensionable job is one in which you will be given a pension when you are too old to continue working.

pen·sion·er /£ˈpent·ʃən·əʳ, $-ɚ/, **old age pen·sion·er**, *Br also abbreviation* **OAP** *n* [C] • A pensioner is a person who receives a pension, esp. the government pension given to old people: *Students and pensioners are entitled to a discount.* • LP› **Age** (I)

pen·sive /ˈpent·sɪv/ *adj* thinking in a quiet way, often with a serious expression on your face • *She became withdrawn and pensive, hardly speaking to anyone.*

pen·sive·ly /ˈpent·sɪv·li/ *adv* • *He gazed pensively at the glass in front of him, lost in thought.*

pent·a·gon SHAPE /£ˈpen·tə·gən, $-t̬ə·gɑːn/ *n* [C] a five-sided shape with five angles • PIC› **Shapes**

Pent·a·gon BUILDING /£ˈpen·tə·gən, $-t̬ə·gɑːn/ *n* [U] **the Pentagon** the building in Washington where the US Defense Department is based, or the US Defense Department itself • *The Pentagon is aiming to cut US forces by over 25 per cent in the next five years.* • *Pentagon* **officials** *said yesterday that there will be no change in policy.*

pent·ath·lon /£penˈtæθ·lɒn, $-lɑːn/ *n* [C] a sporting event in which ATHLETES compete in five different sports • *The pentathlon consists of running, swimming, riding, shooting, and fencing.* • Compare BIATHLON; DECATHLON; HEPTATHLON.

pent·ath·lete /penˈtæθ·liːt/ *n* [C] • A pentathlete is a person who competes in pentathlons.

Pen·te·cost /£ˈpen·tɪ·kɒst, $-t̬ɪ·kɑːst/ *n* [U] (in the Jewish religion) a holy day that comes 50 days after Passover, or (in the Christian religion) a holy day that is the seventh Sunday after Easter • *The Jewish Pentecost celebrates the harvest of the first fruits and the gift of the Torah* (= the holy book of the Jews) *to Moses at Sinai.* • *The Christian Pentecost celebrates the sending of the Holy Spirit to the Apostles.*

Pent·e·cos·tal·i·sm /£ˌpen·tɪˈkɒs·təl·ɪ·zəm, $-ˈkɑː·stəl-/ *n* [U] a modern Christian group which began in the USA in 1901, whose members believe that everything written in the Bible is true • *Pentecostalism emphasizes the importance of the Holy Spirit in the life of the individual and the Church.*

Pen·te·cost·al /£ˌpen·tɪˈkɒs·təl, $-t̬ɪˈkɑː·stəl/ *adj* [not gradable], *n* [C] • *Pentecostal services are characterized by enthusiastic singing and spontaneous exclamations of praise and thanksgiving.* • *There are over 22 million Pentecostals throughout the world.*

pent·house /ˈpent·haʊs/ *n* [C] *pl* **penthouses** /ˈpent ˌhaʊ·zɪz/ a luxurious apartment or set of rooms at the top of a hotel or tall building • *They live in a luxurious penthouse overlooking Central Park.* • *The singer is staying in a penthouse* **suite** (= set of rooms) *in the Hilton.* • PIC› **Accommodation**

pent-up /ˌpentˈʌp/ *adj* (of feelings) not allowed to be expressed or released • *Screaming at the top of your voice is a good way of venting pent-up frustration.* • *The children ran around the garden releasing pent-up excitement.*

pe·nul·ti·mate /£pəˈnʌl·tɪ·mət, $pɪˈnʌl·t̬ə·mət/ *adj* [not gradable], *n* [C] *fml* (something which is) second from the last • *I missed the penultimate episode of the TV series that I was following.* • Compare ANTEPENULTIMATE.

pen·u·ry /£ˈpen·jʊ·ri, $-jɚ·i/ *n* [U] *fml* the state of being extremely poor • *She found moving from her affluent home into student penury a very difficult experience.*

pe·o·ny /ˈpiː·ə·ni/ *n* [C] a garden plant with large red, pink or white flowers

peo·ple /ˈpiː·pl̩/ *pl n* men, women and children • *Many people never take any exercise.* • *We've invited thirty people to our party.* • *Most of her friends are media people* (= people who do this type of work). • You use 'people' when referring to persons in general or everyone: *People will think you've gone mad.* ○ *People like to be made to feel important.* • People is also used to refer to men and women who are involved in a particular type of work or do a particular job: *We'll have to get the people from the tax office to look at these accounts.* • When you say **the** people, you mean the large number of ordinary men and women who do not have positions of power in society: *She claims to be the voice of the people.* ○ *The President has lost the support of the people.* • *(infml)* You sometimes refer to the group of people that you are speaking to as 'people': *Now that we've discussed our problems, are people happy with the decisions taken?* • *(slightly dated infml)* Your people are the people to whom you are related: *Her people come from Scotland originally.* ○ *He wanted to take her home to meet his people.* • *I thought that you,* **of all people** (= especially you, more than anyone else), *would believe me!* • *I'm amazed that Dave,* **of all people** (= in particular), *got married.* • A **man/woman of the people** is a person, usually involved in politics, who is liked by a lot of ordinary people and seems to understand and like them. • LP› **Age**

peo·ple /ˈpiː·pl̩/ *n* [C] • A people is all the men, women and children who live in a particular country: *The French are known as a food-loving people.* • A people is also a society: *Customs similar to this one are found among many peoples of the world.* • *"Let my people go"* (Moses to Pharaoh in the Bible, Exodus 7.16)

peo·ple *obj* /ˈpiː·pl̩/ *v* [T] • If a place is peopled by a particular type of people, those people live there: *These luxurious yachts are peopled by the rich and glamorous.* ○ *(fig.) Her novels are peopled by many eccentric characters.*

pep /pep/ *n* [U] *infml* energy, or a willingness to be active • *Eating the right foods and taking exercise will give you more pep.* • A **pep pill** is a pill containing a drug that gives you more energy and makes you feel happier. • A **pep talk** is a short speech intended to encourage people to work harder or try to win a game or contest: *The boss gave the staff a pep talk this morning in an attempt to boost sales.*

pep up *obj*, **pep** *obj* **up** /pep/ *v adv* [M] • *A good night's sleep will pep you up* (= make you feel more energetic). • *The show needs to be pepped up* (= made more interesting) *with some decent songs.*

pep·per POWDER /£ˈpep·əʳ, $-ɚ/ *n* [U] a greyish black or creamy coloured powder produced by crushing dry PEPPERCORNS, which is used to give a spicy hot taste to food • *Would you like some freshly ground black pepper on your pizza?* • *Please would you pass the* **salt and pepper**. • A **pepper mill** is a small device, the top part of which you turn by hand to crush the PEPPERCORNS inside it to produce pepper. • A *(Br and Aus)* **pepper pot**/*(Am)* **pepper box/shaker** is a small container with several holes in the top that contains pepper: *Salt and pepper pots are often put beside each other on a table.* • A **pepper-and-salt** *(esp. Am* **salt-and-pepper**) pattern is a mixture of black and white: *He has a neatly trimmed pepper-and-salt beard.* • PIC› **Mill**

pep·pery /£ˈpep·ər·i, $-ɚ·i/ *adj* **-ier, -iest** • *This salad has a sharp peppery flavour* (= a spicy flavour like pepper). • A person who is peppery is bad-tempered and easily annoyed: *He was a famously peppery lawyer.*

pep·per VEGETABLE /£ˈpep·əʳ, $-ɚ/ *n* [C] a vegetable that is usually green, red or yellow, has a rounded shape and is hollow with seeds in the middle • *a red/green pepper* • *Peppers are usually fried or baked with other vegetables or* *eaten raw in salads.* • **Red** *peppers are ideal for roasting in the oven.* • PIC> **Vegetables**

pep·per *obj* SCATTER /£'pep·əʳ, $-ɚ/ *v* [T] to hit (something) repeatedly with small objects • *The city's walls were peppered* **with** *bullets.* • *(fig.) Her writing was peppered* **with** (= full of) *quotations from the Koran.*

pep·per·corn /£'pep·ə·kɔːn, $-ɚ·kɔːrn/ *n* [C] a small dried fruit that looks like a seed and is crushed to produce PEPPER • *(Br and Aus)* A **peppercorn rent** is a very small amount of money that you pay as rent: *Michael and Stephanie pay a peppercorn rent for their cottage in the moors.*

pep·per·mint /£'pep·ə·mɪnt, $'-ɚ-/ *n* a strong fresh flavouring obtained from a type of MINT plant, used especially to flavour sweets • *She drinks peppermint-flavoured tea.* [U] • A peppermint is a hard white sweet that has the flavour of peppermint: *You can eat a peppermint as a breath freshener.* [C]

per /£pɜːʳ, $pɜːr/ *prep* (used when expressing rates, prices or measurements) for each • *The meal will cost $20 per person.* • *How many hours do you work per day?* • *The car was travelling at 70 miles per hour (70 mph).* • *There are more cafés per square mile here than anywhere else in the country.* • *This country has the lowest income per head* (= for each person) *in the world.* • *(fml)* If you do something **as per** instructions, you do it following those instructions. • *(infml) I had a shower this morning* **as per usual** (= as I usually do). • *(fml)* In financial and economic matters, **per annum** (*abbreviation* **pa**) means every year: *The country exports goods worth $600 million per annum.* • *(fml)* In financial and economic matters, **per calendar month** (*abbreviation* **pcm**) means every month from the first day of the month to the last day of the month: *The rent for this apartment is $600 per calendar month.* • *(fml)* If you state an amount **per capita**, you mean that amount for each person: *France and Germany invest far more per capita in public transport than Britain.* ○ *The per capita income in the country is very low.* • See also PER CENT. • LP> **Slash**

per·am·bu·late /pə'ræm·bjʊ·leɪt/ *v* [I] *old use* to walk about for pleasure

per·am·bu·lat·or /£pə'ræm·bjʊ·leɪ·təʳ, $-t̬ɚ/ *n* [C] • Perambulator is *fml or dated for* PRAM.

per·ceive *(obj)* SEE /£pə'siːv, $pɚ-/ *v* to see (something or someone), or to become aware of (something that is obvious) • *Bill perceived a tiny figure in the distance.* • *I perceived a note of unhappiness in her voice.* • *Perceiving* **that** *he wasn't happy with the arrangements, I tried to book a different hotel.* [+ *that* clause]

per·ceive *obj* BELIEVE /£pə'siːv, $pɚ-/ *v* [T] to come to an opinion about (something), or have a belief about (something) • *How do the French perceive the British* (= What do they think they are like)? • *Following the recession, people no longer perceive* (= believe) **that** *the value of their houses will continue to rise.* [+ *that* clause] • *Women's magazines are often perceived* (= thought) **to be** *superficial.* [+ obj + *to be* n/adj] • *I perceived him* **to be** (= I thought he was) *a rather shy sort of man.* [+ obj + *to be* n/adj]

per cent, per·cent /£pə'sent, $pɚ-/ *adv* [not gradable] (of rates) for or out of every 100. Per cent can be shown by the symbol %. • *You got 20 per cent of the answers right – that means one in every five.* • *The report states that men are responsible for 95% of cases of drunk driving.* • *Only 40% of people bothered to vote in the election.* • LP> **Mathematics** (PL)

per·cent·age /£pə'sen·tɪdʒ, $pɚ'sen·t̬ɪdʒ/ *n* [C] • *What percentage of women return to work after having a baby?* • *A large percentage of children in the school come from single-parent families.* • *Interest rates have risen by two percentage* **points**. • *(Am and Aus infml)* A percentage is also an advantage: *There's no percentage in working such long hours.*

per·cen·tile /£pə'sen·taɪl, $pɚ'sen-/ *n* [C] *specialized* • A percentile is one of 99 points into which a range of information is divided to make 100 equal-sized groups: *Test scores show that the majority of eleventh graders in the region were in the 60th percentile or above* (= scored 60% or more) *compared with the rest of the country.*

per·cep·ti·ble /£pə'sep·tə·bl̩, $pɚ-/ *adj* that can only just be seen, heard or noticed • *There was a barely perceptible movement in his right arm.* • *The past year has seen a perceptible improvement in working standards.*

per·cep·ti·bly /£pə'sep·tə·bli, $pɚ-/ *adv* • *The mood had changed perceptibly* (= in a way that could be noticed).

per·cep·tion BELIEF /£pə'sep·ʃᵊn, $pɚ-/ *n* [C] a belief or opinion, often held by many people and based on appearances • *We have to change the public's perception that money is being wasted.* • *These photographs will affect people's perceptions of war.*

per·cep·tion SIGHT /£pə'sep·ʃᵊn, $pɚ-/ *n* [U] an awareness of things through the physical SENSES, esp. sight • *Drugs can alter your perception of reality.* • *Psychologists have been studying perception in rats in an attempt to discover more about human mental processes connected with sight.* • A person's perception is their ability to notice and understand things that are not obvious to other people: *I admire her gifts of perception.* • *"If the doors of perception were cleansed everything would appear as it is, infinite"* (from William Blake *The Marriage of Heaven and Hell* 'A Memorable Fancy', 1790-3)

per·cep·tive /£pə'sep·tɪv, $pɚ-/ *adj* • If someone is perceptive, they are very good at noticing and understanding things that many people do not notice: *Her books are full of perceptive insights into the human condition.*

per·cep·tive·ly /£pə'sep·tɪv·li, $pɚ-/ *adv* • *He has spoken perceptively on many subjects.*

per·cep·tive·ness /£pə'sep·tɪv·nəs, $pɚ-/ *n* [U] • *He had enough perceptiveness* (= awareness and understanding) *to realize that I wanted to be alone.*

perch *(obj)* SIT /£pɜːtʃ, $pɜːrtʃ/ *v* to sit or be situated on (something high) or on the edge of (something), or (of a bird) to sit on a branch or other object • *We perched on bar stools and had a beer.* [I] • *The village is perched on top of a high hill.* [T]

perch /£pɜːtʃ, $pɜːrtʃ/ *n* [C] • A bird's perch is a place where it sits, esp. a thin rod in a cage made for the bird to rest on. • A person's perch is a seat or other place high up, often giving a good view of something below: *We watched the parade from our perch on the scaffolding.*

perch FISH /£pɜːtʃ, $pɜːrtʃ/ *n* [C] *pl* **perch** or *Am also* **perches** a fish that lives in lakes and rivers and is eaten as food

per·chance /£pə'tʃɑːnts, $pɚ'tʃænts/ *adv* [not gradable] *old use* by chance; possibly • *Do you know her, perchance?* • *"To sleep: perchance to dream"* (Shakespeare, Hamlet 3.1)

per·ci·pi·ent /£pə'sɪp·i·ənt, $pɚ-/ *adj fml* good at noticing and understanding things • *I always appreciate your percipient comments on my work.*

per·co·late *(obj)* /£'pɜː·kᵊl·eɪt, $'pɜːr-/ *v* to (cause something to) move slowly through a substance with very small holes in it • *Sea water percolates down through the rocks.* [I] • *(fig.) The news has begun to percolate* (= slowly spread) *through the staff.* [I] • To percolate coffee (*infml* **perk**) is to use a machine to make coffee in which hot water passes through crushed coffee beans into a container below. [T]

per·co·lat·or /£'pɜː·kᵊl·eɪ·təʳ, $'pɜːr·kᵊl·eɪ·t̬ɚ/ *n* [C] • A percolator is a device for making coffee in which hot water passes through crushed coffee beans into a container below.

per·cus·sion /£pə'kʌʃ·ᵊn, $pɚ-/ *n* [U] musical instruments that you play by hitting them with your hand or another object such as a stick • *Drums, tambourines and cymbals are all percussion instruments.* • *I thought that the band's percussion section was too loud.* • *Jean plays the guitar and her brother is* **on** *percussion* (= plays percussion instruments). • Compare BRASS MUSICAL INSTRUMENTS; WOODWIND.

per·cus·sion·ist /£pə'kʌʃ·ᵊn·ɪst, $pɚ-/ *n* [C] • A percussionist is a person who plays percussion instruments.

per·cus·sive /£pə'kʌs·ɪv, $pɚ-/ *adj* • *She mixes jazz with percussive rhythms to create a style of music which is all her own.*

per·di·tion /£pə'dɪʃ·ᵊn, $pɚ-/ *n* [U] *literary* a state of endless punishment suffered by evil people after death

per·e·grin·a·tion /ˌper·ə·grɪ'neɪ·ʃᵊn/ *n* [C] *fml* a long journey in which you travel to various different places, esp. on foot • *Our peregrinations took us to some very strange countries.*

per·e·grine fal·con /ˌper·ə·grɪn/ *n* [C] a large bird with a dark back and wings and a lightly coloured front, which catches mice and other small animals • *The peregrine falcon was once used in the sport of falconry.*

per·empt·o·ry /£pə'rem*p*·tᵊr·i, $-tɚ-/ *adj* (of a person or their behaviour) expecting to be obeyed immediately and without questioning • *Sue started giving me peremptory* *instructions on how to drive the car.* • *She was highly critical of the insensitive and peremptory way in which the cases had been handled.*

per·empt·or·i·ly /pəˈremp·trə·li/ *adv* • *"Now," he said peremptorily, "step forward and state your name."*

per·en·ni·al [TIME] /pəˈren·i·əl/ *adj* lasting a very long time, or happening repeatedly or all the time • *The film 'White Christmas' is a perennial favourite.* • *We face the perennial problem of not having enough money.* • Compare ANNUAL; BIENNIAL.

per·en·ni·al·ly /pəˈren·i·ə·li/ *adv* [not gradable] • *She seems to be perennially short of money.*

per·en·ni·al [PLANT] /pəˈren·i·əl/ *n* [C] a plant that lives for several years • *Roses and geraniums are perennials, flowering year after year.*

per·e·stroi·ka /ˌper·əˈstrɔɪ·kə/ *n* [U] the political, social and economic changes which happened in the USSR during the late 1980s • *Perestroika is the Russian word for 'restructuring'.*

per·fect [FAULTLESS] /£ˈpɜː·fekt, $ˈpɜːr-/ *adj* complete and correct in every way, of the best possible type or without fault • *What is your idea of perfect happiness?* • *This church is a perfect example of medieval architecture.* • *You have a perfect English accent.* • *The car is five-years-old but is in almost perfect condition.* • *She thought she had found the perfect man* (= one with all the qualities she wanted). • *(infml)* You use 'perfect' to emphasize the noun that comes after it: *That dog is a perfect nuisance.* ○ *I felt like a perfect fool when I forgot her name.*

per·fect *obj* /£pəˈfekt, $pɜːr-/ *v* [T] • To perfect something is to make it faultless in every way: *He is keen to perfect his golfing technique.*

per·fect·ly /£ˈpɜː·fekt·li, $ˈpɜːr-/ *adv* • *As a couple, they are perfectly* (= completely) *suited.* • *The old house has been restored perfectly* (= as well as it could be). • Perfectly is also used to emphasize the word that follows it: *Your fears are perfectly understandable* (= I do understand them). ○ *I am perfectly* (= very) *happy living on my own.* ○ *That was a perfectly* (= extremely) *horrible thing to say.* • [LP] **Very, completely**

per·fec·tion /£pəˈfek·ʃən, $pə-/ *n* [U] • Perfection is the state of being complete and correct in every way: *In his quest for physical perfection, he spends hours in the gym.* • If you do something **to** perfection, you do it as well as you can: *She played the part of an upper-class Englishwoman to perfection.* ○ *The fish was cooked to perfection.*

per·fect [PAST TENSE] /£ˈpɜː·fekt, $ˈpɜːr-/ *n* [U], *adj* [not gradable] *specialized* (being) the tense of a verb that shows action that has happened in the past or before another time or event • *In English, the perfect is formed with 'have' and the past participle of the verb.* • **Perfect participle** is another word for **past participle**. See at PAST [GRAMMAR]. • [LP] **Tenses**

per·fec·tion·ist /£pəˈfek·ʃən·ɪst, $pə-/ *n* [C] a person who wants everything to be perfect and demands the highest standards possible • *She's such a perfectionist that she notices even the tiniest mistakes.*

per·fec·tion·ism /£pəˈfek·ʃən·ɪ·zəm, $pə-/ *n* [U] • Perfectionism is the wish for everything to be correct: *Obsessive perfectionism can be very irritating.*

per·fid·i·ous /£pəˈfɪd·i·əs, $pə-/ *adj literary* unable to be trusted, or showing a lack of loyalty • *She described the new criminal bill as a perfidious attack on democracy.*

per·fi·dy /£ˈpɜː·fɪ·di, $ˈpɜːr·fə-/ *n* [U] *literary* • Perfidy is behaviour which is not loyal: *Such perfidy cannot be forgiven.*

per·for·ate *obj* /£ˈpɜː·fər·eɪt, $ˈpɜːr·fə·reɪt/ *v* [T] to make a hole or holes in (something) • *He suffered from bruises and a perforated eardrum in the accident.*

per·for·at·ed /£ˈpɜː·fər·eɪ·tɪd, $ˈpɜːr·fə·reɪ·t̬ɪd/ *adj* [not gradable] • If something is perforated, it has a series of small holes made in it, often so that it will tear easily or let in light or air: *You need special perforated paper for this type of printer.* ○ *The windows have been covered with perforated metal screens.*

per·for·a·tion /£ˌpɜː·fərˈeɪ·ʃən, $ˌpɜːr·fəˈreɪ-/ *n* [C] • *A tea bag is full of tiny perforations to let the flavour out, but not the tea leaves.*

per·force /£pəˈfɔːs, $pəˈfɔːrs/ *adv* [not gradable] *fml dated* because it is necessary • *We must perforce be careful about what we say.*

per·form *(obj)* [DO] /£pəˈfɔːm, $pəˈfɔːrm/ *v* to do (an action or piece of work) • *Computers can perform many different tasks.* [T] • *The operation will be performed next week.* [T] • *I can't be expected to perform miracles!* [T] • *The experiment must be performed in a controlled environment.* [T] • If something such as a machine performs well or badly, it operates satisfactorily or does not operate satisfactorily: *The equipment performed well during the tests.* [I] ○ *These tyres perform badly/poorly in hot weather.* [I] • [LP] **Do: verbs meaning 'perform'**

per·for·mance /£pəˈfɔː·mənts, $pəˈfɔːr-/ *n* [U] • The performance of a person or machine is how well they do a piece of work or activity: *Some athletes take drugs to improve their performance.* • *These cars have a reputation for* **poor** *performance.* • **High**-*performance* (= Fast, powerful and easy to control) *cars are the most expensive.* • *This was a very* **impressive** *performance by the young player, who scored 12 points within the first 10 minutes.*

per·form·er /£pəˈfɔː·məʳ, $pəˈfɔːr·mə/ *n* [C] • If you are a particular type of performer, you are able to do the stated thing well or badly: *The British boat was the star performer in the race.*

per·form *(obj)* [ENTERTAIN] /£pəˈfɔːm, $pəˈfɔːrm/ *v* to entertain people by dancing, singing, acting or playing music • *She composes and performs her own music.* [T] • *A major Hollywood star will be performing on stage tonight.* [I] • *The council plans to ban circuses with performing animals.* • The **performing arts** are forms of entertainment such as acting, dancing and playing music.

per·for·mance /£pəˈfɔː·mənts, $pəˈfɔːr-/ *n* • A performance is the action of entertaining other people by dancing, singing, acting or playing music: *They* **gave** *a superb performance* **of** *Arthur Miller's play 'The Crucible'.* [C] • *(esp. Br infml disapproving)* If you describe a person's behaviour as a performance, you mean that they are behaving badly, usually because they are angry or upset: *What a performance! Please stop shouting!* [U] • *(Br)* If something that you do is **a** performance, it involves a lot of work and takes a long time to do: *Cleaning the oven is such a performance.* [U] • A **repeat** performance is when an event or a situation happens again: *The police hope to avoid a repeat performance of last year, when the festivities turned into rioting.* [C] • **Performance art** is a type of theatrical entertainment in which the artist's personality and creative processes form part of the show.

per·form·er /£pəˈfɔː·məʳ, $pəˈfɔːr·mə/ *n* [C] • A performer is a person who entertains people by acting, singing, dancing or playing music: *He is both a talented songwriter and performer.*

per·fume /£ˈpɜː·fjuːm, $pɜːrˈfjuːm/ *n* a liquid with a pleasant smell, usually made from oils taken from flowers or spices, which is often used on the skin • *What perfume are you wearing?* [C] • *She adores French perfume.* [U] • Perfume is also a pleasant natural smell: *The perfume of the roses filled the room.* [U] • [LP] **Shopping goods, Smells** Ⓕ

per·fume *obj* /£ˈpɜː·fjuːm, $ˈpɜːr-/ *v* [T] • *In the evening, the flowers perfume the air* (= make it smell pleasant). • *Is this make-up perfumed or unperfumed* (= does it contain perfume or not)? • *The hall was filled with expensively-perfumed women* (= women wearing expensive perfume) *in silk ballgowns.*

per·func·to·ry /£pəˈfʌŋk·tər·i, $pəˈfʌŋk·tə·i/ *adj* done quickly, without taking care or interest • *His smile was perfunctory.*

per·func·to·ri·ly /£pəˈfʌŋk·tər·əl·i, $pəˈfʌŋk·tə·ə·li/ *adv* • *The two heads of state shook hands perfunctorily for the photographers and then got into their separate cars and drove off.*

per·go·la /£ˈpɜː·gəl·ə, $ˈpɜːr-/ *n* [C] a frame in a garden that climbing plants can grow over and which you can walk through • [PIC] **Garden**

per·haps /£pəˈhæps, £præps, $pəˈhæps/ *adv* [not gradable] used to show that something is possible or that you are not certain about something • *He hasn't written to me recently – perhaps he's lost my address.* • *Perhaps the most important question has not been asked.* • *We plan to travel to Europe – to Spain or Italy perhaps.* • Perhaps is also used to show that a number or amount is approximate: *There were perhaps 500 people at the meeting.* • Perhaps is used when making polite requests or statements of opinion: *Would you like some tea, perhaps?* ○ *"I never remember people's birthdays." "Well, perhaps you should."* • See also MAYBE.

per·il /ˈper·əl/ *n slightly fml* great danger, or something that is very dangerous • *I never felt that my life was* **in** *peril.* [U] • *The journey through the mountains was* **fraught with** *peril*

(=full of dangers). [U] • *Teenagers must be warned about the perils* **of** *unsafe sex.* [C] • *The situation is full of perils* **and pitfalls** (=things that can go wrong). [C] • If you tell someone to do something **at** their peril, you are warning them that this is a very dangerous thing to do: *We underestimate the destructiveness of war at our peril.* [U] • *"For those in peril on the sea"* (The Book of Common Prayer, 1662)

per·il·ous /ˈper·əl·əs/ *adj slightly fml* • Something that is perilous is extremely dangerous: *The country roads are quite perilous.* ○ *The change from dictatorship to democracy is always perilous.*

per·il·ous·ly /ˈper·əl·ə·sli/ *adv slightly fml* • *She* **came** *perilously* **close** *to getting herself killed in her attempt to break the world record.*

pe·ri·me·ter /£pəˈrɪm·ɪ·təʳ, $-ˈrɪm·ə·t̬ɚ/ *n* [C] the outer edge of an area of land or the border around it • *Protesters cut a hole in the perimeter fence.* • *A river runs along one side of the field's perimeter.* • *(specialized)* The perimeter of a shape is the length of its outer edge: *The perimeter of a square is four times the length of one side.*

pe·ri·od TIME /£ˈpɪə·ri·əd, $ˈpɪr·i-/ *n* [C] a length of time • *Her work means that she spends long periods away from home.* • *Unemployment in the first half of 1993 was 2% lower than* **in** *the same period the year before* (=the first half of 1992). • *Fifteen people were killed* **in/over** *a period* **of** *four days.* • *The study will be carried out* **over** *a six-month period.* • *We sell a lot of turkeys* **over** *the Christmas period.* • In school, a period is a division of time in the day when a subject is taught: *We have six periods of science a week.* • A period in the life of a person or in history is a fixed time during that life or history: *Most teenagers go through a rebellious period.* ○ *The house was built during the Elizabethan period.* • A **cooling-off** period is a time when you can change your opinion before you are legally forced to do something: *There is a twenty-day cooling-off period in which the investor can choose to back out of the contract.* • **Peak** periods are times when a lot of people are doing an activity or using a public service: *Trains are very overcrowded in peak periods.* ○ *It's cheaper to travel in* **off-peak** *periods* (=times which are not so busy). • Period **costume/dress/furniture** means the clothes or furniture of the time in history that is being referred to: *They performed Julius Caesar in period dress.* • *(infml)* A **period piece** is something such as a book or a film that is very old-fashioned, often in a way that is amusing to people now: *The play is a whimsical period piece, written in 1938.* • LP **Periods of time**

pe·ri·od BLEEDING /£ˈpɪə·ri·əd, $ˈpɪr·i-/, **men·stru·al pe·ri·od** *n* [C] the bleeding from a woman's womb that happens once a month when she is not pregnant • *Great stress can sometimes cause a woman to miss a period.* • *Do you have regular periods?* • *She's got period pains* (=pain caused by her period).

pe·ri·od MARK /£ˈpɪə·ri·əd, $ˈpɪr·i-/ *n* [C] *esp. Am for* a **full stop**, see at FULL COMPLETE • You say 'period' at the end of a statement to show that you believe you have said all there is to say on a subject and you are not going to discuss it any more: *There will be no more shouting, period!*

pe·ri·od·ic /£ˌpɪə·riˈɒd·ɪk, $ˌpɪr·iˈɑː·dɪk/ *adj* [not gradable] happening repeatedly over a period of time • *He suffers periodic mental breakdowns.*

pe·ri·od·i·cal·ly /£ˌpɪə·riˈɒd·ɪ·kli, $ˌpɪr·iˈɑː·dɪ-/ *adv* [not gradable] • *The equipment should be tested periodically* (=at regular times).

pe·ri·od·i·cal /£ˌpɪə·riˈɒd·ɪ·kəl, $ˌpɪr·iˈɑː·dɪ-/ *n* [C] a magazine or newspaper, esp. on a serious subject, that is published regularly • *The periodical is published every month.* • *She has written for several legal periodicals.* • Ⓔ

pe·ri·od·ic ta·ble *n* [U] **the periodic table** an arrangement of the symbols of chemical elements, usually in rows and columns, showing similarities in chemical behaviour, esp. between elements in the same columns • *Carbon is next to nitrogen on the periodic table.*

per·i·pa·tet·ic /£ˌper·ɪ·pəˈtet·ɪk, $-ˈtet̬-/ *adj* [not gradable] *fml* travelling around to different places, usually because you work in more than one place • *Many schools can only afford to employ peripatetic music teachers.*

pe·ri·phe·ry /£pəˈrɪf·ər·i, $-ˈrɪf·ɚ·i/ *n* [C usually sing] the outer edge of an area • *Houses have been built on the periphery of the factory site.* • *The ring road runs around the periphery of the city centre.* • The periphery is also the less important part of a group or activity: *Many women feel they are being kept on the periphery of the armed forces.*

PERIODS OF TIME

LENGTHS OF TIME

There are only a small number of words referring to exact periods of time.
They are (from largest to smallest):

millennium (1000 years)	**week**
century (100 years)	**day**
decade (10 years)	**hour**
year (365 days)	**minute**
month (12 months in a year)	**second**
(esp *Br*) **fortnight** (2 weeks)	

A century, year and hour are often divided into halves or quarters: *The political changes of the last quarter century* • *Prices rose again in the first quarter (of the year).*

A **generation** is 25–30 years: *It will take a generation for the new trees to grow.*

Some of these words are also used to talk about approximate time periods, and to emphasise how long or short a period is meant:

At this rate it'll take **hours/days/weeks/ months** *to finish the project.*
He's been doing the same job for **years**.
You're late – I've been waiting (for) **ages**!
Filling in these forms seems to take **forever/an eternity**.
I've had these old boots for **quite a while**.
Will builders be here **long**? *They only started a* **short time** *ago.*
She'll be here in a **second/moment/minute**.
Can you wait a minute, I'll be with you **presently/shortly** (= soon).

TIME PERIODS OF THE PAST, PRESENT AND FUTURE

The following words refer to particular periods of time:

Punk music was popular **in the late 1970s** *and* **early 80s**.
Our house was built in the **mid sixties**.
This hospital dates from the **turn of the century** (= around 1900).
Electric lights were invented near **the end of the 19th century**.

You can also talk in a less exact way about periods of time, for example:

The Greek civilisation was one of the most important **in ancient times**.
Medical science has developed enormously **in modern times**.
I love to hear Grandfather talk about **the old days**.
In those days *it was very difficult to travel across Africa.*
After some difficult **times** *the country is entering a new* **era/age** *of peace.*
These days/nowadays *we spend much more time at home than we used to.*
At the moment/at present *she's really busy with her new job.*
I'm **presently/currently** (= now) *studying for an economics degree.*

per·i·pher·al /£pə'rɪf·ᵊr·ᵊl, $-'rɪf·ɚ-/ *adj* • If something is peripheral, it is not as important as something else: *Let's not worry about peripheral issues.* ○ *The book contains a great deal of peripheral detail.* • Peripheral also means happening at the edge of something: *A figure came into my peripheral vision.*

per·i·pher·al /£pə'rɪf·ᵊr·ᵊl, $-'rɪf·ɚ-/ *n* [C] *specialized* • A peripheral is a piece of equipment, such as a printer, that can be connected to a computer.

per·i·scope /£'per·ɪ·skəʊp, $-skoʊp/ *n* [C] a long vertical tube containing a set of mirrors which gives you a view of what is above you when you look through the bottom of the tube • *Periscopes are used in submarines to allow you to look above the surface of the water.* • PIC〉 **Ships and boats**

per·ish /'per·ɪʃ/ *v* [I] (of a person) to die, esp. in an accident or by being killed, or (of a thing) to be destroyed • *Three hundred people perished in the earthquake.* • *He believes that Europe must create closer ties or it will perish.* • *(Br and Aus)* If material such as rubber or leather perishes, it decays and starts to break into pieces: *Being exposed to sunlight has caused the rubber to perish.* • You say **perish the thought** to show that you hope that something that has been suggested will never happen: *Me, get married? Perish the thought!*

per·ish·a·ble /'per·ɪ·ʃə·bl̩/ *adj* • Perishable food is food that decays quickly: *It's important to store perishable food in a cool place.*

per·ish·a·bles /'per·ɪ·ʃə·bl̩z/ *pl n* • Perishables are items of food that decay quickly: *The supermarket has its perishables delivered by air rather than truck to ensure freshness.*

per·ish·ing /'per·ɪ·ʃɪŋ/ *adj* [not gradable] *Br and Aus infml* • If the weather is perishing, it is extremely cold: *Don't go out without your coat, it's perishing out there!* • *(dated)* You can use perishing to show your annoyance about something: *I forgot my perishing keys, didn't I?*

per·ished /'per·ɪʃt/ *adj* [not gradable] *Br and Aus infml* • *I'm perished with cold* (= I am feeling extremely cold).

per·ish·er /£'per·ɪ·ʃəʳ, $-ʃɚ/ *n* [C] *Br dated infml* a child who is being annoying • *Give me my watch back, you little perisher!*

per·i·ton·i·tis /£,per·ɪ·təʊ'naɪ·tɪs, $-t̬ə'naɪ·t̬ɪs/ *n* [U] *specialized* a serious medical condition in which the inside wall of the ABDOMEN becomes very sore and larger than its usual size, esp. because of infection

per·i·wink·le PLANT /'per·ɪ,wɪŋ·kl̩/ *n* [C] an evergreen plant with small blue flowers

per·i·wink·le SEA CREATURE /'per·ɪ,wɪŋ·kl̩/ *n* [C] *Am for* WINKLE

per·jure *obj* /£'pɜː·dʒəʳ, $'pɜːr·dʒɚ/ *v* [T] *law* to cause (yourself) to tell a lie in a law court, after promising formally to tell the truth • *The judge warned the witness not to perjure herself.* • *It was revealed that state witnesses had perjured themselves and that evidence had been suppressed which could have established the men's innocence.*

per·jured /£'pɜː·dʒəd, $'pɜːr·dʒɚd/ *adj* [not gradable] *law* • *The defending attorney accused the police of giving perjured testimony against* (= telling lies about) *her client.*

per·jur·er /£'pɜː·dʒᵊr·əʳ, $'pɜːr·dʒɚ·ɚ/ *n* [C] *law* • *The prosecution accused him of being a perjurer who was motivated by a desire to injure his former employer.*

per·jur·y /£'pɜː·dʒᵊr·i, $'pɜːr·dʒɚ-/ *n* [U] *law* • *She was sentenced to two years in jail for* **committing** *perjury* (= telling lies in a law court). • LP〉 **Crimes and criminals**

perk ADVANTAGE /£pɜːk, $pɜːrk/ *n* [C] *infml* an advantage or benefit, such as money or goods, which you are given because of your job • *Life insurance is a common perk for top company managers.* • *A company car and a mobile phone are some of the perks that come with the job.* • *(fig.) Having such easy access to some of the best cinema and theatre is one of the perks* (= advantages) *of living in Sydney.*

perk *(obj)* MAKE COFFEE /£pɜːk, $pɜːrk/ *v* [I/T] *infml for* PERCOLATE

perk up *(obj)* BECOME HAPPY, **perk** *(obj)* **up** /£pɜːk, $pɜːrk/ *v adv* to (cause to) become happier, more energetic or active • *She perked up* (= became happier) *as soon as I mentioned that Charles was coming to dinner.* [I] • *He perked up* **at** (= became happier when he heard) *the news.* [I] • *Would you like a cup of coffee? It might perk you up a bit* (= make you more energetic). [M] • *If you add a drop of rosemary oil to your bath, it will perk you up* (= make you more active). [M] • *(fig.) Share prices perked up* (= increased) *slightly before the close of trading.* [I]

perk·y /£'pɜː·ki, $'pɜːr-/ *adj* **-ier, -iest** • If someone is perky, they are happy and full of energy: *You look very perky this morning.* ○ *The interview was quite tough, but she managed to remain reasonably perky all the way through it.*

perk·i·ly /£'pɜː·kɪ·li, $'pɜːr-/ *adv* • *"Does anyone want to come out jogging with me?" he said perkily.*

perk·i·ness /£'pɜː·kɪ·nəs, $'pɜːr-/ *n* [U] • *When I went to visit him in hospital, he had lost his former perkiness and was looking much older.*

perk up VOMIT *v adv* [I] *Aus slang* to vomit

perm /£pɜːm, $pɜːrm/, *fml* **per·man·ent wave**, *Am also* **per·man·ent** *n* [C] a chemical process which makes a person's hair wavy or curly for several months, or the hair style which is created in this way • *Is your hair naturally curly or have you had a perm?* • *I think you'd look good with a perm.*

perm *obj* /£pɜːm, $pɜːrm/ *v* [T] • *I'm going to get my hair permed on Saturday.*

per·ma·frost /£'pɜː·mə·frɒst, $'pɜːr·mə·frɑːst/ *n* [U] *specialized* an area of land which is permanently frozen, whose surface melts in the summer and freezes again in the autumn • *Russian scientists have discovered whole mammoths frozen within the Siberian permafrost.*

per·man·ent /£'pɜː·mə·nənt, $'pɜːr-/ *adj* [not gradable] lasting for a long time or forever • *She is looking for a permanent place to stay.* • *Are you looking for a temporary or a permanent job?* LP〉 **Work** • *The disease can cause permanent damage to the brain.* • *Every year in Britain, 30 000 people suffer permanent disabilities as a result of strokes.* • *A semi-permanent hair dye will wash out after about three months.* • *His work is on permanent display in the gallery.* • *He entered the United States in 1988 as a permanent resident because of his marriage to a U.S. citizen.* • *She is an Indian citizen with British permanent-resident status.* • Permanent can also be used to mean that something exists or happens all the time: *Mont Blanc has a permanent snow cap.* ○ *Our office is in a permanent state of chaos.* • *(Br)* A **permanent secretary** is a government official who belongs to the Civil Service (= the official departments responsible for putting government plans into action) rather than an elected government: *He was the permanent secretary at the Department of Health.* • Permanent is also *Am for* PERM. • **Permanent wave** is *fml for* PERM.

per·man·ent·ly /£'pɜː·mə·nənt·li, $'pɜːr-/ *adv* [not gradable] • *Smoking is likely to damage your health permanently* (= forever). • *He and his family have settled permanently* (= forever) *in the States.* • *All three countries seem to be permanently* (= always) *on the brink of war with each other.* • *I seem to be permanently broke* (= I never have any money).

per·man·ence /£'pɜː·mə·nənts, $'pɜːr-/, *fml* **per·ma·nenc·y** /£'pɜː·mə·nənt·si, $'pɜːr-/ *n* [U] • Permanence means remaining the same or continuing for a long time: *A loving family environment gives children that sense of stability and permanence which they need.*

per·me·ate *(obj)* /£'pɜː·mi·eɪt, $'pɜːr-/ *v fml* to spread through (something) and be present in every part of it • *Dissatisfaction with the government seems to have permeated every section of society.* [T] • *A foul smell of stale beer and urine permeated the whole building.* [T] • *The table has a plastic coating which prevents liquids from permeating* **into** *the wood beneath.* [I always + adv/prep]

per·me·a·ble /£'pɜː·mi·ə·bl̩, $'pɜːr-/ *adj fml* • If a substance is permeable, it allows liquids or gases to go through it: *Certain types of sandstone are permeable* **to** *water.* ○ *The solvent passes through the permeable* **membrane** *to the solution.* ○ *Soft and* **gas-permeable** *contact lenses are kinder to the eyes than hard lenses.* ○ *(fig.) Additional guards have been placed along the border and now it is less permeable than it once was* (= fewer people are able to travel across the border illegally).

per·me·a·bil·i·ty /£,pɜː·mi·ə'bɪl·ɪ·ti, $,pɜːr·mi·ə'bɪl·ə·t̬i/ *n* [U] *fml* • Permeability is the ability of a substance to let gases or liquids go through it: *Chalk has a* **high** *permeability* (= It lets liquids pass through it easily). ○ *The treatment uses artificial fever to treat diseases and it has been shown to increase the permeability of the cell membrane.*

per·mit *(obj)* /£pə'mɪt, $pɚ-/ *v* **-tt-** *slightly fml* to allow (something), or make (something) possible • *The regulations do not permit much flexibility.* [T] • *When a child is the care of a local authority, both parents are normally permitted* **access**. [T] • *The prison authorities permit* *visiting only once a month.* [+ v-*ing*] • *The security system will not permit you* **to** *enter without the correct password.* [T + obj + *to* infinitive] • *Flexible working hours permit parents* **to** *spend much more time with their children.* [T + obj + *to* infinitive] • *As it was such a special occasion, she permitted her***self** (= allowed herself the special pleasure of having) *a small glass of champagne.* [+ two objects] • *(fml) The law permits* **of** (= allows) *no other interpretation.* [I always + *of*] • *The Chancellor is looking to lower interest rates, when economic conditions permit.* [I] • *We have arranged to play tennis on Saturday,* **weather** *permitting* (= if the weather is good enough). [I]

per·mit /£ˈpɜː·mɪt, $ˈpɜːr-/ *n* [C] • A permit is an official document that allows you to do something or go somewhere: *a work/travel permit* ○ *You will need a parking permit if you want to park in this street.* ○ *She has managed to obtain a temporary residence permit.* ○ *The council has decided to issue taxi drivers with permits, in an attempt to crack down on unofficial drivers.* ○ *Do you need a permit* **to** *work here?* [+ *to* infinitive]

per·mis·si·ble /£pəˈmɪs·ə·bl̩, $pɚ-/ *adj fml* • If something is permissible, it is allowed: *Is* **it** *permissible* **to** *park my car here?* [+ *to* infinitive] ○ *They have agreed on a permissible* (= acceptable) *level for vehicle exhaust emissions.*

per·mis·sion /£pəˈmɪʃ·ən, $pɚ-/ *n* [U] • If someone is given permission to do something, they are allowed to do it: *You will need permission from the council* **to** *extend your garage.* [+ *to* infinitive] ○ *Official permission has been* **granted** *for huge office developments to be built near the river.* ○ *The authorities have* **refused** *permission for the demonstration to take place.* ○ **Planning** *permission was refused for the hypermarket after a three-week inquiry.*

per·mis·sive /£pəˈmɪs·ɪv, $pɚ-/ *adj* • A person or society that is permissive allows behaviour which other people might disapprove of: *It's a very permissive school where the children are allowed to do whatever they like.* ○ *She wished her parents had a more permissive attitude towards smoking.* ○ *He claims that society has been far too permissive* **towards** *drug taking.* • *(Br and Aus esp. disapproving)* The **permissive society** is the type of society that has existed in most of Europe, Australia and N America since the 1960s, in which there is a great amount of freedom of behaviour, esp. sexual freedom.

per·mis·sive·ness /£pəˈmɪs·ɪv·nəs, $pɚ-/ *n* [U] • *In a famous speech, she attributed the social and economic problems of the 1980s to the permissiveness of the 1960s.* • *He remembers the 1960s as being an era of* **sexual** *permissiveness* (= a period in which there was a great amount of sexual freedom).

per·mu·ta·tion /£ˌpɜː·mjʊˈteɪ·ʃən, $ˌpɜːr·mjuː-/ *n* [C usually pl] *fml* any of the various ways in which a set of things can be ordered • *There are 120 permutations* **of** *the numbers 1, 2, 3, 4 and 5: for example, 1, 3, 2, 4, 5 or 5, 1, 4, 2, 3.* • *He made six separate applications for a total of 39 000 shares, using permutations of his surname and Christian names.* • *(fig.) The company has had five different names in its various permutations* (= different forms) *over the last few years.*

per·ni·cious /£pəˈnɪʃ·əs, $pɚ-/ *adj fml* having a very harmful effect or influence • *The cuts in government funding have had a pernicious effect on local health services.* • *The committee has come to the conclusion that film and television violence has a pernicious influence on society.*

per·nick·e·ty /£pəˈnɪk·ɪ·ti, $pɚˈnɪk·ə·t̬i/, *Am usually* **per·snick·ety** *adj disapproving* giving too much attention to small unimportant details in a way that annoys other people • *Her pernickety style of managing was highly irritating for everyone.* • *As a writer, he is extremely pernickety about using words correctly.*

pe·rox·ide /£pəˈrɒk·saɪd, $pəˈrɑːk-/, *specialized* **hy·dro·gen pe·rox·ide** *n* a liquid chemical used to make hair very pale in colour or to kill bacteria • *Peroxide is a bleach and an antiseptic.* [U] • *Peroxides are found in household detergents.* [C] • *She has dyed her brown hair peroxide* **blonde**. • *(esp. disapproving)* A **peroxide blonde** is a woman who has used peroxide to make her hair very pale yellow which looks unnatural.

per·pen·di·cu·lar /£ˌpɜː·pəmˈdɪk·jʊ·lər, $ˌpɜːr·pənˈdɪk·juː·lɚ/ *adj* [not gradable] *fml or specialized* at an angle of 90° to a horizontal line or surface, or *(specialized)* at an angle of 90° to another line or surface • *We scrambled up the nearly perpendicular side of the mountain.* • *(specialized) The wheel rotates about an axis which is perpendicular* **to** *the plane.*

per·pen·di·cu·lar /£ˌpɜː·pəmˈdɪk·jʊ·lər, $ˌpɜːr·pənˈdɪk·juː·lɚ/ *n specialized* • *Draw a perpendicular* (= a perpendicular line) *from the vertex of the triangle to its base.* [C] • **The** perpendicular is a perpendicular position or direction: *The wall was leaning at an angle of ten degrees to the perpendicular.* [U]

per·pen·di·cu·lar·ly /£ˌpɜː·pəmˈdɪk·jʊ·lə·li, $ˌpɜːr·pənˈdɪk·juː·lɚ-/ *adv* [not gradable] *fml or specialized* • *A grand piano has the strings extending away from the keyboard, whereas an upright piano has the strings set perpendicularly.*

per·pe·trate *obj* /£ˈpɜː·pə·treɪt, $ˈpɜːr-/ *v* [T] *fml* to commit (a crime, or a violent or harmful act) • *In Britain, half of all violent crime is perpetrated by people who have been drinking alcohol.* • *Three businessmen have been charged with perpetrating a massive insurance fraud.* • *Federal soldiers have been accused of perpetrating atrocities* **against** *innocent people.*

per·pe·tra·tion /£ˌpɜː·pəˈtreɪ·ʃən, $ˌpɜːr-/ *n* [U] *fml* • *Human rights activists have accused the country's government of a systematic perpetration of violence* **against** *minority groups.*

per·pe·trat·or /£ˈpɜː·pə·treɪ·tər, $ˈpɜːr·pə·treɪ·t̬ɚ/, *Am dated slang* **perp** /£pɜːp, $pɜːrp/ *n* [C] *fml* • A perpetrator is someone who has committed a crime, or a violent or harmful act: *The perpetrators of the massacre must be brought to justice as war criminals.*

per·pet·u·al /£pəˈpetʃ·u·əl, $pɚˈpetʃ-/ *adj* [not gradable] continuing forever in the same way • *They lived in perpetual fear of being discovered and arrested.* • *Her business has been plagued by perpetual money problems.* • *He has hard, cold eyes and his mouth is set in a perpetual sneer.* • *His father is worried that she will be a perpetual student and never get a proper job.* • Perpetual also means frequently repeated: *All the bus shelters in the town have been taken down because of perpetual vandalism.*

per·pet·u·al·ly /£pəˈpetʃ·u·ə·li, $pɚˈpetʃ-/ *adv* [not gradable] • *Animals and plants are perpetually evolving* (= They are in a continual state of development). • *The family was so poor that they perpetually went hungry* (= they frequently did not eat). • *She's perpetually asking me* (= She frequently asks me) *for money.*

per·pet·u·ate *obj* /£pəˈpetʃ·u·eɪt, $pɚˈpetʃ-/ *v* [T] *fml* • To perpetuate something is to cause it continue: *Increasing the supply of weapons available within the city will only perpetuate the violence and anarchy.* ○ *The aim of the association is to perpetuate the skills of traditional furniture design.*

per·pet·u·a·tion /£pəˌpetʃ·uˈeɪ·ʃən, $ˌpɚ·petʃ-/ *n* [U] *fml* • *The lack of military action from other countries has contributed to the perpetuation* (= continuation) *of the civil war.*

per·pe·tu·i·ty /£ˌpɜː·pəˈtjuː·ə·ti, $ˌpɜːr·pəˈtuː·ə·t̬i/ *n* [U] *fml* • *The council wants the footpaths on the estate to become legal rights of way, which would give the public the right to use them* **in perpetuity** (= for ever).

per·plex *obj* /£pəˈpleks, $pɚ-/ *v* [T] to confuse and worry (someone) slightly by being difficult to understand or solve • *The disease, which affects young children of both sexes, has continued to perplex doctors and public health workers.*

per·plexed /£pəˈplekst, $pɚ-/ *adj* • *The students looked perplexed, so the teacher tried to explain once again.* • *The party's supporters are clearly perplexed by its sudden change in policy.*

per·plex·ing /£pəˈplek·sɪŋ, $pɚ-/ *adj* • *They find the company's attitude perplexing and unreasonable.*

per·plex·i·ty /£pəˈplek·sɪ·ti, $pɚˈplek·sə·t̬i/ *n* [U] • *She stared at the instruction booklet* **in** *perplexity* (= in a confused way), *trying to work out how to programme the video recorder.*

per se /£ˌpɜːˈseɪ, $ˌpɜːr-/ *adv* [not gradable] *fml* by or of itself • *Research shows that it is not divorce per se that harms children, but the continuing conflict between parents.* • *It is not teenage pregnancy per se which government ministers are concerned about, but the financial dependency on the state which it creates.*

per·se·cute *obj* /£ˈpɜː·sɪ·kjuːt, $ˈpɜːr-/ *v* [T usually passive] to treat (someone) unfairly or cruelly over a long period of time because of their race, religion, political beliefs or homosexuality, or to make (someone) anxious and unhappy by refusing to leave them alone • *Religious minorities were persecuted and massacred during the ten-*

year regime. • *His latest film is about the experience of being persecuted* **for** *being gay.* • *Ever since the news broke about her divorce, she has been persecuted by the tabloid press* (= they have refused to leave her alone).

per·se·cu·tion /£ˌpɜː·sɪˈkjuː·ʃən, $ˌpɜːr-/ *n* [U] • *They left the country out of fear of persecution.* • *Thousands of refugees escaping from political persecution have arrived in the United States.* • If someone has a **persecution complex**, they suffer from the feeling that other people are trying to harm them.

per·se·cut·or /£ˈpɜː·sɪ·kjuː·təʳ, $ˈpɜːr·sɪ·kjuː·t̬ɚ/ *n* [C] • *At the start of the revolution, the country's native people rose up against their persecutors* (= the people who had treated them cruelly). • *The clergy were the main persecutors* **of** *witches in the Middle Ages.*

per·se·vere /£ˌpɜː·sɪˈvɪəʳ, $ˌpɜːr·səˈvɪr/ *v* [I] *esp. approving* to try to do or continue doing something in a determined way, despite difficulties • *It looks as if the policy will be a success, providing that the government perseveres and does not give in to its critics.* • *The education director is persevering* **in** *his attempt to obtain additional funding for the school.* • *Despite receiving little support or encouragement, the women are persevering* **with** *their crusade to fight crime in the area.*

per·se·ver·ance /£ˌpɜː·sɪˈvɪə·rənts, $ˌpɜːr·səˈvɪr·ənts/ *n* [U] *esp. approving* • Perseverance is continued effort and determination: *Through hard work and perseverance, he worked his way up from being a teacher in a village school to the headmaster of a large comprehensive.* • *The team's perseverance was finally rewarded when they scored two goals in the last five minutes of the match.*

per·se·ver·ing /£ˌpɜː·sɪˈvɪə·rɪŋ, $ˌpɜːr·səˈvɪr·ɪŋ/ *adj esp. approving* • *She was persevering enough to reach the height of her ambition and become the managing director of the company.*

Per·sian /£ˈpɜː·ʒən, $ˈpɜːr-/ *adj* [not gradable] of the people, language or culture of ancient Persia (now Iran) • A **Persian carpet/rug** is one which comes from esp. Iran and which is made by hand from silk or wool: *Persian carpets are characterized by their geometric designs and rich colours.* • A **Persian cat** is a type of cat with long hair, short thick legs and a round face.

per·sim·mon /pəˈsɪm·ən, $pɚ-/ *n* [C] a very sweet orange-coloured tropical fruit which is edible when it is completely ripe

per·sist /£pəˈsɪst, $pɚ-/ *v* [I] (of something unwanted) to continue to exist, or (of a person) to try to do or continue doing something in a determined but often unreasonable way • *If the pain persists, consult a doctor.* • *The London Weather Centre predicted that the cold weather would persist throughout the week.* • *Despite the general's promises, the climate of fear in the capital persists.* • *If she refuses to answer your phone calls, just persist* (= continue telephoning her) *until she does answer.* • *If he persists* **in** *asking awkward questions, then send him to the boss.* • *The government is persisting* **with** *its ambitious public works programme, despite the massive costs involved.*

per·sis·tence /£pəˈsɪs·tənts, $pɚ-/ *n* [U] • *Most financial analysts have been surprised by the persistence* **of** *the recession* (= the fact that it has continued for so long). • *Her persistence* (= determination) *and enthusiasm have helped the group to achieve its status as an international development agency.*

per·sis·tent /£pəˈsɪs·tənt, $pɚ-/ *adj* • Something that is persistent lasts for a long time or is difficult to get rid of: *a persistent smell/skin rash* ○ *persistent debts/difficulties* ○ *Symptoms of the illness include a high temperature and a persistent dry cough.* ○ *There have been persistent* **rumours** *that the managing director might take early retirement.* • Someone who is persistent continues doing something or tries to do something in a determined but often unreasonable way: *Be persistent – don't give up.* ○ *He has been a persistent critic of the president.* ○ *She is a persistent* **offender** *and has been arrested five times this year for shoplifting.*

per·sis·tent·ly /£pəˈsɪs·tənt·li, $pɚ-/ *adv* • *They have persistently* (= repeatedly) *ignored our advice.* • *A new law is being proposed which will allow children as young as twelve to be locked up if they persistently* (= repeatedly) *break the law.*

per·snick·ety /£pəˈsnɪk·ɪ·ti, $pɚˈsnɪk·ə·t̬i/ *adj Am for* PERNICKETY

per·son /£ˈpɜː·sən, $ˈpɜːr-/ *n* [C] *pl* **people** /ˈpiː·pl̩/ or *fml or law* **persons** a man, woman or child • *Who was the first person to swim the English Channel?* • *Democracy rests on the principle of one person, one vote.* • *A meal at the restaurant costs about $70 for two people.* • *(fml) The aim of the council is to provide temporary accommodation for homeless persons.* • *(law) Four persons have been charged with the murder.* • Person is also used when describing someone and their particular type of character: *She's an extremely kind person.* ○ *He's nice enough* **as a person** (= He has a nice character), *but he's not the right man for this job.* ○ *(infml) I don't think of him as a book person* (= a person who likes books). • If you do something or go somewhere **in person**, you do it or go there yourself so that you are physically present: *He rarely pays visits in person.* ○ *I had seen her before on TV, but she looked very different when I met her in person.* • *(fml) The editorial board has an expert with a world-wide reputation* **in the person of** (= in the form of) *Professor Jameson.* • *(fml)* If someone has something such as weapon **on/about** their **person**, they have it with them, usually hidden in their clothing: *Police officers must check that suspects do not have weapons concealed about their person.* • *(specialized)* In grammar, person is used to describe the verbs and pronouns that refer to the different people in a conversation. The first person ('I' or 'we') refers to the person speaking, the second person ('you') refers to the person being spoken to and the third person ('he', 'she', 'it' or 'they') refers to another person or thing being spoken about or described: *'I' is a first-person pronoun.* ○ *The novel is written in the first person, so that the author and narrator seem to be the same.* ○ *'Are' is the second person plural of the verb 'to be'.* • *(Am and Aus)* A **person-to-person** telephone call is one where you ask the telephone operator to let you speak directly to a particular person. • *(esp. Am)* If you talk to or meet someone **person-to-person**, you talk to or meet them directly. • LP **Age, Sexist language**

-person /£-ˌpɜː·sən, $-ˌpɜːr-/ *combining form pl* **-people** /-ˌpiː·pl̩/ • Sometimes -person is used to combine with nouns to form new nouns which refer to the particular job or duty that someone has. It is often used instead of -man or -woman to avoid making an unnecessary statement about the sex of the particular person: *spokesperson* ○ *chairperson* ○ *salesperson* ○ *townspeople* ○ *business people* • LP **Sexist language**

per·son·al /£ˈpɜː·sən·əl, £ˈpɜːs·nəl, $ˈpɜːr·sən·əl/ *adj* • Personal means relating or belonging to a single or particular person rather than to a group or an organization: *I don't know what anyone else thinks, but my personal* **opinion/view** *is that the students should be doing more work outside the classroom.* ○ *Her uncle takes a personal interest in her progress.* ○ *She has her own personal secretary/bodyguard/fitness instructor.* ○ *Passengers are reminded to take all their personal* **belongings** *with them when they leave the plane.* ○ *He was sacked from his job for abusing his power for personal* **gain** (= using his powerful position to obtain a financial advantage). • A personal action is one which is done by someone directly rather than getting another person to do it: *The health minister made a personal* **appearance** *at the hospital.* ○ *I will give the matter my personal* **attention**. • Personal also means private or relating to someone's private life: *The letter was marked 'Personal. Strictly confidential.'* ○ *Do you mind if I ask you a personal question?* ○ *His resignation was apparently for personal rather than professional reasons.* ○ *For such a famous, wealthy man, his personal* **life** *was surprisingly simple and ordinary.* • Personal also refers to an intentionally offensive remark about someone's character or appearance: *Did you have to make such a personal* **remark/comment** *about her new haircut?* ○ *There's no need to* **get** *personal* (= You should not make such an offensive remark about me). • Personal is also used to refer to your body or appearance: *She is obsessed with personal* **hygiene**. • A **personal ad** is an advertisement that you put in a newspaper or magazine, often in order to find a sexual partner: *He placed/put a personal ad in The Times.* • *(Br specialized)* A **personal allowance** is an amount of money that you can earn before you start to be taxed. • *(Br and Aus)* A **personal column**/*(Am)* **The personals** is the part of a newspaper or magazine which contains short advertisements and private messages: *She placed/put an ad in the personal column which read 'Intelligent, attractive woman seeks humorous man for romance and perhaps marriage.'* • A **personal computer** (*abbreviation* **PC**) is a medium-sized computer which is used mainly by people at home rather than by large organizations. • **Personal effects** are things that you own which are movable, and which you often carry with you, such as keys or clothing: *After she had identified the body of her husband, the police asked her to collect his personal effects.* • **Personal identification number** is *fml for* PIN (NUMBER). • A **personal organizer** (also *trademark* **filofax**) is a small book or electronic device in which information is stored, such as names, addresses, telephone numbers and dates of meetings, and which people use to help them organize their time. • *(specialized)* In grammar, a **personal pronoun** is a word such as 'I', 'you' and 'they' which refers to a person in speech or in writing. • *(law)* **Personal property** is the things you own which are movable, such as money or furniture. • A **personal stereo** (also *trademark* **Walkman**) is a small electronic machine that plays music and which has HEADPHONES so that you can listen to music while you are doing other things. • Something which has the **personal touch** has original or special qualities, or is done for every single person in a group in order to make them feel special: *My hotel room was totally devoid of any personal touch.* ○ *The chairman of the bank believes in the personal touch and always sends a signed letter to each customer.*

per·son·al·ly /£'pɜː·sᵊn·ᵊl·i, £'pɜːs·nə·li, $'pɜːr·sᵊn·ᵊl·i/ *adv* • *Personally (speaking), I think* (= My own opinion is that) *the project is going to be a great success.* • If something has an effect on you personally, it has an effect on you rather than other people: *He believes that parents should be made personally responsible for their children's behaviour.* • If you do something personally, you do it yourself rather than asking someone else to do it: *These figures should be correct because I've checked them personally.* • Personally also refers to a remark about someone's character or appearance that is spoken in an intentionally offensive way or which is understood as being critical: *He seemed personally offended by the comments.* ○ *These are general criticisms which should not be* **taken** *personally* (= They are not meant to criticize any one person in particular).

per·son·al·i·ty /£,pɜː·sᵊn'æl·ə·ti, $,pɜːr·sᵊn'æl·ə·ţi/ *n* • Your personality is the type of person you are, which is shown by the way you behave, feel and think: *She has a very warm personality.* [C] ○ *He is well qualified for the job, but he does lack personality* (= he is a rather boring person). [U] • A personality is also a famous entertainer or sports player etc. who has an attractive, energetic character which makes them popular with the public: *The show is hosted by a popular TV personality.* [C] • A **personality clash** is when two or more people have very different characters and are unable to have a good relationship with each other: *She resigned from the group because of a personality clash with the other people in it.* • *(disapproving)* A **personality cult** is officially organized admiration and love for a particular person, esp. a political leader: *All over the city there are giant posters of the president – evidence of the personality cult that surrounds him.* • *(specialized)* A **personality disorder** is any of a number of mental illnesses, which are characterized by difficulties in relating to your surroundings and to other people, and in maintaining a fixed image of yourself.

per·son·al·ize *obj, Br and Aus usually* **-ise** /£'pɜː·sᵊn·ᵊl·aɪz, $'pɜːr-/ *v* [T] • If you personalize an object, you change it or add to it so that it is obvious that it belongs to or comes from you: *The computer allows you to personalize standard letters by adding a greeting and an address to each one.* ○ *She had done little to personalize her room, except hang a few posters on the walls.* ○ *His car has a personalized number plate – TJ 1.* ○ *When we moved house, we had to have another set of personalized letter paper printed.* • Personalized also means made suitable for the needs of a particular person: *She hired a trainer to create a personalized exercise schedule to get her into shape.* • If you personalize a subject, you make people feel more emotionally involved in it by giving examples about real people: *By telling people about her accident, she personalizes the numbing figure of road accidents that happen every year.* • *(disapproving)* If you personalize an argument or discussion, you start to criticize someone's faults instead of discussing the facts.

per·son·a /£pə'səʊ·nə, $pɚ'soʊ-/ *n* [C] *pl* **personae** /£pə'səʊ·niː, -naɪ, $pɚ'soʊ-/ or **personas** the particular type of character that a person seems to have, which is often different from their real or private character • *He had a shy, retiring side to his personality that was completely at odds with his* **public** *persona.*

per·son·a·ble /£'pɜː·sᵊn·ə·bl̩, $'pɜːr-/ *adj fml* having a pleasant appearance and character • *She is intelligent, hard-working and personable.*

per·son·age /£'pɜː·sᵊn·ɪdʒ, $'pɜːr-/ *n* [C] *fml or humorous* an important or famous person • *I am not used to meeting such elevated personages as bishops and lords.* • (F)

per·son·a non gra·ta /£pə,səʊ·nə,nɒŋ'grɑː·tə, $pɚ,soʊ·nə,nɑːn'grɑː·ţə/ *n* [C] *pl* **persona non grata** *specialized* a person who is not wanted or welcome in a particular country, because they are unacceptable to its government • *Several embassy staff were* **declared** *persona non grata and asked to leave the country within 48 hours.* • *(fig.) His behaviour on the rugby tour to Australia last winter made him persona non grata* **to** (= unpopular with) *the England selectors.* • *(fig.) From the look on their faces, I was obviously persona non grata* (= I was not welcome there).

per·son·i·fy *obj* /£pə'sɒn·ɪ·faɪ, $pɚ'sɑː·nɪ-/ *v* [T] (of a person) to be a perfect example of (a thing or quality) • *The new party leader personifies the modern face of socialism.* • *These louts personify all that is worst in our society today.* • *(specialized)* If a particular quality or idea is personified, it is represented in the form of a human being: *In Greek myth, love is personified by the goddess Aphrodite.*

per·son·i·fi·ca·tion /£pə,sɒn·ɪ·fɪ'keɪ·ʃᵊn, $pɚ,sɑː·nɪ-/ *n* [U] • *In the film, she played a character who was the personification* **of** *evil.* • *During the 1920s, Al Capone was the personification* **of** *organized crime in America.*

per·son·i·fied /£pə'sɒn·ɪ·faɪd, $pɚ'sɑː·nɪ-/ *adj* [after n; not gradable] • *She is charm personified.* • *Rambo is commonly seen as aggressive machismo personified.*

per·son·nel /£,pɜː·sᵊn'el, $,pɜːr-/ *pl n* the people who are employed in a company, organization or one of the armed forces • *The new director of the TV station is likely to make major changes in personnel.* • *The monument was engraved with the names of the 58 000 American military personnel who died in Vietnam.* • **Personnel carriers** are armed transport vehicles used by the army: *The military escort was made up of three tanks and two armoured personnel carriers.*

per·son·nel /£,pɜː·sᵊn'el, $,pɜːr-/ *n* [U] • Personnel is the department of a company or organization that deals with its employees when they first join, when they need training or when they have any problems: *Personnel will help you find a flat to rent.* ○ *For more information about the job, please contact the personnel* **manager**.

per·spec·tive THOUGHT /£pə'spek·tɪv, $pɚ'spek·ţɪv/ *n* [C] a particular way of considering something • *Her attitude lends a fresh perspective to the subject.* • *During the novel, there is a shift in perspective from an adult's view of events to a child's view.* • *He writes* **from** *a Marxist perspective.* • *Due to its geographical position, Germany's perspective* **on** *the situation in Eastern Europe is rather different from Britain's.* • If you **get/keep** a situation or problem **in perspective**, you think about it in a wise and reasonable way: *You must keep things in perspective – the overall situation isn't really that bad.* • If you **put** something **in(to) perspective**, you compare it to other things so that it can be accurately and fairly judged: *Total investments for this year reached £53 million, and to put this into perspective, investments this year were double those made in 1993.* • (CS) (PL) (RUS)

per·spec·tive ART /£pə'spek·tɪv, $pɚ'spek·ţɪv/ *n* [U] (the method of representing in art) the way that objects appear smaller when they are further away and the way parallel lines appear to meet each other at a point in the distance • *In 15th-century Italy, artists rediscovered the rules of perspective.* • *He painted detailed pictures of domestic interiors which are notable for their use of perspective.* • An object or person that is **in perspective** has the correct size and position in comparison with other things in the picture. • An object or person that is **out of perspective** does not have the correct size or position in comparison with other things in the picture, and therefore does not look real or natural. • (CS) (RUS)

Per·spex *Br and Aus* /£'pɜː·speks, $'pɜːr-/, *Am* **Plex·i·glas** *n* [U] *trademark* a strong transparent plastic which is sometimes used instead of glass • *The aircraft's windows are made of toughened Perspex.*

per·spi·ca·cious /£,pɜː·spɪ'keɪ·ʃəs, $,pɜːr-/ *adj fml approving* quick in noticing, understanding or judging things accurately • *His perspicacious grandfather had bought the land as an investment, guessing that there might be gold underground.*

per·spi·cac·i·ty /£ˌpɜː·spɪˈkæs·ə·ti, $ˌpɜːr·spɪˈkæs·ə·t̬i/ *n* [U] *fml approving* • Perspicacity is the ability to understand things quickly and make accurate judgments: *She is a woman of exceptional perspicacity.* ○ *He seems to be guided by prejudice rather than perspicacity.*

per·spire /£pəˈspaɪəʳ, $pɚˈspaɪɚ/ *v* [I] *fml or specialized* to excrete a salty colourless liquid through the skin which cools the body. It is often used to avoid saying SWEAT. • *He was perspiring in his thick woollen suit.* • *The journalists and camera crews began to perspire in the heat as they stood waiting for the president to appear.*

per·spir·a·tion /£ˌpɜː·spəʳˈeɪ·ʃən, $ˌpɜːr·spəˈreɪ-/ *n* [U] *fml or specialized* • *During the break between games, she had a drink of water and wiped the perspiration off her face and arms with a towel.* • **Beads** (=Drops) *of perspiration glistened on his brow.*

per·suade *obj* /£pəˈsweɪd, $pɚ-/ *v* [T] to make (someone) do or believe something by giving them a good reason to do it or by talking to them and making them believe it • *If she doesn't want to go, nothing you can say will persuade her.* • *It's no use trying to persuade him* **(that)** *you're innocent.* [+ obj + (*that*) clause] • *A higher gasoline tax might persuade consumers* **that** *small cars are the best option.* [+ obj + *that* clause] • *He is trying to persuade local and foreign businesses* **to** *invest in the project.* [+ obj + *to* infinitive] • *(fml) The first priority is to persuade the management* **of** *the urgency of this matter.* • *Her legal advisers persuaded her* **into/out of** *mentioning* (=to mention/not to mention) *the names of the people involved in the robbery.* • *(fig.) Using a bunch of bananas, the zoo-keeper patiently persuaded the monkey back* (=made it go back) *into its cage.*

per·sua·sion /£pəˈsweɪ·ʒən, $pɚ-/ *n* [U] • *It took a lot of persuasion to convince the committee of the advantages of the new scheme.* • *She will take you to the airport – she just needs a bit of* **gentle** *persuasion.* • *The occasion will be a test of the senator's* **powers of** *persuasion* (=his ability to persuade people). • See also PERSUASION.

per·suas·ive /£pəˈsweɪ·sɪv, £-zɪv, $pɚˈsweɪ·sɪv/ *adj* • Someone or something that is persuasive makes you want to do or believe a particular thing: *He is an eloquent and persuasive politician.* ○ *She gave a very persuasive speech about the need for more funding for the project.* ○ *He will have to rely on his persuasive powers to convince the government of the need for action.*

per·suas·ive·ly /£pəˈsweɪ·sɪv·li, £-zɪv-, $pɚˈsweɪ·sɪv-/ *adv* • *She spoke very persuasively in favour of a woman's right to abortion.*

per·suas·ive·ness /£pəˈsweɪ·sɪv·nəs, £-zɪv-, $pɚˈsweɪ·sɪv-/ *n* [U] • *Lyndon Johnson's persuasiveness with Congress became legendary.*

per·sua·sion /£pəˈsweɪ·ʒən, $pɚ-/ *n* [C] a particular set of beliefs, esp. political or religious • *She's a politician* **of** *the socialist persuasion.* • *We need a society which welcomes people* **of all** *religious persuasions.* • See also **persuasion** at PERSUADE.

pert /£pɜːt, $pɜːrt/ *adj* **-er, -est** (of a part of the body) attractively small and firm, or (esp. of a young woman) energetic and amusing • *a pert bottom* • *She has an attractive face with a pert nose and huge green eyes.* • *His secretary was a pert brunette called Sylvia.*

per·tain to *obj* /£pɜːˈteɪn, $pɜːr-/ *v prep* [T] *fml* to relate to or have a connection with (something) • *The letters produced in court pertained to the years 1980-1985.* • *We are only interested in the parts of the proposals that pertain to local issues.*

per·ti·nent /£ˈpɜː·tɪ·nənt, $ˈpɜːr·tən·ənt/ *adj fml* • Pertinent means relating directly to the subject being considered: *a pertinent question/remark* ○ *The chapters which are pertinent* **to** *the post-war period are essential reading.* • (NL)

per·ti·na·cious /£ˌpɜː·tɪˈneɪ·ʃəs, $ˌpɜːr·tənˈeɪ-/ *adj fml* very determined and refusing to be defeated by difficulties • *Like most successful politicians, she can be pertinacious and single-minded in the pursuit of her goals.*

per·turb *obj* /£pəˈtɜːb, $pɚˈtɜːrb/ *v* [T] *fml* to cause (someone) to feel worried • *The news that her son had been arrested by the police perturbed her greatly.*

per·tur·ba·tion /£ˌpɜː·təˈbeɪ·ʃən, $ˌpɜːr·t̬ɚ-/ *n fml* • *She displayed signs of increasing perturbation* (=worry) *as she hurried to meet him.* [U] • *(specialized)* A perturbation is also a small change in the regular motion of an object: *Perturbations in the orbit of the planet Uranus led to the discovery of Neptune in 1846.* [C]

per·turbed /£pəˈtɜːbd, $pɚˈtɜːrbd/ *adj fml* • If someone is perturbed, they are worried: *She was perturbed by the news that 50 workers at the factory were going to be made redundant.* ○ *He did not seem* **unduly/overly** *perturbed by the drugs problem until his justice minister was murdered by drugs traffickers.*

per·use *obj* /pəˈruːz/ *v* [T] *fml* to read or look at (something) in a relaxed and not very detailed way • *He opened a newspaper and began to peruse the personal ads.* • *A young woman came into the shop and began perusing the shelves in search of something to read.*

per·us·al /pəˈruː·zəl/ *n* [U] *fml* • *A brief perusal* (=A quick read) *of the document revealed that it was quite controversial.* • *He said that he would send a copy of the report to his fellow-governors for their perusal* (=for them to read).

perv /£pɜːv, $pɜːrv/ *n* [C] *Br and Aus infml for* **pervert**, see at PERVERT

per·vade *obj* /£pəˈveɪd, $pɚ-/ *v* [T] *fml* (of qualities, characteristics or smells) to spread through (a place or thing) and be present in every part of it • *An intense poetic quality pervades her novels.* • *The film is a reflection of the violence that pervades American culture.* • *As she walked through the office, her perfume pervaded the whole room.*

per·vas·ive /£pəˈveɪ·sɪv, $pɚ-/ *adj fml* • If a quality, characteristic or smell is pervasive, it is present or noticeable throughout a thing or place: *The influence of Freud is pervasive in her work.* ○ *There is a pervasive smell of diesel in our garage.* ○ *The government's reforms are being undermined by the* **all-pervasive** *corruption in the country.*

per·vas·ive·ly /£pəˈveɪ·sɪv·li, $pɚ-/ *adv fml* • *In her book, she describes how the desire to be slim is pervasively present in our society.*

per·vas·ive·ness /£pəˈveɪ·sɪv·nəs, $pɚ-/ *n* [U] *fml* • *The book deals with the pervasiveness of television in our culture.*

per·verse /£pəˈvɜːs, $pɚˈvɜːrs/ *adj disapproving* (of a person) intentionally acting in a way that is unreasonable or harmful, or (of an action or feeling) unreasonable or unexpected • *Jack was being perverse and refused to do anything the rest of us wanted to do.* • *After everything I had heard about the city, it would have been perverse to have passed so close by without stopping to visit.* • *She took a perverse* **delight** *in hearing that her sister was getting divorced.* • *The police investigating the case believed that the murderer was a person who took a perverse* **pleasure** *in violence.* • *He felt a sense of perverse* **pride** *in acknowledging that he had made a mistake.*

per·verse·ly /£pəˈvɜː·sli, $pɚˈvɜːr-/ *adv* • *The best way to understand this book is to start, perversely, at the end.* • *She perversely enjoyed the strain of jogging five miles every morning.*

per·ver·si·ty /£pəˈvɜː·sə·ti, $pɚˈvɜːr·sə·t̬i/ *n* [U] • *He found her perversity* (=unreasonable behaviour) *and stubbornness extremely annoying.* • *It took courage and a certain perversity* (=a desire to do something unusual and unexpected) *for her to shave her head.* • See also **perversity** at PERVERT.

per·vert *obj* /£pəˈvɜːt, $pɚˈvɜːrt/ *v* [T] *disapproving* to change (something) so that it is not what it used to be or should be, or to influence (someone) in a harmful way • *The argument has been shamelessly perverted to serve the president's propaganda campaign.* • *His original ideas have been perverted by politicians for their own purposes.* • *One of the history teachers tried to pervert* (=persuade into unacceptable sexual activity) *the boys by showing them pornographic magazines and videos.* • *(law)* If someone **perverts the course of justice**, they act illegally to avoid punishment or to get the wrong person punished: *The two police officers were charged with perverting the course of justice by fabricating evidence in the trial.*

per·vert /£ˈpɜː·vɜːt, $ˈpɜːr·vɜːrt/, *Br and Aus infml* **perv** *n* [C] *disapproving* • A pervert is a person whose sexual behaviour is considered unnatural or unacceptable by most people.

per·vert·ed /£pəˈvɜː·tɪd, $pɚˈvɜːr·t̬ɪd/ *adj disapproving* • Someone or something that is perverted is considered unnatural or unacceptable by most people: *Her photographs of dead babies have been labelled as perverted.* ○ *She told him he had a sick and perverted mind.* ○ *He has been accused of using a perverted form of nationalism to incite racial hatred.*

per·ver·sion /£pəˈvɜː·ʒən, $pɚˈvɜːr-/ *n disapproving* • A perversion is a type of behaviour which is considered unacceptable or unnatural by most people: *The sexual activities that they enjoy would be described as perversions by many people.* [C] ○ *The novels of the Marquis de Sade deal with sexual perversion.* [U] • The perversion of something is the changing of it so that it is not what it used to be or should be: *She has written a report about child abuse and the perversion of childhood innocence.* [U] ○ *His testimony was clearly a perversion of the truth.* [C] ○ *The trial has been described as a gross perversion* **of justice**. [C]

per·ver·si·ty /£pəˈvɜː·sə·ti, $pɚˈvɜːr·sə·t̬i/ *n disapproving* • *The author of the book seems to be obsessed with* **sexual** *perversity and death.* [U] • *The court listened to evidence of the couple's* **sexual** *perversities.* [C] • See also **perversity** at PERVERSE.

pes·ky /ˈpes·ki/ *adj* [before n] **-ier, -iest** *infml* annoying or causing trouble • *The kitchen is full of pesky flies.* • *I have to fill in that pesky form from the tax office.* • *Those pesky kids from next door have let down my car tyres again!*

pes·sim·i·sm /ˈpes·ɪ·mɪ·zᵊm/ *n* [U] the tendency to emphasize or think of the bad part of a situation rather than the good part, or the feeling that bad things are more likely to happen than good things • *An underlying pessimism infuses all her novels.* • *In recent months, there has been a mood of deepening pessimism* **about** *the economy.* • *The United States is not alone in its pessimism* **over** *the future of the island's fragile democracy.* • *The Chancellor expressed* **deep** *pessimism* **that** (= He felt it was extremely unlikely that) *an agreement could be reached.* [+ *that* clause] • Compare OPTIMISM.

pes·sim·ist /ˈpes·ɪ·mɪst/ *n* [C] • *Are you an optimist or a pessimist?* • *The pessimists among us can see no sign of economic recovery in the near future.*

pes·sim·is·tic /£ˌpes·ɪˈmɪs·tɪk, $-t̬ɪk/ *adj* • *The tone of the meeting was very pessimistic.* • *The situation in the capital is so unstable that most commentators are extremely pessimistic.* • *The doctors are pessimistic* **about** *Jane Simpkin's chances of recovery* (= They think she is unlikely to get better).

pes·sim·is·ti·cal·ly /£ˌpes·ɪˈmɪs·tɪ·kli, $-t̬ɪ-/ *adv* • *He talked rather pessimistically about the situation, saying that civil war could erupt at any moment.*

pest /pest/ *n* [C] an insect or small animal which is harmful or which damages crops, or *(infml)* an annoying person, esp. a child • *If you have pests such as rats, mice or cockroaches in your house, you should contact the City Pest Control Department.* • *The insecticide is supposed to kill all the pests that attack the maize plants.* • *(fig. infml) The kids next door are real pests – they keep kicking their football into our garden and then trampling on our plants when they get their ball back.* • *(fig. infml) Put that back, you little pest!* [as form of address] • Ⓙ Ⓢ

pest·er *obj* /£ˈpes·təʳ, $-t̬ɚ/ *v* [T] to behave in an annoying manner towards (someone) by doing or asking for something repeatedly • *Her supervisor, a married man, began to pester her and make unwelcome sexual advances towards her.* • *At the frontier, there were people pestering tourists* **for** *cigarettes, food or alcohol.* • *Her children are always pestering her* **to** *buy them sweets.* [+ obj + *to* infinitive]

pes·ti·cide /£ˈpes·tɪ·saɪd, $-t̬ə-/ *n* a chemical substance used to kill harmful insects, small animals, wild plants and other unwanted organisms • *The pesticides that farmers spray on their crops kill pests but they can also damage people's health.* [C] • *Organic vegetables and crops are grown without the use of pesticide.* [U] • Compare HERBICIDE; INSECTICIDE.

pes·ti·lence /£ˈpes·tɪ·ləns, $-t̬ᵊl·ᵊnts/ *n fml* any very serious infectious disease that spreads quickly and kills large numbers of people • *People were forced to leave their homes because of famine and pestilence.* [U] • *A raging pestilence had broken out in the city, causing the deaths of hundreds each day.* [C] • *(fig.) The report states that vandalism is a pestilence* (= a serious and growing problem) *which must be stamped out.* [C]

pes·tle /ˈpes·l̩/ *n* [C] a heavy stick made of clay, stone or metal, with a thick rounded end, which is used for crushing substances in a MORTAR (= a small strong bowl) by hitting or rubbing them • *Crush the garlic into a paste using a pestle and mortar.*

pes·to /£ˈpes·təʊ, $-toʊ/ *n* [U] a green sauce which is used in Italian cooking, esp. on pasta • *Pesto is made of basil leaves, parmesan cheese, pine nuts, garlic and olive oil which have all been crushed together.*

pet [ANIMAL] /pet/ *n* [C] an animal which is kept in the home as a companion and treated affectionately • *They have several pets – a dog, two rabbits and a guinea pig.* • *As a little girl, she always wanted to* **have** *a parrot* **as a pet.** • *We've run out of pet* **food** *– could you go and get some?* • *He owns a pet* **shop** (= a shop where animals are sold). • *(disapproving)* If you are the pet of a person in authority, they like you very much and treat you better than other people: *The other children hated her because she was the* **teacher's** *pet.* • *(infml approving)* If you describe someone as a pet, you mean that they are a kind person who is easy to like: *He's always sending me flowers – he's a real pet!* ○ *Would you be a pet and make me a coffee?* • *(Br and Aus infml)* Pet is also an affectionate way of addressing someone, esp. a woman or a child: *"Would you like a cup of tea?" "That's very kind of you, pet."* • A pet **theory/subject/hate** is one that is special and important to you: *I just stop listening when he starts talking about his pet theories.* ○ *Football is one of her pet hates.* • A **pet name** is an informal, affectionate name given to someone by their family or friends: *Her pet name was 'Baby' when she was a child, because she was the baby of the family.*

pet *(obj)* [TOUCH] /pet/ *v* **-tt-** to touch (an animal or person) kindly or lovingly with the hands • *Our dog loves to be petted and tickled behind the ears.* [T] • *(fig.) He was such an attractive little boy that people used to pet him and spoil him* (= They were very friendly and kind to him). [T] • *(infml)* If two people are petting, they are kissing and touching each other in a sexual way. See also **heavy petting** at HEAVY [TO A GREAT DEGREE]. [I] • *(Am)* A **petting zoo** is an open area in which small or young animals are kept which children can hold, touch and sometimes feed.

pet·al /£ˈpet·ᵊl, $ˈpet̬-/ *n* [C] any of the usually brightly coloured parts that together form most of a flower • *rose petals* • *(Br regional infml)* Some people use 'petal' as a way of addressing someone that they know and like: *What did you say, petal?* [as form of address] • [PIC] **Flowers and plants**

-pet·alled, *Am usually* **-pet·aled** /£-ˌpet·ᵊld, $-ˌpet̬-/ *combining form* • *a 5-petalled flower* • *a white-petalled rose*

pe·tard /£petˈɑːd, $pɪˈtɑːrd/ *n* [U] **hoist(ed) with your own petard**, see at HOIST

pe·ter /£ˈpiː·tə, $-t̬ɚ/ *n* [C] *esp. Am slang* a penis

pe·ter out /£ˈpiː·təʳ, $-t̬ɚ/, *esp. Br also* **pe·ter a·way** *v adv* [I] to be reduced gradually so that nothing is left • *The fighting which started in the night had petered out by morning.* • *The track petered out after a mile or so, and we were left wondering which way to go.*

Pe·ter Pan /£ˌpiː·təˈpæn, $-t̬ɚ-/ *n* [U] *infml humorous* a man who never seems to look any older although he is no longer young • *Looking two decades younger than his fifty years, the Peter Pan of rock will present the four-part TV series.* • A **Peter Pan collar** is a small collar with rounded ends.

pe·tit bour·ge·ois, *Br also* **pet·ty bour·ge·ois** /£ˌpet·i ˈbɔː·ʒwɑː, $pəˌtiː·bʊrˈʒwɑː/ *adj esp. disapproving* belonging to the lower middle social class, or having the characteristics that are connected with this class, such as obedience to established rules and lack of trust of new or different ideas • *petit bourgeois prejudices/conformity*

pe·tit bour·ge·ois·ie, pet·ty bour·ge·ois·ie /£ˌpet·ɪˌbɔː·ʒwɑːˈziː, $pəˌtiː·bʊr-/ *n* [U + sing/pl v] *esp. disapproving* • The **petit bourgeoisie** are petit bourgeois people considered as a group.

pe·tite /pəˈtiːt/ *adj approving* (of a woman or girl) small and delicate • *She was dark and petite, as all his wives had been.* • The group of clothing sizes for small women is also called petite.

pe·tit four /£ˌpet·iˈfɔːʳ, $ˌpet̬·iˈfɔːr/, *Am also* **pe·tit fours** *n* [C] *pl* **petits fours** /£ˌpet·iˈfɔːz, $ˌpet̬·iˈfɔːrz/ a small cake, biscuit or sweet, usually served at the end of a meal with coffee • [PIC] **Bread and cakes**

pe·ti·tion /pəˈtɪʃ·ᵊn/ *n* [C] a document signed by a large number of people demanding or requesting some action from the government or another authority, or *(law)* a formal letter to a court of law requesting a particular legal action • *I signed a petition* **against** *the proposed closure of the local hospital today.* • *(law) She's* **filing** *a petition* **for** *divorce.*

pe·ti·tion *(obj)* /pəˈtɪʃ·ᵊn/ *v* • *They're petitioning* **for/about** *better facilities for disabled people on public transport.* [I] • *I think we should petition the government* **to** *increase the grant for the project.* [T + obj + *to* infinitive] • *(law) She is petitioning* **for** *a re-trial.* [I]

pe·ti·tion·er /£pə'tɪʃ·ᵊn·əʳ, $-ɚ/ *n* [C] • A petitioner is a person who organizes a petition, or *(law)* a person who is requesting action from a court of law.

pe·tit pois /£ˌpet·i'pwɑː, $pəˌtiː-/ *pl n esp. Br* small PEAS

pet·rel /'pet·rᵊl/ *n* [C] a sea bird with a curved beak, that spends most of its life flying over the sea

pet·ri dish /£'pet·riˌdɪʃ, $'piː·tri-/ *n* [C] a small clear round dish with a cover which is used in scientific tests, esp. for the growing of bacteria

pet·ri·fy *obj* FRIGHTEN /'pet·rə·faɪ/ *v* [T] to frighten (someone) greatly, esp. so that they are unable to move or speak • *I think you petrified poor Jeremy – he never said a word the whole time you were here.*

pet·ri·fied /'pet·rə·faɪd/ *adj* • *She's petrified* **of** *being on her own in the house at night.* • *I stood petrified as the most enormous dog I've ever seen came bounding up to me.*

pet·ri·fy CHANGE TO STONE /'pet·rə·faɪ/, **fos·sil·ize** *v* [I] (of dead things) to change to a substance like stone over a long period of time

pet·ri·fied /'pet·rə·faɪd/, **fos·sil·ized** *adj* [not gradable] • *a petrified tree/shell* • *(literary)* Something that is petrified has stopped changing and developing, and often belongs to the past: *The magazine had an article about that petrified British institution, the gentleman's club.*

pet·ri·fac·tion /ˌpet·rɪ'fæk·ʃᵊn/, **pet·ri·fi·ca·tion** /ˌpet·rɪ·fɪ'keɪ·ʃᵊn/ *n* [U] *specialized*

pet·ro·chem·i·cal /£ˌpet·rəʊ'kem·ɪ·kᵊl, $-roʊ-/ *n* [C] any chemical substance obtained industrially from PETROLEUM or natural gas • *the petrochemical industry* • *a petrochemical company/complex*

pet·ro·dol·lar /£'pet·rəʊˌdɒl·əʳ, $-roʊˌdɑː·lɚ/ *n* [C] a unit of money earned by countries that produce PETROLEUM for sale to other countries • *Petrodollars have maintained Kuwait's wealth.*

pet·rol *Br and Aus* /'pet·rᵊl/, *Am* **gas, gas·o·line** *n* [U] a liquid obtained from PETROLEUM, used esp. as a fuel for cars, aircraft and other vehicles • *a petrol tank/pump* • *lead-free/unleaded/high-octane petrol* • *I'd better* **fill up** *with petrol at the next station.* • *I'm a bit* **low on** (=I haven't got much) *petrol.* • A **petrol bomb** is a bottle filled with petrol or other liquid fuel with a piece of cloth in its top which is set on fire and thrown: *The rioters were throwing petrol bombs.* ○ *Two police-officers were shot and several buildings were* **petrol-bombed** *in the attack.* • **Petrol station** (also **filling station**, *Am* **gas station**) is a place where drivers can buy fuel and oil. • Ⓓ

pe·trol·e·um /£pə'trəʊ·li·əm, $-'troʊ-/ *n* [U] a dark thick oil obtained from under the ground, from which various substances including PETROL, PARAFFIN and DIESEL oil are produced • **Petroleum jelly** is a clear, JELLY-like substance made from petroleum, used as a base for medicines which are rubbed into the skin, and also for making parts in a machine move smoothly against each other.

pet·ti·coat /£'pet·ɪ·kəʊt, $'peţ·ɪ·koʊt/ *n* [C] *dated* a SLIP UNDERWEAR

pet·ti·fog·ging /£'pet·ɪˌfɒg·ɪŋ, $'peţ·ɪˌfɑː·gɪŋ/ *adj dated disapproving* (of people) giving too much attention to small unimportant details in a way that shows a limited mind, or (of rules or details) too small and unimportant to give attention to • *pettifogging lawyers/regulations*

pet·ty /£'pet·i, $'peţ-/ *adj* **-ier, -iest** unimportant and not worth giving attention to • *(disapproving) Prisoners complain that they are subjected to too many petty rules and restrictions.* • *(disapproving) Her latest play shows married life as a tedious succession of petty power struggles.* • **Petty crime** is a group of crimes which are considered as less serious: *Some police officers feel that all their time is spent on petty crime, such as shoplifting and minor traffic offences.* • *(disapproving)* Someone who is petty or **petty-minded** is annoyed and offended by small and unimportant matters in a way that shows a limited and often selfish mind. • **Petty cash** is a small amount of money kept in an office for buying cheap items: *Take the money for stamps out of petty cash.*

pet·ti·ness /£'pet·ɪ·nəs, $'peţ-/ *n* [U] *disapproving* • *It was the pettiness of their arguments that irritated her.*

pet·ty bourge·ois /£ˌpet·i'bʊə·ʒwɑː, £-'bɔː-, $ˌpeţ·i·bʊr'ʒwɑː/ *adj Br for* PETIT BOURGEOIS

pet·ty of·fic·er (*abbreviation* **PO**) *n* [C] a rank in a navy, below the officers but above the ordinary sailors

pe·tu·lant /'pet·jʊ·lᵊnt/ *adj disapproving* bad-tempered or annoyed in a childish and rude way • *One colleague recalled the dancer's petulant refusal to collect an award because his name had been wrongly pronounced.* • Ⓔ Ⓘ

pet·u·lant·ly /'pet·jʊ·lᵊnt·li/ *adv* • *"Well, he didn't invite me to his party so I'm certainly not inviting him to mine!" she said petulantly.*

pet·u·lance /'pet·jʊ·lᵊnts/ *n* [U] • *"I'm angry with you, Emil," she broke out with petulance.*

pe·tu·nia /£pɪ'tjuː·ni·ə, $pə'tuː·njə/ *n* [C] a garden plant grown for its white, pink or purple bell-shaped flowers

pew /pjuː/ *n* [C] a long wooden seat with a high back which a row of people sit on in a church • *Most people were sitting in the back/front pews.* • *(Br and Aus humorous)* Someone might tell you to **take a pew** when you are not in a church, as a way of inviting you to sit down.

pew·ter /£'pjuː·təʳ, $-ţɚ/ *n* [U] a bluish grey metal which is a mixture of TIN and LEAD • *a pewter plate/tankard*

pey·o·te /£peɪ'əʊ·ti, $-'oʊ·ţi/ *n* [C] *Am* a CACTUS (=a plant which stores water in its stem), part of which can be taken as a drug that changes the appearance of reality • See also MESCALIN.

pfft /£fʌt, $fət/ *exclamation Am for* PHUT

PG FILM /ˌpiː'dʒiː/ *adj, n* parental guidance (=(a film) containing slightly sexual or violent parts which parents might not consider suitable for young children) • *Her latest film is classified/rated* **(as)** *PG.* • *The film's a PG* [C] • In the US, **PG-13** marks a film that parents are strongly warned might not be suitable for children under the age of 13. • Compare G FILM; NC-17; U FILM; X FILM.

pg PAGE *n* [C] *esp. Am abbreviation for* page

PGCE /ˌpiː·dʒiː·siː'iː/ *n* [C] *abbreviation for* **Postgraduate Certificate in Education**, see at POSTGRADUATE

pH /ˌpiː'eɪtʃ/ *n* [C usually sing] a number which shows how strongly acid or ALKALINE a substance is, in a range from 0 to 14 • *Below pH 6·5 is acid, above pH 7·5 is alkaline.* • *The soil in our garden has a* **low/high** *pH.* • *I always use a pH-balanced shampoo.*

phag·o·cyte /£'fæg·əʊ·saɪt, $-oʊ-/ *n* [C] *specialized* a type of cell in the body which can surround things and swallow them, esp. a white blood cell which protects the body against infection by destroying bacteria

phal·anx /£'fæl·æŋks, $'feɪ·læŋks/ *n* [C + sing/pl v] *pl* **phalanxes** or **phalanges** /£'fæl·æn·dʒɪz, -dʒiːz, $feɪ'læn-/ *fml* a large group of people standing close to each other, forming a solid mass, usually for the purposes of defence or attack • *Bodyguards had formed a solid phalanx around the singer so that photographers couldn't get to her.* • *(fig.) The government took refuge behind* **a** *phalanx* **of** *obscure rules and regulations.* • *The Greek phalanx dominated battlefields in the ancient world.*

phal·lus /'fæl·əs/ *n* [C] an image or a model of the penis, esp. one representing the power of men to reproduce, or less commonly, a penis • *These primitive peoples are believed to have worshipped the phallus as a symbol of regeneration.*

phal·lic /'fæl·ɪk/ *adj* • Phallic means symbolic of, shaped like, or related to the penis: *phallic symbolism/imagery* ○ *An enormous phallic tower has been erected in the middle of the city.*

phal·lo·cent·ric /£ˌfæl·əʊ'sen·trɪk, $-oʊ-/ *adj literary specialized* having the male or male sexuality as the main subject of interest • *phallocentric eroticism/literature*

phan·ta·sm /'fæn·tæz·ᵊm/ *n* [C] *literary* something which is imagined to exist although it does not in reality, or something which is seen but is not there • *There are hopes that the threatened war will turn out to be a phantasm.*

phan·tas·ma·gor·i·a /£ˌfæn·tæz·mə'gɔː·ri·ə, $-'gɔːr·i-/ *n* [C] *literary* a fast-changing and confused group of real or imagined images, one following the other as in a dream • *Thursday's documentary was less of a narrative and more of a nightmarish phantasmagoria of prison life.*

phan·tom /£'fæn·tᵊm, $-ţᵊm/ *n* [C] a spirit of a dead person believed by some to visit the living as a pale, almost transparent form of a person, animal or other object; GHOST SPIRIT • *Over the years several phantoms have been sighted in the five-hundred-year-old cottage.* • *A phantom coach is said to pass through the grounds of this house when there's a full moon.* • *(humorous) The phantom wine-drinker has been around – this was almost a full bottle when I put it in the fridge* (=an unknown person has been drinking the wine)! • Phantom also means appearing to exist, although in fact it does not: *Although she had to have her leg amputated, she still feels as though she's got a phantom limb.* ○ *They discovered it was a phantom organization set up for the processing of drug profits.* ○ *(Br and Aus) Although she grew bigger and felt ill, she later discovered it was a phantom (Am* **false)** **pregnancy**. • *"Phantom of the Opera"* (title of a musical by Andrew Lloyd Webber based on earlier films, 1987)

pha·raoh /£ˈfeə·rəʊ, $ˈfer·oʊ/ *n* [C] (the title of) a king of ancient Egypt • *Best known of the pharaohs are Tutankhamun (c. 1350 BC), Rameses II and Rameses III.* • *He became Pharaoh when still very young.*

Phar·i·see /£ˈfær·ɪ·siː, $ˈfer-/ *n* [C] a member of an ancient group of Jews, written about in the Bible, who believed in obeying the religious laws very carefully and separated themselves from the ordinary people

phar·ma·ceu·ti·cal /£ˌfɑː·məˈsuː·tɪ·kəl, $ˌfɑːr·məˈsuː·t̬ɪ-/ *adj* [not gradable] connected with the production of medicines • *the pharmaceutical industry* • *a pharmaceutical company/product/journal*

phar·ma·ceu·ti·cal /£ˌfɑː·məˈsuː·tɪ·kəl, $ˌfɑːr·məˈsuː·t̬ɪ-/ *n* [C usually pl] *specialized* • Pharmaceuticals are medicines: *The company manufactures pharmaceuticals.*

phar·ma·cist /£ˈfɑː·mə·sɪst, $ˈfɑːr-/, *Am also* **drug·gist**, *Br and Aus also* **chem·ist** *n* [C] a person who is trained to prepare and sell medicines

phar·ma·cy /£ˈfɑː·mə·si, $ˈfɑːr-/ *n* • A pharmacy (*Am also* **drugstore**, *Br also* **chemist's**) is a shop or a part of a shop in which medicines are prepared and sold. [C] • Pharmacy is also the activity or study of medicine preparation. [U]

phar·ma·col·o·gy /£ˌfɑː·məˈkɒl·ə·dʒi, $ˌfɑːr·məˈkɑː·lə-/ *n* [U] the part of medical science which covers the study of medicines and drugs, including their action, their use and their effects on the body

phar·ma·col·o·gist /£ˌfɑː·məˈkɒl·ə·dʒɪst, $ˌfɑːr·məˈkɑː·lə-/ *n* [C] • A pharmacologist is a person who has studied and has a knowledge of pharmacology.

phar·ynx /ˈfær·ɪŋks/ *n* [C] *specialized* the soft part at the top of the throat which connects the mouth and nose to the OESOPHAGUS (= the tube which takes food to the stomach) and the LARYNX (= the hollow organ between the nose and lungs)

phase /feɪz/ *n* [C] any stage in a series of events or in a process of development • *The project is only in the initial phase as yet, but it's looking quite promising.* • *We're entering a new phase* **in** *international relations.* • If a child or young person goes through a period of strange or difficult behaviour, people sometimes describe it as a phase, meaning that it will stop after a while: *When I was in my early teens I* **went through** *a phase of only ever wearing black.* ○ *He started wearing women's clothes but I thought it was* **just a** *phase and he'd get over it soon.* • The phases of the moon are the regular changes in its shape as it appears to us on Earth. • If two things are happening **in/out of phase** they are reaching the same or related stages at the same time/at different times.

phase *obj* /feɪz/ *v* • If a new system or plan is phased it is introduced in stages over a particular period of time: *The minister said that the reduction in armed forces would be phased over the next five to ten years.* [T] • If you phase **in** something you introduce it gradually: *They will phase the new health care system in over a period of five years.* [M] • If you phase **out** something you remove it or stop using it gradually: *They're phasing the larger coin out because it's too heavy.* [M]

PhD /ˌpiː·eɪtʃˈdiː/, **D Phil** *n* [C] *abbreviation for* doctor of philosophy (= the highest college degree or a person having this) • *She is a PhD.* • *She has a PhD* **in** *physics.* • *a PhD student/thesis* • *He's doing a D Phil in Oxford.* • LP› Schools and colleges

pheas·ant /ˈfez·ənt/ *n pl* **pheasants** or **pheasant** a large bird with a rounded body and long tail, which spends a lot of time on the ground and is often shot for sport and food • *The male pheasant has brightly coloured plumage.* [C] • *roast pheasant* [U] • PIC› Birds

phe·nom /£fəˈnɒm, $-ˈnɑːm/ *n* [C] *Am slang* someone or something extremely successful, esp. someone young in sports who achieves a lot very quickly • *In less than a year, the 23-year-old phenom has gone from being a prospect with great potential to perhaps the best player in baseball.*

phe·nom·e·non EXISTING THING /£fəˈnɒm·ɪ·nən, $-ˈnɑː·mə·nɑːn/ *n* [C] *pl* **phenomena** /£fəˈnɒm·ɪ·nə, $-ˈnɑː·mə-/ something that exists and can be seen, felt, tasted, etc., esp. something which is unusual or something whose cause or origin is a subject of scientific or other interest • *Gravity is a* **natural** *phenomenon.* • *Do you believe in the paranormal and other psychic phenomena?* • *The book which lists all predictable astronomical phenomena for the coming year, such as planetary, lunar, and eclipse data.* • *There's evidence to suggest that child-abuse is not just a recent phenomenon.*

phe·nom·e·non SUCCESS /£fəˈnɒm·ɪ·nən, $-ˈnɑː·mə·nɑːn/ *n* [C] *pl* **phenomena** /£fəˈnɒm·ɪ·nə, $-ˈnɑː·mə-/ or **phenomenons** someone or something extremely successful, often because of unusual qualities or abilities • *The Beatles were a phenomenon – nobody had heard anything like them before.*

phe·nom·en·al /£fəˈnɒm·ɪ·nəl, $-ˈnɑː·mə-/ *adj* • *Her rise to fame was quite phenomenal – in less than two years she was a household name.*

phe·nom·en·al·ly /£fəˈnɒm·ɪ·nəl·i, $-ˈnɑː·mə-/ *adv* • *His first novel was phenomenally successful – it was translated into over thirty languages.*

phen·o·type /£ˈfiː·nəʊ·taɪp, $-noʊ-/ *n* [C] *specialized* the physical characteristics of something living, esp. those which can be seen, as influenced by both its GENES and the environment in which it lives • Compare GENOTYPE.

pher·o·mone /£ˈfer·ə·məʊn, $-moʊn/ *n* [C] *specialized* a chemical substance that animals release which influences the behaviour of other creatures of the same type, for example by attracting them sexually • *male pheromones*

phew /fjuː/ *exclamation infml esp. humorous* an expression of surprise, tiredness or RELIEF (= happiness that something that was causing you anxiety is not going to happen) • *Phew, I think I need to sit down after all that dancing!* • *You've got to feed fifty people? Phew, that's quite a number!* • *So I don't have to give the after-dinner speech after all – phew, what a relief.*

phial *esp. Br dated* /faɪəl/, *Am usually* **vi·al** *n* [C] a small glass bottle, esp. one containing liquid medicine • *a phial of opium*

Phi Be·ta Kap·pa /£ˌfaɪˌbiː·təˈkæp·ə, $-ˌbeɪ·t̬ə-/ *n* a national organization in the US whose members are elected because they have achieved a very high level in their studies at colleges or universities, or a member of this organization • *They were elected to Phi Beta Kappa.* [U] • *He's a Phi Beta Kappa (graduate).* [C]

phil·an·der·er /£fɪˈlæn·dər·əʳ, $-dɚ·ɚ/ *n* [C] *dated disapproving* a man who enjoys having sex with a lot of different women without becoming personally involved with any of them • *My grandfather was a dreadful philanderer, so he and Grandma had some amazing arguments.*

phil·an·der·ing /£fɪˈlæn·dər·ɪŋ, $-dɚ·ɪŋ/ *adj* [not gradable], *n* [U] *dated disapproving* • *The novel focuses on a middle-aged housewife's attempts to punish her philandering husband.*

phil·an·throp·ic /£ˌfɪl·ənˈθrɒp·ɪk, $-ænˈθrɑː·pɪk/ *adj* showing generosity towards other people and a sincere wish to help them, esp. by giving money to poor people • *Few companies offer money purely as a philanthropic gesture – they're usually after something in return.*

phil·an·throp·ist /£fɪˈlænt·θrə·pɪst, $fə-/ *n* [C] • *The housing trust was set up with a donation from a wealthy 19th-century philanthropist.* • *"The Ragged Trousered Philanthropists"* (title of a novel by Robert Tressell, 1914)

phil·an·thro·py /£fɪˈlænt·θrə·pi, $fə-/ *n* [U] • *In the spirit of philanthropy the millionaire donated a large sum of money to the charity.*

phi·lat·e·ly /£fɪˈlæt·əl·i, £fəˈlæt̬-/ *n* [U] *specialized* the collecting and study of postage stamps and postal history as a hobby

phil·ate·list /£fɪˈlæt·əl·ɪst, £fəˈlæt̬-/ *n* [C] *specialized* • A philatelist is a person who collects or studies postage stamps and postal history.

-phile /-faɪl, $-fɪl/ *combining form* someone who enjoys a particular thing or has it as a hobby, or who likes a particular place • *A bibliophile likes books and an oenophile enjoys wine.* • *A Francophile likes France.*

Phil·har·mon·ic /£ˌfɪl·hɑːˈmɒn·ɪk, $-hɑːrˈmɑː·nɪk/ *adj* [before n; not gradable] used in the names of musical groups, esp. ORCHESTRAS • *the Vienna Philharmonic Orchestra*

phil·is·tine /£ˈfɪl·ɪ·staɪn, $-stiːn/ *n* [C] *disapproving* a person who refuses to see the beauty or the value of art, literature, music or culture in any form • *I wouldn't have expected them to enjoy a film of that quality anyway – they're just a bunch of philistines!*

phil·ol·o·gy /£fɪˈlɒl·ə·dʒi, $-ˈlɑː·lə-/ *n* [U] *dated* the study of language, esp. its history and development

phil·o·log·i·cal /£ˌfɪl·əˈlɒdʒ·ɪ·kəl, $-ˈlɑː·dʒɪ-/ *adj* [not gradable] *dated*

phil·os·o·phy /£fɪ'lɒs·ə·fi, $-'lɑː·sə-/ *n* the use of reason in understanding such things as the nature of reality and existence, the use and limits of knowledge and the principles that govern and influence moral judgment • *She studied philosophy at college.* [U] • *René Descartes is regarded as the founder of modern philosophy.* [U] • *He works in the philosophy department.* • The philosophy **of** a subject is a group of theories and ideas related to the understanding of that subject: *the philosophy of education/religion/science* [U] • A philosophy is also a particular system of beliefs, values and principles: *the Ancient Greek philosophy of Stoicism* [C] • *(infml)* Someone might refer to their philosophy meaning their approach to life and their way of dealing with it: *Live now, pay later – that's my philosophy* **of**/*(Br also)* **on** *life!* [C] • See also PHD.

phil·os·o·pher /£fɪ'lɒs·ə·fəʳ, $-'lɑː·sə·fɚ/ *n* [C] • *Plato was a Greek philosopher.* • *(infml) Taxi-driving, with all its opportunities to observe and study human nature, had turned him into a bit of a philosopher.*

phil·o·soph·i·cal /£ˌfɪl·ə'sɒf·ɪ·kəl, $-'sɑː·fɪ-/ *adj* • *philosophical writings/essays* • *They always get into lengthy philosophical debates about morality and such like.* • If you are philosophical in your reaction to something which is not satisfactory you accept it calmly and patiently, understanding that failure and disappointment are a part of life: *You've just got to be a bit philosophical if your plans don't work out first time, and try not to be too discouraged.* ○ *"Life is cruel, you know, it always was and it always will be." "That's very philosophical of you, Dave."*

phil·o·soph·i·cal·ly /£ˌfɪl·ə'sɒf·ɪ·kli, $-'sɑː·fɪ-/ *adv* • Philosophically means calmly accepting a difficult situation: *As she herself remarked quite philosophically, their relationship would have finished sooner or later anyway.*

phil·os·o·phize, *Br and Aus usually* **-ise** /£fɪ'lɒs·ə·faɪz, $-'lɑː·sə-/ *v* [I] *esp. disapproving* • To philosophize is to talk for a long time about subjects such as the nature and meaning of life: *Students, she complained, had nothing better to do than spend whole days philosophizing* **about** *the nature of truth.*

phlegm SUBSTANCE /flem/ *n* [U] a thick MUCUS (= liquid produced in the nose, lungs, etc.) that is produced esp. when you have a COLD (= illness) • *I'm* **coughing up** *a lot of phlegm.*

phlegm CALMNESS /flem/ *n* [U] *fml* the ability to stay calm and not get emotional or excited about things even in a difficult or dangerous situation • *He looked like an English country gentleman but was totally lacking in the phlegm and equanimity associated with one.* • *Such phlegm in the face of adversity could only be admired.*

phleg·mat·ic /£fleg'mæt·ɪk, $-'mæṭ-/ *adj fml* • Someone who is phlegmatic tends not to get emotional or excited about things: *As a footballer his great asset was his calm, phlegmatic manner.*

pho·bi·a /£'fəʊ·bi·ə, $'foʊ·bjə/ *n* [C] an extreme fear of a particular thing or situation, esp. one that cannot be reasonably explained • *I've got a phobia* **about** *worms.*

-pho·bi·a /£-'fəʊ·bi·ə, $-'foʊ·bjə/ *combining form* • *claustrophobia* • *agoraphobia* • *xenophobia*

pho·bic /£'fəʊ·bɪk, $'foʊ-/ *adj, n* [C] • *I wouldn't describe myself as (a) phobic but I don't like heights.* • *Gradual exposure to your fear is the answer to most phobic problems.* • *(fig. infml) Why are so many companies phobic* **about** (= strongly against) *employing fat people?*

phoe·nix /'fiː·nɪks/ *n* [C usually sing] in ancient stories, an imaginary bird which set fire to itself every 500 years and was born again, rising from its ASHES (= black powder left after something has been burnt) • *Much of the town was destroyed by bombs in the war but it was rebuilt and in the following decade rose from the ashes* **like a/the** *phoenix.*

phone /£fəʊn, $foʊn/ *n* [C] a telephone; a device for speaking to someone which sends an electrical signal along a wire to a similar device • *The phone* **rang**. • *Could you* **answer** *the phone?* • **I picked up** *the phone* (= the part that you hold to mouth and ear). • *(Br and Aus) If he's rude to you, just* **put** *the phone* **down** *(also* **hang up**, *Am* **hang up** *the phone)* (= replace the part that you hold). • *(Br and Aus) She* **put** *the phone* **down on** *(also* **hung up on**, *Am* **hung up** *the phone* **on**) *me* (= replaced it before our conversation was finished). • *We speak* **by** *phone about twice a week.* • *You had three phone* **calls** *this morning.* • *If the phone* **lines** *are busy, please try again later.* • *Did you get his phone* **number**? • If a person is **on the phone**, he or she is using the telephone. • *(Br)* To be **on the phone** is also to have a telephone in the home: *Is she on the phone, do you know?* • *(infml)* A **phone book** is a **telephone directory**: *Is he in the (phone) book?* ○ See at TELEPHONE. • *(Br)* A **phone booth** (also **telephone booth**, *Am* **pay/public phone**) is a place in a public building where there is a telephone for use by the public. • *(Br and Aus)* A **phone box** (*Br and Aus also* **telephone box/call box**, *Am* **phone booth**) is a rectangular shelter, found outside in public places, which contains a telephone. • A **phone-in** (*Am* **call-in**) is (a part of) a television or radio programme in which members of the public can telephone the programme to express their opinions or ask questions, and the resulting conversation is broadcast. • **Phone-tapping** is the activity of secretly fitting a special device to someone's telephone in order to listen to their telephone conversations without them knowing. • See also PHONECARD. • LP **Telephone**

phone *(obj)* /£fəʊn, $foʊn/ *v* • *She phoned just after lunch.* [I] • *My sister phoned to tell me all her news.* [I] • *He's phoned me* **(up)** *every day this week.* [T/M] • When people telephone the place where they work they often say that they phone **in**: *She phoned in ill/sick* (= saying that she was ill) *this morning.* [I] • You also phone **in** when you telephone a television or radio programme in order to express your opinion on a matter: *The lines are open until 10 p.m. so please phone in and tell us about your own experience of the problem.* [I] • *"E.T. phone home"* (from the Stephen Spielberg film *E.T.*, 1982)

phone·card /£'fəʊŋ·kɑːd, $'foʊn·kɑːrd/ *n* [C] *Br and Aus* a small card which is used to operate a public telephone that allows you to make telephone calls to the value that you bought the card for • LP **Telephone**

pho·net·ic /£fəʊ'net·ɪk, $foʊ'neṭ-/ *adj* [not gradable] *specialized* using special signs to represent the different sounds made by the voice in speech • *Pronunciations are shown in this dictionary using the International Phonetic Alphabet, which is a standard system.* • A spelling system can be described as phonetic if you can understand how words are pronounced simply by looking at their spelling: *English pronunciation is very difficult because so much of the spelling is not phonetic.* • LP **Pronunciation**

pho·net·i·cal·ly /£fəʊ'net·ɪ·kli, $foʊ'neṭ-/ *adv* [not gradable] *specialized* • *She pronounced 'Leicester' phonetically as 'Ley-ces-ter', but she should have said 'Lester'.*

pho·net·ics /£fəʊ'net·ɪks, $foʊ'neṭ-/ *n* [U] *specialized* • Phonetics is the study of the sounds made by the human voice in speech.

pho·ney, *Am also* **pho·ny** /£'fəʊ·ni, $'foʊ-/ *adj* **phonier**, **phoniest** *infml disapproving* (of a person) not sincere and pretending to be something that he or she is not, or (of a thing) not real, and intended to deceive • *All aerobic instructors seem to have the same phoney American* **accent**. • *He gave the hotel a phoney* **address**. • *A small group of taxpayers had been filing phony or inflated* **claims** *for refunds, and some had been getting away with it.* • *He gives everyone the same phoney 'Mr Nice Guy'* **smile**. • *(Br)* A **phoney war** is a period during a war when there is no fighting and the situation appears calm.

pho·ney, *Am also* **pho·ny** /£'fəʊ·ni, $'foʊ-/ *n* [C] *infml disapproving* • *I don't trust him – I think he's a phoney.*

phon·o·graph /£'fəʊ·nə·grɑːf, $'foʊ·noʊ·græf/ *n* [C] *Am old use for* **record player**, see at RECORD STORE ELECTRONICALLY

pho·nol·o·gy /£fəʊ'nɒl·ə·dʒi, $fə'nɑː·lə-/ *n* [U] *specialized* the study of sounds in a particular language or in languages generally

phon·o·log·i·cal /£ˌfɒn·ə'lɒdʒ·ɪ·kəl, $ˌfoʊ·nə'lɑː·dʒɪ-/ *adj* [not gradable] *specialized*

phoo·ey /'fuː·i/ *exclamation infml humorous* used to express disappointment or a lack of respect for something • *We're supposed to pay sixty pounds a head for tickets? Phooey! No chance!*

phos·phate /£'fɒs·feɪt, $'fɑːs-/ *n* [C] a chemical COMPOUND (= substance consisting of at least two different elements) which contains PHOSPHORUS • *House plant foods are nearly always compound fertilizers containing nitrogen and phosphates.* • *This new detergent claims it won't pollute the water because it's phosphate-free.*

phos·phor·es·cent /£ˌfɒs·fəʳ'es·ənt, $ˌfɑːs·fə'res-/ *adj specialized* (of a substance) giving off light after RADIATION has hit it

phos·phor·es·cence /£ˌfɒs·fəʳ'es·ənts, $ˌfɑːs·fə'res-/ *n* [U] *specialized*

phos·phor·us /£'fɒs·fᵊr·əs, $'fɑːs·fɚ·əs/ *n* [U] a poisonous yellowish white or (more rarely) red or black element that shines in the dark and burns when in the air • *Phosphorus is used in making matches.*

phos·phor·ic /£fɒs'fɒr·ɪk, $fɑːs'fɔːr-/, **phos·phor·ous** /£'fɒs·fə·rəs, $'fɑː·sfɚ·əs/ *adj* [not gradable] • Phosphoric and phosphorous mean of or containing phosphorus: *phosphoric acid*

pho·to PHOTOGRAPH /£'fəʊ·təʊ, $'foʊ·t̬oʊ/ *n* [C] *pl* **photos** *infml* a photograph • *She* **took** *a lot of photos* **of** *the kids.* • *Would you like to see my holiday/wedding photos?* • A **photo album** is a type of book in which you keep photos: *I spent the evening looking at some of my old photo albums.* • A **photo-call/photo opportunity**/*(infml)* **photo op** is a time when esp. a politician, actor or other famous person is present in order to be photographed and appear in newspapers or on television: *The formal visit to the soldier's graves provided the president with the ideal photo opportunity.* • A **photo finish** in a race is a finish in which two or more of the people or animals taking part are so close that a photograph has to be examined in order to discover who has won. • A **photo frame** is a metal rectangle which frames a photo. It usually has an extra part at the back which supports it at an angle on a horizontal surface. • A **photo session** is a short period of time arranged for newspaper photographers to take photographs of politicians, leaders of countries or other famous people. • PIC› **Frame**

pho·to– /£ˌfəʊ·təʊ-, $ˌfoʊ·t̬oʊ-/ *combining form* • Photo- when added to a noun or adjective can mean that the word or phrase is connected with photography: *photogenic* ○ *photojournalism*

pho·to– LIGHT /£ˌfəʊ·təʊ-, $ˌfoʊ·t̬oʊ-/ *combining form* connected with or produced by light • *photoelectric/photosensitive/photosynthesis*

pho·to·cell /£'fəʊ·təʊ·sel, $'foʊ·t̬oʊ-/, **pho·to·el·ec·tric cell**, **e·lec·tric eye** *n* [C] an electrical device which produces a current or a VOLTAGE when light shines on it • *Photocells are used in burglar alarms.*

pho·to·chem·i·cal /£ˌfəʊ·təʊ'kem·ɪ·kᵊl, $ˌfoʊ·t̬oʊ-/ *adj* [not gradable] *specialized* relating to the effect of light on some chemicals • *Ozone, produced by the photochemical* **reaction** *of sunlight with unburnt hydrocarbons, and carbon monoxide emissions are rising inexorably.* • A **photochemical smog** is a fog caused by light from the sun shining on some types of chemicals in the air in areas with a lot of industry and traffic: *Photochemical smogs are worse in summer, when the sun's rays on the cloud of traffic fumes produce a photochemical reaction, creating high levels of ozone.*

pho·to·cop·i·er /£'fəʊ·təʊˌkɒp·i·əʳ, $'foʊ·t̬oʊˌkɑː·pi·ɚ/ *n* [C] a machine which makes copies of pages with printing, writing or drawing on them using a photographic process • PIC› **Office**

pho·to·co·py /£'fəʊ·təʊˌkɒp·i, $'foʊ·t̬oʊˌkɑː·pi/ *n* [C] • A photocopy is a photographic copy of a document made on a photocopier: *I'll just* **make** *a photocopy* **of** *the agreement.*

pho·to·co·py *obj* /£'fəʊ·təʊˌkɒp·i, $'foʊ·t̬oʊˌkɑː·pi/ *v* [T] • *Could you photocopy those three pages for me, please.*

pho·to·el·ec·tric /£ˌfəʊ·təʊ·ɪ'lek·trɪk, $ˌfoʊ·t̬oʊ-/ *adj* [not gradable] of or using an electrical current or VOLTAGE which is produced because of light • A **photoelectric cell** is a PHOTOCELL.

Pho·to·fit (pic·ture) *Br trademark* /£'fəʊ·təʊ·fɪt, $'foʊ·t̬oʊ-/, *Am* **com·pos·ite pho·to·graph**, *Aus* **i·den·ti·kit** *n* [C] a picture which represents as closely as possible a person's memory of a criminal's face, made by putting together photographs of eyes, nose, hair etc. from a set showing different types of facial features • *The police have issued a Photofit (picture) of the man that they are looking for.*

pho·to·gen·ic /£ˌfəʊ·təʊ'dʒen·ɪk, $ˌfoʊ·t̬oʊ-/ *adj* (esp. of a person) having a face that usually looks attractive in photographs • *The event attracted several middle-aged rock-stars and their photogenic girlfriends.*

pho·to·graph /£'fəʊ·tə·grɑːf, $'foʊ·t̬oʊ·græf/, *infml* **pho·to**, **pic·ture** *n* [C] an image of a person, object or view that is produced by using a camera and film • **colour/black-and-white** *photographs* • *aerial photographs* • *nude photographs* • *a signed/autographed photograph* **of** *Elvis Presley* • *My parents* **took** *a lot of photographs* **of** *us when we were small.* • *The world's first photograph was taken in 1826 by a French inventor, J. N. Niépce.* • Ⓓ Ⓕ

pho·to·graph *(obj)* /£'fəʊ·tə·grɑːf, $'foʊ·t̬oʊ·græf/ *v* • *I prefer photographing people rather than places.* [T] • *MacKay was photographed leaving the building.* [T + obj + v-ing] • You can say that a person photographs **well/badly**, meaning that he or she appears attractive/unattractive in photographs. [I always + adv]

pho·tog·raph·er /£fə'tɒg·rə·fəʳ, $-'tɑː·grə·fɚ/ *n* [C] • A photographer is a person who takes photographs, either as a job or as a hobby: *a fashion/press/amateur photographer* ○ *a keen/good photographer*

pho·to·graph·ic /£ˌfəʊ·tə'græf·ɪk, $ˌfoʊ·t̬ə-/ *adj* [not gradable] • *photographic equipment/film/materials* • *photographic skills* • *There is a system which allows you to store up to 100 photographic* **images** *on a CD and watch them on a television or computer screen.* • *The agreement forbids the photographic* **reproduction** *of written, printed, or graphic work.* • *Her paintings are almost photographic in their detail and accuracy.* • If you have a **photographic memory** you are able to remember things in exact detail.

photographi·cally /£ˌfəʊ·tə'græf·ɪ·kli, $ˌfoʊ·t̬ə-/ *adv* [not gradable]

pho·tog·raph·y /£fə'tɒg·rə·fi, $-'tɑː·grə-/ *n* [U] • Photography is the skill or activity of taking or processing photographs or films: *She's doing an evening class in photography.* ○ *The film won an award for its photography.* • *"But o, photography! as no art is,/ Faithful and disappointing!"* (Philip Larkin in the poem *Lines on a Young Lady's Photograph Album*, 1953)

pho·to·jour·nal·i·sm /£ˌfəʊ·təʊ'dʒɜː·nᵊl·ɪ·zᵊm, $ˌfoʊ·t̬oʊ'dʒɜːr-/ *n* [U] the activity of giving news or producing a magazine article by using mainly photographs

pho·to·jour·nal·ist /£ˌfəʊ·təʊ'dʒɜː·nᵊl·ɪst, $ˌfoʊ·t̬oʊ'dʒɜːr-/ *n* [C]

pho·ton /£'fəʊ·tɒn, $'foʊ·tɑːn/ *n* [C] *specialized* a single unit of light

pho·to·sen·si·tive /£ˌfəʊ·təʊ'sent·sɪ·tɪv, $ˌfoʊ·t̬oʊ'sent·sə-/ *adj* reacting to light • *a photosensitive lens/chemical/surface*

Photostat /£'fəʊ·təʊ·stæt, $'foʊ·t̬oʊ-/ *n* [C] *trademark* a machine used esp. in the past to make photographic copies of documents, letters, etc., or a copy made by such a machine

pho·to·stat *obj* /£'fəʊ·təʊ·stæt, $'foʊ·t̬oʊ-/ *v* [T] **-tt-**

pho·to·syn·the·sis /£ˌfəʊ·təʊ'sɪnt·θə·sɪs, $ˌfoʊ·t̬oʊ-/ *n* [U] the process by which a plant uses the energy from the light of the sun to produce its own food from water and **carbon dioxide** • *These plants have an impressive spread of leaves to enable them to produce enough food by photosynthesis to support their size.* • *The scientists say that although the sunlight falling on Mars is only about 43% of that reaching the Earth, this is enough for photosynthesis.* • *Plants' happy knack of swapping carbon dioxide for oxygen during photosynthesis is one of nature's ways of keeping the planet healthy.*

pho·to·syn·the·size *(obj)*, *Br and Aus usually* **-ise** /£ˌfəʊ·təʊ'sɪnt·θə·saɪz, $ˌfoʊ·t̬oʊ-/ *v* [I/T]

phrase GRAMMAR /freɪz/ *n* [C] a group of words which contains an idea, together forming a unit which, in writing, is part rather than the whole of a sentence • *In the sentence, 'I couldn't eat all my dinner', 'I couldn't eat' and 'all my dinner' are both phrases. The first of them is a verb phrase and the second is a noun phrase.* • See also PHRASEBOOK. • Ⓔ Ⓕ ⒼⓇ

phras·al /'freɪ·zᵊl/ *adj* [not gradable] • A **phrasal verb** is a phrase which consists of a verb in combination with a preposition or adverb or both, the meaning of which is different from the meaning of its separate parts: *'Look after', 'work out' and 'make up for' are all phrasal verbs.* • LP› **Compound verbs**

phrase EXPRESSION /freɪz/ *n* [C] a short group of words forming a descriptive expression, esp. one that is cleverly or amusingly expressed or is often used • *We are governed, in Lord Hailsham's famous phrase, by an 'elective dictatorship'.* • *She was fond of the phrase 'it's an opportunity not a risk'.* • LP› **Words used together** Ⓔ Ⓕ ⒼⓇ

phrase *obj* /freɪz/ *v* [T always + adv/prep] • The way that you phrase something is the way in which you express yourself, in the words that you choose to use: *I realize I phrased it badly and I should have been more tactful.* ○ *The last paragraph is ambiguously phrased.*

phras·e·ol·o·gy /£ˌfreɪ·zi'ɒl·ə·dʒi, $-'ɑː·lə-/ *n* [U] • Phraseology is the way in which language is used, especially in the choice of words and expressions:

PHRASES AND CUSTOMS

There are a number of conventional phrases that are very common, and you will feel more comfortable if you can recognize and use them in suitable situations. LP **Meeting someone** at MEET, and **Titles and forms of address** at TITLE.

THANKING British people use *thanks* or *thank you* very often, and it is the usual polite response whenever someone does something for you, even if you pay them. *Thank you* is more formal.

Thanks (a lot/very much).	*That's OK/That's all right.*
Thank you (very much).	*You're welcome.*
(infml) Cheers.	*(esp. Am) No problem.*

SAYING SORRY (you push against someone) *Sorry./Excuse me.*
(you sneeze) *Excuse me.* (When you sneeze, others might say *Bless you!*)
(your stomach makes a noise) *Pardon me.*
(you didn't hear/understand) *(Br)Pardon?/Sorry?/(Am)Pardon me?*
(you are late) *Sorry I'm late/ (fml)I'm so sorry to have kept you waiting.*

SPECIAL DAYS *Happy birthday./Many happy returns (of the day).*
Merry Christmas! Happy New Year!
(on Fridays) *Have a good/nice weekend.*
(before a *(Br and Aus)* holiday/*(Am)* vacation) *Enjoy your holiday/Have a good holiday.*
(wedding, new baby, good exam results) *Congratulations!*
(before new job, exam) *Good luck./All the best.*
(before a long journey) *Have a good trip./Safe journey./Bon voyage.*

PARTICULAR SITUATIONS (drinking alcoholic drinks) *Cheers!*
(eating) English speakers do not usually say anything before eating.
(someone sneezes) *Bless you!*
(you want to use the toilet) *Could I use your bathroom(Br also) loo/toilet, please?* • *Where's the bathroom/loo/toilet/ (Am infml) john, please?*
(something annoys you) *Damn!/Hell!/Heck!*
(something surprises you) *Wow!/Gosh!/ (Am) Gee!/ (Br dated) Blimey!/Crikey!/Strewth!*
(you drop something or make a mistake) *Oops!/Whoops!*

HEALTH (general) *How are you?/How've you been?*
(reply) *Fine/OK/very well, thanks.*
(someone looks unwell) *Are you all right/OK?*
(someone's been ill) *Are you better?/How are you feeling now?*
(someone says they're ill) *I hope you get better soon.*
(you hear someone has died) *I'm terribly sorry to hear about Pat/your brother.*

WEATHER

(It's a) nice/lovely/wonderful day today.	*Yes, isn't it?*
What miserable/awful weather we're having.	*Really awful.*

Journalistic phraseology is sometimes unnecessarily complex.

phras·ing /ˈfreɪ·zɪŋ/ *n* [U] • Phrasing is the way in which something is expressed: *The phrasing of the contract is rather ambiguous.*

phrase MUSIC /freɪz/ *n* [C] *specialized* a small group of notes forming a unit of a tune • *They played the same phrase over and over again.* • Ⓔ Ⓕ ⒼⓇ

phras·ing /ˈfreɪ·zɪŋ/ *n* [U] *specialized* • A singer's or musician's phrasing is the way in which they divide the tune into separate parts: *Her phrasing, as ever, is faultless.*

phrase·book /ˈfreɪz·bʊk/ *n* [C] a small book containing helpful groups of sentences and words in a particular foreign language, intended for people to use in countries where that language is spoken • *a Spanish phrasebook*

phut *Br and Aus* /£fʌt, $fət/ *exclamation* **go phut**/*(Am)* **go pfft** *infml* (of a machine) to stop working • *The washing-machine went phut this afternoon in the middle of a wash.*

phyl·lo (pa·stry) /£ˈfiː·ləʊ, $-loʊ/ *n* [U] FILO (PASTRY)

phys·i·cal BODY /ˈfɪz·ɪ·kəl/ *adj* connected with the body • *physical exercise/strength/disabilities* • *She must have been in a weak physical condition or the blow would not have killed her.* • *There's an element of danger in any sport in which there is a lot of physical* **contact**. • *Jeremy is at the peak of physical* **fitness**. • Physical **activities** are those which involve exercise, hard work, using strength, etc.: *I've never enjoyed sport or other physical activities.* • *(infml) I'm not a very physical sort of person* (= I don't enjoy physical activities). • Physical can be used to avoid saying violent: *The referee stepped in because the game had started to get a bit physical.* • Physical can also mean sexual: *There was obviously a great physical* **attraction** *between them.* ○ *It only started to get physical between us after Ann's party.* • *It was exhausting – I was* **a physical wreck** (= I felt very tired) *by the time I'd finished.* • **Physical education** (*abbreviation* **PE**) refers to the classes at school in which children do exercise and learn to play sport, or the area of study relating to such classes. • *(Br dated humorous)* **Physical jerks** are exercises that people do exercise in order to be healthy. • See also PHYSICAL MATERIAL; **physical** at PHYSICS. Compare MENTAL. • ⒼⓇ

phys·i·cal (ex·am·i·na·tion) /ˈfɪz·ɪ·kəl/, **med·i·cal (ex·am·i·na·tion)**, *Am also* **ex·am**, **ex·am·i·na·tion** *n* [C] • A physical (examination) is an examination of a person's body by a doctor in order to discover if that person is healthy, sometimes done before a person can be accepted for a particular job.

phys·i·cal·ly /ˈfɪz·ɪ·kli/ *adv* • *Physically I find him very attractive, but we don't have the same outlook on life.* • *One person alone couldn't have moved that stone – it's just not physically possible* (= one person would not be strong enough). • *He was creating such a disturbance that he had to be physically removed from the room* (= he was taken away). • *The work is physically* **demanding** (= you have work hard in a way that makes your body tired). • *Special holidays are available for physically* **disabled/handicapped** *people* (= those lacking the full use of part of their body).

phys·i·cal·i·ty /£ˌfɪz·ɪˈkæl·ə·ti, $-ţi/ *n* [U] *literary* • Physicality is the quality of being full of energy and force: *Durante dances with an impassioned physicality.*

phys·i·cal MATERIAL /ˈfɪz·ɪ·kəl/ *adj* existing as or connected with material things that can be seen or felt; not spiritual or mental • *the physical world* • *All physical objects occupy space.* • *The physical and political damage of the war will affect the lives of millions.* • *Insurers are worried about the physical condition of many of the vessels in the world's merchant fleet.* • *Last century flying-machines were considered a physical impossibility.* • **Physical**

geography is the study of the natural features of the Earth, such as mountains and rivers. • See also PHYSICAL [BODY]; **physical** at PHYSICS. • (GR)

phys·i·cian *esp. Am* /fɪ'zɪʃ·ᵊn/, *Br and Aus usually* **doc·tor** *n* [C] a medical doctor, esp. one who has general skill and is not a SURGEON • *Physicians and attorneys can be good role models.* • *"Physician, heal thyself"* (Bible, Luke 4.23) • (D)

phys·ics /'fɪz·ɪks/ *n* [U] the scientific study of matter and energy and the effect that they have on each other • *nuclear physics* • *a physics lab* • *Education experts are claiming that physics is badly taught in our schools.*

phys·i·cal /'fɪz·ɪ·kᵊl/ *adj* • Physical means connected with physics: *physical chemistry* • *physical laws* • The **physical sciences** are the sciences such as physics, chemistry and ASTRONOMY that examine matter and energy and the way the universe behaves. • See also PHYSICAL [BODY]; PHYSICAL [MATERIAL].

phys·i·cist /'fɪz·ɪ·sɪst/ *n* [C] • A physicist is a person who studies physics or whose job is connected with physics: *Two physicists said they had discovered how to make energy by cold fusion.*

phys·i·o /£'fɪz·i·əʊ, $-oʊ/ *n pl* **physios** *Br and Aus infml for* PHYSIOTHERAPY or PHYSIOTHERAPIST • *The complex will house the athletes and their coaches, doctors and physios during the competition.* [C] • *The doctor recommended that I go for some physio on my shoulder.* [U]

phys·i·og·no·my /£ˌfɪz·i'ɒn·ə·mi, $-'ɑː·nə-/ *n* [U] *fml* the physical appearance of something, esp. the face • *Different racial groups can be distinguished to some extent by differences in physiognomy.* • (GR)

phys·i·ol·o·gy /£ˌfɪz·i'ɒl·ə·dʒi, $-'ɑː·lə-/ *n* [U] the scientific study of the way in which the bodies of animals and plants work • *The team has been working on nutritional physiology.* • *The lecture was on* **the** *physiology* **of** *the brain and the transmission of nerve impulses.*

phys·i·o·log·i·cal /£ˌfɪz·i·ə'lɒdʒ·ɪ·kᵊl, $-'lɑː·dʒɪ-/ *adj* [not gradable] • *The cause of stuttering speech is unknown, but several physiological, genetic and psychological factors have been implicated.*

phys·i·ol·o·gist /£ˌfɪz·i'ɒl·ə·dʒɪst, $-'ɑː·lə-/ *n* [C] • A physiologist is a person who studies physiology.

phys·i·o·ther·a·py /£ˌfɪz·i·əʊ'θer·ə·pi, $-oʊ-/, *infml* **phys·i·o** *n* [U] the treatment of stiffness, muscle weakness and pain in the body, esp. by rubbing and moving the sore parts • *It's important for knee injuries that the surgeon who operates on you also supervises the after-care and physiotherapy.* • *He will continue physiotherapy for his back and expects to be able to play again around the end of January.*

phys·i·o·ther·a·pist /£ˌfɪz·i·əʊ'θer·ə·pɪst, $-oʊ-/, *infml* **phys·i·o** *n* [C] • A physiotherapist is someone who treats people using physiotherapy. • *A new video technique has enabled physiotherapists to predict potential injury problems in sports people by monitoring their limb movements.*

phys·ique /fɪ'ziːk/ *n* [C] the appearance, esp. shape and size, of a human body • *His powerful physique and vivid personality identified him with the heroic roles which dominated Soviet ballet in the 1930s.* • *She was of medium height but she had an oddly pear-shaped physique.* • *With natural ability allied to an ideal physique – tall and light, with powerful arms – he quickly developed into an outstanding climber.*

pi, /paɪ/ *n* [U] a Greek letter, esp. used in mathematics as a symbol for the number (approximately 3·14) used to calculate the size of various parts of a circle

pi·an·o /£pi'æn·əʊ, $-oʊ/ *n* [C] *pl* **pianos** a large musical instrument with a row of black and white keys which are pressed to play notes • *We're going to buy a new piano.* • *I play* **the** *piano, but not very well.* • *(esp. Am or specialized) She used to play piano in a jazz band.* • *We all joined in the song, with Pat* **at the** *piano/***on** *piano.* • *Oli opened the piano lid so the children could see how it worked.* • *The balance between orchestra and piano was interesting.* • *Debussy arranged the score for piano himself.* • *It is the piano* **accompaniment** *that makes this piece so enjoyable.* • *I enjoyed the piano* **recital/concerto** *very much indeed.* • *He wrote operas, orchestral works, and songs, but is best known for his piano* **music**. • A **piano stool** is a type of chair without a back or sides which is used when playing the piano. • A **piano tuner** is a person whose job is to make certain that a piano is producing the correct notes by testing it and adjusting the tightness of the strings. • [PIC] **Coverings, Musical instruments**

pi·a·nist /'piː·ᵊn·ɪst/ *n* [C] • A pianist is someone who plays the piano: *a concert pianist* ○ *a jazz pianist*

pi·az·za /£pi'æt·sə, $-'ɑːt-/ *n* [C] an open area with a hard surface in a town, esp. one where there is no traffic • *In Covent Garden, London has its only working piazza, complete with shops, stalls, cafés, jugglers and musicians.* • See also SQUARE.

pic /pɪk/ *n* [C] *infml for* PHOTOGRAPH • *Would you like to see my holiday pics?* • *See main pic on p.2.*

pi·ca·dor /£'pɪk·ə·dɔːʳ, $-dɔːr/ *n* [C] someone, usually a man, who pushes sharp sticks into BULLS during a BULLFIGHT • Compare MATADOR; TOREADOR.

pi·ca·yune /£ˌpɪk·ə'juːn, $'---/ *adj* [not gradable] *Am* having little value or importance • *The misery suffered in this war makes your own problems seem pretty picayune.*

pic·ca·lil·li /£ˌpɪk·ə'lɪl·i, $'----/ *n* [U] small pieces of different vegetables preserved in a yellow sauce, made with MUSTARD, which has a hot taste. It is usually eaten with cold meat.

pic·co·lo /£'pɪk·ə·ləʊ, $-loʊ/ *n* [C] *pl* **piccolos** a musical instrument, like a small FLUTE, which makes a high sound

pick *(obj)* [CHOOSE] /pɪk/ *v* to take some things and leave others; to choose • *We need to pick someone who is good with people.* [T] • *Pick a couple of dates for the party and then we'll see which is the best for most of us.* [T] • *One of my sisters has been picked* **for** *the Olympic team.* [T] • If you pick **and choose** you take some things but not others: *(disapproving) You cannot pick and choose which parts of the job you do – it's all or nothing.* [T] ○ *He was a successful enough actor to pick and choose his roles.* [T] ○ *The universities could pick and choose among students with the best results.* [I] • If you pick something **at random** or pick it **out of a/the hat** you do it without a plan or without knowing what you are doing: *To pick an instance at random, she was late again yesterday.* [T] ○ *Here are half a dozen hotels, picked at random from the latest edition of the guide.* [T] ○ *(disapproving) Some of the material was so unsuitable it seemed to have been picked out of a hat.* [T] • *There are many good reasons to pick* **(on)** (= choose) *Washington for your headquarters.* [T; I + *on*] • *All the puppies were adorable, but we picked* **(out)** (= chose) *the one with the longest, floppiest ears.* [T/M] • *They picked their* **way** (= carefully chose a route) *through the mud/down the broken steps/over the rough ground.* [T] • *So successful has the group been in picking* **winners** (= choosing what will be successful) *that it is held up as a model for other organizations' selection processes.* [T] • *He'd had too much to drink and tried to pick* (= start) *a* **fight** *with the bartender.* [T] • *(disapproving)* If you **pick at** your food you choose only small parts of it to eat without interest or enjoyment: *His guest finally did arrive at the restaurant, only to pick at her food and leave early.* See also **picky**. • Someone with a gun picks **off** a person or animal by shooting only a particular person or animal chosen out of a group, rather than shooting several at one time: *The snipers picked the soldiers off one by one as they ran for cover.* [M] ○ *(fig.) It is relatively easy for newcomers to pick off* (= keep for themselves) *the most lucrative business and ignore the rest.* [M] • When you **pick over** esp. fruit or vegetables, you examine them carefully and choose the best ones or throw away the bad ones: *Pick over the strawberries and keep a few big ones to one side for decoration.* • If you **pick on** someone you frequently treat, criticize or punish the same person unfairly: *He gets picked on because he's small.* ○ *There's one girl at my school who everybody picks on because she doesn't wear what everybody else wears – they're horrible to her.* • *Just leave me alone, will you? Why don't you go and* **pick on someone** *your* **own size** (= fight with someone who is as big you)? • *Could you pick a few books* **(out)** *for me when you go to the library?* [T/M] • *An innocent man she picked* **(out)** *from police photographs was held for 18 days before he was cleared by DNA genetic fingerprinting.* [T/M] • To **pick out** also means to recognize, find or make a choice among items in a group: *Can you pick out the three deliberate mistakes in this paragraph?* ○ *We picked our parents out quite easily in the old photos.* • To **pick out** is also to choose and emphasize, make clearer or HIGHLIGHT: *The series picks out the memorable occasions and issues of each year in the Fifties.* ○ *The critics had picked him out as one of the most outstanding male dancers of the decade.* ○ *She arrived on stage picked out by a spotlight.* ○ *The ship's name was picked out* **in** *bright gold letters along her stern.* • *(Br)* **Pick 'n' mix** is a system in shops where a person can choose a few of several different small things, esp. sweets.

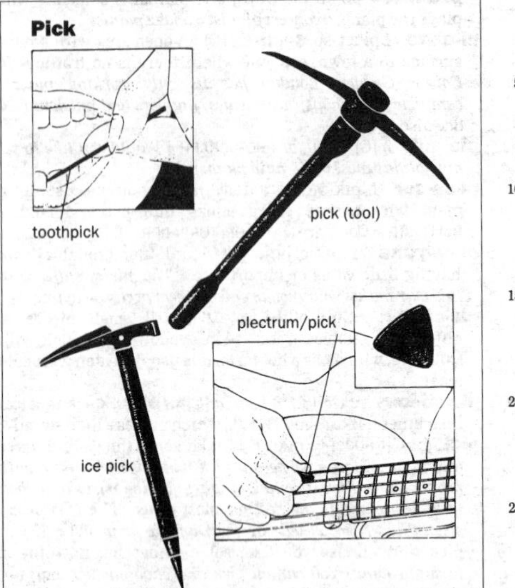

pick /pɪk/ *n* [U] • **Take your pick** means choose anything you want: *There are five sizes and three different colours – just take your pick.* • If you can **have** your **pick of** a set of things you have a large choice: *The plane was fairly empty so we had our pick of seats.* • If something is described as **the pick of** a group of things, it is the best: *The pick* **of** *this year's racehorses is Gandy Dancer.* ○ *(dated) There were many amusing entries, but* **the pick of the bunch** (= the best one) *came from John Robinson.*

pick·er /£ 'pɪk·əʳ, $-ɚ/ *n* [C] *esp. Am* • *Traditional* **stock** *pickers* (= people who select companies in which others should invest) *are being replaced by traders using sophisticated computer programs.*

pick·y /'pɪk·i/ *adj* **-ier**, **-iest** *infml disapproving* • Someone who is picky is very careful about choosing only what they like: *The children are such picky* **eaters**. ○ *Many big companies have frozen recruitment and those that are hiring can afford to be picky.*

pick *(obj)* [REMOVE] /pɪk/ *v* to remove or move (something) with your fingers or hands • *When the fruit has been picked* (= removed from the trees) *it's packed in boxes.* [T] • *He picked the knife* **from/out of** *the drawer.* [T] • *She put down her bag and picked the letters* **off** *the hall table.* [T] • *"Here's a nice ripe one," he said, picking an apple* **off** *the tree.* [T] • *The beetles need to be picked* **off** *the leaves by hand as soon as they emerge.* [T] • *I picked a piece of fluff* **off** *my shiny black suit.* [T] • *He picked* **up** (= lifted) *his case and moved it away from the door.* [M] • *I went to pick* **up** *the phone, but it had stopped ringing.* [M] • *If you need me you just have to pick* **up** *the phone* (= make a telephone call). [M] • *(fig.) She tripped and fell, picked her***self up** (= stood up slowly) *and looked round to see who was watching.* [M] • *A group of us went out to pick* **up** (= lift and remove) *the litter left on the grass after the party.* [M] • *(fig.) Many farmers are just picking themselves* **up off the floor** (= Their lives are beginning to improve) *after the financial blows dealt them by low prices and high interest rates.* [T] • *The child continued picking* **(at)** *a sore on his leg* (= trying to remove parts of it with his fingers). [T; I + *at*] • *The carcass had been picked* **clean** (= all the flesh had been removed) *by other animals and birds.* [T + obj + adj] • *(disapproving) He kept picking* (= removing MUCUS from) *his* **nose** *as he was talking to me.* [T] • When you pick a string on a guitar or similar instrument you pull it quickly and release it suddenly with your fingers to produce a note. [T] • If you **pick** someone's **brains** about a subject, you ask someone who knows a lot about it for information or their opinion: *I've decided to pick Phil's brains about this computer I'm thinking of buying.* ○ *The President is picking the brains of big business executives on this problem.* • *(disapproving)* If you **pick holes in** something you try to find things wrong with it: *They didn't take the proposal seriously and just spent half an hour picking holes in it.* • If you pick **out** a tune, you play it slowly or with difficulty, note by note: *I can't do more than pick out a simple tune on the piano.* [M] • If someone **picks** your **pocket** they steal small objects, esp. money, from your pockets or bag often without you noticing: *Last week I had my pocket picked by the man sitting next to me in the local café.* See also PICKPOCKET. • *(infml)* To **pick up the bill/tab** is to pay for what has been bought: *When a man and a woman are dining together, our waiters are cautioned not to assume that the man is picking up the tab or ordering the wine.* ○ *(fig.) The consumer will be forced to pick up the bill for this ridiculous scheme.* • To **pick up the pieces** is to try to return to a satisfactory situation: *The fire was a blow, but we were determined to pick up the pieces and get the business back on its feet.* ○ *The organization helps separated or divorced people work through these emotions, pick up the pieces of their lives and move on.* • To **pick up the threads** is to start again after an interruption: *Picking up the threads* **of** *our discussion, let's return to the topic of factory farming.* ○ *(fig.) He's stopped seeing Michele, and he's hoping that he and Joan will be able to pick up the threads* **of** *their marriage again.* • A **pick-me-up** is something which makes you feel better, often a drink or a TONIC (= a type of medicine): *In this part of the country, it is traditional to drink brandy with coffee as a morning pick-me-up.* • **Pick your own** (abbreviation **PYO**) is the activity of picking esp. fruit yourself at a farm and then paying for the amount you have picked: *pick-your-own strawberries* ○ *I got some raspberries at that pick-your-own place just outside town.*

pick /pɪk/ *n* [C] • A pick is a PLECTRUM.

pick·er /£ 'pɪk·əʳ, $-ɚ/ *n* [C] • A picker is a person or a machine that picks crops: *fruit pickers* ○ *The grape harvest alone employs 100 000 pickers.*

pick [TOOL] /pɪk/ *n* [C] a PICKAXE or, esp. in combinations, a sharp pointed tool • *picks and shovels* • *He used a pick to break up the concrete path.* • *She cleans her teeth with a toothpick after every meal.* • [PIC]〉**Pick**

pick up *obj* [OBTAIN], **pick** *obj* **up** *v adv* [M] to obtain, get or receive • *These bombs have a guidance system which can pick up signals from targets on the ground.* • *Antennas around the top of the ship pick the radar signals up.* • *Can you pick up* (= receive broadcasts from) *Moscow* **on** *your radio?* • *People see this period as a good time to pick up bargains.* • *The People's Front expect to pick up a lot more votes in this year's elections.* • *He picked up* (= started to suffer from) *malaria when he was visiting the country on business.* • *The nurse had picked up the information from a conversation she overheard.* • *We had picked up* (= learned informally) *enough Russian to be able to read the instructions.* • *There is an instruction manual for the machine, but you can pick up most of what you need to know as you go along* (= learn about it as you work).

pick–up /'pɪk·ʌp/ *n* [C] • A pick-up is a device on an electrical musical instrument or a record player which causes sounds to be produced or made louder.

pick up *obj* [COLLECT], **pick** *obj* **up** *v adv* [M] to collect or to go and get • *When you're in town could you pick up the books I ordered?* • *Whose turn is it to pick up the children after school?* • *Jenny's going to pick me up outside the cinema.* • *We're considering a permit system for all cabdrivers who pick up passengers at the airport.* • *The crew of the sinking tanker were picked up* (= saved from the sea) *by helicopter.* • *When the police picked him up* (= took him to the police station for questioning) *he still had the stolen credit cards in his pocket.* • *(infml)* To pick someone up is to act in a friendly way to a person you meet for the first time in order to persuade them to have esp. a sexual relationship: *He said he'd picked the woman up in a bar.*

pick–up /'pɪk·ʌp/ *n* [C] *infml* • A pick-up is the act of picking up or the place where it happens: *We arranged the pick-up for ten o'clock.* ○ *The pick-up* **point** *for the long-distance coaches is now in the new bus station.* • A pick-up is also the person picked up: *The taxi driver said I was the first pick-up that he'd had all evening.* • *(dated infml)* A pick-up is someone who has an informal, esp. sexual relationship with someone they have met for the first time: *Jerry brought his latest pick-up to the party.* • A **pick-up (truck)** is a small vehicle with an open part at the back in which goods can be carried. • *(Br)* A **pick-up truck** (*Am and Aus* **tow truck**) is also a vehicle which can pull or carry another vehicle which has been involved in an accident or has stopped working during a journey. • [PIC]〉 **Vehicles**

pick up *(obj)* [IMPROVE] *v adv* to improve or increase • *In recent years, new house sales have slowed to a crawl, but builders are starting to see sales pick up again.* [I] • *We don't expect the number of applicants to pick up until at least the* *autumn.* [I] • *His spirits began to pick up when he was told his condition was curable.* [I] • *The truck picked up* **speed** *slowly.* [T] • *(fig.) Her career began to pick up* **speed/momentum** *when she was in her thirties.* [T]

pick–up /ˈpɪk·ʌp/ *n* [U] *Am* • A car with good/bad pick-up can/cannot increase its speed quickly.

pick up *(obj)* START AGAIN, **pick** *(obj)* **up** *v adv* to start again after an interruption • *After lunch shall we pick up* **where** *we* **left off** *yesterday?* [I] • *The author picks up the theme again on page ten.* [M]

pick up *obj* CRITICIZE, **pick** *obj* **up** *v adv* [M] *Br and Aus infml* to stop (someone) in order to correct their behaviour • *His teacher picked him up* **on** *his pronunciation.* • *She was picked up* (= stopped) *by the police* **for** *speeding.*

pick up on *obj v adv prep* [T] to choose (something previously said) as being worth discussion or particular attention • *Originally only one newspaper picked up on the minister's statement, but by the end of the week it was making nationwide headlines.* • *Can I just pick up on the point you made a few minutes ago about personal morality, Archbishop?*

pick·axe, *Am* **pick·ax** /ˈpɪk·æks/, **pick** *n* [C] a tool for breaking hard surfaces which has a long wooden handle fitted into the middle of a curved metal bar with a sharp point • PIC Axe

pick·et /ˈpɪk·ɪt/ *n* [C] a person or group of people who have a disagreement with their employers, stop work and form a line outside their place of work to try to prevent other people entering their place of work until the problem is solved • *They had people scheduled throughout the day to act as pickets outside the factory gates.* • *The group of men had a sign which said 'Official picket'.* • A picket can also be the occasion on which this happens: *a month-long picket* • A **picket line** is a group of workers acting as pickets: *Journalists interviewed the union officials* **on** *the picket line.* ○ *The van drivers refused to* **cross** *the picket line* (= to go past the pickets).

pick·et *(obj)* /ˈpɪk·ɪt/ *v* • *They picketed the restaurant and handed out leaflets to potential customers.* [T] • *The women picketed outside the factory for three months.* [I] • *Picketing miners halted the delivery vans.*

pick·et·er /£ˈpɪk·ɪ·təʳ, $-t̬ɚ/ *n* [C] • A picketer is a person who stands outside a building as part of a picket: *Theatregoers were confronted by picketers with signs declaring 'No Foreign Shows' and 'Stop The Cultural Invasion'.*

pick·et·ing /£ˈpɪk·ɪ·tɪŋ, $-t̬ɪŋ/ *n* [U] • *The proposed new law would ban picketing.*

pick·et fence *n* [C] a low fence made of a row of flat sticks which are pointed at the top and often painted white • *A picket fence can be used to mark the edge of a garden in front of a house.*

pick·ings /ˈpɪk·ɪŋz/ *pl n* money which can be earned easily or dishonestly • *The street-sellers are lured to the town by the* **rich/easy** *pickings that are to be had from foreign tourists.* • *Shoppers who have been waiting for end-of-year bargains will find* **slim** *pickings* (= little available) *in most stores.*

pick·le /ˈpɪk·l̩/ *n* vegetables or fruit which have been preserved in a vinegar sauce or salty water • *a jar of pickle* [U] • *cheese and pickle sandwiches* • *The smoked ham was served with pickles, celery and thin slices of red pepper.* [C] • *Mango pickle is a type of* **sweet** *pickle* (= with sugar added). [U] • *(Am)* A pickle is a preserved CUCUMBER (= long green rounded vegetable): *a sweet/sour pickle* [C] ○ *dill pickles* [C] ○ *pickle spears* (= pickles cut along their length into quarters) ○ *The sandwiches here come with coleslaw and half a pickle.* [C] • *(infml)* If you are **in a (pretty/right) pickle** you are in a difficult situation: *Julie landed herself in a right pickle when she lost her address book.* • Ⓓ

pick·le *obj* /ˈpɪk·l̩/ *v* [T] • *The onions had been pickled* **in** *spiced brine.*

pick·led /ˈpɪk·l̩d/ *adj* • *pickled onions/gherkins/cabbage/walnuts/beetroot* • *pickled eggs/herring* • *(infml)* Pickled also means drunk: *I got really pickled at Pat's party.*

pick·ling /ˈpɪk·l̩.ɪŋ, ˈ-lɪŋ/ *adj* [before n; not gradable] • *pickling onions* (= small onions of a type which are preserved in vinegar) • *pickling spices* (= used to give extra flavour to preserved vegetables)

pick·pock·et /£ˈpɪk,pɒk·ɪt, $-,pɑː·kɪt/ *n* [C] a thief who steals things out of pockets or bags, esp. in a crowd • *Gangs of pickpockets had rushed through the carnival crowds, stealing wallets and purses.* • *Beware of pickpockets!* • LP **Crimes and criminals**

pick·y /ˈpɪk·i/ *adj* See at PICK CHOOSE

pic·nic /ˈpɪk·nɪk/ *n* [C] a usually cold meal taken with you to a place to be eaten outside in an informal way, or an occasion on which such a meal is eaten • *These small packs of fruit juice are ideal for picnics.* • *If the weather's nice we could* **go on** *a picnic on Saturday.* • *If you're going to be away all day, why don't you* **take** *a picnic with you?* • *Do you want to stop at a restaurant on the way, or would you rather take a picnic lunch?* • *picnic tables* • *a picnic area/spot/site* • *a picnic basket/hamper* • If something **seems like a picnic** it is pleasant. If something **is no picnic** it is not pleasant: *The current crisis makes last year's hard work seem like a picnic.* ○ *He has to be there whatever the weather and these damp, dark, cold mornings are no picnic for him.* • PIC **Basket**

pic·nic /ˈpɪk·nɪk/ *v* [I] **picnicking**, *past* **picnicked** • *There were several families picnicking on the river bank.* • *You can visit the gardens, but picnicking is not allowed.* • *The theatre is in a pleasant park where you can picnic before or after the performance.*

pic·nick·er /£ˈpɪk·nɪ·kəʳ, $-kɚ/ *n* [C] • *The grass around the trees was scattered with litter left by picnickers.*

pic·to·ri·al /£pɪkˈtɔː·ri·əl, $-ˈtɔːr·i-/ *adj* presented in the form of a picture • *The police advise homeowners to make a detailed pictorial record of their home by photographing everything that might appeal to burglars.* • *A pictorial history* (= Pictures showing the history) *of the company was exhibited around the room.* • *She is a highly disciplined theatrical artist with a vivid pictorial imagination* (= she can easily change ideas into something that can be seen). • *A pictorial representation of the statistics, a graph perhaps, would make them easier to understand.*

pic·to·ri·al·ly /£pɪkˈtɔː·ri·ə·li, $-ˈtɔːr·i-/ *adv* • *We are trained to think verbally rather than pictorially.*

pic·ture REPRESENTATION /£ˈpɪk·tʃəʳ, $-tʃɚ/ *n* [C] a representation of (someone or something) produced by drawing, painting or taking a photograph • *There was a large picture* **of** *Venice on the wall by the door.* • *He* **drew/painted** *a picture of my dog as a birthday present.* • *Would you like to see the wedding pictures* (= photographs)? • *We* **took** *a picture of* (= photographed) *the children on their new bicycles.* • *I hate having my picture taken* (= being photographed). • A picture is also an image seen on a television or cinema screen: *We can't get a clear picture.* ○ *If you look carefully, you'll see the car appear to the left of the picture.* ○ *The pictures of the earthquake damage were distressing.* ○ *Here are the* **satellite** *pictures of the weather that's on its way.* • A picture is also something you produce in your mind, by using your imagination or memory: *I have a very* **vivid** *picture of the first time I met her.* ○ *All the people were asked to form a* **mental** *picture of the man who had been described and then to match it to photographs.* • *The flowers are blooming and our garden looks as* **pretty as a** *picture* (= extremely pretty). • *(Br)* If something **is a picture**, it is beautiful: *When we visited the garden, the roses were a picture.* ○ *The bride was a picture in her delicate lacy dress.* • *(Br)* If someone's **face is a picture**, they look very surprised or angry: *Her face was a picture when I told her who I'd met.* • If you describe someone as a **picture of** something, you mean that they give a very clear appearance of it: *He sat with his head in his hands, a picture of misery.* ○ *The puppies were the very picture of health.* • A **picture book** is a book, esp. for young children, which has a lot of pictures and not many words. • A **picture frame** is a frame into which a picture fits, or any structure which is designed to hold a picture: *a large gilt picture frame* • A **picture postcard** is a POSTCARD with a picture, usually a photograph of a place, on one side. • Something described as **picture-postcard** is very attractive, in a slightly artificial way: *a picture-postcard cottage/village* • A **picture window** is a large window, esp. in a house or hotel, positioned so that you can see an attractive view: *The upstairs room had a large picture window looking out over the valley.* • *(saying)* 'Every picture tells a story'. • *"One picture is worth a thousand words"* (Frederick R. Barnard writing in *Printers' Ink*, 1927) • *"The Picture of Dorian Gray"* (title of a story by Oscar Wilde, 1891) • PIC **Frame, Room**

pic·tures /£ˈpɪk·tʃəz, $-tʃɚz/ *pl n dated* • **The** pictures is the cinema: *Let's go to the pictures tonight.*

pic·ture *(obj)* /£ˈpɪk·tʃəʳ, $-tʃɚ/ *v* • To picture something is to imagine it: *Picture* **the scene** – *the crowds of people and animals, the noise, the dirt.* [T] ○ *Try to picture yourself lying on a beach in the hot sun.* [+ obj + v-ing] ○

Picture **to** *yourself* **how** *terrible that day must have been.* [+ *wh-* word] • *(fml) He was pictured* (= An artist had painted him) **as** *a soldier in full uniform.* [T]

pic·ture DESCRIPTION /£'pɪk·tʃər, $-tʃɚ/ *n* [U] (a description of) a situation • *She tried to give us a* **vivid** *picture of her life as a child.* • *There is a view of runaways as coming from terrible circumstances, hooked on drugs or pregnant, but this is not an accurate picture.* • *They argue that inconsistencies in the way results are collected prevent any reliable national picture* **emerging**. • To **paint** a picture is to describe a situation: *The experts are painting a* **gloomy/grim** *picture of the current state of the economy.* ○ *They painted a* **rosy** *picture of our chances, saying we couldn't lose.* • *It's true, the picture is brighter* (= the situation is better) *than six months ago.* • *In the report, the inspectors suggest that the* **broad** *picture* (= general situation) *in schools has changed little over the last few years.* • *It's all right, don't say any more – I* **get the picture** (= I understand the situation). • *I've asked Kim to* **keep** *me* **in the picture** (= keep me informed) *about what's happening while I'm abroad.* • *Could you find the file, while I* **put** *Bobby* **in the picture** (= tell him what has happened)? • *At first he appeared to be in line for a place in the team, but he gradually drifted* **out of the picture** (= became less important). • *New systems are being developed for missiles which cut humans* **out of the picture** *altogether* (= make humans unnecessary). • *Above all, keep the press* **out of the picture** (= do not tell them anything) *for as long as possible.*

pic·tur·esque /£ˌpɪk·tʃər'esk, $-tʃə'resk/ *adj* (esp. of a place) attractive in appearance, esp. in an old-fashioned way • *the picturesque narrow streets of the old city* • *a picturesque fishing village*

pic·tur·esque·ly /£ˌpɪk·tʃər'es·kli, $-tʃə'res-/ *adv* • *The cottage was picturesquely situated on the edge of a wood.*

pic·tur·esque·ness /£ˌpɪk·tʃər'esk·nəs, $-tʃə'resk-/ *n* [U] • *The photo didn't fully capture the picturesqueness of the scene.* • *"It is only the old story that progress and picturesqueness do not harmonise"* (Thomas Hardy in *The Dorsetshire Labourer*, 1883)

pid·dle /'pɪd·l̩/ *n* [U] *infml* urine, or an act of urinating • *There was piddle all over the floor of the toilet in the station.* • *Kate was desperate for a piddle all the way through Fionnuala's christening.* • *(infml)* Piddle is also used to express slight annoyance: *Oh piddle! I've broken another glass.*

pid·dle /'pɪd·l̩/ *v* [I] *infml* • *The puppy had piddled all over the rug.*

pid·dling /'pɪd·l̩.ɪŋ, 'pɪd·lɪŋ/ *adj infml disapproving* very small or unimportant • *Their proposals to deal with the situation are piddling in comparison with the problem.* • *Exports were higher this year, though still piddling, at less than $1 billion.* • *I sold my television for the piddling sum of £5.*

pi·dgin /'pɪdʒ·ɪn/ *n* [C] a language which has developed from a mixture of two languages. It is used as a way of communicating by people who do not speak each other's languages. • *In the pidgin of Papua New Guinea, God is referred to as 'Big fella Papa'.* • *They were using pidgin* **English** *to make themselves understood.* • *(infml)* Pidgin is also a simple form of any language used by people who think that someone who speaks another language will find it easier to understand: *"He come quick?" she asked in pidgin* **English**.

pie /paɪ/ *n* a round pastry container in which meat, vegetables or fruit are cooked and which might also be covered with pastry • *pecan/pumpkin/apple pie* [U] • *Would you like some more pork pie?* [U] • *They sell a large selection of hot and cold pies.* [C] • Something which is **pie in the sky** is something you hope will happen but is unlikely to do so: *Their plans to set up their own business are just pie in the sky.* • A **pie chart** is a circle which is divided from its centre into several parts to show how a total amount is divided up: *The pie chart showed that 80% of the money had been spent on staff, 15% on buildings and 5% on equipment.* • A **pie crust** is *(Br)* the pastry on the top of a pie or *(Am and Aus)* the pastry on the top or bottom of a pie: *Bake until the pie crust is golden brown.* ○ *The recipe uses a delicious cheese pie crust.* [U] • *(infml)* **Pie-eyed** means very drunk. • *"You'll get pie in the sky when you die"* (Joe Hill in the song *The Preacher and the Slave*, 1911) • PIC **Bread and cakes**

pie·bald /£'paɪ·bɔːld, $-bɑːld/ *adj* [not gradable] (of an animal, esp. a horse) having a pattern of two different colours on its fur, esp. black and white • *piebald ponies*

piece PART /piːs/ *n* [C] a part of something • *a broken piece* **of** *stone/pottery* • *a torn piece* **of** *cloth/paper* • *a jagged piece* **of** *glass* • *a piece* **of** *bread/cake/pie* • *a piece* **of** *apple* • *chicken pieces* • *This jigsaw puzzle has two pieces missing.* • *The vase lay on the floor* **in** *small pieces* (= broken into small parts). • *The children were told to* **tear** *the paper* **into** *pieces.* • *She tried to* **break/tear** *a small piece* **off** *the edge.* • *We want to sell the business* **in one piece** (= without dividing it into smaller parts). • *The radio had been stolen, but otherwise we got the car back* **(all) in one piece** (= not damaged). • *The building was taken apart, transported across the Atlantic, and reassembled piece by piece* (= one part after another) *in America.* • *(infml)* If something is **a piece of cake**, it is very easy to do: *"Will you be able to fix the car by tomorrow morning?" "No problem – it'll be a piece of cake."* • *(infml) I'm going to* **give** *him/He's going to* **get a piece of** *my* **mind** (= I will make him understand that I am very angry with him). • **To pieces** means into smaller parts: *The cup must have been cracked – it just* **came/fell** *to pieces in my hand.* ○ *(Br) You can* **take** *the bookcase to pieces* (= separate it into the parts that make it up), *so it will fit in the back of your car.* • *(Br)* If something **comes to pieces** *(Am* **breaks down**), it has been designed so that it can be divided into smaller parts: *We've bought a picnic table and chairs that come to pieces for packing.* • If someone **goes/falls to pieces**, they become unable to think clearly and control their emotions because of something unpleasant or difficult that they have experienced: *She just goes to pieces in exams.* ○ *He went* **all** *to pieces after the accident.* • If an organization or system **goes/falls to pieces**, it fails: *Their marriage began to fall to pieces after only a few months.* • *(infml)* If you **pick/pull** someone or something **to pieces**, you criticize them severely: *The theatre critics picked the play to pieces in the papers the next morning.* ○ *The moment she'd left, the rest of the family started to pull her to pieces.* • Ⓕ

piece to·geth·er *obj*, **piece** *obj* **to·geth·er** *v adv* [M] • To piece together is to collect small amounts esp. of information to make a complete story: *We pieced together the details of the day before she died.*

piece ITEM /piːs/ *n* [C] a single item which is one of other similar items • *a piece* **of** *furniture/clothing/equipment* • *a piece* (= whole sheet) *of paper* • *a piece* **of** (= an item made of) *china* • *a piece* **of** *jewellery* • *a piece* **of** *legislation* • *a piece* **of** *software* • *a piece* **of** *information/advice* • *a piece* **of** *evidence* • *You can only take one piece* **of** *baggage with you onto the plane.* • A piece can be something which has been created by someone such as an artist, writer or musician: *an orchestral/piano/instrumental piece* ○ *a descriptive piece* **of** *writing* ○ *an autobiographical piece* ○ *a dramatic piece* **of** *theatre* ○ *a skilful piece of work/research* • A piece is also a single item which forms part of a set: *a chess piece* • A piece is also a coin, of which the value is usually stated: *The figure of Britannia appears on 50 pence pieces.* ○ *Could you swap me a 20p piece for two tens?* • In the past **pieces of eight** were gold coins. • *(slang)* **Piece of skirt/tail/***(esp. Am)* **ass** is used to refer to a woman as a sexually attractive object: *That Carol Ann sure is some piece of ass!* • Ⓕ

-piece /-piːs/ *combining form* • *a five-piece band* (= with five players) • *a four-piece set of saucepans* • *a 36-piece dinner service* • *a one-piece/two-piece swimsuit*

piece GUN /piːs/ *n* [C] *esp. dated or specialized* a gun • *an artillery piece* • *a hand piece* • *(Am slang) He was carrying a piece when he was arrested.* • Ⓕ

pi·èce de ré·sis·tance /piˌes·də·reɪ·zɪ'stɑːs̃/ *n* [C usually sing] *pl* **pièces de résistance** the most important or best thing in a set or group of things, often the last in a series of things • *She is always an entertaining speaker, but her pièce de résistance is the after-dinner speech.* • *The pièce de résistance of his stage act was an Elvis Presley impression.*

piece·meal /'piːs·miːl/ *adv, adj* [not gradable] *sometimes disapproving* not done according to a plan but done at different times in different ways • *Everything is being done piecemeal.* • *Without central funding, we have to push ahead in a piecemeal fashion.*

piece·work /£'piːs·wɜːk, $-wɜːrk/ *n* [U] *specialized* work for which the amount of pay depends on the number of items completed rather than the time spent making them

pied /paɪd/ *adj* [before n; not gradable] *specialized* (used esp. in the names of birds) having markings of two or more different colours, usually black and white • *pied kingfishers* • The **Pied Piper (of Hamelin)** is a character in a children's story who led all the children away from the town of Hamelin by playing beautiful music after the town officials refused to pay him for getting rid of all the RATS.

pied à terre /£pi,eɪ·dæt'eəʳ, $-'er/ *n* [C] *pl* **pieds à terre** a small house or apartment in a town or city which someone owns or rents in addition to their main home and which they use when visiting that town or city for a short time

pier BRIDGE /£pɪəʳ, $pɪr/ *n* [C] a long high structure, similar to a bridge, sticking out from the land into the sea, along which people can walk or to which large boats can be tied and which sometimes has restaurants or buildings with entertaining activities • *The pier has cafés, restaurants, boutiques and an anglers' gallery.* • A pier can also be a smaller lower structure which is situated in a large river and used esp. for getting into and out of boats: *There are daily summer sailings down the River Thames from Westminster Pier at 10.30 am and noon.*

pier COLUMN /£pɪəʳ, $pɪr/ *n* [C] *specialized* a strong thick column used to support a wall, roof or other structure • *brick piers* • *The large beams rest on steel corner posts trimmed with wood to resemble traditional wood piers.*

pierce *(obj)* /£pɪəs, $pɪrs/ *v* to go through (something), esp. in an exact or accurate manner or by making a carefully formed hole • *The needle pierces the fabric and then moves up, leaving a loop of thread beneath the fabric.* [T] • *The gun fires a shell capable of piercing* **(through)** *the armour of an enemy tank.* [T; I + *through*] • *The hole they drilled pierces 6 km* **into** *the earth's crust.* [I always + adv/prep] • *Davis pierced the Spurs defence with a brilliant pass.* [T] • *I couldn't wear these earrings because my ears aren't pierced/ I haven't got pierced* **ears** (= my ears haven't had the necessary holes made in them). [T] • *A few rays of sunlight pierced* (= shone through) *the smoke from the bonfire.* [T] • *The flashbulbs pierced the darkness like fireflies.* [T] • (J)

pierc·ing /£'pɪə·sɪŋ, $'pɪr-/ *adj* • *Troops have been issued with new* **armour**-*piercing anti-tank grenades.* • Piercing usually describes something that is unpleasant or uncomfortable because it goes deeply into something: *We shivered in the piercing wind.* ○ *She hadn't really meant to lie, but their piercing questions had forced her to.* • A piercing sound is high, loud and unpleasant: *The couple at the next table had piercing voices and we couldn't help overhearing.* ○ *A woman was having a baby upstairs and they could hear her groans and occasional piercing shrieks.* • A piercing look/gaze is one in which a person looks carefully at someone or something, esp. when they are trying to discover something, and makes people feel uncomfortable: *Mr Evans was a workaholic with a piercing gaze and a passion for punctuality.* • *(fig.) He looked straight at me with his piercing blue eyes.*

pierc·ingly /£'pɪə·sɪŋ·li, $'pɪr-/ *adv* • *The siren wailed piercingly in the cold morning air.*

pier·head /£'pɪə·hed, $'pɪr-/ *n* [C usually sing] the part of a PIER that is furthest from the land

pi·e·ty /£'paɪ·ə·ti, $'paɪə·t̬i/ *n* [U] *fml* See at PIOUS

pi·ez·o·el·ec·tric /£,piː·zəʊ·ɪ'lek·trɪk, $paɪ,iː·zoʊ-/ *adj* [not gradable] *specialized* producing electrical power by putting pressure on particular types of stone • *a piezoelectric device* • *Some natural crystals such as quartz are piezoelectric, which means they generate an electrical charge when they are pressed or distorted.*

pif·fle /'pɪf·l̩/ *n* [U] *infml dated* nonsense • *Pat really does talk a lot of piffle sometimes.*

pif·fling /'pɪf·l̩·ɪŋ, 'pɪf·lɪŋ/ *adj infml* ridiculously unimportant or small • *piffling details* • *a piffling amount*

pig ANIMAL /pɪg/, *Am also* **hog** *n* [C] a farm animal kept for its meat • *He keeps a few pigs.* • *Pigs have curly tails and make a grunting noise.* • *The meat produced from a pig is called pork, bacon or ham.* • *They're going to sell the pig farm.* • If you buy a **pig in a poke**, you buy something without seeing it or examining it carefully, so it might not be as good as you expected. • *(saying)* 'Pigs might fly' means 'I don't believe it': *"It's taking longer than I thought, but I'll have finished it by tomorrow." "And pigs might fly!"* • *(Br infml)* If you **make a pig's ear of** something you do it badly, wrongly or awkwardly: *He's made a real pig's ear of that bookcase he was supposed to be making.* • See also GUINEA PIG.

pig·gy /'pɪg·i/ *adj infml* • *The actress sued the paper for saying she had 'little piggy* (= small like a pig's) *eyes'.*

pig·gy /'pɪg·i/ *n* [C] *infml* • Piggy is a children's word for pig: *Look at those lovely little piggies!* • **Piggy/pig in the middle** is a game played by throwing a ball between two people over the head of a person who stands between them trying to catch it or *(fig.)* a person who is involved in an argument or disagreement between two groups but does not want to agree with either of them: *(fig.) Jeannie wants to go to Greece and Lesley wants to go to Italy – I'm just piggy in the middle – whatever I say will be wrong!* • When you give someone a **piggy back (ride)** you carry them on your back with their arms round your neck and their legs round your waist. • A **piggy bank** is a small container, sometimes in the shape of a pig, which is used by children for saving money.

pig·let /'pɪg·lət/ *n* [C] • *The sow had eight piglets* (= young pigs).

pig UNPLEASANT PERSON /pɪg/ *n* [C] *infml disapproving* a person who is unpleasant or difficult to deal with • *What a pig! He refused to help, even though he could see we were having trouble.* • *He was a real pig to her.* • *You pig! You knew I didn't want to you to do that.* [as form of address] • *(dated slang)* A pig is also a police officer. • *(Br)* If something is a pig (*Am* **bitch**) **(to** do) it is difficult or unpleasant: *Getting these clips to fit is a pig – as soon as one is on, the other comes off.* ○ *That tune is a pig* **to** *play.* [+ *to* infinitive]

pig BIG EATER /pɪg/ *n* [C] *infml* a person who eats too much • *You* **greedy** *pig! You're not having another chocolate biscuit!* [as form of address] • *They* **made (real) pigs of themselves** (= ate too much) *at the dinner.*

pig *(obj)* /pɪg/ *v* [always + adv/prep] **-gg-** *infml* • *She's always pigging herself* **on** *chocolate.* [T] • *We pigged* **out on** *the delicious cakes and pastries.* [I]

pig–out /'pɪg·aʊt/ *n* [C] *infml* • *Our holiday in France was just a two-week pig-out!*

pi·geon /'pɪdʒ·ən/ *n* a large usually grey bird, which is often seen in towns sitting on buildings in large groups, and is sometimes eaten as food • *wood pigeons* [C] • *roast pigeon* [U] • *pigeon pie* • *I bought some peanuts to feed to the pigeons in the square.* [C] • Some pigeons are kept as pets and take part in competitions to fly from a distant place to their home: *racing/homing pigeons* [C] • *(Br)* A **pigeon loft** is a building in which pigeons are kept. • *(Br)* If you say something **is/is not** your **pigeon** you mean it is/is not your responsibility or problem: *Transport? That's not my pigeon – ask Brian.* ○ *I'm afraid this letter's your pigeon.* • If a person is **pigeon-chested** their chest sticks out more than usual at the front and their shoulders appear to be pushed back. • *(Br and Aus)* A **pigeon fancier** keeps pigeons as pets. • A person who is **pigeon-toed** bends their feet in towards each other when they walk. • PIC **Birds**

pig·eon·hole /£'pɪdʒ·ən·həʊl, $-hoʊl/ *n* [C] one of a set of small boxes, open at the front, in which letters and messages are left for different people, esp. in an office or hotel • *Leave the report in my pigeonhole when you've read it.* • *A letter for Mr Redding? Look in the pigeonhole for 'R'.* • *Joe wants me to check his pigeonhole in the department on my way home* (= to see if there's anything in it). • *(usually disapproving)* If you **put** someone or something **in a pigeonhole** or **put** people or things **in pigeonholes** you make a (too) quick, simple or general decision about what they are like, what they need etc.: *You shouldn't try to put me in a neat pigeonhole – see me as an individual.* ○ *French manufacturers used to put their cars in tight social pigeonholes – Renaults, for example, were working-class cars.*

pig·eon·hole *obj* /£'pɪdʒ·ən·həʊl, $-hoʊl/ *v* [T] • To pigeonhole someone or something is to put them into a group or type: *He is a film producer who can't be conveniently pigeonholed.* • To pigeonhole also means to put away or leave until a later time: *Consultants found the experience frustrating – their reports were only partly implemented, or, worse still, just pigeonholed.*

pig·gy /'pɪg·i/ *adj infml disapproving* selfish • *How piggy! He could see I wanted that parking space, but he just went ahead and took it.*

pig·head·ed /,pɪg'hed·ɪd, '-,–/ *adj disapproving* showing unreasonable support for an opinion or plan of action and refusing to change or listen to different opinions • *Turner describes the main character as practical but very pigheaded – she doesn't listen to people as much as she should.*

pigheadedly /,pɪg'hed·ɪd·li/ *adv disapproving*

pig·head·ed·ness /,pɪg'hed·ɪd·nəs/ *n* [U] *disapproving*

pig i·ron *n* [U] a type of iron which is not pure

pig·let /'pɪg·lət/ *n* [C] See at PIG ANIMAL

pig·ment /'pɪg·mənt/ *n* a substance which gives something a particular colour when it is present in it, added to it or mixed with it • *Melanin is the dark brown* *pigment of the hair, skin and eyes which is present in varying amounts in people of all races.* [C] • *There is concern that some of the modelling clay may contain lead-based colour pigments which produce long-term health hazards.* [C] • *Pigment is mixed into oil, glue, egg, vegetable gum or wax to make paint.* • [U]

pig·men·ta·tion /ˌpɪg·mən'teɪ·ʃᵊn/ *n* [U] • Pigmentation is the natural colour of esp. a living thing: *In response to sunlight, skin increases its degree of pigmentation, making it darker.* ○ *The plant traditionally used for investigating the genetics of flower pigmentation is the petunia.*

pig·ment·ed /£pɪg'men·tɪd, $'pɪg·mən·t̬ɪd/ *adj* • *pigmented tissue/skin/areas*

Pig·my /'pɪg·mi/ *n* [C], *adj* PYGMY

pig·skin /'pɪg·skɪn/ *n* leather made from the skin of pigs • *a pigskin wallet* [U] • *pigskin gloves/shoes* • *(Am infml)* A pigskin is the ball used to play American football. [C]

pig·sty /'pɪg·staɪ/, *Am also* **pig·pen** /'pɪg·pen/ *n* [C] the building and enclosed area where pigs are kept, or *(fig.)* a dirty or untidy place • *(fig.) Your bedroom's a pigsty!*

pig·swill /'pɪg·swɪl/ *n* [U] waste food on which some pigs are fed, or *(fig.)* bad or unpleasant food • *(fig.) I can't eat this pigswill! Take it away!*

pig·tail /'pɪg·teɪl/ *n* [C] a length of hair which is tied at the back of the head and neck or at each side of the head in a PLAIT • *A little girl* **in** *pigtails presented the bouquet.*

pike FISH /paɪk/ *n* [C] *pl* **pike** or **pikes** a large fish which lives in lakes and rivers and eats other fish

pike ROAD /paɪk/ *n* [C] *Am for* TURNPIKE • *the Leesburg Pike*

pike WEAPON /paɪk/ *n* [C] a long sharp stick used in the past as a weapon • *A soldier with a pike could bring down a charging horse.*

pike HILL /paɪk/ *n* [C] *regional* a hill in northern England with a pointed top • Pike is usually used in the names of hills: *Scafell Pike*

pik·er /£'paɪ·kəʳ, $-kɚ/ *n* [C] *Aus infml* a person who avoids getting into difficult or dangerous situations

pike·staff /£'paɪk·stɑːf, $-stæf/ *n* [U] **as plain as a pikestaff**, see at PLAIN CLEAR

pi·lau /£'piː·laʊ, $pɪ'lɔː/, *Am and Aus usually* **pi·laf** /£'piː·læf, $piː'lɑːf/ *n* rice cooked in spicy liquid, often with vegetables or meat added • *chicken pilau* [U] • *I had a delicious mushroom pilau last night.* [C] • *barbecued pork with pilau* **rice**

pil·chard /£'pɪl·tʃəd, $-tʃɚd/ *n* [C] a small edible fish that lives in the sea. It is often preserved in a metal container in sauce. • *a* **tin of** *pilchards* • *pilchards in tomato sauce* • *It's good to include oily fish like mackerel, tuna, sardines and pilchards in your diet.*

pile MASS /paɪl/ *n, v* (to arrange objects, usually of the same type, into) a mass which is high in the middle or which is made from the objects put on top of each other • *a pile* **of** *sand/stones* [C] • *The bookshelves were full and there were piles* **of** *books all over the floor.* [C] • *I'm just working my way through a great pile* **of** *ironing.* [C] • *Wild dogs scavenge through rotting piles* **of** *rubbish.* [C] • *A fierce explosion turned the building into a pile* **of** *rubble and twisted steel.* [C] • *Her clothes lay on the floor* **in** *untidy piles.* [C] • *(infml) I've got piles/a pile* (= a lot) *of things to do today.* [C] • *(infml)* A pile can also be a large amount of money: *He* **made** *a pile selling computers and retired by the time he was forty.* [U] • *They piled more and more logs* **on/onto** *the fire.* [T always + adv/prep] • *Please pile your textbooks neatly* **on** *the table as you leave.* [T always + adv/prep] • *Snow was blowing across the fields and piling* **up** *against walls.* [I always + adv/prep] • *Her plate was piled* **(high) with** *salad.* [T always + adv/prep] • *My work is really piling* **up** (= There is an increasing amount of it to do). [I] • *(esp. Br)* **Pile it high (and) sell it cheap** is said about products which are made in large numbers and sold cheaply: *The lower end of the clothing market still survives by piling it high and selling cheap.* *(infml)* When someone **piles it on** they say too much, esp. giving too much emphasis: *You're really piling it on with the compliments tonight, Gareth, are you all right?* • *(Br infml)* If someone **piles on the agony** they make their problems seem much worse than they really are: *He was piling on the agony about his work situation – he clearly wanted a bit of sympathy.* • A **pile-up** is a traffic accident involving several vehicles which hit each other very hard: *This is the third serious pile-up at the interchange this month.*

pile COLUMN /paɪl/ *n* [C] a strong column or post of wood, steel or concrete which is pushed into the ground to help support a building • A **pile-driver** is a powerful machine which hammers piles into the ground.

pile MOVE /paɪl/ *v* [I always + adv/prep] *infml* (of a group of people) to move together, esp. in an uncontrolled way • *As soon as the train stopped, they all piled* **in.** • *The children piled* **out of/into** *the car excitedly.*

pile SURFACE /paɪl/ *n* [U] the soft surface made by the ends of many short threads on a CARPET (= material for covering a floor) or on cloth such as VELVET • *Come in and see our extensive range of luxurious* **deep-pile** *carpets.*

pile BUILDING /paɪl/ *n* [C] *esp. humorous* a large building • *They've got a great big Victorian pile somewhere out in the country.*

piles /paɪlz/ *pl n infml* HAEMORRHOIDS

pil·fer *(obj)* /£'pɪl·fəʳ, $-fɚ/ *v* to steal (things of small value) • *He was caught pilfering (sweets)* **from** *the shop.* [I/T]

pil·grim TRAVELLER /'pɪl·grɪm/ *n* [C] a person who makes a journey, which is often long and difficult, to a special place for religious reasons

pil·grim·age /'pɪl·grɪ·mɪdʒ/ *n* • A pilgrimage is a special journey made by a pilgrim: *Most Muslims try to* **make/go on** *a pilgrimage* **to** *Mecca at least once in their life.* [C] • *(fig.) For many football fans, the ground is a site* **of** *pilgrimage.* [U]

Pil·grim AMERICA /'pɪl·grɪm/ *n* [C] a member of the group of English people who sailed to America on the ship 'Mayflower' where they formed Plymouth Colony, Massachusetts in 1620

pill /pɪl/ *n* a small solid piece of medicine which a person swallows in one piece; a TABLET • *a sleeping pill* [C] • *My mother* **swallows/takes** *a whole load of pills every morning.* [C] • **The** pill (or *fml* a **contraceptive** pill) is a type of pill which a woman takes regularly, esp. every day, in order to prevent her from becoming pregnant: *Are you* **on the pill?** [U] • To **sweeten/sugar the pill** (*Am also* **sugar-coat** something) is to make something bad seem less unpleasant: *Plans to improve public services are seen as a way of sweetening the pill of increased taxation.* • *(infml)* **Pill-popping** is taking pills, esp. when this is a habit or when the pills are illegal drugs: *It was after the breakdown of her marriage that her pill-popping started to get out of control.* • Ⓙ

pil·lage *(obj)* /'pɪl·ɪdʒ/ *v fml* to steal (something) from (a place or a person) by using violence, esp. during war • *For years waves of invaders pillaged (towns along the coast) without anyone being able to stop them.* [I/T] • *Works of art were pillaged* **from** *many countries in the days of the Empire.* [T]

pil·lage /'pɪl·ɪdʒ/ *n* [U] *fml* • *rape and pillage*

pil·lar /£'pɪl·əʳ, $-ɚ/ *n* [C] a strong column made of stone, metal or wood which supports part of a building, or something generally of this shape • *Reinforced concrete pillars support the bridge.* • *The overhanging first storey rests on a row of pillars.* • *a pillar* **of** *smoke/flame* • *(fig.) Freda is a pillar* (= an active and important member) **of society/of the community/of** *the chess club.* • If someone or something goes **from pillar to post**, they are forced to go repeatedly from one place to another: *My parents were always on the move – my childhood was spent being* **dragged** *from pillar to post.* • *(Br)* A **pillar-box** is a type of POSTBOX found in the street. It looks like a large tube about one and a half metres high, and in Britain is a bright red, sometimes called pillar-box red. • *"The Seven Pillars of Wisdom"* (title of a book by T.E.Lawrence, 1926)

pill·box CONTAINER /£'pɪl·bɒks, $-bɑːks/ *n* [C] a small container which pills are carried in

pill·box BUILDING /£'pɪl·bɒks, $-bɑːks/ *n* [C] a very small building made from strong material, such as concrete, having narrow holes in the walls which guns can be fired through

pil·li·on /£'pɪl·i·ən, $'-jən/ *n* [C] *Br and Aus* a seat or place behind the person riding a motorcycle where a passenger can sit • *a pillion seat/passenger*

pil·li·on /£'pɪl·i·ən, $'-jən/ *adv* [not gradable] *Br and Aus* • *You get a bit uncomfortable after* **riding** *pillion for a couple of hours.*

pil·lock /'pɪl·ək/ *n* [C] *Br slang* a stupid or silly person • *The man's a complete pillock.* • *You pillock, look what you've done!* [as form of address]

pil·lo·ry *obj* /£'pɪl·ᵊr·i, $-ɚ·i/ *v* [T] to severely criticize (someone), esp. in a public way • *Although regularly pilloried by the press as an obnoxious loudmouth, he is, nonetheless, an effective politician.*

pil·low /£ˈpɪl·əʊ, $-oʊ/ *n* [C] a rectangular cloth bag filled with soft material, such as feathers or artificial fibres, used for supporting a person's head when they are in bed • *Do you prefer a feather pillow or a foam pillow?* • Pillow is also *Am for* CUSHION. • **Pillow talk** is conversation which people who love each other have when they are in bed together. • Compare CUSHION. • [PIC] **Beds and bedroom**

pil·low·case /£ˈpɪl·əʊ·keɪs, $-oʊ-/, **pil·low·slip** /£ˈpɪl·əʊ·slɪp, $-oʊ-/ *n* [C] a cloth cover for a PILLOW which can easily be removed and washed

pi·lot [AIRCRAFT] /ˈpaɪ·lət/ *n* [C] a person who flies an aircraft • *a fighter/helicopter/bomber/airline pilot*

pi·lot *obj* /ˈpaɪ·lət/ *v* [T] • *She piloted the aircraft to safety after one of the engines failed.*

pi·lot [TEST] /ˈpaɪ·lət/ *adj* [before n; not gradable] (of a plan, product or system) used to judge how good something is before introducing it or making many of them • *a pilot programme/study* • *If the (Br and Aus) pilot* **scheme**/*(Am) pilot* **program** *is successful many more homes will be offered the new television service.*

pi·lot /ˈpaɪ·lət/ *n* [C] • A pilot is a television programme which is made to introduce and test the acceptance of a suggested television series: *If you'd seen the pilot, you'd know why they decided not to make a complete series of programmes!*

pi·lot *obj* /ˈpaɪ·lət/ *v* [T] • *We shall pilot several new cosmetic products* **to** *selected potential purchasers.*

pi·lot *obj* [INTRODUCE] /ˈpaɪ·lət/ *v* [T always + adv/prep] *esp. Br* to try to introduce (a system or a law) and protect it until it is established • *Twenty years ago he piloted a bill* **through** *Parliament on working conditions.*

pi·lot [SHIP] /ˈpaɪ·lət/ *n* [C] a person with detailed knowledge of an area of water, such as that around a port, who goes onto a ship to direct it safely

pi·lot *obj* /ˈpaɪ·lət/ *v* [T]

pi·lot (light) /ˈpaɪ·lət/ *n* [C] a small flame which burns all the time in a gas device, such as a cooker or a water heater, and which starts the main flame burning when the gas is turned on • [PIC] **Bathroom**

pi·men·to /£pɪˈmen·təʊ, $-toʊ/, *Am usually* **pi·mi·en·to** /£pɪˈmjen·təʊ, $-toʊ/ *n* [C/U] *pl* **pimentos** a sweet red PEPPER (= roundish hollow vegetable)

pimp /pɪmp/ *n* [C] a man who controls PROSTITUTES (= people who are paid to have sex), esp. by finding customers for them, and takes some of the money that they earn

pimp /pɪmp/ *v* [I] • *He eventually fell into the world of robbery, pimping and finally, murder.*

pimple /ˈpɪm·pl̩/ *n* [C] a small raised spot on the skin which is temporary

pimp·ly (**-ier**, **-iest**) /ˈpɪm·pl̩·i, ˈ-pli/, **pim·pled** /ˈpɪm·pl̩d/ *adj* • *a pimply face* • *a pimply adolescent/youth*

pin [METAL STICK] /pɪn/ *n* [C] a thin metal stick with a point at one end, esp. used for temporarily holding pieces of cloth together or used generally for holding things together • *I'll keep the patch in place with pins while I sew it on.* • *a hand-grenade pin* • *a three-pin plug* • A pin can also be decorative and used as jewellery: *a hat/tie pin* • Pin is also *Am for* BROOCH. • *(infml)* **Pin money** is a small amount of extra money which a person earns to buy things they want but do not need. • If someone has **pins and needles** in a part of their body they feel slight sharp pains in it, usually just after they have moved from being still in one position for a long time. • **on pins and needles** is *Am for* **on tenterhooks**. • Compare NEEDLE [SEWING TOOL]. • [PIC] **Pins and needles, Plugs**

pin *obj* /pɪn/ *v* [T] **-nn-** • *A large picture of the president was pinned* **to/(up) on** *the office wall.* • *She wore a white jacket with a little anchor emblem pinned* **on** *the collar.* • *She had pinned* **up** *her lovely long hair.* • If someone **pins** their **hopes on** something or someone they depend on it for success or to help them in some way: *You shouldn't pin all your hopes on getting the job – why don't you apply for some others.* • A **pin-up** is a picture of a sexually attractive, usually famous, person, esp. wearing few clothes or *(infml)* a person who is often seen in such pictures : *Every wall in her bedroom was covered with pin-ups of her favourite pop-star.* ○ *With his perfect college-boy looks he's the latest teenage pin-up.* • *(Am dated)* When a young man pins a young woman, he gives her a piece of jewellery to show that they love each other: *Did you hear that Hugo pinned Kim?*

pin *obj* [KEEP STILL] /pɪn/ *v* [T always + adv/prep] **-nn-** to keep (someone or something) in the same position or place

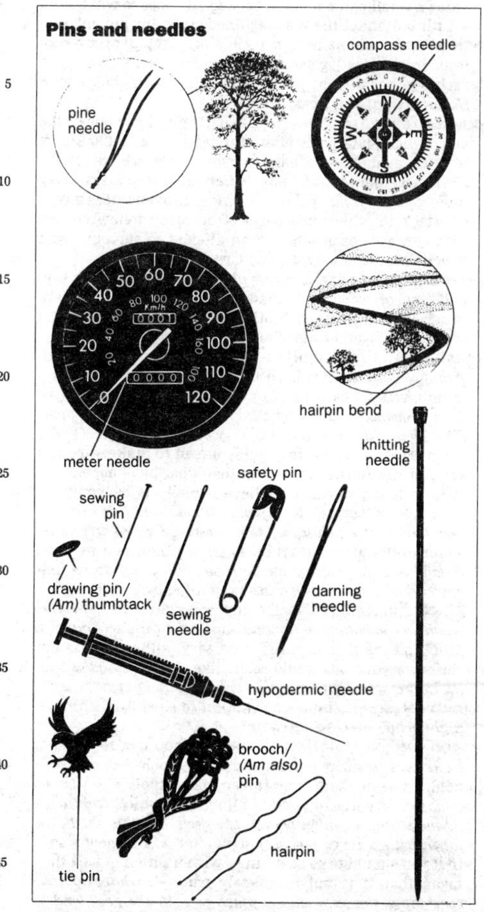

• *Fallen rubble kept her pinned* **to** *the ground until she was rescued.* • *Enemy fire pinned* **down** *a group of soldiers in a bunker.* [M] • *Conner won most of his wrestling matches by pinning* (= holding both shoulders of) *his opponent to the mat.* • *(fig.) You can't pin* (= fix) *the blame* **on** *her – she wasn't there when the accident happened.* • *(Br infml)* If someone tells you to **pin back** your **ears** or **pin** your **ears back**, they are telling you to listen to what they are going to say. • To **pin** someone **down** is to force them to make a decision or provide details: *He's really difficult to pin down – you'll have to be persistent.* • To **pin down** something is to discover exact details about it: *We know there's been a radiation leak, but we can't pin down the place or time of its origin.*

pin /pɪn/ *n* [C] *specialized* • In the game of CHESS, a pin is a special move which stops the other player from moving one of their pieces, because to move it will put another more valuable piece in danger: *That nasty pin stopped me from moving my knight.*

pin [LEG] /pɪn/ *n* [C usually pl] *dated humorous* a leg • *Grandpa's very old now and he's a bit shaky on his pins.*

PIN (num·ber) /pɪn/ *n* [C] *abbreviation for* personal identification number (= a secret number which a person uses together with a special card to obtain money from their bank account from a machine outside the bank) • *I have to write my PIN number down somewhere secret in case I forget it.*

pi·na·fore [LOOSE CLOTHING] /£ˈpɪn·ə·fɔːʳ, $-fɔːr/, *Br and Aus infml* **pinny** *n* [C] a piece of clothing which is worn over the front of other clothes to keep them clean while you are doing something dirty, esp. cooking

pi·na·fore [DRESS] *Br and Aus* /£ˈpɪn·ə·fɔːʳ, $-fɔːr/, *Br* **pi·na·fore dress**, *Am and Aus* **jump·er** *n* [C] a loose dress with no sleeves which is usually worn over other clothing such as a shirt • [PIC] **Clothes**

pin·ball /£ˈpɪm·bɔːl, $ˈpɪn·bɑːl/ *n* [U] a game played on a special machine like a large box on legs in which the player keeps a small ball bouncing between devices to win points • A **pinball machine** is a machine for playing pinball on.

pince–nez /ˌpæ̃ːnsˈneɪ/ *n* [C + sing/pl v] *pl* **pince-nez** (esp. in the past) glasses held on a person's nose by a spring rather than by pieces which fit around their ears • *He wore* **(a pair of)** *pince-nez.*

pin·cer /£ˈpɪnt·sər, $-sɚ/ *n* [C usually pl] either one of the pair of hand-like parts of an animal such as a CRAB or a LOBSTER made of two hard curved pieces which can be closed together to hold things • *Careful of its pincers – they could give you a nasty nip.* • A **pincer movement** is a type of attack in which two parts of an army follow curved paths towards each other in an attempt to surround and then defeat the enemy. • [PIC] **Crustaceans**

pin·cers /£ˈpɪnt·səz, $-sɚz/ *pl n* a tool for pulling esp. nails out of wood. It is made of two curved metal bars which move against each other so that when the handles are pushed together the other ends close tightly. • (J)

pinch *(obj)* [PRESS] /pɪntʃ/ *v* to press (esp. someone's skin) strongly between two hard things such as a finger and a thumb, usually causing pain • *Ouch! Stop pinching (me)!* [I/T] • *She accidentally pinched her hand* **in the front door.** [T] • *These shoes are too tight, they pinch (my feet).* [I/T] • If you say that you have to **pinch** yourself **to make sure** you **are not dreaming**, you mean that what has happened is so good that you cannot believe it really is happening: *I can't believe that he's back from Canada and he's mine – I keep having to pinch myself to make sure I'm not dreaming.* • *(dated)* If you **pinch and scrape** or **pinch pennies** you spend as little money as possible: *When we were first married we had to pinch and scrape to get by.*

pinch /pɪntʃ/ *n* [C usually sing] • *He* **gave** *her a playful pinch on the bottom.* • *(Br and Aus)* **At a pinch**/*(Am)* **In a pinch** means if it is really necessary, although it is not perfect or what one would really like: *I need £2000 to set up the project, but I suppose £1500 would do at a pinch.*

pinch *obj* [STEAL] /pɪntʃ/ *v* [T] *infml* to steal (something) • *Right, who's pinched my chair?*

pinch [AMOUNT] /pɪntʃ/ *n* [C] a small amount of something, such as a powder, esp. the amount which a person can hold between their first finger and thumb • *While the tomatoes are cooking add a pinch* **of** *salt/sugar/dried thyme* • *(fig.) Opinion polls on subjects like this should be taken with a large pinch of scepticism.* • If someone says that you should **take** something **with a pinch of salt** they mean that it is not completely true: *You have to take everything she says with a pinch of salt, she does tend to exaggerate.*

pinched /pɪntʃt/ *adj* (of someone's face) thin and pale • *He had that pinched look which suggests poverty and undernourishment.*

pin·cu·shion /£ˈpɪŋˌkʊʃ·ən, $ˈpɪn-/ *n* [C] a small usually flat bag filled with soft material into which pins can be partly pushed to keep them together

pine (tree) /paɪn/ *n* an evergreen tree that grows in cooler areas of the world • *a plantation of pines* [C] • *ancient woods of pine* (= pine trees) *and fir* [U] • Pine is also the wood of pine trees, which is usually pale in colour: *pine furniture* ○ *Pine is a softwood.* [U] • **Pine cones** are the hard egg-shaped parts of the pine tree which open and release seeds. • **Pine needles** are the thin pointed leaves of a pine tree. • **Pine nuts** (*Br and Aus also* **pine kernels**) are the white seeds of the pine tree, which are often used in cooking. • [PIC] **Cone, Nut, Pins and needles, Tree**

pi·ny, pine·y /ˈpaɪ·ni/ *adj* **pinier, piniest** • *There was a lovely fresh piny smell as we walked into the forest.*

pine (a·way) /paɪn/ *v* [I] to become increasingly thin and weak because of unhappiness, esp. after the death of a loved person • *When Carter died in 1904 after an accident, Leno pined and died in London six months later.*

pine for *obj v prep* [T] to strongly desire (esp. something which is difficult or impossible to obtain) • *It's at this time of year that I start to pine for the snow-topped mountains.* • *As a young girl living in Coventry I always used to pine for a more glamorous existence.*

pine·ap·ple /ˈpaɪnˌæp·l̩/ *n* [C/U] (the juicy yellow flesh of) a large tropical fruit with a rough orange or brown skin and a group of pointed leaves on top • *tinned pineapples* • *pineapple juice* • [PIC] **Fruit**

ping /pɪŋ/ *n, v* [I] (to make) a short sharp sound • *We heard the small stones ping against our window.* • Ping is also *Am and Aus for* PINK [ENGINE NOISE].

Ping–Pong /£ˈpɪŋ·pɒŋ, $-pɑːŋ/ *n* [U] *trademark infml for* **table tennis**, see at TABLE [FURNITURE]

pin·head [END] /ˈpɪn·hed/ *n* [C] a small piece of metal or plastic on the flat end of a pin • *The fault was caused by a hole in the metal no larger than a pinhead.*

pin·head [PERSON] /ˈpɪn·hed/ *n* [C] *infml disapproving* a stupid person

pin·hole /£ˈpɪn·həʊl, $-hoʊl/ *n* [C] a very small hole made by or as if by a pin

pin·ion *obj* [HOLD] /ˈpɪn·jən/ *v* [T] to hold (someone), esp. by the arms, to prevent them from moving • *He was pinioned* **to** *the wall by two men while another one repeatedly punched him.*

pin·ion [DEVICE] /ˈpɪn·jən/ *n* [C] a small wheel with teeth-like parts around its edge which fit against similar parts around the edge of a larger wheel or along the side of a RACK (= bar with teeth-like parts) • *a rack-and-pinion assembly*

pink [COLOUR] /pɪŋk/ *adj, n* **-er, -est** (of) a pale red colour • *pink flowers* • *She's very fond of pink.* [U] • *What a lovely dress you're wearing – it's such a pretty pink.* [C] • *Have you been in the sun? Your nose is a bit pink.* • *(esp. humorous)* If someone is **in the pink** they are in very good health. • *(esp. Am)* If a job is described as **pink-collar** it means it is traditionally done by a woman: *Until recently secretarial work and nursing were very much pink-collar professions.* • *(humorous)* If you say that someone has seen **pink elephants**, you mean that they have imagined seeing something because they were drunk. • The *(Br)* **pink pound**/*(Am)* **pink dollar** is the spending-power of homosexuals: *Companies are just becoming aware of the power of the pink pound, and some are now beginning to target this section of the community.* • *(Am infml)* A **pink slip** is a document given to a person telling them they have been dismissed from their job. • *(Am infml)* If someone or something is **pink-slipped** they are told that what they do, such as work, is no longer needed: *After months of poor viewing figures the series has been pink-slipped.* • (J)

pink·ish /ˈpɪŋ·kɪʃ/ *adj* • Pinkish means slightly pink: *a pinkish blue*

pink·ness /ˈpɪŋk·nəs/ *n* [U]

pink [PLANT] /pɪŋk/ *n* [C] a small garden plant which has sweet-smelling pink, white or red flowers and narrow grey-green leaves, or one of its flowers • (J)

pink [ENGINE NOISE] *Br* /pɪŋk/, *Am and Aus* **ping** *v* [I] (of a car engine) to make a high knocking sound because the fuel is not burning correctly • (J)

pink [POLITICS] /pɪŋk/ *adj* **-er, -est** *dated disapproving* (of a person) partly supporting SOCIALIST ideas and principles • (J)

pink·o /£ˈpɪŋ·kəʊ, $-koʊ/ *n* [C] *pl* **pinkos** or **pinkoes** *dated disapproving* • *Right-wing politicians thought his anti-hanging stance made him a pinko.*

pink·ie /ˈpɪŋ·ki/, **pink·y** *n* [C] *Am, Aus and Scot Eng* the smallest finger of a person's hand

pink·ing shears /ˈpɪŋ·kɪŋ/ *pl n* special SCISSORS (= a type of cutting device) with small V-shaped parts along the blades which make an uneven edge when they cut cloth, so that threads do not easily come out

pin·na·cle [SUCCESS] /ˈpɪn·ə·kl̩/ *n* [C usually sing] the most successful or admirable part of a system or achievement • *Once considered* **the** *pinnacle* **of** *human achievement, climbing Mount Everest now is almost commonplace.* • *The Olympics represent* **the** *pinnacle* **of** *competition and achievement.* • *By the age of thirty-two she had* **reached the** *pinnacle* **of** *her career.*

pin·na·cle [TOP] /ˈpɪn·ə·kl̩/ *n* [C usually pl] a small pointed tower on top of a building, or the top part of a tall pointed tower or a mountain • *The pinnacles of the Himalayas were visible above the clouds.*

pinny /ˈpɪn·i/ *n* [C] *Br and Aus infml for* PINAFORE [LOOSE CLOTHING]

pin·point *obj* [POSITION] /£ˈpɪm·pɔɪnt, $ˈpɪn-/ *v* [T] to give or discover the exact position in space and/or time of (something) • *We are, as yet, unable to pinpoint the source of the transmissions.* • *It is not possible to pinpoint precisely the time of death.* • *(fig.) Emergency workers at the site are still unable to pinpoint* (= discover exactly) *the cause of the explosion.*

pin·point /£ˈpɪm·pɔɪnt, $ˈpɪn-/ *adj* [before n; not gradable] • *These missiles can be fired with pinpoint* (= very exact) **accuracy** *using laser guidance systems.*

pin·point [SMALL AREA] /£ˈpɪm·pɔɪnt, $ˈpɪn-/ *n* [C] a very small area or spot • *a pinpoint* **of** *light*

pin·prick /£ˈpɪm·prɪk, $ˈpɪn-/ *n* [C usually pl] something which is slightly annoying for a short time • *You have to ignore the pinpricks and just get on with the job.*

pin·stripe /ˈpɪn·straɪp/ *n* [U] a usually dark cloth with a pattern of narrow, usually paler, parallel lines • *Jackets, in flannel, pinstripe and tweed, were fitted and usually flared from the waist.* • *He was wearing a pinstripe suit.* • [PIC›] **Patterns**

pin·striped /ˈpɪn·straɪpt/ *adj* [not gradable] • *a pinstriped business suit*

pin·stripes /ˈpɪn·straɪps/ *pl n* • Pinstripes refers to SUITS (= men's matching jackets and trousers) made of pinstriped cloth: *She watched the businessmen walk past in their pinstripes.*

pint /paɪnt/ *n* [C] a measure for liquid equal to about half a litre • *Should I buy one pint* **of milk** *or two?* • *(Br infml)* A pint is also used in a general way to mean (a pint of) beer: *He usually goes out for a pint at lunchtime.* ○ *"Do you want a pint?" "No, just a half for me, thanks."* • *(infml esp. disapproving)* If someone or something is **pint-sized /pint-size**, they are small and not important: *Don't worry about him, he's just a pint-sized nobody.* • [LP›] **Units**

pint·a /£ˈpaɪn·tə, $-t̬ə/ *n* [C] *Br infml dated* a PINT of milk • *"Drinka Pinta Milka Day"* (advertisement for the British Milk Marketing Board by Bertram Whitehead, 1958)

pin·wheel /ˈpɪn·wiːl/ *n* [C] *Am for* WINDMILL (= a child's toy)

pi·o·neer [DISCOVERER] /£ˌpaɪəˈnɪəʳ, $-ˈnɪr/ *n* [C] a person who does something for the first time or discovers how to do something • *He was operated on by Ben Saling, the heart transplant pioneer.* • *The stamp, featuring computer pioneer Charles Babbage, will be launched tomorrow.* • *He is best-known as a pioneer social historian.*

pi·o·neer *obj* /£ˌpaɪəˈnɪəʳ, $-ˈnɪr/ *v* [T] • *Universities that have pioneered new industries in the past are now under severe economic stress.*

pi·o·neer·ing /£ˌpaɪəˈnɪə·rɪŋ, $-ˈnɪr·ɪŋ/ *adj* • *pioneering techniques* • *Her pioneering work with the treatment of chronic pain has given many sufferers renewed hope.*

pi·o·neer [FIRST PERSON] /£ˌpaɪəˈnɪəʳ, $-ˈnɪr/ *n* [C usually pl] one of the first people to live in a new area • *The pioneers cut down forests and planted crops.*

pi·ous [RELIGIOUS] /ˈpaɪ·əs/ *adj* strongly believing in God or a particular religion, and living in a way which shows this belief • *She is a pious follower of the faith, never missing her prayers.*

pi·ous·ly /ˈpaɪ·ə·sli/ *adv*

pi·e·ty /£ˈpaɪ·ə·ti, $ˈpaɪə·t̬i/, **pi·ous·ness** /ˈpaɪ·ə·snəs/ *n* [U] *fml* • *The fame of his piety led to his being appointed the abbot of a monastery at Vicovaro.* • *The reformers attached great importance to personal hygiene, industriousness and piety.*

pi·ous [PRETENDING] /ˈpaɪ·əs/ *adj disapproving* pretending to have sincere feelings • *Quit the pious apologies – I know you don't really care.* • *(Br)* Something which is a **pious hope** is unlikely to happen: *A pay rise this year? That's a rather pious hope, isn't it!*

pi·ous·ly /ˈpaɪ·ə·sli/ *adv*

pip [SEED] /pɪp/ *n* [C] one of the small seeds of an edible fruit such as an apple or an orange • Compare STONE [SEED]. • [PIC›] **Fruit**

pip *obj* [BEAT] /pɪp/ *v* [T] **-pp-** *Br infml* to beat (someone) either by a very small amount or right at the end of a competition • *In this final race the challenger pipped the champion by only five metres.* • *We both wanted the promotion but I was* **pipped at the post** (= beaten) *by the other candidate.*

pip [SOUND] /pɪp/ *n* [C usually pl] *esp. Br* a short high sound, esp. one of a series • *She turned on the radio and heard the five o'clock pips.*

pipe [TUBE] /paɪp/ *n* [C] a long round tube usually made from metal, plastic or concrete, inside which liquid or gas flows to move from one place to another • *a water/gas/sewer pipe* • *a burst/fractured/leaking pipe* • *The old underground system of pipes is now in a serious state of decay.* • [PIC›] **Pipe** Ⓣ

pipe *obj* /paɪp/ *v* [T always + adv/prep, usually passive] • *Hot water is piped* **to** *all apartments from the central boiler room.* • *(esp. disapproving)* **Piped music** is music which has been recorded and is then played quietly and continuously in public places, esp. to make people feel relaxed.

pip·ing /ˈpaɪ·pɪŋ/ *n* [U] • Piping refers to either pipes in general or a particular system of pipes: *He hit her with a piece of lead piping.*

pipe [TOBACCO] /paɪp/ *n* [C] a short narrow tube with a small container at one end, used for smoking esp. tobacco • *I ordered some tea for myself and* **lit** *my pipe.* • *(dated or humorous)* The phrase **put/stick** that **in your pipe and smoke it** is used in anger to mean that what you have just said or done will have to be accepted even though it will not be liked. • A **pipe cleaner** is a piece of wire covered with soft fibres which is used to clean a pipe. • If an idea or a plan is a **pipe dream** it is impossible or very unlikely to happen: *Her plans of becoming an opera singer will never be more than a pipe dream – her voice is really not good enough.* • *"So put that in your pipe, my Lord Otto, and smoke it!"* (The Rev. Richard Harris Barham in the poem "The Lay of St Odille' from *The Ingoldsby Legends*, 1837) • [PIC›] **Pipe** Ⓣ

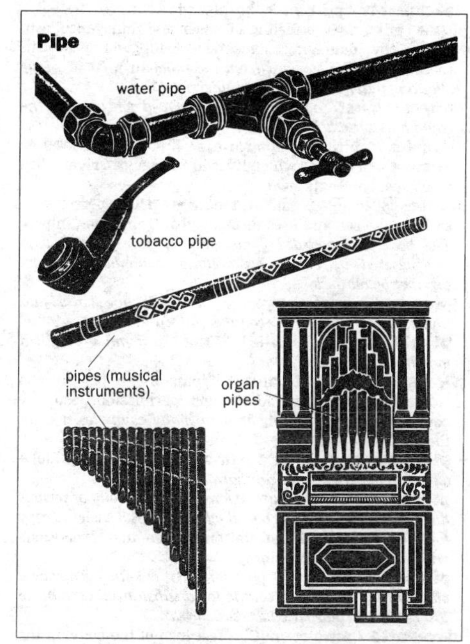

pipe *(obj)* [SPEAK] /paɪp/ *v* to speak, esp. in a high voice and suddenly • *"Don't do that," he piped, in a state of great excitement.* [+ clause] • *To everyone's surprise the child piped* **up** *in protest.* [I] • *(infml) Will you* **pipe down** (= stop talking or making noise), *I'm trying to read!* Ⓣ

pipe [INSTRUMENT] /paɪp/ *n* [C] a simple musical instrument made of a short narrow tube which is played by blowing through it • Pipes are also the metal or wood tubes in an ORGAN (= large musical instrument) which air is pushed through to make sound. • [PIC›] **Pipe** Ⓣ

pipes /paɪps/ *pl n* • Pipes is another word for BAGPIPES.

pip·er /£ˈpaɪ·pəʳ, $-pɚ/ *n* [C] • *We could hear a lone piper* (= BAGPIPE player) *playing.*

pipe·line /ˈpaɪp·laɪn/ *n* [C] a very long large tube, often underground, through which liquid or gas can flow for long distances • Something which is **in the pipeline** is being planned: *The theatre company has several new productions in the pipeline for next season.* • [PIC›] **Energy, Line**

pip·ette /£pɪˈpet, $paɪ-/ *n* [C] a thin glass tube used esp. in biology and chemistry for measuring or moving a small amount of liquid • [PIC›] **Laboratory**

pip·ing [DECORATION] /ˈpaɪ·pɪŋ/ *n* [U] a narrow strip of cloth used to decorate the edges of clothes or furniture, or (*Am* **decoration**) a narrow line of ICING used to decorate a cake • [PIC›] **Bread and cakes**

pip·ing [TEMPERATURE] /ˈpaɪ·pɪŋ/ *adv* [not gradable] **piping hot** *usually approving* (of food or drinks) very hot • *I like my tea piping hot.*

pip·squeak /ˈpɪp·skwiːk/ *n* [C] *infml disapproving* someone who is unimportant and does not deserve respect

pi·quant [INTERESTING] /ˈpiː·kᵊnt, -kɑːnt/ *adj slightly fml* interesting and exciting, esp. because mysterious • *More piquant details of the former official's private life were revealed.*

pi·quan·cy /ˈpiː·kᵊnt·si/ *n* [U] *slightly fml* • *New proposals have added piquancy to the debate.*

pi·quant·ly /ˈpiː·kᵊnt·li, -kɑːnt-/ *adv slightly fml*

pi·quant [SPICY] /ˈpiː·kᵊnt, -kɑːnt/ *adj* having a pleasant sharp or spicy taste • *a piquant mixture of spices*

pi·quan·cy /ˈpiː·kᵊnt·si/ *n* [U]

pi·quant·ly /ˈpiː·kᵊnt·li, -kɑːnt-/ *adv*

pique /piːk/ *n* [U] a feeling of anger and annoyance, esp. caused by damaging someone's feeling of pride in themselves • *He stormed from the room* **in a fit of** *pique shouting that he had been misunderstood.*

piqued /piːkt/ *adj* • *He seemed piqued when I said he could have tried harder.*

pi·ran·ha /£pɪˈrɑː·nə, $pəˈrɑː·njə/ *n* [C] *pl* **piranhas** or **piranha** a fierce fish which lives in S American rivers, has sharp teeth and eats meat

pi·rate CRIMINAL /£ˈpaɪ·rət, $ˈpaɪr·ət/ *n* [C] a person who sails on the sea and uses force to steal from other ships • *The boat was boarded by a gang of four pirates, who overpowered its seven-man crew and handcuffed them together below deck.*

pi·ra·cy /£ˈpaɪ·rə·si, $ˈpaɪr·ə-/ *n* [U] • *Piracy is alive and flourishing on the world's commercial sea-lanes.*

pi·rat·i·cal /£paɪˈræt·ɪ·kᵊl, $-ˈræt̬-/ *adj fml* • *piratical merchants*

pi·rate *obj* STEAL /£ˈpaɪ·rət, $ˈpaɪr·ət/ *v* [T] to use (someone's work) without their permission, esp. by copying and then selling it • *In many countries it's not illegal to pirate software.*

pi·rat·ed /£ˈpaɪ·rə·tɪd, $ˈpaɪr·ə·t̬ɪd/ *adj* [not gradable] • *a pirated video* • *pirated software*

pi·rate /£ˈpaɪ·rət, $ˈpaɪr·ət/ *n* [C] • *One group of pirates has made a small circuit board which makes it easier to copy tapes.* • A pirate radio station is one that broadcasts without official permission.

pi·ra·cy /£ˈpaɪ·rə·si, $ˈpaɪr·ə-/ *n* [U] • *software piracy* • *video piracy* • *Piracy accounts for a substantial amount of lost revenue to video producers each year.*

pi·rou·ette /ˌpɪr·uˈet/ *n* [C] a fast turn of the body on the toes or the front part of the foot, performed esp. by a BALLET dancer • *He swirled round in well-controlled pirouettes before lifting Juliet up and around his body with grace and strength.*

pi·rou·ette /ˌpɪr·uːˈet/ *v* [I] • *(humorous) Lunging for the ball she slipped, pirouetted* (= turned round) *gracelessly and ended up sitting on the grass.*

Pi·sces /ˈpaɪ·siːz/ *n* [not after *the*] the twelfth sign of the ZODIAC, relating to the period 20 February to 20 March, represented by two fish, or a person born during this period • *People born* **under** *Pisces* (= during this period) *are supposed to be very intuitive.* [U] • *Kate's a Pisces.* [C]

Pi·sce·an /£ˈpaɪ·si·ən, £-ˈ--, $ˈpaɪ·si-/ *n, adj* [not gradable] • *Pisceans tend to be dreamy characters.* [C] • *I have most of the typical piscean traits.*

piss URINE /pɪs/ *n, v slang* (to excrete) urine • *What a disgusting toilet – there was piss all over the floor.* [U] • *I'll be with you in a minute, I need (to* **have)** *a* **piss** (= to urinate). [U] • *There was a dog pissing* **on** *our gatepost.* [I] • To **piss yourself** is to lose control and urinate over yourself and the clothes you are wearing or *(fig.)* to laugh very much: *He laughed so much he nearly pissed himself.* ○ *She told such a funny story that we were pissing ourselves (with laughter).* • *(Br)* When a person **takes the piss (out of)** someone or something, they joke about them: *I'm not sure if he was serious or taking the piss when he said he liked the film.* • Someone who is **piss-poor** has very little or no money, something that is **piss-poor** is very low quality: *I'm sick of being piss-poor.* ○ *This film is truly dreadful – a piss-poor production.* • *(Br)* A **piss-take** is an act of joking about something or pretending something: *Is this a piss-take or have I really won £1 000 000?* • *(Br)* If someone **does a piss-take** of another person they copy their behaviour and manner in a way which is amusing because it emphasizes the details of what the person does. • *(Br)* A **piss artist** is either a person who does not do things correctly or someone who is often drunk. See also PISSED.

piss RAIN /pɪs/ *v* [I] *Br and Aus slang* to rain heavily • *It's really pissing* **(down)** *here at the moment.*

piss *(obj)* **a·bout/a·round** *v adv Br and Aus slang* to behave in a foolish way; to waste (someone's) time • *Look we haven't got much time so stop pissing about.* [I] • *Stop pissing me about and just tell me where they are.* [T]

piss a·way *obj*, **piss** *obj* **a·way** *v adv* [M] *slang* to waste (an opportunity) • *You've got another chance to qualify so don't piss away your chances again by not training enough.*

piss off GO *v adv* [I] *Br and Aus slang* to go away • *Let's piss off before the boss gets back and sees what we've done.* • Piss off is often used as an offensive way of telling someone to go away: *Why don't you just piss off – you've caused enough problems already!*

piss off *obj* ANNOY, **piss** *obj* **off** *v adv* [M] *slang* to annoy (someone) • *Her arrogance really pisses me off.*

pissed off /pɪst/, *Am also* **pissed** /pɪst/ *adj* [after v] *Br and Aus slang* • *He was fairly pissed off, to say the least, when all his gear was stolen.*

pissed /pɪst/ *adj* [after v] *Br and Aus slang* drunk • *She was pissed most of the time when she was a student.* • *(Br)* If someone is **pissed as a newt/fart** or **pissed out of** their **head/mind/skull** they are very drunk. • See also **piss artist** at PISS URINE.

piss·er /£ˈpɪs·əʳ, $-ɚ/ *n* [C] *Am taboo slang* something which is unusually or noticeably bad • *There was some pisser of a film about a boy and his dog on TV last night.* • A pisser can also be something extremely good or humorous: *That new comic is a pisser!* ○ *It was a pisser of a party!*

pis·soir /£ˈpɪs·wɑːʳ, $piːˈswɑːr/ *n* [C] a small building in which people, esp. men, can urinate; a public toilet

piss·pot /£ˈpɪs·pɒt, $-pɑːt/ *n* [C] *Aus slang* a person who drinks a lot of alcohol very often • *Patrick's a real pisspot.*

piss–up /ˈpɪs·ʌp/ *n* [C] *Br and Aus slang* an occasion when a lot of alcohol is drunk

pis·tach·i·o (nut) /£pɪˈstɑː·ʃi·əʊ, $-ˈstæʃ·i·oʊ/ *n* [C] *pl* **pistachios** a nut with a hard shell which contains an edible green seed • *salted pistachios* • *pistachio ice cream* • PIC **Nut**

piste /piːst/ *n* [C] an area or track covered with snow which is suitable for SKIING on

pis·tol /ˈpɪs·tᵊl/ *n* [C] a small gun which is held in and fired from one hand • *a loaded pistol* • *an automatic pistol* • *a .25-calibre pistol* • *a pistol shot* • If you **hold/put a pistol to** someone's **head**, you threaten them or force them to do something they do not want to do. • *(Am and Aus)* If you **pistol-whip** someone, you hit them with a pistol: *One cop held him while the other pistol-whipped him.*

pis·ton /ˈpɪs·tᵊn/ *n* [C] a short solid tube or round flat object which moves up and down inside a cylinder in an engine to press the fuel into a small space and to send the power produced by it to the wheels • *a piston engine*

pit HOLE /pɪt/ *n* [C] a large hole in the ground, or a hollow in any surface • *They'd dug a shallow pit and left the bodies in it.* • *The roots are stored in open pits until needed.* • *The holes were identified as ancient* **rubbish** *pits.* • *These deep pits* (= hollows) *in the bone were caused by the disease syphilis.* • *Digital information is imprinted on a compact disc in the form of microscopic rounded hollows called pits.* • A pit can be a coal mine or an area of land from which a natural substance is taken by digging: *a gravel/chalk pit* ○ *The miners were told that three pits would be closed.* ○ *In the past,* **pit ponies** (= small horses) *used to pull carts down the mines.* • In a theatre, **the** pit is the seats at the lowest level. **The** pit (also **orchestra pit**) can also be the area in front of the stage where an ORCHESTRA (= group of musicians) sits. • *(Br dated slang) It's late – I'm off to/going to my pit* (= going to bed). • *(slang disapproving) Your room is a complete pit* (= is very untidy). • The **pit of** the **stomach** is the part of the body in which people say they feel fear: *I got a sick feeling/a knot in the pit of my stomach when the news of the attack was announced.* • A **pit bull (terrier)** is a dog of a fierce, quite small breed that is used for fighting other dogs so that people can risk paying money to guess which one will win, and win more money back if they are right. • See also ARMPIT; SANDPIT.

pit *obj* /pɪt/ *v* [T usually passive] **-tt-** • *He had smallpox as a child and his face was pitted* **with** (= marked with hollows caused by) *pockmarks.*

pit SEED /pɪt/ *n* [C], *v* [T] *Am and Aus also for* STONE SEED

pit·ted /£ˈpɪt·ɪd, $ˈpɪt̬-/ *adj* [not gradable] • Pitted is *Am and Aus also for* STONED.

pit *obj* **a·gainst** *obj v prep* [T] to cause (someone or something) to fight against or be in competition with (someone or something) • *It was a bitter civil war, that pitted neighbour against neighbour.* • *One group of Americans is pitted against another as they squabble over scarce government resources.* • *The climbers pitted themselves against the mountain.* • *The company is pitting the new computer system it has produced against those of its competitors.* • *Would you like to pit your* **wits** *against* (= see if you can be cleverer than) *our quiz champion?*

pitch SPORTS FIELD *Br and Aus* /pɪtʃ/, *Am and Aus* **field** *n* [C] an area marked for playing particular sports, esp. football • *a football/hockey/cricket pitch* • *The club plays on an artificial/synthetic pitch* (= a special strong material which covers the surface of the ground). • *The supporters of the winning team* **invaded** (= ran onto) *the pitch.* • Ⓙ

pitch *(obj)* [MOVE] /pɪtʃ/ *v* [always + adv/prep] to move or be moved suddenly, esp. by throwing • *The bike hit a rut and I was pitched* **onto** *the road.* [T] • *She pitched the stone* **into** *the river.* [T] • *The ship pitched* **up and down/from side to side** *in the rough seas.* [I] • *The bus driver braked sharply and all the passengers pitched* **forward**. [I] • *He pitched the ball* (= in cricket, threw the ball for the player with the bat to hit it) *wide of the stumps, and the batsman didn't play at it.* [T] • *The ball pitched* (= landed after having been thrown) *wide of the stumps.* [I] • *(fig.) He was pitched* **(headlong) into** *despair* (= suddenly became in that state) *by what happened to him in his final year at college.* [T] • Ⓙ

pitch *(obj)* [BASEBALL] /pɪtʃ/ *v* (in baseball) to throw a ball towards the player with the bat in order for them to try to hit it • *Who will be pitching first for the white sox this evening?* [I] • *Mussina has pitched 13 innings* (= thrown the ball in that number of parts of games) *in the last three games.* [T] • Ⓙ

pitch /pɪtʃ/ *n* [C] • In baseball, a pitch is an act of throwing the ball at the player with the bat, who tries to hit it: *That was a* **good** *pitch* (= one that is difficult to hit). ○ *That was a* **bad** *pitch* (= one that is too easy to hit or too far from the player with the bat).

pitch·er /£ˈpɪtʃ·əʳ, $-ɚ/ *n* [C] • In baseball, a pitcher is someone who throws the ball towards the person with the bat who tries to hit it: *Some teams are willing to spend $10 million for a star* **relief** *pitcher* (= one who pitches at the end of games).

pitch [LEVEL] /pɪtʃ/ *n* the degree to which a sound is high or low • *The piano and organ were tuned to the same pitch.* [C] • *The noise reached* **such a** *pitch* (= was so loud) *that people living nearby complained.* [C] • *(fig.) By this time their disagreement had reached* **such a** *pitch* (= was so bad) *that there was no hope of an amicable conclusion.* [U] • *(fig.) It's hard to entertain children and adults, and we need to get* **the** *pitch* **right** (= what we do must be at a level to please both groups). [U] • *The children were* **at fever** *pitch* (= very excited) *the day before the party.* [U] • Ⓙ

pitch *obj* /pɪtʃ/ *v* [T] • *Can you pitch this A* (= sing the note correctly, so that it is not too high or too low)? • *The tune was pitched* (= the notes in it were) *too high for me to reach the top notes.* • *(fig.) We decided to pitch the film* **at**/*(Am also)* **to** (= make it suitable for and of interest to) *young adults.* • *(fig.) The book was pitched* **at**/*(Am also)* **to** (= written so that it was suitable for or of interest to) *children in the higher ability groups.* • *(fig.) "Will farmers be interested in this kind of information?" "It all depends* **at**/*(Am also)* **to** *what* **level** *the leaflet is pitched* (= what level of understanding or interest the people reading it are expected to have)."

-pitched /-ˈpɪtʃt/ *combining form* • *a low-pitched sound* • *a high-pitched voice/scream*

pitch [PERSUASION] /pɪtʃ/ *n* [C] a speech or act which attempts to persuade someone to buy or do something, or *(Br)* a place in a public area where a person regularly sells goods or performs • *He gave me his* **(sales)** *pitch about quality and reliability.* • *The city* **made** *a pitch* **to** *stage the international competition* (= tried to persuade its organizers that it should be held in the city). [+ *to* infinitive] • *She's* **making** *a pitch* **for** (= trying to get) *the job as accounts manager that's been advertised.* • *(Br) The flower seller was at his usual pitch (Am and Aus* **stand***) outside the station every Friday night.* • Ⓙ

pitch *obj* [TENT] /pɪtʃ/ *v* [T] to put up (a tent) and fix it into position • *We pitched camp/our tent in the shade.* • Ⓙ

pitch *Br* /pɪtʃ/, *Am and Aus* **site** *n* [C] • A pitch is the piece of ground on which you CAMP (= stay for a short time in a temporary shelter): *We chose a large level grassy pitch for our tent/caravan/camper van.*

pitch [SLOPE] /pɪtʃ/ *n* [U] the amount of slope, esp. of a roof • *This roof has a very* **steep/low** *pitch.* • *The pitch* **of** *the roof has to be steep so that the snow falls off it.* • Ⓙ

pitch /pɪtʃ/ *v* [I always + adv/prep] • *The roof pitches steeply.*

pitched /pɪtʃt/ *adj* [not gradable] • *The garage has a pitched roof.*

pitch [BLACK SUBSTANCE] /pɪtʃ/ *n* [U] a thick black substance which was used in the past to make esp. wooden ships and buildings waterproof • If something is **pitch-black** or **pitch-dark**, it is very black or dark: *It was pitch-dark in the house* (= there were no lights and it was very dark). ○ *The house was* **in pitch darkness.** • Ⓙ

pitch in *v adv* [I] to start to do something as part of a group, esp. something helpful • *If we all pitch in, it shouldn't take too long.* • *When I bought this house, all my friends pitched in to help fix it up.* • *My brother pitched in* **with** *an offer of transport.* • *After we had seen the video everyone started pitching in* **with** *comments on its faults.*

pitch into *obj v prep* [T] to attack with words or criticize • *He pitched into me as soon as he arrived, asking where the report was.*

pitch up *v adv* [I] *infml* to arrive in a place • *Gerald finally pitched up two hours late.*

pitched bat·tle /pɪtʃt/ *n* [C] a fight in which both sides stay in the same place or *(fig.)* a fierce argument • *A pitched battle* **between** *the two sets of fans developed on the terraces after the match was over.* • *(fig.) The angry shareholders' meeting erupted into a pitched battle.*

pitch·er /£ˈpɪtʃ·əʳ, $-ɚ/ *n* [C] a large container used esp. in the past for holding and pouring liquids or *(esp. Am)* a JUG • *an earthenware pitcher* • *(esp. Am) a pitcher* **of** *water* • See also **pitcher** at PITCH [BASEBALL].

pitch·fork /£ˈpɪtʃ·fɔːk, $-fɔːrk/ *n* [C] a tool with a long handle and two or three large curved metal points used for moving HAY (= cut dried grass) or STRAW (= cut dried stems of crops) • [PIC]▷ **Fork**

pitch·fork *obj* **into** *obj v prep* [T] to cause (someone) to be suddenly in (a particular usually difficult situation), esp. without being ready • *Her father died when she was 22, and she was pitchforked into the running of the estate.*

pi·te·ous /£ˈpɪt·i·əs, $ˈpɪt̬-/ *adj* causing you to feel sad • *He wrote a piteous letter to his parents saying how unhappy he was away from home.* • *The kitten gave a piteous cry.*

pi·te·ous·ly /£ˈpɪt·i·ə·sli, $ˈpɪt̬-/ *adv* • *She wept piteously.*

pi·te·ous·ness /£ˈpɪt·i·ə·snəs, $ˈpɪt̬-/ *n* [U]

pit·fall /£ˈpɪt·fɔːl, $-fɑːl/ *n* [C often pl] an unexpected difficulty • *The store fell into one of the major pitfalls of small business, borrowing from suppliers by paying bills late.* • *"The College Freshman Survival Guide" is a video crammed with good advice and information for new students about pitfalls to avoid.*

pith /pɪθ/ *n* [U] the white substance between the skin and the flesh of CITRUS fruits such as oranges, or the soft white inner part of the stem of some plants

pith·y /ˈpɪθ·i/ *adj* **-ier, -iest** • *a pithy orange* (= an orange with thick pith) • See also PITHY.

pit·head /ˈpɪt·hed/ *n* [C usually sing] *esp. Br and Aus* the area and buildings at the entrance to a MINE (= a place from which natural substances are removed) • *The visitors met the staff at the pithead before going underground.* • *The miners went straight to the pithead baths when they came up from the mine.* • *The issue will be decided by a pithead ballot.* • See also PIT [HOLE].

pith hel·met /pɪθ/, **to·pee** *n* [C] a large white hat made of thick stiff material with a BRIM (= part which sticks out all around). It was worn in the past in hot countries by people who needed to protect themselves from the sun.

pith·y /ˈpɪθ·i/ *adj* **-ier, -iest** (of speech or writing) short and clever; expressing an idea cleverly in a few words • *He gave a pithy summary of his political views: "I want a government that takes less of my money in taxes".* • *As the critics watch a TV programme, they sometimes jot down a pithy phrase or two that sums up their reaction to what they're seeing.* • *Her later books are pithier and contain more critical social commentary.* • See also **pithy** at PITH.

pith·i·ly /ˈpɪθ·ɪ·li/ *adv*

pith·i·ness /ˈpɪθ·ɪ·nəs/ *n* [U]

pi·ti·a·ble /£ˈpɪt·i·ə·bl̩, $ˈpɪt̬-/ *adj* See at PITY

pi·ti·ful /£ˈpɪt·i·fəl, $ˈpɪt̬-/ *adj* See at PITY

pi·ti·less /£ˈpɪt·i·ləs, $ˈpɪt̬-/ *adj* See at PITY

pits [BAD] /pɪts/ *pl n* **the pits** *infml* something that is of extremely low quality • *The hotel we stayed in was the pits!*

pits [REPAIR AREA] /pɪts/ *pl n* **the pits** the area next to a motor race track where the cars are given fuel or repaired during a race

pit /pɪt/ *adj* [before n; not gradable] • *The driver had to* **make** *a pit* **stop**. • *(fig.) We* **made** *a quick pit* **stop** (= stopped to use the toilet, wash, etc.) *in York before continuing on our journey.*

pit·ta (bread), *Am* **pi·ta (bread)** /ˈpɪt·ə/ *n* [U] flat bread, usually in a rounded or oval shape, that is not made with YEAST, and which has a hollow centre into which various fillings can be put • [PIC]▷ **Bread and cakes**

pit·tance /£ˈpɪt·ᵊnts, $ˈpɪt̬-/ *n* [C usually sing] *disapproving* a very small amount of money, esp. money received as payment, income or a present • *He works hard but only earns/is only paid a pittance.* • *Nutritionists have demonstrated that an adequate diet can be maintained* **on** *a pittance.* • *She* **lives on** *the pittance her father left her when he died.* • *$30 billion might seem a lot of money, but it's a* **mere** *pittance in terms of what global capital markets can and do absorb.*

pit·ter–pat·ter /£'pɪt·əˌpæt·əʳ, $'pɪt̬·ɚˌpæt̬·ɚ/ *v, n* (to make) a quick light knocking sound • *The rain pitter-pattered on the roof.* [I] • *We could hear* **the** *pitter-patter* **of** *the rain against the window.* [U] • *Do I hear* **the** *pitter-patter* **of tiny feet** (= the noise of children running)*?* [U]

pit·ter–pat·ter /ˌpɪt·ə'pæt·əʳ, $ˌpɪt̬·ɚ'pæt̬·ɚ/ *adv* [not gradable] • *They ran, pitter-patter* (= making a quick light knocking sound), *along the hall to the door.*

pi·tu·i·ta·ry (gland) /£pɪ'tjuː·ɪ·tᵊr·i, $-'tuː·ə·ter-/ *n* [C] a small organ at the base of the brain which controls the growth and activity of the body by producing HORMONES (= types of chemicals)

pi·ty /£'pɪt·i, $'pɪt̬-/ *n* [U] a feeling of sympathy and understanding for someone else's unhappiness or difficult situation • *Hardly anyone in this story of greed and self-interest has any real claim to our pity.* • *The girl stood gazing* **in/with** *pity at her friend who was so upset.* • *Do you* **feel** *no pity* **for** *all those poor homeless people on such a cold night as this?* • *We* **took** *pity* **on** (= felt sorry for and therefore helped) *a couple of people waiting in the rain for a bus and gave them a lift.* • If something is described as a pity, it is disappointing or not satisfactory: *Can't you go to the party? That's* **a** *pity.* ○ *The children didn't get much attention, which was* **such a** *pity.* ○ *Pity* **(that)** *you didn't remember to give me the message.* [+ (*that*) clause] ○ *The potential readership of this book is huge, and it's* **a** *pity* **(that)** *it's available only as a hardback.* [+ (*that*) clause] ○ **The** *pity was* **that** *such a small crowd turned out to see some of the world's best batsmen in full flow.* [+ *that* clause] ○ *We'll have to leave early,* **more's the** *pity* (= and I am unhappy about it). ○ *"She can't come to see us this week." "***What** *a pity* (= I am unhappy that she can't come)*."* • See also SELF-PITY.

pi·ty *obj* /£'pɪt·i, $'pɪt̬-/ *v* [T] • *Pity* (= Feel sorry for) *the unhappy motorist who has to drive in rush- hour traffic!* • *If you've ever seen one of these devices explode, you'd pity the poor person who survives.*

pi·ti·ful /£'pɪt·i·fᵊl, $'pɪt̬-/, *fml* **pi·ti·a·ble** *adj* • *The refugees arriving at the camp had pitiful stories* (= those that made people feel pity) *to tell.* • Pitiful can also be used to show that you consider something is bad or not satisfactory: *a pitiful state of affairs* ○ *The amount of time and money being spent on researching this disease is pitiful.*

pi·ti·ful·ly /£'pɪt·i·fᵊl·i, $'pɪt̬-/, *fml* **pi·ti·a·bly** /£'pɪt·i·ə·bli, $'pɪt̬-/ *adv* • *The children were pitifully thin and neglected.* • *She only gave a pitifully small amount of money to the charity.*

pi·ti·ful·ness /£'pɪt·i·fᵊl·nəs, $'pɪt̬-/ *n* [U]

pi·ti·less /£'pɪt·i·ləs, $'pɪt̬-/ *adj* • Pitiless means cruel and without pity, or *(fig.)* severe and unpleasant: *the dictator's pitiless rule* ○ *a pitiless critic* ○ *(fig.) He told us his story in pitiless detail.* ○ *(fig.) Few people were out in the pitiless midday sun.*

pi·ti·less·ly /£'pɪt·i·lə·sli, $'pɪt̬-/ *adv*

pi·ti·less·ness /£'pɪt·i·lə·snəs, $'pɪt̬-/ *n* [U]

pi·vot /'pɪv·ət/ *n* [C] a fixed point supporting something which turns or balances • *The rotor blades rest on a pivot.* • A pivot can also be the central or most important person or thing in a situation: *The former guerrilla leader has become the pivot on which the country's emerging political conflict* **turns/revolves.** ○ *The film's emotional pivot is the mother's abandonment of her family.*

pi·vot *(obj)* /'pɪv·ət/ *v* • *Above the stage were large lights which pivoted* (= turned) **on** *brackets.* [T] • *He pivoted* (= turned) *round in his chair as the door opened.* [I] • *The election may pivot* (= its result could depend) **on** *how well Barry gets his supporters to the polls.* [I]

pi·vo·tal /£'pɪv·ə·tᵊl, $-t̬ᵊl/ *adj* • Something which is pivotal is central and important: *a pivotal figure/role/idea*

pi·xel /'pɪk·sᵊl, -sel/ *n* [C] *specialized* the smallest unit of an image on a television or computer screen

pi·xie, pi·xy /'pɪk·si/ *n* [C] (esp. in children's stories) a small imaginary person

piz·za /'piːt·sə/, *Am also* **piz·za pie** *n* (a large circle of) flat bread baked with cheese, TOMATOES and various other things spread on top • *a deep pan pizza* (= one with a thick base) [C] • *an individual pizza* (= one which is of a size suitable for one person) [C] • *Do you want another slice of pizza?* [U] • *You can put a lot of different pizza* **toppings** *on a pizza* **base.** • *We're having* **French-bread** *pizza* (= pizza made with that type of bread) *for lunch.* [U] • *(disapproving slang)* A **pizza-face** is a person whose face has a lot of spots and PIMPLES on it: *Hi, there, pizza-face.* [as form of address] • A **pizza place**/*(Br)* **pizza house**/*(Am also)* **pizza parlor** is a restaurant that sells pizzas. See also PIZZERIA. • [PIC] **Pan**

piz·zazz, p·zazz /pɪ'zæz/ *n* [U] *infml approving* the quality of noticeable and energetic excitement • *Their performance lacked pizzazz.*

piz·ze·ri·a /ˌpiːt·sə'riː·ə/ *n* [C] a restaurant that sells PIZZAS • *They own an 80-seater pizzeria in the main street.*

piz·zi·cat·o /£ˌpɪt·sɪ'kɑː·təʊ, $-t̬oʊ/ *adj, adv* [not gradable] *specialized* played by PLUCKING the strings of a musical instrument such as a VIOLIN or CELLO with the fingers instead of using a BOW (= stick with hairs stretched across it)

pl *n, adj abbreviation for* PLURAL

plac·ard /£'plæk·ɑːd, $-ɑːrd/ *n* [C] a large piece of card, paper, etc. with a message written or printed on it, often carried in public places by people who are complaining about something • *About 1000 people marched past* **carrying** *placards denouncing armed intervention.* • *The protesters waved aloft placards proclaiming 'Hands off our woodland!' and 'No airport here!'*

pla·cate *obj* /£plə'keɪt, $'pleɪ·keɪt/ *v* [T] to stop (someone) from feeling angry • *The letter made him furious, and it took some time to placate him.* • *The new scheme won't placate family-business owners.* • *Outraged minority groups will not be placated by promises of future improvements.*

pla·ca·to·ry /£plə'keɪ·tᵊr·i, $'pleɪ·kə·tɔːr-/ *adj fml* • *To judge from the placatory tone of their letter, I think they may be going to make some concessions.* • *The mood of the negotiations was placatory.*

place [AREA] /pleɪs/ *n* an area, town, building, hotel or shop • *This is the place where they are going to build the new supermarket.* [C] • *Her garden was a cool pleasant place to sit.* [C] • *I like living in Cambridge – it's a nice place.* [C] • *What was the name of that place we drove through on the way to New York?* [C] • *The brochure advertises several different places in Italy.* [C] • *Airports are often busy crowded places.* [C] • *The company owns a big place in the city and several country properties.* [C] • *The hotel was one of those big old-fashioned places.* [C] • *We're staying at a bed-and-breakfast place.* [C] • *They decided to go to a pizza place.* [C] • Your place can be your home: *I'm looking for a place to live.* [C] ○ *They're trying to buy a new place with a bigger garden.* [C] ○ *We'll have the meeting at my place.* [C] ○ *Nice place you've got here.* [C] • Place can also be used to mean a suitable area or building, a suitable situation, or a suitable occasion: *A high-rise tower block is* **no** *place* **to** *bring up young children.* [U + *to* infinitive] ○ *It quickly became clear that university was* **not** *the place* (= a suitable situation) **for** *me, and that I'd have to leave.* [U] ○ *This meeting* **isn't** *the place* (= a suitable occasion) **to** *discuss individual cases – we are considering the broad issues.* [U + *to* infinitive] • *You can buy these T-shirts everywhere – they're* **all over the place** (= in every place). • *(infml) They said that the group was clearly* **going places** (= going to be successful). • *There are several* **places of interest** (= esp. old, important or interesting buildings or areas) *to visit in the area.* • *They phoned his* **place of work** (= the building or area in which he worked) *to tell them about his accident* • A **place of worship** is a building for religious services, such as a church, TEMPLE, etc. • A **place name** is the official name of a town or an area: *York and Toledo are place names.* • (NL)

place [POSITION] /pleɪs/ *n* [C] a position in relation to other things • *This plant needs a warm, sunny place.* • *When you've finished, put the book back* **in** *its place on the shelf.* • *The newspaper seller was* **in** *his usual place outside the station.* • *She spoke to me and I* **lost** *my place in the book* (= I forgot where I had been reading). • Your place in the theatre, in a train, at a table, in a class or in some other organized arrangement is the seat you will sit in on a particular occasion or the seat you usually sit in: *My ticket says 6G but there's someone sitting in my place.* ○ *There are only enough places for ten more people on the bus.* ○ *The waiter showed us to our places and gave us each a menu.* ○ *The children collected their prizes and then went back to their places.* ○ **Save** *me a place* (= Keep a seat for me until I arrive) *near the front.* • A place at a table is also the space where one person will sit and eat. It usually has the plates and utensils you eat with arranged on it: *He* **laid** *six places*

POLISH FALSE FRIENDS (PL)

accumulator *n*	akumulator	car battery
actual *adj*	aktualny	present, current, topical
actually *adv*	aktualnie	at present, currently, nowadays
adapt *v*	adaptować	convert, renovate
advocate *n*	adwokat	solicitor, barrister
angina *n*	angina	tonsilitis
apartment *n*	apartament	hotel suite
arbiter *n*	arbiter	umpire, referee
argument *n*	argument	reasoning
audition *n*	audycja	radio programme
bandit *n*	bandyta	thug
baton *n*	baton	chocolate bar
benzene *n*	benzyna	petrol; gasoline
boot *n*	but	shoe
cabinet *n*	gabinet	surgery (doctor, dentist); manager's office; study
calendar *n*	kalendarz	diary
central *adj*	centrala	telephone exchange; switchboard
chef *n*	szef	chief; leader; boss
chips *n*	chips	potato crisps
civil *adj*	cywil	civilian clothes
colleague *n*	kolega	friend
column *n*	kolumna	loudspeaker
communication *n*	komunikacja	public transport
compositor *n*	kompozytor	composer of music
confectionery *n*	konfekcja	ready-made clothes
confidant *n*	konfident	informer
consequent *adj*	konsekwentny	consistent (of person)
cravat *n*	krawat	tie
delegation *n*	delegacja	business trip
diploma *n*	dyplom	degree
director *n*	dyrektor	headmaster, principal
disposition *n*	dyspozycja	disposal (at your disposal)
divan *n*	dywan	carpet
doping *n*	doping	cheering
dress *n*	dres	tracksuit
emission *n*	emisja	broadcast
eventual *adj*	ewentualny	possible; likely
eventually adv	ewentualnie	possibly; in case
example *n*	egzemplarz	copy (of book)
expedient *n*	ekspedient	sales assistant
fatal *adj*	fatalny	terrible; of poor quality
genial *adj*	genialny	brilliant
golf *n*	golf	polo-neck sweater
gymnasium *n*	gimnazjum	grammar school
gypsum *n*	gips	(medical) plaster
hazard *n*	hazard	gambling
herb *n*	herb	coat of arms
history *n*	historia	story
humour *n*	humor	mood (e.g. to be in a good mood)
hysterical *adj*	histeryczny	uncontrollably emotional
interpret *v*	interpretować	to place a particular meaning on something
lecture *n*	lektura	obligatory reading
local *n*	lokal	cafe, bar; restaurant; premises
lunatic *n*	lunatyk	sleepwalker
machinist *n*	maszynista	engine driver
machinist *n*	maszynistka	typist
mandate *n*	mandat	fine
manifestation *n*	manifestacja	demonstration; parade
mark *n*	marka	make (e.g. car, radio)
marmalade *n*	marmolada	jam
nervous *adj*	nerwowy	irritated; quick-tempered
novel *n*	nowela	short story
obstruction *n*	obstrukcja	constipation
occasion *n*	okazja	bargain
ordinary *adj*	ordynarny	foul-mouthed
pantomime *n*	pantomima	mime show
paragraph *n*	paragraf	clause (of law)
parapet *n*	parapet	window ledge
parasol *n*	parasol	umbrella
pasta *n*	pasta	paste
pathetic *adj*	patetyczny	full of pathos
pension *n*	pensja	salary
per cent *adv*	procent	interest on savings
perspectives *n*	perspektywy	prospects (e.g. job)
practice *n*	praktyka	work experience, training, apprenticeship
preservative *n*	prezerwatywa	condom
problem *n*	problem	concern; responsibility
process *n*	proces	trial
prognosis *n*	prognoza	weather forecast
programme *n*	program	TV channel
project *v*	projektować	to design
proposition *n*	propozycja	proposal
prospect *n*	prospekt	advertising brochure
pupil *n*	pupil	pet, favourite (e.g. teacher's pet)
race *n*	rasa	breed
receipt *n*	recepta	prescription
rent *n*	renta	retirement pension
revenge *n*	rewanż (mecz)	return match (sports)
scene *n*	scena	theatre stage
sclerosis *n*	skleroza	senility
script *n*	skrypt	duplicated handout from teachers
speaker *n*	spiker	(TV, radio, etc.) announcer
stipend *n*	stypendium	student grant; scholarship
sympathetic *adj*	sympatyczny	likeable, friendly
technique *n*	technika	technology
wagon *n*	wagon	railway carriage

at the table. • A place is also a position in a group, organization, system or competition: *They deserve a place* **among** *the country's leading exporters.* ○ *Will you* **keep** *my place* **(in** *the queue)* (= allow me to come back to the same position)? ○ *She has got a place* **at** *university* ○ *She has got a place (Br and Aus)* **on**/*(Am and Aus)* **in** *a fine-arts course.* ○ *The song went from tenth to second place* **in** *the charts.* ○ *Our team finished* **in** *second place.* ○ *He* **took** *third place/(Br also)* **got a** *third place* (= was the third to finish) *in the marathon last year.* ○ *(fig.) Their children always take first place* (= are very important to their parents' decisions)/ *take second place* (= are not very important). • In a list of statements, you can use **the** place to separate and emphasize them: *I don't want to go yet –* **in the first** *place I'm not ready, and* **in the second** *place it's raining.* • *(Am)* Place can be used with words like 'any' and 'some' as a different way of saying 'anywhere,' 'somewhere,' etc.: *I know I left that book some place – now, where was it?* ○ *That bar was like no place I'd ever been before.* • If you make a calculation to a particular number of places **of decimals** or **decimal** places, you have that number of numbers after the **decimal point**: *Pi expressed to five places of decimals is 3·14159.* • If something is **in place**, it is in its usual or correct position. If it is **out of place**, it is in the wrong place or looks wrong: *The chairs are all in place.* ○ *He screwed the shelf in place.* ○ *(fig.) The arrangements are all in place* (= have been made correctly) *for the concert next Thursday.* ○ *The large desk was out of place in such a small room.* ○ *The boy looked uncomfortable and out of place among the adults.* • If something or someone is **in place of** something or someone else, or if they **take the place of** that person or thing, they are used instead: *I invited Jo in place of Les, who was ill.* ○ *You can use margarine in place of butter in some recipes.* • A **place in the sun** is an advantageous position: *He certainly earned his place in the sun.* • If something **takes place**, it happens: *The concert takes place next Thursday.* ○ *When is the training session taking place?* • A **place card** is a card with someone's name on it, which is put in the space at a table where they will sit, esp. at a formal meal: *There was a place card with my name on it on the table, so I knew where to sit.* • A **place mat** is a decorative piece of card, cloth, wood, plastic etc. on which someone's plate and eating utensils are put on a table: *I gave them a set of place mats as a wedding present.* • *(saying)* 'A place for everything and everything in its place' means that the best way to stay tidy and well organized is to keep things in their correct positions. • PIC› **Cutlery** (NL)

place *(obj)* /pleɪs/ *v* • *She placed* (= put) *the letter in front of me.* [T] • *Bowls of flowers had been placed on tables around the room.* [T] • *She placed her name on the list of volunteers.* [T] • *I'd place him among the ten most brilliant scientists of his age.* [T] • *The horse was placed first/second/third in its first race* (= finished the race in first/second/third position). [T + obj + adj] • *I bet on Parker's Mood to place* (= finish in *Br* second or third place/*Am* second place in the horse race). [I] • *The students are placed* (= jobs are found for them) *in companies for a period of work experience.* [T] • *We placed the* **order** *for* (= We ordered) *the furniture six weeks ago.* [T] • *They were placing* **bets** *on* (= risking paying money in order to guess) *who would win.* [T] • *She placed the* **emphasis** *on* (= emphasized) *the word 'soon'.* [T] • *He placed* **importance** *on a comfortable lifestyle* (= It was important to him). [T]

placed /pleɪst/ *adj* [not gradable] • If someone is **highly** placed, they have an important job: *a highly placed official* • *The horse I bet on wasn't even placed* (= did not come in first, second or third position in the race). • *(Br infml)* **How are you placed for** means what is your situation: *How are you placed for money* (=Have you got enough money)*?* ○ *How are you placed for Tuesday night* (=Are you busy or not on Tuesday night)*?*

place·ment /ˈpleɪs·mənt/ *n* • *The placement* (=putting into a particular position) *of the new office building, right in the middle of the town, really spoils the view.* [U] • *I think we can find a placement* (=a job) *for you in the accounts department.* [C] • *They run a* **job/work** *placement* **scheme** *for graduates.*

place *obj* RECOGNIZE /pleɪs/ *v* [T usually in negatives] to recognize (someone) or remember where you have seen them or how you know them • *She looks familiar but I can't place her – did she use to work here?* • (NL)

place DUTY /pleɪs/ *n* [U] *slightly dated* what a person should do or is allowed to do, esp. according to the rules of society • *It's not your place* **to** *tell me what to do.* [+ to infinitive] • *I'm not going to criticize his lordship –* **I know** *my place* (=I know that I am of lower social rank). • *When he tried to take charge, she soon* **put** *him* **in** *his* **place** (=made it clear that he was less important than he thought he was). • (NL)

pla·ce·bo /£pləˈsiː·bəʊ, $-boʊ/ *n* [C] *pl* **placebos** a substance that is not a medicine but that is given to someone who is told that it is a medicine, usually used as a way of testing the effect of a drug given to others • *She was only given a placebo, not the real drug, but she claimed she got better – that's the placebo* **effect**. • *(fig.) These small concessions have been made as a placebo* (=a way of trying to please someone who is not satisfied about something) *to stop the workers making further demands.*

pla·cen·ta /£pləˈsen·tə, $-t̬ə/ *n* [C] *pl* **placentas** or **placentae** /£pləˈsen·tiː, $-t̬iː/ the mass of body tissue which joins a FOETUS (=developing baby) to the inside of its mother's womb

plac·id /ˈplæs·ɪd/ *adj* having a calm appearance or characteristics • *On a warm sunny day the river/lake/sea seems placid and benign, and it's hard to believe it can be dangerous.* • *They mentioned the placid pace of life as their main reason for moving to the village.* • *She was a very placid* (=calm and not easily excited) *child who slept all night and hardly ever cried.*

plac·id·ly /ˈplæs·ɪd·li/ *adv* • *She took the news quite placidly.*

plac·id·ness /ˈplæs·ɪd·nəs/, **pla·cid·i·ty** /£pləˈsɪd·ɪ·ti, $-ə·t̬i/ *n* [U] • *This breed of dogs is known for its placidity.*

pla·giar·ize *(obj)*, *Br and Aus usually* **-ise** /£ˈpleɪ·dʒəʳ·aɪz, $-dʒə·raɪz/ *v* to use (another person's idea or a part of their work) and pretend that it is your own • *They recently discovered that a woman had plagiarized passages* **from** *the book they had written.* [T] • *If you compare the two books side by side, it looks as if the author of the second has plagiarized* **(from** *the first).* [I] • *It is claimed the thesis contains plagiarized material.*

pla·giar·i·sm /£ˈpleɪ·dʒəʳ·ɪ·zəm, $-dʒɚ·ɪ-/ *n* [U] • *Accusations of plagiarism have been made against him.* • *"If you steal from one author, it's plagiarism; if you steal from many, it's research"* (believed to have been said by Wilson Mizner, 1876-1933)

pla·giar·ist /£ˈpleɪ·dʒəʳ·ɪst, $-dʒɚ·ɪst/ *n* [C] • *I was accused of being a plagiarist, but it was just a coincidence that what I wrote was like what she wrote.*

plague *obj* CAUSE PAIN/TROUBLE /pleɪg/ *v* [T] to cause worry, pain or difficulty to (someone or something) over a period of time • *Financial crises have been plaguing their potential new partners.* • *The problem of illegal immigration is one that plagues many parts of Europe.* • *My shoulder's been plaguing me all week.* • *The children plagued him* **with** *questions* (=asked him a lot of them, esp. in a way that was annoying). • *He's been plaguing me* **for** (=continually and and in an annoying way trying to persuade me to give him) *an answer – he called again today.*

plague DISEASE /pleɪg/ *n* a serious disease which kills many people • *Cholera and plague have broken out in the wake of the disaster.* [U] • *She published a history of the plagues which swept across Europe.* [C] • A plague **of** particular things is a large number of things which are unpleasant or likely to cause damage: *Millions of trees are being attacked by a plague of insects in east and southern Africa.* [C] ○ *This week a documentary exposed the current plague of cockroaches in inner-city tower blocks.* [C] ○ *(humorous) A plague of journalists descended on the town.* [C] • *(esp. humorous)* Something which is a plague **on** something is not wanted because it is annoying or causes trouble and difficulty: *The biggest plague on the land is the ubiquitous personal stereo set, he said.* [C] • **The plague** is BUBONIC PLAGUE.

plaice /pleɪs/ *n pl* **plaice** a sea fish with a flat circular body, or its flesh eaten as food • *plaice and chips* [U] • *There were several plaice in the tank.* [C] • PIC› **Fish**

plaid /plæd/ *n* [U] *esp. Am for* TARTAN

plain WITH NOTHING ADDED /pleɪn/ *adj* **-er, -est** not decorated in any way; with nothing added • *She wore a plain black* (=only of that one colour) *dress.* • *The catalogue was sent in a plain brown envelope/wrapper.* • *The room had a plain carpet* (=one without a pattern) *and patterned curtains.* • *I prefer plain (styles of) architecture* (=that/those having no decoration). • *The letter was written on plain* **paper** (=that without lines). • Plain **food** is cooked in a simple way without adding unusual flavours, special sauces, etc.: *My father says he likes* **'good** *plain food'.* ○ *The fish had been grilled and served plain.* ○ *We had apple pie with plain vanilla ice-cream.* ○ *Do you like plain* (=natural and without any added flavouring) **yoghurt***?* • **Plain chocolate** (also **bitter chocolate**, *Am usually* **dark chocolate**) does not contain milk. Compare **milk chocolate** at MILK. • If the police wear **plain clothes**, they are not wearing uniforms while they are doing their job: *There were police* **in** *plain clothes in the crowd.* ○ *A plain-clothes policeman was standing outside the door when I opened it.* • *(Br)* **Plain-coloured** means of one colour only. • *(Br and Aus)* **Plain flour** (*Am* **all-purpose flour**) contains no chemical which makes cakes RISE (=become large when cooked). Compare SELF-RAISING FLOUR. • PIC› **Stationery**

plain·ly /ˈpleɪn·li/ *adv* • *a plainly furnished room*

plain·ness /ˈpleɪn·nəs/ *n* [U]

plain CLEAR /pleɪn/ *adj* **-er, -est** (of expression) obvious, or clear and easy to understand; not complicated • *The reason is* **perfectly** *plain.* • *We must* **make it** *plain* **(that)** *we can't stay too long.* [+ (*that*) clause] • **It's** *plain* **(that)** *they want you to help them.* [+ (*that*) clause] • *The sign was plain* **enough** *– we just didn't see it!* • *There's a plain* **and simple** *way to solve this problem – go and ask him what he wants you to do!* • *"Have I made myself plain* (=Do you understand what I've said)*?" she said in a annoyed tone.* • If something is **(as) plain as the nose on** your **face** or *(Br)* **(as) plain as a pikestaff** is it very obvious. • **Plain English** is clear simple language: *Why can't they write these instructions in plain English?* • If an activity is **plain sailing** (*Am also* **smooth sailing**), it is easy: *The roads were busy as we drove out of town, but after that it was plain sailing.* • Someone who says they believe in **plain speaking** always says clearly and honestly what they think without trying to be polite: *It's time for some plain speaking.* ○ *He's very* **plain-spoken**.

plain·ly /ˈpleɪn·li/ *adv* • Plainly means clearly or obviously: *Every footstep could be plainly heard.* ○ *A group of birds was plainly visible in the distance.* ○ *The average citizen can plainly see the environmental problems.* ○ *The accusation was quite plainly untrue.* ○ *The men had plainly lied.* ○ *Plainly, it is futile to try to persuade her.* ○ *Plainly, a great deal of extra time will be needed for the security checks.* ○ *The incentive to sell more is large – and it plainly works.* ○ *The rail network will* **all too** *plainly make a loss.*

plain·ness /ˈpleɪn·nəs/ *n* [U]

plain COMPLETE /pleɪn/ *adj* [before n; not gradable] (used for emphasis) complete • *It was just plain luck that I ran into her in town, and she told me about this job.* • *Well that was a plain waste of time, wasn't it?* • *The plain* **truth** *is that we can't afford to pay anymore.*

plain /pleɪn/ *adv* **-er, -est** *infml* • *It was* **just** *plain* (=completely) *stupid to give him your address.* • *What she said was* **just** *plain wrong.*

plain NOT BEAUTIFUL /pleɪn/ *adj* **-er, -est** (esp. of a woman or girl) not beautiful • *She had been a very plain child.*

plain·ness /ˈpleɪn·nəs/ *n* [U]

plain LAND /pleɪn/ *n* [U] a large area of flat land • *the coastal plain* • *They live in a farm on the plain.* • *High mountains rise above the plain.*

plains /pleɪnz/ *pl n* • *the Great Plains of the western US* • *They left* **the plains** (=the plain) *when it became hot and spent several months in the hills.*

plain STITCH /pleɪn/ *n* [U] a type of simple stitch in KNITTING (=connecting wool into joined rows) • *a row of plain and two rows of purl*

plain·song /£ˈpleɪn·sɒŋ, $-sɑːŋ/, **plain·chant** /£ˈpleɪn·tʃɑːnt, $-tʃænt/ *n* [U] a type of simple group singing without instruments, used esp. in the past in the Christian church

plain·tiff /£ˈpleɪn·tɪf, $-t̬ɪf/ *n* [C] *law* someone who makes a legal complaint against someone else in court • Compare **defendant** at DEFEND. • [LP]› **Law**

plain·tive /£ˈpleɪn·tɪv, $-t̬ɪv/ *adj* (esp. of a sound) expressing slight sadness • *the plaintive sound of the bagpipes* • *"What about me?" came a plaintive voice.*

plain·tive·ly /£ˈpleɪn·tɪv·li, $-t̬ɪv-/ *adv* • *"I've broken my glasses," he said plaintively.*

plain·tive·ness /£ˈpleɪn·tɪv·nəs, $-t̬ɪv-/ *n* [U]

plait *(obj)* /plæt/, *Am usually* **braid** *v* to join three or more lengths of (string-like material) by putting them over each other in a special pattern. Long hair is often plaited. • *She plaited the horse's tail.* [T] • *My grandfather taught me to plait.* [I] • *He was wearing a plaited leather bracelet/a plaited tie/a plaited belt.*

plait /plæt/, *Am usually* **braid** *n* [C] • A plait is a length of usually hair which has been divided into three parts which have then been crossed over each other in a special pattern: *She usually wears her hair in a plait/in two plaits.* • [PIC]› **Hair**

plan [DECISION] /plæn/ *n* a set of decisions about how to do something in the future • *the country's economic plan* [C] • *a company's business plan* [C] • *a negotiated peace plan* [C] • *contingency plans* [C] • *a three-point plan* [C] • *a five-year plan* [C] • *holiday plans* [C] • *What are your plans* **for** *this weekend?* [C] • *We must* **make** *plans* **for** *next year.* [C] • *Accidents can disrupt the* **best-laid** *plans.* [C] • *My plan is* **to** *hire a car when I arrive in America and travel about.* [C + *to* infinitive] • A plan is also a type of arrangement for financial investment: *a pension plan* [C] • *a savings plan* [C] • *a healthcare plan* [C] • If something **goes according to** plan, it happens in the way you wanted it to: *Events of this type rarely go according to plan.* [U]

plan *(obj)* /plæn/ *v* **-nn-** • *She helped them to plan* (=decide) *their route.* [T] • *If we plan* (=make decisions) *carefully, we should be able to stay within our budget.* [I always + adv/prep] • *Our meeting wasn't planned* (=intended) *– it was completely accidental.* [T] • *I'm planning* (=I intend) **to** *buy a new house.* [+ *to* infinitive] • *I'm not planning* **to** (=I shall not) *stay here much longer.* [+ *to* infinitive] • *We're planning turning the back room into a bedroom for my mother.* [+ v-ing] • *She's already planning* **how** *to spend her prize money.* [+ *wh-* word] • *I've planned* **out** *the day – first we'll take the train up to town, we'll do some shopping, then we'll have a slap-up meal and see a show.* [M] • *They hadn't planned* **on** *the whole family coming.* [I always + adv/prep] • *We were planning* **on** *just having a snack and catching the early train.* [I always + adv/prep] • *We only planned* **for** *six guests but then someone brought a friend.* [I always + adv/prep] • **Planned Parenthood** is a US organization that provides sex education and advice on how to avoid becoming pregnant.

plan·ner /£ˈplæn·əʳ, $-ɚ/ *n* [C] • A planner is a person who makes decisions about how something will be done in the future: *a television programme planner* ○ *a systems planner*

plan·ning /ˈplæn·ɪŋ/ *n* [U] • *Planning isn't his strong point – he just reacts to things as they happen.*

plan [DRAWING] /plæn/ *n* [C] a drawing of a building, town, area, vehicle, machine, etc. which only shows its shape from above and its size and the position of important details • *a street plan* (=a type of map of a town showing the roads) • *a seating plan* (=a drawing which shows where each person will sit) • *We looked at the floor plan to see how we should allocate the offices.*

plans /plænz/ *pl n* • Plans are the drawings from which something is made or built: *The architect showed us the house plans that she had* **drawn up**. ○ *I'll send a set of plans* **for** *the new machine.*

plan *obj* /plæn/ *v* [T] **-nn-** • *The people who planned* (=designed) *Britain's new towns after World War Two had a vision of clean modern housing for everyone.*

plan·ner /£ˈplæn·əʳ, $-ɚ/ *n* [C] • A planner is a person whose job is to decide how land in a particular area is to be used, what is to be built on it, etc.: *a town/city/urban/environmental/local planner*

plan·ning /ˈplæn·ɪŋ/ *n* [U] • Planning is the process of deciding how land in a particular area will be used: *town/environmental/urban/landscape planning* ○ *He works in the planning department of the local council.* • *(Br)* **Planning blight** is the situation of being unable to sell your house, land, etc. because a road, airport etc. is going to be built near to it. • *(Br)* **Planning permission** (*Am and Aus* A **building permit**) is an official agreement that something new can be built or an existing building can be changed.

plane [AIRCRAFT] /pleɪn/ *n* [C] a vehicle designed for air travel, which has wings and one or more engines; an AEROPLANE • *a fighter/transport/cargo/passenger plane* • *a plane ticket* • *What time does the plane arrive?* • *We'll be* **boarding** *the plane in about 20 minutes.* • *He doesn't like travelling* **by** *plane.* • *"Planes, Trains and Automobiles"* (title of a film, 1987) • [PIC]› **Aircraft** Ⓓ

plane [SURFACE] /pleɪn/ *n* [C] *specialized* (in GEOMETRY (=science of shapes and surfaces)) a flat or level surface which continues in all directions • *an inclined plane* • If different points are **in the same** plane, a flat surface will pass through all of them. • Ⓓ

plane /pleɪn/ *adj* [before n; not gradable] *specialized* • *a plane* (=flat) *edge/surface*

plane [LEVEL] /pleɪn/ *n* [C] a particular level or standard • *The poet's treatment of the subject lifts it to a mystical plane.* • *His writing is* **on** *a completely different plane from* (=is much better than) *that of other crime writers.* • *Sometimes I think she's* **on** *a different plane* (=thinks in a different way) *from the rest of us.* • Ⓓ

plane [TOOL] /pleɪn/ *n* [C] a tool which is used to make wooden surfaces and edges flat and smooth by removing small strips of the wood • Ⓓ

plane *obj* /pleɪn/ *v* [T] • *You'll have to plane some more wood off the bottom of the door – it's still sticking.* • *Plane the edge of the frame smooth.* [+ obj + adj]

plane (tree) /pleɪn/ *n* [C] a large tree with wide leaves and spreading branches that grows esp. in towns • [PIC]› **Tools**

plan·et /ˈplæn·ɪt/ *n* [C] an extremely large round mass of rock and metal, such as Earth, or of gas, such as Jupiter, which moves in a circular path around the Sun or another star • *the planet Earth/Venus* • *This technology might allow astronauts to explore areas of Mars and other planets by remote control.* • *Might there be intelligent life on other planets?* • *Sometimes she seems as if she's* **on** *another planet* (=is not giving attention to what is happening around her and is thinking differently from other people). • *"Planet of the Apes"* (film title, 1967)

plan·et·a·ry /£ˈplæn·ɪ·tᵊr·i, $-ɪ·ter-/ *adj* [not gradable] • *planetary science* • *planetary motion* • *a planetary landing* • See also INTERPLANETARY.

plan·et·ar·i·um /£ˌplæn·ɪˈteə·ri·əm, $-ˈter·i-/ *n* [C] *pl* **planetariums** or **planetaria** /£ˌplæn·ɪˈteə·ri·ə, $-ˈter·i-/ a building in which moving images of the sky at night are shown using a special machine

plank [FLAT PIECE] /plæŋk/ *n* [C] a long narrow flat piece of esp. wood, of the type used for making floors • *oak/concrete planks* • *a plank of wood* • *We used a plank to cross the ditch.*

plank·ing /ˈplæŋ·kɪŋ/ *n* [U] • Planking is an area of planks that have been used to form a surface: *rotten planking* ○ *the ship's planking*

plank [PRINCIPLE] /plæŋk/ *n* [C] an important principle on which the activities of esp. a political group are based • *Educational reform was one of the main planks* **of** *their election campaign.* • *The party's policy is based on five* **central** *planks.* • *Equal pay for equal work is an important plank* **of** *feminism.*

plank·ton /ˈplæŋk·tən/ *n* [U] very small plants and animals which float on the surface of the sea and on which other sea animals feed

plant [LIVING THING] /£plɑːnt, $plænt/ *n* [C] a living thing which grows in earth, in water or on other plants. It usually has a stem, leaves, roots and flowers and produces seeds and can make its own food. Trees are plants, but the word is mainly used for those plants which are smaller than trees. • *plants and animals* • *a garden full of exotic plants* • *annual/perennial plants* • *house/indoor plants* • *garden/wild plants* • *a tomato plant* • *(esp. Br)* A **plant pot** (*Aus* **flower pot**, *Am usually* **planter** or **pot**) is a container in which plants are grown. • See also HOUSEPLANT.

plant *obj* /£plɑːnt, $plænt/ *v* [T] • To plant a plant is to put it into the ground or into a container of earth so that it will grow: *We planted trees and bushes* **in** *our new garden.* ○ *If planted* **in** *pots now, the hyacinth bulbs will flower early in the spring.* • If you plant a particular place, you put plants into the ground there: *Potato farmers planted 81 000 acres this year.* ○ *The plot was surrounded by a stone wall and planted* **with** *flowering trees.* ○ *The garden is densely* *planted* (=the plants are close together) *and needs little weeding.* • If you plant something **out**, you put a plant that was grown in a building into the ground outside: *Plant out the geraniums/tomatoes in early June.* [M]

plant·er /£'plɑːn·təʳ, $'plæn·t̬ɚ/ *n* [C] • A planter is someone who grows a particular crop in a hot part of the world: *a tea/sugar/rubber planter* • A planter is a also large container in which plants are grown for decoration or a frame on which to stand such a container. • A planter is also a machine used to plant crops: *a potato planter*

plant·ing /£'plɑːn·tɪŋ, $'plæn·t̬ɪŋ/ *n* • *Heavy spring rain delayed planting in parts of Indiana and Ohio.* [U] • *We organize tree plantings with school groups.* [C]

plant *obj* PUT /£plɑːnt, $plænt/ *v* [T always + adv/prep] to put (something) firmly and strongly in a particular place • *She planted her feet under the table and made it clear she would not move.* • *My brother planted him***self** *on the sofa in front of the television.* • *He planted a kiss on her forehead/a blow on his opponent's jaw.* • To plant an idea or story is to cause it to exist: *The lawyer managed to plant* **doubts** *about his honesty* **in** *the jury's minds.* ○ *Who planted these* **rumours**?

plant *obj* PUT SECRETLY /£plɑːnt, $plænt/ *v* [T always + adv/prep] *infml* to put (something or someone) in a position secretly, esp. in order to deceive someone • *She insisted that the drugs had been planted on her without her knowledge.* • *They're convinced that someone has planted a bugging device in their offices.* • *The government has planted a secret agent in the terrorist group.* • *The bomb was planted in the station waiting room.*

plant /£plɑːnt, $plænt/ *n* [C usually sing] • *He insisted the money was a plant* (=had been secretly given to him by someone who wanted to make him seem guilty of stealing it).

plant BUILDING/MACHINES /£plɑːnt, $plænt/ *n* machines used in industry, or a factory in which such machines are used, or *(Br and Aus)* a large heavy machine or vehicle used in industry, for building roads, etc. • *The industry was accused of having invested little in workers, plant or infrastructure.* [U] • *Two more car-assembly plants* (=factories) *were closed by the strike.* [C] • *They've agreed to allow their nuclear-weapons plants* (=factories) *to be inspected.* [C] • *(Br and Aus) The sign by the roadworks said 'Slow – heavy plant* (=heavy vehicles) *crossing'.* [U] • *(Br and Aus) The firm's main business was plant* **hire**.

plan·ta·tion /£plæn'teɪ·ʃᵊn, £plɑːn-, $plæn-/ *n* [C] a large farm, esp. in a hot part of the world, on which a particular type of crop is grown, or an area where trees are grown for wood • *a tea/coffee/sugar/cotton/rubber plantation* • *plantations of fast-growing conifers*

plaque FLAT OBJECT /plɑːk, plæk/ *n* [C] a flat piece of metal, stone, wood or plastic with writing on it which is fixed to a wall, door or other object • *The small buildings were marked with a modest* **brass** *plaques, stating the name and business of the occupiers.* See also PLATE FLAT PIECE. • *There was a* **bronze** *plaque giving the names of five local men who died in the war.* • *Her Majesty and Her Royal Highness toured the Youth Centre and later* **unveiled** *a* **commemorative** *plaque.* • *On the* **memorial** *plaque these words are* **inscribed**: *'At the rising of the sun, until the setting of the same – we shall remember them'.* • *(Br)* A **blue** plaque on the wall of a house shows that someone famous once lived there: *The blue plaque said 'Charles Darwin, biologist, lived here'.*

plaque SUBSTANCE /plɑːk, plæk/ *n* [U] a substance containing bacteria that forms on the surface of teeth

plas·ma BLOOD /'plæz·mə/, **blood plas·ma** *n* [U] the pale yellow liquid that forms 55% of human blood and contains the blood cells

plas·ma HOT SUBSTANCE /'plæz·mə/ *n* [U] a very hot gas found, for example, inside the Sun and other stars • *solar plasma* • *plasma physics*

plas·ter SUBSTANCE /£'plɑː·stəʳ, $'plæs·t̬ɚ/ *n* [U] a substance which becomes hard as it dries and is used esp. for spreading on walls and ceilings in order to give a smooth surface • *The plaster on the walls had cracked as it dried.* • *A roof leak has damaged a section of ceiling plaster.* • *The wall paintings were frescoes, painted in the traditional way on wet plaster.* • **Plaster of Paris** is a mixture of a white powder and water which becomes hard quickly as it dries and is used esp. to make **plaster casts.** • A **plaster cast** (also **cast**) is a shape made of **plaster of Paris**, either a protective covering for a broken bone or a copy of another object such as a statue. • *(Br)* If a part of the body is **in plaster** (*Am and Aus also* **in a cast**), it has a **plaster cast** around it to protect it while it heals: *When I broke my leg, I had it in plaster for about six weeks.* • See also PLASTERBOARD. • PIC› **Medical equipment**

plas·ter *obj* /£'plɑː·stəʳ, $'plæs·t̬ɚ/ *v* [T] • *We had a professional in to plaster the walls and ceiling.* • *The torrential rain had plastered her hair* (=made it stick in a flat smooth layer) **to** *her head.* • To plaster a surface or an object with something is to cover it completely or thickly: *She had plastered her bedroom walls* **with** *photos of pop stars.* ○ *The car was plastered* **with** *mud.* ○ *The story was plastered* **all over** *the front page of the newspaper* (=it was printed in a very obvious way).

pla·ster·ing /£'plɑː·stᵊr·ɪŋ, $'plæs·tɚ·ɪŋ/ *n* [U] • *There's only the plastering left to be done.*

plas·ter·er /£'plɑː·stᵊr·əʳ, $'plæs·tɚ·ɚ/ *n* [C] • A plasterer is a person whose job is to cover walls and ceilings with plaster: *He's a painter and decorator as well as a plasterer.*

plas·ter STICKY MATERIAL *Br* /£'plɑː·stəʳ, $'plæs·t̬ɚ/, *Br fml* **stick·ing plas·ter**, *Am and Aus trademark* **Band–Aid** *n* a small piece of sticky material used to cover and protect a cut in the skin • *a box of waterproof plasters* [C] • **Put** *a plaster* **on** *it – that way it won't get infected.* [C] • *I need a new* **roll of** *sticking plaster.* [U]

plas·ter·board /£'plɑː·stə·bɔːd, $'plæs·tɚ·bɔːrd/, **wall·board** *n* [U] material consisting of two sheets of heavy paper with a layer of PLASTER between them, used to make walls and ceilings before putting on a top layer of plaster

pla·stered /£'plɑː·stəd, $'plæs·tɚd/ *adj* [after v] *infml* extremely drunk • *They went out to the pub and* **got** *plastered.*

plas·tic SUBSTANCE /'plæs·tɪk, 'plɑː·stɪk/ *n* an artificial substance that can be shaped when soft into many different forms and has many different uses • *Someone had put* **a sheet of** *plastic over the broken window.* [U] • *Those flowers aren't real – they're made of plastic.* [U] • *Most plastics are produced from oil, by a chemical process.* [C]

plas·tic /'plæs·tɪk, 'plɑː·stɪk/ *adj* • *a plastic bag/box* • *The cups and plates were plastic.* • *(disapproving)* Plastic can mean artificial or false: *The food was horribly plastic.* ○ *I hate the hostesses false cheerfulness and plastic smiles.* • A **plastic bullet** is a large bullet made of hard plastic that is intended to hurt but not kill people. • **Plastic (money)** is a general way of referring to any type of **credit card** or **debit card**: *I never bother with cash – I just use plastic (money).* ○ *I'd prefer a restaurant where they take plastic.* ○ See **credit card** at CREDIT PAYMENT; **debit card** at DEBIT. • **Plastic wrap** is *Am and Aus for* CLINGFILM.

plas·tics /'plæs·tɪks, 'plɑː·stɪks/ *n* [U] • Plastics is the process or business of producing plastic: *The company has moved into plastics.* ○ *the plastics industry*

plas·tic SOFT /'plæs·tɪk, 'plɑː·stɪk/ *adj* soft enough to be changed into a new shape • *Clay is a very plastic material.* • *This metal is plastic at high temperatures.* • **Plastic explosive** is a soft explosive substance that is used to make bombs and can be easily formed into different shapes: *They used plastic explosive to blow up the bridge.* ○ *Police discovered a secret cache of automatic weapons and plastic explosives.* • **Plastic surgery** is a medical operation to bring a damaged area of skin, and sometimes bone, back to a usual appearance, or to improve a person's appearance: *Several of the survivors of the crash had to have extensive plastic surgery.* ○ *She had plastic surgery* **on** *her nose, to make it straighter.*

plasticity /£plæs'tɪs·ɪ·ti, £plɑː'stɪs-, $plæs'tɪs·ə·t̬i/ *n* [U]

Pla·sti·cine *trademark* /£'plæs·tə·siːn, £'plɑː·stə-, $'plæs·tɪ-/, *Am trademark* **Play–Doh** /£pleɪ·dəʊ, $-doʊ/ *n* [U] a soft substance produced in different colours, used esp. by children to make shapes and models

plate DISH /pleɪt/, *Am also* **dish** *n* [C] a flat usually round dish with a slightly raised edge on which food is put to be served or eaten • *a china plate* • *paper/plastic plates* • *a dinner/tea* (=large/small) *plate* • *a clean/dirty plate* • *"This looks good," he said, looking at his* **heaped** (=very full) *plate.* • *There's too much food* **on** *my plate!* • A plate (also **plateful**) is an amount of food on a plate: *Stephen ate three plates of spaghetti.* • *(infml)* To **give/hand** something **to** someone **on a plate** is to allow them to get or win something very easily: *The American company was handed the contract on a plate.* ○ *Playing with only ten men, Arsenal handed the game to Spurs on a plate.* • *(infml)* If you have many things **on** your **plate** you are very busy because you have many important things to deal with: *She's got* **a lot** *on her plate – especially with two new projects starting this week.* ○ *The aid agencies working with refugees have* **(more than) enough** *on their plate without looking after unnecessary visitors.* • *(Br)* A **plate rack** (*Am and Aus* **dish rack**) is a frame in which plates can be put vertically, esp. so that they can dry after being washed. • PIC› **Cutlery, Rack** Ⓓ

plate·ful /ˈpleɪt·fʊl/ *n* [C] • *She ate the whole plateful of sandwiches* (= all that was on one plate).

plate FLAT PIECE /pleɪt/ *n* [C] a flat piece of something that is hard and does not bend • *Thick bony plates protected the dinosaur against attack.* • *The ship's deck is composed of* **steel** *plates.* • *On the* **brass** *plate* (= flat rectangle of brass) *outside the building it said Dr B. Singh.* See also PLAQUE FLAT OBJECT. • *The car had German* **(licence/number)** *plates* (= flat pieces of metal or plastic with the car's number on them). • *(specialized)* A plate is also a flat piece of metal with words and/or pictures on it that can be printed: *In the forger's workshop they found the plates he'd used to print the £10 notes.* • **Plate glass** is large sheets of glass used esp. as windows and doors in shops and offices: *a plate-glass window* • See also L-PLATE; TECTONIC PLATE. • PIC› **Car** Ⓓ

plate *obj* THIN LAYER /pleɪt/ *v* [T usually passive] to cover (a metal object) with a thin layer of another metal, esp. gold or silver • *We normally plate the car handles with nickel and then chrome.* • *Tin cans are generally made of steel, very thinly plated* **with** *a layer of tin.* • *The plating may be intended for decoration, or to provide resistance to corrosion.* • Ⓓ

plate /pleɪt/ *n* [U] • *The knives and forks are silver plate* (= ordinary metal with a layer of silver on top). • Plate is also objects, especially plates, dishes and cups, completely made of a valuable metal such as gold or silver: *The thieves got away with £15 000 worth of church plate, some of it dating back to the twelfth century.*

-plat·ed /£-ˈpleɪ·tɪd, $-t̬ɪd/ *combining form* • *The gold-plated earrings are much cheaper than the solid gold ones.*

plate PICTURE /pleɪt/ *n* [C] *specialized* a picture, esp. in colour, in a book • *Hats and caps are illustrated in plate 13.* • *The three birds differ in small features (see Plate 4).* • Ⓓ

plat·eau /£ˈplæt·əʊ, $plætˈoʊ/ *n* [C] *pl Br* **plateaux** /£ˈplæt·əʊz, $plætˈoʊz/ or *Am and Aus* **plateaus** a large flat area of land that is high above sea level • *The town is situated on a plateau high up amongst the mountains of the north.* • A plateau is also a period during which there are no large changes: *The US death rate* **reached** *a plateau in the 1960s, before declining suddenly.*

plate·let /ˈpleɪt·lət/ *n* [C] *specialized* a very small cell in the blood that makes the blood thicker and more solid in order to stop bleeding caused by an injury

plat·form /£ˈplæt·fɔːm, $-fɔːrm/ *n* [C] a flat raised area or structure • *Make a platform from these boxes and put the music system on that.* • *(Br and Aus)* A platform (*Am* **track**) at a railway station is a long flat raised structure where people get on and off trains: *So many times he had stood on* **railway** *platforms waving goodbye to her.* ○ *The train for Cambridge will depart from platform 9.* • A platform is also the raised part of the floor in a large room, from which you make a speech or give a musical performance: *Speaker after speaker* **mounted/took the** *platform to denounce the policy.* ○ *It was the first time a Green politician and a Labour minister had* **shared a** *platform* (= given speeches at the same event). ○ *This brilliant young violinist, still only 13 years old, has appeared on* **concert** *platforms all round the world.* • *(Br)* The platform is also the people who are in the raised part of a room to make speeches: *An elderly lady in the audience stood up and said she had a question for the platform.* ○ *The platform* **party** (= the group on the platform) *applauded loudly.* • A platform is also an opportunity to make your opinion known publicly: *He paid $150 million for a national newspaper and used it as a platform* **for** *airing his personal view on the war.* ○ *By refusing to give us a grant to make this programme, they are denying us a platform.* • A politician's or political party's platform is the things that they say they believe in and that they will achieve, which they hope will persuade people to support and vote for them in an election: *We campaigned on a platform of low taxation and reduced government intervention in the economy.* • **Platform shoes** (also **platforms**) are shoes that have extremely thick bottoms so that the feet are raised more than usual from the ground. • PIC› **Energy**

plat·i·num /£ˈplæt·ɪ·nəm, $ˈplæt·nəm/ *n* [U] an extremely valuable metal that is silvery in colour, does not react easily with other chemicals and is used in jewellery and in industry • *a platinum wedding ring* • *Since the catalytic converters that clean up car emissions are made from platinum, the price of the precious metal has increased.* • A **platinum blonde** is a young woman with hair so pale it is almost white: *It's more common to see platinum blondes/women with platinum blonde hair in countries like Sweden.*

plat·i·tude /£ˈplæt·ɪ·tjuːd, $ˈplæt̬·ə·tuːd/ *n* [C] *disapproving* a remark or statement about something that, although it might be true, is boring and meaningless because it has been said so many times before • *We'll get the usual politicians who'll* **mouth** *the usual platitudes about 'the glories of democracy'.*

plat·i·tud·i·nous /£ˌplæt·ɪˈtjuː·dɪ·nəs, $ˌplæt̬·əˈtuː·dən-/ *adj fml disapproving*

pla·ton·ic /£pləˈtɒn·ɪk, $-ˈtɑː·nɪk/ *adj* (of a relationship or emotion) affectionate but not sexual • *She knew he was sexually interested in her, but she preferred to keep the relationship platonic.*

pla·toon /pləˈtuːn/ *n* [C + sing/pl v] a small group of about 10 or 12 soldiers, with a LIEUTENANT in charge of it • *(fig.) A platoon of demonstrators/clowns/journalists arrived on the scene.*

plat·ter /£ˈplæt·əʳ, $ˈplæt̬·ɚ/ *n* [C] *Am and Aus, or Br old use* a large plate used for serving food • *a fish platter* • *a platter of sliced tomatoes*

plat·y·pus /£ˈplæt·ɪ·pəs, $ˈplæt̬-/, **duck-billed plat·y·pus** *n* [C] an Australian river mammal with a wide beak whose young are born from eggs

plaud·its /£ˈplɔː·dɪts, $ˈplɑː-/ *pl n fml* praise • *The high quality of the photography* **earned/won** *plaudits from all the experts in the audience.*

plaus·i·ble /£ˈplɔː·zə·bl̩, $ˈplɑː-/ *adj* seeming likely to be true; able to be believed • *a plausible explanation/answer/excuse* • *(disapproving)* A person who is plausible appears to be honest and truthful, even if they are not: *He was one of those plausible salesmen.*

plaus·i·bly /£ˈplɔː·zə·bli $ˈplɑː-/ *adv* • *Neither side can plausibly claim to be completely innocent in this conflict.*

plaus·i·bil·i·ty /£ˌplɔː·zəˈbɪl·ɪ·ti, $ˌplɑː·zəˈbɪl·ə·t̬i/ *n* [U] • *In Chapter Two she goes on to test the plausibility of these assumptions.*

play ENJOY /pleɪ/ *v* [I] (esp. of children) to spend time doing an enjoyable and/or amusing activity • *The children spent the afternoon playing in the garden.* • *My daughter used to play* **with** *the kids next door.* • *As a kitten, Puss loved to play* **with** *a ball of string.* • *(humorous) My father is upstairs playing* **with** *his new toy – he's bought a new computer.* • *The children were playing* **at** (= pretending to be) *Batman and Robin.* • To play **at** also refers to doing something for enjoyment or interest, or without much care and effort, rather than in a serious way or as a job: *She's only playing* **at** *being an actress – she's going off to law school next year.* • *(disapproving)* If you ask **what** someone is **playing at**, you express you anger, surprise and disapproval of something they are doing: *What the hell were you playing at – you could have got us all killed!* • To **play along (with** someone) is temporarily to do what they ask you to do: *He was reluctant but he played along, because he wanted to find out more about their plans, before going to the police.* • *(infml disapproving)* If someone who is married or has a serious relationship **plays around**, they have sex with another person or people: *If she finds out he's been playing around* **with** *his secretary, there'll be trouble.* • To **play (around) with** something is to consider various ways of doing something before making a decision about it: *The Committee played around with several ideas before making a final decision.* ○ *Patricia and I were playing with the possibility of moving to Glasgow.* • *(Br and Aus) She accused him of* **playing politics** (= using the relationships between people for his own advantage). • To **play with** your food is to move it around on your plate, rather than eating it, because you do not feel like eating it: *"Stop playing with your food," my mother used to tell me.* • *(infml)* People sometimes say to **play with yourself** in order to avoid saying MASTURBATE (= give yourself sexual pleasure by touching your sexual organs): *He found two of the smaller boys playing with themselves in the boys' toilets.* ○ *(fig.) Oh,* **go** *play with yourself* (= Go away and stop annoying me)! •

If you have a particular amount of time or money to **play with**, you have that amount available to use: *Having only £200 to play with, they bought a second-hand piano.* • *You're* **playing with fire** (=doing something very dangerous), *agreeing to take part in this dishonest business deal.* • **Play-Doh** is *Am trademark for* PLASTICINE (=soft substance used as a toy).

play /pleɪ/ *n* • *If the school gives them a lot of homework, the kids don't get much time for play in the evenings.* [U] • *We watched the dolphins* **at** *play in the sea around the boat.* [U] • A **play on words** is an amusing use of a word with more than one meaning or that sounds like another word: *The name of the shop – 'Strata Various' – is a play on words, because it sounds like 'Stradivarius,' the famous violin maker.*

play·ful /ˈpleɪ·fəl/ *adj* • *a playful* (=not serious) *exchange of insults* • *He was in a playful mood* (=He was being energetic and slightly silly while trying to be amusing).

play·ful·ly /ˈpleɪ·fəl·i/ *adv* • *The child was pulling at her hair playfully.*

play·ful·ness /ˈpleɪ·fəl·nəs/ *n* [U]

play *(obj)* GAME /pleɪ/ *v* to take part in (a game or other organized activity) • *He loves playing football.* [T] • *Do you want to play cards* **(with** *us)?* [T] • *Irene's busy on Saturday so she won't be able to play* **(in** *the match).* [I] • *Which team do you play* **for**? [I] • *Chris plays* **in** *attack.* [I] • *Luke plays centre-forward* (=plays in that position within the team). [I] • If you play a person or team, you compete against them: *Who are Aston Villa playing next week?* [T] • To play the ball or play a shot is to hit or kick the ball: *He played the ball back* **to** *the goalkeeper.* [T] ○ *A good snooker player takes time deciding which shot to play.* [T] • *United and Rangers are playing* **off** *for* (=playing a game to decide which will win) *the championship.* [I] • In a card game, to play a card is to choose it from the ones you are holding and put it down on the table: *She played the ace of spades.* [T] ○ *If you* **play** *your* **cards right** (=act in a way that will bring you an advantage), *you could make quite a lot of money out of this.* • *(infml)* To **play ball** is to agree to work with or help someone in the way they have suggested: *The family wanted him to be looked after at home but the insurance company refused to play ball.* • *(Am)* If you **play both ends against the middle** you try to get opposing people or groups to fight or disagree so that you will gain something from the situation. • *It wasn't really* **playing fair** (=behaving fairly) *not to tell her we'd already decided.* • *She had kicked off her shoes and was* **playing footsie** *(***with** *him)* (=touching his feet with hers under the table, usually in order to show sexual interest). • *We can't sign the agreement yet – we'll have to* **play for time** (=delay until we are ready). • To **play the field** is to maintain an interest in a number of people or things, esp. to become romantically or sexually involved with a number of partners: *In order to remain competitive, the firm continues to play the field and do business with at least six other companies.* ○ *I can't see Becky settling down with just one man, she enjoys playing the field too much.* • *You should have told them – it wasn't* **playing the game** (=behaving fairly) *to keep it secret.* • *Don't* **play games** *(with me)* (=try to deceive me)*!* • *(infml esp. Am)* To **play hardball** is to be firm and determined in order to get what you want: *He's a nice guy but he can play hardball when he needs to.* • A **playing card** is one of a set of 52 small rectangular pieces of stiffened paper each with a number and one of four signs printed on it, used in games. • A **playing field** is a large area of ground where sport is played: *The school playing fields were marked out for football and rugby.* • A **play-off** is an extra game in a competition played between teams or competitors who have both got the same number of points, in order to allow one to become the winner of the competition. • LP **Sports**

play /pleɪ/ *n* • *Rain stopped play* (=the game) *during the final of the National Tennis Championship.* [U] • If a ball is **in/out of** play it is/is not in a position where it can be hit, kicked, etc.: *The ball had gone out of play.* [U] ○ *She managed to keep the ball in play.* [U] • *(Am)* In sports, a play can also be a plan or a small set of actions: *The school football team has been practicing new offensive plays all week.* [C] ○ *The new pitcher made a great play on that throw to first base.* [C] • If you **make a play for** something or someone you try to obtain something, or start a relationship with someone, esp. by using a clever plan: *I wouldn't have made a play for him if I'd known he was married.*

play·er /£ˈpleɪ·əʳ, $-ɚ/ *n* [C] • A player is someone who takes part in a game or sport: *Each player takes three cards.* ○ *The team has many exceptionally talented players.* • *(fig.) She is one of the leading/key players* (=people or groups taking part) *in the reorganization of the health service.*

play *(obj)* ACT /pleɪ/ *v* to perform as (a particular character in a play or film), or to behave or pretend in a particular way, esp. in order to produce a particular effect or result • *In the film version, Kenneth Branagh played the hero.* [T] • *North-West Opera played* **to** *full houses every night.* [I] • *I didn't realize that 'Macbeth' was playing* (=being performed) **at** *the Guildhall.* [I] • *It cannot be right that genetic engineers should play* **God** (=act as if they were in total control of something), *interfering with the basic patterns of Nature.* [T] • *Would you mind playing* **host** (=entertaining the guests)*?* [T] • *(Br)* To **play gooseberry** (*Am* **be a third wheel**) is to be an unwanted third person who is present when two other people, esp. two lovers, want to be alone. • If you **play hard to get**, you avoid accepting someone's suggestions or invitations: *She seems to think that by playing hard to get, she'll make him more interested in her.* • *(infml)* If something **plays (merry) hell with** something else, it damages it or creates confusion: *The power cuts play hell with all our computers.* ○ *Their star strikers played merry hell with the French defence towards the end of the game.* • If you **play it cool**, you behave in a calm, controlled way, often intentionally appearing not to be interested in the thing that you particularly want to get: *After six unsuccessful months of ringing her and asking her out, he finally decided to play it cool.* • *"I can't tell you what to expect." "Don't worry, I'll* **play it by ear** (=decide what to do when I see what is happening, rather than planning in advance)*."* • *To* **play (it) safe** (=To be careful), *let's allow an extra ten minutes, just in case.* • To **play a joke/trick (on** someone) is to deceive them for amusement or in order to get an advantage over them: *She loves to play cruel practical jokes on her friends.* ○ *Raising the price at the last minute was a mean trick to play on the buyers.* ○ *(fig.) The wind played one of its tricks and died down just at the crucial moment.* ○ *(fig.) I thought I heard something – my* **ears** *must have been playing tricks on me* (=causing me to imagine something that was not real or true). • To **play on/upon** someone's feelings is to encourage and make unfair use of these feelings in order to get an advantage for yourself: *The beggars tend to play on one's feelings of guilt and compassion, by having a baby or young child with them.* • If a person or people **play out** something, they act as if it were really happening: *In the psychotherapy group, patients were free to play their fantasies out.* • If a situation **plays** itself **out**, it develops until nothing more can happen and it is no longer very important: *The best thing to do is to stand back and let the crisis play itself out.* ○ See also PLAYED-OUT. • *(esp. Am)* If a situation **plays out**, it happens and develops: *The debate will play out in the meetings and in the media over the next week or two.* • *My thanks to everyone who has* **played a part (in** *saving the hospital)* (=helped to do this). • *(infml) If the tax people ask you any questions, just* **play possum** (=pretend not to know anything or be aware of anything). • *(Br slang)* To **play silly buggers** is to behave in a way that is silly, stupid or annoying: *There'll be a serious accident sooner or later if people don't stop playing silly buggers.* • *That's typical of Tom –* **playing to the gallery** *again* (=behaving in a way intended to attract attention). • To **play up to** someone is to be very polite to them in order to get some advantage for yourself: *Julie knows how to play up to the supervisors – she can always get time off work when she wants it.*

play /pleɪ/ *n* [C] • A play is a piece of writing that is intended to be acted in a theatre or on radio or television: *a radio play* ○ *Lorca wrote several well known plays.* ○ *"Did you see the play* (=the performance of the play) *on Thursday?" "No, I went on Wednesday night."* • *"The play's the thing/ Wherein I'll catch the conscience of the king"* (Shakespeare, Hamlet 2.2) • See also PLAYACTING; PLAYBILL; PLAYHOUSE THEATRE; SCREENPLAY; PLAYWRIGHT.

play·er /£ˈpleɪ·əʳ, $-ɚ/ *n* [C] • *(old use)* A player is an actor. • Players is sometimes used in the name of theatre companies: *the Shakespeare Players*

play *(obj)* PRODUCE SOUNDS/PICTURES /pleɪ/ *v* to perform (music) on (an instrument), or to (cause to) produce (sound or a picture) • *On this recording she plays the sonata much slower.* [T] • *He learned to play the clarinet at the age of ten.* [T] • *She played brilliantly, despite the poorness of the piano.* [I] • *Play us a song then!/Play a song* **for/to** *us then!* [+ two objects] • *The band is playing* (=performing in) *Los Angeles on the 29th and San Francisco on the 31st of the next month.* [T] • *On Radio London they play African and South American music as well as rock and pop.* [T] • *They could hear a jazz band playing in the distance.* [I] • *Play that last few minutes of the video again, and you'll see the robber's face.* [T] • To play **back** something that has just been recorded is to put it through a machine so that you can listen to it or watch it: *When the drummer had done her bit, they played the whole song back and the sound engineers made some changes.* [M] • To **play second fiddle (to** someone else) is to be less important than they are: *I'm not prepared to play second fiddle to Christina any more – I'm looking for another job!* • *"Play it again Sam (Originally – Play it, Sam. Play 'As Time Goes By')"* (said by Ingrid Bergman in the film *Casablanca*, 1942) • See also PLAYBACK.

play·a·ble /ˈpleɪ·ə·bl̩/ *adj* • If a piece of music is playable it is not too difficult for a particular person to play.

play·er /£ˈpleɪ·əʳ, $-ɚ/ *n* [C] • A player is a person who plays a musical instrument: *a cello/flute/piano player* ○ *The ordinary players in the orchestra get paid much less than soloists.* • A player is also a machine: *a CD/tape/video player*

play *(obj)* MOVE /pleɪ/ *v* to move, direct or be directed over or onto something • *A smile played* **across/over/on** *his lips* (=He smiled a little). [I] • *Firefighters played* (=aimed) *their* **hoses onto** *the base of the fire.* [T] • *She could hear the fountain playing* (=sending out water) *in the courtyard outside.* [I]

play /pleɪ/ *n* [U] • *They watched the play of moonlight* **across** *the surface of the water.* • *The play of emotion* **across/on** *his face revealed the conflict going on in his heart.* • If there is play in a rope or in any structure, it is free to move, esp. a small distance: *Aircraft wings are designed to have a certain amount of play in them so that they do not snap under the stresses of flight.* • Play (also **interplay**) is used when talking about the ways in which forces, feelings, objects or people act or have an effect in a particular situation: *The play* **of** *all these factors – of both natural and human origin – determines the final ecological balance in any environment.* • If something **comes into play** or is **brought into play** it starts to have or is given a use and an effect in a particular situation: *In the summer months a different set of climatic factors come into play.* ○ *Even bringing into play all the resources and staff available would not be likely to help resolve the immediate shortfall in production.* • If you **give/allow** your emotions or ideas **full play** or if something or someone **gives/allows full play to** emotions or ideas, they develop and are used completely: *The move from stage to films allowed Gildit to give full play to his sense of the fantastic.*

play *obj* RISK MONEY /pleɪ/ *v* [T] to risk money, esp. on the results of (races or business deals), hoping to win more money • *He plays* **the horses**/*the stock exchange/the (stock) market.*

play down *obj*, **play** *obj* **down** *v adv* [M] to make (something) seem less important or less bad than it really is; to DOWNPLAY • *Military spokespeople tried to play down the seriousness of the disaster, but within a few hours it was clear that at least five ships had been sunk.*

play off *obj*, **play** *obj* **off** *v adv prep* [M] to encourage (one person or group) to compete or argue with another, in the hope of getting some advantage from this situation • *Management policy seemed to be to play one department off* **against** *another.* • See also **play off** and **play-off** at PLAY GAME.

play up *obj* EMPHASIZE, **play** *obj* **up** *v adv* [M] to emphasize (something) or make it seem more important than it really is, usually in order to get a slightly unfair advantage • *The official report plays up the likely benefits of the scheme, but glosses over the costs.*

play *(obj)* **up** CAUSE PAIN *v adv Br and Aus* to cause (someone) trouble or pain, esp. by not working or behaving in the expected way • *(Br and Aus) The starter motor was playing up again.* [I] • *(Br) She has rheumatoid arthritis in her feet and they play her up really badly at this time of year, when it's cold.* [T] • *(Br) There's a group of young hooligans who've been playing (the authorities) up, writing graffiti and starting small fires.* [I/T] • *(Br) The children have been really playing up (their mother) this week.* [I/M]

play·act·ing /£ˈpleɪˌæk·tɪŋ, $-t̬ɪŋ/ *n* [U] pretending; behaviour intended to amuse or to hide your real thoughts and feelings • *Her exaggerated outbursts of anger and joy were part of any adolescent's necessary playacting.* • *Don't take any notice of him – he's just playacting.*

play·back /ˈpleɪ·bæk/ *n* a playing of a recording again, to hear or see something already heard or seen; a REPLAY RECORDING • *Do us a playback of those last few frames.* [C] • *You can see it again on playback.* [U]

play·bill /ˈpleɪ·bɪl/ *n* [C] a piece of paper advertising a play and giving information about where and when it is being performed

play·boy /ˈpleɪ·bɔɪ/ *n* [C] a rich man who spends his time and money on luxuries and a life of pleasure • *The playboys spend the summers on their yachts in the Mediterranean.*

played–out /ˌpleɪdˈaʊt/ *adj infml* tired and no longer having the power or ability to do things • *I'm about played-out, Jack – it's time I retired.* • *(fig.) They won't get people to vote for them with those old played-out policies.* • See also **play out** at PLAY ACT.

play·ful /ˈpleɪ·fəl/ *adj* See at PLAY ENJOY

play·ful·ness /ˈpleɪ·fəl·nəs/ *n* [U]

play·ground /ˈpleɪ·graʊnd/ *n* [C] an area designed for children to play in outside, esp. at a school • *The school playground was a large tarmac rectangle where they played endless games of football.* • *(fig.) The coastal villages are the playground* **of** *the rich and famous* (=rich and famous people spend a lot of time there, enjoying themselves). • Playground is also *Am for* **recreation ground**. See at RECREATION.

play·group *Br also* /ˈpleɪ·gruːp/, **play·school** *n* [C] a group of children aged 3 to 5 years old who play and learn together informally, at regular times in a place outside their homes, which is organized either by their parents or trained leaders • LP› **Schools and colleges**

play·house THEATRE /ˈpleɪ·haʊs/ *n* [C] *pl* **playhouses** /ˈpleɪˌhaʊ·zɪz/ *fml or as part of a name* a theatre • *the La Jolla Playhouse in San Diego, California*

play·house TOY HOUSE /ˈpleɪ·haʊs/, *Br also* **Wen·dy house** *n* [C] *pl* **-houses** /-ˌhaʊ·zɪz/ a small structure that looks like a house, used by children for playing in • *In one corner of the classroom a couple of children were having fun in the playhouse.* • PIC› **Playground**

play·mate /ˈpleɪ·meɪt/ *n* [C] a friend, esp. another child, with whom a child plays often • *We were childhood playmates.* • *Jenny invited three of her playmates to her party.* • *Children often invent* **imaginary** *playmates.* • In some newspapers and magazines, playmate is sometimes used of a sexual partner or esp. a woman who is shown in photographs wearing few clothes: *We can reveal that the popular singer now has a new playmate.* ○ *He plans to marry Playboy's 'playmate' for January and cover girl for August.*

play·pen /ˈpleɪ·pen/ *n* [C] a small structure with bars or a net around the sides but open at the top, within which a baby can be left to play safely

play·room /ˈpleɪ·rʊm, -ruːm/ *n* [C] a room intended for children to play in • *They turned the attic into a playroom.*

play·school /ˈpleɪ·skuːl/ *n* [C] *Br* a PLAYGROUP

play·thing /ˈpleɪ·θɪŋ/ *n* [C] an object used for pleasure or amusement, or someone who is considered or treated without respect and is forced to do things for the enjoyment or benefit of someone else • *"Limousines and yachts – the playthings of the rich", he said dismissively.* • *These men's magazines just treat women as playthings.* • *The United Nations has become the plaything of the major powers.* • Playthings sometimes refers to children's toys and other items that they play with: *I keep all the children's playthings in that big cupboard.*

play·time /ˈpleɪ·taɪm/ *n* [U] a period of time, esp. during school hours, when children can play outside • *You'll have to stay in at playtime today, because it's raining.*

play·wright /ˈpleɪ·raɪt/ *n* [C] a person who writes plays

pla·za /ˈplɑː·zə/ *n* [C] an open area or square in a town, esp. in Spanish-speaking countries, or a group of buildings including shops designed as a single development within a town

plc /ˌpiː·elˈsiː/ *n* [after n] *abbreviation for* public limited company (=a company, esp. in Britain, whose shares can be bought and sold by the public and whose debts are limited if it fails financially) • *J Sainsbury plc* • LP› **Letters**

plea REQUEST /pliː/ *n* [C] *fml* an urgent and emotional request • *He* **made** *a plea* **for** *help/mercy.* • *The Archbishop today* **made** *an emotional plea* **for** *peace.* • *Her*

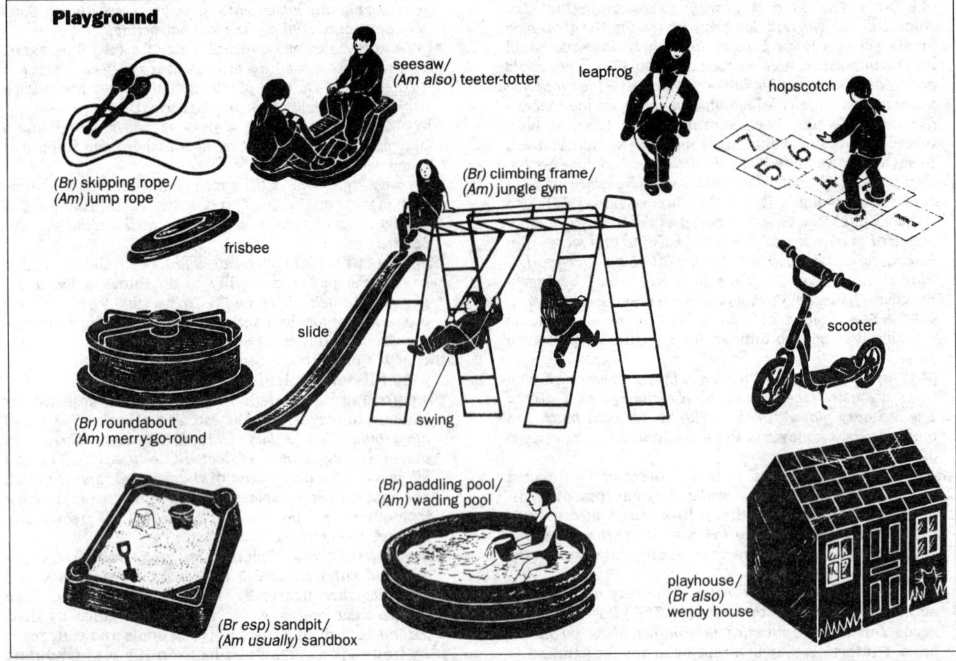

plea **that** *she be allowed to keep the house she was living in went unanswered.* [+ *that* clause]

plea STATEMENT /pliː/ *n* [C] *law* the answer that a person gives in court to the accusation that they have committed a crime • *Mr Wilson* **entered** *a plea of not guilty.* • **Plea bargaining** is the making of an agreement in which a person accused of a crime admits that they are guilty of a less serious crime, so that they will not be charged with a more serious one.

plead REQUEST /pliːd/ *v past* **pleaded** or *Am also* **pled** /pled/ to make an urgent, emotional statement or request for something • *He was on his knees, pleading* **for** *mercy/forgiveness.* [I] • *She appeared on television to plead* **with** *the kidnappers.* [I] • *A middle-aged woman had climbed on the tank to plead* **with** *the soldiers* (= to ask them) *not* **to** *shoot.* [+ *to* infinitive] • *"Give us more time," they pleaded.* [+ clause]

plead·ing /ˈpliː·dɪŋ/ *adj* • *a pleading tone of voice*

plead·ing·ly /ˈpliː·dɪŋ·li/ *adv* • *"Please – try to find me seat on the plane, I must get home tonight," he said pleadingly.*

plead *(obj)* STATE /pliːd/ *v past* **pleaded** or **pled** /pled/ *fml* to make a statement of what you believe to be true, esp. in support of something or someone or in answer to an accusation in a law court • *(law) The seven defendants were paying a high-powered attorney to plead their* **case** (= argue for them in court). [T] • *(law) The defendant pleaded* **guilty/innocent** *to robbery with violence.* [L only + adj] • *(law) The judge ruled her unfit to plead* (= to answer a legal charge) *on the grounds of insanity.* [I] • *He pleaded* **ignorance** *of* (= said he did not know about) *the package they found in his suitcase.* [T] • *A department spokesperson pleaded official difficulties as the reason for the delay.* [T] • *The factory can plead* **that**, *given problems of finance and technology, it is doing the best it can to reduce the noise.* [+ *that* clause]

pleas·ant /ˈplez·ᵊnt/ *adj* enjoyable, attractive or friendly; easy to like • *a pleasant view/climate/smile/person* • *a pleasant meeting/day/surprise* • *The town is very pleasant – full of parks and pretty streets.* • *Harold did his best to be pleasant* **to** *the old man.* • **It** *was pleasant* **to** *sit down after standing for hours.* [+ *to* infinitive]

pleas·ant·ly /ˈplez·ᵊnt·li/ *adv* • *They treated me pleasantly enough.* • *Jacqui was pleasantly surprised to hear she had got a B for history.*

plea·sant·ness /ˈplez·ᵊnt·nəs/ *n* [U]

pleas·ant·ry /ˈplez·ᵊn·tri/ *n* [C usually pl] *fml* a polite and often slightly amusing remark, usually made in order to create a relaxed feeling in other people • *After an exchange of pleasantries, the delegation revealed the purpose of their visit.*

please POLITE REQUEST /pliːz/ *exclamation* used in order to make a request more polite, or in order to add force to a request or demand • *Could I have two cups of coffee and a tea, please?* • *"Please can I have an ice cream?" said the girl.* • *Please, David, put the knife down.* • *Oh, please. Do shut up!* • *"May I see your passports, please (fml* **if you please**)*?" said the customs officer.* • *(Br)* Please is also used esp. by children to a teacher or other adult in order to get their attention: *Please Miss, I know the answer!* • Please is also used when accepting something politely or enthusiastically: *"More potatoes?" "Please."* ○ *"May I bring my husband?" "Please do."* ○ *(esp. Br) "Oh,* **yes** *please," shouted the children, when I suggested a trip to the zoo.*

please *(obj)* MAKE HAPPY /pliːz/ *v* to make (someone) feel happy or satisfied or to give (someone) pleasure • *The presents didn't please her as much as I'd expected.* [T] • *He was always a good boy, very friendly and eager to please.* [I] • **It** *pleases me* **to** *see a well-designed book!* [T + obj + *to* infinitive] • *(slightly fml)* Please also means to want, like or choose, when used with words such as *whatever, whoever,* and *anywhere*: *She'll listen to advice, but in the end she'll do it whichever way she pleases.* [I] ○ *You can do* **as** *you please.* [I] • *(fml)* **Please God** is used to express a strong hope: *It'll be finished by Christmas, please God.* • *(infml)* If you say **please yourself** to someone, you mean that they should do whatever they want to do, but that you disagree with them and do not feel responsible for them: *"I can't stand this place – I'm going home." "Please yourself."*

pleased /pliːzd/ *adj* • *a pleased* (= happy or satisfied) *expression/laugh/smile* • *I told my dad about losing the camera. He wasn't pleased* (= He was annoyed). • *Was the Ambassador pleased* **about** *the news?* • *The company is pleased* **that** *the import restrictions are being relaxed.* [+ *that* clause] • *Are you pleased* **with** *your new car* (= is it satisfactory)*?* • *Simon's looking very pleased* **with** *himself today* (= happy and satisfied about something good that he has done or that has happened to him). • *I'm always so pleased* **to** *get off an aeroplane.* [+ *to* infinitive] • If someone is pleased **to** do something, they are very willing to do it: *The Personnel Manager said she'd be pleased* **to** *offer advice.* [+ *to* infinitive] ○ *I'm* **only too** (= very) *pleased to help.* • *She was* **as pleased as Punch** (= very pleased) *about the news.* • **Pleased to meet you** is a polite way of greeting someone when you meet them for the first time: *"I'm very pleased to meet you," he said as we shook hands.*

pleas·ing /ˈpliː·zɪŋ/ *adj fml* • You describe something or someone as pleasing when it gives you a feeling of satisfaction or enjoyment: *a pleasing performance* ○ *a very* *pleasing piece of architecture* ○ *The music was pleasing* **to** *the ear.* ○ **It** *was pleasing* **to** *know that the presentation had gone so well.* [+ *to* infinitive] ○ **It**'*s pleasing* **that** *so many people could come.* [+ *that* clause]

pleas·ing·ly /ˈpliː·zɪŋ·li/ *adv fml* • *The programme included a pleasingly varied mixture of old and new songs.*

please [ANNOYANCE] /pliːz/ *v fml dated* **if you please** used to express surprise and annoyance • *They're demanding £200, if you please, just to replace a couple of broken windows!* • See also **if you please** at PLEASE [POLITE REQUEST].

pleas·ure /£ˈpleʒ·əʳ, $-ɚ/ *n* (something that gives) enjoyment, happiness or satisfaction • *His visits used to* **give** *his grandparents such pleasure.* [U] • *It's quite common for little boys to* **take** *pleasure* **in** *torturing insects and small animals.* [U] • *"I'm off to the States next week." "Oh,* **business or** *pleasure?"* [U] • *"***It** *was such a pleasure* **to** *meet you," she said politely.* [U + *to* infinitive] • *Seeing him again was a real pleasure* **for** *me.* [U] • *$100? Oh it's worth it* **for** *the pleasure* **of** *hearing Domingo sing.* [U] • *He'd written an article on the pleasures and pains of camping.* [C] • *I hope they don't make me give up smoking – it's one of my few pleasures.* [C] • *"It was so kind of you to give us a lift." "Please don't mention it –* **it was a/my pleasure** (= it was no trouble and I was very willing to do it)*."* • *"Would you mind holding the door open for me, please?" "Oh,* **with pleasure** (= willingly)*."* • *(Br law)* Someone who is put in prison **at the King's/Queen's pleasure** is kept there until it is officially decided that it is safe to release them: *He was declared insane and ordered to be* **detained** *in a mental hospital at Her Majesty's pleasure.* • *"The pleasure is momentary, the position ridiculous and the expense damnable"* (comment on sex believed to have been made by the Earl of Chesterfield, 1694-1773)

pleas·ur·a·ble /£ˈpleʒ·ᵊr·ə·bl̩, $-ɚ·ə-/ *adj slightly fml* • *a pleasurable evening/conversation/meal* • *a pleasurable sensation*

pleat /pliːt/ *n* [C] a narrow fold in a piece of cloth made by pressing or sewing two parts of the cloth together

pleat·ed /£ˈpliː·tɪd, $-t̬ɪd/ *adj* • *a pleated skirt* • *Scottish kilts are pleated.*

pleb /pleb/ *n* [C] *infml disapproving* a person of a low social class

pleb·by /ˈpleb·i/ *adj* **-ier, -iest** *infml disapproving* • *I can't bear her plebby friends.*

ple·be·ian /pləˈbiː·ən/ *adj fml disapproving* of a low social class • *He used to make fun of what he called her 'plebeian origins.'*

pleb·i·scite /£ˈpleb·ɪ·sɪt, $-ə·saɪt/ *n fml* a REFERENDUM

plec·trum (*pl* **plectrums** or **plectra**) /ˈplek·trəm/, *infml* **pick** *n* [C] a small thin piece of plastic, metal etc. which is held between the fingers and thumb and is used for playing instruments such as the guitar • [PIC] **Pick**

pled *Am and Scot Eng* /pled/ *past simple and past participle of* PLEAD

pledge /pledʒ/ *n* [C] a promise, or something that is given as a sign that you will keep a promise, esp. one to give money or to be a friend • *When you* **make** *a pledge, you should always try to* **honour/fulfil** *it.* • *All the candidates have* **given/made** *pledges not* **to** *raise taxes if they are elected.* [+ *to* infinitive] • *He's* **made** *a pledge* **that** *he won't drink any alcohol for a month.* [+ *that* clause] • *Thousands of people* **made** *pledges* (= promised to give money) *to the Children in Need charity campaign.* • *I give you this ring as a pledge* (= sign) **of** *my everlasting love for you.* • *(humorous) What's this then, you're only drinking orange juice – have you* **taken/signed the pledge** (= decided to stop drinking alcohol) *or something?*

pledge *obj* /pledʒ/ *v* [T] • *We are asking people to pledge their support for* (= promise that they will support) *our campaign.* • *If you join the armed forces, you have to pledge allegiance to your country.* • *So far, £50 000 has been pledged* (= people have promised to pay this amount) *in response to the appeal.* • *The government has pledged* **that** *it will spend more money on education.* [+ *that* clause] • *Both sides have pledged* **to** *end the fighting.* [+ *to* infinitive] • *I've been pledged* **to** *secrecy.* • *We've pledged ourselves* **to** *fight for justice.* [+ obj + *to* infinitive]

Pleis·to·cene /£ˈplaɪ·stəʊ·siːn, $-stoʊ-/ *adj* [not gradable], *n* (of) the period in the Earth's history which lasted from about 2 000 000 years ago to about 10 000 years ago, during which much of the northern part of the Earth was covered with ice • *These are thought to be Pleistocene rocks.* • *It was during* **the** *Pleistocene that the earliest humans appeared.* [U]

ple·nary /£ˈpliː·nə·ri, $-nɚ·i/ *adj* [not gradable] *specialized* (of a meeting) having all the members of a group or organization present, esp. at a CONFERENCE • *The issue is expected to be discussed at the plenary* **session** *of the UN Security Council.* • *There will be a plenary* **meeting** *of the planning committee on Friday morning.*

ple·nary /£ˈpliː·nə·ri, $-nɚ·i/ *n* [C] *specialized* • *The hall was packed for the plenary* (= the meeting at which all the members, esp. those who are at a CONFERENCE, are present).

plen·i·po·ten·tia·ry /£ˌplen·ɪ·pəʊˈten*t*·ʃᵊr·i, $-poʊˈten*t*·ʃi·er-/ *n* [C] *dated fml* a person who has the authority to act as the representative of his or her country, esp. in another country • *Ambassadors and plenipotentiaries bowed low as the Emperor and Empress entered.*

plen·ty /£ˈplen·ti, $-t̬i/ *pronoun, n, adv* [not gradable] (the state of having) enough or more than enough, or a large amount • *"Would you like some more wine?" "No thanks, I've had plenty."* • *Don't grab at the balloons, children – there are plenty* **for** *everyone.* • *We've got plenty* **of** *time before we need to leave for the airport.* • *He's had plenty* **of** *opportunities to apologize, but he hasn't done so.* • *They've always had plenty* **of** *money.* • *Have another sandwich – there are plenty* **more**. • *There's plenty to do here.* • *(Am infml) This car cost me plenty* (= a lot of money). • *(fml) In the Bible, Joseph said that in Pharoah's dream, the seven good cows represented Egypt having seven years* **of** *plenty* (= a state of having a large supply of what is needed for life). [U] • *(fml) It doesn't seem fair that in some parts of the world there is food* **in** *plenty* (= there is a lot of food)*, while in other parts, people are starving.* [U] • *(infml) There's plenty* (= a lot) **more** *beer in the fridge.* • *(infml) We can get plenty* **more** *people to help if necessary.* • *(infml) You should always make sure that children's shoes are plenty* (= completely) *big* **enough**. • *(infml) I'm plenty warm* **enough**, *thank you.* • *(Am infml) The movie was plenty* (= very) *good, but I don't want to see it again.* • *"I hear you broke up with Dave." "Yeah, but there are* **plenty more where** *he* **came from** (= it is not important because there are a lot of other men, and I can easily find another partner)*."*

plen·ti·ful /£ˈplen·tɪ·fᵊl, $-t̬ɪ-/ *adj* • *Strawberries are plentiful* (= there are a lot of them) *in the summer.* • *I always make sure I have a plentiful* (= large enough) **supply** *of things to keep the children amused when we go on long journeys.*

plen·ti·ful·ly /£ˈplen·tɪ·fᵊl·i, $-t̬ɪ-/ *adv* • *My uncle is always plentifully* **stocked/supplied** *with* (= has a lot of) *wine.*

pleth·o·ra /£ˈpleθ·ᵊr·ə, $-ɚ·ə/ *n* [U] a very large amount of something, esp. a larger amount than you need, want or can deal with • **A** *plethora* **of** *studies have shown the importance of the pre-school years for a child's later development.* • *There's* **a** *plethora* **of** *restrictions on who can apply for the benefits.* • *I can't believe there's such* **a** *plethora* **of** *books about the royal family.*

pleu·ri·sy /£ˈplʊə·rə·si, $ˈplʊr·ə-/ *n* [U] a serious illness in which the covering of the lungs becomes red and swollen, and which causes sharp pain when breathing

Plex·i·glas /£ˈplek·si·glɑːs, $-glæs/ *n* [U] *trademark, Am for* PERSPEX

pli·able /ˈplaɪ·ə·bl̩/ *adj* (of a substance) easily bendable without breaking or cracking, or (of a person) easily influenced and controlled by other people • *Clay is a pliable substance.* • *Some kinds of plastic become pliable if they're heated.* • *(disapproving) He wanted a sweet, pliable, obedient wife, and that wasn't for me!*

pli·a·bil·i·ty /£ˌplaɪ·əˈbɪl·ɪ·ti, $-ə·t̬i/ *n* [U]

pli·ant /ˈplaɪ·ᵊnt/ *adj* (of a person) easily influenced and controlled by other people, or (of a substance or thing) easily bendable without breaking • *I don't think it's a good thing for children to be too pliant.* • *Don't underestimate the power that advertising has to influence a pliant public.* • *These toys are made of pliant rubber, so they won't break.* • *Fashion models often have tall, pliant bodies* (= bodies which bend easily). • Pliant can also mean being able and willing to accept change or new ideas: *After refusing to back down at first, the management has now adopted a more pliant position, and has agreed to listen to the staff's requests.*

pli·an·cy /ˈplaɪ·ᵊn*t*·si/ *n* [U]

pli·ant·ly /ˈplaɪ·ᵊnt·li/ *adv*

pli·ers /£ˈplaɪ·əz, $-ɚz/ *pl n* a small tool with two handles which you pull apart or press together in order to bring together or separate two specially shaped thick flat pieces of metal at the other end • *You use pliers for pulling out nails, or for bending or cutting wire.* • *Could you pass me that* **pair of** *pliers, please?* • PIC> **Tools**

plight CONDITION /plaɪt/ *n* an unpleasant condition, esp. a serious, sad or difficult one • *Everyone is horrified about the plight* **of** *the starving people.* • *They were* **in a sorry/dreadful** *plight when their money, tickets and passports were stolen while they were on holiday.*

plight *obj* MARRY /plaɪt/ *v* [T] **plight** *your* **troth** *old use or humorous* to (promise to) marry • *So you're finally plighting your troth* (= are going to get married), *are you?* • *Let's all drink to Tess and Jason, who are plighting their troth on Saturday.*

plim·soll *Br* /ˈplɪmp·səl/, *Am and Aus* **sneak·er**, *Aus also* **run·ner**, **sand·shoe** *n* [C] a flat light shoe which has a top made of heavy cloth and a bottom made of rubber, and which is worn esp. for sports • *Plimsolls may either be fastened with laces, or have a strip of elastic at the front so that they can be slipped on.* • PIC> **Shoes**

Plim·soll line, **Plim·soll mark** *n* [C] a line painted on the outside of a ship which shows how deep it is legally allowed to go down into the water when it is loaded

plinth /plɪntθ/ *n* [C] a square block, esp. of stone, on which a column or a statue stands • PIC> **Sculpture**

Pli·o·cene /£ˈplaɪ·əʊ·siːn, $-oʊ-/ *n* [U], *adj* [not gradable] (of) the period in the Earth's history which lasted from about 5 000 000 to about 2 000 000 years ago

PLO /£ˌpiː·elˈəʊ, $-ˈoʊ/ *n* [U] **the PLO** *abbreviation for* the Palestine Liberation Organization (= an organization which has the aim of giving to the Palestinian people the land that was Palestine in the past)

plod WALK /£plɒd, $plɑːd/ *v* [I always + adv/prep] **-dd-** to walk taking slow steps as if your feet are heavy • *We plodded through the mud.* • *Isn't it boring being a police officer, plodding* **along** *the streets all day?* • *Despite the wind and the rain, they plodded* **on** *until they reached the cottage.*

plod WORK /£plɒd, $plɑːd/ *v* [I always + adv/prep] **-dd-** to work slowly and continuously, but without imagination, enthusiasm or interest • *We all sit at our desks, plodding* **away** *in silence.* • *For years, he's plodded* **away at** *the same dull routine job.* • *Alex is just plodding* **along** *at school, making very little progress.* • *"Are you coming for lunch?" "No, I think I'll just plod* **on** (= continue working) *for a bit."*

plod·der /£ˈplɒd·əʳ, $ˈplɑː·dɚ/ *n* [C] • *Dennis always gets the job done, but he's a real plodder* (= someone who works slowly and continuously, without showing any imagination or enthusiasm).

plod·ding /£ˈplɒd·ɪŋ, $ˈplɑː·dɪŋ/ *adj* • *She's one of those dull plodding people, who gets things done but has no imagination.*

plonk SOUND /£plɒŋk, $plɑːŋk/, *Am also* **plunk** *n, adv* [not gradable] *infml* (with) a hollow sound like that made when an object is dropped heavily onto a surface • *The plonk of a tennis ball hitting a racquet always makes me think of summer.* [U] • *I heard something go plonk.* • *An apple fell from the tree and landed plonk* **on** *the ground.*

plonk /£plɒŋk, $plɑːŋk/, *Am also* **plunk** *v* [always + adv/prep] *infml* • *I really enjoy plonking* **away on** *the piano* (= playing, usually not very well, by hitting the keys hard). [I] • *He plonked* **out** *the tune of "Happy birthday to you".* [M]

plonk *(obj)* PUT /£plɒŋk, $plɑːŋk/, *Am usually* **plunk** *v* [always + adv/prep] *infml* to put (something) down heavily and without taking care • *Just plonk the shopping* **(down) on** *the table, and come and have a cup of tea.* [T] • *We spent all evening plonked* (= seated without moving) **on** *the sofa in front of the telly.* [T] • *Come in and plonk your***selves (down)** (= sit down) *anywhere you like.* [T] • *"I'm exhausted," she said, plonking* **down** (= sitting down heavily) **in** *a chair.* [I]

plonk WINE /£plɒŋk, $plɑːŋk/ *n* [U] *esp. Br and Aus infml* cheap wine; wine that is not of good quality • *We had pizza and a bottle of plonk.*

plonk·er /£ˈplɒŋ·kəʳ, $ˈplɑːŋ·kɚ/ *n* [C] *Br slang* a foolish or stupid person • *What did you do that for, you plonker?* [as form of address] • *You're a real plonker sometimes, Rodney.*

plop SOUND /£plɒp, $plɑːp/ *n, adv* [not gradable] *infml* (with) a soft sound like that of something solid dropping lightly into a liquid • *If you drop a stone into water, it falls with a plop.* [U] • *Don't let your bread go plop* **into** *your soup like that.*

plop /£plɒp, $plɑːp/ *v* [I always + adv/prep] **-pp-** *infml* • *The rain plopped* (= fell with a soft sound) **into** *the puddles.*

plop *(obj)* PUT /£plɒp, $plɑːp/ *v* [always + adv/prep] **-pp-** to sit down or land heavily or without taking care, or to put (something) down without taking care • *They ran onto the beach and plopped* **(down) onto** *the sand.* [I] • *He came and plopped* **down** *next to me.* [I] • *She seems so out of place here, it's almost as if she's been plopped* **down** *from another world.* [T]

plot SECRET PLAN /£plɒt, $plɑːt/ *n* [C] a secret plan made by several people to do something that is wrong, harmful or not legal, esp. to do damage to a person or a government • *The plot was discovered before it was carried out.* • *The police have foiled a plot* **to** *assassinate the president.* [+ *to* infinitive] • *The Gunpowder Plot was a secret plan organized by Guy Fawkes to blow up the Houses of Parliament in London in 1605.* • *(humorous saying)* 'The plot thickens' means that a situation has suddenly become more complicated: *"Now there are two men phoning her up all the time." "The plot thickens!"*

plot *(obj)* /£plɒt, $plɑːt/ *v* **-tt-** • *The army is plotting* (= making a secret plan for) *the overthrow of the government.* [T] • *I can't believe that he's plotting* **against** *his own father.* [I] • *They're plotting* **(together) to** *take over the company.* [+ *to* infinitive] • *The prisoners are plotting* **how** *to escape.* [+ *wh-* word] • *(humorous)* Plotting can also be used to mean making a secret plan to do something amusing to or for someone: *She's plotting* **with** *her sister* **to** *play a trick on her brother.* [+ *to* infinitive] ◦ *He's plotting a surprise party for his wife's birthday.* [T]

plot·ter /£ˈplɒt·əʳ, $ˈplɑː·t̬ɚ/ *n* [C] • *The plotters* (= people making a secret plan) *have been arrested.*

plot STORY /£plɒt, $plɑːt/ *n, v* **-tt-** (to write) the story of a book, film, play, etc. • *The film has a very straightforward plot, so it's easy to follow it.* [C] • *The plots* **of** *his books are basically all the same.* [C] • *I've plotted* **(out)** *the story in a rough form, and now I have to fill it in.* [T] • *I thought the* **plot line** (= the story) *of that play was very unconvincing.*

plot *obj* MARK /£plɒt, $plɑːt/ *v* [T] **-tt-** to mark or draw on a piece of paper or a map • If you plot the **course** of a ship, aircraft, etc., you mark it on a map in order to show in what direction it is going or will be going: *Radar operators plotted the course of the incoming missile.* • *We've plotted our projected costs for the coming year* (= drawn them in the form of lines or curves between a series of points on a piece of paper), *and they show a big increase.* • *I've asked Andrew to plot* (= make a record of) *the progress of our sales drive.*

plot·ter /£ˈplɒt·əʳ, $ˈplɑː·t̬ɚ/ *n* [C] • A plotter is a device which marks things, such as the position of a ship or aircraft, on a map or piece of paper.

plot GROUND /£plɒt, $plɑːt/ *n* [C] a small piece of land that has been marked or measured for a particular purpose • *a building plot* • *a vegetable plot* • *There are several plots* **of land** *for sale.* • Plot is also *Am for* **ground plan**. See at GROUND LAND.

plough TOOL, *Am usually* **plow** /plaʊ/ *n* [C] a large farming tool with blades which digs the earth in fields so that seeds can be planted • *Ploughs used to be pulled by horses, but nowadays are usually pulled by tractors.* • *These fields have been* **under the plough** (= crops have been grown on them) *for centuries.* • See also SNOWPLOUGH. • LP> **'-ough' pronunciation** PIC> **Farming**

plough *(obj)*, *Am usually* **plow** /plaʊ/ *v* • *Farmers start ploughing in the spring.* [I] • *We're going to plough the field next week.* [T] • *They ploughed fertilizer* **into** *the field.* [T] • *Sometimes farmers plough* **in/back** *the remains of a crop* (= dig the earth so that the roots etc. of a crop go into it) *to help fertilize the earth.* [M] • *Large areas of grazing land have been ploughed* **up** (= dug so that crops can be grown) *for growing wheat.* [M]

ploughed, *Am usually* **plowed** /plaʊd/ *adj* [not gradable] • *You shouldn't walk over ploughed* **fields** (= fields which have been dug ready for planting seeds).

plough *(obj)* FORCE, *Am usually* **plow** /plaʊ/ *v* [always + adv/prep] to force (your way), or to continue (doing something), although it is difficult • To plough **through** something is to go through it with difficulty: *We ploughed* **through** *the mud.* [I] ◦ *I've got an enormous pile of papers to plough* **through** (= to read, although it will be difficult and take a long time). [I] ◦ *You'll never manage to plough* **through** (= eat) *all that food.* [I] • To plough your **way through** something is the same as to plough through it: *He ploughed his* **way through** *the forest.* [T] ◦ *I've been up all night, ploughing my* **way through** *this report.* [T] • *Although they could hardly see where they were going, they ploughed* **on** (= continued moving) *through the night.* [I] • *He could see that she didn't like what he was saying, but he ploughed* **on** (= continued with it) *regardless.* [I] • *I think it* *would be a mistake to plough* **on** (=continue) **with** *this scheme – we can see that it'll never work.* [I] • If a vehicle ploughs **into** something or someone, it continues moving so that it hits the thing or person, causing damage: *Many people were injured when the train came off the rails and ploughed into the bank.* [I]

plough *obj* INVEST, *Am usually* **plow** /plaʊ/ *v* [T always + adv/prep] to invest (money) in a business, esp. to help make it successful or in order to make more money • *They ploughed all their savings* **into** *their daughter's business.* • *All the profits are being ploughed* **back** *(***into** *the company)* (=are being spent on the company in order to make it more successful). [M]

Plough STARS *Br* /plaʊ/ *n* [U] **the Plough** *(esp. Am* **the Big Dipper***)* a group of seven bright stars, which can only be seen in the northern part of the world

plough·man's (lunch) /ˈplaʊ·mənz/ *n* [C] *pl* **ploughman's (lunches)** *Br and Aus* a small meal eaten in the middle of the day which usually consists of bread, cheese and PICKLE, esp. served in a PUB • *I'd like a ploughman's lunch, please.* • *Can we have two ploughman's?*

plough·share *Br, Am* **plow·share** /£ˈplaʊ·ʃeəʳ, $-ʃer/ *n* [C] the sharp blade of a PLOUGH

plov·er /£ˈplʌv·əʳ, $-ɚ/ *n* [C] *pl* **plovers** or **plover** a bird with a short tail and long legs, which is found mainly by the sea or in grassy areas. There are various types of plover.

ploy /plɔɪ/ *n* [C] something that is done or said in order to get an advantage, often dishonestly • *There are various ploys we can use if necessary.* • *The things he said to her were really just a ploy* **to** *get her into bed.* [+ *to* infinitive] • *I think this is just a government ploy* **to** *deceive the public.* [+ *to* infinitive]

pluck *obj* REMOVE /plʌk/ *v* [T] to pull (something), esp. with a sudden movement, in order to remove it • *He plucked two apples* **from** *the tree and gave them to the children.* • *I'm going to pluck the dead leaves* **off** *this plant.* • *She plucked a loose thread* **from** *her skirt.* • *Caged birds sometimes pluck* **out** *their feathers (***from** *their breasts).* [M] • *Some male models pluck the hairs* **out of** *their chests.* • *He plucked the letter* (=took it quickly) **out of** *my hand, and ran off with it.* • *Do you pluck your eyebrows* (=remove some of the hairs from them to give them a better shape)*?* • To pluck a chicken or other bird is to remove the feathers from it so that it can be cooked and eaten. • *(fig.) She was plucked* **out of** (=suddenly removed from) *the chorus line and became a star.* • If you pluck someone **from** a dangerous or difficult situation, you remove them from it: *The last passengers were plucked* **from** *the ship just seconds before it sank.* • *"Where did you get those figures from?" "Oh, I just* **plucked** *them* **out of the air** (=thought of them, without having any proof for them).*"* • *"Because I would not see thy cruel nails pluck out his poor old eyes"* (Shakespeare, King Lear 3.7)

pluck BRAVERY /plʌk/ *n* [U] *infml* bravery and a strong desire to succeed • *She* **showed** *a lot of pluck in standing up to her boss.* • *It* **took** *pluck to start out on a new career at his age.*

pluck up *obj v adv* [T] *infml* • If you **pluck up** (the/your) **courage** to do something, you make yourself brave enough to do it, although you are frightened or anxious about it: *He finally plucked up courage to ask her to marry him.* ○ *Sophie hasn't yet plucked up the/her courage to try and swim without a float.* ○ *I'd love to do a parachute jump, but I can't pluck up enough courage.*

pluck·y /ˈplʌk·i/ *adj* **-ier, -iest** *infml* • *It was very plucky* (=brave) *of you to chase after the burglar like that.* • *The dog was rescued from the river by two plucky kids.*

pluck *(obj)* MUSIC /plʌk/, *Am also* **pick** *v* [T; I + *at*] to pull with your finger then release the strings of (a musical instrument) in order to play notes • *He sat on the bed, idly plucking* **(at)** *the strings of his guitar.* • *(fig.) I felt a small hand plucking* **(at)** *my jacket* (=taking hold of it and pulling it repeatedly, esp. in order to attract my attention). • *(fig.) It kept plucking* **(at)** (=It repeatedly had an effect on) *my conscience that I hadn't called my mother for weeks.*

plug ELECTRICAL DEVICE /plʌg/ *n* [C] a small plastic or rubber object with two or three metal pins which is fixed to the end of a wire on a piece of electrical equipment, and which is pushed into a special opening in a wall in order to connect the equipment to a supply of electricity • *An American/British/European plug* (=one that is used in this particular country or area) • *Most of the plugs used in Britain are three-pin.* • *If a plug is wired incorrectly, it can be dangerous.* • Plug is also sometimes used to mean SOCKET (=the special opening in a wall through which pieces of electrical equipment are connected to an electricity supply): *Is there a plug in the bedroom that I can use for my hairdryer?* • A plug is also a device which connects a wire from a piece of electrical equipment to a special opening in another piece of equipment: *The keyboard is connected to the computer by means of a plug.* ○ *I think the plug from the cassette player to the amplifier has come loose.* • Plug is also *infml for* **spark plug**. See at SPARK. • Plug is also *Am for* JACK PLUG. • LP **Switching on and off** PIC **Plugs**

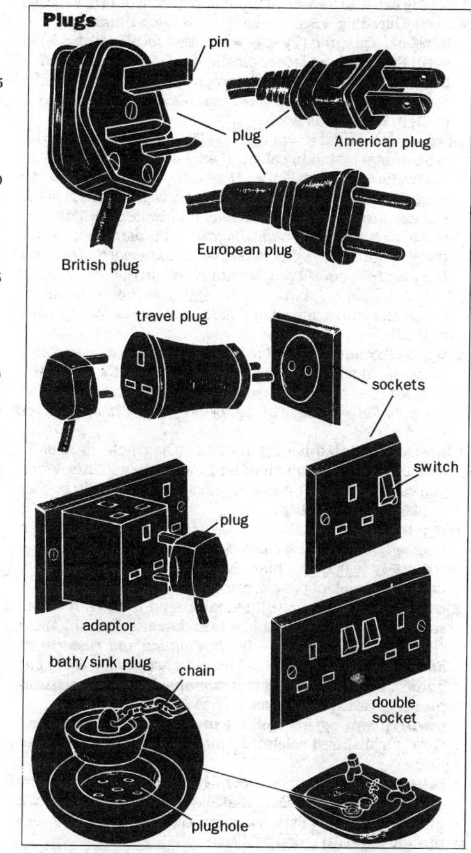

plug *(obj)* /plʌg/ *v* [always + adv/prep] **-gg-** • *Of course the radio isn't working, you haven't plugged it* **in** (=pushed its plug into a special opening in the wall in order to connect it to a supply of electricity). [M] • *I'm trying to plug the kettle* **into** *this socket.* [T] • *Where does the refrigerator plug* **in***?* [I] • To plug **into** an electrical system is to get the use of it by making a connection with it: *You're not supposed to have electrical equipment plugging directly into the mains.* [I] • *I've wired up the stereo system, but I haven't plugged the speakers* **in** (=connected them to the other equipment) *yet.* [M] • *If you plug the video camera* **into** *the television, you can play back the tape you've recorded.* [T] • *The keyboard plugs* **in** *at the back of the computer.* [I] • *Can you show me where the microphone plugs* **into** *the tape recorder?* [I] • *(fig.) I'm sure he only got that job because he was plugged* **into** *the old school* **network** (=because he had connections with people who went to the same school as he did). [T] • *(fig.) This new product line should be able to plug* **into** (=fit into) *our existing distribution* **network**. [I] • *(fig.) Andy is really plugged* **into** (=knows and understands a lot about) *the popular music scene.* [T]

plug HOLE FILLER /plʌg/ *n* [C] a small piece of rubber, plastic, wood, etc. that fits into a hole in order to close it • A plug can be a round piece of usually rubber or plastic that fits into the hole in a SINK, a BASIN or a bath: *Put the plug in the sink before you fill it with water.* ○ *I can't find the bath plug.* • A plug is also a small piece of plastic or wood that you put into a hole in a wall before putting a screw into it. •

A plug can also be a small piece of **cotton wool** that is used to stop bleeding. • See also EARPLUG. • PIC> **Plugs**

plug *obj* /plʌg/ *v* [T] **-gg-** • *We need to plug those holes* (=fill them with a piece of plastic, wood, etc.) *in the wall.* • *Have you plugged that leak* (=stopped it by filling the hole) *in the pipe?* • *To stop someone's nose bleeding, you can plug it* (=fill it) **with** *cotton wool.*

plug *obj* [ADVERTISE] /plʌg/ *v* [T] **-gg-** to advertise (something) by talking about it a lot or praising it, esp. on the radio or television • *The radio stations are really plugging the new U2 single.* • *That interview seemed to me as if it was just a way for him to plug his new book.* • *This new chocolate bar is really being plugged by the manufacturers.*

plug /plʌg/ *n* [C] • *She never misses an opportunity to get in a plug* **for** (=to tell people publicly about) *her new film.*

plug *obj* [SHOOT] /plʌg/ *v* [T] **-gg-** *Am infml* to shoot (someone) with a gun • *Sure, boss, we plugged the guy* **(full of lead)**.

plug a·way *v adv* [I] *infml* to work hard and in a determined way, esp. at something that you find difficult • *"Have you finished the decorating yet?" "No, we're still plugging away."* • *Katie has been plugging away* **at** *her homework for hours.*

plug·hole /£ˈplʌg·həʊl, $-hoʊl/ *n* [C] a hole in a bath, BASIN, etc. through which water flows away and into which you can put a PLUG (=a small round piece of usually rubber or plastic) • PIC> **Plugs**

plug–ug·ly [UGLY] /ˈplʌgˌʌg·li, ˌ-ˈ--/ *adj infml* very ugly • *a plug-ugly old bulldog* • *I may be plug-ugly, but I'm lovable.*

plug–ug·ly [VIOLENT] /ˈplʌgˌʌg·li, ˌ-ˈ--/ *n* [C] *Am infml* an unpleasant violent person, esp. one who lives in a city

plum [FRUIT] /plʌm/ *n* [C] a small round fruit with a thin smooth red, purple or yellow skin, sweet soft flesh, and a single large hard seed • *We had plums and custard for dinner.* • *I love plum jam.* • *There are two plum trees in our garden.* • **Plum pudding** is *Am or dated Br for* **Christmas pudding**. See at CHRISTMAS. • PIC> **Bread and cakes**

plum /plʌm/ *adj* • Something that is plum(**-coloured**) is a dark purplish red colour: *a plum shirt* • *a plum-coloured dress*

plum·my /ˈplʌm·i/ *adj* **-ier**, **-iest** • *This wine has an almost plummy flavour* (=that like a plum). • *Her lipstick was a plummy* (=dark purplish red) *colour.* • See also **plummy** at PLUM [GOOD]; PLUMMY.

plum [GOOD] /plʌm/ *n, adj* **plummer**, **plummest** (something that is) very good and worth having • *The deal was such a plum* (=so good and worth having) *that we had to accept it.* [C] • *How did you manage to get such a plum* **job**? [before n] • *The role of Hamlet is a plum* **part** *for an actor.* [before n] • *The building occupies the plummest site in the city.* [before n]

plum·my /ˈplʌm·i/ *adj infml* • *There's a very plummy* (=good and desirable) **job** *advertised in the paper today.* • See also **plummy** at PLUM [FRUIT]; PLUMMY.

plum·age /ˈpluː·mɪdʒ/ *n* [U] a bird's covering of feathers • *Male peacocks have beautiful plumage.*

plume /pluːm/ *n* [C] • *In Papua New Guinea, the tail plumes* (=large feathers) *of birds of paradise are used to make headdresses.* • *In Edwardian England, women sometimes used to carry fans made of ostrich plumes.* • A plume is also a decoration which looks like several large feathers tied together and which is esp. worn on the heads of horses or the hats of soldiers during particular ceremonies: *The coffin was drawn by horses with black plumes on their heads.* • A plume **of** something like smoke, steam or dust is a mass of it shaped like a feather, which rises up into the sky: *After the explosion, plumes of smoke could be seen in the sky for miles around.* • See also NOM DE PLUME.

plumed /pluːmd/ *adj* [before noun; not gradable] • *The dancers at the Folies-Bergère wore plumed headdresses* (=with a decoration which looked like several large feathers tied together).

plumb *obj* [WATER] /plʌm/ *v* [T] to supply (a building or a device) with water pipes, or to connect (a building or a device) to a water pipe • *We've discovered that our house isn't plumbed properly.* • *I think we can plumb* (=connect) *the new bath* **into** *the existing pipes.* • *Have you plumbed the dishwasher* **in** (=connected it to a water pipe) *yet?* [M]

plumb·er /£ˈplʌm·əʳ, $-ɚ/ *n* [C] • A plumber is a person whose job is to supply and connect, or repair water pipes, baths, toilets, etc.: *When is the plumber coming to mend the burst pipe?* • **Plumber's friend** or **plumber's helper** is *Am for* PLUNGER.

plumb·ing /ˈplʌm·ɪŋ/ *n* [U] • *There's something wrong with the plumbing* (=water and other pipes in a building). • *We did all the plumbing* **(work)** (=the work of connecting water and other pipes in a building) *in our house ourselves.*

plumb [EXACTLY] /plʌm/ *adv* [before adv/prep; not gradable] *infml* exactly • *You can't fail to find the restaurant – it's plumb in the middle of the town.* • *He hit me plumb on the nose.*

plumb [COMPLETELY] /plʌm/ *adv* [not gradable] *Am infml* completely • *I plumb forgot your birthday.* • *You're just plumb crazy, Jack.*

plumb [STRAIGHT] /plʌm/ *adj* [after v; not gradable] *specialized* (esp. of something vertical) exactly straight • *When you hang a door, you need to make sure that it is both level and plumb.* • If something is **out of plumb**, it is not exactly straight. • A **plumb line** is a piece of string with a weight fixed to one end, which is used either to test whether something that is vertical, such as a wall, is exactly straight, or to find the depth of water.

plumb *obj* /plʌm/ *v* [T] • *(specialized)* To plumb is to find the depth of something, esp. water. • *(fig.) Scientists have yet to plumb* (=discover about or understand) *the mystery of the origins of the universe.* • To **plumb the depths** is to reach the lowest point: *Roy plumbed the depths* **of** *despair when his wife left him.* ○ *(humorous) They must be really plumbing the depths* (=must have been unable to find anyone better) *if they're offering the job to her.*

plume /pluːm/ *n* [C] See at PLUMAGE

plumed /pluːmd/ *adj* [before noun] See at PLUMAGE

plum·met /ˈplʌm·ɪt/ *v* [I] to fall very quickly and suddenly • *House prices have plummeted in recent months.* • *A recently published report suggests that national levels of literacy have plummeted.* • *The aircraft's engine failed and it plummeted* **from/out of** *the sky.* • *Several large rocks were sent plummeting* **down** *the mountain.* • *The child fell from the top of the slide and plummeted* **to/towards** *the ground.*

plum·my /ˈplʌm·i/ *adj* **-ier**, **-iest** (of a voice or a way of speaking) low and using lengthened vowels, of a type thought to be typical of the British upper social class • *We were shown round the gallery by a guide with a plummy* **accent/voice**. • See also **plummy** at PLUM [FRUIT]; PLUM [GOOD].

plump /plʌmp/ *adj* **-er**, **-est** having a soft rounded body; slightly fat • *(approving) a nice plump chicken* • *(approving) plump juicy grapes* • *(approving) a child with plump rosy cheeks* • Plump is also used to avoid saying fat: *He's got rather plump since the last time I saw him.* ○ *She's a bit plump in the face.* • Ⓓ

plump *obj* /plʌmp/ *v* [T] • *My aunt is always going round straightening furniture and plumping* **cushions** (=shaking them to make them round and soft). • *Let me plump* **up** *your pillows to make them more comfortable for you.* [M]

plump·ness /ˈplʌmp·nəs/ *n* [U] • *I've always been a bit inclined towards plumpness* (=being slightly fat).

plump down *(obj)*, **plump** *(obj)* **down** *v adv* [always + adv/prep] *infml* to (cause to) sit down suddenly and heavily, or to put (something) down suddenly and without taking care • *She plumped down next to me* **on the sofa**. [I] • *He rushed into the room and plumped* **himself** *down* **in** *a chair.* [T] • *Joan sat down on the bus, and plumped her bags down next to her.* [M]

plump for *obj v prep* [T] *infml* to choose, esp. after taking time for careful thought • *I'm going to plump for the vegetable curry.* • *Which film did you plump for in the end?* • *They finally plumped for Peter as the best candidate for the job.*

plun·der *(obj)* /£ˈplʌn·dəʳ, $-dɚ/ *v* to steal (goods) forcefully from (a place), esp. during a war • *After the president fled the country, the palace was plundered by soldiers.* [T] • *The army is moving from town to town, killing and plundering as it goes.* [I] • *I was horrified to hear about those graves being plundered.* [T] • *It seems that someone has been plundering funds* **from** *the company.* [T] • *(fig.) The future of our planet is in danger if we continue to plunder it* (=take things from it and use them) *as we do.* [T] • Ⓓ

plun·der /£ˈplʌn·dəʳ, $-dɚ/ *n* [U] • *The jewel thieves escaped with their plunder* (=the things they had stolen) *in a waiting van.* • *Residents in the villages under attack have been unable to protect their homes from plunder* (=from having things stolen from them). • *(fig.) We need to put a stop to the plunder* **of** (=things being taken from) *the rain forest.*

plun·der·er /£ˈplʌn·dᵊr·əʳ, $-dɚ·ɚ/ *n* [C]

plunge *(obj)* /plʌndʒ/ *v* to (cause to) move or fall suddenly forward, down or into something • *We ran down to the beach and plunged* **into** *the sea.* [I] • *He lost his footing while he was climbing the mountain, and plunged* **to** *his death.* [I] • *The car went out of control on a bend and plunged* **over** *the cliff.* [I] • *He snatched up the hypodermic syringe and plunged it* **in**. [T always + adv/prep] • *In the opera 'Tosca', Tosca kills Scarpia by plunging a knife* **into** *his breast.* [T always + adv/prep] • *If you burn your hand, you should plunge it* **into** *cold water.* [T always + adv/prep] • *Cook the peas by plunging them* **into** *boiling water.* [T always + adv/prep] • *Niagara Falls plunges* (=falls) *55·5 metres.* [I] • *The fall in demand for the company's products has caused its share prices to plunge* (=fall suddenly and by a large amount). [I] • *Our income has plunged in the last few months.* [I] • *(fig.) The country has been plunged* **into** (=suddenly caused to experience) *recession.* [T always + adv/prep] • *(fig.) We've been spending so much recently that we've plunged ourselves* **into** *debt* (=are suddenly experiencing the condition of being in debt). [T always + adv/prep] • *(fig.) The electricity supply was cut, plunging the town* **into** *darkness* (=making it suddenly dark). [T always + adv/prep] • *(fig.) Peter has really plunged* **into** (=has worked hard and in a determined way at) *his schoolwork this term.* [I] • *(fig.) I asked her how she was and she plunged* **into** (=suddenly started to give) *a long account of how she'd split up with her boyfriend.* [I] • *(fig.) It was very brave of you to plunge* **in** (=suddenly start talking) *and say what you thought like that.* [I] • *(fig.) She'd never dare wear a dress with a* **neckline** *that plunged* (=is shaped low so that it shows part of her breasts) *like that.* [I]

plunge /plʌndʒ/ *n* [C] • *I really enjoyed my plunge* (=jumping in and swimming) **in** *the pool.* • *There has been a plunge* **in** *the (value of the) dollar* (=it has suddenly fallen in value by a large amount) *today.* • *We are expecting a plunge* (=a large fall) **in** *profits this year.* • To **take the plunge** is determinedly to make a decision to do something, esp. after thinking about it for a long time: *I've decided to take the plunge and set up my own business.* ○ *They're finally taking the plunge and getting married.*

plung·ing /ˈplʌn·dʒɪŋ/ *adj* • *The Princess of Wales wore a black dress with a plunging* **neckline** (=a dress shaped low at the neck so that part of her breasts could be seen).

plung·er /£ˈplʌn·dʒəʳ, $-dʒɚ/, *Am also* **plumb·er's friend, plumb·er's help·er** *n* [C] a device consisting of a cup-shaped piece of rubber on the end of a stick, which is used to remove things from a blocked pipe, esp. in a kitchen or bathroom • *You use a plunger by putting the rubber piece over the opening of a blocked pipe, and moving the stick up and down, which produces pressure and suction alternately, dislodging whatever is blocking the pipe.*

plunk /plʌŋk/ *n, v Am for* PLONK [SOUND], PLONK [PUT]

plu·per·fect /£ˌpluːˈpɜː·fekt, $ˈpluːˌpɜːr-/ *n, adj* [not gradable] *specialized for* **past perfect**, see at PAST [GRAMMAR]

plu·ral [GRAMMAR] /£ˈplʊə·rəl, $ˈplʊr·əl/ *(abbreviation* **pl**) *n, adj* [not gradable] (a word or form) expressing more than one • *'Geese' is the plural* **of** *'goose'.* [C] • *"How do you say 'woman'* **in the** *plural?" "You say 'women'."* [U] • *'Cattle' and 'trousers' are both plural nouns.* • Compare SINGULAR [GRAMMAR]. • [LP] **Plurals**

plu·ral·i·ty /£plʊəˈræl·ə·ti, $plʊˈræl·ə·t̬i/ *n* [U] • Plurality is the state of being plural. • See also **plurality** at PLURAL [DIFFERENT].

plu·ral·ize *obj, Br and Aus usually* **-ise** /£ˈplʊə·rə·laɪz, $ˈplʊr·əl·aɪz/ *v* [T] • *Certain nouns, such as 'guilt', cannot be pluralized* (=made into a form in which they express more than one).

plu·ral [DIFFERENT] /£ˈplʊə·rəl, $ˈplʊr·əl/ *adj* [not gradable] consisting of a lot of different types of people or things, or of or for more than one person or thing • *We need to recognize that we are now living in a plural* **society** (=one in which there are a lot of people of different races). • *Very few countries allow people to have plural citizenship* (=to be a CITIZEN of more than one country).

plu·ral·i·sm /£ˈplʊə·rə·lɪ·zəm, $ˈplʊr·əl·ɪ-/ *n* [U] • Pluralism is the existence of different types of people, who have different types of beliefs and opinions, within the same society: *The late 1980s and early 1990s saw the growth of pluralism in many East European countries.* ○ *After years of state control, the country is now moving towards* **political/religious/cultural** *pluralism.* • Pluralism is also the belief that the existence of different types of people within the same society is a good thing: *They are committed to democracy, human rights and pluralism.*

plu·ral·ist /£ˈplʊə·rə·lɪst, $ˈplʊr·əl·ɪst/, **plu·ral·is·tic** /£ˌplʊə·rəˈlɪs·tɪk, $ˌplʊr·əlˈɪs·t̬ɪk/ *adj* • *Most Western European countries are pluralist* (=have a lot of different types of people, with different types of beliefs and opinions, living in them). • *A pluralist society allows its members to express their beliefs freely.* • *We need to take a pluralistic approach* (=one which considers the needs of different types of people) *to education.*

plu·ral·ist /£ˈplʊə·rə·lɪst, $ˈplʊr·əl·ɪst-/ *n* [C] • A pluralist is a person who believes that the existence of different types of people, beliefs and opinions within a society is a good thing.

plu·ral·i·ty /£plʊəˈræl·ə·ti, $plʊˈræl·ə·t̬i/ *n* • *There was* **a** *marked plurality* **of** (=large number of different) *opinions/views/ideas among the people attending the meeting.* [U] • *(specialized)* In politics, if a person or party **has** or **wins** a plurality in an election, they receive more votes than any other person or party, but not more than the total number of votes which the other people or parties have received. [C usually sing] • *(specialized)* A plurality is also the part of a group of voters which is the largest part, but which is not bigger than the total number of other voters: **A** *plurality* **of** *the population has voted for change.* [U] • See also **plurality** at PLURAL [GRAMMAR].

plus [ADDITION] /plʌs/ *prep, conjunction* with the addition of • *What is six plus four?* • *Six plus four is written in figures as 6 + 4.* • *That will be $16·99, plus* (=with the addition of the cost of) *tax.* • *The rent will be £75 a week, plus gas and electricity.* • *(infml) There will be two adults travelling, plus* (=and also) *three children.* • *I don't think we should go on holiday in August – it'll be too hot – plus* **the fact that** *it'll be more expensive.* • *(infml) I don't need a new dress – plus I don't want to spend the money.* • [LP] **Mathematics**

plus /plʌs/ *n* [C] *pl* **pluses** or **plusses** • A plus or a **plus sign** is the sign + which is put between two numbers to show that they are being added together.

plus /plʌs/ *adj* [not gradable] • Plus a number is that number or amount more than zero: *Plus 8 is eight more than zero.* ○ *The temperature today is expected to be no more than plus two degrees.* • Plus is written after a number to show that the real number is more than the number mentioned: *Those cars cost £15 000 plus* (=more than that amount). ○ *It'll take us six plus* (=longer than six) *hours to get there.* ○ *Her eldest son must be 20 plus* (=older than 20) *now.* • Plus is also used by teachers to mark a piece of work done by a student. It is written after particular letters, esp. B,C,D: *I got C plus/C+* (=a mark which is slightly higher than a C) *for my essay.*

plus [ADVANTAGE] /plʌs/ *n* [C] *pl* **pluses** or **plusses** *infml* an advantage or a good feature • *Your teaching experience will be a plus in this job.* • *There are various plusses for us in going to this school – it's near our house, for one.*

plus /plʌs/ *adj* [before n; not gradable] *infml* • *The fact that the house was near the sea was a plus* **factor** *for us.* • *(Br) It was a plus* **point** *that the cheapest flight also went from our nearest airport.* • *"On the plus side* (=An advantage is that), *death is one of the few things that can be done as easily as lying down"* (Woody Allen in the book *Early Essays*, 1976)

plus fours *pl n* loose trousers with wide legs which are pulled in to fit tightly just below the knee, and which are sometimes worn by men playing golf

plush [LUXURIOUS] **(-er, -est)** /plʌʃ/, **plush·y (-ier, -iest)** /ˈplʌʃ·i/ *adj infml* luxurious; expensive, comfortable and of high quality • *We went to a really plush restaurant for dinner.* • *That's a plushy new car you've got.*

plush [CLOTH] /plʌʃ/ *n* [U] thick soft cloth, with a surface like short fur, which is used esp. for covering furniture • *a plush-covered sofa* • *curtains and cushions made of dark blue plush* • *Plush is like velvet.*

Plu·to /£ˈpluː·təʊ, $-t̬oʊ/ *n* [U not after *the*] the planet ninth and most distant from the Sun, after Neptune

plu·toc·ra·cy /£pluːˈtɒk·rə·si, $-ˈtɑː·krə-/ *n* a system of government in which the richest people in a country rule or have power • *It's time we put an end to plutocracy.* [U] • A plutocracy is a country where the richest people have power: *This country is supposed to be a democracy, but it seems to me as if it's becoming more of a plutocracy all the time.* [C] • The plutocracy is the richest people in a country who have power in it: *The area is a favourite winter vacation spot among the plutocracy.* [C]

PLURALS OF NOUNS

Regular plurals

Most nouns have a plural form. Usually the plural is regular, and it is not given in the dictionary. Nouns such as 'assistance' which have no plural are marked [U].

-s/-ss/-sh/-ch/-x/-z	+ es	*bus, buses; mass, masses; wish, wishes; match, matches; box, boxes*
consonant + y	~~y~~ + ies	*baby, babies; university, universities*
other regular nouns	+ s	*hand, hands; play, plays; cat, cats; journey, journeys*

The final 's' of a plural is usually pronounced /z/ but sometimes /s/. LP **Pronunciation** at PRONOUNCE

Plural is the same as the singular (zero plural)

- *aircraft, craft* (=boat), *deer, means* (=method), *series, sheep, spacecraft, species* and some birds and fish.
- **nationality names ending -ese, -sh, -ch**
  Ten Americans and fifteen Japanese attended the conference. Other examples: *Ceylonese, Chinese, Portuguese, Vietnamese.* Nationalities ending in -sh or -ch usually have a plural with -men/-women, as well as a zero plural used with 'the': *We met a couple of Irishmen.* • *The British and the Dutch voted against the proposed change.*
- **some numbers and units of measurement**
  Dozen, hundred, thousand, million, billion when they are used with other numbers: *I counted three* **dozen**. • *two* **hundred** *people* • *four* **thousand** *dollars.* But notice that regular plurals are used with 'of': **Thousands of** *animals were killed by forest fires.*
  Some units of measurement, especially when they are used before another number: *It cost ten* **pound** *fifty.* • *He's five* **foot** *eight tall.* • *(Br) I can't believe I weigh twelve* **stone.**
  Metric units usually have an 's' plural: *two* **metres** *ninety centimetres.*

Noun endings that sometimes have irregular plurals

Some irregular plurals are being replaced by regular forms in situations that are informal or not specialized. This is especially true in the US. Words like this are marked * in the following table.

ending	regular plurals	irregular plurals	
-a	*agendas, dilemmas,encyclopedias, eras, guerrillas, quotas,*	-ae /iː/	*algae, formulae*,lacunae, larvae, personae*, vertebrae*
-eau	*(Am) bureaus, plateaus*	-x /z/	*chateaux, (Br) bureaux, plateaux*
-f/-fe	*beliefs, chiefs, handkerchiefs, mischiefs, proofs, roofs, safes* *Roofs* is often pronounced /ruːvz/	-ves /vz/	*calves, halves, knives, leaves,lives, loaves, selves, shelves, thieves, wives*
-o	Most form the plural with **-s** but the following common nouns take **-es** : *cargoes, echoes, heroes, negroes, potatoes, tomatoes*	-i /iː/	some specialized musical words such as *libretti*, tempi**. These can also have the regular plural form with **-s**
-is	/ɪsɪz/: *irises, metropolises, pelvises, penises* /ɪːz/: *analyses, axes, bases, crises, diagnoses, hypotheses, metamorphoses, neuroses, oases, parentheses, psychoses, syntheses, theses*	**no change:** *chassis* sing /ˈʃæsɪ/ pl /ˈʃæsɪz/	
-ex/-ix	Almost all these nouns have an -es plural: *apexes, complexes, telexes, mixes, sixes*	-ices /ɪsɪz/	*appendices*, indices*, matrices**
-on	Almost all **-on** nouns add -s	-a /ə/	*criteria, phenomena*
-um	Non-specialized words: *albums, museums gymnasiums, stadiums, ultimatums*	-a /ə/	Specialized words: *addenda, bacteria, errata, millennia, spectra, strata*
-us	Most **-us** nouns add **-es** : *bonuses, campuses, choruses, geniuses, prospectuses surpluses*	-i /ɪː/	Specialized words: *bacilli, cacti*, foci*, fungi*, loci, nuclei*, radii*, stimuli,* Notice: *genus,* ***genera***

Plurals of names of animals, fish and birds

These often have a regular plural and also a plural with no change. The regular plural is used to refer to *particular* animals: *We estimate there are 120 elephants in this area.*

The other plural is less common and might be used to refer to a *type* of animal, for example by scientists or hunters: *Ngorongoro Crater is a wildlife range for wildebeest, gazelle and zebra.* • *Mostly they hunt wild boar and antelope.*

But notice that 'fish' is the usual plural, and 'fishes' generally is used to refer to types of fish*: I could see the silver shapes of fish moving in the water.* • *Few freshwater fishes are able to live in these hot salty pools.* This also happens with some names of fish: *He caught two large salmon in the river* • *She's writing a paper on the salmons of the N. American seaboard.*

plu·to·crat /£ˈpluː·təʊ·kræt, $-t̬ə-/ *n* [C] • *The country has long been run by plutocrats* (=people who have power because they are very rich). • *(infml disapproving) The plutocrats* (=very rich people) *who run this company are concerned only with making money for themselves.*

plu·to·crat·ic /£ˌpluː·təʊˈkræt·ɪk, $-toʊˈkræt̬-/ *adj* [not gradable]

plu·to·ni·um /£pluːˈtəʊ·ni·əm, $-ˈtoʊ-/ *n* [U] a metallic element that is used esp. as a fuel in the production of nuclear power, and in nuclear weapons

ply THICKNESS /plaɪ/ *n* [U] a measure of thickness of wool or rope etc., or of PLYWOOD • *What ply* (=thickness of) *wool does this knitting pattern take?* • *I need some four-ply (wool)* (=woollen thread made from four single threads combined together). • *Do you think three-ply (wood)* (=PLYWOOD made from three layers of wood stuck together) *will be strong enough for making a shelf?*

ply *(obj)* WORK /plaɪ/ *v* to work at (esp. a job involving selling things), to sell, or (esp. of a TAXI driver) to drive around or wait in a regular place looking for passengers • *Fishermen in small boats ply their* **trade** (=regularly work at their job) *up and down the coast.* [T] • *Police are trying to crack down on dealers plying* (=selling) *drugs in school playgrounds.* [T] • *The town market was busy with traders loudly plying their* **wares** (=repeatedly trying to persuade people to buy their goods). [T] • *(Br) There are never any taxis plying* **for hire/business/trade** (=driving round or waiting for passengers) *when you want one.* [I] • *In this part of the city, you often see prostitutes plying* **for business/trade** (=waiting for customers). [I]

ply *(obj)* TRAVEL /plaɪ/ *v* (of a form of transport) to travel, esp. making a regular journey • *High-speed trains regularly ply* **between** *Paris and Lyons.* [I always + adv/prep] • *This airline has been plying the transatlantic* **route** *for many years.* [T]

ply *obj* **with** *obj v prep* [T] to keep giving (someone) (something, esp. food or drink or questions) • *John's been plying me with drinks all evening – I don't think I'm capable of driving home.* • *We plied Charlie with questions about his trip round the world.* • *I'm being plied with demands from the tax office.*

ply·wood /ˈplaɪ·wʊd/ *n* [U] wood that consists of several thin layers of wood stuck together, and which is usually not of very good quality • *a box made of plywood* • *a cheap plywood door* • *If it'll be used for flooring, you need 19mm plywood.*

pm TIME, **p.m.** /ˌpiːˈem/ *adv* [not gradable] used when referring to a time in the afternoon or evening or at night • *We'll be arriving at about 4.30 pm.* • *The 6.00 pm train is usually very crowded.* • Compare AM MORNING. • LP **Time**

PM POLITICS /ˌpiːˈem/ *n* [C] *infml abbreviation for* **Prime Minister**, see at PRIME MAIN • *The PM wants to see you.*

PMS /ˌpiː·emˈes/ *n* [U] *abbreviation for* premenstrual syndrome (=a condition in which women experience feelings such as anxiety, anger or unhappiness and feel pains in particular parts of their bodies in the days before they have their monthly flow of blood from the vagina when they are not pregnant)

PMT /ˌpiː·emˈtiː/ *n* [U] *Br abbreviation for* premenstrual tension (=feelings of anxiety that some women experience in the days before their monthly flow of blood from the vagina when they are not pregnant) • *You'll have to excuse her bad mood – she's suffering from PMT.* • *PMT is one of the symptoms of PMS.*

pneu·mat·ic /£njuːˈmæt·ɪk, $nuːˈmæt̬-/ *adj* [not gradable] operated by air pressure, or containing air • *Our car has pneumatic* **brakes** (=they operate by air pressure). • *Pneumatic* **tyres** (=those containing air) *were invented in 1888 by John Dunlop.* • *I've got a headache from listening to that* **pneumatic drill** *(Am and Aus also* **jackhammer***)* (=a powerful tool held in the hand which operates by air pressure and is used esp. for breaking hard surfaces, such as roads) *going on outside all day.*

pneu·mat·i·cal·ly /£njuːˈmæt·ɪ·kli, $nuːˈmæt̬-/ *adv* [not gradable]

pneu·mo·ni·a /£njuːˈməʊ·ni·ə, $nuːˈmoʊ·njə/ *n* [U] a serious illness in which one or both lungs become red and swollen and filled with liquid • *People who are bedridden can easily get pneumonia.* • **Double** *pneumonia is a case of the illness involving both your lungs.* • *(fig.) You'll* **get/catch** *(double) pneumonia* (=will become ill) *if you go out in this cold weather without a coat!*

PO OFFICE /£ˌpiːˈəʊ, $-ˈoʊ/ *n* [C/U] *abbreviation for* **post office**, see at POST LETTERS • A **PO Box** is a numbered box in a **post office** to which someone's letters and parcels can be sent and from which the person can collect them: *Write to P.O. Box 123.*

PO RANK /£ˌpiːˈəʊ, $-ˈoʊ/ *n* [before n] *abbreviation for* PETTY OFFICER • *PO McLintock*

poach *obj* COOK /£pəʊtʃ, $poʊtʃ/ *v* [T] to cook (something, esp. eggs with their shells removed, fish or fruit) by putting it in gently boiling water or other liquid • *We had poached eggs for breakfast.* • *Do you like pears poached in red wine?*

poach *(obj)* TAKE /£pəʊtʃ, $poʊtʃ/ *v* to catch and kill (an animal) without permission on someone else's land, or *(fig.)* to take and use for yourself unfairly or dishonestly (esp. someone else's ideas or a person who works for someone else) • *The farmer claimed that he shot the men because they were poaching on his land.* [I] • *Measures are being taken to try and stop elephants being poached for the ivory from their tusks.* [T] • *(fig.) I don't want to seem as if I'm poaching* **on** *your territory* (=starting to do something that is part of your job)*, but I'd like to handle the advertising for this product myself.* [I] • *(fig.) They were furious when one of their best managers was poached by* (=persuaded to go and work for) *another company.* [T] • *(fig.) Grant has been poached* **from** *England by an Italian team.* [T] • *(fig.) Jeff always poaches my ideas, and then pretends that they're his own.* [T]

poach·er /£ˈpəʊ·tʃəʳ, $ˈpoʊ·tʃɚ/ *n* [C] • *Mountain gorillas are being seriously threatened by poachers* (=people who catch and kill animals illegally). • A **poacher turned gamekeeper** is a person who opposed people in authority in the past who has now become in a position of authority himself or herself.

pock·et BAG /£ˈpɒk·ɪt, $ˈpɑː·kɪt/ *n* [C] a small bag for carrying things in which is made of cloth and sewn esp. into the inside or onto the outside of a piece of clothing • *a jacket/trouser/coat pocket* • *a hip/breast/back pocket* • *a skirt with two* **patch** *pockets* (=squares of material sewn onto the outside of a piece of clothing to form containers) • *I lost my keys when they fell out of a hole* **in** *my pocket.* • *She walked along with her collar turned up and her hands thrust deep* **in/into** *her pockets.* • *He took some coins* **from/out of** *his pocket.* • A pocket is also a container, often made of cloth, which is sewn into or onto a bag or fixed to a seat in a car or on an aircraft: *Sarah put her maps in the outside pocket of her rucksack.* ○ *I want to get one of those bags with lots of zip pockets on it.* ○ *The flight attendant said that we would find the safety instructions in the pocket* **of** *the seat in front of us.* • The pockets on a BILLIARD, SNOOKER or POOL table are the holes around the edge of the table and the small net bags under them into which the balls are hit. • *(infml)* Your pocket is also the amount of money that you have for spending: *These new tax increases will be hard on our pocket* (=will be bad for us financially). ○ *It helps to have* **deep** *pockets* (=a lot of money) *when you're involved in a long law suit like this.* ○ *I paid for my ticket* **out of my own** *pocket* (=with my own money)*, but I can claim the cost of it back from my employer.* • *(disapproving) I don't think it's healthy the way you two* **are/live in** *each other's* **pockets** (=are with each other all the time and are very dependent on each other). • *(disapproving) The head teacher* **has** *the school governors completely* **in** *her* **pocket**/*The school governors* **are** *completely* **in** *the head teacher's* **pocket** (=she has power and control over them)*, so she can do exactly what she wants.* • *Last year's winners again* **have** *the championship firmly* **in** *their* **pocket** (=are certain to succeed in winning it). • If you are **in pocket** or **out of pocket** after an exchange involving money, you have more or less money than you started with: *By the time we've paid all our expenses, we should still be (several hundred pounds) in pocket.* ○ *The last time I went to the pub with you, I ended up seriously out of pocket!* • *All your* **out-of-pocket expenses** (=money you have to pay yourself for things such as food and travel while you are doing a job for someone else) *will be paid when you get back to the office.* • **Pocket-handkerchief** is *fml or dated for* HANDKERCHIEF: • *(Br infml) We have a tiny* **pocket-handkerchief** (=very small and usually square in shape) **garden**. • *My mum gives me £1 a week* **pocket money** *(also* **spending money** *Am also* **allowance***)* (=money given by a parent to a child every week or month, which the child can spend himself or herself). • *Our hotel and food are included in the cost of our holiday, so all we need to take with us is* **pocket money** *(also*

spending money) (=money for spending on personal things). • **Pocket money** can also mean not very much money: *I work really hard at this job, and all I get paid is pocket money.* ○ *Of course, £20 000 is just pocket money to someone like Charles.* • *You can now get* **pocket-sized** *televisions* (=televisions that are very small). • *(infml) I'm not going to be told what to do by some* **pocket-sized** (=small) *kid.* • *(Am) The president's* **pocket veto** (=failure to approve a suggested law before the government completes its business for the year) *avoided a confrontation with Congress before the summer break.* • *"Is that a gun in your pocket, or are you just pleased to see me?"* (Mae West in the film *My Little Chickadee*, 1939)

pock·et *obj* /£'pɒk·ɪt, $'pɑː·kɪt/ *v* [T] • *He carefully pocketed his change* (=put it in his pocket). • *I'll tell them I sold it for £20, not £25, then I can pocket* (=take for myself, esp. dishonestly) *the rest.* • *I expect the Council will just pocket the proceeds of the sale, not spend it on making improvements to the town.* • *Davis pocketed the black* (=hit the black ball into the pocket) *to win the game.*

pock·et /£'pɒk·ɪt, $'pɑː·kɪt/ *adj* [before n; not gradable] • If you describe something as pocket, it means that it is small enough to put in your pocket, or that you regularly carry it in your pocket: • *a pocket dictionary* • *a pocket travel guide* • *a pocket edition of a book* • *a pocket diary* • *a pocket calculator* • *a pocket phone* • *a pocket video game* • *a pocket watch* • Pocket can also mean smaller than usual: *a pocket battleship*

pock·et·ful /£'pɒk·ɪt·fʊl, $'pɑː·kɪt-/ *n* [C] • *She always takes a pocketful* **of** *tissues* (=as many as a pocket will hold) *with her when she goes out with her children.* • If you say someone has **a** pocketful or has pocketfuls **(of money)**, it means they have a lot of money: *They won pocketfuls of money playing cards.*

pock·et GROUP/AREA /£'pɒk·ɪt, $'pɑː·kɪt/ *n* [C] a group, area or mass of something which is separate and different from what surrounds it • *Among the staff there are some pockets* **of** *resistance* (=some small groups of them are opposed) *to the planned changes.* • *Although the President is deeply unpopular, there are still a few pockets* **of** *support for him.* • *Within the city, there are a few pockets* **of** *greenery* (=small areas where plants, trees, etc. grow). • *The captain told us to fasten our seat belts because we were going to encounter a pocket* **of** *turbulence* (=an area of violently moving air).

pock·et·book /£'pɒk·ɪt·bʊk, $'pɑː·kɪt-/ *n* [C] *Am* a woman's HANDBAG • *I want to get a new pocketbook to go with these shoes.* • If you say that something has an effect on someone's pocketbook, or that they decide something with their pocketbook, it means that their personal finances are involved: *These new tax arrangements will hit everyone's pocketbook.* ○ *In this election, people are expected to vote with their pocketbooks.* • Ⓕ ⓃⓁ

pock·et·knife /£'pɒk·ɪt·naɪf, $'pɑː·kɪt-/ *n* [C] *pl* **pocketknives** /£'pɒk·ɪt·naɪvz, $'pɑː·kɪt-/ a PENKNIFE • PIC **Knife**

pock·mark /£'pɒk·mɑːk, $'pɑːk·mɑːrk/ *n* [C] a small hollow on your skin which is left after having had particular diseases, esp. CHICKENPOX or, in the past, SMALLPOX • *a face covered with pockmarks*

pock·marked /£'pɒk·mɑːkt, $'pɑːk·mɑːrkt/, **pocked** /£pɒkt, $pɑːkt/ *adj* • *In Charles Dickens' novel 'Bleak House', Esther becomes badly pockmarked* (=her skin becomes marked with pockmarks) *when she gets smallpox.* • If a surface is pockmarked, it has a lot of hollows in it: *In the parts of the city where the fighting has been the most severe, the buildings are pockmarked* **with** *bullet holes.*

pod PLANT PART /£pɒd, $pɑːd/ *n* [C] a usually thick-skinned long narrow flat part of particular plants, such as beans and PEAS, which contains the seeds • *a seed pod* • *a pea pod* • *a cocoa/vanilla pod*

pod AIRCRAFT PART /£pɒd, $pɑːd/ *n* [C] a long narrow container which is fixed to an aircraft for carrying engines, weapons, extra fuel, etc. • *a missile pod* • *a rocket pod* • *an instrument pod*

podg·y *Br* (**-ier, -iest**) /£'pɒdʒ·i, $'pɑː·dʒi/, *esp. Am* **pud·gy** (**-ier, -iest**) *adj infml esp. disapproving* short and fat • *He's a horrid little man with piggy eyes and a podgy face.*

podg·i·ness *Br* /£'pɒdʒ·ɪ·nəs, $'pɑː·dʒɪ-/, *esp. Am* **pudg·i·ness** *n* [U] *infml*

pod·i·a·trist /£pəʊ'daɪ·ə·trɪst, £pɒd'aɪ-, $pə'daɪ-/ *n* [C] *esp. Am and Aus for* a CHIROPODIST

pod·i·a·try /£pəʊ'daɪ·ə·tri, £pɒd'aɪ-, $pə'daɪ-/ *n* [U] *esp. Am and Aus*

po·di·um /£'pəʊ·di·əm, $'poʊ-/ *n* [C] *pl* **podiums** or **podia** /£'pəʊ·diə, $'poʊ-/ a raised area on which a person stands in order to speak to a large number of people, CONDUCT music or receive a prize in a sports competition • *The conductor Klemperer was a most impressive sight* **on the podium**. • *Tears ran down her face as she stood on the winner's podium, listening to the national anthem being played.* • *(fig.) Austria has rarely been off the podium* (=It has won a lot of prizes) *during this winter's Olympics.* • *(fig.) At the age of 33, she knocked Donald Trump off his podium as* (=she became) *America's youngest billionaire.*

po·em /£'pəʊ·ɪm, $'poʊ·əm/ *n* [C] a piece of writing in which the words are chosen for their sound and the images and ideas they suggest, not just their obvious meaning. The words are arranged in separate lines, often ending in RHYME. • *The poet will recite some of her recent poems.* • *His latest book contains a number of very* **fine** *poems about love.*

po·et /£'pəʊ·ɪt, $'poʊ·ət/ *n* [C] • A poet is a person who writes poems: *The poet and playwright Derek Walcott will be reading from his latest collection of poems.* • In Britain, the **Poet Laureate** (*pl* **Poet Laureates** or *fml* **Poets Laureate**) is a poet specially honoured by the king or queen, who is asked to write poems about important public occasions: *Alfred Lord Tennyson was one of the most famous Poet Laureates.* • A **poet laureate** is also a poet who is honoured for their artistic excellence: *If Kerouac is the Beat Generation's saint, Ginsberg is certainly their poet laureate.*

po·et·ic /£pəʊ'et·ɪk, $poʊ'et̬-/, **po·et·i·cal** /£pəʊ'et·ɪ·kəl, $poʊ'et̬-/ *adj* • Poetic means of or like poetry or poets: *The story is written in richly poetic language.* ○ *She edited an edition of Dryden's poetical works* (=poems). ○ *He ended his speech with a poetical flourish about the glory of the nation's heritage.* • *(approving)* If you describe something as poetic, you mean that it is very beautiful or expressive: *People travel for miles to see these poetic sunsets.* • **Poetic justice** is when something happens to a person that seems particularly fair and deserved, usually because of the bad things that person has done: *Since she's spent her life destroying other people's careers in order to get to the top, it's poetic justice that she should now be pushed out to make way for someone else.* • **Poetic licence** is when a poet or writer changes particular facts and rules to make the story they are telling more interesting or effective: *The author makes use of a certain degree of poetic licence in her account of the time she spent living in rural France.*

po·et·i·cal·ly /£pəʊ'et·ɪ·kli, $poʊ'et̬-/ *adv* • *He speaks very poetically* (=in a way that is like a poem).

po·et·ry /£'pəʊ·ɪ·tri, $'poʊ·ə-/ *n* [U] • Poetry is poems in general as a form of literature: *The actors will be reading from contemporary poetry and prose.* ○ *She started writing poetry at a young age.* ○ *We went to a poetry* **reading** *in which young poets were reading from their latest collections.* • If something has poetry, it is very beautiful or expressive: *This film has a savage poetry and brilliance.* ○ *The young gymnast's moves were poetry* **in motion**.

po–faced /£,pəʊ'feɪst, $,poʊ-/ *adj Br and Aus disapproving* too serious and disapproving • *Two po-faced men came to inspect the house.* • *The film is serious but not po-faced.* • *(infml)* Po-faced also refers to someone whose face shows no expression: *She remained po-faced throughout the evening, even when Bob started to tell a few jokes that had the rest of us in stitches.*

po·go stick /£'pəʊ·gəʊ·stɪk, $'poʊ·goʊ-/ *n* [C] a children's toy made of a long metal stick with a spring at the bottom and a bar on which you put your feet so that you can jump around holding the top of the stick

pog·rom /£'pɒg·rəm, $'poʊ·grəm/ *n* [C] organized cruelty towards or killing of a large group of people because of their race or religion • *The famines and pogroms in 19th-century Eastern Europe forced many Jewish refugees to emigrate.*

poi·gnant /'pɔɪ·njənt/ *adj* causing or having a particularly sharp feeling of sadness • *The photograph awakens poignant memories of happier days.* • **It** *is especially poignant* **that** *he died on the day before his wedding.* [+ *that* clause]

poi·gnant·ly /'pɔɪ·njənt·li/ *adv* • *His father's death is poignantly described in his autobiography.*

poi·gnan·cy /ˈpɔɪ·njənt·si/ *n* [U] • *The poem has a haunting poignancy.*

poin·set·tia /£ˌpɔɪntˈset·i·ə, $-ˈseṭ-/ *n* [C] a tropical plant with groups of bright red leaves that look like flowers, which is often grown as an indoor plant

point [SHARP END] /pɔɪnt/ *n* [C] the sharp end of something, such as a knife • *The knife fell and landed with its point sticking into the floor.* • *Be careful with that knife – it has a sharp point.* • If someone threatens you **at gun/knife point**, they threaten to hurt you with the gun or knife that they are holding: *The prisoner was* **held** *at knife point for two hours.* • A point of land is a long thin area of land that stretches out into the sea: *Many ships had sunk trying to round the rocky point.*

point·ed /£ˈpɔɪn·tɪd, $-ṭɪd/ *adj* • Something pointed has a thin sharp end or becomes much narrower at one end: *He's got funny little pointed ears.* • See also POINTED.

point·y /£ˈpɔɪn·ti, $-ṭi/ *adj* **-ier, -iest** *infml* • *She was wearing a pointy hat* (= a hat which becomes narrower at the top).

point *(obj)* [SHOW] /pɔɪnt/ *v* to direct other people's attention to something by holding out your finger towards it, or to hold (something) in the direction of someone or something • *"Look at that!" she said, pointing* **at** *the hole in the door.* [I] • *Small children are often told that it's rude to point.* [I] • *The soldiers rushed out pointing their guns.* [T] • *He said that the man had pointed a knife* **at** *him.* [T] • If something points in a particular direction, it is turned towards that direction: *The road sign points left.* [I] ○ *All the cars were pointing in the same direction.* [I] ○ *There was an arrow pointing* **to** *the door.* [I] ○ *(fig.) All the evidence points* **to** *suicide* (= suggests that this is the most likely cause of death). [I] • If someone points you **towards/in the direction of** something, they try to persuade you to do or buy that thing: *The salesman was trying to point us in the direction of the most expensive furniture in the showroom.* [T] • If you **point the finger at** someone, you accuse them of being responsible for something bad that has happened: *Unhappy tourists have pointed the finger at unhelpful travel agents.* ○ *When mistakes were made, there was much* **finger-pointing** (= accusations that particular people were to blame). • To **point the way** is to show how something can be done better in the future: *Recent medical discoveries are already pointing the way* **to** *more efficient vaccines.*

point out *obj*, **point** *obj* **out** *v adv* [M] • If you point something out to someone, you direct their attention to it: *The saleswoman pointed out all the new features of the hi-fi.* ○ *If you see her, please point her out* **to** *me.* • If you point out some information to someone, you tell them about it, often because you believe they have forgotten an important fact: *When he told me that he wanted to go mountain-climbing, I pointed out* **that** *he was afraid of heights.* [+ *that* clause] ○ *I feel I should point out* **how** *dangerous it is.* [+ *wh-* word]

point up *obj v prep* [T] *fml* • To point up something is to emphasize it: *The documentary glossed over the important questions while pointing up the trivial ones.* ○ *This accident points up* **how** *important it is to follow safety procedures.* [+ *wh-* word]

point·er /£ˈpɔɪn·təʳ, $-ṭɚ/ *n* [C] • *The performance of the car industry is a pointer* **to** (= shows) *the general economic health of the country.* • A pointer is something that is used for pointing at things, such as a long thin stick that you hold to direct attention to a map or words on a board, or a thin piece of metal that points to numbers on a measuring tool, or a small mark in the shape of an arrow that you can move on a computer screen. • A pointer is also a helpful piece of advice or information: *This booklet gives some useful pointers* **on** *what to expect when you arrive.* • A pointer is also a hunting dog that has been trained to stand very still with its nose pointing towards the animals and birds that are being hunted.

point [IDEA EXPRESSED] /pɔɪnt/ *n* [C] an idea, opinion or piece of information that is said or written • *I'd like to discuss the first point in your essay.* • *You* **made** *some interesting points in your speech.* • *Let's look at your criticisms point by point* (= one after another). • **The** point of something that you say or write, or a person's point, is the most important part of what is being said or written: *The point is, do you really know what you're doing?* ○ *He hasn't got much money, but that's not the point* (= that is not the important thing). ○ *I didn't* **get** *the point of* (= did not understand) *that joke.* ○ *I think you* **missed** (= did not understand) *the point of what she was saying.* ○ *I can* **see** *your point/You've* **got** *a point* **there** (= I understand and perhaps agree with what you are saying). ○ *I* **take** *your point/Point* **taken** (= I believe that what you are saying is true). ○ *Please* **get to** *the point* (= say the thing that is most important to you). ○ *OK, you've* **made** *your point* (= told us your opinion) *– there's no need to go on about it.* • If something is **beside the** point, it has nothing to do with the subject being discussed: *I know you're tired, but that's beside the point.* • If you say **my point exactly** in answer to something that someone has just said, you mean that this is what you believe yourself or what you have just said yourself: *"So even if we got the funding, we still couldn't get the project started." "My point exactly."* • If something is **to the** point, it is very suitable for the subject being discussed: *Her comments on my work were very apt and to the point.* • If you say **that's a point** to someone, you mean that what they have just said is true or important: *"We'll take the bus." "But we haven't got any money for the fare." "That's a point."* • If you **make a point of** doing something, you always do it or you take particular care to do it: *She makes a point of keeping all her shopping receipts.* • *(fml)* A **point of order** is an occasion on which a person in a formal meeting states their belief that a rule of the meeting has been broken: *I would like to* **raise** *a point of order.* ○ **On** *a point of order before the debate, Mr Brown said that at least six people had to be present.*

point [CHARACTERISTIC] /pɔɪnt/ *n* [C] a particular quality or characteristic of a person or thing • *There are various points to look out for when you're judging dogs in a competition.* • *He's boring, but I suppose he has his* **good** *points.* • *I think her kindness is one of her* **strong** *points* (= one of her good qualities). • *Attention to detail is one of his* **weak** *points* (= He is not very careful about detail).

point [TIME OR PLACE] /pɔɪnt/ *n* [C] a particular time, place or stage reached in a process • **At** *that point, a soldier opened fire on the car.* • *I was completely lost at one point* (= at one particular moment). • *This is a good point* (= place) *from which to watch the race.* • *It was so confusing that eventually it* **got to** *the point* **where** *no one knew what was going on.* [+ *wh-* word] • *(dated) I said I'd tell her the bad news, but when* **it came to the point** (= when I actually had to do it), *I couldn't.* • If a substance reaches or is at its **boiling/melting/freezing** point, it has reached the temperature at which this happens. • If something reaches **saturation** point, no more can be added to it because it has received so much already: *Sales of CD players have not yet reached saturation point, but they're slowing down noticeably.* • The **starting** point of something is the place or time where it begins: *Where is the starting point of the walk?* • A **starting** point is also something that is used to begin something else: *This short story was used as the starting point* **for** *a film.* • If you are **on the point of** doing something, you are going to do it very soon: *As we were on the point of giving up hope, a letter arrived.* ○ *She was so tired that she was on the point of collapse.* • If you believe or accept something **up to a point**, you believe or accept it to a limited degree: *Of course there is some truth in all this, but* **only** *up to a point.* • If something works **up to a point**, it works quite well: *The new traffic scheme worked up to a certain point, but it had its problems.* • The **point of no return** is the stage reached when you know that you must continue with what you are doing and you cannot stop: *I knew I had* **passed** *the point of no return and I had to carry on saying what I thought.* • A person's **point of view** (also **viewpoint**) is their own particular way of looking at or considering something, or their opinion about something: *The book looks at college life* **from** *a student's point of view.* ○ *He had been so ill for so long that,* **from** *his point of view, death was a blessing.* ○ **From** *a purely practical point of view, the house is too small.*

point [ADVANTAGE] /pɔɪnt/ *n* [U] purpose or usefulness • *I see little point* **in** *discussing this further.* • *I'd like to write to him, but* **what's the** *point? He never writes back.* • **What's the** *point of complaining now?* • *(infml) There's no point arguing about it – just do as you're told.* [+ v-ing]

point·less /ˈpɔɪnt·ləs/ *adj* • Something that is pointless has no purpose and it is a waste of time doing it: *This is a pointless exercise.* ○ **It** *seemed pointless* **to** *continue.* [+ *to* infinitive] ○ *(infml)* **It's** *pointless arguing with him.* [+ v-ing]

point·less·ly /ˈpɔɪnt·lə·sli/ *adv* • *I tried, rather pointlessly, to change her mind* (= It was a waste of time).

point·less·ness /ˈpɔɪnt·lə·snəs/ *n* [U] • *Many of his poems are about the pointlessness* (= lack of purpose) *of life.*

point [UNIT] /pɔɪnt/ *n* [C] a mark or unit for counting, esp. how much a person or team has scored in a sport • *The* *youngest skier won the most points.* • *San Francisco has* **scored** *31 points in all three of its games.* • *He won the world heavyweight boxing championship* **on** *points* (=as a result of the points that he had won). • *Interest rates have risen by two percentage points* (=2%). • *(specialized)* A point is also a unit used for measuring the size of printed letters. One point is about 0·3 mm: *The large letters are* **in** *7½ point type, and the small letters are* **in** *6 point.*

point [SIGN] /pɔɪnt/ *n* [C] a small round spot that is used in numbers to separate whole numbers from parts of numbers • *One kilogram equals two point two* (=2·2 *pounds.)* • *Someone had moved the* **decimal** *point, completely changing the number.* • [LP]> **Mathematics**

point [ELECTRIC] /pɔɪnt/ *n* [C] *Br and Aus* a SOCKET to which a wire from a piece of electrical equipment is connected in order to supply it with electricity or a radio, television or other signal • *a mains point* • *a TV antenna point* • *There is a telephone point in every room.* • *(specialized)* A point in some car engines is either of two parts that permits or prevents electricity flowing: *I can check your points and plugs, but if it's more serious than that you'll have to bring it to the garage.*

point [MARK] /pɔɪnt/ *n* [C] a small round mark on a line, plan or map to show the position of something, or a mark on a compass which shows direction, such as North, South, East and West • *Join the points A and B together on the diagram with a straight line.* • A point of light is a very small round light that you can see in the distance: *I could just make out the tiny points of a car's headlights far away.* • *"... for a better America, for an enduring dream and a thousand points of light"* (from a speech by President George Bush, 1988)

point–blank [VERY CLOSE] /ˌpɔɪnt'blæŋk, '--/ *adv* [not gradable] (of a gun being fired) from a very close position • *Two bullets had been fired nearly point-blank into the window of the car.* • If someone is shot **at point-blank range**, the gun is almost touching them when it is fired.

point–blank [NOT POLITE] /ˌpɔɪnt'blæŋk, '--/ *adv* saying something very clearly in very few words, without trying to be polite or pleasant • *He asked me to work on the weekend, but I refused point-blank.* • *She asked me point-blank whether I would help her.*

point·ed /£'pɔɪn·tɪd, $-t̬ɪd/ *adj* (of a remark, question or manner) expressing criticism of the person to whom it is directed • *My aunt made a few pointed remarks about my taste in clothes.* • See also **pointed** at POINT [SHARP END].

point·ed·ly /£'pɔɪn·tɪd·li, $-t̬ɪd-/ *adv* • If someone does something pointedly, they do it in a very obvious way: *He pointedly ignored her after the show.*

point·er /£'pɔɪn·təʳ, $-t̬ɚ/ *n* [C] See at POINT [SHOW]

Point·il·li·sm /£'pɔɪn·tɪ·lɪ·zᵊm, £'pwæn-, $'pwæn·tə·lɪ-/ *n* [U] *specialized* a style of painting developed in France at the end of the 19th century in which a painting is created out of small spots of pure colour which seem to mix when seen from far away

Point·il·list /£'pɔɪn·tɪ·lɪst, £'pwæn-, $'pwæn·tə-/ *adj* [not gradable], *n* [C] *specialized* • *Seurat's 'Une Baignade' is a well-known Pointillist painting.* • *Seurat and Signac were two of the most famous Pointillists.*

point·less /pɔɪntlɪs, -ləs/ *adj* See at POINT [ADVANTAGE]

points [FEET] *pl n* the toes of a dancer's shoes • *She is learning how to dance on her points.*

point /pɔɪnt/ *adj* [before n; not gradable] • *I've just bought a new pair of point shoes.* • *We did a lot of point work in our ballet class today.*

points [RAILWAY] /pɔɪnts/, *Am usually* **switch·es** *pl n* a place on a railway track where the RAILS can be moved to allow the train to change from one track to another • *The train rattled as it went over the points.*

point·y /£'pɔɪn·ti, $-t̬i/ *adj* **-ier, -iest** *infml* See at POINT [SHARP END]

poise /pɔɪz/ *n* [U] *approving* calm confidence in a person's way of behaving, or gracefulness and balance in the way a person holds or moves their body • *He looked embarrassed for a moment, then quickly regained his poise.* • *Her confidence and poise show that she is a top model.*

poised /pɔɪzd/ *adj approving* • A poised person is a calm person who is very controlled in their behaviour.

poised /pɔɪzd/ *adj* [after v; not gradable] (of an object or a part of your body) completely still but ready to move at any moment • *My pencil was poised over the page, ready to take down her words.* • If you are poised to do something, you are ready to do it at any moment: *The company is poised* **to** *launch its new advertising campaign.* [+ *to* infinitive] ○ *The military forces are poised* **for** *attack.*

poi·son /'pɔɪ·zᵊn/ *n* a substance that causes illness or death if taken into a living thing, esp. a person's or animal's body • *We thought we had rats in the attic, so we put out bowls of rat poison.* [U] • *The supermarket withdrew thousands of chocolate bars from their shelves after an anonymous caller claimed to have laced them with a* **deadly** *poison.* [C] • *(humorous)* In the past, **name your poison** and **what's your poison?** were ways of offering someone an alcoholic drink. • **Poison gas** is a gas that is used to kill people, esp. in a war: *Soldiers and civilians have been supplied with gas masks to protect them in the event of a poison gas attack.* • **Poison ivy** is a N American plant which climbs up walls and whose leaves contain a substance that causes soreness on the skin if you touch it. • A **poison-pen letter** is a letter that is sent to someone which contains very unkind or unpleasant things about that person in order to offend or upset them: *The writers of poison-pen letters usually remain anonymous.*

poi·son *obj* /'pɔɪ·zᵊn/ *v* [T] • To poison a person or animal is to kill them or make them very ill by giving them poison: *Four members of the family had been poisoned, but not fatally.* ○ *Hundreds of wild animals had been poisoned by the insecticide sprays.* • If you poison someone's food or drink, you put poison in it: *He said that someone had poisoned his coffee.* • If something such as water or air has been poisoned, dangerous chemicals or other harmful substances have been added to it: *The chemical leak had poisoned the water supply.* • If you poison a friendship or another situation, you spoil it by making it very unpleasant: *The long dispute has poisoned relations between the two countries.* • *(disapproving)* If you **poison** someone's **mind** against someone else, you make them believe unpleasant things about the other person which are not true: *Don't believe a word she says about me – she's just trying to poison your mind* **against** *me.* • A **poisoned chalice** is something which seems very good when it is first received, but which in fact does great harm to the person who receives it: *The leadership of the party turned out to be a poisoned chalice.*

poi·son·er /£'pɔɪ·zᵊn·əʳ, $-ɚ/ *n* [C] • A poisoner is a person who has killed or harmed someone using poison.

poi·son·ous /'pɔɪ·zᵊn·əs/ *adj* • Something poisonous is very harmful and can cause illness or death: *Dangerously high levels of poisonous chemicals were found in the river.* ○ *Can you tell the the difference between poisonous mushrooms and edible varieties?* • *(fig.) He said some poisonous* (=very unpleasant) *things to me.*

poke *obj* [PUSH] /£pəʊk, $poʊk/ *v* [T] to push (a finger or other pointed object) quickly into (someone or something) • *I prodded and poked the dog to see if it would move.* • *You'll poke someone* **in** *the eye with that umbrella if you're not careful.* • *Two kids were poking a stick* **into** *the sand.* • *She poked me* **in** *the arm* (=with her finger) *and told me to shut up.* • *(infml)* If you **poke around/about** in a place, you search for something by moving other things about, usually not in a very organized way: *I'm always poking about* **in** *my bag looking for my keys.* • If you **poke fun at** someone, you make them seem ridiculous by making jokes about them or laughing unkindly at them.

poke /£pəʊk, $poʊk/ *n* [C] • *She gave me a poke* **in** *the stomach* (=pushed her finger briefly into my stomach).

poke *(obj)* [APPEAR] /£pəʊk, $poʊk/ *v* [always + adv/prep] to (cause something to) appear or stretch out from behind or through something else • *Cathy poked her* **head** *round the door to say hello.* [T] • *The first green shoots are poking* **through** *the soil.* [I] • *The child's knees were poking* **out of** *his thin trousers.* [I]

po·ker [GAME] /£'pəʊ·kəʳ, $'poʊ·kɚ/ *n* [U] a game played with cards in which people try to win money from each other • *He enjoys playing high-stakes poker.* • *We spent all night playing a game of poker.* • If someone has a **poker face** or is **poker-faced**, their face does not show what they are thinking or feeling: *We all burst out laughing, but Simon's poker face did not show any sign of emotion.* ○ *She sat poker-faced all the way through the film.* • **Poker machine** (*infml* **pokie** or **pokey**) is *Aus for* **slot machine**. See at SLOT [LONG HOLE].

po·ker [TOOL] /£'pəʊ·kəʳ, $'poʊ·kɚ/ *n* [C] a long thin metal stick that you use to move around coal or wood in a fire so that it burns better • [PIC]> **Fires and space heaters**

po·kie, po·key /£'pəʊ·ki, $'poʊ-/ *n* [C] *Aus infml for* **slot machine**, see at SLOT [LONG HOLE]

po·ky SMALL, **po·key** /£ˈpəʊ·ki, $ˈpoʊ-/ *adj* **pokier, pokiest** *infml* (of a room, house or other place) unpleasantly small and uncomfortable • *They live in a poky little flat.* • *The whole family shares one poky room.*

po·ky SLOW, **po·key** /£ˈpəʊ·ki, $ˈpoʊ-/ *adj* **pokier, pokiest** *Am infml* annoyingly slow • *I wish you wouldn't be so poky when you're getting ready.*

po·lar /£ˈpəʊ·ləʳ, $ˈpoʊ·lɚ/ *adj* [not gradable] See at POLE OPPOSITE; POLE PLACE

po·lar·i·ty /£pəʊˈlær·ə·ti, $poʊˈler·ə·t̬i/ *n* [U] See at POLE OPPOSITE.

po·lar·ize *obj, Br and Aus usually* **-ise** /£ˈpəʊ·lə·raɪz, $ˈpoʊ-/ *v* [T]

po·lar·i·za·tion, *Br and Aus usually* **-i·sa·tion** /£ˌpəʊ·lə·raɪˈzeɪ·ʃᵊn, $ˌpoʊ·lɚ·ɪ-/ *n* [U]

Po·lar·oid /£ˈpəʊ·lᵊr·ɔɪd, $ˈpoʊ·lə·rɔɪd/ *n* [C] *trademark* a small camera that takes a picture and prints it after a few seconds, or a photograph taken with this type of camera • *Did you take these with a Polaroid?* • *Please send us your Polaroids and the best ones will be published.* • *A Polaroid picture/snapshot of their baby was stuck on the door.*

Po·lar·oids /£ˈpəʊ·lᵊr·ɔɪdz, $ˈpoʊ·lə·rɔɪdz/ *pl n trademark* SUNGLASSES (= darkened glasses) that have been treated with a substance that reduces the amount of reflected light that reaches the eyes • *I always wear Polaroids when I'm driving.*

pole STICK /£pəʊl, $poʊl/ *n* [C] a long thin stick of wood or metal, often used standing straight up in the ground to support things • *telegraph/electricity poles* • *A flag fluttered from a forty-foot pole.* • *Cross-country skiers use poles to push themselves along over the snow.* • The **pole vault** is a sports competition in which you jump over a high bar using a long stick to push you off the ground: *He's broken his own pole vault record.* ○ *Who's the champion* **pole vaulter** *at the moment?* • See also POLE POSITION. • PIC› **Sports**

pole PLACE /£pəʊl, $poʊl/ *n* [C] either of the two points at the most northern and most southern ends of the Earth, around which the Earth turns • *the North/South Pole* • *Most weather satellites are stationed over the Equator or travel over the poles.* • **The Pole Star** is a star that can be seen by people in the northern part of the world and is always to the north.

po·lar /£ˈpəʊ·ləʳ, $ˈpoʊ·lɚ/ *adj* [not gradable] • *Global warming is expected to melt part of the polar* (= of the area around the poles) *ice caps and raise sea temperatures and levels.* • A **polar bear** is a bear with white fur that lives near the North Pole.

pole OPPOSITE /£pəʊl, $poʊl/ *n* [C] either of two completely opposite or different opinions, positions or qualities • *He has switched from one political pole to another in the past few years.* • *My sister and I are* **poles apart** (= completely opposite) *in personality.*

po·lar /£ˈpəʊ·ləʳ, $ˈpoʊ·lɚ/ *adj* [not gradable] • *The novel deals with the polar* **opposites** (= complete opposites) *of love and hate.*

po·lar·i·ty /£pəʊˈlær·ə·ti, $poʊˈlær·ə·t̬i/ *n* [U] • *The film is based on the polarity* (= quality of being opposite) *of the two main characters.*

po·lar·ize *obj, Br and Aus usually* **-ise** /£ˈpəʊ·lə·raɪz, $ˈpoʊ-/ *v* [T] • If you polarize people or opinions, you cause them to divide into two completely opposing groups: *The debate has become polarized and there seems to be no middle ground.*

po·lar·i·za·tion, *Br and Aus usually* **-i·sa·tion** /£ˌpəʊ·lə·raɪˈzeɪ·ʃᵊn, $ˌpoʊ·lɚ·ɪ-/ *n* [U] • *The polarization of society* **into** *rich and poor can clearly be seen in the city centres.*

pole·axe *obj* /£ˈpəʊ·læks, $ˈpoʊ-/ *v* [T] to hit (someone) so hard that they fall down • *A fight started, and in a matter of seconds one of the men had been poleaxed to the ground.* • If something poleaxes someone, it gives them such a great shock that they do not know what to do: *He was completely poleaxed when his wife left him.*

pole·cat /£ˈpəʊl·kæt, $ˈpoʊl-/ *n* [C] a small wild fierce animal that lives in Europe, Asia and N Africa, which has dark brown fur and a strong and unpleasant smell

po·lem·ic /pəˈlem·ɪk/ *n* [C] *fml* a piece of writing or a speech in which a person strongly attacks or defends a particular opinion, person, idea or set of beliefs • *She has published a fierce anti-war polemic.* • *The angry polemics of US Congressmen will only serve to heighten the tension over this subject.*

po·lem·i·cal /pəˈlem·ɪ·kᵊl/ *adj fml* • *He does not think that novels should be polemical.* • *Her polemical essays are rather naïve and simplistic.*

pole po·si·tion *n* [U] (in motor racing competitions) the starting position for a race on the inside of the front row, which is generally considered to be the best place • *Damon Hill is in pole position for today's Belgian Grand Prix.*

po·lice /pəˈliːs, $poʊ-/ *pl n* the official organization that is responsible for protecting people and property, making people obey the law, finding out about and solving crime, and catching people who have committed a crime • *I think you should call* **the** *police.* • **The** *police are investigating fraud allegations against him.* • *More young people are needed to join* **the** *police* **force**. • Police also refers to members of this organization: *There should be more police patrolling the area on foot.* • A **police officer** is a male or female member of the police force. • *(Br)* A **police constable** (*abbreviation* PC) is a police officer of the lowest rank. • A **police station** is the local office of the police in a town or part of a city: *The man was taken to the police station for questioning.* • *(disapproving)* A **police state** is a country in which the government severely limits people's freedom using the police. • LP› **Crimes and criminals** PIC› **Emergency services** Ⓓ

po·lice *obj* /pəˈliːs, $poʊ-/ *v* [T] • If a public event or area is policed, it is controlled or guarded by members of the police or a similar force: *The march will be heavily policed by an anti-riot unit.* • *(fig.) The use of these possibly dangerous chemicals must be carefully policed* (= controlled).

po·lice·man /pəˈliːs·mən, $poʊ-/ *n* [C] *pl* **-men** a male member of a police force

po·lice·wo·man /pəˈliːsˌwʊm·ən, $poʊ-/ *n* [C] *pl* **-women** a female member of a police force

pol·i·cy PLAN /£ˈpɒl·ə·si, $ˈpɑː·lə-/ *n* [C] a set of ideas or a plan of what to do in particular situations that has been agreed officially by a group of people, a business organization, a government or a political party • *They believe that the European Community needs a common foreign and security policy.* • *The White House said that there will be no change in policy.* • *What is your party's policy* **on** *immigration?* • *A committee of six people is responsible for policy-***making** (= deciding on new policies).

pol·i·cy DOCUMENT /£ˈpɒl·ə·si, $ˈpɑː·lə-/ *n* [C] a document showing an agreement you have made with an INSURANCE company • *You should check your policy to see if you're covered in the case of flooding.* • *Insurance companies blame rising medical bills for high policy costs.*

po·li·o /£ˈpəʊ·li·əʊ, $ˈpoʊ·li·oʊ/, *medical* **po·li·o·my·el·i·tis** /£ˌpəʊl·i·əʊˌmaɪəˈlaɪ·tɪs, $ˌpoʊ·li·oʊˌmaɪəˈlaɪ·t̬əs/ *n* [U] a serious infectious disease that can cause permanent PARALYSIS (= inability to move the body) • *Children used to receive an injection to prevent polio, but now the treatment is usually delivered in drops on a cube of sugar.* • *Before travelling to certain countries, it is advisable to have immunisation for polio, tetanus and typhoid.*

pol·ish *obj* /£ˈpɒl·ɪʃ, $ˈpɑː·lɪʃ/ *v* [T] to rub (something) using a piece of cloth or brush to clean it and make it shine • *You should polish your shoes regularly to protect the leather.* • *Uncut gemstones are rather dull-looking and they have to be cut and polished to make them shine.* • If you polish **up** an object, you make it shine, esp. when it has become very dirty: *Robert was polishing up some old silver candlesticks.* [M] • If you polish **up** a skill that you have, you improve it, esp. when you have allowed it to become less good over a period of time: *I really must polish up my Japanese before we visit Japan next year.* [M]

pol·ish /£ˈpɒl·ɪʃ, $ˈpɑː·lɪʃ/ *n* [U] • *I'll just give my shoes a quick polish* (= I will polish them). • Polish is a cream or other substance that you use to clean something: *shoe/furniture/silver polish* • Someone or something with polish has great style: *This is a musical with polish and wit.*

pol·ished /£ˈpɒl·ɪʃt, $ˈpɑː·lɪʃt/ *adj* • *The dining-room has a highly polished floor.* • If you describe someone as polished, you mean they have style and confidence: *He's suave, polished and charming.* • Something that is polished shows great skill: *The ballet dancer gave a polished performance.*

pol·ish off *obj*, **pol·ish** *obj* **off** *v adv* [M] *infml* to finish (something) quickly and easily • *He polished off a huge pie and a mountain of chips.* • *I polished off three essays last week.* • *Arsenal polished off* (= easily defeated) *Chelsea 5-0 in Saturday's match.*

pol·it·bu·ro /£ˈpɒl·ɪtˌbjʊə·rəʊ, $ˈpɑː·lɪtˌbjʊr·oʊ/ *n* [U] **the politburo** the main government group in a Communist country, which makes all the important decisions

po·lite /pəˈlaɪt/ *adj* behaving in a way that is socially correct and shows awareness of and caring for other people's feelings • *He's a very kind and polite man.* • *She sent me a polite letter thanking me for my invitation.* • *She was too polite to point out my mistake.* • Polite can also mean socially correct rather than friendly: *We kept a polite conversation going for half an hour.* • *(dated)* Polite **society** or **company** is the class of people who consider themselves to be better than ordinary people: *Sex never used to be discussed in polite society.* • LP **Labels, Phrases and customs**

po·lite·ly /pəˈlaɪt·li/ *adv* • *He told them politely to leave him in peace.* • Politely can also mean without enthusiasm: *The audience clapped politely.*

po·lite·ness /pəˈlaɪt·nəs/ *n* [U] • *It was more than an act of politeness – it was genuine friendship.*

pol·i·tic /£ˈpɒl·ɪ·tɪk, $ˈpɑː·lə-/ *adj fml* wise and showing the ability to make the right decisions • **It** *would not be politic* **for** *you* **to** *be seen there.* [+ *to* infinitive]

pol·i·tics /£ˈpɒl·ɪ·tɪks, $ˈpɑː·lə-/ *n* [U] the activities of the government, members of law-making organizations or people who try to influence the way a country is governed • *I'm not interested in politics – I think it's very boring.* • *Joe is very active in left-wing politics.* • Politics is also the job of holding a position of power in the government: *The group is campaigning to get more women into politics.* ○ *He is planning to retire from politics next year.* • Politics also refers to the study of the ways in which a country is governed: *Margaret is reading politics at Leicester University.* • *"Politics is the art of the possible"* (Prince Otto von Bismarck, 1867) • Ⓓ Ⓖⓡ

pol·i·tics /£ˈpɒl·ɪ·tɪks, $ˈpɑː·lə-/ *pl n* • A person's politics are their opinions about how a country should be governed: *Her politics have become more liberal over the past few years.* • The politics of a particular group or organization are the relationships within that group which allow particular people to have power over others: *I don't like to get involved in* **office** *politics.*

po·li·ti·cal /£pəˈlɪt·ɪ·kəl, $-ˈlɪt̬·ə-/ *adj* • Political means relating to politics: *The President met local political leaders last week.* ○ *There are two political parties in the US – the Democratic Party and the Republican Party.* ○ *Education is back at the top of the political* **agenda** (= the matters that the government is considering). • **Political asylum** is the protection given by a government to a foreign person who has left their own country because they disagree with their own government: *The number of people* **seeking** *political asylum in Britain has risen dramatically.* • **Political correctness** is the quality of being **politically correct**: *Political correctness was intended to erase the discrimination that exists in language.* • A **political prisoner** is a person put in prison because they have expressed disapproval of their own government, or because they belong to an organization, race or social group not approved of by that government. • **Political science** is the study of how people obtain or compete for power and how it is used in governing a country. • *"Political power grows from the barrel of the gun"* (speech by Mao Tse-Tung, 1938) • Ⓖⓡ

po·li·ti·cal·ly /£pəˈlɪt·ɪ·kli, $-ˈlɪt̬·ə-/ *adv* • *She is very politically naive.* • If someone is **politically correct** (*abbreviation* **PC**), they believe that language and actions which could be offensive to others, esp. those relating to sex and race, should be avoided. • A word or expression which is **politically correct** (*abbreviation* **PC**) is used instead of another word or expression to avoid being offensive: *Some people think that 'fireman' is a sexist term, and prefer the politically correct term 'firefighter'.* • LP **Sexist language**

pol·i·ti·cian /£ˌpɒl·ɪˈtɪʃ·ən, $ˌpɑː·lə-/ *n* [C] • A politician is a member of a government or law-making organization: *She thinks that politicians cannot be trusted.*

po·li·ti·cize *obj, Br and Aus usually* **-ise** /£pəˈlɪt·ɪ·saɪz, $-ˈlɪt̬·ə-/ *v* [T] • If someone or something becomes politicized, they or it become political or more aware of political matters: *She became politicized in the 1970s and joined the women's movement.* ○ *The whole issue has become increasingly politicized.*

pol·i·tick·ing /£ˈpɒl·ɪ·tɪ·kɪŋ, $ˈpɑː·lə-/ *n* [U] *esp. disapproving* • Politicking is the activity of trying to persuade or even force others to vote for a particular political party or for a person who is trying to obtain a political position.

pol·ka /£ˈpɒl·kə, $ˈpoʊl-/ *n* [C] a fast active dance that was popular in the 19th century, or a piece of music that can be used for this type of dance • *Her father taught her how to dance the polka.* • *Johann Strauss wrote many well-known marches and polkas.*

pol·ka dot *n* [C usually pl] one of a large number of small round spots that are printed on cloth in a regular pattern, esp. on pieces of clothing • *She likes wearing polka dots when she goes to weddings.* • *He was sporting a polka-dot bow tie.* • PIC **Patterns**

poll OPINION /£pəʊl, $poʊl/ *n* [C] a study in which people are asked for their opinions about a subject or person • *A recent poll shows that 70% of British children are regular TV viewers by the age of three.* • *A new nationwide poll suggests there is widespread support for the proposal.* • *We're* **carrying out/conducting** *a poll to find out what people think about abortion.* • *The latest* **opinion** *poll gives the Democrats a clear lead* (= shows that they are the most popular political party).

poll *obj* /£pəʊl, $poʊl/ *v* [T] • When you poll a person, you ask them for their opinion as part of a general study of what people think about a subject: *Half the people polled said they would pay more for environmentally-friendly food.*

poll *obj* ELECTION /£pəʊl, $poʊl/ *v* [T] (of a person or a political party) to receive (a particular number of votes) in an election • *With nearly all the votes counted, Mr Soto had polled 67% of the vote.*

polls /£pəʊlz, $poʊlz/ *pl n* • **The** polls are the places where people vote in a political election: *The TV stations agreed not to announce the projected winner until after the polls closed.* • If people **go to the polls**, they vote: *The country will go to the polls on September 13th.*

poll·ing /£ˈpəʊ·lɪŋ, $ˈpoʊ-/ *adj* [before n; not gradable] • *(Br and Aus)* **Polling day** (*Am usually* **Election day**) is the day when people vote in an election. • *(Br and Aus)* A **polling booth** is a small partly enclosed area in a polling station where you can vote in private. • *(Br and Aus)* A **polling station** (*Am* **polling place**) is a public building where people go to vote in an election.

pol·len /£ˈpɒl·ən, $ˈpɑː·lən/ *n* [U] a powder produced by the male part of a flower that causes the female part of other flowers of the same type to produce seeds • *The bees will carry the pollen from one flower to another.* • A **pollen count** is a measurement of the amount of pollen in the air: *The pollen count is high today, which is bad news for people who suffer from hay fever.* • PIC **Wasps and bees**

pol·lin·ate *obj* /£ˈpɒl·ə·neɪt, $ˈpɑː·lə-/ *v* [T] • *Bees pollinate the plants by carrying the pollen from one flower to another.*

pol·lin·a·tion /£ˌpɒl·əˈneɪ·ʃən, $ˌpɑː·lə-/ *n* [U] • *Many species of tree depend on the wind for pollination.*

pol·lute *obj* /pəˈluːt/ *v* [T] to make (air, water, earth, etc.) dirty or harmful to people, animals and plants, esp. by adding harmful chemicals • *The huge amounts of chemical fertilizers and pesticides used on these farms are polluting the water supply.* • *We won't invest in any company that pollutes the environment.* • *(fig.) The words to the song were so disgusting that she felt they were polluting her house.*

pol·lut·ant /£pəˈluː·tənt, $-t̬ənt/ *n* [C] • *Sulphur dioxide is one of several pollutants that are released into the atmosphere by coal-fired power stations.*

pol·lut·er /£pəˈluː·tər, $-t̬ɚ/ *n* [C] • The **polluter pays** principle is the idea that the person or organization that causes pollution should pay to put right the damage that it causes.

pol·lu·tion /pəˈluː·ʃən/ *n* [U] • *The first task is to clean up the toxic pollution left behind by the weapons factory.* • *People should be more concerned about the continuing pollution* **of** *the environment.*

pol·ly·an·na /£ˌpɒl·iˈæn·ə, $ˌpɑː·li-/ *n* [C] *disapproving esp. Am and Aus* a person who believes that good things are more likely to happen than bad things, even when this is very unlikely

po·lo /£ˈpəʊ·ləʊ, $ˈpoʊ·loʊ/ *n* [U] a game played between two teams of players riding horses who use wooden hammers with long handles to hit a small hard ball in order to try to score goals • *Prince Charles is a keen polo player.* • A **polo neck** (also **roll neck**, *Am usually* **turtleneck**) is a high round collar that folds over on itself and covers the neck, or a SWEATER or shirt with a collar of this type: *She was wearing a (shirt with a) polo neck.* ○ *I've just bought a* *polo-neck (also* **polo-necked***) jumper/sweater/T-shirt.* • A **polo shirt** is a cotton shirt with short sleeves, a collar and some buttons at the neck, worn esp. by people who want to look informal and sporty. • PIC **Clothes**

pol·ter·geist /£ˈpɒl·tə·gaɪst, $ˈpoʊl·t̬ɚ-/ *n* [C] a spirit or force that moves furniture and throws objects around in a house; a type of GHOST

po·ly COLLEGE /£ˈpɒl·i, $ˈpɑː·li/ *n* [C] *infml for* POLYTECHNIC

po·ly– MANY /£ˌpɒl·i-, $ˌpɑː·li-/ *combining form* many • *a polytheistic* (=believing in many gods) *society* • *a polymath* (=person who knows a lot about many different subjects.)

po·ly bag *Br infml* /£ˌpɒl·i, $ˌpɑː·li/, *Am and Aus* **plas·tic bag** *n* [C] a small simple bag made from POLYTHENE (=type of soft plastic) • *He packed his sandwiches in a poly bag.*

pol·y·es·ter /£ˌpɒl·iˈes·tə^r^, $ˌpɑː·liˈes·t̬ɚ/ *n* [U] an artificial cloth • *A polyester shirt would be cheaper and tougher than a cotton one, but it would also be less comfortable next to your skin.*

pol·y·eth·y·lene /£ˌpɒl·iˈeθ·ɪ·liːn, $ˌpɑː·liˈeθ·ə-/ *n* [U] *Am for* POLYTHENE

po·ly·ga·my /pəˈlɪg·ə·mi/ *n* [U] the fact or custom of being married to more than one person at the same time

po·ly·gam·ist /pəˈlɪg·ə·mɪst/ *n* [C]

po·ly·gam·ous /pəˈlɪg·ə·məs/ *adj* [not gradable] • *a polygamous society*

pol·y·glot /£ˈpɒl·ɪ·glɒt, $ˈpɑː·lɪ·glɑːt/ *adj* [not gradable] *fml or specialized* (of a person, book, etc.) speaking or using several different languages, or (of a place) full of people from many distant places • *She was reading a polyglot bible, with the text in English, Latin and Greek.* • *New York is an exciting polyglot city, where you can find almost anything from almost anywhere in the world.*

pol·y·glot /£ˈpɒl·ɪ·glɒt, $ˈpɑː·lɪ·glɑːt/ *n* [C] *fml or specialized* • *My tutor's something of a polyglot – she speaks seven languages.*

pol·y·gon /£ˈpɒl·ɪ·gən, $ˈpɑː·lɪ·gɑːn/ *n* [C] *specialized* a flat shape with three or more straight sides • *Triangles and squares are polygons.* • PIC **Shapes**

pol·y·graph /£ˈpɒl·ɪ·grɑːf, $ˈpɑː·lɪ·græf/ *n* [C] *specialized or esp. Am for* **lie detector**, see at LIE SPEAK FALSELY • *He was interviewed by the police and asked to take a polygraph* **test**.

pol·y·he·dron /£ˌpɒl·iˈhiː·drɒn, $ˌpɑː·liˈhiː·drɑːn/ *n* [C] *specialized* a solid shape with four or more flat surfaces • *A cube is a polyhedron.*

pol·y·math /£ˈpɒl·ɪ·mæθ, $ˈpɑː·lɪ-/ *n* [C] *fml approving* a person who knows a lot about many different subjects • *Thomas Jefferson, one of the great eighteenth-century polymaths, was a politician, architect, philosopher and inventor.*

pol·y·mer /£ˈpɒl·ɪ·mə^r^, $ˈpɑː·lɪ·mɚ/ *n* [C] *specialized* a chemical substance consisting of large MOLECULES (=groups of combined atoms) made from many smaller and simpler molecules • *Some polymers occur naturally but many, such as nylon, are artificial.* • *Proteins and DNA are natural polymers.*

pol·y·mor·phous /£ˌpɒl·ɪˈmɔː·fəs, $ˌpɑː·lɪˈmɔːr-/ *adj fml* having or experiencing many different forms or stages of development • *Intelligence is a polymorphous concept.* • *Pat has an obsession with sadomasochistic sex in all its polymorphous* **perversity**.

pol·yp ANIMAL /£ˈpɒl·ɪp, $ˈpɑː·lɪp/ *n* [C] a small simple tube-shaped water animal

pol·yp GROWTH /£ˈpɒl·ɪp, $ˈpɑː·lɪp/ *n* [C] *specialized* a small mass of diseased cells that grows in the body, and is usually harmless

po·ly·pho·ny /pəˈlɪf·ən·i/ *n* [U] *specialized* music in which several different tunes are played or sung at the same time • *Polyphony had its golden age in the 16th century.*

pol·y·phon·ic /£ˌpɒl·ɪˈfɒn·ɪk, $ˌpɑː·lɪˈfɑː·nɪk/ *adj* [not gradable] *specialized* • *polyphonic music*

pol·y·sty·rene /£ˌpɒl·ɪˈstaɪə·riːn, $ˌpɑː·lɪˈstaɪ-/, *Am usually trademark* **Sty·ro·foam** *n* [U] a light usually white plastic used esp. for putting around delicate objects inside containers to protect them from damage, or for putting around something to prevent it from losing heat • *The computers arrived in large boxes, packed tightly in polystyrene.* • *polystyrene cups* • *When we moved into the house, the ceiling was covered with horrible polystyrene insulation tiles.*

pol·y·syl·lab·ic /£ˌpɒl·ɪ·sɪˈlæb·ɪk, $ˌpɑː·lɪ·sɪ-/ *adj* [not gradable] *specialized* containing three or more syllables • *'Bread' and 'butter' are not polysyllabic words, but 'internationalism' is.*

pol·y·tech·nic /£ˌpɒl·ɪˈtek·nɪk, $ˌpɑː·lɪ-/, *infml* **po·ly** *n* [C] (esp. in Britain before 1992) a college where students study for degrees, esp. in technical subjects, or train for particular types of work • *a polytechnic lecturer/student/course* • *The University of Northumbria used to be Newcastle Polytechnic.* • *I considered applying to university, but I eventually decided to go to the local poly.* • Compare UNIVERSITY. • LP **Schools and colleges**

pol·y·the·i·sm /£ˈpɒl·ɪ·θiː·ɪ·zəm, £ˌ--ˈ--, $ˈpɑː·lɪ-/ *n* [U] *specialized* belief in many different gods

pol·y·the·is·tic /£ˌpɒl·ɪ·θiˈɪs·tɪk, $ˌpɑː·lɪ-/ *adj* [not gradable] *specialized* • *Ancient Egyptian society was polytheistic.*

pol·y·thene /£ˈpɒl·ɪ·θiːn, $ˈpɑː·lɪ-/, *Am also* **pol·y·eth·y·lene** *n* [U] a light usually thin soft plastic, used esp. for making bags or for keeping food or other things dry or fresh • *a polythene bag* • *They covered the broken windows with sheets of polythene.*

pol·y·un·sat·u·rat·ed /£ˌpɒl·i·ʌnˈsætʃ·ər·eɪ·tɪd, $ˌpɑː·li·ʌnˈsætʃ·ə·reɪ·t̬ɪd/ *adj specialized* (of a fat or oil) having a chemical structure that does not easily change into CHOLESTEROL (=a fatty substance that can cause heart disease) • *Most vegetable fats and oils are polyunsaturated.*

pol·y·ur·e·thane /£ˌpɒl·ɪˈjʊə·rə·θeɪn, $ˌpɑː·lɪˈjʊr·ə-/ *n* [U] a plastic used esp. as a type of VARNISH (=substance which protects wood or paint) or as a protection for delicate objects

pom /£pɒm, $pɑːm/, **pom·my** /£ˈpɒm·i, $ˈpɑː·mi/ *n* [C] *Aus infml disapproving* an English person • *A* **whingeing** *pom had made the film, finding fault with everything Australian.* • *I'll get even with you, you pommy bastard!*

po·man·der /£pəˈmæn·də^r^, $ˈpoʊ·mæn·dɚ/ *n* [C] an object containing dried herbs, spices, flowers, etc. that gives a pleasant smell to a room

pom·e·gran·ate /£ˈpɒm·ɪˌgræn·ɪt, $ˈpɑːmˌgræn-/ *n* [C] a round thick-skinned fruit containing a mass of red juicy seeds • PIC **Fruit**

pom·mel ROUND PART /£ˈpɒm·əl, $ˈpʌm-/ *n* [C] the usually rounded part that sticks up at the front of a SADDLE (=seat on a horse), or the rounded part on the end of a sword handle

pom·mel *obj* HIT /£ˈpɒm·əl, $ˈpʌm-/ *v* [T] *Am for* PUMMEL

pomp /£pɒmp, $pɑːmp/ *n* [U] splendid and colourful ceremony, esp. traditional ceremony on public occasions • *I remember the pomp of the Coronation as if it were yesterday.* • *The Prime Minister was received with all the traditional pomp* **and ceremony** *that is laid on for visiting heads of government.* • *Despite all the pomp* **of** *the Archbishop's position, he has only limited powers.* • **Pomp and circumstance** is formal ceremony: *They opened the new shop with great pomp and circumstance.*

pom·pa·dour /£ˈpɒm·pə·dɔː^r^, $ˈpɑːm·pə·dɔːr/ *n* [C] *Am for* QUIFF

pom–pom /£ˈpɒm·pɒm, $ˈpɑːm·pɑːm/ *n* [C] a small ball of wool or other material used as a decoration, esp. on the top of a hat • PIC **Hats**

pom·pous /£ˈpɒm·pəs, $ˈpɑːm-/ *adj disapproving* too serious and full of importance • *He's a pompous arrogant old prig who's totally incapable of taking a joke.* • *The law courts can prohibit government ministers from acting 'in breach of natural justice' – which is just a pompous way of saying 'unfairly'.* • *The dinner was an extremely pompous occasion, with speeches and formal toasts.*

pom·pous·ly /£ˈpɒm·pə·sli, $ˈpɑːm-/ *adv disapproving*

pom·pos·i·ty /£pɒmˈpɒs·ə·ti, $pɑːmˈpɑː·sə·t̬i/, **pom·pous·ness** /£ˈpɒm·pə·snəs, $ˈpɑːm-/ *n* [U] *disapproving*

ponce CRIMINAL /£pɒnts, $pɑːnts/ *n* [C] *Br infml* a man who controls PROSTITUTES and takes a large part of the money that they earn for himself; a PIMP

ponce MAN /£pɒnts, $pɑːnts/ *n* [C] *Br and Aus infml disapproving* a man who does not behave, dress or speak in a traditionally male way, esp. one who behaves in a very careful way • *Don't be such a ponce! Pick the spider up – it won't hurt you!*

ponce a·bout/a·round *v adv* [I] *Br and Aus infml disapproving* • *He was poncing about in a yellow silk dressing gown.*

pon·cy /£ˈpɒnt·si, $ˈpɑːnt-/ *adj* **-ier, -iest** *Br and Aus infml disapproving* • *a poncy flowery shirt*

ponce a·bout/a·round *v adv* [I] *Br infml disapproving* to do something slowly and badly without giving it your full attention • *There's no time for poncing around – we've got to get these boxes packed by this evening.*

pon·cho /£'pɒn·tʃəʊ, $'pɑːn·tʃoʊ/ *n* [C] *pl* **ponchos** a piece of clothing made of a single piece of material, with a hole in the middle through which you put your head, so that it hangs from your shoulders • *Ponchos come originally from South America.*

pond /£pɒnd, $pɑːnd/ *n* [C] an area of water smaller than a lake, often artificially made • *She has a duck pond at the bottom of her garden.* • PIC> **Garden**

pon·der *(obj)* /£'pɒn·dəʳ, $'pɑːn·dɚ/ *v fml* to think carefully about (something), esp. for a noticeable length of time • *She sat back in her chair for a few minutes to ponder her next move in the game.* [T] • *Doctors should ponder a while* **on** *the wisdom of separating babies from their mothers.* [I] • *Many journalists are pondering* **why** *the leading goal-scorer of the World Cup has scored no goals so far this season.* [+ *wh-* word]

pon·der·ous /£'pɒn·dᵊr·əs, $'pɑːn·dɚ-/ *adj fml esp. disapproving* slow and awkward because of being very heavy or large, or (esp. of a book, speech or style of writing or speaking) boring because of being too slow, long or serious • *He had a rather slow and ponderous manner.* • *The ponderous reporting style makes the evening news dull viewing.*

pon·der·ous·ly /£'pɒn·dᵊr·ə·sli, $'pɑːn·dɚ-/ *adv fml, esp. disapproving* • *Ponderously, he got to his feet and began to speak.*

pong /£pɒŋ, $pɑːŋ/ *n, v Br and Aus humorous* (to make) an unpleasant smell • *What a pong!* [C] • *After a couple of days of continuous use the costumes began to pong.* [I]

pon·tiff /£'pɒn·tɪf, $'pɑːn·t̬ɪf/ *n* [C] *fml for* POPE (= leader of the Roman Catholic Church)

pon·ti·fi·cate /£pɒn'tɪf·ɪ·kət, $pɑːn-/ *n* [C] *fml* • *The decision was made during the pontificate* (= period of office) *of Pope John XX.*

pon·ti·fi·cate /£pɒn'tɪf·ɪ·keɪt, $pɑːn-/ *v* [I] *disapproving* to speak or write and give your opinion about something as if you knew everything about it and as if only your opinion was correct • *Grandfather will pontificate* **on/about** *any subject if you let him.*

pon·toon BRIDGE /£pɒn'tuːn, $pɑːn-/ *n* [C] a small flat boat or similarly shaped metal structure used esp. to form or support a temporary floating bridge • *Military engineers hurriedly constructed a pontoon* **bridge** *across the river.*

pon·toon GAME /£pɒn'tuːn, $pɑːn-/ *n* [U] *Br for* BLACKJACK

po·ny ANIMAL /£'pəʊ·ni, $'poʊ-/ *n* [C] a small type of horse • *When she was a young girl, all her weekends were spent riding ponies on a farm.* • A **pony-tail** is a hairstyle in which the hair is tied up high at the back of the head so that it hangs down like a horse's tail: *The only people with pony-tails these days seem to be girls under ten, or men in their fifties who are ageing hippies.* Compare PIGTAIL; PLAIT. • *(Br)* **Pony trekking** is riding ponies through the countryside, esp. as a holiday activity: *How much does it cost to* **go** *pony trekking for an afternoon?* • PIC> **Hair** Ⓓ

po·ny BOOK *Am* /£'pəʊ·ni, $'poʊ-/, *Br* **stud·y aid** *n* [C] a small book containing notes and information about esp. a well-known literary text, often used by students who do not have the time to read the text itself

pooch /puːtʃ/ *n* [C] *infml esp. humorous* a dog • *It was a friendly little pooch, despite its tendency to bite people's legs.*

poo·dle /'puː·dl̩/ *n* [C] a dog with curly hair that is usually cut short, except on its head, tail and legs • *a miniature poodle* • *(Br disapproving humorous)* If you describe someone as a poodle, or as the poodle **of** someone in authority, you mean that they are too willing to support or be controlled by others: *They accused the Labour party of being the unions' poodle.* • PIC> **Dogs**

poof PERSON, **pouf** /pʊf/, **poof·ter** /£'pʊf·təʳ, $'puːf·tɚ/ *n* [C] *esp. Br and Aus disapproving slang* a homosexual man. Some people consider this word offensive.

poof MAGIC /pʊf/ *exclamation Am* used to show that something has happened suddenly or magically • *He waved his hand over the empty box and – poof! – a dove appeared.*

pooh *esp. Br and Aus*, **poo** /puː/, *Am* **poop** *n, exclamation infml* (used esp. by or to children) (a piece of) excrement • *That's horrible – it looks like pooh!* [U] • *Make sure you* **do** *a pooh before we leave – there'll be no toilet for a long time.* [C] • People also sometimes say 'Pooh!' when they smell something unpleasant.

pooh *esp. Br and Aus*, **poo** /puː/, *Am* **poop** *v* [I] *infml* • *Ten minutes after we'd left home, Anna announced that she needed to pooh.*

pooh–pooh *obj* /ˌpuː'puː/ *v* [T] *infml* to express an opinion that (an idea, suggestion etc.) is silly or worthless • *The proposal that safety standards should be raised was pooh-poohed by the committee.*

pool LIQUID /puːl/ *n* [C] a small area of usually still water • *The girls went out to look for crabs in the* **rock** *pools* (= pools of water in hollow places among rocks) *along the sea shore.* • A pool of liquid is a small amount of it on a surface: *a pool of blood* • *a pool of diesel oil* • *(fig.) a pool of light* • A pool is also a **swimming pool**. See at SWIM MOVE IN WATER.

pool COLLECTION /puːl/ *n* [C] an amount of money or a number of people or things collected together for shared use by several people or organizations • *All the local groups put their surplus income in a pool which is kept for emergency use only.* • *Patrick got into terrible trouble at work when he crashed a Ford that he'd borrowed from the* **car** *pool.* • *As unemployment rises, the pool of cheap labour increases.* • In some card games, the pool is an amount of money which is collected from all the players and received by the player who wins the game. • *(Am)* A pool is also the money risked by a number of people on the result of a game or event: *a baseball/football/hockey pool* • *the office pool* • *Who won the pool?*

pool *obj* /puːl/ *v* [T] • *Three schools in Putney have pooled their resources/money in order to buy an area of waste ground and turn it into a sports field.* • *A computer system now exists that enables neighbouring police forces to pool information on crimes.*

pool GAME /puːl/ *n* [U] a game played by two people in which CUES (= long thin poles) are used to hit coloured balls, often with numbers on them, into six holes around the edge of a table which is covered with cloth • *a pool table* • *a pool room/hall* • *(esp. Am infml) Do you want to* **shoot** (= play) *some pool?* • Compare SNOOKER GAME.

pools /puːlz/, **foot·ball pools** *pl n Br* a type of GAMBLING in which people risk a small amount of money and try to guess the results of football matches in order to win a lot of money • *They* **do the** *pools every week but of course they never win any money* **on** *them.*

poop EXCREMENT /puːp/ *n* [U] *infml* excrement, esp. dogs' excrement on the ground in public places • *(infml)* A **poop scoop** (also **pooper scooper**) is a small usually plastic tool like a SPADE, used for picking up and taking away dog excrement from public places.

poop /puːp/ *v* [I] • *Your puppy's just pooped right outside my front door.*

poop INFORMATION /puːp/ *n* [U] *Am slang* information • *Did you get the poop on all the candidates?* • A **poop sheet** is a piece of paper which provides information about a particular subject and is given to everyone in a group who needs this information: *Have you got the poop sheets ready for the press conference?*

poop TIRE /puːp/ *v* [I] *Am and Aus infml* to become very tired • *I'm pooped! I must get some sleep.* • *If I poop* **out** (= have to stop because of tiredness) *can you take over?*

poop·er /£'puː·pəʳ, $-pɚ/ *n* [C] **party pooper**, see at PARTY CELEBRATION

poor NO MONEY /£pɔːʳ, $pʊr/ *adj* **-er, -est** having little money and/or few possessions • *How can they be poor if they have a car and a big house like that?* • *Most of these people are desperately poor.* • *He came from a poor immigrant family and grew up in a poor area of London.* • *Most of the world's poorest countries are in Africa.* • *(fig.) Unfortunately, Iceland is poor* **in** (= has few) *natural resources.* • If you describe one thing, place or person as the **poor relation** of another, you mean that it is similar to but less important than the other, and that people do not think it is so valuable: *The air force and navy were modernised but the army, very much the poor relation, was not.* • *"The rich man in his castle / The poor man at his gate"* (from the hymn *All Things Bright and Beautiful* by Mrs C. Alexander, 1848) • *"It's the same the whole world over, / Ain't it all a blooming shame, / It's the rich that get the pleasure, / It's the poor that get the blame"* (from the song *She was Poor, but she was Honest*, c1915) • *"I've been poor and I've been rich. Rich is better"* (believed to have been said by Sophie Tucker, 1884-1966)

poor /£pɔːʳ, $pʊr/ *pl n* • **The** poor are poor people: *Robin Hood is a mythical character who used to rob the rich in order to give to the poor.*

poor·ly /£ˈpɔː·li, $ˈpʊr-/ *adv* • *The children were all very poorly dressed.* • *In the 1970s the country was so* **poorly off** (=had so little money) *it had to close many of its embassies around the world.* • See also **poorly** at POOR [BAD]; POORLY

poor [BAD] /£pɔːʳ, $pʊr/ *adj* **-er, -est** of a very low quality or standard; not good • *Their defences were poor – the trenches were too shallow and they had very few gun emplacements.* • *If you are a poor mathematician/If you are poor* **at** *maths, you will find physics rather difficult.* • *When my father died he had been in poor health for several years.* • *For Jackie, I'm afraid, money is always of first importance and the children come a poor* (=a very unsatisfactory) *second.* • *Several new varieties of seed have been tried, but with poor results.* • *Labour has attacked the government's poor showing on* (=its lack of effort and success in dealing with) *unemployment.*

poor·ly /£ˈpɔː·li, $ˈpʊr-/ *adv infml* • *A business as poorly managed as that one doesn't deserve to be successful.* • *(slightly dated)* If you **think** poorly **of** someone or something, you have a low opinion of them. • See also **poorly** at POOR [NO MONEY]: POORLY

poor [DESERVING SYMPATHY] /£pɔːʳ, $pʊr/ *adj* [before n; not gradable] deserving sympathy • *Look at that dog – the poor thing has only got three legs.* • *Poor old Norman – did you hear what he died of?* • *The poor bastards/sods went to prison for a crime they didn't commit.* • *"Poor Little Rich Girl"* (title of a song by Noel Coward, 1925)

poor·house /£ˈpɔː·haʊs, $ˈpʊr-/ *n* [C] *pl* **poorhouses** /£ˈpɔːˌhaʊ·zɪz, $ˈpʊr-/ (in the past) a building where extremely poor people could live and be fed. It was paid for by the public. • Compare WORKHOUSE.

poor·ly /£ˈpɔː·li, $ˈpʊr-/ *adj* [after v] **-lier, -liest** *Br and Aus* ill • *He says he's feeling poorly and he's going back to bed.* • *A hospital spokeswoman described her condition as poorly.* • See also **poorly** at POOR [NO MONEY]; POOR [BAD].

pop *(obj)* [SOUND] /£pɒp, $pɑːp/ *v* **-pp-** to (cause to) make a short little explosive sound, often by bursting something • *The kids were popping all the birthday balloons.* [T] • *The proper way to open champagne is not to let the cork pop.* [I] • If your **ears** pop, you experience a strange noise and feeling in your ears as a result of a sudden change in air pressure: *My ears always pop as the plane comes in to land.* [I]

pop /£pɒp, $pɑːp/ *n* [C] • *I heard something – a pop.* • *(fig. humorous) If I eat any more I'm going to* **go pop** (=I can't eat any more because my stomach feels too full already)*!* • *"Pop goes the weasel"* (title of a nursery rhyme)

pop [MOVE] /£pɒp, $pɑːp/ *v* [I] **-pp-** to move quickly and suddenly, esp. from an enclosed space • *When you open the lid of the box, a clown pops* **out**. • *(fig. infml) When she saw the amount written on the cheque her* **eyes (nearly)** *popped* **out of her head** (=she showed extreme surprise). • *(infml)* If someone or something **pops up**, they appear or happen, esp. suddenly or unexpectedly: *She's one of those film stars who pop up everywhere, on TV, in magazines, on Broadway.* ○ *The words 'Hard disk failure – program aborted' popped up on the screen.* ○ *If any problems pop up, just give me a ring.* • *(infml)* If someone is **pop-eyed** their eyes are wide open with surprise or excitement: *The children were pop-eyed* **with** *excitement.* • In baseball, a **pop-up** or **pop fly** is a ball hit very high in the air but not very far. • In computing, a **pop-up** or **pop-down** is a list of choices that is shown on the screen when the user requests it: *Select the option you want from the pop-up/pop-down* **menu**. • A **pop-up** machine, book, etc. is one that has parts that push out from a surface or from inside: *a pop-up toaster* ○ *It's a pop-up children's book with pictures that stand up on their own.*

pop [GO] /£pɒp, $pɑːp/ *v* [I always + adv/prep] **-pp-** *infml* to go to a particular place • *I've just got to pop* **into** *the bank to get some money.* • *I'm afraid Paula's not here – she must have popped* **out** *for a minute.* • *Would you pop* **upstairs** *and see if Grandad is okay?* • *Why don't you pop* **in/over** *and see us this afternoon?* • *(humorous) You're all just waiting till I* **pop off** (=die) *so you can get your hands on my money.*

pop *obj* [PUT] /£pɒp, $pɑːp/ *v* [T always + adv/prep] **-pp-** *infml* to put or take (something) quickly • *If you pop the pizza* **in** *the oven now it should be ready in 15 minutes.* • *He popped his head* **into** *the room/***round** *the door and said "Lunchtime!"* • *Pop your shoes* **on** *and let's go.* • *The nurse came in and asked me, as if I were a child, to pop my clothes* **off**. • *(humorous)* If someone **pops** their **clogs**, they die: *I think I'll leave all my money to charity when I pop my clogs.* • If you **pop pills**, you take pills regularly, esp. ones containing an illegal drug: *A decade of heavy drinking and popping pills ruined her health.* • If you **pop the question**, you ask someone to marry you: *They've been together for six years, but Harry still hasn't popped the question.*

pop [POPULAR] /£pɒp, $pɑːp/ *adj* [before n; not gradable] enjoyed by many people and easy to understand • *Dario Fo, the famous Italian playwright, is a pop Pirandello.* • *'Silence of the Lambs' was pop film-making at its best.* • Pop **culture** is culture that is widely known and/or available, and is enjoyed by many people. • Pop **psychology** consists of theories and advice about people's behaviour that are easily understood and intended to help people improve their lives: *Why is it women that buy the majority of pop psychology, self-help manuals?* • **Pop art** is a type of modern art that started in the 1960s and uses images and objects from ordinary life: *Andy Warhol's pictures of soup cans are a famous example of pop art.*

pop [MUSIC] /£pɒp, $pɑːp/, *fml* **pop·u·lar mu·sic** *n* [U] modern popular music, usually with a strong beat, which is created with electrical or electronic equipment and is easy to listen to and remember • *pop music* • *a pop concert/song/video* • *What do you want to listen to – jazz, classical or pop?* • *There's a lot of awful pop music produced for the 10-15 age group.* • *The song reached No. 32 in the pop* **charts**. • *The Beatles will always be the world's most famous pop* **group** (=small group of people who play and/or sing pop music together). • *She wants to be a pop* **singer/star** *like Madonna.* • [PIC] **Musical instruments**

pop [FATHER] /£pɒp, $pɑːp/ *n* [C] *infml esp. Am* a father • *Hey Pop, can I do anything to help?* [as form of address] • [LP] **Titles and forms of address**

pop [DRINK] /£pɒp, $pɑːp/, *Am usually* **so·da** *n* [U] *dated infml* a sweet fizzy drink, usually flavoured with fruit • *a bottle of pop* • *Would you like some more fizzy pop, Martha?*

pop [OCCASION/ITEM] /£pɒp, $pɑːp/ *n* [C usually sing] *Am and Aus* a particular occasion or item considered as one of a series • *She gives lectures and gets paid $5000* **a** *pop.* • *They cost $200* **a** *pop.*

pop [PEOPLE] /£pɒp, $pɑːp/ *n* [U] *abbreviation for* POPULATION (=number of people living in a place) • *Mauritius, island pop 1023934*

pop·corn /£ˈpɒp·kɔːn, $ˈpɑːp·kɔːrn/ *n* [U] seeds of MAIZE (=a type of grain) that are heated until they burst open and become soft and light. They are usually eaten with salt, butter or a sweet coating. • *At the film, we got some popcorn and an ice-cream each.*

pope /£pəʊp, $poʊp/ *n* [C] (the title of) the leader of the Roman Catholic Church • *Pope John Paul II* • *Many of the greatest Renaissance works of art were commissioned by popes.* • See also PAPACY; PONTIFF.

pop·lar /£ˈpɒp·ləʳ, $ˈpɑː·plɚ/ *n* [C] a tall tree with branches that grow upwards to form a thin pointed shape • *Rows of poplars line the roads through the south of France.*

pop·lin /£ˈpɒp·lɪn, $ˈpɑː·plɪn/ *n* [U] slightly shiny cotton cloth • *She was wearing a summery poplin dress.*

pop·pa·dum, pop·pa·dom /£ˈpɒp·ə·dɒm, $ˈpɑː·pə-/ *n* [C] a very thin flat circular Indian bread that breaks easily into pieces

pop·per *infml* /£ˈpɒp·əʳ, $ˈpɑː·pɚ/ *n* [C] a **press-stud**, see at PRESS [PUSH] • [LP] **Dressing and undressing**

pop·pet /£ˈpɒp·ɪt, $ˈpɑː·pɪt/ *n* [C] *Br and Aus infml* a person, esp. a child, that you like or love • *Come on, poppet, it's time for bed.* [as form of address] • *Oh, Becky's a real poppet – such a sweet personality.*

pop·py /£ˈpɒp·i, $ˈpɑː·pi/ *n* [C] a plant with large, delicate, typically red flowers • *Opium is made from a type of poppy.* • *The top of the loaf was decorated with black poppy seeds.* • *"In Flanders fields the poppies blow / Between the crosses, row on row"* (from the poem *In Flanders Fields*, written about those who died in World War I, by John McCrae, 1915) • [PIC] **Flowers and plants**

pop·py·cock /£ˈpɒp·ɪ·kɒk, $ˈpɑː·pɪ·kɑːk/ *n* [U] *infml dated disapproving* nonsense • *He dismissed the allegations as poppycock.*

Pop·si·cle /£ˈpɒp·sɪ·kl̩, $ˈpɑːp-/ *n* [C] *Am trademark for* **ice lolly**, see at ICE [FROZEN WATER]

pop·sy, pop·sie /£ˈpɒp·si, $ˈpɑːp-/ *n* [C] *Br dated* a young and attractive woman

pop·u·lace /£ˈpɒp·jʊ·ləs, $ˈpɑː·pjə-/ *n* [U + sing/pl v] **the populace** *fml* the ordinary people who live in a particular country or place • *During the first days of the revolution, the populace took to the streets and set up barricades.* • *Some studies show that workers in the nuclear industry are more likely than the general populace to get cancer.*

pop·u·lar LIKED /£'pɒp·jʊ·ləʳ, $'pɑː·pjə·lɚ/ *adj* liked, enjoyed or supported by many people or by most people in a particular group • *Walking is the most popular form of exercise in Britain.* • *The new scheme has proved enormously popular.* • *The North African coast is increasingly popular* **with** *British holidaymakers.* • *How popular is Bruce Springsteen* **among/with** *teenagers?* • *It was a popular song of the 1940s.* • *(infml) Jan wasn't very popular* (=people were annoyed by her) *when she opened all the windows on that cold day.* • **Popular music** is *fml for* POP MUSIC.

pop·u·lar·i·ty /£,pɒp·jʊ'lær·ə·ti, $,pɑː·pjə'ler·ə·ṭi/ *n* [U] • *Movie-going in America is* **enjoying** *an upsurge of popularity* (=it is becoming more popular). • *The increasing popularity of natural produce* **among/with** *middle-class consumers was excellent news for organic farmers.*

pop·u·lar·ize *obj, Br and Aus usually* **-ise** /£'pɒp·jʊ·lə·raɪz, $'pɑː·pjə-/ *v* [T] • *It was Luciano Pavarotti in the 1980s who really popularized opera* (=caused it to become known and enjoyed by many people).

pop·u·lar·i·za·tion, *Br and Aus usually* **-i·sa·tion** /£,pɒp·jʊ·lə·raɪ'zeɪ·ʃᵊn, $,pɑː·pjə·lɚ·ɪ-/ *n* [U]

pop·u·lar GENERAL /£'pɒp·jʊ·ləʳ, $'pɑː·pjə·lɚ/ *adj* [before n; not gradable] *fml* enjoyed, supported or believed by, suitable for, or involving ordinary people rather than specialists or highly educated people • *Until quite recently in Britain, opera was not popular entertainment.* • *The socialists can no longer be sure of the popular vote* (=sure that most ordinary people will vote for them). • *His mistake was to refuse to hold popular elections.* • *The popular myth is that air travel is more dangerous than travel by car or bus.*

pop·u·lar·ize *obj, Br and Aus usually* **-ise** /£'pɒp·jʊ·lə·raɪz, $'pɑː·pjə-/ *v* [T] *fml* • *Television has an important role to play in popularizing new scientific ideas* (=making them known and understood by a lot of ordinary people who are not experts).

pop·u·lar·i·za·tion, *Br and Aus usually* **-i·sa·tion** /£,pɒp·jə·lə·raɪ'zeɪ·ʃᵊn, $,pɑː·pjə·lɚ·ɪ-/ *n* [U] *fml*

pop·u·lar·ly /£'pɒp·jʊ·lə·li, $'pɑː·pjə·lɚ-/ *adv fml* • *BSE is popularly known as Mad Cow Disease* (=Mad Cow Disease is the name by which most ordinary people know it). • *English and Scottish are popularly thought of as more or less the same language, but in fact they are significantly different from each other.*

pop·u·la·tion /£,pɒp·jʊ'leɪ·ʃᵊn, $,pɑː·pjə-/ *n* all the people living in a particular country, area or place • *Ten per cent of* **the** *population lived in poverty.* [U] • *During the Second World War* **the** *population was/were issued with gas masks.* [U + sing/pl v] • **The** *population of* (=number of people living in) *Cairo in 1992 was approximately 6 500 000.* [U] • *The war has led to the biggest movement of population* (=people) *since 1945.* [U] • *Throughout the war, there were horrific casualties amongst the civilian populations of both countries.* [C] • *The UN is investigating new methods of population* **control** (=limiting the growth of the number of people). [U] • *The country is facing a population* **explosion** (=sudden growth in the number of people). [C] • Population is also used to refer to all the people or animals of a particular type or group who live in a particular country, area or place: *There's been a 9% rise in the prison population* (=the number of people in prison). [U] ○ *The measures will affect the entire population of the area.* [U] ○ *The dolphin population has been decimated by tuna fishing.* [U]

pop·u·late *obj* /£'pɒp·jʊ·leɪt, $'pɑː·pjə-/ *v* [T often passive] • *The inner cities are no longer densely populated* (=no longer have many people living in them). • *The river is populated* (=lived in) *mainly by smaller species of fish.*

pop·u·lous /£'pɒp·jʊ·ləs, $'pɑː·pjə-/ *adj fml* • A populous country, area or place has a lot of people living in it, either compared to other areas, or compared to its size: *China is the world's most populous country* (=has the world's largest population). ○ *The most populous areas of the city are now in the suburbs.*

pop·u·lism /£'pɒp·jʊ·lɪ·zᵊm, $'pɑː·pjə-/ *n* [U] *esp. disapproving* political ideas and activities that are intended to represent and satisfy esp. people's more basic and less principled wishes and needs • *Their ideas are simple populism – tax cuts and higher wages.* • *The choice is not just between populism and elitism.*

pop·u·list /£'pɒp·jʊ·lɪst, $'pɑː·pjə-/ *adj, n esp. disapproving* • *a populist manifesto* • *a political party dominated by populists* [C]

p.o.q. /£,piː·əʊ'kjuː, $-oʊ'-/ *v* [I] *Aus infml* to leave hurriedly

por·ce·lain /£'pɔː·sᵊl·ɪn, $'pɔːr-/ *n* [U] a hard but delicate shiny white substance made by heating a special type of clay to a high temperature, used to make cups, plates, decorations, etc., or these cups, plates and decorations themselves • *a porcelain dish* • *The tea cups are (made of) porcelain.* • *He had a fine collection of Meissen porcelain.* • Ⓓⓚ

porch /£pɔːtʃ, $pɔːrtʃ/ *n* [C] a roofed structure in front of the entrance to a building or *(Am)* a VERANDAH (=roofed structure around a building) • *The old church has a porch with a bench in it where you can sit if it's raining.* • PIC **Accommodation**

por·cu·pine /£'pɔː·kjʊ·paɪn, $'pɔːr-/ *n* [C] a small brown mammal with a protective covering of QUILLS (=long sharp points) on its back. It is larger than a HEDGEHOG.

pore /£pɔːʳ, $pɔːr/ *n* [C] a very small hole in the skin of people or other animals or on the surface of plants, rocks or earth • *Sweat passes through the pores and cools the body down.* • *(fig.) He came in and announced, happiness oozing from every pore, that he was going to get married.* • *Rain water falling on a permeable rock such as limestone gradually fills up the pore spaces.*

por·ous /£'pɔː·rəs, $'pɔːr·əs/ *adj* • Something porous has many small holes, so liquid or air can pass through, esp. slowly: *porous soil with good drainage* • *porous brick walls* • *a porous polymer membrane* ○ *(fig.) The home team's defence was so porous* (=weak because of the spaces left for the opposing team to take advantage of) *that they gave away 30 points in the first half.* •.

por·os·i·ty /£pɔː'rɒs·ə·ti, $pɔːr'ɑː·sə·ṭi/ *n* [U] *fml or specialized*

pore o·ver *obj v prep* [T] to look at and study (a book, document, etc.) carefully • *She spends her evenings poring over textbooks.*

pork /£pɔːk, $pɔːrk/ *n* [U] meat from a pig, eaten as food, esp. fresh rather than smoked or salted • *a pork chop* • *pork sausages* • A **pork pie** is a usually small round pastry case filled with cooked pork, eaten cold. • *(Br humorous slang)* **Pork pie** is another word for PORKIE. • *(Br)* **Pork scratchings**/*(Am)* **pork rinds** are small hard pieces of cooked pork skin, usually sold in bags.• Ⓕ Ⓟ

pork·y /£'pɔː·ki, $'pɔːr-/ *adj* **-ier, -iest** *infml disapproving* • *He's been looking porkier* (=fatter) *since he gave up smoking.*

pork·er /£'pɔː·kəʳ, $'pɔːr·kɚ/ *n* [C] • A porker is a pig, esp. one raised to produce meat.

pork–bar·rel /£'pɔːk,bær·ᵊl, $'pɔːrk,ber-/ *adj* [before n; not gradable] *Am disapproving slang* involving the spending of large amounts of money in an area in order to become more popular with local voters • *The new president's trying to discourage high-cost pork-barrel* **projects** *such as the extra lanes planned for the interstate into Washington.*

pork·ie /£'pɔː·ki, $'pɔːr-/, **pork pie** *n* [C usually pl] *Br humorous slang* a lie • *Have you been telling porkies again?*

porn /£pɔːn, $pɔːrn/ *n* [U] *infml for* PORNOGRAPHY • *a porn shop* • *Some of those photos they show in tabloid newspapers are nothing but porn.*

porn /£pɔːn, $pɔːrn/, **porn·o** /£'pɔː·nəʊ, $'pɔːr·noʊ/ *adj* [not gradable] *infml* • *porn* (=PORNOGRAPHIC) *movies* • *porno magazines*

por·nog·ra·phy /£pɔː'nɒg·rə·fi, $pɔːr'nɑː·grə-/, *infml* **porn** *n* [U] *disapproving* books, magazines, films, etc. with no artistic value which describe or show sexual acts or naked people in a way that is intended to be sexually exciting but would be considered unpleasant or offensive by many people • *She's organizing a campaign against pornography and obscenity on TV.* • *He finds all pornography distasteful, whether it's* **hard-core** (=very detailed) *or* **soft-core** (=not very detailed).

por·nog·raph·er /£pɔː'nɒg·rə·fəʳ, $pɔːr'nɑː·grə·fɚ/ *n* [C] *disapproving* • A pornographer is a person who makes or sells pornography.

por·no·graph·ic /£,pɔː·nə'græf·ɪk, $,pɔːr-/, *infml* **porn, porn·o** *adj disapproving* • *The part of the film judged to be pornographic was cut from the final version.*

por·ous /£'pɔː·rəs, $'pɔːr·əs/ *adj* See at PORE

por·poise /£ˈpɔː·pəs, $ˈpɔːr-/ *n* [C] a mammal that lives in the sea, swims in groups and looks similar to a DOLPHIN but has a shorter rounder nose

por·ridge [FOOD] /£ˈpɒr·ɪdʒ, $ˈpɔːr-/ *n* [U] a thick soft food made from OATS (=a type of grain) boiled in milk and/or water • *Porridge is often eaten for breakfast.*

por·ridge [PRISON] /£ˈpɒr·ɪdʒ, $ˈpɔːr-/ *n* [U] *Br slang* a period of time spent in prison • *He* **did** *ten years porridge for armed robbery.*

port [TOWN] /£pɔːt, $pɔːrt/ *n* a town by the sea or by a river which has a HARBOUR (=sheltered area of water where ships can load or unload), or the harbour itself • *a naval/fishing/container port* [C] • *New York is still the second biggest port in the USA.* [C] • *We had a good view of all the ships* **coming into/leaving** *port.* [U] • *The ship was boarded by officials from the Customs and port* **authorities**. • *Five million dollars will be spent on upgrading the port* **facilities**. • A **port of call** is a place where you stop for a short time, esp. on a journey: *When you arrive in the city, your* **first** *port of call should be the tourist office.* • (DK)

port [CONNECTION] /£pɔːt, $pɔːrt/ *n* [C] *specialized* a part of a computer where wires can be connected in order to connect other pieces of equipment, such as a printer • (DK)

port [LEFT] /£pɔːt, $pɔːrt/ *n* [U] *specialized* the left side of a ship or aircraft when viewed from a position inside when you are facing the front • *As we spoke, we saw the ship turn to port.* • *The navigation lights are green on the starboard side of the ship and red on the port* **side**. • (DK)

port [WINE] /£pɔːt, $pɔːrt/ *n* [U] a strong sweet typically dark red wine made in Portugal • (DK)

port [BAG] /£pɔːt, $pɔːrt/ *n* [C] *Aus* a case or bag • (DK)

por·ta·ble /£ˈpɔː·tə·bl̩, $ˈpɔːr·t̬ə-/ *adj* [not gradable] (designed to be) light and small enough to be easily carried or moved • *a portable radio/telephone/computer*

por·ta·bil·i·ty /£ˌpɔː·təˈbɪl·ɪ·ti, $ˌpɔːr·t̬əˈbɪl·ə·t̬i/ *n* [U] • *The advantage of the smaller model is its greater portability.*

Port·a·crib /£ˈpɔː·tə·krɪb, $ˈpɔːr·t̬ə-/ *n* [C] *Am trademark for* CARRYCOT

Port·a·kab·in /£ˈpɔː·təˌkæb·ɪn, $ˈpɔːr·t̬ə-/ *n* [C] *Br trademark* a small building that is designed to be moved from place to place by a vehicle and is used as a temporary office, school or home, esp. when building work is being done

por·tals /£ˈpɔː·tᵊlz, $ˈpɔːr·t̬ᵊlz/ *pl n fml* a large and important-looking entrance to a building • *Passing through the portals of the BBC for the first time, she felt slightly nervous.*

port·cul·lis /£ˌpɔːtˈkʌl·ɪs, $ˌpɔːrt-/ *n* [C] a strong gate made of bars with points at the bottom that hangs above the entrance to a castle and in the past was brought down to the ground in order to close the entrance against enemies

por·tend *obj* /£pɔːˈtend, $pɔːr-/ *v* [T] *fml* to be a sign that (esp. something bad) is likely to happen in the future • *It's a deeply superstitious country, where earthquakes are commonly believed to portend the end of dynasties.*

por·tent /£ˈpɔː·tent, $ˈpɔːr-/ *n* [C] *fml* • *Is it true that cows lying down in a field are a portent* **of** *rain?* • *The report reveals some worrying economic portents for the coming year.*

por·ten·tous /£pɔːˈten·təs, $pɔːrˈten·t̬əs/ *adj fml* • *Recognition of the state's independence would be a portentous step, as it would turn a civil war into an international conflict.* • *The report contains numerous portentous references to a future environmental calamity.*

por·ten·tous /£pɔːˈten·təs, $pɔːrˈten·t̬əs/ *adj fml disapproving* too serious and trying to be very important • *The problem with the book is that it sometimes descends into portentous philosophizing.*

por·ten·tous·ly /£pɔːˈten·tə·sli, $pɔːrˈten·t̬ə-/ *adv fml disapproving*

port·er /£ˈpɔː·təʳ, $ˈpɔːr·t̬ɚ/ *n* [C] a person whose job is to carry things, esp. traveller's bags at railway stations, airports, etc. • *There aren't any porters, so we'll have to find a trolley for the luggage.* • *The expedition was made up of ten professional climbers and thirty porters from local villages.* • *(esp. Br)* A porter (*Am* **doorman**) is also a person whose job is to take care of a building and be present at its entrance in order to help visitors: *The hotel porter opened the door for me and then called a taxi for me.* • *(Am)* A porter is also a person whose job is to help travellers who are spending the night on a train by arranging their bed, looking after their bags, etc.

por·ter·house (steak) /£ˈpɔː·tə·haʊs, $ˈpɔːr·t̬ɚ-/ *n* [C/U] *pl* **porterhouses** /£ˈpɔː·təˌhaʊ·zɪz, $ˈpɔːr·t̬ɚ-/ *Am and Aus* a thick slice of meat containing a T-shaped bone cut from the side of a cow

port·fo·li·o [CASE] /£ˌpɔːtˈfəʊ·li·əʊ, $ˌpɔːrtˈfoʊ·li·oʊ/ *n* [C] *pl* **portfolios** a large thin case used for carrying drawings, papers, etc. • *She opened her portfolio and took out an architect's plan.* • A portfolio is also a collection of drawings, papers, etc. that represent a person's, esp. an artist's, work: *At college, the students build up a portfolio* **of work** *which they can show to employers when they apply for jobs.*

port·fo·li·o [INVESTMENTS] /£ˌpɔːtˈfəʊ·li·əʊ, $ˌpɔːrtˈfoʊ·li·oʊ/ *n* [C] *pl* **portfolios** *specialized* a collection of company shares and other investments that are owned by a particular person or organization • *She has a share portfolio worth about £25 000.* • *The portfolio manager's job is to ensure that there is steady growth in the value of the investments.*

port·fo·li·o [JOB] /£ˌpɔːtˈfəʊ·li·əʊ, $ˌpɔːrtˈfoʊ·li·oʊ/ *n* [C] **portfolios** *specialized* a particular job or area of responsibility of a member of a government • *The Prime Minister offered her the foreign affairs portfolio.* • A minister **without portfolio** is an important government official who is not in charge of a particular department, but who still takes part in the decisions of the government.

port·hole /£ˈpɔːt·həʊl, $ˈpɔːrt·hoʊl/ *n* [C] a small usually round window in the side of a ship or aircraft • [PIC] **Ships and boats**

por·ti·co /£ˈpɔː·tɪ·kəʊ, $ˈpɔːr·t̬ɪ·koʊ/ *n* [C] *pl* **porticoes** or **porticos** a covered entrance to a usually large and splendid building, which is supported by columns

por·tion /£ˈpɔː·ʃᵊn, $ˈpɔːr-/ *n* [C] a part or share of something larger • *A large/major portion* **of** *the company's profit goes straight back into new projects.* • *(fig.) I accept my portion* **of** *the blame* (=I am partly responsible). • A portion is also the amount of a particular food that is served to one person, esp. in a restaurant or a shop which sells food ready to be eaten: *The portions are very* **generous** *in this restaurant.* ○ *A tart that size will probably divide into about ten portions.* ○ *They ordered five portions* **of** *chips.*

por·tion out *obj*, **por·tion** *obj* **out** /£ˌpɔː·ʃᵊn, $ˌpɔːr-/ *v adv* [M] • If you portion something out you share it out: *We'll have to portion the money out* **among/between** *the six of us.* ○ *(fig.) Nobody's going to start portioning out* **blame**. • See also APPORTION.

port·ly /£ˈpɔːt·li, $ˈpɔːrt-/ *adj humorous* (esp. of middle-aged or old men) with a fat stomach and chest • *He arrived at the restaurant, a portly figure in a tight-fitting jacket and bow tie.*

port·man·teau [BAG] /£pɔːtˈmæn·təʊ, $pɔːrtˈmæn·toʊ/ *n* [C] *pl* **portmanteaus** or **portmanteaux** /£pɔːtˈmæn·təʊ, $pɔːrtˈmæn·toʊ/ *dated* a large case for carrying clothes while travelling, esp. one which opens out into two parts

port·man·teau [GENERAL] /£pɔːtˈmæn·təʊ, $pɔːrtˈmæn·toʊ/ *adj* [before n] made up of or covering a wide range of items, usually for a single purpose • *The Official Secrets Act was described as a piece of portmanteau legislation, covering everything from nuclear weapons to army boots.*

por·trait /£ˈpɔː·trɪt, -treɪt, $ˈpɔːr·trɪt/ *n* [C] a painting, photograph, drawing, etc. of a person or, less commonly, of a group of people • *She's commissioned an artist to paint her portrait/paint a portrait* **of** *her.* • *a portrait gallery/painter* • A film or book which is a portrait **of** something is a detailed description or representation of it: *Her latest novel* **gives/paints** *a very vivid portrait of the aristocracy in the 1920s.* • *"A Portrait of the Artist as a Young Man"* (title of a book by James Joyce, 1916)

por·trai·ture /£ˈpɔː·trɪ·tʃə, $ˈpɔːr·trɪ·tʃɚ/ *n* [U] *specialized* • Portraiture is the practice or art of making portraits: *There's an exhibition on the history of portraiture from Tudor times to the present day.*

por·tray *obj* /£pɔːˈtreɪ, $pɔːr-/ *v* [T] to represent or describe (someone or something) in a painting, film, book or other artistic work • *The painting portrays a beautiful young woman and her pet dog.* • *What's the name of the actress who portrays the mother in that film?* • *The writer portrays life in a working-class community at the turn of the century.* • If a person in a film, book, etc. is portrayed **as** a particular type of character, they are represented in that way: *The father in the film is portrayed as a fairly unpleasant character.*

por·tray·al /£pɔːˈtreɪ·əl, $pɔːr-/ *n* [C] • *He won an award for his portrayal* **of** *the tortured musician in Marco Turner's latest film.* • *His latest film is a fairly grim portrayal* **of** *wartime suffering.*

pose *obj* CAUSE /£pəʊz, $poʊz/ *v* [T] to cause (esp. a problem or difficulty) • *I'm glad they're coming to stay, but it does pose the* **problem** *of where they can all sleep.* • *It wasn't as if a fifty-year-old woman posed any* **threat** *to a twenty five-year-old beauty.*

pose *obj* ASK /£pəʊz, $poʊz/ *v* [T] to ask (a question), esp. in a formal situation such as a meeting • *Can we go back to the question that Helena posed earlier concerning the funds for the project?*

pos·er /£ˈpəʊ·zəʳ, $ˈpoʊ·zɚ/ *n* [C] *infml* • A poser is a problem or a question that is difficult to solve or answer: *Who was the last woman to win three Olympic gold medals? – that's quite a poser.*

pose POSITION /£pəʊz, $poʊz/ *v* [I] to move into and stay in a particular position, in order to be photographed, painted, etc. • *We all posed* **for** *our photographs next to the Statue of Liberty.* • *The actress is perhaps better known for posing topless* **for** *the tabloid press.* • A **posing pouch** is a small tight piece of clothing which can be worn by men to support and protect their sex organs when they are wearing no other clothes: *For many years, art schools used male models who hid their genitalia in posing pouches.*

pose /£pəʊz, $poʊz/ *n* [C] • A pose is a particular position in which a person stands, sits, etc. in order to be photographed, painted, etc.: *He* **adopted/assumed/struck** (=moved into) *an elegant pose, one foot placed neatly in front of the other.* ○ *The children were photographed in amusing poses.*

pose PRETEND /£pəʊz, $poʊz/ *v* [I] to pretend to be something that you are not or to have qualities that you do not possess, in order to be admired or attract interest • *He doesn't really know a thing about the theatre – he's just posing!* • *Take your sunglasses off, for goodness' sake, and stop posing!* • If you pose **as** a particular person you pretend to be that person in order to deceive people: *He posed as a health-worker in order to get into the old lady's house, and then stole her money.*

pose /£pəʊz, $poʊz/ *n* [C usually sing] • *She likes to appear as if she knows all about the latest films and art exhibitions, but it's all a pose* (=she's pretending and it's not true).

pos·eur /£ˈpəʊ·zəʳ, $ˈpoʊ·zɚ/, **pos·er** *n* [C] *disapproving* • *You look like a real poseur in your fancy sports car with your expensive clothes!*

pose·y /£ˈpəʊ·zi, $ˈpoʊ-/ *adj* **posier, posiest** *Br infml disapproving* • *I resent paying extra for my drink just because it's in a posey bottle!*

posh /£pɒʃ, $pɑːʃ/ *adj* **-er, -est** *infml* (of places and things) expensive and of high quality, or (*esp. Br* of people and their voices) from a high social class • *Shall I wear my posh new jacket?* • *He takes her to some really posh restaurants.* • *(esp. Br) A woman with a very posh accent telephoned for him earlier – I presumed it was his mother.*

posh /£pɒʃ, $pɑːʃ/ *adv* **-er, -est** *Br not standard* • *She talks dead posh.*

pos·it *obj* /£ˈpɒz·ɪt, $ˈpɑː·zɪt/ *v* [T] *fml* to suggest (something) as a basic fact or principle from which a further idea is formed or developed • *The statistics are based on a set of figures that the government posited.* • *If we posit* **that** *wage rises cause inflation, it follows that we should try to minimize them.* [+ *that* clause]

po·si·tion PLACE /pəˈzɪʃ·ən/ *n* the place where something or someone is, often in relation to other things • *Well, I've found our position on the map if you want to see where we are.* [C] • *It's the position of the house that's so lovely – overlooking the rolling hills.* [C] • *You're* **in** *a good position over there near the window!* [C] • *You've moved the furniture around – the sofa is* **in** *a different position.* [C] • *I didn't know you played hockey – what position* (=place or job in the team) *do you play?* [C] • A position is also the place where people are sent in order to carry out a course of action: *The troops took up their battle positions at the front line.* [C] ○ *As soon as his officers were* **in** *position/had moved* **into** *position, the police commander walked up the path towards the house.* [U] ○ *(fig.) We plan to begin operations in May, but our* **fallback** *position* (=what we shall do if we can't do that) *is to wait until autumn.* [C]

po·si·tion *obj* /pəˈzɪʃ·ən/ *v* [T always + adv/prep] • *I'd carefully positioned that plant near the window so that it got plenty of sunlight.* • *The army had been positioned to the north and east of the city.* • *When it came to seating people for dinner I positioned my***self** *as far away from him as possible.*

po·si·tion·al /pəˈzɪʃ·ən·əl/ *adj* [not gradable] • Positional means relating to position, esp. in sports: *The Brazilian side had made eight changes, six of them positional.*

po·si·tion RANK /pəˈzɪʃ·ən/ *n* [C] a rank or level in a company, competition or society • *Whether or not you're given a car depends on your position* **in** *the company.* • *She devoted her life to improving the position of women* **in** *society.* • *(Br and Aus) She finished the race* **in** *third position.* See also PLACE. • *(Br) At the end of the third round Rik's team are* **in** *first position (esp. Am* **place***), followed by Carla's team and in last place Ben's.* • A position in a company or organization is also a job: *She applied for a position in the firm that I work for.* ○ *Applications are now invited for the position of marketing manager.* ○ *I don't think he was ready to take on a position* **of** *such* **responsibility**. • To **jockey/***(esp. Br)* **jostle for position** is to struggle to obtain an advantage over other people, either in a race or in a situation where there is a struggle for power: *Within any conventional company there's a certain amount of jockeying for position.*

po·si·tion SITUATION /pəˈzɪʃ·ən/ *n* [C usually sing] a situation • *My financial position is rather precarious at the moment.* • *She's* **in** *the fortunate/enviable position of having a large wage and no dependents to support.* • *When two of your best friends argue it* **puts** *you* **in** *a very awkward position.* • *My husband refused to go to the party so I was* **put in** *the embarrassing position of having to make up an excuse for him.* • If you are **in a position to** do something you are able to do it, usually because you have the necessary experience, authority or money: *As I say, I'm not in a position to reveal any of the details of the project at present.* [+ *to* infinitive] ○ *I'm sure they'd like to help her out financially but they're not in a position* **to** *do so.* [+ *to* infinitive] ○ *She'd be in a much better position* **to** *get a job if she had more experience.* [+ *to* infinitive]

po·si·tion OPINION /pəˈzɪʃ·ən/ *n* [C usually sing] *fml* a way of thinking about a particular matter; opinion • *What's the company's position* **on** *recycling?* • *He* **takes** *the position* (=believes) *that individuals have a responsibility to look after themselves.* • *The Labour Party have changed their position* **on** *defence quite radically over the years.*

po·si·tion ARRANGEMENT OF BODY /pəˈzɪʃ·ən/ *n* [C] the way in which the body is arranged • *I go to sleep on my back but I always wake up in a different position.* • *I'm just going to change my position – my legs are a bit stiff.* • *You've got to find the position that's most comfortable for you.* • *Roz was showing me all the different yoga positions she's learned to do.*

pos·i·tive CERTAIN /£ˈpɒz·ə·tɪv, $ˈpɑː·zə·t̬ɪv/ *adj* without any doubt; certain • *"Are you sure it's okay for me to use your mother's car?" "Absolutely positive* (=Yes, I'm certain).*"* • *"It was him – I saw him take it." "Are you positive* **about** *that?"* • *Are you positive* **(that)** *you saw me switch the iron off?* [+ (*that*) clause] • *"Do you reckon she'll come to the party tonight?" "I think so – she seemed quite positive when I asked her last week."* • *It was always suspected that he committed the crime, but they never found any positive proof* (=proof that could not be doubted) *that it was him.*

pos·i·tive·ly /£ˈpɒz·ə·tɪv·li, $ˈpɑː·zə·t̬ɪv-/ *adv* • *He said quite positively that he would come, so I went ahead and saved a place for him.*

pos·i·tive·ness /£ˈpɒz·ə·tɪv·nəs, $ˈpɑː·zə·t̬ɪv-/ *n* [U]

pos·i·tive HOPEFUL /£ˈpɒz·ə·tɪv, $ˈpɑː·zə·t̬ɪv/ *adj* hopeful and confident, or giving cause for hope and confidence • *It's great being with her because she's got such a positive attitude to everything.* • *On a more positive note, we're seeing signs that the housing market is picking up.* • *The past ten years we've seen some very positive developments in East-West relations.* • *There was a very positive response to the samples of the product that we gave out – people seemed very pleased with it.* • *Life doesn't always run smoothly but you've got to* **think** *positive and make the best of it.* • *(Br)* **Positive discrimination** is the practice of giving advantage to those groups in society which are often treated unfairly, usually because of their race or their sex. • *(Br)* **Positive vetting** is the detailed examination of a person's past, political beliefs, etc. in order to discover if they are suitable for a government job which might involve dealing with secret information. • Compare NEGATIVE WITHOUT HOPE.

pos·i·tive·ly /£'pɒz·ə·tɪv·li, $'pɑː·zə·t̬ɪv-/ *adv* • *More positively, we're now seeing companies taking responsibility for the effects of their actions on the environment.* • *I don't respond very positively* (= in a good way) *to being bossed around – it just makes me aggressive.*

pos·i·tive·ness /£'pɒz·ə·tɪv·nəs, $'pɑː·zə·t̬ɪv-/ *n* [U]

pos·i·tive TEST RESULTS /£'pɒz·ə·tɪv, $'pɑː·zə·t̬ɪv/ *adj* [not gradable] (of a medical test) showing the presence of the disease or condition for which the person is being tested • *a positive pregnancy test* • *He's HIV positive.* • *She tested positive for hepatitis.* • Compare NEGATIVE TEST RESULTS.

pos·i·tive·ness /£'pɒz·ə·tɪv·nəs, $'pɑː·zə·t̬ɪv-/ *n* [U]

pos·i·tive COMPLETE /£'pɒz·ə·tɪv, $'pɑː·zə·t̬ɪv/ *adj* [before n; not gradable] (used to add force to an expression) complete • *Far from being a nuisance, she was a positive joy to have around.*

pos·i·tive·ly /£'pɒz·ə·tɪv·li, $'pɑː·zə·t̬ɪv-/ *adv* [not gradable] *infml* • *Nicky positively glows with health.* • *The first assistant I asked wasn't particularly helpful and the second one was positively rude!*

pos·i·tive ABOVE ZERO /£'pɒz·ə·tɪv, $'pɑː·zə·t̬ɪv/ *adj* [not gradable] (of a number or amount) more than zero • *Two is a positive quantity.* • Compare NEGATIVE BELOW ZERO.

pos·i·tive ELECTRICITY /£'pɒz·ə·tɪv, $'pɑː·zə·t̬ɪv/ *adj* [not gradable] being the type of electrical charge which is carried by PROTONS • Compare NEGATIVE ELECTRICITY.

pos·i·tive BLOOD TYPE /£'pɒz·ə·tɪv, $'pɑː·zə·t̬ɪv/ *adj* [not gradable] having the RHESUS FACTOR in the blood • *My blood type is O positive.*

pos·i·tron /£'pɒz·ɪ·trɒn, $'pɑː·zɪ·trɑːn/ *n* [C] *specialized* an extremely small piece of matter with a positive electrical charge, having the same mass as an ELECTRON

poss /£pɒs, $pɑːs/ *adj* [after v; not gradable] *infml for* possible • *If poss, I'd like the whole of it painted.* • *I want it done as soon as poss really.*

pos·se /£'pɒs·i, $'pɑː·si/ *n* [C] a group of people following a person in order to catch him or her, or *(slang)* a group of friends • *A posse of armed policemen made their way to the suspect's address.* • *The disgraced minister walked swiftly from the car to his house pursued by a whole posse of reporters.* • *(slang) Is he one of the posse that you hang out with?*

pos·sess *obj* OWN /pə'zes/ *v* [T not *be possessing*] to have or own (something), or to have (a particular quality) • *She asked me if I had a ball gown that she could borrow, but I'm afraid I don't possess such a thing.* • *(law) They've been charged with possessing guns and explosives.* • *In the past the root of this plant was thought to possess magical powers which could cure impotence.*

pos·sessed /pə'zest/ *adj* [after v; not gradable] *fml or literary* • If you are possessed **of** something you own it or have it as a quality: *He was possessed of a large fortune but sadly no brains to speak of.*

pos·ses·sion /pə'zeʃ·ᵊn/ *n* • *The possession of large amounts of money does not ensure your success with women, but it may help.* [U] • *(fml) I have* **in** *my possession* (= I have or own) *a letter which I think may be of interest to you.* [U] • *(fml) He was found* **in** *possession* **of** *explosives./Explosives were found* **in** *his possession.* [U] • *(fml) Being the only child, he* **came into** *possession of a great deal of property when his father died.* [U] • A possession is something that you own or that you are carrying with you at any time: *She's never really been interested in* **material** *possessions.* [C usually pl] ○ *Will passengers please make sure that they take all their* **personal** *possessions with them on leaving the train.* [C usually pl] ○ *He regards the car as his* **personal** *possession* (= he acts as though it belongs to him, but it belongs to all of us). [C usually pl] • A country's possessions are the countries ruled by it: *a former overseas possession* [C usually pl] • *(law)* You **take/get** possession **of** a building or piece of land when you start to use and control it, whether or not you own it: *We've already bought the house but we won't take possession (of it) until May when the present occupants move out.* [U] • *(saying)* 'Possession is nine points/tenths of the law' means that if you own something, you can control what happens to it, and other people can't take it away from you.

pos·ses·sive /pə'zes·ɪv/ *adj* • If you are possessive **about** something that you own, you do not like lending it to other people or sharing it with other people: *He's a bit possessive about his clothes – I wouldn't dare ask to borrow them.* • Someone who is possessive in his or her feelings and behaviour towards another person wants to have all of that person's love and attention and will not share it with anyone else: *a possessive mother* ○ *He's very possessive* **towards** *his wife.* • In grammar, a possessive word, form etc. shows who or what something belongs to: *In English, the possessive singular of nouns is formed with* **'s**. ○ *'Mine' and 'yours' are possessive* **pronouns**. • LP› **Possessive form**

pos·ses·sor /£pə'zes·əʳ, $-ɚ/ *n* [C usually sing] *fml or humorous* • *I'm pleased to say that I am now the* **proud** *possessor* **of** *a driving licence!*

pos·sess *obj* CONTROL /pə'zes/ *v* [T] (of a desire or an idea) to take control over (a person's) mind, making that person behave in a very strange way • *I'm absolutely dreading making the after-dinner speech – I don't know what possessed me* **to** *agree to it!* [+ obj + *to* infinitive] • *Whatever possessed him* **to** *wear that appalling jacket!* [+ obj + *to* infinitive] • *You actually volunteered to take a class of children ice-skating – what possessed you* (= What made you do it)*?*

pos·sessed /pə'zest/ *adj* [after v; not gradable] • Someone who is possessed is thought to be controlled by an evil spirit. • If you behave **like** someone **possessed** you behave in a wild and uncontrolled manner so that other people do not understand you: *He's been running around the office this morning like a man possessed!*

pos·si·ble ACHIEVABLE /£'pɒs·ə·bl̩, $'pɑː·sə-/ *adj* [not gradable] that can be done or achieved, or that can exist • *I can't get it all done by Friday – it's just not possible.* • **It**'*s just about possible* **to** *fit four people on the seat but it's a squash.* [+ *to* infinitive] • *Is* **it** *possible* **to** *book tickets in advance?* [+ *to* infinitive] • **It**'*s not genetically possible* **for** *two blue-eyed parents* **to** *produce a brown-eyed child.* [+ *to* infinitive] • **If (at all)** *possible I'd like us to get there by midday.* • *We need to send that letter off* **as soon as** *possible.* • *They got as far as was* **humanly** *possible* (= as far as anyone could have) *before turning back.*

pos·si·bly /£'pɒs·ə·bli, $'pɑː·sə-/ *adv* [not gradable] • *He* **can't** *possibly have drunk all that on his own!* • *We did all that we possibly* **could** *to persuade her to come.* • Possibly is sometimes used in polite requests: **Could** *I possibly ask you to move your chair a little?* • Possibly is also sometimes used in polite refusals of offers: *"Have another chocolate." "No, really, I* **couldn't** *possibly."*

pos·si·bil·i·ty /£ˌpɒs·ə'bɪl·ɪ·ti, $ˌpɑː·sə'bɪl·ə·t̬i/ *n* [C] • *We could take on extra staff – that's one possibility* (= one thing that could be done). • *"Have you decided what to do?" "No, I'm still considering the various possibilities."* • *I've looked around the city and from what I've seen I think it* **has** *distinct possibilities* (= things that I will be able to make use of or enjoy).

pos·si·ble UNCERTAIN /£'pɒs·ə·bl̩, $'pɑː·sə-/ *adj* [not gradable] that might or might not happen • **It**'*s possible* **(that)** *Mira might turn up tonight.* [+ (*that*) clause] • *"Do you reckon he'll end up in prison?" "It's very possible."* • *That's one possible solution to the problem.* • **Anything's possible** means that even an unlikely event might happen: *Well,* **if** *your brother can find a woman who's willing to marry him* **then** *I suppose anything's possible.* • Compare PROBABLE.

pos·si·bly /£'pɒs·ə·bli, $'pɑː·sə-/ *adv* [not gradable] • *He may possibly decide not to come, in which case there's no problem.* • Possibly is also used to agree or disagree when some doubt is involved: *"Do you think this skirt might be too small for her?" "(Very) possibly – she has put on a bit of weight."* • *"Will he come?" "Possibly not."*

pos·si·bil·i·ty /£ˌpɒs·ə'bɪl·ɪ·ti, $ˌpɑː·sə'bɪl·ə·t̬i/ *n* [U] • *It's not likely to happen but I wouldn't* **rule out** *the possibility* (= say that it certainly won't happen). • *The forecast said that there's a possibility* **of** *snow* (= it might snow) *tonight.* • *"If she gets there early she'll be locked out." "I wouldn't worry –* **there**'*s not much possibility* **of** *that* (= that's not likely to happen)*!"* • **There**'*s a* **strong** *possibility* **(that)** (= It is likely that) *we may be in France for that week.* [+ (*that*) clause] • *(slightly fml) Is* **there** *any possibility* **(that)** *you could* (= Could you please) *pick me up from the station?* [+ (*that*) clause]

pos·sum /£'pɒs·əm, $'pɑː·səm/, **o·pos·sum** *n* [C] *pl* **possums** or **possum** a small animal which lives in trees and has thick fur, a long nose and a hairless tail. Different types of possums are found in Australia, New Zealand and America.

post LETTERS *esp. Br* /£pəʊst, $poʊst/, *Am and Aus usually* **mail** *n* [U] letters and parcels that are delivered to homes

THE POSSESSIVE FORM

The possessive form of a noun is usually formed by adding 's and is used like a possessive pronoun such as 'my' or 'her'. Possessives are used to show, for example:

possession	*Paul's house; the dog's bowl*
qualities	*the old woman's kindness*
relationships	*Jack's brother; the horse's owner; the King of Spain's daughter*
events	*my aunt's fall; a bird's cry*

WITH NOUNS FOR PEOPLE, ANIMALS AND GROUPS

The possessive form is most typically used with nouns for people and animals (see the examples above); as well as groups of people or animals: *the crowd's reaction; the herd's leader.*

- **Political groups, business companies and countries**:
  the Conservative Party's foreign policy; Sony's profits for the year; France's economy
- **Appearing alone** its function is similar to the personal pronouns 'mine', 'hers' etc.:
  "Whose is this camera?" "Susan's". • Don't use that plate, it's the cat's. • Mine is here and Pete's is over there.
- **With the name of shop-keepers to refer to their shop:**
  I need to go to the hairdresser's/grocer's/newsagent's
  The apostrophe (') is sometimes omitted with names: *Harrods; Debenhams; Lloyds Bank*
- **With family names to refer to homes:**
  I'll call in at Mrs Crawford's. • We're invited to the Smiths' for dinner.
  A family name + s with no apostrophe refers to a family as a group: *The Turners are coming tomorrow.*

WITH OTHER TYPES OF NOUNS

- **To describe qualities, actions, parts:**
  physical objects: *this plant's medicinal properties; the wind's drying effect; the ship's engines; the water's edge*
  abstract things: *the plan's main points; the economy's annual growth*
  the Earth and other planets: *the Earth's atmosphere; the world's energy resources; the sun's rays; Saturn's rings*
- **In time expressions:**
  in a week's time; an hour's walk from here; a good night's sleep; at Tuesday's meeting; the year's profits
- **In some phrases**:
  I saw it in my mind's eye (= imagined it).
  She was at death's door (= very ill).
  It's only a stone's throw away (= not far away).

WHEN THE POSSESSIVE FORM IS NOT USED

English often does not use a possessive form where other languages do. Frequently a compound noun or combination of two nouns is used instead of a possessive. Common examples are:
a family friend; a company car; a shirt sleeve; a chair leg; a truck driver; a rose petal; The Lister Hospital
It is also common to use a phrase with a preposition (often but not always of):
the colour of the sky; the pages in the book; the smile on her face; the money in my account; he has the strength of a bull; it was the chance of a lifetime

WHEN 'S IS NOT USED

Regular plurals ending in s take an apostrophe (') with no extra s: *a boys' school.* With singular nouns and names ending in s, an extra s can be added or omitted: *Dennis' room* or *Dennis's room* (both pronounced /'denɪsɪz/); *James' shoes* or *James's shoes* (/'dʒeɪmzɪz/)

or places of work • *I'd been away for a few days so I had a lot of post waiting for me.* • *Unless it's marked 'private' my secretary usually* **opens** *my post.* • **The** post is a delivery of letters and parcels to any one place: *Has the post* **come/arrived** *yet?* ○ *A couple of letters came for you in the* **second** *post* (= the second delivery of the day). • Post is also the public system that exists for the collecting and delivering of letters: *The cheque is* **in the** *post.* ○ *My letter must have got lost* **in the** *post.* ○ *If you don't want to take it there you can just send it* **by** *post.* • *(Br infml)* If you take a letter or parcel to **the** post, you put it in a special box in the street or in the side of a building from which it will be collected and sent to the address written on it: *I'm just taking these letters to the post.* • A **post office** is a shop where you can buy stamps and other things relating to the post and from where you can send letters and parcels. • In many countries the **Post Office** is the national organization which is in charge of the postal service. • **Post-free/Post-paid** means without having to pay to send something by post: *Send for an educational video post-free.* ○ *The guidebook costs £10·95 post-free.*

post *obj esp. Br, Aus also* /£pəʊst, $poʊst/, *Am and Aus usually* **mail** *v* [T] • To post a parcel or letter is to send it by post: *Did you remember to post my letter?* ○ *I must post that parcel* **(off)** *or she won't get it in time for her birthday.* ○ *Could you post me the details/post the details* **to** *me.* [+ two objects] • *(infml)* If you put any object through a LETTERBOX (= special opening in a door) you can say that you posted it: *Just post the key through the door after you've locked it.*

post·age /£'pəʊ·stɪdʒ, $'poʊ-/ *n* [U] • Postage is the money that you pay for sending letters and parcels through the post: *Enclose £15·99 plus £2 postage.* • *(Br and Aus)* **Postage and packing** (*Am usually* **shipping and handling**) is a charge for the cost of having something packed and then posted to you: *Add £3 for postage and packing.* • A **Postage stamp** is a STAMP [LETTER].

post·al /£'pəʊ·st^{ə}l, $'poʊ-/ *adj* [not gradable] • Postal means relating to post or to the public service that collects and delivers the post: *postal charges* ○ *the postal service* ○ *a postal strike* ○ *postal workers* • *(Br) People who cannot vote in person at the election can take part in a postal* **ballot** *(Am* **absentee ballot***) by sending in a postal* **vote** *(Am and Aus* **absentee vote***).* • *(esp. Br)* A **postal order** (*Am usually, Aus also* **money order**) is a piece of paper with an amount of money written on it, which you send through the post to someone, who can then exchange it for the same amount of money at a post office.

post [POLE] /£pəʊst, $poʊst/ *n* [C] a vertical stick or pole fixed into the ground, usually to support something or mark a position • *Unfortunately he drove the car into a concrete post.* • Post can be used as a combining form: *a lamppost* ○ *a signpost* • In the sport of horse racing, **the** post marks the finishing place or, less often, the place from which the race starts: *The horse I'd put my money on just got beaten* **at** *the post* (= as it was finishing). • *(infml)* In sports such as football, **the** post can be a GOALPOST (= either of two vertical posts marking the area in which the ball is kicked to score points): *Watching the replay, we can see the ball just bounce off the near post.*

post [JOB] /£pəust, $poust/ *n* [C] a position of paid employment in a company or organization; a job • *Teaching posts are advertised in Tuesday's edition of the paper.* • Compare **posting** at POST [PLACE].

post *obj* [STICK] /£pəust, $poust/ *v* [T] *esp. Br and Aus* to stick or pin (a notice) on a wall in order to make it publicly known • *Company announcements are usually posted* **(up) on** *the notice-board.*

post [PLACE] /£pəust, $poust/ *n* [C] the particular place where someone works, esp. where a soldier is told to be for military duty, usually as a guard • *He was* **at** *his post by the door to welcome visitors from 7.30 every day.* • *I was ordered not to leave my post at the information desk until the last customer had left.* • *The soldier was disciplined for* **deserting** *his post.*

post *obj* /£pəust, $poust/ *v* [T usually passive] • To post someone is to send them to a particular place to work: *In his first job at the Foreign Office he was posted* **to** *Abu Dhabi.* ○ *He's been posted* **to** *Pakistan for six months.* ○ *Guards were posted* **at** *all the doors.*

post·ing /£'pəu·stɪŋ, $'pou-/, *Am usually, Aus also* **post** *n* [C] • A posting is a job, often within the same organization that you are working for, which involves going to a different country or town: *If you were offered an overseas posting would you take it?* • Compare POST [JOB].

post *obj* [PAY] /£pəust, $poust/ *v* [T] *Am* to pay (money), esp. so that a person who has been accused of committing a crime can be free until their trial • *She has agreed to post* **bail** *for her brother.*

post– [AFTER] /£pəust-, $poust-/ *combining form* after or later than • *postgraduate* • *postoperative* • *He took a post-lunch nap.* • **Post-coital** means happening or existing after sexual INTERCOURSE: *post-coital satisfaction* ○ *post-coital contraception* • *Britain is struggling to come to terms with the* **post-industrial** *age* (= the present time in Western society, when industries making large machines are no longer very important, and people do many different sorts of work). • **Post-modernism** is used to describe a style of art, writing, music, theatre and esp. ARCHITECTURE (= the designing of buildings), popular in the 1980s and 1990s, which includes features from several different periods in the past or from the present and past: *a* **post-modern** *building* ○ *a* **post-modernist** *critique* • *(specialized)* **Post-traumatic stress disorder** (*abbreviation* **PTSD**) is a mental condition in which a person suffers severe anxiety and DEPRESSION (= sadness) after a very frightening or shocking experience, such as an accident or a war: *Soldiers who'd fought in Vietnam suffered from post-traumatic stress disorder years after they'd come home.*

post·bag *Br* /£'pəust·bæg, $'poust-/, *Am and Aus* **mail** *n* [U] the number of letters received at one time or on one subject • *We've had a huge postbag on the subject of animal rights.* • *It was clear from our postbag that viewers were unhappy about the programme.* • A postbag is also a MAILBAG.

post·box *esp. Br, Aus also* /£'pəust·bɒks, $'poust·bɑːks/, *esp. Br* **let·ter·box**, *Am and Aus* **mail·box** *n* [C] a metal container in the street or other public place in which you can post letters. In Britain it is bright red.

post·card /£'pəust·kɑːd, $'poust·kɑːrd/ *n* [C] a card, often with a photograph or picture on one side, which can be addressed and sent without an envelope • **Drop/Send** *me a postcard from Spain, won't you?*

post·code *Br and Aus* /£'pəust·kəud, $'poust·koud/ *n* [C] a short series of letters and numbers representing a particular area, which contains most of the information in a postal address • *If you put the postcode on the envelope, it'll get there quicker.* • See also **zip code** at ZIP [SPEED]. • [LP] **Letters**

post·date *obj* /£ˌpəust'deɪt, '--, $ˌpoust'deɪt/ *v* [T] to happen or occur after (something) • *Most manuscripts postdate the stories which have circulated by word of mouth for centuries.* • To postdate a document such as a CHEQUE or letter is to write a date on it that is later than the date on which you are writing it, usually to get some advantage: *Luckily, she let me postdate the cheque until the end of the month, so I won't have to pay the money until I get my salary.* • Compare BACKDATE; PREDATE.

po·ster /£'pəu·stəʳ, $'pou·stɚ/ *n* [C] a large printed picture, photograph or notice which you stick or pin to a wall or board • *They've brightened up the place with a few posters.* • *We noticed a poster advertising a circus.* • *The children* **put up** *a poster saying 'Pet mice – get your mouse here'.* • See also POSTER PAINT.

po·ster col·our *n* [C/U] POSTER PAINT

poste res·tante *Br* /£ˌpəust'res·tɑːnt, £-tɑ̃ːnt, $ˌpoust·res'tɑːnt/, *Am* **gen·er·al de·li·ve·ry** *n* [C usually sing] a department in a post office which will receive letters and parcels for a person who is travelling to or around that area and keep them until they can be collected • *There's a poste restante at the main post office.* • *Make sure I give you my poste restante address before I go.*

poste res·tante *Br* /£ˌpəust'res·tɑːnt, £-tɑ̃ːnt, $ˌpoust·res'tɑːnt/, *Am* **gen·er·al de·li·ve·ry** *adv* [not gradable] • *I don't know the name of her hotel, so I'm sending her mail poste restante.*

pos·te·ri·or /£pɒs'tɪə·ri·əʳ, $pɑː'stɪr·i·ɚ/ *adj* [before n; not gradable] *fml* later in time, or positioned at or towards the back • Compare ANTERIOR.

pos·te·ri·or /£pɒs'tɪə·ri·əʳ, $pɑː'stɪr·i·ɚ/ *n* [C] *humorous* • Your posterior is your bottom: *If you would kindly move your posterior just a fraction to the right, I might get by.*

pos·ter·i·ty /£pɒs'ter·ə·ti, $pɑː'ster·ə·t̬i/ *n* [U] *fml* the people who will exist in the future • *Every attempt is being made to ensure that these works of art are* **preserved for** *posterity.*

po·ster paint, po·ster col·our *n* [C/U] a type of paint which is based on GUM (= a sticky substance obtained from trees) and does not contain oil. It is used for painting pictures, and is typically made in bright strong colours. • See also POSTER.

post·grad·u·ate /£ˌpəust'grædʒ·u·ət, £-'græd·ju-, $ˌpoust'grædʒ·u-/, *esp. Am* **grad·u·ate** /'grædʒ·u·ət, £'græd·ju-/ *n* [C] a student who has already obtained one degree and is studying at a university for a more advanced qualification • *He went to Oxford as a postgraduate to study criminology.* • [LP] **Schools and colleges**

post·grad·u·ate /£ˌpəust'grædʒ·u·ət, £-'græd·ju-, $ˌpoust'grædʒ·u-/, *esp. Am* **grad·u·ate** /'grædʒ·u·ət, £'græd·ju-/ *adj* [before n; not gradable] • *postgraduate studies/research* • *a postgraduate degree in microbiology* • A **Postgraduate Certificate in Education** (*abbreviation* **PGCE**) is a one-year teaching qualification taken by people who already have a first degree.

post·haste /£ˌpəust'heɪst, $ˌpoust-/ *adv* [not gradable] *dated fml* as fast as possible • *They travelled posthaste to Rome to collect the award.*

post·hu·mous /£'pɒs·tjʊ·məs, $'pɑːs·tʃə-/ *adj* [not gradable] *fml* happening after a person's death • *The posthumous publication of the actor's memoirs aroused a lot of interest.*

post·hu·mous·ly /£'pɒs·tjʊ·mə·sli, $'pɑːs·tʃə-/ *adv* [not gradable] *fml* • *His last novel was published posthumously.*

Post–It (note) /£'pəust·ɪt, $'poust̬-/ *n* [C] *trademark* a piece of paper which can be written on and can be stuck temporarily to esp. another piece of paper in order to give information • *He wrote some comments on a post-it (note) and stuck it to the front of the report.* • [PIC] **Stationery**

post·man (*pl* **-men**), **post·wo·man** (*pl* **-women**) /£'pəust·mən, $'poust-, -ˌwʊm·ən/, *infml* **pos·tie** /£'pəu·sti, $'pou-/, *Am usually* **mail·man** (**-men**), **let·ter car·ri·er** *n* [C] a person whose job is to deliver and collect letters and parcels that are sent by post

post·mark /£'pəust·mɑːk, $'poust·mɑːrk/ *n* [C] an official mark stamped on a letter or parcel, typically showing the place that it was sent from and the time or date that it was sent • *The postmark is usually put on top of the postage stamp so that the stamp cannot be used more than once.*

post·mark *obj* /£'pəust·mɑːk, $'poust·mɑːrk/ *v* [T usually passive] • *It's postmarked Manchester/the thirtieth of September.* [+ obj + n]

post·mast·er *male, female* **post·mis·tress** /£'pəustˌmɑː·stəʳ, $'poustˌmæs·tɚ, -ˌmɪs·trəs/ *n* [C] a person who is in charge of a post office • *The local postmistress is retiring after forty years.*

post me·ri·di·em /mə'rɪd·i·əm/ *adv* [not gradable] See PM [TIME]

post·mor·tem (ex·am·i·na·tion) /£ˌpəʊstˈmɔː·təm, $ˌpoʊstˈmɔːr·t̬əm/ *n* [C] a medical examination of a dead person's body in order to find out the cause of death; an AUTOPSY, or *(infml)* a discussion of an event after it has happened, esp. of what was wrong with it or why it failed • *A postmortem revealed that the child had died from head injuries.* • *(infml) After we've played a match there's usually a postmortem over a few beers.*

post·na·tal /£ˌpəʊstˈneɪ·tᵊl, $ˌpoʊstˈneɪ·t̬ᵊl/ *adj* [not gradable] relating to the period of time immediately after a baby has been born • *postnatal care* • *postnatal depression* • Compare ANTENATAL.

post·nup·tial /£pəʊstˈnʌp·tʃᵊl, $poʊst-/ *adj* [not gradable] done after or relating to the period after marriage • A **postnuptial agreement** is a legal agreement which shows the rights of married partners, esp. to property, if their marriage comes to an end. See also **prenuptial agreement** at PRENUPTIAL.

post·op·e·ra·tive /£pəʊstˈɒp·ᵊr·ə·tɪv, $poʊstˈɑː·pɚ-/ *adj* [not gradable] *specialized* relating to the period of time which immediately follows a medical operation • *postoperative care* • *postoperative infection*

post·pone *(obj)* /£pəʊstˈpəʊn, £pəst-, $poʊstˈpoʊn/ *v* to delay (an event), esp. arranging for it to take place at a later date or time • *The trip to the museum has been postponed* **until** *Thursday 11th March.* [T] • *They decided to postpone their holiday* **until** *the autumn.* [T] • *We've had to postpone* **going** *to France because Adrian's got an interview for a job that week.* [+ *v-ing*]

post·pone·ment /£pəʊstˈpəʊn·mənt, £pəst-, $poʊstˈpoʊn-/ *n* • *We were disappointed by yet another postponement of our trip.* [C] • *They accepted the need for postponement.* [U]

post·pran·di·al /£pəʊstˈpræn·di·əl, $poʊst-/ *adj* [not gradable] *humorous* happening after LUNCH (=midday meal) or DINNER (=evening meal) • *He took the usual postprandial stroll around the grounds of his house.*

post·script /£ˈpəʊst·skrɪpt, $ˈpoʊst-/ *(abbreviation* **PS***)* *n* [C] a short remark or message added to the bottom of a letter after you have signed your name, usually introduced by the abbreviation PS • *There was the usual romantic postscript at the end of his letter – PS I love you.* • Any written or spoken addition to something already finished can be called a postscript: *As a postscript* **to** *that story I told you last week, it turned out that the woman was his sister-in-law.*

post·sea·son /£pəʊstˈsiː·zᵊn, $poʊst-/ *n* [C], *adj* [not gradable] *esp. Am* (of) games played after the end of the regular sports season • *The three division winners and the second-place team with the best record will advance to the postseason.* • *The Indians have won three straight one-run games in the postseason, including Tuesday's 1-0 state semi-final victory over Woodbridge.* • *The Garden State Bowl kicks off the postseason college football games.* • *A new team can become a postseason power very quickly.*

pos·tu·late *(obj)* /£ˈpɒs·tjʊ·leɪt, $ˈpɑː·stjə-/ *v fml* to suggest (a theory, idea, etc.) as a basic principle from which a further idea is formed or developed • *It was the Greek astronomer, Ptolemy, who postulated* **that** *the Earth was at the centre of the universe.* [+ *that* clause]

pos·tu·late /£ˈpɒs·tjʊ·lət, $ˈpɑː·stjə-/ *n* [C] *fml* • A postulate is an idea that is suggested or accepted as a basic principle before a further idea is formed or developed from it.

pos·ture POSITION OF BODY /£ˈpɒs·tʃəʳ, $ˈpɑːs·tʃɚ/ *n* the way in which someone usually holds their shoulders, neck and back, or a particular position in which someone stands, sits, etc. • *She's got very good/bad posture.* [U] • *Yoga improves* **(the)** *posture.* [U] • *He always* **adopts/ assumes** (=moves into) *the same posture for the cameras.* [C]

pos·ture OPINION /£ˈpɒs·tʃəʳ, $ˈpɑːs·tʃɚ/ *n* [U] a way in which esp. a government or other organization thinks about and/or deals with a particular matter • *For the third time this week the opposition has attacked the government's posture* **on** *defence.* • *The tone of the feminist speakers suggested they were adopting a rather defensive posture.*

pos·tur·ing /£ˈpɒs·tʃᵊr·ɪŋ, $ˈpɑːs·tʃɚ-/ *n* [U] *disapproving* behaviour or speech which is intended to attract attention and interest, or to make people believe something that is not true • *His writing has been dismissed as mere intellectual posturing.*

pos·ture /£ˈpɒs·tʃəʳ, $ˈpɑːs·tʃɚ/ *v* [I]

post·war /£ˈpəʊst·wɔː, $ˈpoʊst·wɔːr/ *adj* [not gradable] happening or existing in the period after a war, esp. the First or Second World War • *postwar Europe* • *postwar rationing* • *the postwar period* • Compare PREWAR.

po·sy /£ˈpəʊ·zi, $ˈpoʊ-/ *n* [C] a small BUNCH of flowers • *a posy of violets* • *The young bridesmaids carried posies of spring flowers.*

pot CONTAINER /£pɒt, $pɑːt/ *n* [C] any of various types of usually round container, esp. one made of clay, metal or glass • *He took a great pot of steaming food out of the oven.* • *There's plenty of cupboard space in the kitchen for all your pots* **and pans**. • A pot can be any of a variety of other containers, with or without a lid: *a pot of cream/jam/paint* • Pot also refers to the amount that is contained inside a pot, esp. a TEAPOT: *I've just drunk a whole pot of tea!* • Pot can also be a combining form and refers to containers of the stated type: *a coffee pot* ○ *a flowerpot* ○ *a plant pot* ○ *a teapot* • A pot can also be a dish, bowl, etc. made by hand out of clay. • *She's got* **pots of money** (= She's very rich). • If a plant is **pot-bound** its roots have filled the container it is growing in and it stops growing well. • *(Br and Aus)* A **pot plant** is a HOUSEPLANT. • A **pot roast** is a piece of BEEF (=meat from cattle) that is cooked slowly in a covered dish with a small amount of liquid and sometimes vegetables: *We usually have a pot roast for Sunday lunch.* • See also FLOWERPOT; TEAPOT. • PIC> **Containers** Ⓙ

pot *obj* /£pɒt, $pɑːt/ *v* [T] **-tt-** • To pot a plant is to put it in a flowerpot which contains earth in order to let it grow: *I'm just going to pot* **(up)** *these seedlings.* • *(esp. Br)* A **potting shed** is a small building in a garden in which plant pots, young plants, seeds, gardening tools, etc. are kept.

pot·ted /£ˈpɒt·ɪd, $ˈpɑː·t̬ɪd/ *adj* [before n; not gradable] • Potted plants are plants which are grown in a pot: *There were potted plants on the windowsill.* • Potted food, esp. meat or fish, is cooked food which is preserved in a closed container: *potted meat/shrimps* • *(Br infml)* A potted form of a story or book is one that has been made shorter and simpler and contains only the main facts or features: *They publish a potted* **version** *of Shakespeare's plays especially for children.* • PIC> **Handicraft**

pot·ter /£ˈpɒt·əʳ, $ˈpɑː·t̬ɚ/ *n* [C] • A potter is a person who makes dishes, plates and other objects from clay, usually by hand on a special wheel. • A **potter's wheel** is a machine with a horizontal spinning disc on which clay is shaped into decorative or useful objects.

pot·te·ry /£ˈpɒt·ᵊr·i, $ˈpɑː·t̬ɚ-/ *n* [U] • Pottery is the activity or skill of making clay objects by hand: *She's doing pottery classes.* • Pottery is also objects that are made out of clay by hand: *She bought a pottery vase* ○ *They sell pottery and other hand-made bits and pieces.*

pot TOILET /£pɒt, $pɑːt/ *n* [C] a POTTY

pot DRUG /£pɒt, $pɑːt/ *n* [U] *dated slang* CANNABIS (=a type of drug which is smoked)

pot *(obj)* SHOOT /£pɒt, $pɑːt/ *v* **-tt-** to shoot (birds or small animals) for food, or to shoot (at) them without taking careful aim • *He strolled through the fields, potting* **(at)** *the occasional rabbit.* [T; I + *at*]

pot *obj* HIT /£pɒt, $pɑːt/ *v* [T] **-tt-** *Br* in games such as SNOOKER, to hit (a ball) so that it falls into one of the holes at the edge of the table

pot /£pɒt, $pɑːt/ *n* [C] *Br* • *Dawson made a difficult pot* (=act of hitting the ball into a hole) *look very easy.*

pot STOMACH /£pɒt, $pɑːt/ *n* [C usually sing] *esp. humorous* a POTBELLY

pot BAD STATE /£pɒt, $pɑːt/ *n* [U] **go to pot** *infml* to be damaged through lack of care or effort • *I used to exercise but I'm afraid I've gone to pot since the baby was born.* • *I let the garden go to pot this summer.*

pot·age /pəˈtɑːʒ, £ˈpɒt·ɪdʒ, $ˈpɑː·t̬ɪdʒ/ *n* [U] *old use* thick soup, esp. one made from vegetables • Ⓙ

pot·ash /£ˈpɒt·æʃ, $ˈpɑː·t̬æʃ/ *n* [U] a white powder containing POTASSIUM which is put on the earth to make crops grow better

po·tas·si·um /pəˈtæs·i·əm/ *n* [U] a silvery-white element which, in combination with other elements, is used in the production of soap, glass and FERTILIZERS (=substances which help crops to grow better). It very easily takes part in chemical reactions.

po·ta·to /£pəˈteɪ·təʊ, $-t̬oʊ/ *n pl* **potatoes** a roundish white vegetable with a light brown, red or pink skin which grows underground and can be prepared and cooked in many different ways, or the plant on which these grow • *boiled/roasted/fried potatoes* [C] • *mashed potato* [U] • A **potato beetle** is a COLORADO BEETLE. • **Potato chip** is *Am* *and Aus for* CRISP. • A **potato crisp** is a CRISP. • **Potato salad** is small pieces of cooked potato mixed with MAYONNAISE. • PIC〉 **Vegetables**

pot·bel·ly /£ˌpɒtˈbel·i, $ˌpɑːt-/, **pot** *n* [C] a noticeably fat, round stomach • *After twenty years of heavy beer-drinking he has a massive potbelly.*

pot·bel·lied /£ˌpɒtˈbel·id, ˈ-ˌ--, $ˌpɑːt-/ *adj* • *Who's that potbellied man sitting over there?*

pot·boil·er /£ˈpɒtˌbɔɪ·ləʳ, $ˈpɑːtˌbɔɪ·lɚ/ *n* [C] *disapproving* an artistic work, usually of low quality, that has been created quickly just to earn money • *Her most recent potboiler was one of last year's bestselling paperbacks.*

po·ten·cy /£ˈpəʊ·tᵊnt·si, $ˈpoʊ·t̬ᵊnt-/ *n* [U] strength, power, force, influence or effectiveness • *This new drug's potency is not yet known.* • *The potency of these weapons is far greater than anything previously available.* • *Although the waste is highly radioactive, its potency declines rapidly, making its eventual disposal relatively easy.* • *He owed his popular support to the potency of his propaganda machine.* • The potency of a man is his ability to have sex: *Consuming large amounts of alcohol can significantly reduce a man's potency.* Compare **impotence** at IMPOTENT SEXUAL PROBLEM.

po·tent /£ˈpəʊ·tᵊnt, $ˈpoʊ·tᵊnt/ *adj* • Something that is potent is very powerful, strong, forceful or effective: *Surprise remains the terrorists' most potent* **weapon**. ○ *The Berlin Wall was a potent* **symbol** *of the Cold War.* ○ *Farmers are still a potent political* **force** *in France.* ○ *In her speech she presented a potent* (=persuasive) **argument** *for increasing taxes.* ○ *He drowned in the hotel swimming pool after drinking a potent* **mix** *of whisky, gin and vodka.* ○ *This is a very potent* **drug** *and can have unpleasant side-effects.* • *"Extraordinary how potent cheap music is"* (from Noel Coward's play *Private Lives*, 1930)

po·tent·ly /£ˈpəʊ·tᵊnt·li, $ˈpoʊ·t̬ᵊnt-/ *adv* • *His arguments were strong, and potently deployed.*

po·ten·tate /£ˈpəʊ·tᵊn·teɪt, $ˈpoʊ·t̬ᵊn-/ *n* [C] *literary, esp. disapproving* a ruler who has a lot of power, esp. one whose power is not limited such as by the existence of a parliament

po·ten·tial /£pəʊˈten·tʃᵊl, $poʊ-/ *adj* [not gradable] possible when the necessary conditions exist • *She is widely regarded as a potential Olympic gold medallist.* • *A number of potential* **buyers** *have expressed interest in the company.* • *Both potential* **bidders** *have experience of the hotel industry.* • *Many potential* **customers** *are waiting for a fall in prices before buying.* • *The accident is a grim reminder of the potential* **dangers** *involved in North Sea oil production.*

po·ten·tial /£pəʊˈten·tʃᵊl, $poʊ-/ *n* [U] • Someone's potential is their ability to develop, achieve or succeed: • *The growth potential* **of** *the company is reflected in the high price of its shares.* ○ *The region has* **enormous** *potential* **for** *economic development but a lot of investment is needed to achieve this.* ○ *I don't feel I'm* **achieving** *my* **full** *potential in my present job.* ○ *You have the potential* **to** *reach the top of your profession if you want to.* [+ *to* infinitive] ○ *The new management intends to* **realize** *the* **untapped** *potential* (=use the potential which is not being used at present) *of the workforce.* • *I think this room has got a lot of potential* (=could be very good if some changes were made to it).

po·ten·ti·al·i·ty /£pəʊˌten·tʃiˈæl·ə·ti, $poʊˌten·tʃiˈæl·ə·t̬i/ *n fml* • The potentiality of a thing or person is an ability for development, achievement or success which is natural or has not been used: *This whole coastline has tremendous potentiality* **for** *hotel development.* [U] • *The army's potentiality* **to** *intervene in politics remains strong.* [U + *to* infinitive] • *The allies' main war objective is to end his country's potentialities as a military threat to neighbouring countries.* [C]

po·ten·tial·ly /£pəʊˈten·tʃᵊl·i, $poʊ-/ *adv* [not gradable] • *Hepatitis is a potentially* **fatal** *disease.* • *Chain saws are potentially the most* **dangerous** *item of garden equipment.* • *This is a potentially* **lucrative** *agreement which could earn us millions of pounds over the next few years.* • *A potentially* **damaging** *situation has been avoided by the government.* • *This crisis is potentially the most* **serious** *in the organization's history.*

pot·head /£ˈpɒt·hed, $ˈpɑːt-/ *n* [C] *dated slang* someone who uses the drug CANNABIS regularly • *Pete's a real pothead – he seems to be permanently stoned.*

pot·hold·er /£ˈpɒtˌhəʊl·dəʳ, $ˈpɑːtˌhoʊl·dɚ/ *n* [C] *esp. Am and Aus* a thick protective piece of material used when removing hot dishes or pans from a cooker

pot·hole ROADS /£ˈpɒt·həʊl, $ˈpɑːt·hoʊl/ *n* [C] a hole in a road surface which results from gradual damage caused by traffic and/or weather • *The car's suspension is so good that when you hit a pothole you hardly notice it.* • *(fig.) The road to economic recovery is full of potholes* (=possible problems).

pot·holed /£ˈpɒt·həʊld, $ˈpɑːt·hoʊld/ *adj* [not gradable] • A potholed road is a road that contains a lot of potholes: *The cottage is situated in the middle of a wood at the end of a narrow potholed lane.*

pot·hole UNDERGROUND /£ˈpɒt·həʊl, $ˈpɑːt·hoʊl/ *n* [C] a deep hole formed underground in LIMESTONE areas by the gradual rubbing and dissolving action of water flowing through the stone

pot·hol·er *Br* /£ˈpɒtˌhəʊ·ləʳ, $ˈpɑːtˌhoʊ·lɚ/, *Br and Aus also* **cav·er**, *Am* **spe·lunk·er**, *Aus also* **spel·e·ol·o·gist** *n* [C] • *Potholers often have to squeeze through tunnels that are only a couple of feet high.*

pot·hol·ing *Br* /£ˈpɒtˌhəʊ·lɪŋ, $ˈpɑːtˌhoʊ-/, *Br and Aus also* **cav·ing**, *Am* **spe·lunk·ing**, *Aus also* **spel·e·ol·o·gy** *n* [U] • Potholing is a sport which involves climbing into and around potholes and underground caves: *She's* **going** *potholing at the weekend.*

po·tion /£ˈpəʊ·ʃᵊn, $ˈpoʊ-/ *n* [C] a drink that is believed to have a good or bad magical effect on the person who takes it, or *(esp. disapproving)* a medicine • *The older women gather fragrant herbs in the mountains for* **love** *potions that are sold to gullible tourists.* • *Asterix is a fictional cartoon character who obtains his superhuman strength from a* **magic** *potion.* • *(esp. disapproving) Americans are said to spend more on pills and potions than any other nation.*

pot luck /£pɒtˈlʌk, $pɑːt-/ *n* [U] anything that is available or is found by chance, rather than something chosen, planned or prepared • *It was just pot luck that I saw his name in the paper and contacted him.* • *I hadn't made a reservation, so I just* **took** *pot luck at the airport and got on the first available flight.* • *We had no idea which hotel would be best, so we just* **took** *pot luck* **with** *the first one on the list.* • *Mary's welcome to stay for dinner if she doesn't mind* **taking** *pot luck* (=having whatever is available). • *(esp. Am)* When people are invited to a pot luck **dinner** or **supper** each guest takes a different dish which is then shared with the other guests.

pot·pour·ri /£ˌpəʊ·pəˈri, $ˌpoʊ-/ *n* a mixture of dried petals and leaves from various flowers and plants that is used to give a room a pleasant smell • *I'm afraid I've knocked your bowl of potpourri on the floor.* [U] • *Their house smelt like a flower shop and had potpourris in every room.* [C] • A potpourri is also an unusual or interesting mixture of things: *Her new TV show will be a potpourri* **of** *arts and media reports.* [C] ○ *The first course was a pot pourri* **of** *all the starters on the menu.* [C]

pot·shot /£ˈpɒt·ʃɒt, $ˈpɑːt·ʃɑːt/, **pot** *n* [C] a shot which is fired carelessly or with little preparation and which takes advantage of an opportunity • *His opponents have* **taken** *potshots* **at** *him, set fire to his house and vandalised his car.* • *The government is not prepared to send troops into a situation in which they would face potshots from both the sides involved in the civil war.* • *(fig.) The recent criticism of his leadership has included potshots* (=spoken or written attacks) *from several leading political journalists.*

pot·ter /£ˈpɒt·əʳ, $ˈpɑː·t̬ɚ/, *Am usually* **put·ter** *v* [I always + adv/prep] to move about without hurrying and in a relaxed and pleasant way • *I spent the afternoon pottering* **around** *the garden doing a few odd jobs.* • *Georgina spends a lot of time pottering* **about** *the house pretending to be busy but doing nothing in particular.* • *He doesn't drive very fast – he tends to potter* **along**. • *Alfred is the elderly bearded man who you often see pottering* **around** *the village.* • *What were you doing pottering* **around** *downstairs in the middle of the night?* • *(fig.) We haven't done anything very exciting recently – we're just pottering* **along** *quite happily.*

pot·ter /£ˈpɒt·əʳ, $ˈpɑː·t̬ɚ/ *n* [U] *Br* • *I'm just going into town for a potter* **round** *the shops.*

pot·ty SILLY /£ˈpɒt·i, $ˈpɑː·t̬i/ *adj* **-ier, -iest** *esp. Br infml* silly or foolish • *I must have been potty* **to** *sell my car so cheaply.* • *He's always coming up with potty ideas about how to change the world.* • *She's slightly potty and eccentric, but that makes her very interesting.* • If you are potty **about** something, you like it very much: *Guy's potty about German beer and sausages.* ○ *She's potty about him, but I* *don't think they'll get married.* • *My parents* **went** *potty* (= became very annoyed) *when I told them I was pregnant.* • Something that **drives** you potty annoys you a lot: *The noise from our next-door neighbours is driving us potty.*

pot·ti·ness /£'pɒt·ɪ·nəs, $'pɑː·t̬ɪ-/ *n* [U] *Br infml* • *He's a strange person to work with, but you get used to his pottiness eventually.*

pot·ty TOILET /£'pɒt·i, $'pɑː·t̬i/, **pot** *n* [C] a plastic bowl with a handle which young children sit on and use as a toilet • *Don't forget to sit Jamie on the potty before you take him to the zoo.* • A child who is **potty-trained** (also **toilet-trained**) knows how to use a potty or toilet and no longer needs to wear a NAPPY to protect its clothing: *By what age are children usually potty-trained?* ○ **Potty-training** (= teaching a child how to use a potty) *is one of the more unpleasant aspects of raising a child.*

pouch /paʊtʃ/ *n* [C] a bag or soft container for a small object or a small amount of something • *All our electric shavers are supplied with a free travel pouch.* • *Food sealed in foil pouches lasts for a long time.* • *"There's plenty more where this came from," said Paul, placing a pouch of gold coins on the table in front of her.* • A pouch is also a pocket on the lower part of the body of some female animals in which their young are carried and protected after they are born: *Animals that carry their young in pouches are called marsupials and include kangaroos and koala bears.* • Some animals have pouches in their mouths that are formed from skin and are used for carrying and storing food.

pouf SEAT, **pouffe** /puːf/, *Am* **ot·to·man** /£'ɒt·əʊ·mən, $'ɑː·t̬ə·mən/ *n* [C] a soft round or square seat with no back or sides, used for sitting on or resting your feet on

pouf HOMOSEXUAL /pʊf/ *n* [C] *esp. Br and Aus disapproving slang* a POOF

poul·tice /£'pəʊl·tɪs, $'poʊl·t̬ɪs/ *n* [C] a piece of cloth covered with a thick warm liquid which is wrapped around an injury to reduce pain or swelling • *The heat from the poultice increases the flow of blood to the injury, resulting in more white blood cells being available to fight infection.*

poul·try /£'pəʊl·tri, $'poʊl-/ *pl n* birds, such as chickens, that are bred for their eggs and meat • *Our poultry live in much better conditions than many other people's.* • *Some poultry farmers keep turkeys and ducks as well as chickens.*

poul·try /£'pəʊl·tri, $'poʊl-/ *n* [U] • Poultry is the meat from birds such as chickens: *Many people who give up eating meat and poultry carry on eating fish.* • *In some countries up to 40 percent of all raw poultry is contaminated with salmonella, which can cause food poisoning.*

pounce /paʊnts/ *v* [I] to jump or move quickly in order to catch or take hold of something • *The cat sat in the tree ready to pounce* **on** *the ducks below.* • *The police were waiting to pounce when he arrived at the airport.* • *(fig.) She pounced* **on** (= accepted enthusiastically) *the money as soon as I offered it to her.* • *(fig.) This gossip is just the sort of thing journalists love to pounce* **on** (= take advantage of eagerly).

pound MONEY /paʊnd/, *symbol* **£** *n* [C] the standard unit of money in the UK, Ireland and some other countries • *There are one hundred pence in a pound.* • *They tied him to a chair and stole jewellery valued at £50 000* (= 50 000 pounds). • *The company made a pre-tax profit of £1·1 million last year.* • *"Have you got any change?" "Sorry, I've only got a five-pound* **note**. • *Can I borrow a pound* **coin** *for the drinks machine?* • *The region has benefited enormously from a* **multi-million** *pound investment by a Japanese car manufacturer.* • *The police failed to catch the killer in spite of spending millions of pounds on the investigation.* • *I've put twenty pounds worth of petrol into the car.* • *Mushrooms cost about a pound* (= one pound in money) *(for) a pound* (= one pound in weight) *at the market.* • *The basic rate of income tax is 25p (Br and Aus)* **in**/*(Am)* **on** *the pound* (= 25p is paid in tax for every pound of income). • *The devaluation of* **the** *pound will make British goods more competitive abroad.* • *On the foreign exchanges* **the** *pound rose two cents against the dollar to $1·52.* • The **pound sign** is the symbol £. • The **pound sterling** is the official name of the pound used in the UK. • *The government has promised to match the money raised by the charity* **pound for pound** (= It will receive one pound from the government for every pound that it collects itself). • *"It does not mean, of course, that the pound here in Britain, in your pocket or purse or in your bank, has been devalued (usually just quoted as 'The pound in your pocket')"* (Harold Wilson in a radio broadcast, 1967) • LP **Money**

pound AMOUNT /paʊnd/ (*abbreviation* **lb**) *n* [C] a unit for measuring weight • *One pound is approximately equal to 454 grams.* • *One kilogram is roughly the same as 2·2 lbs.* • *There are 16 ounces in one pound.* • *Ann's baby weighed eight and a half pounds at birth.* • *I'd like three pounds of bananas and a pound of pears, please.* • *Mushrooms cost about a pound* (= one pound in money) *(for) a pound* (= one pound in weight) *at the market.* • A **pound of flesh** is something which you have the legal right to receive but which is unreasonable to demand from someone: *His boss insisted on getting her pound of flesh from him and forced him to carry on working while his daughter was ill.* • LP **Units**

-pound·er /£-'paʊn·dəʳ, $-dɚ/ *combining form infml* • *"What sort of burger do you want?" "I think I'll have a* **quarter**-*pounder* (= one containing a quarter of a pound of meat)." • *(esp. Am) The newest member of the team is a 23-year-old, 212-pounder* (= person weighing 212 pounds) *from Miami.*

pound *(obj)* HIT /paʊnd/ *v* to hit or beat repeatedly with a lot of force, or to crush by hitting repeatedly • *I could feel my heart pounding as I went on stage to collect the prize.* [I] • *Nearly 50 people are still missing after the storm pounded southern France with torrential rain and powerful winds.* [T] • *Shells, grenades and rockets pounded the town all night but no one was killed.* [T] • *The city was pounded* **to** *rubble during the war.* [T] • *Pound the garlic* **into** *a paste and then fry it with the onions.* [T] • *I locked myself in the bathroom and he pounded* **on** *the door demanding to be let in.* [I] • *He always pounds the table when he's angry.* [T] • *The doorbell rang and she pounded* (= ran with quick loud steps) *downstairs to answer it.* [I] • *She was pounding* **away** *on her typewriter until four in the morning.* [I] • *(fig.) The campaigners have promised to* **keep** *pounding* **away at** (= keep trying to persuade) *the council until the decision to build the road is reversed.* [I]

pound·ing /'paʊn·dɪŋ/ *n* • *The pounding* (= loud noises) *of the guns continued well into the night.* [U] • *The city received heavy poundings* (= attacks) *from the air every night last week.* [C] • *(fig.) After last year's pounding* (= serious defeat) *in the general election, her party was left with only 19 seats.* [C] • *(fig.) The movie* **took** *quite a pounding* (= received a lot of criticism) *from American cinemagoers, but it was a hit in Britain.* [C]

pour *(obj)* CAUSE TO FLOW /£pɔːʳ, $pɔːr/ *v* to make (a substance) flow from a container, esp. into another container, by raising just one side of the container that the substance is in • *Pour the sugar* **into** *the bowl and mix it thoroughly with the other ingredients.* [T] • *Would you like me to pour you some more wine?* [+ two objects] • *Pour yourself a drink and make yourself at home.* [+ two objects] • *Could you pour me* **(out)** *a beer while you're in the kitchen?* [+ two objects] • *Would you like to pour* (= pour a drink into a glass or cup) *while I open some bags of nuts?* [I] • If you pour **out** your worries, problems or emotions to someone you tell them everything, esp. in secret or in private: *He spends every lunchtime pouring out his emotional problems to me and expects me to find a solution.* [M] ○ *I poured my* **heart** *out to him* (= told him about all my feelings) *and then he told all his friends what I'd said.* [M] • To **pour oil on troubled waters** is to try to reduce the amount of disagreement between the people involved in an argument or to make them calmer: *My husband's always arguing with my father, and I'm the one who has to pour oil on troubled waters.*

pour *(obj)* FLOW QUICKLY /£pɔːʳ, $pɔːr/ *v* [always + adv/prep] to (cause to) flow quickly and in large amounts • *The bus was pouring* **out** *thick black exhaust fumes.* [T] • *The government has been pouring money* **into** *inefficient state-owned industries and the country can no longer afford it.* [T] • *(fig.) Critics of the President have been pouring* **scorn on** *the plan* (= repeatedly saying that it is worthless) *ever since it was first proposed.* [T] • *I felt a sharp pain and looked down to see blood pouring* **from** *my leg.* [I] • *Smoke was pouring* **from** *the roof by the time the fire brigade arrived.* [I] • *Refugees have been pouring* **into** *neighbouring countries to escape the civil war.* [I] • *The sweat was pouring* **down** *her face by the end of the race.* [I] • *The rain was pouring* **down** *last night.* [I] • *It looks as though* **it's** *about to pour* **(with rain)**. [I] • *You ought to take an umbrella –* **it's** *really pouring* **down** (= it's raining very heavily) *outside.* [I] • *Many parts of the country have had pouring* **rain** *throughout the day.* • *I was standing in* **the** *pouring* **rain** *for an hour waiting for my bus.*

pout *(obj)* /paʊt/ *v* to push (the lower lip) forward to express annoyance, or to push (both lips) forward in a sexually attractive way • *If Vanessa doesn't get what she wants she just pouts.* [I] • *She pouted for the photographers but refused to talk to any journalists.* [I] • *Caroline always pouts her lips when she's putting on lipstick.* [T] • *Tanner spent most of the evening tending to the gorgeous pouting Tanya, his partner of two months.*

pout /paʊt/ *n* [C] • *She didn't say anything but I could tell from her pout that she wasn't very pleased.*

pov·er·ty /£ˈpɒv·ə·ti, $ˈpɑː·vɚ·t̬i/ *n* [U] the condition of being extremely poor • *Two million people in the city live in* **abject** (= very great) *poverty.* • *He emigrated to Australia to escape the* **grinding** (= very great) *poverty of his birthplace.* • *Helping to* **alleviate** *poverty in developing countries also helps to reduce environmental destruction.* • *(fml)* If there is a poverty of something, there is a lack of it or the quality of it is extremely low: *There is* **a** *disappointing poverty* **of** *creativity in their work.* ○ *The poverty of original ideas for television shows has led to a substantial fall in viewing figures.* • The **poverty line** is the official level of income which is needed to achieve a basic living standard with enough money for things such as food, clothing and housing: *In 1991 almost 36 million Americans were* **living below** *the poverty line.* • A person or place that is **poverty-stricken** is suffering from the effects of being extremely poor: *Some beggars are neither poverty-stricken nor homeless.* ○ *There are few jobs for the peasants who have flooded into the cities from the poverty-stricken countryside in search of work.* • *(Br)* A **poverty trap** is a situation in which someone would be even poorer or only slightly richer if they had a job because they would no longer receive financial help from the government: *He's* **caught in** *the poverty trap and will only be five pounds a week better off if he accepts the job.* • *(saying)* 'When poverty comes in at the door, love flies out of the window'.

POW [PRISONER], *Br also* **PoW** /£ˌpiː·əʊˈdʌb·l̩.juː, $-oʊ-/ *n* [C] *abbreviation for* **prisoner of war**, see at PRISON • *500 PoWs have been released but 60 000 others are still being held in PoW* **camps**.

pow [NOISE] /paʊ/ *exclamation infml* (esp. in children's COMICS) a word which represents the noise of an explosion or a gun being fired • *When I shout "Pow!" that means I've shot you and you've got to pretend to be dead.*

pow·der /£ˈpaʊ·dəʳ, $-dɚ/ *n* a solid substance that consists of extremely small pieces, is soft and easy to divide and tends to have the same shape as the container that it is in • *A packet of white powder was found and police scientists are analysing it.* [U] • *You'll get more flavour from the spices if you* **grind** *them into* **a** *powder beforehand.* [U] • *I love to cover myself with* **talcum** *powder after I've had a bath or shower.* [U] • *Mix the flour,* **baking** *powder, salt and sugar in a bowl.* [U] • *Stir in the* **curry** *powder, ginger and cinnamon and cook for two minutes.* [U] • *(Br) Why are there so many adverts for* **washing** *powders on TV?* [C] • *Do you find a biological powder gets clothes cleaner?* [C] • *You can buy milk in powder form.* • Powder is also a type of make-up which is spread over the skin of the face, often after a layer of FOUNDATION, in order stop the skin from looking oily: *Dust the face lightly with powder.* [U] • Powder is also fallen snow that is loose and has not begun to melt: *Powder is good for skiing on.* [U] • A **powder keg** is a situation or a place that could easily become extremely dangerous: *The build-up of armaments in this region is creating a powder keg.* ○ *(fig.) The new tax is a* **political** *powder keg which could result in widespread violence.* • A **powder puff** is a round piece of soft material which is used for putting powder, often with a sweet smell, on the face or body. • A **powder room** is a usually clean and comfortable room in a public place such as a hotel, restaurant or theatre where women can go to the toilet, wash, put on make-up, etc. • See also GUNPOWDER. • [PIC]› **Cleaning**

pow·der *obj* /£ˈpaʊ·dəʳ, $-dɚ/ *v* [T] • *Powder* (= Put special powder on) *the baby's bottom to stop it chafing.* • *I'll just powder my nose – it's looking a bit shiny.* • Saying that you are going to go and **powder** your **nose** is a polite or humorous way of saying that you are going to go to the toilet: *Would you get me another drink while I go and powder my nose?*

pow·dered /£ˈpaʊ·dəd, $-dɚd/ *adj* [not gradable] • Something that is powdered is in the form of a powder or is covered with a powder: *Shall I put some powdered* **milk** *in your coffee?* ○ *Her face was heavily powdered and she was wearing bright red lipstick.*

pow·der·y /£ˈpaʊ·dᵊr·i, $-dɚ-/ *adj* • *Powdery* **snow** *is excellent for skiing.*

power [CONTROL] /£paʊəʳ, $paʊɚ/ *n* [U] ability to control people and events • *I've got no power* **over** *advertising matters, so you'll have to talk to the publicity department.* • *The unions want more worker power in the company.* • *Once nicotine has you* **in** *its power* (= has control over you), *it's very difficult to stop smoking.* • *I've no power* **over** *him – he takes no notice of anything I say.* • *I don't know why she likes him so much – he just seems to have* **a** *mysterious power* **over** *her.* • Often power is the amount of political control a person or group has in a country: *Does the President have more power than the Prime Minister?* ○ *How long has the Conservative Party been* **in** *power?* ○ *The Liberal Party is expected to be* **returned to** *power in the forthcoming election.* ○ *The army* **seized** *power after five days of anti-government demonstrations.* • *When one politician* **falls from** (= loses) *power, another* **comes to** (= gains) *power in their place.* • A **power base** is an area of a country or a group of people on which someone's power depends: *The industrial cities are the Labour Party's traditional power base.* • *(infml)* A **power breakfast** or **power lunch** is an important business meeting that happens during the meal: *He seems to spend more of his time at power lunches than in the office.* • A **power broker** is someone who has a big influence on decisions about who should possess political power: *There is considerable disagreement among the party's power brokers about who should become the next leader of the party.* • **Power dressing** is a style of dressing in which business people wear formal clothes to make them seem powerful. • **Power politics** is the threat or use of military force to end an international disagreement: *Woodrow Wilson hoped the League of Nations would replace power politics with international cooperation.* • A **power structure** is a way that power is organized or shared in an organization or society: *The president has promised a new constitution and the creation of democratic power structures.* • A **power struggle** is a fierce, unpleasant or violent competition for power: *The power struggle led to the resignation of two of the company's directors.* • A **power vacuum** is a condition that exists when someone has lost control of something and no one has replaced them: *She was quick to* **fill** *the power vacuum that was left by the sudden death of the managing director.* • *"Power to the people"* (phrase used by the political party The Black Panthers, also used as the title of a John Lennon song, 1968)

power·ful /£ˈpaʊə·fᵊl, $ˈpaʊɚ-/ *adj* • *The President is more powerful* (= has more power) *than the Prime Minister.* • *She's the most powerful person in the organisation.* • *The United States is a very powerful nation.*

power·less /£ˈpaʊə·ləs, $ˈpaʊɚ-/ *adj* • *She is a largely powerless constitutional monarch.* • *The villagers are powerless* **against** *the army's modern military equipment.* • *The police seem to be powerless* (= unable) **to** *prevent these attacks.* [+ *to* infinitive]

power·less·ness /£ˈpaʊə·lə·snəs, $ˈpaʊɚ-/ *n* [U] • *An important cause of stress in the workplace is a sense of powerlessness and lack of control.*

power [PERSON WITH CONTROL] /£paʊəʳ, $paʊɚ/ *n* [C] a person, organization or country that has control over others, often because of wealth, importance or great military strength • *Russia is not as important a military power as it used to be.* • *Germany is on its way to becoming a* **world** *power with a permanent seat on the UN Security Council.* • *She is an increasingly important power* **in the** *company.* • A person who is the **power behind the throne** is someone without an official position who is really in control although someone else seems to be: *He remained chairman of the company until his death, but in later years his daughter was the power behind the throne.* • *(literary)* **The powers of darkness** are evil spiritual forces. • **The powers that be** are important people who have authority or control over others but whose names and personal details are unknown: *It's up to the powers that be to decide what should be done next.*

power [OFFICIAL RIGHT] /£paʊəʳ, $paʊɚ/ *n* [U] an official or legal right to do something • *I'd like to help but I don't have the power* **to** *intervene in this dispute.* [+ *to* infinitive] • *It's not* **in** *your power* **to** *cancel the project.* [+ *to* infinitive] • *I can't give you a refund – I'm afraid it's not* **within** *my power.* • *(law)* (A) **power of attorney** is the right to act for someone else in their financial or legal matters, or the document which gives someone this right: *When I went to work abroad I gave power of attorney to my solicitor.* ○ *She* *has a power of attorney ready to sign in case her health gets any worse.*

powers /£ pauəz, $ pauɚz/ *pl n* • *You were acting* **beyond** *your powers when you agreed to give her a pay rise.* • *The latest crime statistics have led to calls for the powers of the police to be strengthened.* • *The army has been given* **full** *powers* **to** *take whatever action is necessary to restore order.* [+ *to* infinitive] • *Visitors to the city are respectfully reminded of the council's powers* **to** *remove illegally parked vehicles.* [+ *to* infinitive]

power ABILITY /£ pauəʳ, $ pauɚ/ *n* [U] a natural skill or an ability to do something • *He was so shocked by what happened to his parents that he lost the power* **of** *speech.* • *Someone who is telepathic has the power* **to** *know what other people are thinking.* [+ *to* infinitive] • *He stared at her with* **an** *almost hypnotic power.* • *The surgeon did everything* **in** *her power* **to** *save him.* [+ *to* infinitive] • *Doctors are predicting that it will soon be* **within** *their power* **to** *cure the disease.* [+ *to* infinitive] • *After forty years, this film still hasn't lost its power* **to** *shock.* [+ *to* infinitive]

powers /£ pauəz, $ pauɚz/ *pl n* • *My mental powers aren't as good as they used to be.* • *Her 1978 recording of the opera was made when she was* **at the height of her** *powers* (= when her ability was greatest).

power STRENGTH /£ pauəʳ, $ pauɚ/ *n* [U] strength or forcefulness • *You need to have tremendous power in your arms and legs to be a good rower.* • *The power of the river when it flooded was enough to wash away several cars.* • *The explosive power of the bomb was the greatest ever used in a terrorist attack.* • *He was a strong leader who managed to control the power of the nationalist movements in his country.* • *Their forces are no match for the military power of an international coalition.* • *The economic power of many Asian countries has grown dramatically in recent years.* • *He's been working too hard and some time off would* **do him a power of good** (= would be extremely good for him). • *(Br and Aus)* **More power to your elbow!** *(Am)* **more power to you!** is an expression of praise or admiration for someone's success or bravery: *"I've decided to quit my job and set up my own business." "Well, good for you. More power to your elbow!"*

power /£ pauəʳ, $ pauɚ/ *v* [I always + adv/prep] • *Halfway through she powered* (= moved quickly and forcefully) *into the lead and went on to the win the race in record time.* • *Everyone's powering* **away** (= working very busily) *trying to get things ready for the official opening.*

power·ful /£ 'pauə·fᵊl, $ 'pauɚ-/ *adj* • *She's an extremely powerful runner.* • *A very powerful* **magnet** *is used to separate the steel and iron from the other scrap metal.* • *The picture quality is bad because the TV signal isn't powerful enough.* • Things that are powerful have a very great effect: *This drug is very powerful and can have unpleasant side-effects.* ○ *Her speech about cruelty to children was very powerful* (= had a great effect on the people listening to her).

power·ful·ly /£ 'pauə·fᵊl·i, $ 'pauɚ-/ *adv* • *He argued powerfully and persuasively against capital punishment for the murder of police officers.* • *She kicked the ball so powerfully that it flew over the hedge and into our neighbour's garden.* • *Dewayne is a very powerfully-***built** *man* (= has a body with large strong muscles) *and is expected to win the fight easily.*

power ELECTRICITY /£ pauəʳ, $ pauɚ/ *n* [U] electricity, particularly when considering its use or production • *You should disconnect the power before attempting any repairs to electrical equipment.* • *The electricity board cut off the power because we hadn't paid the bill.* • *The helicopter crashed after becoming entangled in power* **cables/lines**. • A *(Br and Aus)* **power cut**/*(Am)* **power outage** is an accidental or intentional stoppage in the supply of electricity: *Storms caused power cuts in hundreds of homes in the area last night.* • *(Br and Aus)* A **power point**/*(Am)* **electrical outlet** is a device to which an item of electrical equipment can be connected in order to provide it with electricity: *Most power points are wall sockets but large items such as cookers sometimes have permanent connections.* • A **power station**/*(esp. Am)* **power plant** is a factory where electricity is produced: *For many years coal-***fired** *power stations provided most of the country's electricity.* ○ *Environmentalists have failed to prevent the plans for the* **nuclear** *power plant from going into action.* • A **power tool** is a tool that operates with an electric motor: *We stock a comprehensive range of power tools and DIY equipment.* • LP **Switching on and off** PIC **Energy**

power ENERGY /£ pauəʳ, $ pauɚ/ *n* [U] the rate at which energy is used, or the ability to produce energy • *A car needs a lot of power to accelerate quickly.* • *The ship was only slightly damaged in the collision and was able to sail into port under its own power.* • *(specialized) The output power of a motor depends on the input current.* • *(specialized) The power* **(rating)** *of my amplifier is forty watts per channel.* • **Power(-assisted) steering** is a system for changing the direction in which a road vehicle is moving by using power from the engine to help the driver turn the vehicle: *Power steering, electric windows and central locking are standard features on all models.* • *(specialized)* A **power plant** is an engine or other piece of equipment that supplies power: *The aircraft's power plant is a Rolls Royce Avon engine.*

power *(obj)* /£ pauəʳ, $ pauɚ/ *v* • Something that powers a machine provides it with energy and the ability to operate: *Buses and trucks are usually powered by diesel engines.* [T] ○ *In the future electricity will be used to power road vehicles.* [T] • *(esp. Am)* When something **powers up** or is powered up it is preparing or being prepared to do something that involves the use of a lot of energy or effort: *The computer takes a few seconds to power up after it's been switched on.* ○ *He really needs to power his team up for next Saturday's match.* ○ *The management seems to be powering up for a major confrontation with the unions.* ○ *College baseball teams across the country are powering up for the new season.*

-powered /£ -pauəd, $ -pauɚd/ *combining form* • *a battery-powered radio* • *nuclear-powered submarines* • *My calculator doesn't need batteries because it's* **solar***-powered* (= it obtains its energy from the sun).

power·ful /£ 'pauə·fᵊl, $ 'pauɚ-/ *adj* • *Do you really need a car with such a powerful engine?*

power IMAGE SIZE /£ pauəʳ, $ pauɚ/ *n* [U] the amount by which an image is increased by a device used for seeing things that are very small or a long distance away • *What's the magnification power of your binoculars?* • *You'll need a very high-power microscope to see something as small as that.* • *A low-power telescope is enough if you only want to look at the moon.*

power·ful /£ 'pauə·fᵊl, $ 'pauɚ-/ *adj* • *You'd need an extremely powerful microscope to see something so small.*

power MATHEMATICS /£ pauəʳ, $ pauɚ/ *n* [U] *specialized* the number of times that a number is to be multiplied by itself • *3* **to the** *power 2 is the same as 3 squared and 3* **to the** *power 3 is the same as 3 cubed.* • *2* **to the** *fourth power is 2 times 2 times 2 times 2, which equals 16.* • *3* **to the** *power 4 is usually written as 3^4.* • LP **Mathematics**

power·boat /£ 'pauə·bəut, $ 'pauɚ·bout/ *n* [C] a small boat with a powerful engine which can travel very fast and is used in races • *He started powerboat* **racing** *after he was injured in a motorcycle accident.*

power·house /£ 'pauə·haus, $ 'paur-/ *n* [C] *pl* **powerhouses** /£ 'pauə,hau·zɪz, $ 'paur-/ a country, organization or person with a lot of influence, power or energy • *Germany is the economic powerhouse of the European Community.* • *The university is no longer the academic powerhouse that it once was.* • *She's a powerhouse* **of** *original ideas and solutions to difficult problems.*

pow·wow /'pau·wau/ *n* [C] a meeting or gathering of Native Americans for making decisions or for having spiritual ceremonies or celebrations • *(fig. infml) My brother's getting divorced so I'm going home for a family powwow* (= discussion) *this weekend.*

pox /£ pɒks, $ pɑːks/ *n* [U] **the pox** *dated infml* SYPHILIS • See also CHICKENPOX; COWPOX; SMALLPOX.

po·xy /£ 'pɒk·si, $ 'pɑːk-/ *adj* **-ier, -iest** *Br infml* having little value, importance or influence • *He gets paid a poxy three pounds an hour in that cleaning job.* • *She lives in a poxy little village in the middle of nowhere.*

pp PAGES *pl n fml abbreviation for* pages • *This matter is discussed in more detail on pp 101-123.* • *See pp 34 & 35 for more information.*

pp DOCUMENTS *prep fml* used to show when someone has signed a document for a person who is not available to sign it • *I hope to hear from you soon. Yours sincerely, Chris Smith, pp Rebecca Siobhan.* • LP **Letters**

PPS /,piː·piː'es/ *adv* [not gradable] used when an additional short message is added to the end of a letter after a message has already been added • *PS I forgot to invite you to our party next Sunday at six. PPS Please tell Ellis that he's welcome to come too.* • See also PS.

PR ADVERTISING /£ ,piː'ɑːʳ, $ -'ɑːr/ *n* [U] *abbreviation for* **public relations**, see at PUBLIC PEOPLE • *The company's* *putting out a lot of PR about the new product line.* • *They've decided to hire a PR* **firm** *to improve their public image.* • *These new measures are largely a government PR* **exercise** *and will do little to reduce crime.* • *The new PR* **campaign** *will promote the company's concern for the environment.*

PR VOTING /£ˌpiːˈɑːr, $-ˈɑːr/ *n* [U] *abbreviation for* **proportional representation**, see at PROPORTION • *Do you think a system of PR makes elections fairer?*

prac·ti·ca·ble /£ˈpræk·tɪ·kə·bl̩, $-t̬ɪ-/ *adj fml* able to be done or put into action • *It is the duty of every employer to ensure, so far as is reasonably practicable, the health, safety and welfare of all employees.* • *The troops will be brought home as soon as practicable.* • *It is not practicable* **to** *complete the tunnel before the end of the year.* [+ *to* infinitive]

prac·ti·ca·bil·i·ty /£ˌpræk·tɪ·kəˈbɪl·ɪ·ti, $-t̬ɪ·kəˈbɪl·ə·t̬i/ *n* [U] *fml* • *Many people have expressed doubts about the practicability of the proposed schedule.*

prac·ti·cal EXPERIENCE /£ˈpræk·tɪ·kəl, $-t̬ɪ-/ *adj* relating to experience, reality or action rather than ideas or imagination • *Galileo was one of the first people to apply mathematics to practical problems.* • *Qualifications are important but practical* **experience** *is always an advantage.* • *I think we ought to consider the practical* **difficulties** *of your proposal.* • *The information service offers young people practical* **advice** *on contraception, pregnancy and abortion.* • *What's the use of theoretical knowledge that has no practical* **application?** • *What does this decision mean in practical* **terms?** • *In theory, Dr Frampton is in charge, but* **for all practical purposes** (= in reality) *her assistant runs the office because she's away so much.* • A **practical joke** is a joke which makes someone seem foolish and involves a physical action rather than words: *She stuck her boss's cup and saucer together as a practical joke.* ○ *Some* **practical joker** *has gone and let the air out of my bicycle's tyres.*

prac·ti·cal /£ˈpræk·tɪ·kəl, $-t̬ɪ-/ *n* [C] • A practical is a class or examination in a scientific or technical subject in which students do things rather than just write or talk about them: *We had to dissect a worm in our biology practical today.*

prac·ti·cal·i·ties /£ˌpræk·tɪˈkæl·ɪ·tiz, $-t̬ɪˈkæl·ə·t̬iz/ *pl n* • Practicalities are the conditions which result from an idea becoming reality: *The practicalities of having two young children and working full time meant we had to employ a nanny.* ○ *It sounds like a good idea, but you ought to consider the practicalities before you put it into action.*

prac·ti·cal·ly /£ˈpræk·tɪ·kli, $-t̬ɪ-/ *adv* • *Many people have offered to help, but there is little they can do practically.* • *Theoretically, it's a good idea to live without a car, but practically* **speaking**, *it would be difficult to manage without one.* • See also PRACTICALLY.

prac·ti·cal SUITABLE /£ˈpræk·tɪ·kəl, $-t̬ɪ-/ *adj* suitable for the situation in which something is used • *I tend to wear clothes that are practical rather than fashionable.* • *Heavy boots aren't very practical for running in.* • *Plastic isn't so attractive, but it's more practical than wood for this purpose.*

prac·ti·cal·i·ty /£ˌpræk·tɪˈkæl·ɪ·ti, $-t̬ɪˈkæl·ə·t̬i/ *n* [U] • *I bought these shoes for their practicality not their appearance.*

prac·ti·cal EFFECTIVE /£ˈpræk·tɪ·kəl, $-t̬ɪ-/ *adj approving* able to provide effective solutions to problems • *She has a lot of interesting ideas, but she's not very practical.* • *We need someone practical who can cope with crises.*

prac·ti·cal·i·ty /£ˌpræk·tɪˈkæl·ɪ·ti, $-t̬ɪˈkæl·ə·t̬i/ *n* [U] *approving* • *Jonathan has demonstrated enormous practicality in his management of the shop.*

prac·ti·cal POSSIBLE /£ˈpræk·tɪ·kəl, $-t̬ɪ-/ *adj* able to be done or put into action • *Your ideas are very interesting, but we need practical proposals for getting us out of this mess.* • *It's simply not practical* **to** *divide the work between so many people.* [+ *to* infinitive]

prac·ti·cal·i·ty /£ˌpræk·tɪˈkæl·ɪ·ti, $-t̬ɪˈkæl·ə·t̬i/ *n* [U] • *Your suggestion is appealing in theory, but it lacks practicality.*

prac·ti·cal·ly /£ˈpræk·tɪ·kli, $-t̬ɪ-/ *adv* [not gradable] almost or very nearly • *There's a gun in practically* **every** *American home.* • *Practically* **everything** *she does is a tremendous success.* • *The secret police used to spy on practically* **everyone.** • *People are dying in the violence practically* **all** *the time.* • *Practically the* **entire** *workforce has gone on strike.* • *There has been practically* **no** *improvement in living standards over the past decade.* • *These changes would cost us practically* **nothing.** • *It's practically* **impossible** *to get home in less than an hour when the traffic is heavy.* • *They used to argue all the time and now they've practically* **stopped** *talking to each other.* • See also **practically** at PRACTICAL EXPERIENCE.

prac·tice ACTION /£ˈpræk·tɪs, $-t̬ɪs/ *n* [U] action rather than thought or ideas • *It seemed like a good idea before we started, but* **in** *practice it was a disaster.* • *Officially, Robert's in charge, but* **in** *practice Hannah runs the office.* • *I can't see how your plan is going to work* **in** *practice.* • *How do you intend to* **put** *these proposals* **into** *practice?* • (PL) (RUS)

prac·tice REGULAR ACTIVITY, *Am also* **prac·tise** /£ˈpræk·tɪs, $-t̬ɪs/ *n* something that is usually or regularly done, often as a habit, tradition or custom • *What can European companies learn from Japanese business practices?* [C] • *Traditional religious practices are disappearing in many parts of the world.* [C] • *The new working practices will reduce costs and increase efficiency.* [C] • *This is a cruel practice which should be banned immediately.* [C] • *What is* **standard** *practice* (= What is usually done) *in a situation like this?* [U] • *The aim of the association is to promote the understanding and practice* **of** *homeopathy.* [U] • *Newspaper editors have agreed a new* **code of** *practice on the invasion of privacy.* [U] • *(dated) I'll do your washing for you this time, but I'm not going to* **make a practice of** *it* (= do it regularly). • (PL) (RUS)

prac·tise *obj Br and Aus, Am usually* **prac·tice** /£ˈpræk·tɪs, $-t̬ɪs/ *v* [T] • *The new government has promised all citizens the right to practise their religion.* • *Practising safe sex is an important way of avoiding HIV infection.* • *The company denies that it has practised discrimination against any of its employees.* • If you **practise what** you **preach** you do the things that you advise other people to do: *He's such a hypocrite! He never practises what he preaches.*

prac·tis·ing /£ˈpræk·tɪ·sɪŋ, $-t̬ɪ-/ *adj* [before n; not gradable] • *In fact, he's a practising Muslim.*

prac·tise *(obj)* TRAIN *Br and Aus, Am usually* **prac·tice** /£ˈpræk·tɪs, $-t̬ɪs/ *v* to do or play (something) regularly or repeatedly in order to become skilled at it • *He practises his typing for half an hour every evening.* [T] • *I'm quite good at tennis but I need to practise my service.* [T] • *She practises the violin every day.* [T] • *We'll have to practise that song again before the concert.* [T] • *There's no point having music lessons if you're not going to practise between them.* [I] • *His written French is very good but he needs to practise speak***ing** *it.* [+ *v-ing*]

prac·tice, *Am also* **prac·tise** /£ˈpræk·tɪs, $-t̬ɪs/ *n* • *Will you take me for a driving practice?* [C] • *I need to get some more practice before I take my driving test.* [U] • *Are you coming to cricket practice this evening?* [U] • *She's never at home because she spends all her free time at hockey practices.* [C] • *You'll gradually get better at it – it's just a question of practice.* [U] • *I'm a bit* **out of** *practice* (= I haven't had any recent experience) *but I'd love to play.* [U] • *Do you mind if I have a few practice shots before we start the game?* • *(saying)* 'Practice makes perfect' means the more you try the better you will get at doing something, or that you can't expect to get better at something unless you work hard at it. [U]

prac·tised *Br and Aus, Am usually* **prac·ticed** /£ˈpræk·tɪst, $-t̬ɪst/ *adj* • Someone who is practised has become skilled at doing something by having a lot of experience of it: *She is a confident and practised speaker who always impresses her audience.* ○ *He is practised* **in** *the art of public debate.* ○ *We need someone who is practised* **at** *negotiating business deals.* ○ *He's practised* **in** *getting people to do what he wants.* • *(fml)* Something that is practised has been obtained from a lot of practice: *She performed the song with practised skill.*

prac·tise *(obj)* WORK *Br and Aus, Am usually* **prac·tice** /£ˈpræk·tɪs, $-t̬ɪs/ *v* to work in an important skilled job for which a lot of training is necessary • *He trained as a lawyer but he's no longer practising.* [I] • *How long have you been practising* **as** *a dentist?* [I] • *She practised medicine for twenty years before she became a writer.* [T]

prac·tice, *Am also* **prac·tise** /£ˈpræk·tɪs, $-t̬ɪs/ *n* [C] • *Paul and Steve have just set up a dental practice* (= business) *in Billingham.* • *A new vet is joining the practice next week.* • *A legal practice has just moved into those offices.* • *Our practice is responsible for about five thousand patients.* • *She's decided to leave the Health Service and join a* **private** *practice.*

prac·tis·ing, *Am usually* **prac·tic·ing** /£ˈpræk·tɪ·sɪŋ, $-t̬ɪ-/ *adj* [before n; not gradable] • *The number of practising doctors is falling even though more people are qualifying in medicine.*

prac·ti·tion·er /£præk'tɪʃ·ən·ər, $-ɚ/ *n* [C] *slightly fml* someone involved in a usually skilled job or activity • *A London-based practitioner of traditional Chinese medicine has had remarkable success in the treatment of eczema.* • *The practitioners of many professions are now able to work in any EC country without having to take additional examinations.* • *She is a respected practitioner of the political interview.* • *She was a* **medical** *practitioner* (= a doctor) *before she entered politics.* • See also GP.

prag·mat·ic /£præg'mæt·ɪk, $-'mæṭ-/ *adj esp. approving* solving problems in a way which suits the present conditions rather than obeying fixed theories, ideas or rules • *This pragmatic* **approach** *has made it the oldest and most successful political party in the democratic world.* • *We need someone who is pragmatic rather than ideological, and can respond quickly to changing situations.*

prag·mat·i·cal·ly /£præg'mæt·ɪ·kli, $-'mæṭ-/ *adv esp. approving* • *It is intended that these guidelines should be applied flexibly and pragmatically.*

prag·ma·tism /£'præg·mə·tɪ·zəm, $-ṭɪ-/ *n* [U] *esp. approving* • *The council has operated much more effectively since pragmatism replaced political dogma.*

prag·ma·tist /£'præg·mə·tɪst, $-ṭɪst/ *n* [C] *esp. approving* • *She rose to power by being a political pragmatist who took advantage of every opportunity that presented itself.*

prai·rie /£'preə·ri, $'prer·i/ *n* a wide area of flat land without trees in Canada and the northern US which was originally covered by grass and is now an important farming area • *Prairies stretch as far as the eye can see.* [C] • *When he was a young man he farmed 2500 acres of Nebraska prairie.* [U]

prai·ries /£'preə·riz, $'prer·iz/ *pl n* • *The wheat growers of the Canadian prairies are some of the world's most efficient farmers.* • *Prairies are called 'steppes' in Europe and Asia and 'pampas' in South America.*

praise *obj* [SHOW APPROVAL] /preɪz/ *v* [T] to express admiration or approval about the achievements or characteristics of (a person or thing) • *He should be praised* **for** *his honesty.* • *My parents always praised me when I did well at school and never criticised me when I did badly.* • *I was just praising your cooking, Helen.* • *He was* **highly** *praised for his research on heart disease.* • *She had breast cancer several years ago and made a* **widely** *praised documentary about it.* • *Her first novel was praised* **to the skies** (= praised very strongly).

praise /preɪz/ *n* [U] • *They deserve praise, not condemnation,* **for** *what they have done.* • *I have nothing but praise* **for** *what she's done.* • *His economic policies have* **won** *widespread praise for reducing government debt.* • *The newspaper is a loyal supporter of the President and regularly* **heaps/showers** *praise* **on** *him.* • *Praise from Adrian is praise* **indeed** (= Praise from Adrian is particularly special because he rarely praises anyone).

praise·wor·thy /£'preɪz,wɜː·ði, $-,wɜːr-/ *adj* • *Whether her action was praiseworthy* (= deserving to be praised) *or blameworthy is a matter of opinion.*

praise *obj* [GOD] /preɪz/ *v* [T] to honour, worship and express admiration for (a god) • *In church services hymns are sung to praise God.*

praise /preɪz/ *n* [U] *fml* • *As we* **give** *praise to God let us remember those who are less fortunate than ourselves.*

pral·ine /£'prɑː·liːn, $'preɪ-/ *n* [C/U] a mixture of crushed nuts and burnt sugar that is used in sweet dishes and chocolates • *These chocolates are filled with (an) almond praline.*

pram *Br and Aus* /præm/, *Am* **ba·by car·riage**, *fml or dated* **per·am·bu·lat·or** *n* [C] a vehicle for moving a baby around which consists of a small enclosed bed supported by a frame on four wheels • *At first he was embarrassed to be seen* **pushing** *a pram down the street.*

prance /£prɑːnts, $prænts/ *v* [I] to walk in an energetic way and with more movement than necessary • *It's pathetic to see fifty-year-old rock stars prancing* **around** *on stage as if they were still teenagers.* • *Eric's always prancing* **around** *the bedroom with nothing on.* • *I wish you children would settle down and stop prancing* **about**. • *She pranced into the office and demanded to speak to the manager.* • When a horse prances it moves quickly, raising first its front legs and then its back legs high into the air.

prang *obj* /præŋ/ *v* [T] *Br and Aus infml* to damage (a vehicle) slightly in a road accident • *She pranged her mother's car a week after she passed her driving test.*

prang *Br and Aus* /præŋ/, *Am* **fend·er bend·er** *n* [C] *infml* • *He's already* **had** *two prangs and he only bought the car six months ago.*

prank /præŋk/ *n* [C] a trick that is intended to be amusing but not to cause harm or damage • *When I was at school we were always* **playing** *pranks* **on** *our teachers.* • *I've had enough of your* **childish** *pranks.*

prank·ster /£'præŋk·stər, $-stɚ/ *n* [C] • A prankster is someone who performs pranks on people: *He was very cross when a prankster at work signed him up with a dating agency.*

prat /præt/ *n* [C] *Br infml* someone who behaves stupidly or lacks ability • *He looked a right prat in that pink suit.* • *You've made me spill my drink, you prat!* [as form of address] • *Occasionally I'll have a few too many drinks at a party and* **make a** *prat* **of** *myself* (= behave stupidly).

prat a·bout/a·round /præt/ *v adv* [I] *Br infml* • If you prat about or prat around you behave stupidly, particularly when you should be behaving responsibly: *Just stop pratting around and get on with your work.*

prat·fall /£'præt·fɔːl, $-fɑːl/ *n* [C] *esp. Am* a fall in which a person lands on their bottom, or *(fig.)* an embarrassing defeat or failure • *(fig.) Most of us get over the pratfalls of childhood.*

prat·tle /£'præt·l̩, $'præṭ-/ *v* [I] to talk foolishly or childishly for a long time about something unimportant or without saying anything important • *Many radio listeners are bored with DJs who prattle* **on** *instead of playing music.* • *She'd have prattled* **on about** *her new job for the whole afternoon if I'd let her.*

prat·tle /£'præt·l̩, $'præṭ-/ *n* [U] • *His speech contained nothing new and was full of political prattle and clichés.*

prat·tler /£'præt·l̩.ər, £'-lər, $'præṭ·l̩.ɚ/ *n* [C] • *Fiona's such a prattler – I wish she'd get to the point of what she wants to say.*

prawn /£prɔːn, $prɑːn/ *n* [C] a small edible pink sea animal with a shell and ten legs • *peeled prawns* • *Prawns have a thin flat body and a long tail and are similar to shrimps but bigger.* • *We had a delicious prawn* **cocktail** *for the first course.*

pray *(obj)* [SPEAK TO GOD] /preɪ/ *v* to speak to a god either privately or in a religious ceremony in order to express love, admiration or thanks or in order to ask for something • *Sometimes people pray silently by thinking the words but not actually saying them.* [I] • *Let us pray* **for** *the helpless civilians trapped in this dreadful conflict.* [I] • *(fig.) We're praying* **for** (= hoping very much that there will be) *good weather for tomorrow's cricket match.* [I] • *We've been praying* **to God that** *your son will make a complete recovery.* [+ *that* clause] • *(fig.) I just pray* **to** *God* (= hope very much) **(that)** *you're right about this, because we'll be in serious trouble if you're not.* [+ *(that)* clause] • *I just* **hope and** *pray* **that** *he'll come back in December.* [+ *that* clause] • *I never lost hope and kept on praying* **to be rescued**. [+ *to* infinitive] • *(fml) You must pray* (= ask for) *God's forgiveness for what you have done.* [T] • A **praying mantis** is a MANTIS.

pray·er /£preər, $prer/ *n* • A prayer is the words that someone says or thinks when they are praying: *These prayers have been written specially for people suffering from cancer.* [C] ○ *She always* **says** *her prayers* (= prays) *before she goes to sleep.* [C] ○ *When I was at school we had prayers every morning.* [C] ○ *We thought he had been killed in the war, but our prayers were* **answered** *when he arrived home unexpectedly.* [C] ○ *She carries a prayer* **book** *with her wherever she goes.* • Prayer is also the act or ceremony in which someone prays: *I found her* **kneeling in** *prayer at the back of the church.* [U] ○ *The prisoners find their only solace in prayer.* [U] • *(infml)* Someone who **hasn't a prayer of** doing something has very little chance of doing it: *She hasn't a prayer of winning the competition.* • A **prayer mat/rug** is a small piece of thick cloth on which a Muslim goes down on his knees and bends his body down to the ground when praying.

pray [PLEASE] /preɪ/ *adv* [not gradable] *esp. literary or old use* a formal and emphatic way of saying 'please' • *Pray take a seat.* • *Pray tell your sister that I long to see her.* • *And where have you been, pray* **tell**?

pre- /,priː-/ *combining form* before (a time or an event) • *a pre-flight check* • *a pre-lunch drink* • *pre-industrial societies* • If something is **pre-Columbian**, it belongs to or is from America in the period before Columbus arrived in 1492: *pre-Columbian sculpture* ○ *Most pre-Columbian cultures produced textiles and metalwork.* • *(fml)* If someone or something is **pre-eminent**, they have more good qualities or are more able than anyone else in their situation: *She is the pre-eminent authority in her subject.* ○ *His* **pre-eminence** *in his subject is internationally recognized.* ○ *The arts festival is* **pre-eminently** (=mainly) *a festival of theatre.* • *(slightly fml)* If you **pre-empt** someone, you try to prevent them from doing something or make it worthless for them to do it, by doing it yourself before they can: *In a bid to pre-empt their competitors, they have reduced the price of many of their refrigerators.* • *(slightly fml)* If something is **pre-emptive**, it is done before other people can act, esp. to prevent them from doing something else: *Police have been given powers to take pre-emptive action if they believe a large demonstration is being planned.* ○ *The Treasury has decided to raise interest rates as a pre-emptive* **measure** *against inflation.* ○ *If the country continues building up its supply of weapons, one of the neighboring states may respond with a pre-emptive air* **strike**. • *(fml)* If something **pre-existed**, it existed before (something else): *Some people believe their soul pre-existed before it entered their body.* ○ *Dinosaurs pre-existed human beings* **by** *many millions of years.*

preach *(obj)* SPEAK IN CHURCH /priːtʃ/ *v* (esp. of a priest in a church) to give (a religious speech) • *A bishop preached* **to** *the assembled mourners.* [I] • *Our local priest preached a* **sermon** *on the need for forgiveness.* [T]

preach·er /£'priː·tʃəʳ, $-tʃɚ/ *n* [C] • A preacher is a person, usually a priest, who gives a religious speech: *a lay preacher* ○ *He is a very gifted preacher.*

preach *obj* PERSUADE /priːtʃ/ *v* [T] to try to persuade other people to believe in (a particular belief) or follow (a particular way of life) • *They preach the abolition of established systems but propose nothing to replace them.* • If someone **preaches to the converted**, they try to persuade people to believe things which those people already believe: *You needn't bother telling us how we can change to a greener lifestyle, because you're preaching to the converted.*

preach ADVISE /priːtʃ/ *v* [I] *disapproving* to give unwanted advice, esp. about moral matters, in a boring way • *He's such a pain – he's always preaching* **about** *the virtues of working hard and getting up early.* • *My mother's always preaching* **at/to** *me* **about** *keeping my room tidy.*

pre·am·ble /'priː·æm·bl̩, priː'æm-/ *n specialized* an introduction to a speech or piece of writing • *The preamble* **to** *the document gives details of what it comprises.* [C] • *(fig. infml) I like to get straight down to business, without a lot of preamble* (=talk or activity not connected with business). [U]

pre·ar·ranged /ˌpriː·ə'reɪndʒd/ *adj* [not gradable] arranged in advance • *a prearranged visit* • *At a prearranged* **signal**, *everyone started moving forwards.*

pre·built /priː'bɪlt/ *adj* [not gradable] *Am for* PREFABRICATED

pre·can·cer·ous /£ˌpriː'kænt·sᵊr·əs, $-sɚ·əs/ *adj* [not gradable] *medical* (esp. of cells) showing signs of developing into a CANCER (=an uncontrolled growth of diseased cells in the body) • *Early detection of precancerous* **growths** *is important, because it is at this stage that the disease can be treated.*

pre·car·i·ous /£prɪ'keə·ri·əs, $-'ker·i-/ *adj* in a dangerous state because not safe or firmly fixed • *The lorry was lodged in a very precarious way, with its front wheels hanging over the cliff.* • *Many borrowers now find themselves caught in a precarious financial position.*

pre·car·i·ous·ly /£prɪ'keə·ri·ə·sli, $-'ker·i-/ *adv* • *He lived rather precariously from one day to the next, never knowing where his next meal was coming from.* • *Her suitcase was precariously* **balanced** *on the tiny luggage rack above her head.*

pre·car·i·ous·ness /£prɪ'keə·ri·ə·snəs, $-'ker·i-/ *n* [U] • *The president has been made acutely aware of the precariousness of his position by this latest attempt on his life.* • *The outbreak of civil war in the country has acted as a harsh reminder of the precariousness of the new democracies in eastern Europe.*

pre·cast /£ˌpriː'kɑːst, $'priː·kæst/ *adj* [not gradable] (esp. of concrete) formed into a particular shape and allowed to become solid before being used • *In order to save money, the council has chosen precast concrete slabs rather than stone slabs for the surface of the town square.*

pre·cau·tion /£prɪ'kɔː·ʃᵊn, $-'kɑː-/ *n* [C] an action which is done to prevent something unpleasant or dangerous happening • *Many locals have been stockpiling food as a precaution* **against** *shortages.* • *A quarter of all burglaries are carried out on homes whose owners have failed to* **take** *the basic precaution of locking doors and windows.*

pre·cau·tion·a·ry /£prɪ'kɔː·ʃᵊn·ᵊr·i, $-'kɑː·ʃᵊn·er-/ *adj* [not gradable] • *When her daughter fell down the stairs, she took her to hospital for a precautionary X-ray, to make sure she wasn't seriously injured.* • *The company has withdrawn the drug as a precautionary* **measure** *while further checks are being made.* • *Before he went on holiday, he took the precautionary* **step** *of writing his address on his luggage.*

pre·cau·tions /£prɪ'kɔː·ʃᵊnz, $-'kɑː-/ *pl n* • Precautions is a polite way of referring to CONTRACEPTION (=action taken to prevent a woman from becoming pregnant during sex): *If you're going to have sex, make sure you* **take** *precautions.*

pre·cede *obj* /£prɪ'siːd, $priː-/ *v* [T] to be or go before (something or someone) in time or space • *George Bush preceded Bill Clinton as president of the US.* • *He unlocked the door and preceded them into the bare little room.* • *The introduction of a common currency needs to be preceded by effective political union among the member states.* • *It would be helpful if you were to precede the report* **with** *an introduction.*

pre·ced·ing /£prɪ'siː·dɪŋ, $priː-/ *adj* [before n; not gradable] • *The paintings are a development of ideas she explored in the preceding decade.* • *In conclusion, I hope the preceding arguments have convinced you of the need for action.*

prec·e·dence /£'pres·ɪ·dᵊnts, $-ə·dents/ *n* [U] the condition of being dealt with before other things or of being considered more important than other things • *Precedence must be* **given** *to the injured in the evacuation plans.* • *The government has to decide whether cost or concern for the environment should* **take** *precedence when choosing the route for the new road.* • *Business people often think that fluency and communication* **take** *precedence* **over** *grammar when speaking.* • *(fml)* Precedence is also the order of importance given to people in particular societies, groups or organizations: *The* **order of** *precedence for titled nobility in Britain is duke, marquis, earl, viscount, baron.*

prec·e·dent /£'pres·ɪ·dᵊnt, $-ə·dent/ *n* an action, situation or decision which has already happened and which can be used as a reason why a similar action or decision should be performed or taken • *There are several precedents* **for** *promoting people who do not have formal qualifications.* [C] • *Sadly there are precedents* **of** (=previous examples of) *accidents happening at railway crossings.* [C] • *Some politicians fear that agreeing to the concession would* **set** *a dangerous precedent, since it might allow a whole range of changes to be introduced.* [C] • Precedent is also the way that something has been done in the past which therefore shows that it is the correct way: *Would it be* **breaking with** *precedent for the bride to make a speech?* [U]

pre·cept /'priː·sept/ *n* [C] *fml* a rule for action or behaviour, esp. obtained from moral consideration • *The policy contravenes international law and common precepts of decency.* • *Many Western Buddhists think it is important to be vegetarian because it agrees with the Buddhist precept of not harming any living being.*

pre·cinct SHOPPING AREA /'priː·sɪŋkt/ *n* [C] *Br* part of a city or a town in which vehicles are not allowed and which is used for a special purpose, esp. shopping • *a shopping precinct* • *a pedestrian/pedestrianized precinct*

pre·cinct CITY AREA /'priː·sɪŋkt/ *n* [C] *Am* a division of a city or a town, esp. an area protected by a particular unit of the police or a division used for electoral purposes • *Crime rates in neighboring precincts are much lower.* • *The turnout in precincts with many middle-class voters is expected to be high.*

pre·cincts /'priː·sɪŋkts/ *pl n*, **pre·cinct** *n* [U] *slightly fml* the area which surrounds a building or place, esp. when enclosed by a wall • *A tunnel entrance was found within the precincts of the prison camp.* • *By mid-morning, crowds of souvenir sellers had set up their stalls in the museum precincts.* • *It's so peaceful in the monastery precinct.*

pre·cious VALUABLE /'preʃ·əs/ *adj* of great value because of being rare, expensive or important • *Clean water has become a very precious commodity in many parts of the world.* • *Happiness was the most precious gift I could have given them.* • *Every moment became precious when we heard she was going to die.* • *You're so precious* **to** *me.* • A **precious metal** is a metal which is valuable and usually rare: *Platinum and gold are precious metals.* • A **precious stone** is a valuable stone which is used in jewellery: *The crown, decorated with diamonds and other precious stones, was exhibited in a special case.* • LP **Expensive** Ⓔ

pre·cious [VERY] /ˈpreʃ·əs/ *adv infml* very • *A lot of people will start, but precious* **few** *will finish.* • *Be careful – you'll be precious* **little** *help if you come back injured.* • Ⓔ

pre·cious [PERFECTING] /ˈpreʃ·əs/ *adj disapproving* behaving in a very formal and unnatural way by giving too much attention to unimportant details and trying too hard to be perfect • *He's so precious* **about** *his work that he never gets anything done.* • *Don't you hate the precious* **way** *she speaks, pronouncing each single consonant so precisely.* • Ⓔ

pre·cious·ly /ˈpreʃ·ə·sli/ *adv disapproving* • *He speaks too preciously for my liking.*

pre·cious·ness /ˈpreʃ·ə·snəs/ *n* [U] *disapproving* • *I find her preciousness and her constant criticism of the way I do things extremely irritating.*

pre·cious [DISLIKE] /ˈpreʃ·əs/ *adj* [before n; not gradable] *infml* used to express dislike and/or annoyance • *You and your precious car – it's all you're interested in!* • Ⓔ

prec·i·pice /ˈpres·ɪ·pɪs/ *n* [C] a very steep side of a cliff or a mountain • *The film opens with a shot of a climber dangling from a precipice.* • *We stood at the edge of the precipice and looked down at the valley below.* • A precipice is also a dangerous situation which could lead to disaster or failure: *After years of civil war, the country now stands at the precipice of economic collapse.* ○ *This latest tax increase may push many small companies over the financial precipice.* ○ *Our two countries are* **at the edge of** *the precipice – if we don't pull back it will mean war.*

pre·ci·pi·tous /£prɪˈsɪp·ɪ·təs, $priːˈsɪp·ɪ·t̬əs/ *adj* • If a slope is precipitous, it is very steep: *We slowly made our way down the precipitous mountain path.* ○ *He always chooses the most precipitous slopes to ski down because he loves a challenge.* ○ *The company has suffered from a precipitous* **decline** *in orders.* • If a reduction or increase is precipitous, it is fast or great: *a precipitous rate* ○ *Over the past 18 months, there has been a precipitous* **fall** *in car sales.*

pre·ci·pi·tous·ly /£prɪˈsɪp·ɪ·tə·sli, $priːˈsɪp·ɪ·t̬ə-/ *adv* • *The rate of car crime has risen precipitously* (= greatly) *over the past few years.* • *The price of shares in the company dropped precipitously* (= suddenly and greatly) *with the news of poor sales figures.*

pre·ci·pi·tate *obj* [MAKE HAPPEN] /£prɪˈsɪp·ɪ·teɪt, $-t̬eɪt/ *v* [T] *fml* to make (something) happen suddenly or sooner than expected • *An invasion would certainly precipitate a political crisis.* • *News of possible devaluation of the pound precipitated furious financial trading.* • *Fear of losing her job precipitated* (= suddenly forced) *her* **into** *action.*

pre·ci·pi·tate /£prɪˈsɪp·ɪ·tət, $priːˈsɪp·ɪ·t̬ɪt/, **pre·ci·pi·tous** *adj fml* • If an action is precipitate, it is done sooner or faster that expected and without enough thought or preparation: *Precipitate involvement in the conflict would be foolish.* ○ *Don't be precipitous – stay for another few weeks and then decide if you want to go home.* ○ *I would not wish to act with precipitate* **haste**.

pre·ci·pi·tate·ly /£prɪˈsɪp·ɪ·tət·li, $priːˈsɪp·ɪ·t̬ɪt-/ *adv fml* • *The president has been warned that acting precipitately may lead to a diplomatic row.* • *Scientists are annoyed that the research program has been abandoned so precipitately.*

pre·ci·pi·ta·tion /£prɪˌsɪp·ɪˈteɪ·ʃən, $priː-/ *n* [U] *fml* • *The prime minister has been accused of acting with precipitation* (= too quickly) *over the crisis.* • *The precipitation* (= sudden development) *of the conflict from a minor dispute to full-scale war was brought about by the assassination of a government minister.*

pre·ci·pi·tate *obj* [THROW] /£prɪˈsɪp·ɪ·teɪt, $-t̬eɪt/ *v* [T always + adv/prep] *fml* to throw (someone or something) from a height with great force • *I ran into a brick while riding my bicycle, which precipitated me* **onto** *the road.*

pre·ci·pi·tate [CHEMISTRY] /£prɪˈsɪp·ɪ·tət, $priːˈsɪp·ɪ·t̬ɪt/ *n specialized* a solid substance which is produced from a liquid during a chemical process • *Add the reagent until precipitate begins to form in the flask.* [U] • *After filtration, the precipitate was dried at 90°C.* [C]

pre·ci·pi·tate *(obj)* /£prɪˈsɪp·ɪ·teɪt, $-t̬eɪt/ *v specialized* • *Cooling the beaker helps precipitate the compound* (= helps it to form). [T] • *If any organic salt is formed, it will precipitate* **(out)** *immediately.* [I]

pre·ci·pi·ta·tion /£prɪˌsɪp·ɪˈteɪ·ʃən, $priː-/ *n* [U] *specialized* • *The compound is finally obtained by precipitation.*

pre·ci·pi·ta·tion /£prɪˌsɪp·ɪˈteɪ·ʃən, $priː-/ *n* [U] *specialized* water which falls from the clouds towards the ground, esp. as rain or snow • *Hail and sleet are types of precipitation.* • *The forecast is for dry, cloudy weather with no precipitation expected.*

pré·cis /ˈpreɪ·si/ *n* [C] *pl* **précis** a short form of a text which briefly gives only the important parts • *You have all been given a précis* **of** *the report.*

pré·cis *obj* /ˈpreɪ·si/ *v* [T] • *If I may précis the president's words – "This country will never give in to terrorism."*

pre·cise [EXACT] /£prɪˈsaɪs, $priː-/ *adj* exact and accurate in form, time, detail or description • *The bunker's precise location is a closely guarded secret.* • *The Earth's atmosphere makes the precise observation of faint stars difficult.* • *Precise details about the project are not available as yet, but we do know that it will cost about $400 000.* • *Stop cooking the rice at the precise* **moment** *when its middle still feels a little hard.* • *There was a good turnout for the meeting – twelve of us* **to be precise**. • Ⓔ

pre·cise·ly /£prɪˈsaɪ·sli, $priː-/ *adv* • *The fireworks begin at eight o'clock precisely.* • *What do you think the problem is, precisely?* • Precisely is also used to emphasize the truth or accuracy of what you are saying: *I know precisely what you mean.* ○ *Whenever I tell him to do something, he does precisely the opposite.* ○ *"You look tired – you should go home and rest." "I'm going to do precisely that."* ○ *But it's precisely because of the noise that they're thinking of moving.* ○ *Armed conflict is precisely what the government is trying to avoid.* • You would say 'precisely' if you wanted to express complete agreement with someone or suggest that what they have said is obvious: *"It would be stupid to attempt the journey in the dark." "Precisely," he answered.*

pre·ci·sion /£prɪˈsɪʒ·ən, $priː-/ *n* [U] • *Great precision is required to align the mirrors accurately.*

pre·ci·sion /£prɪˈsɪʒ·ən, $priː-/ *adj* [before n; not gradable] • *Precision* **bombing** *was used to destroy enemy airbases and armaments factories.* • *His comic entrance on stage requires precision* **timing**. • **Precision instruments/tools** are ones which can be controlled very accurately and which produce very accurate results.

pre·cise [CAREFUL] /£prɪˈsaɪs, $priː-/ *adj approving* very careful and accurate, esp. about small details • *Years of doing meticulous research had made her very precise in her working methods.* • Ⓔ

pre·cise·ly /£prɪˈsaɪ·sli, $priː-/ *adv approving* • *He works slowly and precisely whereas I tend to rush things and make mistakes.*

pre·ci·sion /£prɪˈsɪʒ·ən, $priː-/ *n* [U] *approving* • *She organized the conference with great precision.* • *His books are a pleasure to read because he writes with such clarity and precision.* • Ⓟ

pre·clude *obj* /£prɪˈkluːd, $priː-/ *v* [T] *fml* to prevent (something) or make it impossible, or prevent (someone) from doing something • *The large number of demonstrators precluded the option of using force to disperse the rally.* • *The fact that your application was not successful this time does not preclude the possibility of you applying again next time.* • *His contract precludes him* **from** *discussing his work with anyone outside the company.* • *Domestic problems have precluded the government* **from** *pursuing an active foreign policy.*

pre·clu·sion /£prɪˈkluː·ʒən, $priː-/ *n* [U] *fml* • *Your age should not act as a preclusion* **to** *you being accepted on the university course.*

pre·co·cious /£prɪˈkəʊ·ʃəs, $priːˈkoʊ-/ *adj* (of children) showing unusually early mental development or achievement, or *(esp. disapproving)* behaving as if you are much older than you really are • *The child's precocious ability to play chess is astonishing.* • *At the precocious* **age** *of 29 she was made a professor of philology.* • *(esp. disapproving) He's such a precocious little brat that none of the other children want to play with him.*

pre·co·cious·ly /£prɪˈkəʊ·ʃə·sli, $priːˈkoʊ-/ *adv* • *He was a precociously gifted boy who went to university at the age of 14.* • *She decided on a theatrical career at a precociously young age.*

pre·co·cious·ness /£prɪˈkəʊ·ʃə·snəs, $priːˈkoʊ-/, *fml* **pre·coc·i·ty** /£prɪˈkɒs·ə·ti, $priːˈkɑː·sə·t̬i/ *n* [U] • *What is surprising about the new generation of writers is their precociousness, for they all began to write at a very young age.*

pre·cog·ni·tion /£ˌpriː·kɒgˈnɪʃ·ən, $-kɑːg-/ *n* [U] *specialized* knowledge of a future event, esp. when it is obtained by a direct message to the mind, such as in a dream, rather than by reason • *Precognition, telepathy* *and clairvoyance are the three main categories of extrasensory perception.*

pre·cog·ni·tive /£ˌpriːˈkɒg·nɪ·tɪv, $-ˈkɑːg·nɪ·t̬ɪv/ *adj* [not gradable] *specialized* ● *She claims she has precognitive* **abilities** *and that she can foresee events before they actually happen.*

pre·con·ceived /ˌpriː·kənˈsiːvd, ˈ---/ *adj esp. disapproving* (of an idea or an opinion) formed too early, esp. without enough consideration or knowledge ● *I'm not launching this inquiry with any preconceived* **ideas** *– I simply want to gather all the evidence.* ● *You must judge each candidate on their own merits, without any preconceived* **notions** *about what they are like.*

pre·con·cep·tion /ˌpriː·kənˈsep·ʃᵊn/ *n* [C] *esp. disapproving* ● A preconception is an idea or opinion formed before enough information is available to form it correctly: *Try to go into the meeting without too many preconceptions* **about** *what the other group want.*

pre·con·di·tion /ˌpriː·kənˈdɪʃ·ᵊn/ *n* [C] something which must happen or be true before it is possible for something else to happen ● *A halt to the fighting is a precondition* **for** *negotiations.* ● *Sound financial policies are a precondition* **of** *economic growth.* ● *The most important precondition was* **that** *all the participants should agree to a cease-fire.* [+ *that* clause]

pre·cook *obj* /ˌpriːˈkʊk/ *v* [T] to cook (food) in advance so that it can be heated and then eaten at a later time ● *I'll precook the chicken, so all you'll have to do is heat it up.*

pre·cooked /ˌpriːˈkʊkt/ *adj* [not gradable] ● *Sales of precooked* **meals** *have risen sharply over the past few years.*

pre·cur·sor /£ˌpriːˈkɜː·səʳ, $-ˈkɜːr·sɚ/ *n* [C] *slightly fml* something which happened or existed before another thing, esp. if it either developed into it or had an influence on it ● *German World War Two rocket weapons were the precursors* **of** *modern space rockets.* ● *Pure research has often been a precursor* **to** *applications which give economic benefits.*

pre·date *obj* /ˌpriːˈdeɪt, $ˈ--/ *v* [T] *slightly fml* to have existed or happened before (another thing) ● *These cave paintings predate any others which are known.* ● Compare BACKDATE; POSTDATE.

pred·at·or /£ˈpred·ə·təʳ, $-t̬ɚ/ *n* [C] an animal that hunts, kills and eats other animals ● *The antelopes are on their guard against lions and other predators.* ● *(disapproving)* If a person is described as a predator, they try to obtain other people's money or possessions: *In court, he was accused of being a merciless predator who had tricked his grandmother out of her savings.*

pred·at·o·ry /£ˈpred·ə·tᵊr·i, $-tɔːr-/ *adj* ● *The owl is a predatory bird which kills its prey with its claws.* ● *The game involves hunting down your opponents and shooting them with paint, and is designed to appeal to people's predatory* **instincts**. ● *(esp. disapproving)* If a person or organization is predatory, they try to obtain something that belongs to someone else: *The company spent much effort in avoiding takeover bids from predatory competitors.* ● *(disapproving)* A predatory person can also be someone who expresses sexual interest in a very obvious way: *I hate going to bars on my own because men look at you in such a predatory way.* ● *(specialized)* If a company uses **predatory pricing**, it offers goods at such a low price that other companies cannot compete with it: *The airline has reduced its prices so sharply that it has been accused of predatory pricing.*

pre·de·cease *obj* /£ˌpriː·dɪˈsiːs, $-diː-/ *v* [T] *fml or law* to die before (someone else) ● *Her husband predeceased her by five years.* ● *One of the saddest things that can happen in this world is when a parent is predeceased by their child.*

pre·de·ces·sor /£ˈpriː·dɪˌses·əʳ, $ˈpred·ə·ses·ɚ/ *n* [C] someone who had a job or a position before someone else, or something which comes before another thing in time or in a series ● *My predecessor worked in this job for twelve years.* ● *Unlike his predecessor, the present prime minister favours closer political ties with Europe.* ● *The latest Ferrari is not only faster than its predecessors but also more comfortable.* ● Compare **successor** at SUCCEED [FOLLOW].

pre·des·ti·na·tion /£ˌpriː·des·tɪˈneɪ·ʃᵊn, $priː·des·t̬ə-/ *n* [U] the belief that people have no control over events because these things are controlled by God or by FATE ● *He refused to believe in predestination, arguing that every individual was ultimately responsible for their own life and destiny.*

pre·des·tined /£ˌpriːˈdes·tɪnd, $ˌpriːˈdes·t̬ᵊnd/ *adj* [not gradable] ● If an action or event is predestined, it is controlled by God or by FATE: *Many couples would say their meeting was predestined because it was so unlikely to have happened by chance.* ○ *It seems the expedition is predestined* **to** *fail because there have been so many problems.* [+ *to* infinitive]

pre·de·ter·mine *obj* /£ˌpriː·dɪˈtɜː·mɪn, $-diːˈtɜːr·mən/ *v* [T usually passive] *slightly fml* to decide or arrange (something) at an earlier time ● *It is impossible to say how much a person's normal behaviour is predetermined by their genetic make-up.* ● *Time locks can be opened only at certain predetermined times of the day.* ● *At a predetermined* **time**, *three groups of soldiers will simultaneously attack different places.*

pre·de·ter·mi·na·tion /£ˌpriː·dɪˌtɜː·mɪˈneɪ·ʃᵊn, $-diːˌtɜːr·mə-/ *n* [U] *fml* ● *She began to write down her feelings furiously, without any conscious predetermination of what she was going to say.*

pre·de·ter·min·er /£ˌpriː·dɪˈtɜː·mɪ·nəʳ, $-diːˈtɜːr·mə·nɚ/ *n* [C] *specialized* (in grammar) a word which is sometimes used before a determiner to give more information about a noun in a noun phrase ● *In the phrases 'all these children' and 'once a day', the words 'all' and 'once' are predeterminers.* ● [LP] **Determiners**

pre·di·ca·ment /£prɪˈdɪk·ə·mənt, $priː-/ *n* [C] *slightly fml* an unpleasant situation which is difficult to get out of ● *With no money, no job and nowhere to live, he found himself in a real predicament.* ● *She is hoping to get a loan from her bank to help her out of her financial predicament.* ● *I'm in a bit of a predicament because I've accidentally accepted two invitations to dinner on the same night.*

pred·i·cate [SENTENCE PART] /£ˈpred·ɪ·kət, $-kɪt/ *n* [C] *specialized* (in grammar) the part of a sentence which gives information about the subject ● *In the sentence 'We went to the airport', 'went to the airport' is the predicate.*

pred·i·cate *obj* [STATE] /ˈpred·ɪ·keɪt/ *v* [T] *fml* to state that (something) is true ● *It would be unwise to predicate* **that** *the disease is caused by a virus before further tests have been carried out.* [+ *that* clause] ● *(fml)* If an idea or argument is **predicated on** something, it depends on the existence or truth of this thing: *Her theory is predicated on the premise that the birth rate will continue to fall over the next decade.* ○ *The sales forecast is predicated on the assumption that the economy will grow by four per cent this year.*

pre·di·ca·tive /£prɪˈdɪk·ə·tɪv, $priːˈdɪk·ə·t̬ɪv/ *adj* [not gradable] *specialized* (in grammar, esp. of adjectives or phrases) following a verb ● *In the sentence 'She is happy', 'happy' is a predicative adjective.* ● [LP] **Adjectives**

pre·dict *obj* /prɪˈdɪkt/ *v* [T] to say that (an event or action) will happen in the future, esp. as a result of knowledge or experience ● *Nowadays it's possible to predict the time of eclipses with great accuracy.* ● *Anyone who predicts the race result at this stage is either very rash or very gifted.* ● *Who could have predicted* **that** *within ten years he'd be in charge of the whole company?* [+ *that* clause] ● *The storms are predicted* **to** *reach the North of the country tomorrow morning.* [+ obj + *to* infinitive] ● *No one can predict* **when** *the disease will strike again.* [+ *wh-* word]

pre·dic·ta·ble /£prɪˈdɪk·tə·bl̩, $-t̬ə-/ *adj* ● Something which is predictable happens in a way which you know about before it happens: *Comets appear at predictable times.* ● *(disapproving)* Someone who is predictable never shows imagination or does anything which is unexpected: *She's so predictable – she always wants to go to the same old restaurant!*

pre·dic·ta·bly /£prɪˈdɪk·tə·bli $-t̬ə-/ *adv* ● *The American tennis champion predictably beat the British newcomer in the second round of the championship.* ● *Predictably* (= As would be expected), *after the initial media interest, the refugees now seem to have been forgotten.*

pre·dic·ta·bil·i·ty /£prɪˌdɪk·təˈbɪl·ɪ·ti, $-t̬əˈbɪl·ə·t̬i/ *n* [U] ● *He stays in chain hotels when he travels abroad on business, as he appreciates their predictability* (=knowing what they will be like). ● *Although her job is boring and monotonous, she likes the sense of predictability and security that it gives her.* ● *The civil war broke out with such sickening predictability that it is shocking that the rest of the world did not do anything to stop it.*

pre·dic·tion /prɪˈdɪk·ʃᵊn/ *n* ● *To everyone's surprise, his prediction of the severe storm came true.* [C] ● *We are not yet able to* **make** *a prediction* **about** *when the next earthquake will happen.* [C] ● *No one believed her prediction* **that** *the world would end on November 12.* [C + *that* clause] ● *Prediction is a skill which can be enhanced with experience.* [U]

pre·dic·tive /£prɪˈdɪk·tɪv, $-t̬ɪv/ *adj* [not gradable] • *The predictive value* (=The ability to predict things) *of this new method of analysis has still to be proven.*

pre·di·gest·ed /£ˌpriː·daɪˈdʒes·tɪd, $-t̬ɪd/ *adj* [not gradable] *slightly disapproving* (of information) made simpler or easier to understand, esp. by removing any parts which would make a person have to think hard • *The booklet presents information about the project in a predigested form and explains things in an easy, non-technical way.*

pre·di·lec·tion /£ˌpriː·dɪˈlek·ʃᵊn, $ˌpred·ᵊlˈek-/ *n* [C] *slightly fml* a strong liking • *Ever since she was a child, she has had a predilection* **for** *spicy food.*

pre·di·spose *obj* /£ˌpriː·dɪˈspəʊz, $-ˈspoʊz/ *v* [T] *fml* to influence (someone) and make them likely to behave in a particular way • *His family background predisposes him* **to** *support the Democrats.* [+ obj + *to* infinitive] • *The president is predisposed* **towards** (=supports) *negotiation and favours a peaceful way of resolving the crisis.* • If something **predisposes** someone **to** a disease, it makes that person likely to suffer from it: *Smoking predisposes you to lung cancer.* ○ *Researchers have discovered that up to one half of all children born of alcoholics are genetically predisposed to alcoholism.*

pre·di·spo·si·tion /ˌpriː·dɪ·spəˈzɪʃ·ᵊn/ *n* [C] *fml* • Predisposition is the state of being likely to behave in a particular way or to suffer from a particular disease: *She has an annoying predisposition* **to** *find fault wherever she goes.* ○ *There is evidence that a predisposition* **to(wards)** *asthma runs in families.*

pre·dom·i·nant /£prɪˈdɒm·ɪ·nənt, $-ˈdɑː·mə-/ *adj* [not gradable] being the most noticeable, important or largest in number • *Dancers have a predominant role in this performance.*

pre·dom·i·nant·ly /£prɪˈdɒm·ɪ·nənt·li, $-ˈdɑː·mə-/ *adv* [not gradable] • *Public opinion seems to be predominantly* (=Most people are) *in favour of holding a referendum.*

pre·dom·i·nance /£prɪˈdɒm·ɪ·nənts, $-ˈdɑː·mə-/ *n* [U] • If one person or group of people has predominance they have the most importance or power: *We want to avoid any one group having predominance in the negotiations.* • If there is a predominance of one type of person or thing within a set, they are the largest in number: *There is a predominance of people with an arts degree on the board of governors.*

pre·dom·i·nate /£prɪˈdɒm·ɪ·neɪt, $-ˈdɑː·mə-/ *v* [I] • *As with many family businesses, the owner's views predominate* (=have the most influence) *at meetings.* • *In industrial areas, the dark-coloured variety of the moth now predominates* (=is the largest in number).

preem·ie *Am* /ˈpriː·mi/, **prem·ie**, *Aus* **prem·mie** *n* [C] *infml* a baby that is born earlier than expected • *Their baby, who was born three months prematurely, represents a rare success story as only ten per cent of such preemies manage to survive.*

preen *(obj)* MAKE TIDY /priːn/ *v* (of a bird) to clean and arrange (its feathers) using its beak • *The pigeons were too busy preening to notice the bread that had been scattered on the ground for them.* [I] • *There were no ducks on the pond, but she spotted two ducks beneath a tree, preening their* **feathers**. [T] • *(disapproving)* If you preen (yourself), you spend a long time making yourself look tidy: *Roald always spends ages preening himself before he goes out.* [T]

preen·ing /ˈpriː·nɪŋ/ *adj* [not gradable] • *The square was covered with preening pigeons and sparrows searching for crumbs that people had thrown to them.* • *(fig. disapproving) The beach was full of self-obsessed preening people, all trying to get a better suntan than anyone else.*

preen *obj* FEEL PROUD /priːn/ *v* [T] *esp. disapproving* to feel proud or satisfied with (yourself) because of an action or quality • *The government is publicly preening itself* **on** *the latest trade figures.* • *The company preened itself* **for** *having taken on so many new employees last year.*

pre·fab /ˈpriː·fæb/ *n* [C] *infml* a small house which can be built quickly from pieces which have been made in a factory • *After World War Two, lots of prefabs were put up to ease the housing crisis.*

pre·fab·ri·cat·ed /£ˌpriːˈfæb·rɪ·keɪ·tɪd, $-t̬ɪd/, *Am also* **pre·built**, *infml* **pre·fab** /ˈpriː·fæb/ *adj* [not gradable] (esp. of buildings) built from parts which have been made in a factory and can be put together quickly • *The council is using prefabricated* **houses** *as temporary accommodation for homeless families who urgently need housing.*

pre·fab·ri·ca·tion /ˌpriː·fæb·rɪˈkeɪ·ʃᵊn/ *n* [U] • *One of the earliest uses of prefabrication was in the rapid construction of the Crystal Palace in London in 1851.*

pref·ace /ˈpref·ɪs/ *n* [C] something which comes before and introduces something more important, esp. a piece of text at the beginning of a book explaining its aims • *In his preface, the author says that he took eight years to write the book.* • *We're hoping these talks could be a preface* **to** *peace.*

pref·ace *obj* /ˈpref·ɪs/ *v* [T] *fml* • *Both sides must now agree on a statement of principles to preface the new constitution.* • *Each work is prefaced* **by** *a descriptive note and concludes with an author's note.* • *I should like to preface my response* **with** *the following observation.*

pref·a·to·ry /£ˈpref·ə·tᵊr·i, $-tɔːr-/ *adj* [not gradable] *fml* • *After a few prefatory* (=introductory) **comments/ remarks**, *she began her speech.*

pre·fect OFFICIAL /ˈpriː·fekt/ *n* [C] (in some countries) a very important official in the government or the police • *He has been appointed Prefect of Bologna.*

pre·fect STUDENT /ˈpriː·fekt/ *n* [C] (in some schools, esp. in Britain and Australia) an older student who is given some authority and helps to control the younger students • *His job as a prefect was to patrol the school at lunchtime and catch any younger pupils who were smoking.*

pre·fer *(obj)* CHOOSE /£prɪˈfɜːʳ, $priːˈfɜːr/ *v* [not *be preferring*] **-rr-** to choose or want (one thing) rather than another because it would be more pleasant or suitable • *Do you prefer hot or cold weather?* [T] • *We have tea and coffee, but perhaps you'd prefer a cold drink.* [T] • *He prefers* **watching** *rugby* **to** *playing it.* [+ v-*ing*] • *I prefer red wine* **to** *white.* [T] • *She's willing to talk about issues which most other people prefer* **to** *avoid.* [+ *to* infinitive] • *I'd prefer not* **to** *remember what happened that day.* [+ *to* infinitive] • *(fml) I'd prefer you not* **to** *smoke* (=I would like it better if you did not smoke), *please.* [+ obj + *to* infinitive] • *(fml) If it were possible, I would prefer* **that** *the concert was cancelled.* [+ *that* clause] • *Keeping the news secret for a while would be my preferred option.*

pref·er·a·ble /£ˈpref·ᵊr·ə·bl̩, $-ɚ·ə-/ *adj* [not gradable] • *If it would be preferable, we could go on a later train.* • *Surely a diplomatic solution is preferable* **to** *war.*

pref·er·a·bly /£ˈpref·ᵊr·ə·bli, $-ɚ·ə-/ *adv* [not gradable] • *Put the potatoes into boiling water, preferably after peeling them* (=it is best if you do this).

pref·er·ence /£ˈpref·ᵊr·ᵊnts, $ˈ-ɚ-/ *n* • *Her preference is* **for** *comfortable rather than smart clothes.* [U] • *Do you have a preference* **for** *sweet or* **for** *spicy food?* [C] • *What are your preferences* **in** *music.* [C] • *It would be wrong to discriminate against a candidate because of their* **sexual** *preference* (=the sex of the people they are sexually attracted to). [U] • *He studied chemistry* **in preference to** (=rather than) *physics at university.* • A preference is also an advantage which is given to a person or a group of people: *Special preferences were offered initially to encourage investment.* [C] ○ *We give preference* **to** *those who have worked with us for a long time.* [U]

pref·er·en·tial /£ˌpref·ᵊrˈen·tʃᵊl, $-əˈren-/ *adj* [before n] • If you are given something which is preferential, you are given something which is better than what other people receive: *Single mothers have been given preferential access to council housing.* ○ *People who fly regularly with the airline are given preferential seating.* ○ *Inmates claimed that some prisoners had received preferential* **treatment**.

pref·er·en·tial·ly /£ˌpref·ᵊrˈen·tʃᵊl·i, $-əˈren-/ *adv* • *The bank is investigating claims that some borrowers have been treated preferentially.*

pre·fer *obj* ACCUSE *Br law* /£prɪˈfɜːʳ, $priːˈfɜːr/, *Am and Aus* **press** *v* [T] **-rr-** to make (an official accusation) • *The police have decided not to prefer* **charges** *(against them) because there is insufficient evidence.*

pre·fig·ure *obj* /£priːˈfɪg·əʳ, $-jɚ/ *v* [T] *fml* to show or suggest that something will happen in the future • *His paintings prefigure the development of perspective in Renaissance art.* • *The president claims he has sent troops into the capital to supervise the voting, but opponents believe it prefigures an attempt to increase his power.*

pre·fix GRAMMAR /ˈpriː·fɪks/ *n* [C] a letter or group of letters added to the beginning of a word to make a new word • *In the word 'unimportant', 'un-' is a prefix.* • LP **Combining forms**

pre·fix TELEPHONE /ˈpriː·fɪks/ *n* [C] *Br for* **dialling code**, see at DIAL TELEPHONE

preg·nant FEMALE /ˈpreg·nənt/ *adj* [not gradable] (of a woman and some female animals) having young developing inside the womb • *She's five and a half months pregnant.* • *The centre gives advice and prenatal care to pregnant women.* • *My mother stopped smoking when she* **became** *pregnant.* • *She became pregnant* **by** *her boyfriend.* • *He believes that men who* **get** (=make) *young girls pregnant should be severely punished.* • *We moved house when I was* **heavily** *pregnant* (=at a late stage in my pregnancy). • *My sister is pregnant* **with** *twins.* • Ⓒⓢ

preg·nan·cy /ˈpreg·nənt·si/ *n* • *Most women feel sick in the mornings during their first months of pregnancy.* [U] • *My first pregnancy was very straightforward – there were no complications.* [C] • *She gave birth to a healthy baby boy, despite it being an* **ectopic** *pregnancy* (=a pregnancy in which the baby developed outside the womb). [C] • A **pregnancy test** is a chemical test performed on a woman's urine which shows if she is pregnant or not.

preg·nant MEANING /ˈpreg·nənt/ *adj* filled with meaning or importance which has not yet been expressed or understood • *There followed a pregnant* **pause** *in which both knew what the other was thinking but neither knew what to say.* • *The whole area of research is pregnant* **with** *possibilities for future developments.* • Ⓒⓢ

pre·heat *obj* /ˌpriːˈhiːt/ *v* [T] to heat (a cooker) to a particular temperature before putting food in it • *Preheat the oven to 180°C, 350°F, Gas Mark 4.* • *Place the cake in a preheated oven at Gas Mark 5 for 45 minutes.*

pre·hen·sile /£prɪˈhent·saɪl, $priːˈhent·sɪl/ *adj* [not gradable] *specialized* (of parts of the body) able to hold on to things, esp. by curling around them • *Some types of monkey have a prehensile tail which they wrap around branches as they move.*

pre·his·to·ry /£priːˈhɪs·tᵊr·i, $-t̬ɚ·i/ *n* [U] the period of human history before there were written records of events • *Human prehistory is divided into three successive periods: the Stone Age, the Bronze Age and the Iron Age.* • *The book is a history of the visual arts from prehistory to the latest experimental art.*

pre·his·tor·ic /£ˌpriː·hɪˈstɒr·ɪk, $-hɪˈstɔːr-/ *adj* [not gradable] • *Prehistoric* **remains** *have been found by archaeologists investigating the site.* • *The islands are scattered with prehistoric* **sites** *– most of which have not yet been excavated.* • *Painting originated in prehistoric* **times** *with murals drawn on cave walls.* • *(infml disapproving)* If something is described as prehistoric, it is very old-fashioned: *He has prehistoric views about women who have careers.* ○ *She criticized their prehistoric management structures.*

pre·judge *obj* /ˌpriːˈdʒʌdʒ/ *v* [T] *disapproving* to form an opinion about (a situation or a person) before knowing or considering all of the facts • *Let's not prejudge the situation – we need to hear both sides of the story first.* • *His lawyer claims it would be impossible for him to have a fair trial as the media has unfairly prejudged him.*

pre·judg·ment /ˌpriːˈdʒʌdʒ·mənt/, **pre·judge·ment** *n disapproving* • *You shouldn't make any sort of prejudgment about her before you've even met her.* [C] • *The trial was called a classic case of prejudgement, in which public opinion found the men guilty before they even went to court.* [U]

prej·u·dice /ˈpredʒ·ʊ·dɪs/ *n* an unfair and unreasonable opinion or feeling, esp. when formed without enough thought or knowledge • *The TV programme merely confirmed all my prejudices about salespeople.* [C] • *The campaign aims to dispel the prejudice* **that** *AIDS is confined to the homosexual community.* [C + *that* clause] • *He claims that prejudice* **against** *homosexuals would cease overnight if all the gay stars in the country were honest about their sexuality.* [U] • *Many women still encounter* **deep-seated** *prejudice in the workplace which prevents them from achieving top positions.* [U] • *Although* **racial** *prejudice has not yet disappeared, skin colour no longer acts as a bar to advancement.* [U] • *(fml or law)* If a decision or action is made **without prejudice to** a right or claim, it is made without having an effect on that right or claim: *My client accepts the formal apology without prejudice to any further legal action she may decide to take in the future.* ○ *The concessions were made without prejudice to any future territorial arrangements that may be made.*

prej·u·dice *obj* /ˈpredʒ·ʊ·dɪs/ *v* [T] • If someone or something prejudices you, they influence you unfairly so that you form an unreasonable opinion about something: *The prosecutor has been accused of prejudicing the jury and preventing the defendant from getting a fair trial.* ○ *British law prohibits newspapers from publishing information that might prejudice criminal cases before they go to court.* ○ *His unhappy childhood has prejudiced him* **against** *having children.* • *(fml)* If something or someone prejudices something else, they have a harmful influence on it: *The fact that you were late all this week may prejudice your chances of getting a promotion.* ○ *The pursuit of high productivity is prejudicing the quality of service.*

prej·u·diced /ˈpredʒ·ʊ·dɪst/ *adj disapproving* • If someone is prejudiced, they show an unreasonable dislike for something or someone: *The protagonist in the novel is portrayed as prejudiced and hot-tempered.* ○ *The campaign is designed to make people less prejudiced about AIDS and more aware of how to protect themselves against it.* ○ *The media has been accused of presenting a prejudiced* (=unfair) *view of people with disabilities.* • If someone is **prejudiced against** someone or something, they show an unreasonable dislike for them or are unwilling to do something without having a good reason: *He has always been prejudiced against Americans.* ○ *Some companies are prejudiced against taking on employees who are over the age of 40.*

prej·u·di·cial /ˌpredʒ·ʊˈdɪʃ·ᵊl/ *adj slightly fml* • If something is described as prejudicial, it influences people unfairly or is harmful: *An investigation by the police would have a prejudicial* **effect** *on the company's reputation.* ○ *The judge decided that allowing the videotape as evidence would be prejudicial* **to** *the jury in the trial.* ○ *Do we know if chemicals of this type are prejudicial* **to** *health?*

pre·late /ˈprel·ɪt/ *n* [C] an official of high rank in the Christian religion, such as a BISHOP or an ABBOT

pre·lim /ˈpriː·lɪm, prɪˈlɪm/ *n* [C usually pl] *infml* a sports event or an exam which acts as a preparation for a more important event that will follow • *The Australian team did well in the prelims, with all members qualifying.* • *We have prelims in May and the main exams in June.*

pre·li·mi·na·ry /£prɪˈlɪm·ɪ·nᵊr·i, $-ə·ner-/ *adj* [before n; not gradable] coming before a more important action or event, esp. introducing or preparing for it • *In preliminary discussions, American officials rejected the requests.* • *Police say two men have appeared in a preliminary court hearing.* • *Preliminary results show that the tank is not leaking, but this has to be confirmed by detailed tests.*

pre·li·mi·na·ry /£prɪˈlɪm·ɪ·nᵊr·i, $-ə·ner-/ *n* [C usually pl] • *After a few polite preliminaries* (=introductions), *we stated our main ideas and intentions.* • *The French team finished first in the competition preliminaries* (=the first part of the competition).

pre·li·ter·ate /£ˌpriːˈlɪt·ᵊr·ət, $-ˈlɪt̬·ɚ·ət/ *adj* [not gradable] *specialized* (of a society) not having a written language • *He spent a year in Africa, studying the customs and traditions of preliterate tribes.*

prel·ude INTRODUCTION /ˈprel·juːd/ *n* [C usually sing] something that comes before a more important event or action which introduces or prepares for it • *The changes are seen as a prelude* **to** *wide-ranging reforms.* • *Closer social and economic ties between the countries serve as a prelude* **to** *economic and monetary union.*

prel·ude MUSIC /ˈprel·juːd/ *n* [C] *specialized* a short piece of music which introduces the main work • *The concert began with the prelude to Act 1 of Wagner's opera, 'Parsifal'.* • A prelude is also a short independent piece of music written esp. for the piano: *Some of Chopin's preludes are suitable for beginners to play, while others are among the most sophisticated pieces written for the piano.*

pre·mar·i·tal /£ˌpriːˈmær·ɪ·tᵊl, $-ˈmer·ə·t̬ᵊl/ *adj* [not gradable] before marriage • *Attitudes to premarital* **sex** *vary greatly.*

pre·ma·ture /£ˈprem·ə·tʃəʳ, £ˈpriː·mə-, £-tjʊəʳ, £ˌ--ˈ-, $ˌpriː·məˈtʊr/ *adj* happening or done too soon, esp. before the natural or desired time • *His premature retirement was caused by a scandal surrounding his financial affairs.* • *Their criticisms seem premature considering that the results are not yet known.* • *Lack of regular exercise increases the risk of premature death.* • *He's a perfectly healthy baby even though he was (born) six weeks premature.* • *She had a premature* **baby** *which was born at 35 weeks.*

pre·ma·ture·ly /£ˈprem·ə·tʃə·li, £ˈpriː·mə-, £-tjʊə-, £ˌ--ˈ--, $ˌpriː·məˈtʊr-/ *adv* • *Their baby was born prematurely and weighed only 1 kilogram.* • *She has been forced to retire prematurely because of health problems.* • *UVA rays from the sun can prematurely age and wrinkle the skin.* • *His stressful job made him go prematurely grey* (=made his hair turn grey).

pre·med·i·tat·ed /£ˌpriːˈmed·ɪ·teɪ·tɪd, $-t̬ɪd/ *adj* [not gradable] (esp. of a crime or something unpleasant) done after being thought about or carefully planned • *a premeditated attack* • *The murder was premeditated and particularly brutal.*

pre·med·i·ta·tion /ˌpriː·med·ɪˈteɪ·ʃᵊn/ *n* [U] *slightly fml* • *The calculated premeditation of the crime shocked many members of the public.* • *Prosecutors could not prove that he killed her* **with** *premeditation and so had to drop the first-degree murder charge against him.*

pre·men·stru·al /£ˌpriːˈment·stru·əl, $-strəl/ *adj* [before n; not gradable] of the time just before a woman's PERIOD (=monthly bleeding from her vagina when she is not pregnant)

prem·i·er LEADER /£ˈprem·i·əʳ, $prɪˈmɪr/ *n* [C] (esp. used in news reports) the leader of the government of a country, or of a large part of a country • *The talks, chaired by the Canadian Prime Minister, were attended by the premiers of all 10 provinces.* • *Australia's state premiers attended the meeting.*

prem·i·er BEST /£ˈprem·i·əʳ, $prɪˈmɪr/ *adj* [before n; not gradable] best or most important • *Britain's premier festival theatre is based at Chichester.* • *The company had once been among the premier foreign firms in Tokyo.* • *As one of the nation's premier scientists, he is committed to attracting young people to science.*

prem·i·ère /£ˈprem·i·eəʳ, £-ˈ-, $-ˈer/ *n* [C] the first public performance of a play or any other type of entertainment • *The City Theatre is presenting three premières by local playwrights this season.* • *The* **world** *première* **of** *the opera will be at the Metropolitan Opera House in New York.*

prem·i·ère *obj* /£ˈprem·i·eə, $-er/ *v* [T] • *The network will première five new prime-time TV series this fall.* • *The opera was premièred in Paris.*

prem·ise, prem·iss /ˈprem·ɪs/ *n* [C] an idea or theory on which a statement or action is based • *They had clearly started with the premise* **that** *they had to stop Sanders from telling what he knew.* [+ *that* clause] • *The basic premise of their philosophy is* **that** *everyone should be free to do as they please, so long as they do not harm others.* [+ *that* clause] • *The research project is based on the premise stated earlier.*

prem·ise *obj* /prɪˈmaɪz, ˈprem·ɪs/ *v* [T often passive] *slightly fml* • *He premised* (=based) *his argument* **on** *several assumptions which not everyone in the audience shared.* • *The production of the play is premised* **on** *two highly original ideas.* • *This policy is premised* **on** *the expectation that the public will be willing to accept it.* • *(Am)* To premise something is also to make an introductory statement about it: *She premised what she was saying by acknowledging that other interpretations were possible.*

prem·is·es /ˈprem·ɪ·sɪz/ *pl n* the land and buildings owned by someone, esp. by a company or organization • *The company produces kitchen equipment for use in institutional and commercial premises.* • *When his old premises in Birmingham were demolished, he had to relocate his business six miles away.* • *In a survey, 70% of adults thought that supervised activities should be available on school premises up to 6 p.m.* • *The ice cream is made* **on the** *premises* (=in the building where it is sold). • *The security guards escorted the protesters* **off** (=away from) *the premises.*

pre·mi·um EXTRA /ˈpriː·mi·əm/ *n* [C] an amount which is more than usual • *The company is willing to pay a premium in order to get the right person for the job.* • *An organic dairy farmer whose milk earns a premium for* (=costs more because of its) *cleanliness was featured in the magazine.* • *Because of their location, these offices* **attract** *a premium* (=cost more to rent than other offices). • *The modified cars are available* **at** *a (5%) premium* (=a (5%) higher price). • *The modified cars are available* **at** *a premium* **(of** *5%)* **over** (=a price (5%) higher than) *the original price.* • If something is **at a premium**, it is not common and is therefore valuable: *Free time is at a premium for working parents.* • *The premium* **on** (=need for a greater amount of) *space forced the company to establish an out-of-town headquarters.* • *The busy shopper* **puts** *a premium* **on** (=appreciates and will pay more for) *finding everything in one big store.* • *These riverside apartments command premium* (=high) *rents.* • Premium is sometimes used to show that something is of higher than usual quality: *premium pork sausages* ○ *premium ice cream* ○ *premium orange juice* ○ *The building is on a premium site.* • *(Br)* A **premium bond** is part of a government system in which people buy some BONDS (=numbered tickets) and every month have the chance to win a prize of money. • **Premium (gas)** is *Am for* **four-star petrol**. See at FOUR.

pre·mi·um PAYMENT /ˈpriː·mi·əm/ *n* [C] an amount of money paid to obtain INSURANCE (=financial protection in case of accident, having your possessions stolen, etc.) • *Car insurance premiums have increased this year.* • *The premiums* **for** *healthcare plans are high.*

prem·mie /ˈprem·i/ *n* [C] *Aus for* PREEMIE

prem·o·ni·tion /ˌprem·əˈnɪʃ·ᵊn, ˌpriː·mə-/ *n* [C] a feeling that esp. something unpleasant is going to happen • *He had a premonition and rushed out of the kitchen just before an explosion wrecked it.* • *She had a* **sudden** *premonition* **of** *what the future might bring.* • *He stopped playing in competitions because his friend had a premonition* **that** *something dreadful would otherwise happen.* [+ *that* clause]

pre·na·tal /£ˌpriːˈneɪ·tᵊl, $-t̬ᵊl/ *adj* [before n; not gradable] *Am and Aus for* ANTENATAL

pre·nup·tial /ˌpriːˈnʌp·tʃᵊl/ *adj* [not gradable] before getting married • *prenuptial nerves* • *There is growing concern about the increase in the number of prenuptial conceptions.* • In a prenuptial **agreement**, two people who are going to marry agree what will happen to their money and possessions if the marriage ends.

pre·oc·cu·py *obj* /£ˌpriːˈɒk·jʊ·paɪ, $-ˈɑː·kjuː-/ *v* [T] to be the main thought in someone's mind, causing other things to be forgotten • *Economic concerns are preoccupying the voters in this election.* • *This issue has long preoccupied the legal profession in California.*

pre·oc·cup·ied /£ˌpriːˈɒk·jʊ·paɪd, $-ˈɑː·kjuː-/ *adj* • *She's been very preoccupied* (=giving her attention to esp. one thing) *recently because her mother has been very ill.* • *He is so preoccupied* **with** *his own problems that he has been incapable of working in the last few weeks.* • *Why does the media seem to have become so preoccupied* **with** *personal morality and family organization?* • *Preoccupied doctors hurried towards the hospital entrance.*

pre·oc·cu·pa·tion /£priːˌɒk·jʊˈpeɪ·ʃᵊn, $-ˌɑː·kjuː-/ *n* • *My main preoccupation* (=The thing that I am thinking about most) *now is trying to keep life normal for the sake of my two boys.* [C] • *The opening chapter of the book introduces the school staff and their problems and preoccupations, both emotional and academic.* [C] • *Lately, his preoccupation* **with** (=thinking only about) *football had caused his marks at school to slip.* [U] • *Such preoccupation* **with** (=thinking only about) *your work isn't healthy.* [U]

pre·or·dain *obj* /£ˌpriː·ɔːˈdeɪn, $-ɔːr-/ *v* [T usually passive] *fml* (esp. of a power thought to be greater than ordinary people) to decide or fix what will happen in a way that cannot be changed or controlled • *Illness and suffering seemed (to be) preordained* **to be** *her lot.* [+ obj + *to* infinitive] • *From the way these men behave, you'd think* **it** *was preordained* **that** *women could only do certain types of job!* [+ obj + *that* clause] • *The government appears to be preordaining the outcome of the election by promising tax benefits which few voters could resist.* • *His life seems to have followed a preordained path/direction.*

prep SCHOOL WORK /prep/ *n* [U] *Br infml* school work that students do at home; HOMEWORK • *Have you got much prep tonight?* • *(Am)* **Prep-time** is a period when teachers are at school but do not teach, and are therefore able to prepare for later classes.

prep PREPOSITION *abbreviation for* PREPOSITION

pre-packed /ˌpriːˈpækt/, *Am and Aus usually* **pre-pack·aged** /ˌpriːˈpæk·ɪdʒd/ *adj* [not gradable] wrapped or put into a container before being sold • *The nails come prepacked in small boxes.* • *The supermarket sells both loose and prepacked apples.*

pre·paid /ˌpriːˈpeɪd, ˈ--/ *adj* [not gradable] paid in advance • *Admission tickets are $20 prepaid, $25 at the door.*

pre·pare *(obj)* /£prɪˈpeəʳ, $-ˈper/ *v* to make or get (something or someone) ready for something that will happen in the future • *The developers waited three years for the city to prepare the site by installing sewage, water, gas and roads.* [T] • *The MBA is a general management qualification which aims to prepare students* **for** *middle and senior managerial positions.* [T] • *Are the players mentally and physically prepared* **to** *play a tough game?* [T + obj + *to* infinitive] • *The meal took two hours to prepare.* [T] • *The dough had been prepared by hand.* [T] • To prepare also means to expect that something will happen and to be ready for it: *Although the crisis seems to be over, we should prepare* **for** *a time of troubles.* [I] ○ *It almost seems as if she is preparing* **to** *die.* [+ *to* infinitive] ○ *You need to prepare* **yourself for** *a long wait.* [T]

pre·pared /£prɪˈpeəd, $-ˈperd/ *adj* • *We weren't prepared* (=were not expecting and therefore were not ready) **for** *so many guests.* • *They were prepared* **for the worst**. • *The spokesperson read a prepared statement* (=one made previously). • *"Here's one I prepared earlier"* (expression from demonstrations of cookery or model-making on television) • *"Be Prepared"* (motto of the Boy Scouts) • See also PREPARED.

pre·pared·ness /£prɪˈpeəd·nəs, $-ˈperd-/ *n* [U] *slightly fml* • *The army is in a state of preparedness* **for** *war.*

prep·a·ra·tion /£ˌprep·ᵊrˈeɪ·ʃᵊn, $-əˈreɪ-/ *n* • *The course teaches traditional methods of food preparation.* [U] • *Before starting to write a play, he* **does** *a lot of preparation, taking notes and trying ideas out on friends.* [U] • *The teacher didn't seem to have* **done** *much preparation* **for** *the class.* [U] • *The team blamed inexperience, injuries and lack of preparation time for their failure to win in Australia.* • *The writer was assisted* **in the** *preparation* **of** *this article by other members of her family.* [U] • *We are* **making** *preparations* **to** *fly Mr Goodall to the nearest hospital.* [C + *to* infinitive] • A preparation is a mixture of substances, often for use as a medicine: *The company is developing a new pharmaceutical preparation suitable for the treatment of gastric ulcers.* [C]

pre·par·a·to·ry /£prɪˈpær·ə·tᵊr·i, $-ˈper·ə·tɔːr-/ *adj* [not gradable] • *A lot of preparatory work is needed before we can begin the project.* • *Differences over these issues narrowed during the preparatory meetings/talks.* • *These hearings are preparatory* **to** *a trial in two months' time.* • **Preparatory school** is *fml for* **prep school**. See at PREP SCHOOL.

prep·a·ra·tions /£ˌprep·ᵊrˈeɪ·ʃᵊnz, $-əˈreɪ-/ *pl n* • *Preparations* (=Preparation) **for** *the opening ceremony are well under way.*

pre·pared /£prɪˈpeəd, $-ˈperd/ *adj* [after v; always + *to*] willing, happy to agree to • *Would you be prepared* **to** *help me get things ready for the party?* • *People are not really prepared* **to** *talk about these kinds of personal problems.* • *He said he is prepared* **to** *carry on as assistant should a new manager be appointed.* • See also **prepared** at PREPARE.

pre·pon·der·ance /£prɪˈpɒn·dᵊr·ᵊnts, $-ˈpɑːn·dɚ-/ *n* [U] *fml* the largest part or greatest amount • *The preponderance* **of** *the scientific evidence suggests that a diet that is lower in fat and total calories is better for you.* • *Small businesses appear to create the preponderance of new jobs.* • *There is a preponderance* **of** *women* **in** *part-time work.* • *The preponderance* **of** *women* **in** *part-time work means it is often badly paid.*

pre·pon·der·ant /£prɪˈpɒn·dᵊr·ᵊnt, $-ˈpɑːn·dɚ-/ *adj* [not gradable] *fml* • *Music does not play a very preponderant* (=important or large) *role in the school's teaching.*

pre·pon·der·ant·ly /£prɪˈpɒn·dᵊr·ᵊnt·li, $-ˈpɑːn·dɚ-/ *adv* [not gradable] *fml* • *Industry is still a preponderantly male environment.*

pre·pon·der·ate /£prɪˈpɒn·dᵊr·eɪt, $-ˈpɑːn·dɚ-/ *v* [I] *fml* • *Although it was a mixed class, girls preponderated.*

prep·o·si·tion /ˌprep·əˈzɪʃ·ᵊn/ *n* [C] a word which is used before a noun, a **noun phrase** or a pronoun, connecting it to another word • *In the sentences, 'We jumped in the lake', 'There were cheers at the end of the performance' and 'She drove slowly down the track', 'in', 'at', 'of' and 'down' are prepositions.* • LP **Varieties of English**

prep·o·si·tion·al /ˌprep·əˈzɪʃ·ᵊn·ᵊl/ *adj* [not gradable] • A **prepositional verb** is a combination of a verb and a preposition. Often, the meaning of the combination cannot be discovered by knowing the meaning of the different words that form it. • LP **Compound verbs**

pre·pos·sess·ing /ˌpriː·pəˈzes·ɪŋ/ *adj* [usually in negatives] interesting, noticeable or attractive • *He wasn't a very prepossessing sort of person.* • *The box didn't look very prepossessing, but the necklace inside was beautiful.*

pre·pos·ter·ous /£prɪˈpɒs·tᵊr·əs, $-ˈpɑː·stɚ-/ *adj* very foolish or ridiculous • *The idea is preposterous!*

prep·py (**-ier, -iest**), **prep·pie** (**-r, -st**) /ˈprep·i/ *adj, n esp. Am* (belonging to or seeming like) a member of a rich young social group, whose members come from families who have been wealthy for many years, and which is noticeable for its expensive tidy clothes • *preppy clothes* • *The public thinks of him as a pampered preppy who wore blazers and deck shoes and was driven to school in a limousine.* [C]

prep school, *fml* **pre·par·a·to·ry school** *n* [C] a **private school** (=a school paid for by parents not the government), in Britain for children, esp. boys, between the ages of seven and 13, who will then usually go to **public school** (=a similar school for older children), and in the US for children over the age of eleven, which prepares them to go to college • LP **Schools and colleges**

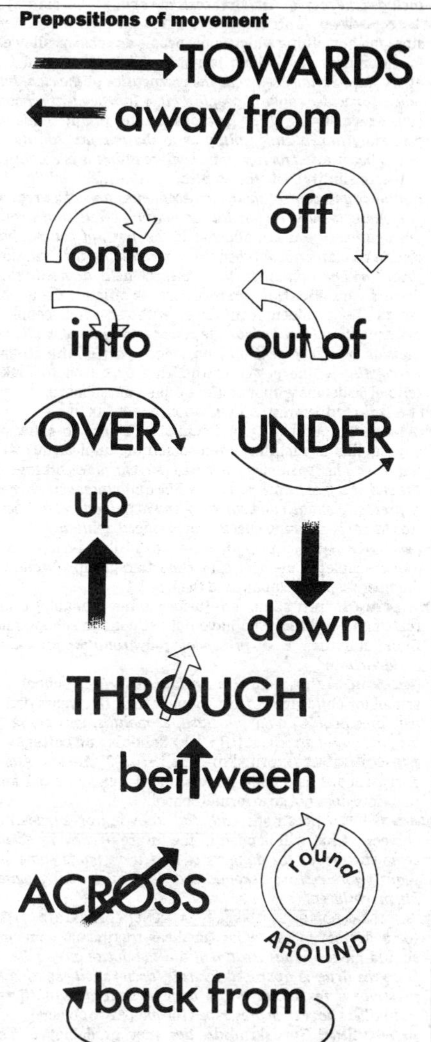

pre·quel /ˈpriː·kwəl/ *n* [C usually sing] a film, book or play which develops the story of an earlier film etc. by telling you what happened before the events in the first film etc. took place • *Jean Rhys's novel 'Wide Sargasso Sea' is a prequel* **to** *Charlotte Bronte's 'Jane Eyre'.* • Compare SEQUEL.

Pre-Raph·ae·lite /£ˌpriːˈræf·ᵊl·aɪt, $ˈ-i·ᵊl-/ *n, adj* [not gradable] a member of a 19th century group of British painters who were influenced by the style of painting of the 14th and 15th centuries, or in the manner of that group • *He has written a survey of British art from Hogarth to the Pre-Raphaelites.* [C] • *Millais, Hunt and Rossetti were famous Pre-Raphaelite painters.* • *She was a woman of Pre-Raphaelite beauty* (=had pale skin and long wavy reddish-brown hair, like the women painted by the Pre-Raphaelites).

pre·re·cord *obj* /£ˌpriː·rɪˈkɔːd, $-ˈkɔːrd/ *v* [T] to record (esp. music or speech) in order to use it at a later time instead of at the time when it was produced • *Is the programme broadcast live, or is it prerecorded?*

pre·req·ui·site /ˌpriːˈrek·wɪ·zɪt/ *n* [C] *fml* something which must exist or happen before something else can exist or happen • *If you want to play golf, club membership is a prerequisite.* • *Public support is a prerequisite* **for/to** *the success of this project.* • *They had to agree to certain conditions as a prerequisite* **of being** *lent the money.* • *The conditions of the loan* *included the prerequisite* **that** *costs were cut.* [+ *that* clause]

pre·rog·a·tive /£prɪ'rɒg·ə·tɪv, $-'rɑː·gə·t̬ɪv/ *n* [C often sing] *fml* something which some people are able or allowed to do or have, but which is not possible or allowed for everyone • *Skiing used to be the prerogative* **of** *the rich, but now a far wider range of people do it.* • *Independent schools can* **exercise/use** *their prerogative* **to** *admit students according to academic ability or to the parents' ability to pay.* • *Defence and foreign policy will remain the prerogative* (= responsibility) **of** *the central authorities, while the republics will control their own economies and resources.* • *"I'm going to make an official complaint." "Well, that's your prerogative* (= you are allowed to do that)*, of course, but couldn't we talk about other ways of resolving the situation first?"* • *The administration recently held a meeting to discuss* **presidential** *prerogatives* (= official decisions which the president can make without other people's agreement). • *He called for the power to declare war to be a decision of Parliament and no longer part of* **the Royal** *Prerogative* (= the power of the king or queen to make official decisions without other people's agreement).

Pres /prez/ *n* [before n] *abbreviation for* PRESIDENT

pres·age *obj* /'pres·ɪdʒ, prɪ'seɪdʒ/ *v* [T] *fml* to show or suggest that (something, often something unpleasant) will happen • *The spokesmen portrayed the reforms as presaging the end of a free health service.* • *The announcement seemed to presage a sudden and startling end to the conflict.* • *There was an early-morning mist which presaged a fine day.*

Pres·by·te·ri·an /£ˌprez·bɪ'tɪə·ri·ən, $-bɪ'tɪr·i-/ *n* [C], *adj* [not gradable] (a member of) a Christian group which has members esp. in Scotland and the US

pre·school /'priː·skuːl/ *adj* [before n; not gradable] of or relating to children who have not yet gone to school, and their activities • *a preschool playgroup* • *preschool children/toys*

pre·school /'priː·skuːl/ *n Am and Aus* • A preschool is a school for children who are younger than five years old: *a new preschool* [C] ○ *Sarina Basu, 22 months, was going to her first day of preschool.* [U] • LP **Schools and colleges**

pre·school·er /£'priːˌskuː·lə^r, $-lɚ/ *n* [C] *Am and Aus* • A preschooler is a child who is under five years old and therefore does not go to formal school.

pres·ci·ent /'pres·i·ənt/ *adj fml* knowing or suggesting correctly what will happen in the future • *Their prescient comments about the dangers of lead were made some six years before research showed that lead in drinking water harms children.*

pre·scribe *obj* GIVE MEDICAL TREATMENT /prɪ'skraɪb/ *v* [T] (of a doctor) to say what (medical treatment) someone should have • *What treatment did the doctor prescribe?* • *Once the drug is approved for sale, doctors will be able to prescribe it* **for** *ulcers.* • *I've been prescribed painkillers/Painkillers have been prescribed* **for** *me.* [+ two objects]

pre·scribed /prɪ'skraɪbd/ *adj* [not gradable] • *The patient was taking a widely prescribed sedative.*

pre·scrip·tion /prɪ'skrɪp·ʃ^ən/ *n* • A prescription (*Aus infml* **script**) is a piece of paper on which a doctor writes the details of the medicine or drugs that someone needs: *More careful control of drug prescriptions can cut costs and reduce overdoses and duplication of medication.* [C] ○ *The demand for prescriptions* **for** *sedatives has decreased.* [C] ○ *(Br and Aus) Doctors were very willing to give* **repeat** *prescriptions* (= another piece of paper allowing more of the same medicine to be given, often without the person seeing the doctor again). [C] ○ *(Am) You've got two* **refills** *left on this prescription* (= You can buy this medicine two more times without talking to your doctor). [C] • Prescription is the act of a doctor writing down that someone needs a particular medicine or drug: *The new drug is only available* **on** *prescription.* [U] • In Britain, a **prescription charge** is the standard amount of money you pay for any medicine prescribed for you by a doctor, which is often not the total cost: *Prescription charges are rising in June.* • A **prescription drug/medicine** is a drug which can only be bought if a doctor orders it for you. Compare **over the counter** at COUNTER SURFACE.

pre·scribe *(obj)* GIVE RULE /prɪ'skraɪb/ *v* to tell someone (what they must have or do); to give (something) as a rule • *Penalties for not paying your taxes are prescribed by law.* [T] • *The law prescribes* **that** *all children must go to school.* [+ *that* clause] • *Grammatical rules prescribe* **how** *words may be used together.* [+ *wh-* word] • *(fml) The First Amendment does not prescribe a duty on the government to ensure easy access to information for members of the press.* [T]

pre·scribed /prɪ'skraɪbd/ *adj* [not gradable] • *The product will have to meet internationally prescribed* (= demanded) *standards.*

pre·scrip·tion /prɪ'skrɪp·ʃ^ən/ *n fml* • *There are no prescriptions* (= instructions/rules) *about what the members of the group can do.* [C] • *He avoids the often crude prescriptions* (= instructions/rules about how to behave) *and statistical comparisons provided by other books about race.* [C] • *Do you think it's possible to give any prescription* **for** (= instruction about how to achieve) *success?* [U]

pre·scrip·tive /£prɪ'skrɪp·tɪv, $-t̬ɪv/ *adj fml esp. disapproving* • Prescriptive means saying exactly what must happen, esp. by giving an instruction or making a rule: • *The working party produced more flexible and less prescriptive guidelines than the previous group and emphasized the importance of creativity.* ○ *"The Bible is not nearly as prescriptive as some people would like it to be," the Archbishop is quoted as saying.*

pres·ent SOMETHING GIVEN /'prez·^ənt/, *Br and Aus infml* **prez·zie, pres·sie** /'prez·i/ *n* [C] something which you are given, without asking for it, on a special occasion, esp. to show friendship, or to say thank you; a GIFT • *a birthday/wedding/retirement/Christmas present* • *They gave me theatre tickets as a present.* • *The present was* **wrapped** *in beautiful shiny paper and tied with a big ribbon.* • *The children couldn't wait to* **unwrap** *their presents.* • *I'll* **make** *you* **a present of** (= give you) *my desk – there's no room for it in my new house.*

pres·ent NOW /'prez·^ənt/ *n* [U] the period of time which is happening now, not the past or the future; now • *That's all for* **the** *present.* • *The play is set* **in the** *present.* • **At present** means now: *"Are you busy?" "Not at present."* ○ *At present she's working abroad.* • *(saying)* 'There's no time like the present' means now is the best time to do whatever you are thinking of doing. • See also PRESENTLY NOW. • LP **Periods of time**

pres·ent /'prez·^ənt/ *adj* [before n; not gradable] • *I'll give you her present address* (= the one she has now) *and you can write to her.* • *Please state your present occupation and salary* (= those you have now) *on your application.* • **Present-day** means existing now: *Present-day leisure facilities are very different from those of 40 years ago.* • The **present continuous** is the tense which you use to refer to actions or events that are happening now or developing: *The sentences 'The children are watching television' and 'The weather is getting colder' are* **in** *the present continuous.* • A **present participle** is a form of a verb which in English ends in '-ing' and comes after another verb to show continuous action. It is used to form the **present continuous**: *In the sentences 'The children are watching television', 'The weather is getting colder' and 'I heard him singing', 'watching', 'getting' and 'singing' are present participles.* • The **present perfect** is the tense which you use to refer to actions or events which have been completed or which have happened in a period of time up to now: *The sentences 'She has broken her leg', 'This is the third time he has asked her to marry him' and 'I have never been to Australia' are all* **in** *the present perfect.* • The **present simple** is the tense which you use to refer to events, actions and conditions which are happening all the time, or exist now: *The sentences 'I live in Madrid', 'She doesn't like cheese' and 'I think you're wrong' are all* **in** *the present simple.* • LP **-ing form of verbs, Tenses**

pres·ent PLACE /'prez·^ənt/ *adj* [after v; not gradable] in a particular place • *We need a list of names of all those who were present at the scene of the accident.* • *There were no children present* (= at the place I am referring to). • **Present company excepted** means 'not the people who are here' and is used to show that criticism or a rude remark does not refer to the people you are talking to: *There hasn't been enough cooperation between the different teams – present company excepted, of course.*

pres·ence /'prez·^ənts/ *n* • *She was overawed by the presence* **of** *so many people.* [U] • *The presence* **of** *pollen in the atmosphere causes hay fever in some people.* [U] • *He's usually quite polite* **in** *my* **presence** (= when I am there). [U] • *The document was signed* **in the presence of** *two witnesses* (= when two people were there). [U] • If you **make** your **presence felt**, you have a strong effect on other people: *The new police chief has really made his presence felt.* • Someone's presence is an feeling that someone is still in a place although they are not there, or cannot be there because they are dead: *His daughter's presence seemed to fill her empty bedroom.* [C] • If a country or organization has a presence in another country, at a meeting, etc., some of its members are there: *The United Nations has maintained a presence in the region for some time.* [C] o *There was a strong police presence at the demonstration.* [C] • *(approving)* If someone **has** presence, they are noticeable in the way they look and behave, and have a strong effect on other people. [U] • *(approving)* **Presence of mind** is the ability to make good decisions and to act quickly and calmly in a difficult situation or an emergency: *When the gunmen came into the bank, she had the presence of mind to press the alarm.*

pres·ent *obj* GIVE /prɪˈzent/ *v* [T] to give, provide or make known • *The winners were presented* **with** *medals.* • *He is going to present the town* **with** *a new hospital in memory of his mother.* • *The letter presented the family* **with** *a* **problem** *that would be difficult to solve.* • *The documentary presented us* **with** *a balanced view of the issue.* • *He presented the report* **to** *his colleagues at the meeting.* • *(fml) The Vice-chair presents his* **apologies**, *but he is unable to attend.* • *The classroom presented a cheerful busy atmosphere* **to** *the visitors* (= appeared to them to have this). • *The school is presenting* (= performing) *'West Side Story' as its end-of-term production.* • *(fml dated) Mr Barney presents his* **compliments** (= gives a greeting). • *(fml or humorous infml) That was an excellent meal. Please present my* **compliments to the chef** (= tell the person who cooked it that I enjoyed it)*!* • If you present **yourself** somewhere, you go there: *He presented himself at the doctor's at 9.30 a.m. as arranged.* • If something presents **itself**, it happens or takes place: *An opportunity suddenly presented itself.*

pres·en·ta·tion /ˌprez·ənˈteɪ·ʃən/ *n* • *The presentation* (= giving) *of prizes and certificates will take place in the main hall.* [C] • *The speaker gave an interesting presentation* (= talk) *on urban transport.* [C] • Presentation is also the way something looks when it is shown to other people, or the way someone looks: *The course places emphasis on presentation and display, which are important skills.* [U]

pres·ent *obj* INTRODUCE /prɪˈzent/ *v* [T] *Br and Aus* to introduce (a television or radio show) or *(fml)* to introduce (a person) • *She presents the late-night news.* • *The chat show host presented his guests* **to** *the audience.* • *(fml) May I present Professor Carter?* • *(fml) Later on I'd like to present you* **to** *the headteacher.*

pre·sent·er /£prɪˈzen·təʳ, $-t̬ɚ/ *n* [C] *Br and Aus* • A presenter is the person who introduces a television or radio show: *a news/sports presenter* • *children's television presenters*

pre·sent·a·ble /£prɪˈzen·tə·bl̩, $-t̬ə-/ *adj* looking suitable or good enough, esp. in the way you are dressed • *I can't answer the door – I'm not presentable.* • *Jeremy was* **looking** *quite presentable for once.* • **Make** *yourself presentable for the interview.* • *She made quite a presentable* (= good) *bookcase at school.* • (RUS)

pre·sen·ti·ment /prɪˈzen·tɪ·mənt/ *n* [C] *fml* a feeling that esp. something unpleasant is going to happen; a PREMONITION • *She had had a presentiment* **of** *what might lie ahead.*

pres·ent·ly SOON /ˈprez·ənt·li/ *adv* [not gradable] soon; not at the present time but after a short time in the future • *I'll do it presently, after I've finished reading the paper.* • *The room was hot and presently her eyes grew heavy and she felt sleepy.* • *There are also several sports personalities on the list, of whom more presently.* • LP **Periods of time**

pres·ent·ly NOW /ˈprez·ənt·li/ *adv* [not gradable] *esp. Br and Aus* now; at the present time • *Of 200 boats, only 20 are presently operational.* • *They are presently trying to pick a suitable successor.* • *Three sites are presently under consideration for the new hotel.*

pre·serve *obj* KEEP /£prɪˈzɜːv, $-ˈzɜːrv/ *v* [T] to keep (something) as it is, esp. in order to prevent it from decaying or being damaged or destroyed; to CONSERVE • *We want to preserve the character of the town while improving the facilities.* • *The agreement preserved our right to limit trade in endangered species.* • *Storing herbs in glass jars in a cool place helps preserve their essential oils, which is what gives them their aromas.* • *Putting varnish on wood is a way of preserving it.* • *Mothers at home with small children need to get out of the house from time to time in order to preserve* (= prevent them from losing) *their* **sanity**. • To preserve food is to treat it in a particular way so that it can be kept for a long time without going bad: *preserved fruit* o *oranges preserved* **in** *brandy* o *Bottling is no longer a common way of preserving fruit and vegetables – deep freezing is now the more usual method.* • See also WELL-PRESERVED.

pre·ser·va·tive /£prɪˈzɜː·və·tɪv, $-ˈzɜːr·və·t̬ɪv/ *n* • *a timber/wood preservative* (= substance used for preventing decay) [C] • *The fence has been treated with preservative.* [U] • Preservatives are chemicals used to keep esp. food from decaying: *This bread is completely free from* **artificial** *preservatives.* [C] o *There was a long list of preservatives on the packet.* [C] o *No added preservatives.* [C] o *Salt and sugar are valuable preservatives.* [C] • (CS) (DK) (F) (PL) (RUS)

pres·er·va·tion /£ˌprez·əˈveɪ·ʃən, $-ɚˈ-/ *n* [U] • *He is one of the world's leading experts in the field of building restoration and preservation.* • *We need to get a timber/wood preservation specialist to look at this roof.* • *There is great public concern about some of the chemicals used in food preservation.* • *The food industry has been moving away from canned packaging and toward preservation methods such as freezing.* • *The cathedral is in a poor state of preservation* (= has not been kept in good condition) *and needs expensive repairs.* • *The prime minister has said that the government is committed to the preservation* (= protection) **of** *the country's national interests.* • *(esp. Am) Volunteers will receive information about architecture and* **historic** *preservation* (= protecting places of historic interest). • *She belongs to the Association for the Preservation of Civil War Sites* • *(Br and Aus)* A **preservation order** is an official decision that a building or area has special value and must be kept in good condition: *Preservation orders have been issued on the three stretches of the town wall which remain.* o *The avenue of mature trees has a preservation order on it.* • See also SELF-PRESERVATION.

pre·serve FOOD /£prɪˈzɜːv, $-ˈzɜːrv/ *n* (a) food made from fruit or vegetables boiled with sugar and water until it becomes like a firm sauce • *apricot preserve* [U] • *green tomato preserve* [U] • *jars of preserves* [C] • See also CONSERVE FOOD.

pre·serve SEPARATE ACTIVITY /£prɪˈzɜːv, $-ˈzɜːrv/ *n* [C] an activity which only one person or a particular type of person does or is responsible for, or something belonging to or used by only one person or a limited number of people • *Owning racehorses is the preserve* **of** (= only done by) *the rich.* • *The gardening is Jo's preserve* (= responsibility). • *You'll have to ask the accounts department about invoices – that's not my preserve* (= responsibility). • *She* **regards** *that cupboard* **as** *her own preserve* (= belonging to her) *and no-one else is allowed to use it.*

pre·serve SEPARATE PLACE /£prɪˈzɜːv, $-ˈzɜːrv/ *n* [C] *esp. Am* for **reserve**, see at RESERVE KEEP SEPARATE

pre·set *obj* /ˌpriːˈset/ *v* [T] **presetting**, *past* **preset** to prepare (a machine) in advance so it will operate or stop later, or to arrange for or agree to (something) in advance • *I'll preset the oven* **to** *come on at 5 p.m.* [+ obj + *to* infinitive] • *The agenda for the meeting has been preset.*

pre·set /ˈpriː·set/ *adj* [not gradable] • *a preset button* • *We have a device which switches the lights on at a preset time when we are out of the house in the evening.* • *The shares will be sold at a preset price.* • *An aircraft's automatic pilot enables it to fly on a preset course/route.*

pre·shrunk /ˌpriːˈʃrʌŋk/ *adj* [not gradable] (of clothes) SHRUNK (= made smaller) by washing before being sold • *preshrunk jeans*

pre·side /prɪˈzaɪd/ *v* [I] to be in charge of or to control a meeting or event • *Who would be the best person to preside* **at** *the public enquiry?* • *Tony will be presiding* **over** *the meeting.* • *(law) Judge Wood is presiding* **over** *the criminal case.* • *The government has presided* **over** *some of the most significant changes in education this century.* • *(humorous) Mother and Grandma were presiding* **over** *lunch, telling everyone else what to do.*

pre·sid·ing /prɪˈzaɪ·dɪŋ/ *adj* [not gradable] *esp. law* • *the presiding judge*

pres·i·dent POLITICS /ˈprez·ɪ·dənt/ *n* [C] (the title given to) the person who has the highest political position in a country which is a REPUBLIC and who, in some of these countries, is the leader of the government • *President Roosevelt* • *the President of France* • *The president gave her approval for the interview.* • *Thank you, Mr/Madam President.* [as form of address]

pres·i·den·tial /ˌprez·ɪˈden·tʃəl/ *adj* [usually before n; not gradable] • *a presidential election*

pres·i·den·cy /ˈprez·ɪ·dənt·si/ *n* • *He has announced that he is standing for the presidency* (= the position or job of being president) **of** *the United States.* [U] • *She has promised improvements during her presidency* (= the period in which she was president). [C]

pres·i·dent ORGANIZATION /ˈprez·ɪ·dᵊnt/ *n* [C] the person who has the highest position in an organization or *(esp. Am)* a company • *a former President of the Royal Society* • *She became president* **of** *the local opera group.* • *(esp. Am) She's a friend of the president* **of** *the bank.*

pres·i·den·tial /ˌprez·ɪˈden·tʃᵊl/ *adj* [before n; not gradable] • *She took 'Art and the community' as the theme of her presidential address to the annual meeting.*

pres·i·den·cy /ˈprez·ɪ·dᵊnt·si/ *n* [C/U]

press *(obj)* PUSH /pres/ *v* to push (something) firmly, esp. in a controlling way, often without causing it to move permanently further away from you • *He pressed the bell/ phone buttons/switch/pedal.* [T] • *She pressed his arm to get his attention.* [T] • *Press the cutter into the pastry several times to make a pattern.* [T] • *We pressed the pieces of the cardboard house out of the book and started to make the model.* [T] • *The crowd pressed against the locked doors trying to get into the building.* [I always + adv/prep] • *Press* **down** *firmly on the lever.* [I always + adv/prep] • *Press the lever firmly* **down**. [M] • If you press fruit, you use force on it with a utensil in order to remove the juice: *When you have pressed the oranges, strain the juice.* [T] • When you press **clothes** you make them smooth by IRONING them. [T] • To press a **record** or CD is to make one: *Emigre pressed 3000 copies and sent some out to college radio stations.* [T] ○ *We'll do a test pressing.* • To press something is also to make it firm and flat by putting it under something heavy: *The children pressed some flowers.* [T] ○ *We've got various types of cold meat, including pressed tongue and pressed turkey breast.* • If you are **(hard)** pressed **(for** something), you are in a difficult situation because you do not have enough of it: *We're rather pressed (for time) – we have to be there in half an hour.* [T] ○ *The research budget is hard pressed for cash.* [T] ○ *They're pressed for space in their little house.* [T] • *(Br and Aus)* A **press-stud** (also **snap fastener**, also *Br* **popper**, *Am* **snap**) is a small clothes fastener with two usually round parts, one of which is pushed into the other. LP➤ **Dressing and undressing** • *(Br)* A **press-up** (*Am and Aus* **push-up**) is a type of physical exercise in which you lie flat with your face towards the floor and try to push up your body with your arms while keeping your legs and your back straight: *Do twenty press-ups every morning.* • LP➤ **Switching on and off** (F) (S)

press /pres/ *n* [C] • *"The machine didn't start." "Just* **give** *the button another press* (= push it again)." • *Don't put the iron away – I want to* **give** *this shirt a quick press* (= make it smooth by IRONING it). • A press is also a piece of equipment which is esp. used to put weight on something to push it down : *a wine press* • *a garlic press* • *a trouser press*

pres·sure /£ˈpreʃ·əʳ, $-ɚ/ *n* • Pressure is the force you produce when you press something: *He put too much pressure on the door handle and it snapped.* [U] ○ *You can stop bleeding by* **applying** *pressure close to the injured area.* [U] • (A) pressure is also the force that a liquid or gas produces when it presses against an area: *gas/water pressure* [U] ○ *The new material allows the company to make gas pipes which withstand higher pressures.* [C] ○ *He described with great precision what happens to a human body* **at/under** *deep-sea pressures.* [C] ○ *The gas is stored* **under** *pressure* (= in a container which keeps it at a higher pressure than it would usually have). [U] • A **pressure cooker** is a cooking pan with a tightly fitting lid which allows food to cook quickly in steam under pressure. • A **pressure point** is a place on the body where an ARTERY (= tube which carries blood from the heart) is close to the surface of the skin so that it can be pressed to partly stop the flow of blood. It is also *(fig.)* a situation which causes difficulty in a relationship.

pres·sur·ize *obj, Br and Aus usually* **-ise** /£ˈpreʃ·ᵊr·aɪz, $-ə·raɪz/ *v* [T] • If a container is pressurized, the air pressure inside it is higher than the air pressure outside it: *a pressurized tank* ○ *There is a* **highly** *pressurized coolant system in the engine.* ○ *Aircraft cabins are pressurized.*

pres·sur·i·za·tion, *Br and Aus usually* **-i·sa·tion** /£ˌpreʃ·ᵊr·aɪˈzeɪ·ʃᵊn, $ˌ-ɚ·ɪˈ-/ *n* [U]

press *(obj)* CONTINUE /pres/ *v* to continue to persuade or encourage (someone), or to continue to take determined action to make certain that (something) is accepted • *The police officer pressed the witness* **to** *identify the man she had seen.* [T + obj + *to* infinitive] • *Letters to the paper pressed newspaper editors not* **to** *intrude into the grief of the missing soldier's families.* [T + obj + *to* infinitive] • *Could I press you a little further* (= persuade you to say more) **on** *what you've just said?* [T] • *They are pressing demands for reform* **on** (= trying to get them accepted by) *the country's leaders.* [T] • *When she saw he was undecided, she pressed* **home** *her advantage/point* (= tried to persuade him to accept her opinion) *by saying that there was absolutely no risk.* [M] • *He presses his* **case** *for promotion* (= continues trying to get it accepted) *at every opportunity.* [T] • *Had the company pressed* (= continued to take action on) **the issue** *and won, it would have been free to impose new wages and benefits on its staff.* [T] • *(law) The family decided not to press* **charges** *against the council* (= they decided not to make their complaint official and have it decided in a court of law). [T] • *Some residents pressed hard* **for** (= tried to get accepted) *a variety of street improvements, such as more trees.* [I] • To press **ahead/on** is to continue in a determined way: *Despite public complaints, the company pressed on* **with** *its plans.* [I] ○ *It was pouring with rain, but we pressed on* **regardless**. [I] • If you **press** something or someone **into service**, you use them because you have no choice, even though they are not really suitable: *The car's broken down so I've had to press my old bike back into service.* • (F) (S)

pres·sure /£ˈpreʃ·əʳ, $-ɚ/ *n* [U] • Pressure is the things that happen to a person which can make them feel anxious and unhappy: *He's got a lot of pressure* **on** *him just now – his wife is ill and he has problems at work.* Compare STRESS WORRY. • Pressure is also the force which causes you to do something: *Pressure* **of** *public opinion forced the government to withdraw the tax.* ○ *It'll be ready on Tuesday, pressure* **of work** *permitting.* ○ *Pressure* **to** *abandon the new motorway is increasing.* [+ *to* infinitive] • Someone who is **under** pressure has one or more things that they must do, usually in a short time, which cause anxiety, or has worry or difficulty in their life: *She doesn't usually shout – she must be under pressure.* ○ *I can't see you this week – I'm under pressure* **to** *get this report finished.* [+ *to* infinitive] • If someone does something **under** pressure, they do it because someone else says that they should: *She only wrote the letter under pressure* **(from** *her sister).* • If you **put** pressure **on** someone/*(fml)* **bring** pressure **to bear on** someone, you strongly persuade them to do something: *They put pressure on her to accept a lower price for the car.* • A **pressure group** is a group of people who work together to try to influence what other people or the government think about a particular subject in order to achieve the things they want.

pres·sures /£ˈpreʃ·əz, $-ɚz/ *pl n* • *He's got a lot of pressures* (= pressure) *on him just now.* • *It'll be ready on Tuesday, pressures* (= pressure) **of work** *permitting.*

pres·sur·ize *obj, Br and Aus usually* **-ise** /£ˈpreʃ·ᵊr·aɪz, $ˈ-ɚ-/, *esp. Am* **pres·sure** *v* [T] • If you pressurize a person, you strongly persuade them to do something they do not want to do: *He was pressurized* **into** *signing the agreement.*

press NEWSPAPERS /pres/ *n* [U] **the press** newspapers and magazines, and those parts of television and radio which broadcast news, or reporters and photographers who work for them • *The story has been all over the press this week.* • *The plane crash has been widely reported* **in** *the press.* • *Press reporters and photographers were waiting outside the presidential palace.* • *The charity invited the press* (= reporters and photographers) *to a presentation of its plans for the future.* • *The press was/were out in force at the awards ceremony.* [+ sing/pl v] • *He said that the* **freedom of** *the press* (= the ability of newspapers to publish news and opinions without being controlled by the government) *must be upheld.* • Press is the judgment that is given of someone or something in the newspapers or on radio or television: *What kind of press has the play had?* ○ *(Br and Aus) The play has* **had a** *good/bad press.* ○ *(Am) The play has* **had** *good/bad press.* • A **press baron** is a person who owns several newspapers and sometimes controls what they publish. • A **press box** is a room or other area kept for reporters to work in, esp. at sports events: *There were three cricket commentators in the press box.* • A **press conference** is a meeting at which a person or organization makes a public statement and reporters can ask questions. • A **press cutting** is a piece cut out of a newspaper: *She kept a scrapbook of press cuttings about the anti-airport campaign.* • The **press gallery**, esp. in a parliament or other place where laws are made, is the upper part of a room where reporters sit to watch what is happening below. • A **press release** is a public statement given to the press to publish if they wish: *The concert promoters put out a press release two weeks before the event, with details of the charities to which they would donate their profits.* • A **press secretary** works for a political leader or organization and makes statements to the press or answers questions for them. • Ⓕ Ⓢ

press [PUBLISHER] /pres/ *n* [C] a business which prints and produces books and similar items • *The family owns a small press which prints leaflets, posters, brochures and similar kinds of material.* • *This dictionary is published by Cambridge University Press.* • Ⓕ Ⓢ

press [PRINTING MACHINE] /pres/ *n* [C] a machine that is used for printing • *a printing press* • *The newspaper will* **go to press** (= start to be printed) *at midnight.* • *We can only* **hold the press** (= wait to start printing a newspaper or stop after starting printing) *for a really sensational news story.* • *My new book is (Br)* **in press**/*(Am)* **on press** (= being printed) *at the moment* • Ⓕ Ⓢ

press *obj* **on** *obj v prep* [T] to give (something) to someone and not allow them to refuse to accept it • *All the children had sweets and presents pressed on them by the visitors.*

press·ing /'pres·ɪŋ/ *adj* urgent or needing to be dealt with immediately • *a pressing social need* • *The fight against drugs is regarded as a pressing issue.* • *The most pressing question is what do we do next?*

pres·tige /pres'tiːdʒ/ *n* [U] respect and admiration given to someone or something, usually because of a reputation for high quality, success or social influence • *The school has immense prestige.* • *Many people are attracted by the prestige of working for a top company.*

pres·tige /pres'tiːdʒ/ *adj* [before n] • *A prestige hotel* (= an expensive and luxurious one) *is to be built outside the town.*

pres·tig·ious /pres'tɪdʒ·əs/ *adj* • *Her first novel won a prestigious* (= greatly respected) *literary prize.*

pre·stressed /ˌpriː'strest/ *adj* [not gradable] (esp. of concrete) made stronger by having tightly stretched wires put inside it

pre·sume *(obj)* [BELIEVE] /£prɪ'zjuːm, $-'zuːm/ *v* to believe (something) to be true because it is very likely, although you are not certain • *I presume* **(that)** *they're not coming, since they haven't replied to the invitation.* [+ (*that*) clause] • *You are Dr Smith, I presume?* [+ clause] • *"Are we walking to the hotel?" "I presume* **not/so.***"* [+ *not/so*] • *The boat's captain is missing, presumed* **dead** (= it is believed that he is dead). [T+ obj + adj/ usually passive] • *In British law, you are presumed innocent until you are proved guilty.* [T+ obj + adj/ usually passive] • *The universe is presumed* **to** *contain many other planets with some form of life.* [T+ obj + *to* infinitive] • *"Dr Livingstone, I presume?"* (Sir Henry Morton Stanley in *How I found Livingstone*, 1872)

pre·sum·a·bly /£prɪ'zjuː·mə·bli, $-'zuː-/ *adv* [not gradable] • You say presumably when you believe that something is very likely: *They can presumably afford to buy a bigger apartment.* ○ *Presumably you've heard the news?*

pre·sump·tion /prɪ'zʌmp·ʃᵊn/ *n* • *The presumption of innocence is central to British law.* [U] • *There is no scientific evidence to support such presumptions.* [C] • *The decision is based on the presumption* **that** *all information must be freely available.* [+ *that* clause]

pre·sume [BE RUDE] /£prɪ'zjuːm, $-'zuːm/ *v* [usually in negatives or questions] to do something although you know that you do not have a right to do it • *I don't wish to presume* (= make a suggestion although I have no right to), *but don't you think you should apologize to her?* [I] • *He presumes* **on** (= takes unfair advantage of) *her good nature by getting her to do all his washing for him.* [I] • *Could I presume* **on** *your time for a moment by asking you a few questions?* [I] • *I wouldn't presume* **to** *tell you how to do your job, but shouldn't this piece go there?* [+ *to* infinitive]

pre·sump·tuous /prɪ'zʌmp·ʃəs/ *adj* • A person who is presumptuous shows a lack of respect for others and does things they have no right to do: *It would be presumptuous of me to comment on the matter.*

pre·sump·tu·ous·ly /prɪ'zʌmp·ʃə·sli/ *adv*

pre·sump·tu·ous·ness /prɪ'zʌmp·ʃə·snəs/, *fml* **pre·sump·tion** *n* [U]

pre·sup·pose *(obj)* /£ˌpriː·sə'pəuz, $-'pouz/ *v* to think that (something) is true in advance without having any proof, or *(fml)* to have (something) as a necessary condition for being true or possible • *You're presupposing* **that** *he'll have told her – but he may not have.* [+ *that* clause] • *(fml) Investigative journalism presupposes some level of investigation.* [T] • *(fml) All this presupposes* **that** *he'll get the job he wants.* [+ *that* clause]

pre·sup·po·si·tion /ˌpriː·sʌp·ə'zɪʃ·ᵊn/ *n* • *Your actions are based on some false presuppositions* (= things that you think without knowing the truth). [C] • *This is all presupposition – we must wait until we have some hard evidence.* [U]

pre·tax /ˌpriː'tæks/ *adj* [not gradable] before tax is paid • *She predicts pretax* **earnings** *of over $13m for the company this year.* • *At least one of the newly privatized industries is expected to announce a huge pretax* **profit/loss** *for the last financial year.*

pre·tend /prɪ'tend/ *v* to behave as if something is true when you know that it is not, esp. in order to deceive people or as a game • *He pretended* **(that)** *he didn't mind, but I knew that he did.* [+ (*that*) clause] • *The children pretended* **(that)** *they were dinosaurs.* [+ (*that*) clause] • *She pretended* **to** *be interested, but I could see she wasn't.* [+ *to* infinitive] • *Let's not pretend any more – we both know what has to be done.* [I] • *(fml)* If you say you do **not** pretend to do something, you do not claim that you can do that thing: *I don't pretend* **to** *remember all the details.* [+ *to* infinitive] • Ⓡⓤⓢ

pre·tence, *Am usually* **pre·tense** /prɪ'tents/ *n* [U] • Pretence is a way of behaving that is intended to deceive people: *They kept up a pretence of normality as long as they could.* ○ *The army has given up any pretence of neutrality in the war.* • See also PRETENTIOUS.

pre·tend·ed /prɪ'ten·dɪd/ *adj* [before n] • *His pretended* (= false) *friendliness didn't fool me for long.*

pre·tend·er /£prɪ'ten·dəʳ, $-dɚ/ *n* [C] a person who claims to have a right to the high position that someone else has, although other people disagree with this • *The rebel forces are led by the pretender* **to** *the throne* (= person who wants to replace the present king or queen).

pre·ten·sion /prɪ'tent·ʃᵊn/ *n* [C usually pl] a claim or belief that you can succeed or that you are important or have serious value • *United's championship pretensions took a dent when they were beaten 5-1 by Liverpool.* • *The Chronicle has pretensions* **to** *being a serious newspaper.* • *He's an actor of modest pretensions, quite content to play small parts.*

pre·ten·ti·ous /prɪ'tent·ʃəs/ *adj disapproving* trying to give the appearance of great importance, esp. in matters of art and literature, in a way that is obviously false • *The novel deals with grand themes, but is never heavy or pretentious.* • *I don't like pretentious rock groups.* • *"Pretentious? Moi?"* (from the British television series *Fawlty Towers*, 1979)

pre·ten·tious·ly /prɪ'tent·ʃə·sli/ *adv disapproving*

pre·ten·tious·ness /prɪ'tent·ʃə·snəs/, **pre·ten·sion** *n* [U] *disapproving* • *I'm sick of his pompousness and pretentiousness.* • *These students have a healthy suspicion of art college pretension.*

pre·ter·nat·u·ral /£ˌpriː·tə'nætʃ·ᵊr·ᵊl, $-t̬ɚ'nætʃ·ɚ-/ *adj fml* more than is usual or natural • *Anger gave me preternatural strength, and I managed to force the door open.*

pre·ter·nat·u·ral·ly /£ˌpriː·tə'nætʃ·ᵊr·ᵊl·i, $-t̬ɚ'nætʃ·ɚ-/ *adv fml* • *The house seemed preternaturally silent.*

pre·text /'priː·tekst/ *n* [C] a pretended reason for doing something that is used to hide the real reason • *The border dispute was used as a pretext* **for** *military intervention.* • **On** *the pretext* **of** *asking to use the phone, she forced her way into my house.* • *Expelling their representatives gave the Americans a pretext* **to** *call off the talks.* [+ *to* infinitive]

pret·ty [PLEASANT] /£'prɪt·i, $'prɪt̬-/ *adj* **-ier, -iest** pleasant to look at, or (esp. of girls or women or things connected with them) attractive or charming in a delicate way • *That's a pretty hat you're wearing.* • *The sofa was covered in very pretty flowery material.* • *She isn't what you'd call pretty, but she's very attractive.* • *(dated)* You can use pretty in particular expressions to refer to something bad: *It's a pretty* **state of affairs** *when you have no privacy in your own home.* • *The average crowd of tourists is* **not a pretty sight** (= is very unpleasant to look at). • *Things are* **at** *or* **have reached/come to a pretty pass** (= the situation is very bad) *when a referee can no longer be trusted.* • *That coat must have cost you/You must have paid* **a pretty penny** (= a lot of money).

pret·ti·ly /£'prɪt·ɪ·li, $'prɪt̬-/ *adv* • *The menus are printed on prettily illustrated cards.*

pret·ti·ness /£'prɪt·ɪ·nəs, $'prɪt̬-/ *n* [U] • *Her designs are never pretty for the sake of prettiness.*

pret·ty [TO A LARGE DEGREE] /£'prɪt·i, $'prɪt̬-/ *adv* [not gradable] *infml* (used to give emphasis) to a large degree • *The house has four bedrooms so it's pretty big.* • *I'm pretty sure I recognized her voice.* • *I've got a pretty good idea of what's going on.* • *(infml)* You say pretty **much/nearly/**

well to mean almost completely: *I've pretty nearly finished packing now.* ○ *She knows pretty well everything there is to know on the subject.*

pret·zel /ˈpret·sᵊl, -zᵊl/ *n* [C] a hard, salty biscuit that has been baked esp. in stick or knot shapes

pre·vail /prɪˈveɪl/ *v* [I] to exist and be accepted among a large number of people, or to get a position of control and influence ● *This is a strange custom that still prevails.* ● *I am sure that common sense will prevail in the end.* ● *Did greed prevail* **over** (= become a more powerful influence than) *generosity?*

pre·vail·ing /prɪˈveɪ·lɪŋ/ *adj* [not gradable] ● Prevailing means existing in a particular place or at a particular time: *The prevailing* **mood** *is one of optimism.* ○ *We will have to look at the offer in the light of prevailing* **circumstances.** ○ *Under prevailing law, the government cannot annul such marriages.* ● A prevailing **wind** is one that usually blows in a particular place: *The town is kept cool by the prevailing westerly winds.*

prev·a·lent /ˈprev·ᵊl·ənt/ *adj* existing very commonly or happening frequently ● *These diseases are more prevalent among young children.* ● *Trees are dying in areas where acid rain is most prevalent.*

prev·a·lence /ˈprev·ᵊl·ənts/ *n* [U] ● *The prevalence of drugs in the inner cities is alarming.*

pre·var·i·cate /£prɪˈvær·ɪ·keɪt, $-ˈver-/ *v* [I] *fml* to avoid telling the truth, making a decision or saying what you think ● *I'm never one to make a decision when I can procrastinate, fudge and prevaricate.* ● *Jane is prevaricating* **over** *whether to buy a new house.*

pre·var·i·ca·tion /£prɪˌvær·ɪˈkeɪ·ʃᵊn, $-ˌver-/ *n* [U] *fml* ● *All my attempts to question the authorities on the subject were met by evasion and prevarication.*

pre·vent *obj* /prɪˈvent/ *v* [T] to stop (something) happening or (someone) doing something ● *Label your suitcases to prevent confusion.* ● *His disability prevents him* **from** *walking.* ● *(Br) Are you trying to prevent me speaking?* [+ obj + v-*ing*] ● ⓘ Ⓟ

pre·vent·a·ble /£prɪˈven·tə·bl̩, $-t̬ə-/ *adj* ● *Many doctors believe that cigarette smoking is the most preventable cause of heart attacks.*

pre·ven·tion /prɪˈvent·ʃᵊn/ *n* [U] ● *The organization is committed to AIDS prevention and education.* ● *(Br saying)* 'Prevention is better than cure' (*Am* 'An ounce of prevention is worth a pound of cure') means that it is better to do something early so that something bad does not happen, rather than try to make it better after it has happened.

pre·ven·tive /£prɪˈven·tɪv, $-t̬ɪv/, **pre·ven·ta·tive** /£prɪˈven·tə·tɪv, $-t̬ɪv/ *adj* [not gradable] ● Preventive actions are intended to stop something before it happens: *In the past 10 years, preventive* **measures** *have reduced levels of tooth decay in children.* ○ *In an ideal world, preventive* **medicine** *would banish premature death.*

pre·view /ˈpriː·vjuː/ *n* [C] an opportunity to see something such as a film or a collection of works of art before it is shown to the public, or a description of something such as a television programme before it is shown to the public

pre·view *(obj)* /ˈpriː·vjuː/ *v* ● *Miller's new play is previewing* (= being performed publicly before it officially opens) *at the Theatre Royal tomorrow.* [I] ● *On page 11, Sally Gaines previews next week's films on TV.* [T]

pre·vi·ous /ˈpriː·vi·əs/ *adj* [before n; not gradable] happening or existing before the one mentioned ● *The previous owner of the house had built an extension on the back.* ● *Training is provided, so no previous experience is required for the job.* ● *That summer she stayed at home, but the previous two summers she had worked abroad.*

pre·vi·ous·ly /ˈpriː·vi·ə·sli/ *adv* [not gradable] ● *She was previously employed as a tour guide.* ● *I had posted the card two months previously.*

pre·war /£ˌpriːˈwɔːʳ, $-ˈwɔːr/ *adj* [not gradable] happening before a war, esp. the Second World War ● *Prewar styles are coming back into fashion.* ● Compare POSTWAR.

prey /preɪ/ *n* [U] a creature that is hunted and killed for food by another animal ● *A hawk hovered in the air before swooping on its prey.* ● If someone or something is prey **to** someone or something unpleasant, they can be harmed by that person or thing: *Small children are prey to all sorts of fears.* ● *Empty houses are prey to squatters and drug-addicts.* ● A person who is **easy** prey is very likely to be approached by someone with bad intentions: *Homeless young people are easy prey for drug-dealers and pimps.* ● If a person **falls** prey **to** someone or something, they receive bad treatment by that person or thing: *Her elderly aunt had fallen prey to a dishonest salesman.*

prey on *obj* /preɪ/ *v prep* [T] ● *The spider preys on* (= kills and eats) *small flies and other insects.* ● If a problem preys on your **mind**, you think about it and worry about it a lot: *The argument we'd had preyed on my mind all day.*

prez·zie /ˈprez·i/ *n* [C] *Br and Aus infml for* PRESENT [SOMETHING GIVEN]

price /praɪs/ *n* [C] the amount of money for which something is sold ● *The price of oil has risen sharply.* ● *House prices have been falling.* ● *What price are apples this week?* ● *We thought they were asking a very* **high/low** *price.* ● *The large supermarkets are offering big price cuts.* ● If you want something **at any price**, you are willing to do anything in order to get it: *We want peace at any price.* ● If you say that you would not do something **at any price**, you mean that you would never do it: *I wouldn't invite her to dinner again at any price.* ● If you can buy or obtain something **at/for a price**, you either have to pay a lot of money or be involved in something unpleasant in order to get it: *You can buy the best of gourmet cuisine here, for a price.* ○ *Forged passports are available, at a price.* ○ *He gained the most powerful position in the company, though many say at a price.* ● If you **pay a price** for something you do or give something in order to get what you want: *This is the price we must pay for a free press.* ○ *Politicians will pay a heavy price* (= will suffer disadvantages) *if they do not listen to the people.* ○ *This sacrifice is a small price to pay.* ● **What price** something means how much do you want it and what are you prepared to do to obtain it: *What price fame?* ● *Shoppers have become very* **price-conscious** *– they compare the prices of two similar products and buy the cheaper one.* ● *The market for these vehicles is* **price-sensitive** *– buyers look for the best deal they can get, comparing prices rather than performance figures.* ● A **price sticker** is a small piece of paper with a price on it which is stuck onto a product. ● The **price tag/ticket** is a piece of paper with a price on which is fixed to a product, or the amount that something costs: *How much is it? – I can't find the price tag.* ○ *These suits have designer names and a price tag to match.* ○ *The price tag for the building project will be around $50 million.* ● *"What Price Glory?"* (title of a play by Maxwell Anderson and Lawrence Stallings, 1924) ● Ⓝⓛ

price *obj* /praɪs/ *v* [T] ● If something is priced **at** a particular amount of money, it costs that much to buy it: *The car is priced at £28 000.* ● *There is a lack of reasonably priced housing for rent.* ● *Could you price* (= put a sign with a price on) *the goods on that shelf next, please.* ● To price something is also to discover how much it costs: *We went around all the travel agents pricing the different tours.* ● To **price out of the market** is to charge so much for a product that no one wants to buy it: *In their desire for large profits they were pricing* **themselves** *out of the market.* ○ *The company has been priced out of the market.*

price·less /ˈpraɪ·sləs/ *adj* ● A priceless object is one that has such a high value, esp. because it is rare, that the price of it cannot be calculated: *A priceless collection of vases was destroyed.* ○ *Her knowledge and experience would make her a priceless asset to the team.*

pric·ey /ˈpraɪ·si/ *adj* **pricier, priciest** *infml* ● *A car like that is too pricey* (= expensive) *for me.* ● [LP]› **Expensive**

prick *obj* [MAKE HOLES] /prɪk/ *v* [T] to make a very small hole or holes in the surface of (something), sometimes in a way which causes pain, or to cause a sudden pain ● *Prick the skin of the potatoes with a fork before baking them.* ● *I accidentally pricked my finger with a needle and it bled.* ● *Watch out for thorns on the roses, they might prick you.* ● *She pricked the balloon with a pin and it burst with a loud bang.* ● *(fig.) They had three extraordinarily successful years and then the recession* **pricked the balloon/bubble** (= spoilt a good situation). ● If something **pricks** your **conscience**, you regret something you have or have not done, or you are caused to do something: *The phone call pricked his conscience – he remembered he had agreed to buy the books but had forgotten all about it.* ○ *This film about the famine pricked our consciences and we decided to send a donation.* ● *"By the pricking of my thumbs,/ Something wicked this way comes"* (Shakespeare, Macbeth 4.1)

prick [BODY PART] /prɪk/ *n* [C] *taboo slang* a penis ● To **prick-tease** (also **cock-tease**) is to behave in a way that causes a lot of sexual interest in a man, and then to refuse to have sex. ● A **prick-teaser** (also **cock-teaser**) is a woman whose behaviour or appearance causes a lot of sexual interest in men but who is not willing to have sex.

prick MAN /prɪk/ *n* [C] *taboo slang* a stupid man, esp. one who pretends to be more clever than he is • *He felt such a prick when she found out he'd been lying.*

prick up *(obj)*, **prick** *(obj)* **up** *v adv* (of an animal) to cause (its ears) to stand up straight because it is listening attentively to something • *The dog pricked its ears up/pricked up its ears when it heard someone at the door.* [M] • *The deer's ears pricked up – it must have heard me.* [I] • A person who pricks up his or her **ears**, or whose ears prick up, suddenly begins to listen very attentively because he or she has heard something interesting: *I pricked up my ears when I overheard them mention my name.* [M]

pri·ckle /ˈprɪk·l̩/ *n* [C] a thin sharp point that sticks out of a plant or animal • *The fruit can be eaten once the prickles have been removed.* • If you feel a prickle on your skin, you feel as if lots of little points are sticking into your body: *I felt a hot prickle of embarrassment spread across my cheeks.*

pri·ckle *(obj)* /ˈprɪk·l̩/ *v* • *Turner started to be worried and felt the back of his neck prickle.* [I] • *She lay on the grass and the stiff dry grass prickled the back of her legs.* [T] • *This sweater is prickling me.* [T]

pri·ckly /ˈprɪk·l̩.i, ˈ-li/ *adj* **-ier, -iest** • *Chestnuts had burst out of their green prickly husks.* • *This cloth is very prickly* (=it makes the skin sore). • *(infml)* A prickly person is someone who becomes angry easily and often: *He becomes prickly and defensive when you ask him about his work.* • **Prickly heat** is a **heat rash**. See at HEAT TEMPERATURE. • A **prickly pear** is a type of CACTUS that has oval edible fruit with prickles on them.

pride SATISFACTION /praɪd/ *n* [U] a feeling of pleasure and satisfaction that you get because you or people connected with you have done or possess something good • *He felt great pride when his youngest daughter won first prize.* • *They feel a sense of pride and relief that the bank was sold for a profit and the problems are finally over.* • If you **take** pride **in** something or someone, you feel very pleased about it or them: *If you don't take professional pride in your work, you're probably in the wrong job.* • *This village is* **the** *pride* **of** *East Sussex* (=people there are very proud of it). • *Her baby son is her pride* **and joy** (=what she is most pleased about). • If something **has/takes pride of place**, it has the most important position in a group of things: *A portrait of the earl takes pride of place in the entrance hall.* • See also PROUD SATISFIED.

pride RESPECT FOR YOURSELF /praɪd/ *n* [U] your feelings of your own worth and respect for yourself • *She has too much pride to accept any help.* • *The country's national pride has been damaged by its sporting failures.* • *"Pride and Prejudice"* (title of a book by Jane Austen, 1813)

pride *obj* /praɪd/ *v* [T] • If you pride **yourself** you value a skill or good quality that you have: *He prides himself* **on** *his loyalty to his friends.* ○ *I pride myself* **(that)** *I've never had a day's illness in my life.* [+ obj + (*that*) clause] • LP> **Reflexive pronouns and verbs**

pride FEELING OF IMPORTANCE /praɪd/ *n* [U] *disapproving* the belief that you are better or more important than other people • *He was motivated by the ordinary human passions of ambition, pride, and greed.* • *It's a tale of paternal passion and* **humbled** *pride.* • *(saying)* 'Pride comes/goes before a fall' means that if you have too high an opinion of yourself, something bad will happen to you as a result. • See also PROUD FEELING IMPORTANT.

pride GROUP /praɪd/ *n* [C] a group of lions

priest /priːst/ *n* [C] a person, usually a man, who has been trained to perform religious duties in the Christian Church, esp. the Roman Catholic Church, or a person with particular duties in some other religions • *Father O'Dooley was ordained a priest in 1949.* • *Many in the Anglican Church are still opposed to women priests.* • *"Will no one rid me of this turbulent priest?"* (remark believed to have been made by King Henry II, and which led to the assassination of St Thomas a Becket, 1139-89)

pries·tess /ˌpriːˈstes, ˈ--/ *n* [C] • A priestess is a woman in particular non-Christian religions who performs religious duties.

priest·hood /ˈpriːst·hʊd/ *n* [U] • *He left the priesthood* (=the position of being a priest) *and got married.*

priest·ly /ˈpriːst·li/ *adj* • *The Brahmans are the Hindu priestly caste.*

prig /prɪg/ *n* [C] *disapproving* a person who obeys the rules of correct behaviour and considers himself or herself to be better than other people

prig·gish /ˈprɪg·ɪʃ/ *adj disapproving* • A priggish person is annoying because they behave as if they are morally better than others: *He is a priggish, domineering man.*

prim /prɪm/ *adj* **primmer, primmest** *disapproving* very formal and correct in behaviour and easily shocked by anything rude • *She's much too prim* **and proper** *to go into a pub.* • KOR

prim·ly /ˈprɪm·li/ *adv* • *She pursed her lips primly.* • *A primly dressed young woman ran up to the car.* • *Morris primly brushed off the seat of the chair before he sat down.*

pri·ma bal·le·ri·na /£ˌpriː·mə·bæl·əˈriː·nə, $-ə˞ˈiː-/ *n* [C] the most important female dancer in a BALLET company

pri·ma·cy /ˈpraɪ·mə·si/ *n* [U] *fml* the state of being the most important thing • *The government insists on the primacy of citizens' rights.*

pri·ma don·na /£ˌpriː·məˈdɒn·ə, $-ˈdɑː·nə/ *n* [C] the most important female singer in an opera company, or *(disapproving)* a person who is difficult to please and whose moods change quickly • *(disapproving) He was behaving like a prima donna, complaining that his champagne was not cold enough.*

pri·ma don·na–ish /£ˌpriː·məˈdɒn·ə·ɪʃ, $-ˈdɑː·nə-/ *adj disapproving* • *prima donna-ish behaviour*

pri·mae·val /ˌpraɪˈmiː·vəl/ *adj* See PRIMEVAL

pri·ma fa·cie /ˌpraɪ·məˈfeɪ·ʃi/ *adj* [before n; not gradable] *fml or law* at first sight (=based on what seems to be the truth when first seen or heard) • *There is prima facie* **evidence** *that he was involved in the fraud.* • *For millions of Americans witnessing the event it was a prima facie* **case** *of police brutality.* • *The prosperous have a moral obligation to assist those who live in poverty and there is a prima facie* **case** *for a transfer of resources from rich countries to poor.*

pri·mal /ˈpraɪ·məl/ *adj* [not gradable] of the earliest time in the existence of a person or thing • *The universe evolved from a densely packed primal inferno.* • *The psychoanalyst encouraged him to relive his primal experiences.*

pri·ma·ry MOST IMPORTANT /£ˈpraɪ·mə·ri, $-mə˞-/ *adj* [not gradable] more important than anything else; main • *The Red Cross's primary concern is to preserve and protect human life.* • *The primary responsibility lies with those who break the law.* • A **primary colour** is one of the three colours red, yellow or blue that can be mixed together in different ways to make any other colour.

pri·mar·i·ly /praɪˈmer·ɪ·li/ *adv* [not gradable] • *We're primarily* (=mainly) *concerned with keeping expenditure down.* • *Soccer is primarily a winter game.*

pri·ma·ry EDUCATION /£ˈpraɪ·mə·ri, $-mə˞·i/ *adj* [before n; not gradable] (in Britain and Australia) of or for the teaching of young children, esp. those between five and eleven years old • *primary education* • *a primary school* • *a primary teacher* • LP> **Schools and colleges**

pri·ma·ry ELECTION /£ˈpraɪ·mə·ri, $-mə˞·i/ *n* [C] (in the United States) an election in which people who belong to a political party choose who will represent that party in an election for political office • *The campaign staff is focussing on the larger state primaries in order to have enough votes to win the nomination.*

pri·mate ANIMAL /ˈpraɪ·meɪt, -mət/ *n* [C] *specialized* a member of the most developed and intelligent group of mammals, including humans, monkeys and APES • *These small but colourful primates are found in the jungles of eastern Brazil.*

pri·mate PRIEST /ˈpraɪ·meɪt, -mət/ *n* [C] *specialized* a priest with the highest position in his country • *He was made the Roman Catholic Primate of All Ireland last year.*

prime MAIN /praɪm/ *adj* [before n; not gradable] most important, or of the very best quality • *Getting on the Olympic team became her prime objective.* • *This town is a prime example of combining old architecture with new.* • *Kelly is our prime suspect.* • *The president is a prime* (=likely) *target for the assassin's bullet.* • *This area of prime land is for sale at a bargain price.* • A **prime minister** (*abbreviation* **PM**) is the leader of the government in some countries. • A person or thing that is the **prime mover** in a situation has a great influence in getting something started: *He was a prime mover* **in** *the campaign to start a theatre in the town.* • *(specialized)* A **prime number** is a number that cannot be divided by any other number except itself and the number 1: *2, 3 and 7 are prime numbers.* • In television and radio broadcasting, **prime time** is the time when the highest number of people are watching or listening: *The interview will be broadcast during prime time, at seven o'clock in the evening.*

prime BEST /praɪm/ *n* [U] the stage in the life or development of esp. a person when they are in the best possible condition, most successful and most powerful • *This is a dancer* **in** *her prime.* • *Middle age can be the prime* **of life** *if you have the right attitude.* • *"The Prime of Miss Jean Brodie"* (title of a book by Muriel Spark, 1961)

prime *obj* PREPARE /praɪm/ *v* [T] to prepare (something) so that it is ready for the next stage in a process • To prime wood is to cover its surface with a special paint before the main paint is put on: *The wooden kitchen units are either primed or fully painted before delivery.* • To prime a bomb or gun is to make it ready to explode or fire: *The incendiary bomb discovered yesterday had not been primed.* • If you prime a person, you give them information about something before it happens: *The board have been carefully primed before answering questions from the public.* • *The body's immune system has cells that are primed* **to** *attack 'foreign' diseased cells.* [+ obj + *to* infinitive]

pri·mer /£'praɪ·məʳ, $-mɚ/ *n* • Primer is a type of paint that you put on a wooden surface before putting on the main paint: *He recommended we should use aluminium primer on bare wood.* [U] ○ *It's best to use a* **coat of** *primer before the top coat.* [U] • *(dated)* A primer is also a small book containing basic facts about a subject, used esp. when you are beginning to learn about that subject: *This little book could be useful as an examination primer.* [C]

pri·me·val, *esp. Br* **pri·mae·val** /praɪ'miː·vəl/ *adj* ancient; existing at or from a very early time • *These were the primeval nebulae from which planets formed.* • *We cycled through primeval forests.*

pri·mi·tive /£'prɪm·ɪ·tɪv, $-t̬ɪv/ *adj* of or typical of a very early stage in the development of a society or the world; simple and not SOPHISTICATED • *Primitive races colonized these islands 2000 years ago.* • *The spiny anteater is a mammal, although a very primitive one.* • *Even today the villagers live in a primitive one-crop economy.* • *(disapproving)* Living conditions that are primitive are basic, unpleasant and uncomfortable: *People are living in tents, without running water and in primitive conditions.*

prim·ly /'prɪm·li/ *adv* See at PRIM

pri·mo·gen·i·ture /£ˌpraɪ·məʊ'dʒen·ɪ·tʃəʳ, $-moʊ'dʒen·ɪ·tʃɚ/ *n* [U] *specialized* the custom by which all of a family's property goes to the oldest son when the father dies

pri·mor·di·al /£praɪ'mɔː·di·əl, $-'mɔːr-/ *adj fml* existing at or since the beginning of the world or the universe, • *The planet Jupiter contains large amounts of the primordial gas and dust out of which the solar system was formed.* • *The trip took us through ancient, primordial rain forest.* • Primordial can also mean basic and connected with an early stage of development: *As she sensed danger, she was overcome with primordial feelings of panic and terror.*

prim·rose /£'prɪm·rəʊz, $-roʊz/ *n* [C] a wild plant with pale yellow flowers • PIC> **Flowers and plants**

pri·mu·la /'prɪm·jʊ·lə/ *n* [C] *specialized* any of a group of wild plants with white, yellow, pink or purple flowers • *The primrose and the cowslip are both types of primula.*

pri·mus (stove) /'praɪ·məs/ *n* [C] *trademark* a small cooker that burns PARAFFIN (= a liquid fuel) • *Primus stoves are often used by people to cook on when they are camping.*

prince /prɪnts/ *n* [C] an important male member of a royal family, esp. a son or grandson of the king or queen • *Prince Edward is Queen Elizabeth's youngest son.* • *Prince Juan Carlos of Spain became king in 1975.* • A prince is also a male ruler of a usually small country: *Prince Rainier is the ruling prince of Monaco.* • If a man is a prince of a particular activity, he is considered to be one of the best people at that activity: *Peter Carey has confirmed his position as a prince* **among** *Australian writers.* • In Britain, the **Prince of Wales** is the oldest son of the king and queen who will become king when they die. • *(infml esp. humorous) Some women seem to spend their lives waiting for a* **Prince Charming** (= a perfect husband or partner). • The husband of a ruling queen is sometimes given the title **Prince Consort**: *Albert, the husband of Queen Victoria, was given the title Prince Consort.* • *(literary)* The **Prince of Darkness** is a name for the Devil (= the main evil spirit in the Christian religion). • *"Some Day my Prince Will Come"* (song from the Walt Disney film *Snow White and the Seven Dwarfs*, 1937)

prin·ci·pal·i·ty /£ˌprɪnt·sɪ'pæl·ɪ·ti, $-ə·t̬i/ *n* [C] • A principality is a country ruled by a prince, or from which a prince takes his title: *Monaco is a principality.*

prince·ly /'prɪnts·li/ *adj fml approving* (esp. of money) very large in amount • *In 1969, they were paying him a princely income of $100 000.* • *(humorous) She acquired the painting at a jumble sale for the princely* (= very small) **sum** *of 25p.*

prin·cess /prɪn'ses, '--/ *n* [C] an important female member of a royal family, esp. a daughter or granddaughter of a king and queen, or the wife of a PRINCE • *Prince Rainier of Monaco has two daughters – Princess Caroline and Princess Stephanie.* • *Lady Diana Spencer became Princess Diana when she married Prince Charles.*

prin·ci·pal MAIN /'prɪnt·sɪ·pəl/ *adj* [before n; not gradable] first in order of importance • *Iraq's principal export is oil.* • *He was principal dancer at the Dance Theatre of Harlem.* • *The principal reason for moving was to find a house in a more peaceful neighbourhood.* • *(Br)* A **principal boy** is the most important male character in a PANTOMIME (= musical play for children), who is usually played by a woman. • (D) (RUS)

prin·ci·pal·ly /'prɪnt·sɪ·pli/ *adv* [not gradable] • Principally means more than anything or anyone else: *Opposition to the changes comes principally from the unions.* ○ *The advertising campaign is aimed principally at women.*

prin·ci·pal PERSON /'prɪnt·sɪ·pəl/ *n* [C] *Am or Aus* the person in charge of a school or college for children aged between approximately 11 and 18 • *If you talk any more in class, I'm sending you off to see the principal.* • (D) (RUS)

prin·ci·pal MONEY /'prɪnt·sɪ·pəl/ *n* [C usually sing] *specialized* an amount of money which someone has invested in a bank or lent to a person or organization so that they will receive INTEREST (= a percentage as profit) on it from the bank, person or organization • *She lives off the interest and tries to keep the principal intact.* • (D) (RUS)

prin·ci·ple BASIC IDEA /'prɪnt·sɪ·pl̩/ *n* [C] a basic idea or rule that explains or controls how something happens or works • *In the first year of your law course, you will study the principles of the criminal justice system.* • *The country is run* **on** *Socialist principles.* • *The machine works according to the principle* **of** *electromagnetic conduction.* • *The* **basic/guiding** *principle* **behind** *the new legislation is* **that** *the rights of the child come first.* [+ *that* clause] • *Working on a new project like this, you need to start from* **first** *principles* (= the simplest and most important truths). • If someone agrees to something **in principle**, they agree with the idea in general, although they may not be able to support it in reality: *In principle I agree that mothers and babies should be together as much as possible, but it's not always so simple in practice.* • If something is possible **in principle**, there is no good reason why it should not happen or be done.

prin·ci·ple MORAL RULE /'prɪnt·sɪ·pl̩/ *n approving* a moral rule or standard of good behaviour • *Jack doesn't have many principles or scruples.* [C] • *She's a woman* **of** *principle* (= a good honest woman). [U] • If you do something **as a matter of principle** or **on principle**, you do it because you believe it is right or the right to do: *I never gamble, as a matter of principle* (= because I believe it is wrong). ○ *She would never ask to borrow money, on principle.*

prin·ci·pled /'prɪnt·sɪ·pl̩d/ *adj fml* • If someone is principled, they behave in an honest and moral way: *He was not the most principled of men, and saw nothing wrong in selling the company the information they wanted.* • Principled behaviour is behaviour based on moral rules which you try to follow: *The Church is taking a principled stand against the conflict.*

print TEXT /prɪnt/ *n* [U] letters, numbers, words or symbols that have been produced on paper by a machine using ink • *The title is in bold print.* • *This novel is available in large print for readers with poor eyesight.* • *The book was rushed* **into** *print* (= was produced and published) *as quickly as possible.* • *The print quality* (= The quality of the text produced) *of the new laser printer is excellent.* • Print also refers to newspapers and magazines: *The debate is still raging, both* **in** *print and on the radio and television.* ○ *She worked in print journalism for a couple of years before joining CBS as a TV broadcaster.* • If a book is **in print/out of print**, it is or is not possible to buy a new copy of it: *"Is 'A Farewell to Arms' still in print?" "Oh yes, classic literature like that will never* **go out of** *print."* • **Print-out** is text produced by a computer printer: *There were pages of* **computer** *print-out all over the desk.* ○ *Would you get me a* *print- out of that document?* • The **print run** of a book is the number of copies produced by the publisher: *This book will have a print run of 20 000.* • LP> **Symbols** (J)

print *(obj)* /prɪnt/ *v* • *The leaflets will be printed* **on** *recycled paper.* [T] • *My letter hasn't printed yet – is something wrong with the printer?* [I] • *We printed* **out** *all the names and addresses of the people in the society.* [M] • *Some newspapers still refuse to print* (= include in the text) *certain rude words.* [T] • To print a newspaper, magazine or book is to produce it in large quantities: *20 000 copies of the novel will be printed in hardback.* [T]

print·a·ble /£'prɪn·tə·bl̩, $-t̬ə-/ *adj* [not gradable] • If something that you say is not printable, it is too rude or offensive to be included in a newspaper or magazine: *He let out a torrent of abuse, none of it printable in a respectable daily newspaper.*

print·ed /£'prɪn·tɪd, $-t̬ɪd/ *adj* [not gradable] • **The printed word** is information in the form of books, newspapers and magazines: *Children who watch TV all the time have no real interest in the printed word.* • *(specialized)* A **printed circuit (board)** is a set of electrical connections made by thin lines of metal fixed onto a surface. • *(specialized)* **Printed matter** is documents or books that can be sent by post at a special low cost.

print·er /£'prɪn·tə^r, $-t̬ɚ/ *n* [C] • A printer is a person whose job it is to print books, newspapers and magazines: *He has been a printer all his life.* • A printer is also a machine that is connected to a computer and prints onto paper using ink: *a bubble-jet/dot-matrix/laser printer* • PIC> **Office**

print·ing /£'prɪn·tɪŋ, $-t̬ɪŋ/ *n* • *She has written a book on the history of printing.* [U] • A printing is the number of copies of a book which the publishers have produced: *The publishers produced a first printing of 2500.* [C] • *She runs her own printing business.* • *Printing costs are estimated at $50 000.* • A **printing press** is a machine that prints books, newspapers or magazines: *The printing presses were in constant use.*

print PICTURE /prɪnt/ *n* [C] a photographic copy of a painting, or a picture made by pressing paper onto a special surface covered in ink, or a single photograph from a film • *I've got a lovely Matisse print on my bedroom wall.* • *A signed print* **of** *Hockney's would cost you thousands of pounds.* • *When you have a film developed, do you get prints or slides?* • *I would like a second set of prints of this film, please.* • (J)

print *obj* /prɪnt/ *v* [T] • *Photographs are better if they are printed* **from** *the original negative.*

print PATTERN /prɪnt/ *n* [C] any type of pattern produced using ink on a piece of clothing • *This style of dress comes in a floral or a paisley print.* • (J)

print *obj* /prɪnt/ *v* [T] • *The design has been printed onto the fabric by hand.*

print *(obj)* WRITE /prɪnt/ *v* to write without joining the letters together • *Children are often taught to print before they learn joined-up writing.* [I] • *Please print your name clearly below your signature.* [T] • (J)

print FINGER /prɪnt/ *n* [C] *infml for* FINGERPRINT • *The burglar had left his prints all over the window.* • (J)

print·wheel /'prɪnt·wiːl/ *n* [C] a DAISYWHEEL

pri·or EARLIER /£praɪə^r, $praɪr/ *adj, adv slightly fml* earlier than or before something else, or earlier than or before a particular time • *She has denied prior knowledge of the meeting.* • *They had to refuse the dinner invitation because of a prior* **engagement** (= something already planned for that time). • *He had showed no signs of being in pain prior* **to** (= before) *suffering a heart attack and collapsing.* • See also **prior** at PRIORY.

pri·or MORE IMPORTANT /£praɪə^r, $praɪr/ *adj* [before n; not gradable] *fml* more important • *Mothers with young children have a prior* **claim** *on funds.* • See also **prior** at PRIORY.

pri·or·i·ty /£praɪ'ɒr·ɪ·ti, $-'ɔːr·ə·t̬i/ *n* something that must be dealt with as soon as possible and before other less important things • *The management did not seem to consider office safety to be a priority.* [C] • *My* **first/top** *priority is to find somewhere to live.* [C] • *You have to learn to* **get** *your priorities* **right/straight** (= decide which are the most important jobs or problems and deal with them first). [C] • *Mending the lights is a priority task* (= more important than other jobs). • *Banks normally* **give** *priority* **to** *large businesses when deciding on loans* (= They deal with large businesses first and give them preferential treatment). [U] • *Official business requirements obviously* **take/have** *priority* **over** *personal requests* (= Official business matters will be dealt with first and given preferential treatment). [U]

pri·or·i·tize *(obj), Br and Aus usually* **-ise** /£praɪ'ɒr·ɪ·taɪz, $-'ɔːr·ə-/ *v* • To prioritize a list of things to be done is to put them into order of importance so that the most important ones are done first: *When you have twenty tasks for the day, all of them urgent, it's not easy to prioritize them.* [T] ○ *You must learn how to prioritize.* [I]

pri·o·ry /£'praɪə·ri, $praɪr·i/ *n* [C] a building where MONKS (= religious men) or NUNS (= religious women) live, work and pray • *A priory is similar to but smaller and less important than an abbey.*

pri·or /£praɪə^r, $praɪr/, *female* **pri·or·ess** /£'praɪə·rəs, $'praɪr·əs/ *n* [C] • A prior is the person in charge of a priory or the person who is second in charge of an ABBEY. • See also PRIOR EARLIER; PRIOR MORE IMPORTANT.

prise *obj* /praɪz/ *v* [T] *Br and Aus for* PRIZE LIFT

pri·sm /'prɪz·ᵊm/ *n* [C] a transparent glass or plastic object which separates white light that passes through it into different colours • *In a prism, you can see all the colours of the rainbow.*

pri·son /'prɪz·ᵊn/ *n* a building where criminals are forced to live as a punishment • *Conditions in the prison are said to be appalling.* [C] • *It was a* **maximum-security** *prison* (= intended to be especially difficult to escape from). [C] • *It was somehow obvious that he had spent time* **in** *prison.* [U] • *She* **went to/was sent to** *prison for six months.* [U] • *He was given a long prison* **sentence** *for robbing a bank.* • *Prison* **warders** *have threatened to go on strike.* • Prison also refers to the time that someone spends inside a prison as a punishment: *Prison hadn't changed him at all.* [U] • A prison is also a situation or relationship from which it is difficult to escape: *She felt that her marriage had become a prison.* [C] • A **prison camp** is a place where people, usually prisoners of war or political prisoners, are forced to stay: *He was captured by enemy forces and sent to a prison camp for the rest of the war.* • LP> **Crimes and criminals**

pri·son·er /£'prɪz·ᵊn·ə^r, $-ɚ/ *n* [C] • A prisoner is a person who is kept in prison as a punishment: *Prisoners climbed onto the prison roof to protest at the awful conditions inside the prison.* ○ *Civil rights groups are demanding the release of all* **political** *prisoners* (= people who are kept in prison because their political beliefs are different from those of the government). • If someone is **taken prisoner**, they are caught by enemy forces: *Of 10 000 troops, 7000 were killed, wounded or taken prisoner.* • If someone is **held/kept prisoner**, they are caught and guarded so that they cannot escape: *The pilot and several passengers were held prisoner by the gunmen for 57 hours.* • If someone is a prisoner **of** a situation, their possible choices of action and the ways in which they can improve the situation are very limited: *The Minister for Trade and Industry is just as much a prisoner of the situation as the union leaders.* • A **prisoner of conscience** is someone kept in prison because their political or religious beliefs are different from those of the government. • A **prisoner of war** (*abbreviation* **POW**) is a member of the armed forces who has been caught by enemy forces during a war.

pris·sy /'prɪs·i/ *adj* **-ier, -iest** *disapproving* (of a person) always behaving and dressing in a way that is considered correct and that does not shock • *She is a very prim and prissy woman.* • *I know it sounds prissy, but I do wish you wouldn't wear such short skirts.*

pris·si·ly /'prɪs·ɪ·li/ *adv disapproving*

pris·tine /£'prɪs·tiːn, $prɪ'stiːn/ *adj fml approving* new or almost new, and in very good condition • *They moved into a pristine new office which had brand new furniture and polished floors.* • *Washing machine for sale – only 2 months old and in pristine condition.*

pri·vate PERSONAL /'praɪ·vət/ *adj* for the use of or belonging to one particular person or group, not to other people • *She has a small office which is used for private discussions.* • *I caught him looking through my private papers.* • *The sign on the gate said 'Private* **Property** *– No Admittance.'* • *I have something to say to Miranda and I'm afraid it's private* (= secret) *– so could you leave us alone for a minute?* • Private activities are ones which involve personal matters or relationships and are not connected with your work: *The President has refused to talk about his private* **life**, *especially the rumour that he and his wife are getting divorced.* • Your private thoughts and opinions are ones which are secret and which you do not discuss with other people: *Although I support the project in public, my* *private opinion is that it will fail.* • A private place is a place where you are alone: *He looked for somewhere private where he could think in peace.* • A private person is someone who does not like to talk about their personal feelings and thoughts and who enjoys being alone: *Shaun is a very private sort of person.* • If you talk to someone or do something **in private**, you do it without other people being present because the subject or activity is something you do not want other people to know about: *I knocked on the door and asked if I could talk to her in private.* • **Private parts** (*infml* **privates**) is a polite way to avoid saying sexual organs: *He grabbed a towel to cover his private parts.* • Ⓘ Ⓟ

pri·vate·ly /ˈpraɪ·vət·li/ *adv* • *She spoke privately* (= without other people present) *with the Director and told him the true facts of the case.* • *Despite his public support, privately* (= secretly) *he was worried.*

pri·va·cy /£ˈprɪv·ə·si, $ˈpraɪ·və-/ *n* [U] • *The new law is designed to protect people's privacy* (= their right to keep their personal matters and relationships secret). • Privacy is the state of being alone: *I needed some privacy* (= I needed to be alone) *to read the letter properly and understand it.*

pri·vate NOT OFFICIAL /ˈpraɪ·vət/ *adj* [not gradable] not connected with, controlled by or paid for by the government • *Going to a private doctor is going to cost you a lot of money.* • *Banks should be supporting small private businesses.* • *The President attended the funeral as a private citizen* (= not as an official duty). • *The paintings were gathered from museums and private* **collections** (= collections of works of art owned by ordinary people). • *The finance for the project will come mainly from the government but also from* **the private sector** (= private businesses). • A **private detective** (also **private investigator**, *infml* **private eye**, *Am infml* **gumshoe** or **dick**) is a person whose job it is to discover information about people. A private detective is not a government employee or a police officer: *She* **hired** *a private detective to follow her husband and find out where he was going.* • **Private enterprise** is industry and businesses owned by ordinary people, not by the government. • *(esp. Br)* If someone has a **private income** or **private means** (*Am usually* **independent means**), they have money from their family, or from investments, property or land, rather than from a job. • A **private school** is a school which does not receive financial support from the government: *People who send their children to private schools must pay fees.* • LP **Schools and colleges** Ⓘ Ⓟ

pri·vate·ly /ˈpraɪ·vət·li/ *adv* [not gradable] • *Privately-owned businesses are often more efficient than state-owned ones.*

pri·va·tize *obj, Br and Aus usually* **-ise** /ˈpraɪ·və·taɪz/ *v* [T] • If a government privatizes an industry, company or service that it owns and controls, it sells it so that it becomes privately owned and controlled: *I bought shares in British Gas when it was privatized.*

pri·va·tiz·a·tion, *Br and Aus usually* **-i·sa·tion** /£ˌpraɪ·vɪ·taɪˈzeɪ·ʃən, $-t̬ɪ-/ *n* [U] • *The last few years have seen the privatization of many industries previously owned by the state.*

pri·vate SOLDIER /ˈpraɪ·vət/ *n* [C] a soldier of the lowest rank in an army • Ⓘ Ⓟ

pri·va·tion /praɪˈveɪ·ʃən/ *n fml* a lack of the basic things that are necessary for an acceptable standard of living • *Economic privation is pushing the poor towards crime.* [U] • *Several villages* **suffered** *serious privations during their long isolation during the war.* [C]

pri·vet /ˈprɪv·ɪt/ *n* [U] an evergreen bush, which is often grown in gardens as a HEDGE • *A high privet hedge blocked the view from the ground-floor windows.*

pri·vi·lege /ˈprɪv·əl·ɪdʒ/ *n* a special advantage, opportunity or honour possessed by a particular person or group • *As a senior executive, you will* **enjoy** *certain privileges, such as free health insurance and the right to buy shares in the company.* [C] • *As a teenager, she felt that living in Manhattan was a privilege she was lucky to* **have**. [C] • *I had the privilege* **of** *interviewing Picasso in the 1960s.* [C] • *It would be a privilege* **to** *be taught by such a famous violinist.* [C + to infinitive] • *(humorous) We had a pretty awful dinner at the hotel and had to pay £40* **for** *the privilege.* [C] • *The children of the rich and powerful experience privilege from birth.* [U] • The official privilege possessed by people in authority allows them to do or say things that other people are not allowed to do: *She* **has/enjoys** *diplomatic privilege and so she cannot be prosecuted in the normal way.* [U]

pri·vi·leged /ˈprɪv·əl·ɪdʒd/ *adj* • *As an ambassador, she enjoys a very privileged status.* • *I have been privileged* **to** *work with the pioneers of silicon technology.* [+ to infinitive] • *We are privileged* **in having** *with us in tonight's show one of the world's greatest comedians, Mr. Les Dennis.* • *(specialized)* Information that is privileged is secret: *Any communication between doctors and their patients is privileged.*

priv·y AWARE /ˈprɪv·i/ *adj* [not gradable] **privy to** *fml* aware of or knowing about (something secret) • *Only top members of the Cabinet were privy to secret information about the safety of the nuclear industry.*

priv·y TOILET /ˈprɪv·i/ *old use* a toilet, esp. in a very small building in the garden of a house

Priv·y Council /ˌprɪv·i-/ *n* [C] (in Britain) a group of people of high rank in politics who sometimes advise the king or queen but who do not have much power

Priv·y Coun·cil·lor /ˌprɪv·i-/ *n* [C]

prize REWARD /praɪz/ *n* [C] something valuable, such as an amount of money, that is given to someone who succeeds in a competition or game or that is given to someone as a reward for doing very good work • *Did you* **win** *a prize in the raffle?* • *In the national lottery, the* **first** (= main) *prize is $1 000 000.* • *At school, I* **received** *several prizes* **for** *chemistry and physics.* • *The prize* **money** *for literary competitions can be as high as £20 000.* • A prize is also something which is considered important or which is difficult to achieve or obtain: *Three companies have been struggling to win the same prize – the TV franchise for the north-west.* • *He must* **take the prize for** (= He is responsible for) *the most boring speech this year.* • **There are no prizes for guessing** (= It is obvious) *who will be the next Prime Minister.* • See also NOBEL PRIZE. • Ⓝ

prize /praɪz/ *adj* [before n] • A prize animal, flower or vegetable is one that has won or deserves to win a prize in a competition because it is of very good quality: *a prize bull* • *a prize marrow* • *(infml slightly dated)* Prize also refers to something which is a very good example of something: *Which prize* **idiot** (= extremely foolish person) *forgot to lock the door?*

prize *obj* /praɪz/ *v* [T usually passive] • If something is prized, it is valued greatly: *The 1961 vintage is* **highly** *prized among wine connoisseurs.* • A prized possession is one that is very important to you: *Has she ever shown you her prized collection of antique clocks?*

prize *obj* LIFT, *Br and Aus also* **prise** /praɪz/ *v* [T] to move or lift (something) by pressing a tool against a fixed point • *I prized the lid* **off** *with a spoon.* [M] • *A thief had prized the window* **open** *with a jemmy.* [+ obj + adj] • *(fig.) He's so secretive – you'll have a hard time prizing* (= obtaining) *any information* **out of** *him.* • Ⓝ

prize·fight·er /£ˈpraɪzˌfaɪ·tər, $-t̬ɚ/ *n* [C] a boxer who fights to win money

prize·fight /ˈpraɪz·faɪt/ *n* [C] • A prizefight is a boxing competition in which people fight to win money.

prizewin·ning /ˈpraɪzˌwɪn·ɪŋ/ *adj* [before n; not gradable] that has won a prize • *There are some prizewinning films in the festival.* • *Gabriel Garcia Marquez is a Nobel-prizewinning novelist.*

pro- SUPPORT /£prəʊ-, $proʊ-/ *combining form* supporting or approving of something • *The population of Gibraltar is very pro-British.* • *Pro-democracy demonstrations took place in the capital this weekend.* • Compare ANTI-.

pro /£prəʊ, $proʊ/ *adj, prep* • *Are you pro or anti* (= Do you support or are you against) *the new bill?*

pro SPORTSPERSON /£prəʊ, $proʊ/ *n* [C] *pl* **pros** *infml* a person who plays sport as a job rather than as a hobby • *She's a tennis pro.* • *He's a pro golfer.* • *When you get to pro level, competition is extremely fierce.* • In a **pro-am** competition, the teams include professionals (= people who compete as a job) and AMATEURS (= people who compete for pleasure): *a pro-am golf competition*

pro ADVANTAGE /£prəʊ, $proʊ/ *n* [C] *pl* **pros** an advantage or a reason for doing something • *One of the big pros of living in Madrid is the exciting night life.* • *We considered all the pros* **and cons** *very carefully before deciding to buy a bigger house.* • Ⓚ

pro·ac·tive /£ˌprəʊˈæk·tɪv, $ˌproʊˈæk·t̬ɪv/ *adj* taking action yourself, rather than waiting for something to happen and then acting as a result of it • *He is critical of other firms for not being more enterprising and taking a proactive attitude towards exporting.*

pro·ac·tive·ly /£ˌprəʊˈæk·tɪv·li, $ˌproʊˈæk·t̬ɪv-/ *adv*

prob·a·ble /£ˈprɒb·ə·bl̩, $ˈprɑː·bə-/ *adj* likely to be true or likely to happen • *The doctor said that the most probable cause of death was heart failure.* • *An election in June seems increasingly probable.* • **It** *is probable* **that** *electronic books will start to replace paper ones in the near future.* [+ *that* clause] • Compare POSSIBLE [UNCERTAIN].

prob·a·bly /£ˈprɒb·ə·bli, $ˈprɑː·bə-/ *adv* • *The play finishes at 11.30, so I'll probably be* (= I am likely to be) *home about midnight.* • *There are lots of possible reasons for these symptoms, but it's probably* (= likely to be) *nothing serious.*

prob·a·bil·i·ty /£ˌprɒb·əˈbɪl·ɪ·ti, $ˌprɑː·bəˈbɪl·ə·t̬i/ *n* • The probability of something happening or being true is how likely it is that it will happen or be true: *I'm afraid there is a high/strong probability* (= it is very likely) **(that)** *something has gone wrong.* [C + (*that*) clause] • *The probability* **of** *her* **making** *a full recovery is quite good* (= She is likely to get better). [U] • *The probability* **of getting** *all the answers correct is only about one in ten.* [U] • *Until yesterday, the project was just a possibility, but now it has become a real probability* (= it is likely that it will happen). [C] • *They realized too late that* **in all probability** (= almost certainly) *he was not guilty of the crime.*

pro·bate /£ˈprəʊ·beɪt, $ˈproʊ-/ *n* [U] *law* the legal process of deciding whether or not a person's WILL (= document stating who they want their property to be given to after their death) has been made correctly and that the information it contains is correct • *Before probate can be* **granted**, *all business assets have to be identified and valued.* • Probate is also *Aus for* **death duty**. See at DEATH.

pro·ba·tion /£prəʊˈbeɪ·ʃən, $proʊ-/ *n* [U] a period of time during which you must behave well or do good work • If a person who has committed a crime is **on** probation, they are not sent to prison but must see a **probation officer** regularly and must not commit more crimes: *He served a year in prison and was then* **let out** *on probation.* • If a new employee is **on** probation, they are being watched and tested in order to see if their work is good enough and if they are the right person for the job. • *(Am)* If a student is **on** probation, they must behave well or improve their work. • A **probation officer** is a person whose job it is to see people regularly who have committed crimes and who are on probation and to help them live honestly.

pro·ba·tion·a·ry /£prəʊˈbeɪ·ʃən·ər·i, $proʊˈbeɪ·ʃən·er-/ *adj* [not gradable] • *Our new recruit did well in her probationary period.*

pro·ba·tion·er /£prəʊˈbeɪ·ʃən·əʳ, $proʊˈbeɪ·ʃən·ɚ/ *n* [C] • A probationer is a criminal on probation. • A probationer is also a person such as a police officer or teacher who has recently passed their final exams and who is doing their first year of work: *At the teachers' centre, they met other probationers for training sessions on a wide range of different subjects.*

probe *(obj)* /£prəʊb, $proʊb/ *v* to try to discover information that other people do not want you to know, by asking questions in an indirect careful way • *Detectives questioned him for hours, probing* **for** *any inconsistencies in his story.* [I] • *The official enquiry will probe* **into** *alleged corruption within the Defence Ministry.* [I] • *The article probes* (= tries to describe and explain) *the mysteries of nationalism in modern Europe.* [T] • To probe something **with** a tool is to examine it, esp. in order to find something that is hidden: *They probed* **in/into** *the mud with a special drill, looking for a long-buried shipwreck.* [I] ○ *Using a special instrument, the doctor probed the wound* **for** *the bullet.* [T]

probe /£prəʊb, $proʊb/ *n* [C] • A probe is an attempt to discover information: *In their official probe* **into** *malpractice, federal officials have found evidence of corruption within the company.* • *(specialized)* A probe is also a long thin metal tool used by doctors to examine inside someone. • *(specialized)* A probe is also a device that is put inside something to test or record information: *Scientists inserted a probe into the muscle of the fish in order to measure its body temperature.* • Probe is also another word for **space probe**. See at SPACE [BEYOND EARTH].

prob·ing /£ˈprəʊ·bɪŋ, $ˈproʊ-/ *adj* • A probing question is one that is difficult to answer without telling the truth: *She kept asking me probing questions in order to find out what was really happening.*

prob·ing *n* [C] • A probing is an attempt to discover information: *The Tax Office's probings* **into** *the firm's accounts revealed nothing illegal.*

pro·bi·ty /£ˈprəʊ·bɪ·ti, $ˈproʊ·bə·t̬i/ *n* [U] *fml* complete honesty • *Her probity and integrity are beyond question.*

prob·lem /£ˈprɒb·ləm, $ˈprɑː·bləm/ *n* [C] a situation, person or thing that needs attention and needs to be dealt with or solved • *Our main problem is lack of cash.* • *No one has* **solved** *the problem* **of** *what to do with radioactive waste.* • *The very high rate of inflation* **poses/presents** (= is) *a serious problem for the government.* • *The city* **faces** *worsening social and economic problems.* • *When is the government going to* **tackle** (= deal with) *the problem of poverty in the inner cities?* • *Modern educational theory stresses the importance of developing the problem-***solving** *capacity of children.* • *Did you have any problems* (= difficulties) *getting here?* [+ v-*ing*] • If someone has a **drink/drinking** problem, they have a habit of drinking too much alcohol which they cannot control. • If someone has a **weight** problem, they have a habit of eating too much and are too fat. • A problem **child/person** finds it difficult to have good relationships and behaves badly as a result. • A problem is also a question in mathematics which needs an answer: *In the maths lesson, the children were given problems to solve.* • *(infml)* If someone asks if you will do something and you answer **no problem**, you mean that you will do it: *"Can you get me to the station by 11.30?" "No problem."* • *(infml)* If someone thanks you for something you have done for them and you answer **no problem**, you mean that it did not cause you much trouble to do it: *"Oh, how kind of you!" "No problem."* • (PL) (RUS)

prob·lem·a·tic·al /£ˌprɒb·ləˈmæt·ɪ·kəl, $ˌprɑː·bləˈmæt̬-/, **prob·lem·a·tic** /£ˌprɒb·ləˈmæt·ɪk, $ˌprɑː·bləˈmæt̬-/ *adj* • Something that is problematical is difficult and is not certain to have a successful or satisfactory result: *Restoring the house to its original condition would be problematical because of its age and bad condition.*

prob·lem·a·tic·al·ly /£ˌprɒb·ləˈmæt·ɪ·kli, $ˌprɑː·bləˈmæt̬-/ *adv*

pro·bos·cis /£prəˈbɒs·ɪs, $proʊˈbɑː·sɪs/ *n* [C] *pl* **probosces** /£prəˈbɒs·iːz, $proʊˈbɑː·siːz/ *specialized* the long movable nose of some animals, or the long tube-like mouth of some insects • *An elephant's trunk is a proboscis.* • *(humorous)* A proboscis can also be a person's nose, esp. a large or long one.

pro·ce·dure /£prəˈsiː·dʒəʳ, $-dʒɚ/ *n* a set of actions which is the accepted way of doing something • *You can't just do it however you like – you must follow procedure.* [U] • *There is a complicated procedure* **for** *setting up the printer.* [C] • *Social workers have standard procedures which they must* **follow** *when they are taking children away from their parents.* [C] • *(specialized)* In computing, a procedure is part of a program which performs a particular job and which is operated by the main part of the program when it is needed. [C]

pro·ce·dur·al /£prəˈsiː·djʊ·rəl, $-dʒɚ·əl/ *adj* • *There are procedural difficulties in getting this bill through Parliament.*

pro·ceed /£prəʊˈsiːd, $proʊ-/ *v* [I] *slightly fml* to start or continue, esp. after a pause or delay • *After a year of arguments, preparations for the festival are now proceeding smoothly.* • *Shall we proceed* **with** *the plan as agreed?* • *She accepted a lift in my car and then proceeded* (= began) **to** *lecture me on how people shouldn't own cars because they damage the environment.* [+ *to* infinitive] • *(fml)* If someone proceeds or proceeds **with** something, they continue to do something which they have already started: *You should ask a lawyer for advice on how to proceed from here.* • *(fml)* To proceed is also to move forward or travel in a particular direction: *The warning signs above the road said 'Proceed with caution'.* ○ *Train drivers have to stop and telephone the control room for permission to proceed.*

pro·ceed a·gainst *obj v prep* [T] *law* to take legal action against (someone) • *Lack of evidence meant that the Council could not proceed against Mr Naylor.*

pro·ceed·ings /£prəʊˈsiː·dɪŋz, $proʊ-/ *pl n law* • If you take/start **legal** or **disciplinary** proceedings against someone, you take legal action against them: *Allegations of sexual harassment have led to disciplinary proceedings being taken* **against** *three naval officers.*

pro·ceed·ings /£prəʊˈsiː·dɪŋz, $proʊ-/ *pl n fml* a series of events that happen in a planned and controlled way • *Millions of people watched the proceedings on television – eager to see the new Queen being crowned.* • *The Chairperson opened the proceedings with a short speech.* • The proceedings **of** a meeting are a complete written record of what is said or done during it. Compare MINUTES.

pro·ceeds /£prəʊ'siːdz, $proʊ-/ *pl n* **the proceeds** the amount of money received from a particular event or activity or when something is sold • *The proceeds* **of** *today's festival will go to several local charities.*

pro·cess /£'prəʊ·ses, $'prɑː-/ *n* [C] a series of actions or events that are part of a system or a continuing development, or a series of actions that are done to achieve a particular result • *Could you explain how the digestive process works?* • *Increasing the number of women in top management jobs will be a slow process.* • *This decision may delay the process* **of** *European unification.* • *The party has begun the* **painful** (= difficult) *process of rethinking its policies and strategy.* • *Going to court to obtain compensation can be a long and* **painful** (= difficult) *process.* • *She arrived at the correct answer by a process* **of** *elimination* (= by deciding against each answer that was unlikely to be correct until only one was left). • *We are still* **in the process of** (= have not finished) *redecorating the house.* • *She won the 10 000 metres by five seconds and broke the world record* **in the process** (= at the same time). • A process is also a method of producing goods in a factory by treating raw materials: *They have developed a new process for extracting aluminium from bauxite.* • Ⓒⓢ Ⓟⓛ

pro·cess *obj* /£'prəʊ·ses, $'prɑː-/ *v* [T] • To process information or documents is to deal with them officially: *Visa applications take a minimum of two months to be processed by Embassy staff.* • If a computer processes information, it performs a particular series of operations on the information, such as a set of calculations: *My new laptop can process information much more quickly than my old computer.* • To process raw materials is to change them industrially: *The raw materials such as coal and iron are processed in local factories.* • To process photographic film is to make pictures from it: *The shop offers high-quality processing at a reasonable price.*

pro·cessed /£'prəʊ·sest, $'prɑː-/ *adj* [not gradable] • Processed food has been treated with chemicals that preserve it or give it extra taste or colour: *processed cheese*

pro·ces·sor /£'prəʊ·ses·əʳ, $'prɑː·ses·ɚ/ *n* [C] • *The firm is one of the largest processors of seal skins and fur.* • A processor is also the part of a computer that performs operations on the information that is put into it. See also MICROPROCESSOR.

pro·ces·sion /prə'seʃ·ᵊn/ *n* [C] a line of people who are all walking or travelling in the same direction, esp. in a formal way as part of a religious ceremony or public celebration • *a wedding/funeral procession* • *The festival will open with a procession led by the mayor.* • *He imagined a procession* (= line) **of** *cars stretching away towards the horizon.* • *(fig.) And on the evening news there was a procession* (= series) **of** *journalists giving 'expert' opinions.*

pro·ces·sion·al /prə'seʃ·ᵊn·ᵊl/ *adj* [before n; not gradable] • *There was tight security along the processional route* (= the route of the procession).

pro·cess /prə'ses/ *v* [I] *fml* • *The priest, followed by the choir, processed* (= walked) *slowly through the church.*

pro–choice /£ˌprəʊ'tʃɔɪs, $ˌproʊ-/ *adj* [not gradable] supporting the belief that a pregnant woman should have the freedom to choose an ABORTION (= an operation to end a pregnancy) if she does not want to have a baby • *pro-choice activists/advocates/demonstrators* • *The President is known to be pro-choice.* • Compare **anti-choice** at ANTI-; PRO-LIFE.

pro·claim *(obj)* ANNOUNCE /£prəʊ'kleɪm, $proʊ-/ *v fml* to announce (esp. something positive) publicly or officially • *All the countries have proclaimed their loyalty to the alliance.* [T] • *Republican party members were confidently proclaiming victory even as the first few votes came in.* [T] • *That was the famous speech in which he proclaimed* **that** *socialism was dead.* [+ *that* clause] • *She was proclaimed Queen at the age of thirteen after the sudden death of her father.* [T + obj + n]

pro·cla·ma·tion /£ˌprɒk·lə'meɪ·ʃᵊn, $ˌprɑː·klə-/ *n* [C] • *to issue a proclamation* • *Eventually, his books were banned in a royal proclamation of June 1555.* • *A bloody civil war followed the proclamation of an independent state.*

pro·claim *obj* SHOW /£prəʊ'kleɪm, $proʊ-/ *v* [T] *literary* to show (something) or make it clear • *Wearing scarves and hats which proclaimed their allegiance, the football fans flooded into the bar.*

pro·cla·ma·tion /£ˌprɒk·lə'meɪ·ʃᵊn, $ˌprɑː·klə-/ *n* [C] *literary*

pro·cli·vi·ty /£prə'klɪv·ɪ·ti, $-ə·t̬i/ *n* [C] *fml* a tendency to behave in a particular way, esp. one which shocks other people, or a tendency to like something, esp. something bad or unacceptable • *The tabloid papers are obsessed with the* **sexual** *proclivities of famous people.* • *His proclivity* **for** *alcohol was almost as well-known as his poetry.*

pro·cras·tin·ate /£prəʊ'kræs·tɪ·neɪt, $proʊ-/ *v* [I] to keep delaying something that must be done, often because it is unpleasant or boring • *I know I've got to deal with the problem at some point – I'm just procrastinating.*

pro·cras·ti·na·tion /£prəʊˌkræs·tɪ'neɪ·ʃᵊn, $proʊ-/ *n* [U]

pro·cre·ate /£'prəʊ·kri·eɪt, $'proʊ-, ˌ--'-/ *v* [I] *fml or specialized* to produce young • *While priests were denied the right to marry and procreate, he said, their situation would remain impossible.*

pro·cre·a·tion /£ˌprəʊ·kri'eɪ·ʃᵊn, $ˌproʊ-/ *n* [U] *fml or specialized* • *Some people believe that sex should only be for the purpose of procreation.*

pro·cre·a·tive /£ˌprəʊ·kri'eɪ·tɪv, $ˌproʊ·kri'eɪ·t̬ɪv/ *adj* [not gradable] *fml or specialized* • *The purpose of sexuality is to be procreative, says a lecturer in sociology at the University of California.*

proc·tor *(obj)* /£'prɒk·təʳ, $'prɑːk·t̬ɚ/ *v* [I/T] *Am for* INVIGILATE

procure *(obj)* /£prə'kjʊəʳ, $-'kjʊr/ *v fml* to obtain (something) esp. after an effort • *She's managed somehow to procure his telephone number.* [T] • *He'd procured us seats in the front row.* [+ two objects] • *(fml)* Someone who procures obtains PROSTITUTES for people who want to have sex with them. [I]

pro·cure·ment /£prə'kjʊə·mənt, $-'kjʊr-/ *n* [U] *fml* • *They are reported to have a substantial budget for the procurement of military supplies.* • Procurement is the buying of supplies: *He's in charge of procurement for the army.*

pro·cur·er /£prə'kjʊə·rəʳ, $-'kjʊr·ɚ/ *n* [C] *fml* • A procurer is a person who obtains PROSTITUTES for men who want to have sex with them.

prod *(obj)* /£prɒd, $prɑːd/ *v* **-dd-** to push (something or someone) with your finger or with a pointed object, or *(fig.)* to encourage (someone) to take action, esp. when they are being slow or unwilling • *I felt someone prod me in the back, so I turned round to see who it was.* [T] • *She prodded the cake with her fork to see if it was cooked.* [T] • *He prodded* **at** *the fish with his fork a few times, but he didn't eat a mouthful.* [I] • *(fig.) He gets things done, but only after I've prodded him* **into** *doing them.* [T] • *(fig.) After much prodding from my wife, I'm finally sorting out the mess in the garage.*

prod /£prɒd, $prɑːd/ *n* [C] • *He* **gave** *her a prod in the ribs.* • *(fig.) I think she's forgotten to order that book for me – I must* **give** *her a prod* (= encourage her to remember).

prod·dy /£'prɒd·i, $'prɑː·di/ *n* [C] *Aus infml for* PROTESTANT

prod·i·gal /£'prɒd·ɪ·gᵊl, $'prɑː·dɪ-/ *adj fml* wasteful with money; tending to spend large amounts without thinking of the future • *There have been rumours that he has been prodigal with company funds.* • The **prodigal son** is a man or boy who has left his family in order to do something that the family disapprove of and has now returned home feeling sorry and regretful for what he has done: *(fig.) Manchester City football club sees the return of the prodigal son tonight with Black once again in the side after a season away.*

prod·i·gal·i·ty /£ˌprɒd·ɪ'gæl·ɪ·ti, $ˌprɑː·dɪ'gæl·ə·t̬i/ *n* [U] *fml*

prod·i·gal·ly /£'prɒd·ɪ·gli, $'prɑː·dɪ-/ *adv fml*

pro·di·gious /prə'dɪdʒ·əs/ *adj fml* extremely great in ability, amount or strength • *She wrote a truly prodigious number of novels.* • *She was a prodigious musician.* • *He had a prodigious appetite for both women and drink.*

pro·di·gious·ly /prə'dɪdʒ·ə·sli/ *adv* • *He was a prodigiously gifted artist.*

prod·i·gy /£'prɒd·ɪ·dʒi, $'prɑː·də-/ *n* [C] someone with a very great ability which usually shows itself when that person is a young child • *The 16-year old tennis prodigy is the youngest player ever to reach the Olympic finals.* • *He read in the paper about a mathematical prodigy who was attending university at the age of 12.* • A **child/infant prodigy** is a young child that has very great ability in something: *He was a child prodigy who made his first professional tour as a pianist when he was six.*

pro·duce *obj* MAKE /£prə'djuːs, $-'duːs/ *v* [T] to make (something) or bring it into existence • *France produces a great deal of wine for export.* • *Red blood cells are produced in the bone marrow.* • *She produces the most wonderful paintings and she's only six.* • *She works for a company that* *produces* (= makes for sale) *electrical goods.* • *I was wondering whether I could produce a meal out of what's left in the fridge.* • *She's asked me to produce a report on the state of the project.* • When animals produce young they give birth to them: *Our cat produced four kittens during the course of the night.* ○ *(humorous) All our friends seem to be busy producing offspring at the moment.*

pro·duce /£'prɒd·juːs, $'prɑː·djuːs/ *n* [U] • Produce is food or any other substance or material that is grown or obtained through farming, esp. that which is produced in large amounts and *(Am)* esp. fruit and vegetables: *agricultural/dairy/fresh produce*

pro·duc·er /£prə'djuː·sər, $-'duː·sɚ/ *n* [C] • A producer is a company, country or person that provides goods, esp. those which are produced by an industrial process or grown or obtained through farming, usually in large amounts: *egg/gas/oil producers*

prod·uct /£'prɒd·ʌkt, $'prɑː·dʌkt/ *n* • A product is something that is made to be sold, usually something that is produced by an industrial process or, less commonly, something that is grown or obtained through farming : *Nowadays there's such a range of skin-care products to choose from.* [C] ○ *If you don't believe in your company's product it's very hard to sell it.* [U] ○ *I'm trying to cut down on* **dairy** *products.* [C] • A product **of** something can also be a result of it: *A figure like that is usually the product of many hours spent in the gym.* [C] ○ *She had a very happy childhood, and I guess her confidence is a product of that.* [C] • See also BY-PRODUCT.

pro·duc·tion /prə'dʌk·ʃən/ *n* [U] • Production is the process of making or growing goods to be sold: *Coke is used in the production of steel.* ○ *We saw a quick film showing the various stages in the production of glass.* ○ *The company's new model will be* **going into** *production early next year.* • Production can also refer to the amount of something that is made or grown by a country or a company: *Swedish industrial production has fallen steadily this year.* ○ *Wheat production has risen over the years.* • A **production line** is a factory system in which different parts of a product are sent to a series of different places at each of which another stage of work is completed, either by hand or by machine.

pro·duc·tive /£prə'dʌk·tɪv, $-t̬ɪv/ *adj* • Something which is productive results in or can provide a large amount or supply of something: *In order to turn the deserts into fertile and productive land, engineers built an 800-mile canal.* ○ *He had an amazingly productive five years in which he managed to write four novels.* • More generally, productive can be used to mean having positive results: *We had a very productive meeting – I felt we sorted out a lot of problems.* ○ *Theirs was a very productive partnership.*

pro·duc·tive·ly /£prə'dʌk·tɪv·li, $-t̬ɪv-/ *adv* • *Their working system is based on the belief that people work more productively* (= produce better results) *in a team.*

prod·uc·ti·vi·ty /£ˌprɒd·ʌk'tɪv·ɪ·ti, $ˌproʊ·dək'tɪv·ə·t̬i/ *n* [U] • A company's or country's productivity is the rate at which it makes goods, and is usually judged in connection with the number of people and the amount of materials necessary to produce the goods: *Studies show that if a working environment is pleasant, productivity increases.* ○ *a productivity bonus/incentive* ○ *Productivity in the steel industry improved by 5% last year.*

pro·duce *obj* FILM/BROADCASTING /£prə'djuːs, $-'duːs/ *v* [T] to organize the practical and financial matters connected with the preparation of (a film, play or television or radio programme) • Compare DIRECT CONTROL.

pro·duc·er /£prə'djuː·sər, $-'duː·sɚ/ *n* [C] • *a film/Hollywood/movie producer* • Compare **director** at DIRECT CONTROL..

pro·duc·tion /prə'dʌk·ʃən/ *n* • *She's hoping to get into television production.* [U] • *Disney's latest production* (= film) *looks likely to be their most successful ever.* [C] • A production of a theatrical entertainment such as a play or opera is a particular series of performances of it: *They're doing a new production* **of** *Macbeth at the National Theatre.* [C]

pro·duce *obj* RECORDING /£prə'djuːs, $-'duːs/ *v* [T] to be in charge of making (a musical recording) and to be responsible for the arrangement of the music, the combination of the different instruments or voices and the general sound of it

pro·duc·er /£prə'djuːs, $-'duːs/ *n* [C] • *a record producer*

pro·duc·tion /prə'dʌk·ʃən/ *n* [U] • The production on a record is the preparation and general quality of its sound and shows the way in which the music was recorded rather than the quality of the singing and the music: *George Martin* **did** *the production* **on** *the Beatles records.*

pro·duce *obj* BRING OUT /£prə'djuːs, $-'duːs/ *v* [T] to bring (something) out from somewhere and show it • *He produced a letter from his desk which he asked me to read.* • *Quite unexpectedly he produced a beautifully wrapped present from his inside pocket.* • *It was only when she produced a knife that I took her threats seriously.*

pro·duc·tion /prə'dʌk·ʃən/ *n* [U] *fml* • *Entry to the club is only permitted* **on** *production of a membership card.*

pro·duce *obj* CAUSE /£prə'djuːs, $-'duːs/ *v* [T] to cause (a reaction or result) • *The prime minister's speech produced an angry response from the opposition.* • *Her remarks produced an awkward silence.* • *If used on delicate skin this cream may produce a stinging sensation.*

pro·duce *obj* RESULT IN /£prə'djuːs, $-'duːs/ *v* [T] to result in or discover (esp. proof) • *A lengthy police investigation didn't produce any evidence on which the suspect could be convicted.*

prod·uct /£'prɒd·ʌkt, $'prɑː·dʌkt/ *n* [C] *specialized* the result obtained when two or more numbers are multiplied together • *The product of six and three is eighteen.* • See also **product** at PRODUCE MAKE.

prof /£prɒf, $prɑːf/ *n* [C] *abbreviation for* PROFESSOR • *Prof Tina Pritchard* • *(infml humorous) Morning, prof.* [as form of address] • *(infml) Most of the profs in our department should have retired years ago.*

pro·fane AGAINST RELIGION /prə'feɪn/ *adj fml* showing a lack of respect for a god or a religion, often through language • *Viewers had complained that the programme contained 'obscene and profane language'.* • *Funny, profane and fearless, she has become one of America's biggest television celebrities.*

pro·fan·i·ty /£prə'fæn·ɪ·ti, $-ə·t̬i/ *n fml* • Profanity is (an example of) showing a lack of respect for a god or a religion, esp. through language: *His latest film, obviously aimed at a family audience, contains no profanity, sex or violence.* [U] • A profanity can also be a word or words which are offensive or OBSCENE: *It was the song's opening line, a series of profanities, that caused the record to be banned on the radio station.* [C]

pro·fane NOT SPIRITUAL /prə'feɪn/ *adj fml* not connected with religion or spiritual matters; relating to life on Earth; SECULAR • *sacred and profane art* • *What was once a church is now a profane museum of the village's history.*

pro·fess *(obj)* /prə'fes/ *v* to claim (something), sometimes in a way which is not sincere • *She professes not* **to** *be interested in money.* [+ *to* infinitive] • *I don't profess* **to** *know all the details about the case.* [+ *to* infinitive] • *She professes ignorance of the whole affair, though I'm not sure I believe her.* [T]

pro·fessed /prə'fest/ *adj* [before n; not gradable] • A professed belief is one which someone has made known: *She is a professed monarchist.* • A professed belief or feeling can also be one which is not sincerely claimed to be held or felt: *His professed love of women seems a little odd when you consider how he treats them.*

pro·fes·sion /prə'feʃ·ən/ *n* [C] • *The government's professions of commitment to the environment seem less believable every day.*

pro·fes·sion /prə'feʃ·ən/ *n* [C] any type of work which needs a special training or a particular skill, often one which is respected because it involves a high level of education • *He left the teaching profession in 1965 to set up his own business.* • *He is a plumber* **by** *profession.* • *The report notes that forty per cent of lawyers* **entering** *the profession are women.* • *Teaching as a profession is very underpaid.* • Some types of work which need special training and skill, such as being a doctor or lawyer, but not work in business or industry, are sometimes called **the** professions. • Profession also refers to the people employed in a particular type of work: *There's a feeling among the nursing profession that their work is undervalued.* • LP› **Work**

pro·fes·sion·al /prə'feʃ·ən·əl/ *adj* • Professional means related to work that you do as a job: *Chris, you're a nurse, so can I ask your professional* **opinion** *on bandaging ankles?* ○ *Both doctors have been charged with professional* **misconduct** (= bad or unacceptable behaviour in their work). • Professional is often used to mean having the qualities that you connect with trained and skilled people, such as effectiveness, skill, organization and seriousness of manner: *(approving) It would look more professional if the letter was typed rather than hand-written.* ○ *She always* *looks very professional in her smart suits.* ○ *You've done a very professional job stripping that floor!* ● You describe someone as professional if they do as a job what people usually do as a hobby: *She's a professional dancer/ photographer.* ○ *He's a runner who's just* **turned** *professional.* (= His running used to be a hobby, but now it's his job.) ● Professional is also used to mean having the type of job that is respected because it involves a high level of education and training: *Room for rent in shared house – would suit professional person.* ○ *It's the sort of bar that's full of young professional types in suits.* ● *(infml) She's a professional liar* (= She lies a lot). ● When people talk about taking **professional advice** they usually mean advice from a lawyer or an ACCOUNTANT (= someone who deals with money matters). ● In football a **professional foul** is an intentional FOUL (= act which breaks the rules), esp. one which is intended to prevent the other team from scoring a goal. ● **Professional help** is sometimes used to avoid saying help from a PSYCHIATRIST (= a doctor trained in treating mental problems): *Personally, I think he should get some professional help.* ● Compare AMATEUR.

pro·fes·sion·al /prəˈfeʃ·ᵊn·ᵊl/ *n* [C] ● A professional is a person who has the type of job that needs a high level of education and training: *It's the sort of ad that is intended to appeal to teachers, lawyers, doctors and other professionals.* ● *(infml)* You can describe someone as a professional if they have worked hard in the same type of job for a long time and have become skilled at dealing with any problem that might happen: *I thought the whole meeting was going to fall apart but you rescued that situation like a true professional!* ● Professional can refer to a person who does as a job what people usually do as a hobby: *He's only been playing football as a professional for two years.* ● A professional is also a sportsperson, esp. a golf or tennis player, who is employed by a CLUB to train its members in a particular sport. ● Compare AMATEUR.

pro·fes·sion·al·ly /prəˈfeʃ·ᵊn·ᵊl·i, -nə·li/ *adv* ● *I think next time we need any decorating we'll get it done professionally* (= by skilled people). ● *He started to sing professionally* (= for money) *after leaving college.* ● *Are you asking for my opinion of him personally or professionally?*

pro·fes·sion·al·i·sm /prəˈfeʃ·ᵊn·ᵊl·ɪ·zᵊm/ *n* [U] ● Professionalism is the combination of all the qualities that are connected with trained and skilled people: *The director claims that the company's success is mainly due to the professionalism of his staff.*

pro·fes·sor /£prəˈfes·ər, $-ɚ/ (*abbreviation* **prof**) *n* [C] a teacher of the highest rank in a department of a British university, or a teacher of high rank in an American university or college ● *Professor Stephen Hawking* ● *a professor of sociology* ● *a sociology professor* ● *She was a lecturer at the university for 20 years before she became a professor.*

pro·fes·sor·i·al /£ˌprɒf·əˈsɔː·ri·əl, $ˌprɑː·fəˈsɔːr·i-/ *adj* [not gradable] *fml* ● *She's applying for a professorial post at a Scottish university.*

pro·fes·sor·ship /£prəˈfes·ə·ʃɪp, $ˈ-ɚ-/ *n* [C] ● A professorship is the position of professor in a university: *She has applied for a professorship in biochemistry at Warwick University.*

prof·fer *obj* /£ˈprɒf·əʳ, $ˈprɑː·fɚ/ *v* [T] *fml* to offer (something) by holding it out, or to offer (advice or an opinion) ● *He shook the warmly proffered hand.* ● *I didn't think it wise to proffer an opinion.* ● Ⓘ

pro·fi·cient /prəˈfɪʃ·ᵊnt/ *adj* skilled and experienced ● *a proficient swimmer* ● *It takes a couple of years of regular driving before you become proficient* **at** *it.* ● *I can make myself understood in French, but I wouldn't say I was really proficient* **in** *the language.*

pro·fi·cien·cy /prəˈfɪʃ·ᵊnt·si/ *n* [U] ● *It said in the job ad that they wanted proficiency* **in** *at least two languages.*

pro·file SIDE VIEW /£ˈprəʊ·faɪl, $ˈproʊ-/ *n* [C] a side view of a person's face ● *Drawing profiles is somehow easier than drawing the full face.* ● *She has a good strong profile* (= Her features look good and strong from the side). ● *The actor is photographed* **in profile** (= from the side), *smoking a cigarette.*

pro·file SHORT DESCRIPTION /£ˈprəʊ·faɪl, $ˈproʊ-/ *n* [C] a short description of someone containing all the most important or interesting facts about them ● *Some journalist had written a profile about him in which some of the facts were untrue.*

pro·file *obj* /£ˈprəʊ·faɪl, $ˈproʊ-/ *v* [T] ● *Every week in the books section of the paper they profile a different author.*

pro·file ATTENTION /£ˈprəʊ·faɪl, $ˈproʊ-/ *n* [C] the amount of public attention and notice that something receives ● *This court case, which has attracted a lot of publicity, has done a lot to raise the issue's profile with the public.* ● *There is a growing number of women in* **high**-*profile positions* (= positions where they are noticed) *in the government.* ● If you **keep a low** profile you intentionally avoid doing anything which attracts attention: *He's been in a bit of trouble recently so he's trying to keep a low profile.* ○ *No incidents were reported during the march and the police kept a low profile* (= not many were seen).

prof·it /£ˈprɒf·ɪt, $ˈprɑː·fɪt/ *n* money which is earned in trade or business, esp. after paying the costs of producing and selling goods and services ● *She* **makes** *a big profit from selling waste material to textile companies.* [C] ● *A year ago the Tokyo company had a* **pretax** *profit of 35 million yen.* [C] ● *You don't expect to make much profit within the first couple of years of setting up a company.* [U] ● *Company profits are down on last year's figures.* [C] ● *He bought his house a long time ago so he sold it* **at a profit**. [U] ● Profit is also the benefit or advantage that can be achieved by a particular action or activity: *There's no profit to be* **gained** *from endlessly discussing where we went wrong.* [U] ● A **profit margin** is the profit that can be made in a business after the costs have been subtracted: *Many small companies operate on very narrow profit margins.* ● **Profit sharing** is the system of sharing the profits that a company makes between all the people who work for it.

prof·it /£ˈprɒf·ɪt, $ˈprɑː·fɪt/ *v* [I always + prep] ● To profit **by/from** something is to achieve an advantage from it: *I certainly profited from the two years I spent in that company.* ○ *I profited enormously from working with her.* ● *(esp. Am)* To profit **by/from** something is also to earn money from it: *A lot of companies will profit from the fall in interest rates.*

prof·it·a·ble /£ˈprɒf·ɪ·tə·bl̩, $ˈprɑː·fɪ·t̬ə-/ *adj* ● Profitable means resulting in or likely to result in a profit or an advantage: *Over the years it has developed into a highly profitable business.* ○ *I made profitable use of my time* (= used my time to get advantages or benefits), *mixing with a lot of different people and practising my Spanish.*

prof·it·a·bly /£ˈprɒf·ɪ·tə·bli, $ˈprɑː·fɪ·t̬ə-/ *adv* ● *It took several months before the company started to trade profitably.* ● *I spent my time profitably* (= used it to get advantages or benefits), *reading a lot and learning a new language.*

prof·it·a·bil·i·ty /£ˌprɒf·ɪ·təˈbɪl·ɪ·ti, $ˌprɑː·fɪ·t̬əˈbɪl·ə·t̬i/ *n* [U] ● *The company needs to return to profitability extremely soon.*

prof·it·eer /£ˌprɒf·ɪˈtɪəʳ, $ˌprɑː·fɪˈtɪr/ *n* [C] *disapproving* ● A profiteer is a person who takes advantage unfairly of a situation in which other people are suffering to make a profit, often by selling at an unusually high price goods which are difficult to obtain: *a war profiteer*

prof·it·eer·ing /£ˌprɒf·ɪˈtɪə·rɪŋ, $ˌprɑː·fɪˈtɪr·ɪŋ/ *n* [U] *disapproving* ● *The pharmaceutical company has been charged with profiteering from the AIDS crisis.*

pro·fi·te·role /£prəˈfɪt·ᵊr·əʊl, $ˈfɪt̬·ə·roʊl/ *n* [C usually pl] a small pastry cake with a cream filling and a covering of chocolate sauce, usually served in a pile

prof·li·gate /£ˈprɒf·lɪ·gət, $ˈprɑː·flɪ-/ *adj fml* wasteful with money ● *She is well-known for her profligate spending habits.*

prof·li·ga·cy /£ˈprɒf·lɪ·gə·si, $ˈprɑː·flɪ-/ *n* [U] *fml* ● *The profligacy of the West shocked him.*

pro form·a /£ˌprəʊˈfɔː·mə, $ˌproʊˈfɔːr-/ *adj, adv fml* (of words or actions) usual or done in the usual way ● *After the attack, other countries expressed the predictable pro-forma condemnation that is the usual response to such incidents.* ● *The interview was conducted pro forma, even though they had already decided to give her the job.*

pro form·a (in·voice) /£ˌprəʊˈfɔː·mə, $ˌproʊˈfɔːr-/ *n* [C] *fml* a list of items that have been ordered which is sent with their prices to a customer so that the items can be paid for before they are delivered ● *A pro forma invoice is always sent out by the publisher before books are supplied to the customer.*

pro·found EXTREME /prəˈfaʊnd/ *adj* felt or experienced very strongly or deeply; extreme ● *His mother's death when he was aged six had a very profound* **effect** *on him.* ● *The invention of the contraceptive pill brought about profound changes in the lives of women.* ● *Those two lines of poetry express perfectly the profound sadness of loss.* ● *My grandfather has a profound mistrust of anything new or* *foreign.* • *There was a note of profound irritation in his voice.* • LP **Very, completely**

pro·found·ly /prəˈfaʊnd·li/ *adv* • *Society has changed so profoundly over the last fifty years.* • *She detested her mother's second husband whom she described as arrogant and profoundly ignorant.* • *We are all profoundly grateful for your help and encouragement.*

pro·fun·di·ty /£prəˈfʌn·dɪ·ti, $-də·t̬i/ *n* [U] *fml*

pro·found SHOWING UNDERSTANDING /prəˈfaʊnd/ *adj* showing a clear and deep understanding of serious matters • *profound truths/wisdom* • *The review that I read said that it was 'a thoughtful and profound film'.* • *"Dying is easy – it's living that's the problem." "That was very profound of you, Steven."*

pro·fun·di·ty /£prəˈfʌn·dɪ·ti, $-də·t̬i/ *n fml* • *I don't doubt the profundity of this wisdom.* [U] • A profundity is also a remark or thought that shows great understanding or is intended to: *We would sit all afternoon exchanging profundities.* [C]

pro·fuse /prəˈfjuːs/ *adj* in large amounts • *She was admitted to St Mary's Hospital with profuse bleeding.* • *The company accepted blame and sent us profuse* **apologies**.

pro·fuse·ly /prəˈfjuː·sli/ *adv* • *She apologized/thanked us profusely.* • *He was bleeding/sweating profusely.*

pro·fu·sion /prəˈfjuː·ʒən/ *n* [U] *fml* • A profusion **of** something is an extremely large amount of it: *I was remarking on the recent profusion of books and articles on the subject of sex.* ○ *She'd never seen flowers so beautiful and* **in** *such profusion.*

pro·gen·i·tor /£prəʊˈdʒen·ɪ·təʳ, $proʊˈdʒen·ɪ·t̬ɚ/ *n* [C] *fml or specialized* a person who first thinks of something and causes it to happen • *Marx was the progenitor of communism.*

prog·e·ny /£ˈprɒdʒ·ə·ni, $ˈprɑː·dʒə-/ *n* [U + sing/pl v] *fml* the young or OFFSPRING of a person, animal or plant • *His numerous progeny are scattered all over the country.*

pro·ges·te·rone /£prəʊˈdʒes·tər·əʊn, $proʊˈdʒes·tə·roʊn/ *n* [U] a female HORMONE (=chemical substance produced in the body) which causes the womb to prepare for pregnancy • *Some women take progesterone to treat menstrual problems or prevent miscarriage.*

prog·no·sis /£prɒgˈnəʊ·sɪs, $prɑːgˈnoʊ-/, **prog·nos·ti·ca·tion** /£prəgˌnɒs·tɪˈkeɪ·ʃən, $prɑːgˌnɑː·stɪ-/ *n* [C] *pl* **prognoses** /£prɒgˈnəʊ·siːz, $prɑːgˈnoʊ-/ *fml* a doctor's judgment of the likely or expected development of a disease or of the chances of getting better or, more generally, a statement of what is judged likely to happen in the future, esp. in connection with a particular situation • *The prognosis after the operation was for a full recovery.* • *I was reading a* **gloomy** *economic prognosis in the paper this morning.* • PL RUS

pro·gram /£ˈprəʊ·græm, $ˈproʊ-/ *n* [C] a series of instructions which can be put into a computer in order to make it perform an operation, or *(Aus usually and Am)* a PROGRAMME • *a* **computer** *program* • *She's* **written** *a program to find words which frequently occur together.*

pro·gram *obj* /£ˈprəʊ·græm, $ˈproʊ-/ *v* [T] **-mm-** • If you program a computer you write a series of instructions which make the computer perform a particular operation: *She programmed the computer* **to** *calculate the rate of exchange in twelve currencies.* [+ obj + *to* infinitive] • Program is also *Am and Aus for* PROGRAMME INSTRUCT.

pro·gram·mer /£ˈprəʊ·græm·əʳ, $ˈproʊ·græm·ɚ/ *n* [C] • A **(computer)** programmer is a person whose job is to produce computer programs.

pro·gramme BROADCAST *Br, Am and Aus* **pro·gram** /£ˈprəʊ·græm, $ˈproʊ-/ *n* [C] a broadcast on television or radio • *It's one of those arts programmes late at night in which people discuss the latest films and books.* • *It's my favourite TV programme – I never miss an episode.* • PL RUS

pro·gramme THIN BOOK *Br, Am and Aus also* **pro·gram** /£ˈprəʊ·græm, $ˈproʊ-/ *n* [C] a thin book or piece of paper giving information about a play or musical or sporting event, usually bought at the theatre or place where the event happens • *Look in the programme and see what they're going to play next.* • PL RUS

pro·gramme PLAN *Br, Am and Aus also* **pro·gram** /£ˈprəʊ·græm, $ˈproʊ-/ *n* [C] a plan of activities to be done or things to be achieved • *The school offers an exciting and varied programme of social events.* • *He played an important part in the development of the French nuclear power programme.* • *The rail system is to put twenty million pounds into its modernisation programme.* • *I'm running three mornings a week – it's all part of my fitness programme.* • PL RUS

pro·gramme *obj* INSTRUCT *Br, Am and Aus* **pro·gram** *obj* /£ˈprəʊ·græm, $ˈproʊ-/ *v* [T + obj + *to* infinitive] to instruct (a device or system) to operate in a particular way or at a particular time • *The central heating is programmed* **to** *come on for six hours of the day.* • If a person is programmed to do something he or she is trained mentally to do a particular thing without thinking about it: *I'm programmed* **to** *wake up at seven.* ○ *Children in that society are programmed* **to** *work extremely hard from a very early age.* • PL RUS

pro·gram·ma·ble /£prəʊˈgræm·ə·bl̩, £ˈprəʊ·græm-, $ˈproʊ·græm·ə-/ *adj*

pro·gress /£ˈprəʊ·gres, $ˈprɑː-/ *n* [U] advancement to an improved or more developed state, or to a forward position • *Technological progress has been so rapid over the last few years.* • *How are your driving lessons going – do you feel you're* **making** *progress?* • *I'm afraid we're* **making** *rather slow progress in the kitchen – lunch will be a little later than usual.* • *The doctor said that she was* **making** *good progress* (=getting better after a medical operation or illness) *and she would probably be out of hospital by next week.* • *The recent free elections mark the next step in the country's progress towards democracy.* • *The yacht's crew said that they were* **making** *relatively slow progress north-easterly.* • *(fml)* If something is **in** progress it is happening or being done now: *Repair work is in progress on the south-bound lane of the motorway and will continue until June.* • *At the end of each term the parents go to the school to discuss their child's progress* **report**.

pro·gress /prəˈgres/ *v* [I] • *My Spanish never really progressed* (=improved) *beyond the stage of being able to order drinks at the bar.* • *As the war progressed* (=developed) *more and more countries became involved.* • *As the holiday progressed, we became increasingly annoyed with each other.* • *We started off talking about the weather and gradually the conversation progressed* **to** *politics.* • Compare REGRESS.

pro·gres·sion /prəˈgreʃ·ən/ *n* [U] • *The new medication slows down the progression of the disease, but it cannot cure it.* • *The novel follows the progression of a woman from youth to middle age.* • *She'd always worked with old people so becoming a nurse was a* **natural** *progression.*

pro·gres·sive /prəˈgres·ɪv/ *adj* • *There's been a progressive* (=gradually developing) *decline in the standard of living over the past few years.* • A progressive disease is one that gets worse. • Progressive ideas or systems are new and modern, encouraging change in society or in the way that things are done: *The left of the party is pressing for a more progressive social policy.* ○ *He went to one of those progressive schools where there's no discipline and you call teachers by their first name.* • Progressive **tax** is a tax system in which the rate of tax is higher on larger amounts of money. • The progressive form of a verb is used to show that the action is continuing. It is formed with the verb 'be' followed by the present participle (=*-ing* form of the verb): *'He's working hard at the moment' is an example of the* **present** *progressive form of the verb 'work'.* ○ *'I was eating when the phone rang' is an example of the* **past** *progressive.* • LP **-ing form of verbs, Continuous form, Tenses**

pro·gres·sive /prəˈgres·ɪv/ *n* [C] • A progressive is a person who supports new ideas and social change, especially one who belongs to a political party: *Religion, like politics, has its progressives.* • Compare REACTIONARY.

pro·gres·sive·ly /prəˈgres·ɪv·li/ *adv* • *My eyesight has got progressively worse over the years.*

pro·hi·bit *obj* /prəˈhɪb·ɪt/ *v* [T] to forbid (something), esp. by law, or to prevent (a particular activity) by making it impossible • *Motor vehicles are prohibited* **from** *driving in the town centre.* • *The government introduced a law prohibiting tobacco advertisements on TV.* • *Parking is* **strictly** *prohibited between these gates.* • *The loudness of the music prohibits serious conversation in most nightclubs.*

pro·hi·bi·tion /£ˌprəʊ·hɪˈbɪʃ·ən, $ˌproʊ-/ *n* • *London Transport has announced a prohibition* **on** *smoking on buses.* [C] • *The environmental group is demanding a complete prohibition* **against** *the hunting of whales.* [C] • *It's my feeling that the money spent on drug prohibition would be better spent on information and education.* [U] • Prohibition was the period from 1920 to 1933 when the production and sale of alcohol was forbidden in the US. [U; not after *the*]

pro·hib·i·tive /£prəˈhɪb·ɪ·tɪv, $-t̬ɪv/ *adj* • If the cost of something is prohibitive it is so expensive that it prevents people from buying or paying for it: *Hotel prices in the major cities are high but not prohibitive.*

pro·hib·i·tive·ly /£prəˈhɪb·ɪ·tɪv·li, $-t̬ɪv-/ *adv* • *Property in the area tends to be prohibitively* **expensive** (= so expensive that you can not buy it).

proj·ect [PIECE OF WORK] /£ˈprɒdʒ·ekt, $ˈprɑː·dʒekt/ *n* [C] a piece of planned work or activity which is completed over a period of time and intended to achieve a particular aim • *He was employed by the company to work on the Kings Cross housing project.* • *Her latest project is a film based on the life of a nineteenth-century music hall star.* • *Less and less money is being put into scientific research projects.* • *There's the living room still to be decorated, so that's my next project.* • A project can also be a study of a particular subject done over a period of time, especially by students: *He's doing a school project on pollution.* ○ *In our third year at college everyone had to do a special project.* • (PL) (RUS)

proj·ect *obj* [CALCULATE] /prəˈdʒekt/ *v* [T + obj + *to* infinitive; usually passive] to calculate (an amount or number expected in the future) from information already known • *Revenue from tourism this year is projected* **to** *total £3 billion.* • *Retail prices for milk and cheese are projected* **to** *rise 3 percent by the end of the year.* • (PL) (RUS)

pro·ject·ed /£prəˈdʒek·tɪd, $-t̬ɪd/ *adj* • *The projected* (= planned) *extension to the motorway is going to cost over £4 million.* • *The princess's projected* (= planned) *tour of the islands has been postponed.*

pro·jec·tion /prəˈdʒek·ʃən/ *n* [C] • *The company has failed to achieve last year's sales projections by thirty percent.* • *The number of people leaving the country will amount to over three million, according to recent government projections.* • See also PROJECTION; **projection** at PROJECT [MAKE AN IMAGE], PROJECT [STICK OUT].

proj·ect *obj* [THROW] /prəˈdʒekt/ *v* [T] to throw or direct (something) forward, with force • *Ninety percent of the projected missiles will hit their target.* • *(fig.) It's a big theatre so you really have to project your voice* (= speak or sing loudly) *if you're going to be heard at the back.* • *(fig.) It's difficult to project your mind into the future* (= imagine the future) *and think what your life will be like in a few years' time.* • (PL) (RUS)

pro·jec·tile /£prəˈdʒek·taɪl, $-t̬əl/ *n* [C] *specialized* • A projectile is an object that is thrown or fired forwards, esp. from a weapon: *The second projectile exploded after hitting a tank.*

proj·ect *obj* [MAKE AN IMAGE] /prəˈdʒekt/ *v* [T] to cause (a film, image or light) to appear on a screen or other surface • *We don't have a screen but we can project the slides* **onto** *the back wall.* • *On the back wall of the stage is a projected image of Christ.* • If you project your emotions **onto** someone else you imagine that they are feeling the same way as you without understanding that this is what you are doing: *He accuses me of being bored with the relationship when all he's doing is projecting his dissatisfaction onto me!* • The way that you project yourself is the way that you represent yourself to other people through your speech, behaviour and appearance: *Recently the president has sought to project a much tougher* **image**. • (PL) (RUS)

pro·jec·tion /prəˈdʒek·ʃən/ *n* [U] • *Part of the display involves the projection of a series of images.* • See also PROJECTION; **projection** at PROJECT [CALCULATE], PROJECT [STICK OUT].

pro·jec·tion·ist /prəˈdʒek·ʃən·ɪst/ *n* [C] • A projectionist is a person whose job is to operate a projector in a cinema.

pro·jec·tor /£prəˈdʒek·təʳ, $-t̬ɚ/ *n* [C] • A projector is a device for showing films or images on a screen or other surface.

proj·ect [STICK OUT] /prəˈdʒekt/ *v* [I] to stick out over an edge • *One of the features of the hotel is that its dining room projects* **(out)** *over the sea.* • (PL) (RUS)

pro·jec·tion /prəˈdʒek·ʃən/ *n* [C]

pro·jec·tion /prəˈdʒek·ʃən/ *n* [C] *specialized* a drawn representation of a solid shape or a line as seen from a particular direction • See also **projection** at PROJECT [CALCULATE], PROJECT [MAKE AN IMAGE], PROJECT [STICK OUT].

pro·lapse /£ˈprəʊ·læps, $ˈproʊ-/ *n* [C] a medical condition in which an organ has moved down out of its usual position • *a rectal prolapse/a prolapse of the rectum*

pro·lapsed /£ˈprəʊ·læps, $ˈproʊ-/ *adj* • *He called in a vet to treat a sheep that had a prolapsed womb.*

pro·le·ta·ri·at /£ˌprəʊ·lɪˈteə·ri·ət, £ˌprɒl·ɪ-, $ˌproʊ·ləˈter·i-/ *n* [U + sing/pl v] **the proletariat** the class of people who do unskilled jobs in industry and own little or no property • *His novels can be read as an account of the lives of the oppressed industrial proletariat.* • *"What I did that was new was to prove ... that the class struggle necessarily leads to the dictatorship of the proletariat"* (Karl Marx in a letter, 1852)

pro·le·tar·i·an /£ˌprəʊ·lɪˈteə·ri·ən, £ˌprɒl·ɪ-, $ˌproʊ·ləˈter·i-/, *infml usually humorous* **prole** /£prəʊl, $proʊl/ *n* [C], *adj* [not gradable] • *proletarian revolution*

pro–life /£ˌprəʊˈlaɪf, $ˌproʊ-/ *adj* [not gradable] opposed to the belief that a pregnant woman should have the freedom to choose an ABORTION (= an operation to end a pregnancy) if she does not want to have a baby • *The pro-life, anti-abortion movement has supporters in all the major political parties.* • Compare PRO-CHOICE.

pro·li·fer·ate /£prəˈlɪf·ər·eɪt, $-ə·reɪt/ *v* [I] to increase greatly and suddenly in number • *Small businesses have proliferated in the last ten years.*

pro·li·fer·a·tion /£prəˌlɪf·əˈreɪ·ʃən, $-əˈreɪ-/ *n* [U] • *Over the past two years we have witnessed the proliferation of TV channels.*

pro·lif·ic /prəˈlɪf·ɪk/ *adj* • Prolific means producing a great number or amount of something: *He was probably the most prolific song-writer of his generation.* ○ *Rabbits and other rodents are prolific* (= have a lot of babies).

pro·lix /£ˈprəʊ·lɪks, $ˈproʊ-/ *adj fml disapproving* using too many words and therefore boring or difficult to read or listen to; VERBOSE • *The author's prolix style has done nothing to encourage sales of the book.*

pro·logue, *Am also* **pro·log** /£ˈprəʊ·lɒg, $ˈproʊ·lɑːg/ *n* [C] an introductory part at the beginning of a play, story or long poem, often giving information about events that have happened before the time when the play, story or poem begins • *The prologues* **to** *many plays of this period were actually spoken on stage by the actors.* • *(fig. infml) A series of internal struggles was the prologue* **to** (= the events that led to) *full-scale civil war.* • Compare EPILOGUE.

pro·long *obj* /£prəˈlɒŋ, $-ˈlɑːŋ/ *v* [T] to make (something) last a longer time • *We were having such a good time that we decided to prolong our stay by another week.* • *She chewed each delicious mouthful as slowly as she could, prolonging the pleasure.*

pro·lon·ga·tion /£ˌprəʊ·lɒŋˈgeɪ·ʃən, $ˌproʊ·lɑːŋ-/ *n* [U] • *Research strongly suggests that we can contribute to the prolongation of healthy life by altering our diets.*

pro·longed /£prəˈlɒŋd, $-ˈlɑːŋd/ *adj* • *Prolonged use of the drug is known to have harmful side-effects.* • *The decision was finally made after a prolonged debate in the Senate.*

prom [PARTY] /£prɒm, $prɑːm/ *n* [C] *Am* a formal party held for older students at the end of the school year, at which there is dancing • *Who are you taking to the Senior Prom?*

prom [PATH] /£prɒm, $prɑːm/ *infml for* PROMENADE

prom·e·nade /£ˌprɒm·əˈnɑːd, $ˌprɑː·məˈneɪd/, *infml* **prom** *n* [C] a path for walking on, esp. *(Br)* one built next to the sea at a town beside the sea • *We strolled along on the promenade eating ice-creams.*

prom·e·nade /£ˌprɒm·əˈnɑːd, $ˌprɑː·məˈneɪd/ *v* [I] *dated* • To promenade is to walk slowly along a road or path for relaxation and pleasure.

prom·i·nent /£ˈprɒm·ɪ·nənt, $ˈprɑː·mə-/ *adj* very noticeable, well known or important • *The recent fraud scandal involved and discredited a number of the country's most prominent politicians.* • *The government should be playing a more prominent role/part in promoting human rights.* • Something might be prominent because it sticks out from a surface: *She has a rather prominent chin/nose.* • Something might also be prominent because it is in a position in which it is easily seen: *New books were displayed in a prominent* **position** *on tables at the front of the shop.*

prom·i·nent·ly /£ˈprɒm·ɪ·nənt·li, $ˈprɑː·mɪ-/ *adv*

prom·i·nence /£ˈprɒm·ɪ·nənts, $ˈprɑː·mə-/ *n* [U] • *Most of the papers* **give** *prominence* **to** (= put in a noticeable position) *the same story this morning.* • *It's the first time that a lawyer of such prominence* (= fame and importance) *has been given the freedom to air his views on TV.* • *Elton was one of the comedians who* **came to/rose to/gained** *prominence* (= became famous) *in the 1980s.*

pro·mis·cu·ous /prəˈmɪs·kju·əs/ *adj disapproving* (of a person) having a lot of different sexual partners or sexual relationships, or (of sexual habits) involving a lot of different partners • *I suppose I was quite promiscuous in my* *youth.* • *It's an often repeated fallacy that homosexual men have more promiscuous life-styles than heterosexuals.* • *The sixties are synonymous with promiscuous sex and free living.*

pro·mis·cu·ous·ly /prə'mɪs·kju·ə·sli/ *adv*

prom·is·cu·i·ty /£ˌprɒm·ɪ'skjuː·ɪ·ti, $ˌprɑː·mɪ'skjuː·ə·ti/ *n* [U] • *The Health Secretary stated that a dramatic decline in promiscuity would greatly reduce the number of cases of HIV and AIDS.*

prom·ise *(obj)* /£'prɒm·ɪs, $'prɑː·mɪs/ *v* to tell (someone) that you will certainly do something • *Do you promise never* **to** *repeat what I've just said?.* [+ *to* infinitive] • *I've got to go – I promised* **to** *be home by 10 o'clock.* [+ *to* infinitive] • *The government have promised* **that** *they'll reduce taxes.* [+ *that* clause] • *Promise me* **(that)** *you'll never leave me!* [+ obj + (*that*) clause] • *Promise me* **(that)** *if you go bald you'll never try to hide it.* [+ obj + (*that*) clause] • *"I won't do anything dangerous." "You promise?" "I promise."* [I] • *"I won't have time to take you shopping this afternoon." "But you promised!"* [I] • *I'll have a look for some while I'm at the shops but I'm not promising anything.* [T] • *Can I have that book back when you've finished because I've promised it* (= I've said I'll give it) **to** *Sara.* [T] • *Her husband promised her a new bedroom suite if she'd lose weight.* [+ two objects] • *I've promised myself a long bath when I get through all this work.* [+ two objects] • *'I'll come round and see you every day,' she promised.* [+ clause] • If you say that a future situation promises **to** be interesting, enjoyable, etc., you mean that you expect it will be interesting, enjoyable, etc.: *The men's final this afternoon promises to be a very exciting match.* [+ *to* infinitive] • *(infml)* If you **promise** (someone) **the earth/moon** you say that you will do much greater things than you will ever be able to achieve: *Like most governments in their first term of office they promised the earth.* • In the Bible, **the Promised Land** is the land of Canaan, promised by God to Abraham and his race: *(fig.) America was the Promised Land for many immigrant families.*

prom·ise /£'prɒm·ɪs, $'prɑː·mɪs/ *n* • *If I* **make** *a promise I like to* **keep** *it* (= do what I said I would). [C] • *You've* **broken** *your promise, Dad – you said you'd take me swimming this week and you haven't!* [C] • *I'll tidy my things away tonight – and that's a promise!* [C] • *I'll try to get back in time but I'm not* **making** *any promises.* [C] • *(infml)* You can say **promises, promises** to tell someone, humorously, that you think they are making a promise that they cannot or are not likely to keep: *"When I've got some time I'll show you everything." "Promises, promises!"* • Promise also refers to positive signs for future development: *His English teacher had written on his report that he* **showed** *great promise.* [U] ○ *As a child I was quite a good dancer but I didn't fulfil my early promise.* [U] ○ *The morning sky was clear and held great promise.* [U]

prom·is·ing /£'prɒm·ɪ·sɪŋ, $'prɑː·mɪ-/ *adj* • Something which is promising shows signs that it is going to be successful or enjoyable: *They won the award for the most promising new band of the year.* ○ *"How's your new venture going?" "It's looking quite promising."* ○ *It's a strange restaurant because it doesn't look at all promising from the outside.*

prom·is·ing·ly /£'prɒm·ɪ·sɪŋ·li, $'prɑː·mɪ-/ *adv* • *The film starts promisingly enough but it doesn't maintain the interest level.*

prom·is·so·ry note /£ˌprɒm·ɪ·sᵊr·i-, $ˌprɑː·mɪ·sɔːr-/ *n* [C] *specialized* a document which contains a promise to pay a stated amount of money to a stated person either on a fixed date or when the money is demanded

pro·mo /£'prəʊ·məʊ, $'proʊ·moʊ/ *n* [C] *pl* **promos** *infml* a short film which is made to advertise a product, esp. a record of modern popular music • *It's a short promo, made to accompany the release of the group's latest record.* • *(Am and Aus)* A promo is also an advertisement, broadcast announcement, discussion with a writer, film producer, actor, etc. which is designed to give attention to a book or film in order to increase sales: *In Chicago she'll appear on two talk shows and sign books at Doubleday as promos for her new novel.*

pro·mon·to·ry /£'prɒm·ən·tri, $'prɑː·mən·tɔːr-/, **head·land** *n* [C] a narrow area of high land that sticks out into the sea • *There's a castle built on the promontory overlooking the cliffs.*

pro·mote *obj* ENCOURAGE /£prə'məʊt, $-'moʊt/ *v* [T] to encourage the popularity, sale, development or existence of (something) • *Advertising companies are always having to think up new ways to promote products.* • *The government have announced plans for a new campaign to promote safe sex.* • *The Institute is intended to promote an understanding of the politics and culture of the Arab world.* • *Greenpeace works to promote awareness of the dangers that threaten our planet today.* • *It has long been known that regular exercise promotes all-round good health.* • *A report recently suggested that sugary foods promote breast cancer.* • (CS)

pro·mot·er /£prə'məʊ·təʳ, $-'moʊ·t̬ɚ/ *n* [C] • *The bishop stressed the ever-increasing role of the church as a promoter of peace between nations.* • Promoter often refers to a person who organizes and arranges finance for sporting and musical events: *a boxing/rock concert promoter*

pro·mo·tion /£prə'məʊ·ʃᵊn, $-'moʊ-/ *n* • *As part of their* **sales** *promotion they're giving away a free pair of sunglasses with each holiday.* [C] • *There was a promotion in the supermarket and they were giving away free glasses of wine.* [C] • *Obviously as sales manager he'll be very involved in the promotion and marketing of the product.* [U]

pro·mo·tion·al /£prə'məʊ·ʃᵊn·ᵊl, $-'moʊ-/ *adj* • *Part of the bank's recent promotional campaign has involved trying to persuade young people to open an account with them.* • *The writer recently went on a promotional tour of his homeland.*

pro·mote *obj* RAISE /£prə'məʊt, $-'moʊt/ *v* [T] to raise (someone) to a higher or more important rank or position • *If I'm not promoted within the next two years I'm going to change jobs.* • *She's just been promoted which means a company car and an extra five thousand.* • *He was promoted from Captain* **to** *Commodore in 1939.* • *If Coventry City win this match they'll be promoted* **to** *the Premier League.* • *(Am)* If a student is promoted, they go up to the next higher GRADE (= level of schooling) at the end of the school year after completing their work during the year successfully: *The fifth graders did very well this year and all have been promoted* **to** *grade six.* • Compare DEMOTE. • (LP) **Sports** (CS)

pro·mo·tion /£prə'məʊ·ʃᵊn, $-'moʊ-/ *n* • *Did Steve* **get**/ *Was Steve* **given** *the promotion he wanted?* [C] • *She's been recommended for promotion by her boss.* [U] • *The job offers excellent promotion* **prospects**. [U] • *Internal promotions are usually posted on the notice board.* [C] • *Fiorentina's win against Palermo last night has considerably increased their chances of promotion this season.* [U] • (CS) (D)

prompt *obj* CAUSE /£prɒmpt, $prɑːmpt/ *v* [T] to cause or tell (someone) to say or do something • *What prompted you* **to** *say that?* [+ obj + *to* infinitive] • *Revelations over the minister's affair with a young actress have prompted calls for his resignation.* • *The bishop's speech has prompted an angry response from both political parties.* • *The recent worries over the president's health have prompted speculation over his political future.* • *Seeing the children in the park prompted thoughts of his own sons on the other side of the Atlantic.* • Someone prompts an actor or speaker while they are performing or speaking by reading out the word or phrase that the speaker has forgotten: *The leading actress had to be prompted twice!*

prompt /£prɒmpt, $prɑːmpt/ *n* [C] • On a computer screen a prompt is a sign which shows that the computer is ready to receive your instructions. • In the theatre a prompt is either the words which are spoken to an actor who has forgotten what he or she is meant to say, or (also **prompter**) a person whose job is to supply forgotten words to an actor.

prompt·ing /£'prɒmp·tɪŋ, $'prɑːmp-/ *n* • *Kids of that age really shouldn't need prompting* **to** *say thank you for things.* [U + *to* infinitive] • *Amazingly – without any prompting – my husband actually said how nice I looked in my new dress!* [U] • *I didn't once compliment him, despite repeated promptings to do so.* [C]

prompt QUICK /£prɒmpt, $prɑːmpt/ *adj* **-er, -est** (of an action) done quickly and without delay, or (of a person) acting quickly or arriving at the arranged time • *They've written back already – that was a very prompt reply.* • *It's a fairly serious problem which requires prompt action.* • *They're usually fairly prompt in dealing with enquiries.* • *Try to be prompt because we'll be very short of time.*

prompt /£prɒmpt, $prɑːmpt/ *adv* [not gradable] • *She said that they were leaving at six o'clock prompt* (= certainly no later than six o'clock). • *Classes start at ten o'clock prompt.*

prompt·ly /£'prɒmpt·li, $'prɑːmpt-/ *adv* • *We'll have to leave fairly promptly if we want to catch that train.* • *We try to answer reader's letters as promptly as we can.* • *She asked* *to borrow my car and promptly* (= immediately after) *went and smashed it up!*

prom·ul·gate *obj* ANNOUNCE /£'prɒm·ᵊl·geɪt, $'prɑː·məl-/ *v* [T] *fml* to announce publicly, esp. at the start of (a new law) • *The new law was finally promulgated in the autumn of last year.*

prom·ul·ga·tion /£ˌprɒm·ᵊl'geɪ·ʃᵊn, $ˌprɑː·məl-/ *n* [U] *fml* • *Under the present law, death sentences cannot be carried out within ten days of their promulgation.*

prom·ul·gate *obj* SPREAD /£'prɒm·ᵊl·geɪt, $'prɑː·məl-/ *v* [T] *fml* to spread (beliefs or ideas) among a lot of people • *It's all part of the propaganda machine which promulgates the belief that men are superior to women.*

prom·ul·ga·tion /£ˌprɒm·ᵊl'geɪ·ʃᵊn, $ˌprɑː·məl-/ *n* [U] *fml*

pron *abbreviation for* PRONOUN

prone TENDING /£prəʊn, $proʊn/ *adj* [after v; always + *to*] tending to suffer from an illness or show a particular negative characteristic • *You're more prone* **to** *illnesses when you're tired and your body is run-down.* • *As a child he was very prone* **to** *nose and throat infections.* • *You have to bear in mind that Angela is rather prone* **to** *exaggeration.* • *Mists are prone* **to** *come rolling in at the end of the day.* [+ *to* infinitive]

-prone /£-prəʊn, $-proʊn/ *combining form* • *accident-prone* (= often having accidents) • *injury-prone* (= often getting injuries)

prone LYING DOWN /£prəʊn, $proʊn/ *adj, adv* [not gradable] *fml* lying on the front with the face down • *The photograph showed a man lying prone on the pavement, a puddle of blood about his head.* • Compare SUPINE.

prong /£prɒŋ, $prɑːŋ/ *n* [C] one of two or more long sharp points on an object, esp. a fork

-pronged /£-prɒŋd, $-prɑːŋd/ *combining form* • A two/three-pronged plan involves two/three different ways of achieving the same aim: *The government evolved a three-pronged strategy to beat inflation.*

pro·noun /£'prəʊ·naʊn, $'proʊ-/ *n* [C] a word which is used instead of a noun or a noun phrase • *Pronouns are often used to refer to a noun that has already been mentioned.* • *'She', 'it' and 'who' are all examples of pronouns.*

pronominal /£prəʊ'nɒm·ɪ·nəl, $proʊ'nɑː·mə-/ *adj* [not gradable] *specialized*

pro·nounce *obj* MAKE SOUND /prə'naʊnts/ *v* [T] to say a word or a letter in a particular way • *How do you pronounce your surname?* • *She pronounced his name so badly he didn't even recognise it.* • *Sade, pronounced shah-day, is a singer.*

pro·nun·ci·a·tion /prəˌnʌnt·si'eɪ·ʃᵊn/ *n* • *English pronunciation is notoriously difficult.* [U] • *As a newsreader she became famous for her very exact pronunciation of foreign names.* [U] • *There are two different pronunciations of this word.* [C] • *His knowledge of English is good but he has problems with pronunciation.* [U] • LP **Pronunciation, Varieties of English**

pro·nounce *(obj)* TO STATE /prə'naʊnts/ *v fml* to state something officially or with certainty • *He was taken to the hospital where he was pronounced dead on arrival.* [T + obj + n/adj] • *When the vicar says "I now pronounce you man and wife" and the newly-married couple kiss, I always start to cry!* [T + obj + n/adj] • *The jury pronounced him guilty.* [T + obj + n/adj] • *He gazed vacantly while the verdict and sentence were pronounced.* [T] • *She surveyed the building and pronounced herself pleased with their work.* [T + obj + n/adj] • *The government pronounced* **that** *they are no longer a nuclear state.* [+ *that* clause] • *"Have I met him?" "You have indeed – I recall you pronounced the man* (= said that he was) *a fool."* [T + obj + n/adj] • *The dessert was tried and pronounced delicious.* [T + obj + n/adj] • *I'd rather not go pronouncing* **on/upon** (= making judgments on) *a subject that I know so little about.* [I]

pro·nounce·ment /prəʊ'naʊnt·smənt/ *n* [C] • *The treasurer has been taking a more optimistic view of economic recovery in his recent public pronouncements.* • *I think we're all sick of politicians* **making** *pronouncements on the decline of moral values.*

pro·nounced /prə'naʊntst/ *adj* very noticeable or certain • *I'm told I have a very pronounced English accent when I speak French.* • *She's a woman of very pronounced views which she is not afraid to air.*

pron·to /£'prɒn·təʊ, $'prɑːn·t̬oʊ/ *adv* [not gradable] *infml* quickly and without delay • *I'll send those off pronto, before I forget.*

proof SHOWING TRUTH /pruːf/ *n* one or more reasons for believing that something is or is not true • *Do they have any proof* **that** *it was Hampson who stole the goods?* [U + *that* clause] • *I have a suspicion that he's having an affair, though I don't have any* **concrete** *proof.* [U] • *If anyone needs proof* **of** *Andrew Davies' genius as a writer, this novel is it.* [U] • *"How old are you?" "Twenty-one." "Have you got any proof on you?"* [U] • *Keep your receipt as proof* **of** *purchase.* [U] • *It has always seemed to me that there are two proofs of* (= arguments that show) *the existence of God given by philosophers that seem convincing.* [C] • *(saying)* 'The proof of the pudding (is in the eating)' means that you can only judge the quality of something after you have tried, used or in some way experienced it. • **Proof positive** is facts that cannot be doubted: *The strength of negative reaction to the article is proof positive that this is a very important issue.* • See **burden of proof** at BURDEN.

prove *obj* /pruːv/ *v* [T] *past* **proved**, *past part esp. Am* **proven** /'pruː·vᵊn, £'prəʊ-/ • *They suspected that she'd killed him but they could never actually prove* **that** *it was her.* [+ *that* clause] • *They proved him innocent/guilty.* [+ obj + adj] • *Under the present system you're innocent until proven guilty.* [+ obj + adj] • *You've got to prove to me* **that** *I can trust you.* [+ *that* clause] • *(infml) "I spent thirty pounds in the pub last night." "That just* **goes to** *prove* **what** *an idiot you are!"* [+ *wh-* word] • *Computers have been used to prove mathematical theorems.* • *If you don't believe that I stayed at my parents' house last night I'll prove it!* • *That theory was proved false.* [+ obj + adj] • *He's so aggressive – it's as if he's always trying to prove something.* • See also PROVE SHOW.

pro·ven /'pruː·vᵊn, £'prəʊ-/ *adj* [not gradable] • *You've got a proven work record which gives you a big advantage.*

-proof PROTECTED /-pruːf/ *combining form* protecting against; not damaged by • *a bullet-proof vest* • *a waterproof jacket* • *It's a warm coat but it's not wind-proof.* • *You need to buy terracotta pots that are frost-proof.*

proof /pruːf/ *adj fml* • *No household security devices are proof* **against** (= protect completely against) *the determined burglar.* • *Her virtue would be proof* **against** *his charms.*

proof *obj* /pruːf/ *v* [T] • If you proof a surface you treat it with a substance which will protect it against something, esp. water: *The jackets are proofed with a special substance which makes them resistant to water and oil.*

proof PRINTED COPY /pruːf/ *n* [C] a printed copy of something which is examined and corrected before the final copies are printed • *He had worked for a publisher during the summer vacation, correcting proofs and making the tea.* • *We chose two photos for enlargement from the five proofs the photographer showed us.*

proof ALCOHOL /pruːf/ *adj* [after n; not gradable] of the stated alcoholic strength, a higher number meaning a greater amount of alcohol • *It says on the bottle that it's 60 proof.*

proof·read *(obj)* /'pruːf·riːd/ *v* to find and correct mistakes in PROOFS (= copies of printed text) before the final copies are printed • *Judith proofreads (poetry books) for a small publishing company.* [I/T]

proof·read·er /£'pruːfˌriː·dəʳ, $-dɚ/ *n* [C] • A proofreader is a person whose job is to correct mistakes in books before they are printed.

proof·read·ing /'pruːfˌriː·dɪŋ/ *n* [U] • *Most of the errors were corrected at the proofreading stage.*

prop SUPPORT /£prɒp, $prɑːp/ *v* [I always + adv/prep] **-pp-** to support something physically, often by leaning it against something else or putting something under it • *I left my bike propped* **(up) against** *the wall.* • *He was sitting upright in his hospital bed, propped* **up** *by pillows.* • *She was sitting at the desk with her chin propped on her hands.* • *There were the usual bunch of drinkers propped* **up** *at the bar.* • *This window keeps on closing – I'll have to prop it* **open** *with something.* • *(fig.) How long is that government likely to survive without the US military force there to keep it propped* **up**?

prop /£prɒp, $prɑːp/ *n* [C] • A prop is an object which is used to support something by holding it up: *I need some sort of a prop to keep the washing line up.* • *(fig.) A lot of people use cigarettes as a sort of social prop* (= to make them feel more confident).

prop FILM/THEATRE /£prɒp, $prɑːp/ *n* [C usually pl] an object that is used in a play or film • *The set is minimal and the only props used in the show are a table, a chair and a glass of water.* • *She's the props mistress at the local theatre.*

PRONUNCIATION

• Types of English pronunciation given in the dictionary

A particular way of pronouncing a language is called an accent. This dictionary gives information on the two most important English accents:

BBC pronunciation is the standard British accent used by educated, professional people in Britain, particularly in the south.

General American is the standard accent in the United States, especially in the central and western parts of the country.

• Pronunciation symbols

Inside the back cover of the dictionary there is a complete list of the symbols used to show the pronunciation of a word. Mostly these symbols are taken from the International Phonetic Alphabet. The following notes give more information about some of these symbols.

• Syllable division

Many words can be divided into several spoken parts which are called syllables. In the pronunciation given in the dictionary, the syllables in a word are separated by a raised dot (·) or by one of the stress marks (ˈor ˌ). The stress marks show the primary (= main) stress (ˈ) and also the secondary stress (ˌ). For example **expectation** /ˌek·spekˈteɪ·ʃᵊn/ has four syllables: /ek/, /spek/, /teɪ/ and /ʃᵊn/. (For more information on primary and secondary stress LP **Stress in pronunciation**.)

The division of words into syllables is based on this rule: with some exceptions, as many consonants as possible are placed in the following syllable, except where this would produce a combination of sounds that could not be pronounced. For example **selfishness** /ˈsel·fɪʃ·nəs/, **helplessness** /ˈhel·plə·snəs/.

When writing words, we can also divide them into syllables according to the spelling. These written syllables are separated by a raised dot, for example **ex·pec·ta·tion, help·less·ness**. Notice that the divisions are not always in the same place as in the pronunciation.

• The symbol ᵊ

Most syllables in English have a vowel, but sometimes a syllable can be formed just from one or two consonants, as for example the last syllable in the words nation and special. The consonants n, m, l and r are often used in this way, and are called syllabic consonants. They can be pronounced in two different ways: simply as a consonant, or with a /ə/ before them. For example nation can be pronounced /ˈneɪ·ʃn/ or /ˈneɪ·ʃən/, and special can be pronounced /ˈspeʃ·l̩/ or /ˈspeʃ·əl/. In the dictionary this is shown by putting a small raised 'ə' before the consonant. So these words are shown as /ˈneɪ·ʃᵊn/ and /ˈspeʃ·ᵊl/.

• Sounds that can be omitted

When a sound within a word can be left out, that sound is printed in *italic*. For example, the word **lunch** can be pronounced with or without a /t/ so the pronunciations /lʌntʃ/ and /lʌnʃ/ are both used. This is shown as /lʌn*t*ʃ/.

• Alternative pronunciations

Some words are commonly pronounced in more than one way. In these cases the pronunciations are shown in the order:

1. the most common British pronunciation (marked £ if found only in British English)
2. other important standard British pronunciations
3. the most common American pronunciation (marked $ if found only in American English)

Pronunciations which are both British and American are left unmarked. Alternative pronunciations are not shown in full, but parts of the pronunciation which do not change are shown with a – symbol. For example, **dagger** is pronounced /ˈdæg·eʳ/ in British English and /ˈdæg·ɚ/ in American English. This is shown as **dagger** /£dæg·əʳ, $–ɚ/.

• Alternative patterns of stress

Sometimes it is only the pattern of stress which is different between two alternative pronunciations. In such cases a dash is written to represent each syllable and the alternative stress pattern is shown by marking these dashes with stress symbols. For example **fifteenth** /ˌfifˈtiːnθ, ˈ--/.

• Words pronounced with /ə/ or /ɪ/

There are very many words which have an unstressed syllable which can be pronounced either /ə/ or /ɪ/. For example, **become** can be pronounced /bəˈkʌm/ or /bɪˈkʌm/. Both pronunciations are acceptable, but in order to save space only the most common is shown in the dictionary.

• Pronunciation of regular word forms

The dictionary shows all *irregular* forms of words and their pronunciation. It does not give the pronunciation of regular word forms such as regular plurals or past forms. The rules are as follows:

'-s' endings of nouns and verbs

Regular plurals of nouns, and the third person singular of the present tense of regular verbs, are formed with '-s'. Their pronunciation depends on the sound at the end of the word:

ending in a sibilant sound (s, ʃ, tʃ, z, ʒ, dʒ) — /ɪz/ *horses; raises*

not ending in a sibilant

- ending in a voiced sound (a vowel or b, d, g, v, ð, l, l̩, r, m, n, ŋ) — /z/ *boys; dogs; falls*
- ending in a voiceless sound (p, t, k, f, θ) — /s/ *gates; stops*

'-d' endings of verbs

The past simple and past participle of regular verbs are formed with '-d'.

ending in /t/	/£tɪd/, /$t̬ɪd/	*parted*
ending in /d/	/dɪd/	*mended*
not ending in /t/ or /d/:		
ending in a voiced sound or dʒ	/d/	*banned; judged*
ending in a voiceless sound or s, ʃ, tʃ, z	/t/	*coughed; tapped passed; bunched*

prop [AIRCRAFT/SHIP] /£prɒp, $prɑːp/ *n* [C] *infml for* PROPELLER

prop·a·gan·da /£ˌprɒp·əˈgæn·də, $ˌprɑː·pə-/ *n* [U] *esp. disapproving* information, ideas, opinions or images, often only giving one part of an argument, which are broadcast, published or in some other way spread with the intention of influencing people's opinions • *wartime propaganda* • *At school they were fed communist/right-wing propaganda and they believed a good deal of it.* • *During this time the television was just another propaganda weapon.* • *One official dismissed the ceasefire as a mere propaganda exercise.*

prop·a·gan·dist /£ˌprɒp·əˈgæn·dɪst, $ˌprɑː·pə-/ *n* [C], *adj disapproving* • *Communist/Nazi/Republican/right-wing propagandists* • *The government have recruited the usual army of image-makers and propagandists.* • *The papers were full of the most blatant propagandist nonsense.*

prop·a·gan·dize, *Br and Aus usually* **-ise** /£ˌprɒp·əˈgæn·daɪz, $ˌprɑː·pə-, ˈ---/ *v* [I] *fml disapproving*

prop·a·gate *(obj)* /£ˈprɒp·ə·geɪt, $ˈprɑː·pə-/ *v* to produce a new plant from a parent plant, or *(fml)* (of a plant or animal) to reproduce • *Most house plants can be propagated from stem cuttings.* [T] • *Many plants propagate themselves using the wind to carry their seeds.* [T] • *The plant needs certain conditions to propagate.* [I] • *Some single-celled animals propagate by division rather than sexual reproduction.* [I] • *(fml)* To propagate opinions, lies or religions is to spread them among a lot of people: *The government tried to propagate the belief that this is a decent war.* [T] ○ *Such lies are propagated in the media.* [T] • (CS)

prop·a·ga·tion /£ˌprɒp·əˈgeɪ·ʃᵊn, $ˌprɑː·pə-/ *n* [U] • *Propagation is generally best in spring or early summer.*

prop·a·gat·or /£ˈprɒp·ə·geɪ·təʳ, $ˈprɑː·pə·geɪ·t̬ɚ/ *n* [C] • A propagator is a small, sometimes heated, box with a transparent cover in which seeds or young plants are grown.

pro·pane /£ˈprəʊ·peɪn, $ˈproʊ-/ *n* [U] a colourless gas used as fuel, esp. in cooking and heating • *a propane stove/torch* • *Propane is so clean-burning that there is almost no smoke.*

pro·pel *obj* /prəˈpel/ *v* [T] **-ll-** to cause something to move forwards • *a rocket propelled grenade* • *The Kon-Tiki sailed across the Pacific Ocean propelled by wind power.* • *(fig.) Mr Jovis said that the country was being propelled* (=pushed) *towards civil war.* • *(Br and Aus)* A **propelling pencil** (*Am* **mechanical pencil**) is a pencil in which the LEAD (=part that writes) can be pushed forward by turning or pressing a part of the pencil.

pro·pel·lant /prəˈpel·ənt/ *n* • A propellant is an explosive substance or fuel which causes something to move forwards: *The factory produces propellant for ballistic missiles.* • A propellant is also a gas which is used in AEROSOLS to force the liquid out in very small drops.

pro·pel·ler /£prəˈpel·əʳ, $-ɚ/, *infml* **prop** *n* [C] • A propeller is a device which causes a ship or aircraft to move, consisting of two or more blades which turn round at high speed.

pro·pul·sion /prəˈpʌl·ʃᵊn/ *n* [U] • *wind propulsion* • *a propulsion system* • See **jet propulsion** at JET [AIRCRAFT]. • [PIC]> **Blade, Ships and boats**

pro·pen·si·ty /£prəˈpen·sɪ·ti, $-sə·t̬i/ *n* [U] *fml* a tendency towards a particular way of behaving, esp. a bad one • *She's inherited from her mother a propensity* **to** *talk too much.* [+ *to* infinitive] • *He's well-known for his natural propensity* **for** *indiscretion.*

prop·er [REAL] /£ˈprɒp·əʳ, $ˈprɑː·pɚ/ *adj* [not gradable] real, satisfactory, suitable or correct • *This is Sara's first proper job – she usually does temporary work just for the money.* • *If you're going to walk those sort of distances you need proper walking boots.* • *I would have done the job myself but I didn't have the proper equipment.* • *She never seems to eat a proper meal – she just nibbles on peanuts and chocolate.* • *She likes everything to be in its proper place.* • *(specialized)* A **proper fraction** is a FRACTION in which the number below the line is larger than the number above it: ½ *and* ¾ *are proper fractions.* • *(specialized)* A **proper noun** is the name of a particular person, place or object and it is spelt with a capital letter: *Examples of proper nouns in English are Joseph, Vienna and the White House.* Compare **common noun** at COMMON [SHARED]. • [LP]> **Capital letters** (D) (DK) (S)

prop·er /£ˈprɒp·əʳ, $ˈprɑː·pɚ/ *adv* [not gradable] *Br not standard esp. humorous* • Proper is sometimes used as an adverb, usually when someone is being humorous and trying to copy a way of speaking which is not standard: *She's dead posh you're girlfriend, ain't she – she* **speaks** *real proper like!* ○ *You should* **talk** *proper, like what I do.*

prop·er·ly /£ˈprɒp·ᵊl·i, $ˈprɑː·pɚ·li/ *adv* [not gradable] • *It's still not working properly.* • *I'm not properly dressed for this sort of weather.* • *I think you should take it somewhere to have it mended properly.* • *I was so drunk I couldn't even walk properly let alone dance.* • *Come on, Evie, speak properly – you're not a baby any more!* • *(fml) It's not,* **properly speaking**, *champagne but it tastes just like it.*

prop·er [SOCIALLY ACCEPTABLE] /£ˈprɒp·əʳ, $ˈprɑː·pɚ/ *adj* showing standards of behaviour that are socially and morally acceptable • *In those days* **it** *was considered not quite proper for young ladies* **to** *be seen talking to men in public.* [+ *to* infinitive] • *She was very proper, my grandmother – she'd never go out without wearing her hat and gloves.* • (D) (DK) (S)

prop·er·ly /£ˈprɒp·ᵊl·i, $ˈprɑː·pɚ·li/ *adv fml* • *Most vegetables should be eaten with a fork but asparagus can be properly* (=politely) *eaten with the fingers.*

pro·pri·e·ty /£prəˈpraɪə·ti, $-t̬i/ *n* [U] *fml* • Propriety is moral correctness of behaviour or of actions: *The director insisted that there was no question as to the propriety of how the funds were raised.* ○ *My mother is very concerned with propriety – I think she'd be horrified if I was living with a man that I wasn't married to.* • (F)

pro·pri·e·ties /£prəˈpraɪə·tiz, $-t̬iz/ *pl n fml* • **The proprieties** are the rules of polite social behaviour: *Because they'd invited us to dinner, we thought we'd better* **observe** *the proprieties and invite them back, even though we found them very boring.*

prop·er [MAIN] /£ˈprɒp·əʳ, $ˈprɑː·pɚ/ *adj* [after n; not gradable] belonging to the main, most important or typical part • *It's a suburb of Manchester really – I wouldn't call it Manchester proper.* • *They're a wing of the Conservative party – they're not the Conservative party proper.* • (D) (DK) (S)

prop·er [COMPLETE] /£ˈprɒp·əʳ, $ˈprɑː·pɚ/ *adj* [not gradable] *Br infml* complete • *You've got yourself into a proper mess there!* • *I'll look a proper prat in those trousers!* • (D) (DK) (S)

prop·er·ty [THINGS OWNED] /£ˈprɒp·ə·ti, $ˈprɑː·pɚ·t̬i/ *n* something or a number of things owned by someone, esp. buildings and land • *He seems to have absolutely no respect for other people's property – he's already smashed up two cars belonging to other people.* [U] • *Both books have 'property of Her Majesty's Government' stamped inside them.* [U] • *The club does not accept responsibility for loss of or damage to club members'* **personal** *property.* [U] • *The notice said 'Private Property, Keep Off.'* [U] • *(Br) My boyfriend is in property (Am and Aus* **real estate**) (=his job is related to buildings and land). [U] • *He owns some extremely valuable properties* (=buildings or land) *in the centre of London.* [C] • *The property report showed that house prices had fallen by 1% last month.* • *(fml or humorous) Yes, I've bought my own house – I'm now a* **man of** *property!* [U] • *(specialized)* Property is also the legal right to own and use something. [U] • A **property developer** is a person whose job involves buying and selling buildings and land, and arranging for new buildings to be built. • *"Property is theft"* (Pierre-Joseph Proudhon, 1840) • [LP]> **Borrow**

prop·er·ty [QUALITY] /£ˈprɒp·ə·ti, $ˈprɑː·pɚ·t̬i/ *n* [C] a quality in a substance or material, esp. one which means that it can be used in a particular way • *One of the properties of copper is that it conducts heat and electricity very well.* • *We use herbs in cooking but we forget that they also have medicinal properties.*

proph·e·cy /£ˈprɒf·ə·si, $ˈprɑː·fə-/ *n* a statement that says what is going to happen in the future, esp. one which is based on what you believe about a particular matter rather than existing facts • *The minister suggested that the dire prophecies of certain leading environmentalists were somewhat exaggerated.* [C] • *These doom and gloom prophecies are doing little to help the economy.* [C] • *Well, your prophecy* **that** *I would end up with a rich older man hasn't exactly come true, has it!* [C] • *Nostradamus was a French doctor and astrologer who wrote a book of prophecies.* [C] • *Ask Sara – she's a genius at the art of prophecy.* [U]

proph·e·sy *(obj)* /£ˈprɒf·ə·saɪ, $ˈprɑː·fə-/ *v* • *Few could have prophesied this war.* [T] • *He prophesied* **that** *the present government would only stay four years in office.* [+ *that* clause] • *I wouldn't like to prophesy* **what** *will happen to that marriage!* [+ *wh-* word] • *I've been proved wrong too many times – this time I'm not going to prophesy.* [I]

proph·et, *female also* **proph·et·ess** /£'prɒf·ɪt, $'prɑː·fɪt, £ˌprɒf·ɪ'tes, $ˌprɑː·fɪ'ţes/ *n* [C] • A prophet is a person who is believed to have a special power which allows them to say what a god wishes to tell people, esp. about things that will happen in the future : *an Old Testament prophet* ○ *Let us hear the words of the prophet Isaiah on the coming of the Prince of Peace.* • A prophet can also be a person who supports a new system of beliefs and principles: *Rousseau, that great prophet of the modern age* • **The Prophet** is Mohammed, the man who made Islam known to the world through the Koran. • *(disapproving)* A **prophet of doom** is a person who emphasizes the bad side of a situation and continually states that something bad is going to happen: *The prophets of doom have been predicting the end of the European cinema for the last ten years.*

pro·phet·ic /£prə'fet·ɪk, $-'feţ-/ *adj* • *Much of Orwell's writing now seems grimly prophetic* (=true). • *"There are bad days ahead for all of us," he said with prophetic gloom.*

pro·phet·i·cal·ly /£prə'fet·ɪ·kli, $-'feţ-/ *adv* • *He told her, prophetically, that she wouldn't be a success until she was thirty.*

proph·y·lac·tic /£ˌprɒf·ɪ'læk·tɪk, $ˌprɑː·fɪ'læk·ţɪk/ *adj* [not gradable] *specialized* preventing disease • *Some dentists are convinced that the addition of fluoride in water is ineffective as a prophylactic treatment.*

proph·y·lac·tic /£ˌprɒf·ɪ'læk·tɪk, $ˌprɑː·fɪ'læk·ţɪk/ *n* [C] *specialized* • A prophylactic is something which is intended to prevent disease or *(esp. Am)* pregnancy, esp. a CONDOM: *After a long period of decline, sales and public acceptance of prophylactics are both rising due to AIDS.*

pro·pi·ti·ate *obj* /prə'pɪʃ·i·eɪt/ *v* [T] *fml* to please and make calm (a god or person who is annoyed with you) • *In those days people might sacrifice a goat or sheep to propitiate an angry god.* • *The radicals in the party were clearly sacked to propitiate the conservative core.*

pro·pi·ti·a·tion /prəˌpɪʃ·i'eɪ·ʃᵊn/ *n* [U] *fml*

pro·pi·ti·a·to·ry /£prəˌpɪʃ·i'eɪ·tᵊr·i, $prə'pɪʃ·i·ə·tɔːr-/ *adj* [not gradable] *fml* • *a propitiatory gesture*

pro·pi·tious /prə'pɪʃ·əs/ *adj fml* likely to result in or showing signs of success • *With the economy in the worst recession for thirty years, it was scarcely the most propitious time to start up a company.* • *He'd been woken up that morning by a furious telephone call from his wife – it was not a propitious start to the day.*

pro·pi·tious·ly /prə'pɪʃ·ə·sli/ *adv fml*

pro·po·nent /£prə'pəʊ·nənt, $-'poʊ-/ *n* [C] a person who speaks publicly in support of a particular idea or plan of action • *Portillo is one of the leading proponents* **of** *capital punishment.* • Compare OPPONENT.

pro·por·tion /£prə'pɔː·ʃᵊn, $-'pɔːr-/ *n* a part or share of the whole, or a compared number, amount or level • A proportion is often the number, amount or level of one thing when compared to another: *The proportion of women* **to** *men at my college was about five women to one man.* [C] ○ *The proportion of fat* **to** *flour is different in pastry and sponge.* [C] ○ *The chart shows how weight increases* **in** *proportion* **to** *height* (=the increase in weight depends on the increase in height). [U] ○ *The level of crime in an area is almost always in* **direct** *proportion* **to** *the number of unemployed.* [U] • A proportion can also be the number or amount of a group or part of something when compared to the whole: *A higher proportion of women are now working.* [C] ○ *The report shows that poor families spend a large proportion of their income on food.* [C] • If something is big, small, long, short, etc. **in** proportion **to** another related thing it is big, small, etc. compared to the other thing: *You're lucky in that your legs are very long in proportion to your height.* [U] ○ *Her head is ridiculously big in proportion to her body.* [U] • Proportion also refers to the correct or most attractive relationship between the size of different parts of the same thing: *My head was much nearer the camera than the rest of me so I'm all* **out of** *proportion.* [U] ○ *"My legs are short." "They're not – they're in proportion to the rest of your body."* [U] • Proportion is used in particular phrases to mean importance and seriousness: *You've got to keep a* **sense of** *proportion* (=the ability to understand what is important and what is not). [U] ○ *It's ridiculous – we have a tiny disagreement and you blow the whole thing up* **out of** *proportion* (=treat the matter far too seriously)*!* [U] ○ *Of course when the papers get hold of a story it's blown out of all proportion.* [U] ○ *I think a certain amount of worry about work is very natural but you've got to keep it* **in** *proportion* (=judge correctly its seriousness). • See **inverse proportion** at INVERT.

pro·por·tion·ed /£prə'pɔː·ʃᵊnd, $-'pɔːr-/ *adj* • *We wandered through the beautifully proportioned rooms* (=with all the parts in exactly the right and most attractive size in relation to each other) *of the Winter Palace.* • *She has the dancer's finely proportioned physique.* • *The generously proportioned* (=fat) *singer has to have all his garments specially made.*

pro·por·tion·al /£prə'pɔː·ʃᵊn·ᵊl, $-'pɔːr-/, **pro·por·tion·ate** /£prə'pɔː·ʃᵊn·ət, $-'pɔːr-/ *adj* • *The degree of punishment is meant to be proportional* **to** *the seriousness of the crime.* • **Proportional representation** (also **PR**) is an electoral system in which political parties are represented in parliament according to the number of people who voted for them.

pro·por·tion·al·ly /£prə'pɔː·ʃᵊn·ᵊl·i, $-'pɔːr-/, **pro·por·tion·ate·ly** *adv* • *Proportionally* **to** *her income she spends far more on holidays than I do.* • *Unemployment is proportionally much higher in the north of the country.*

pro·por·tions /£prə'pɔː·ʃᵊnz, $-'pɔːr-/ *pl n* • The proportions of something refers to the size of all its different parts and how they compare with and match each other: *I'm not very good at drawing people – I can never get the proportions right.* ○ *(humorous) She's a woman of generous proportions* (=she is fat). • *(fig.) A small worry in the back of your mind can for no apparent reason* **assume/take on** *massive proportions* (=seem much more serious) *in the middle of the night.*

pro·pose *(obj)* SUGGEST /£prə'pəʊz, $-'poʊz/ *v* to offer or state (a possible plan or action) for other people to consider • *I propose* **that** *we wait until the budget has been announced before committing ourselves to any expenditure.* [+ *that* clause] • *He proposed* **dealing** *directly with the suppliers.* [+ v-*ing*] • *She proposed a boycott of the meeting.* [T] • *He proposed a* **motion** *that the chairman resign.* [T] • To propose someone is to suggest them for a position or for membership of an organization: *To be nominated for union president you need one person to propose you and another to second you.* [T] • If you propose **(to a person)** you ask someone to marry you: *I remember the night your father proposed to me.* [I] ○ *She felt sure he was going to propose.* [I]

pro·pos·al /£prə'pəʊ·zᵊl, $-'poʊ-/ *n* [C] • A proposal is a suggestion, sometimes a written one: *Congress has rejected the latest economic proposal* **put forward** *by the president.* ○ *There has been an angry reaction to the government's proposal* **to** *reduce unemployment benefit.* [+ *to* infinitive] ○ *Have you read Steve's proposals for the new project?* ○ *There was anger at the proposal* **that** *a UN peace-keeping force should be sent to the area.* [+ *that* clause] • A proposal is also an offer of marriage: *She refused his marriage proposal/proposal of marriage.*

pro·pos·er /£prə'pəʊ·zəʳ, $-'poʊ·zɚ/ *n* [C] • A proposer is a person who suggests a subject for discussion: *The proposer of the motion tonight is Jonathan Hesk.* • A proposer is also a person who suggests someone's name for a position or for membership of an organization.

prop·o·si·tion /£ˌprɒp·ə'zɪʃ·ᵊn, $ˌprɑː·pə-/ *n* [C] • A proposition is a suggestion or a statement offered for consideration: *He wrote to me last week regarding a business proposition he thought might interest me.* ○ *I've put my proposition to the company director for his consideration.* ○ *They were debating the proposition that 'All people are created equal'.* • A proposition might also be an offer of sex: *I certainly wasn't expecting him to* **make** *me a proposition!*

prop·o·si·tion *obj* /£ˌprɒp·ə'zɪʃ·ᵊn, $ˌprɑː·pə-/ *v* [T] *infml* • To proposition someone with whom you are not having a sexual relationship is to ask them if they would like to have sex with you: *I've just been propositioned by a dirty old man at the bar!*

pro·pose *obj* INTEND /£prə'pəʊz, $-'poʊz/ *v* [T] *fml* to intend to do something • *How do you propose* **to** *complete the project in such a short time scale?* [+ *to* infinitive] • *How do you propose* **tackling** *this problem?* [+ v-*ing*] • *I do not propose* **to** *reveal details at this stage.* [+ *to* infinitive] • *What we are proposing is a radical change in approach.*

pro·posed /£prə'pəʊzd, $-'poʊzd/ *adj* [not gradable] • *There have been huge demonstrations against the proposed factory closure.*

pro·pose *obj* EXPRESS GOOD WISHES /£prə'pəʊz, $-'poʊz/ *v* [T] **propose a toast** to ask people gathered at a formal social occasion to express their good wishes, admiration or respect for someone by holding up their glasses of wine at the same time and then drinking from them • *Now, if you'd all please raise your glasses, I'd like to propose a toast* **to** *the bride and groom.*

pro·pound *obj* /prəˈpaʊnd/ *v* [T] *fml* to suggest (a theory, belief or opinion) for other people to consider • *He's written a new book in which he propounds his vision of social reform.* • *It was Ptolemy who propounded the theory that the earth was at the centre of the universe.*

pro·pri·e·tor, *female dated also* **pro·pri·e·tress** /£prəˈpraɪə·təʳ, $-t̬ɚ, -trɪs/ *n* [C] a person who owns a particular type of business, esp. a hotel, a shop or a company that makes newspapers • *The proprietors of the hotel are being taken to court over failures to meet various safety regulations.*

pro·pri·e·tor·i·al /£prə,praɪəˈtɔː·ri·əl, $-ˈtɔːr·i-/ *adj* • *He put a proprietorial arm around her* (=as if he owned her).

pro·pri·e·ta·ry /£prəˈpraɪə·tri, $-ter·i/ *adj* • *I just assumed he owned the place – he had a proprietary air about him.* • Proprietary goods are those which are made and sent out by a company which can legally do so and whose name is on the product: *proprietary medicines*

pro·pri·e·ty /£prəˈpraɪə·ti, $-t̬i/ *n* [U] See at PROPER [SOCIALLY ACCEPTABLE]

pro·pri·e·ties /£prəˈpraɪə·tiz, $-t̬iz/ *pl n*

pro·pul·sion /prəˈpʌl·ʃᵊn/ *n* See at PROPEL

pro ra·ta /£,prəʊˈrɑː·tə, $,proʊˈreɪ·t̬ə/ *adj, adv* [not gradable] *fml* (of payments, pay increases, etc.) calculated according to a fixed rate • *It's £20 thousand pro rata but I'm doing half the full number of hours so I'll be getting ten thousand.*

pro·sa·ic /prəˈzeɪ·ɪk/ *adj fml* lacking interest, imagination and variety; boring • *I felt the book was spoilt by its prosaic dialogue.* • *If only she'd been called 'Camilla' or 'Flavia' instead of the prosaic 'Jane'.* • *He asked if I'd got my black-eye in a fight – I told him the prosaic truth that I'd banged my head on a door.*

pro·sciut·to /£prəˈʃuː·təʊ, $-t̬oʊ/ *n* [U] Italian HAM (=meat from a pig's leg), served in very thin slices • *I had my favourite prosciutto and melon for starters.*

pro·scribe *obj* /£prəʊˈskraɪb, $proʊ-/ *v* [T] *fml* (of a government or other authority) to forbid (something) • *The Broadcasting Act allows ministers to proscribe any channel that offends against good taste and decency.* • *The Athletics Federation have banned the runner from future races for using proscribed drugs.*

pro·scrip·tion /£prəʊˈskrɪp·ʃᵊn, $proʊ-/ *n* [U] *fml* • *Last year saw the proscription of the political party because of their terrorist links.*

pro·scrip·tive /£prəʊˈskrɪp·tɪv, $proʊˈskrɪp·t̬ɪv/ *adv fml disapproving* • *They still have very proscriptive laws governing the sale and consumption of alcohol.* • *The handbook aims to give guidelines on the use of non-sexist language without being overtly proscriptive.*

prose /£prəʊz, $proʊz/ *n* [U] written language in its ordinary form rather than poetry • *I've always preferred reading prose to poetry.* • Compare VERSE.

pros·e·cute *(obj)* [LEGAL] /£ˈprɒs·ɪ·kjuːt, $ˈprɑː·sɪ-/ *v* to officially accuse (someone) of committing a crime in a court of law, or (of a lawyer) to try to prove that a person accused of committing a crime is guilty of that crime • *Shoplifters will be prosecuted.* [T] • *Most of the civil servants involved in the affair have been successfully prosecuted and dismissed.* [T] • *He was prosecuted* **for** *fraud.* [T] • *Any manufacturer who does not conform to the standards could be prosecuted under the Consumers Protection Act, 1987.* [T] • *The victim has said that she will not prosecute.* [I] • Compare DEFEND.

pros·e·cu·tion /£,prɒs·ɪˈkjuː·ʃᵊn, $,prɑː·sɪ-/ *n* • *A number of the cases have resulted in successful prosecution.* [U] • *Doctors guilty of neglect are* **liable to** *prosecution.* [U] • *The proprietor has been given until the end of the week to clean his kitchens or he will* **face** *prosecution.* [U] • **The** prosecution refers to the lawyers in a trial who try to prove that a person accused of committing a crime is guilty of that crime: *His plea of guilty to manslaughter was not accepted by the prosecution.* [U] ○ *The prosecution alleged that he lured the officer to his death by making an emergency call.* [U] • *There have been a large number of fraud prosecutions recently.* [C]

pros·e·cut·or /£ˈprɒs·ɪ·kjuː·təʳ, $ˈprɑː·sɪ·kjuː·t̬ɚ/ *n* [C] • A prosecutor is a legal representative who officially accuses someone of committing a crime, esp. in a court of law.

pros·e·cute *obj* [CONTINUE] /£ˈprɒs·ɪ·kjuːt, $ˈprɑː·sɪ-/ *v* [T] *fml* to continue to take part in a planned group of activities, esp. a war • *He seemed convinced that the US would prosecute the* **war** *to its end.*

pros·e·cu·tion /£,prɒs·ɪˈkjuː·ʃᵊn, $,prɑː·sɪ-/ *n* [U] *fml* • (I)

pros·e·lyt·ize, *Br and Aus usually usually* **–ise** /£ˈprɒs·ᵊl·ɪ·taɪz, $ˈprɑː·sə·lɪ-/ *v* [I] *fml disapproving* to try to persuade someone to change their religious or political beliefs or their way of living to your own • *He was also remarkable for the proselytizing zeal with which he wrote his political pamphlets.* • *The television has provided the Evangelists with yet another platform for their proselytizing.*

pros·e·lyt·iz·er, *Br and Aus usually usually* **–iser** /£,prɒs·ᵊl·ɪˈtaɪ·zəʳ, $,prɑː·səl·ɪ·taɪ·zɚ/ *n* [C] *fml* • *This particular sect are the most active proselytizers, sending out missionaries to convert people to their faith.*

pros·pect [POSSIBILITY] /£ˈprɒs·pekt, $ˈprɑː·spekt/ *n* a possibility or likelihood of something happening • **There***'s a reasonable prospect* **of** *reaching the trapped child before it gets dark.* [C] • *With* **not much** *prospect* **of** *settling the dispute, the talks were halted.* [U] • *There's not much prospect* **that** *this war will be over soon.* [U + *that* clause] • *A recurrence of the illness was a prospect which terrified him.* [C] • *She enjoyed contemplating the prospect* **of** *being away from her job for a month.* [U] • *The prospect* **of** *having to be pleasant to all those boring people is far from enticing.* [U] • A prospect can also be a person who might be chosen, for example as an employee: *We'll be interviewing four more prospects for the secretarial job this afternoon.* [C] • (CS) (PL) (RUS)

pros·pects /£ˈprɒs·pekts, $ˈprɑː·spekts/ *pl n* • *Prospects* **of/for** (=Opportunities for) *employment remain bleak for most people in the area.* • *If she can bring in a few more good customers like that, her prospects* (=possibility of achieving success) *with this company look excellent.*

pro·spec·tive /£prəˈspek·tɪv, $-t̬ɪv/ *adj* [not gradable] • *We have received letters of application from several prospective* (=possible) *candidates.* • *Always be polite to prospective buyers.*

pros·pect [SEARCH] /prəˈspekt/ *v* [I] to search for gold, oil or other valuable substances on or under the surface of the earth • *to prospect* **for** *oil/gold* • *He spends the summers prospecting in the mountains.* • (CS) (PL) (RUS)

pro·spec·tor /£prəˈspek·təʳ, $-t̬ɚ/ *n* [C]

pros·pect [VIEW] /£ˈprɒs·pekt, $ˈprɑː·spekt/ *n* [C] *literary* a good view of a large land area or of a city • *From the restaurant there was a marvellous prospect* **of/over** *Sienna and the countryside beyond.* • (CS) (PL) (RUS)

pro·spec·tus /prəˈspek·təs/ *n* [C] a document giving details of a college, school or business and its activities • *I picked up a really impressive prospectus for Shirley Heath Junior School.*

pros·per /£ˈprɒs·pəʳ, $ˈprɑː·spɚ/ *v* [I] (of a person or a business) to be or become successful, esp. financially • *A lot of microchip manufacturing companies prospered at that time.* • *Perhaps he'll prosper as a painter now the initial problems seem to be over.*

pros·per·i·ty /£prɒsˈper·ɪ·ti, $prɑːˈsper·ə·t̬i/ *n* [U] • *A country's future prosperity depends, to an extent, upon the quality of education of its people.* • *The war was followed by a long period of peace and prosperity.*

pros·per·ous /£ˈprɒs·pᵊr·əs, $ˈprɑː·spɚ-/ *adj* • *She was the second daughter of a prosperous merchant banker.* • *It's hard to believe that in this prosperous country, hunger could be a serious problem.*

pros·per·ous·ly /£ˈprɒs·pᵊr·ə·sli, $ˈprɑː·spɚ-/ *adv*

pros·tate (gland) /£ˈprɒs·teɪt, $ˈprɑː·steɪt/ *n* [C] an organ in male mammals situated near to the penis which produces a liquid that mixes with and carries sperm • *He has prostate trouble.*

pros·the·sis /£ˈprɒs·θiː·sɪs, $ˈprɑːs-/ *n* [C] *pl* **prostheses** /£ˈprɒs·θiː·siːz, $ˈprɑːs-/ *specialized* an artificial body part, such as an arm, foot or tooth, which replaces a missing part

pros·thet·ic /£prɒsˈθet·ɪk, $prɑːsˈθet̬-/ *adj* [not gradable] *specialized* • *a prosthetic hand*

pros·ti·tute [PERSON], **male pros·ti·tute** /£ˈprɒs·tɪ·tjuːt, $ˈprɑː·stɪ·tuːt/ *n* [C] a person, usually a woman, who has sex with someone, usually a man, for money

pros·ti·tute *obj* /£ˈprɒs·tɪ·tjuːt, $ˈprɑː·stɪ·tuːt/ *v* [T] *fml* • *She prostituted* **herself** (=had sex for money) *because she had no other means of making money.*

pros·ti·tu·tion /£,prɒs·tɪˈtjuː·ʃᵊn, $,prɑː·stɪˈtuː-/ *n* [U] • *Poverty drove her to prostitution* (=earning money by having sex). • *Prostitution is common in many parts of the city.*

pros·ti·tute *obj* USE BADLY /£ˈprɒs·tɪ·tjuːt, $ˈprɑː·stɪ·tuːt/ *v* [T] *fml disapproving* to use (yourself or your abilities or beliefs) in a way which does not deserve respect, esp. in order to get money • *Some critics say he prostituted his musical skills by going into pop rather than staying with classical music.*

pro·strate OBEDIENT /£ˈprɒs·treɪt, £-ˈ-, $ˈprɑː·streɪt/ *adj* lying with the face down and arms stretched out, esp. in obedience or worship • *She* **lay** *prostrate on the cold chapel floor while the other nuns sat in silence.* • *We could see a man prostrate on the ground with two policemen standing over him holding guns.*

pro·strate *obj* /£prɒsˈtreɪt, $ˈprɑː·streɪt/ *v* [T] • *He prostrated him***self before** *the golden statue.*

pro·stra·tion /£prɒsˈtreɪ·ʃᵊn, $prɑːˈstreɪ-/ *n* [C/U]

pro·strate VERY TIRED /£ˈprɒs·treɪt, £-ˈ-, $ˈprɑː·streɪt/, **pro·strat·ed** /£prɒsˈtreɪ·tɪd, $ˈprɑː·streɪ·t̬ɪd/ *adj* having lost all strength or all determination because of an illness or an extremely bad experience • *Rescuers found her prostrate* **with** *exhaustion and cold on the snow-covered mountain.*

pro·tag·on·ist SUPPORTER /prəˈtæg·ᵊn·ɪst/ *n* [C] an (important) supporter of an idea or political system • *Key protagonists* **of** *the revolution were hunted down and executed.* • *She is the main/chief protagonist* **of** *change in our department.* • Compare **antagonist** at ANTAGONISM.

pro·tag·on·ist CHARACTER /prəˈtæg·ᵊn·ɪst/ *n* [C] an important character in a story or a play • *This is one of the few successful films this year in which the protagonists are all female.*

pro·te·an /£prəʊˈtiː·ən, $ˈproʊ·t̬i-/ *adj literary* easily (and continually) changing; variable • *He was so protean as an artist that the critics could never categorize his work.*

pro·tect *obj* /prəˈtekt/ *v* [T] to keep (someone or something) safe from injury, damage or loss • *These gloves will protect your hands* **against** *the cold.* • *She's learning self-defence so she can protect* **herself** *if she's ever attacked.* • *Surely the function of the law is to protect everyone's rights.* • *Will this type of sun block protect me* **from** *ultraviolet light?* • *Of course the company will act to protect its financial interests in the country if war begins.* • *Patients' names have been changed to protect their privacy.* • *Public pressure to protect the environment is strong and growing.* • If a government protects a part of its country's trade or industry, it helps it by taxing goods from other countries. • If an INSURANCE agreement protects a person **against** something, such as having possessions stolen, being injured or being killed, then that person or someone they have named will receive money if one of these things happens.

pro·tect·ed /£prəˈtek·tɪd, $-t̬ɪd/ *adj* • *Dolphins are a protected* **species** (=it is illegal to harm or kill them). • *Government leaflets advise you always to have protected* **sex** (=to use a CONTRACEPTIVE when having sex).

pro·tec·tion /prəˈtek·ʃᵊn/ *n* [U] • *Round-the-clock police protection is given to all senior politicians.* • *Their flimsy tent gave/offered hardly any protection* **against** *the severe storm.* • *New legislation still does not offer adequate protection* **for** *many endangered species.* • *There is growing evidence that environmental protection makes good business sense.* • *Always wear goggles as a protection* **for** *your eyes when using the machines.* • *The insurance policy provides protection* (=will make a financial payment) *in case of accidental loss of life or serious injury.* • *(infml)* If criminals offer protection they take money from people in exchange for agreeing not to hurt them or damage their property: *Organized gangs in the area extort protection* **money** *from local business people who are too frightened to refuse.* ○ *These thugs ran a vast protection* **racket** (=system) *with which all property-owners had to co-operate if they hoped to prosper, or survive.* • (CS) (RUS)

pro·tec·tive /£prəˈtek·tɪv, $-t̬ɪv/ *adj* • *Firefighters have to wear protective clothing to stop them getting burned.* • *She is charming, stylish, sensuous and fiercely protective* **of** (=wishing to protect) *the man she married 29 years ago.* • *On the other hand it's easy to be too protective* **towards/of** *your children.* • If someone is in **protective custody** they are kept in a safe place by the police, sometimes prison, for their own safety.

pro·tec·tive·ly /£prəˈtek·tɪv·li, $-t̬ɪv-/ *adv* • *He put an arm around her shoulder protectively.*

pro·tec·tive·ness /£prəˈtek·tɪv·nəs, $-t̬ɪv-/ *n* [U] • *There seems to be very little maternal protectiveness about her.*

pro·tec·tion·i·sm /prəˈtek·ʃᵊn·ɪ·zᵊm/ *n* [U] *disapproving* • Protectionism is the actions of a government to help its country's trade or industry by taxing goods bought from other countries.

pro·tec·tion·ist /prəˈtek·ʃᵊn·ɪst/ *adj* [not gradable] *disapproving* • *South Korea is looking for new markets in an increasingly protectionist world.*

pro·tec·tor /£prəˈtek·təʳ, $-t̬ɚ/ *n* [C] • A protector is someone who protects someone or something: *Philip II considered himself the protector of the Catholic Church.* ○ *She has a reputation for being an ardent protector of individuals' liberties.* • A protector is also a device that protects someone: *All flat jockeys are required to wear a back and chest protector.*

pro·tec·tor·ate /£prəˈtek·tᵊr·ət, $-tɚ-/ *n* [C] • A protectorate is a country which is generally controlled and defended by a more powerful country: *The Tunisian president negotiated this former French protectorate's independence in 1956.*

prot·é·gé /£ˈprɒt·eʒ·eɪ, $ˈprɑː·t̬eʒ-/ *n* [C] someone who is helped and taught by an important or more experienced person • *Shapur's restaurant is full every night as trendy Londoners enjoy the wonders of his young protégé, chef Glyn Fussell.* • *Within a few years the protégé was teaching his master.* • Compare MENTOR.

pro·tein /£ˈprəʊ·tiːn, $ˈproʊ-/ *n* any of a large group of chemicals which are necessary to and found in all living things • *protein molecules* • *Meat and nuts are good sources of protein.* [U] • *We use this technique to study the structure of proteins.* [C] • *Prolonged protein deficiency in the diet can cause health problems.* [U]

pro tem /£ˌprəʊˈtem, $ˌproʊ-/ *adv* [not gradable] now and for only a short period after; temporarily

pro·test /£ˈprəʊ·test, $ˈproʊ-/ *n* a strong complaint expressing disagreement, disapproval or opposition • *Protests have been* **made/registered** *by many people who would be affected by the proposed changes.* [C] • *Conservation groups have united* **in** *protest* **against** *the planned new road.* [U] • *A formal protest was made by the German team* **about** *their disqualification from the relay final.* [C] • If something is done **under protest** it is done unwillingly: *All right, I'll go to the meeting, but only under protest.* • A **protest (march)** is a march, usually made by many people, to show disagreement, disapproval or worry, esp. about a political decision or subject. • A **protest song** is a song which expresses disapproval, usually about a political subject. • *"The Lady doth protest too much"* (Shakespeare, Hamlet 2.1)

pro·test *(obj)* /prəˈtest, $ˈproʊ·test/ *v* • *A lot of people protested* **about** *the new working hours.* [I] • *Several demonstrators protesting* **against** *cuts in health spending were arrested.* [I] • *They protested bitterly to their boss, but he wouldn't change his mind.* [I] • *All through the trial he protested his* **innocence** (=strongly said he was not guilty), *insisting he had not robbed the shop.* [T] • *But he protests* (=says strongly) **that** *he knows nothing about the guns or the explosives.* [+ *that* clause] • *(Am)* If a person protests something, they protest against or about it: *Outside, a group of students were protesting research cuts.* [T] • If a person **protests too much**, they agree or disagree with something so strongly that their sincerity becomes doubted.

pro·test·er, **pro·tes·tor** /£prəˈtes·təʳ, $-tɚ/ *n* [C] • *Protesters met in front of the embassy to demand the release of all political prisoners.*

pro·tes·ta·tion /£ˌprɒt·esˈteɪ·ʃᵊn, $ˌprɑː·t̬esˈteɪ-/ *n* [C usually pl] • *Ignoring my protestations* (=strong expressions of disagreement), *they went ahead and chopped the tree down.* • *Their protestations* (=strong expressions) **of** *loyalty seem rather hollow in view of the way they behaved.* • *The minister's protestations* (=strongly expressed claims) **that** *she never knew about the cover-up are hard to believe.* [+ *that* clause]

Prot·e·stant /£ˈprɒt·ɪ·stᵊnt, $ˈprɑː·t̬ɪ-/ *n* [C], *adj* [not gradable] (a member) of the parts of the Christian Church which separated from the Roman Catholic Church during the 16th century • *At the age of thirty-three he became a Protestant (minister).* • *She has been brought up with the* **Protestant work ethic** (=the belief that work is valuable as an activity as well as for what it produces).

Prot·es·tant·i·sm /£'prɒt·ɪ·stᵊn·tɪ·zᵊm, $'prɑː·t̬ɪ-/ *n* [U]

prot(o)- /£'prəʊ·təʊ-, $'proʊ·t̬oʊ-/ *combining form* first, esp. from which other similar things develop; original • *protoplasm* • *a prototype*

pro·to·col [RULES] /£'prəʊ·tə·kɒl, $'proʊ·t̬ə·kɑːl/ *n* [U] the system of rules and acceptable behaviour used at official ceremonies and occasions • *a breach of protocol* • *Protocol would require detailed preparations and notification of appropriate authorities in advance of a royal visit.* • (GR)

pro·to·col [AGREEMENT] /£'prəʊ·tə·kɒl, $'proʊ·t̬ə·kɑːl/ *n* [C] a formal international agreement • *The Geneva Protocol of 1925 prohibits the use in war of 'asphyxiating, poisonous or other gases, and . . . all analogous liquids, materials or devices'.* • (GR)

pro·ton /£'prəʊ·tɒn, $'proʊ·tɑːn/ *n* [C] a type of **elementary particle** (= very small piece of matter) which has a positive electrical charge and is found in the NUCLEUS (= central part) of all atoms • Compare ELECTRON; NEUTRON.

pro·to·pla·sm /£'prəʊ·tə·plæz·ᵊm, $'proʊ·t̬ə-/ *n* [U] the transparent liquid which is inside all living cells

pro·to·type /£'prəʊ·tə·taɪp, $'proʊ·t̬ə-/ *n* [C] the first example of something, such as a machine or other industrial product, from which all later forms are developed • *The prototype crashed on its first flight.* • *A prototype* **of** *the system was unveiled at an agricultural-engineering conference in Paris last month.* • *The robot, initially designed to help draw detailed maps of the ocean floor, may serve as a prototype* **for** *mining and construction vehicles.*

pro·to·zo·an /£ˌprəʊ·təʊ'zəʊ·ən, $ˌproʊ·t̬ə'zoʊ-/ *n* [C] *pl* **protozoans** or **protozoa** /£ˌprəʊ·təʊ'zəʊ·ə, $ˌproʊ·t̬ə'zoʊ-/ any of various types of very small, usually single-celled animal which do not have a BACKBONE (= a row of bones along the centre of an animal's back) • *Amoebas are protozoans.*

pro·to·zo·an /£ˌprəʊ·təʊ'zəʊ·ən, $ˌproʊ·t̬ə'zoʊ-/ *adj* [not gradable]

pro·tract·ed /£prə'træk·tɪd, $-t̬ɪd/ *adj* lasting for a long time or made to last longer • *protracted negotiations* • *a protracted argument/discussion* • *A protracted struggle in the Australian courts about whether the book can be published there remains unresolved.*

pro·tract *obj* /prə'trækt/ *v* [T] • *Please don't protract the suspense – tell me if I passed or not.*

pro·trac·tion /prə'træk·ʃᵊn/ *n* [U]

pro·trac·tor /£prə'træk·təʳ, $-t̬ɚ/ *n* [C] a device used for measuring and drawing angles. It is usually in the form of half a circle made from transparent plastic with degrees marked on it. • (LP) **Mathematics**

pro·trude /prə'truːd/ *v* [I] to stick out from or through something • *a protruding jaw* • *A rotting branch protruded* **from** *the swamp like a ghostly arm.* • *They made a pitiful sight with their shaved heads and protruding collar bones and ribs.*

pro·tru·sion /prə'truː·ʒᵊn/ *n* • *The condition results in weight loss, rapid heart beat and protrusion of the eyes* (= eyes which stick out). [U] • *What are these protrusions* (= things sticking out) *along its back?* [C]

pro·tu·ber·ance /£prə'tjuː·bᵊr·ᵊnts, $-'tuː-/ *n* [C] *fml* a swelling from a surface • *If the plant has been infected you will see dark protuberances along the stems.*

pro·tu·ber·ant /£prə'tjuː·bᵊr·ᵊnt, $-'tuː·bɚ-/ *adj fml* • *He stared at me with his heavy-lidded, protuberant* (= sticking out) **eyes.**

proud [SATISFIED] /praʊd/ *adj* **-er, -est** feeling satisfaction and pleasure because of something which has been done or is owned • *He's very proud* **of** *his daughter's achievements.* • *Dr Schmidt is particularly proud* **of** *the environmental record of his company.* • *She says she is a feminist and proud* **of** *it.* • *It's always a proud moment for a coach seeing someone they've trained be presented with a medal.* • *When she received her prize I think I was the proudest parent on the face of the Earth.* • *I am proud* **to** *have played a part in what has been, in a very real sense, a team effort.* [+ *to* infinitive] • *I'm so proud* **(that)** *my son's been chosen for the national team.* [+ *(that)* clause] • *(Br and Aus dated)* If you **do** someone **proud** you treat them very well, esp. by giving them lots of good food and making them very comfortable: *We had a lovely tea – Sheila did us proud.* • *(Am)* To **do** someone **proud** is also to please them by doing well: *Our daughter's performance with the chorus did us proud.* • See also HOUSEPROUD; PRIDE [SATISFACTION].

proud·ly /'praʊd·li/ *adv* • *He proudly held out his trophy for us to admire.* • *Elaine and Ian Gibson proudly* **announce** *the birth of their son, John Maurice.* • *There were photographs of all her children proudly* **displayed** *on the mantelpiece.*

proud [RESPECTING YOURSELF] /praʊd/ *adj* **-er, -est** *approving* having or showing self-respect • *We Albanians are a proud people.* • *He might be poor but he's also proud, and he won't be pushed around by anyone.* • See also PRIDE [RESPECT FOR YOURSELF].

proud·ly /'praʊd·li/ *adv*

proud [FEELING IMPORTANT] /praʊd/ *adj* **-er, -est** *disapproving* (of a person) feeling better and more important than other people without good reason to do so • *He's silly not coming to our meetings – he has nothing to be proud about – we're all the same.* • *She knows she's lost, but she's too proud* **to** *admit it.* [+ *to* infinitive] • See also PRIDE [FEELING OF IMPORTANCE].

proud·ly /'praʊd·li/ *adv*

proud [STICKING OUT] /praʊd/ *adj* **-er, -est** *specialized, esp. Br* sticking out from the surrounding area • *Sand the surface with abrasive paper until no flakes of paint stand proud* **of** *the surface.*

prove *(obj)* [SHOW] /pruːv/ *v past* **proved**, *past part Am also* **proven** /'pruː·vᵊn, £'prəʊ-/ to show after a time or by experience that (something or someone) has a particular quality • *During the rescue she proved* **herself (to be)** *a highly competent climber/highly competent as a climber.* [T + obj + *(to be)* n/adj] • *The dispute over who has rights to the song could prove impossible to resolve.* [L] • *The operation on his broken leg proved a complete success.* [L] • *Working with children proved* **to** *require more patience than he'd expected.* [+ *to* infinitive] • *Yes, the new safety procedures have so far proved* **(to be)** *satisfactory.* [L + *(to be)* n/adj] • A **proving ground** is a situation or place where something such as a new theory or machine can be tested. • (P)

prove *obj* [TRUE] /pruːv/ *v* [T] *past* **proved**, *past part esp. Am* **proven** See at PROOF [SHOWING TRUTH] • (P)

prov·e·nance /£'prɒv·ᵊn·ənts, $'prɑː·vᵊn-/ *n* [U] *fml* the place of origin of something • *There is no guarantee that all or any of the manuscripts of* **unknown/uncertain** *provenance originated in Italy.* • *I don't need to see a label to identify the provenance of a garment that someone is wearing.*

prov·erb /£'prɒv·ɜːb, $'prɑː·vɜːrb/ *n* [C] a short sentence, etc., usually known by many people, stating something commonly experienced or giving advice • *The appetite, says the proverb, grows with eating.* • *There is an old Arab proverb* **that** *everything you write or speak should pass through three gates: Is this kind? Is this necessary? Is this true?* [+ *that* clause] • (LP) **Words used together**

pro·ver·bi·al /£prə'vɜː·bi·əl, $-'vɜːr-/ *adj* • *She's got as much chance of winning as* **the** *proverbial snowball in hell.* (The expression "a snowball's chance in hell" is commonly understood to mean something with no chance of success.) • *His proverbial* (= known by many people) *good humour never fails to cheer me up.*

pro·ver·bi·al·ly /£prə'vɜː·bi·ə·li, $-'vɜːr-/ *adv* • *The locals are proverbially* (= widely known to be) *unwelcoming to strangers.*

pro·vide *(obj)* [SUPPLY] /prə'vaɪd/ *v* to give (someone) or arrange for (someone) to have (something which is useful or desirable or which they will need) • *All meals are provided throughout the residential course.* [T] • *We will not be able to provide the same standard of teaching if there are funding cuts.* [T] • *The author provides no documentary references to support her assertions.* [T] • *We have concerns about whether the government will be able to provide viable social services* **for** *poorer families/provide poorer families* **with** *viable social services.* [T] • *Putting more police on patrol doesn't provide a real solution to the problem of increasing violence.* [T] • *(fml) Beach operators do not have a legal obligation to provide* **against** (= make arrangements to prevent) *injury or drowning.* [I always + prep] • *He has two young daughters and he has to provide* **for** *them* (= give them all of the things necessary for life). [I always + prep] • *In the event of your death the policy ensures that your partner will be provided* **for** *financially* (= will be given enough money) *for the rest of their life.* [I always + prep] • *(fml) Engineers provided* **for** (= considered and made arrangements to allow for) *every conceivable accident scenario when they designed the containers.* [I always + prep]

• *(fml)* If a law or a decision **provides for** something it allows it to happen: *Current legislation provides for the detention of those suspected of terrorism.*

pro·vid·er /£prəˈvaɪ·dəʳ, $-dɚ/ *n* [C] • *The bank is now a major provider of financial services to industry.* • *Until her illness she was the main provider* (= earner of money) *in the family.* • *(slightly fml) The company's medical plan allows you to choose your* **health-care** *provider* (= doctor).

pro·vi·sion /prəˈvɪʒ·ᵊn/ *n* • *The provision* **of** *good public transport will be essential for developing the area.* [U] • *Of course there's provision in the plan* **for** *population increase.* [U] • *He* **made** *financial provision* **for** *his wife if he should die young.* [U] • *When designing buildings in this area you have to* **make** *provision(s)* **against** *earthquakes.* [C/U] • See also PROVISIONS.

pro·vide [LAW] /prəˈvaɪd/ *v* [+ *that* clause] *fml* (of a law or decision) to state that (something) must happen if particular conditions exist • *Section 17 provides* **that** *all decisions must be circulated in writing.*

pro·vi·sion /prəˈvɪʒ·ᵊn/ *n* [C] • A provision is a statement within an agreement or a law that a particular thing must happen or be done, esp. before another can be: *We have inserted certain provisions into the treaty to safeguard foreign workers.* ○ *She accepted the job with the provision* **that** *she would be paid expenses for relocating.* [+ *that* clause]

pro·vid·ed (that) /prəˈvaɪ·dɪd/, **pro·vid·ing (that)** /prəˈvaɪ·dɪŋ/ *conjunction* if, or only if • *Provided (that) there are no objections, we will begin with item three on the agenda.* • *He says he'll go parachuting provided/providing (that) you do too.* • [LP]> **Conditionals**

prov·i·dence /£ˈprɒv·ɪ·dᵊnts, $ˈprɑː·və-/ *n* [U] an influence which is not human in origin and is thought to control whether or not people receive the things which they need • *As a monk he trusts to* **divine** *providence that he will receive food.*

prov·i·dent /£ˈprɒv·ɪ·dᵊnt, $ˈprɑː·və-/ *adj fml approving* making arrangements for future needs, esp. by saving money

prov·i·dent·ly /£ˈprɒv·ɪ·dᵊnt·li, $ˈprɑː·və-/ *adv fml approving*

prov·i·den·tial /£ˌprɒv·ɪˈden·tʃᵊl, $ˌprɑː·və-/ *adj fml* happening exactly when needed but without being planned • *It was providential, my meeting you – I wanted to have a word with you.*

prov·i·den·tial·ly /£ˌprɒv·ɪˈden·tʃᵊl·i, $ˌprɑː·və-/ *adv fml*

prov·ince [REGION] /£ˈprɒv·ɪnts, $ˈprɑː·vɪnts/ *n* [C] an area which is governed as part of a country or an empire • *The province of Milan includes the city and surrounding communities in the middle of Lombardy.*

pro·vin·cial /prəˈvɪn·tʃᵊl/ *adj* • *As Canada's federal government cuts back on arts spending, provincial* **governments** *are finding ways to make up the shortfalls.* • See also **provincial** at PROVINCES.

prov·ince [SUBJECT] /£ˈprɒv·ɪnts, $ˈprɑː·vɪnts/ *n* [U] *slightly fml* a subject or activity of special interest, knowledge or responsibility • *Renaissance art is not really his province – he specializes in the modern period.* • *Marketing is within the province* **of** *the sales department.*

prov·in·ces /£ˈprɒv·ɪnt·sɪz, $ˈprɑː·vɪnt-/ *pl n* **the provinces** the parts of a country outside its capital city • *There are compensations for living in the provinces – it's easy to get into the countryside for one.*

pro·vin·cial /prəˈvɪn·tʃᵊl/ *n* [C] *esp. disapproving* • A provincial is a person who comes from somewhere in a country outside its capital city.

pro·vin·cial /prəˈvɪn·tʃᵊl/ *adj* • *The majority of young professionals in the capital have moved there from provincial* **towns**. • *It's a city that, despite having a population as large as New York's, has regularly been dismissed as a provincial backwater.* • *(disapproving)* Provincial also means having manners and ideas which are dated and simple: *provincial attitudes* • See also **provincial** at PROVINCE [REGION].

pro·vin·cial·i·sm /prəˈvɪn·tʃᵊl·ɪ·zᵊm/ *n* [U] *disapproving* • *Despite its obvious provincialism, the arts festival was a huge success.*

pro·vi·sion·al /prəˈvɪʒ·ᵊn·ᵊl/ *adj* for the present time but likely to change; temporary • *a provisional government* • *Provisional figures for the three months to November showed a 6% increase in sales.* • *(Br and Aus)* A **provisional licence** (*Am* **learner's permit**) is a LICENCE (= an official document giving permission to do something) which someone has to obtain before they can learn to drive.

pro·vi·sion·al·ly /prəˈvɪʒ·ᵊn·ᵊl·i/ *adv* • *Club members have provisionally agreed to the changes, which will not become permanent until they have seen the full report.*

pro·vi·sions /prəˈvɪʒ·ᵊnz/ *pl n* supplies of food and other necessary things • *All provisions for the camp have to be flown in by helicopter.*

pro·vi·sion *obj* /prəˈvɪʒ·ᵊn/ *v* [T] *fml* • *We started the voyage by provisioning our boat at the quay.*

pro·vi·so /£prəˈvaɪ·zəʊ, $-zoʊ/ *n* [C] *pl* **provisos** a statement in an agreement saying that a particular thing must happen before another can • *There was one proviso – unless there was a decision by midnight on Friday, the offer would be withdrawn.* • *I'll come,* **with/on** *the proviso* **that** *you'll pay my fare.* [+ *that* clause]

pro·voke *obj* [ANGER] /£prəˈvəʊk, $-ˈvoʊk/ *v* [T] to make or try to make (a person or an animal) angry or annoyed • *If you provoke that dog too much it'll bite you.* • *She attacked the boy because he provoked her* **into** *a state of rage.* • *Police asked demonstrators to move away from the mourners who were provoked* **by** *their presence.*

prov·o·ca·tion /£ˌprɒv·əˈkeɪ·ʃᵊn, $ˌprɑː·və-/ *n* • *People* **under** *provocation can react in unexpected ways.* [U] • *Her comments weren't constructive criticism, they were blatant provocation!* [U] • *The constant noise from his neighbours was more provocation than he could bear – it's no wonder he complained.* [U] • *Ignore the letter – it's just a provocation to see if you're really serious.* [C]

pro·voc·a·tive /£prəˈvɒk·ə·tɪv, $-ˈvɑː·kə·t̬ɪv/ *adj* • *a provocative comment* • *In a deliberately provocative speech, she criticised the whole system of government.* • If behaviour or clothing is provocative it is intended to cause sexual desire: *She slowly leaned forward in a provocative way.*

pro·voc·a·tive·ly /£prəˈvɒk·ə·tɪv·li, $-ˈvɑː·kə·t̬ɪv-/ *adv* • *"You looking at me punk?" he snarled provocatively* (= intending to cause anger). • *She* **dresses** *very provocatively* (= intending to cause sexual desire).

pro·voke *obj* [CAUSE REACTION] /£prəˈvəʊk, $-ˈvoʊk/ *v* [T] to cause (a reaction, esp. a negative one) • *The prospect of increased prices has already provoked confrontation/an outcry.* • *He provoked outrage by calling the TV programmes "talking wallpaper".* • *Test results have provoked worries that the reactor could overheat.* • *It is the combination of styles which provokes surprise.*

pro·voc·a·tive /£prəˈvɒk·ə·tɪv, $-ˈvɑː·kə·t̬ɪv/ *adj* • Provocative means causing thought about interesting subjects: *The programme will take a detailed and provocative look at the problem of homelessness.*

pro·voc·a·tive·ly /£prəˈvɒk·ə·tɪv·li, $-ˈvɑː·kə·t̬ɪv-/ *adv*

prov·ost /£ˈprɒv·əst, $ˈprɑː·vəst/ *n* [C] *(Br)* (in some universities) the person in charge of a particular college, or *(Am)* a person of high rank who helps to run a college • *the provost of Queen's College*

prow /praʊ/ *n* [C] the front part of a boat or ship; BOW [FRONT PART]

prow·ess /ˈpraʊ·es/ *n* [U] *slightly fml* great ability or skill • *He's always boasting about his* **sexual** *prowess.* • *So what explains the* **sporting** *prowess of a nation of barely 17 million people?* • *Undergraduates at the college are more often known for their prowess* **in** *sport rather than academic activities.* • *Although the resistance groups do not show great military prowess they frequently penetrate deep into the interior.*

prowl *(obj)* /praʊl/ *v* to move around quietly in (a place) trying not to be seen or heard, such as when hunting • *There have been reports of a masked man prowling in the neighbourhood.* [I] • *At night, adult scorpions prowl the desert* **for** (= trying to catch) *insects.* [T] • *(infml) Unable to sleep he prowled* (= walked without purpose) **(about/around)** *the hotel corridors.* [I/T]

prowl /praʊl/ *n* • *(infml) After a prowl* (= walk) *around the exhibition I went for a coffee.* [C] • *(fig.) After two years of famine, death is* **on the** *prowl* (= many people are dying) *throughout the villages.* [U]

prowl·er /£ˈpraʊ·ləʳ, $-lɚ/ *n* [C] • *A prowler who had molested several women was caught by police last night.*

prox·i·mi·ty /£prɒkˈsɪm·ɪ·ti, $prɑːkˈsɪm·ə·t̬i/ *n* [U] *fml* the state of being near in space or time • *No longer is it the case that national suppliers, because of their proximity, are favoured over foreign ones.* • *The house is* **in** *close proximity* **to** *the shops and the station.*

prox·y /£ˈprɒk·si, $ˈprɑːk-/ *n* authority given to a person to act for someone else, such as by voting for them in an election, or the person who this authority is given to • *a proxy vote* • *My brother's voting for me* **by proxy** *in the club elections.* [U] • *Can I nominate someone as a proxy to sign for me?* [C]

prude /pru:d/ *n* [C] *disapproving* a person who is easily shocked by rude things, esp. those of a sexual type • *"We're not prudes," he said, "but we've had enough of the filth and violence that pollute much of the media."*

pru·dish /ˈpru:·dɪʃ/ *adj disapproving* • *I don't consider myself prudish but I do think one or two of the sex scenes in the film were a bit excessive.*

pru·dish·ly /ˈpru:·dɪʃ·li/ *adv disapproving*

pru·dish·ness /ˈpru:·dɪʃ·nəs/, **pru·de·ry** /£ˈpru:·dᵊr·i, $-dɚ-/ *n* [U] *disapproving*

pru·dent /ˈpru:·dᵊnt/ *adj slightly fml* avoiding risks and uncertainties; careful • **It** *would be prudent* **to** *read the contract properly before signing it.*

pru·dent·ly /ˈpru:·dᵊnt·li/ *adv slightly fml* • *You should spend the money prudently – it's all you'll have for a long time.*

pru·dence /ˈpru:·dᵊnts/ *n* [U] *slightly fml* • *The firm was commended for its financial prudence.*

prune *obj* CUT /pru:n/ *v* [T] to cut off branches from (trees, bushes or plants), esp. so that they will grow better in future • *She spent the afternoon pruning roses.* • *(fig.) Many museums have pruned* (= got rid of items from) *their collections, believing this will improve them.* • *(fig.) Arco has reacted to the loss in revenue by pruning* **(back)** *its expansion plans.* [T/M] • **Pruning shears** is *Am for* SECATEURS (= a tool for pruning). • PIC› **Garden** Ⓕ

prune FRUIT /pru:n/ *n* [C] a dried whole PLUM (= fruit) which is purplish black and can be kept for a long time before it has to be eaten • Ⓕ

pru·ri·ent /£ˈprʊə·ri·ənt, $ˈprʊr·i-/ *adj fml disapproving* unusually interested in the details of another person's sexual behaviour or in unpleasant things • *He showed a very prurient interest in the assault.*

pru·ri·ent·ly /£ˈprʊə·ri·ənt·li, $ˈprʊr·i-/ *adv fml disapproving* • *These newspapers delve pruriently into people's private lives.*

pru·ri·ence /£ˈprʊə·ri·ənts, $ˈprʊr·i-/ *n* [U] *fml disapproving*

prus·sic ac·id /ˈprʌs·ɪk/ *n* [U] *dated* a very poisonous acid, a type of CYANIDE

pry ASK QUESTIONS /praɪ/ *v* [I] *disapproving* to try to obtain private facts about a person • *"I thought I'd just told you not to pry* **into** *my affairs," he said, getting up again.* • *As a reporter, I was paid to pry* **into** *other people's lives, a requirement that frequently made me uncomfortable.* • *I don't wish to pry but has your boyfriend ever lived with anyone before?* • *The experimental installation is hidden from prying* **eyes** (= people who want to look at it or discover things about it) *by a tall bank of earth.*

pry *obj* OPEN /praɪ/ *v* [T] *esp. Am for* PRIZE LIFT • *The car trunk had been pried* **open** *and all her equipment was gone.* [+ obj + adj] • *(fig.) Eventually they pried the information* **out** *of him.*

PS /ˌpi:ˈes/ *n abbreviation for* POSTSCRIPT. It is written at the end of a letter after it has been signed to introduce extra text. • *...Yours sincerely, R. Langdale. P.S. Give my best wishes to your father.* • A PS is a POSTSCRIPT: *Don't rewrite the letter – just add a PS.* [C]

psalm /sɑ:m/ *n* [C] a holy poem or song, esp. one of the 150 grouped together in the Bible

pseud /su:d/ *n* [C] *Br infml disapproving* a person who tries to seem to have detailed knowledge or excellent judgment of a subject, esp. in art, literature, music etc. • *He's such a pseud, with his talk of 'lambent harmonies' and 'melting arpeggios'.*

pseud·y /ˈsu:·di/ *adj* **-ier, -iest** *Br infml disapproving* • *I have to say, I don't have much time for the pseudy vocabulary of wine snobs.*

pseud(o)– /£ˈsu:·dəʊ, $-doʊ/ *combining form esp. disapproving* not real; pretended • *pseudo-religious* • *a pseudo-intellectual* • A system of thought or a theory is **pseudo-science** if it is not formed in a scientific way: *Some people feel economics will always be a pseudo-science.*

pseu·do·nym /ˈsu:·də·nɪm/ *n* [C] a name which a person, such as a writer, uses instead of their real name, esp. on their work • *She uses a pseudonym on her articles criticizing medical research because she works for a pharmaceutical company.* • *George Orwell was a pseudonym – his real name was Eric Blair.*

pseu·do·nym·ous /£su:ˈdɒn·ɪ·məs, $-ˈdɑ:·nɪ-/ *adj* [not gradable] *specialized* • *pseudonymous literature*

psor·i·a·sis /səˈraɪə·sɪs/ *n* [U] a disease in which areas of skin turn red and are covered with small dry pieces of skin • *Psoriasis can be very itchy.*

psst /pst/ *exclamation* a sound made to get someone's attention, esp. without other people noticing • *Psst, let me have a look at what you've written.* • Ⓒⓢ

psych out *obj*, **psych** *obj* **out** /saɪk/ *v adv* [M] *infml* to behave in a very confident or forceful way in order to make (another competitor, esp. in a sports event) less confident • *Both athletes were trying to psych each other out on TV before the race.*

psych *obj* **up** /saɪk/ *v adv* [T] *infml* to prepare (someone) for something, esp. mentally • *I always spend about half an hour psyching* **myself** *up before I go on stage and give a performance.*

psy·che /ˈsaɪ·ki/ *n* [C] the mind, or the deepest thoughts, feelings or beliefs of a person or group • *The instinct to avoid conflict was deeply lodged in his psyche by his parents frequently arguing when he was a child.* • *Peru is a very traditional country and embedded in its psyche is a love of ceremony.*

psy·che·del·ic /ˌsaɪ·kəˈdel·ɪk/ *adj* (of a drug) causing effects on the mind such as feelings of deep understanding or seeing strong images • *psychedelic drugs* • Psychedelic art or clothing has bright colours and strange patterns of a type which might be experienced by taking psychedelic drugs: *a psychedelic shirt* • *psychedelic music*

psy·chi·a·try /saɪˈkaɪə·tri/ *n* [U] the part of medicine which studies mental illness • Compare PSYCHOLOGY.

psy·chi·at·ric /ˌsaɪ·kiˈæt·rɪk/ *adj* [not gradable] • *psychiatric treatment* • *a psychiatric patient* • *There are fears that we may have to close the hospital's psychiatric unit.* • A **psychiatric hospital** is a place where people with mental illnesses stay and receive treatment: *A lot of the large psychiatric hospitals are now being closed down in favour of smaller, more specialized units.*

psy·chi·at·ri·cal·ly /ˌsaɪ·kiˈæt·rɪ·kli/ *adv* [not gradable] • *psychiatrically disturbed*

psy·chi·a·trist /saɪˈkaɪə·trɪst, sɪ-/ *n* [C] • A psychiatrist is a doctor who is also trained in psychiatry: *She's very depressed – I think she should see a psychiatrist.* • *"Anyone who goes to see a psychiatrist ought to have his head examined"* (believed to have been said by the film producer Sam Goldwyn, 1884-1974)

psy·chic KNOWING /ˈsaɪ·kɪk/ *adj* having or being knowledge and mental abilities impossible to explain using present scientific understanding • *Her grandmother's psychic – she sometimes has dreams about the future which come true.* • *I'm not psychic and I don't know what you're thinking, so if you want me to do something, you'll have to ask me first!*

psy·chic /ˈsaɪ·kɪk/ *n* [C] • *a gifted psychic* (= person with these abilities)

psy·chi·cal /ˈsaɪ·kɪk·ᵊl/ *adj* [before n] • *The Society for Psychical Research is investigating reports of a ghost at the old vicarage.*

psy·chi·cal·ly /ˈsaɪ·kɪ·kli/ *adv* • *They seem psychically connected by a deep intuitive understanding.*

psy·chic MENTAL /ˈsaɪ·kɪk/, *rare* **psy·chi·cal** *adj* (esp. of an illness) of the mind rather than the body • *psychic problems*

psy·chi·cal·ly /ˈsaɪ·kɪ·kli/ *adv* • *psychically disorienting*

psy·cho /£ˈsaɪ·kəʊ, $-koʊ/ *n* [C], *adj pl* **psychos** *infml for* PSYCHOPATH and PSYCHOPATHIC • *In the film, she's attacked and raped by a psycho.* • *He suddenly* **went** *psycho and started shooting in all directions.*

psych(o)– /£ˈsaɪ·kəʊ, $-koʊ/ *combining form* of the mind or mental processes • *psychopharmacology* (= the study of drugs which effect the mind)

psy·cho·a·nal·y·sis /£ˌsaɪ·kəʊ·əˈnæl·ə·sɪs, $-koʊ-/ *n* [U] any of a number of the theories of the human personality, which attempt to examine a person's unconscious mind to discover the hidden causes of their mental problems • *Sigmund Freud is known as the father of psychoanalysis.*

psy·cho·an·a·lyse *obj Br, Am and Aus* **psy·cho·an·a·lyze** /£ˌsaɪ·kəʊˈæn·ᵊl·aɪz, $-koʊ-/ *v* [T] • To psychoanalyse someone is to examine or treat them using psychoanalysis.

psy·cho·an·a·lyst /£ˌsaɪ·kəʊˈæn·ᵊl·ɪst, $-koʊ-/, *Am also* **an·al·yst** *n* [C]

psy·cho·bab·ble /£ˈsaɪ·kəʊˌbæb·l̩, $-koʊ-/ *n* [U] *disapproving infml* language using lots of words and expressions taken from PSYCHOLOGY (=the study of the mind)

psy·cho·ki·nes·is /£ˌsaɪ·kəʊ·kɪˈniː·sɪs, $-koʊ-/ *n* [U] changing the state of a physical object, such as moving it, using only the power of the mind

psy·cho·ki·net·ic /£ˌsaɪ·kəʊ·kɪˈnet·ɪk, $-koʊ·kɪˈneṭ-/ *adj*

psy·chol·o·gy /£saɪˈkɒl·ə·dʒi, $-ˈkɑː·lə-/ *n* [U] the scientific study of the way the human mind works and how it influences behaviour, or the influence of a particular person's character on their behaviour • *She studied psychology at Harvard.* • *John Lambie is a lecturer in psychology.* • *These arguments do not take into account the psychology* **of** *the ordinary soldier, like his close bond with a 'buddy'.* • *The article is persuasive, but it omits that little-understood factor, the golfer's psychology.* • Compare PSYCHIATRY.

psy·cho·log·i·cal /£ˌsaɪ·kəlˈɒdʒ·ɪ·kəl, $-kəˈlɑː·dʒɪ-/ *adj* • *The report says a high proportion of consultations with doctors involve psychological* **problems** (=mental health problems, such as anxiety and deep unhappiness). • *The doctor says my headaches are purely psychological* (=have no physical cause). • Sometimes psychological refers to the mental effects of something on someone: *The constant aircraft noise had a bad psychological effect on the residents.* ○ *The company is concerned with the physical and psychological well-being of its employees.* ○ *The decision to reassess the evidence has given the campaign a huge psychological* **boost** (=has given great encouragement to the people involved). • A psychological book or film is one in which there is a lot of attention to the way people influence each other's behaviour: *Her new psychological* **thriller** *will be published next month.* • *The success of the new model will depend on it being introduced it at the right* **psychological moment** (=the time when it is most likely to be accepted). • A **psychological profile** (*specialized* **offender profile**) is a description of the likely character, behaviour and interests of a violent criminal which is based on information about the crime that he or she has committed: **Psychological profiling** *is often more helpful to detectives than statements from eye-witnesses.* • **Psychological warfare** is the use of activities which cause fear and anxiety in the people you want to influence without hurting them physically.

psy·cho·log·i·cal·ly /£ˌsaɪ·kəlˈɒdʒ·ɪ·kli, $-kəˈlɑː·dʒɪ-/ *adv* • *Serial killers are usually psychologically* **disturbed** *men* (=men with mental problems). • *Unemployment is expected to hit the psychologically* **important** (=important for emotional rather than practical reasons) *two million level next month.*

psy·chol·o·gist /£saɪˈkɒl·ə·dʒɪst, $-ˈkɑː·lə-/ *n* [C] • A psychologist is someone who studies the human mind and human emotions and behaviour, and how different situations have an effect on them: *Proper training by* **child** *psychologists should be given to social workers dealing with abused children.* ○ *She has spent 15 years as a* **clinical** *psychologist with the Northumberland Health Authority.* ○ **Educational** *psychologists claim that reading standards among young children have declined during the past year.* • *(infml) You need to be a bit of a psychologist* (=someone who understands the way people behave) *to handle these temperamental singers and actors.*

psy·cho·path /ˈsaɪ·kə·pæθ/, *infml* **psy·cho** *n* [C] a person, usually suffering from a mental illness, who violently attacks or kills people • *The vast majority of these prisoners are not dangerous psychopaths.* • *Only a psychopath could be responsible for these terrible crimes.* • *(specialized)* In PSYCHOLOGY a psychopath is a person who continually gets into trouble with society, has no feeling for other people, does not think about the future and does not feel bad about anything they have done in the past.

psy·cho·path·ic /ˌsaɪ·kəˈpæθ·ɪk/, *infml* **psy·cho** *adj* • *A series of unsolved murders on the island has raised fears that a psychopathic* **serial killer** *is on the loose.*

psy·cho·pa·thol·o·gy /£ˌsaɪ·kəʊ·pəˈθɒl·ə·dʒi, $-koʊ·pəˈθɑː·lə-/ *n* [U] the study of mental illnesses • *She's doing an M.Phil in psychopathology.*

psy·cho·sis /£saɪˈkəʊ·sɪs, $-ˈkoʊ-/ *n pl* **psychoses** /£saɪˈkəʊ·siːz, $-ˈkoʊ-/ *medical* any of a number of the more severe mental illnesses • *She fell into a* **drug-induced** *psychosis.* [C] • *He was suffering from severe psychosis when he killed the man.* [U]

psy·chot·ic /£saɪˈkɒt·ɪk, $-ˈkɑː·ṭɪk/ *adj medical* • *a psychotic killer* • *a psychotic disorder* • *His dislike of women bordered on the psychotic.*

psy·cho·so·mat·ic /£ˌsaɪ·kəʊ·səˈmæt·ɪk, $-koʊ·soʊˈmæṭ-/ *adj* (of an illness) caused by anxiety and worry and not by an infection or injury • *a psychosomatic illness/disorder/condition* • *psychosomatic symptoms*

psy·cho·ther·a·py /£ˌsaɪ·kəʊˈθer·ə·pi, $-koʊ-/ *n* [U] the treatment of mental illness by discussing the problems which caused it with the sufferer, instead of using drugs or operations • *All the survivors of the disaster needed counselling, and the worst affected received psychotherapy.*

psy·cho·ther·a·pist /£ˌsaɪ·kəˈθer·ə·pɪst/ *n* [C] • *He's been seeing a psychotherapist ever since his wife was murdered.*

pt PART *n* [C] *abbreviation for* PART SEPARATE PIECE • Pt can be used as an abbreviation for 'part' when referring to a section of a document: *See pt 3 for further details.*

pt MEASUREMENT *n* [C] *abbreviation for* PINT (=0.57 litres or 0.47 litres) • *a 4-pt jug* • *Add 1 pt of water and bring to the boil.* • *No milk today, 2 pts tomorrow please.* • LP **Units**

pt POINT *n* [C] *abbreviation for* POINT • Sometimes pt refers to a position: *Fix the shelf to the wall at pts A and B.* • On a map, Pt refers to a small thin piece of land which is surrounded by sea: *Pt of Ayre* • *Dreswick Pt* • In sport, pt refers to a score: *He needs a good high jump to score more than 9000 pts.*

PTA /ˌpiː·tiːˈeɪ/ *n* [C] *abbreviation for* **parent-teacher association**, see at PARENT • *Are you going to the PTA meeting tonight?*

pter·o·dac·tyl /£ˌter·əˈdæk·tɪl, $-ṭəl/ *n* [C] a very large flying animal that lived a long time ago • *The pterodactyl is an extinct reptile that existed at the same time as the dinosaurs.*

PTO INSTRUCTION /£ˌpiː·tiːˈəʊ, $-ˈoʊ/ *abbreviation for* please turn over • *PTO is usually written at the bottom of a page to show that there is more information on the other side.*

PTO SCHOOL ORGANIZATION /£ˌpiː·tiːˈəʊ, $-ˈoʊ/ *n* [C] *esp. Am abbreviation for* **parent-teacher organization**, see at PARENT • *I became a member of the PTO when Katy joined the school.*

Pty *adj* [after n] *abbreviation for* PROPRIETARY, which is used in the names of private companies in Australia, New Zealand and South Africa whose owners are responsible for only a limited amount of the companies' debts • *She has been working for Mackenzie Investments Pty for the past five years.* • LP **Letters**

pub *Br and Aus* /pʌb/, *Br fml* **pub·lic house**, *Am usually* **bar** *n* [C] a building with one or more rooms where alcoholic drinks can be bought and drunk and where food is often available • *Children younger than 14 are not allowed in some pubs.* • *The traditional British pub usually has two bars* (=rooms where drinks are sold) *– a public bar, popular with the regulars and sometimes with cheaper prices, and a saloon bar or lounge bar, with more comfortable seats.* • *This beer is very popular in the pubs* **and clubs** *of northern England.* • *Shall we* **go to**/*(infml)* **go down** *the pub after work?* • *My* **local** *pub does good bar meals.* See also LOCAL BUILDING. • *They took me out for a pub* **lunch/meal**. • *(infml)* If you go on a **pub crawl**, you visit several pubs one after the other, having a drink at each one: *I* **went on** *a pub crawl with Sally on Saturday night.* • See also PUBLICAN

pu·ber·ty /£ˈpjuː·bə·ti, $-bɚ·ṭi/ *n* [U] the stage in a person's life when they develop from a child into an adult because of changes in their body that make them able to have children • **At** *puberty, pubic hair develops and girls begin to menstruate.* • LP **Age**

pu·bes·cent /pjuːˈbes·ənt/ *adj* [not gradable] • Someone who is pubescent is at the stage in their life when they are developing from a child into an adult and becoming able to have children: *The new magazine is targetted at pubescent girls.* ○ *Many parents want more sex education for* **pre-***pubescent children.*

pubes /pjuːbz/ *pl n* [C] short curly hairs which grow around the sexual organs on the outside of the body of a person who is old enough to reproduce

pu·bic /ˈpjuː·bɪk/ *adj* [before n; not gradable] of or near the sexual organs on the outside of a person's body • *pubic hair* • *the pubic area*

pub·lic PEOPLE /ˈpʌb·lɪk/ *adj* [not gradable] relating to or involving people in general, rather than being limited to a particular group of people • *Public pressure was successful in getting the speed limit reduced outside the school.* • *All the* *hotel's public rooms, such as the dining room, are very luxuriously furnished.* • *They wanted to increase public awareness of the dangers of AIDS.* • *The disclosure of information will not be a criminal offence if it can be shown that it was in the public* **interest** (= that people ought to know about it). • *Peaceful demonstrations that do not cause a public* **nuisance** (= do not harm other people) *are a fundamental right in any truly democratic country.* • *There has been a change in public* **opinion** (= what people think) *over recent years and provision for smokers has been reduced in public places.* • *A recent public* **opinion poll** *revealed that many people prefer houses with gardens, however small.* • *The results will not be* **made** *public* (= told to everyone) *until tomorrow.* • *We will not* **go** *public* **with** (= tell people in general) *the results until tomorrow.* • If something, esp. information or knowledge, is **in the public domain** it is available for everyone to use without needing permission. • If you are **in the public eye** you are a famous person who is written about in newspapers and magazines and seen on television. • A **public address** (*abbreviation* **PA**) **(system)** is equipment used to make voices or music loud so that many people can hear them: *I heard my name being called over the public address.* • A **public bar** is a drinking room in a PUB with plainer furniture and sometimes lower prices than in the other drinking rooms. • A **public company** is a business which is owned by many people who have bought shares in it. • *(esp. Br and Aus fml)* A **public convenience** is a building containing toilets that are available for everyone to use. • Computer programs that are **public domain** are available without charge for everyone to use. • **Public enemy number one/no. 1** is a person or organization that has committed a serious crime: *Their policy on dumping waste has made the company public enemy no. 1.* • A **public figure**, or someone who is **in public life**, is famous because of what they do, and is written about in newspapers and magazines or is often on television or the radio. • A **public holiday** is a day when almost everyone in a particular country does not have to go to work or school: *New Year's Day is a public holiday in many countries.* • *(Br)* **Public house** is *fml for* PUB. • **Public relations** (*abbreviation* **PR**) is the activity of keeping good relationships between an organization and the people outside it: *Environmentalists attacked the company's ad as a public-relations* **exercise.** • In England, a **public school** is a **private school** (= paid for by parents not the government) at which girls aged from 11 to 18 and boys aged from 13 to 18 usually live while they study. Compare **public school** at PUBLIC [GOVERNMENT]. Ⓕ Ⓘ LP **Schools and colleges** • *(approving)* If you do something which is **public-spirited**, you do something good for society without expecting a reward: *The supermarket has made a public-spirited donation towards the repair of the church.* • **Public transport** (*Am usually* **public transportation** or **mass transit**) is a system of vehicles such as buses and trains which operate at regular times on fixed routes and are used by the public: *Greater investment in public transport would keep more cars off the roads.*

pub·lic /ˈpʌb·lɪk/ *n* [U + sing/pl v] • **The** public is all the people, esp. all those in one country: *The public isn't/aren't interested in the sex life of a second-rate pop star.* ○ *The palace and its grounds are* **open to** *the public* (= people can visit if they wish) *during the summer months.* ○ *The consumer electronics industry will soon have lots of new products to entice the British public.* ○ *(Br infml often humorous) I'm all for members of the* **Great British** *Public* (= British people) *knowing more about what goes on behind the scenes in government.* • **The** public is also all the people who do not belong to a particular group or organization: *The company has made a decision and informed its employees, but it won't be announced to the public till next week.* ○ *This product is not yet available to the* **general** *public* (= all ordinary people). ○ **Members of** *the public were asked about their shopping habits.* • Your public is the group of people who are involved with you or your organization, esp. in a business relationship: *The newspapers publish these outrageous stories because they know what their public wants.* • Something which is done **in public** is not done secretly, and most people know about it. Compare **in private** at PRIVATE [PERSONAL].

pu·blic·ly /ˈpʌb·lɪ·kli/ *adv* [not gradable] • If something is done publicly, it is done so that everyone can know about it: *The company publicly apologized and agreed to contribute some money to charity.* ○ *A price hasn't been publicly disclosed.* ○ *Her contribution to the company's success has never been publicly* **acknowledged.** ○ *She decided to divorce her husband after she was publicly* **humiliated** *by his affair with his secretary.*

pub·lic [GOVERNMENT] /ˈpʌb·lɪk/ *adj* [not gradable] provided by the government from taxes to be available to everyone • *public broadcasting* • *public buildings* • *the public highway* • *a public library* • *the Government's public spending plans* • *She works in* **the public sector** (= for a government organization). • *He is unlikely to* **hold** *public* **office** (= have an important job in national or local government). • *The company has been* **taken into** *public* (= government) *ownership.* • **Public housing** is *Am and Aus for* **council housing**, see at COUNCIL. • *(law)* A **public prosecutor** is a lawyer who acts for the government against a criminal in court. • *(esp. Br and Aus)* If something is provided from **the public purse** it is paid for by the government, and the person speaking usually disapproves of it: *People should provide for their own retirement and not expect to be supported by the public purse.* • In Scotland, Australia and the US, a **public school** is a free school provided by the government. Compare **public school** at PUBLIC [PEOPLE]. Ⓕ Ⓘ LP **Schools and colleges** • **Public servants** (= Government employees) *must have high standards of honesty.*

pu·blic·ly /ˈpʌb·lɪ·kli/ *adv* [not gradable] • *The new railway will not be publicly* **funded.**

pub·lic [OPEN] /ˈpʌb·lɪk/ *adj* allowing anyone to see or hear what is happening • *It's too public here – let's go back to my room to talk.* • *This is a very public place – you must be careful what you say.*

pu·blic·ly /ˈpʌb·lɪ·kli/ *adv* • *It was embarrassing to be seen to be disagreeing so publicly.*

pub·li·can /ˈpʌb·lɪ·kən/ *n* [C] *Br and Aus* the manager of a PUB

pub·li·ca·tion /ˌpʌb·lɪˈkeɪ·ʃᵊn/ *n* the act of making information or stories available to people in a printed form, or a book, magazine, newspaper or document in which information or stories are published • *The brochure will be ready* **for** *publication in September.* [U] • *Will you arrange the publication* **of** *the names of the winners?* [U] • *Our latest publication is a magazine for health enthusiasts.* [C] • *When is the publication* **date** (= When will the book be available to buy)? • See also PUBLISH.

pu·bli·ci·ty /£pʌbˈlɪs·ɪ·ti, $-ə·t̬i/ *n* [U] the activity of making certain that someone or something attracts a lot of interest or attention from many people, or the attention received as a result of this activity • *The concert wasn't given much* **advance** *publicity, so many tickets remained unsold.* • *He attracted a lot of* **adverse** *publicity with his speech about unmarried mothers.* • *Many public relations people believe there is no such thing as* **bad** *publicity.* • *Her first novel was published last year* **in a blaze of** (= with a lot of) *publicity.* • *We have planned an exciting publicity* **campaign** *with our advertisers.* • *The publicity* **generated** *by the court case has given a welcome boost to our sales.* • *His mother's fame has made him used to* **the glare of** *publicity.* • *The publicity* **material** *sent out by the company stressed their concern for the environment.* • *The company's continued use of such dangerous chemicals has* **attracted** *a lot of* **negative** *publicity.* • *The normally publicity-***shy** *director will be making several public appearances for the launch of the movie.* • *The enormous publicity* **surrounding the case** *will make it very difficult to hold a fair trial.* • *The pop group's arrival by hot-air balloon was just a publicity* **stunt** (= an unusual way of attracting the public's attention). • *(saying)* 'Any publicity is good publicity'.

pub·li·cist /ˈpʌb·lɪ·sɪst/ *n* [C] • A publicist is someone who arranges publicity for a person or organization by giving information to reporters and broadcasters and arranging public meetings and special events: *After the dismal sales of her second novel, she's decided to employ a publicist to promote her new book.* ○ *The festival has become little more than a platform for egotists and* **self-***publicists* (= people wanting to attract a lot of attention to themselves and their activities).

pub·li·cize *obj, Br and Aus usually* **-ise** /ˈpʌb·lɪ·saɪz/ *v* [T] • If you publicize something, you make information about it generally available: *We'll need to publicize the date of the meeting well in advance because it's a busy time of year.* ○ *The teacher was criticized by the education authority for publicizing his complaints.* ○ *Attitudes seem to be changing as a result of recent* **highly** *publicized* **cases** *of sexual harassment.* ○ *The resort's popularity has declined since the* **much-***publicized death of a German tourist there* *last year.* ○ *The event was* **well** *publicized all over town.* ○ *The work of the charity has been* **widely** *publicized throughout the media.*

pub·lish *obj* /ˈpʌb·lɪʃ/ *v* [T] to make (information) available to people, esp. in a book, magazine or newspaper, or to produce and sell (a book, magazine or newspaper) • *The newspaper has published many articles and letters about the effect of the new tax on their readers.* • *The Government publishes figures every six months showing how many people are unemployed.* • *The names of the winners of the competition will be published in June.* • *She was only 19 when her first novel was published.* • *The organization publishes more than 30 specialized newsletters as well as books, directories and maps.* • *"Publish and be damned"* (The Duke of Wellington when a former mistress tried to get him to pay her money to leave him out of her autobiograpy, 1769-1852) • See also PUBLICATION.

pub·lish·er /£ˈpʌb·lɪ·ʃəʳ, $-ʃɚ/ *n* [C] • A publisher is an organization which publishes printed texts or music: *The publisher of this dictionary is Cambridge University Press.* • Sometimes a publisher is an employee of such an organization who has responsibility for deciding what is published: *I was an editor for seven years before I was promoted to publisher.*

pub·lish·ing /ˈpʌb·lɪ·ʃɪŋ/ *n* [U] • *She's hopes to pursue a career in publishing.* • A **publishing house** is a company which publishes books.

puce /pjuːs/ *n* [U], *adj* (being) a dark purplish red colour • *Her face turned puce with rage and she started shouting at me.*

puck /pʌk/ *n* [C] a small hard rubber disc which is used instead of a ball in **ice hockey** (= a game played on ice)

puck·er *obj* /£ˈpʌk·əʳ, $-ɚ/ *v* [T] to tighten (skin or cloth) until small folds appear • *She puckered her lips and kissed him.* • *This hem hasn't been sewn properly – it's all puckered* **(up)**. [T/M]

puck·er /£ˈpʌk·əʳ, $-ɚ/ *n* [C] • *The seam is very badly stitched and full of puckers.*

puck·ish /ˈpʌk·ɪʃ/ *adj* typical of someone who plays harmless tricks • *She had a puckish grin.* • *His puckish* **humour** *endeared him to everyone he met.*

pud /pʊd/ *n Br infml* PUDDING • *What's for pud?* [U] • *We have roast beef and Yorkshire pud for lunch every Sunday.* [U] • *I like a nice steak-and-kidney pud.* [C]

pud·ding [SWEET FOOD] /ˈpʊd·ɪŋ/, *Br infml* **pud** *n* a sweet and usually hot dish made with pastry, flour, bread or rice and often fruit, or *(Br)* the final part of a meal when this or other sweet dishes are eaten • *He made a delicious* **toffee** *pudding for his dinner party.* [C] • *Is there any more* **treacle** *pudding?* [U] • *(Br)* **What's for** *pudding?* [U] • *(Br) I thought we'd* **have** *trifle* **for** *pudding.* [U] • *(Br dated infml humorous) I hear Sally's* **in the pudding club** (= pregnant) *again.* • A **pudding basin** is a large bowl which is used for making puddings. • A **pudding-basin haircut** is a short hairstyle which is not fashionable and looks as though it has been created by placing a pudding basin over your head and cutting round the edge of it: *I'm not going to that barber again! They gave me a real pudding-basin haircut last time.* • Ⓓ Ⓙ

pud·ding [SAVOURY FOOD] *esp. Br* /ˈpʊd·ɪŋ/, *Br infml* **pud** *n* a savoury dish made with pastry or flour which contains or is eaten with meat • *I've made a* **steak and kidney** *pudding for dinner.* [C] • *Would you like some more* **suet** *pudding?* [U] • Ⓓ Ⓙ

pud·dle /ˈpʌd·l̩/ *n* [C] a small pool of liquid on the ground, esp. water which is left in a hole after it has rained • *a puddle* **of** *water* • *He crashed into a tree after skidding on a puddle of oil in the middle of the road.* • *The children were splashing through the puddles in the street.* • *The river had dried up leaving only a few muddy puddles.*

pud·gy /ˈpʌdʒ·i/ *adj* **-ier, -iest** *esp. Am for* PODGY • *I was a very pudgy child.*

pudg·i·ness /ˈpʌdʒ·ɪ·nəs/ *n* [U]

pue·rile /£ˈpjʊə·raɪl, $ˈpjʊr·ɪl/ *adj disapproving* showing or expressing silliness that is unsuitable for an adult • *He can be very puerile when he's had a couple of drinks.* • *I find her sense of humour rather puerile.*

pue·ril·i·ty /£pjʊəˈrɪl·ɪ·ti, $, $pjʊrˈɪl·ə·t̬i/ *n* [U] *disapproving* • *Some of your colleagues have been complaining about your puerility in the office.*

puff *(obj)* [BREATHE] /pʌf/ *v* to breathe quickly and deeply, usually as a result of an activity which needs a lot of physical effort • *Alfred was puffing and drenched with sweat after his half-hour jog.* [I] • *Old Mr. Carmichael came puffing up and stood beside her until he had enough breath to speak.* [I] • *"I ran all the way home," she puffed* (= said while puffing). [+ clause] • *The men were* **puffing and panting** (= taking a lot of deep breaths) *as they pulled the box across the room.*

puff /pʌf/ *n infml* • *"Would you mind just having a puff* (= blowing) *into this breathalyser, sir?" said the policewoman.* [C] • *(Br) I can't talk at the moment – I'm* **out of** *puff* (= I need to breathe more air in). [U]

puffed *Br* /pʌft/, *Am and Aus* **pooped** /puːpt/ *adj* [after v] *infml* • If you are puffed **(out)**, you are breathing with difficulty because you have been making a lot of physical effort: *I can't walk any further – I'm puffed!*

puff *(obj)* [SMOKE] /pʌf/ *v* to smoke (tobacco) • *One per cent of the people questioned had puffed their first cigarette by the age of four.* [T] • *Pattie, puffing an imaginary cigar, did a brilliant imitation of Brian's way of walking.* [T] • *He puffed* **(away)** *thoughtfully* **on**/*(Br also)* **at** *his pipe and gazed out of the window.* [I always + adv/prep] • *The railway carriage was full of cigar-puffing businessmen.* • *"Puff the Magic Dragon"* (title of children's song written by Peter Yerrow and Leonard Lipton, 1963)

puff /pʌf/ *n* [C] • A puff is an act of smoking: *If you just* **take** *fewer puffs* **on**/*(Br also)* **at** *each cigarette you'll reduce your smoking without really missing it.* ○ *You get the most tar and nicotine from the last few puffs because the tobacco itself acts as a filter.*

puff [SMALL AMOUNT] /pʌf/ *n* [C] a small amount of smoke, air or something that can rise into the air in a small cloud • *Sean blew a puff* **of smoke** *at his reflection in the mirror.* • *He hit the ground with his stick and a puff* **of** *dust rose up into the air.* • *Humans blink their eyes in response to a puff* **of** *air directed towards them.*

puff *(obj)* /pʌf/ *v* [always + adv/prep] • *He puffed a cloud of cigarette smoke into my eyes.* [T] • *The battered old bus was puffing* **out** *clouds of smoke.* [M] • *The old steam train whistled and puffed* (= produced smoke as it moved) *out of the station.* [I]

puf·fer /£ˈpʌf·əʳ, $-ɚ/ *n* [C] • *You can apply the powder with a puffer* (= a small soft bottle that blows out its contents when pressed). • *(Br)* **Puffer train** is a child's word for a steam train.

puff *(obj)* [SWELL] /pʌf/ *v* [always + adv/prep] to increase in size; to make or become larger • *The child puffed* **out** *his cheeks to make himself look like the fat man.* [M] • *With all its feathers puffed* **out** *the bird looked twice its normal size.* [M] • *My leg puffed* **up** *all round the insect bite.* [I] • *Naan bread traps steam while it cooks so it puffs* **up** *to a larger size.* [I] • *(sometimes disapproving)* If someone **puffs** themselves **with pride** or is **puffed up** they are very pleased with themselves: *Her parents puffed themselves with pride when they heard that she'd won.* ○ *He came back from the meeting very puffed up because he'd made a successful deal.*

puff /pʌf/ *n* [C] • A puff is a type of sweet cake or savoury food which is made from **puff pastry** and is filled with different substances: *a cream puff* ○ *a jam puff* ○ *cheese puffs* • A **puff adder** is a poisonous African snake which swells to a larger size when it is attacked. • **Puff pastry** is pastry with lots of thin layers which swells to a larger size when cooked. • **Puff sleeves** are short sleeves which swell out into a ball shape.

puf·fy /ˈpʌf·i/ *adj* **-ier, -iest** • If something is puffy it has swollen to a larger than usual size: *The prisoner's face was bruised and puffy, and it was obvious he had been beaten.* ○ *I could tell he had been crying because his eyes were red and puffy.* ○ *Bake the pastry until it's golden brown and puffy.*

puff [PRAISE] /pʌf/, *Am also* **puff piece** *n* [C] *infml usually disapproving* a piece of writing or speech which praises something • *I was annoyed to see part of my article being used as a puff* **for** *a novel.* • *The interviewer tried to prevent him* **giving** *a puff to his new invention.*

puff *obj* /pʌf/ *v* [T] *infml usually disapproving* • *I heard him puffing his latest film on a chat show.* • *The restaurant is usually busy thanks to it being regularly puffed by travel writers.*

puf·fer·y /£ˈpʌf·ᵊr·i, $ˈ-ɚ-/ *n* [U] *infml usually disapproving* • Puffery is praise which is too forcefully expressed and is intended to make people buy something: *In spite of all the media puffery, her latest novel has failed to make it into the bestseller list.*

puff·ball /£ˈpʌf·bɔːl, £-bɑːl/ *n* [C] a large white round edible FUNGUS

puf·fin /ˈpʌf·ɪn/ *n* [C] a sea bird which lives in northern parts of the world and has a large brightly coloured beak

pug /pʌg/ *n* [C] a small dog with a flat face and a short wide nose

pug·na·cious /pʌgˈneɪ·ʃəs/ *adj fml* willing to start an argument or fight, or expressing an argument or opinion very forcefully • *She became very pugnacious as a result of being bullied at school.* • *Her pugnacious speech convinced her opponents that she was still a threat to them.* • *When he became a lawyer, he sprang to the defence of his clients with the same pugnacious attitude that had characterised his childhood.*

pug·nac·i·ty /£pʌgˈnæs·ɪ·ti, $-ə·t̬i/, **pug·na·cious·ness** /pʌgˈneɪ·ʃə·snəs/ *n* [U] *fml* • *Her reputation was based on her pugnacity as an interviewer.*

puke /pjuːk/ *v slang* to vomit • *His baby puked all down my shirt.* [I] • *He puked* **(up)** *all over the floor.* [I] • *She puked her dinner* **up**/*puked* **up** *her dinner after eating too much.* [M] • If something or someone **makes you (want to) puke** it greatly upsets or disgusts you: *Doesn't it make you want to puke when you see animals being treated so badly?* ○ *You really make me puke! How could you do such a terrible thing?*

puke /pjuːk/ *n* [U] *slang* • *The floor was covered with puke* (= vomit).

puk·ka /ˈpʌk·ə/ *adj dated* totally correct, sincere or acceptable • *With his lordly manner, he seems like the epitome of the pukka Englishman.* • *She has lost most of her wealth, but she has retained her pukka accent.* • *The certificates that are issued at the end of the course are practically worthless and are no substitute for pukka qualifications.*

pull *(obj)* MOVE TOWARDS YOU /pʊl/ *v* to move (something) towards yourself, sometimes with great physical effort • *Could you help me move this bookcase over there? You pull and I'll push.* [I] • *He pulled the chair away from the desk.* [T] • *He pulled the heavy box across the floor to the door.* [T] • *He pulled the door open.* [T + obj + adj] • *The car was pulling a caravan.* [T] • *When you fire a gun, you should pull the trigger gently.* [T] • *The sun was so strong we had to pull* **down** *the blinds.* [M] • *She pulled* **out** *the drawer.* [M] • If you pull **at** something you pull it briefly and often repeatedly: *The child pulled at his sleeve to catch his attention.* [T] ○ *He pulled at his ear as he spoke.* [T] • If you **pull** something **out of the bag/hat**, you do something unexpected which improves a bad situation: *The football club, almost bankrupt just a short while ago, has pulled £1 million out of the hat by selling a star player.* • If you **pull the carpet/rug from under** someone, you stop them doing what they were planning to do: *We've managed to pull the rug* **out** *from under our competitors with this new product.* ○ *He really pulled the carpet from under her* **feet** *when he secretly applied for and was given the promotion that she had wanted.* • If you **pull a face**, you make an unusual expression with your face: *You must have pulled a very frightening face if you made him cry.* ○ *She's always laughing and joking and pulling funny faces.* ○ *"This tastes disgusting," said Tom, pulling a face* **at** *his cup of coffee.* ○ *He pulled a* **long** (= disappointed) *face when I said he couldn't borrow my car.* • *(infml)* If someone **pulls** your **leg**, they deceive you in a way that is intended to be humorous: *Stop pulling my leg – you haven't been having lunch with the President!* • *(infml humorous)* **Pull the other one** or **Pull the other leg (it's got bells on)** is a way of saying that you do not believe what someone is telling you and that they should stop trying to deceive you: *"I'll be a millionaire by the time I'm thirty." "Oh, pull the other one!"* • If you **pull the plug**, you cause something to stop, often by making public something which was being kept secret: *They are willing to continue production long after other companies would have pulled the plug.* ○ *The newspaper pulled the plug* **on** *a fraud that duped people into spending nearly £80 to collect £15.* • People who do not **pull** their **punches** speak in an open and honest way without trying to be kind or gentle: *Her image is that of an investigative reporter who doesn't pull her punches.* ○ *He is a barrister who never pulls any punches and is well-known for the fierceness of his cross-examinations.* • To **pull rank** is to use the advantage that is yours because you have a higher rank: *He pulled rank* **on** *me and insisted that he should get the free tickets that were given to the office.* • *(infml)* If you **pull** your **socks up**, you return to your usual level of effort after making less effort for a while: *Your work hasn't been up to your usual standard recently and you're going to have to pull your socks up.* • When you **pull out all the stops**, you make a lot of effort to do something well: *They pulled out all the stops for their daughter's wedding.* • To **pull strings** is to use people that you know to help you to do something that you could not do without their special help: *I couldn't get a ticket, but my uncle works there, so he pulled a few strings and got one for me.* • Someone who is **pulling the strings** is in control of something, often secretly: *I want to know who's pulling the strings around here.* • If a group of people **pull together**, they help each other to achieve a particular result: *There isn't much time to get the display ready, but if we all pull together we should finish it by the end of this week.* • If someone tells you to **pull yourself together**, they want you to behave in a less emotional way and take control of what you are doing: *Just pull yourself together. There's no point crying about it.* • Someone who does not **pull** their **weight** does not do the fair share of work that other people think they should do: *The others complained because Sarah wasn't pulling her weight.* ○ *If you want to move in with us, you'll have to pull your weight and do your share of the cooking and cleaning.* • To **pull the wool over** someone's **eyes** is to persuade them to believe something which is not true in order to hide the truth from them: *She pulled the wool over his eyes, making him think she was a faithful wife when in fact she was having a passionate love affair.* • A **pull-out** table/bed/unit is one that can be pulled into position when you want to use it and folded away when you do not. • **Pull-tab** is *Am for* **ring-pull**. See at RING CIRCLE.

pull /pʊl/ *n* • **Give** *the rope a hard pull* (= pull it). [C] • *(fig.) I've still got quite a bit of pull* (= influence) *in the club, so I think I could get you elected.* [U] • A pull is also something that you pull to make something work or to open something: *a curtain pull* ○ *a drawer pull* [C]

pull *obj* REMOVE /pʊl/ *v* to take (something) out of or away from a place, esp. using physical effort • *He pulled* **off** *his wet clothes and laid them out to dry in the sun.* [M] • *I hadn't seen the dentist for three years, and she had to pull two of my teeth* **out**. [M] • *He put his hands on the side of the pool and pulled himself* **out** *of the water.* [T] • *I spent the morning pulling* **up** *the weeds in the flowerbeds.* [M] • *The old woman pulled herself* **up** *the stairs with difficulty, holding on to the rail.* [T] • To **pull down** something, esp. a building, is to destroy it: *They pulled down the warehouse to build a new supermarket.* ○ *They set fire to the flag and pulled the dictator's statue down.* • *(Br dated) That virus she had two months ago really* **pulled** *her* **down** (= made her feel ill and weak) *– she still hasn't fully recovered.* • If you **pull a gun on** someone, you remove it from its holder and point it at them to threaten them: *He suddenly pulled a gun on me and said he'd shoot me if I didn't give him my bag.* • **Pull date** is *Am and Aus for* **sell-by date**. See at SELL MONEY. • A **pull-out** in a magazine or newspaper is a set of pages that are intended to be taken out and used separately: *a 16-page pull-out* ○ *There's a pull-out on hair care in next week's issue.*

pull *(obj)* ATTRACT /pʊl/ *v* to attract (a person or people) • *The show has certainly pulled* **(in) the crowds**. [T/M] • *(Br and Aus infml)* If you pull someone, you start to have a sexual relationship with them: *He certainly knows how to pull* **the birds** (= attract female sexual partners). [T] ○ *Did Tracy pull at the nightclub last night?* [I] • A person or thing's **pulling power** is their ability to attract people to see them: *Although she hasn't made a movie for four years, her pulling power is as great as ever.* ○ *Circuses don't seem to have much pulling power these days.*

pull /pʊl/ *n* • A pull is something which attracts people: *"How can we persuade people to come to the meeting?" "A glass of wine is quite a good pull."* [C] • Pull is the physical or emotional power to attract: *The greater the mass of an object, the greater its* **gravitational** *pull.* [U] ○ *The movie's all-star cast should give it a lot of pull.* [U] • *(Br infml)* Someone who is **on the pull** is actively looking for a sexual partner: *Sally was out on the pull again last night.*

pull MOVE /pʊl/ *v* [I always + adv/prep] (esp. of a vehicle or its driver) to move in the stated direction • *During the last lap of the race one of the runners began to pull* **ahead**. • *There was a roar and a cloud of smoke as the car pulled* **away** *from the traffic lights.* • *Our armies are pulling* **back** *on all fronts.* • *The driver pulled* **into** *the empty parking space.* • *We waved as the train pulled* **into/out of** *the station.* • *The bus pulled* **out** *into the line of traffic.* • *Just pull* **over/in** (= move to the side of the road and stop) *here, and I'll get out and walk the rest of the way.* • If you **pull back from** something or from doing something, you do not do something you were going to do: *He seemed quite interested in sharing the house to start with, but he pulled back from it when it was time to sign the lease.* • *The car/driver* **pulled up** (=stopped) *outside the cinema.* • If you **pull up short**, you stop suddenly in a vehicle: *I almost skidded when a dog ran across the road and I had to pull up short.* ○ *(fig.) It pulled me up short* (=surprised me greatly) *when I saw Chris with all her hair cut off.* • *(Br infml)* A **pull-in** (*Am* **rest stop**) is a place at the side of a road where vehicles can stop and where it is sometimes possible to buy food and drinks: *There's a pull-in further along the road where you can get a marvellous view of the valley.* • PIC› **Driving**

pull *obj* INJURE /pʊl/ *v* [T] to injure (esp. a muscle) by stretching it too much or too quickly • *Mary pulled a* **hamstring** *and couldn't play in the finals.*

pull /pʊl/ *n* [C] • *He's suffering from a groin pull.*

pull *obj* PERFORM /pʊl/ *v* [T] *slang* to perform (an action which is dishonest or intended to deceive) • *The gang that pulled the bank robbery were all arrested.* • *No one's gonna pull that kind of trick* **on** *me!* • To **pull a fast one** is to trick someone: *He really pulled a fast one* **on** *those pensioners when he persuaded them to invest in a non-existent company.*

pull down *obj v adv* [T] *Am infml* to earn (an amount of money) • *Between them they must be pulling down over $100 000 a year.*

pull in *obj*, **pull** *obj* **in** *v adv* [M] *esp. Am infml* to arrest (someone) • *The police pulled in scores of protesters during the demonstration.*

pull off *obj*, **pull** *obj* **off** *v adv* [M] *infml* to succeed in doing (something difficult or unexpected) • *It's a clever plan and his colleagues think he may have a chance of pulling it off.* • *The central bank has pulled off one of the biggest financial rescues of recent years.* • *The football club pulled off their first away win of the season this Saturday.*

pull out *(obj)*, **pull** *(obj)* **out** *v adv* to (cause to) leave or no longer take part • *The fighting's getting too fierce – we're going to have to pull our troops out.* [M] • *He pulled out* (**of** *the deal) at the last moment, leaving the rest of us to make up his share of the money.* [I]

pull–out /ˈpʊl·aʊt/ *n* [C] • A pull-out is the removal of soldiers from an area where there has been fighting: *The troop withdrawal will be completed within 21 days, and a pull-out from the city is expected within four days.*

pull through *(obj)* LIVE *v adv*, *v prep* to become well again after (a serious illness), esp. when you might have died • *They said the operation had been successful and they expected his wife to pull through.* [I] • *Their baby's just pulled through a bout of pneumonia.* [T]

pull *(obj)* **through** *(obj)* MANAGE *v adv*, *v prep* to help (someone to) deal with (a difficult situation) • *During their time in government they have pulled through several crises.* [T] • *Her friends helped her pull through after her sister was killed in a car crash.* [I] • *He'd never have managed on his own, but his colleagues have pulled him through.* [T]

pull *obj* **up** *v prep* [T] *infml* to criticize (someone) • *She's always pulling me up* **for/over** *my bad spelling.*

pul·ley /ˈpʊl·i/ *n* [C] a piece of equipment for moving heavy objects up or down, consisting of a small wheel over which a rope or chain fixed to the object can be easily pulled or released slowly • *The blocks of stone had to be lifted into position with a system of pulleys.*

pull·over /£ˈpʊlˌəʊ·və(r), $-ˌoʊ·vɚ/, *Am usually* **sweat·er**, *Aus usually* **jump·er** *n* [C] a piece of clothing which is made of a warm material such as wool, has long sleeves, and is worn over the top part of the body and put on by pulling it over your head

pul·mo·na·ry /£ˈpʊl·mə·nə·ri, $-ner·i/ *adj* [not gradable] *medical* relating to the lungs • *The pulmonary veins carry oxygenated blood from the lungs to the heart.*

pulp /pʌlp/ *n* a soft wet mass, often produced by pressing things until they lose their shape and firmness • *Mash the bananas* **to a** *pulp and then mix in the yoghurt.* • Pulp is also small pieces of paper, cloth or wood mixed with water until they form a soft wet mass. It is used for making paper: *wood pulp* [U] ○ *a pulp mill* ○ *The company manufactures pulp and paper products.* • *(disapproving)* Pulp can also refer to books and magazines which are of low quality in the way they are produced and the stories and articles they contain: *pulp fiction* ○ *a pulp writer* • *(infml)* If you **beat** someone **to (a)** pulp, you seriously injure them by hitting them a lot: *The gang threatened to beat the boy to a pulp.* • *(infml)* Someone or something that **reduces** you **to (a)** pulp frightens you: *One look at his face reduced me to pulp.*

pulp *obj* /pʌlp/ *v* [T] • *Cook the apples and then pulp them.* • *The old newspapers were pulped and recycled.*

pul·pit /ˈpʊl·pɪt/ *n* [C] a raised place in a church, with steps leading up to it, from which the priest speaks to the worshippers • *It's difficult to imagine people's reactions when he first arrived in the city and began to preach his radical sermons from the pulpit.*

pul·sar /£ˈpʌl·sɑː(r), $-sɑːr/ *n* [C] *specialized* a very small dense star that sends out radio waves • *Pulsars have a mass similar to the sun, but a diameter of about 10 km.*

pul·sate /£pʌlˈseɪt, $ˈ--/ *v* [I] to make a sound or move with a regular rhythm • *Music pulsated from loudspeakers in every corner of the bar.* • *The pulsating drumbeats penetrated the silence of the forest.* • *The dancers pulsated* **to** *the festive beat of traditional folk songs.* • *I was kept awake by neon signs pulsating* (=flashing on and off repeatedly) *outside my window.* • *(fig.) Rue St. Denis is the pulsating* (=very active and energetic) *heart of French street life in Montreal.*

pul·sa·tion /pʌlˈseɪ·ʃ(ə)n/ *n* • *Their instruments picked up pulsations coming from a distant galaxy.* [C] • *The pulsation of the drums worked itself up to a climax.* [U]

pulse BEAT /pʌls/ *n* [C] the regular beating of the heart, esp. when it is felt at the wrist or side of the neck • *The child's pulse was* **strong/weak**. • *Running fast increases your pulse* **rate**. • If you **take** someone's pulse, you hold their wrist and count how many times their heart beats in one minute: *The doctor took her pulse and looked worried.* ○ *(fig.) The opinion poll will take the pulse of* (=discover the general feelings of) *the nation to find out whether people will accept the new tax.* • If something **sets** your pulse **racing** or **quickens** your **pulse**, it excites you or makes you very interested in it: *This is a movie that will set your pulse racing.* ○ *There's nothing in the book to quicken your pulse.* • Someone who has their **finger on the pulse**, knows everything about something: *You ought to hear what she has to say, because she's someone* **with** *her finger on the pulse of the city.* ○ *The situation changes daily, so it's really important to* **keep** *your finger on the pulse.* • A pulse is also a short burst of energy which is repeated regularly, such as a brief loud sound or a brief flash of light: *The data, normally transmitted electronically, can be changed into pulses of light.*

pulse /pʌls/ *v* [I] • *With the TV and radio news pulsing* (=sounding loudly and regularly) **through** *the house all day there is no protection for anyone from the real world.* • *The music had a pulsing rhythm.*

pulse SEED /pʌls/ *n* [C] *specialized* (an edible ripe seed of) a plant belonging to the bean family • *Pulses grow in cases called pods.* • *Pulses include peas, lentils and chickpeas and are an important part of a vegetarian diet.*

pul·ver·ize *obj*, *Br and Aus usually* **–ise** /£ˈpʌl·v(ə)r·aɪz, $-və·raɪz/ *v* [T] to press or crush (something) until it becomes powder or a soft mass • *Divers found an area of pulverized rock on the sea bed.* • *Chicken stock cubes are often made from pulverised remnants of unwanted day-old chicks.* • *(infml)* Pulverize also means to damage badly: *Mirta said the storm pulverized their trailer home.*

pul·ver·i·za·tion, *Br and Aus usually* **–i·sa·tion** /£ˌpʌl·v(ə)r·aɪˈzeɪ·ʃ(ə)n, $-vɚ·ɪ-/ *n* [U]

pu·ma /ˈpjuː·mə/ *n* [C] a COUGAR (=large wild cat) • PIC› **Cats**

pu·mice (stone) /ˈpʌm·ɪs/ *n* [U] a type of grey light stone which is used in pieces or as a powder for rubbing things to make them smooth • *Pumice is produced in volcanic eruptions.* • *Some people use pumice in the bath to remove dry skin from their feet.*

pum·mel *obj* /ˈpʌm·(ə)l/, *Am also* **pom·mel** *v* [T] **-ll-** or *Am usually* **-l-** to hit (someone or something) repeatedly, esp. with your FISTS • *The boxer had pummelled his opponent* **into** *submission by the end of the fourth round.* • If you pummel someone, you attack or criticize them or almost defeat them: *When we switched the tennis on, he was pummelling the champion.* ○ *Pro-life candidates for governor are being pummeled* **on** (=severely criticized because of their opinions about) *abortion.*

pum·mell·ing, *Am usually* **pum·mel·ing** /ˈpʌm·(ə)l·ɪŋ/ *n* [C] • *(fig.) As a newcomer he really* **took** *a pummelling* (=was severely criticized) *at his first meeting.*

pump DEVICE /pʌmp/ *n* [C] a piece of equipment which is used to cause liquid, air or gas to move from one place to another • *a water/electric/hand/bicycle/fuel pump* • *a (Br and Aus) petrol/(Am) gas pump* • A **pump-action** device operates by forcing something, esp. air, in or out of an enclosed space or container: *a pump-action shotgun/toilet* • PIC⟩ **Bicycles** Ⓣ

pump *obj* /pʌmp/ *v* [T] • *Our latest machine can pump a hundred gallons a minute.* • *The new wine is pumped* **into** *storage tanks.* • *The heart pumps blood* **through** *the arteries/***round** *the body.* • *The oil and gas are pumped* **(up)** *from under the seabed.* • *We took turns pumping* **out** *the boat* (=removing water using a pump). [M] • *(infml disapproving)* To pump something **out** is also to produce a lot of something, esp. speech or music, continuously: *The government keeps pumping out the same old propaganda.* [M] ○ *The car radio was pumping out music with a heavy beat.* [M] • If a person or their stomach is **pumped out**, a poisonous substance is sucked out through a tube: *He took an overdose of sleeping pills and they had to pump him out.* ○ *She had to be taken to the hospital to have her stomach pumped out.* • If you **pump up** something, you fill it with air using a pump: *She pumped up the airbed/balloon.* ○ *I must remember to pump my bike tyres up.* • *(infml)* When you pump someone, you ask them for information, esp. in an indirect way: *She was pumping me* **(for** *details)* **about** *the new family next door.* • If you **pump** someone's **hand**, you hold it and move it up and down in order to greet them, as if you were using an old type of pump: *He rushed over to me and pumped my hand as though I were an old friend.* • *(infml)* To **pump iron** is to lift heavy weights for exercise: *In gritty television commercials, he pumps iron and talks tough about working out.* • If you **pump money into** something, you spend a lot of money trying to make it operate successfully: *They had been pumping money into the business for some years without seeing any results.* • A **pumping station** is a building with machinery for pumping large amounts of water.

pump SHOE /pʌmp/ *n* [C] *Br and Aus* a women's shoe with low heels and no fastenings • Pump is also *Am and Aus for* **court shoe**. See at COURT ROYALTY. • Ⓣ

pum·per·ni·ckel /£'pʌm·pə,nɪk·l̩, $-pɚ-/ *n* [U] a type of firm dark brown bread made from RYE

pump·kin /'pʌmp·kɪn/ *n* [C] a large round vegetable with hard yellow or orange flesh • *pumpkin pie* • *To celebrate Halloween, people remove the inside of a pumpkin and make the shell into a light by putting a candle inside.* • *I'll* **turn into a pumpkin** (= be very late) *if I don't leave now.* • PIC⟩ **Vegetables**

pun /pʌn/ *n* [C] an amusing use of a word or phrase which has several meanings or which sounds like another word • *Pat's always telling bad jokes and* **making** *dreadful puns.* • *This is a well-known joke based on a pun: "What's black and white and red* (= read) *all over?" "A newspaper."* • *I love fish. The sole exception –* **no pun intended/excuse the** *pun – is mackerel.* • *"When I am dead, I hope it may be said:/ His sins were scarlet, but his books were read."* (a pun by Hilaire Belloc in *On His Books*, 1923)

pun /pʌn/ *v* [I] • *In almost every article she puns* **on** (=makes a pun about) *the name of the person she's writing about.*

pun·ster /£'pʌn·stəʳ, $-stɚ/ *n* [C] • A punster is a person who makes puns.

punch HIT /pʌntʃ/ *n* [C] a forceful hit with a FIST (=hand with the fingers bent in) • *a knockout punch* • *He lashed out with kicks and punches and the other man fell to the floor.* • *She gave him a punch (Br and Aus)* **on***/(Am)* **in** *the nose.* • *The boxer was* **landing** *punches* **to** *the head before his opponent knew what was going on.* • *(Br)* A **punch ball** (*Aus also and Am* **punching bag**) is an air-filled leather bag hung from a frame or fixed to a stand: *Boxers practise with punch balls.* • *(Am)* A **punch ball** is a rubber ball filled with air which is hit with your FIST when playing a game similar to baseball. • A boxer who is **punch-drunk** is behaving in a way that suggests his brain has been damaged as a result of being hit repeatedly on the head: *Boxers who are punch-drunk sometimes have speech problems.* • If you are **punch-drunk**, you are tired and confused after putting a lot of mental effort into an activity, and you find it difficult to think clearly: *She was punch-drunk after she lost the vote.*

punch *obj* /pʌntʃ/ *v* [T] • *I punched him* **in** *the stomach.* • *He had been punched* **and kicked**, *leaving both eyes badly injured and his nose and cheekbone broken.* • *An American businessman was punched unconscious by two muggers in a city street this afternoon.* [+ obj + adj] • *(esp. Am)* If you punch buttons on a telephone or keys on a keyboard, you hit them hard and quickly with your fingers: *I punched* **out** *an angry reply to his letter on my portable typewriter.* [M] • If you punch a clock or a **time clock**, you put a card into a special machine to record the times you arrive at and leave work: *After 17 years of punching the clock, he just took off one morning and was never heard from again.* • *(esp. Br)* If you **have/get into** a **punch-up** with someone, you have a fight with them: *He got into a punch-up* **with** *the man who bumped his car.*

punch EFFECT /pʌntʃ/ *n* [U] the power to be interesting and have a strong effect on people • *He gave the song plenty of punch.* • *The performance/speech/presentation* **lacked** *punch.* • A **punch line** is the last part of a story or a joke which explains the meaning of what has happened previously or makes it amusing: *The punchline for the joke "How do you know an elephant has been in your fridge?" is "You can see its footprints in the butter!"* ○ *It's a long story, but you can see the punch line coming a mile off.*

punch·y /'pʌn·tʃi/ *adj* **-ier**, **-iest** • *a punchy speech/song/rhythm/tune* • *By and large the new look for the magazine strikes me as punchy and effective.*

punch DRINK /pʌntʃ/ *n* a cold or hot drink made by mixing fruit juices, pieces of fruit and often wine or other alcoholic drinks • *One of the best-known punches is Spanish sangria, which is based on red wine.* [C] • *Would you like some fruit punch/a glass of punch?* [U] Ⓙ • A **punch bowl** is a large bowl in which punch is served: *Glasses are filled from a punch bowl with a type of large spoon called a ladle.*

punch TOOL /pʌntʃ/ *n* [C] a piece of equipment which cuts holes in a material by pushing a piece of metal through it • *a ticket punch* • *a metal punch* • *There are several types of punch that are designed for different materials.* • *Have you seen the* **hole** *punch anywhere?* • PIC⟩ **Stationery**

punch *obj* /pʌntʃ/ *v* [T] • *If you punch some holes in these sheets of paper you'll be able to keep them in your ring binder.* • *This belt's too big – I'll have to punch an extra hole in it.* • *My ticket was punched three times on the journey!*

Punch IMAGINARY PERSON /pʌntʃ/, **Mr Punch** *n* [not after *the*] an imaginary man with a long nose who appears as a PUPPET (=a small model of a person) in a famous children's entertainment • A **Punch and Judy show** is a traditional children's entertainment in which Mr Punch argues with his wife Judy. It is performed in Britain at children's parties and in towns by the sea in summer.

punc·til·i·ous /pʌŋk'tɪl·i·əs/ *adj fml* very careful to behave correctly or to give attention to details • *She is very punctilious* **about** *hygiene.* • *The mistake was spotted immediately by their punctilious lawyer.*

punc·til·i·ous·ly /pʌŋk'tɪl·i·ə·sli/ *adv fml* • *He punctiliously stood up as she entered the room.* • *The article had been punctiliously edited.*

punc·til·i·ous·ness /pʌŋk'tɪl·i·ə·snəs/ *n* [U] *fml*

punc·tual /'pʌŋk·tju·əl/ *adj* arriving, doing something or happening at the expected, correct time; not late • *a punctual start to the meeting* • *a very punctual person* (=a person who never arrives late)

punc·tual·ly /'pʌŋk·tju·ə·li/ *adv* • *The meeting started punctually at 10.00 a.m.*

punc·tu·al·i·ty /£,pʌnk·tju'æl·ɪ·ti, $-ə·ṱi/ *n* [U] • *The boss does expect punctuality from us.* • *"Punctuality is the politeness of princes"* (believed to have been said by Louis XVIII of France, 1755-1824)

punc·tu·ate *obj* /'pʌŋk·tju·eɪt/ *v* [T] *slightly fml* (to cause) to happen repeatedly while something else is happening; to interrupt repeatedly • *Brilliant piano solos punctuate the songs.* • *Cries of "Yeah! Tell it like it is!" and "Right on!" punctuated her speech.* • *The President spoke at length in a speech punctuated* **by** *constant applause.* • *He chatted freely, punctuating his remarks as often as possible* **with** *the interviewer's first name.* • See also **punctuate** at PUNCTUATION.

punc·tu·a·tion /,pʌŋk·tju'eɪ·ʃən/ *n* [U] (the use of) special marks that you add to a text to show the divisions between phrases and sentences, and to make the meaning clearer • *His letter was completely without punctuation.* • *Punctuation and spelling were never really taught at my school.* • A **punctuation mark** is a mark that you add to a text to show the divisions between different parts of it: *Full stops/Periods, commas, semicolons, question marks and brackets are all different types of punctuation mark.* • LP⟩ **Symbols** PIC⟩ **Mark**

punc·tu·ate *obj* /£'pʌŋk·tjuː·eɪt, $-tuː-/ *v* [T] • *Please punctuate* (= put punctuation in) *your writing otherwise it is very difficult to understand.* • See also PUNCTUATE.

punc·ture /£'pʌŋk·tʃəʳ, $-tʃɚ/ *n* [C] a small hole made by a sharp object, esp. in a tyre • *My bike has* **had** *two* *punctures in the last three weeks.* • *I* (=My car tyre) **had** *a puncture when I was driving back from Keele.* • *(Br) The front tyre is looking a bit flat – it may have a* **slow** *puncture (Am* **slow leak***).* • *She had a puncture* **wound** *in her arm, from a wasp sting.* • (KOR)

punc·ture *(obj)* /£ˈpʌŋk·tʃəʳ, $-tʃɚ/ *v* • *The new tyres are made of a stronger rubber so that they puncture less easily.* [I] • *She had used a screwdriver to puncture two holes in the lid of a paint tin.* [T] • *Several broken ribs and a punctured lung were the worst injuries.* [T] • *(fig.) The collapse of the Soviet Union punctured* (=caused the end of) *most people's faith in Communism.* [T] • *(fig.) Most of the players are tough working-class lads, so any inflated egos tend to be quickly punctured* (=made smaller). [T]

pun·dit /ˈpʌn·dɪt/ *n* [C] a person who knows a lot about a particular subject and is therefore often asked to give an opinion about it • *a political/foreign-policy/sports pundit*

pun·gent /ˈpʌn·dʒᵊnt/ *adj* (of a smell or taste) very strong, sometimes in an unpleasant way, or *(fig. literary)* (of speech or writing) very strongly felt and expressed and often critical • *the pungent whiff of a goat* • *I sat down to a cup of wonderfully pungent Turkish coffee.* • *(fig. literary) He's the author of a pungent political comedy.* • *We need journalism with a cutting, pungent style for this new magazine.*

pun·gent·ly /ˈpʌn·dʒᵊnt·li/ *adv* • *(fig. literary) She made her points pungently.*

pun·gen·cy /ˈpʌn·dʒᵊnt·si/ *n* [U] • *The different sorts of chilli peppers vary in pungency.*

pun·ish *obj* CRIME /ˈpʌn·ɪʃ/ *v* [T] to cause (someone who has done something wrong or committed a crime) to suffer, by hurting them, forcing them to pay money, sending them to prison, etc. • *He punished the class* **by** *giving them extra work.* • *The oil company was found guilty on ten counts of pollution, and was punished* **with** *a $250 million fine.* • *Those responsible for this violence should be brought to court and punished* **severely**. • To punish a crime means to punish the person or people who commit it: *Drunken driving can be punished* **with** *a prison sentence.* • See also PUNITIVE. • LP **Crimes and criminals**

pun·ish·a·ble /ˈpʌn·ɪ·ʃə·bl̩/ *adj* • *a punishable offence* • *The two men are charged with second-degree murder, punishable* **by** *up to life in prison.*

pun·ish·ment /ˈpʌn·ɪʃ·mənt/ *n* • *Punishment* **for** *some crimes can sometimes take the form of community service.* [U] • *Many people think that the death penalty is too severe a punishment* **for** *any crime.* [C] • *(fml) It was always our father who* **administered/meted** *out punishments.* [C] • *"My object all sublime / I shall achieve in time – / To let the punishment fit the crime"* (W.S.Gilbert in the operetta *The Mikado*, 1885)

pun·ish *obj* TREAT BADLY /ˈpʌn·ɪʃ/ *v* [T] to use or treat badly, violently or without care • *Her car engine won't last long if she carries on punishing it like that.* • *He really punishes that horse of his.*

pun·ish·ing /ˈpʌn·ɪ·ʃɪŋ/ *n* [U] • *You have to expect the shock absorbers to* **take a** *punishing* (=to be damaged by bad treatment) *on gravel and mud roads.* • *Both boxers* **took** *quite* **a** *punishing* (=both were hurt badly).

pun·ish·ing /ˈpʌn·ɪ·ʃɪŋ/ *adj* • *During peak periods she has a punishing* (=very tiring) *schedule of five presentations a day.* • *Ground troops endured a week of punishing* (=very destructive) *air strikes from evening bombers.*

pun·ish·ing·ly /ˈpʌn·ɪ·ʃɪŋ·li/ *adv* • *a punishingly heavy workload* (=a very large amount of work)

pun·ish·ment /ˈpʌn·ɪʃ·mənt/ *n* [U] • *These trucks are designed to take a lot of punishment* (=be used in very bad conditions) *without breaking down.*

pu·ni·tive /£ˈpjuː·nɪ·tɪv, $-t̬ɪv/ *adj* intended as a punishment • *The teacher has taken punitive action against the children who broke the rules.* • *The UN has imposed punitive sanctions on the invading country.* • *(law) She is suing the newspaper for $5 million punitive* **damages** *claiming they knew the article about her was untrue.* • *(fig.) The President has threatened to impose punitive* (=very severe and so causing difficult conditions) *import duties/tariffs on a range of foreign goods.*

pu·ni·tive·ly /£ˈpjuː·nɪ·tɪv·li, $-nə·t̬ɪv-/ *adv* • *The men were given a punitively heavy sentence by the judge.* • *(fig.) Rents in the city are punitively high* (=so high they cause difficulty).

punk CULTURE /pʌŋk/ *n* [U] a culture popular among young people, esp. in the late 1970s, involving opposition to authority expressed through shocking behaviour, clothes and hair, and through fast loud music • *Punk had an amazing influence, even on the conventional fashion industry.* • **Punk (rock)** is a type of fast, loud, often offensive music that was originally popular among young people in the late 1970s: *When punk was fashionable everybody seemed to be listening to the Sex Pistols.* • (J)

punk (rock·er) /pʌŋk/ *n* [C] • *A couple of punks with orange and green hair got up and started dancing madly.*

punk /pʌŋk/ *adj* [before n] • *a punk band* ○ *a punk hairstyle*

punk CRIMINAL /pʌŋk/ *n* [C] *esp. Am slang* a young person who fights and is involved in criminal activities • *Listen to me, you little punk – I'll break your neck if you do that again.* • *He grew up as a street punk in a poor neighbourhood in Brooklyn.* • (J)

pun·net /ˈpʌn·ɪt/ *n* [C] *Br and Aus* a small square or rectangular box in which particular types of fruit are sold • *This punnet contains a pound of strawberries.* • *The raspberries cost £1·50 a punnet.* • *I'd like two punnets* **of** *peaches, please.* • Punnet can also be used to refer to the amount of fruit contained in a punnet: *Add a punnet* **of** *blackcurrants to the egg mixture.*

pun·ster /£ˈpʌn·stəʳ, $-stɚ/ *n* [C] See at PUN

punt BOAT /pʌnt/ *n* [C] a long narrow boat with a flat bottom and a square area at each end, which is moved by a person standing on one of the square areas and pushing a long pole against the bottom of the river • *Punts can only be used in relatively shallow water.*

punt *(obj)* /pʌnt/ *v* • *We punted* (=moved a punt with a pole) *up the river.* [I] • *It's a lovely afternoon – let's* **go** *punting.* [I] • *I've been punting you* (=moving a punt in which you are sitting) *for over half an hour – it's your turn now.* [T] • *I don't think I can punt this boat* (=move it with a pole) *any further – my arms are really aching.* [T]

punt·er /£ˈpʌn·təʳ, $-t̬ɚ/ *n* [C] • A punter is a person who punts. • See also PUNTER.

punt *obj* KICK /pʌnt/ *v* [T] (in RUGBY or American football) to kick (the ball) after you have dropped it from your hands and before it touches the ground, or (in football) to kick (the ball) powerfully so that it goes a long way

punt /pʌnt/ *n* [C] • A punt is a way of kicking the ball in RUGBY or American football, by dropping it from your hands and kicking it before it hits the ground, or a powerful kick in football which causes the ball to go a long way.

punt·er RISK MONEY /£ˈpʌn·təʳ, $-t̬ɚ/ *n* [C] *Br and Aus specialized* a person who makes a BET (=risks paying money in order to guess the result of a race, competition, game etc. in the hope of winning more money if the guess is correct) • *Bookmakers are offering punters odds of 6-1 on the horse Red Devil winning the race.* • *The average punter at the casino will spend £200 to £300 an evening.* • See also **punter** at PUNT BOAT.

punt·er CUSTOMER /£ˈpʌn·təʳ, $-t̬ɚ/ *n* [C] *Br infml* a customer; a user of services or buyer of goods • *Punters queued outside the cinema for two hours to get tickets for the film.* • *Many hotels are offering discounts in an attempt to attract punters/pull in the punters.* • *The newspaper editor claimed that she always tries to give the punters what they want.* • A punter is also a person who uses the services of a PROSTITUTE (=person who has sex for money): *She was last seen getting into a punter's car at Euston station.*

pu·ny /ˈpjuː·ni/ *adj* **-ier, -iest** small; weak; not effective • *You'll never be able to lift that heavy box with your puny muscles.* • *My car only has a puny little engine.* • *The party's share of the vote rose from a puny 11% in the last election to 21% this time.* • *His puny attempts/efforts at producing a financial plan for the department did not impress his boss.*

pup /pʌp/ *n* [C] the young of particular animals, or a PUPPY • *a seal pup* ○ *an otter pup* • *We got him when he was just a pup and now look what a huge dog he is!*

pu·pa /ˈpjuː·pə/ *n* [C] *pl* **pupas** or **pupae** /ˈpjuː·piː/ an insect in the stage of development which happens before it is completely developed, during which it is contained in a COCOON (=a protective covering) and does not move • *a moth pupa* ○ *a mosquito pupa* • *Female wasps lay their eggs in the pupae* **of** *various flies.* • See also CHRYSALIS.

pu·pal /ˈpjuː·pᵊl/ *adj* [not gradable] • *the pupal* **stage** *of development*

pu·pil STUDENT /ˈpjuː·pᵊl/ *n* [C] a person, esp. a child at primary school, who is being taught • *a second-year pupil* ○ *a third-grade pupil* ○ *a primary-school pupil* ○ *a year four pupil* • *The school has over 400 pupils.* • *There is a very relaxed atmosphere between staff and pupils at the school.* •

Her school report described her as a very promising pupil. • A pupil is also someone who is being taught a skill, esp. such as painting or music, by an expert: *The painting is believed to be by a pupil* **of** *Titian.* • LP **Schools and colleges** (PL)

pu·pil EYE /'pjuː·pəl/ *n* [C] the circular black area in the centre of your eye, through which light enters • *Your pupils contract in bright light, and dilate in darkness.* • LP **Eye and seeing** (PL)

pup·pet /'pʌp·ɪt/ *n* [C] a type of toy which is caused to move by a person using strings or putting their hand inside it • *Punch and Judy are famous puppets in Britain.* • *We took the children to a puppet* **show/theatre**. • *(disapproving)* A puppet is also a person or group whose actions are controlled by someone else: *She said that she was nobody's puppet* **(on a string)**. ○ *The article described the country's government as an American puppet.* ○ *Western powers have been accused of trying to establish a puppet* **regime/state** *in the divided country.* ○ *He is no more than a puppet* **president/prime minister/king**.

pup·pet·eer /£ˌpʌp·ɪ'tɪəʳ, $-ə'tɪr/ *n* [C] • A puppeteer is a person who entertains with puppets.

pup·py /'pʌp·i/, **pup**, **pup** *n* [C] a young dog • *Our dog has just had six puppies.* • *He follows her around like a little puppy-***dog**. • *(Br and Aus infml)* **Puppy fat** (*Am* **baby fat**) is fat which a child sometimes has, and which disappears as the child grows older. • *(infml)* **Puppy love** is romantic love which a young person feels for someone else, and which usually disappears as the young person becomes older.

pur·chase *obj* BUY /£'pɜː·tʃəs, $'pɜːr-/ *v* [T] *slightly fml* to buy • *The museum is trying to raise enough money to purchase a painting by Van Gogh.* • *To be eligible for the lower fare, you must purchase your tickets 21 days in advance.* • *Except under clearly defined circumstances, it is illegal in Britain for a company to purchase its own shares.* • *I'm interested in purchasing a bicycle* **for** *my son – could you show me what you have that might be suitable?* • *She purchased her first house* **with** *the money that her uncle left her when he died.* • **Purchasing power** is the value of money considered as the amount of goods it will buy. A person's purchasing power is their ability to buy goods: *The purchasing power* **of** *the average hourly wage has risen in the last five years.* ○ *The purchasing power* **of** *people living on investment income has fallen as interest rates have gone down.* • *"I wish to complain about this parrot what I purchased not half an hour ago"* (from the television programme *Monty Python's Flying Circus*, 1969)

pur·chase /£'pɜː·tʃəs, $'pɜːr-/ *n fml* • *How do you wish to pay for your purchases* (= the things you have bought), *sir?* [C] • A purchase is also an act of buying: *A house is the most expensive purchase that most people ever* **make**. [C] • Purchase can also mean the act of buying: *New restrictions have been placed on the purchase* **of** *guns.* [U] ○ *This product may be frozen. If required, freeze on day of purchase.* [U] ○ *No purchase is necessary for you to enter this competition.* [U] • *(Br) When land is needed for building a road, if necessary the government can buy it by* **compulsory** *purchase.* [U] • *The purchase* **price** *of the company was about $70 million.*

pur·chas·er /£'pɜː·tʃə·səʳ, $'pɜːr·tʃə·sɚ/ *n* [C] *fml* • *We haven't been able to find a purchaser* (= someone who buys something) **for** *our house yet.* • *Japan is the second biggest purchaser* **of** *the country's manufacturing products.*

pur·chase HOLD /£'pɜː·tʃəs, $'pɜːr-/ *n* [U] *fml* a firm hold which allows someone or something to be pulled or lifted without sliding or falling • *These tyres are so worn that they don't provide much purchase* **on** *the road.* • *Dancers sometimes use a special powder on their shoes to help them* **get** *a better purchase* **on** *the floor.* • *The climber* **gained** *a purchase* **on** *the rock and hauled himself up.* • *(fig.) I just couldn't* **get** *any purchase* **on** (= understand) *what he was saying.*

pur·dah /£'pɜː·də, $'pɜːr-/ *n* [U] (the condition of following) the custom, found in some Muslim and Hindu cultures, of women not allowing their faces to be seen by male strangers, either by staying in a special part of the house or by wearing a covering over their faces • *Purdah is practised in many parts of the Middle East.* • *The women in the village live* **in (strict)** *purdah.* • *In this region women seldom venture* **out of** *purdah, and talk of the shame of strange men seeing their faces.* • *(fig.) Jeff has* **gone into** *purdah* (= is not seeing or speaking to anyone) *while he's preparing for his exams.*

pure NOT MIXED /£pjʊəʳ, $pjʊr/ *adj* **-r, -st** not mixed with anything else • *a pure cotton shirt* • *pure orange juice* • *pure English honey* • *a pure Arab horse* • *Police have confiscated 90 kilos of pure heroin/cocaine.* • A pure colour is one which is is not mixed with any other colour: *One of the swans was a pure white adult, but the other still showed small patches of brown among its white feathers.* • A pure sound is not mixed with other sounds and does not shake: *He played the saxophone with a soft, pure tone.* ○ *Because it stores music in the form of numbers, a compact disc produces pure music, with no surface noise.* • Pure also means clean and free from harmful substances: *The mountain air was wonderfully pure.* ○ *Tap water is never chemically pure.* • *Adolf Hitler wanted to create a pure Aryan race* (= one which was not mixed with any other race and which did not contain weak or less able people).

pu·ri·fy *obj* /£'pjʊə·rɪ·faɪ, $'pjʊr-/ *v* [T] • *One of the functions of the kidneys is to purify* (= remove harmful substances from) *the blood.* • *She went on a three-day fast to purify her body.* • *Travellers to this part of South America are advised to take water-purifying tablets with them.* • *The Office de la Langue Française was created in 1961 in Quebec to preserve the French language and purify it* (= remove from it the harmful influence) **of** *English words.* • *Government records show that Winston Churchill wanted to purify the British race* (= remove weak or less able people from British society, or forbid them from having children) *to make it strong enough to stand up to other nations.*

pu·ri·fi·ca·tion /£ˌpjʊə·rɪ·fɪ'keɪ·ʃən, $ˌpjʊr-/ *n* [U] • Purification is the act of removing harmful substances from something: *a water purification plant* • *an air purification system*

pu·ri·fi·er /£'pjʊə·rɪ·faɪ·əʳ, $'pjʊr·ɪ·faɪ·ɚ/ *n* [C] • A purifier is a machine or a substance which removes harmful substances from something: *a water purifier* • *an air purifier* ○ *In traditional medicine, certain herbs are used as blood purifiers.*

pu·ri·ty /£'pjʊə·rɪ·ti, $'pjʊr·ə·t̬i/ *n* [U] • Purity is the state of not being mixed with anything else: • *One of the underlying causes of the war was a belief in* **racial/ethnic** *purity, and a desire to drive all immigrants out of the country.* ○ *Her singing has purity, clarity and strength.* ○ *The ballet company are good, if not yet of real classical purity.* • Purity also means cleanness or freedom from harmful substances: *The drinking water in several regions of the country does not meet European purity standards.* ○ *Many advertisements for skin-care products emphasise their purity.*

pure MORALLY GOOD /£pjʊəʳ, $pjʊr/ *adj* **-r, -st** behaving in a morally good way, or not having sex • *Mr Singh has taken a Sikh vow to lead a pure life, and not to drink, smoke or eat meat.* • *In his sermon, the priest encouraged the members of his congregation to think only pure thoughts.* • *He invited me up to his flat for coffee, but I didn't think that his motives were entirely pure, and I said no.* • *In many cultures, it is considered important for a woman to keep herself pure* (= not to have sex) *until she marries.* • If someone is **(as) pure as the driven snow**, they behave in a morally very good way, or do not have sex: *It's all very well for you to criticize my behaviour, but you're not exactly as pure as the driven snow yourself.* • *"Blessed are the pure in heart"* (Bible, St Matthew 5.8)

pu·ri·fy *obj* /£'pjʊə·rɪ·faɪ, $'pjʊr-/ *v* [T] • *One of the main teachings of Buddhism is that you should try and purify* (= remove immoral thoughts from) *your mind.* • *Some Jewish people go to the mikveh, a ritual bath, to purify themselves* (= remove from themselves morally harmful influences or the effects of having acted immorally).

pu·ri·fi·ca·tion /£ˌpjʊə·rɪ·fɪ'keɪ·ʃən, $ˌpjʊr-/ *n* [U] • In some religions, purification is the act of a removing from a person, usually by a ceremony, the bad effects that they are suffering because they have broken a religious or moral law.

pu·ri·ty /£'pjʊə·rɪ·ti, $'pjʊr·ə·t̬i/ *n* [U] • Purity means moral goodness or the state of not having sex: *For Christians, the Virgin Mary is a symbol of purity.*

pure COMPLETE /£pjʊəʳ, $pjʊr/ *adj* [before n] **-r, -st** complete; only • *It was pure* **coincidence/chance** *that I met Gail at the theatre.* • *The minister dismissed the newspaper reports as pure* **speculation/invention**. • *The police think that the killer may have fled the country, but that's pure* **guesswork/conjecture**. • *Her dancing is a pure* **delight**. • *After a tiring day's work, relaxing in a hot bath was pure* **bliss**. • *She looked at him with pure* **hate/malice**

in her eyes. • *This last month has been pure* **hell** *for us.* • *I thought that what he said was pure* **and utter** *rubbish.* • *That film was pure Disney* (=was like the films that only Disney has made). • A pure area of study is one that is studied only for the purpose of developing theories about it, not for the the purpose of using those theories in a practical way: *pure mathematics* • *pure economics* • *pure geometry* ○ *She has always been more interested in pure research than in applied science.* • *He is motivated by greed,* **pure and simple** (=and nothing else).

pure·ly /£ˈpjʊə·li, $pjʊr-/ *adv* [not gradable] • *Any resemblance of any of the characters in the film to any person, living or dead, is purely* (=completely • only) *coincidental.* • *On a purely practical level, it is difficult to see how such proposals would work.* • *Checks are being carried out purely as a precautionary measure.* • *We made this decision purely for financial reasons.* • *They decided to close the museum* **purely and simply** (=only) *because it cost too much to run.*

pure·bred /£ˈpjʊə·bred, $ˈpjʊr-/ *adj* [not gradable] (an animal or type of animal) with parents which are both of the same breed • *purebred cattle* • *a purebred stallion* • *a purebred strain of cat* • See also THOROUGHBRED.

pu·rée *obj* /£ˈpjʊə·reɪ, $ˌpjʊˈreɪ/ *v* [T] (of food, esp. fruit or vegetables) to make into a thick, soft sauce • *Purée the strawberries in the liquidizer and add the the lightly whipped cream.* • *He puréed the garlic by pressing it through a sieve.* [T] • *The first solid food she gave her baby was puréed carrot.* [T]

pu·rée /£ˈpjʊə·reɪ, $pjʊˈreɪ/ *n* • *a fruit purée* [C] ○ *spinach purée* [U] ○ *a purée* **of** *apple* [C] • *Add two tablespoonsful of tomato purée.* [U] • *Place all the ingredients in a food processor and blend them to a* **fine** *purée.* [C]

pur·ga·tive /£ˈpɜː·gə·tɪv, $ˈpɜːr·gə·t̬ɪv/ *n* [C] a substance which makes you excrete the contents of your bowels • *Castor oil is a strong purgative.* • *Prunes can have a purgative effect.* • See also LAXATIVE.

pur·ga·to·ry /£ˈpɜː·gə·tri, $ˈpɜːr·gə·tɔːr·i/ *n* [U] the place to which Roman Catholics believe that the spirits of dead people go and suffer for the evil acts that they did while they were alive, before they are able to go to heaven • *The priest asked the members of his congregation to pray for the souls of people in Purgatory.* • *(infml)* Purgatory is also an extremely unpleasant experience which causes suffering: *He described his experience of combat in Vietnam as* **sheer** *purgatory.* ○ *The parents of the missing child have been* **going through** *purgatory for the last few days.* ○ *(humorous) I've been on a diet for two weeks now, and it's purgatory!*

purge *obj* REMOVE PEOPLE /£pɜːdʒ, $pɜːrdʒ/ *v* [T] to free (esp. a political group) from (unwanted people) by removing them from office or, sometimes, by killing them • *Party leaders have undertaken to purge the party* **of** *extremists.* • *The new prime minister is expected to purge his cabinet* **of** *ministers from his predecessor's government.* • *Hard-liners are expected to be purged* **from** *the administration.*

purge /£pɜːdʒ, $pɜːrdʒ/ *n* [C] • *Between 1934 and 1938, Stalin mounted a massive purge* **of** (=an act of forcefully removing unwanted members from) *the Communist Party, the government and the armed forces in the Soviet Union.* • *In a purge* **of** *the army, at least eight colonels and a major have been removed from their posts.*

purge *obj* REMOVE EVIL /£pɜːdʒ, $pɜːrdʒ/ *v* [T] to make free of (something evil or harmful) • *Roman Catholics go to confession to purge them***selves***/purge their souls* **(from/of** *sin).* • *The new state governor has promised to purge the police force* **of** *corruption.* • *The philosopher, Francis Bacon, wrote that one of the first tasks of a scientist was to purge him***self** *of prejudices and predispositions.*

pu·ri·fi·er /£ˈpjʊə·rɪ·faɪ·əʳ, $ˈpjʊr·ɪ·faɪ·ɚ/ *n* [C] See at PURE NOT MIXED

pu·rist /£ˈpjʊə·rɪst, $ˈpjʊr·ɪst/ *n* [C] a person who believes that it is very important to do things in the correct way or to have things without any additions • *Although purists may object to split infinitives, like 'to boldly go', they are commonly used.* • *Purists eat smoked salmon with nothing more than lemon and black pepper.* • *Some purists have complained that the repairs to the building have not restored it to its original form.*

pu·ri·sm /£ˈpjʊə·rɪ·zᵊm, $ˈpjʊr·ɪ-/ *n* [U]

pu·ri·tan /£ˈpjʊə·rɪ·tᵊn, $ˈpjʊr·ɪ·t̬ᵊn/ *n* [C] a member of an English religious group in the 16th and 17th centuries which wanted to make church ceremonies simpler, and who believed that self-control and hard work were important and that pleasure was wrong or unnecessary, or, more generally, a person who has these beliefs • *During the seventeenth century, the Puritans destroyed many decorations in English churches.* • *The Puritans did not approve of the theatre because of the pleasure that seeing plays gave to the audience.* • *Despite his apparent liberal views, he's really something of a puritan/he has a puritan streak.*

pu·ri·tan·i·cal /£ˌpjʊə·rɪˈtæn·ɪ·kᵊl, $ˌpjʊr·ɪ-/ *adj* • Puritanical means believing or involving the belief that self-control and hard work are important and that pleasure is wrong or unnecessary: *She is very puritanical about sex.* ○ *Puritanical readers will be horrified by the amount of bad language that the book contains.* ○ *As a teenager, he rebelled against his puritanical upbringing.*

pur·i·tan·i·cal·ly /£ˌpjʊə·rɪˈtæn·ɪ·kli, $ˌpjʊr·ɪ-/ *adv*

pur·i·tan·i·sm /£ˈpjʊə·rɪ·tᵊn·ɪ·zᵊm, $ˈpjʊr·ɪ.t̬ᵊn-/ *n* [U] • Puritanism is the beliefs and ways of behaving of a Puritan, or, more generally, the belief that self-control and hard work are important and that pleasure is wrong or unnecessary.

purl /£pɜːl, $pɜːrl/ *n* [U] a type of stitch which you make when you KNIT by putting the needle into the front of the first stitch on the other needle • *a purl stitch* • *Knit a row of plain, followed by a row of purl.*

purl *(obj)* /£pɜːl, $pɜːrl/ *v* • To purl is to KNIT a purl stitch: *Knit one, purl one.* [T] ○ *I know how to do plain knitting, but I can't purl.* [I]

pur·loin *obj* /£pəˈlɔɪn, $pɚ-/ *v* [T] *fml or humorous* to steal • *He was accused of purloining company profits.* • *She complained that her daughter was always purloining her clothes.* • *"That's a nice pen. Where did you get it?" "Oh, I purloined it* **from** *the office."*

pur·ple /£ˈpɜː·pl̩, $ˈpɜːr-/ *adj, n* (of) a dark reddish blue colour • *purple pansies* • *purple plums* • *a dark purple bruise* • *The early morning sun cast* **deep** *purple shadows.* • *She wore a dress of dark purple.* [U] • *The evening sky was full of purples and reds.* [C] • If a person is purple **(in the face)**, their face is a dark red colour because they are angry or are making a lot of physical effort: *She was purple with rage.* ○ *He* **went** *purple in the face trying to lift the heavy weights.* • *(Br and Aus)* Purple is also used to refer to a style of writing or speaking which is unnecessarily complicated and contains too much detail: *His speech contained a lot of purple* **passages/patches**. ○ *Despite occasional patches of purple* **prose**, *the book is mostly clear and incisive.* • Purple can also be used to refer to writing or speaking that contains a lot of offensive or taboo words: *The book 'Lady Chatterly's Lover' is full of purple* **prose**. • The **Purple Heart** is an American MEDAL (=metal disc given as a reward) given to soldiers who have been injured in war: *His military decorations included the Bronze Star and four awards of the Purple Heart.* • (RUS)

pur·ple·ness /£ˈpɜː·pl̩·nəs, $ˈpɜːr-/ *n* [U]

pur·plish /£ˈpɜː·pl̩·ɪʃ, £-plɪʃ, $ˈpɜːr-/ *adj* • *He has a purplish* (=slightly purple) *birthmark on his cheek.* • *The curtains are a purplish pink colour.*

pur·port CLAIM /£pəˈpɔːt, $pɜːrˈpɔːrt/ *v* [+ *to* infinitive] *fml* to claim, not necessarily in a way that is believable • *They purport* **to** *represent the wishes of the majority of parents at the school.* • *The study purports* **to** *show an increase in the incidence of the disease.* • *The tape recording purports* **to** *be of a conversation between the princess and a secret admirer.*

pur·port GENERAL MEANING /£ˈpɜː·pɔːt, $ˈpɜːr·pɔːrt/ *n* [U] *fml* the general meaning of someone's words or actions • *I didn't read it all but I think the purport of the letter was that he will not be returning for at least a year.*

pur·pose REASON /£ˈpɜː·pəs, $ˈpɜːr-/ *n* an intention or aim; a reason • *The purpose* **of** *the research is to try and and find out more about the causes of the disease.* [C] • *At the airport, the immigration office asked me what was the purpose* **of** *my visit to the US.* [C] • *The purpose* **of** *this organization is to help homeless people.* [C] • *His only purpose* **in life** *seems to be to enjoy himself.* [C] • *Her main/primary purpose* **in** *suing the newspaper for libel was to clear her name.* [C] • *I came to Brighton* **for/with** *the* **express** *purpose* **of** *seeing you.* [C] • *Letters whose* **sole** *purpose is to make a political viewpoint will not be published.* [C] • *She had the operation entirely* **for** *cosmetic purposes.* [C] • Purpose can also mean determination or a feeling of having a reason for what you do: *I've always admired her for her strength of purpose.* [U] ○ *He decided* *early in life what he wanted, and, thanks to his great determination and singleness of purpose, he succeeded in getting it.* [U] ○ *There seems to be a lack of purpose among the team at the moment.* [U] ○ *In 1956, he met his future wife, who transformed his life, giving him a sense of purpose and personal happiness.* [U] • A purpose can also be a need: *The firm has not yet managed to find new premises that are suitable for their purposes.* [C] ○ *The fabric I bought isn't exactly what I wanted, but it will* **serve** *my purposes* (= fulfil my needs). [C] • If you do something **on purpose**, you do it intentionally, not accidentally: *I'm sorry I broke the glass – I didn't do it on purpose.* • *The college was the first* **purpose-built** (= specially designed and originally built for a particular use) *teacher training college in the country.*

pur·pose·ful /£'pɜː·pəs·fᵊl, $'pɜːr-/ *adj* • *What the company needs is a strong and purposeful* (= determined • having a clear intention) *manager.* • *The atmosphere in the meeting room was serious and purposeful.* • *She said that she wanted to lead a more purposeful existence.*

pur·pose·ful·ly /£'pɜː·pə·sfᵊl·i, $'pɜːr-/ *adv* • *He strode purposefully into the room.*

pur·pose·ful·ness /£'pɜː·pə·sfᵊl·nəs, $'pɜːr-/ *n* [U]

pur·pose·less /£'pɜː·pə·sləs, $'pɜːr-/ *adj* • An action which is purposeless is done without clear intention: *This purposeless fighting has been going on for far too long.* ○ *He said that people's television viewing is often purposeless.*

pur·pose·less·ly /£'pɜː·pə·slə·sli, $'pɜːr-/ *adv* • *They are continuing their campaign purposelessly, without any hope of success.*

pur·pose·less·ness /£'pɜː·pə·slə·snəs, $'pɜːr-/ *n* [U]

pur·pose·ly /£'pɜː·pə·sli, $'pɜːr-/ *adv* • *The trial has been purposely* (= intentionally) *delayed.* • *I purposely avoid making train journeys during the rush hour.*

pur·pose USE /£'pɜː·pəs, $'pɜːr-/ *n* (a) use or result or effect • *It seems that the money has not been used for the purposes for which it was intended.* [C] • *I don't think children should waste their time at school doing things which don't have any real purpose.* [U] • *"I can see no* **useful** *purpose* **in** *continuing this conversation," he said.* [U] • *The sunglasses are said to be suitable for* **general** *purpose use, but they transmit too much light.* • *This is a* **multi-/all-***purpose kitchen knife.* • *These comics will* **serve** *the purpose* (= achieve the result) **of** *keeping the children occupied during the journey.* [U] • *All the doctors' efforts to save his life turned out to be* **to no** *purpose* (= were not successful). [U] • *Several mothers complained that the play equipment in the park was not safe for their children, but their complaints were* **to little** *purpose* (= did not have any effect). [U] • *She gave each of her grandchildren some money, telling them to be sure to use it* **to good** *purpose* (= well). [U]

purr /£pɜː, $pɜːr/ *v, n* (to make) a quiet, continuous, slightly shaking sound • *The cat purred as I stroked its fur.* [I] • *The engine of my old car rattled all the time, but my new one purrs.* [I] • *We could hear the sound of a lawnmower purring in the back garden.* [I] • *A black limousine purred* **up** (= drove up making a quiet, continuous, slightly shaking sound) *outside the hotel.* [I] • *He purred with satisfaction* (= expressed pleasure by making a quiet sound) *as she massaged his back.* [I] • *"This is the life," she purred* (= said in a way expressing pleasure) *contentedly, as she lay by the pool in the sunshine, sipping her drink.* [+ clause] • *"Can I help you at all, madam?" purred* (= said in a quiet, comforting way) *the shop assistant.* [+ clause] • *When I stroked the cat, it gave a low purr.* [C] • *I heard the gentle purr* **of** *an engine outside the house.* [C]

purse BAG /£pɜːs, $pɜːrs/ *n* [C] a small bag used esp. by women for carrying money in • *She opened her purse and took out some money to pay the bus driver for her ticket.* • Purse is also *Am for* HANDBAG. • **The purse strings** means the spending of money by a family or a company or a country: *A recent survey showed that in 53% of families, women* **hold/control** *the purse strings.* ○ *If the country's economic position continues to get worse, it will be necessary for the government to* **tighten** *the national purse strings still further.* • Compare WALLET. • PIC **Bags**

purse AMOUNT OF MONEY /£pɜːs, $pɜːrs/ *n* [C] an amount of money which is offered as a prize in a sporting competition, or the total amount of money which esp. a country has available for spending • *The players in the golf tournament are competing for a purse* **of** *£525 000.* • *Having a lot of people out of work places a large drain on the* **public** *purse.*

purse *obj* MOVE LIPS /£pɜːs, $pɜːrs/ *v* [T] to bring (your lips) tightly together so that they form a rounded shape, usually as an expression of disapproval • *"I don't approve of that kind of language," she said, pursing* **(up)** *her lips.* • *The teacher looked at Billy with pursed lips. "Stop that immediately," he said.*

purs·er /£'pɜː·səʳ, $'pɜːr·sɚ/ *n* [C] an officer on a ship who deals with the ship's accounts, or a person on a passenger ship or aircraft who is responsible for taking care of passengers

pur·sue *obj* FOLLOW /£pə'sjuː, $pɚ'suː/ *v* [T] to follow or search for (someone or something), in order to catch or kill them • *The Romans, Saxons and Normans pursued hare, deer and wild boar for enjoyment.* • *The hunters spent hours pursuing their prey/quarry.* • *He was killed by the driver of a stolen car who was being* **hotly** *pursued by the police.* • *(fig.) Ben has been pursuing* (= trying to form a romantic relationship with) *Elaine for months, but she won't go out with him.* • *(fig.) The company has been pursuing* (= offering a job to) *Holton for some time, but so far he has rejected all their offers.* • To pursue a matter is to consider it or ask questions about it: *The police are currently pursuing several lines of inquiry into the case.* ○ *I don't think this idea is worth pursuing any further.* ○ *The newspapers have relentlessly pursued the story.*

pur·su·er /£pə'sjuː·əʳ, $pɚ'suː·ɚ/ *n* [C] • *She made a sudden right turn off the road in order to escape her pursuers* (= the people who were following her and trying to catch her). • *The team are ten points ahead of their closest pursuers in the league.*

pur·suit /£pə'sjuːt, $pɚ'suːt/ *n* • *Three people have been killed in high-speed pursuits* (= acts of chasing) *by the police recently.* [C] • *The robbers fled the scene of the crime, with the police* **in** *pursuit after them.* [U] • The pursuit **of** someone or something is the act of following it in order to catch or kill them: *The dog set off across the field* **in** *pursuit* **of** *the rabbit.* [U]

pur·sue *obj* ATTEMPT /£pə'sjuː, $pɚ'suː/ *v* [T] to try to achieve • *She is ruthless in pursuing her goals/aims/objectives.* • *He suggested that Churchill was wrong not to have pursued peace with Hitler in 1941.*

pur·su·ance /£pə'sjuː·ənts, $pɚ'suː-/ *n* [U] *fml* • *She has devoted herself to the pursuance* **of** (= the act of trying to achieve) *justice for her son.* • **In** *pursuance* **of** *his aims, he has decided to stand for parliament.*

pur·su·er /£pə'sjuː·əʳ, $pɚ'suː·ɚ/ *n* [C] • *He described himself as a pursuer* **of** (= someone who tries to achieve) *truth and justice.*

pur·suit /£pə'sjuːt, $pɚ'suːt/ *n* [U] • *In the Declaration of Independence, Thomas Jefferson said that human rights included the preservation of life, liberty and the pursuit* **of** (= the activity of trying to achieve) *happiness.* • *The company is ruthless* **in** *its pursuit* **of** *profit.* • *The union is on strike* **in** *pursuit* **of** (= the act of trying to achieve) *a 10% pay increase.* • *The terrorists insist on their right to use violent means* **in** *pursuit* **of** *their goals.* • **In** *pursuit* **of** *a healthier diet, Americans are eating more fish than they used to.*

pur·sue *obj* PERFORM /£pə'sjuː, $pɚ'suː/ *v* [T] to perform; to continue to do • *The government is proposing to pursue a policy/programme of radical economic reform.* • *We need to decide soon what marketing strategy we should pursue for these new products.* • *Many women find it difficult to combine pursuing a career with having children.* • *Mr Macintyre is leaving the company to pursue his own business interests.* • *I used to enjoy photography, but I no longer have enough time for pursuing any hobbies.*

pur·su·ance /£pə'sjuː·ənts, $pɚ'suː-/ *n* [U] *fml* • *The action was taken* **in** *pursuance* **of** *the country's obligations under the terms of the international treaty.*

pur·su·ant /£pə'sjuː·ənt, $pɚ'suː-/ *adj* [after v; not gradable] *fml or specialized* • *The fact that a person acted pursuant* **to** (= following) *an order of his government does not relieve him from responsibility under international law.* • *"The movement of goods, services, capital and persons between Member States has been liberalized pursuant to this Treaty"* (The Maastricht Treaty, 1992)

pur·suit /£pə'sjuːt, $pɚ'suːt/ *n* • *He has a reputation for intelligence and ruthlessness* **in** *the pursuit* **of** (= when acting according to) *his policies.* [U] • A pursuit is an activity that you spend time doing, usually when you are not working: *I enjoy* **outdoor** *pursuits, like hiking, climbing and riding.* [C] ○ *She said that she didn't have much opportunity for* **leisure** *pursuits, but that when she had the time, she liked painting.* [C]

pur·vey *obj* /£pə'veɪ, $pɚ-/ *v* [T] *fml* to provide (goods or services) as a business, or to provide (information) •

Fortnum and Mason is a well-known shop in London which purveys fine foods and wines. • *This company has purveyed clothing* **to** *the armed forces for generations.* • *The prime minister's speech was intended to purvey a message of optimism.* • *The newspaper has been accused of purveying fictions instead of truth.*

pur·vey·or /£pəˈveɪ·əʳ, $pɚˈveɪ·ɚ/ *n* [C] *fml* • A purveyor (also **purveyors**) is a business which provides goods or services: *a purveyor* **of** *fine china* ○ *a purveyor* **of** *leather goods* ○ *purveyors* **of** *seafood* ○ *(in Britain) Purveyors of Jams and Marmalades to Her Majesty the Queen* • *Both candidates have presented themselves to the voters as purveyors* **of** (=people who provide) *new ideas.* • *Radio stations are not just purveyors* **of** *music, they're purveyors* **of** *information, companionship, entertainment, ideas, wit.*

pur·view /£ˈpɜː·vjuː, $ˈpɜːr-/ *n* [U] *fml* the limit of someone's responsibility, interest or activity • *This case falls* **outside** *the purview* **of** *this particular court.* • *Some of the bank's lending operations come* **under/within** *the purview* **of** *the deputy manager, and some are handled directly by the manager.*

pus /pʌs/ *n* [U] thick yellowish liquid that forms in and comes from an infected cut or injury in the body • *a pus-filled wound*

push *(obj)* USE PRESSURE /pʊʃ/ *v* to use physical pressure or force, esp. with your hands, in order to move (something) into a different position, usually one that is further away from you • *We should be able to move this table if you push and I pull.* [I] • *You're not allowed to ride your bicycle on this path, so you'll have to get off and push.* [I] • *This window sticks, so you have to push* **hard** *to open it.* [I] • *When my car broke down, a passing motorist stopped and helped me push it off the road.* [T] • *In Greek mythology, Sisyphus was condemned to push a large rock up a hill from where it always rolled down again.* [T] • *He pushed his plate away from him. "I can't possibly eat any more," he said.* [T] • *"Where shall I put the shopping?" "Oh, just push those cups out of the way and put it on the table."* [T] • *She pushed her hair out of her eyes.* [T] • *I tried push the door open, but it was one that you had to pull.* [T] • *It isn't clear whether he fell off the balcony, or was pushed.* [T] • *Daddy, Matthew pushed me* **over**. [T] • *To turn the television on, you just push* (=press) *this button.* [T] • *Push the raspberries* (=Force them with a utensil) *through a sieve, then mix them with the yoghurt.* [T] • *He pushed the money into my hand* (=forcefully gave me the money). *"Please take it," he said.* [T] • *We pushed the boat* **off** *from* (=moved the boat forward by using pressure against) *the river bank.* [T] • *(esp. Br)* If you are pushed (Am usually **pressed**) **for** something, esp. time or money, you do not have enough of it: *I'm sorry, I can't stop and chat now, I'm a bit pushed* **(for time)**. [T] ○ *I wouldn't stop her now – she looks rather pushed.* [T] ○ *No, I can't lend you any money – I'm rather pushed* **(for cash)** *myself.* [T] • *(esp. Br)* To **be pushed** *(Am and Aus* **be pressed**) is also to find it difficult to do something: *At this rate, we'll be pushed* **to** *get to Brighton by six o'clock.* [+ *to* infinitive] ○ *I'm* **hard** *pushed to know what* **to** *do for the best.* [+ *to* infinitive] • To **be pushing** a stated age or speed is to be nearly that age or to be travelling at nearly that speed: *My grandmother is pushing 70, but she's still very active.* ○ *"You're driving too fast." "No I'm not, I'm barely pushing 50."* • **If/When push comes to shove** (=If/When we're in a situation of special need), *we can always ask Dad to lend us the money.* • *(infml) If you think you can* **push** *me* **around/about** (=try to control me by telling me what to do in a rude and unpleasant way) *like that, you're mistaken.* • *(Br infml)* If you **push the boat out**, you spend a lot of money, esp. on making something enjoyable: *Jack's parents really pushed the boat out* **on** *a big party to celebrate his 18th birthday.* ○ *The publishers are pushing the boat out* **on** *promoting her latest book.* • *(humorous)* To **push up (the) daisies** is to be dead and buried: *"Is your Uncle Fred still alive?" "Oh no, he's been pushing up the daisies for years now."* • *My boss let me have a day off last week, so I don't think I can* **push** *my* **luck/push it** (=foolishly risk trying to achieve something that I know is not reasonable) *and ask for more time off this week.* • People also sometimes say "Don't push your luck" or "Don't push it" to someone who is behaving badly. • *Have you noticed that keys on a* **push-button** *telephone* (=a telephone which is operated by pressing buttons) *are numbered from the top downwards, but numbers on a computer keyboard are the other way round?* • If your car needs a **push start** (also **bump start**), it will not start by turning the key and someone will have to push it to try to make it start. If you **push start** (also **bump start**) a car you start it in this way. • **Push-up** is *esp. Am and Aus for* **press-up**. See at PRESS PUSH. • LP **Switching on and off**

push /pʊʃ/ *n* [C] • *"Will you* **give** *me a push* (=an act of using esp. your hands to move something into a position that is away from you), *Daddy?" said his daughter as she climbed onto the swing.* • *I* **gave** *the door a* **hard** *push, but it still wouldn't open.* • *It's a terrifying thought that we now have the kind of weapons which make it possible for the world to be destroyed* **at** *the push* **of a** *button.* • If you say that you can do something **at a push**, you mean that it might be possible for you to manage it, although it would be difficult: *I don't think I can get to the meeting at 7.00, but at a push I could make 7.30.* • *(Br and Aus) I hear Nick* **got/was given the push** (=was dismissed) *from his job last week.* • *(Br and Aus infml) She'd been going out with him for a long time and we all thought they'd get married, but she's* **given** *him* **the push**/*he's* **got the push** (=she has ended her relationship with him). • **If/when it comes to the push** (=if a situation of special need happens), *we can get a lawyer to handle the situation.*

push *(obj)* TAKE STRONG ACTION /pʊʃ/ *v* [always + adv/prep] to (cause to) move in a particular direction by taking strong and determined action • *The government has two weeks to push this piece of legislation through parliament before the current session ends.* [T] • *Measures that will have to be taken to push the nation towards recovery could worsen things over the short term.* [T] • *His rivals are trying to push him out of the running.* [T] • *We're rather behind on our schedule. Has anyone got any suggestions as to how we can push things* **ahead/along/forward/on**? [T] • If you push **ahead/forward/on**, you continue with an activity in a determined way: *It seems as if the president is going to push ahead and sign the treaty.* [I always + adv/prep] ○ *They are pushing on* **with** *their campaign for improved childcare facilities.* [I always + adv/prep] • *"You've been driving for a long time – do you want to stop for a rest?" "No, we're nearly there – let's push* **on/ahead/forward** (=continue with our journey)." [I always + adv/prep] • *We can't just push these problems* **aside** (=ignore them) *– we have to deal with them.* [M] • *He claimed that he had been pushed* **aside** (=not given a job) *in favour of a younger person.* [T] • *Their research has pushed* **forward** *the frontiers of knowledge.* [M] • *I want to make quite sure that I push my point* **home**. [T] • *She said she had the strong impression that she was no longer wanted in her job, and that her boss was trying to push her* **out** (=dismiss her unfairly). [M] • *We are trying to push this deal* **through** (=cause it to be accepted) *as quickly as possible.* [M] • *The president is trying to push* **through** *tax reforms.* [M] • *Rising demand tends to push prices* **up**, *and falling demand pushes them* **down**. [M] • *The rise/fall in interest rates has pushed the value of my investments* **up/down**. [M] • To **push for** something is to demand it repeatedly or to take strong action to make it happen: *They are pushing for greater equality of opportunity for women.* ○ *Local residents are pushing for the road to be made safer.*

push /pʊʃ/ *n* [C] • *The country is* **making** *a push* **for** (=taking strong action to try and achieve) *independence.* • *We should make sure that any push* **to** *cut costs does not affect our efforts to improve quality and performance.* [+ *to* infinitive]

push *(obj)* MOVE FORCEFULLY /pʊʃ/ *v* to move forcefully, esp. in order to cause someone or something that is in your way to move, so that you can go through or past them • *Stop pushing – wait your turn.* [I] • *We pushed through the undergrowth.* [I] • *She pushed through the crowd of people that had gathered at the scene of the accident, saying "I'm a doctor – let me through."* [I] • *I'm sorry – I didn't mean to push in front of you.* [I] • *The minister pushed past the waiting journalists, refusing to speak to them.* [I] • *They pushed* (=forcefully made) *their* **way** *to the front of the queue.* [T always + adv/prep] • *In the final lap of the race, he managed to push* (=move strongly) **ahead**. [I] • *I was waiting in the bus queue when two men pushed* **in** (=unfairly moved forcefully into a position in front of someone who is waiting in a line) *in front of me.* [I] • If you push **off**, you move yourself or a boat away from the side of a pool or lake or river by using pressure against the side: *He pushed off from the side of the pool and swam slowly to the other side.* [I] • *Weeds push* (=grow strongly) **up** *through the cracks in the concrete.* [I] • If an army pushes, it advances: *The invading troops have pushed* *further into the north of the country.* [I] ○ *The US Marines have succeeded in pushing* **through** *the enemy defences.* [I]

push /pʊʃ/ *n* [C] ● *The army is continuing its push* (= advance) *towards the capital.*

push *obj* PERSUADE FORCEFULLY /pʊʃ/ *v* [T] forcefully to persuade or direct (someone to do or achieve something) ● *She said that she thought it was better for children to be allowed to learn at their own pace, rather than being pushed.* ● *Her parents pushed her* **into** *marrying him when she didn't really want to.* ● *The school manages to push most of its students* **through** *their exams.* ● *If we want an answer from them by Friday, I think we're going to have to push them* **for** *it.* ● *We had to push them* **to** *accept our terms, but they finally agreed to the deal.* [+ obj + *to* infinitive] ● *When I pushed him* (= asked him for more information), *he admitted that he hadn't actually seen what had happened.* ● *You'll never be successful if you don't push yourself* (= work) *harder.* ● People also sometimes say "don't push yourself" to someone who is being lazy or not being helpful: *"I've finished reading the paper now – is there anything you want me to do?" "Oh, don't push yourself."*

push·y /ˈpʊʃ·i/ *adj disapproving* ● Someone who is pushy tries strongly to persuade someone else to do something or achieve something: *A pushy salesperson tried to persuade us to buy a new car that we didn't really want.* ○ *His teachers said that many of his problems stemmed from being the child of pushy parents.*

push·i·ly /ˈpʊʃ·ɪ·li/ *adv disapproving*

push·i·ness /ˈpʊʃ·ɪ·nəs/ *n* [U] *disapproving*

push *obj* ATTRACT ATTENTION /pʊʃ/ *v* [T] to attract attention forcefully to (something or someone), esp. in order to persuade people to buy or accept them ● *The manufacturers are really pushing this new shampoo.* ● *The company has spent a lot of money on pushing their new image.* ● *They've been pushing this particular argument for months.* ● *He tries to push his own ideas* **forward**, *but he's not willing to listen to anyone else's.* ● *She's always pushing* **herself forward** *at work and not letting anyone else have a chance to take any responsibility.*

push /pʊʃ/ *n* [C] ● *This film is unlikely to attract large audiences unless it* **gets**/*it is* **given** *a big push in the media.* ● *The company plans to* **make** *a big push into the European market next spring.* ● *The hotel is* **making** *a major push* **to** *attract customers.* [+ *to* infinitive]

push·y /ˈpʊʃ·i/ *adj* **-ier**, **-iest** *infml disapproving* ● Someone who is pushy is always trying to attract attention and to do or achieve more than other people: *He only got promoted because he's so pushy.*

push·i·ly /ˈpʊʃ·ɪ·li/ *adv infml disapproving*

push·i·ness /ˈpʊʃ·ɪ·nəs/ *n* [U] *infml disapproving*

push *obj* SELL DRUGS /pʊʃ/ *v* [T] *infml* to sell (illegal drugs) ● *He was arrested for pushing drugs* **to** *schoolchildren.*

push·er /£ˈpʊʃ·əʳ, $-ɚ/ *n* [C] ● *Many of the empty buildings in the neighbourhood are being used by (drug) pushers* (= people who sell illegal drugs). ● LP **Crimes and criminals**

push a·long/off *v adv* [I] *infml* to leave ● *Thanks for the tea – it's time I was pushing along now.* ● *Well, I must push off – nice to have seen you.*

push off *v adv* [I] *slang* to go away. Some people consider this not to be polite. ● *He told me to push off.* ● *Push off and leave me alone.*

push·bike /ˈpʊʃ·baɪk/ *n* [C] *Br and Aus infml* a bicycle

push·chair *Br* /£ˈpʊʃ·tʃeəʳ, $-tʃer/, *Br* **bug·gy**, *Am and Aus* **strol·ler** *n* [C] a small, usually folding, chair on wheels which a baby or small child sits in and is pushed around in ● *a child's/folding pushchair* ● PIC **Chair**

push·over /£ˈpʊʃˌəʊ·vəʳ, $-ˌoʊ·vɚ/ *n* [C usually sing] *infml* something that is easy to do or to win, or someone who is easily persuaded or influenced or defeated ● *I was very nervous about the job interview, but it turned out to be a pushover.* ● *Julie's dad will give us some money to go out tonight – he's a real pushover.* ● *We won the first three rounds of the competition easily, but the team we're playing in the next round won't be such a pushover.* ● *I'm sure Jean will look after Harry for us while we go out – she's a real pushover* **for** (= is easily persuaded to do things for) *babies.*

push·pin /ˈpʊʃ·pɪn/ *n* [C] *Am* a small pin with a small ball-shaped piece of plastic on one end, used esp. for fixing notices, pictures etc. to a board or a wall

pu·sil·lan·i·mous /ˌpjuː·sɪˈlæn·ɪ·məs/ *adj fml* weak and cowardly; frightened of taking risks ● *He's too pusillanimous to stand up to his opponents.*

pu·sil·la·ni·mi·ty /£ˌpjuː·sɪ·ləˈnɪm·ɪ·ti, $-ə·t̬i/ *n* [U] *fml* ● *The American government has been accused of pusillanimity for pulling its troops out of the area of conflict.*

pu·sil·lan·i·mous·ly /ˌpjuː·sɪˈlæn·ɪ·mə·sli/ *adv fml* ● *They behaved pusillanimously in allowing such injustice to go unchallenged.*

puss /pʊs/ *n* [C] *infml* a cat ● *Here, puss.* [as form of address] ● *Isn't she a beautiful puss?*

pus·sy CAT /ˈpʊs·i/, **pus·sy–cat** /ˈpʊs·i·kæt/ *n* [C] *infml* (used esp. by or to children) a cat ● *Now then, don't pull the nice pussy's tail, George.* ● *(fig.) He likes to make out that he's tough, but he's a pussy-cat* (= is gentle and kind) *really.* ● **Pussy willow** is a tree which has small greyish furry flowers in the spring. Pussy willow is also used to refer to the flowers.

pus·sy SEX /ˈpʊs·i/ *n taboo slang* a woman's vagina, or sex with a woman ● *The stripper took off her top, but kept her pussy covered.* [C] ● *He said he wanted to get himself some pussy* (= to have sex with a woman). [U]

pus·sy·foot /ˈpʊs·i·fʊt/ *v* [I] *infml disapproving* to avoid making a decision or taking action because you are uncertain or frightened about doing so ● *We've been pussyfooting for far too long – it's time we decided what to do.* ● *Stop pussyfooting* **around/about** *and tell me what you really think.*

pus·tule /ˈpʌs·tjuːl/ *n* [C] *specialized* a small raised area on the skin which contains PUS (= thick yellowish liquid)

put *obj* MOVE /pʊt/ *v* [T always + adv/prep] **putting**, *past* **put** to move (something or someone) into the stated place, position or direction ● *Put your clothes* **in** *the cupboard.* ● *Do you think people should be put* **in** *prison for drinking and driving?* ● *She put him* **in** (= made certain that he got in) *a taxi, then went home.* ● *Sam will eat anything you put* **in front of** *him.* ● *He put salt* **into** *the sugar bowl by mistake.* ● *(fig.) No, I'm not getting married – whatever put that idea/notion* **into** *your head* (= made you think that)*?* ● *When you lay the table, put the soup spoons* **next to** *the knives.* ● *She put her coffee cup* **on** *the table.* ● *I'm going to put some clean sheets* **on** *the bed.* ● *Don't forget to put a stamp* **on** *the envelope.* ● *I need to put* (= sew) *a new button* **on** *these trousers.* ● *The film was so frightening that she put her hands* **over** *her eyes.* ● *She put her arm* **round** *him to comfort him.* ● *(fig.) I'm sorry to put you* **through** (= make you suffer) *this ordeal.* ● *I always put the children* **to bed** *at 7.00 p.m.* ● If you put some time **aside/away/on one side/to one side**, you make sure that you are able to use it for a special purpose: *He always puts some time aside each evening to read to his children.* [M] ● If you put some money **aside/away/on one side/to one side**, you save it: *We're putting aside some money each week to pay for our holiday.* [M] ● If you put a disagreement or problem **aside/on one side/to one side**, you ignore it temporarily so that it does not prevent you doing what you want to do: *Let's put our disagreements/differences aside and make a fresh start.* [M] ○ *Can we put that question/matter/issue to one side for now, and come back to it later?* ● *Come on, it's time to put these toys* **away** (= move them into the place or container in which they are kept). [M] ● If you put something **back**, you return it to where it was before it was moved: *Will you put the books back when you've finished with them?* [M] ○ *"OK, Mr Hall," said the doctor, "you can put your clothes back* **on** (= get dressed again) *now."* ○ *The vase is broken into so many pieces that it'll be impossible to put it back* **together** *again* (= repair it). ● *(fig.) We put* **back** *all our profits* **into** (= invest them in) *the company.* [M] ● To put the clock(s) **back** (*Am also* **set the clock(s) back**) is to change the time shown on a clock or watch so that it is an hour earlier. To put them **forward** (*Am* also **set the clock(s) ahead**) is to change the time shown so that it is an hour later: *Most European countries put the clocks back in the autumn and forward in the spring.* [M] ● If you put money **by**, you save it to use it later: *I try to put by a few pounds every week.* [M] ● *This bag's too heavy for me to carry – I'll have to put it* **down** (= move it into a position in which I am no longer carrying it). [M] ● *"Put me* **down**, *Daddy," squealed his three-year-old daughter as he lifted her high in the air.* ● *It was such a good book that I couldn't put it* **down** (= I continued reading it without stopping until I reached the end). ● If you put a baby **down**, you move it into the place where it sleeps: *We always put Dorothy down for a nap in the middle of the morning.* ● *(Br)* To put **down** (*Am, Br also* **bring down**) a price or a charge is to reduce it: *Shops are being forced to put their prices down in order to attract customers.* [M] ○ *It's time that the government put down interest rates.* [M] ● *I've* *put a deposit* **down** *on a new car* (= paid part of the cost and promised to pay what is left later.) [M] • *We'll have to let everyone know that we've put the time of the party* **forward** (= moved it to an earlier time) *to 6.00 p.m.*. [M] • *Our house was in a terrible mess when we were having the central heating put* **in**. [M] • *We always put the cat* **out** (= outside the house) *at night.* [M] • *In the winter, they put food* **out** (= outside) *for the birds.* [M] • *Every night, she puts* **out** *her clothes* (= takes them from where they are kept so that they are ready) *for the next day.* • To put **out** your hand or your tongue is to move it forward away from your body: *She put out her hand to shake mine.* ○ *Don't put your tongue out – it's rude.* [M] • *(Br)* If you put work **out** (**to** someone) (*esp. Am and Aus* **contract** work **out**), you employ someone outside your organization to do it: *The council has put the job of street-cleaning out to a private firm.* [M] • To put a telephone caller **through** (**to** someone) is to connect them so that they can speak to that person: *Hold the line, please, I'm just putting you through.* ○ *Could you put me through to customer services, please?* • To put someone **through** school, college or university is to pay for that person to study there: *It's costing them a lot of money to put their children through school.* ○ *She's putting her***self** *through college.* • *Model aeroplanes come in pieces which you have to put* **together** (= fix to each other to form the whole objects). [M] • *If we put the c irs a bit closer* **together** (= move them nearer to each other), *we should be able to get another one round the table.* • *(fig.) It takes about three weeks to put the magazine* **together** (= prepare and produce it). [M] • *(fig.) The management are putting* **together** (= preparing and producing) *a plan/proposal/package/strategy to rescue the company.* [M] • *If you put* **together** (= mix) *yellow and blue paint you get green.* • You use **put together** after a phrase referring to a group of people or things to show that you are thinking of them as a group rather than separately: *She earns more than all the rest of us put together.* ○ *The population of the US is bigger than that of Britain, France and Germany put together.* • To put something **up** is to fix it to a vertical surface: *We've put up some new curtains in the living room.* [M] ○ *Posters advertising the concert have been put up all over the town.* [M] • To put something **up** is also to raise it or fix it in a raised position: *Why don't you put up your hood/umbrella* (= raise it over your head)*?* [M] ○ *Sam put his hand up* (= raised it into the air) *to ask the teacher a question.* [M] ○ *Helen's going to put her hair up* (= fix it into a position on the top of her head) *for her wedding.* [M] ○ *The nurse put up a drip* (= fixed it in a raised position) *to give the patient some fluids.* [M] ○ *(fig.) I'm just going to put my feet up* (= rest and relax) *for a little while.* [T] ○ *(fig.) I see they've put up* (= increased) *the price of fuel again.* [M] • To put something **up** is also to build it: *They're planning to put a hotel up where the museum used to be.* [M] ○ *Local residents are opposing the plans to put up a new supermarket.* [M] ○ *We're going to put up a new fence around our garden.* [M] • *The prisoners were put* **up against** (= moved into a position next to) *a wall and shot.* • *(Br infml)* If you **put it about** or **put** your**self about**, you have sex with a lot of different people: *I find it hard to respect people who put it about.* ○ *He's been putting himself about a bit since he split up with Pat.* • If you **put** someone **away**, you move them into a mental hospital or similar place: *Aunt Edith is worried about being put away (in an old people's home).* • *(slang) After what he did, he deserves to be* **put away** (= sent to prison) *for life.* • *(Br) The match has been* **put back** (= delayed) *to next Wednesday because the pitch is waterlogged.* • If you **put** something **behind** you, you try to forget or ignore something unpleasant: *I'm going to put all that's happened behind me, and think about the future.* • If you **put** your**self in** someone's **place/position/shoes**, you imagine that you are in the difficult situation that they are in: *Put yourself in my place – what else could I have done?* • *"So, do we have a deal?" "Sure,* **put it there** (= shake my hand to show that we have made an agreement)*."* • To **put** part of your body **out** is to cause it to be moved out of its correct position: *He put his knee out playing football.* ○ *I've put my shoulder out.* • *Grandma gave me some money to* **put towards** (= to use as part of the cost of) *a new coat.*

put *obj* WRITE /pʊt/ *v* [T always + adv/prep] **putting**, *past* **put** to write down or record • *You should put your name* **in** *your textbooks in case anyone borrows them.* • *Put a cross* **next to** *the name of the candidate you want to vote for.* • *He asked me to put my objections* **(down) on** *paper.* [T/M] • *Make sure you put the date of the party* **down** *in your diary.* [M] • If you put someone **down for** something, you arrange for their name to be recorded on the list of people who want to be involved with it: *Do you want me to put you down for the trip to London?* ○ *I've put my***self** *down for the office football team.* ○ *If you want to get your children into that school, you'll have to put their* **names** *down for it at birth.* • If a person is put **down for** a sum of money, a record is made that they have promised to pay it to someone collecting money to help people in need: *Put me down for a £10 donation, and you can put my husband down for the same.* • *Alex has been* **put down as** (= is considered to be) *a trouble-maker at school.* • *I* **put** *the children's bad behaviour* **down to** (= thought that it was caused by) *the fact that they were tired.* • *I know I've made a big mistake, but I'm going to* **put it down to experience** (= consider it as forming part of my experience of life). • *That article about solar heating was very interesting, but I wish they'd put* **in** *more information* (= included more information) *about the costs.* [M]

put *obj* EXPRESS /pʊt/ *v* [T] **putting**, *past* **put** to express (something) in words • *She wanted to tell him that she didn't want to see him any more, but she didn't know* **how** *to put* **it**. • *We're going to have to work very hard, but* **as** *Chris so succinctly put* **it**, *there's no gain without pain.* • *"Shall we all go out for a pizza tonight?" "I don't know. I'll put* **it to** (= suggest the idea to) *Jim and see what he says."* • *(fml) I put* **it to** *you* (= I believe it to be true), *Ms Dawson,* **that** *you were in the building at the time of the murder.* [+ obj + *that* clause] • *Why do you always have to put things so crudely?* • *He has difficulty putting his* **feelings into words**. • *Has everyone had a chance to put their point of view?* • To put something **about/around** is to tell a lot of people something that isn't true: *I'd like to know who put the rumour around that Chris and I are getting divorced.* [M] • *Mary's been putting* **it** *about* **that** *Dan is planning to leave, but he isn't.* [+ obj + *that* clause] • *A good teacher has to be able to put things* **across/over** (= give information to people) *clearly.* [M] • *We have a proposal/plan we'd like to put* **before** (= suggest for consideration by) *the committee.* • *The minister has put* **out** (= produced or broadcast) *a statement/press release denying the allegations.* [M] • *The police have put a warning* **out** *that the escaped prisoner could be dangerous.* [M] • *I have a suggestion/question/idea I want to put* **to** *you* (= to tell or ask you about). • You say **to put it bluntly/simply/briefly/mildly** or **putting it bluntly/simply/briefly/mildly** to describe the way you are expressing an opinion: *To put it bluntly, Pete, you're just no good at the job.* ○ *It's putting it mildly to say that Dad was annoyed* (= He was extremely angry).

put *obj* CONDITION /pʊt/ *v* [T] **putting**, *past* **put** to cause to be in the stated condition or situation • *Are you prepared to put your children* **at risk**? • *This puts me* **in** *a very difficult position.* • *What has put you* **in/into** *such a bad mood?* • *This election is a chance for the country to put a new government* **in** (= elect a new government). [M] • *Let's give her the chance to put her ideas* **into** *practice.* • *Put your shoes* **on** (= Cover your feet with them) *– we're going out.* [M] LP **Dressing and undressing** • *Could you put the light* **on/out** (= cause it to operate/not to operate), *please?* [M] LP **Switching on and off** • *The terrorists were put* **on** *trial* (= Their case was judged in a law court) *six years after the bombing.* • *Please put your cigarettes* **out** (= stop them burning). [M] • *Wilson was put* **out** *(of the competition)* (= was defeated) *by Clarke in the second round.* • *How much did it cost to have the television put* **right** (= repaired)*?* [+ obj + adj] • *I originally thought he was Australian, but he soon put me* **straight** (= corrected me) *and explained he was from New Zealand.* [+ obj + adj] • To put something **out** is to produce it so that it can be sold: *The factory puts out millions of pairs of shoes a year.* [M] • If something puts your mathematical calculations **out**, it causes them to be wrong: *That mistake put the figures out by several thousand pounds.* • *I know she's gone forever, but I just can't put her* **out of** *my mind/head* (= forget her). • *He's putting me* **under** *pressure to change my mind.* • To **put/throw** someone who is trying to find someone or something **off the scent/track/trail** is to cause them to look in the wrong place: *The police were put off the scent by the postmark on the letter.* • To **put** someone **to** something is to cause them to experience or do it: *Your generosity puts me to* **shame**. ○ *I've put the children to* **work** *clearing the snow from the path.* ○ *I hope we're not putting you to any* **inconvenience**. ○ *Having the roof repaired will put us to great* **expense**. ○ *(slightly fml) Ruth Ellis was the last woman to be put to* **death** (= killed as a punishment) *by* *hanging in Britain.* ○ *We need to put this proposal to a* **vote/discussion** (= make a decision about it by voting on it or discussing it).

put *obj* OPERATION /pʊt/ *v* [T always + adv/prep] **putting**, *past* **put** to bring into operation; to cause to be used • *When the drugs failed to cure her, she put her* **faith/trust** *in herbal medicine.* • *The school puts a lot of* **emphasis** *on teaching children to read and write.* • *He's putting* **pressure** *on me to change my mind.* • *The events of the last few weeks have put a real* **strain** *on him.* • *In the story of Sleeping Beauty, the wicked fairy puts a* **spell/curse/***(Am)* **hex** *on the baby princess.* • *You know the accident was your fault, so don't try and put the* **blame** *on anyone else.* • *The government is expected to put a new* **tax** *on cars.* • *The new tax will put 8%* **on** *fuel prices* (= increase them by 8%). • *She's never put* **a bet/money on** *a race before.* • *(fig. infml) I'll put* **money** *on it* (= I'm certain) *that he won't stay in that job for long.* • *We've put a lot of effort/energy/time* **into** *making the house look nice.* • *He put everything he had* **into** (= He used all his abilities and strength in) *the final game.* • *The more you put* **into** *something, the more you get out of it* (= The harder you work at something, the more satisfying it is). • *They put* (= invested) *a lot of money* **into** *the family business.* • If you put a price/value/figure **on** something, you say what you think its price or value is: *The agent has put a price of £60 000 on our house.* ○ *You can't put a value on friendship* (= say what it is worth). ○ *"Yes, officer, I definitely saw her getting into the car." "Could you put a time on that* (= say when that was), *sir?"* • *The President is trying to put* **through** (= bring into operation) *reforms of the country's economic system.* [M] • *She told her children to put* **an end to/a stop to** *their fighting* (= to stop fighting). • *(slang) My landlord is* **putting the heat/screws on** *me* (= trying to force me, esp. by using threats or violence) *to pay my rent.* • *(slang)* If you **put the squeeze on**/*(Am also)* **put the arm/bite on** someone, you ask them to give you money: *She put the squeeze on her mother* **for** *a hundred bucks.* ○ *The insurance company put the bite on me* **for** *a huge increase in my premium after I crashed the car.* • If you say that you cannot **put** a face **to** a name, or **put** a date **to** an event, you mean that you cannot remember what someone with that name looks like, or the date on which that event happened: *"Do you know Anna Jones?" "I know the name, but I can't put a face to it."* ○ *We've been to Scotland quite recently, but I couldn't put a precise date to it.*

put *obj* JUDGE /pʊt/ *v* [T always + adv/prep] **putting**, *past* **put** to judge (something or someone) in comparison with other similar things or people • *I'd put him* **among** *the top six tennis players of all time.* • *The value of the painting has been put* **at** *£1 million.* • *I'd put her* **at** (= guess that her age is) *about 35.* • *Although it can't be put* **in** *the same category/class as a Rolls Royce, this is still a luxury car.* • *Drama critics have put her* **on** *a level/par with the great Shakespearean actresses.* • *He always puts the needs of his family first/last* (= they are the most/least important thing to him). • *She puts her job* **before/above** *everything else* (= treats it as the most important thing in her life).

put *obj* THROW /pʊt/ *v* [T] **putting**, *past* **put** to throw (a heavy metal ball) in a sporting competition • *He won the gold medal for* **putting the shot** (= the sport of throwing a metal ball as far as possible). • See also **shot put** at SHOT METAL BALL.

put SAIL /pʊt/ *v* [I always + adv/prep] **putting**, *past* **put** to travel in a boat or ship across the sea • *Our mast broke, so we had to put* **about** (= turn round) *and return to port.* • *The ship put* **in at** (= stopped at) *Cape Town for fresh supplies.* • *We put* **to sea** (= began our sea journey) *at dawn.*

put *obj* **a·cross** *obj v prep* [T], **put** *obj* **o·ver on** *obj v adv prep* [T] *infml* to cause (something that is not true) to be believed by (someone) • *My dad's really smart – you can never put anything across him.* • *You didn't manage to put that story over on the tax people, did you?* • *I think she's put* **one** *over on you* (= has tricked you), *Ken.*

put a·way *obj*, **put** *obj* **a·way** *v adv* [M] *infml* to eat (a lot of food) • *I don't know how she manages to put so much food away.* • *He felt very sick after he put away a whole box of chocolates in one evening.*

put back *obj*, **put** *obj* **back** *v adv* [M] *infml esp. Br* to drink (esp. a large amount of alcohol) quickly • *He regularly puts back six pints a night – I don't know how he does it.*

put down *obj* STOP, **put** *obj* **down** *v adv* [M] to stop or limit (political opposition) • *Police used tear gas to put the* **riot** *down.* • *The Prime Minister first needs to put down the* **opposition** *to his proposals within his own party.* • *Thousands of troops were needed to put down the* **uprising**.

put *obj* **down** INSULT *v adv* [T] *infml* to make (someone) feel foolish and unimportant • *Why did you have to put me down in front of everybody like that?* • *I don't know why she stays with him – he's always putting her down.*

put-down /ˈpʊt·daʊn/ *n* [C] *infml* • A put-down is an unkind remark that makes someone seem foolish: *One of the big put-downs of the American presidential election campaign was the comment that he was 'no Jack Kennedy'.*

put down *obj* KILL, **put** *obj* **down** *v adv* [M] to kill (an animal that is old, ill or injured) to prevent suffering • *Animals are usually put down with a painless injection.* • *If a horse breaks its leg, it usually has to be put down.* • *The vet says that our dog is so ill that it would be kinder if we put her down.*

put for·ward *obj*, **put** *obj* **for·ward**, *fml esp. Am* **put forth** *obj*, **put** *obj* **forth** *v adv* [M] to suggest (an idea) for consideration • *The* **proposals** *that you have put forward deserve serious consideration.* • *None of the* **ideas** *that I put forward have been accepted.* • *I wasn't convinced by any of the* **arguments** *that he put forward.* • *Many* **suggestions** *have been put forward, but a decision is unlikely until after next year's general election.* • *The peace* **plan** *put forward last August has been revived for the latest round of negotiations.* • *He put forth a clear, logical argument for allowing homosexuals in the armed forces.* • *She has decided to put her* **name**/*put her***self** *forward* (= said that she is willing to be considered) *as a candidate.*

put in *(obj)* OFFER, **put** *(obj)* **in** *v adv* to offer (something or yourself) for consideration • *My insurance company wanted to know if I'd put any claims in before.* [M] • *She has put in an application to the college.* [M] • *He's put in a request for a week's holiday.* [M] • *They've put in a bid for the company/a bid to buy the company.* [M] • *I'm putting in* **for** *a job at the hospital.* [always + prep] • *Richard has finally put in* **for** *his driving test.* [always + prep]

put in *obj* DO, **put** *obj* **in** *v adv* [M] to do (work), to use (effort) or to spend (time) • *You've obviously put a lot of work in* **on** *your garden.* • *She's put in a lot of effort* **on** *this piece of work.* • *If I put in some extra hours* (= spend some extra hours working) *today, I can have some time off tomorrow.*

put in SAY *v adv* to say (something which adds to or interrupts what is already being said) • *"But I don't think she's the right kind of person for this job," put in Jane.* [+ clause] • *Then William put in* **that** *we'd need to check whether our car insurance covered us for driving abroad.* [+ *that* clause]

put off *obj* DELAY, **put** *obj* **off** *v adv* [M] to delay or move to a later time or date, or to stop or prevent (someone) from doing something • *We've been putting off the decision about whether to have a baby or not.* • *The meeting has been put off* **for** *a week/***for** *the time being.* • *I can't put off go***ing** *to the dentist any longer.* [+ v-ing] • *(saying) Never put off until tomorrow what you can do today.* • *I really don't want to go out with Helen and Greg tonight – can't we put them off* (= stop our planned meeting with them)? • *He keeps asking me out, and I keep putting him off.* • *You're not going to put me off* (= stop me asking questions) **with** *excuses – I want an explanation.*

put *obj* **off** *(obj)* TAKE ATTENTION AWAY *v adv, v prep* [T] to take (someone's) attention away from (what they want to be doing or should be doing) • *Once she's made up her mind to do something, nothing will put her off.* • *Could you be quiet please – I'm trying to concentrate and you're putting me* **right** *off.* • *The phone keeps ringing and it's putting me off my revision.* • *The sudden flash of the camera put the runners off their stride/put the players off their game.* • To **put** someone **off** their **stride/***(Br and Aus also)* **stroke** is to take someone's attention away from what they are doing, so that they stop doing it, or do it wrong: *He completely put me off my stride when he interrupted my speech.*

put off *obj* DISLIKE, **put** *obj* **off** *(obj) v adv, v prep* [T] to cause (someone) to dislike (someone or something), or to discourage (someone) from doing something • *The smell of hospitals always puts me off.* • *The long and anti-social hours demanded by this job put off many people.* [M] • *We'd like to have gone to the concert, but we were put off by the cost of the tickets.* • *His attitude put me* **right** *off him.* • *I didn't think the film was very good, but don't let that put you off* going. [+ obj + v-*ing*] • *Seeing how the hens were kept was enough to put you off eating chicken* **for life**. [+ obj + v-*ing*]

put on *obj* PROVIDE, **put** *obj* **on** *v adv* [M] *esp. Br* to provide (something), esp. for the benefit of other people • *Whenever we go and see my aunt, she puts on a wonderful meal for us.* • *Because the trains aren't running, buses have had to be put on instead.*

put on *obj* ADD, **put** *obj* **on** *v adv* [M] to add or increase • *I'd expected to put* **weight** *on when I gave up smoking, but I didn't.* • *He's put on 10 pounds* (= become 10 pounds heavier) *in the last month.* • *Christie put on a spurt in the last few metres to win the race.*

put on *obj* PRETEND, **put** *obj* **on** *v adv* [M] to appear to have (a feeling or way of behaving that is not real or not natural for you) • *Why are you putting on that silly voice?* • *There's no need to put on that injured expression – you know you're in the wrong.* • *They give the impression of coming from a wealthy background, but it's all put on really.* • *I can't tell whether he's really upset, or if he's just* **putting it on** (= pretending to feel that way).

put–on /£'pʊt·ɒn, $-ɑːn/ *n* [C] *Am infml* • *She's not really angry – it's just a put-on* (= she is pretending that she is angry).

put *obj* **on** DECEIVE *v adv* [T] *infml esp. Am* to try to deceive (someone) into believing something that is not true • *I thought Chris was putting me on when she said she was planning to give her house to a charity for the homeless.* • *"I hear Joe's left his wife." "No, you're putting me on!"*

put–on /£'pʊt·ɒn, $-ɑːn/ *n* [C] *Am infml* • *Is this one of your put-ons, Matt, or have I really been fired?*

put *obj* **out** ANNOY *v adv* [T] to annoy, upset or inconvenience (someone) • *We were rather put out when they turned up two hours late for our dinner party.* • *Would it put you out if we came tomorrow instead of today?* • *Brian's always willing to put him***self** *out* (= make an effort, even if it is inconvenient) *for other people.*

put out HAVE SEX *v adv* [I] *Am slang* (esp. of a woman) to have sex willingly • *He's one of those guys who expects a woman to put out if he buys her dinner.* • *You put out* **for** *a man, and what happens – he has no respect for you any more.*

put up *obj* SHOW OPPOSITION *v adv* [T] to show or express (opposition) to something • *The villagers were unable to put up any* **resistance** *to the invading troops.* • *I'm not going to let them build a road here without putting up a* **fight**. • *No one has yet put up any* **objections** *to the proposal.*

put up *obj* PROVIDE HOUSING, **put** *obj* **up** *v adv* [M] to provide (someone) with a place to stay temporarily • *Sally is putting me up* **for** *the weekend.* • *Mike wants to know if we can put up a friend of his* **for** *the night.*

put up *obj* PROVIDE MONEY, **put** *obj* **up** *v adv* [M] to provide or lend (money) so that an aim can be achieved • *Dad put £1000 up to help me buy a car.* • *The* **money** *to build the new hospital was put up by an anonymous donor.* • *His brother has agreed to put up* **bail** *for him.*

put up *obj* SUGGEST, **put** *obj* **up** *v adv* [M] to suggest (an idea) or make (someone) available for consideration • *They've put up this really crazy scheme.* • *Alan has put up the argument that the proposal will cost too much.* • *Each party is allowed to put one* **candidate** *up.* • *William has been put up* **as** *a candidate for the committee.* • *Is Chris willing to be put up* **for** *election?*

put–up /£'pʊt·ʌp, $'pʊṭ-, -'-/ *adj* [not gradable] *infml* arranged in advance in order to deceive or cheat • *The scheme looked like a good investment, but it turned out that the whole thing was just put-up/a put-up* **job**.

put *obj* **up to** *obj v adv prep* [T] to encourage (someone) to do (esp. something wrong) • *This sort of behaviour isn't like you, Sarah. Who put you up to it?* • *I think he was put up to it by his friends.*

put up with *obj v adv prep* [T] to be willing to accept (something that is unpleasant or not desirable) • *He's finding it difficult to put up with the pain.* • *I can put up with the house being untidy, but I hate it if it's not clean.* • *I don't know why she puts up with him* (= is willing to accept his unpleasant behaviour). • *They have a lot to put up with* (= They have a lot of difficulties).

put u·pon *obj v prep* [T usually passive] *infml* to treat (someone) badly by taking advantage of their helpfulness • *I'm fed up with being put upon by my boss all the time.*

put–u·pon /£'pʊt·ə·pɒn, $'pʊṭ·ə·pɑːn/ *adj infml* • *I don't mind helping them, but I can't help* **feeling** *a bit put-upon* (= that they are using me for their own advantage). • *She always gets her poor put-upon secretary to make her coffee for her.*

pu·ta·tive /£'pjuː·tə·tɪv, $-ṭə·ṭɪv/ *adj* [before n; not gradable] *fml* generally thought to be or to exist, whether or not this is really true • *There have been many attempts to track down the putative Loch Ness monster.* • *The putative leader of the terrorist organization was arrested by police in Birmingham yesterday.*

pu·ta·tive·ly /£'pjuː·tə·tɪv·li, $-ṭə·ṭɪv-/ *adv* • *There remain many social injustices in putatively egalitarian societies.*

pu·tre·fy /'pjuː·trɪ·faɪ/ *v* [I] to decay, producing a strong unpleasant smell • *The river is badly polluted and full of dead putrefying fish.* • *The body had putrefied beyond recognition.*

pu·tre·fac·tion /ˌpjuː·trɪ'fæk·ʃən/ *n* [U] *specialized or fml* • *Putrefaction* (= Decay) *had destroyed the body's features, and it could not be identified.* • *The rubbish dump is turning into a heap of putrefaction* (= decaying matter).

pu·trid DECAYED /'pjuː·trɪd/ *adj* very decayed and having an unpleasant smell • *We came across the putrid body of a dead fox while we were walking in the woods.* • *What's that putrid* **smell**?

pu·trid UNFAIR /'pjuː·trɪd/ *adj slightly dated* causing moral offence, esp. by being unfair • *That was a pretty putrid trick to play on someone!*

pu·trid WORTHLESS /'pjuː·trɪd/ *adj infml slightly dated* worthless; lacking value or quality • *Your last essay was a putrid effort, James. You really must try harder.*

putsch /pʊtʃ/ *n* [C] a sudden secretly planned attempt to remove a government by force • *Although the putsch in the USSR which attempted to overthrow President Gorbachev was unsuccessful, it accelerated the country's disintegration.*

putt *(obj)* /pʌt/ *v* to hit (a golf ball) gently across an area of short and even grass towards or into a hole • *Palmer putted the ball straight into the hole.* [T] • *You need to use a special club for putting.* [I] • A **putting green** is a small area of short grass on which people can gently hit golf balls into a series of holes for entertainment or to practise for a game of golf.

putt /pʌt/ *n* [C] • *She won the competition with an impressive six-metre putt* (= a gentle hit across short grass which sends a ball towards or into a hole).

put·ter /£'pʌt·əʳ, $'pʌṭ·ɚ/ *n* [C] • A putter is a stick with a short handle and metal end which is specially designed for putting: *A putter is a type of golf club.* • A putter is also someone who putts: *You need to be a good putter to be a successful golfer.* • PIC **Sports**

put·ter /£'pʌt·əʳ, $'pʌṭ·ɚ/ *v, n Am for* POTTER • *He really enjoys puttering around in the garden.*

put·ty /£'pʌt·i, $'pʌṭ-/ *n* [U] a soft oily clay-like substance which is used esp. for fixing glass into window frames or for filling small holes in wood • *My house was broken into twice within 24 hours – the putty used to repair the broken window was still wet when they broke in the second time.* • *Jim will do whatever Emma wants – he's* **(like) putty in** *her* **hands** (= is easily influenced and controlled by her).

putz /pʌtz/ *n* [C] *Am slang* a stupid person • *He got me really angry so I told him he was a putz.*

puz·zle *(obj)* /'pʌz·l̩/ *v* to cause (someone) to feel confused and slightly worried because they cannot understand something, or to think hard about something in order to understand it • *The findings of the survey puzzle me – they're not at all what I would have expected.* [T] • **It** *puzzles me* **why** *she said that.* [+ *wh-* word] • *We're still puzzling* **about** *how the accident could have happened.* [I always + adv/prep] • *Scientists are puzzling* **over** (= thinking hard about) *the results of the research on the drug.* [I always + adv/prep] • To **puzzle** something **out** is to find it out by thinking hard: *We haven't managed to puzzle out the solution to our problem yet.* ○ *I can't puzzle out* **how** *I managed to spend so much money last month.*

puz·zle /'pʌz·l̩/ *n* [C] • *Their son is a puzzle* **to** *them* (= they cannot understand him). • *The police are trying to* **solve** *the puzzle* (= the matter that is difficult to understand) **of** *who sent them the letter.* • A puzzle is also a game or toy in which you have to fit separate pieces together, or a problem or question which you have to answer by using your skill or knowledge: *a jigsaw puzzle* • *a crossword puzzle* • *a puzzle book*

puz·zled /'pʌz·l̩d/ *adj* • *The students sat with puzzled expressions/looks* (= expressions showing that they did not understand) *on their faces as their lecturer tried to explain the theory.* • *She's puzzled* **about** *what would be the best thing to do.* • *I'm rather puzzled* **by** *her refusal to get *involved. She's usually very keen to help.* • *I'm puzzled* **that** *I haven't heard from Liz for so long.* [+ *that* clause]

puz·zle·ment /ˈpʌz·l̩.mənt/ *n* [U] • *He turned to her* **in** *puzzlement* (=a state of being unable to explain or understand something). • *She* **expressed** *puzzlement* **at** *being excluded from the team.*

puz·zler /£ˈpʌz·ləʳ, £-l̩·əʳ, $-lɚ/ *n* [C] *infml* • A puzzler is something or someone that is difficult to explain or understand: *What happened to the missing money is quite a puzzler.* ○ *You can be a real puzzler sometimes, Emily.*

puz·zling /ˈpʌz·l̩.ɪŋ, ˈ-lɪŋ/ *adj* • *I found that film very puzzling* (=difficult to understand). • *It's a puzzling situation.*

PVC /ˌpiː·viːˈsiː/ *n* [U] *abbreviation for* polyvinyl chloride (=a type of plastic which is used esp. for making clothes, floor coverings and bags) • *She was carrying a brightly coloured PVC shopping bag.* • *The floor tiles were (made of) PVC.*

pw *adv* [not gradable] *Br abbreviation for* per week (=for every week) • *I am writing to inform you that your rent will be increased to £60 p.w. from October 1st.*

PWA /ˌpiː·dʌb·l̩.juːˈeɪ/ *n* [C] *abbreviation for* person with AIDS

PX /ˌpiːˈeks/ *n* [C] a shop at an American **military base** (=place where soldiers live and work)

Pyg·my, Pig·my /ˈpɪg·mi/ *n* [C] a member of one of several groups of very small people who live in central Africa • *Pygmies average about 1·5 metres in height.* • *(disapproving)* If a person is described as a pygmy, it means that they are not important or have little skill: *Criticism from these* **political** *pygmies doesn't worry me at all.*

pyg·my, pig·my /ˈpɪg·mi/ *adj* [before n; not gradable] • A pygmy animal or bird is one of a type which is smaller than animals or birds of that type usually are: *a pygmy hippopotamus* • *a pygmy owl*

py·jam·as *esp. Br and Aus, Am usually* **pa·ja·mas** /pɪˈdʒɑː·məz/ *pl n* soft loose clothing which is worn in bed and consists of trousers and a type of shirt • *pink/striped pyjamas* • *silk pyjamas* • *I need a new* **pair of** *pyjamas.* • *Would you like some new pajamas for your birthday?* • PIC〉 **Beds and bedroom**

py·jam·a *esp. Br and Aus, Am usually* **pa·ja·ma** /pɪˈdʒɑː·mə/ *adj* [before n; not gradable] • *I always wear pyjama bottoms* (=trousers) *in bed, but never a pyjama top.*

py·lon /£ˈpaɪ·lɒn, $-lɑːn/ *n* [C] a tall steel structure to which wires carrying electricity are fixed so that they are safely held high above the ground • *Those* **electricity** *pylons have ruined the view of the valley.* • A pylon is also a tall tower or post which shows where aircraft should land. • PIC〉 **Energy**

PYO /£ˌpiː·waɪˈəʊ, $-ˈoʊ/ *abbreviation for* pick your own • *PYO is written on signs outside farms where people can pick their own fruit, and sometimes vegetables, and so pay less than they would in a shop.*

py·ra·mid /ˈpɪr·ə·mɪd/ *n* [C] a solid object with a flat, often square, base and four flat triangular sides which slope inwards and meet to form a point at the top • The Pyramids in Egypt are stone structures of this shape which were built in ancient times as places to bury esp. kings and queens: *The Great Pyramid is made of 2·5 million stone blocks.* • A pyramid is also a pile of things which has this shape: *The acrobats formed a pyramid by standing on each other's shoulders.* • *Many organizations have a pyramid* **structure** (=there are fewer people at the top levels of them than there are at the bottom). • *(Am)* A **pyramid scheme** is a way of deceiving investors in which money that a company receives from new customers is not invested for their benefit, but is used instead to pay debts owed to existing customers. • *(Br and Aus)* In business, **pyramid selling** is when someone buys the right to sell a company's goods, and then sells part of that right to someone else for a profit. • PIC〉 **Shapes**

py·ram·i·dal /pɪˈræm·ɪ·dᵊl/ *adj specialized* • *It is claimed that pyramidal containers* (=in the shape of a pyramid) *keep razor blades sharp and prolong the life of fruit and vegetables.*

pyre /£paɪəʳ, $paɪr/ *n* [C] a large pile of wood on which a dead body is ceremonially burnt in some parts of the world • *A traditional Indian custom used to involve widows burning themselves alive on their husbands'* **funeral** *pyres.* • *"... and our love become a funeral pyre. Come on baby light my fire"* (song *Light My Fire* by The Doors, 1967)

Py·rex /ˈpaɪ·reks/ *n* [U] *trademark* a type of glass that does not break when it is heated, so it is used for making containers that are used for cooking • *a Pyrex dish/bowl* • *a plate made of Pyrex*

py·ro·ma·ni·a /£ˌpaɪ·rəʊˈmeɪ·ni·ə, $-roʊ-/ *n* [U] a mental illness in which a person feels an uncontrollable desire to start fires

py·ro·ma·ni·ac /£ˌpaɪ·rəʊˈmeɪ·ni·æk, $-roʊ-/ *n* [C] • A pyromaniac is someone who suffers from pyromania: *Large areas of the forest were destroyed when pyromaniacs set fire to it last summer.*

py·ro·tech·nics /£ˌpaɪ·rəʊˈtek·nɪks, $-roʊ-/ *pl n* a public show of FIREWORKS (=explosives that produce bright coloured patterns) • *(fig.)* Pyrotechnics are also a show of great skill, esp. by a musician or someone giving a speech: *His verbal pyrotechnics held his audience spellbound.*

py·ro·tech·nic /£ˌpaɪ·rəʊˈtek·nɪk, $-roʊ-/ *adj* [before n; not gradable] • *The concert finished with a spectacular pyrotechnic display.*

Pyr·rhic vic·tory /ˈpɪr·ɪk/ *n* [C] a victory which is not worth winning because the winner has lost so much in winning it • *She won the court case, but it was a Pyrrhic victory because she had to pay so much in legal fees.*

py·thon /ˈpaɪ·θᵊn/ *n* [C] *pl* **pythons** or **python** a very large snake that kills animals for food by wrapping itself around them and crushing them • PIC〉 **Reptiles and amphibians**

p·zazz /pəˈzæz/ *n* [U] *infml* PIZZAZZ

Q q

Q LETTER (*pl* **Q's** or **Qs**), **q** (*pl* **q's** or **qs**) /kjuː/ *n* [C] the 17th letter of the English alphabet

q QUESTION *n* [C] *abbreviation for* QUESTION ASKING • *Answer Q6 in a separate answer book.* • *(esp. Am) The textbook has a* **Q and A** (=question and answer) *section at the end of each chapter.*

QC /ˌkjuːˈsiː/ *n* [C] *abbreviation for* **Queen's Counsel** (=a high-ranking British lawyer who is allowed to represent a person in court, or the title given to such a lawyer when a queen is ruling) • *A QC is a senior barrister.* • *She was one of the first women to be made a QC.* • *Charles Gordon, Q.C.* • Compare KC.

QED /ˌkjuː·iːˈdiː/ *abbreviation for* quod erat demonstrandum (=Latin for 'which was to have been proven'). Written after an argument in mathematics to show that you have proven something that you wanted to prove. • *(infml)* QED is also used to show that something you have just said or done is the solution to a problem or the answer to a question: *Well, if you want to get into the final, all you have to do is beat everyone in all the heats. QED.*

qt *n* [C] *abbreviation for* QUART

Q-Tip /ˈkjuː·tɪp/ *n* [C] *Am trademark* **cotton bud**, see at COTTON

qu *n* [C] *abbreviation for* QUESTION ASKING

qua /kwɑː/ *prep fml* as (a); when considered as being (a) • *Qua musician, he lacks skill, but his playing is lively and enthusiastic.* • *I have little interest in television qua television, though I do watch the occasional programme.*

quack SOUND /kwæk/ *v* [I] to make the usual sound of a DUCK • *The ducks started quacking loudly when we threw them some bread.*

quack /kwæk/ *n* [C] • *The duck gave a warning quack as we got close to her nest.*

quack DISHONEST PERSON /kwæk/ *n* [C] *disapproving* a person who dishonestly pretends to have medical skills or knowledge • *He went to see a quack who said he could cure him with some kind of strange herbs.* • *I can't believe that quack treatment will work.* • *(Br and Aus infml)* A quack is also a doctor: *Have you seen your quack about that cough?*

quack·e·ry /£ˈkwæk·ᵊr·i, $ˈ-ɚ-/ *n* [U] *disapproving* • *Traditional Western medicine tends to regard alternative remedies such as homeopathy as quackery* (=methods that do not work and are only intended to make money for the people that sell them).

quad [PERSON] /£kwɒd, $kwɑːd/ *n* [C] *infml for* QUADRUPLET • *She had quads after taking fertility drugs.*

quad [SQUARE SPACE] /£kwɒd, $kwɑːd/, *fml* **quad·rang·le** /£ˈkwɒd·ræŋ·gl̩, $ˈkwɑː·dræŋ-/ *n* [C] a square or rectangular space outside which has buildings on all four sides, esp. in a school or college • *Small groups of students had gathered in the ancient quad.*

quad·rant [PART OF CIRCLE] /£ˈkwɒd·rənt, $ˈkwɑː·drənt/ *n* [C] *specialized* a quarter of a circle • *(fig.) The southwest quadrant* (= quarter) *of the M25, near Heathrow Airport, is the busiest road in Britain.*

quad·rant [DEVICE] /£ˈkwɒd·rənt, $ˈkwɑː·drənt/ *n* [C] *specialized* a device for measuring the height of stars in the sky which was used in the past for calculating directions when travelling across the sea

quad·ra·phon·ic, *Br and Aus also* **quad·ro·phon·ic** /£ˌkwɒd·rəˈfɒn·ɪk, $ˌkwɑː·drəˈfɑː·nɪk/ *adj* [not gradable] (of an electronic system of recording, playing or receiving sound) having sound coming from four different directions • *Quadraphonic sound systems make recordings of musical performances more realistic, but they tend to be complicated and expensive.* • Compare MONO [SOUND]; STEREO.

quad·rat·ic e·qua·tion /£ˌkwɒdˈræt·ɪk, $-ˈræt̬-/ *n* [C] an EQUATION (= mathematical statement) which includes an unknown value that is multiplied by itself only once, and which does not include an unknown value multiplied by itself more than once • *In the quadratic equation,* $2y^2+3y=14$*, y=2 or y=*$-3\frac{1}{2}$*.*

qua·dri·lat·e·ral /£ˌkwɒd·rɪˈlæt·ər·əl, $ˌkwɑː·drɪˈlæt̬-/ *n* [C] *specialized* a flat shape with four straight sides • *Squares and rectangles are quadrilaterals.*

quad·ri·ple·gic, *Aus* **quad·ru·ple·gic** /£ˌkwɒd·rəˈpliː·dʒɪk, $ˌkwɑː·drə-/ *n* [C] a person who is permanently unable to move any of their arms or legs, often because their SPINE has been injured • *The multiple sclerosis that has already made her a quadriplegic is beginning to destroy her lungs.*

quad·ru·ped /£ˈkwɒd·rʊ·ped, $ˈkwɑː·drə-/ *n* [C] *specialized* any animal that has four legs • *Horses, lions and dogs are quadrupeds, but humans are bipeds.* • Compare BIPED.

quad·ru·ple *(obj)* /£kwɒdˈruː·pl̩, $kwɑːˈdruː-/ *v* to become four times as big, or to multiply (a number or amount) by four • *The number of students at the college has quadrupled in the last ten years.* [I] • *We expect to quadruple our profits this year.* [T]

quad·ru·ple /£ˈkwɒd·rʊp·l̩, $ˈkwɑː·druː·pl̩/ *adj, adv* [not gradable] • *a quadruple measure* (= one four times as big as usual) • *We have had quadruple the number of applicants we expected.* • *Cows have quadruple-chambered stomachs* (= stomachs with four parts).

quad·ru·plet /£kwɒdˈruː·plət, $kwɑːˈdruː-/, *infml* **quad** *n* [C] any of four children who are born to the same mother at the same time • *Looking after quadruplets must be very hard work.*

quaff *(obj)* /£kwɒf, $kwæf/ *v* to drink (something) quickly or in large amounts • *In Shakespeare's play 'King Henry IV', Falstaff and Bardolph are often seen quaffing in the Boar's Head Tavern.* [I] • *He's always quaffing these strange herbal medicines, which he thinks will make him more healthy.* [T]

quaf·fa·ble /£ˈkwɒf·ə·bl̩, $ˈkwæf-/ *adj infml* • If an alcoholic drink is quaffable, it is easy and pleasant to drink a lot of it: *This wine is very quaffable, isn't it? Would you like some more?*

quag·mire /£ˈkwɒg·maɪəʳ, $ˈkwæg·maɪr/ *n* [C] an area of soft wet ground which you sink into if you try and walk on it • *At the end of the match, the pitch was a real quagmire.* • *(fig.) Since the coup, the country has sunk deeper into a quagmire* (= difficult and complicated situation) *of violence and lawlessness.*

quail [BIRD] /kweɪl/ *n pl* **quails** or **quail** (the meat of) a small brown bird with a round body, small head, short neck and short tail, which is shot for sport or food • *Quail are similar to partridges, but smaller.* [C] • *Quails' eggs are considered to be a delicacy.* [C] • *We had roast quail for dinner last night.* [U]

quail [SHOW FEAR] /kweɪl/ *v* [I] *literary* to feel or show fear; to want to able to move away from something because you fear it • *I was quailing* **with** *fear as I opened the envelope containing my exam results.* • *Charlie quailed* **at** *the sound of his mother's angry voice.* • *She quailed* **before** *her boss's anger.*

quaint /kweɪnt/ *adj* **-er, -est** attractive because of being unusual and esp. old-fashioned • *a quaint country pub* • *a quaint old cottage* • *a quaint little village* • Quaint can also be used to show that you do not approve of something, esp. an opinion, belief or way of behaving, because it is strange or old-fashioned: *"How quaint!/What a quaint idea!" she said, laughing at him.* ○ *He's full of these quaint* **notions** *about giving up his job and going to live on a remote Scottish island.*

quaint·ly /ˈkweɪnt·li/ *adv* • *A lot of his ideas about family life are quaintly old-fashioned.*

quaint·ness /ˈkweɪnt·nəs/ *n* [U] • *It's easy to be charmed by the quaintness of the village.*

quake [SHAKE] /kweɪk/ *v* [I] to shake because you are very frightened or very amused, or to feel or show great fear • *Every time I get on a plane, I quake* **with fear.** • *She quaked* **at** *the prospect of having to tell him what she'd done.* • *Charlie stood outside the head teacher's office, quaking* **in** *his* **boots/shoes** (= feeling very frightened). • *The play was so funny, we were all quaking* **with laughter.**

quake [EARTH MOVEMENT] /kweɪk/ *n* [C] *infml for* EARTHQUAKE • *The most extensive damage occurred in small towns near the quake's epicenter, 80 miles south of San Francisco.*

Quak·er /£ˈkweɪ·kəʳ, $-kɚ/, **Friend** *n, adj* [not gradable] (a member) of a Christian group called the Society of Friends, which does not have formal ceremonies or a formal system of beliefs, and which is strongly opposed to violence and war • *Quakers emphasize the importance of simplicity in all things.* [C] • *Quaker meetings are often held in silence.*

qua·li·fy *(obj)* [STANDARD] /£ˈkwɒl·ɪ·faɪ, $ˈkwɑː·lɪ-/ *v* to (cause someone to) achieve or have the standard of skill, knowledge or ability that is necessary for doing or being something • *I hope to qualify* (= successfully complete a training course) *at the end of the year.* [I] • *Chris has just qualified* **as** *a doctor* (= passed the exams necessary to become a doctor). [I] • *Ann's disappointed that she hasn't qualified* **for** (= has not played well enough to be able to take part in) *the next round in the tennis competition.* [I] [LP] **Sports** • *England has to win tonight's qualifying match to go through to the next round of the competition.* • *In what way do you think your experience in publishing qualifies you* **for** (= has given you the necessary skills and knowledge for) *this job?* [T] • *Just because you've done a short course on cookery, that doesn't qualify you* **as** *an expert chef.* [T] • *Simply knowing a lot about a subject doesn't qualify you* **to** *teach it.* [T + obj + *to* infinitive]

qua·li·fi·ca·tion /£ˌkwɒl·ɪ·fɪˈkeɪ·ʃən, $ˌkwɑː·lɪ-/ *n* • A qualification is an official record that a person has achieved the necessary standard of knowledge or skill in a subject, usually after studying or training and passing an exam: *You'll never get a good job if you don't have any qualifications.* [C] • *Do you have any teaching/legal/medical/secretarial/academic qualifications?* [C] • *I haven't got any qualifications* **in** *science.* [C] • A qualification is also an ability, characteristic or experience that makes you suitable for a particular job or activity: *Some nursing experience is a necessary qualification* **for** *this job.* [C] ○ *One of the qualifications you need* **to** *work here is a sense of humour!* [C + *to* infinitive] • *Qualification* (= The process of qualifying) **as** *a doctor takes several years.* [U] • [LP] **Schools and colleges**

qua·li·fied /£ˈkwɒl·ɪ·faɪd, $ˈkwɑː·lɪ-/ *adj* • *Tim is now a qualified architect* (= has an official record that he has completed the necessary training). • *What makes you think that you are qualified* **for** (= that you have the necessary skills, knowledge or experience for) *this job?* • *I'm not qualified* **to** *give advice on such matters.* [+ *to* infinitive]

qua·li·fi·er /£ˈkwɒl·ɪ·faɪ·əʳ, $ˈkwɑː·lɪ·faɪ·ɚ/ *n* [C] • A qualifier is a person or team who have won part of a competition and are therefore competing in the next part of it: *The qualifiers from the first round will go into the quarter final.* • A qualifier is also a game from which the winner will go on to compete in the next part of a competition: *Belgium and Italy are playing in tonight's qualifier.*

qua·li·fy *(obj)* [RIGHT] /£ˈkwɒl·ɪ·faɪ, $ˈkwɑː·lɪ-/ *v* to (cause someone to) have the legal right to have or do something because of the situation you are in • *I asked if I could apply for free dental treatment, but I was told that I didn't qualify.* [I] • *She doesn't qualify* **for** *maternity leave because she hasn't been in her job long enough.* [I] • *Being a single parent qualifies you* **for** *extra benefits.* [T] • *(fig.) He thinks the fact *that he's worked here longer than the rest of us qualifies him* (= gives him the right) **to** *tell us all what to do.* [T + obj + *to* infinitive]

qua·li·fy *obj* LIMIT /£ˈkwɒl·ɪ·faɪ, $ˈkwɑː·lɪ-/ *v* [T] to limit the strength or meaning of (a statement) • *I'd like to qualify what I just said about the school's failings, by adding that it's a very happy place.* • *He qualified his statement/remarks when he realised they might cause offence.* • *(specialized)* In grammar, a word or phrase which qualifies another word or phrase limits its meaning and makes it less general: *In the sentence 'He walked quickly along the road', 'quickly' and 'along the road' qualify 'walked'.*

qua·li·fi·ca·tion /£ˌkwɒl·ɪ·fɪˈkeɪ·ʃᵊn, $ˌkwɑː·lɪ-/ *n* [C] • *After certain qualifications* (= After it was limited in particular ways), *the proposal was accepted.* • *The doctor said I can leave hospital today, but with the qualification* **that** *I've got to come back every day to have the dressing changed.* [+ *that* clause]

qua·li·fied /£ˈkwɒl·ɪ·faɪd, $ˈkwɑː·lɪ-/ *adj* • *There seems to be qualified* (= limited) *support for the idea.*

qua·li·fi·er /£ˈkwɒl·ɪ·faɪ·əʳ, $ˈkwɑː·lɪ·faɪ·ɚ/ *n* [C] *specialized* • In grammar, a qualifier is a word or phrase, such as an adjective or adverb, which limits the meaning of another word or phrase, or makes it less general.

qua·li·ty STANDARD /£ˈkwɒl·ɪ·ti, $ˈkwɑː·lə·t̬i/ *n* [U] the standard of excellence of something, often a high standard • *Sam's schoolwork has shown a marked improvement in quality this year.* • *These shoes are of good/high/poor/low quality.* • *I only buy good-quality wine.* • *The quality* **of** *the picture on our television isn't very good.* • *He's not interested in quality* (= a high standard of excellence). *All he cares about is making money.* • *All the members of the orchestra are musicians of real quality* (= are excellent musicians). • **Quality control** is the process of looking at goods when they are being produced to make certain that all the goods are of the intended standard. • *My* **quality of life** (= the level of enjoyment, comfort and health that I have in my life) *has improved tremendously since I moved to the country.* • *"Never mind the quality, feel the width"* (title of a British television programme, 1967-9)

qua·li·ty /£ˈkwɒl·ɪ·ti, $ˈkwɑː·lə·t̬i/ *adj* [before n; not gradable] • *The market for quality cars* (= cars of a high standard) *remains strong.* • *(infml) That's a real quality* (= very good) *job you've done there, Bob.* • *(esp. Br and Aus) The story received little coverage in the quality* **newspapers/papers/dailies/press** (= newspapers which are generally thought to give serious accounts of news, business matters, subjects of social interest, sport and the arts). • **Quality time** is time that you are able to spend developing your relationships with members of your family: *Although we did things like shopping and housework together, our marriage suffered because we had very little quality time.*

qua·li·ta·tive /£ˈkwɒl·ɪ·tə·tɪv, £-teɪ-, $ˈkwɑː·lɪ·teɪ·t̬ɪv/ *adj* • *Is there any qualitative difference* (= difference in quality) *between these two video recorders?* • *We have to make a qualitative judgement about the two candidates* (= decide which one is best).

qua·li·ty CHARACTERISTIC /£ˈkwɒl·ɪ·ti, $ˈkwɑː·lə·t̬i/ *n* [C] a characteristic or feature of someone or something • *I don't think he has the right qualities to be a politician.* • *The school has many excellent qualities.* • *Do you think she possesses the necessary managerial qualities to do this job?* • *We're looking for someone with the qualities* **of** *patience, tolerance and understanding.* • *This cheese has a rather rubbery quality (to it)* (= it is like rubber). • *His paintings have an almost childlike quality.* • *"The quality of mercy is not strained"* (Shakespeare, Merchant of Venice 4.1)

qua·li·ta·tive /£ˈkwɒl·ɪ·tə·tɪv, £-teɪ-, $ˈkwɑː·lɪ·teɪ·t̬ɪv/ *adj* • *Her book is a qualitative study of people's wartime experiences* (= is about what they were like). • *There has been a qualitative change in the relationship between the two sides in the conflict* (= the characteristics of the relationship have changed). • Compare **quantitative** at QUANTITY.

qua·li·ta·tive·ly /£ˈkwɒl·ɪ·tə·tɪv·li, £-teɪ-, $ˈkwɑː·lɪ·teɪ·t̬ɪv-/ *adv* • *The research suggests that the ways in which adults and children learn languages are qualitatively* **different**.

qualm /kwɑːm/ *n* [C usually pl] an uncomfortable feeling of doubt about whether you are doing the right thing • *Most parents have occasional qualms* **about** *whether they're doing the best thing for their children.* • *She had* **no** *qualms* **about** *lying to the police.*

quan·dary /£ˈkwɒn·dri, $ˈkwɑːn-/ *n* [C usually sing] a state of not being able to decide what to do about a situation in which you are involved • *I've had two job offers, and I'm* **in a real quandary about** *which one to accept.* • *We're* **in a quandary over** *which school to send our children to.*

quan·go /£ˈkwæŋ·gəʊ, $-goʊ/ *n* [C] *pl* **quangos** *often disapproving* an organization which is established by a government to consider a subject of public importance, but which is independent from the government • *There is considerable public concern about the lack of accountability of many quangos.*

quan·ti·fy *obj* /£ˈkwɒn·tɪ·faɪ, $ˈkwɑːn·t̬ə-/ *v* [T] to measure or judge the size or amount of (something) • *It's* **difficult to** *quantify how many people will be affected by the change in the law.*

quan·ti·fi·a·ble /£ˈkwɒn·tɪ·faɪ·ə·bl̩, $ˈkwɑːn·t̬ə-/ *adj* • *The benefits of the new policy are not easily quantifiable.*

quan·ti·fi·ca·tion /£ˌkwɒn·tɪ·fɪˈkeɪ·ʃᵊn, $ˌkwɑːn·t̬ə-/ *n* [U] • *The quantification of the materials that will be needed should be as accurate as possible.*

quan·ti·fi·er /£ˈkwɒn·tɪ·faɪ·əʳ, $ˈkwɑːn·t̬ə·faɪ·ɚ/ *n* [C] *specialized* • A quantifier is a word or phrase which is used before a noun to show the amount of it that is being considered: *'Some', 'many', 'a lot of' and 'a few' are examples of quantifiers that are used in English.* • LP **Quantity words**

quan·ti·ty /£ˈkwɒn·tɪ·ti, $ˈkwɑːn·t̬ə·t̬i/ *n* the amount of something that can be measured, weighed, counted, etc. or a fixed amount or number • *Luckily I'd brought with me in my toilet bag a quantity* **of** (= some) *cotton wool.* [C] • *Police found a* **large/small** *quantity* **of** *drugs in his possession.* [C] • *The* **sheer** *quantity* (= large amount) **of** *equipment needed for the trip is staggering.* [C] • *Between us we consumed a* **vast** *quantity of food.* [C] • *This recipe is only for four so I usually do double the quantity if I'm cooking for my family.* [U] • *British wines will never be cheap because they cannot be produced* **in** *the same quantity* (= in such large amounts) *as many of their foreign rivals.* [U] • Quantity is often compared to quality, in saying that it is better to have a little of something good than a lot of something that is not very good: *It's quality not quantity that really counts.* [U] • *(Br)* A **quantity surveyor** is a person whose job is to calculate the cost of the materials and work needed for future building work. • LP **Measurements**

quan·ti·ta·tive /£ˈkwɒn·tɪ·tə·tɪv, £-teɪ-, $ˈkwɑːn·t̬ə·teɪ·t̬ɪv/ *adj specialized* • Quantitative means relating to numbers or amounts: *Quantitative analysis shows that 36% of the population carry this gene.* ○ *The data can reveal quantitative as well qualitative results about the population of the district.* • Compare **qualitative** at QUALITY CHARACTERISTIC.

quan·ti·ta·tive·ly /£ˈkwɒn·tɪ·tə·tɪv·li, £-teɪ-, $ˈkwɑːn·t̬ə·teɪ·t̬ɪv-/ *adv specialized*

quan·tum /£ˈkwɒn·təm, $ˈkwɑːn·t̬əm/ *n* [C] *pl* **quanta** /£ˈkwɒn·tə, $ˈkwɑːn·t̬ə/ *fml* the smallest amount or unit of esp. energy • *quantum theory* • A **quantum leap** is a great improvement or important advance in something: *The appointment of a female director is a quantum leap for women's equality.* • *(specialized)* In physics, **quantum mechanics** is a theory that explains the behaviour of **elementary particles**, both separately and in groups.

qua·ran·tine /£ˈkwɒr·ᵊn·tiːn, $ˈkwɔːr-/ *n* [U] a period of time during which a person or animal that might have a disease is kept away from other people or animals so that the disease cannot spread • *The horse had to spend several months* **in** *quarantine when it reached Britain.*

qua·ran·tine *obj* /£ˈkwɒr·ᵊn·tiːn, $ˈkwɔːr-/ *v* [T] • *He had to be quarantined for a few days to prevent the infection from spreading.*

quark /£kwɑːk, $kwɑːrk/ *n* [C] *specialized* one of the most basic forms of matter that make up the heavier **elementary particles** • *Atoms are made up of smaller particles – protons, neutrons and electrons – some of which are made up of even smaller ones, called quarks.*

quar·rel /£ˈkwɒr·ᵊl, $ˈkwɔːr-/ *n* [C] an angry disagreement between two or more people or groups • *They had a quarrel three years ago and haven't spoken to each other since.* [C] • *A bitter quarrel* **over** *border territory has broken out between the two countries.* [C] • *We have no quarrel* **with** *the people of your country* (= We have no reason to disagree with them). • *They seem to have* **patched up** *their quarrel* (= finished their disagreement and started to be friendly) *since the last time we saw them.* [C]

QUANTITY WORDS

Words like 'some', 'little', 'few' show what quantity is being referred to, and are sometimes called quantity determiners (LP on **Determiners** for other types of determiners). Some of these are used mainly with nouns that have a plural [C] while others are used with nouns that have no plural [U]; some words can be used with either type.

The common quantity words are given below. The table shows whether the word is generally used with singular [C] nouns, plural nouns, or with [U] nouns

		singular [C] nouns	plural [C] nouns	[U] nouns
• **total amount or quantity:**				
(more than two things):				
every	*Every child needs affection.*	•		
all	*All children should receive eduction.*		•	
	All meat is rich in protein.			•
(two things):				
each	*He had a cup of coffee in each hand.*	•		
both	*She held on to the rope with both hands.*		•	
(every thing in a group of two or more, considered separately):				
each	*He checked each document carefully.*	•		
• **amount or quantity that is indefinite or not complete:**				
'any' is mostly used in negative statements and questions				
some	*I had some problems, but not too many.*		•	
	I'd like some sugar, please.			•
any	*Do you have any suggestions?*		•	
	I doubt if we've got any glasses left.		•	
	We don't have any information.			•
• **large amount or quantity:**				
many	*Many tourists visit here every year.*		•	
most	*Most trains arrive on time.*		•	
	Most gold is used to make jewellery.			•
much	*Will it take much time?*			•
lots of/a lot of	*I eat lots of apples/fruit every day.*		•	
	I've got a lot of work to do.			•
• **small amount or quantity:**				
'Few' and 'little' have negative meanings, 'almost no' and 'not much'. 'A few' and 'a little' have positive meaning, 'some'.				
few	*Few people realized who she was.*		•	
a few	*We've invited a few friends to dinner.*		•	
several	*Hanna gets several letters a week.*		•	
little	*The windows let little light into the room.*			•
a little	*Drink a little water and you'll feel better.*			•
• **amounts or quantities being compared**:				
(the superlative form is given in brackets)				
more (most)	*I think I made the most mistakes in the exam.*		•	
	Kim's got more bags/luggage than me.			•
fewer (fewest)	*You must take fewer expensive trips abroad.*		•	
less (least)	*I had less money than I thought.*			•
• **sufficient amount:**				
enough	*You look cold, do you have enough clothes on?*		•	
	There isn't enough furniture in my room.			•
• **negative amount or quantity:**				
no	*I had no chance to talk to my boss.*	•		
	He left no instructions.		•	
	There's no ice in the fridge.			•

[U] nouns can be combined with some other nouns like 'piece' or 'item' and then behave like [C] nouns: *a few items of news; some pieces of fruit; many bits of information.* Words for containers and units of measurement also have this effect: *several bottles of oil; a few kilos of fruit.*

QUANTITY WORDS WITH 'OF'

'Of' must normally be added to quantity determiners when they are used before another determiner such as 'the', 'this', 'me', 'her', 'which' or a possessive form like 'Harry's', 'somebody's'.

Neither person is to blame.	*Neither of us is to blame.*
Eat some bread.	*Eat some of Josie's bread.*
We have no accurate information.	**None** *of this information is accurate.*
Every tree is marked with a cross.	**Every one** *of the trees is marked with a cross.*
Each person sang a different song.	**Each (one)** *of us sang a different song.*

QUANTITY WORDS USED AS PRONOUNS

Most of these quantity determiners can also be used as pronouns: *Tell me all.* • *Do you want any?* • *Some will complain.* • *I've had enough.* • *Each gave five pounds.* But notice that *'every'*, *'lots of'* and *'no'* cannot be used as pronouns. *Every, any, some* and *no* form pronouns with *-body, -thing* and *-one*:

She tested every student.	*She tested* **everybody/everyone**.
Every item is checked by machine.	*The machines check* **everything**.
We have no work to do.	*We have* **nothing** *to do.*
Were there lots of people there?	*Yes,* **lots**. / *Yes,* **a lot**.

quar·rel /£ˈkwɒr·ᵊl, $ˈkwɔːr-/ *v* [I] **-ll-** or *Am usually, Aus also* **-l-** • *Stop quarrelling, you two!* • *What did you quarrel* **about/over***?*

quar·rel·some /£ˈkwɒr·ᵊl·səm, $ˈkwɔːr-/ *adj disapproving* • A quarrelsome person repeatedly argues with other people: *They've got very quarrelsome kids, as I remember.*

quar·ry [PLACE] /£ˈkwɒr·i, $ˈkwɔːr-/ *n* [C] a large artificial hole in the ground where stone, sand, etc. is dug out of the ground for use as building material • *a granite/limestone/marble/slate quarry*

quar·ry *obj* /£ˈkwɒr·i, $ˈkwɔːr-/ *v* • *It's in the mountains above Verona that the red limestone is quarried.* [T]

quar·ry [PERSON/ANIMAL] /£ˈkwɒr·i, $ˈkwɔːr-/ *n* [C] a person or animal being hunted or looked for • *They pursued their quarry into an empty warehouse.*

quart /£kwɔːt, $kwɔːrt/ (*abbreviation* **qt**) *n* [C] a unit of measurement for liquids equal to, in Britain, 1·14 litres or, in the US, 0·95 litres • *A quart is so-called because it is a quarter of a gallon.*

quar·ter [FOURTH PART] /£ˈkwɔː·təʳ, $ˈkwɑː·t̬ɚ/ *n* [C] one of four equal or almost equal parts of something; ¼ • *About a quarter of the British own their home outright, while another 45 per cent have a mortgage.* • *My house is situated one and three-quarter miles/a mile and three-quarters from here.* • *The book focuses on events from the last quarter of a century.* • A quarter of an hour is 15 minutes: *I waited a quarter of an hour and then went home.* • A quarter **to**/*(Am also)* **of** the hour means 15 minutes before the stated hour: *It's a quarter to three.* • A quarter **past**/*(Am also)* **after** the hour means 15 minutes after the stated hour: *I'll meet you at a quarter past five.* [LP>] **Time** • A quarter of a year is a period of three months: *There was a fall in unemployment in the second quarter of the year.* ○ *The electricity bill is sent each quarter.* [LP>] **Periods of time** • A quarter is also one of four periods in a game of American football: *At the end of the first quarter the Giants led the Packers 21 to 3.* • **Quarter note** is *Am for* CROTCHET.

quar·ter *obj* /£ˈkwɔː·təʳ, $ˈkwɑː·t̬ɚ/ *v* [T] • *You will need two medium tomatoes, quartered* (= cut into four pieces each).

quar·ter·ly /£ˈkwɔː·tᵊl·i, $ˈkwɑː·t̬ɚ·li/ *adj, adv* [not gradable] • *a quarterly magazine* • *The magazine will be published quarterly* (= four times a year).

quar·ter [MONEY] /£ˈkwɔː·təʳ, $ˈkwɑː·t̬ɚ/ *n* [C] in the US and Canada, a coin worth 25 CENTS • *I put another quarter in the machine.* • [LP>] **Money**

quar·ter [AREA] /£ˈkwɔː·təʳ, $ˈkwɑː·t̬ɚ/ *n* [C] an area of a town where a particular group of people live or work or where a particular activity happens • *The family lives in the Muslim quarter of east Jerusalem.* • *This is the bustling commercial quarter of the city.*

quar·ter [PERSON] /£ˈkwɔː·təʳ, $ˈkwɑː·t̬ɚ/ *n* [C] a person or group of people who provide help, information or a particular reaction to something but who are not usually named • *Help came from an unexpected quarter.* • *There is a feeling* **in certain/some** *quarters* (= Some people consider) *that a change is needed.*

quar·ter [KINDNESS] /£ˈkwɔː·təʳ, $ˈkwɑː·t̬ɚ/ *n* [U] *literary* a show of sympathy towards a person that you have defeated, esp. in allowing them to live • *We can expect no quarter from our enemies.*

quar·ters /£ˈkwɔː·təz, $ˈkwɑː·t̬ɚz/ *pl n* a room or house that has been provided, esp. for servants or soldiers and their families, to live in • *He's a soldier so he lives* **in** *quarters.* • *The army's* **married** *quarters are just outside the town.* • *The original house had* **servants'** *quarters on the top floor.*

quar·ter *obj* /£ˈkwɔː·təʳ, $ˈkwɑː·t̬ɚ/ *v* [T always + adv/prep] • *The soldiers were quartered with* (= they lived with) *local villagers during the war.*

quar·ter·back /£ˈkwɔː·tə·bæk, $ˈkwɑː·t̬ɚ-/ *n* [C] *esp. Am* (in American football) the player who receives the ball at the start of every play and tries to move it along the field by carrying it or throwing or handing it to other members of his team • *The most famous quarterback in the world is probably Joe Montana, who played his best football with the San Francisco 49ers.* • **Rookie** (= new and without much experience) *quarterback Harold Matthews led his side to a 20-17 win over the Minnesota Vikings last weekend.*

quar·ter·deck /£ˈkwɔː·tə·dek, $ˈkwɑː·t̬ɚ-/ *n* [C] the highest part of the DECK at the back of a ship • *The quarterdeck is usually reserved for officers.*

quar·ter·fi·nal /£ˌkwɔː·təˈfaɪ·nəl, $ˌkwɑː·t̬ɚ-/ *n* [C] any of the four games in a competition that decides which players or teams will play in the two **semi-finals**

quar·tet /£kwɔːˈtet, $kwɔːr-/ *n* [C] four people who play musical instruments or sing as a group, or a piece of music written for four people • *A string quartet was playing Mozart.* • *He has composed 14 quartets and 11 symphonies.*

quartz /£ˈkwɔːts, $ˈkwɔːrts/ *n* [U] a hard colourless MINERAL substance, used in making electronic equipment and accurate watches and clocks • *Although it is colourless, quartz is often tinted by impurities and is found in a variety of colours, such as purple, brown, yellow and pink.*

qua·sar /£ˈkweɪ·zɑːʳ, $-zɑːr/ *n* [C] *specialized* the centre of a very distant GALAXY (= group of stars), producing large amounts of energy • *Quasars seem to emit about 100 times as much energy as an average galaxy.*

quash *obj* [REFUSE] /£kwɒʃ, $kwɑːʃ/ *v* [T] to state officially that something, esp. an earlier official decision, is no longer to be accepted • *His* **conviction** *was quashed in March 1986 after his counsel argued that the police evidence showed inconsistencies.* • *He was found guilty, but the* **verdict** *was quashed on appeal.* • *He had his five-year* **sentence** *quashed by the court and was released.*

quash *obj* [STOP] /£kwɒʃ, $kwɑːʃ/ *v* [T] to stop; to CRUSH [DESTROY] • *Troops moved swiftly to quash any unrest yesterday.* • *The company moved quickly to quash* **rumours/speculation** *that it is losing money.* • *All my hopes are quashed.*

qua·si– /ˈkweɪ·zaɪ-, ˌ-–/ *combining form* used to show that something is almost, but not completely, the thing described • *The school uniform is quasi-military in style.* • *Somehow the idea has got around that the environment isn't a normal political issue, but a quasi-religious crusade.* • *He describes the quasi-mystical experiences induced by drugs.*

qua·train /£ˈkwɒt·reɪn, $ˈkwɑː·treɪn, -ˈ-/ *n* [C] *specialized* a group of four lines in a poem

qua·ver [SHAKE] /£ˈkweɪ·vəʳ, $-vɚ/ *v* [I] (of a person's voice) to sound shaky, esp. because of emotion • *Her* **voice** *began to quaver and I thought she was going to cry.*

qua·ver /£ˈkweɪ·vəʳ, $-vɚ/ *n* [U] • *There was a quaver in her voice as she thanked her staff for all their support.*

quav·er·y /£ˈkweɪ·vᵊr·i, $-vɚ-/ *adj* • *She spoke in a small quavery* **voice**.

qua·ver MUSICAL NOTE *esp. Br and Aus* /£ˈkweɪ·vəʳ, $-vɚ/, *Am usually* **eigh·th note** *n* [C] *specialized* a musical note that is half as long as a CROTCHET

quay /kiː/ *n* [C] a long structure, usually built of stone, where boats can be tied up and load and unload their goods

quay·side /ˈkiː·saɪd/ *n* [C usually sing] the edge of a QUAY, beside the water • *The animals were unloaded on/at the quayside.*

quea·sy /ˈkwiː·zi/ *adj* **-ier, -iest** likely to vomit • *She was two months' pregnant and* **feeling** *slightly queasy in the mornings.* • *I started to* **feel** *queasy as soon as the boat left the harbour.* • *I can't watch operations on TV – it makes me feel too queasy.*

quea·si·ly /ˈkwiː·zɪ·li/ *adv*

quea·si·ness /ˈkwiː·zɪ·nəs/ *n* [U]

queen WOMAN /kwiːn/ *n* [C] a woman who rules a country because she has been born into a royal family, or a woman who is married to a king • *How long did Queen Victoria* **reign**? • *The Queen is meeting the Prime Minister today.* • A queen is also any woman who is considered to be the best at what she does: *She's the* **reigning** *queen* **of** *crime writers.* • In the game of CHESS, the queen is the most powerful piece on the board. • In a group of insects, a queen is a single large female that produces eggs: *a queen* **bee** ○ *a queen* **ant** ○ *a queen* **wasp** • A queen in a set of playing cards is a card with a picture of a queen on it. It is usually worth less than a king. LP› **Cards** • The **Queen Mother** is the mother of the king or queen who is ruling. • **Queen Anne's lace** is *esp. Am for* **cow parsley**; see at cow (ANIMAL). • PIC› **Flowers and plants, Games, Wasps and bees**

queen HOMOSEXUAL /kwiːn/ *n* [C] *slang esp. disapproving* a homosexual man, esp. an older man, whose manner is noticeable and artificial • *James is such an* **old** *queen.*

queen·side /ˈkwiːn·saɪd/ *n* [U], *adj* [not gradable] *specialized* (in the game of CHESS) (on) the side of the board on which your queen is placed at the start of the game • *I very rarely castle on the queenside.* • *McDonald built up a strong queenside attack/defence.*

queer UNNATURAL /£kwɪəʳ, $kwɪr/ *adj* **-er, -est** *dated* unusual, strange or not expected • *She had a queer expression on her face.* • *What a queer thing to say!* • *I'm feeling rather queer* (= ill), *may I sit down?*

queer HOMOSEXUAL /£kwɪəʳ, $kwɪr/ *n, adj slang* (of) a homosexual, esp. a homosexual man • Queer is sometimes used disapprovingly: *He is quoted as having said, "We can't have queers in the government".* ○ *Do you think he's queer?* • Queer is also used in a way that is not offensive, esp. by homosexuals. • **Queer-bashing** is the activity of physically attacking and hurting people because they are homosexual.

queer *obj* SPOIL /£kwɪəʳ, $kwɪr/ *v* [T] **queer** *someone's* **pitch** *Br and Aus infml* to spoil a chance or an opportunity for someone, often on purpose • *If she asks Ian for a pay rise before I do she/it will probably queer my pitch.*

quell *obj* /kwel/ *v* [T] to stop (something), esp. by using force • *Police in riot gear were called in to quell the* **disturbances/unrest**. • *This latest setback will have done nothing to quell the growing* **doubts** *about the future of the club.* • *The army quelled the* **rebellion** *in September, arresting dozens of the participants.*

quench *obj* /kwentʃ/ *v* [T] to satisfy (your thirst) by having a drink • *When it's hot it's best to quench your* **thirst** *with water.* • *(fig.) Her thirst for knowledge will never be quenched.* • *(fig. literary) The flames were quenched* (= stopped) *by heavy rain.*

quer·u·lous /ˈkwer·jʊ·ləs/ *adj* often complaining, esp. in a weak high voice • *He became increasingly dissatisfied and querulous in his old age.*

que·ru·lous·ly /ˈkwer·jʊ·lə·sli/ *adv*

que·ry /£ˈkwɪə·ri, $ˈkwɪr·i/ *n* [C] a question, often expressing doubt about something or looking for an answer from an authority • *If you have any queries about this document, please let me know.* • *I'll hand you over to Peter Jackson who should be able to* **answer** *your queries.*

que·ry *(obj)* /£ˈkwɪə·ri, $ˈkwɪr·i/ *v* • *I queried the wisdom of* (= expressed doubt about) *spending so much money.* [T] • *She queried* (= asked) **whether** *three months was long enough.* [+ *wh-* word] • *"Any chance of a cup of tea?" he queried* (= asked) *hopefully.* [+ clause]

quest /kwest/ *n* [C] *literary* a long search for something that is difficult to find, or an attempt to achieve something difficult • *Nothing will stop them* **in** *their quest* **for** *truth.* • *I don't think she went to India* **on** *any spiritual quest, but she came back a very changed person.* • *She does aerobics four times a week in her quest* **to** *achieve the perfect body.* [+ to infinitive]

ques·tion ASKING /ˈkwes·tʃən/ *n* [C] a sentence or phrase used to find out information • *Are there any questions you would like to* **ask**? • *Why won't you* **answer** *my question?* • *To* **answer** *your question/In* **answer** *to your question about road safety, improvements have been made.* • *The question is* (= What needs to be known is), *are they telling the truth?* • In an exam, a question is a problem that tests a person's knowledge or ability: **Answer/Do** *as many questions as you can in the allotted time.* • A **question mark** is a written or printed sign (?) that is put at the end of a phrase or sentence to show that it is a question: *(fig.) A question mark* **hangs over** *the future of the company* (= There is doubt about its future). • *There will be a* **question-and-answer** *session/a* **question time** (= a period when questions can be asked and will be answered) *at the end of the seminar.* • LP› **Auxiliary verbs, Short forms** PIC› **Mark**

QUESTION MARK [?]

A question mark is used:

- **at the end of a direct question.** Indirect questions do not have a question mark.
  How much does it cost?
  She asked how much it cost.
  "You're studying law, aren't you?" I asked.
  I asked if she was studying law.
- **to show that a sentence with the form of a statement is meant as a question**
  I beg your pardon?
  So, you're leaving tomorrow?
- **to show doubt**
  Sidney Morgan (1898?–1972) was little known until after his death .
  "Richard? Is that you?"
- **in informal or humorous writing ?? or ?! might be used to show great surprise**
  Did you hear that Mark is going to marry Pat?! Is he completely mad??

ques·tion *(obj)* /ˈkwes·tʃən/ *v* • If you question a person, you ask them about something, esp. officially: *Several men were questioned by police yesterday about the burglary.* [T] ○ *When questioned about the issue, the Foreign Minister declined to comment.* [T] ○ *68% of those questioned in the poll thought noise levels had increased.* [T] • If you question something, you express doubts about its value or whether it is true: *Experts have questioned the usefulness of vitamin pills.* [T] ○ *I questioned the wisdom of such a move.* [T] ○ *Two months ago, results from a European study questioned* **whether** *early treatment with the drug really improved survival.* [+ *wh-* word] ○ *She gave me a questioning look* (= as if she wanted an answer from me).

ques·tion·a·ble /ˈkwes·tʃə·nə·bl/ *adj* • Something that is questionable is not certain or is wrong in some way: **It** *is questionable* **whether** *this goal can be achieved.* [+ *wh-* word] ○ *Much of late-night television is of questionable value.* • *Some of his jokes were in questionable* **taste** (= were quite rude).

ques·tion·er /£ˈkwes·tʃə·nəʳ, $-nɚ/ *n* [C] • *I'm afraid I don't know how to respond in a way which will satisfy the questioner* (= the person who asked the question).

ques·tion·ing /ˈkwes·tʃə·nɪŋ/ *n* [U] • *Three suspects were taken in for questioning at Hereford police station.*

ques·tion PROBLEM /ˈkwes·tʃən/ *n* any matter that needs to be dealt with or considered • *There is still the question of the missing money.* [C] • *The article* **raises** *the vexed question of human rights.* [C] • *What are your views on the Northern Irish question?* [C] • **It's** *simply* **a question of** *getting* (= you must get) *your priorities right.* • Question also means doubt or uncertainty: *There's no question* **about** (= It is certain) *whose fault it is.* [U] ○ *Whether children are reading fewer books is* **open to** *question* (= there is some doubt about it). [U] ○ *He's competent – there's* **no** *question* **about** *that.* [U] ○ *Her loyalty is* **beyond** *question* (= There is no doubt about it). • *I stayed at home on the night* **in**

question (= the night being discussed). • If you say that something is **out of the question** or that there is **no question of** it happening, you mean there is no possibility of it happening: *A trip to New Zealand is out of the question this year.* ○ *There's no question of agreeing to their demands.*

ques·tion·naire /£ˌkwes·tʃə'neəʳ, $-'ner/ *n* [C] a written list of questions that a number of people are asked to complete so that information can be collected • *Visitors to the country have been asked to* **fill in** *a detailed questionnaire.*

queue *esp. Br and Aus* /kjuː/, *Am usually, Aus also* **line** *n* [C] a line of people, usually standing or in cars, waiting for something • *There was a long queue of traffic stretching down the road.* • *If you want tickets you'll have to* **join** *the queue at the ticket office.* • *There was such a long queue* **for** *the toilets that I couldn't be bothered to go.* • If you say that there is a queue for something, you mean that there are a lot of people wanting that thing: *Our bank said that there was a long queue* **for** *loans.* ○ *There's a queue of companies wanting to make the product.* • *(disapproving)* **Queue-jumping** is the act of positioning yourself further towards the front of a queue than you should be: *Hey, no queue-jumping!* • PIC **Line, Supermarket**

queue *Br and Aus* /kjuː/, *Aus also and Am* **line up** *v* [I] • To queue **(up)** is to wait in a line of people, often to buy something: *Dozens of people were queueing to buy sausages.* ○ *We had to queue for three hours to get tickets.* • If a lot of people are queueing **up** to do something, large numbers of them want to do it: *There are thousands of young women queueing up to be models.*

quib·ble /'kwɪb·l̩/ *v* [I] *disapproving* to argue about, or say you disapprove of, something very small and unimportant • *There's no point quibbling* **about** *a couple of dollars.* • *I might quibble* **over** *some of the finer points of the staging but overall it's a very impressive production.*

quib·ble /'kwɪb·l̩/ *n* [C] • *My only* **minor** *quibble* **with** *the novel* (= small complaint about it) *is that it's a bit short.*

quiche /kiːʃ/ *n* [C] an open pastry case filled with a mixture of eggs, cream and other savoury things that is baked and eaten hot or cold • *asparagus/broccoli quiche*

quick FAST /kwɪk/ *adj* **-er, -est** happening or done with great speed, or lasting only a short time • *It's a surprisingly quick train ride from London to Peterborough.* • *I only had time for a quick glance at the paper this morning.* • *He scored three goals in quick* **succession** (= happening one after the other in a short time). • *Could I have a quick* **word** (= speak to you for a short time)*?* • If you are quick **to** do something, you do it immediately: *She was quick to point out that it wasn't her fault.* [+ *to* infinitive] • A person might be described as quick if they are clever and understand or notice things quickly: *She was quick* **at** *understanding what we wanted her to do.* ○ *He has a quick mind.* ○ *Glyn's quick* **thinking** (= ability to solve problems with speed) *averted what could have been a disaster.* ○ See also **quick-witted.** • *(disapproving)* A **quick fix** is something that seems to be a fast and easy solution to a problem but is in fact not very good or long-lasting: *He warned against any quick-fix solutions.* • *(infml)* If you invite someone to have a **quick one** with you, you ask them to have a drink, usually alcoholic, with you just before going somewhere else: *Do we have time for a quick one before the train arrives?* • A **quick-tempered** person or one with a **quick temper** is someone who becomes angry very easily. • A person who is **quick-witted** is clever and able to understand things easily: *She was quick-witted enough to reply with biting sarcasm.*

quick /kwɪk/ *exclamation* • *Quick! Close the door before the cat comes in!*

quick·en *(obj)* /'kwɪk·ᵊn/ *v* • *This is music that will make your* **pulse** *quicken.* [I] • *We'll have to quicken the* **pace** *if we want to keep up with him.* [T] • *The basic problem is that without fresh foreign capital South Africa has little chance of quickening its economic growth.* [T] • *(literary) Peter walked in the room and her heart quickened.* [I]

quick·ly /'kwɪk·li/ *adv* • *We'll have to walk quickly to get there on time.* • *You ate that up quickly!* • *Quickly now, you two, daddy's waiting in the car!*

quick BODY PART /kwɪk/ *n* [U] the area of skin at the edge of your fingernails and toenails where the nails join the skin • *He's bitten his nails* **to the** *quick* (= very short).

quick·fire /£'kwɪk·faɪəʳ, $-faɪr/ *adj* [not gradable] happening at great speed • *The most exciting part of the drama is the quickfire dialogue.* • *The quiz includes a quickfire round, when you will have to answer as many questions as you can in sixty seconds.*

quick·ie /'kwɪk·i/ *n* [C] *infml* something done or had quickly, esp. a sexual act or an alcoholic drink • *Shall we just* **have** *a quickie?* • *Just 33 days after his actress wife was granted a quickie divorce citing 'unreasonable behaviour', the magazine's editor, Anthony Collins, is to re-marry.*

quick·sand /'kwɪk·sænd/ *n* [U] deep wet sand that sucks in anyone trying to walk across it • *(fig.) We will run into moral quicksand* (= great difficulties) *if we follow this argument to its logical conclusion.*

quick·sil·ver /£'kwɪkˌsɪl·vəʳ, $-vɚ/ *n old use* MERCURY METAL

quick·step /'kwɪk·step/ *n* [C/U] **the quickstep** a dance with a lot of quick steps, or the music for this

quid /kwɪd/ *n* [C] *pl* **quid** *Br infml* a POUND MONEY; £1 • *Could you lend me twenty quid* (= £20)*, mate?* • If you are **quids in**, you have just made, or are likely to make, a lot of money: *If the paintings sell I'll be quids in.* ○ *If the European publishing deal comes off, we'll be quids in.* • LP **Money**

quid pro quo /£ˌkwɪd·prəʊ'kwəʊ, $-proʊ'kwoʊ/ *n* [C] *pl* **quid pro quos** *fml* something that is given to a person in return for something they have done • *The government has promised food aid as a quid pro quo for the stopping of violence.*

qui·es·cent /kwi'es·ᵊnt/ *adj literary* quiet and at rest • *The political situation was now relatively quiescent.*

qui·et /kwaɪət/ *adj* **-er, -est** making very little noise • *She spoke in a quiet voice.* • *This new vacuum cleaner is very quiet.* • *Please be quiet* (= stop talking)*!* • *I felt quiet* **satisfaction** (= I was pleased but did not say much about it) *when I was proved right.* • *(approving)* A quiet place or event is one where there is very little activity or excitement: *They wanted to have a quiet wedding, with just a few friends and relations.* • *It's a quiet, peaceful little village.* • A quiet person is one who does not talk much: *He was a quiet, almost taciturn, young man.* • If you **keep** quiet, you do not make any noise: *The children were told to keep quiet.* • If you **keep** something quiet, you try to hide it from other people: *She managed to keep the operation quiet for a while.* ○ *Davies kept quiet* **about** *the amount of money being spent.* • LP **Sound**

qui·et down *(obj)*, **qui·et** *(obj)* **down** /kwaɪət/ *v adv Am* • *Alright, boys and girls, I want everyone to quiet down* (= be quiet) *now.* [I] • *He tried to quiet her down and get back to sleep.* [T] • See also QUIETEN.

qui·et·ly /'kwaɪət·li/ *adv* • If you do something quietly, you make very little noise as you do it: *I slipped quietly out of the back door.* • *He is a quietly* **spoken** (= He speaks quietly)*, thoughtful man.*

qui·et /kwaɪət/ *n* [U] • Quiet means the state of being silent: *Let's have* **some** *quiet!* ○ *I go camping for some* **peace and** *quiet* (= absence of activity and excitement). • *(infml disapproving)* If you do something **on the quiet**, you do it secretly or in such a way that most other people do not notice it: *He was accepting bribes on the quiet.*

qui·et·ness /'kwaɪət·nəs/ *n* [U] • Quietness means making very little noise, and is often used of machinery: *This car offers safety, comfort, quietness and speed.*

qui·et·en *(obj)* /£'kwaɪə·tᵊn, $-t̬ᵊn/ *v esp. Br* to become or be made calmer and less noisy • *The barking dogs quietened when they recognized me.* [I] • *A public meeting was held to quieten the tension.* [T] • *The cheering crowds eventually quietened* **down.** [I] • See also **quiet down** at QUIET.

qui·et·i·sm /£'kwaɪə·tɪ·zᵊm, $-t̬ɪ-/ *n* [U] *fml* the belief that it is best to accept things in life and not try to change them

qui·et·ude /£'kwaɪə·tjuːd, $-tuːd/ *n* [U] *fml* calm and peacefulness • *In many of his poems the poet reflects on the quietude of the countryside.*

quiff *Br* /kwɪf/, *Am* **pom·pa·dour** *n* [C] a hairstyle, worn usually by men, in which the hair at the front of the head is brushed up and back so that it stands up above the FOREHEAD • *With his quiff and long jacket, he looks like something out of the 1950s.*

quill (pen) /kwɪl/ *n* [C] a pen made from a bird's feather that was used in the past • *A few quill pens lay on the antique writing table.* • *(fig. humorous) She is a gifted writer from whose quill we expect much.*

quill /kwɪl/ *n* [C] any of the long sharp points that can rise up stiffly on the body of a PORCUPINE

quilt /kwɪlt/ *n* [C] a decorative cover for a bed • *She exhibited one of her* **patchwork** *quilts at the local craft fair.* • A quilt (*Am also* **comforter**) is also a DUVET. • PIC **Beds and bedroom, Coverings**

quilt·ed /£ˈkwɪl·tɪd, $-t̬ɪd/ *adj* (esp. of cloth) filled with thick soft material which is sewn in place • *She wore a quilted satin jacket.*

quince /kwɪnts/ *n* [C] a hard fruit that looks like an apple and has a strong sweet smell • *quince jam*

quin·ine /£ˈkwɪn·iːn, $ˈkwaɪ·naɪn/ *n* [U] a drug used to treat fevers such as MALARIA

quin·tes·sen·tial /£ˌkwɪn·tɪˈsent·ʃᵊl $-t̬e-/ *adj* [not gradable] *fml* representing the most typical example or most important part of something • *This is the quintessential English village.* • *Roasted garlic with sheep's milk cheese is the quintessential Corsican meal.*

quin·tes·sen·tial·ly /£ˌkwɪn·tɪˈsent·ʃᵊl·i, $-t̬e-/ *adv* [not gradable] *fml* • *Sherry before dinner is quintessentially* (= typically) *English.* • *Zappa's music was quintessentially weird.*

quin·tes·sence /kwɪnˈtes·ᵊnts/ *n* [U] *fml* • *An American football game is* **the** *quintessence* (= most typical example) **of** *machismo.*

quin·tet /kwɪnˈtet/ *n* [C] five people who play musical instruments or sing as a group, or a piece of music written for five people • *He was a drummer in the Miles Davis Quintet.*

quin·tu·plet /kwɪnˈtuː·plət,ˈkwɪn·tjʊ-, $-ˈtuː·plɪt/, **quin** /kwɪn/ *n* [C] any of five children born at the same time to the same mother

quip /kwɪp/ *n* [C] an amusing and clever remark • *It was Oscar Wilde who made the famous quip about life, in the end, mimicking art.*

quip *obj* /kwɪp/ *v* [T] **-pp-** *esp. Am* • *When asked earlier why he seemed to be so relaxed, Mr McCarthy quipped: "It's the drugs".* [+ clause]

quirk /£kwɜːk, $kwɜːrk/ *n* [C] an unusual part of someone's personality or habit, or something that is strange and unexpected • *You have to get used to other people's quirks and foibles.* • *There is a quirk in the rules that allows you to invest money without paying tax.* • **By** *some strange quirk*/**By** *an odd quirk* **of fate** (= unexpectedly), *we ended up on the same train.*

quirk·y /£ˈkwɜː·ki, $ˈkwɜːr-/ *adj* **-ier, -iest** • Someone or something quirky is unusual in an attractive and interesting way: *He was tall and had a quirky off-beat sense of humour.*

quisl·ing /ˈkwɪz·lɪŋ/ *n* [C] a person who helps the enemy army that has taken control of his or her country; TRAITOR

quit *(obj)* /kwɪt/ *v* **quitting**, *past* **quit** or *Am also* **quitted** to stop doing (something) or leave (a job or a place) • *The director has threatened to quit.* [I] • *Would you quit your job if you inherited lots of money?* [T] • *I'm going to quit smok***ing** *next week.* [+ v-ing] • *Quit wast***ing** *my time!* [+ v-ing] • *I quit London last year and went to live in the country.* [T] • LP› **Work** Ⓓ

quit·ter /£ˈkwɪt·əʳ, $ˈkwɪt̬·ɚ/ *n* [C] *disapproving* • A quitter is a person who gives up easily instead of finishing something: *I'm no quitter.*

quite NOT VERY /kwaɪt/ *adv* [not gradable], *predeterminer* to a particular extent, but not very • *I was feeling quite pleased with myself.* • *She's not black-haired like her brother but she's quite dark.* • *There was quite a lot of traffic today but yesterday was even busier.* • *He's quite pleasant-looking but he's not what you'd call handsome.*

quite COMPLETELY /kwaɪt/ *adv* [not gradable] completely; to a large degree or very much • *The two brothers are quite different in character.* • *Quite* **honestly/frankly**, *the thought of it terrified me.* • *Nobody is quite sure how many bikes there are in Cambridge.* • *It would be quite wrong to suggest that she told a lie.* • *The colours almost match but not quite.* • *I enjoyed her new book though it's* **not** *quite* **as** *good as her last one.* • You use quite with a negative to express uncertainty: *I don't quite know what to say.* ○ *I didn't quite catch what he said.* • *(Br)* You can say quite or quite **so** to show that you agree with what someone has just said: *"You'd think he could spare some money – he's not exactly poor." "Quite."* • LP› **Very, completely**

quits /kwɪts/ *adj* [after v] *infml* no longer owing money to someone or to each other • *I paid for the tickets and you bought dinner so we're quits, I reckon.* • *Am I quits* **with** *you now?*

qui·ver SHAKE /£ˈkwɪv·əʳ, $-ɚ/ *v* [I] to shake slightly, often because of strong emotion • *Lennie's bottom lip quivered and tears started in his eyes.* • *She was quivering with frustration and rage.*

qui·ver /£ˈkwɪv·əʳ, $-ɚ/ *n* [C] • *The opening bars of the music sent* **a** *quiver* **of** *excitement through the crowd.*

qui·ver CONTAINER /£ˈkwɪv·əʳ, $-ɚ/ *n* [C] a long thin container for carrying arrows

qui·xot·ic /£kwɪkˈsɒt·ɪk, $-ˈsɑː·t̬ɪk/ *adj literary* having ideas that are not practical or likely to succeed, esp. in trying to help other people • *This is a vast, exciting and perhaps quixotic project.*

quix·o·ti·cally /£kwɪkˈsɒt·ɪ·kli, $-ˈsɑː·t̬ɪ-/ *adv* **-ier, -iest** *literary* • *The minister pushes quixotically ahead with his reform programme in the face of vehement opposition.*

quiz /kwɪz/ *n* [C] a game or competition in which you answer questions • *There are so many inane television quiz* **shows**. • *He hosts a pop quiz show on television.* • *(Br) A lot of pubs have quiz* **nights** *once or twice a week.* • *I was looking at a quiz in a magazine titled "Thirty questions to help you discover if you are really in love".* • A quiz is also a short informal test: *I often start the class with a short quiz to revise some vocabulary items.* ○ *(Am) There was a* **pop** (= surprise) *quiz in history at school today.*

quiz *obj* /kwɪz/ *v* [T] **-zz-** • If you quiz someone about something, you ask them questions about it: *She spent an hour being quizzed by journalists.*

quiz·zi·cal /ˈkwɪz·ɪ·kᵊl/ *adj* seeming to ask a question without saying anything • *She gave me a quizzical* **look**.

quiz·zi·cal·ly /ˈkwɪz·ɪ·kli/ *adv* • *People stared at me quizzically as if trying to decide whether I was mad.*

quoits /kɔɪts/ *n* [U] a game in which you throw rings over a small post, often played on ships

quok·ka /£ˈkwɒk·ə, $ˈkwɑː·kə/ *n* [C] a small WALLABY (= an animal with a long tail and strong legs for jumping with) which in the past used to be found in great numbers in Western Australia

QUOTATION MARKS [' ' and " "]

Quotation marks are also called *(infml)* quotes or *(Br)* inverted commas. They may be single '. . .' (this is usual in Britain) or double ". . ." (this is usual in America). Some writers prefer to use double quotation marks only to enclose words that were spoken. Quotation marks are used:

- **in direct speech to enclose the words that were spoken.** Notice that sentences in quotation marks do not end with a *(Br)* full stop/*(Am)* period if the main sentence continues. The sentence in quotation marks begins with a capital letter.
  "My car's broken down again," he said. "Do you want some help?" I replied.
  She kept saying "Hurry up".
  Notice also the position of the commas and full stops in these examples.
- **to enclose short pieces of text written by someone else**
  Mackie argues that 'there can be no simple solution to such a complex problem' but we hope to show that he is wrong.
- **to emphasize a word or phrase that the writer believes is untrue, morally wrong or humorous**
  So why didn't your 'friends' come to see you in hospital? (= you are wrong to call them friends)
  I saw Tina dancing with her 'man'. (= I do not like Tina calling her boyfriend her man)
- **to enclose new, unusual, slang or foreign words**
  A computer keeps your work on small disks or 'floppies'.
  Maria cooked 'enchiladas verdes' for us.
  My 8-year-old son calls anything big 'ginormous'.
- **to refer to the titles of books, films, television programmes and so on**
  Tolstoy's 'Anna Karenina'
  Have you ever seen Hitchcock's 'Psycho'?
  You must watch 'Sports Special' tonight.

Quon·set hut /£ˈkwɒn·sɪt, $ˈkwɑːn-/ *n* [C] *Am trademark* a usually military shelter with the roof and walls made in a curved shape out of CORRUGATED steel sheets • *Refugees were sleeping in Quonset huts normally used as barracks for Marines.* • See also NISSEN HUT.

quo·rum /£ˈkwɔː·rəm, $ˈkwɔːr·əm/ *n* [C] the smallest number of people needed to be present at a meeting before it can be allowed to begin • *Four members walked out of the session, with the result that the committee did not have a quorum and could not take any decisions.*

quor·ate /£ˈkwɔː·reɪt, $ˈkwɔːr·eɪt/ *adj* [not gradable] *specialized* • A quorate meeting has the necessary number of people present for decisions to be allowed to be made.

quo·ta /£ˈkwəʊ·tə, $ˈkwoʊ·t̬ə/ *n* [C] a fixed amount or number that is officially allowed, esp. of goods that can be brought into a country • *Spanish producers are subject to quotas* **on** *wine and milk.* • *America* **cut** *its sugar* **import** *quota by 25% this year to only 758 000 tons, against some 3m tons in 1984.* • *Most of India's coffee exports are restricted by an* **export** *quota fixed under the rules of the International Coffee Agreement.* • *The country's* **production** *quotas of 1·1 million barrels a day has been doubled.* • *(esp. Am) He rejects mandatory* **racial** *quotas as ineffective in dealing with discrimination.* • *(fig.) The class contains the usual quota* (= number) *of troublemakers.*

quote *(obj)* SAY /£kwəʊt, $kwoʊt/ *v* to repeat the words that someone else has said or written • *"If they're flexible, we're flexible", the official was quoted* **as saying.** [T] • *He's always quoting* **from** *the Bible.* [I] • *She worked,* **to** *quote her daughter, "as if there was no tomorrow".* [T] • *Can I quote you* **on** *that* (= Can I repeat to other people what you have just said)*?* [T] • If you quote a fact or example, you refer to it in order to add force to what you are saying: *Quote me one organization that doesn't have some bad managers.* [T] • *(infml)* You can say 'quote' or '**quote, unquote**' to show that you are repeating someone else's words, esp. if you do not fully believe them or agree with them: *She's been seeing, quote, 'an older man'.* ○ *He says he's been on a quote, unquote 'high-protein diet'.* ○ *They are quote 'just good friends' unquote.*

quo·ta·tion /£kwəʊˈteɪ·ʃən, $kwoʊ-/, *infml* **quote** /£kwəʊt, $kwoʊt/ *n* [C] • A quotation is a phrase or short piece of writing taken from a longer work of literature, poetry, etc. or what someone else has said: *At the beginning of the book there is a quotation from Abraham Lincoln.* • *(infml) I'd like to include a quote from Shakespeare, "Fools rush in where angels fear to tread".* • **Quotation marks** (*also* **quote marks**, *Br also* **inverted commas** or *infml* **quotes**) are the pair of printed marks put at the beginning or end of a word or phrase to show that someone else has written or said it. • LP **Words used together** PIC **Mark**

quote *obj* PRICE /£kwəʊt, $kwoʊt/ *v* [T] to give a price, esp. that will be charged for doing a piece of work • *The architect has quoted £3000 to build an extension.* • *Small shareholders own only 215 of the shares quoted on the stock exchange.*

quo·ta·tion /£kwəʊˈteɪ·ʃən, $kwoʊ-/, *infml* **quote** /£kwəʊt, $kwoʊt/ *n* [C] • A quotation is the price that a person will charge to do a piece of work: *You should* **get** *quotations from several plumbers for having a shower put in.* • *(infml) Could you* **give** *me a quote for the work?*

quoth /£kwəʊθ, $kwoʊθ/ *v old use or humorous* said • *"Point taken, Kingers," quoth I.*

quo·ti·di·an /£kwəʊˈtɪd·i·ən, $kwoʊ-/ *adj* [not gradable] *fml* ordinary; EVERYDAY • *Television has become part of our quotidian existence.*

quo·tient /£ˈkwəʊ·ʃənt, $ˈkwoʊ-/ *n* [C] the particular degree of something • *This is a car with a high head-turning quotient* (= a lot of people turn to look at it). • *(specialized)* If one number is divided by another, the result is the quotient.

Qur'an /£kɒrˈɑːn, $kəˈrɑːn/ *n* [U] **the Qur'an** the Koran

R r

R LETTER (*pl* **R's** or **Rs**), **r** (*pl* **r's** or **rs**) /£ɑːʳ, $ɑːr/ *n* [C] the 18th letter of the English alphabet • LP **Silent letters**

R ROYAL PERSON /£ɑːʳ, $ɑːr/ (used after the name of a king or queen) *abbreviation for* Rex (= king) or Regina (= queen) • *Elizabeth R* • *George R*

R DIRECTION *adj, adv, n abbreviation for* RIGHT DIRECTION • *R eye: 3.20/L eye: 3.25* [before n] • *Go r. at the traffic lights.* • *Take the second road on r.* [U]

R RIVER *n abbreviation for* RIVER, used in writing before or after the name of a river • *R Thames* • *Mississippi R*

R ROYAL *adj abbreviation for* ROYAL, used in the names of organizations • *RAF* • *RAC* • *WRVS* • *WRNS*

R FILM /£ɑː, $ɑːr/ *adj Am abbreviation for* **restricted**, see at RESTRICT • R is used to show that people under 17 years of age may see a film only if a parent or GUARDIAN is with them.

rab·bi /ˈræb·aɪ/ *n* [C] (the title given to) a teacher and religious leader in the Jewish religion • *the Chief Rabbi* • *Rabbi Jonathan Sacks* • *Rabbi Julia Neuberger* • *Excuse me, Rabbi/Rabbi Gryn.* [as form of address] • *As an orthodox rabbi, he felt that it was his role to protect traditional Jewish Orthodox values.* • *A rabbi's job involves giving help and care to the members of the community in which he or she works, as well as holding religious services.*

rab·bi·ni·cal /rəˈbɪn·ɪ·kəl/ *adj* [not gradable] • *a rabbinical student/college* • *rabbinical literature/law*

rab·bit ANIMAL /ˈræb·ɪt/ *n* [C] a small animal with long ears and large front teeth, which moves by jumping on its long back legs. In some places, rabbits are kept as pets or eaten as food, although in other places they are considered as being harmful to farming. There are various types of rabbit. • *a wild rabbit* • *rabbit stew/pie* • *He demonstrated how to kill and* **skin** *a rabbit.* • *The dogs barked enthusiastically when they found a new rabbit* **burrow/hole.** • *The hillside was a huge rabbit* **warren** (= area of holes and underground passages in which wild rabbits live). • *Whose turn is it to clean out the rabbit* **hutch** (= box with a wire front in which a pet rabbit is kept)*?* • *The child stood at the edge of the swimming pool like a* **frightened/petrified** *rabbit* (= he or she was frightened and could not move). • *My family* **breeds like** *rabbits* (= My relatives keep having lots of babies)*!* • See also BUNNY (RABBIT). • PIC **Wild animals in Britain**

rab·bit TALK /ˈræb·ɪt/ *v* [I] *Br and Aus infml disapproving* to continue talking about something, esp. something which is uninteresting to the listener • *He's always rabbiting* **(on) about** *his stamp collection.*

rab·ble /ˈræb·l̩/ *n* [U] *disapproving* a large noisy uncontrolled group of people • *The defeated army returned home as* **a** *demoralized rabble.* • *He views his opponents as* **a** *mindless rabble.* • *The coach has the job of turning* **a** *rabble* **of** *a team into a strong playing force.* • **The rabble** are people of a low social position: *Her speech stirred the emotions of the rabble.* • A **rabble-rouser** is a person who makes speeches that make people excited or angry, esp. in a way that causes them to act as the person wants them to: *Johnson was unpopular with the management because he was a well-known rabble-rouser/was always making* **rabble-rousing** *speeches.*

rab·id /ˈræb·ɪd, ˈreɪ·bɪd/ *adj esp. disapproving* expressing strong feelings • *A rabid baseball fan, he pores over the sports pages to chart the exploits of his favorite teams and players.* • *Even the survey's most rabid* **critics** *acknowledge the utility of this kind of data.* • *She is a rabid* **feminist** *who believes that all men want to exercise power over women.* • *These attacks are believed to have been carried out by a rabid* **nationalist/racist/anti-semitic** *group.* • See also **rabid** at RABIES.

rab·id·ly /ˈræb·ɪd·li, ˈreɪ·bɪd-/ *adv esp. disapproving* • *Articles in the more rabidly nationalistic newspapers have been demanding that immigrants be sent back to the countries they came from.*

ra·bies /ˈreɪ·biːz/, *specialized* **hy·dro·pho·bi·a** *n* [U] a disease of the nervous system of dogs and other animals, which can also cause a type of madness and death in humans who are bitten by a diseased animal • *Dogs, cats, foxes and bats can all* **carry** *rabies.*

rab·id /ˈræb·ɪd, ˈreɪ·bɪd/ *adj* [not gradable] • *a rabid* (= suffering from rabies) *dog* • See also RABID.

RAC /£ˌɑː·reɪˈsiː, $ˌɑːr·eɪ-/ *n* [U + sing/pl v] **the RAC** *abbreviation for* the Royal Automobile Club (= an

PRONUNCIATION OF 'R' IN BRITISH AND AMERICAN ENGLISH

The following rules explain when 'r' is pronounced:

- In British English when a word is spoken by itself, 'r' is pronounced *only* when it comes before a vowel sound. It is *not* pronounced if it comes at the end of a word or before a consonant:

  ✔ round /raʊnd/
  ✘ car /kɑː/
  ✘ actor /ˈæk·tə/
  ✘ hard /hɑːd/

- In American English 'r' is *always* pronounced when it is present in the spelling:

  ✔ round /raʊnd/
  ✔ car /kɑːr/
  ✔ actor /ˈæk·tɚ/
  ✔ hard /hɑːrd/

  The /ɚ/ sound is only found in American English. It is the /ə/ sound with an 'r'-like quality.

- In British English when words are linked together in a phrase, the 'r' at the end of the first word might be pronounced. This happens when it is followed by another word beginning with a vowel sound:

  her arm /hɜːr ɑːm/
  far away /fɑːr əˈweɪ/
  four eggs /fɔːr egz/
  mother is /ˈmʌð·ər ɪz/

  This type of 'r' is sometimes called **linking r**. In the dictionary this is shown as a small raised 'r' at the end of the pronunciation. For example 'her' is shown as /hɜːʳ/. This means that 'her' has two possible British pronunciations, as in *her leg* /hɜː leg/ and *her arm* /hɜːr ɑːm/.

- In British English an 'r' is pronounced at the end of some words which have no 'r' in their spelling. This is called **intrusive r**; it is not shown in the dictionary. If a word ends with the vowels /ɔː/ or/ə/ British speakers add /r/ when the following word begins with a vowel. Compare the pronunciation of the following phrases:

  law and order /lɔːr ənd ˈɔː·də/ — law court /lɔː kɔːt/

  Anna is /ˈæn·ər ɪz/ — Anna was /ˈæn·ə wɒz/

organization in Britain which gives help and information to drivers who are members of it)

rac·coon, ra·coon /rækˈuːn/, *esp. Am infml* **coon** *n* [C] a small N American animal with black marks on its face and a long tail with black rings on it

race [COMPETITION] /reɪs/ *n* [C] a competition involving an attempt to do or finish something before others or before a time limit • *Do you know who* **won** *the race?* • *Let's* **have** *a race to see who can get home first.* • *The Oxford and Cambridge boat race takes place on the River Thames.* • *She ran in the cross-country race every year and often won.* • *The race is* **run** *through all five boroughs of New York.* • *They're taking part in a race* **to** *the top of Ben Nevis.* • *Kieran and Andrew are involved in a race* (= are competing) **for** *promotion.* • *Another candidate has now* **entered** *the presidential/governor's race* (= attempt to be elected to that position). • *The newspapers are involved in a race* (= are trying to be the first) **to** *publish the story.* [+ *to* infinitive] • *It will be a race* **against** *time/the clock* (= an attempt to do something quickly in order to finish it in the available time) **to** *get this project finished by the end of September.* [+ *to* infinitive] • A *(Br and Aus)* **race meeting**/*(Am)* **race meet** is a set of horse/car/running races on one day in one place. • [LP]> **Sports** (CS) (PL) (RUS)

race *(obj)* /reɪs/ *v* • *He has been racing* (= competing in races) *for over ten years.* [I] • *I used to race* **(against)** *him when we were boys.* [T; I + *against*] • *Come on, I'll race you home.* [T] • *He's racing three of his dogs* (= causing them to take part in a race) *on Saturday.* [T]

ra·cer /£ˈreɪ·səʳ, $-sɚ/ *n* [C] • A racer is a person or thing that races: *Three racers finished with almost exactly the same time.* ○ *In a high-speed crash, a downhill racer has about a 50% chance of injury.* ○ *This car is a* **custom-built** (= made for a particular person) *racer.* • A racer (also **racing bike**) is a bicycle designed for speed with a light frame and HANDLEBARS which curve downwards.

rac·es /ˈreɪ·sɪz/ *pl n* • The races are a series of competitions in a particular place on one day involving horses racing at fixed times: *He often has* **a day at** *the races.*

ra·cing /ˈreɪ·sɪŋ/ *n* [U] • *I enjoy cycling, but I'm not interested in racing.* • *I like watching* **horse/motor** *racing on television.* • Racing is sometimes used to refer to horse races: *Sean has written several books about racing.* ○ *He always reads the racing pages in the paper.* ○ *Have you got any racing tips* (= suggestions about which horse might win a race) *for me?* • A **racing bike/cycle** is a **racer**. • A **racing car** is a low car with a powerful engine and wide wheels which is designed for use in races. • A **racing driver** is a driver who drives a **racing car**. • **Racing pigeons** are PIGEONS that take part in races in which they are timed to see how long it takes them to fly home from the place where they have been released. • If you have a **racing start**, you have an advantage when you are doing something because you start it more quickly than other people: *We* **had** *a racing start* **over** *our competitors.* • [PIC]> **Bicycles, Vehicles** (T)

race [PEOPLE] /reɪs/ *n* a group, esp. of people, with particular similar physical characteristics, who are considered as belonging to the same type, or the fact of belonging to a particular such group • **Members** *of several races live together in Britain today.* [C] • *Discrimination on grounds of race should not be allowed.* [U] • *An increasing number of people in the country are of* **mixed** *race* (= with parents of different races). [U] • Race is sometimes used to mean a group of people who share the same language, history, characteristics, etc.: *The British are an island race.* [C] ○ *The French race is/are sometimes said to have a strong interest in food.* [C + sing/pl v] ○ *Dick said that his army captain seemed to want to turn the soldiers into a race* **of** *super-beings.* [C] • *(specialized)* Race can also mean a group of animals or plants which have special characteristics that make them different from other animals or plants which are otherwise of the same type: *They are trying to breed crops which are resistant to different races* **of** *pest.* [C] • **Race relations** are the relationship between the members of different races: *These measures are being taken in an attempt to improve race relations in the area.* ○ *She is employed as a race relations officer.* • [LP]> **Nations and nationalities** (CS) (PL) (RUS)

ra·cial /ˈreɪ·ʃəl/ *adj* [not gradable] • Racial means connected with a person's race: *a racial tradition* ○ *They are members of a minority racial group/a racial minority.* • Racial also means involving the members of different races: *He had a vision of a society in which the members of different races could live together in racial harmony.* ○ *There is a lot of racial tension/unrest/violence in the area.* ○ *Mahatma Gandhi, the political leader, led protests against racial* **discrimination** *in South Africa in the early 20th century.* ○ *A lot of racial* **prejudice** *still exists.* ○ *Police think that the attack was racial* (= caused by a dislike of people from other races).

ra·cial·ly /ˈreɪ·ʃəl·i/ *adv* [not gradable] • *a racially mixed child* • *The number of racially* **motivated** *attacks/assaults on Asians and Afro-Caribbeans in this country has increased dramatically in the last decade.*

race *(obj)* [HURRY] /reɪs/ *v* [always + adv/prep] to move or go fast • *The boys raced/came racing* **across** *the playground.* [I] • *He shouted "Hurry up" and then raced* **on/off/away**. [I] • *She raced* **for** *the bus.* [I] • *The ambulance raced* (= quickly took) *the injured* **to** *a nearby hospital.* [T] • *The summer seems to have raced* **by** (= passed very quickly). [I] • *I need to get my car's engine fixed – it's racing* (= working faster than it should) *all the time.* [I] • *He raced the car engine* (= made it work faster than it needed to) *as he sat waiting impatiently.* [T] • [LP]> **Driving** (CS) (PL) (RUS)

race·course *esp. Br and Aus* /£'reɪs·kɔːs, $-kɔːrs/, *esp. Am* **race·track** *n* [C] a wide, usually circular, path with a grass surface, on which horses race, or the whole area in which this path is situated, including buildings

race·horse /£'reɪs·hɔːs, $-hɔːrs/ *n* [C] a horse bred and trained for racing

race·track /'reɪs·træk/ *n* [C] a usually circular path or road, usually with a hard surface and often divided into LANES (=marked strips), on which competitors, esp. runners, cars or bicycles, race, or the whole area in which this path is situated, including buildings • *The racetrack has been freshly marked out in white paint.* • *We met at the racetrack.* • Racetrack is also *esp. Am for* RACECOURSE.

ra·ci·ly /'reɪ·sɪ·li/ *adv* See at RACY

ra·ci·ness /'reɪ·sɪ·nəs/ *n* [U] See at RACY

ra·ci·sm /'reɪ·sɪ·zᵊm/, *Br dated* **ra·cial·i·sm** /'reɪ·ʃᵊl·ɪ·zᵊm/ *n* [U] *disapproving* the belief that people's qualities are influenced by their race and that the members of other races are not as good as the members of your own, which results in the other races being treated unfairly • *We hope to counter racism and prejudice with information and education.* • *The authorities are taking steps to combat/fight/tackle racism in schools.* • *She said that she had encountered* **overt** *racism when she was trying to get a job.* • *The report made it plain that* **institutionalized** *racism is deep-rooted in the country and that immigrants face discrimination in education, training, and employment.* • *He said that racialism is* **endemic** *in the rural areas of the country.*

ra·cist /'reɪ·sɪst/, *Br dated* **ra·cial·ist** /'reɪ·ʃᵊl·ɪst/ *n* [C] *disapproving* • A racist is someone who believes that other races are not as good as their own and therefore treats them unfairly: *He is a racist who refuses to employ blacks.*

ra·cist /'reɪ·sɪst/ *adj* • *His views on the immigration question can only be described as racist.* • *They were the victims of a vicious racist attack.*

rack [FRAME] /ræk/ *n* [C] a frame or shelf, often formed of bars, which is used to hold things • *a wire rack* • *a vegetable rack* • *a magazine rack* • *a plate rack* • *a soap rack* • *a car roof rack* • *a luggage rack* • *racks of children's clothing* • *Electronic books take up less space and one rack of discs replaces a roomful of paper books.* • [PIC> **Rack**

rack *obj* [CAUSE PAIN] /ræk/ *v* [T] to cause physical or mental pain, or trouble, to • *Even at the end, when cancer racked his body, he was calm and cheerful.* • *The dog was already racked* **by/with** *the pains of old age.* • *He was racked* **by/with** *doubts/guilt.* • *A similar sort of scandal racked the government some years ago.* • *They hope the plan will curb the violence that has racked the region this year.* • *The firm, which has been racked* **by** *resignations, is losing five more partners.* • *The city still has crumbling, rat-infested apartments, and housing estates racked* **by/with** *heroin.* • To **rack** your **brains** is to think very hard: *I've racked my brains all day but I still can't remember her name.*

rack /ræk/ *n* [C usually sing] • In the past, **the** rack was a device to which people were tied and which stretched their bodies by pulling their arms in one direction and their legs in the other direction, usually used as a way of getting information from them. • If you are **on the rack**, you are suffering great physical or mental pain: *A couple of years ago he was on the rack, following accusations of fraud and corruption.*

–racked /-rækt/ *combining form* • *a pain-racked gesture* • *a guilt-racked society*

rack·ing /'ræk·ɪŋ/ *adj* • *a racking* (=very painful) *headache/toothache*

rack [MACHINE] /ræk/ *n* [C] a bar with tooth-like parts along one edge which fits into a PINION (= a wheel with tooth-like parts), allowing change between circular and straight-line movement

rack [DECAY], *esp. Am and Aus* **wrack** /ræk/ *n* [U] **rack and ruin** a bad state; decay • *The whole farm was* **going to** *rack and ruin without Clive around to keep the hedges in trim and the buildings repaired.* • *The recession has meant rack and ruin for many small businesses.*

rack up *obj*, **rack** *obj* **up** *v adv* [M] *esp. Am infml* to gradually increase in number or amount; to ACCUMULATE • *Astronomical* **losses** *were racked up by airlines during this period.* • *Still greater* **sales** *are racked up by putting the designer's name on accessories such as perfume and glasses.* • *The show has racked up 450 performances and been seen by about three million fans in the US, Europe and South America.*

rack·et [SPORT], **rac·quet** /'ræk·ɪt/ *n* [C] an object consisting of a net fixed tightly to an oval frame with a long handle, used in various sports for hitting a ball • *a tennis/squash/badminton racket* • [PIC> **Sports**

rack·et [NOISE] /'ræk·ɪt/ *n* [U] *infml* an unpleasant loud continuous noise • *There was such* **a** *racket going on outside that I couldn't get to sleep.* • *What* **a** *racket these pop groups* **make!** • *Stop that racket!* • *I couldn't hear him over the racket* **of** *the engine.*

rack·et [CRIME] /'ræk·ɪt/ *n* [C] *infml* a dishonest or illegal activity that makes money • *They're involved in a drug-***smuggling** *racket.* • *He was caught* **running** *a* **prostitution** *racket in London.* • *They claimed that the business was the victim of a* **protection** *racket* (= was being forced to pay money to a criminal in order to prevent them being damaged by that criminal). • *Telephone chat lines are* **a bit of a** *racket*/**a real** *racket* (= are considered dishonest although they are not illegal).

rack·et·eer /£ˌræk·ə'tɪəʳ, $-'tɪr/ *n* [C] *disapproving* • *There are reports that babies in the country are being sold to foreigners by racketeers.* • *Racketeers are threatening violence to store owners who refuse to pay them money.*

rack·et·eer·ing /£ˌræk·ə'tɪə·rɪŋ, $-'tɪr·ɪŋ/ *n* [U] *disapproving* • *The men were charged with racketeering, and face stiff prison sentences if they are found guilty.*

rac·on·teur /£ˌræk·ɒn'tɜːʳ, $-ɑːn'tɜːr/ *n* [C] someone who tells amusing or interesting stories • *He knew many jokes and was an excellent/witty/brilliant raconteur.*

ra·coon /ræk'uːn/ *n* [C] a RACCOON

ra·cy /'reɪ·si/ *adj* **-ier**, **-iest** (of speech or writing) exciting, esp. because of being about sex, or (of someone or something) having an exciting, interesting and attractive appearance, sometimes in a sexual way • *a racy story* • *a racy style* • *a racy advertisement* • *racy swimwear* • *She is trying to create a racier image for herself.*

ra·ci·ly /'reɪ·sɪ·li/ *adv*

ra·ci·ness /'reɪ·sɪ·nəs/ *n* [U]

ra·dar /£'reɪ·dɑːʳ, $-dɑːr/ *n* [U] a system which uses radio waves to find the position of objects which cannot be seen • *Even small ships now have radar.* • *The new fighter plane is designed to be invisible to radar.* • *Radar satellites are used to track targets through clouds and at night.* • *Other vessels in the area show up on the ship's radar* **(screen).** • *Bats have a radar* **system** *which allows them to locate and catch small insects.* • A **radar trap** is a system, using radar, which the police use to catch vehicles that are travelling too fast: *We were caught in a radar trap as we drove home.*

ra·di·al (tyre) /'reɪ·di·əl/ *n* [C] a tyre which has cords inside the rubber that go across the edge of the wheel at an angle of 90° rather than along it • *Radials/Radial tyres can help give a car better control.*

ra·di·ant /'reɪ·di·ənt/ *adj* obviously very happy, or very beautiful • *He gave a radiant* **smile** *when he heard the news.* • *The bride looked radiant, as brides are supposed to do.* • *You were at your most radiant that evening.* • *The dancers gave a radiant* (= beautiful) *performance.* • *It was a radiant* (= beautiful) *autumn day.* • See also **radiant** at RADIATE [PRODUCE HEAT/LIGHT].

ra·di·ance /'reɪ·di·ənts/ *n* [U] • *He was struck by the radiance of her smile.*

ra·di·ate *(obj)* [PRODUCE HEAT/LIGHT] /'reɪ·di·eɪt/ *v* to produce (heat and/or light), or (of heat or light) to be produced • *The planet Jupiter has an internal source of heat, and radiates twice as much heat from inside as it receives from the Sun.* [T] • *The engine was so hot that we could feel the heat radiating.* [I] • *A single beam of light radiated* **from** *the lighthouse.* [I]

ra·di·ant /'reɪ·di·ənt/ *adj* [before n] • *a radiant heater* • *the radiant heat of the sun* • *Plants absorb radiant energy from sunlight.* • See also RADIANT.

ra·di·ance /'reɪ·di·ənts/ *n* [U] • *We basked in the radiance of the African sun.*

ra·di·ate *(obj)* [EXPRESS] /'reɪ·di·eɪt/ *v* to show that you are feeling or have (a particular emotion or quality), or (of an emotion or quality) to be expressed or possessed (by someone) • *He was radiating joy and happiness.* [T] • *She always radiates such energy and enthusiasm.* [T] • *Bad vibes were radiating* **from** *him.* [I]

ra·di·ate [SPREAD] /'reɪ·di·eɪt/ *v* [I always + adv/prep] to spread out in all directions (from a central point) • *The Romans built a network of over 80 000 km of usually straight roads radiating* **(out) from** *ancient Rome.* • *Flows of lava radiated* **from** *the volcano's crater.* • *Just before the*

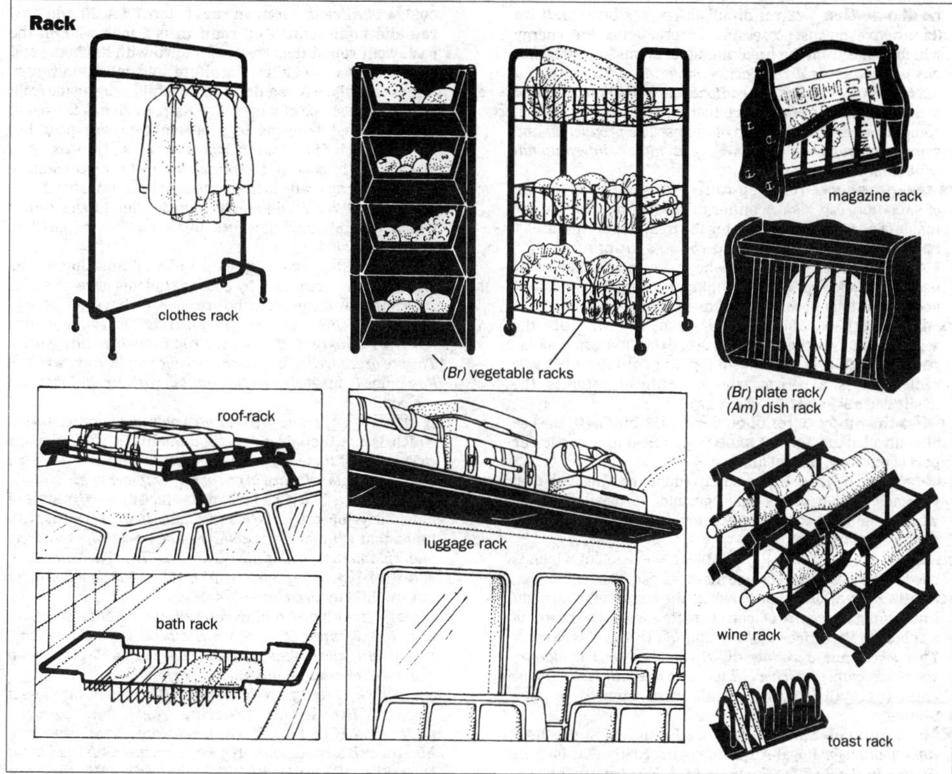

breeding season, these birds radiate outwards to warmer climates.

ra·di·al /ˈreɪ·di·əl/ *adj* [not gradable] • *a radial road system* (= one spreading out from a central point)

ra·di·al·ly /ˈreɪ·di·əl·i/ *adv* [not gradable]

ra·di·a·tion /ˌreɪ·diˈeɪ·ʃən/ *n* [U] heat, light, or **elementary particles** (= the most simple parts of matter) produced by an object • *microwave/ultraviolet/electromagnetic radiation* • *With nuclear power, there is always the fear that there will be an escape of* **harmful** *radiation.* • *Many servicemen suffered radiation* **sickness** *after being present without protection at the early atomic tests.*

ra·di·a·tor /£ˈreɪ·di·eɪ·təʳ, $-t̬ɚ/ *n* [C] a device, usually a container filled with water, that sends out heat, often as part of a cooling or heating system • *When we installed the central heating, we put a radiator in every room.* • *My car engine overheated because the water had leaked out of the radiator.*

rad·i·cal SUPPORTING CHANGE /ˈræd·ɪ·kəl/ *adj* believing or expressing the belief that there should be great or extreme social or political change • *He was known as a radical reformer/thinker/politician.* • *These people have very radical views.* • *She works for a radical newspaper/bookshop.* • *These proposals have been strongly opposed by the radical right.*

rad·i·cal /ˈræd·ɪ·kəl/ *n* [C] • *She was a radical* (= a person who supports great social and political change) *all her life.*

rad·i·cal·i·sm /ˈræd·ɪ·kəl·ɪ·zəm/ *n* [U] • *The high prices of the 1790s threatened the standard of living of the rural poor and gave rise to radicalism.* • *The protests of these students is nothing like the militant left-wing* **political** *radicalism of students in the 1960s.*

rad·i·cal EXTREMELY IMPORTANT /ˈræd·ɪ·kəl/ *adj* relating to the most important parts of something or someone; complete or extreme • *He made a radical mistake when he changed his job.* • *We need to take a radical look at our operating procedures.* • *The* **changes/reforms** *you're suggesting are rather radical, aren't they?* • *There is a radical* **restructuring** *of the company going on.* • *She has had to undergo radical* **surgery** (= that aimed at removing the cause of a disease).

rad·i·cal·ly /ˈræd·ɪ·kli/ *adv* • *Barker introduced no radically new ideas but encouraged some of the younger people to make suggestions for change.* • *Her views are not radically different from my own.* • *The industry has* **altered/changed** *radically as a result of the increased use of electronic systems.*

rad·i·i /ˈreɪ·di·aɪ/ *pl of* RADIUS

ra·di·o /£ˈreɪ·di·əʊ, $-oʊ/ *n pl* **radios** a device for receiving, and sometimes broadcasting, sound messages that travel in the form of **electromagnetic** waves, or the receiving or sending of sound messages in this way • *a portable radio* [C] • *Could you* **turn/switch** *the radio* **on/off**, *please.* [C] • *I heard a good programme* **on the** *radio last night.* [U] • *They were able to send a message back to shore* **over** *the ship's radio.* [C] • *We received the message* **by** *radio.* [U] • *The children had radio-***controlled** *cars* (= toy cars which move when they receive **electromagnetic** waves) *as birthday presents.* • Radio can be used to refer to the work of broadcasting sound programmes for the public to listen to: *She's got some kind of job in radio.* [U] • Radio can also be used to refer to the sound programmes broadcast by **electromagnetic** waves: I don't listen to radio much. [U] ○ *Many local businesses advertise on* **local** *radio.* [U] ○ *Which radio* **station** *do you mostly listen to?* ○ *We heard the news on a radio* **broadcast/programme.** • A **radio alarm (clock)** (also **clock radio**) is a radio which can be switched on by a clock at a particular time, usually to wake someone up. • A **radio telescope** is a device for receiving, for scientific study, the **electromagnetic** waves sent out by objects in space. • PIC> **Clocks and watches, Emergency services** Ⓕ

ra·di·o *(obj)* /£ˈreɪ·di·əʊ, $-oʊ/ *v* **radioing**, *past* **radioed** • *We'll have to radio* (= send a message by using **electromagnetic** waves) *for more supplies.* [I] • *They radioed* **(to)** *their base for help.* [T; I + prep] • *Can we radio* (= send a message by using electrical waves to) *the shore from here?* [T]

ra·di·o·ac·ti·vi·ty /£ˌreɪ·di·əʊ·ækˈtɪv·ɪ·ti, $-oʊ·ækˈtɪv·ə·t̬i/ *n* [U] the quality that some atoms have of producing energy, which may be harmful even in very small amounts • *Becquerel was one of the first scientists to study radioactivity.* • Radioactivity is also used to refer to the energy produced by atoms: *A spokesperson said that there was no danger of a* **leak/escape** *of radioactivity from the nuclear power station.* ○ *There is concern about the amount of radioactivity being* **released** *into the environment.*

ra·di·o·ac·tive /£ˌreɪ·di·əʊ'æk·tɪv, $-oʊ-/ *adj* • Radioactive means possessing or producing the energy which comes from the breaking up of atoms: *a radioactive gas ○ Uranium is a radioactive material. ○ The core of a nuclear reactor is highly radioactive.* • Radioactive also means resulting from the production of the energy which comes from the breaking up of atoms: *The production and storage of radioactive* **waste** *is a major international environmental issue.*

ra·di·o·graph·y /£ˌreɪ·di'ɒg·rə·fi, $-'ɑː·grə-/ *n* [U] the use of RADIATION, esp. X-RAYS, either to produce a picture of the inside of people or objects, or for the treatment of disease

ra·di·o·graph·er /£ˌreɪ·di'ɒg·rə·fəʳ, $-'ɑː·grə·fɚ/ *n* [C] • A radiographer is a person who operates a machine that uses RADIATION, esp. X-RAYS, to take pictures of the inside of people or things, or for the treatment of disease.

ra·di·ol·o·gy /£ˌreɪ·di'ɒl·ə·dʒi, $-'ɑː·lə-/ *n* [U] the scientific study of the medical use of RADIATION, esp. X-RAYS

ra·di·ol·o·gist /£ˌreɪ·di'ɒl·ə·dʒɪst, $-'ɑː·lə-/ *n* [C] • A radiologist is a person who scientifically studies the medical use of RADIATION, esp. X-RAYS.

ra·di·o·ther·a·py /£ˌreɪ·di·əʊ'θer·ə·pi, $-oʊ-/ *n* [U] the use of controlled amounts of RADIATION, aimed at a particular part of the body, to treat disease

rad·ish /'ræd·ɪʃ/ *n* [C] a small round or finger-shaped vegetable which grows underground, is usually red or white in colour, and is usually eaten raw, esp. in SALADS • PIC **Vegetables** (1)

ra·di·um /'reɪ·di·əm/ *n* [U] a RADIOACTIVE element which is used in the treatment of some diseases, esp. CANCER

ra·di·us /'reɪ·di·əs/ *n* [C] *pl* **radii** (the length of) a straight line joining the centre of a circle to its edge or the centre of a sphere to its surface • *The radius of this wheel is 30 cm.* • *This wheel* **has** *a* **radius of** *30 cm.* • *(fig.) The station, shopping centre and school lie within a one-mile radius of the house* (= are all less than a mile away from it). • PIC **Shapes**

RAF /£ˌɑː·reɪ'ef, $ˌɑːr·eɪ-, ræf/ *n* [U + sing/pl v] **the RAF** *abbreviation for* Royal Air Force (= the British air force) • *He was in the RAF for thirty years.* • See also **air force** at AIR [AREA].

Raf·fer·ty's rules /£'ræf·ə·tiz, $-ɚ·t̬iz/ *pl n Aus slang* (esp. used when referring to a competition or an organization which is not well organized) no rules

raf·fi·a, *Br also* **raf·i·a** /'ræf·i·ə/ *n* [U] long narrow pieces of pale yellow, dried leaf, esp. from a type of PALM tree, used as string or for making hats, containers, etc.

raf·fish /'ræf·ɪʃ/ *adj* not following usual social standards of behaviour or appearance, esp. in a careless way • *He has a certain raffish elegance.* • *She seems to have had a raffish past.* • *They live in a rather raffish part of town.*

raf·fish·ness /'ræf·ɪʃ·nəs/ *n* [U]

raf·fle /'ræf·l̩/ *n* [C] an activity in which people buy numbered tickets, some of which are later chosen to win prizes, which is arranged in order to make money for a good social purpose • *I have never won anything* **in a raffle**. • *The raffle* **prizes** *include a bottle of wine and a basket of fruit.* • *I sell raffle* **tickets** *for several charities every year.*

raf·fle *obj* /'ræf·l̩/ *v* [T] • *We are going to raffle* **(off)** *a car* (= offer it as a prize in a raffle) *for the hospital appeal.* [T/M] • See also DRAW [CHOOSE].

raft [FLOATING STRUCTURE] /£rɑːft, $ræft/ *n* [C] a flat floating structure for travelling across water, often made of pieces of wood tied roughly together and moved along with a PADDLE (= pole with a flat end), or used as a place on which swimmers can land • *We lashed together anything that would float to make a raft.* • *We swam out to the raft and lay there sunbathing for a while, before diving back into the sea and returning to the shore.* • A raft is also a small rubber or plastic boat that can be filled with air: *a rubber raft ○ an inflatable raft*

raft *(obj)* /£rɑːft, $ræft/ *v* • *They rafted* (= transported on a raft) *their supplies down the river.* [T] • *We rafted* (= travelled on a raft) *through the rapids.* [I] • *Have you ever been* **white water** *rafting?* [I]

raft [MANY] /£rɑːft, $ræft/ *n* [C always + *of*] *esp. Am* a large number or range; a lot • *I've got a raft* **of** *papers to read for the meeting tomorrow.* • *The band has recorded rafts* **of** *albums.* • *We have designed* **a whole** *raft* **of measures** *to improve the transport system.*

raft·er /£'rɑːf·təʳ, $'ræf·tɚ/ *n* [C] any of the large specially shaped pieces of esp. wood which support a roof

rag [CLOTH] /ræg/ *n* [C] a torn piece of old cloth • *I keep these rags for cleaning the car.* • Rag is also *Am for* **duster**. See at DUST. • *Their clothes were* **in rags** (= torn). • A *(Br and Aus)* **rag and bone man**/*(Am)* **ragman** is a man who, in the past, went round the streets of a town with his horse and cart to buy old clothes, furniture and other unwanted things cheaply. • A **rag doll** is a soft child's toy, made from cloth, in the shape of a person. • **Rags-to riches** is used to describe what happens to a person who was poor but becomes rich: *She told a rag-to-riches story of a child brought up in poverty becoming owner of a hotel chain.* • *(infml)* The **rag trade** is the clothes-making industry.

rag *obj* [JOKE] /ræg/ *v* [T] **-gg-** *dated infml* to say things which are amusing but a little unkind • *They ragged him* **about** *his girlfriend.*

rag [AMUSEMENTS] /ræg/ *n* [C] a series of amusing events and activities organized by college students once a year to collect money for people who are poor, ill, have nowhere to live, etc. • *This year's rag is collecting money for famine relief.* • *I've agreed to be on the rag committee this year.* • *They've organized a fancy dress parade for rag* **day/week**. • *Rag* **mags** (= magazines) *often contain rather rude jokes and cartoons.*

rag [NEWSPAPER] /ræg/ *n* [C] *infml* a newspaper or magazine which is not thought to be good quality • *The combined circulation of these rags is more than 20 million a week.* • *I read about this software in one of the computer rags.*

rag [MUSIC] /ræg/ *n* [C] a piece of RAGTIME music (= a style of music developed by black musicians in N America with tunes that are not on regular beats) • *Scott Joplin wrote many piano rags, including his famous 'The Entertainer'.*

rag·a·muf·fin /'ræg·əˌmʌf·ɪn/ *n* [C] *infml dated* a dirty untidy child in torn clothes

rag·bag /'ræg·bæg/ *n* [C usually sing] a confused mixture of different types of things • *His book is just a ragbag, without any clear ideas or conclusions in it.* • *He produced* **a** *ragbag* **of** *excuses for missing my party.*

rage [ANGER] /reɪdʒ/ *n* (a period of) extreme or violent anger • *Her sudden* **towering** *rages were hard to understand.* [C] • *I was frightened because I had never seen him* **in** *such* **a rage** *before.* [C] • *She reacted with rage to his suggestion.* [U] • *(dated) This hairstyle is* **(all) the rage** (= very popular at the moment).

rage /reɪdʒ/ *v* [I always + adv/prep] • *He raged* **at** (= spoke angrily to) *us for forgetting to order a replacement.* • To rage is also to happen in strong or violent way: *The storm raged* **outside**/*raged* **around** *us.* ○ *A flu epidemic is raging* **in/through** *local schools.* ○ *The argument rages* **on** (= continues strongly).

rag·ing /'reɪ·dʒɪŋ/ *adj* [not gradable] • Raging means very severe or extreme: *a raging toothache ○ a raging thirst ○ a raging bore ○ He's got a raging* (= high) **temperature**. • Raging also means very strong or violent: *a raging temper ○ The rains had turned the stream into a raging* **torrent**. ○ *We got caught in a raging storm.*

rage [EVENT] /reɪdʒ/ *n* [C usually sing] *Aus infml* an exciting or entertaining event involving a lot of activity • *The party was a rage.*

rag·ga /'ræg·ə/ *n* [U] a type of music which combines elements of REGGAE, RAP [MUSIC] and dance-club music, mostly played by Afro-Caribbean people • *As with punk and grunge, ragga is associated with a particular set of styles, fashions and attitudes.*

ragg·ed /'ræg·ɪd/ *adj* not in good condition; torn or uneven • *The children were wearing dirty ragged clothes.* • *The bottoms of the legs of my jeans are rather ragged.* • *Two ragged* (= untidy and dirty and wearing old torn clothes) *children stood outside the station begging for money.* • *Rats had gnawed ragged* (= uneven) *holes in the rug.* • *This part of the coastline is rather ragged* (= uneven). • *The leaves of this plant have ragged* (= uneven) **edges**. • *The patient's* **breathing** *was ragged* (= not regular) *and uneven.* • *A ragged* (= not organized) *line of people were waiting at the bus stop.* • Ragged can also mean not performing well, because of not being organized: *The team were rather ragged in the first half of the match, but improved in the second half.* ○ *The acting was good, but the play itself was somewhat ragged.*

ragg·ed·ly /'ræg·ɪd·li/ *adv*

ragg·ed·ness /'ræg·ɪd·nəs/ *n* [U]

rag·lan /'ræg·lən/ *adj* [not gradable] (being or having a sleeve) not having a join at the shoulder; being sewn to the body in two straight lines from the neck to a point under the arm • *a sweater with raglan sleeves* • *a raglan sweater*

rag·out /ræg'uː/ *n* a dish consisting of small pieces of meat or fish and vegetables cooked together • *I've made a ragout* of *veal for dinner.* [C] • *Would you like some more ragout?* [U]

rag·time /ˈræg·taɪm/ *n* [C] a type of popular music, developed by black musicians in N America in the early 1900s, with tunes that are not on regular beats

raid /reɪd/ *n* [C] a sudden unexpected attack, usually by a small group of people • *The commandos* **made** *a daring raid* **(on** *the enemy).* • *The air force has* **carried out** *a low-level* **bombing** *raid.* • *Two robbers* **staged** *a* **dawn** *raid* **on** (= an act of stealing from) *a restaurant in Western Street, tied up a security guard and escaped with about 30 bottles of brandy and wine.* • *Millions of dollars were stolen in a* **bank** *raid* (= an act of stealing from a bank) *last night.* • *The drugs were found during a raid by the police/a* **police** *raid* (= a sudden entering of a building by the police, esp. when they are looking for criminals or illegal activities). • *(fig.) I'm going to have to* **make** *a raid* **on** (= take money from) *my savings to pay for the repairs to my car.*

raid *(obj)* /reɪd/ *v* • *The soldiers raided* (= attacked) *the enemy camp.* [T] • *The post office was raided* (= people entered it illegally and stole things) *late at night.* [T] • *During the riots people were looting and raiding* (= entering places illegally). [I] • *Police officers from the organized crime branch have raided* (= entered in order to look for criminals or illegal activity) *solicitors' offices in central London.* [T] • *(fig.) The boys raided* (= took food from) *the* **larder/fridge**. [T] • *(fig.) The children raided* (= took money from) *their mother's purse to get money to buy sweets.* [T]

raid·er /£ˈreɪ·dəʳ, $-dɚ/ *n* [C] • *"Raiders of the Lost Ark"* (title of a film starring Harrison Ford as Indiana Jones, 1981)

rail TRAINS /reɪl/ *n* the system of transport which uses trains, or one of the two metal bars fixed to the ground on which trains travel • *Rail competes with road, and to some extent with air, for passenger and freight transport within Britain.* [U] • *Environmentalists argue that more goods should be transported* **by rail**. [U] • *Rail* **passengers** *are complaining about the recent increase in rail* **fares**. • *The country has an excellent rail* **system/network**/*excellent rail* **links**. • *Do not cross the rails.* [C] • *A train left/went off the rails and crashed into the bank, killing several passengers.* [C] • To **go off the rails** is to behave in a way that is not generally acceptable, esp. dishonestly or illegally. • PIC〉 **Rail**

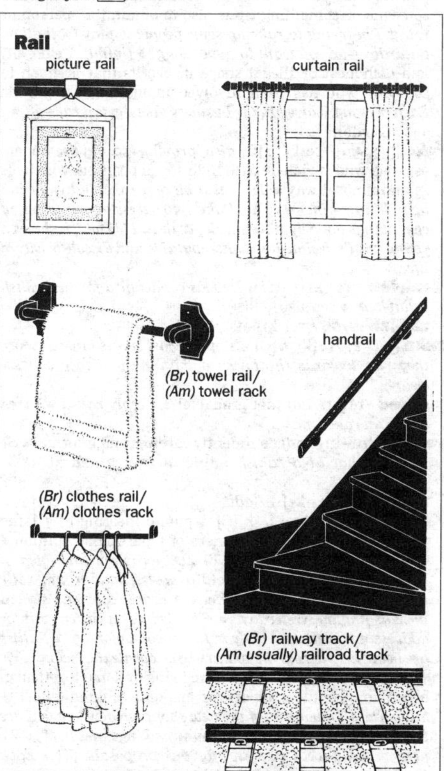

rail ROD /reɪl/ *n* [C] a straight bar or rod fixed in position, esp. to a wall or to vertical posts, used to enclose something, as a support, or to hang things on • *Will spectators please stay behind the rail.* • *Gitano placed his hand on the top rail of the fence.* • *Hold onto the rail so that you don't fall.* • *They were leaning on the deck rail.* • *The* **(clothes)** *rail in her wardrobe was crammed full of dresses.* • *He folded the towels neatly and hung them on the* **towel** *rail (Am* **rack**) • *A portrait of her great-grandmother hung from the* **picture** *rail.* • PIC〉 **Bathroom**

rail *obj* ENCLOSE /reɪl/ *v* [T always + adv/prep] to enclose (something), esp. using RAILINGS • *Part of the playing field had been railed* **off** *for use as a car park.*

rail COMPLAIN /reɪl/ *v* [always + prep] *fml* to complain angrily • *He railed* **against/at** *the injustices of the system.*

rail·card /£ˈreɪl·kɑːd, $-kɑːrd/ *n* [C] (in Britain) a card which you can buy and then use to buy train tickets more cheaply • *a young person's railcard* • *a family railcard*

rail·ing /ˈreɪ·lɪŋ/ *n* [C usually pl] a vertical, usually metal or wooden post, which is used together with other such posts to form a fence • *The park is surrounded by iron railings.* • *Tourists pressed their faces against the palace railings.* • *I chained my bike to a railing.*

rail·ler·y /£ˈreɪ·lᵊr·i, $-lɚ·i/ *n* [U] *fml* joking or laughing at someone in a friendly way; TEASING

rail·road *obj* FORCE /£ˈreɪl·rəʊd, $-roʊd/ *v* [T always + adv/prep] to force something to happen or force someone to do something, esp. quickly or unfairly • *He railroaded the proposed change* **through** *the staff meeting.* • *We were railroaded* **into** *signing the agreement.*

rail·road TRAIN /£ˈreɪl·rəʊd, $-roʊd/ (*abbreviation* **RR**) *n* [C] *Am for* RAILWAY

rail·way /ˈreɪl·weɪ/, *Am usually* **rail·road** *n* [C] a metal track on which trains run, or the whole system of such tracks, stations and trains • *Be careful when you cross the railway.* • *I cross the railway bridge every day on my way to school.* • *We live close to the railway* **(line)**. • *Repairs are being carried out on the railway* **(line)** (= the route of the track) *between Birmingham and Newcastle this weekend.* • *She travelled on the Trans-Siberian/trans-continental railway* (= route). • *He worked* **on the railway(s)**/*was a railway worker* (= worked for the system of transport using trains) *for forty years.* • *I'll meet you at the railway* **station**. • *Have you got a railway* **timetable** *I could borrow?* • *There were several trains in the railway* **sidings**. • PIC〉 **Line, Rail**

rai·ment /ˈreɪ·mənt/ *n* [U] *old use* clothes

rain /reɪn/ *n, v* (to fall as) drops of water from clouds • *Rain is forecast for tomorrow.* [U] • *Come inside out of* **the** *rain.* [U] • *We had* **heavy/light** *rain all day.* [U] • *The barbecue was ruined by a* **downpour of** (= a lot of) *rain.* [U] • *We got caught in* **pouring/torrential** (= a lot of) *rain without either raincoats or umbrellas.* [U] • *There will be* **showers of** *rain/rain* **showers** (= short periods of rain) *in the east.* [U] • *Rain* **fell (heavily)** *all night.* [U] • **It looks like** *rain* (= as if rain is going to fall). [U] • *I think* **it's** *starting to rain.* [I] • **It**'*s raining* **hard** (= a large amount of rain is falling). [I] • *The tennis match was rained (Br)* **off**/*(Am)* **out** (= was stopped because of rain). [T] • *(Br) The organizers rained the match* **off** (= stopped it because of rain). [M] • Rain can also mean fall in a large amount: *Debris from the explosion rained* **down** *the slope.* [I] ○ *Streamers and balloons rained* **down on** *the party guests.* [I] ○ **Bombs/Shells** *rained* **down on** *the city.* ○ *(fig.) The children rained* **(down)** *questions* **on** *their teacher* (= asked a lot of them). [T/M] ○ *(fig.) Her attacker rained blows* **(down) on** *her* (= hit her repeatedly). [T/M] • **Come rain or shine** means whatever happens: *Come rain or shine, I'll see you on Thursday.* • *(Am and Aus infml)* To **take a rain check (on** something) is to do something later: *I won't have that coffee just now, but can I take a rain check on it?* • A **rain forest** is a forest in a tropical area which receives a lot of rain: *Cutting down* **tropical** *rain forests is altering the earth's climate.* ○ *Large areas of rain forest are being destroyed.* • A **rain gauge** is a device for measuring how much rain falls. • **Rain water** is water than has fallen as rain, rather than water which has come from a TAP: *I collect rain water to water my plants.* • *(saying)* 'It never rains but it pours' means that when something bad happens it is always something very bad. • *"The rain in Spain stays mainly on the plain"* (song from the musical *My Fair Lady*, 1956)

rains /reɪnz/ *pl n* • **The rains** are the season of the year in tropical countries when there is a lot of rain: *Villagers are now waiting for the rains to* **come** *so that the rice will* *grow.* ○ *This is the third year in a row that the rains have failed.*

rain·y /ˈreɪ·ni/ *adj* **-ier, -iest** • *We had three rainy days on holiday, but otherwise it was sunny.* • *She had saved/kept some money for* **a rainy day** (= a time when money might unexpectedly be needed).

rain·bow [ARCH] /£ˈreɪm·bəʊ, $ˈreɪn·boʊ/ *n* [C] a many-coloured arch seen in the sky when rain is falling and the sun is shining • *The tropical butterfly's beautiful wings were shimmering with* **all colours of the** *rainbow.* • *"Somewhere over the Rainbow"* (from the song *Over the Rainbow* sung by Judy Garland in the film *The Wizard of Oz*, 1939) • *"My heart leaps up when I behold / A rainbow in the sky"* (William Wordsworth in the poem *My Heart Leaps Up*, 1807)

rain·bow [GIRL] /£ˈreɪm·bəʊ, $ˈreɪn·boʊ/ *n* [C] a girl aged between 5 and 7 years old who is a member of the international youth organization for young women called the Guides

rain·coat /£ˈreɪŋ·kəʊt, $ˈreɪn·koʊt/ *n* [C] a waterproof coat worn for protection against rain • *He took a* **plastic** *raincoat with him in case it rained.* • If someone refers to people, esp. men, in **dirty** raincoats, they can mean people who have an unpleasant interest in sex, often in a secretive way.

rain·drop /£ˈreɪn·drɒp, $-drɑːp/ *n* [C] a single drop of rain • *"Raindrops Keep Falling on my Head"* (title of a song written by Hal David, 1969)

rain·fall /£ˈreɪn·fɔːl, $-fɑːl/ *n* [U] rain, or the amount of rain that falls • *Heavy rainfall ruined the match.* • *The average annual rainfall in this region: 750 mm.*

rain·storm /£ˈreɪn·stɔːm, $-stɔːrm/ *n* [C] a weather condition with strong wind and heavy rain

rain·y /ˈreɪ·ni/ *adj* See at RAIN

raise [LIFT] /reɪz/ *v* [T] to cause (something) to rise or become bigger or better • *He raised the window and leaned out.* • *Mary Quant was the first fashion designer to raise hemlines.* • *The teacher raised her hand to tell the children to be quiet.* • *Never* **raise** *your* **hand to/against** (= hit) *a child.* • *He raised his* **eyebrows** (= lifted them in order to express surprise) *when I told him what had happened.* • *Her behaviour* **raised** *(a few)* **eyebrows** (= caused surprise or shock). • *I had to raise my* **voice** (= speak more loudly) *in order to make myself heard over the noise in the classroom.* • *She raised her***self to** *her full height* (= stood in such a way as to make herself as tall as possible). • *I was delighted when my salary was raised* (= increased). • *The president has said that there are no plans to raise* (= increase) **taxes.** • *The campaign is designed to raise* (= increase) *public* **awareness** *of the issue.* • *The report says that* **standards** *at the school need to be raised* (= improved). • *Our little chat has really raised my* **spirits** (= made me feel happier/braver). • *(humorous) I think it's time we raised* **the tone (of these proceedings)** (= became more serious/polite). • A person who is raised **from the dead** is made alive again or *(infml)* shows new activity in some way. • If you raise another player in a game of cards, you risk more money than that player has done: *I'll raise you.* • *I'll raise you $50.* [+ two objects] • One number raised **to the power of** another number is the first number multiplied by itself the amount of times of the second number: *Ten to the power of six* (= ten multiplied by itself six times) *is one million.* • To **raise the roof/raise hell** is to be very angry: *My mother really raised the roof* **with** *me when I came home late.* • To **raise the roof** is also to make a lot of noise.

raise *obj* [EXIST] /reɪz/ *v* [T] to cause to exist • *Her answers raised* **doubts/fears/suspicions** *in my mind.* • *This discussion has raised many important* **issues/problems.** • *The announcement raised a* **cheer/laugh/murmur.** • *I want to raise* (= talk about) *two problems/questions* **with** *you.* • *I want to start my own business if I can raise* (= obtain) *the* **money/cash/capital.** • *This year we are raising* **funds** (= obtaining money) *for three charities.* • *(fml) The chapel was raised* (= built) *as a memorial to her son.*

-rais·er /£-ˌreɪ·zəʳ, $-zə˞/ *combining form* • A -raiser is a person or thing that causes the stated thing to exist or be obtained: *a money-raiser* ○ *These new taxes are designed to be a revenue-raiser.*

raise *obj* [DEVELOP] /reɪz/ *v* [T] to take care of until completely grown • *Her parents died when she was a baby and she was raised by her grandparents.* • *The lambs had to be raised by hand* (= fed artificial milk by people) *when their mother died.* • *The farmer raises* (= breeds) *chickens and pigs.* • *The soil around here isn't good enough for raising* (= growing) *crops.*

raise *obj* [END] /reɪz/ *v* [T] to end or stop • *They agreed to raise the trade embargo if three conditions were met.* • *After three weeks the siege was raised.*

raise *obj* [COMMUNICATE] /reɪz/ *v* [T] to communicate with, esp. by telephone or radio • *I've been trying to raise Jack/Tokyo all day.*

raise [PAY] /reɪz/ *n* [C] *Am and Aus for* RISE (= higher pay) • *She asked the boss for a raise.*

rai·sin /ˈreɪ·zᵊn/ *n* [C] a dried black GRAPE (= type of fruit), often used in cakes • *I bought a packet of nuts and raisins.* • Ⓕ

rai·son d'êt·re /£ˌrez·ɑ̃ːˈdet·rə, $ˌreɪ·zɑːn-/ *n* [C usually sing] *pl* **raisons d'être** /£ˌrez·ɑ̃ːˈdet·rə, $ˌreɪ·zɑːn-/ reason for existence • *After his wife died, his children became his raison d'être.* • *Her job is her raison d'être.*

Raj /rɑːdʒ/ *n* [U] **the Raj** the period of British rule in India • *the days of the Raj*

ra·jah /ˈrɑː·dʒə/ *n* [C] a male Indian ruler • See also RANI.

rake [TOOL] /reɪk/ *v, n* (to use) a tool with a long handle and long pointed, usually metal, parts sticking out in a row at the bottom, esp. a garden tool for making earth level and even or for gathering leaves etc. • *In the autumn I rake* **(up)** *the dead leaves.* [T/M] • *Rake* **(over)** *the soil before planting the seeds.* [T/M] • *In the spring I use the rake to make a good seed bed.* [C] • *Never leave a rake leaning with its points facing outwards because someone could tread on them and be hit in the face by the handle.* [C] • To **rake about/around** somewhere or to **rake through** something is to search: *He raked about* **in** *the drawer looking for his passport.* ○ *I've raked through the cupboard but I can't find my tennis racket.* • If you **rake in** a sum of money, esp. a large one/**rake** a sum of money **in**, you earn it: *He rakes in over £100 000 a year.* ○ *She's really raking* **it in** (= earning a lot of money). • *(Br)* If you **rake out** something/**rake** something **out**, you look for it and find it: *I raked this old blanket out for camping.* • If you **rake over** esp. something unpleasant/**rake** esp. something unpleasant **over**, you keep talking or thinking about it: *He keeps on raking over his divorce, when really he should be getting on with his life.* • To **rake up** something/**rake** something **up** is to talk about something which should be forgotten: *She's always raking up the past/that old quarrel.* • To **rake up** someone or something/**rake** someone or something **up** is also to obtain that person or thing: *I'm trying to rake up some people to play football on Saturday – do you want to come along?* • *(infml)* A **rake-off** is a dishonest or illegal share in profits that is given to someone who has been involved in making the profits: *Each person involved in the business takes/gets a rake-off.* • [PIC] **Garden**

rake [PERSON] /reɪk/ *n* [C] *disapproving esp. old use* a man, esp. one who is rich or with high social position, who lives in an immoral way • *Jerry is a bit of a rake, but you can't help liking him.* • *'The Rake's Progress' is a series of engravings done by William Hogarth in 1735 which shows a young man's decline into a disreputable and dissolute way of life.*

rak·ish /ˈreɪ·kɪʃ/ *adj* • *He was condemned for his rakish behaviour.* • See also RAKISH.

rak·ish·ness /ˈreɪ·kɪʃ·nəs/ *n* [U]

rake [SLOPE] /reɪk/ *n* [C] a slope • *Most stages have a rake – they rise towards the back so that the audience can see clearly.*

raked /reɪkt/ *adj* [not gradable] • *steeply raked* • *raked wings* • *a raked mast*

rak·ish /ˈreɪ·kɪʃ/ *adj* confidently careless and informal • *He wore his hat at a rakish* **angle.** • See **rakish** at RAKE [PERSON].

rak·ish·ly /ˈreɪ·kɪʃ·li/ *adv*

ral·ly [MEETING] /ˈræl·i/ *n* [C] a public meeting of a large group of people, esp. supporters of a particular opinion • *The police broke up a rally* **of** *2000 people in the town of Nandaime.* • *5000 people* **held** *a protest march and rally* **against** *sexual discrimination.* • *A peace rally was* **staged** *in Washington yesterday.* • *The prime minister will be addressing an election rally in Liverpool tomorrow.* • *Rallies are being held across the country* **to** *celebrate the victory.*

ral·ly *(obj)* [SUPPORT] /ˈræl·i/ *v* to bring or come together in order to provide support or make a shared effort • *Supporters/Opponents of the new shopping development are trying to rally local people* **in favour of/against** *it.* [T] • *We need to rally local* **support** *for our proposals.* [T] • *Each candidate will have to rally their supporters* **to** *vote.* [T + obj

+ *to* infinitive] • *The general rallied his forces* **to** *defend the town.* [T + obj + *to* infinitive] • *The prime minister has called on the public to rally* **to/behind** *the government.* [I] • *Father's death rallied the family* **around/round** *Mother.* [T] • *(infml) When I'm ill, my friends always rally* **round** (= help me). [I] • *'Workers of the world unite' was their rallying* **cry/call**.

ral·ly RACE /ˈræl·i/ *n* [C] a car or motorcycle race, esp. over long distances on public roads • *The French driver has taken the lead in the Paris-Dakar rally.* • *The cars raced in rallies are supposed to be the same as those you can buy from the car showroom.* • *A rally driver was injured yesterday.*

ral·ly SPORT /ˈræl·i/ *n* [C] a continuous exchange of shots between players in tennis, SQUASH or BADMINTON • *Mike won the point after a ten-stroke rally.*

ral·ly IMPROVE /ˈræl·i/ *v, n* (to return to) a better condition • *The nurse said my mother had rallied after a poor night.* [I] • *The team played badly in the first half of the match, but rallied in the second.* [I] • *The pound rallied* **against** *the dollar in trading today.* [I] • *Share prices fell again today after yesterday's rally.* [C]

ram *(obj)* HIT /ræm/ *v* **-mm-** to hit or push with force • *Someone rammed* **(into)** *my car while it was parked outside my house.* [T; I + *into*] • *He rammed the sweets/his pipe* **into** *his mouth.* [T] • To ram esp. an idea or an opinion **into** someone is to force them to accept it: *Parents should not try to ram their own opinions into their children.* [T] ○ *It's time someone rammed a bit of* **sense** *into you.* [T] ○ *He rammed* **it** *into his daughter* **that** *she shouldn't speak to strangers.* [T] • *I rammed* **down** *the soil around the fence post.* [M] • *The prisoners who were being force-fed had tubes rammed* **down** *their throats.* [T] • *For years I've had his political views* **rammed down** *my* **throat** (= forced on me). • *She slammed the door and rammed* **home** *the bolt.* [M] • *(fig.) He thumped the desk as he rammed his point* **home** (= emphasized his point). [M] • A **ram-raid** is an act of stealing from a shop after entering it by driving a stolen car through its front window. To **ram-raid** is to do this: *Televisions, radios and music systems were stolen in a ram-raid late last night.* ○ *Youths ram-raided several shops in the city centre.* ○ *The police are increasing their efforts to prevent car thefts and subsequent ram-raiding.* ○ *His car was stolen by* **ram-raiders** (= people who steal in this way)

ram /ræm/ *n* [C] • *They used a ram (also* **battering ram***) to break down the door.* • In a machine, the ram is a moving part which puts pressure or force on something.

ram ANIMAL /ræm/ *n* [C] an adult male sheep which can breed

RAM COMPUTER /ræm/ *n* [U] *specialized abbreviation for* Random Access Memory (= a type of computer memory which can be searched in any order and changed as necessary) • Compare ROM.

Ram·a·dan /£ˈræm·ə·dæn, $ˌræm·əˈdɑːn/ *n* [C] the ninth month of the Muslim year, during which believers have no food or drink during the day

ram·ble WALK /ˈræm·bl̩/ *v* [I] to walk for pleasure, esp. in the countryside • *I love to ramble* **through** *the fields and lanes in this part of the country.* • *Shall we* **go** *rambling this afternoon?*

ram·ble /ˈræm·bl̩/ *n* [C] • *We go for a ramble* (= a long walk) **over** *the hills/***through** *the woods every Saturday.*

ram·bler /£ˈræm·bləʳ, $-blɚ/ *n* [C] • *These hills are very popular with ramblers* (= people who enjoy going for long walks in the countryside).

ram·bling /ˈræm·blɪŋ/ *n* [U] • *I used to enjoy rambling, but I don't have the time to do it very much now.*

ram·ble TALK /ˈræm·bl̩/ *v* [I] to talk or write in a confused way, often for a long time • *Sorry, I'm rambling – let me get back to the point.* • *You were rambling in your sleep last night.* • *I got really bored listening to her rambling* **on.** • *My granddad is always rambling* **on about** *how things were better when he was a boy.*

ram·bler /£ˈræm·bləʳ, $-blɚ/ *n* [C] • A rambler is someone who talks in a confused way for a long time.

ram·bling /ˈræm·blɪŋ/ *adj* • *I really don't want to have to listen to another of his long, rambling* (= confused and lacking order) *speeches.* • *I've just had this rambling, incoherent letter from my sister.* • *His book was criticized for being long and rambling.* • *We got involved in a rather rambling discussion about politics.*

ram·blings /ˈræm·blɪŋz/ *pl n* • *We had to sit for hours listening to his ramblings* (= the long and confused things that he was saying).

ram·ble SPREAD /ˈræm·bl̩/ *v* [I] (esp. of a plant, a path or a stream) to go in many different directions • *An old clematis rambles* **over** *the garden wall.* • *There's a little stream that rambles* **through** *the valley.*

ram·bler /£ˈræm·bləʳ, $-blɚ/ *n* [C] • A rambler is a rambling rose.

ram·bling /ˈræm·blɪŋ/ *adj* • A rambling plant is one which grows in many different directions: *a rambling rose* • A rambling place or building is one which is large, does not have a regular shape and spreads out in many directions: *They live in a rambling old farmhouse.*

Ram·bo /£ˈræm·bəʊ, $-boʊ/ *n* [C] *pl* **Rambos** someone who uses, or threatens to use, strong and violent methods against their enemies • *The Americans responded, Rambo-***style/***Rambo-***like, *by threatening to attack immediately if their conditions were not met.* • Rambo was originally a film character known for his violence, who was played by Sylvester Stallone in several films.

Ram·bo·esque /£ˌræm·bəʊˈesk, $-boʊ-/ *adj* • *A decade of weightlifting had made his physique Ramboesque* (= having strong muscles). • *In a free society, attitudes, Ramboesque* (= forceful and violent) *or other, cannot and should not be controlled by governments.*

ram·i·fi·ca·tions /ˌræm·ɪ·fɪˈkeɪ·ʃᵊnz/ *pl n* the possible results of an action • *Have you considered all the ramifications* **of** *your suggestion?*

ramp /ræmp/ *n* [C] an artificial slope • *To get to the cinema foyer, you have to push the wheelchair up the ramp.* • *(Br)* Ramps are also raised strips built into a road to make vehicles drive more slowly: *Local residents have been asking the council to have ramps put in on the High Street.* • Ramp is *Am for* **slip road**. See at SLIP SLIDE. • PIC〉 **Motorway**

ram·page /ræmˈpeɪdʒ/ *v* [I] to make a wild or violent advance • *The demonstrators rampaged* **through** *the town, smashing windows and setting fire to cars.* • *Several villages were destroyed by rampaging soldiers.* • *(fig.) The government is taking steps to deal with rampaging* (= fast increasing) *inflation.*

ram·page /ˈræm·peɪdʒ/ *n* • *Several people were injured in the rampage* (= act of violent behaviour) *that followed the team's defeat.* [C] • *He confessed to having killed men, women and children during a 10-year rampage across at least 16 US states.* [C] • *Rioters* **went on** *a rampage through the city.* [C] • *There's no more alarming sight than an angry rhinoceros* **on** *the rampage.* [U]

ram·pant INCREASING /ˈræm·pᵊnt/ *adj* (of something bad) getting worse quickly and in an uncontrolled way • *Rampant inflation means that our wage increases soon become worth nothing.* • *He said that he had encountered rampant prejudice in his attempts to get a job.* • *Disease is rampant in the overcrowded city.*

ram·pant STANDING /ˈræm·pᵊnt/ *adj* [after n; not gradable] *specialized* (of an animal represented on a COAT OF ARMS) standing on its back legs with its front legs raised • *a lion rampant*

ram·part /£ˈræm·pɑːt, $-pɑːrt/ *n* [C] a large wall built round a town, castle, etc. to protect it • *an earth rampart*

ram·parts /£ˈræm·pɑːts, $-pɑːrts/ *pl n* • Ramparts are a rampart: *Soldiers patrolled the castle ramparts.*

ram·rod /£ˈræm·rɒd, $-rɑːd/ *n* [C] a long thin rod used for pushing explosives, bullets, etc. into old types of gun • *The old lady's back is still* **as stiff/straight as a ramrod** (= very straight).

ram·shack·le /ˈræmˌʃæk·l̩/ *adj disapproving* badly or untidily made and likely to break or fall down easily • *There's a ramshackle old shed at the bottom of the garden* • *(fig.) England's ramshackle* (= not well organized) *defence had soon conceded two goals.* • *(fig.) We need to reorganize this ramshackle* (= not well organized) *system.*

ran /ræn/ *past simple of* RUN

ranch /£rɑːntʃ, £ræntʃ/ *n* [C] (esp. in N and S America) a very large farm on which animals are kept • *a cattle ranch* • *a sheep ranch* • *He went to work* **on** *a ranch.* • *The rancher and his wife live in the* **ranch house** (= house on a ranch in which the people who own the ranch live, and which usually has only one level and a roof that does not slope much). • *(Am)* A **ranch house** or **ranch-style house** is a house which usually has only one level, and a roof that does not slope much, esp. one in a town or city.

ranch·er /£ˈrɑːn·tʃəʳ, $ˈræn·tʃɚ/ *n* [C] • A rancher is someone who owns or works on a ranch.

ranch·ing /£ˈrɑːn·tʃɪŋ, $ˈræn-/ *n* [U] • Ranching is the activity of keeping animals on a ranch.

ran·cid /ˈrænt·sɪd/ *adj* (of butter, oil, etc.) tasting or smelling unpleasant because not fresh

ran·cour *Br and Aus,* *Am and Aus* **ran·cor** /£ˈræŋ·kəʳ, $-kɚ/ *n* [U] *fml* a feeling of bitterness and hate • *They cheated me, but I feel no rancour* **towards/against** *them.* • *Can't we settle this disagreement* **without rancour?**

ran·cor·ous /£ˈræŋ·kᵊr·əs, $-kɚ·əs/ *adj fml* • *a rancorous dispute*

R and D /£ˌɑː·rᵊnˈdiː, $ˌɑːr·ᵊnd-/ *n* [U] *abbreviation for* research and development (=activities related to inventing new products, new methods of making things, etc.) • *If we want to get ahead of our competitors, we ought to invest more in R and D.*

ran·dom /ˈræn·dəm/ *adj* happening, done, or chosen by chance rather than according to a plan • *We asked a random* **sample/selection** *of people what they thought.* • *This is the latest in a sequence of seemingly random crimes/attacks/killings.* • *The choice of poems included in the collection seems somewhat random.* • *(Aus)* **A random breath test** (*abbreviation* **RBT**) is a test given by the police to drivers chosen by chance, to measure the amount of alcohol the drivers have in their blood.

ran·dom /ˈræn·dəm/ *n* [U] • *We wandered* **at random** (=without any organization or plan) *through the streets of the city.* • *The winning entry will be the first correct answer drawn* **at random** (=by chance).

ran·dom·ly /ˈræn·dᵊm·li/ *adv* • *The books were randomly arranged on the shelves.*

ran·dy /ˈræn·di/ *adj* **-ier, -iest** *infml* full of sexual desire

ran·di·ness /ˈræn·dɪ·nəs/ *n* [U]

ra·nee /ˈrɑː·niː, ˌ-ˈ-/ *n* [C] a RANI

rang /ræŋ/ *past simple of* RING

range LIMIT /reɪndʒ/ *n* [U] the levels or area within or to which something is limited • *The temperature range was* **between** *eight* **and/to** *twelve degrees Celsius.* • *The value of sterling fluctuated within a* **narrow** *range yesterday.* • *The coat was expensive and well* **outside/beyond/out of** *my* **price** *range.* • *They said that that particular issue had not been* **within** *the range* **of** *the research.* • *This type of work is* **outside/beyond/out of** *my range* **(of** *experience).* • *The high notes are rather* **out of** *my range* (=the total amount of difference between the highest and lowest notes that I can sing or play). • *The range* **of** *the missiles* (=distance within which they could operate) *was 30 miles.* • *An agreement has been signed limiting the development of new* **short-/medium-/long-***range* (=operating distance) *weapons.* • Range can also mean the distance within which you can see or hear someone: *Although she had a loud voice, she was too far away and* **outside/beyond/out of** *my range* **(of** *hearing).* • Range can also be used to refer to the period of time in the future within which something is planned or expected to happen: *long-range plans* ○ *short-/medium-/long-range weather forecasting* • A vehicle's or aircraft's range is the distance that it can travel without having to stop for more fuel: *short-/medium-/long-range airliners* • The range at which someone or something is shot is the distance from which they are shot: *She was shot at* **close/point-blank** *range.* • A **range finder** is an instrument which you use for measuring the distance of an object when you are shooting at it or taking a photograph of it. • Ⓙ

range /reɪndʒ/ *v* [I always + adv/prep] • *Dress sizes range* **from** *petite* **to** *extra large.* • *Prices range* **between** *$50 and $250.*

range SET /reɪndʒ/ *n* [C] a set of similar things • *I offered her a range* **of** *options.* • *There is a* **wide/broad** *range of opinions on this issue.* • A range (*Am also* **line**) can also be the goods made by one company or goods of one particular type that are sold in a shop: *We stock the whole range* **of** *model railway accessories.* • *This jacket is part of our autumn/spring range.* • *Our* **full range of** *cars is on display in our showroom.* • A group of hills or mountains is called a range: *a mountain range* ○ *the Pennine Range* ○ *We could see a low range* **of** *hills in the distance.* • Ⓙ

range *obj* GROUP /reɪndʒ/ *v* [T always + adv/prep] to position (people or things) together, esp. in rows; to ARRANGE PUT IN POSITION • *The crowd ranged* **itself** *along the route of the procession.* • *The troops were ranged before the commanding officer.* • To range people is also to cause them to join together with other people against something or someone else: *We are trying to range local people* **against** *the proposed building of the new supermarket.* • To range **yourself** with other people in to put yourself in the same group as them: *She ranged herself* **with** (=agreed with the opinions of) *my opponents.* • Ⓙ

range MOVE /reɪndʒ/ *v* [I always + adv/prep] to move or travel freely • *The hens range freely* **about/over** *the farm.* • *The walkers ranged* **through/over** *the hills all day.* • When used of a piece of writing or speech, range means to deal with: *Our discussion ranged* **over** *many current issues.* ○ *The findings of a* **wide-ranging** (=including many subjects) *survey of young people's attitudes are published today.* • Ⓙ

range WEAPONS AREA /reɪndʒ/ *n* [C] an area where people can practise shooting or where bombs or other weapons can be tested • *The soldiers were practising on the* **rifle/shooting** *range.* • *The bomb was tested on a* **missile** *range in the desert.* • Ⓙ

range LAND /reɪndʒ/ *n* [C] *Am* land for animals to feed on • *The cowboys were herding the cattle* **on** *the range.* • Ⓙ

range COOKER /reɪndʒ/ *n* [C] *(Br)* esp. in the past, a set of cookers burning wood or coal, or heated by a fire, or *(Am)* a cooker • *a kitchen range* • PIC **Kitchen** Ⓙ

rang·er OFFICER /£ˈreɪn·dʒəʳ, $-dʒɚ/ *n* [C] a person whose job is to protect a forest or natural park • *a park ranger*

Rang·er YOUNG WOMAN /£ˈreɪn·dʒəʳ, $-dʒɚ/, **Rang·er Guide** *n* [C] a young woman aged 14-19 who belongs to the international youth organization for young women called the Guides

ra·ni, ra·nee /ˈrɑː·niː, ˌ-ˈ-/ *n* [C] a female Indian ruler or the wife of an Indian ruler

rank POSITION /ræŋk/ *n* a position higher or lower than others, showing the importance or the degree of responsibility of the person having it • *A soldier taken as a prisoner of war only needs to give his name, rank, and number.* [C] • *She has just been promoted to the rank* **of** *captain.* [C] • *Ministers of Cabinet rank receive a higher salary than other ministers.* [U] • *He said that there were few members of ethnic minorities in senior legal ranks.* [C] • *She seems to be destined for the top rank of government.* [C] • *Having a large income is one of the advantages of rank* (=high position). [U] • **The rank and file** (also **the ranks**) are all the soldiers who are not officers, or the members of an organization who are not part of the leadership, or *(humorous)* less important people generally: *Conscripts form the bulk of the army's rank and file.* ○ *The party leadership seems to be losing the support of the rank and file.* ○ *A new law requires companies to offer comparable health benefits to top executives and rank-and-file workers.* ○ *These statistics concern rank-and-file citizens as well as economists.*

rank *(obj)* /ræŋk/ *v* [always + adv/prep] • *A duchess ranks* (=has a position) **above** *a marchioness in social importance.* [I] • *My entry was ranked third* (=placed in that position) *in the flower show.* [T] • *He is currently ranked/He currently ranks second in the world* (=has that position) *as a tennis player.* [T/I] • *She ranks* **among/alongside** (=is considered to be one of) *the theatre's greatest actors.* [I] • *Which type of Scotch whisky do you rank* (=consider) **as** *the best?* [T] • *She said that 1989 must rank* **as** (=be) *the most remarkable year for change in Europe since 1848.* [I] • *She ranked the bottles* (=arranged them in a particular order) **in** *order of size along the shelf.* [T] • *Consumer preferences were placed in* **rank order/ranking order** *from 1 (very unpopular) to 5 (most popular).*

rank·ing /ˈræŋ·kɪŋ/ *adj* [before n; not gradable] *Am* • *General Steinberger is the ranking officer* (=officer of highest rank) *present.*

ranks /ræŋks/ *pl n* • The ranks are the membership of a group or organization: *Party ranks have swelled by nearly 300 000.* ○ *There is great concern about safety among the ranks* **of** *racing drivers.* ○ *John has* **joined** *the ranks* **of** *the* (=become) *unemployed.* • **The ranks** are also **the rank and file**: *He rose from the ranks to become a director of the company.*

rank ROW /ræŋk/ *n* [C] a row, esp. of people or things standing side by side • *The front rank* **of** *the riot squad raised their shields.* • *In Cambridge, ranks* **of** *bikes line the streets outside the colleges.* • *The* **serried** *ranks* (=many rows) **of** *fir trees showed serious signs of damage by pollution.* • *There were no taxis at the* **taxi/cab** *rank* (=the place where these vehicles wait for passengers).

rank EXTREME /ræŋk/ *adj* [before n; not gradable] (esp. of something bad) complete or extreme • *The horse that won the race was a rank* **outsider**. • *It was rank* **stupidity** *to drive so fast on an icy road.*

rank GROWN /ræŋk/ *adj* **-er, -est** (esp. of plants) producing too much growth; OVERGROWN • *The rank growth of the* *creepers choked the less vigorous plants.* • *The abandoned garden was rank* **with** *weeds.*

rank SMELL /ræŋk/ *adj* **-er, -est** smelling strong and unpleasant • *His body was rank* **with** *sweat.*

rank·le /ˈræŋ·kl̩/ *v* to cause annoyance or anger which lasts a long time • *The unkind way in which his girlfriend left him still rankled* **(with** *him) long after.* [I] • **It** *still rankles* **that** *she got promoted, and I didn't.* [+ *that* clause]

ran·sack *obj* /ˈræn·sæk/ *v* [T] to search violently and carelessly for something, often leaving things untidy • *The burglars ransacked the house but found nothing valuable.* • *I ransacked the cupboard* **for** *my ski boots.*

ran·som /ˈrænt·sᵊm/ *n* something, esp. a large sum of money, demanded in exchange for someone or something which has been taken • *They* **demanded** *a huge ransom* **for** *the return of the little girl whom they had kidnapped.* [C] • *The kidnappers specified that the ransom* **money** *should be left at the bus station.* • *The gang* **held** *the racehorse (esp. Br)* **to**/*(Am usually)* **for** *ransom* (= took it and demanded money in exchange for it). [U] • *(fig.) Some people regarded the miners' strike as the union* **holding** *the nation (esp. Br)* **to**/*(Am usually)* **for** *ransom* (= put the nation in the position of having to agree to unreasonable demands). [U] • LP **Crimes and criminals**

ran·som *obj* /ˈrænt·sᵊm/ *v* [T] • *Her father ransomed her* **for** (= got her back from someone who had taken her away by paying a ransom of) *a million dollars.*

rant /rænt/ *v* to speak or shout in a loud uncontrolled or angry way, often saying things that are foolish or have no meaning • *He's always ranting* **(on) about** *the government.* [I] • *I get fed up with my mother ranting* **and raving** *(***about** *my clothes) all the time.* [I] • *He ranted* **that** *young people today take everything for granted.* [+ *that* clause]

rant /rænt/ *n* • *He went into a long rant* (= angry and meaningless speech) **about** *the phone company not having repaired his phone yet.* [C] • *The minister's speech descended into a rant* **against** *his political opponents.* [C] • *What she said was just rant.* [U]

rant·ing /£ˈræn·tɪŋ, $-t̬ɪŋ/ *n* [U] • *Do we really have to sit and listen to his mindless ranting all evening?*

rant·ings /£ˈræn·tɪŋz, $-t̬ɪŋz/ *pl n* • Rantings are **ranting.**

rap MUSIC /ræp/ *n* [U], *v* [I] **-pp-** (esp. among black people) (to produce) a type of rhythmic talking, which is spoken with a strong beat to music, often without preparation, as entertainment • *a rap musician* • *a rap song* • *a rap artist* • *Do you like rap?* • *They were rapping about powerful black women.*

rap *(obj)* HIT /ræp/ *v* **-pp-** to hit or say (something) suddenly and forcefully • *We heard him rap* **on** *the door.* [I] • *She rapped the table to get everyone's attention.* [T] • *The colonel rapped* **(out)** *an order to his men.* [T/M] • *(fig.) He'll* **get** *rapped* **over the knuckles/get his knuckles** *rapped* (= be criticized or punished) *for that mistake.* [T] • *(fig.) The headline read 'Judge raps* (= criticizes) *police'.* [T]

rap /ræp/ *n* [C] • A rap is a sudden short noise, esp. one made by hitting a hard surface: *There was a series of raps* **on** *the window.* ○ *(fig.) I got/was given a rap* **on/over the knuckles** (= was spoken to severely as a punishment) *for not finishing my essay on time.*

rap PUNISHMENT /ræp/ *n esp. Am slang* (a) punishment • *He got a* **bum rap** *from the judge.* [C] • *The police caught him, but somehow he managed to* **beat** *the rap* (= escape punishment). [U] • *I'm not going to* **take** *the rap* **for** *you* (= be punished for something you did). [U]

rap JUDGMENT /ræp/ *n* [C] *Am slang* a judgment or a reaction • *The new show got a* **bum/bad** *rap in all the papers.*

rap ANYTHING /ræp/ *n* [U] *infml* the smallest amount; anything • *She* **doesn't care a** *rap for what her father says.*

ra·pa·cious /rəˈpeɪ·ʃəs/ *adj fml* having or showing a strong desire to take or get something for yourself, or forcefully to get something for yourself • *a rapacious landlord/businessperson* • *a rapacious appetite* • *Rapacious soldiers looted the houses in the defeated city.*

ra·pa·cious·ly /rəˈpeɪ·ʃə·sli/ *adv fml*

ra·pa·cious·ness /rəˈpeɪ·ʃə·snəs/ *n* [U] *fml*

ra·pac·i·ty /£rəˈpæs·ə·ti, $-t̬i/ *n* [U] *fml*

rape *(obj)* FORCE /reɪp/ *v* to force (someone) to have sex when they are unwilling, using violence or threatening behaviour • *The girl was dragged from the car and raped.* [T] • *It's difficult to understand what causes a man to rape.* [I] • Ⓕ

rape /reɪp/ *n* • Rape is (an example of) the crime of forcefully having sex with someone against their wish: *He had* **committed** *several rapes.* [C] ○ *He was convicted of rape.* [U] ○ *(fig.) The road builders were accused of the rape* (= severe damage) *of the countryside.* [U]

ra·pist /ˈreɪ·pɪst/ *n* [C] • *The police have caught the rapist* (= a man who rapes).

rape PLANT /reɪp/, **oil·seed rape** *n* [U] a plant with yellow flowers from which oil and animal food are produced • PIC **Cereals** Ⓕ

rap·id /ˈræp·ɪd/ *adj* quick or sudden • *I was startled by a rapid movement to my left.* • *His response to the accusation was rapid.* • *There has been a rapid* **growth/rise/increase/expansion** *in the number of people who have home computers.* • *The industry is currently undergoing rapid* **change.** • *Since we began our campaign, we have* **made** *rapid* **strides** (= advanced quickly). • *We were woken by the sound of rapid* **fire** (= shooting). • *As a comedian, he's a master of* **rapid-fire** *jokes* (= those coming quickly one after another). • *There are plans to build a new* **rapid transit** *system* (= a system of fast moving trains) *in the city.*

ra·pi·di·ty /£rəˈpɪd·ɪ·ti, $-ə·t̬i/ *n* [U] *fml*

rap·id·ly /ˈræp·ɪd·li/ *adv*

rap·ids /ˈræp·ɪdz/ *pl n* a dangerous part of a river which flows very fast because it is steep and sometimes narrow • *There are many rapids and falls on this part of the river, which make it difficult to navigate.* • *They* **shot** (= travelled through) *the rapids in a canoe.*

ra·pi·er /£ˈreɪ·pi·əʳ, $-ɚ/ *n* [C] a sword with a long, thin blade • *(fig.) He has a rapier(-like)* **tongue/wit** (= says funny and clever things).

rap·pel /ræpˈel / *v* [I], *n* [C] *Am for* ABSEIL

rap·port /£ræpˈɔːʳ, $-ˈɔːr/ *n* [U] close agreement or sympathy with someone else • *After working with Jane for many years, we had developed a* **close/good** *rapport.* • *There was a* **close** *rapport* **between** *us.* • *She* **has** *an excellent rapport* **with** *her staff.* • Ⓢ

rap·proche·ment /£ræpˈrɒʃ·mɑ̃ːŋ, $ˌræp·rɔːʃˈmɑ̃ːŋ/ *n fml* (an) agreement reached by opposing groups or people • *The two sides involved in the conflict seem to be drawing closer to a rapprochement.* [C] • *There are signs of rapprochement* **between** *George and his son.* [U]

rapt /ræpt/ *adj* giving complete attention, or showing complete involvement, or (of attention) complete • *She sat with a rapt expression reading her book.* • *He gazed rapt at the stars.* • *They held the* **audience** *completely rapt.* • *The children watched with rapt* **attention.** • *(Aus infml)* Rapt means **wrapped.** See at WRAP.

rap·ture /£ˈræp·tʃəʳ, $-tʃɚ/ *n* [U] extreme pleasure and happiness • *He listened to the music with an expression of pure rapture on his face.* • *"This is rapture," she said as she sank back into the hot bath.* • *The prime minister's supporters greeted her speech with rapture.* • *"The first fine careless rapture"* (Robert Browning describing a bird's song in the poem *Home-Thoughts, from Abroad,* 1845)

rap·tures /£ˈræp·tʃəz, $-tʃɚz/ *pl n* • *She* **went into** *raptures* (= an expression of extreme happiness and pleasure) **at** *the news of her success.* • *She was* **in** *raptures* **about/over** *her first visit to Paris.*

rap·tur·ous /£ˈræp·tʃᵊr·əs, $-tʃɚ-/ *adj* • *The audience gave the new play a rapturous reception.* • *The play was greeted with rapturous applause.*

rap·tur·ous·ly /£ˈræp·tʃᵊr·ə·sli, $-tʃɚ-/ *adv* • *The audience received the play rapturously.*

rare NOT COMMON /£reəʳ, $rer/ *adj* **-r, -st** not common and therefore sometimes valuable • *My visits to the dentist are more rare than they should be.* • *He's suffering from a rare disease/illness.* • *The museum is full of rare and precious treasures.* • *The wildlife documentary described the rare* **species** *found in Madagascar.* • *These sheep are a* **relatively/comparatively/extremely** *rare* **breed.** • *This exhibition provides a rare* **opportunity** *to see all the painter's work together in one place.* • *He likes to be alone, and only goes out on very rare* **occasions.** • *Having breakfast in bed is a rare* **treat (for** *me).* • **It**'*s rare* **for** *me* **to** *have this time to watch television.* [+ *to* infinitive] • **It**'*s rare* **to** *find these birds in England, but there is a small population of them in the north-west.* [+ *to* infinitive] • The atmosphere or air around you at the top of a mountain is rare when it contains less oxygen and you find it harder to breathe. See also RAREFIED. • *He's that* **rare bird** (= unusual person), *a barman who doesn't drink alcohol.* • *(dated) While their parents were out, the young people* **had a rare old time** (= enjoyed themselves). • *(dated) We* **had a rare**

old time (=had difficulty) *trying to get tickets on the Orient Express because it was so heavily booked.*

rare·ly /£'reə·li, $'rer-/ *adv* • *I rarely* (=not often) *have time to read a newspaper.* • *(fml) Rarely have I seen such a beautiful sunset.* • *He rarely comes* (=He doesn't often come) *here any more, does he?* • See also SELDOM.

ra·ri·ty /£'reə·rə·ti, $'rer·ə·ṭi/ *n* • *The rarity* (=something which is not common) *in the concert was a little-known piece by Sibelius.* [C] • *Men who do the cooking are* **something of a** *rarity.* [C] • *Diamonds are valuable because of their rarity* (=quality of being not common). [U] • *These cars have (a) rarity* **value** (=they are valuable because so few were produced).

rare COOKED /£reəʳ, $rer/ *adj* **-r, -st** (esp. of meat) not cooked for very long; still red • *I'd like my* **steak** *rare, please.* • Compare MEDIUM VALUE.

ra·re·fied, ra·ri·fied /£'reə·rı·faıd, $'rer·ə-/ *adj* (of air) with little oxygen • *It is hard to breathe in the rarefied air of the mountains.* • *(fig.) In the rarefied* (=limited) *atmosphere/circles of college life, he lost touch with reality.*

rar·ing /£'reə·rıŋ, $'rer·ıŋ/ *adj* [after v; + *to* infinitive] very enthusiastic or eager • *After three months abroad I was raring* **to** *get home.* • *I had been preparing for the expedition for a year and now I was raring* **to go** (=eager to start).

ras·cal /£'rɑː·skᵊl, $'ræs·kᵊl/ *n* [C] a person, esp. a child or a man, who does things of which you disapprove, but whom you still like • *I caught those* **little/young** *rascals dressing up in my clothes.* • *What's that* **old** *rascal been up to now?* • *(old use)* A rascal is also a dishonest person.

ras·cal·ly /£'rɑː·skᵊl·i, $'ræs·kᵊl-/ *adj*

rash WITHOUT THOUGHT /ræʃ/ *adj* **-er, -est** careless or unwise, without thought for what might happen or result • *That was a rash move/decision – you didn't think about the costs involved.* • *That was very rash* **of** *you.* • *I think* **it** *was a bit rash* **of** *them* **to** *get married when they'd only known each other for a few weeks.* [+ *to* infinitive] • **In a** *rash* **moment**, *I said I'd lead the group.* • Ⓓ

rash·ness /'ræʃ·nəs/ *n* [U] • **In a moment of** *rashness, I agreed to do a parachute jump for charity.* • *He suddenly realized the rashness* **of** *what he had said.*

rash·ly /'ræʃ·li/ *adv* • *I rashly agreed to help organize the village summer fête.*

rash SKIN CONDITION /ræʃ/ *n* [C] an appearance of a lot of spots on skin • *I've got a strange rash all over my chest.* • *He* **came out/up in** *a rash after he fell in a patch of nettles.* • *My skin* **came out/up in** *an* **itchy** *rash when I used that cream on my face.* • *If you stay in the sun too long you'll get a* **heat** *rash.* • Ⓓ

rash LARGE NUMBER /ræʃ/ *n* [U] **a rash of** a large number of • *A rash of ugly new houses has been built for commuters near the railway station.* • *There has been a rash of robberies/accidents/complaints in the last two months.* • Ⓓ

rash·er /£'ræʃ·əʳ, $-ɚ/ *n* [C] a thin flat piece of BACON (=type of pig meat)

rasp TOOL /£rɑːsp, $ræsp/ *n* [C] a tool with a rough blade, used for shaping wood or metal

rasp *obj* /£rɑːsp, $ræsp/ *v* [T] • *The horse rasped* (=rubbed roughly) *my hand with his tongue as I fed him the apple.*

rasp SOUND /£rɑːsp, $ræsp/ *n* [U] an unpleasant noise, like metal being rubbed against metal • *There was* **the** *rasp* **of** *a bolt and the door suddenly opened.*

rasp *(obj)* /£rɑːsp, $ræsp/ *v* • *The bolt rasped and the door suddenly opened.* [I] • *(fig.) Her voice rasped* **on** (=had an unpleasant effect on) *me/my nerves.* [I] • *The gunman rasped* **(out)** *an urgent order* (=gave it in an unpleasant-sounding voice) *to the other members of the gang.* [T/M] • *The gunman gave an order in a rasping* (=unpleasant-sounding) *voice.*

rasp·ber·ry FRUIT /£'rɑːz·bᵊr·i, $'ræz·ber-/ *n* [C] a small soft red fruit, or the bush on which it grows • *raspberries and ice cream* • *raspberry jam* • *a raspberry bush* • PIC Berries

rasp·ber·ry SOUND /£'rɑːz·bᵊr·i, $'ræz·ber-/ *n* [C] *infml* a rude sound made by sticking the tongue out and blowing • *The boy turned and* **blew** *a raspberry at the teacher before running off.*

ras·ta·fa·ri·an /£ˌræs·tə'feə·ri·ən, $-ṭə'fer·i-/, *infml* **ras·ta** /£'ræs·tə, $-ṭə/ *n, adj* [not gradable] (a member) of a religious group which originated in Jamaica and which worships a previous ruler of Ethiopia • *Rastafarians follow strict rules about what they eat, and usually wear their hair in dreadlocks.* [C] • *Do you like Rastafarian music?*

ras·ta·fa·ri·an·i·sm /£ˌræs·tə'feə·ri·ə·nı·zᵊm, $-ṭə'fer·i-/ *n* [U]

rat ANIMAL /ræt/ *n* [C] a small RODENT (=type of animal), larger than a mouse, which is considered to be harmful. There are various types of rat. • *Rats carry disease.* • *I think we've* **got** *rats* (=there are rats in our house or other building). • *He decided to get out of the* **rat race** (=competition for success), *and went to work on a farm.* • *(infml)* If you are *(Br)* **rat-arsed**/*(Am)* **rat-assed**, you are extremely drunk: *I got completely rat-arsed at the party.*

rat /ræt/ *v* [I] **-tt-** *infml* • To rat is to be not loyal to someone, esp. by giving away secret information about them, or to fail to do something that you said you would do: *He's ratted* **on** *us.* ○ *They ratted* **on** *the deal/their promise.*

rat PERSON /ræt/ *n* [C] an unpleasant person who deceives or is not loyal • *He's a real rat!* • *You cheated me, you* **dirty** *rat!* [as form of address]

rat·a·tou·ille /£ˌræt·ə'tuː·i, $ˌræṭ-/ *n* [U] a savoury dish made from cooking vegetables, such as TOMATOES, PEPPERS and AUBERGINES, in liquid at a low heat

rat·bag /'ræt·bæg/ *n* [C] *esp. Br and Aus infml* a person who is unpleasant and does not have good qualities • *My brother's a little ratbag – he's always going into my room and taking my things.*

rat·chet /'rætʃ·ıt/ *n* [C] a part of a machine which allows movement in one direction only. It is usually a wheel with teeth-like parts which either slide over or lock against the free end of a bar.

rate MEASURE /reıt/ *n* [C] a level of speed with which something happens or changes, or the number of times it happens or changes, within a particular period • *Although she's recovering from her illness, her rate* **of** *progress is quite slow.* • *I told my assistants to work* **at their own** *rate/* **at a steady** *rate.* • *The taxi was going* **at a tremendous** *rate.* • *The rate* **of** *application for this garden weed-killer is 1 litre per 10 square metres.* • *The* **growth** *rate/rate* **of** *growth of the country's economy/population was 3% last year.* • *The government's economic policies are directed towards keeping the* **inflation** *rate/rate* **of inflation** *low.* • *The* **unemployment** *rate/rate* **of unemployment** (=number of people without jobs) *in the region has risen.* • *This form of meningitis has a very high* **mortality** *rate* (=many people die from it). • *As a lawyer, she has a high* **success** *rate in* (=is successful in a large number of) *the cases she handles.* • *The school has a very low* **dropout** *rate* (=number of students failing to complete courses). • *(Br) She got through her work* **at a rate of knots** (=very fast) *so that she could go and play tennis.* • **At this rate** (=If the situation stays as it is), *we'll never be home by midnight.* • *Well, I'm not going* **at any rate** (=whatever happens). • People also say **at any rate** as a way of showing that they are going to say something more exactly: *I don't think they liked my idea. At any rate, they weren't very enthusiastic about it.* • See also **rate** at RATES. • Ⓓ

rate PAYMENT /reıt/ *n* [C] an amount or level of payment • *We agreed a rate with the painter before he started work.* • *What's the* **going** (=standard) *rate* **for** *this type of work.* • *Do you pay your mortgage on a* **fixed** *or* **variable** *rate?* • *We're paying quite a low* **mortgage** *rate at the moment.* • *The country has a high* **taxation** *rate/rate* **of taxation**. • **Interest** *rates/Rates* **of interest** *have risen again.* • The **rate of exchange** is the **exchange rate**. See at EXCHANGE. • See also **rate** at RATES. • Ⓓ

rate *(obj)* VALUE /reıt/ *v* to judge the value or worth of; to ASSESS • *How do you rate him* **as** *a footballer?* [T] • *She is rated very* **highly** *by the people she works for.* [T] • *(infml) "What do you think of her as a singer?" "I don't really rate her* (=I do not think that she is very good)." [T] • *She rates him* (=considers him to be) *among her closest friends.* [T] • *I rate cars* **as** (=I consider that cars are) *one of the worst polluters of the environment.* [T] • *That rates* **as** (=I consider it to be) *the worst film I've ever seen.* [I always + adv/prep] • *On a scale of one to ten, I'd rate his book* (=consider it to have the value of) *a five.* [T + obj + n] • *Car crashes are so frequent that they don't rate* **a mention** (=are not considered to be worth reporting) *in the newspaper unless a lot of people are killed.* [T] • See also **rate** at RATES; UNDERRATE; OVERRATE. • Ⓓ

-rate /-reıt/ *combining form* • *His suggestions are always* **first**-*rate* (=very good). • *This company produces* **second/third**-*rate* (=not very good) *goods.*

ra·ting /£'reɪ·tɪŋ, $-t̬ɪŋ/ *n* • *The government's rating* (= people's judgment of its quality) *in the opinion polls sank to an all-time low.* [C] • *What's your rating* (= judgment) **of** *our chances of winning.* [U]

rat·ings /£'reɪ·tɪŋz, $-t̬ɪŋz/ *pl n* • Ratings are a record of the number of people who watch each television broadcast during the week, in order to judge which are the most and the least popular: *Advertisers are interested in ratings.* ○ *The serial has fallen in the ratings this week.*

rates /reɪts/ *pl n* a local tax paid in Australia, and in Britain in the past, by the owners of houses and other buildings

rate *obj* /reɪt/ *v* [T] *Br* • In Britain in the past, a building was rated to decide how much local tax the owner should pay. • See also RATE.

rate·a·ble /£'reɪ·tə·bl̩, $-t̬ə-/ *adj* [not gradable] *Br* • In the past in Britain, a **rateable value** was an official value given to a building, based partly on its size and type, which decided the amount of local tax that the owner should pay.

ra·ther SMALL AMOUNT /£'rɑː·ðəʳ, $'ræð·ɚ/ *adv* [not gradable] quite; to a slight degree • *It's rather cold/difficult.* • *Let me give you a different book – I think you'll find it rather easier.* • *The train was rather too crowded for a comfortable journey.* • *The dress was rather more expensive than I was expecting it would be, so I didn't buy it.* • *She answered the telephone rather sleepily.* • *I've rather foolishly lost their address.* • *I rather think you should consider the trouble this decision will cause.* • *I rather doubt I'll be able to come to your party.*

ra·ther VERY /£'rɑː·ðəʳ, $'ræð·ɚ/ *adv* [not gradable], *predeterminer* very; to a large degree • *I was rather pleased to be invited to the wedding.* • *Actually, I did rather well in my exams.* • *She's rather ill.* • *He's a rather nice man.* • *He's rather a nice man.* • *I've got rather a lot of work to do at the moment.* • *It's rather a shame that you can't come to the party.*

ra·ther MORE EXACTLY /£'rɑː·ðəʳ, $'ræð·ɚ/ *adv* more accurately; more exactly • *She'll go to London on Thursday,* **or** *rather, she will if she has to.* • *He's my sister's friend really, rather* **than** *mine.* • *The dress is rather pink* **than** *purple.* • Rather can also be used to express an opposite opinion: *The ending of the war is not a cause for celebration, but rather for regret that it ever happened.* ○ *No, I'm not tired. Rather the opposite in fact.*

ra·ther PREFERENCE /£'rɑː·ðəʳ, $'ræð·ɚ/ *adv* **rather than** in preference to; instead of • *I think I'd like to stay at home this evening rather than going out.* • *Why don't you wear the black shoes rather than the brown ones?* • *He likes starting early rather than staying late.* • **Rather** one person **than** another person means that the second person certainly does not want to do what the first person is doing: *"I've got to have two teeth out next week." "Rather you than me."*

ra·ther YES /£ˌrɑː'ðɜːʳ, $ˌræð'ɜːr/ *exclamation esp. Br infml* certainly; yes • *"Do you want to come out for dinner with us this evening?" "Rather!"*

rat·i·fy *obj* /£'ræt·ɪ·faɪ, $'ræt̬·ə-/ *v* [T] *fml* (esp. of governments or organizations) to agree, in writing, to act according to (a set of rules), or officially to approve (a decision or plan made by another organization) • *Many countries have now ratified the UN convention on the rights of the child.* • *The* **decision** *will have to be ratified* (= approved) *by the executive board.*

rat·i·fi·ca·tion /£ˌræt·ɪ·fɪ'keɪ·ʃən, $ˌræt̬·ə-/ *n* [U] *fml*

ra·ti·o /£'reɪ·ʃi·əʊ, $-oʊ/ *n* [C] *pl* **ratios** the relationship between two groups or amounts, which expresses how much bigger one is than the other • *The ratio* **of** *men* **to** *women at the conference was ten to one/10:1.* • *The school is trying to improve its pupil-teacher ratio* (= the number of teachers compared with the number of students). • Ⓓ

ra·tion /'ræʃ·ən/ *n* [C] a limited amount (of something) which one person is allowed to have, esp. when there is not much of it available • *During the war, no one was allowed more than their ration* **of** *food, clothing and fuel.* • *By Wednesday I had already eaten my weekly ration* **of** *chocolate* (= the amount of it I allow myself to have in a week). • *(fig.) We've had more than our ration* **of** (= had a lot of) *problems recently.*

ra·tion *obj* /'ræʃ·ən/ *v* [T] • To ration something is to limit the amount of it that each person is allowed to have: *Do you remember when petrol was rationed* **to** *five gallons a week?* ○ *My children would watch television all day long, but I ration it.* • To ration someone is to limit the amount of something that they have: *My children would watch television all day, but I ration them.* • To ration something **out** is to divide it between a group of people so that each person gets a small amount: *Ann rationed out the cake* **between** *the children.* [M]

rat·ion·ing /'ræʃ·ən·ɪŋ/ *n* [U] • Rationing is a system of limiting the amount of something that each person is allowed to have: *A speed limit was introduced to try to avoid the need for fuel rationing.*

ra·tions /'ræʃ·ənz/ *pl n* • Rations are the total amount of food that is given to someone to be eaten during a particular activity and in a particular period of time, esp. that given to soldiers when they are fighting: *The soldiers' daily rations were limited.* ○ *Can I share your rations?*

ra·tion·al /'ræʃ·ən·əl/ *adj* showing clear thought or reason • *She was too upset to be rational.* • *We need to decide what would be the most rational course of action.* • *There must be a* **perfectly** *rational* **explanation** *for what happened.* • Ⓓ

rat·ion·al·i·sm /'ræʃ·ən·əl·ɪ·zəm/ *n* [U] • Rationalism is the belief or principle that actions and opinions should be based on reason rather than on emotion or religion.

rat·ion·al·ist /'ræʃ·ən·əl·ɪst/ *n* [C] • A rationalist is someone whose actions and decisions are based on reason rather than emotions or beliefs. • *Descartes, Leibniz and Spinoza are considered to be the most important of the rationalists.*

rat·ion·al·ist /'ræʃ·ən·əl·ɪst/, **ra·tion·al·is·tic** /ˌræʃ·ən·əl'ɪs·tɪk/ *adj* • *His view of the world is rationalist.* • *Descartes was a rationalist philosopher.*

rat·ion·al·i·ty /£ˌræʃ·ən'æl·ɪ·ti, $-ə·t̬i/ *n* [U]

ra·tion·al·ly /'ræʃ·ən·əl·i/ *adv* • *Can we talk about this rationally* (= in a way based on reason rather than emotion)*?* • *Rationally, he knows that she won't ever go back to him, but emotionally he can't accept it.*

rat·ion·ale /£ˌræʃ·ə'nɑːl, $-'næl/ *n* the reasons or intentions for a particular set of thoughts or actions • *I don't understand the rationale* **behind** *the council's housing policy.* [C] • *Could you* **provide** *me with a clear rationale* **for** *taking this course of action?* [C] • *The plans have been criticized for their lack of rationale.* [U]

ra·tion·al·ize *obj* EXPLAIN, *Br and Aus usually* **-ise** /'ræʃ·ən·əl·aɪz/ *v* [T] to provide an explanation, esp. one based on reason, for (something) • *He rationalized his decision to resign by saying that he wanted to spend more time with his family.* • *She rationalized the expense by saying that the costly carpet she had bought would last longer than a cheaper one.* • *Tom's parents sometimes find it difficult to rationalize his behaviour.*

rat·ion·a·liz·a·tion, *Br and Aus usually* **-i·sa·tion** /ˌræʃ·ən·əl·aɪ'zeɪ·ʃən/ *n* [U/C]

ra·tion·al·ize *(obj)* CHANGE, *Br and Aus usually* **-ise** /'ræʃ·ən·əl·aɪz/ *v* to make (a company, way of working, etc.) more effective, usually by combining or stopping particular activities, or (of a company, way of working, etc.) to become more effective in this way • *We rationalized the production system so that one operator could control all three machines.* [T] • *The recession is forcing the company to rationalize and it is halving its workforce.* [I]

rat·ion·a·liz·a·tion, *Br and Aus usually* **-i·sa·tion** /ˌræʃ·ən·əl·aɪ'zeɪ·ʃən/ *n* [U/C]

rat·tle SOUND /£'ræt·l̩, $'ræt̬-/ *n* a sound similar to a series of quickly repeated knocks, or an object containing many small solid pieces, which makes this sound when it is shaken • *From across the town came the rattle* **of** *machine gun fire.* [U] • *The baby was waving around a plastic rattle* (= a toy which makes a noise like a series of knocks) *and laughing.* [C] • *In those days, rattles* (= wooden devices that when turned round and round produce a noise like a series of knocks) *were a common sight at football matches.* [C] • A rattle is also the part of a RATTLESNAKE's tail that produces a noise. [C]

rat·tle *(obj)* /£'ræt·l̩, $'ræt̬-/ *v* • *The cups rattled* (= made a noise like a series of knocks) *as the waitress laid the table.* [I] • *The dying man's voice rattled in his throat.* [I] • *The explosion rattled the cups* (= caused them to make a noise like a series of knocks) *on the shelf.* [T] • *The car rattled* (= made a noise as it travelled) **along** *the road*/**down** *the street*/**over** *the cobblestones.* [I] • *My car engine is making a strange rattling noise.* • To **rattle off** something/**rattle** something **off** is to say it quickly: *She rattled off the names of the people who were coming to the party.* • To **rattle on/away** is to talk for a long time, esp. about things that are not important: *My sister rattles on for hours on the phone to her friends.* • If you **rattle through** something, you do or say it quickly: *I'm going to rattle through my work today so that I can go home early.* ○ *He rattled through the list of* *countries he had visited.* • *"Will the people in the front seats clap your hands? All the rest of you, if you'll just rattle your jewellery"* (John Lennon at The Royal Variety Performance, 1963)

rat·tle *obj* WORRY /£'ræt·l̩, $'ræţ-/ *v* [T] to worry or make nervous • *The quiet deliberate footsteps approaching my door really rattled me/got me rattled.* • *She was obviously rattled by the question.*

rat·tle·snake /£'ræt·l̩.sneɪk, $'ræţ-/, *infml* **rat·tler** /£'ræt·lər, $'ræţ·lɚ/ *n* [C] a poisonous snake found in southern parts of the US which, when annoyed, produces a loud noise by shaking its tail • PIC **Reptiles and amphibians**

rat·ty /£'ræt·i, $'ræţ-/ *adj* **-ier, -iest** *infml* bad-tempered; IRRITABLE • *Watch out for Mum, she's a bit ratty today.* • *What's made you so ratty?* • *He's in a bit of a ratty mood today.*

rau·cous /£'rɔː·kəs, $'rɑː-/ *adj* sounding loud and unpleasant; HARSH • *I heard the raucous call of the crows.* • *I think their music is rather raucous.* • *Raucous* **laughter** *came from the next room.* • *The party was becoming rather raucous* (=noisy). • *The match was played before a raucous* (=noisy) *crowd.*

rau·cous·ly /£'rɔː·kə·sli, $'rɑː-/ *adv*

rau·cous·ness /£'rɔː·kə·snəs, $'rɑː-/ *n* [U]

raunch·y /£'rɔːn·tʃi, $'rɑːn-/ *adj* **-ier, -iest** having to do with sex in a very clear and obvious way • *a raunchy magazine/video* • *Sally is offended when the conversations get too raunchy.*

raunch·i·ly /£'rɔːn·tʃɪ·li, $'rɑːn-/ *adv*

raunch·i·ness /£'rɔːn·tʃɪ·nəs, $'rɑːn-/ *n* [U]

rav·age *obj* /'ræv·ɪdʒ/ *v* [T] to cause great damage to • *Many trees were uprooted in the worst storm of the decade, which ravaged the forests in the south.* • *An incurable skin disease has ravaged his once-handsome face.* • *The area has been ravaged by drought/floods/war.*

rav·ag·es /'ræv·ɪ·dʒɪz/ *pl n* • **The ravages of** something are the great damage caused by that thing: *The ravages of war/the fire showed in the splintered woodwork and blistered paint of the houses.* ○ *Their business plans were ruined by the ravages of inflation.* ○ *Few of us manage to escape the ravages of* **time**.

rave SPEAK FOOLISHLY /reɪv/ *v* to speak in an uncontrolled way, esp. saying things that have no meaning, usually because you are upset or angry, or because you are (mentally) ill. • *He's raving, ignore him.* [I] • *In his distress, he even raved* **against** *his friends.* [I] • *He raved* **(on) about** *the tax system for hours.* [I] • *My mother is always raving* **(on) at** *me* **about** *staying out late.* [I] • *She was* **ranting and** *raving* **about** *some imagined insult.* [I] • *He raved* **that** *no one would listen to him.* [+ *that* clause] • See also RAVING. • DK

ra·ving /'reɪ·vɪŋ/ *n* [U] • *They found it hard to listen to his raving* (=saying meaningless things, esp. because of being angry or (mentally) ill). • See also RAVING.

rav·ings /'reɪ·vɪŋz/ *pl n* • *The things he said are simply the ravings* (=meaningless statements) *of a deranged/disturbed mind.* • See also RAVING.

rave ENTHUSIASTIC /reɪv/ *adj* [before n] *infml* admiring; giving praise • *The show has received rave* **reviews/ notices** *in all the papers.* • DK

rave /reɪv/ *v infml* • *She raved* **about** (=praised greatly) *the clothes she had seen at the Paris fashion shows.* [I] • *Everyone is raving* **about** *that new restaurant in town.* [I] • *"It's an absolutely brilliant play," she raved* (=said enthusiastically). [+ clause] • See also RAVING.

rave PARTY /reɪv/ *n* [C] *esp. Br infml* a party which takes place in a large building or open space where people dance and sometimes take illegal drugs • *an all-night/open-air rave* • *rave music* • *the rave scene* • *A mother told how her 18-year-old son began taking drugs when he started going to rave* **parties**. • DK

rav·el *(obj)* /'ræv·əl/ *v* **-ll-** or *Am usually* **-l-** to (cause to) become gathered together untidily or twisted into a ball • *This wool has all ravelled* **(up)**. *What shall I do about it?* [I] • *The cat has been playing with the wool and has ravelled it* **up**. [T]

ra·ven BIRD /'reɪ·vən/ *n* [C] the largest bird in the CROW family, with shiny black feathers

ra·ven BLACK /'reɪ·vən/ *adj* [before n] *literary* (esp. of hair) shiny black • *Her pale face was framed by raven locks.*

ra·ven·ing /'ræv·ən·ɪŋ/ *adj* [not gradable] *literary* (esp. of wild animals) fiercely hunting for food • *ravening wolves* • *(fig.) She said that she was tired of being pursued by ravening journalists* (=those who were forcefully trying to reach her).

rav·en·ous /'ræv·ən·əs/ *adj* extremely hungry • *I'm ravenous – where's supper?* • *Growing boys have ravenous appetites.*

rav·en·ous·ly /'ræv·ən·ə·sli/ *adv* • *He looked ravenously at the buffet table.* • *I'm ravenously hungry.*

ra·vine /rə'viːn/ *n* [C] a deep narrow valley with steep sides

ra·ving /'reɪ·vɪŋ/ *adj* [before n], *adv* [not gradable] *infml* complete or extreme, or completely or extremely • *He must be a raving idiot/lunatic to drive that far without a break.* • *Her last book was a raving best-seller/success.* • *The last couple of weeks have been a raving nightmare* (=extremely difficult). • *She's a raving* **beauty** (=extremely beautiful). • *I think you're* **(stark)** *raving* (=completely) **mad** *to agree to do all that extra work without being paid for it.* • *My father went* **(stark)** *raving* (=completely) **mad** *when he heard I'd crashed his car.* • See also **raving** at RAVE SPEAK FOOLISHLY.

rav·ings /'reɪ·vɪŋz/ *pl n* See at RAVE SPEAK FOOLISHLY

rav·i·o·li /£,ræv·i'əʊ·li, $-'oʊ-/ *n* [U] small square cases of pasta filled with meat or cheese, which are cooked in boiling water

rav·ish *obj* PLEASE /'ræv·ɪʃ/ *v* [T] to give great pleasure to • *I was utterly ravished by the way she smiled.*

rav·ish·ing /'ræv·ɪ·ʃɪŋ/ *adj* • *She* **looked** *ravishing/She was a ravishing* **sight** (=She looked very beautiful) *in her wedding dress.* • *The countryside around here is quite ravishing* (=beautiful). • *He made an absolutely ravishing dessert* (=one having a very pleasant taste).

rav·ish *obj* FORCE /'ræv·ɪʃ/ *v* [T] *old use or humorous* to force (a woman) to have sex against her wish

raw NOT PROCESSED /£rɔː, $rɑː/ *adj* [not gradable] not processed, treated, or (of food) cooked • *She was wearing a jacket made of raw silk.* • *Oil is an important raw* **material** *which can be processed into many different products, including plastics.* • *They claimed that raw* **sewage** *was being pumped into the sea.* • *Some dried beans are poisonous if they are eaten in their raw* **state**. • *I prefer to eat vegetables raw, not cooked.* • *Sushi is a Japanese dish made from raw fish.* • Raw is also used to refer to information which has been collected but has not yet been studied in detail: *raw data* ○ *raw evidence* ○ *raw figures* • A person who is raw is not trained or is without experience: *I would prefer not to leave this job to John while he's still a raw* **recruit/ beginner**. • Feelings or qualities that are raw are those which you do not control in any way: *We were struck by the raw* **energy/power** *of the dancers' performances.* ○ *Her emotions are still a bit raw after her painful divorce.* • A piece of writing that is raw is one which does not try to hide anything about its subject: *His new play is a raw drama about family life.* • *(Aus)* To **come the raw prawn** is to try to deceive someone, esp. by pretending that you have no knowledge of something: *Don't come the raw prawn* **with** *me – you know exactly what happened.*

raw /£rɔː, $rɑː/ *n* [U] *infml* • **In the raw** means without clothes: *They sunbathed in the raw.* • **In the raw** also means plainly and honestly with nothing hidden: *The film really showed you prison life in the raw.*

raw·ness /£'rɔː·nəs, $'rɑː-/ *n* [U]

raw PAINFUL /£rɔː, $rɑː/ *adj* sore or painful because of being rubbed or damaged • *The shoe had rubbed a raw place on her heel.* • If the weather is raw, it is very cold and sometimes wet: *a raw morning* ○ *a raw wind* ○ *The evening was cold and raw.* • **A raw deal** is bad or unfair treatment: *He said that many children in the city's schools were* **getting/being given** *a raw deal by being taught in classes that were too large.* • When you **touch/strike/hit/expose a raw nerve/spot**, or *(Br and Aus also)* **touch** someone **on the raw**, you upset someone: *Her remarks about his failure to get the job he wanted touched a raw nerve.* • A **raw-boned** animal is one that has little flesh on its bones so that its bones can be seen clearly.

raw·ness /£'rɔː·nəs, $'rɑː-/ *n* [U]

ray BEAM /reɪ/ *n* [C] a narrow beam of light, heat, etc. travelling in a straight line from its place of origin • *The sun's rays streamed through the gap in the clouds.* • *Light rays bend as they pass from air to water.* • *(fig.) The news of her safe arrival was a ray* **of sunlight** (=the only good thing) *in an otherwise gloomy situation.* • *(fig.) Our new secretary is a real ray* **of sunshine** (=a happy person). • A ray is also a small amount: *There was nothing I could do to offer her even the smallest ray* **of comfort**. ○ *There's still a ray* **of hope** *that the missing child will be found alive.* • In science fiction stories, a **ray gun** is a gun which produces rays that kill people or make them unable to move.

ray [FISH] /reɪ/ *n* [C] a large flat sea fish with a long narrow tail. There are various types of ray. • *a manta ray* • *a sting ray*

ra·yon /£'reɪ·ɒn, $-ɑːn/ *n* [U] (cloth made from) a type of artificial thread • *Rayon is a synthetic cellulose fibre used to make silky cloth.* • *This skirt is made of cotton and rayon.* • *She was wearing a rayon blouse.* • (NL)

raze *obj* /reɪz/ *v* [T] to destroy (a building, city, etc.) completely • *A series of earthquakes struck northern China, killing at least 29 people, injuring hundreds and razing about 8000 homes.* • *The town was razed* **to the ground** *in the bombing raid – not a building was left standing.*

raz·or /£'reɪ·zəʳ, $-zɚ/ *n* [C] a small device for SHAVING (=removing hair), esp. from the face or legs • *According to the advertisement, this new razor will give you an extra smooth shave.* • *Do you use an* **electric** *razor or the kind that you have to put a razor* **blade** *in?* • *In a 100 metres race, there's often just a* **razor's edge** (=a very small division) *between first and second place.* • **Razor knife** is *Am for* STANLEY KNIFE. • *These animals have* **razor-sharp** (=very sharp) *teeth.* • *She's got a* **razor-sharp** (=clear and quick) *brain.* • *The president won the election by a* **razor-thin** (=very narrow) *margin.* • **Razor wire** is strong wire with pieces of sharp metal fixed closely together across it, which is often arranged in a pile of circles on top of walls, such as those surrounding a prison, to stop people climbing over the walls. • [PIC〉] **Blade, Edge, Knife, Tools**

raz·or *obj* /£'reɪ·zəʳ, $-zɚ/ *v* [T] • *My hairdresser always razors* (=cuts with a razor) *my fringe to give a soft effect.*

raz·zle /'ræz·l̩/ *n* [U] **on the razzle** *Br infml* enjoying yourself, visiting bars and dancing, etc. • *I was* **(out)** *on the razzle last night, and I'm rather tired this morning.* • *On New Year's Eve we're* **going (out)** *on the razzle.* • *We're having* **a night** *on the razzle tonight – are you coming?*

raz·zle–daz·zle /ˌræz·l̩'dæz·l̩, '–ˌ–/ *n* [U] *esp. Am* (confusion caused by) very noisy and noticeable activity or very colourful appearance, intended to attract attention • *Amid all the razzle-dazzle of the party convention, it was easy to forget about the real political issues.*

razz·ma·tazz /'ræz·mə·tæz/, **raz·za·ma·tazz** /'ræz·ə·mə·tæz/ *n* [U] noisy and noticeable activity which intentionally attracts attention • *The new car was launched with great razzmatazz: champagne, food, free gifts and dancers.*

RBT /£ˌɑː·biː'tiː, $ˌɑːr-/ *n* [C] *Aus abbreviation for* **random breath test**, see at RANDOM

RC /£ˌɑː'siː, $ˌɑːr-/ *adj, n* [C] *abbreviation for* Roman Catholic

RCMP /£ˌɑː·siː·em'piː, $ˌɑːr-/ *pl n* **the RCMP** *abbreviation for* Royal Canadian Mounted Police (=a Canadian police force known for specialist police services and for ceremonial appearances in red uniform and on horses)

Rd *n* [C] *abbreviation for* road (used in writing after the name of a road) • *Shaftesbury Rd*

re [ABOUT] /riː/ *prep fml* (esp. in business letters) about; on the subject of • *Re your communication of 15 February...* • [LP〉] **Letters**

re– [DO AGAIN] /ˌriː-/ *combining form* used to add the meaning 'do again', esp. to verbs • *rebuild* • *remarry* • *redecorate* • *reusable carrier bags* • *The film was re-released ten years later and became an instant success.* • *Angie has re-covered* (=put new material on) *the purple settee in the front room.* • Re- can also include the meaning of returning something to its original state: *The reafforestation of* (=planting of new trees in) *areas where all the trees have been chopped down is progressing well.*

're /£ᵊr, $ɚ/ *short form of* are • *You're very late.* • *We're going swimming this afternoon.* • *They're coming to see us next week.*

reach *obj* [ARRIVE] /riːtʃ/ *v* [T] to arrive at or come to • *He reached my house at ten o'clock.* • *How long will it take this letter to reach Italy?* • *The news of your accident has only just reached me.* • *The temperature is expected to reach 25°C today.* • *He's just reached the grand old age of 95.* • *Athletes often reach the height of their powers in their twenties.* • *She reached the* **conclusion** *that there was no more she could do.* • *I've finally reached the* **decision** *that I should find a new job.* • *We haven't yet been able to reach an* **agreement** *on the terms of the contract.* • *The jury took four days to reach a* **verdict**. • *I've reached the* **point** *where I'm not going to put up with her criticisms of me any more.* • *I think we've reached* **the point of no return** (=the state from which we have to advance) *with our car, and we're going to have to get a new one*

reach *(obj)* [STRETCH] /riːtʃ/ *v* to stretch out your arm, esp. in order to get or touch (something) • *She's grown so tall that she can reach the door handle now.* [T] • *Could you get that book down from the shelf for me, please – I can't reach.* [I] • *He reached* **for** *the phone and knocked over a glass.* [I] • *The cowboy reached* **for** *his gun and said "Reach* **for the skies** (=put your hands up)." [I] • *She reached* **over/across** *and took his hand in hers.* [I] • *The child reached* **down/out** *and picked up the kitten.* [I] • *He reached his hand* **out** *for the money.* [M] • *(fig.) The organizers of the appeal are reaching* **out to** *the public for* (=trying to communicate with them in order to get) *their help.* • *Helen reached* **up** *and took a glass from the cupboard.* [I] • *(Br) Can you reach me* **(down)** (=stretch out your arm and get) *that book/reach that book* **(down) for** *me?* [+ two objects] • If an object reaches **(to)** something, the top or bottom of it touches that thing: *The ladder won't quite reach the top of the wall.* [T] ○ *The snow reached almost to the children's knees.* [I] ○ *She was wearing a dress that reached to her ankles.* [I] • To reach someone who is in a different place is also to communicate with them, esp. by telephone or post: *The only way to reach them in the place where they're staying is* **by** *mail.* [T] ○ *I've been trying to reach you* (=talk to you on the telephone) *all day.* [T] [LP〉] **Telephone** • To reach someone is also to understand and communicate with them: *He's a strange child and his teachers find it difficult to reach him.* • If you **reach for the stars**, you want or try to get something that is difficult or impossible to get.

reach /riːtʃ/ *n* • Your reach is the distance within which you can stretch out your arm and touch something: *I like to keep a notebook and pencil* **within (arm's)** *reach.* [U] ○ *He's grown so much that now even the top shelf is* **within** *(his) reach.* [U] ○ *The apples were on a branch just* **out of** *(my) reach.* [U] ○ *Make sure that you keep all dangerous substances* **out of** *the reach* **of** *the children.* [U] • Reach can also be the distance that can be travelled, esp. easily: *We live* **within (easy)** *reach of the station.* [U] • Your reach is also the limit within which you can achieve something: *The exam was rather* **beyond/out of** *my reach* (=I found it difficult to do). ○ *I came* **within** *reach* **of** *solving* (=I almost solved) *the crossword, but there was one clue that I couldn't work out.* [U] ○ *An expensive trip like that would be completely* **beyond/out of** *(my) reach* (=I would not have enough money to pay for it). [U] ○ *After years of saving, the car was at last* **within** *(her) reach* (=she had enough money to pay for it). [U] • Your reach can also be the distance you can stretch out your arm: *You've got quite a long reach – can you get that box down from the top shelf for me?* [C] • A reach is an act of stretching out your arm: *He made a sudden reach* **for** *his gun.* [C] ○ *(fig.) It takes (quite) a reach* **of** *the imagination* (=It is very difficult) *to believe that story.* [C] • *"Ah, but a man's reach should exceed his grasp,/ Or what is heaven for?"* (Robert Browning in the poem *Andrea del Sarto*, 1855)

reach·es /riːtʃ/ *pl n* a part of a river or part of an area of land • *The expedition set out for the* **upper** *reaches* **of** *the Amazon.* • *There was little snow on the* **lower** *reaches* **of** *the ski run.* • *We know very little about the* **farthest/outermost** *reaches* **of** *the universe.* • *(fig.) The news has shocked the* **upper** *reaches* (=highest levels) **of** *the government.*

re·act /ri'ækt/ *v* [I] to act in a particular way as a direct result of something else • *How did she react when you told her you were leaving?* • *She slapped him and called him names, but he didn't react.* • *The judge reacted angrily* **to** *the suggestion that it hadn't been a fair trial.* • *He reacted* **against** (=intentionally behaved in a different way from) *everything he had been taught.* • *Many people react* **(badly) to** (=are made ill by) *penicillin.* • *This perfume seems to have reacted* (=had a bad effect) **on** *my skin.* • *(specialized) Potassium reacts* (=changes when mixed) **with** *water.*

re·ac·tant /ri'æk·tᵊnt/ *n* [C] *specialized* • A reactant is a substance which has been part of a chemical reaction.

re·ac·tion /ri'æk·ʃᵊn/ *n* [C] • A reaction is behaviour, a feeling or an action that is a direct result of something else: *I love to watch people's reactions when I say who I am.* /*There has been an immediate/widespread/hostile reaction* **against** *the government's proposed tax increases.* ○ *Reactions* **to** *the proposal so far have been* **adverse/favourable/mixed**. ○ *His reaction* **to** *the news was one of complete amazement.* ○ *What was his reaction* **towards** *you when you told him you were leaving him?* • A reaction is also a type of behaviour or opinion that is produced or held with the intention of being different from something: *The current fashion for floaty dresses is a reaction* **against** *last year's severe suits.* ○ *Her left-wing views are a reaction* **against** *the conservatism of her parents.* • A reaction can also be an unpleasant effect resulting from eating particular things or taking particular drugs: *Some people* **have** *an* **allergic** *reaction* **to** *shellfish.* • A **chemical** reaction is two or more substances reacting with and changing each other. • *"To every action there is an equal and opposite reaction." (Isaac Newton)* • See also REACTION.

re·ac·tions /ri'æk·ʃənz/ *pl n* • Your reactions are your ability to act quickly when something happens: *Driving a car after drinking is dangerous because alcohol slows the body's reactions.* ○ *You need to have* **quick** *reactions to play these computer games.*

re·ac·tion /ri:'æk·ʃən/ *n* [U] *disapproving* the belief or principle that there should be no social or political change, and the attempt to stop such change from happening • *We must not allow reaction to stand in the way of progress.* • *The proposed changes in the way young offenders are dealt with have been opposed by* **the forces of** *reaction* (=people opposed to political and social change).

re·ac·tion·a·ry /£ri'æk·ʃən·ər·i, $-er-/ *n* [C] *disapproving* • *Reactionaries* (=people who are opposed to political or social change or new ideas) *are preventing reforms.* [C] • Compare **progressive** at PROGRESS.

re·ac·tion·a·ry /£ri:'æk·ʃən·ər·i, $-er-/ *adj* • *Daryl accused the government of being ineffective and reactionary.* • *My father is* **deeply** *reactionary.* • *Reactionary* **forces/elements** *in the industry are preventing its progress.* • Compare **progressive** at PROGRESS.

re·ac·ti·vate *(obj)* /£ri'æk·tɪ·veɪt, $-t̬ɪ-/ *v* to bring or come back into action or use • *Seeing the old photographs reactivated a lot of memories for her.* [T] • *There are plans to reactivate the former railway line.* [T] • *The police file was reactivated because of new evidence.* [T] • *The virus can reactivate at any time.* [I]

re·ac·tor /£ri'æk·təʳ, $-t̬ɚ/, **nu·cle·ar re·ac·tor** *n* [C] a device in which atoms are either divided or joined in order to produce power

read *(obj)* UNDERSTAND /ri:d/ *v past* **read** /red/ to obtain meaning or information, esp. by looking at printed or written words or symbols • *He spent a pleasant afternoon reading (the newspaper/a book).* [I/T] • *As a teenager, I read all his books* **avidly**. [T] • *Children of that age tend to read* **voraciously** (=many books of all kinds). [I] • *I read* **about** *the family's success in the local paper.* [I] • *It was too dark to read our map and we took a wrong turning.* [T] • *Can you read music?* [T] • *Your handwriting is so untidy I can't read it.* [T] • *I've read in the newspapers* **(that)** *there is a threat of war.* [+ *(that)* clause] • *She read the instructions* **to** *find out how to use the computer.* [T] • *Put your plastic card in the slot, and the machine will read it and identify who you are.* [T] • *Many children can read* (=have learnt the skill of obtaining information from printed or written words) *by the age of four.* [I] • *The letter reads* (=seems when you read it) **as if**/*(Am also, Br not standard)* **like** *it was written in a hurry.* [I] • *Her latest novel reads well* (=is written in an attractive way). [I] • To read is also to say the words that are printed or written: *She read (the poem) slowly and quietly.* [I/T] ○ *Their teacher always read them a story/read a story* **to** *them at the end of the day.* [+ two objects] ○ *Children love to have stories read* **(aloud/out loud/out) to** *them.* [M] ○ *Every night when I was a child my father* **read** *me* **to sleep** (=read aloud to me until I went to sleep). • To read also means to understand or INTERPRET written information: *She missed the train because she read 18.30* **as** *8.30 p.m. instead of 6.30 p.m.* [T] ○ *On page 19,* **for** *Blitish, please read British.* [T] ○ *If I've read the situation* **aright**, *we should have some agreement on the contract by the end of the week.* [T] • *(Br fml)* To read is to study at university or for some professional qualifications: *They're both reading history at Cambridge.* [T] ○ *(law) She's reading* **for the Bar** (=studying to become a type of lawyer called a BARRISTER). [I] • Read is used, esp. when communicating by radio, to mean 'hear and understand': *Do you read me?* [T] ○ *I read you loud and clear.* [T] • To read **over/through** something means to read it quickly from the beginning to the end: *I read your proposal through last night and I think we'll agree to it.* [M] • To read **up about/up on** something is to read in order to find out information about it: *It's a good idea to read up on a company before going for an interview.* [I] • To **read between the lines** is to find hidden meanings or intentions in what has been said or written: *She said they were busy on that day but, reading between the lines, they just didn't want to come to the presentation.* • To **read** something **into** something is to find meanings in an activity that were possibly not intended: *Don't read too much into her leaving so suddenly – she probably just had a train to catch.* ○ *I think you're reading more into their refusal than is justified.* • To **read** someone's **lips** is to follow the movements of their lips in order to understand what they are saying, esp. if you are unable to hear them speak: *She read his lips across the busy conference hall – "Time to go".* ○ *(fig.) Read my lips* (=Make sure you understand what I am saying). *No more ice cream today!* See also **lip-read** at LIP. • If someone comes to your house to **read the meter**, they look at a piece of measuring equipment to see how much electricity/gas has been used: *They read the meter once a quarter.* ○ *We had the meter read before we moved house.* • To **read** someone's **mind/thoughts** is to know what they are thinking without them telling you. • To **read** someone's **palm** is to look at the lines on a person's hand as a way of finding out what will happen to them in the future, esp. for payment as part of a group of entertainment activities: *They passed the shooting range and a couple of food stalls and finally reached the tent where a gypsy was reading palms.* • When someone **reads the Riot Act**, they demand that something such as noise or bad behaviour should stop immediately: *Her mother rushed into the room and read the Riot Act* **to** *Sal and her friends, demanding that they turned the music down and tidied the place up.* • *(Br)* If you **read the runes** you understand from what is taking place at present what will happen in the future: *He was the first of the eastern leaders to read the runes and make political changes to stay in power.* • *"Read my lips – no new taxes"* (President George Bush in a speech, 1988)

read *Br and Aus* /ri:d/ *n* [U] • *I always find spy-thrillers* **a good** *read* (=enjoyable to read). • *(infml) Could I* **have a** *read* **of** (=Could I read) *your newspaper, if you've finished with it?*

read /red/ *adj* • *It's a* **widely** *read newspaper* (=it has many readers). • *(Br)* If you **take** something **as read**, you accept it without having read, expressed or talked about it in detail: *We will take the minutes of the last meeting as read and go on to the next business.* ○ *He took it as read that anyone who applied for the course would have the necessary qualifications.*

read·a·ble /'ri:·də·bl̩/ *adj* • Readable means easy or enjoyable to read because of interesting language and/or clear writing, printing, etc.: *It is an excellent and* **highly** *readable account of the army today.* ○ *They have packed 150 years of complex history into some hundred clear and readable pages.*

-read·a·ble /-'ri:·də·bl̩/ *combining form* • **Machine/Computer**-readable means in a form which is able to be used by a computer: *Machine-readable passports will permit precise identity-checking.*

read·er /£'ri:·dəʳ, $-dɚ/ *n* [C] • A reader is someone who reads for pleasure, esp. a person who reads a lot: *He's a* **great** *reader* (=reads many books). ○ *She's an* **avid** *reader* **of** *historical novels.* • The people who read a particular newspaper or magazine are called its readers: *We asked our readers to write in and give us their views.* ○ *The magazine conducted a reader survey recently.* ○ *She described him as a typical Guardian reader.* • *(specialized)* At British universities, a reader is a teacher just under the rank of PROFESSOR: *a Reader* **in** *History* **at** *Liverpool.* • *(specialized)* A reader is also a person whose job is to give advice to a publisher on whether or not a book should be published. • A reader can also be a device that helps you to read very small writing, or a machine that can recognize printed material: *a microfilm/microfiche reader* ○ *an optical character reader* • *"Reader, I married him"* (Jane Eyre of Mr Rochester in the book *Jane Eyre* by Charlotte Brontë, 1847)

read·er·ship /£'ri:·də·ʃɪp, $-dɚ-/ *n* [C] • A readership is the group of people who regularly read a particular newspaper, magazine, etc.: *The magazine has a readership* **of** *over 250 000.* ○ *It's a newspaper with a large right-wing readership.*

read·ing /'ri:·dɪŋ/ *n* • Reading is the skill or activity of getting information from books: *Reading and tennis are my favourite pastimes.* [U] ○ *The early years at school concentrate on the teaching of reading and writing.* [U] ○ *The diaries* **make good (bedtime)** *reading* (=are good to read (in bed at night)). [U] ○ *These books are* **compulsory/required** *reading for students of architecture.* [U] • A reading is an occasion when something written, esp. a literary work, is spoken to an audience: *Later in his life, the poet rarely gave readings of his work.* [C] o *The society often arranges* **poetry** *readings and musical evenings.* [C] • In a parliament, a reading of a new law is one of the stages of discussion before it is approved: *The Housing Bill was given its second reading in Parliament today.* [C] • Your reading of something is the way in which you understand it: *My reading of the situation is that John wanted any excuse to resign.* [U] o *The usual reading of this passage stresses the hero's failure.* [C] • If you have a **reading knowledge** of a language, you can read it, but you can't speak it: *I've got a good reading knowledge of Spanish.* • A **reading list** is list of books that esp. students are expected to read as part of their course. • A **reading room** is a room, in a library, hotel or other building, which is for people who want to read quietly and where conversation is not usually allowed.

read [STATE] /riːd/ *v* (of something written or printed) to have or give the stated information or meaning • *The start of the American Constitution reads 'We, the people of the United States...'* [+ clause] • *The thermometer is reading 40°C in the shade.* [L] • *A sign reading 'No Smoking' was stuck on the wall.* [+ clause] • A **read-out** is information produced by electronic equipment, shown in print, on a screen or by sound: *In electronic calculator displays and digital watch read-outs, the digits are made up from diodes.* o *The operators control the working life of the mine without seeing it, the computer giving a read-out on the status of each vehicle.* o *The computerized map has a voice read-out, so it'll say "Turn left in 200 yards".*

read·ing /ˈriː·dɪŋ/ *n* [C] • *a thermometer reading*

re·ad·dress *obj* /ˌriː·əˈdres/ *v* [T] to write a different address (on an envelope) because the person for whom it is intended has moved to another place • *We readdressed all his letters* **to** *Australia for years after he had emigrated.*

read·ies /ˈred·iːz/ *pl n* **the readies** *Br slang for* MONEY • *I'm a bit short of the readies.*

re·ad·just *(obj)* /ˌriː·əˈdʒʌst/ *v* to change again to fit a different situation or to correct something • *After living abroad for so long, he found it difficult to readjust* **to** *life at home.* [I] • *He readjusted his tie.* [T] • *The clock automatically readjusts when you enter a new time zone.* [I] • *The machines were old and constantly needed readjusting* (= repairing slightly). [T]

re·ad·just·ment /ˌriː·əˈdʒʌst·mənt/ *n* [C] • *President Gorbachev's policies led to a major readjustment in the way the West viewed the USSR.*

read·y [PREPARED] /ˈred·i/ *adj* [not gradable] prepared and suitable for immediate activity • *"The dinner's ready," she called out.* • *"Are you ready? Hurry up – we're late."* • *I quickly finish dressing in the morning when my mother says, "***Get** *ready. We have to leave."* • *The concert hall was* **made** *ready* (= prepared) **for** *the performance.* • *The waiter came over to the table and asked, "Are you ready* **to** *order?"* [+ *to* infinitive] • *He looked ready* **to** (= as if he would very soon) *collapse.* [+ *to* infinitive] • **Ready to** also means willing to: *What good friends you have – they're always ready to help you out.* [+ *to* infinitive] o *They weren't ready to lend me the money.* [+ *to* infinitive] • *(disapproving)* If you are **too** ready **with** something you are too eager to do it: *He's too ready with* (= too eager to give) *his advice.* • *Secret information allowed the police to be ready* **and waiting** (= waiting and prepared to act) *when the robbers came out of the bank.* • *The sheriff slept with his gun ready* **to hand** (= close to him and prepared for use) *under his pillow.* • *He stood by the phone, pencil* **at the ready** (= prepared to write). • *(Br)* **Ready, steady, go!** is said at the start of a race, esp. one for children. • Clothes that are **ready-to-wear** (*Br and Aus also* **off-the-peg**, *Am also* **off-the-rack**) are produced in standard sizes and not made to fit a particular person. • If something is **ready-made** it has been found or bought in a finished form or is available to use immediately: *ready-made frozen meals* o *I didn't make the birthday cake myself – I bought it ready-made.* o *When she married Giles, she acquired a ready-made family – two teenage sons and a daughter.* • *(dated infml)* **Ready money** is money that is available to be spent immediately. See also **readies**. • *"No cucumbers in the market, not even for ready money"* (Oscar Wilde in the play *The Importance of Being Earnest*, 1895)

read·i·ly /ˈred·ɪ·li/ *adv* • Readily means quickly, immediately, willingly or without any problem: *He readily* (= quickly and willingly) *agreed to help.* o *Larger sizes are readily available* (= can be obtained easily).

read·i·ness /ˈred·ɪ·nəs/ *n* [U] • *The company has declared its readiness* **to** *fight a challenge in the courts.* [+ *to* infinitive] • *The readiness of the authorities* **to** *embrace tourism as a means of preserving the nation's heritage has resulted in the conservation of some of the finest historic sites.* [+ *to* infinitive] • *The scaffolding has been put up* **in** *readiness* **for** *the repair work on the building.*

read·y [QUICK] /ˈred·i/ *adj* [before n; not gradable] *esp. approving* mentally clever, esp. quick with answers, jokes, solutions, etc. • *She's got a ready* **mind/tongue/wit**. • *He had a ready* **reply** *to every question.*

re·af·firm *obj* /£ˌriː·əˈfɜːm, $-ˈfɜːrm/ *v* [T] to give (your support) to a person, plan idea etc. for a second time • *The government yesterday reaffirmed its* **commitment** *to the current peace process.* • *These events reaffirm my* **belief** *in the need for better information.* • *The latest reports only served to reaffirm the people's* **opposition** *to these unpopular measures.*

re·af·for·est *obj* /£ˌriː·əˈfɒr·ɪst, $-ˈfɔːr·ɪst/ *v* [T] *Br and Aus for* REFOREST

re·af·for·es·ta·tion /£ˌriː·əˌfɒr·ɪˈsteɪ·ʃən, $-ˌfɔːr·ɪ-/ *n* [U] • Reafforestation is *Br and Aus for* **reforestation**. See at REFOREST.

re·ag·ent /ˌriːˈeɪ·dʒənt/ *n* [C] *specialized* a substance which acts on another in a chemical reaction • *Mix the two reagents in the flask.*

real [NOT IMAGINARY] /£rɪəl, $riː·əl/ *adj* existing in fact; not imaginary • *Assuring the patient that she has a real and not imaginary problem is the first step.* • *There is a real threat that he will lose his job.* • *The possibility of defeat is only too real.* • *Wages grew by 2·9% in the year to September – the biggest increase for 20 months – but real* **earnings/incomes/wages** *still fell by 1·3%* (= although it appeared to increase, in fact the buying power of the money was reduced). • If you tell someone to **get real**, you mean that they should behave according to the situation as it is, not as they would like it to be: *Get real! He's never going to lend you £5000.* • **In real terms** means existing in fact, despite what appears to be the situation: *A family man's earnings rose 5% in real terms after deducting income tax, insurance, child allowances etc.* • **Real life** is what happens in human situations rather than in a story, film, etc.: *It's a good plot but not exactly like real life.* o **In** *real life the star of the film is a devoted husband and father.* o *The film is based on a real-life story.* • **Real-time** computing systems are able to deal with and use new information immediately and therefore influence or direct the actions of the objects supplying that information: *Real-time programs are used by air traffic controllers to direct aircraft.* • **The real world** is the set of situations most humans have to deal with in their lives, rather than what happens in stories, films, specially protected ways of life, etc.: *The humour of most of his 20 books is based on confronting intellectuals with the real world.* o **In** *the real world Christine, the play's main character, would hardly be able to sustain her reign of terror so effortlessly.* o *Wolves in European folk tales are destructive human-killers, not the intelligent, social creatures that we know them to be* **in** *the real world.* • (D) (P)

real·i·sm /£ˈrɪə·lɪ·zəm, $ˈriː·ə-/ *n* [U] • Realism is a way of thinking and acting based on the facts of a situation and what appears to be possible, rather than on hopes for things which are unlikely to happen: *In his decision to move his business into the school market he showed a shrewd, down-to-earth realism – schools always needed paper and books.* • *(specialized)* Paintings, films, books etc. that try to represent life as it really is are in the artistic tradition of realism: *The anti-drugs adverts were shot using hand-held camera techniques to add to the* **gritty** *realism of the situations.* • *(specialized)* In science and PHILOSOPHY, realism is the belief that objects continue to exist in the world even when no one is there to see them: *Like some quantum theorists, Berkeley sought to undermine realism as a philosophical position.* • Compare **idealism** at IDEAL [PRINCIPLE].

re·al·ist /£ˈrɪə·lɪst, $ˈriː·ə-/ *n* [C] • A realist is someone who hopes for or accepts only what seems possible or likely and does not have too high hopes or expectations: *I'm a realist – I knew there was no way I could win, so I swam for a good finish, for points.* o *Only dreamers believe that barriers between the two countries will fall soon – realists hope that progress to a frontier-free situation will be made in the next five years.* • *(specialized)* A realist is an artist, writer, etc. who represents life as it really is, rather than in an imagined way: *Courbet was one of the first Realists/realist painters.*

re·al·is·tic /£ˌrɪə'lɪs·tɪk, $ˌriː·ə-/ *adj* • Realistic means accepting things as they are in fact and not basing decisions on unlikely hopes for the future: *Let's be realistic – I just can't afford to pay that much money.* ○ *You have to be realistic* **about** *how long the job is going to take.* ○ *Is this a realistic* **prediction/estimate** (=one that has been carefully considered and is based on the facts)? • *It isn't realistic* **to** *expect people to work for so little money.* [+ to infinitive] • Realistic also means appearing to be existing or happening in fact: *The scene in the film where the dinosaur hatches from the egg was incredibly realistic.* • See also REALPOLITIK.

re·al·is·ti·cally /£ˌrɪə'lɪs·tɪ·kli, $ˌriː·ə-/ *adv* • *Realistically speaking, he hadn't a hope, but that didn't stop him trying.* • *He was made up very realistically – he looked just like an old woman.*

re·al·i·ty /£ri'æl·ɪ·ti, $-ə·t̬i/ *n* • Reality is the state of things as they are, rather than as they are imagined to be: *The reality* **of** *the situation is that unless we find some new funding soon, the youth centre will have to close.* [U] ○ *He* **escaped from** *reality by going to the cinema every afternoon.* [U] ○ *He seemed very young, but he was* **in reality** (= in fact) *older than all of us.* [U] ○ *His account of the event* **bore very little resemblance to** *reality* (= was not similar to what happened in fact). ○ *"You're* **out of touch with** *reality* (= Your decisions are not based on the facts of the situation)," *said his boss, "you're not living in the real world."* [U] • Realities are facts: *The book* **confronts** *the social, political and economic realities of the world today.* [C] ○ *The trouble with these suggestions is that they almost completely* **ignore** *the realities of most of our schools.* [C] ○ *Once you've left school you have to face up to life's* **harsh** *realities.* [C] ○ *Her childhood ambition* **became a** *reality* (= happened in fact) *when she was made a judge.* [C]

re·al·ize *obj, Br and Aus usually* **-ise** /£'rɪə·laɪz, $'riː·ə-/ *v* [T] • To realize something is to cause it to be real or to exist or happen in fact: *Lots of money, a luxury house, a fast car – Danny had realized all his ambitions by the age of 25.* ○ *Ten years later her worst fears were realized.* • *(law)* To realize **assets** is to change property, etc. into money: *He had to realize all his assets to pay off his debts.* • See also REALIZE. • Ⓕ

re·al·iz·a·ble, *Br and Aus usually* **-is·a·ble** /£'rɪə·laɪ·zə·bl̩, $'riː·ə-/ *adj* • *He doubted whether the plan was realizable in practice.* • *(specialized) realizable assets*

re·al·i·za·tion, *Br and Aus usually* **-i·sa·tion** /£ˌrɪə·laɪ'zeɪ·ʃən, $ˌriː·ə-/ *n* [U] • *To win the Olympic gold medal was the realization of his life's dream.* • *(law) Even the realization of all his assets* (= changing property into money) *would not be enough to prevent financial ruin.* • See also **realization** at REALIZE.

real·ly /£'rɪə·li, $riː·ə-/ *adv* • *What really happened on that day?* • *He isn't really cross – he's just pretending.* • *You don't really expect them to refuse, do you?* • Really is used to express great certainty: *Thank you, but I really couldn't eat another thing.* ○ *He's really going to do it this time.*

real NOT FALSE /£rɪəl, $riːl/ *adj* [before n] not false; being what it appears to be; GENUINE • *a real leather bag* • *These spoons are made of real silver.* • *(humorous) He's not a real* **man** *– real men like sport and fast cars, and real men definitely don't eat quiche!* • *(Br approving)* Real is used, esp. with foods, to mean produced using traditional methods and without artificial substances: *The Real Meat Company* ○ *The pub sells several kinds of real* **ale** (= beer). • *(infml)* When something is **for real** it is not false and is what it appears to be: *Is this letter a joke or is it for real?* ○ *Is this a practice or is it for real?* • **The real thing** is the original, best or most typical example of something: *After weeks of slight flurries, this at last was the real thing, a heavy fall of snow.* ○ *He was wearing an 'ultra-suede' jacket – it's a synthetic material which looks like the real thing.* ○ *'Coca-Cola, it's the real thing!' is the company's advertising slogan.* ○ *"We didn't know if it was the real thing or a practice, so we pulled on the respirators and followed the drill," said a soldier.* • **The real McCoy** is the original or the best example of something: *The caviar was the real McCoy too – not the stuff we buy in the supermarket at home.* • *"This Time I Know it's for Real"* (song by Donna Summer, 1989) • Ⓓ Ⓟ

real IMPORTANT /£rɪəl, $riːl/ *adj* [before n] the most important; the main • *Bullies and ruffians, swaggerers and drunks occasionally invade these places, but they are never the real danger.* • *The real difficulty was the language, because my children don't speak English.* • *The commander was said to be unavailable – it turned out that the real problem was that none of his men wanted to risk disturbing him.* • *The Bishop concedes that the film's artistic merit is of little interest to him – his real interest is censorship.* • *Novelty value may be a part of it, but the real reason people like our paper is that it speaks the truth.* • *The real threat to the species is loss of habitat as towns spread into the countryside.* • Ⓓ Ⓟ

real VERY GREAT /£rɪəl, $riː·əl/ *adj* [before n] very great or to a great degree • *He's a real gentleman/Christian.* • *She's a real beauty.* • *How to get there by public transport is a real problem.* • *He can be a real bastard.* • Ⓓ Ⓟ

real /£rɪəl, $riː·əl/ *adv* [not gradable] *esp. Am infml* • *I like this homemade lemonade, it's real good!* • *My uncle bought me a real neat model kit.*

real·ly /£'rɪə·li, $'riː·ə-/ *adv* [not gradable] *infml* • *This room is really hot.* • *It's a really difficult decision.* • *We had a really good time.* • *Things became really serious when the plane's second engine stopped.* • *The film was quite good really* (= it was good, but not very good). • *"A Really Useful Engine"* (phrase from the *Thomas the Tank Engine* books by The Rev. W. Awdry, 1946-) • LP> **Very, completely**

real·ly /£'rɪə·li, $'riː·ə-/ *exclamation* • Really is used to express interest, surprise or annoyance: *"I'm getting married to Fred." "Really? When?"* ○ *"She's agreed to do a parachute jump for charity." "Really? Do you think she'll do it?"* ○ *"He hasn't brought the book back." "Oh, really! That's the second time I've asked him!"* ○ *"Well really! I think he might have put some clothes on!"*

real es·tate, *Br law* **real prop·er·ty** *n* [U] *esp. Am and Aus* property in the form of land or buildings • *We're going to buy a piece of real estate.* • **Real estate agent** is *Am and Aus for* **estate agent**. See at ESTATE PROPERTY. • **Real estate broker** is *Aus for* **estate agent**.

re·al·ign *obj* /ˌriː·ə'laɪn/ *v* [T] to put into a new or correct position • *She realigned the books along the edge of the shelf.* • *Several politicians left the party and realigned themselves* **with** *the opposition.*

re·align·ment /ˌriː·ə'laɪn·mənt/ *n* [U] • *This war will inevitably lead to a realignment* **of/within** *European politics.* • *Car wheels need occasional realignment by a mechanic.*

re·al·ize *(obj), Br and Aus usually* **-ise** /£'rɪə·laɪz, $'riː·ə-/ *v* to understand (a situation), sometimes suddenly • *They didn't realize the danger they were in.* [T] • *"Do you realize* **(that)** *this is the third time you've forgotten?" she said angrily.* [+ (that) clause] • *I realize* **how** *difficult it's going to be, but we must try.* [+ wh- word] • *I didn't* **fully** *realize what an enthusiastic father Nigel would be.* [+ wh- word] • *As he watched the TV play, he* **suddenly** *realized* **(that)** *he'd seen it before.* [+ (that) clause] • *"You're standing on my foot." "Sorry, I didn't realize."* [I] • See also **realize** at REAL NOT IMAGINARY.

re·al·i·za·tion, *Br and Aus usually* **-i·sa·tion** /£ˌrɪə·laɪ'zeɪ·ʃən, $ˌriː·ə-/ *n* [C usually sing] • *The realization was* **dawning** (= They were starting to realize) **that** *this was a major disaster.* [+ that clause] • *The novel revolves around the hero's growing realization* **of** *financial corruption.* • *The realization* **that** *he would never see her again broke his heart.* [+ that clause] • *The letter came as a* **sobering** *realisation* (= showed him) **that** *he could not depend on everyone's support.* [+ that clause] • Ⓕ

realm AREA /relm/ *n* [C] an area of interest or activity • *The differences between the two groups are quite profound, both in the realm of ideology and in the realm of practical policy.* • *Several other similar stories have entered the public realm, unnoticed and unchecked.* • *We knew that the music was leading us into new realms of pleasure.* • *The change in people's attitudes will slowly move from the realm of theory into the sphere of practice.* • *Some dramatic successes in the realm of foreign policy marked the last six years of his time in office.* • *The story remains in the realms of fantasy but is presented as an adult dream.* • *A new building for the school is not* **within the realms of possibility** (= definitely not possible).

realm COUNTRY /relm/ *n* [C] *fml or literary* a country ruled by a king or queen • *a peer/knight of the realm* • *coins of the realm* • *the defence of the realm* • *The matter was hotly debated in all the towns of the realm.* • *In a realm as large as medieval Germany, the king faced a huge task.* • *"This blessed plot, this earth, this realm, this England"* (Shakespeare, Richard II 2.1)

re·al·pol·i·tik /£reɪ'ɑːl,pɒl·ɪ·tiːk, $-poʊ·lɪ-/ *n* [U] practical politics, decided more by the immediate needs of the country, political party etc., than by morals or principles

re·al·tor /£'rɪəl·təʳ, $'riː·əl·tɔːr/, **real es·tate a·gent/brok·er** *n* [C] *Am and Aus for* **estate agent**, see at ESTATE [PROPERTY]

ream /riːm/ *n* [C] *specialized* 500 sheets of paper, or *(infml)* a lot of something, esp. writing • *I ordered three reams of the best typing paper.* • *(infml) She's written reams of poetry.*

ream out *obj*, **ream** *obj* **out** *v adv* [M] *Am slang* to express severe disapproval to (someone) • *He reamed them out for sleeping on the job.*

ream·er /£'riː·məʳ, $-mɚ/ *n* [C] *specialized* a tool used to make holes larger or to an exact size

reap *(obj)* /riːp/ *v* to cut and collect by hand (crops such as wheat) using a tool with a curved blade or, more generally, to obtain or receive (something) as a result of your own actions • *The villagers were out in the fields all day, reaping (the corn).* [I/T] • *We sold them most of their modern weapons and now we are reaping the bitter* **harvest**. [T] • *Lawyers are reaping a rich* **harvest** *from the current trend for suing the minute something goes wrong.* [T] • *She studied every evening and reaped the* **benefit** *at exam time.* [T] • *In retirement he reaped the* **rewards** *of his earlier investments.* [T] • To **reap what** you **have sown** is to benefit or lose as a result of something you did in the past. • *"They have sown the wind and they shall reap the whirlwind* (= any bad thing that you do, no matter how small, might lead to something very dangerous)*"* (Bible, Hosea 8.7)

reap·er /£'riː·pəʳ, $-pɚ/ *n* [C] • A reaper is a person who cuts and collects crops by hand, using a tool with a curved blade. • In the past, a reaper was a machine pulled by horses that cut crops, and a **reaper-binder** was a machine which cut and collected crops.

re·ap·pear /£,riː·ə'pɪəʳ, $-'pɪr/ *v* [I] to appear again or return after a period of time • *As the clouds finally drifted away the moon reappeared.* • *Ten minutes later she reappeared from the storeroom holding the paint.*

re·ap·pear·ance /£,riː·ə'pɪə·rənts, $-'pɪr·ənts/ *n* [C] • *Her reappearance in the news was not unexpected.*

rear [BACK] /£rɪəʳ, $rɪr/ *adj* [before n; not gradable], *n* (at) the back (of something) • *Is the puncture in the front or rear wheel?* • *There's a sticker on the rear door/window.* • *She doesn't like sitting in the rear seat.* • *He tipped the chair back on its rear legs.* • *The horse has strained one of its rear (also* **hind**) *legs.* • *The rear end of the car is sometimes hard to control in sharp cornering.* • *(Am infml)* To **rear-end** is to hit the back of one car with another in an accident: *My new car was rear-ended while it was parked outside the station.* • *(dated)* The part of your body on which you sit is sometimes called your **rear (end)**, in order to avoid saying bottom: *The ad showed a female rear in a pair of red trousers.* [C] ○ *He said, "I worked my* **rear end off** (= very hard) *to help elect the President."* • **The rear** is the back part: *Many people avoid sitting in the rear of a train, because they are worried about a crash.* ○ *We tried to get round to the rear of the house.* ○ *Two police motorcyclists* **brought up** *the rear* (= formed the last part) *of the demonstration.* • A **rear admiral** is an officer of very high rank in the navy. • A **rear view mirror** is a mirror which allows a driver to see what is happening behind the car: *She saw a flashing light in her rear view mirror.* • If a car has **rear-wheel drive**, the engine provides power to the back wheels. • See also REARGUARD. • [PIC] **Car**

rear·most /£'rɪə·məʊst, $'rɪr·moʊst/ *adj* [before n; not gradable] *fml* • Rearmost means furthest to the back or the last in a row: *the rearmost seats on the bus*

rear *obj* [CARE FOR] /£rɪəʳ, $rɪr/ *v* [T] to care for (young animals or children) until they are able to care for themselves, or to care for (animals) in order to use them for food • *Some women have made a deliberate choice to rear a* **child** *alone.* See also **child-rearing** at CHILD. • *He describes how these birds rear their* **chicks**. • *The farmer's wife* **hand-***reared* (= fed and cared for) *the tiny lambs when their mother died.* • *The scientists tracked one lot of infected meat back to the farms where the* **animals/cattle/pigs/etc.** *had been reared* (= in order to be used as food).

rear *(obj)* [RISE] /£rɪəʳ, $rɪr/ *v* to rise up or to lift up • *The horse reared* **(up)** (= suddenly rose onto its back legs) *when it heard the gun shot.* [I] • *The lion slowly reared its head* (= lifted it up) *and looked around.* [T] • *The familiar spectre of drought and famine* **reared its (ugly) head** (= appeared) *again.* • If something or someone **rears above/over** something or someone else, they appear very tall and big in comparison: *The mountain reared above the village.* ○ *He reared over his little opponent.*

rear·guard /£'rɪə·gɑːd, $'rɪr·gɑːrd/ *n* [U] the people who are the last in a row or group, esp. in a military situation • A **rearguard action** is a final and probably hopeless attempt to prevent something from happening: *The unions were determined to* **fight** *a rearguard action* **against** *the government's plans to strip them of their powers.*

re·arm *(obj)* /£,riː'ɑːm, $-'ɑːrm/ *v* to supply (yourself or others) with new weapons, esp. in order to become a strong military power again • *They cannot be sure whether their opponents want a lasting peace or just a chance to rearm.* [I] • *They patrolled the sea between there and the island to stop the guerrillas being rearmed.* [T]

re·ar·ma·ment /£ri'ɑː·mə·mənt, $-'ɑːr-/ *n* [U] • *The post-war constitution forbade rearmament.*

rear·range *obj* /,riː·ə'reɪndʒ/ *v* [T] to change the order, position or time of (arrangements already made) • *The new sofa was bigger than the old one, so they had to rearrange the rest of the* **furniture**. • *He rearranged his limbs into a more comfortable position.* • *Janey's going to be late, so we'll have to rearrange the order of the speakers.* • *I'm busy tomorrow – could we rearrange the meeting* **for** *Monday* (= have it on Monday instead)*?*

re·ar·range·ment /,riː·ə'reɪndʒ·mənt/ *n* [C] • *As students of chemistry know, even small rearrangements* **of** *a molecule's structure can produce a compound that acts differently.* • *Going on a long trip always means lots of rearrangements* **to** *my schedule.*

rea·son [EXPLANATION] /'riː·zᵊn/ *n* something suggested as the cause of an event or situation or which provides an excuse or explanation • *The reason* **for** *the disaster was engine failure, not human error.* [C] • *The reasons* **for** *her actions remained unclear.* [C] • *The reason* **why** *grass is green was a mystery to the little boy.* [C + *wh-* word] • *The reason* **(that)** *I'm asking is (that) I wondered if you'd be able to help me.* [C + *(that)* clause] • *(not standard) The reason I walked out was* **because** *I was bored.* [C] • *She* **has no** *reason* **to** *go, but she feels it's the right thing to do.* [U + *to* infinitive] • *The police* **have (every good)** *reason* **to** *believe that he is guilty.* [U + *to* infinitive] • *She was furious, and* **with** *reason* (= with good cause). [U] • **For some** *reason*/**For** *reasons* **best known to** *himself* (= For reasons no one else knows about) *he's decided to leave his job.* [C] • *(fml) He's always asked to these occasions* **by reason of** (= because of) *his position.* • *"Reasons to be Cheerful"* (title of a song by Ian Dury, 1979)

rea·son [JUDGMENT] /'riː·zᵊn/ *n* [U] the ability of a healthy mind to think and make judgments, esp. based on practical facts • *We humans assert that we are the only animals to have* **the power of** *reason.* • *(esp. Br dated) He* **lost** *his reason* (= became mentally ill) *when both his parents were killed in the crash.* • What is **within** reason is what is practical or acceptable: *You can choose you own gift, within reason.* • If what someone says or does **is/goes beyond all reason**, it is unacceptable: *The awful things she said went beyond all reason.* • To **listen to/see reason** is to listen to good advice and act according to it: *Friends tried to persuade them to change their minds but neither man would listen to reason.*

rea·son *(obj)* /'riː·zᵊn/ *v* • To reason is to try to understand and to make judgments based on practical facts: *From the presence of a giraffe in the garden, Gerald reasoned* **(that)** *the circus had arrived in town.* [+ *(that)* clause] ○ *Newton reasoned* **(that)** *there must be a force such as gravity, when an apple fell on his head.* [+ *(that)* clause] ○ *I spent hours reasoning* **out** *the solution to the puzzle.* [M] • If you reason someone **into/out of** doing something, you persuade them to do/not to do something based on good judgment: *I reasoned him into being sensible.* [T always + adv/prep] • *We couldn't reason him out of his panic.* [T always + adv/prep] • To reason **with** someone is to argue with and try to persuade them, esp. to act wisely: *The police reasoned with the hijackers* **to** *at least let the children go.* [I] ○ *She reasoned with her sons* **that** *they needed to work harder if they were going to pass their exams.* [+ *that* clause] ○ *There's no reasoning with somebody who's prejudiced.* [I] • *"Theirs not to make reply,/ Theirs not to reason why,/ Theirs but to do and die"* (Alfred, Lord Tennyson in the poem *The Charge of the Light Brigade*, 1854)

rea·son·a·ble /'riː·zᵊn·ə·bl̩/ *adj* • Reasonable means based on or using good judgment and therefore fair and practical: *If you tell him what happened I'm sure he'll understand – he's a reasonable man.* ○ *He went free because* *the jury decided there was (a) reasonable* **doubt** *about his guilt.* ○ *Is* **it** *reasonable* **to** *believe that the president really knew nothing about this decision?* [+ *to* infinitive] ○ *"I want another $500 by tomorrow." "Be reasonable – you know I can't manage that."* • Reasonable also means acceptably good: *We had a reasonable journey.* ○ *It's a reasonable book.* ○ *Tomatoes are very reasonable/a reasonable* **price** (= not too expensive) *at this time of year.* ○ *We have a strong team and a reasonable chance of winning the game.*

rea·son·a·ble·ness /ˈriː·zᵊn·ə·bl̩·nəs/ *n* [U]

rea·son·a·bly /ˈriː·zᵊn·ə·bli/ *adv* • *Stop shouting and let's discuss this reasonably* (= using good judgment). • Reasonably also means acceptably: *She writes reasonably good children's books.* ○ *I live reasonably close* (= not far from) *to the airport.* ○ *I bought a reasonably priced* (= not expensive) *radio.*

rea·soned /ˈriː·zᵊnd/ *adj* • A **(well)** reasoned **argument** is one that is clear and carefully considered.

rea·son·ing /ˈriː·zᵊn·ɪŋ/ *n* [U] • *The reasoning behind her conclusion is impossible to fault.*

re·as·sure *obj* /£ˌriː·əˈʃɔːʳ, $-ˈʃʊr/ *v* [T] to comfort (someone) and stop them from worrying • *The meeting was designed to reassure parents whose children were taking exams that summer.* • *I was nervous on my first day at college, but I was reassured* **to** *see some friendly faces.* [+ *to* infinitive] • *He reassured me* **(that)** *my cheque would arrive soon.* [+ obj + (*that*) clause] • *The bank says it is doing everything it can to reassure people* **(that)** *their savings are safe.* [+ obj + (*that*) clause]

re·as·sur·ing /£ˌriː·əˈʃɔː·rɪŋ, $-ˈʃʊr·ɪŋ/ *adj* • *He smiled at me in a reassuring fashion.* • *I found her speech highly reassuring.*

re·as·sur·ing·ly /£ˌriː·əˈʃɔː·rɪŋ·li, $-ˈʃʊr·ɪŋ-/ *adv* • *"Don't worry," he said reassuringly. "Everything will be alright."*

re·as·sur·ance /£ˌriː·əˈʃɔː·rənts, $-ˈʃʊr·ᵊnts/ *n* • *I felt I couldn't cope with the situation and was in desperate need of some reassurance.* [U] • *Despite her father's reassurances* (= things said to comfort her) *she was still frightened of the dark.* [C]

re·bate /ˈriː·beɪt/ *n* [C] an amount of money which is returned to you, esp. by the government, for example when you have paid too much tax • *He managed to get a rebate of £800 for overpaid tax which had been deducted from his bank account.* • *Major car manufacturers are offering rebates of up to $600 on new models.*

reb·el /ˈreb·ᵊl/ *n* [C] a person who is opposed to the political system in their country and tries to change it using force, or a person who shows their disagreement with the ideas of people in authority or of society by behaving differently • *The prime minister left the capital after learning that the rebels were planning an imminent attack.* • *Rebel forces have taken over the capital and set up a new government.* • *She has successfully led a rebel backbench campaign against the government's education bill.* • *He was a bit of a rebel when he was a teenager and dyed his hair pink and had his nose pierced.* • *"Rebel without a Cause"* (title of a film in which James Dean played a teenager searching for something to believe in, 1955)

reb·el /rɪˈbel/ *v* [I] **-ll-** • *The people rebelled* **against** *the harsh new government.* • *Jacob rebelled* **against** *his parents' plans for him and left school at the age of 16.* • *Research has shown that if talented children's potential is wasted, they may rebel and become delinquent.* • *(fig.) My conscience rebelled* **at** *the thought of keeping the money I had found in the street* (= I thought it would be morally wrong to keep it). • If part of your body rebels, it is no longer able to bear the pain that it is experiencing: *My stomach rebelled* **at** *the idea of any more food.* • *"What are you rebelling against?' 'What've you got?'"* (from the film *The Wild One* starring Marlon Brando, 1951)

re·bel·li·on /rɪˈbel·i·ən/ *n* • Rebellion is violent action organized by a group of people who are trying to change the political system in their country: *The government has brutally crushed the rebellion.* [C] ○ *They stirred up open rebellion among the people* **against** *the government.* [U] • Rebellion is also action against the leaders of an organization by people who are in the organization because they disagree with the way in which it is being controlled: *The party's rebellion* **against** *the prime minister's unpopular foreign policy led to his fall from power.* [C]

re·bel·li·ous /rɪˈbel·i·əs/ *adj* • If a group of people is rebellious, they oppose the ideas of the people in authority and plan to change the system, often using force: *The government has sent another 200 troops to the border region to control the rebellious population.* • If someone is rebellious, they are difficult to control and do not behave in the way they are expected to: *Her teachers regard her as a rebellious, trouble-making girl.* ○ *He believes that a certain amount of rebellious behaviour is normal among teenagers.*

re·bel·li·ous·ly /rɪˈbel·i·ə·sli/ *adv* • *They were rebelliously plotting the overthrow of the government.*

re·bel·li·ous·ness /rɪˈbel·i·ə·snəs/ *n* [U] • *At times his parents found him difficult to cope with as he opposed all their decisions and acted out his teenage rebelliousness.*

re·birth /£ˌriːˈbɜːθ, $-ˈbɜːrθ/ *n* [U] a new period of growth of something or an increase in popularity of something that was popular in the past • *English drama has enjoyed* **a** *rebirth since the 1950s with John Osborne, Harold Pinter and Tom Stoppard.* • *The rebirth of nationalism in Europe has caused widespread consternation.*

re·bound /ˌriːˈbaʊnd/ *v* [I] to bounce back after hitting a hard surface • *The ball rebounded* **off** *the wall at a difficult angle, but she still managed to hit it.* • If one of your actions rebounds on you, it does not have its desired effect but has an unpleasant effect on you instead: *His continual demands for sympathy rebounded* **on** *him because his friends finally stopped listening.*

re·bound /ˈriː·baʊnd/ *n* [U] • *I hit the ball* **on the** *rebound* (= after it had hit the wall or ground once). • *(infml)* If someone is **on the rebound**, they have just finished a close loving relationship with someone and are still unhappy and upset: *She was on the rebound when she met Jack, so she was still rather vulnerable and gullible.* ○ *A month after her boyfriend had left her, she married another man on the rebound.*

re·buff *obj* /rɪˈbʌf/ *v* [T] *fml* to refuse to accept (a helpful suggestion or offer) and answer in an unfriendly way • *She rebuffed all suggestions that she should resign.* • *Mr Sullivan has been rebuffed by shareholders in his efforts to become a director of the company.* • *I went down on my knees to apologize, but he still rebuffed me* (= he refused to listen to me).

re·buff /rɪˈbʌf/ *n* [C] *fml* • *Her desperate request for help was met with a rebuff.* • *He is still suffering from the rebuff he received from the senate finance committee.*

re·build *obj* /ˌriːˈbɪld/ *v* [T] *past* **rebuilt** /ˌriːˈbɪlt/ to build (something) again that has been damaged or destroyed • *The cathedral was completely rebuilt in 1425 after it had been destroyed by fire.* • *He bought a vintage car and completely rebuilt the engine* (= he separated all the parts of the engine, replaced the broken parts and put it back together). • If you rebuild a system or organization, you develop it so that it works effectively: *During the election campaign, the party claimed it would rebuild the country's economy through a national reinvestment programme.* • If someone rebuilds their life after something unpleasant has happened to them, they try to return to the good situation that they were in before the unpleasant event happened to them: *Many people have difficulty in rebuilding their lives when they come out of prison.*

re·buke *obj* /rɪˈbjuːk/ *v* [T] *fml* to speak angrily to (someone) because you disapprove of what they have said or done • *Her mother rebuked her* **for** *frightening her brother.*

re·buke /rɪˈbjuːk/ *n fml* • *Her sudden withdrawal from the team drew an immediate and angry rebuke from the club's chairman.* [C] • *He received a stern rebuke from the manager* **for** *arriving at work an hour late.* [C] • *He seems unlikely to escape rebuke* **for** *his actions.* [U]

re·but *obj* /rɪˈbʌt/ *v* [T] **-tt-** *fml* to argue that (a statement or claim) is not true • *He has written numerous letters to the company rebutting their claims.* • *She has rebutted charges that she has been involved in any financial malpractice.*

re·but·tal /£rɪˈbʌt·ᵊl, $-ˈbʌt̬-/ *n* [C] *fml* • A rebuttal is a statement which says that a claim or criticism is not true: *She issued a point-by-point rebuttal of the company's accusations.*

re·cal·ci·trant /rɪˈkæl·sɪ·trᵊnt/ *adj fml* (of a person) unwilling to obey orders, or (of an animal) refusing to be controlled • *She claims that the company has shown itself to be recalcitrant and unwilling to take appropriate action to correct serious health hazards.* • *The donkey was of a recalcitrant temperament and had to be pulled around wherever it went.*

re·cal·ci·trance /rɪ'kæl·sɪ·trᵊnts/ *n* [U] *fml* • *The company has shown a resistance to modernization and a recalcitrance to any idea of change.*

re·call *(obj)* REMEMBER /£rɪ'kɔːl, $'riː·kɑːl/ *v* [not *be recalling*] to bring back (the memory of a past event) into your mind, and often to give a description of what you remember • *The old man recalled the city as it had been before the war.* [T] • *She recalls with horror the night that her husband was involved in road accident.* [T] • *"As I recall," he said with some irritation, "you still owe me £150."* [I] • *"My parents sent me to stay with some friends in Yorkshire in 1942," she recalled.* [+ clause] • *He recalled* **(that)** *he had sent the letter over a month ago.* [+ (*that*) clause] • *Can you recall* **what** *happened last night?* [+ *wh-* word] • *He cannot recall* **how** *he got the car home, but he arrived late on Sunday night and went straight to bed.* [+ *wh-* word] • *She recalled seeing him outside the shop on the night of the robbery.* [+ v-*ing*] • If something or someone recalls an event, situation or style, it makes you think of that event, situation or style: *His paintings recall the style of Picasso.* [T] • LP **Memory**

re·call /£rɪ'kɔːl, $'riː·kɑːl/ *n* [U] • Your recall is your ability to remember things: *Old people often have astonishing* **powers of** *recall.* ○ *My brother has* **total** *recall* (= He can remember every detail of past events).

re·call *obj* CALL BACK /£rɪ'kɔːl, $'riː·kɑːl/ *v* [T] to order the return of (a person who belongs to an organization or products made by a company) • *The ambassador was recalled when war broke out.* • *The company recalled thousands of tins of baby food after an anonymous caller claimed to have put rat poison in several tins.*

re·call /£rɪ'kɔːl, $'riː·kɑːl/ *n* [C usually sing] • *There was an emergency recall of Parliament following the economic crisis.* • *Earlier this week, the company recalled its 100mg version of the antibiotic, and then expanded the recall to the 50mg capsules of the same drug.*

re·cant *(obj)* /rɪ'kænt/ *v fml* to announce in public that (your past beliefs or statements) were wrong and that you no longer agree with them • *In the past, the Church ordered people charged with heresy to be burned to death if they did not recant.* [I] • *After a year in spent in solitary confinement, he publicly recanted his views.* [T]

re·can·ta·tion /ˌriː·kæn'teɪ·ʃᵊn/ *n fml* • *The Church published Galileo's recantation throughout Europe to demonstrate their power to make people recant.* [C] • *Recantation was not enough to appease the company and she was sacked a few days later.* [U]

re·cap *(obj)* /'riː·kæp, ˌ-'-/ *v* **-pp-** *infml for* RECAPITULATE • *The teacher recapped the main points of the lesson.* [T] • *To recap, our main aim is to increase sales by 12% this year.* [I]

re·cap /'riː·kæp/ *n* [C] *infml* • *Could you give me a quick recap on what happened in the meeting?*

re·ca·pit·u·late *(obj)* /ˌriː·kə'pɪt·jʊ·leɪt/, *infml* **re·cap** *v* to repeat the main points of (an explanation or description) • *Let us recapitulate before concluding.* [I] • *She recapitulated her speech for the benefit of latecomers.* [T] • *The second scene of the play recapitulates the central points of the first scene.* [T]

re·ca·pit·u·la·tion /ˌriː·kəˌpɪt·jʊ'leɪ·ʃᵊn/, *infml* **re·cap** *n* • *His latest movie is a recapitulation of all his most personal themes and preoccupations.* [C] • *They devoted a series of concerts to* **a** *recapitulation of musical developments during the 19th century.* [U]

re·cap·ture *obj* /£ˌriː'kæp·tʃəʳ, $-tʃɚ/ *v* [T] to take (something) into your possession again, esp. by force • *The army recaptured the town* **from** *the rebels.* • If something recaptures a previous emotion or style, it makes you experience that emotion again or it repeats that style: *They took a second honeymoon and tried to recapture their earlier happiness.* ○ *The film successfully recaptures the joyful style of the 1940s Hollywood musical.*

re·cast *obj* /£ˌriː'kɑːst, $-'kæst/ *v* [T] *past* **recast** to change the form of (something), or to change (an actor) in a play or film • *The agreement has been recast to include the rebel faction.* • *She recast her novel* **as** *a musical comedy.* • *In despair, the theatre director recast the leading role.*

rec·ce /'rek·i/ *n* [C] *infml for* RECONNAISSANCE • *I didn't know the area, so I did a quick recce of the shops.*

re·cede /rɪ'siːd/ *v* [I] to move further away into the distance, or to become less clear or less bright • *The road to the island only appears when the tide has receded.* • *As the boat picked up speed, the coastline receded* **into** *the distance until finally it became invisible.* • *The painful memories gradually receded in her mind.* • If a man has a **receding hairline**, he is losing the hair from the front of his head.

re·ceipt /rɪ'siːt/ *n* [C] a piece of paper which proves that money, goods or information have been received • *Make sure you are given a receipt for everything you buy.* • *Shops will not normally give you a refund for goods unless you show them a receipt.* • See also **receipt** at RECEIVE GET. • PIC **Supermarket** CS D I N P PL RUS S

re·ceipts /rɪ'siːts/ *pl n* the amounts of money received during a particular period by a business • *The theatre's receipts for the winter were badly down.*

re·ceive *obj* GET /rɪ'siːv/ *v* [T] to get or be given (something) • *Did you receive my letter?* • *I received a phone call from your mother.* • *They received a visit from the police.* • *She died after receiving a blow to the head.* • *He received a knighthood for his services to industry.* • *Members of Parliament received a 4·2% pay increase this year.* • When a radio or television receives signals, it changes them into sounds and pictures. See also RECEPTION RADIO/TELEVISION. • If you say receiving you when communicating with someone by radio, you mean that you can hear the other person's message: *I'm receiving you* **loud and clear.** • To be **on/at the receiving end (of** something) is to suffer something unpleasant: *Sales assistants are often at the receiving end of verbal abuse from customers.*

re·ceiv·er /£rɪ'siː·vəʳ, $-vɚ/ *n* [C] • A receiver is a piece of equipment that changes radio and television signals into sounds and pictures. • A **(telephone) receiver** is the part of the telephone that you hold to your ear and mouth: *She picked up the receiver and dialled his number.* ○ *Remember to replace the receiver when you have finished your call.* • *(Br and Aus law)* A receiver **(of stolen goods)** is a person who buys and sells property which they know has been stolen. • See also RECEIVER; RECIPIENT. • LP **Telephone**

re·ceipt /rɪ'siːt/ *n* [U] *fml* • Receipt is the act of receiving money or goods: *We are awaiting receipt of the money.* • *Goods will be delivered* **on** *receipt of payment* (= once the money is received). • *I wrote to* **acknowledge** *receipt of* (= to say that I had received) *the cheque.* • *He was charged with being in receipt of stolen goods* (= possessing stolen goods). • See also RECEIPT.

re·ceive *obj* WELCOME /rɪ'siːv/ *v* [T] to welcome (someone or something) • If you receive something or someone in a particular way, you react to it or them in a way that shows how you feel about it or them: *The prime minister's speech was well/warmly received by the conference delegates.* ○ *Her suggestions were coldly received.* • If you receive a visitor or guest, you welcome them in a formal way: *She stood by the entrance to receive her guests as they arrived.* ○ *The returning soldiers were received* **as** *heroes.* • If someone is received into an organization, they are made a member of it: *He was received* **into** *the church.* • See also RECEPTION WELCOME.

re·ceived /rɪ'siːvd/ *adj* [before n; not gradable] *fml* generally accepted as being right or correct because it is based on authority • *You should be original and challenge received* **ideas.** • *According to received* **wisdom,** *exposure to such low levels of radioactive fall-out is harmless.* • *(specialized)* **Received Pronunciation** (*abbreviation* **RP**) is the standard way in which middle class speakers of southern British English pronounce words. • LP **Pronunciation**

re·ceiv·er /£rɪ'siː·vəʳ, $-vɚ/, *Br and Aus also* **of·fi·cial re·ceiv·er** *n* [C] a person who officially deals with the business matters of companies who cannot pay their debts • *The company went bankrupt and was* **put into the hands of** *the receivers.* • See also **receiver** at RECEIVE GET.

re·ceiv·er·ship /£rɪ'siː·və·ʃɪp, $-vɚ-/ *n* [U] • *Since the beginning of the year, over a hundred medium-sized companies have been forced* **into** *receivership* (= have been forced to stop doing business because of financial problems).

re·cent /'riː·sᵊnt/ *adj* having happened or been made a short time ago in the past • *He told me all about his recent trip to France.* • *Have you been following recent political* **events?** • *The article described recent* **developments** *in the search for a cure for AIDS.* • **In** *recent* **times,** *there has been an increase in the amount of violence shown on television.*

re·cent·ly /'riː·sᵊnt·li/ *adv* • *Have you seen any good films recently?* • *Our car has only recently been repaired.* • *I had only recently returned and was still feeling tired from the journey.*

re·cep·ta·cle /rɪ'sep·tə·kl̩/ *n* [C] *fml* a container used for storing or putting objects in • *Householders are given four* *separate receptacles* **for** *their rubbish: one for food, one for plastics, one for paper and one for tins and bottles.* • *(fig.) My father knows the position of every football team in the league and is a receptacle* **for** *all sorts of useless knowledge* (=he knows a lot of useless facts).

re·cep·tion WELCOME /rɪ'sep·ʃᵊn/ *n* the act of welcoming someone or something • *The new hospital was ready for the reception of its first patients.* [U] • A reception is also a formal party at which important people are welcomed: *The President gave a reception for the visiting heads of state.* [C] • The reception of something or someone is the way in which people react to it or them: *Her first book got a wonderful/warm reception from the critics.* [U] ○ *His speech received* **a** *frosty reception* (=It was unpopular). [U] • The reception or the **reception area/desk** in a place such as a hotel, office or hospital is the area where you go when you first arrive and where you ask for information and where your requests will be dealt with: *I'll meet you at reception in half an hour.* [U] ○ *You can leave a message with reception.* [U] • *(Br)* The first year of **infant school** is sometimes called reception: *He will be in the reception* **class** *when he starts school.* ○ *She is a reception* **teacher**. • A **(wedding) reception** is a party to celebrate the marriage ceremony of two people: *The wedding will be held at St Martins Church and the reception at Crathorne Hotel.* • *(Br fml)* (esp. in descriptions of houses for sale) A **reception room** is a room in a house where people can sit together: *The house has two bedrooms and three reception rooms – a living room, a study and a dining room.* • See also RECEIVE WELCOME.

re·cep·tion·ist /rɪ'sep·ʃᵊn·ɪst/ *n* [C] • A receptionist is a person who works in a place such as a hotel, office or hospital, who welcomes and helps visitors and answers the telephone.

re·cep·tion RADIO/TELEVISION /rɪ'sep·ʃᵊn/ *n* [U] the degree to which radio or television sounds and pictures are clear • *We live on top of a hill and so we get excellent radio reception.* • See also RECEIVE GET.

re·cep·tive /rɪ'sep·tɪv/ *adj* willing to listen to and accept new ideas and suggestions • *She is fairly receptive* **to** *most suggestions.* • *The government is not receptive* **to** *the idea that the general public should have free access to information.*

re·cep·tive·ness /£rɪ'sep·tɪv·nəs, $-t̬ɪv-/, **re·cep·tiv·i·ty** /£,riː·sep'tɪv·ɪ·ti, $-ə·t̬i/ *n* [U] • *He has shown some receptivity* **to** *certain aspects of alternative medicine.*

re·cep·tor /£rɪ'sep·təʳ, $-tɚ/ *n* [C] *specialized* a nerve ending that reacts to a change, such as heat or cold, in the body by sending a message to the central **nervous system**

re·cess PAUSE /rɪ'ses, 'riː-/ *n* [C] a period of time in the year when the members of a parliament are not meeting • *Congress* **goes into** *recess between sessions.* • *Parliament was* **recalled from** *recess.* • *(Am and Aus)* In schools, recess is a period of time between classes when children do not study: *They used to meet once a week during recess or after school.*

re·cess SPACE /rɪ'ses, 'riː-/ *n* [C] a small area in a room which is formed by one part of a wall being set back further than other parts • *The room has a recess designed to hold bookshelves.* • *(literary)* A recess is also a secret or hidden place: *Psychoanalysts aim to explore the* **deepest/innermost** *recesses of the mind.*

re·cessed /rɪ'sest/ *adj* [not gradable] • Recessed means built in a space in a wall: *We have a recessed fireplace in our living room.*

re·ces·sion /rɪ'seʃ·ᵊn/ *n* a period when the economy of a country is not successful, business conditions are bad, industrial production and trade are at a low level and there is a lot of unemployment • *Many businesses are failing because of the continuing recession.* [C] • *He claims that the recession is much* **deeper** *than the government is prepared to admit.* [C] • *In times of recession, more graduates seek careers in the public sector because they perceive it as offering greater job security.* [U] • *The latest report confirms that the economy is* **in** *recession.* [U] • *"It's a recession when your neighbour loses his job: it's a depression when you lose yours"* (Comment by President Harry S Truman, 1958)

re·ces·sive /rɪ'ses·ɪv/ *adj* [not gradable] *specialized* (of GENES and the physical qualities they control) only appearing in a child if both parents supply the controlling GENE • *Recessive characteristics such as blue eyes or red hair can reappear after being hidden for a generation.*

re·charge *(obj)* /£,riː'tʃɑːdʒ, $-'tʃɑːrdʒ/ *v* to give (a BATTERY) the ability to supply electricity again by connecting it to a piece of electrical equipment and filling it with electricity • *The batteries last for four hours and recharge in 2·5 hours.* [I] • *An electric car needs to have its battery recharged approximately every 150 kilometres.* [T] • To **recharge** your **batteries** is to have a period of rest and relaxation so that you feel energetic again: *She took a trip to the South of France to recharge her batteries.*

re·charge·a·ble /£riː'tʃɑː·dʒə·bl̩, $-'tʃɑːr-/ *adj* [not gradable] • *a rechargeable battery*

re·cher·ché /£rə'ʃeə·ʃeɪ, $-'ʃer-/ *adj fml* unusual and not generally known about, or chosen or planned with extreme care • *He writes with a great command of detail on the most recherché topics.* • *The restaurant prides itself on its recherché menu.*

re·cid·i·vist /rɪ'sɪd·ɪ·vɪst/ *n* [C] a criminal who continues to commit crimes even after they have been punished • *She claims that our prison system seems to create recidivists rather than discouraging criminals from reoffending.* • *Recidivist offenders will face fines of up to £800 000 and life imprisonment.*

re·cid·i·vi·sm /rɪ'sɪd·ɪ·vɪ·zᵊm/ *n* [U] • *The report showed that the rate of recidivism among people who were sent to special centres was about 25% below that of those who went to prison.*

re·ci·pe /'res·ɪ·pi/ *n* [C] a set of instructions telling you how to prepare and cook food, including a list of what food is needed for this • *That soup was delicious – could you give me your recipe?* • *For real Indian food, just follow these recipes.* • *The recipe says you need four eggs and 250g of chocolate.* • *Do you know a good recipe* **for** *wholemeal bread.* • *Do you have a vegetarian recipe* **book**? • A **recipe for** something is an idea, situation or method that is likely to result in this: *A defence spokesperson said that lifting the arms embargo would be a recipe for bloodshed in the warring country.* ○ *Despite its reorganization, the company still seems to lack a recipe for growth.* ○ *The opposition declared the government's plans a recipe for* **disaster**. • Ⓟ

re·cip·i·ent /rɪ'sɪp·i·ənt/ *n* [C] *fml* a person who receives something • *This latest cut in government spending will affect income support recipients and their families.* • *He was a recipient* **of** *the Civilian Service Award for his work in restructuring the Defense Department's communications system.*

re·ci·pro·cate *(obj)* /rɪ'sɪp·rə·keɪt/ *v fml* to share the same feelings as someone else, or to behave in the same way as someone else • *He loved and admired her and felt that his love was reciprocated.* [T] • *If you show trust to somebody, that trust will be reciprocated.* [T] • *We invited them to dinner and a week later they reciprocated.* [I] • If a part of a machine reciprocates, it moves backwards and forwards: *Some electric razors have reciprocating heads.*

re·ci·pro·cal /rɪ'sɪp·rə·kᵊl/ *adj fml* • A reciprocal action or arrangement involves two people or groups of people who behave in the same way or agree to help each other and give each other advantages: *The two superpowers agreed to a reciprocal reduction of nuclear weapons.* ○ *Many states have passed laws that will allow nationwide reciprocal banking.*

re·ci·pro·cal·ly /rɪ'sɪp·rə·kli/ *adv fml*

re·ci·pro·ca·tion /rɪ,sɪp·rə'keɪ·ʃᵊn/ *n* [U] *fml* • *She had loved him almost all her life without reciprocation* (=he did not have the same feelings for her).

re·ci·proc·i·ty /£,res·ɪ'prɒs·ɪ·ti, $-'prɑː·sə·t̬i/ *n* [U] *fml* • Reciprocity is behaviour in which two people or groups of people give each other help and advantages: *The two countries have signed a new agreement based on reciprocity in trade.*

re·ci·tal /£rɪ'saɪ·tᵊl, $-t̬ᵊl/ *n* [C] a performance of music or poetry, usually given by one person or a small group of people • *Would you like to come to a piano recital?* • *He is* **giving** *a recital* **of** *Bach's sonatas.* • See also **recital** at RECITE.

re·cite *(obj)* /rɪ'saɪt/ *v* to say (a piece of writing) aloud from memory, or to state in public (a list of things) • *She proudly recited the Oath of Allegiance.* [T] • *He gets nervous whenever he recites in front of an audience.* [I] • *The opposition party recited a litany* (=a long list) *of national failings: a collapsing health system, a failing educational system, homelessness, crime and unemployment.* [T]

re·ci·tal /£rɪ'saɪ·tᵊl, $-t̬ᵊl/ *n* [C] • A recital is a detailed description of something or a list of things: *She gave us a long, boring recital of all her troubles.* • See also RECITAL.

re·ci·ta·tion /,res·ɪ'teɪ·ʃᵊn/ *n* [C] • Recitation is saying a piece of writing aloud from memory: *He gave a beautiful* *recitation* **of** *some poems by Blake.* ○ *The end-of-term concert consisted of songs and recitations of poetry.*

re·ci·ta·tive /ˌres·ɪ·təˈtiːv/ *n specialized* • In an OPERA, recitative is words that are sung as though they are being spoken: *Italian serious opera of the 18th and early 19th century exhibited a rigid separation of aria and recitative.* [U] ○ *In the production, the recitatives are eliminated and replaced with much crisper spoken dialogue.* [C]

reck·less /ˈrek·ləs/ *adj* showing a lack of care about risks or danger, and acting without thinking about the results of your actions • *She claimed the company had shown a reckless disregard for its employees safety.* • *He drives with all the reckless abandon* (= lack of control and care) *of someone who does not think about the future.* • *He was found guilty of reckless* **driving,** *fined $1000 and disqualified from driving for three months.* • LP› **Crimes and criminals**

reck·less·ly /ˈrek·lə·sli/ *adv* • *She tried to avoid travelling in a car with Patrick because he drove so recklessly.*

reck·less·ness /ˈrek·lə·snəs/ *n* [U] • *The council was keen to avoid charges of financial recklessness and took severe measures to bring its budget under control.*

reck·on THINK /ˈrek·ᵊn/ *v* [I] *infml* to think or believe • *What do you reckon – will it rain today?* • *"I think you've got a good chance of getting that job." "Do you reckon* (= Do you think it is likely)?" • *How much do you reckon* **(that)** *it's going to cost?* [+ (*that*) clause] • *I reckon* **(that)** *you won't see her again, not after the way you've treated her.* [+ (*that*) clause] • *"Can you fix my car today?" "I reckon not/so* (= probably not/probably)." [+ *not/so*]

reck·on *obj* CONSIDER /ˈrek·ᵊn/ *v* [T] to consider or have the opinion that something is as stated • *I don't reckon much (Br)* **to**/*(Am and Aus)* **of** *their chances of winning* (= I do not think they will win). • *Many people reckon him* **to be** *a great footballer.* [+ obj + *to be* n/adj] • *She was widely reckoned* **(to be)** *the best actress of her generation.* [+ obj + (*to be*) n/adj]

reck·on *obj* CALCULATE /ˈrek·ᵊn/ *v* [T] to calculate (an amount) based on facts or on your expectations • *Angela quickly reckoned the amount on her fingers.* • *My pay is reckoned* **from** *the middle of the month.* • *The organisers reckoned* **(that)** *there had been 50 000 demonstrators on the march.* [+ (*that*) clause] • *The inflation rate is now reckoned* **to be** *10%.* [+ obj + *to be* n/adj] • If you reckon **in** an amount, you include it in your calculations: *When you reckon in all my overtime, my total pay is quite good.* • If you reckon **on** something, you feel that it is likely to happen and base your plans on the expectation that it will happen: *We're reckoning on having sales of 2000 cars a month.* ○ *I don't reckon on him ever coming back.* ○ *I'm reckoning on* (= depending on) *your continued support.* • If you reckon **up** something, you calculate the total amount: *She can reckon up a bill faster than any calculator.* • To **reckon with** something or someone is to deal with it or them: *If you harm her, you're going to have the police to reckon with.* • If someone is **to be reckoned with,** you have to deal with them which will be difficult because they are strong or powerful: *Margaret was a woman to be reckoned with.* ○ *Since the government limited their powers, the unions are no longer* **a force** *to be reckoned with* (= they are no longer very strong). • If you had **reckoned without** something, you had not considered or expected it and so were not prepared for it: *The authorities wanted to build a nuclear power station in the region, but they reckoned without the opposition of local people.*

reck·on·ing /ˈrek·ᵊn·ɪŋ/ *n* • A reckoning is a calculation which you make: *By my reckoning, we should arrive in ten minutes.* [U] • *Your reckoning is out* (= wrong) *by £10.* [C] • *"Never think that you're not good enough yourself ... My belief is that in life people will take you very much at your own reckoning* (= share your own opinion of yourself)*"* (Anthony Trollope in the book *The Small House at Allington,* 1864)

re·claim *obj* /rɪˈkleɪm/ *v* [T] to take back (something that was yours) • *Foreign tourists who have paid tax on goods they have bought can reclaim it when they leave the country.* • *I went to the station to reclaim my suitcase* **from** *the left luggage office.* • If land is reclaimed, it is made suitable for building or farming: *The Dutch have reclaimed a lot of land* **from** *the sea by draining it and enclosing it with sea walls.* • If you reclaim waste materials, you treat them to obtain useful materials, such as glass or paper, that can be used again. • Ⓓ Ⓘ (RUS)

rec·la·ma·tion /ˌrek·ləˈmeɪ·ʃᵊn/ *n* [U] *fml* • Reclamation is the attempt to make land suitable for building or farming: *The government has launched a programme of land reclamation for industrial use.* ○ *The southern part of the reclamation area will be developed into a major commercial centre.* • Reclamation is also the treatment of waste materials to obtain useful materials from them. • Ⓓ Ⓘ

re·cline (*obj*) /rɪˈklaɪn/ *v fml* to lean or lie back with the upper part of your body in a nearly horizontal position • *She was reclining elegantly* **on** *the sofa.* [I] • *He reclined his head* **against/on** *my shoulder.* [T] • If you recline a chair, you change the position of its back so that it is in a leaning position: *She reclined her seat and went to sleep.* [T]

re·clin·ing /rɪˈklaɪ·nɪŋ/ *adj* [before n; not gradable] • *He lay on the bed in a reclining position.* • *The coach has air conditioning and reclining seats.*

re·clin·er /£rɪˈklaɪ·nəʳ, $-nɚ/ *n* [C] • A recliner is a chair in which you can lean back at different angles.

re·cluse /rɪˈkluːs/ *n* [C] a person who lives alone and avoids going outside or talking to other people • *She has led the life of a recluse since her husband died.* • *He is a millionaire recluse who refuses to give interviews.* • Ⓘ

re·clus·ive /rɪˈkluː·sɪv/ *adj* • *He lived alone in a small apartment and became increasingly reclusive.*

re·cog·nize *obj* KNOW, *Br and Aus usually* **-ise** /ˈrek·əg·naɪz/ *v* [T] to know (someone or something) because you have seen, heard or experienced them or it before • *I hadn't seen her for 20 years, but I recognized her immediately.* • *"Do you recognize this song?" "Yes. It's 'Yesterday' by the Beatles."* • *Doctors are trained to recognize the symptoms of different diseases.* • LP› **Memory**

re·cog·niz·a·ble, *Br and Aus usually* **-is·a·ble** /ˈrek·əg·naɪ·zə·bl̩/ *adj* • Recognizable means easy to recognize: *Caroline has very recognizable handwriting.* ○ *The Eiffel Tower in Paris is an instantly recognizable landmark.*

re·cog·niz·a·bly, *Br and Aus usually* **-is·a·bly** /ˈrek·əg·naɪ·zə·bli/ *adv* • *At seven weeks, an embryo is recognizably human.* • *The magazine has a style of writing that is smart, cultivated and recognizably American.*

re·cog·ni·tion /ˌrek·əgˈnɪʃ·ᵊn/ *n* [U] • *The quick recognition of disease is vital for effective treatment.* • *Computerized voice recognition systems respond to people's voices.* • *When he returned to his home town after the war, he found it had* **changed out of all/beyond all** *recognition* (= it had changed so much that he no longer recognized it).

re·cog·nize (*obj*) ACCEPT, *Br and Aus usually* **-ise** /ˈrek·əg·naɪz/ *v* to accept that (something) is legal, true or important • *You must recognize the seriousness of the problems we are facing.* [T] • *The international community has refused to recognize* (= officially accept the existence of) *the newly independent nation state.* [T] • *He sadly recognized* **(that)** *he would die childless.* [+ (*that*) clause] • If a person's achievements are recognized, official appreciation is shown for them: *The Prime Minister recognized her services to her country by awarding her an MBE.* [T]

re·cog·nized /ˈrek·əg·naɪzd/ *adj* • If someone or something is recognized, it is generally accepted that they have a particular position or quality: *Professor Jones is a recognized authority on ancient Egypt.*

re·cog·ni·tion /ˌrek·əgˈnɪʃ·ᵊn/ *n* [U] • Recognition is an acceptance that something is true or legal: *The country is hoping for diplomatic recognition from the international community.* ○ *There's a growing recognition* **that** *this country can no longer afford to be a nuclear power.* [+ *that* clause] • If you are given recognition, people show appreciation of your achievements: *The artist Van Gogh achieved little public recognition while he was alive.* ○ *Ella complained that the company never gave her any recognition* **for** *her work.* ○ *He was presented with a gold watch* **in** *recognition* **of** (= to show appreciation of) *his years as club secretary.*

re·coil /rɪˈkɔɪl/ *v* [I] to move back because of fear or disgust • *She turned round to greet him then recoiled in horror when she saw the state he was in.* • *He recoils in disgust* **at** *the mere mention of her name.* • *(fig.) She recoiled* **at** *the idea of paying $70 for a theatre ticket* (= She thought it was unacceptable).

re·coil /ˈriː·kɔɪl/ *n* [U] • The recoil of a gun is the sudden movement back that it makes when it is fired: *He raised the gun with both hands, pulled the trigger, and the force of the recoil almost broke his wrist.*

re·col·lect (*obj*) /£ˌrek·ᵊlˈekt, £ˈ---, $ˌrek·əˈlekt/ *v* [not *be recollecting*] *fml* to remember (something) • *Can you* *recollect his name?* [T] • *As far as I can recollect, his name is Edward.* [I] • *She suddenly recollected* **(that)** *she had left her handbag in the restaurant.* [+ (*that*) clause] • *Do you recollect* **where** *she went?* [+ *wh-* word] • *He does not recollect* **seeing** *her at the party.* [+ v-*ing*] • *"Poetry is ... emotion recollected in tranquillity"* (William Wordsworth in the Preface to *Lyrical Ballads*, 1802) • LP **Memory**

re·col·lec·tion /£ˌrek·əlˈek·ʃən, $-əˈlek-/ *n fml* • A recollection is a memory of something: *I have many pleasant recollections of the time we spent together.* [C] • Recollection is also the ability to remember things: *His powers of recollection are extraordinary.* [U] • **To the best of** *my* **recollection** (= I think that) *I have never seen her before.*

re·com·mend *obj* /ˌrek·əˈmend/ *v* [T] to suggest that (someone or something) would be good or suitable for a particular job or purpose, or to suggest that (a particular action) should be done • *I recommend the chicken in mushroom sauce – it's the chef's speciality.* • *Can you recommend any reasonably-priced hotels in Amsterdam?* • *She has been recommended* **for** *promotion.* • *The headmistress agreed to recommend the teachers' proposals* **to** *the school governors.* • *We went to see 'The Lion King' yesterday and I* **highly** *recommend it.* • *He recommends* **(that)** *I take more exercise.* [+ (*that*) clause] • *The doctor recommended* **(that)** *she should stop smoking immediately.* [+ (*that*) clause] • *The city has* **much to** *recommend it* (= It has a lot of pleasant qualities). • *The area near the station is dirty and run-down and has* **little to** *recommend it* (= it has very few pleasant qualities).

re·com·mend·ed /ˌrek·əˈmen·dɪd/ *adj* • *It is dangerous to take more than the recommended dose of this medicine.* • *She is a* **highly** *recommended architect.* • *(esp. Am)* The **recommended daily allowance** (*abbreviation* **RDA**) of a substance such as a VITAMIN is the amount you should have every day.

re·com·men·da·tion /ˌrek·ə·menˈdeɪ·ʃən/ *n* • A recommendation is a suggestion that something is good or suitable for a particular purpose or job: *I bought this computer* **on** *John's recommendation* (= because John told me that it was good). [C] ○ *I got the job* **on** *Sam's recommendation* (= because she told her employers that I was suitable for the job). [C] ○ *My university tutor wrote me a letter of recommendation to support my job application.* [U] • A recommendation is also advice telling someone what the best thing to do is: *The government has* **accepted** *the key recommendation in Lord Justice Woolf's recently published report.* [C] ○ *She is likely to* **make** *a recommendation in a few days time on whether the company should file a law suit.* [C] ○ *The jury followed the judge's recommendation* **that** *they should take into account the extenuating circumstances.* [C + *that* clause]

re·com·pense /ˈrek·əm·pents/ *n* [U] *fml* a present given to someone to thank them for their help, or payment given to someone because of inconvenience or because of the loss of or damage to their property • *I gave her some flowers and chocolates as recompense* **for** *looking after me while I was ill.* • *I received £500 from the local council* **in** *recompense* **for** *the damage to my garden.* • *The farmers received minimal recompense* **for** *the loss of their land.* • *"There is no sufficient recompense for an unjust slander"* (Thomas Fuller, 1732)

re·com·pense *obj* /ˈrek·əm·pents/ *v* [T] *fml* • *The bank has undertaken to recompense customers immediately when money erroneously disappears from an account.* • *The court awarded the women $100 000 each to recompense them* **for** *nine years of lost wages and missed employment opportunities.*

re·con /£ˈriː·kɒn, $-kɑːn/ *n* [C] *Am infml for* RECONNAISSANCE

re·con·cile *obj* /ˈrek·ən·saɪl/ *v* [T] to find a way in which (two situations or beliefs that are opposed to each other) are in agreement, or to become friendly with (someone) after you have argued with them • *It's difficult to reconcile different points of view.* • *How can you reconcile your fur coat* **and** *your love of animals?* • *My brother and I were finally reconciled* **with/to** *each other, after not speaking for over five years.* • If you reconcile yourself **to** something unpleasant, you accept it although you do not like it: *She must reconcile herself to the fact that she must do some work if she wants to pass her exams.* ○ *He was reconciled to living a solitary life.*

re·con·cil·i·a·tion /ˌrek·ənˌsɪl·iˈeɪ·ʃən/ *n* • Reconciliation is the process of making two people or groups of people friendly again after they have argued: *It took hours of negotiations to* **bring about** *a reconciliation* **between** *the two sides.* [C] • Reconciliation is also the process of making two things in agreement which seem to be opposed: *The reconciliation* **of** *the facts* **with** *the theory is not always easy.* [U]

re·con·dite /ˈrek·ən·daɪt/ *adj fml* not known about by many people and difficult to understand • *We had to work from material that was both complex and recondite.* • *She believes that poetry should be part of the everyday, not a recondite preoccupation of academics.*

re·con·di·tion *obj* /ˌriː·kənˈdɪʃ·ən/ *v* [T] to repair (a machine or piece of equipment) and return it to good condition • *The containers can be crushed and recycled or they can be reconditioned for reuse.* • *The shop sells reconditioned vacuum cleaners and washing machines.*

re·con·nais·sance /£rɪˈkɒn·ɪ·sənts, $-ˈkɑː·nə-/, *infml* **rec·ce**, *Am also infml* **re·con** *n specialized* the process of obtaining information about enemy forces or positions by sending out small groups of soldiers or by using aircraft • *Two soldiers were sent on a reconnaissance* **of** *the enemy position.* [C] • **Aerial** *reconnaissance showed that the enemy was about to attack.* [U] • *US forces were not directly involved in the fighting but American reconnaissance* **planes** *later flew over the area.*

re·con·noit·re *(obj)*, *Am usually* **re·con·noit·er** /£ˌrek·əˈnɔɪ·təʳ, $ˌriː·kəˈnɔɪ·t̬ɚ/ *v specialized* (of soldiers or military aircraft) to obtain information about (an area or the size and position of enemy forces) • *A small group of soldiers reconnoitred the territory before the attack.* [T] • *Their ground forces were able to manoeuvre and reconnoitre without any danger of air attack.* [I]

re·con·si·der *(obj)* /£ˌriː·kənˈsɪd·əʳ, $-kɑːnˈsɪd·ɚ/ *v* to think again about (a decision or opinion) and decide whether you want to change it • *He begged her to reconsider but she would not.* [I] • *We have reconsidered your proposals and we have decided to go ahead with the deal.* [T]

re·con·si·der·a·tion /£ˌriː·kənˌsɪd·əˈreɪ·ʃən, $-kɑːn-/ *n* [U] • *The committee's recommendations will go the President and he will then approve them or return them for reconsideration.* • *The authority's decision was quashed and sent back for further investigation and reconsideration.*

re·con·sti·tute *obj* /£ˌriːˈkɒn·stɪ·tjuːt, $-ˈkɑːn·stə·tuːt/ *v* [T] to change (food that has been dried) into its original form by adding water, or to form (an organization) in a different way • *The milk is transported in powdered form to be reconstituted at the factory.* • *reconstituted soup/orange juice* • *The army has been called in to protect the capital while the government is being reconstituted.* • *The Health Education Council has been reconstituted* **as** *the Health Education Authority.*

re·con·struct *obj* /ˌriː·kənˈstrʌkt/ *v* [T] to build or create again (something that has been damaged or destroyed) • *The stadium has been reconstructed at a cost of $850 million.* • *We had no computer backup and had to rely on old paper files to reconstruct the records.* • *The post-war government had the enormous task of reconstructing the country's economy* (= making the economy grow again). • If you reconstruct a system or organization, you change it completely so that it works more effectively: *They were given the task of reconstructing the city's public transport system.* • If you reconstruct something that has happened in the past, you combine a lot of information to obtain a complete description of what happened: *The police tried to reconstruct the crime using the statements of witnesses and clues that they had found.*

re·con·struc·tion /ˌriː·kənˈstrʌk·ʃən/ *n* • Reconstruction is the process of building or creating something again that has been damaged or destroyed: *The only acceptable redevelopment of the buildings is a scheme of internal reconstruction which preserves all the external architectural features.* [U] ○ *Economic reconstruction in the country must begin with the resumption of agricultural production.* [U] • The reconstruction of a country after a war is the process of returning it to the good state that it was in before the war, by making its economy grow again and by building things such as towns and factories again that have been destroyed or damaged: *The government has borrowed a large amount of money to finance its post-war reconstruction.* [U] • The reconstruction of an event is an attempt to obtain a complete description of what happened using the information available, or an attempt to repeat what happened during the event: *A dramatized reconstruction of the robbery was shown on television to try to make people remember any vital pieces of information that would help the police.* [C]

re·con·struc·tive /£ˌriː·kᵊnˈstrʌk·tɪv, $-t̬ɪv/ *adj* [not gradable] • *After the accident, he underwent reconstructive* **surgery** *to rebuild his face.*

re·cord *(obj)* STORE INFORMATION /£rɪˈkɔːd, $-ˈkɔːrd/ *v* to keep (information) for the future, by writing it down or storing it on a computer • *She records everything that happens to her in her diary.* [T] • *The proceedings of the meeting will be recorded in the minutes.* [T] • *The temperature fell very low today, with -14°C being recorded in some places.* [T] • *Unemployment is expected to keep rising through the summer, when it is likely to reach the highest total recorded since records began 100 years ago.* [T] • *In his journal he records* **that** *he and his companions were weakened by lack of food.* [+ *that* clause] • *(law) The coroner recorded* (= gave) *a verdict of accidental death.* [T] • If a device records a measurement, it shows that measurement: *The thermometer recorded a temperature of 30 degrees Celsius.* [T] • (I) (RUS)

re·cord /£ˈrek·ɔːd, $-ɚd/ *n* • A record is a piece of information or a description of an event which is written on paper or stored on a computer: *The weather centre keeps a record* **of** *the weather.* [C] ○ *All births, marriages and deaths are entered in the official records.* [C] ○ *This summer has been the hottest* **on** *record* (= the hottest summer known about). [U] • A record of someone or something is information about that person or thing which is stored by the police or by a doctor: *The police investigated the records of an earlier crime.* [C] ○ *A person's* **medical** *records are confidential.* [C] ○ *He is well known to the police and has a long* **criminal** *record* (= the police have a list of crimes for which he has been found guilty in a court of law). [C] • A person's or company's record is the facts that are known about them and the actions they have done in the past: *He is a very brave man, as you can see from his excellent* **war** *record* (= he has done a lot of brave actions). [C] ○ *I won't fly with an airline that has a bad* **safety** *record* (= whose aircraft have often had accidents). [C] • If you say something **for the record**, you want it to be made publicly known and remembered: *I want to say for the record that I am totally opposed to this new tax.* • If you **go on record** or if you **are on record** as saying something, you state it publicly and officially and it is written down: *The team manager went on record as saying that he had never seen any team play as badly as his team had done during that match.* • If someone says something **off the record**, they do not want it to be known publicly: *The Ambassador said he would talk to us, but strictly off the record.* • If you **set/put the record straight**, you write or say something in order to make the true facts known: *I'm going to put the record straight in the meeting tomorrow.* ○ *She's decided to write her memoirs to set the record straight once and for all* (= finally).

re·cord·ed /£rɪˈkɔː·dɪd, $-ˈkɔːr-/ *adj* [not gradable] • *The last recorded* (= known) *case of smallpox was in the 1970s.* • *The level of recorded* **crime** (= crime that is reported to the police) *has decreased by 5% this year.* • *(Br)* If a letter is sent by **recorded delivery**, the person who receives it must write their name in a book to show that they have received it.

re·cord *obj* STORE ELECTRONICALLY /£rɪˈkɔːd, $-ˈkɔːrd/ *v* [T] to put (sounds or moving pictures) onto usually a magnetic TAPE using electronic equipment so that they can be heard or seen later • *Cliff Richard has recorded more number one hit songs than any other British pop star.* • *Did you record that film on TV last night?* • *We recorded their wedding on our video camera.* • *I recorded the interview* **on tape**. • (I) (RUS)

re·cord /£ˈrek·ɔːd, $-ɚd/ *n* [C] • A record is a flat plastic disc on which music is recorded: *Music is mostly recorded on CDs and cassettes rather than records.* ○ *Would you like to listen to some records?* ○ *He has a very large record* **collection** *worth hundreds of pounds.* ○ *She works for a record* **company**. • A record is also a song or music which has been recorded and which is available for the public to buy: *The Beatles' first hit record was 'Love Me Do'.* • A **record player** is a machine on which records can be played.

re·cord·ed /£rɪˈkɔː·dɪd, $-ˈkɔːr-/ *adj* [not gradable] • *I tried to phone her, but all I got was a recorded message saying that she was away for the weekend.* • If a performance or programme is recorded, it is made before being broadcast on the television or radio: *Was the concert recorded or live?*

re·cord·er /£rɪˈkɔː·dəʳ, $-ˈkɔːr·dɚ/ *n* [C] • A recorder is a **tape recorder** or a **video recorder**.

re·cord·ing /£rɪˈkɔː·dɪŋ, $-ˈkɔːr-/ *n* • A recording is a record, disc or TAPE on which you can hear speech or music or watch moving pictures: *I bought a recording* **of** *Maria Callas singing Verdi.* [C] ○ *New legislation will allow the use of videotaped evidence in court, including recordings of police interviews.* [C] • Recording is also the process or business of putting sounds, esp. music, onto records or magnetic TAPES using electronic equipment: *The recording of their latest album took over two months.* [U] ○ *She has signed a new recording* **contract** (= an agreement to allow her songs to be recorded and sold to the public) *with the record company.* ○ *The players had not met as a full orchestra until their first recording* **session**.

re·cord BEST /£ˈrek·ɔːd, $-ɚd/ *n* [C] the best or fastest ever done • *He ran the 100 metres in 9·91 seconds and* **broke/smashed** *the* **world** *record.* • *She* **set/established** *a new European record in the high jump.* • If something is **record-breaking**, it is better than anything else: *Company profits are rising and it looks as though this is going to be a record-breaking year.* • (I) (RUS)

re·cord /£ˈrek·ɔːd, $-ɔːrd/ *adj* [not gradable] • Record means at a higher level than ever achieved before: *The long hot summer has led to a record harvest this year.* ○ *Inflation has reached record levels.* ○ *We finished the work in record time* (= faster than had ever been done before).

re·cord·er INSTRUMENT /£rɪˈkɔː·dəʳ, $-ˈkɔːr·dɚ/ *n* [C] a musical instrument of the WOODWIND group consisting of a wooden or plastic tube with holes which are covered or left open in order to play different notes

re·cord·er JUDGE /£rɪˈkɔː·dəʳ, $-ˈkɔːr·dɚ/ *n* [C] *Br* a person chosen from among experienced lawyers to work sometimes as a judge

re·count *(obj)* DESCRIBE /rɪˈkaʊnt/ *v fml* to describe how something happened; to tell a story • *I listened to him recount an* **anecdote/story/tale** *about a woman he'd met on a train.* [T] • *He was recounting his* **adventures** *since he had left home.* [T] • *She recounted her* **experiences** *working as a nurse in a refugee camp.* [T] • *He was fond of recounting* **how** *he had played for Manchester United when he was 19.* [+ *wh-* word]

re·count *obj* COUNT AGAIN /ˌriːˈkaʊnt/ *v* [T], *n* [C] (to make) a second or another count, esp. of the number of votes in an election • *They recounted the votes.* • *They* **demanded** *a recount.*

re·coup *obj* /rɪˈkuːp/ *v* [T] to get back money that you have spent or lost • *It takes a while to recoup the initial* **costs** *of starting up a business.* • *The gambler recouped his* **losses** *in the next game.*

re·course /£rɪˈkɔːs, $ˈriː·kɔːrs/ *n* [U] *fml* the possibility of using something or someone as a way of obtaining help, esp. in a difficult or dangerous situation • *It is hoped that the dispute will be settled* **without** *recourse* **to** *litigation.* • *I'd prefer to buy the house myself* **without** *recourse* **to** *my parents.* • *If the businesses collapse, investors* **have** *no recourse for compensation from the island's government.*

re·cov·er *(obj)* /£rɪˈkʌv·əʳ, $-ɚ/ *v* to get back something lost, esp. health, ability, possessions etc. • *It took her a long while to recover* (= become completely well again) **from/after** *her heart operation.* [I] • *He never really recovered* **from** *the shock of his wife dying* (= He was never happy after his wife died). [I] • *Have you recovered* (= Are you feeling better) *after your ten-hour flight yet?* [I] • *She went into a coma and died without recovering consciousness* (= without becoming conscious again). [T] • *She was astonished to see me, but she soon recovered* **herself**/*her voice*/*her composure* (= soon gave the appearance of being calm). [T] • *It took a long time for the economy to recover* (= improve) **after** *the slump.* [I] • *The country is in a state of decline and very unlikely to recover* (= get back) *its former prosperity.* [T] • *Police only recover* (= get back) *a very small percentage of stolen goods.* [T] • *The initial outlay of setting up a company is considerable and it takes a while to recover those* **costs** (= get back what you have spent). [T] • See also **re-cover** at RE-.

re·cov·er·y /£rɪˈkʌv·ᵊr·i, $-ɚ-/ *n* • *Mira* **made** *a* **full** *recovery* **from/after** (= became completely well again after) *the operation.* [C] • *We wished her a* **speedy** *recovery from her illness* (= that she would get better quickly). [C] • *At last the economy is showing* **signs of** *recovery* (= is starting to improve). [U] • *I certainly don't think we're going to see a miraculous* **economic** *recovery in the next* *five years.* [C] • *The police arranged the recovery* (=the getting back) **of** *her body from the river.* [U]

re·cre·a·tion /ˌrek·riˈeɪ·ʃᵊn/ *n* (a way of) enjoying yourself when you are not working • *His favourite recreations are golf and playing scrabble.* [C] • *Emma's only form of recreation seems to be shopping.* [U] • *The university campus has excellent exercise and recreation* **facilities.** • A **recreation ground** is a piece of publicly owned land (esp. in a town) used for sports and games. • *(Am)* A **recreation center** is a building open to the public where meetings are held, sports are played and special services are available for young and old people.

re·cre·a·tion·al /ˌrek·riˈeɪ·ʃᵊn·ᵊl/ *adj* • *recreational activities/facilities/interests* • **Recreational vehicle** (abbreviation **RV**) is *Am for* **camper van**. See at CAMP [TENTS/BUILDINGS].

re·cri·mi·na·tion /rɪˌkrɪm·ɪˈneɪ·ʃᵊn/ *n* [U], **re·cri·mi·na·tions** /rɪˌkrɪm·ɪˈneɪ·ʃᵊnz/ *pl n* argument between people who are blaming each other • *The peace talks broke down and ended in* **mutual** *recrimination.* • *It's the story of a lovelorn girl whose suicide provokes* **bitter** *recriminations.*

re·cri·mi·na·to·ry /£rɪˈkrɪm·ɪ·nə·tᵊr·i, $-ə·nə·tɔːr-/ *adj* • *Recriminatory remarks increase the bitterness on both sides.*

re·cru·des·cence /ˌriː·kruːˈdes·ᵊnts/ *n* [U] *fml* a sudden new appearance and growth, esp. of something dangerous and unpleasant • *There has been an unwelcome recrudescence* **of** *racist attacks.*

re·cruit /rɪˈkruːt/ *n, v* (to persuade someone to become) a new member of an organization, esp. the army • *The* **raw** *recruits* (=new soldiers) *were trained for six months and then sent to the war front.* [C] • *Charities such as Oxfam are always trying to recruit volunteers to help in their work.* [T] • *Even young boys are now being recruited* **to** *the army.* [T] • *a recruiting centre/officer*

re·cruit·ment /rɪˈkruːt·mənt/ *n* [U] • *The recession has forced a lot of companies to cut down on graduate recruitment.* • *It's all part of a recruitment* **drive** *intended to increase the party's falling numbers.* • *He works for a recruitment consultancy in London.*

rec·tal /ˈrek·tᵊl/ *adj* [not gradable] *specialized* See at RECTUM

rec·tang·le /ˈrek·tæŋ·gl̩/ *n* [C] a flat shape with four 90 degree angles and four sides, with opposite sides of equal length • [PIC] **Shapes**

rec·tan·gu·lar /£rekˈtæŋ·gjʊ·ləʳ, $-gjə·lɚ/ *adj* • *The painting consists of four rectangular blocks of colour.*

rec·ti·fy *obj* [CORRECT] /ˈrek·tɪ·faɪ/ *v* [T] *slightly fml* to correct or make right • *I am determined to take whatever action is necessary to rectify the* **situation.** • *Every effort is made to rectify any* **errors/mistakes** *before the book is printed.* • *(specialized)* In chemistry, if you rectify substances, you make them pure.

rec·ti·fi·ca·tion /ˌrek·tɪ·fɪˈkeɪ·ʃᵊn/ *n* [C/U] *fml*

rec·ti·fy *obj* [ELECTRIC CURRENT] /ˈrek·tɪ·faɪ/ *v* [T] *specialized* to change an **alternating current** (=flow of electricity in two directions) to **direct current** (=one direction)

rec·ti·fi·er /£ˈrek·tɪ·faɪ·əʳ, $-ɚ/ *n* [C] *specialized* • *You use the rectifier* (=electronic device) *to change an alternating current to direct current.*

rec·ti·li·ne·ar /£ˌrek·tɪˈlɪn·i·əʳ, $-təˈlɪn·i·ɚ/ *adj* [not gradable] *fml* moving in or formed from straight lines • *a rectilinear street plan*

rec·ti·tude /£ˈrek·tɪ·tjuːd, $-tə·tuːd/ *n* [U] *fml* honesty and moral correctness of a person's character and behaviour • *An austere man of unquestioned* **moral** *rectitude, Nava inspired deep devotion in those who worked for him.*

rec·tor /£ˈrek·təʳ, $-tɚ/ *n* [C] (in the Church of England) a priest in charge of a PARISH (=area) • At some colleges in Scotland the rector is an important official elected by the students. • *(Am)* A rector can also be the person in charge of a university or school. • Ⓓ ⒹⓀ Ⓢ

rec·tory /£ˈrek·tᵊr·i, $-tɚ-/ *n* [C] • A rectory is the house in which a rector lives.

rec·tum /ˈrek·təm/ *n* [C] the lowest end of the bowels down which excrement travels before leaving the body through the ANUS

rec·tal /ˈrek·tᵊl/ *adj specialized* • *rectal prolapse*

rec·tal·ly /ˈrek·tᵊl·i/ *adv specialized* • *They took his temperature rectally.*

re·cum·bent /rɪˈkʌm·bənt/ *adj literary* lying down • *She looked at the recumbent* **form** *beside her.*

re·cu·pe·rate /£rɪˈkjuː·pᵊr·eɪt, $-ˈkuː·pə·reɪt/ *v* [I] *slightly fml* to become well again after an illness; to get back your strength, health, etc. • *She spent a month in the country recuperating after the operation.* • *He was in hospital recuperating* **from** *his injuries at the time.*

re·cu·pe·ra·tion /£rɪˌkjuː·pᵊrˈeɪ·ʃᵊn, $-ˌkuː·pəˈreɪ-/ *n* [U] *slightly fml* • *He returned to work in November after a lengthy period of rest and recuperation.*

re·cu·pe·ra·tive /£rɪˈkjuː·pᵊr·ə·tɪv, $-ˈkuː·pɚ·ə·ţɪv/ *adj fml* • Recuperative means helping you to become well again after illness: *The doctor reminded her of the recuperative power of a good night's sleep.*

re·cur /£rɪˈkɜːʳ, $-ˈkɜːr/ *v* [I] **-rr-** to happen again or happen many times; return • *The* **themes** *of freedom and independence recur throughout much of his writing.* • *If the* **problem** *recurs I shall go and see my doctor about it.* • A **recurring number** (or *specialized* **recurring/repeating decimal**) is a number that repeats itself forever following a **decimal point**, such as 3·3333....

re·cur·ring /£rɪˈkɜː·rɪŋ, $-ˈkɜːr·ɪŋ/, **re·cur·rent** /£rɪˈkʌr·ᵊnt, $-ˈkɜːr-/ *adj* • *The father-daughter relationship is a recurring* **theme/motif** *throughout all of her work.* • *For much of his life he suffered from recurring* **bouts** *of depression.* • *A recurring back* **problem** *has put Brinkworth out of action for most of this season.* • *I have this recurring* **dream** *in which I'm running through the streets of my home town completely naked.* • *LeFanu suffered all his life from a recurrent* **nightmare** *that he was trapped in a falling house.*

re·cur·rence /£rɪˈkʌr·ᵊnts, $-ˈkɜːr-/ *n* • *The doctor told him to go to the hospital if there was a recurrence* **of** *his symptoms.* [C] • *There has been a 40 per cent fall in recurrence of breast cancer among women taking the drug.* [U]

re·cycle *obj* /ˌriːˈsaɪ·kl̩/ *v* [T] to collect and treat (rubbish) to produce useful materials which can be used again • *Companies are now trying to recycle their* **waste** *or find other ways of disposing of their by-products.* • *The Japanese recycle more than half their waste paper.* • *All restaurants will be equipped with recycling* **bins** *for plastic items.* • *There's no point in recycling plastics if it does more harm than good.*

re·cy·cla·ble /ˌriːˈsaɪ·klə·bl̩/ *adj* • *Most of the rubbish on this site is recyclable* (=able to be recycled). • *recyclable household waste*

re·cyc·led /ˈriːˌsaɪ·kl̩d/ *adj* • *This newspaper is made of recycled* **paper.**

red [COLOUR] /red/ *adj, n* **redder, reddest** (of) the colour of fresh blood • *She was wearing bright red lipstick.* • *As the strawberries ripened they* **turned** *red.* • *The woman was (dressed) all* **in** *red.* [U] • *I could see five different reds in the picture.* [C] • *To make the colour pink you mix red and white.* [U] • If someone's hair is red it is a colour between red, brown and orange. • If you **are/turn/go** red, blood goes to your face esp. because of anger or embarrassment: *Look, you've embarrassed her – she's gone* **bright** *red.* • If your eyes are red, the white part of your eyes and the skin around your eyes is red, because of crying, tiredness, drunkenness, etc. • *(infml)* If you or your bank account are **in the red**, you owe money (to the bank). Compare **in the black** at BLACK [DARK IN COLOUR]. • *Announcing that you're a Communist is* **like a red rag to a bull** *to him* (=certain to produce an angry or violent reaction in him). • A **red admiral** is a BUTTERFLY with black wings and red and white marks. • A **red alert** is (the state of being ready to deal with) a sudden dangerous situation: *The army was* **on** *red alert against the possibility of an attack.* • A **red blood cell** (also *specialized* **red corpuscle**) is any of the cells that carry oxygen around the body. • If you call someone **red-blooded**, you mean that they seem to be full of confidence or sexual strength: *a red-blooded American male* • **The red carpet** is a special official welcome that is given to an important guest, esp. in which a long red floor covering is put down for them to walk on: *We'll* **roll out** *the red carpet for the Senator.* ○ *The minister was given the red carpet* **treatment.** • *(Am infml)* If you **don't give a red cent for** something, you don't give it any value: *I wouldn't give a red cent for their chances of winning.* • The **Red Crescent** is an international organization in Muslim countries that takes care of people suffering because of war, hunger, illness, etc. • The **Red Cross** is an international organization that takes care of people suffering because of war, hunger, illness, etc.: *The Red Cross is/are supplying food and medicine to the famine victims.* • A **red deer** is a deer with brown fur which changes to a different brown or brownish-red colour in summer. [PIC〉] **Wild animals in Britain** • *(esp. Am infml)* A **red-eye** is a flight taken at night: *We caught the red-eye from LA and got to New York at five this morning.* • A **red flag** is used as a sign of danger or REVOLUTION: *You're not allowed to swim when the red flag is flying.* ○ *The song of some parties of the political* LEFT *is called* **The Red Flag**. • A **red giant** is a very large cool star that gives out a reddish light. • If someone is caught/found/discovered **red-handed**, they are found in the act of doing something illegal. • A **red herring** is a fact, idea or subject that takes people's attention away from the central point being considered: *The police investigated many clues, but they were all red herrings.* • If metal is **red-hot**, it is so hot that it has turned red, or (more generally) it is too hot to touch: *(fig.) red-hot enthusiasm* ○ *red-hot news, straight from the war zone* • *(taboo dated)* A **Red Indian** is a **Native American**. See at NATIVE. • A **red-letter day** is a special, happy and important day that you will always remember: *The day I first set foot in America was a red-letter day for me.* • A **red light** is used as a signal meaning danger or stop: *The police stopped her for* **driving through/jumping** *a red light.* • The **red-light district** of a city is the part where there are many people and businesses selling sex. • **Red meat** is meat from mammals, which is dark brown in colour after it has been cooked. • A **red pepper** is the red ripe fruit of the CAPSICUM plant, eaten as a vegetable, and **red pepper** is a red powder made from these fruits that gives a spicy taste to food. • *(disapproving)* **Red tape** means official rules and processes that seem unnecessary and delay the getting of results: *My passport application is stuck in red tape.* ○ *We must* **cut through** *the red tape.* • *"I'm the last of the red-hot mamas"* (title of a song by Sophie Tucker, 1928) • *"Little Red Riding Hood"* (title of a fairy story) • *"Red sky at night, shepherd's delight / Red sky in the morning, shepherd's warning"* (traditional rhyme about the weather)

red·dish /ˈred·ɪʃ/ *adj* • If something is reddish it is slightly red in colour: *Nicki's got reddish-brown hair.*

red·den *(obj)* /ˈred·ᵊn/ *v* • If something reddens, it becomes or is made more red than it was: *The cold wind had reddened her cheeks.* [T] ○ *His face reddened with embarrassment.* [I]

red·ness /ˈred·nəs/ *n* [U] • *Her scar healed, but the redness remained for a long time.*

Red [POLITICAL] /red/ *n* [C], *adj* [not gradable] *esp. disapproving* (a person) having **left wing** political opinions; SOCIALIST or COMMUNIST • *In the 1950s people's fear and hatred of communism were expressed in phrases such as "Better dead than Red."* • The **Red Army** was the name of the Soviet army.

red·brick /ˈreb·brɪk, ˌ-ˈ-/ *adj, n* [C] (being) any of the British universities built in the late 19th and early 20th centuries in cities such as Liverpool and Manchester, and not one of the older ones such as Oxford or Cambridge • *Ben actually chose to go to a redbrick* **university** *because he didn't like the elitism of Oxford and Cambridge.* • Compare OXBRIDGE.

red·cur·rant /£ˈredˌkʌr·ᵊnt, $-ˌkɜːr-/ *n* [C] (a bush producing) a very small round red edible fruit • *redcurrant wine/jam/jelly*

re·deem *obj* [IMPROVE] /rɪˈdiːm/ *v* [T] *fml* to make something or someone (seem) less bad • *A poor game was partially redeemed in the second half by a couple of superb goals from Anthony Edwards.* • *He was an hour late, but he redeemed him***self** *in her eyes by giving her a huge bunch of flowers.* • *She's trying to redeem her* **reputation** *by working extra hard.* • *She took me to see a really dull film, the only redeeming* **feature** *of which* (=the only thing which prevented it from being completely bad) *was the soundtrack.* • *As far as I can see the man is appalling – he has absolutely no redeeming* **qualities** (= there is nothing to like or admire in him).

re·demp·tion /rɪˈdemp·ʃᵊn/ *n* [U] • If something or someone is **beyond/past** redemption, they are so bad that it would be impossible to improve or save them: *She took her car to the garage but they said it was beyond redemption.*

re·deem *obj* [GET BACK] /rɪˈdiːm/ *v* [T] to get (something) back • *She managed to save enough money to redeem her jewellery* **from** *the pawn shop.*

re·deem *obj* [FULFIL] /rɪˈdiːm/ *v* [T] to fulfil (a promise) or pay back (a debt) • *I thought it was time to redeem my* **promises** *to Linda and marry the girl.* • *If you redeem a* **coupon** *or* **voucher** *you exchange it for money or goods.* • *Since 1986 Australia has used its surplus to redeem foreign debt.* • *The amount required to redeem the mortgage, including the arrears, was £358 587.*

re·deem *obj* [RELIGION] /rɪˈdiːm/ *v* [T] (in Christianity) to free people from SIN • *"Jesus," said the priest, "saved and redeemed mankind by taking our sins upon himself."*

Re·deem·er /£rɪˈdiː·məʳ, $-mɚ/ *n* [C] • In Christianity, the Redeemer is Jesus Christ.

re·demp·tion /rɪˈdemp·ʃᵊn/ *n* [U] • *His is a tragic view of life because it sees no redemption from the pain and suffering of life.*

re·demp·tive /£rɪˈdemp·tɪv, $-t̬ɪv/ *adj fml* • *This is essentially a story about the redemptive* **power** *of love.*

re·de·vel·op *obj* /ˌriː·dɪˈvel·əp/ *v* [T] to change an area (of a town) by replacing old buildings, roads, etc. with new ones

re·de·vel·op·ment /ˌriː·dɪˈvel·əp·mənt/ *n* [C/U]

red·head /ˈred·hed/ *n* [C] *infml* a person, esp. a woman, whose hair is a colour between red, brown and orange

re·di·rect *obj* /ˌriː·daɪˈrekt/ *v* [T] to change the direction of (something), esp. to send (a letter) to a new address • *Could you ask him to redirect any* **mail** *that arrives for me to my address in Ottawa.* • *Resources must be redirected into the many under-funded areas of education.*

re·di·stri·bute *obj* /ˌriː·dɪˈstrɪb·juːt, -strɪˈbjuːt/ *v* [T] to share out differently from before • *As president he would redistribute the country's* **wealth**. • *He intends to redistribute income from the middle class to poorer paid employees and pensioners.*

re·di·stri·bu·tion /ˌriː·dɪ·strɪˈbjuː·ʃᵊn/ *n* [U]

red·neck /ˈred·nek/ *n* [C] *esp. Am infml* a poor white person without education, esp. one living in the countryside in the southern US, who has **prejudiced** (= unfair and unreasonable) ideas and beliefs

red·ness /ˈred·nəs/ *n* [U] See at RED [COLOUR]

red·o·lent /ˈred·ᵊl·ᵊnt/ *adj* [after v] *literary* smelling strongly of something or having qualities (esp. smells) that make you think of or remember something else • *The mountain air was redolent* **with** *the scent of pine needles.* • *We entered a dark cavern redolent* **with** *manly scents – gun oil and cigar smoke and boot polish.* • *His image is redolent* **of** *the smell of old leather, old money and class.*

re·dou·ble *obj* /ˌriːˈdʌb·l̩/ *v* [T] to make (something) much more than before; increase • *The government, he said, must redouble their* **efforts** *to beat crime.*

re·doubt /rɪˈdaʊt/ *n* [C] *fml* something which maintains or defends a belief or a way of life, esp. one that is disappearing or threatened • *The party's reputation as a staunch redoubt* **of** *high moral probity has taken a bit of a knock since the scandal.* • *He described British public schools as 'the* **last** *redoubt* **of** *upper-class privilege'.* • *(specialized)* A redoubt is also a small, often hidden, building in which soldiers can hide themselves while they are fighting: *He spoke of secret underground redoubts, from which troops would pour when enemy tanks tried to pass.*

re·doubt·a·ble /£rɪˈdaʊ·tə·bl̩, $-t̬ə-/ *adj literary or humorous* very strong, esp. in character; producing respect and a little fear in others • *Tonight Villiers faces the most redoubtable opponent of his boxing career.* • *Little did he realize that he had the redoubtable Sally Palmer to deal with.*

re·dress /rɪˈdres/ *v* [T], *n* [U] *fml* (to put right a wrong or give) payment for a wrong that has been done • *Her employers redressed her* **grievances** *by increasing her salary.* • *Most managers, politicians and bosses are men – how can women redress* **the (im)balance** (=make the situation fairer and more equal)*?* • *He went to the industrial tribunal to* **seek** *redress for the way his employers had discriminated against him.* • *Unfortunately, providing better* **legal** *redress against harassment does not always help.*

red·skin /ˈred·skɪn/ *n* [C] *taboo dated* a **native American**, see at NATIVE

re·duce *obj* /£rɪˈdjuːs, $-ˈduːs/ *v* [T] to make less in size, amount, degree, importance, etc., or bring into a different, usually worse, state • *Do nuclear weapons really reduce the risk of war?* • *The plane reduced speed as it approached the airport.* • *I reduced (my) weight by going on a diet.* • *We bought a television that was reduced* **(from** *£500* **to** *£350) in the sales.* • *To make a thicker sauce, reduce the ingredients by boiling for 5 minutes.* • *I reduced the problem* **to** *a few simple questions.* • *Allied bombing reduced the city* **to** *ruins.*

• *I was reduced* **to tears** (= made to cry) *seeing the mess that they had made.* • *The sergeant was reduced* **to the ranks** (= made an ordinary soldier) *for his cowardice.* • If you are **reduced to doing** something, you are forced to do it because you have no other choice: *I'd run out of cigarettes and was reduced to smoking the butts left in the ashtrays.* • *(dated) She claims she is a duchess living in* **reduced circumstances** (= living in a poorer way than before). • If someone who works at a factory or in an office is on **reduced time** (also **short time**), they are working fewer days or hours than usual for less money because there is not much work to do: *He's been put* **on** *reduced time because business is so quiet.*

re·duc·tion /rɪ'dʌk·ʃᵊn/ *n* • *His advice about tight cash management and cost reduction has been noted.* [U] • *Last week, the airline cut its overseas service by half because of a sharp reduction* **in** *traffic.* [C] • *There are huge (price) reductions in many shops during the summer sales.* [C]

re·dun·dant NOT EMPLOYED /rɪ'dʌn·dᵊnt/ *adj Br and Aus* (of a worker) having lost his or her job because the employer no longer needs or is able to pay them • *To keep the company alive half the workforce is being* **made** *redundant* (= dismissed from employment). • *The newly redundant workers were furious to see robots doing their old work.* • *New technology often* **makes** *old skills and even whole communities redundant.* • LP> **Work**

re·dun·dan·cy /rɪ'dʌn·dᵊnt·si/, *Aus also* **re·trench·ment** *n Br and Aus* • *He hates his job but on the other hand he's terrified of redundancy.* [U] • *The depression has meant 10 000 redundancies* (= people made redundant) *in the North-East.* [C] • *Some of the staff will be encouraged to take early retirement and others* **voluntary** *redundancy.* [U] • A **redundancy payment** is money that a company pays to workers who have lost their jobs because they are no longer needed.

re·dun·dant EXTRA /rɪ'dʌn·dᵊnt/ *adj* (esp. of a word, phrase etc.) unnecessary because it is more than is needed • *In the sentence 'She is a single unmarried woman' the word 'unmarried' is redundant.*

re·dun·dan·cy /rɪ'dʌn·dᵊnt·si/ *n* [U]

red·wood /'red·wʊd/ *n* [C/U] a CONIFEROUS tree of California that grows very tall, or the valuable wood of this tree

reed /riːd/ *n* [C] (the hollow stem of) any of various types of tall stiff grass-like plants growing together in groups near water • *The villagers wove dried reeds together to make the roof.* • **Reed instruments** such as the CLARINET or OBOE have a thin piece of wood or metal, called a reed, which shakes very quickly to produce sound when the musician blows over it.

reed·y /'riː·di/ *adj* **-ier, -iest** • A place that is reedy has many reeds growing there: *the reedy river banks* • *(disapproving)* If you describe a sound, esp. someone's voice, as reedy, you mean that it is thin and high and not pleasant to listen to.

reef /riːf/ *n* [C] a line of rocks or sand just above or just below the surface of the sea, often dangerous to ships • *Eleven million gallons of oil were dumped when one of the company's tankers ran into an underwater reef.* • *The* **coral** *reefs, food and habitat for many fish, could also be devastated by the oil slick.*

reef·er /£'riː·fəʳ, $-fɚ/ *n* [C] *infml dated* a hand-rolled cigarette containing the drug MARIJUANA

reef·er (jack·et) /£'riː·fəʳ, $-fɚ/ *n* [C] a jacket made of thick material and often worn by sailors

reef knot, *Am also* **square knot** *n* [C] a strong knot tied twice that does not come unfastened easily

reek /riːk/ *v* [I], *n* [U] *infml* (to have) a strong, esp. unpleasant smell • *Her breath reeked* **of/with** *garlic.* • *The room was filled with the reek* **of** *stale beer and cigarettes.* • *(fig.) His promotion reeks* **of** (= seems to be a result of) *favouritism.* • LP> **Smells**

reel HOLDER /rɪəl/ *n* [C] a round wheel-shaped object on which sewing thread, fishing wire, cinema film, etc. can be rolled, or the amount of thread, film, etc. stored on one of these • *I put a new reel of film in my camera.* • *The projectionist played the last reel of the film first, which ruined it for me.* • PIC> **Reel**

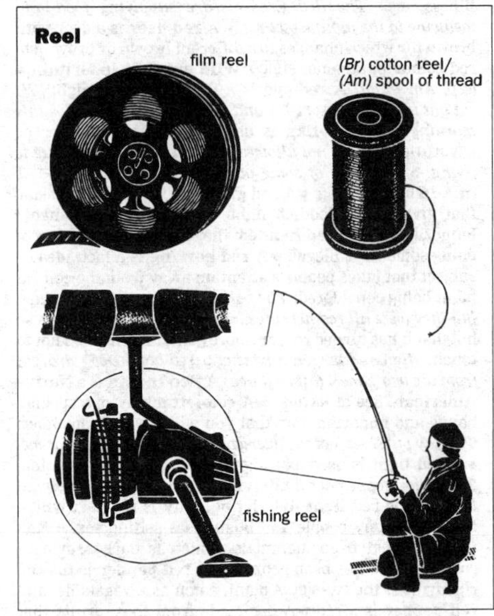

reel MOVE /rɪəl/ *v* [I] to walk moving from side to side and looking like you are going to fall • *At closing time he reeled* **out of** *the pub and across the road.* • *She hit him so hard that he reeled* **across** *the room/reeled* **back**. • If the place where you are reels, what you are looking at seems to go round and round in front of you: *A stone hit his head and the street reeled before his eyes.* • If you reel, or your mind or brain reels, you feel very confused or shocked and unable to act: *We were reeling* **(in** *amazement/shock/delight)* **from/with** *the news that we had won all that money.*

reel DANCE /rɪəl/ *n* [C] (the music for) a fast Scottish or Irish dance

reel in/out *obj*, **reel** *obj* **in/out** *v adv* [M] to pull in, take or give out by turning something round and round • *Slowly the fisherman reeled in his line, bringing the fish ashore.* • *The firemen reeled out the hoses from their fire engine.* • *(fig.) The old man reeled off* (= said without pausing to remember) *the names of his twenty-two grandchildren.*

ref SPORT /ref/ *n* [C] *infml abbreviation for* REFEREE (= person in charge of a game) • *Come on, ref, get your glasses on!* [as form of address]

ref BUSINESS /ref/ *n* [C] *abbreviation for* **reference**, see at REFER SEND • *Your ref. JW/155/C/1991*

re·fec·to·ry /£rɪ'fek·tᵊr·i, $-tɚ-/ *n* [C] *fml or old use* a large room in a MONASTERY, college, school, etc. where meals are eaten

re·fer to *obj* TALK ABOUT /£rɪ'fɜːʳ, $-'fɜːr/ *v prep* [T] **-rr-** to mention, describe or involve (someone or something) • *In her autobiography she often refers to her unhappy schooldays.* • *He always refers to his wife* **as** *'the old woman'.* • *The new salary scale only refers to company managers and directors.* • *Does this (information) refer to me?*

ref·er·ence /£'ref·ᵊr·ənts, $'-ɚ-/ *n* • *Knowing what had happened I avoided* **making** *any reference* **to** (= mentioning) *weddings.* [C] • *I notice in her book she makes only a* **passing** (= brief) *reference* **to** *her first husband.* [C] • *His speech was full of biblical references.* [C] • *(fml) I am writing to you* **with/in** *reference* **to** (= in connection with) *your letter of 15 March.* [U] • See also REFERENCE.

re·fer *obj* **to** *obj* SEND /£rɪ'fɜːʳ, $-'fɜːr/ *v prep* [T] **-rr-** to send (someone or something) to (a different place or person having more knowledge and power) for information, help, a decision, etc. • *My doctor referred me to a hospital specialist.* • *The High Court has referred the* **case** *to the Court of Appeal.* • *The reader is constantly referred* **back** *to the introduction.*

re·fer·ral /£rɪ'fɜː·rəl, $-'fɜːr·ᵊl/ *n* • *The doctor gave him a referral* **to** (= arranged for him to see) *the consultant.* [C] • *Immediate referral of urgent cases* **to** *the hospital is essential.* [U]

ref·er·ence /£'ref·ᵊr·ənts, $'-ɚ-/ *n* [C] • *Academic books and articles usually have* **a list of** *references at the end that tell you where the author found his information.* • Business letters usually have a reference that tells you who to speak to or where to look for more information: *In all future letters on this subject please* **use/quote** *our reference JW/155/C/1991.* • See also REFERENCE.

re·fer to *obj* LOOK AT /£rɪ'fɜːʳ, $-'fɜːr/ *v prep* [T] **-rr-** to look at (something) for information and help, or instruct (someone) to look at something for information or help •

She spoke for an hour without once referring to her notes. • *He referred to a history book to find out the dates of the French Revolution.*

ref·er·ence /£ˈref·ᵊr·ənts, $ˈ-ɚ-/ *n* [U] • *These books are for reference purposes only and must not be removed from this room.* • A **reference book** is a book of facts, such as a dictionary or an ENCYCLOPEDIA, which you look at to discover particular information. • A **reference library** is (a place for looking at) a collection of books that must be read only where they are kept and not taken away. • See also REFERENCE.

ref·e·ree [JUDGE] /ˌref·əˈriː/ *n* [C] a person in charge of a game who makes certain the rules are followed, or (more generally) any person or organization that helps to find a fair answer to a disagreement • *Liverpool only lost because the referee was biased.* • *A senior judge is acting as referee in the pay dispute between the trade union and management.* • [LP] **Sports**

ref·e·ree *(obj)* /ˌref·əˈriː/ *v* • *They had to ask one of the spectators to referee (the match).* [I/T]

ref·e·ree [SUPPORTER] *Br and Aus* /ˌref·əˈriː/, **ref·er·ence** *n* [C] a person who knows you and who is willing to describe and, usually, praise you, to support you when you are trying to get a job, etc. • *She* **gave** *her college tutor* **as** *her referee to the interviewer.*

ref·er·ence /£ˈref·ᵊr·ᵊnts, $ˈ-ɚ-/ *n* [C] a letter describing and, usually, praising you, to support you when trying to get a job, etc. • *My old headteacher said he would* **write** *me a* **glowing** (= very good) *reference.* • *I'm applying for a new job and I'm hoping my ex-boss will* **give** *me a reference.* • *I've got a reference from my bank saying that my financial situation is fine.* • See also **reference** at REFER [TALK ABOUT], REFER [SEND], REFER [LOOK AT].

ref·e·ren·dum /£ˌref·əˈren·dəm/, *fml* **pleb·i·scite** *n* [C] *pl* **referendums** or *fml* **referenda** /ˌref·əˈren·də/ a vote in which all the people in a country or an area are asked to give their opinion about or decide an important (political) question • *Is it more truly democratic to* **hold a** *referendum, rather than let the government alone decide an important issue?*

re·fer·ral /£rɪˈfɜː·rəl, $-ˈfɜːr·ᵊl/ *n* [C] See at REFER TO [SEND]

re·fill /ˈriː·fɪl/ *n* [C] (a container holding) an amount of some material needed to fill up again an object which has become empty • *My pen seems to be running out of ink – I need a refill.* • *(infml) Chuck, you've nearly finished your drink – do you want a refill?*

re·fill *obj* /ˌriːˈfɪl/ *v* [T] • *He got up and refilled their* **glasses.**

re·fine *obj* /rɪˈfaɪn/ *v* [T] to make pure or improve, esp. by removing unwanted material • *Crude oil is industrially refined to purify it and separate out the different elements, such as benzene.* • If you refine **(on)** your ideas/methods you make small changes that make them more correct and clear.

re·fined /rɪˈfaɪnd/ *adj* • *Many doctors say it's unhealthy to eat only refined foods such as white bread and white sugar which are almost empty of original goodness.* • *The new computer software is highly refined* (= complicated and made with great skill) *and can do much more than the old version.* • If you call someone refined you mean that they have a very delicate manner and seem to be extremely polite: *Delia is so terribly refined – I really can't imagine her using foul language.*

re·fine·ment /rɪˈfaɪn·mənt/ *n* • *The accuracy of the machine has been greatly increased through corrections and refinements.* [C] • *The refinement of raw opium yields other drugs, such as morphine.* [U] • *Clearly, the hypothesis does need some refinement.* [U] • *(fig.) She's the personification of culture and refinement* (= politeness and delicacy). [U]

re·fin·e·ry /£rɪˈfaɪ·nᵊr·i, $-nɚ-/ *n* [C] • A refinery is a factory where raw substances such as oil or sugar are made pure: *There were two huge* **oil** *refineries on the coast.*

re·fit *(obj)* /ˌriːˈfɪt/ *v* **refitting**, *past* **refitted** or *Am also* **refit** to put (esp. a ship) back into good condition by repairing or adding new parts to it • *The ship sailed into the dock to refit/to be refitted.* [I/T]

re·fit /ˈriː·fɪt/ *n* [C] • *After a long sea voyage the boat needed a refit.*

re·flate *(obj)* /ˌriːˈfleɪt/ *v* (in economics) to increase the amount of money in use in (a country's) economy • *The government hopes to increase consumer demand and therefore industrial production by reflating (the economy).* [I/T]

re·fla·tion /ˌriːˈfleɪ·ʃᵊn/ *n* [C/U]

re·fla·tion·a·ry /£ˌriːˈfleɪ·ʃᵊn·ᵊr·i, $-er-/ *adj* [not gradable]

re·flect *(obj)* [RETURN] /rɪˈflekt/ *v* to send back (light, heat, etc.) • *It is a good idea to wear white clothes in hot countries because they will reflect the sun's heat, rather than absorb it.* [T] • *He saw himself reflected* **in** *the water/mirror/shop window.* [T] • *The light reflected* **off** (= hit and returned from) *the surface of the water.* [I]

re·flec·tive /£rɪˈflek·tɪv, $-t̬ɪv/ *adj* • A reflective surface is one that can be seen easily when a light shines on it.

re·flec·tion /rɪˈflek·ʃᵊn/ *n* • *In Greek mythology, Narcissus fell in love with his own reflection which he saw in a pool of water.* [C] • *He put silver foil around the fire to increase heat reflection.* [U]

re·flec·tor /£rɪˈflek·təʳ, $-t̬ɚ/ *n* [C] • Bicycles, cars, and other vehicles have red reflectors at the back which shine when a light touches them to show the vehicle's position. • A reflector is also *Am for* **cat's eye**. See at CAT. • [PIC] **Bicycles, Motorway**

re·flect *obj* [SHOW] /rɪˈflekt/ *v* [T] to show, express or be a sign of (something) • *His unhappy face reflected his inner despair.* • *Her rough, red hands reflected a life of hard physical work.* • *The skill of the new players was soon reflected* **in** (= was shown by) *the team's high scores and rapid improvement.* • *Alfred's courage in facing and overcoming his disease reflects* **(great) credit on** *him* (= shows that we should admire him). • *(fig.) When one player behaves disgracefully it* **reflects (badly) on/upon** (= gives a similar (bad) reputation to) *the whole team.*

re·flec·tion /rɪˈflek·ʃᵊn/ *n* • *Putting soldiers on the streets is a reflection* **of** *how terrified the government is.* [C] • *His unhappiness is a reflection* **of** *his mistaken marriage.* [C] • *This young girl is now a heroin addict – what a (terrible) reflection* **on** *her parents* (= it makes them look bad). [U]

re·flect [THINK] /rɪˈflekt/ *v* to think deeply and carefully, esp. about possibilities and opinions • *The manager demanded time to reflect* **(on** *what to do).* [I] • *She reflected* **that** *this was probably the last time she would see him.* [+ *that* clause]

re·flec·tion /rɪˈflek·ʃᵊn/ *n* • *After thirty years as a judge, her reflections* **on/about** *life and justice were well worth listening to.* [C] • **On/After** *reflection* (= after considering it), *Paul decided he had been wrong to refuse the job in London.* [U]

re·flec·tive /£rɪˈflek·tɪv, $-t̬ɪv/ *adj* • *After hearing the news they sat in a quiet, reflective silence.*

re·flec·tive·ly /£rɪˈflek·tɪv·li, $-t̬ɪv-/ *adv* • *"Mm," I said reflectively.*

re·flex /ˈriː·fleks/ *n* [C] an uncontrollable physical reaction to something • *The doctor hit me just below the knee to test my reflexes.* • *Psychologists have studied* **conditioned** *reflexes* (= reactions which are learned rather than natural) *in people and animals for over a hundred years.* • *I'm sorry I punched him, it was a reflex* **action/response.**

re·flex·ive /rɪˈflek·sɪv/ *adj Am* • *I hadn't meant to answer her, it was simply reflexive.*

re·flex·ive·ly /rɪˈflek·sɪv·li/ *adv Am* • *My arm went up reflexively.*

re·flex·ive /rɪˈflek·sɪv/ *n, adj* [not gradable] (a word) describing a situation in which the person who does the action also feels its effect • *In the sentence, 'He prides himself on doing a good job', 'prides' is a* **reflexive verb** *and 'himself' is a* **reflexive pronoun.**

re·flex·ive·ly /rɪˈflek·sɪv·li/ *adv* [not gradable]

re·flex·ol·o·gy /£ˌriː·flekˈsɒl·ə·dʒi, $-ˈsɑː·lə-/ *n* [U] a treatment in which the bottom part of the foot is rubbed gently in order to improve the blood flow and help the person relax

re·for·est *obj* /£ˌriːˈfɒr·ɪst, $-ˈfɔːr-/, *esp. Br and Aus* **re·af·for·est** *v* [T] to plant trees on (an area of land which has become bare or spoiled)

re·for·es·ta·tion /£ˌriː·fɒr·ɪˈsteɪ·ʃᵊn, $-fɔːr·ɪ-/ *n* [U] *esp. Am*

re·form /£rɪˈfɔːm, $-ˈfɔːrm/ *v, n* (to make) an improvement, esp. by changing a person's behaviour or the structure of something • *Who will reform Britain's unfair electoral system?* [T] • *For years I was an alcoholic, but I reformed when the doctors gave me six months to live.* [I] • *Some reforms to the system will be necessary.* [C] • *The government is committed to* **carrying out** *a programme of* **social** *reform.* [U] • *The education system in Britain was crying out for reform.* [U] • (J)

REFLEXIVE PRONOUNS AND REFLEXIVE VERBS

A reflexive pronoun is used when the object and subject of a verb refer to the same person or thing: *He describes himself as a socialist.* • *It was dark and they found themselves in a strange part of town.* • *Please drive more carefully or you'll kill yourself.* • *We saw ourselves in the mirror.* • *The city defended itself from attack.* • *Why do I set myself such impossible goals?*

• **Verbs that require a reflexive pronoun** These are uncommon, and usually formal. This dictionary shows these verbs by marking **-self** in an example sentence: *The headteacher prides* **himself** *on knowing* (= is pleased that he knows) *the names of all 430 of his students.*
acquit, comport, conduct (= behave); absent; avail; pride

With 'behave' the pronoun can be omitted: *The children are behaving themselves* (= being good). • *Will you please behave!*

• **Verbs used with a reflexive meaning** Notice that English often uses intransitive verbs where other languages use reflexive forms, for example: imagine, remember, apologize, move, sit down, wonder.

With verbs for the following common actions that you do to yourself, a reflexive pronoun can be used but is usually omitted: dressing, shaving, washing, bathing, showering: *I shaved and went down to breakfast.* (Notice that 'bath' and 'dress' are rather formal; it is more usual to say *take/have a bath* and *get dressed.*) If a reflexive pronoun is used, this suggests that the person found it difficult to do the action: *He's only three but he can dress himself.*

• **Emphasis** Reflexive pronouns are often used to emphasize that an action is done by one particular person instead of another: *Please don't wash my cup, I'll do it myself.* • *The President himself will attend the meeting.* • *She was trying to calm Mrs Hogan but I noticed she herself was very upset.*

• **'by myself'** Notice that the combinations 'by myself', 'by herself' and so on have a special meaning and can be replaced by 'alone' or 'on my own', 'on her own' etc.:

I'll carry it myself.
(I, rather than another person, will carry it)
I can carry it by myself.
(I can carry it alone, without another person's help)

• **'each other'** Reflexive pronouns are not used where 'each other' is needed. Compare:

Nick and Jon talked to each other (Nick talked to Jon, Jon talked to Nick)
Nick and Jon talked to themselves (Nick talked to himself, Jon talked to himself)

LP **Each other**

re·for·ma·tion /£ˌref·əˈmeɪ·ʃən, $-ər-/ *n* [C] • *He's undergone a reformation – he's a changed man.*

re·formed /£rɪˈfɔːmd, $-ˈfɔːrmd/ *adj* [before n] • *a reformed alcoholic/criminal* (= someone who was previously an alcoholic/criminal, but is not now) • *I can't believe how much he's changed – he's a* **reformed character** (= a completely different, better person).

re·form·er /£rɪˈfɔː·mər, $-ˈfɔːr·mər/ *n* [C] • *Wilberforce was a great British* **social** *reformer who fought for the abolition of the slave trade in the late 18th and early 19th century.*

re·for·mist /£rɪˈfɔː·mɪst, $-ˈfɔːr-/ *adj* • *a reformist, rather than a revolutionary approach to government*

re·for·ma·tion /£ˌref·əˈmeɪ·ʃən, $-ər-/ *n* [U] **the Reformation** the 16th-century religious ideas and activity in Europe which tried to change and improve the Catholic Church, and resulted in the establishment of the Protestant Churches

re·fract *obj* /rɪˈfrækt/ *v* [T] *specialized* (of water, glass, etc.) to change the direction of (light, sound, etc.) or to cause it to separate when it travels through • *The glass prism refracted the white light* **into** *the colours of the rainbow.*

re·frac·tion /rɪˈfræk·ʃən/ *n* [U] • *You can see refraction of light in action by placing a drinking straw in a glass of water.*

re·frain NOT DO /rɪˈfreɪn/ *v* [I] *fml* to avoid or not let yourself do something; not do • *We refrained* **from** *talking until we knew that it was safe.* • *The sign on the wall said "Please refrain* **from** *smoking."*

re·frain SONG /rɪˈfreɪn/ *n* [C] a short part of a song or poem that is repeated, esp. between the VERSES (= the separate parts) or, *(fml)* anything that is often repeated • *(fml) "I'm only an ignorant old lady", was her* **constant** *refrain.*

re·fresh *obj* /rɪˈfreʃ/ *v* [T] to give new energy and strength to (someone) or make (someone) less hot • *It was such a hot night that I had a cold shower to refresh* **myself**. • *I looked the word up in the dictionary to* **refresh** *my* **memory** *of* (= help me to remember) *its exact meaning.* • *"Refreshes the parts other beers cannot reach"* (advertisement for Heineken beer, 1975-)

re·freshed /rɪˈfreʃt/ *adj* • *I feel so refreshed after my holiday.*

re·fresh·er /£rɪˈfreʃ·ər, $-ər/ *n* [C] • *Most airlines give pilots one-day refreshers* (= courses to practise skills again after a period of not using them) *every year.* • *I went on a refresher* **course** *on new techniques in design to bring myself up to date.*

re·fresh·ing /rɪˈfreʃ·ɪŋ/ *adj* • *There's nothing more refreshing on a hot day than a cold beer.* • **It**'s *refreshing/a refreshing change* (= pleasant because unusual) **to** *see a losing team shaking hands and smiling after a match.* [+ to infinitive]

re·fresh·ing·ly /rɪˈfreʃ·ɪŋ·li/ *adv* • *a woman with refreshingly original ideas*

re·fresh·ment /rɪˈfreʃ·mənt/ *n* • *He stopped at a bar for a little refreshment* (= a drink or some food). [U] • **Light** *refreshments* (= drinks and small amounts of food) *will be available.* [C]

re·fri·ge·rate *obj* /£rɪˈfrɪdʒ·ər·eɪt, $-ə·eɪt/ *v* [T] to make or keep (esp. food or drink) cold so that it stays fresh, esp. in a FRIDGE • *Fresh orange juice should be refrigerated after opening and drunk within three days.*

re·fri·ge·ra·tion /£rɪˌfrɪdʒ·əˈreɪ·ʃən/ *n* [U]

re·fri·ge·ra·tor /£rɪˈfrɪdʒ·ər·eɪ·tər, $-ə·eɪ·t̬ər/ *n* [C] • Refrigerator is *(Br fml)* or *Am and Aus for* FRIDGE. • **Refrigerator-freezer** is *Am for* **fridge-freezer**. See at FRIDGE • PIC **Kitchen**

re·fuge /ˈref·juːdʒ/ *n* (a place which gives) protection or shelter from danger, trouble, unhappiness, etc. • *Many people escaping persecution are* **seeking/taking** *refuge in this country.* [U] • *The climbers slept in a mountain refuge.* [C] • *The woman had fled from her violent husband to a* **women's** *refuge in Chelmsford.* [C]

re·fug·ee /ˌref·jʊˈdʒiː, $ˈ---/ *n* [C] • *Thousands of refugees* (= people escaping their country for religious or political reasons) *fled across the border.* • A **refugee camp** is a place where people who have escaped their own country can live, usually in bad conditions and only expecting to stay for a limited time.

re·fund /ˌriːˈfʌnd/ *v, n* (to give) a returned sum of money • *When I went on business to Peru, the office refunded my expenses.* [T] • *When the holiday trip was cancelled, the travel agency refunded everybody the price of the tickets.* [+ two objects] • *I returned the useless radio to the shop where I bought it and* **demanded/got** *a refund.* [C]

re·fund·a·ble /ˌriːˈfʌn·də·bl/ *adj* [not gradable] • *a refundable deposit*

re·fur·bish *obj* /£ˌriːˈfɜː·bɪʃ, $-ˈfɜːr-/ *v* [T] *fml* to make (something) look new and bright again • *The developers refurbished the house inside and out.*

re·fur·bished /£ˌriːˈfɜː·bɪʃt, $-ˈfɜːr-/ *adj* [before n] • *a curious mix of slums, trendy shops and the refurbished homes of the rich*

re·fur·bish·ment /£ˌriːˈfɜː·bɪʃ·mənt, $-ˈfɜːr-/ *n* • *The office looks so much better following its refurbishment.* [U] • *Our company carries out refurbishments on shops and offices all over the North-East of England.* [C]

re·fuse *(obj)* SAY NO /rɪˈfjuːz/ *v* to say no (to); to (choose to) not accept, allow or do (something) • *He asked me to give him another loan, but I refused.* [I] • *I know he's in trouble but he's refused all (my offers of) help.* [T] • *On cold mornings the car always refuses* **to** *start.* [+ *to* infinitive] • *The local council refused him planning permission to build an extra bedroom.* [+ two objects] • LP Two objects Ⓘ

re·fus·al /rɪˈfjuː·zᵊl/ *n* • *Our request for permission to travel* **met with/received** *a* **flat/blunt/point-blank** *refusal from the authorities.* [C] • *The government's refusal* **to** *see that the maintenance of the environment must be our first priority today is a great tragedy.* [U + *to* infinitive]

re·fuse RUBBISH /ˈref·juːs/ *n* [U] *fml* unwanted waste material, esp. material that is regularly thrown away from a house, factory, etc.; rubbish • *garden/kitchen refuse* • **Refuse collector** is *Br fml for* DUSTMAN. • A **refuse dump** is a place where a town's rubbish is put. • Ⓘ

re·fute *obj* /rɪˈfjuːt/ *v* [T] *fml or law* to say or prove that (a person, statement, opinion, etc.) is wrong or false • *to refute a person/theory/argument* • *The barrister used new evidence to refute the* **charges** *and clear the defendant.*

re·fu·ta·tion /ˌref·jʊˈteɪ·ʃᵊn/ *n* [C/U] *fml or law*

reg /redʒ/ *n* [C] *infml for* **registration (number)**, see at REGISTER

re·gain *obj* /rɪˈgeɪn/ *v* [T] to take or get possession of (something) again or *(fml or literary)* to reach or return to (a place), esp. after difficulty or danger • *The government has regained control of the capital* **from** *rebel forces.* • *She made an effort to regain her self-control.* • *(fml or literary) The swimmers struggled to regain the shore.* • *(fml or literary) We'll drive on little roads for a while, and regain the main road later.*

re·gal /ˈriː·gᵊl/ *adj* extremely splendid; of, like, or suitable for a king or queen • *a regal manner* • *He made a regal entrance.*

re·gal·ly /ˈriː·gᵊl·i/ *adv*

re·gale *obj* **with** *obj* /rɪˈgeɪl/ *v prep* [T] *esp. humorous* to entertain (someone) with (stories, jokes, etc.) • *The sailor regaled us all night with stories of his adventures.*

re·ga·li·a /rɪˈgeɪ·li·ə/ *n* [U + sing/pl v] official and traditional special clothes and decorations, esp. those worn or carried on ceremonial occasions, or (more generally and humorously) any set of special clothes • *The queen's regalia at her coronation included her crown and sceptre.* • *The biker was dressed* **in full** *regalia, with shiny black leather and lots of chains.* • Ⓘ

re·gard *obj* /£rɪˈgɑːd, $-ˈgɑːrd/ *v* [T always + adv/prep] to consider or have an opinion about, or *(fml)* to look carefully at • *Local people regard this idea of a motorway through their village* **with** *horror.* • *Her parents always regarded her* **as** *the cleverest of their children.* [+ obj + *as* n/adj] • *(fml) The bird regarded me curiously/angrily/***with** *suspicion when I walked up to its nest.* • *There is no problem* **as regards** (= in connection with) *the financial arrangements.*

re·gard /£rɪˈgɑːd, $-ˈgɑːrd/ *n* [U] *fml* • *He* **has** *no regard* **for** (= has no care or thought for) *other people's feelings.* • *The company* **holds** *her talents* **in low/the highest** *regard* (= does not respect them/respects them very much). • *I am writing to you* **with regard to** (= in connection with) *your letter of 15 March.* • *He wants to speak to you* **in regard to** (= in connection with) *your financial situation.* • *The union is the largest in the country and* **in this/that regard** *is best placed to serve its members.*

re·gard·ing /£rɪˈgɑː·dɪŋ, $-ˈgɑːr-/ *prep* • *The company is being questioned regarding* (= about) *its employment policy.*

re·gard·less /£rɪˈgɑːd·ləs, $-ˈgɑːrd-/ *adv* [not gradable] • *The plan for a new office tower went ahead regardless* **of** (= despite) *local opposition.* • *She knew it was dangerous to visit him except at night, but she set out regardless.*

re·gards /£rɪˈgɑːdz, $-ˈgɑːrdz/ *pl n* greetings • *Please* **give/send/convey** *my regards to your mother if you see her.* • *"Give my Regards to Broadway"* (title of a song written by George M. Cohan, 1904) • LP Letters

re·gat·ta /£rɪˈgæt·ə, $-ˈgɑː·t̬ə/ *n* [C] a sports event consisting of boat races • *the Henley Regatta*

re·gen·e·rate *obj* IMPROVE /£rɪˈdʒen·ᵊr·eɪt, $-ə·eɪt/ *v* [T] to improve (a place or system), esp. by making it more active or successful • *The new minister has promised to regenerate the inner cities.*

re·gen·e·ra·tion /£rɪˌdʒen·ᵊrˈeɪ·ʃᵊn, $-əˈeɪ-/ *n* [U] • *The council is committed to a programme of* **urban** *regeneration.*

re·gen·e·ra·tive /£rɪˈdʒen·ᵊr·ə·tɪv, $-ə·ə·t̬ɪv/ *adj fml* • *Their action has been needlessly destructive rather than regenerative.*

re·gen·e·rate *(obj)* GROW /ˌriːˈdʒen·ə·reɪt/ *v* to grow again • *Tissue regenerates after skin is scratched.* [I] • *A lizard can regenerate its tail.* [T]

re·gen·e·ra·tion /ˌriː·dʒen·əˈreɪ·ʃᵊn/ *n* [U]

re·gen·e·ra·tive /£rɪˈdʒen·ᵊr·ə·tɪv, $-ə·ə·t̬ɪv/ *adj specialized*

re·gent /ˈriː·dʒᵊnt/ *n, adj* a person who rules a country only for a limited period, because the king or queen is absent or too young or too ill, etc. • *In the UK, it is customary for the next heir to the throne to be regent.* [C] • *George IV became* **Prince** *Regent in 1811, because of his father's insanity.* [after n]

re·gen·cy /ˈriː·dʒᵊnt·si/ *n* [C], *adj* [not gradable] • A regency is a period of time when a country is ruled by a regent. • Regency refers to the style of buildings, furniture, literature, etc. in Britain from 1811 to 1820.

reg·gae /ˈreg·eɪ/ *n* [U] a type of popular music from Jamaica with a strong second and fourth beat

reg·i·cide /ˈredʒ·ɪ·saɪd/ *n* [C/U] a person who kills a king, or the act of killing a king

re·gime /reɪˈʒiːm/ *n* [C] *esp. disapproving* a particular government or a system or method of government • *We want to overthrow this corrupt, totalitarian regime.* • *The regime in this office is hard work and more hard work.* • Ⓕ

reg·i·men /ˈredʒ·ɪ·mən/ *n* [C] *fml* any set of rules about food and exercise that someone follows, esp. in order to improve their health • *After his heart attack the doctor put him on a strict regimen.*

reg·i·ment /ˈredʒ·ɪ·mənt/ *n* [C + sing/pl v] a large group of soldiers, or (more generally) any large number of things or people • *Regiments are usually commanded by a colonel and are sometimes made up of soldiers from a particular city or part of the country.* • *There's a* **whole** *regiment* **of** *people here to see you, Doctor.*

reg·i·men·tal /£ˌredʒ·ɪˈmen·tᵊl, $-əˈmen·t̬ᵊl/ *adj* • *a regimental tie/uniform* • *(disapproving) Her style of teaching is too regimental* (= organized) *and predictable.*

reg·i·men·ta·tion /£ˌredʒ·ɪ·menˈteɪ·ʃᵊn, $-ə·mən-/ *n* [U] *disapproving* • Regimentation is extreme organization and control of people.

reg·i·ment·ed /£ˈredʒ·ɪ·men·tɪd, $-ə·men·t̬ɪd/ *adj disapproving* • *a regimented* (= extremely controlled) *school/society/lifestyle*

re·gion /ˈriː·dʒᵊn/ *n* [C] a particular area or part (of the world, of the body, etc.) or any of the large official areas into which a country is divided • *the semi-desert regions of Australia* • *the Birmingham region* • *He said he had sharp pains* **in** *the stomach region/the region of the stomach.* • *They estimate that the temperature yesterday was (somewhere)* **in the region of** (= approximately) *-30°C.* • LP World regions

re·gion·al /ˈriː·dʒᵊn·ᵊl/ *adj* [not gradable] • *The disc jockey had a strong regional* **accent** *that I couldn't identify.* • LP Varieties of English

re·gion·al·ly /ˈriː·dʒᵊn·ᵊl·i/ *adv* [not gradable]

reg·i·ster LIST /£ˈredʒ·ɪ·stəʳ, $-stɚ/ *v, n* (to put information, esp. your name, into) an official list or record • *She bought a new car and registered it in her name.* [T] • *Within two weeks of arrival all foreigners had to register* **with** *the local police.* [I] • *Students have to register* **for** *the new course by the end of April.* [I] • *If you don't have a job, to claim money from the government, you must first register* **(as** *unemployed)* **at** *the Job Centre.* [I] • *(fig. infml) I did mention the address but I'm not sure that it registered* **(with** *him)* (= was heard and remembered by him). [I] • When you register a letter or parcel, you send it using a special postal service, so that it will be handled carefully and not lost. • *Is your name on the register of voters?* [C] • *Guests write their names in the* **(hotel)** *register.* [C] • A register is also a book used to record whether a child is present at school: *If a child is absent the teacher notes it down in the* **(class)** *register.* [C] • A **register office** is a **registry office**. • Ⓚ

reg·i·stered /£ˈredʒ·ɪ·stəd, $-stɚd/ *adj* [not gradable] • *a registered* (= officially listed and accepted) *nurse/charity/trademark* • If something is sent by *(Br and Aus)* **registered post**/*(Am)* **registered mail** it is sent using a special postal service so that it will be handled carefully and not lost: *a registered letter* • LP Symbols

reg·i·stra·tion /ˌredʒ·ɪˈstreɪ·ʃᵊn/ *n* [U] • *With an election approaching, both political parties are encouraging voter registration.* • A road vehicle's **registration (number)** (*infml* **reg**) (*Am usually* **license plate number**) is the official set of numbers and letters shown on the front and back: *Police are looking for a small blue car with the* *registration number K17 EMW.* ○ *It's not bad for a K registration/reg* (=vehicle with the letter K showing the year when it was registered).

reg·is·try /ˈredʒ·ɪ·stri/ *n* [C] *esp. Br* ● A registry is a place where official records are kept: *a land/business/electoral registry* ● *(esp. Br)* A **registry office** (also **register office**) is a place where births, deaths and marriages are officially recorded and where you can get officially married, without a religious ceremony.

reg·is·ter *(obj)* SHOW /£ˈredʒ·ɪ·stəʳ, $-stɚ/ *v* to record, show or express (something) ● *The geiger counter registered a dangerous level of radioactivity.* [T] ● *The earthquake was too small to register* **on** *the Richter scale.* [I] ● *Thousands of miners demonstrated in the streets to register their opposition to the government's plans to close five coal mines.* [T] ● *(fml) His face registered extreme disapproval of what he had witnessed.* [T] ● (KOR)

reg·is·ter RANGE /£ˈredʒ·ɪ·stəʳ, $-stɚ/ *n* [C] all the notes that a musical instrument or a person's voice can produce, from the highest to the lowest ● *music written mainly for the* **lower/higher** *register of the clarinet* ● (KOR)

reg·is·ter LANGUAGE STYLE /£ˈredʒ·ɪ·stəʳ, $-stɚ/ *n specialized* the style of language, grammar and words used for particular situations ● *People chatting at a party will usually be talking in (an) informal register.* [C/U] ● LP **Labels** (KOR)

reg·is·ter MONEY /£ˈredʒ·ɪ·stəʳ, $-stɚ/ *n* [C] *Am for* TILL MONEY DRAWER ● *a cash register* ● (KOR)

reg·is·trar RECORD KEEPER /£ˌredʒ·ɪˈstrɑːʳ, $ˈredʒ·ɪ·strɑːr/ *n* [C] a person whose job is to keep official records, esp. of births, deaths and marriages ● At some colleges the officials in charge of exams, keeping records and admitting new students are called registrars.

reg·is·trar DOCTOR /£ˌredʒ·ɪˈstrɑːʳ, $ˈredʒ·ɪ·strɑːr/ *n* [C] *Br and Aus* a type of hospital doctor ● *A hospital registrar is of a lower rank than a consultant.*

re·gress /rɪˈgres/ *v* [I] *fml* to return to a previous and less advanced or worse state, condition or way of behaving ● *She suffered brain damage from the car accident and regressed* **to** *the mental age of a five-year-old.* ● Compare PROGRESS.

re·gres·sion /rɪˈgreʃ·ᵊn/ *n* [U] *fml*

re·gres·sive /rɪˈgres·ɪv/ *adj fml* ● *This new system of taxation is regressive, hurting poor people more than rich.*

re·gret /rɪˈgret/ *v, n* **-tt-** (to have or express) a feeling of sadness about something sad or wrong or about a mistake that you have made, and (to have or express) a wish that it could have been different and better ● *Is there anything in your past life that you regret?* [T] ● *I had too much to drink last night, and I'm really regretting it this morning.* [T] ● *I have always regretted not having studied harder at school.* [+ v-*ing*] ● *I really regret leaving* (=I am sorry that I have to leave) *the party so early like this.* [+ v-*ing*] ● *(fml) The council regrets* **(that)** *the money to subsidise the youth club is no longer available.* [+ *(that)* clause] ● *(fml) British Airways regret* **to** *announce the cancellation of flight BA205 to Madrid.* [+ *to* infinitive] ● *I left school at 16, but I've had a great life and I* **have no** *regrets.* [C] ● *My* **only** *regret* **is that** *I never got the chance to go to America.* [C + *that* clause] ● *The manager expressed deep regret* **at/for** *the number of staff reductions.* [U] ● *We think,* **much to** *our regret* (=and we regret this very much), that we will not be able to visit you next year. [U] ● *We had five party invitations while we were in Greece, so we had to* **send** *our* **regrets** (=send letters of polite refusal) *to all of them.*

re·gret·ful /rɪˈgret·fᵊl/ *adj* ● *a regretful* (=expressing regret) *goodbye/glance/smile*

re·gret·ful·ly /rɪˈgret·fᵊl·i/ *adv* ● *I left New York regretfully after only a week.*

re·gret·ta·ble /£rɪˈgret·ə·bl̩, $-ˈgreţ-/ *adj* ● *a most/deeply regrettable* (=very bad) *mistake* ● *We feel* **it** *is* **(deeply)** *regrettable* **that** *the government refuses to listen to our ideas on road safety.* [+ *that* clause]

re·gret·ta·bly /£rɪˈgret·ə·bli, $-ˈgreţ-/ *adv* ● *Regrettably, there will be no school play this year, because of lack of money.* ● *He is regrettably slow to understand.*

reg·u·lar EVEN /£ˈreg·jʊ·ləʳ, $-lɚ/ *adj* existing or happening repeatedly in a fixed pattern, with equal or similar amounts of space or time between one and the next; even or frequent ● *a regular customer/churchgoer/reader of newspapers/user of a dictionary* ● *Her heartbeat was regular.* ● *She had slow and regular breathing.* ● *The gardeners planted the trees at regular intervals.* ● *I take regular exercise.* ● *Top footballers make regular appearances on TV.* ● *I suggest that we have regular meetings/meet* **on a** *regular* **basis.** ● *He's a man of regular* **habits** – *he always does the same things on the same days.* ● *We* **keep** *regular* **hours** (=wake up and go to sleep at a similar time every day). ● If you say someone is regular, you mean they excrete the contents of their bowels frequently enough or (of women) that their PERIOD (=monthly bleeding from the womb) is always at approximately the same time: *The doctor asked if I was regular/if my bowel movements were regular.* ● *In this country the trains run/are* **(as) regular as clockwork** (=never late).

reg·u·lar /£ˈreg·jʊ·ləʳ, $-lɚ/ *n* [C] ● *He's one of the regulars* (=people who are frequently present) *at the Rose and Crown pub.*

reg·u·lar·i·ty /£ˌreg·jʊˈlær·ə·ti, $-ˈler·ə·ţi/ *n* [U] ● *The same familiar faces reappear in the law courts* **with** *depressing regularity.*

reg·u·lar·ly /£ˈreg·jʊ·lə·li, $-lɚ-/ *adv* ● *The competitors set off at regularly spaced intervals.* ● *Accidents regularly occur on this bend.*

reg·u·lar SIMILAR /£ˈreg·jʊ·ləʳ, $-lɚ/ *adj* the same on both or all sides ● *He has shining, regular teeth and handsome, regular features.* ● *A square is a regular quadrilateral.*

reg·u·lar·ly /£ˈreg·jʊ·lə·li, $-lɚ-/ *adv* ● *a regularly divided cake*

reg·u·lar USUAL /£ˈreg·jʊ·ləʳ, $-lɚ/ *adj* usual or ordinary ● *Why do you never do things the regular way?* ● *Do you have a work permit – are your work arrangements regular?* ● *Her regular secretary was off sick for a week.* ● *(esp. Am) I bought a regular size tee-shirt, rather than extra large.* ● *(specialized)* A regular verb, noun or adjective follows the usual rules in the structure of its various forms: *'To gain' is a regular verb but 'to be' is not.* LP **Forms of words** ● *(esp. Am approving)* A regular **(sort of) guy** is an honest, ordinary man. ● A regular **army** is an army that exists all the time.

reg·u·lar /£ˈreg·jʊ·ləʳ, $-lɚ/ *n* [C] ● A **regular (soldier)** is someone whose job is being a soldier.

reg·u·lar·ize *obj, Br and Aus usually* **-ise** /£ˈreg·jʊ·lᵊr·aɪz, $-lɚ-/ *v* [T] ● *Some people want to regularize the English spelling system* (=change it so that all words follow the same rules for spelling). ● *The position of our formerly illegal workers has now been regularized* (=made legal and official).

reg·u·lar·i·za·tion, *Br and Aus usually* **-i·sa·tion** /ˌreg·jə·lə·raɪˈzeɪ·ʃᵊn/ *n* [U]

reg·u·lar COMPLETE /£ˈreg·jʊ·ləʳ, $-lɚ/ *adj* [before n; not gradable] *infml esp. humorous* real; complete ● *The situation here now is becoming a regular disaster.* ● *(dated) That child is a regular charmer/little nuisance.*

reg·u·late *(obj)* /ˈreg·jʊ·leɪt/ *v* to control, esp. by making something work in a particular way ● *You can regulate the temperature in the house by adjusting the thermostat and the radiators.* [T] ● *Her mother strictly regulates* **how** *much TV she can watch.* [+ *wh*-word] ● *She has a* **well-regulated** *lifestyle.*

reg·u·la·tion /ˌreg·jʊˈleɪ·ʃᵊn/ *n* ● A regulation is an official rule or the act of controlling: *safety/health/traffic/fire/security regulations* [C] ○ *We have to observe a million petty regulations* **on/about** *the way we do business.* [C] ○ *The correct procedure is laid down in the* **rules and** *regulations.* [C] ● *Regulation* (=official testing) *of all the machines must take place every month.* [U]

reg·u·la·tion /ˌreg·jʊˈleɪ·ʃᵊn/ *adj* [not gradable] ● *Most people were in tee-shirts, but the businessmen were still wearing (the) regulation* (=usual, or ordered by the rules) *pin-stripe suits.* ● *It's regulation to wear suits at the office.*

reg·u·lat·or /£ˈreg·jʊ·leɪ·təʳ, $-ţɚ/ *n* [C] ● A regulator is a device used to control things such as the speed of a clock, the temperature in a room, etc.

reg·u·lat·o·ry /ˌreg·jʊˈleɪ·tri, $ˈreg·jʊ·lə·tɔːr·i/ *adj fml* ● *a regulatory* (=controlling) *body/organization*

re·gur·gi·tate *obj* /£rɪˈgɜː·dʒɪ·teɪt, $-ˈgɜːr·dʒə-/ *v* [T] to bring back (swallowed food) into the mouth ● *Owls regurgitate partly digested food to feed their young.* ● *(fig. disapproving) He speaks well, but he's just regurgitating* (=repeating) *information that he's heard but not really understood.*

re·ha·bil·i·tate *obj* /ˌriː·həˈbɪl·ɪ·teɪt/ *v* [T] to return (someone or something) to a good or healthy condition, state or way of living ● *The prison service should try to rehabilitate prisoners so that they can lead normal lives when they leave prison.* ● *We want to rehabilitate the victims* *of the accident.* • *After 20 years in official disgrace, she's been rehabilitated.*

re·ha·bil·i·ta·tion /ˌriː·həˌbɪl·ɪˈteɪ·ʃᵊn/ *n* [U] • *the rehabilitation of derelict buildings* • *a drug rehabilitation clinic*

re·hash /ˈriː·hæʃ/ *n* [C] *infml disapproving* writing or speech that uses old ideas as if they were new • *His new book is just a rehash* **(of** *his previous ones).*

re·hash *obj* /ˌriːˈhæʃ/ *v* [T] *infml disapproving* • *Some students merely rehash what they've heard in lectures.*

re·hearse *(obj)* /£rɪˈhɜːs, $-ˈhɜːrs/ *v* to practise (a play, a piece of music, etc.) in order to prepare it for public performance • *The musicians rehearsed (the symphony) for the concert.* [I/T] • *(fig.) On her way to her interview she silently rehearsed what she would say.* • *(fml)* When someone rehearses a story or an argument they repeat it with all the details: *These are arguments that I've heard rehearsed at meetings many times before.* [T]

re·hear·sal /£rɪˈhɜː·sᵊl, $-ˈhɜːr-/ *n* • *They didn't have time for (a) rehearsal before the performance.* [C/U] • *He's a producer with three plays* **in** *rehearsal* (= being practised). [U]

re·house *obj* /ˌriːˈhaʊz/ *v* [T usually passive] to move (someone) to a new and usually better place to live in • *The local residents demanded to be rehoused.*

reich /raɪk/ *n* [U] **the Reich** (in the past) the German state or KINGDOM • *Hitler intended the* **Third Reich** *(1933-45) to last for a thousand years.*

reign /reɪn/ *v* [I] to be the king or queen of a country or to be the most noticeable or most powerful person or thing • *Queen Victoria reigned from 1837 to 1901.* • *The bomb attacks produced a panic which reigned* **over** *the city.* • *Love reigned supreme in her heart.*

reign /reɪn/ *n* [C] • *the reign of Henry VIII* • A **reign of terror** is a period of political violence and the organized killing of any opposition.

reign·ing /ˈreɪ·nɪŋ/ *adj* [before n; not gradable] • *Bjorn Borg was the reigning* **champion** *at Wimbledon for five years.*

re·im·burse *obj* /£ˌriː·ɪmˈbɜːs, $-ˈbɜːrs/ *v* [T] *fml* to pay (someone) back esp. money that they have spent for you or lost because of you • *The airline reimbursed me* **for** *the amount they had overcharged me.* • *She was reimbursed by the gas company* **for** *the damage to her house.*

re·im·burse·ment /£ˌriː·ɪmˈbɜː·smənt, $-ˈbɜːr-/ *n* [C/U]

rein /reɪn/ *n* [C usually pl] a long thin piece of material, esp. leather, which helps you to control and direct a horse, or *(Br)* something similar used to control and direct young children • *You pull (on) both reins to stop or slow a horse, but only the left rein to turn left.* • *(Br) She always put the reins on her little son when they went for walks.* • If you **give free rein to** someone or something, you allow them freedom to act: *The young film-makers were given free rein to experiment with new themes and techniques.* • If you **keep a tight rein on** someone or something or **keep** someone or something **on a tight rein** you firmly control them: *My father always kept us on a tight rein.*

rein *obj* /reɪn/ *v* [T always + adv/prep] • If you rein **in/back** a horse or rein a horse **in/back**, you make it go more slowly or stop it. • *(fig.) We tried to rein in our excitement and curiosity.*

re·in·car·na·tion /£ˌriː·ɪŋ·kɑːˈneɪ·ʃᵊn, $-ɪn·kɑːr-/ *n* the belief that a dead person's spirit returns to life in another body, or a person or animal in whose body a dead person's spirit returns to life • *Hindus and Buddhists believe in reincarnation.* [U] • *She thinks that she's a reincarnation of Cleopatra.* [C]

re·in·car·nate *obj* /£ˌriː·ɪŋ·kɑːˈneɪt, $-ɪnˈkɑːr·neɪt/ *v* [T usually passive] • If a person or animal is reincarnated as someone or something else, their spirit returns to life in that person or animal: *If you had a choice, what animal would you like to be reincarnated* **as**? • If something is reincarnated, it appears in a different form, esp. after it has disappeared for a period of time: *Compared to the old model, the reincarnated Mini Cooper has a more powerful engine and looks more streamlined.*

rein·deer /£ˈreɪn·dɪəʳ, $-dɪr/ *n* [C] *pl* **reindeer** a type of deer with large horns, which lives in the northern parts of Europe, Asia and America • *The female reindeer is the only type of female deer to have antlers.* • *Father Christmas travels in a sleigh pulled by reindeer.* • *Radioactive fallout from the Chernobyl disaster contaminated the reindeer feeding grounds in northern Scandinavia.* • *"Rudolph, the Red- Nosed Reindeer / Had a very shiny nose, / And if you ever saw it, / You would even say it glows"* (song *Rudolph the Red-Nosed Reindeer* written by Johnny Marks, 1949)

re·in·force *obj* /£ˌriː·ɪnˈfɔːs, $-ˈfɔːrs/ *v* [T] to make (something) stronger • *The pockets on my jeans are reinforced* **with** *double stitching.* • *His behaviour merely reinforced my dislike of him.* • *One of the unforeseen consequences of the reforms was that they reinforced differences between the north and south of the country.* • If something reinforces an idea or opinion, it provides more proof or support for it and makes it seem true: *Official denials just reinforced the impression that some huge fraud was being kept secret.* ○ *The final technical report into the accident reinforces the findings of initial investigations.* • To reinforce an army is to provide it with more soldiers or weapons to make it stronger: *The UN is sending 800 troops to reinforce the army patrolling the border area.* ○ *The defence minister has announced that the garrison is to be reinforced* **with** *another battalion of soldiers.* • **Reinforced concrete** is concrete that contains metal rods inside it to make it stronger.

re·in·force·ment /£ˌriː·ɪnˈfɔː·smənt, $-ˈfɔːr-/ *n* [U] • *The harbour walls need urgent reinforcement* (= They need strengthening). • *The report stated that the highway collapsed because it was supported by columns that lacked steel reinforcement* (= they contained no steel to strengthen them). • *The government's latest economic policy is a reinforcement of* (= a way to strengthen) *their earlier attempts to conquer inflation.* • *The government has agreed to the reinforcement of UN troops in* (= to send in more soldiers and weapons to) *the war zone.*

re·in·force·ments /£ˌriː·ɪnˈfɔː·smənts, $-ˈfɔːr-/ *pl n* • Reinforcements are soldiers sent to join an army to make it stronger: *More reinforcements have been sent to the border area.*

re·in·state *obj* /ˌriː·ɪnˈsteɪt/ *v* [T] *fml* to give (someone) back their previous job or position, or to cause (something) to exist again • *A month after being unfairly dismissed, he was reinstated* **in** *his job.* • *The Supreme Court reinstated the death penalty in 1976.*

re·in·state·ment /ˌriː·ɪnˈsteɪt·mənt/ *n* [U] *fml* • *He claims the reinstatement of the tax would have damaging effects on many small businesses.* • *The union demanded the immediate reinstatement of a factory worker who had been forced to resign because of her criticism of the company's safety standards.*

re·is·sue *obj* /ˌriːˈɪʃ·uː/ *v* [T] to print or produce (something) again • *Her two major novels have recently been reissued.* • *The recording has been reissued to celebrate the conductor's 80th birthday.*

re·is·sue /ˌriːˈɪʃ·uː/ *n* [C usually sing] • *The music is now available in a reissue on CD.*

re·i·te·rate *obj* /£riˈɪt·ᵊr·eɪt, $-ˈɪt̬·ə·eɪt/ *v* [T] *fml* to say (something) again, once or several times • *The government has reiterated its refusal to compromise with terrorists.* • *She reiterated* **that** *she had never seen him before.* [+ *that* clause]

reiteration /£riˌɪt·ᵊrˈeɪ·ʃᵊn, $-ˌɪt̬·əˈreɪ-/ *n fml* • *Several of these issues warrant explicit reiteration.* [U] • *When she had completed her lecture, she summed up with reiterations of the same theme.* [C]

re·ject *obj* /rɪˈdʒekt/ *v* [T] to refuse to accept, use or believe (something or someone) • *The appeal was rejected by the High Court.* • *Coin-operated machines in England reject Irish money.* • *The prime minister rejected the suggestion that it was time for him to resign.* • *Both children have rejected their parents' religion and have become Buddhists.* • *The agency sent five possible candidates for the job and we rejected two.* • *I applied for a job as a mechanic in a local garage, but I was rejected* (= I was not offered the job). • *The football coach rejected him* **for** *the first team* (= He was not offered a place in the team). • If you reject someone who expects love and affection from you, you treat them in an unkind or cruel way and do not show them the love they want or were expecting: *When she was sent to boarding school, she felt as though her parents had rejected her.* • *(specialized)* If your body rejects an organ that has been put in by an operation, it fails to accept it and tries to attack and destroy it: *The doctors gave him a new kidney, but his body rejected it.*

re·ject /ˈriː·dʒekt/ *n* [C] • A reject is an object which is damaged or faulty: *These two plates are factory rejects because they're slightly cracked in the middle.* • A reject is also a person who has not been accepted by an organization or by society: *She dismisses the idea that the university takes* *in a lot of Oxbridge rejects* (= students who have not been offered a place at the universities of Oxford or Cambridge). ○ *He says that he has always considered himself as one of life's rejects.* • A **reject shop** sells damaged or faulty products that cannot be sold at the full price.

rejection /rɪˈdʒek·ʃᵊn/ *n* • *I've applied for ten jobs, but all I've got is rejections.* [C] • *He was never able to ask her to marry him out of fear of rejection* (= because of the fear that she would not agree to marry him). [U]

re·jig *obj Br and Aus* /ˌriːˈdʒɪɡ/, *Am usually* **re·jig·ger** /£ˌriːˈdʒɪɡ·əʳ, $-ɚ/ *v* [T] **-gg-** *infml* to change and improve the arrangement of (something) • *She spent the afternoon rejigging the furniture.* • *European Finance Ministers have been discussing whether to rejig the rates for several currencies inside the European Monetary System.*

re·joice /rɪˈdʒɔɪs/ *v* [I] *fml or literary* to feel or show great happiness about something • *Everyone rejoiced* **at** *the news of his safe return.* • *She rejoiced* **in** *meeting the challenge of her new job.* • *I rejoiced* **to** *see that she had made such a quick recovery.* [+ *to* infinitive] • *(dated humorous)* If someone **rejoices in the name of** something, they have that particular name and it seems unusual or silly.

re·joic·ing /rɪˈdʒɔɪ·sɪŋ/ *n* [U] *fml or literary* • *There was much rejoicing* **at** *the good news.* • *The end of the war was a* **cause for** *great rejoicing.*

re·join *obj* RETURN /ˌriːˈdʒɔɪn/ *v* [T] to return to (a person or place) • *She rejoined her husband in Toronto after spending six months in Paris.* • *When war broke out, he rejoined his regiment in Edinburgh.* • *Take the turning off to Bath and then rejoin the motorway at Bristol.*

re·join ANSWER QUICKLY /rɪˈdʒɔɪn/ *v* [+ clause] *fml or literary* to give a quick answer to something that someone has said, in an angry or amusing way • *"No, I do not have time to help you," he rejoined impatiently.*

re·join·der /£rɪˈdʒɔɪn·dəʳ, $-dɚ/ *n* [C] *fml or literary* • A rejoinder is a quick and often angry or amusing answer: *She always has a witty rejoinder* **to/for** *any question.*

re·juv·e·nate *obj* /rɪˈdʒuː·vᵊn·eɪt/ *v* [T] to make (someone) look or feel young and energetic again • *She felt rejuvenated by her fortnight in the Bahamas.* • If you rejuvenate an organization or system, you make it more efficient and modern by introducing new methods and ideas: *He has decided to rejuvenate the team by bringing in a lot of new, young players.* ○ *Since taking over the family firm, they have completely rejuvenated it.*

re·juv·e·na·tion /rɪˌdʒuː·vᵊnˈeɪ·ʃᵊn/ *n* [U] • *She is one of the people behind the rejuvenation of the company* (= She is responsible for making it more modern and efficient).

re·lapse /rɪˈlæps/ *v* [I] *fml* to return to a previous condition or a worse way of life after making an improvement • *She managed to stop using drugs for a month, but then relapsed.* • *He talked for a short while and then relapsed* **into** *silence* (= he became silent again).

re·lapse /ˈriː·læps/ *n* [C] *fml* • If someone who is getting better after an illness **has/suffers a relapse**, they become ill again: *She was looking quite healthy on Friday, but she suffered a relapse over the weekend and was taken back into intensive care.*

re·late *obj* CONNECT /rɪˈleɪt/ *v* [T] to find or show the connection between (two things) • *Some education advisers have related the drop in the standard of students' performances* **and/with** *the increase in the size of classes.* • If something **relates to** a particular subject, it is connected with or deals with that subject: *Chapter nine relates to the effects of inflation on consumers.* • If something **relates to** a particular person or group of people, it has an effect on them: *I do not understand how your proposal relates to me* (= what effect it will have on me). ○ See also RELATE TO. • **Relating to** means connected with: *Anything relating to maths is a complete mystery to me.*

re·lat·ed /£rɪˈleɪ·tɪd, $-t̬ɪd/ *adj* [not gradable] • If two things are related, there is a connection between them: *We discussed inflation, unemployment and related issues.* ○ *Experts believe that the large number of cancer cases in the area are* **directly** *related* **to** *the new nuclear power station.* • If people are related, they belong to the same family: *She claims she is related* **to** *royalty.* ○ *Jim and I are related* **by** *marriage.* • If different types of animal are related, they originate from the same type of animal: *The cat and the lion are related species.*

re·la·tion /rɪˈleɪ·ʃᵊn/ *n* • The relation between two things is the connection or similarity between them: *The relation* **between** *the original book* **and** *this new film is very faint.* [U] ○ *She* **bears** *no relation* **to** (= She is not similar to) *her brother.* [U] • Someone who is your relation is a member of your family: *She's a relation* **by marriage** *because she married my cousin.* [C] ○ *The funeral was attended by friends and relations.* [C] • **In/With relation to** means in connection with: *She used the map to discover where she was in relation to her surroundings.* • See also **relations** at RELATE TO. • Ⓕ

re·la·tion·ship /rɪˈleɪ·ʃᵊn·ʃɪp/ *n* [C] • The relationship between two things is the way in which they are connected: *Scientists have established the relationship* **between** *lung cancer* **and** *smoking.* • The relationship between people is their family connection: *The judge asked the witness what the relationship was between her and the victim, and she replied, "He's my son."* • See also **relationship** at RELATE TO. • LP **Relationships**

rel·a·tive /£ˈrel·ə·tɪv, $-t̬ɪv/ *adj* [not gradable] • *(fml)* If something is relative **to** a particular subject, it is connected with it: *The documents are relative to the discussion.* • *(specialized)* A **relative clause** is part of a sentence which cannot exist independently and which describes a noun which comes before it in the main part of the sentence: *In the sentence 'The woman whom I met was wearing a brown hat', 'whom I met' is a relative clause.* • *(specialized)* A **relative pronoun** is a pronoun such as *which, who* or *that* which is used to begin a **relative clause**: *In the sentence 'The woman whom I met was wearing a brown hat', 'whom' is a relative pronoun.*

rel·a·tive /£ˈrel·ə·tɪv, $-t̬ɪv/, *Aus infml* **rel·lie** *n* [C] • A relative is a member of your family: *I haven't got many* **blood** *relatives* (= people related to me by birth rather than by marriage). ○ *All her* **distant** *relatives* (= people who were not closely related to her) *came to the wedding.*

re·late *(obj)* TELL /rɪˈleɪt/ *v fml or literary* to tell (a story) or describe (a series of events) • *She related the events of the past week* **to** *the police.* [T] • *He relates* **how** *at the age of 23 he was interned in a prison camp.* [+ *wh-* word]

re·late to *obj v prep* [T] to understand and sympathize with (someone) • *Many parents find it hard to relate to their children when they are teenagers.* • *My father cannot relate to* (= cannot understand or accept) *the idea of working with computers.* • See also **relate to** at RELATE CONNECT.

re·la·tions /rɪˈleɪ·ʃᵊnz/ *pl n* • Relations between two people or groups of people are the way in which they feel and behave towards each other: *Relations* **between** *him and his new wife are rather strained.* ○ *Britain* **enjoys** *friendly relations* **with** *the Canada.* ○ *The country has decided to restore full* **diplomatic** *relations with the United States.* • *(fml)* To **have sexual relations with** someone is to have sex or a sexual relationship with them: *The couple had been having sexual relations for a year prior to the divorce.* • See also **relation** at RELATE CONNECT.

re·la·tion·ship /rɪˈleɪ·ʃᵊn·ʃɪp/ *n* [C] • The relationship between two people or groups of people is the way in which they feel and behave towards each other: *They have a very good business relationship.* • A relationship is also a close romantic friendship between two people, which is often sexual: *She's just finished a six-year relationship.* ○ *Have you had any relationships in the past year?* • See also **relationship** at RELATE CONNECT. • LP **Relationships**

rel·a·tive /£ˈrel·ə·tɪv, $-t̬ɪv/ *adj* [not gradable] *fml* being judged or measured in comparison with something else • *We weighed up the relative advantages of driving there or going by train.* • Relative can also mean that something is true to a certain degree when it is being compared with other things: *Since I got a job, I've been living in relative comfort* (= I am now living in a more comfortable way than I was in the past). • If something is relative **to** something else, it varies according to the speed or level of the other thing: *The amount of petrol a car uses is relative to its speed* (= depends on the speed at which the car moves). ○ *How rich I feel is relative to what things cost in the shops.* • *(specialized)* **Relative density** is the mass of a particular volume of a substance when compared with the mass of an equal volume of water at 4°C. • The **relative humidity** of the air is the amount of water that is present in the air compared to the greatest amount it would be possible for the air to hold at that temperature: *The temperature is due to reach 32°C and the relative humidity will be 83%.* • See also **relative** at RELATE CONNECT.

rel·a·tive·ly /£ˈrel·ə·tɪv·li, $-t̬ɪv-/ *adv* [not gradable] • *We had expected bloodshed, but there was relatively little violence* (= There was not as much violence as we were expecting). • *He's a relatively good squash player* (= He plays quite well in comparison with other players). • You say **relatively speaking** when you want to judge one thing in comparison with other things: *Relatively speaking, Britain is a poor European country.*

rel·a·tiv·i·ty /£ˌrel·əˈtɪv·ɪ·ti, $-ə·t̬i/ *n* [U] *fml* • Relativity is the state of being judged in comparison with other things and not by itself.

rel·a·tiv·i·ty /£ˌrel·əˈtɪv·ɪ·ti, $-ə·t̬i/ *n* [U] *specialized* either of two very important theories of physics giving the relationship between space, time and energy, esp. for two objects moving in different ways • *According to Einstein's Theory of Relativity, the amount of energy in an object depends on its mass and the speed of light.*

re·lax *(obj)* /rɪˈlæks/ *v* to (cause someone to) become less active and more calm, or to (cause a part of the body to) become less stiff • *You shouldn't work so hard – you should relax more.* [I] • *I like to relax* **by doing** *the gardening.* [I] • *After work she relaxed* (= enjoyed herself calmly) **with** *a cup of tea and the newspaper.* [I] • *A good massage will relax your tired muscles.* [T] • *He relaxed his* **grip** *on my arm* (= He began to hold it less tightly). [T] • *(fig.) The Mafia has relaxed its* **grip/hold** *on* (= reduced its tight control of) *local businesses.* [T] • When rules or controls are relaxed, they are made less severe: *Two weeks after the police relaxed security at the airports, there was a bomb attack.* [T] • Ⓕ

re·lax·a·tion /ˌriː·lækˈseɪ·ʃᵊn/ *n* • *I go fishing* **for** *relaxation* (= in order to relax). [U] • Relaxation is also the act of making rules or the control of something less severe: *I cannot allow any relaxation* **in/of** *the rules.* [U] • A relaxation is a pleasant activity which makes you become calm and less worried: *Yoga is one of my favourite relaxations.* [C]

re·laxed /rɪˈlækst/ *adj* • *I feel so relaxed when I'm by the sea.* • *It's a very friendly bar with a relaxed* (= informal) *atmosphere.* • If someone is relaxed **about** something, they are not worried about it: *My parents are fairly relaxed about me staying out late.*

re·lax·ing /rɪˈlæk·sɪŋ/ *adj* • *I find swimming very relaxing.* • *I spent a relaxing holiday on the beach, reading and sunbathing.*

re·lay *obj* REPEAT /ˌriːˈleɪ/ *v* [T] to repeat (something) you have heard, or to broadcast (a signal, message or programme) on television or radio • *I was told the news first and then I relayed it* **to** *the others.* • *TV pictures of the war were relayed around the world by satellite.*

re·lay TEAM /ˈriː·leɪ/ *n* [C] a group of people who continue an activity that others from the same team or organization have been doing previously • *Relays of workers kept the machines going through the night.* • *After the landslide, volunteers worked* **in** *relays to rescue people buried under the rubble.* • A **relay (race)** is a running or swimming race between two or more teams in which each person in the team runs or swims part of the race: *The Jamaican relay* **team** *won the gold for the 400m relay.*

re·lay EQUIPMENT /ˈriː·leɪ/ *n* [C] a device that reacts to a small change in an electrical current by moving switches or other devices in an electrical CIRCUIT • *The high-voltage lines are activated by relays.*

re·lease *obj* MAKE FREE /rɪˈliːs/ *v* [T] to give freedom or free movement to (someone or something) • *He was released* **from** *prison after serving two years of a five-year sentence.* • *The zoo keepers released the lions* **from** *their cage.* • *(fig.) The medicine released him* **from** *years of pain* (= It stopped him suffering pain). • *She was arrested for shoplifting but was released* **on bail** (= after paying a sum of money to the law court). • If you release a device, you move it from a fixed position and allow it to move freely: *She released the handbrake and the car jumped forwards.* • If you release a bomb or a MISSILE, you fire it or allow it to fall: *The plane released its bombs at 10 000 feet.* • If you release a gas, you cause it to leave an enclosed area and enter the surrounding area: *Oil and coal power stations release sulphur dioxide* **into** *the atmosphere.* • *(fml)* If you release a feeling which you have been trying not to show, you express it.

re·lease /rɪˈliːs/ *n* [U] • *Diplomatic efforts are being made to secure the release of the hostages.* • *Her early release* **from** *prison led to a demonstration.* • *The accident at the power station caused the release of radioactivity into the atmosphere.* • *I noticed a release* **of** *tension when he left the room.* • *Pull the release cord to open the parachute.* • Release is also a feeling that you are free from something unpleasant: *After she resigned, she experienced a strong feeling of release.* ○ *After years of suffering, his death came as a merciful release.*

re·lease *obj* MAKE PUBLIC /rɪˈliːs/ *v* [T] to let (something) be shown in public or available for use • *The police have released a picture of the man they want to question.* • *The minister has released a statement explaining the reasons for his resignation.* • *I'm afraid I have no authority to release* (= give) *these documents* **to** *you.* • If a company releases a film or musical recording, it allows the film to be shown in cinemas, or makes the musical recording available for the public to buy: *The band's latest album will be released next week.*

re·lease /rɪˈliːs/ *n* • *The government has refused to be governed by strict rules on the release of official information.* [U] • A release is a written statement which gives information to be broadcast or published: *The Department of Transport has issued a* **press** *release about the proposals for the new motorway.* [C] • A release is also a musical recording which is made available for the public to buy: *Her latest release is a song about hopeless love.* [C] • If a film is *(Br and Aus)* **on**/*(Am)* **in** general release, it is available to be shown in cinemas: *The latest film from Disney goes on general release next month.* [U]

rel·e·gate *obj* /ˈrel·ɪ·geɪt/ *v* [T usually passive] to put (something or someone) into a lower or less important rank or position • *The story was relegated* **to** *the middle pages of the paper.* • *She resigned from the company when she was relegated* **to** *a role of financial consultant.* • *They complained that the financial cost of the project had been relegated* **to** *the margins of the debate, when it should have been central.* • *(Br)* If a football team is relegated, it is moved down to a lower division: *If Arsenal lose again they may be relegated* **from** *the Premier League* **to** *the First Division.* ○ Compare PROMOTE RAISE. • LP Sports

rel·e·ga·tion /ˌrel·ɪˈgeɪ·ʃᵊn/ *n* [U] • *(Br)* Relegation is the act of moving a football team to a lower division: *The threat of relegation has hung over Everton all season.* ○ *Arsenal* **face** *relegation if they lose again.*

re·lent /rɪˈlent/ *v* [I] *slightly fml* to act in a less severe way towards someone and allow something that you had refused to allow before • *Her parents had initially refused to let her go to the party, but eventually they relented* (= they allowed her to go). • *There is no sign of the warring parties relenting* (= stopping the fighting) *on the ground, whatever assurances they gave during the negotiations.*

re·lent·less /rɪˈlent·ləs/ *adj* • Relentless means continuing in a severe or determined way: *He believes that the relentless push for economic growth is deeply damaging to the environment.* ○ *The main symptom of anorexia is a relentless pursuit of thinness by starving yourself.* ○ *With all the money and glamour of a film career in Hollywood comes the relentless pressure to succeed.* ○ *The pool was a delightfully cool spot in the relentless summer heat.*

re·lent·less·ly /rɪˈlent·lə·sli/ *adv* • *She has campaigned relentlessly to secure her husband's release from prison.* • *Demand for places in the college has been rising relentlessly over the past few years.*

rel·e·vant /ˈrel·ə·vᵊnt/ *adj* connected with what is happening or being discussed • *For further information, please refer to the relevant leaflet.* • *All evidence relevant* **to** *this trial must be given to police.* • *That point is* **highly** *relevant* **to** *the discussion.* • *I'm sorry but your personal wishes are not relevant* (= important) *in this case.* • Relevant also means correct or suitable for a particular purpose: *The Board of Education has announced plans to make schooling more relevant and prepare students better for life beyond high school.* • Ⓔ Ⓘ

rel·e·vance /ˈrel·ə·vᵊnts/, **rel·e·van·cy** /ˈrel·ə·vᵊnt·si/ *n* [U] • *I'm afraid I don't understand the relevance of your question.* • *What relevance does that point have* **to** *the discussion?* • *He believes that Marx's ideas do not have much relevance* (= are not important or useful) **to/for** *us today.*

re·li·a·ble /rɪˈlaɪə·bl̩/ *adj* See at RELY ON

re·li·ance /rɪˈlaɪ·ənts/ *n* [U] See at RELY ON

re·li·ant /rɪˈlaɪ·ənt/ *adj* See at RELY ON

rel·ic /ˈrel·ɪk/ *n* [C] an object, tradition or system from the past which has survived and continues to exist • *During the dig, the archeological team found some relics* **from** *the Stone Age.* • *The country's employment system is a relic* **of** *the 1960s when jobs were scarce.* • *Since returning from imprisonment, he has seemed like a relic* **of** *the past, clinging to his outdated beliefs.* • A relic is also a part of the body or clothing or one of the belongings of a SAINT (= a holy person): *These bones are the relics of a 12th-century saint.* •

RELATIONSHIPS

The Language Portrait on **the family** explains simple family relationships such as wife, father, brother and so on. More complicated relationships happen, for example when one partner in a marriage dies and the other marries again. There are also important words referring to relationships between people who are not married.

• People who are single (not married)

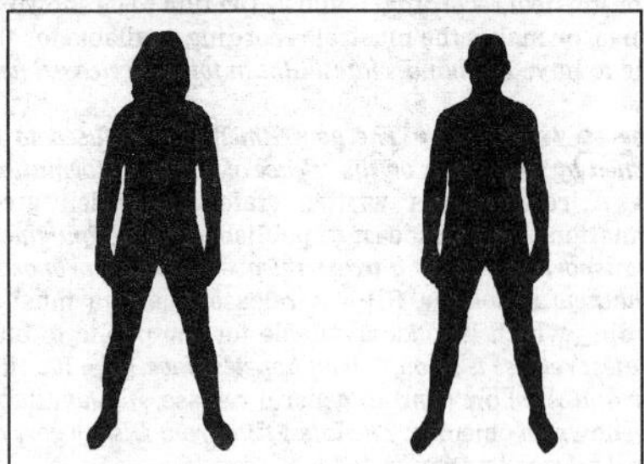

Your **boyfriend** or **girlfriend** is someone with whom you are having a romantic or sexual relationship. The word **lover** can be used if the relationship is sexual.

If a **couple** (= two people in a relationship) are **engaged** they have formally agreed to marry. The person to whom you are engaged is your *(male)* **fiancé** / *(female)* **fiancée**: *Have you met Peter, my fiancé? We got engaged a couple of months ago.*

An **unmarried couple** are in a sexual relationship and **live together** but are not married. The two people are **partners**: *I've been living with my partner Jessie for three years now and we're thinking of getting married one day.*

If a couple have children they are **unmarried parents**. If one unmarried person has a child whom they are looking after, they are a **single parent/mother/father** or a **lone parent**.

• People who are married

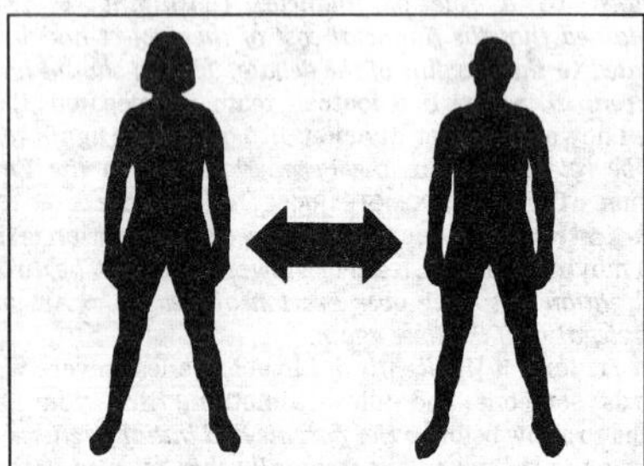

A person's husband or wife is their *(fml or law)* **spouse**: *Guests may bring their spouse or partner or a friend.*
The two people are a **(married) couple**: *Do you know the Browns? They're a very interesting couple.*

In informal conversation people might speak of their **hubby** (= husband) or **missus** (= wife): *I'm taking the missus and the kids on holiday to Portugal this year.*

(For the use of the titles *Mr, Mrs, Ms, Miss* and other forms of address LP **Titles and forms of address** at TITLE.)

• If a marriage ends

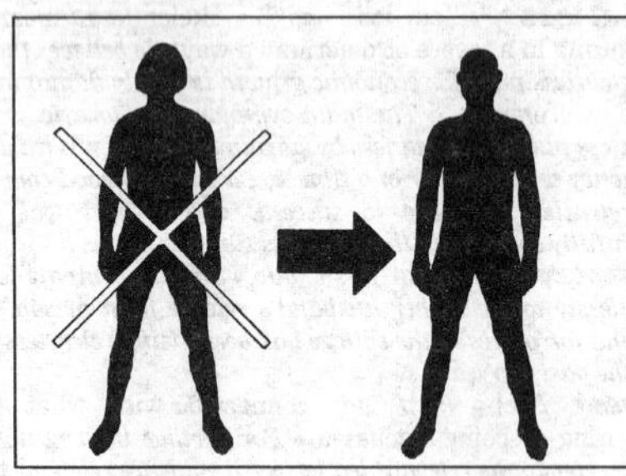

If someone's husband or wife has died, they are a *(female)* **widow**/*(male)* **widower** and the dead person is called their **late** husband/wife.

A child whose parents are both dead is an **orphan**. He or she might be **adopted** or **fostered** by another couple (see below).

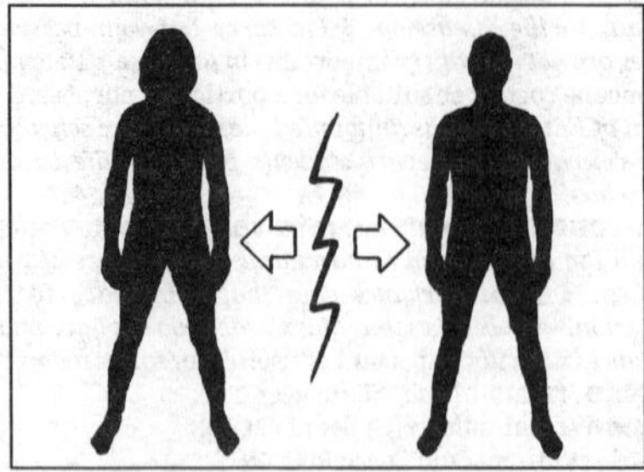

When a couple **divorce** they end their marriage by an official or legal process. If they **separate** they stop living together, often as a part of a legal arrangement: *The marriage didn't work out so they separated for a while and then decided to get divorced.*

People who are divorced can refer to the person who was their husband or wife as their **ex-husband** or **ex-wife**.
Your *(infml)* **ex** is someone who is no longer your wife, husband, lover, etc.: *I gather that my ex has just moved in with his new girlfriend.*
A divorced person who has children but no partner living with them is a **lone parent**.

• If there is a new marriage

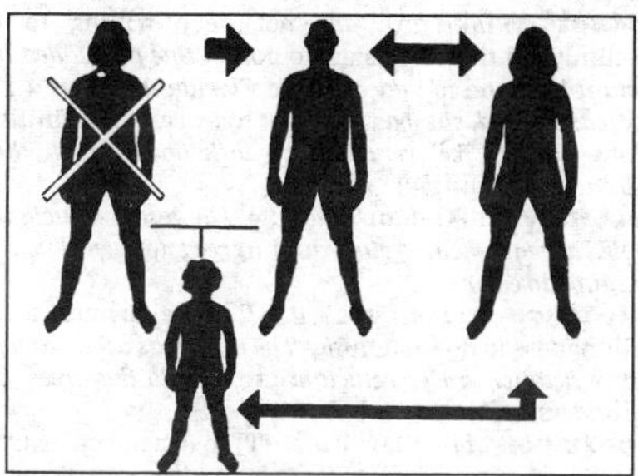

When someone **re-marries** this might cause some new relationships.

In the example a couple had a daughter and then the mother died. The man married again. His new wife is the **stepmother** of his daughter, and his daughter is the **stepdaughter** of his new wife. They do not have any **blood** relationship (=family relationship by birth).

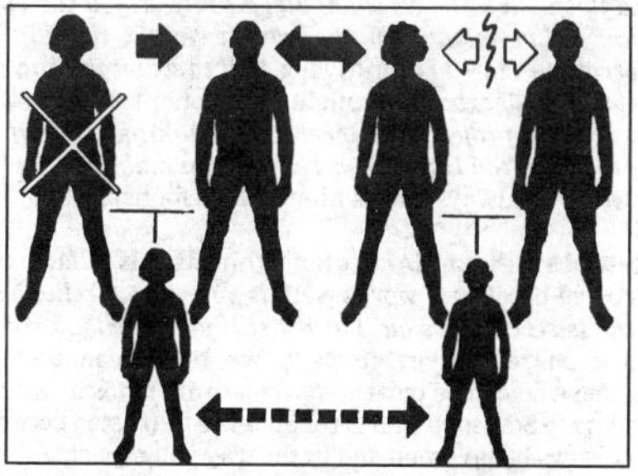

In the second example both husband and wife have a child from a previous marriage. These children have no blood relationship: they are **stepbrother** or **stepsister** to each other.

(Notice that *stepmother, stepchild* etc. are not words that would be used often within the family. They would probably refer to each other as *my new mother/daughter/brother* etc.)

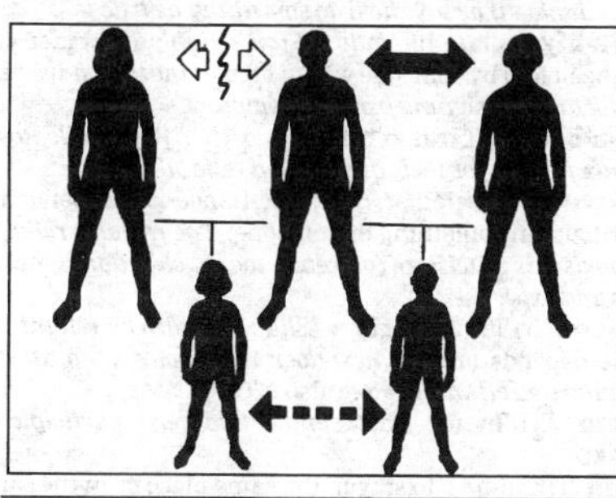

In the third example there is a child from a previous marriage, and the couple also have another child together. These children have some relationship by blood because they have one parent who is the same: they are **half-brother** or **half-sister** to each other.

• If a couple take a child into their own family

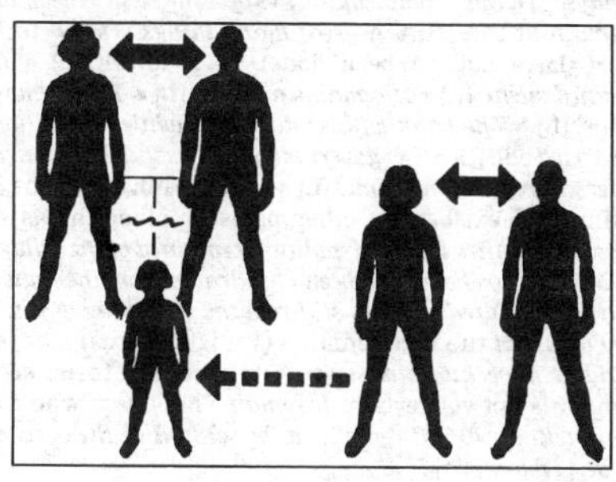

A person's **natural** mother and father are the parents who caused them to be born, although they may not be their legal parents or the parents who raised them.

When a couple **adopt** a child they take another person's child into their own family and legally raise him or her as their own child. They are **adoptive parents** and the child is their **adopted son/daughter**.

When a couple **foster** a child they take care of him or her, usually for a limited time, without being the child's legal parents. They are **foster parents** and the child is their **foster son/daughter**.

(Notice that these words would not often be used within the family.)

(humorous) A relic can be a very old or old-fashioned thing or person: *He's still driving around in that* **old** *relic of his.*

re·lief HELP /rɪˈliːf/ *n* food, money or services which provide help for people in need • *Pop stars have raised millions of pounds for* **famine** *relief in Africa.* [U] • *Relief* **agencies** *are trying to provide emergency water supplies in the area.* • *Relief* **supplies** *have been flown out to the refugee camps.* • *When the driver was taken ill, a relief* (= a new driver) *was sent to take his place.* [C] • *(Br) A relief* (= special) *bus service was provided during the rail strike.* • *(fml)* The relief of a town that has been surrounded by an enemy army is the freeing of it using force. [U] • *(Am infml)* If someone is **on** relief, they receive money from the government because they are poor. [U] • *(Br)* A **relief road** is a road that drivers can use to avoid driving on very busy main road. • *"For this relief much thanks"* (Shakespeare, Hamlet 1.1)

re·lieve *obj* /rɪˈliːv/ *v* [T] • *The government has agreed to provide £11 million of emergency food aid to help relieve the famine.* • To relieve someone is to take their place and continue doing their job or duties: *I'm on duty until 2p.m. and then Peter is coming to relieve me.* • *(fml)* If you relieve someone of something heavy, you take it from them to help them: *May I relieve you* **of** *that heavy bag?* ○ *(humorous) The pickpocket delicately relieved him* **of** (= stole) *his wallet.* • *(fml)* If you relieve someone of their job or position, you dismiss them: *She was relieved* **of** *her post after five years of service.* • *(fml)* If an army relieves a place that has been surrounded by an enemy army, it frees that place by force: *Enemy troops had besieged the town and an armoured battalion was sent to relieve it.*

re·lief HAPPINESS /rɪˈliːf/ *n* [U] a feeling of happiness that something unpleasant has not happened or has ended • *The ceasefire was greeted with relief by people living in the* *capital which has been under siege for two years.* • **It** *was such* **a** *relief* **to** *hear that Glen had been found safe and well.* [+ *to* infinitive] • *She breathed* **a sigh of** *relief when she found out she had passed her exams.* • *After he left the room, I felt an incredible* **sense of** *relief.*

re·lieve *obj* /rɪˈliːv/ *v* [T] • If something relieves an unpleasant feeling, such as pain or worry, it makes it less strong: *She was given a shot of morphine to relieve the pain.* ○ *The good news relieved my anxiety.* ○ *She relieved her boredom at home by learning how to type.* ○ *He relieved his feelings of frustration by kicking the desk.* • If something relieves an unpleasant situation, it improves it: *The council is considering banning vehicles from the town centre to relieve congestion.* ○ *She claims that the pressure on public hospitals could be relieved by combining medical resources in the public and private sectors.* • *(dated)* To relieve your**self** is to urinate.

re·lieved /rɪˈliːvd/ *adj* • If someone is relieved, they are happy that something unpleasant has not happened or has ended: *I'm so relieved* **to** *find you – I thought you'd already gone.* [+ *to* infinitive] ○ *She wore a relieved expression.* ○ *My family were relieved* **at** *the news of my safe arrival.* ○ *He was relieved* **to** *see Jeannie reach the other side of the river safely.* [+ *to* infinitive] ○ *I was relieved* **to** *hear that I'd passed my exams.* [+ *to* infinitive] ○ *I'm relieved* **(that)** *you didn't tell her.* [+ *that* clause]

re·lief RAISED AREA /rɪˈliːf/ *n* a method of raising shapes above a flat surface so that they appear to stand out slightly from it • *Coins have pictures on them* **in** *relief.* [U] • A relief is a SCULPTURE made from a flat surface in which the forms are raised above the background: *The bronze reliefs on the doors of the Baptistery in Florence were designed by Ghiberti in the 15th century.* [C] • If something stands out **in** relief, its shape is very clear and noticeable: *The mountain stood out in* **sharp** *relief against the evening sky.* [U] • **A relief map** is a map that shows the hills, valleys and mountains of a particular area or country.

re·li·gion /rɪˈlɪdʒ·ᵊn/ *n* the belief in and worship of a god or gods, or any such system of belief and worship • *She loves to discuss religion.* [U] • *He* **practises** *the Jewish religion.* [C] • If an activity is a religion for you, you are extremely enthusiastic about it and do it regularly: *Golf is a religion* **for** *Susan.* [C]

re·li·gious /rɪˈlɪdʒ·əs/ *adj* • *The government wants to increase the amount of religious education in schools.* • If someone is religious, they have a strong belief in a god or gods: *He's* **deeply** *religious and goes to church twice a week.*

religiously /rɪˈlɪdʒ·ə·sli/ *adv* • *India is quite diverse, both politically and religiously.* • If you do something religiously, you do it regularly: *He visits his mother religiously every week.*

re·lin·quish *obj* /rɪˈlɪŋ·kwɪʃ/ *v* [T] *fml* to give up (something such as a responsibility or claim) • *He has relinquished his claim to the throne.* • *She relinquished responsibility for the family investments* **to** *her son.* • If you relinquish your hold on an object, you stop holding it: *She relinquished her* **hold/grip** *on the steering wheel.*

rel·ish *(obj)* ENJOY /ˈrel·ɪʃ/ *v slightly fml* to like or enjoy (something) • *I always relish a challenge.* [T] • *I don't relish tell***ing** *her that her son has been arrested.* [+ v-*ing*] • If you relish the idea or thought of something, you feel pleasure that it is going to happen: *I had enjoyed writing the first book, and relished the thought of working on the second.* [T] ○ *She's relishing the prospect of studying in Bologna for six months.* [T]

rel·ish /ˈrel·ɪʃ/ *n* [U] *slightly fml* • Relish is the enjoyment you get from doing something: *She ate her cake slowly and* **with** *relish.* ○ *I have no relish* **for** *hunting and killing animals.*

rel·ish SAUCE /ˈrel·ɪʃ/ *n* a type of sauce which is eaten with food to add flavour to it • *Ann made a tomato and onion relish.* [C] • *Would you like some relish on your burger?* [U]

relive *obj* /ˌriːˈlɪv/ *v* [T] to remember clearly (an experience that happened in the past) • *Whenever I smell burning, I relive the final moments of the crash.*

rel·lie /ˈrel·i/ *n* [C] *Aus infml for* **relative**, see at RELATE CONNECT.

re·load *(obj)* /£ˌriːˈləʊd, $-ˈloʊd/ *v* to put more bullets in (a gun) • *He reloaded and fired a second shot.* [I] • *The police said that type of pistol is not often used in crimes because it has to be reloaded after every shot.* [T]

re·lo·cate *(obj)* /£ˌriː·ləʊˈkeɪt, $-ˈloʊ·keɪt/ *v* to (cause a person or company to) move to a new place • *The company has relocated* **to** *Liverpool.* [I] • *My company relocated me* **to** *Paris.* [T]

re·luc·tant /rɪˈlʌk·tᵊnt/ *adj* not very willing to do something and therefore slow to do it • *She persuaded her reluctant husband to take a trip to Florida with her.* • *The party was so good, she was reluctant* **to** *leave.* [+ *to* infinitive] • *Many parents feel reluctant* **to** *talk openly with their children.* [+ *to* infinitive]

reluctantly /rɪˈlʌk·tᵊnt·li/ *adv* • *The losers reluctantly accepted defeat.* • *She reluctantly agreed to step down as managing director.*

re·luc·tance /rɪˈlʌk·tᵊnts/ *n* [U] • Reluctance is an unwillingness to do something: *The offer was accepted with great reluctance.* ○ *Her reluctance* **to** *talk to the Press was quite understandable.* [+ *to* infinitive]

re·ly on/u·pon *obj* /rɪˈlaɪ/ *v prep* [T] to depend on or trust (someone or something) • *British weather can never be relied upon – it's always changing.* • *I rely on you* **for** *good advice.* • *I'm relying on the garage* **to** *fix the car by tomorrow.* [+ obj + *to* infinitive] • *Don't rely on find***ing** *me here when you get back* (= I might have gone). [+ v-*ing*] • *The success of this project relies on everyone mak***ing** *an effort.* [+ obj + v-*ing*] • *You can always rely on him mak***ing** *a fool of himself* (= He always makes himself look foolish). [+ obj + v-*ing*]

re·li·a·ble /rɪˈlaɪə·bl̩/ *adj* • Something that is reliable can be trusted because it works well: *Is your watch reliable?* ○ *My car is seven years old but it's still fairly reliable.* ○ *We have it on reliable* **evidence** (= We have been told by someone who can be trusted) *that there are plans to build a road here.* • Someone who is reliable can be trusted because they always behave well and in the way you expect: *John is very reliable – if he says he'll do something he'll do it.*

re·li·a·bly /rɪˈlaɪə·bli/ *adv* • *I am reliably* **informed** (= I have been told by someone whom I trust) *that you have been talking about resigning from the company.*

re·li·a·bil·i·ty /£rɪˌlaɪəˈbɪl·ɪ·ti, $-ə·t̬i/ *n* [U] • *Rolls-Royce cars are famous for their quality and reliability.*

re·li·ance /rɪˈlaɪ·ənts/ *n* [U] • Reliance is a dependence on or trust in something or someone: *The region's reliance* **on** *tourism is unwise.* ○ *You* **place** *too much reliance* **on** *her ideas and expertise.*

re·li·ant /rɪˈlaɪ·ənt/ *adj* • *She's completely reliant* **on** (= She depends on) *her next-door neighbour to do all her shopping and cleaning.* • See also SELF-RELIANT.

re·made /ˌriːˈmeɪd/ *past simple and past participle of* REMAKE

re·main /rɪˈmeɪn/ *v* to stay in the same place or in the same condition • *The doctor ordered him to remain in bed for a few days.* [I] • *Most commentators expect the basic rate of tax to remain at 25%.* [I] • *A great many things remain* **to** *be done* (= have not yet been done). [+ *to* infinitive] • *He remained silent.* [L] • *It remains a secret.* [L] • *They remain friends.* [L] • *The bank will remain open while renovations are carried out.* [L] • *The government insists that it wants the borders to remain the same.* [L] • If something remains, it continues to exist when other parts or other things no longer exist: *After the flood, nothing remained of the village.* [I] • *Most troops have now been withdrawn from the region, but a few hundred soldiers still remain.* [I] • *I know you're sorry now, but* **the fact remains** (= it is still true) *that you shouldn't have hit your sister.* • **It remains to be seen** means it is not yet certain: *It remains to be seen* **who** *will win.* [+ *wh-* word] ○ *It remains to be seen* **what** *the outcome will be.* [+ *wh-* word]

re·main·der /£rɪˈmeɪn·dəʳ, $-dɚ/ *n* [U] • The remainder of something is the part that is left after the other parts have gone, been used or been taken away: *We ate most of the food and gave the remainder to the dog.* ○ *It rained the first day but the remainder of the trip was lovely.* • *(specialized)* In mathematics, the remainder is the amount that is left when one number cannot be exactly divided by another: *9 divided by 4 is 2, remainder 1.* • See also REMAINDER.

re·main·ing /rɪˈmeɪ·nɪŋ/ *adj* [before n; not gradable] • If something is remaining, it continues to exist or is left after other parts or things have been used or taken away: *Six of the team's remaining nine matches are away from home.* ○ *Bernstein's two remaining lectures will take place on January 22 and 23.* ○ *Wheat was planted in two of the fields and the remaining land was dug over and left bare.*

re·mains /rɪˈmeɪnz/ *pl n* • Remains are pieces or parts of something which continue to exist when most of it has been used, destroyed or taken away: *The remains of lunch were still on the table.* ○ *The remains of a 12th-century* *monastery can still be seen on the site.* • *(fml)* A person's remains are that person's dead body: *Fifty years after he died, his remains were returned to his homeland.* ○ *Human remains have been found in a shallow grave in the woods.*

re·main·der *obj* /£rɪˈmeɪn·dəʳ, $-dɚ/ *v* [T usually passive] to sell (a book) cheaply because it has not sold well and no more copies of it will be produced • *His autobiography never sold very well and was soon remaindered.* • See also **remainder** at REMAIN.

re·make *obj* /ˌriːˈmeɪk/ *v* [T] *past* **remade** /ˌriːˈmeɪd/ to make (a new film) with a similar story and title to an old one • *The French film 'Trois Hommes et un Bébé' was remade in Hollywood* **as** *'Three Men and a Baby'.*

re·make /ˈriː·meɪk/ *n* [C] • *Do you prefer the remake of 'King Kong' to the original?*

re·mand *obj* /£rɪˈmɑːnd, $-ˈmænd/ *v* [T usually passive] *law* to send (a person accused of committing a crime) away from a law court to wait until their trial begins • *He was remanded* **on** *theft charges.* • *The report has proposed a ban on remanding boys* **to** *adult prisons.* • *The accused was remanded* **in custody** (=kept in prison before the trial began) *for a week.* • If someone accused of a crime is **remanded on bail**, they are allowed to leave the law court and go to a particular place, usually their home, to wait until their trial begins, after they have paid a sum of money to the court which will not be given back if they do not appear at the trial.

re·mand /£rɪˈmɑːnd, $-ˈmænd/ *n* [U] *law* • *In 1981, custodial remand* (=keeping people in prison before their trial begins) *for 14-year-old boys was ended.* • If someone is **on** remand, they are waiting until their trial begins: *He was* **held** *on remand in Brixton prison for 18 months before his trial began.* • *(Br and Aus)* A **remand centre** (*Am* **detention home** or **detention center**) is a place where young people accused of committing a crime are sent to wait until their trial begins.

re·mark /£rɪˈmɑːk, $-ˈmɑːrk/ *v* to give a spoken statement of an opinion or thought • *"I think it's going to rain," she remarked.* [+ clause] • *Dr Johnson once remarked* **(that)** *"When a man is tired of London, he is tired of life."* [+ (*that*) clause] • If you remark **on** something, you notice it and say something about it: *All his friends remarked on the change in him since his marriage.* [I]

re·mark /£rɪˈmɑːk, $-ˈmɑːrk/ *n* [C] • *Her remarks* **on** *the employment question led to a heated discussion.* • *He finished his speech with the remark* **(that)** *"Education must be our priority."* [+ (*that*) clause] • *She stunned her audience with the remark* **that** *she was committed to pursuing reform through the party.* [+ *that* clause] • *The children* **made/passed** *rude remarks* **about** *the old man.*

re·mark·a·ble /£rɪˈmɑː·kə·bl̩, $-ˈmɑːr-/ *adj* • If someone or something is remarkable, they are unusual or special and therefore surprising and worth mentioning: *Nelson Mandela is a truly remarkable man.* ○ *Meeting you here in Rome is a remarkable coincidence.* ○ *The 20th century has been remarkable* **for** *its inventions.* ○ **It** *is quite remarkable* **(that)** *no one was hurt in the accident.* [+ (*that*) clause]

remarkably /£rɪˈmɑː·kə·bli, $-ˈmɑːr-/ *adv* • *It is a remarkably noisy and crowded city.* • *Remarkably* (=Surprisingly), *she wasn't hurt in the crash.*

rem·e·dy /ˈrem·ə·di/ *n* [C] a successful way of curing an illness or dealing with a problem or difficulty • *Effective herbal remedies exist* **for** *headaches and migraines.* • *The best remedy* **for** *grief is hard work.* • *(law)* A **legal** remedy is a way of solving a problem or instructing someone to make a payment for harm or damage they have caused, using a decision made in a court of law: *We have pursued and exhausted all possible legal remedies* **for** *this injustice.*

rem·e·dy *obj* /ˈrem·ə·di/ *v* [T] *fml* • If you remedy something that is wrong, you do something to correct or improve it: *This mistake must be remedied.*

re·me·di·al /rɪˈmiː·di·əl/ *adj fml* • A remedial action is one which is intended to correct something that is wrong or to improve a bad situation: *The report stated that cigarette smoking was a health hazard of sufficient importance to warrant appropriate remedial action.* • Remedial exercises are one which are intended to improve someone's health when they are ill. • *(Br and Aus)* **Remedial teaching/lessons** are intended to help people who have difficulties in reading or writing: *He's been having remedial lessons and is now starting to read.* ○ *She is a teacher of remedial English.*

re·mem·ber *(obj)* /£rɪˈmem·bəʳ, $-bɚ/ *v* [not be *remembering*] to be able to bring back (a piece of information) into your mind, or to keep (a piece of information) in your memory • *"Where did you park the car?" "I can't remember."* [I] • *I never remember her birthday.* [T] • *I find it easy to remember people's faces, but not their names.* [T] • *I've suddenly remembered* **(that)** *I've got to leave.* [+ (*that*) clause] • *I don't remember signing a contract.* [+ *v-ing*] • *I remember you screaming for hours when you were a baby.* [T + obj + *v-ing*] • *Can you remember* **what** *her telephone number is?* [+ *wh-* word] • *I (can) remember* **when** *there were horse-drawn carriages in London.* [+ *wh-* word] • *I remember him* **as** (=I thought he was) *a rather annoying man.* [T] • If you remember to do something, you do it: *Did you remember* **to** *do the shopping?* [+ *to* infinitive] ○ *I remembered* **to** *buy you some stamps.* [+ *to* infinitive] • *(infml)* If you say 'you remember' to someone when you are talking to them, you are telling them something that they already know: *We went and had tea in the little café on Primrose Hill – you remember, the one next to the bookshop.* • If someone is remembered for a particular quality or action, it is because of that action or quality that they will be kept in people's memories: *She will be remembered* **for** *her courage.* [T] • If you remember a past event or someone who has died, you hold a special ceremony to honour them: *On November 11th, the British remember those who died in the two World Wars.* [T] • If you remember someone whom you love or who has provided good service to you, you give them a present or a sum of money: *My Granny always remembers me* (=sends me a present) *on my birthday.* [T] ○ *My cousin remembered me* **in** *her will* (=She left money for me after her death). [T] • *(fml)* If you ask someone to **remember** you **to** another person, you ask them to give your greetings to that other person: *Please remember me to your parents.* • *"You must remember this, a kiss is still a kiss, A sigh is just a sigh; / The fundamental things apply, /As time goes by."* (song written by Herman Hupfield, used in the film *Casablanca*, 1931) • *"Do you remember an Inn, Miranda?"* (from the poem *Tarentelle* by Hilaire Belloc, 1923) • Compare REMIND. • LP **Memory**

re·mem·brance /rɪˈmem·brᵊnts/ *n fml* • *A church service was held* **in** *remembrance* **of** (=to honour) *the victims.* [U] • A remembrance is a memory of something that happened in the past: *He has published his remembrances of the author in a memoir entitled 'Sylvia Plath: Last Encounters'.* [C] • In Britain, **Remembrance Day** is November 11, and **Remembrance Sunday** is the closest Sunday to that date, when people honour those who were killed in the two World Wars.

re·mind *obj* /rɪˈmaɪnd/ *v* [T] to make (someone) aware of something they have forgotten or might have forgotten • *Could you remind Paul* **about** *dinner on Saturday?* • *This hot summer reminds me* **of** *my years in Kenya.* • *Your hair and eyes remind me* **of** *your mother.* • *Please remind me* **to** *post this letter.* [+ obj + *to* infinitive] • *I am always reminding my children* **to** *say please and thank you.* [+ obj + *to* infinitive] • *I rang Jill and reminded her* **(that)** *the conference had been cancelled.* [+ obj + (*that*) clause] • *"These Foolish Things Remind Me of You"* (title of a song written by Holt Marvell, 1935) • Compare REMEMBER. • LP **Memory**

re·mind·er /£rɪˈmaɪn·dəʳ, $-dɚ/ *n* [C] • A reminder is a letter, note or message which tells someone to do something: *When he forgot to pay his rent, his landlady sent him a reminder* (=a note asking for payment). ○ *She gave her secretary a* **gentle** *reminder* **that** *she needed the documents by 5 o'clock.* [+ *that* clause] ○ *She let me go, with a final reminder* **to** *be back before 11pm.* [+ *to* infinitive] • A reminder is also a person or thing which makes you think of a particular person or event: *He described the monument as a chilling reminder* **of** *a tragedy that must never be repeated.*

rem·i·nisce /ˌrem·ɪˈnɪs/ *v* [I] *fml* to talk or write about past experiences which you remember with pleasure • *My grandfather used to reminisce* **about** *his years in the navy.*

re·mi·nis·cence /ˌrem·ɪˈnɪs·ᵊnts/ *n* [U] *fml* • Reminiscence is the act of remembering events and experiences from the past: *His descriptions of the village are sewn with reminiscence of his own childhood.*

re·mi·nis·cen·ces /ˌrem·ɪˈnɪs·ᵊnt·sɪz/ *pl n fml* • A person's reminiscences are the experiences they remember from the past which they write in a book: *She published a book of her reminiscences.* ○ *The novel contains endless reminiscences* **of/about** *the author's youth.*

re·mi·nis·cent /ˌrem·ɪˈnɪs·ənt/ *adj fml* • If something is reminiscent of another person or thing, it reminds you of that person or thing: *That song is so reminiscent* **of** *my adolescence.*

re·miss /rɪˈmɪs/ *adj* [after v] *fml* careless and not doing a duty well enough • *You have been remiss* **in** *your duties.* • *It was remiss* **of** *me* **to** *forget to give you the message.* [+ to infinitive]

re·mis·sion ILLNESS /rɪˈmɪʃ·ən/ *n fml* a period of time when an illness is less severe • *This is his second remission* **from** *his cancer.* [C] • *Her cancer has been* **in** *remission for several years.* [U] • See also **remission** at REMIT REDUCE.

re·mis·sion RELIGION /rɪˈmɪʃ·ən/ *n* [U] *fml* forgiveness for breaking religious laws or rules • *He believes that redemption is based on remission of sin.* • See also **remission** at REMIT REDUCE.

re·mit *obj* REDUCE /rɪˈmɪt/ *v* [T] **-tt-** *Br law* to reduce (the time that someone spends in prison) • *She has had part of her sentence remitted.* • *His prison sentence was remitted* **to** *two years.*

re·mis·sion /£rɪˈmɪt·ənts, $-ˈmɪţ-/ *n* [U] *Br law* • A remission is a reduction of the time that a person has to stay in prison: *He was given three months' remission for good behaviour.* • See also REMISSION ILLNESS; REMISSION RELIGION.

re·mit *obj* SEND /rɪˈmɪt/ *v* [T] **-tt-** *fml* to send (money) to someone, or to refer (a matter) to someone in authority to deal with • *He worked as a builder in Chicago and remitted half his monthly wage* **to** *his family in the Philippines.* • *She remitted the case* **to** *a new tribunal for reconsideration.* • *The case was remitted* **to** *the Family Division to consider whether or not the two children should be returned to their families.*

re·mit·tance /£rɪˈmɪt·ənts, $-ˈmɪţ-/ *n fml* • A remittance is a sum of money which you send to someone: *She sends a small remittance home to her parents each month.* [C] • Remittance is payment sent to someone: *The prospect of imminent war caused plunging stock prices and a failure of remittance from overseas.* [U]

re·mit AREA /ˈriː·mɪt/ *n* [U] the area which a person or group of people in authority has responsibility for or control over • *The council, whose remit covers matters of sex, violence and decency in television programmes, has considered over 50 complaints in the past six months.* • *The remit* **of** *this official inquiry is to investigate the reasons for the accident.*

rem·nant /ˈrem·nənt/ *n* [C] a small piece or amount of something that is left from a larger original piece or amount • *a carpet remnant* • *remnants* **of** *a meal* • *remnants* **of** *the city's former glory*

re·mod·el *obj* /£ˌriːˈmɒd·əl, $-ˈmɑː·dəl/ *v* [T] **-ll-** or *Am usually* **-l-** to give a new shape or form to • *We've remodelled the kitchen because there was no room for the dishwasher.*

re·mould /£ˌriːˈməʊld, $-ˈmoʊld/ *v, n Br for* RETREAD

re·mon·strate /£ˈrem·ən·streɪt, $rɪˈmɑːnt-/ *v* [I] *fml* to complain to someone or about something • *I went to the boss to remonstrate* **against** *the new rules.* • *The barrister remonstrated* **with** *the judge* **about** *the amount of the fine.*

re·mon·strance /£rɪˈmɒnt·strənts, $-ˈmɑːnt-/ *n* [C/U] *fml*

re·morse /£rɪˈmɔːs, $-ˈmɔːrs/ *n* [U] *fml* a strong feeling of guilt and regret about something you have done • *He felt no remorse* **for/about** *the murders he had committed.* • *She* **was filled with** *remorse after the argument.*

re·morse·ful /£rɪˈmɔː·sfəl, $-ˈmɔːr-/ *adj fml* • *Is he remorseful* (= feeling regret and guilt) **for** *what he has done?*

re·morse·ful·ly /£rɪˈmɔː·sfəl·i, $-ˈmɔːr-/ *adv fml*

re·morse·less /£rɪˈmɔː·sləs, $-ˈmɔːr-/ *adj fml* • *remorseless* (= severe and lacking feelings of guilt) *cruelty/violence* • *a remorseless* (= severe) *judge/punishment* • Something bad that cannot be stopped can be called remorseless: *the hurricane's remorseless approach*

re·morse·less·ly /£rɪˈmɔː·slə·sli, $-ˈmɔːr-/ *adv fml*

re·mort·gage *(obj)* /£ˌriːˈmɔː·gɪdʒ, $-ˈmɔːr-/ *v* to arrange a second MORTGAGE (= an agreement with a bank or similar organization in which you borrow money to buy property), or increase the first mortgage, esp. in order to obtain more money • *Robin decided to remortgage his house to pay off his debts.* [T] • *Home buyers are considering remortgaging to cut interest rates.* [I]

re·mort·gage /£ˈriː·mɔː·gɪdʒ, $-mɔːr-/ *n* [C] • *The building society will arrange a remortgage for a fee of £100.*

re·mote /£rɪˈməʊt, $-ˈmoʊt/ *adj* **-r, -st** far away in distance, time or relation; not close • A remote area/house/ village is a long way from any towns or cities: *The house was very remote and I felt lonely all the time.* • *It happened in the remote* **past**, *so no one worries about it any more.* • *It may happen sometime in the remote* **future**. • If someone's behaviour is remote, they are not very friendly or interested in others: *Her manner was remote and cool.* • *The* **chances** *of a visit by Martians to the Earth are remote* (= it's unlikely). • *"Who's that?" "I* **haven't the remotest idea** (= I don't know)*."* • **Remote control** is a system or a device for controlling something such as a machine or vehicle from a distance, by using electrical or radio signals: *He changed channels on the TV with the remote control.* ○ *a* **remote-controlled** *model aircraft* • PIC Room

re·mote·ly /£rɪˈməʊt·li, $-ˈmoʊt-/ *adv* [not gradable] • *a remotely situated farmhouse* • *a woman remotely related to my father* • *I've never tasted a fruit remotely* (= not even slightly) *like this before.* • *I'm afraid we're not remotely* (= even slightly) *interested in your proposal.*

re·mote·ness /£rɪˈməʊt·nəs, $-ˈmoʊt-/ *n* [U]

re·move *obj* /rɪˈmuːv/ *v* [T] to take (something) away (from a place) • *The men came to remove the rubbish* **(from** *outside the house).* • *(fml) She angrily asked him to remove* **himself from** (= leave) *the room.* • *This detergent will remove all stains from your clothes.* • *She had her legs waxed to remove unwanted hair.* • *It got so hot that he removed his tie and jacket.* LP **Dressing and undressing** • *(fig.) Hearing your opinion has removed* (= got rid of) *my last doubts/fears/suspicions about her.* • *(fml)* If someone is removed from their position or job, they are dismissed: *He was removed* **from office** (= dismissed from an official position) *following the scandal.*

re·move /rɪˈmuːv/ *n* [C] *fml* • *We are* **at one remove from** (= close to) *war.* • *What you have said is* **several/many removes (away) from** (= has very little relation to) *the truth.*

re·mov·a·ble /rɪˈmuː·və·bl̩/ *adj* [not gradable] • *a removable stain* • *a coat with removable sleeves*

re·mov·al /rɪˈmuː·vəl/ *n* [U] • *the removal of a tyrant* **from** *power* • *stain removal* • *a removal van* (= vehicle used to transport furniture and other possessions when people move to a new home)

re·mov·als /rɪˈmuː·vəlz/ *pl n* • *Does your firm do removals* (= transport furniture and other possessions when people move to a new home)*?*

re·moved /rɪˈmuːvd/ *adj fml* • *What you've said is* **far** *removed* **from** (= different from) *the truth.* • A **cousin** once, twice, etc. removed is a cousin separated from you by one, two, etc. GENERATIONS (= same family age groups): *Your first cousin once removed is a cousin of your parents, a cousin of your children or the child of one of your cousins.*

re·mov·er *Br* /£rɪˈmuː·vəʳ, $-vɚ/ *n* • *Have you got any nail-varnish remover?* [U] • *There are plenty of good stain removers available.* [C] • *(Br)* A **(furniture) remover** (*Am* **mover**, *Aus* **removalist**) is a person who helps people to move their furniture and other possessions when they move to a new home: *Unskilled removers can do as much damage to themselves as to the furniture.* [C]

re·mu·ne·rate *obj* /£rɪˈmjuː·nər·eɪt, $-nə·reɪt/ *v* [T] *fml* to pay (someone) for work or services • *He is poorly remunerated* **for** *all the hard work he does.*

re·mu·ne·ra·tion /£rɪˌmjuː·nərˈeɪ·ʃən, $-nəˈreɪ-/ *n fml* • *They demanded adequate remuneration* **for** *their work.* [U] • *We are offering a free flat and a small remuneration for some caretaking duties in the office block.* [C]

re·mu·ne·ra·tive /£rɪˈmjuː·nər·ə·tɪv, $-nə·reɪ·ţɪv/ *adj fml* • *a highly remunerative* (= well paid) *job* • *Charity work is not very remunerative.*

re·nais·sance /rəˈneɪ·sɑ̃ːnts/ *n* [C] a new growth of (interest in) something, esp. art, literature or music • *There's a renaissance* **of** *theatre in Britain at the moment.* • *Opera in Britain is enjoying a long-awaited renaissance.* • **The Renaissance** was (the period of) a new growth of interest and activity in the areas of art, literature and ideas in Europe, esp. N Italy, during the 14th, 15th and 16th centuries: *Renaissance art/music/painting* • *(esp. humorous)* A **Renaissance man** is someone who does many different things very well: *He's a writer, politician, musician and athlete – a real Renaissance man.*

re·nal /ˈriː·nəl/ *adj* [not gradable] *specialized* of the KIDNEYS (= bodily organs for waste liquid) • *a renal unit* • *a renal transplant* • *renal dialysis*

rend *obj* /rend/ *v* [T] *past* **rent** /rent/ or *Am also* **rended** *esp. old use or literary* to break (something) violently; tear •

With one stroke of his sword he rent his enemy's helmet **in** *two.* • *She screamed and wept and rent her garments* (**into** *pieces).* • *Firemen had to rend him* **free** (=pull him out) *of the burning car.* [+ obj + adj] • *(fig.) A terrifying scream rent the air.*

rend·er *obj* CAUSE /£'ren·dəʳ, $-dɚ/ *v* [T] *fml* to cause (someone or something) to be in a particular state • *His rudeness rendered me speechless.* [+ obj + adj] • *New technology has rendered my old computer obsolete.* [+ obj + adj] • *She is rendering the book* **into** *English from French* (=changing it from French to English). • *(specialized)* To render a wall is to put a first layer of PLASTER or CEMENT on it. • *(specialized)* To render fat **down** or to render **down** fat means to melt it and make it purer. [M]

ren·der·ing /£'ren·dᵊr·ɪŋ, $-dɚ-/ *n* [C] • *a new rendering of the Bible* **into** *modern English*

rend·er *obj* GIVE /£'ren·dəʳ, $-dɚ/ *v* [T] *fml* to give (something, esp. a performance of a song, poem etc.) • *The singers rendered the song with enthusiasm.* • *I have to* **render an account of** (=explain) *my expenses* **to** *my boss.* • *"Render therefore unto Caesar the things which are Caesar's; and unto God the things that are God's"* (The Bible, Matthew 22.21)

ren·der·ing /£'ren·dᵊr·ɪŋ, $-dɚ-/, **ren·di·tion** /ren'dɪʃ·ᵊn/ *n* [C] • *Her rendering of the song* (=the way she performed it) *was delightful.*

ren·dez·vous /£'rɒn·deɪ·vuː, $'rɑːn-/ *n* [C] *pl* **rendezvous** (an arrangement for) a meeting, esp. a secret one, at a particular place and time, or the place itself • *We have a rendezvous* **for** *next week, don't we?* • *I was afraid that you wouldn't be able to come to our rendezvous.* • *The lovers met at a secret rendezvous in the park.* • A rendezvous is also a place where a particular group of people often go or meet, by arrangement or habit: *This restaurant is a popular rendezvous* **for** *local artists.*

ren·dez·vous /£'rɒn·deɪ·vuː, $'rɑːn-/ *v* [I] • *The police arranged to rendezvous* **with** *their informant at a disused warehouse.*

ren·e·gade /'ren·ɪ·geɪd/ *n, adj fml or literary disapproving* a person who has changed their loyalties from one political, religious, national, etc. group to a new one • *A band of renegades had captured the prince and were holding him to ransom.* [C] • *a renegade soldier/priest* [before n]

re·nege /rɪ'neɪg/ *v* [I] *fml* to not do what you previously agreed to do; to fail to keep a promise, an agreement, etc. • *If you renege* **on** *the deal now, I'll fight you in the courts.*

re·new *obj* REPEAT /£rɪ'njuː, $-'nuː/ *v* [T] to begin doing (something) again • *The kidnappers renewed their threats.* • *She renewed her efforts to escape.*

re·newed /£rɪ'njuːd, $-'nuːd/ *adj* [not gradable] • *renewed interest/enthusiasm* • *Some of the concerns of the 1960s, such as environmentalism, are receiving renewed support today.*

re·new *obj* MAKE NEW /£rɪ'njuː, $-'nuː/ *v* [T] to increase the life of or replace (something old) • *Every year I renew my membership of the Sports Club.* • *I must remember to renew my British Rail season ticket.* • *I bought some material and renewed the covers on the chairs.*

re·new·a·ble /£rɪ'njuː·ə·bl̩, $-'nuː-/ *adj* [not gradable] • *Renewable energy sources like sun, wind and waves will not run out, unlike oil and coal.* • An official document that is renewable is one whose use can be lengthened for an extra period of time: *a renewable passport/contract*

re·new·al /£rɪ'njuː·əl, $-'nuː-/ *n* • *Renewal of a passport in Britain can be done at any post office.* [U] • *Do you deal with season-ticket renewals here?* [C]

ren·net /'ren·ɪt/, *Am also* **ren·nin** /'ren·ɪn/ *n* [U] a substance used for thickening milk, esp. to make cheese • *Most cheese is made with rennet, which comes from the stomach lining of calves, and is therefore not vegetarian.*

re·nounce *obj* /rɪ'naʊnts/ *v* [T] *fml* to say formally or publicly that you no longer own, support, believe in or have a connection with (something) • *Her ex-husband renounced his claim to the family house.* • *Gandhi renounced the use of violence.* • *She renounced family and country* **for** *a life of adventure abroad.* • *"I should renounce the devil and all his works"* (The Book of Common Prayer, 1662)

re·nun·ci·a·tion /rɪˌnʌnt·si'eɪ·ʃᵊn/ *n* [U] • *the renunciation* **of** *violence*

ren·o·vate *obj* /'ren·ə·veɪt/ *v* [T] to repair and improve (esp. a building) • *He renovates old houses and sells them at a profit.*

ren·o·va·tion /ˌren·ə'veɪ·ʃᵊn/ *n* • *The museum is closed for renovation.* [U] • *If we buy this house we will need to make extensive renovations.* [C]

re·nown /rɪ'naʊn/ *n* [U] *fml or literary* the state of being famous • *a woman of great renown* • *Her renown spread across the country.* • *Neil Armstrong won* **great** *renown for being the first man on the moon.*

re·nowned /rɪ'naʊnd/ *adj fml or literary* • *Marco Polo is a renowned explorer/is renowned* **as** *an explorer.* • *The region is renowned* **for** *its outstanding natural beauty.*

rent PAYMENT /rent/ *n* a fixed amount of money paid or received regularly for the use of a room, house, car, television, etc. that is owned by someone else • *We let the spare room at a monthly rent of £55.* [C] • *I pay a higher rent/more rent than the other tenants because my room is bigger.* [C/U] • *Rents in the centre of London are ridiculously high.* [C] • If something is **for rent** the owner is offering its use for money. • *(Br infml)* A **rent boy** is a young male PROSTITUTE (=person who sells sex for money) used by other men. • If a house is **rent-free** or if you are living or staying **rent-free**, it means that the owner is not asking for payment. • A **rent strike** is a refusal to pay rent, esp. by all the people living in a particular house or houses: *The tenants organized a rent strike to force the landlord to repair the central heating.* • LP› **Borrow** (CS) (D) (PL) (RUS)

rent *obj* /rent/ *v* [T] • To rent is to pay or receive a fixed amount of money for the use of a room, house, car, television, etc.: *I had a week in London so I rented a car* **from** *a garage and drove all around the city.* ○ *The old lady rented us her spare bedroom/rented her spare room* **to** *us* **for** *£55 a week.* [+ two objects] ○ *My Dad has a cottage by the sea which he rents* **out to** *tourists.* [M] • *(Br disapproving)* A **rent-a-**person or thing or group of people seem as if they have been rented for a particular purpose and are not sincere: *The protest was mostly attended by rent-a-mob and few people turned up to support the real issue.* ○ *(humorous) I don't know anyone at this party, it must be rent-a-crowd.* • *(humorous) Old rent-a-quote is always turning up on TV to give his opinions about political developments.*

rent·al /£'ren·tᵊl, $-t̬ᵊl/ *n* • *Property rental* (=renting apartments or houses) *is quite expensive here.* [U] • *Video and television rentals have decreased this year.* [C] • *The car rental* **companies** (=companies offering cars to rent) *had offices at the airport.*

rent TEAR /rent/ *n* [C] *esp. old use* a large hole torn in a piece of material • *After he'd climbed over the fence he noticed a rent in his coat.* • (CS) (D) (PL) (RUS)

rent TORN /rent/ *past simple and past participle of* REND • (CS) (D) (PL) (RUS)

ren·tier /£'rɒn·ti·eɪ, $rɑ̃ːn'tjeɪ/ *n* [C] *fml esp. disapproving* a person whose income is from investments and who therefore does not have to work • *the rentier class*

re·nun·ci·a·tion /rɪˌnʌnt·si'eɪ·ʃᵊn/ *n* [U] See at RENOUNCE

rep BUSINESS /rep/ *n* [C] *infml* a **sales representative**, see at SALE

rep THEATRE /rep/ *n* [U] *infml for* REPERTORY

re·paid /rɪ'peɪd/ *past simple and past participle of* REPAY

re·pair *obj* /£rɪ'peəʳ, $-'per/ *v* [T] to put (something damaged, broken or not working correctly) back into good condition or make it work again; MEND • *repair (the surface of) the road* • *repair a roof after a storm* • *My son breaks all his toys but I do my best to repair them.* • *The garage said the car was so old it wasn't worth repairing.* • If you repair something wrong or harmful that has been done, you do something to make it right: *Is it too late to repair the damage we have done to our Earth?* ○ *She tried to repair their friendship by inviting him to dinner.* • (P)

re·pair /£rɪ'peəʳ, $-'per/ *n* • *My car is in the garage for repairs.* [C] • *Repairs* **to** *the roof will be expensive.* [C] • *The mechanic pointed out the repair* (=repaired place) *on the front of my car from the previous crash.* [C] • *This section of motorway will be* **under** *repair* (=being repaired) *until January.* [U] • *The house is* **in good/bad repair** (= in good/bad condition). • *This computer system is* **in a** *terrible/excellent* **state of repair** (= bad/good condition).

re·pair·a·ble /£rɪ'peə·rə·bl̩, $-'per·ə-/ *adj* • *My old watch was not repairable.*

re·pair to *obj v prep* [T] *old use* to go to (another place) esp. as a group • *After dinner we repaired to the lounge for coffee.*

re·par·a·tion /£ˌrep·ə'reɪ·ʃᵊn/ *n fml esp. law* payment for harm or damage • *The company was forced to* **make** *reparation* **to** *the victims for ill health caused by chemical pollution.* [U] • *They have promised to make full reparations to war victims.* [C] • (E)

re·par·tee /£ˌrep·ɑːˈtiː, $-ɑːr-/ *n* [U] quick, usually amusing answers and remarks in conversation • *Oscar Wilde's plays are full of witty repartee.*

re·past /£rɪˈpɑːst, $-ˈpæst/ *n* [C] *fml or literary* a meal

re·pat·ri·ate *obj* /£riːˈpæt·ri·eɪt, $-ˈpeɪ·tri-/ *v* [T] to send or bring (someone or something) back to their own country • *The government repatriated him because he had no visa.*

re·pat·ri·a·tion /£ˌriː·pæt·riˈeɪ·ʃᵊn, $rɪˌpeɪ·tri-/ *n* [U]

re·pay *obj* /rɪˈpeɪ/ *v* [T] *past* **repaid** /rɪˈpeɪd/ to pay back or to reward • *He had to sell his car to repay the loan from the bank.* • *She repaid her mother the loan./She repaid the loan* **to** *her mother.* [+ two objects] • *How can I ever repay you* **for** *all your kindness?* • *The team repaid their manager's faith* **with** *a series of wins.* • *She repaid his love* **by** *selling all the sordid details of the affair to the papers.* • *(esp. Br) You should read this article – it would* **repay** *your* **interest/attention/time** (= be worth the effort).

re·pay·a·ble /rɪˈpeɪ·ə·bl̩/ *adj* [not gradable] • *The loan is repayable* (= must be repaid) *over six months.*

re·pay·ment /rɪˈpeɪ·mənt/ *n* • *mortgage repayments* [C] • *The bank demanded immediate repayment.* [U]

re·peal *obj* /rɪˈpiːl/ *v* [T] (of a government) to make (a law) no longer have any legal force

re·peal /rɪˈpiːl/ *n* [U] • *We're campaigning for a/the repeal* **of** *the abortion laws.*

re·peat *obj* /rɪˈpiːt/ *v* [T] to say, tell or do again • *Would you mind repeating what you just said?* • *She repeated* **that** *she had no intention of standing for President.* [+ *that* clause] • *The boy learned his poem by heart and repeated it (aloud)* **to** *the class.* • *This is a secret, and if you repeat it* **to** *anyone I'll kill you.* • *It was a boring speech because he repeated* **himself** *a lot* (= said the same things again and again). • *Some historians think that history repeats itself.* • *This is an offer never to be repeated.* • *Johnny had to repeat a year/a class* (= do that year of school again). • If a business repeats an **order** for something, it supplies it again. • *(infml)* If you say that food **repeats on** you, you mean that the taste of it comes up again into the mouth: *Cucumber always repeats on me.* • Ⓣ

re·peat /rɪˈpiːt/ *n* [C] • *All this is a repeat/a repeat performance of what happened last year.* • *There's nothing on television but repeats* (= broadcasts that have been shown before).

re·peat·ed /£rɪˈpiː·tɪd, $-t̬ɪd/ *adj* [not gradable] • *repeated attempts/mistakes/warnings* (= happening again and again)

re·peat·ed·ly /£rɪˈpiː·tɪd·li, $-t̬ɪd-/ *adv* [not gradable] • *He telephoned repeatedly* (= many times), *begging her to return.*

re·pe·ti·tion /ˌrep·əˈtɪʃ·ᵊn/ *n* • *These statements are just repetitions of what was said last year.* [C] • *His books are full of repetition and useless information.* [U] • (RUS)

re·pet·i·tive /£rɪˈpet·ə·tɪv, $-ˈpet̬·ə·t̬ɪv/, **re·pe·ti·tious** /ˌrep·əˈtɪʃ·əs/ *adj* • *I find this kind of work boringly repetitive.* • **Repetitive strain injury** (*abbreviation* **RSI**) is a painful medical condition which can cause damage to the hands, wrists, upper arms and backs of esp. people who use computers and other forms of keyboard.

re·pel *obj* [FORCE AWAY] /rɪˈpel/ *v* [T] **-ll-** to force away (something unwanted) • *This coat has a special surface that repels moisture.* • *(fml) The defenders repelled the attack without losing any men.* • *(specialized) Similar poles of magnets repel each other.*

re·pel·lent /rɪˈpel·ᵊnt/ *n* • *Use insect repellent* (= a substance used to keep insects away) *to avoid getting bitten.* [U] • *There are many different mosquito repellents available in the shops.* [C]

re·pel *obj* [CAUSE STRONG DISLIKE] /rɪˈpel/ *v* [T] **-ll-** to make you not want to be near, see or think about something; to cause disgust • *She was repelled by his ugliness.* • *Her arrogance repels many people.*

re·pel·lent /rɪˈpel·ᵊnt/ *adj* • *repellent behaviour/beliefs/appearance* • *I find any cruelty to children utterly repellent.*

re·pent /rɪˈpent/ *v fml* to be very sorry for and wish that you had not done something bad, in the past • *He repented (of his sins) just hours before he died.* [I] • *She repented shouting at the children and promised never to do it again.* [+ *v-ing*]

re·pen·tance /rɪˈpen·tᵊnts/ *n* [U] • *It was not only the crime's extreme violence that attracted attention, but the boy's complete lack of repentance.*

re·pen·tant /rɪˈpen·tᵊnt/ *adj fml* • *The priest tried to make him feel repentant.*

re·per·cus·sion /£ˌriː·pəˈkʌʃ·ᵊn, $-pɚ-/ *n* [C usually pl] the usually bad indirect effect of an event, action or decision • *President Kennedy's assassination had far-reaching repercussions.*

re·per·toire /£ˈrep·ə·twɑːʳ, $-ɚ·twɑːr/ *n* [C] all the things (esp. music or plays) that someone or something knows or can do or perform • *The Royal Shakespeare Company also have many modern plays* **in** *their repertoire.* • *There is an extensive repertoire of music written for the flute.* • Ⓕ

re·per·to·ry /£ˈrep·ə·tᵊr·i, $-ɚ·tɔːr-/, *infml* **rep** /rep/ *n* [U] the repeated performance of several plays one after the other by one company of actors • A **repertory company** is a theatre company that performs repertory. • *She's working* **in** *repertory* (= with a repertory theatre group). • *'Macbeth' is* **in** *repertory* (= being performed on particular days) *at the RSC.*

re·pe·ti·tion /ˌrep·ɪˈtɪʃ·ᵊn/ *n* [C/U] See at REPEAT

re·pet·i·tive /£rɪˈpet·ə·tɪv, $-ˈpet̬·ə·t̬ɪv/, **re·pe·ti·tious** *adj*

re·phrase *obj* /ˌriːˈfreɪz/ *v* [T] to say or write (something) again in a different (and clearer) way • *Could you rephrase your question please?*

re·pine /rɪˈpaɪn/ *v* [I] *fml or literary* to feel sad about or complain at something, esp. a bad situation • *She was alone and unloved, but she did not repine.*

re·place *obj* [CHANGE FOR] /rɪˈpleɪs/ *v* [T] to take the place of (something) or put something or someone in the place of (something or someone else) • *Ugly new offices have replaced the house where I lived as a child.* • *The factory replaced most of its workers* **with** *robots.* • *Tourism has replaced agriculture as the nation's main industry.* • If you replace something broken, damaged or lost you provide a new one: *I promised to replace the plate that I'd dropped.*

re·place·ment /rɪˈpleɪs·mənt/ *n* • *the replacement of paper and pencil* **with/by** *computers* [U] • *The agency sent a replacement* **for** *the secretary who resigned.* [C]

re·place·a·ble /rɪˈpleɪ·sə·bl̩/ *adj* [not gradable] • *Don't worry – all that stolen stuff is replaceable.*

re·place *obj* [PUT BACK] /rɪˈpleɪs/ *v* [T] to put (something) back where it was before • *The librarian replaced the books correctly on the shelves.*

re·play *obj* [COMPETITION] /ˌriːˈpleɪ/ *v* [T] to play again (a game, esp. of football, that neither team won the first time) • *Following today's 1:1 draw, the match will be replayed next Thursday.*

re·play /ˈriː·pleɪ/ *n* [C] • *The semi-final replay will be on Saturday.*

re·play *obj* [RECORDING] /ˌriːˈpleɪ/ *v* [T] to play again (esp. music or film recorded already) • *The police replayed the video of the robbery in court.*

re·play /ˈriː·pleɪ/ *n* [C] • *a slow-motion replay* • *a television/video replay*

re·plen·ish *obj* /rɪˈplen·ɪʃ/ *v* [T] *fml* to fill up (something) again • *Food stocks were replenished* **by/with** *imports from the USA.* • *Does your glass need replenishing?* (= Do you want some more to drink?)

re·plen·ish·ment /rɪˈplen·ɪʃ·mənt/ *n* [U]

re·plete /rɪˈpliːt/ *adj* [after v] *fml* full, esp. with food, or well supplied • *After two helpings of dessert he was replete.* • *This car has an engine replete* **with** *the latest technology.*

rep·li·ca /ˈrep·lɪ·kə/ *n* [C] an exact copy of an object • *His hobby is building replicas of vintage cars.* • *The ship is an exact replica* **of** *the original Golden Hind.* • Ⓘ

rep·li·cate *(obj)* /ˈrep·lɪ·keɪt/ *v fml* • *Chromosomes replicate* (= make exact copies of themselves) *before cells divide and multiply.* [I] • *Researchers tried many times to replicate* (= repeat in exactly the same way) *the original experiment.* [T]

rep·li·ca·tion /ˌrep·lɪˈkeɪ·ʃᵊn/ *n* [C/U] *fml*

re·ply /rɪˈplaɪ/ *v, n* (to make) an answer • *She asked him how old he was but he didn't reply.* [I] • *"Where are you going?" I asked. "Home," he replied.* [+ clause] • *I replied* **that** *it was 12 o'clock.* [+ *that* clause] • *I try to reply* **to** *letters the day I receive them.* [I] • *(fig.) She replied* (= reacted) **to** *the threats by going to the police.* [I] • *He made/gave no reply* **to** *my anxious questioning.* [C] • *We advertised the job but received very few replies.* [C] • *She just shrugged her shoulders* **in** *reply (to their questions).* [U] • *(Br)* A letter that is **reply-paid** is paid for by the sender.

re·port *(obj)* [TELL] /£rɪˈpɔːt, $-ˈpɔːrt/ *v* to give a description of (something) or information about it to someone • *We immediately rang the insurance company to report the theft.* [T] • *Our correspondent in the capital city reports heavy fighting.* [T] • *The assassination was reported* *in all the newspapers.* [T] • *Spies reported seeing a build-up of soldiers.* [+ v-ing] • *The government reported* **that** *inflation had fallen.* [+ that clause] • *He was reported missing in action.* [T + obj + adj] • *The British Ambassador reported* **on** *the situation* **to** *the Prime Minister/reported* **to** *the Prime Minister* **on** *the situation.* [I] • *The inquiry into alleged police brutality reports* (= will officially make its results publicly known) *next week.* [I] • *I want you to report* **on** *progress* (= on what you have done until then) *every Friday.* [I] • *You will report directly* **to** *the boss* (= you will be directly responsible to him or her). [I] • If something is reported to be true, people are saying that it is true without having real proof: *The storm is reported* **to** *have killed five people.* [T + obj + *to* infinitive] • If you report someone **for** something bad, or you report someone **to** a person in authority, you make a complaint about it or them: *My neighbours reported me to the police for firing my rifle in the garden.* [T] • If you report **back** to someone, you bring information to them: *Find out their names and report back (to me) tomorrow.* [I] • Ⓘ Ⓙ

re·port /£rɪˈpɔːt, $-ˈpɔːrt/ *n* [C] • *newspaper reports* **of** *the disaster* • *a weather report* • *a company's financial/annual report* • *a progress report* **on** *what has happened so far* • *I gave/made/submitted a report* **of** *the theft to the insurance company.* • *She sent weekly/yearly reports* **on** *the situation.* • *(not standard) The report* **into** *the fire at Crossley Station is being published tomorrow.* • *According to* **reports** (= stories without real proof) *there has been an earthquake in Los Angeles.* • A **(school)** report (*Am also* **report card**) is the teachers' written statement to the parents about a child's ability and performance at school.

re·port·age /£ˌrep·ɔːˈtɑːʒ, $rɪˈpɔːr·t̬ɪdʒ/ *n* [U] *fml* • Reportage is the activity of or style of reporting events: *The book is part travel literature, part reportage, and part history.*

re·port·ed /£rɪˈpɔː·tɪd, $-ˈpɔːr·t̬ɪd/ *adj* [not gradable] • *There has been a reported* (= unofficial news about a) *hijack in Tel Aviv this morning.* • *(specialized)* **Reported speech** is the same as **indirect speech**. See at INDIRECT NOT STRAIGHT.

re·port·ed·ly /£rɪˈpɔː·tɪd·li, $-ˈpɔːr·t̬ɪd-/ *adv* [not gradable] • *New York is reportedly* (= People say that New York is) *a very exciting place to live.*

re·port·er /£rɪˈpɔː·təʳ, $-ˈpɔːr·t̬ɚ/ *n* [C] • A reporter is a person whose job is to discover information about news events and describe them for a newspaper or magazine or for radio or television: *Reporters rushed to the scene of the accident to interview the victims.*

re·port GO /£rɪˈpɔːt, $-ˈpɔːrt/ *v* [I always + adv/prep] to go to a place or a person and say that you are there • *I report* **for** (= am ready for and at) *work/duty at the agency at 8 a.m. every morning.* • *Some foreign visitors have to report* **to/at** *the police station once a month.* • Ⓘ Ⓙ

re·port NOISE /£rɪˈpɔːt, $-ˈpɔːrt/ *n* [C] *fml* the loud noise of a shot • *We heard the loud/sharp report of a rifle.* • Ⓘ Ⓙ

re·pose *(obj)* /£rɪˈpəʊz, $-ˈpoʊz/ *v* [always + adv/prep] *fml* to rest, lie or place • *She reposed on the sofa.* [I] • *The necklace reposed in its case.* [I] • *My grandparents now repose* (= are buried) *in a cemetery in Jamaica.* [I] • To repose **trust/confidence/hope** in someone or something is to place your trust or hopes in them: *We repose a lot of hope* **in** *this project.* [T]

re·pose /£rɪˈpəʊz, $-ˈpoʊz/ *n* [U] *fml* • *Your face is so beautiful* **in** *repose* (= when resting).

re·pos·i·to·ry /£rɪˈpɒz·ɪ·tᵊr·i, $-ˈpɑː·zɪ·tɔːr-/ *n* [C] *fml* a place where things are stored and can be found • *The lost manuscript was found in a repository in France.* • *(fig.) My diary is a repository* **for** *all my secret thoughts.* • *(fig.) She's a repository* **of** *knowledge about our family history.*

re·pos·sess *obj* /ˌriː·pəˈzes/ *v* [T] to take back possession of (something, esp. property not completely paid for) • *When I failed to make my mortgage repayments the building society repossessed my house.*

re·pos·ses·sion /ˌriː·pəˈzeʃ·ᵊn/ *n* • *The number of* **house/mortgage** *repossessions in the last six months has doubled on the same period last year.* [C] • *When mortgagers default on their debts, repossession may be the only answer.* [U]

rep·re·hen·si·ble /ˌrep·rɪˈhent·sə·bl̩/ *adj fml* (of a person's behaviour) extremely bad; not acceptable; deserving blame • *reprehensible conduct/attitude/actions*

rep·re·hen·si·bly /ˌrep·rɪˈhent·sɪ·bli/ *adv fml*

rep·re·sent *obj* ACT FOR /ˌrep·rɪˈzent/ *v* [T] to speak, act or be present officially for (another person or people) • *The accident victims chose a famous barrister to represent them in court.* • *Union officials representing the teachers met the government today.* • *Our company is represented in New York by Ms Taylor.* • *Mr Smythe represents Barnet* (= is the Member of Parliament for that area). • *Women were* **well/poorly** *represented at the conference* (= there were many/few present).

rep·re·sent·a·tion /ˌrep·rɪ·zenˈteɪ·ʃᵊn/ *n* [U] • *The government pays for a lawyer when people are too poor to pay for* **legal** *representation.* • *"No taxation without representation" was the American slogan of refusal to pay taxes to Britain without having a voice in Parliament.*

rep·re·sent·a·tive /£ˌrep·rɪˈzen·tə·tɪv, $-t̬ə·t̬ɪv/ *adj* • *a representative system of government* • *The school has a representative committee of elected students and teachers.* • Ⓓ

rep·re·sent·a·tive /£ˌrep·rɪˈzen·tə·tɪv, $-t̬ə·t̬ɪv/ *n* [C] • *Members of Parliament are the* **elected** *representatives of the British people.* • *The firm has two representatives in every European city.* • In the US, a representative is also someone who has been elected to the US House of Representatives.

rep·re·sent *obj* DESCRIBE /ˌrep·rɪˈzent/ *v* [T] to show or describe (something); to be a sign or symbol of (something) • *This picture represents the Battle of Waterloo.* • *The statue represents St George killing the dragon.* [+ obj + v-ing] • *In this dictionary the word 'noun' is represented by the letter n.* • *The report represents the current situation in our schools.* • *To many people the Queen represents the former glory of Britain.* • *(fml)* If you represent something **to** someone, you express or complain about something to them: *We represented our grievances/demands to the boss.* • *(fml) He represents himself* **as** *an expert, but he knows nothing.*

rep·re·sent·a·tion /ˌrep·rɪ·zenˈteɪ·ʃᵊn/ *n* • *This statue is a representation of Hercules.* [C] • *He gave a talk on the representation of women in 19th-century art.* [U] • *(fml) We* **made a representation to/made representations to** (= we complained to) *the boss* **about** *the long hours we had to work.*

rep·re·sent·a·tion·al /ˌrep·rɪ·zenˈteɪ·ʃᵊn·ᵊl/ *adj* • *Picasso painted few pictures that were representational* (= showing things as they are ordinarily seen) *in the traditional sense.*

rep·re·sent·a·tive /£ˌrep·rɪˈzen·tə·tɪv, $-t̬ə·t̬ɪv/ *adj* • *Are your opinions representative* (= typical) **of** *all the workers here?* • A representative **sample/cross-section/selection** is one that is typical of the larger group.

rep·re·sent BE /ˌrep·rɪˈzent/ *v* [L only + n] to be the result of (something) or to be (something) • *This book represents ten years of thought and research.* • *This offer represented an increase of 10% on the previous one.* • *Louis Armstrong's playing represented* (= was an example of) *the best of traditional jazz.*

re·press *obj* /rɪˈpres/ *v* [T] to not allow (esp. feelings) to be expressed • *He repressed a sudden desire to cry.*

re·pressed /rɪˈprest/ *adj* • *repressed anger/emotion/sexuality* • *English people are notoriously repressed and don't talk about their feelings.*

re·pres·sion /rɪˈpreʃ·ᵊn/ *n* [U] • *The* **political** *repression* (= extreme control) *in this country is enforced by terror.* • Repression is also the process and effect of keeping particular thoughts and desires out of your conscious mind in order to defend or protect it: *She attacked what she saw as an attitude of unhealthy sexual repression in the school.*

re·pres·sive /rɪˈpres·ɪv/ *adj* • *a repressive* (= cruel) *military regime*

re·pres·sive·ness /rɪˈpres·ɪv·nəs/ *n* [U]

re·prieve /rɪˈpriːv/ *v, n* (to make) an official order stopping or delaying the punishment, esp. by death, of a prisoner • *He was sentenced to death but was granted a last-minute reprieve.* [C] • *(fig.) The injection provided only a temporary reprieve* **from** (= delay before) *the pain.* [C] • *(fig.) The government has reprieved the hospitals threatened with closure, and they will now stay open until next year.* [T]

rep·ri·mand *obj* /£ˈrep·rɪ·mɑːnd, $-rə·mænd/ *v* [T] to express to (someone) your strong official disapproval of them; to TELL OFF • *She was reprimanded by her teacher* **for** *biting another girl.*

rep·ri·mand /£ˈrep·rɪ·mɑːnd, $-rə·mænd/ *n* [C] • *His boss gave him a severe reprimand* **for** *being late yet again.*

re·print *(obj)* /ˌriːˈprɪnt/ *v* to print (a book) again, or (of a book) to be printed again • *The first edition sold out so we are reprinting it/it is reprinting.* [I]

re·print /ˈriː·prɪnt/ *n* [C] • *The book has gone through many reprints* (= It has been reprinted many times).

re·pri·sal /rɪˈpraɪ·zᵊl/ *n* (an example of) activity against another person, esp. as a punishment by military forces or a political group • *Ten houses were burnt down as a reprisal* **for** *the killing of a soldier.* [C] • *He is unwilling to give his real name* **for fear of** *reprisals from the authorities.* [C] • *They promised that individuals would be free to live as they chose* **without fear of** *reprisal from the military.* [U] • *The attack was* **in** *reprisal* **for** *the kidnapping of one of the local leaders.* [U] • *The protestors called for economic reprisals to be* **taken** *against the aggressor states.* [C]

re·prise /rɪˈpriːz/ *n* [C] *specialized* a repeat of (a part of) a piece of music • *At the end of every verse there's a reprise of the chorus.*

re·proach *obj* /£rɪˈprəʊtʃ, $-ˈproʊtʃ/ *v* [T] to criticize (someone), esp. for not being successful or not doing what is expected • *She reproached the government* **with** *failing to help the poor.* • *Stop reproaching yourself* **for** *what was not your fault.* • *His mother reproached him* **for** *not eating all his dinner.*

re·proach /£rɪˈprəʊtʃ, $-ˈproʊtʃ/ *n* • *The look of reproach on his face made her feel guilty.* [U] • *Your behaviour today has been* **above/beyond** *reproach* (= blameless). [U] • *The recent drop in passenger numbers should be* **a** *reproach* **to** *the airline* (= they should be ashamed of it). [U] • *Your reproaches are useless – what's done is done.* [C]

re·proach·ful /£rɪˈprəʊtʃ·fᵊl, $-ˈproʊtʃ-/ *adj* • *reproachful looks/words*

re·proach·ful·ly /£rɪˈprəʊtʃ·fᵊl·i, $-ˈproʊtʃ-/ *adv* • *Don't look at me so reproachfully.*

re·pro·bate /£ˈrep·rəʊ·beɪt, $-rə-/ *n* [C] *fml or humorous* a person of bad character and habits • *Every time I see you, you're drunk, you old reprobate.* [as form of address]

re·pro·cess *obj* /£ˌriːˈprəʊ·ses, $-ˈprɑː-/ *v* [T] to put (a material that has been used) through another industrial process to change it so that it can be used again • *The nuclear waste is sent abroad to be reprocessed.* • A **reprocessing plant** is a place where materials are changed so that they can be used again: *Here at the* **nuclear** *reprocessing plant we extract plutonium from spent atomic fuel rods.*

re·pro·duce *(obj)* PRODUCE YOUNG /£ˌriː·prəˈdjuːs, $-ˈduːs/ *v* (of living things) to produce young • *If this generation of young women don't start reproducing soon there will be a fall in the population.* [I] • *Some creatures were better at surviving and reproducing* **themselves** *than others, so they thrived at the others' expense.* [T] • *These plants can reproduce sexually and asexually.* [I]

re·pro·duc·tion /ˌriː·prəˈdʌk·ʃᵊn/ *n* [U] • *The group is researching reproduction* **in** *elephants/***the** *reproduction* **of** *elephants.* • *Teaching about human reproduction was widespread in schools but only half of all 16-year-olds had discussed 'personal relationships' in the classroom.* • *Sexual reproduction involves the formation and fusion of specialized gametes, such as sperm and egg.* • *The reproduction rate is the rate at which a population produces new members by birth.*

re·produc·tive /£ˌriː·prəˈdʌk·tɪv, $-t̬ɪv/ *adj* [not gradable] • *reproductive organs* • *reproductive behaviour*

re·pro·duce *(obj)* COPY /£ˌriː·prəˈdjuːs, $-ˈduːs/ *v* to produce a copy of (something) or to show or do (something) again • *The map was reproduced on T-shirts and scarves.* [T] • *His work was reproduced on posters, leaflets and magazines and reached far beyond the art gallery.* [T] • *They said the printing was too faint to reproduce well.* [I] • *In the last race he reproduced the high speeds of the day before.* [T] • *The car design unfortunately reproduced some of the problems of the earlier model.* [T]

re·pro·duc·tion /ˌriː·prəˈdʌk·ʃᵊn/ *n* • *The book contains excellent* **colour** *reproductions of Monet's paintings.* [C] • *The exhibition also has on display facsimile reproductions of several old documents.* [C] • *One of the boats is an elegant reproduction of a 1905 steam yacht.* [C] • *The* **sound** *reproduction on your system is great.* [U] • Cheap copies of ANTIQUE furniture are called **reproduction furniture**.

re·prove *obj* /rɪˈpruːv/ *v* [T] *fml* to tell (someone) that you disapprove of their wrong or foolish behaviour • *The teacher gently reproved the boys* **for** *not paying attention.*

re·prov·ing /rɪˈpruː·vɪŋ/ *adj* • *Why do you look so reproving?* • *She* **threw him an angry and reproving look/glance.**

re·proof /rɪˈpruːf/ *n fml* • *She got a sharp reproof* **for** *being late.* [C] • *He picked up the broken vase without a word of reproof to his son.* [U]

rep·tile /ˈrep·taɪl/ *n* [C] an animal which produces eggs and uses the heat of the sun to keep its blood warm • *Snakes and crocodiles are reptiles.* • *Reptiles are usually covered by scales or bony plates.*

rep·til·i·an /repˈtɪl·i·ən/ *adj* [not gradable] • *(specialized)* Reptilian means of or like a reptile: *The fossil bird shows several reptilian features, for example sharp teeth on both jaws.* • *(disapproving)* If you describe a person as reptilian, you are saying that they look or seem to be very unpleasant: *He intimidated the questioner with a cold, reptilian gaze.*

re·pub·lic /rɪˈpʌb·lɪk/ *n* [C] a country without a king or queen, usually governed by elected representatives of the people and a president • *the People's Republic of China* • *America is a republic, but Britain is not.*

re·pub·li·can /rɪˈpʌb·lɪ·kən/ *n, adj* [not gradable] • *He's a republican* (= a supporter of government by the people), *and hates monarchies.* • *The people demanded a republican system of government.* • In America, a **Republican** is a member or supporter of the **Republican Party** (= one of the two largest political parties in the USA). • A **Republican** is also a person who believes that Northern Ireland should become part of the Irish Republic.

re·pub·li·can·i·sm /rɪˈpʌb·lɪ·kə·nɪ·zᵊm/ *n* [U]

re·pu·di·ate *obj* /rɪˈpjuː·di·eɪt/ *v* [T] *fml* to refuse to accept (something or someone) as true, good or reasonable; to DENY or REJECT • *He repudiated the allegation/charge/claim that he had tried to deceive them.* • *He used his position to repudiate the policies/views of the leadership.* • *The demand was for the group to repudiate and renounce terrorism.* • *I utterly repudiate those remarks.* • *They agreed it was not in their interest to repudiate the treaty.*

re·pu·di·a·tion /rɪˌpjuː·diˈeɪ·ʃᵊn/ *n* [U] • *They were surprised by his sudden repudiation of all his former beliefs.*

re·pug·nant /rɪˈpʌg·nənt/ *adj fml* (often of behaviour or beliefs) very unpleasant, esp. causing a feeling of disgust • *a repugnant smell* • **It** *is repugnant* **for** *these essential services* **to** *rely on charity.* [+ to infinitive] • *I* **find** *your attitude towards these women repugnant and ridiculous.* • *The idea of cheating in an exam is morally repugnant* **to** *me.* • **It** *is repugnant* **that** *a child could be treated so unkindly.* [+ *that* clause]

re·pug·nance /rɪˈpʌg·nənts/ *n* [U] *fml* • *The thought of eating meat fills me* **with** *repugnance.*

re·pulse *obj* /rɪˈpʌls/ *v* [T] *fml* to successfully stop (esp. an attack), or to push away or refuse (someone or something unwanted) • *The enemy attack was quickly repulsed.* • *Guards had to repulse looters from the damaged shops.* • *Better for a child to offend a genuinely kind stranger than risk danger by being too polite to repulse an advance.* • If something repulses you, it causes you to have a strong feeling of dislike, disapproval or disgust: *We're not compatible – he likes all the things that repulse me.* ○ *The tourists were repulsed by the filthy conditions.*

re·pulse /rɪˈpʌls/ *n* [C] • *The author tells the story of the conflict, from the repulse of the first offensive to the end of the war in June.*

re·pul·sion /rɪˈpʌl·ʃᵊn/ *n* [U] • *His badly scarred face produced an involuntary feeling of repulsion* (= disgust) *in her.* • *(specialized)* The force in physics that pushes two objects apart is called repulsion: *magnetic repulsion*

re·pul·sive /rɪˈpʌl·sɪv/ *adj* • If you say that something or someone is repulsive, you mean that you feel they are very unpleasant: *What a repulsive old man!* ○ *I think rats and snakes are repulsive and disgusting.*

re·pu·ta·tion /ˌrep·jʊˈteɪ·ʃᵊn/ *n* what people in general think or say about someone or something; how much someone or something is generally liked, admired or respected, based on past behaviour, character, etc. • *She has the reputation* **of** *being a good doctor.* [U] • *The company has a worldwide reputation* **for** *quality.* [C] • *His reputation was destroyed when he was caught stealing some money.* [C] • *The hotel has a bad reputation.* [C] • *He* **established/gained/acquired** *a reputation* (= behaved in a way that caused him to become recognized) **as** *an entertaining speaker.* [C] • *She* **made a** *reputation* **for herself** (= behaved in a way that caused her to become recognized) **as** *an expert manager.* [C] • *I find it impossible to* **live up to** *my reputation* (= behave as well as people now expect of me). [C] • If you **know** someone or something **by**

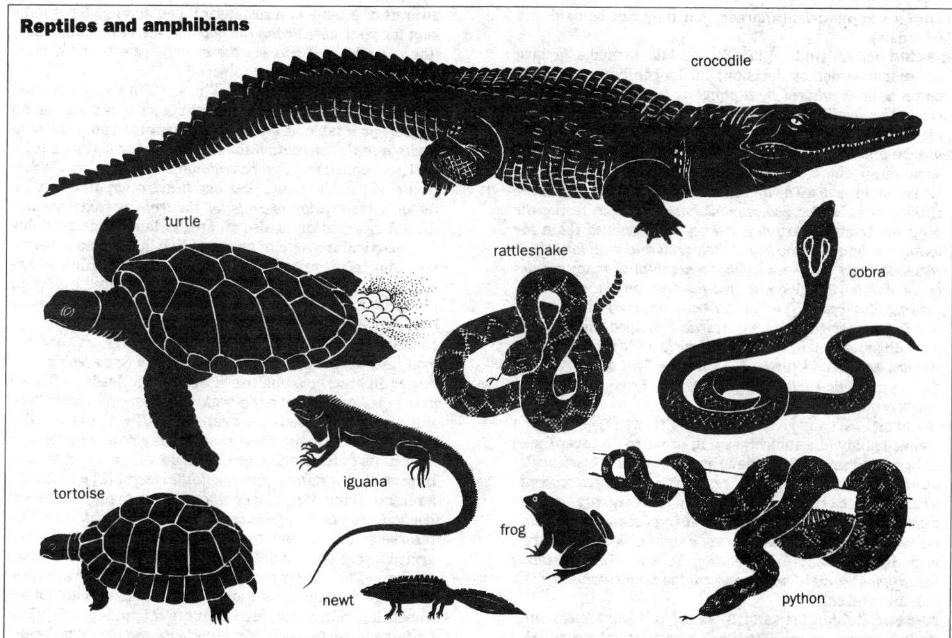

reputation, you only know them indirectly, by hearing what other people say about them. [U]

re·pu·ta·ble /£'rep·jʊ·tə·bl̩, $-t̬ə-/ *adj* • A reputable person or company has a good reputation and can be trusted.

re·pu·ta·bly /£'rep·jʊ·tə·bli, $-t̬ə-/ *adv* • *a reputably established firm*

re·pute /rɪ'pjuːt/ *n* [U] • *a place* **of ill/evil/good** *repute* (= with a bad/good reputation) • *My father was* **held in high** *repute* (= greatly respected) *by his colleagues.*

re·put·ed /£rɪ'pjuː·tɪd, $-t̬ɪd/ *adj* [not gradable] • If something or someone is reputed to be something, people say that this is the case, although it is not known to be certain and is not always believed to be likely: *She is widely reputed* **to** *be 25 years younger than her husband.* [+ *to* infinitive] ○ *They employed him because of his reputed skill in dealing with the press.*

re·put·ed·ly /£rɪ'pjuː·tɪd·li, $-t̬ɪd-/ *adv* [not gradable] • *He's reputedly* (= is said to be) *the strongest man in Britain.*

re·quest /rɪ'kwest/ *n* an act of asking; a polite demand for something • *They received hundreds of requests (asking)* **for** *more information.* [C] • *We made repeated requests* **for** *help with our debts to our bank.* [C] • *The boss refused our request* **to** *leave work early.* [C + *to* infinitive] • *We submitted a request* **that** *cars should be banned after midnight.* [C + *that* clause] • *Don't blame me – I did it* **at** *my boss's request* (= my boss asked me to do it). [U] • *An application form will be sent to you* **on** *request* (= if you ask). [U] • At a show or on the radio, a request can be something, such as a song, which someone has asked for: *The next song is a request* **from/for** *Roz in Totteridge.* [C] • In Britain, a **request stop** is a bus stop at which buses stop only if someone waiting there signals to them to do so. • Compare ORDER [INSTRUCTION]. • Ⓟ

re·quest *(obj)* /rɪ'kwest/ *v* • *We requested* **(of** *the chairman)* **that** *the next meeting be held on a Friday.* [+ *that* clause] • *Visitors are requested not* **to** *walk on the grass.* [T + obj + *to* infinitive] • *(fml) I requested* (= ordered) *a taxi for 8 o'clock.* [T]

re·qui·em (mass) /'rek·wi·əm/ *n* [C] (a piece of music written for) a MASS (= Christian religious ceremony) at which people honour and pray for a dead person

re·quire *(obj)* /£rɪ'kwaɪəʳ, $-'kwaɪr/ *v* to need or make necessary • *Please telephone this number if you require any further information.* [T] • *(fml) "Will you be requiring* (= Do you need) *anything else, sir?", asked the waiter.* [T] • *Skiing at 80 miles per hour requires total concentration.* [T] • *Marathons require incredible stamina* **(of** *the runners).* [T] • *Success in this job requires anticipat***ing** *the whims of the public.* [+ v-ing] • *Working here requires you* **to** *have a sense of humour.* [T + obj + *to* infinitive] • *Bringing up children often requires you* **to** *put their needs first.* [T + obj + *to* infinitive] • *You are required by law to stop your car after an accident.* [T + obj + *to* infinitive] • *The rules require* **that** *you can only bring one guest to the dinner.* [+ *that* clause]

re·quire·ment /£rɪ'kwaɪə·mənt, $-'kwaɪr-/ *n* [C] • *A good degree is a minimum requirement* **for** *many jobs.* • *It is a legal requirement* **that** *you have insurance for your car.* [+ *that* clause] • *Students who fail to* **meet** *the requirements* **(of** *the course) will fail.* • *My requirements* **from/in** *life are a well-paid job and a fast car.*

req·ui·site /'rek·wɪ·zɪt/ *adj* [before n; not gradable] *fml* necessary; needed for a particular purpose • *You must produce the requisite documents to prove that you're the owner, before we can let you have the car.*

req·ui·site /'rek·wɪ·zɪt/ *n* [C usually pl] *fml* • A requisite is an important necessary item: *A good book is a requisite for long journeys.* ○ *Self-esteem, self-judgment and self-will are said to be the three requisites of independence.* ○ *The kiosks sell all the requisites for a Japanese in Paris – Japanese newspapers, take-away sushi, green tea and much more.*

req·ui·si·tion *obj* /ˌrek·wɪ'zɪʃ·ᵊn/ *v* [T] to officially request or take • *The army requisitioned all the cars and trucks they could find.*

req·ui·si·tion /ˌrek·wɪ'zɪʃ·ᵊn/ *n* • *They expected government requisition of fuel supplies.* [U] • *The staff* **made** *a requisition* **for** (= sent a written request for) *new chairs and desks.* [C]

re·quite *obj* /rɪ'kwaɪt/ *v* [T] *fml* to give or do something in return for (something) • *You can't force a person to requite your* **love**. • *There is a mistaken belief that requited* **love** *is all you need to sustain a long-term relationship.* • *Society craves for more and costlier physical objects that can never requite the toil it takes to acquire them.*

re·route *obj* /ˌriː'ruːt, $-'raʊt/ *v* [T] to change the route of • *Where scheduled fights are cancelled or rerouted, travellers will be offered alternative flights.* • *Computers recognize numbers and uses them to reroute phone calls.*

re·run *obj* /ˌriː'rʌn/ *v* [T] **rerunning**, *past simple* **reran** /ˌriː'ræn/, *past part* **rerun** to show (a film, play, television programme, etc.) again • *The James Bond films are always being rerun on television.*

re·run /ˌriː'rʌn/ *n* [C] • *The films this week are all reruns.* • *The theatre put on a rerun* **of** *'Gone With the Wind'.* • *(fig.) The situation looks like a rerun* **of** *the Twenties and early Thirties, when money policies produced disastrous results.*

re·sat /ˌriː'sæt/ *past simple and past participle of* RESIT

re·sched·ule *obj* /£ˌriː'ʃed·juːl, $-'skedʒ·uːl/ *v* [T] to agree a new and later date for (something) to happen • *I rescheduled my doctor's appointment for later in the week.* • *(specialized) Banks have rescheduled the* **debts** *of many* *third-world countries* (=agreed that they can be paid at a later date).

re·scind *obj* /rɪˈsɪnd/ *v* [T] *fml or law* to make (a law, agreement, order or decision) no longer have any legal power • *He is advised by a panel as to whether he should rescind or modify deportation decisions in cases where no right of appeal exists.*

res·cue *obj* /ˈres·kjuː/ *v* [T] to help (someone or something) out of a dangerous, harmful or unpleasant situation; to save • *The lifeboat rescued the sailors* **from** *the sinking boat.* • *The government has refused to rescue the company* **from** *bankruptcy.* • *They were rescued* **from** *the locked hut by a boy who heard their cries and went for help.*

res·cue /ˈres·kjuː/ *n* • *Lifeboats accomplish many rescues every month.* [C] • *We huddled together on the cliff ledge, waiting for rescue.* [U] • *I didn't know anybody at the party, but the hostess* **came to** *my rescue* (=helped me out of a difficult situation) *by introducing me to a few people.* [U]

res·cu·er /£ˈres·kjuː·əʳ, $-ɚ/ *n* [C] • *Two of the rescuers died in a second earthquake.* • *After the crisis was over, he publicly thanked his rescuers.*

re·search /£rɪˈsɜːtʃ, £ˈriː·sɜːtʃ, $ˈriː·sɜːrtʃ/ *n* [U] a detailed study of a subject, esp. in order to discover (new) information or reach a (new) understanding • *scientific/medical/historical/linguistic research* • *a research student/assistant* • *a research laboratory* • *They are* **doing/carrying out/conducting/pursuing** *some fascinating research* **into/on** *the language of dolphins.* • *The* **research and development** *(abbreviation* **R and D***) department investigated ways of improving engine performance.* • LP Schools and colleges

re·search *(obj)* /rɪˈsɜːtʃ, $-ˈsɜːrtʃ/ *v* • *She's researching* **in** *18th-century poetry.* [I] • *She's researching* **into** *possible cures for AIDS.* [I] • *Journalists were frantically researching the new Prime Minister's background, family, interests and everything else about him.* [T] • *The article in the newspaper was well-researched* (=provided accurate information).

re·search·er /£rɪˈsɜː·tʃəʳ, $-ˈsɜːr·tʃɚ/ *n* [C]

re·search·es /£rɪˈsɜː·tʃɪz, £ˈriː·sɜː-, $ˈriː·sɜːr-/ *pl n* • *His researches* (=research) *in the field of disease prevention produced unexpected results.*

re·sem·ble *obj* /rɪˈzem·bl̩/ *v* [T not *be resembling*/no passive] to look or be like; be similar esp. in appearance to (someone or something) • *You resemble your mother very closely.* • *After the earthquake the city resembled a battlefield.*

re·sem·blance /rɪˈzem·bləns/ *n* • *His nose is similar to his father's but there the resemblance ends.* [U] • *There was a clear* **family** *resemblance* **between** *all the brothers.* [C] • *These prices* **bear** *no resemblance* **to** (=are completely different from) *the ones I saw printed in the newspaper.* [U]

re·sent *(obj)* /rɪˈzent/ *v* to be angry about and to dislike being forced to accept (something or someone annoying) • *She bitterly resented her father's new wife.* [T] • *He resents having to explain his work to other people.* [+ v-*ing*]

re·sent·ful /rɪˈzent·fəl/ *adj* • *a resentful look* • *She was resentful* **of** *anybody's attempts to interfere in her work.*

re·sent·ful·ly /rɪˈzent·fəl·i/ *adv*

re·sent·ful·ness /rɪˈzent·fəl·nəs/ *n* [U]

re·sent·ment /rɪˈzent·mənt/ *n* [C/U] • *He feels/harbours (a) deep resentment* **against/at/towards** *his parents for his miserable childhood.*

res·er·va·tion /£ˌrez·əˈveɪ·ʃən, $-ɚˈ-/ *n* a doubt or feeling of not being able to agree with or accept something completely • *Workers and employees shared deep reservations* **about** *the wisdom of the government's plans for the industry.* [C often pl] • *I approved of my mother's new husband,* **with** *reservations.* [C often pl] • *He accepted my advice* **without** *reservation.* [U] • See also **reservation** at RESERVE KEEP SEPARATE.

re·serve /£rɪˈzɜːv, $-ˈzɜːrv/ *n* [U] • *(fml) I can recommend him to you* **without** *reserve.* • *She agreed to the plan, but I detected some reserve.* • *Articles which present the situation only from the perspective of the landowners must be treated with considerable reserve.* • See also RESERVE KEEP SEPARATE; RESERVE BEHAVIOUR.

re·serve *obj* KEEP SEPARATE /£rɪˈzɜːv, $-ˈzɜːrv/ *v* [T] to keep (something) for a particular purpose or time • *I reserve Mondays* **for** *tidying my desk and answering letters.* • *These seats are reserved* **for** *the elderly and women with babies.* • *He reserved* **the right** *to veto any future plans he disagreed with.* • *I reserve* **judgment** *(on this issue)* (=I won't give an opinion on it now) *until we have more information.* • If you reserve something such as a seat on an aircraft or a table at a restaurant, you arrange for it to be kept for your use: *I rang the hotel to reserve a double room* **(for** *a week).* ○ *If you get there early, reserve me a seat/reserve a seat* **for** *me.* [+ two objects]

res·er·va·tion /£ˌrez·əˈveɪ·ʃən, $-ɚˈ-/ *n* • A reservation is an arrangement to have something such as a seat on an aircraft or a table at a restaurant kept for you: *I'd like to* **make** *a table reservation* **for** *two people* **for** *9 o'clock.* [C] ○ *Will you* **confirm** *your reservation in writing by Friday, please.* [C] ○ *She* **cancelled** *her ticket reservations.* [C] ○ *Advance reservation of seats for the train is recommended.* [U] • A reservation is also an area of land made available for a particular group of people to live in, or (also **reserve**, *esp. Am also* **preserve**) in which wild animals are protected: *The family lives* **on** *a Native American reservation.* [C] ○ *He's the chief warden of a big-game reservation.* [C] • See also RESERVATION.

re·serve /£rɪˈzɜːv, $-ˈzɜːrv/ *n* • *I have a reserve of food/food reserves in case of emergencies.* [C] • *She keeps a little money* **in** *reserve* (=for use if and when needed). [U] • *I asked the librarian to put a book* **on** *reserve (for me)* (=keep it for me when it becomes available). [U] • A reserve (also **reservation**, *esp. Am* also **preserve**) is also an area of land kept in its natural state, esp. for wild animals to live in to be protected: *a nature/game/wildlife reserve* [C] • In sports, a reserve is an extra player who is ready to play if needed: *We had two reserves in case anyone was injured.* [C] • The reserve(s) are people that are not permanently in the armed forces but are used only if needed: *He's in the naval reserve.* ○ *They will call up the reserves.* • **A reserve (price)** is the lowest amount of money the owners will accept for something being sold, esp. at AUCTION (=public sale): *The painting failed to reach its reserve price and was withdrawn.* ○ *We put a reserve* **of** *£50* **on** *the picture.* [C]

re·served /£rɪˈzɜːvd, $-ˈzɜːrvd/ *adj* • *a reserved seat/table/place* • *May I sit here, or is this seat reserved?*

re·ser·vist /£rɪˈzɜː·vɪst, $-ˈzɜːr-/ *n* [C] • A reservist is a person who is trained as a soldier and is ready to fight in the army if needed.

re·serve BEHAVIOUR /£rɪˈzɜːv, $-ˈzɜːrv/ *n* [U] the habit of not showing your feelings or thoughts • *He was a man of such impenetrable reserve that not even his closest friends really understood him.* • *I took her out for a drink and tried to break through her reserve.*

re·served /£rɪˈzɜːvd, $-ˈzɜːrvd/ *adj* • *The English have a reputation for being reserved.*

res·er·voir /£ˈrez·ə·vwɑːʳ, $-ɚ·vwɑːr/ *n* [C] a place for storing liquid, esp. a natural or artificial lake providing water for a city or other area • *The big storms in August refilled the reservoirs.* • *(fig.) Over the years the department had built up a reservoir* (=large supply for use when needed) **of** *expert knowledge.*

re·set·tle *(obj)* /£ˌriːˈset·l̩, $-ˈseţ-/ *v* to (be helped or forced to) move to another place to live • *His family originally came from Ireland, but resettled* **in** *the US in the 19th century.* [I] • *The US government resettled the Native Americans* **in** *reservations.* [T]

re·set·tle·ment /£ˌriːˈset·l̩.mənt, $-ˈseţ-/ *n* [U] • *Voluntary organizations are helping with the resettlement of refugees.*

re·shuf·fle *obj* /ˌriːˈʃʌf·l̩/ *v* [T] to change the positions of people or things within (a group) • *When the Prime Minister reshuffled his Cabinet five ministers lost their jobs.*

re·shuf·fle /ˈriːˌʃʌf·l̩/ *n* [C] • *They expect a Cabinet reshuffle in the summer.*

re·side /rɪˈzaɪd/ *v* [I always + adv/prep] *fml* to live, have your home or stay (in a place) • *The family resides in southern France.* • *He came back to England from Ghana and has resided here ever since.* • *The jewellery normally resides in the bank.* • If a power or quality **resides in** someone or something, they have that power or quality: *The power to sack employees resides in the Board of Directors.* ○ *Nationhood does not reside only in institutions and religion.*

res·i·dence /ˈrez·ɪ·dənts/ *n fml* • A residence is a home: *That big building is the Governor's official residence.* [C] ○ *The tourist guide described it as a well-preserved Georgian residence.* [C] • *She* **took up** *residence* (=went to live) **abroad/***in South America.* [U] • *The Queen is* **in** *residence* (=officially staying) **at** *the Palace this week.* [U] • An author/poet/artist/etc. **in** residence at a school, college, etc. is employed there for a short period. • RUS

res·i·denc·y /ˈrez·ɪ·dənt·si/ *n* [U] *fml* • *She took up permanent residency* (=went to live permanently) *abroad.*

res·i·dent /ˈrez·ɪ·dᵊnt/ *n* [C] • A resident is a person who lives or has their home in a place: *a resident of the UK/the United States/Australia* ○ *The local residents were angry at the lack of parking spaces.* • *The hotel bar was only open to residents* (= to people staying at the hotel).

res·i·dent /ˈrez·ɪ·dᵊnt/ *adj* [not gradable] • *She's resident abroad/***in** *Moscow.* • *She is the university's resident expert* (= their own expert) *on Italian literature.* • *(humorous) Tony is the company's resident clown and scapegoat.* • (RUS)

res·i·den·tial /ˌrez·ɪˈden·tʃᵊl/ *adj* [not gradable] • A residential road, area, etc. has only private houses, not offices and factories. • A residential job, position, course, etc. is one for which you live at the same place where you work or study. • *You must satisfy the residential qualifications* (= You must have lived in this country for a particular length of time) *to get a work permit.*

res·i·due /£ˈrez·ɪ·djuː, $-ə·duː/ *n* [C usually sing] *fml* the part that is left after the main part has gone or been taken away • *She cut off the best meat and threw away the residue.* • *The white residue* **in/on** *the kettle is a result of minerals in the water.* • *(law)* The residue is the part of a dead person's money and property that is left after taxes, debts and presents have been paid: *The residue* (**of** *the estate) went to her granddaughter.*

re·si·dual /£rɪˈzɪd·ju·əl, $-ˈzɪdʒ-/ *adj* [not gradable] • *Residual* **income** *is your income after tax.* • *Only residual* (= a little remaining) *opposition to the government troops now exists.* • *I still felt some residual* (= a little remaining) *bitterness ten years after my divorce.*

re·sign *(obj)* /rɪˈzaɪn/ *v* to give up (a job or position) by telling your employer that you are leaving • *He resigned* (**from** *the company) in order to take a more challenging job.* [I] • *She resigned* **as** *director.* [I] • *She resigned the directorship.* [T] • In the game of chess you resign when you cannot see any way to avoid being beaten: *Timman resigned a hopeless position.* [T] ○ *After she had taken my rook, there was nothing I could really do except resign.* [I] • LP› **Work**

res·ig·na·tion /ˌrez·ɪgˈneɪ·ʃᵊn/ *n* • *With the news of the scandal came the call for his resignation.* [U] • *I* **handed in/ gave in/sent in** *my resignation this morning.* [C]

re·sign *obj* **to** *obj v prep* [T] to make (yourself) accept (something unpleasant) calmly • *After his wife died he resigned himself* **to** *a lonely old age.* • *He resigned* **himself** *to living alone.* • *They were resigned to* **being** *criticized.*

res·ig·na·tion /ˌrez·ɪgˈneɪ·ʃᵊn/ *n* [U] • *She showed an attitude of quiet resignation* **to** *her fate.* • *They received the news* **with** *resignation.*

re·signed /rɪˈzaɪnd/ *adj* • *a resigned look/expression/ tone* • *With three men injured we became resigned* **to losing** (= we expected to lose) *the game.*

re·sign·ed·ly /rɪˈzaɪn·ɪd·li/ *adv* • *"We're going to be late again," he said resignedly.*

re·sil·i·ent /rɪˈzɪl·i·ənt/ *adj* able to quickly return to a previous (good) condition • *This rubber ball is very resilient and immediately springs back into shape after you've squashed it.* • *She's a resilient girl – she won't be unhappy for long.* • *She seems to be resilient* **to** *stress.*

re·sil·i·ence /rɪˈzɪl·i·ənts/, **re·sil·i·en·cy** /rɪˈzɪl·i·ənt·si/ *n* [U]

res·in /ˈrez·ɪn/ *n* [U] a sticky substance that becomes yellow and hard after it is taken from particular trees or plants such as PINES or FIRS, or any of various similar substances produced chemically for use in industry

res·in·ous /ˈrez·ɪ·nəs/ *adj*

re·sist *(obj)* /rɪˈzɪst/ *v* to fight against (something or someone); to not be changed by or to refuse to accept (something) • *The soldiers resisted (the enemy attacks) for two days.* [I/T] • *The party leader resisted demands for his resignation.* [T] • *He tried to run away from the police and was later charged with (the crime of) resisting* **arrest**. [T] • *The new hybrid crops are much better at resisting* (= not being damaged by) *disease.* [T] • *I can't resist temptation/ chocolate/the urge to go home early* (= I want to do something so much that I will do it). [T] • *She couldn't resist* (= stop herself from) *laughing at him in those clothes.* [+ *v-ing*]

re·sis·tance /rɪˈzɪs·tᵊnts/ *n* • *Government troops offered no resistance (***to** *the rebels).* [U] • *When he was caught he put up a* **determined/stiff** *resistance.* [C] • *There's a lot of resistance* (= opposition) **to** *the idea of a united Europe.* [U] • *The car's speed was reduced by* **air/wind** *resistance.* [U] • *A good diet helps the body to build up (a) resistance* **to** *disease.* [U] • *(specialized)* Resistance is the degree to which a substance prevents the flow of an electric current through it: *Copper has (a) low resistance.* [U] • *I took the* **path/***(Br usually)* **line of least resistance** (= easiest way) *and agreed with the others.* • **The Resistance** is an organization that secretly fights against an enemy that has taken control of its country.

re·sis·tant /rɪˈzɪs·tᵊnt/ *adj* • *Why are you so resistant* **to** *change?* • *a stain-resistant carpet* • *a water-resistant polish* • *a disease-resistant variety of tomato*

re·sis·tor /£rɪˈzɪs·təʳ, $-tɚ/ *n* [C] *specialized* • *We decreased the resistance in the electric circuit by using a copper wire as the resistor.*

re·sit *obj* /ˌriːˈsɪt/ *v* [T] **resitting**, *past* **resat** /ˌriːˈsæt/ *esp. Br* to take (an exam) again • *If you fail these exams you can resit them next year.*

re·sit /ˈriː·sɪt/ *n* [C] • *She's got to do resits* **in/for** *French and German.*

res·o·lute /£ˈrez·ᵊl·uːt, $-ə·luːt/ *adj fml* (of people) determined in character, action or ideas • *Why are you so resolute (***in** *your refusal to apologise)?* • *She's a resolute believer in the benefits of spanking children.* • *Their resolute opposition to the introduction of new methods was difficult to overcome.* • *I admired her resolute optimism in those difficult times.*

res·o·lute·ly /£ˈrez·ᵊl·uːt·li, $-ə·luːt-/ *adv* • *She resolutely refused to learn about computers.*

res·o·lu·tion /£ˌrez·ᵊlˈuː·ʃᵊn, $-əˈluː-/, **res·o·lute·ness** /£ˈrez·ᵊl·uːt·nəs, $-ə·luːt-/ *n* [U] *approving* • *I admired her resolution* (= determination). • *He showed great resolution* **in** *facing the robbers.*

re·solve *obj* SOLVE /£rɪˈzʌlv, $-ˈzɑːlv/ *v* [T] to solve or end (a problem or difficulty) • *We need to resolve this dispute quickly.* • *Have you resolved the problem of transport yet?* • *The crisis resolved* **itself** *when the unions saw they couldn't win.* • *The couple resolved their* **differences** *and made an effort to get along.*

res·o·lu·tion /£ˌrez·ᵊlˈuː·ʃᵊn, $-əˈluː-/ *n* [U] *fml* • *Your information has made the resolution* **of** *this problem possible.*

re·solve DECIDE /£rɪˈzʌlv, $-ˈzɑːlv/ *v fml* to make a decision formally or with determination • *She resolved* **that** *she would never speak to him again.* [+ *that* clause] • *After an hour of argument they resolved* **on/against** *going to the party.* [I always + adv/prep] • *The company resolved* **to** *take no further action against the thieves.* [+ *to* infinitive] • See also RESOLUTE.

re·solve /£rɪˈzʌlv, $-ˈzɑːlv/ *n* [U] *fml* • Resolve is strong decision or determination: *The experience increased her resolve to change her job.*

re·solved /£rɪˈzʌlvd, $-ˈzɑːlvd/ *adj* [after v] *fml* • *He was resolved* **to** *ask her to marry him the next day.* [+ *to* infinitive]

res·o·lu·tion /£ˌrez·ᵊlˈuː·ʃᵊn, $-əˈluː-/ *n* [C] • If a group of people **passes/rejects** a resolution, it agrees/disagrees with a suggested course of action or statement of opinion: *The United Nations passed a resolution* **to** *increase aid to the Third World.* [+ *to* infinitive] • *The member nations voted on the resolution* **banning** *whaling.* [+ *v-ing*] • *I proposed the resolution* **that** *military spending (should) be cut.* [+ *that* clause] • If you **make** a resolution, you make a promise to yourself to do or to not do something: *I made a resolution* **to** *give up chocolate.* [+ *to* infinitive] • LP› **Holidays**

re·solve into *obj v prep* [T] *specialized* to separate into parts • *There was a blur of sound, which slowly resolved* **itself** *into different words.* • *The computer program resolves sentences into their component parts.*

res·o·lu·tion /£ˌrez·ᵊlˈuː·ʃᵊn, $-əˈluː-/ *n* [U] *specialized* • *the resolution of oil* **into** *bitumen and tar* • A television/ computer screen or a MICROSCOPE (= a scientific instrument) that has **high** resolution can show things clearly and with a lot of detail.

res·o·nate *(obj)* /ˈrez·ᵊn·eɪt/ *v* to produce, increase or fill with sound, by VIBRATING (= shaking slightly and quickly) objects which are near • *His voice resonated in the empty church.* [I] • *The noise of the bell resonated* **through** *the building.* [I] • *The concert hall resonated* **with** *the power of the tenor's last notes.* [I] • *Some species of fish make sounds by resonating the swim bladder.* [T] • *(fig.) The building resonates* **with** *historic significance.* [I] • *(fig.) The significance of those great stories resonate down the years.* • If an experience or memory resonates, it reminds you of another similar one: *Her experiences resonate powerfully* **with** *me, living, as I do, in a similar family situation.* [I] • *(esp. Am) When we're in conversation together, I always seem* *to resonate* **with** (= share an understanding of) *what Jody says.* [I] • Compare RESOUND.

res·o·nance /ˈrez·ᵊn·ənts/ *n* • *The acoustic analysis was based on physical measurement of resonance.* [U] • *My mother read this poem to me when I was a child – it has many resonances* (= connected thoughts and memories) *for me.* [C]

res·o·nant /ˈrez·ᵊn·ənt/ *adj* • Resonant means (causing sounds to be) clear and loud: *a resonant concert hall* ○ *a deep, resonant voice* • Resonant also means reminding you of a similar experience or memory: *Having studied Soviet politics, we felt privileged to be the first group of Western visitors to enter the historic palace, resonant* **with** *past conflicts.* • See also RESOUND.

res·o·nat·or /£ˈrez·ᵊn·eɪ·təʳ, $-t̬ɚ/ *n* [C]

re·sort /£rɪˈzɔːt, $-ˈzɔːrt/ *n* [C] a place that many people go for rest, relaxation or another stated purpose • *a ski resort* • *a seaside/beach resort* • *a (Br and Aus) holiday/(Am) vacation resort* • *a health resort* • *In recent years this little town has grown into a fashionable resort.* • See also **resort** at RESORT TO.

re·sort to *(obj) v prep* to use (something) for help, because you cannot find any other way of acting • *I had to resort to violence/threats to get my money.* [T] • *When she didn't answer the telephone I resorted to standing outside her window and calling up to her.* [+ v-*ing*]

re·sort /£rɪˈzɔːt, $-ˈzɔːrt/ *n* [U] • *He got hold of the money legally, without resort* **to**/*without* **having** *resort* **to** *violence.* • *You have to help me – you're my* **only/last resort** (= the only person who could possibly help/save me). • See also RESORT.

re·sound /rɪˈzaʊnd/ *v* [I] to sound loudly or for a long time, or (of a place) to be filled with sound • *The noise of the fire alarm resounded* **through/throughout** *the building.* • *The concert hall resounded* **with** *cheers and applause.* • *(fig.) The California student movement resounded through the world and continues to echo today.* • See also RESONATE.

re·sound·ing /rɪˈzaʊn·dɪŋ/ *adj* [before n] • *Supporters gave the team three resounding cheers.* • Resounding also means very great: *The plan was a resounding success/failure.*

re·sound·ing·ly /rɪˈzaʊn·dɪŋ·li/ *adv*

re·source /£rɪˈzɔːs, £ˈriː·sɔːs, $ˈriː·sɔːrs/ *n* [C usually pl] a useful or valuable possession or quality of a country, organization or person • *The country's greatest resource is the dedication of its workers.* • *A big company like IBM has huge resources* **of** *money and skills.* • *Britain's* **mineral** *resources include oil, coal and gas deposits.* • *He can't cope with difficult situations on his own – he has no* **inner** *resources* (= he does not have the ability to help himself). • *The school has a resource* **room** *where video and audio equipment is stored.* • Resource is also *fml* for **resourcefulness**.

re·source *obj* /£rɪˈzɔːs, £ˈriː·sɔːs, $ˈriː·sɔːrs/ *v* [T] • To resource an organization or department is to provide it with money or equipment: *The school must be resourced* **with** *musical instruments and audio equipment.*

re·sourced /£rɪˈzɔːst, £riː·sɔːst, $ˈriː·sɔːrst/ *adj* • *He has always showed concern for those less resourced* (= those people with less money) *and less privileged than himself.* • *The hospital needs additional funding to give patients access to* **adequately**-*resourced health services.* • *They are a* **well**-*resourced organization with access to research, training and information.* • *She claims that a* **poorly** *resourced education system is demoralising for both students and teachers.* • *It is widely acknowledged that the welfare system is* **under**-*resourced.*

re·source·ful /£rɪˈzɔː·sfᵊl, $-ˈsɔːr-/ *adj approving* • Someone who is resourceful is good at solving problems and making decisions on their own: *She's a very resourceful manager.*

re·sour·ce·ful·ly /£rɪˈzɔː·sfᵊl·i, $-ˈzɔːr-/ *adv approving*

re·source·ful·ness /£rɪˈzɔː·sfᵊl·nəs, $-ˈzɔːr-/, *fml* **re·source** *n* [U] *approving* • Resourcefulness is the ability to make decisions and act on your own: *She showed great resourcefulness* **at** *problem solving.* ○ *(fml) He demonstrated great resource* **in** *finding a solution to the company's problems.*

re·spect [ADMIRATION] /rɪˈspekt/ *n* [U] admiration felt or shown for someone or something that you believe has good ideas or qualities • *I* **have** *great/the greatest respect* **for** *his ideas, although I don't agree with them.* • *She is a formidable figure who* **commands** *a great deal of respect* (= who is greatly admired by others). • *New teachers have to* **earn/gain** *the respect* **of** *their students.* • *She was often attacked for her outspoken comments, but over the years she* **gained** *people's* **grudging** *respect.* • *"R-E-S-P-E-C-T, /Find out what it means to me"* (Song by Aretha Franklin, 1967) • See also SELF-RESPECT.

re·spect *obj* /rɪˈspekt/ *v* [T] • If you respect someone or something that you believe has good ideas or qualities, you feel or show admiration for them: *I deeply respect David* **for** *what he has achieved.* • If you respect your**self**, you have pride in your own qualities or achievements.

re·spect·ed /£rɪˈspek·tɪd, $-t̬ɪd/ *adj* • Someone or something that is respected is admired by many people for their qualities or achievements: *He is well respected in the business world.* ○ *She is a highly respected politician who has campaigned for the rights of the disabled.* ○ *The country's most respected daily newspaper has published a critical article about the government.*

re·spect·ful /rɪˈspekt·fᵊl/ *adj* • Respectful means showing admiration for someone or something: *"We're so pleased to meet you at last," he said in a respectful tone of voice.*

re·spect·ful·ly /rɪˈspekt·fᵊl·i/ *adv* • *The audience clapped respectfully as she stood up to speak.*

re·spect [HONOUR] /rɪˈspekt/ *n* [U] politeness and honour shown towards someone or something that is considered important • *She told him that he should treat his parents with more respect.* • *He took off his hat* **out of** *respect* **for** (= to honour) *the dead man.* • *She* **has** *no respect* **for** *other people's property* (= She does not treat it well). • If you have respect for the law, you think it is important to obey it: *She startled to grumble about how young people seemed to have no respect for the law.* • If you show respect for something which has been formally agreed or established, you accept that it is right or important and do not attempt to change it or harm it: *The UN has imposed sanctions on the country for the lack of respect which it has shown for ethnic rights.* ○ *In their senseless killing of innocent people, the terrorists have shown their lack of respect for human life* (= shown that they do not think human life is important and valuable). • If you have/show respect for different customs or cultures, you accept that they are different from your own and behave in a way which would not cause offence: *She teaches the students to have respect for different races and appreciate the diversity of other cultures.* • You can say **with great/with the greatest of/with all due respect** to express polite disagreement in a formal situation: *With all due respect, Minister, I cannot agree with your last statement.*

re·spect *obj* /rɪˈspekt/ *v* [T] • If you respect something or someone, you treat it or them with kindness and care: *We should respect the environment and not pollute it.* • If you respect someone's rights or customs, you accept their importance and do nothing that would harm them or cause that person offence: *The agreement will respect the rights of both nations.* ○ *The president has pledged to respect the existing frontiers between the two countries.* ○ *I would appreciate it if you would respect my* **privacy** (= accept that I want to be alone and do not interrupt me). • If you **respect** someone's **wishes**, you do what they asked to have done: *His children respected his last wishes and held a simple funeral for him.*

re·spec·ter /£rɪˈspek·təʳ, $-tɚ/ *n* [C] • *He is a great respecter of tradition* (= He thinks tradition is very important). • *Air pollution is* **no** *respecter* **of** *national frontiers* (= It is a problem in every country).

re·spect·ful /rɪˈspekt·fᵊl/ *adj* • Respectful means showing politeness or honour to someone or something: *There was a respectful two-minute silence as we remembered the soldiers who had died in the war.* • To be respectful **of** something is to accept its importance and not try to change it or cause offence: *He taught his children to be respectful of other cultures.*

re·spect·ful·ly /rɪˈspekt·fᵊl·i/ *adv* • *His former pupils still respectfully* (= politely) *call him 'Sir'.* • *When she was asked if she had any ambition to become prime minister, she respectfully* (= politely) *declined to answer the question.* • *As the body of the religious leader was carried through the crowd, people drew back respectfully* (= to show their honour). • **Respectfully yours** is a very formal way of ending a letter.

re·spects /rɪˈspekts/ *pl n fml* • Respects are polite formal greetings: *Please* **convey/give** *my respects* **to** *your parents.* ○ *We* **paid** *our respects* **to** *our new neighbours* (= We visited them in order to welcome them). ○ *Friends and relatives came to* **pay** *their* **last respects** *to Mr Cohen* (= to honour him after his death).

re·spect FEATURE /rɪ'spekt/ *n* [C] a particular feature or detail • *This proposal differs from the last one* **in many** *important respects.* • **In most** *respects* (= In many ways) *the new film is better than the original.* • *The house is in a fairly good condition and,* **in this** *respect, contrasts with the rest of the street which is in a state of disrepair.* • *(fml)* **In respect of/With respect to** is used to mean in connection with: *I am writing with respect to your letter of 15 June.*

re·spec·ta·ble /rɪ'spek·tə·bl̩/ *adj* considered to be socially acceptable because of having a good character or appearance or behaving in a way that is approved of • *She is a respectable young woman from a good family.* • *This part of the city has become quite respectable in the last ten years.* • *I wore my boring, respectable suit to the interview.* • *He wanted to become a writer, but his father didn't think it was a respectable profession.* • If you say that an amount or quality is respectable, you mean that it is large enough or of a good enough standard to be acceptable: *She earns a respectable salary.* ○ *The final score was a respectable 2:1.* ○ *They succeeded in getting members of Parliament to take their resolution seriously and a respectable number agreed to give their support.* • *(humorous)* If you **make yourself respectable**, you put on some clothes so that you are in a suitable state to meet someone: *Can you wait for a few minutes while I make myself respectable?*

re·spec·ta·bly /rɪ'spek·tə·bli/ *adv* • *She had been worried that he might say something to offend her parents, but he behaved quite respectably all through dinner.* • If something does respectably, it achieves a reasonable result: *The car performs respectably on the motorway, although it is slightly noisy.* ○ *It is a small-budget film, but it has done respectably at the box office* (= it has been quite popular).

re·spec·ta·bil·i·ty /£rɪˌspek·tə'bɪl·ɪ·ti, $-ə·t̬i/ *n* [U] • *The company operates out of modern offices and expensive hotel suites to create an air of respectability.* • *The country has restored diplomatic relations with its neighbours in an attempt to* **gain** *international respectability.* • *Her ideas* **gained** *respectability when they were taken up by a well-respected member of the council.*

re·spec·tive /£rɪ'spek·tɪv, $-t̬ɪv/ *adj* [before n; not gradable] relating to the people or things in the same order as you have just mentioned them • *Neil came down from Sydney for the meeting and Lisa flew in from Perth, and when the meeting had finished, they returned to their respective homes* (= John returned to Sydney and Lisa to Perth).

re·spec·tive·ly /£rɪ'spek·tɪv·li, $-t̬ɪv-/ *adv* [not gradable] • *In the 200 metres, Lizzy and Sarah came first and third respectively* (= Lizzy won the race and Sarah was third).

re·spire /£rɪ'spaɪəʳ, $-'spaɪr/ *v* [I] *fml or specialized* to breathe • *Fish respire through their gills.*

res·pi·ra·tion /ˌres·pɪ'reɪ·ʃən/ *n* [U] *fml or specialized* • *The diaphragm is the principle muscle of respiration* (= breathing). • *Her respiration was slow and difficult.* • *One of the accident victims was given* **artificial** *respiration by a member of the ambulance crew* (= they blew air into the person's lungs to help them start breathing again).

res·pi·ra·tor /£'res·pɪ·reɪ·təʳ, $-t̬ɚ/ *n* [C] • A respirator is artificial breathing equipment: *Her lungs were so weak that she couldn't breathe without a respirator.* ○ *Doctors put the patient* **on** *a respirator.* • A respirator is also a device worn over the mouth and nose to prevent harmful substances from being breathed in: *The fire fighter was wearing a respirator to help him breathe in the smoke-filled house.*

res·pi·ra·tory /£rɪ'spɪr·ə·tri, $'res·pɚ·ə·tɔːr·i/ *adj* [before n; not gradable] *fml or specialized* • *Smoking can cause respiratory diseases.* • The **respiratory system** is the organs which allow breathing to happen: *In humans and other mammals, the respiratory system includes the lungs, the diaphragm and the windpipe.*

res·pite /'res·paɪt/ *n* [U] *fml* a pause or rest from something difficult or unpleasant • *We worked for hours without respite.* • *Although neither side was satisfied with the treaty, both sides recognised that some respite from two years of conflict was necessary.* • *The sunshine is a welcome respite* **from** *this morning's rain.* • If you have a respite before something unpleasant happens, there is a useful delay before it happens: *Their teacher was away, so they had* **a** *day's respite before their essays were due.*

re·splen·dent /rɪ'splen·dənt/ *adj fml or literary* having a very bright or splendid appearance • *The queen's resplendent purple robes and crown were on display in the museum.* • *I saw Anna at the other end of the room, resplendent* **in** *a red sequined cocktail dress.*

re·splen·dent·ly /rɪ'splen·dənt·li/ *adv fml or literary* • *He was resplendently dressed in a soft grey three-piece suit and red silk cravat.*

re·splen·dence /rɪ'splen·dənts/ *n* [U] *fml or literary* • *Now that the renovations are complete, visitors have the opportunity to admire the resplendence of the hall, with its marble floors and gilded ceilings.*

re·spond /£rɪ'spɒnd, $-'spɑːnd/ *v* to say or do something as a reaction to something that has been said or done • *To every question the police officer asked, he responded "I don't know."* [+ clause] • *When the tax office wrote to me demanding unpaid income tax, I responded* **that** *I had been working abroad since 1988.* [+ *that* clause] • *I asked her what the time was, but she didn't respond.* [I] • *He responded* **by** *marching off and slamming the door behind him.* [I] • *How did she respond* **to** *the news?* [I] • *The car suddenly stopped responding* **to** *the controls.* [I] • *Many people wonder why the international community cannot respond* **to** *the current crisis in a unified way.* [I] • *The government has responded* **to** *public pressure* **by** *abolishing the new tax.* [I] • *She responded* **to** *his suggestion* **with** *a stony silence.* [I] • *The police respond* **to** (= arrive and are ready to deal with) *emergencies in just a few minutes.* [I] • If a disease from which a person is suffering responds **to** treatment, the treatment has begun to cure the disease: *Her cancer has responded to treatment.* [I] ○ *For patients who do not respond to drug treatment, surgery is a possible option.* [I]

re·spon·dent /£rɪ'spɒn·dənt, $-'spɑːn-/ *n* [C] • *(specialized)* A respondent is a person who answers a request for information: *In a recent opinion poll, a majority of respondents were against nuclear weapons.* • *(law)* In a **civil law** case (= a case which deals with matters that are not criminal), the respondent is the person against whom a PETITION (= a formal letter to the court requesting a particular action) is made, esp. in a divorce case: *She divorced the respondent on the grounds of unreasonable behaviour.* Compare CO-RESPONDENT.

re·sponse /£rɪ'spɒnts, $-'spɑːnts/ *n* • A response is an answer or reaction: *Responses* **to** *our advertisement have been disappointing.* [C] ○ *The appeal for help produced/elicited a positive response worldwide.* [C] ○ *Her proposals have met with an enthusiastic response.* [C] ○ *His comments provoked an angry response from the government.* [C] ○ *I looked in her face for some response, but she just stared at me blankly.* [U] ○ *Management have granted a 10% pay rise* **in** *response* **to** *union pressure.* [U] ○ *The company has changed some of its working practices* **in** *response* **to** *criticism by government inspectors.* [U] • In some religious ceremonies, a response is any of those parts sung or said by the people in answer to the parts said or sung by the priest. [C]

re·spon·sive /£rɪ'spɒnt·sɪv, $-'spɑːnt-/ *adj* • Responsive means making a positive and quick reaction to something or someone: *The new car has a very responsive engine.* ○ *We had a wonderfully responsive audience for last night's performance.* ○ *She wasn't responsive* **to** *questioning.* ○ *The disease has proved responsive* **to** *the new treatment.*

re·spon·sive·ly /£rɪ'spɒnt·sɪv·li, $-'spɑːnt-/ *adv*

re·spon·sive·ness /£rɪ'spɒnt·sɪv·nəs, $-'spɑːnt-/ *n* [U] • *The audience's responsiveness* (= The degree to which people respond) *is a key part of any performance.* • *The disease causes a loss of normal emotional responsiveness in the sufferer* (= a loss in their ability to respond).

re·spon·si·ble BLAME /£rɪ'spɒnt·sɪ·bl̩, $-'spɑːnt-/ *adj* having done a particular action or caused a particular situation, esp. a harmful or unpleasant one • *Who is responsible* **for** *this terrible mess?* • *He* **holds** *last month's bad weather responsible* (= He blames the bad weather) **for** *the crop failure.* • *I will* **hold** *you personally responsible* (= I will blame you) *if anything goes wrong in this project.* • *The judge agreed that the defendant had been depressed and was therefore not fully responsible* **for** *her actions* (= she was not in control of herself and so could not be completely blamed for her actions).

re·spon·si·bil·i·ty /£rɪˌspɒnt·sɪ'bɪl·ɪ·ti, $-ˌspɑːnt·sə'bɪl·ə·t̬i/ *n* [U] • *Terrorists have* **claimed** *responsibility* **for** (= stated that they caused) *yesterday's bomb attack.* • *The minister* **took/accepted** *full responsibility* **for** (= admitted that he was to blame for) *the disaster and resigned.*

re·spon·si·ble DUTY /£rɪ'spɒnt·sɪ·bl̩, $-'spɑːnt-/ *adj* having control and authority over something or someone and the duty of taking care of it or them • *Paul is directly responsible* **for** *the efficient running of the office.* • *Her department is responsible* **for** *overseeing the councils.* • *In Australia, the Prime Minister and the Cabinet of Ministers are responsible* **to** (=are controlled by) *the House of Representatives.*

re·spon·si·bil·i·ty /£rɪˌspɒnt·sɪ'bɪl·ɪ·ti, $-ˌspɑːnt·sə'bɪl·ə·ţi/ *n* • A responsibility is a duty that you have because of your job or position: *She takes her responsibilities as a nurse very seriously.* [C] ○ *My responsibility is* **to** *collect the rent.* [C + *to* infinitive] ○ *It's her responsibility* **to** *ensure the project finishes on time.* [C + *to* infinitive] • If you have a responsibility **to** someone who is in a position of authority over you, it is your duty to work for them or help them: *The company says it cannot cut its prices any more because it has a responsibility to its shareholders.* [C] • If you **have** responsibility **for** someone or something, you have authority over them and it is your duty to make sure that certain things are done: *Who* **has** *responsibility here?* [U] ○ *You* **have** *responsibility* **for** *clearing up the room after the class.* [U]

re·spon·si·ble GOOD JUDGMENT /£rɪ'spɒnt·sɪ·bl̩, $-'spɑːnt-/ *adj* having good judgment and the ability to act correctly and make decisions on your own • *Is he responsible enough for this job?* • *He wrote her a reference saying she was a hardworking and responsible employee.* • *Let's be calm about the situation and try to behave/act like responsible adults.* • *Many big companies that have been destroying the environment are now becoming more responsible* **about** *the way they operate.* • A responsible job or position is one which involves making important decisions or doing important things.

re·spon·si·bly /£rɪ'spɒnt·sɪ·bli, $-'spɑːnt-/ *adv* • *When he saw the crash, the young boy acted very responsibly and called the police.*

re·spon·si·bil·i·ty /£rɪˌspɒnt·sɪ'bɪl·ɪ·ti, $-ˌspɑːnt·sə'bɪl·ə·ţi/ *n* [U] • *He has no sense of responsibility.* • *The job* **carries** *a lot of responsibility* (=It involves making important decisions) *and is open to applicants with at least three years relevant experience.* • *(fml) She* **acted on** *her* **own** *responsibility* (=She made the decision to act).

rest *(obj)* STOP /rest/ *v* to (cause to) stop doing a particular activity or stop being active for a period of time in order to relax and get back your strength • *He looked away from the computer screen to rest his eyes.* [T] • *She invited him in to rest his tired feet.* [T] • *I'm exhausted – let's rest for a few minutes.* [I] • *The doctor told him that he should rest for a few days.* [I] • *She promised that she would not rest* (=would not stop looking) *until the murderer of her son was caught and imprisoned.* [I] • *(Am) Why don't you take a nap to rest* **up** (=relax in order to have strength) **for** *the party?* [I] • *(infml)* An actor who is resting does not have any work. It is another way of saying unemployed: *Over 90% of professional actors are resting at any given time.* [I] • If you **let** a subject rest, you do not talk about it or mention it: *After he had told his friends he was writing a novel, they wouldn't let the subject rest.* [I] ○ *(infml) "Why won't you let me come with you?" "Oh, let it rest* (=Do not mention it)*!"* [I] • **Rest in peace** (*abbreviation* **RIP**) is often written on a stone put above a person's GRAVE (=a place where a dead person is buried), or is said of a person who has recently died. • If you say about someone who has died 'may he/she/they rest in peace' you are showing respect for them and expressing the hope that their spirit has finally found peace. • A **resting-place** is a place where someone is buried: *His* **last/final** *resting-place was in the churchyard in the village in which he was born.* • Ⓘ Ⓟ

rest /rest/ *n* • A rest is a period of time in which you relax and are not active: *After five miles, my legs were desperate for a rest.* [C] ○ *After they had carried the piano up the stairs, they stopped for a rest* **from** *their exertions.* [C] • Rest is the state in which you are relaxing and not doing anything active: *The doctor prescribed some pills and told her to get a week's rest.* [U] ○ *What you need is a good/decent night's rest* (=enough sleep). [U] ○ *The boss* **gives us no** *rest* (=keeps us working all the time). [U] • *(specialized)* In music, a rest is a period of silence between notes, or a symbol which represents this. [C] • **At rest** means not doing anything active or not moving: *Her heartbeat is only 55 at rest* (=when she is not moving). • If someone is **at rest**, it is another way of saying that they are dead: *Your father was a very troubled man, but he's at rest now.* • If something that is moving **comes to rest** in a particular place, it stops in that place: *The car hit the kerb, rolled over and came to rest in a ditch.* • *(infml)* If you tell someone who has mentioned something annoying to **give it a rest**, you mean you do not want them to talk about it: *I wanted to tell her about my motorbike, but she just said "Give it a rest!"* • A **rest cure** is a long period of relaxation which people take as part of their medical treatment to cure anxiety or tiredness. • A **rest home** is a place where old people live and are cared for. • A **rest room** is a room in a public building in which there are toilets. • *(Am)* A **Rest stop** (*Aus* **Rest area**) is a LAY-BY ROAD. • PIC〉 **Road**

rest·ed /'res·tɪd/ *adj* • If you feel rested, you feel healthy and active after a period of relaxation: *I came back from my trip to California feeling rested and rejuvenated.*

rest·ful /'rest·fᵊl/ *adj* • Something that is restful produces a feeling of calmness and relaxation: *I love the restful sound of the wind in the trees.*

rest·ful·ly /'rest·fᵊl·i/ *adv*

rest·ful·ness /'rest·fᵊl·nəs/ *n* [U] • *She always thought of the house as being a place of great peace and restfulness* (=calmness and relaxation).

rest·less /'rest·ləs/ *adj* • If someone is restless, they are unwilling or unable to stay still or be happy because they are worried or bored: *He's a restless type – he never stays in one country for long.* ○ *I get restless on Sundays when nothing happens and all the shops are closed.* ○ *She spent a restless night* (=She did not sleep well), *tossing and turning with worry.*

rest·less·ly /'rest·lə·sli/ *adv* • *She shifted restlessly in her chair.* • *He moved about restlessly, lighting a cigarette with fumbling fingers and then stubbing it out.*

rest·less·ness /'rest·lə·snəs/ *n* [U] • *Symptoms of the disease include periods of restlessness and exaggerated movements of the arms and legs.* • *The children showed signs of growing restlessness as they waited for their food to arrive.*

rest REMAIN /rest/ *v* [I] *fml* to remain in a particular place or state, or remain under the control of a particular person or organization • *We must talk to the council about the problem – the matter cannot be allowed to rest here* (=further action must be taken). • *The authority to call an emergency meeting rests* **with** *the president* (=The president is the only person who has the authority to do this). • *It rests* **on** *her to decide* (=She must decide) *whether to press charges against him.* • *(fml or literary)* If your eyes rest **on** a particular object or person, you look at it or them for a long time: *As she looked around her, her eyes rested on a small wooden box at the back of the shop.* • If you tell someone to **rest easy/rest assured**, you are telling them not to worry and that you are in control of the situation: *I told her to rest easy and that I would take care of everything.* ○ *"Rest assured, Mrs. Cooper" said the police officer. "We will find your son for you."* • *(law)* In a law court, when lawyers say **I rest my case/my case rests**, they mean that they have finished the explanation of their case. • Ⓘ Ⓟ

rest *(obj)* SUPPORT /rest/ *v* [always + adv/prep] to lie or lean on something, or to put (something) on something else so that its weight is supported • *She rested her head* **on** *my shoulder.* [T] • *The bicycle was resting* **against** *the wall.* [I] • *The palaces of Venice are resting* **on** (=supported by) *a marsh.* [I] • *(fig.) Our success rests* **on** (=depends on) *an increase in sales.* [I] • *(fig.) Our hopes rest* **with** (=depend on) *you.* [I] • If someone **rests on** their **laurels**, they are satisfied with their achievements and do not make an effort to do anything else: *Just because you've got your degree doesn't mean you can rest on your laurels.* • If an idea or belief **rests on** something, it is based on that thing or it depends on that thing in order to be thought true or to exist: *Christianity rests on the belief that Jesus was the son of God.* ○ *The prosecution's case rests almost entirely on the evidence of one witness who is a convicted criminal.* • Ⓘ Ⓟ

rest /rest/ *n* [C] • A rest is an object which supports the weight of something: *Each seat has a headrest and armrests for your comfort.* ○ *I used a pile of books as a rest* **for** *my telescope.*

rest OTHER PART /rest/ *n* [U + sing/pl v] **the rest** the other things, people or parts that are left or that have not been mentioned • *I've got two bright students, but the rest are average.* • *I'll keep a third of the money and the rest is for you.* • *Have you got anything planned for the rest* **of** *the day?* • *He spent the rest* **of** *his life regretting that he hadn't married her.* • **For the rest** is used when introducing a phrase to mean that you have already mentioned the important parts and you now want to mention the other less important parts: *The salary in my new job is great, but (as) for the rest, I'm not impressed.* • *(infml)* **(And) all the**

rest is used at the end of a phrase or list to refer to other things or people that belong to the same set or group and that you have not had time to mention: *Bob, June and Alison and all the rest are coming to dinner tonight.* • *The Beatles had their first hit record in 1962 and* **the rest is history** (= everything which has happened to them since them is well known). • *"The rest is silence"* (Prince Hamlet's dying words in Shakespeare's Hamlet 5.2) • Ⓘ Ⓟ

re·state *obj* /ˌriːˈsteɪt/ *v* [T] to say (something) again or in a different way • *He restated his belief that sanctions should be allowed sufficient time to work.*

re·state·ment /ˌriːˈsteɪt·mənt/ *n* • *Her recent speech was merely a restatement of her widely publicised views.* [C] • *The meeting involved much discussion of policy and restatement of the party's aims.* [U]

res·tau·rant /£ˈres·tᵊr·ɑ̃ː, £-ɒnt, $-tə·rɑːnt/ *n* [C] a place where meals are prepared and served to customers • *(Br)* A **restaurant car** (*esp. Am and Aus* **dining car**) is a carriage of a train in which passengers are served meals. • Ⓣ

res·tau·ra·teur /£ˌres·tɒr·əˈtɜːʳ, $-tɚ·əˈtɜːr/ *n* [C] *fml* • A restaurateur is a person who owns and manages a restaurant.

res·ti·tu·tion /£ˌres·tɪˈtjuː·ʃᵊn, $-ˈtuː-/ *n* [U] *fml* the return of items stolen or lost, or *(law)* payment made for damage or loss • *The government is now demanding the restitution of its ancient treasures that were removed from the country in the 16th century.* • *(law) The defendant presented a cheque for $80 000 to the court as restitution* **to** *her former employer.* • *(law) The chemicals company has promised to* **make** *full restitution* **to** *the victims* **for** *the injury to their health.*

res·tive /£ˈres·tɪv, $-t̬ɪv/ *adj* unwilling to be controlled or be patient • *The dogs were feeling restive because they sensed a storm was in the air.* • *The audience was becoming restive as they waited for the performance to begin.*

res·tive·ly /£ˈres·tɪv·li, $-t̬ɪv-/ *adv* • *I stirred restively in my seat, wishing the journey would end.*

res·tive·ness /£ˈres·tɪv·nəs, $-t̬ɪv-/ *n* [U] • *There were increasing signs of restiveness within the party.*

re·store *obj* /£rɪˈstɔːʳ, $-ˈstɔːr/ *v* [T] to return (something or someone) to an earlier condition or position • *The badly neglected furniture and paintings have all been carefully restored.* • *He buys old cars and restores them* **to** *their original condition.* • *After a week in bed, she was fully restored* **to** *health* (= she felt healthy again). • *The former leader was today restored* **to** *power in the first free elections for twenty years.* • If you restore a quality or ability that someone has not had for a long time, you make it possible for them to have that quality or ability again: *Doctors have restored his sight.* ○ *The government is trying to restore public confidence* (= make the public have confidence again) *in its management of the economy.* • If you restore something that has been absent for a period of time, you bring it back: *Some people are in favour of restoring capital punishment for murderers.* • *(fml)* If something that has been lost or stolen is restored **to** its owner, it is given back to that person: *The painting was restored to its rightful owner.*

res·to·ra·tion /£ˌres·tᵊrˈeɪ·ʃᵊn, $-təˈreɪ-/ *n* • The restoration of something is the act or process of returning it to its earlier condition or position: *The first task following the disaster was the restoration of clean water supplies.* [U] ○ *Restoration work on the Sistine Chapel ceiling is now complete.* [U] ○ *A large majority of the population is demanding the restoration of the former government.* [U] ○ *She is an expert in 17th-century paintings and has done a number of first-class restorations.* [C] • **The Restoration** is the event in British history when Charles II was made King of Britain in 1660 after a period in which there was no king or queen. • Restoration refers to the style of art that was popular during the period in which Charles II was king: *Restoration comedy/architecture/art*

res·tor·a·tive /£rɪˈstɒr·ə·tɪv, $-ˈstɔːr·ə·t̬ɪv/ *n* [C] *fml* • A restorative is something which makes you feel better or more energetic if you are feeling tired or ill: *After a hard day at the office, a hot bath is a welcome restorative.* ○ *Ginseng has been used for over 5000 years in the Orient as a restorative and preventive remedy.*

re·stor·er /£rɪˈstɔː·rəʳ, $-ˈstɔːr·ɚ/ *n* [C] • A restorer is a person who restores buildings, furniture or paintings to their original condition: *She's a furniture restorer.*

re·strain *obj* /rɪˈstreɪn/ *v* [T] to control the actions or behaviour of (someone) by force, esp. in order to stop them from doing something, or to limit the growth or force of (something) • *When he started fighting, it took four police officers to restrain him.* • *One of the patients became violent and had to be physically restrained by two of the nurses.* • *You should try to restrain your ambitions and be more realistic.* • *The five members of the UN Security Council have agreed on a set of guidelines designed to restrain arms sales.* • *The report states that the growth in car ownership could be restrained by increasing taxes.* • *She was so angry that she could hardly restrain* **herself**. • *I had to restrain* **myself from** *laughing at his hideous tie.* • *He was wild and unpredictable, but she acted as a restraining influence on him.* • *(law)* A **restraining order** is a written instruction made by a court which forbids a particular action until a decision has been made by the judge about the matter: *She obtained a restraining order forbidding her partner from seeing their two children.*

re·strained /rɪˈstreɪnd/ *adj* • Someone who is restrained acts in a calm and controlled way: *She was restrained, despite the anger that welled up inside her.* • Something that is restrained is controlled: *The tone of his poetry is restrained and unemotional.* ○ *Banks and building societies say that they have now adopted a more restrained policy on mortgage lending.*

re·straint /rɪˈstreɪnt/ *n* • Restraint is calm and controlled behaviour: *He showed admirable restraint, and refused to be provoked.* [U] ○ *The federal government appealed for restraint, insisting the crisis could be resolved without the use of force.* [U] ○ *The security forces* **exercised** (= used) *great restraint by not responding to hostile attacks or threats.* [U] • A restraint is something which limits the freedom of someone or something, or which prevents something from growing or increasing: *Government spending restraints mean that the plans to develop the harbour area have had to be delayed for several years.* [C] ○ *The political reforms have been accompanied by an easing of restraints* **on** *the press.* [C] ○ *A lack of space is the main restraint* **on** *the firm's expansion plans.* [C] ○ *During the recession, the government opted for a policy of pay/wage restraint rather than a reduction in public investment.* [U] • If a violent person is **kept/placed under restraint**, they are kept in a way that prevents them from moving freely: *The two prisoners were kept under restraint while they were transported between prisons.*

re·strict *obj* /rɪˈstrɪkt/ *v* [T] to limit the movements or actions of (someone), or to limit (something) and reduce its size or prevent it from increasing • *The government has restricted freedom of movement into and out of the country.* • *Congress is considering measures to restrict the sale of cigarettes.* • *This new law restricts freedom of speech.* • *The growth of television exports is restricted* **to** *10% a year.* • If you restrict yourself **to** one particular thing or activity, you limit yourself to that thing or activity: *When I'm driving, I restrict* **myself** *to one glass of wine.*

re·strict·ed /£rɪˈstrɪk·tɪd, $-t̬ɪd/ *adj* • Something that is restricted is limited: *Building in this area of town is restricted.* ○ *The seats were cheap because our view of the stage was restricted.* ○ *It's a cheap restaurant and the choice is rather restricted* (= small). • *Membership is restricted* **to** (= It is only for) *chief executive officers.* • *In the state games she will be competing only in the swimming, because athletes are restricted* **to** *one sport.* • A restricted **area** is one which you need official permission to enter because the authorities want to keep it secret or because it is considered dangerous. • A restricted **document** is one which you need official permission to read because the authorities want to keep it secret.

re·stric·tion /rɪˈstrɪk·ʃᵊn/ *n* • *import/export/currency restrictions* [C] • *He travelled everywhere by bicycle because of the wartime restriction* **on** *the use of cars.* [C] • *At the turn of the century, Congress* **imposed/placed** *a height restriction of 13 stories* **on** *all buildings in Washington.* [C] • *The president has urged other countries to* **lift** *the trade restrictions.* [C] • *The council has introduced* **speed** *restrictions in residential areas to try to prevent road accidents.* [C] • *The government tried to control the population through restriction* **on** *emigration.* [U]

re·stric·tive /£rɪˈstrɪk·tɪv, $-t̬ɪv/ *adj* • *(often disapproving)* Something that is restrictive limits the freedom of someone or prevents something from growing: *He is self-employed because he finds working for other people too restrictive.* ○ *The college is not able to expand because of restrictive planning laws.* • *(Br specialized)* In industry or business, a **restrictive practice** is an action taken by a union which limits the freedom of workers or employers:

Management has accused the union of restrictive practices. • *(specialized)* In business, **restrictive trade practices** are agreements between companies to control prices or the areas in which goods are sold, preventing fair competition.

re·struc·ture *obj* /£ˌriːˈstrʌk·tʃəʳ, $-tʃɚ/ *v* [T] to organize (a company, business or system) in a new way to make it operate more effectively • *A new managing director has been appointed to restructure the company.* • *The government restructured the coal industry before selling it to private owners.*

re·struc·tur·ing /£ˌriːˈstrʌk·tʃᵊr·ɪŋ, $-tʃɚ·ɪŋ/ *n* • *The company has undergone restructuring and 1500 workers have lost their jobs.* [U] • *The industry has split off its two main businesses into two new companies as part of a major restructuring.* [C] • *A restructuring* **plan** *involving a 12% reduction in costs will be put in place next year.*

re·sult /rɪˈzʌlt/ *n* something that happens or exists because of something else • *The road has been widened, but* **the** *result is just more traffic.* [U] • *The records show that her arrest was the result* **of** *questionable legal practices.* [U] • *His broken leg is the* **direct** *result* **of** *his own carelessness.* [U] • *Profits have declined* **as a result of** (= because of) *the recent drop in sales.* [U] • *Compensation will be paid to people who have suffered physical damage* **as a result of** *vaccination.* [U] • *Both parents were working,* **with the** *result* **that** (= this meant that) *their children were cared for by their grandparents.* [U] • *We worked for hours with no result/ without result.* [U] • *I tried to repaint the kitchen walls* **with** *disastrous results.* [C] • *We began this project without knowing what the* **end** (= final) *result would be.* [U] • *The results of* (= The answers given in) *the opinion poll showed that most women supported this action.* [C] • *To ensure* **good/the best** *results, use Italian tomatoes and fresh basil.* [C] • Results are good or pleasing effects: *We've spent a lot of money on advertising and we're beginning to see the results.* [C] ○ *She's an excellent coach who knows how to* **get** (= obtain) *results.* [C] • The results of something is also the success or failure of the people involved in a competitive activity, such as a sports competition or an election: *The results of the local elections have been a disaster for the Conservatives.* [C] ○ *The football results are printed in the back of the newspaper.* [C] ○ *We were expecting to win, so a draw was a disappointing result for us.* [C] ○ *(Br infml) The team needs a result* (= a win) *to go through to the semi-finals.* [C] • Your results are the marks you have got after you have taken an exam: *I finished my exams yesterday, but I won't know the results until August.* [C] • In mathematics, a result is the answer to a calculation: *We used different methods to solve the calculation, but we both got the same result.* [C]

re·sult /rɪˈzʌlt/ *v* [I] • *Teachers were not fully prepared for the major changes in the exam system, and chaos resulted* (= was caused). • If something results **from** an event or activity, it is caused by that event or activity: *His difficulty in walking results* **from** *a childhood illness.* • If something results **in** a particular situation, it causes that situation to happen: *The fire resulted* **in** *damage to their property.* ○ *Environmental pollution is resulting* **in** *the forests* **dying**.

re·sult·ing /rɪˈzʌl·tɪŋ/, *fml* **re·sul·tant** /rɪˈzʌl·tᵊnt/ *adj* [before n; not gradable] • A resulting situation is one which is caused by something which you have just mentioned: *The tape was left near a magnetic source, and the resulting damage was considerable.* ○ *The economy has been hit by high inflation and its resultant problems.*

re·sume *(obj)* /£rɪˈzjuːm, $-ˈzuːm/ *v fml* to start again after a pause • *The wind died down for an hour but then resumed its assault.* [T] • *Airline services will be disrupted during the expansion of the airport, but normal services will be resumed in the spring.* [T] • *She took a break from her work to make herself some coffee and then resumed* (= began working again) *a few minutes later.* [I] • *He stopped to take a sip of water and then resumed speak***ing**. [+ v-*ing*] • If you resume a place or position which you have left for a period of time, you return to it: *The second half of the performance will begin in two minutes, and you are kindly asked to resume your seats.* [T] ○ *He resumed his advisory role for the presidential elections, but never returned to full-time government service.* [T] • Ⓕ Ⓢ

re·sump·tion /rɪˈzʌmp·ʃᵊn/ *n* [U] • *Congress has vetoed the resumption of military aid to the rebels.* • *The president called for an immediate ceasefire and* **a** *resumption of negotiations between the two sides.*

ré·sum·é /£rɪˈzjuːm, $-ˈzuːm/ *n* [C] a short statement of the important details of something • *She gave us a brief résumé* **of** *the history of the project so far.* • Résumé is also *Am and Aus for* CV: *She sent her résumé to fifty companies, but didn't even get an interview.*

re·sur·face *obj* COVER /£ˌriːˈsɜː·fɪs, $-ˈsɜːr-/ *v* [T] to put a new surface on (a road) • *Drivers will experience delays on the road while stretches of it are being resurfaced.*

re·sur·face APPEAR /£ˌriːˈsɜː·fɪs, $-ˈsɜːr-/ *v* [I] to rise to the surface of the water again • *When the divers did not resurface after an hour, three members of the crew dived down to look for them.* • If an object resurfaces, it appears again after it has been lost or stolen: *She asked the police to contact her if any of the paintings that had been stolen resurfaced.* • If a memory resurfaces, you remember it again after you had forgotten about it: *Memories of his childhood resurfaced when he saw the photographs.* • If a person resurfaces after they have been busy or absent for a period of time, they start seeing their friends again or start working again: *Jill resurfaced last week, after spending the past few months doing research in the library.* ○ *Three months after his catering business collapsed, he resurfaced as a financial consultant.*

re·sur·gence /£rɪˈsɜː·dʒᵊnts, $-ˈsɜːr-/ *n* [U] *fml* a new increase of activity or interest in a particular subject or idea which had been forgotten for some time • *The creation of independent states has led to* **a** *resurgence* **of** *nationalism.* • *Law-enforcement officials say that the past few months have seen* **a** *resurgence* **in** *heroin use.* • *The band enjoyed* **a** *resurgence* **in** *popularity when a compilation of their greatest hits was released last year.*

re·sur·gent /£rɪˈsɜː·dʒᵊnt, $-ˈsɜːr-/ *adj fml* • Resurgent means increasing or becoming popular again: *Many people have been critical of the resurgent militarism in the country.* ○ *In his article, he talks of the resurgent fundamentalism in many religious movements.*

res·ur·rect *obj* /£ˌrez·ᵊrˈekt, $-əˈrekt/ *v* [T] to bring back (someone) to life, or bring back (something) into use or existence that had disappeared • *Almost all Christians believe that Jesus was resurrected* **from** *the dead.* • *With the recent change in leadership, several members of the party have resurrected the idea of constitutional change.* • *His aim is to resurrect the kind of approach to furniture making that was pioneered in the 1950s.* • *Over the past few months, she has been busily trying to resurrect* (= start again) *her career in Hollywood.*

res·ur·rec·tion /£ˌrez·ᵊrˈek·ʃᵊn, $-əˈrek-/ *n* [U] • *The court has permitted the resurrection of these laws, if they meet certain procedural requirements.* • *His victory in this week's final represents the triumphant resurrection of a career which last year looked as though it had finished.* • In the Christian religion, **the Resurrection** is Jesus Christ's return to life on the third day after his death, or the return of all people to life at the end of the world: *The Resurrection is one of the most crucial doctrines of Christianity.*

re·sus·ci·tate *obj* /rɪˈsʌs·ɪ·teɪt/ *v* [T] to bring (someone) back to life or consciousness • *Her heart had stopped, but the doctors successfully resuscitated her.* • If you resuscitate something that has been forgotten or that is in a bad situation, you bring it back to the attention of the public or you help to improve it: *The theatre group has won praise for resuscitating several lesser-known works of world literature.*

re·sus·ci·ta·tion /rɪˌsʌs·ɪˈteɪ·ʃᵊn/ *n* [U] • *The patient suffered a cardiac arrest and died, despite an attempt at resuscitation.* • *When he stopped breathing, one of the paramedics tried* **mouth-to-mouth** *resuscitation* (= breathing into his mouth to start his breathing again). • *(fig.) The prime minister said that small businesses would play a full part in the resuscitation of the economy* (= in helping the economy to grow). • PIC **Emergency services**

re·tail /ˈriː·teɪl/ *n* [U], *adj* [not gradable] (relating to) the activity of selling goods to the public, usually in small quantities • *The job is open to applicants with over two years' experience in retail.* • *The clothing company has six retail* **outlets** (= shops) *in south-eastern Australia.* • *This price represents a saving of $13 off the manufacturer's recommended retail* **price**. • *Retail* **sales** *were lower than expected this year.* • *(Br)* The **retail price index** (*abbreviation* **RPI**, *Am and Aus* **cost of living index**, *Am and Aus also* **consumer price index**) is a measurement of the changes in the cost of basic goods and services: *The retail price index is used as the main indicator of inflation.* • Compare WHOLESALE SELLING.

re·tail *(obj)* /ˈriː·teɪl/ *v* • To retail is to sell goods to the public in shops or by post: *The company makes and retails* *moderately priced sportswear.* [T] ○ *This model of computer is retailing* **at/for** (= being sold for) *£650.* [I]

re·tail /ˈriː·teɪl/ *adv* [not gradable] ● *It's much cheaper to buy wholesale than retail.*

re·tail·er /£ˈriː·teɪ·ləʳ, $-lɚ/ *n* [C] ● A retailer is a person or business that sells goods to the public: *Retailers must be sensitive to the needs of their customers.* ○ *The big electronics retailer said that its profits were up by 24% this year.*

re·tain *obj* /rɪˈteɪn/ *v* [T] *slightly fml* to keep or continue to have (something) ● *She has lost her battle to retain control of the company.* ● *He managed to retain his dignity throughout the performance.* ● *She succeeded in retaining her lead in the second half of the race.* ● *He is hoping to retain his title for the 800m* (= to win the race again) *in the Commonwealth Games.* ● *The British Library retains the right to a copy of every new book published in the UK.* ● *I have a good memory and am able to retain* (= remember) *facts easily.* ● *The wall of this dam retains* (= holds in place) *5 000 000 cubic metres of water.* ● If a substance retains something, such as heat or water, it continues to hold or contain it: *The sea retains the sun's warmth longer than the land.* ● *(law)* To retain a lawyer is to obtain their services by paying them in advance.

re·tain·er /£rɪˈteɪ·nəʳ, $-nɚ/ *n* [C] ● *(specialized)* A retainer is an amount of money which you pay to someone in advance so that they will work for you when you need them to: *I pay my lawyer a retainer every month so that she's always available if I need her.* ● *(old use)* A retainer is a servant who has usually been with the same family for a long time.

re·ten·tion /rɪˈten·tʃᵊn/ *n* [U] *slightly fml* ● Retention is the continued use, existence or possession of something or someone: *The retention of old technology has slowed the company's growth.* ○ *Two influential senators have argued for the retention of the unpopular tax.* ○ *To aid staff recruitment and retention, the education authority has increased the number of nursery places available for teachers' children.* ○ *The sea's retention of heat is greater than the land's.* ○ *She suffers from* **water retention** (= the continued presence of too much water in the body).

re·ten·tive /£rɪˈten·tɪv, $-t̬ɪv/ *adj slightly fml* ● *She has a retentive* **memory** (= She is able to remember things easily).

re·take *obj* /ˌriːˈteɪk/ *v* [T] to take (something) again ● If you retake an exam, you take it again because you failed it the first time: *15% of first year students fail their exams and have to retake them.* ● If you retake a place or position that you have lost, you take it into your possession again, often by force: *In the battle to retake the village, over 150 soldiers were killed.* ○ *She was pushed back into third place but fought back to retake the lead in the closing laps of the race.*

re·take /ˈriː·teɪk/ *n* [C] ● A retake is an exam which you take again because you failed it the first time: *I'm going back to college in September and doing my retakes next summer.* ● A retake is also a part of a film that must be photographed again to change or improve it: *It took seven retakes to get the scene exactly right.*

re·tal·i·ate /rɪˈtæl·i·eɪt/ *v* [I] to hurt someone or do something harmful to them because they have done or said something harmful to you ● *Her mother taught her never to retaliate if someone insulted her, as it would only make the situation worse.* ● *The demonstrators threw rocks at the police, who retaliated* **by** *firing blanks into the crowd.* ● *She retaliated* **to** *his insults* **by** *slapping his face.* ● *The terrorists retaliated* **against** *the government* **with** *a bomb attack.*

re·tal·i·a·tion /rɪˌtæl·iˈeɪ·ʃᵊn/ *n* [U] ● *The uprising was followed by massive retaliation from the authorities, who arrested and imprisoned anyone suspected of being involved in it.* ● *The bomb attack was* **in** *retaliation* **for** *the recent arrest of two well-known members of the terrorist organization.*

re·tal·i·a·to·ry /£rɪˈtæl·i·ə·tri, $-tɔːr·i/ *adj* [not gradable] ● A retaliatory action is a harmful one against someone who has done something to harm you: *He urged people not to resort to retaliatory violence after one of the worst terrorist attacks in the country's history.*

re·tard *obj* /£rɪˈtɑːd, $-ˈtɑːrd/ *v* [T] *fml or specialized* to make (something) slower ● *Icy roads retarded their progress through the mountains.* ● *A rise in interest rates would severely retard economic growth.*

re·tar·dant /£rɪˈtɑː·dᵊnt, $-ˈtɑːr-/ *n, adj* ● *fire/flame retardant furniture* (= furniture that does not burn easily) ● *Pot plants are commonly treated with (a) growth retardant* (= substance that slows growth) *so that they retain their shape.* [C/U]

re·tard /£ˈriː·tɑːd, $-tɑːrd/ *n* [C] *Am taboo slang* ● *I'm not playing with him, he's a total retard* (= stupid or mentally slow person). ● *Get out of my way, retard!* [as form of address] ● This word is considered offensive by many people.

re·tard·ed /£rɪˈtɑː·dɪd, $-ˈtɑːr-/ *adj* ● *(dated)* A person who is retarded has had a slower mental development than other people of the same age. This word is considered offensive by most people: *mentally/emotionally retarded*

re·tard·ed /£rɪˈtɑː·dɪd, $-ˈtɑːr-/ *pl n* ● **The** retarded are people with slow mental development: *The program offers long-term care for the elderly and intermediate care for the* **mentally** *retarded.*

re·tar·da·tion /£ˌriː·tɑːˈdeɪ·ʃᵊn, $-tɑːr-/ *n* [U] *fml* ● Retardation is the process of making something happen or develop more slowly than it should: *The drugs taken by the women while they were pregnant caused growth retardation in their children.* ● **Mental** retardation is slow mental development: *The principles of care for people with mental retardation have undergone radical changes over the past 20 years.* ● Retarded and retardation are no longer used as specialized terms in the care of people with slow mental development, and some people find them offensive.

retch /retʃ/ *v* [I] to react in a way as if you are vomiting ● *The sight of blood makes him retch.*

retd *adj* [after n; not gradable] *abbreviation for* **retired**, see at RETIRE [STOP WORKING] ● Retd is written after someone's name to show that they are no longer in one of the armed forces: *The meeting will be chaired by Colonel E. Smith (retd).*

re·ten·tion /rɪˈten·tʃᵊn/ *n* [U] See at RETAIN

re·think *(obj)* /ˌriːˈθɪŋk/ *v past* **rethought** /£ˌriːˈθɔːt, $-ˈθɑːt/ to think again about (a plan, idea or system) in order to change or improve it ● *Her family's disapproval made her rethink her plans.* [T] ● *I don't think we should go ahead with this idea – it's far better to wait and rethink.* [I] ● *The European Commission is having to rethink* **how** *it can maintain farmers' incomes while cutting costs and excess production.* [+ *wh*-word]

re·think /ˈriː·θɪŋk/ *n* [U] ● *This new information means we should have* **a** *rethink.*

ret·i·cent /£ˈret·ɪ·sᵊnt, $ˈret̬·ə-/ *adj fml* unwilling to speak about your thoughts or feelings ● *She is a reticent woman.* ● *He is very reticent* **about** *his past.* ● *Most of the students were reticent* **about** *answering questions, but were quite happy to get on with their own writing.*

ret·i·cent·ly /£ˈret·ɪ·sᵊnt·li, $ˈret̬·ə-/ *adv fml*

ret·i·cence /£ˈret·ɪ·sᵊnts, $ˈret̬·ə-/ *n* [U] *fml* ● *His reticence* **about** *his past made them very suspicious.*

re·tic·u·la·tion /rɪˌtɪk·jʊˈleɪ·ʃᵊn/ *n* [C] *specialized* a net-like pattern of lines and squares, or a structure of pipes or wires ● *They installed a water reticulation in the gardens so that the huge area could be watered easily.*

re·ti·cu·lat·ed /£rɪˈtɪk·jʊ·leɪ·tɪd, $-t̬ɪd/, **re·ti·cu·late** /£rɪˈtɪk·jʊ·lət, $-lɪt/ *adj* [not gradable] *specialized* ● *The plant has broad leaves with a reticulate vein structure.*

ret·i·na /£ˈret·ɪ·nə, $-ᵊn·ə/ *n* [C] *pl* **retinas** or **retinae** /£ˈret·ɪ·niː, $-ᵊn·iː/ the area at the back of the eye that receives light and sends pictures of what the eye sees to the brain ● *If a person is short-sighted, images are focused in front of their retina, and if a person is long-sighted, images are focused beyond their retina.*

ret·i·nal /£ˈret·ɪ·nəl, $-ᵊn·ᵊl/ *adj* [not gradable] ● *The disease can result in retinal damage and the loss of vision.*

ret·i·nue /£ˈret·ɪ·njuː, $-ᵊn·uː/ *n* [C + sing/pl v] a group of helpers and followers who travel with an important person ● *When she travels, the President has a large retinue of aides and bodyguards.*

re·tire *(obj)* [STOP WORKING] /£rɪˈtaɪəʳ, $-ˈtaɪr/ *v* to (cause to) leave your job or stop working because of old age or ill health ● *They came back to England in 1991 to retire.* [I] ● *Since she retired* **from** *the company, she has begun to work as a volunteer for a charity.* [I] ● *He is due to retire* **as** *chief executive next year.* [I] ● If an employer retires an unwanted employee, they dismiss that person: *He was retired with a generous pension.* [T] ○ *Over 300 people have been retired* **from** *the factory in the past year.* [T] ● If someone retires from a race or competition, they stop taking part in it because of illness or injury: *She retired injured* **from** *the competition after the first day.* [I] ● [LP] **Work** Ⓟ (RUS) Ⓣ

re·tired /£rɪˈtaɪəd, $-ˈtaɪrd/ *(abbreviation* **retd***)* *adj* [not gradable] ● If someone is retired, they have stopped working: *Both my parents are retired.* ○ *He is a retired airline pilot.*

re·tir·ee /£rɪˌtaɪəˈriː, $-ˈtaɪ·riː/ *n* [C] *Am* • A retiree is a person who has stopped working: *The neighborhood is a mixture of young couples, retirees and single professionals.* ○ *Almost two-thirds of current retirees rely on the Social Security system for more than half of their income.* • [LP] Age

re·tire·ment /£rɪˈtaɪə·mənt, $-ˈtaɪr-/ *n* • Retirement is the point at which someone stops working or the period in their life when they have stopped working: *She* **went into** *retirement last year.* [U] ○ *Many teachers over the age of 50 are* **taking** *early retirement.* [U] ○ *There have been three retirements this month at the office.* [C] ○ *What is the normal retirement* **age** *in this country?* ○ *He's living happily* **in** *retirement, with his retirement* **pension.** [U]

re·tir·ing /£rɪˈtaɪə·rɪŋ, $-ˈtaɪr·ɪŋ/ *adj* [before n; not gradable] • Retiring refers to someone who plans to leave their job: *She will succeed the retiring Ian Dixon as chief executive of the company.* ○ *The match ended in disappointment for the retiring captain, Viv Richards.* • See also RETIRING.

re·tire [LEAVE A PLACE] /£rɪˈtaɪəʳ, $-ˈtaɪr/ *v* [I] *fml* to leave a room or group of people and go somewhere quiet or private • *After dinner our host said, "Shall we retire* **to** (= go to) *the drawing room?"* • To retire also means to go to bed: *It had been a long day, so I retired early.* • Ⓟ Ⓡⓤⓢ Ⓣ

re·tir·ing /£rɪˈtaɪə·rɪŋ, $-ˈtaɪr·ɪŋ/ *adj fml* unwilling to be noticed or to be with other people • *He's a retiring author who hates parties and publicity.* • See also **retiring** at RETIRE [STOP WORKING].

re·tort /£rɪˈtɔːt, $-ˈtɔːrt/ *v, n slightly fml* (to make) a quick annoyed or clever answer • *She offered to help me but I retorted* **that** *I could do it myself.* [+ *that* clause] • *"If I were your wife I'd put poison in your coffee," she said. – "And if I were your husband I'd drink it," he retorted.* [+ clause] • *He made an angry retort.* [C]

re·touch *obj* /ˌriːˈtʌtʃ/ *v* [T] to make small changes to (a picture, photograph, etc.) esp. in order to improve it • *We had the wedding photos retouched to make it seem like a sunny day.*

re·trace *obj* /rɪˈtreɪs/ *v* [T] to go back over (a path, series of past actions, etc.) • *She walked straight past her office and then had to* **retrace** *her* **steps.** • *When he realised he had lost his keys he retraced in his mind his movements that day.*

re·tract *(obj)* /rɪˈtrækt/ *v fml* to take back or admit as false (an offer, statement, etc.), or to pull (something) back or in • *retract an offer/promise/invitation/confession* [T] • *When questioned on TV, the minister retracted (his allegations).* [I/T] • *The wheels retracted after the aircraft took off.* [I] • *The cat retracted its claws.* [T]

re·trac·ta·ble /£rɪˈtræk·tə·bl̩, $-t̬ə-/ *adj* [not gradable] • *Cats have retractable claws.*

re·trac·tion /rɪˈtræk·ʃən/ *n* [C] • *He was forced to issue a retraction (of his accusations).* • *The newspaper printed a retraction for their previous error.*

re·tread /ˌriːˈtred/, *Br* **re·mould**, *Am* **re·cap** *v, n* (to put) a new rubber surface on the outer part of esp. a worn tyre, or the renewed tyre • *You'll have to have those tyres retreaded.* [T] • *Are those new tyres or retreads?* [C]

re·treat /rɪˈtriːt/ *v* [I] to go away from a person or place, esp. because unwilling to fight any more; to WITHDRAW • *Attacks by enemy aircraft forced the tanks to retreat* (**from** *the city*). • *When she came towards me shouting, I retreated (behind my desk).* • *(fig.) I retreated* **to** *a place in the mountains to put my thoughts on paper.* • *(fig.) When he's afraid he retreats under the blankets/to his bedroom/into himself/into a fantasy world.* • *(fig.) The government is retreating* **from** (= failing to keep to) *its principles/beliefs/promises.*

re·treat /rɪˈtriːt/ *n* • *Thousands of soldiers died on the retreat.* [C] • *(fig.) The professor's speech marked/signalled a retreat* **from** *his usual extreme views.* [C] • *Enemy soldiers are now* **in** *(full) retreat.* [U] • A retreat is also a private and safe place: *Mike has a small comfortable retreat by the lake.* [C] • A retreat is also a period of time used to pray, study, or think carefully: *We went on a retreat at a monastery.* [C]

re·trench [TO BE CAREFUL] /rɪˈtrentʃ/ *v* [I] *fml* (of governments, companies, etc.) to start to be more careful about spending money; to reduce costs • *The company had to retrench because of falling orders.*

re·trench·ment /rɪˈtrentʃ·mənt/ *n* • *Retrenchment not expansion is now the policy of most companies.* [U] • *The depression is forcing us to make a series of retrenchments.* [C]

re·trench *obj* [DISMISS] /rɪˈtrentʃ/ *v* [T] *Aus* to dismiss (a worker) from their job as a means of reducing costs

re·trench·ment /rɪˈtrentʃ·mənt/ *n* [C] *Aus* • A retrenchment is the dismissal of a worker: *The downturn in business has resulted in many retrenchments.*

re·tri·al /ˈriː·traɪəl/ *n* [C] a new trial of a law case • *The discovery of new evidence forced a retrial.*

ret·ri·bu·tion /ˌret·rɪˈbjuː·ʃən/ *n* [U] *fml* deserved and severe punishment • *Some people saw her death as* **divine** *retribution* **for** *her crimes.* • *Retribution swiftly overtook him* (= He was soon found and punished). • Ⓔ Ⓘ

re·tri·bu·tive /£rɪˈtrɪb·ju·tɪv, $-t̬ɪv/ *adj* [before n] *fml*

re·trieve *obj* /rɪˈtriːv/ *v* [T] to find and bring back (something) • *We taught our dog to retrieve a ball.* • *Matthew retrieved his kite from the tree.* • *Computers are used to store and retrieve information efficiently.*

re·triev·al /rɪˈtriː·vəl/ *n* [U] • *Information coming from the camera is converted to digital format and stored on disc for later retrieval.*

re·triev·er /£rɪˈtriː·vəʳ, $-vɚ/ *n* [C] a type of big golden or black dog

ret·ro– [BACKWARDS] /£ˌret·rəʊ-, $-roʊ-/ *combining form* going backwards • A **retro-rocket** is a rocket on a spacecraft or an aircraft that fires in the opposite direction to the direction in which the vehicle is travelling, in order to slow it down.

ret·ro– [PAST] /£ˌret·rəʊ-, $-roʊ-/ *combining form* looking towards or copying the past • *Retro-mania is sweeping the country causing normally sane people to collect junk from the past.* • *Retro-pop nostalgia* (= Love of popular music from the past) *is common among young people.*

ret·ro /£ˈret·rəʊ, $-roʊ/ *adj* • *retro clothes* • *a retro style*

ret·ro·ac·tive /£ˌret·rəʊˈæk·tɪv, $-roʊ-/, **ret·ro·spec·tive** *adj* [not gradable] *fml* (esp. of a law) having effect from a date before the law was approved • *The first British law to have retrospective effect made possible the trial of suspected Nazis for crimes committed fifty years ago.* • *Your pay rise is retroactive* **to** *the beginning of last year.*

ret·ro·ac·tive·ly /£ˌret·rəʊˈæk·tɪv·li, $-roʊ-/ *adv*

ret·ro·grade /£ˈret·rəʊ·greɪd, $-rə-/ *adj fml* returning to older and worse conditions, methods, ideas, etc. • *The development of new nuclear weapons may be considered a retrograde* **step.**

ret·ro·gress /£ˌret·rəʊˈgres, $ˈret·rə·gres/ *v* [I] *fml* to return to an older and worse state • *There is a time in the history of many great civilisations when they begin to retrogress.*

ret·ro·gres·sion /£ˌret·rəʊˈgreʃ·ən, $-rə-/ *n* [U]

ret·ro·gres·sive /£ˌret·rəʊˈgres·ɪv, $ˈret·rə·gres-/ *adj* • *retrogressive and disastrous policies*

ret·ro·spect /£ˈret·rəʊ·spekt, $-rə-/ *n* [U] **in retrospect** thinking now about something in the past • *In retrospect I think my marriage was doomed from the beginning.* • *I'm sure my university days appear happier in retrospect than they actually were at the time.*

ret·ro·spec·tion /£ˌret·rəʊˈspek·ʃən, $-rə-/ *n* [U] • *Too much retrospection makes me sad.*

ret·ro·spec·tive /£ˌret·rəʊˈspek·tɪv, $-rə-/ *adj, n* • *A retrospective influence pervaded the whole production of the ballet.* • A retrospective is also a show of the work an artist has done in their life so far: *The museum is putting on a Hockney retrospective/a retrospective of Hockney's work.* [C]

ret·ro·spec·tive·ly /£ˌret·rəʊˈspek·tɪv·li, $-rə-/ *adv* • *Retrospectively it's obvious how we went wrong.*

ret·si·na /retˈsiː·nə/ *n* [U] a Greek wine that tastes strongly of the RESIN (= juice) of particular trees

re·turn [GO BACK] /£rɪˈtɜːn, $-ˈtɜːrn/ *v* [I] to come or go back to a previous place, subject, activity or condition • *Odysseus returned home/returned* **to** *his home after many years of travelling.* • *She left South Africa at the age of 15 and has never returned.* • *David returned* (**from** *work*) **to** *find his house had burned down.* [+ *to* infinitive] • *Every five minutes he returned* **to** (= again started speaking about) *the same subject.* • *Gandhi urged Indians to return* **to** *spinning their own yarn.* • *Within two days of the end of the fighting the situation had returned* **to** *normal.* • *After his mother died he returned* **to** *his old ways and bad habits.* • *He promised that he would go to the doctor if the pain returned.*

re·turn /£rɪˈtɜːn, $-ˈtɜːrn/ *n* [C] • *The whole town came out to celebrate his return* (**from** *the war*). • **On** *her return* (= When she came back) *she went straight to the office.* • *Some environmentalists argue for a return* **to** *a pre-industrial society.* • *Most sensible people have welcomed her return* **to power/office.** • *Will we ever see the return* **of/***a return* **to** *comfortable fashion clothes?* • *(Br and Aus)* A **return (ticket)** (*Am* **roundtrip ticket**) is a ticket for travel to a place and back again: *May I have a return to Birmingham, please.* • *(Am)* A **return ticket** is a ticket for the returning part of a journey. • *"Return of the -"* (Common phrase in film titles, such as *Return of the Jedi, Return of the Living Dead, Return of the Dragon*)

re·turn /£rɪˈtɜːn, $-ˈtɜːrn/ *adj* • *a return envelope* • *The return journey was two hours longer because of the strong winds.* • *The touring company will do a return performance of that opera* (= they will perform it again).

re·turn *obj* PUT BACK /£rɪˈtɜːn, $-ˈtɜːrn/ *v* [T] to send, take, give, put, etc. (something) back to where it came from • *Both tax forms must be filled out and returned* **to** *this office.* • *The new TV broke within a week so they returned it to the shop.* • *He returned two books he had borrowed from me in 1963.* • *She carefully returned the book to its place on the shelf.* • *"Return to sender, address unknown"* (song by Elvis Presley, 1962)

re·turn /£rɪˈtɜːn, $-ˈtɜːrn/ *n* [C] • *She answered my letter (Br and Aus)* **by return (of post)**/*(Aus also)* **by return mail** (= She sent her letter in the first post collection that left after she got my letter). • *(Am)* **Returns** are the results of voting in an ELECTION (= a political competition). • **Returns** are also goods that are taken back to where they came from, often from the customer back to the shop where they were bought.

re·turn·a·ble /£rɪˈtɜː·nə·bl̩, $-ˈtɜːr-/ *adj* • *a returnable bottle*

re·turn *obj* EXCHANGE /£rɪˈtɜːn, $-ˈtɜːrn/ *v* [T] to give, do or get (something) in exchange • *to return an invitation/greeting* • *I returned his angry stare until his eyes dropped.* • *My boss said how pretty I was looking so I returned* **the compliment** *and said what a nice suit he was wearing.* • *I gave her a ride when her car broke down and now she is returning* **the favour** (= doing something to help me because I helped her). • *The terrorists in the house started shooting and the police returned (their/the)* **fire** (= started shooting back). • *My investments* **return a high/low rate of interest** (= give a large/small profit).

re·turn /£rɪˈtɜːn, $-ˈtɜːrn/ *n* • *Her return of serve was the strongest part of her tennis game.* [C] • *America helped the rebels* **in** *return* **for** *their promise to support democracy.* [U] • **In** *return* **for** (= in exchange for) *your cooperation we will give you a free gift.* • *The return/returns* (= profit) **on** *the money we invested was/were very low.* [C] • *We enjoyed the game so much that we arranged a* **return match** (= another match) *for the next week.*

re·turn *obj* DECIDE /£rɪˈtɜːn, $-ˈtɜːrn/ *v* [T] *law or fml* to decide on (something such as a judgment or decision) • *The jury* **returned a verdict of** (= said that their opinion was of) *not guilty.*

re·turn COMPUTER /£rɪˈtɜːn, $-ˈtɜːrn/ *n* [U] the key on a computer keyboard that is used to say that the words or numbers on the screen are correct or that an instruction should be performed or to move down a line on the screen • *Press return twice to leave a blank line.*

re·un·ite *obj* /ˌriː·juːˈnaɪt/ *v* [T] to bring together again • *reunite a divided family/country/organization/world* • *Sarah was finally reunited* **with** *her children at the airport.* • Ⓟ

re·un·ion /£ˌriːˈjuː·ni·ən, $ˈ-njən/ *n* [C] • *We had a family reunion where I saw relatives I hadn't seen for 20 years.*

re·use *obj* /ˌriːˈjuːz/ *v* [T] to use (something) again, or to RECYCLE (something) • *To conserve resources please reuse this carrier bag.*

re·us·a·ble /ˌriːˈjuː·zə·bl̩/ *adj* • *reusable packaging*

Rev PRIEST /rev/ *n* [before n] *abbreviation for* REVEREND

rev SPEED /rev/ *n* [C usually pl] a REVOLUTION (= one complete turn of a part in an engine) • *Keep the revs up* (= the engine speed high) *or the engine will stall.* • See also RPM.

rev *(obj)* /rev/ *v* **-vv-** • To rev an engine is to increase its speed while the vehicle is not moving (usually to warm it to the correct temperature). • *He nervously revved* **(up)** *the engine before driving off.* [T] • *The noise of the car revving* **(up)** *woke the whole neighbourhood.* [I]

re·val·ue *obj* /ˌriːˈvæl·juː/ *v* [T] to change or consider again the value of (something) • *The company's assets are periodically revalued.*

re·vamp *obj* /ˌriːˈvæmp/ *v* [T] *infml* to change, remake or arrange (something) again in order to improve it • *The words have been revamped but the song's still no good.* • *We revamped all the management system, but the business is doing no better than it was before.*

Revd *abbreviation for* REVEREND

re·veal *obj* /rɪˈviːl/ *v* [T] to make known, show or allow to be shown (something usually secret or hidden) • *He was jailed for revealing secrets to the Russians.* • *(literary) A glance at the clock revealed* **that** *it was almost ten.* [+ *that* clause] • *Her biography revealed* **that** *she was not as rich as everyone thought.* [+ *that* clause] • *A gap in the clouds revealed the Atlantic far below.* • *He would not reveal* **where** *he had hidden her chocolate eggs.* [+ *wh-* word]

re·veal·ing /rɪˈviː·lɪŋ/ *adj* • Revealing clothes show more of the body than is usual: *a revealing dress/shirt* • *A joke can be very revealing* **of** *what someone's really thinking.*

re·veal·ing·ly /rɪˈviː·lɪŋ·li/ *adv*

re·veille /£rɪˈvæl·i, $ˈrev·ə·li/ *n* [U] a musical signal played to wake up soldiers in the morning

rev·el *(obj)* /ˈrev·əl/ *v* **-ll-** or *Am usually* **-l-** *literary or humorous* to dance, drink, sing, etc. at a party or in public, esp. in a noisy way • *They revelled all day and all night after their exams.* [I] • To revel **in** a situation or an activity is to get great pleasure from it: *After the long hot summer we revelled in the rainstorm.* [T] • *She's revelling in her newly found freedom.* [T]

rev·el·ler /£ˈrev·əl·əʳ, $-ɚ/ *n* [C] • *On New Year's Eve thousands of revellers fill Trafalgar Square.*

rev·el·ry /ˈrev·əl·ri/ *n* • *Sounds of revelry came from next door.* [U] • *The revelries next door kept me awake all night.* [C usually pl]

rev·e·la·tion /ˌrev·əlˈeɪ·ʃən/ *n* making known something that was secret, or a fact made known • *It was a revelation* **of** *the President's involvement in secret arms deals that shocked the nation.* [U] • *That method was a revelation* **to/for** *her and she was eager to try it again.* [C] • *His wife divorced him after the revelation* **that** *he was having an affair.* [C + *that* clause] • *Shocking revelations appeared in the papers about the private life of the royal family.* [C]

re·venge /rɪˈvendʒ/ *n* [U] harm done to someone as a punishment for harm that they have done to someone else; VENGEANCE • *She* **took/got/exacted** *(her) revenge* **on** *him* **for** *leaving her by smashing up his car.* • *He is believed to have been shot by a rival gang* **in** *revenge* **for** *the shootings last week.* • *The semi-final will be a chance for the losing team to* **get** *their revenge* **on** *the winning team (for their earlier defeat).* • *(saying)* "Revenge is sweet" means it is satisfying to do harm to someone who has done harm to you. • Ⓒⓢ Ⓟⓛ Ⓡⓤⓢ

re·venge *obj* /rɪˈvendʒ/ *v* [T] • *to revenge a defeat/injury/injustice* • *The red team revenged themselves* **on** *the blue team by winning the semi-final.*

re·ven·ge·ful /rɪˈvendʒ·fəl/ *adj* • *She felt bitter and revengeful* (= wanting to punish him) *after he stole her money.*

rev·e·nue /£ˈrev·ən·juː, $-ə·nuː/ *n* [U] the income that a government or company receives regularly • *Taxes provide most of the government's revenue.*

rev·e·nues /£ˈrev·ən·juːz, $-ə·nuːz/ *pl n* • *Government revenues have fallen dramatically with four million people out of work.*

re·ver·be·rate /£rɪˈvɜː·bəʳ·eɪt, $-ˈvɜːr·bɚ·eɪt/ *v* [I] *literary* (of sound) to continue to be heard around an area; to ECHO repeatedly • *The narrow street reverberated* **with/to** *the sound of the workmen's drills.* • *(fig.) News of the disaster reverberated* **through/around** (= quickly moved through) *the organization.*

re·ver·be·ra·tion /£rɪˌvɜː·bəʳˈeɪ·ʃən, $-ˌvɜːr·bəˈreɪ-/ *n literary* • *She felt the reverberation(s) in her chest.* [U/C usually pl]

re·vere *obj* /£rɪˈvɪəʳ, $-ˈvɪr/ *v* [T] *fml* to greatly respect and admire (someone or something) • *I revere Nelson Mandela (***for** *his brave fight against apartheid).* • *We all revere Shakespeare's plays as great literature.*

rev·e·rence /£ˈrev·əʳ·ənts, £ˈ-rənts, $-ɚ·ənts/ *n* [U] *fml* • *She has/shows/feels great reverence* **for** *her professors.*

rev·e·rent /£ˈrev·əʳ·ənt, £ˈ-rənt, $-ɚ·ənt/ *adj fml* • *The Bishop's sermon was received in reverent silence.*

rev·e·rent·ly /£ˈrev·əʳ·ənt·li, £ˈ-rənt-, $-ɚ·ənt-/ *adv fml* • *He gazed reverently down at the body in the coffin.*

rev·e·ren·tial /£ˌrev·əˈrent·ʃəl, $-əˈrent-/ *adj fml* • *He opened the ancient book with reverential care.*

Rev·e·rend /£ˈrev·əʳ·ənd, £ˈ-rənd, $-ɚ·ənd/ *(abbreviation* **Rev, Revd***)* *n* a title for a member of the Christian CLERGY (= official workers of the church) • *the Reverend H. Clark* • *(fml) the Reverend Mr H. Clark*

rev·e·rie /£ˈrev·əʳ·i, $ˈ-ɚ-/ *n literary* (a state of having) pleasant dream-like thoughts • *He was lost* **in** *reverie until* *he suddenly heard someone behind him.* [U] *She was enjoying pleasant reveries* **about** *her schooldays.* [C]

re·vers /£rɪˈvɪəʳ, $-ˈvɪr/ *n* [C usually pl] *pl* **revers** /£rɪˈvɪəz, $-ˈvɪrz/ *specialized* an edge of a coat, shirt, dress, etc. that is folded back on the chest

re·verse *(obj)* /£rɪˈvɜːs, $-ˈvɜːrs/ *v* to (cause to) go backwards, or to change the direction, order, position, result, etc. of (something) to its opposite • *(esp. Br and Aus) She reversed (Am usually* **backed***) (the car) into the parking space.* [I/T] • *(Br and Aus) I was almost knocked off my bike by a car reversing (Am* **backing up***) out of a garage.* [I] • *The new manager hoped to reverse the decline in the company's fortunes.* [T] • *Why don't you reverse the order so that I play first and she plays second?* [T] • *Now that you have a job and I don't, our situations are reversed.* [T] • *The Court of Appeal reversed the earlier judgment and set him free.* [T] • To **reverse the charges** (*Am also* **call collect**) is to make a telephone call that is paid for by the person receiving it. • [LP] **Telephone** [PIC] **Driving**

re·verse /£rɪˈvɜːs, $-ˈvɜːrs/ *n* • *I win at chess by doing* **the** *reverse of what my opponent expects.* [U] • *The teachers say my son is slow but I believe* **the** *reverse (is true).* [U] • *To stop the engine you repeat the same procedures, but* **in** *reverse* **(order)**. [U] • *To drive a vehicle backwards you must put it* **in/into** *reverse (gear).* [U] • *(fig.) The trend towards home ownership has* **gone into** *reverse* (= the opposite of this is now true). [U] • *(fml)* A reverse is a defeat or failure: *They suffered a serious military/financial/political reverse.* [C] • **The reverse** of a coin, MEDAL, etc. is the back of it: *The English £1 coin has a royal coat of arms on the reverse.* • **Reverse discrimination** (*Br and Aus also* **positive discrimination**) is when an advantage is given to people who are typically thought to be treated unfairly, usually because of their race or sex.

re·ver·sal /£rɪˈvɜː·səl, $-ˈvɜːr-/ *n* [C] • *He demanded a reversal* (= change to be the opposite) *of a previous decision/policy.* • *(fig. infml) We have suffered a couple of minor reversals* (= problems or failures).

re·vers·i·ble /£rɪˈvɜː·sɪ·bl̩, $-ˈvɜːr-/ *adj* • *It might be a good idea to buy a reversible raincoat because then it can be worn with either side out.*

re·vers·ion /£rɪˈvɜː·ʃən, $-ˈvɜːr·ʒən/ *n* [U] *fml* a change back to a previous and often worse condition, or *(law)* a return of something to its previous owner • *The new procedures are being seen as a reversion to old, inefficient ways of working.*

re·vert to *obj* /£rɪˈvɜːt, $-ˈvɜːrt/ *v prep* [T] to go back to (a previous and often worse condition, way of life, etc.), or to talk again about (something) • *After their mother left the room the children soon reverted to their naughty ways.* • *Why does the conversation have to revert to money every five minutes?* • *When they divorced, she reverted to using her maiden name.* [+ v-ing] • *(law) When I die, the house will revert to* (= become again the property of) *my sister.*

re·view *obj* /rɪˈvjuː/ *v* [T] to consider (something) in order to make changes to it, give an opinion on it or to study it • *The committee is reviewing the situation/its current arrangements/its decision.* • *Let's review what has happened so far.* • *He reviewed his options before making a final decision.* • *She is reviewing* (= studying) *the notes for her speech.* • If critics review a book, play, film, etc. they write their opinion of it: *I only go to see films that are reviewed favourably.* • When an important person reviews a large group of military forces, they formally visit and look at them: *The Queen reviewed the troops on her recent visit.* • Review is also *Am for* REVISE [STUDY]. • *"I never read a book before reviewing it; it prejudices a man so"* (believed to have been said by Rev. Sydney Smith, 1771-1845)

re·view /rɪˈvjuː/ *n* • *an annual review of company performance* [C] • *Perhaps we could have a quick review of the progress made so far?* [C] • *Salary levels are* **under** *review* (= being reconsidered) *at the moment.* [U] • *Your licence will* **come up for** *review* (= will be reconsidered) *every July.* [U] • *A review* (= programme or article giving the important events) *of the year's top news stories will be shown on television later tonight.* [C] • *Derek writes film/theatre/literary reviews* (= articles giving opinions on films/plays/literature) *for the newspapers.* [C] • *The play got excellent reviews* (= comments from critics) *when it was first seen.* [C] • A review is also a (part of a) newspaper or magazine that has articles on films, books, travel, famous people, etc.: *Could you pass me the review* **(section** *of the paper), please?* • *Many diplomats will attend the naval review* (= formal military ceremony) *next month to mark the anniversary of the end of the war.* • Review is another word for REVUE. • *(Am) Their teacher distributed a review* (= information or a practice exercise about the subject to be studied) *for the exam.*

re·view·er /£rɪˈvjuː·əʳ, $-ɚ/ *n* [C] • A reviewer is someone who writes articles expressing their opinion of a book, play, film, etc.

re·vile *obj* /rɪˈvaɪl/ *v* [T] *fml* to criticize (someone) strongly or say unpleasant things to or about (someone) • *The judge has been reviled in the newspapers* **for** *his opinions on rape.*

re·vise *obj* [CHANGE] /rɪˈvaɪz/ *v* [T] to look again at (an idea, a piece of writing, etc.) in order to make corrections or improvements to it • *His helpfulness today has made me revise my original opinion/impression of him.* • *(Br and Aus) Government estimates of the cost of the war are being revised* **upwards/downwards** (= increased/decreased). • *His publishers forced him to revise his manuscript three times.*

re·vised /rɪˈvaɪzd/ *adj* [not gradable] • *The researchers made many corrections to the revised edition.*

re·vi·sion /rɪˈvɪʒ·ən/ *n* • *These proposals will need a lot of revision.* [U] • *He was forced to make several revisions to his speech.* [C] • (RUS)

re·vise *(obj)* [STUDY] *Br and Aus* /rɪˈvaɪz/, *Am* **re·view** *v* to study again (something already learned) in preparation for an exam • *We are revising (algebra)* **for** *the test tomorrow.* [I/T]

re·vi·sion /rɪˈvɪʒ·ən/ *n* [U] • *She did no revision but she still got a very high mark.*

re·vi·sion·i·sm /rɪˈvɪʒ·ən·ɪ·zəm/ *n* [U] the questioning of, and attempts to change, the existing beliefs of a political or religious system, esp. the Marxist political system

re·vis·ion·ist /rɪˈvɪʒ·ən·ɪst/ *n* [C] • *Revisionists within the Communist Party are trying to create a moderate new ideology.*

re·vis·ion·ist /rɪˈvɪʒ·ən·ɪst/ *adj* • *revisionist ideas*

re·vi·tal·ize *obj, Br and Aus usually* **-ise** /£ˌriːˈvaɪ·təl·aɪz, $-t̬əl-/ *v* [T] to give new life, energy, activity or success to (something) • *Japanese investment has revitalized this part of Britain.*

re·vive *(obj)* /rɪˈvaɪv/ *v* to come or bring (something) back to life, health, existence, or use • *revive our hopes/confidence/fortunes* [T] • *My plants revived as soon as I gave them a little water.* [I] • *The lifeguard revived the swimmer with oxygen.* [T] • *She tried to revive herself with a hot shower and a cup of tea.* [T] • *Public interest in the shipwreck has been revived by these incredible photographs.* [T] • *Traditional skills are being revived by local craftsmen.* [I] • *The director is reviving a play that hasn't been performed since 1952.* [T]

re·viv·al /rɪˈvaɪ·vəl/ *n* • *Recntly, there has been some revival* **of (interest in)** *ancient music.* [U] • *An economic/artistic revival is sweeping the country.* [C] • *We're staging a revival* (= performance of a play which has not been seen for a long time) *of a 1950s play.* [C] • A revival is also a time of renewed interest in religion or meetings intended to encourage this to happen. [C]

re·vi·vi·fy *obj* /ˌriːˈvɪv·ɪ·faɪ/ *v* [T] *fml* to give new energy and strength to (an event or activity) • *It would need a leader with real charisma to revivify the political party.*

re·voke *obj* /£rɪˈvəʊk, $-ˈvoʊk/ *v* [T] *fml* to say officially that (an agreement, permission, a law, etc.) is no longer in effect • *The authorities have revoked their original decision to allow development of this rural area.*

re·volt [FIGHT] /£rɪˈvəʊlt, £-ˈvʌlt, $-ˈvoʊlt/ *v* [I] (esp. of a large number of people) to refuse to be controlled or ruled; to take often violent action against authority • *The people in the north have revolted* **against** *foreign rule and established their own government.*

re·volt /£rɪˈvəʊlt, £-ˈvʌlt, $-ˈvoʊlt/ *n* • *They were accused of trying to incite/stir up/start a revolt.* [C] • *Troops were called in to crush/put down the revolt.* [C] • *The army is* **in** *revolt* **(against** *its commanders).* [U] • See also REVOLUTION.

re·volt *obj* [DISGUST] /£rɪˈvəʊlt, £-ˈvʌlt, $-ˈvoʊlt/ *v* [T] to make (someone) feel unpleasantly shocked or disgusted • *We were revolted* **by** *the dirt and mess in her house.* • *It revolts me to know that the world spends so much money on arms, yet millions of people are dying of hunger.* • See also REVULSION.

re·volt·ing /£rɪˈvəʊl·tɪŋ, £-ˈvʌl-, $-ˈvoʊl·t̬ɪŋ/ *adj* • *What a revolting smell of rotting cabbage.* • *Picking your nose is a revolting* **habit**.

re·volt·ing·ly /£rɪˈvəʊl·tɪŋ·li, £-ˈvʌl-, $-ˈvoʊl·t̬ɪŋ-/ *adv* • *a revoltingly dirty kitchen*

rev·o·lu·tion /£ˌrev·əlˈuː·ʃən, $-əˈluː-/ *n* (a) sudden and great change, esp. a violent change of a system of government • *win/carry out/defeat/crush a revolution* [C] • *The French Revolution changed France from a monarchy to a republic.* [C] • *The country seems to be heading towards revolution.* [U] • *(specialized) Marxists believe that revolution* (= change, esp. through violence in the parts of a society that are important to its economic activities) *will eventually occur in all capitalist countries.* [U] • *The discovery of penicillin produced a revolution* **in** *medicine.* [C] • See also **revolution** at REVOLVE.

rev·o·lu·tion·a·ry /£ˌrev·əlˈuː·ʃən·ər·i, $-əˈluː·ʃən·er-/ *n* [C], *adj* • *Lenin was a revolutionary.* • *revolutionary leaders/parties/wars/tendencies* • *Penicillin was a revolutionary drug.* • *This new process is revolutionary* (= completely new and likely to have a great effect) *and will double our profits.*

rev·o·lut·ion·ize *obj*, *Br and Aus usually* **–ise** /£ˌrev·əlˈuː·ʃən·aɪz, $-əˈluː-/ *v* [T] • *Newton's discoveries revolutionized* (= completely changed) *physics.*

re·volve *(obj)* /£rɪˈvʌlv, $-ˈvɑːlv/ *v* to (cause to) move round a central point or line • *The Earth revolves (Br)* **round/***(Am and Aus)* **around** (= moves around) *the sun in an ellipse.* [I] • *The gun turret revolved until the gun was aimed at the advancing soldiers.* [I] • *The platform is revolved by a small electric motor.* [T] • *(fig.) His life revolves* **around** (= He's only interested in) *football.* [I] • *(fig.) All the questions revolved* **around** (= were connected with) *what she had been doing on the night of the robbery.* [I] • A **revolving door** is a set of doors which you go through by pushing them round in a circle. • PIC **Doors**

rev·o·lu·tion /£ˌrev·əlˈuː·ʃən, $-əˈluː-/ *n* • Revolution is circular movement: *The revolution of the Earth (Br)* **round/***(Am and Aus)* **around** *the sun was proposed by Copernicus.* [U] • A revolution is also one complete circular movement: *The moon makes one revolution* **of/around** *the Earth in approximately 29½ days.* [C] ○ *The speed of an engine can be measured in revolutions per minute (abbreviation* **rpm***).* [C] • See also REVOLUTION.

re·volv·er /£rɪˈvʌl·vər, $-ˈvɑːl·vɚ/ *n* [C] a type of small gun held in one hand that can be fired several times without putting more bullets in it

re·vue /rɪˈvjuː/, **re·view** *n* [C] a not very serious theatrical show with songs, dances, and jokes and short plays often about recent events

re·vul·sion /rɪˈvʌl·ʃən/ *n* [U] a strong often sudden feeling that something is extremely unpleasant; disgust • *I turned away* **in** *revulsion (from the dead body on the steps).* • *She looked at him* **with** *revulsion.* • *She felt revulsion* **at** *his appearance.* • *He expressed his revulsion* **at/against/towards** *the whale hunting.* • See also REVOLT DISGUST.

re·ward /£rɪˈwɔːd, $-ˈwɔːrd/ *n* something given in exchange for good behaviour or good work, etc. • *My mother used to give me chocolate as a reward when I was good.* [U] • *There's a reward* **for** *whoever finishes first.* [C] • *The rewards of motherhood outweigh the anguish.* [C] • *She got a percentage of the profits* **in reward for** *having thought of the original idea.* [U] • A reward is also an amount of money given to someone who helps the police or who helps to return stolen property to its owner: *The police offered a reward* **for** *any information about the robbery.* [C]

re·ward *obj* /£rɪˈwɔːd, $-ˈwɔːrd/ *v* [T] • *He was rewarded* **for** *his years of service to the company* **with** *a grand farewell party and several presents.* • *(slightly fml) All his hard work was rewarded* (= was made worth it) *when he saw his book in print.* • *(fml) He rewarded their kindness* **with** *hostility and contempt.* • *(fml) I think this book will reward* (= be worth) *your attention/time.*

re·ward·ing /£rɪˈwɔː·dɪŋ, $-ˈwɔːr-/ *adj* • *For me, studying Spanish has been a very rewarding experience.* • A job that is rewarding is one that gives a lot of satisfaction, but possibly not much money.

re·wind *obj* /ˌriːˈwaɪnd/ *v* [T] *past* **rewound** /ˌriːˈwaʊnd/ to put (a TAPE recording) back to the beginning • *Will you rewind the tape so we can hear it again?*

re·wind /ˈriː·waɪnd/ *adj* [not gradable] • *a rewind button*

re·wire *obj* /£ˌriːˈwaɪər, $-ˈwaɪr/ *v* [T] to put a new system of electric wires into (a building or machine) • *You really should have the whole house rewired – the existing wiring isn't safe.*

re·word *obj* /£ˌriːˈwɜːd, $-ˈwɜːrd/ *v* [T] to write (something) again in different words • *She reworded sensitive areas of the report so that it wouldn't be so controversial.*

re·work *obj* /£ˌriːˈwɜːk, $-ˈwɜːrk/ *v* [T] to change (a speech or a piece of writing) in order to improve it or make it more suitable for a particular purpose • *She reworked her speech for a younger audience.*

re·work·ing /£riːˈwɜː·kɪŋ, $-ˈwɜːr-/ *n* [C] • *His latest book is a reworking of material from his previous short stories.*

re·wound /ˌriːˈwaʊnd/ *past simple and past participle of* REWIND

re·write *obj* /ˌriːˈraɪt/ *v* [T] **rewrote** /£ˌriːˈrəʊt, $ˌriːˈroʊt/ or **rewritten** /£ˌriːˈrɪt·ən, $-ˈrɪt̬-/ to write (something such as a book or speech) again or in a different way in order to improve it or change it because new information is available • *The news of the revolt meant she had to rewrite her speech.*

re·write /ˈriː·raɪt/ *n* [C] • *The producer disliked the script and demanded a rewrite.*

rhap·so·dy /ˈræp·sə·di/ *n* [C] *fml* a speech or piece of writing that contains powerful feelings and enthusiasm • *The novel is highly emotional and yet does not contain any of those extravagant rhapsodies that often spoil the works of descriptive writers.* • *(specialized)* A rhapsody is also a piece of music which has no formal structure and which expresses powerful feelings: *One of my favourite pieces of music is Rachmaninov's 'Rhapsody on a Theme of Paganini'.* • If you **go into rhapsodies** about/over something, you express enthusiasm and admiration for it: *She went into rhapsodies over the chocolate cake.* ○ *(Br) Some Americans go into rhapsodies when they hear an English accent.*

rhap·so·dic /£ræpˈsɒd·ɪk, $-ˈsɑː·dɪk/ *adj fml* • If a speech or piece of writing is rhapsodic, it expresses great enthusiasm about something: *The advertising brochure sent to prospective customers is written in a rhapsodic style.*

rhap·so·dize, *Br and Aus usually* **–ise** /ˈræp·sə·daɪz/ *v* [I] *fml* • If you rhapsodize about/over something, you express great enthusiasm for it: *He rhapsodized about the joys of having children.*

rhe·os·tat /£ˈriː·əʊ·stæt, $-oʊ-/ *n* [C] a device that controls the flow of electric current in a machine • *A rheostat can be used to control the brightness of electric lights.*

rhe·sus /ˈriː·səs/, **rhe·sus mon·key** *n* [C] a small short-tailed monkey from northern India • *Rhesus monkeys are often used in scientific experiments.*

rhe·sus fac·tor /ˈriː·səs/, **Rh fac·tor** *n* [U] *specialized* a substance found in the red blood cells of most people which causes the production of ANTIBODIES in the blood • *People whose blood contains the rhesus factor are Rh+ and those whose blood does not contain it are Rh-.* • See also POSITIVE BLOOD TYPE; NEGATIVE BLOOD TYPE.

rhet·or·ic /£ˈret·ər·ɪk, $ˈret̬·ɚ-/ *n* [U] speech or writing which is intended to be effective and persuasive, or *(specialized)* the study of the ways of using language effectively • *I was swayed by her rhetoric into donating all my savings to the charity.* • *How far the president will be able to translate his campaign rhetoric into action remains to be seen.* • *(specialized) He is a professor of rhetoric at the University of Naples.* • *(disapproving)* Rhetoric is also clever and persuasive language which is not sincere or has no real meaning: *The politician's speech was full of* **empty** (= meaningless) *rhetoric.*

rhe·tor·i·cal /£rɪˈtɒr·ɪ·kəl, $-ˈtɔːr·ɪ-/ *adj* • An action or speech which is rhetorical is intended to seem important or persuasive: *She threw her arms open in a grand rhetorical gesture.* • A **rhetorical question** is a question that is asked in order to make a statement and which does not expect an answer: *"Why do these things always happen to me?" is a rhetorical question.*

rhe·tor·i·cal·ly /£rɪˈtɒr·ɪ·kli, $-ˈtɔːr·ɪ-/ *adv* • *"Why has he gone to the meeting when there is nothing new to discuss?" she asked rhetorically.*

rhe·to·ri·cian /£ˌret·ərˈɪʃ·ən, $ˌret̬·əˈrɪʃ-/ *n* [C] *fml* • A rhetorician is a person who is good at speaking in public. • *(specialized)* A rhetorician is also a person who teaches the skill of speaking and writing in an effective and persuasive way: *Lucian was a famous Greek rhetorician.*

rheum·a·ti·sm /ˈruː·mə·tɪ·zəm/ *n* [U] a medical condition that causes stiffness and pain in the joints or muscles of the body, particularly in the shoulders and back • *She suffers from rheumatism.* • *Rheumatism is common in older people.* • *I can't play the piano anymore because I have rheumatism* **in** *my fingers.*

rheum·a·tic /£ruːˈmæt·ɪk, $-ˈmæt̬-/ *adj* • *She has a rheumatic hip.* • *Peppermint oil can be used to soothe* *rheumatic pains.* • **Rheumatic fever** is a serious disease that causes fever, swelling of the joints, and possible heart damage: *Rheumatic fever is common in children and adolescents.*

rheum·a·toid arth·ri·tis /'ruː·mə·tɔɪd/ *n* [U] a disease that causes stiffness, swelling and pain in the joints of the body • *He suffers from severe rheumatoid arthritis which came on suddenly at the age of 35.*

Rh fac·tor *n* [U] *abbreviation for* RHESUS FACTOR

rhine·stone /£'raɪn·stəʊn, $-stoʊn/ *n* [C] a bright, colourless artificial jewel which is often sewn onto clothes • *She wore a leather jacket studded with rhinestones.*

rhi·noc·e·ros (*pl* **rhinoceros** or **rhinoceroses**) /£raɪ'nɒs·ᵊr·əs, $-'nɑː·sɚ-/, *infml* **rhi·no** /£'raɪ·nəʊ, $-noʊ/ *n* [C] a very large thick-skinned animal from Africa or Asia, which has one or two horns on its nose • *Rhinoceroses are hunted for their horns which are ground into powder and used as a medicine.* • *There are only 3 000 black rhinos left in the world, and at the present rate of poaching, they will be extinct in five years.*

rhi·zome /£'raɪ·zəʊm, $-zoʊm/ *n* [C] *specialized* a stem of some plants which grows horizontally along or under the ground and which produces roots and leaves • *Bracken is a type of fern which often grows in woods and heaths where it may cover extensive areas by means of its rhizomes.*

rho·do·den·dron /£ˌrəʊ·də'den·drən, $ˌroʊ-/ *n* [C] a large evergreen bush with large usually bright pink, purple or white flowers • *The drive was lined with rhododendrons.*

rhom·bus /£'rɒm·bəs, $'rɑːm-/ *n* [C] *pl* **rhombuses** or **rhombi** /£'rɒm·baɪ, $'rɑːm-/ *specialized* a flat shape which has four sides that are all of equal length

rhu·barb FOOD /£'ruː·bɑːb, $-bɑːrb/ *n* [U] a plant which has long red and green stems that are cooked and eaten in sweet dishes • *We grow rhubarb and gooseberries in our garden.* • *Rhubarb can be rather bitter and needs a lot of sugar added before it is eaten.* • *Have you ever eaten rhubarb crumble?*

rhu·barb SOUND /£'ruː·bɑːb, $-bɑːrb/ *exclamation* a word which is repeated many times in order to produce the sound of people talking when the meaning of the word is not important • *Actors often say 'rhubarb' over and over again when they want to sound like a crowd of people talking.*

rhu·barb ARGUMENT /£'ruː·bɑːb, $-bɑːrb/ *n* [C] *Am slang* a loud argument

rhyme *(obj)* /raɪm/ *v* [not *be rhyming*] (of words) to have the same last sound • *'Blue' and 'flew' rhyme.* [I] • *The poet rhymed the words 'verse' and 'worse'.* [T] • *Can you think of a word that rhymes* **with** *'orange'?* [I] • **Rhyming slang** is slang which is used instead of a word or phrase and which rhymes with it: *In Cockney rhyming slang, you say 'apples and pears' to mean 'stairs'.* ○ *In Australian rhyming slang, you say 'elephant's (trunk)' to mean 'drunk'.*

rhyme /raɪm/ *n* • A rhyme is a word which has the same last sound as another word: *The rhyme in the last line of the poem doesn't work.* [C] • A rhyme is also a short poem, esp. for young children: *As a child, he used to love learning rhymes and songs.* [C] ○ See also **nursery rhyme** at NURSERY FOR CHILDREN. • Rhyme is the use of rhymes in poetry: *This poem is her first attempt at rhyme.* [U] ○ *Although each line rhymes with another, the poem has no fixed rhyme* **scheme**. • If a piece of writing is written **in** rhyme, it is written as a poem so that the word at the end of a line has the same last sound as a word at the end of another line: *A lot of modern poetry is not written* **in** *rhyme.* [U] • If you say that something has no **rhyme or reason**, you mean that you can see no obvious explanation for it: *Government money was given out to some people and not to others, apparently* **without** *rhyme or reason.* ○ *There is* **no** *rhyme or reason* **to** *her behaviour.*

rhy·thm /'rɪð·ᵊm/ *n* a strong pattern of sounds, words or musical notes which is used in music, poetry and dancing • *He beat out a jazz rhythm on the drums.* [C] • *She captures the rhythm of the poem exactly.* [C] • *I've got no sense of rhythm, so I'm a terrible dancer.* [U] • Rhythm is also a regular movement: *She was lulled to sleep by the gentle rhythm of the boat in the water.* [C] ○ *The rhythm of the boat's motor became faster as it left the harbour.* [C] ○ *By the second game, she was hitting the ball so hard that she didn't give the German player the opportunity to establish any rhythm.* [C] • Rhythm is also a regular pattern of change, esp. one which happens in nature: *the rhythm of the seasons* [C] ○ *Breathing and sleeping are examples of* **biological** *rhythms in human beings.* [C] • **Rhythm and blues** (also **R & B**) is a type of popular music of the 1940s and 1950s which has a strong beat: *Rhythm and blues grew out of blues music and developed into rock and roll.* • The **rhythm method** is a way of preventing pregnancy in which partners have sex on those days when the woman is unlikely to become pregnant: *The rhythm method is one of the least successful methods of birth control.* • The **rhythm section** of a dance or jazz group is the instruments that give a strong beat to the music: *The drums and double bass usually form the rhythm section of a jazz group.*

rhyth·mic /'rɪð·mɪk/, **rhyth·mi·cal** /'rɪð·mɪ·kᵊl/ *adj* • A sound which is rhythmic has a regular movement or beat which is repeated: *The rhythmic sound of the train sent him to sleep.*

rhyth·mi·cal·ly /'rɪð·mɪ·kli/ *adv* • *She tried to breathe deeply and rhythmically.*

rib BONE /rɪb/ *n* [C] a bone that curves round from your back to your chest • *People and animals have 12 ribs on each side of their bodies.* • *My son broke a rib when he fell off a ladder.* • A rib is also a piece of meat taken from this part of the animal: *He cooked a tasty rib of lamb for Sunday lunch.* ○ *She ordered prime rib and a baked potato even though she wasn't hungry.* • The ribs of a boat or roof are the curved pieces of metal or wood which support the structure of the boat or roof. • If you **poke/dig** someone **in the ribs**, you push your finger quickly into their chest, usually to make them notice something or to stop them from doing or saying something. • Your **rib cage** is the structure of ribs that protects your heart and lungs in your chest. • *(infml)* If a story or joke is **rib-tickling** or **rib-ticklingly funny**, it is very amusing.

rib *obj* JOKE /rɪb/ *v* [T] **-bb-** *infml* to joke and laugh about (someone) in a friendly way • *His brothers ribbed him* **about** *his new girlfriend.*

rib·bing /'rɪb·ɪŋ/ *n* [C usually sing] *infml* • *They gave him a ribbing about his accent.* • See also **ribbing** at RIB PATTERN.

rib PATTERN /rɪb/ *n* [U] a method of KNITTING that makes a pattern of raised parallel lines

rib·bed /rɪbd/ *adj* [not gradable] • *Do you prefer plain or ribbed tights?*

rib·bing /'rɪb·ɪŋ/ *n* [U] • Ribbing is a pattern of raised lines on a piece of woollen clothing: *He liked the ribbing on the cuffs of the sweater.* • See also **ribbing** at RIB JOKE.

ri·bald /'rɪb·ᵊld, £'raɪ·bᵊld, $'raɪ·bɔːld/ *adj dated* (of language) referring to sex in a rude but humorous way • *He loves entertaining his friends with ribald stories.*

ri·bald·ry /'rɪb·ᵊl·dri, £'raɪ·bᵊl-, $'raɪ·bɔːl-/ *n* [U] *dated* • Ribaldry is language that refers to sex in a rude but humorous way: *His speech was greeted with whistles and shouts that contained something more than the traditional ribaldry.*

rib·bon /'rɪb·ᵊn/ *n* a long narrow strip of material used to tie things together or as a decoration • *My daughter wears a ribbon in her hair.* [C] • *She tied a yellow ribbon round her hat.* [C] • *He tied up the present with ribbon.* [U] • *(fig.) A narrow ribbon* (= strip) *of road stretched ahead of us across the desert.* [C] • A ribbon is also a small piece of coloured material given to someone in the armed forces to show appreciation for their brave actions. [C] • *(specialized)* A ribbon is also the narrow strip of material that contains the ink for a TYPEWRITER (= a keyboard machine that produces letters that look like printed text): *My typewriter needs a new ribbon.* [C] • If something is **in ribbons**, it is torn into narrow strips: *Her coat was in ribbons.* ○ *His shirt hung in tattered ribbons about him.* • If something is **cut/torn into ribbons**, it is cut or torn many times and is badly damaged: *Our new kitten has torn the living room carpet into ribbons.* ○ *(fig.) The attacking soldiers were cut to ribbons* (= killed) *by machine-gun fire.* • *(Br and Aus)* **Ribbon development** happens when long rows of buildings are built along main roads leading out of towns: *Ribbon development was common in the 1920s and 1930s.*

ri·bo·flav·in /£ˌraɪ·bəʊ'fleɪ·vɪn, $'raɪ·bə·fleɪ-/, **vi·ta·min B2** *n* [U] *specialized* a natural substance that exists in meat, fish, milk, eggs and green vegetables, which is important for health and the production of energy in the body

rice /raɪs/ *n* [U] a grass grown in warm, wet places, or the small seeds of this grass which are cooked and eaten as food • *Rice is an important part of many people's diet.* • *Do you prefer brown rice or white rice?* • *We had boiled rice and fish for lunch.* • A **rice paddy** is a field full of water in which rice is grown. • **Rice paper** is a thin edible paper that is used in cooking and in painting. • **Rice pudding** is a sweet dish made by cooking rice in milk and sugar. • PIC> **Cereals**

rich MONEY /rɪtʃ/ *adj* **-er, -est** having a lot of money or valuable possessions • *He is one of the richest men in Britain.* • *Japan is the world's richest nation.* • *She became very rich by making some shrewd investments.* • *He is determined to get rich quickly.* • *She despised the* **get-rich-quick** *mentality of the 1980s.* • *Pickpockets are attracted to large crowds because of rich* **pickings** (= being able to steal things easily). • If land is rich **in** a valuable natural substance such as coal, oil or wood, it contains a lot of that substance: *The region is rich in minerals and coal deposits.* • *The country has vast oil reserves and rich* (= large) *deposits of other minerals such as sulphur and phosphates.* • Earth that is rich contains a large amount of substances which help plants to grow: *Crops grow very well in this region because the soil is so rich.* ○ *Their farm contains some of the richest arable land in the country.* • Material that is rich is very beautiful and valuable: *She was wearing a velvet skirt and a rich brocade jacket.* • If the style of something such as a piece of furniture or a building is rich, it contains a lot of decoration: *The temple dates from the 8th century and is noted for its rich carvings.* • If something is rich **in** a particular quality, esp. a desirable one, it contains a lot of that quality: *Van Eyck's paintings are very rich in detail.* ○ *Pineapple juice is rich in vitamins A and B.* ○ *The English language is rich in vocabulary.* • If someone's life or the history of a place is rich, it is very interesting because a lot of exciting things happened to that person or in that place: *He has written a book about the island's rich history.* ○ *Starting college can be an exciting and rich* (= interesting and beneficial) *experience.*

-rich /-rɪtʃ/ *combining form* • -rich means containing a large amount of a valuable substance: *Kuwait is an oil-rich country.* ○ *We now consume less milk and calcium-rich food which helps to build strong bones.*

rich /rɪtʃ/ *pl n* • **The rich** are people who have a lot of money or valuable possessions: *The resort is frequented by the rich and famous during the winter.* ○ *She believes that the gap between the rich and the poor is growing.*

rich·es /ˈrɪtʃ·ɪz/ *pl n* • Riches is a large amount of money or valuable possessions: *She has donated a sizeable portion of her riches to children's charities.* ○ *He was persuaded to invest in the company with the promise of great/untold riches.* ○ *(fig.) The arrival of a new coach brought the team three years of unparalleled riches* (= great success). • Riches is also a large quantity of a valuable natural substance: *The country has great oil riches, a resource which as yet has not been tapped.*

rich·ly /ˈrɪtʃ·li/ *adv* • *The facade of the church is richly decorated in green and white marble.* • *A richly* (= extremely) *detailed portrait of the author appears from his autobiography.* • *They have a richly-stocked wine cellar* (= It contains a large quantity of wine). • If something is richly deserved or earned, you strongly believe that someone deserves it or has earned it: *She has finally obtained the recognition which she so richly deserves.* • If someone is richly rewarded for something, they are given something which is valuable or desirable: *The cake takes two hours to cook, but your patience will be richly rewarded because it tastes delicious.*

rich·ness /ˈrɪtʃ·nəs/ *n* [U] • *Her richness* (= wealth) *has been a cause of jealousy among her friends.* • *We were impressed by the great richness of detail* (= the large quantity of detail) *in her painting.* • *He claims he wrote the book to reveal something of the sheer richness* (= variety) *of art history.* • See also **richness** at RICH FOOD, RICH COLOUR/SOUND.

rich FOOD /rɪtʃ/ *adj* **-er, -est** (of food) containing a large amount of oil, butter, eggs or cream • *Rich food can be very bad for you if you eat it in large amounts.* • *This chocolate mousse is too rich for me.* • See also **richness** at RICH MONEY, RICH COLOUR/SOUND.

rich·ness /ˈrɪtʃ·nəs/ *n* [U] • *The richness of the food made him feel slightly ill.*

rich COLOUR/SOUND /rɪtʃ/ *adj* **-er, -est** (of a colour, sound, smell or taste) strong in a pleasing or attractive way • *This lipstick offers long-lasting rich colour.* • *Her bedroom was painted a rich, dark blue.* • *The countryside was bathed in a rich red-gold light from the setting sun.* • *He has a rich, resonant voice.* • *She produced a rich, deep tone from her clarinet.* • *The wine has a rich aromatic flavour.*

rich·ness /ˈrɪtʃ·nəs/ *n* [U] • *I loved the richness of the colours in which the house was painted.* • *The wine has a surprising richness of flavour.* • See also **richness** at RICH MONEY, RICH FOOD.

rich CRITICISM /rɪtʃ/ *adj* [after v] **-er, -est** (of a criticism) not suitable because it relates to your own actions or faults • *The education minister's criticism of the new exam system seems rich considering it was the government who was responsible for changing the system.* • *(infml)* **That's rich** can be said to or about someone who has just criticized another person for a fault which they themselves have: *"He said I was looking rather fat." "That's a bit rich coming from him."*

Rich·ter scale /£ˈrɪk·tə·skeɪl, $-t̬ɚ-/ *n* [U] a system used to measure the strength of an EARTHQUAKE • **The** *Richter scale ranges from 0 to 8.* • *The earthquake in Mexico City registered 7·1 on the Richter scale.*

rick PILE /rɪk/ *n* [C] a large pile of STRAW (= dried wheat stems) or HAY (= dried grass) that has been built in a regular shape

rick *obj* TWIST /rɪk/ *v* [T] *Br and Aus infml* to twist (a part of your body) and hurt it • *I ricked my neck while I was playing squash.*

rick·ets /ˈrɪk·ɪts/ *n* [U] a disease that children can get in which the bones become soft because of a lack of VITAMIN D • *People can suffer from rickets if they do not eat a balanced diet or if their skin is not exposed to enough sunlight.*

rick·e·ty /£ˈrɪk·ɪ·ti, $-ə·t̬i/ *adj* in bad condition and therefore weak and likely to break • *Careful! That chair's a bit rickety.* • *We travelled around Europe on a rickety old bus.* • *She slowly climbed the rickety wooden* **steps**. • *The hut was a rickety* **structure** *that looked as if it might collapse at any moment.* • *(fig.) A few rickety* (= old) *pop stars took part in the farewell concert.*

rick·shaw, rick·sha /£ˈrɪk·ʃɔː, $-ʃɑː/ *n* [C] a small covered passenger vehicle with two wheels which is usually pulled by one person • *Rickshaws are used in some parts of Asia.*

ri·co·chet /ˈrɪk·ə·ʃeɪ/ *v* [I] (of a ball or bullet) to hit a surface and bounce away from it at an angle • *He kicked the ball fiercely into the penalty area, causing it to ricochet* **off** *the goalkeeper into the net.*

ri·co·chet /ˈrɪk·ə·ʃeɪ/ *n* [C] • *He was hit in the arm by a ricochet from a stray bullet.* • *In squash, you have to learn to play the ricochets* (= balls which bounce off the wall at an angle).

ri·cot·ta /£rɪˈkɒt·ə, $-ˈkɑː·t̬ə/ *n* [U] soft white Italian cheese which does not have a strong taste • *I ate ravioli stuffed with spinach and ricotta.*

rid *obj* /rɪd/ *v* [T] **ridding**, *past* **rid** or **ridded** to make (a person or place) free of someone or something unpleasant or harmful • *Our aim is to rid this government* **of** *corruption.* [always + *of*] • *I didn't enjoy marking those papers and I was glad to be rid* **of** *them.* [always + *of*] • To **get rid of** something unwanted is to remove it or throw it away: *That cream got rid of my skin rash.* ○ *I used weedkiller to get rid of the weeds in the garden.* • To **get rid of** someone annoying is to send them away or persuade them to leave: *We got rid of our unwelcome guests by saying we had to go to bed.* • *(infml)* To **get rid of** an old possession, such as a car or piece of furniture, is to sell it: *Have you managed to get rid of your old Volvo yet?*

rid·dance /ˈrɪd·ᵊnts/ *n infml* • **Good riddance** is used to express happiness that someone or something unwanted has gone: *The tax is due to be abolished at the end of the month – and good riddance.* ○ *Some of his colleagues might be tempted to* **bid** *him good riddance.* • *(saying)* 'Good riddance to bad rubbish' means you are pleased that someone bad or something of poor quality has gone: *We've got rid of the old computer system, and good riddance to bad rubbish is what I say.*

rid·den RIDE /ˈrɪd·ᵊn/ *past participle of* RIDE

-rid·den FULL OF /-ˌrɪd·ᵊn/ *combining form* full of (something unpleasant or bad) • *It is a superstition-ridden community.* • *She was guilt-ridden when she discovered that the business had failed because of her.* • *An independent organisation is to be set up to regulate the country's scandal-ridden financial markets.*

rid·dle QUESTION /ˈrɪd·l̩/ *n* [C] a type of question which describes something in a difficult and confusing way and which has a clever or amusing answer • *Can you solve this riddle?* • A riddle is also something which is confusing or a problem which is difficult to solve: *There is no clear solution to the riddle of how much reform is needed or how* *fast the plan should be implemented.* • If someone **talks/ speaks in riddles**, they say things in a confusing way.

rid·dle *obj* MAKE HOLES /ˈrɪd·l̩/ *v* [T] to make a lot of holes in (something) • *The anti-aircraft guns riddled the the plane's wings* **with** *bullets.* [always + *with*]

rid·dled /ˈrɪd·l̩d/ *adj* [not gradable] • *He wore an old jacket riddled* **with** (= full of) *holes.* • If a plan or system is riddled with undesirable features such as mistakes, it is full of them: *Your plan is riddled* **with** *errors.*

ride *(obj)* /raɪd/ *v past simple* **rode** /£rəʊd, $roʊd/, *past part* **ridden** /ˈrɪd·ᵊn/ to sit on (a horse or a bicycle) and travel along on it controlling its movements, or to travel in a vehicle, such as a car, bus or train • *I learned to ride a bike when I was six.* [T] • *We rode the train from Sydney to Perth.* [T] • *I ride my bicycle to work.* [T] • *I ride to work* **on** *my bicycle.* [I] • *I rode home from work* **by** *bike.* [I] • *He hasn't got a car so he rides to work* **on** *the bus.* [I] • *She rides* (= rides horses) *every weekend.* [I] • *He rides well/badly* (= He can ride horses well/badly). [I] • *The hunters came riding* **by/past** *on their horses.* [I] • *They rode the waves at the beach.* [T] • *(literary) The ship rode the waves.* [T] • *(fig.) The Prime Minister is* **riding (on) a wave of** *popularity* (= is very popular). • *(Am)* To ride someone is to try to control them and force them to work: *Your boss is riding you much too hard at the moment.* [T] • *(infml)* If you **let** something **ride**, you do not take any action to stop it. • If someone is **riding for a fall**, their behaviour is likely to lead them into trouble: *She spends far more than she earns and is riding for a fall.* • If someone is **riding high**, they are very successful: *Now that he's managing director, he's really riding high.* • If the success of something **rides on** something else, it depends on it: *The future of the company is* **riding on** *the new managing director.* • *I have a lot of money* **riding on** *that horse* (= I will win or lose money if that horse wins or loses the race). • If a ship rides **out** a period of bad weather, it continues to float during it: *The ship managed to ride out the storm.* [M] ○ *(fig.) Many companies did not manage to ride out* (= survive during) *the recession.* [M] • To **ride roughshod over** someone is to do what you want without giving any attention to other people or their wishes. • If an item of clothing **rides up**, it moves up out of position: *His T-shirt rode up when he bent over.* ○ *Your skirt has ridden up at the back.* • *"She's got a Ticket to Ride"* (song by The Beatles, 1965) • Ⓘ

ride /raɪd/ *n* [C] • A ride is a journey on a horse or bicycle, or in a vehicle: *It's a short bus ride to the airport.* ○ *I went for a (horse) ride last Saturday.* ○ *Do you want to come for a ride* **on** *my motorbike?* ○ *Alex had a ride* **on** *a donkey along the beach.* ○ *I gave my niece a ride* **on** *my shoulders.* • A ride is also a free journey in a car to a place where you want to go: *He asked me for a ride into town.* • A ride is also a machine in an amusement park which people travel in or are moved around by for entertainment: *My favourite ride is the Ferris wheel.* • *(infml)* If someone **takes you for a ride**, they deceive or cheat you: *Be careful or he'll take you for a ride.*

ri·der /£ˈraɪ·dəʳ, $-dɚ/ *n* [C] • A rider is a person who travels along on a horse or bicycle: *One of the riders was thrown off his horse.* • *"Riders on the Storm"* (title of a song by The Doors, 1971) • See also RIDER.

ri·der·less /£ˈraɪ·də·ləs, $-dɚ-/ *adj* [not gradable] • *The sight of the riderless horse worried us.*

ri·ding /ˈraɪ·dɪŋ/ *n* [U] • Riding is the sport or activity of riding horses: *Have you ever been riding?* ○ *She loves horses and was given some riding* **boots** *and a riding* **hat** *for her birthday.* • *(old use)* A **riding habit** is a long skirt and jacket or a long dress which women wore in the past when they rode horses. • A **riding school** is a place where you can learn to ride horses.

ri·der /£ˈraɪ·dəʳ, $-dɚ/ *n* [C] *fml* a statement that is added to what has already been said or decided, or an addition to a government BILL (= a written plan for a law) • *I should like to add a rider* **to** *the judgment of the court.* • See also **rider** at RIDE.

ridge /rɪdʒ/ *n* [C] a long narrow raised part of a surface, esp. a high edge along a mountain • *We walked along the narrow mountain ridge to reach the summit.* • *A ridge* (= narrow area) *of high pressure will bring good weather to the north east this afternoon.* • The ridge of a roof is where the sloping sides join at the top. • *(Aus)* If you **have been around the ridges**, you have a lot of experience.

ri·di·cule /ˈrɪd·ɪ·kjuːl/ *n* [U] unkind words or actions that make someone or something look foolish or worthless • *She was treated with scorn and ridicule by her colleagues when she applied for the job.* • *He was regarded as an* **object of** *ridicule* (= a person who was foolish or worthless). • *Her plans were* **held up to** *ridicule* (= people laughed at them). • *If you continue believing that, you will* **lay** *yourself* **open to** *ridicule* (= people will laugh at you).

ri·di·cule *obj* /ˈrɪd·ɪ·kjuːl/ *v* [T] • To ridicule someone is to laugh at them in an unkind way: *She rarely spoke her mind out of fear of being ridiculed.* ○ *He was ridiculed* **for** *his ideas.*

ri·di·cu·lous /rɪˈdɪk·jʊ·ləs/ *adj* • Someone or something that is ridiculous is foolish or unreasonable and deserves to be laughed at: *You look ridiculous in that old hat.* ○ *Don't be so ridiculous! I can't possibly afford to go on holiday.* ○ *It was so ridiculous of them to have a party starting at 10pm.* ○ **It's** *ridiculous* **to** *expect a two-year-old to be able to read.* [+ *to* infinitive]

ri·di·cu·lous·ly /rɪˈdɪk·jʊ·lə·sli/ *adv* • *Hotel rooms in the city are ridiculously overpriced during the festival.* • *I had to pay a ridiculously high amount to insure my car.* • *He danced ridiculously* (= in a foolish and amusing way) *around the room, waving his arms in the air.*

ri·ding /ˈraɪ·dɪŋ/ *n* [U] See at RIDE

rife /raɪf/ *adj* [after v; not gradable] *fml* (of something unpleasant) very common or frequent • *Dysentery and malaria are rife in the refugee camps.* • *He leads a party in which corruption is rife.* • If a place is rife **with** something unpleasant, it is full of it: *The office was rife with rumours that the chairman was thinking of resigning.*

riff /rɪf/ *n* [C] (in popular music) a simple tune that is used as a starting point to invent other music from which does not have a formal structure • *The song is punctuated by long guitar riffs.*

riff–raff /ˈrɪf·ræf/ *pl n disapproving* people with a bad reputation or of a low social class • *She thinks that by charging such high prices for the tickets she's going to keep the riff-raff out.*

ri·fle GUN /ˈraɪ·fl̩/ *n* [C] a type of gun with a long BARREL (= cylindrical part), which is fired from the shoulder • *Rifles are designed to be accurate at long distances.* • A **rifle-range** is a place where you can practise shooting with a rifle.

ri·fle·ry /£ˈraɪ·flə·ri, $-flɚ·i/ *n* [U] *Am* • Riflery is shooting at TARGETS (= objects intended to be hit) with a rifle.

ri·fle *(obj)* SEARCH /ˈraɪ·fl̩/ *v* to search quickly through (something), often in order to steal something • *The safe had been rifled and the diamonds were gone.* [T] • *He rifled* **through** *the papers on the desk, but the photographs were nowhere to be seen.* [I]

rift /rɪft/ *n* [C] a narrow space in the ground or in rock • *The stream had cut a deep rift* **in** *the rock.* • A rift is also something which separates two people who have been friends and prevents their friendship continuing: *The marriage caused a rift* **between** *the brothers and they didn't speak to each other for ten years.* • A **rift valley** is a valley with steep sides formed by movements of the Earth's surface.

rig *obj* ARRANGE /rɪg/ *v* [T] **-gg-** to arrange dishonestly for the result of (something such as an election) to be changed • *All previous elections in the country have been rigged by the ruling party.* • To **rig the market** is to make the price of shares go up or down in order to make a profit.

rig·ging /ˈrɪg·ɪŋ/ *n* [U] • *Opposition parties have protested over alleged vote rigging in the election.* • *Party leaders have been accused of ballot rigging in an attempt to increase the power of the trade unions in the party.* • See also **rigging** at RIG FIX IN PLACE.

rig *obj* FIX IN PLACE /rɪg/ *v* [T] to fix (a piece of equipment) in place • *We rigged* **up** *a tent between two trees.* [M] • *I rigged* **up** (= made) *a temporary radio aerial from a coat hanger.* [M] • *The sailors rigged the ship* **with** *new sails.*

rig·ging /ˈrɪg·ɪŋ/ *n* [U] • Rigging is the ropes which support and control a ship's sails. • See also **rigging** at RIG ARRANGE.

rig STRUCTURE /rɪg/ *n* [C] a large structure which is used for removing oil or gas from the ground or the bottom of the sea • *Safety precautions on* **oil** *rigs are designed to cope with fires and small-scale explosions.* • PIC **Energy**

rig TRUCK /rɪg/ *n* [C] *esp. Am* a truck consisting of two or more parts which bend where they are joined in order to help the vehicle turn corners

rig out *obj*, **rig** *obj* **out** *v adv* [M] *infml* to put a particular type of clothing on (someone) • *We rigged ourselves out in tracksuits and running shoes for the race.*

rig–out /ˈrɪg·aʊt/, *dated infml* **rig** *n* [C] *infml* • A rig-out is a set of clothes: *I want to get myself a new rig-out for the party.*

right CORRECT /raɪt/ *adj* [not gradable] correct • *Four of your answers were right and two were wrong.* • *You* **got** *three answers right and two wrong.* • *Did you* **get** *that calculation right?* • *Do you know what the right time is?* • *I set the clock to the right time.* • *Were you given the right change?* • *"Is that Mrs Kramer?" "Yes, that's right."* • *"You should give up smoking." "Yes, you're right, I should."* • *Am I right* **in thinking** (=Is it true) *that you will be at the conference?* • *It was quite right* **of** *you to come and see me.* • *You're right* **to** *be annoyed – you've been treated very badly.* [+ *to* infinitive] • *You must* **put** *matters right* (=make the situation better) *by telling the truth.* • If you are right **about** something or someone, you are correct in your judgment or statement about it or them: *You were right* **about** *him – he is a troublemaker.* • *(infml)* If you **put** someone **right** on something, you stop them believing something which is not true, or you correct them by telling them the truth: *She thought she wouldn't have to work hard, but we soon put her right* **on** *that.* ○ See also **put** someone **right** at RIGHT HEALTHY. • *"The lark's on the wing / The snail's on the thorn / God's in His heaven,/ All's right with the world"* (Robert Browning in the poem *Pippa Passes*, 1841) • Compare WRONG NOT CORRECT.

right /raɪt/ *adv* [not gradable] • *Why does he never do anything right?*

right *obj* /raɪt/ *v* [T] • If you right a situation or a mistake, you make it better or correct it: *It's a terrible situation and we should right it as soon as possible.* • If a boat rights itself, it turns itself back to its correct position in the water: *The boat will right itself if it capsizes.*

right·ly /ˈraɪt·li/ *adv* [not gradable] • *"What's the quickest way from here to the library?" "I don't rightly know* (=I am not certain)*."*

rights /raɪts/ *pl n* • If you **put/set something to rights**, you improve it or correct it: *The company needs over a million dollars to set its finances to rights.*

right SUITABLE /raɪt/ *adj* [not gradable] suitable or desirable, or as it should be • *He's the right person for the job.* • *Are you sure we're going in the right direction?* • *I think you've made the right decision.* • *She always tries to do the right thing.* • *You must do things in the right order.* • *The temperature of the swimming pool was just* (=exactly) *right.* • *That hat looks just right on you* (=It suits you). • *He thought the time was right* **to** *let his intentions be known.* [+ *to* infinitive] • *The lid has to go on* **the right way** *(Br and Aus)* **round**/*(Am)* **around** (=one particular part has to be at the front) *or it won't fit.* • Right is also used to describe a person who is considered to be socially important or a place that is considered socially desirable: *She knows all the right people.* ○ *He likes to be seen in the right clubs and restaurants.* • *The key to success is to be* **in the right place at the right time** (=in the best position or place to take advantage of an opportunity). • Compare WRONG NOT SUITABLE.

right /raɪt/ *adv* [not gradable] • If something **goes** right, it is successful or happens in a way that you hoped it would: *Things have been going right for me since I got my present job.*

right MORALLY ACCEPTABLE /raɪt/ *adj* [after v], *adv* [not gradable] considered fair or morally acceptable by most people • *I don't believe they should have put him in prison. It isn't right.* • **It**'s *not right* **to** *criticize someone behind their back.* [+ *to* infinitive] • **It** *is right and proper* **that** *the government should ensure that taxpayers' money is used properly.* [+ *that* clause] • **It** *is only right* **that** *men and women should be paid the same if they are doing the same work.* [+ *that* clause] • *(infml)* If you say that someone is **right-on**, you mean that you approve of them because they have ideas and political beliefs characteristic of someone who supports the political LEFT. • *(dated slang)* **Right on** is an expression of agreement or approval: *"D'you want to listen to some Jimi Hendrix?" "Right on."* • *(approving)* If someone is **right-minded/right-thinking**, they have reasonable beliefs: *Every right-minded person is against terrorism.* • Compare WRONG IMMORAL.

right /raɪt/ *n* • Right is what is considered to be morally good or acceptable: *Your conscience should tell you the difference between right and wrong.* [U] ○ *I don't care about the rights* **and wrongs** *of the matter* (=who is right or wrong) *– I just want you both to stop arguing.* [C] ○ *They discussed* **the rights and wrongs of** (=the moral arguments for and against) *abortion.* • A right is the claim which a person or animal has to be treated in a fair, morally acceptable or legal way, or to have the things that are necessary for life: *She campaigned for women's rights during the 1960s.* [C] ○ *He's a gay rights activist.* [C] ○ *She believes that adequate health care is a basic human right.* [C] ○ *Everyone has a right* **to** *education.* [C] ○ *He demanded the right* **to** *a fair trial.* [C] ○ *Once a person is arrested, they have the right* **to** *call their lawyer.* [C + *to* infinitive] ○ *Britain and Spain have been arguing over fishing rights* (=who is legally allowed to catch fish in a particular place). [C] ○ *She has no more right* **to** *a company car than I have* (=She does not deserve one more than I do). [C] ○ *You're not my boss, so what right* (=authority) *have you got* **to** *criticize me?* [C + *to* infinitive] ○ *You have* **every** *right* (=You have a good reason) **to** *complain.* [C + *to* infinitive] • **By rights** (=If the situation was fair), *I should go before you.* • *She spoke first,* **by right of** (=because of) *her position as director.* • If you are **in the right**, what you are doing is morally or legally correct. • If someone has a position **in** their **own right**, they have earned it or obtained it by themselves and not because of anyone else: *She's a millionaire* **in** *her* **own right.** • If you are **within** your **rights** to do something, you are legally allowed to do it: *I think I'm quite within my rights* **to** *demand a full refund.* [+ *to* infinitive] • When a vehicle or a person has **(the) right of way** on a road, other vehicles and drivers must allow them to go first, for example where roads cross: *Vehicles coming from the left have right of way.* • A **right of way** is also a path or road over private land which people are legally allowed to walk along: *Some farmers illegally plough up rights of way which go across their fields.* • If you believe in a person's **right-to-die**, you support the belief that a person should be allowed to die naturally rather than being kept alive by medical methods when they are unlikely to get well again. • If you believe in a person's **right-to-life**, you are against ABORTION (=the act of ending a pregnancy, usually by a medical operation).

right·ly /ˈraɪt·li/ *adv* [not gradable] • *They quite rightly complained to the manager.* • *(Whether) rightly or wrongly, she has been given the post of managing director.*

right·ness /ˈraɪt·nəs/ *n* [U] • *He is convinced of the rightness of his actions* (=that they are morally or legally correct).

right·ful /ˈraɪt·fəl/ *adj* [not gradable] • A rightful position or claim is one which is morally or legally correct: *He felt he had lost his rightful place as the head of the family.* ○ *Don't forget that I am the rightful owner of this house.*

right·ful·ly /ˈraɪt·fəl·i/ *adv* [not gradable] • *The furniture rightfully belongs to you.*

rights /raɪts/ *pl n* • The rights of a book is the legal authority over the book: *They own the* **foreign** *rights of the book* (=They are allowed to sell it in different languages). ○ *He has acquired the* **film** *rights to the book* (=He is allowed to make a film of the story).

right DIRECTION /raɪt/ *adj, adv* [not gradable], *n* (on or towards) a position that is the opposite of 'left', for example in the word 'the', 'h' is on the right of 't' and 'e' is on the right of 'th' • *Most people write with their right hand.* • *English is written and read from left to right.* [U] • *I've found the right glove, but do you know where the left one is?* • **Turn/Go** *right* (=Turn into the road on the right side) *at the first traffic lights.* • *(Am) I* **took/made/***(infml)* **hung** *a right* (=turned into the next road on the right side) *after crossing the bridge.* • *King's Avenue is the first right* (=the first road on the right side). • *Take the second right* (=Turn into the second road on the right side). • *In this photo, my wife is the woman standing* **on/to** *my right.* [U] • *(infml)* If you say that you would **give** your **right hand/arm** to do something, you mean you would like to do it very much: *I would give my right arm* **to** *meet the President.* [+ *to* infinitive] • *He spends money* **right, left and centre** (=He spends a lot of money). • A **right angle** is an angle of 90°: *A square has four right angles.* ○ *A right angle is one quarter of a full rotation.* • A *(Br and Aus)* **right-angled triangle**/ *(Am)* **right triangle** is a triangle which has one angle of 90°. • **Right field** is the area of a baseball field beyond the BASES (=places to which players run) and between first and second base. • **Right-hand** means on or to the right: *The pictures are all displayed on the right-hand page.* ○ *In North America, vehicles drive on the right-hand* **side** *of the road.* • A **right-hand drive** vehicle has the controls on the right side, and the vehicle is driven on the left side of the road: *In Britain and Australia, people have right-hand drive cars.* •

Someone who is **right-handed** or is a **right-hander** uses their right hand to write with and do most things: *She's right-handed.* ○ *He is a right-handed tennis player.* • *(infml)* A **right-hander** (also a **right**) is a hit made with the right hand: *He gave a vicious right-hander to the man's stomach.* • Someone's **right-hand man** is their most trusted and important helper and supporter: *The president's right-hand man, the Finance Minister, has resigned after a scandal over political donations.* • Compare LEFT [DIRECTION].

right [POLITICS] /raɪt/ *n, adj* (political parties or people) having traditional opinions, and believing in low taxes, private ownership of property, business and industry, and less help for the poor • *In Britain,* **the** *Right has/have been in power since 1979.* [U + sing/pl v] • *The two parties* **on the** *right are planning to unite in the next election.* [U] • *He's a man of the* **far** (= extreme) *right.* [U] • If someone is **right-wing** or is on the **right wing**, they support the political right: *She's* **on** *the right wing* **of** *the party.* ○ *He's extremely right-wing and wants to abolish the benefit system.* • If a belief is **right-wing**, it follows the principles of the political right: *Her views are fairly right-wing.* • A **right-winger** is someone who supports the beliefs of the political right. • Compare LEFT [POLITICS].

right·ist /£'raɪ·tɪst, $-t̬ɪst/ *n* [C], *adj* [not gradable] • A rightist politician or government is one that supports the beliefs of the political right: *He continued to serve the Communist cause in its fight against a succession of rightist governments.* • A rightist is a politician who supports the beliefs of the political right: *She is trying to persuade the rightists into forming a coalition with her party.*

right [HEALTHY] /raɪt/ *adj, adv* [not gradable] healthy, or working correctly • *Since eating that food last night, I haven't felt quite right.* • *The garage said they had fixed my car but the engine's still not right.* • *Something isn't quite right with the brakes on your bike.* • *Something's gone wrong with my computer – could you* **put** *it right* (= make it work correctly) *for me?* • *(infml)* If someone is **as right as rain**, they are healthy, esp. after they have been ill for a period of time: *I was suffering from flu for several weeks, but I'm as right as rain now.* • If someone is **not in** their **right mind**, they are not thinking clearly or they are mentally ill: *My poor old Granny is not in her right mind half the time.* • *(infml)* If someone is **not (quite) right in the head**, you think they are mentally ill because they behave in a strange way. • If something **puts/sets** you **right**, it makes you feel better: *A good night's sleep will soon put you right.* ○ See also **put** someone **right** at RIGHT [CORRECT].

right [AGREEMENT] /raɪt/ *exclamation* used to express agreement with someone or to show that you have understood what someone has said • *"Johnny, you climb up first." "Right."* • *(dated) "Give me a shout when you're ready."* "**Right you are/Right oh.**" • *(Br infml) "You can't do anything in this town if you haven't got any money."* "**Too right** (= I agree completely)." • *(Aus infml)* Right is also used to comfort someone and try to persuade them that there is not a problem: *"I'm worried about Lauren. It's after 10 and she hasn't come back." "She'll be right."* • You can also say right when you want to make a group of people notice you, esp. so that you can start an activity: *Right, you lot. Could you all stop talking, and then we'll begin.*

right [EXACTLY] /raɪt/ *adv* [before adv/prep; not gradable] exactly or directly • *I've got a pimple right on the end of my nose.* • *I filled the bath right up to the top.* • *They built a row of hotels right along the sea-front.* • *I fell asleep right in the middle of her speech.* • *She came up right behind me.* • If someone is **right behind** you, they give you their complete support: *My whole family are right behind me.* • *I'll be right back/I'll be right with you* (= I will return very soon). • *We're very busy right* **now** (= at the present time). • *You must leave right* **now/away** (= immediately). • *She knew the answer* **right away/right off** (= immediately). • Right can also be used to emphasize the qualities that something has: *The car ran right* (= completely) *out of fuel.* ○ *The roof blew right* (= completely) *off the barn.* ○ *She walked right* (= all the way) *past me without noticing me.* ○ *This government is corrupt right* **through** (= completely).

right /raɪt/ *adj* [before n] *infml* • *He's a right* (= total) *idiot.* • If you say **we've got a right one here** about someone who is near you, you mean that you think they are very foolish.

right [TITLE] /raɪt/ *adv* [not gradable] used as part of the title of particular people, such as BISHOPS (= a priest of high rank) and some members of Parliament • *Our new bishop is the Right Reverend James Taylor.* • *The committee will be chaired by the Right Honourable Sarah Bast, MP.*

right·eous /'raɪ·tʃəs/ *adj fml* (of a person) behaving in a way that is morally correct, or (of an action or emotion) considered to be morally correct by the person responsible for the action or emotion • *He was regarded as a righteous and holy man.* • *The government has shown an outburst of righteous anger at the attack.* • See also SELF-RIGHTEOUS.

right·eous /'raɪ·tʃəs/ *pl n fml* • **The righteous** are people who behave in a way that is morally correct. • *"The souls of the righteous are in the hand of God"* (from *The Wisdom of Solomon* in the Apocrypha to the Bible, c.A.D.40)

right·eous·ly /'raɪ·tʃə·sli/ *adv fml* • *Although he was quite prepared to resort to dubious tricks himself, he was righteously incensed if one was used against him.*

right·eous·ness /'raɪ·tʃə·snəs/ *n* [U] *fml*

right·ful /'raɪt·fəl/ *adj* [not gradable] See at RIGHT [MORALLY ACCEPTABLE]

right·ful·ly /'raɪt·fəl·i/ *adv* [not gradable]

ri·gid /'rɪdʒ·ɪd/ *adj* stiff or fixed; not able to be bent, moved, changed or persuaded • *a rigid structure* • *a rigid frame* • *I was rigid* **with** (= stiff and unable to move because of) *pain/fear/etc.* • *When I was studying for exams, I kept to a rigid routine/schedule.* • *(disapproving) We were disappointed that they insisted on such a rigid interpretation of the rules.* • *(disapproving) He lives by his own severe and rigid principles.*

ri·gid·ly /'rɪdʒ·ɪd·li/ *adv esp. disapproving* • *Why do you have to rigidly adhere* (= keep) *to such out-dated ideas?*

ri·gid·i·ty /£rɪ'dʒɪd·ɪ·ti, $-ə·t̬i/ *n* [U] • *These bars are bolted to the structure to add rigidity.* • *(disapproving) Their answer revealed their dogmatic rigidity.*

rig·ma·role /£'rɪg·mə·rəʊl, $-roʊl/ *n* [U] *disapproving* a long set of actions or words without any real purpose • *The customs officials twice made us* **go through the (whole)** *rigmarole of opening up our bags for inspection.*

ri·gor mor·tis /£ˌrɪg·ə'mɔː·tɪs, $-ɚ'mɔːr·t̬ɪs/ *n* [U] *specialized* the stiffness of the joints and muscles of a dead body • *Rigor mortis usually* **sets in** *between two and four hours after death.*

ri·gour [SEVERITY] *Br and Aus, Am and Aus* **ri·gor** /£'rɪg·əʳ, $-ɚ/ *n* [U] severity or difficulty • *She was punished with unusual rigour.*

ri·gours *Br and Aus, Am and Aus* **ri·gors** /£'rɪg·əz, $-ɚz/ *pl n* • *They survived the rigours* (= severe conditions) *of the winter.*

ri·gor·ous /£'rɪg·ᵊr·əs, $'-ɚ-/ *adj* • *It's a rigorous survival course in the mountains.*

ri·gor·ous·ly /£'rɪg·ᵊr·ə·sli, $'-ɚ-/ *adv*

ri·gour [EXACTNESS] *Br and Aus, Am and Aus* **ri·gor** /£'rɪg·əʳ, $-ɚ/ *n* [U] *approving* care and exactness • *The article fails to explore the issues with any real rigour.* • *They considered that, as a method, it lacked intellectual rigour.* • *This passage is remarkable for the rigour of its argument and its language.*

ri·gor·ous /£'rɪg·ᵊr·əs, $'-ɚ-/ *adj approving* • *rigorous testing/checking* • *rigorous methods* • *She has a scientifically rigorous approach.*

ri·gor·ous·ly /£'rɪg·ᵊr·ə·sli, $'-ɚ-/ *adv approving* • *He rigorously notes down every penny he spends.* • *They monitored the traffic flow rigorously.*

rig–out /'rɪg·aʊt/ *n* [C] *infml* See at RIG OUT

rile *obj* /raɪl/ *v* [T] *infml* to make angry • *The new policy riled existing customers and didn't win many new ones.* • *Don't let her rile you.* • *It's not in your best interests to* **get** *him riled.*

rim /rɪm/ *n* [C] the outer, often curved or circular, edge of something • *The rim of the cup was chipped and broken.* • *There was a pattern of flowers all around the rim of the plate.* • *His reading glasses had gold/plastic/horn/wire rims.* • *The village is just below the rim of the crater.* • *The company supplies systems for clients on the Pacific rim* (= countries on the edge of the Pacific ocean). • [LP]› **World regions** [PIC]› **Edge**

rim *obj* /rɪm/ *v* [T] **-mm-** • *The garden was rimmed with* (= surrounded by) *a high stone wall.*

rim·less /'rɪm·ləs/ *adj* [not gradable] • *He's got new rimless reading glasses.*

–rimmed /-rɪmd/ *combining form* • *gold-rimmed glasses* • *horn-rimmed spectacles* • *He had red-rimmed eyes from crying.*

rind /raɪnd/ *n* [U] the hard outer layer or covering of particular fruits and foods • *lemon/orange rind* •

watermelon rind • *bacon/cheese rind* • *Add the* **grated** *rind of a lemon to the cake mixture.* • Compare PEEL [REMOVE SKIN]. • [PIC] **Fruit**

ring [CIRCLE] /rɪŋ/ *n* [C] a small circle of any material, or any group of things or people in a circular shape or arrangement • *The game involved throwing metal rings over a stick.* • *I need some more of these plastic rings for the shower curtain.* • *The wet glass left a ring* (= circular mark) *on the table.* • *The children sat in a ring around the teacher.* • *Stonehenge is made up of several rings of huge ancient stones.* • A ring is also a circular piece of jewellery worn esp. on your finger: *She wore a gold wedding ring.* ○ *He bought her a diamond/emerald ring* (= a ring with a jewel fixed to it). [PIC] **Jewellery** • A ring is also a group of people who help each other, often secretly and in a way which is to their advantage: *a drug ring* ○ *an antiques ring* ○ *a spy ring* • See also RINGLEADER. • *(Br)* A ring (*Am and Aus usually* **element**) is also a circular piece of material often made of metal that can be heated in order to be used for cooking: *a gas ring* ○ *an electric ring* • A ring is also an enclosed space where people perform or compete: *a boxing ring* ○ *a circus ring* • *The boxers climbed into the ring.* • *The horses trotted round the ring.* • See also RINGSIDE. • If someone **runs rings round** you they are very much better, faster, or more successful at something than you are: *Our girls' hockey team have run rings round all their opponents this year.* • A **ring binder** is a piece of stiff folded cardboard with metal rings inside, used to keep loose pages in position. [PIC] **Stationery** • Your **ring finger** is the finger nearest to your **little finger**. People often wear a ring on their ring finger to show that they are married or are planning to get married. • *(Br and Aus)* A **ring-pull** (*Am* **pull-tab**) is a metal ring which must be lifted to open a closed metal container, esp. of drink: *a ring-pull can* • *(Br and Aus)* A **ring road** (*Am usually* **beltway**) is a main road that goes around the edge of a town, allowing traffic to avoid the town centre. • [PIC] **Ring**

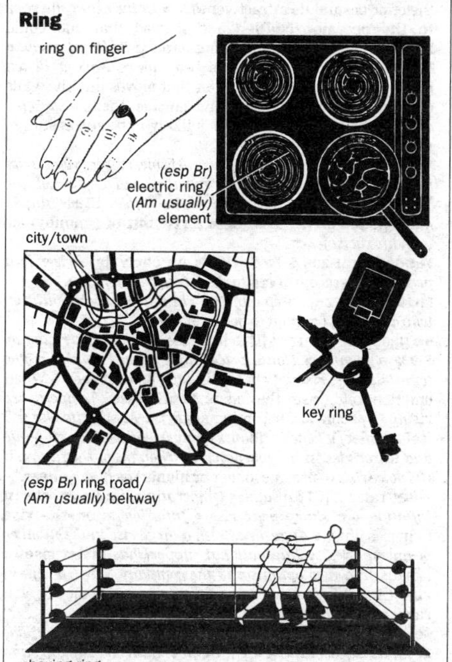

ring *obj* /rɪŋ/ *v* [T] • To ring something is to surround it: *Armed police ringed the hijacked plane.* • *(Br)* To ring (also **circle**) something is also to draw a circle round it: *Students should ring the correct answers in pencil.* ○ *The harbour is dangerous – it's ringed* **by/with** *rocks and reefs.* • To ring something, esp. an animal, is also to put a ring on it: *The farmer ringed the bull* (= put a ring through its nose). ○ *We ringed the birds* (= put rings around their legs) *so that we could identify them later.* • *(Aus infml)* A **ring-in** is a person included in an activity at a late stage.

ring *(obj)* [TELEPHONE] *esp. Br* /rɪŋ/, *Am usually* **call** *v past simple* **rang** /ræŋ/, *past part* **rung** /rʌŋ/ to make a telephone call to (someone) • *I ring home once a week to tell my parents I'm okay.* [I] • *There's been an accident – can you ring* **for** *an ambulance?* [I] • *I'm busy now – could you ring (me)* **back** *later, please.* [I/T] • *I've been trying to ring you all week, but there's been no answer.* [T] • *The boss rang* **(in)** *to say he'll be back at 4.30.* [I] • *I rang* **down/through to** *(hotel) reception* **to** *ask for some sandwiches.* [I] • *(Br) I rang* **round** *the* (= I telephoned many) *airlines to find out the cheapest price.* [I] • *Why don't you ring* **(up)** *Simon and ask him to the party?* [T/M] • *Mother rang* **up** *while you were out.* [I] • *(Br)* When you **ring off** (*Am and Aus* **hang up**), you end a telephone conversation and put down the RECEIVER (= the part of the telephone you hold to your ear): *She said "No, thank you" and rang off hurriedly.* • [LP] **Telephone**

ring *esp. Br* /rɪŋ/, *Am usually, Br and Aus also* **call** *n* [U] • *I'll* **give** *you* **a** *ring* (= telephone you) *tomorrow.* • *Give me a ring sometime.*

ring *(obj)* [SOUND] /rɪŋ/ *v past simple* **rang** /ræŋ/, *past part* **rung** /rʌŋ/ to (cause to) make the sound of a bell • *The doorbell/telephone rang.* [I] • *Anne's alarm clock rang for half an hour before she woke.* [I] • *The church bells were rung after the wedding.* [T] • *She tapped the glass bowl with a knife to make it ring* (= produce a continuous sound). [I] • *I rang the bell but nobody came to the door.* [T] • *My head is/My ears are still ringing* (= are full of a ringing noise) *from the sound of the military band.* [M] • *The church bells rang* **in** (= rang to announce the beginning of) *the New Year.* [M] • *The bells are ringing* **out** (= ringing to announce the end of) *the old year.* [M] • To ring **out** is also to sound loudly and clearly: *A cry of warning rang* **out**. [I] ○ *A shot rang* **out**. [I] • If a place rings **with** a sound, it is full of it: *The room rang with his screams.* [I] • *The name* **rang a bell** (= sounded familiar) *but I couldn't remember where I had heard it before.* • To **ring the changes (on** something) is to do something in different ways in order to make it interesting: *For variety, ring the changes on packed lunches using different types of bread and spicy fillings.* • *Since I knew she was jealous, her words of praise* **rang hollow** (= seemed insincere). • *Her explanations* **rang true/false** (= seemed to be true/false). • If someone **rings up** a price on a **cash register** (= a machine that calculates and records a sale) they record the money that has been paid by a customer: *I'm sorry, I've rung up the wrong amount.* • *"Ring out the old, ring in the new / ... Ring out the false, ring in the true"* (from the poem *In Memoriam* by Alfred, Lord Tennyson, writing about ringing church bells to mark the New Year, 1850)

ring /rɪŋ/ *n* • *There was a ring at the door.* [C] • *He gave a ring at the door.* [C] • *(fig.) Your name has* **a** *familiar ring* (= I think I have heard it before). [U] • *(fig.) This story has* **a/the** *ring* **of truth** (= it seems to be true). [U]

ring·lead·er /£ˈrɪŋˌliː·dəʳ, $-dɚ/ *n* [C] the person who seems to be leading a group of people who might be dangerous or cause trouble • *Once they caught the ringleader, it was easy to round up the rest of the gang.*

ring·let /£ˈrɪŋ·lət, $-lɪt/ *n* [C usually pl] a curled piece of long hair • *Her hair hung about her shoulders* **in** *ringlets.*

ring·side /ˈrɪŋ·saɪd/ *adj* [not gradable], *n* [C] (at) the edge of an enclosed space where people compete or perform • *We had seats by* **the** *ringside for the boxing match.* [U] • *We managed to get ringside seats for the circus.*

ring·toss /£ˈrɪŋ·tɒs, $-tɑːs/ *n* [U] *Am for* HOOPLA [GAME]

ring·worm /£ˈrɪŋ·wɜːm, $-wɜːrm/ *n* [U] a disease that causes red rings on the skin

rink /rɪŋk/ *n* [C] a large flat surface, of ice or other hard material, for SKATING (= a sport using special boots to move along), or the area or building which contains this • *an ice rink* • *a roller-skating rink* • [PIC] **Winter sports**

rink·y-dink /ˈrɪŋ·ki·dɪŋk/ *adj Am infml* having little importance or influence; of poor quality or old-fashioned • *Their family business is a rinky-dink operation.*

rinse *obj* /rɪnts/ *v* [T] to use water to clean the soap or dirt from (something) • *First apply shampoo to hair and then rinse* **thoroughly**. [I] • *Don't forget to rinse* **(off)** *the suds from the dishes.* [T/M] • *She rinses* **(out)** *her mouth every morning to prevent bad breath.* [T/M] • *There was no soap, so I just quickly rinsed my hands with water/(Br also)* **under the tap**. [T]

rinse /rɪnts/ *n* [U] • *She gave the towel* **a** *quick rinse.* • *The washing machine has a* **cold/hot** *rinse cycle.* • A rinse is also a temporary colouring of or for the hair: *My* *grandmother has* **a blue** *rinse every month.* ○ *a bottle of blue rinse*

ri·ot /ˈraɪ·ət/ *n* a noisy, violent, and uncontrolled public gathering • *Inner-city riots erupted when a local tax was increased.* [C] • *Police in riot* **gear** (= protective clothes and equipment) *lined up at the end of the street.* • **Riot police** *were called to the scene to control the angry mob.* • *The soldiers held up their riot* **shields** *and advanced slowly towards the crowd.* • *Jim's roses are a* **riot of colour(s)** (= extremely bright and colourful). • *(infml)* A riot is also a very funny or entertaining occasion, event, or person: *The festival was a riot.* [U] ○ *We had a riot of a time at the party.* [U] ○ *My younger brother's a riot* (= very amusing). [U]

ri·ot /ˈraɪ·ət/ *v* [I] • *Students are rioting in the streets of the capital.* • *The road was blocked by a rioting mob.*

ri·ot·er /£ˈraɪ·ə·tər, $-t̬ɚ/ *n* [C] • *The police and rioters clashed violently.*

ri·ot·ing /£ˈraɪ·ə·tɪŋ, $-t̬ɪŋ/ *n* [U] • *The government is afraid of further serious rioting today.*

ri·ot·ous /£ˈraɪ·ə·təs, $-t̬əs/ *adj* • *The neighbours complained about their riotous behaviour.* • *We went to a riotous* (= full of loud fun) *party and danced all night.* • Ⓘ

ri·ot·ous·ly /£ˈraɪ·ə·tə·sli, $-t̬ə-/ *adv*

ri·ot·ous·ness /£ˈraɪ·ə·tə·snəs, $-t̬ə-/ *n* [U]

RIP DEAD /£ˌɑː·raɪˈpiː, $ˌɑːr·aɪ-/ *abbreviation for* **rest in peace**, see at REST STOP • *Esmerelda McClellan RIP*

rip *(obj)* TEAR /rɪp/ *v* **-pp-** to pull apart; to tear or be torn violently and quickly • *His new trousers ripped when he bent down.* [I] • *I ripped my shirt on a nail.* [T] • *I saw her ripping the note into little pieces.* [T] • *She excitedly ripped the parcel* **open.** [T + obj + adj] • *The explosion ripped* **open** *the side of the house.* [T + obj + adj] • *The wind ripped the flag* **to/into shreds** (= into little pieces). [T] • To rip **up** something is to tear it into small pieces: *That's all wrong – rip it* **up** *and start again.* [M] ○ *She ripped* **up** *his letters and burned the pieces.* [M] • To rip is also to do something quickly and esp. without much care: *I wish the old fireplaces hadn't been ripped* **out** (= removed). [M] ○ *They ripped* **off** (= removed) *their clothes and ran into the sea.* [M] ○ *The explosion ripped* **through** (= moved through) *the hotel.* [M] ○ *We ripped* **up** (= removed) *the carpets and laid a new wooden floor.* [M]

rip /rɪp/ *n* [C] • *Your sleeve has got a rip in it.*

rip off *obj* CHEAT, **rip** *obj* **off** *v adv* [M] *infml* to cheat (someone) by charging them too much money • *We didn't know how much it was likely to cost and they just ripped us off.* • *Everybody else is paying less – I think we've been ripped off.*

rip–off /£ˈrɪp·ɒf, $-ɑːf/ *n* [C] • *$300 for that shirt? – That's a complete rip-off.*

rip off *obj* STEAL, **rip** *obj* **off** *v adv* [M] *slang* to steal (something) or steal from (somebody) • *He ripped the radio off yesterday.* • *She rips off old people all the time.*

rip·cord /£ˈrɪp·kɔːd, $-kɔːrd/ *n* [C] a cord that you pull to open a PARACHUTE (= large piece of cloth used to make you fall more slowly from the sky)

ripe /raɪp/ *adj* **-r, -st** (of fruit or crops) fully developed ready to be collected or eaten • *Those bananas aren't ripe yet – they're still green.* • *Fields of ripe wheat were ready for harvesting.* • If cheese is described as ripe, it has developed a strong, or too strong, flavour: *I like ripe cheese – it is best when it's strong and smelly.* ○ *(fig.) There was a ripe* (= strong and unpleasant) *smell from his socks.* • *(dated humorous)* Language that is ripe is rude: *a ripe joke* • Ripe **for** means ready for or needing: *This country is ripe for change.* ○ *The company is ripe for takeover.* • **The time is ripe** (= It is the right time) **to** *invest*/**for** *investing in new technology.* [+ *to* infinitive; + v-*ing*] • *My grandmother died at the* **ripe old age** (= great age) *of 92.*

ri·pen *(obj)* /ˈraɪ·pᵊn/ *v* • *The sunshine in August ripened the tomatoes.* [T] • *These tomatoes are ripening nicely.* [I] • *(fig.) My plans are ripening – now all I need is official approval.* [I]

ripe·ness /ˈraɪp·nəs/ *n* [U] • *The yellowness of the bananas showed their ripeness.*

ri·poste /£rɪˈpɒst, $-ˈpoʊst/ *n* [C] a quick and clever remark, often made in answer to a criticism • *She made a sharp/witty/neat riposte.*

ri·poste /£rɪˈpɒst, $-ˈpoʊst/ *v* • *Marshall riposted* **that** *they did not have the money to go to court.* [+ *that* clause] • *"And you'll pay for us all, will you?" she riposted.* [+ clause]

rip·ple /ˈrɪp·l̩/ *n* [C] a small continuous movement, esp. on the surface of water • *The stone she threw caused ripples to spread across the lake.* • *A ripple* **of** *laughter/applause* (= a continuous sound which gets louder and then quieter) **ran through** *the crowd.* • *A ripple* **of** *excitement/unease* (= an emotion that comes and goes quickly) **ran through** *her body.* • *(fig.) News of the war hardly caused a ripple* (= caused no increase of interest or activity). • Ripple is also plain ice cream with thin layers of chocolate or other flavours mixed into it: *chocolate ripple* ○ *raspberry ripple* • A **ripple effect** is a spreading effect or a series of things which happen as the result of a certain action or event: *The bank crash has had a ripple effect on the whole community.*

rip·ple *(obj)* /ˈrɪp·l̩/ *v* • *The breeze rippled the water.* [T] • *The field of wheat rippled in the breeze.* [I] • *His muscles rippled under his skin.* [I]

rip–roar·ing /£ˌrɪpˈrɔː·rɪŋ, $-ˈrɔːr·ɪŋ/ *adj infml* wild, noisy, and exciting • *He's a rip-roaring, extravagant sort of a person.* • *The party was a rip-roaring, riotous success.*

rise MOVE UP /raɪz/ *v* [I] *past simple* **rose** /£rəʊz, $roʊz/, *past part* **risen** /ˈrɪz·ᵊn/ to move upwards • *The balloon rose gently* **(up)** *into the air.* • *She rose* **from** *her chair* (= stood up) *to welcome us.* • *Murmurs of disapproval rose* **from** (= came from) *the crowd.* • *He rose* **to** *his* **feet** (= stood up) *to deliver his speech.* • *My grandfather rises* (= gets out of bed) *at 5 every morning to do his exercises.* • *The River Cam rises* (= first comes out of the ground) **in/at** *a place called Ashwell.* • *When you put yeast in bread and bake the bread, it rises.* • *(fml specialized) Parliament/The court/The meeting rose* (= stopped work) *at 6 pm.* • *We watched the sun rise* (= move up into the sky). • *The fish aren't rising* (= coming to the surface) *today.* • *New buildings are rising* (= being built) *throughout the city.* • *He* **rose above** (= was successful or able to manage despite) *his pain/bad luck/difficulties.* • *They were unkind to me but I tried to* **rise above** *it* (= not allow it to trouble me) *and stay calm.* • *Christians believe that Jesus* **rose from** *the dead/***rose again** (= came back to life) *after he was killed.* • *He* **rose through the ranks** (= kept being moved up to more important positions) *to become a General.* • *He* **rose to fame** (= became famous) *as a TV presenter.* • *They offered a good salary, but I didn't* **rise to the bait** (= I didn't accept the offer despite its attractiveness). • *In the exam she* **rose to the occasion/challenge** (= showed that she could handle a difficult situation) *and wrote a brilliant essay.* • **Rise and shine** (= Get out of bed), *we're leaving in ten minutes.* • **Rising damp** is water that moves into the walls of buildings from the ground and damages them. • *She's the* **rising star** (= the person who is likely to be successful) *of the organisation.*

rise /raɪz/ *n* [U] • *Her rapid rise to fame/power/popularity meant that she made many enemies.* • *The rise of the Worker's Party was as rapid as its fall.* • *Steve always manages to* **get/***(Br also)* **take a rise out of** (= annoy) *me with his racist jokes.*

ri·ser /£ˈraɪ·zər, $-zɚ/ *n* [C] • *An* **early/late** *riser is a person who gets out of bed early/late in the morning.*

ri·sing /ˈraɪ·zɪŋ/ *prep esp. Br* • *The school accepts children who are rising* (= about to become) *five.*

rise INCREASE /raɪz/ *v* [I] to increase • *Inflation is rising by 2·1% a month.* • *House prices have risen rapidly.* • *The wind/storm is rising* (= beginning to get stronger). • When emotions etc. rise, they start to increase: *Tempers are rising* (= people are becoming angry). ○ *My spirits rise* (= I feel happier) *whenever I think of my friends.* ○ *She felt panic and terror rise* **in** *her whenever she thought of the future.* ○ *His voice rose* (= became louder or higher) *as he got angry.*

rise /raɪz/ *n* [C] • *a sudden temperature rise* • *a 5% rise* **in** *inflation* • *a sharp price rise* • *Inflation is* **on the rise** (= increasing). • *August has seen a large rise in the number of unemployed.* • *International support has* **given rise to** (= caused) *a new optimism in the company.* • A *(Br)* **(pay) rise**/*(Am)* **(pay) raise** is an increase in the money you earn: *I asked the boss for a rise and he refused.*

rise BECOME HIGHER /raɪz/ *v* [I] to become higher • *The ground rises over there.* • *The castle is built on rising ground* (= ground higher than areas around it). • *You can see the Alps rising* (= showing as a higher area) **in** *the distance/***above** *the clouds.*

rise /raɪz/ *n* [C] • A rise is a small hill or slope: *The castle is built on a slight rise above the town.* ○ *My house is hidden by a rise in the road.*

ri·ser /£ˈraɪ·zər, $-zɚ/ *n* [C] • *(specialized)* A riser is the vertical part of a step.

ris·ers /£ˈraɪ·zəz, $-zɚz/ *pl n Am* • Risers are a group of steps on which people sit or stand to see or to be seen better.

rise BE OPPOSED TO /raɪz/ *v* [I always + adv/prep] to begin to oppose or fight (esp. a bad government or ruler) as a group • *The people rose* **(up) against** *the oppressor/tyrant/dictator.*

ri·sing /ˈraɪ·zɪŋ/ *n* [C] • A rising is an UPRISING: *He left the country after the unsuccessful rising.*

ri·si·ble /£ˈrɪz·ə·bl̩, £ˈraɪ·zə-, $ˈrɪz·ə-/ *adj fml disapproving* causing laughter or deserving to be laughed at • *She's been making risible attempts to write a novel.*

risk /rɪsk/ *n* (an example of) danger of loss, harm, etc. • *In this business, the risks and the rewards are high.* [C] • *Leaving my job was a risk, but it has worked out well.* [C] • *There's a risk* **of** *another accident happening in this fog.* [C] • *The risk* **(that)** *we might fail made us work twice as hard.* [C + (*that*) clause] • *It's always a risk starting up a new business.* [C] • *This wire is a safety/fire risk* (= it's dangerous). [C] • *His employers thought he was a security risk* (= he might tell their secrets to a competitor). [C] • *He's a* **bad/high** *risk* (= he is likely to cause failure, damage, etc.). [C] • *The company is quite a* **good** *risk* (= safe to lend money to). [C] • *We want clean rivers and lakes, where you can swim* **without** *risk* **to** *your health.* [U] • *It's a* **low-***risk* (= safe) *strategy.* • *A young woman out alone at night is* **at risk** (= in a dangerous situation). • *(fml)* **At the risk of** *seeming rude* (= Even if I do seem rude), *I'm afraid I have to leave now.* • *If you take my car, it's* **at** *your* **own risk** (= you are responsible for any damage or difficulty). • *The notice said 'Cars parked* **at** *their owners'* **risk***'* (= the owners are responsible for any damage or difficulty). • *A policeman often has to* **run/take** *risks* (= do dangerous things). • *If we don't take more money with us, we* **run the risk of** *running out* (= it is possible we will not have enough) *over the weekend.*

risk *(obj)* /rɪsk/ *v* • *"It's dangerous to cross here." "I'll just have to risk* **it** (= accept the danger of doing it).*"* [T] • *She was prepared to risk everything* **on** *a last throw of the dice.* • *He risked* **losing** *his house when his company went bankrupt.* [+ v-*ing*] • *I'm not risking* (= taking the chance of losing) *my* **life/***(infml)***neck** *in that old car.* [T] • *He risked* **life and limb** *to get the cat down from the tree* (= it was a dangerous thing to attempt). [T]

risk·y /ˈrɪs·ki/ *adj* **-ier, -iest** • *Parachuting is a risky sort of thing to do.* • **It's** *risky* **to** *buy a car without some good advice.* [+ *to* infinitive]

ri·sot·to /£rɪˈzɒt·əʊ, $-ˈzɑː·t̬oʊ/ *n* [C/U] *pl* **risottos** (a dish of) cooked rice, with added vegetables, meat, etc.

ris·qué /ˈrɪskeɪ/ *adj* (of jokes or stories) slightly rude or shocking, esp. because about sex

ris·sole /£ˈrɪs·əʊl, $-oʊl/ *n* [C] a type of food made from meat or vegetables cut into small pieces and then pressed together and cooked in fat • *chicken rissoles* • *lentil rissoles*

rite /raɪt/ *n* [C usually pl] (a usually religious ceremony with) a set of fixed words and actions • *funeral/marriage/fertility rites* • *You have to go through an initiation rite before you become a full member.* • *A priest administered the* **last rites** *to the dying man.* • A **rite of passage** is an official ceremony or informal activity which marks an important stage or occasion in a person's life esp. becoming an adult.

ri·tual /£ˈrɪt·ju·əl, $ˈrɪtʃ·u-/ *n* a set of fixed actions and sometimes words performed regularly, esp. as part of a ceremony • *My father is in the kitchen conducting his morning ritual – reading the newspaper and sipping his coffee.* [C] • *Football players have a ritual of touching and hugging each other after a goal.* [C] • *The birds were performing a mating ritual.* [C] • *In traditional societies the ties between people were formed by symbol, myth and religious ritual.* [U] • *The group were accused of ritual* **abuse/murder** (= as part of a ceremony).

ri·tual·is·tic /£ˌrɪt·ju·əlˈɪs·tɪk, $ˌrɪtʃ·u·əlˈɪs·t̬ɪk/ *adj*

ri·tual·is·ti·cal·ly /£ˌrɪt·ju·əlˈɪs·tɪ·kli, $ˌrɪtʃ·u·əlˈɪs·t̬ɪ-/ *adv*

ritz·y /ˈrɪt·si/ *adj* **-ier, -iest** *infml dated* expensive, fashionable, and luxurious • *This is a ritzy hotel.* • *That's a ritzy dress.*

ri·val /ˈraɪ·vəl/ *n* [C] a person, group, etc. competing with others for the same thing or in the same area • *Jack and Colin were* **arch** (= very great) *rivals.* • *He beat his* **closest/nearest** *rival by 20 marks.* • *We were business rivals/rivals* **in** *business.* • *Sporadic fighting has continued between forces of the two rival* **factions**. • *The companies produce rival versions of the toy.*

ri·val *obj* /ˈraɪ·vəl/ *v* [T] **-ll-** or *Am usually* **-l-** • *No computer can rival* (= equal) *a human brain* **for/in** *complexity.* • *The beauty of the country is only rivalled by* (= is equal to) *the violence of its politics.*

ri·val·ry /ˈraɪ·vəl·ri/ *n* • *There's such rivalry* **among/between** *my three sons.* [U] • *The brothers competed with* **friendly** *rivalry.* [U] • *There's fierce rivalry* **for** *the job/***to** *get the job.* [U] • *There was deadly rivalry to be the first to market the product.* [U] • *The incident revived old/ancient rivalries.* [C]

ri·ven /ˈrɪv·ən/ *adj* [after v; not gradable] *literary* violently divided • *It was a community/nation/family riven* **by** *jealousy, hatred and bitterness.*

ri·ver /£ˈrɪv·əʳ, $-ɚ/ *n* [C] a natural wide stream of fresh water flowing across the land into the sea, a lake, or another river • *They took a walk by the river.* • *We sailed* **up** *the river/***up river** *to its* **source** (= where it starts). • *I rowed* **down** *the river/***down river** *to its* **mouth** (= where it flows into the sea). • River is used usually before, sometimes after, the name of a river: *the River Thames* ○ *the River Nile* ○ *the Yellow River* • **Rivers of** means a large amount of (a liquid): *If there's a revolution, rivers of* **blood** *will flow.* ○ *Rivers of sweat ran down his back.* • A **river bank** is the land at either edge of a river: *The river flows between its steep banks.* ○ *We sat on the (river) bank and had a picnic.* • A **river-bed** is the ground over which a river usually flows: *a stony river-bed* ○ *a dry river-bed* • A **river boat** is a large passenger boat which travels up and down a river. • *"A River Always Runs Through"* (title of a book by Norman Maclean, 1979) • See also RIVERSIDE. Compare STREAM SMALL RIVER. • PIC Mouth

ri·ver·side /£ˈrɪv·ə·saɪd, $ˈ-ɚ-/ *n* [U] the land along the edges of a river • *a riverside restaurant*

ri·vet /ˈrɪv·ɪt/ *n* [C] a metal pin used to fasten flat pieces of metal, and other thick materials such as leather, together

ri·vet *obj* /ˈrɪv·ɪt/ *v* [T] • *Many parts of an aircraft are riveted* **together**. • *(fig.) When she pulled out a gun, I was riveted* **to the spot** (= unable to move). • *If you or your attention is riveted by/***on** *something, you are very interested in it: I was riveted/My attention was riveted by my grandmother's stories.* ○ *His eyes were riveted* (= fixed) **on** *the television.*

ri·vet·ing /£ˈrɪv·ɪ·tɪŋ, $-t̬ɪŋ/ *adj infml* • *It was a riveting* (= extremely interesting) *story/film/book.*

riv·i·e·ra /£rɪ·viˈeə·rə, $-ˈer·ə/ *n* [C] an area of coast, esp. one where there are holiday towns with beaches • *the French/Italian/Cornish riviera*

ri·vu·let /£ˈrɪv·jʊ·lət, $-lɪt/ *n* [C] *literary* a very small stream • *(fig.) Rivulets of sweat/rain/blood ran down his face.*

RN *n* [U] (used after the names of naval officers) *abbreviation for* **Royal Navy**, see at ROYAL • *Captain H. Doughty, RN*

RNA /£ˌɑː·renˈeɪ, $ˌɑːr·en-/ *n* [U] *specialized abbreviation for* ribonucleic acid (= an important chemical present in all living cells)

roach FISH /£rəʊtʃ, $roʊtʃ/ *n* [C] *pl* **roach** a European fish that lives in fresh water • *The river contains large quantities of roach and bream.*

roach INSECT /£rəʊtʃ, $roʊtʃ/ *n* [C] *Am infml for* COCKROACH

roach CIGARETTE /£rəʊtʃ, $roʊtʃ/ *n* [C] *slang* the end part of a cigarette made of MARIJUANA (= an illegal drug), that is not smoked

road /£rəʊd, $roʊd/ *n* a long piece of hard ground that people can drive along from one place to another • *Roads usually have a tarmac surface.* [C] • *We live on a busy/quiet road.* [C] • *Take the next road on the left.* [C] • *There's a bank on the other side of the road.* [C] • *You must always remember to look both ways before crossing the road.* [U] • *The road* **from** *here* **to** *Adelaide runs/goes through some beautiful countryside.* [C] • *All roads* **into** *the town were blocked by the snow.* [C] • *I hate flying so I go everywhere* **by** *road or rail.* [U] • *I live (Br and Aus)* **in***/(Am)* **on** *Mill Road.* [C] • *My address is 82 Mill Road.* [U] • *I don't like cycling along* **main** *roads.* [C] • *I prefer driving along* **minor** *roads.* [C] • *Is this the Oxford Road* (= the road that goes to Oxford)*?* [C] • *Do you have a recent road* **map***?* • *That road* **sign** *said 'No Entry'.* • A road **accident** is an accident involving a vehicle: *Most road accidents are caused by people driving too fast.* [C] • The **back** roads are the smaller, less busy roads which you can use to avoid travelling along busy major roads: *We travelled down to Tours on the back roads.* [C] • A **dirt** road is a road with a rough surface made of earth. [C] • *(Am infml) If he would* **get out of the/my road** (= stop blocking my way) *I could pass.* • *My car was in the garage for a week, but it's now back* **on the road** (= working

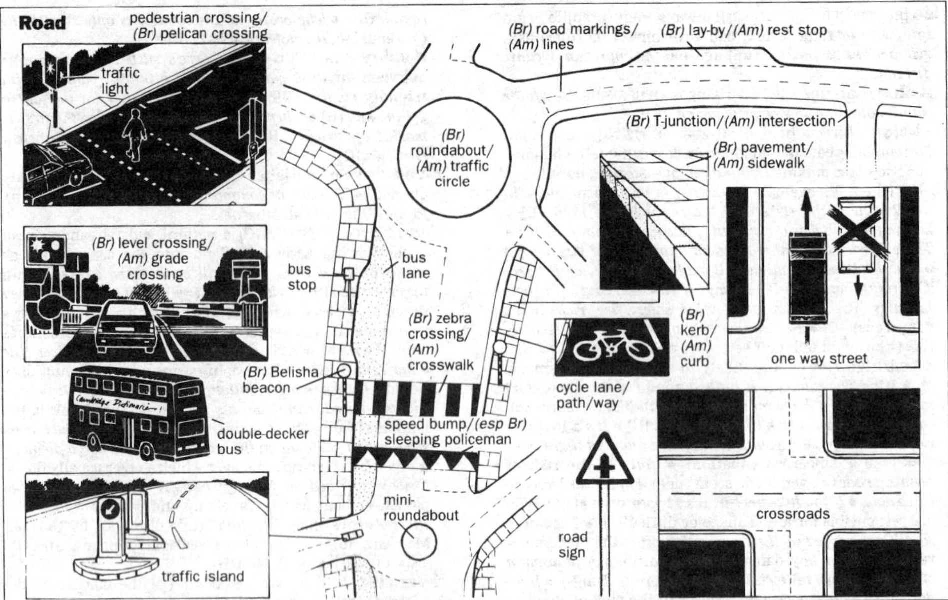

again). • *After two days* **on the road** (= driving for two days), *they reached the coast.* • *Most rock groups spend two or three months a year* **on the road** (= travelling to different places to perform). • *The doctors say she's* **on the road to** (= likely to achieve) *recovery.* • *He's* **on the road to** (= likely to achieve) *success.* • *(Br) These results show that we are* **on the right** *(Br)* **road**/*(Am)* **track** (= going to be successful). • *My relationship with Jeannie has* **come to the end of the road** (= finished). • *(dated) Before I went home, she persuaded me to have* **one for the road** (= an alcoholic drink just before leaving). • Someone's **road to Damascus** is an experience they have had which they consider to be very important and may change their life: *Meeting Martin Luther King was a road to Damascus for many people.* • *After a short visit, they* **took to the road** (= began to travel). • *(infml disapproving)* A **road hog** is a selfish and dangerous driver. • **Road safety** is teaching people how to behave safely when driving or crossing the road: *The government has launched a new road safety campaign in an attempt to reduce the number of road accidents.* • If you have good **road sense**, you have the ability to drive carefully or walk carefully and skilfully through traffic: *It's not surprising he's had so many accidents, he's got no road sense.* • In Britain, you must pay **road tax** on your vehicle before you are allowed to drive it on the roads. • If you give a car a **road test**, you drive it to test its safety or how well it works. • *(Am)* A **road test** is also a test of a driver's ability to control a vehicle, which must be passed in order to obtain official permission to drive. • *(Aus)* A **road toll** is the number of people who have died in road accidents. • *(Am)* If someone, esp. a sports team, takes a **road trip**, they travel to other places to play games against other teams or for business reasons: *Baltimore won seven of the nine games they played on this three-city road trip.* ○ *George is on an extensive road trip for his company, covering eight cities in three states.* • *(saying)* 'All roads lead to Rome' means that all the methods of doing something will achieve the same result in the end. • *(saying)* 'The road to hell is paved with good intentions' means that you must not simply intend to behave well but you must act according to your intentions, because you will have problems or be punished if you do not. • *"The Road to Wigan Pier"* (title of a book by George Orwell, 1937) • *"How many roads must a man walk down / Before you can call him a man?"* (Bob Dylan in the song *Blowin' in the Wind*, 1962) • LP› **Capital letters** PIC› **Road**

road·block /£ˈrəʊb·blɒk, $ˈroʊd·blɑːk/ *n* [C] a temporary structure put across a road to stop traffic • *Police put up/set up road blocks on all roads out of the town in an effort to catch the bombers.*

road·house /£ˈrəʊd·haʊs, $ˈroʊd-/ *n* [C] *pl* **roadhouses** /£ˈrəʊd,haʊ·zɪz, $ˈroʊd-/ *esp. Am dated* a restaurant or bar on a main road leading out of a city

road·ie /£ˈrəʊ·di, $ˈroʊ-/ *n* [C] *infml* someone who works for travelling entertainers, esp. setting up and taking care of their equipment

road·run·ner /£ˈrəʊd,rʌn·əʳ, $ˈroʊd,rʌn·ɚ/ *n* [C] a bird from the SW United States and Mexico with a long tail and feathers which stand up on the top of its head, which runs very fast

road·show /£ˈrəʊd·ʃəʊ, $ˈroʊd·ʃoʊ/ *n* [C] a group of people who travel around the country in order to give shows for public entertainment, or the show itself • *The roadshow is coming to town.*

road·side /£ˈrəʊd·saɪd, $ˈroʊd-/ *n* [U] the edge of a road • *The car pulled in* **at/by/on** *the roadside.* • *We stopped at a roadside café for lunch.*

road·ster /£ˈrəʊd·stəʳ, $ˈroʊd·stɚ/ *n* [C] *dated* a car without a roof and only two seats

road·way /£ˈrəʊd·weɪ, $ˈroʊd-/ *n* [U] the part of the road on which vehicles drive • *An overturned bus was blocking the roadway.*

road·works *Br and Aus* /£ˈrəʊd·wɜːks, $ˈroʊd·wɜːrks/ *pl n, Am* **road·work** /£ˈroʊd·wɜːk, $ˈroʊd·wɜːrk/ *n* [U] building or repair work on a road • *There are delays on the M4 because of roadworks.*

road·wor·thy /£ˈrəʊd,wɜː·ði, $ˈroʊd,wɜːr-/ *adj* (of a vehicle) in good enough condition to be driven without danger

roam *(obj)* /£rəʊm, $roʊm/ *v* to move about or travel, esp. without any real purpose • *After the pubs close, gangs of youths roam the city streets, drinking and fighting.* [T] • *She roamed* **around** *America for a year, working in bars and restaurants.* [I always + adv/prep]

roan /£rəʊn, $roʊn/ *n* [C] a horse which is red, black or brown with some white hairs mixed in

roar *(obj)* /£rɔːʳ, $rɔːr/ *v* to make a long, loud, deep sound • *We could hear the lions roaring at the other end of the zoo.* [I] • If a vehicle or aircraft roars somewhere, it moves there very quickly making a lot of noise: *She looked up as a plane roared overhead.* [I] ○ *The street was full of boys roaring up and down on their motorbikes.* [I] • If a person roars, they shout loudly: *"Stop that!" he roared.* [+ clause] ○ *As the team came out on the pitch, their fans roared their support.* [T] • If someone roars **with** an emotion, such as laughter or anger, they express it noisily: *She roared with laughter when she saw what he was wearing.* [I]

roar /£rɔːʳ, $rɔːr/ *n* • A roar is a loud, deep sound: *The lion let out a loud roar.* [C] ○ *His apartment was on a main road and there was a constant roar of traffic from down below.* [U]

roar·ing /£ˈrɔː·rɪŋ, $ˈrɔːr·ɪŋ/ *adj, adv* • *We couldn't get any sleep because of the roaring traffic outside our window.* • A roaring fire is one which has very large flames and is very hot: *We sat by the roaring fire listening to the rain outside.* • *(infml)* If someone is **roaring drunk**, they are very drunk and noisy: *They came back from the pub roaring drunk.* • *(infml)* If something is a **roaring success**, it is very successful: *The party/film was a roaring success.* • *(infml)* If someone is doing **a roaring trade**, they are selling a lot of goods very quickly: *It was a hot sunny day and the ice-cream sellers were doing a roaring trade.* • The **roaring forties** are the parts of the Atlantic Ocean about 40 degrees north of the Equator where it is often stormy. • The **roaring twenties** are the years between 1920 and 1930 when society was returning to normal after World War I and the general mood of the people was positive.

roast *(obj)* /£rəʊst, $roʊst/ *v* to cook (food) using dry heat in an OVEN or over a fire • *You should roast the chicken for two hours.* [T] • *(fig.) We lay on the beach and roasted in the Mediterranean sun.* [I] • If you roast nuts or coffee beans, you dry them using heat so that they turn brown: *Coffee beans have to be roasted to acquire a rich flavour.* • A roasting **pan**/*(Br also)* **tin** is a flat dish with low sides in which meat and vegetables are cooked inside an OVEN. • PIC› **Cooking, Pan**

roast /£rəʊst, $roʊst/, **roast·ed** /£'rəʊ·stɪd, $'roʊ-/ *adj* [before n; not gradable] • *We had roast beef, roast potatoes, and peas for lunch.* • *Kate made pasta and roasted red pepper sauce for supper.* • *Do you prefer pale, medium or dark roast coffee?*

roast /£rəʊst, $roʊst/ *n* [C] • A roast is a large piece of roasted meat: *We had an enormous roast for Sunday lunch.*

roast·ing /£'rəʊ·stɪŋ, $'roʊ-/ *adj, adv* [not gradable] • If something is roasting, it is very hot: *On a roasting hot summer day, the city was bustling with tourists.* ○ *(infml) I'm roasting* (= I am very hot) *out here – let's go inside and have a cool drink.*

roast·ing /£'rəʊ·stɪŋ, $'roʊ-/ *n* [C usually sing] *infml* • If you get or are given a roasting, you are severely criticized: *I got a real roasting from my Mum for coming back so late last night.*

rob *obj* /£rɒb, $rɑːb/ *v* [T] **-bb-** to take money or property illegally from (a place, organization or person), often using threats or violence • *The terrorists financed themselves by robbing banks.* • *My wallet's gone! I've been robbed!* • *They robbed the company* **of** *£2 million.* • If someone is robbed of something they deserve or want, it is taken away from them: *A last-minute injury robbed me* **of** *my place on the team.* • *(saying)* 'To rob Peter to pay Paul' means to borrow money from one person to pay back money you borrowed from someone else. • *"We was robbed"* (Joe Jacobs after the boxer he was manager for lost a fight, 1932) • LP› **Crimes and criminals**

rob·ber /£'rɒb·əʳ, $'rɑː·bɚ/ *n* [C] • *The robbers shot a policeman before making their getaway.* • *He's a famous* **bank** *robber.*

rob·be·ry /£'rɒb·ᵊr·i, $'rɑː·bɚ-/ *n* • *The gang admitted they had* **committed** *four recent bank robberies.* [C] • *He is in prison for armed robbery.* [U] • *(Br and Aus law) He was found guilty of robbery* **with violence**. [U] • *(infml) £90 for a meal? That's* **daylight** *(Am also* **highway***) robbery* (= much too expensive)*!* [U]

robe /£rəʊb, $roʊb/ *n* [C] a long, loose-fitting piece of clothing worn on very formal occasions, or a loose-fitting piece of clothing which is worn before or after a bath or on top of clothing that is worn in bed • *The Queen wore a long velvet robe at her Coronation.* • *Judges wear black robes when they are in court.* • *She wrapped a robe (also* **bathrobe***) around herself before answering the door.*

robed /£rəʊbd, $roʊbd/ *adj* [not gradable] *fml* • *She was robed* (= dressed) **in** *scarlet.*

rob·in /£'rɒb·ɪn, $'rɑː·bɪn/, *literary* **rob·in red·breast** /'red·brest/ *n* [C] a small brown European bird with a red front, or a similar but slightly larger brown bird of N America • *Robins mostly appear in the winter and are commonly pictured on Christmas cards.*

ro·bot /£'rəʊ·bɒt, $'roʊ·bɑːt/ *n* [C] a machine used to perform jobs automatically which is programmed and controlled by a computer • *Some types of robot can walk and talk, but they cannot think like humans.* • *Robots are commonly used in factories to assemble machinery such as cars.* • *(disapproving)* If you describe someone as a robot, you mean that they do things in a very quick and effective way but never show their emotions: *She plays the piano like a robot – perfectly but without any feeling.* • In South Africa, a robot is also a traffic light. • *"The three fundamental Rules of Robotics...One, a robot may not injure a human being, or, through inaction, allow a human being to come to harm ...Two ... a robot must obey the orders given it by human beings except where such orders would conflict with the First Law ... three, a robot must protect its own existence as long as such protection does not conflict with the First or Second Laws"* (From *I, Robot* by Isaac Asimov, 1950)

ro·bot·ic /£rəʊ'bɒt·ɪk, $roʊ'bɑː·t̬ɪk/ *adj* • *It is a remote-controlled device armed with cameras and a robotic arm.* • *(disapproving) He is a slightly robotic actor* (= He does not show emotion when he acts). • Robotic dancing is a type of dancing in which you make short sudden movements with your arms and legs like the actions of a robot.

ro·bot·ics /£rəʊ'bɒt·ɪks, $roʊ'bɑː·t̬ɪks/ *n* [U] • Robotics is the science of making and using robots.

ro·bust /£rəʊ'bʌst, $roʊ-/ *adj* (of a person or animal) strong and healthy, or (of an object) strong and unlikely to break • *You need to be robust to go rock climbing.* • *He looks healthier than he did six months ago – a little heavier and more robust.* • *She's just bought herself a robust pair of walking boots to go hiking in the Pyrenees.* • *(fig.) The company's finances are fairly robust at the moment* (= The company has made a large profit).

ro·bust·ly /rə'bʌst·li/ *adv* • If you do something robustly, you do it in a determined way: *Some of his colleagues felt he could have defended himself more robustly.*

ro·bust·ness /rə'bʌst·nəs/ *n* [U] • *Her robustness* (= strength) *and energy made her an ideal candidate for the expedition.* • *(fig.) The robustness of the dollar* (= Its ability to keep its value) *has surprised many financial analysts.*

rock STONE /£rɒk, $rɑːk/ *n* the dry solid part of the Earth's surface, or any large piece of this which sticks up out of the ground or the sea • *Mountains and cliffs are formed from rock.* [U] • *They had to drill through several metres of rock to find oil.* [U] • *The houses along the shore have been built into the rock.* [U] • *I spent the day turning over rocks by the sea, looking for crabs.* [C] • *The boat struck a rock outside the bay and sank.* [C] • *Ayers Rock is one of the most famous sights of central Australia.* [C] • *Do you enjoy rock* **climbing**? • *He scaled the sheer rock* **face** (= a steep area of rock). • *(Am and Aus)* A rock is also a small piece of rock which you can pick up in your hand: *The demonstrators were hurling rocks at the police.* [C] • Rock is also *Am slang for* DIAMOND: *She sure has some beautiful rocks.* [C often pl] • A **stick of** rock (*Am usually* **rock candy**) is a long tube-shaped hard sweet, sold esp. in towns next to the sea. [U] • *(Am)* **Rock candy** is also boiled sugar in large, hard lumps. • If someone is **between a rock and a hard place**, they are in a very difficult situation and have to make a hard decision. • *(infml)* If a price or level is at **rock bottom**, it is at its lowest possible level: *Prices have reached rock bottom.* ○ *The prime minister's opinion poll ratings have* **hit** *rock bottom.* ○ *Confidence in the government is* **at** *rock bottom.* • *(infml)* If someone is at **rock bottom**, they feel very unhappy and completely without hope. • *I can't eat this cake – it's* **rock hard** (= completely hard). • *I've fixed the table – it's* **rock solid** *(also* **solid as a rock***)* (= very firm) *now.* • *Their marriage is* **solid as a rock** (= very strong). • *(Br and Aus)* A **rock cake** or **rock bun** is a small cake with a rough surface which is made with dried fruit. • **Rock garden** is another word for ROCKERY. • **A rock pool** is a small area of sea water contained by the rocks around it. • **Rock salt** is salt that is taken from the ground, not the sea. • *"Rock of Ages, cleft for me, / Let me hide myself in Thee"* (hymn by Augustus Montague Toplady, 1740-1778) • PIC› **Garden, Stick**

rocks /£rɒks, $rɑːks/ *pl n* • Rocks are a line of large stones sticking up from the ground or the sea: *The storm forced the ship onto the rocks.* ○ *I found him sitting on the rocks along the shore.* • *(infml)* If something is **on the rocks**, it is likely to fail soon: *I think their marriage is on the rocks.* • If you have an alcoholic drink **on the rocks**, you have it with lumps of ice: *I'll have a whisky on the rocks, please.* • *(taboo slang)* To **get** your **rocks off** is to have sex.

rock·y /£'rɒk·i, $'rɑː·ki/ *adj* **-ier, -iest** • *She scrambled along the rocky path.* • *The desert road winds through rocky gorges and hills.* • If you are on a rocky path/road, you are experiencing a difficult period in your life and have a lot of problems. • See also **rocky** at ROCK MOVE.

rock *(obj)* MOVE /£rɒk, $rɑːk/ *v* to (cause someone or something to) move backwards and forwards or from side to side in a regular way • *He picked up the baby and gently rocked her* **to sleep**. [T] • *If you rock* **back** *on that chair, you're going to break it.* [I] • If a building is rocked by an explosion, the force of the explosion makes the building shake: *The explosion, which rocked the city, killed a number* *of passers-by and damaged many buildings.* [T] • If an event rocks a group of people or society, it causes feelings of shock and fear: *The managing director's resignation rocked the whole company.* [T] ○ *The program has been rocked by allegations of fraud and mismanagement.* [T] • *(infml)* If you **rock the boat**, you do or say something that will upset people or cause problems: *A small number of MPs are determined to speak out against the bill, even if this means rocking the boat.* • A **rocking chair** (also **rocker**) is a chair built on two pieces of curved wood so that you can move forwards and backwards on it as you sit in it. • A **rocking horse** is a wooden toy horse that children can make move backwards and forwards as they sit on it. • *"The hand that rocks the cradle / Is the hand that rules the world"* (from a poem by W.D.Wallace, 1865) • PIC **Chair, Toy**

rock·er /£'rɒk·əʳ, $'rɑː·kɚ/ *n* [C] • A rocker is one of the two curved pieces of wood under a **rocking chair** that allow it to move backwards and forwards. • Rocker is another word for **rocking chair**. • *(infml)* If you say that someone is **off** their **rocker**, you mean that they are behaving in a very strange or foolish way: *He says he's going to give up his job and become a sheep farmer in Wales – he must be off his rocker!* • See also **rocker** at ROCK MUSIC.

rock·y /£'rɒk·i, $'rɑː·ki/ *adj* **-ier, -iest** • *After two months in a hospital bed, I felt a bit rocky* (=I could not balance very well) *on my feet.* • *(fig.) Their relationship got off to a rocky* (= uncertain) *start but they're very close now.* • *(infml)* If something such as a relationship is rocky, it is in a very bad state and is unlikely to last very long. • See also **rocky** at ROCK STONE.

rock MUSIC /£rɒk, $rɑːk/ *n* [U] a type of popular music with a strong loud beat which is usually played with electric guitars and drums • *Do you prefer rock or pop?* • *Nirvana is a famous rock* **group**. • *Bruce Springsteen is an American rock* **star**. • **Rock 'n' roll/Rock and roll** is a style of popular dance music that began in the 1950s in the United States and has a strong loud beat and simple repeated tunes: *Elvis Presley was one of the greatest rock 'n' roll singers.* • *"Rock around the Clock"* (song by Bill Haley and the Comets, 1955) • *"It's only rock'n'roll"* (song by the Rolling Stones, 1974)

rock·er /£'rɒk·əʳ, $'rɑː·kɚ/ *n* [C] • A rocker is a singer of rock music or rock 'n' roll music: *He helped start the careers of some of the first British rockers, such as Cliff Richard, Adam Faith and Marty Wilde.* • *(Am)* A rocker is also a rock song or a person who really likes rock music. • *(dated)* A rocker is also a young person, esp. in Britain in the 1950's, who wore leather clothes, rode a motorcycle and listened to rock and roll music. • See also **rocker** at ROCK MOVE.

rock·er·y *Br and Aus* /£'rɒk·ᵊr·i, $'rɑː·kɚ-/, *Am usually* **rock gar·den** *n* [C] a garden or an area within a garden that has plants growing between piles of stones • PIC **Garden**

rock·et DEVICE /£'rɒk·ɪt, $'rɑː·kɪt/ *n* [C] a cylindrical object which moves very fast by forcing out burning gases, and which is used for space travel or as a weapon • *They have launched a rocket to the planet Venus.* • *The rebels were firing anti-tank rockets at the government forces.* • *More than 200 mortar shells and rocket-propelled grenades had been pounding the village since Monday night.* • *The shuttle uses a mixture of kerosene and oxygen as rocket* **fuel**. • *They have recently acquired two rocket* **launchers** *with a range of over 2000 metres.* • A rocket (also **skyrocket**) is also a type of FIREWORK (=an explosive which produces bright coloured patterns) that flies up into the air before exploding. • *(Br and Aus infml)* If someone **gives** you **a rocket**, they criticize you severely: *Her Mum gave her a rocket for tearing her new jeans.* ○ *He got a rocket from his boss for coming into work so late.* • *(Am)* A **rocket ship** is a spacecraft which is powered by a rocket. • *"Rocket Man"* (song by Elton John, 1972)

rock·et /£'rɒk·ɪt, $'rɑː·kɪt/, **sky·rock·et** *v* [I] *infml* • If something rockets, it rises extremely quickly: *House prices in the north are rocketing* **up**. ○ *Their team rocketed* **to** *the top of the League.* ○ *Sharon Stone rocketed* **to** *fame* (= became very famous) *in the film 'Basic Instinct'.*

rock·et PLANT /£'rɒk·ɪt, $'rɑː·kɪt/ *n* [U] a plant whose long green leaves are used in salads • *She made a green salad using rocket and cos lettuce.*

rock·fall /£'rɒk·fɔːl, $'rɑːk·fɑːl/ *n* [C] a mass of stones that is falling or has already fallen • *The hikers were killed in a rockfall.* • *The road was blocked by a rockfall.*

rock·mel·on /£'rɒk,mel·ən, $'rɑːk-/ *n* [C] *Aus for* CANTALOUPE

ro·co·co /£rəʊ'kəʊ·kəʊ, $rə'koʊ·koʊ/ *adj, n* [U] (relating to) the highly decorated and detailed style in buildings, art and furniture that was popular in Europe in the 18th century • *Rococo is a delicate style of interior decoration that is characterized by the use of scrolls and the asymmetrical arrangements of curves.* • *Watteau is the most famous Rococo painter.*

rod /£rɒd, $rɑːd/ *n* [C] a long thin pole made of wood or metal • *He was given a fishing rod for his birthday.* • *Reinforced concrete has long steel rods in it to strengthen it.* • *(Br)* If you **make a rod for** your **own back**, you act in a way which creates more problems for yourself in the future: *By giving in to the terrorists' demands, the government will simply be making a rod for its own back.*

rode /£rəʊd, $roʊd/ *past simple of* RIDE

ro·dent /£'rəʊ·dᵊnt, $'roʊ-/ *n* [C] any of various small mammals with large sharp front teeth • *Mice, rats, squirrels and rabbits are all rodents.*

ro·de·o /£rəʊ'deɪ·əʊ, £'rəʊ·di-, $'roʊ·di·oʊ/ *n* [C] *pl* **rodeos** (in N America) a sport and public entertainment in which COWBOYS (= people who take care of cattle) show different skills by riding wild horses and catching cattle with ropes

roe /£rəʊ, $roʊ/ *n* [U] the eggs of a female fish or the sperm of a male fish, which is often eaten as food • *Cod's roe is used to make the Greek dish taramasalata.*

roe deer /£rəʊ, $roʊ/ *n* [C] *pl* **roe deer** a small European and Asian deer • PIC **Wild animals in Britain**

ro·ent·gen /£'rɒnt·gən, $'rent-/ *n* [C] *specialized* a RONTGEN

rog·er UNDERSTOOD /£'rɒdʒ·əʳ, $'rɑː·dʒɚ/ *exclamation* used in radio communications to mean that a message has been received and understood • *"You are clear to land." "Roger, I'm coming in to land now."*

rog·er obj HAVE SEX /£'rɒdʒ·əʳ, $'rɑː·dʒɚ/ *v* [T] *Br and Aus taboo slang dated* to have sex with (someone)

rogue /£rəʊg, $roʊg/ *n* [C] *dated* a dishonest or immoral person • *He was known as being a bit of a rogue who had left his wife and run off with his secretary.* • A rogue is also a person who jokes and behaves in a way which you do not approve of but whom you do not want to criticize because you like them too much: *"What an old rogue you are," she said, blushing.* ○ *He's a likeable rogue.* • A rogue animal is a fierce, dangerous animal that lives apart from the rest of its group. • A **rogues' gallery** is a collection of photographs of criminals kept by the police: *(fig.) He occupies a prominent position in the rogues' gallery of the financial world.*

rogu·ish /£'rəʊ·gɪʃ, $'roʊ-/ *adj* • *His eyes were bright blue with a roguish twinkle in them.*

rogu·ish·ly /£'rəʊ·gɪʃ·li, $'roʊ-/ *adv*

rogu·ish·ness /£'rəʊ·gɪʃ·nəs, $'roʊ-/ *n* [U] • *There is a slight roguishness* (= a tendency to behave in a way which is not approved of) *about him which women find irresistible.*

role DUTY /£rəʊl, $roʊl/ *n* [C] the position of a person or group of people in a particular situation and the degree to which they are involved in it, or the duty or use which someone or something is expected to perform or have • *What is his role* **in** *this project?* • *Does religion have a role to* **play in** *society today?* • *The future role of local authorities* **in** *providing housing for the homeless is uncertain.* • *She has played a crucial/decisive role* **in** *securing a $2 million deal for the company.* • *Six people have been put on trial for their role* (= involvement) **in** *the anti-government demonstrations.* • A **role model** is a person whom someone admires and whose behaviour they try to copy: *My elder brother has always been a role model for me.* • **Role reversal** is when two people exchange their usual duties or positions: *Men are starting to take a break from continuous full-time employment for further education or for role reversal in the home* (= taking care of their children and doing jobs around the home while their wives return to employment).

role REPRESENTATION /£rəʊl, $roʊl/ *n* [C] the person whom an actor represents in a film or play • *He has* **played** *some of the great Shakespearean roles, including Hamlet and Henry V.* • *She's got the* **leading** (= main) *role in the school play.* • *He won an Oscar for his* **supporting** *role in the film.* • **Role play** is a method of acting out particular ways of behaving or pretending to be other people in order to teach people how to deal with new situations: *Role play is used in training courses, language-learning and psychotherapy.* ○ *They used role play to train us how to deal with aggressive customers.*

roll *(obj)* MOVE /£rəʊl, $roʊl/ *v* to (cause to) move or move along by turning over and over or from side to side • *The vase rolled off the edge of the table and smashed.* [I always + adv/prep] • *The dog rolled over onto its back.* [I always + adv/prep] • *I rolled the wheel along the side of the road back to the car.* [T always + adv/prep] • Roll is sometimes used to mean move as if turning over and over: *A tear rolled down his cheek.* [I always + adv/prep] ○ *The truck rolled to a stop.* [I always + adv/prep] ○ *A wave of cigarette smoke rolled towards me.* [I always + adv/prep] ○ *The piano's on wheels, so we can roll it into the room.* [T always + adv/prep] ○ *(fig.) They years rolled by* (= The years passed) *and I didn't see her again until she was married with two children.* [I always + adv/prep] • If an aircraft or a ship rolls, it leans to one side and then to the other because of the wind or waves. [I] • If a machine is rolling, it is operating: *Just as the television cameras started rolling, it began to pour down with rain.* [I] • If you roll your eyes, you move them up and then round in a circle. [T] • If you roll your eyes when someone says or does something which you consider stupid or foolish, you move them around in a circle: *When he suggested they should buy a new car, she rolled her eyes* **in disbelief**. [T] • *(infml)* If money is **rolling in**, it is being received in large amounts: *Once our business gets started, the money will be rolling in.* • *(infml)* If someone is **rolling in it/rolling in money**, they are extremely rich: *If they can afford a yacht, they must be rolling in it.* • *(infml) The comedian had the audience* **rolling in the aisles** (= laughing uncontrollably). • *(Br and Aus infml)* If you say **roll on** something, you want it to happen sooner: *Roll on the weekend!* • *(infml)* If you **roll up** somewhere, you arrive there: *They rolled up at the party two hours late and rather drunk.* • *(Br and Aus)* If someone says **Roll up! Roll up!**, they want you to come and look at something unusual or interesting: *Roll up! Roll up! Come and see the amazing bearded lady!* • *(Am infml)* If someone **rolls with the punches**, they are able to deal with a series of difficult situations: *Even though things keep going wrong, she's able to roll with the punches.* • A **roll-on** is a small container with a moving ball at the top which is used for storing DEODORANT (= a chemical substance that prevents or hides unpleasant body smells). • *(Br and Aus)* A **roll-on roll-off** ship (*infml* **ro-ro**) is a ship built so that vehicles can drive on at one end and off at the other. • **Rolling stock** is the engines and carriages that are used on a railway. • *(dated saying)* 'A rolling stone gathers no moss' means that a person who is always travelling and changing jobs has the advantage of having no responsibilities, but also has the disadvantage of having no permanent place to live. • *"Roll over Beethoven"* (song written by Chuck Berry, 1956) • *"Let the Good Times Roll"* (title of a song written by Sam Theard and Fleecie Moore, 1946) • *"The rolling English drunkard made the rolling English road"* (G.K. Chesterton in the poem *The Rolling English Road*, 1914) • *"How does it feel / To be on your own / With no direction home / Like a complete unknown / Like a rolling stone"* (from the song *Like a Rolling Stone* by Bob Dylan, 1965)

roll /£rəʊl, $roʊl/ *n* • *The dog went for a roll in the grass.* [C] • The roll of a ship or aircraft is its movement from side to side in the water or air: *The roll of the ship changed as it left the harbour.* [U] • *(infml)* If someone is **on a roll**, they are successful or lucky for a short period of time: *When he won one game after another, it was obvious he was on a roll.* • A **roll bar** is a metal bar across the roof of a car that protects the people inside if the car turns over.

rol·ler /£ˈrəʊ·ləʳ, $ˈroʊ·lɚ/ *n* [C] • A roller is a tube-shaped object in a machine that turns over and over in order to carry things along or press them together: *As the hot metal passed between the huge rollers it was pressed into thin sheets.* • A roller is also a large long wave in the sea: *The beach is very popular with surfers because of the rollers.* • Rollers (also **curlers**) are tube-shaped objects, often heated, that women use to curl their hair: *She answered the door in her dressing gown and rollers.* • *(Br and Aus)* A **roller blind** (*Am* **(window) shade**) is a piece of material fixed onto a wooden or metal roller that can be pulled down to cover a window. • A **roller coaster** (*Br and Aus also* **big dipper**) is a type of small railway in an amusement park with carriages that travel very quickly along a narrow track that slopes and bends suddenly. ○ *(fig.) He's been* **on** *an* **emotional** *roller coaster* (= experiencing many different strong feelings) *in the last few weeks.* • *(Am)* A **roller derby** is a race between two teams of **roller skaters** (= people wearing shoes with small wheels on the bottom) around a circular track. • A **roller skate** is a device with four wheels on the bottom that you tie onto your shoe or a type of boot with four wheels on the bottom which you wear in order to travel along quickly for enjoyment: *I got some new roller skates for my birthday.* ○ *Have you ever tried* **roller-skating**? ○ *She* **roller-skated** *to the shops.* • A **roller towel** is a piece of cloth joined at both ends which is fixed onto a wooden or metal roller and which you use for drying your hands. • See also **roller** at ROLL SMOOTH. • PIC› **Hair, Skate**

roll *(obj)* TURN OVER /£rəʊl, $roʊl/ *v* to (cause something to) turn over onto itself to form a cylindrical or spherical shape • *He rolled the clay* **into** *a ball in his hands.* [T] • *Could you roll* **up** *that string for me?* [M] • *As I got closer, the hedgehog rolled itself* **up into** *a ball.* [T] • If you roll a cigarette, you make one by wrapping a piece of paper around some tobacco. [T] • If you roll a piece of clothing or material, you fold it over to make it shorter: *We rolled* **back** *the carpet to see the floorboards.* [M] ○ *(fig. Am) The furniture dealer is rolling* **back** (= reducing) *the prices on all beds for this week only.* [M] ○ *I rolled* **up** *my sleeves and began to wash the dishes.* [M] • *(infml)* If you **roll up** your **sleeves**, you prepare for hard work: *There's a lot of work to do, so roll up your sleeves and get busy.* • If someone or something has several qualities **rolled into one**, they have all of those qualities: *He is a father, sales manager, and athlete all rolled into one.* • *(Br and Aus)* If a piece of jewellery is **rolled gold** (*Am* **gold-plated**) it is made out of cheap metal covered with a thin layer of gold: *She wanted 9-carat gold earrings but she could only afford rolled-gold ones.*

roll /£rəʊl, $roʊl/ *n* [C] • A roll of film, paper or cloth is a piece of it rolled into the shape of a tube: *a toilet roll* (= a roll of toilet paper) • If a person or animal has rolls of fat on their body, they are very fat: *The dog had rolls of fat along its neck.* • **Roll neck** is another word for **polo neck**. See at POLO. • A **roll-top desk** is a type of writing table with a movable cover that you can push back or pull down. • A *(Br)* **roll-up**/*(Aus)* **roll-your-own** is a cigarette which you make by wrapping a piece of paper around some tobacco. • PIC› **Bathroom**

roll *obj* SMOOTH /£rəʊl, $roʊl/ *v* [T] to make (something) smooth and flat • *He spends hours rolling the grass before a cricket match.* • *She borrowed a garden roller to roll the grass flat.* [+ obj + adj] • *When you have rolled* **out** *the pastry, place it in a pie dish.* [M] • **Rolled oats** are OATS (= a type of grain) that have had their outer covering removed and have been flattened. • A **rolling mill** is a factory or machine in which metal is rolled into flat pieces. • A **rolling pin** is a tube-shaped object with handles on each end that is used for making pastry flat and thin before cooking it. • PIC› **Kitchen**

rol·ler /£ˈrəʊ·ləʳ, $ˈroʊ·lɚ/ *n* [C] • A roller is a heavy machine used to make surfaces smooth and flat: *The men used a roller to flatten the tarmac.* • See also STEAMROLLER VEHICLE; **roller** at ROLL MOVE.

roll *(obj)* SOUND /£rəʊl, $roʊl/ *v* to make a continuous repeated sound • *The drums rolled as the acrobat walked along the tightrope.* [I] • If you roll your r's, you pronounce them with your tongue moving quickly and repeatedly against the top of the mouth: *The Italians roll their r's.* [T]

roll /£rəʊl, $roʊl/ *n* [C usually sing] • *A drum roll signalled the beginning of the national anthem.* • *There was a deafening roll of thunder and then it started to pour down with rain.*

roll LIST /£rəʊl, $roʊl/ *n* [C] an official list of names • *Is your name on the electoral roll* (= the list of people who can vote)? • If you **take/call the roll**, you read aloud the names of all the people on the list to make certain that they are present: *The teacher called the roll to see if any students were absent.* • If someone does a **roll call**, they read aloud the names of all the people on the list to make certain that they are present. • *(Br and Aus)* A **roll of honour** (*Am and Aus also* **honor roll**) is a list of people who should be remembered for their brave actions: *The names of the dead were carved in a roll of honour on the church wall.*

roll BREAD /£rəʊl, $roʊl/, **bread roll** *n* [C] a small loaf of bread for one person • *Would you like a roll and butter with your soup?* • *(Br and Aus) I bought a cheese roll (Am cheese on a roll)* (= a small loaf of bread filled with cheese) *for lunch.* • PIC› **Bread and cakes**

Rol·ler·blade /£ˈrəʊ·lə·bleɪd, $ˈroʊ·lɚ-/, *Am and Aus also* **in-line skate** /ˌɪn·laɪn/ *n* [C] *trademark* a type of shoe with a single row of small wheels on the bottom which you wear in order to travel along quickly for enjoyment • *She tried out her new Rollerblades in the park.* • PIC> **Skate**

roll·ing GRADUAL /£'rəʊ·lɪŋ, $'roʊ-/ *adj* [before n; not gradable] gradual • *The plan is for a rolling extension of the tax over the next ten years.*

roll·ing HILL /£'rəʊ·lɪŋ, $'roʊ-/ *adj* [before n; not gradable] (of hills) gently rising and falling • *The train journey took us through a deep valley past rolling hills.*

roll·mop /£'rəʊl·mɒp, $'roʊl·mɑːp/ *n* [C] *Br and Aus* a piece of HERRING (= a type of fish) with the bones removed that has been rolled up and preserved in vinegar

ro·ly-po·ly /£,rəʊ·li'pəʊ·li, $,roʊ·li'poʊ-/ *adj infml humorous* (of people) short and round • *He was a roly-poly sort of man, bulging out of his clothes.*

ro·ly-po·ly (pud·ding) /£,rəʊ·li·pəʊ·li, $,roʊ·li·poʊ-/ *n Br* a sweet dish made with thick pastry spread with JAM, which is rolled up and cooked • *Do you like jam roly-poly?* [U] • *She made a delicious roly-poly pudding.* [C]

ROM /£rɒm, $rɑːm/ *n* [U] *specialized abbreviation for* Read Only Memory (= a type of computer memory which holds information that can be used but not changed or added to) • *ROM is used for storing computer programs or the operating system of a computer.* • Compare RAM COMPUTER.

ro·maine /rə'meɪn/ *n* [C] *Am for* COS (LETTUCE)

Ro·man CITY /£'rəʊ·mən, $'roʊ-/ *adj* [not gradable] relating to the city of Rome and its empire in ancient times • *The Roman Empire once extended over most of Europe.* • *The museum houses some impressive Roman antiquities.* • Roman also means relating to the modern city of Rome: *Are Roman hotels quite expensive to stay in?* • The **Roman alphabet** (also **Latin alphabet**) is the alphabet used for writing most western European languages, including English. • A **Roman candle** is a type of FIREWORK (= a small container filled with explosive chemicals) which produces brightly coloured stars when it explodes. • A **Roman Catholic** (also **Catholic**) is a person who is a member of the Roman Catholic Church: *Our guest is the Roman Catholic Bishop of London.* • The **Roman Catholic Church** is the part of the Christian religion which is ruled by the Pope in Rome. • **Roman Catholicism** is the beliefs and activities of the Roman Catholic Church. • *(law)* **Roman law** is the system of laws of the ancient Romans, on which some modern legal systems are based. • A **Roman nose** is a nose that is higher than usual at its top end. • **Roman numerals** are the letters that the ancient Romans used to write numbers, for example I (= 1), II (= 2), III (= 3), V (= 5), X (= 10), L (= 50), C (= 100), D (= 500), M (= 1000). ○ *Some modern clock and watch faces have roman numerals.* ○ Compare **Arabic numerals** at ARAB. • (J)

Ro·man /£'rəʊ·mən, $'roʊ-/ *n* [C] • Romans were the people who lived in Rome or the Roman Empire in ancient times: *The Romans ruled over most of Europe.* • A Roman is also a person who lives in the modern city of Rome. • *"When in Rome do as the Romans do"* (St Ambrose, 339-397)

Ro·man·o- /£rə'mɑː·nəʊ-, $-'mæn·oʊ-/ *combining form* • *She has written a book about Romano-British architecture in the 3rd century AD.*

ro·man PRINT STYLE /£'rəʊ·mən, $'roʊ-/ *n* [U], *adj* [not gradable] (having) small vertical letters, like the letters used for these words • *Roman type is the most common style of printed letters.* • *In this book, definitions are set* in roman. • (DK) (S)

ro·mance LOVE /£rəʊ'mænts, £'rəʊ·mænts, $roʊ'-/ *n* a close relationship between two people who are in love with each other but are not married • *They got married last year after a* **whirlwind** (= very short and unexpected) *romance.* [C] • *(fig.) America's long-running romance* **with** (= feelings of affection for) *Hollywood seems to be over.* [C] • A romance is also a story about love: *She loves reading romances.* [C] ○ *Mills and Boon is one of the world's biggest publishers of romances.* [C] • A romance is also a story of exciting events, esp. one written in the Middle Ages: *The absence or unobtainability of the beloved is an important part of medieval romances.* [C] • Romance is the feeling of love and pleasure that you experience when you are with someone whom you love: *I felt as though all the romance had gone out of my marriage.* [U] • Romance is also the feeling of excitement or mystery that you have from a particular experience or event: *He loves the romance of travelling on a steam train.* [U] • LP> **Relationships**

ro·mance *(obj)* /£rəʊ'mænts, £'rəʊ·mænts, $roʊ'-/ *v* • To romance is to tell stories that are not true or to describe an event in a way that makes it sound better than it was: *He's always romancing* **(about)** *his childhood.* [I/T]

ro·man·tic /£rəʊ'mæn·tɪk, $roʊ'mæn·t̬ɪk/ *adj* Romantic means relating to love or a close loving relationship: *a romantic novel/comedy* ○ *Barbara Cartland is a writer of romantic fiction.* • If something is romantic, it is exciting and mysterious and has a strong effect on your emotions: *We thought that Egypt was an incredibly romantic country.* • *(slightly disapproving)* If you describe someone as romantic, you might mean that they are not practical and have a lot of ideas which are not related to real life: *She has a romantic idea of what it's like to be a struggling young artist.* • See also **Romantic** at ROMANTICISM.

ro·man·ti·cally /£rəʊ'mæn·tɪ kli, $roʊ'mæn·t̬ɪ-/ *adv*

ro·man·tic /£rəʊ'mæn·tɪk, $roʊ'mæn·t̬ɪk/ *n* [C] *slightly disapproving* • If someone is a romantic, they are not practical and have ideas which are not related to real life: *You're a hopeless/incurable romantic.* • See also **Romantic** at ROMANTICISM.

ro·man·ti·ci·sm /£rəʊ'mæn·tɪ·sɪ·zᵊm, $roʊ'mæn·t̬ə-/ *n* [U] • *He is an excellent travel writer, whose descriptions contain a vivid streak of romanticism* (= a tendency to describe things in a way that makes them sound more exciting or mysterious that they really are). • See also ROMANTICISM.

ro·man·ti·cize, *Br and Aus usually* **-ise** /£rəʊ'mæn·tɪ·saɪz, $roʊ'mæn·t̬ə-/ *v* [I] • If you romanticize about something, you talk about it in a way that makes it sound better than it really is, or you believe that it is better than it really is: *Stop romanticizing! Nothing's that perfect.* ○ *She has rather a romanticized idea of married life.*

Ro·mance LANGUAGE /£rəʊ'mænts, $roʊ-/ *adj* [before n; not gradable] *specialized* (of a language) developed from Latin • *French, Italian, Spanish, Catalan, Portuguese and Romanian are all Romance languages.*

Ro·man·esque /£,rəʊ·mə'nesk, $,roʊ-/ *adj* [not gradable], *n* [U] *specialized* (relating to) the style of building which was common in W and S Europe from the 10th to the 12th centuries • *Romanesque architecture is characterized by large vaults and round arches.* • *Durham Cathedral is a famous Romanesque cathedral.* • (I)

Ro·man·ti·ci·sm /£rəʊ'mæn·tɪ·sɪ·zᵊm, $roʊ'mæn·t̬ə-/ *n* [U] *specialized* a style of art, music and literature that was common in Europe in the late 18th and early 19th centuries, which describes the beauty of nature and which emphasizes the importance of human emotions • *Goethe, Hugo, Keats and Shelley were all important writers associated with Romanticism.* • See also **romanticism** at ROMANCE LOVE. Compare CLASSICISM.

Ro·man·tic /£rəʊ'mæn·tɪk, $roʊ'mæn·t̬ɪk/ *adj* [not gradable], *n* [C] *specialized* • *Wordsworth was one of the greatest English Romantic poets.* • *Turner and Constable were the leading Romantic painters in Britain.* • *Beethoven, Schumann and Chopin were leading Romantic composers.* • See also **romantic** at ROMANCE LOVE.

Ro·ma·ny /£'rəʊ·mə·ni, $'rɑː·mə-/ *n* [C/U] a GYPSY (= member of a race who travel from place to place) or the language of the gypsy people

Ro·me·o /£'rəʊ·mi·əʊ, $'roʊ·mi·oʊ/ *n* [C] *pl* **Romeos** *humorous or disapproving* a man who thinks he is attractive to women and has sexual relationships with many women • *a high-school Romeo*

romp /£rɒmp, $rɑːmp/ *v* [I] to play roughly, excitedly and noisily • *The children romped happily* **around/about** *in the garden.* • *(Br) She is riding the fastest horse and is certain to* **romp home/in** (= win the race easily). • *Rory expected to* **romp through** *the test and interviews* (= succeed in them without any effort).

romp /£rɒmp, $rɑːmp/ *n* [C usually sing] • A romp is an amusing, energetic and often sexual entertainment or situation: *The new production at the National Theatre takes us on a romp* **through** *the rudest bits of Shakespeare.* ○ *The newspaper headline was 'Vicar Caught In Sex Romp'.*

romp·ers /£'rɒm·pəz, $'rɑːm·pɚz/ *pl n*, **romp·er suit** *n* [C] a single piece of clothing consisting of a top part and trousers worn esp. by babies and very young children

ron·do /£'rɒn·dəʊ, $'rɑːn·doʊ/ *n* [C] *pl* **rondos** *specialized* a piece of music that repeats the main tune several times and often forms part of a longer piece

röntgen, **ro·ent·gen** /£'rɒnt·gən, $'rent-/ *n* [C] *specialized* a unit of measurement for showing the amount of RADIATION received by a person over a period of time

roo /ruː/ *n* [C] *pl* **roos** *Aus infml for* KANGAROO

rood screen /'ruːd·skriːn/ *n* [C] *specialized* a decorative wooden or stone wall that in some Christian churches separates the area near the ALTAR (=a table used for religious ceremonies) from the other parts of the church

roof /ruːf/ *n* [C] the covering that forms the top of a building, vehicle, etc. • *From my window I have a lovely view out over the red roofs of the city.* • *The house has a sloping/flat/tiled/thatched roof.* • *Put the luggage* **on** *the roof of the bus.* • *I'll put these empty boxes* **in** *the roof* (=the space below the top of the building) *until we need them.* • *The roof* (=upper surface) *of the cave is 50 metres up.* • *This cake is so dry that it sticks to the roof* **of** *your* **mouth** (=upper surface of the mouth). • *She gave him enough money to get* **a roof over** *his* **head** (=a place to live). • *I refuse to live* **under the same roof** *as* (=in the same place as) *that horrible man.* • *Prices have* **gone through the roof** (=risen to a very high level). • *When I was expelled from school, my parents* **went through the roof/hit the roof** (=got very angry). • *With their last, triumphant piece, the musicians* **raised the roof** (=played/sang very loudly and enthusiastically). • A **roof garden** is a garden on the roof of a building. • A **roof-rack** is a frame fixed on top of the roof of a vehicle, for carrying large objects. • PIC> **Accommodation, Rack**

roof *obj* /ruːf/ *v* [T] • *She's having her house roofed* **with** *slates.* • If you roof an area or place **in/over**, you put a roof on it: *The council has decided to roof over the open-air swimming pool.* [M]

-roofed /-ruːfd/ *combining form* • *a slate-roofed house*

roof·er /£ˈruː·fəʳ, $-fɚ/ *n* [C] • A roofer is a person whose job is to put new roofs on buildings or to repair damaged roofs.

roof·ing /ˈruː·fɪŋ/ *n* [U] • Roofing is material used for making roofs: *Slates, tiles and shingles are the commonest roofing materials.*

roof·less /ˈruː·fləs/ *adj* [not gradable] • *a ruined and roofless* (=without a roof) *church*

roof·top /£ˈruːf·tɒp, $-tɑːp/ *n* [C usually pl] the outside surface of the roof of a building • *We had a magnificent view of the rooftops and church spires from our hotel room.* • *Police marksmen with rifles were stationed on the rooftops.* • *About thirty students were involved in the rooftop protests.* • If you **shout/proclaim** something **from the rooftops**, you say it publicly.

rook [BIRD] /rʊk/ *n* [C] a large black bird similar to a CROW

rook·e·ry /£ˈrʊk·ᵊr·i, $ˈ-ɚ-/ *n* [C] • A rookery is several rooks' nests, high up in the branches of a group of trees.

rook [GAME PIECE] /rʊk/, *infml* **cas·tle** *n* [C] (in the game of CHESS) a piece that can move along any number of squares in straight lines parallel to the sides of the board • PIC> **Games**

rook *obj* [CHEAT] /rʊk/ *v* [T] *infml dated* to cheat (someone) out of some money • *He feels the garage rooked him* **of** *about £100.*

rook·ie /ˈrʊk·i/ *n* [C] *esp. Am and Aus infml* a person who is new to an organization or an activity • *These rookie cops don't know anything yet.*

room [PLACE] /ruːm, rʊm/ *n* [C] an area within a building that has its own walls, floor, ceiling, doors, etc. and that usually has a particular use • *He calls it his country cottage, but it has 20 rooms!* • *She's waiting for you in the conference room upstairs.* • *The room smelled of cigarette smoke.* • *The room was empty.* • *The front room (of the house) gets the sun.* • *She's upstairs in her room* (=her private room, where she sleeps). • Room is also used as a combining form: *a bedroom* ○ *a bathroom* ○ *a dining-room* ○ *living-room* • *I'm looking for a hotel room/a cheap room to rent.* • *He booked a single/double room* (=a room for one person/two people in a hotel). • *I'd like a room for the night, please.* • *"Where's Cindy?" "She's in the* **next** *room* (=the room connected to this one)*."* • *(fig.) The whole room* (=All the people in the room) *turned and looked at her.* • *(Am) When I went to school I had to pay* **room and board** (=for a place to live and meals). • In a hotel, **room service** is the serving of food and drink to customers in their room, or the people who do this work. • *"Room at the Top"* (title of a book by John Braine, 1957)

room /ruːm, rʊm/ *v* [I always + adv/prep] *Am* • To room is to rent a room from someone or share a rented room with someone: *At college he rooms* **with** *this guy from Nebraska.* ○ *I roomed* **with** *her when I was at the university.* • **Rooming house** is *Am for* **boarding house**, see at BOARD [STAY]. • *(Am)* **Rooming-in** is an arrangement in some hospitals where new babies stay with their mothers rather than being taken to a separate room for special care.

room·er /£ˈruː·məʳ, $-mɚ/ *n* [C] • Roomer is *Am for* **lodger**, see at LODGE [STAY].

room·ful /ˈruːm·fʊl/ *n* [C usually sing] • A roomful is as many or as much as a room will hold: *a roomful* **of** *people/guests/boxes*

rooms /ruːmz, rʊmz/ *pl n Br dated* • Rooms are a set of rented rooms, esp. in a college or university.

room [SPACE] /ruːm, rʊm/ *n* [U] the amount of space that someone or something needs • *That sofa would* **take up** *too much room in the flat.* • *How much room will the new desk take up?* • *He's fainted! Don't crowd him – give him room.* • *Is there (enough/any) room* **for** *me* **in** *the car?* • *There's* **plenty of** *room in the car.* • *James took the books off the little table to* **make** *room* **for** *the television.* • *There were so many people in the lift that there wasn't room* **to** *move.* [+ to infinitive] • *(fig.) I feel the company has little room* **for manoeuvre** (=only a few possible plans of action to choose from). • *(saying)* 'There's no/not (enough) room to swing a cat' means that a particular place or space is very small. • *(fig.) In a small company like this, there is no room* **for** (=no possibility of having) *lazy staff.* • *There is little room* **for** (=little possibility of) *doubt about what happened.* • *Her writing has improved but there is still* **room for improvement** (=the possibility or hope that it will get better). • See also HEADROOM; LEGROOM. • LP> **Measurements**

room·y /ˈruː·mi/ *adj* **-ier, -iest** *approving* • If something such as a house or car is roomy, it has a lot of space inside it.

room·mate /ˈrʊm·meɪt, ˈruːm-/ *n* [C] a person with whom you share a room for a period of time, or *(Am)* a person with whom you share an apartment or house • *"So how did you meet Karen?" "She was my roommate during our first year at university."* • *(Am) Brian's moving out next month, so we're looking for another roommate to share our apartment.*

roost /ruːst/ *n* [C] a place, such as a branch of a tree, where birds rest or sleep

roost /ruːst/ *v* [I] • *The birds found a tree to roost* (=stay) *in for the night.* • *All his earlier mistakes are* **coming back/home to roost** (=returning to cause problems).

roost·er /£ˈruː·stəʳ, $-stɚ/ *n* [C] *Am and Aus for* COCK [BIRD]

root [PLANT PART] /ruːt/ *n* [C] the part of a plant which grows down into the earth to obtain water and food and which holds the plant firm in the ground • *The girl carefully pulled up the weed by its roots* (=pulled all of it out). • *In the desert, he lived on roots and berries.* • *Irises have* **shallow** *roots* (=Their roots do not grow very deep). • *I've planted some saplings, but it'll be a while before they* **send out roots/take root** (=start growing). • *(fig.) Communism has never* **taken root** (=become established) *in Britain.* • *(fml) Racism must be eliminated,* **root and branch** (=completely). • In America, **root beer** is a fizzy drink without alcohol that is flavoured with the roots of various plants. • *(Am)* A **root cellar** is an area, often underground, for storing root crops and vegetables. • A **root crop** is a plant such as potatoes or CARROTS that is grown because its roots are eaten. • The root of a hair, tooth, or nail is the hidden part that connects it to the body: *The dentist pulled out her tooth by the roots* (=pulled all of it out). • The root of something bad is the cause or origin of it: *We must get to the root of* (=discover the cause of) *this problem.* ○ *What* **lies at** *the root* **of** *the* **problem** *is their lack of interest.* ○ *The high crime rate has its roots* **in** *unemployment and poverty.* ○ *The root* **(cause)** *of your anxiety is probably your mother's neglect of you as a child.* ○ *The main message of my sermon is that money is the root* **of all evil**. • *(specialized)* The root of a word is its most basic form, to which other parts, such as AFFIXES, can be added: *The root of the word 'sitting' is 'sit', and the root of 'friendliness' is 'friend'.* ○ *'Merchant'* **comes from/is derived from** *the Latin root 'merx'.*

root *(obj)* /ruːt/ *v* • *The trees failed to root* (=grow roots) *and so died.* [I] • *I suggest you root* **up/out** *the weeds* (=take out the whole plant including the roots) *before they take hold.* [M] • To **root out** something/someone/**root** something/someone **out** is to make an effort to find and remove them: *His friends went upstairs to root him out of his bedroom.* ○ *I've rooted out an old pair of shoes that might fit you.* ○ *Ms Campbell has been appointed to root out inefficiency* (=remove it completely) *in this company.*

root·ed /£ˈruː·tɪd, $-t̬ɪd/ *adj* [not gradable] • *There is a* **deep-***rooted* (=firm and strong) *distrust of any form of*

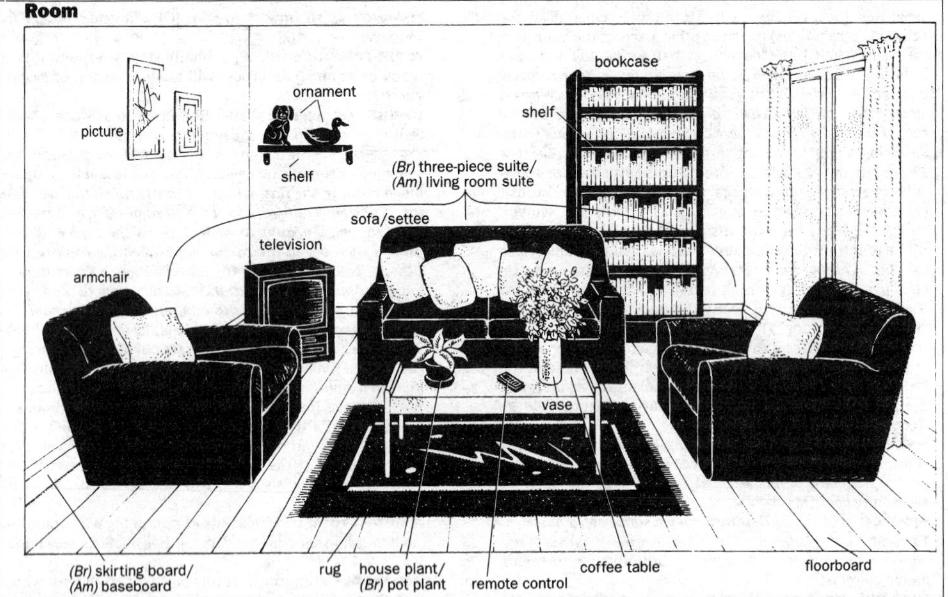

change. • *Their distrust is* **firmly** *rooted* **in** (= caused by) *fear and ignorance.* • *She was* **rooted to the spot** (= unable to move) *with fear/amazement.*

root·less /ˈruːt·ləs/ *adj* [not gradable] • A rootless person is someone without a home to return to.

root·less·ness /ˈruːt·lə·snəs/ *n* [U]

roots /ruːts/ *pl n* • *They quickly* **put down (new)** *roots in their new town* (= found a home, friends, activities in which to join, etc.). • Roots can also mean origins: *She's visiting Africa to discover her roots.* ○ *The city of Tours can* **trace** *its roots* **back to** *Roman times.* ○ *The book gives a detailed account of the Korean War and its* **historical** *roots.* • See also GRASSROOTS.

root MATHEMATICS /ruːt/ *n* [C] *specialized* a solution of some EQUATIONS (= mathematical statements) • *The roots of the equation x^2-1=0 are -1 and +1.* • A root **of** a particular number is another number which, when multiplied by itself one or more times, reaches that number: *The* **square** *root of 64 is 8, and the* **cube** *root of 64 is 4.* ○ *5 x 5 x 5 x 5 = 625, so 5 is the fourth root of 625.* • LP **Mathematics**

root LOOK /ruːt/ *v* [I always + adv/prep] to look for something by turning things over • *She rooted* **through/among** *the papers on her desk.* • *The pigs rooted* **for** *acorns in the forest.*

root for *obj v prep* [T] *esp. Am infml* to give your support to (someone), or to show your support for (someone) • *I'll be rooting for you in the election.* • *Most of the crowd were rooting for the home team.*

rope /£rəʊp, $roʊp/ *n* (a piece of) strong, thick cord made of long pieces of HEMP (= a plant with strong fibres) or other material twisted together • *A sailor threw a rope ashore and we tied the boat to a post.* [C] • *(fig.) Round her neck hung a thick rope* (= several strings twisted together) *of pearls.* [C] • *(fig.) a rope of garlic* (= several pieces tied together) [C] • *Coils of rope lay untidily all over the ship's deck.* [U] • A **rope ladder** is a LADDER (= a frame with steps for climbing up or down) made of two long pieces of rope connected by short pieces of rope, metal, wood, etc. • A **rope bridge** is a bridge made of long pieces of rope knotted together, and wooden boards for people to walk on, used esp. in the past or for children's games. • PIC **Bridge**

ropes /£rəʊps, $roʊps/ *pl n* • The ropes are a fence made of rope enclosing esp. a **boxing ring**: *The champion has his opponent up against the ropes.* • *(infml)* If you say that someone or something is **on the ropes**, you mean that they are doing badly and are likely to fail. • *When the new teacher arrived I spent a day* **showing/teaching** *her* **the ropes** (= explaining the job, etc. to her). • *Our new recruits all go on a six-week training course to* **learn the ropes** (= learn the job).

rope *(obj)* /£rəʊp, $roʊp/ *v* [always + adv/prep] • *I'll rope* (= join with a rope) *my horse* **to** *your car and pull you out.* [T] • *The climbers roped* **up**/*roped themselves* **together**. [I/T] • If you rope an area **off**, you enclose it with ropes to keep people out: *The police had roped off the scene of the crime.* [M] • If you rope someone **in**, you persuade them to do something for you that they did not really want to do: *At the last minute we roped in a couple of spectators to complete the team.* [M] • If you **rope** someone **into** something you persuade them to do something: *We roped a couple of spectators into playing for our team.*

rope·y, rop·y /£ˈrəʊ·pi, $ˈroʊ-/ *adj* **ropier, ropiest** *esp. Br and Aus infml* in bad condition or of low quality • *Your tyres look a bit ropey, don't they?* • *That car has ropy tyres.* • *I usually feel rather ropey* (= ill) *the morning after a big party.*

rort *obj* /£rɔːt, $rɔːrt/ *v* [T] *Aus infml* to take unfair advantage of (a public service) for your own benefit • *Gary's been rorting the system, getting both a student allowance and unemployment benefit.*

rort *n* [C] *Aus infml* • A rort is a plan to take unfair advantage of a public service for your own benefit: *She's come up with a new rort to get more money out of the social security system.*

ro·sa·ry /£ˈrəʊ·zᵊr·i, $ˈroʊ·zɚ-/ *n* [C] a string of BEADS (= little decorative balls) used esp. by Roman Catholics to count prayers, or the prayers themselves • *wearing a rosary* • *telling/saying/reciting her rosary*

rose RISE /£rəʊz, $roʊz/ *past simple of* RISE

rose PLANT /£rəʊz, $roʊz/ *n* [C] a garden plant with pleasant-smelling flowers and THORNS (= sharp points) on its stems, or a flower from this plant • *a rose bush* • *a rose garden* • *rose petals* • *Your roses are looking lovely, Gertrude.* • *She sent him a bunch of red/white/pink/yellow roses.* • *(fig.) A brisk walk will* **put the roses (back) into** *your* **cheeks** (= make your face look healthier). • If something is **coming up roses**, it is happening successfully. • When you say that a situation is **not all roses/not a bed of roses**, you mean that there are unpleasant things to deal with as well as the pleasant ones: *Being an actress is not all roses, you know.* • **Rose hips** are the fruit produced by rose bushes: *rose-hip syrup/tea/wine* • **Rose-water** is a liquid with a pleasant smell made from roses, used on the skin as a PERFUME or to flavour food. • A **rose window** is a round window, esp. in a church, with coloured glass in it. • *"A rose by any other name would smell as sweet"* (Shakespeare, Romeo and Juliet 2.2) • *"It was roses, roses, all the way"* (Robert Browning in the poem *The Patriot*, 1855) • *"The Yellow Rose of Texas"* (traditional American song, 1850s) • PIC **Berries, Flowers and plants**

rose /£rəʊz, $roʊz/ *adj* [not gradable] • *The houses were painted various shades of rose* (= pink). • If you **look at/see/view** a situation **through rose-coloured/tinted glasses**/*(Br and Aus also)* **spectacles**, you see only the pleasant things about it and don't see the reality of the situation: *She has always looked at life through rose-tinted spectacles.*

ros·y /£'rəʊ·zi, $'roʊ-/ *adj* **-ier, -iest** • *(literary) The white walls of the house were turned a rosy colour* (=between red and pink) *by the evening sunlight.* • *(approving) Your rosy* **cheeks** *always make you look so healthy.* • *(approving) A rosy-***cheeked** *girl was planting flowers in the garden.* • *(fig.) Our financial position is rosy* (=hopeful). • *"Rosy-fingered Dawn"* (Homer, 8th century BC) • See **paint a rosy picture** at PAINT.

rose DEVICE /£rəʊz, $roʊz/ *n* [C] a circular device with small holes in it which is put on the end of a **watering can** (=a container for pouring)

ros·é /£'rəʊ·zeɪ, $roʊ'zeɪ/ *n* [U] a pink wine

rose·ate /£'rəʊ·zi·ət, $'roʊ·zi·ɪt/ *adj poetic* pink • *The roseate buds of the apple blossom swayed in the breeze.*

rose·bud /£'rəʊz·bʌd, $'roʊz-/ *n* [C] the beginning stage of a rose flower

ro·sel·la /£rəʊ'zel·ə, $roʊ-/ *n* [C] *Aus* one of the brightly-coloured PARROTS of esp. eastern Australia

rose·ma·ry /£'rəʊz·mə·ri, $'roʊz·mer·i/ *n* [U] a small bush whose leaves are used as flavouring in cooking and used in some PERFUMES (=pleasant smelling liquids), or the leaves themselves • PIC› **Herbs and spices**

ro·sette /£rəʊ'zet, $roʊ-/ *n* [C] a flower-shaped decorative object cut into wood or stone or one made of RIBBON (=narrow silk strips) worn as a sign that you support a particular team or political party or that you have won a race, etc. • *They were all wearing red rosettes pinned to their jackets.* • *The winning horse had a rosette fixed to its bridle.*

rose·wood /£'rəʊz·wʊd, $'roʊz-/ *n* [U] a hard dark-coloured wood used esp. for making high-quality furniture

ros·in /£'rɒz·ɪn, $'rɑː·zən/ *n* [U] yellow hardened RESIN (=a thick, sticky liquid from some trees), used esp. on the hairs of BOWS (=a long thin piece of wood with hairs from a horse stretched across it) of stringed musical instruments to prevent the hairs from sliding over the strings

ros·ter /£'rɒs·təʳ, $'rɑː·stɚ/ *n* [C] *esp. Am and Aus* a list of people's names, often with the jobs they have been given to do • *If you look on the* **duty** *roster, you'll see when you're working.*

ros·trum /£'rɒs·trəm, $'rɑː·strəm/ *n* [C] *pl* **rostrums** or **rostra** /£'rɒs·trə, $'rɑː·strə/ a small PLATFORM (=raised area) on which a public speaker or a music CONDUCTOR (=leader) stands

rot *(obj)* /£rɒt, $rɑːt/ *v* **-tt-** to (cause to) decay • *The meat lay rotting in the hot sun.* [I] • *Rain has got in and rotted* **(away)** *the woodwork.* [T/M] • *Sweet foods rot your teeth and gums.* [T] • *The room was full of the smell of rotting fruit.* • *You should buy a bag of well-rotted manure and spread it on the garden.* • *(fig.) She was* **left to** *rot* (=left and forgotten about) *in jail for most of her life.* [I]

rot /£rɒt, $rɑːt/ *n* [U] • *Rot has got into the furniture.* • *(infml) The* **rot set in** (=Things began to go wrong) *when his parents divorced and he started taking drugs.* • *We must try to* **stop the rot** (=take action against something bad) *before the whole school is corrupted.* • *(dated infml)* If you say that the things someone is saying are rot, you mean that they are nonsense: *"Don't talk rot!"*

rot·ten /£'rɒt·ᵊn, $'rɑː·tᵊn/ *adj* • *The room smelled of rotten vegetables.* • *(fig.)* **It** *was rotten* (=very bad) **of** *you* **to** *leave without saying goodbye.*

ro·ta *esp. Br* /£'rəʊ·tə, $'roʊ·t̬ə/, *Am and Aus usually* **ros·ter** *n* [C] a list of things that have to be done and of the people who will do them • *a weekly rota* • *a rota for cleaning*

ro·tate *(obj)* /£rəʊ'teɪt, $'roʊ·teɪt/ *v* to (cause to) turn in a circle, esp. around a fixed point • *Rotate the handle by 180° to open the door.* [T] • *The wheel rotates* **around** *an axle.* [I] • *The satellite slowly rotates as it circles the earth.* [I] • If a job rotates or if a group of people rotate their jobs, the jobs are done at different times by different people. [T] • When farmers rotate crops, they regularly change which crops they grow in a particular field. [T]

ro·ta·tion /£rəʊ'teɪ·ʃᵊn, $roʊ-/ *n* • *The earth completes 366 rotations* **about** *its axis in every leap year.* [C] • *With this drill it's possible to adjust the speed of rotation.* [U] • *There are ten employees and they do the various jobs* **in rotation** (=they take turns to do them). • **Crop** *rotation is an important way of maintaining the fertility of farmland.* [U]

ro·ta·ry /£'rəʊ·tᵊr·i, $'roʊ·t̬ɚ-/ *adj* [not gradable] • *a rotary engine/mower/pump* • *A helicopter flies by the rotary* (=circular) *movement of its blades.* • KOR

rote /£rəʊt, $roʊt/ *n* [U] *usually disapproving* memory or habit, rather than understanding • To **learn** something **by rote** or **rote learning** means learning something in order to be able to repeat it from memory, rather than learning it in order to understand it: *She learned the equations by rote.*

ro·tis·se·rie /£rəʊ'tɪs·ᵊr·i, $roʊ'tɪs·ɚ-/ *n* [C] (a shop or restaurant which contains) a device for cooking meat, esp. chicken, by turning it round slowly near a flame or cooker • *The boy stared in fascination at the rotating meat on the rotisserie.* • *The rotisserie on the corner of Waldorf Street stays open until midnight.*

rot·or /£'rəʊ·təʳ, $'roʊ·t̬ɚ/ *n* [C] a part of a machine that spins, esp. the device supporting the spinning blades of a HELICOPTER • *A helicopter needs a tail rotor to produce a sideways thrust that stops the whole machine spinning round in the opposite direction to the main rotor.*

rot·ten /£'rɒt·ᵊn, $'rɑː·tᵊn/ *adj* See at ROT

rot·ter /£'rɒt·əʳ, $'rɑː·t̬ɚ/ *n* [C] *infml humorous esp. Br* someone who is very unpleasant or does very unpleasant things • *"She'd been really rude to me, so I told the boss that she'd been phoning her boyfriend when she should have been working." "You rotter!"*

rott·weil·er /£'rɒt,waɪ·ləʳ, £-,vaɪ-, $'rɑːt,waɪ·lɚ/ *n* [C] a large, fierce and sometimes dangerous type of dog • *(fig.) Jenkins is one of the new breed of political rottweilers* (=fierce political fighters) *in his party.*

ro·tund /£rəʊ'tʌnd, $roʊ-/ *adj* (esp. of a person) round or rounded in shape

ro·tun·da /£rəʊ'tʌn·də, $roʊ-/ *n* [C] (part of) a building which is round in shape, and often has a DOME (=rounded roof) on top • *The company's headquarters are made up of a central rotunda and four tower blocks which surround it.*

rouge /ruːʒ/ *n* [U] *dated* a red powder put on the CHEEKS (=the sides of the face) to make the face look more attractive • KOR

rough UNEVEN /rʌf/ *adj* **-er, -est** uneven or not smooth, often because of being in bad condition • *It was a rough mountain road, full of stones and huge holes.* • If a surface such as paper or skin is rough, it does not feel smooth when you touch it: *His hands were rough from years as a mechanic.* ○ *The rough side of the paper absorbed the ink better.* • If you describe a drink, such as wine, as rough, you mean that it tastes cheap and usually also strong. • Something that is rough is not very well or carefully made: *I made a rough table out of some old boxes.* • A rough voice or sound is hard and loud: *He had a rough accent.* • Rough **ground** is ground that is not used for any particular purpose and is uneven and full of wild plants: *The boys played football on a patch of rough ground next to the old factory.* • If something such as a machine is **running** rough or **sounds** rough, it is in bad condition: *My engine's been sounding rough ever since I started using unleaded fuel.* • **Rough and ready** means simple, esp. because of having been hurriedly arranged: *There was no luxury, but we lived in rough and ready comfort.* • *(Br and Aus)* A **rough diamond** (*Am* **diamond in the rough**) is a person who is kinder and more pleasant than they seem to be from their appearance and manner. • *The roof was supported by* **rough-hewn** (=shaped but not given a smooth surface) *wooden pillars.* • *(fig.) She's an experienced politician with a* **rough-hewn** *style* (=She does not make an effort to follow the usual rules of polite behaviour). • LP› **'-ough' pronunciation**

rough·en *obj* /'rʌf·ᵊn/ *v* [T] • *I roughened both surfaces a little before gluing them together.*

rough·ly /'rʌf·li/ *adv* • *Roughly* **chop** *the coriander and mix it with the garlic.*

rough /rʌf/ *n* [U] • In golf, **the rough** is the uneven ground with long grass: *My ball landed in the rough.* • If you tell someone that they must **take the rough with the smooth**, you mean that they must accept the unpleasant as well as the pleasant things in a particular situation.

rough NOT EXACT /rʌf/ *adj* [before n] **-er, -est** fairly correct but not exact or detailed; approximate • *I've made a rough drawing of what I had in mind for the cupboards in the kitchen.* • *This is only a rough guess.* • *She made a rough estimate/calculation of the likely cost.* • *This is just a rough* **copy** *of the press release – I'll get you a properly printed-out version.* • *The tests are a rough* **guide** *to students' progress.* • *The guidebook gave me a rough* **idea** *of what the weather would be like in Spain.* • *Her rough* **work** (=early ideas written down) *showed how her ideas had developed.* • *His first plans were drawn up* **in rough** (=simply, without details). • *I quickly thought up a* **rough and ready** (=quickly produced and not detailed) *plan.* • *(Br) She did her first calculations on* **rough paper** (=paper used to do incomplete or undetailed work). • LP› **Approximate numbers**

rough /rʌf/ *n* [C] • A rough is a first quick drawing of something.

rough *obj* /rʌf/ *v* [T always + adv/prep] • If you rough a drawing **out/in**, you draw the basic lines, without the detail. [M] • If you rough **out** something such as a plan or suggestion, you give someone your first ideas for it. [M]

rough·ly /ˈrʌf·li/ *adv* • *The world's population is roughly* **about** *5·25 billion.* • *Roughly speaking it's 5·25 billion.* • *We have roughly similar tastes/roughly the same tastes.*

rough VIOLENT /rʌf/ *adj* **-er, -est** violent, hard or difficult; not calm or gentle • *a rough-looking drunkard* • *a rough* (= often violent) *area of town* • *The other boys were rough, always looking for a fight.* • *It's a rough and dangerous life, being a fisherman.* • *I'm always sea-sick if the water/wind/sea/weather is rough* (= stormy). • *(infml) You look a bit rough* (= ill) *– how much did you have to drink last night?* • *(infml) She's had a rough* (= difficult and unlucky) *time/month/year, what with her divorce and then her father dying.* • *(infml) This month's been rough* **on** (= difficult for) *her.* • *(infml)* **It** *must be rough* **to** *have two kids and nowhere to live.* [+ to infinitive] • *It seems* **rough justice/luck** (= unfair) **on** *him that every penny he earns is taken in taxes.* • *(dated infml) The boss* **gave** *me* **the rough side of** *her* **tongue** (= criticized me severely). • *(infml) The boss* **gives** *me* **a rough time/ride** (= criticizes me severely) *if I make any mistakes.* • *(slang)* **Rough trade** are male PROSTITUTES who have sex with men and who give the appearance of being from the lower social classes: *He went to the docks to pick up a bit of rough trade.*

rough /rʌf/ *adv* • *The Hull team had a bad reputation for playing rough.* • *When we ran out of money we* **slept** *rough* (= slept outside on the ground) *for a week.*

rough /rʌf/ *n* • A rough is a violent person: *a gang of drunken young roughs* [C] • *Two chairs got broken in the boys'* **rough and tumble** (= not very serious fighting). • *(fig.) She enjoys the* **rough and tumble** *of politics.*

rough *obj* /rʌf/ *v* [T] • *(infml) While the house was being decorated we* **roughed it** (= lived in basic conditions) *in a tent.* • *(infml) A gang of youths caught me outside the garage and* **roughed** *me* **up** (= beat me up).

rough·ly /ˈrʌf·li/ *adv* • *He pushed the children roughly to one side.* • *"And what's going on here?" he said roughly.*

rough·age /ˈrʌf·ɪdʒ/ *n* [U] FIBRE FOOD

rough·cast /£ˈrʌf·kɑːst, $-kæst/ *n* [U] *specialized* a mixture of water, sand, LIME and small stones which is used to cover the outside of buildings

rough·house *(obj)* /ˈrʌf·haʊs/ *v infml* to fight, often playfully • *A couple of boys were roughhousing (each other) in the park.* [T]

rough·house /ˈrʌf·haʊs/ *n* [C usually sing] *pl* **roughhouses** /ˈrʌfˌhaʊ·zɪz/ *infml* • *There was a bit of a roughhouse* (= fight) *in the restaurant last night, and the furniture got wrecked.*

rough·neck /ˈrʌf·nek/ *n* [C] a worker on an **oil rig** (= a large piece of equipment for getting oil from underground) or *(esp. Am and Aus infml)* a person who is rough and rude, usually a man

roul·ette /ruːˈlet/ *n* [U] a game of chance in which a small ball is dropped onto a wheel that is spinning and the players guess in which hole it will finally stop

round CIRCULAR /raʊnd/ *adj* **-er, -est** shaped like a ball, circle, curve or cylinder • *a round table/pot/plate/pie/pizza/hole/stone/wheel* • *Her eyes were round/She was* **round-eyed** *with amazement/terror.* • *The Earth is round.* • *Tennis balls and oranges are round.* • *Her face seemed round and white in the moonlight.* • *The baby's plump round arms and legs made me laugh.* • *Along the row of pointed windows there was one round arch.* • *(Br)* **Round brackets** (also **brackets** or **parentheses**) are a pair of signs () used in text to enclose some information: *You can give that information in round brackets at the end of the sentence, or as a footnote at the bottom of the page.* LP› **Brackets** • A **round number** is a whole or complete number: *2·8 to the nearest round number is 3.* ○ *I need eleven books for tomorrow's class – I'd better make that a* **round dozen** (= exactly 12). ○ *"I've got 95 bottles here for you." "Could you make it a* **round hundred**, *please?"* ○ *How much is it in* **round figures** (= to the nearest number ending in zero)? • A **round robin** is a letter, usually of demands or complaints, which is signed by many people. • A **round robin** is also a competition in which all the players play against each other at least once. • If you describe someone as **round-shouldered**, you mean that their shoulders curve down and forward: *He had become round-shouldered from years of sitting in front of a computer.* • A **round-table** discussion/meeting is one where people meet and talk in conditions of equality. • If you make a **round trip**, you go on a journey and return to where you started from: *The round trip from France to Australia is very expensive.*

round *obj* /raʊnd/ *v* • To **round** a number **up/down** or **round up/down** a number is to increase/reduce it to the nearest whole or simple number: *I owe you $48·90 but I'll round it up* **to** *$50 for you.*

round·ed /ˈraʊn·dɪd/ *adj* • Something that is rounded has become round or curved: *The little boy stared at the pregnant woman's rounded belly.* ○ *The kitchen table has rounded edges.*

round AROUND *esp. Br* /raʊnd/, *Br also, Am and Aus usually* **a·round** *prep, adv* [not gradable] in a circular way or position; around • *The Moon goes round* (= travels in a circle about) *the Earth.* • *We ran round (the outside of the house) to the back, looking for the dog.* • *Drive round the corner and take the second road on the left.* • *As we came round a bend (in the road) we could suddenly see the sea.* • *As the bus left, Ann turned round and waved goodbye to us.* • *The children turned round and round until they made themselves dizzy and fell over.* • *That tune has been going round and round in my head all day* (= I can't stop singing it silently to myself). • *We'd gone 200 miles when one engine stopped and we had to turn round and fly home.* • *She walked round* (= walked everywhere in) *the room, pointing at my pictures.* • *The landlord showed me round* (= showed me the rooms of the house). • *We had a look round* (= spent time in) *the museums while we were in London.* • *I spent a year travelling round* (= visiting various parts of) *Africa and the Middle East.* • *I had to go* **all/right** *round* (= everywhere in) *the town to find a hotel that was open.* • *This virus has been going round (the school)* (= many people have had it). • *You must come round (to my house) sometime soon.* • *We'll be at your house round* **about** (= at approximately) *10 o'clock.* • *(fig.) I know how we can* **get round** (= solve) *this problem.* • *(fig.) There's no* **way round** (= solution to) *this problem.* • *There aren't enough pencils to* **go round** (= enough for each person to have one). • *He put the wheel on the* **right/wrong way round** (= facing the right/wrong way). • See **theatre in the round** at THEATRE. • PIC› **Prepositions of movement**

round *obj* /raʊnd/ *v* [T] • *When we rounded* (= went around) *the Cape of Good Hope we had a party on the ship.* • To round something **off/out** is to complete it in the best possible way: *To round off her education, her father sent her to a Swiss finishing school.* [M] ○ *We rounded the meal off* **with** *a chocolate and rum cake.* [M] • If you **round on** someone or something, you suddenly turn and attack them: *The fox rounded on its pursuers.* ○ *(fig.) The Prime Minister rounded on his critics with a very forceful speech.* • To **round** people or animals **up** is to gather them together into one place: *The cowboys rounded up the cattle.* ○ *Why don't you round some friends up, and we'll have a party?*

round SURROUNDING *esp. Br* /raʊnd/, *Br also, Am and Aus usually* **a·round** *prep, adv* [not gradable] on all or some sides of something • *There are trees all round the house.* • *The house has trees all round.* • *We sat round the fire.* • *There were 40 of us round the table.* • *Round* (= In the area of) *the city there are lots of jobs.* • *The rope had already been tied round his neck.* • *I wrapped my towel round me before answering the door.* • *They walked along with their arms round each other's waists.* • *The pyramid is 50 metres high and 100 metres round (the base).* • *Everyone for a mile round heard the explosion.*

round DIRECTION *esp. Br* /raʊnd/, *Br also, Am and Aus usually* **a·round** *prep, adv* [not gradable] in a particular direction • *The garden is round the back (of the house).* • *I used to live round* (= near) *here when I was a child.* • *There's a great restaurant just* **round the corner** (= very near here). • *(Br and Aus not standard) We're going round* (= to) *the pub for a quick drink.*

round GROUP /raʊnd/ *n* [C] a number of things or group of events • *He didn't have enough money to buy a round* **(of drinks)** (= to pay for an esp. alcoholic drink for everyone in a group of people). • *(Br)* A round **of toast** is one whole slice of it, and a round **of sandwiches** is a sandwich made from two whole slices of bread: *He ordered five rounds of sandwiches.* • *Russia and America will hold another round* **of talks** *next month.* • *The singer got a big round* **of applause** (= the people watching clapped a lot). • *When we* *were young life was just one long round of parties/pleasure.* • *(dated) I get exhausted just by* **the/my daily round** (= the things I have to do every day). • *(Br and Aus)* A round (*Am* **route**) is also a set of regular visits that you make to a number of places or people, esp. as part of your job: *He has/does a* **milk/paper** *round* (= he delivers newspapers to houses). ○ *The doctor's* **out on** *his* **rounds** (= visiting ill people). • *I've* **made/done the rounds** *of* (= talked/been to) *all the agents, but nobody has any tickets left.* • *That story has* **gone the rounds** (= been passed on from person to person) *in our office.* • In many sports, a round is a part of a competition: *She was knocked out of the championship in the third round.* [LP〉] **Sports** • In boxing or WRESTLING, a round is a period of time during which the competitors are fighting: *He lasted two rounds against the champion.* • In golf, a round is a complete game: *Do you fancy a round of golf after lunch?* • *(specialized)* In music, a round is a song for several singers, who begin singing one after the other at various points in the song.

round [BULLET] /raʊnd/ *n* [C] a bullet or other single piece of AMMUNITION (= material used to destroy property, people, etc. in a war) • *They fired off several rounds to scare the birds.* • *The soldiers had only twenty rounds left.*

round·a·bout [CIRCULAR OBJECT] *Br and Aus* /ˈraʊnd·ə·baʊt/, *Am* **traf·fic cir·cle** *n* [C] a place where three or more roads join and traffic must go in one direction around a circular area in the middle, rather than straight across • *In Britain, vehicles must give way to traffic that's already on a roundabout.* • *(Br)* A roundabout (*esp. Am* **merry-go-round**, *Am also* **carousel**) is also a large machine in an amusement park which has model animals, cars, etc. on it for children to sit on and be carried round and round. • *(Br and Aus)* A roundabout (*Am* **merry-go-round** or **carousel**) is also a flat round piece of equipment in play areas on which children sit or stand and are pushed round and round. • [PIC〉] **Playground, Road**

round·a·bout [INDIRECT] /ˈraʊnd·ə·baʊt/ *adj* not in a simple, direct or quick way • *We took a roundabout route to avoid the accident.* • *He asked me, in a roundabout way, if he could have a salary increase.*

roun·del /ˈraʊn·dᵊl/ *n* [C] a circular decoration, esp. a coloured circle on a military aircraft that shows its nationality

round·ers /£ˈraʊn·dəz, $-dɚz/ *n* [U] a British game similar to baseball, in which you try to hit a ball and score a point if you run round all four sides of a large square area

round·ly /ˈraʊnd·li/ *adv fml* severely • *The government is being roundly criticized for its education policy.* • *The home team were roundly* (= completely) *defeated.*

round·up /ˈraʊnd·ʌp/ *n* [C] a gathering together of people, cattle, things, etc. • *a cattle roundup* • *The President ordered the roundup and imprisonment of all opposition politicians.* • A **news** roundup is a statement of the main items of news on the radio or television. • See also **round up** at ROUND [CIRCULAR], ROUND [AROUND].

round·worm /£ˈraʊnd·wɜːm, $-wɜːrm/ *n* [C] any of various types of WORM with a round body that can live in the bowels of people and particular animals, esp. pigs, and often cause disease • *Roundworms are parasitic.* • *a roundworm infestation* • [PIC〉] **Worm**

rouse *obj* /raʊz/ *v* [T] to wake (someone) up or make (someone) more active or excited • *(fml) I promised to rouse the others at 5 am.* • *He roused himself* **(from** *a pleasant day dream) and got back to work.* • *The speaker attempted to rouse the crowd with a cry for action.*

rous·ing /ˈraʊ·zɪŋ/ *adj* • *She delivered a rousing speech full of passion and hope.* • *We sang a last rousing chorus of the national anthem.*

roust·a·bout *Am* /ˈraʊst·ə·baʊt/, *Aus* **rouse·a·bout** /ˈraʊz·ə·baʊt/ *n* [C] a person whose job involves heavy unskilled work

rout *obj* /raʊt/ *v* [T] *fml* to defeat (an enemy) completely and force them to run away • *The cavalry charge utterly routed the enemy.* • *(fig.) The Russian teams have routed all the rest.* • If you **rout** someone **out**, or **rout out** someone, you make them come out of the place where they are: *His wife had to rout him out* **of** *the crowd.*

rout /raʊt/ *n* [C] • *The battle/election was a complete and utter rout.*

route /ruːt/ *n* [C] a particular way or direction between places • *The route we had planned took us right across the country.* • Shipping routes, bus routes, etc. are fixed paths between places: *I live* **on** *a bus route so I can easily get to work.* • *(Am)* A route is also a ROUND: *a (news)paper route* ○ See at ROUND [GROUP]. • *(fig.) I've come to these conclusions by a rather complicated/indirect route.* • In America, **Route** is used before the names of main roads between cities: *Route 66* • A **route march** is a long, difficult and tiring walk, esp. one done by soldiers as part of their training. • *"Get your kicks, on Route 66"* (song *Route 66* written by Nelson Riddle, 1966) • Ⓕ

route *obj* /ruːt/ *v* [T always + adv/prep] • *The company routes* (= sends) *its deliveries via/by way of London.*

rou·tine /ruːˈtiːn/ *n* (a) habitual or fixed way of doing things • *There's no* **set/fixed** *routine at work – every day is different.* [C] • *He checks under the car for bombs as a* **matter of** *routine.* [U] • *An* **exercise/dance** *routine is a set of particular movements.* [C] • *He went into his usual "I'm the head of the family" routine* (= habitual way of speaking). [C] • *(specialized)* A routine is also computer program that does a particular operation. [C]

rou·tine /ruːˈtiːn/ *adj* • *a routine* (= regular) *task/inspection/medical checkup* • *a routine* (= ordinary) *case of appendicitis* • *(disapproving) My job is so routine and boring – I hate it.*

rou·tine·ly /ruːˈtiːn·li/ *adv* • *Health and safety rules are routinely* **flouted/ignored** *on the building site.*

roux /ruː/ *n* [C/U] *pl* **roux** a mixture made from equal amounts of fat and flour, used esp. to thicken a sauce or soup

rove /£rəʊv, $roʊv/ *v* to move, travel or look around esp. a large area; to WANDER • *(literary) His eye/gaze roved hungrily about the room.* [I always + adv/prep] • *He spent most of his life roving the world in search of his fortune.* [T] • *And now a live report from our roving* **reporter** *Martin Jackson.* • *(dated humorous)* If you say that someone **has a roving eye**, you mean that they are always sexually interested in men or women other than their partner.

row [LINE] /£rəʊ, $roʊ/ *n* [C] a line of things, people, animals, etc. arranged next to each other • *a row of houses/books/plants/people/horses* • *They were holding hands in the back row* (= line of seats) *of the cinema.* • *We stood* **in a** *row/***in** *rows to receive our certificates from the Chancellor.* • *She's been voted Best Actress three times* **in a row** (= three times without anyone else winning). • Row is also used in the names of some roads: *Prospect Row* • **Row house** is *Am for* **terraced house**. See at TERRACE [HOUSE]. • [PIC〉] **Accommodation**

row [ARGUMENT] /raʊ/ *n* [C] *esp. Br and Aus* a noisy argument or fight • *My parents often have rows, but my dad does most of the shouting.* • *What was a political row* **over** *government policy on Europe is fast becoming a diplomatic row* **between** *France and Britain.* • *I can't concentrate because of the row* (= noise) *the builders are making.*

row /£raʊ/ *v* [I] *esp. Br infml* • *My parents are always rowing* **(about/over** *money).*

row *(obj)* [MOVE THROUGH WATER] /£rəʊ, $roʊ/ *v* to cause (a boat) to move through water by pushing against the water with OARS (= long poles with flat ends) • *The wind dropped, so we had to row (the boat) back home.* [I/T] • *The sailors rowed us and the supplies ashore/to land/across the lake.* [T] • [PIC〉] **Water sports**

row·ing /£ˈrəʊ·ɪŋ, $ˈroʊ-/ *n* [U] • *I love rowing.* • *Rowing can be a wonderful team sport.* • A **rowing-boat** (*Am* **rowboat**) is a small boat that is moved by pulling OARS (= long poles with flat ends) through the water. • [PIC〉] **Ships and boats**

row /£rəʊ, $roʊ/ *n* [C usually sing] • *They've gone for a row to the island.*

row·er /£ˈrəʊ·əʳ, $ˈroʊ·ɚ/ *n* [C] • *The Cambridge rowers have won the boat race.*

ro·wan /£ˈrəʊ·ən, $ˈroʊ-/ *n* [C] a small tree with small bright red fruit

row·dy /ˈraʊ·di/ *adj* **-ier, -iest** *disapproving* noisy and possibly violent • *a rowdy party* • *rowdy teenagers on the streets* • *rowdy behaviour* • *The football team got a rowdy welcome when they came home after the cup final.*

row·di·ly /ˈraʊ·dɪ·li/ *adv disapproving* • *The children were behaving very rowdily.*

row·di·ness /ˈraʊ·dɪ·nəs/ *n* [U] *disapproving* • *an increasing level of rowdiness on the streets*

row·dy·i·sm /ˈraʊ·di·ɪ·zᵊm/ *n* [U] *disapproving* • *disgraceful rowdyism in the House of Commons*

row·lock /£ˈraʊ·lɒk, $ˈrɑː·lək/, *Am* **oar·lock** *n* [C] a U-shaped device or hole on each side of a **rowing-boat** in which the OARS (= long poles with flat ends) are held

roy·al /ˈrɔɪ·əl/ *adj* [not gradable] belonging or connected to a king or queen or a member of their family • *the royal* *family* • *a royal visit* • *the royal yacht* • *The law has not yet received the* **royal assent** (= approval of the ruling king or queen). • The colour **royal blue** is a medium bright blue. • In card games, if you have a **royal flush**, you have a set of all the five highest cards in one SUIT (= one of the four types of cards). • When you speak to a member of the family of a king or queen, you address them as **Royal Highness**: *"Thank you,* **Your** *Royal Highness."* ○ **His** *Royal Highness, Prince Andrew* • The **Royal Navy**, the **Royal Society**, etc., are organizations that serve or have the support of the British king or queen. • A **royal pardon** is an official order given by a king or queen to stop the punishment of a person accused of a crime: *Historically, the royal pardon stems from an era when the monarch was considered to function on a higher plane than the courts.* Compare **free pardon** at FREE [NOT IN PRISON]. • The **royal prerogative** is the special rights of the ruling king or queen. • Royal can also mean good or excellent as if intended for or typical of royalty: *a royal reception/welcome* • *in royal spirits* • *(esp. Am)* Royal can also be used to mean 'big' or 'great': *a royal pain/a royal mess*

roy·al /'rɔɪ·əl/ *n* [C usually pl] *infml* • *The photographers follow the royals* (= members of the royal family) *everywhere, on the look-out for scandal.*

roy·al·ist /'rɔɪ·ə·lɪst/ *n, adj* • A royalist is a person who supports a ruling king or queen or who believes that a king or queen should rule their country: *He's an old royalist – he fought against the republicans.* [C] ○ *She's very royalist.*

roy·al·ty /£'rɔɪ·əl·ti, $-t̬i/ *n* [U + sing/pl v] • Royalty are the people who belong to the family of a king and queen. *She believes she's related to royalty* • See also ROYALTY.

roy·al·ty /£'rɔɪ·əl·ti, $-t̬i/ *n* [C usually pl] a payment made to writers, inventors, owners of property, etc. every time their books, devices, land, etc. are bought or used by others • *The BBC intend to reissue old material on video, with appropriate royalties for the musicians, actors and scriptwriters.* • *She gets a royalty cheque every time her play is shown on TV.* • See also **royalty** at ROYAL.

RP /£,ɑː'piː, $,ɑːr-/ *n* [U] *abbreviation for* **Received Pronunciation**, see at RECEIVED

RPI /£,ɑː·piː'aɪ, $,ɑːr-/ *n* [U] **the RPI** *Br abbreviation for* **retail price index**, see at RETAIL

rpm /£,ɑː·piː'em, $'ɑːr-/ *abbreviation for* revolutions per minute (= measurement of the number of times something goes round during a minute)

RR [TRAIN] *n* [C] *Am abbreviation for* RAILROAD

rr [POST] *n* [C] *Am abbreviation for* rural route (= a postal delivery area)

RSVP /£,ɑː·res·viː'piː, $,ɑːr·es-/ *abbreviation for* répondez s'il vous plait (= French for 'please answer'), often written on invitations • *RSVP by October 9th.*

Rt Hon *adj* [before n] *abbreviation for* Right Honourable (= used as part of the title of members of the Privy Council, a group of high-ranking politicians and others that advises the British queen or king) • *the Rt. Hon. Judith Smith MP*

rub *(obj)* /rʌb/ *v* **-bb-** to press or be pressed against (something) with a circular or up and down repeated movement • *She yawned and rubbed her eyes sleepily.* [T] • *I caught him rubbing his bald head with hair restorer.* [T] • *He rubbed* **(at)** *the stain on his trousers and made it worse.* [T; I + *at*] • *We rubbed some polish* **into** *the surface of the wood.* [T] • *First rub the baking tray well* **with** *butter.* [T] • *Alice rubbed the blackboard* **clean** *for the teacher.* [T + obj + adj] • *Your cat keeps on rubbing itself* **(up) against** *my leg.* [T] • *She was rubbing her hands* **(together)** *at the thought of winning.* [T] • *The branches rubbed* **against** *each other in the wind.* [I] • *The chair legs have rubbed holes in the carpet.* [T] • *My new shoes are rubbing* **(against/on** *my toe) and now I've got blisters.* [I] • *(Br infml)* If two people **rub along (together)**, they work or live together in a satisfactory way: *My flat-mate and I rub along okay (together).* • If you **rub down** something, or **rub** something **down**, you clean it, smooth it, or rub it until it shines: *We rubbed down the walls with soap and hot water/with sandpaper.* • If you **rub down** a person or animal, or **rub** a person or animal **down**, you dry them: *I took a towel to rub down my dog.* • *She gently rubbed the ointment* **in**. [M] • *You may think I made a mistake, but you don't have to* **rub it in** (= repeatedly tell me about it). • *These marks will never rub* **off** (= be cleaned off). [I] • *Alice rubbed the sums* **off** (= cleaned them off) *the blackboard for the teacher.* [T] • *(infml) His parents are lovely, but it's a shame that none of their honesty and kindness has* **rubbed off on(to)** *him!* (= he has not learnt from their good example). • *It's in pencil, so you can* **rub** *it* **out** (= remove the marks) *if you need to.* • *(Am slang) He was* **rubbed out** (= murdered) *by the Mafia.* • *(infml) She claims that she* **rubs shoulders with** *(Am also* **rubs elbows with***)* (= meets) *royalty all the time.* • *Just to* **rub** *her* **nose in it/the dirt** (= tell her of something in order to make her feel unhappy), *I put my certificate up on the wall.* • *As soon as they met they started to (Br and Aus)* **rub** *each other* **up the wrong way**/*(Am)* **rub** *each other* **the wrong way** (= to annoy each other without intending to). • **Rubbing alcohol** is *Am for* **surgical spirit** (= alcohol used to clean injuries). • A **rub-down** is an act of cleaning or smoothing something or drying a person or animal: *a cold shower and a rub-down with a towel*

rub /rʌb/ *n* [C] • *He gave her hair a good rub to dry it.* • *(dated literary) You can't get a job unless you have experience, but there's* **the rub** (= the difficulty), *you can't get experience unless you have a job.*

rub·ber [SUBSTANCE] /£'rʌb·əʳ, $-ɚ/ *n* an elastic substance made either from the juice of particular tropical trees or artificially • *Tyres are almost always made of rubber.* [U] • *a bouncy rubber ball* • *waterproof rubber boots* • *the rubber industry* • *Rubber seals on pipes or machines make joints waterproof.* • *(Br and Aus)* A rubber is an **eraser**. [C] See at ERASE [RUB AWAY]. • *(esp. Am slang)* A rubber is a CONDOM (= covering worn on the penis when having sex to prevent pregnancy or disease). [C] • A **rubber band** (also **elastic band**) is a thin ring of rubber used for holding things together: *She put a rubber band around my papers for me.* • A **rubber dinghy** is a small rubber boat which has air in it to keep its shape. • A **rubber plant** is a plant with dark green shiny leaves that comes originally from Asia and is now grown and kept inside. • A **rubber-stamp** is a small device with raised letters made of rubber that is used for printing the date, name of an organization, etc. on documents. • *(disapproving)* If a person or organization **rubber-stamps** something, they give automatic approval to it: *The boss makes the decisions and the committee just rubber-stamps them.* • A **rubber tree** is a type of tropical tree from which LATEX (= liquid which is used to make rubber) is obtained. • [PIC> **Stationery**

rub·bers /£'rʌb·əz, $-ɚz/ *pl n* • Rubbers is *Am for* OVERSHOES.

rub·ber·y /£'rʌb·ᵊr·i, $'-ɚ-/ *adj* **-ier, -iest** • *Octopus can taste a bit rubbery – tough and difficult to chew.* • *My legs felt all rubbery* (= weak) *after the race.*

rub·ber [GAME] /£'rʌb·əʳ, $-ɚ/ *n* [C] a series of three or five games between two teams, esp. in cricket or card games • *We played a rubber of bridge.* • *The West Indies won the rubber against England's cricketers.*

rub·bish *esp. Br* /'rʌb·ɪʃ/, *esp. Am and Aus* **gar·bage**, *Am also* **trash** *n* [U] waste material or unwanted or worthless things • *I forgot to put the rubbish out for collection this morning.* • *Put the carrot peelings in the rubbish* **bin**. • *Have you got a rubbish* **bag** *I can put all these old shoes in?* • *Take the old furniture to the rubbish* **dump**. • *(fig. infml) His ideas are* **a load of (old)** *rubbish* (= nonsense). • *(fig. infml) The film was rubbish* (= bad).

rub·bish *obj* /'rʌb·ɪʃ/ *v* [T] *Br and Aus* • *Why does everyone rubbish* (= criticize) *my ideas?*

rub·bish·y /'rʌb·ɪ·ʃi/ *adj esp. Br and Aus infml* • *a rubbishy* (= bad) *film/piece of architecture*

rub·ble /'rʌb·l̩/ *n* [U] the piles of broken stone and bricks, etc. that are left when a building falls down or is destroyed • *The bomb* **reduced** *the house* **to rubble**. • Rubble is also small pieces of stone or rock used for building: *The walls were filled with rubble and faced with cement.*

ru·bel·la /ruː'bel·ə/ *n* [U] *medical for* GERMAN MEASLES

ru·bi·cund /£'ruː·bɪ·kənd, $-bə·kʌnd/ *adj dated literary or humorous* having a red face

ru·bric /'ruː·brɪk/ *n* [C] *fml* a set of instructions, etc., esp. on an exam paper and usually printed in a different style or colour • *Read/Follow the rubric carefully.* • (N)

ru·by /'ruː·bi/ *n* [C] a dark red jewel • *The ring was set with two rubies.* • *She had ruby* (= ruby-coloured) *lips.*

ruched /ruːʃt/ *adj* [not gradable] (of cloth) in tight elastic folds • *elegant ruched curtains* • *a ruched collar*

ruck [CROWD] /rʌk/ *n* a large group (of people) who are not being successful or (things) which are ordinary • *Her brilliant second novel lifted her* **out of the** *ruck (of average writers).* [U] • *(specialized)* In RUGBY, a ruck is a group of players all together around the ball. [C]

ruck [FOLD] /rʌk/ *n* [C] a fold • *The blankets were caught up in rucks around his feet.*

ruck up *(obj)*, **ruck** *(obj)* **up** *v adv* • *The blankets had rucked up* (= piled up in folds) *around his feet.* [I] • *Her dress was rucked up* (= pushed up in folds) *at the back.* [T]

ruck·sack /ˈrʌk·sæk/, *Am usually* **back·pack** *n* [C] a large bag used esp. by walkers and climbers to carry things on their back • *a frame rucksack with a belt and shoulder straps* • PIC› **Luggage**

ruck·us /ˈrʌk·əs/ *n* [C usually sing] *esp. Am infml* a noisy situation or argument; a RUMPUS

ruc·tions /ˈrʌk·ʃənz/ *pl n esp. Br and Aus infml* a noisy argument or angry complaint • *There'll be ructions if I'm not home by midnight.*

rud·der /£ˈrʌd·əʳ, $-ɚ/ *n* [C] a flat piece of wood or metal at the back of a boat or aircraft, which is moved from side to side in order to control the direction of travel • PIC› **Ships and boats** Ⓓ

rud·der·less /£ˈrʌd·ə·ləs, $ˈ-ɚ-/ *adj*

rud·dy COLOUR /ˈrʌd·i/ *adj* **-ier, -iest** red • *ruddy-cheeked* • *(approving) Her face was ruddy and healthy-looking.* • *(literary) The red lampshade threw a ruddy light around the room.*

rud·dy EXPRESSION /ˈrʌd·i/ *adj* [before n], *adv Br and Aus dated infml* used to avoid saying BLOODY to express anger or annoyance • *that ruddy man* • *Ruddy hell!* • *It's ruddy well raining again.*

rude NOT POLITE /ruːd/ *adj* **-r, -st** not polite; offensive or embarrassing • *a rude man* • **It's** *rude not* **to** *say "Thank you" when you are given something.* [+ to infinitive] • *He's got no manners – he's rude* **to** *everyone.* • *He told a rude joke/story about three women and a donkey.* • *The children made rude noises behind their hands.* • LP› **Labels** Ⓔ

rude·ly /ˈruːd·li/ *adv* • *He pushed past me rudely.* • *She rudely interrupted my speech.*

rude·ness /ˈruːd·nəs/ *n* [U]

rude SUDDEN /ruːd/ *adj* [before n] **-r, -st** sudden and unpleasant • *It was a rude* **shock/surprise** *to us to learn the awful truth about our son.* • *We had a rude* **awakening** (= unpleasant shock) *when we saw the amount of our phone bill.* • Ⓔ

rude·ly /ˈruːd·li/ *adv* • *The news rudely pushed her into the glare of world-wide publicity.*

rude SIMPLE /ruːd/ *adj* **-r, -st** *old use or literary* simply and roughly made • *We built a rude shelter from rocks on the beach.* • Ⓔ

rude·ly /ˈruːd·li/ *adv* • *a rudely constructed table and chairs*

ru·di·ments /ˈruː·dɪ·mənts/ *pl n* **the rudiments** the simplest and most basic facts about a subject or activity • *It only took me an hour to learn/pick up the rudiments* **of** *French grammar/***of** *skiing.*

ru·di·men·ta·ry /£ˌruː·dɪˈmen·tər·i, £ˈ-tri, $-tɚ-/ *adj fml* • *She's only had time to pick up a rudimentary knowledge/grasp of the language.* ○ *Her knowledge is still only rudimentary.* • Rudimentary methods, equipment, systems, etc. are simple and not highly developed. • *(specialized) Some unusual fish have rudimentary* (= small and not developed) *legs.*

rue *obj* /ruː/ *v* [T] *old use or literary* to feel sorry about (an event) and wish it had not happened; regret • *(sometimes humorous) She'll* **rue the day** *she bought that house* (= regret it very much).

rue·ful /ˈruː·fəl/ *adj literary* • *He turned away with a rueful laugh/smile.*

rue·ful·ly /ˈruː·fəl·i/ *adv literary* • *She ruefully contemplated the end of her marriage.*

ruff /rʌf/ *n* [C] a large stiff white collar with many folds worn in Europe in the 16th and 17th centuries, or a circle of hair or feathers growing round a bird or animal's neck

ruf·fi·an /ˈrʌf·i·ən/ *n* [C] *dated* a violent, wild and unpleasant person, usually a man • *(slightly humorous) "Stop beating your sister up, you young ruffian," said his dad.*

ruf·fle *(obj)* MOVE /ˈrʌf·l̩/ *v* [T] to make (something that is smooth) uneven • *She affectionately ruffled his hair with her hand as she passed.* • *The birds ruffled their feathers* **(up)** *in alarm.* [T/M] • *(fig.) Nothing ever ruffles* (= upsets) *her self-confidence.* • *(fig.) He's easily ruffled* (= made nervous or annoyed) *by criticism.* • *She knows how to* **ruffle** *his* **feathers** (= upset or annoy him) *with her teasing.*

ruf·fle FOLD /ˈrʌf·l̩/ *n* [C] a series of small folds made in a piece of cloth or sewn onto it, as decoration • *The dress had lace ruffles at the neck and wrists.*

rug /rʌg/ *n* [C] a piece of thick heavy cloth smaller than a CARPET used for covering the floor or for decoration • *My dog loves lying on the rug in front of the fire.* • *They have a Persian silk rug hanging on the wall.* • *(Br) He put a* **travelling** *rug* (= rug that can be used outside) *around her shoulders/knees to keep her warm.* • Rug is also *Am slang for* TOUPEE. • PIC› **Room** Ⓝ

rug·by /ˈrʌg·bi/, *fml* **rug·by foot·ball**, *infml* **rug·ger** /£ˈrʌg·əʳ, $-ɚ/ *n* [U] a sport where two teams try to score points by carrying an oval ball across a particular line or kicking it over and between an H-shaped set of posts • In **Rugby League** there are 13 players in each team, and in **Rugby Union** there are 15. • LP› **Sports**

rug·ged UNEVEN /ˈrʌg·ɪd/ *adj* (of land) uneven and wild; not easy to travel over • *rugged landscape/terrain/hills/cliffs*

rug·ged STRONG /ˈrʌg·ɪd/ *adj* strong and simple; not delicate • *Jeeps are rugged vehicles, designed for rough conditions.* • If you describe a man's face as rugged, you mean that it is strongly and quite roughly formed: *She fell for his charm and his rugged good looks.*

rug·ged·ly /ˈrʌg·ɪd·li/ *adv* • *She always falls for ruggedly handsome men.*

ru·in *obj* /ˈruː·ɪn/ *v* [T] to spoil or destroy severely or completely • *Tourism has ruined this once unspoiled coastline.* • *The previous owners ruined the house by covering the outside with plastic bricks.* • *Rain ruined my trip.* • *Her injury ruined her chances of winning the race.* • *Cheap imported goods are ruining many businesses* (= forcing them to close).

ru·in /ˈruː·ɪn/ *n* • *Many companies are* **on the edge/brink/verge of** *ruin.* [U] • *Many companies are* **facing** *ruin.* [U] • *The car accident meant* **the ruin of** *all her hopes.* [U] • *They let the palace* **fall into** *ruin* (= become ruined). [U] • *Alcohol was my ruin* (= the thing that destroyed me). [U] • *We visited a Roman ruin.* [C] • *the ruins of Carthage* [C] • *After the war this town was a ruin.* [C] • *The town lay* **in ruins** (= destroyed) *after years of bombing.* • *His life/career/reputation lies/is* **in ruins** (= destroyed).

ru·ined /ˈruː·ɪnd/ *adj* [not gradable] • *an ancient ruined castle* • *My life/career/reputation is ruined.*

ru·in·a·tion /ˌruː·ɪˈneɪ·ʃən/ *n* [U] • *Drink was the ruination of him* (= drinking alcohol destroyed his life).

ru·in·ous /ˈruː·ɪ·nəs/ *adj* [not gradable] • *ten ruinous* (= causing great harm and destruction) *years of terrorism* • *The cost was ruinous* (= destructive because so expensive).

ru·in·ous·ly /ˈruː·ɪ·nə·sli/ *adv* [not gradable] • *Having an accident without insurance can be ruinously expensive.*

rule INSTRUCTION /ruːl/ *n* [C usually pl] an accepted principle or instruction that states the way things are or should be done, and tells you what you are allowed or are not allowed to do • *When she started at her new school she had to learn a whole new set of rules.* • *A referee must know all the rules of the game.* • *The first/most important rule is always to appear confident.* • *Before you start your own business you should be familiar with the government's rules* **and regulations.** • *You must* **follow/obey/observe** *the rules.* • *You must not* **break** *the rules.* • *We have a family rule not* **to** *speak during meals.* [+ to infinitive] • *It's* **against** *the rules* **(of/in** *boxing) to hit below the belt.* • *The rules of English grammar often seem ridiculously complicated.* • *It's a club rule* **that** *new members must sing a song.* [+ that clause] • *The authorities will always* **bend/stretch** *the rules* (= break them slightly) *for royalty.* • *You can trust Ruth because she always* **plays (it) by/goes by/does things by** *the rules* (= follows instructions, standards, or rules). • *A good* **rule of thumb** (= a practical and approximate way of doing or measuring something) *is that a portion of rice is two and a half handfuls.* • **As a (general) rule** (= Usually), *I only read detective novels.* • *In England, it often seems that rain is* **the rule** (= usual) *all the year round.* • *I* **make it a rule** (= I always try) *not to eat fatty foods.* • A **rule book** is a book containing the official rules for an organization or activity. • *(saying)* 'Rules are made to be broken' means it is natural or necessary to disobey particular rules sometimes.

rule *(obj)* CONTROL /ruːl/ *v* to control, or to be the person in charge of (a country) • *Emperors and dictators rule their countries.* [T] • *Most modern kings and queens rule only in a formal way, without real power.* [I] • *She rules her household* **with an iron hand/fist** (= severely). [T] • *For years he has ruled (his country)* **with a rod of iron** (= complete and severe control). [I/T] • *(fig.) The desperate desire to go to Moscow ruled their lives.* [T] • *(fig.) Love ruled supreme* **in** *her heart.* [I] • *(Br and Aus) The graffiti on the wall said 'Liverpool* **rules OK**' (= is the best). • *If you're wise you'll* **be**

ruled by (=take the advice of) *your father.* • *In that family it is the grandma who* **rules the roost** (=controls everyone else). • *"Rule, Britannia, Britannia rule the waves; / Britons never, never, never shall be slaves"* (song based on lines from *Alfred: a Masque* by James Thomson, 1740)

rule /ruːl/ *n* [U] • *The period of foreign/Fascist rule is one people try to forget.* • *We don't want one-party rule – we want rule* **by** *the people.* • *(fml) Everyone is subject to* **the rule of law** (=must obey the laws). • See also MISRULE.

ru·ler /£ˈruː·ləʳ, $-lɚ/ *n* [C] • *The country was without a ruler after the queen died.*

ru·ling /ˈruː·lɪŋ/ *adj* [before n; not gradable] • *The ruling* **body** (=group) *of the Labour Party were united in their condemnation of the Home Secretary.* • *The Communists are the ruling* **party** *at the moment.* • The **ruling class/ruling classes** are the most powerful people in a country. • *His* **ruling passion** (=most important interest) *is music.*

rule *(obj)* DECIDE /ruːl/ *v* to decide officially • *Only the Appeal Court can rule* **on** *this point.* [I] • *The judge ruled* **for/in favour of/against** *the defendant.* [I] • *The government has ruled* **that** *the refugees must be deported.* [+ *that* clause] • *The courts have ruled his brave action illegal.* [T + obj + n/adj] • *The police haven't yet* **ruled out** (=stopped considering the possibility of) *murder.* • *I won't* **rule out** (=state the impossibility of) *a June election.* • *This recent wave of terrorism has* **ruled out** (=prevented) *any chance/possibility of peace talks.* • See also OVERRULE.

ru·ling /ˈruː·lɪŋ/ *n* [C] • *The court's final ruling* (=decision) **on** *the case was* **that** *the companies had acted illegally.* [+ *that* clause]

rule *obj* DRAW /ruːl/ *v* [T] to draw (a straight line) using something that has a straight edge • *She ruled two red lines under the title/across the page.* • *She ruled* **off** (=drew lines to separate) *a space for the picture.* [M] • *I bought a pad of ruled* (=lined) *paper for writing shopping lists.* • PIC **Stationery**

ru·ler /£ˈruː·ləʳ, $-lɚ/, *dated or formal* **rule** /ruːl/ *n* [C] • A ruler is a long, narrow, flat piece of plastic, metal or wood with straight edges marked in centimetres or INCHES (=a unit for measuring length), or both. It is used for measuring things and for drawing straight lines. • LP **Mathematics**

rum DRINK /rʌm/ *n* a strong alcoholic drink made from the juice of the **sugar cane** plant • *I'll have a (glass of) rum.* [C/U] • *Rum and coke is my favourite drink.* [U] • *"Fifteen men on the dead man's chest / Yo-ho-ho and a bottle of rum"* (pirate song from Robert Louis Stevenson's adventure story *Treasure Island*, 1883)

rum STRANGE /rʌm/ *adj* **rummer, rummest** *Br dated or regional infml* strange; PECULIAR • *She's a rum girl/lass/one.* • *The bride was in a red dress – the whole wedding was a bit of a* **rum do** (=strange occasion).

rum·ba /ˈrʌm·bə/ *n* [C] a type of dancing, originally from Cuba, or the music for this.

rum·ble SOUND /ˈrʌm·bl̩/ *v* [I] to make a continuous low sound • *Please excuse my stomach rumbling – I haven't eaten all day.* • *The tanks rumbled* (=moved slowly and noisily) *across the battlefield.* • A **rumble strip** is one of a set of raised strips on a road that makes a low sound when vehicles drive over it to warn drivers to slow down or change direction because they are approaching something.

rum·ble /ˈrʌm·bl̩/ *n* [U] • *We could hear the rumble of distant guns/thunder.*

rum·blings /ˈrʌm·bl̩·ɪŋz, ˈ-blɪŋz/ *pl n* • *rumblings of distant guns/thunder*

rum·ble *obj* DISCOVER /ˈrʌm·bl̩/ *v* [T] *Br infml* to discover the true facts about (someone or something secret and often illegal) • *I'm afraid our little tax dodge has been rumbled.*

rum·ble FIGHT /ˈrʌm·bl̩/ *v* [I] *Aus infml* to take part in a physical fight

rum·bling /ˈrʌm·bl̩·ɪŋ, ˈ-blɪŋ/ *n* [C usually pl] a sign of dissatisfaction or that a situation is becoming worse • *There are rumblings* **of** *annoyance throughout the workforce.* • *Most people had heard rumblings* (=suggestions) *of the war months before it happened.*

ru·mi·nate THINK /ˈruː·mɪ·neɪt/ *v* [I] *fml* to think slowly and deeply about (something) • *She ruminated for weeks about whether to tell him or not.*

ru·mi·na·tive /£ˈruː·mɪ·nə·tɪv, $-neɪ·t̬ɪv/ *adj fml* • *You're wearing a very ruminative expression* (=you look as if you're thinking deeply)!

ru·mi·nate EAT /ˈruː·mɪ·neɪt/ *v* [I] *specialized* (of particular types of animal) to bring up food from the stomach and chew it again

ru·mi·nant /ˈruː·mɪ·nənt/ *n* [C], *adj* [not gradable] *specialized* • *Cows, sheep, and deer are ruminants/ruminant animals.*

rum·mage /ˈrʌm·ɪdʒ/ *v* [I always + adv/prep] to search for something by moving things around without care and looking into, under and behind them • *She rummaged* **in/through** *all the drawers, looking for a pen.*

rum·mage /ˈrʌm·ɪdʒ/ *n* [U] • *I had a rummage* **around/about** *(the house), but I couldn't find my certificate anywhere.* • *(esp. Am)* A **rummage sale** (*Br* **jumble sale**) is a sale of used clothing, books, etc.

rum·my /ˈrʌm·i/ *n* [U] any of various card games in which two or more players try to collect cards which have the same value or whose numbers follow an ordered series

ru·mour *Br and Aus, Am and Aus* **ru·mor** /£ˈruː·məʳ, $-mɚ/ *n* an unofficial interesting story or piece of news that might be true or invented, which quickly spreads from person to person • *an atmosphere of rumour and suspicion* [U] • *Rumours are* **going round** *(the school)* **about** *why the teacher left her previous school.* [C] • *She's* **circulating/spreading** *rumours* **that** *the manager is going to resign.* [C + *that* clause] • *They refused to confirm or deny the rumour of planned job losses.* [C] • **Rumour has it** (=people are saying) **(that)** *you're going to be the next managing director. Is it true?* • A **rumour-monger** is a person who spreads rumours. • Ⓟ

ru·moured *Br and Aus, Am and Aus* **ru·mored** /£ˈruː·məd, $-mɚd/ *adj* [not gradable] • *The rumoured stock market crash has yet to take place.* • **It's** *rumoured in my family* **that** *we have relations in Australia.* [+ *that* clause] ○ *The president is rumoured* **to** *be seriously ill.* [+ *to* infinitive]

rump /rʌmp/ *n* [C] the back end of an animal, or *(humorous)* a person's bottom • *I've bought* **rump steak** (=meat taken from the back end of a cow) *for dinner tonight.* • *(humorous) Fred fell down suddenly, his fat rump going in the mud.* • A rump is also those few members of a group or organization who stay after the others have left or been forced out: *The council was reduced to a rump of 10.*

rum·ple *obj* /ˈrʌm·pl̩/ *v* [T] to make (something) become CREASED (=not smooth) or untidy • *You'll rumple your jacket if you don't hang it up properly.*

rum·pled /ˈrʌm·pl̩d/ *adj* • *a rumpled suit/sheet/bed* • *He looked tired and her hair was rumpled.*

rum·pus /ˈrʌm·pəs/ *n* [U] *infml* a lot of noise, esp. a loud and often confused argument or complaint • *There was a real rumpus* **(going on)** *in the house next door last night.* • *You should* **raise a rumpus** (*Br also* **kick up a rumpus**) (=make a complaint) *about the lack of safety routines here.* • *(Am and Aus)* A **rumpus room** is a room in a house intended for games and entertainment.

run *(obj)* GO QUICKLY /rʌn/ *v* **running**, *past simple* **ran** /ræn/, *past part* **run** (of people and some animals) to move along, faster than walking, by taking quick steps in which each foot is lifted before the next foot touches the ground • *The children had to run to keep up with their father.* [I] • *People came running at the sound of shots.* [I] • *I'm not fit enough to run up those stairs.* [I] • *The sheep ran* **away/off** *in fright.* [I] • *I ran to catch/ran* **for** *the bus.* [I] • *A little girl ran* **up to** (=came quickly beside) *me, crying for her daddy.* [I] • *I go running every evening.* [I] • *I can run a mile in 5 minutes.* [T] • *Are you running* **against** *each other or* **against** *the clock?* [I] • *The Olympic champion ran a terrible race.* [T] • If you run an animal **in** a race, you cause it to take part: *Thompson Stables are running three horses in the next race.* [T] • *The first two races will be run* **(off)** (=will happen) *in 20 minutes.* [T/M] • To run is also to go quickly or in a hurry: *I spent the day running* **all over** *town/* **around** *town looking for Christmas presents.* [I] ○ *Would you run* **out/over/round to** *the post office and get me some stamps?* [I] ○ *I ran* **out of** *the house without even a coat.* [I] • *She got suddenly furious and* **ran at** *me* (=ran towards me and attacked) *with a bread knife.* • *The doctor's advice is to let the fever* **run its course** (=develop and finish naturally). • If you are **running a fever**, your body is hotter than it should be, probably because you are ill. • *After school he* **runs errands** (=goes out to buy or do something) **for** *his father.* • *When the shooting started we* **ran for it/ran for** *our* **lives/ran for cover** (=ran away to save ourselves). • *(Br) "Are you going to ask him to marry you?" "Oh no, he'd* **run a mile**! (=do anything to avoid it)." • If you **run on the spot**, you move your legs as if running, but you stay in one place: *I run on the spot to warm up before I play football.* • *(infml)* If you **run** someone **ragged** you tire them out, usually by giving them too much work or work that is too demanding: *The kids have run me ragged this week – I'm glad they're going back to school tomorrow.* • *(Br) Peter's been* **running round in circles** *(Am* **running around in circles***)* (= been very active but with few results) *since half his department resigned.* • If you **run** someone **to ground/** *(Br also)* **earth** you find them after a lot of searching and difficulties: *Detectives finally ran the terrorists to ground in an apartment building in Chicago.* • *(infml)* If you have a **run-in with** someone, you have a serious argument with them or you get into trouble with them: *I had a run-in with the boss/the law/the police yesterday.* • A **run-off** is an extra competition or election to decide the winner, because the leading competitors have finished equal: *a run-off race* ○ *a run-off election* ○ *In a run-off* **for** *the presidency of the assembly, Santos beat Gutierez.* • In some sports, a **run-up** is a period or distance of running that you do in order to be going fast enough to perform a particular action: *The longer and faster your run-up is, the higher you can jump.* ○ *(fig. esp. Br) Everyone is very busy during the run-up* **to** (= final period of time before) *publication.* • *"Run rabbit run"* (song written by Noel Gay and Ralph Butler, 1939) • *"He can run, but he can't hide"* (the boxer Joe Lewis of the opponent before a fight, 1946)

run /rʌn/ *n* [C] • *We go for/do a three-mile run every evening after work.* • *If you set off* **at a run**, *you'll be exhausted later.* • *They* **broke into** *a run* (= started to run) *when they saw the police coming.* • *While she's away, I've got* **the run of** (= freedom to use) *her house.* • *After a month* **on the run** (= living secretly, trying to avoid being caught), *the prisoners were finally recaptured by the police.* • *Since the children are older now and involved in their own activities, it seems they are always* **on the run** (= hurrying from one activity to the next). • *When I am rushed in the mornings, I eat breakfast* **on the run** (= while hurrying to get somewhere). • *I've achieved a lot in my life and I feel I've* **had a good run for** *my* **money** (= had a good enough time). • *We're going to* **give** *the other candidate* **a run for** *her* **money** (= not let her win easily).

run·ner /£ˈrʌn·əʳ, $-ɚ/ *n* [C] • *The runners in today's Olympic marathon come from 37 different countries.* • A runner can be a horse running in a race: *All the runners and riders for today's races are in the newspaper.* • Runner is also *Aus for* PLIMSOLL (= kind of shoe). • A runner can also be a person who works for someone by taking messages, collecting money, etc.: *I worked as a runner for a ticket seller.* • See also RUNNER-UP.

run·ning /ˈrʌn·ɪŋ/ *n* [U] • *running shoes/shorts* • *Road running is bad for your knee joints.* • *(Br infml) He's been following me around, so I just told him to go and* **take a running jump** (= to go away and stop being annoying). • PIC› **Shoes**

run *(obj)* TRAVEL /rʌn/ *v* **running**, *past simple* **ran** /ræn/, *past part* **run** to (cause to) travel, move or continue in a particular way • *Trains are still running, despite the snow.* [I] • *A bus runs* (= goes on a particular route at particular times) *three times a day between here and there.* [I] • *Skis are waxed on the bottom so that they run smoothly over the snow.* [I] • *She left the engine running* (= left the car's engine switched on) *while she went into the shop.* [I] • *The route/railway/road runs* (= goes) **across** *the border/***into** *Italy/* **through** *the mountains.* [I] • *A climbing rose bush runs* (= grows) **around** *the front door.* [I] • *The road runs* **along** *the coast.* [I] • *There's a beautiful cornice running* **around/ round** *all the ceilings.* [I] • *The film runs* (= lasts) **for** *two hours.* [I] • *The show/course/film runs* (= continues) **for** *another week.* [I] • *A magazine subscription usually only runs* (= can be used) **for** *one year.* [I] • *Buses are running an hour* **late**, *because of an earlier accident.* [I] • *The truck's brakes failed and it ran* (= went) **off** *the road.* [I] • *Trains run* **on** *rails* (= move along on top of them). [I] • *Electricity is running* **through** (= moving along within) *this cable.* [I] • *An angry muttering ran* **through** (= went through) *the crowd.* [I] • *A shiver of fear ran* **through** *her (body).* [I] • *(fig.) The game/luck is really running* **against** *you tonight!* (= despite your efforts, you're losing). [I] • *She ran her finger* **along/down** *the page/list, looking for her name.* [T always + adv/prep] • *Could you run the tape/film/video* **back** *to the beginning, please?* [T always + adv/prep] • *Could you possibly run me* (= take me in your car) **home/to** *the station?* [T always + adv/prep] • *He ran his fingers* **through** *his hair and looked up at me.* [T always + adv/prep] • If a ship or boat **runs aground/ashore/onto the rocks**, it hits the coast, sometimes becoming stuck there. • *Inflation is* **running at** *10%* (= is at the rate of 10%). • *She got 90%, but Fred* **ran** *(her)* **close** (= did nearly as well), *with 87%.* • *Can I have a copy of the article to* **run** *my* **eye over** (= examine), *before it's printed?* • *Intelligence* **runs in** *that* **family** (= is common in that family). • *I've had that tune* **running in** *my* **head** (= I've been singing it in my mind) *all day.* • *(esp. Am infml) The sheriff and his men* **ran** *the horse thieves* **out of town** (= forced them to leave town). • *This show* **will run and run** (= be performed successfully for a long time).

run /rʌn/ *n* [C] • A run is a journey: *The number of aircraft on the New York-Moscow run is being increased.* ○ *(dated) Let's go for a run* **(out)** *in the car somewhere.* ○ *The plane swooped in on its* **bombing** *run* (= attack). • A run **of** something is a continuous period during which it lasts or is repeated: *a run of successes/defeats/bad luck* ○ *The long run of bad weather has ruined the harvest.* • A play's run is the period during which it is performed: *Stoppard's latest play had an extended 25-week run on Broadway.* ○ *The musical's London run was a disaster.* • *The company is planning a first run* (= production) *of 10 000 red teddy bears.* • *My mother always told me that* **in the long run** (= in the distant future) *I would be glad I didn't give up the piano.* • *This may save money* **in the short run** (= in the near future), *but it's going to be expensive* **in the long run**. • *(infml)* A **dummy/ dry run** is a practice of a particular activity or performance in preparation for the real event: *The local elections can be seen as a dummy run* **for** *the national election next year.*

run·ning /ˈrʌn·ɪŋ/ *adj* • *You've been late three days running* (= for three continuous days, without a day of not being late between them). [after n] • *I've had a* **running battle** (= long continuing argument) *with the neighbours over whose responsibility that fence is.* • *As they climbed the final 100 metres they gave us a* **running commentary** (= continuous description of what was happening). • A **running stitch** is a type of sewing stitch made by passing a needle in and out of material repeatedly and evenly.

run *(obj)* OPERATE /rʌn/ *v* **running**, *past simple* **ran** /ræn/, *past part* **run** to (cause to) operate, or to manage • *Keep clear of the machines while they're running.* [I] • *The car is running well since I had it serviced.* [I] • *The government is planning desperate measures to keep the economy running.* [I] • *Some calculators run* **on** (= use as power) *solar power.* [I] • *They had the new computer system* **up and** *running* (= working) *within an hour.* [I] • *(fig.) Work is running* **smoothly** *at the moment.* [I] • *Do you know how to run this sort of machinery?* [T] • *The mechanic asked me to run* (= switch on and allow to work) *the engine for a minute.* [T] • *Change this part of the program and run it again.* [T] • *We can leave the program to run overnight.* [I] • *We've run the computer program, but nothing happens.* [T] • *We're running* (= doing) *an experiment to prove that monkeys can learn to talk like humans.* [T] • *He's been running* (= managing) *a restaurant/his own company since he left school.* [T] • *The local college runs* (= provides) *a course in self-defence.* [T] • *I can't afford to run* (= have and use) *a car.* [T] • *(fig.) Some people run their lives* (= live in particular ways) *according to the movements of the stars.* [T] • *a well-run/badly-run organization/business/course* • *If you need instructions, ask Mark – he's* **running the show** (= directing the operation, project, etc.).

run·ning /ˈrʌn·ɪŋ/ *n* [U] • *She has control of the day-to-day running of the business.* • *I had to sell the car when I could no longer afford the* **running costs** (= the cost of fuel, repairs, etc.). • *(Br)* If you **make/take the running** in a situation, you do the best and most work: *British companies have often made all the running in developing new ideas, but have then failed to market them successfully.*

run *(obj)* FLOW /rʌn/ *v* **running**, *past simple* **ran** /ræn/, *past part* **run** to flow, produce liquid, or (esp. of colours in clothes) to come out or spread • *I can feel trickles of sweat running* **down** *my neck.* [I] • *When the sand has run through the egg-timer, it'll be five minutes.* [I] • *Don't cry, or your make-up will run* (= become liquid and move down your face). [I] • *The walls were running* **with** *damp.* [I] • *The river runs* **(down) to/into** *the sea.* [I] • *The hot tap is running cold* (= producing cold water)! [I] • *He ran a little cold water* **into** *the bath.* [T] • *You should run some cold water* **on** *that burn.* [T] • *I'll run you a hot bath* (= fill a bath with water for you). [+ two objects] • *My nose and eyes have been running all week because of hay fever.* [I] • *After 12 hours at her word processor, the words began to run* **into** *one another.* [I] • *I* *must have washed my dress at too high a temperature, because the colour has run.* [I] • *If the first layer isn't dry before you add the next one, the colours will run* **into** *each other* (=mix). [I] • *During the revolution the streets were* **running with blood** (=there was a lot of fighting and many people were hurt). • *She said mice* **made** *her* **blood run cold** (=made her very frightened). • *"Sweet Thames, run softly, till I end my song"* (Edmund Spenser in his poem *Prothalamion*, 1596)

run·ning /ˈrʌn·ɪŋ/ *adj* [before n; not gradable] • *It's usually safer to drink from running* **water** *than the still water in a pond or lake.* • *Some of these houses still don't have running* **water** (=water supplied by pipes). • A **running sore** is an injury that will not heal and keeps producing liquid.

run [BECOME] /rʌn/ *v* [L only + adj] **running**, *past simple* **ran** /ræn/, *past part* **run** to be or become • *Differences between the two sides run* **deep** (=are serious). • *The river/reservoir/well ran* **dry** (=its supply of water finished). • *Supplies are running* **low**. • *We're beginning to run* **short of** *money/Money is beginning to run* **short** (=there's not much left). • *Feelings are* **running high** (=people are angry or excited). • *Those children are allowed to* **run wild** (=do anything that they want to do).

run *obj* [SHOW] /rʌn/ *v* [T] **running**, *past simple* **ran** /ræn/, *past part* **run** to show in a newspaper or magazine, on television, etc. • *All the papers ran* (=printed) *stories about the new peace talks.* • *Channel 4 is running a series on the unfairness of the legal system.*

run [POLITICS] /rʌn/ *v* [I] **running**, *past simple* **ran** /ræn/, *past part* **run** to try to get elected; to be a CANDIDATE • *Mrs Thatcher wanted to run a fourth time.* • *He's going to run* **against** *Smith*/**for** *President*/**for** *election.*

run·ning /ˈrʌn·ɪŋ/ *n* [U] • *Half the vote has been counted, and our candidate is still* **in the running** (=still has a reasonable chance of winning). • *Her poor health has put her* **out of the running** *(for election)* (=taken away her chance of being elected). • In America, a **running mate** is a political partner chosen for a politician who is trying to get elected: *If a candidate for president wins the election, his/her running mate becomes the vice president.*

run *obj* [TAKE] /rʌn/ *v* [T] **running**, *past simple* **ran** /ræn/, *past part* **run** to take (guns or drugs) illegally from one place to another • *He was arrested for running drugs* **across** *the border* **into** *America.*

run·ner /£ˈrʌn·əʳ, $-ɚ/ *n* [C] • *a gun-runner*

run [BUY OR SELL] /rʌn/ *n* [C usually sing] an eager wish by many people to buy or sell something • *There's been a run* **on** *umbrellas* (=many have been bought) *because of all this rain.* • *A sudden run* **on** *the dollar* (=many people selling it) *has lowered its value.* • *Economists fear a run* **on** *the bank* (=many people wanting to take their money out of the bank at the same time).

run [ORDINARY] /rʌn/ *n* [U] a particular type • *Their food is not* **the general/usual run of** (=it is better than ordinary) *hotel cooking.* • *It's just a* **run-of-the-mill** (=not special) *war film.*

run [AREA] /rʌn/ *n* [C] an area of ground of limited size for keeping animals • *a sheep/chicken/hen run*

run [POINT] /rʌn/ *n* [C] (in cricket and baseball) a single point, scored by running from one place to another • *England need 105 runs to win the game.* • *a home run*

run [HOLE] /rʌn/ *n* [C] a long vertical hole in TIGHTS and STOCKINGS (=underwear for the legs) • *I've got a run in my tights from the nail on my chair.*

run /rʌn/ *v* [I] **running**, *past simple* **ran** /ræn/, *past part* **run** • *Oh no, my tights have run!*

run a·cross *obj v prep* [T] to meet (someone or something) unexpectedly • *I ran across several old friends when I went back to my hometown.* • *We've run across a slight problem with the instruction manual.*

run af·ter *obj v prep* [T] to chase • *Why do dogs run after cats?* • *They ran after the taxi.* • *She ran after me to hand me some papers I'd dropped.* • *(fig.) She has spent her life running after* (=trying to achieve) *fame and fortune.* • *(infml disapproving) He's always running after* (=trying to get into sexual relationships with) *women.*

run a·long *v adv* [often in commands] *infml rather dated* (used esp. to a child) to go away • *Run along now, children – go and play outside while I'm working.* • *It's late – I'd better be running along.*

run a·round with *obj v adv prep* [T] to spend a lot of time with (someone) • *She's running around with Micky and his friends these days.*

run a·way *v adv* [I] to leave a place or person secretly and suddenly • *He ran away* **to** *sea*/**from** *home*/**from** *school when he was only 12.* • *Malcolm and my sister are planning to run away* **together** *to get married.* • *My sister is planning to run away* **with** *Malcolm (to get married).* • *She accused him of running away* **from** (=not dealing with) *the situation/his responsibilities.*

run a·way with *obj v adv prep* [T] to take control of (something or someone) and carry it away • *Her horse ran away with her.* • *Don't let your imagination/enthusiasm run away with you.* • *Don't let the idea of winning all that money run away with you.* • *(fig.) She ran away with* (=easily got) *four first prizes.*

run *obj* **by** *obj v prep* [T] to tell (someone) about (something), esp. in order to discover their opinion of it • *Can I run this/my idea by you?* • *Run that by me one more time.*

run down *obj* [CRITICIZE], **run** *obj* **down** *v adv* [M] *infml* to criticize, often unfairly • *He's always running himself down.* • *I think it's bad manners to run down your parents.*

run down *(obj)* [REDUCE], **run** *(obj)* **down** *v adv Br* to reduce (a business, organization, etc.) in size, importance, etc., or to become reduced • *They claim that the government is secretly running down the Youth Training Schemes.* [T] • *The fishing industry is running down but the government does nothing.* [I]

run-down /ˈrʌn·daʊn/ *n* [U] • *The Union is protesting at the proposed rundown of the Youth Training Scheme.*

run down *obj* [HIT], **run** *obj* **down** *v adv* [M] (of a vehicle or its driver) to hit and hurt (a person or large animal), esp. intentionally • *Two masked men on motorbikes tried to run me down.* • If a large ship runs down a smaller one, it hits it.

run down *(obj)* [WORSEN], **run** *(obj)* **down** *v adv* to (cause to) be in an increasingly worse condition • *These batteries can be recharged when they run down* (=lose power). [I] • *You'll run the battery down* (=cause it to lose power) *if you leave your (car) lights on.* [M] • *Since he took that extra job, he's really run himself down.* [T]

run–down /ˌrʌnˈdaʊn/ *adj* • *a run-down building/cemetery* • *My doctor said I was looking run-down and ought to take some time to rest.* • See also RUN-DOWN.

run down *obj* [FIND], **run** *obj* **down** *v adv* [M] to find after a lot of searching • *I finally ran Mr Green down* **in/to** *a house in the country.*

run in *obj* [CATCH], **run** *obj* **in** *v adv* [M] *infml* to catch (someone) and take them to a police station • *Well, officer, are you going to run me in or not?*

run in *obj* [USE CAREFULLY] *Br and Aus*, **run** *obj* **in**, *Am* **break in** *v adv* [M] to use (a new engine) carefully, until it is working completely and correctly • *I'm still running the engine/car in, so I won't drive fast.*

run *(obj)* **into** *obj* [HIT] *v prep* [T] to accidentally drive (a vehicle) into (something) • *I had to stop suddenly, and the car behind ran into me.* • *He ran his motorbike into a tree.* • If you **run yourself into the ground**, you make yourself very tired by working too hard.

run into *obj* [MEET] *v prep* [T] to meet (someone) by chance • *Graham ran into someone he knew at school the other day.* • *(fig.) We've run into bad weather/debt/trouble/difficulties.*

run into *obj* [REACH] *v prep* [T] to have (an amount, esp. a cost) as a total • *The repairs will probably run into thousands of pounds.* • *The number of books we produce runs into the 100 000 range.*

run off [LEAVE] *v adv* [I] to leave suddenly • *You can't run off (home) now, just when I need you!* • *My wife has run off and left me/run off* **with** *another man.*

run off *obj* [PRODUCE], **run** *obj* **off** *v adv* [M] to print (copies) of something, or to invent (a piece of poetry, music, etc.) • *Could you run me off five copies of this/run off five copies of this* **for** *me, please?* [+ two objects] • *Kate can run off a sonnet in half an hour on any subject you like.*

run off with *obj v adv prep* [T] to steal • *He ran off with $10 000 of the company's money.*

run on *v adv* [I] to continue, esp. after the expected finishing time • *The game/speech/discussion ran on for too long/for hours.* • **Time**'s *running on* (=is passing quickly) – *let's hurry up!*

run out [FINISH] *v adv* [I] to finish or be finished; to be used completely • *I've run out* **of** *milk/money/ideas/patience.* • *"Have you got any milk?" "Sorry, I've run out."* • *The milk has run out.* • *My patience is beginning to run out.* • *My passport/licence runs out* (=can no longer be used) *next month – I must get it renewed.* • **Time** *is running out* **for** *the men trapped under the rubble* (=they have not got much time left and the danger is increasing). • *The peace talks seem to have* **run out of steam** (= lost their original energy and success).

run out *obj* [CRICKET], **run** *obj* **out** *v adv* [M] to end the turn of (a player to hit the ball) by throwing the ball at the WICKET (= set of three sticks) they are running towards and hitting it before they can reach it • *Their best batsman was run out* **for/on** *99.*

run out on *obj v adv prep* [T] to leave (a person or place) without warning, esp. when you have a responsibility to stay • *She ran out on him two months ago, leaving him to look after their two children.* • *Two men had run out on their restaurant bill, knocking over the table as they left.*

run o·ver *obj* [HIT], **run** *obj* **o·ver** *v adv* [M] (of a vehicle or its driver) to hit and drive over the top of (someone or something) • *I'm afraid we've just run a rabbit over.* • *She was run over and killed by a train.*

run o·ver *obj* [REPEAT] *v prep* [T] to repeat (something said or done before), esp. for practice • *I'll just run over what's been said so far,* **for** *the latecomers.* • *She quickly ran over* (= practised) *her speech before going on-stage.* • If you run over something **with** someone else, you examine it with them, to get their help or their opinion on it.

run o·ver *obj* [CONTINUE] *v adv, v prep* [I/T] to continue beyond (the expected finishing time) • *I'm afraid we're starting to run over (time), so could you make your speeches short please.*

run o·ver [FLOW OVER] *v adv* [I] to flow over the edges of something, because there is too much liquid • *The water/The bath is running over – quick, turn the taps off.*

run through *obj* [PRACTISE], **run** *obj* **through** *v prep, v adv* [T] to practise (something); to REHEARSE • *The director wants us to run through the first act this morning.*

run–through /ˈrʌn·θruː/ *n* [C] • *We've got time for one more run-through before the concert.*

run through *obj* [DEAL WITH] *v prep* [T] to look at, examine or deal with (a set of things), esp. quickly • *I ran through the list, but none of the machines seemed any good.* • *I'd like to run through these points/questions* **with** *you, if that's okay, because you've made several mistakes.*

run through *obj* [EXIST] *v prep* [T no passive] to be in all parts of (something) • *Melancholy runs through all her stories.* • *Racism runs right through society.* • If something **runs through** your **mind/head**, you suddenly or continuously think about it.

run through *obj* [SPEND] *v prep* [T] to spend (money) quickly, esp. on useless things • *It took him just 6 months to run through all the money his father left him.*

run *obj* **through** [ATTACK] *v adv* [T] to push a pointed weapon right through (a person or animal) • *He drew his sword and ran the villain/wolf through.*

run to *obj v prep* [T usually in negatives; not *be running to*] to reach (a particular amount, level, size, etc.) • *I can lend you £1000, but I can't run to/my salary won't run to more than that.* • *I'm afraid my cooking skills don't run to fancy cakes and desserts.* • *The new encyclopedia runs to several thousand pages.*

run up *obj* [INCREASE], **run** *obj* **up** *v adv* [M] to make (a BILL, debt, etc.) increase • *She stayed two weeks at the hotel and ran up a bill which she couldn't pay.*

run–up /ˈrʌn·ʌp/ *n* [C] *Am* • A run-up is a sudden increase in something, such as prices or engine speed.

run up *obj* [PRODUCE], **run** *obj* **up** *v adv* [M] to make (something such as clothes) quickly • *I got out my sewing machine and ran up a pink skirt for the wedding.* • *She can run you up a dress/run up a dress* **for** *you in less than a day.* [+ two objects]

run up *obj* [RAISE], **run** *obj* **up** *v adv* [M] *Br and Aus* to raise (a flag) • *They've run up a British flag on the roof.*

run up a·gainst *obj v adv prep* [T] to meet (unexpected difficulty) • *The community scheme has run up against strong local opposition.*

run·a·bout /ˈrʌn·ə·baʊt/, **run·a·round** *n* [C] a small car for short journeys

run·a·round /ˈrʌn·ə·raʊnd/ *n* [U] **give** *someone* **the runaround** to refuse to help (someone) and to send (them) on to someone or somewhere else to get help • *I'm trying to get a visa/information but, the embassy staff keep giving me the runaround.*

run·a·way /ˈrʌn·ə·weɪ/ *adj* [not gradable] out of control or escaped from somewhere • *a runaway bus/horse speeding through the streets* • *a runaway child sleeping on the streets* • *Her first novel's runaway* (= surprisingly big) *success came as a great surprise.*

run·a·way /ˈrʌn·ə·weɪ/ *n* [C] • *We're searching for a couple of runaways* **from** *the young offenders' institution.*

run–down /ˈrʌn·daʊn/ *n* [C] a detailed report • *Here's a run-down* **on/of** *the activities of our ten biggest competitors.* • See also RUN DOWN [WORSEN].

rune /ruːn/ *n* [C] any of the letters of an ancient alphabet cut into stone or wood by the peoples of N Europe, or any similar mark with a secret or magic meaning

run·ic /ˈruː·nɪk/ *adj* • *a runic letter/alphabet/message*

rung [RING] /rʌŋ/ *past participle of* RING [TELEPHONE]; RING [SOUND]

rung [STEP] /rʌŋ/ *n* [C] any of the short bars that form the steps of a LADDER (= a device used for climbing up) • *Half-way up I had to stop because several rungs were broken.* • *(fig.) I started my life on the* **lowest/bottom rung of the ladder** (= at the lowest level) *in this company.*

run·ner [BLADE] /£ˈrʌn·əʳ, $-ɚ/ *n* [C] one of two blades under a SLEDGE (= snow vehicle) which allow it to move along easily, or one of two similar long narrow parts under something to allow it to move backwards or forwards

run·ner [STEM] /£ˈrʌn·əʳ, $-ɚ/ *n* [C] a long stem of a plant which grows along the ground in order to put down roots in a new place • *Strawberry plants spread by putting out runners.* • *(Br)* A **runner bean** (*Am* **scarlet runner**) is a climbing bean with long green PODS (= seed containers) which are eaten as a vegetable.

run·ner–up /£ˌrʌn·əˈrʌp, $-ɚˈʌp/ *n* [C] a person who completes a race or competition but who does not win • *There were 150 runners-up and they all got a small sum of money for participating.* • [LP] **Sports**

run·ning /ˈrʌn·ɪŋ/ *n, adj* [not gradable] See at RUN [GO QUICKLY]; RUN [TRAVEL]; RUN [OPERATE]; RUN [FLOW]; RUN [POLITICS] • (J)

run·ny /ˈrʌn·i/ *adj* **-ier, -iest** more liquid than usual • *a runny egg yolk* • *I like French cheese when it is strong and runny.* • *The sauce looked runny so I added some more flour.* • If your nose or eyes are runny, usually because you are ill, they are producing more MUCUS (= liquid) than usual: *I've got a runny nose.*

runs /rʌnz/ *pl n* **the runs** *infml* a condition of the bowels in which the contents are excreted too frequently and in a form which is too liquid; DIARRHOEA

runt /rʌnt/ *n* [C] the smallest and weakest animal of a group born at the same time to the same mother, or *(slang)* a small or weak person whom you dislike

run·way /ˈrʌn·weɪ/ *n* [C] a long level piece of ground with a specially prepared smooth hard surface on which aircraft take off and land • *They've extended the runway, to take larger jets.*

rup·ture *(obj)* /£ˈrʌp·tʃəʳ, $-tʃɚ/ *v* to burst or break, or cause this to happen • *His appendix ruptured and he had to be rushed to hospital.* [I] • *The pipes/boiler may easily rupture under this pressure.* [T] • *(fig.) This news has ruptured the delicate peace between the enemy parties.* [T] • If you rupture your**self**, you cause the wall which keeps your stomach and your bowels from getting outside the ABDOMEN to break apart, usually by lifting something too heavy. [T]

rup·ture /£ˈrʌp·tʃəʳ, $-tʃɚ/ *n* [C] • *a rupture of the pipeline* • *(fig.) a rupture* (= an end to a friendly relationship) *between the families* • *You're going to give yourself a rupture if you lift that.* See also HERNIA.

ru·ral /£ˈrʊə·rəl, $ˈrʊr·əl/ *adj* in, of or like the countryside • *Rural life is usually more peaceful than city life.* • *He paints pictures of rural scenes.* • *The area is still very rural and undeveloped.* • Compare URBAN.

ruse /ruːz/ *n* [C] a trick intended to deceive someone • *His ruse to get an extra week's pay failed completely.*

rush *(obj)* [HURRY] /rʌʃ/ *v* to (cause to) hurry; to (cause to) go or do (something) very quickly • *Whenever I see him, he seems to be rushing* **(about/around).** [I] • *She's always rushing to finish first/rushing* **through** *her work.* [I] • *I rushed up the stairs/to the office/to find a phone.* [I] • *The clouds were rushing towards us at a great speed.* [I] • *When she turned it upside down the water rushed out.* [I] • *We shouldn't rush* **to** *blame them.* [+ *to* infinitive] • *You can't rush a job like this.* [T] • *Don't rush me!* [T] • *Don't rush your food* (= eat it too quickly)*!* [T] • *The United Nations has rushed medical aid and food to the famine zone.* [T] • *She was rushed to hospital with a burst appendix.* [T] • *He rushed the children off to school so they wouldn't be late.* [T] • *Supper was rushed since the family had to go out that evening.* [T] • If a group of people rush an enemy or the place where an enemy is, they attack suddenly and all together: *We rushed the palace gates and killed the guards.* [T] • In American

RUSSIAN FALSE FRIENDS

English	Russian	Meaning
accord *n*	аккорд	musical chord
accumulator *n*	аккумулятор	storage battery
actual *adj*	актуальный	present, current, topical
advocate *n*	адвокат	solicitor, barrister
affect *n*	аффект	fit of passion
agitate *v*	агитировать	to campaign; to persuade
alimentary *adj*	алименты *n*	alimony
ambitious *adj*	амбициозный	pretentious, pompous
angina *n*	ангина	tonsilitis
apartment *n*	апартамент	luxury apartment
argument *n*	аргумент	reasoning
artist *n*	артист	actor
aspirant *n*	аспирант(ка)	post-graduate
barracks *n*	барак	temporary building
basin *n*	бассейн	swimming pool
baton *n*	батон	thin oval loaf
cabinet *n*	кабинет	office, study
camera *n*	камера	cell, ward, chamber
candidate *n*	кандидат	Doctor of Philosophy; nominee
capital *n*	капитал	money, wealth
chef *n*	шеф	chief; leader; boss
civil *adj*	цивилизованный	civilized
combination *n*	комбинация	scheme; petticoat
command *n*	команда	sports team, crew
commission *n*	комиссия	committee, board
communication *n*	коммуникация	military line of communication
complexion *n*	комплекция	build, constitution, physique
compositor *n*	композитор	composer of music
concourse *n*	конкурс	competition
concurrent *n*	конкурент	competitor, rival
conserve *n*	консервы	tinned food
control *n*	контроль	inspection, supervision
cravat *n*	кровать	bed
cylinder *n*	цилиндр	top hat
delicate *adj*	деликатный	tactful, polite
director *n*	директор	manager, headmaster
divan *n*	диван	couch, sofa
drape *n*	драп	thick cloth
dress *n*	дрессура	training, taming
example *n*	экземпляр	copy
extravagant *adj*	экстравагантный	eccentric
fabric *n*	фабрика	factory
faggot *n*	фагот	bassoon
focus *n*	фокус	magic act
gallantry *n*	галантерея	haberdashery, fancy goods shop
genial *adj*	гениальный	brilliant
gymnasium *n*	гимназия	grammar school
gypsum *n*	гипс	plaster
hazard *n*	азарт	excitement
herb *n*	герб	coat of arms; national emblem
history *n*	история	story
hymn *n*	гимн	national anthem
hysterical *adj*	истерический	uncontrollably emotional
intelligent *adj*	интеллигент	educated, sophisticated
lunatic *n*	лунатик	sleepwalker
machine *n*	машина	car, lorry, vehicle
machinist *n*	машинист(ка)	engine, driver; typist
magazine *n*	магазин	shop
manifest *v*	манифест *n*	written declaration
(RUS)		
manufacture *n*	мануфактура	textile mill; textiles
marmalade *n*	мармелад	fruit sweets
nervous *adj*	нервозный	irritated, quick-tempered
novel *n*	новелла	short story; amendment (of a law)
obligation *n*	облигация	bond
occasion *n*	оказия	opportunity
order *n*	ордер	warrant
ordination *n*	ординатура	post graduate course in internal medicine
original *adj*	оригинал *n*	eccentric person
pamphlet *n*	памфлет	lampoon
panel *n*	панель	prefabricated concrete slab
pantomime *n*	пантомима	mime show
paragraph *n*	параграф	clause (of law); section mark
partisan *n*	партизан	guerilla
party *n*	партия	batch of goods; game (of chess)
pasta *n*	паста	paste
pathetic *adj*	патетический	full of pathos, passionate
perspective *n*	перспектива	prospects, plans
practice *n*	практика	training, apprenticeship
presentable *adj*	презентабельный	reliable and good looking
preservative *n*	презерватив	condom
pretend *v*	претендовать	to aspire
principal *adj*	принципиальный	high-principled
problem *n*	проблема	concern, responsibility
prognosis *n*	прогноз	weather forecast
programme *n*	программа	TV channel
project *n*	проект	plans, scheme, draft
prospect *n*	проспект	avenue, boulevard
protection *n*	протекция	favouritism, patronage
race *n*	раса	breed
receipt *n*	рецепт	prescription; recipe
reclaim *v*	рекламировать	to advertise
record *n*	рекорд	(sports) record
rent *n*	рента	annuity
repetition *n*	репетиция	rehearsal
residence *n*	резиденция	seat of Royal family
resident *n*	резидент	head of an office
retire *v*	ретироваться	to withdraw
revenge *n*	реванш	return match (sports)
revision *n*	ревизия	inspection
scene *n*	сцена	theatre stage
scenery *n*	сценарий	script, scenario
sentence *n*	сентенция	maxim
smoking *n*	смокинг	dinner jacket
speculate *v*	спекулировать	to profiteer, gamble; to misuse
spleen *n*	сплин	melancholy
stipend *n*	стипендия	student grant, scholarship
stool *n*	стул	chair
sympathetic *adj*	симпатичный	pretty, pleasant
technique *n*	техника	engineering; technology; equipment, machinery
transparent *adj*	транспарант *n*	banner
trivial *n*	тривиальный	commonplace, hackneyed
urn *n*	урна	dustbin
wagon *n*	вагон	railway/tram carriage

football, to rush is to carry the football forward across the **line of scrimmage** (= place on the field at which play begins). Also, a member of the opposite team rushes when they force their way to the back of the field quickly to catch the player carrying the football. [I] • If you **rush into** something such as a job, you start doing it without having really decided if it is the right thing to do or having considered the best way to do it. • If someone **rushes** you **into** doing something, they forcefully persuade you to do it without giving you time to really decide. • *When the war started, several publishers* **rushed out** (= produced quickly in order to satisfy a sudden popular demand) *books on the conflict.* • *The factory* **rushed** *the new toy* **through** *production* (= produced it very quickly).

rush /rʌʃ/ *n* • *Slow down! What's the rush* (= need to be so hurried)*?* [U] • *Why is it always such a rush* (= hurry) *to get ready in the mornings?* [U] • *If seating is not assigned there's always a rush* (= sudden and quick movement of people) **for**/*to get to the best seats.* [C] • *She made a rush at him to get his gun, but he just pointed it at her and fired.* [C] • *I hate driving during the 5 o'clock rush* (= busy and crowded period). [C] • *I try to do my shopping before the Christmas rush.* [C] • *There's been a rush* **for** (= sudden popular demand for) *tickets.* [C] • *There was a rush* (= quick movement) **of** *air as she opened the door.* [C] • A rush is also a sudden strong emotion or physical feeling: *The memory of who he was came back to him with a rush.* [C] ○ *I had my first cigarette for a year and felt a sudden rush (of dizziness).* [C] • A rush is also a sudden movement of people to a certain area, usually because of some economic advantage: *the California gold rush* [C] • In American football, a rush is an attempt to rush the ball or a player from the opposing team carrying the ball. [C] See at RUSH [HURRY] *v.* • The **rush hour** is the busy part of the day when towns and cities are crowded, either in the morning when people are travelling to work, or in the evening when people are travelling home: *rush hour traffic* • *The book was a bit of a* **rush job** (= a quick and therefore not very good piece of work).

rush·ing /ˈrʌʃ·ɪŋ/ *adj* [not gradable] • *I stretched out and listened to the sound of the rushing stream.*

rush [PLANT] /rʌʃ/ *n* a grass-like plant that grows in or near water and whose long thin hollow stems can be dried and made into floor coverings, containers, etc. • *a rush mat* • *rush matting*

rusk /rʌsk/ *n* [C] a type of very hard dry biscuit, esp. eaten by babies

rus·set /ˈrʌs·ɪt/ *n* [U], *adj esp. literary* reddish brown • *russet and golden autumnal leaves*

Rus·sian roul·ette /ˌrʌʃ·ᵊn-/ *n* [U] a very dangerous game of chance where each player aims at their own head with a gun which has one bullet in it and five empty CHAMBERS (=spaces where bullets could go), after having first spun the chambers

rust DECAY /rʌst/ *n* [U] a reddish brown substance that forms on the surface of iron and steel as a result of decay caused by reacting with air and water • *The mechanic said that older cars of this type were prone to rust.* • Rust is also used to mean of a reddish brown colour like that of rust.

rust *(obj)* /rʌst/ *v* • *It'll rust if you leave it out in the rain.* [I] • *Years of being left out in the rain had rusted the metal chairs.* [T] • *The floor of the car had rusted* **away/through** (=been destroyed by rust), *so I was careful where I put my feet.* [I]

rust·y /ˈrʌs·ti/ *adj* **-ier, -iest** • *If the underside of the car is rusty, I wouldn't buy it.* • *(fig.) I'm afraid my Italian is a bit rusty* (=not very good because I've forgotten a lot of it). • *(fig.) I'm always a bit rusty* (=not quick and skilful because lacking practice) *for the first few games of the football season.* • Ⓓ

rust DISEASE /rʌst/ *n* [U] any of various plant diseases that cause reddish brown spots

rus·tic /£ˈrʌs·tɪk, $-t̬ɪk/ *adj* simple and often rough in appearance; typical of the countryside • *a rustic bench/cabin* • *The landlord had tried to give the pub a rustic appearance by putting horseshoes and old guns on the walls.*

rus·ti·ci·ty /£rʌsˈtɪs·ɪ·ti, $-t̬ɪs·ə·t̬i/ *n* [U]

rus·tle *(obj)* NOISE /ˈrʌs·l̩/ *v* to make or cause to make soft sounds • *The leaves rustled in the breeze.* [I] • *Her skirt rustled as she walked.* [I] • *He rustled his papers* (=noisily moved them about) *to hide his embarrassment.* [T]

rus·tle /ˈrʌs·l̩/ *n* • *I heard a rustle – do you think it's a mouse?* [C] • *The rustle of paper broke his concentration.* [U]

rus·tling /ˈrʌs·l̩.ɪŋ, ˈ-lɪŋ/ *n, adj* [not gradable] • *I could hear (a) rustling in the bushes.* [C/U] • *A small animal was making rustling noises among the leaves.*

rus·tle *obj* STEAL /ˈrʌs·l̩/ *v* [T] *esp. Am and Aus* to steal (cattle, horses, etc.)

rus·tler /£ˈrʌs·l̩.əʳ, £ˈ-ləʳ, $ˈ-lɚ/ *n* [C]

rus·tle up *obj*, **rus·tle** *obj* **up** *v adv* [M] *infml* to make (esp. food) quickly • *Give me a minute and I'll rustle up a salad for your supper.*

rust·proof /ˈrʌst·pruːf/ *adj* [not gradable] protected against RUST (=metal decay)

rust·proof *obj* /ˈrʌst·pruːf/ *v* [T] • *Painting steel is a good way to rustproof it.*

rust·y /ˈrʌs·ti/ *adj* See at RUST DECAY

rut HOLE /rʌt/ *n* [C] a deep narrow mark made in soft ground esp. by a wheel • *The farmer's tractors had made/worn deep ruts in the road.* • If a person, organization, etc. is **in a rut**, they have become fixed in one particular type of job, activity, method, etc.: *I've got to change jobs – after 15 years here I feel I'm* **(stuck)** *in a rut.* ○ *The company is in a rut and it's up to us to get it out.*

rut·ted /£ˈrʌt·ɪd, $ˈrʌt̬-/ *adj* [not gradable] • *a deeply/badly rutted road*

rut SEXUALLY ACTIVE PERIOD /rʌt/ *n* [U] the period of the year during which particular animals, esp. the male deer, sheep, etc. are sexually active • *During* **the** *rut, the stags can be seen fighting for females.* • *When the male deer is* **in rut** (=sexually excited) *it may fight its rivals for the female.*

rut·ting /£ˈrʌt·ɪŋ, $ˈrʌt̬-/ *adj* [not gradable] • *rutting stags* • *the rutting season*

rut·a·ba·ga /£ˌruː·təˈbeɪ·gə, $-t̬ə-/ *n* [C] *Am for* SWEDE • PIC› **Vegetables**

ruth·less /ˈruːθ·ləs/ *adj* without thinking or caring about any pain caused to others; cruel • *ruthless ambition* • *ruthless efficiency* • *a ruthless plan/order* • *He's a ruthless dictator, responsible for the murder of thousands of innocent people.* • *It would be a ruthless decision to stop supporting the arts.* • *Some people think to succeed in this world you have to be ruthless.*

ruth·less·ly /ˈruːθ·lə·sli/ *adv*

ruth·less·ness /ˈruːθ·lə·snəs/ *n* [U]

RV /£ˌɑːˈviː, $ˌɑːrˈviː/ *n* [C] *abbreviation for* **recreational vehicle**, see at RECREATION

Rx /£ˌɑːˈreks, $ˌɑːrˈeks/ *n* [C] *Am and Aus abbreviation for* a medical **prescription** (=a written order by a doctor describing what medicine a person should receive)

rye /raɪ/ *n* [U] a type of CEREAL (=grass-like plant), grown in many quite cold areas, the grain of which is used to make flour or WHISKY (=a strong alcoholic drink) or to feed animals • **Rye bread** is dark brown bread made with rye. • Rye is also the name of WHISKY made with rye: *a glass of rye* • *"Catcher in the Rye"* (title of a book by J.D.Salinger, 1951) • PIC› **Cereals**

S s

S LETTER (*pl* **S's**), **s** (*pl* **s's**) /es/ *n* [C] the 19th letter of the English alphabet • An **S-bend** in a road is a bend which is in the shape of the letter S. • LP› **Silent letters**

s SECOND *n* [C] *pl* **s** *abbreviation for* SECOND TIME • *His time for the 100m was 10·1s.*

S SOUTH, *Br also* **Sth**, *Am also* **So** *n* [U], *adj abbreviation for* SOUTH or SOUTHERN

S SMALL /es/ *adj* (esp. used on clothing to show its size) *abbreviation for* SMALL LIMITED

S SATISFACTORY *n* [C] *Am* (given as a mark for an exam or course) *abbreviation for* SATISFACTORY

-s NOUN PLURALS /-s, -z/, **-es** /-ɪz/ *combining form* used to form the plural of nouns • *books* • *jackets* • *sandwiches* • *one tree – two trees* • LP› **Plurals, Pronunciation**

-'s LETTER PLURALS /-s, -z/ *combining form* used to form the plural of numbers, letters, abbreviations, etc. • *seven 6's* • *a line of m's* • *the 40's* (also *the 40s*) • *several MP's* (also *several MPs*)

-'s BELONGING TO SINGULAR /-s, -z/ *combining form* used to show that the following thing belongs to the person or thing named • *the cat's tail* • *Patricia's dress* • *James's* (also *James'*) *shoes* • *today's paper* • *the policemen's helmets* • -'s also means the house or shop belonging to the stated person: *The boys are at Alison's.* ○ *I got it at the greengrocer's.* • -'s is used to form the possessive of singular nouns and of plural nouns which do not end in *-s*, and sometimes of names which end in *-s*. • LP› **Possessive form**

-s' BELONGING TO PLURAL /-s, -z/ *combining form* used to show that the following thing belongs to the people or things named • *the girls' books* • *employees' rights* • -s' is used to form the possessive plural of most nouns. • LP› **Possessive form**

-'s IS OR HAS /-z/ *short form of* is or has • *He's having his lunch.* • *It's in the cupboard.* • *Bernard's not here today.* • *She's gone home.* • *Where's he put the coffee jar?*

-'s DOES /-z/ *infml* (in questions) *short form of* does • *When's she hope to leave?* • *What's he think of the new car?* • *How's this thing work?*

-'s US /-s/ (only after *let*) *short form of* us • *Let's see what he thinks.* • *Let's go swimming this afternoon.*

Sab·bath /ˈsæb·əθ/ *n* [C] the day of the week kept by some religious groups for rest and worship (Sunday for most Christians, Saturday for Jews and Friday for Muslims) • *We always* **observed/kept the** *Sabbath when I was a child.* • *My grandmother never* **broke the** *Sabbath.*

sab·bat·i·cal /£səˈbæt·ɪ·kəl, $-ˈbæt̬-/ *adj* [not gradable], *n* (of or being) a period of time when college or university teachers are allowed to stop their usual work in order to study or travel, usually while continuing to be paid • *a sabbatical year/term* • *sabbatical leave* • *Some lecturers* **take/have** *a sabbatical every seven years.* [C] • *She isn't here this year – she's* **on** *sabbatical, finishing off her book.* [U]

sa·ble /ˈseɪ·bl̩/ *n* [U] the fur of a small dark-brown animal of N Asia and N Europe which can be made into expensive clothes • *She always refuses to wear mink or sable* (=clothes made of this). • *She had on a long sable coat.*

sab·o·tage *obj* /ˈsæb·ə·tɑːʒ/ *v* [T] to prevent the success of an enemy or competitor by damaging or destroying (their buildings, weapons or equipment), or to intentionally prevent the success of (a plan or action) • *The rebels had tried to sabotage the oil pipeline.* • *Terrorists have attempted to sabotage the nuclear power station.* • *This was a deliberate attempt to sabotage* (=prevent the success of) *the ceasefire.* • *The rain effectively sabotaged* (=prevented the success of) *their efforts to win the match.* • *By telling them I'd been in prison, he sabotaged*

SWEDISH FALSE FRIENDS (S)

afterthought *n*	eftertanke	reflection, meditation; consideration
announce *v*	annonsera	to advertise
announcer *n*	annonsör	advertiser
art *n*	art	kind, sort; nature; character; species
arty *adj*	artig	polite, courteous, attentive
bassoon *n*	basun	trombone; trumpet
beef *n*	biff	steak
befall *v*	befalla	to command, order
benzene *n*	bensin	petrol; gasoline
blade *n*	blad	leaf, sheet; petal; paper; page
blanket *n*	blankett	blank; form
bucket *n*	bukett	bouquet, posy, nosegay
burst *v*	borsta	to brush
cake *n*	kaka	pastry, biscuit
censure *n*	censur	censorship
chef *n*	chef	chief; leader; boss
cling *v*	klinga	to ring, sound, resound, jingle, chink, clink
coal *n*	kål	cabbage,
cock *n*	kock	cook, chef
communal *adj*	kommunal	civic, local, municipal
commune *n*	kommun	municipality
companion *n*	kompanjon	(business) partner,
compositor *n*	compositor	composer of music
concept *n*	koncept	rough draft, outline, plan
conjunctive *adj*	konjunktiv	subjunctive mood (grammar)
corn *n*	korn	grain, barley
crave *v*	krava	to demand, call for, require, need
cunning *adj*	kunnig	skilful, capable, competent, proficient, well-informed
deck *n*	dack	tyre
delicate *adj*	delikat	delicious, tasty
eventual *adj*	eventuell	(if) any; possible; prospective
example *n*	exemplar	specimen, copy (of book)
expedition *n*	expedition	office; department; serving (of customers); carrying out; dispatching
fabric *n*	fabrik	factory, works, plant, mill
fasten *v*	fastna	to get caught, catch, stick, get stuck, jam, get wedged
filial *adj*	filial (n.)	branch
fur *n*	fura	pine
gage *n*	gage	fee
gang *n*	gång	walking; gait, walk; pace; going, moving; running; working; motion; action; progress; course; passage, corridor, aisle, gangway; subway, duct; canal; time
genial *adj*	genial	brilliant, ingenious
geniality *n*	genialitet	genius, brilliance
genie *n*	genie	genius
genteel *adj*	gentil	fine; stylish; generous; handsome
gentle *adj*	gentil	stylish; fine; generous; handsome
gift *n*	gift	poison, toxin
give out *v*	ge ut	to publish; to spend,
glance *v*	glänsa	to shine, glitter, glisten,
gracious *adj*	graciös	graceful
halt *v*	halta	to limp
handicraft *n*	handkraft	manual strength
harm *n*	harm	indignation; resentment, annoyance, vexation
history *n*	historia	story; thing; business; affair
inconsequential *adj*	onkonsekvent	inconsistent
island *n*	Island	Iceland
magazine *n*	magasin	storehouse, warehouse; shop, boutique
map *n*	mapp	file, folder,
mask *n*	mask	worm, grub, caterpillar, maggot
merit *n*	merit	qualification
motion *n*	motion	exercise
motion *v*	motionera	to exercise; to take exercise; to move (make a proposal, propose a motion)
nap *n*	napp	teat; nipple; dummy; comforter; bite, nibble
nosy *adj*	nosig	cheeky, pert
novel *n*	novell	story, thing, business, affair
obligation *n*	obligation	bond
offer *n*	offer	sacrifice, offering; victim, casualty
pack up *v*	packa upp	to unpack, unwrap
pest *n*	pest	plague, pestilence
press *n*	press	pressure
proper *adj*	proper	tidy, neat, clean
rapport *n*	rapport	report, account
receipt *n*	recept	prescription; recipe
rector *n*	rektor	headmaster, president, vice chancellor
resume *v*	resumera	to sum up, give a summary of
roman *n*	roman	novel
salad *n*	sallad	lettuce
sax *n*	sax	scissors, shears; trap
semester *n*	semester	holiday(s)
sensible *adj*	sensibel	sensitive
sin *n*	sinne	sense, mind, temperament, nature, soul, heart, taste, inclination
slang *n*	slang	tube, hose
smoking *n*	smoking	dinner jacket, tuxedo
spectacle *n*	spektakel	row, scandal; trouble; ridicule
spiritual *adj*	spirituell	brilliant, witty
stark *adj*	stark	strong, powerful, solid, durable, firm
strand *n*	strand	beach, seashore, seaside
swamp *n*	svamp	fungus, mushroom, toadstool; sponge
sympathetic *adj*	sympatisk	likeable, pleasant; attractive
tax *n*	tax	dachshund
tax *n*	taxa	rate; charge, fare, fee
technique *n*	teknik	(pl.) technics, engineering, technology
tips *n*	tips (sing.)	tip-off; hint; football pools
toll (house) *n*	tullhus	custom-house
tree *n*	tra	wood, timber
under *prep*	under	during, in the course of
under *prep*	under (n)	wonder, marvel, miracle
uproar *n*	uppror	rebellion, mutiny, sedition
uproarious *adj*	upprorisk	rebellious, mutinous, seditious
villa *n*	villa	house, bungalow, cottage; illusion, delusion; confusion
wink *v*	vinka	to beckon, signal, wave
wink *n*	vink	wave; hint; signal
wrist *n*	vrist	instep; ankle; bones in ankle

(=prevented the success of) *my chances of getting the job.* • Ⓙ

sab·o·tage /ˈsæb·ə·tɑːʒ/ *n* [U] • *The sabotage of the main bridge stopped the enemy advancing.* • *They began a campaign of industrial and economic sabotage.*

sab·o·teur /£ˌsæb·əˈtɜːʳ, $-ˈtɜːr/ *n* [C] • A saboteur is a person who sabotages something: *Saboteurs are being sent across the border to cause destruction in enemy towns.* ○ *Hunt saboteurs try to disrupt fox hunts because they disapprove of fox-hunting.*

sa·bre *esp. Br and Aus, Am usually* **sa·ber** /£ˈseɪ·bəʳ, $-bɚ/ *n* [C] one of two types of sword, either a heavy sword with a wide, usually curved blade, used in the past by soldiers on horses, or a light pointed sword with one sharp edge used in the sport of FENCING • *The cavalry rode into battle brandishing their sabres.* • *The Russian team won the sabre event in the latest Olympics.* • *(disapproving) The dictator's speech was mere* **sabre-rattling** (=talk threatening military action) *and not to be taken seriously.* • The **sabre-toothed tiger** was a large wild cat which lived in the past, with two long curved front teeth.

sac /sæk/ *n* [C] *specialized* a part of a plant or animal which is like a bag and often contains liquid

sac·cha·rin /£ˈsæk·ᵊr·ɪn, $ˈ-ɚ-/ *n* [U] a very sweet artificial substance which is used to replace sugar, esp. by people who want to lose weight or who must not eat sugar • *saccharin tablets*

sac·cha·rine /£ˈsæk·ᵊr·aɪn, $ˈ-ɚ-/ *adj disapproving* too sweet or too polite • *I don't trust her, with her saccharine smiles.* • *He can't bear that sort of saccharine, sentimental love story.*

sach·et /£ˈsæʃ·eɪ, $-ˈ-/ *n* [C] a small closed container, often made of paper or plastic, containing a small amount of something, usually enough for only one occasion • *a sachet of sauce/sugar* • *There was a free sachet of shampoo on the front of my* *magazine.* • *I keep a sachet of pot pourri in the wardrobe.*

sack [BAG] /sæk/ *n* [C] a large bag, usually made of strong cloth, paper or plastic, used to store large amounts of something • *The corn was stored in large sacks.* • *There was a sack* **of** (= one containing) *potatoes/coal/flour in the corner of the barn.* • *(Am)* A sack is a paper or plastic bag used to carry items bought in a food shop: *a sack of groceries* • In a **sack race**, people jump along with both legs in a cloth sack, which they hold up with their hands. • See also HAVERSACK; KNAPSACK; RUCKSACK. • [PIC] **Bags, Outdoor games for children** Ⓟ

sack·ful /ˈsæk·fʊl/, **sack·load** /£ˈsæk·ləʊd, $-loʊd/ *n* [C] • A sackful is the amount contained in a sack: *(fig.) He got a whole sackful* **of** (= very many) *letters from listeners following the show.*

sack [BED] /sæk/ *n* [U] **the sack** *Am and Aus infml* bed • *It was late by the time we jumped into the sack.* • *He was very good/bad* **in the sack** (= was/was not sexually skilled). • Ⓟ

sack out *v adv* [I] *Am infml* • *It's late – I'm going to sack out* (= go to bed).

sack *obj* [DISMISS] /sæk/ *v* [T] to dismiss (someone) from a job, usually because they have done something which their employer does not like or because their work is not good enough • *Thirty workers were sacked because they went on strike over the staff cuts.* • [LP] **Work** Ⓟ

sack /sæk/ *n* [U] • **The sack** is the condition of being dismissed from your job: *She* **got**/*She* **was given** *the sack* **for** *stealing money from her employer.*

sack·ing /ˈsæk·ɪŋ/ *n* [C] • *There was a* **mass** *sacking at the car plant today, when seven hundred workers lost their jobs.*

sack *obj* [STEAL] /sæk/ *v* [T] to steal all the valuable things from (buildings, towns etc.) and possibly destroy them, usually during a war • *The invaders sacked every village they passed on their route.* • Ⓟ

sack /sæk/ *n* [U] • **The sack** (= destruction) **of Rome** *by the Barbarians occurred in the 5th century.*

sack·cloth /£ˈsæk·klɒθ, $-klɑːθ/, **sack·ing** *n* [U] the thick rough material used to make SACKS (= large strong bags) • To **be in/wear sackcloth and ashes** is to be or to appear to be extremely sorry, esp. much more sorry than is necessary, when you have done something wrong.

sac·ra·ment /ˈsæk·rə·mənt/ *n* [C] an important religious ceremony in the Christian Church • *Baptism and Communion are two of the sacraments.* • **The** sacrament is the holy bread and wine eaten at **Holy Communion** (= a religious ceremony): *They went up to the altar to* **receive** *the holy sacrament at the Eucharist.*

sac·ra·men·tal /£ˌsæk·rəˈmen·tᵊl, $-t̬ᵊl/ *adj*

sa·cred /ˈseɪ·krɪd/ *adj* considered to be holy and deserving respect, esp. because of a connection with God or a god • *They visited the sacred places of Islam.* • *This box holds the sacred relics of a saint.* • *They have occupied our land, stolen our freedom and violated everything we* **held** *sacred.* • *This area is sacred* **to** *the Apaches.* • Sacred can also mean connected with religion: *sacred music* • *sacred writings* • Sacred is sometimes also used to mean regarded as too important to be changed: *His daily routine is absolutely sacred* **to** *him.* • *(humorous) The cricketers wore blue, not their usual white – is* **nothing** *sacred?* • *(disapproving)* A **sacred cow** is a belief, custom, etc. that people support and do not question or criticize: *They did not dare to challenge the sacred cow of parliamentary democracy.*

sa·cred·ness /ˈseɪ·krɪd·nəs/ *n* [U]

sac·ri·fice *(obj)* [KILL] /ˈsæk·rɪ·faɪs/ *v* to kill (an animal or a person) ceremonially and offer them to a god or gods • *The ancient Aztecs sacrificed people* **to** *the gods.* [T] • *It was the practice of these people to sacrifice* **to** *their gods when rain had not fallen.* [I] • *(fig.) There are fears that the company's traditions of service and quality will be sacrificed* **on the altar of** (= given up in order to achieve) *profit.* [T]

sac·ri·fice /ˈsæk·rɪ·faɪs/ *n* [C] • *The people offered a lamb on the altar as a sacrifice* **for** *their sins.*

sac·ri·fi·cial /ˌsæk·rɪˈfɪʃ·ᵊl/ *adj* [not gradable] • *The priest held up the head of the sacrificial goat.* • *(fig.) It's unfair that Ted has been made a sacrificial* **victim** (= one who has to suffer because of something that someone else has done) *– it was his boss who should have been dismissed.* • A **sacrificial lamb** is someone or something put forward to people in authority with the expectation that they will remove or destroy it, esp. in order to prevent someone or something else being removed or destroyed : *We knew the department would be a sacrificial lamb when it came time to cut staff.*

sac·ri·fi·cial·ly /ˌsæk·rɪˈfɪʃ·ᵊl·i/ *adv* [not gradable]

sac·ri·fice *obj* [GIVE UP] /ˈsæk·rɪ·faɪs/ *v* [T] to give up (something that is valuable to you) in order to help another person • *The people are prepared to sacrifice everything to achieve victory.* • *Many women sacrifice interesting careers* **for** *their family.* • *They were prepared to sacrifice their immediate needs* **to** *the long- term goal of equal opportunity.* • In the game of CHESS, you might sacrifice a piece to gain time or a positional advantage: *Karpov sacrificed a knight on move twenty-eight, going on to mate his opponent in seven moves.* • *"We ... sacrificed most of our lives, / We gave her everything money can buy"* (from the song *She's Leaving Home* by The Beatles, 1967)

sac·ri·fice /ˈsæk·rɪ·faɪs/ *n* • *We had to* **make** *sacrifices and go without things in order to pay for our children's education.* [C] • *They cared for their handicapped son for 27 years,* **at** *great personal sacrifice.* [U] • *If you become a soldier, you may have to* **make the ultimate/supreme sacrifice** (= die) *for your country.*

sac·ri·lege /ˈsæk·rɪ·lɪdʒ/ *n* (an act of) treating something holy or important without respect • *Muslims consider it sacrilege to wear shoes inside a mosque.* [U] • **It** *would be a sacrilege* **to** *put a neon sign on that beautiful old building.* [C + *to* infinitive] • *(humorous) He's one of those people who thinks* **it**'*s sacrilege* **to** *put ice in wine.* [U + *to* infinitive]

sac·ri·le·gious /ˌsæk·rɪˈlɪdʒ·əs/ *adj* • *sacrilegious practices/acts*

sac·ri·le·gious·ly /ˌsæk·rɪˈlɪdʒ·ə·sli/ *adv*

sac·ri·sty /ˈsæk·rɪ·sti/ *n* [C] a VESTRY

sac·ro·sanct /ˈsæk·rə·sæŋkt/ *adj esp. humorous* thought to be too important or too special to be changed • *I'm willing to help on any weekday, but I'm afraid my weekends are sacrosanct.* • *He lives by the sacrosanct rule/principle that nothing is sacrosanct!*

sad [NOT HAPPY] /sæd/ *adj* **sadder**, **saddest** unhappy or sorry • *Why are you looking so sad?* • *I've just received some very sad news.* • *That was a very sad book/story/film.* • *She gave a rather sad smile.* • *It's sad* **about** *your trip being cancelled.* • *I'm so/very sad* **(that)** *you can't come.* [+ *(that)* clause] • **It**'*s so/very sad* **(that)** *you can't come.* [+ *(that)* clause] • *I'm sad* **to** *see so many failures this year.* [+ *to* infinitive] • **It**'*s sad* **to** *see so many failures this year.* [+ *to* infinitive] • *He's a sad* **case** (= He deserves sympathy). • *(fig. humorous) Give those flowers some water – they're looking a bit sad* (= as though they have not been cared for). • *After his bike accident, he was* **sadder but wiser** (= he had learned from the painful experience). • *"A sadder and a wiser man/ He rose the morrow morn* (= the next morning)*"* (Samuel Coleridge in *The Rime of the Ancient Mariner*, 1798)

sad·ly /ˈsæd·li/ *adv* • *"He's gone away for six months," she said sadly.*

sad·ness /ˈsæd·nəs/ *n* [U] • *(fml) It was* **with great** *sadness that I heard of your husband's death.*

sad·den *obj* /ˈsæd·ᵊn/ *v* [T usually passive] • *I was saddened* **to** *hear of the death of your brother.* [+ obj + *to* infinitive] • **It** *saddens me* **to** *think that we'll never see her again.* [+ obj + *to* infinitive] • *We are* **deeply** *saddened by this devastating tragedy.*

sad [UNPLEASANT] /sæd/ *adj* [before n] **sadder**, **saddest** unacceptable; not satisfactory • *The sad* **fact/truth** *is we can't afford to provide homes for all.* • *It's a sad* **reflection/comment** *on our society that many old people die of the cold each winter.* • *This is the sad* **state of affairs** *facing film-makers today.* • **Sad to say**, (= It is a cause for regret) *the ring was never found.*

sad·ly /ˈsæd·li/ *adv* • *Her garden looks sadly neglected.* • *Sadly,* (= It is a cause for regret that) *there just aren't enough doughnuts for everybody.* • *If you think she'll let you do that, you're sadly* (= completely) **mistaken.**

SAD /ˌes·eɪˈdiː/ *n* [U] *abbreviation for* seasonal affective disorder (= a medical condition in which a person lacks energy and enthusiasm during the winter because of the reduced period of natural light)

sad·dle [SEAT] /ˈsæd·l̩/ *n* [C] a seat, often made of leather, used on a horse, bicycle, motorcycle, etc. • *He swung himself into the saddle and rode off.* • *I've been* **in the saddle** (= riding) *all day.* • **In the saddle** also means in charge or in control: *The chairman is back in the saddle after his heart attack.* • A **saddle-bag** is a small bag which you fix to the back of your bicycle saddle, or one of a pair of bags you put over the back of a horse or over the back wheel of a bicycle or motorcycle. • **Saddle-sore** means having a sore bottom from riding on a saddle for a long time. • See also SIDESADDLE. • PIC **Bicycles**

sad·dle *(obj)* /ˈsæd·l̩/ *v* • *She saddled* **(up)** (= put a saddle on the back of) *the horse for her friend.* [T/M] • *Saddle* **up** (= Put a saddle on the back of your horse)*! It's time we were off!* [I]

sad·dler /£ˈsæd·ləʳ, $-lɚ/ *n* [C] • A saddler is a person who makes, sells and repairs saddles and other leather objects for horses.

sad·dler·y /£ˈsæd·lə·ri, $ˈ-lɚ·i/ *n* [U] • Saddlery is leather objects, such as saddles and BRIDLES, for horses.

sad·dle MEAT /ˈsæd·l̩/ *n* a large piece of meat taken from the middle of the back of an animal • *She bought a saddle of venison.* [C] • *We had saddle of lamb for dinner.* [U]

sad·dle *obj* **with** *obj v prep* [T] *infml* to give (someone) (a responsibility or problem which they do not want) • *I've been saddled with the job of leading the club.* • *They've saddled me with send***ing** *out the invitations.* [+ obj + v-*ing*] • *Why did you saddle your***selves** *with such a large loan?* • *The company is saddled with* **debt**.

sa·di·sm /£ˈseɪ·dɪ·zᵊm, $ˈsæd·ɪ-/ *n* [U] the obtaining of pleasure, sometimes sexual, from being cruel to or hurting another person • *The violence, sadism and brutality in the film was horrific.*

sa·dist /£ˈseɪ·dɪst, $ˈsæd·ɪst/ *n* [C] • *These killings seem to be the work of a sadist.* • *Our teacher's a real sadist* (= a cruel or unkind person), *making us stand outside in the pouring rain.*

sa·dis·tic /səˈdɪs·tɪk/ *adj* • *a sadistic smile* • *sadistic behaviour* • *a sadistic tyrant*

sa·dis·ti·cal·ly /səˈdɪs·tɪ·kli/ *adv* • *We heard him laugh sadistically as he locked us in and threw away the key.*

sa·do·mas·o·chi·sm /£ˌseɪ·dəʊˈmæs·ə·kɪ·zᵊm, $ˌsæd·oʊ-/ (*abbreviation* **SM**, **S and M** /ˌes·əˈnem/) *n* [U] the obtaining of sexual pleasure from SADISM (= hurting other people) and from MASOCHISM (= being hurt) • *The pornographic magazines that the police found when they searched the man's home indicated that he was* **into** *sadomasochism.*

sa·do·mas·o·chist /£ˌseɪ·dəʊˈmæs·ə·kɪst, $ˌsæd·oʊ-/ *n* [C]

sa·do·mas·o·chis·tic /£ˌseɪ·dəʊˌmæs·əˈkɪs·tɪk, $ˌsæd·oʊ-/ *adj* [not gradable]

sae /ˌes·eɪˈiː/, **SAE** *n* [C] *abbreviation for* stamped addressed envelope or self-addressed envelope (= an envelope which has on it a stamp and the address of the person who sends it) • *Please write, enclosing an s.a.e., and we will send you details immediately.* • Compare SASE.

sa·fa·ri /£səˈfɑː·ri, $-ˈfɑːr·i/ *n* an organized journey to look at, or sometimes hunt, wild animals, esp. in Africa • *For his winter vacation this year, he's decided to* **go on** *a safari.* [C] • *They're currently* **on** *safari in Kenya.* [U] • A **safari jacket** is a jacket made of light cloth with short sleeves, pockets on the chest and a belt. A **safari suit** is such a jacket with matching trousers or a matching skirt. • A **safari park** is a large enclosed park where wild animals are kept and can move freely, and can be watched by visitors driving through in their cars.

safe NOT IN DANGER /seɪf/ *adj* **-r**, **-st** not causing danger or not in danger • *a safe play-area for children* • *I don't like going in a car with him – he's not a safe driver.* • *Watch out! That ladder isn't safe – it's going to fall down.* • *She wished us a safe journey.* • *Is this medicine safe* **for** *children?* • **It's** *safe* **to** *come out now – the danger's past.* [+ *to* infinitive] • *Your secret's safe* **with** *me* (= I will not tell anyone what you have told me). • *In some cities you don't* **feel** *safe going out alone at night.* • *We're safe* **from** *attack now – the enemy planes have gone.* • *I know I put it* **somewhere** *safe* (= where it could not be damaged, stolen or lost) *but I just can't find it.* • *Don't lose your passport – keep it in a safe* **place** (= where it cannot be damaged, stolen or lost). • Safe can also be applied to things which do not involve any risk: *Almost all the votes have been counted now, so I think* **it's** *safe* **to** *say* (= there is little risk of being wrong if we say) *that we've won.* [+ *to* infinitive] ○ *He's never remembered my birthday in his life, so it's a safe* **bet** (= I am certain) *he'll forget it again this time!* ○ *The interviewers made the safe* **choice** (= one that was not risky) *and gave the job to the man they knew.* • If an official position in parliament is safe, it is likely to be won by the political party which has won it at previous elections: *She's been chosen as a candidate for a safe Conservative* **seat**. • *Dr Bailey is doing the operation, so your wife is* **in safe hands** (= she is being cared for by someone skilled). • *(Br) If you invest your money with us, it will be* **as safe as houses** (= you are very unlikely to lose it). • *I'm sure it won't rain, but I'll take an umbrella* **(just) to be on the safe side** (= to be ready if it does rain). • *After three days lost in the mountains, all the climbers arrived home* **safe and sound** (= completely without injury). • (A) **safe-conduct** is (a document giving) official protection from harm while travelling through an area: *They* **issued** *us with safe-conducts so that we could pass through enemy country.* ○ *In exchange for the hostages, the terrorists demanded safe-conduct out of the country.* • A **safe house** is a house where someone can hide or shelter: *The authorities discovered our safe house and captured two of our agents there.* • The **safe period** is the few days just before and during a woman's PERIOD (= monthly bleeding) when she is unlikely to become pregnant. • **Safe sex** is the use of CONDOMS or other methods of avoiding catching a disease, esp. AIDS, from sexual contact with someone else.

safe·ly /ˈseɪ·fli/ *adv* • *The house was safely locked up.* • *They all arrived safely, thank God.* • *Drive safely* (= Do not take any risks)*!* • *I think we can safely* (= with no risk of being wrong) *say they won't find us now.*

safe·ty /£ˈseɪf·ti, $-ţi/ *n* [U] • *With no thought for his own safety, he ran into the burning building to save the child.* • **For** *your (comfort and) safety, we recommend you keep your seat belt loosely fastened during the flight.* • *Journalists may enter the danger zone but unfortunately we cannot* **guarantee/assure** *their safety.* • *Refugees should be allowed to return* **in** *safety to their own homes.* • *The crew of the ship were winched to safety by a rescue helicopter.* • *As the gunman opened fire, they all* **ran/dived for** *safety behind trees.* • *You wouldn't get me on skis – I prefer to watch on TV* **from** *the safety* **of** *my own armchair.* • *Many people are worried about the safety* **of** *the nuclear industry* (= think it might be dangerous). • *Police are* **concerned for** *the safety* **of** (= think that something bad might have happened to) *a five-year-old who disappeared while playing in a wood near his home.* • *The boy led the escaped prisoner to* **a place of** *safety* (= somewhere he would not be in danger, esp. of being found). • Safety can be used to describe something which protects a person or thing from a particular danger: *safety checks/measures* • *a safety device* • *a safety harness/helmet* ○ *Among the safety features of this car are anti-lock brakes and airbags.* ○ *Safety regulations stipulate that the machine should be covered while it is in operation.* • A **safety belt** is a **seat belt**. See at SEAT FURNITURE. • A **safety catch** is a special part on something dangerous, esp. a machine or a gun, which prevents people from using it unintentionally. • In a theatre, the **safety curtain** is a curtain made of material which will not burn and which comes down between the stage and the part where people sit to prevent any fire that might happen from spreading. • A **safety deposit box** is a **safe deposit box**. See at SAFE BOX. • **Safety-first** means not showing a willingness to take risks: *A safety-first attitude is best when it comes to driving.* • **Safety glass** is a type of glass, used esp. for car windows, that either stays in one piece in an accident, or breaks into small pieces which are not sharp. • **Safety glasses** are special pieces of strong glass or plastic in a frame which fits tightly to a person's face to protect their eyes from dangerous chemicals or machines. • A **safety lamp** (also **Davy lamp**) is a light used in a MINE (= underground passage) which can show if there is dangerous gas in a place, without any risk of causing the gas to explode. • A **safety match** is a match that will only start burning if you rub it along a special surface on its box. • A **safety net** is put below people performing at a great height to catch them and stop them from getting hurt if they fall: *There was a safety net below the acrobats at the circus.* ○ *(fig.) No one dies of hunger there because the government provides a safety net* (= help for people in a difficult situation) *of payments to the unemployed.* • A **safety pin** is a pin which has a round end into which the sharp point fits so that it is covered and cannot therefore stick into you. It is used for fastening things, esp. cloth. • A **safety razor** is a device for cutting hair on the face which has a blade that is partly covered, to prevent it from cutting the skin. • A **safety valve** is a small part on a machine or device which allows steam or gas to escape if the pressure inside becomes too high: *(fig.) For many people who suffer from stress at work, sport is a safety valve* (= way of getting rid of strong feelings without hurting other people). • *(saying)* 'There's safety in numbers' means that we will be or feel safer or more confident as a group. • PIC› **Laboratory, Pins and needles**

safe·ness /ˈseɪf·nəs/ *n* [U] • *I'm a bit worried about the safeness of this machine for* (= whether this machine will cause any danger to) *children.*

safe BOX /seɪf/ *n* [C] a strong box or cupboard with special locks where valuable things, esp. money or jewels, are kept • *Thieves* **broke into/cracked** (= opened by force) *the safe and stole everything in it.* • A **safe deposit box** (also **safety deposit box**) is a strong box in a bank where you can keep money or valuable things.

safe·break·er *Br and Aus* /£ˈseɪfˌbreɪ·kəʳ, $-kɚ/, *Am* **safe·crack·er** /£ˈseɪfˌkræk·əʳ, $-ɚ/ *n* [C] someone who opens SAFES using force and steals the valuable things from inside

safe·guard *obj* /£ˈseɪf·gɑːd, $-gɑːrd/ *v* [T] to keep (something) safe from, or protect it against, harm or destruction • *People hope their savings will safeguard them* **against** *poverty in their old age.* • *The re-armament programme will safeguard the country* **from** *attack.* • *The union safeguards the* **interests** *of all its members employed in the electricity industry.*

safe·guard /£ˈseɪf·gɑːd, $-gɑːrd/ *n* • *The new chemicals factory has many built-in safeguards* (= systems of protection), *so if there is an accident, the public will be in no danger.* [C] • *Does the new law provide an adequate safeguard* (= protection) **for** *consumers?* [C] • *Is there sufficient safeguard* **against** *the possibility of abuse?* [U]

safe·keep·ing /ˌseɪfˈkiː·pɪŋ/ *n* [U] protection from harm or loss • *Can I leave my watch with you* **for** *safekeeping while I'm swimming?* • *He left his CD player and video* **in** *my safekeeping while he was away.*

saf·flower /£ˈsæf·laʊəʳ, $-flaʊr/ *n* [C] a plant with sharp points on its leaves, from which the seeds are used for making an oil which is used in cooking • *Safflower* **oil** *is low in the sort of fats that are considered to be bad for people's health.*

saf·fron SPICE /£ˈsæf·rɒn, $-rən/ *n* [U] a dark yellow substance obtained from a flower and used as a spice to give colour and flavour to food • *saffron rice* • *saffron buns* • *Add some saffron to the paella for that authentic Spanish flavour.*

saf·fron COLOUR /£ˈsæf·rɒn, $-rən/ *adj* dark yellow • *The Buddhist monks were wearing saffron* **robes.**

sag /sæg/ *v* [I] **-gg-** to drop down to a lower level in the middle • *a sagging roof/floor/bed* • *His cheeks sagged and he walked with a stoop.* • *The shelf sagged* **under** *the weight of the heavy books.* • *(fig.) Her spirits sagged* (= She felt unhappy) *at the thought of all the work she had to do that evening.* • *(fig.) The dollar held up well this morning but the pound sagged* (= was reduced in value). • *(fig.) Halfway through the lecture my interest began to sag* (= I began to lose interest). • A **sag bag** is a large BEANBAG.

sag /sæg/ *n* [U] • *a sag in the roof* • *(fig.) a sag* (= fall) *in sales*

sa·ga /ˈsɑː·gə/ *n* [C] a long story about several past events or people, originally one told in the Middle Ages in Iceland or Norway • *the Volsunga Saga* • *'The Forsyte Saga' by John Galsworthy tells the story of several generations of the same family.* • *(disapproving)* A saga is also a long complicated series of related events: *It was just another episode in the* **ongoing** *saga* **of** *corruption in this company.* ○ *It was the latest twist in this* **long-running** *saga* **of** *fraud and scandal.* ○ *He made me listen to the* **whole sorry** *saga* **of** *his lost cat.*

sa·ga·cious /səˈgeɪ·ʃəs/ *adj fml* having or showing understanding and the ability to make good judgments; wise • *a sagacious person/comment/choice*

sa·ga·cious·ly /səˈgeɪ·ʃə·sli/ *adv fml*

sa·gac·i·ty /£səˈgæs·ɪ·ti, $-ə·ţi/ *n* [U] *fml* • *It required a statesman's foresight and sagacity to make the decision.*

sage WISE /seɪdʒ/ *adj* [not gradable] *literary* wise, esp. as a result of great experience • *sage advice* • *my sage old grandfather*

sage /seɪdʒ/ *n* [C] *literary or humorous* • A sage is a person, esp. an old man, who is wise: *The sages will tell you that when you can see those distant hills, it's going to rain.*

sage·ly /ˈseɪdʒ·li/ *adv literary* • *He nodded his head sagely.*

sage PLANT /seɪdʒ/ *n* [U] a plant whose greyish green leaves are used as a herb to give flavour to some foods • *sage-and-onion stuffing* • *His trousers were* **sage-green** (= a greyish-green colour). • PIC› **Herbs and spices**

Sag·it·ta·ri·us /£ˌsædʒ·ɪˈteə·ri·əs, $-ˈter·i-/ *n* [not after *the*] the ninth sign of the ZODIAC, relating to the period 22 November to 22 December and represented by a CENTAUR (= half human, half horse) shooting an arrow, or a person born during this period • *She was born* **under** *Sagittarius* (= during this period). [U] • *My brother's a Sagittarius.* [C]

Sag·it·ta·ri·an /£ˌsædʒ·ɪˈteə·ri·ən, $-ˈter·i-/ *n* [C] • *Sagittarians are supposed to be outgoing and hardworking.*

sa·go /£ˈseɪ·gəʊ, $-goʊ/ *n* [U] small white grains that are obtained from part of the trunk of a particular tree and which are used in cooking • *sago pudding*

said SAY /sed/ *past simple and past participle of* SAY

said ALREADY MENTIONED /sed/ *adj* [before n; not gradable] *law* (of a person or thing) already mentioned • **The** *said Joseph Brown was seen breaking into the car on the night of January 15th.*

sail *(obj)* TRAVEL /seɪl/ *v* to (cause (a boat) to) travel across water using sails or an engine • *I learned to sail when I was only eight.* [I] • *We sailed up/down the river.* [I] • *The boat sailed along/down the coast.* [I] • *As the ship sailed by/past, everyone on deck waved.* [I] • *She sailed around the world single-handed in her yacht.* [I] • *The ship was sailing* **to** *China.* [I] • *When do we sail* (= When does our ship leave)*?* [I] • *Their ship sails* (= leaves) **for** *Bombay next Friday.* [I] • *The oil tanker was sailing* **under** *a foreign flag* (= was officially using another country's flag). [I] • *It'll be a slow journey – we're sailing* **against the wind** (= the wind is blowing towards us). [I] • *He's* **sailing against the wind** (= opposing the ideas of most people) *in his fight to stop women using the club.* • *You were* **sailing** *a bit* **close to the wind** *there* (= taking a risk by doing something that was dangerous, illegal or unacceptable) *when you made those remarks about his wife.* • *The children were sailing their toy yachts on the pond in the park.* [T] • *Thor Heyerdahl sailed* **(across)** *the Pacific in the Kon-Tiki in 1947.* [T; I + *across*] • *They* **go** *sailing* (= take part in the sport of using boats with sails) *every weekend.* [I] • *"They sailed away for a year and a day,/ To the land where the Bong-tree grows"* (from the poem *The Owl and the Pussy-Cat* by Edward Lear, 1870) • *"In fourteen hundred and ninety-two / Columbus sailed the ocean blue"* (verse by Winifred Sackville Stoner Jr.)

sail /seɪl/ *n* [U] • *It's two days' sail/It's a two-day sail* (= a journey of two days by sea) *from here to the nearest island.* • *Who feels like* **coming/going** *for a sail* (= a journey in a boat, often quite short and for pleasure) *this afternoon?*

sail·ing /ˈseɪ·lɪŋ/ *n* • Sailing is the sport or activity of using boats with sails: *a sailing club* • *a sailing dinghy* ○ *She loves sailing.* [U] • A sailing is when a ship leaves a port: *There are frequent sailings from Dover.* [C] • *(Br and Aus)* A **sailing boat** (*Am* **sailboat**) is a small boat with sails. • PIC› **Water sports**

sail·or /£ˈseɪ·ləʳ, $-lɚ/ *n* [C] • A sailor is a person who works on a ship, esp. one who is not an officer: *His brother's a sailor in the Australian navy.* • A sailor is also a person who often takes part in the sport of using boats with sails: *Roger is a* **keen** *sailor – he sails with his club every Saturday.* • If you are a **good/bad** sailor, you do not/ do usually feel ill when you travel by boat. • A **sailor suit** is a set of clothes, esp. for a child, in the style of a sailor's uniform, usually blue with a large white collar at the back.

sail MATERIAL /seɪl/ *n* [C] a sheet of material fixed to a vertical pole on a boat to catch the wind and make the boat move • *Sails were traditionally made of canvas, but now they are usually made of synthetic material.* • *They* **hoisted/lowered** *the sails.* • To **set sail** is to begin a boat journey: *We set sail* **from** *Kuwait.* ○ *They set sail* **for** (= in order to travel to) *France.* • *After ten hours* **under sail** (= being moved by wind pushing sails), *they reached dry land.* • On a WINDMILL, a sail is any of the wide blades which are turned by the wind in order to produce power.

sail MOVE SMOOTHLY /seɪl/ *v* [I always + adv/prep] (usually of a person) to move smoothly, confidently and quite quickly • *She was sailing* **along** *on her bike, singing at the top of her voice.* • *She sailed* **into** *the room, waving her exam results triumphantly.* • *He wasn't looking where he was going, and just sailed* **straight into** *her.* • To **sail into** someone is to attack them using words: *The President sailed into her opponents with an angry speech.* • *The ball went sailing* **over** *the wall.* • *They won three matches and sailed confidently* **on** (= continued easily) **to** *victory in the final.* • To **sail through** (something) is to succeed in it without difficulty: *Rachel sailed through (the exam) with Distinction in all the papers.*

sail·board /£'seɪl·bɔːd, $-bɔːrd/ *n* [C] a WINDSURFER • PIC> Water sports

sail·boat /£'seɪl·bəʊt, $-boʊt/ *n* [C] *Am for* **sailing boat**, see at SAIL TRAVEL

saint /seɪnt, sᵊnt/ (*abbreviation* **St**) *n* [C] (the title given to) a person who has received an official honour by the Christian, esp. the Roman Catholic, Church for having lived in a good and holy way • *Margaret Clitherow, who died in 1586, was* **made** *a saint in 1970.* • *Saint Peter was one of Christ's disciples.* • The names of saints are sometimes used in naming places and buildings: *Saint Andrew's Road* • *Saint Matthew's School* • *Saint Paul's Cathedral* • *the Saint Lawrence Seaway* • *(fig.) She must be a* **real** *saint* (= very kind and patient) *to stay with him all these years.* • *(fig.) Oh you are a saint* (= are kind to me), *fetching my slippers for me.* • *(fig. esp. humorous) I don't know why she thinks she has the right to criticize other people's behaviour – she's* **no** *saint* (= does not behave in a good or moral way) *herself.* • In Roman Catholic countries, people often celebrate their **saint's day** (= the day on which the saint, whose name they have, was born).

saint·ed /£'seɪn·tɪd, $-t̬ɪd/ *adj* [not gradable] • Sainted means CANONIZED (= given the title of 'saint' in honour of a holy life): *(fig.) My sainted* (= extremely good) *mother worked cleaning offices so that I could go to a good university.*

saint·hood /'seɪnt·hʊd/ *n* [U] • *The Pope has taken the first step in* **conferring** *sainthood* **on** *the cardinal.*

saint·ly /'seɪnt·li/ *adj* • *He led a virtuous, almost a saintly* (= very good and holy) *life.* • *Her saintly manner concealed a devious mind.*

saint·li·ness /'seɪnt·lɪ·nəs/ *n* [U]

sake HELP /seɪk/ *n* [C] **for the sake of** *someone*/**for** *someone's* **sake** in order to help or bring advantage to (someone) • *Please do it, for my/his/her/their/David's sake.* • *John and Mary only stayed together for the sake of the children.* • *I hope for both our sakes that you're right!*

sake REASON /seɪk/ *n* [U] **for the sake of** *something*/**for** *something's* **sake** because of, or for the purpose of, (something) • *Let's not disagree for the sake of* (= because of) *a few pounds.* • *The company has decided for economy's sake* (= for the purpose of saving money) *to close down this department.* • *Let's say, just for the sake of argument/for argument's sake* (= for the purpose of this discussion), *that prices rise by 3 per cent this year.* • *You're only arguing for the sake of arguing* (= because you like arguing).

sake EMPHASIS /seɪk/ *n* [U] **for** *something's/someone's* **sake** used to emphasize requests or orders and when you are angry or have lost patience • **For goodness/Pete's/heavens/pity's sake** can be used in ordinary conversation: *For goodness sake don't let her know I told you!* • **For God's/Christ's sake** might be considered offensive or taboo by some people: *For Christ's sake, turn that music off!*

sa·ke DRINK, **sa·ki** /'sɑː·ki/ *n* a Japanese alcoholic drink made from rice and usually drunk warm • *He offered me some sake.* [U] • *We'll have two sakes* (= containers of sake) *please.* [C]

sa·laam /sə'lɑːm/ *v* [I] (esp. in Muslim countries) to greet someone by bending deeply from the waist with the front of the right hand against the top of the face • *He entered the room and salaamed* **to** *the visitors.*

sa·laam /sə'lɑːm/ *n, exclamation* • *He* **made** *a salaam* **of greeting** *and walked on.* [C] • *"Salaam!" he said and went on his way.*

sal·a·ble /'seɪ·lə·bl̩/ *adj esp. Am for* **saleable**, see at SALE

sa·la·cious /sə'leɪ·ʃəs/ *adj disapproving* causing or showing a strong interest in sexual matters • *a salacious film/book/joke/comment* • *Some newspapers try to attract more readers with their salacious articles and pictures of nude women.*

sa·la·cious·ly /sə'leɪ·ʃə·sli/ *adv disapproving*

sa·la·cious·ness /sə'leɪ·ʃə·snəs/ *n* [U] *disapproving*

sal·ad /'sæl·əd/ *n* a mixture of usually raw vegetables, eaten either as a separate dish or with other food • *She made a* **mixed** *salad with lettuce, cucumber, tomato and pepper and* **tossed** *it in* (= mixed it with) *a vinaigrette dressing.* [C] • *Do help yourself to some more* **green** *salad* (= a mixture of green leaves, esp. LETTUCE, and green vegetables, esp. CUCUMBER and PEPPER.) [U] • **Cheese/chicken/egg/ham** salad is cheese/chicken/egg/ham with salad: *That late in the evening, all they could offer me was cold chicken salad.* [U] ○ *If you didn't want meat, the only choice was a cheese salad.* [C] • *I'll serve the quiche and then you can help yourself from the salad* **bowl**. • A **salad bar** is a type of table where different prepared salads are served in a restaurant or shop. • *(Br)* **Salad cream** is a thick, cream-coloured liquid, similar to MAYONNAISE but sweeter, which may be eaten with salad. • **Salad dressing** is a mixture of oil, vinegar and flavourings, which is added to salads to give flavour. • *(dated) I met her* **in my salad days** (= when I was young and had little experience). • PIC> **Cutlery, Food preparation** Ⓓ ⒹⓀ Ⓕ Ⓢ

sal·a·man·der /£ˌsæl·ə'mæn·dəʳ, $-dɚ/ *n* [C] a small animal which looks like a LIZARD but has soft skin and lives both on land and in water

sa·la·mi /sə'lɑː·mi/ *n* [U] a large SAUSAGE made from meat and spices which has a strong taste and is usually eaten cold in slices

sal·a·ry /£'sæl·ᵊr·i, $'-ɚ-/ *n* [C] a fixed amount of money agreed every year as pay for an employee, part of which, that is left once tax has been paid, is usually paid directly into his or her bank account every month • *She has an* **annual** *salary of £20 000* **gross**. • *His net* **monthly** *salary is £1500.* • *She* **earns/gets/is on** *quite a good/high/decent salary in her present job.* • *The boss* **put up/raised** *everyone's salary by $4000 last year, because profits were good.* • *He* **took a drop in** (= accepted a lower) *salary in order to help the firm.* • *The report is certain to fuel the storm over the huge salary* **increase** *awarded to the chairman.* • **Top** *salary* **earners** (= People with high salaries) *will in future face a much heftier tax bill.* • *She negotiated a salary (Br)* **rise**/*(Am)* **raise** *with her employer.* • Compare WAGE MONEY. • LP> **Money**

sal·a·ried /£'sæl·ᵊr·id, $'-ɚ-/ *adj* [not gradable] • *salaried employees/workers/staff* • *There are relatively few salaried* **posts** *in the company – most employees work freelance.*

sale SELL /seɪl/ *n* an act of exchanging something for money • *The sale* **of** *cigarettes to children is forbidden in many countries.* [U] • *He gave the* **proceeds from** *the sale of his drawings to several worthwhile causes.* [U] • *I didn't sell a single car yesterday, but I've* **made** *a sale* (= sold one) *this morning.* [C] • *The company is expecting a* **large/record** *sale* **of** (= to sell a lot of/the most ever of) *the new model.* [C] • *Sales of cars were* **up/down** *this week.* [C] • A sale is also an occasion when things are sold, esp. by an organization such as a school or church, in order to make money for the organization: *Our school is* **holding** *a sale next week to raise money for a new computer.* [C] • *Can you help at the charity sale/Christmas sale/book sale?* [C] • A sale is also an AUCTION: *a sale of antique furniture* [C] ○ *a cattle sale* [C] • If something is **for sale**, it is available to be bought: *Is this painting only on display or is it for sale?* ○ *There was a small stall outside the house with plants and vegetables for sale.* ○ *The house next door is being sold – the For Sale sign went up yesterday.* ○ *Our neighbours* **put** *their house* **up** *for sale* (= started to advertise that they want to sell it) *last week.* • *(Br and Aus)* If goods are **on sale** they are available to be bought in a shop: *This week's 'Radio Times' is on sale now.* ○ *Prices of video recorders have come down – we paid £250 for ours and now it's on sale for only £150.* • *(Br)* **Sale or return** is a system by which goods are supplied to shops which can return them if they are not sold within a particular period of time: *Newspapers are supplied to the shop on sale or return.* • See also SELL.

sales /seɪlz/ *pl n* • Sales are the number of items sold: *Sales this year exceeded the total for the two previous years.* ○ *This month's sales figures are good.* • Sales/The sales **department** is the department of a company that organizes and does the selling of the things it makes: *He works in Sales.* • *(Br and Aus fml)* A **sales assistant** (*Am* **salesclerk**) is someone who works in a shop serving customers. • *We're having a* **sales drive** (= a special effort to sell more than usual) *this week.* • *He's got a good* **sales pitch** (= special way of talking to possible buyers). • A **sales representative** (also **sales rep**) travels to different places trying to persuade people to buy the things their company produces. The **sales force** of a company consists of all the sales representatives of that company. • **Sales resistance** is unwillingness to buy: *In the early years of satellite television there was a lot of sales resistance amongst the public.* • **Sales slip** is *Am for* RECEIPT. • *I don't believe a word she says about the beauty cream – it's just* **sales talk** (= talking to persuade you to buy something). • *(Am) The President has introduced a new 5%* **sales tax** (= tax on things people buy in shops). See also VAT. • See also TELESALES.

sale·a·ble, *esp. Am* **sal·a·ble** /ˈseɪ·lə·bl̩/ *adj* • Saleable means easy to sell or suitable for selling: *Expensive watches are not very saleable items in a little shop like this.* ○ *These cute badges are easily saleable.*

sale CHEAP PRICE /seɪl/ *n* [C] an occasion when goods are sold at a lower price than usual • *a mid-season/end-of-season sale* • *a clearance sale* • *a closing-down sale* • *There's a sale on this week at the dress shop.* • *The DIY shop has got a sale on this week.* • *I bought this in a sale.* • *Are these dresses (Br and Aus)* **in** *the sale/(Am)* **on sale** (=reduced in price)? • *Sale* **goods** *are on the racks over there.* • *Usual price £10·99 – sale* **price** *£6·99!*

sales /seɪlz/ *pl n* • **The sales** are the period when many shops sell goods at a lower price than usual: *I bought this in the* **January/summer** *sales.*

sales·clerk /£ˈseɪlz·klɑːk, $-klɜːrk/ *n* [C] *Am for* **sales assistant**, see at SALE SELL

sales·per·son (*pl* **-people**), **sales·man** (*pl* **-men**), **sales·wo·man** (*pl* **-women**), *dated also* **sales·girl** /£ˈseɪlzˌpɜː·sᵊn, $-ˌpɜːr-, -mən, -ˌwʊm·ən, £-gɜːl, $-gɜːrl/ *n* [C] a person whose job is selling things in a shop or directly to customers • *a car salesperson* • *a computer salesperson* • *a travelling salesperson* • *He got a job as a* **door-to-door** *salesman with a double-glazing company.* • *Well, she was certainly a good saleswoman – she nearly talked me into buying that coat!* • *I asked the salesgirl if they had a larger size.*

sales·man·ship /ˈseɪlz·mən·ʃɪp/ *n* [U] • Salesmanship is skill in selling: *Clever salesmanship can persuade you to buy things you don't really want.*

sa·li·ent /ˈseɪ·li·ənt/ *adj* [not gradable] most noticeable or important • *Remind me of the salient* **features** *of the proposal.* • *The article presented the salient* **facts** *of the dispute clearly and concisely.* • *I don't need to know everything that he talked about, just give me the salient* **points.**

sa·line /ˈseɪ·laɪn/ *adj* [not gradable] *specialized* containing or consisting of salt • *saline deposits* • *saline springs* • *a saline lake* • *The Gulf is more saline than the Indian Ocean.*

sa·line /ˈseɪ·laɪn/ *n* [U] *medical* • Saline is a liquid mixture of salt and pure water, which helps to kill bacteria or can be used to replace liquid lost from the body: *Saline can be used for cleaning contact lenses.* ○ *If you have a sore throat, you can gargle with a saline* **solution.** ○ *In hospital they put her on a saline* **drip** *to restore her body fluids.*

sa·lin·i·ty /£səˈlɪn·ɪ·ti, $-ə·t̬i/ *n* [U] *specialized* • *The high salinity of the land near the coast makes farming difficult.*

sa·li·va /səˈlaɪ·və/ *n* [U] the natural watery liquid that keeps your mouth wet and helps to prepare food for digestion • *Saliva* **dribbled** *from the baby's mouth.*

sa·li·va·ry /£səˈlaɪ·vᵊr·i, $-vɚ-/ *adj* [not gradable] • The **salivary glands** in your mouth produce saliva.

sal·i·vate /ˈsæl·ɪ·veɪt/ *v* [I] *specialized or humorous* • *The thought of all that delicious food made me salivate* (=produce saliva).

sal·low /£ˈsæl·əʊ, $-oʊ/ *adj* **-er, -est** (of white-skinned people) yellowish and looking unhealthy • *a sallow complexion/face* • *sallow skin/cheeks*

sal·low·ness /£ˈsæl·əʊ·nəs, $-oʊ-/ *n* [U]

sal·ly /ˈsæl·i/ *v, n* (to make) a sudden attack on an enemy, esp. when they are surrounding you, and then return to your position of defence • *The troops* **made** *a sally into enemy territory, returning with ten prisoners.* [C] • *(fig.) The minister sallied* **forth** (=went out bravely) *to face the angry crowd.* [I]

Sal·ly Ar·my /£ˌsæl·iˈɑː·mi, $-ˈɑːr-/, *Aus infml* **the Sal·lies** /ˈsæl·iz/ *n* [U] *Br infml for* **Salvation Army**, see at SALVATION.

sal·mon /ˈsæm·ən/ *n pl* **salmon** a medium-sized silvery fish with pink flesh that is valued as a food, which lives in the sea and swims up rivers to produce its eggs • *fresh/tinned salmon* [U] • *pink/red salmon* [U] • *salmon mousse/fishcakes* • *She passed round a plate of* **smoked** *salmon sandwiches.* • *He caught two large salmon in the river.* [C] • *They went salmon fishing while they were in Scotland.* • A **salmon trout** is a large TROUT which has pink flesh and looks like a salmon. • *He was wearing a* **salmon-pink** (=orange pink) *T-shirt.* • PIC **Fish**

sal·mo·nel·la /ˌsæl·məˈnel·ə/ *n* [U] a group of bacteria, some types of which live in food and cause illness in people who eat the food, or *(infml)* the illness caused • *(infml) The outbreak of salmonella/salmonella* **poisoning** *resulted from people eating undercooked chicken.*

sal·on SHOP /£ˈsæl·ɔ̃ː, $səˈlɑːn/ *n* [C] a shop where you can obtain a particular service, esp. connected with beauty or fashion • *a beauty salon* • *a hairdressing/hair salon*

sal·on MEETING /£ˈsæl·ɔ̃ː, $səˈlɑːn/ *n* [C] *literary* a meeting of writers, painters, etc., at the house of someone famous or important • *Flaubert was often a guest at the* **literary** *salons of nineteenth-century Paris.*

sa·loon CAR *Br, Am and Aus* **se·dan** /səˈluːn/ *n* [C] a type of car with seats at the front and the back and a separate closed space for bags, etc. • *a family saloon* • PIC **Vehicles**

sa·loon ROOM /səˈluːn/ *n* [C] a public bar, esp. in the past in the United States • *The cowboys burst into the saloon and shot wildly at the drinkers.* • *(Br and Aus dated)* The **saloon bar** in a PUB (=place where you buy and drink alcoholic drinks) or hotel is a bar which is more comfortable than the other bars, and in which you sometimes pay a little more for your drink. Compare **public bar** at PUBLIC PEOPLE. • KOR

salt FOOD /£sɒlt, $sɑːlt/ *n* [U] a common white substance found in sea water and in the ground, which is used esp. to add flavour to food or to preserve it • *Pass the salt* **(and pepper)** *please!* • *There were* **grains** *of salt all over the tablecloth.* • *Add* **a pinch of** (=small amount of) *salt to the sauce.* • *Simmer the soup for 15 minutes and add salt* **to taste** (=as much as you like). • *The recipe uses garlic/celery salt* (=salt flavoured with these things). • *I'm on a salt-***free** *diet* (=I am not allowed to eat any salt). • *Utah and Nevada have large salt* **flats** (=flat areas of land with a layer of hard dried salt). • *Special plants grow on salt* **marshes** (=land near the sea which is always wet and salty). • *The area is famous for its salt* **mines** (=places where salt is dug from the ground). • *The technical name for salt is sodium chloride.* • Salt helps to kill bacteria and cause wounds to heal: *Having salt* **baths** *will help your leg to heal.* ○ *Bathe your eye in a mild salt* **solution** *to help reduce the infection.* ○ See also SALINE. • *(fig. dated) You can be sure she'll always add salt to the conversation* (=make it more interesting)*!* • *People like Bartow and Marianne are* **the salt of the earth** (=good people that you can always depend on). • **Salt-and-pepper** is *esp. Am for* **pepper-and-salt.** See at PEPPER POWDER. • A **salt cellar** (*Am and Aus also* **saltshaker**) is a small container for salt, usually with one hole in the top. • A **salt-lick** is a lump of salty substance which animals rub with their tongues.

salt *obj* /£sɒlt, $sɑːlt/ *v* [T] • *Don't forget to salt* (=add salt to) *the potatoes.* • *My granny used to salt* **(down)** (=preserve in salt) *green beans each summer for eating in the winter.* [T/M] • *When it's icy the city salts* (=puts salt on) *the* **roads** *to thaw the ice.*

salt /£sɒlt, $sɑːlt/ *adj* [before n; not gradable] • Salt water is sea water: *salt water lakes/lagoons* ○ *salt water fish/plants* ○ *The estuary – a partially enclosed bay where fresh and salt water mix – took its present form about 3000 years ago.* • Salt water is also water to which salt has been added: *The cooked eggs are kept in salt water for a few days.* • Salt meat has been preserved in salt: *salt beef/pork*

salt·ed /£ˈsɒl·tɪd, $ˈsɑːl·t̬ɪd/ *adj* [not gradable] • *salted peanuts* • *lightly salted butter*

salt·i·ness /£ˈsɒl·tɪ·nəs, $ˈsɑːl·t̬ɪ-/ *n* [U] • *If you put a raw potato into the soup, it will remove some of the saltiness.*

salt·y /£ˈsɒl·ti, $ˈsɑːl·t̬i/ *adj* **-ier, -iest** • *This bacon is too salty for me.*

salt CHEMICAL /£sɒlt, $sɑːlt/ *n* [C] *specialized* a chemical substance which is a combination of a metal or a BASE with an acid • *Potassium nitrate, potassium sulphate and potassium chloride are potassium salts.*

salt a·way *obj*, **salt** *obj* **a·way** *v adv* [M] *infml* to save (something, esp. money) secretly • *He salted away a fortune over the years and no one ever knew!*

salt·pe·tre *Br and Aus, Am* **salt·pe·ter** /£ˌsɒltˈpiː·tər, $ˈsɑːltˌpiː·t̬ɚ/ *n* [U] a salty-tasting white powder used to preserve meat and also used in the production of explosives and of substances which help plants grow better • *The technical name for saltpetre is potassium nitrate.*

sa·lu·bri·ous /səˈluː·bri·əs/ *adj fml or humorous* (esp. of places) socially or morally acceptable; RESPECTABLE • *He doesn't live in a very salubrious part of town.* • *Most of the attacks took place in the city's less salubrious suburbs.*

sal·u·ta·ry /£ˈsæl·jʊ·tri, $-ter·i/ *adj fml* causing improvement of behaviour or character • *The experience of nearly killing a child was salutary – he never drove too fast again.* • *The war is a salutary* **reminder** *of how dangerous* *the world has become.* • *Their experience offers a salutary* **lesson** *to the rest of Europe.*

sal·u·ta·tion /ˌsæl·jʊˈteɪ·ʃᵊn/ *n old use or fml* a greeting in words or actions, or the words used at the beginning of a letter or speech • *(fml) She raised her hand* **in** *salutation.* [U] • *(fml) 'Dear Sir' or 'Dear Madam' are the usual salutations at the start of a letter to someone whose name you do not know.* [C]

sa·lute *(obj)* SHOW RESPECT /səˈluːt/ *v* (esp. of people in the armed forces) to make a formal sign of respect to (someone), esp. by raising the right hand to the side of the head • *Whenever you see an officer, you must salute.* [I] • *The soldiers saluted the colonel when he arrived.* [T]

sa·lute /səˈluːt/ *n* [C] • *The soldier* **gave** *a salute and the officer* **returned** *it.* • *They* **fired** *a salute* (= fired guns) *to welcome the President.* • *Full military honours and a* **21-gun** *salute* (= 21 guns fired at the same time) *marked his funeral.* • When a person of high rank **takes the salute**, they stand and watch while soldiers march past saluting them: *The Queen took the salute at the parade.*

sa·lute *obj* PRAISE /səˈluːt/ *v* [T] *fml* to honour or express admiration publicly for (a person or an achievement) • *On this memorable occasion we salute the wonderful work done by the Association.* • *We salute you* **for** *your courage and determination.* • *He was saluted* **as** *the saviour of his country.* [+ obj + *as* n]

sal·vage *obj* /ˈsæl·vɪdʒ/ *v* [T] to save (goods) from damage or destruction, esp. from a ship that has sunk or been damaged or a building that has been damaged by fire or flooding • *The ship was lying in deep water, but we managed to salvage some of its cargo.* • *After the fire, there wasn't much furniture left worth salvaging.* • *(fig.) At the meeting today, foreign ministers will attempt to salvage something from the failure of the peace mission.* • *(fig.) After the fraud scandal he had to make great efforts to salvage his* **reputation.** • *(fig.) The Party was desperately attempting to salvage some of its lost* **credibility** *and is not going to give up power without a struggle.* • *(fig.) It was desperate last-ditch attempt to salvage the* **situation.**

sal·vage /ˈsæl·vɪdʒ/ *n* [U] • *The museum director said that the first step in salvage was to get any party with a claim to the wreck to relinquish it to the museum.* • *The salvage* **company** *said the job was made more difficult by the position of the ship.* • *They mounted a salvage* **operation** *after the fire.*

sal·vag·a·ble /ˈsæl·vɪdʒ·ə·bl̩/ *adj* • *There is nothing that is salvagable in the building – we have lost everything.*

sal·va·tion /sælˈveɪ·ʃᵊn/ *n* [U] (a way of) being saved from danger, loss or harm • *That blanket was my salvation when my car broke down in the snow.* • *The company is in trouble and the latest plan for its salvation has few supporters.* • *Getting to know Mary was his salvation – she made him laugh and forget all his troubles.* • In the Christian religion, salvation of a person or their spirit is the state of being saved from evil and its effects by the death of Jesus Christ on a cross: *The Gospel message is one of* **personal** *salvation.* • The **Salvation Army** (*Br infml* **Sally Army**, *Aus infml* **Sallies**), is an international Christian organization whose members have military-style ranks and uniforms, have meetings with music, and work to help poor people: *It's a Salvation Army* **hostel** *for homeless men and women.*

salve /£sælv, $sæv/ *n* [C] an oily substance used on a damaged, sore or dry place on your body to make it hurt less and encourage new skin to grow; OINTMENT • *(esp. old use) The plant has an old herbal use in salves for treating cuts.* • *(fig.) She created this fantasy* **as a salve to** *her hurt feelings* (= way of making her feelings hurt less). [C] • *(fig.) I hadn't written to her for months so I sent her a little present* **as a salve to** *my* **conscience** (= to make me feel less guilty).

salve *obj* /£sælv, $sæv/ *v* [T] • *(fig.) The new agreement was intended to salve the wound/pain/sting of previous conflicts.* • *(fig.) He salves his* **conscience** (= makes himself feel less guilty) *by giving money to charity.*

sal·ver /£ˈsæl·vəʳ, $-vɚ/ *n* [C] a large metal plate used to bring food, drinks or letters to people, esp. in a formal situation • *The servant brought the letter in on a* **silver** *salver.*

sal·vo /£ˈsæl·vəʊ, $-voʊ/ *n* [C] *pl* **salvos** or **salvoes** a firing of several guns at the same time, either in a war or in a ceremony • *a salvo of guns/rockets* • *They* **fired** *a salvo and it was quickly returned by the enemy over the river.* • *(fig.) In his* **opening** *salvo* (= attack in words) *the speaker fiercely attacked the Government's record on health care.* • *(fig.) Every joke the comedian made was greeted by a salvo* (= large amount) *of laughter from the audience.*

SAM /sæm/ *n* [C] *abbreviation for* **surface-to-air missile**, see at SURFACE

sa·mar·i·tan /£səˈmær·ɪ·tᵊn, $-ˈmer·ɪ·t̬ᵊn/ *n* [C] a **good Samaritan**, see at GOOD MORAL RIGHT • *If it wasn't for the assistance of that unknown samaritan, I might still be stuck on the country road.*

Sa·mar·i·tans /£səˈmær·ɪ·tᵊnz, $-ˈmer·ɪ·t̬ᵊnz/ *pl n* **the Samaritans** a British organization you can telephone if you are very worried about something and need to talk to someone

Sa·mar·i·tan /£səˈmær·ɪ·tᵊn, $-ˈmer·ɪ·t̬ᵊn/ *n* [C] • *Working at night as a Samaritan you get many calls from people saying they want to kill themselves.*

sam·ba /ˈsæm·bə/ *n* [C] (music for) an energetic dance originally from Brazil

same EXACTLY LIKE /seɪm/ *adj* [before n; not gradable] exactly like another or each other • *My twin sister and I have got* **the** *same nose,* **the** *same hair, and* **the** *same tastes in clothes.* • *My school reports all said* **the** *same thing – 'could do better'.* • *I was wearing* **exactly the** *same dress* **as** *she was – it was most embarrassing.* • *Hilary's* **the** *same age* **as** *me.* • *Every year, 50 000 books are published in Britain and* **roughly the** *same number in America.* • *He accused her of appalling neglect of the child and suggested that nobody would treat a dog in* **the** *same* **way.** • *Prison governors may be given powers to control their own budgets in* **much** (= approximately) **the** *same* **way** *that head teachers now can.* • *She brought up her children in* **just** (= exactly) **the** *same* **way** *her mother did.* • *Some of them said "We feel* **the** *same* **way** (= like you do), *but what can we do?"* • *I need two more of* **the** *same-***sized** *boxes.* • *They all wore* **the** *same-***coloured** *dresses.* • **By the same token** is used to mean that something you are about to say is also true, for the same reasons as what has just been said: *I don't think that prices will go up really sharply but, by the same token, I don't see them going down much lower either.* • *The family history is a sad one, and I'm afraid that he will* **go the same way** *as his parents* (= the same things will happen to him as to his parents). • **It all amounts/comes to the same thing** means that any of several different actions will all produce the same result: *It doesn't matter whether you do it first or last – it all amounts to the same thing.* • *(infml)* **Same difference** is used when you agree that what you said was not exactly correct, but you think the difference is unimportant: *"Did you see that bus?" "Actually it was a coach." "Same difference."* • Compare SIMILAR.

same /seɪm/ *pronoun* • *We both think* **the** *same – the house is too expensive.* • *People say I look* **just the** *same* **as** *my sister.* • *After all these years you look* **exactly the** *same – you haven't changed a bit.* • *I'm hopeless at physics, and* **it's the same** *with chemistry – I get it all wrong.* • *With the arrival of their first baby they realized that* **life/things** *would* **never be the** *same* **again.** • If something or someone is **never the same again**, they will never be as good as they were before: *That heart attack really shook him – he'll never be the same again.* • If you say that a group of things or people are **all the same**, you mean that they all have a common quality which is usually bad: *Men are all the same* (= all have the same weaknesses). • *It rained every day of our holiday –* **all the same** (= despite this) *we had a good time.* • **If it's all the same to** you, it is not important to you which of several things is chosen: *I don't care whether we go to the Lake District or North Wales – it's all the same to me.* ○ *I'll have tea –* **if it's all the same to you.** • **All the same** is used when you are thanking someone for an offer but want to refuse it politely: *"Do you want to come round for supper?" "No, I won't tonight, but* **thanks** *all the same."* Compare NEVERTHELESS. • *People feel that, whichever party wins the election, its just going to be* **more of the same** (= things are not going to change). • If something is **not the same**, it is not as good: *I went back to our old house – but it wasn't the same* **without** *David.* ○ *You can make shortbread with margarine instead of butter but it isn't the same.* • You say **same again** when you want another drink of the same sort as you have just had: *"What are you having, David?" "Same again, please."* • *(infml)* **Same here** means that you agree with what has been said or you have done the same thing as they have: *"I thought that film was awful!" "Same here!"* ○ *"I've spent all my money!" "Same here!"* • **Same to you** is used as an answer to someone who has greeted or insulted you in order to wish the same thing to them: *"Have* *a good holiday." "Same to you* (= I hope you have a good holiday too)*!"* ○ *"You're a pathetic idiot!" "Same to you!"* ● *She's* **the same as ever** – *I don't believe anything could change her.* ● *(fml)* Same is often used to mean the thing just mentioned when making a calculation of the cost of some work for a customer or when requesting payment for the work: *Estimate for repairs to windows and repainting of same – £300.*

same /seɪm/ *adv not standard* ● *These two machines look different but they're operated* **the** *same* (= in the same way). ● *(infml) I need some time to myself, same* **as** (= like) *anybody else.*

same·ness /ˈseɪm·nəs/ *n* [U] ● *She was struck by the sameness of the houses.* ● *(disapproving) Life in prison gives an experience of routine stifling sameness.*

same·y /ˈseɪ·mi/ *adj Br and Aus infml disapproving* ● *His paintings all look a bit samey* (= uninteresting because they are very similar).

same NOT ANOTHER /seɪm/ *adj* [before n; not gradable] not another different one ● *My brother and I sleep in* **the** *same room.* ● *Our teacher always wears* **the** *same pullover.* ● *Rachel's still going out with* **the** *same boyfriend.* ● *I'd like* **the** *same book* **as** *my friend.* ● *She wore* **the** *same hat* **as** *yesterday.* ● *She wore* **the** *same hat* **(that)** *she'd worn the day before.* ● **That (very)** *same day, he heard he'd passed his exam.* ● *They suggested I quit, but twelve months earlier* **those** *same people had been urging me to stay on.* ● *He's* **the** *same* **old** *Geoff* (= just as he has always been) – *not a bit changed by his move up in the world.* ● *I would do* **the** *same* **thing** *again if I had the chance.* ● *The men both tried to talk* **at the** *same* **time** (= each talked while the other was talking). ● *No-one likes war, but* **at the same time** (= despite this) *we are making money out of it.* ● *(Br) The latest statistics show that sales of new cars are up by 12%* **on the** *same* **time** (= compared with the same period) *last year.* ● To be **in the same boat** is to be in the same usually unpleasant situation: *I've got no money, my friends have got no money – we're all in the same boat.* ● **In the same breath** is used when someone says two things that seem to be opposites: *How can he say he's got no money and in the same breath say he's buying a new car?* ● To be **in the same league**/*(Br also)* **in the same street** is to be of the same standard: *Her golf is brilliant – I'm not in the same league.* ● *At every meeting you see* **the same old faces** (= the same people who come regularly). ● *It's* **the same old story** (= bad things never change) – *the rich get richer and the poor get poorer.* ● *I'll see you next week,* **same time, same place.** ● Things or people that are **one and the same** are not something or someone else: *I was amazed to discover that Mary's husband and Jane's son are one and the same person.* ○ *You're not allowed to be a citizen of the United States and another country at one and the same* **time.**

same /seɪm/ *pronoun* ● *(humorous) "Was that Marion on the phone?"* **"The (very)** *same* (= Yes, it was)." ● Things or people that are **one and the same** are not something or someone else: *Nutrasweet and aspartame are one and the same, but Nutrasweet is a trade name.* ○ *"Did you know Mary had married Julian Roberts?" "Jane Roberts' son?" "One and the same."*

sa·mo·sa /£səˈməʊ·zə, $-ˈmoʊ·sə/ *n* [C] a small Indian triangular pastry case usually filled with vegetables or meat and spices and cooked in deep oil

sam·o·var /£ˈsæm·ə·vɑːʳ, $-vɑːr/ *n* [C] a large metal container used, esp. in Russia, to heat water for tea

sam·pan /ˈsæm·pæn/ *n* [C] a small boat with a flat bottom used along the coasts and rivers of China and SE Asia

sam·ple SMALL AMOUNT /£ˈsɑːm·pl̩, $ˈsæm-/ *n* [C] a small amount of something which shows you, or which can be tested to show you, what the rest is or should be like ● *Please bring some samples* **of** *your work to the interview.* ● *There was a* **free** *sample* **of** *shampoo attached to the front of the magazine.* ● *The nurse said she would* **take** *a* **blood** *sample and* **test** *it.* ● *Olympic athletes often have to* **give** *a* **urine** *sample to prove that they have not been taking drugs.* ● *They were giving away sample* **bottles/jars/sachets** *of the product.* ● *The book contains sample* **questions and answers,** *which will help you to pass the exam.* ● A sample of people or things is a group which is chosen out of a larger number and is questioned or tested in order to obtain information about the larger group : *We talked to a* **random** *sample* **of** *voters* **drawn from** *selected regions of the country.* ○ *The survey was based on a nationally* **representative** *sample* **of** *200 schools.* ● (J)

sam·ple *obj* /£ˈsɑːm·pl̩, $ˈsæm-/ *v* [T] ● *As the food looked so good, he decided to sample* (= take and try) *a little from each dish.* ● *(fig.) So you're going to sample* (= experience) *the* **delights/pleasures** *of the new restaurant?* ● *We sampled* **opinion** *among 600 doctors* (= asked them what they thought in order to know what most doctors might think).

sam·ple *obj* MUSIC /£ˈsɑːm·pl̩, $ˈsæm-/ *v* [T] *specialized* to make a recording of small sections or single parts of existing tunes or songs and use these recordings to make a new piece of music ● *If we sample the snare-drum sound from this Bowie track, I think it would go nicely with the melody we've already got.* ● (J)

sam·pler /£ˈsɑːm·pləʳ, $ˈsæm·plɚ/ *n* [C] *specialized* ● A sampler is a device which allows you to record parts of other people's music and then use these parts to construct different tunes.

sam·pler /£ˈsɑːm·pləʳ, $ˈsæm·plɚ/ *n* [C] a piece of cloth with letters, words, pictures etc. stitched on it to show how well you can sew, made esp. in the past and often hung on the wall like a picture

sam·u·rai /£ˈsæm·ʊ·raɪ, $-ʊr·aɪ/ *n* [C] *pl* **samurai** or **samurais** a member of a military class of high social rank in the 11th to 19th century in Japan ● *a samurai sword* ● *Samurai warriors*

san·a·to·ri·um /£ˌsæn·əˈtɔː·ri·əm, $-ˈtɔːr·i-/, *Am also* **san·i·ta·ri·um** *n* [C] *pl* **sanatoriums** or **sanatoria** /£ˌsæn·əˈtɔː·ri·ə, $-ˈtɔːr·i-/ a special type of hospital, usually in the countryside, where people can have treatment and rest, esp. when getting better after a long illness ● *I had TB and spent several months in a sanatorium in the mountains.*

sanct·i·fy *obj* /£ˈsæŋk·tɪ·faɪ, $-t̬ɪ-/ *v* [T] *fml* to make (an event or place) holy ● *At one time, marriages were always sanctified by the church, but this is not the case now.* ● *Each side in the religious conflict believed that it had been sanctified by the grace of God.* ● *(fig.) This system has been sanctified* **by** *years of practice* (= made acceptable because it has been done for many years). ● See also SANCTITY.

sanct·i·fi·ca·tion /£ˌsæŋk·tɪ·fɪˈkeɪ·ʃən, $-t̬ɪ-/ *n* [U] *fml*

sanct·i·mo·ni·ous /£ˌsæŋk·tɪˈməʊ·ni·əs, $-t̬ɪˈmoʊ-/ *adj fml disapproving* acting as if morally better than others ● *We can do without sanctimonious lectures on the evils of promiscuous sex from government ministers who themselves have fathered illegitimate children.*

sanct·i·mo·ni·ous·ly /£ˌsæŋk·tɪˈməʊ·ni·ə·sli, $-t̬ɪˈmoʊ-/ *adv fml disapproving*

sanct·i·mo·ni·ous·ness /£ˌsæŋk·tɪˈməʊ·ni·ə·snəs, $-t̬ɪˈmoʊ-/ *n* [U] *fml disapproving*

sanc·tion APPROVAL /ˈsæŋk·ʃən/ *n* [U] approval or permission, esp. formal or legal ● *The council refused to* **give** *its sanction* **to** *the building scheme.* ● *He tried to get* **official** *sanction* **for** *his scheme.* ● (T)

sanc·tion *obj* /ˈsæŋk·ʃən/ *v* [T] ● *The government was reluctant to sanction intervention in the crisis.* ● *Slavery was once socially sanctioned* (= generally thought to be acceptable).

sanc·tion PUNISHMENT /ˈsæŋk·ʃən/ *n* [C] a strong action taken in order to make people obey a law, rule or custom, or a punishment given when they disobey ● *Without realistic sanctions, some teachers have difficulty keeping order in the classroom.* ● *They had to resort to the* **ultimate** *sanction of legal action against the company.* ● Sanctions can be actions, such as the stopping of trade, which are taken against a country in order to make it obey international law: *Many nations have* **imposed** *sanctions* **on** *that country because of its attacks on its own people.* ○ **Trade/economic** *sanctions will only be* **lifted** (= stopped) *when the aggressor nation withdraws its troops.* ● **Sanctions-busting** is trading with a country with which trade has been forbidden. ● (T)

sanct·i·ty /£ˈsæŋk·tɪ·ti, $-tə·t̬i/ *n* [U] holiness, or a condition of deserving great respect ● *The claim that supporters of abortion have no respect for the sanctity of* **life.** ● *They believe in the sanctity of marriage – that there should be no sex between people before they are married.*

sanct·u·a·ry /£ˈsæŋk·tʃʊə·ri, $-tʃu·er·i/ *n* protection or a safe place, esp. for someone or something being chased or hunted ● *There will be no sanctuary* **for** *criminals this side of the border.* [U] ● *The illegal immigrants* **found/sought/took** *sanctuary in a local church.* [U] ● *(fig.) If I want some peace and quiet, I* **take** *sanctuary in my study.* [U] ● A sanctuary is a place where birds or animals can live and be protected, esp. from hunters or dangerous conditions: *a* *wildlife/ bird sanctuary* [C] • *(fig.) The island was his sanctuary when he felt the need to escape from the stress of life.* [C]

sanct·um /ˈsæŋk·təm/ *n* **inner sanctum**, see at INNER

sand [SMALL GRAINS] /sænd/ *n* [U] (a mass of) very small grains which used to be rock and which form deserts and some beaches • *a grain of sand* • *coarse/fine sand* • *The children played all day* **in/on** *the sand with their buckets (Am* **sandpails***) and spades.* • Sand is also used in building work: *Lay the slabs for the path on a thick layer of sand.* ○ *They mixed sand and cement to make mortar.* • A **sand dune** is a hill of sand made by the wind on the coast or in a desert: *We looked for a sheltered spot in the sand dunes to do some sunbathing.* • **Sand trap** is *Am for* BUNKER [HOLLOW AREA].

sands /sændz/ *pl n* • *There were miles of* **golden** *sands* (= sand, esp. large flat areas of sand beside the sea). • Sands is also used as part of a name of a bank of sand under the sea which you can see when the water is low: *the Maplin Sands* • *the Goodwin Sands* • *(fml literary)* If you say **the sands of time are running out**, you mean that not much time is left in which to do something.

sand·y /ˈsæn·di/ *adj* **-ier, -iest** • *I prefer a sandy beach to a pebbly one.* • *Carrots grow well in a sandy soil.* • Sandy hair is pale brownish orange in colour.

sand *obj* [MAKE SMOOTH] /sænd/ *v* [T] to make (something) smooth by rubbing it with something rough, esp. SANDPAPER (= strong paper with sand fixed to it) • *The wooden shelves were rather rough so we sanded them.* • *Sand the door* **(down)** *thoroughly before starting to paint.* [T/M] • See also SANDPAPER.

sand·er /£ˈsæn·dəʳ, $-dɚ/, **sand·ing ma·chine** /ˈsæn·dɪŋ·məˌʃiːn/ *n* [C] • A sander is an electrical machine to which a sheet or disc of rough paper is attached with the purpose of rubbing other surfaces in order to make them smoother: *They used a sander to sand the floorboards before varnishing them.*

san·dal /ˈsæn·dᵊl/ *n* [C] a light shoe, esp. worn in warm weather, consisting of a bottom part held onto the foot by straps • *a pair of sandals* • *open-toed sandals* • [PIC] **Shoes**

san·dal·wood /ˈsæn·dᵊl·wʊd/ *n* [U] the hard light-coloured wood of a tree that grows in SE Asia and Australia • *Sandalwood has a pleasant smell and its oil is used in making perfume and soap.*

sand·bag /ˈsæm·bæg/ *n* [C] a bag filled with sand which is used as a defence against flooding, explosions etc. • *When the river started rising we piled sandbags outside the door.*

sand·bag *obj* /ˈsæm·bæg/ *v* [T] **-gg-** • *They sandbagged* (= put sandbags in front of) *the doors to stop the water coming in.*

sand·bank /ˈsæm·bæŋk/ *n* [C] a raised area of sand below the surface of the sea or a river, which you can only see when the water level is low • *They waded out to the sandbank at low tide.*

sand·bar /£ˈsænd·bɑːʳ, $-bɑːr/ *n* [C] a long raised area of sand below the surface of the water, esp. where a river enters the sea, usually formed by moving currents • *Many boats have run aground on the sandbar at the river mouth.*

sand·blast *obj* /£ˈsænd·blɑːst, $-blæst/ *v* [T] to clean or decorate (stone, metal or glass) with a machine that blows sand out at a high speed • *They sandblasted the cathedral and restored the beautiful golden colour of the stone.*

sand·cas·tle /£ˈsændˌkɑː·sḷ, $-ˌkæs·ḷ/ *n* [C] a model castle of sand, usually made by children playing on the beach

sand·man /ˈsænd·mæn/ *n* [U] **the sandman** (used by or to children) an imaginary man who throws sand into children's eyes to make them go to sleep • *The sandman's* **coming** (= It's time to get into bed and go to sleep)*!*

sand·pail /ˈsænd·peɪl/ *n* [C] *Am for* BUCKET

sand·pa·per /£ˈsændˌpeɪ·pəʳ, $-pɚ/ *n* [U] strong paper with sand or a similar rough substance stuck to one side, used for rubbing a surface in order to make it smoother • *coarse/fine sandpaper*

sand·pa·per *obj* /£ˈsændˌpeɪ·pəʳ, $-pɚ/ *v* [T] • *You'll have to sandpaper that door before painting it.*

sand·pit *Br and Aus* /ˈsænd·pɪt/, *Am* **sand·box** /£ˈsænd·bæks, $-bɑːks/ *n* [C] a hole in the ground, or a box, filled with sand in which children can play • [PIC] **Playground**

sand·shoe /ˈsænd·ʃuː/ *n* [C] a light shoe, usually made of cloth, worn esp. on the beach • Sandshoe is also *Aus for* PLIMSOLL.

sand·stone /£ˈsænd·stəʊn, $-stoʊn/ *n* [U] a type of rock formed from sand • *Most houses in the area are built of sandstone.*

sand·storm /£ˈsænd·stɔːm, $-stɔːrm/ *n* [C] a strong wind in a desert carrying a large amount of sand

sand·wich /ˈsæn·wɪdʒ, -wɪtʃ/ *n* [C] two pieces of bread, sometimes spread with butter or MARGARINE, with some other usually cold food between them • *a tuna/ham sandwich* • *Would you like a* **toasted** *sandwich* (= one which is heated until the bread is brown and hard and the food inside is hot)*?* • *(Br) I'll make you* **a round of** *sandwiches* (= sandwiches made from two whole slices of bread, then usually cut into two or four pieces). • *He took his lunch with him in a plastic sandwich* **box**. • *Egg and cress or cheese and tomato are typical sandwich* **fillings**. • *(Br and Aus)* A **sandwich bar** is a small shop where you can buy sandwiches, esp. to eat during the working day. • A **sandwich board** is a pair of connected boards which a person hangs over their shoulders and walks around with in public places to advertise something. • *(Br)* A **sandwich (cake)** consists of two thin round cakes with a filling such as cream between them: *a jam and cream sandwich* ○ *a Victoria sandwich* • *(Br)* A **sandwich course** at a college consists of periods of study with periods of work between them so that students get practical experience.

sand·wich *obj* /ˈsæn·wɪdʒ, -wɪtʃ/ *v* [T always + adv/prep] • To sandwich two things together is to put a layer of something between them which sticks them together: *I sandwiched the cakes together with chocolate butter cream.* • *(infml)* To sandwich one person or thing between others is to fit it in with difficulty: *On the train I was sandwiched between two very large men.* ○ *She managed to sandwich the repairs in between taking the kids to school and starting work.*

sand·y /ˈsæn·dɪ/ *adj* **-ier, -iest** See at SAND [SMALL GRAINS]

sane /seɪn/ *adj* **-r, -st** having a healthy mind and not mentally ill, or showing good judgment and understanding • *In the doctor's opinion he was sane at the time of the murder.* • *(esp. humorous) The only thing which* **keeps** *me sane after a hard day in the office is jogging!* • *She seemed a sane, well-balanced sort of person.* • *It was a sane decision and one we all respected.* • *(esp. humorous) No sane person would want to ride on the back of his motorbike!*

san·i·ty /£ˈsæn·ɪ·ti, $-ə·ṭi/ *n* [U] • *He'd been behaving so strangely that they began to* **doubt/question** *his sanity.* • *Her sanity was in question after the shooting.* • *Maybe Jenny can* **bring some** *sanity* **into** (= think and act with good judgment in) *this crazy situation.* • *We shall continue to hope for* **a return to** *sanity* (= sensible behaviour) *in the housing market.* • *(esp. humorous) It's hard to* **keep/preserve/retain** *your sanity in this madhouse of an office.*

sang /sæŋ/ *past simple of* SING

sang·froid /£ˌsɒ̃ˈfwɑː, $ˌsɑːŋ-/ *n* [U] *fml* ability to stay calm in a difficult or dangerous situation • *She showed great sangfroid in dealing with the panic-stricken victims of the accident.*

sang·ri·a /£ˈsæŋ·gri·ə, $sɑːnˈgriː-/ *n* [U] a cold Spanish drink made from red wine, fruit juice, fizzy water, and sometimes BRANDY (= a strong alcoholic drink)

san·guine /ˈsæŋ·gwɪn/ *adj fml* (of someone or their character) positive and hopeful • *He's sanguine* **about** *getting the work finished on time.* • *Some people are hopeful of a drop in the inflation figures, but others are* **less** *sanguine.* • See also **optimistic** at OPTIMISM.

san·i·ta·ri·um /£ˌsæn·ɪˈteə·ri·əm, $-ˈter·i-/ *n* [C] *pl* **sanitariums** or **sanitaria** /£ˌsæn·ɪˈteə·ri·ə, $-ˈter·i-/ *Am for* SANATORIUM

san·i·ta·ry /£ˈsæn·ɪ·tri, $-ter·i/ *adj* clean and not dangerous for the health, or protecting health by the removal of dirt and waste, esp. human waste • *Cholera thrives in poor sanitary* **conditions**. • *The sanitary* **conditions/facilities** (= toilet arrangements) *were the most primitive imaginable – a bucket which kept overflowing.* • *His kitchen didn't look very sanitary* (= clean). • *(Br)* **Sanitary fittings** *(Am and Aus* **bathroom fittings***)* are the items which are in a bathroom, such as a toilet, bath, etc. • Sanitary also refers to the items which are used by women during their PERIOD (= monthly bleeding): *sanitary protection* ○ *disposable sanitary products* • A *(Br)* **sanitary towel**/*(Am)* **sanitary napkin**/*(Aus)* **sanitary pad** is a soft absorbent paper product worn by a woman between her legs during her PERIOD (= monthly bleeding).

san·i·ta·tion /ˌsæn·ɪˈteɪ·ʃᵊn/ *n* [U] the systems for taking dirty water and other waste products away from buildings in order to protect people's health • *Many illnesses in these* *temporary refugee camps are the result of bad/poor/inadequate sanitation.* • **Sanitation worker** is *Am for* DUSTMAN.

san·i·tize *obj* CLEAN, *Br and Aus usually* **–ise** /ˈsæn·ɪ·taɪz/ *v* [T] *esp. Am* to make completely clean and free from bacteria • *This lavatory has been sanitized for your protection.*

san·i·ti·za·tion, *Br and Aus usually* **–i·sa·tion** /ˌsæn·ɪ·taɪˈzeɪ·ʃᵊn/ *n* [U] *esp. Am*

san·i·tize *obj* CHANGE, *Br and Aus usually* **–ise** /ˈsæn·ɪ·taɪz/ *v* [T] *disapproving* to change (something) in order to make it less strongly expressed, less harmful or less offensive • *Some acts of genocide have been sanitized by calling them 'war', including the aerial bombardment of civilians.* • *The committee was given what one member called a 'sanitized' briefing on the talks between the terrorists and the government.* • *The military wants to allow only a sanitized* **report/version** *of the incident to become public.*

san·i·ti·za·tion, *Br and Aus usually* **–i·sa·tion** /ˌsæn·ɪ·taɪˈzeɪ·ʃᵊn/ *n* [U] *disapproving*

san·i·ty /£ˈsæn·ɪ·tɪ, , $-ə·t̬i/ *n* [U] See at SANE

sank /sæŋk/ *past simple of* SINK

San·ta Claus /£ˈsæn·tə˛klɔːz, $-t̬ə˛klɑːz/, *infml* **San·ta**, *Br also* **Fa·ther Christ·mas** /£ˌfɑː·ðəˈkrɪs·məs, $-ðɚ-/ *n* [not after *the*] the imaginary old man with long white hair and a BEARD and a red coat who is believed by children to bring them presents at Christmas, or a person who dresses as this character for children • *Go to sleep quickly or Santa Claus won't come!* • *(Br)* **Santa's grotto** is a place where children can receive presents from a person dressed as Santa: *They're having a Santa's grotto at the school fair.* ○ *Most of the big stores have a Santa's grotto in the weeks before Christmas.* • LP› **Holidays**

sap *obj* WEAKEN /sæp/ *v* [T] **-pp-** to weaken (someone) or take away (strength) from someone, esp. over a long period of time • *Constant criticism saps you* **of** *all your confidence.* • *Looking after her dying mother sapped all her energy.*

sap·ping /ˈsæp·ɪŋ/ *adj* • *This hot weather is very sapping – it makes me feel tired all the time.*

sap LIQUID /sæp/ *n* [U] liquid that carries food to all parts of a plant • *Maple syrup is obtained from the sap of the sugar maple tree.* • *It was spring, and the sap was* **rising** *in the trees.*

sap PERSON /sæp/ *n* [C] *infml* a stupid person who can easily be tricked or persuaded to do something • *He's a sap for* (= He can easily be persuaded to buy) *any new machine.*

sap·py /ˈsæp·i/ *adj* **-ier**, **-iest** *Am and Aus infml* • If someone is sappy, they are very foolish: *She's so sappy, you could probably convince her the moon is made of green cheese.* • If something is sappy, it is extremely emotional in a rather embarrassing way: *It's a sappy film – take some tissues when you go to see it.*

sap·ling /ˈsæp·lɪŋ/ *n* [C] a young tree

Sap·phic /ˈsæf·ɪk/ *adj* [not gradable] a type of poetry with four lines, which is like that written by Sappho, a poet in Ancient Greece

sap·phire /£ˈsæf·aɪəʳ, $-aɪr/ *n* [C] a transparent, usually bright blue, precious stone • *The necklace was set with diamonds and sapphires.* • *She was given a sapphire ring for her birthday.* • Sapphire also means a bright blue colour: *She has sapphire blue eyes.*

sar·ca·sm /£ˈsɑː·kæz·ᵊm, $ˈsɑːr-/ *n* [U] (the use of) remarks which clearly mean the opposite of what they say, and which are made in order to hurt someone's feelings or to criticize something in an amusing way • *"You have been working hard", he said with* **heavy/biting** *sarcasm, as he looked at the empty page.* • *(saying)* 'Sarcasm is the lowest form of wit' means that sarcasm is the most unkind type of humour. • Compare IRONY FIGURATIVE SPEECH.

sar·cas·tic /£sɑːˈkæs·tɪk, $sɑːr-/, *Br and Aus infml* **sar·ky** (**-ier**, **-iest**) *adj* • *a sarcastic person/comment* • *Are you being sarcastic?* • *She has a sarcastic tongue* (= She is sarcastic).

sar·cas·ti·cal·ly /£sɑːˈkæs·tɪ·kli, $sɑːr-/ *adv* • *"Thanks so much for your help," Tim said sarcastically.*

sar·co·ma /£sɑːˈkəʊ·mə, $sɑːrˈkoʊ-/ *n* [C] *pl* **sarcomas** or *fml* **sarcomata** /£sɑːˈkəʊ·mə·tə, $sɑːrˈkoʊ·mə·t̬ə/ *medical* a CANCER (= uncontrolled and diseased growth of cells) in esp. the bones, muscles and joints • *The main cancer that affects AIDS sufferers is Kaposi's sarcoma.*

sar·coph·a·gus /£sɑːˈkɒf·ə·gəs, $sɑːrˈkɑː·fə-/ *n* [C] *pl* **sarcophaguses** or **sarcophagi** /£sɑːˈkɒf·ə·gaɪ, $sɑːrˈkɑː·fə-/ a stone COFFIN (= box for a dead body), which was used in ancient times and is often decorated • *Archaeologists found a sarcophagus in the burial chamber.*

sar·dine /£sɑːˈdiːn, $sɑːr-/ *n* [C] a small young sea fish which can be eaten • *Sardines can be eaten fresh but are often preserved in oil or tomato sauce in tins.* • If people are **packed/squashed like sardines**, they are positioned very close together so that they cannot move: *We were squashed like sardines in the rush-hour train.* • PIC› **Containers**

sar·don·ic /£sɑːˈdɒn·ɪk, $sɑːrˈdɑː·nɪk/ *adj* showing a lack of respect in a humorous but unkind way, often because you think that you are too important to consider a matter or to talk to a person seriously • *She gave him a sardonic smile/look.* • *His words often had a bitter, sardonic edge to them.*

sar·don·i·cal·ly /£sɑːˈdɒn·ɪ·kli, $sɑːrˈdɑː·nɪ-/ *adv*

sarge /£sɑːdʒ, $sɑːrdʒ/ *n* [C] *infml for* SERGEANT • *I'll be there straight away, sarge.* [as form of address] • *Look out, the sarge is coming!*

sa·ri, **sa·ree** /£ˈsɑː·ri, $ˈsɑːr·i/ *n* [C] a dress, worn esp. by Indian and Pakistani women, consisting of a very long piece of thin cloth wrapped around the body

sar·ky /£ˈsɑː·ki, $ˈsɑːr-/ *adj* **-ier**, **-iest** *Br and Aus infml* **sarcastic**, see at SARCASM • *"That's enough of your sarky comments," she said.*

sar·nie *Br* /£ˈsɑː·ni, $ˈsɑːr-/, *Aus* **sang·er** *n* [C] *infml* a SANDWICH

sa·rong /£səˈrɒŋ, $-ˈrɑːŋ/ *n* [C] a long piece of thin cloth which is worn wrapped around the waist • *The sarong is traditionally worn by Malaysian men and women.* • *People in the West sometimes wear sarongs on the beach.* • *She was wearing a sarong-style skirt.*

sarsa·pa·ril·la /ˌsɑː·spəˈrɪl·ə, ˌsæs·pə-/ *n* [U] a plant with large roots and heart-shaped leaves which climbs up walls, or a drink which is flavoured with the root of this plant • *The dried roots of the sarsaparilla are used to make a drug to treat rheumatism.* • *Would you like a glass of sarsaparilla?*

sar·to·ri·al /£sɑːˈtɔː·ri·əl, $sɑːrˈtɔːr·i-/ *adj* [not gradable] *fml or humorous* relating to the making of clothes, usually men's clothes, or to a way of dressing • *He was renowned for his sartorial elegance.*

SASE /ˌes·eɪˌesˈiː/ *n* [C] *Am abbreviation for* self-addressed stamped envelope (= an envelope which has a stamp on it and the address of the person who sends it) • *Please enclose an SASE with your application.* • Compare SAE.

sash CLOTHING /sæʃ/ *n* [C] a long narrow piece of cloth worn round the waist and fastened at the back, or a strip of cloth worn over the shoulder, which is often worn with a uniform at official ceremonies • *She was wearing a white dress with a red sash.* • *The president was wearing a sash of office.* • Ⓙ

sash WINDOW /sæʃ/ *n* [C] a frame with a piece of glass in it which is used to make windows and doors • A **sash window** is a window which has two frames fixed one above the other that open by being moved up and down on **sash cords** (= ropes with weights at the end). • PIC› **Window** Ⓙ

sash·ay /£ˈsæʃ·eɪ, $-ˈ-/ *v* [I always + adv/prep] to walk smoothly, stylishly and in a way that attracts attention • *She sashayed down the stairs, into the hall.*

sas·quatch /£ˈsæs·kwɒtʃ, $-kwɑːtʃ/ *n* [C] BIGFOOT

sass /sæs/ *n* [U] *esp. Am infml* talk or behaviour which is rude and lacking respect • *You just sit there and shut up – I don't want to hear any more of your sass.*

sass *obj* /sæs/ *v* [T] *esp. Am infml* • *Don't you sass your father like that!*

sas·sy /ˈsæs·i/ *adj* **-ier**, **-iest** *esp. Am infml* • *a sassy young girl* • Sassy can also mean lively, funny and confident: *She has a sassy self-confidence that suggests she has spent her whole life in front of television cameras.* ○ *The company takes pride in its sassy management style.*

Sass·e·nach /ˈsæs·ə·næk/ *n* [C] *pl* **Sassenaches** /ˈsæs·ə·næks/ *Scot Eng esp. disapproving* an English person • *She was invited on a Radio Scotland programme in which, as a Sassenach, she was asked to comment on Anglo/Scottish attitudes.*

sat SIT /sæt/ *past simple and past participle of* SIT

Sat DAY OF THE WEEK *n* [U] *abbreviation for* SATURDAY

SAT IN BRITISH EDUCATION /ˌes·eɪˈtiː/ *n* [C] *Br abbreviation for* Standard Assessment Task (= tests introduced in Britain in 1991 to be taken by children at the ages of 7, 11 and 14) • *The SATs results show great improvement this year.*

SAT [IN US EDUCATION] /ˌes·eɪˈtiː/ *n* [C] *Am trademark abbreviation for* Scholastic Aptitude Test (=test for entry into college)

Sa·tan /ˈseɪ·tᵊn/ *n* [not after *the*] *fml or specialized* the name used by Christians and Jews for **the Devil** (=the originator of evil and the enemy of God)

sa·tan·ic /səˈtæn·ɪk/ *adj* • *a satanic cult/practice/rite* • *It was suggested that some children have recently been the victims of satanic* **abuse** (=cruel treatment by people who worship Satan). • *(fig.) He gave a satanic smile* (=a smile which looked very evil). • *"And was Jerusalem builded here/ Among these dark, satanic mills?"* (from the hymn *Jerusalem* by William Blake, 1804-10)

Sa·tan·i·sm /ˈseɪ·tᵊn·ɪ·zᵊm/ *n* [U] • Satanism is the worship of Satan.

Sa·tan·ist /ˈseɪ·tᵊn·ɪst/ *n* [C] • A Satanist is a person who worships Satan.

sat·chel /ˈsætʃ·ᵊl/ *n* [C] a rectangular bag with a long strap, which is used for carrying books • *Children often carry their books to school in satchels.* • PIC› **Bags**

sate·d /£ˈseɪ·tɪd, $-t̬ɪd/ *adj* [not gradable] *fml* having had more of something than you can easily have at one time • *He fell onto his bed, sated* **with** *drink.*

sat·el·lite /£ˈsæt·ᵊl·aɪt, $ˈsæt̬-/ *n* [C] a natural object moving round a larger object in space, or an artificial object sent up into space to travel round the earth • *The moon is the satellite of the Earth.* • *The World Cup was transmitted around the world* **by** *satellite.* • *Satellite communication is widely used nowadays.* • A country can use **spy** satellites to collect information about other countries, esp. its enemies. • **Weather** satellites are used to collect information about the weather. • A **satellite dish** is an object fixed in place outside a house or building to receive the signals for **satellite television** (=television broadcast over long distances using a satellite) or to receive other signals from satellites. • A **satellite state** is a country controlled by or dependent on a more powerful country. See also **client state** at CLIENT. • PIC› **Accommodation, Energy**

sat·i /ˈsæt·iː/, **sut·tee** *n* [U] the Hindu custom, which is no longer legal, of a woman being burnt alive in the same fire as that in which her dead husband's body is burnt

sa·ti·ate *obj* /ˈseɪ·ʃi·eɪt/ *v* [T usually passive] *fml* to completely satisfy (yourself or your needs), esp. with food or pleasure, so that you could not have any more • *He drank greedily until his thirst was satiated.* • *The company can hardly produce enough of these toys to satiate public demand.*

sat·in /£ˈsæt·ɪn, $ˈsæt̬·ᵊn/ *n* [U] a type of cloth, sometimes made of silk, which is shiny on one side but not on the other • *She wore a cream satin dress.* • **Satin (finish)** paint is paint which is slightly shiny when it dries: *Did you use matt or satin finish paint for the walls?* • *"Nights in White Satin"* (title of a song by The Moody Blues, 1967)

sat·in·y /£ˈsæt·ɪ·ni, $ˈsæt̬·ᵊn·i/ *adj* • Something that is satiny is smooth and soft: *She has satiny skin like a child.*

sat·ire /£ˈsæt·aɪəʳ, $-aɪr/ *n* a way of criticizing people or ideas in a humorous way to show that they have faults or are wrong, or a piece of writing or play which uses this style • *George Orwell's 'Animal Farm' is a work of* **political** *satire.* [U] • *Her play was a* **biting/cruel** *satire on life in the 80s.* [C]

sa·ti·ri·cal /səˈtɪr·ɪ·kᵊl/ *adj* • *'Private Eye' is a British satirical magazine which makes fun of contemporary public figures.*

sat·i·rist /£ˈsæt·ɪ·rɪst, $ˈsæt̬·ɚ·ɪst/ *n* [C] • A satirist is a person who writes satire: *Voltaire was a famous French satirist.*

sat·i·rize *obj, Br and Aus usually* **-ise** /£ˈsæt·ɪ·raɪz, $ˈsæt̬·ə·raɪz/ *v* [T] • *'Spitting Image' is a British television programme which satirizes the political events of the past week.*

sat·is·fac·tion /£ˌsæt·ɪˈsfæk·ʃᵊn, $ˌsæt̬-/ *n* the pleasant feeling you get when you receive something you wanted, or when you have done or are doing something you wanted to do • *She looked at the finished painting* **with** *satisfaction.* [U] • *She derived/obtained great satisfaction* **from/out of** *watching her children gradually become independent.* [U] • *I did it* **just for** *the satisfaction* **of** *seeing him smile.* [U] • *She* **had** *the satisfaction* **of** *being the first British woman to go into space.* [U] • *We aim to* **give** *full satisfaction to all our customers.* [U] • *Do you get* **job** *satisfaction from your work?* [U] • *Nursing may be difficult, but it does* **have its** *satisfactions* (=things that make it worth doing). [C] • *(fml) You have sold me a faulty product and I* **demand** *satisfaction* (=you must return my money or give me a new product). [U] • *The boy explained* **to the** *satisfaction* **of** *the court why he had lied* (=They completely believed his explanation). [U] • *"I can't get no satisfaction"* (the Rolling Stones, from the song *Satisfaction*, 1965)

sat·is·fac·to·ry /£ˌsæt·ɪˈsfæk·tᵊr·i, $ˌsæt̬·ɪˈsfæk·tɚ-/ *adj* good or good enough for a particular need or purpose • *The teachers said his work was satisfactory but there was still room for improvement.* • *We are hoping there will soon be a satisfactory end to the crisis.* • *The result of the match was* **highly** *satisfactory* (=very pleasing).

sat·is·fac·to·ri·ly /£ˌsæt·ɪˈsfæk·tᵊr·ᵊl·i, $ˌsæt̬·ɪˈsfæk·tɚ-/ *adv* • *The central heating system is working satisfactorily.* • *I'm sure these problems can be satisfactorily resolved.*

sat·is·fy *obj* /£ˈsæt·ɪˈsfaɪ, $ˈsæt̬-/ *v* [T not *be satisfying*] to please (someone) by giving them what they want or need • *Why are some people never satisfied?* • *I offered him $10 000 to keep quiet, but that didn't satisfy him and he wanted even more.* • *Many countries cannot satisfy the* **needs** *of* (=provide what is necessary for) *their people.* • *She satisfied the court* (=The court believed) **that** *she was innocent.* [+ obj + *that* clause] • *(fml) The authorities were satisfied* **of**/ *satisfied* **as to** (=they accepted) *the seriousness of his situation.* • *Come on, satisfy my* **curiosity** (=tell me what I want to know), *tell me when your wedding is!* • If you satisfy the **requirements** for something, you are considered suitable enough for it or you have the qualifications necessary for it: *She satisfied the entrance requirements for the college and was accepted as a student.* ○ *There are three main conditions you must satisfy if you wish to be a member of this club.* • *(Br fml)* To **satisfy the examiners** means to pass an examination.

sat·is·fied /£ˈsæt·ɪ·sfaɪd, $ˈsæt̬-/ *adj* • *When she had finished her meal, she gave a satisfied smile.* • *I am not fully satisfied* **with** *the standard of your work.* • *Rachel is always asking for more clothes – she's never satisfied* **with** *what she's got.*

sat·is·fy·ing /£ˈsæt·ɪ·sfaɪ·ɪŋ, $ˈsæt̬-/ *adj* • Something that is satisfying gives pleasure: *The election produced a satisfying result for us.* ○ *It's an immensely satisfying job.* ○ *Potatoes are a satisfying food – they make you feel full.* ○ *He had the satisfying* **experience** *of beating her in the match.* ○ **It** *is very satisfying* **to** *know that we were the ones who brought Sarah and Stephen together.* [+ *to* infinitive]

sat·su·ma /£ˌsætˈsuː·mə, $ˈsæt·sə·mɑː/ *n* [C] *Br and Am* a fruit like a small orange with skin that can be removed easily • *(Aus)* A **satsuma plum** is a small round fruit with a thin smooth dark red skin, sweet soft flesh, and a single large hard seed in the middle. • PIC› **Fruit**

sat·u·rate *obj* /£ˈsæt·jʊ·reɪt, $-jʊr·eɪt/ *v* [T often passive] to make (something or someone) completely wet • *The grass has been saturated by overnight rain.* • *He had cut his leg badly, and his trousers were saturated* **with/in** *blood.* • To saturate a thing or place is to fill it completely so that no more can be added: *A major accident in this area could saturate medical facilities.* ○ *The police saturated* (=A large number of police officers were sent into) *the area in an attempt to find the missing child.* • When a **market** is saturated, so many people have bought a product that there are not enough people left to sell the product to: *Since the US market has now been saturated, the drug dealers are looking to Europe.*

sat·u·rat·ed /£ˈsæt·jʊ·reɪ·tɪd, $-jʊr·eɪ·t̬ɪd/ *adj* • *It's pouring down outside – I'm absolutely saturated* (=completely wet)*!* • A saturated **fat** or **oil** contains particular types of chemicals which are thought to be unhealthy: *Butter and cream contain a lot of saturated fats.* ○ See also POLYUNSATURATED. • *(specialized)* In chemistry, a **saturated solution** is a SOLUTION (=a liquid containing a solid) in which as much solid as possible is dissolved.

sat·u·ra·tion /£ˌsæt·jʊˈreɪ·ʃᵊn, $-jʊrˈeɪ-/ *n* [U] • If something reaches **saturation point**, it reaches a stage where no more can be added, contained or accepted: *Households have* **reached** *saturation point in the number of magazines they are prepared to buy.* ○ *Demand for cars in the developed world will have* **reached** *saturation point within 20 years.* • *After six hours of* **saturation bombing** (=extremely severe military attack), *no building in the city remained standing.*

Sat·ur·day /£ˈsæt·ə·deɪ, $ˈsæt̬·ɚ-/ (*abbreviation* **Sat**) *n* the day of the week after Friday and before Sunday • *Saturday morning/afternoon/evening* • *"What's today?"*

Satur Saturday." [U] • *Ben is going to London* **on** *Saturday.* [U] • *(infml) He's leaving Saturday* (= on Saturday). [U] • *I hate Saturdays – they're always so busy in our house.* [C] • *Most football matches are played* **on** *Saturdays.* [C] • *Joel was born on* **a** *Saturday.* [C] • *We had a party* **last** *Saturday.* [U] • *Would you like to come to dinner* **next** *Saturday?* [U] • *We've got to visit my parents next weekend, but we're free* **the following** *two Saturdays.* [C] • *Rachel passed her driving test on the Wednesday and crashed our car on* **the** *Saturday* (= on the Saturday of that particular week). [C] • *I can't come* **this** *Saturday* (= the first one from now), *but I am free (Br and Aus) Saturday* **week** (= the second one from now). [U] • *(Br)* Saturday **staff** are people who work in a shop only on Saturdays. • *(Am infml)* A **Saturday night special** is a type of small gun. • *"Saturday Night Fever"* (title of a film, 1977) • LP› **Calendar**

Sat·urn /£'sæt·ən, $'sæţ·ɚn/ *n* [U not after *the*] the planet sixth in order of distance from the Sun, after Jupiter and before Uranus • *Saturn is large and has rings around it.*

Sat·ur·na·li·a /£ˌsæt·ə'neɪ·li·ə, $ˌsæţ·ɚ-/ *n* [C] *pl* **Saturnalia** or **Saturnalias** an ancient Roman celebration which happened in December, or *(literary)* a party where people behave in an uncontrolled way

sat·ur·nine /£'sæt·ə·naɪn, $'sæţ·ɚ-/ *adj literary* serious and unfriendly • *a saturnine character/look/frown*

sat·yr /£'sæt·əʳ, $'sæţ·ɚ/ *n* [C] a god in Greek literature who is half man and half goat

sauce THICK LIQUID /£sɔːs, $sɑːs/ *n* a thick liquid eaten with food to add flavour • *a savoury/sweet sauce* [C] • *A well-flavoured sauce can improve an ordinary meal.* [C] • *He puts tomato sauce on everything he eats.* [U] • *(Am slang)* Sauce is also alcohol: *Bukowski had been hitting the sauce very hard* (= drinking a lot of alcohol). [U] • *(saying)* 'What's sauce for the goose is sauce for the gander' means if one person is allowed to behave in a particular way, then another person can behave in that way too. • Ⓓ Ⓕ Ⓝⓛ

sauce RUDENESS /£sɔːs, $sɑːs/ *n* [U] *dated* remarks which are rude or which lack respect • *That's enough of your sauce, my girl!* • *What* **a** *sauce, telling me I'm getting fat.* • Ⓓ Ⓕ Ⓝⓛ

sau·cy /£'sɔː·si, $'sɑː-/ *adj* **-ier, -iest** *dated* Saucy means rude and lacking respect, or referring to sex, esp. in a humorous way: *a saucy remark/manner/look* ○ *a saucy postcard/magazine* • *(Br)* Saucy **underwear** is underwear that shows more of the body than is usual.

sauce·pan /£'sɔː·spən, $'sɑː-/ *n* [C] a deep round pan with straight sides, usually with a handle and a lid, used for cooking things over heat • *Guy has just bought a* **set** *of green saucepans.* • PIC› **Containers, Coverings, Pan**

sau·cer /£'sɔː·səʳ, $'sɑː·sɚ/ *n* [C] a small curved plate which you put a cup on • *a cup and saucer* • *She gave the cat a saucer* **of** *milk* (= a small amount of milk on a saucer).

sau·er·kraut /£'saʊə·kraʊt, $'saʊr-/ *n* [U] CABBAGE (= a large round leafy vegetable) which has been cut into small pieces and preserved in vinegar

sau·na /£'sɔː·nə, $'saʊ-/ *n* [C] (a period of time spent in) a room or small building, often with wood fixed to the walls, which is heated to a high temperature, usually with steam • *I* **went for/had** *a sauna this morning, so now I feel really relaxed.*

saun·ter /£'sɔːn·təʳ, $'sɑːn·ţɚ/ *v* [I always + adv/prep] to walk in a slow and relaxed way, often in no particular direction • *He sauntered* **by**, *looking very pleased with himself.*

saun·ter /£'sɔːn·təʳ, $'sɑːn·ţɚ/ *n* [C usually sing] • *Let's go for a saunter along the river.*

sau·sage /£'sɒs·ɪdʒ, $'sɑː·sɪdʒ/ *n* a thin tube-like case containing meat which has been cut into very small pieces and, mixed with spices and sometimes bread • *Sausages are usually made from pork or beef.* [C] • *Some sausages are raw and must be cooked, while others are already cooked and are eaten cold.* [C] • *Do you prefer fried or grilled sausages?* [C] • *I'll have sausage, egg and chips, please.* [U] • *Could I have half a pound of garlic sausage, please.* [U] • *(Br humorous dated)* **Not a sausage** means nothing: *"Did you find anything out?" "No, not a sausage."* • *(Br infml)* A **sausage dog** is a DACHSHUND (= a small dog with a long body and short legs). • *(Br) That school's just a* **sausage machine** (= They deal with children as if they were all the same, like products in a factory). • **Sausage meat** is the meat mixture used to make sausages. • *(Br and Aus)* A **sausage roll** consists of a pastry case filled with **sausage meat**.

sau·té *obj* /£'səʊ·teɪ, $soʊ'teɪ/ *v* [T] *past* **sautéd** /£'səʊ·teɪd, $soʊ'teɪd/ or **sautéed** /£'səʊ·teɪd, $soʊ'teɪd/ to cook (food) in oil or fat over heat, usually until it is brown • *Sauté the meat for a few minutes over a medium heat before adding the wine.*

sau·té /£'səʊ·teɪ, $soʊ'teɪ/ *adj* [before n; not gradable] • *The chicken was served with sauté* **potatoes** *and green beans.*

sav·age /'sæv·ɪdʒ/ *adj* (of an animal) wild and fierce, or (of a remark or action) violently cruel • *a savage dog/wolf* • *savage criticism/anger/remarks* • *It was a particularly brutal and savage* **attack**. • *He made a savage* **attack** *on the policies of the government.* • Savage also means very large: *The savage* **cuts** *in education spending will mean bigger classes and fewer books.* • Ⓕ

sav·age *obj* /'sæv·ɪdʒ/ *v* [T] • If an animal savages someone, it attacks them violently and badly hurts them: *The child was savaged by a dog.*

sav·age /'sæv·ɪdʒ/ *n* [C] • Savages are people whose way of life is at a very early stage of development. This word is considered offensive by most people: *Twelve thousand years ago, your ancestors were primitive savages living in caves.* ○ *(humorous) My two-year-old daughter is a real little savage* (= Her behaviour is very bad)*!*

sav·age·ly /'sæv·ɪdʒ·li/ *adv* • Savagely means violently or in a cruel way: *She was savagely murdered at the age of 22.* ○ *"What do you want?" he demanded savagely.*

sav·ag·e·ry /'sæv·ɪdʒ·ri/ *n* • Savagery is violent cruelty: *The prisoners were treated with great savagery by the secret police.* [U] ○ *The savagery in his voice made her step back in terror.* [U] ○ *Savageries* (= Acts of violent cruelty) *like this massacre make you ashamed to be a human being.* [C]

sa·van·nah, sa·van·na /sə'væn·ə/ *n* [C/U] a large flat area of grassy land, usually with few trees, which is found in hot countries, esp. in Africa

save *obj* MAKE SAFE /seɪv/ *v* [T] to make or keep (someone or something) safe from danger or harm • *Wearing seat belts has saved many lives.* • *Her leg was badly crushed in the accident but the surgeons were able to save it.* • *He fell in the river but his friend saved him* **from** *drowning.* • *She needs saving* **from herself** (= protecting from the results of her own stupid actions). • *We tried to save our* **marriage** (= continue our relationship), *but in the end we decided we couldn't live together.* • *It was an exciting point in the tennis match, and the former champion was serving to save the* **match** (= to win the next point so that the other player did not win the competition). • To save someone is also to help them escape from a difficult or unpleasant situation: *Thanks for helping me with that report – you saved my* **life** (= helped me when I was in a very difficult situation)*!* ○ *(infml) You* **saved** *my* **bacon/neck** (= helped me avoid getting into trouble)*!* • If someone **saves the day/situation**, they act in a way which makes a bad situation better: *The business was heading for financial disaster but the arrival of an excellent new manager saved the situation.* • If you **save** your **own skin/hide**, you protect yourself from danger or difficulty, without worrying too much about other people. • *(infml) "Can you cook?"* **"Not to save** *my* **life** (= No)*!"* • *The film's* **(only/one) saving grace** (= the one thing that stops it being completely bad) *is the photography.*

save *(obj)* KEEP /seɪv/ *v* to keep (something, esp. money) for use in the future • *I've been saving for almost a year and I've got nearly $900 in the bank.* [I] • *I save all my old letters in case I want to read them again.* [T] • *Some people save postage stamps or milk bottle tops and give them to charities who sell them to make money.* [T] • *Save me a place at your table, will you?* [T] • *She's saving* **(up) for** *a new bike.* [I] • *I save* **with** (= I keep my money in) *the Cooperative Bank.* [I] • *(specialized)* To save information on a computer is to put it onto a computer disc: *I forgot to save the work I did on the computer this morning.* [T]

save·r /£'seɪ·vəʳ, $-vɚ/ *n* [C] • A saver is a person who saves money regularly: *Savers will be pleased about the rise in interest rates.*

sa·vings /'seɪ·vɪŋz/ *pl n* • Your savings is the money which you keep in an account in a bank or similar financial organization: *He spent all his savings on an expensive car.* • A **savings account** is an account in a bank or similar financial organization which earns INTEREST (= profit obtained from investing money with a financial organization). See also **current account** at CURRENT NOW. • **Savings and loan association** is *Am for* **building society**. See at BUILDING. • A **savings bank** is a bank which only offers accounts where your money earns INTEREST. • LP Money

save *(obj)* NOT WASTE /seɪv/ *v* to prevent (time, money or effort) being wasted or spent • *You'll save time if you take the car.* [T] • *Thanks for your help – it saved me a lot of work/saved a lot of work* **for** *me.* [+ two objects] • *The tax changes save me £9 a week/save £9 a week* **for** *me.* [+ two objects] • *I'll lend you a bag for your trip – it'll save you* **buying** *one specially.* [+ obj + v-*ing*] • *I'll lend you a bag for your trip – it'll save you* **from buying** *one specially.* [I] • *It was a warm winter, so we saved* **on** *electricity.* [I] • *He's saving himself* (= keeping his strength) **for** *the big match.* [T] • *(humorous) She's saving herself for the right man* (= waiting to find the perfect man before having a sexual relationship). [T] • *(infml) Can you save* **it** *for later* (= tell me your news later when I am less busy)*?* [T] • *(infml)* If you **save your breath**, you do not talk to someone because you know that they will not listen to you: *I don't know why I bother speaking to him – I might as well save my breath.*

-sav·er /£-ˌseɪ·vəʳ, $-vɚ/ *combining form* • A -saver is something that makes it possible for you to use less of the stated thing: *A washing machine is a time-saver.* ○ *That special offer is a money-saver.*

-sav·ing /-ˌseɪ·vɪŋ/ *combining form* • -saving means making it possible to use less of the stated thing: *a time-saving recipe* ○ *a money-saving offer* ○ *a labour-saving device*

sav·ing /ˈseɪ·vɪŋ/ *n* [C] • *You can* **make** *huge savings* (= save a lot of money) *by buying food in bulk.*

save *obj* SPORT /seɪv/ *v* [T] (esp. in football) to stop (the ball) from going into the goal when a player on the other team has kicked or hit it • *Schmeichel managed to save the penalty.*

save /seɪv/ *n* [C] • *The goalkeeper* **made** *a great save in the last minute of the match.*

save EXCEPT /seɪv/, **save for** *prep fml or dated* but or except (for) • *They found all the lost documents save one.*

sa·vi·our *Br and Aus, Am and Aus* **sa·vi·or** /£ˈseɪ·vjəʳ, $-vjɚ/ *n* [C] a person who saves someone from danger or harm • *They regarded him as the saviour* **of** *their country.*

sav·oir–faire /£ˌsæv·wɑːˈfeəʳ, $-ˈfer/ *n* [U] *fml* the ability to do and say the right thing in any social situation • *She possesses* **great** *savoir-faire.* • *He is a man of* **great** *savoir-faire.*

sa·vour *obj Br and Aus, Am and Aus* **sa·vor** /£ˈseɪ·vəʳ, $-vɚ/ *v* [T] to enjoy (food or an experience) slowly, in order to appreciate it as much as possible • *It was the first chocolate he'd tasted for over a year, so he savoured every mouthful.* • *It's the first day of the holidays, so I'm savouring my freedom.*

sa·vour *Br and Aus, Am and Aus* **sa·vor** /£ˈseɪ·vəʳ, $-vɚ/ *n* [U] • *She felt that life had lost most of its savour* (= pleasure and interest).

sa·vour of *obj Br and Aus, Am and Aus* **sa·vor of** *v prep* [T no passive] to possess particular characteristics or qualities that make people think of (something unpleasant) • *His behaviour savours of hypocrisy.*

sa·vou·ry *Br and Aus, Am and Aus* **sa·vo·ry** /£ˈseɪ·vᵊr·i, $-vɚ-/ *adj* (of food) salty or spicy and not sweet in taste • *savoury dumplings/pancakes* • *Do you prefer sweet or savoury food?* • If you say that something is not savoury, you mean that it is not pleasant or socially acceptable: *That hotel doesn't have a very savoury* **reputation**.

sa·voy /səˈvɔɪ/ *n* [C] a type of CABBAGE (= large round leafy vegetable) with curly leaves

sav·vy /ˈsæv·i/ *n* [U] *infml* practical knowledge and ability • *She's got a lot of savvy.* • *She hasn't got much savvy.* • *He decided to apply some business savvy to the situation.* • *She will need all the political savvy she can muster to win the next election.*

saw SEE /£sɔː, $sɑː/ *past simple of* SEE

saw TOOL /£sɔː, $sɑː/ *n* [C] a tool with a long or round blade and a row of sharp points along one edge, which is used for cutting hard materials, such as wood or metal • *a hand/power/chain/circular saw* • See also FRETSAW; HACKSAW; JIGSAW. • PIC Tools

saw *(obj)* /£sɔː, $sɑː/ *v past simple* **sawed**, *past part* **sawn** /£sɔːn, $sɑːn/ *or esp. Am* **sawed** • *She spent the morning sawing* (= cutting with a saw). [I] • *I sawed* **off** *the dead branches of the tree.* [M] • *I'll saw the logs* **up** *into smaller pieces.* [M] • *We'll have to saw that tree* **down** (= cut it down). [M] • To saw also means to play a musical instrument badly, as though you were playing it with a saw: *He was sawing* **away** *at his violin, making a terrible noise!* [I]

sawn–off /£ˌsɔːnˈɒf, $ˌsɑːnˈɑːf/, *Am also* **sawed–off** /£ˌsɔːdˈɒf, $ˌsɑːdˈɑːf/ *adj* [before n; not gradable] • A **sawn-off shotgun** is a gun with most of the BARREL (= the long part of the gun shaped like a tube) cut off: *Sawn-off shotguns are sometimes carried by criminals because they are easier to hide than normal shotguns.*

saw·dust /£ˈsɔː·dʌst, $ˈsɑː-/ *n* [U] the dust and small pieces of wood which are produced when you cut wood with a SAW

saw·mill /£ˈsɔː·mɪl, $ˈsɑː-/ *n* [C] a factory where trees are cut up into pieces with machines

sax /sæks/ *n* [C] *infml for* SAXOPHONE • *She plays* **alto/tenor** *sax.* • *Charlie Bird Parker was a famous sax* **player**. • Ⓢ

Sax·on /ˈsæk·sᵊn/ *adj* [not gradable] relating to or belonging to a people who were originally from Germany and who came to live in Britain in the fifth and sixth centuries

sax·o·phone /£ˈsæk·sə·fəʊn, $-foʊn/, *infml* **sax** *n* [C] a musical instrument made of metal which is curved at the bottom, and which is played by blowing through a REED (= a thin piece of wood) and pressing the metal keys to produce notes • *The saxophone is used mainly in jazz and dance music.* • *He plays the saxophone in a jazz band.* • PIC Musical instruments

sax·o·phon·ist /£sækˈsɒf·ᵊn·ɪst, $-ˈsɑː·fᵊn-/, *infml* **sax play·er** *n* [C] • *We've got two saxophonists in our dance band.*

say *(obj)* SPEAK /seɪ/ *v past* **said** /sed/ to pronounce (words or sounds), to express (a thought, opinion, or suggestion), or to state (a fact or instruction) • *Small children find it difficult to say long words.* [T] • *How do you say your name in Japanese?* [T] • *"How do you say 'goodbye' in French?" "Au revoir."* [T] • *Ben never forgets to say "Please" and "Thank you".* [T] • *I'm sorry, what did you say?* [T] • *What did you say* **to** *him?* [T] • *What did they say* **about** *the house?* [T] • *"I'm going shopping," she said. "Do you want to come?"* [+ clause] • *I talked to my boss and said* **(that)** *I needed some time off.* [+ (*that*) clause] • *Experts say* **that** *restoring the country's water supply will take three more weeks.* [+ *that* clause] • *I've got* **something** *to say to you.* [T] • *"Do you have* **anything** *to say?" the judge asked, turning to the accused.* [T] • **Nothing you can** *say will make me stay.* [T] • *I seem to have* **nothing** *to say to him nowadays – we're like strangers.* [T] • *"I've* **nothing more** *to say," he insisted.* [T] • *If you've got* **nothing better** *to say, then keep quiet.* [T] • *She said* **goodbye** *to all her friends and left.* [T] • *(fig.) If Europe fails to agree on this, we can say goodbye to* (= give up hope of) *any common foreign policy.* [T] • *Did you say* **yes** *to* (= accept) *her invitation?* [T] • *The offer was so good that I couldn't say* **no** (= refuse). [T] • *(infml) "Would you like another drink?"* **"I wouldn't say no** (= I would like one).*"* • Say can be used to mean think or believe: *People/They say* **(that)** *he's over 100.* [+ (*that*) clause] ○ **It** *is said* **(that)** *he's over 100.* [+ (*that*) clause] ○ *He's said* **to** *be over 100.* [+ *to* infinitive] ○ *"It's going to be a very hot summer."* **"So** *they say* (= That is what people believe).*"* [+ *so*] ○ *"Is Spanish a difficult language to learn?" "They say* **not** (= People believe it is not difficult).*"* [+ *not*] ○ *She is a firm leader, too firm* **some might** *say* (= some people believe that she is too severe). [I] • *"Is it possible?"* **"Who can** *say?* (= No one knows.)*"* [I] • *"Who do you think will get the job?" "I'd rather not say* (= express an opinion).*"* [I] • *I think we should tell him –* **what do** *you say* (= what is your opinion)*?* [T] • *What are you saying, exactly* (= What do you mean)*?* [T] • *What do you think the artist is trying to say* (= What ideas is he/she trying to express) *in this painting?* [T] • *The look on his face said* (= showed) **(that)** *he knew what had happened.* [+ (*that*) clause] • *What would/do you say* **to** (= Would you like) *a trip to the seaside?* [T] • *(infml) What do you say we* (= What do you think about the idea that we should) *sell the car?* [T] • *We've been driving all day – I say* (= I suggest) **(that)** *we start looking for a hotel now.* [+ (*that*) clause] • *Try and finish the work by,* **let's** *say* (= I suggest), *Friday.* [T] • *Say/***Let's** *say* (= If we accept) **(that)** *the journey takes three hours, that means you'll arrive at 2 o'clock.* [+ (*that*) clause] • *Take any writer, say* (= for example) *Thomas Hardy, and study the way they portray the emotions of the main character.* [T] • *Please don't say anything* **against** *him* (= criticize him or say unpleasant things about him) *to my father.* [T] • *"Where was he going?" "He didn't say* (= He did not tell me).*"* [I] • *(infml) He said* (= told me) **to** *meet him here.* [+ *to* infinitive] • *(infml) Did she say* (= tell you) **where** *to meet her?* [+ *wh-* word] • *Did she say* (= tell you) **why** *she wasn't coming?* [+ *wh-* word] • *"Why can't I go out to play?"*

SAY, TELL, TALK AND SPEAK

Examples	Use	say	tell	talk	speak
"Hello," she said, "I'm Mavis. I work here." *"I'm Mavis. I work here," she told him.*	direct speech	•	•		
She said **that** *her name was Mavis.* *She said* **where** *she worked.* *She told him* **that** *her name was Mavis.* *She told him* **where** *she worked.*	reported speech (with 'tell' the listener is usually mentioned)	•	•		
My daughter is learning to talk/speak. *There were a couple of men talking.*	used without an object ('speak' is more formal than 'talk')			•	•
I can speak Spanish. *They were talking* **(in)** *French.*	used with languages			•	•
He told me **about** *his trip to Mexico.* *We talked* **about** *the future.* *He spoke* **of** *his plans for the company.*	used with 'about' and 'of' ('of' is more formal)		•	•	•
Say something **to** *him. Talk/speak* **to** *me.* *(esp. Am)Can I speak* **with** *Andy, please?*	used with 'to'	•		•	•
The sign said **that** *the road was closed.* *The label told us nothing about the contents.*	used to mean 'give information'	•	•		
It is said **(that)** *she earns £100,000.* *She is said* **to** *earn £100,000.* *We were told* **(that)** *she earns £100,000.*	used in passive sentences	•	•		
Then I said, "How do you know?"	used with questions*	•			
"Good grief!" he said, "You nearly killed me."	used with exclamations	•			
"Be careful with those boxes!" said Morris. *"Be careful with those boxes!" Morris told me.*	used with orders	•	•		
Morris told me **to** *be careful with the boxes.* *I was told* **to** *be careful with the boxes.*	other common patterns of 'tell'				

Some common phrases	
	He said yes (=agreed). *They said no* (=refused). *Tell (someone) the truth/a lie. Tell (someone) a story/a joke.* *They're talking nonsense. They never talk sense.*

* The common verb used with questions is 'ask'. This is similar to 'tell' – but notice it is not used in the pattern *tell someone* **that**... [+ obj + *that* clause]

"Because I say **so** (=Because I am telling you that you cannot)!*"* [+ *so*] • *She said little* **of** (=gave little information about) *her family history.* [T] • 'Who shall I say is calling?' is used by people in business when asking the name of a telephone caller or visitor. [+ *wh-* word] • If you say a formal set of words such as a prayer, you speak them aloud: *Let's say grace.* [T] ○ *Say your prayers, then get into bed.* [T] ○ *If you want to be an actor, you'll have to learn to say your lines with a lot of expression.* [T] • If you say something **to yourself**, you think it: *Then she said to herself, "What a fool I am!"* [+ clause] • *(dated)* **Before you can/could say Jack Robinson** means very quickly: *Before you could say Jack Robinson, she'd jumped into the car and driven away.* • *(disapproving)* If you **have a lot to say for** yourself, you talk too much and seem to have a high opinion of yourself. • If you **have nothing to say for yourself**, it means that you are not very willing to take part in conversations or express your opinions. • *Well, you've ruined my car –* **what have you got to say for** *yourself* (=what excuse are you going to give)? • *He forgets most things, but* **having said that** (=despite what I say), *he always remembers my birthday.* • **I'll say** is used to show that you agree very strongly with what has been said: *"Does he eat a lot?" "I'll say!"* • **I must say** (=I must admit), *I don't think much of her dress.* • *Of course,* **it goes without saying** (=it is obvious) **that** *you'll be paid for the extra hours you work.* • **It says a lot for** *her determination* (=It shows how determined she is) *that she practises her cello so often.* • If someone will *(Br and Aus)* **not say boo to a goose**/*(Am)* **not say boo**, they are very shy and nervous. • *It would be unwise,* **not to say** (=and possibly even) *stupid, to leave your first job after only six months.* • **Say no more** is used to show that you understand exactly what the other person is suggesting: *"I saw him coming out of her flat." "Say no more!"* • *Just* **say** *your* **piece** (=say what you are obviously wanting to say) *and then go.* • *The way he drives* **says something/a lot about** *his character* (=shows what his character is like). • *(Am)* To **say uncle** means to admit failure. • **Say what you like** (=Even if you disagree with me), *I still can't believe she would do a thing like that.* • You can say **say when** when you are pouring a drink for someone and you want them to tell you when to stop pouring. • *You only have to/Just* **say the word**, *and I'll come and help* (=You only have to ask me to do something and I will do it willingly). • **Says you/Says who?** is used to show that you do not believe what someone has just said: *"I'm certain to win." "Says you!"* • *Our friends,* **that is to say** (=or more exactly) *our son's friends, will meet us at the airport.* • If you say **there's something/a lot to be said for** something, you mean that it has advantages: *There's a lot to be said for living alone.* • If you say **there's little to be said for** something, you mean that it has disadvantages:

Personally, I think there's little to be said for such a policy. • **To say the least** is used to show that what you are describing is in fact much more serious than you have suggested. • *It would be an enormous amount of work,* **to say nothing of** (= and in addition there is) *the cost.* • **What I say, goes** (= Whatever I say must be obeyed). • **When all is said and done** (= The most important thing to remember is that) *you can only do your best.* • *(infml)* **You don't say** is used either to express surprise or lack of surprise in a humorous and slightly unkind way: *"He's lost his job." "You don't say!"* • *(infml) "How stupid of me to lend him that money!"* "**You said it!**" (= I did not want to say that, but I agree with you.) • *(saying)* 'That's not saying much' means that what has been said is not special. • *(saying)* 'You can say that again' means I completely agree with you. • *(Br saying)* 'You can't say fairer than that' means that that is a very good offer or arrangement. • *"What Can I Say After I've Said I'm Sorry"* (song written by Abe Lyman and Walter Donaldson, 1926) • LP> **Say**

say /seɪ/ *n* [U] • *Can't you keep quiet for a minute and let me* **have** *my say* (= say what I think). • To **have (a) say in** a matter is to be involved in making a decision about it: *When he's 18, he'll begin to have a/some say in the running of the family business.* ○ *The staff had little/no say* (= were not involved) *in the restructuring of the company.*

say *(obj)* [GIVE INFORMATION] /seɪ/ *v past* **said** /sed/ (of a sign, piece of writing or device) to give information • *My watch says 3 o'clock.* [T] • *Can you read what that notice says?* [T] • *It says in the paper* **(that)** *they've found the man who did it.* [+ *(that)* clause] • *It says on the bottle* **to** *take three tablets a day.* [+ *to* infinitive]

say [EXPRESSION] /seɪ/ *exclamation* used to express surprise or pleasure, or to attract attention to what you are about to say • *(Am) Say, that's really good of you!* • *(Am) Say, how about going out tonight?* • *(Br dated or humorous) I say, what a splendid hat you're wearing!* • *(Br dated or humorous) I say, how about a round of golf?*

say·ing /ˈseɪ·ɪŋ/ *n* [C] a well-known and wise statement, which often has a meaning that is different from the meanings of the words it contains • *As the saying* **goes**, *'Don't count your chickens before they're hatched'.* • LP> **Words used together**

say–so [STATEMENT] /£ˈseɪ·səʊ, $-soʊ/ *n* [U] *infml* a statement made by someone without proof • *Don't just believe it* **on** *my say-so – find out for yourself.*

say–so [PERMISSION] /£ˈseɪ·səʊ, $-soʊ/ *n* [U] *infml* an instruction to do something, or permission given by someone to do something • *She's not allowed to do anything without her father's say-so.*

scab [SKIN COVERING] /skæb/ *n* a rough surface made of dried blood which forms over a cut or broken skin while it is healing • *A big scab* **formed** *on her knee.* [C] • *You shouldn't* **pick** *scabs* (= try to remove them with your fingers). [C] • Scab is also a plant or animal disease which causes roughness on the skin: *sheep scab* [U] ○ *Apples, pears and potatoes can all* **suffer from** *different types of scab.* [U] • Compare SCAR. • (N)

scab·by /ˈskæb·i/ *adj* **-ier, -iest** • *a scabby knee* • *scabby potatoes*

scab [WORKER] /skæb/ *n* [C] *infml disapproving* a person who continues working while other people in the organization are on STRIKE (= are not working because of a disagreement with their employers) • *"You dirty scab!" shouted the pickets at the factory gate.* [as form of address] • (N)

scab·bard /£ˈskæb·əd, $-ɚd/ *n* [C] a long thin cover for the blade of a weapon, esp. a sword, which is usually fixed to a belt • PIC> **Knife**

sca·bies /ˈskeɪ·biːz/ *n* [U] a skin disease which causes your skin to become rough and uncomfortable • *Scabies is a contagious disease which is caused by a parasite.*

sca·brous /ˈskeɪ·brəs/ *adj literary* offensive or shocking, because describing or showing sex • *The book includes some memorably seedy characters and scabrous descriptions.*

scads /skædz/ *n* [C usually pl] *Am and Aus infml* a large number or amount • *He earns scads* **of** *money.* • **Scads of** *people came to the party.*

scaf·fold /£ˈskæf·əʊld, -əld, $-oʊld/ *n* a flat raised structure on which criminals are punished by having their heads cut off or by being hung with a rope around the neck until they die • *A scaffold was erected in the town square.* [C] • *King Charles I died* **on** *the scaffold* (= He was killed by having his head cut off). [U]

scaf·fold·ing /ˈskæf·əl·dɪŋ/ *n* [U] a structure of wooden boards and metal poles put against a building for workers to stand on when they want to reach the higher parts of the building • *Scaffolding has been* **erected** *around the tower and repair work will start next week.* • *Many public buildings in the city are covered in scaffolding and closed to the public.* • PIC> **Building and construction**

scal·a·wag /ˈskæl·ɪ·wæg/ *n* [C] *Am for* SCALLYWAG

scald *obj* /£skɔːld, $skɑːld/ *v* [T] to burn (the skin) with boiling liquid or steam • *I dropped a pan of boiling water and scalded my leg.* • To scald something is also to put it in boiling water or steam in order to make it completely clean: *Scald the jars and then fill with the jam.* ○ *Scald the needles to sterilize them.* • *(specialized)* To scald a liquid is to heat it until it almost boils: *Scald the milk and then add it to the egg and sugar mixture.*

scald /£skɔːld, $skɑːld/ *n* [C] • A scald is an injury to the skin caused by boiling liquid or steam: *This cream helps to soothe burns and scalds.*

scald·ing /£ˈskɔːl·dɪŋ, $ˈskɑːl-/ *adj, adv* • If a liquid is scalding, it is extremely hot: *scalding tea* ○ *scalding* (= extremely) *hot water* • If criticism is scalding, it is very strong or fierce.

scale [MEASURE] /skeɪl/ *n* a set of numbers or other system used to measure or compare things • *I want a thermometer that is marked with both the Centigrade and the Fahrenheit scales.* [C] • *How would you rate his work* **on a scale of** *1 to 5?* [U] • *"What scale is your map?" "It's* **large** *scale* (= things are shown in detail) – *1:25 000, that's about two and a half inches to the mile."* [U] • *My parents used to entertain friends* **on a large/small** *scale* (= they had large/small parties). [U] • *His scale* **of values** (= belief about what is good, moral, important etc.) *is different from mine.* [C] • If you make a scale **model** or scale **drawing** of something, you make or draw it with exactly the same relationship between height, width and depth as the real thing, but much smaller: *He was building a scale model of Concorde.* • Scale also means size or amount, esp. when this is large: *The sheer scale of the Grand Canyon amazed them – it was so much larger than they had expected.* [U] ○ *The candidate was surprised and delighted by the scale of her success.* [U] ○ *For bigger companies, there are* **advantages/economies** *of scale.* [U] • *Is this drawing of the bridge* **to scale** (= does it show the exact shape of the bridge, but much smaller)*?* • PIC> **Scales** (GR)

scale *obj* /skeɪl/ *v* [always + adv] • *My company is scaling* **up/down** (= increasing/reducing) *its operations in the Middle East.* [M]

scale [MUSIC] /skeɪl/ *n* [C] a set of notes played or sung in order, going up or down • *a major/minor/chromatic scale* • *Start by playing a G major scale* (= a scale starting and ending on the note G). • *You must* **practise** *your scales every day.* • PIC> **Music, Scales** (GR)

scale [SKIN] /skeɪl/ *n* [C usually pl] any of the many very small flat pieces which cover the skin of fish, snakes etc. • *Wash the fish and scrape off the scales with a sharp knife.* • *(literary)* If **the scales fall from** your **eyes**, you are suddenly able to know the truth. • PIC> **Fish, Scales** (GR)

scal·y /ˈskeɪ·li/ *adj* **-ier, -iest** • If your **skin** is scaly, it has small hard dry areas which fall off in tiny pieces.

scal·i·ness /ˈskeɪ·lɪ·nəs/ *n* [U]

scale [COVERING] /skeɪl/, *Br also* **lime·scale** /ˈlaɪm·skeɪl/ *n* [U] a hard white or grey layer of material which forms on the inside of pipes or containers that heat water • *Can you recommend a way of removing the scale from this kettle?* • *Scale consists mainly of calcium carbonate.* • (GR)

scal·i·ness /ˈskeɪ·lɪ·nəs/ *n* [U]

scal·y /ˈskeɪ·li/ *adj* **-ier, -iest**

scale *obj* [CLEAN TEETH] /skeɪl/ *v* [T] *specialized* to remove TARTAR (= hard white substance) and PLAQUE (= soft substance in which bacteria breed) from (teeth) • *The dentist scaled and polished my teeth last week.* • (GR)

scale *obj* [CLIMB] /skeɪl/ *v* [T] to climb up (a steep surface, such as a wall or the side of a mountain), often using special equipment • *The prisoner scaled the high prison wall and ran off.* • *(fig.) At the age of 35 she had already scaled the* **heights** *of her profession* (= risen to a very important position in her work). • (GR)

scales /skeɪlz/ *pl n, Am* **scale** *n* [C] a device for weighing things or people • *He's just moved into a new house and he wants some* **kitchen** *and* **bathroom** *scales for his birthday.* • Scales used in hospitals have a raised area on which a person stands while someone weighs them by moving a weight along a horizontal metal bar until the bar balances.

• A **pair of** scales is a weighing device with two containers attached to a metal bar which is free to move up and down about its fixed central point. An object of known weight is placed in one container and the thing to be weighed is placed in the other. When their weights are equal, the scales balance. • PIC〉 **Bathroom, Scales**

scal·li·on /ˈskæl·i·ən/ *n* [C] *Am for* **spring onion**, see at SPRING [SEASON] • PIC〉 **Vegetables**

scal·lop /£ˈskɒl·əp, $ˈskɑː·ləp/ *n* [C] an edible sea creature which lives inside two joined flat round shells

scal·ly·wag, *Am usually* **scal·a·wag** /ˈskæl·i·wæg/ *n* [C] *infml humorous* someone, esp. a child, who has behaved badly but who is still liked • *He's a real scallywag and always getting into mischief.* • *Get back into bed immediately, you young scallywag!* [as form of address]

scalp [HEAD] /skælp/ *n* [C] the skin on the top of a person's head where hair usually grows • *a dry/oily/itchy scalp* • *Some tribes used to collect scalps to prove how many of the enemy they had killed in battle.* • *(fig.) Although they are expected to take some important scalps* (= defeat some important people) *in the election, they are unlikely to form the next government.* • If someone is **out for/after** your **scalp**, they want to defeat you in some way, esp. to make you lose your job: *After what happened to his daughter, I'm not surprised he's out for the doctor's scalp.*

scalp *obj* /skælp/ *v* [T] • *After killing enemy soldiers, they would scalp them* (= cut off their scalps) *as a sign of victory.* • *(fig. humorous) She's just been to the hairdresser's and he's scalped her* (= cut her hair very short).

scalp *obj* [SELL] /skælp/ *v* [T] *Am and Aus infml* to buy (things such as theatre tickets) at the usual prices and then sell them, when they are difficult to obtain, at greatly increased prices • *He was scalping tickets for the match and made a huge profit for himself.*

scal·per /£ˈskæl·pəʳ, $-pɚ/ *n* [C] *Am and Aus infml* • *A scalper offered me a $10 ticket for the final match for $70.*

scal·pel /ˈskæl·pᵊl/ *n* [C] a very sharp knife that is used for cutting through skin and flesh during an operation • PIC〉 **Knife, Medical equipment**

scam /skæm/ *n* [C] *infml* a plan or action for making money which is dishonest, illegal and often clever • *He burnt his own house down so that he could claim the insurance money – what a scam!*

scamp /skæmp/ *n* [C] *dated* a badly behaved but playful child • *She can be a real scamp sometimes, but she doesn't mean any harm.* • *Give me back my gloves, you little scamp!* [as form of address]

scam·per /£ˈskæm·pəʳ, $-pɚ/ *v* [I always + adv/prep] (esp. of small children and animals) to run with small quick steps, playfully or in fear • *The children scampered* **off** *into the garden.* • *The rabbit scampered* **down** *its hole as soon as it saw me.*

scam·pi /ˈskæm·pi/ *n* [U] large PRAWNS (= edible animals from the sea) which are usually fried • *I'll have scampi and chips, please.*

scan *(obj)* [LOOK] /skæn/ *v* **-nn-** to look at (something) usually carefully, with the eyes or with a machine, in order to obtain information • *She anxiously scanned the faces of the men leaving the train in the hope of finding her husband.* [T] • *The radar scanned the sea* **for** *any sign of enemy ships.* [T] • *She scanned* **the horizon** *for the boat, but she could not see it anywhere.* [T] • To scan a text can also be to look through it quickly in order to find a piece of information that you want or to get a general idea of what the text contains: *I scanned* **through** *the booklet but I couldn't find the address anywhere.* [I] ○ *Scan the newspaper article quickly and make a note of the main points.* [T]

scan /skæn/ *n* [C] • *I gave the book a quick scan* (= I looked through it quickly), *but it seemed rather technical so I decided not to buy it.* • A scan is also a medical examination in which an image of the inside of the body is made using a special machine: *He was understandably worried when his doctor told him he would have to have a* **brain** *scan.* ○ *A pregnant woman often has an* **ultrasound** *scan to check that her baby is developing normally.*

scan·ner /£ˈskæn·əʳ, $-ɚ/ *n* [C] • A scanner is a device for making images of the inside of the body or for reading information into a computer system: *an ultrasound scanner* ○ *Waiting times at supermarket checkouts have been reduced by the introduction of bar code scanners.*

scan [FOLLOW A PATTERN] /skæn/ *v* [I] **-nn-** *specialized* (of a poem) to follow a pattern of regular beats • *This line doesn't scan – it's got too many syllables.*

scan·dal /ˈskæn·dᵊl/ *n* (an action or event that causes) a public feeling of shock and strong moral disapproval • *a financial/political/sex scandal* [C] • *Nothing sells a newspaper quite like a nice* **juicy** *scandal* (= one that is unusually shocking and often sexual). [C] • *The minister was forced to resign after a scandal* **involving** *him and another minister's wife.* [C] • *The company is implicated in the growing scandal* **surrounding** *the collapse of the bank.* [C] • *She was* **at the centre of** *a public scandal last year.* [C] • *If there is the slightest* **suggestion/hint** *of scandal, the public will no longer trust us.* [U] • *Their affair* **caused/created** *a scandal in the office.* [C] • *The government has done its best to* **cover up/hush up** *the scandal.* [C] • *One of the newspapers* **uncovered/exposed** *the scandal.* [C] • *The scandal* **broke** (= became public knowledge) *right at the beginning of the Conservative Party Conference.* [C] • Scandal is reports about actions or events that cause shock and disapproval: *Some magazines contain nothing but scandal and gossip.* [U] ○ *Who's been* **spreading** *scandal* **about** *me?* [U] ○ *(humorous) What's the latest scandal then?* (= What's the most recent news about people's personal lives?) [U] • A scandal is also a situation that is shockingly bad: *It's a scandal* **that** *in such a rich country there are so many beggars on the streets.* [C + *that* clause] • *The way they treat their children is a scandal.* [C]

scan·dal·ize *obj*, *Br and Aus usually* **–ise** /ˈskæn·dᵊl·aɪz/ *v* [T usually passive] • If you are scandalized by someone's behaviour, you disapprove of it and are shocked by it because you think it is immoral: *The whole village was scandalized by her marriage to a man who was young enough to be her grandson.* ○ *His colleagues were scandalized when they discovered he'd been having an affair with his assistant.*

scan·dal·ous /ˈskæn·dᵊl·əs/ *adj* • *His name has appeared in several scandalous stories recently.* • **It's** *scandalous* (= very annoying and upsetting) **that** *we do so little to prevent homelessness.*

scan·da·lous·ly /ˈskæn·dᵊl·ə·sli/ *adv* • *The charge for using the phone in your hotel room can be scandalously* (= extremely and shockingly) *high.*

scan·dal·mong·er /£ˈskæn·dᵊlˌmʌŋ·gəʳ, $-gɚ/ *n* [C] *disapproving* a person who creates or spreads reports about actions and events that cause public shock and disapproval

Scan·di·na·vi·an /ˌskæn·dɪˈneɪ·vi·ən/ *n, adj* [not gradable] (a person) coming from Sweden, Norway, Denmark, Iceland or Finland • *Many Scandinavians speak excellent English.* [C] • *Have you ever visited any Scandinavian* **countries?** • LP› **World regions**

scant /skænt/ *adj* [before n] **-er, -est** very little and not enough • *There is still scant* **evidence** *of an improvement in business and consumer confidence.* • *Many mothers pay scant* **attention** *to their own needs when their children are small* (= they think much more about their children's needs than their own). • *That man has scant* **regard** *for the truth* (= he lies if he needs to). • Scant can also mean almost: *Add a scant half litre* (= almost half a litre) *of milk to the mixture and stir well.*

scan·ty /£ˈskæn·ti, $-t̬i/ *adj* **-ier, -iest** smaller in size or amount than is considered necessary or desirable • *scanty vegetation* • *a scanty lunch* • *I haven't got a good enough figure to wear such a scanty dress* (= a dress which covers so little of my body). • *There is scanty* **evidence** *to support their accusations.* • *Unfortunately, her decision was based on rather scanty* **information.**

scan·ti·ly /£ˈskæn·tɪ·li, $-t̬ɪ-/ *adv* • *I received very little training so I felt scantily equipped for the work I was expected to do.* • Someone who is scantily **clad** or scantily **dressed** is wearing very little clothing: *He's one of those singers who always appear on TV surrounded by scantily-clad dancers.* ○ *The authorities are planning to ban scantily-dressed tourists from entering the church.*

–scape /-skeɪp/ *combining form* used to form nouns referring to a wide view of a place, often one represented in a picture • *a landscape* • *a seascape* • *a cityscape* • *a moonscape*

scape·goat /£ˈskeɪp·gəʊt, $-goʊt/ *n* [C] a person who is blamed for something that someone else has done • *The captain* **became** *a scapegoat* **for** *the team's failure to win the cup that year.* • *His friends* **made** *a scapegoat* **of** *him because they knew that he wouldn't dare tell on them.* • *Workers are often* **made into/used as** *scapegoats* **for** *the failures of management.* • *The party began* **searching for** *scapegoats immediately after their election defeat.* • *Instead of* **looking for** *scapegoats for what went wrong, we should be trying to prevent it happening again.*

scap·u·la /ˈskæp·jʊ·lə/ *n* [C] *medical for* **shoulder blade**, see at SHOULDER

scar /£skɑːʳ, $skɑːr/ *n* [C] a mark left on part of the body after an injury such as a cut after it has healed • *a prominent/noticeable/ugly scar* • *That burn will* **leave** *a nasty scar.* • *Scar* **tissue** *forms very quickly in small children.* • *(fig.) Every village* **bears** *the scars* **of** *war* (= the signs that there has been a war). • *(fig.) His early years in the refugee camp* **left** *a deep* **psychological** *scar* (= had a very bad effect on his mind). • Compare SCAB [SKIN COVERING].

scar *(obj)* /£skɑːʳ, $skɑːr/ *v* **-rr-** • *Her face was scarred by smallpox.* [T] • *He was scarred as a result of the fire.* [T] • *The cut will scar* **(over)** *quickly.* [I] • *The accident left her scarred* **for life** (= physically damaged, or *fig.* mentally upset, for the rest of her life). • *(fig.) His experiences in the army left him* **deeply** *scarred* (= had a great mental effect on him).

scarce /£skeəs, $skers/ *adj* **-r, -st** not easy to find or obtain • *Firewood is scarce in many parts of the world.* • *Scarce* **resources** *should be used sensibly.* • *(infml) Dad's really angry with you, so you'd better* **make yourself scarce** (= go away to avoid trouble).

scar·ci·ty /£ˈskeə·sɪ·ti, $ˈsker·sə·t̬i/ *n* [U] • *The scarcity* **of** *skilled workers is worrying the government.*

scarce·ly [ONLY JUST] /£ˈskeə·sli, $ˈsker-/, *literary* **scarce** /£skeəs, $skers/ *adv* [not gradable] only just or almost not • *I was scarcely able to move my arm after the accident.* • *I had scarcely sat down/(fml) Scarcely had I sat down to eat* **when** *the phone rang.* • *I* **could** *scarcely* **believe** *it when she said she wanted to marry me.* • *"And even the ranks of Tuscany / Could scarce forbear to cheer"* (Thomas Macaulay *Lays of Ancient Rome* 'Horatius', 1842)

scarce·ly [NOT] /£ˈskeə·sli, $ˈsker-/ *adv* [not gradable] certainly not • *I'd scarcely have done it if I didn't think it was absolutely necessary.* • *His wife died last week, so it's scarcely* **surprising** *that he seems unhappy.* • *He would scarcely have said a thing like that* (= I don't believe he did).

scare *(obj)* /£skeəʳ, $sker/ *v* to (cause to) feel frightened • *Sudden noises scare me.* [T] • *She's very brave – she doesn't scare easily.* [I] • *Don't make too much noise or you'll scare* **away/off** *the birds* (= make them fly away by frightening them). [M] • *(fig.) If you charge as much as that you'll scare the customers* **away/off** (= discourage them from buying anything). [M] • If you scare someone **into/out of** doing something, you persuade them to do/not to do something by frightening them: *The two boys scared the old man into handing over his wallet.* [T] ○ *We scared her out of telling the teacher what had happened.* [T] • *He scared me* **out of** *my* **wits/witless** (= made me extremely frightened) *when he tried to overtake a car while a bus was coming in the opposite direction.* • *Meeting new people scares me* **stiff/to death** (= makes me extremely nervous and anxious). • *She scared* **the pants off/the life out of** *me* (= frightened me very much) *when she crept up behind me and shouted in my ear.* • *(taboo) Coming face to face with the burglar* **scared** *me* **shitless** (= made me extremely frightened).

scare /£skeəʳ, $sker/ *n* [C] • *I* **got/had** *a scare* (= I was very worried) *when I looked at my bank statement this morning!* • *You* **gave** *us a real scare* (= frightened us) *when you fainted, you know.* • *The Tories accused Labour of planning higher taxes, but Labour said the Tories were* **using/employing** *scare* **tactics** (= frightening people in order to win support for themselves). • When there is a scare **about** a subject, that subject receives a lot of public attention and worries many people, often unnecessarily: *There have been quite a few scares about food poisoning recently.* ○ *The health minister said it was irresponsible of the press to print scare* **stories** *about the mystery virus.*

scared /£skeəd, $skerd/ *adj* • *She had a scared look on her face.* • *He's scared* **of** *spiders/snakes/the dark.* • *I'm scared* **of telling** *her what really happened.* • *He's scared* **to** *tell her what really happened.* [+ to infinitive] • *I was scared* (= very worried) **(that)** *you might not be there.* [+ (*that*) clause] • *There were hundreds of people at the meeting, and I was scared* **to death** *while I was waiting to speak.* • *I was scared* **stiff/witless/***(taboo)* **shitless** (= extremely frightened) *during that horror movie.* • *The newspapers accused him of* **running** *scared* (= of being frightened and trying to escape his responsibilities).

scare·dy (cat) /£ˈskeə·di·kæt, $ˈsker-/ *n* [C] *infml disapproving* • A scaredy (cat) is someone who is frightened: *Come on, scaredy – it won't bite you!* [as form of address] • *"Scaredy cat, scaredy cat, sitting on the doormat!"* (Children's rhyme, used to make fun of other children)

scar·y, *Br also* **scar·ey** /£ˈskeə·ri, $ˈsker·i/ *adj* **scarier, scariest** *infml* • *I like that story because it's a bit scary* (= frightening).

scare up *obj*, **scare** *obj* **up** *v adv* [M] *Am infml* to find or make (something) with difficulty because of a limited supply of things • *There's hardly any food in the house, but I'll scare something up* **from** *these leftovers.*

scare·crow /£ˈskeə·krəʊ, $ˈsker·kroʊ/ *n* [C] a model of a person dressed in old clothes and put in a field of growing crops to frighten birds away • PIC› **Farming**

scare·mong·er /£ˈskeəˌmʌŋ·gəʳ, $ˈskerˌmʌŋ·gɚ/ *n* [C] *disapproving* a person who spreads stories that cause public fear • *Eventually, the scaremongers were taken seriously and the mineral water was removed from the shops and tested.*

scare·mong·er·ing /£ˈskeəˌmʌŋ·gᵊr·ɪŋ, $ˈskerˌmʌŋ·gɚ-/ *n* [U] *disapproving* • *All these stories in the papers about dogs attacking children are just scaremongering.* • *He accused the government of scaremongering* **tactics.**

scarf [CLOTH] /£skɑːf, $skɑːrf/ *n* [C] *pl* **scarves** /£skɑːvz, $skɑːrvs/ or **scarfs** /£skɑːfs, $skɑːrfs/ a strip, square or triangle of cloth, worn around the neck, head or shoulders to keep you warm or to make you look attractive • *a knitted/woollen/silk scarf* • *A* **school/college/university** *scarf has its own special colours or pattern which show where you are a student.*

scarf obj [EAT] /£skɑːf, $skɑːrf/ *v* [T] *Am for* SCOFF [EAT]

scar·la·ti·na /£ˌskɑː·ləˈtiː·nə, $ˌskɑːr-/ *n* [U] *medical for* **scarlet fever**, see at SCARLET

scar·let /£ˈskɑː·lət, $ˈskɑːr-/ *adj, n* bright red • *He* **went** *scarlet with shame and embarrassment.* • *The band was dressed in scarlet.* [U] • **Scarlet fever** (*medical* **scarlatina**) is an infectious illness of children which causes a sore throat, a high body temperature and red spots on the skin. • *(disapproving dated)* A **scarlet woman** is a woman who has behaved immorally and shamefully by having sex with a lot of men.

scar·per /£ˈskɑː·pər, $ˈskɑːr·pɚ/ *v* [I] *Br and Aus slang* to leave very quickly, often to avoid getting into trouble • *The police are coming! We'd better scarper.*

sca·ry /£ˈskeə·ri, $ˈsker·i/ *adj* **-ier, -iest** See at SCARE

scat [GO AWAY] /skæt/ *exclamation infml* said to an animal, esp. a cat, or to a person to make them go away quickly

scat [SINGING] /skæt/ *n* [U] a type of jazz singing that uses words with no meaning • *Betty Carter is one of the best scat* **singers** *ever.*

scath·ing /ˈskeɪ·ðɪŋ/ *adj* severely and unkindly critical • *a scathing attack/remark/review* • *scathing criticism* • *Mr Parkinson was scathing* **about** *the report, denouncing it as out of date and biased.*

scath·ing·ly /ˈskeɪ·ðɪŋ·li/ *adv* • *She spoke scathingly of the poor standard of work done by her predecessor.*

scat·o·log·i·cal, *Br also* **scat·a·log·i·cal** /£ˌskæt·əˈlɒdʒ·ɪ·kəl, $ˌskæt̬·əˈlɑː·dʒɪ-/ *adj disapproving* showing an extreme and unpleasant interest in excrement and sex • *a scatological joke* • *William Hogarth's scatological* **humour** *shocked many of the people who saw his drawings.*

scat·ter *(obj)* /£ˈskæt·ər, $ˈskæt̬·ɚ/ *v* to (cause to) move far apart in different directions, or to cover (a surface) with things that are far apart and in no particular arrangement • *The policeman blew his whistle and the students scattered in all directions.* [I] • *The protesters scattered at the sound of gunshots.* [I] • *The soldiers came in and scattered the crowd.* [T] • *Scatter some of this powder* **round** *the plants and they will grow better.* [T] • *I scattered grass seed all* **over** *the lawn.* [T] • *I scattered the whole lawn* **with** *grass seed.* [T] • *(literary)* To **scatter** something **to the (four) winds** is to cause or allow it to be blown away: *(fig.) It was the finest collection of paintings in Denmark, but during the last war it was broken up and scattered to the four winds* (=parts of it went to different places, so it no longer exists). • **Scatter rugs** and *(Br and Aus)* **scatter cushions** are small decorative RUGS and CUSHIONS that are designed to be moved around: *Why don't we hide that stain on the carpet with a scatter rug?* ○ *(Br and Aus) A few scatter cushions would help to brighten up that old sofa.* • *"We plough the fields and scatter / The good seed on the land"* (harvest hymn by James Montgomery Campbell, translated from a German hymn by Matthias Claudius, 1861) • (I)

scat·tered /£ˈskæt·əd, $ˈskæt̬·ɚd/ *adj* • *After the concert hundreds of wine bottles and beer cans were left scattered on the grass.* • *My family is scattered* **all over** *the world.* • *The number of refugees scattered* **throughout** *the world is growing.* • *The window was open and all the papers that she'd left on her desk were scattered* **about/around** *the room.* • *In the south of the island there are just a few scattered* (=widely separated) **villages/settlements**. • *The weather forecast said there would be scattered* **showers** *tomorrow.*

scat·ter·ing /£ˈskæt·ər·ɪŋ, $ˈskæt̬·ɚ-/ *n* [C] • *Why is there only a scattering* (=small number) **of** *female Members of Parliament in this country?*

scat·ter·brain /£ˈskæt·ə·breɪn, $ˈskæt̬·ɚ-/ *n* [C] a person who forgets things easily or does not think seriously about things, but is likeable despite this • *I'm such a scatterbrain – I'm always leaving my umbrella behind.* • *He likes to give the impression of being a bit of a scatterbrain, but he's actually extremely efficient and well-organized.*

scat·ter·brained /£ˈskæt·ə·breɪnd, $ˈskæt̬·ɚ-/ *adj* • *I find I'm becoming more scatterbrained as I get older.*

scat·ty /£ˈskæt·i, $ˈskæt̬-/ *adj* **-ier, -iest** *Br and Aus infml* rather silly and forgetful • *a scatty child* • *scatty behaviour* • *The noise made by the builders next door is* **driving** *me scatty* (=annoying me so much that I'm finding it difficult to think).

scav·enge *(obj)* /ˈskæv·ɪndʒ/ *v* to look for or obtain (food and other objects) in or from other people's unwanted rubbish, or (of animals) to feed on the flesh of dead decaying animals • *We were so poor we had to scavenge through rubbish dumps* **for** *old furniture.* [I] • *The flood has left villagers and animals desperately scavenging* **for** *food.* [I] • *We managed to scavenge a lot of furniture* **from** *the local rubbish dump.* [T] • *Those cats aren't fed by anybody – they just live in the open and scavenge.* [I]

scav·eng·er /£ˈskæv·ɪn·dʒər, $-dʒɚ/ *n* [C] • A scavenger is a bird or animal which feeds on dead animals which it has not killed itself: *Vultures are scavengers.*

scen·ar·i·o /£sɪˈnɑː·ri·əʊ, $səˈner·i·oʊ/ *n* [C] *pl* **scenarios** a description of possible actions or events in the future, or a written plan for a performance such as a play or film, with brief details about the story and characters • *A nuclear attack could be started by mistake, and that could lead to the Third World War – it's a* **horrific/nightmare** *scenario.* • *In the* **worst-case** *scenario* (=the worst situation we can imagine), *the whole town would be under water.* • *In the original scenario, he died in the last scene, but in the actual film he survived.* • (NL)

scene [THEATRE/FILM] /siːn/ *n* [C] a part of a play or film in which the action stays in one place for a continuous period of time • *the funeral/wedding scene* • *She refused to appear in the film because there were so many nude scenes.* • *What impressed me most about the movie were the scenes filmed in New York.* • *A play is divided into acts, which are themselves divided into scenes.* • *Juliet dies in Act IV, Scene iii of Shakespeare's 'Romeo and Juliet'.* • *In the second half of the opera, the scene* **shifts to** (=the action starts to happen in) *a city street at night.* • A scene can also be an event in real life which seems like something in a play or film: *There were scenes* **of** *great joy as the hostages were re-united with their families.* ○ *The police arrived to find a scene* **of** *horrifying destruction.* ○ *When we reached the top of the mountain a scene* **of** *unparalleled beauty lay before us.* ○ *Lowry painted street scenes.* ○ *The strongest evidence against him was the fact that his blood sample matched bloodstains found at the scene* **of the crime** (=the place where the crime had been committed). • When something happens **behind the scenes**, it is not generally known that it is happening: *Diplomats have been* **working** *hard behind the scenes in preparation for the peace talks.* ○ *The armed forces have a long history of exerting powerful behind-the-scenes* **influence** *during times of civilian rule.* • *I phoned the police and they were* **on the scene** (=they arrived) *within minutes.* • To **set the scene** is to describe a situation where something is about to happen: *First, let's set the scene – it was a dark, wet night with a gale blowing in from the sea.* • (PL) (RUS)

scen·ic /ˈsiː·nɪk/ *adj* [before n; not gradable] • *She's interested in a career in scenic design* (=designing and decorating theatre stages so that they are suitable for particular plays).

scene [AREA] /siːn/ *n* [U] a particular area of life and all the things connected with it • *the pop/political/business/drugs/gay scene* • *(infml) I'd rather go to a jazz concert – I'm afraid opera isn't really my scene* (=is not the type of thing I like). • *(Am dated infml) It was a really* **bad** *scene* (=bad situation) *when his ex-girlfriend turned up at his engagement party.* • *(fig.) He* **disappeared/vanished/departed from** *the scene* (=no longer appeared in public) *after failing to win the presidency in 1987.* • *(fig.) Rap music* **arrived on/came on/appeared on/burst upon** *the scene* (=suddenly appeared and became popular) *in the early 1980s.* • (PL) (RUS)

scene [ARGUMENT] /siːn/ *n* [C] (an occasion when there is) an expression of great anger or similar feelings, often between two people • *Please don't* **make** *a scene.* • *Through the wall I could hear Bob and Jayne* **having** *a scene.* • (PL) (RUS)

scen·e·ry [COUNTRYSIDE] /£ˈsiː·nər·i, $-nɚ-/ *n* [U] the general appearance of natural surroundings, esp. when these are beautiful • *beautiful/breathtaking/picturesque/spectacular/wild scenery* • *bleak moorland scenery* • *They stopped at the top of the hill to* **admire** *the scenery.* • *(fig.) A secret agent has to be able to* **blend into** *the scenery* (=able to avoid being noticed). • (RUS)

scen·ic /ˈsiː·nɪk/ *adj* • Something that is scenic has or allows you to see beautiful natural features: *a scenic drive/photo/railway* ○ *The pamphlet contains full details of the national park's scenic attractions.* • If you say that you **took the** scenic **route**, you mean that you travelled on a road with beautiful countryside around it, or *(humorous)* that you lost your way and took a much longer route than you needed to.

scen·e·ry THEATRE /£ˈsiː·nᵊr·i, $-nɚ-/ *n* [U] the painted backgrounds used on a theatre stage to represent the place where the action is • *I'm in charge of the scenery for the play.* • (RUS)

scene·shift·er /£ˈsiːnˌʃɪf·təʳ, $-t̬ɚ/ *n* [C] a person who changes the SCENERY (=background) in a theatre

scent /sent/ *n* a pleasant natural smell, or a smell produced by an animal which acts as a signal to other animals • *The evening air was full of the scent of roses.* [C] • *The hounds had been on the scent* (=following the smell) *of the fox for several miles, but they lost it near the river.* [C] • *"We're* **on the scent of** (=close to discovering) *something big," said the police chief.* • If you **throw/put** someone **off the scent**, you do something to prevent them from discovering something that you do not want them to know about. • Scent can also be PERFUME, esp. when it is cheap or low in quality: *a bottle of scent* [U] • *She put on/was wearing scent.* [U] • LP› **Shopping goods, Smells**

scent *obj* /sent/ *v* [T] • If an animal scents something, it knows it is there because it can smell it. • If a person scents something, they have a feeling that they are about to experience it: *We could scent danger/trouble/success.* ○ *Halfway through the match, the team could already scent* **victory**. ○ *From the look on his face, she scented* (=was caused to believe) **(that)** *something was wrong.* [+ *(that)* clause]

scent·ed /£ˈsen·tɪd, $-t̬ɪd/ *adj* • *scented soap/notepaper* • *pine-scented mountain air* • *Wild carnations have pink, strongly-scented flowers.* • *The air was scented* **with** *lavender.*

scep·tic, *Am usually and Aus also* **skep·tic** /ˈskep·tɪk/ *n* [C] a person who doubts the truth or value of an idea or belief • *They tried hard to convince the sceptics of the truth of what they said.*

scep·ti·cal, *Am usually and Aus also* **skep·ti·cal** /ˈskep·tɪ·kᵊl/ *adj* • *Some people think the economy will improve soon, but many experts* **remain** *sceptical* **about/of** *this.*

scep·ti·cal·ly, *Am usually and Aus also* **skep·ti·cal·ly** /ˈskep·tɪ·kli/ *adv* • *The union has reacted sceptically to the management's assurances that there would be no more job losses.*

scep·ti·ci·sm, *Am usually and Aus also* **skep·ti·ci·sm** /ˈskep·tɪ·sɪ·zᵊm/ *n* [U] • *Senior ministers have* **expressed** *scepticism about the practicality of the proposals.* • *The company's environmental claims have been* **greeted with** *scepticism by conservationists.* • *I think it's important to* **treat** *his claims* **with** *a degree of skepticism.* • *She maintained* **a healthy** *scepticism* **about** (=was wisely unwilling to believe in) *her chances of winning.*

scep·tre *Br and Aus* /£ˈsep·təʳ, $-tɚ/, *Am* **scep·ter** *n* [C] a decorated stick which is carried by a queen or king during some official ceremonies as a symbol of their authority

schad·en·freude /ˈʃɑː·dᵊnˌfrɔɪ·də/ *n* [U] pleasure or satisfaction obtained from someone else's misfortune • *I had a curious feeling of schadenfreude when my ex-girlfriend got divorced.*

sched·ule /ˈʃed·juːl, ˈsked-/ *n* [C] a list of planned activities or things to be done showing the times or dates when they are intended to happen or be done • *a production schedule* • *a fixed/flexible schedule* • *a punishing/hectic/gruelling/tight* (=very busy) *schedule* • *A complete schedule* **of** *the events commemorating the city's 500th anniversary can be obtained from the tourist information office.* • *The prime minister had a* **full/heavy** *schedule of engagements for every day of the conference.* • *We've* **drawn up/planned** *our teaching schedule for the next six months.* • *Everyone must* **keep to/stick to**/*not* **depart from** *this schedule.* • *We expect the building work to be completed* **ahead of/on/behind** *schedule* (=early/on time/late). • *Everything went* **according to** *schedule* (=as planned). • *(esp. Am)* An **airline/bus/train** schedule (*Br and Aus* **timetable**) is a list of places and the times and days when aircraft/buses/trains arrive at and leave those places. • *(fml)* A schedule can also be an official list of things: *My accountant wants me to prepare a schedule* **of** *my business expenses for the tax office.*

sched·ule *obj* /ˈʃed·juːl, ˈsked-/ *v* [T often passive] • *The meeting has been scheduled* **for** *tomorrow afternoon.* • *They've scheduled Ian* **to** *speak at three o'clock.* [+ obj + *to* infinitive] • *The train is scheduled* **to** *arrive at 8.45, but it's running twenty minutes late.* [+ obj + *to* infinitive] • *The restoration work is scheduled* **to begin** *early next year.* [+ obj + *to* infinitive] • *The general election,* **originally** *scheduled* **for** *29th September, is to be postponed until December.*

sched·uled /ˈʃed·juːld,ˈsked-/ *adj* [not gradable] • *One of the scheduled events at the fair is a parachute drop by the local club.* • A **scheduled flight** is a regular flight organized by the company which owns the aircraft.

sched·ul·er /£ˈʃed·juː·ləʳ, ˈsked-, $-lɚ/ *n* [C] • A scheduler is a person who works for a broadcasting company putting the various programmes for the day, week, month, etc. into a particular order: *Schedulers at ITV have decided to put the programme back half an hour from its usual 7.30 slot on Wednesdays to avoid losing viewers to BBC1.*

schem·a·tic /£skɪˈmæt·ɪk, $-ˈmæt̬-/ *adj* showing the main form and features of something, usually in the form of a drawing, which helps people to understand it • *It's only a schematic* **diagram** – *it doesn't show all the details.*

schem·a·ti·cal·ly /£skɪˈmæt·ɪ·kli, $-ˈmæt̬-/ *adv*

scheme /skiːm/ *n* [C] a plan for obtaining an advantage for yourself, esp. by deceiving others • *He's got a* **hare-brained/crazy/daft** *scheme* **for** *getting rich before he's 20.* • *They've devised a scheme* **to** *defraud the government of millions of dollars.* [+ *to* infinitive] • *(esp. Br)* A scheme can also be any officially organized plan or system: *a training/housing scheme* • *a pension/savings scheme* ○ *There's a new scheme in our town* **for** *recycling plastic bottles.* ○ *The council is* **organizing** *a* **play** *scheme for 7- to 11-year-olds.* • A **scheme of things** is what is thought about the organization or state of everything in a particular situation: *When he became president he tried to change the structure of government to fit into his scheme of things.* ○ *I was disappointed not to get the job, but it's not that important in the* **great** *scheme of things* (=when all things are considered). • (D)

scheme *(obj)* /skiːm/ *v disapproving* • Someone who schemes makes clever secret plans which often deceive others: *All her ministers were scheming* **for** *her downfall.* [I] ○ *Half the party seems to be scheming* **for**, *and half* **against**, *the leader.* [I] ○ *He was scheming* **to** *get the top job from the moment he joined the firm.* [+ *to* infinitive] ○ *What are you scheming* (=secretly planning) *now?* [T]

schem·er /£ˈskiː·məʳ, $-mɚ/ *n* [C] *disapproving* • *He's a schemer who always finds a way of getting what he wants.*

schem·ing /ˈskiː·mɪŋ/ *adj disapproving* • *The president is a secretive and scheming politician.*

scher·zo /£ˈskeət·səʊ, $ˈskert·soʊ/ *n* [C] *pl* **scherzos** a fast and happy piece of music for instruments, often part of a longer piece

schi·sm /ˈskɪz·əm/ *n* [C] a division into two groups caused by a disagreement about ideas, esp. in a religious organization • *During the Great Schism in the Roman Catholic Church, from 1378 to 1417, there was a Pope in Avignon and a Pope in Rome.* • *The schism* **in/within** *the Socialist Party will damage its chances of being reelected.* • (GR)

schiz·o /£ˈskɪt·səʊ, $-soʊ/ *n* [C] *pl* **schizos** *infml disapproving* a person with very strange and usually violent or threatening behaviour • *He turns into a real schizo when he's had too much to drink.*

schiz·oid /ˈskɪt·sɔɪd/ *n, adj medical* (a person who is) suffering from or behaving as if suffering from SCHIZOPHRENIA • *schizoid behaviour* • *a schizoid personality* • *The stress of fighting in the war turned him into a schizoid.* [C]

schi·zo·phre·nia /ˌskɪt·səˈfriː·ni·ə/ *n* [U] *medical* a mental illness • *Symptoms of schizophrenia can include delusions, hallucinations, thought disorder, and strange behaviour and emotions.* • *He was discharged from the Royal Navy after he was found to be suffering from* **paranoid** *schizophrenia.* • *(infml)* Schizophrenia sometimes refers to behaviour in which a person appears to have two different personalities: *My boss's schizophrenia can be difficult to cope with – one day he's really friendly, and the next he completely ignores me.*

schi·zo·phren·ic /ˌskɪt·səˈfren·ɪk/ *n, adj* • *(medical) The most violent prisoners are often men who have been diagnosed as psychopaths or schizophrenics.* [C] • *(medical) He was only 15 when he was diagnosed as schizophrenic.* • *(infml) Her style of management is somewhat schizophrenic – she often changes her mind from one day to the next.*

schi·zo·phren·i·cal·ly /ˌskɪt·səˈfren·ɪ·kli/ *adv*

schlep *(obj)* /ʃlep/, **schlepp**, **shlep** *v* [always + adv/prep] **-pp-** *Am infml* to move (yourself or an object) with effort and difficulty • *I've just spent the afternoon schlepping* **around** *town trying to find a birthday present for my girlfriend.* [I] • *Do I really have to schlep all that junk* **down** *to the cellar?* [T]

schlock /£ʃlɒk, $ʃlɑːk/ *n* [U] *infml disapproving esp. Am* goods or artistic works which are cheap or low in quality • *The jewelry she bought at the market was real schlock, and it fell apart a week later.* • *Women's popular fiction is often described as slush or schlock, but it's still not easy to write.* • *They sit at home in the afternoon watching all the schlock TV shows.*

schlock·y /£'ʃlɒk·i, $'ʃlɑː·ki/ *adj infml disapproving esp. Am*

schmaltz, schmalz /£ʃmɒlts, $ʃmɑːlts/ *n* [U] *infml disapproving* popular artistic works, such as music or writing, which are intended to cause strong sad or romantic feelings, but which lack any real artistic value • *Her first album had some depth to it, but her second one was pure schmaltz.*

schmaltz·y (**-ier, -iest**), **schmalz·y** (**-ier, -iest**) /£'ʃmɒlt·si, $'ʃmɑːlt-/ *adj infml disapproving* • *They seem to spend most of their time together listening to schmaltzy love songs.*

schmuck /ʃmʌk/ *n* [C] *infml disapproving esp. Am* a stupid or foolish person • *Her husband was a complete schmuck and was always being unfaithful.*

schnapps /ʃnæps/ *n* a colourless strong alcoholic drink made in eastern and northern parts of Europe, usually from grain, potato or fruit • *We brought a bottle of schnapps back from our holiday in Germany.* [U] • *Would you like a schnapps* (= a glass of this)*?* [C]

schnit·zel /'ʃnɪt·səl/ *n* [C] a thin slice of meat, usually VEAL (= young cow), which is covered in egg and very small pieces of bread before being fried

schnor·kel /£'ʃnɔː·kəl, $'ʃnɔːr-/ *n* [C] *Aus for* SNORKEL

schol·ar /£'skɒl·əʳ, $'skɑː·lɚ/ *n* [C] a person who studies a subject in great detail, esp. at a university • *a classics/history scholar* • *Dr Miles was a* **distinguished** *scholar* **of** *Russian history and government.* • *(infml)* A scholar is also someone who is clever or good at learning by studying: *a good/bad scholar* ○ *I'm not much of a scholar myself – I left school at 16 and I've worked as a plumber ever since.*

schol·ar·ly /£'skɒl·ə·li, $'skɑː·lɚ-/ *adj* • Scholarly means containing a serious detailed study of the subject concerned: *a scholarly article/book/work/journal* • Someone who is scholarly studies a lot and knows a lot about what they study: *She was a scholarly woman who had specialized in Italian literature at university.*

schol·ar·ship /£'skɒl·ə·ʃɪp, $'skɑː·lɚ-/ *n* • *Her book on Chinese verbs is a work of great scholarship* (= serious detailed study). [U] • *Recent historical scholarship has contradicted many commonly held ideas about the Roman invasion.* [U] • A scholarship is an amount of money given by a school, college, university or other organization to pay for a person with great ability but little money to study: *He* **won** *a scholarship* **to** *Eton.* ○ *He won a scholarship* **to study at** *Eton.* [C + *to* infinitive] ○ *She's been* **awarded** *a Rhodes scholarship.* [C] ○ *Paula went up to Oxford* **on** *a scholarship.* [C]

scho·las·tic /skə'læs·tɪk/ *adj* [not gradable] relating to school and education • *My scholastic achievements* (= the qualifications I got at school and college) *were not very impressive.*

scho·las·ti·cal·ly /skə'læs·tɪ·kli/ *adv*

school [EDUCATION] /skuːl/ *n* a place where people, esp. young people, are educated • *a primary/secondary school* [C] • *Milton Road School* [C] • *Harrow School* [C] • *the school bus* • *school uniform* • *school meals/dinners/lunches* • *a school report* • *school buildings* • *school fees* • *They're building a new school in the village.* [C] • *The headteacher knows the names of all 430 pupils at the school.* [C] • *The girl left the school at 3 p.m. and has not been seen since.* [C] • *She drives the kids to school every morning.* [U] • *(Br) I was* **at** *school* **with** (= I went to the same school at the same time as) *the Prime Minister.* [U] • *There is no playing field* **at the** *school.* [C] • *Is Emily* **in** *school today or is she still ill?* [U] • *Jenny's got two school-***age** *children/children* **of** *school* **age**. • *Sex education only recently became a compulsory part of the school* **curriculum**. • *Which school do you* **go to**/*(fml)* **attend***?* [C] • *Does Lisa* **go to**/*(fml)* **attend** *school yet?* [U] • *We want to* **send** *our children* **to** *a good school.* [C] • *Some children pass through the entire school* **system** *without gaining a single qualification.* • *(Am) My sister* **teaches** *school* (= teaches children in a school) *in New York City.* [U] • *In Britain, the school* **year** *starts in September and ends in July.* See also **academic year** at ACADEMIC. • *British children* **start/begin** *school at the age of four or five.* [U] • *I love/hate school* (= the activities that are done at school). [U] • *What do you want to do when you* **leave** *school* (= finish studying at school)*?* [U] • *(Br and Aus)* A **school leaver** is a young person who is about to leave or has just left **secondary school** (= a school for children aged 11 to 16 (or 18) years). • *(Br and Aus)* The **school-leaving age** is the lowest age at which a person can leave school: *The school-leaving age in Britain and Australia is 16.* • *The whole school* (= all the children and teachers at the school) *is/are delighted about Joel's success in the championships.* [C + sing/pl v] • School also means the time during the day when children are studying in school: *before/after school* [U] ○ *School starts at 9 a.m. and finishes at 3.30 p.m.* [U] • A school is also a part of a college or university specializing in a particular subject or group of subjects: *The School of Oriental and African Studies is part of the University of London.* [C] ○ *She went to medical school in Edinburgh.* [U] • A school can also be a place where people, esp. adults, can study a particular subject either some of the time or all of the time: *a driving/dancing school* [C] ○ *She's studying marketing at the London Business School.* [C] • School is also *Am for* UNIVERSITY: *They went to school together at Stanford and started the business before they graduated.* [U] ○ *We first met at* **graduate** *school* (= while doing a university course for a second or third degree). [U] • If you learn from the **school of life**, you learn from the good and bad experiences that you have had. • If you learn something in the **school of hard knocks**, you learn it as a result of often unpleasant experience. • *"And then the whining schoolboy, with his satchel, / And shining morning face, creeping like snail/ Unwillingly to school"* (Shakespeare, As You Like It 2.7) • *"School's out for summer"* (from the song *School's Out* by Alice Cooper, 1972) • See also PLAYSCHOOL. • [LP] **Schools and colleges**

school *obj* /skuːl/ *v* [T] *fml* • *It takes a lot of patience to school* (= train) *a dog/horse.* • *You must school yourself* **in** *tolerance.* • *You must school yourself* **to be tolerant**. [+ obj + *to* infinitive] • *Her children are* **well** *schooled* **in** (= have been taught to have) *correct behaviour.*

school·ing /'skuː·lɪŋ/ *n* [U] • *His grandparents paid for his schooling.* • *He didn't* **receive** *much* **formal** *schooling* (= education at school), *but he did learn a lot about the world when he was travelling with his parents.* • *In Britain,* **compulsory** *schooling begins at the age of five.*

school [GROUP] /skuːl/ *n* [C] a group of painters, writers, thinkers, etc. whose work is similar, esp. similar to that of a particular leader • *the Flemish School* • *the School of Raphael* • *the Frankfurt School* • *Her work has been greatly influenced by the Impressionist school* **of** *painting.* • A **school of thought** is (a group of people who share) a set of ideas or opinions about a matter: *According to one school of thought, the increase in divorce reflects the higher standards expected of marriage.* ○ *There are two opposing schools of thought on how to reduce unemployment.*

school [SEA ANIMALS] /skuːl/ *n* [C] a large number of fish or some other sea animals swimming in a group; a SHOAL [FISH] • *a school of dolphins/whales*

school·child (*pl* **-children**), **school·boy**, **school·girl**, *infml* **school·kid** /'skuːl·tʃaɪld, -bɔɪ, £-gɜːl, $-gɜːrl, -kɪd/ *n* [C] a child who goes to school • *I must say I find his schoolboy* (= childish) *humour rather tiresome.* • *She's got a schoolgirl* **crush** *on* (= she has strong romantic feelings for) *one of her teachers.* • *We just sat there giggling like* **naughty** *schoolchildren.* • **As every schoolboy/schoolchild knows** (= As everyone, including very young people, knows), *the earth revolves around the sun.*

school·days /'skuːl·deɪz/ *pl n* the period a child spends at school • *His schooldays were very unhappy.* • *My parents say your schooldays are the best days of your life, but I'm not so sure.*

school·house /'skuːl·haʊs/ *n* [C] *pl* **schoolhouses** /'skuːl,haʊ·zɪz/ *esp. Am* a building used as a school, esp. in a village • *They're planning to turn the old schoolhouse into a community centre.*

school·ie /'skuː·li/ *n* [C] *Aus infml* a teacher in a school • *Like an old schoolie, he couldn't resist using the blackboard.*

school·marm /£'skuːl·mɑːm, $-mɑːrm/ *n* [C] *(disapproving)* a very formal and severe woman who likes to control other people and is easily shocked, or *(Am dated)* a female school teacher

SCHOOLS AND COLLEGES

Primary and secondary education

UK			year that child is...	US	
playgroup, playschool, nursery school			3	playgroup, nursery school	
kindergarten (optional)			4	preschool, kindergarten	
infant school			5		
		lower	6		
		school	7	elementary/	
junior	primary		8	primary school	
school	school		9		primary
		middle	10		school
		school	11		
			12		
secondary/high			13	junior	
school			14	high school	
(comprehensive/		upper	15		high
grammar)		school	16	high school	school
	sixth form		17	(prep school)	
	college		18		

Grammar schools take students selected for their ability. **Comprehensive** schools take students of all abilities. **Private/independent** schools charge money and are called **boarding** schools if students live in them. In the US, Australia and Scotland, **public schools** are free schools provided by the government. In England *private* schools are called public schools; **prep/** *(fml)* **preparatory schools** are private schools for younger children.

Types of student

- **at school:** schoolgirls/schoolboys/schoolchildren; pupils
- **at university or college:**
  - **Undergraduates** are studying for their first degree and become **graduates** when they **graduate** (= obtain their degree).
  - **Postgraduates/** *(Am also)* **graduate students** already have a first degree and are studying for a higher qualification.

Students **attend** (= go to) a school/college/university. At school they have **lessons**, and at college **lectures**. Postgraduates often attend **seminars**.

school·mar·mish /£'sku:lˌmɑ:·mɪʃ, $-ˌmɑːr-/ *adj disapproving* • *Stop being so schoolmarmish and bossy.*

school·mas·ter *male, female* **school·mis·tress** /£'sku:lˌmɑ:·stəʳ, $-ˌmæs·tɚ, -ˌmɪs·trəs/ *n* [C] *dated* someone who teaches children in a school • *The competition was won by James Brown, a* **retired** *schoolmaster from Dorset.* • *Her teaching career began as a* **village** *schoolmistress in rural Pennsylvania.*

school·mate /'sku:l·meɪt/ *n* [C] a friend who is at the same school as you at the same time • *He spends more time with his schoolmates than he does with his family.* • *Pat and I were schoolmates in the sixties.*

school·teach·er /£'sku:lˌti:·tʃəʳ, $-tʃɚ/ *n* [C] someone who teaches children in a school

school·work /£'sku:l·wɜ:k, $-wɜ:rk/ *n* [U] studying done by a child at school or at home • *I hope the training for the swimming competition won't affect her schoolwork.*

school·yard /£'sku:l·jɑ:d, $-jɑ:rd/ *n* [C] *esp. Am* an outside area next to a school where children can play games or sport when they are not studying

schoon·er /£'sku:·nəʳ, $-nɚ/ *n* [C] a sailing ship with two or more MASTS and with its sails parallel to the length of the ship, rather than across it • *The schooners of the past were often large and fast.*

sci·at·i·ca /£saɪ'æt·ɪ·kə, $-'æṭ-/ *n* [U] pain in the lower part of the back and esp. the back of the legs • *My sciatica's playing me up again.*

sci·ence /saɪənts/ *n* (knowledge obtained from) the systematic study of the structure and behaviour of the physical world, involving experimentation and measurement and the development of theories to describe the results of these activities • *pure/applied science* [U] • *a science course/lesson/teacher* • *a science laboratory* • *There is a shortage of maths and science graduates.* • *Developments in science* **and technology** *have made possible a great many improvements in areas such as health and public safety.* [U] • *Space travel is* **one of the marvels/wonders of modern** *science.* [U] • A science is a particular subject that is studied using scientific methods: *Physics and chemistry are sciences, and history and literature are arts subjects.* [C] ○ *Girls seem to be more interested in the arts than* **the** *sciences.* [C] ○ *Economics is not an* **exact** *science because it has to take account of political and social considerations.* [C] ○ *Advances in* **medical** *science mean that people are living longer.* [U] • **The** science **of** something is the whole body of knowledge that has been built up about it: *the science of climatology* [C] • **Science fiction** (also *infml* **sci fi**, *abbreviation* **SF**) consists of books, films and cartoons about an imagined future, esp. about space travel or other worlds: *John Wyndham's 'Day of the Triffids' is a science-fiction* **novel/ story**. • *(esp. Br)* A **science park** is an area, often started or supported by a college or university, where companies involved in scientific work and new TECHNOLOGY are based. • *"The great tragedy of Science: the slaying of a beautiful hypothesis by an ugly fact"* (Thomas Huxley) • *"Whenever science makes a discovery, the devil grabs it while the angels are debating the best way to use it"* (A.Valentine)

sci·en·ti·fic /ˌsaɪən'tɪf·ɪk/ *adj* • *a scientific discovery/ experiment/theory* • *scientific evidence/knowledge/method/ research/terminology* • *scientific instruments/journals* • *The project has attracted considerable criticism from* **the** *scientific* **community** (=from scientists). • *(infml) I've made a note of which plants I've put in the garden, but I haven't been very scientific* (=systematic) **about** *it, I'm afraid!*

sci·en·ti·fi·cally /ˌsaɪən'tɪf·ɪ·kli/ *adv* • *Has this phenomenon ever been studied scientifically?* • *The foundation was set up in 1967 to provide scientifically-***based** *information about nutrition.* • *I'm afraid I'm not very scientifically-***minded** (=not very interested in or good at science). • *Claims that vitamins and minerals speed up the healing process have not been scientifically* **proven**. •

Higher education

Age	UK	Exam	US
18			junior college
19	university		college/
20	(3 or more years)		university
21		BA/BSc degree	(4 years)
22			
23	university	MA/MSc (1-2yrs)	graduate
24		PhD (3–7 years)	college/university
25			

Many students in Britain **attend** colleges of further/higher education. These usually give **training** in more practical subjects than universities and award **diplomas** or **certificates** such as the HNC (Higher National Certificate). In the US there is a great variety of specialist schools and colleges which award qualifications.

Qualifications
The names of degrees are used as titles in writing: *George Wright, MSc.* In conversation, people with a PhD are given the title Doctor: *Have you shown this to Dr Graham?*

- **first degrees** (American degrees are in the right column)

BA	Bachelor of Arts	BA/AB	Bachelor of Arts
BEd	Bachelor of Education	BAEd	Bachelor of Arts in Education
MB	Bachelor of Medicine	BM	Bachelor of Medicine
LLB	Bachelor of Laws	LLB/BL	Bachelor of Laws
BSc	Bachelor of Science	BSc /BS	Bachelor of Science

- Students are **awarded** these qualifications if they pass their examinations: *Kate is* **studying for/taking/doing** *a BA* **in** *Modern History.* Science students usually **receive** a BSc. People studying **the arts** (= subjects such as English, history and social sciences) receive a BA.
- For some jobs, such as doctors and lawyers, graduates must obtain further **professional qualifications** before they are fully **qualified** to do the job.

- **second/postgraduate/higher degrees** (*Am also* **graduate degrees**)

MA	Master of Arts
MSc/*(Am also)* MS	Master of Science
PhD	Doctor of Philosophy

Postgraduates must write a **thesis**. The detailed study of a subject for a higher degree is called **research.**

Scientifically **(speaking)** (= According to scientific opinion), *this chemical is a salt, although you wouldn't want to eat it.*

sci·en·tist /ˈsaɪən·tɪst/ *n* [C] • A scientist is an expert who studies or works in one of the sciences: *a research/nuclear scientist* • *Scientists discovered the atomic nucleus in 1909.*

sci fi /ˈsaɪ·faɪ/ *n* [U] *infml for* **science fiction**, see at SCIENCE

sci·mi·tar /£ˈsɪm·ɪ·tər, $-t̬ɚ/ *n* [C] a sword with a curved blade which is sharp only on its outer edge and which widens towards its pointed end • *Scimitars were used in the past by the Turks and the Persians.*

scin·til·la /sɪnˈtɪl·ə/ *n* [C usually sing; usually in negatives and questions] *fml* the slightest amount • *I can make that prediction without a scintilla* **of** *doubt in my mind.* • *There's not a scintilla* **of** *truth* **in** *what he says.*

scin·til·lat·ing /£ˈsɪn·tɪ·leɪ·tɪŋ, $-t̬əl·eɪ·t̬ɪŋ/ *adj* interesting, exciting and clever • *scintillating wit/repartee* • *a scintillating personality/speech* • *I'm looking forward to some scintillating* **conversation** *at your dinner party tomorrow night.*

scin·til·late /£ˈsɪn·tɪ·leɪt, $-t̬əl·eɪt/ *v* [I] *esp. literary* • *Cynthia simply scintillated* (= spoke and behaved very excitingly and amusingly) *at the party last night.*

sci·on /ˈsaɪ·ən/ *n* [C] *literary* a young member of a rich and famous family • *He's the scion* **of** *a newspaper-publishing family and the heir to a fortune of half a billion dollars.*

sci·roc·co /£sɪˈrɒk·əʊ, $-ˈrɑː·koʊ/ *n* [C] a SIROCCO

scis·sors /£ˈsɪz·əz, $-ɚz/ *pl n* a device used for cutting materials such as paper, cloth and hair, consisting of two sharp blades which are joined in the middle in a way that allows them to move against each other • *nail/manicure scissors* • *kitchen scissors* • *dressmaking scissors* • *a pair of scissors* • *Could you pass me those scissors, please.* • *These scissors are rather* **blunt**/*(Am also)* **dull** – *I'll have to get them sharpened.* • *(disapproving)* If a book or television programme is a **scissors and paste** job, it is not original, but made up from parts of other books or programmes. • PIC〉 **Cosmetics, Nail**

scis·sor /£ˈsɪz·ər, $-ɚ/, **scis·sors** [before n] • *a scissor blade* • *a scissor/scissors case* • A **scissor jump/kick** or **scissors jump/kick** in sports such as swimming and football is a jump or kick in which the legs are brought together quickly.

scle·ro·sis /£skləˈrəʊ·sɪs, $-ˈroʊ-/ *n* [U] *medical* a medical condition which causes a hardening of body tissue or organs, esp. the ARTERIES (= tubes which carry blood from the heart) • *(fig.) economic sclerosis* (= extremely slow economic development) • (PL)

scle·rot·ic /£skləˈrɒt·ɪk, $-ˈrɑː·t̬ɪk/ *adj* [not gradable] *medical* • *sclerotic arteries* • *(fig. disapproving) The tax cuts are designed to bring growth to a sclerotic* (= slowly developing and not easily changed) *economy.*

scoff [LAUGH] /£skɒf, $skɑːf/ *v* [I] to speak about someone or something in a way which shows that you have no respect for them • *Don't scoff – what I've just said is absolutely true.* • *The Prime Minister scoffed* **at** *the suggestion that he was about to resign.* • *Years ago people would have scoffed* **at the idea/notion** *that cars would be built by robots.*

scoff /£skɒf, $skɑːf/ *n* [C usually pl] • *Despite the scoffs* (= remarks that lack respect) *of her colleagues, the experiment was completely successful.*

scof·fer /£ˈskɒf·ər, $ˈskɑː·fɚ/ *n* [C usually pl] • *I was able to prove the scoffers wrong.* • *The idea of democracy has more believers than scoffers.*

scoff *obj* [EAT] /£skɒf, $skɑːf/, *Am also* **scarf** *v* [T] *infml* to eat (something) quickly and eagerly • *I baked two huge cakes this morning, and those greedy children have scoffed* *them both.* • *I left two platefuls on the table and the dog scoffed the lot.*

scold *obj* /£skəʊld, $skoʊld/ *v* [T] to criticize angrily (someone who has done something wrong) • *He didn't scold her, but he demanded to know how the accident had happened.* • *His mother scolded him* **for** *breaking her favourite vase.* • *The president was scolded* **publicly** *for the environmental pollution his country has caused.* • *He endured years of criticism from her scolding tongue.*

scold·ing /£'skəʊl·dɪŋ, $'skoʊl-/ *n* [C] • *He* **gave** *his son a scolding* **for** *coming home so late.* • *Her country was the target of a public scolding by the US Secretary of State last week.*

sconce /£skɒnts, $skɑːnts/ *n* [C] *specialized* a device which is fixed to a wall to hold electric lights or candles

scone /£skɒn, $skɑːn/ *n* [C] a small, usually round, bread-like cake made from flour, milk and a little fat • *plain/fruit/cheese scones* • *He brought out a large plate of scones with lots of jam and cream.* • *Later that afternoon we had tea and scones in the garden.*

scoop TOOL /skuːp/ *n* [C] a tool with a deep bowl-shaped end which is used to dig out and move a soft or powdery substance • *a measuring scoop* • *an ice-cream scoop* • A scoop is also the amount held by a scoop: *Just one scoop of mashed potato for me, please.* • A **scoop-neck** piece of women's clothing is one which is cut low around the neck in a U-shape leaving a larger than usual area of skin uncovered: *Do you think it'll be warm enough at the barbecue to wear a scoop-neck dress?* • (J)

scoop *obj* /skuːp/ *v* [T] • If you scoop something, you move it with a scoop or with something used as a scoop: *Scoop* **out** *the flesh of the melon with a spoon, and fill the centre with fruit salad.* [M] ○ *He scooped the sand into a bucket with his hands.* ○ *(fig.) She scooped the children* **up** (= lifted them protectively) *into her arms and ran with them to safety.* [M] ○ *(fig.) As predicted, the film scooped* (= won) *half of the awards at the festival.* ○ *(fig.) The socialist party is expected to scoop* **up** (= win easily) *the majority of the working-class vote.* [M] • *(Br and Aus infml)* If you **scoop the pool**, you win all the prizes that are available: *Cuba scooped the pool in the boxing at this year's Olympics.*

scoop NEWS /skuːp/ *n* [C] a story or piece of news discovered and published by one newspaper before all the others • *Getting that story was the scoop of a lifetime for the young journalist.* • *The paper managed to secure a major scoop and broke the scandal to the world.* • (J)

scoop *obj* /skuːp/ *v* [T] • *Just as we were about to publish the story, we were scooped by a rival paper* (= it published the story before we managed to).

scoot /skuːt/ *v* [I] *infml* to go quickly • *I'm scooting off to St Andrews for a few days' golf.* • *I'll have to scoot* (= leave quickly) *or I'll miss my train.* • *(Am)* To scoot is also to slide while sitting: *Scoot over and make room for your sister.*

scoot·er TOY /£'skuː·tər, $-t̬ɚ/ *n* [C] a child's vehicle with two or three small wheels joined to the bottom of a narrow board and a long vertical handle fixed to the front wheel. It is ridden by standing with one foot on the board and pushing against the ground with the other foot. • PIC› **Playground, Toy**

scoot·er MOTORCYCLE /£'skuː·tər, $-t̬ɚ/ *n* [C] a **motor scooter**, see at MOTOR CAR • *The best way to get around the island is to hire a scooter for $20 a day.* • PIC› **Bicycles**

scope RANGE /£skəʊp, $skoʊp/ *n* [U] the range of a subject covered by a book, programme, discussion, class, etc. • *I'm afraid that problem is* **beyond/outside the** *scope* **of** *my lecture.* • *Oil painting does not come* **within the** *scope* **of** *a course of this kind.* • *We would now like to* **broaden/widen the** *scope* **of** *the enquiry and look at more general matters.* • *His study of juvenile crime was very* **narrow/broad in** *scope.* • (GR) (I)

scope OPPORTUNITY /£skəʊp, $skoʊp/ *n* [U] the opportunity for doing something • *There is* **limited** *scope* **for** *further reductions in the workforce.* • *The government is hoping there will be* **plenty of** *scope* **for** *tax cuts before the next election.* • *This is a large old house with* **much/considerable** *scope* **for** *improvement.* • *I asked at the job interview whether there would be any scope* **for me to** *use my Japanese.* [+ *to* infinitive] • (GR) (I)

-scope TOOL /£-skəʊp, $-skoʊp/ *combining form* used to form nouns that refer to devices for looking at or discovering and measuring things • *a microscope* • *a telescope* • *a stethoscope*

scorch *(obj)* BURN /£skɔːtʃ, $skɔːrtʃ/ *v* to (cause to) change colour with dry heat, or to burn slightly • *The iron was too hot and he scorched the shirt.* [T] • *The surrounding area was scorched by the heat of the explosion.* [T] • *Don't stand too near the fire or your clothes will scorch.* [I]

scorch /£skɔːtʃ, $skɔːrtʃ/ *n* [C] • *Is there any way of getting rid of the scorch on this shirt?* • *We managed to put the fire out before it did any serious damage, but it still left scorch* **marks** *halfway up the wall.*

scorched /£skɔːtʃt, $skɔːrtʃt/ *adj* [not gradable] • *The countryside was scorched* (= dry and brown) *after several weeks of hot sun.* • If a country at war has a **scorched-earth policy**, it removes or destroys things such as food, buildings or equipment which could be useful to an advancing enemy.

scor·cher /£'skɔː·tʃər, $'skɔːr·tʃɚ/ *n* [C] *infml* • *Yesterday was a real scorcher* (= an extremely hot and sunny day).

scorch·ing /£'skɔː·tʃɪŋ, $'skɔːr-/ *adj, adv* • Scorching means very hot: *scorching weather* ○ *scorching heat* ○ *a scorching summer day* ○ *A dozen women carrying sacks of oranges sat under a scorching* **sun**, *waiting patiently to catch a bus to the local market.* • *It was scorching* (= extremely) *hot inside the greenhouse, and the plants were beginning to wilt.*

scorch DRIVE FAST /£skɔːtʃ, $skɔːrtʃ/ *v* [I always + adv/prep] *infml dated* (esp. of motorcycles and cars) to travel or be driven very fast • *A motorbike scorched* **down** *the road at a terrifying speed.* • *The sports car scorched* **past** *and disappeared into the distance.*

score *(obj)* WIN /£skɔːr, $skɔːr/ *v* to win or obtain (a point, goal etc.) in a competitive activity, such as a sport or game, or in an exam, or *(Br)* to record the number of points won by competitors • *Has either team scored yet?* [I] • *United narrowly avoided defeat when Richardson scored the equalizer thirty seconds before the end of the match.* [T] • *In a low-scoring game, Italy beat France 1-0.* • *Ireland scored* **against** *Wales two minutes into the second half.* [I] • *Botham scored a* **century** (= 100 points) *in yesterday's cricket match.* [T] • *Lineker scored a* **goal** *in the last minute of the match.* [T] • *Oakland scored three* **runs** *on five hits in the seventh inning.* [T] • *In American football, a touchdown scores* (= is worth) *six points.* [T] • *Penny did very well to score 18 out of 20 in the spelling test.* [T] • *Ann scored well/badly/high/low in the test.* [I] • *Two of the machines we tested scored high marks on running costs and friendliness to the environment.* [T] • *Could you* **keep** *score* (Br also *score)* (= record the points won) *at this afternoon's match?* [I] • *(fig.) You have a lot of patience – that's where you score* (= have an advantage) **over** *your opponents.* [I] • *(fig.) This new CD player really scores* (= is better than the others) *in terms of sound quality.* [I] • *(fig.) You certainly scored* (= were appreciated) *with that wonderful meal you cooked!* [I] • *(fig.) Nearly every bomb scored* **a hit** (= destroyed something). [T] • *(fig.) She has certainly scored* (= achieved) **a success** *with her latest novel.* [T] • *(fig.) The communists scored* (= achieved) *a surprise* **victory** *in the election.* [T] • *(Am and Aus infml)* Sometimes when you score something you obtain it: *I managed to score a couple of tickets to the World Cup final.* [T] • *(slang)* To score is also to obtain illegal drugs: *You need a lot of money to score every day.* [I] ○ *She was arrested by an undercover cop when she tried to score some dope in a nightclub.* [T] • *(slang)* If someone scores, they have a brief sexual relationship with someone that they have usually just met: *He scored* **with** *her after the party on Saturday night.* [I] • *I hate Alan – he's always trying to* **score (points) off/over** *people* (= make them look foolish in arguments by making clever remarks). • LP› **Sports**

score /£skɔːr, $skɔːr/ *n* [C] • A score is the number of points, goals, etc. achieved in a game or competition: *a high/low score* ○ *Have you heard the latest cricket score?* ○ *It was their highest score of the season.* ○ *Anna got an average score of 67 in her exams.* ○ *Add up your score and let's see who's won.* ○ *At half time, the score* **stood at** (= was) *two all.* ○ *The* **final** *score was 3-0.* ○ *Could you* **keep** (= record) *the score at this afternoon's match?* • *That goal was absolutely brilliant. I've never seen a score* (= act of scoring) *like it.* • *(fig. infml) So what's the score* (= what are the facts of this situation), *doctor? Is it serious?*

score·less /£'skɔː·ləs, $'skɔːr-/ *adj* [not gradable] • In a scoreless game, no goals or points are scored: *After a scoreless first half, United went on to win 2-0.*

scor·er /£'skɔː·rər, $'skɔːr·ɚ/, *Am usually* **score·keep·er** /£'skɔːˌkiː·pər, $'skɔːrˌkiː·pɚ/ *n* [C] • A scorer is the person who records the score in a game. • *(esp. Am)* A scorer is someone who scores a point or goal in a game. • *"For when the One Great Scorer comes to write against your name, / He marks – not that you won or lost – but how you played the Game"* (Grantland Rice in the poem *Alumnus Football*, 1941)

score MUSICAL TEXT /£skɔːʳ, $skɔːr/ *n* [C] a piece of written music with the parts for all the instruments and voices arranged on separate lines, or the music written for a film, play, etc. • *an orchestral score* • *a film score* • *How can someone be a conductor if they can't read the score?* • *Rodgers wrote the score* **of/to** *'Oklahoma!' and Hammerstein wrote the lyrics.*

score *obj* /£skɔːʳ, $skɔːr/ *v* [T] • To score a piece of music is to write or adjust it for particular instruments or voices: *This piece is scored* **for** *strings and woodwind.* ○ *Stravinsky scored the piece* **for** *wind instruments.*

score *obj* MARK /£skɔːʳ, $skɔːr/ *v* [T] to make a mark or cut on the surface of (something hard) with a pointed tool, or to draw a line through (writing) • *Score the cardboard along the dotted line and then fold it.* • *If you score the tile first, it will be easier to break.* • *He scored* **out/through** *two names on the list.* [M] • See also UNDERSCORE.

score ARGUMENT /£skɔːʳ, $skɔːr/ *n* [C] an argument or disagreement that has existed for a long time • *It's time these* **old** *scores were forgotten.* • If you **settle** a score, you punish someone for something wrong which they did to you in the past, and which you cannot forgive: *"I've got a score to settle with you," he said, "and this time you're not going to get away."* ○ *More than 60 gangsters have been shot dead in the settling of* **old** *scores over the past few years.*

score REASON /£skɔːʳ, $skɔːr/ *n* [C] a reason or matter • *I'll let you have the money, so there's nothing to worry about* **on that** *score* (= there is no reason to worry about money). • *"The team has great determination to win," declared the coach. "I've* **no doubts** *on that score* (= about that matter)." • *It is important to maintain healthy growth in the economy, and* **on that/this score** (= in connection with that/this), *our policy has succeeded.* • *(fml) The play was banned* **on the** *score* **of** (= because of) *its sexual explicitness.*

score TWENTY /£skɔːʳ, $skɔːr/ *n* [C] *pl* **score** *esp. fml* (a set or group of) 20 or approximately 20 • *We ordered three score* (= 60) *boxes.* • *He lived to be three score years and ten* (= until he was 70 years old). • *The play has only been performed* **a** *score* **of** (= approximately 20) *times.* • **A** *score* **of** *countries have been quick to recognise the new state.* • *People are leaving the Nationalist Party* **by the score** (= in large numbers). • *"The days of our years are three score years and ten"* (Bible, Psalm 90.10)

scores /£skɔːz, $skɔːrz/ *pl n* • If there are scores of people or things, there is a lot of them: • *Benjamin received cards from scores* **of** *local well-wishers.* ○ *There have been five more deaths and scores* **of** *injuries in the past three days.* ○ *There were scores* **of** *tourists at the memorial when we visited it.* ○ *The problem is one of scores that we've experienced over recent months.*

score·board /£'skɔː·bɔːd, $'skɔːr·bɔːrd/ *n* [C] a large board on which the score of a game is shown • *The election results were flashed up on a giant electronic scoreboard that had been erected outside the town hall.*

score·card /£'skɔː·kɑːd, $'skɔːr·kɑːrd/ *n* [C] a small card for recording the score while watching or taking part in a game, race or competition

scorn /£skɔːn, $skɔːrn/ *n* [U] a very great lack of respect for someone or something that you think is bad or worthless • *She* **feels/has** *nothing but scorn* **for** *people who condemn lying but tell lies themselves.* • *His stupid suggestion* **filled** *her* **with** *scorn.* • *Why do you always* **pour/heap** *scorn* **on** (= criticize severely and unfairly) *my suggestions?* • If you are **the** scorn **of** other people, you are treated with scorn by them: *After cheating in the test, he was the scorn of all his classmates.*

scorn *obj* /£skɔːn, $skɔːrn/ *v* [T] • *Does he respect the press and media, or does he secretly scorn them?* • *She scorned the view that inflation was already beaten.* • If you scorn advice or an offer, you refuse it because you are too proud: *She scorned all my offers of help, so that's the last chance she'll get!* • *"Hell hath no fury like a woman scorned"* (based on lines from William Congreve's play *The Mourning Bride*, 1697)

scorn·ful /£'skɔːn·fᵊl, $'skɔːrn-/ *adj* • *a scornful look/remark/laugh/tone* • *They are openly scornful* **of** *the idea of life on other planets.*

scorn·ful·ly /£'skɔːn·fᵊl·i, $'skɔːrn-/ *adv* • *His proposals were scornfully* **dismissed** *by his boss.*

Scor·pi·o /£'skɔː·pi·əʊ, $'skɔːr·pi·oʊ/ *n* [not after *the*] *pl* **Scorpios** the eighth sign of the ZODIAC, relating to the period 23 October to 21 November and represented by a SCORPION, or a person born during this period • *I was born* **under** *Scorpio* (= during this period), *so I'm supposed to be cunning and ambitious.* [U] • *Frances and her boyfriend are Scorpios.* [C]

scor·pi·on /£'skɔː·pi·ən, $'skɔːr-/ *n* [C] a small insect-like creature which lives in hot dry areas of the world and has a long body and a curved tail with a poisonous sting

Scot, **Scots·man** (*pl* **-men**), **Scots·wo·man** (*pl* **-women**) /£skɒt, $skɑːt, £'skɒts·mən, £'skɒts,wʊm·ən, $'skɑːts-/ *n* [C] a person who comes from Scotland • *My mother/father was a Scot.* • *The Scots are used to cold weather.* • *It's often asked what's under a Scotsman's kilt!* • LP **Britain**

Scots /£skɒts, $skɑːts/, **Scot·tish** /£'skɒt·ɪʃ, $'skɑː·t̬ɪʃ/ *adj* [not gradable], *n* • Scots means of or from Scotland, and is used esp. of people: *Her husband is Scots.* • Scots is a form of the English language that is spoken in Scotland: *They still speak broad Scots even though they left Scotland twenty years ago.* [U]

Scotch COUNTRY /£skɒtʃ, $skɑːtʃ/ *adj* [not gradable] (esp. of products) of or from Scotland. In Scotland, 'Scottish' or 'Scots' is preferred to 'Scotch' when referring to people and language. • **Scotch broth** is a thick soup which usually contains BEEF (= meat from cattle), vegetables and BARLEY (= a type of grain). • A **Scotch egg** is a boiled egg that has been covered with a mixture of crushed meat, spices and bread and then fried. • **Scotch mist** is a mixture of thin fog and light rain. • *(trademark)* **Scotch tape** is *Am and Aus for* SELLOTAPE. • A **Scotch terrier** is a type of small active dog with short legs and rough fur. • See also SCOTTISH. • PIC **Dogs**

Scotch (whis·ky) /£skɒtʃ, $skɑːtʃ/ *n* • **Scotch (whisky)** is a strong alcoholic drink made in Scotland: *a bottle of Scotch* [U] ○ *I'll have a Scotch* (= a glass of this)/*a* **double** *Scotch/a Scotch* **and soda**/*a Scotch* **on the rocks** (= with ice). [C]

scotch *obj* PREVENT /£skɒtʃ, $skɑːtʃ/ *v* [T] *slightly fml* to prevent (something) from being believed or being done • *The announcement will scotch the rumours of a takeover that have plagued the company for the past 18 months.* • *He was keen to scotch suggestions that he would be unable to play in the rugby match on Saturday.* • *Her remarks were clearly intended to scotch speculation about a possible change in party leadership.* • *The rain scotched our plans for a picnic.* • Ⓕ

scot–free /£,skɒt'friː, $,skɑːt-/ *adv* [not gradable] without receiving the deserved or expected punishment or without being harmed • *The court* **let** *her* **off** *scot-free* (= did not punish her). • *She* **got off** *scot-free* (= received no punishment).

Scot·land Yard /£,skɒt·lᵊnd'jɑːd, $,skɑːt·lᵊnd'jɑːrd/ *n* [U not after *the*] the main office of the London police force, or the officers who work there, esp. those involved in solving serious crimes • *Scotland Yard is the headquarters of the Metropolitan Police.* • *Scotland Yard have/has been* **called in** *to investigate the murder.* [+ sing/pl v]

scoun·drel /'skaʊn·drəl/ *n* [C] *dated or humorous* a person, esp. a man, who treats other people very badly and has no moral principles • *He's an absolute scoundrel – he took our antique vase to get it valued and we haven't seen him since.* • *I'll see you in court, you filthy scoundrel!* [as form of address] • *"Every man over forty is a scoundrel"* (George Bernard Shaw in *Maxims for Revolutionists*, 1903)

scour *obj* CLEAN /£skaʊəʳ, $skaʊr/ *v* [T] to remove dirt from (something) by rubbing with something rough • *The plates were easy to wash, but the saucepans needed scouring.* • *You'll have to scour* **(out)** *those old cooking pots before you use them.* [M] • *I had to use scouring* **powder** *to get those stains off the sink.* • *(fig.) The fast-moving water had scoured* **(out)** (= formed by flowing continuously) *a channel in the rock.* [M] • *(fig.) She had scoured* **away** (= hidden or removed) *all evidence of nervousness and appeared completely calm.*

scour /£skaʊəʳ, $skaʊr/ *n* [U] • *The bath's absolutely filthy. I'll have to* **give it a good** *scour before Sheila comes to stay.*

scour·er /£'skaʊə·rəʳ, $'skaʊr·ɚ/, **pan scour·er**, *Am and Aus usually* **scour·ing pad** /£'skaʊə·rɪŋ, $'skaʊr·ɪŋ/ *n* [C] • A scourer is a small ball or rectangle of metal or stiff plastic netting which is used to clean dirt off surfaces: *You should use a nylon scourer rather than a metal one to clean non-stick pans.*

scour *obj* SEARCH /£skaʊəʳ, $skaʊr/ *v* [T] to search (a place or thing) very carefully in order to try to find something • *The police are scouring the fields* **for** *the missing child.* • *I scoured the shops* **for** *a blue and white shirt, but I couldn't find one anywhere.*

scourge /£skɜːdʒ, $skɜːrdʒ/ *n* [C usually sing] something or someone that causes great suffering or a lot of trouble • *One of the roles of the United Nations is to save succeeding generations from the scourge of war.* • *Aids has been described as the scourge* **of** *the modern world.* • *He is the* **self-appointed** *scourge of the educational establishment and has angered many teachers with his criticism of their work.*

scourge *obj* /£skɜːdʒ, $skɜːrdʒ/ *v* [T usually passive] • *The country has been scourged* **by** (= has suffered very much because of) *famine in recent years.*

Scouse /skaʊs/, **Scous·er** /£ˈskaʊ·səʳ, $-sɚ/ *n* [C] *infml* a person who comes from the Liverpool area, in north-west England • *The Beatles were Scouses.*

Scouse /skaʊs/ *n, adj* [not gradable] • Scouse is the form of English spoken by a person from Liverpool: *Many southerners can't understand Scouse.* [U] ○ *She's got a Scouse accent.*

scout SOLDIER /skaʊt/ *n* [C] a person, esp. a soldier, sent out to get information about where the enemy are and what they are doing

scout *(obj)* SEARCH /skaʊt/ *v* to go to look in (various places) for something you want • *He's scouting* **about for** *somewhere better to live.* [I always + adv/prep] • *Could you scout* **around/round** *and see whether there's somewhere we could get a coffee?* [I always + adv/prep] • *We've been sent to scout London's principal theatres* **for** *new talent.* [T] • *She's opened an office in Connecticut to scout* **out** (= discover information about) *the east coast housing market.* [M]

scout /skaʊt/ *n* [U] *infml* • *I'd better have* **a** *quick scout* (= search) **around** *and make sure I haven't left anything behind.*

scout /skaʊt/ *n* [C] • A scout is a person employed to look for people with particular skills, esp. in sport or entertainment: *Manchester United's chief scout spotted him when he was playing for his school football team.*

Scouts /skaʊts/ *pl n* **the Scouts** an international organization, which encourages young people of all ages to take part in activities outside and to become responsible and independent • Compare GUIDES.

scout /skaʊt/, *Am* **Boy Scout**, **Girl Scout** *n* [C] • A Scout is a young person aged between 10 and 16 years old who is a member of the Scouts: *A group of Scouts in scout uniform were waiting outside the scout hut.* ○ *We're appointing a new scout leader.* ○ *They've started a new scout* **troop** (= group). ○ *Sarah's going to/is on Scout* **camp** *next week.* ○ *Baden Powell founded the Scout* **Movement**. • *(esp. humorous)* You can say **scout's honour** when you are trying to make someone believe that you are telling the truth: *I didn't break it. Scout's honour!*

scout·er /£ˈskaʊ·təʳ, $-t̬ɚ/, **scout lead·er** *n* [C] • A scouter is the adult leader of any of the age groups which are part of the Scout organization.

scout·ing /£ˈskaʊ·tɪŋ, $-t̬ɪŋ/ *n* [U] • *I have fond memories of my scouting days* (= the time when I was a scout).

scowl /skaʊl/ *v* [I] to have a bad-tempered and angry expression on your face • *The boy scowled* **at** *her and reluctantly followed her back into school.*

scowl /skaʊl/ *n* [C] • *She looked at him* **with** *a scowl.* • *He wore a permanent scowl on his face.*

scrab·ble MOVE QUICKLY /ˈskræb·l̩/ *v* [I] *infml* to move your fingers or toes quickly, usually to search for something which you cannot see • *She scrabbled* **around** *in her bag, trying to find her keys.* • *He was scrabbling* **about** *on the gravel searching for the ring.* • *He scrabbled* **through** *piles of photographs to find the one he wanted.* • *He hung from the rock ledge, desperately scrabbling* **with** *his toes for a foothold.* • *Paul scrabbled* (= climbed quickly and not carefully) *up the cliff, dislodging several small stones.* • *(fig.) Several companies are scrabbling* (= competing with each other) **for** *a share in this rapidly-expanding market.*

Scrab·ble ® GAME /ˈskræb·l̩/ *n* [not after *the*] *trademark* a game played on a board covered in squares in which players win points by creating words from letters with different values and connecting these words with ones already on the board • *Do you fancy* **a game of** *Scrabble?* • *Scrabble ® is a registered trademark of J.W. Spear & Sons plc.* • PIC〉 **Games**

scrag·gly /ˈskræg·li/ *adj* **-ier**, **-iest** *esp. Am and Aus infml* growing in an untidy and irregular way • *scraggly vegetation* • *a scraggly beard/moustache* • *long scraggly hair*

scrag·gy /ˈskræg·i/ *adj* **-ier**, **-iest** *disapproving* so thin that the bones stick out • *He was wearing a high-necked pullover to hide his scraggy neck.* • *The scraggy old animals looked sad and neglected.*

scram /skræm/ *v* [I usually in commands] **-mm-** *infml* to go away quickly • *Stop hanging around my house, you lot. Scram!* • *We'd better scram!*

scram·ble MOVE QUICKLY /ˈskræm·bl̩/ *v* to move or climb quickly but with difficulty, often using the hands • *There were a lot of people waiting to scramble* **aboard** *the small boat.* [I always + adv/prep] • *She scrambled* **up/down** *the steep hillside and* **over** *the rocks.* [I always + adv/prep] • *We were scrambling* **through** *the thick undergrowth when we suddenly came across a fast-flowing stream.* [I always + adv/prep] • *He scrambled* **into** *his clothes* (= put them on quickly) *and raced to fetch a doctor.* [I always + adv/prep] • *As the burning plane landed, the terrified passengers scrambled* **for** *the door* (= tried to reach the door quickly). [I always + adv/prep] • *After waiting for over an hour, they scrambled madly* **to** *get the best seats.* [+ *to* infinitive] • *(fig.) Cuts in funding have sent arts groups scrambling* **to** *find* (= searching urgently for) *new sources of income.* [+ *to* infinitive]

scram·ble /ˈskræm·bl̩/ *n* [U] • *It was* **a** *real scramble to the top of the hillside.* • *(fig.) There was* **a mad/wild** *scramble* (= act of hurrying) **to get** *the best tickets.* [+ *to* infinitive] • *(fig.) After the death of the dictator there was* **an** *unseemly scramble* **for** (= hurried attempt to get) *power among the generals.*

scram·ble *obj* MIX EGGS /ˈskræm·bl̩/ *v* [T] to mix together the transparent and yellow parts of (eggs) with a little milk and butter while cooking them, so that they form a solid yellow mixture • *Should I scramble the eggs or poach them?* • *We had scrambled eggs on toast for breakfast.*

scram·ble *obj* CHANGE SIGNAL /ˈskræm·bl̩/ *v* [T] to change (a radio or telephone signal) while it is being sent so that it can only be understood using a special device • *Our radio signals were routinely scrambled to prevent the enemy discovering our plans.*

scram·bler /£ˈskræm·bləʳ, $-blɚ/ *n* [C] • A scrambler is an electronic device which scrambles radio or telephone messages.

scram·ble *(obj)* TAKE OFF /ˈskræm·bl̩/ *v specialized* to (cause to) take off very quickly • *The Mountain Rescue Team was alerted at 10.30pm, and a helicopter scrambled immediately.* [I] • *Orders were given to scramble the planes as soon as we received news of the missile attack.* [T]

scram·bling /ˈskræm·blɪŋ/ *n* [U] MOTOCROSS

scram·ble /ˈskræm·bl̩/ *n* [C] • *We're planning a scramble* (= a MOTOCROSS event) *through the forest next weekend.*

scrap *obj* THROW AWAY /skræp/ *v* [T] **-pp-** to get rid of (something which is no longer useful or wanted) • *There's no point keeping this kettle if it doesn't work. Why don't you scrap it?* • *We had to scrap the car after the accident as it was very badly damaged.* • *They're considering scrapping the tax and raising the money in other ways.* • *The proposed international treaty would scrap all short-range nuclear missiles by the end of the decade.* • *Under the new system, student grants would be scrapped and replaced by loans.* • *We scrapped our* **plans** *for a trip to France because we had to stay and look after my grandmother.*

scrap METAL /skræp/ *n* [U] old or used material, esp. metal, that has been collected in one place, often in order to be treated so that it can be used again • *scrap iron/metal* • *What is the ship's scrap* **value**? • *We've sold our old car* **for** *scrap.* • A **scrap dealer** (*Br also* **scrap merchant**) buys and sells scrap. • A **scrap heap** is a pile of scrap: *(fig.) Many actresses complain of being* **on the** *scrap heap* (= no longer wanted or needed) *at the age of 40.* ○ *(fig.) Some people believe that Communism has been* **consigned to the** *scrap heap* **of history** (= got rid of and forgotten about). ○ *(fig.) Those who lost their jobs felt that their commitment to the education service was being* **thrown on the** *scrap heap* (= ignored and not valued). • A **scrap yard** is a place where scrap is collected and either sold or prepared for being used again.

scrap SMALL PIECE /skræp/ *n* [C] a small and often irregular piece (of something) • *Have you got a scrap* **of**

paper I could write on? • *I mended the tear in my jeans with scraps* **of** *material from an old pair.* • *I've read* **every** *scrap of information I can find on the subject.* • *There's* **not a** *scrap* **of** (= no) *evidence to suggest that he committed the crime.* • *(fig.) She's just* **a** *scrap* **of a** *girl* (= very small and thin). • **Scrap paper** (*Am also* **scratch paper**) is loose sheets of paper, often partly used, for writing notes on.

scraps /skræps/ *pl n* • Scraps are small bits of food which have not been eaten and which are usually thrown away: *We give all our scraps to our cat.*

scrap ARGUMENT /skræp/ *v, n* **-pp-** (to have) a fight or argument, esp. a quick noisy one about something unimportant • *Stop scrapping* **over** *who's going to help. Just come and dry the dishes!* [I] • *Three dogs were* **having** *a scrap right outside my door.* [C]

scrap·py /ˈskræp·i/ *adj* **-ier, -iest** *Am* • *He's feeling scrappy today* (= He wants a fight or an argument), *so be careful what you say.*

scrap·book /ˈskræp·bʊk/ *n* [C] a book with empty pages where you can stick newspaper articles, pictures, etc. which you have collected and want to keep • *When I was young I* **kept** *a scrapbook and put train tickets and postcards from all our family trips in it.*

scrape *(obj)* REMOVE /skreɪp/ *v* to remove (an unwanted covering or a top layer) from (something), esp. using a sharp edge or something rough • *These are new potatoes, so scrape them rather than peel them.* [T] • *Scrape your boots clean before you come in.* [T + obj + adj] • *Jackie scraped her knee* **on** *the wall as she was climbing over it.* [T] • *The gateway was narrow, and he scraped the side of the car* **against** *it.* [T] • *We'll have to scrape the snow* **off** *the car before we go out in it.* [T] • *Emily scraped* **away** *the dead leaves to reveal the tiny shoot of a new plant.* [M] • *Stop scraping* (= pulling without lifting) *your feet* **along** *the floor, Joel – walk properly.* [T] • *Don't scrape* (= make an unpleasant noise by rubbing) *your chairs on the floor like that!* [T] • *I was woken up by the branches scraping* (= rubbing noisily) **against** *my bedroom window.* [I always + adv/prep] • *There was a long slow scraping sound of the raft against the mud.* • *(fig.) The company barely scraped* (= earned) *a profit this year.* [T] • To **scrape (the bottom of) the barrel** is to use the worst people or things because that is all that is available: *Richard's in the team? – You really are scraping the barrel!*

scrape /skreɪp/ *n* • *I haven't hurt myself seriously – it's just a scrape* (= a slight injury in which some skin has been removed). [C] • *I hate the scrape* (= unpleasant noise) *of chalk on a blackboard – it really sets my nerves on edge.* [U] • *(fig.) The injuries he suffered in the crash were quite serious, but despite this scrape* **with** (= despite being very close to) *disaster, he refused to give up racing.* [C] • *(infml)* A scrape is also a difficult situation which you cause by your own foolishness: *She's always getting into silly scrapes – I do wish she'd think before she does things.* [C]

scrap·er /£ˈskreɪ·pər, $-pɚ/ *n* [C] • *Using a scraper* (= tool for scraping) *to remove wallpaper can be very time-consuming.*

scrap·ing /ˈskreɪ·pɪŋ/ *n* [C] • *"Is there any mashed potato left?" "Just a scraping/Just the scrapings* (= Just what is left on the bottom and sides of the container)."

scrape SUCCEED /skreɪp/ *v* [I always + adv/prep] to only just be successful in getting • *She scraped* **into** *university on very low grades.* • *He managed to scrape* **through** (= only just pass) *his exam with 52%.* • To **scrape by/along** is to only just reach an acceptable standard: *I only learnt Spanish for three years but I can just scrape by in most situations.* ○ *I work 50 hours a week and still only earn enough to scrape by on.* ○ *He lost his job, so the family had to scrape along on £95 a week.* • *(Br and Aus)* To **scrape home** is to win by a very small amount in a competitive situation: *The reigning champion scraped home just 2·9 seconds ahead of his nearest rival.* • *(Br)* If you **scrape a living**, you only just earn enough money to provide yourself with food, clothing and housing: *He settled in Paris, where he scraped a living writing short stories and magazine articles.* ○ *The economy is still largely a peasant one, with most families scraping a living from the land.* • To **scrape together** something/**scrape** something **together** or **scrape up** something/**scrape** something **up** is to gather something together with great difficulty: *In ten years, they only once scraped together enough money for a week by the sea.* ○ *If we scrape enough people together, we can hire a bus.* ○ *Do you think we can scrape up a team for the match on Saturday?*

scrap·ie /ˈskreɪ·pi/ *n* [U] a viral disease of sheep and goats which usually results in death • *Scrapie affects the central nervous system and causes severe itching or drowsiness.*

scrap·py /ˈskræp·i/ *adj* **-ier, -iest** badly arranged or planned and consisting of parts which fit together badly • *I'm afraid your last essay was a very scrappy piece of work.*

scrap·pi·ly /ˈskræp·ɪ·li/ *adv* • *I wasn't impressed by that report they produced for us. It was very scrappily put together.*

scratch *(obj)* CUT /skrætʃ/ *v* to cut or damage (a surface) slightly with or on something sharp or rough • *We scratched the paintwork trying to get the bed into Martha's room.* [T] • *Be careful not to scratch your***self on** *the roses.* [T] • *CDs are better than records because it doesn't matter if they get scratched.* [T] • *I don't like this sweater – it scratches* (= makes the skin sore). [I] • *(esp. Br) This pen scratches* (= does not write smoothly). [I] • *A few chickens were scratching* **about/around** (= searching with their beaks) *in the yard* **for** *grain.* [I] • *(fig.) The editor of the local paper says he's really scratching* **around for** (= having difficulty finding) *stories this week.* [I] • If you scratch something on or off a surface, you add it or remove it by scratching: *People have been scratching their names* **on** *this rock for years.* [T] ○ *I'm afraid I scratched some paint* **off** *the door as I was getting out of the car.* [T] • If an animal scratches, it rubs something with the nails on its toes: *Don't worry about the cat. She doesn't scratch.* [I] ○ *The dog's scratching* **at** *the door – he wants to be let in.* [I] • If you scratch your skin, you rub it with the nails on your fingers: *Those mosquito bites will itch even more if you scratch them.* [T] ○ *Hannah scratched her head thoughtfully and wondered what she should do next.* [T] ○ *(fig.) A lot of people must be* **scratching** *their* **heads** (= thinking very hard) *and wondering how they will afford the tax increases.* ○ *Would you scratch my back for me? I've got a dreadful itch and I can't reach it.* [T] • *The councillors gave the building contract to the company who had offered them financial support for their election campaign – it was a case of* **you scratch my back and I'll scratch yours** (= I'll help you if you'll help me). • To **scratch beneath the surface** is to look beyond what is obvious: *If you scratch beneath the surface you'll find she's really a very nice person.* • A **scratch-and-sniff** picture is one which releases a smell if you rub it.

scratch /skrætʃ/ *n* [C] • *Where did all the scratches* (= marks made by scratching) *on this table come from? It's ruined.* • *Her legs were covered in scratches and bruises after her walk through the forest.* • *The development of CDs means that the problem of scratches on conventional records is becoming a thing of the past.* • *That dog's* **giving itself/having** *a good scratch* (= rubbing itself with its nails). *It must have fleas.* • *Amazingly, he survived the accident* **without a** *scratch* (= without suffering any injuries). • **Scratch paper** is *Am for* **scrap paper**. See at SCRAP SMALL PIECE.

scratch·y /ˈskrætʃ·i/ *adj* **-ier, -iest** • *We spent the evening listening to her scratchy old jazz records.* • *Using fabric conditioner when you wash your pullover should make it less scratchy* (= rough on your skin). • *(esp. Br) This pen's scratchy* (= not writing smoothly). *Have you got another one?* • *(esp. Br) I hope you can read my scratchy* (= uneven) *writing.* • *(fig.) She's bad-tempered and scratchy* (= easily annoyed) *if she doesn't get enough sleep.*

scratch GOOD /skrætʃ/ *n* [U] **up to scratch** reaching an acceptable standard • *You didn't play the piece too badly this time, so we should be able to* **bring** *it up to scratch before next week's concert.* • *Your last essay wasn't up to scratch/didn't* **come** *up to scratch* (= was not as good as usual). *You really ought to make more effort.*

scratch START /skrætʃ/ *n* [U] **from scratch** completely from the beginning • *I learned Russian from scratch at university.* • *At my restaurant we try to make everything from scratch.* • *Should we try and correct these problems, or would it be better to* **start again** *from scratch?*

scratch /skrætʃ/ *adj* [before n; not gradable] • A scratch group of people is one that is brought together in a hurry to play together: *a scratch team/side/orchestra*

scratch *(obj)* REMOVE /skrætʃ/ *v* to remove (yourself or another person or an animal) from a competition before the start • *The world champion scratched* **from** *the 800m after falling ill three hours earlier.* [I] • *They scratched the horse* **from** *the race because she had become lame.* [T]

scratch·pad /ˈskrætʃ·pæd/ *n* [C] *Am and Aus* a set of sheets of paper which have been joined together along one edge and are used for writing notes on

scrawl /£skrɔːl, $skrɑːl/ *v, n* (to produce in) untidy and careless writing • *Hilary was out, so I scrawled a note* **to** *her and put it under the door.* [T] • *The graffiti scrawled* **across** *the wall was removed with chemicals.* [T] • *I hope you can decipher my scrawl!* [C] • *The walls of the cell were covered with the scrawls of the prisoners that had been held there over the years.* [C]

scrawn·y /£ˈskrɔː·ni, $ˈskrɑː-/ *adj* **-ier, -iest** bony and unpleasantly thin; SCRAGGY • *He came home after three months at college looking terribly scrawny.*

scream *(obj)* /skriːm/ *v* to cry or say (something) loudly and usually on a high note, esp. because of strong emotions such as fear or excitement or anger • *The baby was still screaming at two in the morning.* [I] • *A spider landed on her pillow and she screamed.* [I] • *Her fans screamed hysterically as she walked on stage.* [I] • *Everyone started screaming and yelling when they heard England had won.* [I] • *Two youths had dragged the man* **kicking and** *screaming into a field and stabbed him repeatedly in the chest.* [I] • *Through the smoke, the rescuers could hear people screaming* **for** *help.* [I] • *He was screaming* **in/with** *pain and begging for anaesthetic.* [I] • *They screamed* **with** *laughter when I tripped and fell over.* [I] • *Ken screamed* **(out)** *a warning telling people to get out of the way.* [M] • *(fig.) 'Royal Plane Disaster!' screamed* **(out)** (=was printed in large letters in) *the newspaper headlines the next day.* [+ clause] • *(fig.) This matter is screaming* **out** *for* (=urgently needs) *attention.* [I] • *Mrs Brown screamed* (=shouted angrily) **at** *Joel* **for** *dropping the test-tube.* [I] • *I've never found screaming* **(and shouting)** (=shouting angrily) **at** *my staff to be very effective.* [I] • *"I wish you were dead!" she screamed* (=shouted angrily). [+ clause] • *I tried to apologize, but he just screamed* **abuse/obscenities** *at me.* [T] • *(fig.) The ambulance raced down the road with its* **sirens** *screaming.* [I] • *(fig.) The cars screamed* (=travelled very quickly and noisily) **round** *the bend/***past** *the spectators.* [I] • If you say that two colours are screaming at each other, you think that they do not look attractive or pleasant together: *You can't wear that pink jacket with your orange skirt. They'll just scream at each other.* [I] • *"You can* **scream** *yourself* **hoarse/scream** *your* **head off/scream the place down** (=scream very loudly), *but no one will hear you," said the kidnapper.* • *"In space, no one can hear you scream"* (advertisement for the film *Alien*, 1979)

scream /skriːm/ *n* [C] • *a scream of pain/rage/joy/laughter* • *No one heard their screams.* • *She* **let out** *a* **piercing/shrill** *scream.* • *(infml)* A scream is also a person, thing or situation which is very amusing: *Jane's such a scream – she's always telling funny stories.* ○ *Go and see Woody Allen's latest film – it's an* **absolute** *scream.*

scream·ing·ly /ˈskriː·mɪŋ·li/ *adv* extremely • *I'm not screamingly popular at home at the moment, since I crashed Dad's car.* • *She told me a screamingly* **funny** *story about the time she got stuck in an elevator.* • *It was screamingly* **obvious** *to me that we couldn't afford to do it.*

scree /skriː/ *n specialized* (an area on the side of a mountain covered with) large loose broken stones • *She fell over and twisted her ankle as she was scrambling down the scree.* [C] • *Scree is formed by the action of rain and frost on rock.* [U]

screech /skriːtʃ/ *v, n* (to make) a long loud high noise, which is usually unpleasant to hear • *She let out a loud screech.* [C] • *The truck stopped with a screech of brakes.* [C] • *It was so upsetting to see the monkeys screeching in the cage.* [I] • *I was woken by a barn owl screeching outside my window.* [I] • *He was screeching* **with** *pain/laughter.* [I] • *The children screeched* **with** *delight when they saw Father Christmas.* [I] • *(humorous) That woman's screeching, not singing!* [I] • *"Don't you dare touch me!" she screeched.* [+ clause] • *The car screeched* **to a halt/came to a** *screeching* **halt**/*screeched* **to a standstill** (=the BRAKES or wheels made a loud high noise as the car stopped suddenly). [I] • *(fig.) The economic recovery is likely to screech* **to a halt** (=stop suddenly) *if taxes are increased.*

screed /skriːd/ *n* [C] a long and usually boring piece of writing • *She's written screeds (and screeds)* (=a lot) *on the subject, but hardly any of it is worth reading.*

screen PICTURE /skriːn/ *n* [C] a flat surface in a cinema or on a television or a computer system on which pictures or words are shown • *a multi-screen/twelve-screen cinema* • *Our television has a 19-inch screen.* • *The TV coverage of the concert was* **displayed** *on giant video screens so that everyone in the stadium could see it.* • *I find it really irritating watching foreign films with subtitles* **flashing** *across the bottom of the screen.* • *Coming to your screens* (=cinemas) *shortly, the amazing adventures of "Robin Hood".* • *Her ambition is to write for* **the** *screen* (=for television and films). • *He prefers to* **adapt** *his novels* **for the** *screen himself.* • *I spend most of the day working in front of a* **computer** *screen.* • *Write the letter on the computer, then you can make changes easily* **on screen.** • Sometimes television is called **the small** screen and cinema is called **the big** screen: *You've made several films for the small screen, but this is your first one for the big screen, isn't it?* • **Screen printing** is a method of printing by forcing ink through a pattern cut into a piece of cloth stretched across a frame. • On a computer, a **screen saver** is a program which protects the screen by automatically covering a still image with a moving image if the computer has not been used for a few minutes: *One popular screen saver shows winged toasters flying across the screen, accompanied by slices of toast.*

screen *obj* /skriːn/ *v* [T usually passive] • When a film or television programme is screened, it is shown or broadcast: *Her new movie opens in London tomorrow and will be screened nationwide next month.* ○ *As a result of intervention by the Foreign Office, the programme was not screened on British television.*

screen·ing /ˈskriː·nɪŋ/ *n* [C] • *There will be three screenings* (=showings) *of the film – at 3, 5 and 7 p.m.* • *The movie was given an enthusiastic reception at its press screening last week.*

screen *obj* EXAMINE /skriːn/ *v* [T] to test or examine (someone or something) to discover if there is anything wrong with them • *All women over 50 will be screened* **for** *breast cancer.* • *The FBI screened* (=looked at the records of) *all applicants for the job to see whether any of them was a security risk.* • *Completely unsuitable candidates were screened* **out** (=tested and refused) *at the first interview.* [M] • *All luggage is screened* (=tested with a special machine) *at the airport to make sure it contains nothing illegal or dangerous.*

screen·ing /ˈskriː·nɪŋ/ *n* • *Studies are under way to see if the interval between* **breast** *screenings should be shorter than the recommended three years.* [C] • *Many of these cancer deaths could be avoided by regular* **cervical** *screening.* [U] • *The screening process for political refugees has been criticized by human rights organisations for being too restrictive.*

screen SEPARATE /skriːn/ *n* [C] something vertical which separates one thing from another, esp. to hide something, or to protect you from something unpleasant or dangerous • *The nurse pulled a screen around the bed so that the doctor could examine the patient in private.* • *A screen of trees at the bottom of the garden hid the ugly factory walls.* • *Put a screen in front of the fire when the children are playing in here.* • *(fig. esp. Am) That café's just a screen* (=something that looks harmless but is used to hide something bad) **for** *their criminal activities.* • *(Am and Aus)* A **screen door** is a door consisting of a wire net with very small holes stretched over a frame which allows air but not insects to move through it. • See also SUNSCREEN; WINDSCREEN.

screen *obj* /skriːn/ *v* [T] • *She raised her hand to screen* (=protect) *her eyes* **from** *the bright light.* • *We can screen* **off** *part of the room* (=separate part of the room with a movable wall) *and use it as a temporary office.* [M] • *(fig. esp. Am) The husband says he's the murderer but we think it was his wife – he's just screening* (=protecting) *her.*

screen·play /ˈskriːn·pleɪ/ *n* [C] the text for a film with the words to be spoken by actors and usually instructions for the cameras • *Who wrote/did the screenplay* **for/of/to** *the film 'Chariots of Fire'?*

screen·writ·er /£ˈskriːnˌraɪ·təʳ, $-t̬ɚ/ *n* [C] someone who writes the story for a film • *Only by becoming directors can screenwriters retain control over their work.*

screw METAL OBJECT /skruː/ *n* [C] a small straight thin metal object with a raised edge twisting round along its length, a flat circular top with a cut in it, and usually a pointed end, which is used to join esp. pieces of wood together • *Would it be better to use screws or nails to make the bookcase?* • *You* **tighten (up)/loosen** *a screw with a screwdriver.* • A screw is also a twist or turn made to fasten or tighten something: *Give it another screw to make sure the lid doesn't come off while we're travelling.* • *(infml humorous)* If you say that someone **has a screw loose**, you mean that they behave in a strange way and seem slightly mentally ill: *Did you know she cuts her hedge with scissors? I think she's got a screw loose.* • *(infml)* To **put/tighten the screws on** someone is to use force or threats to make someone do what you want: *They put the screws on him until he was forced to resign.* ○ *Tightening the screws on business drivers would have an immediate effect on traffic congestion.* • If a container has a **screw top** or is **screw-topped**, it has a lid which fastens by being turned: *a screw top jar* ○ *This bottle is screw-topped but the other one has a push-on lid.* • See also CORKSCREW.

screw *(obj)* /skruː/ *v* [always + adv/prep] • *Screw this piece of wood* (= Fasten it using a screw) **to** *the wall so that we can fix the curtain rail to it.* [T] • *Screw these two pieces* **together** *and then fit the top on afterwards.* [T] • If you screw something with a raised edge along its length and a pointed end like a screw into something else, you push and turn it into the other thing so that it becomes fastened to the other thing: *If we want to hang this picture up, we'll have to screw a hook* **into** *the wall.* [T] • To screw something **up/on** is to fasten it by turning it or twisting it: *Screw the nut up tightly.* [T] ○ *Screw the lid firmly on to the jar and shake well.* [T] • If something screws **in/together**, it fits or fastens together by being turned: *This light bulb screws in, but the bulb with a bayonet fitting pushes in.* [I] ○ *At present the steel rods screw together, but in future they will have hinged connections.* [I] • *(fig.) She screwed* (= twisted) *her head right* **round** *so that she could see the back of the hall.* [T] • *(Br infml)* If you screw something **out of** someone you obtain it by using force or threats: *The police took five hours to screw a confession out of him.* [T] ○ *We'll screw* **every last penny** *out of him.* [T] ○ *They were able to screw increasingly large amounts of money out of the government because of what they knew.* [T] • To **screw up** your **courage** is to force yourself to be brave: *I screwed up my courage and went in to see the director.*

screw *obj* CHEAT /skruː/ *v* [T] *infml* to cheat or deceive (someone) • *It was only after we'd had the car for a few days that we realised we'd been screwed.* • *He got screwed when he bought that antique chest.* • *They screwed her* **for** *five thousand quid over that business deal.*

screw *(obj)* HAVE SEX /skruː/ *v taboo slang* to have sex, or to have sex with (someone) • *They were caught screwing underneath the desk in her office.* [I] • *They say he's screwing the boss's wife.* [T] • If you screw **around**, you have sex with a lot of people or with people other than your husband or wife: *She threatened to divorce him after she discovered he'd been screwing around on business trips.* [I] • *(taboo slang)* **Screw it/you/them!** is an expression of extreme anger and annoyance: *"Screw it!" he said. "If they won't give us the money, we'll just take it."* ○ *You don't like it? Well, screw you!*

screw /skruː/ *n* [C] *taboo slang* • A screw is either the act of sex or a sexual partner: *I never feel like a screw when I wake up in the morning.* ○ *Chris is a really good screw!*

screw PRISON GUARD /skruː/ *n* [C] *slang* a prison guard • *I got beaten up for making friends with one of the screws.*

screw (up) *obj*, **screw** *obj* **(up)** *v adv* [T] to crush (esp. paper or cloth) roughly in the hand, or to tighten the muscles of (part of) the face • *She screwed the letter (up) into a ball and threw it angrily in the bin.* [T/M] • *The children screwed their faces up in disgust at the horrible smell.* [M] • *Julian screwed up his eyes when he came out into the bright sunlight.* [M] • *Her face was all screwed up with the effort of cycling up such a steep hill.*

screw up *(obj)*, **screw** *(obj)* **up** *v adv infml* to cause (something) to fail or be spoiled, or to cause (someone) to become anxious and unhappy • *I reckon I've passed the physics exam, but I'm sure I screwed chemistry up.* [M] • *Having the car stolen completely screwed up our holiday plans.* [M] • *We really screwed up when we invited Jane and two of her ex-boyfriends to the party.* [I] • *It really screwed him up when he saw his friend get killed.* [M]

screwed up /skruːd/ *adj infml* • *He's been really screwed up since his wife died.*

screw·ball PERSON /£'skruː·bɔːl, $-bɑːl/ *n* [C] *esp. Am infml* a person who behaves in a strange and amusing way • *You'll love Chris – she's a real screwball!*

screw·ball BALL /£'skruː·bɔːl, $-bɑːl/ *n* [C] *Am* a ball which is thrown during a baseball game so that it curves to one side

screw·dri·ver /£'skruːˌdraɪ·vəʳ, $-vɚ/ *n* [C] a tool for turning screws, consisting of a handle joined to a metal rod shaped at one end to fit in the cut in the top of the screw • *I'll need that large screwdriver to loosen these screws.* • PIC **Tools**

screws /skruːz/ *pl n* THUMBSCREW

screw·y /'skruː·i/ *adj* **-ier, -iest** *infml dated* very strange, foolish or unusual • *Pat's always coming up with screwy ideas.* • *This is the screwiest book I've ever read.* • *It might seem screwy to you, but it makes perfect sense to me.*

scrib·ble *(obj)* /'skrɪb·l̩/ *v* to write or draw (something) quickly or carelessly • *The baby's just scribbled* **all over/on** *my new dictionary!* [I] • *I'll just scribble Dad a note/ scribble a note* **to** *Dad to say we're going out.* [+ two objects] • *"Another damned, thick, square book! Always scribble, scribble, scribble! Eh! Mr Gibbon?"* (William Henry, Ist Duke of Gloucester (1743-1805) to the writer Edward Gibbon)

scrib·ble /'skrɪb·l̩/ *n* • *What are all these scribbles doing on the wallpaper?* [C] • *I hope you can read my scribble!* [U] • PIC **Writing**

scrib·bler /£'skrɪb·ləʳ, $'-lɚ/ *n* [C] *disapproving or humorous* • A scribbler is a bad or unimportant writer of books or articles in newspapers or magazines: *He dismissed the economists as teenage scribblers who wanted to get their names in the newspapers.*

scrib·bly gum /'skrɪb·li·gʌm/ *n* [C] *Aus* a type of EUCALYPTUS tree whose smooth BARK (= hard covering) is marked by irregular patterns left by insects

scribe /skraɪb/ *n* [C] a person employed before the invention of printing to make copies of documents • In Biblical times, a scribe was a teacher of the religious law.

scrimp /skrɪmp/ *v* [I] to save money by spending less than is necessary to reach an acceptable standard • *When we were first married, we had to scrimp* (**on** *food and clothes*), *so now we're really enjoying having some money.* • *There is a risk that the debt-ridden airline that may be tempted to scrimp* **on** *maintenance or security.* • If you **scrimp and save**, you manage to live on very little money in order to pay for something: *I've been scrimping and saving all year for our holiday, and now you've wasted it all on that stupid old car!*

script TEXT /skrɪpt/ *n* [C] a written or printed record of the words to be performed or presented in a film, play, broadcast or speech • *All members of the cast must* **keep to/stick to**/*not* **depart from** *the script.* • Script is also *Aus for* **prescription**. See at PRESCRIBE GIVE MEDICAL TREATMENT. • CS PL

script *obj* /skrɪpt/ *v* [T usually passive] • *He's a very good actor, but the part was scripted for an older person.*

script·ed /£'skrɪp·tɪd, $-t̬ɪd/ *adj* [not gradable] • *He read from a scripted speech* (= one written down in advance) *and refused to answer any questions at the end of it.*

script EXAM /skrɪpt/ *n* [C] *Br and Aus* an answer paper written by a student in an exam • *I've got 200 scripts to mark before Monday!* • CS PL

script WRITING /skrɪpt/ *n* writing, esp. when well formed, or a special system of writing • *Arabic/Cyrillic script* [U] • *The invitation was written in beautiful italic script.* [U] • *They can write out your invitations in a choice of scripts.* [C] • CS PL

scrip·ture /£'skrɪp·tʃəʳ, $-tʃɚ/ *n* the holy writings of a religion • *the Hindu/Buddhist/Muslim scriptures* [C] • *According to* **Holy Scripture** (= the Bible), *God created the world in six days.* [U] • *The Scriptures say* (= The Bible says) *that the love of money is the root of all evil.* [C]

scrip·tur·al /£'skrɪp·tʃəʳ·əl, $-tʃɚ-/ *adj specialized* • *scriptural texts/passages* • *He challenged his opponents to support their case with scriptural evidence.*

script·writ·er /£'skrɪptˌraɪ·təʳ, $-t̬ɚ/ *n* [C] a person who writes the texts for films or radio or television broadcasts

scroll PAPER /£skrəʊl, $skroʊl/ *n* [C] a long roll of paper or similar material with usually official writing on it • *The ancient Egyptians stored information on scrolls, which could be carried around more easily than clay tablets.* • *(fig.) The tops of the marble pillars were decorated with scrolls* (= shapes like scrolls).

scroll MOVE TEXT /£skrəʊl, $skroʊl/ *v* [I always + adv/prep] to move text or other information on a computer screen in order to view a different part of it • *Scroll* **to** *the end of the document.* • *Using the search facility saves you having to scroll* **through** *a document to find what you are looking for.* • *Scroll* **up/down/to the right/to the left** *to see if you can find the information you want.*

scrooge /skruːdʒ/ *n* [C] *disapproving* someone who spends as little money as possible and is not generous •

He's a mean old scrooge! • Scrooge is a character in the book 'A Christmas Carol' by Charles Dickens.

scro·tum /£'skrəʊ·təm, $'skroʊ·t̬əm/ *n* [C] *pl* **scrotums** or *fml* **scrota** /£'skrəʊ·tə, $'skroʊ·t̬ə/ *specialized* a bag of skin near the penis which contains the TESTICLES in most male mammals

scrounge *(obj)* /skraʊndʒ/ *v infml* to obtain (things, esp. money or food) by asking for them instead of buying them or working for them • *Peter never buys anything – he just scrounges* **(off** *his friends).* [I] • *She's always scrounging drinks* **(off/from** *me).* [T] • To scrounge **around** is to look for something which may or may not be there: *Scrounge around* **in** *the toolbox for a tack or nail to hang the notice up with.* [I] • To scrounge **up** something is to make it or put it together using only what is available: *I haven't gone shopping but I'm sure I can scrounge up something for dinner.* [M]

scrounge /skraʊndʒ/ *n* [U] *disapproving or humorous* • Someone who is **on the scrounge** is trying to obtain something without having to pay for it: *Patrick's on the scrounge again. Has anyone got a spare cigarette for him?*

scroung·er /£'skraʊn·dʒəʳ, $-dʒɚ/ *n* [C] *disapproving* • *You're such a scrounger, Pat. Why don't you buy your own drink for once?* • *He thinks that people who receive state benefits are scroungers.*

scrub *(obj)* CLEAN /skrʌb/ *v* **-bb-** to rub (something) hard in order to clean it, esp. using a stiff brush, soap and water • *I used to scrub the kitchen floor every Monday.* [T] • *She scrubbed* **(at)** *the mark on the wall for ages, but it wouldn't come off.* [T; I + *at*] • *He scrubbed the old saucepan clean, and it looked as good as new.* [T + obj + adj] • *Surgeons have to* **scrub up** (= wash their hands and arms very carefully) *before performing an operation.* • A **scrubbing brush** (*Am also* **scrub brush**) is a stiff brush used for scrubbing floors. • PIC› **Brush**

scrub /skrʌb/ *n* [U] • *Children, give your hands* **a good** *scrub and come and get your tea!*

scrub *obj* STOP /skrʌb/, *Am usually* **scratch** *v* [T] **-bb-** *infml* to decide not to do (something you had planned to do); to CANCEL • *We were going to modernize our kitchen, but we had to scrub the idea when I lost my job.* • *Take the first turning on the left – no, scrub that* (= ignore what I just said) *– take the second on the left.* • *(Br infml)* If you **scrub round** something, you avoid it or take no notice of it: *We can scrub round the rules.*

scrub PLANTS /skrʌb/ *n* [U] (an area of land covered with) short trees and bushes, growing on dry earth of low quality • *The area where we set up camp was just scrub and sand.*

scrub·by /'skrʌb·i/ *adj* **-ier, -iest** • *scrubby vegetation*

scruff NECK /skrʌf/ *n* [U] **by the scruff of** *the/your* **neck** by the skin at the back of the neck • *Cats carry their kittens by the scruff of the neck.* • *I* **took/grabbed** *him by the scruff of his neck and threw him out of the hall.*

scruff PERSON /skrʌf/ *n* [C] *Br infml* a dirty and untidy person • *Those old jeans make you look a terrible scruff!*

scruf·fy /'skrʌf·i/ *adj* **-ier, -iest** • Someone or something that is scruffy is untidy and dirty: *They live in a rather scruffy part of town.* ○ *He glanced up and saw a small, scruffy-***looking** *man gazing at him curiously.*

scruf·fi·ly /'skrʌf·ɪ·li/ *adv* • *She was too scruffily dressed for such a formal occasion.*

scrum /skrʌm/, **scrum·mage** /'skrʌm·ɪdʒ/ *n* [C] (in the sport of RUGBY) a group of attacking players from each team who come together with their heads down and arms joined, and push against each other, trying to take control of the ball • *(fig.) It was the first day of the sales, and as the shop doors opened, there was a terrible scrum* (= everyone pushed to try to get what they wanted).

scrum·mag·er /£'skrʌm·ɪ·dʒəʳ, $-dʒɚ/ *n* [C] • *The New Zealand forwards are brilliant scrummagers.*

scrum-half /£,skrʌm'hɑːf, $-'hæf/ *n* [C] *pl* **scrumhalves** /£,skrʌm'hɑːvz, $-'hævz/ a RUGBY player who throws the ball into the SCRUM

scrump *obj* /skrʌmp/ *v* [T] *Br dated infml* to steal fruit (esp. apples) from trees • *We used to scrump apples from our neighbour's orchard when we were little.*

scrump·tious /'skrʌmp·ʃəs/, *Br infml* **scrum·my** (**-ier, -iest**) /'skrʌm·i/ *adj* tasting extremely pleasant; DELICIOUS • *scrumptious cream cakes*

scrump·y /'skrʌm·pi/ *n* [U] *Br* an alcoholic drink made from apples • *Scrumpy is a type of strong cider.*

scrunch *(obj)* MAKE A NOISE /skrʌntʃ/ *v* to make the noise produced by hard things being pressed together, or to press (hard things) together so that they make a noise; to CRUNCH • *The pebbles/gravel/snow scrunched beneath our feet.* [I] • *We scrunched the pebbles/gravel/snow under our feet.* [T]

scrunch *obj* CRUSH /skrʌntʃ/ *v* [T] to crush (material such as paper or cloth) into a rough ball in the hand • *If you're in a rush, you can leave your hair to dry naturally, simply scrunching it into curls with your hands.* • *She scrunched the letter* **up** *and threw it in the bin.* [M] • *(fig. esp. Am) He had to scrunch* **up** *his shoulders* (= bring them close together) *to get through the narrow gap.*

scrunch·y /'skrʌn·tʃi/ *n* [C] • A scrunchy is a piece of elastic covered in often brightly-coloured cloth which is used to hold long hair at the back of the head and away from the face. • PIC› **Hair**

scru·ple /'skruː·pl̩/ *n* a feeling that prevents you from or makes you uncertain about doing something you think is morally wrong • *Robin Hood* **had** *no scruples* **about** *robbing the rich to give to the poor.* [C] • *If the use of force is left in the hands of those with* **no moral** *scruples, then there will be no justice in the world.* [C] • *She has moral and religious scruples which prevent her from eating meat.* [C] • *He is a man* **without** *scruple – he has no conscience.* [U]

scru·ple /'skruː·pl̩/ *v* [+ *to* infinitive; usually in negatives] *fml* • *He wouldn't scruple* **to** *cheat his own mother* (= He would cheat her without worrying about it) *if there was money in it for him.*

scru·pu·lous /'skruː·pjʊ·ləs/ *adj* extremely honest, or doing everything correctly and exactly as it should be done • *A scrupulous politician would not lie about her business interests.* • *The nurse told him to be scrupulous* (= extremely careful) **about** *keeping the wound clean.* • Ⓓ

scru·pu·lous·ly /'skruː·pjʊ·lə·sli/ *adv* • *She is always scrupulously* **honest/fair**. • *They have scrupulously* **avoided** *being seen in public together.* • *A hospital must be kept scrupulously* **clean**.

scru·tin·eer /£,skruː·tɪ'nɪəʳ, $-t̬ən'ɪr/ *n* [C] *Br and Aus* a person who counts votes in an election or who makes certain that the counting has been done correctly

scru·tin·ize *obj, Br and Aus usually* **-ise** /£'skruː·tɪ·naɪz, $-t̬ən·aɪz/ *v* [T] to examine (something) very carefully in order to discover information • *He scrutinized the men's faces* **carefully/closely**, *trying to work out who was lying.*

scru·tin·y /£'skruː·tɪ·ni, $-t̬ən·i/ *n* [U] • Scrutiny is the careful and detailed examination of something in order to obtain information about it: *The Government's record will* **be subjected to/come under close** *scrutiny in the weeks before the election.* ○ *His work will not* **stand up to/bear (close)** *scrutiny* (= If it is examined carefully, mistakes will be found).

scu·ba div·ing /'skuː·bə-/ *n* [U] the sport of swimming under water with special breathing equipment • PIC› **Water sports**

scu·ba div·er /'skuː·bə-/ *n* [C] • *The scuba divers put on their oxygen tanks and set off to explore the coral reef.*

scud /skʌd/ *v* [I always + adv/prep] **-dd-** (esp. of clouds and ships) to move quickly and smoothly in a straight line • *It was a windy day, and small white clouds were scudding* **across** *the blue sky.*

scuff *obj* /skʌf/ *v* [T] to make a rough mark on (a smooth surface), esp. on a shoe or floor • *Please wear trainers in the gym, to avoid scuffing the floor.* • *She's always scuffing her* **shoes** *in the playground.* • *Have you got anything for getting rid of scuff* **marks?** • *If you scuff your feet* (= pull your shoes along the ground as you walk) *like that, you'll ruin your shoes.*

scuffed /skʌft/ *adj* • *The book's a bit scuffed, but it was the only copy left in the shop.* • *She's had the same scuffed old handbag for twenty years.* • *The edges of the cupboards were all scuffed where the children had kicked a football against them.*

scuf·fle /'skʌf·l̩/ *v, n* (to take part in) a short and sudden fight, esp. one involving a small number of people • *There was a brief scuffle, and a man fell to the ground.* [C] • *Two police officers were injured in scuffles with fans at Sunday's National Football League contest.* [C] • *The boys scuffled* **with** *the policeman, then escaped down the lane.* [I]

scul·le·ry /£'skʌl·ər·i, $'-ɚ-/ *n* [C] a room next to the kitchen, usually in a large old house, where pans are washed and vegetables are prepared for cooking • *a scullery maid*

scull·ing /'skʌl·ɪŋ/ *n* [U] the sport of ROWING in a small narrow boat designed for one, two or four people, who use two small OARS each, rather than one large one, to move the boat

sculp·ture /£'skʌlp·tʃəʳ, $-tʃɚ/ *n* the art of forming solid objects out of a material such as wood, clay, metal or stone, or an object made in this way • *Tom teaches sculpture at the local art school.* [U] • *The museum houses an abstract sculpture as well as several life-sized sculptures* **of** *people and animals.* [C]

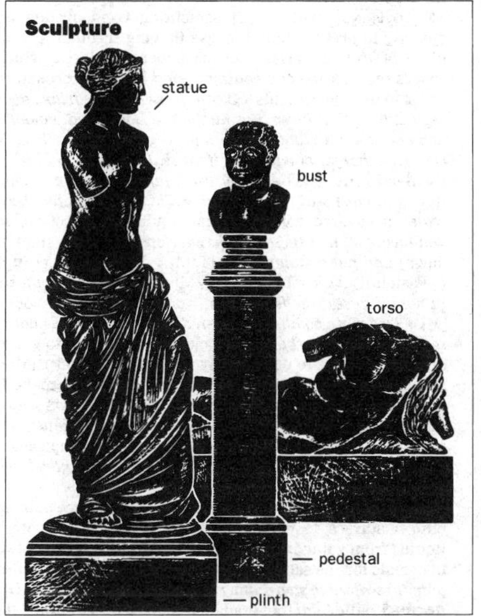

sculp·ture *obj* /£'skʌlp·tʃəʳ, $-tʃɚ/, **sculpt** /skʌlpt/ *v* [T] • *She sculptures statues* **out of/from** *the local stone.* • *(fig.) The dripping water had sculpted* (= formed) *strange shapes* **out of** *the rocks/sculpted the rocks* **into** *strange shapes.*

sculp·tured /£'skʌlp·tʃəd, $-tʃɚd/ *adj* • *The exhibition includes a wonderful group of animals sculptured* **in** *wax.* • *(fig.) Some women admire his (beautifully) sculptured* (= shaped like a sculpture) *features.*

sculp·tur·al /£'skʌlp·tʃə·rəl, $-tʃɚ-/ *adj specialized* • *Her delicate sculptural* **pieces** (= works of art) *are now selling in the USA, Europe and Japan.*

sculpt·or /£'skʌlp·təʳ, $-tɚ/ *n* [C] • A sculptor is someone who creates sculptures: *Henry Moore, who died in 1986, is one of Britain's best-known sculptors.*

scum [DIRT] /skʌm/ *n* [U] a layer of unpleasant or unwanted material that has formed on the top of a liquid • *The lake near the factory was covered with grey, foul-smelling scum.* • *Look at the scum round the bath – you must have been very dirty!* • *Bring the beans to the boil, then remove the scum with a spoon.*

scum·my /'skʌm·i/ *adj* **-ier, -iest** • *I wish you wouldn't leave the bath in such a scummy state.*

scum [IMMORAL PERSON] /skʌm/ *n pl* **scum** *disapproving slang* a very bad or immoral person or group of people • *Anyone who could do something like that is scum.* [U] • *People who organize dog fights are scum in my opinion!* [U] • *Do you know what that scum has done now?* [C] • *Those scum have been robbing old people.* [C] • *You scum! How dare you accuse me of lying!* [as form of address] • *His boss treats him* **like scum** (= very badly). [U] • *Those men are* **the scum of the earth** (= the worst type of people that can be imagined).

scum·bag /'skʌm·bæg/ *n* [C] *slang* a person of little value who has done something dishonest or immoral • *What a scumbag! I gave him a lift in my car and he's stolen my coat!* • *(humorous) Now look what you've done. You've got mud all over my homework, you scumbag!* [as form of address]

scup·per *obj* [SINK] /£'skʌp·əʳ, $-ɚ/ *v* [T] to sink (your own ship) on purpose • *Rather than face capture by the enemy, they scuppered the ship and escaped by night in the lifeboats.*

scup·per *obj* [SPOIL] /£'skʌp·əʳ, $-ɚ/ *v* [T] to cause (esp. a plan or a chance) to fail • *Arriving late for the interview scuppered my chances of getting the job.* • *The vote will scupper the school's reorganization plans.* • *The whole hospital project will be scuppered if we can't find more money.*

scurf /£skɜːf, $skɜːrf/ *n* [U] very small bits of dry dead skin which fall off the head esp. at the same time as hair; DANDRUFF • *The collar of his black jacket was covered with scurf – it looked horrible!*

scur·ri·lous /£'skʌr·ɪ·ləs, $'skɜːr-/ *adj fml* expressing unfair or false criticism which is likely to damage someone's reputation • *a scurrilous remark/attack/article*

scur·ri·lous·ly /£'skʌr·ɪ·lə·sli, $'skɜːr-/ *adv*

scur·ry /£'skʌr·i, $'skɜːr-/ *v* [I always + adv/prep] to move quickly, with small short steps • *The mouse scurried* **across** *the floor and disappeared through a hole in the wall.* • *We all scurried* **for** *shelter when the storm began.* • *Suddenly, he jumped to his feet and scurried* **out of** *the room.* • *The noise of the explosion* **sent** *the villagers scurrying* **back** *into their homes.*

scur·ry /£'skʌr·i, $'skɜːr-/ *n* [U] • *We heard* **a/the** *scurry* **of** *little feet from the children's bedroom.*

scur·vy /£'skɜː·vi, $'skɜːr-/ *n* [U] an illness of the body tissues which is caused by a lack of VITAMIN C • *In the past, sailors often suffered from scurvy on long journeys because they were not able to eat enough fresh fruit and vegetables.*

scut·tle [RUN] /£'skʌt·l̩, $'skʌt̬-/ *v* [I always + adv/prep] to move quickly, with small short steps, esp. in order to escape • *A crab scuttled* **away** *under a rock as we passed.* • *The children scuttled* **off** *as soon as the headmaster appeared.*

scut·tle *obj* [SINK] /£'skʌt·l̩, $'skʌt̬-/ *v* [T] to sink (a ship, esp. your own) intentionally by making holes in it, esp. in order to prevent an enemy from capturing it • *In 1942, the French fleet was scuttled at Toulon to prevent it being captured by the Germans.* • *(fig.) The projected costs were so high that we decided to scuttle the expansion plan* (= not to put it into action).

scut·tle [CONTAINER] /£'skʌt·l̩, $'skʌt̬-/ *n* [C] a **coal scuttle**, see at COAL • [PIC] **Fires and space heaters**

scuz·zy /'skʌz·i/ *adj* **-ier, -iest** *Am infml* (usually of people) unpleasant, dirty and probably unable to be trusted • *Who's that scuzzy-***looking** *guy in the corner?*

scythe /saɪð/ *n* [C] a tool with a long sharp curved blade and a long handle held in two hands, used esp. to cut down long grass • Compare SICKLE.

scythe *(obj)* /saɪð/ *v* • *He was scything* **(down)** *the long grass beside the road.* [T/M] • *(fig.) The racing car left the track at 120 mph and scythed* **(a path) through** (= violently crashed into) *the crowd of spectators, killing ten.* [I/T]

SDI /ˌes·diː'aɪ/, *infml* **Star Wars** *n* [U] *abbreviation for* Strategic Defense Initiative (= a 1980s plan to defend the US from enemy nuclear weapons by destroying them in space)

SDLP /ˌes·diːˌel'piː/ *n* [U] **the SDLP** *abbreviation for* Social and Democratic Labour Party (= a political party in N Ireland which supports union with the Republic of Ireland by peaceful methods)

SE *n* [U], *adj abbreviation for* SOUTHEAST or SOUTHEASTERN

sea /siː/ *n* the salty water which covers a large part of the surface of the Earth, or a large area of salty water, smaller than an OCEAN, which is partly or completely surrounded by land • *the North Sea* [U] • *the Mediterranean Sea* [U] • *the Caspian Sea* [U] • *The Atlantic isn't a sea – it's an ocean.* [C] • *We went swimming* **in the** *sea.* [U] • *There were lots of small yachts sailing* **on the** *sea.* [U] • *When we moved to the US, we sent our things/travelled there* **by** *sea* (= in a ship). [U] • *I'd love to live on an island in the middle of* **the** *sea!* [U] • *Moscow is a long way* **from the** *sea.* [U] • *The River Nile flows* **into the** *sea near Alexandria.* [U] • *The barrels of nuclear waste fell off the ship and are now lying* **at the bottom of the** *sea.* [U] • *The sea was* **calm/smooth/choppy/rough** *when we crossed the Channel.* [U] • **Choppy** *seas can often make travelling between the islands difficult.* [C] • *Is* **the** *sea* (= the water) *clean enough to swim in here?* [U] • *We spent a lovely week* **by the sea** (= on the coast) *this year.* [U] • *Soon we had left the river estuary and were heading towards* **the open** *sea* (= the part of the sea a long way from land). [U] • *The refugees were* **at sea** (= in a boat on the sea a long way from land) *for forty days before reaching land.* [U] • *I'm all/completely* **at sea with** (= confused by) *the new coins.* • *She stood motionless, staring* **out to** *sea* (= over the sea into the distance). [U] • A sea is also one of the large flat areas on the moon which in the past were thought to be seas: **The** *Sea* **of** *Showers* [C] • A sea of something is a lot of it: *The teacher looked down and saw* **a** *sea* **of** *smiling faces.* [C] • *The boats will* **put (out) to sea** (= leave) *on this evening's high tide.* • *My grandfather* **ran away to sea/went to sea** (= became a sailor) *when he was twelve.* • Sometimes **-on-sea** or **-by-sea** is used in the name of a town on the coast: *Southend-on-Sea* ○ *Goring-by-Sea* • A **sea anemone** is a soft, brightly coloured sea creature which looks like a flower and often lives on rocks under the water. • A **sea breeze** is a light cool wind blowing from the sea onto the land. • A **sea captain** is a person in charge of a ship, esp. one used for trading rather than for military purposes. • *There will have to be a* **sea change** (=a complete change) *in people's ideas if public transport is ever to replace the private car.* • *(literary or humorous)* A **sea dog** is an old sailor with many years of experience at sea: *His grandfather had the weather-beaten features of an* **old** *sea dog.* • *A ship usually travels in a* **sea lane** (=along a fixed route across the sea). • A person's **sea legs** are their ability to keep their balance while walking on a moving ship and not be ill: *How are your sea legs? I think it's going to be a rough crossing.* • **Sea level** is the average height of the sea where it meets the land: *The top of Mount Everest is 8 848m* **above** *sea level.* ○ *Much of Holland* **lies at or below** *sea level.* • A **sea lion** is a large SEAL from the North Pacific Ocean which has large ears and can move on land: *Sea lions often perform in entertainments such as circuses.* • A **sea urchin** is a small edible sea animal which lives in water that is not very deep, and has a spherical shell that is covered with sharp points like needles. • A **sea wall** is a wall that protects land from being flooded or damaged by the sea or protects a port from the action of powerful waves. • *"The Owl and the Pussy-Cat went to sea / In a beautiful pea-green boat"* (opening of the nonsense poem *The Owl and the Pussy-Cat* by Edward Lear, 1871) • *"I must down to the seas again, to the lonely sea and the sky / And all I ask is a tall ship and a star to steer her by"* (John Masefield in the poem *Sea Fever*, 1902) • *"Speed, bonnie boat, like a bird on the wing ... / Over the sea to Skye"* (*Skye Boat Song* in Sir Harold Edwin Boulton's 'National Songs and Some Ballads', 1908) • Ⓓ

sea·bed /'siː·bed/ *n* [U] **the seabed** the solid surface of the Earth which lies beneath the sea • *The ship has been lying on the seabed for more than 50 years.*

sea·bird /£'siː·bɜːd, $-bɜːrd/ *n* [C] a bird that lives near the sea and obtains its food from it • *Gulls, kittiwakes and terns are seabirds that are found along the British coast.*

sea·board /£'siː·bɔːd, $-bɔːrd/ *n* [C usually sing] the long thin area of a country which is next to the sea • *She lives* **on** *the* **Atlantic** *seaboard.* • *The hurricane was moving* **along** *the* **Eastern** *seaboard with gusts of up to 138mph yesterday as holidaymakers and residents fled inland.*

sea·borne /£'siː·bɔːn, $-bɔːrn/ *adj* [not gradable] carried on the sea in a ship • *seaborne trade/goods* • *seaborne missiles/troops/reinforcements*

sea·far·ing /£'siːˌfeə·rɪŋ, $-ˌfer·ɪŋ/ *adj* [before n; not gradable] *esp. literary* connected with travelling by sea • *a seafaring man* (=a sailor) • *a seafaring life* (=a life spent working on a ship) • *Portugal is a seafaring nation* (=The sea is an important part of Portuguese life).

sea·food /'siː·fuːd/ *n* [U] edible animals from the sea, esp. fish and creatures with shells • *Mary refuses to eat meat, but she'll eat seafood.* • *There's an excellent seafood* **restaurant** *near here.*

sea·front /'siː·frʌnt/, **front** *n* [C usually sing] the part of a coastal town next to the beach, often with a wide road or path and a row of houses and shops facing the sea • *We rented a house* **on** *the seafront for a couple of weeks.* • *After dinner we went for a stroll* **along** *the seafront.* • *The town has some marvellous seafront cafés.*

sea·go·ing /£'siːˌgəʊ·ɪŋ, $-ˌgoʊ-/ *adj* [before n; not gradable] (of ships) built for use on journeys across the sea, not just for coastal and river journeys • *Tougher safety regulations need to be introduced for seagoing vessels.*

sea·gull /'siː·gʌl/, **gull** *n* [C] a bird which lives near the sea and has short legs, long wings and grey, or black, and white feathers • *a flock of seagulls* • *The gulls circled overhead as the boats sailed into the port.*

sea·horse /£'siː·hɔːs, $-hɔːrs/ *n* [C] a small fish which swims in a vertical position and has a head like that of a horse • PIC〉 **Fish**

seal ANIMAL /siːl/ *n* [C] a large fish-eating mammal which lives partly in the sea and partly on land or ice • Ⓙ

seal·ing /'siː·lɪŋ/ *n* [U] • *Environmental groups are campaigning against sealing* (=the hunting and killing of seals) *in the North Sea.*

seal MARK /siːl/ *n* [C] an official mark on a document, sometimes made with wax, which shows that it is legal or has been officially approved • *The lawyer stamped the certificate with her seal.* • *The Government has* **given** *the proposal its* **seal of approval** (=said it approves of it). • *This meeting has* **set/put the seal on** (=made certain the results of) *the negotiations.* • *The party at the embassy* **set/put the seal on** (=was a suitable way to end) *the president's official visit.* • **Sealing wax** is a type of wax which is used for making a seal because it melts easily and hardens quickly. • Ⓙ

seal COVERING /siːl/ *n* [C] something fixed around an opening to prevent liquid or gas flowing through it, or a piece of thin material such as paper or plastic which covers the opening of a container and has to be broken in order to use the contents • *Clean the seal on the fridge door regularly so that it remains airtight.* • *Doors and windows don't close tightly unless they have a good seal on them.* • *Don't use that jar of baby food if the seal is broken.* • Ⓙ

seal *obj* /siːl/ *v* [T] • *If you want jam to keep for a long time, you must seal the jars well.* • *This floor has just been sealed* (=covered with a special liquid to protect it), *so don't walk on it!* • *He sealed the envelope* **(down)** (=stuck it down) *and put a stamp on it.* [T/M] • *Seal the parcel* **(up)** (=Fasten it) *with sticky tape.* [T/M] • *Fry the meat quickly in hot oil to seal the flavour* **in** (=preserve all its flavour). [M] • *Two more bombs have been discovered since the police sealed* **off** *the area/building* (=closed and started to guard all the entrances to prevent anyone going in or out). [M] • If you seal something such as an agreement, you make it more certain or approve it formally: *The two leaders sealed their agreement* **with** *a handshake/***by** *shaking hands.* • If your **fate** is sealed, nothing can stop some unpleasant thing happening to you: *From the time she was introduced to the drug ring her fate was sealed.*

seal·ant /'siː·lənt/ *n* • (A) sealant is a substance painted onto a surface to make it waterproof or to stop other liquids from going into it, or put in the space between two materials for the same reason: *The stone floor was painted with (a) sealant to stop damp rising up into the room.* [C/U]

sealed /siːld/ *adj* [not gradable] • *The teacher opened the sealed envelope containing the exam papers.* • **Sealed orders** are instructions given to a member of the armed forces which are not to be opened until a particular time.

seal·skin /'siːl·skɪn/ *n* [U] the skin or fur of a SEAL, esp. when it is used for making clothing • *sealskin boots* • *a sealskin coat*

seam JOIN /siːm/ *n* [C] a line where two things join, esp. a line of sewing joining two pieces of a material such as cloth or leather • *The bags we sell have very strong seams, so they will last for years.* • *How embarrassing! I've split the seam on my trousers.* • *My old coat is* **falling/coming apart at the** *seams* (=it is in a very bad condition). • *(fig.) Their marriage is* **falling/coming apart at the** *seams* (=going wrong). • *(fig.) Now that they've got six children, their little house is* **bursting/bulging at the** *seams* (=too full).

seamed /siːmd/ *adj* [not gradable] *literary* • *The old man's face was seamed* (=covered in lines) *and wrinkled.*

seam·less /'siːm·ləs/ *adj* [not gradable] • *seamless stockings/tights*

seam LAYER /siːm/ *n* [C] a long thin layer of esp. coal which has formed between layers of other rocks • *a coal seam* • *a seam of coal* • *a seam of iron ore* • *(fig.) The world of finance, with all its complexity, colour and character, is a* **rich** *seam for novelists to mine* (=subject for them to write about).

sea·man /'siː·mən/ *n* [C] *pl* **-men** a sailor, esp. one who is not an officer

sea·man·ship /'siː·mən·ʃɪp/ *n* [U] skill in managing a ship • *As a result of his seamanship they avoided the rocks and the ship was saved from disaster.*

seam·stress /'sem·strəs/ *n* [C] *dated* a woman whose job is sewing and making clothes

seam·y /'siː·mi/ *adj* **-ier, -iest** (of a situation) unpleasant because of a connection with immoral things such as dishonesty, violence and illegal sex • *The film vividly portrays the seamy* **side of life** *in the London of the early 70s.* • *He did not want to be involved in the seamier* **side** *of the gaming world.*

séance /'seɪ·ɑ̃ːns/ *n* [C] a meeting where people, esp. spiritualists, try to talk with dead people • *They're holding/attending a séance this evening.* • Ⓕ

sea·plane /'siː·pleɪn/ *n* [C] an aircraft that can take off from and land on water • PIC〉 **Aircraft**

sea·port /£'siː·pɔːt, $-pɔːrt/ *n* [C] (a city or town with) a port which can be used by ships • *Ostend is the most important seaport and largest seaside resort in Belgium.*

sear *obj* /£sɪəʳ, $sɪr/ *v* [T] to burn the surface of (something) with sudden very strong heat • *The heat from the explosion seared their hands and faces.* • If you sear a piece of meat, you fry it quickly at a high temperature in order to prevent liquid and flavour escaping from it: *Sear the steak and then fry it over a low heat for three minutes.* • *(fig.) The disaster is indelibly seared* **into** *the villagers' memory* (= They will never be able to forget it).

sear·ing /£'sɪə·rɪŋ, $'sɪr·ɪŋ/ *adj* • *The searing* **heat** *of the midday sun was almost unbearable.* • *(fig.) A searing* **pain** (= very bad pain which felt like a burn) *shot up her arm.* • Searing also means very emotional and powerful: *Her latest novel is a searing tale of love and hate.* ○ *It was sung with searing intensity.*

sear·ing·ly /£'sɪə·rɪŋ·li, $'sɪr·ɪŋ-/ *adv*

search *(obj)* /£sɜːtʃ, $sɜːrtʃ/ *v* to look (somewhere) carefully in order to find something • *The police failed to find any evidence when they searched the office.* [T] • *I've been searching all day, but I can't find my ring anywhere.* [I] • *This computer programme is able to search text* **for** *spelling mistakes.* [T] • *He searched* **(in/through)** *his pockets* **for** *some change.* [T; I + prep] • *The police are searching the woods* **for** *the missing child.* [T] • *She searched his face* **for** *some sign of forgiveness, but it remained expressionless.* [T] • *I've searched* **high and low** (= everywhere), *but I can't find my birth certificate.* [I] • *The detectives searched the house* **from top to bottom** (= all over it), *but they found no sign of the stolen goods.* [T] • A police officer who searches you or your possessions looks for something you might be hiding: *They were searched* **for** *guns and then released.* [T] • If you search **out** something or someone, you find them after searching: *Despite the warm weather we managed to search some snow out and do some skiing.* [M] ○ *I searched out several old school friends by putting adverts in a newspaper.* [M] • *(fig.) She searched her* **mind/memory for** (= tried to remember) *the man's name, but she couldn't remember it.* [T] • *(fig.) Search your* **heart/conscience** (= think honestly) *and ask yourself whether you are really doing as much as you could to help the poor.* [T] • *(fig. fml) People who are searching* **after** (= trying to obtain by mental effort) *inner peace sometimes turn to religion.* [I] • *(infml) "Where's Jack?"* "**Search me!** (= I don't know!)"

search /£sɜːtʃ, $sɜːrtʃ/ *n* [C] • *After a long search, they eventually found the missing papers.* • *We're* **doing** *a (computer) search* **for** *all words beginning with 'high'.* • *The police* **conducted a thorough/exhaustive** *search* **of** *the premises, but they failed to find any drugs.* • *A* **land and sea** *search is* **under way** *in the north of the island to try to find the missing aircraft.* • *She was shot by a sniper when she went out* **in search of** (= to try to find) *firewood.* • A **search party** is a group of people who look for someone who is lost: *After they had been missing in the mountains for 3 hours, a search party was sent out to look for them.* • A **search warrant** is an official document which gives police officers the authority to search a building for stolen property, illegal goods or information which might help to solve a crime.

search·ing /£'sɜː·tʃɪŋ, $'sɜːr-/ *adj* • Searching means intended to find out the often hidden truth about something: *She gave him a searching* **look**, *wondering whether he was telling her the truth.* ○ *I think we need to ask some searching* **questions** *about how the money has been spent.*

search·ing·ly /£'sɜː·tʃɪŋ·li, $'sɜːr-/ *adv*

search·light /£'sɜːtʃ·laɪt, $'sɜːrtʃ-/ *n* [C] a light with a very bright beam that can be turned in any direction, used esp. to guard prisons or to see the movements of enemy aircraft in the sky • *The powerful searchlights around the prison made it very difficult for prisoners to escape at night.*

sear·ing /£'sɪə·rɪŋ, $'sɪr·ɪŋ/ *adj* See at SEAR

sea·scape /'siː·skeɪp/ *n* [C] a painting of a view of the sea • *Turner painted many seascapes.*

sea·shell /'siː·ʃel/ *n* [C] the empty shell of a small sea creature, often one found lying on the beach • *My children love collecting seashells.* • *'She sells seashells on the seashore and the shells that she sells are seashells I'm sure' is a humorous saying which is difficult to pronounce.*

sea·shore /£'siː·ʃɔːʳ, $-ʃɔːr/ *n* [U] the land along the edge of the sea • *As we walked along* **the** *seashore we saw several different sorts of seaweed and lots of tiny crabs.*

sea·sick /'siː·sɪk/ *adj* vomiting or having the feeling you will vomit because of the movement of a ship you are travelling in • *I* **was/felt** *seasick so I went up on deck for some fresh air.*

sea·sick·ness /'siː,sɪk·nəs/ *n* [U]

sea·side /'siː·saɪd/ *n* [U] the area near the sea, esp. where people spend their holidays and enjoy themselves • *a seaside holiday/hotel/resort* • *Let's go to* **the** *seaside at the weekend!* • *"I do like to be beside the seaside"* (title of a song written by J. Glover-Kind, 1909)

sea·son PART OF YEAR /'siː·zᵊn/ *n* [C] a part of a year, esp. spring, summer, autumn and winter • *Each season is associated with a particular type of weather and with natural events that are affected by the weather.* • A season is also the period of the year when something that happens every year happens: *How long does the* **dry/hurricane/monsoon/rainy** *season last?* ○ *These plants have a very long* **flowering** *season.* ○ *Some animals become very aggressive during the* **mating** *season.* • A season is also the period of the year during which a particular sport is played: *The British football season begins in August and ends in May.* ○ *He has decided to retire from cricket at the end of the season.* ○ *(Am) Reggie played well during the* **regular** *season* (= the part of the sports season when the winners of each division are decided). See also POSTSEASON. • The season is the period when most people take their holidays, go to visit places or do a leisure activity: *Air fares are more expensive during the* **(holiday/summer/tourist)** *season.* ○ *Most hotels in the ski resort are full* **at the height of** (= the busiest part of) *the season.* ○ *Hotel rooms are more expensive* **in season** (= at the busiest period of year). ○ *The cross-Channel ferries are cheaper* **out of season** (= during the period when fewer people want to travel). ○ *I find* **out-of-season** *seaside resorts rather depressing.* • *(Br and Aus)* A season is also a period of planned entertainment, esp. when a set of programmes, plays or musical events are broadcast or performed: *There will be more documentaries and fewer quiz shows in the autumn season on TV.* ○ *There's a season (Am and Aus* **festival***)* **of** *1960s French films at the Arts Cinema next month.* • Fruit and vegetables that are **in season** can be obtained easily because they are from recent local crops, esp. those grown outside: *Strawberries are cheaper when they're in season and don't need to be imported from a hotter country.* ○ *Tomatoes are* **out of season** (= not available from local crops) *in the winter.* • A female animal that is **in season** is willing to have sex and able to become pregnant. • An animal that is **in season** can be hunted legally during a particular period of time: *You'll have to wait until salmon are in season before you can go fishing again.* ○ *There are heavy fines for hunting deer* **out of season**. • **Season's Greetings** is sometimes written on a Christmas card as a way of expressing a Christmas greeting, esp. to someone who is not from a Christian culture. • **The season of goodwill** is the period around Christmas. It is often used when showing a difference between what is considered as a happy time and what the situation really is: *Here we are in the season of goodwill and every shop door has homeless people sleeping in it at night.* • *(Br and Aus)* A **season ticket** is a ticket which can be used many times within a limited period and is cheaper than paying separately for each use: *I have a season ticket for all Manchester United's games.* ○ *Long-distance rail commuters face massive rises in the cost of their annual season ticket (Am* **commutation ticket***).* ○ *We usually buy season tickets (Am and Aus* **subscription (tickets)***) for the Opera House.*

sea·son·a·ble /'siː·zᵊn·ə·bl/ *adj* • Seasonable means expected at or suitable for a particular time: *September brought some far from seasonable snow showers.* ○ *(fml) His father gave him some seasonable advice* (= that showing good judgment).

sea·son·al /'siː·zᵊn·ᵊl/ *adj* • Something that is seasonal relates to or happens during a particular period in the year: *The stalls in the market were piled high with seasonal* **fruit** *and* **vegetables**. ○ *Britain has cool summers and mild winters with relatively modest seasonal* **variation**. ○ *Some students supplement their incomes with seasonal farm* **work** *during the summer vacation.* ○ *After seasonal* **adjustments** *last month's unemployment figure fell by almost 10 000.*

sea·son·al·i·ty /£,siː·zᵊn'æl·ɪ·ti, $-ə·ṭi/ *n* [U] • *The seasonality of the tourist industry makes it difficult to find a permanent job in the town.*

sea·son·al·ly /'siː·zᵊn·ᵊl·i/ *adv* • *Although total unemployment has decreased, the seasonally* **adjusted** *figure has risen slightly.*

sea·son *obj* FLAVOUR /'siː·zᵊn/ *v* [T] to improve the flavour of (savoury food) by adding small amounts of salt, herbs or spices when cooking or preparing it • *Lightly season the salad before serving.* • *Drain the rice, stir in the* *salmon and season* **to taste** (=until it has the taste you like). • *Processed foods tend to be heavily seasoned* **with** *salt.*

sea·son·ing /ˈsiː·zᵊn·ɪŋ/ *n* • Seasoning is a substance that is added to savoury food to improve its flavour: *Taste the soup and adjust the seasoning, adding more salt or pepper as desired.* [U] ○ *Bake for twenty minutes, remove from the oven and sprinkle on herbs and seasoning.* [U] ○ *Add the tomatoes, salt and other seasonings of your choice.* [C]

sea·son *obj* HARDEN WOOD /ˈsiː·zᵊn/ *v* [T] to harden (wood) to make it ready for use by drying it gradually • *These days wood is rarely seasoned in the traditional way and is treated with preservative instead.*

sea·soned /ˈsiː·zᵊnd/ *adj* skilled in an activity because of having a lot of experience of it • *She is a seasoned* **campaigner** *for human rights, which she has been involved with for twenty years.* • *Most of the restaurants in the square are expensive tourist traps that are avoided by seasoned* **travellers.**

seat FURNITURE /siːt/ *n* [C] an item of furniture that has been designed for someone to sit on • *Chairs, stools, sofas and benches are different types of seat.* • *All the chairs are taken – I'm afraid you'll have to use this table as a seat.* • *A car usually has a* **driver's** *seat, a* **front/passenger** *seat and* **back/rear** *seats.* • *Why don't you sit down* **on** *that seat over there while we're waiting?* • *The hall's quite full – I can't see any* **empty** *seats.* • *My ticket says 22D but there's already someone* **in** (=sitting on) *that seat.* • *Is this seat* **free/taken** (=Is anyone using it)*?* • *Would you* **keep** (=stop anyone else from sitting in) *my seat* **(for** *me) while I go to the buffet car?* • *Please keep your seats* (=remain seated) *during the interval.* • *(fml) Please* **keep** *your seats* (=stay sitting down) *until asked to leave.* • *Could I* **book** *two seats* (=arrange for a seat to be officially kept for me) *for tomorrow evening's performance?* • *I'd like to* **reserve** *a seat* (=arrange for a seat to be officially kept for me) *on the midday train from Newcastle to London.* • *(infml) We hope our decision to show more popular films will increase the number of (Br and Aus)* **bums on seats** *(Am* **fannies in the seats***)* (=people who pay to watch). • If you tell someone to **have/take a seat** you are asking them politely to sit down: *Have a seat, Mr Jones, and tell me what I can do for you.* ○ *Just calm down, take a seat, and describe what happened.* • *We arrived late and weren't allowed to* **take** *our* **seats** (=go to our seats to watch the performance) *until the interval.* • A **seat belt** (also **safety belt**) is a belt which fastens around someone travelling in a vehicle or aircraft and, by holding them in their seat, reduces the risk of them being injured in an accident: *You've forgotten to* **fasten** *your seat belt.* ○ *The air hostess showed the passengers how to* **undo/ unfasten** *their seat belts.* ○ *He would have survived the car crash if he had been* **wearing** *his seat belt.* • PIC **Bathroom**

–seat /-siːt/ *combining form* • *The 2000-seat theatre is due to close at the end of the year.*

seat *obj* /siːt/ *v* [T] • *The waiter greeted me with a big smile and seated us* (=gave us a place to sit) *by the window.* • *"I'm so glad to see you!" she said, seating* **herself** (=sitting down) *between Eleanor and Marianne.* • *The new concert hall seats* (=has enough seats for) *1500 people.* • *They converted the old barn into a small theatre seating* (=with enough seats for) *250 people.*

seat·ed /£ˈsiː·tɪd, $-t̬ɪd/ *adj* [not gradable] • Seated means sitting: *The woman seated opposite him refused to stop staring at him.* ○ *You are requested to* **remain** *seated during takeoff.* ○ *The research suggests that seated passengers are no safer than standing passengers when a train crashes.*

–seat·er /£-ˌsiː·təʳ, $-t̬ɚ/ *combining form* • *a 50000-seater stadium* • *Her car is a four-seater* (=has space for four people to sit down)*, but we could probably squeeze five people in.* • *We bought a two-seater bench* (=one with space for two people to sit down).

seat·ing /£ˈsiː·tɪŋ, $-t̬ɪŋ/ *n* [U] • Seating is the seats which are provided in a place: *Apart from the rather cramped seating, we had an excellent flight.* ○ *The huge auditorium has modern, comfortable seating.* ○ *The car has seating* **for** *six.* ○ *The theatre has a seating* **capacity** *of* (=there are enough seats for) *2000 people.* • Seating also refers to how or where people will sit: *Recent design improvements include a seating position that allows the rider to make more efficient use of the bike.* ○ *Have you worked out the seating* **arrangements/plan** *for the wedding reception?*

seat BOTTOM AREA /siːt/ *n* [C usually sing] the part of an item of furniture or clothing on which a person sits • *I've spilt some coffee on the seat of the armchair.* • *I like those chairs with the* **cane/upholstered/wooden** *seats.* • *The seat of those trousers looks rather tight, sir – Would you like to try a larger size?* • *Stand up straight with your chest out and your seat* (=bottom) *in.* • If you do something **by the seat of** your **pants,** you do it using your own experience and trusting your own judgment: *He had no formal qualifications or training, and managed the business by the seat of his pants.* ○ *She has a* **seat-of-the-pants** *ability to find the best way out of a crisis.* • PIC **Chair**

seat OFFICIAL POSITION /siːt/ *n* [C] an official position as a member of a group of people who control something or possess power • *She has a seat* **on** *the board of directors.* • *He is expected to* **lose** *his seat* **on** *the council in next month's elections.* • *She* **won** *her first* **parliamentary** *seat in 1979.* • *He is the MP for the most* **marginal** (=most likely to be lost) *seat in the country, and had a majority of only eleven votes at the last election.* • *The Conservative Party's seats in the south of England are the* **safest** (=the least likely to be lost in an election).

seat BASE /siːt/ *n* [C] a place which acts as a base or centre for an important activity • *St Petersburg was the seat* **of** *the Russian Revolution.* • *In the 14th century, Barcelona was the seat* **of** *a Mediterranean empire that stretched to Naples and Athens.* • *The seat* **of government** *in the US is in Washington, DC.* • *(fml) The Sorbonne is a part of the University of Paris and a world-famous* **seat of learning** (=a place where people are educated).

sea·weed /ˈsiː·wiːd/ *n* [U] a green, brown or dark red plant that grows in the sea or on land very close to the sea

sea·wor·thy /£ˈsiːˌwɜː·ði, $-ˌwɜːr-/ *adj* in a condition that is good enough to travel safely on the sea • *The ship underwent emergency repairs and was declared seaworthy for a voyage to Germany, where permanent repairs will be made.*

sea·wor·thi·ness /£ˈsiːˌwɜː·ðɪ·nəs, $-ˌwɜːr-/ *n* [U] • *There are serious doubts about the seaworthiness of the vessel.*

se·ba·ceous gland /sɪˈbeɪ·ʃəsˌglænd/ *n* [C] *specialized* a very small organ in the skin which produces an oily substance that makes hair shiny and prevents skin from becoming dry • *The neck is one of the first areas to show signs of ageing because its skin has few sebaceous glands and tends to dry out, causing lines and wrinkles.*

sec /sek/ *n* [C] *abbreviation for* SECOND TIME • *She completed the marathon in 4 hrs 15 mins 28 secs.* • *(infml)* A sec is any brief period of time: *Would you mind waiting for me – I'll only be a couple of secs.* ○ *I'd like to have a word with you when you've* **got** *a sec.*

sec·a·teurs *Br and Aus* /£ˌsek·əˈtɜːz, $-ˈtɚz/, *Am* **prun·ing shears** /£ˈpruː·nɪŋˌʃɪəz, $-ˌʃɪrz/ *pl n* a garden tool which has two short sharp blades and is used for cutting plant stems • *You'll need* **a pair of** *secateurs to prune the roses.* • PIC **Garden**

se·cede /sɪˈsiːd/ *v* [I] *fml* to become independent of a country or governmental area • *There is likely to be civil war if the region tries to secede.* • *Many Scots would like their country to secede* **from** *the United Kingdom.*

se·ces·sion /sesˈeʃ·ᵊn/ *n* [U] *fml* • *In a referendum in 1993 the people of Eritrea voted for secession* **from** *Ethiopia.*

se·ces·sion·ist /sesˈeʃ·ᵊn·ɪst/ *n* [C], *adj* [not gradable] *fml* • *Almost everyone in the southern half of the country supports the war against the secessionists in the north.* • *The break-up of the country is likely to encourage secessionist* **movements** *in other areas.*

se·clud·ed /sɪˈkluː·dɪd/ *adj* quiet and private by being situated away from people, roads or buildings • *We used to sunbathe on a secluded beach that was completely cut off when the tide came in.* • *They have their own helicopter to take them to their secluded house in the forest.*

se·clu·sion /sɪˈkluː·ʒᵊn/ *n* [U] • *He's been living* **in** *seclusion since he retired from acting.* • *The victim's family remained* **in** *seclusion yesterday and refused to talk to reporters.* • *After being with a tour group all week I was glad to return to the seclusion of my own home.* • *If you want a little more seclusion for sunbathing the answer is a high garden fence.* • The seclusion **of** women is a traditional practice in some countries which keeps women separate from men in daily life. • A **seclusion cell/room** is a place where a prisoner is kept separate from other people as a punishment.

sec·ond [POSITION] /ˈsek·ᵊnd/ *determiner, pronoun, adj, adv* immediately after the first and before any others • *Is Brian her second or third child?* • *She's in the second year of a three-year chemistry course at Cambridge University.* • *This is only the second time I've been to Germany.* • *Sheila was the second of the four interview candidates.* • Second is the position in which a person finishes a race or competition if they finish immediately behind the winner: *Robertson won the race and Cameron* **was/came/finished** *second.* ○ *Halfway through the race she was in second* **place**, *but she finished fifth.* ○ *First prize is a fortnight in Barbados and second* **prize** *is a weekend in Rome.* ○ *Although he failed to win first prize he (Br and Aus)***came a good**/*(Am and Aus)* **was a strong** *second* (= his performance in achieving second place was very good). ○ *In this business, money comes first and principles* **come** *a very* **poor** *second* (= they are much less important). • Second is used to show that only one thing is better, bigger, etc. than the thing mentioned: *Japan is* **the world's** *second industrial power.* ○ *St Petersburg is Russia's second* **(biggest/largest)** *city.* ○ *Iraq's oil reserves are second* **only to** *Saudi Arabia's.* ○ *The conditions that these prisoners are kept in are second* **to none** (= better than all others). • Second sometimes means another: *She is often described as the second Marilyn Monroe.* ○ *You really ought to make the most of the opportunity, because you won't get a second* **chance**. ○ *Richard and Liz have a second* **home** *in France.* ○ *Pay attention to what she's saying because she won't explain it a second* **time** (= again). • Second sometimes means ALTERNATE or happening only once out of every two possible times: *We've decided to hold the conference* **every** *second year.* • **Second thoughts** are a change of opinion: *You're not* **having** *second thoughts* **about** *getting married, are you?* ○ *I'd like a cup of coffee, please – (Br and Aus)* **on** *second thoughts/(Am and Aus)* **on second thought** (= I've changed my opinion), *I'll have a beer.* • If you do something **without a second thought** you do it immediately without having any doubts about it: *When I asked to borrow some money, she gave me £100 without a second thought.* • **Second best** is not as good the best and is therefore less desirable: *She's always striving for excellence, and refuses to* **settle for** *second best.* ○ *Their position is so weak that they're bound to* **come off** *second best* (= be defeated) *in any power struggle.* ○ *He tends to* **feel** *second best because he's her stepfather.* • Someone who is in their **second childhood** has started to behave like a child, esp. because of mental weakness caused by old age: *Her grandfather's in his second childhood and talks nonsense most of the time.* ○ *(humorous) He's started playing with his train set when he comes home from work – it's as if he were in his second childhood.* • **The Second Coming** is the return of Jesus Christ to Earth from heaven that Christians expect will happen one day. • Your **second cousin** is any person who is a first cousin of your mother or father, or a child of your first cousin. • In a vehicle, **second (gear)** is the GEAR (= part of the engine) which combines power with limited speed and is used when increasing or reducing speed or when travelling up or down a steep hill: *You'll have to* **change (down) into** *second for this roundabout, because the car will stall if you stay in third.* • If you **second-guess**, you try to say in advance what someone will do: *I wouldn't like to second-guess how the committee will deal with the issue.* ○ *She's always trying to second-guess me.* • *(Am)* To **second-guess** a person or thing is also make a criticism or judgment about an event after it has happened: *Of course it's easy to second-guess the management of the election campaign, but I do think serious mistakes were made.* • **Second-hand** means not new and having been used in the past by someone else: *This bike is second-hand but it's still in good condition.* ○ *The children were dressed in second-hand* **clothes**. • The **second floor** is the floor which is *(Br and Aus)* two floors/*(Am and Aus)* one floor above the ground. • *(humorous)* A **second honeymoon** is a holiday taken by a husband and wife who have been married for some time, esp. in order to try to improve a relationship which is failing: *A second honeymoon is a way of revitalizing a marriage through fun, frolics and romance – qualities experienced in the early days.* ○ *A second honeymoon on a Greek island earlier this year gave their 18-year marriage a much needed boost.* • A **second-in-command** is someone who is almost as important as the person in charge: *Well, if the manager isn't available I'd like to speak to the second-in-command.* ○ *He was Johnson's second-in-command.* • A **second language** is a language that a person can speak which is not the first language they learnt naturally as a child: *German is my second language.* ○ **English as a** *second language is English taught to people whose language is not English but who are living in an English-speaking country.* • Your **second name** is either your family name or a second given (also **middle**) name: *She's called Maureen something – I can't remember her second* (= family) *name.* ○ *"Have you got a second* (= middle) *name?" "No, just plain Andrew, nothing else."* • If something is **second nature** to you, you are so familiar with it that you can do it easily without needing to think very much about it: *I used to hate computers, but using them is second nature* **to** *me now.* • **Second-rate** means not very good: *a second-rate film* • Someone who has **second sight** is thought to have an unusual natural ability to know without being told what will happen in the future or what is happening in a different place: *I once met a woman with second sight who told me I was about to lose my job, and I did the very next day.* • **Second wind** is a return of strength or energy that makes it possible to continue in an activity that requires a lot of effort: *We started to feel we couldn't walk any further but when we saw the village in the distance we* **got** *our second wind.* • [LP] **Two** (KOR)

sec·ond /ˈsek·ᵊnd/, **sec·ond·ly** *adv* [not gradable] • *There are two good reasons why we can't do it. First, we can't afford it, and second, we don't have time.*

sec·ond /ˈsek·ᵊnd/, **sec·ond class de·gree** *n* [C] *Br* • A second is a British university degree of a quality which is almost as good as the best that can be achieved: *The majority of students leave university with seconds.* • Seconds are usually divided into **upper** second (also **two-one**) and **lower** second (also **two-two**): *He was delighted when he got an upper second.*

sec·ond·ly /ˈsek·ᵊnd·li/, **sec·ond** *adv* [not gradable] • Secondly is used when stating the second of two or more reasons or pieces of information: *I want two things from my boss – firstly, a pay rise, and secondly, a longer contract.*

sec·onds /ˈsek·ᵊndz/ *pl n* • *(infml)* Seconds are an extra serving of food that is given after the first serving has been eaten: *Would anyone like seconds* **of** *ice cream?*

sec·ond [TIME] /ˈsek·ᵊnd/ (*abbreviation* **sec** /sek/, **s**) *n* [C] a short unit of time which is equal to a sixtieth of a minute • *There are sixty seconds in a minute and sixty minutes in an hour.* • *She completed the race in 4 minutes 22 seconds.* • *He won the race easily and sliced a tenth of a second off his personal record.* • *These computers perform complex calculations for things such as weather forecasts by processing millions of instructions* **per** *second.* • *The new system can trace a phone call in a* **fraction** *of a second.* • A second is also a brief period that is not of any particular length: *He tripped and banged his head against the wall, and seconds later he was dead.* ○ *"Come on, hurry up!" "I'll* **just/only** *be a second – I've got to lock the back door."* ○ *Have you got a second, Paul? I'd like to have a word with you.* ○ *It won't take a second* (= It will be very quick) *to do and it'll save you a lot of effort in the long run.* • A **second hand** is the small pointer on some clocks that shows how many seconds have past. • [LP] **Periods of time, Time** (KOR)

sec·ond *obj* [SUPPORT] /ˈsek·ᵊnd/ *v* [T] to make a formal statement of support for (a suggestion made by someone else during a meeting) so that a discussion or vote can take place • *The* **motion** *was proposed by the club's chairwoman and seconded by the secretary.* • *(infml) "I could do with a drink." "I'll second that* (= I agree with you)*!"* • (KOR)

sec·ond·er /£ˈsek·ᵊn·dəʳ, $-dɚ/ *n* [C] • *There was no seconder for* (= person who was willing to second) *the motion so it could not be debated.*

sec·ond *obj* [SEND] /£sɪˈkɒnd, $-ˈkɑːnd/ *v* [T] *Br and Aus* to send (an employee) to work somewhere else temporarily, either to increase the number of workers or to replace other workers, or to exchange experience or skills • *During the dispute, many police officers were seconded* **from** *traffic duty* **to** *the prison service.* • *Professor Barnes was seconded* **from** *Florida State University to work with a team of scientists in Budapest.* • (KOR)

sec·ond·ment /£sɪˈkɒnd·mənt, $-ˈkɑːnd-/ *n Br and Aus* • *We hope that having academics working* **on** *secondment with us will improve their understanding of the industry.* [U] • *His involvement with the project began when he was on a three-year secondment* **from** *NASA* **to** *the European Space Agency.* [C]

sec·ond [MEASUREMENT] /ˈsek·ᵊnd/ *n* [C] the smallest unit used for measuring an angle • *There are 3600 seconds in a degree.* • (KOR)

sec·ond DAMAGED PRODUCT /ˈsek·ᵊnd/ *n* [C] a product that is sold cheaply because it is damaged or not in perfect condition • *This jacket was sold as a second because it had some buttons missing.* • *These towels are cheaper because some of them are* **slight** *seconds* (= they have small faults). • (KOR)

sec·ond HELPER /ˈsek·ᵊnd/ *n* [C] a person who takes care of someone who is taking part in a boxing competition or, in the past, in a DUEL (= organized fight) • *The seconds are leaving the ring as we approach the start of Round One.* • *Seconds away/out – Round Two!* • (KOR)

sec·on·da·ry LESS IMPORTANT /£ˈsek·ᵊn·dri, $-der·i/ *adj* [not gradable] less important than related things • *Her health is what matters – the cost of the treatment is of secondary importance.* • *The need for secrecy is secondary* **to** *the need to take immediate action.* • *Our priority is to have an efficient transport system, and clean air is a secondary* **consideration.** • *Apart from the hero's family, the play has few secondary characters.*

sec·on·dar·i·ly /£ˌsek·ᵊnˈdeə·rɪ·li, $-ˈder·ɪ-/ *adv* [not gradable]

sec·on·da·ry EDUCATION /£ˈsek·ᵊn·dri, $-der·i/ *adj* [before n; not gradable] relating to the education of children approximately between the ages of 11 and 18 years old • *The proposed reforms include making secondary* **education** *compulsory up to the age of 18.* • *Funding has not been equally divided between the primary and secondary* **phase/level.** • *There has been a drop in the number of children* **of** *secondary* **age.** • *Marcus has just started at secondary* **school.** • LP **Schools and colleges**

sec·on·da·ry COMING AFTER /£ˈsek·ᵊn·dri, $-der·i/ *adj* [not gradable] developing from something similar that existed earlier • *The drug is not very effective against AIDS, though it may be used to treat secondary viral* **infections.** • *You can't just rely on secondary* **sources** *for your research into her life history – you ought to look at primary sources such as her letters and diaries.* • *A deep voice and facial hair are secondary sexual characteristics.*

se·cret /ˈsiː·krət/ *n* [C] a piece of information that is only known by one person or a few people and should not be told to others • *Don't tell anyone about this – it's a secret.* • *Why did you have to go and tell Bob about my illness? You just can't* **keep** *a secret, can you?* • *We have no secrets* **from** *each other.* • *The couple were alleged to have* **sold** *military secrets* **to** *the enemy.* • *The negotiators were meeting* **in secret** (= without other people knowing) *for several months before the peace agreement was reached.* • *He says he loathes her, but I think* **in secret** (= without telling other people) *he really likes her.* • *Aren't you going to* **let me in on** (= tell me) *the secret?* • *There's no secret* (= everyone knows) *about his homosexuality.* • *She* **makes** *no secret of her dislike of her father.* • *That restaurant is one of the* **best-kept** *secrets in London.* • *The role of nuclear weapons in the crisis is a* **closely-guarded** *secret.* • *Did Caroline* **divulge** (= tell you) *any secrets about her love-life when you last saw her?* • *The discovery of this diary is very important as it reveals some of her* **innermost** *secrets.* • *(fig.) James Watson and Francis Crick unlocked the secrets* (= solved the mysteries) *of DNA in 1953.* • *(fig.) So what's* **the secret of** (= what are the knowledge and skills needed for) *being a good cook?*

se·cret /ˈsiː·krət/ *adj* • *The President escaped through a secret passage underneath the parliament building.* • *When they are released, the hostages will be taken to a secret location to be reunited with their families.* • *Hamilton became a secret smoker after he promised his parents he would give up cigarettes.* • *We ought to keep these proposals secret* **from** *the chairman for the time being.* • *This is* **top** (= extremely) *secret information.* • *Do you think we'll manage to* **keep** *the party secret* **from** *Mum until her birthday?* • *(humorous)* A **secret admirer** is a person who likes another person but does not say so openly: *Who sent you those flowers – have you got a secret admirer?* • A **secret agent** is a government employee whose job involves obtaining secret information about the governments of unfriendly foreign countries: *The book has some interesting stories about the activities of spies and secret agents during that difficult period.* • A **secret ballot** is a method of voting in which each person writes their choice on a piece of paper so that no one else knows how they have voted: *The election of the government is carried out* **by secret ballot.** • The **secret police** of a country is a police force which secretly gathers information about people who oppose the government and weakens such opposition, often using illegal or unfair methods: *Hundreds of political prisoners have been tortured by the secret police.* • The **secret service** of a country is a government organization that is responsible for things such as the safety of important politicians and for preventing secret government and military information being discovered by possible enemy countries: *A network of police informers and secret service* **agents** *has kept the government in touch with the growing demands for reform.* • A **secret society** is an organization which prevents people who are not members from finding out about its activities and customs. • A **secret weapon** is something which will give you a clear advantage when you use it: *His secret weapon is the information he could give to the authorities about who helped him and why.* ○ *Mary was their secret weapon – she knew more about the system than anyone else.* • (D)

se·cre·tive /£ˈsiː·krə·tɪv, $-t̬ɪv/ *adj esp. disapproving* • People who are secretive hide their feelings, thoughts, intentions and actions from other people: *Julian is a very private, almost secretive, person.* ○ *Her secretive behaviour made us very suspicious.* ○ *He's being very secretive* **about** *his new girlfriend.*

se·cre·tive·ly /£ˈsiː·krə·tɪv·li, $-t̬ɪv-/ *adv esp. disapproving* • *Why are you behaving so secretively at the moment?*

se·cre·tive·ness /£ˈsiː·krə·tɪv·nəs, $-t̬ɪv-/ *n* [U] *esp. disapproving* • *I don't like all this secretiveness – I want to be kept fully informed about everything that's happening.*

se·cret·ly /ˈsiː·krət·li/ *adv* • *She said she didn't care about it, but I believe she was secretly* **delighted.** • *He was convicted on the evidence of secretly* **recorded** *telephone conversations.* • *It was recently revealed that the two leaders* **met** *secretly for peace talks in Geneva last year.*

se·cre·cy /ˈsiː·krə·si/ *n* [U] • *His obsessive secrecy about his private life is a defence against the pressures of being a superstar.* • *The content of her report is* **shrouded in** *secrecy* (= being kept secret). • *I'd love to tell you about it, but Martin's* **sworn** *me* **to** *secrecy* (= made me promise not to tell anyone). • *There has been strong criticism of the* **veil of** *secrecy surrounding the negotiations.*

sec·re·tar·y OFFICE /£ˈsek·rə·tri, $-ter·i/ *n* [C] someone who works in an office and writes letters, makes telephone calls, arranges meetings and organizes documents for a particular person or for a company, organization etc. • *My secretary will phone you to arrange a meeting.*

sec·re·tar·i·al /£ˌsek·rəˈteə·ri·əl, $-ˈter·i-/ *adj* [not gradable] • *The new secretarial* **college** (= where people learn to be secretaries) *offers courses in shorthand, typing, word-processing and office management.* • *We've decided to create a new secretarial* **post** *(Am and Aus usually* **position***) in the publicity department.* • *The duties of the post are mainly secretarial.* • *Computerization has enabled us to reduce our secretarial* **staff.** • *I'm looking for part-time secretarial* **work** *at the moment.*

sec·re·tar·y GOVERNMENT /£ˈsek·rə·tri, $-ter·i/ *n* [C] the head of a government department • In the UK, a secretary (also *fml* **Secretary of State**) is a Member of Parliament who belongs to the ruling party and is in charge of a government department: *She became Secretary of State for Education after spending three years as Environment Secretary.* ○ *In the UK, the Foreign Secretary is the minister in charge of the Foreign Office.* ○ *Was the conference a success, Foreign Secretary?* [as form of address] • In the US, a secretary is chosen by the president and is not a member of a law-making body: *the Secretary of Health and Human Services* • In the US, the **Secretary of State** has responsibility for relations with other countries. • Compare MINISTER POLITICIAN.

sec·re·tar·y OFFICIAL /£ˈsek·rə·tri, $-ter·i/ *n* [C] an official who has responsibility for the general management of an organization • *The* **company** *secretary has written to all the shareholders to apologise for the mistake.* • *The* **honorary** *secretary of the charity is Lady Castleton.* • *He recently became the* **general** *secretary of the National Union of Teachers.* • The **Secretary-General** of an organization is its most important official: *My moral duty as Secretary-General of the United Nations is to do everything possible to avoid war.* ○ *The secretary-general of the Arts Council has welcomed the increase in government funding.* ○ *The Prime Minister's most likely successor is the secretary-general of his party.*

sec·re·tar·i·at /£ˌsek·rəˈteə·ri·ət, $-ˈter·i-/ *n* [C + sing/pl v] • A secretariat is the office or people responsible for the management of an organization, particularly an international or political one: *He worked at the Secretariat of the United Nations for forty years.*

se·crete *obj* PRODUCE /sɪˈkriːt/ *v* [T] *specialized* (of animals or plants or their cells) to produce and release (a liquid) • *Saliva is a liquid secreted by glands in or near the mouth.* • *The thyroid gland secretes hormones which affect growth.*

se·cre·tion /sɪˈkriː·ʃᵊn/ *n specialized* • *The excessive secretion of gastric juices in the gut causes ulcers.* [U] • *The insect causes damage to plants by direct feeding and by its toxic secretions.* [C]

se·crete *obj* HIDE /sɪˈkriːt/ *v* [T] *fml* to put (something) in a place where it is unlikely to be found • *He was arrested at the airport with two kilos of heroin secreted* **in** *his clothing.* • *She secreted millions of dollars* **in** *foreign bank accounts to try to reduce her tax bill.*

se·cre·tive /£ˈsiː·krə·tɪv, $-t̬ɪv/ *adj* See at SECRET

se·cret·ly /ˈsiː·krət·li/ *adv* See at SECRET

sect /sekt/ *n* [C] *usually disapproving* a religious group which has developed from a larger religion and is considered to have extreme or unusual beliefs or customs • *When he was sixteen he ran away from home and joined a* **religious** *sect.*

sec·tar·i·an /£sekˈteə·ri·ən, $-ˈter·i-/ *n, adj esp. disapproving* (a person) strongly supporting a particular religion group, esp. in such a way as not to be willing to accept other beliefs • *Let us put aside our sectarian differences.* • *He called on terrorists on both sides of the sectarian divide to end the cycle of violence.* • *The shooting appears to be drugs-related rather than a sectarian murder.* • **Non**-*sectarian education is vital for long-term peace.* • *Sectarians on both sides of the conflict are refusing to compromise.* [C]

sec·tar·i·an·i·sm /£sekˈteə·ri·ə·nɪ·zᵊm, $-ˈter·i-/ *n* [U] *disapproving* • *These appalling murders represent sectarianism of the most evil kind.*

sec·tion PART /ˈsek·ʃᵊn/ *n* [C] one of the parts that something is divided into or made up of • *Have you finished reading the arts section of the paper?* • *Jonathan plays in the wind section of the orchestra.* • *They were killed on a notoriously dangerous section of the motorway.* • *Does the restaurant have a non-smoking section?* • *Only the tail section of the plane remained intact during the crash.* • *An extra £1 billion is to be targeted at the poorest sections of the community over the next five years.* • *He was charged* **under** *section 17 of the 1968 Firearms Act* (= according to that part of the law) *with possessing an imitation firearm at the time of committing a theft.* • The sections of a fruit such as an orange are the parts that it is naturally divided into. • See also SUBSECTION.

sec·tion·al /ˈsek·ʃᵊn·ᵊl/ *n* [C] *Am* • A sectional is a piece of furniture that is made up of parts which can be arranged in various ways: *All of our sectionals, love seats and sofas are on sale this week.*

sec·tion·al /ˈsek·ʃᵊn·ᵊl/ *adj* [not gradable] • Interests or aims that are sectional are limited to a particular group within an organization, society or country and do not consider other groups: *The national interest is more important than the sectional and personal interests of individual politicians.*

sec·tion CUT /ˈsek·ʃᵊn/ *n* a cut, esp. *(medical)* one made in part of the body in an operation or *(specialized)* one made in order to show the structure of something • *(medical) The new technique involves the insertion of a miniature video camera into the stomach through the mouth, eliminating the need for a section.* [C] • *(medical) The section* (= cutting) *of the nerve fibres is the most delicate part of the operation.* [U] • *(medical)* A section is also a CAESAREAN SECTION. [C] • *(specialized) Make* **transverse** *and* **longitudinal** *sections of the tissue to show the numbers and areas of the blood vessels.* [C] • *(specialized)* A section is also a very thin slice of a part of an animal, plant or other object made in order to see its structure: *Each section is mounted on a slide and numbered before being examined under the microscope.* [C] • *(specialized)* A section is also a drawing or model which shows the structure of something by cutting part of it away: *This* **vertical** *section of the soil shows four basic soil layers.* [C] ○ *The first diagram is a view of the shop from the street, and the second shows it* **in section**. • A section is also the shape of a flat surface that is produced when an object is cut into separate pieces. [C]

sec·tor ECONOMIC AREA /£ˈsek·tər, $-tɚ/ *n* [C] one of the areas into which the economic activity of a country is divided • *Every sector of the economy has been affected by the recession.* • *In the* **financial** *sector, banks and insurance companies have both lost a lot of money.* • *The new government's policy is to transfer state industries from the* **public** *sector to the* **private** *sector.* • *Job creation in the* **service** *sector* (= hotels, restaurants, leisure activities and other services) *is failing to match job losses in the* **manufacturing** *sector* (= companies making products). • *Much community care of old people is undertaken by the* **voluntary** *sector* (= people who are not paid to do it).

sec·tor CONTROLLED AREA /£ˈsek·tər, $-tɚ/ *n* [C] an area of land or sea that has been divided from other areas and is controlled by a particular country • *At the end of the war, Germany was divided into four sectors, and the Soviet sector became East Germany.* • *What is the total oil output from the British sector of the North Sea?*

sec·u·lar /£ˈsek·jʊ·lər, $-jə·lɚ/ *adj* not having any connection with religion • *We live in an increasingly secular* **society**, *in which religion has less and less influence on our daily lives.* • *I want my children to have a secular* **education** *and be allowed to make up their own minds about religion.* • *He's just one of those fanatical right-wing preachers who blame everything on* **secular humanism** (= a set of beliefs placing the greatest importance on individuals rather than religion).

sec·u·lar·i·sm /£ˈsek·jʊ·lᵊr·ɪ·zᵊm, $-jə·lɚ-/ *n* [U] • Secularism is the belief that religion should not be involved with the ordinary social and political activities of a country.

sec·u·lar·ist /£ˈsek·jʊ·lᵊr·ɪst, $-jə·lɚ-/ *n* [C], *adj* • *The secularists have more support in the cities than in the traditional rural communities.* • *The country's constitution was founded on secularist principles.*

sec·u·lar·ize *obj, Br and Aus usually* **-ise** /£ˈsek·jʊ·lᵊr·aɪz, $-jə·lə·raɪz/ *v* [T] • When something is secularized, religious influence, power or control is removed from it: *He claims that Western secularized society makes it difficult to live as a Christian.*

se·cure PROTECTED /£sɪˈkjʊər, $-ˈkjʊr/ *adj* **-r, -st** (esp. of objects, situations etc.) able to avoid being harmed by any risk, danger or threat • *Car manufacturers ought to produce vehicles which are more secure* **against** *theft.* • *Endangered species need to be* **kept** *secure* **from** *poachers.* • *Some insurance companies offer lower premiums to people who* **make** *their houses more secure.*

se·cure *obj* /£sɪˈkjʊər, $-ˈkjʊr/ *v* [T] • *How can we secure the factory* **against** *vandals?* • *The wall was built to secure the village* **from** *attack.* • *The building has only one main entrance and is easy to secure.* • *(fig.) This form of investment is an excellent way of securing your children's financial future* (= making sure they will have enough money in the future).

se·cure·ly /£sɪˈkjʊə·li, $-ˈkjʊr-/ *adv* • *There are 15 000 kilometres of railway track, and it is impossible to guard it securely against terrorist attacks.* • *This certificate is an important document, and should be kept securely* (= in a place where it cannot be lost or stolen).

se·cur·i·ty /£sɪˈkjʊə·rɪ·ti, $-ˈkjʊr·ə·t̬i/ *n* [U] • Security is protection of a person, building, organization or country against threats such as crime, criminals and attacks by foreign countries: *The station was closed for two hours because of a security* **alert**. ○ *The banks deny that cash-machine withdrawals can be made as a result of computer error or internal* **breaches** *of security.* ○ *I can't let you into the building without security* **clearance**. ○ *Thirty demonstrators were killed in clashes with the security* **forces** *over the weekend.* ○ *The tighter security* **measures** *include video cameras in the city centre.* ○ *The students were deported because they posed a threat to* **national** *security.* ○ *Extra security* **precautions** *are being taken to protect public buildings against bomb attacks.* ○ *The proposed national identity card system would help to* **tighten** *security against fraud.* • Security is also the group of people responsible for protecting a building: *You'll need to notify security if you want to work late in the office.* [+ sing/pl v] • *(Br)* A **security blanket** is protection for a person or place threatened by a violent attack which involves preventing details of an activity from being discovered by the public: *A security blanket was thrown around the President's visit because of the bomb threats.* See also **security blanket** at SECURE CONFIDENT. • The **Security Council** of the United Nations is an organization with five permanent and ten temporary members whose purpose is to prevent war and maintain peace: *The five permanent members of the UN Security Council are China, France, Russia, the UK and the US.* ○

Failure to comply with the Security Council **resolution** *will result in sanctions being imposed.* • A **security guard** is someone whose job involves preventing people going into places without permission, delivering and collecting large amounts of money, or protecting goods from theft: *To reassure the public, there are now two security guards at every entrance to the complex.* • A **security risk** is something or someone likely to cause danger or difficulty: *Excavations so close to the Parliament buildings were regarded as presenting an unacceptable security risk.* ○ *The only reason she was considered a security risk was because her husband was a foreigner.*

se·cure [FIXED] /£sɪˈkjʊəʳ, $-ˈkjʊr/ *adj* **-r, -st** fixed, fastened or locked into a position which prevents movement; not likely to move or change • *That ladder doesn't look very secure to me.* • *Just check that the door is secure – the lock doesn't always work properly.* • *The prosperity of the country depends on a stable and secure peace.* • *Her promotion has made her position in the company more secure.* • *The museum has been promised £22 million by the government, so its future is relatively secure.* • *I wasn't sure if I was going to keep my job, so I wasn't financially secure.* • A secure place is one that it is difficult to get out of or escape from: *He killed the man just a month after his release from a secure mental hospital.*

se·cure *obj* /£sɪˈkjʊəʳ, $-ˈkjʊr/ *v* [T] • If you secure one object to another you fasten it firmly to that object: *The gate won't stay open, so we'll have to secure it* **to** *that post.*

se·cure·ly /£sɪˈkjʊə·li, $-ˈkjʊr-/ *adv* • *Please ensure that your seatbelts are fastened securely.* • *I'd locked my bike securely to a lamp-post but someone still managed to steal it.* • *For a moment it looked as if he would drop the ball, but he held it securely.* • *The election result leaves her securely in office until the end of the decade.* • *He has given up political power, but he remains securely in control of the army.*

se·cur·i·ty /£sɪˈkjʊə·rɪ·ti, $-ˈkjʊr·ə·t̬i/ *n* [U] • *She has security of* **tenure** *at the university, which means she can work there for as long as she likes.* • *If it's a choice between higher pay and* **job** *security, I'd prefer to keep my job.* • *I've been unemployed for two years and have absolutely no financial security* (= no certainty of having enough money to live on). • *The most dangerous criminals are held in* **maximum***-security prisons* (= prisons that are as difficult as possible to escape from).

se·cure *obj* [OBTAIN] /£sɪˈkjʊəʳ, $-ˈkjʊr/ *v* [T] *fml* to get something, sometimes with difficulty • *He was clearly disappointed by his failure to secure the top job with the bank.* • *His secret mission to secure the release of the hostages ended in failure.* • *The change in the law will make it harder for the police to secure* **convictions**.

se·cure [CONFIDENT] /£sɪˈkjʊəʳ, $-ˈkjʊr/ *adj* **-r, -st** having few worries or doubts about yourself and your personal relationships • *Children need to feel secure to do well at school.*

se·cur·i·ty /£sɪˈkjʊə·rɪ·ti, $-ˈkjʊr·ə·t̬i/ *n* [U] • *She said that she believes it to be important for children to have the security of a stable family life.* • A **security blanket** is a soft object such as a small piece of cloth or a toy which is very familiar to a baby or young child and makes it feel secure: *(fig.) He never goes anywhere without his hat – it seems to be his security blanket.* See also **security blanket** at SECURE [PROTECTED].

se·cure *obj* [FINANCIAL] /£sɪˈkjʊəʳ, $-ˈkjʊr/ *v* [T] to make certain that (money that has been lent) will be paid back by giving the lender the right to own things which belong to the borrower if the money is not paid back • *Her bank loan is secured* **against** *some shares that she inherited from her aunt.* • *Large loans need to be secured by strong collateral.* • *His business loan is secured* **on** *his house, so he could end up homeless if he doesn't repay it.* • *If you wanted to borrow more than $5000, the bank would only be able to offer you a secured* **loan**.

se·cur·i·ty /£sɪˈkjʊə·rɪ·ti, $-ˈkjʊr·ə·t̬i/ *n* [U] • *She used her shares in the company* **as** *security* **against** *a £23 million bank loan.* • *The hotel held onto our baggage* **as** *security while we went to the bank to change money to pay the bill.*

se·cur·i·ty /£sɪˈkjʊə·rɪ·ti, $-ˈkjʊr·ə·t̬i/ *n* [C] *specialized* an investment in a company or in government debt which can be traded on the financial markets and which produces an income for the investor • *Securities include government bonds, which pay interest, and company shares, which pay dividends.*

se·dan /sɪˈdæn/ *n* [C] *Am and Aus for* SALOON [CAR] • *If you're looking for an inexpensive family car, this well-equipped sedan deserves serious consideration.* • [PIC] **Vehicles**

se·dan chair /sɪˈdæn/ *n* [C] an enclosed seat for one person with horizontal poles at either side so that it can be lifted and carried by two people with one person at the front of the seat and the other at the back

se·date [CALM] /sɪˈdeɪt/ *adj* tending to avoid excitement or great activity and to be calm and relaxed • *The fight against a chemical storage site has transformed a normally sedate village into a battleground.* • *Opponents of the government are calling for a more sedate* **pace** *of economic reform.* • *The speed limit in many areas is a sedate 55 mph.*

se·date·ly /sɪˈdeɪt·li/ *adv*

se·date *obj* [DRUG] /sɪˈdeɪt/ *v* [T] to cause (someone) to be calm or go to sleep by giving them a drug • *The nurse said we could visit him, but he's* **heavily** *sedated and probably won't recognize us.*

se·da·tion /sɪˈdeɪ·ʃᵊn/ *n* [U] • *She's* **under** *strong sedation and should not be disturbed.*

sed·a·tive /£ˈsed·ə·tɪv, $-t̬ɪv/ *n* [C] • *He was hysterical after the accident and had to be* **given** *a sedative* (= a substance which calms people). • *This drug has a sedative* **effect** *and should not be taken when driving.*

sed·en·ta·ry /£ˈsed·ᵊn·tri, $-ter·i/ *adj* involving little exercise or physical activity • *My doctor says I should start playing sport because my* **lifestyle** *is too sedentary.* • *Many people in sedentary* **occupations** *do not take enough exercise.*

sed·i·ment /ˈsed·ɪ·mənt/ *n* [U] a soft substance that is like a wet powder and consists of very small pieces of a solid material which have fallen to the bottom of a liquid • *They devised an efficient method for the removal of sediment from the water.* • *There was a brown sediment in the bottom of the bottle.* • *Scientists have found a large amount of lead in the sediment in the North Sea.*

sed·i·ments /ˈsed·ɪ·mənts/ *pl n* • *It is hoped that the oil slick will sink to the seabed where it would be covered within a few years by sediments* (= sediment) *and eventually decompose.*

sed·i·men·ta·ry /£ˌsed·ɪˈmen·tᵊr·i, $ˈ-t̬ɚ·i/ *adj* [not gradable] • Sedimentary **rock** is rock made from sediment left by water, ice or wind: *Sedimentary rock forms the top geological layer in much of southern Britain.*

sed·i·men·ta·tion /ˌsed·ɪ·menˈteɪ·ʃᵊn/ *n* [U] • *Heavy rain has washed a lot of soil into the river, causing sedimentation.*

se·di·tion /sɪˈdɪʃ·ᵊn/ *n* [U] language or behaviour that is intended to persuade other people to oppose their government • *The president has charged eight people with sedition and closed a radio station which broadcast a discussion that criticized the government.*

se·di·tious /sɪˈdɪʃ·əs/ *adj* • *She was arrested after making a speech that the government considered to be seditious.*

se·duce *obj* [PERSUADE] /£sɪˈdjuːs, $-ˈduːs/ *v* [T] to persuade in a traditional romantic way (someone who is usually younger and has little experience of sex) to have sex with you • *Pete lost his virginity at 15 when he was seduced by his best friend's mother.* • *He seduced her* **into** *an affair that had tragic consequences for both of them.*

se·duc·er *male, female* **se·duc·tress** /£sɪˈdjuː·səʳ, $-ˈduː·sɚ, -ˈdʌk·trəs/ *n* [C] • *The play tells the story of a fabulously wealthy woman who seeks revenge on her seducer.* • *In the film she played a seductress who ensnares her lover into killing her husband.*

se·duc·tion /sɪˈdʌk·ʃᵊn/ *n* • *The film depicts the seduction of a schoolgirl by a middle-aged man.* [U] • *His seductions involve the usual expensive dinner and witty conversation.* [C]

se·duc·tive /£sɪˈdʌk·tɪv, $-t̬ɪv/ *adj* • *The advertisement for the car was banned because of its gratuitous portrayal of a nude woman in a seductive* **pose**.

se·duc·tive·ly /£sɪˈdʌk·tɪv·li, $-t̬ɪv-/ *adv* • *He leaned across the table to whisper seductively in her ear.*

se·duc·tive·ness /£sɪˈdʌk·tɪv·nəs, $-t̬ɪv-/ *n* [U]

se·duce *obj* [ATTRACT] /£sɪˈdjuːs, $-ˈduːs/ *v* [T often passive] to cause (someone) to do something that they would not usually consider doing by being very attractive and difficult to refuse • *Don't be seduced by the low price – the more expensive one is much better.* • *Many voters have been seduced by his charm and wit.* • *She has refused to be seduced by modern technology and prefers a traditional lifestyle.* • *Many east Europeans who were seduced by the glamour and prosperity of the West have become* *disillusioned with its superficiality.* • *They were seduced* **into** *buying the washing machine by the offer of a free flight to the United States.* • *Almost every visitor to Edinburgh is seduced* (=attracted and pleased) *by its splendid architecture.*

se·duc·tion /sɪˈdʌk·ʃᵊn/ *n* • *The movie begins with the seduction of newly qualified young lawyer by a top law firm with an offer that's impossible to refuse.* [U] • *The seduction of life in a warm climate has led to many Britons buying homes around the Mediterranean.* [U] • *It's impossible to resist the seductions* (=attractions) *of French cuisine.* [C]

se·duc·tive /£sɪˈdʌk·tɪv, $-t̬ɪv/ *adj* • *Television confronts the viewer with a succession of glittering and seductive* **images.** • *The* **argument** *that sanctions should be given more time to work is seductive but fatally flawed.*

se·duc·tive·ly /£sɪˈdʌk·tɪv·li, $-t̬ɪv/ *adv* • *The seductively rich taste of Greek yoghurt depends on it being made with whole milk.*

se·duc·tive·ness /£sɪˈdʌk·tɪv·nəs, $-t̬ɪv-/ *n* [U]

see *(obj)* USE EYES /siː/ *v* [not usually *be seeing*] *past simple* **saw** /£sɔː, $sɑː/, *past part* **seen** /siːn/ to be aware of what is around you by using your eyes • *They used to say that eating carrots helped you see in the dark.* [I] • **I can't** *see very well without my glasses.* [I] • *"***Can** *you see any empty seats?" "Yes, I* **can** *see a couple in the third row."* [T] • *There were so many people in front of us we weren't able to see* **what** *was happening.* [+ *wh-* word] • *I can't believe what I'm seeing – is that car really yours?* [T] • *The film crew didn't want to be seen.* [T] • *Standing by the station entrance, he saw his mother before she saw him.* [T] • *The teacher could see* **(that)** *the children had been fighting.* [+ *(that)* clause] • *The woman said she saw the van park outside her house at ten o'clock.* [T + obj + infinitive without *to*] • *From the window we could see the children* **playing** *in the playground.* [T + obj + v-*ing*] • *You were seen* **to** *enter the building at 8.30.* [T + obj + *to* infinitive; passive] • *She didn't want to be seen* **visiting** *the doctor.* [T + obj + v-*ing*] • *(fig.) The government didn't want to be seen* **to** (=to appear to) *be making concessions to terrorists.* [T + obj + *to* infinitive; passive] • *His parents saw him* **awarded** *the winner's medal.* [+ obj + v-*ed*] • *See* (=Look at) *p. 23 for prices and flight details.* [T] • *See* **over** (=Look at the next page) *for further information.* [I] • *Did you see that documentary on homelessness on Channel Four last night?* [T] • *(fig.) This summer has seen the end of water restrictions in the area* (=They have ended this summer) *thanks to a new reservoir.* [T] • *(fig.) I don't know* **what** *you see* **in** (=find attractive about) *him.* [T] • If something **has seen better days**, it is now old and in bad condition: *That jacket's seen better days. Why don't you get a new one?* • *(humorous saying)* 'You ain't seen nothing yet' means that more surprising or exciting things are likely to happen. • *No one else had expected the factory to close, but we* **saw/could see it coming** (=we expected it to happen). • *(Br)* If you **can't see** someone **for dust**, they leave quickly in order to avoid something, or they show very little enthusiasm: *If you let him know that Margaret's coming, you won't see him for dust.* ○ *They were all very interested until I asked for volunteers, and then you couldn't see them for dust.* • If someone **can't see further than/can't see beyond the end of** their **nose**, they do not notice what is happening around them. • *The mess the burglars left behind* **had to be seen to be believed** (=was difficult to believe, but really did exist). • If you **see red**, you become very angry: *She saw red when she heard that he had left without finishing the job.* ○ *People like that really make me see red.* • If you **see stars**, you are partly unconscious because you have been hit on the head. • To **see the colour of** someone's **money** is to make certain that a person is going to pay for something: *He said he'd buy my bike, but I'll wait until I see the colour of his money!* ○ *"I'll have one of those." "Let's see the colour of your money first!"* • If you are pleased to **see the last of** (*Br and Aus also* **see the back of**) someone or something, you are pleased that you no longer have to be involved with them: *I was* **glad** *to see the back of that essay – I'd been working on it for weeks.* ○ *The hotel staff couldn't wait to see the back of such a difficult guest.* • If you are **seeing things**, you are imagining that things are happening when they are not: *Didn't Marie come in just now? I must have been seeing things.* • *(infml) I* **wouldn't be seen dead** *wearing* (=I certainly would not wear) *a dress like that.* • **Seeing-Eye dog** is *Am and Aus trademark for* **guide dog**. See at GUIDE. • Something which is **see-through** is transparent: *see-through partitions* • A piece of clothing which is **see-through** is very thin and light, and other clothes or the body can be seen under it: *a see-through blouse* • *(saying)* 'Seeing is believing' means if you see something yourself you will believe it to exist or be true, despite the fact that it is extremely unusual or unexpected: *"I never thought Simon would get out of bed before lunchtime on a Saturday, but seeing is believing!"* • *(saying)* 'What you see is what you get' means that there is nothing hidden. See also WYSIWYG. • LP **Eye and seeing**

see *(obj)* UNDERSTAND /siː/ *v* [not *be seeing*] *past simple* **saw** /£sɔː, $sɑː/, *past part* **seen** /siːn/ to understand, know or be aware • *I see* **(that)** *the social club is organising a theatre trip next month.* [+ *(that)* clause] • *He couldn't see* **what** *difference it made to come* (=He didn't think it was important if he came) *on Thursday instead of Friday.* [+ *wh-* word] • *I can't see* **why** *you didn't write to him.* [+ *wh-* word] • *They didn't see* **the need/any need** (=understand that it was important) *to notify their members of the changes in writing.* [T] • *They only refused to help because they're too busy, but he seems to see more* **in** *it than that.* [T] • *It'll be easier if you hold it this way – do you see* **what** *I mean?* [+ *wh-* word] • *"I'm tired." "***So** *I see – you've been yawning all afternoon."* [T] • *The chairwoman thought the new scheme was a great improvement, but I couldn't see it myself* (=couldn't understand why it was thought to be good, or didn't agree). [T] • *I was surprised that they couldn't see my point of view.* [T] • *After she read his book she started to see the issue* **in another/a different/a new light** (=differently). [T] • If someone says they can see **(into) the future** they think they know what is going to happen: *The election will turn on how people see the future for themselves and their families.* [T] ○ *We see a bright future over the next 10 to 15 years for this part of the country.* [T] ○ *If she could have seen into the future, she wouldn't have done what she did.* [I] • *My sister didn't* **see eye to eye with** *me* (=agree with me) *about the arrangements.* • *We talked to her for an hour, but we couldn't make her* **see sense/reason** (=understand what we thought was the best thing for her to do). • If you **see the light** you understand something you didn't understand before: *The children struggled with the puzzle for a while, until one of them suddenly saw the light – the red pieces fitted into the blue pieces.* See also **see the light of day** at SEE MEET. • *They couldn't* **see the point of** (=understand the importance of or the reason for) *further training.* • *Everyone else laughed loudly but I didn't* **see the joke** (=understand what everyone was laughing about). • If you **can't see the** *(Br and Aus)* **wood**/*(Am)* **forest for the trees** you are looking at a situation too closely and this prevents you from understanding it. • If you **see through** someone or their behaviour you are aware that they are acting to get some advantage for themselves, although it appears otherwise: *They were very friendly, but I quickly saw through them.* ○ *She saw through his excuse at once.* • *Could you lend me £10? The bank's closed now and I need to do some shopping,* **you see** (=I hope you understand).

see *(obj)* CONSIDER /siː/ *v* [not *be seeing*] *past simple* **saw** /£sɔː, $sɑː/, *past part* **seen** /siːn/ to consider or think about, esp. to think about (someone or something) in a particular way, or to imagine (someone) doing a particular activity • *We didn't see him* **as** *a potential leader.* [T] • *She didn't see herself* **as** *brave.* [T] • *The library didn't see the Wilson collection* **as** *valuable.* [T] • *It was easy to see the gift* **as** *a sort of bribe.* [T] • *I can't see her* **accepting** (=I don't think she will accept) *the job in the present circumstances.* [T + obj + v-*ing*] • *As I see* **it/things/the situation**, *we'll have to get extra help.* [T] • *Try and see it my* **way** *– I'll be left without any help if you go to Edinburgh tomorrow.* [T] • *"Do you think there'll be time to stop for meal?"* **'I'll/We'll (have to) see** (=I will think about it and make a decision later).*"* • *"Can we have fish and chips tonight, Dad?"* **"We'll see about that (later)."** • *He wants to park his car on my lawn? Well,* **we'll (soon) see about** *that* (=I will (try to) prevent it)*!* • *"Do you know a shop that sells sports clothes?"* **'Let me see/Let's see** (=I must think about it briefly) *– I think there's one near the station."* • If you **see fit** to do something, you think it is good or necessary to do it: *You can leave it here or take it home with you, whichever you see fit.* ○ *She saw fit to take her son away from the school.* • *Could you* **see** *your* **way (clear) to** *letting us* (=consider agreeing to allow us to) *borrow the machine on Wednesday?*

see *(obj)* MEET /siː/ *v past simple* **saw** /£sɔː, $sɑː/, *past part* **seen** /siːn/ to meet or come into CONTACT with (someone), or to visit (a place) • *We're seeing friends at the weekend.* [T] • *I've only seen her twice in the last three years.* [T] • *How long has she been seeing him* (=been having a romantic relationship with him)? [T] • *My mother is seeing the doctor again next week.* [T] • *I haven't seen Jerry* **around** *in the last few weeks.* [T] • *No one has seen* **much of** *Darryl since he got married.* [T] • *They see* **a lot of** *each other* (= are often together) *at weekends.* [T] • *The children wanted to see the dolphins.* [T] • *The agent said they could see the house (Br also* **see round/through**/*Aus usually* **over the house**) *at 3 p.m.* [T/I] • **Be seeing you**, **See you** and **See you later** are informal ways of saying goodbye. • *(infml)* Someone might say they have to **see a man about a dog** when they don't want to tell you what they are really doing, esp. when they are going to the toilet: *I've just got to see a man about a dog. I'll be back in a minute.* ○ *"Where are you going this afternoon?" "Oh, just to see a man about a dog."* • *(infml) I haven't* **seen hide nor hair of** *her* (= haven't met her on any occasion) *since last Friday.* • *(esp. Br)* If you would **see** someone **in hell** before you would do something, you are determined not to do it: *I'd see her in hell before I'd agree to an arrangement like that.* ○ *He said he'd see her in hell first.* • To **see life** is to experience many different and often unexpected things: *As a volunteer on the childcare project, I really saw life.* • When something **sees the light of day** it appears for the first time: *The relic first saw the light of day in the thirteenth century in the Middle East, and quickly became an object of veneration.*

see *obj* GO WITH /siː/ *v* [T always + adv/prep] *past simple* **saw** /£sɔː, $sɑː/, *past part* **seen** /siːn/ to go with (someone) to the stated place • *He saw his visitors* **to the door.** • *Her friends saw her* **home.** • *The security guard saw the protesters* **off** *the premises.* • *My parents saw me* **off** *at the airport* (= went to the airport with me to say goodbye). [M] • *She saw me* **out of** *the building.* • If you **see in the New Year**, you do not go to bed on 31 December until after 12 o'clock at night in order to celebrate the start of a new year. • If you **see** someone or something **off**, you defeat them or deal with them effectively so that they can no longer cause harm: *England saw off Luxembourg 5-0.* ○ *He may not have seen off the challengers for the leadership of the party, but he has at least silenced them for a while.*

see TRY TO DISCOVER /siː/ *v* [+ *wh-* word] *past simple* **saw** /£sɔː, $sɑː/, *past part* **seen** /siːn/ to try to discover • *Will you see* **if** *you can get anyone to help?* • *We were just seeing* **how** *much room was left in this cupboard.* • *I'll see* **what** *I can do.* • *I'll see* **if** *I can find him for you.*

see *obj* MAKE CERTAIN /siː/ *v* [+ *(that)* clause] *past simple* **saw** /£sɔː, $sɑː/, *past part* **seen** /siːn/ to make certain (that something happens) • *See (that) you're ready by five.* • *The receptionist said he'd see (that) she got the message.* • *(Br and Aus infml)* To **see** someone **right** is to make certain that someone is helped or treated well: *Ask Mrs Martin at the desk over there about the invoices – she'll see you right.*

see a·bout *obj v prep* [T] *infml for* SEE TO • *It's getting late – I'd better see about* (= prepare) *lunch.* • *You should see about* **getting** *your hair cut.* [+ v-*ing*]

see out *obj*, **see** *obj* **out** *v adv* [M] to wait or last until the end of (something) • *The besieged town hasn't enough food to see the month out.* • *They saw out the storm in the best shelter they could find.*

see to *obj v prep* [T] to do (something which is waiting to be dealt with) • *"These letters need posting." "I'll see to them later."* • *Mrs Chapman asked for some help with the orders – could you see to it?* • *Please see to* **it that** *no-one comes in without identification.* [+ obj + *that* clause]

seed PLANT /siːd/ *n* a small esp. round or oval object which forms inside a fruit or the case of a vegetable such as a bean and from which, when it is planted, a new plant can grow • **Sow** *parsley seeds now, covering them with a little soil.* [C] • *The chemical will stop all seeds from* **sprouting** *for the rest of the year.* [C] • *(fig.) Revolutions often contain within themselves the seeds* (= beginning) **of** *future disaster.* [C] • *(fig.) He may be* **sowing** *the seeds* **of** (= creating the reasons for) *his own destruction in the long term by using violence against his own people.* [C] • *(fig.) The seeds* **of** *friendship were sown early, and they remained lifelong companions.* [C] • *(specialized)* Seed is an amount of seeds: *Fresh seed of hardy primulas can be* **sown** *outside now.* [U] ○ *Keep the sown seed at a steady 21°C until germination.* [U] ○ *The farmers grow these crops for seed* (= for planting to grow more crops, rather than for eating). [U] • *Write to the address below for a free seed catalogue.* • If a plant, esp. one which is grown for food, **goes/runs to** seed it produces flowers and seeds because it has not been picked early enough: *In the hot weather the lettuces suddenly ran to seed.* [U] ○ *When we got home from holiday the onions had gone to seed.* [U] ○ *(fig.) After he retired he really went to seed* (= stopped caring for his appearance). [U] • Seed is also *Am infml for* SEMEN. [U] • **Seed corn** is grain which is kept for planting to produce new plants, or *(fig.)* something which is important because it is the starting point for future development: *(fig.) Investment is the seed corn of economic progress.* • *(Am and Aus)* **Seed money** is money used to start a development or activity. • **Seed potatoes** are potatoes which are planted so that a plant will grow and more potatoes will be produced. • PIC〉 **Fruit**

seed *(obj)* /siːd/ *v* • *Pull up annual weeds before they seed* (= let their seeds fall), *which most of them do in August.* [I] • *Sycamores seed* **freely** (= produce a lot of seeds). [I] • *The plants have seeded themselves* (= their seeds have fallen) *into the cracks between the paving stones.* [T] • To seed (also **deseed**) a fruit or vegetable is to remove its seeds: *Wash, seed and cut the pepper into small pieces.* [T] • If you seed something **with** something, you provide it with that thing to help it to start: *The project was seeded with money from the company, which has been very generous over the years.* [T] ○ *The machine's memory can be seeded with a simple program that copies itself many times in one run.* [T]

seed·ed /ˈsiː·dɪd/ *adj* [not gradable] • *Garnish with peeled, seeded* (= with the seeds removed) *and diced tomatoes.* • Seeded is sometimes the opposite of **seedless**: *black seeded grapes*

-seed·ed /-ˌsiː·dɪd, ˈ--/ *combining form* • *The walnut is a hard-seeded fruit.*

seed·less /ˈsiːd·ləs/ *adj* [not gradable] • *seedless grapes* • *a seedless satsuma*

seed·ling /ˈsiːd·lɪŋ/ *n* [C] • A seedling is a young plant which has grown from a seed: *The seeds* **sprout** *into small, hair-like seedlings resembling young grass.* ○ **Raise** *the seedlings in the greenhouse, and transplant when the weather becomes warmer.*

seed SPORT /siːd/ *n* [C] (esp. in tennis) a good player who is given a place on the list of those expected to win games in a particular competition because of the way they have played in the past • *She is ranked fifth in the world and is the top seed is this competition.* • *Turner's opponent in the quarter-finals of the snooker is the No. 1 seed.*

seed *obj* /siːd/ *v* [T usually passive] • *I was disappointed not to be seeded this year.* • *Jones, seeded second, has closeted herself with her coaches to concentrate on the next rounds.* [+ obj + adj] • *He was angered to be seeded 11th in the nationals, two below his world ranking of No. 9.* [+ obj + adj]

-seed·ed /-ˌsiː·dɪd, ˈ--/ *combining form* • *The 5th-seeded Browne crushed the defending champion, who was seeded second.*

seed·y /ˈsiː·di/ *adj* **-ier**, **-iest** being in bad condition or having a dirty and unpleasant appearance and likely to be involved in immoral activities • *a seedy hotel/cafe* • *the seedy 1930s-style business district* • *Their offices are in the seedier end of town.* • *The documentary delves into the seedy world of massage parlours.* • *I didn't like the look of those seedy characters who were hanging around outside the bar.*

seed·i·ness /ˈsiː·dɪ·nəs/ *n* [U]

see·ing (that) /ˈsiː·ɪŋ/, *infml* **see·ing as**, *not standard* **see·ing as how** *conjunction* considering or accepting the fact that; as • *Seeing that we need to arrive by twelve o'clock, we'd better leave at nine.* • *We may as well go to the concert, seeing as (how) we've already paid for the tickets.*

seek *obj* SEARCH /siːk/ *v* [T] *past* **sought** /£sɔːt, $sɑːt/ *fml* to search for, look for or try to find or obtain (esp. something which is not a physical object) • *Most of the posts would be taken by the short-term unemployed, the group that is* **actively** *seeking jobs.* • *The refugee crisis worsened yesterday, with hundreds seeking* **refuge/asylum** *in foreign embassies in the capital.* • *Watson said yesterday that he would not seek* **re-election** *next year.* • *They are victims of a legal system in which the odds are heavily stacked against the individual seeking* **damages/redress** *for a medical injury.* • If you seek advice/help/approval/permission, you ask for it: *They suggested she should seek advice from the legal department.* ○ *Approval should be sought before doctors carry out such operations.* • If you seek someone or something **out** you look for them (and find them): *After the meeting he sought out the person who had spoken about the plans.* [M] ○ *While he was at the library he decided to seek some information out on accommodation in the area.* [M] • *"Seek, and ye shall find"* (Bible, Matthew 7.7.)

seek·er /£ˈsiː·kər, $-kɚ/ *n* [C esp. in combinations] • *asylum seekers* • *publicity seekers* • *job-seekers* • *Sun-seekers* *should visit this island paradise.* • *He described them as 'compulsive seekers* **of**/(Br also) **after** *lost youth'.*

-seek·ing /-ˌsiː·kɪŋ, '-/ *combining form* • *pleasure-seeking* • *attention-seeking* • *The adventure-seeking youngster had climbed up the tree but couldn't get down again.* • See also SELF-SEEKING.

seek [TRY] /siːk/ *v* [+ *to* infinitive] *past* **sought** /£sɔːt, $sɑːt/ *fml* to try or attempt • *They sought* **to** *reassure broadcasters that the new rules would not mean certain news programmes disappearing from television schedules.* • *Mr Taylor is seeking* **to** *recover money he believes he is owed by the insurance company.*

seem /siːm/ *v* [not *be seeming*] to give the effect of being; to be judged to be • *You seem very quiet today.* [L] • *He's 16, but he seems* **(to be)** *younger.* [L (+ *to be*)] • *She didn't seem* **(to be)** *particularly happy at home.* [L (+ *to be*)] • *The news seemed* **(to be)** *too good to be true.* [L (+ *to be*)] • *The children seemed* **(as if/as though** *they were) tired.* [L; I always + adv/prep] • *He seemed* **(to be)** *such a nice man – I was amazed to hear he'd murdered his wife.* [L (+ *to be*)] • *They seemed* **(like)** *such friendly people, but they never returned our invitation.* [L; I always + adv/prep] • *You seem* **as if/as though/like** *you don't want to get involved.* [I always + adv/prep] • *I suspect his claims are not* **all** *they seem – he tends to exaggerate.* [L] • *She was not* **what** *she seemed – it turned out that she had a husband and five children.* [L] • *Things are seldom* **as/how** *they seem.* [I always + adv/prep] • *I know* **how** *this must seem, but could you lend me some more money?* [I always + adv/prep] • *I seem* **to** *know more about him than anyone else.* [+ *to* infinitive] • *I was met by someone who seemed* **to** *be the group leader.* [+ *to* infinitive] • *They seem* **to** *be taking a long time to decide.* [+ *to* infinitive] • **It** *seems* **(that)** *she can't come.* [+ (*that*) clause] • **It** *seems* **to me** *(that)* (= I think that) *he isn't the right person for the job.* [+ (*that*) clause] • *(fml)* **It would** *seem* **(that)** *we need to be at the airport two hours before takeoff.* [+ (*that*) clause] • **There** *seems* **to** *have been a mistake – my name isn't on the list.* [+ *to* infinitive] • *Patients said* **there** *didn't seem* **to** *be time to ask the doctor questions.* [+ *to* infinitive] • *The car doesn't seem* **to** *have suffered much damage.* [+ *to* infinitive] • *(fml) The car seems not* **to** *have suffered much damage.* [+ *to* infinitive] • **It** *seems* **(that)** *the eastern Swiss ski resorts are subject to a different weather pattern from those in central and western Switzerland.* [+ (*that*) clause] • *"There's no reply – they've all gone home."* **"So** *it seems."* [after *so*] • *"Was a decision made?" "It seems* **not/so.***"* [+ *not/so*] • [LP]> **It, There**

seem·ing /'siː·mɪŋ/ *adj* [before n; not gradable] *fml* • *Their seeming reluctance to demand better treatment was puzzling.* • *He said, with seeming embarrassment, that he would have to cancel the meeting.*

seem·ing·ly /'siː·mɪŋ·li/ *adv* [not gradable] • *He remains confident and seemingly untroubled by our recent problems.* • *The factory closure is seemingly inevitable.* • *Seemingly she's gone off to live with another man.* • *March 13 was a welcome interlude between many days of seemingly* **endless** *rain.*

seem·ly /'siːm·li/ *adj* **-ier, -iest** *old use* socially suitable; not unpleasantly noticeable

seen /siːn/ *past participle of* SEE • *"Have you seen my diary anywhere?" "I saw it on your desk this morning."*

seep /siːp/ *v* [I always + adv/prep] to move or spread slowly and gradually from one place to another • *The level of nitrates and pesticides in water supplies increases as chemicals seep* **out of** *the farmland.* • *The foul-smelling flood water seeped* **into** *the room and we used blankets as a makeshift dam.* • *The seawater seeped* **through** *the pebbles.* • *The suburbs of the city continue to seep* **into** *the surrounding rural areas.* • *Given the intense secrecy of the arms business, information only seeps* **out** *in company literature.*

seep·age /'siː·pɪdʒ/ *n* [U] • *Oil spills and seepage from refineries are common.* • *The damp patches on the floor had been caused by seepage.* • *There is* **a** *natural seepage of scientific ideas from the specialist down to the lay person through newspaper articles and TV programmes.*

seer /£sɪəʳ, $sɪr/ *n* [C] *literary* a person who is able to say what will happen in the future • *Briseida, daughter of a seer who had foreseen the Trojan demise, was exiled from Troy into the Greek camp.* • *The seer who predicts oil prices into the twenty-first century is either brave or foolish.*

seer·suck·er /£'sɪəˌsʌk·əʳ, $'sɪrˌsʌk·ɚ/ *n* [U] a light cloth which has a pattern of raised and flat strips on it

see·saw /£'siː·sɔː, $-sɑː/, *Am also* **tee·ter–tot·ter** *n* [C] a board balanced on a central point. A child sits on each end and they make the board go up and down by pushing off the ground with their feet. • *Prices have gone up and down like a seesaw this year.* • [PIC]> **Playground**

see·saw /£'siː·sɔː, $-sɑː/ *v* [I] • To seesaw is to go up and down or backwards and forwards between two places: *(fig.) Nobody knows what effect this new information will have on those committee members who have seesawed back and forth* (= whose opinions have regularly changed) *on this issue.*

see·saw /£'siː·sɔː, $-sɑː/ *adj* [before n] • *The stock market's recent seesaw movements have made many investors nervous.*

seethe [FEEL ANGER] /siːð/ *v* [I] to feel anger without expressing it • *The residents seethed when the council first began charging vehicles to park.* • *The class positively seethed* **with** *indignation when Julia won the award.* • *She seethes* **with** *anger at the idea that Mrs. Austin's case should be investigated before hers.* • *By the end of the meeting he was seething.*

seeth·ing /'siː·ðɪŋ/ *adj* [before n] • *Their seething resentment led to angry jostling between team-mates.*

seethe [MOVE] /siːð/ *v* [I] (of a large number or amount) to move about energetically in a small space • *The water seethed and bubbled as it boiled in the pan.* • *The streets were seething* (= busy or crowded) **with** *tourists.* • *(fig.) The violence that seethes so close to the surface is partly explained by the unhappy lives so many of the people live.*

seeth·ing /'siː·ðɪŋ/ *adj* • *Packed hotels and seething crowds in the town are a thing of past.* • *A seething* **mass** *of children crowded around the tables.*

seg·ment /'seg·mənt/ *n* [C] any of the parts into which something (esp. a circle or sphere) can be divided or into which it is naturally divided • *People over the age of 85 make up the fastest-growing segment of the elderly.* • *The salad was decorated with orange segments.* • [PIC]> **Fruit**

seg·ment *(obj)* /£seg'ment, $'--/ *v* • *The replies to the questionnaire segment broadly* **into** *three groups.* [I] • *Amex segmented the market by issuing gold and platinum cards to customers who have higher incomes than those qualifying for green cards.* [T]

seg·men·ta·tion /ˌseg·men'teɪ·ʃᵊn/ *n* [U] • *The key to increased profitability is market segmentation, or carving out services that will appeal to particular groups of travellers.*

seg·re·gate *obj* /'seg·rɪ·geɪt/ *v* [T] to cause to become separate or to keep apart, often for social reasons and esp. because of race or sex • *Girls and boys were segregated* **into** *different dining rooms for meals and not allowed to mix at break time.* • *The systems will have to be able to segregate clients' money* **from** *the firm's own cash.*

seg·re·ga·tion /ˌseg·rɪ'geɪ·ʃᵊn/ *n* [U] • *The system of* **racial** *segregation that used to exist in South Africa was called apartheid.* • *Police security was tight for the match between Everton and Manchester United, and segregation of the opposing fans was strictly observed.*

seg·re·gat·ed /£'seg·rɪ·geɪ·tɪd, $-t̬ɪd/ *adj* • *segregated schools* • *segregated swimming* • *Eagle Harbor was established as a summer resort for well-to-do blacks at a time when most of the state's beaches were segregated.* • *I could not go to see him because the psychiatric section is segregated* **from** *the rest of the prison.*

seis·mic /'saɪz·mɪk/ *adj* relating to or caused by an EARTHQUAKE (= sudden violent movement of the Earth's surface), or *(fig.)* having very great and damaging effects • *Geological studies show that the area has been free of seismic activity for a long time.* • *(fig.) The news that the chairman would resign set off seismic waves in the business community.* • *(fig.) When the story became public, the reactions from parents were of seismic proportions.*

seis·mo·graph /£'saɪz·mə·grɑːf, $-græf/ *n* [C] *specialized* a piece of equipment which measures and records the strength of an EARTHQUAKE (= sudden violent movement of the Earth)

seis·mol·o·gy /£saɪz'mɒl·ə·dʒi, $-'mɑː·lə-/ *n* [U] the scientific study of the sudden violent movements of the Earth connected with EARTHQUAKES

seis·mol·o·gist /£saɪz'mɒl·ə·dʒɪst, $-'mɑː·lə-/ *n* [C]

seize *obj* /siːz/ *v* [T] to take (something) quickly and keep or hold it • *I seized his arm and made him turn to look at me.* • *Journalists seized the* **opportunity** *provided by the liberalization to investigate previously taboo subjects.* • *He seized the* **chance** *of a free flight* **with both hands** (= with eagerness or enthusiasm). • *Advertisers agree they need to seize* **the initiative** *rather than just react to criticism.* • Seize can also mean to take using sudden force: *The rebels* *seized the soldiers earlier this week and have been holding them as hostages.* ○ *Economic collapse and political instability helped the army to seize* **power**. ○ *Troops yesterday seized* **control** *of the broadcasting station.* • If police or other officials seize something, they take possession of it with legal authority: *Customs officers at Heathrow have seized 60 kilos of heroin with an estimated street value of £8 million.* ○ *An international treaty exists enabling police and courts to ask their counterparts in foreign countries to seize* **assets/property**.

sei·zure /£'siː·ʒəʳ, $-ʒɚ/ *n* • *the seizure of power/property/control* [U] • *Seizures of illicit drugs have increased by 30% this year.* [C]

seize on/u·pon *obj v prep* [T] to use, accept or take advantage of (something) eagerly or enthusiastically • *The story was seized on by the tabloid press who printed it under huge headlines.* • *The loopholes in the law have already been seized upon by unscrupulous car dealers.*

seize up *v adv* [I] *infml* to stop being able to move or work in the usual way • *The washing machine seized up on Thursday and they can't come to repair it till next week.* • *The traffic had seized up for miles because of the roadworks.* • *After a couple of hours of working on the figures his brain started to seize up.* • *If the banking system collapses, the whole economy could seize up because of a lack of credit.*

sei·zure /£'siː·ʒəʳ, $-ʒɚ/ *n* [C usually sing] • *If the oil gets inside the mechanism, it will block all the tubes and cause a seizure of some of the pipes.*

seize with *obj v prep* [T usually passive] to feel (a strong emotion or pain) suddenly • *While at university he became involved in politics and was seized with ambition.* • *I was suddenly seized with a feeling of great insecurity and loneliness.*

sei·zure /£'siː·ʒəʳ, $-ʒɚ/ *n* [C] a very sudden attack of an illness involving unconsciousness or violent movement • *an epileptic seizure* • *He suffered the head injury when he was 4, and he's been* **having** *seizures ever since.* • *(old use)* A seizure is also a sudden failure of the heart: *His aunt died of a seizure.* ○ *(fig. humorous) When I told her how much it cost she nearly had a seizure* (= she was greatly shocked)*!*

sel·dom /'sel·dəm/ *adv* almost never • *I seldom get a letter from my son these days.* • *Now that we have a baby, we seldom get the chance to go to the cinema.* • *(fml) Seldom do we receive any apology when mistakes are made.*

se·lect *(obj)* CHOOSE /sɪ'lekt/ *v* to choose (a small number of things), or to choose by making careful decisions • *There was a choice of four prizes, and the winner could select one of them.* [T] • *Winners will be able to select* **from** *a range of prizes – cars, free flights and mountain bikes.* [I] • *I'm surprised Chris was selected for the job. Pat was a much better candidate.* [T] • *A mouse is a device which makes it easier to select different options* **from** *computer menus.* [T] • *The methods used to select people* **for** *promotion were explained to every employee.* [T] • *He was selected* **to** *play for Australia at the age of only 18.* [T + obj + *to* infinitive] • *(fml) The supermarket's policy is to select* **out** (= choose) *the best fruit and discard the rest.* [M]

se·lect /sɪ'lekt/ *adj* • A **select committee** is a group of people chosen by a parliament or other law-making body to consider a particular matter: *She is a member of the Commons Select Committee* **on** *education.*

se·lec·tion /sɪ'lek·ʃᵊn/ *n* • *Success is achieved by the careful selection* (= choosing) *of projects.* [U] • *We are keen to see if Robley still has the international qualities to justify selection* (= being chosen) **for** *the national team.* [U] • *Some schools operate a system of selection* (= choosing students for their ability). [U] • *After some discussion, we* **made** *our selection* (= chose what we wanted). [C] • *We apply several different tests during the selection* **process**. • A selection is a choice, range or variety of something: *Most schools would have* **a** *good selection* **of** *these books in their libraries.* [C] ○ *The larger shops are able to stock* **a** *wider selection* **of** *goods.* [C] • A selection is also an item or person which has been or will be chosen: *Their music was a mix of old stuff and selections* **from** *the new album.* [C] ○ *These players are automatic selections* **for** *the team.* [C]

se·lec·tive /£sɪ'lek·tɪv, $-t̬ɪv/ *adj* • Selective means intentionally choosing some things and not others: *As a teacher she was very selective, accepting only a small number of exceptionally gifted pupils.* ○ *It is unfair to present the evidence in such a selective fashion.* ○ *He seemed to have a very selective recall of past events.* ○ *Few insecticides now marketed are adequately selective, so some harmless insects are killed as well as pests.*

se·lec·tive·ly /£sɪ'lek·tɪv·li, $-t̬ɪv/ *adv*

se·lec·tiv·i·ty /£,sɪl·ek'tɪv·ɪ·ti, $sə,lek'tɪv·ə·t̬i/, **se·lec·tive·ness** /£sɪ'lek·tɪv·nəs, $-t̬ɪv-/ *n* [U] • *We're introducing an element of selectivity into the placement of children in schools.* • *The author omits nothing, but a thoughtful selectiveness would have suited his purpose better.*

se·lec·tor /£sɪ'lek·təʳ, $-t̬ɚ/ *n* [C] • *This vacuum cleaner has a four position carpet height selector.* • *His performance should have persuaded the selectors* (= people who choose a sports team) *that he should be included in the side to tour New Zealand.*

se·lect BEST QUALITY /sɪ'lekt/ *adj* of only the best type or highest quality, and usually small in size or amount • *It's a very select club – I've been trying unsuccessfully to join it for years.* • *These activities should be available to all pupils, not just a select* **few**. • *Hamilton lives in a very select part of London.*

self PERSONALITY /self/ *n pl* **selves** /selvz/ the set of someone's characteristics, such as personality and ability, which are not physical and make that person different from other people • *For the hero of the film, combat is the ultimate experience that allows him to* **find** *his* **true** *self.* [C] • *When I saw them this afternoon they were more like their* **old/normal** *selves* (= as they were in the past). [C] • *This transformation cannot be achieved without discarding your old timid self.* [C] • *(fml) These nurses seem to be able to put the needs of self* (= their own needs) *a long way after the demands of those they care for.* [U] • *(saying)* 'Unto thine own self be true' means only do what you think is right.

self PERSONAL ADVANTAGE /self/ *n* [U] *disapproving* interest in your own advantage • *Her reply was typical of her constant regard for self.* • If you **think only of** self or if you **are all for** self you are only interested in what will be good for you and not whether it will be good for other people.

self·ish /'sel·fɪʃ/ *adj disapproving* • Someone who is selfish only thinks of their own advantage: *The judge told him: "Your attitude shows a selfish disregard for others".* ○ *I know it sounds selfish, but what I'm really worried about is what will happen to me.*

self·ish·ly /'sel·fɪʃ·li/ *adv disapproving* • *He selfishly took all the best cakes for himself.*

self·ish·ness /'sel·fɪʃ·nəs/ *n* [U] *disapproving* • *Their decision seems to have been motivated by greed and selfishness.*

self·less /'sel·fləs/ *adj approving* • Someone who is selfless only thinks of other people's advantage: *Selfless* **devotion** *to the service and undeniable bravery have marked out lifeboat crews throughout our history.*

self·less·ly /'sel·flə·sli/ *adv approving*

self·less·ness /'sel·flə·snəs/ *n* [U] *approving*

self– YOURSELF /self-/ *combining form* of or by yourself or itself • *self-aggrandizement* • *self-critical* • *self-educated* • *self-incriminating* • *a self-winding watch*

self–ab·sorbed /£,self·əb'zɔːbd, $-'zɔːrbd/ *adj usually disapproving* only interested in yourself and your own activities • *The theatres are in decline because directors are too self-absorbed.* • *The public's interest in this self-absorbed but powerful family is still strong.*

self–ab·sorp·tion /£,self·əb'zɔːp·ʃᵊn, $-'zɔːrp-/ *n* [U] • *Her self-absorption is total – you can't get her to talk about anyone else's problems.*

self–ad·dressed /,self·ə'drest/ *adj* [not gradable] (esp. of an envelope) addressed to the person who has sent it • *Send a self-addressed* **envelope** *for our free catalogue.* • See also SAE ; SASE

self–ap·point·ed /£,self·ə'pɔɪn·tɪd, $-t̬ɪd/ *adj* [not gradable] *disapproving* behaving as if you had responsibility or authority without having been chosen by other people • *She seems to have become the self-appointed manager of the department.* • *The newspaper has become the self-appointed guardian of public morals.*

self–as·sem·bly *esp. Br* /,self·ə'sem·bli/ *adj* [not gradable] designed to be made at home from a set of prepared parts by the person who buys it • *a manufacturer of self-assembly kitchens*

self–as·sess·ment /,self·ə'ses·mənt/ *n* a judgment, which is sometimes for official purposes, made by yourself about your abilities, principles or decisions • *The tax authorities are introducing a system of self-assessment for self-employed people's income tax.* [U] • *The students' self-assessments were regarded as important, but more guidance was needed for them to be effective.* [C]

self–as•sured /£ˌself·əˈʃɔːd, $ˈʃɜːrd/ *adj approving* having confidence in your own abilities • *The interview showed her as a self-assured and mature student.*

self–as•sur•ance /£ˌself·əˈʃɔː·rənts, $-ˈʃɜːr·ənts/ *n* [U] *approving* • *She came on stage with the dignity and self-assurance of a great opera star.*

self–a•ware•ness /£ˌself·əˈweə·nəs, $-ˈwer-/ *n* [U] good knowledge and judgment about yourself • *Everyone has inner conflicts that they need to sort out for themselves, taking small steps towards self-awareness.*

self–a•ware /£ˌself·əˈweəʳ, $-ˈwer/ *adj*

self–ca•ter•ing /£ˌselfˈkeɪ·tᵊr·ɪŋ, $-t̬ɚ-/ *adj* [not gradable] *Br and Aus* (of a holiday) having a kitchen so that you can cook meals for yourself rather than having them provided for you • *Long-stay holiday makers have the option of six weeks in self-catering apartments/accommodation.* • *As the prime setting for a self-catering family holiday I can hardly fault it.* • *We decided to go for self-catering rather than stay in a hotel.*

self–cen•sor•ship /£ˌselfˈsent·sə·ʃɪp, $-sɚ-/ *n* [U] control of what you say or do in order to avoid annoying or offending others, but without being told officially that such control is necessary • *These writers knew that unless they practised a form of self-censorship, the authorities would persecute them.*

self–cen•tred *Br and Aus, Am* **self–cen•tered** /£ˌselfˈsen·təd, $-t̬ɚd/ *adj disapproving* only interested in yourself and your own activities • *We live in a time when our economy rewards the self-centred and the selfish while penalizing those who work for the good of others.* • *Robert is a self-centered, ambitious and bigoted man.*

self–cer•ti•fi•ca•tion /£ˌselfˌsɜː·tɪ·fɪˈkeɪ·ʃᵊn, $-ˌsɜːr·t̬ɪ-/ *n* [U] *Br fml* an official statement that you make about yourself, esp. in connection with tax or illness • *You are able to notify up to eight days' illness by self-certification.* • *Non-taxpayers will be able to receive their interest gross provided they have filled in a self-certification form.*

self–con•fessed /ˌself·kənˈfest/ *adj* [before n; not gradable] admitting willingly to having a characteristic which is considered to be bad or not desirable • *New evidence from a self-confessed* **liar** *was not enough to justify a retrial.* • *She had a self-confessed fear of heights, so we shouldn't have made her go up to the top.*

self–con•fid•ent /£ˌselfˈkɒn·fɪ·dᵊnt, $-ˈkɑːn-/ *adj approving* behaving calmly because you have no doubts about your ability or knowledge • *At school he was popular and self-confident, and we weren't surprised at his later success.*

self–con•fid•ent•ly /£ˌselfˈkɒn·fɪ·dᵊnt·li, $-ˈkɑːn-/ *adv approving* • *The little girl showed the visitors round the school self-confidently.*

self–con•fid•ence /£ˌselfˈkɒn·fɪ·dᵊnts, $-ˈkɑːn-/ *n* [U] *approving* • *He had the self-confidence to argue his case with the so-called experts.*

self–con•grat•u•lat•o•ry /£ˌself·kənˌgræt·jʊˈleɪ·tᵊr·i, $-t̬ɚ-/ *adj disapproving* praising yourself or saying how well you have done something • *When it was all over, the officials were self-congratulatory about how well the conference had gone.*

self–con•grat•u•la•tion /ˌself·kənˌgræt·jʊˈleɪ·ʃᵊn/ *n* [U] *disapproving* • *No profession, not even journalism, is quite as fond of self-congratulation as acting.*

self–con•scious /£ˌselfˈkɒn·ʃəs, $-ˈkɑːn-/ *adj* uncomfortably or unnaturally aware of yourself and your actions • *He looked uncomfortable, like a self-conscious adolescent who's gate-crashed the wrong party.*

self–con•scious•ly /£ˌselfˈkɒn·ʃə·sli, $-ˈkɑːn-/ *adv*

self–con•scious•ness /£ˌselfˈkɒn·ʃə·snəs, $-ˈkɑːn-/ *n* [U] • *As she grew up, she gradually lost her self-consciousness.*

self–con•tained /ˌself·kənˈteɪnd/ *adj* [not gradable] containing or having everything that is needed within itself • *The government wants to encourage viable self-contained rural communities.* • *The block consists of 50 self-contained apartments.* • A person who is self-contained does not have a large number of relationships with other people or does not depend on others for support: *(disapproving) Neighbours described him as a self-contained young man who seldom spoke to anyone.* ○ *She's very self-contained and isn't at all worried about moving to a big city where she won't know anybody.*

self–con•tra•dict•o•ry /£ˌselfˌkɒn·trəˈdɪk·tᵊr·i, $-ˌkɑːn·trəˈdɪk·tɔːr·i/ *adj fml* expressing one thing which is the opposite of another thing already said; saying two things which cannot both be correct • *He is described as a Texas oil millionaire and environmentalist, which might appear to be self-contradictory.* • *I have to say I find your argument self-contradictory.*

self–con•trolled /£ˌself·kənˈtrəʊld, $-ˈtroʊld/ *adj usually approving* having strong control over your emotions and actions • *He's always seemed very self-controlled, so I was amazed by his sudden outburst in the office.*

self–con•trol /£ˌself·kənˈtrəʊl, $-ˈtroʊl/ *n* [U] *usually approving* • *It took incredible self-control not to cry out with pain.*

self–de•cep•tion /ˌself·dɪˈsep·ʃᵊn/ *n* [U] hiding the truth from yourself • *His claim to be an important and unjustly neglected painter is sheer self-deception – he's no good at all.*

self–de•clared /£ˌself·dɪˈkleəd, $-ˈklerd/ *adj* [before n; not gradable] stated or announced by yourself • *The self-declared guardians of law and order held a press conference.* See also SELF-STYLED. • *The corporation failed to meet its self-declared target of completing the deal by the end of this week.*

self–de•feat•ing /£ˌself·dɪˈfiː·tɪŋ, $-t̬ɪŋ/ *adj* preventing or damaging something which was intended to be helped • *Well-intentioned but self-defeating regulations have reduced the amount of property available for rent.*

self–de•fence *Br and Aus* /ˌself·dɪˈfents/, *Am* **self–de•fen•se** *n* [U] protection of yourself, either by fighting or discussion • *He used the gun* **in** *self-defence.* • **In** *self-defence, I have to say that I only did what you asked me to do.* • The **art** of self-defence is the skill of fighting without weapons to protect yourself.

self–de•lu•sion /ˌself·dɪˈluː·ʒᵊn/ *n* (an act of) allowing yourself to believe something that is not true • *It's self-delusion if he thinks he'll be offered a better contract.* [U] • *The company claimed to offer equal opportunities, but closer investigation of complaints showed this to be a self-delusion.* [C]

self–de•ni•al /ˌself·dɪˈnaɪ·əl/ *n* [U] the act of not taking or having something which you would like, esp. because you think it is good for you not to have it • *I felt sure that his self-denial, as he handed me the last chocolate, was prompted less by selflessness than by a fear of getting fat.*

self–dep•re•cat•ing /£ˌselfˈdep·rɪ·keɪ·tɪŋ, $-t̬ɪŋ/, **self–dep•re•ca•to•ry** /£ˌselfˌdep·rɪˈkeɪ·tᵊr·i, $-kə·tɔːr-/ *adj fml* saying or showing that you do not have a good opinion of yourself • *a self-deprecating manner/remark* • *self-deprecating humour/jokes*

self–dep•re•cat•ing•ly /£ˌselfˈdep·rɪ·keɪ·tɪŋ, $-t̬ɪŋ/ *adv fml* • *"It's just a modest little daub," he said self-deprecatingly. "It only took me an afternoon to paint."*

self–dep•re•ca•tion /ˌselfˌdep·rɪˈkeɪ·ʃᵊn/ *n* [U] *fml* • *Her autobiography is full of witty self-deprecation.*

self–de•struct /ˌself·dɪˈstrʌkt/ *v* [I] to be destroyed from within, esp. in a way planned during the process of being made • *Synthetic materials derived from petroleum do not self-destruct and are producing mountains of waste.* • *An investigation is underway after a missile self-destructed shortly after it was launched.* • *(fig.) At least he reached the semi-final before hitting the self-destruct* **button** (= doing something that destroyed his chance of success).

self–de•struc•tion /ˌself·dɪˈstrʌk·ʃᵊn/ *n* [U] • *All moving images before the 1950s were shot on nitrate film, a highly inflammable medium which inevitably tends to self-destruction.* • *It was fierce clan loyalty that set the country on its path of self-destruction.*

self–de•struc•tive /£ˌself·dɪˈstrʌk·tɪv, $-t̬ɪv/ *adj* • *It was an unusual viewpoint from a man who has been rebellious, aggressive and at times self-destructive.*

self–de•ter•min•a•tion /£ˌself·dɪˌtɜː·mɪˈneɪ·ʃᵊn, $-ˌtɜːr-/ *n* [U] the ability or power to make decisions for yourself, esp. the power of a nation or people to decide how it will be governed • *Is armed struggle the only way to achieve self-determination?*

self–dis•ci•pline /ˌselfˈdɪs·ɪ·plɪn/ *n* [U] *approving* the ability to make yourself do things you know you should do even when you do not want to • *You need a lot of self-discipline when you're doing research work on your own.*

self–dis•ci•plined /ˌselfˈdɪs·ɪ·plɪnd/ *adj approving* • *You need to be very self-disciplined in this job, because there's nobody telling you what you should be doing.*

self–dis•cov•er•y /£ˌself·dɪˈskʌv·ᵊr·i, $ˈ-ɚ-/ *n* [U] learning about yourself and your beliefs • *Her own* **journey/voyage** *of self-discovery started as she was recovering from a severe illness.* • *You have to understand* *the Canadian need for national self-discovery, the constant need to define how they are different from Americans.*

self–doubt /ˌself'daʊt/ *n* [U] a lack of confidence in your abilities and decisions • *He admits to moments of self-doubt, and wonders if he is focussing on the most important issues.*

self–drive /'self·draɪv/ *adj* [not gradable], *n Br* (the provision of a car) that you rent and drive yourself, rather than being driven by someone else • *The tour company provides a self-drive hire car at the airport and pre-booked hotels along a wide variety of routes.* • *Self-drive is the best way to travel on the island, as bus and train services are severely restricted.* [U]

self–ef·fac·ing /ˌself·ɪ'feɪ·sɪŋ/ *adj* not making yourself noticeable; not trying to get the attention of other people; modest • *The captain was typically self-effacing when questioned about the team's successes, giving credit to the other players.*

self–ef·fac·ing·ly /ˌself·ɪ'feɪ·sɪŋ·li/ *adv*

self–ef·face·ment /ˌself·ɪ'feɪ·smənt/ *n* [U]

self–em·ployed /ˌself·ɪm'plɔɪd/ *adj* [not gradable] not working for an employer but finding work for yourself or having your own business • *He was a self-employed builder.* • *Do you pay less tax if you're self-employed?*

self–em·ployed /ˌself·ɪm'plɔɪd/ *pl n* • *They run an advice centre for* **the** *self-employed.*

self–em·ploy·ment /ˌself·ɪm'plɔɪ·mənt/ *n* [U]

self–es·teem /ˌself·ɪ'stiːm/ *n* [U] belief and confidence in your own ability and value • *This type of unsympathetic approach can destroy a child's confidence and self-esteem.* • *The compliments she received after the presentation boosted her self-esteem.*

self–ev·i·dent /ˌself'ev·ɪ·dənt/ *adj* clear or obvious without needing any proof or explanation • *Solutions which seem self-evident* **to** *humans are often beyond the grasp of computers.* • *Most of us feel that our moral beliefs are quite simply self-evident.*

self–ev·i·dent·ly /ˌself'ev·ɪ·dənt·li/ *adv* • *Any growth in unemployment is self-evidently a matter of extreme seriousness.*

self–ex·plan·a·to·ry /£ˌself·ɪk'splæn·ə·tri, $-tɔːr·i/ *adj* easily understood from the information already given and not needing further explanation • *I've left you a list of things to do. It should be self-explanatory, but ask Bob if there's anything that isn't clear.*

self–ex·pres·sion /ˌself·ɪk'spreʃ·ən/ *n* [U] expression of your personality, emotions or ideas, esp. through art, music or acting • *He regarded poetry as sentimental self-expression.*

self–fi·nanc·ing /ˌself'faɪ·nænt·sɪŋ/ *adj* [not gradable] paid for only by the money that an activity itself produces • *Fees will have to treble to make the courses self-financing, now that government support has been withdrawn.*

self–ful·fill·ing /ˌself·fʊl'fɪl·ɪŋ/ *adj* [not gradable] happening because it is expected to happen • *Pessimism is self-fulfilling – expect the worst and it happens.* • A self-fulfilling **prophecy** causes something expected to happen: *The expectation of lower prices becomes a self-fulfilling prophecy as people wait for prices to fall before buying.*

self–ful·fil·ment /ˌself·fʊl'fɪl·mənt/ *n* [U] a feeling of satisfaction that you have achieved what you wanted • *When the options are unemployment or a dead-end job, having babies can seem like the only means of self-fulfilment.*

self–ful·filled /ˌself·fʊl'fɪld/ *adj*

self–gov·ern·ment /£ˌself'gʌv·ən·mənt, £-əm-, $-ə·n-/ *n* [U] the control of a country or an area by the people living there being allowed to choose their own government, or control of an organization by a group of people independent of central or local government • *The poll showed that 80% of the population supported regional self-government.*

self–gov·ern·ing /£ˌself'gʌv·ən·ɪŋ, $-ə·nɪŋ/ *adj* [not gradable] • *self-governing trusts/schools*

self–help /ˌself'help/ *adj* [not gradable], *n* (the activity of) providing what you need for yourself and others with similar experiences or difficulties without going to an official organization • *self-help groups* • *a self-help manual* [before n] • *It is mainly a group providing social events and self-help for single parents.* [U]

self–im·age /ˌself'ɪm·ɪdʒ/ *n* [C] the way a person feels about his or her personality, achievements and value to society • *Having a decent job contributes to a good self-image, to status and esteem.*

self–im·por·tance /£ˌself·ɪm'pɔː·tənts, $-'pɔːr·t̬ənts/ *n* [U] *disapproving* the belief that you are more important or have a higher value than other people • *He's a modest, mild-mannered man, without a trace of self-importance.*

self–im·por·tant /£ˌself·ɪm'pɔː·tənt, $-'pɔːr·t̬ənt/ *adj disapproving*

self–im·por·tant·ly /£ˌself·ɪm'pɔː·tənt·li, $-'pɔːr·t̬ənt-/ *adv disapproving*

self–im·posed /£ˌself·ɪm'pəʊzd, $-'poʊzd/ *adj* [not gradable] decided by yourself, without being influenced or ordered by other people • *The end of the year was their self-imposed deadline for finishing the building work.* • *After the military coup, the family left for self-imposed* **exile** *in America.*

self–in·duced /£ˌself·ɪn'djuːst, $-'duːst/ *adj* [not gradable] caused by yourself • *self-induced vomiting* • *self-induced hysteria*

self–in·dul·gent /ˌself·ɪn'dʌl·dʒənt/ *adj* allowing yourself to have or do anything that you enjoy • *I know it's self-indulgent of me, but I'll just have another chocolate.*

self–in·dul·gence /ˌself·ɪn'dʌl·dʒənts/ *n* [U] • *Lying on a sunbed for an hour can be very expensive, and few people can afford such self-indulgence.*

self–in·flict·ed /£ˌself·ɪn'flɪk·tɪd, $-t̬ɪd/ *adj* [not gradable] (of something bad) done to yourself • *self-inflicted pain/damage*

self–in·ter·est /£ˌself'ɪn·tər·est, $-t̬ə-/ *n* [U] considering the advantage to yourself when making decisions, and acting for your own benefit • *The company's donation was surely* **motivated by** *self-interest as it attracted a lot of media attention.* • *Their environmental concern is just* **enlightened** *self-interest.*

self–in·ter·est·ed /£ˌself'ɪn·tər·es·tɪd, $-t̬ə·es·t̬ɪd/ *adj* • *There were months of self-interested arguing between landowners and the building company.*

self·ish /'sel·fɪʃ/ *adj* See at SELF [PERSONAL ADVANTAGE]

self·less /'sel·fləs/ *adj* See at SELF [PERSONAL ADVANTAGE]

self–made /ˌself'meɪd/ *adj* [not gradable] rich and successful as a result of your own work and not because of family wealth • *a self-made man/millionaire/tycoon/businesswoman* • *"He is a self-made man, and worships his creator"* (John Bright about the Prime Minister, Disraeli, c.1868)

self–ob·sessed /ˌself·əb'sest/ *adj* only interested in yourself and your own activities • *a self-obsessed teenager* • *If you go for therapy, you may be judged neurotic, mad or self-obsessed.*

self–o·pin·ion·at·ed /£ˌself·ə'pɪn·jə·neɪ·tɪd, $-t̬ɪd/ *adj* [not gradable] *disapproving* having and expressing very strong feelings and beliefs, and believing that your own ideas are the only correct ones • *She's very self-opinionated and refuses to listen to anyone else's point of view.*

self–per·pet·u·at·ing /£ˌself·pə'pet·juː·eɪ·tɪŋ, $-pə'pet·juː·eɪ·t̬ɪŋ/ *adj disapproving* having a system which avoids change and produces new things which are very similar to the old ones • *The fighting between the different social groups has become a self-perpetuating spiral of death and hatred.* • *The judicial system is dominated by a self-perpetuating élite which appoints people who come from a background similar to that of existing members.*

self–pi·ty /£ˌself'pɪt·i, $-'pɪt̬-/ *n* [U] *disapproving* too much sympathy and feeling for your own problems • *He faced his illness bravely and without any hint of self-pity.*

self–pi·ty·ing /£ˌself'pɪt·i·ɪŋ, $-'pɪt̬-/ *adj disapproving* • *The article begins with a self-pitying and disgruntled tirade about his talent having gone unnoticed.*

self–port·rait /£ˌself'pɔː·treɪt, $-'pɔːr·trɪt/ *n* [C] a picture, photograph or piece of writing of or about yourself • *a Rembrandt self-portrait* • *The book is described as a highly romantic self-portrait of the author.*

self–pos·ses·sion /ˌself·pə'zeʃ·ən/ *n* [U] the characteristic of being calm and in control of your emotions at all times • *He looked surprised but soon recovered his self-possession.* • *She has a rare self-possession which allows her to approach life untroubled by such negative emotions as embarrassment or regret.*

self–pos·sessed /ˌself·pə'zest/ *adj* • *She is a confident and self-possessed public speaker.*

self–pres·er·va·tion /£ˌselfˌprez·ə'veɪ·ʃən, $-ə·'-/ *n* [U] behaviour based on the characteristics or feelings which warn people or animals to protect themselves from difficulties or dangers • *It was his instinct for self-*

preservation that led him to abandon his former friends and transfer his allegiance to the new rulers.

self–pro·claimed /ˌself·prəˈkleɪmd/ *adj* [not gradable] *esp. disapproving* said or announced about yourself • *He's a self-proclaimed expert on national defense, international politics and just about everything else.*

self–pro·fessed /ˌself·prəˈfest/ *adj* [not gradable] said, announced or admitted about yourself • *a self-professed gambler* • *She's a self-professed supporter of prison reform.*

self–pro·pelled /ˌself·prəˈpeld/ *adj* [not gradable] able to move by its own power • *self-propelled artillery/guns*

self–pro·tec·tion /ˌself·prəˈtek·ʃən/ *n* [U] keeping yourself safe from injury or damage • *They claimed that they needed the weapons for self-protection.*

self–rais·ing flour *Br and Aus* /ˌselfˈreɪ·zɪŋ/, *Am* **self–ri·sing flour** /ˌselfˈraɪ·zɪŋ/ *n* [U] flour that contains a substance which makes cakes swell when they are cooked • Compare **plain flour** at PLAIN [WITH NOTHING ADDED].

self–reg·u·la·tion /ˌself·reg·jʊˈleɪ·ʃən/ *n* [U] making certain yourself that you or your employees act according to the rules, rather than having this done by other people • *They favour the self-regulation of the industry, and strict codes of conduct have already been issued by the Advertising Association.*

self–reg·u·lat·ing /£ˌselfˈreg·jʊ·leɪ·tɪŋ, $-t̬ɪŋ/, **self–reg·u·lat·o·ry** /£ˌself·reg·jʊˈleɪ·tər·i, $-tɔːr-/ *adj* [not gradable] • *a self-regulating body/organization*

self–re·li·ant /ˌself·rɪˈlaɪ·ənt/ *adj approving* not needing help or support from other people • *Lone parents have to be self-reliant, resilient and inventive.*

self–re·li·ance /ˌself·rɪˈlaɪ·ənts/ *n* [U] *approving* • *The course focussed on building the young people's self-reliance and personal responsibility.*

self–re·spect /ˌself·rɪˈspekt/ *n* [U] respect for yourself which shows that you value and admire yourself • *He felt what he was being asked to do took away his dignity and self-respect.* • *(fig.) The first thing a decaying inner-city must rebuild is its self-respect.*

self–re·spect·ing /£ˌself·rɪˈspek·tɪŋ, $-t̬ɪŋ/ *adj* [before n] • **No** *self-respecting government can allow such atrocities to be done in its name.* • Self-respecting often means good and effective: **No** *self-respecting chief executive could do without a strategic-planning staff.* ○ **No** *self-respecting garden should be without the splendid and delicious herbs of summer.*

self–re·straint /ˌself·rɪˈstreɪnt/ *n* [U] control of your own actions • *He was angry but managed, with great self-restraint, to reply calmly.*

self–right·eous /ˌselfˈraɪ·tʃəs/ *adj disapproving* believing that your ideas and behaviour are morally better than those of other people, in a way that other people find unacceptable • *He's so self-righteous – you'd think he'd never done anything wrong in his life.*

self–right·eous·ly /ˌselfˈraɪ·tʃə·sli/ *adv disapproving* • *The newspaper published details about her private life which it now self-righteously claims was in the public interest.*

self–right·eous·ness /ˌselfˈraɪ·tʃə·snəs/ *n* [U] *disapproving*

self–rule /ˌselfˈruːl/ *n* [U] the ability of a country or part of a country to choose its own government and control its own activities • *It was agreed that the country would move to self-rule after an election for a state assembly in September.* • *The region should have internal self-rule, while the national government would handle its defence and foreign affairs.* • See also SELF-GOVERNMENT.

self–sac·ri·fice /ˌselfˈsæk·rɪ·faɪs/ *n* [U] *approving* giving up what you want so that other people can have what they want • *People say this is a selfish society, but frankly I've seen too much kindness, self-sacrifice and generosity to believe that.* • *The job requires a lot of enthusiasm, dedication and self-sacrifice.*

self–sac·ri·fic·ing /ˌselfˈsæk·rɪ·faɪ·sɪŋ/ *adj approving* • *She's a tremendously loyal, self-sacrificing and heroic person who's never betrayed anyone.*

self–same /ˈself·seɪm/ *adj* [before n; not gradable] exactly the same or extremely similar • *The self-same car has been parked outside three times this week.* • *It's funny when you walk into a room and see another woman wearing the self-same 'exclusive' outfit.*

self–sat·is·fied /£ˌselfˈsæt·ɪs·faɪd, $-ˈsæt̬-/ *adj disapproving* very pleased with and not critical of yourself • *She was very* **smug and** *self-satisfied about getting the promotion.*

self–sat·is·fac·tion /£ˌselfˌsæt·ɪsˈfæk·ʃən, $-ˌsæt̬-/ *n* [U] *disapproving* • *Her evident delight at winning was not accompanied by any feeling of self-satisfaction.*

self–seek·ing /ˌselfˈsiː·kɪŋ/ *n, adj fml disapproving* (the characteristic of) being interested in your own advantage in everything that you do • *The article accused senior officials of self-seeking and arrogance.* [U] • *The army felt that the politicians of the day were just self-seeking opportunists.*

self–ser·vice /£ˌselfˈsɜː·vɪs, $-ˈsɜːr-/ *n, adj* [not gradable] (esp. in a shop or other place which sells things) not being served or helped by an employee but collecting goods or making use of things yourself • *a self-service salad bar* • *self-service (Br and Aus) petrol/(Am) gas pumps* • *a self-service store* • *They argue that packaging makes self-service in shops possible and guarantees the safety and hygiene of food and drink.* [U]

self–serv·ing /£ˌselfˈsɜː·vɪŋ, $-ˈsɜːr-/ *adj* [not gradable] *fml disapproving* working or acting for your own advantage • *There is growing dissatisfaction with this generation of politicians who are seen as old-fashioned, corrupt and self-serving.*

self–start·er /£ˌselfˈstɑː·tər, $-ˈstɑːr·t̬ɚ/ *n* [C] a person who is able to work efficiently without regularly needing to be told what to do • *The successful applicant for the position will be a well-motivated self-starter who has excellent communication skills.*

self–styled /ˈself·staɪld/ *adj* [before n] *usually disapproving* given a name or title by yourself without any official reason for it • *The media appears to be full of self-styled 'experts' who are happy to give their views on subjects that they actually know very little about.*

self–suf·fi·cient /ˌself·səˈfɪʃ·ənt/ *adj* able to provide everything you need, esp. food, for yourself without the help of other people • *The programme aims to make the country self-sufficient* **in** *food and to cut energy imports.* • *The motorist is not a particularly self-sufficient creature, and emergency calls to breakdown organizations are increasing.*

self–suf·fi·cien·cy /ˌself·səˈfɪʃ·ənt·si/ *n* [U] • *They're heavily into self-sufficiency, and grow nearly all their own vegetables.*

self–sup·port·ing /£ˌself·səˈpɔː·tɪŋ, $-ˈpɔːr·t̬ɪŋ/ *adj* [not gradable] earning or having enough money to pay for your activities without receiving financial help from other people • *The government will make available £5 million over the next four years, after which the service is planned to be self-supporting.* • *The vast majority of students here are self-supporting.* • See also SELF-FINANCING.

self–willed /ˌselfˈwɪld/ *adj disapproving* determined to base your actions on your own decisions without listening to advice from other people • *She is usually described as a tough woman who is courageous and astute, as well as bossy and self-willed.*

self–worth /£ˌselfˈwɜːθ, $-ˈwɜːrθ/ *n* [U] the value you give to your life and achievements • *Many people derive their self-worth from their work.*

sell *(obj)* [MONEY] /sel/ *v past* **sold** /£səʊld, $soʊld/ to give (a possession, product or service to someone else) in return for money • *I sold him my car/I sold my car to him* **for** *£600.* [+ two objects] • *We'll be selling the tickets* **at/for** *£50 each.* [T] • *The stall sells drinks and snacks.* [T] • *These baskets sell well* (= a lot of them are bought). [I] • If you sell something **off (cheap)** you charge a low price for it to encourage people to buy it: *They're selling off last year's stock at half price.* [T] ○ *Fears about a rise in interest rates triggered a general* **sell-off** *of shares in leading companies.* ○ *The* **sell-offs** *of nationalised industries have raised billions of pounds for the government.* • When you sell **out (of)** something you have none of it left to sell: *We sold out of the T-shirts in the first couple of hours.* [I] ○ *I'm sorry, we've sold out.* [I] ○ *We couldn't get seats – the concert was sold out.* [T] ○ *(approving) The concert was a* **sell-out** (= all the tickets were sold). ○ *a* **sell-out** *season at New York's Lincoln Center* • When you sell **(out) to** someone, or *(Br and Aus)* sell **up**, you sell your company, shares or property and are not involved with them any more: *They decided to sell out to their competitors.* [I] • *(Br and Aus)* You can also say that you are selling **up** if you sell your house, esp. as part of a big change in your life: *We're going to sell up and retire to the West Country at the end of the year.* [I] • *(infml disapproving)* If you sell (someone) **out** you do something which fails to satisfy people's hopes and expectations and which they feel you have only done because of the money or other reward you will receive: *The government appears to be ready to sell the teachers out.* [M] ○ *They've sold out* **to** *the road transport lobby* (= done what these people wanted). [I] ○ *He's sold out* **on us** (= disappointed us by not doing what we expected). [I] ○ *The majority of farmers felt the subsidy agreement was a* **sell-out**. ○ *They see the peace accord as a* **sell-out** *to the guerrillas whose ultimate aim is an independent state.* • To **sell** someone **down the river** is to put them in a difficult situation because you have done something different to what you promised or suggested you would do. • You **sell** someone or something **short** by putting too low a value on them and what they do: *It's important that employees who negotiate their own contracts do not sell themselves short.* ○ *I'm fed up with people selling this country short.* • If you **sell** your **soul (to the devil)** you are persuaded to do something, esp. something bad, because of the money or other reward you will receive for doing it. • *(Br and Aus)* If you **sell** someone **a pup** (*Am* **sell someone a bill of goods**) you deceive them into buying something which is no good. • *(Br)* A **sell-by date** (*Am and Aus* **pull date**) is a date marked on a product such as food after which it should not be sold. • A **selling point** is a characteristic of a product which will persuade people to buy it: *Its best selling point is the price – it's the cheapest on the market.* ○ *They attached too little importance to design and missed an important selling point in the export market.* • See also SALE [SELL].

sell /sel/ *n* [U] • *The computer is proving to be* **a** *hard/tough sell* (= difficult to sell) *because of its high price.* • *(specialized) The company's profits have fallen dramatically, and most stockbrokers reckon its shares are* **a** *sell* (= they think investors should sell their shares in the company).

sel·ler /£'sel·əʳ, $-ɚ/ *n* [C] • A seller is a person who is selling something: *flower/newspaper/souvenir sellers* ○ *street sellers* (= people who sell things at the side of a road rather than in a shop) ○ *The identity of the seller of the painting was kept secret.* ○ *Do you think the seller will accept £69 000 for the house?* • A seller is also a product which a lot of people buy: *Fax modems are one of the hottest sellers in the personal computer market today.* ○ *Of the ten top sellers, six are women's magazines.* ○ *This car is our* **biggest** *seller at the moment.*

sell *obj* [PERSUADE] /sel/ *v* [T] *past* **sold** /£səʊld, $soʊld/ to persuade someone that (an idea or plan) is a good one and likely to be successful • *My boss is very old-fashioned and I'm having a lot of trouble selling the idea of working at home occasionally.* • *The chance of greater access to European markets would help sell the scheme to the President/the President the scheme.* [+ two objects] • *Selling employers* **(on)** *the proposal to give their workers more time off is a real challenge.* [T (+ two objects)] • *She's really sold* **on** *the idea of buying a new car* (= She thinks it's a very good idea). [T]

Sel·lo·tape *Br trademark* /'sel·ə·teɪp/, *Am and Aus trademark* **Scotch–tape**, *Aus and Br infml* **stick·y tape** /'stɪk·i·teɪp/ *n* [U] a long thin strip of sticky and usually transparent material which is sold in a roll and is used for joining together things such as paper or card • *a roll of sellotape* • *Put some sellotape across the back of the envelope.* • *I stuck the note to the door* **with** *Sellotape.* • [PIC] **Stationery**

sel·lo·tape *obj Br* /'sel·ə·teɪp/, *Am and Aus* **Scotch–tape** *v* [T] • *She sellotaped the torn pages back into the book.* • *When I got home, I found a mysterious message sellotaped* **to** *the front door.*

selt·zer /£'selt·səʳ, $-sɚ/ *n* [C/U] *Am for* fizzy **mineral water**, see at MINERAL

selves /selvz/ *pl of* SELF • *They hope meditation will help them find their* **true** *selves* (= discover what sort of people they really are).

se·man·tic /£sɪ'mæn·tɪk, $-t̬ɪk/ *adj* [not gradable] connected with (the study of) meaning in language • *Words are the smallest semantic units that can combine to form new sequences with different meanings.* • *Semantic and syntactic information should both be taken into account when considering meanings.*

se·man·ti·cal·ly /£sɪ'mæn·tɪ·kli, $-t̬ɪk-/ *adv* [not gradable] • *The idea of the book is to present words that are semantically* **related** *together in the same place.*

se·man·tics /£sɪ'mæn·tɪks, $-t̬ɪks/ *n* [U] • Semantics is the study of meanings in a language: *Syntax describes the rules by which words can be combined into sentences, while semantics describes what they mean.* ○ *I want to find solutions to these problems instead of discussing the semantics* (= detailed meanings) *of bureaucratic terminology.*

sem·a·phore /£'sem·ə·fɔːʳ, $-fɔːr/ *n* [U] a system of communication using two mechanical arms or hand-held flags which are moved into different positions to represent different letters, numbers or symbols • *Semaphore was widely used at sea, before the advent of electricity.* • *(fig.) When I lived opposite her we would send semaphore* **signals** (= messages without speaking) *to each other from our bedroom windows.*

sem·blance /'sem·blənts/ *n* [U] *slightly fml* a situation or condition which is similar to what is wanted or expected, but is not exactly as desired • *The city has now returned to* **some** *semblance* **of** *normality after last night's celebrations.* • *Mike has the job of creating* **some** *vague semblance* **of** *organization out of this chaos.* • *In spite of her disability, she has been able to maintain* **a** *semblance* **of** *normal life.* • *He was executed without even* **the** *semblance* **of** *a fair trial* (= without anyone trying to make it seem that there had been a fair trial).

se·men /'siː·mən/ *n* [U] a thick sticky liquid containing sperm which is produced by men and male animals as a result of sexual activity • *The virus which causes AIDS can be transmitted in semen.* • See also SEMINAL [LIQUID].

se·mes·ter /£sɪ'mes·təʳ, $sə'mes·tɚ/ *n* [C] one of the two or three periods into which a year is divided at a college or university, esp. in the US and Australia • *the first/second semester* • *the spring/fall semester* • Compare TERM [TIME]; TRIMESTER.

sem·i– [HALF] /'sem·i-, '-ɪ-, '-aɪ-/ *combining form* half or partly • *semi-literate* • *semi-permanent* • *semi-retirement* • *semi-rural/semi-urban* • *semi-skilled workers* • *a semi-autobiographical novel* • Something which is **semi-automatic** is partly automatic: *a semi-automatic gearbox* • A **semi-automatic** weapon is one which automatically puts bullets into position ready for firing, but it can only fire one bullet at a time: *a semi-automatic pistol* • A **semi-circle** is half a circle: *We arranged the chairs* **in** *a semi-circle.* ○ *The chairs were placed in a* **semi-circular** *arrangement.* • A **semi-detached (house)** (*Br and Aus infml* **semi**) is one of a pair of houses which are joined together: *They live in a semi-detached (house).* ○ *Their house is semi-detached.* Compare **detached** at DETACH. • A **semi-final** (*infml* **semi**) is one of the two games that are played to decide who will take part in the final game of a competition: *She's the youngest player ever to* **get through to/advance to** (= win enough matches to play in) *a semi-final.* [LP] **Sports** • A **semi-precious** stone is one which is used for making jewellery but is not very valuable: *Jade and turquoise are semi-precious stones.* • People who are **semi-professional** are paid for an activity which they take part in but do not do all the time: *semi-professional musicians/rugby players* • *a semi-professional cook* • [LP] **Two** [PIC] **Accommodation, Shapes**

sem·i [HOUSE] /'sem·i/ *n* [C] *pl* **semis** *Br and Aus infml for* **semi-detached house**, see at SEMI- [HALF] • *I'm hoping to buy a three-bed semi* (= with three bedrooms) *near the station.*

sem·i [VEHICLE] /'sem·i/ *n* [C] *pl* **semis** *Am and Aus infml* an ARTICULATED truck

sem·i [COMPETITION] /'sem·i/ *n* [C] *pl* **semis** *infml for* **semi-final**, see at SEMI- [HALF] • *You did very well to make it to the semis.* • *I knew it would be a tough semi and that I couldn't afford to make any mistakes.* • [LP] **Sports**

sem·i·breve *esp. Br and Aus* /'sem·i·briːv/, *Am usually* **whole note** *n* [C] *specialized* a musical note with a time value equal to two MINIMS or four CROTCHETS

sem·i·co·lon /£ˌsem·i'kəʊ·lɒn, $'sem·iˌkoʊ·lən/ *n* [C] a sign (;) used in formal writing between two parts of a sentence, usually when each of the two parts could form grammatical sentences on their own • Semicolons can also be used to separate the items in a list.

sem·i·con·duc·tor /£ˌsem·i·kən'dʌk·təʳ, $-t̬ɚ/ *n* [C] a material, such as SILICON, which allows electricity to move through it more easily when its temperature increases, or an electronic device made from this material • *Semiconductors are used for making integrated circuits and computers.*

sem·i·con·duct·ing /£'sem·i·kənˌdʌk·tɪŋ, $-t̬ɪŋ/ *adj* [before n; not gradable] • *These highly sophisticated devices use semiconducting compounds which respond to infrared light.*

SEMICOLON [;]

The semicolon is more commonly used in formal writing. A semicolon can be used:

- **to join two parts of a sentence which could be two separate sentences, but which you prefer to keep together.** A comma should not be used in this way.
  Rachel's eyes began to close; Dan, too, was feeling tired.
  Francis Bacon, a truly great painter, is well known; his paintings have great insight and feeling.

  When two clauses are connected by a conjunction a semicolon is not normally used:
  My eyes began to close **but** *Paul was wide awake.*
- **instead of a comma to divide parts of sentences, especially lists, that already have commas in them**
  Send this letter to McAllister, Dewey and Sturton; Baxter; and Hough.
  Her first three books are about politics, power and male attitudes; American women in the 60s; and women in education.

LP › **Colon** and **Comma**

sem·i·nal [IMPORTANT] /ˈsem·ɪ·nəl/ *adj fml* containing important new ideas and being very influential on later work • *It took her ten years to collect and check all the material that has gone into this seminal* **work**. • *She wrote a seminal* **article** *on the subject while she was still a student.* • *He played a seminal role in the formation of the association.*

sem·i·nal [LIQUID] /ˈsem·ɪ·nəl/ *adj* [before n; not gradable] *specialized* connected with SEMEN • *seminal fluid*

sem·i·nar /£ˈsem·ɪ·nɑːʳ, $-nɑːr/ *n* [C] an occasion when a teacher or expert and a group of people meet to study and discuss something • *I* **attended** *practically every lecture and seminar when I was a student.* • *I'm* **giving** *a seminar* **on** *the latest developments in genetic engineering next week.* • *I think we ought to* **hold** *a seminar* **on** *communication skills for our sales team.* • *Did you get the message about the* **training** *seminar?* • *a seminar* **room** • Compare LECTURE. • LP› **Schools and colleges**

sem·in·ary /£ˈsem·ɪ·nə·ri, $-ner·i/ *n* [C] a college for training people to become priests • *So many young Poles wanted to become priests that the seminaries could not accommodate them, and a lot had to be turned away.*

sem·i·qua·ver *esp. Br and Aus* /£ˈsem·iˌkweɪ·vəʳ, $-vɚ/, *Am usually* **six·teenth note** *n* [C] a musical note which has a time value of half a QUAVER or one-sixteenth of a SEMIBREVE

Se·mi·tic /£sɪˈmɪt·ɪk, $səˈmɪt̬-/ *adj* [not gradable] relating to the Arab and Jewish races or their languages • *Hebrew and Arabic are Semitic* **languages**. • Semitic can also refer to races such as the Babylonians and Phoenicians that existed in ancient times. • Sometimes Semitic refers only to Jews. • See also **anti-Semitic** at ANTI-.

sem·i·tone /£ˈsem·i·təʊn, $-toʊn/, *Am also* **half step**, *Am and Aus also* **half tone** *n* [C] the smallest difference in sound between two notes which are next to each other in the western musical SCALE • *There is one semitone between B flat and B.* • *The middle note in a minor chord is a semitone lower than in a major chord.*

sem·o·lina /ˌsem·əlˈiː·nə/ *n* [U] a powder made from crushed wheat which is used for making pasta and, esp. in Britain in the past, for making sweet dishes by mixing it with milk and baking it • *semolina pudding*

Sem·tex /ˈsem·teks/ *n* [U] *trademark* a very powerful explosive made in the Czech Republic • *Semtex is very difficult to detect and is used by terrorist organizations.* • *The police said 100lb of Semtex were used to make the bomb.*

Sen *n* [before n] *abbreviation for* **senator**, see at SENATE • *The legislation is sponsored by Sen. Bennett Johnston.*

SEN /ˌes·iːˈen/ *pl n abbreviation for* **Special Educational Needs**, see at SPECIAL [NOT USUAL] • *an SEN teacher* • *SEN funding* • *The child received an SEN statement.*

sen·ate /ˈsen·ət/ *n* [U] the more important of the two groups of politicians who make laws in some countries, and which in the United States is responsible for approving officials put in office by the President • **the** *French/Australian Senate* • *The US Senate has 100 members.* • *The law has no chance of being passed by* **the** *Senate.* • **The** *Senate is/are debating the issue next week.* [+ sing/pl v] • *Senate Republicans have distorted the budget proposals.* • Senate sometimes refers to the group of people which controls a college or university: *Cambridge University has a Senate.* ○ *Is she a member of Senate?*

sen·a·tor /£ˈsen·ə·təʳ, $-t̬ɚ/ (*abbreviation* **Sen**) *n* [C] • A senator is a politician who has been elected to a Senate: *Only two senators voted against the bill.* ○ *Senator Moynihan will see you now, Madam.* ○ *It's a pleasure to meet you, Senator.* [as form of address]

sen·a·tor·i·al /£ˌsen·əˈtɔː·ri·əl, $-ˈtɔːr·i-/ *adj* [not gradable] *esp. Am fml* • *a senatorial candidate/committee*

send *(obj)* [POST] /send/ *v past* **sent** /sent/ to cause (something) to go from one place to another, esp. by post • *I'll send her a letter/fax/parcel/postcard next week.* [+ two objects] • *We'll send it* **by post/airmail/sea**. [T] • *Should I send this letter first or second class?* [T] • *Could you send a reply* **to** *them as quickly as possible.* [T] • *Please send a stamped addressed envelope with your application.* [T] • *The news report was sent by satellite.* [T] • *We had to send* **(off) to** (= send a request to) *Ireland to get a replacement.* [I] • *We sent* **(away/off) for** (= sent a request for) *the holiday brochure as soon as we saw it advertised.* [I] • *She sent a message with John to say that she couldn't come.* [T] • *They sent her flowers for her birthday.* [+ two objects] • *Maggie sends her love and hopes you'll feel better soon.* [T] • *The magazine asked its readers to send* **(in)** *their comments/views/opinions about the new style of presentation.* [M] • *I'll send* **(off)** *the application form tomorrow/I'll send the form* **(off)** *tomorrow.* [M] • *Paul's moved back to New York and he's asked me to send* **on** *his letters/send his letters* **on** (= send them from his old address to his new address). [M] • *We sent* **(out)** *the wedding invitations about three weeks ago.* [M] • *(fml or literary)* To **send word** is to send a message: *She sent word with her secretary* **that** *she would be unable to attend the meeting.* [+ *that* clause]

send·er /£ˈsen·dəʳ, $-dɚ/ *n* [C] • *The winner of the competition will be the sender of the first correct entry that is drawn at random by the editor.* • *Postage stamps were introduced in Britain in 1840 as a way of showing that the sender had paid for the letter to be delivered.* • *The letter came back with* '**return to** *sender – not known at this address' written on it.*

send *obj* [CAUSE TO GO] /send/ *v* [T] *past* **sent** /sent/ to cause or order (someone) to go and do something • *We're sending the children* **to** *stay with my parents for a couple of weeks.* [+ obj + *to* infinitive] • *They sent a courier* **to** *deliver the documents.* [+ obj + *to* infinitive] • *The commander has asked us to send reinforcements.* • *They've sent their son* **(away)** *to school in Scotland.* • *He was trying to explain but she became impatient and sent him away* (= told him to leave). • *In expensive hotels you can* **send down for** (= order) *drinks and meals to be brought to your room.* • *There's not much to eat in the fridge. Should I* **send out for** (= telephone a restaurant and ask them to deliver) *a pizza?* • *I've asked for some samples to be* **sent up** (= brought up) *from the stores so that you can look at them.* • *(Br)* A student who is **sent down** is asked to leave college or university without finishing the course because they have done something wrong. • Someone who has committed a crime is *(Br)* **sent down**/*(Am)* **sent up** by being sent to prison: *He was sent down for five years.* • *(Br and Aus)* A player who is **sent off** (*Am* **ejected**) during a game is told to leave the playing area by the REFEREE because they have done something wrong. • *(infml)* If you **send** someone **packing** you ask them to leave immediately: *There were some kids at the door asking for money but I sent them packing.*

send–off /£ˈsend·ɒf, $-ɑːf/ *n* [C] • A send-off is an occasion at which people can express good wishes and say goodbye to someone who is leaving a place: *We'll have to give her a good send-off when she leaves the office.*

send *obj* [CAUSE TO HAPPEN] /send/ *v* [T] *past* **sent** /sent/ to cause (someone or something) to do the stated thing, or to cause (something) to happen • *Watching the television always sends me to sleep.* • *The explosion sent the crowd into a panic.* • *(Br) His untidiness sends her crazy/mad/wild.* [+ obj + adj] • *The announcement of the fall in profits sent the company's share price* **plummeting** (= caused it to go down a lot). [+ obj + v-*ing*] • *The disappointing trade statistics sent the pound* **down** (= caused it to fall in value) *against all the leading currencies.* • *The dry weather has sent vegetable* *prices* **soaring** (= caused them to increase a lot). [+ obj + v-*ing*] • *The rise in oil prices is bound to send manufacturers' costs* **up**. • *The draught from the fan sent papers flying all over the room.* [+ obj + v-*ing*] • *The news sent him running back to the house.* [+ obj + v-*ing*] • *The rise in interest rates should* **send a signal to** (= tell) *financial institutions that the government is serious about reducing inflation.* • If a group of people **send** someone **to Coventry** they refuse to speak to that person, usually as a punishment for something he or she has done to upset the group: *We sent him to Coventry for two weeks because he told the teacher who had broken the window.*

send out *obj*, **send** *obj* **out** *v adv* [M] to produce (something) in a way that causes it to spread out from a central point • *The equipment sent out a regular high-pitched signal.* • *It was a mild winter and by February the bushes were sending out new shoots.*

send up *obj*, **send** *obj* **up** *v adv* [M] *infml* to cause other people to laugh about someone (or something) esp. by copying their behaviour in an unkind way • *The show was very funny – they were sending up sports commentators/ sending sports commentators up.*

send–up /'send·ʌp/ *n* [C] *infml* • *He does a brilliant send-up of the President.*

sen·ile /£'siː·naɪl, $'sen·aɪl/ *adj* showing a lack of mental ability because of old age, esp. a lack of ability to think clearly and make decisions • *He spent many years caring for his senile mother.* • *He was too senile to stand trial as a war criminal.* • *I'm always losing my keys these days. I think I must be* **going senile**. • *Alzheimer's disease is the commonest form of* **senile dementia** (= the medical condition of being senile).

se·nil·i·ty /£sɪ'nɪl·ɪ·ti, $-ə·t̬i/ *n* [U] • *Senility is perhaps the worst prospect of old age, both for the people affected and for those who care for them.*

sen·i·or OLDER /£'siː·ni·əʳ, $-njɚ/ *n, adj* [not gradable] (someone) older • *(fml) She's my senior by three years* (= She is three years older than me). • *There are four classes in the senior part of the school* (= the part for older students). • *Senior pupils are expected to set an example to the younger children.* • A **senior citizen** (*Am also* **senior**, *Br and Aus also* **old age pensioner**) is a person who has reached the official age when they can stop working regularly. Senior citizen is used to avoid saying 'old person': *Discounts are available for senior citizens.* • *(Am)* A senior is someone in their final year of high school or university. • You can add Senior (*abbreviation* **Sr** or *Br and Aus* **Snr**) to the name of the older of two men in a family who have the same name, or to the family name of parents who have married sons of the same name: *The letter's addressed to James Grafton Snr – it's for you, Dad.* ○ *We're inviting the Furlongs and the Wisemans Senior* (= the parents rather than their married son's family). • A **senior statesman/stateswoman** is an experienced politician who is usually no longer working in government: *They found a senior statesman to head the project – someone who could make the worlds of politics and business work together.* See also **elder statesman** at ELDER. • Compare JUNIOR YOUNGER. • LP **Age**

sen·i·or·i·ty /£,siː·ni'ɒr·ɪ·ti, $siː'njɔːr·ə·t̬i/ *n* [U] • *Older employees complain about new policies that reward youth and innovation more than seniority.* • *Male power apparently increases with seniority, but women's decreases.*

sen·i·or HIGH RANK /£'siː·ni·əʳ, $-njɚ/ *n, adj* (someone) high or higher in rank • *She's senior* **to** *me, so I have to do what she tells me.* • *senior management* • *It's important to impress your seniors if you want to be promoted.* [C] • *a senior government minister* • *He was my senior officer when I was in the army.* • *(Br and Aus)* A **senior nursing officer** (*Am* **head nurse**, *Br and Aus dated* **matron**) is the person in charge of all the nurses in a hospital. • Compare JUNIOR LOW RANK.

sen·i·or·i·ty /£,siː·ni'ɒr·ɪ·ti, $siː'njɔːr·ə·t̬i/ *n* [U] • *In future, promotion will be based on merit not seniority.* • *They chose him for the top military job over more than two dozen generals and admirals who have greater seniority.*

sen·sa·tion FEELING /sen'seɪ·ʃᵊn/ *n* the ability to feel something physically, esp. by touching, or a physical feeling that results from this ability • *The disease causes a loss of sensation in the fingers.* [U] • *The exhibition allows visitors to share the sensation* **of** *flying like Superman.* [C] • *Nerve impulses convey the sensation* **of** *pain to the brain.* [C] • *After a while the burning sensation began to subside and my skin looked less red and sore.* [C] • A sensation is also a general feeling caused by something that happens to you, esp. a feeling which you cannot describe exactly: *I had the eerie/strange/weird sensation* **of** *being completely isolated from the events going on around us.* [C] ○ *I had the odd sensation that someone was following me.* [+ *that* clause] ○ *I can remember the first time I went sailing – it was a wonderful sensation.* [C] • LP **Feelings and pains**

sen·sa·tion EXCITEMENT /sen'seɪ·ʃᵊn/ *n* [C] something very exciting or interesting, or something which causes great excitement or interest • *He* **caused** *a sensation when he held a press conference and confessed to having an affair with his secretary.* • *A German produced the sensation of the championships yesterday by beating the world champion to win the women's 100 metres in record time.* • *Great dance routines, lively songs, a classic villain and a happy ending – no wonder the show was an* **overnight** *sensation* (= was very successful immediately). • *The books have been a publishing sensation on both sides of the Atlantic, and they have spent months on the best-seller lists.*

sen·sa·tion·al /sen'seɪ·ʃᵊn·ᵊl/ *adj* • *(approving)* Sensational means very good, exciting or unusual: *a sensational sports car/dress* ○ *She looks sensational* (= extremely attractive) *in her new dress.* • *(disapproving)* News reports and articles that are sensational are intended to excite or shock people rather than be serious and factual: *It was a sensational piece of reporting that did considerable damage to his reputation.* ○ *Some of the more sensational Japanese newspapers have given a lot of coverage to the scandal.* ○ *After a sensational trial* (= a trial which attracted a lot of public interest) *the Baroness was cleared of the killing.*

sen·sa·tion·al·ly /sen'seɪ·ʃᵊn·ᵊl·i/ *adv* • Sensationally means extremely. It is used with adjectives and adverbs relating to good or positive things: *sensationally popular/ successful* ○ *The book sold sensationally well.* • Sensationally also means in an extremely interesting or exciting way: *The show ended sensationally with fireworks.*

sen·sa·tion·al·i·sm /sen'seɪ·ʃᵊn·ᵊl·ɪ·zᵊm/ *n* [U] *disapproving* • *The newspaper has been accused of sensationalism* (= trying to excite or shock people) *in its coverage of the murders.*

sen·sa·tion·al·ist /sen'seɪ·ʃᵊn·ᵊl·ɪst/ *adj disapproving* • *sensationalist newspapers* • *a sensationalist headline*

sen·sa·tion·al·ize *obj*, *Br and Aus usually* **–ise** /sen'seɪ·ʃᵊn·ᵊl·aɪz/ *v* [T] • *It's important not to sensationalize crimes when they are reconstructed for television programmes.*

sense GOOD JUDGMENT /sents/ *n* [U] the characteristic of having good judgment, esp. when it is based on practical ideas or understanding • *I hope they'll* **have the (good)** *sense/***have enough** *sense* **to** *shut the windows before they leave.* [+ *to* infinitive] • **There's no sense in** *waiting* (= It is not practical to wait) – *the next train isn't for two hours.* [+ v-*ing*] • **Where's/What's the** *sense* (= There would be no advantage) **in** *paying someone when you could get a volunteer?* [+ v-*ing*] • **It makes (good)** *sense* **to** (= It shows good judgment to) *buy a large packet because it works out cheaper in the end.* [+ *to* infinitive] • See also **make sense** at SENSE MEANING. • *Planning so far ahead* **makes no** *sense* (= does not show good judgment) – *so many things will have changed by next year.* • *You're not* **making/ talking** *sense* (= showing good judgment) – *you know I can't come with you.* • Ⓙ

sen·ses /'sent·sɪz/ *pl n* • *Have you* **taken leave of** *your senses* (= Have you lost your ability to make a good judgment)*?* • *It's time you* **came to** *your senses* (= started to use your good judgment) *and realised that they are not going to help you.* • *The accident* **brought** *him* **to** *his senses* (= caused him to use his good judgment again) *and made him stop drinking.*

sen·si·ble /'sent·sɪ·bl̩/ *adj* • Sensible means based on or acting on good judgment and practical ideas or understanding: *a sensible answer/approach/compromise/ option* ○ *an eminently sensible solution* ○ *a sensible person* ○ *The sensible place to start is at the beginning.* ○ *I think the sensible thing to do is phone before you go and ask for directions.* ○ **It** *would be sensible* **to** *take an umbrella.* [+ *to* infinitive] ○ *"I'll go by train." "That seems sensible – the traffic will be terrible over the Christmas weekend."* • Sensible clothes or shoes are practical and suitable for the purpose they are needed for, rather than being attractive or fashionable: *We'll be doing quite a lot of walking so make sure you bring some sensible shoes.* ○ *It could be cold and wet so pack some sensible clothes.*

sen·si·bly /'sent·sɪ·bli/ *adv* • *She was always telling the children to behave more sensibly.* • *The police praised motorists for driving sensibly in appalling conditions.* • *She wasn't very sensibly dressed for hiking across the moors.*

sense·less /'sent·sləs/ *adj* • Something that is senseless lacks good or intelligent judgment or a good or useful purpose: *senseless killings/violence/deaths* ○ *It's a senseless argument, because homelessness is not usually based on choice.* ○ *He said it would be senseless to educate a generation for unemployment.* • See also **senseless** at SENSE [ABILITY], SENSE [MEANING].

sense [ABILITY] /sents/ *n* [C] an ability to understand, recognize, value or react to something, esp. any of the five physical abilities to see, hear, smell, taste and feel • *Sight is one of the five senses.* • *With her keen sense* **of** *smell, she could tell if you were a smoker from the other side of the room.* • *My cold is so bad I've* **lost** *my sense* **of** *smell/taste* (=I can't smell/taste anything). • A **sense organ** is a part of the body which makes it possible to experience the physical characteristics of a situation: *Your ears, eyes, tongue, nose and skin are your sense organs.* • A sense is also a general feeling or understanding: *I had a sudden sense that I was needed at home.* ○ *Did you get any sense of how they might react?* ○ *The helicopters hovering overhead added to the sense* **of** *urgency.* ○ *Are we doing enough to* **instil** *a sense* **of** *social responsibility in young people?* ○ *All sports have their special language that gives players a cosy sense* **of** *belonging and mystifies outsiders.* • *(esp. Br)* Someone who has a **sense of fun** (*Am and Aus usually* **sense of humor**) enjoys life and is not too serious: *He has a crazy but harmless sense of fun.* ○ *Don't be angry – it was just a joke – where's your sense of fun?* • Your **sense of humour** is your ability to understand amusing things: *We had a good laugh about what had happened – we have the same sense of humour.* ○ *I'd rather marry a man who had a good sense of humour than one who was stunningly attractive.* • *(Br and Aus)* A **sense of occasion** is the feeling people have when there is a very important event or celebration: *The decorations, flowers and crowds gave the town a real sense of occasion.* • (J)

sense *obj* /sents/ *v* [T] • To sense something is to be aware of it or experience it without being able to explain exactly how: *Although she said nothing, I could sense her anger.* ○ *She sensed someone was approaching.* ○ *He sensed something was about to happen.* ○ *He sensed* **(that)** *his guests were bored, although they were listening politely.* [+ (*that*) clause] ○ *Could you sense* **what** *was likely to happen?* [+ *wh*-word] • (I)

sense·less /'sent·sləs/ *adj* • Senseless means unconscious: *Pat was* **beaten** *senseless by the burglars.* ○ *Ambulances ploughed through the chaos, carrying away those* **knocked** *senseless by the blast.* • See also **senseless** at SENSE [GOOD JUDGMENT], SENSE [MEANING].

sense [MEANING] /sents/ *n* [C] one of the possible meanings of a word or phrase • *They are not immigrants, at least not in any sense that I understand.* • *The packaging is green – in both senses of the word* (= it is green in colour and it is good for the environment). • *Security defined* **in the broad/broadest** *sense* **of** *the term means getting at the root causes of trouble and helping to reduce regional conflicts.* The opposite of *the broad sense* is *the* **narrow** *sense.* • *The word 'bastard', used* **in** *its* **literal** *sense of a child born to unmarried parents, is less common than it used to be.* • *It's a book which is,* **in every sense** (=in every way), *about different ways of seeing the world.* • *She's right,* **in a/one sense** (=She is partly right) *because we did agree to wait, but only until June.* • *We are* **in no sense** (=We certainly are not) *obliged to agree to this.* • *This passage doesn't* **make (any)** *sense* (=the meaning is not clear). • *I've read the letter twice, but I can't* **make (any)** *sense* **of** *it* (=I can't understand it). • See also **make sense** at SENSE [GOOD JUDGMENT]. • (J)

sen·si·bil·i·ty /£ˌsent·sɪ'bɪl·ɪ·ti, $-sə'bɪl·ə·t̬i/ *n* [U] an awareness, understanding or ability to decide about what is good or valuable, esp. in connection with artistic or social activities • *literary/musical/artistic/theatrical/aesthetic sensibility* • *No-one with taste and sensibility would buy the book.* • *The author has applied* **a** *modern sensibility* (=way of understanding things) *to the social ideals of an earlier age.*

sen·si·bil·i·ties /£ˌsent·sɪ'bɪl·ɪ·tiz, $-sə'bɪl·ə·t̬iz/ *pl n* • *To understand American sensibilities* (=feelings) *in this regard, think how the British would feel if the BBC was owned by foreign corporations.* • *In a multicultural society we need to show respect for the sensibilities* (=feelings) **of** *others.*

sen·si·ble /'sent·sɪ·bl̩/ *adj fml or literary* having an awareness or understanding of a situation • *He did not appear to be sensible* **of** *the difficulties that lay ahead.* • (D) (DK) (E) (F) (I) (P) (S)

sen·si·tive [KIND] /£'sent·sɪ·tɪv, $-sə·t̬ɪv/ *adj* understanding what other people need, and being helpful and kind to them • *Dr Abraham said he hoped teachers would be sensitive* **to** *signs of stress in children at exam time.* • *Representatives of the company claim their plan will be sensitive* **to** *local needs.* • *We are sensitive* **to** *the needs and expectations of our customers.* • *In the movie, he plays a concerned and sensitive father trying to bring up two teenage children on his own.*

sen·si·tive·ly /£'sent·sɪ·tɪv·li, $-sə·t̬ɪv-/ *adv* • *This is a very delicate situation and it needs to be handled sensitively.*

sen·si·tive·ness /£'sen·sɪ·tɪv·nəs, $-sə·t̬ɪv-/ *n* [U]

sen·si·tiv·i·ty /£ˌsent·sɪ'tɪv·ɪ·ti, $-sə't̬ɪv·ə·t̬i/ *n* • *She counselled people who were dying with great care and sensitivity.* [U] • *He was loved for his human sensitivities, his gentle wit and his warmth.* [C]

sen·si·tize *obj, Br and Aus usually* **-ise** /'sent·sɪ·taɪz/ *v* [T] • *The association aims to sensitize employers* **to** (=make them aware of) *the problems faced by left-handed people in the workplace.*

sen·si·tive [UPSET] /£'sent·sɪ·tɪv, $-sə·t̬ɪv/ *adj* (of people) easily upset, esp. by things that are said or done, or (of things) causing people to be upset or producing a difficult or embarrassing situation • *Her reply showed that she was very sensitive* **to** *criticism.* • *He was very sensitive* **about** *his scar and thought everyone was staring at him.* • *Sex education and birth control are sensitive* **issues** *for the anti-abortion movement.* • *A car from the army base at Aldershot has been stolen together with military documents described as very sensitive.* • *The scandal comes at an especially sensitive time for the government.*

sen·si·tive·ness /£'sen·sɪ·tɪv·nəs, $-sə·t̬ɪv-/ *n* [U]

sen·si·tiv·i·ty /£ˌsent·sɪ'tɪv·ɪ·ti, $-sə't̬ɪv·ə·t̬i/ *n* • *Such is the sensitivity of the information that only two people are allowed to know it.* [U] • *A military response is unlikely, given Western political sensitivities about casualty rates.*

sen·si·tive [REACTING EASILY] /£'sent·sɪ·tɪv, $-sə·t̬ɪv/ *adj* easily influenced, changed or damaged, esp. by a physical activity or effect • *Some people's teeth are highly sensitive* **to** *cold.* • *Their products include facial cleansers and moisturizers for sensitive* **skin.** • Sensitive equipment is able to record small changes: *The patient's responses are recorded on a sensitive piece of equipment which gives extremely accurate readings.*

-sen·si·tive /£-'sent·sɪ·tɪv, $-sə·t̬ɪv/ *combining form* • *The device is controlled by light-/heat-sensitive detectors.*

sen·si·tiv·i·ty /£ˌsent·sɪ'tɪv·ɪ·ti, $-sə'tɪv·ə·t̬i/, **sen·si·tive·ness** /£'sent·sɪ·tɪv·nəs, $-sə·t̬ɪv-/ *n* [U] • *One of the side effects of the drug is an increased sensitivity* **to** *sunlight.*

sen·si·tize *obj, Br and Aus usually* **-ise** /'sent·sɪ·taɪz/ *v* [T] • *It seems very likely that air pollutants are sensitizing people so that they become allergic to pollen.*

sen·sor /£'sent·səʳ, $-sɚ/ *n* [C] a device which is used to record the presence of something or changes in something • *The security device has a heat sensor which detects the presence of people and animals.* • *The toaster has an* **electronic** *sensor for even browning.*

sen·so·ry /£'sent·sᵊr·i, $-sɚ-/ *adj* [before n; not gradable] *specialized* connected with the physical SENSES of touch, smell, taste, hearing and seeing • *A sensory perception that occurs without any stimulation of the appropriate sense organ is called a hallucination.* • *While experimenting on the effects of sensory* **deprivation,** *he submerged his assistants in flotation tanks.* • *Using small electrical shocks applied to her feet, they were able to monitor sensory* **nerves.** • *Sharks have sensory* **organs** *that can detect faint electrical fields from other fish.*

sen·su·al /'sent·sjuəl/ *adj* expressing or suggesting physical, esp. sexual, pleasure or satisfaction • *For many people, eating chocolate is a very sensual* **experience.** • *A woman with a sensual voice answered the phone.* • *He is elegant, sensual, conscious of his body.* • *He noticed her high cheekbones, the sensual mouth and the way her brown eyes fixed on him directly as he talked.* • *He was looking at her with an odd, flickering smile, faintly sensual and appreciative.*

sen·su·al·i·ty /£ˌsent·sju'æl·ɪ·ti, $-ə·t̬i/ *n* [U] • *She found his innocent sensuality irresistible.*

sen·su·ous /'sent·sjʊəs/ *adj* giving or expressing pleasure through the physical SENSES, rather than pleasing the mind or the intelligence • *She luxuriated in the sensuous feel of the silk sheets.* • Sensuous is very often used to mean SENSUAL: *He had a very sensuous mouth.*

sen·su·ous·ly /'sent·sjʊə·sli/ *adv*

sen·su·ous·ness /'sent·sjʊə·snəs/ *n* [U] • *He is famous for the sensuousness he brings to his performances.*

sent /sent/ *past simple and past participle of* SEND • *"Have you sent Mum a birthday card?" "Yes, I sent it last week."*

sen·tence [PUNISHMENT] /'sen·tənts/ *n* [C] a punishment given by a judge in court to a person or organization after they have been found guilty of doing something wrong • *He got a* **heavy/light** *sentence* (= He was severely/not severely punished). • *The offence* **carries** *a* **jail/prison/life/5-year** *sentence.* • *He was given a* **non-custodial/suspended** *sentence.* • *The judge will* **pronounce sentence** (= say officially what the punishment will be) **on** *the defendant this afternoon.* • A sentence **of death** or **death sentence** is the legal punishment of being killed. • LP› **Crimes and criminals** (RUS)

sen·tence *obj* /'sen·tənts/ *v* [T] *law* • *He was sentenced* **to** *life imprisonment.* • *The judge sentenced her* **to** *three years in prison.*

sen·tence [WORD GROUP] /'sen·tənts/ *n* [C] a group of words, usually containing a verb, which expresses a thought in the form of a statement, question, instruction or exclamation and starts with a capital letter when written • *He's very impatient and always interrupts me mid-sentence.* • *Your conclusion is good, but the final sentence is too long and complicated.* • LP› **Full stop** (RUS)

sen·ten·tious /sen'ten·tʃəs/ *adj fml disapproving* trying to appear wise, clever and important • *The document was sententious and pompous.*

sen·ten·tious·ly /sen'ten·tʃə·sli/ *adv*

sen·tient /'sen·tɪ·ənt/ *adj fml* able to experience physical and possibly emotional feelings • *They failed to offer sound moral justifications for treating sentient creatures as mere research tools.* • *It is hard for a sentient person to understand how any parents could treat their child so badly.*

sen·ti·ment [IDEA] /£'sen·tɪ·mənt, $-t̬ə-/ *n fml* a thought, opinion or idea based on a feeling about a situation, or a way of thinking about something • *The* **prevailing** *sentiment in the school is that Andrew did not steal the money.* [U] • *It seems that* **public/popular** *sentiment is shifting in favour of nursery education for all children.* [U] • *Nationalist sentiment/sentiments has/have increased in the area since the bombing.* [U; C] • *Joan said she needed a few days' holiday and that sentiment was immediately* **echoed** *by her friend.* [C] • *Several other people have* **expressed** *rather* **similar** *sentiments.* [C] • *I don't think she* **shares** *my sentiments.* [C] • *It remains to be seen whether his* **lofty/worthy** *sentiments will be put into action.* [C] • *His son was overwhelmed by the sentiments* **of** *love and support in the cards and letters he received.* [C] • *(fml) "It's a very bad situation." "My sentiments exactly* (= I completely agree)." [C]

sen·ti·ment [FEELINGS] /£'sen·tɪ·mənt, $-t̬ə-/ *n* [U] gentle feelings of love, sympathy, or caring about sad or romantic events, esp. when thought to be foolish or not suitable • *The bronze statue of a child holding a begging bowl appeals to sentiment.* • *The film is flawed by slightly treacly sentiment.*

sen·ti·men·tal /£ˌsen·tɪ'men·tᵊl, $-t̬ə'men·t̬ᵊl/ *adj* • If you are sentimental, you are strongly influenced by emotional feelings, esp. about happy memories of past events or relationships with other people, rather than by careful thought and judgment based on facts: *Why* **be** *sentimental* **about** *that old coat? There's no point in keeping it just because you were wearing it when you first met me.* ○ *He had no sentimental* **attachment** *to his working class roots.* ○ *The film is the ultimate sentimental* **journey**, *a trip back to the days when the sun seemed to shine all the time and family quarrels were unknown.* ○ *She kept the book for sentimental* **reasons**. ○ *It's a cheap ring but it has great sentimental* **value** *for me.* • *(disapproving)* Sentimental also means too strongly influenced by emotional feelings: *sentimental songs/stories*

sen·ti·men·tal·ly /£ˌsen·tɪ'men·tᵊl·i, $-t̬ə'men·t̬ᵊl-/ *adv*

sen·ti·men·tal·i·sm /£ˌsen·tɪ'men·tᵊl·ɪ·zᵊm, $-t̬ə'men·t̬ᵊl-/ *n* [U] *disapproving fml* • Sentimentalism is the tendency to be sentimental: *Caring for animals is not sentimentalism – it reinforces our respect for life.* • Sentimentalism is also sentimentality.

sen·ti·men·tal·ist /£ˌsen·tɪ'men·tᵊl·ɪst, $-t̬ə'men·t̬ᵊl-/ *n* [C] *disapproving fml* • *Sentimentalists hark back to the last century as a time when genius flowered unsupported by the state.*

sen·ti·men·tal·i·ty /£ˌsen·tɪ·men'tæl·ɪ·ti, $-t̬ə·men'tæl·ə·t̬i/ *n* [U] *disapproving* • Sentimentality is the expression of feelings that are too sentimental: *"What do you think of his songs?" "The tunes are great, but I can't stand the sentimentality of his lyrics."* • Sentimentality is also sentimentalism.

sen·ti·men·tal·ize *obj, Br and Aus usually* **-ise** /£ˌsen·tɪ'men·tᵊl·aɪz, $-t̬ə'men·t̬ə·laɪz/ *v* [T] *disapproving* • *Her book sentimentalizes parenthood and completely ignores the disadvantages of it.* • *The film is a sentimentalized version of what actually happened.*

sen·ti·nel /£'sen·tɪ·nᵊl, $-t̬ɪ-/ *n* [C] *esp. old use or literary* a person employed to guard something; a SENTRY • *At every gate that we passed through, we saw a watchman – on every bridge a sentinel.* • *A policeman* **stood** *sentinel at the entrance.* • *(esp. Am)* Sentinel is also used in the names of some newspapers: *the Fort Lauderdale Sun-Sentinel* • *the Fitchburg Sentinel*

sen·try /'sen·tri/ *n* [C] a soldier who guards a place, usually by standing at its entrance • *As usual, a group of tourists were taking pictures of the sentries outside the palace.* • *My squad were on sentry* **duty** *last night.* • A **sentry box** is a shelter in which a sentry stands while guarding a place: *At night I park the car outside the Polish embassy, within sight of a sentry box, to deter thieves.*

sep·a·rate /£'sep·ᵊr·ət, $'-ɚ-/ *adj* existing or happening independently or in a different physical space • *The arts department and the main college are two separate buildings.* • *Two other youths were shot and killed in separate incidents.* • *On two separate occasions I've had to ask them to turn their music down.* • *Under the plan, each of the three broadcast services is to remain a separate entity.* • *I have my public life and my private life, and as far as possible I try to* **keep** *them separate.* • *It was agreed that the detainees should be kept separate* **from** *the other prisoners.* • *Like most other places in Japan, restaurants rarely have the space for separate non-smoking sections.* • *In 1963 Kuwait was recognized as a separate state.* • *From as early as I can remember my parents had separate bedrooms.* • If two or more people **go** their **separate ways** they stop being together: *In 1983 the group disbanded and went their separate ways.*

sep·a·rate *(obj)* /£'sep·ᵊr·eɪt, $-ə·reɪt/ *v* • *At school they always tried to separate* (= keep apart) *Jane and me because we were trouble-makers.* [T] • *Somehow in the rush to get out of the building I got separated* **from** (= I lost) *my mother.* [T] • *The police have separated the two sides' supporters* **into** *different parts of the ground.* [T] • *They were fighting so fiercely that it took five of us to separate them* (= pull them apart). [T] • *Perhaps we should separate* (= go to different places) *now and meet up later when we've each finished our shopping.* [I] • *The older brothers look so alike I can't separate them* (= consider them as two different people) *in my mind.* [T] • *You can't separate* (= consider independently) *morality* **from** *politics.* [T] • *The north and south of the country are separated by* (= have between them) *a mountain range.* [T] • *You can get a special device for separating* (= dividing) *egg whites* **from** *yolks.* [T] • If a liquid separates it becomes two different liquids, one of them thinner and more liquid and the other, a thicker more solid substance. [I] • If two married people separate, they stop living together as husband and wife, often as a part of a legal arrangement: *My parents separated when I was six and divorced a couple of years later.* [I] • LP› **Relationships**

sep·a·ra·ble /£'sep·ᵊr·ə·bl̩, $'-ɚ-/ *adj slightly fml* • Separable means able to be separated from each other: *He regarded art as very much a part of life and not something separable* **from** *it.* ○ *Political rights were not separable* **from** *other rights.* • Compare INSEPARABLE.

sep·a·rate·ly /£'sep·ᵊr·ət·li, $'-ɚ-/ *adv* • Separately means not together: *Detectives interviewed the men separately over several days.* ○ *I tend to wear the jacket and skirt separately rather than as a suit.* ○ *I think we'd better deal with these two points separately.* ○ *Perhaps I should wash the new towels separately* (= not with the other clothes) *in case the colour comes out.*

sep·a·rates /£'sep·ᵊr·əts, $'-ɚ-/ *pl n* • In shops, separates are pieces of women's clothing that are bought singly and not as part of a SUIT: *Ladies separates are on the next floor, madam.*

sep·a·ra·tion /£ˌsep·ᵊr'eɪ·ʃᵊn, $-ə'reɪ-/ *n* • *During the war many couples had to endure long periods of separation* (=not being together). [U] • *After many years the government finally abandoned its apartheid system of racial separation.* [U] • *The law involved the separation of the population* **into** *whites and non-whites.* [U] • *He firmly believes in the separation* (=independent existence) *of church and state.* [U] • A separation is an often legal arrangement by which two married people stop living together as husband and wife: *Couples may agree to divorce each other after a separation.* [C] ○ *They're considering separation as an option.* [U]

sep·a·rat·i·sm /£'sep·ᵊr·ə·tɪ·zᵊm, $-ɚ·ə·t̬ɪ-/ *n* [U] • Separatism is the belief held by a racial, religious or other group within a country that they should be independent and have their own government or in some way live apart from other people: *Quebec/Basque separatism* ○ *I consider myself a feminist, but I hate the labels and separatism.*

sep·a·rat·ist /£'sep·ᵊr·ə·tɪst, $-ɚ·ə·t̬ɪst/ *n* [C] • *Twenty Punjab villagers kidnapped by Sikh separatists on Friday have been released unharmed.* • *There is resentful talk about how "women's centres have been taken over by radical separatists".* • *It is difficult to establish how much of the Kurdish population sympathises with the separatist movements.*

se·pi·a /'siː·pi·ə/ *adj* of the reddish brown colour of photographs in the past • *She showed me an old sepia* **photograph** *of her grandmother, dated 1911.* • *Carey is the woman on the sepia-toned album cover.*

sep·sis /'sep·sɪs/ *n* [U] *medical* a severe medical condition in which bacteria enter the blood after an operation or accident

Sep·tem·ber /£sep'tem·bəʳ, $-bɚ/ (*abbreviation* **Sept**) *n* the ninth month of the year, after August and before October • *23(rd) September/September 23(rd)/23(rd) Sept/Sept 23(rd)* [U] • *We're leaving for France* **on** *September the ninth/the ninth of September/(Am) September ninth.* [U] • *Claudia started school* **last** *September/is starting school* **next** *September.* [U] • *My mother's birthday is* **in** *September.* [U] • *We went to Greece two Septembers ago.* [C] • [LP]〉 **Dates**

sep·tet /sep'tet/ *n* [C + sing/pl v] seven people who play musical instruments or sing as a group, or a piece of music written for seven people

sep·tic /'sep·tɪk/ *adj* (of a part of the body) infected by bacteria which produce PUS (=a poisonous yellowish substance) • *I had my ears pierced and one of them* **went** *septic.* • *Antibiotics have failed to help the injury to Fiennes's foot, which is thought to have started as a septic blister.* • A **septic tank** is a large, esp. underground, container usually in a countryside area in which excrement and urine are dissolved by the action of bacteria.

sep·ti·cae·mi·a *Br and Aus, Am and Aus* **sep·ti·ce·mi·a** /ˌsep·tɪ'siː·mi·ə/ *n* [U] *medical for* **blood poisoning**, see at BLOOD [LIQUID]

sep·tu·a·ge·na·ri·an /£ˌsep·tjʊə·dʒɪ'neə·ri·ən, $-tu·ə·dʒə'ner·i-/ *n* [C] a person who is between 70 and 79 years old

sep·ul·chre, *Am also* **sep·ul·cher** /£'sep·ᵊl·kəʳ, $-kɚ/ *n* [C] *old use* a stone structure where someone is buried

se·pul·chral /sɪ'pʌl·krᵊl/ *adj literary* • Sepulchral means suggesting death or places where the dead are buried: *The curtain rose to reveal a gloomy, sepulchral set for the play.* ○ *Not a whisper broke the sepulchral silence.* ○ *"There are punishments worse than death," he said, in his hollow, sepulchral voice.*

se·quel /'siː·kwᵊl/ *n* [C] a book, film or play which continues the story of a previous book etc. • *I'm reading the sequel* **to** *'Gone with the Wind'.* • *Seven of the 40 top-earning films in American cinema have been sequels* **of** *earlier box-office successes.* • A sequel is also an event which happens after and is the result of an earlier event: *There was a dramatic sequel* **to** *last Thursday's scandalous revelations when the minister for trade suddenly announced his resignation.* • Compare PREQUEL.

se·quence [ORDERED SERIES] /'siː·kwənts/ *n* a series of related things or events, or the order in which they follow each other • *The first chapter describes the strange sequence* **of events** *that lead to his death.* [C] • *It all happened a long time ago and I can't remember the precise sequence* **of events.** [U] • *A good aerobics instructor will teach you the basic sequence of moves which you then simply repeat.* [C] • *Is there a particular sequence in which you have to perform these tasks?* [C] • *For the sake of convenience the photographs are shown* **in** *chronological sequence* (=in the order in which they were taken). [U]

se·quenc·ing /'siː·kwənt·sɪŋ/ *n* [U] *specialized* • Sequencing is the process of deciding the correct or existing order of things: *A common sign of dyslexia is that the sequencing of letters when spelling words may be incorrect.* ○ *Dr Gilbert's team are working on new methods of gene-sequencing.*

se·quen·tial /sɪ'kwen·ʃᵊl/ *adj fml or specialized* • Sequential means following a particular order: *The publishers claim that the book constitutes 'the first sequential exposition of events and thus of the history of the revolution'.*

se·quen·tial·ly /sɪ'kwen·ʃᵊl·i/ *adv fml or specialized* • *The sections are ordered sequentially.*

se·quence [FILM PART] /'siː·kwənts/ *n* [C] a part of a film that shows a particular event or a related series of events • *The film's* **opening** *sequence is of a very unpleasant murder.* • *In the next sequence you see the blonde woman getting into Robert De Niro's car.*

se·ques·ter *obj* [TAKE] /£sɪ'kwes·təʳ, $-tɚ/, **se·ques·trate** /'siː·kwə·streɪt/ *v* [T usually passive] *law* to take temporary possession of (someone's property) until they have paid back the money that they owe or obeyed a court order • *Their own small estate was sequestered by the Tsar for the family's part in the uprising.*

se·ques·tra·tion /ˌsiː·kwes'treɪ·ʃᵊn/ *n* [U] *law*

se·ques·ter *obj* [KEEP SEPARATE] /£sɪ'kwes·təʳ, $-tɚ/ *v* [T usually passive] *Am law* to keep (a JURY) (=group of people deciding a legal case) together as a group and not allow them to discuss the case or read or hear news reports about it

se·ques·tra·tion /ˌsiː·kwes'treɪ·ʃᵊn/ *n* [U] *Am law*

se·ques·tered /£sɪ'kwes·təd, $-tɚd/ *adj literary* (of a place) peaceful; situated away from people • *I found a sequestered spot at the bottom of the garden and lay down with my book.*

se·quin /'siː·kwɪn/ *n* [C] a small shiny metal or plastic disc sewn onto clothes for decoration • *And to think, every single sequin on Carlene's dress was sewn on by hand by her mother, Doreen!* • *Sequins were very popular in the 1970s.*

se·quined /'siː·kwɪnd/ *adj* • *She appeared in the doorway, wearing a shimmering blue sequined dress which made her resemble a mermaid.*

se·quoi·a /sɪ'kwɔɪ·ə/ *n* [C] a large Californian evergreen tree that can reach a height of more than 90 metres

se·ra /£'sɪə·rə, $'sɪr·ə/ *pl of* SERUM

ser·aph /'ser·əf/ *n* [C] *pl* **seraphim** /'ser·ə·fɪm/ or **seraphs** an ANGEL (=a good spiritual creature) of the highest rank, often represented as the winged head of a child • *At the highest point in the ceiling is a figure of Christ, flanked by two seraphim.*

ser·a·phic /sə'ræf·ɪk/ *adj literary approving* beautiful in a way that suggests goodness and purity • *a seraphic smile*

ser·aph·i·cal·ly /sə'ræf·ɪ·kli/ *adv literary approving*

Serb·i·an /£'sɜː·bi·ən, $'sɜːr-/, **Serb** /£sɜːb, $sɜːrb/ *n* [C], *adj* [not gradable] (a person) of or from Serbia

Serb·i·an /£'sɜː·bi·ən, $'sɜːr-/ *n* [U] • *He speaks Serbian* (=the language of Serbia).

ser·e·nade *obj* /ˌser·ə'neɪd/ *v* [T] to play a piece of music or sing for (someone, esp. a woman) at night, while standing outside her house • *There's that lovely bit in the film where Romeo serenades Juliet in the moonlight.* • *(fig.) Nowadays in the classier stores, shoppers are serenaded with live piano music.*

ser·e·nade /ˌser·ə'neɪd/ *n* [C] • A serenade is a song or piece of music sung or played for someone, esp. a woman, traditionally at night while standing outside her house. • A serenade is also a piece of gentle CLASSICAL music in several parts: *'Moonlight Serenade'*

ser·en·di·pi·ty /£ˌser·ᵊn'dɪp·ɪ·ti, $-ə·t̬i/ *n* [U] *fml* the lucky tendency to find interesting or valuable things just by chance • *The actress Lana Turner, it is said, was discovered by serendipity at Schwab's Hollywood drug store.*

ser·en·di·pi·tous /£ˌser·ᵊn'dɪp·ɪ·təs, $-t̬əs/ *adj fml* • *Reading should be an adventure, a personal experience full of serendipitous surprises.*

se·rene /sɪ'riːn/ *adj* **-r, -st** peaceful and calm; troubled by nothing • *She has a lovely serene face.* • *What amazes me is his serene* **indifference** *to all the trouble around him.*

se·rene·ly /sɪˈriːn·li/ *adv* • *She smiled serenely and said nothing.*

se·ren·i·ty /£sɪˈren·ɪ·ti, $-ə·ţi/ *n* [U] • *She has a Madonna-like serenity.* • *I admired her serenity in the midst of so much chaos.*

serf /£sɜːf, $sɜːrf/ *n* [C] a member of a low social class in MEDIEVAL times (= between about 1000 and 1500) who worked on the land and was the property of the person who owned it.

serf·dom /£ˈsɜːf·dəm, $ˈsɜːrf-/ *n* [U] • Serfdom refers either to the state of being a serf or to the system by which the land was farmed by serfs.

serge /£sɜːdʒ, $sɜːrdʒ/ *n* [U] a strong woollen cloth which is used esp. to make jackets and coats

ser·geant SOLDIER /£ˈsɑː·dʒᵊnt, $ˈsɑːr-/ (*abbreviation* **Sgt**, *infml* **sarge**) *n* [C] (in armies and air forces) a soldier of middle rank • *Sergeant Lewis* • *Dismiss the men, sergeant.* [as form of address] • **Sergeant major** is a military rank.

ser·geant POLICE OFFICER /£ˈsɑː·dʒᵊnt, $ˈsɑːr-/ (*abbreviation* **Sgt**, *infml* **sarge**) *n* [C] (in Britain) a police officer whose rank is above CONSTABLE and below INSPECTOR, or (in the US) a police officer whose rank is below a CAPTAIN

se·ri·al STORY /£ˈsɪə·ri·əl, $ˈsɪr·i-/ *n* [C] a story on television or radio or in a newspaper etc. which is broadcast or printed in separate parts • *Most of her novels have been made into* **television** *serials at some time.* • *The Sunday Times bought the serial* **rights** *to* (= the right to publish in parts) *her autobiography.*

se·ri·al·ize *obj, Br and Aus usually* **-ise** /£ˈsɪə·ri·ᵊl·aɪz, $ˈsɪr·i·ə·laɪz/ *v* [T usually passive] • If a book is serialized, it is made into a number of television or radio programmes or published in a newspaper or a magazine in parts: *'The Adventures of Sherlock Holmes' was serialized in the Strand Magazine.*

se·ri·al·i·za·tion, *Br and Aus usually* **-i·sa·tion** /£ˌsɪə·ri·ᵊl·aɪˈzeɪ·ʃᵊn, $ˌsɪr·i·əl-/ *n* • *This year has seen the serialization of a number of popular classics on TV.* [U] • *There have been several book serializations in the Sunday papers lately.* [C]

se·ri·al REPEATED /£ˈsɪə·ri·əl, $ˈsɪr·i-/ *adj* [before n; not gradable] repeated, one after another • A **serial killer/murderer** is a person who murders many people one after another: *She wrote a thriller about a brutal serial killer and the policewoman assigned to track him down.* ○ *This month's best-seller is a book about London's unsolved* **serial murders.** • *(humorous)* **Serial monogamy** is the tendency to have a series of sexual relationships one after another, but never more than one at a time: *Me, I'm into serial monogamy.* • A **serial number** is a number that is printed on one of a large number of the same items, each of which has a different number, in order to be able to recognize which is which.

se·ries SET OF EVENTS /£ˈsɪə·riːz, $ˈsɪr·iːz/ *n* [C] *pl* **series** a number of similar or related events or things, one following another • *A series* **of** *scandals over the past year has not helped public confidence in the government.* • *There has been a series* **of** *sexual attacks on women in the area.* • *He wrote a series* **of** *articles devoted to modern farming methods.* • *She gave a series* **of** *lectures at Warwick University last year on contemporary British writers.* • A series is also a number of games played by two teams: *England won the Test series against Australia by two matches to one.* ○ *The Yankees have a four-game series against the Orioles at home, after which they start a two-week road trip.* See also **World Series** at WORLD THE EARTH. • Parts of an electrical system that are **in series** are arranged in a single line so that the current flows through each part, one after another.

se·ries SET OF BROADCASTS /£ˈsɪə·riːz, $ˈsɪr·iːz/ *n* [C] a set of television or radio broadcasts on the same subject or using the same characters but in different situations • *Tonight sees the start of 'Soldier, Soldier', a new documentary series about the lives of servicemen.* • *The footballer Paul Gascoigne is to host a Channel 4* **television** *series on soccer skills* • *Have you seen the new comedy series that's set in a health club?* • *I missed the second episode of the series so I don't know what's going on now.*

se·ries SET OF BOOKS /£ˈsɪə·riːz, $ˈsɪr·iːz/ *n* [C] a set of books published by the same company which deal with the same subject • *They do a series* **on** *architecture throughout the ages.*

se·ri·ous BAD /£ˈsɪə·ri·əs, $ˈsɪr·i-/ *adj* severe in effect; bad • *It's a serious illness – you can die of it.* • *Windows were smashed and missiles thrown but there were no reports of serious injuries.* • *The new tax regulations have landed some of the smaller companies in serious trouble.* • *Drugs have become a serious problem in a lot of schools.* • *The possession of drugs is a very serious offence.* • *The situation is very serious and yet the government doesn't seem to be taking any notice.* • *He's been taken to hospital where his condition is described as serious but stable.* • Ⓓ

se·ri·ous·ly /£ˈsɪə·ri·ə·sli, $ˈsɪr·i-/ *adv* • *Badly cooked shellfish can make you seriously ill.* • *You can seriously damage your knees running on roads.* • *He wasn't seriously injured – he just got a few cuts and bruises.*

se·ri·ous·ness /£ˈsɪə·ri·ə·snəs, $ˈsɪr·i-/ *n* [U] • *I don't think he has any notion of the seriousness of the situation.*

se·ri·ous NOT JOKING /£ˈsɪə·ri·əs, $ˈsɪr·i-/ *adj* not joking or intended to amuse • *Please don't laugh – I'm being serious.* • *Ian's got such a strange manner – I can never tell if he's being serious.* • *He was wearing a very serious expression and I knew something was wrong.* • *Are you telling me that ball was outside the line? You can't be serious* (= It was not)*!* • *On the surface it's a very funny novel but it does have a more serious underlying theme.* • *I know he's amusing when he's in company, but he has a more serious side to him in private.* • A serious person is quiet, thinks deeply about things and does not laugh a lot: *I remember her as a very serious child – she always looked worried.* • *"You cannot be serious!"* (phrase used by the tennis player John McEnroe, 1980s) • Ⓓ

se·ri·ous·ly /£ˈsɪə·ri·ə·sli, $ˈsɪr·i-/ *adv* • *Seriously, though, did he really say that or are you just being silly?* • *No, seriously, I know it sounds funny, but it's no joke when you're woken up at three o'clock every morning.* • *Are you seriously trying to tell me that if you were offered all that money you'd refuse?* • *You're not seriously thinking of leaving, are you?*

se·ri·ous·ness /£ˈsɪə·ri·ə·snəs, $ˈsɪr·i-/ *n* [U] • **In all** *seriousness now – joking aside – I do think there's a problem here that we've got to get sorted.*

se·ri·ous NEEDING ATTENTION /£ˈsɪə·ri·əs, $ˈsɪr·i-/ *adj* [before n] needing complete attention • *That's quite an interesting job offer – I'd give it some serious consideration if I were you.* • *I've been doing some serious thinking recently about what I want out of life.* • *We've got some serious talking to do, you and me.* • Ⓓ

se·ri·ous·ly /£ˈsɪə·ri·ə·sli, $ˈsɪr·i-/ *adv* • If you **take** a subject, situation or person seriously you consider it or them to be important and worth a lot of attention or respect: *The police have to take any terrorist threat seriously.* ○ *You don't take anything seriously, do you? It's all one big joke to you.* ○ *She's sick of being seen as a sex symbol and wants to be taken seriously as an actress.* ○ *These young actors take them***selves** *so seriously!*

se·ri·ous DETERMINED /£ˈsɪə·ri·əs, $ˈsɪr·i-/ *adj* [after v] determined to follow a particular plan of action • *If you're serious* **about** *becoming an actress you need proper training.* • *Is she serious* **about** *going to live abroad?* • If two people who have a loving relationship are serious **about** each other they intend to stay with each other for a long time and possibly marry: *She's had a lot of boyfriends but Simon's the only one she's been serious about.* • Ⓓ

se·ri·ous EXTREME /£ˈsɪə·ri·əs, $ˈsɪr·i-/ *adj infml* extreme in degree or amount • *We did some fairly serious walking over the weekend.* • *Hey, that's a serious* (= very short) *haircut you've got there!* • *I mean we're talking serious* (= a large amount of) *money, right?* • Serious can mean very good of its type: *This is a serious wine, Annabelle, you've just got to try some.* ○ *That's a serious jacket, man!* • Ⓓ

se·ri·ous·ly /£ˈsɪə·ri·ə·sli, $ˈsɪr·i-/ *adv infml* • Seriously means very: *They do some seriously good desserts there.* ○ *That boy is seriously stupid.* • LP **Very, completely**

ser·mon /£ˈsɜː·mən, $ˈsɜːr-/ *n* [C] a part of a Christian church ceremony in which a priest gives a talk on a religious or moral subject, often based on something written in the Bible • *The Reverend William Cronshaw* **delivered/preached** *the sermon.* • *Today's sermon was* **on** *the importance of compassion.* • *(disapproving)* A sermon is also a long talk in which someone advises other people how they should behave in order to be better people: *I really don't think it's a politician's job to go delivering sermons on public morality.* • *"Tongues in trees, books in* *the running brooks / Sermons in stones, and good in everything"* (Shakespeare, As You Like It 2.1)

ser·mon·ize, *Br and Aus usually* **-ise** /£ˈsɜː·mə·naɪz, $ˈsɜːr-/ *v* [I] *disapproving* • To sermonize is to give a long talk to people, telling them how they should behave in order to be better people: *My grandmother's all right until she starts sermonizing and then she's unbearable.*

ser·pent /£ˈsɜː·pᵊnt, $ˈsɜːr-/ *n* [C] *old use* a snake

ser·pen·tine /£ˈsɜː·pᵊn·taɪn, $ˈsɜːr-/ *adj literary* • Serpentine means curving and twisting like a snake: *We followed the serpentine course of the river.* ○ *I watched his serpentine movements on the dance-floor.* ○ *(fig.) His explanation was even more serpentine* (= complicated and difficult to follow).

ser·rat·ed /£sɪˈreɪ·tɪd, $-t̬ɪd/ *adj* [not gradable] having a row of sharp points along the edge • *You really need a knife with a serrated edge for cutting bread.*

ser·ried /ˈser·id/ *adj literary* pressed closely together, usually in lines • *The soldiers marched past in their serried* **ranks**. • *We flew over the city with its serried* **ranks** *of identical grey houses.*

se·rum /£ˈsɪə·rəm, $ˈsɪr·əm/ *n pl* **serums** or **sera** /£ˈsɪə·rə, $ˈsɪr·ə/ the watery, colourless part of the blood, or this liquid taken from an animal and put into a human in order to fight an infection • *cholesterol levels in blood serum* [U] • *an anti-venom serum* [C]

ser·vant /£ˈsɜː·vᵊnt, $ˈsɜːr-/ *n* [C] a person who is permanently employed in another person's house, doing jobs such as cooking and cleaning • *In the 19th century, far more people had servants than is the case now.* • *The novel is really about the master-servant relationships.*

ser·vice /£ˈsɜː·vɪs, $ˈsɜːr-/ *n* [U] • A person who is **in** service is employed as a servant: *My grandmother was in service for most of her life.*

serve *obj* DEAL WITH CUSTOMER /£sɜːv, $sɜːrv/ *v* [T] (esp. of a person working in a shop, restaurant or hotel) to deal with (a customer) by taking their order, showing or selling them goods etc. • *Are you being served, madam?* • *If I'm not served within the next five minutes I'm leaving.* • *That's the restaurant in which they refused to serve Giles because he was abusive to one of the waiters.*

ser·vice /£ˈsɜː·vɪs, $ˈsɜːr-/ *n* [U] • *The only trouble with this café is that the service is so slow.* • *Can I have some service please – I've been waiting here fifteen minutes!* • *Is service* (= an amount of money charged for dealing with the customer) *included in the bill or should I leave the waiter a tip?* • A **service charge** is an amount of money added to the basic price of something to pay for the cost of dealing with the customer: *With the service charge, our restaurant bill came to more than £120.* ○ *If you order the tickets by phone you have to pay a $2 service charge as well as $13·50 for each ticket.*

serve *(obj)* PROVIDE FOOD/DRINK /£sɜːv, $sɜːrv/ *v* to provide (food or drinks) • *Do they serve meals in the bar?* [T] • *Breakfast is served in the restaurant between 7.00 a.m. and 9 a.m.* [T] • *Alcohol will not be served between 3.00 p.m. and 8.00 p.m.* [T] • *We would like to remind our customers that the snack bar is now open serving tea, coffee and light snacks.* [T] • *"Dinner is served* (= is ready to eat)*," announced the butler.* [T] • *You can serve* (= put the food onto plates) *since you've got the spoon in your hand.* [I] • *As a first course, we were served quails eggs.* [+ two objects] • *We arrived at the hotel and were served* **with** *champagne and canapés.* [T] • *Coffee was served* **to** *us in tiny little cups.* [T] • *All recipes in this book, unless otherwise stated, will serve* (= be enough for) *4 to 5 people.* [T] • *Serve the tarts hot with custard or whipped cream.* [T + obj + adj] • *Drain the pasta, transfer to a warmed bowl, stir in the sauce and serve.* [I] • *It says on the packet serve hot or cold.* [I] • If you serve **up** or **out** food you put it on plates for people to eat: *If you can get everyone to sit at the table I'm ready to serve up the food.* [M] • A serving **bowl/spoon** or other utensil is one that is intended to be used for holding food before it is put onto plates, or for putting food onto plates. • LP› **Two objects** PIC› **Cutlery**

serv·ing /£ˈsɜː·vɪŋ, $ˈsɜːr-/ *n* [C] • A serving is an amount of one type of food which is given to one person: *The quantities given in the recipe should be enough for four servings.*

serv·er /£ˈsɜː·vər, $ˈsɜːr·vɚ/ *n* [C] • A server is a utensil that is used for serving food: **salad** *servers* • PIC› **Cutlery**

serve *(obj)* WORK /£sɜːv, $sɜːrv/ *v* to work (for); to do your duty to • *He served* **in** *the army in India for twenty years.* [I] • *She has served* **on** *the committee for the last fifteen years.* [I] • *The younger Mr Wang will continue to serve* **on** *the board.* [I] • *He served* **under** *Harold Wilson for two years as Transport Minister.* [I] • *Believe it or not, I joined the police force because I wanted to serve the public.* [T] • *The civil service is there to serve the public.* [T] • *There's no doubt that these deals serve the West's interests.* [T] • *(fig.) I think he was called Brian, if my memory serves me* **(right)** (= is correct). [T] • *(infml)* If you say that something bad **serves** someone **right**, you mean that they deserve it: *"He hit me!" "It serves you right. You shouldn't have been rude to him."* • *"They also serve who only stand and wait"* (John Milton in the poem *On his blindness*, 1673)

ser·vant /£ˈsɜː·vᵊnt, $ˈsɜːr-/ *n* [C] • **Public** *servants/ Servants of the state* (= People who work for the government) *should be incorruptible.*

ser·vice /£ˈsɜː·vɪs, $ˈsɜːr-/ *n* • *She was given the award for a lifetime of* **public** *service.* [U] • *The battleship has been* **in** *service* (= used) *since 1965.* [U] • *(fig.) These boots have* **seen** *some service*/**given good** *service* (= have been used over a long period)*!* [U] • *(fml) I may be needing the services* **of** *a surveyor* (= I might need one to do some work for me) *soon as I'm buying a house.* [C] • *You've* **done me a great** *service* (= helped me greatly) – *I'm really very grateful.* [C] • *"Thank you so much for doing that bit of shopping for me." "It's a pleasure – I'm just glad to have* **been of** *service* (= helped in some way)*."* [U] • *(humorous) "Could you fetch me my glasses from the kitchen, Rozzie?"* **"At your** *service* (= It is my duty to help you), *madam."* [U] • A service is also a government department that is responsible for a particular area of activity: *the diplomatic service* • *the security services* [C]

serv·ing /£ˈsɜː·vɪŋ, $ˈsɜːr-/ *adj* [before n; not gradable] • *The new government is packed with serving and retired military officers.* • *Sir Wynn is the* **longest***-serving minister at the Welsh Office.*

serve *obj* SPEND TIME /£sɜːv, $sɜːrv/ *v* [T] to spend a period of time doing something • *He served four years* **in prison** *for robbery.* • *After he'd served his* **apprenticeship** *he found work overseas.* • *Osman, aged 59, is the longest-serving prisoner in Britain.* • *How many* **terms** *did he serve as president?* • *(infml) He's* **serving time** (= in prison) *for drugs offences.*

serve *(obj)* HELP ACHIEVE /£sɜːv, $sɜːrv/ *v* to help achieve or result in (something, esp. something useful or positive) • *The minister said she did not consider that a public enquiry would serve any useful* **purpose**. [T] • *What possible* **purpose** *do eyebrows serve, I wonder?* [T] • *Mr Sykes said that unions served a useful* **function** *for both workers and management.* [T] • *The problem with roadblocks is that they only serve* **as** *a deterrent for as long as they are in place.* [I] • *The judge said that the fine would serve* **as** *a warning to other motorists who drove without due care and attention.* [I] • *Menendez's fate in the last election, she said, would serve* **as** *a reminder to all politicians that popularity does not last.* [I] • *In the absence of anything better the settee would serve* (= could be used) **as** *a bed for a couple of nights.* [I] • *Nothing serves* **to** *explain the violent fighting we have seen recently.* [+ to infinitive] • *My umbrella will serve* **for** *a weapon, should the occasion arise.* [I] • *Is this old penknife all you've got? It will serve, I suppose, but I really need something sharper.* [I]

serve *obj* PROVIDE SOMETHING NECESSARY /£sɜːv, $sɜːrv/ *v* [T] to provide (an area or group of people) with something that is needed • *Two other Church of England schools would continue to serve the inner city.* • *London's hospitals, so says the report, are out of touch with the communities that they serve.*

ser·vice /£ˈsɜː·vɪs, $ˈsɜːr-/ *n* • A service is a system or organization that provides for a basic public need: *the ambulance/health/postal/prison service* • *a counselling service* [C] • Service can also refer to the operation of that system: *There isn't any railway service on Christmas day.* [U] ○ *We hope to be* **operating** *a normal service as soon as possible.* [C] • A service **industry** or the service **sector** is an area of business that provides something for people but does not result in the production of goods: *More than 70% of jobs in the borough are in service industries, ranging from hotels to banking.* • A **service road** is a small road which is parallel to a bigger road and is used mainly by people travelling locally. • A **service station** is building or group of buildings near a road which sells fuel and might also sell food, drinks and other items that people want on their journey, or *(Am)* which repairs cars. • PIC› **Motorway**

ser·vi·ces /£ˈsɜː·vɪs·ɪz, $ˈsɜːr-/ *pl n* • Services are an establishment beside a large road at which fuel, food, drink and other items that people want on their journey are sold: *The sign said 'Next services 5 miles'/'No services on motorway'.*

serve *(obj)* [HIT BALL] /£sɜːv, $sɜːrv/ *v* (in tennis and other RACKET sports) to hit the ball to the other player as a way of starting the game • *Whose turn is it to serve?* [I] • *That's the third ace you've served this game.* [T]

serve /£sɜːv, $sɜːrv/ *n* [C] • *It's your serve.* • *He has a very strong serve and I just can't seem to return it.*

ser·vice /£ˈsɜː·vɪs, $ˈsɜːr-/ *n* [U] • Service means the same as the noun 'serve': *Whose service is it?* ○ *She's got a very fast service.*

serve *obj* [DELIVER DOCUMENT] /£sɜːv, $sɜːrv/ *v* [T] *law* to deliver (a legal document) to (someone), demanding that they go to a court of law or that they obey an order • *Less than two weeks ago Gough finally served* **a writ on** *Slater, claiming damages for alleged loss of royalties.* • *Each person served* **with** *a summons will be given six weeks before they have to appear in the magistrates court.*

serv·er /£ˈsɜː·vəʳ, $ˈsɜːr·vɚ/ *n* [C] *specialized* a central computer from which other computers obtain information • *a client/network/file server*

ser·vice [ARMED FORCES] /£ˈsɜː·vɪs, $ˈsɜːr-/ *n* (work in) the armed forces • *He joined the air force in 1964 and spent ten years* **in** *the service.* [C] • *All men under thirty-five were told to report for* **military** *service within three days.* [U] • *Ten men died and thirteen others were injured* **on active** *service* (=while fighting). [U] • *Service personnel are subject to the Official Secrets Act.* • *I hadn't planned a career in* **the services** (=the army, navy and/or air force). • (J) (KOR)

ser·vice·man *(pl* **-men***)*, **ser·vice·wo·man** *(pl* **-women***)* /£ˈsɜː·vɪs·mən, $ˈsɜːr-, -ˌwʊm·ən/ *n* [C] • *Yesterday's announcement brings to twelve the number of British servicemen* (=men in the armed forces) *killed on active service in this region.*

ser·vice [RELIGIOUS CEREMONY] /£ˈsɜː·vɪs, $ˈsɜːr-/ *n* [C] a formal religious ceremony • *A* **memorial** *service is being* **held** *on Sunday for victims of the bomb explosion.* • *We always go to the Christmas Eve service at the cathedral.* • *Do you remember Albert's funeral? It was a lovely service, wasn't it.* • (J) (KOR)

ser·vice *obj* [REPAIR] /£ˈsɜː·vɪs, $ˈsɜːr-/ *v* [T] to examine (a machine) and repair any faulty parts • *I'm taking the car in to have it serviced this afternoon.* • (J) (KOR)

ser·vice /£ˈsɜː·vɪs, $ˈsɜːr-/ *n* [C] *esp. Br* • *He took the car in for a service yesterday and there's about £600 worth of repairs to be done.*

ser·vic·ing /£ˈsɜː·vɪs·ɪŋ, $ˈsɜːr-/ *n* [U] *esp. Am* • *Dad brought the car in for servicing, so she won't be able to drive us today.*

ser·vice [FOOD UTENSILS] /£ˈsɜː·vɪs, $ˈsɜːr-/ *n* [C] a set of items such as plates, cups or other utensils that are used in providing and eating food • *a 24-piece dinner service* • *a tea service* • *a silver service* • (J) (KOR)

ser·vice·a·ble /£ˈsɜː·vɪ·sə·bl̩, $ˈsɜːr-/ *adj* suitable for the situation in which something is used; effective • *You're wearing some serviceable-looking footwear, Johnny.* • (I)

ser·vi·ette /£ˌsɜː·viˈet, $ˌsɜːr-/ *n* [C] *esp. Br* a square piece of cloth or paper used while you are eating for protecting your clothes or cleaning your mouth and fingers; a NAPKIN • *paper serviettes*

ser·vile /£ˈsɜː·vaɪl, $ˈsɜːr·vəl/ *adj disapproving* too eager to serve and please someone else in a way that shows a lack of respect for yourself • *As a waiter you want to be pleasant to people and tend to their needs without appearing totally servile.*

ser·vil·i·ty /£sɜːˈvɪl·ɪ·ti, $sɜːrˈvɪl·ə·t̬i/ *n* [U] *fml disapproving* • *She found the servility of the hotel staff embarrassing.*

ser·vi·tude /£ˈsɜː·vɪ·tjuːd, $ˈsɜːr·vɪ·tuːd/ *n* [U] *fml* the state of being under the control of someone else and of having no freedom • *In the past, the majority of women were consigned to a lifetime of servitude and poverty.*

ser·vo /£ˈsɜː·vəʊ, $ˈsɜːr·voʊ/ *n* [C] *pl* **servos** *specialized* a SERVOMOTOR or SERVOMECHANISM

ser·vo·mech·a·ni·sm /£ˈsɜː·vəʊˌmek·ə·nɪ·zəm, $ˌsɜːr·voʊˈmek-/ *n* [C] *specialized* a system that uses a small amount of power to control the power of a larger machine

ser·vo·mo·tor /£ˈsɜː·vəʊˌməʊ·təʳ, $ˈsɜːr·voʊˌmoʊ·t̬ɚ/ *n* [C] *specialized* a motor which provides the power for a SERVOMECHANISM

ses·a·me /ˈses·ə·mi/ *n* [U] a herb grown for its small oval seeds and its oil • *sesame oil/seeds* • *"Open, sesame"* (magic words to open a door in the traditional story *Ali Baba and the Forty Thieves*)

ses·sion [FORMAL MEETING] /ˈseʃ·ən/ *n* a formal meeting or series of meetings of an organization such as a parliament or a law court • *The* **parliamentary** *session is due to end on May 27th.* [C] • *The UN Security Council met* **in** *emergency session to discuss the crisis.* [U]

ses·sion [ACTIVITY] /ˈseʃ·ən/ *n* [C] a period of time or meeting arranged for a particular activity • *The 21-year-old runner twisted his ankle in a* **training** *session last Friday.* • *As the European heads of state gathered the press were allowed in for a* **photo** *session.* • *The vocals were added at a* **recording** *session the following Thursday.* • *There'll be a question-and-answer session at the end of this morning's lecture.* • *We're having a brainstorming session this afternoon to try to get a few ideas together for the project.* • *(infml) Rob and I had a* **heavy** *session last night* (=we drank a lot of alcohol), *and my head's a bit delicate this morning.*

ses·sion [COLLEGE PERIOD] /ˈseʃ·ən/ *n* [C] *Am and Scot Eng* (at a college) any of the periods of time that a teaching year or day is divided into, or the teaching year itself • *The session begins on 1 October.* [C] • *Access to these buildings is restricted when school is* **in** *session.* [U]

set *obj* [POSITION] /set/ *v* [T always + adv/prep] **setting**, *past* **set** to put (something) in the stated place or position • *He set a vase of flowers* **on** *the table.* • *The child set one toy brick carefully* **on top of** *another.* • *Our cat brought in a dead mouse and set it proudly* **in front of** *us.* • *The campsite is set* (=is in a position which is) **in** *the middle of a pine forest.* • *Our house is set* **back from** (=is in a position which is away from) *the road.* • If a story, film, etc. is set in a particular time or place, the action in it happens in that time or place: *'West Side Story' is set* **in** *New York* **in** *the late 1950s.* ○ *The film 'Gone with the Wind' is set* **against the background of** (=during the events of) *the American Civil War.* • If you set some time **aside/on one side/to one side**, you make sure that you are able to use it for a special purpose: *He always sets some* **time** *aside every day to read to his children.* [M] • To set money **aside/on one side/to one side** is to save it: *We try and set aside a bit of money every week.* [M] • If you set a disagreement or problem **aside/on one side/to one side**, you forget it or ignore it: *If we're going to work together successfully, we'll have to set our* **differences** *aside.* [M] • To set a matter **aside/on one side/to one side** is also temporarily not deal with it: *Setting aside the question of cost, what do you think of the idea in principle?* [M] • To **set aside** a decision or a judgment, esp. a legal one, which someone else has made, or to **set** a decision of this kind **aside**, is to state that it was wrong or not reasonable: *The Court of Appeal set aside his conviction.* • To set **down** a plane is to land it: *It will be difficult for the pilot to set the plane down in that small space.* [M] • If a vehicle sets **down** a passenger, it stops so that the passenger can get out: *The taxi set us down a long way from our hotel, and we had to walk.* [M] • To set something **down** is also to write or print it: *The rules of the club are set down in the members' handbook.* [M] • If you **set** something **against** something else, you consider the first thing in relation to the second: *You have to set the advantages of the scheme against the disadvantages.* ○ *The cost of business travel and entertainment can be set against* **tax** (=can be recorded as an item on which tax does not have to be paid). • If something is **set apart (from** something else), it is shown to be different from something else, esp. by having a particular good characteristic: *The separation of words into sense groupings is one of the things that sets this dictionary apart.* ○ *What set her apart* **from** *the other candidates for the job was that she had a lot of original ideas.* • If you **set back** something/**set** something **back**, you delay it: *The opening of the new swimming pool has been set back by a few weeks.* ○ See also SET BACK; SETBACK. • To **set back** something/**set** something **back** is also to cause it to stop advancing: *This result has set back their* **chances** *of winning the competition.* ○ *This act will set the nationalist* **cause** *back by several years.* ○ See also SET BACK; SETBACK. • To **set out** something/**set** something **out** is to arrange it: *The market was full of brightly coloured vegetables set out on stalls.* ○ *Every evening Michael sets out the breakfast things on the table, ready for the morning.* ○ *The grounds of the house are attractively set out.* • If you are **set to work**, you are given work to do: *When I started my new job, I was just set to work without anyone explaining to me what I was* *supposed to be doing.* • To **set up** something/**set** something **up** is to prepare it for use, esp. by putting parts together: *We arrived early so that we could set up our display for the flower show.* • **Set-aside** is land for which farmers are paid in order not to grow crops on it. • (I)

set·ting /£'set·ɪŋ, $'seṭ-/ *n* [C usually sing] • The setting of a house or other building is its position: *The villa* **has** *a beautiful setting overlooking the sea.* ○ *Their cottage is* **in** *an idyllic rural setting.* ○ *This would be a lovely setting* **for** (= place to have) *a wedding.* • *After years of working in an office setting* (= his job being in an office), *David has now got a job out of doors.* • The setting of a book, film, play, etc. is the time and the place in which the action of the book etc. happens: *The film '2001' has a spaceship as its setting.* ○ *The play* **has** *its setting* **in** *a wartime prison camp.*

set *obj* CONDITION /set/ *v* [T] **setting**, *past* **set** to cause to be in the stated condition or situation • *It is believed that the building was set* **alight/ablaze/on fire** *deliberately.* • *My new boss has set a lot of changes* **in motion** *in our department.* • *The government believes that these measures will set the country* **on the road to** *economic recovery.* • *After years in prison, the men who had wrongfully been found guilty of the bombing were finally set* **free**. [+ obj + adj] • *If I've made a mistake, then it's up to me to set it* **right** (= correct it). [+ obj + adj] • *Thank you for setting me* **straight** (= correcting my mistake) *about the time of next week's meeting.* [+ obj + adj] • If you set someone or something do**ing** something, you cause them to start doing it: *His remarks set me thinking.* [+ obj + v-*ing*] ○ *The thunderstorm set the radio crackling.* [+ obj + v-*ing*] • If something sets someone **against** someone else, it causes them to oppose that person: *Something happened which set Julie against her father.* ○ *This war has set neighbour against neighbour.* • If someone **sets the world** */(Br also)* **the Thames on fire/alight/ablaze**, they are very noticeable and attract attention because they are successful. The names of other places are sometimes also used instead of 'the world': *He's a good student, but I don't think he's going to set the world on fire.* ○ *The band really set the stadium alight with their concert last night.* • (I)

set *obj* GET READY /set/ *v* [T] **setting**, *past* **set** to get (something) ready so that it comes into operation or can be used • *We've got mice in our cellar, so we've set a* **trap**. • *I don't know how to set the cruise control on the car.* • *The heating is set* **to** *come on at 5.00 p.m.* [+ obj + *to* infinitive] • *Have you set* **up** *the video recorder* (= got it ready so that it comes into operation or can be used)*?* [M] • *I usually set my watch* (= make it show the right time) **by** *the time signal on the radio.* • *He set the alarm* **for** (= arranged the controls on it so that it would ring at) *7.00 a.m.* • *Will you set the table* (= put plates and utensils on it ready for use), *please?* • When someone sets a stage, they put furniture and other items on it so that it represents the time and the place in which the action of a play, film or television programme is going to happen: *During the interval the stage was set* **for** *the second act.* • If you say that **the scene/stage is set**, or that something has **set the scene/stage**, it means that conditions have been made advantageous for something to happen, or that something is likely to happen: *The stage looks set* **for** *a repeat of last year's final.* ○ *This weekend's talks between the two leaders have set the scene* **for** *a peace agreement to be reached.* • (I)

set /set/ *adj* [after v] • *Shall we go now – is everyone* **(all)** *set* (= ready)*?* • *Is everything* **(all)** *set* **for** *the party?* • *At the beginning of a race, the starter often says "On your marks,* **get** *set, go" or "Ready,* **get** *set, go".* • *We were just* **getting** *set* **to** *leave when Ben said he had something important to tell us.* [+ *to* infinitive] • *Gemma is set* (= has made the necessary preparations) **to** *go to college in September.* [+ *to* infinitive] • *He looks set* (= likely) **to** *become world champion again this year.* [+ *to* infinitive] • *(Br) The weather looks set* **fair** (= seems likely to be good) *for the rest of the week.*

set /set/ *n* [C] • The set of a play, film or television programme is the furniture and other items put on a stage to represent the place in which the events are happening, or the place where a film is being made: *a film set* ○ *a stage set* ○ *a set designer* ○ *As the curtain rose, the audience applauded the set.* ○ *After a long day* **on** *the set, the actors were all very tired.*

set·ting /£'set·ɪŋ, $'seṭ-/ *n* [C] • A setting on a machine is a position into which the controls can be arranged: *My hairdryer has three settings – high, medium and low.* ○ *This camera is automatic, so you don't need to* **adjust** *the setting every time you take a photograph.* • A setting (also **place setting**) is also is also a group of the plates and utensils which one person needs for eating a meal, arranged on a table. • PIC> **Cutlery**

set *obj* ESTABLISH /set/ *v* [T] **setting**, *past* **set** to establish or cause to exist • *The school has been criticized for failing to set high enough* **standards** *for its students.* • *The government has set new* **limits** *on public spending.* • *The* **fashion** *for short skirts was first set in the 1960s.* • *Lewis has set/(Br also) set* **up** *a new world* **record**. • *The court's decision has set/(Br also) set* **up** *a legal* **precedent**. • *Parents should set their children a good* **example**/*set a good* **example to** *their children.* [+ two objects] • *He's set himself the* **goal/target**/*set the* **goal/target for** *himself of making his first million by the time he's 30.* [+ two objects] • *My teacher has set me a* **deadline**/*set a* **deadline for** *me of next Friday for handing in my essay.* [+ two objects] • *This painting is so valuable, I wouldn't like to try to set a price* **on** *it* (= decide or guess what its price should be). • (I)

set *(obj)* FIX /set/ *v* **setting**, *past* **set** to fix or make firm • *Has a* **date/time** *been set for the meeting yet?* [T] • **Bail** *was set* **at** *$5000.* [T] • *The* **price** *of the house has been set* **at** *£125 000.* [T] • *Each October, the company sets its* **budget** *for the following year.* [T] • If a precious stone is set **in/into** a piece of jewellery, or a piece of jewellery is set **with** a precious stone, the stone is fixed firmly to the piece of jewellery: *a gold tiepin with a diamond set into it* [T] ○ *a brooch set with rubies and pearls* [T] • When a doctor sets a broken bone, he or she puts it into a fixed position so that it will heal. [T] • When a broken bone sets, it heals in a fixed position: *Your leg is setting nicely, Mr Hirst.* [I] • If you have your **hair** set, you have it arranged while it is wet so that it will be fixed in a particular style when it is dry. [T] • If you set a part of your body, you tighten the muscles around it in order to show that you are determined about something: *"I'm never going back to him," she said, setting her* **jaw** *firmly.* [T] ○ *His face was set in determination.* [T] • If a liquid or soft material sets, it becomes firm or hard: *Leave the jelly in the fridge to set.* [I] ○ *Don't walk on the concrete until it has set.* [I] • *"This precious stone set in the silver sea ... this England"* (Shakespeare, Richard II 2.1) • (I)

set /set/ *adj* • *My piano teacher says that I should practise for a set number of hours a week.* • *Small babies have no set routine.* • *If I go out in the evening, my parents say I have to be home by a set time.* • *The restaurant does a set lunch* (= a meal which is offered at a fixed price, but with little or no choice about what you have to eat) *on Sundays.* • *The receptionist had a bright set* (= fixed and not sincere) *smile on his face, but I could tell that he was bored.* • A set **expression/phrase** is one in which the words are always used in the same order. • If you are set **on/upon** something, you are determined to do it. If you are set **against** it, you are determined not to do it: *Despite all the opposition from her family, she seems set on marrying him.* ○ *Why are you so set against going to college?* ○ *They are* **dead** *set against* (= strongly opposed to) *the plans to close the local hospital.* • *My father has very set opinions/views* (= is not likely to change them). • *As people get older, they often become* **set in** *their* **ways** (= their ideas, habits and ways of living become fixed). • A **set piece** is part of a film, play, etc. which is exciting and attracts attention, but is often not a necessary part of the story or does not cause the story to develop: *The musical has no real story – it just consists of a series of set pieces.*

set /set/ *n* • **The** set **of** a part of your body is the position in which you hold it: *I could tell from the set of his jaw that he was angry.* [U] ○ *She wore a jacket with padded shoulders that made the set of her shoulders look very square.* [U] • A set is the act of having your hair arranged while it is wet so that it becomes fixed in a particular position when it dries: *I'd like to make an appointment for a* **shampoo and** *set, please.* [C]

set·ting /£'set·ɪŋ, $'seṭ-/ *n* [C] • A setting is the piece of metal in a ring, or other item of jewellery, into which a precious stone is fixed: *Her engagement ring consisted of a single diamond in a plain gold setting.* • PIC> **Jewellery**

set *obj* GIVE WORK *esp. Br and Aus* /set/, *Am usually* **as·sign** *v* [T] **setting**, *past* **set** to give or provide (a piece of work) • *The students' examinations are set by people outside their college.* • *I don't like my science teacher – she always sets a lot of homework.* • *We set the kids the task of clearing the snow from the front path.* [+ two objects] • *What books have been set* (= have been chosen for students to study) *for this term?* • (I)

set /set/ *adj* [before n; not gradable] • *The students are reading 'Lord of the Flies' as one of their set* **books/texts** (=books that they have to study) *this year.*

set *obj* [MUSIC] /set/ *v* [T] **setting**, *past* **set** to write or provide music for (a poem or other words) so that they can be sung • *The musical 'Cats' consists of poems by T.S. Eliot set* **to music** *by Andrew Lloyd Webber.* • Ⓘ

set·ting /£'set·ɪŋ, $'seṭ-/ *n* [C] • *He sang Schubert's setting* **of** *a Goethe poem.*

set [SUN] /set/ *v* [I] **setting**, *past* **set** (of the sun, moon or planets) to go down below the HORIZON (=the line at which the Earth seems to join the sky) • *We sat on the beach and watched the sun set.* • *The setting sun cast long shadows across the lawn.* • *(fig.) It used to be said that Britain ruled an empire* **on** *which the sun would never set* (=which would never end). • *"His Majesty's dominions, on which the sun never sets"* (Christopher North in *Noctes Ambrosianae*, 1829) • See also SUNSET. • Ⓘ

set [GROUP] /set/ *n* [C] a group of similar things or people that belong together in some way • *We bought Charles and Mandy a set* **of** *cutlery/a cutlery set as a wedding present.* • *I always keep a set* **of** *tools/a tool set in the back of my car.* • *His job is selling sets* **of** *encyclopaedias.* • *There was an advertisement on the television for a three-CD set* **of** *Cole Porter songs.* • *A new* **box(ed)** *set* **of** *Beatles music has just been released on CD and cassette.* • *The doctor said that he hadn't seen this particular set* **of** *symptoms before.* • *We need to establish a new set* **of** *priorities.* • A set is also a number of items or pieces of equipment needed for a particular activity, esp. playing a game: *a chess set* ○ *a train set* ○ *a chemistry set* • A set is also a group of people who have similar interests and ways of living: *the fashion set* ○ *the London set* ○ *the tennis set* ○ *She's got in with a very arty set.* ○ *The* **smart** *set is/are going to the Caprice restaurant this season.* [+ sing/pl v] • *(specialized)* In mathematics, a set is a group of objects with stated characteristics. • Ⓘ

set [TELEVISION] /set/ *n* [C] a television • *We need a new* **television** *set.* • *They've got a colour set in their living room and a black-and-white set in their bedroom.* • *There is some interference on the signal – do not adjust your set.* • Ⓘ

set [PART] /set/ *n* [C] a part of a game of tennis, or a musical performance which forms part of a CONCERT, esp. one of **popular music** or jazz • *The person who wins the most sets in tennis wins the match.* • *The American player won the first set by six games to three.* • *They won in* **straight** *sets* (=did not lose any). • If a tennis player **has a set point**, it means that if they win the next point, they will win the set. • *The charity concert in 1985 included sets by many famous rock musicians.* • *The band's opening set lasted 45 minutes.* • Ⓘ

set a·bout *(obj)* [START TO DO] *v prep* to start to do or deal with • *The teacher told the class to work out the area of a circle, but some of them didn't know how to set about* **it**. [T] • *I've no idea how to set about changing a tyre on a car.* [+ v-ing] • *I tried to apologize, but I think I set about* **it** (=dealt with it) *the wrong way.* [T]

set a·bout *obj* [ATTACK] *v prep* [T] *infml* to attack • *Her attacker set about her* **with** *a knife.*

set *obj* **back** *(obj) v adv* [T] *infml* to cost (someone) (a large amount of money) • *Buying that suit must have set you back.* • *That new car looks as if it set you back a bit, Geoff.* • *The holiday set us back over £1000.* • See also **set back** at SET [POSITION]; SETBACK.

set forth *obj*, **set** *obj* **forth** *v adv* [M] *fml for* SET OUT [GIVE DETAILS]

set in *v adv* [I] (of something unpleasant) to begin and to be likely to continue to exist • *We need to have the roof repaired before the bad weather sets in.* • *This rain looks as if it has set in* **for** *the rest of the day.* • *If you get bitten by a dog, you have to make sure the wound is properly cleaned, or an infection could set in.* • *Despair seems to have set in among the England team.* • *After a few days, exhaustion set in and the climbers were forced to give up their attempt to reach the top of the mountain.*

set off/out *v adv* [I] to start a journey • *What time will we have to set off tomorrow?* • *Jenny set off down the road on her new bike.* • *It's time we were setting off* **for** *the station.* • *They've just set off* **on** *a round-the-world cruise.*

set off *obj* [CAUSE] *v adv* [T] to cause (esp. some type of activity or an explosion) to begin or to happen • *The court's initial verdict in the police officers' trial set off serious riots.* [M] • *Reports that a doctor had died from AIDS set off a panic among his former patients.* [M] • *Terrorists set off a bomb in the city centre, killing two children.* [M] • *If you drop a lighted cigarette, you could set off a fire.* [M] • *Somebody set the alarm off* (=made it ring) *on my car.* [M] • To set someone off (doing something) is to cause them to start to do it: *Every time I think about that joke I heard, it sets me off laughing.* [+ obj + v-ing] ○ *She's finally stopped crying – now don't set her off again.*

set off *obj* [MAKE NOTICEABLE], **set** *obj* **off** *v adv* [M] to make (something) look noticeable or attractive by providing a comparison for or CONTRAST with it • *She set off her suntan by wearing a white dress.* • *The blue cushions nicely set off the blue of the chair covers.*

set *obj* **on** *obj* [CAUSE TO ATTACK] *v prep* [T] to cause (someone or something) to attack (someone) • *The security guards set their dogs on the intruders.* • *If you do that again, I'll set my big brother on you!*

set on *obj* [ATTACK], **set u·pon** *obj v prep* [often passive] to attack • *The child was set on by a lion at the zoo.* • *As he left the theatre, the singer was set upon by fans* (=they tried to get hold of him in order to attract his attention).

set out [START ACTION] *v adv* to begin a plan of action, esp. with a particular aim • *She set out* **with** *the aim of becoming the youngest ever winner of the championship.* [I] • *They set out* **to** *discover a cure for cancer.* [+ *to* infinitive] • *He set out* **to** *break the world record for the 1500 metres.* [+ *to* infinitive] • *Like so many young people before them, they set out* **to** *change the world.* [+ *to* infinitive]

set out *obj* [GIVE DETAILS], **set** *obj* **out**, *fml* **set forth** *v adv* [M] to give the details of or to explain (something), esp. in writing, in a clear, reasoned way • *The management board has set out its goals/plans/proposals for the coming year.* • *Your contract will set out the terms and conditions of your employment.* • *The instructions for using the computer are set out in an accompanying handbook.*

set to [START WORKING] *v adv* [I] to start working or dealing with something in an energetic way • *If we all set to, we should be able to finish the job in a week.*

set to [START FIGHTING] *v adv* [I] *infml* to begin to fight • *The boys argued all afternoon, then suddenly they set to with fists, feet and elbows.*

set–to /'set·tuː, ,-'-/ *n* [C] *infml* • A set-to is a short argument or fight: *Dad* **had** *a bit of a set-to* **with** *the neighbours about their playing loud music all the time.* ○ *Tom* **had** *a set-to* **with** *some other kids in the playground at school.*

set up *obj* [ESTABLISH], **set** *obj* **up** *v adv* [M] to establish or arrange • *A committee has been set up to organize social events in the college.* • *She plans to set up her own business.* • *The government has agreed to set up a public enquiry.* • *They've set up a fund for victims of the earthquake.* • *We need to set up a meeting to discuss the proposals.* • *In some people this drug sets up* (=causes) *a reaction.* • If you set someone up, you establish them in a business: *After he left college, his father set him up* **in** *the family business.* ○ *She set* **herself** *up* **as** *an interior designer.* • To set yourself up **as** a particular type of person is also to claim that you are that type of person: *He sets himself up as an expert on vegetable growing, but he doesn't seem to me to know much about it.*

set–up /£'set·ʌp, $'seṭ-/ *n* [C] • *When I started my new job, it took me a while to get used to the set-up* (=way things are organized). • *"Nice little set-up you've got here* (=Things are comfortably and attractively arranged)*," he said as we showed him round the house.*

set up *obj* [EQUIP], **set** *obj* **up** *v adv* [M] to cause to be healthy and strong, or to cause to have what is needed for life • *You need to make sure that you eat well to set yourself up after your illness.* • *I think we're set up* **with** *everything we need for the journey.* • *Winning the lottery has set them up* **for life** (=provided them with all the money they need for the rest of their lives).

set up *obj* [DECEIVE], **set** *obj* **up** *v adv* [M] *infml* to cause (someone) to seem to have done something wrong when they have not, or to deceive (someone) • *They claimed that they weren't selling drugs, but that they'd been set up by the police.* • *We sent in our money in response to an advertisement we saw in the paper, but it turned out that the company didn't really exist and we were just being set up* (=deceived).

set–up /£'set·ʌp, $'seṭ-/ *n* [C] *infml* • *He was arrested following a scuffle with an undercover police officer, which his colleagues say was a secret service set-up* (=had been arranged secretly by them as a trick). • *When drugs were found in her luggage, she claimed it was a set-up.*

set·back /'set·bæk/ *n* [C] something that happens which delays or prevents a process from advancing • *Sally had* *been recovering well from her operation, but yesterday she* **experienced/suffered** *a setback.* • *Their hopes of winning the championship have* **received** *a serious setback.* • *Teachers' opposition to the proposed changes to the education system has been a setback* **for** *the government.* • *There has been a slight/temporary setback* **in** *our plans.* • *These events are a major setback* **to** *the establishment of a peaceful settlement of the conflict.* • See also **set back** at SET [POSITION]; SET BACK.

set·square *Br and Aus* /£'set·skweər, $-skwer/, **tri·an·gle** *n* [C] a flat piece of metal or plastic in the shape of a triangle with one angle of 90°, which is used for drawing angles • Compare T-SQUARE. • [LP]> **Mathematics**

set·tee /set'iː/ *n* [C] a SOFA • *Come and sit next to me* **on** *the settee.* • *(Am)* A settee is also a long wooden seat which has a back.

set·ter /£'set·ər, $'set̬·ɚ/ *n* [C] a long-haired dog, which is sometimes trained to help hunters find birds or animals to shoot. There are various types of setter. • *an Irish setter* • *a red setter* • *When they find an animal for a hunter, setters stand motionless with their noses pointing towards the animal.*

set·tle *(obj)* [MAKE COMFORTABLE] /£'set·l̩, $'set̬-/ *v* [always + adv/prep] to (cause to) get into a comfortable position • *After dinner we settled* **in front of** *the television for the evening.* [I] • *The dentist told her patient to settle* **back** *in the chair.* [I] • *Settle* **down** *on the sofa, and I'll bring you a cup of tea.* [I] • *He settled him***self down** *with a newspaper, and waited for the train to arrive.* [T] • If you **settle down** in, or **settle into**, somewhere, you become familiar with it and feel comfortable in it: *She quickly settled down in her new house/job/school.* ○ *It took Ed a long time to settle into living in London.* • To **settle in** is to become familiar with a new house, job, school, etc., and to feel comfortable and happy in it: *Once we've settled in, you must come round for dinner.* ○ *It takes time for the children to settle in at the beginning of a new school year.* • If you **settle in** someone/**settle** someone **in**, you help them become familiar with a new job, place, school, etc.: *The nurse will be with you soon – she's settling a new patient in at the moment.*

set·tled /£'set·l̩d, $'set̬-/ *adj* [after v] • *Now that the children are settled at school* (= have become familiar with it and feel comfortable and happy there), *we don't really want to move again.* • *Although I worked there for over a year, I never really felt settled.*

set·tle *(obj)* [QUIET] /£'set·l̩, $'set̬-/ *v* to (cause to) become quiet and calm • *He's one of those very active children who finds it difficult to settle.* [I] • *The weather is expected to settle towards the end of the week.* [I] • *I'll call you back as soon as I've settled the children for the night.* [T] • *Before a performance, she takes three deep breaths to settle her nerves.* [T] • *I need something to settle my stomach after drinking so much alcohol last night.* [T] • *We're very busy this week, but things should settle* **(down)** *a bit after the weekend.* [I] • *The teacher told the children to settle* **down** *and get on with their work.* [I] • *They settled* **down** *to watch* (= became quiet and calm in order to give all their attention to) *the film.* [I] • *(Br and Aus) Joe's parents are very worried about him because he doesn't seem to be able to settle* **to** (= to give his whole attention to) *anything.* [I]

set·tled /£'set·l̩d, $'set̬-/ *adj* • *It looks as if we are in for a settled spell* (= as if the weather will be calm) *this week.*

set·tle *(obj)* [AGREE] /£'set·l̩, $'set̬-/ *v* to reach a decision or an agreement (about), or to end (a disagreement) • *We might go to London for the weekend, but it's not settled yet.* [T] • *Good, that's all settled – you send out the invitations for the party, and I'll organize the food.* [T] • *They haven't yet settled* **wh***en the wedding is going to be.* [+ *wh-* word] • **It***'s been settled* **that** *Jake will present the report to the committee.* [+ *that* clause] • *"The tickets are £40 each." "Well,* **that** *settles* **it/that** *then – I can't afford that much."* [T] • *I'd like to get this matter settled* **once and for all** (= to reach a final decision on it). [T] • *Have you settled* (= decided) **on/upon** *a name for the baby?* [I] • If you settle **for** something, you agree to it, or decide to have it, or accept it, although it might not be exactly what you want: *I'll settle for the chicken and chips.* [I] ○ *He never settles for second best.* [I] ○ *They were hoping to sell their car for £2000, but settled* **for** *£1500.* [I] • To settle something is also to arrange it: *The details of the contract have not yet been settled.* [T] ○ *Three officials in the US Embassy were told they had a week to settle their* **affairs** *and leave.* [T] • *Our lawyer advised us that it would be better to settle* **out of court** (= reach an agreement in a legal case without it being decided in a court of law). [I] • *The management/workers are expected to agree to settle* (= reach an agreement or end their disagreement) *today.* [I] • *It took months to settle* (= bring to an end) *the dispute/strike.* [T] • *My father and I have agreed finally to settle our* **differences** (= stop arguing). [T] • *(fml)* To **settle** your **affairs**, is to decide what will happen to your possessions after your death, usually by making a legal document. • If you **settle a score/settle (old) scores (with** someone), you harm them because they have harmed you in the past: *The President used his speech to settle some old scores with his opponents.*

set·tle·ment /£'set·l̩.mənt, $'set̬-/ *n* • *Following the settlement* **of** (= the agreement ending) *the strike, the train service is now back to normal.* [U] • *It now seems unlikely that it will be possible to* **negotiate** *a peaceful settlement* **of** *the conflict.* [C] • *We hope to be able to* **reach** *a settlement* **with** *the strikers soon.* [C] • *(esp. Br) The government is urging companies to keep their pay settlements* (= agreements about how much workers will be paid) *low this year.* [C] • *As part of their divorce settlement, Geoff agreed to let Polly keep the house.* [C] • A settlement can be an arrangement to end a disagreement involving a law having been broken, without taking it to a court of law. It is also an amount of money paid as part of such an arrangement: *They* **reached** *an* **out-of-court** *settlement.* [C] ○ *The actor accepted a settlement* **of** *£100 000 from the newspaper.* [C]

set·tle *(obj)* [PAY] /£'set·l̩, $'set̬-/ *v* to pay (esp. money owed or claimed) • *Please settle your* **account/bill** *without further delay.* [T] • *It took the insurance company months to settle my* **claim.** [T] • *I don't know when I'm going to be able to settle all my* **debts.** [T] • *(fml) Payment of your account is now overdue, and we must ask you to settle* (= pay the money you owe) *immediately.* [I] • *Would you like to settle* **up** (= pay the money you owe) *now, sir?* [I] • *You buy the tickets and I'll settle* **(up) with** (= pay what I owe) *you later.* [I] • *(law)* If someone settles money or property **on** someone, they formally give it to them: *When my uncle died, he settled £1000 a year on me.* [T] • *(fig.)* If you **settle an account (with** someone), you harm them in some way because they have harmed you in the past: *This match will be an opportunity for France to settle their account with Brazil.* [T] ○ *Police think that the killings may be a result of accounts being settled between local gangs.* [T]

set·tle·ment /£'set·l̩.mənt, $'set̬-/ *n* • *The settlement* (= paying) **of** *his debts took him several months.* [U] • *I enclose a cheque* **in** *settlement* (= as payment) **of** *your claim.* [U] • *We try to send all settlements* (= money owed) *out as soon as possible after receiving the claims.* [C] • *(law) Her mother made a settlement* **on** *her* (= made a formal arrangement to give her money) *when she started college.* [C]

set·tle *(obj)* [LIVE] /£'set·l̩, $'set̬-/ *v* to go and live (in), esp. permanently • *After they got married, they settled* **in** *Brighton.* [I always + adv/prep] • *These people are descendants of migrants who settled* (= went, esp. from another country, to establish a new place to live) *the continent some 40 000 years ago.* [T] • *America was first settled* (= people went, esp. from another country, to establish a new place to live there) *by people who came across from Asia over 25 000 years ago.* [T] • If you **settle down**, you go and live permanently in one place, esp. because you have responsibilities such as a job or a family: *Eventually I'd like to settle down and have a family, but not yet.*

set·tled /£'set·l̩d, $'set̬-/ *adj* • *After many years of travelling around, we're now enjoying a more settled* (= living in one place) *life.*

set·tle·ment /£'set·l̩.mənt, $'set̬-/ *n* • *A large Roman settlement* (= a place where people lived during that period in history) *has been discovered just outside the town.* [C] • *There has been continuous settlement* (= There have been people living) *in this area since the 16th century.* [U] • *Many Native Americans were killed during the settlement* **of** *the American West by Europeans* (= the process of people from Europe going to establish new places to live there) *in the nineteenth century.* [U]

set·tler /£'set·lər, $'set̬-/ *n* [C] • *Some of the earliest free settlers in Australia* (= people who went esp. from another country to establish new places to live there) *were sheep farmers.*

set·tle [MOVE LOWER] /£'set·l̩, $'set̬-/ *v* [I] to move to a lower level and stay there; to drop • *The house had been empty for years, and dust had settled* **on** *all the surfaces.* • *Do* *you think the snow will settle* (= stay on the ground without melting after it has fallen)? • *The butterfly settled* (= landed) *lightly* **on** *a leaf.* • *He poured the wine into another bottle and left it to settle* (= for any solid matter in it to fall to the bottom of the bottle). • *The contents of this packet may settle* (= become closer together by falling towards the bottom of the container and staying there, so that the container seems to contain less than it really does). • *Cracks appeared in the wall as it began to settle* (= the bricks moved downwards and pressed more closely together). • *The dry weather has caused the ground to settle* (= sink to a lower level). • *(fig.) After the recent riots, an uneasy calm has settled* **on** *the city* (= the city has become calm). • *(fig.) A peaceful expression settled* (= appeared and stayed) **on** *her face.* • *(fig.) The pound rose slightly against the dollar today, then settled* **at** (= stayed at a value of) *$1·53.*

set·tle·ment /£'set·l̩.mənt, $'seţ-/ *n* [U] • Settlement is the process of the slow sinking of a building or the ground.

sev·en /'sev·ən/ *determiner, pronoun, n* (the number) 7 • *five, six, seven, eight, nine* • *"How many grandchildren do you have now?" "I've got seven (grandchildren)."* • *They played seven-a-side rugby* (= a game with seven players in each team). • *We're open seven days a week* (= every day). • *You can find our house easily because there's a large brass seven on the door.* [C] • The **seven deadly sins** are those faults in a person's character which are thought to be the cause of all evil actions. They are anger, COVETOUSNESS, ENVY, GLUTTONY, LUST, pride and SLOTH. • *(infml humorous)* If a married person has the **seven-year itch**, they are feeling dissatisfied with their marriage after seven years, and are considering having a sexual relationship with someone who is not their wife or husband.

sev·enth /'sev·ənθ/ *determiner, pronoun, adj, adv* [not gradable], *n* • *Gary is in the seventh grade.* • *It's the seventh (of May) today.* • *Our team was/came seventh.* • *Can we divide the bar of chocolate up into sevenths* (= seven equal parts)? [C] • *(infml humorous) Since they got married, they've been* **in seventh heaven** (= extremely happy). • A **Seventh-Day Adventist** is a member of a Christian group which believes that Jesus Christ will return to the Earth soon, and which has Saturday as its day for worship: *a Seventh-Day Adventist church/group* • *"And on the seventh day God ...rested"* (Bible, Genesis 2.2)

sev·en·teen /ˌsev·ən'tiːn, '---/ *determiner, pronoun, n* (the number) 17 • *sixteen, seventeen, eighteen* • *There are seventeen days to go till my birthday.* • *"How old are you?" "(I'm) seventeen (years old)."* • *Is that a seventeen on the front of that bus?* [C]

sev·en·teenth /ˌsev·ən'tiːnθ, '---/ *determiner, pronoun, adj, adv* [not gradable], *n* • *Sweden was in seventeenth place in the Olympic medal table.* • *"When's our next meeting?" "The seventeenth (of October)."* • *Laura was/came seventeenth out of twenty in her class.* • A seventeenth is one of seventeen equal parts of something. [C]

sev·en·ty /£'sev·ən·ti, $-ţi/ *determiner, pronoun, n* (the number) 70 • *sixty, seventy, eighty* • *seventy-one, seventy-two, seventy-three* • *This house was built seventy years ago.* • *There are seventy* (= seventy people) *coming to the party.* • *There was a seventy on the door of our hotel room.* [C] • A **seventy-eight** (also **78**) is an old-fashioned record which was played by being turned around 78 times every minute: *I've got some old Billie Holiday 78s.*

sev·en·ties /£'sev·ən·tiz, $-ţiz/ *pl n* • **The** seventies is the range of temperature between 70° and 79°: *The temperature is expected to be reach the seventies tomorrow.* • **The** seventies is also the period of years between 70 and 79 in any century: *Flared trousers and platform shoes were fashionable* **in** *the seventies* (= between 1970 and 1979). • A person's seventies are the period in which they are aged between 70 and 79: *He's very active considering he's* **in** *his seventies.*

sev·en·ti·eth /£'sev·ən·ti·əθ, $-ţi-/ *determiner, pronoun, adj, adv* [not gradable], *n* • *Today is the seventieth anniversary of his death.* • *She is (ranked) seventieth in the world.* • A seventieth is one of seventy equal parts of something. [C]

sev·er *obj* /£'sev·ər, $-ɚ/ *v* [T] to break or separate, esp. by cutting • *The knife severed an artery and he bled to death.* • *The doctors think that she may have severed her spinal cord.* • *Her foot was severed* **from** *her leg in a car accident.* • *Surgeons have been able to sew his severed hand back on.* • *Electricity cables have been severed by the storm.* • *(fig.) The company has severed* (= ended) *its connection/links/relationship/ties with its previous partners.* • *(fig.) The US severed* (= ended) **diplomatic relations** *with Cuba in 1961.* • *(fig.) It has been decided to sever* (= stop sending) *aid to all countries involved in the conflict.*

sev·er·ance /£'sev·ər·ənts, $'-ɚ-/ *n* [U] • Severance is money paid by an employer to an employee whose job the employer has had to bring to an end: *The management have offered employees one week's severance* **(pay)** *for each six months they have worked at the company.* ○ *A severance agreement/deal/package has been accepted by the workers.* • *(fml)* Severance is also the act of ending a connection, relationship, etc. or of being separated from a person, place, etc.: *The minister announced the severance* **of** *aid to the country.* ○ *He said that when he went away to school for the first time, the hardest thing to cope with was the severance* **from** *his family.*

sev·er·al [SOME] /£'sev·ər·əl, $'-ɚ-/ *determiner, pronoun* some; an amount that is not exact but is fewer than many • *I've seen 'Gone with the Wind' several times.* • *Several people have complained about the scheme.* • *It's several hundred miles from Paris to Lyon.* • *Several* **of** *my friends are learning English at language schools in Cambridge.* • *You can take one of these brochures if you want to – we've got several.* • [LP] **Approximate numbers, Quantity words**

sev·er·al [SEPARATE] /£'sev·ər·əl, $'-ɚ-/ *adj* [before n; not gradable] *fml or literary* separate; different; RESPECTIVE • *We are striving to reach an agreement which will satisfy the several interests of the parties concerned.*

sev·er·al·ly /£'sev·ər·əl·i, $'-ɚ-/ *adv* [not gradable] *fml or literary*

se·vere [VERY SERIOUS] /£sɪ'vɪər, $-'vɪr/ *adj* **-r, -st** causing very great pain, difficulty, anxiety, damage, etc.; very serious • *He's suffering from a severe chest infection/a severe leg injury/severe toothache.* • *She said that the pain was becoming increasingly severe.* • *People who have severe disabilities/handicaps often get special allowances.* • *This is a school for children with severe learning difficulties.* • *After the accident they were in (a state of) severe shock.* • *Lesley has been under severe strain/pressure recently.* • *In parts of Africa there is a severe food/water shortage.* • *There is expected to be a severe frost tonight.* • *The storm has done severe damage.* • *We are in the middle of a severe recession.* • *Severe cutbacks in public spending have been announced.* • *This result is a severe setback for the team.* • A competition, test etc. that is severe is one which is difficult, and is likely to cause failure: *Competition for places at the school is very severe.* ○ *This will be a severe test of our strength.*

se·vere·ly /£sɪ'vɪə·li, $-'vɪr-/ *adv* • *Their daughter was severely injured in a car accident.* • *He is severely disabled/handicapped.* • *Smoking severely damages your health.* • *Job opportunities are severely limited/restricted at the moment.* • [LP] **Very, completely**

se·ver·i·ty /£sɪ'ver·ɪ·ti, $-ə·ţi/ *n* [U] • *The police said that they had never previously witnessed an attack of such severity.* • *Even the doctors were shocked by the severity* **of** *his injuries.* • *It has not yet been possible to assess the severity* **of** *the damage.* • *I don't think you quite understand the severity* **of** *our financial problems.* • *He was put off applying for the job by the severity* **of** *the competition.*

se·vere [NOT KIND] /£sɪ'vɪər, $-'vɪr/ *adj* not kind or sympathetic; not willing to accept other people's mistakes or failures • *Laura's teacher is so severe that she's afraid of him.* • *She spoke in a severe voice.* • *My parents were always very severe* **with** *me and my brother.* • *The government is currently facing severe criticism.* • *The judge said that he was passing the most severe sentence that the law allowed.* • *There are severe penalties for failing to declare all your income to the tax authorities.*

se·vere·ly /£sɪ'vɪə·li, $-'vɪr-/ *adv* • *I was severely reprimanded by my boss.* • *Many people have severely criticized the handling of the affair.* • *"I will not allow that kind of behaviour in my class," the teacher said severely.*

se·ver·i·ty /£sɪ'ver·ɪ·ti, $-ə·ţi/ *n* [U] • *He spoke with great severity.* • *The severity* **of** *the punishment should match the seriousness of the crime.*

se·vere [PLAIN] /£sɪ'vɪər, $-'vɪr/ *adj* completely or too plain and without decoration • *She wore a severe black dress, and plain black shoes.* • *I don't like these severe modern buildings.*

se·vere·ly /£sɪ'vɪə·li, $-'vɪr-/ *adv* • *He always dresses rather severely.* • *She had her hair severely pulled back from her face.*

se·ver·i·ty /£sɪ'ver·ɪ·ti, $-ə·ţi/ *n* [U]

sew *(obj)* /£səʊ, $soʊ/ *v past simple* **sewed**, *past part* **sewn** /£səʊn, $soʊn/ *or* **sewed** to join together (esp.

pieces of cloth), or to fix (something) to esp. a piece of cloth, by putting thread through it with a needle • *My grandmother taught me to sew.* [I] • *Did you sew this seam by hand or by machine?* [T] • *I made this skirt just by sewing two pieces of material* **together**. [M] • *He sewed* (=fixed) *the badge neatly onto his uniform.* [T] • *It's time you learned to sew* **on** *your own buttons* (=fix them to your clothes). [M] • *His finger was cut off when he caught it in a machine, but the surgeon was able to sew it back* **on**. [T] • *I've got to sew* **(up)** (=repair) *a hole in my jeans.* [T/M] • *(infml) A nurse will come and sew* **up** *that wound for you soon.* [M] • *(fig. infml) It's going to take another week or two to sew* **up** (=satisfactorily arrange) *this deal.* [M] • *(fig. infml) The Democrats appear to have the election sewn* **up** (=it seems likely that they will win it). [T] • To sew a piece of clothing or other item made from cloth is to make it by joining pieces of cloth together by putting thread through them with a needle: *She sews all her children's clothes.* [T]

sew·ing /£'səʊ·ɪŋ, $'soʊ-/ *n* [U] • *I've got some sewing* (=making or repairing clothes or other items made from cloth) *I want to finish before I go to bed.* • *She put her sewing* (=clothes or other items made from cloth that are in the process of being made or repaired) *down.* • Sewing is also the skill of making or repairing clothes or other items made from cloth: *I'm not very good at sewing.* ○ *Are you enjoying your sewing class?* • A **sewing machine** is a machine which is used for joining together pieces of cloth, and which has a needle that is operated either by turning a handle, or by electricity. • PIC› **Handicraft**

sew·er /£sʊəʳ, $'suː·ɚ/ *n* [C] a large artificial passage or a large pipe, usually underground, which is used for carrying waste water and human waste, such as urine and excrement, away from buildings to a place where they can be safely got rid of • *a sewer pipe* • *a sewer rat* • *sewer services* • *A complicated system of sewers runs under the city.* • An **open** sewer is a channel for carrying away waste water and waste from the human body which is above the ground and is not covered.

sew·age /'suː·ɪdʒ/ *n* [U] • *Some cities in the world do not have proper facilities for the disposal of sewage* (=waste matter such as water or human urine or excrement). • **Raw/untreated** *sewage is being pumped into the sea, from where it pollutes our beaches.* • *If properly* **treated**, *sewage can be used as fertilizer.* • A **sewage (treatment) plant** (also **sewage farm**/*Br also* **sewage works**) is a place where sewage is treated so that it can be safely got rid of or changed into FERTILIZER.

sew·er·age /£'sʊə·rɪdʒ, $'suː·ɚ·ɪdʒ/ *n* [U] • Sewerage is the system of carrying away waste water and human waste from houses and other buildings through large underground pipes or passages: *a sewerage system* • *sewerage services* • Sewerage is also another word for SEWAGE.

sex MALE OR FEMALE /seks/ *n* the state of being either male or female, or all males, or all females, considered as one group • *What sex is your cat?* [C] • *Some tests enable you to find out the sex* **of** *your baby before it's born.* [C] • *It's illegal to discriminate against people on the basis of sex* (=of whether they are male or female). [U] • *She accused her employer of sex discrimination* (=of treating her unfairly because she was a woman). • *Do you think sex differences* (=differences between men and women) *in behaviour are inborn or learned?* • *Under a new sex-equality law* (=a law intended to make certain that men and women are treated equally), *all-male clubs would be banned.* • *He found it difficult to fit into the male sex* **role** (=to behave in the ways thought to be typical of and suitable for a man). • *Giving birth is something which can be done only by the female sex* (=all females considered as a group). [C] • *She seems to regard all* **members of** *the male sex as inferior.* [C] • *Members of the* **opposite** *sex are not allowed in students' rooms overnight.* [C] • *The play 'Lysistrita' is partly about the* **battle of the** *sexes* (=the disagreements that typically exist between men and women). [C] • A **sex change (operation)** is an operation which, together with HORMONE treatment, gives a man many of the characteristics of a woman, or a woman many of the characteristics a man: *After his sex change, Gerald became known as Geraldine.* • If something is **sex-linked**, it is found only among men or only among women: *Haemophilia is a sex-linked disease.* • LP› **Sexist language**

sex *obj* /seks/ *v* [T] • *How do you sex these fish* (=know whether they are male or female)*?*

sex·less /'sek·sləs/ *adj* • A living thing that is sexless does not have working sexual organs and cannot produce young. Compare NEUTER.

sex·u·al /'sek·sjʊəl/ *adj* • *Sexual equality* (=equality between males and females) *will not be achieved until there is more provision for child-care.* • *Some steps have been taken towards ending sexual discrimination* (=treating people unfairly because of which sex they are). • *According to sexual stereotypes* (=characteristics considered to be typical of males and females), *men are aggressive and women are gentle.*

sex·u·al·ly /'sek·sjʊə·li/ *adv* • *a sexually segregated school* (=a school which separates boys and girls) • *sexually stereotyped behaviour* (=behaviour which is considered to be typical of a male or a female)

sex ACTIVITY /seks/ *n* [U] activity involving causing or experiencing pleasurable feelings in your body, usually centred on your penis or vagina, esp. the activity of a man putting his penis into a woman's vagina • *In some religions, sex that is not for the purpose of reproduction is considered a sin.* • *His first experience of sex was when he was 17.* • *They said that they were going on holiday looking for sun, sand, and sex.* • *All these kids are interested in is sex and drugs and rock and roll.* • *I don't think that there should be so much sex and violence on television.* • *Sex before/outside marriage is strongly disapproved of in some cultures.* • *Young people are often pressured to* **have** *sex before they're ready.* • *It turned out that she had been* **having** *sex* **with** *a colleague at work for years.* • *Most young people now receive sex* **education** *in school.* • *The film was banned because it contained too many* **explicit** *sex* **scenes.** • *In many countries, people are not as strongly criticized as they used to be for engaging in* **extramarital/premarital** *sex.* • *He often hangs around in bars, looking for* **casual** *sex* (=hoping to find someone he does not know with whom he can have sex). • *There used to be severe penalties against* **gay** *sex* (=sexual activity between people of the same sex). • *She didn't like the idea of* **group** *sex* (=sexual activity involving more than two people). • *If you don't want to get pregnant, don't have* **unprotected** *sex* (=sex without a CONTRACEPTIVE). • Sex is also used to refer to things involved in the process by which young are produced: *Oestrogen is a female sex* **hormone**. ○ *The penis, the vagina and the womb are all sex* **organs.** • A **sex aid** (also **sexual aid** or *humorous* **marital aid**) is an item that people use to increase their sexual pleasure, such as a DILDO or a VIBRATOR. • *He has about as much* **sex appeal** (=sexual attractiveness) *as a wet fish.* • *(dated)* A **sex kitten** is a young woman who is sexually exciting or attractive, esp. in a playful way. Some people, esp. women, might consider this offensive. • *Many new parents find that having a baby seriously affects their* **sex life** (=their sexual activities). • *(humorous) My brother's a real* **sex maniac** (=is extremely interested in sex and likes to have a lot of sexual activity). • *I think he just regards me as a* **sex object** (=he is only interested in my giving him sexual pleasure, not in my character or abilities). • **Sex offenders** (=people who commit crimes involving sex) *are often kept in separate parts of a prison.* • *Local residents are opposed to the opening of a* **sex shop** (=a shop which sells products connected with causing sexual pleasure, such as magazines, clothing and equipment) *in their neighbourhood* • Someone who is **sex-starved** feels that they do not have, or have not recently had, enough opportunity for sexual activity. • *Marilyn Monroe is one of the cinema's most famous* **sex symbols** (=people who have the characteristics that are very sexually attractive or exciting). • *They're having* **sex therapy**/*seeing a* **sex therapist** (=talking to a person whose job is to help people who have problems with their sexual activities) *to try and sort out their marital problems.* • *"Sex and drugs and rock and roll"* (song by Ian Dury, 1977) • *"Sex, Lies and Videotape"* (title of film, 1989) • *"No Sex Please, we're British"* (title of a play by Anthony Marriott and Alistair Foot, 1971) • *"Continental people have a sex life; the English have hot-water bottles"* (George Mikes in the book *How to be an Alien*, 1946) • LP› **Relationships**

-sexed /-sekst/ *combining form* • *highly-sexed* (=having a large amount of sexual desire or interest) • *over-sexed/under-sexed* (=having too much/too little sexual desire or interest)

sex·less /'sek·sləs/ *adj* • *She's a pleasant, attractive girl, but utterly sexless* (=not sexually attractive or exciting).

sex·u·al /'sek·sjʊəl/ *adj* • *Most people always remember their first sexual experience* (=experience involving causing or experiencing feelings of pleasure in their bodies, centred on their penis or vagina). • *They denied that they were in/having a sexual relationship.* • *He was charged with sexual* **assault.** • *Many women suffer sexual* **harassment** *at work.* • *(fml) He denied having sexual* **intercourse** *with the woman against her will.* • *I don't think that people should be discriminated against on the basis of their sexual* **orientation/preference** (= of whether they choose to have sex with men or women, or both). • Sexual **reproduction** is the reproduction of young by the combining of a cell from a male with a cell from a female. • **Sexual abuse** is the activity of having sex with a child or old person or someone who is mentally ill, against their wishes or without their agreement: *She claimed that as a child she had been the victim of sexual abuse.* • The **sexual revolution** is the change in people's ideas about sex which happened in western countries in the 1960s. • *"Sexual Healing"* (title of a song by Marvin Gaye, 1980) • *"Sexual intercourse began / In nineteen sixty-three / (Which was rather late for me)"* (Philip Larkin in the poem *Annus Mirabilis*, 1974)

sex·u·al·i·ty /£ˌsek·sju'æl·ɪ·ti, $-ə·ṭi/ *n* [U] • Your sexuality is your ability to experience or express sexual feelings: *She was uncomfortably aware of her son's developing sexuality.* ○ *Freud thought that many psychological problems were caused by repressed sexuality.*

sex·u·al·ly /'sek·sjʊə·li/ *adv* • *She's fun to be with, but I don't find her sexually* **attractive** (= do not want to have sex with her). • *He's always making sexually suggestive remarks* (= those which suggest a desire for sex). • *He claimed that she told him she was sexually experienced* (= that she had previous experience of sex). • A **sexually transmitted disease** (*abbreviation* **STD**) is one which people become infected with during sexual activity: *AIDS is a sexually transmitted disease.*

sex·y /'sek·si/ *adj* **-ier, -iest** *infml* • Someone or something that is sexy is sexually attractive: *I think your boyfriend's dead sexy.* ○ *She had a sexy way of wiggling her hips when she walked.* ○ *He bought his wife some sexy underwear for her birthday.* • You can also call something sexy if it is attracts a lot of interest and attention: *For a lot of people grammar isn't a very sexy subject, though some people find it fascinating.*

sex·i·ly /'sek·sɪ·li/ *adv infml*

sex·a·ge·na·ri·an /£ˌsek·sə·dʒɪ'neə·ri·ən, $-'ner·i-/ *n* [C] a person who is between 60 and 69 years old

sex·i·sm /'sek·sɪ·zᵊm/ *n* [U] *disapproving* (actions based on) the idea or belief that the members of one sex are less intelligent, able, skilful, etc. than the members of the other sex, esp. that women are less able than men, and that particular jobs and activities are suitable for women and others are suitable for men • *Do you think that all women are victims of sexism?* • *She claimed that it was because of sexism that she had not been promoted.* • *The university has been accused of sexism because it has so few women professors.* • *She said that she had encountered covert/overt sexism in her job.* • **It's** *blatant sexism* **that** *the company has no female directors.* [+ *that* clause] • See also HETEROSEXISM. • [LP] **Sexist language**

sex·ist /'sek·sɪst/ *adj, n disapproving* • *I wish you'd stop making sexist remarks/comments/jokes/statements* (= those which suggest that women are less able than men or which direct attention to women's sexuality) *all the time.* • *I think it's extremely sexist having all these photographs of naked women in the newspapers.* • *My uncle is a real sexist* (= believes that women are less able than men or gives too much attention to women's sexuality). [C]

sex·ol·o·gist /£sek'sɒl·ə·dʒɪst, $-'sɑː·lə·ɪst/ *n* [C] a person who studies human sexual behaviour

sex·pot /£'seks·pɒt, $-pɑːt/ *n* [C] *infml* a woman who is sexually exciting or is very interested in sex. Some people, esp. women, consider this offensive. • *Mae West and Marilyn Monroe were sexpots of the film industry.* • *She's a real little sexpot.* • *Have you met Andy's sexpot girlfriend?*

sex·tant /'sek·stᵊnt/ *n* [C] a device used on a ship or aircraft for measuring angles, such as those between stars or that between the sun and the Earth, in order to discover the exact position of the ship or aircraft

sex·tet /sek'stet/ *n* [C] a group of six musicians or singers who play or sing together, or a piece of music for six players or singers • *a jazz sextet* • *the Miles Davis Sextet* • *a sextet* **for** *strings, oboe and flute*

sex·ton /'sek·stᵊn/ *n* [C] a person whose job is to take care of a church building and its GRAVEYARD, and sometimes to ring the church bells

sex·tu·plet /£sek'stjuː·plɪt, $-'stuː-/ *n* [C] any of six children born to the same mother at the same time

sex·u·al·i·ty /£ˌsek·sju'æl·ɪ·ti, $-ə·ṭi/ *n* [U] See at SEX [ACTIVITY]

sex·y /'sek·si/ *adj* See at SEX [ACTIVITY]

SF /ˌes'ef/ *n* [U] *abbreviation for* **science fiction**, see at SCIENCE • *an SF book/comic/movie*

Sgt *n* [before n] *abbreviation for* SERGEANT

sh, shh, ssh /ʃʊʃ/, **shush** *exclamation* used to tell someone to be quiet; HUSH • *Sh, you'll wake the baby!* • *Sh, don't cry.* • *Shh, the film's started!*

Shab·bat /ʃæb'æt/ *n* [U not after *the*] the day of the week (Saturday) kept for rest and religious worship by Jews

shab·by [BAD CONDITION] /'ʃæb·i/ *adj* **-ier, -iest** looking old and in bad condition because of wear or lack of care • *He wore a shabby old overcoat, dirty and full of holes.* • *Her home is a rented one-bedroom flat in a shabby part of town.* • *The refugees were shabby* (= wore old clothes in bad condition) *and hungry.*

shab·bi·ly /'ʃæb·ɪ·li/ *adv* • *A crowd of shabbily dressed children had gathered.*

shab·bi·ness /'ʃæb·ɪ·nəs/ *n* [U] • *I was shocked by the shabbiness of the room.*

shab·by [NOT FAIR] /'ʃæb·i/ *adj* **-ier, -iest** not honourable or fair; unacceptable • *a shabby compromise* • *She spoke out about the shabby way the case had been handled.* • *The whole shabby story of cheating began to come out.*

shab·bi·ly /'ʃæb·ɪ·li/ *adv* • *The hostages were shabbily* (= not well or fairly) **treated** *when they came home.*

shack /ʃæk/ *n* [C] a very simple and small building made from bits of wood, metal or other materials • *These families live in one-room shacks which they made out of cardboard, wood and tin.*

shack up /ʃæk/ *v adv* [I] *infml* to start to live together as sexual partners without being married • *I hear Tony and Helen have shacked up* **together.** • *She's decided to shack up* **with** *her boyfriend.*

shacked up /ʃækt/ *adj* [after v; not gradable] • *"Is Alan still living with Maria?" "No, he's shacked up* **with** (= is living with as a sexual partner, though is not married to) *someone else now."*

shack·les /'ʃæk·l̩z/ *pl n* a pair of metal rings connected by a chain and fastened to a person's wrists or the bottom of their legs to prevent them from escaping, or *(fig.)* anything that prevents you from doing what you want to do • *Wardens bound Mr Wang with handcuffs and shackles.* • *(fig.) The press, once heavily censored, has managed to shake off its shackles.*

shack·le *obj* /'ʃæk·l̩/ *v* [T usually passive] • If you are shackled by something you are unable to do what you want to do because of this thing: *The government is shackled by its own debts.*

shade [SLIGHT DARKNESS] /ʃeɪd/ *n* slight darkness and coolness caused by something blocking the direct light from the sun • *The sun was hot, and there were no trees to offer us shade.* [U] • *There is almost no shade in the desert.* [U] • *These plants like partial shade.* [U] • *I always try to park my car* **in the** *shade.* [U] • *The children played* **in/under the** *shade* **of** *a large beach umbrella.* [U] • A shade is a covering that is put over an electric light in order to make it less bright: *The lamps all had matching purple shades.* [C] • *(specialized)* Shade (also **shading**) is also the parts of a picture or painting that the person who made the picture or painting has made slightly darker than the other parts: *A good artist can produce a very realistic effect using only* **light and shade.** [U] ○ *(fig.) The orchestra's playing brought out the* **light and** *shade* (= variety) *in the music.* [U] • Shade is also *Am for* **roller blind**. See at ROLL [TURN OVER]: *It was getting dark so I pulled down the shades.* [C] • If someone or something **puts/leaves** someone or something else **in the shade**, they are so good that they make the other person or thing seem unimportant and not worth very much: *Although I thought I'd done well, my sister's exam results put mine in the shade.* • *(Am and Aus) Red maples make excellent* **shade trees** (= trees which are planted in order to provide slight darkness and coolness). • See also SUNSHADE.

shade *obj* /ʃeɪd/ *v* [T] • To shade something is to prevent direct light from shining on it: *I shaded my* **eyes** *from the glare of the sun.* ○ *The broad avenues are shaded by splendid trees.* • To shade **(in)** a picture is to make parts of it a darker colour: *The artist has shaded the background of the portrait (in) so that the subject's face stands out clearly.* [T/M]

USING LANGUAGE THAT IS NOT SEXIST

Sometimes the use of particular words can support unfair or untrue attitudes towards a particular sex, usually women. For example using the pronoun *he* to refer to a doctor, when you do not know if they are male or female, might support the belief that it is not normal for women to be doctors. Many people speaking or writing English today prefer to avoid using language that is sexist. This modern *non-sexist* use of language is sometimes called *inclusive language*.

Old-fashioned sexist language	Modern non-sexist language
Male pronouns *he, his* and *him* are used even though the sex of the person is not known.	You can often avoid unnecessary male pronouns by using the plural pronouns *they, them* etc. instead. Male pronouns can also be replaced by combinations like *she or he, him or her, her or his.** Sometimes a pronoun can be avoided completely.
"Someone's on the phone." "What does **he** *want?"* *The television viewer hardly ever leaves* **his** *chair.* *A gardener is usually proud of* **his** *garden.* *A child needs to feel that* **he** *is liked by* **his** *friends.*	*"Someone's on the phone." "What do* **they** *want?"* *Television viewers hardly ever leave* **their** *chairs.* *A gardener is usually proud of* **his or her** *garden.* *A child needs to feel liked by friends.*
Words formed from 'man' are used when referring to people generally. (But notice that many words like *manager* or *manufacture* are not connected with 'man' at all.)	Use other words when referring to both men and women.
Man/mankind *is polluting the Earth.* **Man** *is not the only animal that uses tools.* *No* **man** *has ever climbed this mountain before.* *Who's* **manning** *the office?* *This is the largest* **man-made** *lake in Europe.*	**People** *are*/**Humanity** *is*/**Humankind** *is polluting...* **Human beings/Humans** *are not the only animals...* **No one** *has ever climbed this mountain before.* *Who's* **staffing/running** *the office?* *This is the largest* **artificial** *lake in Europe.*
Many jobs or activities are strongly connected with a particular sex.	Use expressions or pronouns that do not support sexist assumptions.
The teacher must not be late for **his** *class.* *A manager has a duty towards* **his** *workers.* *The fall in prices is great news for* **housewives**. *A* **mother** *should never leave a baby alone in the house.* **He** *might hurt* **himself**.	*Teachers must not be late for* **their** *classes.* *A manager has a duty towards* **his or her** *workers.* *... is great news for* **consumers/shoppers**. **Parents** *should never leave babies alone in the house.* **They** *might hurt* **themselves**.
Job names are used which refer unnecessarily to the sex of the person.	Use job names that apply equally to women and men.
We're meeting a group of **businessmen**. *The* **chairman** *cannot vote.* *Jane is a* **camerawoman**. *She's a very talented* **authoress/lady writer**. *John is training as a* **male nurse**. *workman; salesman/saleslady; airline stewardess*	*...a group of* **business people/executives**. *The* **chairperson/chair** *cannot vote.* *Jane is a* **camera operator**. *She's a very talented* **author/writer**. *John is training as a* **nurse**. *worker; sales representative/agent; flight attendant*
Male words are frequently put before female words in common combinations.	Try to balance the ordering of male and female pairs.
men and women; boys and girls; husband and wife; brother and sister; his and her; he or she	*men and women; girls and boys; husband and wife; mother and father*
The words used for men and women in the same situation are not equal. For example the title *Miss* tells you that the woman is not married, but *Mr* applies to married and unmarried men.	Use equal male and female terms.
Ted and Angela are **man** *and* **wife**. *I have three* **girls** *and two* **men** *working for me.* **Mr** *Lewis and* **Miss** *Masters.*	*Ted and Angela are* **husband** *and* **wife**. *I have three* **women** *and two* **men** *working for me.* **Ms** *Masters and* **Mr** *Lewis.*

* Notice that these combinations might sound awkward, and generally should not be repeated often in a piece of writing or conversation. The written forms *he/she, (s)he, s/he, her/him* etc. are also possible.

shad·ed /ˈʃeɪ·dɪd/ *adj* • *Nothing will grow in the shaded part of the garden.* • *The shaded areas of the plans show where the houses will be built.*

shades /ʃeɪdz/ *pl n infml* • Shades are SUNGLASSES: *She was wearing a black leather jacket and shades.*

shad·ing /ˈʃeɪ·dɪŋ/ *n* [U] • *On a print or photograph, an artist can define the shape of the face by adding small amounts of shading* (= by making some areas of the picture slightly darker than others).

shad·y /ˈʃeɪ·di/ *adj* **-ier, -iest** • A shady place is one that is sheltered from direct light from the sun: *We sat on the shady grass for our picnic.* • *(infml)* A shady person or action is one that appears to be dishonest or illegal: *They know some very shady characters.* ○ *He was involved in shady deals in the past.*

shade [DEGREE] /ʃeɪd/ *n* [C] a variety or degree of a colour • *Their kitchen is painted an unusual shade* **of** *yellow/an unusual yellow shade.* • *This hair colouring comes in several shades* (= varieties of colour). • *What shade* **of** *lipstick do you use?* • *The room has been decorated in* **pastel** *shades* (= soft and light colours) *throughout.* • *(fig.) For him everything is black or white, there are no shades* **of grey** (= things that are uncertain). • Shade can also mean type or variation: *They are hoping to satisfy all shades* **of** *public* **opinion**. ○ *There are several shades* **of meaning** *in that sentence.* • **A shade** means slightly: *Don't you think those trousers are a shade too tight?* ○ *"I've been waiting over an hour for you," he said, a shade crossly.* ○ *I think he took that joke just a shade too far.* ○ *The journey took us a shade* **over/under** *three hours.* ○ *Our new car cost us a shade* **more/less** *than we were expecting it to.*

shade /ʃeɪd/ *v* [I always + adv/prep] • *At sunset, the sky shaded* (= changed colour gradually) **from** *pink* **into** *dark red.* • *At the horizon, the hills shade* **off into** *a pale purple.* • *(fig.) Over time, her despair shaded away* **into** (= changed gradually so that it became) *acceptance of the situation.* • *(fig.) Their views shade* **into** (= are in some ways similar to) *the policies of the extreme left of the party.*

shades /ʃeɪdz/ *pl n* **shades of** *infml* similarities with • *There are shades of an earlier era in the way the school is run.* • You say 'shades of' to mean that something or someone makes you remember something or someone similar in the past: *In his speech he said – shades of Martin Luther King Jr. – that he had a dream.*

shad·ow [DARKNESS] /£ˈʃæd·əʊ, $-oʊ/ *n* (an) area of darkness, caused by light being blocked by something, which usually has a similar shape to the object that is blocking the light and which appears to be joined to it • *The children were playing, jumping on each other's shadows.* [C] • *Jamie followed his mother around all day like a shadow.* [C] • *The sun shone through the leaves,* **casting** *shadows* **on** *the lawn.* [C] • *The house next door* **casts** *a shadow* **over** *our garden.* [C] • If something unpleasant **casts** a shadow, it makes something else less happy or good than it would otherwise have been: *Her father's illness cast a shadow* **over** *the birth of her baby.* [C] ○ *Memories of the war still cast a* **long/dark** *shadow* **over** *relations between the two countries.* [C] • *A swinging bare electric bulb* **threw** *sinister shadows* **across** *the wall of the darkened room.* [C] • *Our cat's so nervous, it's* **afraid/frightened/scared of** *its* **own** *shadow* (= is always extremely nervous and is easily frightened). [C] • *(fig.) You'll* **wear** *yourself* **to** *a shadow* (= will become thin, tired and weak) *if you keep working so hard.* [C] • *(fig.) The new minister is a* **pale** *shadow* **of** (= is less powerful or influential or effective than) *his predecessor.* [C] • *This corner of the room is always* **in** *shadow* (= darkness). [U] • A shadow is also a small dark area of skin under your eye: *She put on some make-up to cover the* **dark** *shadows under her eyes.* [C] • If a shadow is **hanging over** you, something unpleasant is influencing you: *The team has the shadow* **of** *four successive defeats hanging over them.* [C] • *She has always been* **in/under** *her sister's* **shadow** (= Her sister has always seemed better than she is, and has attracted more attention than she has.) • *They live in a charming house* **in/under the shadow of** (= close to) *the cathedral.* • If you are **in/under the shadow of** something unpleasant, that thing either seems likely to happen and to have a bad effect on your life, or is already having a bad effect on your life: *We are all living under the shadow of war.* ○ *He is under the shadow of investigation for illegal business activities.* • If you are a **shadow of** your **former self**, you have less strength or influence or weight than you did before: *The former world boxing champion is now only a shadow of his former self.* ○ *Since she had cancer, she's become a shadow of her former self.* • To **shadow-box** is to fight an imaginary enemy by hitting the air with your hands: *Boxers often shadow-box when they are training.* ○ *(fig.) A lot of* **shadow-boxing** (= making a suggestion in order to find out what someone else's opinions or intentions are) *goes on in parliament.* • *"Me and My Shadow"* (title of a song written by Billy Rose, 1927)

shad·ow *obj* /£ˈʃæd·əʊ, $-oʊ/ *v* [T] • *The wide brim of her hat shadowed* (= made an area of darkness on) *her face.* • *We came across a glade shadowed* (= made dark) *by large trees.*

shad·ows /£ˈʃæd·əʊz, $-oʊz/ *pl n* • **The shadows** are an area of darkness in which people and things cannot be seen: *Someone jumped* **out of** *the shadows and grabbed my handbag.* ○ *A man peered out of the window, then stepped back* **into** *the shadows.*

shad·ow·y /£ˈʃæd·əʊ·i, $-oʊ-/ *adj* • *She was startled by a sudden movement in the shadowy hallway* (= one in which there were areas of darkness). • *The only photograph I have of my grandfather is this rather shadowy* (= dark and not clear) *one.* • Shadowy can also be used to refer to someone or something about which little is known: *The English king, Arthur, is a somewhat shadowy* **figure** *who may not have even existed.* ○ *He has a rather shadowy past.* ○ *They are members of some shadowy extremist group.*

shad·ow *obj* [FOLLOW] /£ˈʃæd·əʊ, $-oʊ/ *v* [T] to follow closely • *The police think that the robbers shadowed their victims for days before the crime.* • *His every move to and from his house was shadowed by a private detective.* • *Every time Carter got control of the ball, he was shadowed by Lynch.* • *Your first week in the job will be spent shadowing one of our more experienced employees.* • *The Swiss franc has closely shadowed the D-mark.*

shad·ow /£ˈʃæd·əʊ, $-oʊ/ *adj* [before n; not gradable] • In Britain and Australia, shadow refers to a politician belonging to the party which is not in government, who represents the opinions of his or her party on the work done or decisions made by a particular member of the government, and who says what his or her party would do if it were in government: *the Shadow Home Secretary* • *the Shadow Foreign Secretary* • *a Shadow Minister* • *the Shadow Cabinet*

shad·ow /£ˈʃæd·əʊ, $-oʊ/ *n* [C] • *I think we have a shadow* (= a person, such as a police officer, who secretly follows someone in order to discover what they are doing) *on our tail.* • *Ever since he was able to walk, Stephen has been his older brother's shadow* (= has followed him and copied his actions). • In industry, a shadow is a person who follows someone else while they are at work in order to learn about that person's job.

shad·ow [SMALL AMOUNT] /£ˈʃæd·əʊ, $-oʊ/ *n* [usually in negatives] a small amount • *There isn't a shadow* **of doubt** *that you've made the right decision.* • *There wasn't even a shadow* **of** *remorse on his face.*

shaft [POLE] /£ʃɑːft, $ʃæft/ *n* [C] a pole or rod which forms the handle of a tool or weapon, or which forms part of a machine • *the shaft* **of** *a hammer* • *the shaft* **of** *a golf club* • A shaft is the part of an arrow or SPEAR (= a long pole with a sharp point used as a weapon) to which the point is fixed. • A shaft is also a rod which forms part of a machine such as an engine, and which turns round and round in order to pass power on to the machine: *the drive shaft of a car* ○ *the propeller shaft of an aircraft* ○ *He used an electric tool, which had hundreds of strong metal teeth on a rotating shaft, to clear the soil of weeds.* • *(fig.) A shaft* (= beam) **of (sun)light** *came through the open door.* • See also CRANKSHAFT.

shaft [PASSAGE] /£ʃɑːft, $ʃæft/ *n* [C] a long, either vertical or sloping, passage through a building or through the ground • *a (Br and Aus) lift/(Am) elevator shaft* • *a ventilation/air shaft* • *a well shaft* • *In tin mining today, workers excavate tunnels horizontally from a vertical shaft.* • *It is proposed to dump nuclear waste down shafts that have been* **sunk** *into the sea bed.*

shaft [REMARK] /£ʃɑːft, $ʃæft/ *n* [C] *esp. literary* a clever remark, esp. one that is intended as an attack on someone or something • *We were all startled by her opening shaft.* • *I couldn't bear his shafts* **of** *scorn.* • *John came out with an unexpected shaft* **of** *wisdom.*

shaft *obj* [TREAT UNFAIRLY] /£ʃɑːft, $ʃæft/ *v* [T usually passive] *Am and Aus infml* to cheat or trick; to treat unfairly or cruelly • *She was shafted over the film rights to her book.* • *We were shafted* **(out of** *thousands of dollars) on that deal.*

shaft /£ʃɑːft, $ʃæft/ *n* [U] *Am infml* • **The shaft** is unfair treatment: *After years of loyal service, his boss* **gave him the**

shaft by firing him just before he would have qualified for a pension.

shag *obj* [HAVE SEX] /ʃæg/ *v* [T] **-gg-** *Br and Aus taboo slang* to have sex with

shag /ʃæg/ *n* [C] *Br and Aus taboo slang* • A shag is an act of having sex, or a sexual partner: *He just came up to me and said "Fancy a shag?"* • *So was he a good shag* (= sexual partner), *then?*

shag [LONG THREADS] /ʃæg/ *adj* [before n; not gradable] (of a CARPET or RUG) made of long thick threads • *a shag carpet* • *shag* **pile** (= the soft surface formed by cut threads)

shag [BIRD] /ʃæg/ *n* [C] a large sea bird which has dark feathers, a long neck and body, and a curved beak • *(Aus slang)* **Like a shag on a rock** means completely alone: *They walked out of the room and left me like a shag on a rock.*

shagged out /ʃægd/ *adj* [after v] *Br and Aus taboo slang* extremely tired • *I'm too shagged out to go out tonight.*

shag·gy /ˈʃæg·i/ *adj* **-ier, -iest** having or covered with long, rough and untidy hair, or (of hair) long, rough and untidy • *a shaggy dog* • *a shaggy pony* • *a shaggy, bearded youth* • *the shaggy coat of a sheep* • *a lion's shaggy mane* • *a shaggy rug* • A **shaggy dog story** is a long joke which has an intentionally silly or meaningless ending.

shag·gi·ness /ˈʃæg·ɪ·nəs/ *n* [U]

Shah /ʃɑː/ *n* [C] (the title of) a ruler of Iran in the past

shake *(obj)* [MOVE] /ʃeɪk/ *v past simple* **shook** /ʃʊk/, *past part* **shaken** /ˈʃeɪ·kᵊn/ to (cause to) move backwards and forwards or up and down in quick, short movements • *A young boy climbed into the apple tree and shook the branches so that the fruit fell down.* [T] • *Babies like toys that make a noise when they're shaken.* [T] • *The explosion shook buildings for miles around.* [T] • *He said that the reason he'd shaken his baby daughter so violently was because she wouldn't stop crying.* [T] • *The dog shook* **itself** *as it climbed out of the river.* [T] • *People in southern California were shaken awake by an earthquake.* [T + obj + adj] • *She shook her hair* **loose** *from its ribbon.* [T + obj + adj] • *Anna shook some powdered chocolate* **over** *her coffee.* [T] • *He shook the rain* **off/from** *his umbrella.* [T] • *Potatoes should be dug up and the earth shaken* **off** *without damaging the skin.* [T] • *She removed her new dress from the box in which it had been packed and shook it* **out** (= made it smooth by moving it quickly backwards and forwards). [M] • *I'll just shake* **out** *this duster* (= move it from side to side in order to remove dirt from it). [M] • *Put all the sweets together in one bag, shake them* **up** (= mix them together by moving the container in which they are held from side to side), *and then each of you pick one out.* [M] • *I'll have a martini, please, shaken* (= mixed by putting liquid into a container and moving the container quickly from side to side) **not stirred**. [T] • *Every time one of these big trucks goes through the village, all the houses shake.* [I] • *The stadium shook* **with** *a roar as the winning goal was scored.* [I] • *The child's body was shaking* **with** *sobs.* [I] • If you are shaking, your body makes quick short movements, or you feel as if it is doing so, because you are frightened or nervous: *She was shaking as she opened the letter.* [I] ○ *He picked up the phone with a shaking hand, expecting bad news.* [I] ○ *Her voice shook as she spoke about the person who attacked her.* [I] ○ *I was shaking* **in my shoes/boots** (= very nervous) *about having to tell Dad what I'd done.* [I] ○ *I was shaking* **like a leaf**/*(Br and Aus)* **like a jelly** (= very nervous) *before my exam.* [I] • If you shake someone's **hand**, or shake **hands** (**with** someone), or shake someone **by the hand**, you hold someone's hand in your own for a short time, often also slightly moving it up and down a few times, as a greeting, or to say goodbye, or to show that you have made an agreement, or to express that they have done something well: *"Pleased to meet you," he said, shaking my hand.* [T] ○ *At the end of the tennis match, the two players shook hands.* [T] ○ *The Princess has been photographed shaking hands with AIDS victims.* [T] ○ *It seems that we have a deal, so let's shake (hands)* **on it**. [I] ○ *"Congratulations," she said, shaking the winner by the hand.* [T] • If you shake your **head**, you move it from side to side, in order to express disagreement, sadness, or that you do not believe something: *When I asked Tim if he'd seen Jackie lately, he shook his head.* [T] ○ *The doctor shook her head and said "I'm sorry, there's nothing more I can do".* [T] ○ *She stood shaking her head as she looked at the damage the fire had caused.* [T] ○ *"That's incredible!" he said, shaking his head in disbelief.* [T] • If you shake your **fist**, you hold your hand up with your fingers and thumb bent, and move your lower arm strongly backwards and forwards, to show that you are angry: *The demonstrators shouted their demands and shook their fists.* ○ *He shook his fist* **at** *the driver who pulled out in front of him.* • *(infml) I don't know why you need to buy more shoes – you've already got* **more than you can shake a stick at** (= very many). • *(infml) Come on, Nick,* **shake a leg** (= hurry or act more quickly), *or we'll never be ready in time.* • *"Shake, Rattle and Roll"* (song by Bill Haley and his Comets, 1954)

shake /ʃeɪk/ *n* [C] • *She gave the box a shake* (= moved it from side to side or up and down), *to see if there was anything inside it.* • *"No, no, no," he said with a shake* **of** *his head.* • Shake is *Am infml for* **milk shake**. See at MILK. • *(infml) I'll be with you in* **two shakes (of a duck's/lamb's tail)/a couple of shakes** (= very soon).

shak·er /£ˈʃeɪ·kəʳ, $-kɚ/ *n* [C] • A shaker is a container with a tightly fitting lid in which liquids can be mixed together by moving the container quickly from side to side: *a cocktail shaker* • A shaker is also a container with holes in its lid from which a powdery substance can be put onto a surface by holding the container upside down and moving it up and down: *a salt/pepper shaker* • A shaker is also a container into which DICE are put and moved quickly from side to side before being thrown onto a flat surface, usually during a game involving chance. • [PIC] **Games**

shakes /ʃeɪks/ *pl n infml* • **The shakes** are short quick movements from side to side that your body makes because you are ill, frightened or have drunk too much alcohol: *"What seems to be the matter, Mrs Davis?" "Well, doctor, I feel really hot and I've* **got** *the shakes."* ○ *Before my driving test, I was so nervous that I* **got** *the shakes.*

shak·y /ˈʃeɪ·ki/ *adj* **-ier, -iest** • Shaky means moving with quick, short movements from side to side, not in a controlled way: *Soon after it was born, the calf got up and tried to stand on its shaky legs.* ○ *The child wrote her name in large shaky letters.* ○ *He sang well, but his voice was a bit shaky* (= not controlled) *on the top notes.* ○ *She's recovering well from her operation, but she's still a little shaky* **on** *her* **feet**.

shak·i·ly /ˈʃeɪ·kɪ·li/ *adv* • *The old man stood up and walked shakily across the room.*

shak·i·ness /ˈʃeɪ·kɪ·nəs/ *n* [U]

shake *obj* [UPSET] /ʃeɪk/ *v* [T] *past simple* **shook** /ʃʊk/, *past part* **shaken** /ˈʃeɪ·kᵊn/ to cause to feel upset and troubled • *The child seemed nervous and visibly shaken.* • *He was badly shaken by the scandal.* • *I think she was quite shaken* **(up)** *by the accident.* [T/M] • *The news has shaken the whole country.* • *'Ten days that shook the world' is the title of John Reed's book about the 1917 Russian Revolution.*

shak·y /ˈʃeɪ·ki/ *adj* **-ier, -iest** • *The news left me feeling a little shaky* (= upset).

shake *obj* [WEAKEN] /ʃeɪk/ *v* [T] *past simple* **shook** /ʃʊk/, *past part* **shaken** /ˈʃeɪ·kᵊn/ to make less certain or firm or strong; to weaken • *No evidence seems to shake their faith in the rightness of their cause.* • *What has happened has shaken the foundations of her belief.* • *After six defeats in a row, the team's confidence has been badly shaken.* • *His unexpected failure has shaken his complacency.* • *This discovery may shake* **(up)** *traditional theories on how mountains are formed.* [T/M]

shak·y /ˈʃeɪ·ki/ *adj* **-ier, -iest** • *The building's foundations are rather shaky* (= not firm or strong), *and it could collapse at any time.* • *The government is taking these steps to try to improve the country's shaky economy.* • *The talks got off to a shaky start, but now seem to be going well.* • *Their marriage looks pretty shaky to me.* • *His English is rather shaky.* • *I think you're on very shaky* **ground** *with that argument.*

shak·i·ly /ˈʃeɪ·kɪ·li/ *adv*

shak·i·ness /ˈʃeɪ·kɪ·nəs/ *n* [U]

shake *obj* [GET RID OF] /ʃeɪk/ *v* [T] *past simple* **shook** /ʃʊk/, *past part* **shaken** /ˈʃeɪ·kᵊn/ to get rid of; to escape from • *I just can't seem to shake* **(off)** *this cold.* [T/M] • *He has been struggling to shake* **(off)** *a chest infection.* [T/M] • *It's very difficult to shake* **(off)** *the habit of a lifetime.* [T/M] • *The company has so far been unable to shake* **(off)** *its reputation for being old-fashioned.* [T/M] • *The actor said that he was trying to shake* **(off)** *his 'bad guy' image.* [T/M] • *Mr O'Donnell was arrested after driving through red lights in an attempt to shake* **off** *the police officer who was chasing him.* [M] • *I have no doubt that we will be able to shake* **off** *the challenge from our rivals.* [M] • *She is one of those intelligent, educated women who have gratefully shaken* **off** *the shackles of family life.* [M]

shake down *obj* THREATEN, **shake** *obj* **down** *v adv* [M] *Am infml* to get money from (someone) by using threats or tricks • *The gang would shake down local businesses, demanding protection payments that would insure against 'accidents'.*

shake·down /ˈʃeɪk·daʊn/ *n* [C] *Am infml* • *He'd been expecting a shakedown, but $1000 a month was more than he could possibly pay.*

shake down BECOME ORGANIZED *v adv* [I] *infml* to be in, or to complete, the process of becoming organized • *Give the new arrangements time to shake down – I'm sure they'll be OK.*

shake·down /ˈʃeɪk·daʊn/ *adj* [before n; not gradable] *Am* • *The new administration is still in the shakedown period.*

shake down STAY *v adv* [I always + adv/prep] *infml* to use a particular place for sleeping in temporarily • *My girlfriend's kicked me out – can I shake down with you for a couple of nights?*

shake up *obj*, **shake** *obj* **up** *v adv* [M] to cause large changes to (something), esp. in order to make improvements • *The Cultural Revolution completely shook up China's economy and society.* • *Technological changes have shaken up many industries.* • *The first thing the new chairman of the company did was to shake up the management.* • *Several new players have been brought in to shake up the team.* • *We're looking for ways of shaking our campaign up.* • *The country still needs more shaking up, more competition, more choice before it can face the future with confidence.*

shake–up /ˈʃeɪk·ʌp/ *n* [C] • *The company is undergoing a radical shake-up* (= a large change in the way it is organized). • *The planned management shake-up is likely to result in the loss of several jobs.* • *They seem to be getting along much better after a major shake-up* **in** *their relationship.* • *The arrival of the new baby caused a thorough shake-up* **of** *their family life.*

shake-out /ˈʃeɪk·aʊt/ *n* [C] a situation in which people lose their jobs, or companies stop doing business, because of economic difficulties • *In a continuing shakeout, two more newspapers have been forced to close.* • *The shakeout in the labour market after Christmas usually makes January a bad month for unemployment.* • *The merger of the two companies is likely to produce a shakeout* **of** *staff.* • *This is not a shakeout* **of** *inefficient organizations, but a case of good companies being unable to survive any longer in a harsh economic climate.*

shale /ʃeɪl/ *n* [U] a type of soft grey rock, usually formed from hardened clay, which breaks easily into thin layers

shall FUTURE TENSE /ʃæl/ *v aux* [+ infinitive without *to*; not *be shalling*] *slightly dated* used instead of 'will' when the subject is 'I' or 'we' • *I shall be late home tonight.* • *If you do that one more time, I shall be very cross.* • *I shall never forget you.* • *I shall have to call you back – there's someone at the front door.* • *Next month I shall* **have** *worked here for five years.* • *Shall we be able to get this finished today, do you think?* • *I'm afraid I shall not/shan't be able to come to your party.* • *(fml) I shall hope to hear from you again soon.* • *(fml) I shall look forward to meeting you next week.* • *So we'll see you at the weekend, shall we* (= is that right)? • *We shall* (= intend to) *let you know as soon as there's any news.* • *This is an important point in my argument, and I shall* (= intend to) *come back to it.* • *"We shall not be moved"* (title of a civil rights song, 1931) • *"We shall overcome"* (title of a song by various people including Pete Seeger, used in the civil rights movement in the 1960s) • In the past, the future tense in English was formed with 'shall' in the first person ('I shall go', 'we shall go') and 'will' in the second and third persons ('you will go', 'Charlie will go', 'they will go'). In modern English, it is much more common to use 'will' for all three persons ('I will go' etc.), although some people still keep the difference between 'shall' and 'will'. • LP› **Tenses**

shall SUGGEST /ʃæl/ *v aux* [+ infinitive without *to*; not *be shalling*] used, with 'I' or 'we', to make a suggestion • *"I'm cold." "Shall I close this window?"* • *Shall we go out for dinner tonight?* • *Shall I* (= Do you want me to) *pick the children up from school today?* • *What shall* (= What do you suggest that) *we do about this broken window?* • *Which restaurant shall we* (= would you like us to) *go to?* • LP› **Auxiliary verbs**

shall CERTAINLY WILL /ʃæl/ *v aux* [+ infinitive without *to*; not *be shalling*] he/she/it **shall** used to say that something certainly will or must happen, or that you are determined that something will happen • *Don't worry, I shall be there to meet the train.* • *I'm determined that she shall not be allowed to suffer.* • *(fml) The school rules state that no child shall be allowed out of the school during the day, unless accompanied by an adult.* • *You shall* (= I promise that you will) *go to the ball, Cinderella.*

shal·lot /£ʃəˈlɒt, $-ˈlɑːt/ *n* [C/U] a type of small onion • PIC› **Vegetables**

shal·low NOT DEEP /£ˈʃæl·əʊ, $-oʊ/ *adj* **-er, -est** having only a short distance from the top to the bottom • *The stream was quite shallow so we were able to walk across it.* • *She told her children to stay in the shallow end (of the swimming pool).* • *The body was found in a shallow grave.* • *Fry the onions in a shallow pan.* • *He ran a shallow bath* (= did not put very much water in the bath). • *These beech trees have shallow roots* (= roots which do not go very deep into the ground). • Shallow **breathing** is a way of breathing in which you only take a small amount of air into your lungs with each breath: *The doctors are worried because her breathing has become very shallow.* • To **shallow-fry** food is to cook it in a very small amount of oil or fat: *shallow-fried fish/bacon*

shal·low·ly /£ˈʃæl·əʊ·li, $-oʊ-/ *adv* • *He's been breathing shallowly for several hours now.*

shal·low·ness /£ˈʃæl·əʊ·nəs, $-oʊ-/ *n* [U] • *Because of the shallowness* **of** *the water, we could see the fish in it very clearly.* • *The shallowness* **of** *her breathing concerned the doctors.*

shal·lows /£ˈʃæl·əʊz, $-oʊz/ *pl n* • **The shallows** are the shallow part of an area of water: *Ships must be careful to avoid the shallows.* ○ *Alligators live* **in** *the shallows.*

shal·low NOT SERIOUS /£ˈʃæl·əʊ, $-oʊ/ *adj* **-er, -est** not showing serious or careful thought • *I thought that play/book/film was rather shallow.* • *He seemed to have only a shallow understanding of his subject.* • *I don't accept that shallow explanation.* • *The better I got to know her, the more shallow I realized she was.*

shal·low·ly /£ˈʃæl·əʊ·li, $-oʊ-/ *adv* • *The book was criticized for being shallowly written.*

shal·low·ness /£ˈʃæl·əʊ·nəs, $-oʊ-/ *n* [U] • *The fine performances of the actors hide the shallowness* **of** *the play's script.*

shal·low NOT STRONGLY FELT /£ˈʃæl·əʊ, $-oʊ/ *adj* **-er, -est** not strongly felt or experienced • *Theirs is only a shallow friendship.* • A person who is shallow is not able to form strong relationships: *He's a shallow, selfish individual who only ever thinks of himself.*

shal·low·ly /£ˈʃæl·əʊ·li, $-oʊ-/ *adv*

shal·low·ness /£ˈʃæl·əʊ·nəs, $-oʊ-/ *n* [U]

sha·lom /£ʃəˈlɒm, $-ˈlɑːm/ *exclamation* a form of greeting or a way of saying goodbye, used by Jewish people

shalt /ʃælt/ *v aux* **thou shalt** *dated or biblical* you shall • Thou shalt is sometimes used in a humorous way: *He's one of those people who believes that thou shalt not serve red wine with fish.* • *"Thou shalt not kill"* (Bible, Exodus 20.13)

sham /ʃæm/ *n disapproving* someone or something that is not what it pretends to be, or pretence • *It turned out that he wasn't a real doctor at all – he was just a sham.* [C] • *They claimed that the election had been fair, but really it was a sham.* [C] • *She appears to be rich with her fine clothes, but it's only a sham.* [C] • *The American dream is a sham.* [C] • *I have no time for all this sham* (= pretence). [U]

sham /ʃæm/ *adj* [not gradable] *disapproving* • *They made a fortune through some sham* (= false) *property deal.* • *He's been involved in making sham loans.* • *That jewellery looks sham to me.* • *I've had enough of your sham sympathy.* • *She's trapped in a sham* (= not real) *marriage.*

sham *(obj)* /ʃæm/ *v* **-mm-** *disapproving* • *He isn't really upset – he's just shamming* (= pretending). [I] • *I think she's shamming sickness so that she doesn't have to go to school.* [T]

sham·an /ˈʃeɪ·mən/ *n* [C] (in particular religions) a person who has special powers to control or influence good and evil spirits, and who can therefore discover the cause of illness or other bad luck • *A shaman of the Wayana tribe may use over 100 different plant species as medicine.*

sham·an·i·sm /ˈʃeɪ·mən·ɪ·zᵊm/ *n* [U] • Shamanism is a form of religion which includes a belief in the power of the shaman to control and influence good and evil spirits.

sham·an·is·tic /ˌʃeɪ·məˈnɪs·tɪk/ *adj* [not gradable]

sham·ble /ˈʃæm·bl̩/ *v* [I] to walk slowly and awkwardly, without lifting your feet correctly • *Sick patients shambled along the hospital corridors.* • *He was a strange, shambling figure who wandered from place to place trying to sell books* *he wrote himself.* • *With a shambling* **gait** *she came into the room, looking older than the last time we had seen her.*

sham·bles /ˈʃæm·blz/ *n* [U] *infml* (a place, event or situation which is in) a state of confusion, of not being well organized or of untidiness • *The new bookkeeper says the accounts are* **a** *shambles.* • *The morning after the party, the house was* **a total/complete** *shambles.* • *The match* **degenerated into**/*was* **reduced to a** *shambles.* • *The country's economy is* **in a** *shambles.* • *The way these files are arranged is the biggest shambles I've ever seen.*

sham·bol·ic /£ʃæmˈbɒl·ɪk, $-ˈbɑː·lɪk/ *adj Br infml* • *Things are often a bit shambolic* (= confused and not well organized) *at the beginning of the school year.* • *The country's shambolic civil service is about to be reorganized, with the loss of several thousand jobs.* • *Anna is far too shambolic to be able to run a business.* • *Sorry, the kitchen's a bit shambolic – I haven't had time to tidy it up yet.*

sham·bol·i·cal·ly /£ʃæmˈbɒl·ɪ·kli, $-ˈbɑː·lɪ-/ *adv Br infml*

shame BAD FEELING /ʃeɪm/ *n* [U] an uncomfortable feeling of guilt or of being ashamed because of your own or someone else's bad behaviour • *She was full of shame about having deceived her friend.* • *He said that he felt no shame for what he had done.* • *Many people were filled with a* **deep (sense of)** *shame at the actions taken by their government.* • *The children* **hung/bowed** *their* **heads in** *shame.* • *The shame* **of** *the scandal was so great that he shot himself a few weeks later.* • *If anyone found out that I who took the money, I'd* **die of** *shame.* • *It should be a matter of shame* **to** *the government that so many of the country's children don't have enough to eat.* • **To** *my shame,* (= I feel ashamed because) *I never wrote and thanked Mary for her present.* • *It* **puts** *me* **to** *shame* (= I feel ashamed) *that it's taken me so long to write David the letter I owe him.* • *You can't go out dressed like that –* **have** *you* **no** *shame* (= ability to feel ashamed because you are not dressed in an acceptable way)*?* • Shame can also be loss of honour and respect: *He thinks there's great shame in being out of work, and unable to provide for his family.* ○ *In some societies, if a woman leaves her husband, it* **brings** *shame* **on** *her and her family.* • *Shame* **on** *you* (= You should feel ashamed) *for being so unkind.* • *(humorous) You mean you were in town and you didn't come and see us – shame* **on** *you!* • People sometimes say 'Shame!' to express disapproval of something that is being said by a public speaker: *To cries of 'Shame!', the minister announced that taxes were being increased.*

shame *obj* /ʃeɪm/ *v* [T] • *Years ago in England, villagers used to clang pots and pans to shame a violent man* (= cause him to feel ashamed). • *It shames me that I treated her so badly.* • *The city is shamed by the large number of homeless people living on its streets.* • *The behaviour of a few children has shamed* (= caused a loss of honour to) *the whole school.* • If you shame someone **into** or **out of** an action, you cause them to do it or not to do it because they feel ashamed: *The number of people out of work has shamed the government into taking action to prevent further job losses.* ○ *She's trying to shame her husband out of drinking so heavily, but without much success.*

shame·ful /ˈʃeɪm·fᵊl/ *adj disapproving* • Shameful means deserving of blame or being a reason for feeling ashamed: *He treated her in a shameful way.* ○ *I didn't think that there was anything shameful in what I had done.* ○ *The crime figures are shameful.* ○ *The family have kept their shameful secret for years.* ○ **It's** *shameful* **that** *his own country did not fully appreciate his talent until it was recognized abroad.* [+ *that* clause]

shame·ful·ly /ˈʃeɪm·fᵊl·i/ *adv disapproving* • *The children had been shamefully neglected.* • *Both of you have behaved shamefully.* • *I'm shamefully behind in my work.*

shame·ful·ness /ˈʃeɪm·fᵊl·nəs/ *n* [U] *disapproving*

shame·less /ˈʃeɪm·ləs/ *adj disapproving* • Shameless means not ashamed, esp. about something generally considered unacceptable: *She is quite shameless* **about** *her ambition.* ○ *He has a shameless desire for power.* ○ *They seem to have a shameless disregard for truth.* ○ *The magazine printed a shameless article about the singer's private life.* • Shameless also means behaving in a way intended to attract sexual interest, without feeling ashamed about it: *She's a shameless* **hussy**.

shame·less·ly /ˈʃeɪm·lə·sli/ *adv disapproving* • *The government has shamelessly abandoned its principles.* • *They are shamelessly trying to exploit their advantage.* • *He shamelessly admits that his main interest is in making money.* • *She's shamelessly having an affair with her friend's husband.*

shame·less·ness /ˈʃeɪm·lə·snəs/ *n* [U] *disapproving*

shame MISFORTUNE /ʃeɪm/ *n* [U] an unlucky situation • **It's a (great)** *shame* **that** *we have had to cancel the concert, but we just didn't sell enough tickets.* [+ *that* clause] • **It's a crying** (= very great) **shame that** *the hospital has been forced to close.* [+ *that* clause] • *Have some more vegetables –* **it** *would* **be a** *shame* **to** *waste them.* [+ *to* infinitive] • *"Douglas is having to miss the school concert because he's ill." "Oh,* **what a** *shame/***that's a** *shame!"* • **What a** *shame* **that** *you couldn't come to party.* [+ *that* clause]

shame *obj* COMPARE WELL /ʃeɪm/ *v* [T] to cause (something) by comparison to seem not to be of a high standard • *Our neighbour's garden shames ours.* • *The school's examination results shame those of the other schools in the area.*

shame /ʃeɪm/ *n* [U] • *Your cooking* **puts** *mine* **to** *shame* (= makes it seem not good). • *Mexico City's clean, cheap and user-friendly subway system could* **put** *New York's* **to** *shame.*

shame·faced /ˌʃeɪmˈfeɪst, ˈ--/ *adj* awkward and embarrassed; ashamed • *He looked somewhat shamefaced when he realized his mistake.* • *Two shamefaced children came to apologize for kicking their ball into my garden and damaging my flowers.*

shame·fa·ced·ly /ˌʃeɪmˈfeɪst·li, ˈ-ˌ--, -ˈfeɪ·sɪd-, ˈ-ˌ---/ *adv* • *"I'm sorry for what I said," she said shamefacedly.*

sham·my (leath·er) /ˈʃæm·i/ *n* [C/U] See at CHAMOIS

sham·poo /ʃæmˈpuː/ *n pl* **shampoos** (a) soapy liquid used for washing hair, or for washing particular objects or materials • *an anti-dandruff shampoo* • *a carpet shampoo* • *a car shampoo* • *suede shampoo* [C] • *Directions: wet hair, apply shampoo and massage into rich lather.* [U] • *This frequent-wash shampoo and conditioner is not tested on animals.* [U] • A shampoo is also an act of washing something, esp. your hair, with shampoo: *My hair/The rug/The dog needs a shampoo.* [C] • *She went to the hairdressers for a shampoo* **and set**. [C]

sham·poo *obj* /ʃæmˈpuː/ *v* [T] he/she/it **shampoos**, **shampooing**, *past* **shampooed** • *When I went to the hairdresser's, Duncan shampooed my hair* (= washed it with shampoo) *before Tracy cut it.* • *I had to shampoo the sofa because I spilled a cup of coffee on it.*

sham·rock /£ˈʃæm·rɒk, $-rɑːk/ *n* a plant which has three round leaves, arranged in a triangular pattern, on each stem • *The shamrock is the national emblem of Ireland.* [U] • *A clump of shamrocks was growing in the lawn.* [C]

shan·dy /ˈʃæn·di/ *n esp. Br and Aus* a drink made by mixing together beer and LEMONADE or sometimes **ginger beer** • *Do you want lager or shandy?* [U] • *Two shandies* (= glasses of this drink)*, please.* [C]

shan·ghai /ˌʃæŋˈhaɪ, ˈ--/ *n* [C] *Aus for* CATAPULT

Shan·gri–La /ˌʃæŋ·grɪˈlɑː/ *n* [not after *the*] an imaginary distant beautiful place, where everything is pleasant • *New York is a shopper's Shangri-La.*

shank STRAIGHT PART /ʃæŋk/ *n* [C] the long thin straight part of a device or tool, which connects the end of the device or tool that you hold with the end of it which operates, or the long thin straight part of particular objects • *the shank* **of** *a screwdriver* • *the shank* **of** *a key* • *the shank* **of** *a nail*

shank LEG /ʃæŋk/ *n* [C] *dated or humorous* the leg of a person or animal, esp. the part below the knee

shanks's po·ny /£ˌʃæŋk·sɪzˈpəʊ·ni, $-ˈpoʊ-/, **shank's mare** /£ˌʃæŋk·sɪzˈmeəʳ, $-ˈmer/ *n* [U] *infml* walking as a way of travelling • *As there's no public transport, I suppose we'll have to use Shanks's pony.*

shan't /£ʃɑːnt, $ʃænt/ *short form of* shall not • *I shan't be able to come to your party.* • *"Pick those books up immediately." "Shan't* (= I refuse to)*!"*

shan·ty HOUSE /£ˈʃæn·ti, $-ţi/ *n* [C] a small, badly built house, usually made from pieces of wood or metal or cardboard, in which poor people live, esp. in a city • *Over 3 million people in the city live in shanties without a proper water supply.* • A **shanty town** is an area in or on the edge of a city, in which poor people live in small, badly built houses: *Many people have been forced to live in squalid shanty towns near the factories where they work.*

shan·ty SONG /£ˈʃæn·ti, $-ţi/, *Am usually* **chan·ty**, *Am also* **chan·tey** *n* [C] a song which sailors sang in the past while they were working on a ship • *There's a well-known* **(sea)** *shanty that begins 'What shall we do with the drunken sailor?'.*

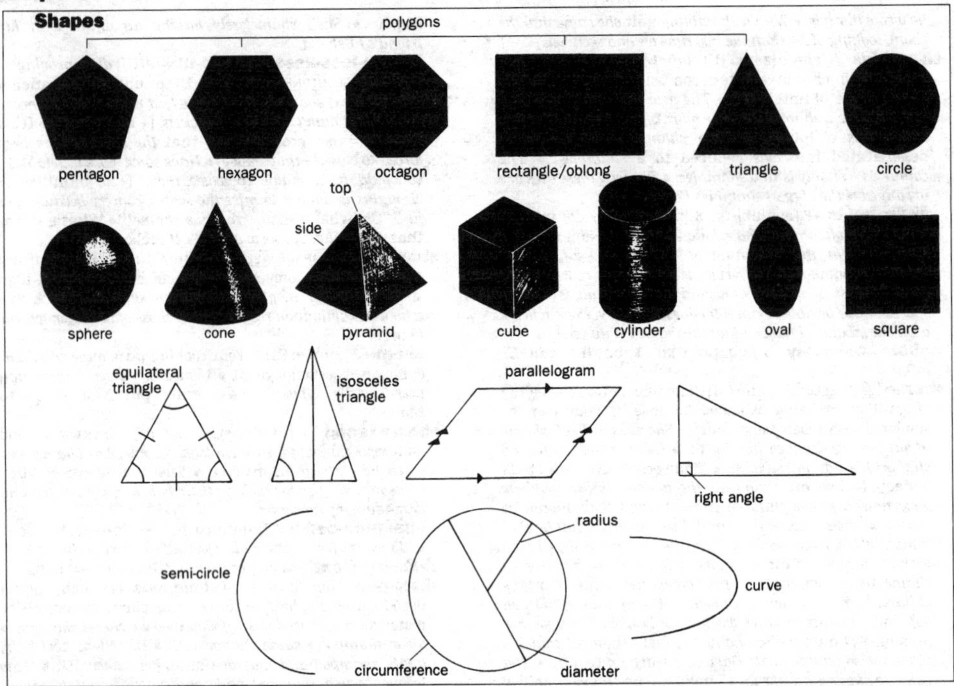

shape FORM /ʃeɪp/ *n* the outer form or appearance that something has • *Apples and oranges have* **a** *round shape.* [C] • *Our table is oval* **in** *shape.* [U] • *My bicycle wheel has got bent* **out of** *shape.* [U] • *We watched the vase begin to* **take** *shape* (= have its characteristic form) *in the potter's hands.* [U] • *This T-shirt has been washed so many times that it's* **lost** *its shape* (= has become loose and lost its form). [U] • *Clay can be moulded into almost any shape.* [C] • *These wine bottles have very distinctive shapes.* [C] • *It's difficult to build a wall straight if the bricks are all different shapes.* [C] • *In 1953 Watson and Crick discovered the shape* **of** *DNA.* [C] • *The shape* **of** *the landscape is constantly changing.* [C] • *Kim's birthday cake was* **in the** *shape* **of** *a train.* [C] • **In the shape of** means appearing as: *I was worried when my car broke down late at night, but luckily help arrived in the shape of a police officer.* ○ *We had a nice surprise yesterday, in the shape of a call from a friend we hadn't seen for years.* • A shape is also an arrangement that is formed by joining lines together in a particular way: *A triangle is a shape with three sides.* [C] ○ *To make jam tarts, you need to roll out the pastry, then cut circular shapes* (= pieces in the form of circles) *out of it.* [C] ○ *The children made patterns by sticking shapes onto paper.* [C] • *(fig.) Life on Earth* **takes** *many shapes* (= There are many types of living being on Earth). [C] • *(fig.) In the story of Faust, Faust is tempted by the devil, who has* **taken the** *shape* **of** (= made himself look like) *a man.* [C] • A shape is also a person or object that you cannot see clearly because it is too dark, or because the person or object is too far away: *Through the window, I could see a dark shape in the street outside.* [C] ○ *A huge shape suddenly appeared out of the mist.* [C] • **All shapes and sizes** means many different types: *We sell all shapes and sizes* **of** *teddy bear.* ○ *Cars* **come in** *all shapes and sizes.* ○ *Teachers have to be aware that children* **come in** *all shapes and sizes, and can't all be treated exactly the same.* • *I'm opposed to war* **in any shape or form** (= of any type).

shape *obj* /ʃeɪp/ *v* [T] • *She uses a special brush to shape her hair* (= give it a particular appearance). • *The skirt has been shaped* (= made in a particular form) *so that it hangs loosely.* • *When you've made the dough, shape it* **into** (= give it the form of) *two loaves.* • *Early humans shaped* (= made) *tools* **out of** *stone.*

shaped /ʃeɪpt/ *adj* [not gradable] • *She was wearing sunglasses with lenses shaped* **like** *hearts.* • *This carrot is rather unusually shaped.* • *Jackie has a perfectly shaped figure.* • *Although he only came fourth this time, he is shaped* **like** (= looks as if he will be) *a future winner.*

-shaped /-ʃeɪpt/ *combining form* • *She was wearing sunglasses with heart-shaped lenses* (= those in the form of a heart). • *I've just bought an oval-shaped table* (= one in the form of an oval). • *Our kitchen is L-shaped* (= in the form of an L).

shape·less /ˈʃeɪp·ləs/ *adj* • Shapeless means without a clear form or structure: *I was trying to make a clay pot, but it ended up just a shapeless lump.* ○ *His ideas are interesting, but they're rather shapeless.* ○ *The child seems to be suffering from all sorts of shapeless fears.* ○ *She was wearing a shapeless black dress.*

shape·less·ly /ˈʃeɪ·plə·sli/ *adv* • *Her clothes hung shapelessly* (= loosely and without fitting well) *on her.*

shape·less·ness /ˈʃeɪ·plə·snəs/ *n* [U]

shape·ly /ˈʃeɪ·pli/ *adj* **-ier, -iest** *approving* • Shapely means having an attractive form. It is often used of a woman's body or parts of a woman's body: *shapely legs* • *a shapely mouth* • *a shapely bone structure* ○ *Car manufacturers have been criticized for using shapely models to advertise their cars.*

shape·li·ness /ˈʃeɪ·pli·nəs/ *n* [U]

shape CHARACTER /ʃeɪp/ *n* [U] the way something is organized; the general character or nature of something • *We need to have the main shape* **of** *the proposals decided by early April.* • *Technological developments have changed the shape* **of** *industry.* • *There have been some disagreements about what the future shape* **of** *the newspaper should be.* • *I think we need to change the shape* **of** *our campaign.* • *Our ideas are beginning to* **take** *shape* (= become formed). • *I hope the fashions pictured in this magazine are not* **the shape of things to come** (= a sign of what is likely to be popular in the future).

shape *obj* /ʃeɪp/ *v* [T] • To shape a belief or an idea is to decide or influence its form: *He said that he thought religion had lost much of its influence in shaping the way people think.* ○ *They come from a generation whose attitudes were shaped during the Vietnam war.* ○ *My relationship with my father played a major part in shaping my attitude towards men.* ○ *Many people are not able to shape their own destinies.* ○ *He had a great influence on the shaping of the government's economic policy/strategy.* ○ *We are all shaped* (= What our characters are like is influenced or decided) *by the times in which we live.*

shape CONDITION /ʃeɪp/ *n* [U] (good) condition or state of health • *It's taken us five years to* **get** *our house* **into** *shape* (= good condition). • *He made his money by buying up businesses that were* **in** *bad/poor shape* (= condition), *then selling them off bit by bit.* • *She runs six miles every day to help keep herself* **in** *shape* (= in good physical condition). • *She found it hard to* **get back into** *shape* (= good physical condition) *after the birth of her baby.* • *I haven't had any* *exercise for weeks, and I'm really* **out of** *shape* (= not in good physical condition). • *She had a major operation last week, so she's not* **in** *very good shape* (= state of health) *at the moment.* • *You're* **in** *no shape* (= not in a good enough state of health) *to go to work today.* • *"How are you?" "Oh, I'm* **in** *great shape* (= I'm very well)*"* • *(fig.) All our bags are packed, and we don't have to leave for another hour, so we're* **in** *good shape* (= in a good situation). • If you **knock/lick/** *(Am usually)* **whip something or someone into shape**, you take action to cause them to be in the good condition that you want them to be in: *The prime minister's main aim is to knock the economy into shape.* ○ *Sam is rather a difficult child, but his teacher will soon lick him into shape.* • See also SHIPSHAPE.

shape up *v adv* to develop • **How** *are your plans shaping up?* [I] • *Things seem to be shaping up nicely.* [I] • *Colin is shaping up quite well in his new job.* [I] • *The election is shaping up* **to** *be* (= seems likely to be) *a close contest.* [+ to infinitive] • *This is shaping up* **as** *a difficult month.* [I] • If you tell someone to shape up, you want them to improve their behaviour or performance: *I've been told that if I don't shape up, I'll lose my job.* [I] ○ **Shape up or ship out** (= Improve your performance or leave)*!*

shard /£ ʃɑːd, $ ʃɑːrd/ *n* [C] a piece of a glass, cup, plate, bowl or metal object which has been broken • *After the accident, a shard* **of** *metal had to be removed from his leg.* • *Shards* **of** *glass have been cemented into the top of the wall to stop people climbing over it.*

share PART /£ ʃeəʳ, $ ʃer/ *n* the part of a larger amount, which has been divided between several people, that belongs to or is owed to or has to be done by a particular person • *The total bill comes to £80, so our share is £20.* [C] • *I think you've had more than your* **(fair)** *share* **of** *that ice cream.* [C] • *We must make sure that everyone gets equal shares* **of** *the food.* [C] • *The managing director said that the company had increased its share* **of** *the market this year.* [C] • *The party's share* **of** *the vote fell from 39% to 24%.* [C] • *Middle-class students take up a large share* **of** *university places.* [C] • *We have a quarter share* **in** *a house in Spain.* [C] • *All of us had a share* **in** *making the decision.* [C] • *She's not doing her share* **of** *the work.* [C] • *He should take his share* **of** *the blame for what happened.* [C] • *We must all accept some share* **of** *the responsibility.* [U] • *Why don't we* **go shares** (= divide the cost between us) **on** *lunch?* • If you have your **share of** something, you have a lot of it: *We've certainly got our share of problems at the moment.* ○ *They've had more than their* **(fair)** *share of troubles recently.* ○ *She's had her* **fair** *share of tragedies in her life.*

share *(obj)* /£ ʃeəʳ, $ ʃer/ *v* • *Our house isn't big enough for the children each to have their own room, so they have to share* (= to use a room together). [I] • *Let Harry play with your toys as well, Clare – you must learn to share* (= to allow other people to use something which is yours). [I] • *Bill and I shared* (= worked together in) *an office for years.* [T] • *I share a house* (= live in a house together) **with** *four other people.* [T] • *She knew that he was the person she wanted to share her life* (= experience it together) **with**. [T] • If two or more people share an activity, they each do some of it: *Shall we share the driving?* [T] ○ *If we share the preparation for the party* **between** *us, it won't be so much work for one person.* [T] ○ *Anna and Max share* **(in)** *the housework and childcare.* [T; I + *in*] • *Lyn and Josh share a birthday/share the same birthday* (= they both have their birthday on the same day). [T] • If two or more people or things share a feeling, quality, etc., they both or all have the same feeling, quality, etc.: *We share an interest in sailing.* [T] ○ *All hospitals share some common characteristics.* [T] ○ *I don't share your views/beliefs.* [T] ○ *Lucy and I have shared many experiences.* [T] ○ *We share your concern about what happened.* [T] ○ *We share* **(in)** *your sorrow at the death of your father.* [T; I + *in*] • If you share food, money, goods, etc., you divide them and give part of them to someone else: *Will you share your sandwich* **with** *me?* [T] ○ *We'll share the sweets* **(out) among** *everyone.* [T/M] ○ *When my uncle died, his things were shared* **(out) between** *all the members of the family.* [T/M] ○ *All the employees in the company share* **(in)** *the profits.* [T; I + *in*] ○ *We should share* **(in)** *the reward.* [T; I + *in*] • If you share your thoughts, feelings, ideas, etc., you tell someone else about them: *He's not very good at sharing his worries.* [T] ○ *I have an idea I'd like to share* **with** *you.* [T] ○ *It's nice to have someone you can share your problems* **with**. [T] ○ *Come on, Bob, share the joke.* [T] • *Don't keep all those chocolates to yourself –* **share and share alike** (= let everyone have an equal amount of them). • *(Br and Aus)* A **share- out** is an act of dividing something between several people: *Everyone benefited from the share-out* **of** *the profits.* ○ *We need to organize a share-out* **of** *the tasks that still need to be done.* • *(saying)* 'A problem shared is a problem halved' means that if you tell someone about a problem, that makes it easier to deal with. [T]

shared /£ ʃeəd, $ ʃerd/ *adj* [not gradable] • *The company is in shared ownership* (= is owned by more than one person). • *She and her husband have many shared interests* (= have many of the same interests) • *We all sat and talked about our shared experiences* (= those which we had all had) *of India.*

share PART OF A BUSINESS /£ ʃeəʳ, $ ʃer/ *n* [C] one of the equal parts into which the ownership of a company is divided and which can be bought by members of the public • *The value of my shares has risen/fallen by 8%.* • *We've got some shares* **in** *British Telecom.* • *They made all their money investing in* **stocks and** *shares.* • *Share* **prices** *showed little change today.* • *The FTSE 100 share* **index** (= record of the value of shares) *closed 25·3 points down.*

share·crop·per /£ ˈʃeəˌkrɒp·əʳ, $ ˈʃerˌkrɑː·pɚ/ *n* [C] *Am* a farmer who rents land and who gives part of his or her crop as rent

share·crop·ping /£ ˈʃeəˌkrɒp·ɪŋ, $ ˈʃerˌkrɑː·pɪŋ/ *n* [U] *Am*

share·hold·er /£ ˈʃeəˌhəʊl·dəʳ, $ ˈʃerˌhoʊl·dɚ/, *esp. Am* **stock·hold·er** *n* [C] a person who owns some of the equal parts into which the ownership of a company is divided • *Shareholders have seen the value of their shares fall by one fifth since last July.* • *Shareholders will be voting on the proposed merger of the companies next week.*

share·ware /£ ˈʃeə·weəʳ, $ ˈʃer·wer/ *n* [U] computer programs that you are allowed to use for a short period before you decide whether or not to buy them • *Shareware and public domain software is often just as good as commercial software costing much more.* • *Shareware firms will usually sell you an upgraded version of their software for a little extra.*

sha·ri·a /ʃəˈriː·ə/, **sha·ri·ah** *n* [U] the holy laws of Islam, which cover all parts of a Muslim's life

shark /£ ʃɑːk, $ ʃɑːrk/ *n* [C] *pl* **shark** or **sharks** a very large fish that has sharp teeth and a vertical triangular part on its back which can sometimes be seen above the water. There are various types of shark. • *He was attacked by a man-eating shark.* • *The movie 'Jaws' is about a shark that kills people in the ocean off the coast of the US.* • *(infml disapproving)* A shark is also a dishonest person, esp. one who persuades other people to pay too much money for something: *Often the image of a lawyer in popular films is of a shark in a smart suit.* ○ *People who need a place to live can often find themselves at the mercy of local property sharks.* • *(Aus)* A **shark fence** is a fence, often made of wire net, which surrounds an open swimming area to protect swimmers from sharks. • PIC **Fish**

shark·skin /£ ˈʃɑːk·skɪn, $ ˈʃɑːrk-/ *n* [U] a type of shiny material, made from artificial fibres, which is used for making clothing • *a sharkskin jacket* • *a sharkskin suit*

shark·spot·ter /£ ˈʃɑːkˌspɒt·əʳ, $ ˈʃɑːrkˌspɑː·t̬ɚ/ *n* [C] *Aus* a HELICOPTER which flies along an area of coast so that the person flying it can warn swimmers if there are SHARKS in the sea

sharp ABLE TO CUT /£ ʃɑːp, $ ʃɑːrp/ *adj* **-er, -est** having a thin edge or point which can cut something or make a hole in it, or producing a feeling of pain as if you have been cut • *Chop the spinach with a sharp knife.* • *To cut steak, you need a knife with a sharp edge/blade.* • *A shark has sharp teeth.* • *The point of this pencil isn't sharp enough.* • *Her fingernails are very sharp.* • *I stepped on a sharp stone.* • *She nudged me with a sharp elbow, to tell me to be quiet.* • If you describe parts of someone's face as sharp, you mean that they are pointed: *He had a thin face with a sharp nose.* See also **sharp-nosed** at SHARP CLEVER. ○ *She had lively blue eyes set in sharp features.* • *I have this sharp* **pain** (= one which feels as if I am being cut) *in my chest, doctor.* • If someone is sharp or makes a sharp statement, they speak or act in a severe and angry way, which can hurt other people: *He was rather sharp* **with** *me when I asked if he could help me.* ○ *The government's proposals have come in for some sharp* **criticism**. ○ *Her comments drew the sharp words from Alan that she didn't know what she was talking about.* ○ *He delivered a sharp rebuke to his son.* ○ *Jane has rather a sharp* **tongue**/*Jane is rather sharp-***tongued** (= often speaks in a severe and critical way). • If something is sharp, or has a sharp taste, it has a strong taste which

Sharp

sharp bend

sharp blade

sharp

causes a feeling in your mouth as if your tongue is being cut: *This cheese is rather sharp.* ○ *Lemons have a sharp taste.* • *(Br)* **The sharp end** is the part of an activity, such as a job, where the most problems are likely to be found: *A job like hers would be much too demanding for me, but she enjoys being at the sharp end.* ○ *These people are at the sharp end* **of** *the industry.* • *Building contractors are subject to rules aimed at protecting customers from* **sharp practice** (= a way of behaving in business that is dishonest but not illegal). • Compare BLUNT [NOT SHARP]. • [PIC> **Sharp** (KOR)

sharp·en *obj* /£ˈʃɑː·pᵊn, $ˈʃɑːr-/ *v* [T] • *This knife needs to be sharpened* (= made sharp or sharper). • *My pencil is blunt – I'll have to sharpen it.* • *He was attacked by a gang carrying sharpened sticks.* • *The company has cut production costs in an attempt to sharpen its competitive edge.* • See also SHARPEN.

sharp·en·er /£ˈʃɑː·pᵊn·əʳ, $ˈʃɑːr·pᵊn·ɚ/ *n* [C] • A sharpener is a machine or tool for making esp. pencils or knives sharper: *a pencil/knife sharpener*

sharp·ly /£ˈʃɑː·pli, $ˈʃɑːr-/ *adv* • *a sharply* (= in a way which will cut or make a hole) *pointed nail* • Sharply also means severely and angrily: *He spoke sharply to his daughter.* ○ *The television company received several sharply-worded letters of complaint about the commercial.* ○ *The police have been sharply criticized for their handling of the affair.*

sharp·ness /£ˈʃɑːp·nəs, $ˈʃɑːrp-/ *n* [U] • *the sharpness* **of** *a knife/needle/pain* • *the sharpness* **of** *his comments/attack*

sharp [SUDDEN] /£ʃɑːp, $ʃɑːrp/ *adj* **-er, -est** happening suddenly and quickly and strongly • *There will be a sharp drop in temperature tonight.* • *Many young plants were killed by the sharp* **frost**. • *The changes to the country's economy have resulted in a sharp deterioration in people's standard of living.* • *The sharp change in her mood surprised all of us.* • *There has been a sharp* **rise/increase** *in the number of cases of the illness recently.* • *Many companies have experienced a sharp* **fall/decline** *in profits this year.* • *He crashed his car driving too fast round a sharp* **bend**. • *After the traffic lights, there's a sharp* **right/left turn** *into Cromwell Road.* • *She suffered a sharp* **blow** *to her head when she fell off her bike.* • *A* **sharp** *noise woke me with a start.* • [PIC> **Sharp**

sharp /£ʃɑːp, $ʃɑːrp/ *adv* **-er, -est** • *Go past the church, then make a sharp* **left/right** (= a sudden left/right) *turn.*

shar·pish /£ˈʃɑː·pɪʃ, $ˈʃɑːr-/ *adv Br infml* • *I think we'd better get out of here pretty sharpish* (= quickly).

sharp·ly /£ˈʃɑː·pli, $ˈʃɑːr-/ *adv* • *Inflation has* **risen/fallen** *sharply.* • *His health has* **improved/deteriorated** *sharply this week.* • *She looked up sharply when she heard someone come into the room.* • *As you go down the hill, the road bends sharply to the left.* • [LP> **Very, completely**

sharp·ness /£ˈʃɑːp·nəs, $ˈʃɑːrp-/ *n* [U] • *the sharpness* **of** *the increase/fall* • *the sharpness* **of** *a blow* • *the sharpness* **of** *a curve*

sharp [CLEAR] /£ʃɑːp, $ʃɑːrp/ *adj* **-er, -est** clear; easy to see or understand • *Our new television has a very sharp picture.* • *On a clear day, the mountains stand* **in** *sharp* **contrast** *to the blue sky.* • *Sales this month have shown a slight increase,* **in** *sharp* **contrast** *to those of the last few months.* • *The incident has again brought* **into** *sharp* **focus** *the potential influence of what children watch on how they behave.* • *There is a sharp* **distinction** *between crimes which involve injury to people and those which don't.* • *The terrorist attack was a sharp* **reminder** *of how dangerous the world can be.*

sharp·en *(obj)* /£ˈʃɑː·pᵊn, $ˈʃɑːr-/ *v* • *How do you sharpen* (= make clearer) *the focus on this camera?* [T] • See also SHARPEN.

sharp·ly /£ˈʃɑː·pli, $ˈʃɑːr-/ *adv* • *a sharply* **focused** *photograph* • *Men contrasted sharply with women on the issues they considered important.* • *We have sharply differing views.*

sharp·ness /£ˈʃɑːp·nəs, $ˈʃɑːrp-/ *n* [U] • *the sharpness* **of** *a photograph/image*

sharp [CLEVER] /£ʃɑːp, $ʃɑːrp/ *adj* **-er, -est** quick to notice; clever • *Bird-watchers need to have sharp ears and eyes.* • *She has a sharp eye for a bargain.* • *Make sure you keep a sharp eye/watch on the children when you go swimming.* • *The mistake was spotted by a sharp-***eyed** *secretary.* • *Our new director is very sharp.* • *She manages to combine a sharp* **mind/intellect** *with a sympathetic manner.* • *She's the type of student who is always asking sharp questions.* • *She is a sharp student.* • *He will be remembered as a politician of sharp* **wit** *who always spoke his mind.* • *You need to be very sharp-***witted** *in this job.* • *Patrick has a sharp sense of humour.* • *The play was full of sharp one-liners.* • *Many of Woody Allen's films are sharp comedies.* • Someone who is **sharp-nosed** is good at dealing with money, and making advantageous financial arrangements: *a sharp-nosed banker*

sharp·en *obj* /£ˈʃɑː·pᵊn, $ˈʃɑːr-/ *v* [T] • *I want go to university not only to broaden my knowledge and experience, but also to sharpen my mind.* • *Our opponents on this issue have some strong arguments, so we'll need to sharpen our* **wits** *if we're going to defeat them.* • See also SHARPEN.

sharp·ly /£ˈʃɑː·pli, $ˈʃɑːr-/ *adv* • *Her ears are sharply attuned to her baby's cry.* • *During the discussion, Simon made several sharply observant comments.*

sharp·ness /£ˈʃɑːp·nəs, $ˈʃɑːrp-/ *n* [U] • *At 71, he worries about losing his sharpness.* • *She has a remarkable sharpness* **of** *mind.*

sharp [FASHIONABLE] /£ʃɑːp, $ʃɑːrp/ *adj* **-er, -est** *infml* fashionable • *Tony is a very sharp dresser.* • *He was wearing a sharp blue suit.* • *The hotel bar was full of sharp-***suited** *business executives.*

sharp·ly /£ˈʃɑː·pli, $ˈʃɑːr-/ *adv* • *He was sharply dressed.*

sharp·ness /£ˈʃɑːp·nəs, $ˈʃɑːrp-/ *n* [U] • *Even when I wear jeans and a denim shirt, I still have shoulder pads because I like sharpness and elegance – I don't like to look scruffy.*

sharp [MUSIC] /£ʃɑːp, $ʃɑːrp/ *adj, adv* **-er, -est** (in music) higher than the correct or stated note • *The E string on my guitar is a bit sharp.* • *This concerto is in the key of C sharp* (= the set of musical notes a SEMITONE higher than the one based on the note C). [after n] • *She sang sharp* (= slightly higher than she should have) *on the top notes.* • Compare FLAT [MUSIC]; NATURAL [MUSIC]. • [PIC> **Music, Sharp**

sharp /£ʃɑːp, $ʃɑːrp/ *n* [C] • A sharp is (the sign for) a note that is slightly higher than the stated note.

sharp·en *obj* /£ˈʃɑː·pᵊn, $ˈʃɑːr-/ *v* [T] • *The A string on your violin needs to be sharpened.*

sharp [EXACTLY] /£ʃɑːp, $ʃɑːrp/ *adv* [not gradable] exactly at the stated time • *Dad says I've got to be home by midnight sharp.* • *The performance will start at 7.30 sharp.*

sharp·en *obj* /£ˈʃɑː·pᵊn, $ˈʃɑːr-/ *v* [T] to make stronger • *Recent changes in the law have sharpened competition between the airlines.* • *That long walk has certainly sharpened my appetite.* • *The riots at the prison have sharpened the debate about how prisons should be run.* • *Hearing the story about ghosts sharpened my son's fear of the dark.* • Sharpen can also mean improve: *I'm going on a course which I hope will help me sharpen my computer skills.* ○ *After six defeats in a row, it's time the team sharpened* **(up)** *its performance a bit.* [T/M] ○ *(fig.) She told me to sharpen* **(up)** *my* **act** (= improve my behaviour or performance). [T/M] • *If the company doesn't soon* **sharpen up** (= improve its performance), *it will go out of business.* • See also **sharpen** at SHARP [ABLE TO CUT]; SHARP [CLEAR]; SHARP [CLEVER].

sharp·shoot·er /£ˈʃɑːpˌʃuː·təʳ, $ˈʃɑːrpˌʃuː·t̬ɚ/ *n* [C] a person who is skilled at firing a gun and accurately hitting what they are aiming at

shat /ʃæt/ *past simple and past participle of* SHIT

shat·ter *(obj)* /£ˈʃæt·əʳ, $ˈʃæt̬·ɚ/ *v* to (cause to) break suddenly into very small pieces • *The glass shattered* **into** *a* *thousand tiny pieces.* [I] • *A stone thrown up from the road by the wheel of a passing car shattered the windscreen.* [T] • *His leg was shattered in the accident.* [T] • Shatter can also mean to end or damage: *The book shattered all her* **illusions** *about the Romans.* [T] ○ *All his* **dreams** *have been shattered.* [T] ○ *Noisy motorbikes shattered* **the peace.** [T]

shat·tered /£ˈʃæt·əd, $ˈʃæṭ·ɚd/ *adj* • *The family were shattered* (=extremely upset) *at the news of Annabel's suicide.* • *I am shattered* **that** *this decision has been made without any consultation or discussion.* [+ *that* clause]

–shat·ter·ing /£-ˌʃæt·ər·ɪŋ, $-ˌʃæṭ·ɚ-/ *combining form* • *a record-shattering movie* (=one which breaks previous records) • *a confidence-shattering defeat* (=one which destroys confidence) • See also **earth-shattering** at EARTH [PLANET].

shat·tered /£ˈʃæt·əd, $ˈʃæṭ·ɚd/ *adj Br infml* (of a person) extremely tired • *I had a meeting after work so by the time I got home I was shattered.*

shat·ter·ing /£ˈʃæt·ər·ɪŋ, $ˈʃæṭ·ɚ-/ *adj* • *We have a shattering* (=extremely tiring) *schedule of seven meetings in two days.*

shat·ter·proof /£ˈʃæt·ə·pruːf, $ˈʃæṭ·ɚ-/ *adj* [not gradable] (esp. of glass or plastic) made so that it will not break into small pieces • *a shatterproof windscreen*

shave *(obj)* /ʃeɪv/ *v* to remove (hair) from (the body, esp. a man's face) by cutting it close to the skin with a RAZOR (=a device with a blade) or **shaver**, so that the skin feels smooth • *John needs to shave* (=remove the hair from his face) *twice a day.* [I] • *The barber will shave you* (=remove the hair from your face) *as well as cut your hair, if you want.* [T] • *"It's easier if you shave your legs in the bath," she said.* [T] • *Do you shave* **under** *your arms?* [I] • *When my dad shaved his beard* **(off)**, *he looked ten years younger.* [T/M] • If you shave an amount **off/from** an object or surface, you cut a very thin piece from it: *She shaved a few millimetres off the bottom of the door, so that it would open more easily.* [T] • To shave something by an amount, or shave an amount **off** something, is to reduce it by that amount: *Our prices have been shaved by 5%!* [T] ○ *The new high speed trains will shave 25 minutes* **off** *the journey time* (=reduce it by 25 minutes). [T] • [LP]> **Reflexive pronouns and verbs**

shave /ʃeɪv/ *n* [C] • A shave is the act of removing hair from someone's, esp. a man's, face: *I* **need** *a shave.* ○ *He washed his face and* **had** *a shave.*

shav·en /ˈʃeɪ·vən/ *adj* [not gradable] • *All the women in the band had shaven heads* (=those with hair removed from them).

shav·er /£ˈʃeɪ·vər, $-vɚ/ *n* [C] • A shaver is an electric device used for shaving hair from the face or body. • A *(Br)* **shaver point**/*(Am)* **shaver outlet** is a special opening in a wall, often in a bathroom, into which the plug of a shaver can be put in order to connect it with a supply of electricity. • Compare RAZOR. • [PIC]> **Bathroom**

shav·ing /ˈʃeɪ·vɪŋ/ *adj* [not gradable] • *a shaving kit* • *a shaving brush* • *shaving cream/foam*

shav·ing /ˈʃeɪ·vɪŋ/ *n* [C usually plural] • *The floor of the workshop was covered in wood shavings* (=small very thin pieces). • [PIC]> **Brush**

shawl /£ʃɔːl, $ʃɑːl/ *n* [C] a large piece of cloth worn esp. by women or girls over their shoulders and/or head

she /ʃiː/ *pronoun* used to refer to a woman, girl or female animal that has already been mentioned • *I asked my mother if she'd lend me some money, but she said no.* • *Harriet isn't very good at sport, but she's the best chess player in the school.* • *She's such a cute dog!* • She is also sometimes used instead of 'it' to refer to something, such as a country or vehicle, that has already been mentioned: *After India became independent, she chose to be a member of the Commonwealth.* ○ *Look at my new car – isn't she beautiful?* ○ *Bless this ship and all who sail in her.* • *"She who must be obeyed"* (title of a queen in Rider Haggard's book *She*, 1887) • [LP]> **Sexist language**

she /ʃiː/ *n* [C] • *It took us a while to realize the kitten was a she* (=a female) *not a he.*

she– /ʃiː-/ *combining form* • *a she-goat* (=a female GOAT) • *a she-wolf* (=a female WOLF) • A **she-devil** is a woman who is considered to be dangerous or evil.

s/he *pronoun* used in writing instead of 'she or he' to refer to a person whose sex is not known • *If any employee needs to take time off, s/he should contact the Personnel Department.* • See also THEY. • [LP]> **Sexist language**

sheaf /ʃiːf/ *n* [C] *pl* **sheaves** /ʃiːvz/ a number of things, esp. pieces of paper or plant stems, held or tied together • *A lawyer walked in, carrying a sheaf* **of** *papers in her hand.* • *The corn was cut, tied in sheaves and left to dry.*

shear *obj* [CUT] /£ʃɪər, $ʃɪr/ *v* [T] *past simple* **sheared**, *past part* **sheared** or **shorn** /£ʃɔːn, $ʃɔːrn/ to cut the wool off (a sheep) or *(esp. literary)* to cut (the hair on a person's head) close to the skin • *The farmer taught her how to shear sheep.* • *(esp. literary) He recalled the humiliation of having his hair shorn and being forced to exchange his clothes for the prison uniform.* • *(esp. literary) The men had all been shorn* **of** *their hair* (=had it cut close to their skin). • If you are shorn **of** something, you have it taken away from you: • *The ex-President, although shorn of his official powers, still has a lot of influence.*

shear·ing /£ˈʃɪə·rɪŋ, $ˈʃɪr·ɪŋ/ *n* [U] • *Sheep shearing is a very busy time on the farm.*

shear *(obj)* [BREAK] /£ʃɪər, $ʃɪr/ *v specialized* (esp. of metal parts) to break into two pieces, esp. because of a sideways force • *The old screws holding the engine casing had sheared* **(off).** [I]

shears /£ʃɪəz, $ʃɪrz/ *pl n* very large SCISSORS (=cutting tool) • *gardening shears* • *dressmaking shears* • *They use electric shears for sheep shearing.* • [PIC]> **Garden**

sheath /ʃiːθ/ *n* [C] a close-fitting protective covering • *The cable has a copper wire surrounded by a plastic sheath.* • *The nerves are surrounded and protected by thin sheaths of fatty tissue.* • A sheath is also a container into which a knife fits closely so that the blade cannot cut someone when it is not being used: *He drew the sword from its jewelled leather sheath.* • *(Br)* A sheath is also a CONDOM. • A **sheath knife** is a knife with a fixed blade: *He suddenly attacked the doctor with a sheath knife.*

sheathe *obj* /ʃiːð/ *v* [T] • *She sheathed the knife* (=put it back inside its sheath). • *The ships' hulls were sheathed* **in/with** *copper* (=covered with COPPER as a protection). • *The landscape was sheathed* (=covered) **in** *ice.*

sheath·ing /ˈʃiː·ðɪŋ/ *n* • *The concrete frame of the building is covered by a glass and metal sheathing* (=protective cover). [C] • *They use specially treated plywood as roof sheathing* (=protective outer covering). [U]

sheaves /ʃiːvz/ *pl of* SHEAF

she·bang /ʃɪˈbæŋ/ *n* [U] **the whole shebang** *esp. Am and Aus infml*, see at WHOLE

shed [BUILDING] /ʃed/ *n* [C] a building, often made of wood, for storing things such as garden tools, or a large simple building used for a particular activity • *a garden shed* • *a tool shed* • *a bicycle shed* • *The lambing shed was a huge concrete place.* • [PIC]> **Garden**

shed *obj* [GET RID OF] /ʃed/ *v* [T] **shedding**, *past* **shed** to get rid of (something not needed or wanted) • *The company yesterday announced that 900 jobs will be shed over the next few months.* • *Psychotherapy helped him to shed some of his insecurity/inhibitions.* • *The trees shed their leaves in autumn* (=they fall off naturally). • *In spring, when the weather is warmer, many animals shed their thicker winter coats* (=their hair falls out naturally). • *I'm going on a diet to see if I can shed* (= become thinner by losing) *a few kilos.* • *They ran down to the sea, shedding* (=taking off) *clothes as they went.* • *(Br) A lorry had shed* (=dropped by accident) *a load of gravel across the road.*

shed *obj* [PRODUCE] /ʃed/ *v* [T] **shedding**, *past* **shed** to produce (esp. tears, light or blood) • *She shed a few tears at her daughter's wedding.* • *The fluorescent bulbs shed a harsh light on the workbenches.* • *So much blood has been shed* (=So many people have been badly hurt or killed) *in this particular war.*

sheen /ʃiːn/ *n* [U] *approving* smooth brightness of a surface • *The conditioner gives the hair* **a** *beautiful soft sheen.* • *Using this polish will restore the sheen to your furniture/car.* • *(fig.) Her appearance is always perfect, with the sheen* (=well cared-for attractive appearance) *that only money can buy.*

sheep /ʃiːp/ *n* [C] *pl* **sheep** a farm animal, with thick esp. whitish-coloured hair, that eats grass, and which is kept for its hair, skin and meat • *Wool comes from sheep.* • *There was a* **flock** (=group) *of sheep on the hillside.* • *We heard the sheep* **bleating/baaing** *in the field.* • *(disapproving)* If you say that a group of people are **(like) sheep**, you mean that they all behave in the same way or all behave as they are told, because they are not able or do not want to think or act independently: *The politicians are like sheep, all afraid to act first, waiting to be told what to do.* • *(Br and Aus)* To **separate/tell/sort (out) the sheep from the goats** is to make clear which people in a particular group are of a higher ability than the others: *The uphill stages of the race* *will sort the sheep from the goats.* • *(Aus)* A **sheep station** is a large farm on which sheep are kept. • See also EWE; LAMB; MUTTON; RAM.

sheep·dip /ˈʃiːp·dɪp/ *n* a liquid in which sheep are washed in order to kill harmful insects living in their hair, or the container in which the liquid is put • *Fears have been expressed that sheepdip might be harmful to farmers.* [U] • *The sheep had to be forced into the sheepdip* (= container). [C]

sheep·dog /£ˈʃiːp·dɒg, $-dɑːg/ *n* [C] a dog trained to help a farmer control sheep and move them in the desired direction • *Two sheepdogs* **herded** *the sheep into pens.*

sheep·ish /ˈʃiː·pɪʃ/ *adj* embarrassed because you know that you have done something wrong or silly • *She gave me a sheepish smile and apologized.*

sheep·ish·ly /ˈʃiː·pɪʃ·li/ *adv* • *He sheepishly admitted he had lost the money in a card game.*

sheep·ish·ness /ˈʃiː·pɪʃ·nəs/ *n* [U]

sheep·shear·ing /£ˈʃiːpˌʃɪə·rɪŋ, $-ˌʃɪr·ɪŋ/ *n* [C/U] the act or occasion of cutting the wool of sheep

sheep·skin /ˈʃiːp·skɪn/ *n* the skin of a sheep with the wool still connected to it, which has been removed from its body • *We've got a rug made from (a) sheepskin.* [C/U] • *He was wearing a sheepskin coat.*

sheer [COMPLETE] /£ʃɪəʳ, $ʃɪr/ *adj* **-er, -est** (used for emphasis) nothing except; complete • *The suggestion is sheer nonsense.* • *The engine's sheer size would make it difficult to transport.* • *It was because of sheer willpower/determination/cussedness that he succeeded.* • *It was the sheerest coincidence that we met.*

sheer [STEEP] /£ʃɪəʳ, $ʃɪr/ *adj* **-er, -est** extremely steep; almost vertical • *a sheer mountain side* • *a sheer cliff* • *a sheer drop of 100 metres*

sheer /£ʃɪəʳ, $ʃɪr/ *adv* [not gradable] • *(literary) The cliffs fall sheer* (= vertically) *into the valley below.*

sheer [THIN] /£ʃɪəʳ, $ʃɪr/ *adj* **-er, -est** (esp. of clothes) very thin, delicate and weighing very little • *sheer nylon tights* • *She was wearing a dress of the sheerest silk.*

sheer [TURN] /£ʃɪəʳ, $ʃɪr/ *v* [I always + adv/prep] to change direction suddenly • *It looked as if the boats were going to collide, but one sheered* **off/away** *at the last second.*

sheet /ʃiːt/ *n* [C] a large thin flat esp. rectangular piece of something, esp. a piece of cloth used for sleeping on or a piece of paper • *One of the things I like about staying in hotels is that they put clean sheets on the bed every day.* • *Several typewritten sheets* (= pieces of paper) *lay on his desk.* • *The application form was a single sheet* **of paper.** • *It took five or six sheets* **of** *wrapping paper to cover the TV that we were giving Dad as a present.* • *She was nervously carrying a large sheet* **of glass.** • *They fixed a* **polythene/plastic** *sheet over the broken window.* • *Sheet* **metal** *is used to make car bodies and things like the outsides of fridges and stoves.* • A sheet is also a piece of paper with something printed on it: *The tourist office provides a weekly information sheet about things that are happening in the town.* ○ *The model aeroplane came with an instruction sheet about how to put it together.* • *A thick sheet* (= layer) **of** *ice had formed over the water.* • *(fig.) A sheet* (= wide mass) **of** *flame shot up into the air immediately after the explosion.* • *The rain was coming down* **in sheets** (= it was raining very hard). • **Sheet lightning** is lightning that lights up a large part of the sky. • **Sheet music** is music in its printed or written form, esp. single sheets of paper not formed into a book. • PIC› **Beds and bedroom**

sheet /ʃiːt/ *v* [usually + adv/prep] • If it/rain is sheeting **(down)**, it is raining very hard: *We can't go out yet, it's sheeting down outside.* • *The rain was sheeting* **against** *the windows.*

sheet·ing /£ˈʃiː·tɪŋ, $-t̬ɪŋ/ *n* [U] • Sheeting is thin material, esp. cloth, plastic or metal.

sheikh /ʃeɪk, ʃiːk/ *n* [C] an Arab ruler or head of a TRIBE (= a group of families)

sheikh·dom /ˈʃeɪk·dəm, ˈʃiːk-/ *n* [C] • A sheikhdom is an area of land or a country ruled by a sheikh.

shei·la /ˈʃiː·lə/ *n* [C] *Aus slang* a girl or a woman. Some people consider this offensive.

shek·els /ˈʃek·ᵊlz/ *pl n slang humorous* money

shelf /ʃelf/ *n* [C] *pl* **shelves** /ʃelvz/ a long flat board fixed horizontally usually against a wall or inside a cupboard so that objects can be stored on it • *One wall had shelves from floor to ceiling, crammed with books.* • *She has some glass shelves in her living room, with photographs of her family* **on** *them.* • *He's got a temporary job* **stacking** (= putting goods onto) *shelves at the supermarket.* • *Shops have removed all jars of the baby food from their shelves* (= made them not available for sale) *following reports that it has been contaminated.* • *(specialized)* A shelf is also a flat area of rock underwater or on a cliff. • If a product can be bought **off the shelf**, it does not need to be specially made or requested: *It's often cheaper if you buy wallpaper off the shelf/if you buy off-the-shelf wallpaper, rather than having to order it.* • If something is, or is left, **on the shelf**, no notice is taken of it and it is not used for anything: *Many of their wedding presents have just been left on the shelf.* • *(esp. Br and Aus infml)* If you say that someone, esp. a woman, is **on the shelf**, you mean that they are now too old for anyone to want to marry them: *In those days, if you hadn't married by the time you were 30, you were definitely on the shelf.* • The **shelf life** of a product, esp. food, is the length of time it can be kept in a shop before it becomes too old to be sold or used. • **Shelf space** is the amount of space on shelves that is available to be used: *The bookstore is devoting a lot of shelf space to the former prime minister's autobiography.* • See also BOOKSHELF. • PIC› **Room, Supermarket**

shelve *obj* /ʃelv/ *v* [T] • *I'm going to shelve* (= fix shelves, esp. to a wall, in) *the garage to give me more space for storing things.* • See also SHELVE [DELAY]; SHELVE [SLOPE].

shelv·ing /ˈʃel·vɪŋ/ *n* [U] • *They paid a carpenter to put up some shelving* (= shelves) *in the living room.*

shell [COVERING] /ʃel/ *n* the hard outer covering of something, esp. nuts, eggs and some animals • *I found a nutcracker to break the shells open.* [C] • *The little birds' eggs had pretty blue shells.* [C] • *When I was making the cake, a piece of shell from an egg fell into the mixture.* [U] • *Tortoises, snails and crabs all have shells to protect them.* [C] • *Some small sea creatures have wonderful delicate shells.* [C] • *He wore a shell necklace* (= a piece of jewellery made out of the shells of small sea animals). • The shell of a building or vehicle is its basic outer structure, esp. when the inner parts have been destroyed or taken or have not yet been made: *The soldiers sheltered in a shell of a burnt-out farmhouse.* [C] ○ *The shells of most modern cars are still mainly made of steel.* [C] • If someone **comes out of** their **shell** or someone **brings** them **out of** their **shell**, they become more interested in other people and more willing to talk and take part in social activities: *Marrying Margot seems to have brought Derek out of his shell!* • If someone **crawls/goes/retreats/retires into** their **shell**, they become less interested in other people and less willing to talk and take part in social activities: *The more they tried to get her to talk about her experiences, the further she retreated* **back** *into her shell.* • A **shell suit** is a light TRACKSUIT (= informal loose top and trousers). • See also EGGSHELL; NUTSHELL; SEASHELL; SHELLFISH. • PIC› **Nut**

shell *obj* /ʃel/ *v* [T] • If you shell PEAS, nuts, etc., you remove them from their shell or their natural protective covering. • PIC› **Food preparation**

shell [EXPLOSIVE] /ʃel/ *n* [C] a container usually with a pointed end, which is filled with explosives and fired from a large gun • **Artillery** *and* **mortar** *shells were landing in the outskirts of the city.* • **Shell-shock** is mental illness caused by experiences of war: *It's not surprising that soldiers who saw their friends die in front of them suffered from shell-shock.* ○ *The nurses had to deal with* **shell-shocked** *civilians* (= those suffering from shell-shock) *as well as soldiers.* • Someone can also be **shell-shocked** if they are extremely tired and nervous or frightened, esp. after an unpleasant and unexpected event: *After the crash, the passengers were shell-shocked but there were no serious injuries.* ○ *They were shell-shocked by the news.*

shell *obj* /ʃel/ *v* [T] • *They were under orders to shell* (= fire shells at) *the hospital and the Town Hall.*

shell·ing /ˈʃel·ɪŋ/ *n* [U] • *Shelling of enemy lines has gone on all day.*

shell [BOAT] /ʃel/ *n* [C] a type of boat used for racing, powered by people using OARS

shell out *obj*, **shell** *obj* **out** *v adv* [M] *infml* to pay (money), esp. unwillingly • *Why is it that whenever we go to the movies, it's always me who has to shell out* **for** *the tickets?*

shel·lack·ing /ʃəˈlæk·ɪŋ, ˈʃel·æk-/ *n* [C usually sing] *Am and Aus infml* a complete defeat or beating • *The Dodgers* **took** *a shellacking* (= were defeated by many points). • *His dad* **gave** *him a shellacking* (= beating) *for stealing the money.*

shell·fish /ˈʃel·fɪʃ/ *n pl* **shellfish** a small animal that lives in water and has a shell • *Lobsters, crabs, prawns, mussels and oysters are all shellfish that are commonly* *eaten as food.* [C] • *I think these nice bits in the stew are some kind of shellfish.* [U]

shel·ter /£ˈʃel·təʳ, $-t̬ɚ/ *n* (a building designed to give) protection from bad weather, danger or attack • *an air-raid shelter* [C] • *They have opened a shelter to provide temporary housing for homeless people in the city.* [C] • *We* **found/took** *shelter* **for** *the night in an abandoned house.* [U] • *The trees* **gave/provided** *some shelter* **from** *the rain.* [U]

shel·ter /£ˈʃel·təʳ, $-t̬ɚ/ *v* • *We were caught in a thunderstorm, without anywhere to shelter* (=protect ourselves). [I] • *A group of us were sheltering* **from** *the rain under the trees.* [I] • *Local people risked their own lives to shelter resistance fighters* **from** *the army* (=to give them secret hiding places so the army would not catch them). [T]

shel·tered /£ˈʃel·təd, $-t̬ɚd/ *adj* • *We found a sheltered* **spot** (=a place protected from wind, rain, etc.) *to have our picnic.* • *(disapproving)* If someone has had a sheltered **life**, they have had a (too) quiet life, protected from anything dangerous, painful or exciting: *Until going to University, she had led a very sheltered life.* • *(Am)* If you shelter income, you legally avoid paying taxes on it: *Their accountant suggested some novel ways of sheltering their retirement income.* • **Sheltered accommodation/ Sheltered housing** is housing specially designed for old people or people with mental or physical difficulties to live in, in which each person has their own apartment, and someone is employed to help them if they need help. • *(Br and Aus)* A **sheltered workshop** is a factory, or similar place of work, specially designed for people with mental or physical difficulties to work in.

shelve *(obj)* DELAY /ʃelv/ *v* [T] to not take action on (something) until a later time • *I've had to shelve my* **plans** *to buy a new car because I can't afford it at the moment.*

shelve SLOPE /ʃelv/ *v* [I] (of the bottom of the sea) to slope down gradually • *The sea bed shelves gently for several hundred metres.*

shelve *obj* SHELF /ʃelv/ *v* [T] See at SHELF

shelves /ʃelvz/ *pl of* SHELF

she·nan·i·gan /ʃɪˈnæn·ɪ·gənz/ *n* [C] *infml disapproving* a complicated, dishonest activity, intended to bring advantages by deceiving people • *Another business shenanigan was exposed in the newspapers today.*

shep·herd, *female also* **shep·her·dess** /£ˈʃep·əd, $-ɚd, £-ə·des, $ˈ-ɚ-/ *n* [C] a person whose job is to take care of sheep and move them from one place to another • *a shepherd boy* • **Shepherd's pie** (also **Cottage pie**) is a food consisting of a layer of small pieces of meat covered with a thick layer of potato. • *"The Lord is my shepherd; I shall not want"* (Bible, Psalm 23.1) • *"While shepherds watched their flocks by night, / All seated on the ground, / The Angel of the Lord came down, / And glory shone around"* (hymn from *New Versions of the Psalms* by Nahum Tate, 1700)

shep·herd *obj* /£ˈʃep·əd, $-ɚd/ *v* [T always + adv/prep] • *The dogs shepherded the sheep* (=made them move) *into the pens.* • To shepherd a group of people is to make them move to where you want them to go, in a pleasant, careful way: *He shepherded the old people towards the dining room.*

sher·bet /£ˈʃɜː·bət, $ˈʃɜːr-/ *n* [U] *Br and Aus* an artificial fruit-flavoured powder eaten as a sweet or used to make a drink, esp. for children • Sherbet is also *Am for* SORBET. • (J)

sher·iff /ˈʃer·ɪf/ *n* [C] (in the US) an official, sometimes elected, whose job is to be in charge of performing the orders of the law courts and making certain that the laws are obeyed within a particular COUNTY (=large local area) • In England and Wales, a sheriff is a person who represents the king or queen in a particular county, and who has mainly ceremonial duties. • In Scotland, a sheriff is the most important judge of a county. • *"I Shot the Sheriff"* (title of a song written by Bob Marley, 1974)

Sher·pa /£ˈʃɜː·pə, $ˈʃɜːr-/ *n* [C] a member of a Himalayan people who are skilled mountain climbers and who are often employed as GUIDES by visiting climbers

sher·ry /ˈʃer·i/ *n* a usually brownish or yellowish alcoholic drink made from GRAPES which is stronger than wine and is drunk in small glasses, esp. before a meal • *Sherry came originally from Spain.* [U] • *We have both* **sweet** *and* **dry** *sherry.* [U] • *Would you like a glass of sherry/some sherry?* [U] • *Would you like a sherry* (=a glass of sherry)*?* [C]

Shet·land po·ny /£ˈʃet·lənd,pəʊ·ni, $,-poʊ-/ *n* [C] a very small rough-haired horse

Shi·a /ˈʃiː·ə/, **Shi·ite** *n* [C] a member of the second largest religious movement within Islam, which is based on the belief that Ali, a member of Mohammed's family, and the teachers who came after him, were the true religious leaders • *The majority of people in Iran are Shias.*

Shi·i·sm /ˈʃiː·ɪ·zᵊm/ *n* [U] • Shiism is the religious movement of which Shias are members.

shi·at·su /£ʃiˈæt·su, $-ˈɑːt-/ *n* [U] a treatment for pain or illness, originally from ancient Japan, in which particular places on the body are pressed • *Shiatsu and acupuncture both use the same pressure points on the body, but in shiatsu, you apply pressure with the hands and in acupuncture, you push thin needles into the skin.*

shib·bo·leth /ˈʃɪb·ᵊl·eθ/ *n* [C] *fml* a belief or custom that is not now considered as important and correct as it was in the past • *They still cling to many of the old shibboleths* **of** *education.*

shic·er /£ˈʃaɪ·səʳ, $-sɚ/ *n* [C] *Aus infml* a **swindler**, see at SWINDLE

shield /ʃiːld/ *n* [C] something that is used as, or provides, protection, esp. a large slightly curved piece of metal, wood, plastic, etc. used by soldiers in the past, or by police officers • *The police held up their riot shields against the flying rocks and bricks and homemade petrol bombs.* • *The anti-personnel mines were laid as a protective shield around the town.* • *The ozone layer is a shield which protects the earth against the sun's radiation.* • *Anger can function as a shield* **against** (=a way of avoiding suffering) *even more painful emotions of loss and hurt.* • A shield is also a flat object with two straight sides, a rounded or pointed lower edge and usually a straight top edge, on which there is a **coat of arms**. • A shield is also an object shaped like a shield, which is given as a prize, or used as a BADGE: *Our school won the county football shield this year.* ○ *The Cambridge University Press shield has four lions on it.* • (NL)

shield *(obj)* /ʃiːld/ *v* [T] • *Plastic sheeting should be wrapped around the tree in winter to shield* (=protect) *it* **from** *the wind and the frost.* • *Several officials are accused of trying to shield the General* **from** *US federal investigators.* • *She held her hand above her eyes to shield them* **from** *the sun.*

shift *(obj)* MOVE OR CHANGE /ʃɪft/ *v* to (cause to) move or change from one position or direction to another, esp. slightly • *She shifted (her weight) uneasily* **from** *one foot* **to** *the other.* [I/T] • *If we shift the furniture against the walls, we'll have more space to dance.* [T] • *The wind is expected to shift* **(to the east)** *tomorrow.* [I] • *Media attention has shifted recently* **onto** *environmental issues.* [I] • *He tried to shift* **the blame onto** *his sister.* [T] • *The government's economic policy has been to shift* **the emphasis** *from the public sector to the private sector wherever possible.* [T] • *(esp. Am) In cars that are automatics, you don't have to bother with shifting* **gears** (=moving them into different positions in order to make the car go faster or slower). [T] • *He's annoying to argue with because he keeps* **shifting** *his* **ground** (=changing his opinion). • *Come on, there's work to be done –* **shift** *yourself* (=hurry and do it). • *(dated)* If you **shift for yourself**, you earn your own income or buy and cook your own food, etc.: *He left home at 18 and had to shift for himself.* • *(specialized)* The **shift key** is a key on a computer or a TYPEWRITER which you press at the same time as you press a letter key in order to produce a capital letter. • See also MAKESHIFT. • LP **Driving** PIC **Office**

shift /ʃɪft/ *n* [C] • *A shift* (=change) **in** *the wind/ temperature is expected tonight.* • *This shift* **in** *the balance of power in the region has had far-reaching consequences.* • *There has been a* **dramatic** *shift* **in** *public opinion* **away from** *support for the war and* **towards** *opposition to it.* • *A* **fundamental/radical** *shift* **in** *people's attitudes to drinking and driving has taken place.* • *There was an abrupt shift* **of** *economic policy in November.*

shift·ing /ˈʃɪf·tɪŋ/ *adj* [not gradable] • *They lost their way in the shifting* (=always changing) *sands of the Sahara.* • *It's hard to pursue a consistent policy in a shifting political world.*

shift GROUP /ʃɪft/ *n* [C + sing/pl v] a group of workers who do a job for a period of time during the day or night, or the period of time itself • *As the* **night** *shift leave/leaves, the* **day** *shift arrive/arrives.* • *Are you on the* **night** *shift or the* **day** *shift* (=Do you work during the night period or the day period)*?*

shift·work /£ˈʃɪft·wɜːk, $-wɜːrk/ *n* [U] • *The factory is run on shiftwork* (=with different groups of workers working at different times of the day and night). • *I hate shiftwork* (=working at different times of the day and night).

shift [DRESS] /ʃɪft/ *n* [C] a simple dress that hangs straight from the shoulders

shift *obj* [GET RID OF] /ʃɪft/ *v* [T] *Br and Aus infml* to get rid of (something), or to sell (something) • *Modern detergents will shift most stains, such as blood, oil and food.* • *The people at the toy shop expect to shift* (=sell) *a lot of stock in the run-up to Christmas.*

shift·less /ˈʃɪft·ləs/ *adj disapproving* lazy and lacking determination or a firm purpose • *He called the young people shiftless, lazy and good-for-nothing.*

shift·y /ˈʃɪf·ti/ *adj* **-ier**, **-iest** (of a person or their appearance) seeming dishonest • *I wouldn't trust anyone with such shifty eyes/who was so shifty-***eyed**. • *You're* **looking** *very shifty. What have you been up to?* • *There were a couple of shifty-***looking** *people standing on the corner of the street.*

shif·ti·ly /ˈʃɪf·tɪ·li/ *adv*

shif·ti·ness /ˈʃɪf·tɪ·nəs/ *n* [U]

Shi·i·sm /ˈʃiː·ɪ·zᵊm/ *n* [U] See at SHIA

Shi·ite /ˈʃiː·aɪt/ *n* [C] a SHIA

shil·ling /ˈʃɪl·ɪŋ/ *n* [C] a unit of money used in Britain until 1971, equal to 12 old PENCE or 5 new PENCE

shil·ly shal·ly /ˈʃɪl·iˌʃæl·i, ˌ–ˈ–/ *v* [I] *infml disapproving* to spend too much time doing something or making a decision because you do not know what is the right thing to do • *Stop shilly-shallying and make a decision now!*

shim·mer /£ˈʃɪm·əʳ, $-ɚ/ *v* [I] to shine softly and unevenly, in such a way that the light seems to shake slightly and quickly • *She could see her reflection in the water, shimmering in the moonlight.* • *We drove across the desert, through the shimmering heat haze.* • *(fig.) This week, the ballet company launches a shimmering* (=bright and attractive) *new production of 'A Midsummer Night's Dream'.*

shim·mer /£ˈʃɪm·əʳ, $-ɚ/ *n* [U] • *Across the shimmer of the lake, we could see the dark shape of the mountain.* • *(fig.) The first movement of the symphony ends in a shimmer of sound* (=a soft, slightly shaking sound).

shim·my /ˈʃɪm·i/ *n, v* (to do) a dance in which you shake your hips and shoulders • *Almost a hundred people were shimmying on the dance floor.* [I] • *He watched her do* **the** *shimmy.* [C] • To shimmy is also to move quickly, esp. by moving from side to side: *He shimmied through the door.* [I] • *(Am)* If a car shimmies, it has a very light shaking movement which is not the usual movement of the car. [I]

shin [BODY PART] /ʃɪn/ *n* the front part of your leg between your knee and your foot • *She's got a nasty bruise on her shin.* [C] • A shin is also a joint of meat from the lower leg of a cow: *(a) shin of beef* [C/U] • **Shin splints** are severe pains in the area of your shin, happening esp. to runners and other people who do exercise involving a lot of running or jumping. • [PIC] **Body**

shin [CLIMB] /ʃɪn/, *Am and Aus also* **shin·ny** *v* [I always + adv/prep] **-nn-** to climb something such as a tree, using your hands and legs to move along quickly • *Several of us shinned* **up** *lampposts so that we could see over the top of the crowds.*

shin·bone /£ˈʃɪm·bəʊn, $ˈʃɪn·boʊn/ *n* [C] the bone at the front of your leg, between the knee and the foot

shin·dig /ˈʃɪn·dɪg/ *n* [C] *infml* a noisy event or situation, esp. a large, energetic party, celebration, etc. • *Are you going to that shindig at the Town Hall tonight?* • *(esp. Br and Aus)* A shindig is also a noisy argument.

shine *(obj)* /ʃaɪn/ *v past* **shone** /£ʃɒn, $ʃɑːn/ or **shined** to (cause to) be bright either by sending out or reflecting light • *Can you stop the light shining* **in** *our eyes?* [I] • *The* **sun** *shone all afternoon.* [I] • *He polished the brass till it shone* **brightly/brilliantly**. [I] • *Their bodies were shining* **with** *sweat.* • *(fig.) Her* **eyes/face** *shone* **with** *happiness and excitement* (=she looked very happy and excited). [I] • *(fig.) Her honesty and sincerity shine* **out** *of her* (=are obvious). [I] • If you shine a light in a particular direction, you point it there: *The policeman walked along the street, shining a torch into every car.* [T] • If you shine something, you make it bright by rubbing it: *He ironed his shirt and shined his* **shoes** *for the interview.* [T] • If you shine **at/in** an activity or skill, you are extremely and obviously good at it: *She's hopeless at languages, but she shines at science.* [I] • *"How far that little candle throws his beams! So shines a good deed in a naughty world"* (Shakespeare, Merchant of Venice 5.1)

shine /ʃaɪn/ *n* [U] • *How do you get that wonderful shine* **on** *your furniture?* • *(infml)* If you **take a shine to** someone, you quickly decide that you like them very much.

shin·er /£ˈʃaɪ·nəʳ, $-nɚ/ *n* [C] • Shiner is *infml for* **black eye**. See at BLACK [DARK IN COLOUR].

shi·ni·ness /ˈʃaɪ·nɪ·nəs/ *n* [U]

shin·ing /ˈʃaɪ·nɪŋ/ *adj* • *a shining silver cup* • *She looked at him with shining* (=bright and happy) *eyes.* • *These pictures are shining* (=excellent) **examples** *of great photography.*

shin·y /ˈʃaɪ·ni/ *adj* **-ier**, **-iest** • *a shiny surface* • *She gave me a shiny* **bright** *silver dollar.* • *His hands were shiny* **with** *oil.*

shin·gle [STONES] /ˈʃɪŋ·gl̩/ *n* [U] small round stones covering a beach or by the edge of a river • *a shingle beach* • *We sat listening to the noise of the waves on the shingle.*

shin·gly /ˈʃɪŋ·gl̩·i/ *adv* **-ier**, **-iest** • *It was uncomfortable walking barefoot on the shingly beach.*

shin·gle [PIECE] /ˈʃɪŋ·gl̩/ *n* [C] a thin flat TILE usually made of wood, that is fixed in rows to make a roof or wall covering

shin·gles /ˈʃɪŋ·gl̩z/ *n* [U] a disease caused by a virus that infects particular nerves and that produces a line or lines of painful red spots, esp. around the waist

shin·ny /ˈʃɪn·i/ *v* [I] *Am and Aus for* SHIN [CLIMB]

Shin·to /£ˈʃɪn·təʊ, $-toʊ/, **Shin·to·i·sm** /£ˈʃɪn·təʊ·ɪ·zᵊm, $-toʊ-/ *n* [U] a Japanese religion in which people worship past members of their family and various gods that represent nature

ship [BOAT] /ʃɪp/ *n* [C] a large boat for travelling on water, esp. across the sea • *a sailing ship* • *a merchant/naval ship* • *a ship-to-shore phone* • *We've decided to go* **by ship**, *rather than flying.* • *They* **boarded** (=went on to) *a ship that was* **sailing** (=leaving) *the next day.* • *"The Ship of Fools"* (title of a book by Sebastian Brant, 1494) • *"Ships that pass in the night, and speak each other in passing"* (The poet H.W.Longfellow in *Tales of a Wayside Inn*, 1874) • (NL)

ship *obj* /ʃɪp/ *v* [T] **-pp-** • To ship esp. a large object to a distant place is to send it there: *The company paid for her luggage to be shipped* **over** *from the US.* ○ *(fig.) The children had already been shipped* **off** (=sent) *to stay with their grandparents.*

ship·per /£ˈʃɪp·əʳ, $-ɚ/ *n* [C usually pl] • A shipper is a person or company whose job is to organize the sending of goods from one place to another: *wine shippers*

ship·ping /ˈʃɪp·ɪŋ/ *n* [U] • Shipping is ships considered as a group, or the sending of goods from one place to another, esp. by ship: *This stretch of water is heavily used by shipping.* ○ *The cost is $205 plus $3 for shipping* (=the sending of goods). ○ *The fruit is picked and artificially ripened before shipping* (=being sent from one place to another). • (T)

-ship [RANK] /-ʃɪp/ *combining form* having the rank, position, skill or relationship of the stated type • *lordship* • *partnership* • *craftsmanship* • *friendship*

ship·board /£ˈʃɪp·bɔːd, $-bɔːrd/ *adj* [not gradable] happening or used on a ship • *shipboard activities* • *a shipboard news conference* • *a shipboard romance* • *a shipboard transmitter*

ship·build·er /£ˈʃɪpˌbɪl·dəʳ, $-dɚ/ *n* [C] a person or company that builds ships

ship·build·ing /ˈʃɪpˌbɪl·dɪŋ/ *n* [U] • *The economy was based on traditional industries such as shipbuilding, steel production and coalmining.*

ship·mate /ˈʃɪp·meɪt/ *n* [C] a sailor working on the same ship as another sailor • *Police interviewed the dead man's relatives, friends and shipmates.*

ship·ment /ˈʃɪp·mənt/ *n* a large amount of goods sent together to a place, or the act of sending them • *A shipment* **of** *urgent medical supplies is expected to arrive very soon.* [C] • *The supplies are ready but there have been problems arranging shipment* (=the act of sending them) *from the port.* [U]

ship·shape /ˈʃɪp·ʃeɪp/ *adj infml* tidy and with everything in its correct place • *It took a while to* **get** *things shipshape, after the builders had finished in the house.*

ship·wreck /ˈʃɪp·rek/, **wreck** *n* the destruction or sinking of a ship in an accident at sea, esp. by hitting rocks, or a ship which has been destroyed or sunk in such an accident • *The danger of shipwreck is much greater in fog.* [U] • *There have been many shipwrecks along this dangerous stretch of coastline.* [C] • *They hope to find gold and other treasure aboard the shipwreck, buried 50 metres deep in mud on the sea floor.* [C]

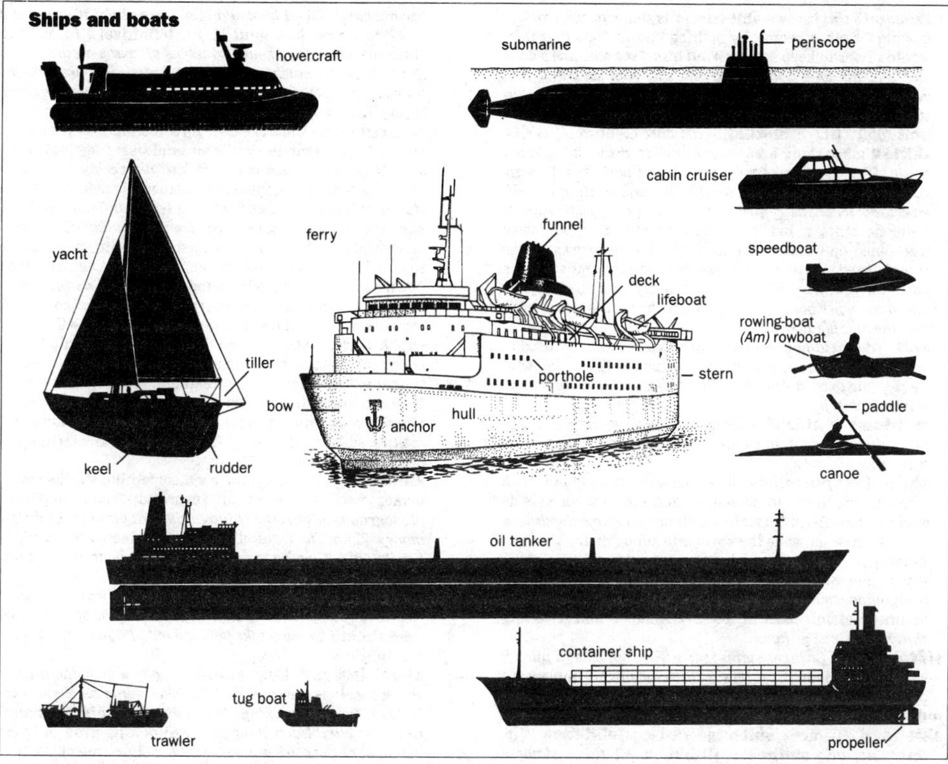

ship·wreck *obj* /ˈʃɪp·rek/ *v* [always passive] • *They were shipwrecked* **off** *the coast of Newfoundland.* • *The story tells the adventures of a group of shipwrecked sailors living on a desert island.*

ship·yard /£ˈʃɪp·jɑːd, $-jɑːrd/ *n* [C] a place where ships are built or repaired

shire /£ʃaɪəʳ, $ʃaɪr/ *n* [C] (in the past in Britain) a COUNTY (= local area)

shire horse *n* [C] a large strong English horse which has long hair on its feet

shirk *(obj)* /£ʃɜːk, $ʃɜːrk/ *disapproving* to avoid (esp. difficult or unpleasant work, duties or responsibilities) • *If you shirk your* **responsibilities/duties** *now, the situation will just be that much harder to deal with next month.* [T] • *The president has said that the country will not shirk the use of military force, should it be necessary.* [T] • *I shall not shirk* **from** *my obligations.* [I]

shirk·er /£ˈʃɜː·kəʳ, $ˈʃɜːr·kɚ/ *n* [C] • A shirker is someone who avoids something, esp. work: *We have no room for shirkers in this office.* ○ *She is no shirker* **of** *a tough decision.*

shirt /£ʃɜːt, $ʃɜːrt/ *n* [C] a piece of clothing worn esp. by men on the upper part of the body, made of a light cloth and usually having a collar and buttons at the front • *a denim shirt* • *a silk shirt* • *a striped shirt* • *Jack was wearing jeans and a white long-sleeved shirt.* • *You've spilled something down your shirt front.* • *He rolled up his shirt sleeves and got to work.* • If someone, esp. a man, is **in** (their) **shirt-sleeves**, they are not wearing anything, such as a jacket, on top of their shirts. This is often considered to be an informal way of dressing: *Because it was so hot, the men were all in their shirt-sleeves.* ○ *People were sitting around* **shirt-sleeved** (= not wearing anything on top of their shirts) *in the sunshine.* • *(Br infml)* If you **put** your **shirt on** something, you feel very sure that it will happen: *I'm putting my shirt on the President being re-elected* (= I think that that is extremely likely). • *(infml)* **The shirt off** your **back** is the last thing that you have left: *She says she's my friend but she'd* **have** *the shirt off my back if she had the chance.* ○ *He's the kind of man who'd* **give** *you the shirt off his back.* • See also NIGHTSHIRT; SWEATSHIRT; T-SHIRT. • PIC Clothes Ⓙ Ⓚⓞⓡ

shirt·tail /£ˈʃɜːt·teɪl, $ˈʃɜːrt-/ *n* [C usually pl] one of the two long parts of a shirt which come below the waist of the person wearing it • *He tucked his shirttails into his trousers.*

shirt·y /£ˈʃɜː·ti, $ˈʃɜːr·ţi/ *adj* **-ier, -iest** *Br and Aus infml* annoyed or angry, esp. in a rude way • *Don't get shirty* **with** *me – this is your fault, not mine.*

shish ke·bab /£ˈʃiːʃ·kɪˌbæb, $ˈʃɪʃ·kəˌbɑːb/ *n* [C] a KEBAB

shit /ʃɪt/ *n taboo slang* excrement; the contents of the bowels that are excreted • *The little kid stepped right in a pile of dog shit.* [U] • *(Br) I need to* **have**/*(Am)* **take a** *shit* (= excrete the contents of my bowels). [U] • *(disapproving)* Shit can also be used to refer to someone or something you do not like, esp. because they are unpleasant or of low quality: *Pollock is a* **little** *shit – he's been complaining to the boss about me.* [C] ○ *Everything that journalist writes is* **a load of** *shit.* [U] ○ *What's all this shit* (= nonsense) **about** *Janet being fired?* [U] • *(disapproving)* Shit is also insults, criticism or unkind or unfair treatment: *Nikki* **gets** *a lot of shit* **from** *his parents about the way he dresses.* ○ *Jackie doesn't* **take** *(any) shit* **from** *anyone* (= does not allow anyone to treat her badly). • *(Am)* Shit is also used in negatives to mean 'anything': *He doesn't know shit about what's going on.* • If you **don't give a shit**, you do not care: *Derek doesn't give a shit (***about** *what other people think).* • *(esp. Am approving)* To **have/get** your **shit together** is to be or become effective, organized and skilful: *She really has her shit together.* • If you say **no shit**, you are expressing surprise or lack of surprise about information you have just heard: *"Richard's got the job in New York!" "No shit!"* • *(Am disapproving)* If you say that someone has **shit for brains**, you mean that they are extremely stupid: *Old Jack must have shit for brains – he gets it wrong every time.* • When **(the) shit hits the fan** or when **the shit flies**, a situation suddenly causes trouble for someone: *If Dad finds out how much money you spent, the shit will really hit the fan.* • Adding **the shit out of** when you are describing an action that happened to someone is a way of emphasizing the degree of force with which the action happened: *He got into an argument with some soldiers, who proceeded to* **beat/knock/kick** *the shit out of him.* ○ *I wish you wouldn't creep up on me like that – you* **scared/frightened/terrified** *the shit out of me.* • *(Am slightly disapproving)* If you say that someone has a **shit-eating grin**, you mean that they are looking extremely satisfied and happy about something: *When the news came through, she looked at us all* **with** *a shit-eating grin.* • *(Am)* If you are on someone's **shit list**, they do not like you and consider you or your opinions unpleasant or wrong: *How did we get on the Vice-*

President's shit list? • A **shit stirrer** is someone who makes trouble for other people, by making known facts that they would prefer to keep secret: *What a shit stirrer – she's gone and told his wife about what she saw him and that girl getting up to at the Christmas party.* ○ *I hate all the shit-stirring that goes on in this office.* • See also BULLSHIT; SHITE.

shit *(obj)* /ʃɪt/ *v* **shitting**, *past* **shit** or **shat** /ʃæt/ or **shitted** *taboo slang* • *The dog has shat in the living room again!* [I] • *(esp. Am) I need to shit real bad.* [I] • To **shit yourself** is to be very frightened: *She was shitting herself, especially when he pulled out a gun.* [T] • *(esp. Am)* If someone **shits a brick** or **shits bricks**, they are very frightened or worried: *We were all shitting bricks as the truck missed the car by inches.* • *(disapproving)* If someone **shits on** you, they treat you very badly and unkindly: *In my opinion, her boss shat on her badly by not allowing her to take the time off after all.*

shit /ʃɪt/ *exclamation taboo* • Shit is a swear word used to express annoyance, anger, disgust or surprise: *Oh shit, we're going to be late again!* • *Don't do it that way! Shit, now you've broken it!*

shit·load /£ˈʃɪt·ləʊd, $-loʊd/ *n* [U] *taboo slang* • *You'll be in a shitload* (= a lot) **of** *trouble if you don't finish that job by tomorrow.*

shits /ʃɪts/ *pl n taboo slang* • **The shits** is DIARRHOEA (= a medical condition in which contents of the bowels is excreted too often): *Something I ate has given me the shits.* • *(Aus)* To **give** someone **the shits** is to annoy them.

shit·ty /£ˈʃɪt·i, $ˈʃɪţ·i/ *adj* **-ier, -iest** *taboo slang* • *I think you've had really shitty* (= unfair and unkind) *treatment from management.* • *Jack had had a shitty* (= difficult and/or unsuccessful) *week at work.* • *Anna, if you're feeling shitty* (= ill), *just go home.*

shite /ʃaɪt/ *n Br taboo slang* SHIT • *The film was (a pile of) shite* (= not good). [U] • *He's a little shite* (= an unpleasant person). [C]

shit·faced /ˈʃɪt·feɪst/ *adj taboo slang* extremely drunk

shit·head /ˈʃɪt·hed/, **shit·bag** /ˈʃɪt·bæg/, **shit·face** /ˈʃɪt·feɪs/, *Am also* **shitheel** /ˈʃɪt·hiːl/ *n* [C] *taboo slang* a stupid, unpleasant and unpopular person • *That little shithead has screwed things up again.*

shit·house /ˈʃɪt·haʊs/ *n* [C] *pl* **shithouses** /ˈʃɪt,haʊ·zɪz/ *Am taboo slang* a small building containing a toilet • If you are **in the shithouse**, you are in trouble.

shi·ver /£ˈʃɪv·əʳ, $-ɚ/ *v* [I] (of a person or animal) to shake slightly because of feeling cold, ill or frightened • *The poor dog – it's shivering!* • *He shivered* **with** *cold in his thin cotton shirt.*

shi·ver /£ˈʃɪv·əʳ, $-ɚ/ *n* [C] • *I felt a shiver as I looked out at the dark expanse of sea.* • *(literary) There was a breeze, and a shiver ran through the leaves* (= the leaves shook). • *(infml)* People sometimes say that they feel **a shiver/shivers (up and) down** their **spine** when they are frightened or excited: *At its most terrifying, his writing* **sends** *shivers up and down my spine.* ○ *Whenever that music is played, I feel a shiver down my spine.*

shi·vers /£ˈʃɪv·əz, $-ɚz/ *pl n* • *She's aching and she's* **got** *the shivers* (= she is shivering), *so I've sent her to bed.* • *(infml)* If something or someone **gives** you **the shivers**, you are very frightened of it or them: *I don't like him – he gives me the shivers.*

shi·ver·y /£ˈʃɪv·ᵊr·i, $ˈ-ɚ-/ *adj* **-ier, -iest** *infml* • If you are shivery, you are shaking slightly because you feel cold, frightened or ill: *She's feeling hot and cold and she's shivery, so I think she must have flu.*

shi·voo /ʃɪˈvuː/ *n* [C] *pl* **shivoo** *Aus infml* a party or a celebration • *We're having a shivoo round at our place tonight – do you want to come?*

shoal FISH /£ʃəʊl, $ʃoʊl/ *n* [C + sing/pl v] a large number of fish swimming as a group • *In the shallower water, we could see shoals of tiny fish darting about.* • *Piranhas often feed* **in** *shoals.* • *(infml)* A shoal is also a large number of things or people: *Shoals of angry letters have come in over the past few weeks about the programme.* ○ *In the summer, tourists visit the city* **in** *shoals.*

shoal RAISED AREA /£ʃəʊl, $ʃoʊl/ *n* [C] *specialized* a raised bank of sand or rocks under the surface of the water which gradually moves

shock SURPRISE /£ʃɒk, $ʃɑːk/ *n* (the emotional or physical reaction to) a sudden, unexpected and usually unpleasant event or experience • *Her mother's death* **came as**/*was a great shock – it was so unexpected.* [C] • *It was such a loud crash –* **it gave me/I got** *quite a shock.* [C] • *It was several years before she recovered from the shock* **of** *losing her husband.* [C] • *I know I'd been warned but* **it** *was still a shock* **to** *see her look so ill.* [C + *to* infinitive] • *I was* **in (a state of)** *shock for about two weeks after the accident, so I can't remember much about it.* [U] • *(infml) He burst into my bedroom completely without warning – it gave me the shock* **of my life** (= a very great shock)*!* [C] • *(infml) It's really hard getting back to work after three months off – it's quite* **a shock to the system** (= it is an unpleasant feeling). • *(Br and Aus) The French team are still recovering from their shock* **defeat** (= completely unexpected defeat) *by the Italian side at the weekend.* • Shock is also *infml for* **electric shock**: *Ow! – I just* **got** *a shock from that plug!* [C] ○ See at ELECTRICITY. • Shock is also a medical condition caused by severe injury, pain, loss of blood or fright which slows down the flow of blood around the body: *She died from shock.* [U] ○ *Several passengers from the wrecked vehicle were taken to hospital* **suffering from** *shock.* [U] • If you use **shock tactics**, you do something unexpected in order to shock someone or to get an advantage over them. • **Shock therapy/treatment** is the treatment of particular mental illnesses by sending electric currents through the brain. • **Shock troops** are soldiers who are specially trained for making sudden attacks. • *"The Shock of the New"* (title of a book by Ian Dunlop, 1972)

shock *(obj)* /£ʃɒk, $ʃɑːk/ *v* • If something shocks you, it makes you feel upset or surprised: *Those appalling photographs of starving children shocked people* **into** *giving money.* [T] ○ *The news of the accident* **deeply** *shocked the family.* [T] ○ *'How To Stay Healthy' is a book that can shock, but it's always readable.* [I]

shocked /£ʃɒkt, $ʃɑːkt/ *adj* • *There was a shocked silence as people tried to take in what had happened.* • *We were shocked* **to** *see smoke pouring out of a hole in our roof.* [+ *to* infinitive]

shock·ing /£ˈʃɒk·ɪŋ, $ˈʃɑː·kɪŋ/ *adj* • If something is shocking, it is surprising: *The news came as a shocking blow.* ○ *Becker's shocking 1985 victory made him Germany's first-ever Wimbledon champion.* • **Shocking pink** is a very bright dark pink. • See also SHOCKING; **shocking** at SHOCK OFFEND.

shock·ing·ly /£ˈʃɒk·ɪŋ·li, $ˈʃɑː·kɪŋ-/ *adv* • *The film is shockingly true to life.* • *The restaurant charges shockingly high prices for its food.*

shock *(obj)* OFFEND /£ʃɒk, $ʃɑːk/ *v* to offend or upset (someone) by doing or saying something which they consider is immoral or unacceptable • *The advertisements were designed to shock – that was the whole point of the campaign.* [I] • *I think it shocks him* **to** *hear women talking about sex.* [T + obj + *to* infinitive] • *It still shocks me* **when** *I hear young children swear.* [T + obj + *wh-* word]

shock /£ʃɒk, $ʃɑːk/ *n* [U] • *You should have seen the look of shock on her face when she saw how short your skirt was!* • *(humorous)* **Shock, horror** is sometimes said to express a pretend feeling of shock and anxiety: *Shock, horror! Carl James was seen talking to a woman and it wasn't his wife.*

shock·a·ble /£ˈʃɒk·ə·bl̩, $ˈʃɑː·kə-/ *adj infml* • *I have to be careful what I say to my mother – she's very shockable* (= easily offended).

shock·er /£ˈʃɒk·əʳ, $ˈʃɑː·kɚ/ *n* [C] *infml* • A shocker is something that is likely to offend, esp. something new or newly announced: *The local newspaper's headlines contained the shocker 'Vicar swears on TV'.* ○ *When the film first came out in the late 1960s, it was a real shocker.*

shock·ing /£ˈʃɒk·ɪŋ, $ˈʃɑː·kɪŋ/ *adj* • If something is shocking, it offends or upsets people because they think it is immoral or unacceptable: *Warning: the following film contains language that some viewers may find shocking.* ○ *The sex scenes in the book were considered very shocking at the time when it was published.* ○ *There are few crimes more truly shocking than the murder or abuse of children.* • See also SHOCKING; **shocking** at SHOCK SURPRISE.

shock·ing·ly /£ˈʃɒk·ɪŋ·li, $ˈʃɑː·kɪŋ-/ *adv* • *Horror stories of abused and battered children are shockingly familiar.*

shock DAMAGING EFFECT /£ʃɒk, $ʃɑːk/ *n* [U] the effect of one object violently hitting another, which might cause damage or a slight movement • *If you're running on hard roads, it's important that your shoes have extra cushioning so as to* **absorb** (= reduce) *the shock.* • A **shock absorber** is a device on a vehicle, esp. a car or an aircraft, which is intended to reduce the effects of travelling over rough ground or to improve the smoothness of the landing. • A **shock wave** is an area in which there is a sudden increase in pressure or temperature, caused by an explosion, an

EARTHQUAKE or an object moving faster than the speed of sound: *Aircraft flying at supersonic speeds produce shock waves in the air around the aircraft.* ○ *(fig.) The assassination of the president* **sent** *shock waves* (= caused strong reactions) *across the world.*

shock [HAIR] /£ʃɒk, $ʃɑːk/ *n* [U] a large and noticeable mass of hair • *She's got a* **shock of** *bright red hair.*

shock·ing /£ˈʃɒk·ɪŋ, $ˈʃɑː·kɪŋ/ *adj esp. Br infml* extremely bad or unpleasant, or of very low quality • *What shocking weather!* • *My memory is shocking.* • *The food in the first hotel we stayed in was shocking.* • See also **shocking** at SHOCK [SURPRISE], SHOCK [OFFEND].

shock·ing·ly /£ˈʃɒk·ɪŋ·li, $ˈʃɑː·kɪŋ-/ *adv esp. Br infml* • *The service was shockingly* (= extremely) *bad.*

shock·proof /£ˈʃɒk·pruːf, $ˈʃɑːk-/ *adj* [not gradable] (esp. of a watch) not easily damaged if hit or dropped

shod /£ʃɒd, $ʃɑːd/ *past simple and past participle of* SHOE • *Her feet were shod in leather cowboy boots.* • *I'm not very well-shod for this sort of weather* (= My shoes are not suitable).

shod·dy [BADLY MADE] /£ˈʃɒd·i, $ˈʃɑː·di/ *adj* **-ier, -iest** *disapproving* badly and carelessly made, using low quality materials • *If you look at the way the furniture has been put together, it's fairly shoddy.*

shod·di·ly /£ˈʃɒd·ɪ·li, $ˈʃɑː·dɪ-/ *adv disapproving* • *These clothes are very shoddily made considering how expensive they are.*

shod·di·ness /£ˈʃɒd·ɪ·nəs, $ˈʃɑː·dɪ-/ *n* [U] *disapproving* • *In its attempt to cut costs, the company has drifted towards short cuts and shoddiness* (= producing badly made goods).

shod·dy [NOT RESPECTFUL] /£ˈʃɒd·i, $ˈʃɑː·di/ *adj* **-ier, -iest** *disapproving* showing a lack of respect, consideration and care • *They didn't even give him any sick-pay when he was off ill which is a fairly shoddy way to treat an employee.*

shod·di·ly /£ˈʃɒd·ɪ·li, $ˈʃɑː·dɪ-/ *adv disapproving* • *I think you've been treated very shoddily by the company.*

shod·di·ness /£ˈʃɒd·ɪ·nəs, $ˈʃɑː·dɪ-/ *n* [U] *disapproving*

shoe /ʃuː/ *n* [C] one of a pair of coverings for your feet, which has an upper part made of a strong material such as leather, a base made of thick leather or plastic, and usually a HEEL (= a raised part which supports the heel of the foot) • *I need some new gym/tennis shoes.* • *Do you prefer flat or high-heeled shoes?* • *I need to get my shoes repaired because the soles are wearing rather thin.* • *I've just bought a new* **pair of** *winter shoes.* • *I'll just* **do up/lace up** *my shoes and then I'll be ready.* • *He works in a shoe shop.* • Shoe is also another word for HORSESHOE (= a curved piece of metal fixed under a horse's foot). • *(infml)* If you say that you **wouldn't like to be in** someone's **shoes**, you mean that you would not like to be in their situation: *I wouldn't like to be in Mike's shoes – imagine the trouble he's going to be in!* • *(infml)* People sometimes say **if I were in your shoes** when they want to tell you what they would do in your situation: *If I were in your shoes, I think I'd write to her rather than try to explain over the phone.* • If you **step into/fill** someone's **shoes**, you take their place, often by doing the job they have just left: *Who do you think will step into Sarah's shoes when she goes?*

shoe *obj* /ʃuː/ *v* [T] **shoeing**, *past* **shod** /£ʃɒd, $ʃɑːd/ or *Am also* **shoed** • If you shoe a horse, you nail a HORSESHOE (= a curved piece of metal) to one or each of its feet.

shoe·horn /£ˈʃuː·hɔːn, $-hɔːrn/ *n* [C] a smooth, curved piece of plastic or metal which you hold in the back of your shoe when putting the shoe on in order to help the foot slide into it more easily • [PIC] **Shoes**

shoe·horn *obj* /£ˈʃuː·hɔːn, $-hɔːrn/ *v* [T usually passive] *infml* • If something is shoehorned into a place, it fits there tightly, often between two other things: *This tiny restaurant is situated right in the heart of the city, shoehorned between two major banks.*

shoe·lace /ˈʃuː·leɪs/, **lace**, *Am also* **shoe·string** *n* [C often pl] a thin cord or strip of leather used to fasten shoes • *One of your shoelaces has come undone.* • **Do up/Tie (up)** *your shoelaces, Rosie.*

shoe·string /ˈʃuː·strɪŋ/ *n* [C often pl] *Am for* SHOELACE • *(infml)* If you do something **on a shoestring**, you do it with a very small amount of money: *The film was made on a shoestring.* • **Shoestring potatoes** are long, very thin pieces of potato which have been fried and which are usually eaten hot.

shoe·tree /ˈʃuː·triː/ *n* [C] a piece of wood or metal, shaped like the inside of a shoe, which is put inside a shoe when it is not being worn in order to preserve its shape

shone /£ʃɒn, $ʃɑːn/ *past simple and past participle of* SHINE

shonk·y /£ˈʃɒŋ·ki, $ˈʃɑːŋ-/ *adj* **-ier, -iest** *Aus infml* of low quality

shoo /ʃuː/ *exclamation* said to animals or children to make them go away • *"Shoo!" she shouted at the cat. "Get out of my garden!"*

shoo *obj* /ʃuː/ *v* [T always + adv/prep] he/she/it **shoos**, **shooing**, *past* **shooed** *infml* • If you shoo animals or children somewhere, you make sounds and movements in order to send them away: *Go and shoo that cat* **away** *before it catches a bird.*

shook /ʃʊk/ *past simple of* SHAKE

shoot *(obj)* [WEAPON] /ʃuːt/ *v past* **shot** /£ʃɒt, $ʃɑːt/ to fire (a bullet or an arrow), or to hit, injure or kill (a person or animal) by firing a bullet from a gun • *If he's not armed, don't shoot.* [I] • *The kids were shooting arrows* **at** *a target.* [T] • *She was shot three times in the head.* [T] • *The dog picked up a rabbit that had been shot.* [T] • *He has a licence to shoot pheasants on the farmer's land.* [T] • *Most people can remember what they were doing on the night that Kennedy was shot.* [T] • *A policeman was shot* **dead** *in the city centre last night.* [T + obj + adj] • *Only in the most desperate circumstances are the police ordered to shoot* **on sight**. [I] • *Troops had been given orders to shoot* **to kill**. [I] • *(fig.) He shot* **questions** *at me* (= He asked me questions) *so quickly that I didn't even have time to answer.* [T] • *(infml)* If you say that someone should be shot for doing something, you think that their actions are extremely unreasonable: *They should be shot for selling drinks at that price!* [T] • If you shoot **at** someone or something, you try to shoot them by aiming your gun at them and firing: *The police shot at him but he escaped.* [I] • *(Am)* If you **shoot at/for** something, you try to do it: *If you're going to ask for a raise in salary, you might as well shoot for* **the moon** (= ask for the best or the most you could hope for) *and ask for a promotion as well.* • *(infml)* If you have **shot** your **bolt**, you have already achieved all that you have the power, ability or strength to do and can do nothing more: *He started off the game well but seemed to have shot his bolt by half-time.* • *(Am infml)* If you **shoot the breeze**, you talk with someone or a group of people about unimportant things: *We sat out on the porch until late at night, just shooting the breeze.* • *(Am infml)* If you **shoot darts at** someone, you look at them in a very angry way: *He was shooting darts at me in the meeting, so I shut up quick.* • If someone **shoots down** an aircraft, they destroy it or force it out of the sky by shooting it: *He was killed during the war when his plane was shot down.* • *(infml)* If someone **shoots down (in flames)** one of your suggestions or ideas, they refuse to accept it without giving it any consideration. • If you **shoot a glance** at someone, you look at them quickly: *She shot him a glance as he entered the room.* • *(infml)* If you **shoot yourself in the foot**, you unintentionally do something which spoils the situation for you: *I really shot myself in the foot when I introduced him to my wife, because two months later she left me and went to live with him!* • *(taboo slang)* If a man or boy **shoots** his **load**/*(Am also)* **shoots his wad**, he EJACULATES (= sperm comes out through his penis). • *(slang)* If you **shoot** your **mouth off**, you talk too much in a loud and uncontrolled way: *It's just like Richard to go shooting his mouth off* **about** *other people's affairs.* • If something, such as a piece of writing, is **shot through with** a particular emotion or quality, that emotion or quality is noticeable all the way through it: *Her novel is shot through with a haunting lyricism.* ○ *The report was shot through with inaccuracies.* ○ See also **shoot through** at SHOOT [MOVE QUICKLY]. • *(Am infml)* If you **shoot the works**, you use all your money or make the greatest effort you can: *I emptied by bank account, took out a loan and shot the works on a trip to Mauritius.* • A **shoot-out**, esp. in the US, is a fight in which two people or two groups of people shoot at each other with guns. • *"Please don't shoot the pianist. He is doing his best."* (sign in a bar reported by Oscar Wilde in *Impressions of America, Leadville,* 1883) • *"They Shoot Horses, Don't They?"* (title of a book by Horace McCoy, 1935)

shoot /ʃuːt/ *n* [C] • A shoot is an occasion on which a group of people go to an area of the countryside in order to shoot animals.

shoot·er /£ˈʃuː·tər, $-t̬ɚ/ *combining form* • Shooter is used in combinations to mean a gun or other device which shoots: *a rifleshooter/peashooter* • See also TROUBLESHOOTER.

shoot·ing /£ˈʃuː·tɪŋ, $-t̬ɪŋ/ *n* • *She'd heard some shooting in the night and a noise that sounded like a bomb exploding.* [U] • A shooting can be an occasion on which

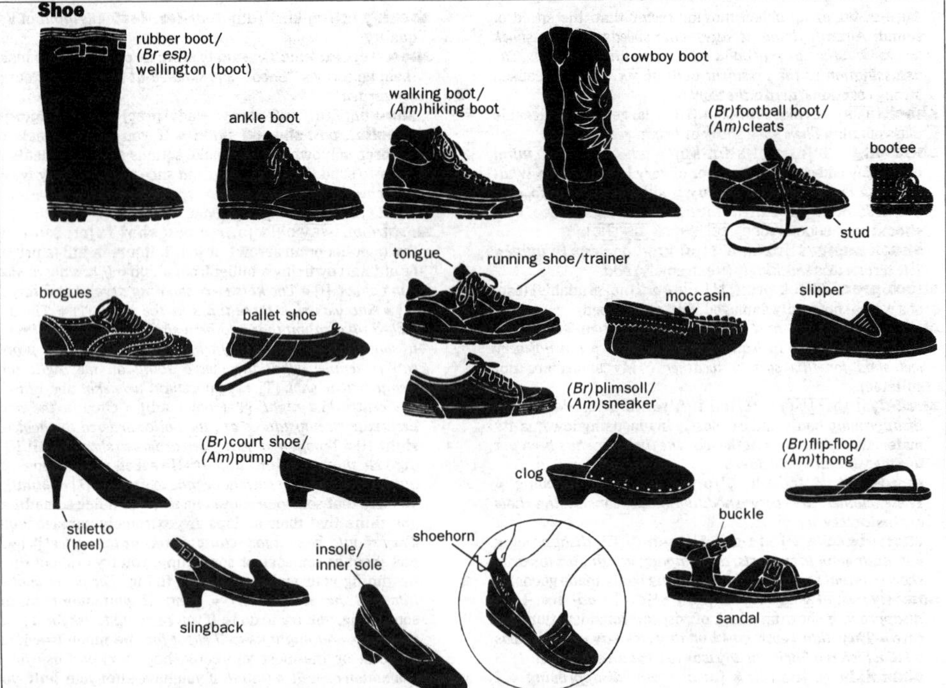

someone is injured or killed by a bullet fired from a gun: *There have been a number of shootings in the capital this week.* [C] • Shooting is also the sport of shooting animals or birds: *pheasant/grouse shooting* [U] ○ *He* **goes** *shooting most weekends.* [U] • A **shooting gallery** is an enclosed area in which people shoot guns at TARGETS (= objects intended to be hit), either for entertainment or in order to improve their shooting skills. See also **shooting gallery** at SHOOT DRUG. • A **shooting star** (also **falling star** or *specialized* **meteor**) is a bright moving line of light in the sky, caused by a small piece of matter travelling through space which burns as it enters the Earth's air. • A **shooting stick** is a walking stick which can also be used outside as a seat, having a sharp point to put in the ground at one end and a piece of folding material to sit on at the other.

shot /£ʃɒt, $ʃɑːt/ *n* [C] • A shot is the action of firing a gun or another weapon: *Did you hear a shot?* ○ *He* **fired** *four shots at the car as it drove off.* • You might also describe someone as a **good** or **poor** shot if they are skilled or not skilled at aiming and firing a gun. • *(infml)* If you do something **like a shot**, you do it extremely quickly: *The moment I let go of the dog, she's off like a shot.* • *(infml)* You might describe a guess as **a shot in the dark** when you have no information or knowledge about the subject and therefore cannot possibly know what the answer is.

shoot SPORT /ʃuːt/ *v* [I] *past* **shot** /£ʃɒt, $ʃɑːt/ (in sports involving a ball) to kick, hit or throw the ball in an attempt to score points for yourself or your team • *He shot from the middle of the field and still managed to score.*

shoot·er /£ˈʃuː·təʳ, $-t̬ɚ/ *n* [C] • *He's thought to be the best shooter in the league.*

shot /£ʃɒt, $ʃɑːt/ *n* [C] • In sports involving a ball such as cricket, football, tennis or golf, a shot is a kick, hit or throw of the ball which is intended to score points: *And that was a great shot by Lineker!* ○ *Graf drove a forehand shot down the line to win the match.* ○ *His tee shot finished a few centimetres away from the hole.*

shoot MOVE QUICKLY /ʃuːt/ *v* [I always + adv/prep] *past* **shot** /£ʃɒt, $ʃɑːt/ to move in a particular direction very quickly and directly • *She shot past me several metres before the finishing line.* • *He shot out of the office a minute ago – I think he was late for a meeting.* • *We were meant to be following Anna's car, but she shot ahead at the traffic lights and we lost her.* • *They were just shooting off to town so we didn't stop to speak.* • *We heard that Jenny had been in a car accident, and so shot* **over** (= went quickly) *to see her in hospital.* • *Sylvester Stallone shot* **to fame** (= became famous suddenly) *with the film 'Rocky'.* • *Inflation has shot* **up** (= risen very noticeably) *over the last two years.* • *(infml)* If a child shoots **up**, he or she grows a lot very suddenly: *David has really shot up since I saw him last.* ○ See also **shoot up** at SHOOT DRUG. • *(Aus infml)* If you shoot **through** somewhere, you leave that place very quickly. ○ See also **shot through with** at SHOOT WEAPON. • **Shooting pains** are sudden severe pains which move through the body: *I get shooting pains up my spine whenever I try to move.*

shoot *(obj)* FILM /ʃuːt/ *v past* **shot** /£ʃɒt, $ʃɑːt/ to film or photograph (something) • *When the lights come up, we're ready to shoot.* [I] • *We shot* (= used) *four reels of film in Egypt.* [T] • *The first half of the film was shot* **on location** *in Southern India.* [T]

shoot /ʃuːt/ *n* [C] • When photographers **do** a shoot, they take a series of photographs, usually of the same person or people in the same place: *We did a shoot on the beach in which the girls were modelling swimwear.*

shot /£ʃɒt, $ʃɑːt/ *n* [C] • A shot is a photograph: *I* **got/took** *some really good shots of the harbour at sunset.* • A shot is also a short piece in a film in which there is a single action or a short series of actions: *Do you remember that shot at the beginning of the film where the tall guy gives a package to the blonde woman?*

shoot *obj* PLAY /ʃuːt/ *v* [T] *past* **shot** /£ʃɒt, $ʃɑːt/ *esp. Am infml* to play a game of (POOL or CRAPS) • *Pat and I would hang around the local bars, drinking beer and shooting pool.*

shoot *(obj)* DRUG /ʃuːt/ *v past* **shot** /£ʃɒt, $ʃɑːt/ *slang* to take (an illegal drug) by INJECTING yourself with it (= putting it directly into your blood using a special needle) • *By the time he was sixteen, he was shooting heroin twice a day.* [T] • *She saw a girl shooting* **up** *in the toilets.* [I] • *(slang)* A **shooting gallery** is a place where people go to INJECT illegal drugs: *Police raided a lower East Side shooting gallery on Thursday night.* ○ See also **shooting gallery** at SHOOT WEAPON.

shot /£ʃɒt, $ʃɑːt/ *n* [C] *infml* • A shot **of** a drug is the amount of a particular drug, whether medical or illegal, which is put into the body by a single INJECTION (= putting a drug directly into the blood using a special needle): *She would do anything for a shot of heroin.* ○ *The doctor* **gave** *him a shot of morphine.* ○ *(fig.) The senator's presidential campaign needs to be injected with a shot of professionalism* (= It needs to be organized in a more serious and effective way). • A **shot in the arm** is something which has a sudden and positive effect on something, providing encouragement and new activity: *Fresh investment in our* *major industries would provide the shot in the arm that the nation so badly needs.*

shoot *obj* MOVE PAST /ʃuːt/ *v* [T] *past* **shot** /£ʃɒt, $ʃɑːt/ to move through or past (something) quickly • *(infml) He shot three sets of* **traffic lights** (= He went past them when they gave the signal to stop) *before the police caught up with him.* • *We spent an exhilarating morning shooting* **the rapids** (= travelling along the dangerous part of a river where the water flows very fast).

shoot PLANT /ʃuːt/ *n* [C] the first part of a plant to appear above the earth as it develops from a seed, or any new growth on an already existing plant • *Two weeks after we'd planted the seeds, little green shoots started to appear.* • *(fig.) The prime minister has commented that the green shoots of economic recovery have started to appear* (= that the economy is starting to grow again).

shop PLACE TO BUY THINGS /£ʃɒp, $ʃɑːp/, *Am usually* **store** *n* [C] a building or a room in a building where you can buy goods or obtain services • *a book/clothes/record/sweet shop* • *a barber's/betting shop* • *She spent the afternoon gazing in the shop windows.* • *While I was in the shop, I picked up a couple of magazines.* • *I need to go to the shops at some point – we've got no food in the house.* • *(Br and Aus)* Shop can also refer to the act of shopping, esp. of shopping for food and other things needed in the house: *I usually* **do** *the* **weekly** *shop on a Monday.* • *His latest novel will be* **in the shops** (= will be available to be bought) *by Christmas.* • *(Br and Aus)* A **shop assistant** (*Am* **salesclerk** or **salesperson**) is a person who works in a shop, serving customers. • A **shop front** is the outside of a shop which faces the street.

shop /£ʃɒp, $ʃɑːp/ *v* [I] **-pp-** • *I like to shop* **at** *Marks and Spencers for clothes.* • *If I'm just shopping* **for** *food, I tend to go to the local supermarket.* • To shop **around** is to compare the price and quality of the same or a similar item in different shops before you decide which one to buy: *When you're buying a flight, you should always shop around for the best deal.*

shop·per /£ˈʃɒp·əʳ, $ˈʃɑː·pɚ/ *n* [C] • A shopper is a person who is buying things from a shop or a number of shops: *We tried to make our way through the crowds of* **Christmas** *shoppers.*

shop·ping /£ˈʃɒp·ɪŋ, $ˈʃɑː·pɪŋ/ *n* [U] • Shopping is the activity of buying things from shops: *The department store is open for late night shopping on Wednesdays.* ○ *I'm* **going** *shopping this afternoon.* ○ *She* **does** *the shopping for the old lady who lives next door.* ○ *There are only sixteen shopping* **days** (= days on which the shops are open) *left until Christmas.* ○ *I haven't done any* **Christmas** *shopping yet.* • Shopping also refers to goods which you have bought from shops, esp. food: *She had so many* **bags of** *shopping that she could hardly carry them.* ○ *Did you remember to bring the shopping* **list?** • *(Br)* A **shopping bag** is any bag intended to carry items bought in shops, esp. one bought for this purpose and used many times: *a plastic/string shopping bag* • **Shopping bag** is also *Am for* **carrier (bag)**. See at CARRY TRANSPORT. • *(Br)* A shopping **basket** is a wide container with a handle, which is made of thin bendable strips of wood woven together and which is used for carrying things you have bought, esp. food. • A shopping *(Br)* **centre**/*(Am and Aus)* **mall** is an enclosed area in which there is a variety of shops. • A **shopping** *(Am)* **center**/*(Aus)* **centre** is a group of shops with a common area for cars to park, which usually provides goods and services for local people. • PIC **Bags** KOR

shop WORK AREA /£ʃɒp, $ʃɑːp/ *n* [C] a place where a particular type of thing is made or repaired • *an engineering shop* • *He runs an auto-tyre repair shop.* • The **shop floor** refers to the ordinary workers in a factory: *There is great concern on the shop floor* (= among the ordinary workers) *over job security.* • A **shop steward** is a worker elected by workers in a factory or business to represent them in discussions with the management.

shop BUSINESS /£ʃɒp, $ʃɑːp/ *n infml* a business • If someone **sets up shop**, they start their own business: *She set up shop back in 1965 with a very small restaurant in the Kings Road.* • *(Br and Aus)* If you **shut up shop** (*Am usually* **close up shop**), you stop doing business, either for a short period or permanently: *They were forced to shut up shop because they weren't getting enough customers.*

shop *obj* GIVE INFORMATION /£ʃɒp, $ʃɑːp/ *v* [T] **-pp-** *Br slang* to give the police information about (a criminal) • *His ex-wife shopped him to the police.*

shop·keep·er /£ˈʃɒpˌkiː·pəʳ, $ˈʃɑːpˌkiː·pɚ/, *Am usually* **store·keep·er** *n* [C] a person who owns and manages a small shop • *The new parking restrictions have angered both shopkeepers and residents.* • *Small independent shopkeepers believe that the new supermarket will drive business away from the town centre.* • *"England is a nation of shopkeepers"* (believed to have been said by Napoleon I, 1769-1821)

shop·lift·ing /£ˈʃɒpˌlɪf·tɪŋ, $ˈʃɑːpˌlɪf·t̬ɪŋ/ *n* [U] the illegal act of taking goods from a shop without paying for them • *He was charged with shoplifting.* ○ LP **Crimes and criminals**

shop·lift /£ˈʃɒp·lɪft, $ˈʃɑːp-/ *v* [I] • *He was caught shoplifting by a store detective.*

shop·lift·er /£ˈʃɒpˌlɪf·təʳ, $ˈʃɑːpˌlɪf·t̬ɚ/ *n* [C] • *Shoplifters will be prosecuted.*

shop·per /£ˈʃɒp·əʳ, $ˈʃɑː·pɚ/ *n* [C] See at SHOP PLACE TO BUY THINGS

shop·ping /£ˈʃɒp·ɪŋ, $ˈʃɑː·pɪŋ/ *n* [U] See at SHOP PLACE TO BUY THINGS

shop·soiled *Br and Aus* /£ˈʃɒp·sɔɪld, $ˈʃɑːp-/, *Am* **shop·worn** *adj* (of goods sold in shops) slightly dirty or damaged and therefore reduced in price • *I managed to get this shirt for only £15 because it's slightly shopsoiled.*

shop·talk /£ˈʃɒp·tɔːk, $ˈʃɑːp·tɑːk/ *n* [U] talking about work or business with the people you work with when you are in a social situation • See also **talk shop** at TALK.

shop·worn /£ˈʃɒp·wɔːn, $ˈʃɑːp·wɔːrn/ *adj Am for* SHOPSOILED • A shopworn story or joke is one which is boring or uninteresting because it is so familiar to people: *She told him that shopworn story about the time she broke her leg while skiing.*

shore /£ʃɔːʳ, $ʃɔːr/ *n* the land along the edge of a sea, lake or wide river • *You can walk for miles along the shore.* [C] • *Seals die in their thousands on these polluted north European shores.* [C] • *The boat was about a mile from/off (the) shore when the engine suddenly died.* [U] • *(fig.) In 1992, Britain played host to the first multi-racial South African team to visit these shores* (= to come to this country). [C] • **On shore** means on the land and not in a ship: *We waited until we were on shore before repairing the sails.* • See also ONSHORE; OFFSHORE.

shore·line /£ˈʃɔː·laɪn, $ˈʃɔːr-/ *n* [C usually sing] • The shoreline is the edge of a sea, lake or wide river: *The oil from the wrecked tanker polluted more than 40 miles of the Normandy shoreline.*

shore up *obj*, **shore** *obj* **up** /£ʃɔːʳ, $ʃɔːr/ *v adv* [M] to make (something) stronger by supporting it • *Boundary walls have had to be shored up.* • *We will have to shore the wall up.* • *(fig.) As public relations manager, she is now faced with the difficult task of shoring up* (= trying to improve) *the company's troubled image.*

shorn /£ʃɔːn, $ʃɔːrn/ *past participle of* SHEAR CUT

short DISTANCE /£ʃɔːt, $ʃɔːrt/ *adj* **-er, -est** small in length, distance or height • *Both long and short skirts are fashionable this year.* • *I wish I didn't have such short legs.* • *Her hair is much shorter than it used to be.* • *It's only a short walk to the station.* • *Could you write a short report about the meeting?* • *I'm quite short but my brother's very tall.* • Short is used with adjectives ending in -ed formed from nouns: *a short-haired dog* (= a dog with short hair) ○ *a short-sleeved shirt* (= a shirt with short sleeves) • *Her name's Jo – it's short* **for** (= the shorter form of) *Josephine.* • *Her name's Josephine, or Jo* **for short.** • *(infml)* To **draw/get the short straw** is to have to do the least enjoyable of a range of duties, often because you have been chosen to do it: *Colin, I'm afraid you've drawn the short straw – you're cleaning out the toilets.* • *(slang)* If you **have (got)** someone **by the short and curlies/by the short hairs**, you have them in your power. • A **short back and sides** is an old-fashioned hairstyle for men in which the hair is cut short at the back and sides, showing the ears. • A **short-circuit** (*infml* **short**) in an electrical system is a wrong electrical connection which causes the current to flow in the wrong direction, often having the effect of stopping the power supply. A machine that goes wrong in this way **short-circuits**: *If those two wires touch, the appliance will short-circuit and probably go up in flames.* • A **short cut** is a route which leads from one place to another which is quicker and more direct than the usual route: *I know a short cut* **to** *town through the back streets.* ○ *(fig.) When you're cooking every night for seven people, you quickly get to learn the short cuts* (= quickest methods). J • If someone has a **short fuse**, they get angry very easily: *He has a short*

SHOPPING GOODS

Large stores have parts called **departments** or **counters** where particular types of goods are sold. They often use formal names for the types of things they sell. For example, *cutlery* is knives and forks for eating with, and *knitwear* means knitted woollen clothes.

CLOTHES

Shops often use *wear* to mean clothes: *children's wear, sportswear, school wear*
beachwear/swimwear: swimming costumes, trunks, bikinis, swimsuits
maternity wear: for women who are going to have a baby
leisurewear: for relaxing in - sweatshirts, tracksuits
casuals: informal clothes not suitable for work – jeans, slacks, pullovers
knitwear: knitted woollen clothes - jumpers, sweaters, jerseys
underwear: to wear under other clothes – underpants, bras
lingerie: women's clothes for sleeping in and underclothes – bras, nightdresses
hosiery: thin clothes worn on the legs by women – stockings, tights
coordinates: women's clothes in matching colours
accessories: handbags, shoes, gloves, umbrellas
fabrics: cloth used to make clothes
haberdashery: cloth, wool and tools for making clothes and for sewing
Words like *fashion, style* and *trend* refer to clothes in a popular and modern style.

GOODS FOR THE HOUSE AND GARDEN

Shops use *domestic, home* and *household* to refer to the house.
furnishings: furniture, curtains, carpets
(Br) soft furnishings/(Am) soft goods: curtains, furniture coverings
(Br) drapery/(Am) dry goods: cloth and cloth goods, esp. for making curtains
appliances: devices or machines for cleaning, cooking etc.
kitchenware: plates, bowls, knives, forks
ovenware: dishes and other containers in which food can be cooked
cutlery: knives, forks, spoons
silverware, glassware: articles made of silver or glass
china or *chinaware:* plates, cups and ornaments made of china
linens: cotton items like bed sheets and table cloths
homecare: substances and tools for cleaning the house
DIY (abbreviation for do it yourself*):* materials and tools for decorating and improving your house or garden
hardware, (Br also) ironmongery: tools or equipment used in house or garden

OTHER TYPES OF GOODS

greetings cards: printed cards for birthdays, weddings
stationery: pens, paper, envelopes
handicrafts: materials and tools for sewing, weaving
needlework: materials and tools for sewing
luggage/travel goods: bags and articles used while travelling - suitcases, holdalls
cosmetics: substances used to improve your appearance - lipstick, eye liner
perfumes/fragrances: pleasant-smelling substances – scent, perfume
confectionery: sweet foods - chocolate, *(Br)* sweets/*(Am)* candy
toiletries: used to clean or tidy yourself – soap, toothpaste, hair brushes

fuse, and is liable to be rude to colleagues who disagree with him. • A **short list** is a list of people who have been judged the most suitable for a job or prize, made from a longer list of people originally considered, and from which one person will be chosen: *We've* **drawn up** (=decided) *a short list for the job.* ○ *She's* **on** *the short list for a teaching post.* • *His latest novel has been* **short-listed** *for the Booker prize.* • **Short-range** means reaching a short distance or relating to a short time: *short-range missiles/weapons* • *a short-range weather forecast* • Someone who is **short-sighted** (*Am also* **near-sighted**, *specialized* **myopic**) can only see objects clearly which are close to them. Compare **long-sighted** at LONG [DISTANCE]. • **Short-sightedness** (*Am also* **near-sightedness**, *specialized* **myopia**) is an inability to see distant things clearly. [LP> **Eye and seeing** • *(disapproving)* A **short-sighted** action or way of thinking is one that will not bring help or advantage in the future but only considers the effects it will have in the present: *It's very short-sighted of the government not to invest in technological research.* • A **short story** is an invented story which is no more than about 10 000 words in length: *He has just published a book of short stories.*

short·en *(obj)* /£'ʃɔː·tᵊn, $'ʃɔːr·t̬ᵊn/ *v* • *As you grow older, your spine shortens by about an inch.* [I] • *I've asked him to shorten my grey trousers.* [T] • *The name 'William' is often shortened* **to** *'Bill'.* [T]

short·ish /£'ʃɔː·tɪʃ, $'ʃɔːr·t̬ɪʃ/ *adj* • *She's got shortish* (=quite short) *black hair.* • See also **shortish** at SHORT [TIME].

short·ness /£'ʃɔːt·nəs, $'ʃɔːrt-/ *n* [U] • *He raised his eyebrows in surprise when he saw the shortness of her skirt.* • *He feels that he has been discriminated against because of his shortness.* • See also **shortness** at SHORT [TIME], SHORT [LACKING].

short·y /£'ʃɔː·ti, $'ʃɔːr·t̬i/, *Br also slang* **short-arse** /£'ʃɔːt·ɑːs, $'ʃɔːrt̬·æs/ *n* [C] *infml* • Shorty is an offensive way of addressing or referring to a short person: *That coat reaches your ankles, shorty!* • [PIC> **Clothes**

short [TIME] /£ʃɔːt, $ʃɔːrt/ *adj* **-er, -est** being an amount of time which is less than average or usual • *It's quite a short film.* • *He's grown so much in such a short time.* • *I can work better if I give myself short breaks every hour or so.* • *I will have to cancel this afternoon's class – I'm sorry it's such short* **notice** (=so near the time). • If books, letters and other examples of writing are short, they do not contain many words and do not take much time to read: *It's a very short book – you'll read it in an hour.* • *(Br infml)* If you are **caught/taken short**, you suddenly and unexpectedly need to go to the toilet, especially when it is not convenient for you to do so: *I was caught short at the station and had to use their revolting toilets.* • If you **make short work** of something, you deal with it quickly. • *My grandfather is in favour of the* **short sharp shock** *treatment* (=quick, effective punishment) *for young offenders.* • *(infml humorous) This morning's lecture was* **short and sweet** (=surprisingly or pleasingly short). • If a feeling or experience is **short-lived**, it only lasts for a short time: *I had a few relationships at college, most of which were fairly short-lived.* • If someone has a **short memory**, they forget things easily. • If you get or are given **short shrift** by someone, you are treated without sympathy and given little attention: *He'll* **get** *short shrift from me if he starts*

SHORT FORMS OF VERBS (CONTRACTIONS)

In everyday speech and in informal writing, some combinations of a verb with a pronoun or with *not* are given in a short form.

• short forms with I

I'm	I am	*I'm sorry I'm late.*
I've	I have	*I've got a cold.*
I'd	I had	*It was after I'd been.*
	I would	*I'd like some tea.*
I'll	I will	*I'll do it tomorrow.*

• short forms with she, he or it

she's	she is	*She's writing a letter.*
	she has	*She's opened an account.*
she'd	she had	*If only she'd known.*
	she would	*She'd soon be ready.*
she'll	she will	*She'll see you now.*

The forms *it'd* and *it'll* are not usually written.

We, *you* and *they* have an additional short form with **'re**: **We're** (= we are) *still looking*

• short forms with other pronouns The following are common:

here's	here is/has
that'll	that will
that's	that is/has
there's	there is/has
what's	what is/has
where's	where is/has
who'd	who would/had
who's	who is/has

Many more short forms are used in spoken English: *My camera's broken.* • *Why'd you do that?* (= why did) • *This'll* (= this will) *last for a long time.* • *Let's* (= let us) *go outside.*

• short forms with *not* Some verb forms have two short forms. That given first is the more common. The other form is especially used when you want to emphasize that something is being denied: *He's* **not** *the person we need.*

Full form	*Short form*	*Pronunciation*
am not	**I'm not**	aım
are not	**aren't (–'re not)**	
cannot	**can't**	£kɑːnt, $kænt
could not	**couldn't**	
dare not	**daren't**	
did not	**didn't**	
does not	**doesn't**	
do not	**don't**	£dəʊnt, $doʊnt
has not	**hasn't (–'s not)**	
have not	**haven't (–'ve not)**	
had not	**hadn't (–'d not)**	
is not	**isn't (–'s not)**	
might not	**mightn't**	
must not	**mustn't**	'mʌs·ᵊnt
need not	**needn't**	
ought not	**oughtn't**	
(*esp. Br*) shall not	**shan't**	£ʃɑːnt, $ʃænt
should not	**shouldn't**	
was not	**wasn't**	
were not	**weren't**	
will not	**won't (–'ll not)**	£wəʊnt, $woʊnt
would not	**wouldn't (–'d not)**	

An important use of short forms with *not* is in questions: *Aren't you hungry?* • *Didn't you talk to him?* • *Can't you find it?* The full forms of the verbs would only be used in very formal situations. Notice that the question form of *I'm not* is *Aren't I?*

Short forms with *not* are also used at the end of questions to check or confirm a fact: *You're over 18, aren't you?* • *She really surprised us, didn't she?* • *I can go in here, can't I?* Short forms used in this way are often called question tags.

• short forms with *have* In spoken English, when *have* follows a short form or an auxiliary verb it is often said as **'ve**: *If only you'd've told me earlier.* • *Really, you needn't've bothered.* • *Who'd've expected it?* • *I should've guessed it was Rita.*

• non-standard short forms In non-standard or very informal spoken English, the following are common:

ain't (eınt) am/is/are/has/have not	*I ain't coming till eight.*
dunno (£də'nəʊ, $də'noʊ) don't know	*"Who's that?" "Dunno."*
gimme ('gım·i) give me	*Gimme a chance, will you?*
gonna (£'gɒn·ə, 'gən·ə, $'gɑː·nə) going to	*I'm gonna win this time.*
gotta (£'gɒt·ə, $'gɑː·tə) got to	*We've gotta get out of here.*
wanna (£'wɒn·ə, $'wɑː·nə) want to	*I don't wanna go home.*

complaining about money again, now I know how much he earns! • If you **make short shrift of** something, you deal with or get rid of it quickly: *You two made short shrift of* (=ate quickly) *that cheesecake!* • If someone who works at a factory or in an office is on **short time** (also **reduced time**), they are working fewer days or hours than usual for less money because there is not much work to do: *He's been put on short time because business is so quiet.*

short /£ʃɔːt, $ʃɔːrt/ *n* [C] • A short is a short film, esp. one which is made for showing before the main film at a cinema. • **In short** can be used to introduce something you are going to say in as few words and as directly as possible: *He's disorganized, he's inefficient, he's never there when you want him – in short, the man's hopeless.*

short·ish /£ˈʃɔː·tɪʃ, $ˈʃɔːr·ṭɪʃ/ *adj* [not gradable] • *"Is it a short film?" "Well, shortish* (=not long but not very short)*."* • See also **shortish** at SHORT DISTANCE.

short·ly /£ˈʃɔːt·li, $ʃɔːrt-/ *adv* [not gradable] • *Shortly after you left, a man came into the office looking for you.* • *We will shortly be arriving in King's Cross Station. May I remind all passengers to take their luggage with them.*

short·ness /£ˈʃɔːt·nəs, $ˈʃɔːrt-/ *n* [U] • *They were constantly aware of the shortness of time they had left in which to finish the project.* • See also **shortness** at SHORT DISTANCE, SHORT LACKING.

short LACKING /£ʃɔːt, $ʃɔːrt/ *adj* **-er, -est** lacking • *We're a bit short* **of** *coffee – I must remember to get some more.* • *We're a bit short* **of** *space in this apartment.* • *I'm a little short* **of** *time over the next few days, but perhaps we could schedule an appointment for next week.* • *The bill comes to £85 but we're £15 short.* • *Computers are in rather short* **supply** *in this office* (=There are not enough). • *(infml) She's like her mother – a bit short* **on** *brains* (=She is not very clever). • *I'm a little short* (=I do not have much money) *this week – could you lend me ten dollars?* • If someone is **short of breath**, they cannot breathe very well because they have been running or doing some sort of energetic exercise: *She's always short of breath when she climbs the stairs.* • *(Br and Aus infml) He's* **not short of a bob or two** (=He is wealthy). • If someone **short-changes** you when you are buying something, they give you back less money than you are owed: *I think I was short-changed in the pub last night, because I've only got £5 in my purse when I should have £10.* ○ *(fig. infml) There weren't many boys at my college – I think I was short-changed* (=it was rather unfair) *in that respect.* • **Short-staffed** is *Br and Aus for* SHORTHANDED: *We've got a few people off sick at the moment so we're a bit short-staffed.*

short /£ʃɔːt, $ʃɔːrt/ *adv* **-er, -est** • *(esp. Br)* To **go** short of something is to lack it, esp. when it is something you need in order to live: *My parents didn't have much money, although we didn't go short of anything.*

short·age /£ˈʃɔː·tɪdʒ, $ˈʃɔːr·ṭɪdʒ/ *n* [C] • If there is a shortage in a supply of something, there is not enough of it: *Relief workers are concerned at the shortage* **of** *food and shelter in the refugee camps.* ○ *The long hot summer has led to serious water shortages.*

short·ness /£ˈʃɔːt·nəs, $ˈʃɔːrt-/ *n* [U] • *The disease may cause cold sweating, nausea, vomiting and shortness* **of breath** (=difficulties in breathing). • See also **shortness** at SHORT DISTANCE, SHORT TIME.

short NOT PATIENT /£ʃɔːt, $ʃɔːrt/ *adj* [after v] **-er, -est** saying little but showing a slight lack of patience or annoyance in the few words that you say • *I'm sorry if I was a bit short* **with** *you on the phone this morning – I was just in a bad mood.* • If someone is **short-tempered**, they get angry easily, often for no good reason.

short DRINK /£ʃɔːt, $ʃɔːrt/ *n* [C] *Br infml* a drink of SPIRITS (=type of strong alcohol) without water or any other liquid added • *She doesn't like beer or wine and only drinks shorts.*

short ELECTRICITY /£ʃɔːt, $ʃɔːrt/ *n* [C], *v* [I] *infml for* **short-circuit**, see at SHORT DISTANCE

short EARLY /£ʃɔːt, $ʃɔːrt/ *adv* **-er, -est** before the arranged or expected time or place • *We had to* **cut** *short our holiday* (=finish it early) *because Richard was ill.* • *Although we still have a lot to discuss in this meeting, I'm going to have to* **stop** *you short there* (=stop the discussion) *because we only have this room until midday.*

short·age /£ˈʃɔː·tɪdʒ, $ˈʃɔːr·ṭɪdʒ/ *n* [C] See at SHORT LACKING

short·bread /£ˈʃɔːt·bred, $ˈʃɔːrt-/, **short·cake** *n* [U] a type of thick sweet biscuit which contains a lot of butter • *Scottish shortbread* • *Would you like a shortbread finger* (=a piece of shortbread)*?* • PIC› **Bread and cakes**

short·cake /£ˈʃɔːt·keɪk, $ˈʃɔːrt-/ *n* SHORTBREAD, or *(esp. Am)* a type of cake which is often served in layers with fruit and cream • *(esp. Am) Do you like* **strawberry** *shortcake?* [U] • *(esp. Am) For dessert, there was a hot caramel shortcake with ice cream.* [C] • Ⓙ

short·com·ing /£ˈʃɔːtˌkʌm·ɪŋ, $ˈʃɔːrt-, ˌ-ˈ--/ *n* [C usually pl] a failure to reach a particular standard • *Whatever his shortcomings as a husband, I think he was a good father to his children.* • *Like any political system, it has its shortcomings.*

short·crust (pa·stry) /£ˈʃɔːt·krʌst, $ˈʃɔːrt-/ *n* [U] a type of soft pastry • *The base of the pie should be made from shortcrust pastry.*

short·en·ing /£ˈʃɔː·tᵊn·ɪŋ, $ˈʃɔːrt·nɪŋ/ *n* [U] *Am and Aus* butter or other fat which is used in cooking, esp. to make pastry soft and CRUMBLY (=easily broken) • *For the cake, you need flour, shortening, eggs, milk and sugar.*

short·fall /£ˈʃɔːt·fɔːl, $ˈʃɔːrt·fɑːl/ *n* [C] an amount which is less than the level that was expected or needed • *Lack of rain in this area has caused serious shortfalls* **in** *the food supply.*

short·hand *Br and Aus* /£ˈʃɔːt·hænd, $ˈʃɔːrt-/, *Am* **ste·no·graph·y** *n* [U] a system of fast writing which uses lines and simple signs to represent words and phrases • *Their conversations were taken down* **in** *shorthand by a secretary.* • *He learnt how to* **do** *shorthand when he was a journalist.* • *He picked up a shorthand* **pad** *and a pen and went into her office.* • A short simple phrase which is used instead of a longer and more complicated phrase might be said to be shorthand **for** that phrase. • *(Br and Aus)* A **shorthand typist** (*Am or Br dated* **stenographer**) is someone who does shorthand and typing as a main part of their job. • PIC› **Writing**

short·hand·ed /£ˌʃɔːtˈhæn·dɪd, $ˌʃɔːrt-/, *Br and Aus also* **short–staffed** /£ˌʃɔːtˈstɑːft, $ˌʃɔːrtˈstæft/ *adj* (of a company or organization) lacking the usual or necessary number of workers • *Some hospitals are so shorthanded that nurses and doctors are having to work twenty-hour shifts.*

short·ly /£ˈʃɔːt·li, $ˈʃɔːrt-/ *adv* [not gradable] See at SHORT TIME

short·ness /£ˈʃɔːt·nəs, $ˈʃɔːrt-/ *n* [U] See at SHORT DISTANCE, SHORT TIME, SHORT LACKING

shorts /£ʃɔːts, $ʃɔːrts/ *pl n* trousers that end above the knee or reach the knee, which are often worn by children or by adults in hot weather, and when relaxing or playing sport • *tennis shorts* • *She put on a* **pair of** *shorts and a T-shirt.* • *(Am)* Shorts are also men's UNDERPANTS (=a short piece of underwear worn below the waist).

short·y /£ˈʃɔː·ti, $ˈʃɔːr·ṭi/ *n* [C] *infml* See at SHORT DISTANCE

shot SHOOT /£ʃɒt, $ʃɑːt/ *past simple and past participle of* SHOOT

shot METAL BALL /£ʃɒt, $ʃɑːt/ *n* a heavy metal ball thrown in a sports competition, or a mass of small metal balls which are fired from a gun • *The shot weighs over 7kg when used in men's competitions and over 3kg when used in women's.* [C] • *Shotgun cartridges contain lead shot.* [U] • The **shot put** is a sports competition in which a heavy metal ball is thrown from the shoulder as far as possible: *He's practising for* **the** *shot put.* • A **shot putter** is a person who competes in the shot put. • PIC› **Sports**

shot ATTEMPT /£ʃɒt, $ʃɑːt/ *n* [U] *infml* an attempt to do or achieve something that you have not done before • *Many ambitious executives faced a long wait before they could hope for* **a** *shot* **at** *one of the top jobs in the company.* • *I can't get the last two answers in this crossword – here, you* **have** *a shot.* • *I thought I'd* **have** *a shot* **at** *making my own wine since we've got all these grapes.* • *I've never tried hang-gliding before, but I thought I'd* **give** *it a shot.* • *I know you won't win, but just* **give** *it your* **best** *shot* (=do as well as you can).

shot AMOUNT OF DRINK /£ʃɒt, $ʃɑːt/ *n* [C] a small amount of an alcoholic drink • *Would you like a shot* **of** *whisky?*

shot GET RID OF /£ʃɒt, $ʃɑːt/ *n* [U] **get/be shot of** *Br infml* get rid of or leave something • *I can't wait to get shot of this office for a week.* • *I suspect he left home to get shot of that awful mother of his.*

shot WOVEN /£ʃɒt, $ʃɑːt/ *adj* [not gradable] (of silk) woven in such a way that the colour appears to change depending on the angle at which the material is seen • *Her evening dress is made of green shot silk.*

shot DESTROYED /£ʃɒt, $ʃɑːt/ *adj* [not gradable] *infml* no longer working or effective • *It's no good – these gears are shot.* • *I can't carry on working in this office – my nerves are shot!*

shot·gun /£ˈʃɒt·gʌn, $ˈʃɑːt-/ *n* [C] a long gun which fires a large number of small metal bullets at one time, which is intended for the shooting of birds and animals • *The robbers used a (Br and Aus)* **sawn-off**/*(Am)* **sawed-off** *shotgun in the raid.* • *(infml dated)* A **shotgun wedding**/*(Am also)* **shotgun marriage** is a marriage which is arranged very quickly and suddenly because the woman is pregnant.

should DUTY /ʃʊd/ *v aux* [+ infinitive without *to*; not *be shoulding*] he/she/it **should** used to show when it is necessary, desirable, advisable or important to perform the activity referred to by the following verb • *If you're annoyed with him, you should tell him.* • *You should change trains at Peterborough if you're going to Newcastle.* • *"Should I apologize to him?" "Yes, I think you should."* • *"I'm very sorry about crashing your car." "And so you should be."* • *You should be ashamed of yourselves.* • *This computer isn't working as it should.* • *Everything is as it should be.* • *Can you think of any reason why we shouldn't do it?* • *You really should see her new play if you get the chance.* • *People like that should be sent to prison for the rest of their lives.* • *It's essential that the project should not be delayed any further.* • *There should be an investigation into the cause of the disaster.* • *She* **recommended** *that there should be an investigation.* • *You should see a doctor about it.* • *He* **suggested** *that I should see a doctor.* • *I should* **have** *written to her but I haven't had time.* • *She says she is very sorry and realizes she shouldn't* **have** *done it.* • *It's very kind of you but you really shouldn't* **have** *bothered.* • *Chocolates! How kind – you really shouldn't* **have** (= there was no need for you to have given them to me). • *You should* **have** *seen her* (= Seeing her would have interested or amused you) – *she was really angry.* • *Where should* (= do you suggest that) *we meet tonight?* • *It's rather cold in here. Should I* (= Do you want me to) *turn the heating on?* • *(humorous) She should worry* (= does not need to worry)*! She hasn't a problem in the world.* • LP **Auxiliary verbs**

should PROBABLE /ʃʊd/ *v aux* [+ infinitive without *to*; not *be shoulding*] he/she/it **should** used to show when something is likely or expected • *My dry cleaning should be ready this afternoon.* • *There shouldn't be any problems.* • *First-class letters should arrive the next day if you post them before five o'clock.* • *"How much milk do you need for the recipe?" "Oh, half a litre should be enough."* • *You should find this guidebook helpful.* • *She says it won't work in very cold conditions, and she should* (= is expected to) *know because she invented it.* • *I wonder what's happened to Annie. She should be* (= It was expected that she would be) *here by now.* • *"Where's Daryl?" "How should I know?* (= Why do you expect me to know?) *He's hardly ever in the office these days."* • *"Could you have the report ready by Friday?" "Yes, I should think so* (= it is likely that it will be ready)*."* • *"This shirt's made of very good quality silk." "I should think it is* (= I would expect it to be)*, considering how much it cost."* • *"I bought her some flowers to say thank you." "I should think so too* (= I think it would have been bad not to do this)*."* • *"I don't like to drink more than one bottle of wine in an evening." "I should think not* (= I would not expect you to)*."* • *"Colleen wants to see us in her office immediately." "This should be good* (= This is likely to be interesting or amusing)*!"* • *(infml) "You might win first prize." "I should be so lucky* (= That is not likely)*."*

should POSSIBILITY /ʃʊd/ *v aux* [+ infinitive without *to*; not *be shoulding*] he/she/it **should** *fml* used when referring to a possible event in the future • *It seems very unlikely to happen, but if it should, we need to be well-prepared.* • *If anyone should ask for me, I'll be in the manager's office.* • *Should you* (= If you) *ever need anything, please don't hesitate to contact me.* • *He would be most welcome to pay us a visit, should he be coming* (= if he ever comes) *to Cambridge at all.*

should MIGHT /ʃʊd/ *v aux* [+ infinitive without *to*; not *be shoulding*] he/she/it **should** used after 'that' and after some adjectives and nouns which show an opinion or reaction, and after 'that' and some verbs showing agreement, instruction, intention, decision, etc., to suggest that a situation possibly exists or might come into existence • *It's odd that she should think I would want to see her again.* • *It's strange that he shouldn't* **have** *contacted us by now.* • *It's so unfair that she should* **have** *died so young.* • That he should be so generous came as a great surprise. • *(esp. Br) It worries me that he should drive all that way on his own.* • *(esp. Br fml) I suggest that you should leave.* • *(esp. Br fml) I prefer that Jane should do it.* • Should is used after 'so that' and 'in order that' to show purpose: *He took his umbrella so that he shouldn't get wet.* • *(fml)* Should is also used after 'for fear that', 'in case' and 'lest': *He took his umbrella in case it should rain.* • You use 'should' in sentences like this when you are imagining a situation that might exist, but allowing for the possibility that it does not exist. Compare 'It's strange that she thinks that' (= She does think that, which is strange) and 'It's strange that she should think that' (= If she thinks that, and it seems that she does, it is strange). When it is used in connection with events that have happened already, as in 'It's so unfair that she should have died so young', 'should' suggests the idea that they might not have happened, although in fact they did. After a verb and 'that', it is usual to use the SUBJUNCTIVE (I suggest that you leave), but in formal British English, you use 'should' (I suggest that you should leave).

should SURPRISE /ʃʊd/ *v aux* [+ infinitive without *to*; not *be shoulding*] he/she/it **should** used to express surprise in sentences that are in the form of questions • *I was just getting off the bus when who should I see but my old school friend Pat Grantham!*

should WOULD /ʃʊd/ *v aux* [+ infinitive without *to*; not *be shoulding*] *fml slightly dated* used instead of 'would' when the subject is 'I' or 'we' • *I should like a whisky before I go to bed.* • *I shouldn't expect you to pay, of course.* • *We should like to invite you for dinner next week.* • *We should have come sooner if we'd known how ill he was.*

should ADVISE /ʃʊd/ *v aux* [+ infinitive without *to*; not *be shoulding*] used after 'I' when giving advice • *I shouldn't worry about it if I were you.* • *I shouldn't* (= I advise you not to) *let it worry you.*

should REASON /ʃʊd/ *v aux* [+ infinitive without *to*; not *be shoulding*] he/she/it **should** used after 'why' when giving or asking the reason for something • *Why should anyone want to eat something so horrible?* • *Why shouldn't she buy it if she can afford it?* • *Why should he* **have** *said it if he didn't mean it?*

shoul·der BODY PART /£ˈʃəʊl·dəʳ, $ˈʃoʊl·dɚ/ *n* [C] one of the two parts of the body at each side of the neck which join the arms to the rest of the body • *I rested my head on her shoulder.* • *Then she put her arm round my shoulder and gave me a kiss.* • *She walked along the street with her shoulders* **hunched** *and her hands in her pockets.* • *He couldn't take his exams because he'd* **dislocated** *his shoulder in a rugby match.* • *"I don't know what to do about it," said Martha,* **shrugging** *her shoulders.* • *"I'll see you tomorrow," said Brian,* **slinging** *his jacket* **over** *his shoulder.* • *She* **glanced** *nervously* **over** *her shoulder to make sure no one else was listening.* • *His team mates* **carried** *him shoulder-***high** (= carried him on their shoulders) *through the city centre.* • *The police are looking for a white man in his early twenties with brown eyes and shoulder-***length** *blonde hair* (= hair that touches his shoulders). • The shoulder of a bottle is the part that curves out below its opening. • Shoulder is *Am and Aus for* **hard shoulder**. See at HARD SOLID. PIC **Motorway** • A **shoulder to cry on** is someone who is willing to listen to your problems and give you sympathy, emotional support and encouragement: *I wish you'd been here when my mother died and I* **needed** *a shoulder to cry on.* • When people are **shoulder to shoulder**, they are close together and next to each other: *The refugees were packed shoulder to shoulder on the boat.* ○ *The British fought shoulder to shoulder* **with** *the Americans during the battle.* ○ *(fig.) The chairman has promised to* **stand** *shoulder to shoulder* **with** (= to act in support of) *the managing director throughout the investigation.* • A **shoulder bag** is a bag that hangs on a strap from the shoulder, esp. one used for carrying small personal items. • A **shoulder blade** (*specialized* **scapula**) is one of the two large flat triangular bones on each side of the body which are situated over the upper part of the back and which help to increase the range of movement of the arms. • **Shoulder pads** are small pieces of a soft material that are put into the shoulders of a piece of clothing in order to raise them or improve their shape. • A **shoulder strap** is a narrow strip of material on a bag or a piece of clothing which hangs from the wearer's shoulder and holds the bag or clothing in position: *I want to buy a large rucksack with padded shoulder straps.* • PIC **Bags**

shoul·der *obj* /£ˈʃəʊl·dəʳ, $ˈʃoʊl·dɚ/ *v* [T] • *Shouldering her pack* (=putting it on her shoulders to carry it), *she strode off up the road.* • To shoulder something can also be to push it with one of your shoulders: *She was carrying two suitcases and had to shoulder the door open.* ○ *Her bodyguards shouldered her fans out of the way as she walked up the steps.* ○ *He shouldered his* **way** (=formed a way through by pushing with his shoulders) *to the front of the crowd to get a better look.* ○ *(fig.) She has shouldered* **aside** (=ignored) *many of her colleagues who disagreed with her.* [M]

-shoul·dered /£-ˌʃəʊl·dəd, $ˌʃoʊl·dɚd, -ˈ--/ *combining form* • *He was an unimpressive figure, short and narrow-shouldered* (=with a narrow upper back).

shoul·ders /£ˈʃəʊl·dəz, $ˈʃoʊl·dɚz/ *pl n* • Your shoulders are the top part of your back: *He was about six feet tall with* **broad** *shoulders and a thick black beard.* ○ *(fig.) Responsibility for the dispute* **rests** *squarely* **on** *the shoulders of the president* (=he or she is completely responsible). ○ *(fig.) A huge* **burden** *was* **lifted** *from my shoulders* (=I became much less worried and anxious) *when I told my parents about my problem.* • The shoulders of a piece of clothing are the parts which cover the wearer's shoulders: *The shoulders look a bit tight. Do you want to try a larger size?* ○ *She thinks that a jacket with* **padded** *shoulders will make her look more important.*

shoul·der MEAT /£ˈʃəʊl·dəʳ, $ˈʃoʊl·dɚ/ *n* a piece of meat which includes the upper part of an animal's front leg • *I've bought a shoulder of* **lamb** *for Sunday lunch.* [C] • **Pork** *shoulder is on special offer at the moment.* [U]

shoul·der *obj* ACCEPT RESPONSIBILITY /£ˈʃəʊl·dəʳ, $ˈʃoʊl·dɚ/ *v* [T] to accept responsibility for (a demand which involves great effort or expense); to bear • *It is women who shoulder the major* **responsibility** *for the care of elderly and disabled relatives.* • *Religious groups shoulder much of the* **burden** *for sheltering homeless people.* • *Teachers cannot be expected to shoulder all the* **blame** *for poor exam results.* • *Not many parents can afford to shoulder the* **cost** *of educating their children privately.*

should·n't /ˈʃʊd·ᵊnt/ *short form of* should not • *You shouldn't do things like that.*

shout *(obj)* USE LOUD VOICE /ʃaʊt/ *v* to speak or say with a very loud voice, often as loud as possible • People shout when they want to make themselves heard in noisy situations or when the person they are talking to is a long way away or cannot hear very well: *There's no need to shout, I can hear perfectly well.* [I] ○ *She shouted down* **to** *us from the bedroom window.* [I] ○ *"I'll see you tomorrow," shouted Martha* **above** *the noise of the helicopter.* [+ clause] ○ *He shouted from the bottom of the garden* **that** *he'd be finished in about half an hour.* [+ *that* clause] • Sometimes people shout to express strong emotions such as anger, fear or excitement: *Dad really shouted* **at** *me when I broke the window.* [I] ○ *Hundreds of protesters shouting anti-war* **slogans** *gathered outside the embassy yesterday evening.* [T] ○ *He shouted* **abuse** *at the judge after being sentenced to five years imprisonment.* [T] ○ *We shouted ourselves* **hoarse** *at the demonstration.* [T + obj + adj] ○ *Even before the beginning of the concert the fans were screaming and shouting* **out** *the names of the band members.* [M] ○ *I shouted* **at** *him* **to** *put the gun down, but he took no notice.* [+ *to* infinitive] ○ *"I wish you'd stop this childish nonsense!" he shouted furiously.* [+ clause] • People sometimes shout to attract attention: *I heard them shouting* **for help** *but there was absolutely nothing I could do for them.* [I] ○ *(fig.) It's the charities that shout* **loudest** (=attract the most public attention) *that often get given the most money.* [I] ○ *(fig.) Her clothes absolutely shout* (=obviously show that she has) *money.* [T] • When people **shout down** someone who is speaking at a meeting, they prevent them from being heard by shouting: *She was shouted down when she tried to speak on the issue of abortion.* • Something **to shout about** is something that causes the expression of strong feeling, esp. of pleasure or excitement: *At last, a 5-0 victory gives England's supporters* **something** *to shout about.* ○ *Our pay increase this year is* **nothing** *to shout about* (=is small), *but it's better than last year's.* • LP **Exclamation mark**

shout /ʃaʊt/ *n* [C] • *Her speech was frequently interrupted by* **angry** *shouts from the audience.* • *(infml)* **Give** *me a shout* (=Tell me) *when you've finished in the bathroom.*

shout·ing /£ˈʃaʊ·tɪŋ, $-t̬ɪŋ/ *n* [U] • *I heard a lot of shouting and yelling and thought it was just kids mucking around.* • *We could hear shouting* **and screaming** *going on in the street outside.* • If you are **within/in shouting distance** of something, you are very near to it: *Living within shouting distance* **of** *the station is very convenient.* ○ *The management and unions are said to be within shouting distance* **of** *a three-year pay agreement.* • *(disapproving)* A **shouting match** is an argument which involves people shouting at each other because they have very strong opinions: *Nobody had expected the meeting to solve anything, and it soon degenerated into a shouting match.* ○ *(fig.) The dispute is the latest in a series of shouting matches* (=disagreements) *between the two countries over trade.*

shout DRINKS /ʃaʊt/ *n* [C] *Br and Aus infml* (a turn to buy) a set of drinks for a group of people • *"Would you like another drink?" "Yes I would, but you bought the last ones, so it's my shout."* • *Who's going to get the next shout?*

shout *obj* /ʃaʊt/ *v* [T + two objects] *Aus infml* • *I'll shout you a drink* (=buy one for you).

shove *(obj)* PUSH /ʃʌv/ *v* to push forcefully • *She was jostled and shoved by an angry crowd as she left the court.* [T] • *Just wait your turn – there's no need to shove.* [I] • *Reporters* **pushed and** *shoved as they tried to get close to the princess.* [I] • *The bus came really close to me as it was overtaking and almost shoved me off the road.* [T] • *(fig.) A rise in interest rates could shove the already weak economy* (=cause it to move) *into recession.* [T] • If you shove someone **around**, you push them forcefully in an unpleasant and threatening way: *He had a miserable time at school because the older boys were always shoving him around.* [T] ○ *(fig.) Don't let them shove you around* (=tell you what to do and ignore your wishes). *You've got to stand up for your rights.* [T] • *(slang)* If someone tells you to **shove it**, they are expressing extreme lack of respect for you or what you have said: *When I told him he'd have to work harder, he said I could take the job and shove it.*

shove /ʃʌv/ *n* [C] • *Would you help me* **give** *the piano a shove?* • *It's nearly in position. It just needs a couple more shoves.*

shove *obj* PUT /ʃʌv/ *v* [T always + adv/prep] *infml* to put (something) somewhere in a hurried or careless way • *I'll just shove this laundry* **in** *the washer before we go out.* • *Shove the shopping* **on** *the table and I'll sort it out later.* • *"Where should I put this suitcase?" "Shove it* **down** *there for the moment."* • *Just shove those books* **aside** *and make some space for yourself on the desk.* • *They can't just shove motorways anywhere they like, you know.* • *(Br) I didn't have time to do the essay properly, so I had to shove* **down** (=write) *the first thing that came into my head.* [M]

shove MOVE /ʃʌv/ *v* [I always + adv/prep] *infml* to move your body to make space for someone else • *Shove* **over/along**, *Martha, and make some room for me.* • *(Br) Why don't you shove* **up** *so that Brian can sit next to you?*

shove off GO AWAY *v adv* [I] *slang* to go away or leave. This is often said in an angry way. • *I wish you'd shove off and let me get on with my work.* • *Just shove off, Chris, and leave me alone.*

shove off LEAVE LAND *v adv* [I] to leave land in a boat, esp. by pushing against the land with a foot or an OAR • *She jumped into the dinghy and shoved off.*

shov·el /ˈʃʌv·ᵊl/ *n* [C] a tool consisting of a wide square metal or plastic blade, usually with raised sides, fixed to a handle, which is used esp. for moving loose material, such as sand, stones, coal or snow, rather than for digging • *The builders used shovels to put the sand and rubble into the hole they had dug.* • *Armed with pickaxes and shovels, the police began the hunt for his body yesterday morning in a small wood behind his house.* • *The shovel* (=part for picking up and holding material) *of the earth-moving machine is capable of moving a large amount of earth in one go.* • A shovel is also a **shovelful**.

shov·el *(obj)* /ˈʃʌv·ᵊl/ *v* **-ll-** or *Am usually* **-l-** • *Do you want to give me a hand shovelling the snow away from the garage door?* [T] • *He stopped shovelling for a few moments to get his breath back.* [I] • *(fig.) Have you seen the horrid way he shovels* (=hurriedly puts) *his lunch into his mouth?* [T]

shov·el·ful /ˈʃʌv·ᵊl·fʊl/, **shov·el** *n* [C] • A shovelful of something is the amount of it that can fit on a shovel: *He put a shovelful* **of** *snow in Kate's bed as a practical joke.* ○ *Should I put another shovelful* **of** *coal on the fire?*

show *obj* MAKE SEEN /£ʃəʊ, $ʃoʊ/ *v past simple* **showed**, *past part* **shown** /£ʃəʊn, $ʃoʊn/ to make it possible for (something) to be seen • *Let me show you this new book I've just bought.* [T + two objects] • *Remember to have your passport ready to show at the border.* [T] • *On this map, urban areas are shown* **in** *grey.* [T] • *You ought to show that* *rash* **to** *your doctor.* [T] • *Why won't you show me* **what** *you've got in your hand?* [T + obj + *wh-* word] • *She sent us a map which showed* **where** *her house is.* [+ *wh-* word] • *The secretly filmed video shows the prince and princess kiss***ing** *and cuddl***ing**. [T + obj + v-*ing*] • *We watched a film showing* **how** *people live in the desert.* [+ *wh-* word] • *These photographs show the* **effects** *of the chemical on the trees.* [T] • *The locks showed* **signs** *of having been tampered with, but no one had managed to get into the building.* [T] • *Within 24 hours of receiving the new drug he was showing remarkable* **signs** *of recovery.* [T] • *It's showing signs of* (= It looks likely to) *rain, so I'd rather not go out tonight.* [T] • *"I've got a Victorian gold coin here." "Have you? Show me* (= Allow me to see it)*."* [T] • *He used to have a very youthful appearance, but after the accident he started to show his* **age** (= look as old as he really was). [T] • If you **show** your **face** in a place, you go there when you were not expected to because you had done something bad: *I don't know how you* **dare** *show your face in here after you said all those dreadful things.* • If you **show** your **hand**, you let people know about intentions that you had previously kept secret: *Following the coup, tourists were advised to avoid the country until the new régime had shown its hand.* • If you **show off** something that you are proud of, you encourage people to see it so that they can admire it: *Caroline was proudly showing off her portable phone in the restaurant.* ○ *I reckon she only came to the party so she could show her new boyfriend off.* See also SHOW OFF. • *(infml)* If you say **that will show** someone, you are making it clear that you disapprove of them or what they have done: *The next time she's late home, I'll throw her dinner away. That'll show her!* • If you have something **to show for** your work or effort, you have achieved something or benefited from it: *I worked for her for two weeks, and fifty pounds was all I had to show for it.* ○ *I've been trying to write this essay all day and I've got* **nothing** *to show for it.* ○ *You've had this job for five years, and what have you got to show for your* **efforts**? • *(Am and Aus)* **Show-and-tell** is a school activity for young children in which a child brings an object into the class and talks to the other children about it: *He displayed the pistol as proudly as a schoolboy at show-and-tell.*

show [BE NOTICEABLE] /£ʃəʊ, $ʃoʊ/ *v* [I] *past simple* **showed**, *past part* **shown** /£ʃəʊn, $ʃoʊn/ to be able to be seen or noticed • *"Oh no, I've spilt red wine on my jacket!" "Don't worry, it doesn't show."* • *Whatever she's thinking she never lets it show.* • *Your scar doesn't show as much as it used to.* • *Areas of land with trees and plants show blue on these photographs.* • *I've painted over the graffiti twice, but it still shows* **through**. • *The drug does not show* **up** *in blood tests because it only needs to be taken in very small quantities to be effective.* • *The company's improved efficiency is starting to show* **up** *in increased profits.* See also SHOW UP. • *When we moved in, the house hadn't been decorated for twenty years, and* **it showed** (= it was very obvious).

show *obj* [FAIL TO HIDE] /£ʃəʊ, $ʃoʊ/ *v* [T] *past simple* **showed**, *past part* **shown** /£ʃəʊn, $ʃoʊn/ to fail to hide, or to make it possible to see or know, (something that is not intended to be seen or known) • *Your shirt's so thin that it shows your bra.* • *The carpet in the bedroom is white and shows all the dirt.* • *She's an investigative journalist who specialises in showing* **up** *corruption scandals.* [M] • *He should be shown* **up** *for being a cheat.* [M] • *His failure in the exams shows* **up** *just* **how** *bad his teachers are.* [+ *wh-* word]

show *obj* [DIRECT] /£ʃəʊ, $ʃoʊ/ *v* [T + obj + *wh-* word] *past simple* **showed**, *past part* **shown** /£ʃəʊn, $ʃoʊn/ to make (someone) aware of (something) by directing their attention to it • *Show me* **where** *it hurts.* • *Can you show me* **where** *you live on this map?* • *Show me* **which** *one you want.*

show *obj* [LEAD] /£ʃəʊ, $ʃoʊ/ *v* [T always + adv/prep] *past simple* **showed**, *past part* **shown** /£ʃəʊn, $ʃoʊn/ to lead (someone) somewhere within a building • *Would you show Dr Foster into the living room?* • *Would like me to show you* **to** *your seats, or can you find them on your own?* • *I'm sorry you have to leave so soon. I'll show you* **to the door**. • *Don't stand up. I'll show my***self out** (= I will leave the house alone, without anyone coming to the door with me). • When you **show** someone **the door**, you make it obvious that you do not want them to be present and that they should leave: *When I told my bank manager that I wanted to borrow £100 000, she showed me the door.* • When you **show** someone **round/around** (a place that they have not visited before), you go round it with them so that they can look at it: *I'll show you around the house after lunch.* ○ *Let me know when you're coming to Cambridge and I'll show you around.* • *(Br and Aus)* If you **show** someone **over** a place that they are making a formal or official visit to, you lead them around it while telling them about it: *Would you like me to show you over the scene of the murder?* ○ *I've shown fifteen people over the house, but none of them has expressed any interest in buying it.*

show *obj* [RECORD] /£ʃəʊ, $ʃoʊ/ *v* [T] *past simple* **showed**, *past part* **shown** /£ʃəʊn, $ʃoʊn/ to record or express (a number or measurement) • *The company showed a loss of £2 million last year.* • *The right-hand dial shows the temperature, and the left-hand one shows the air pressure.* • *The clock in the office never shows the right time.* • *The latest crime figures show a sharp rise in burglaries over the past year.*

show *obj* [EXPLAIN] /£ʃəʊ, $ʃoʊ/ *v* [T] *past simple* **showed**, *past part* **shown** /£ʃəʊn, $ʃoʊn/ to explain (something) to (someone) by doing it or by giving instructions or examples • *Can you show me* **how** *to set the video recorder?* [+ obj + *wh-* word] • *There ought to be a diagram that shows* **how** *to fit these pieces together.* [+ *wh-* word] • *This dictionary contains many examples that show* **how** *words are actually used.* [+ *wh-* word] • *Would you show me the* **way** *to get this computer going?* • *Could you show me the* **way** *to the bus station?* • If you **show the way**, you do something original which others are likely to copy: *Sweden has shown the way* **forward** *on energy efficiency.*

show *obj* [PROVE] /£ʃəʊ, $ʃoʊ/ *v* [T] *past simple* **showed**, *past part* **shown** /£ʃəʊn, $ʃoʊn/ to prove (something) or make the truth or existence of (something) known • *All the evidence shows the murder* **to** *have been committed by the defendant.* [+ obj + *to* infinitive] • *He has shown him***self (to be)** *completely useless at his job.* [+ obj + (*to be*) n/adj] • *This vicious attack shows him* **to be** *even more dangerous than we had imagined.* [+ obj + *to be* n/adj] • *She has shown her***self (to be)** *a highly competent manager.* [+ obj + (*to be*) n/adj] • *His diaries show him* **to have been** *an extremely insecure person.* [+ obj + *to be* n/adj] • *Show me* **(that)** *I can trust you.* [+ obj + (*that*) clause] • *The diaries show* **(that)** *he was very insecure.* [+ (*that*) clause] • *Opinion polls show* **(that)** *most Americans would readily pay more tax in return for better schools.* [+ (*that*) clause] • *Her refusal to help shows* **how** *mean she really is.* [+ *wh-* word] • *Our research has shown (us)* **how** *little we know about this disease.* [+ obj + *wh-* word] • *The team's performance today shows* (= allows people to understand) **why** *they are bottom of the league.* [+ *wh-* word]

show *obj* [EXPRESS] /£ʃəʊ, $ʃoʊ/ *v* [T] *past simple* **showed**, *past part* **shown** /£ʃəʊn, $ʃoʊn/ to express (ideas or feelings) using actions or words • *He finds it difficult to show affection.* • *She showed enormous courage when she rescued him from the fire.* • *I'd like to give you these flowers to show my gratitude for what you did for me.* • *Your essay fails to show a detailed knowledge of the novel.* • *You should show your parents more respect/show more respect* **to** *your parents.* [+ two objects]

show /£ʃəʊ, $ʃoʊ/ *n* • *His refusal to attend the meeting was described as a childish show* **of** *defiance.* [C] • *Despite its public show* **of** *unity, the royal family had its share of disagreements just like any other.* [C] • *In an unexpected show* **of** *solidarity, the management and workers have joined forces to campaign against the closure of the factory.* [C] • *Over 100 military vehicles had paraded in a show of* **strength** *through the middle of the capital.* [C] • *She may not have won the race, but she nevertheless put up a* **good** *show* (= appeared to try very hard). [U] • A **show of hands** is a vote in which people raise one of their hands to show that they support a suggestion: *He was elected secretary by a unanimous show of hands.* ○ *Her re-election to the committee was defeated* **on** *a show of hands.*

show [PUBLIC EVENT] /£ʃəʊ, $ʃoʊ/ *n* [C] an event at which a group of related things are available for the public to look at • *They had some amazing new car designs at the motor show.* • *Are you going to the Chelsea Flower Show this year?* • *There's a show* **of** *her photographs at the city library this week.* • *He works behind the scenes at* **fashion** *shows.* • *She organized a* **retrospective** *show of his work at the National Museum of American Art in Washington.* • *He gave a fascinating lecture which was followed by a* **slide** *show of his latest Arctic expedition.* • Something that is **on show** has been made available for the public to look at: *Her sculptures will be on show at the museum until the end of the month.* • *(Br)* A **show home/show house** (*Am* **model house**) is a house or apartment which forms part of a group of similar houses or apartments and which has been decorated and filled with furniture as if someone lived in it, so that possible buyers of similar homes can see what their house or apartment might look like if they were living in it. • See also AIRSHOW; **peepshow** at PEEP LOOK; ROADSHOW; SHOW JUMPING; SIDESHOW.

show *(obj)* /£ʃəʊ, $ʃoʊ/ *v past simple* **showed**, *past part* **shown** /£ʃəʊn, $ʃoʊn/ • *Our aim is to make it easier for young unknown artists to show their work* (=make it available for the public to see). [T] • *The paintings and etchings will be shown in the National Gallery until May 24.* [T] • To show a film is to cause it to appear on a cinema screen or to be broadcast on television: *I'd really like to go and see that film, but they're only showing it at 11 o'clock, which is too late for me.* [T] ○ *It's the first time this film has been shown on British television.* [T] ○ *The 'Evening News' provides a complete guide to what's showing at the cinemas in the area.* [I] ○ *Now showing at a cinema near you!* [I]

show·ing /£'ʃəʊ·ɪŋ, $'ʃoʊ-/ *n* [C] • A showing is an opportunity for the public to see something: *This is the film's first showing on British television.* ○ *The exhibition is the first substantial showing of her paintings for 20 years.*

show ENTERTAINMENT /£ʃəʊ, $ʃoʊ/ *n* [C] a theatrical performance or a television or radio programme which is entertaining rather than serious • *Why don't we go to London on Saturday and see a show?* • *We had to raise £60 000 to* **stage** *the show.* • *It was a* **stage** *show long before it was made into a film.* • *Although Annie's had several* **radio** *shows in the past, this is the first time she's had her own* **television** *show.* • *Why are there so many* **quiz** *shows and* **game** *shows on TV?* • *He's always wanted to be a* **game** *show* **host** (=person who introduces the programme). • *I'm thinking of organizing a* **puppet** *show for Jamie's birthday party.* • **Show business** (*infml* **showbiz**) is the part of the entertainment business which is considered to be the most popular, but is often the least artistic or serious: *Some of the biggest names in the entertainment world turned out to honor his 40th year* **in** *show business.* • *(saying)* 'The show must go on' means that even if someone is experiencing difficulties, they must still continue with what they are doing. • See also ROADSHOW.

show FALSE APPEARANCE /£ʃəʊ, $ʃoʊ/ *n* [C] an appearance of something which is not really sincere or real • *They* **put on** *a show* **of** *being interested, but I don't think they really were.* • *His father* **makes** *a show* **of** *liking me, but I'm sure he doesn't really.* • Something that is **for show** has no practical value and is used only to improve the appearance of something else: *Do the lights on this cassette deck have any useful function or are they* **just/only** *for show?* • *(Aus)* A **show pony** is a person who appears to perform well, but has no real ability. • A **show trial** is a trial organized by a government which appears to be interested in matters of justice but which is really intended to have an effect on the opinions of the public and reduce political opposition: *The show trials demonstrated the government's resistance to political reform and resulted in the imprisonment of 19 people.*

show ACTIVITY /£ʃəʊ, $ʃoʊ/ *n* [U] *infml* an activity, business or organization, considered in relation to who is managing it • *Who will* **run** *the show when Meg retires?* • *She doesn't like working for other people and prefers to be* **in charge of** *her own show.* • *The wedding is their show – let them do it their way.* • *Come on, let's* **get the/this show on the road** (= begin what we have planned) *or we'll be late.*

show off *v adv* [I] to behave in a way which is intended to attract attention or admiration, and which other people often find annoying • *She only bought that sports car to show off and prove she could afford one.* • *He's always showing off and trying to impress his classmates.*

show–off /£'ʃəʊ·ɒf, $'ʃoʊ-ɑːf/, *Am also* **show·boat** *n* [C] • *Jane's such a show-off, she always wants to be the centre of attention.*

show up *obj* BEHAVE EMBARRASSINGLY, **show** *obj* **up** *v adv* [M] to behave in a way which makes (someone else) feel ashamed or embarrassed • *I wish you wouldn't show me up in front of my parents by getting so drunk.* • *He's always telling rude jokes and showing up his girlfriend when they're with her friends.*

show up ARRIVE, *esp. Am and Aus* **show** *v adv* [I] *infml* (esp. of a person or people other than yourself or the group of which you are a member) to arrive at a place, esp. late or when other people are not expecting them • *I invited him for eight o'clock, but he didn't show up until nine-thirty.* • *We were expecting thirty people to come, but half of them never showed up.* • *Gangs of men routinely show up at his house and threaten his family with knives and guns.* • *She* **failed** *to show up for the meeting because she missed her train.*

show·biz /£'ʃəʊ·bɪz, $'ʃoʊ-/ *n* [U] *infml for* **show business**, see at SHOW ENTERTAINMENT • *The charity's fund-raising dinner was attended by a host of showbiz* **personalities.**

show·boat·ing /£'ʃəʊˌbəʊ·tɪŋ, $'ʃoʊˌboʊ·t̬ɪŋ/ *n* [U] (esp. in sport) a slightly annoying form of behaviour which is intended to attract attention or admiration because it is very skilful • *When he scored his fourth goal of the afternoon, you were forced to forgive his showboating and other antics.*

show·boat /£'ʃəʊ·bəʊt, $'ʃoʊ·boʊt/ *n* [C] • *He's a showboat outfielder who's famous for his flamboyant catches.*

show·case CONTAINER /£'ʃəʊ·keɪs, $'ʃoʊ-/ *n* [C] a container with glass sides in which valuable or important objects are kept so that they can be looked at without being touched, damaged or stolen • *Showcases are used for displaying objects in shops and museums.*

show·case OPPORTUNITY /£'ʃəʊ·keɪs, $'ʃoʊ-/ *n* [C] a situation or event which makes it possible for the best features of something to be seen • *The Venice Film Festival has always been the showcase* **of** *Italian cinema.* • *The exhibition is an annual showcase* **for** *British design and innovation.* • *The war acted as a showcase* **for** *the products of weapons manufacturers.*

show·case *obj* /£'ʃəʊ·keɪs, $'ʃoʊ-/ *v* [T] • *The main aim of the exhibition is to showcase British design* (=allow its best features to be seen).

show·down /£'ʃəʊ·daʊn, $'ʃoʊ-/ *n* [C] an important argument which is intended to end a disagreement that has existed for a long time • *The President is preparing for a showdown with his advisers* **over** *his plans to reform the economy.* • *I'd like to avoid a showdown* **with** *my boss if I possibly can.* • *Millions of dollars were spent on lawyers in a courtroom showdown* **between** *the two companies.*

sho·wer RAIN /£ʃaʊəʳ, $ʃaʊr/ *n* [C] a brief period when it is raining or snowing • *You're soaked! Did you get caught in the shower?* • *Showers of rain, hail and sleet are likely across the region tomorrow.* • *Overnight there will be* **thundery** *showers over many parts of the country.* • *Scattered* **wintry** *showers are likely in the north.* • **Snow** *showers are expected at the end of the week.* • **Heavy/Light** *showers will become more* **widespread** *over the next 36 hours.*

sho·wer·proof *Br and Aus* /£'ʃaʊə·pruːf, $'ʃaʊr-/, *Am* **wa·ter–re·pel·lent** *adj* • A piece of clothing that is showerproof does not absorb water when it is raining lightly: *This coat is not waterproof but it is showerproof.*

sho·wer·y /£'ʃaʊə·ri, $'ʃaʊr·i/ *adj* • *The forecast is for showery weather over the weekend.*

sho·wer BRIEF FALL /£ʃaʊəʳ, $ʃaʊr/ *n* [C] a brief gentle fall of a lot of small objects or drops of liquid • *A shower* **of** *confetti fell on the newly-married couple outside the church.* • *Suddenly the television went bang, sending a shower* **of sparks** *into the air.* • *The pipe burst, sending out a shower* **of** *water.* • *(fig.) Her handling of the dispute brought a shower* (= a lot) **of praise** *from her colleagues.*

sho·wer *(obj)* /£ʃaʊəʳ, $ʃaʊr/ *v* [always + adv/prep] • *I heard a massive explosion, and seconds later fragments of glass were showering* (=falling) *down on us.* [I] • *She shook the bottle violently and showered us* **with** *champagne.* [T] • *The town has been showered* **with** *missiles over the past 24 hours.* [T] • If you shower someone **with** something, or shower something **on** someone, you give them a lot of it: *She only sees her niece occasionally, so she showers her with* **presents** *when she does.* [T] ○ *His boss showered him with* **praise** *for everything he had done for the company.* [T] ○ *They showered* **compliments** *on her for the meal she had cooked for them.* [T]

sho·wer WASHING DEVICE /£ʃaʊəʳ, $ʃaʊr/ *n* [C] a device which releases drops of water through a lot of very small holes and which a person stands under in order to wash their body • *She stood under the shower letting the hot water run all over her.* • *Many British homes have a shower* **attachment** *fixed to the bath taps.* • *Pull the shower* **curtain** *before you turn on the shower to stop water splashing on the floor.* • A shower is also a wash using such a device: *"Have I got time to* **take** *a shower before we go out?" "Not really. Why don't you* **have** *one when we get back?"* • A shower is also the place, usually in a bathroom, where such a device is situated: *She's in the shower at the moment. Would you like her to phone you back?* • **Shower**

cream/ gel is a type of thick liquid soap used for washing the body. • PIC› **Bathroom**

sho·wer /£ʃaʊəʳ, $ʃaʊr/ *v* [I] • *I always shower every morning.* • LP› **Reflexive pronouns and verbs**

sho·wer PARTY /£ʃaʊəʳ, $ʃaʊr/ *n* [C] *Am* a party held for a woman just before she gets married or gives birth to a child, at which presents are given to her for her future home or baby • *I bought the cutest baby clothes to take to Jacey's* **baby** *shower.* • *(Aus)* A **shower tea** is a party held for a woman just before she gets married, at which usually female friends, give her presents for her future home.

sho·wer·head /£ˈʃaʊə·hed, $ˈʃaʊr-/ *n* [C] the part of a SHOWER (=washing device) from which water flows and which is usually movable so that the water can be directed towards different parts of the body

show·girl /£ˈʃəʊ·gɜːl, $ˈʃoʊ·gɜːrl/ *n* [C] a young woman who sings or dances in a musical theatrical entertainment

show·i·ly /£ˈʃəʊ·ɪ·li, $ˈʃoʊ-/ *adv* See at SHOWY

show·i·ness /£ˈʃəʊ·ɪ·nəs, $ˈʃoʊ-/ *n* [U] See at SHOWY

show·ing /£ʃəʊɪŋ, $ʃoʊɪŋ/ *n* [C usually sing] the quality of someone's performance in a competitive activity • *Although he didn't win, he* **made** *a* **strong** *showing and came a close second.* • *She managed a* **good** *showing in the world championship, but was knocked out in the semi-final.* • *Few people believe she will be re-elected following her* **dismal** *showing in the opinion polls.*

show jump·ing *n* [U] a sport which involves riding horses in competitions which test their ability to jump quickly over large objects such as walls and fences

show jump·er *n* [C] • A show jumper is a rider or horse that takes part in show jumping.

show·man /£ˈʃəʊ·mən, $ˈʃoʊ-/ *n* [C] *pl* **-men** *esp. approving* a man who performs, esp. something which is usually serious, in an entertaining way that attracts a lot of attention • *He was a real showman whose eccentric behaviour brought thousands of people to the sport.*

show·man·ship /£ˈʃəʊ·mən·ʃɪp, $ˈʃoʊ-/ *n* [U] *esp. approving* • *Muhammad Ali's showmanship in the ring shouldn't detract from his considerable skill.*

shown /£ʃəʊn, $ʃoʊn/ *past participle of* SHOW

show·piece /£ˈʃəʊ·piːs, $ˈʃoʊ-/ *n* [C] an extremely good example of something, which deserves to be admired • *The hospital will be the new showpiece of the health service when it opens next year.* • *An inquiry has been launched into what went wrong at a showpiece jail where prisoners went on the rampage causing £500 000 worth of damage.*

show·room /£ˈʃəʊ·rʊm, £-ruːm, $ˈʃoʊ·ruːm, $-rʊm/ *n* [C] a large shop in which people are encouraged to look at the goods that are on sale before buying them • *Our complete range of carpets is on display in our showroom.* • *The level of business in* **car** *showrooms is usually a good indicator of the state of the economy.*

show·stop·per /£ˈʃəʊˌstɒp·əʳ, $ˈʃoʊˌstɑː·pɚ/ *n* [C] an item in a stage performance that is so admired by the people watching that their clapping and shouts of approval interrupt the performance

show·stop·ping /£ˈʃəʊˌstɒp·ɪŋ, $ˈʃoʊˌstɑː·pɪŋ/ *adj* [before n; not gradable]

show·y /£ˈʃəʊ·i, $ˈʃoʊ-/ *adj* **-ier, -iest** attracting a lot of attention by being very colourful or bright, but lacking any real beauty • *a showy production of a play* • *Her dress was too showy for such a formal occasion.*

show·i·ly /£ˈʃəʊ·ɪ·li, $ˈʃoʊ-/ *adv*

show·i·ness /£ˈʃəʊ·ɪ·nəs, $ˈʃoʊ-/ *n* [U]

shrank /ʃræŋk/ *past simple of* SHRINK

shrap·nel /ˈʃræp·nᵊl/ *n* [U] small pieces of metal that are scattered by a bomb or similar weapon when it explodes and are intended to injure people • *Twelve people were* **hit** *by shrapnel in the attack.* • *He was killed by a shrapnel* **wound** *to the chest.*

shred *obj* CUT /ʃred/ *v* [T] **-dd-** to cut or tear (something) roughly into long thin strips • *Shred the lettuce and arrange it around the edge of the dish.* • *Add some shredded carrot to the salad.* • *He ordered the shredding of important documents* (=destroying them by tearing them into strips) *when government inspectors began to investigate his business affairs.* • PIC› **Food preparation**

shred /ʃred/ *n* [C usually pl] • *Peel the carrots and cut them into shreds.* • *My shirt was* **in** *shreds when I took it out of the washer.* • *(fig.) The report has left the reputation of the prison governor* **in** *shreds* (=badly damaged). • *My trousers were* **ripped/torn to** *shreds when I fell off my bike.* • *(fig.) There's no point trying to argue with him – he'll* **tear** *you* **to** *shreds* (=completely defeat you).

shred·der /£ˈʃred·əʳ, $-ɚ/ *n* [C] • A shredder is a tool or machine that is used for cutting things into very small pieces: *Much of the documentary evidence against her had been put through the shredder before she was arrested.* ○ *A decent* **garden** *shredder should be able to cope with branches as thick as 5 cm.*

shred SMALL AMOUNT /ʃred/ *n* [U] a very small amount of something • *There's still* **a** *shred* **of** *hope that a peace agreement can be reached.* • *There isn't* **a** *shred* **of evidence** *to support her accusation.* • *He lost* **every** *shred* **of** (=all) *credibility when he posed nude for the magazine.* • *She was sunbathing without* **a** *shred* **of** (=any) *clothing on.*

shrew ANIMAL /ʃruː/ *n* [C] an animal which is like a small mouse, but has a longer pointed nose and small eyes • *Shrews often live near water and some have a poisonous bite.* • PIC› **Wild animals in Britain**

shrew WOMAN /ʃruː/ *n* [C] *disapproving* a woman who is bad-tempered or unwilling to share her possessions • *Her former husband describes her as a greedy and manipulative shrew.* • *"Taming of the Shrew"* (title of a play by Shakespeare, 1592)

shrew·ish /ˈʃruː·ɪʃ/ *adj disapproving* • *The battles within the women's movement contributed to the shrewish image of feminism that still lingers today.*

shrewd /ʃruːd/ *adj* **-er, -est** *approving* possessing or based on clear understanding and good judgment of a situation, resulting in an advantage • *He was shrewd* **enough** *not* **to** *take the job when there was the possibility of getting a better one a few months later.* [+ *to* infinitive] • **It** *was shrewd* **of you** *to make that investment.* [+ *to* infinitive] • *She is a shrewd* **politician** *who wants to avoid offending the electorate unnecessarily.* • *She has a reputation for shrewd management* **decisions**. • *It was a shrewd* **move** *to buy your house just before property prices started to rise.* • *She has a shrewd* **eye** *for publicity and rarely misses an opportunity to appear in the media.*

shrewd·ly /ˈʃruːd·li/ *adv approving* • *She shrewdly predicted the stock market crash.* • *Coming just a week before the election, the government's decision to increase the state pension is shrewdly* **timed**.

shrewd·ness /ˈʃruːd·nəs/ *n* [U] *approving* • *With her latest film, she has proven herself to be a director of considerable shrewdness and imagination.*

shriek /ʃriːk/ *n* [C] a short, loud, high cry, esp. one produced suddenly as an expression of a powerful emotion • *All of a sudden he let out a* **piercing** *shriek, and I dashed upstairs to see what the matter was.* • *"This is the best birthday present I've ever had," said Brenda with a shriek of* **delight**. • *All was quiet except for the shriek of the seagulls.*

shriek *(obj)* /ʃriːk/ *v* • *We shrieked* **with laughter** *when we realised how stupid we'd been.* [I] • *She was shrieking* **in** *pain and clutching her arm where she'd broken it.* [I] • *I tried to apologize for breaking the window, but he just shrieked* **abuse** *at me.* [T] • *"Don't you dare do that ever again!" she shrieked.* [+ clause]

shrill /ʃrɪl/ *adj* **-er, -est** sounding loud and high in a way that is unpleasant or painful to listen to • *She had a shrill high-pitched voice that quickly became irritating.* • *(fig.) He launched a shrill* (=strongly complaining) *attack on the Prime Minister shortly after his resignation.*

shril·ly /ˈʃrɪl·li/ *adv*

shrill·ness /ˈʃrɪl·nəs/ *n* [U]

shrimp ANIMAL /ʃrɪmp/ *n pl* **shrimps** or **shrimp** a small pink sea animal with a shell, ten legs, a thin flat body and a long tail, or its flesh eaten as food • *Shrimps are a popular type of seafood.* [C] • *The speciality of the restaurant is a seafood platter that includes lobster and fresh shrimp.* [U] • PIC› **Crustaceans**

shrimp PERSON /ʃrɪmp/ *n* [C] *infml disapproving* an unusually short person • *Randy's such a shrimp that we couldn't see him in the middle of the crowd.*

shrine /ʃraɪn/ *n* [C] a place for worship which is holy because of a connection with a holy person or object • *Islam's most sacred shrine is at Mecca in Saudi Arabia.* • A shrine can also be a place where a famous person who has died is honoured: *She's turned her bedroom into a shrine* **to** *the dead pop star and covered the walls with pictures of him.* ○ *The exact location of his grave is being kept secret to prevent it becoming a shrine* **for** *neo-fascists.*

shrink *(obj)* BECOME SMALLER /ʃrɪŋk/ *v past simple Br and Aus* **shrank** /ʃræŋk/ or *esp. Am* **shrunk** /ʃrʌŋk/, *past part* **shrunk** /ʃrʌŋk/ or *Am also* **shrunken** /ˈʃrʌŋ·kən/ to (cause to) become smaller • *Your sweater will shrink if you wash it at too high a temperature.* [I] • *I shrank another shirt* *at the launderette today.* [T] • *The programme's audience has shrunk dramatically in the last few months.* [I] • *The introduction of a national lottery will help shrink the budget deficit.* [T] • *The company's profits have shrunk* **from** *£5·5 million* **to** *£1·25 million.* [I] • *The productivity improvements have shrunk our costs* **by** *25%.* [T] • **Shrink-wrap** is a thin transparent plastic material which is shrunk to fit the shape of the thing that it is wrapped around and which is used for protecting goods when they are being transported or sold: *Why is everything I buy these days covered in shrink-wrap?* ○ *Most of the fresh food sold in supermarkets is* **shrink-wrapped**. • *"Honey, I Shrunk the Kids"* (film title, 1989) • See also SHRUNKEN.

shrink·age /ˈʃrɪŋ·kɪdʒ/ *n* [U] • *Synthetic fabrics are less susceptible to shrinkage than natural ones.* • *How can the shrinkage of the economy be reduced?*

shrink BE FRIGHTENED /ʃrɪŋk/ *v* [I always + adv/prep] *past simple Br and Aus* **shrank** /ʃræŋk/ or *Am and Aus* **shrunk** /ʃrʌŋk/, *past part* **shrunk** /ʃrʌŋk/ or *Am also* **shrunken** /ˈʃrʌŋ·kən/ *literary* to move away (from someone or something) because you are frightened • *The child shrank behind the sofa as his father shouted at him.* • *She shrank* **at** *his touch.* • *When she was younger she would shrink* **(away) from** *me whenever I spoke to her.* • If you **shrink from** something, you avoid it because you think it is unpleasant or difficult: *We must not shrink from our responsibilities.* ○ *The president has said that she will not shrink from increasing taxes if such a move were to become necessary.* • *(infml)* A **shrinking violet** is a person who is very shy or modest and does not like to attract attention.

shrink DOCTOR /ʃrɪŋk/ *n* [C] *infml* a PSYCHIATRIST or PSYCHOANALYST • *I was so depressed that I ended up going to see a shrink.*

shri·vel *(obj)* /ˈʃrɪv·ᵊl/ *v* **-ll-** or *Am usually* **-l-** to (cause to) become dry, smaller and covered with lines as if by crushing or folding • *The lack of rain has shrivelled the crops.* [T] • *You ought to pick those lettuces before they shrivel* **(up)** *and die.* [I] • *Those oranges were looking a bit old and shrivelled, so I threw them out.* • *(fig.) Profits are shrivelling* (=becoming smaller) *as the recession bites deeper.* [I]

shroud CLOTH /ʃraʊd/ *n* [C] a cloth or long loose garment that is used to wrap a dead body before it is buried

shroud *obj* HIDE /ʃraʊd/ *v* [T often passive] to hide (something) by covering or surrounding it • *Many visitors have complained about the scaffolding that shrouds half the castle.* • *Because of restoration work, many of the historic buildings in the old town are shrouded* **in** *scaffolding.* • *Suddenly all the lights went out and the house was shrouded in* **darkness**. • *Skiing was impossible because the mountains were shrouded in* **fog**. • *The* **mist** *shrouding the valley had lifted by eight o'clock.* • *(fig.) Her reason for confessing to a crime that she never committed remains shrouded in* (=not able to be known because of) **mystery**. • *(fig.) Her whereabouts have been shrouded in* (=not able to be known because of) **secrecy** *since she received the death threat.*

shroud /ʃraʊd/ *n* [C] • *It was years since anyone had been in the attic, and everything was covered in a thick shroud* (=covering) **of** *dust.* • *(fig.) The truth about the accident remains hidden beneath a shroud* **of** *secrecy* (=a situation which prevents it from being known).

Shrove Tues·day /£ʃrəʊv, $ʃroʊv/ *n* [not after *the*] the day before the Christian period of Lent begins • *Shrove Tuesday is also called Pancake Day because of the custom of making pancakes to use up eggs and cooking fat which traditionally were not eaten during Lent.* • LP› **Holidays**

shrub /ʃrʌb/ *n* [C] a plant, esp. grown in gardens, with many small branches growing either directly from the ground or from a hard woody stem, giving the plant a rounded shape • *Bushes and shrubs are often the same plants, but tend to be called 'shrubs' when they are intentionally cultivated in gardens and 'bushes' when they grow wild or in an uncontrolled way.* • *She planted some roses and other* **flowering** *shrubs.* • *Shrubs can live for many years and the different species vary in size from a few centimetres to several metres tall.* • *I'd like some advice about planting a shrub border at the end of my garden.*

shrub·be·ry /£ˈʃrʌb·ᵊr·i, $ˈ-ɚ-/ *n* • A shrubbery is a part of a garden where a lot of shrubs have been planted: *There's a strange man lurking in the shrubbery.* [C] • Shrubbery is a group of shrubs: *We've decided to remove some shrubbery so we can enlarge the lawn.* [U]

shrug *(obj)* /ʃrʌg/ *v* **-gg-** to raise (your shoulders) and then lower them in order to express a lack of knowledge, certainty, interest or care • *"Where's Dad?" "How should I know?" replied my brother, shrugging his* **shoulders**. [T] • *He shrugged his* **shoulders** *as if to say that there was nothing he could do about it.* [T] • *(fig.) Thousands of people are starving to death while the world shrugs its* **shoulders** (=does nothing to help). [T] • *"I feel sorry for homeless people, but what can I do to help them?" said Chris, shrugging.* [I] • If you **shrug off/aside** something or **shrug** something **off/aside**, you treat it as if it is not important or not a problem: *The stock market shrugged off the economic gloom and rose by 1·5%.* ○ *There's no point telling her she's doing it wrong because she just shrugs off* **criticism**. ○ *You're a father and you can't simply shrug off your* **responsibility** *for your children.* • If you **shrug off** something or **shrug** something **off**, you get rid of something that you do not want: *I hope I manage to shrug off this cold before I go on holiday.* ○ *The city is trying to shrug off its industrial image and promote itself as a tourist centre.*

shrug /ʃrʌg/ *n* [C] • *"I'm afraid there's nothing I can do about your problem," she said with a shrug* **of** (=an act of raising and lowering) *her shoulders.* • *"Well, I suppose we'll just have to do what he says," said Kim with a shrug* **of** (=an act of raising and lowering her shoulders to express) *resignation.*

shrunk /ʃrʌŋk/ *past simple and past participle of* SHRINK • See also PRESHRUNK.

shrunk·en /ˈʃrʌŋ·kən/ *adj* smaller than before • *The company faces shrunken profits for the third year in succession.* • *The man who has dominated American politics and world affairs for the past four years is now a shrunken and humbled figure.* • See also SHRINK BECOME SMALLER.

shtuck, schtuck, shtook /ʃtʊk/ *n* [U] **in shtuck** *Br slang* experiencing trouble, problems or difficulties • *You'll be in shtuck if you don't pay him the money back.*

shuck *obj* /ʃʌk/ *v* [T] *Am* to remove the shell or natural covering from (something that is eaten) • *The farmers shuck corn by hand and haul the grain themselves.* • *When I started training to be a chef I was shucking oysters all day long.* • *(fig.) They seem to be able to just shuck guilt* **off** (=get rid of it). [M] • If you shuck your clothes, you remove them: *He urged them to shuck their old-fashioned suits and start dressing stylishly.*

shucks /ʃʌks/ *exclamation Am infml* an expression of modesty, embarrassment, disappointment, regret or annoyance • *"You played brilliantly in the concert." "Aw, shucks, do you honestly think so?"* • *"Randy likes you a lot, you know." "Shucks, does he really?"* • *Shucks, I wish I could have gone to the party with Martha.* • See also AW-SHUCKS.

shud·der /£ˈʃʌd·əʳ, $-ɚ/ *v* [I] to shake suddenly with very small movements because of a very unpleasant thought or feeling • *The coffee was so bitter that it made me shudder.* • *The sight of so much blood made him shudder.* • *She shuddered* **at the thought of** *kissing him.* • *He still shudders* **at the memory** *of his car accident.* • When an object shudders, it shakes violently and quickly: *I heard a massive explosion and the ground shuddered beneath me.* ○ *Suddenly there was a screech of brakes and we were all thrown forward as the bus shuddered* **to a halt**. ○ *(fig.) The economy has shuddered to a halt* (=suddenly stopped) *because of the civil war.* • If you say **I shudder to think**, you mean that you are anxious about something: *I shudder to think what my parents will say when I tell them I've failed my exams.* ○ *I shudder to think what would have happened if the brakes had failed.*

shud·der /£ˈʃʌd·əʳ, $-ɚ/ *n* [C] • *He* **gave** *a slight shudder as he considered how near he had come to death.* • *She recalled with a shudder how her boss had once tried to kiss her.* • *"He's the most unpleasant person I've ever had the misfortune to meet," said Wendy with a shudder* **of** *disgust.* • *When I think of what might have happened in the accident, it* **sends** *shudders* **down** *my* **spine**. • *(fig.) The thought of him being elected* **sends** *a shudder* **down the spines of** (=causes great fear and worry among) *those who remember the atrocities committed by his father.* • *(fig.) Britain's second biggest supermarket chain has* **sent** *a shudder through* (=has had a strong effect on) *its rivals by slashing its prices.*

shuf·fle *(obj)* MIX CARDS /ˈʃʌf·l̩/ *v* to mix (a set of playing cards), without seeing their values before beginning a game, so that their order is unknown to any of the players • *I wish you'd remember to shuffle before you deal.* [I] • *It's your turn to shuffle the cards.* [T] • LP› **Cards**

shuf·fle /ˈʃʌf·l̩/ *n* [C] • *Make sure you give the cards a good shuffle before you deal.*

shuf·fle *obj* MOVE AROUND /ˈʃʌf·l̩/ *v* [T] to move (things) from one place to another, often to give an appearance of activity when nothing useful is being done • *She shuffled her* **papers** *nervously on her desk as she waited for the phone call.* • *The company is hopelessly inefficient and has too many offices and* **paper**-*shuffling employees.* • *He never actually repays any of the money – he just shuffles his debts between different bank accounts.* • *Many prisoners have to be shuffled around police stations because of prison overcrowding.*

shuf·fle /ˈʃʌf·l̩/ *n* [C] • *She gave her papers a quick shuffle.* • *(esp. Am and Aus)* A shuffle is a change in the people who are governing a country or managing an organization: *The cabinet shuffle is intended to improve the President's popularity in the opinion polls.* ○ *She lost her seat on the board of directors during a management shuffle.* See also RESHUFFLE.

shuf·fle *(obj)* WALK /ˈʃʌf·l̩/ *v* to walk by pulling (your feet) slowly along the ground rather than lifting them • *Don't shuffle your feet like that! Lift them properly.* [T] • *They shuffled through the snow, weighed down with their luggage.* [I always + adv/prep] • *He shuffled into the kitchen, leaning on his walking stick.* [I always + adv/prep] • *I like to spend Sunday morning shuffling around in my slippers and reading the newspapers.* [I always + adv/prep] • *(fig.) The economy is only shuffling along* (= advancing slowly) *at the moment.* [I always + adv/prep] • To shuffle is also to move your feet or bottom around, while staying in the same place, esp. because you are uncomfortable, nervous or embarrassed: *The play was really good, but it was spoilt by a woman in front of me who was shuffling around in her seat all the way through.* [I always + adv/prep] ○ *When I asked him where he'd been he just looked down at the ground and shuffled his feet.* [T]

shuf·fle /ˈʃʌf·l̩/ *n* [U] • *He's got arthritis and walks with a shuffle.*

shuf·fle off *obj*, **shuf·fle** *obj* **off** *v adv* [M] to get rid of (something unwanted), esp. by giving it to someone else • *Not until this turbulent region can shuffle off the burdens of the past will it be able to settle peacefully into the community of nations.* • *The local authority may then try to shuffle these responsibilities off* **onto** *another authority.* • *(humorous)* When someone **shuffles off this mortal coil**, they die: *My children can't wait for me to shuffle off this mortal coil so they can get their hands on their inheritance.*

shuf·ti, **shuf·ty** /ˈʃʊf·ti/ *n* [U] *Br dated infml* a brief look • *Can I have* **a** *shufti* **at** *your paper?*

shun *obj* /ʃʌn/ *v* [T] **-nn-** to determinedly avoid (someone or something); to refuse to accept (someone or something) • *He was shunned by his parents when they discovered he was gay.* • *She has shunned publicity since she retired from the theatre.*

shunt *obj* TRAINS /ʃʌnt/ *v* [T] to move (a train or carriage) between the tracks in or near a station using a special railway engine designed for this purpose • *The first-class carriages are shunted into the sidings when they are not in use.*

shunt /ʃʌnt/ *n* [C usually sing] • *Our train broke down and had to be* **given** *a shunt into the station.*

shunt·er /£ˈʃʌn·təʳ, $-t̬ɚ/ *n* [C] • A shunter is a small railway engine that is used for moving carriages around on the tracks rather than making journeys between stations.

shunt *obj* MOVE /ʃʌnt/ *v* [T always + adv/prep] to move (someone or something) to a particular place, often without any consideration of any unpleasant effects that this might have • *I spent most of my childhood being shunted* **between** *my parents who had divorced when I was five.* • *He shunts his parents* **off** *to the south coast every summer.* • *She was expecting to be promoted but ended up being shunted* **aside** *to make way for a younger person.* • *Many viewers are fed up with their favourite sitcoms being shunted* **to** *later times because of live football coverage.* • *Can you help me shunt this wardrobe into the other bedroom?*

shush /ʃʊʃ/ *exclamation infml* used to tell someone to be quiet; SH • *Shush! I want to listen to the news.*

shush *(obj)* /ʃʊʃ/ *v infml* • *I wish you children would shush* (= stop talking or making a noise) *and let me read the paper in peace.* [I] • *Don't you shush* (= say "SH" or "shush" *to me! I'll make as much noise as I like.* [T]

shut *(obj)* CLOSE /ʃʌt/ *v* **shutting**, *past* **shut** to (cause to) move so that an opening is covered or blocked • *Would you shut the door as you go out, please?* [T] • *Please shut the gate.* [T] • *Don't forget to shut all the windows and lock the back door before you go out.* [T] • *I can't get this window to shut.* [I] • If you shut your eyes, you lower the pieces of skin that cover the top parts of your eyes so that you are unable to see anything: *I've got a surprise for you! Shut your eyes* **tightly** *and hold out your hand.* [T] • *Until now the President has* **shut** *his* **eyes to** (= ignored) *the homelessness problem.* • If you shut a book that is open, you bring the two sides of it together so that the pages can no longer be read: *As I walked into the room, Mary shut her book and put it down on the table.* [T] • *(slang)* **Shut** your **mouth!**/**Shut** your **face!**/**Shut** your **gob!**/**shut it** means stop talking or say nothing: *He told me to shut my mouth or there'd be trouble.* ○ *"You're a lazy slob!" "You shut your mouth* (= Don't talk to me like that"*!)*

shut /ʃʌt/ *adj* [after v; not gradable] • *I suspected something was wrong when I noticed her curtains were still shut at lunchtime.* • *The doors slid shut and the train pulled out of the station.* • *When the witch bent down to peer inside the oven, Gretel gave her a tremendous push and* **slammed** *the oven* **door** *shut.* • *(fig.) The government ought to have opened the door to Japanese investment instead of* **slamming** *it shut.* • See **with** your **eyes closed/shut** at EYE; **open-and-shut** at OPEN NOT CLOSED.

shut *obj* PREVENT MOVEMENT /ʃʌt/ *v* [T always + adv/prep] **shutting**, *past* **shut** to prevent (someone or something) leaving or entering a place • *He was so upset that he shut himself* **in** *his bedroom and refused to come out for the rest of the evening.* • *The gunman shut us* **in** *the bathroom and left us there for four hours.* • *The children hate being shut* **in** (= inside a house or other building) *all day.* • *Steve was off work for a week after he shut his hand* **in** *the car door* (= caught his hand between the door and the frame). • *The double glazing shuts* **out** (= prevents people from hearing) *most of the traffic noise.* [M] • *She pulled the duvet over her head to try to shut* **out** (= prevent herself from seeing) *the light.* [M] • *The wind blew the door closed behind me and now I'm shut* **out** (= unable to get back inside a house or other building). • *(fig.) She finds it impossible to shut* **out** *the memory of* (= stop remembering) *the accident.* [M] • *(fig.) What are are chances of peace if the terrorists are shut* **out of** (= not included in) *the negotiations?* • *(fig.) The electoral system means that the two left-wing parties, who have 53 per cent of the vote, remain shut* **out of** *power.* • If you **shut away** someone/**shut** someone **away**, you put them in a place which they cannot leave: *He was six years old when he was shut away in an asylum for stealing an apple.* ○ *The jury was shut away for a week to consider its verdict.* • If you **shut** yourself **away**, you put yourself in a place that you are unwilling to leave and where you do not want to be interrupted by other people: *Andy shuts himself away in his studio for hours on end when he's recording a song.* • To **shut off** someone or something/**shut** someone or something **off** is to separate them from their surroundings: *When her husband died she seemed to shut herself off* **from** *her friends and family.* ○ *The houses are shut off* **from** *the outside world by high walls and hedges.* • To **shut up** a person or an animal/**shut** a person or an animal **up** is to keep them in an enclosed place: *She can't spend her whole life shut up in her office.* ○ *I think it's cruel to keep animals shut up in cages.*

shut *(obj)* STOP OPERATING /ʃʌt/ *v* **shutting**, *past* **shut** (to cause something) to stop operating or being in service, either temporarily or permanently • *The shops shut at eight o'clock on Wednesday evenings.* [I] • *It's a shame they shut that shop – it was in a really convenient location.* [T] • *Two thousand people will lose their jobs if the factory shuts* **(down)**. [I] • *The company recently announced plans to shut* **(down)** *two factories and reduce its workforce by 4000.* [T/M] • *By mistake, the crew shut* **down** (= stopped operating) *the right-hand engine of their aircraft when a fire broke out in the left-hand one.* [M] • *The engine shuts* **off** (= stops operating) *automatically when the desired speed is reached.* [I] • *Gas supplies were shut* **off** (= stopped operating) *for four hours while the leak was repaired.* [T] • *The UN is powerless to prevent the local military commanders shutting* **off** *humanitarian aid* (= stop it being delivered) *whenever they want.* [M] • *The release of this protein by the brain shuts* **off** *nerve signals that stimulate the desire to eat* (= stops these signals being sent). [M] • *A good personal stereo will have an automatic* **shut-off** (= will turn itself off when the disc or other recording ends) *to save on batteries.* • *(Br and Aus)* When someone **shuts up (shop)** (*Am usually* **closes up (shop)**), they get ready to go home and lock their shop when business is finished for the day: *The robbers attacked just as I was shutting up for the night.* ○ *(fig.) Many international companies are considering shutting up shop* (=stopping their business activities) *in this country and transferring production to low wage economies.* • LP> **Switching on and off**

shut out *obj*, **shut** *obj* **out** *v adv* [M] *Am* to prevent (your competitor in a sports competition) from scoring any points • *She had shut out two of her first four Wimbledon opponents by identical 6-0, 6-0 scores.* • See also SHUTOUT.

shut *(obj)* **up** *v adv infml* to stop talking or making a noise, or to make (someone) do this • *I wish you'd shut up for a moment and listen to what the rest of us have to say.* [I] • *Just shut up and get on with your work!* [I] • *My dad never stops talking. It's impossible to shut him up!* [T] • *I wish someone would shut that baby up. It's making a dreadful racket.* [T] • *(fig.) The kids were complaining that they were hungry, so their father gave them some biscuits to shut them up* (=stop them complaining). [T] • *(fig.) If you breathe a single word to the police we'll come round and shut you up for good* (=kill you). [T]

shut·down /ˈʃʌt·daʊn/ *n* [C] a stopping of operation • *North Sea oil output has been affected by shutdowns for maintenance in all the major British oilfields.* • *The emergency shutdown procedure was activated by the release of 30 000 litres of radioactive water.*

shut·eye /£ˈʃʌt·aɪ, $ˈʃʌt̬-/ *n* [U] *dated infml* sleep • *You look exhausted! Try to* **get** *some shuteye on the train.*

shut·out /£ˈʃʌt·aʊt, $ˈʃʌt̬-/ *n* [C] *Am* a situation in a sports competition in which a player or team wins without the other player or team scoring any points • *He didn't win a single game – it was the first shutout in the history of World Championship chess.*

shut·ter PHOTOGRAPHY /£ˈʃʌt·əʳ, $ˈʃʌt̬·ɚ/ *n* [C] the part of a camera which opens temporarily to allow light to reach the film when a photograph is being taken • *Have you taken the photo already? I didn't hear the shutter* **click**. • *You'll need a high shutter* **speed** *to photograph racing cars, otherwise they'll come out blurred.* • *Photographs of the meteor shower can be taken by using a fast film and leaving the shutter* **open** *for several minutes.*

shut·ter WINDOW COVER /£ˈʃʌt·əʳ, $ˈʃʌt̬·ɚ/ *n* [C] a wooden cover on the outside of a window which prevents light or heat from going into a room or heat from leaving it • *Shutters usually come in pairs and are hung like doors on hinges.* • *She opened the shutters and the sun came streaming in through the window.* • A shutter is also a metal covering which protects the windows and entrance of a shop from thieves when it is closed: *Many shopkeepers pull down their shutters during August and go on holiday.* • PIC> **Window**

shut·tered /£ˈʃʌt·əd, $ˈʃʌt̬·ɚd/ *adj* [not gradable] • *houses with white-shuttered windows* • *Many shops are closed and shuttered on Saturday afternoons during the summer.*

shut·tle VEHICLE /£ˈʃʌt·l̩, $ˈʃʌt̬-/ *n* [C] a vehicle or aircraft that travels regularly between two places • *To get across town, you can* **take** *the shuttle from Times Square to Grand Central.* • *There is an air shuttle* **(service)** *from New York to Washington.* • *The American* **(space)** *shuttle can be used many times to put payloads in space.* • *The Secretary General of the United Nations was involved in weeks of* **shuttle diplomacy** (=discussions to try and make peace between two or more opposed countries, in which someone travels between the countries involved, carrying messages and suggesting ways of dealing with problems).

shut·tle *(obj)* /£ˈʃʌt·l̩, $ˈʃʌt̬-/ *v* [always + adv/prep] • *In some airports, there are small trains which shuttle* (=travel backwards and forwards) **from** *the main area* **to** *the area from which the planes take off.* [I] • *Passengers are shuttled by bus* (=are moved by bus) **from** *the bus stop* **to** *the airport.* [T]

shut·tle THREAD /£ˈʃʌt·l̩, $ˈʃʌt̬-/ *n* [C] (in weaving) a device which is used to carry the thread that goes across the cloth between the threads that go down the cloth, or (in a sewing machine) a device which carries the lower thread to meet the upper thread, making a stitch • PIC> **Handicraft**

shut·tle·cock /£ˈʃʌt·l̩.kɒk, $ˈʃʌt̬·l̩.kɑːk/, *infml* **shut·tle** *n* [C] a small light object with a rounded end to which real or artificial feathers are fixed and which is hit over the net in the game of BADMINTON • PIC> **Sports**

shy NERVOUS /ʃaɪ/ *adj* **shyer, shyest** nervous and uncomfortable with other people; TIMID • *He was too shy to ask her to dance with him.* • *She gave a shy smile.* • *Children are often shy* **of/with** *people they don't know.* • *The deer were shy* (=unwilling to be near people) *and hid behind some trees.*

shy /ʃaɪ/ *v* [I] • *The horse shied* (=suddenly moved sideways or backwards, esp. because of fear) **at** *the fence.* • *There's a lot of traffic on the road – I'm sure my horse is going to shy.*

-shy /-ʃaɪ/ *combining form* • *camera-shy* (=not liking being photographed) • *publicity-shy* (=not liking receiving public attention) • *workshy* (=not liking work)

shy·ly /ˈʃaɪ·li/ *adv* • *She smiled shyly at him.*

shy·ness /ˈʃaɪ·nəs/ *n* [U] • *His face went red with shyness* (=the condition of being shy) *when he walked into the crowded room.*

shy *obj* THROW /ʃaɪ/ *v* [T always + adv/prep] *dated infml* to throw suddenly, often in a sideways movement • *Two small boys were shying stones* **at** *a tree.*

shy /ʃaɪ/ *n* [C] *dated infml* • *The children were* **having/taking** *shies* **at** *a bottle floating on the pond.* • *(fig.) The newspaper report* **took a shy at** (=attacked with words) *the government.*

shy LACKING /ʃaɪ/ *adj* [after n; not gradable] less than; lacking • *We're only £100 shy* **of** *the total amount we've been trying to raise.*

shy a·way from *obj v adv prep* [T] to avoid (something) because of dislike, fear, or lack of confidence • *I've never shied away from hard work.*

shy·ster /£ˈʃaɪ·stəʳ, $-stɚ/ *n* [C] *infml* a dishonest person, esp. a lawyer or politician • *He's a real shyster.* • *What are those shyster politicians doing now?*

SI /ˌesˈaɪ/ *n* [U] *abbreviation for* Système International (=French for 'International System (of Units)'; a set of units of measurement used for scientific and technical work all over the world) • LP> **Units**

Si·am·ese cat /ˈsaɪ·ə·miːz/ *n* [C] a short-haired cat with pale fur, darker ears, tail and feet, and blue eyes

Si·am·ese twins /ˈsaɪ·ə·miːz/ *pl n* two babies with the same mother who were born at the same time, with some part of their bodies joined together • *The Siamese twins who were born joined at the arm had an operation to separate them.*

sib·ling /ˈsɪb·lɪŋ/ *n* [C] *fml* a brother or sister • *I have four siblings: three brothers and a sister.* • *There was great sibling* **rivalry** (=competition) *between Peter and his brother.*

sib·yl /ˈsɪb·əl/ *n* [C] *literary* any of several women in the ancient world who were thought to be able to see into the future • *At the beginning of the war the king asked the sibyl which side she thought would win.*

sic /sɪk/ *adv* [not gradable] a word written in BRACKETS after a word or phrase that has been copied from somewhere else and is spelled or used wrongly. Writers use this word to tell readers that they know that the original text contains a mistake. • *The notice outside the cinema said 'Closed on Wedensday' (sic)* (=Wednesday is spelled wrong).

sick ILL /sɪk/ *adj* **-er, -est** physically or mentally ill; not well or healthy • *He's not at work today because he's looking after his sick child.* • *My father has been sick for a long time.* • *The farmer called the vet to visit his sick cow.* • *Anyone who could hurt a child like that must be sick* (=mentally ill). • *The old woman* **fell/took/was taken** *sick* (=became ill) *while she was away and had to come home.* • *Mr. Jones is not here today – he's* **off sick/on the sick-list** (=absent because of illness). • *Sarah* **called in/reported** *sick* (=told her employer that she was unable to go to work because of illness) *because she had a bad cold.* • A **sick day** is a day for which an employee will receive pay while absent from work because of illness. • A **sick headache** is a severe pain in the head, esp. a MIGRAINE. • *Mark is not in the office today. He broke his leg yesterday, so he's on/he's taken* **sick leave** (=he has permission to be absent from work because of illness). • **Sick pay** is money given by an employer to someone who cannot work because of illness. • *(fig.) High rates of crime are considered by some people to be a sign of a sick society.* • *(fig.) My car won't start – the engine sounds sick* (=as if it is not working as it should). • See also HEARTSICK; HOMESICK; LOVESICK.

sick /sɪk/ *pl n* • *It's better for* **the sick** (=people who are ill) *to be cared for at home rather than in hospital.*

sick·en /ˈsɪk·ən/ *v* [I] • *The child sickened and died.* • *(Br) "You look feverish. Are you sickening* **for** (=about to become ill with) *something?"* • *(fig.) Eventually she* *sickened* **of** (=became tired of) *the demands made by her employer, and left her job.*

sick·ly /ˈsɪk·li/ *adj* **-ier, -iest** • Someone who is sickly is weak, unhealthy and often ill: *He was a very sickly child.* ○ *Her face was a sickly* (=unhealthily pale) *colour when she came out of the dentist's.* ○ *(fig.) That plant looks rather sickly* (=weak). *Shouldn't you give it some water?*

sick·ness /ˈsɪk·nəs/ *n* [U] • *There's a lot of sickness* (=the condition of being ill) *around this winter.* • *(fig.) The politician argued that the high number of failing businesses is a sign of the economic sickness of our society.* • *(Br and Aus)* **Sickness benefit** is money paid by the government to someone who cannot work because of illness.

sick VOMIT /sɪk/ *adj* [after v] **-er, -est** feeling ill as if you are going to vomit • *She was sick after she ate too much chocolate.* • *Lucy* **felt** *sick* (=felt likely to vomit) *the morning after the party.* • *If you eat any more of that cake, you'll* **make** *yourself sick.* • *(Am and Aus) I was* **sick as a dog** (=very sick) *after last night's meal.* • *(Am) I'm (feeling)* **sick** *my* **stomach** (=likely to vomit). • See also AIRSICK; CARSICK; SEASICK. • LP **Feelings and pains**

sick /sɪk/ *n* [U] *Br infml* • *I woke up in the morning to find a bowl full of sick* (=vomit) *next to my bed.*

sick·ly /ˈsɪk·li/ *adj* **-ier, -iest** • *A sickly* (=causing a sick feeling) *smell of decaying fish came from the dirty river.* • *The chocolate cake was sickly* **sweet**. • *(fig.) The book is a sickly* (=too emotional) *story about a little boy and his faithful dog.*

sick·ness /ˈsɪk·nəs/ *n* [U] • *Drinking unclean water can cause diarrhoea and sickness.*

sick up *obj*, **sick** *obj* **up** /sɪk/ *v adv* [M] *Br infml* • *The baby sicked up* (=vomited) *some milk on her aunt's shoulder.*

sick UNPLEASANT /sɪk/ *adj* [after v] **-er, -est** causing or expressing unpleasant feelings • *(infml) I'm very sick* **about/***(Br)* **at/***(Am)* **over** (=unhappy about) *not getting that job.* • *(Br humorous) He was* **sick as a parrot** (=very disappointed) *when his team lost the match.* • *(literary) David was* **sick at heart** (=very unhappy) *about having to leave his family behind when he went to work abroad.* • *(infml) It* **makes** *me sick* (=makes me very angry) *to see people wearing fur coats.* • *(Br infml) It's sick-***making** (=very annoying) *that she's being paid so much for doing so little.* • *(infml) I'm sick* **(and tired/to death) of** (=very annoyed about) *the way you're behaving.* • *(infml) She was* **worried** *sick* (=very worried) *when her daughter didn't come home on time.* • *(infml) Joan was not amused by the sick* (=cruel, offensive) **joke/story** *her brother told. She didn't share his liking for sick* **humour**. • *(infml) I* **felt** *sick* (=felt shocked, disgusted) *when I heard about the prisoners being beaten.* • *(Am infml) It* **makes** *me* **sick to** *my* **stomach** (=feel very unpleasant) *when I remember my car accident.*

sick·en *obj* /ˈsɪk·ən/ *v* [T] • *The violence in the film sickened me.* • *He was sickened* **by/at** *the number of people who were hurt in the crash.*

sick·en·ing /ˈsɪk·ən·ɪŋ/ *adj* • *The slaves were treated with sickening* (=extremely unpleasant) *cruelty.* • *There was a sickening thud when the child fell from the tree and hit the ground.* • *The wound on his leg was a sickening sight.* • *(fig.) It's sickening* (=annoying) *that I can't go to the party.*

sick·en·ing·ly /ˈsɪk·ən·ɪŋ·li/ *adv*

sick·bay /ˈsɪk·beɪ/ *n* [C] a room with beds for people who are ill, esp. on a ship or in a school • *Mark fainted during the biology lesson, so he's* **in the sickbay**.

sick·bed /ˈsɪk·bed/ *n* [C] the bed of a person who is ill • *We visited my grandmother* **on** *her sickbed.*

sick·le /ˈsɪk·l̩/ *n* [C] a tool with a short handle and a curved blade, used for cutting grass and grain crops • Compare SCYTHE.

sick·le–cell a·nae·mi·a, *esp. Am* **sick·le–cell a·ne·mi·a** /ˌsɪk·l̩.sel/ *n* [U] a medical condition, given from parent to child and found esp. in black people, in which the red blood cells are curved in shape, and which causes pain and fever

sick·o /£ˈsɪk·əʊ, $-oʊ/ *n* [C], *adj* [not gradable] *pl* **sickos** *slang* (connected with) someone, esp. a man, who is mentally ill or performs unpleasant, often sexual, acts • *She's afraid of being attacked in the park by a sicko.* • *Those perverts indulge in some really sicko activities.*

sick·room /ˈsɪk·rʊm, -ruːm/ *n* [C] a room in which someone who is ill lies in bed

side SURFACE /saɪd/ *n* [C] a surface of something that is not the top, the bottom, the front or the back; a surface of a flat object • *The door of the house is at the side.* • *The names of ships are usually painted on their sides.* • *Many tourists go to see the white horse cut into the side of a hill in southern England.* • *Please write on one side of the paper only.* • *I've already written four sides* (=pages of writing) *for my essay.* • *Canadian coins have a picture of the Queen's head on one side.* • *Pin the pattern to the right side of the material.* • *Have you listened to both sides of the new record?* • **The other side of the coin** is a different way of considering a situation, making it seem either better or worse than it did originally: *The snow caused terrible traffic problems, but the other side of the coin was that we got a day off work.* ○ *I like having a white car, but the other side of the coin is that it soon gets dirty.* • *The election is next week, so you'll have to* **come down on one side of the fence or other** (=make a decision between two choices) *by then.* • A **side drum** is a drum with an upper surface which is hit with sticks, and a lower one with metal strings fixed to it. • **Side-wheeler** is *Am for* **paddle steamer**. See at PADDLE POLE.

side /saɪd/ *adj* [before n; not gradable] • *The side view* (=the view of the side) *of the house isn't very attractive.* • *Please use the side entrance* (=the entrance at the side).

side–on /£ˌsaɪdˈɒn, $-ˈɑːn/ *adv* [not gradable] • *The bus hit the car side-on* (=on its side).

–sid·ed /-ˈsaɪ·dɪd, -ˌ-–/ *combining form* • *a steep-sided hill* • *A cube is a six-sided polyhedron.*

side EDGE /saɪd/ *n* [C] an edge or border of something • *A square has four sides.* • *After our long walk, we rested by the side of the river.* • *There are trees on both sides of the road.* • *Tom and Sally sat on opposite sides of the table.* • *They were surrounded* **on all** *sides/***on every** *side by curious children.*

–sid·ed /-ˈsaɪ·dɪd, -ˌ-–/ *combining form* • *A square is a four-sided figure.*

side NEXT TO /saɪd/ *n* [U] a place next to something • *I have a small table* **at/by** *the side of* (=next to) *my bed.* • *He stayed* **at/by** *her side* (=with her) *throughout her long illness.* • *He makes a little money* **on the side** (=in addition to his usual activities) *by cleaning windows in his spare time.* • *I think he has another woman* **on the side** (=is having a sexual relationship with a woman who is not his wife). • *(esp. Am) I'd like some sauce* **on the side** (=in a container separate from the plate on which my meal is served), *please.* • *We have* **put/laid** *some money* **on/to one** *side* (=kept for later use) *to pay for our holiday.* • *Can we* **put/leave** *that* **on/to one** *side for now* (=leave it for consideration later)? • *Bill's father* **took/led** *him* **on/to one** *side* (=had a private talk with him) *and told him to stop behaving so badly.* • *The children sat* **side by side** (=next to each other) *watching television.* • See also ALONGSIDE; ASIDE TO ONE SIDE; BESIDE. • PIC **Cutlery**

side /saɪd/ *adj* [before n] • *I'd like a side* **dish/***(esp. Am) side* **order** *of potatoes, please* (=some potatoes in a separate container from the plate on which the main meal is served). • *Would you like a side salad with your meal?* • *When you set the table, don't forget side plates for the rolls.* • *We parked the car on a side* **street/road** (=a small road, esp. that joins on to a main road). • *Does this drug have any* **side effects** (=often unwanted effects which happen in addition to an intended effect)? • *I think that's a side* **issue** (=a question which is separate from the main one) *which we should talk about later.*

side PART /saɪd/ *n* [C] a part of something, esp. in relation to a real or imagined central line • *She cut the left side of her face when she fell through the window.* • *He likes to sleep on the right side of the bed.* • *In Britain, cars drive on the left side of the road.* • *I have a pain in my right-hand side* (=the part of the body from under the arm to the top of the leg). • *There were three sides of lamb* (=half of an animal's body, considered as meat) *in the butcher's shop.* • *(Br) What side* (=television station) *is 'Coronation Street' on?* • *Look* **from side to side** (=from left to right/right to left) *before you cross the road.* • *There is no money* **on** *my mother's* **side (of the family)** (=My mother's family is not wealthy). • *I could just see Joan* **on the far** *side* **of** *the room.* • *The swimming pool is* **on the other** *side* **of** *town from where we live.* • *Now that Colin lives* **on the other** *side* **of** *the country/world, we rarely see him.* • *Children came running* **from/on all sides/every side** (=from all directions) *when Santa Claus and his reindeer arrived in the town square.* • *When Clare was a teenager, she was always getting* **on the wrong side of** (=annoying, upsetting and disagreeing with) *her mother, but they're very good friends now.* • *Sara* **got/kept on the right side of** (=pleased) *her teacher by doing as she was told.* • *He has always been* **on the right/wrong side of the law** (=has always obeyed/broken the law). • *She looks to* *me as if she's* **on the right/wrong side of** *50* (= looks as if she's younger/older than 50). • *I can't believe she's* **this side of** *50* (= is younger than 50). • *We don't expect to see him* **this side of** (= before) *Christmas.* • *This is the best pizza I've tasted* **this side of** (= anywhere other than) *Italy.* • *Parenting is the hardest, yet most rewarding thing I will do* **this side of the grave** (= in life). • *This dress is rather* **on the large/small side** (= too large/small) *for me.* • *"I've looked at life from both sides now, / From win and lose and still somehow / It's life's illusions I recall; / I really don't know life at all"* (from the song *Both Sides Now* by Joni Mitchell, 1967)

side·ways /ˈsaɪd·weɪz/ *adv, adj* [not gradable] • *The fence is leaning sideways.* • *If you would move sideways to the left* (= to the left side), *I can get everyone on the picture.*

side [OPPOSING GROUP] /saɪd/ *n* [C + sing/pl v] one of two or more opposing groups or people • *This is a war which neither side can win.* • *Our side* (= team) *lost again on Saturday.* • *"Whose/which side are you* **on** (= which team are you playing for)?" *"I'm* **on** *Liverpool's side* (= I am playing for Liverpool)." • *Don't be angry with me – I'm* **on** *your side* (= I want to help you). • *My mother never* **takes sides** *when my brother and I argue* (= She never supports one of us rather than the other). • *My mother always* **takes** *my brother's* **side** (= supports my brother) *when I argue with him.* • *(esp. Br) Sam's behaviour really* **let the side down** (= caused trouble for his family or team). • *(fig.) I thought I would get the job, but the other person who was being considered for it had experience* **on** *his side* (= had the advantage of experience). • See **time on** your **side** at TIME [MINUTES/DAYS/YEARS]. • [LP] **Sports**

side /saɪd/ *v* [I always + adv/prep] • *Peter always sides* **with/against** *me* (= supports me/doesn't support me) *in an argument.*

side [OPINION] /saɪd/ *n* [C] an opinion held in an argument; way of considering • *There are at least two sides* **to** *every question.* • *Let's look at all sides* **of** *the picture before we make a decision.* • *I've listened to your side* **of the story**, *but I still think you were wrong to do what you did.* • *"Is man an ape or an angel? Now I am on the side of the angels."* (Benjamin Disraeli in a speech about evolution, 1864)

-sid·ed /-ˈsaɪ·dɪd, -ˌ-–/ *combining form* • *a many-sided question* • *a one-sided argument*

side [CHARACTER] /saɪd/ *n* [C] a part of someone's character • *She seems quite fierce, but actually she has a gentle side.* • *We've only seen his bad side so far, but he can behave well.*

side·arm /£ˈsaɪd·ɑːm, $-ɑːrm/ *n* [C] a weapon worn on the side of the body, esp. a small gun or sword

side·bar /£ˈsaɪd·bɑːʳ, $-bɑːr/ *n* [C] *Am* a short news story in a newspaper or magazine that relates to a longer main story, giving details or extra information

side·board /£ˈsaɪd·bɔːd, $-bɔːrd/ *n* [C] a piece of furniture with a flat top and cupboards at the bottom, usually used for holding glasses, plates, etc.

side·burns /£ˈsaɪd·bɜːnz, $-bɜːrnz/, *Br also* **side·boards** /£ˈsaɪd·bɔːdz, $-bɔːrdz/ *pl n* areas of hair grown down the sides of a man's face in front of the ears • [PIC] **Hair**

side·car /£ˈsaɪd·kɑːʳ, $-kɑːr/ *n* [C] a small one-wheeled vehicle fixed to the side of a motorcycle to hold a passenger

side·kick /ˈsaɪd·kɪk/ *n* [C] *infml* a person who works with someone who is more important than they are • *I've been his sidekick for long enough – it's time I found myself something better to do.*

side·light [LIGHT] *Br* /ˈsaɪd·laɪt/, *Am and Aus* **park·ing light** *n* [C] either of the two smaller lights fixed on the front of a car • *It's sensible to leave your sidelights on when you park in a dark street.* • Compare HEADLIGHT. • [PIC] **Car**

side·light [INFORMATION] /ˈsaɪd·laɪt/ *n* [C] a piece of additional, less important, information • *What he said threw an interesting sidelight* **on** *what had happened.*

side·line [JOB] /ˈsaɪd·laɪn/ *n* [C] an activity that is additional to your main job • *Jim works in a bank, but teaches French in the evenings* **as** *a sideline.* • *Our business is selling cars, but we have a sideline* (= another type of business in addition to the main one) **in** *bicycles.*

side·line [SPORT] /ˈsaɪd·laɪn/ *n* [C] *esp. Am* a line marking the side areas of play esp. for football • *The ball fell just outside the sideline.* • *In tennis, ball boys wait* **on** *the sidelines* (= the area just outside the area of play) *to pick up balls that have been played.* • *(fig.) Our party has been* **on the** *political* **sidelines** (= has not been in control) *for too long – we must now work towards getting into power.* • *(fig.) I don't really like joining in things, I'd rather watch* **from** *the sidelines* (= I'd prefer not to be directly involved).

side·line *obj* /ˈsaɪd·laɪn/ *v* [T] • If a sports player is sidelined they are prevented from playing or competing, and can only watch: *Johnson has been sidelined through injury.* • If you sideline someone you stop paying attention to their opinions: *The minister was sidelined after he criticized party policy.*

side·long /£ˈsaɪd·lɒŋ, $-lɑːŋ/ *adj* [before n], *adv* [not gradable] (directed) to or from the side • *He gave her a sidelong glance.* • *He glanced at her sidelong and smiled.*

side·real /£saɪˈdɪə·ri·əl, $-ˈdɪr·i-/ *adj* [before n; not gradable] *specialized* of or calculated by the stars • **Sidereal time** is based on the movement of the Earth in relation to the stars.

side·sad·dle /ˈsaɪdˌsæd·l̩/ *n* [C], *adv* [not gradable] (on) a SADDLE (= a seat on a horse) used by women, on which the rider sits with both legs on the same side of the horse • *The Queen rode on a sidesaddle/rode sidesaddle when she inspected the soldiers.*

side·show /£ˈsaɪd·ʃəʊ, $-ʃoʊ/ *n* [C] a small show or attraction in addition to the main entertainment • *Carol won a large soft toy at a sideshow at the fair.* • *At the circus, the clowns put on a very clever side-show.* • *(fig.) As a sideshow* **to** (= a less serious or important activity than) *the adult events, we have the children's races.*

side·spin /ˈsaɪd·spɪn/ *n* [U] a spinning motion given to a ball to make it turn repeatedly in the air • *The batter was beaten by the sidespin on the ball.*

side·split·ting /£ˈsaɪdˌsplɪt·ɪŋ, $-ˌsplɪţ-/ *adj* extremely amusing • *a sidesplitting joke/story/film*

side·step *(obj)* /ˈsaɪd·step/ *v* **-pp-** to step to the side in order to avoid (something, esp. being hit) • *The player sidestepped his opponent and kicked the ball into the net.* [T] • *He avoided the blow by sidestepping.* [I] • *The speaker sidestepped* (= avoided) *the question by saying that it would take him too long to answer it.* [T]

side·stroke /£ˈsaɪd·strəʊk, $-stroʊk/ *n* [U] any of various ways of swimming lying on one side • *Can you do/swim (the) sidestroke?* • *She swam* **a** *slow sidestroke up and down the pool.*

side·swipe [REMARK] /ˈsaɪd·swaɪp/ *n* [C] a remark attacking something made while talking about something else • *While talking about her flights overseas, she made several sideswipes* **at** *the food served by the airline.*

side·swipe *obj* [HIT] /ˈsaɪd·swaɪp/ *v* [T] to hit on the side • *The motorcycle turned the corner too quickly, and sideswiped a car coming towards it.*

side·swipe /ˈsaɪd·swaɪp/ *n* [C] • *The motorcycle gave the car a sideswipe.*

side·track *obj* /ˈsaɪd·træk/ *v* [T] to direct (a person's) attention away from an activity or subject towards another one which is often less important • *Ruth was looking for an envelope in a drawer when she was sidetracked by some old letters.* • *The students sidetracked their teacher into talking about her hobby.* • *I'm sorry I'm late – I* **got** *sidetracked.*

side·track /ˈsaɪd·træk/ *n* [C] • *That's an interesting sidetrack* (= a less important subject than the main one), *but I don't think we can follow it now.*

side·walk /£ˈsaɪd·wɔːk, $-wɑːk/ *n* [C] *esp. Am for* PAVEMENT • [PIC] **Road**

side·ways /ˈsaɪd·weɪz/ *adv, adj* [not gradable] See at SIDE [PART]

sid·ing [MATERIAL] /ˈsaɪ·dɪŋ/ *n* [U] *Am* material which covers the surface of the outer walls of a building, usually in angled layers • *vinyl/aluminum/wood siding*

sid·ing [RAILWAY] /ˈsaɪ·dɪŋ/ *n* [C] a short railway track connected to a main track, where carriages are kept when they are not being used

sid·le /ˈsaɪ·dl̩/ *v* [I always + adv/prep] to move uncertainly or nervously • *Tim sidled* **up/over to** *the pretty girl in the bar and asked if he could buy her a drink.* • *She sidled* **past** *him, pretending that she had not seen him.*

siege /siːdʒ/ *n* [C] the surrounding of a place by an armed force in order to defeat those defending it • *The siege of Mafeking lasted for eight months.* [C] • *After a three-day siege, the terrorists who had seized the restaurant gave themselves up to the police.* [C] • *The castle was* **under** *siege/in a state of siege for months.* [U] • *(fig.) In those days Brigitte Bardot was* **under siege** *by photographers at Cannes.* • *The soldiers* **laid** *siege* **to** (= started a siege of) *the city.* [U] • *Ever since that unfortunate incident he has been suffering from a* **siege mentality** (= a fearful or defensive attitude). • See also BESIEGE.

si·en·na /si'en·ə/ *n* [U] a type of earth which is used to colour paint • **Raw sienna** is a brownish yellow colour. • **Burnt sienna** is a reddish brown colour.

si·er·ra /£si'eə·rə, $-'er·ə/ *n* [C] a range of steep mountains, esp. in N and S America and Spain • *In the high sierras there is not much oxygen in the air.* • *'The Treasure of the Sierra Madre' is a 1948 film with Humphrey Bogart as one of three men searching for gold in the mountains of southwestern USA.*

si·es·ta /si'es·tə/ *n* [C] a rest or sleep taken at the beginning of the afternoon, esp. in hot countries

sieve /sɪv/ *v, n* (to put something through) a tool consisting of a wood, plastic or metal frame with a wire or plastic net fixed to it. You use it either to separate solids from a liquid, or you rub larger solids through it to make them smaller. • *He sieved the sand from the bottom of the river, hoping to find pieces of gold.* [T] • *It took a long time to sieve* **out** *all the lumps from the flour.* [T] • *When making soup, you can put it through a sieve to remove any lumps.* [C] • *My son has a* **memory/mind like a sieve** (= He forgets things easily). • PIC> **Kitchen**

sift *obj* SEPARATE /sɪft/ *v* [T] to separate as if putting a loose solid substance through a SIEVE (= a tool with a net attached) in order to remove lumps • *When the cake is cooked, sift some icing sugar over the top of it.* • *She lay on the beach, sifting the sand through her fingers.* • PIC> **Food preparation**

sift·er /£'sɪf·tə^r, $-ţə/ *n* [C usually as combining form] • A sifter is a container with many small holes in its lid for sifting powdery substances, usually foods: *a flour-sifter* ○ *a sugar-sifter.*

sift *obj* EXAMINE /sɪft/ *v* [T] to make a close examination of (something) • *The police are sifting the material very carefully to try and find the guilty person.* • *(fig.) After my father's death, I had to sift* **through** *all his papers.*

sigh /saɪ/ *v, n* (to breathe out) a deep breath that can be heard, expressing tiredness, sadness, pleasure, boredom, etc. • *James sighed when Ann told him that she would not go to the dance with him.* [I] • *"Time for another chemistry lesson," sighed the boy* (= the boy said with a sigh). [+ clause] • *Angela sighed* **with** *disappointment/sadness when she was told that she had not got the job.* [I] • *(fig.) She lay on her back, listening to the sound of the wind sighing through the trees.* [I] • *(fig. fml) Thinking about where she had lived before, she* **sighed for** (= felt a desire for something that is lost or far away) *the friends she had left behind.* • *After his tiring journey home, he sat down on the chair with a sigh.* [C] • *The student* **heaved/let out/gave** *a sigh* **of relief** *when he finished the examination.* [C]

sight ABILITY TO SEE /saɪt/ *n* [U] the ability to see • *The mother took her baby to have his sight tested.* • *If your sight is poor, you should not drive a car.* • *The old woman has lost her sight* (= has become blind). • If you can **sight-read**, you have the ability to play or sing written music the first time you see it: *You have to be able to sight-read to pass the exam.* [I] ○ *She picked up the piece of music and sight-read it effortlessly.* [T] ○ *She's an expert* **sight-reader**. ○ *I've never been any good at* **sight-reading**. • See also EYESIGHT. • LP> **Eye and seeing**

-sight·ed /£-ˌsaɪ·tɪd, $-ţɪd, -'--/ *combining form* • You can add -sighted to a word to mean a particular type of vision: *short-sighted/(esp. Am) near-sighted* (= unable to see far) *long-sighted/(esp. Am) far-sighted* (= unable to see close) • You can also add -sighted to a word to mean a particular way a person considers matters: *a far-sighted/(Am also) long-sighted view* (= considering matters according to possible future concerns) • *a short-sighted/(Am also) near-sighted approach* (= considering matters only according to present concerns)

sight·ed /£'saɪ·tɪd, $-ţɪd/ *adj* [not gradable] • Sighted people are those who are able to see.

sight·less /'saɪt·ləs/ *adj* [not gradable] • Sightless people are those who are blind.

sight VIEW /saɪt/ *n* something that is in someone's view • *The rope marking the end of the race was a welcome sight for the runners.* [C] • *The flowers at the annual flower show were a beautiful sight.* [C] • *Her face after the accident was* **not a pretty sight** (= her appearance was spoiled). • *You should always* **keep** *sight* **of** *your bags* (= have them where you can see them) *while you're at the airport.* [U] • *(infml) You can't go out in those clothes – you look* **a real** *sight* (= look untidy or silly)! [U] • *The child laughed* **at the** *sight* **of** (= when she saw) *the clockwork toy.* [U] • *Have you seen all* **the sights** (= places of interest, esp. to visitors)? • *(fml) The lawyer requested sight* **of** (= to see) *the papers.* [U] • *I dare not let the children* **out of** *my sight* (= go where I cannot see them) *in this park.* [U] • *(infml)* **Get out of my sight!** (= go away!) • *The police officer was hidden* **out of** *sight* (= where she could not be seen) *behind a tree.* [U] • *Put the presents* **out of** *sight so we can surprise her.* [U] • *The price of the house we like is* **out of sight** (= extremely high and beyond what we could manage to pay). • *(slang) The group's new record is* **out of sight** (= excellent)! • *The castle came* **into** *sight* (= started to be able to be seen) *as we went round a bend in the road.* [U] • *We're looking for a house which is* **within** *sight* **of** (= from which it is possible to see) *the mountains.* [U] • *(fig.) The building was* **in/within** *sight* **of** *being finished* (= almost finished). [U] • *The train left the station and* **disappeared from** *sight* (= went where it could not be seen). [U] • *I've been learning music for a long time, but I still can't play it* **on/at** *sight* (= the first time I see it). [U] • *I* **caught** *sight* **of** (= saw for a moment) *my former teacher while I was out shopping today, but she turned a corner and I* **lost** *sight of* (= could no longer see) *her.* [U] • *(fig.) We're paying so much attention to the details that we have* **lost sight of** (= have forgotten about) *our aims.* • *(fig.)* **In the** *sight* **of** *the law, all people are equal.* [U] • *"Do you know David Wilson?" "I haven't met him, but I know him* **by** *sight* (= I recognize him, but do not know him personally)." [U] • *(saying)* 'Out of sight, out of mind' means that when something or someone cannot be seen, it is forgotten about. • *(infml) "You're* **a sight for sore eyes** (= I'm very pleased to see you/You look very attractive)!" • *I never buy anything* **sight unseen** (= without seeing it first). • *(infml) She hated/loathed* **the** *sight* **of** (= had a strong dislike for) *her former husband.* [U] • *(infml) I'm* **sick of the** *sight of your mess – I wish you'd tidy up a bit.* [U] • *(infml) They used to be very good friends, but now they* **can't bear/stand the** *sight of each other.* [U] • *The question seemed easy* **at first** *sight* (= when he first saw it), *but when the student tried to answer it, he discovered how difficult it was.* [U]

sight *obj* /saɪt/ *v* [T] • *After several days at sea, the sailors finally sighted* (= suddenly saw) *land.*

sight·ing /£'saɪ·tɪŋ, $-ţɪŋ/ *n* [C] • *This is the first sighting of this particularly rare bird* (= the first time it has been seen) *in this part of the country.*

sight MUCH /saɪt/ *n* [U] **a sight** *infml* a lot; much • *Food is* **a** *(darn/damn) sight* **more** *expensive than it used to be.* • *He's a sight better than he was yesterday.*

sight GUN PART /saɪt/ *n* [C] part of a gun or other device through which you look to help you aim at something • *Make sure you line up the sights before you fire the gun.* • *(fig.) Jenny has* **set** *her* **sights on** *being* (= is trying very hard to be) *top of the class.* • *(fig.) He had hoped to become a doctor, but he had to* **lower** *his* **sights** (= accept something less than he wanted) *because of his disappointing exam results.*

sight·see·ing /'saɪtˌsiː·ɪŋ/ *n* [U] the visiting of interesting places, esp. by people on holiday • *We went sightseeing in Rome.* ○ *We went on a sightseeing trip to Rome.*

sight·se·er /£'saɪtˌsiː·ə^r, $-ə/ *n* [C]

sign MARK /saɪn/ *n* [C] a written or printed mark which has a standard meaning • *+ and – are mathematical signs.* • *£ is the sign for the British pound.* • A **sign (of the Zodiac)** is any of the twelve divisions of the year in ASTROLOGY (= the study of the sun, moon, stars and planets and their influence on life): *"What* **(star)** *sign is Guy?" "He was born on May 30th, so that means he's a Gemini."* • LP> **Symbols** (I) (J) (KOR)

sign NOTICE /saɪn/ *n* [C] a notice giving information, directions, a warning etc. • *a road sign* • *a traffic sign* • *a shop sign* • PIC> **Road** (I) (J) (KOR)

sign BODY MOVEMENT /saɪn/ *n* [C] a movement of the body which gives information or an instruction • *Don't cross the road yet – wait till I give you a sign.* • *She pointed to her watch* **as a** *sign* **that** *it was getting late and she wanted to leave.* [+ *that* clause] • *She made/gave a sign to her husband* **to** *stop talking.* [+ *to* infinitive] • *The priest made the sign* **of the cross** (= made the shape of a cross by moving his hand between four points on his chest) *when he entered the church.* • **Sign language** is a system of hand and body movements representing words, which is used by and to people who cannot hear or talk, or the movements which people sometimes make when talking to someone whose language they do not speak. • See also SIGNAL ACTION. • (I) (J) (KOR)

sign *(obj)* /saɪn/ *v* • *He signed the waiter* **to** *bring him another drink* (= gave an order or information, or made a request, using hand and body movements). [T + obj + *to* infinitive] • *He signed* **for/to** *the waiter to bring him another drink.* [I] • *He signed* **to** *the waiter* **that** *he wanted another drink.* [+ *that* clause] • To sign is also to use sign language. [I/T]

sign SHOWING /saɪn/ *n* [C] something showing that something else exists or might happen or exist in the future • *His inability to handle the situation is a sign* **of** *weakness.* • *The fact that he's eating more is a sign* **that** *he's feeling better.* [+ *that* clause] • *Those black clouds are a* **sure** *sign of rain.* • *Billy's work at school has* **shown signs of** *improvement this year, and he has* **shown every sign/all the signs that** *he has found it interesting.* • *I've searched for my hat, but there's* **no** *sign* **of** *it anywhere* (= I can't find it). • *The search team could not find* **any** *sign* **of** *the climbers* (= could not find them or any evidence of where they had been). • *The doctor listened to the old man's heart, but she could find no sign* **of life**. • *(usually disapproving) "I only bought this car last month, and already I'm having problems with it." "Well, that's* **a sign of the times** (= something that is typical of the (bad) way things are now)." • See also SIGNAL SHOWING. • (I) (J) (KOR)

sign *(obj)* WRITE /saɪn/ *v* to write your name, usually on a written or printed document, to show that you agree with its contents or have written it yourself • *to sign a letter/cheque/contract/lease/agreement* [T] • *Sign here, please.* [I] • *He signed his name at the end of the letter.* [T] • *He signed* **himself** *'Mark Taylor'.* [T + obj + n] • *She said the painting was by Picasso, but it wasn't signed.* [T] • *The football club has just signed* (= signed an employment agreement with) *a new player.* [T] • *He was very disappointed when he heard that his favourite player was going to sign* **for/with** (= sign an employment agreement with) *another team.* [T] • *(infml) Now that the papers are* **signed and sealed/signed, sealed and delivered** (= all the necessary signing has been completed), *we can plan the future of the business.* • *(infml) If you want to join the club, all you have to do is* **sign on the dotted line** (= agree to do something, esp. by signing). • *(infml) She* **signed** *her* **own death warrant** (= did something that would be harmful to her position) *by refusing to do what her employer asked.* • To sign something **away** is to give up your rights to it by signing a paper: *Under the treaty, both sides will sign away a third of their nuclear weapons.* [M] • *I had to sign* **for** *the parcel* (= sign a form to show that I had received it) *when I collected it from the post office.* [I] • *For safety reasons, please sign* **in** (= sign your name in a book or on a form) *when you arrive at the building, and sign* **out** *when you leave.* [I] • *(fig. infml) The broadcaster signed* **off** (= ended) *the radio show by wishing all the listeners good night.* [I] • *(infml) His letter ended: "I'd better sign* **off** (= end the letter) *now. Love, James."* [I] • *(fig. infml) As it's Friday, I think I'll sign* **off** (= stop work) *early today.* [I] • *(Am) The president signed* **off on** (= gave his approval to) *a proposal put forward by his advisors.* [I] • *My brother has signed* **on/up** (= signed an agreement to work) *as a soldier.* [I] • *Julie has signed* **on/up** *for* (= signed a document to show that she wants to study) *courses on English and French this year.* [I] • *(Br infml)* To sign **on** is to report to a government unemployment office that you are unemployed and wish to receive **unemployment benefit** (= money paid by the government to the unemployed). [I] • *You have to sign books* **out**/*sign* **out** *books* (= record that you have taken them) *when you borrow them from the library.* [M] • To sign something **over**/sign **over** something is to give your rights to it or ownership of it to someone else by formally signing a document. [M] • (I) (J) (KOR)

sign·ing /ˈsaɪ·nɪŋ/ *n* [C] • A signing is a sportsman or -woman who has been bought from one team by another: *At the news conference, Manchester United proudly showed off their new/recent signing from Leeds United, Eric Cantona.*

sig·nal ACTION /ˈsɪg·nəl/ *n* [C] an action, movement or sound which gives information, a message, a warning or an order • *When she gave (them) the signal, they all cheered.* • *The driver gave a signal* **that** *he was going to turn right.* [+ *that* clause] • *The police officer gave us a signal* **to** *stop.* [+ *to* infinitive] • *The police officer held up his hand* **as a** *signal (for us to stop).* • *The signal* **for** *a race to start is often the firing of a gun.* [C] • Signal is also *Am for* **indicator**. See at INDICATE SIGNAL.

sig·nal *(obj)* /ˈsɪg·nəl/ *v* **-ll-** or *Am usually* **-l-** • *Flashing lights on a parked car usually signal a warning (to other motorists).* [T] • *He signalled left, but turned right.* [T] • *He was signalling* (= giving a signal) *with a red flag.* [I] • *She signalled* **for** *help.* • *The teacher signalled* **for** *the examination to begin.* [I] • *She signalled* **that** *we were going the wrong way.* [+ *that* clause] • *The children's mother signalled them* **to** *be quiet.* [T + obj + *to* infinitive] • *The children's mother signalled* **to/for** *them* **to** *be quiet.* [+ *to* infinitive] • *The children's mother signalled* **to** *them* **that** *they should be quiet.* [+ *that* clause]

sig·nal SHOWING /ˈsɪg·nəl/ *n* [C] something which shows that something else exists or is likely to happen • *The changing colour of the leaves on the trees is a signal* **that** *it will soon be autumn.* [+ *that* clause] • *The fact that few people went to the performance is a* **clear** *signal* **that** *there is little interest in the play.* [+ *that* clause]

sig·nal *(obj)* /ˈsɪg·nəl/ *v* **-ll-** or *Am usually* **-l-** • *The union has signalled* (= given a signal) **that** *the workers will strike.* [+ *that* clause] • *The union has signalled the workers' intention to strike.* [T] • *The death of Chairman Mao signalled* (= marked) *the end of an era in Chinese history.* [T] • LP › **Driving**

sig·nal EQUIPMENT /ˈsɪg·nəl/ *n* [C] equipment, esp. on the side of a railway or road, often with lights, which tells drivers whether they can go, must stop, or should move more slowly • *a railway signal* • *a traffic signal* • *a road signal* • A **signal box** (*Am* **signal tower**) is a building from which railway signals can be operated. • PIC › **Box**

sig·nal WAVE /ˈsɪg·nəl/ *n* [C] a series of electrical or radio waves which send a sound, picture or message • *The air traffic controller received a signal from the aircraft.* • *"The TV signal in our area isn't very strong." "Really? Our signal strength is excellent."*

sig·nal IMPORTANT /ˈsɪg·nəl/ *adj* [before n] *fml* noticeable; not ordinary • *a signal success* • *a signal failure* • *a signal victory*

sig·nal·ly /ˈsɪg·nə·li/ *adv* • *The council signally* (= noticeably) *failed to deal with the problem of keeping the streets clean.*

sig·nal·ize *obj, Br and Aus usually* **-ise** /ˈsɪg·nə·laɪz/ *v* [T] *fml* to make noticeable; DISTINGUISH • *Her willingness to work hard is what signalizes her from the other students.*

sig·nal·man /ˈsɪg·nəl·mən, -mæn/ *n* [C] *pl* **-men** someone who operates a railway signal

sig·na·to·ry /£ˈsɪg·nə·tri, $-tɔːr·i/ *n* [C] a person, organization or country which has signed an agreement • *Most western European nations are signatories* **to/of** *the North Atlantic Treaty Organization.* • *The signatory states have agreed to talks about reducing their supplies of weapons.*

sig·na·ture /£ˈsɪg·nɪ·tʃəʳ, $-tʃɚ/ *n* [C] (the act of writing) your name written by yourself, always in the same way, usually to show that something has been written, read, etc. by you • *The doctor's signature was difficult to read.* • *We collected hundreds of signatures in support of not allowing cars into the city centre.* • *These letters are ready for your signature.* • A **signature tune** is a short tune used in broadcasting at the beginning and/or end of a particular programme or to mark the appearance of a particular performer. • Compare AUTOGRAPH. • LP › **Letters** PIC › **Writing**

sig·net ring /ˈsɪg·nɪt/ *n* [C] a finger ring with a flat piece at the front, which usually has a pattern cut into it • PIC › **Jewellery**

sig·ni·fi·cant IMPORTANT /sɪgˈnɪf·ɪ·kənt/ *adj* important; CONSIDERABLE • *There has been a significant increase in the number of women students at Cambridge University in recent years.* • *The sales department has made a significant contribution to the company's performance this year.* • *The talks between the USA and the USSR were very significant* **for** *the relationship between the two countries.*

sig·ni·fi·cance /sɪgˈnɪf·ɪ·kənts/ *n* [U] • *The discovery of the new drug is* **of** *great significance* (= importance) **for/to** *people suffering from heart problems.*

sig·ni·fi·cant·ly /sɪgˈnɪf·ɪ·kənt·li/ *adv* • *My piano playing has improved significantly* (= a lot) *since I've had a new teacher.*

sig·ni·fi·cant SPECIAL MEANING /sɪgˈnɪf·ɪ·kənt/ *adj* having a special meaning • *She looked at him across the table and gave him a significant smile.* • *Do you think* **it's** *significant* **that** *he hasn't replied to my letter yet?* [+ *that* clause]

sig·ni·fi·cance /sɪgˈnɪf·ɪ·kənts/ *n* [U] • *At first I thought that his remark meant that he was angry, but now I don't think that it had any significance* (= special meaning).

sig·ni·fi·cant·ly /sɪgˈnɪf·ɪ·kənt·li/ *adv* • *He said that he would be bringing a friend with him, but, significantly* (= in a way that had a special meaning), *didn't say who it was.*

sig·ni·fi·ca·tion /ˌsɪg·nɪ·fɪˈkeɪ·ʃən/ *n* [C] *specialized* the meaning (of a word)

sig·ni·fy *(obj)* MEAN /ˈsɪg·nɪ·faɪ/ *v fml* to be a sign of (something); to mean • *Red often signifies danger.* [T] • *Nobody really knows what the marks on the ancient stones signify.* [T] • *The number 30 on a road sign signifies* **that** *the speed limit is 30 miles an hour.* [+ *that* clause]

sig·ni·fy *(obj)* MAKE KNOWN /ˈsɪg·nɪ·faɪ/ *v* to make (something) known; to show • *All those in favour, please signify.* [I] • *She signified her agreement by nodding her head.* [T] • *She signified* **(that)** *she was in agreement by nodding her head.* [+ *(that)* clause]

sig·ni·fy *(obj)* BE IMPORTANT /ˈsɪg·nɪ·faɪ/ *v fml* to have importance; MATTER BE IMPORTANT • *Don't worry about being late – it doesn't signify.* [I]

sign·post /£ˈsaɪm·pəʊst, $ˈsaɪn·poʊst/ *n* [C] a pole at a point where two or more roads meet, which has signs at the top of it pointing to places along the roads and showing the distances to them • *The signpost said 'London 18 miles'.* • *(fig.) My teacher has given me some signposts* (= directions) **towards** *what I should study next.*

sign·post *obj* /£ˈsaɪmn·pəʊst, $ˈsaɪn·poʊst/ *v* [T] *usually passive* • *The road wasn't very well signposted* (= provided with signposts). • *We found where we were going very easily, because it was signposted* (= the direction was shown by signposts) *all the way.* • *(fig.) The minister signposted the way for the future of the government's defence policy* (= said how it was likely to develop).

Sikh /siːk/ *n* [C] a member of the Indian religion Sikhism which developed from Hinduism in the sixteenth century and which teaches that there is only one God

si·lage /ˈsaɪ·lɪdʒ/ *n* [U] grass or other green plants cut and stored, without being dried first, to feed cattle in winter

si·lence QUIET /ˈsaɪ·lənts/ *n* [U] an absence of sound; complete quiet • *There was silence in the theatre as the curtain rose.* • *A loud crash of thunder broke the silence of the night.* • *Silence* **reigned** (= There was complete silence) *in the church.* • *"The Silence of the Lambs"* (film title, 1990) • *"The Sound of Silence"* (title of a song by Simon and Garfunkel, 1966)

si·lent /ˈsaɪ·lənt/ *adj* • *The empty house was completely silent* (= without any sound). • *"Silent Night"* (Christmas carol written by Joseph Mohr and Franz Gruber, 1818) • LP> **Silent letters, Sound**

si·lent·ly /ˈsaɪ·lənt·li/ *adv*

si·lence NO SPEAKING /ˈsaɪ·lənts/ *n* a state of not speaking or writing or making a noise • *Her silence* **on/about** *what had happened to her surprised everyone.* [U] • *The soldiers listened* **in** *silence as their captain gave the order to attack.* [U] • *"Silence!"* (= Stop talking) *shouted the teacher.* [U] • *My request for help was* **met with** *silence* (= I received no answer). [U] • *Their mother's angry words* **reduced** *the children* **to** *silence.* [U] • *After three years' silence* (= three years in which she has not spoken or written to me), *I don't expect to hear from her again.* [U] • *Silence will be considered to mean agreement* (= if no-one says anything it will be considered that everyone agrees with what has been said). [U] • A silence is a period of time in which there is complete quiet or an absence of speaking: *On Remembrance Sunday every year in Britain there is a one minute's silence in honour of those killed in the two world wars.* [C] ○ *There was a long silence after she had finished speaking.* [C] ○ *Their conversation was punctuated by uncomfortable silences.* [C] • *(saying)* 'Silence is golden' means it is often better not to say anything. • *"A period of silence on your part would be welcome"* (letter from Clement Attlee to Harlold Laski, 1945)

si·lence *obj* /ˈsaɪ·lənts/ *v* [T] • *The teacher raised his voice to silence the noisy class* (= to make them quiet). • *Her remark about his appearance completely silenced him* (= made him unable to answer). • *Al Capone silenced his opponents* (= prevented them from opposing him) *by killing them.* • *The government silenced its critics* (= stopped them expressing opposing opinions) *by changing the tax system.* • *(fig.) The enemy's guns were silenced* (= made to stop firing) *in a surprise attack.*

si·lent /ˈsaɪ·lənt/ *adj* • *The police officer told the criminal that he had* **the right to remain silent.** • *She whispered a silent* (= not spoken) *prayer that her wounded brother would not die.* • *The minister was silent* **on/about** *his plans for the future..* • *Arthur has always been the* **strong, silent type** (= a type of person, usually a man, who says very little). • *A few people have spoken in favour of the plans to build a new car park, but I'm sure the* **silent majority** (= the mass of people who have not expressed an opinion) *are against it.* • *'Battleship Potemkin' is a famous* **silent film** (= a film without any spoken words), *made by Eisenstein.* Compare TALKIE. • A **silent letter** in a word is one which is written but not pronounced, such as the 'b' in 'doubt'. • **Silent partner** is *Am for* **sleeping partner**. • *"It is time for the great silent majority of Americans to stand up and be counted"* (Richard Nixon in a speech, 1970)

si·lent·ly /ˈsaɪ·lənt·li/ *adv*

si·len·cer /£ˈsaɪ·lənt·səʳ, $-sɚ/ *n* [C] a part of a gun, or *(Br)* a part of a vehicle (*Am and Aus* **muffler**), which reduces noise

sil·hou·ette /ˌsɪl·uˈet/ *n* a dark shape seen against a light background • *The bare branches of the trees formed silhouettes* **against** *the winter sky.* [C] • *A silhouette of a deer on a road sign warns drivers that there may be wild animals on the road.* [C] • *Plants can sometimes be recognized by the silhouette* (= shape) *of their leaves.* [C] • *I looked for her through the window, but the curtains were drawn and I could only see her* **in** *silhouette.* [U]

sil·hou·ette *obj* /ˌsɪl·uˈet/ *v* [T always + prep; usually passive] • *The goats high up in the mountains were silhouetted* (= formed silhouettes) **against/on** *the snow.*

si·li·ca /ˈsɪl·ɪ·kə/ *n* [U] a MINERAL (= chemical substance formed naturally under the ground) which exists in various forms, including sand, QUARTZ and FLINT, and which is used to make glass and CEMENT (= a building material)

si·li·cate /ˈsɪl·ɪ·kət/ *n* [C; U] any of a large number of common MINERALS (= chemical substances) formed of SILICA, oxygen and one or more other elements

si·li·con /ˈsɪl·ɪ·kən/ *n* [U] a grey element, not metal, which is found combined with oxygen in a large number of common MINERALS (= chemical substances formed naturally in the ground), and which has unusual electrical characteristics • A **silicon chip** is a small piece of silicon which is used in computers, calculators and other electronic machines.

si·li·cone /£ˈsɪl·ɪ·kəʊn, $-koʊn/ *n* [U] any of a number of COMPOUNDS (= combinations of elements) of SILICON that are used in making paint, POLISH and VARNISH (= clear liquid which dries to form a hard surface) • A **silicone implant** is used to replace or increase the size of body parts that can be seen: *The controversy over leaking silicone* **breast** *implants is likely to end up in court.*

si·li·co·sis /£ˌsɪl·ɪˈkəʊ·sɪs, $-ˈkoʊ-/ *n* [U] a lung disease caused by breathing in SILICA dust, esp. found among **coal miners** and STONEMASONS

silk /sɪlk/ *n* a delicate, soft cloth made from a thread produced by SILKWORMS, or the thread itself • *a silk dress* • *a silk shirt* • *a silk scarf* [U] • *Her clothes were made of the finest silk.* [U] • In the British legal system, a **silk** is a Queen's Counsel (= senior lawyer). [C] • In the British legal system, to **take silk** is to become a Queen's Counsel. • **Silk screen** printing is a method of printing by forcing ink through a pattern cut into silk or, more usually now, other similar cloth, stretched across a frame. To **silk screen** (something) is to use the silk screen method of printing. • *(saying)* 'You can't make a silk purse out of a sow's ear' means that you can't make something good out of something that is naturally bad.

silk·en /ˈsɪl·kən/ *adj* [usually before n] *usually approving* • *(literary) The princess in the fairy story had long silken hair* (= soft, smooth and shiny, like silk). • *(old use) She wore a silken dress* (= made of silk). • *(fig.) The actor delivered his speech in a silken* (= soft and smooth) *voice.*

silk·y /ˈsɪl·ki/ *adj* **-ier, -iest** *usually approving* • *Advertisements claim that using hand cream keeps your hands smooth and silky* (= soft and smooth, like silk). • *Persian cats have long, silky fur.* • *(fig.) I could listen to that broadcaster's silky* (= soft and smooth) *voice all night.*

silk·i·ness /ˈsɪl·kɪ·nəs/ *n* [U]

silk·worm /£ˈsɪlk·wɜːm, $-wɜːrm/ *n* [C] a type of CATERPILLAR (= a small tube-shaped insect with many legs) which produces threads of silk from which it makes a COCOON (= a covering for its body)

sill /sɪl/ *n* [C] a flat piece of usually wood or stone which forms the base of a window or door • See also WINDOWSILL.

sil·ly FOOLISH /ˈsɪl·i/ *adj* **-ier, -iest** showing a lack of thought or judgment; foolish • *Don't do that, you silly boy!* • *I made a silly mistake in the examination.* • *That was a silly thing to say.* • *It was silly* **of** *you to go out in the hot sun without a hat.* • *She looked silly wearing such a short skirt.* • *I feel silly in this dress.* • *My aunt wore a silly-looking hat for*

SILENT LETTERS

The following letters may be silent in the pronunciation of some words: b, c, d, e, g, h, k, l, n, p, r, s, t, w.

In most cases their silence depends on their relationship to the letters that surround them, and their position in the word itself.

Rules are given where possible with the examples below:

b: 'b' is silent in the combination 'mb' at the end of a word:
bomb numb limb thumb dumb lamb tomb womb comb climb succumb aplomb crumb
and in the word **plumber**
'b' is also silent in 'bt' at the end of a word: **debt doubt** and also in **subtle**

c: 'c' is silent in 'sc' at the beginning of a word before the letters 'i', 'e' and 'y':
scene scent sceptre scientist scissors scythe but not *sceptic* /'skep·tɪk/
'c' is silent also in the combination 'scle' at the end of a word: **muscle corpuscle**

d: 'd' is usually silent in these words: **handkerchief handsome**

e: 'e' is silent at the end of a word when it follows a single consonant, as in 'bite' or 'shine'. The final 'e' changes the vowel in the middle of the word from a short to a long sound: 'a' is pronounced /eɪ/ as in 'pale', 'e' is /iː/ as in 'Pete', 'i' is /aɪ/ as in 'fine', 'o' is /£əʊ/ or /$oʊ/ as in 'note', and 'u' is /uː/ as in 'flute' or /juː/ as in 'use'.

g: 'g' is silent in 'gm' at the end of a word: **diaphragm paradigm phlegm**
'g' is also silent in 'gn' at the beginning or end of a word:
gnome gnaw gnash gnat gnarled • sign design resign consign assign ensign campaign foreign malign deign reign benign impugn and in the word **champagne**

h: 'h' is silent in 'rh' at the beginning of a word:
rhyme rhythm rhinoceros rheumatism rhetoric
'h' is also silent in the combination 'wh' at the beginning of a word before the letters 'a', 'e', 'i' and 'y'
why what where when which while whiskey whisper whimper whine whinge whale whip wheat wheel white whistle
'h' is silent in these words too: **exhibition exhaust heir honest honour hour scheme school vehicle**

k: 'k' is silent in 'kn' at the beginning of a word: **knee knife knit knock knot know**

l: 'l' is often silent before the letters 'f', 'd', 'k' and 'm' at the end of a word:
half calf behalf • should could would • talk stalk yolk chalk walk folk • palm calm

n: 'n' is silent in the combination 'mn' at the end of a word: **autumn column damn condemn hymn solemn**

p: 'p' is silent in 'ps' and 'pn' at the beginning of a word, and in the word **cupboard**:
psychologist psychiatrist psychosis psychic psychopath psalm pseudonym • pneumatic pneumonia

r: In British English 'r' is not pronounced if it comes at the end of a word (as in **car**) or before a consonant (as in **part**). In American English 'r' is pronounced in all positions. LP **Pronunciation of 'r' in British and American English** at R
hardworking sincere organised careless popular superior but not in words like *direct*; *superior*

s: 's' is silent in these words: **aisle corps island**

t: 't' is silent in words ending in 'stle' and 'sten':
castle whistle wrestle thistle • listen fasten christen hasten chasten glisten moisten
't' is also silent in these words: **Christmas mortgage soften**
In some words ending in '-et' the final 't' is silent. LP **Pronunciation of 'et'** at ET

w: 'w' is silent in the combination 'who' at the beginning of a word: **who whole whose whom whore wholly** but not in 'whoosh', 'whopper', and 'whoop' (the first 'h' is silent in these words).
'w' is also silent in 'wr' at the beginning of a word: **wrong wrist wrap wrinkle wreck wretched wrath writhe wraith writ write wrench** and in: **answer sword two**

the wedding. • *(Br and Aus slang) Stop* **playing silly buggers** (= not behaving responsibly) *and do some work.* • The **silly season** is the time of year, usually in the summer, when newspapers are full of unimportant stories because there is no important, esp. political, news.

sil·ly (bil·ly) /'sɪl·i/ *n* [C] *infml* • *Come here, you (big) silly* (= silly person), *and tell me what's wrong.* • *You're being a silly billy, now stop it.*

sil·li·ness /'sɪl·ɪ·nəs/ *n* [U]

sil·ly NOT THINKING CLEARLY /'sɪl·i/ *adj* [after v] **-ier, -iest** unable to think clearly or behave with good judgment • *I* **laughed** *myself silly* (= laughed a lot) *at his jokes.* • *One of the boys who was fighting* **knocked** *the other one silly* (= hit him very hard). • *We were all* **bored** *silly* (= very much) *by the play.*

si·lo /£'saɪ·ləʊ, $-loʊ/ *n* [C] *pl* **silos** a large round tower on a farm for storing grain or winter food for cattle, or a large underground place for storing and firing MISSILES (= large explosive flying weapons) • PIC **Farming**

silt /sɪlt/ *n* [U] sand or earth which is carried along by flowing water and then dropped esp. at a bend in a river or at a river's opening

silt up *(obj)*, **silt** *(obj)* **up** /sɪlt/ *v adv* • To silt up is to (cause to) become blocked with silt: *Mud has silted up the part of the river where we used to keep our boat.* [M] ○ *The harbour silted up many years ago.* [I]

sil·van, syl·van /'sɪl·vən/ *adj old use or literary* of or having woods • *a silvan scene* • *a silvan glade* (= an open space without trees in a wood)

sil·ver /£'sɪl·vəʳ, $-vɚ/ *n* [U] a valuable shiny white metal that is used for making utensils, jewellery, coins and decorative objects • *We gave Alison and Tom a dish made of* **solid** *silver as a wedding present.* • *The silver mines of South America played an important part in the economy of sixteenth-century Europe.* • *Cleaning* **the** *silver* (= silver objects) *is a dirty job.* • *Shall we use* **the** *silver* (= utensils made of silver) *for dinner tonight?* • *I need some silver* (= coins made of silver or a metal of similar appearance) *for the ticket machine in the car park.* • Ⓙ

sil·ver /£'sɪl·vəʳ, $-vɚ/ *adj* • *He had a silver photograph frame* (= made of silver) *on his desk, with a picture of his daughter in it.* • *My grandmother has silver hair* (= the colour of silver). • A **silver birch** is a common type of BIRCH tree, which has a silver-coloured trunk and branches. • *Queen Elizabeth II had her* **silver jubilee** (= a date that is exactly 25 years after the date of an important event) *in 1977.* • *Britain won a* **silver (medal)** (= a coin-like piece of silver given to a person who comes second) *in the* *swimming competition.* • **Silver paper/Silver foil** is shiny silver-coloured paper: *Bars of chocolate are usually covered in silver paper.* • **Silver plate** (= objects made of metal with a thin covering of silver) *is less valuable than solid silver.* • *She gave them* **silver-plated** *cutlery as a wedding present.* • *Katharine Hepburn and Spencer Tracy were big stars of the* **silver screen** (= cinema). • *(literary)* If you are **silver-tongued**, you speak in a way that charms or persuades people. • *We had a party for my parents'* **silver wedding (anniversary)** (= the date exactly 25 years after the date of a marriage) *last week.*

sil·ver *obj* /£ˈsɪl·vəʳ, $-vɚ/ *v* [T] • *Some of the windows in the new building are silvered* (= the glass has been covered with a thin layer of silver-coloured material to turn it into a mirror).

sil·ver·y /£ˈsɪl·vᵊr·i, $-vɚ-/ *adj* **-ier, -iest** *literary* • *We were woken early by the peal of silvery bells* (= those having a pleasant clear musical sound). • *"By the Light of the Silvery Moon"* (title of a song written by Gus Edwards and Edward Madden, 1909)

sil·ver·fish /£ˈsɪl·və·fɪʃ, $-vɚ-/ *n* [C] *pl* **silverfish** or **silverfishes** a silvery-white insect without wings which lives in houses and feeds on pieces of food and paper

sil·ver·side /£ˈsɪl·və·saɪd, $-vɚ-/ *n* [U] *Br and Aus* part of a leg of BEEF (= meat from cattle)

sil·ver·smith /£ˈsɪl·və·smɪθ, $-vɚ-/ *n* [C] a person who makes or sells silver articles

sil·ver·ware /£ˈsɪl·və·weəʳ, $-vɚ·wer/ *n* [U] articles, esp. utensils, made of silver • *(Am)* Silverware is also utensils made of steel or other materials. • LP **Shopping goods**

si·mi·an /ˈsɪm·i·ən/ *adj* [not gradable], *n* [C] *fml* (of or like) a monkey

si·mi·lar /£ˈsɪm·ɪ·ləʳ, $-ə·lɚ/ *adj* looking or being almost, but not exactly, the same • *My father and I have similar views on politics.* • *I bought some new shoes which are very similar* **to** *a pair I had before.* • *Paul is very similar* **in** *appearance* **to** *his brother.*

si·mi·lar·i·ty /£ˌsɪm·ɪˈlær·ɪ·ti, $-əˈler·ə·t̬i/ *n* • *There was a lot of similarity* **between** *the two books.* [U] • *There were no* **points of** *similarity between the politicians' arguments.* [U] • *I can see the similarity* **between** *you and your mother.* • *English cooking has few similarities* **to/with** *French cooking.* [C]

si·mi·lar·ly /£ˈsɪm·ɪ·lə·li, $-ə·lɚ-/ *adv* • *The children were similarly dressed.* • *Cars must stop at red traffic lights: similarly* (= in a similar way), *bicycles should stop too, but they don't always do so.*

si·mi·le /ˈsɪm·ɪ·li/ *n* (the use of) an expression comparing one thing with another; the use of 'as' or 'like' • *She described her child's dirty face using the simile "as black as coal".* [C] • *The lines 'She walks in beauty, like the night...' from Byron's poem contain a simile.* [C] • *The poem was rich in simile.* [U]

sim·mer *(obj)* /£ˈsɪm·əʳ, $-ɚ/ *v* to cook (something liquid, or with liquid in it) at a temperature slightly below boiling • *Leave the vegetables to simmer for a few minutes.* [I] • *Simmer the soup until it becomes thick.* [T] • *(fig.) I left her simmering* **with** *anger/fury/rage* (= almost unable to control her anger) *after our disagreement.* [I] • *(fig.) The strike has been simmering for weeks* (= seeming likely to happen, but not doing so). [I] • *(infml) New York simmered* (= was very hot) *in the summer heat.* [I] • *(infml) After all the trouble there was last week, things have* **simmered down** (= become calm) *now.*

sim·mer /£ˈsɪm·əʳ, $-ɚ/ *n* • *Bring the potatoes to a simmer.*

sim·per /£ˈsɪm·pəʳ, $-pɚ/ *v* [I] to smile in a foolish or silly way • *She simpered* **at** *her teacher.* ○ *She gave her teacher a simpering smile.*

sim·per /£ˈsɪm·pəʳ, $-pɚ/ *n* • *"Oh, I couldn't do that!", she said with a simper.*

sim·ple PLAIN /ˈsɪm·pl̩/ *adj* **-r, -st** without decoration; plain • *I like simple food better than fancy dishes.* • *She looked very pretty in a simple dress.*

sim·pli·ci·ty /£sɪmˈplɪs·ɪ·ti, $-ə·t̬i/ *n* [U] • *The book was written with* **a** *simplicity of style that I greatly admired.*

sim·ply /ˈsɪm·pli/ *adv* • *The restaurant was known for its good, simply prepared food.*

sim·ple EASY /ˈsɪm·pl̩/ *adj* **-r, -st** easy to understand or do; not difficult • *The instructions were written in simple English.* • *If you go by train, the journey is very simple.* • **It**'s *simple* **to** *find our house.* [+ to infinitive] • *I wish I could buy a new car, but it's not as simple as that.* • *There is no simple solution to the problem.* • *That's a simple question to answer.* • *I want an explanation, but* **keep/make it** *simple.* • *Riding a bicycle is simple* **when you know how.** • *The* **deceptively** *simple idea proved to be hugely successful.* • *The installation is a* **relatively** *simple and inexpensive procedure.*

sim·pli·ci·ty /£sɪmˈplɪs·ɪ·ti, $-ə·t̬i/ *n* [U] • *The advantage of the plan is its simplicity.* • **For the sake** *of simplicity* (= to make things easy), *we will take the questions one at a time.* • *The examination was simplicity* **itself** (= very easy).

sim·pli·fy *obj* /£ˈsɪm·plɪ·faɪ, $-plə-/ *v* [T] • *Could you simplify* (= make easier) *what you've just said?*

sim·pli·fi·ca·tion /ˌsɪm·plɪ·fɪˈkeɪ·ʃᵊn/ *n* • *The newspaper report of the politician's speech was a simplification* (= a more simple description) *of what he really said.* [C] • *The teacher's simplification of the argument helped the students to understand it.* [U]

sim·plis·tic /sɪmˈplɪs·tɪk/ *adj disapproving* • *The scientist's explanation of the results of the study was considered to be simplistic* (= made the results seem simpler than they really were).

sim·ply /ˈsɪm·pli/ *adv* • *The teacher explained the point as simply as she could* (= in as easy a way as she could), *but the students still did not understand it.* • *The book was simply written* (= written in a way that was easy to understand).

sim·ple ONE PART /ˈsɪm·pl̩/ *adj* [before n] **-r, -st** having or made of only one or a few parts, rather than several • *A hammer is a simple tool.* • *Simple toys are often the best.* • *Pastry is made from a simple mixture of flour, fat and water.* • *Simple forms of life have only one cell.* • *(specialized)* A **simple sentence** is one that has only one verb.

sim·ple NO MORE THAN /ˈsɪm·pl̩/ *adj* [before n; not gradable] without anything more or other • *I didn't break the window – that's the simple truth.* • *We didn't go swimming for the simple reason that the water was too cold.* • *The simple fact is that you're late and we've missed the start of the show.* • **Simple interest** is money that is paid only on an original amount of money that has been borrowed or invested, and not on the additional money that the original sum earns. Compare COMPOUND COMBINATION. • A **simple fracture** is one in which the broken bone does not go through the flesh. Compare **compound fracture** at COMPOUND COMBINATION.

sim·ply /ˈsɪm·pli/ *adv* [not gradable] • *I don't like my job – I simply* (= just) *do it for the money.* • *I simply* (= really) *don't know what happened.* • *You look simply* (= really) *beautiful in that dress.* • *The hunger in parts of Africa is terrible – there's (quite) simply* (= without question) *no other word for it.* • *"Simply the Best"* (title of a song by Tina Turner, 1989)

sim·ple NATURAL /ˈsɪm·pl̩/ *adj* **-r, -st** *usually approving* natural; ordinary; without experience of the ways of society and fashion • *He was just a simple fisherman.* • *Her behaviour was simple and childlike.* • *Gandhi was a man of simple tastes.* • *The simple things in life are the best.* • *I've lived in the city for years, but I have a secret wish for* **the** *simple* **life** (= a quiet life, without many possessions).

sim·pli·ci·ty /£sɪmˈplɪs·ɪ·ti, $-ə·t̬i/ *n* [U] • *The old people led a life of great simplicity* (= with few possessions and little money).

sim·ply /ˈsɪm·pli/ *adv* • *The child's picture was simply drawn* (= drawn in a natural way). • *He lived simply* (= with few possessions and little money) *in a small hut in the middle of a forest.*

sim·ple FOOLISH /ˈsɪm·pl̩/ *adj* **-r, -st** foolish; easily deceived; not experienced • *I can't believe you were simple enough to give him your money.* • *In the film 'Ryan's Daughter', John Mills played the part of a simple man* (= a man without the ability to reason and understand). • *(infml) My brother became rather* **simple-minded** (= lacking ability to reason and understand) *after he suffered brain damage in a car accident.* • *(infml disapproving) Stephen always takes such a* **simple-minded approach** *to problems* (= an approach showing a limited ability to reason and understand).

sim·ple·ton /£ˈsɪm·pl̩·tᵊn, $-t̬ən/ *n* [C] *dated infml disapproving* a person without the usual ability to reason and understand • *Their second child was a simpleton.* • *(infml disapproving) Don't do that, you simpleton!* (= foolish person)

si·mu·la·crum /ˌsɪm·jʊˈleɪ·krəm/ *n* [C] *pl* **simulacrums** or **simulacra** /ˌsɪm·jʊˈleɪ·krə/ *fml* something that looks like or represents something or someone else • *The plan of a Christian church is often a simulacrum* **of** *a cross.*

si·mu·late *obj* /ˈsɪm·jʊ·leɪt/ *v* [T] to give the appearance of (something different) • *In cheap furniture, plastic is often* *used to simulate wood.* • *Anne simulated pleasure at seeing Simon, but really she wished he hadn't come.* • *Some driving teachers use computers to simulate* (=represent) *different road conditions for learners to practise on.*

si·mu·lat·ed /£'sɪm·jʊ·leɪ·tɪd, $-t̬ɪd/ *adj* [not gradable] • *She was wearing a coat of simulated* (=artificial) *fur.* • *The actor shouted loudly in simulated anger.*

si·mu·la·tion /ˌsɪm·jʊ'leɪ·ʃᵊn/ *n* • *The manager prepared a* **computer** *simulation* (=a model of a problem or course of events, esp. in business or science) **of** *likely sales performance for the rest of the year.* [C] • *It was difficult to tell which of the jewels were real, and which were simulations* (=artificial). [C] • *I was quite deceived by her simulation* **of** *sorrow.* [U]

si·mu·lat·or /£'sɪm·jʊ·leɪ·təʳ, $-t̬ɚ/ *n* [C] • *People learning to fly often practise on a* **flight** *simulator* (=equipment which represents real conditions esp. in an aircraft or spacecraft).

sim·ul·cast /£'sɪm·ᵊl·kɑːst, $'saɪ·mᵊl·kæst/ *n* [C] *esp. Am and Aus* a broadcast by a radio and a television station of the same programme at the same time

si·mul·tan·e·ous /£ˌsɪm·ᵊl'teɪ·ni·əs, $ˌsaɪ·mᵊl-/ *adj* [not gradable] happening or being done at exactly the same time • *There was a simultaneous broadcast of the concert on the radio and the television.* • *The arrival of the train from Scotland was simultaneous* **with** *the departure of the one for Wales.*

si·mul·tan·e·ous·ly /£ˌsɪm·ᵊl'teɪ·ni·ə·sli, $ˌsaɪ·mᵊl-/ *adv* [not gradable] • *Two children answered the teacher's question simultaneously.*

si·mul·tan·e·ous·ness /£ˌsɪm·ᵊl'teɪ·ni·ə·snəs, $ˌsaɪ·mᵊl-/, **si·mul·tan·e·i·ty** /£ˌsɪm·ᵊl·tə'neɪ·ɪ·ti, $ˌsaɪ·mᵊl·tə'neɪ·ə·t̬i/ *n* [U]

sin OFFENCE /sɪn/ *n* the offence of breaking, or the breaking of, a religious or moral law • *Adultery is considered by some people to be a sin.* [C] • *Parents teach their children not to* **commit** *sins.* [C] • *Roman Catholics* **confess** *their sins to their priests.* [C] • *My sister is guilty of the sin* **of** *pride.* [C] • *He thinks a lot about sin.* [U] • *(infml) I think* **it's a sin** (=is morally wrong) **to** *waste food, when so many people in the world are hungry.* [C + *to* infinitive] • *(fig. infml)* **It** *would be a sin* (=the wrong thing to do) **not** *to go out on such a nice day.* [C + *to* infinitive] • *(infml) He's* **as** *miserable/ugly* **as sin** (=very unhappy/ugly). • *(humorous) For my sins* (=As if it were a punishment), *I'm organizing the office party this year.* [C] • *(Br and Aus slang)* In some sports, a **sin-bin** is an area off the field where a player who has committed an act which is against the rules can be sent to, for a stated length of time: *The referee sent him to the sin-bin for ten minutes for not allowing the wing man to play the ball.* • *(Am infml)* A **sin tax** is a tax on items such as cigarettes, alcohol, and GAMBLING (=playing games for money) and other things which are considered unnecessary luxuries in life. • Ⓟ Ⓢ

sin /sɪn/ *v* [I] **-nn-** • *As a good Christian, you may sometimes sin, but you must repent of sinning.* • *"I am a man / More sinned against than sinning"* (Shakespeare, King Lear 3.2)

sin·ful /'sɪn·fᵊl/ *adj* • *He confessed that he had sinful thoughts.* • *(infml) Buying that new car was a sinful waste of money* (=it was morally wrong to spend so much money on it). • *(fig. infml) This cream cake is sinful* (=tastes very good, but is bad for you)*!*

sin·ful·ly /'sɪn·fᵊl·i/ *adv*

sin·ful·ness /'sɪn·fᵊl·nəs/ *n* [U]

sin·less /'sɪn·ləs/ *adj* [not gradable]

sin·less·ness /'sɪn·lə·snəs/ *n* [U]

sin·ner /£'sɪn·əʳ, $-ɚ/ *n* [C] • *The painting represented the repentant sinner brought back to the fold.* • *"We are sinners all"* (Shakespeare, Henry VI pt 2, 3.3)

sin MATHEMATICS /sɪn/ *n* [C] *abbreviation for* SINE

since TIME /sɪnts/ *adv* [not gradable] from a particular time in the past until a later time, or until now • *Emma went to work in New York a year ago, and we haven't seen her since.* • *My mother was seriously ill last month, but she has since got better.* • *I went to Maxim's restaurant in December, and have not had a better meal* **before or** *since.* • *He started working for the company when he left school, and has been there* **ever** *since* (=and is still there). • *I've* **long** *since* (=long ago) *forgotten any Latin I ever learned.*

since /sɪnts/ *prep* • *England have not won the World Cup in football since 1966.* • *I haven't seen her since the birth of her baby.* • *That was the best film I've seen since 'Gone with the Wind'.*

since /sɪnts/ *conjunction* • **Ever** *since she started her new job* (=continuously from then up to the present), *she has been much happier.* • *It's a year now since we went to France.* • *I've been very busy since I came back from holiday.*

since BECAUSE /sɪnts/ *conjunction* because; as • *Since we've got a few minutes to wait for the train, let's have a cup of coffee.*

sin·cere /£sɪn'sɪəʳ, $-'sɪr/ *adj* (of a person, feelings or behaviour) not pretending; without falseness; honest • *He offered a sincere apology for his behaviour.* • *I don't think the politician was being completely sincere when he said he supported the government's plans.* • *Mr and Mrs Baker send their sincere regrets that they are unable to attend the dinner on Friday.* • *She is sincere* **in** *her political beliefs.*

sin·cere·ly /£sɪn'sɪə·li, $-'sɪr-/ *adv* • *I'm sincerely* (=honestly or without falseness) *grateful for all the help you've given me.* • *I disagree with my brother's religious beliefs, but they are sincerely held.* • **(Yours) sincerely/** *(Am)* **Sincerely (yours)** is a common way of ending a formal letter which is addressed to a named person. • LP› **Letters**

sin·cer·i·ty /£sɪn'ser·ɪ·ti, $-ə·t̬i/ *n* [U] • *The priest was a man of deep sincerity* (=honesty). • *Her sincerity was recognized by everyone.* • **In all** *sincerity, I thought your speech was excellent.*

sine /saɪn/ (*abbreviation* **sin**) *n* [C] *specialized* (in a triangle that has one angle of 90°) the RATIO of the length of the side opposite an angle less than 90° divided by the length of the HYPOTENUSE (=the side opposite the 90° angle • Compare COSINE; TANGENT TRIANGLE.

si·ne·cure /£'sɪn·ɪ·kjʊəʳ, $'saɪ·nə·kjʊr/ *n* [C] a position which involves little work, but for which the person is paid

sine qua non /£ˌsɪn·eɪ·kwɑː'nəʊn, $-'noʊn/ *n* [C] *fml* a necessary condition • *A sense of humour is a sine qua non* **for** *a job in our office!* • *An interest in children is a sine qua non* **of** *teaching.*

si·new /'sɪn·juː/, *specialized* **ten·don** *n* a strong cord in the body connecting a muscle to a bone • *Muscles need strong sinews to work effectively.* [C] • *(fig.) We will fight with all our sinew* (=strength). [U] • *(fig.) These steel posts form the sinews of the building* (=method of support and strength). [C] • *(esp. Br literary)* The **sinews of war** are the money needed for weapons and supplies during a war.

si·new·y /'sɪn·ju·i/ *adj* • *This meat is rather sinewy* (=difficult to cut or eat). • *The fighter had a strong, sinewy body* (=a body with strong muscles but little fat).

sin·ful /'sɪn·fᵊl/ *adj* See at SIN OFFENCE

sing *(obj)* MAKE MUSIC /sɪŋ/ *v past simple* **sang** /sæŋ/ or *Am also* **sung** /sʌŋ/, *past part* **sung** /sʌŋ/ to make musical sounds with the voice, usually producing words to match a tune • *I like to sing while I'm cleaning the house.* [I] • *The children sang two songs by Schubert at the school concert.* [T] • *We were woken early by the sound of the birds singing.* [I] • *Your grandmother would like you to sing* **for/to** *her.* [I] • *Will you sing us a song/sing a song* **to** *us?* [+ two objects] • *She sang her baby* **to sleep** *every night.* [T] • *Pavarotti is singing Rodolfo* (=singing the part of Rodolfo) *in 'La Boheme' at La Scala this week.* [T] • *Sing (Br and Aus)* **up/***(Am)* **out**, *we can't hear you.* [I] • *The newspapers have been* **singing the praises of** (=praising) *Italy's new football player.* • *"Sing Something Simple"* (title of a song written by Herman Hupfeld, 1930) • *"Singing the Blues"* (title of a song written by Melvin Endsley, 1954)

sing·er /£'sɪŋ·əʳ, $-ɚ/ *n* [C] • *Kiri Te Kanawa is a famous singer from New Zealand.* • *We heard the sound of carol singers outside the door.*

sing RING /sɪŋ/ *v* [I] *past simple* **sang** /sæŋ/ or *Am also* **sung** /sʌŋ/, *past part* **sung** /sʌŋ/ to make or be filled with a (high) ringing sound • *My ears are still singing from the noise of that explosion.* • *The kettle is singing on the stove.* • *A bullet sang* **past** *the top of the soldier's head.*

sing SINGULAR /sɪŋ/ *n, adj abbreviation for* singular

sing·a·long /£'sɪŋ·ə·lɒŋ, $-lɑːŋ/, *Br dated* **sing·song** *n* [C] a very informal musical event, where people sing well-known songs with each other • *It's nice to have a good old-fashioned singalong now and again.*

singe *(obj)* /sɪndʒ/ *v* **singeing** to burn slightly on the surface, without producing flames • *Chris laid his cigarette on the table and singed the top of it.* [T] • *The cat singed its fur by waving its tail too close to the fire.* [T] • *My hair singed when I leaned over a burning candle.* [I]

singe /sɪndʒ/ *n* [C] • *The hot iron left a slight singe* (=burn) *on my dress.*

Singh·al·ese /ˌsɪŋ·gəˈliːz/ *adj* [not gradable], *n* [U] SINHALESE

sin·gle ONE /ˈsɪŋ·gl̩/ *adj* [before n; not gradable] one only • *A single red rose stood in a glass on the table.* • *He knocked his opponent down with a single blow.* • **Not a** *single person offered to help her.* • *You haven't been listening to a single word I've been saying.* • *Single flowers have only one set of petals – double flowers have two sets.* • *A single yellow line painted on the side of the road means that you can only park there at certain times.* • *A* **single bed** (= A bed for only one person) *is too narrow for me.* • *Jack bought a new* **single-breasted** *coat* (= a coat which fastens in the centre with one row of buttons). • *(Br)* **Single cream** *(Am and Aus* **light cream)** is a type of thin cream. • *The two soldiers met in* **single combat** (= a fight between two people, usually with weapons). • A **single-decker** (bus) is a bus which has only one level. • *The schoolchildren were told to walk* **(in) single file** (= one behind the other). • **Single-handed** means without any help from anyone else: *Sir Francis Chichester was a sailor who made a single-handed voyage/sailed* **single-handedly** *round the world in 1966-7.* • **Single-minded** means having or showing only one aim: *My brother has always taken a single-minded approach to everything he does – he works* **single-mindedly**. • A **single-sex** school is a school for either girls or boys, not both: *My daughter goes to a single-sex school.* • *I'd like a* **single room** *please* (= a room in a hotel for one person). • Compare DOUBLE TWICE. • LP **One** Ⓟ

sin·gly /ˈsɪŋ·gli/ *adv* [not gradable] • *Doctors usually see their patients singly* (= one at a time).

sin·gle /ˈsɪŋ·gl̩/ *n* [C] • *(Br and Aus) May I have a single (ticket)* (= a ticket for a journey to a place, not there and back) *to London, please.* • *Please could I have $50* **in** *singles* (= in $1 notes). • A single is also a record which has only one main popular song on it: *Have you heard Michael Jackson's new single?* • In cricket, a single is one RUN: *The West Indies players hit several quick singles in the last few minutes before play ended for the day.* • In baseball, a single is a hit which allows the player to reach first base.

sin·gle /ˈsɪŋ·gl̩/ *v* [I] • A baseball player singles by hitting a ball that allows him to reach first base.

sin·gle·ness /ˈsɪŋ·gl̩·nəs/ *n* [U] • *He showed great singleness* **of mind/purpose** (= attention to one thing) *in dealing with the problem.*

sin·gles /ˈsɪŋ·gl̩z/ *n* [C] *pl* **singles** • Singles is a game, esp. in tennis, played between one player on one side and one on the other: *Martina Navratilova won the ladies' singles at Wimbledon nine times.* Compare **doubles** at DOUBLE TWICE.

sin·gle SEPARATE /ˈsɪŋ·gl̩/ *adj* [before n; not gradable] considered on its own; separate from other things • *Patience is the single most important quality needed for this job.* • *She lost every single thing when her house burned down.* • Ⓟ

sin·gle NOT MARRIED /ˈsɪŋ·gl̩/ *adj* [not gradable] not married • *a single woman/man/person* ○ *a single mother/father/parent* • *He's been single for so long now, I don't think he'll ever marry.* • *The number of single-parent* **families** *dependent on the state has risen enormously in recent years.* • *"Sex and the Single Girl"* (title of a book by Helen Gurley Brown, 1962) • LP **Relationships** Ⓟ

sin·gles /ˈsɪŋ·gl̩z/ *pl n* • *Last year I went on a tour organised by a club for singles* (= people who are not married). • *A new* **singles bar** (= a bar for people who are not married) *has just opened in Soho.*

sin·gle out *obj*, **sin·gle** *obj* **out** /ˈsɪŋ·gl̩/ *v adv* [M] to choose for special attention • *I was very pleased when the teacher singled my work out.* • *She singled him out* **as** *being a good person for the job.* • *It's not fair the way my sister is always singled out* **for** *special treatment.*

sin·glet /ˈsɪŋ·glət/ *n* [C] *esp. Br and Aus* a sleeveless piece of clothing worn on the top part of the body under clothes, or for playing particular sports

sin·gle·ton /£ˈsɪŋ·gl̩·tən, $-ṭən/ *n* [C] *specialized* a playing card which is the only one of that SUIT (= set of cards) held by a player • *Jack has a singleton* **in** *hearts.*

sing·song MUSICAL VOICE /£ˈsɪŋ·sɒŋ, $-sɑːŋ/ *n* [U] a voice rising and falling in level • *She spoke in a singsong.*

sing·song /£ˈsɪŋ·sɒŋ, $-sɑːŋ/ *adj* [before n] • *Welsh people are often described as having singsong voices.*

sing·song SINGING *Br and Aus* /£ˈsɪŋ·sɒŋ, $-sɑːŋ/, *Am* **song·fest**, **sing–a·long** *n* [C] the informal singing of songs by a group of people • *We had a singsong on the bus on the way back from the football match.*

sin·gu·lar GRAMMAR /£ˈsɪŋ·gjʊ·ləʳ, $-lɚ/ *adj* [not gradable], *n* (of or being) the form of a word used to talk about one thing • *a singular noun/verb/form/ending* • *The word 'woman' is singular.* • *The singular* (= The form representing only one) **of** *'children' is 'child.'* [U] • *The word 'teeth' is plural –* **in the** *singular it's 'tooth'.* [U]

sin·gu·lar NOTICEABLE /£ˈsɪŋ·gjʊ·ləʳ, $-lɚ/ *adj* [before n] *fml* of an unusual quality or standard; noticeable • *She was a woman of singular beauty.* • *He showed a singular lack of skill in painting.*

sin·gu·lar·ly /£ˈsɪŋ·gjʊ·lə·li, $-lɚ-/ *adv* • Singularly means to an unusual degree: *She was a singularly beautiful woman.* ○ *He wanted to become a painter, but he was singularly unskilled.*

sin·gu·lar STRANGE *fml* /£ˈsɪŋ·gjʊ·ləʳ, $-lɚ/ *adj* unusual or strange; not ordinary • *My father has singular views on politics.* • *What happened after you left was most singular.*

sin·gu·lar·i·ty /£ˌsɪŋ·gjʊˈlær·ɪ·ti, $-ˈler·ə·ṭi/ *n* [U] *fml* • *He has been behaving with great singularity* (= strangeness).

sin·gu·lar·ly /£ˈsɪŋ·gjʊ·lə·li, $-lɚ-/ *adv fml* • *He has been behaving most singularly* (= strangely).

si·nis·ter /£ˈsɪn·ɪ·stəʳ, $-stɚ/ *adj* suggesting that someone or something is evil, or that something evil is going to happen • *The ruined house had a sinister appearance.* • *A sinister-looking man sat in the corner of the room.* • *(infml) "The personnel director wants to see you." – "Oh dear, that sounds sinister* (= as if there is going to be trouble)*."*

sink *(obj)* GO DOWN BELOW /sɪŋk/ *v past simple* **sank** /sæŋk/ or **sunk** /sʌŋk/, *past part* **sunk** /sʌŋk/ to (cause to) go down below the surface or to the bottom of a liquid or soft substance • *The Titanic was a passenger ship which sank* **(to the bottom of the ocean)** *in 1912.* [I] • *I thought the cardboard box would float on the water, but it sank.* [I] • *The legs of the garden chair sank* **into** *the soft ground.* [I] • *The dog sank her teeth* **into** (= bit) *the ball and ran off with it.* [T] • *She sank* (= put) *her spoon* **into** *the large bowl of cream.* [T] • *We sank* (= put) *all our money* **into** *my brother's business.* [T] • *My employer gave me no help when I started my new job – I was just left to* **sink or swim** (= to fail or succeed by my own efforts, without help from others). • *Jill's suggestion that we all play tennis* **sank like a stone/a lead balloon** (= received no support). • *Since his last book five years ago, he seems to have* **sunk without (a) trace** (= disappeared from public notice). • See also SUNKEN.

sink·er /£ˈsɪŋ·kəʳ, $-kɚ/ *n* [C] • A sinker is a weight fixed to a fishing net or line to keep it under the water.

sink *(obj)* FALL /sɪŋk/ *v past simple* **sank** /sæŋk/ or **sunk** /sʌŋk/, *past part* **sunk** /sʌŋk/ to (cause to) fall or move to a lower level • *After the heavy rains, the level of the flood waters did not sink for weeks.* [I] • *The sun glowed red as it sank slowly below the horizon.* [I] • *Student numbers have sunk considerably this year.* [I] • *The pound sank* (= lost value) *two cents against the dollar today.* [I] • *(Br and Aus infml) We sank* (= drank) *a bottle of wine each last night.* [T] • To sink a ball is to hit it into a hole or pocket, esp. in golf or SNOOKER. [T] • *The wounded soldier sank* (= fell) **to** *the ground.* [I] • *I was so tired when I got home that all I wanted to do was sink* **into** (= sit or lie in) *bed/an armchair/a hot bath.* [I] • *Certain drugs can make you sink* **into** (= become so that you are in) *a deep sleep.* [I] • *He sank* **into** *deep despair* (= became very unhappy) *when he lost his job.* [I] • *The child's voice* **sank to a whisper** (= The child lowered her voice to a very low level) *as she admitted that she had broken the window.* • *He* **sank** (= lowered) **his voice to a whisper** *as he entered the church.* • *My* **spirits sank**/*My* **heart sank** (= I was very disappointed) *when I realised I couldn't afford the new car I wanted.* • *When I woke up this morning, I had a* **sinking feeling** (= a feeling that something bad was going to happen) *that it was going to be a difficult day.* • *(esp. Br) My father is always complaining about* **sinking standards** (= falling standards) *in public services.* • *Mrs Jones is* **sinking fast** (= Her health is getting much worse), *and the doctor doesn't think she'll live much longer.* • *I can't believe you would* **sink to such a level/sink to such depth(s)/sink so low** (= do something so wrong). • *Rodin's sculpture 'The Thinker' is the image of a man* **sunk in thought** (= thinking deeply). • *He* **sank in** *my* **estimation** (= My opinion of him fell) *when he failed to do as he promised.* • *(Br) Paul and Mark agreed to* **sink their differences** (= forget their disagreement) *and be friends.*

sink *obj* DIG /sɪŋk/ *v* [T] *past simple* **sank** /sæŋk/ or **sunk** /sʌŋk/, *past part* **sunk** /sʌŋk/ to dig (a hole) in the ground, or to put (something) into a hole dug into the ground • *Sinking more wells is the best way of supplying the population with clean drinking water.* • *The first stage of building the fence is sinking the posts* **into** *the ground.* • See also SUNKEN.

sink *obj* FAILURE /sɪŋk/ *v* [T] *past simple* **sank** /sæŋk/ or **sunk** /sʌŋk/, *past part* **sunk** /sʌŋk/ to cause to fail or be in trouble • *This rain could sink our plans for the garden party.*

sink GO THROUGH /sɪŋk/ *v* [I always + adv/prep] *past simple* **sank** /sæŋk/ or **sunk** /sʌŋk/, *past part* **sunk** /sʌŋk/ (of a liquid or soft substance) to pass into a solid object through its surface • *You'd better wipe up that coffee you spilled on the carpet before it sinks* **in**. • *Rub the cream gently on your face until it has all sunk* **into** *your skin.* • *(fig.) I don't think her loss has quite sunk* **in** *yet* (= She has not fully understood it yet). • *(fig. infml) How many times do I have to tell you something before it sinks* **into** *your head* (= before you understand it)*?*

sink CONTAINER /sɪŋk/ *n* [C] a large open container in a kitchen which holds water, has pipes to supply and remove water and is used esp. for washing dishes • *a kitchen sink* • *Leave the dishes in the sink – I'll deal with them in the morning.* • *I want to buy a new* **sink unit** (= a piece of furniture into which a sink is fitted), *but I can't find one that I like.* • Sink is also *Am for* WASHBASIN.

sink·ing fund /ˈsɪŋ·kɪŋ/ *n* [C] *specialized* money saved by a company or government for the payment of future debts

sin·less /ˈsɪn·ləs/ *adj* See at SIN OFFENCE

Sinn Fein /ˌʃɪnˈfeɪn/ *n* [U + sing/pl v] an Irish political party that wants Northern Ireland to become part of the Republic of Ireland • *Many people consider Sinn Fein to be the political wing of the IRA.*

Si·no– /£ˈsaɪ·nəʊ-, $-noʊ-, ˌ--/ *combining form* of or connected with China • *He is studying sinology.* • *There are signs that Sino-Cuban relations* (= the relationship between China and Cuba) *are becoming worse.*

si·nol·o·gy /£saɪˈnɒl·ə·dʒi, $-ˈnɑː·lə-/ *n* [U] the study of Chinese language, literature, history, society, etc.

si·nol·o·gist /£saɪˈnɒl·ə·dʒɪst, $-ˈnɑː·lə-/ *n* [C]

si·nu·ous /ˈsɪn·ju·əs/ *adj* moving in a twisting, curving or indirect way, or having many curves • *He enjoyed watching the sinuous bodies of the dancers.* • *The walkers followed the sinuous path through the trees.*

si·nu·ous·ly /ˈsɪn·ju·ə·sli/ *adv* • *The snake moved sinuously* (= in a curving and indirect way) *over the branches of the tree.*

si·nus /ˈsaɪ·nəs/ *n* [C] any of the hollow spaces in the bones of the face that open into the nose • *I always have sinus trouble/problems in the summer.*

sip /sɪp/ *v, n* **-pp-** (to drink) a very small amount of a drink • *This tea is very hot, so sip it carefully.* [T] • *She slowly sipped* **(at)** *her wine.* [T; I + prep] • *The child took several sips of the milk before she decided that she didn't like it.* [C]

si·phon, sy·phon /ˈsaɪ·fᵊn/ *n* [C] a tube that is bent in the shape of an 'n', with each end in a separate container at two different levels, so that liquid can be pulled up into it from the higher container and go down through it into the lower container • A siphon (also **soda siphon**) is also a bottle for filling water with gas and forcing it out under pressure to use in drinks.

si·phon *obj*, **sy·phon** /ˈsaɪ·fᵊn/ *v* [T always + adv/prep] • *When we ran out of petrol we had to siphon some* **from**/ *siphon some out* **of** *another car.* • *(fig.) He lost his job when it was discovered that he had been siphoning off* (= removing) *money from the company for his own use.*

sir MAN /£sɜːʳ, $sɜːr/ *n* [as form of address] *fml* used as a formal and polite way of speaking to a man, esp. one whom you are providing with a service or who is in a position of authority • *What would you like, Sir?* • *"Did you hear what I said?" – "Yes, sir."* • '**Dear Sir**' is the usual way of beginning a formal letter to a man whose name you do not know. '**Dear Sirs**' can be used when writing to a company. • '**Dear Sir or Madam**' is used when you do not know whether the person you are writing to is a man or a woman. • Sir is sometimes used instead of the name of a male teacher: *Please Sir, I don't understand.* • *(Am infml) I'm not going to ride the subway,* **no sir** (= certainly not)*!* • *"To Sir, with Love"* (title of a book by E.R. Braithwaite and also of a film and song, 1959) • Compare MADAM; MISS. • LP **Titles and forms of address**

Sir TITLE /£sɜːʳ, $sɜːr/ *n* used as the title of a KNIGHT • Sir is used with a man's first name, or with his first and family names, but never with just his family name: *Sir Walter (Scott)*

sire FATHER /£saɪəʳ, $saɪr/ *n* [C] a father, esp. of a horse • *That young horse should race well – its sire won many events.* • *(old use) His sires* (= past members of his family) *have lived in the same village for hundreds of years.*

sire *obj* /£saɪəʳ, $saɪr/ *v* [T] • *The foal was sired by a cup-winning racehorse.* • *(old use or humorous) At the age of 70, he married a much younger woman and went on to sire two more children.*

sire KING /£saɪəʳ, $saɪr/ *n* [C] *old use* used as a form of address to a MASTER or king • *I will serve you always, sire.*

si·ren DEVICE /£ˈsaɪə·rən, $ˈsaɪr·ən/ *n* [C] a device for making a loud warning noise • *In big cities you hear police sirens all the time.* • *The ship sounded its siren in the fog.* • *The siren went off in the middle of the night to warn that there was going to be an air attack.*

si·ren WOMAN /£ˈsaɪə·rən, $ˈsaɪr·ən/ *n* [C] (in ancient Greek literature) one of the creatures who were half woman and half bird, whose beautiful singing tempted sailors to sail into dangerous waters where they died • *Odysseus and his sailors managed to escape the sirens.* • *(fig.) That woman is a real siren* (= a dangerous beautiful woman).

sir·loin (steak) /£ˈsɜː·lɔɪn, $ˈsɜːr-/ *n* the best meat from the lower back of cattle • *I'd like a piece of sirloin, please.* [U] • *We have a very good sirloin today, madam.* [C]

si·roc·co, sci·roc·co /£sɪˈrɒk·əʊ, $-ˈrɑː·koʊ/ *n* [C] *pl* **siroccos** or **sciroccos** a hot wind which blows from the Sahara Desert to southern Europe • *Siroccos are dry as they pass over North Africa but wet by the time they reach southern Europe.*

sir·rah /ˈsɪr·ə/ *n old use* a not respectful form of address used to a man • *Come here, sirrah!*

sis /sɪs/ *n* [U] *esp. Am infml for* SISTER • *Have you met my sis?* • *Hello, Sis! How are you?* [as form of address]

si·sal /£ˈsaɪ·sᵊl, $ˈsɪs·ᵊl/ *n* [U] (a tropical plant whose leaves produce) strong threads which are used for making rope and floor coverings

sis·sy /ˈsɪs·i/, **cis·sy** *n* [C] *infml disapproving* a boy who looks or behaves like a girl or who lacks qualities considered as male, or a person who is weak and cowardly • *Kevin is such a sissy.* • *Can't you climb that tree, you big sissy?* [as form of address]

sis·sy (-ier, -iest) /ˈsɪs·i/, **cis·sy** *adj* • *I'm not going to play that sissy game.*

sis·ter /£ˈsɪs·təʳ, $-tɚ/ *n* [C] a female who has the same parents as another person • *Sophie and Emily are sisters.* • *Emily is Sophie's younger/little/older/big sister.* • *Lyn's such a good friend – she's* **like a** *sister* **to** *me* (= she treats me in the kind way that a sister would). • *We must continue the fight, sisters* (= women who share a common interest, esp. that in improving women's rights). [as form of address] • *(Am infml dated)* Sister is sometimes used to address a woman: *OK, sister, move it!* • *(Br and Aus)* A sister is also a nurse who is in charge of a department of a hospital: *There are two sisters on duty tonight.* ○ *(Br and Aus) Sister Jones was very kind to my mother when she was in hospital.* [as form of address] • A sister is also a female member of a religious group, esp. a NUN: *The sisters are spending an hour in private prayer.* ○ *Sister Catherine is leading the prayers this morning.* [as form of address] • *Our sister* **company** (= a company with the same owner) *in Australia has had a very successful year this year.* • *The US battleship Missouri has been joined by her sister* **ship**, *Wisconsin.* • *(Br) John is a true* **sister under the skin** (= a man who supports women's action to improve their rights). • *"Sisters are doing it for themselves"* (title of a song by The Eurythmics and Aretha Franklin, 1985) • LP **Relationships** PIC **Family tree**

sis·ter·hood /£ˈsɪs·tə·hʊd, $-tɚ-/ *n* • *It was sisterhood* (= the relationship between sisters) *that made her care for me as she did.* [U] • Sisterhood is a strong feeling of companionship and support among women who are involved in action to improve women's rights: *Every year, on International Women's Day, millions of women celebrate the idea of sisterhood.* [U] ○ **The sisterhood** (= women involved in action to improve their rights) *agree/agrees that further campaigning is necessary on this issue.* • A sisterhood is a society of women living a religious life: *She is a member of a sisterhood in northern France.* [C]

sis·ter–in–law /£ˈsɪs·tə·rɪn·lɔː, $-tɚ·ɪn·lɑː/ *n* [C] *pl* **sisters-in-law** or *Br also* **sister-in-laws** • A person's **sister-in-law** is the wife of their brother, or the sister of their husband or wife, or the wife of the brother of their husband or wife.

sis·ter·ly /£'sɪs·tᵊl·i, $-tɚ·li/ *adj* • *That's not a very sisterly* (=like a sister) *way to behave.* • *I felt quite sisterly towards him, but I couldn't marry him.*

sit *(obj)* BE SEATED /sɪt/ *v* [usually + adv/prep] **sitting**, *past* **sat** /sæt/ to (cause to) be in a position in which the lower part of the body is resting on a seat or other type of support, with the upper part of the body vertical • *to sit* **at** *a table/desk* [I] • *to sit* **in** *an armchair/tree* [I] • *to sit* **on** *a chair/a horse/the ground* [I] • *Are you sitting comfortably?* [I] • *He came and sat* **(down)** (=got into a seated position) *next to me.* [I] • *(infml) Sit your***self down** *and have a cup of tea.* [T] • *The child's father sat her* **(down) on** *a chair and told her not to move.* [T] • *(fig.) I think we should sit* **(down)** *and talk about this* (=get together and have a serious talk). [I] • *Everybody was already sitting* **(down)** (=seated) **at** *the table when we arrived.* [I] • *"Have you read Jeffrey Archer's new book?" "No, I bought a copy a few months ago, but it's still sitting* **on** *my shelf* (=it's still on the shelf and not being read)*."* [I] • *The village sits* (=is in a position) **at/in** *the bottom of a valley.* [I] • *(dated) That coat sits very well* **on** *you* (=fits/suits you very well). [I] • *Monet's wife sat* (=acted as a painter's model) **for** *him many times.* [I] • *(esp. Br) It's a lovely day today, why don't we sit* **out** (=sit outside). [I] • *I don't think I can sit* **through** (=stay seated until the end of) *this film, it's much too long.* [I] • *How many times do I have to tell you children to sit* **up (straight)** (=sit with a straight back)*?* [I] • *Let me sit you* **up** (=help you move from a lying position into a sitting position) *so you'll be more comfortable.* [T] • *(dated) Lunch is ready, come and sit* **up to** *the table* (=come and sit at the table). [I] • *We're trying to train our dog to sit* (=to move into a position with its back legs bent and its tail end on the ground). [I] • *Can you see that bird sitting* (=resting with its feet) **on** *the fence?* [I] • *Hens should not be disturbed while they are sitting (Am usually* **setting***)* (=they are covering their eggs with their bodies to keep them warm before they HATCH). [I] • To sit is also to BABYSIT: *Have you found anyone to sit* **for** *you tonight?* • *When my grandfather was at Princeton, he* **sat at the feet of** (=was a student of) *Einstein himself.* • *I don't know why he thinks he can* **sit in judgment on/over** *us* (=make a judgment, esp. without having any right to do so) *like that.* • *You can't* **sit on the fence** (=delay making a decision) *any longer – you have to make a decision.* • *She just* **sits on** *her* **hands**/*(slang)* **sits on** *her (Br)* **arse**/*(Am)* **ass**/ *(Aus)* **bum** (=does nothing) *all day, while I do all the work.* • *(Am) Their decision/answer didn't* **sit right/well** *with me* (=I did not agree/was not pleased with it). • *You'd better* **sit tight** (=stay where you are) *and I'll call the doctor.* • *(fig.) My parents tried to persuade me not to go alone, but I* **sat tight** (=refused to change my mind). • *(Am) He* **sat under** (=received teaching from) *the most influential teacher/preacher in his field/the church.* • *With their bullets all gone, the soldiers were* **sitting ducks** *for the enemy* (=it was easy for the enemy to attack them). • *We bought our house while prices were low, so we're* **sitting pretty** (=are in a good position). • *(infml) You look tired. Why don't you come and have a* **sit-down** (=a rest in a seated position) *for a few minutes.* • *The workers are holding a* **sit-down (strike)** (=they have stopped work and are refusing to leave their place of work until their demands have been met). • *We are having a* **sit-down meal** (=a meal served to people seated at a table) *at our wedding.* • *(esp. Br)* A **sitting-room** (also **living room**) is the room usually used for relaxing and entertaining in a private house: *Please come into the sitting-room.* • *If you don't lock your doors and windows, you'll be a* **sitting target** *for* (=you'll have no protection against) *burglars.* • *(Br) We can't sell our house because we have* **sitting tenants** (=people renting it from us who have a legal right to stay). • A **sit-up** is a type of exercise in which someone sits up from a lying position and which makes the stomach muscles stronger.

sit·ter /£'sɪt·ɚ, $'sɪṭ·ɚ/ *n* [C] • A sitter is someone who is having their PORTRAIT (=picture of their face or body) painted. • A sitter is also a **babysitter**. See at BABYSIT.

sit·ting /£'sɪt·ɪŋ, $'sɪṭ-/ *n* [C] • *When the hotel is full, dinner is served in two sittings* (=periods in which a number of people eat a meal). • *I enjoyed the book so much that I read it all* **at/in** *one sitting* (=without stopping). • *The portrait was finished after only three sittings* (=periods spent by a model being painted).

sit MEET /sɪt/ *v* [I] **sitting**, *past* **sat** /sæt/ to hold an official meeting of a parliament, council or court • *The court will sit tomorrow morning.* • *As an MP, I see much less of my family when Parliament is sitting.*

sit·ting /£'sɪt·ɪŋ, $'sɪṭ-/ *n* [C] • *There will be no more sittings* (=meetings) *of the legislature now until the autumn.*

sit BE A MEMBER /sɪt/ *v* [I] **sitting**, *past* **sat** /sæt/ to be a member of an official group • *I'm going to be sitting* **on** *the committee for one more year.* • *Our member of Congress has sat* **for** *this town for years.* • *(Am) All of the federal judges currently sitting* (=in office) *in Maryland hail from Baltimore.* • *(Br) The* **sitting member** (=The present Member of Parliament for the area) *will not be contesting her seat at the next election.*

sit *obj* EXAMINATION /sɪt/ *v* [T] **sitting**, *past* **sat** /sæt/ *esp. Br* to take (an examination) • *After I've sat my exams, I'm going on holiday.* • *(Aus) I sat* **for** *my exams today.*

sit a·round *(obj)*, *Br also* **sit a·bout** *v adv infml* to sit doing nothing • *I've had to sit about all day waiting for someone to come and repair the television.* [I] • *We sat around most of the evening, drinking beer.* [I] • *He just sits around the house all the time, when he should be doing something useful.* [T]

sit back *v adv* [I] to sit comfortably with your back against the back of a chair • *Sit back and make yourself comfortable.* • *We have a wonderful show for you tonight, ladies and gentlemen, so please sit back* **and enjoy** *it.* • *(fig.) I can't just sit back* (=take no action) *and do nothing when there are so many homeless people on the streets.*

sit by *v adv* [I] to fail to take action to stop something wrong happening • *I can't just sit by while this government destroys the health service.*

sit in COMPLAIN *v adv* [I] to make a complaint or express dissatisfaction by moving into a public building, stopping its usual activities, and refusing to leave until your demands have been met • *The students are sitting in as a protest about the increase in their fees.*

sit–in /£'sɪt·ɪn, $'sɪṭ-/ *n* [C] • *The union has decided to stage a sit-in as part of a campaign against the job losses.*

sit in BE PRESENT *v adv* [I] to go to a meeting or a class without taking part • *I'm interested in how you teach your class. May I sit in and watch?* • *We were not allowed to sit in* **on** *the council's private meeting.*

sit in for *obj v adv prep* [T] *dated* to take the place of • *Mr Baker is ill today, so Miss Dixon is sitting in for him (***as** *your teacher).*

sit on *obj* DELAY *v prep* [T] *infml* to delay taking action about • *The company has been sitting on my letter for weeks without dealing with my complaint.* • *I think we should sell the silver now, rather than sit on it and hope its value increases.*

sit on *obj* CONTROL *v prep* [T] *infml* to force (someone) into silence or inactivity • *That child's behaviour is so bad that someone should firmly sit on him.*

sit on *obj* FOOD *v prep* [T] *infml* to make (the stomach) feel full of food • *That chocolate cake we had for tea is sitting heavily on my stomach.*

sit out *obj*, **sit** *obj* **out** *v adv* [M] to stay seated during and not take part in (a dance), or to stay seated until the end of (a performance that you are not enjoying) • *I'm feeling rather tired, so I think I'll sit out the next dance.* • *We didn't enjoy the concert very much, but we sat it out because Kim was performing in it.*

sit up NOTICE *v adv* [I] *infml* to show interest or surprise • *The news that he was getting married really made her sit up.* • *She* **sat up and took notice** *when she heard he was getting married.*

sit up STAY AWAKE *v adv* [I] to stay awake late; to not go to bed • *The book was so interesting that I sat up all night reading it.* • *I'll be late tonight, so don't sit up* **for** *me.*

si·tar /£'sɪt·ɑːʳ, $sɪ'tɑːr/ *n* [C] an Indian musical instrument, with a round body, a long neck and two sets of strings

sit·com /£'sɪt·kɒm, $-kɑːm/ *n* [C/U] a **situation comedy**, see at SITUATE

site /saɪt/ *n* [C] a place where something is, was, or will be built, or where something happened, is happening, or will happen • *The council haven't yet chosen the site* **for** *the new hospital.* • *A monument marks the site* **of** *the battle.* • *This is the site* **of** *the accident.* • *There are many archaeological sites in southern England.* • *We're meeting the builders* **on site** (=at the place where they are building) *tomorrow.*

site *obj* /saɪt/ *v* [T always + adv/prep] • *The hotel is sited on a cliff above the sea.* • *We sited our tent under a tree.*

si·tu·ate *obj* /'sɪt·ju·eɪt/ *v* [T always + adv/prep] to put in a particular position • *They plan to situate their vegetable garden* **between** *the fence and the trees.* • *At first the garden table was situated under the apple tree, but it had to be* *moved.* • *To understand this issue, it must first be situated* **in** *its context.*

si·tu·at·ed /£'sɪt·ju·eɪ·tɪd, $-ţɪd/ *adj* [after v; not gradable] • *The school is situated* (= in a position) *near to the station.* • *Could you tell me* **where** *St John's Church is situated?* • *(slightly fml) My brother is rather badly situated since he lost his job* (= has no money and no hope of finding a new job). • *(slightly fml) With this new product, we are well situated* **to** *beat* (= we have a good chance of beating) *our competitors.* [+ *to* infinitive] • *(slightly fml) How are you situated* **(for time)***?* (= How much time do you have?)

si·tu·a·tion /ˌsɪt·ju'eɪ·ʃᵊn/ *n* [C] • *The situation* (= What is happening) *is making her very unhappy.* • *"Would you get involved in a fight?" "It would* **depend on the** *situation* (= the particular conditions)*."* • *I'll worry about it* **if/when/as the** *situation* **arises** (= if/when/as it happens). • *The current economic and political situation* (= set of conditions) *shows little sign of improving.* • *I'm not very good* **in** *social situations* (= at social events). • *There are organizations which can help people* **in** *your situation* (= people who are experiencing the same unpleasant thing as you). • *(old use) My sister has a good situation* (= job) **as** *a teacher in the local school.* • *(Br and Aus) I look at the* **situations vacant** *section of the newspaper* (= the part in which jobs are listed) *every day, but I still can't find a job.* • *The house is in an attractive situation* (= position) *in a river valley.* • *The best situation for growing tomatoes is one which gets plenty of sun.* • **Situation comedy** (also *infml* **sitcom**) is a form of amusing television or radio show in which the same characters appear in each programme in a different story: *I don't like sitcoms much.* [C] ○ *The careers of many movie stars began in situation comedy.* [U]

six /sɪks/ *determiner, pronoun, n* (the number) 6 • *There were six horses in the field.* • *I'd like six, please.* • *Look for a bus with a (number) six on the front of it.* [C] • *The crowd cheered when Richards hit a six* (= six points in cricket, scored when the player hits the ball to the edge of the playing area without it touching the ground first). [C] • *Alan is a six-***footer** (= is six feet or 1.83 metres tall) *already and he's only fifteen.* • *(infml) We've been* **at sixes and sevens** (= in a confused, badly organized or undecided situation) *this week.* • *(infml) "Shall we go by car or train?" "I don't know, it's* **six of one and half a dozen of the other** (= there is no difference)*."* • *(Br dated infml) Ian was given* **six of the best** (= a beating, usually of six hits with a stick, given to a student at school as a punishment) *for misbehaving.* • *(humorous)* Someone who is **six feet under** has died and been buried: *There's no point worrying about it – we'll both be six feet under when the oil runs out.* • *Why don't you bring a* **six-pack** (= a set of six CANS or bottles of a drink, esp. beer, sold in a plastic or cardboard container) *round and we'll watch football on television.* • *Pulling his* **six-shooter** (= a small gun which holds six bullets) *from his belt, the sheriff fired three shots at the horse thieves.*

sixth /sɪksθ/ *determiner, pronoun, adj, adv* [not gradable], *n* • *That's the sixth time I've asked you that question.* • *I have to return my library books on the sixth (of July).* • *England were/came sixth in the 100 metres.* • *Cut the cake into sixths* (= six equal parts)*, then there'll be an extra piece for anyone who wants it.* [C] • The **sixth form** in a British school consists of the highest two classes, and contains students of age 16-18: *The* **sixth form** *students are preparing to take their A levels.* • A **sixth former** is a student in the sixth form. • *I had a* **sixth sense** (= an ability to know something without using the five SENSES of sight, hearing, smell, touch and taste) *that the train was going to crash.* • LP› **Schools and colleges**

six·pence /'sɪks·pᵊnts/ *n* (a small silver-coloured coin used in Britain until 1971 which was worth) the sum of six old PENNIES • *I can remember when a sixpence would buy quite a lot.* [C] • *There used to be a time when a loaf of bread cost sixpence.* [U]

six·teen /ˌsɪk'stiːn, '--/ *determiner, pronoun, n* (the number) 16 • *fifteen, sixteen, seventeen* • *We've got sixteen (people) coming for lunch.* • *He bought her a birthday card with a big gold sixteen on the front.* [C] • *"Happy Birthday, Sweet Sixteen"* (title of a song by Neil Sedaka, 1962)

six·teenth /ˌsɪk'stiːnθ, '--/ *determiner, pronoun, adj, adv* [not gradable], *n* • *the sixteenth floor* • *the sixteenth of August* • *She was/came sixteenth in the class in the exams.* • A sixteenth is one of sixteen equal parts of something. [C] • **Sixteenth note** is *Am for* SEMIQUAVER.

six·ty /'sɪk·sti/ *determiner, pronoun, n* (the number) 60 • *fifty, sixty, seventy* • *There are sixty (people) coming to the wedding.* • *I want to buy a card with a sixty on it for my uncle.* [C] • *(infml) So will she marry him? That's the* **sixty-four-thousand-dollar question** (= an important or difficult question, the answer to which might not be known and on which a lot depends).

six·ties /'sɪk·stiz/ *pl n* • **The** sixties is the range of temperature between 60° and 69°: *The temperature is usually around the sixties at this time of year.* **The** sixties is also the period of years between 60 and 69 in any century: *The Beatles made their first records* **in** *the sixties* (= between 1960 and 1969). • A person's sixties are the period in which they are aged between 60 and 69: *Many people retire* **in** *their sixties.*

six·ti·eth /'sɪk·sti·əθ/ *determiner, pronoun, adj, adv* [not gradable], *n* • *My grandmother's celebrating her sixtieth birthday on Sunday.* • *"How many exam papers have you marked now?" "This is the sixtieth."* • *They were/came finished sixtieth out of a hundred.* • A sixtieth is one of sixty equal parts of something. [C]

size LARGENESS /saɪz/ *n* (a degree of) largeness or smallness • *The value of a piece of land depends on where it is rather than on its size.* [C] • *The size of our business has been decreasing steadily for some time.* [C] • *We are concerned about the size of our debt.* [C] • *Certain trees grow to a huge size.* [C] • *What is the size* **of** (= how big is) *that window?* [C] • *Over the last ten years, the school has greatly increased* **in** *size.* [U] • *The field was about ten acres* **in** *size.* [U] • *He had a lump on his head the size* **of** (= the same size as) *an egg.* [C] • *"Look at the size of that dog!* (= Look how big it is!)*" "Yes, it's* **about the size of** (= approximately as large as) *a small horse!"* • *(dated) Ann and Ruth are* **(both) of a** *size* (= are the same size). [U] • *Is there a hotel* **of any** *size* (= a large hotel) *near here?* [U] • *The baby is* **a good** *size* (= quite large). [U] • *The theatre was* **a good** *size* **for** (= a suitable size for) *concerts.* [U] • *(infml) "So you mean you won't come to the party with me?" "Yes,* **that's about the size of it** (= that's exactly what I mean)*."* • LP› **Measurements**

size·a·ble, **siz·a·ble** /'saɪ·zə·bḷ/ *adj* • *a sizeable* (= large) *amount/area/house*

-sized /-saɪzd/ *combining form* • *a medium-sized house* (= a house of medium size) • *a good-sized* (= large) *garden* • *a child-sized chair* (= a chair of a size suitable for a child) • *a pocket-sized mobile phone* (= one small enough to fit into a pocket)

size MEASURE /saɪz/ *n* [C] one of the standard measures according to which goods are made or sold • *a size 12 dress* • *a size 15 collar/shirt* • *a size 7 shoe* • *Do these shoes come* (= Are they made) *in children's sizes?* • *What size are you?/What is your size?/What size do you take?* • *What size shirt/shoe/dress do you take?* • *I'm a size 10./I take a size 10.* • *The orange juice comes in 1 litre, 2 litre, or 3 litre sizes.* • *This shirt is a couple of sizes too big/small (for me). I need a smaller/bigger size.* • *Would you like to* **try the coat (on) for** *size* (= see how well it fits you)*, sir?* • *We'll need to get the carpet cut* **to** *size* (= cut so that it fits).

size *obj* GLUE /saɪz/ *n* [U], *v* [T] (to cover or treat with) a glue-like substance which gives stiffness and a hard shiny surface to cloth, paper, etc.

size up *obj*, **size** *obj* **up** /saɪz/ *v adv* [M] to examine carefully and form an opinion of • *We must size up the situation before we decide what to do.* • *The two cats walked in circles around each other, sizing each other up.*

siz·zle /'sɪz·ḷ/ *v* [I] to make a sound like food cooking in hot fat • *The sausages are sizzling in the pan.* • *Hot coals sizzle when water is poured onto them.* • *(fig.) It's a sizzling hot day today!*

siz·zler /£'sɪz·ləʳ, $-lɚ/ *n* [C] • *(infml) We haven't had a sizzler* (= a very hot day) *like that since last summer.*

skate BOOT /skeɪt/ *n* [C] either of a pair of boots with metal blades fixed to the bottom so that the wearer can move smoothly over ice, or with four small wheels fixed to the bottom so that the wearer can move over a hard surface • *I've just got some new* **ice/roller** *skates, but I can't balance very well on them yet.* • *(Br infml)* **Get/Put** *your* **skates on** (= Hurry)*, or we'll be late.* • PIC› **Skate, Winter sports**

skate *(obj)* /skeɪt/ *v* • *The ice on the river is thick enough to skate* (= move on skates) **on/across/over**. [I] • *Shall we* **go** *skating tomorrow?* [I] • *Everyone cheered as she skated a perfect figure of eight.* [T] • *(fig.) Hurrying to catch the bus, she skated* (= ran quickly) *down the road.* [I] • *He's* **skating on thin ice** (= doing something risky or dangerous) *by lying to the police.* • PIC› **Winter sports**

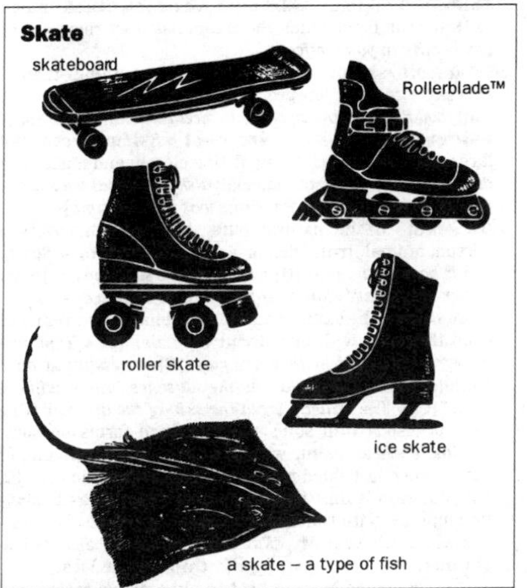

a skate – a type of fish

skat·er /£ˈskeɪ·təʳ, $-t̬ɚ/ *n* [C] • *There are lots of skaters* (= people on skates) *in the park today.*

skat·ing /£ˈskeɪ·tɪŋ, $-t̬ɪŋ/ *n* [U] • Skating is the activity or sport of moving on skates: *ice/roller skating* ○ *figure/speed skating* ○ *a skating club* • *a skating competition* • *a skating skirt* • *a skating boot* • A **skating rink** is an area of natural or specially prepared ice for using ice skates on, or a smooth hard area for using **roller skates** on.

skate FISH /skeɪt/ *n pl* **skate** or **skates** a large flat sea fish, which can be eaten as food • *Skate live at the bottom of the sea.* [C] • *Can I have some skate, please?* [U] • PIC› **Fish, Skate**

skate o·ver *obj, Am and Aus* **skate a·round** *obj, Br* **skate round** *obj v prep* [T] to avoid dealing completely with; to fail to pay enough attention to • *Providing homeless people with somewhere to stay when the weather is cold only skates round the problem, it doesn't solve it.* • *I didn't understand what the teacher said about prepositions, because she only skated over it.*

skate through *(obj) Br and Aus, Br and Aus* **sail through** *(obj) v adv* to be successful in (a test or exam) without experiencing any problems • *Kate skated through her French exam.* [T] • *Don't worry about your driving test, you'll skate through.* [I]

skate·board /£ˈskeɪt·bɔːd, $-bɔːrd/ *n* [C] a short flat narrow board with two small wheels under each end, which a person stands on and moves forward by pushing one foot on the ground • *Nigel sped down the hill on his skateboard.* • PIC› **Skate**

skate·board·er /£ˈskeɪtˌbɔː·dəʳ, $-ˌbɔːr·dɚ/ *n* [C] • *We watched the skateboarders* (= people riding on skateboards) *racing round the park.*

skate·board·ing /£ˈskeɪtˌbɔː·dɪŋ, $-ˌbɔːr-/ *n* [U] • *I'm not very good at skateboarding* (= the activity or sport of riding on a skateboard).

ske·dad·dle /skɪˈdæd·l̩/ *v* [I] *infml* to run away quickly • *OK, children, skedaddle!* • *The teacher's coming, let's skedaddle!*

skein THREAD /skeɪn/ *n* [C] a length of wool or thread loosely wound into the shape of a ring

skein BIRDS /skeɪn/ *n* [C] a large group of wild birds such as GEESE or DUCKS in flight

skel·e·tal /£ˈskel·ɪ·tᵊl, £skɪˈliː-, $-t̬ᵊl/ *adj* of or like a SKELETON (= frame of bones) • *Her body was skeletal* (= very thin). • *He suffered serious skeletal injuries in the accident.* • *(fig.) The newspaper report gave only a skeletal account of the debate* (= an account providing only the main points, without many details).

skel·e·ton /£ˈskel·ɪ·tᵊn, $-t̬ən/ *n* [C] the frame of bones supporting a human or animal body • *Children should drink milk to help them develop strong skeletons.* • *The farmer found an old skeleton when he was digging his field.* • *Her long illness* **reduced** *her* **to** *a skeleton* (= made her very thin). • *(fig.) After years in the prison camps, the prisoners were just skeletons* (= were extremely thin). • *(fig.) The skeleton* **of** *the office block* (= a frame onto which something is to be built or added) *has been built very quickly, but it will take longer to add the walls.* • *(fig.) The skeleton* **of** *my book is written/My book is* **in** *skeleton* **form** – *now I just have to add the details.* • *The hospital has a* **skeleton staff** (= the smallest number of people needed to keep it working) *at weekends.* • *The local bus company only runs a* **skeleton service** (= a limited number of bus rides or routes) *on Sundays.* • A **skeleton key** is one which will open several doors. • *(fig.) Most families have one or two* **skeletons (in the cupboard/***Am also* **closet)** (= secrets which would cause embarrassment if they were known).

skep·tic /ˈskep·tɪk/ *n* [C] *Am and Aus for* SCEPTIC

sker·rick /ˈsker·ɪk/ *n* [U; usually in negatives] *Aus* a very small amount • *There wasn't* **a** *skerrick left – they'd eaten everything!*

sketch DRAWING /sketʃ/ *n* [C] a simple, quickly-made drawing which does not have many details, or a short written or spoken story which does not have many details • *My mother made a (pencil) sketch* **of** *my brother reading a book.* • *The introduction to the book provides a sketch* **of** *its contents.* • A **sketch map** is one that has only a few details, and is usually drawn by hand. • PIC› **Drawing and painting**

sketch *(obj)* /sketʃ/ *v* • *The art students were each told to sketch* (= make a sketch of) *a tree.* [T] • *When I have some spare time, I like to sketch.* [I] • *The artist has sketched* **out** (= has made a sketch of) *a design for the new school.* [M] • *The artist has sketched* **in** (= has added to a sketch) *some people to show the size of the building.* [M] • *(fig.) The guide sketched* **out** *for the tourists* (= gave them a short description of) *what activities were planned for the week.* [M] • *(fig.) I don't understand what you're saying. Could you sketch* **in** *a few more details* (= provide additional information)*?* [M]

sketch·er /£ˈsketʃ·əʳ, $-ɚ/ *n* [C] • *The ruined church is a popular subject with sketchers* (= people who make sketches).

sketch·y /ˈsketʃ·i/ *adj* **-ier, -iest** • A story which is sketchy does not contain many details: *So far we only have sketchy information about what caused the explosion.*

sketch·i·ly /ˈsketʃ·ɪ·li/ *adv*

sketch HUMOROUS PERFORMANCE /sketʃ/ *n* [C] a short humorous part of a longer show or entertainment on stage, on television, or on the radio • *I thought the sketch about Queen Victoria was very funny.*

sketch·pad /ˈsketʃ·pæd/, **sketch·book** /ˈsketʃ·bʊk/ *n* [C] a number of sheets of plain paper fixed together for drawing on

skew *obj* /skjuː/ *v* [T] to cause to be not straight or exact; to twist; to DISTORT • *The company's results for this year are skewed because not all our customers have paid their bills.*

skew /skjuː/ *adj* [after v], *adv* [not gradable] • *I think that picture is skew/is hanging skew* (= not straight). • *(Br and Aus infml)* Something that is **skew-whiff** is sloping instead of being horizontal or vertical: *You've got your hat on skew-whiff.*

skew·bald /£ˈskjuː·bɔːld, $-bɑːld/ *n, adj* (an animal, esp. a horse) having large white and brown coloured areas on the hair on its body • *Fiona's horse is a skewbald.* [C] • *Fiona has a skewbald horse.* • See also PIEBALD.

skew·er *obj* /£skjʊəʳ, $ˈskjuː·ɚ/ *v, n* (to fasten or make a hole in pieces of food, esp. meat with) a long thin metal pin • *You'll have to skewer that meat before you cook it or it will fall apart.* [T] • *Would you skewer the chicken to see if it's cooked?* [T] • *Kebabs are made by putting pieces of meat and vegetables onto a skewer.* [C]

ski /skiː/ *n* [C] either of a pair of long, flat narrow pieces of wood, metal or plastic, which curve up at the front, and are fastened to boots so that the wearer can move quickly and smoothly over snow • *I've just bought a new pair of skis.* • *ski boots* • *a ski club/resort* • The **ski jump** is a competition in which people on skis move very fast down a specially made steep slope which turns up at the end, and jump off from the bottom of it, landing on a lower level. • A **ski lift** is a machine consisting of seats hanging down from a continuously moving wire, which carries people on skis to the top of slopes which they then ski down. • **Ski pants** are a pair of tight trousers, usually for women, which are made from a material that stretches easily and are held firmly in place by an elastic strap worn under each foot. • **Ski poles** *(Br also* **ski sticks)** are short pointed poles which are held one in each hand by people on skis to help them balance. • PIC› **Clothes, Winter sports**

ski /skiː/ *v* [I] he/she/it **skis, skiing,** *past* **skied** • *I'm learning to ski* (= to move over snow on SKIS). • *We went* *skiing in the French Alps last year.* • *He skied* **down** *the hill,* **past** *the forest, and* **into** *the village.*

ski·er /£'skiː·ər, $-ɚ/ *n* [C] • *After the heavy snow, there were lots of skiers* (= people on skis) *on the mountain.*

ski·ing /'skiː·ɪŋ/ *n* [U] • (= Skiing is the activity or sport of moving on skis:) *Shall we go skiing?* ○ *a skiing trip* ○ *a skiing instructor* ○ *skiing equipment* • PIC› **Winter sports**

ski·bob /£'skiː·bɒb, $-bɑːb/ *n* [C] a vehicle like a bicycle with skis instead of wheels, used for races

skid /skɪd/ *v* [I] **-dd-** (esp. of a vehicle) to slide unintentionally on a surface • *The roads are icy this morning, so be careful you don't skid.* • *My bicycle skidded* **on** *some oil that had been spilled on the road.* • *The car skidded and hit a tree.*

skid /skɪd/ *n* [C] • *The best way of dealing with a skid* (= an act of sliding) *is to turn the front wheels in the direction of the skid.* • *She was riding too fast on a wet road, and the motorbike* **went into a** *skid* (= started to slide). • *There were* **skid marks** (= black marks made by the tyres of a car which slid) *on the road where a car had braked suddenly.* • Skids are long flat pieces under some aircraft such as helicopters, which help the aircraft to land. • A skid is also a support, often made of wood, for raising heavy objects off the ground or moving them. • *(esp. Am infml)* **Skid row** is a poor and dirty part of a town where many jobless, homeless and drunk people live: *William Kennedy wrote several books about life* **on** *skid row.* • *(infml)* Something that is **on the skids** is experiencing difficulties and is unlikely to continue successfully: *Lots of small businesses are on the skids* (= likely to close) *at the moment.* ○ *Their marriage seems to be on the skids* (= likely to end). • *(Br and Aus infml) Local residents have* **put the skids under** *plans to build a new shopping centre* (= have caused the plans to fail). • PIC› **Driving**

skid·pan /'skɪd·pæn/ *n* [C] *Br* a specially prepared surface on which drivers can practise controlling SKIDDING (= unintentionally sliding) vehicles

skiff /skɪf/ *n* [C] a small light boat for ROWING (= moving through water using special poles) or sailing, usually by only one person

skif·fle /'skɪf·l̩/ *n* [U] a type of music popular in the 1950s, a mixture of jazz and FOLK music, in which players often perform on instruments they have made themselves

skill /skɪl/ *n* a special ability to do something • *Sewing is a skill that I don't possess.* [C] • *I have no skill* **at/in** *sewing.* [U] • *His writing skills helped him to get a job working on a newspaper.* [C] • *She was an executive* **with** *good negotiating skills.* [C] • *Picasso was a painter* **of** *great skill.* [U] • *The old skill* **of** *basket-making has almost disappeared now.* [C]

skil·ful *Br and Aus, Am* **skill·ful** /'skɪl·fᵊl/ *adj* • *Police officers have to be skilful drivers.* • *Miss Jones is quite skilful* **at** (= has special ability for) *dealing with difficult customers.*

skil·ful·ly *Br and Aus, Am* **skill·ful·ly** /'skɪl·fᵊl·i/ *adv* • *I thought you answered that question very skilfully* (= with great skill).

skilled /skɪld/ *adj* • *My mother is very skilled* **at/in** *dress-making.* • *Nursing is a highly skilled job* (= a job for which one has to be trained). • **The skilled** (= people who have been trained for a job) *usually earn more than the unskilled.*

skil·let /'skɪl·ɪt/ *n* [C] *Am for* **frying pan**, see at FRY • PIC› **Containers, Pan**

skim *(obj)* MOVE ABOVE /skɪm/ *v* **-mm-** to (cause to) move quickly just above (a surface) without, or only occasionally, touching it • *The birds skimmed* **(across/along/over)** *the tops of the waves, then dipped beneath them to catch fish.* [T; I + prep] • *The plane skimmed* **along** *just above the surface of the fjord, until they sighted the village.* [I] • *We watched a child skimming (Am and Aus also* **skipping)** *stones on the lake* (= throwing small flat stones so that they touched the surface of water, and rose up into the air again, several times). [T]

skim *(obj)* CONSIDER QUICKLY /skɪm/ *v* **-mm-** to read or consider (something) quickly to understand the main points, without studying it in detail • *I've only skimmed* **(through/over)** *his letter, I haven't read it carefully yet.* [T; I + prep] • *We've only skimmed* **the surface of** (= considered a small part of) *the problem.* [T]

skim *obj* REMOVE /skɪm/ *v* [T] **-mm-** to remove (something solid) from the surface of a liquid • *Skim the* **cream** *carefully* **from** *the milk.* • *Strain the cooking liquid and skim* **off the fat**. [M] • *(fig.) We've skimmed* **off** *the six people who seem to be the most suitable for the job* (= we have chosen six people and are considering them for the job). [M]

skimmed /skɪmd/, **skim** *adj* • *Would you like* **skimmed milk** (= milk from which the cream has been removed) *or whole milk in your coffee?*

skimp *(obj)* /skɪmp/ *v* to use less of (something) than is necessary to do a job properly • *Many old people skimp* **(on)** *food and heating in order to meet their bills.* [T/I + *on*]

skimp·y /'skɪm·pi/ *adj* **-ier, -iest** • Skimpy means not large enough, or of clothing, fitting closely and made with only a small amount of material: *a skimpy meal* ○ *a skimpy letter* ○ *skimpy shorts* ○ *The dress was rather skimpy.*

skin /skɪn/ *n* the natural outer layer which covers a person, animal, fruit, etc., or any outer covering • *Strong sun is bad for the skin.* [U] • *Babies have soft skins.* [C] • *My father has a rare skin disease.* • *Native Americans used to trade skins* (= the skins of animals that have been removed from the body, with or without the hair). [C] • *Tomatoes have red skins when they are ripe.* [C] • *He slipped on a banana skin.* [U] • *Would you like sausages with or without skins?* [C] • *The bullet pierced the skin of the aircraft.* [C] • Skin is also a thin solid surface which forms on some liquids, such as paint, when they are left in the air, or others, such as heated milk, when they are left to cool. [U] • If your skin is thin/thick you are easily/not easily made unhappy by criticism: *I don't worry about what he says – I've got thick skin/My skin is thick.* ○ See also **thick-skinned** at THICK NOT THIN; **thin-skinned** at THIN NOT THICK. • *He escaped* **by the skin of** *his* **teeth** (= he only just escaped). • *We had no umbrellas so we got* **drenched/soaked/wet to the skin** (= extremely wet) *in the pouring rain.* • *Jack really* **gets under** *my* **skin** (= annoys me) – *he never buys anyone a drink.* • *The loud noise made me* **jump/leap out of** *my* **skin** (= surprised me very much). • *It's* **no skin off** *my* **nose**/*(Am also)* **back/teeth** (= It will not have a negative effect on me) *if we don't go to the football match.* • *She was (nothing but/all/just)* **skin and bone(s)** (= extremely thin). • *(disapproving)* **Skin-deep** means not carefully considered or deeply felt: *They believe that public concern is only skin-deep.* ○ *Beauty is only skin-deep.* ○ *After the first half-hour she realised that her new-found confidence was no more than skin-deep.* • **Skin-diving** is swimming under water with only limited breathing equipment and without a special suit: *The sea was warm and clear, perfect for skin-diving.* ○ *We saw a lot of* **skin-divers** *while we were in the Caribbean.* • *(infml) Our local cinema shows* **skin flicks** *late at night* (= films with a lot of sex in them). • A **skin graft** is skin from one part of the body that is used to replace damaged skin in another part: *After the fire, he had to have a skin graft on his burnt arm.* • **Skin-tight** is used to refer to clothes that fit tightly around the body: *skin-tight jeans* ○ *a skin-tight dress* • PIC› **Fruit** Ⓙ

skin *obj* /skɪn/ *v* [T] **-nn-** • To skin something is to remove its skin: *The hunters skinned the deer they had killed.* ○ *You can skin tomatoes by putting them briefly in hot water.* ○ *I skinned my knee* (= I hurt my knee by rubbing skin off it) *when I fell down the steps.* • *(esp. humorous) My mother will* **skin** *me* **alive** (= will punish me severely) *for being so late home.*

skin·less /'skɪn·ləs/ *adj* [not gradable] • *skinless, boneless fillets of fish* • *Use skinless orange and grapefruit segments to decorate the dessert.* • *I like skinless* **sausages**.

–skin /-skɪn/ *combining form* • *I've got an old sheepskin coat/pigskin bag.* • *The shop had a range of ostrich skin bags and purses.*

–skinned /-skɪnd/ *combining form* • *I'm quite* **fair**/ **dark**-*skinned* (= my skin is pale/dark in colour).

skin·flint /'skɪn·flɪnt/ *n* [C] *infml disapproving* a person who dislikes spending money • *He's a real skinflint.*

skin·ful /'skɪn·fʊl/ *n* [U] *slang* an amount of alcohol that is enough to make a person drunk • *By ten o'clock he'd* **had** *a skinful.* • *My head aches from the skinful I* **had** *last night.*

skin·head /'skɪn·hed/ *n* [C] *disapproving* a young person, esp. a man, who has very short hair, or no hair, and is part of a group which can sometimes be violent • PIC› **Hair**

skink /skɪŋk/ *n* [C] a small lizard found in various hot parts of the world

skin·ny /'skɪn·i/ *adj* **-ier, -iest** *esp. disapproving* very thin • *You should eat more, you're much too skinny.*

skin·ny–dip /'skɪn·i·dɪp/ *v* [I] *infml* to swim while naked • *Jean and I skinny-dipped at night, when most of the other campers were asleep.*

skin·ny–dip·ping /'skɪn·iˌdɪp·ɪŋ/ *n* [U] • *We sometimes* **go** *skinny-dipping.*

skint /skɪnt/ *adj* [after v] **-er, -est** *Br slang* having no money • *I get paid each Friday, and by Tuesday I'm always skint.*

skip MOVE /skɪp/ *v* [I] **-pp-** to move lightly and quickly with small dancing or jumping steps • *The lambs were skipping* **about** *in the field.* • *She watched her little granddaughter skip* **down** *the path.* • *(fig.) This record must be scratched – the needle keeps skipping* (=failing to play part of the record). [I]

skip /skɪp/ *n* [C] • *She gave a little skip* (=a small, light dancing or jumping step) *of joy.* • *a hop, skip and jump*

skip JUMP /skɪp/, *Am* **jump rope, skip rope** *v* [I] **-pp-** to jump lightly over a rope that is held in both your hands, or by two other people, and swung repeatedly under your legs and over your head as exercise or a game • *Sports players often train by skipping.* • *Several children were skipping in the playground.* • *Let's play with the* **skipping rope** *(Am also* **jump rope***)* (=a rope used for skipping). • *The children were chanting a* **skipping rhyme** (=a type of poem which is said as you skip). • PIC› **Playground**

skip *(obj)* LEAVE /skɪp/ *v* **-pp-** to leave (one thing or place), esp. quickly, in order to go to another • *This part of the book isn't very interesting, so I'm going to skip* **(over)** *it.* [T; I + prep] • *The teacher kept skipping* **from** *one subject* **to** *another so it was difficult to follow what he was saying.* [I] • *We're skipping* **over/across/off** (=making a quick journey) *to France for the day.* [I] • *The police think that the bank robbers must have skipped* (=left) **the country** *by now.* [T] • *She skipped* **off/out** (=left quickly and/or secretly) *without saying goodbye.* [I]

skip *obj* AVOID /skɪp/ *v* [T] *infml* to not do or have; avoid • *I'm trying to lose weight, so I'm skipping* (=not eating) **lunch** *today.* • *How do you always manage to skip* (=avoid) *doing the housework?* [+ v-ing] • *"Are you coming to the talk – or shall we skip it?"* • *(esp. Am) "Shall I go through the details again for you?" "Oh, (let's) skip it* (=not do it)*, I'm tired and it's too late."*

skip CONTAINER *Br and Aus* /skɪp/, *Am trademark* **Dump·ster** *n* [C] a large metal container into which people put unwanted items or building or garden waste, and which is brought to and taken away from a place by a special truck when requested • *We hired a skip over the weekend for all the old window frames.* • *They dumped the hedge cuttings in their neighbour's skip.* • PIC› **Building and construction**

skip·per /£ˈskɪp·əʳ, $-ɚ/ *n, v* (to be) the CAPTAIN (=person in charge) of a ship or boat, a sports team, or an aircraft • *The report criticises the skippers* **of** *both vessels involved in the collision for failing to keep a proper lookout.* [C] • *John is (the) skipper* **of** *the cricket team this year.* [C] • *John is skippering the cricket team this year.* [T] • *Ready to go, Skipper.* [as form of address] • LP› **Sports**

skir·mish /£ˈskɜː·mɪʃ, $ˈskɜːr-/ *n* [C] a small fight which is usually short and not planned, and which happens away from the main area of fighting in a war • *We are receiving reports of several skirmishes in the surrounding countryside.* • *(fig.) There was a* **short** *skirmish* (=a short exchange of arguments between opposing groups) **between** *the political party leaders when the government announced it was to raise taxes.*

skir·mish /£ˈskɜː·mɪʃ, $ˈskɜːr-/ *v* [I] • *The rebels are still skirmishing in the hills.* • *Small groups of soldiers were skirmishing* **with** *each other long after the war had ended.* • *(fig.) There was angry skirmishing* (=arguing) *at the meeting yesterday.*

skir·mish·er /£ˈskɜː·mɪʃ·əʳ, $ˈskɜːr·mɪʃ·ɚ/ *n* [C] • *A teacher had to separate the two skirmishers* (=children who were fighting) *in the school playground.*

skirt CLOTHING /£skɜːt, $skɜːrt/ *n* [C] a piece of women's clothing that hangs from the waist and does not have legs • *Short skirts are fashionable again this year.* • The skirt of certain machines is an outer covering or protective part: *The hovercraft was taken out of service when its skirt was damaged.*

skirt *(obj)* EDGE /£skɜːt, $skɜːrt/ *v* to be on or move along the edge (of something) • *Take the road which skirts* **(around/round)** *the village, not the one which goes through it.* [T; I + prep] • *The car had to skirt* **(around/round)** *a large hole in the road.* [T; I + prep] • *(fig.) She skirted* **(around/round)** (=avoided) *the question of what she had been doing the night before.* [T; I + prep]

skirt·ing board *Br and Aus* /£ˈskɜː·tɪŋ, $ˈskɜːr·t̬ɪŋ/, *Am* **base·board** *n* [C/U] (a piece of) wood fixed along the bottom of a wall where it meets the floor • PIC› **Room**

skit /skɪt/ *n* [C] a short amusing play which makes a joke of something • *I thought the skit* **on** *politicians was really funny.*

skit·ter /£ˈskɪt·əʳ, $ˈskɪt̬·ɚ/ *v* [I always + adv/prep] (esp. of a small animal, bird or insect) to move very quickly and lightly • *When I lifted the log, there were lots of beetles skittering* **about/around** *under it.*

skit·tish /£ˈskɪt·ɪʃ, $ˈskɪt̬-/ *adj* (of people and animals) nervous or easily frightened, or (of a person) energetic and restless • *The sale of technology stocks shows just how skittish investors are* **about** *the impact of an economic downturn.* • *My horse is rather skittish, so I have to keep him away from traffic.* • *The first thing he realized was that Marilyn was a complete child, playful and skittish one moment, sulky and withdrawn the next.*

skit·tish·ly /£ˈskɪt·ɪʃ·li, $ˈskɪt̬-/ *adv*

skit·tish·ness /£ˈskɪt·ɪʃ·nəs, $ˈskɪt̬-/ *n* [U]

skit·tle /£ˈskɪt·l̩, $ˈskɪt̬-/ *n* [C] one of a set of bottle-shaped objects which are knocked down with a ball as part of a game • *Peter knocked down six skittles with one throw.* • *Lots of pubs in the West Country have a skittle* **alley** (=a special area for playing the game).

skit·tles /£ˈskɪt·l̩z, $ˈskɪt̬-/ *n* [U] • Skittles is a game played esp. in Britain in which players roll a ball at bottle-shaped objects to try to knock them down and score points. • *"Life isn't all beer and skittles"* (Thomas Hughes in the book *Tom Browne's Schooldays*, 1857)

skive /skaɪv/ *v* [I] *Br infml* to avoid work of any type, esp. by staying away or leaving it early • *I can't find Martin anywhere in the office, he must be skiving.* • *Tom and Mike have skived* **off** *school today to watch the football match.*

skiv·er /£ˈskaɪ·vəʳ, $-vɚ/ *n* [C] *Br infml* • *I bet those skivers* (=people who are avoiding work) *are at home watching telly.*

skiv·vies /ˈskɪv·iz/ *pl n Am infml* men's underwear

skiv·vy SERVANT /ˈskɪv·i/ *n* [C] *Br infml* a person, in the past a female servant, who does the dirty and unpleasant jobs in a house, such as cleaning • *If you think I'm going to be your skivvy and do all the cleaning, you're mistaken.* • *They treat me like a skivvy.*

skiv·vy /ˈskɪv·i/ *v* [I] *Br infml* • *I'm not going to skivvy* (=do the dirty, unpleasant jobs in the house) **for** *you any more.*

skiv·vy CLOTHING /ˈskɪv·i/ *n* [C] *Aus* a tight-fitting item of clothing, made of KNITTED cotton, with a high round collar

skol *obj* /£skɒl, $skɑːl/ *v* [T] **-ll-** *Aus infml* to drink (something, esp. beer) all at once without a pause

sku·a *Br*/ˈskjuː·ə/, **jaeg·er** /£ˈjeɪ·gəʳ, $-gɚ/ *n* [C] a type of large sea bird which lives in the north Atlantic and steals food from other birds

skul·dug·ge·ry *Br and Aus, Am* **skull·dug·ger·y** /£ˌskʌlˈdʌg·ər·i, $-ɚ-/ *n* [U] secret and dishonest behaviour • *There's so much skulduggery in political life these days that you don't know who to trust or believe.* • *There must have been some skulduggery going on for him to have got that job.*

skulk /skʌlk/ *v* [I always + adv/prep] to hide or move around as if trying not to be seen, usually with bad intentions • *I thought I saw someone skulking* **in** *the bushes – perhaps we should call the police.* • *He was skulking over there behind the shed.* • *As I skulked up to the window, I heard the sound of voices.*

skull /skʌl/ *n* [C] the bony part of the head, which surrounds the brain • *The soldiers discovered piles of human skulls and bones.* • *He* **fractured** *his skull in a car accident.* • *(infml) How many times do I have to tell you something before it finally* **gets into your (thick) skull** (=before you understand it). • A **skull and crossbones** is a picture of a skull with two long bones crossing each other underneath it, which warns of death or danger: *A skull and crossbones on a bottle usually means that it contains poison.* ○ *Pirate ships used to* **fly** *the* **skull and crossbones** (=a flag with this sign on it).

skull·cap /ˈskʌl·kæp/ *n* [C] a small round hat that fits closely on the top of the head, worn esp. by religious Jewish men or high-ranking Roman Catholic priests • PIC› **Hats**

skunk /skʌŋk/ *n* [C] a small black and white N American animal that makes a strong unpleasant smell as a defence when it is attacked • *We drove past several squashed skunks.* • *(fig. infml) He's such a skunk* (=an unpleasant, unkind person) *he'd rob his own grandmother.*

sky /skaɪ/ *n* [U] the area above the tallest structures on the Earth, in which clouds, the sun, etc. can be seen • *Can you see those birds high up in the sky?* • *The sky is so clear tonight that you can see lots of stars.* • *We* **looked up** *into the* *sky at the sound of the plane.* • *A dark sky is a sign that it's going to rain.* • *There are tall buildings all around our house, so we can't see very much sky.* • **The sky's the limit** (= There is no limit) *to what you can win in our competition.* • *She was wearing a pretty* **sky-blue** *dress* (= a dress of the bright blue colour of the sky on a sunny day). • *The explosion blew the building* **sky-high** (= blew the pieces up into the sky). • *(fig.) House prices are* **sky-high** (= very high) *this year.* • ⒹⓀ Ⓝ

skies /skaɪz/ *pl n* • *The skies* (= sky) *over the city were* **clear** *for the first time in weeks.* • *It was a sunny Sunday, with* **cloudless blue** *skies* (= weather conditions) *and a pleasantly refreshing breeze.* • *(fig.)We're off to the sunny skies* (= weather conditions) *of Spain.* [C]

sky·cap /ˈskaɪ·kæp/ *n* [C] *Am* a person who carries passengers' bags at an airport or receives them for loading onto an aircraft

sky·div·ing /ˈskaɪˌdaɪ·vɪŋ/ *n* [U] a sport in which a person jumps from an aircraft and falls for as long as possible before opening a PARACHUTE (= a circular cloth with ropes) which allows the jumper to land safely

sky·div·er /£ˈskaɪˌdaɪ·vəʳ, $-vɚ/ *n* [C]

sky·jack *obj* /ˈskaɪ·dʒæk/ *v* [T] to take control of (a flying aircraft) by force, usually in order to make political demands • See also HIJACK.

sky·jack·er /£ˈskaɪˌdʒæk·əʳ, $-ɚ/ *n* [C]

sky·jack·ing /ˈskaɪˌdʒæk·ɪŋ/ *n* • *The number of skyjackings has risen alarmingly this year.* [C] • *Skyjacking has become a major problem for the airlines.* [U]

sky·lark [BIRD] /£ˈskaɪ·lɑːk, $-lɑːrk/ *n* [C] a LARK [BIRD]

sky·lark [ACTIVITY] /£ˈskaɪ·lɑːk, $-lɑːrk/ *v* [I] *dated* to LARK [ACTIVITY]

sky·light /ˈskaɪ·laɪt/ *n* [C] a window built into a roof to let in light • *New skylights made the attic seem bigger and brighter.* • [PIC> **Window**

sky·line /ˈskaɪ·laɪn/ *n* [C] a shape or pattern made against the sky, esp. by buildings • *You get a good view of the New York skyline from the Statue of Liberty.* • [PIC> **Line**

sky·rock·et /£ˈskaɪˌrɒk·ɪt, $-ˌrɑː·kɪt/ *v* [I] to ROCKET

sky·scrap·er /£ˈskaɪˌskreɪ·pəʳ, $-pɚ/ *n* [C] a very tall modern building, usually in a city

sky·ward /£ˈskaɪ·wəd, $-wɚd/, **sky·wards** *adv, adj* [not gradable] in the direction of the sky • *The player hit the ball skyward.* • *He raised his eyes slowly skyward.* • *(fig.) At the news, share-prices shot skyward* (= increased suddenly). • *a skyward direction*

slab /slæb/ *n* [C] a thick, flat piece of a solid substance, such as stone, wood, metal, food, etc., which is usually square or rectangular • *They were housed in a striking white building made of massive* **concrete** *slabs/slabs* **of** *concrete.* • *The top of the table was a polished* **marble** *slab/slab* **of** *marble.* • *We have just laid some* **paving** *slabs in our garden to make a path.* • *He ate a slab* **of** *cheese with some bread.*

slack [NOT TIGHT] /slæk/ *adj* **-er, -est** not tight; loose • *As you grow older your muscles start to get slack.* • *These tent ropes are too slack – they need tightening.* • *People stared in* **slack-jawed** *amazement* (= showed great surprise) *at the light show.*

slack·en *(obj)* /ˈslæk·ᵊn/ *v* • *Slacken* (= loosen) *the reins or you'll hurt the horse's mouth.* [T] • *The paper came off the parcel when the string that had been tied round it slackened* (= became loose). [I]

slack /slæk/ *n* [U] • *There's too much slack* (= looseness) *in these ropes.* • *The men pulled on the ropes to* **take up** *the slack* (= to tighten them). • To **pick up/take up the slack** is to improve a situation in a suitable way: *If the children's parents can't afford the fare, a teacher and I pick up the slack* (= pay the money). • *Some companies have had to look to the home and office furniture markets to pick up the slack* (= find new customers).

slack·ly /ˈslæk·li/ *adv*

slack·ness /ˈslæk·nəs/ *n* [U]

slack [NOT ACTIVE] /slæk/ *adj* showing a lack of activity; not busy or happening in a positive way • **Business** *is always slack at this time of year.* • *The company is to axe 184 jobs because of slack demand for its products.* • *(disapproving) Discipline in Mr Brown's class has become very slack recently.* • *(disapproving) The auditors also found slack procedures in cash offices.* • *(disapproving) The job is taking a long time because the workmen are so slack.*

slack *(obj)* /slæk/ *v infml* • *Everyone slacks* **off/up** *a bit at the end of the week.* [I] • *You'll need to slack* **off/up** (= go more slowly) *as you near the next bend.* [I] • *Slack off speed* (= go more slowly) *as you approach the corner.* [T] • *(disapproving)* It's time you stopped slacking and did some work. [I] • *(disapproving) You'll be in trouble if you're caught slacking on the job like that.* [I]

slack·en *(obj)* /ˈslæk·ᵊn/ *v* • *He stooped to pick it up, without slackening his* **pace** (= without walking more slowly). [T] • *The pace of trading slackened* (= became less) *during the winter months.* [I] • *We expect demand to slacken* **(off)** (= become less) *in the New Year.* [I] • *The car's speed slackened* **(off)** (= became less) *as it went up a steep hill.* [I] • *The plane slackened* **(off)** (= reduced) *speed as it approached the airport.* [T; I + **off**] • *Most people slacken* **off/up** (= work more slowly) *at the end of a day's work.* [I]

slack·er /£ˈslæk·əʳ, $-ɚ/ *n* [C] *infml disapproving* • *Those slackers* (= people who do not work hard enough) *have gone home early again.*

slack·ness /ˈslæk·nəs/ *n* [U] • *Low sales figures were partly because of normal mid-summer slackness in demand.* • *(disapproving) The inspector criticized slackness and incompetence in staff.*

slack [COAL] /slæk/ *n* [U] very small pieces and dust from coal • *The fire won't burn very well if you only put slack on it.*

slacks /slæks/ *pl n dated* a pair of trousers, usually of a type that fit loosely • *He wore smart grey slacks and a dark blue jacket.* • *a pair of slacks*

slag [WASTE] /slæg/ *n* [U] waste material produced when coal is dug from the earth, or a substance produced by mixing chemicals with metal that has been heated until it is liquid in order to remove unwanted substances from it • *The huge heaps of slag warned us that we were approaching a mining area.* • *On cooling, slag becomes glass-like and brittle, and is broken away from the purified metal.* • See also SLAGHEAP.

slag [WOMAN] /slæg/ *n* [C] *Br taboo* a woman whose appearance and behaviour, esp. sexual, are considered unacceptable

slag *obj* [CRITICIZE] /slæg/ *v* **-gg-** *slang* to criticize (someone) • *I don't like the way Ian is always slagging people* **(off)** *when they're not there to defend themselves.* [M]

slag [LIQUID] /slæg/ *n* [U] *Aus infml for* **spit**, see at SPIT [FORCE OUT]

slag·heap /ˈslæg·hiːp/ *n* [C] *esp. Br* a hill made from the waste material from a MINE (= place where coal etc. is removed from underground)

slain /sleɪn/ *past participle of* SLAY

slake *obj* /sleɪk/ *v* [T] to satisfy (a thirst or a desire) • *After our long game of tennis, we slaked our* **thirst** *with a beer.* • *I don't think Dick will ever manage to slake his lust for power.*

slal·om /ˈslɑː·ləm/ *n* [C] a race for people on SKIS (= long flat pieces of wood fastened to boots for moving over snow) or in CANOES (= a long light narrow boat) in which they have to follow a route that bends in and out between poles

slam *(obj)* /slæm/ *v* **-mm-** to (cause to) move against a hard surface with force and usually a loud noise • *The wind made the* **door** *slam.* [I] • *The shutter slammed against the wall.* [I] • *The window slammed* **shut**. [I] • *Close the door carefully, don't slam it.* [T] • *He slammed the* **brakes on** (= used them quickly and with force) *when a child ran in front of his car.* [M] • *She was so angry, she slammed the* **phone down** *on him.* [M] • *I had to stop suddenly, and the car behind slammed* **into** *the back of me.* [I] • *(fig. infml) Although the reviewers slammed* **(into)** *the play* (= strongly criticized it), *the audience loved it.* [T; I + *into*] • If you **slam dunk** (also **dunk**) a BASKETBALL (= a ball used in this game) you score by jumping up and forcing it down into the net: *(fig. Am disapproving) This committee follows democratic procedures – you can't slam dunk* (= force through) *your proposals.*

slam /slæm/ *n* [U] • *The door shut with a slam* (= a sudden loud noise)

slam·mer /£ˈslæm·əʳ, $-ɚ/ *n* [U] **the slammer** *slang* prison • *He's doing five to ten years in the slammer.*

slan·der /£ˈslɑːn·dəʳ, $ˈslæn·dɚ/ *n* a false spoken statement about someone which damages their reputation, or the making of such a statement • *The doctor is* **suing** *his partner* **for** *slander/bringing a slander* **action** *against his partner, on the grounds that she had publicly accused him of sexual harassment.* [U] • *He complained of a systematic campaign of slander against the agency.* [U] • *The article said there is no universally accepted distinction between libel and slander.* [U] • *She regarded his remarks as a slander on her good name.* [C] • Compare LIBEL. • [LP> **Crimes and criminals**

slan·der *obj* /£ˈslɑːn·dəʳ, $ˈslæn·dɚ/ *v* [T] • *The shop assistant was found guilty of slandering* (=harming by speaking a false statement about) *his employer.*

slan·der·er /£ˈslɑːn·dᵊr·əʳ, $ˈslæn·dɚ·ɚ/ *n* [C] • *He wrote to the newspaper, in a furious reply to his organization's slanderers.*

slan·der·ous /£ˈslɑːn·dᵊr·əs, $ˈslæn·dɚ-/ *adj* • *The reporter is said to have made slanderous accusations/allegations* (=remarks containing slander) *about the owner of the newspaper he worked for.*

slan·der·ous·ly /£ˈslɑːn·dᵊr·ə·sli, $ˈslæn·dɚ-/ *adv*

slang [INFORMAL LANGUAGE] /slæŋ/ *n* [U] informal language, which might include words and meanings which are not polite and which might stay in use only for a short time. It is used by particular groups of people who know each other, and is usually spoken rather than written. • *schoolboy slang* • *army slang* • *British slang* • *a slang word* • *a slang expression* • *'Chicken' is slang* **for** *someone who isn't very brave.* • LP **Labels** Ⓢ

slang·y /ˈslæŋ·i/ *adj infml* • *His language is very slangy* (=he uses a lot of slang expressions).

slang *obj* [ATTACK] /slæŋ/ *v* [T] *Br and Aus* to attack with angry, uncontrolled language • *The football players started slanging each other in the middle of the game.* • *The politicians started a* **slanging match** (=an argument in which both people use angry, uncontrolled language) *in the middle of the debate.* • Ⓢ

slant *(obj)* /£slɑːnt, $slænt/ *v* to (cause to) lean in a diagonal position; to (cause to) slope • *Italic writing slants* **to** *the right.* [I] • *That picture needs to be slanted slightly* **to** *the left.* [T] • *The evening sun slanted* (=shone diagonally) **through** *the narrow window.* [I] • *(fig. disapproving) The report on the accident at the power station was slanted* (=expressed in a way that is advantageous to a particular person, group or situation) *to conceal who was responsible.* [T]

slant /£slɑːnt, $slænt/ *n* • *The path has no slant* (=slope) **(to** *it).*/*There is no slant* **to** *the path so water can't run off it.* [U] • *In very old houses the floors and windows are often* **on/at a** *slant* (=are not straight). [U] • *(fig.) I've just read a new book on Mozart which has a very unusual slant* (=way of expressing facts or a situation) **on** *his music.* [C] • *(fig.) Most newspapers have a particular political slant.* [C]

slant·ed /£ˈslɑːn·tɪd, $ˈslæn·t̬ɪd/ *adj* • *They sat relaxed, their slanted fishing-lines taut across the side of the boat.* • *(fig. disapproving) Joe's account of what happened was very slanted.* • *(fig. disapproving) Slanted media coverage is directly influencing how the public responds to the war.*

slant·ing /£ˈslɑːn·tɪŋ, $ˈslæn·t̬ɪŋ/ *adj* • *Swiss chalets have steeply slanting roofs, so that snow does not settle on them.* • *He went out, with a little shiver, into the hard slanting rain.*

slant·wise /£ˈslɑːnt·waɪz, $ˈslænt-/, *Am also* **slant·ways** /£ˈslɑːnt·weɪz, $ˈslænt-/ *adv*

slap [HIT] /slæp/ *n* [C] a quick hit with the flat part of the hand or other flat object, esp. one which makes a noise • *She gave her son a quick slap for behaving badly.* • *We could hear the slap of the waves against the side of the boat.* • *(infml) It was a real* **slap in the face** (=an action showing lack of care or respect) *for him when she refused to go out to dinner with him.* • *(infml) He's won – give him a* **slap on the back** (=show pleasure or praise for what he has done). See also BACKSLAPPING. • *(infml) Lyn was given a* **slap on the wrist** (=a gentle warning or punishment) *for not wearing her seat belt.* • *(Br infml humorous) I think there's a bit of* **slap and tickle** (=playful sexual behaviour) *going on in the back of that car over there.*

slap *obj* /slæp/ *v* [T] **-pp-** • *The mother slapped her son for pulling her daughter's hair.* • *She slapped his face when he put his hand on her knee.* • *She slapped him* **across** *the face.* • *(infml) Her husband has been slapping her* **around** (=hitting her repeatedly), *but she's afraid to go to the police.* • *His friends slapped him* **on the back** *when he said he was getting married* (=hit him lightly on the back in a friendly way to express pleasure at what he had done). • *He slapped the doormat* **against** *the wall to get the dust out.* • *When her ideas were rejected, she slapped her report* **(down)** *on the table and stormed out of the meeting.* • *(fig.) We want to sell our house, so we've slapped some paint* **on** *the outside* (=put it on quickly without taking a lot of care) *to make it look better.*

slap [EXACTLY] /slæp/, *Br also* **slap–bang** /ˌslæpˈbæŋ/ *adv* [not gradable] *infml* directly or right • *The football player kicked the ball slap into the middle of the net.* • *The child sat down slap in the middle of the floor and refused to move.* • See also SMACK [EXACTLY].

slap down *obj*, **slap** *obj* **down** *v adv* [M] to stop (someone) talking or making suggestions, often in an unpleasant way • *I tried to suggest ways in which the plans could be improved, but I was slapped down.*

slap *obj* **on/on·to** *obj v prep* [T] to cause (esp. something unpleasant) to happen • *The government has slapped more tax on cigarettes.* • *The librarian slapped a fine on him* (=caused him to pay money) *for returning the books late.* • *They slapped an injunction on the BBC to prevent them showing the programme.*

slap·dash /ˈslæp·dæʃ/ *adj infml disapproving* done or made in a hurried and careless way • *He gets his work done quickly, but he's very slapdash.* • *Her face was made up in a rather slapdash way.*

slap·hap·py /ˈslæpˌhæp·i/ *adj infml* happily careless and irresponsible • *He's slaphappy in his approach to rules and regulations.*

slap·stick /ˈslæp·stɪk/ *n* [U] a type of amusing acting in which the actors behave in a silly way, such as by throwing things, falling over, etc. • *There's a lot of slapstick in Marx Brothers' films.*

slap–up /ˈslæp·ʌp/ *adj* [not gradable] *Br and Aus infml* (esp. of a meal) large and good • *We went for a slap-up meal on our wedding anniversary.*

slash *(obj)* [CUT] /slæʃ/ *v* to cut with a sharp blade used in a quick strong swinging action • *The museum was broken into last night and several paintings were slashed.* [T] • *Jack the Ripper slashed the bodies of the women he killed.* [T] • *She tried to commit suicide by slashing her* **wrists**. [T] • *We had to slash* **(our way) through** *the long grass to clear a path.* [I/T] • *The gardener slashed* **at** *the overgrown bushes to cut them down.* [I] • *(fig.) You'll never hit the ball if you keep slashing* **at** *it* (=using a careless swinging action) *like that.* [I] • *(fig.) Julie wore a dress with a slashed skirt* (=a skirt made with a decorative cut in it to show a different coloured material in the opening). [T] • *(fig. infml) There are fears that the government is planning to slash* (=strongly reduce) *spending on education.* [T] • *(fig. infml) Prices have been slashed* (=strongly reduced) *by 50%!* [T]

SLASH MARK [/]

The slash mark is also called the stroke or *(Br)* oblique. It is used:

- **to mean 'or'**
  On Tuesdays Kay/Colin will open the mail.
  A doctor gets to know his/her patients quite well.
  Payment by cash/cheque/credit card only.
- **to show that two expressions mean the same**
  Add 8oz/225g sugar and bake at 200°C/400°F.
- **as one way of separating the numbers when writing dates**
  (Br) 16/7/75 (= 16 July 1975)
  (Am) 10/22/90 (= October 22 1990)
- **to mean 'for each' when talking of amounts, prices** (This is spoken as 'per' or 'a'.)
  Standard rates $20/hour or $100/day.
  My car doesn't use much petrol. It does about 40 miles/gallon.
- **to separate lines of poetry when they are not written on different lines**
  The stars must make an awful noise / In whirling round the sky . . .

slash /slæʃ/ *n* [C] • *He has a deep slash* **across** *his face*/**on** *his arm*/**in** *his side, where he was hit by flying glass.* • *(fig.) Ben took a wild slash* (=a long swinging hit) **at** *the ball, and luckily managed to hit it.* • *(fig.) My new dress is pale blue, with a dark blue slash* (=a decorative opening showing a different colour in it) *in the sleeves.* • A slash is also a sloping line used in printing or writing to separate letters or numbers: *You often write a slash between alternatives, as in and/or.* ○ *My reference number is 10/T.*

slash·er /£ˈslæʃ·əʳ, $-ɚ/ *n* [C] *infml* • *The passage describes the slasher* (=person who damages or kills by using a knife) *breaking into a house after midnight to find a* *girl asleep.* • A slasher **book/movie** is a book/film which contains a lot of violence esp. against women who are often seen having their throats cut.

slash [URINATION] /slæʃ/ *n* [U] *Br and Aus slang* the act of excreting urine from the body; urination • *"I need a* **slash***" is an expression used usually by men.*

slat /slæt/ *n* [C] a thin narrow piece of wood, plastic or metal used to make floors, furniture, window coverings, etc. • *Wooden slats cut out the light so that only a soft gloom entered the offices.* • *In today's pig factories, the floors are either metal slats or concrete.* • *The base of the bed was made of slats.*

slat·ted /£ˈslæt·ɪd, $ˈslæt̬-/ *adj* [not gradable] • Slatted means made with slats: *a slatted fence* ○ *slatted floors/doors/windows* ○ *We have a slatted bed.*

slate [ROCK] /sleɪt/ *n* a dark grey rock that can be easily divided into thin pieces • *The trucks were taking slate from the quarry.* [U] • *Several slates* (= small thin square pieces of slate used to cover a roof) *blew off our roof during last night's storm.* [C] • *Our house has a slate roof.*

slate *obj* /sleɪt/ *v* [T] • *We're having our roof slated* (= covered with slates).

slat·y /£ˈsleɪ·ti, $-t̬i/ *adj* **-ier, -iest** • *My new car is a slaty* (= of or like slate) *grey colour.*

slate [FOR WRITING] /sleɪt/ *n* [C] esp. in the past, a small thin rectangular piece of SLATE [ROCK], usually in a wooden frame, on which esp. a school child wrote • *(Br and Aus infml) Could you* **put** *these drinks* **on the slate** (= make a record of them so that they can be paid for later)? • *He served six months in prison for cheating his employer, but is now going back to work with the* **slate wiped clean** (= with his past crimes forgotten).

slate *obj* [CHOOSE] /sleɪt/ *v* [T] *Am and Aus* to choose • *Geoff is slated* **to** *be the next captain of the football team.* [+ obj + *to* infinitive] • *He was made deputy director and is slated* **for** *the directorship when the current director retires.* • *The election is slated* **for** (= the chosen day is) *next Thursday.*

slate /sleɪt/ *n* [C] *Am and Aus* • A slate is the group of people who are chosen by a particular party to take part in an election: *The Republicans are expected to announce their slate tomorrow.* ○ *The senator has not got a full slate* **of** *delegates in New York.*

slate *obj* [ATTACK] /sleɪt/ *v* [T] *Br and Aus infml* to attack by criticizing; to write or say that something is very bad • *Lucy's last book was slated by the critics.*

slath·er *obj* /£ˈslæð·əʳ, $-ɚ/ *v* [T] *esp. Am* to spread thickly or wastefully on • *She slathered lotion* **on/all over** *her body.* • *She slathered her toast* **with** *butter.* • *(fig. Am) He has a habit of slathering his money* **around** (= spending it wastefully).

slat·tern /£ˈslæt·ɜːn, $ˈslæt̬·ɚn/ *n* [C] *old use* a dirty, untidy woman • *(Am)* A slattern is also a woman who has many sexual partners, for pleasure or payment.

slat·tern·ly /£ˈslæt·ɜːn·li, $ˈslæt̬·ɚn-/ *adv* • *slatternly behaviour*

slaugh·ter /£ˈslɔː·təʳ, $ˈslɑː·t̬ɚ/ *n* [U] the killing of many people or animals, often cruelly and unfairly, or in a war • *Hardly anyone escaped the slaughter that followed when the rebels were defeated.* • *We must find ways of reducing the slaughter which takes place on our roads* (= death of many people in motor accidents) *every year.* • *The geese are being fattened for slaughter* (= killing for meat). See also SLAUGHTERHOUSE. • *(fig. infml) Saturday's game was absolute slaughter* (= one team was very easily defeated by the other).

slaugh·ter *obj* /£ˈslɔː·təʳ, $ˈslɑː·t̬ɚ/ *v* [T] • *Thousands of people were slaughtered* (= killed cruelly and wrongly) *in the civil war.* • *Many people believe it is wrong to slaughter animals to make fur coats.* • *In the past, farmers used to slaughter their pigs* (= kill them for meat) *in the autumn, so that they had meat for the winter.* • *(fig. infml) Germany slaughtered* (= easily defeated) *England in last night's football match.*

slaugh·ter·house /£ˈslɔː·tə·haʊs, $ˈslɑː·t̬ɚ-/ *n* [C] *pl* **slaughterhouses** /£ˈslɔː·təˌhaʊ·zɪz, $ˈslɑː·t̬ɚ-/ *esp. Am for* ABATTOIR

Slav /slɑːv/ *n* [C] a member of any of the E European peoples who speak Slavic languages

Slav /slɑːv/, **Slav·ic** /ˈslɑː·vɪk, ˈslæv·ɪk/, **Sla·von·ic** /£sləˈvɒn·ɪk, $-ˈvɑː·nɪk/ *adj* [not gradable]

slave /sleɪv/ *n* [C] a person who is legally owned by someone else, who works as a servant for that person, and who has no personal freedom • *Black slaves used to work on the cotton plantations of the southern United States.* • *I'm tired of being* **treated like a** *slave.* • *(fig.) Since Alan bought a computer, he's become a real slave* **to** *it* (= has become dependent on it). • *(fig.) She's a slave* **of/to** (= is strongly influenced by) *fashion.* • *(infml) My father is a real* **slave driver** (= a person who makes other people work very hard). • *In the past,* **slave labour** (= work done by slaves) *was used in the sugar fields of the West Indies.* • *(infml) It's* **slave labour** (= hard work for little money) *working in that office.* • **The slave trade** was the catching, transporting and selling of Africans as slaves, which happened esp. from the 16th to 19th centuries.

slave /sleɪv/ *v* [I always + adv/prep] *infml* • To slave is to work hard with little or no rest: *We slaved* **(away) at** *the housework and got it done quickly.* • *(humorous) I've been slaving* **over** *a hot stove* (= cooking) *all morning.* • See also ENSLAVE.

slav·er /£ˈsleɪ·vəʳ, $-vɚ/ *n* [C] • In the past, a slaver was a ship used for carrying slaves, or a person who sold slaves. • See also SLAVER.

sla·ve·ry /£ˈsleɪ·vəʳr·i, $ˈ-ɚ-/ *n* [U] • *Slavery* (= the activity of having slaves) *was abolished by the British in 1833.* • *Millions of Africans were sold* **into** *slavery* (= the condition of being a slave) *between the 17th and 19th centuries.*

sla·vish /ˈsleɪ·vɪʃ/ *adj* • *Since he joined the army, Ken has developed a slavish devotion to it* (= he works hard for it and is completely obedient to and dependent on it). • A slavish **translation** or copy of something is exactly like it, without any new characteristics.

sla·vish·ly /ˈsleɪ·vɪʃ·li/ *adv* • *My son slavishly* (= enthusiastically and without criticism) *supports our local football team.*

slav·er /£ˈslæv·əʳ, $-ɚ/ *v* [I] to let liquid come out of the mouth, esp. because of excitement or hunger • *The dog slavered with excitement when told it was time for a walk.* • *(fig. usually disapproving) The gambler was slavering* **over** (= was showing great happiness and excitement about) *all the money he had won.*

slaw /£slɔː, $slɑː/ *n* [U] *Am and Aus infml for* COLESLAW

slay *obj* /sleɪ/ *v* [T] *past simple* **slew** /sluː/ or **slayed**, *past part* **slain** /sleɪn/ *(Br and Aus old use or literary)* to kill in a violent way, or *(Am)* to murder • *(Br esp. old use or literary) St George slew the* **dragon**. • *(Br esp. old use or literary) He became king after slaying Duncan* **in battle** *near Elgin, and in 1050 went on a pilgrimage to Rome.* • *(Am) More than half the 23 438 who died as a result of gun incidents were slain by people they knew.* • *(Am) He was found slain in an alley in the 900 block of P Street NW, in the city's Shaw section.* • *(Am) They tried to organize a memorial service for students slain in the rioting.*

slay·ing /ˈsleɪ·ɪŋ/ *n* [C] *esp. Am* • *The suspect had moved to the Baltimore area several months before the girl's slaying* (= murder).

sleaze·bag /ˈsliːz·bæg/, *Am* **sleaze·ball** /£ˈsliːz·bɔːl, $-bɑːl/, **sleaze** *n* [C] *slang* a person of low standards of honesty or morals

sleaz·y /ˈsliː·zi/ *adj* **-ier, -iest** dirty, cheap and not socially acceptable, esp. relating to moral or sexual matters • *This part of town is full of sleazy bars and restaurants.*

sleaze /sliːz/ *n* • *I didn't enjoy that film – there was too much sleaze* (= activity of a low moral standard) *in it for my liking.* [U] • *(Am slang) A sleaze is a* SLEAZEBAG. [C] • The **sleaze factor** is a part of a situation, esp. a political one, which is of a low standard of honesty or morality.

sled /sled/ *n* [C] *esp. Am for* SLEDGE

sledge *esp. Br* /sledʒ/, *Am usually* **sled** *n* [C] an object used for travelling over snow and ice, which is either a low frame on which people sit or goods are carried, or (also **sleigh**) a carriage-like vehicle, pulled by animals, esp. horses or dogs, with long narrow strips of wood or metal under it instead of wheels • *The children raced down the snow-covered hill on sledges.* • *In the past, sledges were used in Russia for carrying people and goods during the winter.* • PIC› **Winter sports**

sledge /sledʒ/ *v esp. Br* • *It's been snowing, shall we go sledging* (= riding on sledges for pleasure or sport)? [I] • *In some parts of the world the sea freezes in winter, so goods can be sledged across it.* [T]

sledge·ham·mer /£ˈsledʒˌhæm·əʳ, $-ɚ/ *n* [C] a large heavy hammer with a long handle, used for breaking stones or other heavy material, or for hitting posts into the ground, etc. • *(fig.) He tends to tackle problems with a sledgehammer* (= not act carefully or considering other people). • *(fig.) They accused him of sledgehammer tactics.* • If you use **a sledgehammer to crack a nut** you use much more force than is needed: *Fifty police officers to arrest two unarmed men is surely a case of* **using** *a sledgehammer to crack a nut.*

sleek /sliːk/ *adj* **-er, -est** (esp. of hair, clothes or shapes) smooth, shiny and lying close to the body, and therefore looking well cared for; not untidy or with parts sticking out • *The cat had sleek fur.* • *She wore a sleek little black dress.* • *Who owns that sleek black car parked outside your house?* • *(disapproving) He's one of those fat, sleek* (=rich-looking) *businessman types.*

sleek *obj* /sliːk/ *v* [T] • *The cat sleeked her hair* (=made it smooth, shiny and flat) *with her tongue.* • *Before going to the party, he sleeked* **back/down** *his hair* (=made it smooth, shiny and flat) *with hair cream.* [M]

sleek·ly /ˈsliː·kli/ *adv* • *The submarine rose sleekly above the waves.* • *Robert, a sleekly groomed 22-year-old, told us he was our guide for the day.* • *The car is a sleekly styled, comfortable, front-wheel-drive hatchback.*

sleek·ness /ˈsliːk·nəs/ *n* [U]

sleep RESTING STATE /sliːp/ *n* the resting state in which the body is not active and the mind is unconscious • *He reckons he only needs six hours sleep a night.* [U] • *I must* **get** *some sleep – I'm exhausted.* [U] • To **get to** sleep is to succeed in sleeping: *I finally got to sleep at four o'clock this morning.* [U] ○ *I couldn't get to sleep last night for worrying.* [U] • *You'll find that your baby usually* **goes to** (=starts to) *sleep after a feed.* [U] • A sleep is a period of sleeping: *You must be tired after all that driving – why don't you have a little sleep?* [C] ○ *He* **fell into a deep** *sleep.* [C] • *(infml)* You can also say that your arm or leg has **gone to sleep** if you cannot feel or control it, often because you have been sitting or lying for too long in a strange position. • When a pet animal that is ill is killed painlessly because its owners do not want it to suffer, it is sometimes said to be **put to sleep**, to avoid saying it has been killed. • *(infml) Why don't you just* **go back to sleep**? (=It is obvious that you were not listening carefully). • *"The Big Sleep* (=death)*"* (title of a book by Raymond Chandler, 1939) • See also SLEEPWALKER.

sleep *(obj)* /sliːp/ *v past* **slept** /slept/ • *I couldn't sleep because of all the noise next door.* [I] • *I only slept (for) four hours last night.* [I] • *I slept* **late** *on Saturday.* [I] • *We had dinner with Ann and Charles and slept* **the night** *(with them)* (=at their home). [I] • *How can Jayne sleep* **at night** *with all that on her mind!* [I] • If a vehicle, tent, etc. is said to sleep a particular number of people it means that it provides enough space or beds for that number of people to be able to sleep in it: *The caravan sleeps four comfortably.* [T] • If you sleep **in** you sleep until later than usual: *I usually sleep in at the weekends.* [I] • *(infml)* If you sleep **like a log** you sleep very well. [I] • If you say that you are going to sleep **on** a decision you mean that you are going to allow yourself until the next day before you make the final decision about what to do: *We're all tired and none of us can think straight so why don't we go home and sleep on it, eh?* [I] • If you sleep **off** a pain you get rid of it by sleeping: *I can usually sleep off a hangover/headache.* [M] • *(infml)* To sleep **over** is to stay the night in someone else's home: *If you don't want to catch a train home at that time of night you're welcome to sleep over.* [I] ○ See also **sleep-over**. • *(Br)* Someone who sleeps **rough** sleeps outside because they have no home and no money: *Hundreds of kids are sleeping rough in the capital.* [I] • If you sleep **through** a lot of noise or an activity it does not wake you, or keep you awake: *I never heard the storm last night – I slept through it.* [I] ○ *I was so bored that I slept through the second half of the film.* [I] • *(infml)* Someone who **sleeps around** has sex with a lot of different people without having a close or long relationship with any of them. • *(infml)* If two people **sleep together** they have sex: *They started sleeping together a couple of weeks after they met.* • *(infml)* If you **sleep with** someone you have sex with them, usually spending the night with them: *He found out that his wife had been sleeping with his best friend.* • A **sleep-over** is a type of party when several young people stay for the night at a friend's house. • See also OVERSLEEP; SLEEPOUT.

sleep·er /£ˈsliː·pər, $-pɚ/ *n* [C] • *I'm a* **light** *sleeper – the slightest noise wakes me.* • *Don't worry – you won't wake him – he's a* **heavy** *sleeper.* • A sleeper is also a carriage in a train with beds for passengers to sleep in, or one of the beds in this carriage, or the type of train which has these carriages: *I'm travelling overnight so I've booked a sleeper.* ○ *The 11.45 is a sleeper.* • A sleeper is also a person or thing that is suddenly and surprisingly successful after a long period of not achieving anything and sometimes refers to a SPY who only becomes active a long time after being placed in an organization. • See also SLEEPER RING; SLEEPER BLOCK.

sleep·ing /ˈsliː·pɪŋ/ *adj* [not gradable] • *She looked lovingly at the sleeping child.* • A **sleeping bag** is a large thick bag for sleeping in. • A **sleeping car** (also **sleeper**) is a railway carriage containing beds for passengers to sleep in. • *(Br)* A **sleeping partner** *(Am and Aus* **silent partner**) is a partner in a company who does not take an active part in its management, esp. one who provides some of the money. • A **sleeping pill/tablet** is a pill which you take to help you to sleep better. • *(Br)* A **sleeping policeman** is a raised part built across a road which is intended to make people drive more slowly. • **Sleeping sickness** is an African disease which causes fever, severe lack of energy, weight loss and sometimes death. • See also ASLEEP. • PIC› **Road**

sleep·less /ˈsliː·pləs/ *adj* • *I've spent so many sleepless* **nights** (=nights without sleep) *worrying about him.* • *Alone and sleepless* (=not able to sleep) *she stared miserably up at the ceiling.*

sleep·y /ˈsliː·pi/ *adj* **-ier, -iest** • If you are sleepy you are tired and want to sleep: *I had two glasses of wine at lunch and it's made me feel really sleepy.* • A sleepy place is quiet and without much activity or excitement: *They retired to a sleepy little village in the west of Yorkshire.* • See also SLEEPYHEAD.

sleep·i·ly /ˈsliː·pɪ·li/ *adv* • *She stumbled sleepily into the bathroom.*

sleep SUBSTANCE /sliːp/ *n* [U] *infml* a yellowish green substance sometimes found in the corners of the eyes after sleeping • *You haven't washed properly, Lola, you've still got sleep in your eyes.* • *(fig.) I was just* **rubbing/wiping the sleep out of** *my* **eyes** (=waking) *when you called.* • LP› **Feelings and pains**

sleep·er RING /£ˈsliː·pər, $-pɚ/ *n* [C] *Br and Aus* a small gold or silver ring which is worn in an ear which is PIERCED (=has a hole in it) to stop the hole from closing while other EARRINGS are not being worn • *a pair of gold sleepers* • See also **sleeper** at SLEEP RESTING STATE; SLEEPER BLOCK. • PIC› **Jewellery**

sleep·er BLOCK /£ˈsliː·pər, $-pɚ/ *n* [C] *Br and Aus* one of the heavy horizontal blocks that supports a railway track • See also **sleeper** at SLEEP RESTING STATE; SLEEPER RING.

sleep·out /ˈsliːp·aʊt/ *n* [C] *Aus* a small building in a garden or an enclosed outside part of a house which is used for sleeping in

sleep·walk·er /£ˈsliːpˌwɔː·kər, $-ˌwɑː·kɚ/ *n* [C] a person who gets out of bed and walks around while they are sleeping • *My sister is a sleepwalker.*

sleep·walk·ing /£ˈsliːpˌwɔː·kɪŋ, $-ˌwɑː-/ *n* [U] • *Sleepwalking can be very dangerous – people have been known to fall down flights of stairs and out of windows.*

sleep·walk /£ˈsliːp·wɔːk, $-wɑːk/ *v* [I]

sleep·y·head /ˈsliː·pi·hed/ *n* [C] *infml* a person, esp. a child, who is tired and looks as if they want to sleep • *Come on, sleepyhead, let's get you to bed.* [as form of address]

sleet /sliːt/ *n* [U] wet, partly melted falling snow • *The snow had turned to sleet.* • *Driving snow and sleet brought more problems to the county's roads last night.*

sleet /sliːt/ *v* [I] • **It**'*s sleeting.*

sleet·y /£ˈsliː·ti, $-t̬i/ *adj* **-ier, -iest** • *sleety rain*

sleeve ARM COVER /sliːv/, **arm** *n* [C] the part of a piece of clothing that covers some or all of the arm • *I wore that black mini-dress with the short sleeves.* • *You'd better* **roll** *your sleeves* **up** *or you'll get them dirty.* • *(infml)* If you **have** something **up** your **sleeve** you have secret plans or ideas: *If I know Mark he'll have one or two tricks up his sleeve.*

-sleeved /-sliːvd/ *combining form* • *a short/long-sleeved blouse*

sleeve·less /ˈsliːv·ləs/ *adj* [not gradable] • A piece of clothing which is sleeveless has no sleeves: *a sleeveless blouse/dress/jacket*

sleeve PROTECTIVE COVER /sliːv/ *n* [C] *esp. Br* a protective cover • *(Br) Can you put the record back in its sleeve (Am and Aus* **jacket**), *please?* • *(Br)* **Sleeve notes** *(Am* **liner notes**) are information about a performer or a performance that is supplied with a sound recording: *According to the sleeve notes, she recorded all the songs at home in her attic.* • A sleeve is also a tube-shaped protective covering for a part of a machine.

sleigh /sleɪ/ *n* a type of SLEDGE, pulled by animals, esp. horses or dogs • *"To hear sleigh bells in the snow"* (from the song *White Christmas* written by Irving Berlin, 1942)

sleight of hand /slaɪt/ *n* [U] quickness and skill of the hand when performing tricks, or *(fig.)* a piece of skilful trickery • *Most of these conjuring tricks depend on sleight of hand.* • *(fig.) By some statistical sleight of hand the government have produced figures showing that unemployment has recently fallen.*

slen·der /£ˈslen·dəʳ, $-dɚ/ *adj* thin and delicate, often in a way that is attractive • *He put his hands around her slender waist.* • *He had the longer slender fingers of a pianist.* • *The plant's leaves are long and slender.* • Slender can also be used to mean small in amount or degree: *a man of slender* **means** (=without much money) ○ *The chances of settling this dispute through talks seem increasingly slender.*

slen·der·ize *(obj)* /£ˈslen·dᵊr·aɪz, $-dɚ-/ *v Am infml* • If you slenderize you try to get thinner or make a part of your body thinner by eating less food and doing more exercise: *No dessert for me, Krystle, I'm trying to slenderize.* [I] ○ *I've really got to slenderize my legs if I'm going to get into my new pants.* [T]

slen·der·ness /£ˈslen·də·nəs, $-dɚ-/ *n* [U]

slept /slept/ *past simple and past participle of* sleep

sleuth /sluːθ/ *n* [C] *infml* (esp. in films) a DETECTIVE • *Tonight on Channel 4 sees the return of Hercule Poirot, Agatha Christie's famous sleuth.*

sleuth·ing /ˈsluː·θɪŋ/ *n* [U] *infml* • *A bit of sleuthing from our investigative reporter uncovered some interesting information on Mr. Parkinson.*

slew SLAY /sluː/ *past simple of* SLAY

slew LARGE AMOUNT /sluː/ *n* [C usually sing] *Am infml* a large amount or number • *Mr Savino has been charged with three murders as well as a* **whole** *slew* **of** *other crimes.*

slew *(obj)* TURN ROUND *Br and Aus, Am* **slue** /sluː/ *v* [always + adv/prep] to turn or be turned round suddenly and awkwardly • *The car hit a patch of ice and slewed* **around** *violently.* [I] • *He slewed the van to the left to avoid the dog.* [T]

slewed /sluːd/ *adj* [after v] *dated slang* drunk • *By this time I was totally slewed and could scarcely stand up!*

slice PIECE /slaɪs/ *n* [C] a flat, often thin, piece of food that has been cut from a larger piece • *a slice* **of** *bread/cake* • *cucumber/lemon slices* • *Would you like another slice of ham/beef?* • *(fig.) We agreed before we did the deal that we'd both take an equal slice* (= part) *of the profit.* • A slice is also a kitchen utensil with a wide blade which is used for serving pieces of food: *a cake/fish slice* • A film, piece of literature or a play might be described as **a slice of life** if it describes or shows the ordinary details of real life. • *(Aus infml)* If you want a **slice of the cake**, you want a share of any money that is being made from an activity. See also **piece/slice of the action** at ACTION.

slice *obj* /slaɪs/ *v* [T] • *Slice* (= Cut into thin flat pieces) *the onions thinly and fry in butter.* • *Could you slice me a very thin piece of cake/slice a very thin piece of cake* **for** *me?* [+ two objects] • *She sliced* **off** *a piece of sausage.* [M] • *He accidentally sliced the top* **off** *his finger while he was cutting vegetables.* [M] • *(fig.) She watched his slim strong body as it sliced effortlessly through the water* (= moved through it in the way that a knife cuts through something). • *(fig.) Portillo won the race, slicing a magnificent three seconds* **off** (= reducing by three seconds) *the world's fastest time.* [M] • *(esp. Am infml)* **Any way you slice it/No matter how you slice it** means in whatever way the matter is considered: *He shouldn't have hit her, any way you slice it.* • PIC› **Food preparation**

sliced /slaɪst/ *adj* [not gradable] • *sliced bread/ham/tomato* • PIC› **Bread and cakes**

slic·er /£ˈslaɪ·səʳ, $-sɚ/ *n* [C] • A slicer is a machine or other device for slicing particular types of food: *an egg/bread/meat slicer*

slice *obj* HIT /slaɪs/ *v* [T] (in the sports of golf and baseball) to hit a ball so that it goes to one side rather than straight in front • *Sara sliced the ball, sending it a hundred metres or so to the left.* • *In golf, left-handed people slice the ball to the left, but hook it to the right – the opposite is true for right-handed people.* • If you slice the ball in a game of tennis, you hit the bottom of the ball so that it doesn't bounce very high when it hits the ground.

slice /slaɪs/ *n* [C] • *That wonderful backhand slice of Peter's sends the ball where his opponent just can't reach it.*

slick SKILFUL /slɪk/ *adj* **-er, -est** operating or performing skilfully and effectively, without faults and without seeming to need effort • *Manilow gave the slick, polished performance that we've come to expect from his shows.* • *The set for the show is spectacular and there are some impressively slick scene-changes.* • *A slick pass from Eaves to Brinkworth placed the ball neatly in the shooting area.* • *(disapproving)* Slick can mean skilful and effective but lacking sincerity or value: *It was the usual slick production with well-rehearsed, competent performances but without any depth or insight.* ○ *I've learned to mistrust the slick packaging of the modern presidential election campaign.* ○ *It's precisely that sort of slick sales-talk that I mistrust.*

slick OIL /slɪk/ *n* [C] an **oil slick**, see at OIL

slick *obj* MAKE SMOOTH /slɪk/ *v* [T] to cause (hair) to be smooth and close to the head by brushing it flat, often using a substance to make it stick • *He'd slicked his hair* **back** *and he was wearing a new suit.* • *Slick your hair* **down** *with a bit of gel.*

slick MAGAZINE /slɪk/ *n* [C] *Am for* **glossy magazine**, see at GLOSS COVERING • *Hers was the sort of flawless beauty that you only usually saw on the covers of the slicks.*

slick·er /£ˈslɪk·əʳ, $-ɚ/ *n* [C] a **city slicker**, see at CITY

slide *(obj)* MOVE SMOOTHLY /slaɪd/ *v past* **slid** /slɪd/ to (cause to) move smoothly over a surface • *When I was little I used to like sliding on the polished floor in my socks.* [I] • *We've got one of those doors in the kitchen that slides open.* [I] • *He slid the letter into his pocket while no one was looking.* [T] • *We've got sliding* **doors** *in the kitchen.* • A **sliding scale** is a system in which the rate at which something is measured varies as a result of other conditions: *UK income tax is paid on a sliding scale which means that the rate at which you pay tax increases with the level of your income.* • A **slide rule** is a long, narrow device for calculating numbers with a middle part which slides backwards and forward. • LP› **Mathematics**

slide /slaɪd/ *n* [C] • A **mud** or **rock** slide is a sudden movement of a large mass of MUD (= earth) or rock down a hill. • A slide is also a structure for children to play on which has a slope for them to slide down and usually a set of steps leading up to the slope: *Do you want to play on the slide, Joe?* • On a musical instrument or a machine a slide is a part that moves smoothly backwards and forward: *the slide on a trombone* • See also LANDSLIDE FALLING EARTH. • PIC› **Playground**

slide GET WORSE /slaɪd/ *v* [I] *past* **slid** /slɪd/ to go into a worse state, often through lack of control or care • *The dollar slid against other major currencies.* • *Car exports slid by 40% this year.* • *He managed to work quite hard for a while but I fear he's sliding* **back** *into his old habits.* • *I was doing really well with the diet and the exercise at the start of the year but I'm afraid I've* **let it** *slide* (= not tried as hard) *recently.* • See also BACKSLIDE.

slide /slaɪd/ *n* [C usually sing] • *There has been a lot of concern in the City about the pound's recent slide.* • *The government must take measures, he said, to* **halt** *the country's slide* **into** *recession.* • *What we are witnessing is the country's slow slide* **into** *civil war.*

slide PHOTOGRAPHIC FILM /slaɪd/, *specialized* **trans·par·en·cy** *n* [C] a small piece of photographic film in a frame which, when light is passed through it, shows a larger image on a screen or plain surface • *My dad showed us some colour slides of us when we were children.* • *We're going to have a slide show.*

slide PIECE OF GLASS /slaɪd/ *n* [C] a small piece of glass on which you put something in order to look at it through a MICROSCOPE

slide DEVICE FOR HAIR *Br and Aus* /slaɪd/, *Br and Aus* **hair slide**, *Am* **bar·rette** *n* [C] a small, often decorative, fastener which women and girls use in their hair, esp. to hold it back off the face • PIC› **Hair**

slight SMALL IN AMOUNT /slaɪt/ *adj* **-er, -est** small in amount or degree • *There's been a slight improvement in the situation.* • *I've got a slight headache.* • *I haven't the slightest* **idea** *what he's talking about* • *'Does it worry you?' 'Not in the slightest.'* (= Certainly not).

slight·ly /ˈslaɪt·li/ *adv* • *She's slightly taller than her sister.* • *This wine is slightly warm – shall I put it back in the fridge?*

slight THIN /slaɪt/ *adj* **-er, -est** (of people) thin and delicate • *Like most long-distance runners she is very slight.*

slight·ly /ˈslaɪt·li/ *adv* • *He is small and slightly built.*

slight·ness /ˈslaɪt·nəs/ *n* [U]

slight *obj* INSULT /slaɪt/ *v* [T] to insult (someone) by not paying them any attention or treating them as if they are not important • *Observers recalled other times he'd slighted* *his wife, by neglecting to introduce her.* • *It is a powerful job, but he thinks he deserves better and considers that he has been slighted by the company.*

slight /slaɪt/ *n* [C] • *'I'm so sorry I forgot your name just now.' 'It's all right – I didn't take it as a slight.'*

slight·ed /£ˈslaɪ·tɪd, $-t̬ɪd/ *adj* • *I'm afraid I just didn't recognise him – I hope he didn't* **feel** *slighted.* • *The slighted players spoke to the newspapers about their disappointment at having been dropped from the team.*

slim THIN /slɪm/ *adj* **slimmer, slimmest** *approving* (esp. of people) attractively thin • *slim hips/legs* • *She's got a lovely slim figure.* • *How do you keep so slim – is it all the exercise you do?* • *It's quite a slim* **volume** (= thin book) *so it's not too heavy to carry around in your bag.* • *They've only a slim* **chance** *of winning* (= It's not very likely that they'll win). • **Slim pickings** refers to lack of success in obtaining or achieving something: *Buyers who have waited for bargains at the end of the year will* **find** *slim pickings.* ○ *Students who specialize in such fields as accounting, systems analysis and electrical engineering are in demand, she said, but others* **find** *slim pickings.*

slim /slɪm/ *v* [I] **-mm-** • If you slim you try to get thinner by eating less food and taking more exercise: *You haven't got much lunch – are you slimming?* • *He's really slimmed* **down** (= got thinner) *over the last few months.*

slim·mer /£ˈslɪm·əʳ, $-ɚ/ *n* [C] • A slimmer is a person who is trying to get thinner by eating less and doing more exercise: *It's one of the most delicious cakes I've ever tasted but it's certainly not one for slimmers!*

slim·ming /ˈslɪm·ɪŋ/ *n* [U] • *With all the diet-food and books on the market, slimming is big business these days.*

slim·ming /ˈslɪm·ɪŋ/ *adj* • *slimming aids/clubs/magazines* • *(infml)* If people describe a particular food as slimming they mean that it is the type of food that you can eat without getting fat: *Have a salad – that's slimming.*

slim·ness /ˈslɪm·nəs/ *n* [U] • *For dancers, the emphasis is on height and slimness.*

Slim DISEASE /slɪm/ *n* [U] *E African for* AIDS

slime /slaɪm/ *n* [U] a sticky liquid substance which is unpleasant to touch, such as the liquid produced by fish and SLUGS and the greenish brown substance found near water • *The ceiling was mouldy and there was a revolting green slime in between the bathroom tiles.* • *You could see trails of slime where the slugs had been.* • *(slang disapproving)* A **slime ball** is a very unpleasant man whose friendly manner is not sincere in a way that causes you not to trust him: *How can she go out with him – he's such a slime ball!*

slim·y /ˈslaɪ·mi/ *adj* **-ier, -iest** • *I can't stand the slimy feel of seaweed underneath my feet.* • *Although snakes look slimy their skin is actually dry to the touch.* • *(disapproving)* If you describe a person or their manner as slimy you mean that they appear to be friendly in a way that you find unpleasant: *He was the very worst sort of slimy salesman.*

sli·mi·ness /ˈslaɪ·mɪ·nəs/ *n* [U]

slim·line /ˈslɪm·laɪn/ *adj* [not gradable] (of liquid added to an alcoholic drink to make it last longer) containing little or no sugar • *I'll have a gin and slimline* **tonic** *please.*

sling *obj* THROW /slɪŋ/ *v* [T always + adv/prep] *past* **slung** /slʌŋ/ *infml* to throw or drop (something) carelessly • *Don't just sling your bag on the floor!* • *If any of the letters aren't interesting just sling them in the bin.* • *(infml) I'll just sling* **together** *a few things* (= put what I need to take with me in a bag) *and I'll be ready to go.* [M] • *(fig.) She was slung* **out of** (= caused to leave) *college because she never did any work.* • *(infml)* If you sling something to someone you give it or throw it: *Sling me a pen, will you?* [+ two objects] • *(Br slang)* If you **sling** your **hook** you leave somewhere: *She told him to sling his hook.* ○ *Sling your hook, will you!*

sling *obj* HANG /slɪŋ/ *v* [T always + adv/prep] *past* **slung** /slʌŋ/ to hang (something) over something • *I usually sling my jacket* **over** *the back of my chair.* • *Standing by the roadside were groups of soldiers, their rifles slung* **over** *their shoulders.* • *She sat next to him on the sofa, her long legs slung* **over** *his.*

sling SUPPORTING DEVICE /slɪŋ/ *n* [C] a device which uses a strap, piece of cloth, or ropes for supporting, lifting or carrying objects • *His gun was held on his back in a sling.* • *The cylinder was lifted from the seabed in a sling.* • A sling is a device for supporting a broken or damaged arm in which the arm is held in front of the body in a piece of cloth which is tied around the neck: *I had my arm* **in a** *sling after I broke it playing football.* • A sling is also a bag-like device for carrying a baby which is tied to the front or the back of the adult's body: *When Nicki goes shopping, she takes the baby in a sling.* • Sling also refers to a simple weapon used mainly in the past in which a strap held at the ends was used for throwing stones. • *"Whether 'tis nobler in the mind to suffer/ The slings and arrows of outrageous fortune"* (Shakespeare, Hamlet 3.1) • PIC **Medical equipment**

sling·backs /ˈslɪŋ·bæk/ *pl n* women's shoes with a strap around the back of the heel instead of a full covering • *a pair of slingbacks* • PIC **Shoes**

sling·back /ˈslɪŋ·bæk/ [before n] • *slingback sandals*

sling·shot /£ˈslɪŋ·ʃɒt, $-ʃɑːt/ *n* [C] *Am and Aus for* CATAPULT

slink /slɪŋk/ *v* [I always + adv/prep] *past* **slunk** /slʌŋk/ to walk away from somewhere quietly so that you are not noticed • *I tried to slink out of the office so that nobody would see me.* • *(disapproving) He usually slinks off* (= leaves) *at about 3.30 p.m.*

slink·y /ˈslɪŋ·ki/ *adj* **-ier, -iest** *infml* (of music or dancing) slow and suggesting sex, or (of women's clothes) made of delicate or luxurious cloth and fitting the body closely in a way that is sexually attractive • *There's some very slinky dancing going on tonight!* • *The record opens with a slinky ballad.* • *She's bought herself a slinky black dress for the party.*

slink /slɪŋk/ *v* [always + adv/prep] *past* **slunk** *infml* • If a person, esp. a woman, slinks they move in a way that is intended to be sexually attractive: *She slunk (her way) past the admiring customers at the bar.* [T/I]

slip SLIDE /slɪp/ *v* [I] **-pp-** to slide unintentionally • *I held her firmly by the arm in case she slipped on the ice.* • *Careful you don't slip – there's water on the floor.* • *She slipped while she was getting out of the bath.* • *My foot slipped off the pedal and I grazed my leg on my bike.* • *The razor slipped while he was shaving and he cut himself.* • A **slipped disc** is a medical condition in which one of the DISCS (= flat pieces of body tissue between the bones in the back) slides out of its usual place, causing pain in the back. • **Slip-ons** are shoes with no fastenings which can be quickly put on and taken off: *a pair of slip-ons* ○ *slip-on shoes* • PIC **Motorway** Ⓓ Ⓔ Ⓕ Ⓖⓡ Ⓘ Ⓙ

slip·py /ˈslɪp·i/ *adj* **-ier, -iest** *infml* • A surface that is slippy causes you to slip easily because it is wet, smooth or oily: *Careful – I've just polished the floor and it's a bit slippy.* • See also SLIPPERY.

slip *(obj)* DO QUICKLY /slɪp/ *v* **-pp-** to go somewhere or carry out an action quickly, often so that you are not noticed • *Just slip out of the room while nobody's looking.* [I] • *I'm just going to slip to the shops before lunch.* [I] • *If you could wait two minutes I'm just going to slip* **into** *a smarter dress.* [I] • *She slipped* **into** *the cool cotton sheets and was soon asleep.* [I] • *She slipped her hand* **into** *his.* [T] • *He slipped a piece of paper* **into** *my hand with his address on it.* [T] • *You don't need to go into the changing rooms – just slip the jacket* **on** *over your sweater.* [T] • *If nobody's at home just slip the key through the letter box.* [T] • *If you slip the waiter some money/slip some money* **to** *the waiter he'll give you the best table.* [+ two objects] • *"Excuse me while I slip into something more comfortable"* (said by Jean Harlow in the film *Hell's Angels*, 1930) • Ⓓ Ⓔ Ⓕ Ⓖⓡ Ⓘ Ⓙ

slip GET WORSE /slɪp/ *v* [I] **-pp-** to go into a worse state, often because of lack of control or care • *Their standard of living has slipped steadily over the last ten years.* • *Productivity in the factory has slipped quite noticeably in the last year.* • Ⓓ Ⓔ Ⓕ Ⓖⓡ Ⓘ Ⓙ

slip·page /ˈslɪp·ɪdʒ/ *n* [U] • Slippage is reduction in the rate, amount or standard of something: *A faulty machine has caused slippage in the tunnel-building project.* ○ *The party leader is said to be concerned at the slippage* (= loss of popularity) *in the recent opinion polls.*

slip PIECE OF PAPER /slɪp/ *n* [C] a small piece of paper • *She wrote my address on a slip* **of paper**. • *If you want to order a book fill in the green slip (also* **form**). • *(dated) Keep that slip (also* **receipt**) *somewhere safe as proof of purchase.* • Ⓓ Ⓔ Ⓕ Ⓖⓡ Ⓘ Ⓙ

slip MISTAKE /slɪp/ *n* [C] a small mistake • *She's* **made** *one or two slips – mainly spelling errors – but it's basically well written.* • *I suffered the embarrassment of calling her new boyfriend by her previous boyfriend's name – it was just a* **slip of the tongue** (= mistake made by using the wrong word). • A **slip-up** is a mistake or something which goes wrong: *Make sure all the arrangements are correct – I don't want any slip-ups.* • Ⓓ Ⓔ Ⓕ Ⓖⓡ Ⓘ Ⓙ

slip up *v adv* [I] • *These figures don't make sense – have we slipped up somewhere?*

slip [UNDERWEAR] /slɪp/ *n* [C] a piece of underwear for a woman or girl which is like a dress or skirt, or a pair of UNDERPANTS for a man or a boy • (D) (E) (F) (GR) (I) (J)

slip *obj* [ESCAPE] /slɪp/ *v* [T] **-pp-** to get free from, leave or escape (something) • *The ship slipped its moorings.* • *Write the name down so that you remember or it'll* **slip through the crack** (= be forgotten). • If you let an opportunity or a person **slip through** your **fingers** you lose it or them through lack of care or effort: *You're surely not going to let a job/man like that slip through your fingers!* • If something **slips** your **memory/mind** you forget it: *I forgot I'd arranged to meet Richard last night – it completely slipped my mind.* • A *(Br)* **slip road** (*Am and Aus* **ramp**) is a short road by which you enter or leave a MOTORWAY (= a main road for fast travel). • (D) (E) (F) (GR) (I) (J)

slip /slɪp/ *n* [U] *infml* • If you **give** someone **the slip** you escape from them: *If you're not interested in a bloke you can always give him the slip in a bar as crowded as that.*

slip [SMALL] /slɪp/ *n* [U] **slip of a** *dated* small and thin, usually because young • *I knew her when she was but a slip of a* **girl**. • *She was just a little slip of a* **thing**. • (D) (E) (F) (GR) (I) (J)

slip·case /ˈslɪp·keɪs/ *n* [C] a protective case for a book, usually made of cardboard, with one open end

slip·co·ver /£ˈslɪpˌkʌv·əʳ, $-ɚ/ *n* [C] a removable cover for a chair or SOFA (= chair for two or more people)

slip·knot /£ˈslɪp·nɒt, $-nɑːt/ *n* [C] a knot that can easily be untied by pulling one of its ends

slip·per /£ˈslɪp·əʳ, $-ɚ/ *n* [C] a type of soft comfortable shoe for wearing inside the house • *a pair of slippers* • *furry slippers* • *He came to the door in an old dressing gown and slippers.* • [PIC] **Shoes** (D)

slip·pe·ry /£ˈslɪp·ᵊr·i, $ˈ-ɚ-/ *adj* **-ier, -iest** wet, smooth or oily so that it slides easily or causes something to slide • *slippery soap* • *It had been raining and the road was slippery.* • *(infml disapproving)* A person who is slippery is one you do not feel you can trust: *He's as slippery* **as an eel** *– you can never get a straight answer out of him.* ○ *He's a slippery* **customer** (= person), *that Tim, I've never felt comfortable with him.* • A **slippery slope** is a bad situation or habit which, after it has started, is likely to get very much worse: *You're* **on a**/*It's a slippery slope once you start drinking alcohol on your own!*

slip·shod /£ˈslɪp·ʃɒd, $-ʃɑːd/ *adj disapproving* (esp. of a piece of work) showing lack of effort and attention; without care • *She complained that the solicitor's work had been slipshod.*

slip·stream /ˈslɪp·striːm/ *n* [C] a current of air behind a quickly moving object such as a car travelling extremely fast or an aircraft

slip·way /ˈslɪp·weɪ/ *n* [C] a slope from which boats are put into or taken out of the water, or a place where they are built

slit *obj* /slɪt/ *v* [T] **slitting**, *past* **slit** to make a long straight narrow cut in (something) • *He slit open the envelope with a knife.* • *She killed herself by slitting her wrists.* • *He was found the next day with his throat slit.* • *She was wearing one of those skirts that's slit up the front.*

slit /slɪt/ *n* [C] • A slit is a long straight narrow cut or opening in something: *There was an unfortunate slit in the back of his trousers.* ○ *I could see that it was getting light through the slits in the blind.*

sli·ther /£ˈslɪð·əʳ, $-ɚ/ *v* [I always + adv/prep] to move (the body) smoothly while twisting or curving • *She watched the lizard as it slithered over the rock.* • *She watched the passers-by outside as they slipped and slithered on the ice.* • *It is the slithering motion of the snake that frightens me.*

sli·ver /£ˈslɪv·əʳ, $-ɚ/ *n* [C] *fml* a very small thin piece of something, usually broken off something larger • *She found a sliver* **of** *glass where she had dropped the bowl the night before.* • *Just a sliver* **of** *cake for me, please – I shouldn't really be having any.*

Sloane (Rang·er) /£sləʊn, $sloʊn/ *n* [C] *Br infml disapproving* a young person from a high social class who lives usually in or near London, wears expensive, traditional clothes and speaks with an **upper-class** voice • *We went to this dreadful restaurant full of Sloanes.*

Sloane·y /£ˈsləʊ·ni, $ˈsloʊ-/ *adj* **Sloanier, Sloaniest** *Br infml disapproving* • *She was wearing one of those Sloaney green jackets.*

slob /£slɒb, $slɑːb/ *n* [C] *infml disapproving* a lazy person, esp. one who is untidy and unattractive • *He's a big* **fat** *slob of a man – I can't stand him.* • *"I didn't get up till midday." "You slob!"* [as form of address]

slob a·round /£slɒb, $slɑːb/, **slob a·bout** *v adv* [I] *infml esp. disapproving* • If you slob around you behave very lazily, doing very little: *We didn't do much on Sunday – just slobbed around in front of the TV.* ○ *He won't get a job and just slobs around all day.*

slob·bish /£ˈslɒb·ɪʃ, $ˈslɑː·bɪʃ/ *adj infml disapproving*

slob·ber /£ˈslɒb·əʳ, $ˈslɑː·bɚ/ *v* [I] *disapproving* to let SALIVA (= the liquid in the mouth) or food run out of the mouth • *My grandmother is rather old and senile and she tends to slobber* **over** *her dinner.* • *(fig. infml)* To slobber **over** someone is to show too much admiration and liking for them in a way that shows a lack of pride or control of yourself: *All the blokes were slobbering over Amanda's sister who happens to be very pretty and blonde.*

slob·ber·y /£ˈslɒb·ᵊr·i, $ˈslɑː·bɚ-/ *adj* **-ier, -iest** *disapproving* • *He gave me a big slobbery* (= wet) **kiss** *on the lips – I nearly died!*

sloe /£sləʊ, $sloʊ/ *n* [C] a small blueish-black fruit which tastes sour • **Sloe gin** is a drink made from GIN with sloes in it. • [PIC] **Berries**

slog [WORK HARD] /£slɒg, $slɑːg/ *v* [I always + adv/prep] **-gg-** *infml* to work hard, physically or mentally, over a long period, esp. doing work that is not interesting • *I've been slogging* **away** *for days on the same piece of work and I'm still no nearer finishing.* • *We slogged* **on** *with the digging until it grew dark.* • *I'm afraid we've still got to slog* **on** (= keep on walking or travelling) *for another six miles yet.*

slog /£slɒg, $slɑːg/ *n* [U] *infml* • *The exams were* **a** *real* **hard** *slog but I'm glad I did them.* • *That last hill before the finishing-line was* **a** *long slog!*

slog *obj* [HIT HARD] /£slɒg, $slɑːg/ *v* [T] **-gg-** *infml* in the sports of cricket and boxing, to hit (the ball or the other boxer) hard and often in an uncontrolled way • *Thompson slogs the ball right out of the ground!*

slog /£slɒg, $slɑːg/ *n* [C] *infml* • A slog is a very hard, and often uncontrolled hit: *And that was a real slog from Kumar.*

slog·ger /£ˈslɒg·əʳ, $ˈslɑː·gɚ/ *n* [C] *infml* • In cricket or boxing a slogger is a person who hits the ball or the person he is boxing against very hard.

slo·gan /£ˈsləʊ·gən, $ˈsloʊ-/ *n* [C] a short easily remembered phrase intended to bring an idea or a product to public notice • *'Coke, it's the real thing' is an example of a slogan.*

slo·gan·eer·ing /£ˌsləʊ·gəˈnɪə·rɪŋ, $ˌsloʊ·gəˈnɪr·ɪŋ/ *n* [U] *esp. Am disapproving* • *Without a coherent set of policies to persuade the electorate, the Republicans have resorted to sloganeering and empty rhetoric.*

slop *(obj)* /£slɒp, $slɑːp/ *v* **-pp-** (of a liquid) to SPILL (= pour out by mistake) over the edge of a container, or to cause this to happen through lack of care or rough movements • *Careful, you've just slopped coffee all over the carpet!* [T] • *Oh hell, I've slopped wine all down my new shirt!* [T] • *Water slopped out of the bucket as he carried it up the stairs.* [I always + adv/prep] • See also SLOPS.

slop a·round, **slop a·bout** *v adv* [I] *infml* to relax and do very little • *Jeans are all right just for slopping around the house but I don't wear them for work.*

slop out *v adv* [I] *Br* (esp. of prisoners) to empty the containers used as toilets during the night

slope /£sləʊp, $sloʊp/ *n* [C] a surface which lies at angle to the horizontal so that some points on it are higher than others • *The garden was on a south-facing slope which caught the sun.* • *The roof is at a slope* (= at an angle to a horizontal surface) *of 30°.* • A slope is also (part of) the side of a hill or mountain: *Snow had settled on some of the higher slopes.* ○ *There's a very* **steep** *slope just before you reach the top of the mountain.* ○ *There are some nice* **gentle** *slopes that we can ski down.* ○ *It was a beautiful day and there were lots of people on the* **ski** *slopes.*

slope /£sləʊp, $sloʊp/ *v* [I] • *The path slopes* **up/down** *to the house.* • *Our school football pitch sloped at the south end, so one half of the game always had to be played uphill.* • *Her hair is cut so that it slopes forward* (= is longer at the front than the back).

slop·ing /£ˈsləʊ·pɪŋ, $ˈsloʊ-/ *adj* • *sloping handwriting/shoulders* • *The bedroom is in the roof so it's got a sloping ceiling.*

slope off *v prep* [I] *Br and Aus infml* to leave somewhere quietly so that you are not noticed, esp. in order to avoid work • *I saw you sloping off just after lunch yesterday!*

slope·head /£ˈsləʊp·hed, $ˈsloʊp-/, **slope** *n* [C] *Am and Aus taboo slang* a person from SE Asia. This word is considered offensive by most people.

slop·py TOO WET /£ˈslɒp·i, $ˈslɑː·pi/ *adj* **-ier, -iest** *infml disapproving* (of a substance) more liquid than it should be, often in a way that is unpleasant • *The mixture was a bit sloppy so I added some more flour.* • A sloppy **kiss** is a wet kiss: *He planted a big sloppy kiss on my hand – it was revolting.* • See also SLOPPY LACKING CARE and SLOPPY EMOTIONAL.

slop·py LACKING CARE /£ˈslɒp·i, $ˈslɑː·pi/ *adj* **-ier, -iest** *disapproving* lacking care or effort • *Spelling mistakes always look sloppy in a formal letter.* • *Another sloppy pass like that might lose them the whole match.* • A sloppy piece of clothing is large, loose and informal: *At home I tend to wear big sloppy jumpers and jeans.*

slop·pi·ly /£ˈslɒp·ɪ·li, $ˈslɑː·pɪ-/ *adv disapproving* • *Their clothes are so sloppily made – they fall to bits after you've worn them a couple of months.*

slop·pi·ness /£ˈslɒp·ɪ·nəs, $ˈslɑː·pɪ-/ *n* [U]

slop·py EMOTIONAL /£ˈslɒp·i, $ˈslɑː·pi/ *adj* **-ier, -iest** *disapproving* expressing feelings of love in a way that is silly or embarrassing • *People were dancing to sloppy love songs.*

slops /£slɒps, $slɑːps/, **slop** *n* [U] liquid or wet food waste, esp. that which is fed to animals • *We feed the slops to the pigs.* • *There's a tray under each tap to catch the beer slops.* • *(infml disapproving)* Slop can refer to food that is unpleasant and more liquid than it should be: *Have you tried the slop that they call curry in the canteen?*

slosh /£slɒʃ, $slɑːʃ/ *v* [always + adv/prep] *infml* (of a liquid) to move around noisily in the bottom of a container, or to cause liquid to move around in this way by making rough movements • *When you go round a corner you can hear the petrol sloshing about in the tank.* [I] • *I could hear you sloshing around in the bath.* [I] • *We sloshed through the puddles.* [I] • *I'm just sloshing the water* **about** *in my glass so that the tablet dissolves.* [T] • *(infml) She sloshed* (= poured without care) *some more brandy into her glass.* [T]

sloshed /£slɒʃt, $slɑːʃt/ *adj* [after v] *slang* drunk • *He looks sloshed to me.*

slot LONG HOLE /£slɒt, $slɑːt/ *n* [C] a long narrow hole, esp. one for putting coins into or for fitting a separate piece into • *I put my money in the slot and pressed the button but nothing came out.* • *The frame has slots into which you can fit the shelves.* • A **slot machine** (also **one-armed bandit**, *Br and Aus also* **fruit machine**, *Aus also* **poker machine**) is a machine that you try to win money from by putting coins into it and operating it, often by pressing a button or pulling a handle. • *(Br and Aus)* A **slot machine** is also a **vending machine**. See at VENDING.

slot *(obj)* /£slɒt, $slɑːt/ *v* **-tt-** • *I see – the legs of the chair are meant to slot* **into** *the hole at the back.* [I] • *Slot piece A* **into** *piece B, taking care to keep the two pieces at right angles.* [T]

slot·ted /£ˈslɒt·ɪd, $ˈslɑː·t̬ɪd/ *adj* [not gradable] • A slotted kitchen utensil or tool has long narrow holes in it: *a slotted spoon/spatula/screw*

slot AMOUNT OF TIME /£slɒt, $slɑːt/ *n* [C] an amount of time which is officially allowed for a single event in a planned order of activities or events • *We had to fly around the airport waiting for a landing slot.* • *The programme will occupy that half-hour slot before the nine o'clock news.* • *It's becoming increasingly difficult to fill the advertising slots.*

slot *obj* /£slɒt, $slɑːt/ *v* [T] **-tt-** • *Doctor Meredith is busy this morning but she might be able to slot you* **in** (= find time to talk to you) *around one o'clock.*

sloth NO EFFORT /£sləʊθ, $sloʊθ/ *n* [U] *literary* unwillingness to work or make any effort; LAZINESS • *The report criticizes the government's sloth in tackling environmental problems.* • *By mid-afternoon Sunday I'm usually overcome by sloth and spend the rest of the day in bed.* • *Sloth is one of the seven deadly sins.*

sloth·ful /£ˈsləʊθ·fᵊl, $ˈsloʊθ-/ *adj literary* • *The woman in the tent next to us seemed to spend half the day shouting at her two slothful adolescent sons.*

sloth ANIMAL /£sləʊθ, $sloʊθ/ *n* [C] an animal with long arms which moves slowly and spends much of its time hanging upside down from the branches of a tree • *the three-toed sloth* • *Sloths live in Central and South America.*

slouch /slaʊtʃ/ *v* [I] to stand, sit or walk with the shoulders hanging forward and the head bent slightly over so that you look tired and bored • *Straighten your back – try not to slouch.* • *A couple of boys were slouched over the table reading magazines.* • *A group of teenagers were slouching around outside the building.* • *"And what rough beast, its hour come round at last, / Slouches towards Bethlehem to be born?"* (W.B.Yeats in the poem *The Second Coming*, 1920)

slouch /slaʊtʃ/ *n* • *He's developed a slouch from leaning over his books all day.* • *(infml)* If you say that someone **is no slouch** at a particular activity you mean that they work hard at it and produce good results: *She's no slouch when it comes to organizing parties.*

slouch hat *n* [C] *Am and Aus* a hat made from soft material which has a soft brim and is worn esp. by soldiers

slough /slaʊ/ *n literary* a mental state of deep sadness and hopelessness • *She seems unable to pull herself out of this deep slough* **of** *self-pity.* • *"The name of the slough was Despond"* (John Bunyan in *Pilgrim's Progress*, 1678)

slough *obj* **off** /slʌf/ *v prep* [T] *(literary)* to get rid of (something not wanted), or *(specialized)* (of snakes and other REPTILES) to get rid of (the old skin) • *(literary) He seemed to want to slough off* (= get rid of) *all his old acquaintances.*

slo·ven·ly /ˈslʌv·ᵊn·li/ *adj* untidy and dirty • *She's got that slightly slovenly appearance – I don't think she ever brushes her hair or irons her clothes.* • *I'll have to improve my slovenly habits – my mother's coming to stay.*

slo·ven·li·ness /ˈslʌv·ᵊn·lɪ·nəs/ *n* [U]

slow /£sləʊ, $sloʊ/ *adj* **-er, -est** moving or happening without speed • *I noticed how slow her movements were.* • *We're making rather slow progress with the decorating.* • *She's the slowest driver I've ever seen.* • *If I walk any slower, I'll be going backwards!* • *The service in here is so slow – I've been waiting for a coffee for fifteen minutes!* • *The slow train takes twenty minutes more than the express because it stops at so many stations.* • *Unfortunately the government was very slow* **to** *react to the problem.* [+ *to* infinitive] • *Business is always slow during those months because everyone's on holiday.* • *I drive in the slow* **lane** *of the motorway* (= the one intended for cars driving slowly). • You might describe a film, book, play, etc. as slow if it lacks excitement and action: *His films are so slow they send me to sleep.* • A person might be described as slow if they are not very clever and do not understand or notice things quickly: *He's so slow – I have to explain everything fifty times!* ○ *I feel so slow when I'm with Andrew – he's so much brighter than me.* ○ *I was a bit slow* **off the mark/on the uptake** *there – I didn't follow his reasoning at all.* ○ See also **slow-witted**. • If a clock or watch is slow, it shows a time that is not correct and is earlier than the real time: *That clock is ten minutes slow.* ○ *I think my watch must be slow.* • *(esp. Am)* A **slow burn** is a slow, controlled show of anger and deep dissatisfaction: *When it was first suggested that the park might be built on, the citizens* **did** *a slow burn.* • *(Br)* A **slow handclap** is a slow, regular clap, used by a crowd watching a performance, football match etc. to show their annoyance. • **Slow motion** (*esp. Am* **slow-mo** or **slo-mo**) is action that is intentionally made to appear slower than it was when it happened: *They showed the goal* **in** *slow motion.* ○ *We watched a slow motion film of a ballet dancer doing pirouettes.* • Someone who is **slow-witted** is not clever and does not notice or understand things quickly: *She's very nice but I'm afraid rather slow-witted.* • *"I'd love to get you / On a slow boat to China, / All to myself, alone"* (from the song *Slow Boat to China* written by Frank Loesser, 1948) • PIC› **Motorway**

slow /£sləʊ, $sloʊ/ *adv* **-er, -est** • *If the action in a film is too slow-***moving** *I get fed up with it.* • *Who was the slow-speaking bloke with the dark hair and glasses?* • *He walks so slow it drives me mad.*

slow /£sləʊ, $sloʊ/ *v* • To slow is to reduce speed or activity: *All the cars have to slow at the bend.* [I] ○ *The traffic slowed* **to a crawl** (= went so slowly it almost stopped) *at the roadworks.* [I] ○ *Drivers on main roads are to be slowed to 50 mph in the first reduction in national speed limits since the 1970s.* [T] ○ *Last year, growth in the economy slowed* **to** *2%* (= only increased by 2% after larger increases before). [I] ○ *This year the issue of new models has slowed* **to a trickle** (= very few have been produced). [I] ○ *Slow* **down/up**, *you two, you're walking too fast!* [I] ○ *Slow* **down/up** *– I can't follow what you're saying when you speak so fast!* [I] ○ *We slowed* **down/up** *because we saw the police.* [I] ○ *The doctor has told him to slow* **down/up** (= be less active and relax more) *or he'll have a heart-attack.* [I] ○ *If I run with Christina she tends to slow me* **down/up** (= make me run more slowly). [T] ○ *They slowed the film* **down** *to see if they could identify any of the faces.* [M] • See also SLOWDOWN.

slow·ly /£ˈsləʊ·li, $ˈsloʊ-/ *adv* • *She speaks very slowly.* • *The traffic is moving very slowly ahead of us.* • **Slowly but surely** means carefully in order to avoid problems: *Slowly but surely we made our way down the hillside.*

slow·coach *Br and Aus* /£ˈsləʊ·kəʊtʃ, $ˈsloʊ·koʊtʃ/, *Am* **slow·poke** /£ˈsləʊ·pəʊk, $ˈsloʊ·poʊk/ *n* [C] *infml* someone, esp. a child, who is walking or doing something too slowly • *Come on, slowcoach, we haven't got all day you know!* [as form of address]

slow·down /£ˈsləʊ·daʊn, $ˈsloʊ-/ *n* [C] a reduction in speed, activity or the rate that things are produced • *The president anticipated a worldwide economic slowdown.* • Slowdown is also *Am for* **go-slow**. See at GO OPERATE.

slow·worm /£ˈsləʊ·wɜːm, $ˈsloʊ·wɜːrm/ *n* [C] a small brownish-grey LIZARD with no legs, found in Europe

SLR (cam·era) /£ˌes·elˈɑːʳ, $-ɑːr/ *n* [C] single lens reflex camera

sludge /slʌdʒ/ *n* [U] soft wet earth or earth-like matter • *We seemed to spend the last mile of the walk knee-deep in sludge.* • *Sometimes a mixture of* **sewage** *sludge is spread directly on farmland as fertilizer.*

sludg·y /ˈslʌdʒ·i/ *adj* **-ier, -iest** *disapproving* • *The lasagne turned out to be a sludgy mess of overcooked pasta and bland sauce.*

slue *(obj)* /sluː/ *v* [I/T always + adv/prep] *Am for* SLEW TURN ROUND

slug CREATURE /slʌg/ *n* [C] a small, usually black or brown, creature with a long soft body and no arms or legs, like a SNAIL but with no shell • *I found a slug in my lettuce!* • *(esp. Am infml)* A slug is a slow-moving, lazy person: *Come on, do something for once – you're such a slug!* ○ See also SLUGGISH. • **Slug pellets** are small hard pieces of a substance which is poisonous to slugs. • PIC **Mollusc, Worm**

slug BULLET /slʌg/ *n* [C] *infml* a bullet • *The poor guy wound up with a slug in his stomach.*

slug AMOUNT OF DRINK /slʌg/ *n* [C] *infml* a mouthful of drink, esp. strong alcoholic drink • *I had a slug* **of** *vodka to give me courage.*

slug *obj* HIT /slʌg/ *v* [T] **-gg-** *infml* to hit (someone) hard with the FIST (= closed hand) • *She slugged him and he fell against the bar.* • *(Aus) They slugged me* (= charged me a lot of money) *for the car repairs.* • If two people **slug it out** they fight or argue fiercely until one of them wins: *If a couple can't settle these matters between them they tend to slug it out in the courts.*

slug COIN /slʌg/ *n* [C] *Am* a piece of metal used instead of a coin for putting in machines

slug·gish /ˈslʌg·ɪʃ/ *adj* moving or operating more slowly than usual and with less energy or power • *A heavy lunch makes me sluggish in the afternoon.* • *Something is wrong with the car – the engine feels a bit sluggish.* • *The housing market has been very sluggish these past few years.*

slug·gish·ly /ˈslʌg·ɪʃ·li/ *adv*

slug·gish·ness /ˈslʌg·ɪʃ·nəs/ *n* [U]

sluice /sluːs/, **sluice·way** /ˈsluːs·weɪ/ *n* [C] an artificial channel for carrying a quickly flowing current of water, which has an opening at one end to control the flow of the water • *The water rushed through the sluice* **gates** *of the dam.* • NL

sluice *(obj)* /sluːs/ *v* • If water sluices out from somewhere it flows in large amounts: *Water sluiced out from the pipes.* [I always + adv/prep] • If you **sluice down/out** something you wash it with large amounts of running water: *We had to sluice out the garage to get rid of the smell of petrol.* [M]

slum /slʌm/ *n* [C] a very poor and crowded area, esp. of a city, where the houses are in an extremely bad state and the living conditions are very low • *She was brought up in the slums of Lima.* [C] • *Slums housing many of the city's 2 million residents are swelling alarmingly.* [C] • *Most of the villages in the north of the country are virtually rural slums.* [C] • *Over half of the inhabitants of this city live in slum conditions.* [U] • *(infml disapproving)* A slum can also be a very untidy or dirty place: *This flat would be an absolute slum if I wasn't here to clean it.* [C]

slum /slʌm/ *v* [I] **-mm-** *infml* • To slum **(it)** is to stay in conditions which are much lower than the standard that you are used to: *We ran out of money towards the end of the holiday so we had to slum it in cheap hostels.*

slum·my /ˈslʌm·i/ *adj* **-ier, -iest** • *She found herself in a slummy back street.*

slum·ber /£ˈslʌm·bəʳ, $-bɚ/ *n* [U] *poetic* sleep • *I was lulled back into slumber by the gentle sound of the river.* • *(fig.) Sharp cuts in interest rates have failed to bring the economy out of its slumber.*

slum·bers *pl n poetic* • *I didn't want to rouse you from your slumbers* (= wake you).

slum·ber /£ˈslʌm·bəʳ, $-bɚ/ *v* [I] *poetic* • *He slumbered after lunch, under the willow tree.*

slump REDUCE SUDDENLY /slʌmp/ *v* [I] (of prices, values or sales) to fall suddenly • *The value of property has slumped.* • *Car sales have slumped dramatically over the past year.*

slump /slʌmp/ *n* [C] • *There has been a slump in demand for beef ever since the recent health scare.* • *The hotel industry, like most industries, is currently* **in a slump.** • Slump is another word for DEPRESSION (= a period when the economy is in a bad state and there is a lot of unemployment): *There are fears that we are entering another economic slump as bad as the 1930's.*

slump SIT/FALL /slʌmp/ *v* [I always + adv/prep] to sit or fall heavily and suddenly • *She slumped into the chair, exhausted.*

slumped /slʌmpt/ *adj* • *He sat slumped* (= sitting with round shoulders and head low as if extremely tired) *over his desk, staring vacantly at the keyboard.*

slung /slʌŋ/ *past simple and past participle of* SLING

slunk /slʌŋk/ *past simple and past participle of* SLINK

slur *obj* PRONOUNCE BADLY /£slɜːʳ, $slɜːr/ *v* [T] **-rr-** to pronounce (the sounds of a word) in a way which is unclear, uncontrolled or wrong • *The brace on his teeth made him slur his s's slightly.* • *Her* **speech** *was slurred but she still denied she was drunk.*

slur /£slɜːʳ, $slɜːr/ *n* [U] • *The drug affected her vision and made her speak with* **a** *slur.*

slur CRITICISM /£slɜːʳ, $slɜːr/ *n* [C] a critical remark which is likely to have a harmful effect on the reputation of the person it is made about • *Her letter contained several outrageous slurs* **against/on** *her former colleagues.* • *His comments* **cast** *a slur* **on** *the integrity of his employees.*

slur *obj* /£slɜːʳ, $slɜːr/ *v* [T] **-rr-** • *The report fails to give a complete picture of the school and slurs both the teachers and pupils.*

slurp *(obj)* /£slɜːp, $slɜːrp/ *v infml* to drink (a liquid) noisily as a result of sucking air into the mouth at the same time as the liquid • *Do try not to slurp.* [I] • *I wish you wouldn't slurp your soup like that.* [T] • *He stuffed the sandwich into his mouth and slurped* **down** *his coffee.* [M] • When a thick liquid slurps, it moves slowly, making loud noises: *The lava is slurping down the mountainside, burying everything in its path.* [I]

slurp /£slɜːp, $slɜːrp/ *n* [C] *infml* • *She paused to take a slurp* **of** *tea and then ate the rest of her cake.*

slur·ry /£ˈslʌr·i, $ˈslɜːr-/ *n* [U] a mixture of water and small pieces of a solid, esp. such a mixture used in an industrial or farming process • *To produce the paper used for printing newspapers, wood chips are mixed with water and ground to a slurry.* • *Farm slurry is a mixture of animal excrement, urine and water which can be used as fertilizer.*

slush SNOW /slʌʃ/ *n* [U] snow that is lying on the ground and has started to melt • *In summer, skiing is limited to the higher glaciers, but even here the snow turns to slush by noon.*

slush·y /ˈslʌʃ·i/ *adj* **-ier, -iest** • *The snow on the lower slopes is hard in the early morning, but slushy by the afternoon.*

slush ROMANTIC LANGUAGE /slʌʃ/ *n* [U] language or writing that is too emotional and romantic and lacks any real importance or meaning • *When she recorded the song, she rewrote the lyrics and replaced the* **sentimental** *slush with something more meaningful.*

slush·y /ˈslʌʃ·i/ *adj* **-ier, -iest** • *There's nothing I like more than curling up in bed with a slushy novel.*

slush fund *n* [C] a sum of money that is available for paying for dishonest or illegal activities in politics or business • *He used his party's slush fund to buy votes in the election.*

slut SEXUALLY ACTIVE WOMAN /slʌt/ *n* [C] *disapproving* a woman who has sexual relationships with a lot of men without any emotional involvement • *If a man sleeps with a lot of women he's called a stud, but if a woman sleeps with a lot of men she's called a slut.* • *I saw you coming out of his room, you slut!* [as form of address]

slut·tish /£ˈslʌt·ɪʃ, $ˈslʌṭ-/, **slut·ty** /£ˈslʌt·i, $ˈslʌṭ-/ *adj disapproving* • *She was very glamorous when she was younger, but now she wears too much make-up and is starting to look sluttish.*

slut [LAZY WOMAN] /slʌt/ *n* [C] *disapproving* a woman who is habitually untidy and lazy • *She's a real slut and never does any housework.*

slut·tish /£ˈslʌt·ɪʃ, $ˈslʌt̬-/, **slut·ty** /£ˈslʌt·i, $ˈslʌt̬-/ *adj disapproving*

sly [SECRETIVE] /slaɪ/ *adj* **slyer, slyest** avoiding letting other people know what you are thinking or intending to do or have done • *"You'll find out eventually," said Mary with a sly* **smile**. • *He's a sly* **one**! *He kept his inheritance secret for ten years.* • *When he referred to people not paying their fair share, I think he was having a sly* (= not openly expressed) *dig at me.* • *(Aus infml)* **Sly grog** is illegally sold alcoholic drink.

sly /slaɪ/ *n* [U] • If you do something **on the sly** you do it secretly because you should not be doing it: *He drives his mother's car on the sly while she's out at work.*

sly·ly /ˈslaɪ·li/ *adv* • *She grinned slyly and refused to tell me where the money came from.*

sly·ness /ˈslaɪ·nəs/ *n* [U]

sly [DECEIVING] /slaɪ/ *adj* **slyer, slyest** *disapproving* able to deceive people in a clever way • *Upton's a sly old devil. I wouldn't trust him with my money.*

sly·ly /ˈslaɪ·li/ *adv disapproving* • *She slyly slipped a shot of vodka into his beer when he wasn't looking.*

sly·ness /ˈslaɪ·nəs/ *n* [U] *disapproving*

sly·boots /ˈslaɪ·buːts/ *n* [C] *pl* **slyboots** *infml* a person who avoids letting other people know what he or she is thinking or intending to do or has done • **You** *old slyboots! Why didn't you tell us about your new girlfriend?* [as form of address]

SM /ˌesˈem/ *n* [U], *adj abbreviation for* SADOMASOCHISM or SADOMASOCHISTIC • *The vast majority of people who enjoy SM fantasies do not inflict real pain on each other.*

smack *obj* [HIT FORCEFULLY] /smæk/ *v* [T] to hit (someone) forcefully with your hand when it is flat, producing a brief loud noise, esp. in order to punish a child • *I never smack my children, no matter how naughty they are.* • *I'll smack your* **bottom** *if you don't behave yourself.* • *(esp. Am infml)* To smack something is to hit it forcefully: *Trammell smacked the ball deep into the left-field seats for a home run.* • ⓘ

smack /smæk/ *n* [C] • *You're going to get a smack* **on** *the bottom if you don't stop being such a naughty boy.* • *(infml)* Sometimes if you **give** someone a smack, you hit them with your hand closed: *He was being cheeky, so I gave him a smack* **on** *the jaw.* • *(infml)* If someone **gives** you a smack **on** the cheek, lips, etc., they kiss you briefly on the face, producing a loud noise: *"Thank you very much," said Frank, giving his aunt a loud smack on the cheek.*

smack *obj* [PUT NOISILY] /smæk/ *v* [T always + adv/prep] to put (something which is hard and not easily broken) forcefully onto a hard surface, producing a brief loud noise • *She smacked her books* **down** *on the table and stormed out of the room.* • If you **smack** your **lips** you close and open your mouth loudly to express a strong desire to eat something you like a lot: *"I adore chocolate cake," said Susannah, smacking her lips.* • ⓘ

smack /smæk/ *n* [C] • *She slammed her case down on the desk with a smack.*

smack [EXACTLY] /smæk/, *Br also* **smack–bang** /ˈsmæk·bæŋ, ˌ-ˈ-/, *Am also* **smack–dab** /ˈsmæk·dæb/ *adv* [before adv/prep; not gradable] exactly in a place • *She lives smack in the middle of London.* • ⓘ

smack [DIRECTLY] /smæk/, *Br also* **smack–bang** /ˈsmæk·bæŋ, ˌ-ˈ-/, *Am also* **smack–dab** /ˈsmæk·dæb/ *adv* [before adv/prep; not gradable] directly and forcefully, producing a brief loud noise • *I wasn't looking where I was going and walked smack into a lamppost.* • *He lost control of the car and drove smack into the garden gate.* • ⓘ

smack [DRUG] /smæk/ *n* [U] *slang* HEROIN • *How long has she been* **on** *smack?* • *He's had a smack* **habit** *since he was seventeen.* • A **smack head** is a person who regularly takes HEROIN. • ⓘ

smack of *obj v prep* [T] to seem to possess (a characteristic or quality that is not considered to be desirable) • *He doesn't want a long-term relationship and avoids* **anything** *that smacks of commitment.* • *The minister's unexpected statement smacked of desperation.* • *The whole affair smacks of mismanagement and incompetence.*

smack·er [MONEY] /£ˈsmæk·əʳ, $-ɚ/ *n* [C usually pl] *infml* a POUND or DOLLAR • *It cost me fifty smackers to get that window fixed.*

smack·er [KISS] /£ˈsmæk·əʳ, $-ɚ/ *n* [C] a loud or long kiss • *I was really embarrassed when she gave me a smacker in front of my parents.*

smack·er [LIPS] /£ˈsmæk·əʳ, $-ɚ/ *n* [C] *Am* the lips or the outer part of the mouth • *She was so rude about my dress that I hit her* **on** *the smacker.* • *He was really surprised when I gave him a kiss* **on** *the smacker.*

small [LIMITED] /£smɔːl, $smɑːl/ *adj* **-er, -est** limited in size or amount when compared with what is typical or average • *I'd rather live in a village or small town than a big city.* • *People in richer countries tend to have smaller families.* • *San Marino is the world's oldest and smallest republic.* • *That jacket's too small* **for** *you.* • *He's small* (= not tall) **for** *his age.* • *I really like mushrooms, especially small ones.* • *A replacement would be very expensive, but it would cost a* **relatively** *small* **amount** *of money to repair it.* • *The government has promised to reduce the tax burden on small* **businesses**. • *Small* **doses** *of ultra-violet radiation cause sunburn, and larger doses cause skin cancer and eye cataracts.* • *So far, they've raised only a small* **fraction** *of the money needed to restore the church.* • *The size of the military budget is only a small* **percentage** *of national income.* • *The number of women in parliament is* **pitifully** (= extremely and disappointingly) *small.* • *I'm on a diet, so I only want a small* **portion** *of potatoes.* • *Only a small* **proportion** *of people who have been baptized are practising Christians.* • *Liqueurs have a high alcohol content, and are usually drunk* **in** *small* **quantities** *after a meal.* • *He admitted possession of a small* **quantity** *of cannabis and was fined £75.* • *The city's medieval streets are* **too small to** *handle so much traffic.* • If someone should be **grateful/thankful for small mercies**, they should be grateful for something although it is not as good as they would like: *We've only raised a quarter of the money we needed, but I suppose we must be thankful for small mercies.* • The **small of** your **back** is the narrow part in the middle of the lower back where it curves in slightly: *He punched me* **in** *the small of my back.* • *(infml)* **A small fortune** is a large sum of money: *She'll inherit a small fortune when her father dies.* ○ *You'll have to* **spend** *a small fortune in legal fees if you decide to sue for compensation.* • **Small arms** are small light guns that are designed to be held in the hand when fired: *The helicopter made a crash landing after being hit by small arms* **fire**. • **Small change** is money that is in the form of coins of low value: *Remember to take some small change to use at the launderette.* ○ *(fig.) Fuel costs are small change* (= not particularly expensive) *compared to the other expenses of running a car.* • **Small claims** are legal actions that are taken against people who owe or are believed to owe a small amount of money: *The shop only agreed to give me a refund when I threatened to take them to the small claims* **court**. • The **small hours** are the early hours of the morning, between twelve o'clock at night and the time when the sun rises: *She was up until* **the** *small hours of the morning trying to finish her essay.* ○ *It was well into the* **wee** *small hours before we arrived home.* • The **small intestine** is the upper part of the bowels in which food is digested before it travels to the lower part of the bowels where water is removed from it. • *(disapproving)* Someone who is **small-minded** has a limited view of the world and refuses to consider ideas which do not suit their own opinions: *It's small-minded of you not to support the campaign.* ○ *He has some very small-minded opinions about foreigners.* ○ *She moved to London to get away from the* **small-mindedness** *of the people in the village where she grew up.* • **Small print** (also **fine print**) is text in a formal agreement which is printed smaller than the rest of the text partly in the hope that it will not be noticed because it contains rules or information that will be disadvantageous to the person signing the agreement: *Don't sign anything until you've* **read** *the small print.* ○ *The details of the extra charges were buried in the small print.* • The **smallest room** is *Br and Aus infml for* the toilet. • The **small screen** is television, esp. when compared with cinema: *She has had countless roles in movies and plays but her new detective series will be her debut on the small screen.* • *The film explores the life of* **small-town** *America* (= life in small American towns where ordinary simple people live) *in the 1930s.* • *(saying)* People say 'It's a small world' to show their surprise that people or events in different places are connected: *So you know my old science teacher! Well, it's certainly a small world, isn't it?* • *"Small is Beautiful"* (*A Study of Economics as if People Mattered* by E.F. Schumacher, 1973) • PIC **Body** Ⓓ (DK)

small /£smɔːl, $smɑːl/ *adv* **-er, -est** • *The instructions are printed so small I can hardly read them.*

small·ness /£ˈsmɔːl·nəs, $ˈsmɑːl-/ *n* [U] • *The smallness of the city often surprises first-time visitors.*

small YOUNG /£smɔːl, $smɑːl/ *adj* **-er, -est** being a very young child that is older than a baby • *Looking after small children can be very tiring.* • *You used to love fish fingers when you were small.* • *She's too small to understand what she's done.* • (D) (DK)

small LACKING IMPORTANCE /£smɔːl, $smɑːl/ *adj* **-er, -est** not having much importance or effect • *Talking to her always makes me* **feel** *small* (= unimportant and stupid). • *He's always trying to make me* **look** *small* (= foolish and unimportant) *in front of my girlfriend.* • *It was small* **consolation** (= not very comforting) *that three of her colleagues had also lost their jobs.* • *After five years with the company she hadn't been promoted. Small* **wonder** (= It is not surprising) *then that she decided to quit her job and become self-employed.* • *(infml)* If something is **small beer** or *(Am)* **small potatoes** it seems unimportant when it is compared to something else: *The insurance premium is small beer* **compared** *to what we'd have to pay if the house burnt down.* • **Small fry** are people or things that are not considered to be important: *The police have failed to catch the leaders of the gang, although they have arrested some of the small fry.* • **Small talk** is social conversation about unimportant things, often between people who do not know each other well: *I don't enjoy parties where I have to* **make** *small talk with complete strangers.* • Someone or something that is **small-time** has limited involvement in an activity and is therefore not very important: *He's well-known to the police as a small-time* **crook**. ○ *He built up his leisure empire from a small-time restaurant.* ○ *The police are arresting the* **small-timers** *when they should be going for the ringleaders.* • (D) (DK)

small LIMITED ACTIVITY /£smɔːl, $smɑːl/ *adj* [before n] **-er, -est** limited in the amount of an activity • *The government should give more help to small businessmen and women* (= people whose businesses are of a limited size). • *Chris is quite a small* **eater** *so he won't want much.* • *If you can help us in a small* **way** (= to a limited degree) *it would be greatly appreciated.* • (D) (DK)

small LETTER SIZE /£smɔːl, $smɑːl/ *adj* [before n; not gradable] (of a letter) having the size and shape that in Western writing is not usually used at the beginning of a sentence or name • *The poet e. e. cummings preferred his name to be written with small letters, not capital letters.* • *(fig.) It's been claimed that most trade unionists are conservatives, with a small 'c'* (= they like the established ways of doing things, but do not support the Conservative party). • (D) (DK)

small·hold·ing /£ˈsmɔːlˌhəʊl·dɪŋ, $ˈsmɑːlˌhoʊl-/ *n* [C] *Br* an area of land that is used for farming but which is much smaller than a typical farm • *For thirty years she has grown strawberries and raspberries on her five-acre smallholding.*

small·hold·er /£ˈsmɔːlˌhəʊl·dəʳ, $ˈsmɑːlˌhoʊl·dɚ/ *n* [C] *Br* • *Many smallholders will be unable to afford the rent increases.*

small·pox /£ˈsmɔːl·pɒks, $ˈsmɑːl·pɑːks/ *n* [U] an extremely infectious viral disease which causes a fever, spots that leave marks on the skin and sometimes death • *In 1979, as a result of a worldwide vaccination effort, it was declared that smallpox had been eradicated from the planet.*

smalls /£smɔːlz, $smɑːlz/ *pl n Br dated infml humorous* underwear, esp. when being washed or about to be washed • *Have you got any smalls that need washing?*

smarm·y /£ˈsmɑː·mi, $ˈsmɑːr-/ *adj* **-ier, -iest** *infml disapproving* extremely polite, respectful or helpful in a way which is intended to be attractive but which fails to seem sincere • *She was trying to be friendly, but she just seemed smarmy and insincere.* • *He has a smarmy charm that some women find irresistible.*

smarm *obj* /£smɑːm, $smɑːrm/ *v* [T] • *He's always trying to smarm his way into a promotion.*

smar·mi·ly /£ˈsmɑː·mɪ·li, $ˈsmɑːr-/ *adv infml disapproving* • *"Certainly, madam," he replied smarmily.*

smart STYLISH /£smɑːt, $smɑːrt/ *adj* **-er, -est** *Br and Aus, or Am dated* having a clean, tidy and stylish appearance • *Guy* **looks** *very smart in his new suit, doesn't he?* • *Is this jacket smart enough for my interview?* • *They looked very attractive in their smart uniforms.* • *The clothes are designed to appeal to professional women who want to look smart but sexy.* • *She works in a very smart* **new office** *overlooking the River Cam.* • People who belong to the **smart set**, or to **smart society** or **smart circles**, are stylish, fashionable, rich and often artistic or well educated: *The nightclub is popular with Berlin's smart set.* ○ *His plays were popular with the masses but frowned upon by smart society.* ○ *It's not the kind of music that I would admit to listening to in smart circles.* • A place or event that is smart attracts fashionable, stylish or rich people: *Chris took me to a very smart restaurant to celebrate our wedding anniversary.* ○ *We went to a very smart party on New Year's Eve.* • (J) (T)

smart·ly /£ˈsmɑːt·li, $ˈsmɑːrt-/ *adv Br and Aus, or Am dated* • *We're expected to* **dress** *smartly for work.* • *Paul's always very smartly* **dressed**.

smart·ness /£ˈsmɑːt·nəs, $ˈsmɑːrt-/ *n* [U] *Br and Aus, or Am dated* • *Interviewers are usually impressed by a candidate's smartness.*

smar·ten up *(obj)*, **smar·ten** *(obj)* **up** /£ˈsmɑː·tᵊn, $ˈsmɑːr·t̬ᵊn/ *v adv* • If you smarten something up you make it smart: *She's really smartened* **herself** *up since she left university.* [T] • *You'll have to smarten up if you want to work in television.* [I] • *A lot of money has been spent on smartening up the town centre.* [M] • *The car wasn't in very good condition when we bought it, but we've managed to smarten it up quite nicely.* [M] • *Why are you always so late for work? You'll have to* **smarten up** *your* **act** (= make more effort) *if you want to keep your job.*

smart CLEVER /£smɑːt, $smɑːrt/ *adj* **-er, -est** intelligent, or able to think quickly or cleverly in difficult situations • *Gemma's teacher says she's one of the smartest kids in the school.* • *Why don't you fix it if you're so smart?* • *I ain't smart enough to understand computers.* • *He's smart enough to know he can't run the business without her.* • *Quitting that job was the smartest* **move** *I ever made.* • *(infml)* A **smart alec/aleck** is someone who annoys other people by trying to appear to be cleverer and more knowledgeable than them: *I'm fed up with being bossed around by those smart alecs from the university.* ○ *He's just a smart-aleck know-all who thinks he's got all the answers.* • *(infml)* A **smart ass**/*(Br and Aus also)* **smart arse** is a clever or highly qualified person who thinks he or she knows the solutions to everyone's problems and is too eager to tell other people what to do: *I don't want some smart ass from the city telling me how to manage my farm.* ○ *He's a real smart arse and reckons he knows all the answers.* ○ *I've had enough of your smart-assed remarks about how I should live my life.* • A **smart bomb** is a bomb which is directed to the object it is intended to hit by a television signal or a LASER. • A **smart card** is a small plastic electronic card with a computer memory which can be carried conveniently and is used to make payments and to store personal information which can be read when connected to a computer system: *The smart card has quite a large memory so that it can record every purchase that is made with it.* ○ *A smart card is necessary to decode some satellite television broadcasts.* • **Smart drugs** are drugs which are designed to make you more intelligent or help you think more clearly. • **Smart money** is money that is invested by experienced investors who know a lot about what they are doing: *The smart money is* **on** *a rise in the stock market over the next year.* ○ *(fig.) The smart money says* (= The experts believe) *she will win the world championship.* ○ *(fig.) The smart money is* **on** *humans landing on Mars in the first half of the 21st century.* • *(Am infml)* If someone says you have a **smart mouth** they mean you are too clever and lack respect in what you say: *I don't want to hear any more of your smart mouth for the rest of the afternoon!* • (J) (T)

smart·y–pants /£ˈsmɑː·ti·pænts, $ˈsmɑːr·t̬i-/ *n* [C] *pl* **smarty-pants** *infml* • A smarty-pants is someone who wants to appear to be clever: *He makes out he's such a smarty-pants, but I reckon he's pretty stupid.* ○ *Okay, smarty-pants, tell me how to do it.* [as form of address]

smart QUICK /£smɑːt, $smɑːrt/ *adj* [before n] **-er, -est** done quickly with a lot of force or effort • *She gave him a smart smack on the bottom and told him not to be so rude.* • *We'll have to work at a smart pace if we're going to finish on time.* • (J) (T)

smart·ly /£ˈsmɑːt·li, $ˈsmɑːrt-/ *adv* • *I cuffed him smartly on the ear and sent him home.* • *The good economic news caused share prices to rise smartly this afternoon.* • *The Prime Minister has* **moved** *smartly to minimise the effects of the scandal.*

smart STING /£smɑːt, $smɑːrt/ *v* [I] to cause someone to feel a stinging pain • *My eyes were still smarting* **from** *the tear gas the day after the demonstration.* • *(fig.) Be nice to*

Bob – he hasn't stopped smarting **from** (=being upset about) *Mary's criticism of his advertising campaign.* • *(fig.) Conservationists are* **still** *smarting from their failure to prevent the road being built through ancient woodland.* • *(fig.) France are still smarting* **at** *their defeat in the European championship by Italy.* • LP **Feelings and pains** Ⓙ Ⓣ

smash *(obj)* BREAK NOISILY /smæʃ/ *v* (to cause something) to break noisily into a lot of small pieces • *Fragments of a guitar smashed by the late American rock star Jimi Hendrix have been auctioned for £29 700.* [T] • *The burglar broke in by smashing a pane of* **glass** *in the back door.* [T] • *The police were powerless as the rioters ran through the city centre, smashing shop* **windows**. [T] • *She dropped her cup and watched it smash* **to pieces/to smithereens** *on the stone floor.* [I] • *He threatened to come and smash the place* **up** *if I didn't pay him the money.* [M] • *In the sixties he was famous for taking drugs and smashing* **up** *hotel rooms.* [M] • *The aid workers arriving in the smashed-up villages cannot believe the scale of the devastation.* • *(fig.) How did you feel when you smashed* (=broke, esp. by a large amount) *the world record for the 100 metres?* [T] • *Nuclear bombs are designed to* **smash the atom** (=divide an atom into the parts that it consists of). • *(Br and Aus)* During a **smash-and-grab raid** thieves break the window of a shop and steal the things behind it before running or driving away very quickly.

smash /smæʃ/ *n* [U] • *I was woken by the smash of glass.*

smash *(obj)* MOVE FORCEFULLY /smæʃ/ *v* (to cause something) to move with great force against something hard, usually causing damage or injury • *Several boats were smashed against the rocks during the storm.* [T] • *When I locked myself in the bathroom, he became really angry and tried to smash the door* **down**. [M] • *Bulldozers were used to smash* **through** *a barricade of vehicles that had been built by the demonstrators.* [I] • *The car was travelling very fast when it smashed* **into** *the tree.* [I] • *He tried to smash me* **in the face** *with a glass because I trod on his foot.* [T] • *He threatened to smash* **my face in** *if I didn't give him the money.* [T] • *The batsman smashed the ball* (=hit it very hard) *to the boundary for four.* [T] • In tennis, to smash the ball is to hit it quickly and forcefully before it bounces by raising the arm high above the head and then quickly bringing it down towards the ground: *Her opponent tested her with a lob, and she decided to smash (it).* [I/T]

smash /smæʃ/ *n* [C] • *The cars collided with a loud smash.* • A smash or a **smash-up** is a road or train accident: *He hasn't driven since his* **car** *smash two years ago.* ○ *The inquiry will establish whether the smash was due to driver error or signal failure.* ○ *There was a terrible smash-up on the motorway this morning.* • In tennis, a smash is made by hitting the ball down quickly and forcefully from a position high above the head: *Heacock won the match with a powerful smash from the baseline.*

smash *obj* DESTROY /smæʃ/ *v* [T] to defeat or destroy completely (an activity or organization that is disapproved of) • *The company is determined to smash all opposition to the factory closures.* • *The government has said it will take whatever action is necessary to smash the rebellion by separatist guerrillas.* • *Petersen smashed the 400m record by over half a second.*

smash (hit) /smæʃ/ *n* [C] an extremely popular and successful song, play or film • *The film grossed over $100 million, making her the first woman to direct a smash hit in Hollywood.* • *Her first movie was an international* **box-office** *smash.* • *Seats for Woodford's latest smash-hit production are booked up months in advance.*

smashed /smæʃt/ *adj* [after v] *slang* extremely drunk or powerfully affected by illegal drugs • *I feel like going out and* **getting** *really smashed tonight.* • *He was so smashed he could hardly stand up.*

smash·ing /ˈsmæʃ·ɪŋ/ *adj dated infml, esp. Br* extremely good, attractive, enjoyable or pleasant • *There's a smashing view from her office.* • *Jonathan would make a smashing dad.* • *You've made a smashing* **job** *of the wallpapering.* • *He* **looks** *smashing in his dinner suit.* • *This wine is smashing value at £3·50 a bottle.* • *We had some smashing parties when I was a student.*

smash·er /£ˈsmæʃ·əʳ, $-ɚ/ *n* [C] *Br dated infml* • A smasher is someone who is very attractive: *Aunt Eva thinks Adrian's a real smasher.*

smat·ter·ing /£ˈsmæt·ər·ɪŋ, $ˈsmæt̬·ɚ-/ *n* [C usually sing] a very small amount or number • *She speaks fluent French and has a basic smattering* **of** *German.* • *I've only got a smattering of experience with computers.* • *There's only a smattering of people who oppose the proposal.*

smear *obj* SPREAD /£smɪəʳ, $smɪr/ *v* [T always + adv/prep] to spread (a thick liquid or a soft sticky substance) over a surface • *In protest at their treatment, the prisoners smeared excrement* **on** *the walls of their cells/smeared the walls of their cells* **with** *excrement.* • *It cost me $300 to remove the paint that some vandal had smeared* **over** *my car.* • *Can you explain why the front of your car is smeared* **with** *blood?*

smear /£smɪəʳ, $smɪr/ *n* [C] • *You'd look very stylish if it wasn't for that smear* **of** *ketchup on your shirt.* • A **smear (test)** (*Am and Aus* **pap smear**) is an examination of cells contained in the thick liquid on the surface of a woman's CERVIX (=entrance to the womb) to discover if there is any disease: **Cervical** *smears help to show abnormalities which might lead to cancer before any obvious symptoms have appeared.*

smear ACCUSATION /£smɪəʳ, $smɪr/ *n* [C] an accusation which is unpleasant, unreasonable or unlikely to be true and which is made publicly with the intention of harming a person's reputation • *Throughout the election he had to contend with smears about his illegitimacy.* • *The minister has dismissed the allegations of an affair with her chauffeur as smears and innuendo.* • *She claims she was the victim of a smear* **campaign** *that was conducted against her by a rival candidate.* • *He was very upset that smear* **tactics** *had been used to destroy his professional reputation.*

smear *obj* /£smɪəʳ, $smɪr/ *v* [T] • *She decided to sue for libel after the newspaper smeared her private life.*

smell ABILITY /smel/ *n* [U] the ability of the nose to discover the presence of a substance in the air • *Smell is one of the five senses.* • *Dogs have a very good* **sense of** *smell.* • *She lost her sense of smell after the accident.*

> **SMELLS**
>
> There are several words meaning a *smell*. Some usually refer to pleasant smells: *aroma, fragrance*, while others are used for unpleasant smells: *(Br) odour/(Am) odor, stink, stench. Perfume* usually means a pleasant-smelling liquid worn by women. Only the words *smell, reek* and *stink* are used as verbs meaning to smell **of** something. In the following list, more pleasant smells are at the top.
>
> *A wonderful* **aroma** *of fresh coffee/baking bread/wine filled the room.*
> *The little shop was full of* **aromatic** *plants/herbs/spices.*
> *I could smell the* **fragrance** *of Isabel's expensive French* **perfume**.
> *She loved* **fragrant** *flowers/fruits/spices/food.*
> *Police dogs are very good at following a person's* **scent**.
> *The garden had a sweet* **scent** *of flowers/fruit/herbs.*
> *Most animals can recognise many more (Br)* **odours**/*(Am)* **odors** *than we can.*
> *There was a strong (Br)* **odour**/*(Am)* **odor** *of smoke/excrement/chemicals.*
> *Pure water is completely (Br)* **odourless**/*(Am)* **odorless** (= has no smell).
> *What's the lovely/awful* **smell** *in here?*
> *Our new house* **smells** *of paint.*
> *(infml) She kept complaining about Bill's* **smelly** *clothes.*
> *Len was* **reeking** *of alcohol – he was completely drunk again.*
> *There was a dreadful* **stink** *of tobacco smoke and body* **odour/odor**.
> *The* **stench** *of dead animals/rotting garbage/dirty toilets made me feel sick.*

smell /smel/ *v* [I] *past Br and Aus* **smelt** /smelt/ or *esp. Am* **smelled** /smelt, smeld/ • *Humans can't smell as well as dogs.* • *I've been able to smell a lot better since I gave up smoking.* • *What I hate most about having flu is not being able to smell.*

smell CHARACTERISTIC /smel/ *n* [C] the characteristic of something that can be recognized or noticed using the nose • *Do you like* **the** *smell* **of** *this perfume?* • *What's your favourite smell?* • *The smell of cabbage pervaded the whole apartment.* • *I got very drunk on rum when I was 16, and now the mere smell of it makes me feel nauseous.* • *Mmmm, what are you cooking? There's a* **delicious** *smell in here.* • *Is it possible to remove the musty smell from books that have been in storage for a long time?* • *When she arrived home, there was a pungent smell of curry in the kitchen.* • *The room was filled with the putrid smell of rotting meat.* • *(fig.) The government has the smell of decay about it – it can't last more than a few months.* • *(fig.) She's still enjoying the* **sweet** *smell* (= pleasant experience) **of success** *after her victory in the world championships.* • Sometimes a smell is unpleasant, although this might not be shown by an adjective: *I wish we could get rid of that smell in the bathroom.* ○ *What a smell! Do you mind if I open the window?*

smell /smel/ *v past Br and Aus* **smelt** /smelt/ or *esp. Am* **smelled** /smelt, smeld/ • *My hands smell* **of** *onions.* [I] • *The drain's blocked and smells disgustingly of rotten fish.* [I] • *This bag's made of plastic, but something's been added to make it smell* **like** *leather.* [I] • *That cake smells good.* [L only + adj] • *There's something in the fridge that smells mouldy.* [L only + adj] • *Your feet smell* (= have an unpleasant smell). *Why don't you wash them?* [I] • *As I'm your best friend, I think I should tell you that your breath smells.* [I] • If you **come up smelling of roses**, a difficult, embarrassing or unpleasant situation has not had a bad effect on you when it was expected that it would: *When the results of the fraud investigation were announced last week, the staff came up smelling of roses.* • If a situation **smells fishy** to you, you believe that there might be some dishonest activity happening: *Webber's account of what happened smells distinctly fishy* **to** *me.* • When something **smells out** a place/**smells** a place **out** (*Am also* **smells up**), it makes the place unpleasant by filling it with its smell: *That aftershave of yours is smelling out the whole house.*

-smell·ing /-ˌsmel·ɪŋ, ˈ--/ *combining form* • *The prisoners are being held in an* **evil***-smelling barn* (= one which has an unpleasant smell) *near the police headquarters.* • *When we got back to the apartment the place was full of* **foul***-smelling smoke.* • *Bowls of* **sweet***-smelling flowers had been placed on the table.*

smel·ly /ˈsmel·i/ *adj* **-ier, -iest** • Someone or something that is smelly has an unpleasant smell: *The toilets in that restaurant were horribly smelly and* **dirty**. ○ *Don't let him take his shoes off. He's got really smelly* **feet**.

smell *(obj)* DISCOVER /smel/ *v past Br and Aus* **smelt** /smelt/ or *Am and Aus also* **smelled** /smelt, smeld/ to become aware of or to discover about (something) using the nose • *Just smell this perfume! Isn't it wonderful?* [T] • *Can you smell* **burning***?* [T] • *I can smell lunch cook***ing** *from up here.* [+ obj + v-ing] • *Didn't you smell* **that** *the pie was burning?* [+ *that* clause] • *You should be able to smell* **wh***en the bread is ready.* [+ *wh-* word] • *I can smell something nasty in the bottom of the fridge.* [T] • *(fig.) Brenda can smell trouble a mile off.* (= She knows a long time in advance when there is going to be trouble.) [T] • If you **smell blood**, you recognize an opportunity to attack or take advantage of someone who is in a difficult situation: *When she smells blood, you don't get a second chance.* • *(esp. Br)* To **smell out** something/**smell** something **out** (*Am usually* **sniff out**) is to discover where it is by smelling: *At customs, dogs are used to smell out drugs in passengers' luggage.* ○ *(fig.) If there's a bargain to be had, you can be sure Jonathan will smell it out.* • If you **smell a rat** you recognize that something is not as it appears to be or that something dishonest is happening: *She smelled a rat because he said he was working late at the office but he wasn't there when she tried to phone him.* • **Smelling salts** are a chemical with a strong smell in a small bottle which is put under the nose of people who have lost consciousness: *People used to be revived with smelling salts when they had fainted.*

smell /smel/ *n* [U] • *Have* **a** *smell* **of** (= Smell) *this perfume.*

smelt SMELL *Br and Aus* /smelt/ *past simple and past participle of* SMELL • *Her bathroom always smelt of disinfectant.*

smelt *obj* OBTAIN METAL /smelt/ *v* [T] to obtain (a metal) from rock by heating it to a very high temperature, or to melt (objects made from metal) in order to use the metal to make something new • *Learning to smelt iron from its ores was a major step in human civilization.*

smel·ter /£ˈsmel·təʳ, $-t̬ɚ/ *n* [C] • A smelter is a factory or machine in which metal is smelted.

smelt·ing /£ˈsmel·tɪŋ, $ˈsmel·t̬ɪŋ/ *n* [U] • *Silver is a by-product of tin smelting.* • *The new lead smelting plant will recycle the lead from car batteries.*

smidg·en, smidg·in, smidg·eon /ˈsmɪdʒ·ɪn/ *n* [U] *infml* a very small amount • *Could I have* **a** *smidgen more wine?* • *Chris tends to wear a smidgeon too much make-up.* • *It was five years since I'd last seen him, but he hadn't changed a smidgeon.* • *When I took it back to the shop, they agreed to replace it without a smidgin* **of** *fuss.*

smile /smaɪl/ *n* [C] a facial expression in which the ends of the mouth curve up slightly, often with the lips moving apart so that the teeth can be seen • *A smile usually expresses a positive feeling such as happiness, pleasure, amusement or friendliness, but it can sometimes express sadness or regret.* • *It's nice to be able to* **bring** *a smile* **to** *people's faces* (= make people smile). • *A* **broad** *smile lit up her face.* • *He walked into the room with a* **cheery** *smile and announced that he had some good news for us.* • *"Maybe," she said, with an* **enigmatic** *smile.* • *Our efforts to cheer her up failed to produce even a* **flicker** *of a* (= a small) *smile.* • *She* **gave** *her father a* **big** *smile and told him not to worry.* • *"It's nice to see you again," she said, without the slightest* **hint** *of a smile.* • *We exchanged* **knowing** *smiles as Caroline told yet another person about her trip on the Trans-Siberian express.* • *"That's the best steak I've ever eaten," he said, leaning back in his chair with a* **satisfied** *smile.* • *"I've finished at last!" she announced with a smile of* **satisfaction**. • *I don't know what you're looking so pleased about – you can* **wipe that** *smile* **off your face** (= stop smiling) *this instant.* • *"I used to go dancing with your father every weekend when we were young," she said with a* **wistful** *smile.* • *He lay back, his face* **wreathed in** *smiles* (= he was smiling very happily). • *"The more we quarrel, the more we love each other," she said with a* **wry** *smile.* • Someone who is **all smiles** looks very happy and friendly or pleased: *Understandably, she was all smiles when she spoke about breaking the world record.*

smile *(obj)* /smaɪl/ *v* • *I couldn't help smiling when I thought of how pleased she was going to be.* [I] • *When he smiled* **at** *me I knew everything was all right.* [I] • *"We're here to help you," he said, smiling* **benignly**. [I] • *In one photograph she was smiling* **broadly** *at the camera, in the other she was looking away from it.* [I] • *He smiled* **politely** *as Mary apologised for the state of her drunken friends.* [I] • *She smiled* **wryly** *as she thought about all the money she'd lost.* [I] • *He smiled the* **smile** *of a man who knew victory was within reach.* [T] • *He smiled* **to himself** *as he thought about his new girlfriend.* [I] • *He smiled* (= expressed with a smile) *his congratulations and left without another word.* [T] • *"Don't you worry about a thing. Everything's going to be just fine," smiled Robin reassuringly.* [+ clause] • If you **smile on** something, you feel positive about it or treat it in a very positive way: *The government began to smile on small businesses when it realised that they were the key to economic growth.* ○ *Americans tend to smile tolerantly on the misdemeanors of their presidents.* ○ *(fig.) Fate has been smiling on him ever since he won the world championship last year.* ○ *(fig.) The gods smiled on us and we had brilliant sunshine throughout the day.*

smiley /ˈsmaɪ·li/ *adj* **smilier, smiliest** *infml* • A smiley person or someone who has a smiley face looks friendly and smiles a lot: *He's a very smiley, friendly man – I'm sure you'll get on with him.*

smil·ing /ˈsmaɪ·lɪŋ/ *adj* • *I really miss seeing their happy smiling* **faces**.

smil·ing·ly /ˈsmaɪ·lɪŋ·li/ *adv* • If someone does something smilingly, they smile as they are doing it: *When I complained about how long we'd had to wait for our food, the bill was whisked away and smilingly returned without the service charge.*

smirk /£smɜːk, $smɜːrk/ *n* [C] *disapproving* a smile that expresses satisfaction or pleasure about having done something or knowing something which is not known by someone else • *"Maybe your husband does things that you don't know about," he said with a smirk.* • *"I told you it would end in disaster," said Polly with a* **self-satisfied** *smirk on her face.*

smirk /£smɜːk, $smɜːrk/ *v disapproving* • *I don't like the way he winks and smirks* **at** *me whenever he sees me.* [I] • *Would you like to explain to the rest of the class what you're smirking about?* [I] • *"Have you heard about Mary's affair with her husband's brother?" smirked Brian.* [+ clause]

smite *obj* /smaɪt/ *v* [T] *past simple* **smote** /£sməʊt, $smoʊt/, *past part* **smitten** /£'smɪt·ᵊn, $'smɪţ-/ *literary* to hit (someone) forcefully or to have a sudden powerful or destructive effect on (someone) • *We shall smite the evil invaders and tear them to pieces.* • *The last time we met she had just been smitten by cancer.* • *Employment was hard to find in the recession-smitten thirties.*

smith /smɪθ/ *n* [C], *combining form* someone who makes things out of metal, esp. by heating and hammering it to shape it • *My grandfather was a goldsmith.* • A smith can also be someone who is inventive in writing things: *a wordsmith* ○ *a tunesmith* • See also BLACKSMITH.

smith·y /'smɪð·i/ *n* [C] • A smithy is a place where things are made out of metal, esp. iron or steel, by heating and hammering.

smith·e·reens /£ˌsmɪð·ᵊr'iːnz, $-ə'riːnz/ *pl n* a lot of very small broken pieces • *Our city was bombed* **to** *smithereens during the war.* • *So many films nowadays involve everyone and everything being* **blown** *to smithereens.* • *The vase lay* **in** *smithereens on the floor.*

smit·ten /£'smɪt·ᵊn, $'smɪţ-/ *adj* [after v] having suddenly started to like something very much or to be in love with someone • *She was smitten* **with** *jazz at a very early age.* • *The novel tells the story of a man smitten with love for his wife's cousin.* • *He was so smitten* **by** *her that he promised to become a vegetarian to please her.* • *"Why's David being so nice to everyone at the moment?" "I think he's smitten* (= in love)*."*

smock /£smɒk, $smɑːk/ *n* [C] a piece of clothing like a long shirt which is worn loosely over other clothing to protect it when working, or a piece of women's clothing that is similar to this • *"We've done the best we can for him," said the surgeon, as she removed her mask and green smock.* • *He has a fascinating collection of artist's smocks.*

smock·ing /£'smɒk·ɪŋ, $'smɑː·kɪŋ/ *n* [U] decoration on a piece of clothing consisting of cloth which has been gathered into tight folds that are held in position with decorative stitching

smog /£smɒg, $smɑːg/ *n* a type of air pollution in some large cities that is caused either by smoke from burning wood and coal mixing with water in the air to produce a type of dirty fog or by chemicals produced by road vehicles reacting with bright light from the sun • *Smog is a major problem in Los Angeles.* [U] • *Such high levels of smog would not normally be expected in a coastal city, where sea breezes should help to disperse it.* [U] • *As we flew into the airport, we could see a murky yellow smog hovering over the city.* [C]

smog·gy /£'smɒg·i, $'smɑː·gi/ *adj* **-ier, -iest** • *Mexico City is one of the world's smoggiest capitals.*

smoke CLOUDY AIR /£sməʊk, $smoʊk/ *n* [U] a cloudy grey or black mixture of air and very small pieces of carbon that is produced by something that is burning • **Cigarette** *smoke contains thousands of harmful chemicals.* • *This tragedy could have been avoided if they'd had a smoke* **detector**. • *Ten of us were crammed into a tiny smoke-***filled** *office.* • *The forest fires are the worst for a quarter of a century and millions of trees have* **gone up in** *smoke* (= been destroyed by burning). • Something that **goes up in smoke** fails to produce the desired result: *When the business went bankrupt, twenty years of hard work went up in smoke.* • *Nobody died in the fire, but twelve people were treated for minor injuries and smoke* **inhalation**. • *The fire produced a massive* **pall** (= large mass) *of smoke that was visible twenty miles away.* • **Plumes** *of smoke* **billowed** *from the blazing house.* • *She leaned back thoughtfully and blew* **a puff of** (= a small amount of) *smoke into the air.* • *(fig.) One moment he was standing behind me, the next he had* **vanished in** *a puff of smoke* (= suddenly disappeared completely). • *Exposure to* **tobacco** *smoke can cause cancer in non-smokers.* • *A* **wisp of** *smoke spiralled skywards from the chimney.* • *(esp. Am)* Something that is described as **smoke and mirrors** is intended to take attention away from an embarrassing or unpleasant situation: *Instead of cutting expenditure, the government's relying on smoke and mirrors to make it seem as though it's doing something.* • A **smoke bomb** is a device which produces a lot of smoke instead of exploding: *Several protesters were arrested for throwing smoke bombs at the police.* • A **smoke-filled room** is a place where politicians have discussions and make agreements in secret: *The whole business stinks of political corruption and decisions made in smoke-filled rooms.* • A **smoke signal** is a message in the form of amounts of smoke of various sizes that represent words, which can be seen from a long distance. • *(saying, esp. Br and Aus)* 'There's no smoke without fire' or *(esp. Am)* 'Where there's smoke, there's fire' means that if unpleasant things are said about someone or something, there is probably a good reason for it, or that if small problems are discovered, there are probably larger ones still to be discovered: *She says the accusations are not true, but there's no smoke without fire.* ○ *Satisfying the police of my innocence is not enough, as the general public will reckon that where there's smoke, there's fire.* • *"Smoke Gets in Your Eyes"* (title of a song written by Otto Harbach, 1933)

smoke /£sməʊk, $smoʊk/ *v* [I] • Something that smokes produces smoke as a result of industrial activity or of something such as an electrical fault: *The views of the city are dominated by smoking factory chimneys.* ○ *Suddenly the TV went blank and started smoking.* • A **smoking gun** is information which proves who committed a crime: *The tape recordings provided prosecutors with the smoking gun they needed to prove he'd been involved in the conspiracy.* • If you **smoke out** an animal or person that is hiding, or you **smoke** them **out**, you force them to leave the place where they are by filling it with smoke: *(fig.) The finance minister has promised a tougher approach to smoking out* (= finding) *tax dodgers.*

smoked /£sməʊkt, $smoʊkt/ *adj* • **Smoked glass** is glass that has been darkened by a process involving smoke: *She works in a very smart office with smoked-glass windows.*

smoke·less /£'sməʊk·ləs, $'smoʊk-/ *adj* • *(Br) If you live in a smokeless* **zone** *you have to use smokeless* **fuels** *such as gas instead of wood and coal.* • *(Am)* Smokeless **tobacco** is tobacco which is chewed or placed in the mouth.

smok·y, smoke·y /£'sməʊ·ki, $'smoʊ-/ *adj* **smokier, smokiest** • If a place is smoky there is a lot of smoke in it: *This café's too smoky for me – I'm starting to get a sore throat.* ○ *The fire's very smoky. Do you think the chimney needs to be swept?* • Sometimes smoky describes something which appears to be similar to smoke: *Her new car is a smoky blue colour.* ○ *Our red wine of the week has a delicious smoky flavour.* ○ *A mysterious smoky mist surrounded the cottage.*

smoke *(obj)* BREATHE SMOKE /£sməʊk, $smoʊk/ *v* to breathe smoke into the mouth or lungs from (burning tobacco, such as cigarettes) • *Do you mind if I smoke?* [I] • *I used to smoke a packet of cigarettes a day.* [T] • *Is smoking cigars or a pipe safer than cigarettes?* [T] • *What are the long-term effects of smoking marijuana?* [T]

smoke /£sməʊk, $smoʊk/ *n* • *I really enjoy* **a** *smoke* (= an act of smoking) *at the end of a meal.* [U] • *I always* **have** *a smoke with my coffee.* [U] • *(infml) Would you buy me some smokes* (= cigarettes) *while you're out?* [C]

smok·er /£'sməʊ·kəʳ, $'smoʊ·kɚ/ *n* [C] • A smoker is someone who smokes tobacco regularly: *Although the number of* **cigarette** *smokers is falling in the West, it is rising in industrializing countries.* • *Do many* **ex-***smokers start smoking again?* • *Chris is a* **heavy** *smoker* (= smokes a lot). • **Non-***smokers are less likely to contract lung cancer than smokers.* • *Why are so few women* **pipe** *smokers?* • *(dated)* A smoker is also a train carriage in which people are allowed to smoke tobacco: *There's a couple of empty seats in a smoker at the other end of the train.*

smok·ing /£'sməʊ·kɪŋ, $'smoʊ-/ *n* [U] • *Smoking is not permitted anywhere in this theatre.* • *The airline was the first to introduce a smoking* **ban** *on all its flights.* • *The nicotine patches are designed to help people* **give up/quit/stop** *smoking.* • **Cigarette** *smoking kills thousands of people every year.* • **Non-***smoking vegetarian wanted to share house with two female students.* • **No** *smoking, please.* • *I avoid going to restaurants that don't have a* **no-smoking** *area.* • *(dated)* A **smoking jacket** is a comfortable coat for a man that is made from a soft material and is worn when relaxing at home, traditionally when smoking: *He was wearing a pair of red leather slippers and a velvet smoking jacket richly embroidered in gold.* • ⒸⓈ Ⓓ Ⓕ Ⓘ ⓇⓊⓈ Ⓢ

smoke *obj* PRESERVE /£sməʊk, $smoʊk/ *v* [T] to preserve and add a smoky flavour to (meat, fish or cheese) using smoke from burning wood • *People in the Middle East, India and Egypt were salting, drying and smoking fish and meat 6000 years ago.* • *She had champagne and smoked* **salmon** *sandwiches at her birthday party.* • *The soup is made to a traditional Corsican recipe with beans, cabbage, smoked* **ham** *and potatoes.*

smoke CITY /£sməʊk, $smoʊk/ *n* [U] **the smoke** *infml* any large city, esp. as compared with the countryside • *He was a naive young lad of 16 when he first came to the smoke to look for work.*

smoke·screen /£'sməʊk·skriːn, $'smoʊk-/ *n* [C] something which hides the truth about a person's intentions • *This job creation scheme is just a smokescreen to divert attention from the government's poor record on unemployment.* • *Instead of doing something about the problem, the council is hiding* **behind** *a smokescreen of jargon and bureaucracy.* • *This is an outrageously offensive book which is being published* **under** *the smokescreen of free speech.* • A smokescreen is also an artificial cloud of smoke that is used to hide the movements or positions of soldiers from the enemy: *Nowadays, smokescreens need to block not only visible light but also the infra-red sights that soldiers use to spot targets.*

smoke·stack /£'sməʊk·stæk, $'smoʊk-/ *n* [C] a tall vertical pipe which takes smoke or steam into the air from an engine powered by steam or from a factory • *The smokestacks of the power station tower above the town.* • *Smokestack* **emissions** *are reduced by burning coal more efficiently.* • *(esp. Am)* **Smokestack industries** are traditional industries that produce large machines or materials used in other industries and create a lot of pollution in doing so: *The trade union movement has been weakened by the decline in smokestack industries such as shipbuilding and steel.*

smol·der /£'sməʊl·dəʳ, $'smoʊl·dɚ/ *v* [I] *Am for* SMOULDER • *The fire was still smoldering the next morning.*

smooch /smuːtʃ/ *v* [I] *infml* to kiss, hold and touch someone very affectionately • *The photographs show them smooching next to a swimming pool.* • *Didn't I see you smooching* **with** *Mark at Kim's party?* • *(Br)* Sometimes when two people are smooching, they are dancing slowly and very close together to slow romantic music: *The dance floor was full of middle-aged couples smooching* **to** *slushy ballads.*

smooch /smuːtʃ/ *n* [C usually sing] *infml* • *I was so embarrassed when I walked in on them* **having a** *smooch on the sofa.* • *(Br) Kate* **had a** *smooch* (= romantic dance) *with a very attractive young man at the Christmas party.*

smooch·y /'smuː·tʃi/ *adj* **-ier, -iest** *infml* • *She put her arm around him and gave him a smoochy kiss.* • *(Br) He gets really embarrassed about dancing to smoochy music.*

smooth REGULAR /smuːð/ *adj* **-er, -est** having a surface or substance which is perfectly regular and has no holes or lumps or areas that rise or fall suddenly • *Mix together the butter, sour cream and sugar until smooth.* • *Her skin was* **as** *smooth* **as silk** (= very smooth). • *The top of his head was completely bald, and* **as** *smooth* **as a baby's bottom** (= very smooth). • *Crumble the yeast into the milk, stir in the honey and mix to a smooth* **paste**. • *This cream will help to keep your* **skin** *smooth.* • *Use fine sandpaper to obtain a smooth* **surface** *before varnishing.* • *The best ice cream that we tasted had a natural vanilla colour, a smooth* **texture** *and a distinctive flavour.*

smooth *obj* /smuːð/ *v* [T] • *You should smooth the cracks* **over** *with some filler before you paint the wall.* [M] • *He straightened his tie nervously and smoothed* **(down)** *his hair.* [T/M] • If you **smooth away** irregularities, or you **smooth** them **away**, you remove them from something: *She had a face-lift to smooth away her wrinkles.* ○ *Recent developments have smoothed away the jerkiness of diesel engines.* ○ *(fig.) The surprise fall in inflation has helped smooth away some of the economic gloom.* • If you **smooth out** differences or changes in something, or you **smooth** them **out**, you reduce or get rid of them: *The camcorder detects tiny movements caused by unsteady hands and uses an earlier image to smooth out the picture.* ○ *By investing small amounts regularly, you can smooth out the effects of sudden rises and falls in the stock market.*

smooth·ness /'smuːð·nəs/ *n* [U] • *I just love the smoothness of silk.*

smooth NOT INTERRUPTED /smuːð/ *adj* **-er, -est** happening without any sudden changes, interruption, inconvenience or difficulty • *The car's improved suspension gives a much smoother* **ride** *than earlier models.* • *We had a very smooth* **flight** *with no turbulence at all.* • *The bill has all-party support which will ensure it has a smooth* **passage** *through parliament.* • *An efficient transport system is vital to the smooth* **running** *of a country's economy.* • *He has the unenviable task of bringing about a smooth* **transition** *to democracy after 21 years of military rule.*

smooth *obj* /smuːð/ *v* [T] • *We encourage parents to help smooth their children's* **way** *through school.* • *Their friendship smoothed the* **way** *for an amalgamation of their businesses.* • *We must do more to smooth the country's* **path** *to democratic reform.* • When you **smooth over** problems, difficulties or disagreements, or **smooth** them **over**, you make them less serious or easier to solve, esp. by talking to the people involved: *Would you like me to try to smooth* **things** *over between you and your parents?*

smooth·ly /'smuːð·li/ *adv* • *Oil is used to make the parts of a machine* **move** *smoothly when they rub together.* • *The road was blocked for two hours after the accident, but traffic is now* **flowing** *smoothly again.* • *Lead is added to fuel to make car engines* **run** *more smoothly.* • *It's wonderful to work in such a smoothly-***run** *office.* • *The pregnancy's* **gone** *very smoothly so far.* • **If all goes** *smoothly, we should arrive by nine o'clock.*

smooth·ness /'smuːð·nəs/ *n* [U] • *The smoothness* **of** *the ride is remarkable for such an inexpensive car.* • *We can thank Paul's efficient organization for the smoothness of the demonstration.*

smooth TASTING PLEASANT /smuːð/ *adj* **-er, -est** having a pleasant flavour which is not sour, acidic or bitter • *This wine is lovely and smooth.*

smooth·ness /'smuːð·nəs/ *n* [U] • *The wine possesses a smoothness and balanced depth which is rare at such a low price.* • *Freshness and smoothness are very important in a cigar.* • *The smoothness of the beans is sharpened with the tang of the spinach.*

smooth POLITE /smuːð/ *adj* **-er, -est** very polite, confident and persuasive in a way that lacks sincerity • *The foreign minister is so smooth that many of his colleagues distrust him.* • *In job interviews, the successful candidates tend to be the smooth* **talkers** *who know exactly how to make the right impression.* • *She fell for his smooth* **talk** *and handed over £5000 for him to invest.* • *You ought to be careful with her. She's a very smooth* **operator** *who can make you agree to almost anything.*

smooth·ie, smooth·y /'smuː·ði/ *n* [C] *disapproving* • A smoothie is a man who is so polite, confident and tidily dressed that he does not seem sincere: *He was a real smoothy who persuaded me to lend him a lot of money.* ○ *American TV audiences love his smoothie charm and witty one-liners.*

smooth *obj* RUB /smuːð/ *v* [T always + adv/prep] to cover the surface of something with (a liquid, cream or wax) using gentle rubbing movements • *Pour some oil into the palm of your hand and then smooth it over your arms and neck.*

smor·gas·bord /£'smɔː·gəs·bɔːd, $'smɔːr·gəs·bɔːrd/ *n* [C] a mixture of many different hot and cold Scandinavian dishes which are arranged so that you can serve yourself with as much as you want and which are eaten at the start of a meal or as the main part of it • *The smorgasbord table was laden with fresh baked salmon, salads, pickled herring, fruit, cheese, bread and desserts.* • *(fig.) The discounts are limited to certain resorts, but there is still a smorgasbord* (= wide range) **of** *cheap destinations to choose from.*

smote /£sməʊt, $smoʊt/ *past simple of* SMITE

smo·ther *obj* COVER /£'smʌð·əʳ, $-ɚ/ *v* [T] to cover most or all of the surface of (something) by existing in a large amount • *Her bedroom wall is smothered* **with** *photographs of him.* • *Pasta is not very fattening unless it is smothered* **in** *a creamy sauce.* • *During the summer months, the city is smothered* **in** *smog and choking with traffic.* • *Once it has sunk to the bottom of the sea, the oil can kill plants by smothering them.*

smo·ther *obj* PREVENT /£'smʌð·əʳ, $-ɚ/ *v* [T] to prevent the development, growth or continued existence of (something or someone) • *The robber didn't manage to smother his cough and was discovered by security guards.* • *The latest violence has smothered any remaining hopes for an early peace agreement.* • *Daisies grow in short grassland and lawns where regular mowing prevents them from being smothered by taller vegetation.* • If you smother someone you love, you make them feel that they have lost their independence and freedom by giving them too much affection and attention: *I think she broke off their engagement because she felt smothered by him.* • To smother someone is to kill them by covering their face so that they cannot breathe: *He was so ill and in such pain that the kindest thing to do would have been to smother him with a pillow.* ○ *They held guns to our heads and threatened to smother us with plastic bags.* • When you smother a fire, you stop it burning by covering it with something which prevents air from reaching it: *I threw a blanket over him to smother the flames.*

smoul·der, *Am usually* **smol·der** /£'sməʊl·dəʳ, $'smoʊl·dɚ/ *v* [I] to burn slowly with smoke but without flames • *Two firefighters stayed at the scene to keep an eye on the smouldering remains.* • *Safety regulations prevent the sale of any furniture that will catch fire from a smouldering cigarette.* • *Volcanoes can smoulder for many years without erupting.* • *(fig.) The civil war has been smouldering* **on** *for the past fifteen years.* • *(fig.) The dispute is* **still** *smouldering, five years after the negotiations began.* • If a strong emotion smoulders, it exists, but is prevented from being expressed: *She was smouldering* **with** *rage as she explained how her son had been killed.* ○ *The farmers' smouldering resentment has finally developed into a powerful protest movement.* • A person who smoulders has strong sexual or romantic feelings but does not express them: *She said nothing, but it was obvious from the way she smouldered that she found Chris very attractive.* • *He gazed at her with smouldering* **eyes**, *wishing she wasn't married.* • *Much of his success is due to his smouldering good looks.*

smudge /smʌdʒ/ *n* [C] a mark with no particular shape that is caused, usually accidentally, by rubbing something such as ink or a dirty finger across a surface • *The police identified the murderer from a smudge of blood on his victim's shirt.* • *Her hands were covered in coal dust and she had a black smudge on her nose where she had scratched it.* • *(fig.) She said we were nearly there, but the island was still no more than a distant smudge on the horizon.*

smudge *(obj)* /smʌdʒ/ *v* • *It was raining heavily and her mascara had smudged.* [I] • *She managed to eat a massive hamburger without smudging her lipstick.* [T]

smudged /smʌdʒd/ *adj* • *The signature was smudged and impossible to decipher.* • *(fig.) The line between erotica and pornography is badly smudged* (= very unclear).

smudg·ing /'smʌdʒ·ɪŋ/ *n* [U] • *Fixative is a special liquid that can be sprayed over charcoal and chalk drawings to prevent smudging.*

smudg·y /'smʌdʒ·i/ *adj* **-ier**, **-iest** • *I could tell it was a forged note because the ink was smudgy.*

smug /smʌg/ *adj* **smugger**, **smuggest** very pleased or satisfied in an annoying way about something you have achieved or something you know • *She did very well to get the job, but I wish she wasn't so damned smug* **about** *it.* • *I reckon she has good reason to feel smug.* • *There was a hint of smug* **self-satisfaction** *in her voice as she explained why her investments had been so successful.* • *He's been* **unbearably** *smug since he gave up smoking.* • *It's difficult to tell people about exam results that are as good as mine without sounding smug.*

smug·ly /'smʌg·li/ *adv* • *He is smugly confident that he'll be re-elected.* • *On a motorbike you can smugly weave between the cars stuck in a traffic jam.*

smug·ness /'smʌg·nəs/ *n* [U] • *I get a tremendous feeling of smugness from being a blood donor.*

smug·gle *obj* /'smʌg·l̩/ *v* [T] to take (things or people) to or from a country or place illegally and/or secretly • *When import taxes on goods are high, there is a greater chance that they will be smuggled.* • *Tougher measures are needed to prevent drugs being smuggled into prisons.* • *He was arrested when he tried to smuggle a knife into the House of Commons.* • *To avoid complex and time-consuming official procedures, some couples who are desperate to adopt children try to smuggle them into Britain.* • *She has admitted to trying to smuggle 26 kilos of heroin* **out of** *the country.* • *They allegedly smuggled 75 tons of cocaine* **into** *the United States in the 1980s.* • *He was sentenced to 13 years in jail for smuggling* **arms** *and* **explosives**. • *Smuggling* **illegal aliens** *into the United States has become big business.* • [LP]> **Crimes and criminals**

smug·gler /£'smʌg·ləʳ, $-lɚ/ *n* [C] • *The police raid on the house was part of an operation to track down international* **drug** *smugglers.*

smug·gling /'smʌg·lɪŋ/ *n* [U] • *The murdered man is thought to have been involved in* **drug** *smuggling.*

smut [SEXUAL MATERIAL] /smʌt/ *n* [U] *disapproving* magazines, books, pictures, films, jokes or conversations which might offend some people because they relate to sexual activity or nakedness and are intended to be entertaining, exciting or amusing rather than artistic or educational • *There's an awful lot of smut on television these days.* • *Patrick's conversations are always full of smut.*

smut·ty /£'smʌt·i, $'smʌt̬-/ *adj* **-ier**, **-iest** *disapproving* • *People seem to laugh at anything as long as it's smutty.* • *What should you do if you find a pile of smutty magazines under your son's bed?* • *I was really embarrassed by his smutty* **jokes**.

smut·ti·ness /£'smʌt·ɪ·nəs, $'smʌt̬-/ *n* [U]

smut [DIRT] /smʌt/ *n* (a very small piece of) black powder that is floating in the air or forming a dirty mark on something and has been produced by something burning • *We were showered with smut as the locomotive got up steam.* [U] • *The washing is covered with smuts from the bonfire.* [C]

snack /snæk/ *n* [C] a smaller than usual meal or a small amount of food that is eaten between meals, often something produced specially for this purpose • *I had a huge lunch, so I only want a snack for dinner.* • *The British Dental Association wants a ban on television advertisements which encourage children to eat sugary snacks between meals.* • *Snack* **foods** *tend to be high in salt and fat, which we ought to be eating less of.* • *Today's busy lifestyles mean that people are eating more snack* **meals** *than ever before.* • *The pub's new owners have promised to improve the beers and widen the range of* **bar** *snacks.* • A **snack bar** is a small informal restaurant where small meals can be eaten or bought to take away: *We've arranged to meet at the railway station snack bar in Lausanne next week.* • (J)

snack /snæk/ *v* [I] • *You ought to eat proper meals instead of snacking all the time.* • *If you eat three good meals a day, you'll be less likely to snack* **on** *cakes, biscuits, confectionery and other high-fat foods.*

snaf·fle *obj* /'snæf·l̩/ *v* [T] *Br and Aus infml* to obtain or take (something) in a way that prevents someone else from having or using it • *Who's snaffled my pen? It was on my desk a moment ago.* • *Martha snaffled* (= ate) *all the peanuts before the party had even begun!* • *Susannah's snaffled* **up** (= bought) *a few bargains in the sales.* [M] • *The company grew by snaffling* **up** (= taking control of) *several smaller businesses.* [M]

snaf·u /snæf'uː/ *n* [C] *Am and Aus infml* a situation, which is often expected, in which nothing has happened as planned • *The company isn't wholly to blame for the snafu.* • *A single snafu* (= serious mistake) *by an airline can leave a lasting impression on travelers.*

snag [PROBLEM] /snæg/ *n* [C] a problem, difficulty or disadvantage • *The snag* **with** *helicopters is that they are noisy, slow, expensive to operate and not as safe as conventional aircraft.* • *What are the possible snags* **with** *this proposal?* • *We don't anticipate any snags* **in** *the negotiations.* • *What are the snags* **for** *a woman working in such a male-dominated industry?* • *It's a great idea, but* **the** *snag* **is that** *we can't afford to do it at present.* • *The drug is very effective. The* **only** *snag is that it cannot yet be produced in large quantities.* • *Their plans to build a factory in France have* **hit** *a major snag.* • *I'm afraid I've* **run into** *a snag with our holiday arrangements.*

snag *(obj)* /snæg/ *v* **-gg-** *esp. Am* • *Financial problems have snagged* (= caused difficulties for) *the project for the past six months.* [T] • *The negotiations have snagged* **on** (= had problems because of) *a dispute about who should chair them.* [I]

snag [DAMAGE] /snæg/ *n* [C] a tear, hole or loose fibre in a piece of clothing or cloth caused by a sharp or rough object • *This sweater's full of snags.*

snag *obj* /snæg/ *v* [T] **-gg-** • *Be careful not to snag your coat* **on** *the barbed wire.* • *An American submarine snagged the boat's nets while it was fishing in the Irish Sea.*

snag *obj* [OBTAIN] /snæg/ *v* [T] **-gg-** *Am infml* to obtain or catch (something) by acting quickly • *The ball was hit well, but Silverman snagged it for the final out of the inning.* • *She did very well to snag the first prize.* • *He hasn't stopped boasting since he snagged that job.* • *They'd have gone bust if they hadn't snagged that contract* **from** *their rivals.* • *He recently snagged the exclusive rights to promote the Moscow Circus in North America.*

snag [FOOD] /snæg/ *n* [C] *Aus infml for* SAUSAGE

snail /sneɪl/ *n* [C] a small thin animal that moves very slowly, eats plants and has a wet skin, no bones, eyes supported on stems, and a shell which protects its important organs • *Snails are a traditional French dish.* • *Snails can hide in their shells when they face danger.* • *Thrushes like eating* **garden** *snails, whose shells they break against rocks.* • *Ordinary snails live on land or in fresh water, but there are many types of* **marine** *snail, such as limpets and whelks.* • *The roads were full of traffic and we were travelling* **at a snail's pace** (= extremely slowly) *for two hours.* • [PIC]> **Mollusc**

snake [ANIMAL] /sneɪk/ *n* [C] an animal with a long cylindrical body and no legs which grows a new skin several times a year and has a mouth that can open very wide to allow it to swallow food that is much bigger than its head • *He's terrified of being* **bitten** *by a snake.* • *Between thirty and forty thousand people die each year from snake* **bites**. • *The organization aims to promote the development of medicines from natural substances such as snake* **venom**. • A **snake (in the grass)** is an unpleasant person who cannot be trusted: *You're a lousy, two-timing snake in the grass and I can't imagine why I ever married you.* • A **snake charmer** is an entertainer who controls the movements of snakes by playing music: *Indian snake charmers use cobras in their performances.* • **Snakes and ladders** is a game consisting of a board that is divided into 100 squares with pictures of snakes and LADDERS connecting some of the squares. Each player moves a piece up the ladders and down the snakes, and the player who reaches the end first wins.

snake [TWIST] /sneɪk/ *v* [I always + adv/prep] to move along a route that includes a lot of twists or bends • *The river snakes through some of the most spectacular countryside in France.* • *In many offices, computer cables snaking across the floor pose a considerable safety hazard.* • *The queue for tickets snaked all the way around the block.* • Something that **snakes** its **way** moves or is arranged in a twisting way: *A long queue had formed, snaking its way downstairs and out into the street.*

snak·y /ˈsneɪ·ki/ *adj* **-ier, -iest** • *Take care on those mountain roads – some of them are very snaky* (= have a lot of bends).

snak·y /ˈsneɪ·ki/ *adj* **-ier, -iest** *Aus infml* annoyed or angry

snap *(obj)* [BREAK] /snæp/ *v* **-pp-** (to cause something which is thin and can be bent or stretched slightly) to break suddenly and quickly with a cracking sound • *You'll snap that ruler if you bend it too far.* [T] • *Some vandal's gone and snapped* **off** *my car aerial again.* [M] • *The gales caused some power cables to snap, leaving hundreds of homes without electricity for several hours.* [I] • *(fig.) After ten years of abuse from her husband, her* **patience** *finally snapped, and she stabbed him to death while he was asleep.* [I]

snap /snæp/ *n* [C usually sing] • *She broke the broom handle over her knee with a loud snap* (= cracking sound). • *He slaughtered the turkey with a quick snap of its neck* (= by breaking its neck quickly). • A **snap fastener** (*Am also* **snap**) is a **press stud**. See at PRESS [PUSH]. • **Snap pea** is *Am and Aus for* MANGETOUT. • *"Snap, crackle and pop"* (advertisement for Rice Crispies breakfast cereal)

snap *(obj)* [MOVE QUICKLY] /snæp/ *v* [always + adv/prep] **-pp-** to move into a position quickly, producing a brief noise as if breaking • *Tendons store elastic energy by stretching and then snapping* **back** *into shape like rubber bands.* [I] • *(fig.) After substantial losses last year, the company has snapped* **back** *to profitability* (= started making profits again). [I] • *The dog chased him down the street,* **snapping at** *his* **heels** (= trying to bite him) *all the way.* • *(fig.) With so many younger women* **snapping at** *her* **heels** (= competing strongly with her), *this year may be her last chance to win the championship.* • If you **snap** your **fingers** you make a brief noise by pushing your second finger hard against your thumb and then releasing it suddenly so that it hits the base of your thumb: *Chris snapped her fingers to attract the waiter's attention.* ○ *(fig.) She just has to snap her fingers and he'll do whatever she wants.* • If you **snap out of** an unpleasant condition, you force yourself to stop experiencing it: *He just can't snap out of the depression he's had since his wife died.* ○ *(fig.) Nearly half the companies in the survey said they were about to snap out of the recession.* ○ *What's wrong with you? Your work's been very poor recently – you're going to have to snap out of* **it**. ○ *Now come on, snap out of* **it**. *Losing that money isn't the end of the world.* • If something **snaps shut** or is snapped shut, it closes quickly with a sudden sharp sound: *She snapped her notebook* **shut** *and put it back in her pocket.* ○ *Her mouth snapped* **shut** *when she realized he'd heard everything she'd said about him.* • If you tell someone to **snap to it** or *(Am)* **snap it up** you want them to do something more quickly: *We're leaving in five minutes so you'd better snap to it and finish your breakfast.* • If you **snap up** something that you want a lot, or you **snap it up**, you buy or obtain it quickly and enthusiastically: *Her book had been rejected by five other publishers, but we snapped it up as soon as we were offered it.* ○ *The tickets for the concert were snapped up within three hours of going on sale.* ○ *The fall in property prices means that there are a lot of bargains waiting to be snapped up.*

snap·py /ˈsnæp·i/ *adj* **-ier, -iest** • If you tell someone to **make it snappy**, you want them to do something immediately and to do it quickly: *I'd like my bill please, waiter, and make it snappy – I've already been waiting half an hour for it.* ○ *You've got just enough time to phone her before the train leaves, but you'll have to look snappy.* • See also SNAPPY [STYLISH]; SNAPPY [EFFECTIVE].

snap *(obj)* [SPEAK] /snæp/ *v* **-pp-** to speak short sentences in an annoyed and unfriendly way • *There's no need to snap* **at** *me like that. It's not my fault that you lost your wallet.* [I] • *She seems to be happiest when he's snapping* **out** *instructions to people.* [M] • *"Well, I hate you too!" she snapped.* [+ clause] • *I only asked her what she'd done over the weekend and she snapped* **back that** *it was none of my business.* [+ *that* clause] • If you **snap** someone's **head off** you answer them in an unreasonably angry way: *There's no point trying to discuss anything with him if all he's going to do is snap your head off.*

snap·pish /ˈsnæp·ɪʃ/ *adj* • Someone who is snappish tends to be bad-tempered and to speak in an angry way: *He's very snappish when he arrives at work in the morning.*

snap·pish·ly /ˈsnæp·ɪʃ·li/ *adv* • *"Of course I know what I'm doing!" she said, snappishly.*

snap [PHOTOGRAPH] /snæp/, **snap·shot** /£ˈsnæp·ʃɒt, $-ʃɑːt/ *n* [C] *infml* an informal photograph which is not particularly skilful or artistic and which is usually taken with a simple camera • *Would you like to see my (Br and Aus)* **holiday**/*(Am)* **vacation** *snaps?* • *Did you* **take** *many snaps while you were away?* • *The photographs were just a collection of* **family** *snapshots and failed to provide any clues.*

snap *(obj)* /snæp/ *v* **-pp-** • If you snap photographs, you take a lot of them quickly: *He was arrested for snapping photos of a military parade.* [T] ○ *She's very pleased with her new camera and was snapping* **away** *the whole time we were abroad.* [I]

snap [GAME] /snæp/ *n* [U] a card game in which the players compete to call out the word 'snap' when they see two cards that have the same value • *In a* **game of** *snap, the person who says 'snap' first wins the cards on the table, and the game continues until one person has all the cards.*

snap /snæp/ *exclamation* • 'Snap!' is what you say when two cards of the same value have been played. • *(fig.) Snap! We're wearing the same shirts!*

snap [SOMETHING EASY] /snæp/ *n* [U] *Am infml* something that can be done without any difficulty • *"Will you finish on time?" "Sure thing. It's* **a snap**." • *Talking to girls is a snap* **for** *him, but I'm always tongue-tied.*

snap [DONE SUDDENLY] /snæp/ *adj* [before n] done suddenly without allowing time for careful thought or preparation • *He always makes snap* **decisions** *and never thinks about their consequences.* • *The Prime Minister has decided to take advantage of his popularity in the opinion polls, and called a snap* **election** *for next month.*

snap·drag·on /ˈsnæpˌdræg·ən/, **an·tir·rhi·num** *n* [C] a garden plant with white, yellow, pink or red flowers whose petals are shaped like a pair of lips which open when they are pressed

snap·per /£ˈsnæp·əʳ, $-ɚ/ *n* [C] an edible fish that lives in warm seas

snap·py [STYLISH] /ˈsnæp·i/ *adj* **-ier, -iest** *infml approving* (esp. of a man's clothes or some feature of his appearance) modern and stylish; SHARP [FASHIONABLE] • *He's a snappy* **dresser**. • *That's a very snappy new suit you've got, Peter.* • See also **snappy** at SNAP [MOVE QUICKLY].

snap·pi·ly /ˈsnæp·ɪ·li/ *adv infml approving* • *The sales team are usually fairly snappily dressed.*

snap·py [EFFECTIVE] /ˈsnæp·i/ *adj* **-ier, -iest** *approving* immediately effective in getting people's attention or communicating an idea • *The magazine will be launched in September with a snappy design.* • *They're looking for a snappy slogan to communicate the campaign's message.* • *The play contained some good snappy dialogue.* • See also **snappy** at SNAP [MOVE QUICKLY].

snap·pi·ly /ˈsnæp·ɪ·li/ *adv approving* • *Do you think that if the book had been more snappily titled, it would have sold any more copies?*

snare /£sneəʳ, $sner/ *n* [C] a device for catching small animals and birds, usually with a rope or wire which tightens around the animal, or *(fig.)* a trick or situation which deceives you or involves you in some problem of which you are not aware • *He shoots rabbits and he* **sets** *snares for them.* • *(fig.) The legal system is full of snares for those who are not wary.*

snare *obj* /£sneəʳ, $sner/ *v* [T] • *We used to snare small birds such as sparrows and robins.* • *(fig.) She grew up in the days when a woman's main aim was to snare a (preferably rich) husband.*

snare drum, side drum *n* [C] a drum with twisted wires stretched across the bottom which shake against it when it is hit • *The snare drum is the most important drum in a drum kit.* • PIC› **Musical instruments**

snarl *(obj)* /£snɑːl, $snɑːrl/ *v* (esp. of dogs) to make a deep rough sound while showing the teeth, usually in anger, or (of people) to speak or say something angrily and fiercely • *The dogs had started to snarl* **at** *each other so I thought I'd better separate them.* [I] • *"Go to hell!", he snarled.* [+ clause] • *There was an old drunk sitting on a bench snarling* **at** *passers-by.* [I]

snarl /£snɑːl, $snɑːrl/ *n* [C] • *The dog gave a low snarl so I quickly drew my hand back.* • *"Take your hands off me!" she said with a snarl.*

snarled /£snɑːld, $snɑːrld/ *adj* (of a long line of traffic) unable to go forward because of something blocking the road • *Traffic was snarled* **(up)** *in both directions for ten miles.*

snarl /£snɑːl, $snɑːrl/ *n* [C] • *The accident had created a huge traffic* **snarl/snarl-up** (= a situation in which a long line of traffic is unable to move) *during the evening rush hour.*

snatch *(obj)* TAKE QUICKLY /snætʃ/ *v* to take hold of (something) suddenly and roughly • *He snatched the photos out of my hand before I had a chance to look at them.* [T] • *Small children are often told not to snatch because it is rude.* [I] • *The six-year-old girl was snatched* (= taken away by force) *from a playground and her body found two days later.* [T] • *She had her purse snatched* (= stolen) *while she was in town.* [T] • *Running the best race of his career, Fletcher snatched* (= only just won) *the gold medal from the Canadian champion.* [T] • To snatch an amount of time is to use it quickly for what you want to do: *I managed to snatch a minute for a quick sandwich at the station.* [T] • To snatch something that is to your advantage is to take it quickly: *Perhaps you'll be able to snatch a couple of hours' sleep before dinner.* [T] • If you snatch **at** something, you attempt to take hold of it or take advantage of it quickly before it is too late: *Try not to snatch at the ball.* [I] ○ *A man snatched at my bag, but he didn't get it.* [I] ○ *I was desperate to find a way out of teaching so when this job came along I snatched at it.* [I] • To **snatch victory (from the jaws of defeat)** is to win a surprising victory at the last moment possible, when it had previously seemed certain that you were going to lose: *In the last ten minutes of the game, Germany scored two goals, snatching victory from the jaws of almost certain defeat.*

snatch /snætʃ/ *n* [C] • *I felt someone behind me* **make** *a snatch at my bag.*

snatch·er /£ˈsnætʃ·əʳ, $-ɚ/ *n* [C] • *You have to watch out for bag/purse snatchers* (= people who steal bags/PURSES).

snatch BRIEF PART /snætʃ/ *n* [C] a brief part (of something) • *I tried hard to listen to what they were saying, but I only managed to catch a few snatches.* • *There were a few snatches* **of** *music between the scenes in the play.*

snatch VAGINA /snætʃ/ *n* [C] *taboo slang* the VULVA

snaz·zy /ˈsnæz·i/ *adj* **-ier, -iest** *infml* modern and stylish in a way that attracts attention • *Paula's wearing a very snazzy pair of shoes!* • *He designs snazzy new graphics for software packages.*

snaz·zi·ly /ˈsnæz·ɪ·li/ *adv* • *I like to be a bit more snazzily dressed for a party.*

sneak *(obj)* MOVE SECRETLY /sniːk/ *v* [always + adv/prep] *past* **sneaked** or *esp. Am* **snuck** /snʌk/ to go somewhere or take (someone or something) somewhere secretly • *I managed to sneak* **in** *through the back door while she wasn't looking.* [I] • *Jan hasn't got a ticket but I thought we might sneak her* **in** *somehow.* [T] • *I have a feeling that he's been sneaking* **into** *my room and reading my diary while I'm out.* [I] • *Could you sneak a bottle of his precious wine* **out of** *the house, or would he notice?* [T] • *I thought I'd sneak* **up on** *him* (= move close to him without him seeing) *and give him a surprise.* [I] • *Rather naughtily, I sneaked* **a look** (= looked secretly) *at what he'd written after he left the office.* [T] • A **sneak preview** is an opportunity to see (a part of) something new before the rest of the public see it: *Clare's husband produced the film so we saw a sneak preview of it.*

sneak·y /ˈsniː·ki/ *adj* **-ier, -iest** • *"I had a look in the files while no-one was around." "That was very sneaky of you!"*

sneak·i·ly /ˈsniː·kɪ·li/ *adv* • *I rather sneakily looked in her diary when she was out last night.*

sneak TELL SECRETLY *Br slang disapproving* /sniːk/, *Am* **snitch**, *Aus* **dob** *v* [I] to secretly tell someone in authority, esp. a teacher, that someone else has done something bad, often in order to cause trouble • *She was one of those dreadful children who was always sneaking* **on** *other kids in the class.* • *Have you been sneaking again?*

sneak *esp. Br slang disapproving* /sniːk/, *Am* **snitch, tat·tle·tale** /£ˈtæt·l̩.teɪl, $ˈtæt̬-/, *Aus* **dob·ber** *n* [C] • *You told Mrs Cooper that it was me who tipped the paint over, didn't you – you nasty little sneak!*

sneak·er /£ˈsniː·kəʳ, $-kɚ/, *infml* **sneak** *n* [C] *Am for* PLIMSOLL • PIC› **Shoes**

sneak·ing /ˈsniː·kɪŋ/ *adj* [not gradable] (of feelings such as respect and admiration) unwilling or secret, usually because felt for a person whose basic character or moral principles you do not like or trust, or (of a belief, esp. an unpleasant one) not certain but probably true • *I don't like the woman and I certainly don't like what she stands for, but I do have a sneaking admiration for her.* • *I've got a sneaking* **feeling/suspicion** *that we're going the wrong way.*

sneer *(obj)* /£snɪəʳ, $snɪr/ *v disapproving* to express or show in your facial expression a very strong lack of respect (for someone or something you consider to be of little value or interest), esp. in a way that is unkind and rude • *You may sneer, but a lot of people like this kind of music.* [I] • *She'll probably sneer* **at** *my new shoes because they're not leather.* [I] • *Some people sneer* **at** *the sixties generation with their banners of love and peace.* [I] • *"Is that the best you can do?" he sneered.* [+ clause]

sneer /£snɪəʳ, $snɪr/ *n* [C] *disapproving* • *"How much did you say you earned last year – was it fifteen thousand?" she said with a sneer.*

sneer·ing /£ˈsnɪə·rɪŋ, $ˈsnɪr·ɪŋ/ *adj disapproving* • *I don't like that superior, sneering tone of his.*

sneer·ing·ly /£ˈsnɪə·rɪŋ·li, $ˈsnɪr·ɪŋ-/ *adv disapproving*

sneeze /sniːz/ *v* [I] to send air out from the nose and mouth explosively, in a way that you cannot control • *I keep sneezing – I hope I'm not getting another cold.* • *Cats make him sneeze – I think he's allergic to the fur.* • *'Bless you' is often said to people who have just sneezed.* • *(infml, often humorous)* If you say that something, esp. an amount of money, is **not to be sneezed at** you mean that it is a large enough amount to be worth having: *Well, a 5% pay-increase means an extra £700 a year which is not to be sneezed at!* • LP› **Phrases and customs**

sneeze /sniːz/ *n* [C] • *He's got all the classic symptoms of a cold – the coughs and sneezes and the sore throat.*

snick *obj* /snɪk/ *v* [T] *Br and Aus* (in sports, esp. cricket) to hit the ball off the edge of the BAT • *Carlton snicked the ball low and fast to Lynch's right.*

snick /snɪk/ *n* [C] *Br and Aus*

snick·er /£ˈsnɪk·əʳ, $-ɚ/ *v* [I] *Am for* SNIGGER

snide /snaɪd/ *adj* **-r, -st** (esp. of remarks) containing unpleasant and indirect criticism • *She made one or two snide* **remarks** *about their house which I thought was a bit unnecessary.*

snide·ly /ˈsnaɪd·li/ *adv* • *She referred to him rather snidely as "a small man in a large suit".* • *'Well, she's certainly better looking than her mother,' she said snidely.*

snide·ness /ˈsnaɪd·nəs/ *n*

sniff *(obj)* /snɪf/ *v* to take air in through your nose noisily and in one action, usually to stop the liquid inside the nose from flowing out, or to smell something by taking air in through your nose • *Blow your nose properly but don't keep sniffing, Emily!* [I] • *You were sniffing a lot – I presumed you had a cold.* [I] • *She sniffed miserably, and wiped a tear from the corner of her eye.* [I] • *He sniffed* (= smelt) *his socks to see if they needed washing.* [T] • *Dogs love sniffing* (= smelling) *each other.* [T] • *He was expelled from school for sniffing glue* (= taking in the gas from glue because of the pleasurable feelings that that gives). [T] • *She sniffed* **(at)** *her glass of wine before tasting it.* [T; I + *at*] • *(fig.) A few computer firms are sniffing* **at** (= showing an interest in) *the project already.* [I] • If you **sniff at** something, you show a low opinion of it: *She sniffed at my new job, saying she couldn't imagine why I would want to do it.* ○ *A two million pound profit is* **not to be** *sniffed at* (= is worth having). • *Dogs are sometimes used at airports to sniff* **out** (= find by smelling) *drugs in people's luggage.* [M] • *(fig.) Her job is to go round the big fashion shows sniffing* **out** (= discovering) *talent for a modelling agency.* [M] • *(fig.) "They didn't even serve wine at dinner!"*

she sniffed (= said unpleasantly and in a way expressing a low opinion). [+ clause]

sniff /snɪf/ *n* [C] • *He* **took** *a deep sniff of the country air.* • *Have a sniff of this medicine – it smells revolting, doesn't it?* • *"I don't think much of that idea," she said with a sniff* (= an expression of a low opinion).

snif·fer /£'snɪf·əʳ, $-ɚ/ *n* [C] • *My cousin is a* **glue** *sniffer* (= a person who takes in the gas from glue because of the pleasurable feelings that that gives). • A **sniffer dog** is a dog that is trained and used by the police or army to find hidden drugs and bombs by smelling them.

snif·fy /'snɪf·i/ *adj* **-ier, -iest** *infml* • *She's a bit sniffy* **about** (= She shows that she has a low opinion of) *my taste in music.*

snif·fle /'snɪf·l̩/, **snuf·fle** *v* [I] to SNIFF quietly and repeatedly, usually because you are crying or because you have a COLD (= an infection of the nose, throat, etc.) • *I left her sniffling into her handkerchief.* • *You're sniffling a lot today – have you got a cold?*

snif·fle /'snɪf·l̩/, **snuf·fle** *n* [C] • *There were a few sniffles* (= acts of crying) *in the audience at the end of the play.* • If you have **a sniffle/the sniffles**, you have a slight COLD: *I had a cold a couple of weeks ago and it's left me with a bit of a sniffle.*

snif·ter DRINK /£'snɪf·təʳ, $-t̬ɚ/ *n* [C] *dated infml* a small drink of something alcoholic • *How about a snifter before dinner?*

snif·ter GLASS /£'snɪf·təʳ, $-t̬ɚ/ *n* [C] *Am* a bowl-shaped glass which is narrower at the top and has a short stem, used for drinking BRANDY (= a strong alcoholic drink)

snig·ger /£'snɪg·əʳ, $-ɚ/, *esp. Am* **snick·er** *v* [I] to laugh at someone or something childishly and often unkindly • *They spent half the time sniggering* **at** *the clothes people were wearing.* • *What are you two sniggering* **at/about**?

snig·ger /£'snɪg·əʳ, $-ɚ/ *n* [C] • *We were* **having** *a snigger at the bride who was rather large and dressed in a tight pale pink dress.* • *Now and again a swear word raises a few schoolboy sniggers.*

snip *obj* CUT /snɪp/ *v* [T] **-pp-** to cut something, usually with one or two short quick actions, using a pair of SCISSORS or another device with two blades • *I asked the hairdresser just to snip the ends of my hair.* • *Have you seen the scissors? I want to snip* **off** *this loose thread.*

snip /snɪp/ *n* [C] • *Give it a snip with the scissors.* • *(Br infml humorous)* The snip is a VASECTOMY.

snip CHEAP ITEM /snɪp/ *n* [U] *Br infml* an item which is being sold cheaply, for less than you would expect • *The sunglasses are now available in major stores,* **a snip at** *£60 a pair.* • Snip can also be used humorously of items which are extremely expensive: *'What did you say you got your dress for in the sale? – £350 reduced from £500?' 'Yes, it was* **a** *snip!'*

snipe SHOOT /snaɪp/ *v* [I] to shoot at someone from a position where you cannot be seen, or *(fig.)* to criticize someone unpleasantly • *Another of the rebels' tactics has involved sniping* **at** *and indiscriminately shelling civilians.* • *(fig.) The former minister has been making himself unpopular recently, sniping* **at** *his ex-colleagues.*

snip·er /£'snaɪ·pəʳ, $-pɚ/ *n* [C] • *He was shot and fatally injured by a sniper on the outskirts of the city.* • *Sniper fire has claimed countless lives these past few weeks.*

snipe BIRD /snaɪp/ *n* [C] *pl* **snipe** or **snipes** a bird with a long straight beak which lives near rivers and MARSHES (= low land that is wet and sometimes flooded) • *The 11 000-acre estate on the Isle of Lewis offers grouse and snipe shooting and trout fishing.*

snip·pet /'snɪp·ɪt/ *n* [C] *infml* a small and often interesting bit of esp. news, information or conversation • *I heard an interesting snippet on the radio this morning.* • *I like being on public transport because you overhear these fascinating snippets* **of** *conversation.* • *My husband meets a few actors in his job, so I get to hear lots of little snippets* **of** *gossip that you don't get in the magazines.*

snit /snɪt/ *n* [C] *Am and Aus infml* an angry mood • *He was* **in** *a snit this morning and I didn't dare approach him.* • *My mother's always getting* **into** *snits.*

snitch TELL SECRETLY /snɪtʃ/ *v* [I] *slang disapproving* to secretly tell someone in authority that someone else has done something bad, often in order to cause trouble • *He snitched* **to** *my boss that I'd been making long-distance calls on her phone after she had left the office!* • *Snitching* **on** *your friends is generally regarded as fairly low behaviour.*

snitch *obj* STEAL /snɪtʃ/ *v* [T] *infml* to steal, or to take dishonestly • *"Where did you get that money?" "I snitched it* **from** *my dad when he wasn't looking."* • *He's always snitching my ideas and pretending they're his own.*

sni·vel /'snɪv·ᵊl/ *v* [I] **-ll-** or *Am usually* **-l-** to cry slightly in a way that is weak and does not make other people feel sympathy for you • *He's sitting in his bedroom snivelling because he was told off for not doing his homework.*

sni·vel·ling, *Am usually* **sni·vel·ing** /'snɪv·ᵊl·ɪŋ/ *adj infml dated* • Snivelling can be used to describe someone whom you do not like because they are weak and unpleasant: *That snivelling creep/coward!*

snob /£snɒb, $snɑːb/ *n* [C] *esp. disapproving* a person who respects and likes to be with only those people who are of a high social class, or a person who has extremely high standards in a particular (usually stated) thing and is not satisfied by the things that ordinary people like • *He's a frightful snob – if you haven't been to the right school he probably won't even speak to you.* • *I suppose you wouldn't buy clothes from an ordinary high street shop, would you, Polly – you're such a snob!* • *I'm afraid I'm a bit of a wine snob/a snob where wine is concerned.* • *You pay an extra $50 just for the designer label – for some reason it has some snob* **appeal/value**.

snob·bish /£'snɒb·ɪʃ, $'snɑː·bɪʃ/, *infml* **snob·by** /£'snɒb·i, $'snɑː·bi/ *adj esp. disapproving* • *My brother is very snobbish about cars.* • *He seems only to write for a small audience of people who share his snobbish literary views.*

snob·bish·ly /£'snɒb·ɪʃ·li, $'snɑː·bɪʃ-/, **snob·bi·ly** *adv* • *"We only eat at the best restaurants," she said snobbishly.*

snob·be·ry /£'snɒb·ᵊr·i, $'snɑː·bɚ-/, **snob·bish·ness** /£'snɒb·ɪʃ·nəs, $'snɑː·bɪʃ-/ *n* [U] *esp. disapproving* • *She accused me of snobbery because I sent my sons to a private school.* • *Why are certain colleges rated more highly than others – is it just* **intellectual** *snobbery?*

snog *(obj)* /£snɒg, $snɑːg/ *v* **-gg-** *Br infml* to kiss and hold a person in a sexual way • *I saw them snogging on the back seat of a bus.* [I] • *I've never snogged* **(with)** *a man with a beard.* [T; I + *with*]

snog /£snɒg, $snɑːg/ *n* [C] *Br infml* • *He caught us* **having** *a snog.*

snook /£snuːk, $snʊk/ *n* [U] **cock a snook**, see at COCK SHOW LACK OF RESPECT

snook·er GAME /£'snuː·kəʳ, $-kɚ/ *n* [U] a game played by two people on a cloth-covered table in which CUES (= long thin poles) are used to hit coloured balls into six holes around the table in a fixed order • *Do you want a game of snooker?* • Compare POOL GAME. • LP **Sports**

snook·er *obj* PREVENT /£'snuː·kəʳ, $-kɚ/ *v* [T usually passive] *Br and Aus* to prevent (someone) from completing an intended plan of action • *We had intended to go driving around Scotland, but unless I can get my licence we're snookered.* • *(Am)* To snooker (someone) is to deceive or trick them.

snoop /snuːp/ *v* [I] *infml disapproving* to look round (somewhere belonging to someone else) secretly, in order to discover things about the place or about its owner's private life • *People were sent out to snoop* **on** *factories in order to check that banned missiles were not being produced.* • *We'd better tell Joe that the police have been snooping* **about/around**. • *She's the sort of person you can imagine snooping* **about/around** *your room when you're not there.* • To snoop is also to try to find out about other people's private lives: *I don't mean to snoop, but is there something wrong?* ○ *Clara's husband is snooping* **on** *her because he thinks she is seeing another man.*

snoop /snuːp/ *n* [C] *infml* • *I think someone's been* **having** *a snoop* (= secret look) *around my office – I didn't leave that drawer open.* • A snoop is also a **snooper**.

snoop·er /£'snuː·pəʳ, $-pɚ/, **snoop** *n* [C] *infml disapproving* • *The government employ snoopers whose job is to secretly follow people who are suspected of claiming unemployment benefit while working.* • *Most journalists are snoopers by nature.*

snoot /snuːt/ *n* [C] *Am slang* a nose • *Give your snoot a wipe, honey.*

snoot·y /£'snuː·ti, $-t̬i/ *adj* **-ier, -iest** *infml* seeming by your manner to think that you are better than everyone else, esp. because you are from a higher social class • *She was one of those really snooty sales assistants that you often find in expensive shops.* • *I hope Alex doesn't bring that girlfriend of his along – she's really snooty.*

snoot·i·ly /£'snuː·tɪ·li, $-t̬ɪ-/ *adv infml* • *"I don't want to sit at a table with those people," she said snootily.*

snooze /snuːz/ *v* [I] *infml* to sleep lightly for a short while • *When I got there Mark was snoozing on a blanket in the* *garden.* • *The dog's snoozing in front of the fire.* • A **snooze button** is a button on an **alarm clock** (= a clock for waking you up) that you press, after the bell has woken you up, if you want to sleep for a few minutes more before being woken up again, by the bell ringing another time.

snooze /snuːz/ *n* [C] *infml* • *I* **had** *a nice little snooze in the back of the car.*

snore /£snɔːʳ, $snɔːr/ *v* [I] to make loud noises as you breathe while you are sleeping • *Sometimes my husband snores so loudly, it keeps me awake at night.* • *Do you know any cures for snoring?* • *Snoring is caused by the soft palate vibrating.* • (NL)

snore /£snɔːʳ, $snɔːr/ *n* [C] • *I could hear loud snores coming from Jim's bedroom.*

snor·er /£'snɔː·rəʳ, $'snɔːr·ɚ/ *n* [C] • *He's a terrible snorer.*

snor·kel /£'snɔː·kəl, $'snɔːr-/, *Aus also* **schnor·kel** *n* [C] a tube which allows a swimmer under but near the surface of the water to breathe, fitting into the mouth at one end and sticking out above the water at the other • *I've got a mask with a snorkel attached.* • PIC› **Water sports**

snor·kel·ling *Br, Am* **snor·kel·ing** /£'snɔː·kəl·ɪŋ, $'snɔːr-/ *n* [U] *Aus also* **schnorkelling** • *We went snorkelling along the Great Barrier Reef.* • PIC› **Water sports**

snort *(obj)* /£snɔːt, $snɔːrt/ *v* to make an explosive sound by forcing air quickly up or down the nose • *He did an impression of a horse snorting.* [I] • *Camille snorts when she laughs.* [I] • *(infml) By this time I was snorting* **with** *laughter* (= laughing a lot and loudly) *and quite out of control.* • To snort an illegal drug is to take it by breathing it in through the nose: *I saw a man in the toilets snorting what looked like cocaine.* [T] • To snort is also to suddenly express strong feelings of annoyance, disapproval or impatience, either by speaking or in a sound that you make: *"And you call that a first class service?" snorted one indignant customer.*

snort /£snɔːt, $snɔːrt/ *n* [C] • *The minister's speech drew loud snorts of derisive laughter.*

snot /£snɒt, $snɑːt/ *n* [U] *infml* the greenish yellow substance produced in the nose; MUCUS

snot·ty /£'snɒt·i, $'snɑː·t̬i/ *adj* **-ier, -iest** *infml* • *You could have told me I had a snotty nose!* • *I don't want to use your snotty handkerchief!*

snot·ty /£'snɒt·i, $'snɑː·t̬i/ *adj* **-ier, -iest** *infml disapproving* tending to behave rudely to other people in a way that shows that you believe yourself to be better than them • *The only difficult bit about working in a shop is when you get a snotty customer that you have to deal with.* • *She's got a rather snotty manner which can be a bit off-putting.*

snout /snaʊt/ *n* [C] the nose and mouth which stick out from the face of some animals • *a pig's snout* • *I felt a dog's snout nuzzling my leg.* • Snout is also *slang for* a person's nose: *George has an enormous snout.*

snow WEATHER /£snəʊ, $snoʊ/ *n* the small soft white bits of ice which sometimes fall from the sky when it is cold, or the white layer on the ground and other surfaces which it forms • *Outside the snow was* **falling**. [U] • *He came in, stamping the snow off his boots.* [U] • *Let's go and play in the snow!* [U] • *We went sledging in the snow.* [U] • *I think the snow is starting to melt/thaw.* [U] • **A blanket of** *snow lay on the ground.* [U] • *Her hair was jet-black, her lips ruby-red and her skin* **as white as** *snow.* [U] • A snow is a single fall of snow: *We haven't had many heavy snows this winter.* [C] • *(esp. Am)* A **snow bank** is a large pile of snow. See also SNOWDRIFT. • **Snow blindness** is a temporary loss of sight which is caused by the GLARE (= brightness) of light reflected by large areas of snow. • *Halfway up the mountain I suddenly went* **snow-blind**. • **Snow-capped** mountains and hills have snow on the top of them. • A **snow pea** is *Am and Aus for* MANGETOUT. • A *(Br)* **snow tyre**/*(Am)* **snow tire** is a tyre with a pattern of raised lines which are thicker than usual in order to stop a vehicle from sliding on ice or snow. • *As an old lady, her hair was* **snow-white** (= pure white). • *"Snow White and the Seven Dwarfs"* (title of fairy tale) • *"Where are the snows of yesteryear?"* (François Villon *Le Grand Testament*, 1461) • PIC› **Peas and beans**

snow /£snəʊ, $snoʊ/ *v* [I] • **It's** *snowing, mummy!* • **It** *had snowed overnight and a thick white layer covered the ground.* • If you are snowed **in/up**, you are prevented from travelling from a place because of very heavy snow: *We were snowed in for four whole days last winter – the kids couldn't even go to school.* • *(fig.)* If you are **snowed under**, you have too much work, esp. of the type that involves writing and papers.

snow·y /£'snəʊ·i, $'snoʊ-/ *adj* **-ier, -iest** • *We've had a very snowy winter this year.* • *I remember him as an old man with a snowy-***white** (= pure white) *beard.*

snow *obj* CHARM /£snəʊ, $snoʊ/ *v* [T] *Am and Aus* to deceive or trick (someone) by charming and persuasive talk or by giving them a lot of information • *It's hoped that the electorate won't be snowed into supporting that measure.* • A **snow-job** is an attempt to persuade someone to do something, esp. by praising them and using charm: *My boss* **did** *a snow-job* **on** *me.*

snow DRUG /£snəʊ, $snoʊ/ *n* [U] *slang* COCAINE (= a drug) used illegally for pleasure

snow·ball /£'snəʊ·bɔːl, $'snoʊ·bɑːl/ *n* [C] a ball of snow pressed together in the hands, esp. for throwing • *Someone* **threw** *a snowball at me from behind.* • *A bunch of kids were having a snowball fight.* • *(esp. Am and Aus infml)* If something does not have **a snowball's chance in hell** of succeeding, there is no chance of it succeeding: *If he can't afford a good lawyer, he doesn't have a snowball's chance in hell of winning the case.* • A **snowball effect** is a situation in which something increases in size and importance very quickly: *This new project has had a snowball effect in creating a lot of new possibilities for the company.*

snow·ball *obj* /£'snəʊ·bɔːl, $'snoʊ·bɑːl/ *v* [T] • If a plan snowballs, it grows in size, importance and influence with increasing speed: *Last year we started raising money locally for the hospital, then the campaign went nationwide and the whole thing just snowballed.*

snow·bound /£'snəʊ·baʊnd, $'snoʊ-/ *adj* (of vehicles or people) prevented from or having difficulties travelling because of heavy snow, or (of roads) not able to be travelled on or reached because of heavy snow • *Several snowbound vehicles have already been rescued on this stretch of the motorway.* • *Large areas of Scotland and Northern Ireland are still snowbound.*

snow·drift /£'snəʊ·drɪft, $'snoʊ-/ *n* [C] a bank of deep snow formed by the wind • *Snowdrifts are causing problems for drivers in this region.*

snow·drop /£'snəʊ·drɒp, $'snoʊ·drɑːp/ *n* [C] a plant which produces small white bell-shaped flowers in the early spring • PIC› **Flowers and plants**

snow·fall /£'snəʊ·fɔːl, $'snoʊ·fɑːl/ *n* the amount of snow that falls in a particular area during a particular period, or a fall of snow • *The annual snowfall for this region is the largest across the whole of the country.* [U] • *Isola had heavy snowfall yesterday making skiing conditions difficult.* [U] • *Heavy snowfalls* (= falls of snow) *are predicted for tonight and tomorrow.* [C]

snow·flake /£'snəʊ·fleɪk, $'snoʊ-/ *n* [C] one of the small soft masses of ice CRYSTALS that fall as snow • *She looked up into the sky and saw the snowflakes whirling down.*

snow·line /£'snəʊ·laɪn, $'snoʊ-/ *n* [U] **the snowline** the level on a mountain above which snow is found for most or all of the year

snow·man /£'snəʊ·mæn, $'snoʊ-/ *n* [C] *pl* **-men** a model of a person made of snow • *I helped the kids to build a snowman.* • *"Frostie the snowman was a jolly happy soul"* (from the song *Frostie the Snowman* written by Steve Nelson and Jack Rollins, 1951)

snow·mo·bile /£'snəʊ·məˌbiːl, $'snoʊ-/ *n* [C] a vehicle for travelling on snow and ice which moves using a chain of flat metal pieces which are fastened over its wheels and is directed using a pair of SKIS at the front

snow·plough VEHICLE *Br, Am* **snow·plow** /£'snəʊ·plaʊ, $'snoʊ-/ *n* [C] a vehicle or device for clearing snow from roads or railways

snow·plough SPORT *Br, Am* **snow·plow** /£'snəʊ·plaʊ, $'snoʊ-/ *n* [C usually sing] (in SKIING) a way of turning or stopping in which the points of the SKIS are turned inwards and the person's weight on one or other of the skis influences the direction of movement

snow·shoe /£'snəʊ·ʃuː, $'snoʊ-/ *n* [C] a flat frame with straps of material stretched across it which can be fixed to a boot to allow a person to walk on the snow without sinking in

snow·storm /£'snəʊ·stɔːm, $'snoʊ·stɔːrm/ *n* [C] a heavy fall of snow which is blown by strong winds

snow·suit /£'snəʊ·suːt, $'snoʊ-/ *n* [C] an item of winter clothing for a child which is warm and covers most of the body

snow·y /£'snəʊ·i, $'snoʊ-/ *adj* See at SNOW WEATHER

Snr, *esp. Am* **Sr** *adj* [after n; not gradable] *abbreviation for* SENIOR [OLDER]. Used after a man's name to refer to the older of two people in the same family who have the same name.

snub *obj* [INSULT] /snʌb/ *v* [T] **-bb-** to insult (someone) by not giving them any attention or treating them as if they are not important • *I think she felt snubbed because Anthony hadn't bothered to introduce himself.*

snub /snʌb/ *n* [C] • *I didn't say hello because I simply didn't recognize her and apparently she took it as a snub.*

snub [NOSE] /snʌb/ *adj disapproving* (of a nose) short, flat and turned slightly up at the end • *She has a snub* **nose**/*is* **snub-nosed**, *but she's quite pretty.* • A **snub-nosed** gun is one with a very short BARREL (= tube): *a snub-nosed revolver*

snuck *esp. Am* /snʌk/ *past simple and past participle of* SNEAK [MOVE SECRETLY]

snuff [POWDER] /snʌf/ *n* [U] tobacco in the form of a powder for breathing into the nose • *a* **pinch of** *snuff* • *She gave me an antique snuff* **box** *for my birthday.* • *Very few people* **take** *snuff nowadays.*

snuff *obj* [PUT OUT] /snʌf/ *v* [T] to put out (a flame, esp. from a candle), usually by covering it with something so that it has no oxygen • *One by one she snuffed* **(out)** *the candles.* [T/M] • *It will take weeks to snuff* **out** *the burning grassland.* [M] • To snuff something **out** is also to end it: *Italy's fourth goal well and truly snuffed out any hopes that England may have had of winning this game.* [M] ○ *The country has been able to celebrate the return of its independence so brutally snuffed out in 1940.* [M] ○ *(Am) In the end they hoped his life would be snuffed out* (= he would die) *so he wouldn't suffer any more.* [M] • *(esp. Br and Aus dated infml)* To **snuff it** it is to die. • *(infml)* A **snuff movie** is a PORNOGRAPHIC film (= sex film) in which one of the actors or actresses is really murdered in order to provide the viewer with extra excitement: *Links have been suggested between the death of several boys in the London area and the alleged making of child 'snuff movies'.*

snuf·fle /ˈsnʌf·l̩/ *v* [I] SNIFFLE

snug /snʌg/ *adj* **snugger, snuggest** (of a person) feeling warm, comfortable and protected, or (of a place, esp. a small place) giving feelings of warmth, comfort and protection • *We curled up in bed, all snug and warm, and listened to the wind in the trees outside.* • *I bet your feet are nice and snug in your fur-lined boots!* • *I like the smaller room for the winter because it's nice and snug with the fire blazing.* • Snug also means fitting closely: *That green skirt is a snug* **fit** *now but if I put on any weight I'll never be able to get into it.* • *(humorous saying)* '(As) snug as a bug in a rug' means feeling very warm, comfortable and protected.

snug·ly /ˈsnʌg·li/ *adv* • *She's curled up snugly in the armchair, reading a book.* • *If we put the washing-machine over there the fridge will* **fit** *snugly* (= closely) *into this space.*

snug /snʌg/ *n* [C] *Br* • A snug (also **snuggery**) is a small room or enclosed area in a PUB where only a few people can sit.

snug·gle /ˈsnʌg·l̩/ *v* [I always + adv/prep] to move yourself into a warm and comfortable position, esp. one in which your body is against another person or covered by something • *The children snuggled* **up** *to their mother to get warm.* • *I was just snuggling* **down** *into my warm duvet when the telephone rang.*

so [TO SUCH A DEGREE] /£səʊ, $soʊ/ *adv* [not gradable] to such a great degree • *She's so beautiful.* • *Your hair is so soft.* • *Thank you for being so patient.* • *Don't be so stupid!* • *What are you looking so pleased about?* • *I didn't know she had so many children!* • *I've never seen so much food in all my life.* • *You can only do so much to help* (= There is a limit to how much you can help). • *(infml) She's* **ever** *so kind and nice.* • *I'm so tired* **(that)** *I could sleep in this chair!* [+ adj + (*that*) clause] • *That soup was so filling* **(that)** *I don't think I'll want a main course.* [+ adj + (*that*) clause] • *You were so rude to her* **(that)** *I don't think she'll be coming back!* [+ adj + (*that*) clause] • *He's* **not** *so stupid* **as** *he looks.* • *I'm* **not** *so desperate* **as to** *agree to that.* • *The word itself is so rare* **as to be** *almost obsolete.* • *I've never been to so expensive* **a** *restaurant* (= such an expensive restaurant) *before.* • *(old use or literary) So fair* **a** *face* (= such a beautiful face) *he could not recall.* • *(esp. literary)* So is sometimes used at the end of a sentence to mean to a very great degree: *Is that why you hate him so?* ○ *And I love you so.* ○ *You worry so!* • See also SO-AND-SO; SO-CALLED; SO-SO.

so [SIMILARLY] /£səʊ, $soʊ/ *adv* [not gradable] used usually before the verbs 'have', 'be' or 'do', and other **auxiliary verbs** to express the meaning 'in the same way' or 'similarly' • *"I've got an enormous amount of work to do." "So have I."* • *"I'm allergic to nuts." "So is my brother."* • *"I love Australian wine." "So do I."* • *Neil left just after midnight and so did Roz.* • *"I'd love to go to India." "So would I."* • *"You look really tired." "So would you if you'd just worked for 15 hours without a break."* • *Just* **as** *you like to have a night out with the lads, so I like to go out with the girls now and again.*

so [SENTENCE BEGINNING] /£səʊ, $soʊ/ *conjunction* used at the beginning of a sentence to connect it with something that has been said or has happened previously • So can be used as a way of making certain that you or someone else understand something correctly, often when you are repeating the important points of a plan: *So we leave on the Thursday and get back the next Tuesday, yes?* ○ *So now, you're getting the shopping while I pick up the kids – is that what we said?* ○ *So we're not going away this weekend after all?* • So can also be used to refer to a discovery that you have just made: *So that's what he does when I'm not around!* ○ *So that's where all the biscuits keep going – you feed them to the wretched dog!* ○ *So that's why she made an excuse and left early!* • You might say 'so' to return to a conversation that you were having a short time earlier: *So, there I was standing at the edge of the road with only my dressing-gown on ...* ○ *So, you were saying...* ○ *So, just to finish what I was saying earlier...* • So can be used as a brief pause, sometimes to emphasize what you are saying: *And so, finally, to the tax reforms, the topic that has dominated the news these past few days.* ○ *So, here we are again – just you and me.* • So can also be used before you introduce a subject of conversation that is of present interest, esp. when you are asking a question: *So, when am I going to see you again?* ○ *So who's coming tonight?* ○ *So, who do you think is going to win the election?* ○ *So you're going to hire the German nanny – I think that sounds like a good decision.* • *(infml)* So is sometimes used to show that you agree with something that someone has just said, but you do not think that it is important: *So the car's expensive – well, I can afford it.* • *(infml)* So/**So what** is used to mean 'it's not important' and 'I don't care.': *"She might complain to your manager." "So what (if she does)? – I know I'm in the right!"* ○ *So what* **if** *I'm 35 and I'm not married – I lead a perfectly fulfilling life!* ○ *"Andrew won't like it, you know." "So? – I don't care what Andrew thinks!"* • [LP] **Clauses**

so [IN ORDER THAT] /£səʊ, $soʊ/ *conjunction, adv* [not gradable] used before you give an explanation for the action that you have just mentioned • *I deliberately didn't have lunch so* **(that)** *I would be hungry tonight.* • *I warned her you'd be late so* **(that)** *she wouldn't start worrying.* • *Leave the keys out so* **(that)** *I remember to take them with me.* • *I always keep fruit in the fridge so* **(that)** *the insects keep off it/***so as to** *keep insects off it.*

so [THEREFORE] /£səʊ, $soʊ/ *conjunction* and for that reason; therefore • *I was getting tired so I came home.* • *My knee started hurting so I stopped running.* • *I was lost so I bought a street map.* • *I couldn't find you so I left.* • *He's in a very delicate state at the moment so you've got to be gentle with him.* • *(infml humorous)* **So there**! is used for emphasis, or to show that something is being done in opposition to someone else's wishes: *Mine's bigger than yours, so there!* ○ *No, I won't help you, so there!*

so [IT IS THE SITUATION] /£səʊ, $soʊ/ *adj* [after v], *adv* [not gradable] used instead of repeating something that has just been mentioned, to mean it is the situation • *"Anthony and Mia don't get on very well." "Is that so?"* • *"You're not allowed in here." "Really? Could you tell me why that's so?"* • *"The forecast says it might rain." "If so we'll have the party inside."* • *Do let me know if you're not coming because if so we'll give your place to someone else.* • *Carla's coming over this summer or so I've heard.* • So is often used in this way with a verb of thinking, hoping or saying: *"I hope they stay together." "I hope so too."* ○ *"Do you think he's upset?" "I don't think so."* ○ *"Is it true that we're not getting a pay increase this year?" "I'm afraid so."* ○ *James is coming tonight, or so he said* ○ *"Dina's business collapsed." "So I believe."* • So can also be used in this way to give certainty to a fact that has just been stated: *"My eyes are slightly different colours." "So they are."* ○ *"That's her brother – he looks like James Dean." "So he does."* ○ *"There, I told you there was a sculpture outside the restaurant." "So there is – how strange I hadn't noticed it."* ○ *"I'm sorry I'm late." "So you should be."* • So can be used instead of repeating an adjective that has already been mentioned: *Of all the sweet-natured and kind people that I know, nobody is more so than*

Mira. ○ *He's incredibly generous – in fact so much so that it's embarrassing.* ○ *She's quite reasonable to work with – more so than I was led to believe.* ○ *He's quite bright – well, certainly more so than his brother.* • *(Am infml)* So is used, esp. by children, to argue against a negative statement: *'You didn't even see the movie.' 'I did so!'*

so IN THIS WAY /£səʊ, $soʊ/ *adv* [not gradable] in this way; like this • *The pillars, which are outside the building, are so placed in order to provide the maximum space inside.* • *I've so arranged my trip that I'll be home on Friday evening.* • So can be used when you are showing how something is done: *Just fold this piece of paper back, so, and make a crease here.* ○ *Gently fold in the eggs* **like** *so.* • So is also used when you are representing the measurements of something: *"How tall is he next to you?" "Oh, about so big," she said, indicating the level of her neck.* ○ *"The table that I liked best was about so wide," she said, holding her arms out a metre and a half.*

so TIDY /£səʊ, $soʊ/ *adj* [not gradable] **just/exactly so** perfectly tidy and well arranged • *He's a perfectionist about the house – everything has to be just so.*

soak *(obj)* MAKE WET /£səʊk, $soʊk/ *v* to make very wet, or (of liquid) to be absorbed in large amounts • *The wind had blown the rain into the bedroom and soaked the bed.* [T] • *You'd better wipe up that red wine you've spilt before it soaks* (= is absorbed) **into** *the carpet.* [I] • *Blood had soaked* (= been absorbed) **through** *both bandages.* [I] • To soak something or allow it to soak is also to (cause it to) be left in liquid, esp. in order to clean it, or soften it, or change its flavour: *I thought I'd* **leave** *my trousers to soak for a while to get the worst of the dirt out.* [I] ○ *You can usually soak* **out** *a stain.* [M] ○ *Leave the beans to soak overnight.* [I] ○ *You soak the fruit* **in** *brandy for a few hours before you add it to the mixture.* [T] • If a dry material or substance soaks **up** a liquid, it absorbs it through its surface: *I tried to soak up most of the spilt milk with a cloth.* [M] ○ *You should have some food to soak up all that alcohol you've drunk!* [M] ○ *Damage to the environment has reduced the capacity of trees to soak up heavy rainfall.* [M] ○ *(fig.) Given the right environment, children are like sponges and will soak up* (= take in) *information.* [M] ○ *(fig.) The visitor can walk along these bustling streets during the fiesta and just soak up* (= take in and enjoy) **the atmosphere**. [M] ○ *(fig.) She's one of these people who finds it enough to just lie on the beach all day and soak up* **the sun**. [M]

soak /£səʊk, $soʊk/ *n* [C] • *Most dried beans need a soak before they're cooked.* • *Showers are all right but there's nothing like a good long soak in the bath.*

soaked /£səʊkt, $soʊkt/ *adj* • Soaked means extremely wet: *I'm going to have to take these clothes off – I'm soaked* **to the skin**! ○ *My shoes are soaked* **through**. ○ *His T-shirt was soaked* **in** *sweat.* ○ *A bottle of wine had broken in my suitcase and half my clothes were soaked.*

soak·ing /£'səʊ·kɪŋ, $'soʊ-/ *adj* • *It's so hot outside – I've only been walking ten minutes and my shirt is soaking* **(wet)**!

soak DRINKER /£səʊk, $soʊk/ *n* [C] *dated infml* a person who is habitually drunk • *Grandpa was a real old soak.*

so–and–so NAMELESS PERSON /£'səʊ·ənd·səʊ, $'soʊ·ənd·soʊ/ *n* [C] *pl* **so-and-sos** *infml* used instead of a particular name to refer to someone or something, esp. when the real name is not important or you have forgotten it • *She always keeps me up to date with the latest gossip – you know, so-and-so from down the road is having a baby and so-and-so's just bought a car.*

so–and–so UNPLEASANT PERSON /£'səʊ·ənd·səʊ, $'soʊ·ənd·soʊ/ *n* [C] *infml* an unpleasant person • So-and-so is used of an unpleasant person to avoid using a more offensive or less polite word: *Oh, he was a right old so-and-so that Mr Baker – he hadn't got a nice word to say about anyone!*

soap /£səʊp, $soʊp/ *n* a substance used for washing the body which is usually hard, often has a pleasant smell, and produces a mass of bubbles when rubbed with water, or a piece of this • *a soap dish/dispenser* [U] • *Have you washed your hands properly, Anna – with soap?* [U] • *He was clean-shaven and smelt of soap.* [U] • *I hate that liquid soap that you get in public lavatories.* [U] • *We need another* **bar/tablet of** *soap in the bathroom.* [U] • *She bought me a box of prettily coloured soaps.* [C] • *Blow me a soap* **bubble**, *daddy!* • **Soap flakes** are small flat pieces of soap used for washing clothes, esp. by hand: *a box of soap flakes* • PIC **Bar**

soap *obj* /£səʊp, $soʊp/ *v* [T] • *Have you soaped* (= put soap on) *yourself all over, Alice?* • *Let me soap your back.*

soap·y /£'səʊ·pi, $'soʊ-/ *adj* **-ier, -iest** • *I soaked it in some soapy water and the stains came out.* • *I used to think avocados tasted soapy* (= like soap) *when I was a child.*

soap·box /£'səʊp·bɒks, $'soʊp·bɑːks/ *n* [C] a rough wooden box used, esp. in the past, for storing and carrying goods in and traditionally used as a raised surface for people to stand on while making informal public speeches • *We used to go to Speaker's Corner in Hyde Park and watch people making speeches on their soapboxes.* • *(fig. disapproving) If we're not careful he'll* **get on** *his* **soapbox** (= start to express his opinions with force) *again and start lecturing us on the evils of the modern world!*

soap op·e·ra /£'səʊp,ɒp·rə, $'soʊp,ɑː·prə/, *infml* **soap** *n* [C] a series of television or radio programmes about the lives and problems of a particular group of characters. The series continues over a long period and is broadcast (several times) every week. • *She used to watch all the American soaps.* • *Soap operas are called soap operas because they were originally sponsored in the US by soap manufacturers.*

soap·stone /£'səʊp·stəʊn, $'soʊp·stoʊn/ *n* [U] a soft stone which feels slightly oily

soap·suds /£'səʊp·sʌdz, $'soʊp-/, **suds** *pl n* the mass of small bubbles that form on the surface of soapy water • *I'd just been washing some clothes and my arms were covered in soapsuds.*

soar RISE QUICKLY /£sɔːʳ, $sɔːr/ *v* [I] to rise very quickly to a high level • *All night long fireworks soared into the sky.* • *Temperatures will soar into the eighties over the weekend say the weather forecasters.* • *Housing prices had soared a further twenty per cent.* • *Soaring property prices have put many people off buying.* • *(fig.) Year after year skiers flock to the slopes of this spectacular mountain whose snow-capped peak soars* (= reaches the height of) *15 771 feet into the sky.*

soar FLY /£sɔːʳ, $sɔːr/ *v* [I] (of a bird or aircraft) to rise high in the air while flying without moving the wings or using power • *She watched the gliders soaring effortlessly above her.*

S.O.B. /£,es·əʊ'biː, $,-oʊ'-/ *n* [C usually sing] *esp. Am abbreviation for* **son of a bitch**, see at SON • *Man, he's a real S.O.B.!*

sob *(obj)* /£sɒb, $sɑːb/ *v* **-bb-** to cry noisily, taking in deep breaths • *I found her sobbing in the bedroom because she'd broken her favourite doll.* [I] • *You're not going to help matters by lying there sobbing!* [I] • *She sobbed* **herself** *to sleep* (= made herself go to sleep by crying) *the night that you left.* [T] • *She was* **sobbing** *her* **heart out** (= crying a lot)!

sob /£sɒb, $sɑːb/ *n* [C] • *I could hear her sobs from the next room.* • *(infml disapproving)* A **sob story** is a story or piece of information that someone tells you or writes about themselves which is intended to make you feel sad and sympathetic towards them: *She came out with some sob story about not having enough money to go and see her father who was ill.* • **Sob-stuff** is spoken or written stories which are intended to cause strong feelings, esp. sad ones, in people: *They heard sob-stuff from one man about his deprived childhood in an institution.*

so·ber NOT DRUNK /£'səʊ·bəʳ, $'soʊ·bɚ/ *adj* not under the influence of alcohol; not drunk • *Are you sober enough to drive, Jim?* • *Ask me to explain it to you when I'm sober.* • *I'd only had one glass of wine all evening so I was* **stone cold** (= completely) *sober.* • *Me, I'm as sober* **as a judge** (= completely sober).

so·ber *(obj)* /£'səʊ·bəʳ, $'soʊ·bɚ/ *v* • *I went for a walk to try to sober* **up** (= become less drunk). [always + *up*] • *Have a black coffee – that should sober you* **up** (= make you less drunk)! [T]

so·bri·e·ty /£sə'braɪ·ɪ·ti, $-ə·ţi/ *n* [U] *fml or humorous* • *I'd just drunk my third cup of coffee, and was well on the way to sobriety.* • *(Am) The police said his car had been weaving all over the road, so they pulled him over and gave him a sobriety* **test**.

so·ber SERIOUS /£'səʊ·bəʳ, $'soʊ·bɚ/ *adj* serious and calm • *In fact the whole wedding was a sober affair – no dancing, just people standing around in groups chatting politely.* • *Anthony was in a very sober mood – I scarcely heard him laugh all night.* • *On a more sober* (= serious) *note, there have been one or two break-ins in the building recently.* • *The fashionable colours this autumn are very sober* (= not bright) *– dull greys and greens and dark browns predominate.*

so·ber /£'səʊ·bəʳ, $'soʊ·bɚ/ *v* [I] • *He was quite wild as a youth but like most people he has sobered* **(up)** (=become more serious and calm) *over the years.* [I]

so·ber·ly /£'səʊ·bᵊl·i, $'soʊ·bɚ·li/ *adv* • *She was dressed very soberly in a plain grey suit.* • *They behaved very soberly for a bunch of young lads – I was quite impressed.*

so·ber·ing /£'səʊ·bᵊr·ɪŋ, $'soʊ·bɚ-/ *adj* • Something which is sobering makes you feel serious or makes you think about serious matters : *In ten years' time, he himself would probably have a wife and children – it was a sobering* **thought**. ○ *Manchester City's shock defeat had a sobering effect on the fans.*

so·bri·e·ty /£sə'braɪ·ɪ·ti, $-ə·ṭi/ *n* [U] *fml* • *We had the priest sitting at our table which instilled a little sobriety into the occasion.*

sob·er·sides /£'səʊ·bə·saɪdz, $'soʊ·bɚ-/ *n* [C usually sing] *pl* **sobersides** *infml* a serious person

so·bri·quet, **sou·bri·quet** /£'səʊ·brɪ·keɪ, $'soʊ-/ *n* [C] *fml or humorous* a name given to someone or something which is not their real or official name • *These charms have earned the television programme's presenter the sobriquet 'the thinking woman's crumpet.'*

so–called /£,səʊ'kɔːld, $,soʊ'kɑːld/ *adj* [not gradable] believed or thought to have a particular position or relationship but not suitable or deserving of being described in that way • *It was one of his so-called friends who supplied him with the drugs that killed him.* • *Our so-called 'leaders' couldn't lead children into a sweet-shop, it seems.* • So-called can also be used to introduce a new word or phrase which is not yet known by many people: *AIDS is characterized by one or more so-called opportunistic infections.*

soc·cer *esp. Am* /£'sɒk·əʳ, $'sɑː·kɚ/, *esp. Br* **foot·ball** *n* [U] a game in which two teams of 11 players try to kick or use their heads to send a round ball into the goal of the opposing side • *I had a game of soccer with the lads.*

so·cial /£'səʊ·ʃᵊl, $'soʊ-/ *adj* relating to activities in which you meet and spend time with other people and which happens during the time when you are not working • *I had such a good social* **life** *when I was at college.* • *I'm a social drinker – I only ever drink when I'm in company.* • *He's one of those people who use alcohol as a sort of social prop.* • *There are quite a few interesting things on the social calendar this month.* • *Most British schools organize social events for the students.* • *I've just become a member of the company's sports and social club.* • See also **social** at SOCIETY [PEOPLE].

so·cial·ly /£'səʊ·ʃᵊl·i, $'soʊ-/ *adv* • *I chat to him at work now and then but I've never seen him socially.* • *Socially, she's a disaster – she's always offending someone or picking a fight.* • *Socially they're a great company to work for – I've never been to so many parties in my life.*

so·cial /£'səʊ·ʃᵊl, $'soʊ-/, *Am also* **so·cia·ble** *n* [C] *dated* • A social is an occasion when the members of a group or organization meet informally to enjoy themselves: *Every year the club has a social – it's usually around Christmas-time.*

so·cia·ble /£'səʊ·ʃə·bḷ, $'soʊ-/ *adj approving* • Someone who is sociable likes to meet and spend time with other people: *He's a very sociable bloke, Roger – he likes his parties.* ○ *I had a headache and I wasn't feeling very sociable.*

so·cial·ite /£'səʊ·ʃᵊl·aɪt, $'soʊ·ʃə·laɪt/ *n* [C] • A socialite is a person, usually of high social class, who is famous because they go to a lot of parties and social events which are reported in the newspapers: *He and his wife Susan, who is 17 years younger than him, are both prominent Manhattan socialites.* ○ *It's one of those glossy magazines with endless pictures of minor celebrities and socialites attending balls.*

so·cial·ize, *Br and Aus usually* **–ise** /£'səʊ·ʃᵊl·aɪz, $'soʊ·ʃə·laɪz/ *v* [I] • To socialize is to spend the time, when you are not working, with friends or with other people in order to enjoy yourself: *I tend not to socialize* **with** *my colleagues.* ○ *I hope Adrian's actually doing some work at college – he seems to spend all his time socializing!*

so·cial·i·sm /£'səʊ·ʃᵊl·ɪ·zᵊm, $'soʊ-/ *n* [U] the set of beliefs which states that all people are equal and should share equally in the wealth of the country, or the political systems based on these beliefs • Compare CAPITALISM; COMMUNISM.

so·cial·ist /£'səʊ·ʃᵊl·ɪst, $'soʊ-/ *adj, n* • *socialist policies* • *He was a socialist all his life.* [C] • *She joined the Young Socialists.* [C]

so·cial·ized med·ic·ine /£'səʊ·ʃᵊl·aɪzd, $'soʊ·ʃə·laɪzd/ *n* [U] *Am* medical services provided or paid for by the government for anyone who needs them

so·ci·e·ty [PEOPLE] /£sə'saɪ·ə·ti, $-ṭi/ *n* a large group of people who live together in an organized way, making decisions about how to do things and sharing the work that needs to be done. All the people in a country, or in several similar countries, can be referred to as society. • *a classless/multicultural/capitalist/civilized society* [C] • *These changes strike at the heart of British/American/European society.* [U] • *There's a danger that we will end up blaming innocent children for society's problems.* [U] • *We must also consider the needs of the younger/older* **members of** *society.* [U] • *These facilities are used by all* **sectors of** *society.* [U] • Society (also **high society**) also refers to the group of people who are rich and powerful in a country and to their activities: *a society hostess/ball/function* [U] • *(fml)* Society can also mean being together with other people: *She prefers her own society* (=likes to be alone). [U]

so·cial /£'səʊ·ʃᵊl, $'soʊ-/ *adj* [before n] • *social classes/groups* • *social disorder/trends/change/equality/justice/differences* • *Seals are social* **animals** *– they live in organized groups.* • *(disapproving) She's a terrible* **social climber** (=someone who tries to move into a higher class in society). • If you have a **social conscience**, you worry about people who are poor, ill, old, etc. and try to help them. • In Britain, a **Social Democrat** is a person who was a member of the **Social Democratic Party** which existed from 1981-1990 and which was a centre party. • **Social engineering** is the artificial controlling or changing of the groupings within society. • **Social science** is the study of all the features of society. When the features, such as politics and economics, are considered separately they are called **the social sciences.** • **Social security** is *(Br and Aus)* a system of payments made by the government to people who are ill or poor or who have no job, or *(Am)* a system of payments made by the government to old people, people whose husbands or wives have died and people who are unable to work because of illness or who have no job: *He's* **on** *social security.* • The **social services** are services provided by local or national government to help people who are old or ill or need support in their lives. The work they and some private organizations do is called **social work.** • A **social worker** is a person who works for the social services or for a private organization providing help and support for people who need it. • See also SOCIAL.

so·cial·ly /£'səʊ·ʃᵊl·i, $'soʊ-/ *adv* • *Drinking and driving is no longer socially acceptable.* • *Private education is often regarded as socially divisive.* • *The scheme will pay £10 a week in addition to benefits for socially useful work, such as improving the environment.*

so·cial·ize *obj*, *Br and Aus usually* **–ise** /£'səʊ·ʃᵊl·aɪz, $'soʊ·ʃə·laɪz/ *v* [T] • To socialize people or animals is to train them to behave in a way that others in the group think is suitable: • *Here at the special school we make every effort to socialize these young offenders.*

so·cial·i·za·tion, *Br and Aus usually* **–i·sa·tion** /£,səʊ·ʃᵊl·aɪ'zeɪ·ʃᵊn, $,soʊ·ʃᵊl·ɪ'-/ *n* [U]

so·ci·e·ty [ORGANIZATION] /£sə'saɪ·ə·ti, $-ṭi/ *n* [C] an organization to which people who share similar interests can belong • *an amateur dramatic society* • *the Royal Society for the Protection of Birds*

so·ci·o·ec·o·nom·ic /£,səʊ·si·əʊ,ek·ə'nɒm·ɪk, $,soʊ·si·oʊ,iː·kə'nɑː·mɪk/ *adj* [not gradable] of the differences between groups of people caused mainly by their financial situation • *socioeconomic groups/groupings* • *socioeconomic factors* • *College Board officials said the difficulties arise more from socioeconomic than from ethnic differences.*

so·ci·o·ec·o·nom·i·cal·ly /£,səʊ·si·əʊ,ek·ə'nɒm·ɪ·kli, $,soʊ·si·oʊ,iː·kə'nɑː·mɪ-/ *adv* [not gradable]

so·ci·ol·o·gy /£,səʊ·si'ɒl·ə·dʒi, $,soʊ·si'ɑː·lə-/ *n* [U] the study of the relationships between people living in groups, esp. in industrial societies • *She has a degree in sociology and politics.* • *He specializes in the sociology* **of** *education/medicine/law/the family.*

so·ci·o·log·i·cal /£,səʊ·si·ə'lɒdʒ·ɪ·kᵊl, $,soʊ·si·ə'lɑː·dʒɪ-/ *adj* [not gradable] • *sociological theory/research*

so·ci·o·log·i·cal·ly /£,səʊ·si·ə'lɒdʒ·ɪ·kli, $,soʊ·si·ə'lɑː·dʒɪ-/ *adv* [not gradable]

so·ci·ol·o·gist /£,səʊ·si'ɒl·ə·dʒɪst, $,soʊ·si'ɑː·lə-/ *n* [C] • *She is an eminent sociologist.* • *Sociologists disagree about whether sociology is a science or not.*

so·ci·o·path /£'səʊ·si·əʊ·pæθ, $'soʊ·si·ə-/ *n* [C] a person who is completely unable or unwilling to behave in a way that is acceptable to society • *I'm telling you he's a complete/total sociopath.*

sock CLOTHES /£sɒk, $sɑːk/ *n* [C] *pl* **socks** or *Am also* **sox** /£sɒks, $sɑːks/ a piece of clothing made from soft material which covers your bare foot and lower part of the leg • *nylon/woollen/cotton socks* • *thermal socks* • *ankle/knee socks* • *a pair of socks* • *Put on your* **shoes and** *socks.* • *The little boy was wearing* **odd/(Am usually) mismatched** *socks* (= they were different colours). • *(infml humorous)* **Put a sock in it!** means be quiet or stop making such a lot of noise.

sock *obj* HIT /£sɒk, $sɑːk/ *v* [T] *dated slang* to hit (someone) • *He socked the policeman* **on** *the jaw/***in** *the eye.* • *(Am)* In baseball, if you sock the ball you hit it very powerfully: *Remember the game when Reggie socked three homers in three at-bats?*

sock /£sɒk, $sɑːk/ *n* [C usually sing] *dated slang* • *a sock* **on** *the jaw*

sock·et /£'sɒk·ɪt, $'sɑː·kɪt/ *n* [C] the part of esp. a piece of electrical equipment into which another part fits • *I really need a* **double** *socket so I can use the kettle and the radio at the same time.* • *He had forgotten to plug the television into the* **wall/(Br) mains** *socket.* • *The air freshener plugs into a car's* **lighter** *socket.* • Some parts of the body into which other parts fit are referred to as sockets: *a* **tooth/eye** *socket* ○ *a* **ball-and-***socket joint like the hip joint* • A **socket set** is a set of metal tools of different sizes, which fix onto one handle and are used to fasten and unfasten NUTS on pieces of equipment. • LP **Switching on and off** PIC **Plugs, Tools**

sod UNPLEASANT /£sɒd, $sɑːd/ *n* [C] *Br taboo slang* something or someone considered unpleasant or difficult • *She was explaining to her friends what a sod the photographer had been to work for.* • *What did you do that for, you stupid sod?* [as form of address] • *I can't get this thing to unscrew – it's a real sod!* • *It was a sod* **of** *a car to repair.* • Sod is sometimes used to show that you think that someone has done better than they should: *He's won again – the lucky sod!* • Sod can also be used to show that you are sympathetic: *the poor old sod* • If you couldn't or don't **care/give a sod**, you are not worried about other people's opinions or actions: *I don't give a sod* **(about)** *what Margaret said, I can't finish it today.* • **Sod all** means nothing: *Ann's just been chatting on the phone all morning – she's done sod all.* • **Sod's law** is MURPHY'S LAW.

sod *obj* /£sɒd, $sɑːd/ *v* [T] *Br taboo slang* • People use sod to show their anger: *Sod this drawer – it's stuck!* ○ *Sod you/him!* ○ *Oh sod* **it** *– I've left my glasses behind!* • **Sod off** means go away: *Oh sod off, you stupid git!* ○ *She told him to sod off.*

sod·ding /£'sɒd·ɪŋ, $'sɑː·dɪŋ/ *adj* [before n; not gradable] *Br taboo slang* • *Stupid sodding thing, why won't it move?*

sod GRASS /£sɒd, $sɑːd/ *n* [C] *specialized* a rectangular piece which has been cut from an area of grass • *He worked fast, cutting and slicing the turf neatly, heaving the sods to one side.* • *(literary) She sleeps beneath the sod* (= She is dead and has been buried).

so·da (wa·ter) /£'səʊ·də, $'soʊ-/, *Am also* **club so·da**, **seltzer** *n* [U] a type of fizzy water, often mixed with alcoholic drinks • *a whisky and soda* (= a glass of these drinks mixed together) • *(Am)* Soda (also **soda pop**) is also any type of sweet fizzy drink which is not alcoholic: *an ice-cream soda* (= a sweet fizzy drink with some ice cream added) ○ *"What kind of soda do you want?" "I'd like a root beer, please."*

sod·den /£'sɒd·ᵊn, $'sɑː·dᵊn/ *adj* (of something which can absorb water) extremely wet • *sodden muddy grass* • *Her thin coat quickly became sodden.*

so·di·um /£'səʊ·di·əm, $'soʊ-/ *n* [U] a soft silverish white chemical element that occurs in salt • *(specialized)* **Sodium bicarbonate** is a white powder which dissolves in water and is used esp. in cooking and in medicines. • *(specialized)* **Sodium chloride** is salt.

sod·o·my /£'sɒd·ə·mi, $'sɑː·də-/ *n* [U] *fml or law* the sexual act of putting the penis into a man's or woman's ANUS • *(Am law)* Sodomy can also be the sexual act of FELLATIO (= putting the penis into a person's mouth).

sod·om·ize *obj*, *Br and Aus usually* **-ise** /£'sɒd·ə·maɪz, $'sɑː·də-/ *v* [T usually passive]

so·fa /£'səʊ·fə, $'soʊ-/, **set·tee** *n* [C] a long soft seat with a back and usually arms, on which more than one person can sit at the same time • *Their offices have small upholstered sofas and comfortable chairs.* • A **sofa bed** is a sofa which has a part that opens to form a bed. • PIC **Beds and bedroom, Room**

soft NOT HARD /£sɒft, $sɑːft/ *adj* **-er, -est** not hard or firm; changing its shape when pressed • *soft ground/sand* • *a soft pillow/mattress* • *soft contact lenses* • *soft cheese* • *a soft-boiled* (= cooked for a short time) *egg* • *I like chocolates with soft centres.* • *Soft* **tissue**, *such as flesh, allows X-rays through.* • Some things, esp. parts of the body, which are soft are not hard or rough and feel pleasant and smooth when touched: *soft lips/cheeks/skin/hair* ○ *soft leather* • *(fig.) Look at you! You need more exercise. You're* **going/getting** *soft* (= in bad bodily condition and not fit). • *(infml)* If you say someone is soft or is **(going) soft in the head**, you mean that they are losing or have lost their ability to make good judgments and are being stupid: *Don't put it there, you great soft thing!* • *(esp. Br)* **Soft fruit** is a general name for small fruits such as STRAWBERRIES, RASPBERRIES and BLACKCURRANTS which do not have a thick skin. • *(Br and Aus)* **Soft furnishings/***(Am)* **soft goods** is a general name for curtains, furniture coverings and other items made of cloth which decorate a room. LP **Shopping goods** • *(infml)* If you **soft-soap** someone, you try to persuade them to do what you want by saying pleasant things to them. • A **soft top** is a **convertible**. See at CONVERT. • *(Br)* **Soft toys** (also *Am* **stuffed animals**) are toys, often in the shape of animals, which are made from cloth with a soft filling and which are pleasant to hold.

soft·en *(obj)* /£'sɒf·ᵊn, $'sɑː·fᵊn/ *v* • *You can soften the butter by warming it gently.* [T] • *These dried apples will soften* **(up)** *if you soak them in water.* [I]

soft·en·er /£'sɒf·ᵊn·əʳ, $'sɑː·fᵊn·ɚ/ *n* • (A) softener is a substance used to make something soft: *(a) fabric softener* [C/U]

soft·ness /£'sɒft·nəs, $'sɑːft-/ *n* [U] • *Our fabrics are carefully selected for their softness, to ensure they won't irritate a baby's skin.*

soft GENTLE /£sɒft, $sɑːft/ *adj* **-er, -est** not forceful, loud or easily noticed • *a soft voice/sound* • *soft music* • *a soft glow* • *soft lighting* • *(disapproving)* If you are (too) soft or you **go** soft or you **take a soft line** you are not forceful or STRICT enough, esp. in criticizing or punishing someone who has done something wrong: *This government for too long has been too soft* **on** *firms that break the sanctions.* ○ *They have accused him of going soft* **on** *the independence issue.* • Someone who is **soft-hearted** is kind, gentle and thinks about what other people need. Compare **hard-hearted** at HARD SEVERE. • If you **soft-pedal** something, you treat it as less important or less urgent than you think it is: *This is a rather sensitive issue – I think we'd better soft-pedal it for the moment.* • If someone uses a **soft sell**, they try to sell something to someone by being gently persuasive: *The training brochure deliberately adopts a soft sell approach.* • Someone who is **soft-spoken** has a quiet pleasant voice. • *(Am)* If you are **soft on** someone you love them or like them very much: *I think Walter must be soft on Marj – he keeps sending her flowers and cards.* • If you have a **soft spot** for someone, you like them more than other people: *She's always had a soft spot* **for** *her younger nephew.*

soft·en *(obj)* /£'sɒf·ᵊn, $'sɑː·fᵊn/ *v* • *The news will upset him – we must think of a way to soften* **the blow** (= make the news less unpleasant for him). [T] • *Would you say the government's stance on law and order has softened?* [I] • *She tried to* **soften up** (= persuade) *her sister by buying her some chocolates.*

sof·tie, **soft·y** /£'sɒf·ti, $'sɑːf-/ *n* [C] *infml esp. approving* • A softie is a kind, gentle person who is not forceful, looks for the pleasant things in life and can be easily persuaded to do what you want them to: • *For all his tough manner, he's just a* **(big)** *softie.*

soft·ly /£'sɒft·li, $'sɑːft-/ *adv* • *She speaks softly but usually gets her own way.* • *(Br and Aus)* If you take a **softly-softly** approach, you are not forceful and try to solve a problem in a quiet and reasonable way.

soft·ness /£'sɒft·nəs, $'sɑːft-/ *n* [U]

soft EASY /£sɒft, $sɑːft/ *adj* **-er, -est** not difficult; easier than other things of the same type • *You kids have had a soft time of it recently, but I warn you, your new teacher's very strict.* • *He's got a pretty soft job – he hardly seems to do anything all day.* • A **soft landing** is when a person or vehicle comes down from the air to the ground without difficulty or damage. • *(Br and Aus disapproving)* A **soft option** (*Am usually* **easy option**) is the easier of two choices: *When he realised how much a shared house was going to cost, he took the soft option and lived at home.* • A

soft target is something that is easy to attack or get advantage from: *Major tourist attractions are a soft target for pickpockets.* • If someone is a **soft touch**, it is easy to make them do what you want, esp. to give you money: *He thought his mother would be a soft touch.*

soft NOT HARMFUL /£sɒft, $sɑːft/ *adj* [before n] **-er, -est** not causing great harm; of less strength or less unpleasant than other things of the same type • A **soft drink** is a cold, usually sweet drink which does not contain alcohol: *Could I have a soft drink, please? I'm driving.* • A **soft drug** is one which is taken for pleasure and does not cause you to keep wanting more of it. • **Soft porn** is books and films showing sexual activity which are less extreme than other material of the same type. • **Soft water** does not contain CHALK (= soft white rock) and allows soap to produce bubbles easily: *a soft-water area*

soft·back /£'sɒf*t*·bæk, $'sɑːf*t*-/, *Am usually* **soft·co·ver** /£'sɒf*t*ˌkʌv·əʳ, $'sɑːf*t*ˌkʌv·ɚ/ *adj* [not gradable], *n* [C] (a book) with a bendable cover • Compare HARDBACK; PAPERBACK.

soft·ball /£'sɒf*t*·bɔːl, $'sɑːf*t*·bɑːl/ *n* [U] a game similar to baseball but played with a larger softer ball

soft·ware /£'sɒf*t*·weəʳ, $'sɑːf*t*·wer/ *n* [U] the instructions which control what a computer does; computer programs • *We are writing software to analyse the text.* • A **software house** is a company which writes and sells software. • A **software package** is a computer program that is sold together with instructions on how to use it: *A new software package is now on the market which controls traffic flow in cities.* • Compare HARDWARE COMPUTER.

soft·wood /£'sɒf*t*·wʊd, $'sɑːf*t*-/ *n* wood from evergreen trees like PINE which grow quickly, or a tree of this type • *The window frames were made from softwood.* [U] • *The mattress is supported on a softwood frame.* [U] • *A 200000-acre forest site will be replanted with softwoods to supply the paper and pulp mill.* [C] • Compare HARDWOOD.

sog·gy /£'sɒg·i, $'sɑː·gi/ *adj* **-ier, -iest** (of things which can absorb water, often of food) extremely wet and soft • *soggy ground/shoes* • *I dropped my magazine in the bath and now it's all soggy.* • *Will you answer the phone for me or my cereal will* **go** *soggy.* • *The pasta was limp and soggy, topped with flavourless chicken in tomato sauce.* • *Food industry research shows that 20% of consumers say their microwave makes items soggier.* • *(Am) In Houston, the soggy* (= very wet • HUMID) *summer heat can make you want to die.* • *(esp. Br) The soggy* (= rainy) *summer is all set to continue into August and it might well rain until September.*

sog·gi·ly /£'sɒg·ɪ·li, $'sɑː·gɪ-/ *adv*

sog·gi·ness /£'sɒg·ɪ·nəs, $'sɑː·gɪ-/ *n* [U]

soil EARTH /sɔɪl/ *n* the material on the surface of the ground in which plants grow; earth • *light/heavy/strong/fertile soil* [U] • *sandy or chalky soils* [C] • *soil-borne diseases* • *(fml or literary)* **The** soil sometimes means the activity of farming: *The government is trying to encourage a return to the soil.* [U] • *(fml)* Soil is sometimes a country: *It was the first time we had set foot on foreign/French/American soil* (= gone to a foreign country/France/America). [U] ○ *She didn't want to leave her* **native** *soil* (= the country where she was born). [U] • **Soil science** is the scientific study of soils.

soil *(obj)* MAKE DIRTY /sɔɪl/ *v fml* to make dirty • *soiled sheets/towels/clothes* • *The company said that miles of beaches had been soiled by the 11-million-gallon oil spill.* [T] • Soil often refers to making dirty with human or animal excrement: *soiled nappies/diapers* ○ *The kittens had soiled (on) the carpet.* [I/T] • *(fig.) Steal from my employers? I wouldn't soil my* **hands with** *a thing like that* (= I wouldn't do something I thought was bad). [T] • *(fig.) Her* **reputation** *was soiled* (= spoilt) *by the excesses of her youth.* [T]

soir·ee, soir·ée /£'swʌr·eɪ, $swɑː'reɪ/ *n* [C] *fml or humorous* an evening party, often with musical entertainment

so·journ /£'sɒdʒ·ən, $'sɑː·dʒɜːrn/ *n* [C] *literary or humorous* a short period when a person stays in a particular place • *My sojourn* **in** *the youth hostel was thankfully short.*

so·journ /£'sɒdʒ·ən, $'sɑː·dʒɜːrn/ *v* [I always + adv/prep] *literary*

sol·ace /£'sɒl·ɪs, $'sɑː·lɪs/ *n* [U] help and comfort when you are feeling sad or worried • *I know it isn't much solace, but several people did worse in the exam than you.* • *I'm sorry to say that when his wife left him, he* **found** *solace* **in** *the bottle* (= drank alcohol).

sol·ace *obj* /£'sɒl·ɪs, $'sɑː·lɪs/ *v* [T] • *She solaced herself* **with** *the thought that the term was nearly over.*

so·lar /£'səʊ·ləʳ, $'soʊ·lɚ/ *adj* [before n; not gradable] of or from the sun, or using the energy from the sun to produce electric power • *solar radiation* • *solar flares* • *a solar cell/panel* • *solar heating* • The **solar system** is the sun and the group of planets which move around it. • *(specialized)* The **solar year** is the time it takes for the Earth to go round the sun, just over 365 days. • PIC› **Energy**

so·lar·i·um /£sə'leə·ri·əm, $soʊ'ler·i-/ *n* [C] *pl* **solariums** or **solaria** /£sə'leə·ri·ə, $soʊ'ler·i-/ a room in which you can TAN (= make brown) your skin using either light from the sun or special equipment • Solarium is also *Am for* CONSERVATORY.

so·lar plex·us /£ˌsəʊ·lə'plek·səs, $ˌsoʊ·lɚ-/ *n* [U] the front part of the body below the chest • *a punch in* **the** *solar plexus*

sold /£səʊld, $soʊld/ *past simple and past participle of* SELL

sol·der /£'səʊl·dəʳ, $'sɑː·dɚ/ *n* [U] soft metal used when melted to join together pieces of metal so that they stick together when it cools and becomes hard again

sol·der *obj* /£'səʊl·dəʳ, $'sɑː·dɚ/ *v* [T] • A **soldering iron** is the tool which you use for heating when you solder things together.

sol·dier /£'səʊl·dʒəʳ, $'soʊl·dʒɚ/ *n* [C] a person who is in an army and wears its uniform, esp. someone who fights when there is a war • *Soldiers were patrolling the streets.* • A **soldier of fortune** is someone who fights for anyone who will pay, not necessarily for their own country.

sol·dier·ing /£'səʊl·dʒᵊr·ɪŋ, $'soʊl·dʒɚ-/ *n* [U] • *a life of soldiering*

sol·dier on /£'səʊl·dʒəʳ, $'soʊl·dʒɚ/ *v adv* [I] to continue doing something although it is difficult • *I admired the way she soldiered on when her business ran into trouble.*

sole ONLY /£səʊl, $soʊl/ *adj* [before n; not gradable] being one only; single • *My sole purpose/objective/concern is to make the information more widely available.* • *The sole* **survivor** *of the accident was found in the water after six hours.* • *His sole* **surviving relative** *is an elderly aunt.* • *I like flowers – the sole* **exception** *is lilies* (= they are the only flowers I don't like). • Sole also means that only one person or organization is involved in an activity: *She had sole* **responsibility** *for locking the shop each night.* ○ *Nanny wanted to take sole* **charge** *of* (= be the only person caring for) *Amanda, 4, and John, 2, during the day.* • LP› **One**

sole·ly /£'səʊl·li, $'soʊl-/ *adv* [not gradable] • *The regulations are solely* (= only) *designed to control dangerous practices – they can't eliminate them.* • *She was solely* **responsible** *for causing the accident.*

sole BOTTOM PART /£səʊl, $soʊl/ *n* [C] the bottom part of a foot which touches the ground when you stand or walk, or the front part of the bottom of a shoe • *a cut on the sole of her foot* • *shoes with rubber soles* • PIC› **Body**

-soled /£-səʊld, $-soʊld/ *combining form* • *leather-soled shoes* • *rope-soled sandals*

sole *obj* /£səʊl, $soʊl/ *v* [T] • *Can I leave these shoes to be soled* (= have new soles put on) *and heeled?*

sole FISH /£səʊl, $soʊl/ *n* [C] *pl* **sole** or **soles** a flat round fish which is eaten as food. There are different types of sole. • *lemon sole* • *Dover sole*

sol·e·cism /£'sɒl·ɪ·sɪ·zᵊm, $'sɑː·lə-/ *n* [C] *fml* an act of breaking what are generally considered to be the rules of esp. behaving or speaking

sol·emn /£'sɒl·əm, $'sɑː·ləm/ *adj* serious and without any amusement • *a solemn face/voice* • *This is a far from solemn book – it is a rich mix of pleasures and information, and is full of surprises.* • *A car arrived with three distinguished, grey-haired men in dark suits, looking solemn.* • *The chant was accompanied by solemn* (= serious and carefully produced) *ritual gestures.* • A solemn **promise/commitment/undertaking** is an agreement which you make in a serious way and expect to fulfil.

sol·emn·ly /£'sɒl·əm·li, $'sɑː·ləm-/ *adv*

so·lem·ni·ty /£sə'lem·nɪ·ti, $-nə·t̬i/, **sol·emn·ness** /£'sɒl·əm·nəs, $'sɑː·ləm-/ *n* [U] • *the solemnity* **of** *a funeral service*

so·lem·ni·ties /£sə'lem·nɪ·tiz, $-nə·t̬iz/ *pl n* • The solemnities are the ways of behaving or the activities which are considered suitable for a serious formal social ceremony, such as a funeral.

sol·em·nize *obj, Br and Aus usually* **-ise** /£'sɒl·əm·naɪz, $'sɑː·ləm-/ *v* [T] *fml or specialized* • To solemnize a **marriage** is to perform the official marriage ceremony, esp. as part of a religious ceremony in a church.

sol·em·ni·za·tion, *Br and Aus usually* **-i·sa·tion** /£ˌsɒl·əm·naɪˈzeɪ·ʃᵊn, $ˌsɑː·ləm·nɪ-/ *n* [U] *fml or specialized*

so·li·cit *obj* /səˈlɪs·ɪt/ *v* [T] *fml* to ask formally for (something, esp. money) • *The ads solicited donations for the American Heart Disease Foundation and the Cancer Fund of America.* • *It is illegal for public officials to solicit gifts or money in exchange for favours.*

so·li·ci·ta·tion /səˌlɪs·ɪˈteɪ·ʃᵊn/ *n fml* • *The solicitation of business was regarded as unethical.* [U] • *They endured regular telephone solicitations by double glazing companies.* [C]

so·li·cit·ing /£səˈlɪs·ɪ·tɪŋ, $-t̬ɪŋ/ *n* [U] *law* • If someone, esp. a woman, is accused of soliciting, she has been asking men to have sex with her in exchange for payment.

so·li·ci·tor /£səˈlɪs·ɪ·təʳ, $-t̬ɚ/ *n* [C] *Br and Aus* a type of lawyer in Britain and Australia who is trained to give advice about the law and sometimes to represent people in court • *a* **firm of** *solicitors* • Compare BARRISTER; LAWYER. • [LP] **Law**

so·li·ci·tous /£səˈlɪs·ɪ·təs, $-t̬əs/ *adj fml* showing care and helpful attention to someone • *He made a solicitous enquiry after her health.* • *The restaurant is noted for its solicitous service.*

so·li·ci·tous·ly /£səˈlɪs·ɪ·tə·sli, $-t̬ə-/ *adv fml*

so·li·ci·tude /£səˈlɪs·ɪ·tjuːd, $-tuːd/, **so·li·ci·tous·ness** /£səˈlɪs·ɪ·tə·snəs, $-t̬ə-/ *n* [U] *fml*

sol·id [HARD] /£ˈsɒl·ɪd, $ˈsɑː·lɪd/ *adj, adv* hard or firm, keeping a clear shape • *a solid surface/base* • *a solid object* • *a solid structure* • Solid is also used to mean completely hard or firm all through an object, or without any spaces or holes: *solid rock* ○ *a solid oak table* ○ *solid doors/walls* ○ *a solid line of traffic* ○ *The lecture hall was* **packed** *solid* **(with** *students).* ○ *The hotel was* **booked** *solid from Dec 23 to Jan 6* **(with** *tour groups from the United States).* • If a metal or colour is described as being solid, it is pure, and does not have anything else mixed together with it: *solid gold/silver candlesticks* ○ *a white rose on a solid blue background* • *(specialized)* In a **solid-state** electronic device, the flow of electrical current is through solid material and not through a VACUUM (= space without air). • (D)(F)

sol·id /£ˈsɒl·ɪd, $ˈsɑː·lɪd/ *n* [C] *specialized* • A solid is an object with three DIMENSIONS (= height, width and length): *A cube and a pyramid are both solids.*

sol·id·ly /£ˈsɒl·ɪd·li, $ˈsɑː·lɪd-/ *adv* • *The house seems very solidly built.*

so·li·di·ty /£səˈlɪd·ɪ·ti, $-ə·t̬i/, **sol·id·ness** /£ˈsɒl·ɪd·nəs, $ˈsɑː·lɪd-/ *n* [U]

sol·id [NOT LIQUID/GAS] /£ˈsɒl·ɪd, $ˈsɑː·lɪd/ *n* [C], *adj* [not gradable] (a substance which is) not liquid or gas • *Liquid and solid waste is collected in the tank.* • *Freeze for about 3 hours or so until solid.* • *It compresses hot gases to densities greater than those of solids at room temperature.* • Solid **food** (also **solids**) is food which is not in liquid form, esp. used to refer to such food when it is given to babies or people who are ill: *Babies can start to take solids at 4-6 months.* ○ *That rice pudding was the first solid food he's eaten since his operation.* • **Solid fuel** is coal or a similar type of fuel, not oil or gas: *a solid-fuel boiler* • (D)(F)

so·li·di·fy *(obj)* /səˈlɪd·ɪ·faɪ/ *v* • If something solidifies it becomes solid: *Molten volcanic lava solidifies as it cools.* [I] ○ *The chemical reaction solidifies the resin.* [T]

so·li·di·fi·ca·tion /səˌlɪd·ɪ·fɪˈkeɪ·ʃᵊn/ *n* [U] • *a process of gradual solidification*

so·li·di·ty /£səˈlɪd·ɪ·ti, $-ə·t̬i/ *n* [U] • *Coal is abundant, but its solidity makes it inconvenient to use – gas is less trouble.*

sol·id [CERTAIN] /£ˈsɒl·ɪd, $ˈsɑː·lɪd/ *adj* **-er, -est** certain or safe; of a good standard; giving confidence or support • *"I obviously would have preferred to see our highway funding program on more solid financial* **footing,***" he said.* • *The drama course gives students a solid* **grounding** *in the basic techniques of acting.* • *The orchestra gave a good solid professional* **performance**. • *We have received solid* **support** *from all sections of the community.* • (D)(F)

sol·id·ly /£ˈsɒl·ɪd·li, $ˈsɑː·lɪd-/ *adv* • *The economy has been growing solidly for five years now.* • *My colleagues are solidly* **behind** *me* (= they support me) *on this issue.*

so·li·di·fy *(obj)* /səˈlɪd·ɪ·faɪ/ *v* • *He solidified his commitment to the treaty by giving a forceful speech in favour of it.* [T] • *Support for the policy is solidifying.* [I]

so·li·di·ty /£səˈlɪd·ɪ·ti, $-ə·t̬i/, **sol·id·ness** /£ˈsɒl·ɪd·nəs, $ˈsɑː·lɪd-/ *n* [U] • *The agreement would give a new solidity to military co-operation between the two countries.* • *The orchestra gave a performance of great solidity but little excitement.*

sol·i·dar·i·ty /£ˌsɒl·ɪˈdær·ɪ·ti, $ˌsɑː·lɪˈder·ə·t̬i/ *n* [U] agreement between and support for the members of a group, esp. a political group • *The situation raises important questions about solidarity among member states of the UN.* • *The lecturers joined the protest march to show solidarity* **with** *their students.*

so·li·lo·quy /səˈlɪl·ə·kwi/ *n* [C] a speech in a play which the character speaks to him- or herself or to the people watching rather than to the other characters • *Hamlet's soliloquy "To be or not to be"*

sol·ip·si·sm /£ˈsɒl·ɪp·sɪ·zᵊm, $ˈsɑː·lɪp-/ *n* [U] *specialized* the belief that only one's own experiences and existence can be known with absolute certainty

sol·ip·sis·tic /£ˌsɒl·ɪpˈsɪs·tɪk, $ˌsɑː·lɪp-/ *adj* [not gradable] *fml disapproving* • *This is a highly solipsistic book – but at least the author cannot be accused of a lack of self-knowledge.*

sol·i·taire [JEWEL] /£ˌsɒl·ɪˈteəʳ, £ˈ---, $ˈsɑː·lə·ter/ *n* [C] a single jewel which is part of a piece of jewellery, esp. a ring, or the ring itself • *a solitaire diamond*

sol·i·taire [CARDS] /£ˌsɒl·ɪˈteəʳ, £ˈ---, $ˈsɑː·lə·ter/ *n* [U] *Am for* PATIENCE (= card game for one person)

sol·i·ta·ry /£ˈsɒl·ɪ·tri, $ˈsɑː·lə·ter·i/ *adj* being the only one, or not being with other similar things, often by choice • *Injury denied the runner the chance to add to her solitary Olympic title.* • *On the hill, a solitary figure is busy chopping down trees.* • *Just after dawn he went for a solitary stroll* (= walked alone) *through the gardens.* • *She wasn't happy to walk down such a solitary path/to be in such a solitary place* (= where there were no other people) *late at night.* • *Fishing and walking are the two pleasures of the solitary* **life** *he enjoys.* • *He's a solitary little boy, quite happy to play on his own.* • Someone who is in **solitary confinement** (also *infml* **solitary**) is kept in a room alone, esp. in a prison: *The woman was diagnosed as clinically depressed after weeks of being* **kept in** *solitary confinement.* • [LP] **One**

sol·i·tude /£ˈsɒl·ɪ·tjuːd, $ˈsɑː·lə·tuːd/ *n* [U] the situation of being alone without other people • *We were worried that he might find his reception rather overwhelming after months of solitude at sea.* • *People need a chance to reflect on spiritual matters* **in** *solitude.* • *The hotel guests provided me with company whenever solitude began to turn to loneliness.*

so·lo /£ˈsəʊ·ləʊ, $ˈsoʊ·loʊ/ *adj* [before n], *adv* [not gradable] alone; without other people • *a solo performance/flight* • *to sail/fly solo* • *She did nine months' solo walking in Japan.* • *He used to play with a group but now he's* **going** *solo/pursuing a solo career.*

so·lo /£ˈsəʊ·ləʊ, $ˈsoʊ·loʊ/ *n* [C] *pl* **solos** • A solo is a musical performance done by one person alone, or a musical performance in which one person is featured: *a piano solo* ○ *Parker's solo on 'A Night in Tunisia' was so amazing that the pianist backing him simply stopped playing.*

so·lo·ist /£ˈsəʊ·ləʊ·ɪst, $ˈsoʊ·loʊ-/ *n* [C] • *The soloist* (= person performing solo) *in the violin concerto was Yehudi Menuhin.*

sol·stice /£ˈsɒl·stɪs, $ˈsɑːl-/ *n* [C] either of the two occasions in the year when the sun is directly above either the furthest point north or the furthest point south of the equator that it ever reaches. These are the times in the year, in the middle of the summer or winter, when there are the longest hours of day or night. • *the summer/winter solstice* • Compare EQUINOX.

so·lu·tion /səˈluː·ʃᵊn/ *n specialized* a liquid into which a solid has been mixed and has dissolved • *an aqueous solution of salts* [C] • *two solutions of different concentrations* [C] • *copper sulphate* **in** *solution* (= dissolved in water) [U] • *The oranges are preserved in sugar solution.* [U] • See also **solution** at SOLVE.

sol·u·ble /£ˈsɒl·jʊ·bl̩, $ˈsɑːl-/ *adj* • Something that is soluble is able to be dissolved to form a solution: *I find soluble aspirins easier to take than the ones you have to swallow whole.*

sol·u·bil·i·ty /£ˌsɒl·jʊˈbɪl·ɪ·ti, $ˌsɑːl·jəˈbɪl·ə·t̬i/ *n* [U]

solve *obj* /£sɒlv, $sɑːlv/ *v* [T] to find an answer to (a problem) • *Just calm down – it won't solve anything to get hysterical.* • *The rescue plan could cause more problems than it solves.* • *Ms Cook's version of the affair solves many of the story's puzzling inconsistencies.* • *Did you solve the* **crime** (= discover who committed it) *before the end of the book?*

so·lu·tion /səˈluː·ʃᵊn/ *n* [C] • *It's too big for the box – what's the solution?* • *"We could just leave it out." "That's no solution."* • *When you finish doing the crossword, the solution is on the back page.* • *They help you talk through your problems but they don't give you any solutions.* • See also SOLUTION.

solv·a·ble /£ˈsɒl·və·bḷ, $ˈsɑːl-/, **sol·u·ble** *adj* • *The problem isn't solvable.*

sol·vent [HAVING MONEY] /£ˈsɒl·vənt, $ˈsɑːl-/ *adj* (esp. of companies) having enough money to pay all that you owe to other people • *Many of the insurance companies are under pressure to increase premiums to* **stay** *solvent.* • *The court was told that the firm was "***barely** *solvent."* • *(infml) I'll be solvent* (=have enough money) *again at the end of the month.*

sol·ven·cy /£ˈsɒl·vᵊnt·si, $ˈsɑːl-/ *n* [U] • *Only those firms that have passed honesty, competence and solvency tests are allowed to do business.*

sol·vent [LIQUID] /£ˈsɒl·vənt, $ˈsɑːl-/ *n* [C] a liquid in which solids will dissolve • *The use of industrial solvents to extract fat from the waste products has now been abandoned.* • *(esp. Br) The poster warned against solvent* **abuse** (=the dangerous activity of breathing in particular chemicals to get a feeling of pleasure and excitement). • See also DISSOLVE [BE ABSORBED].

som·bre, *Am usually* **som·ber** /£ˈsɒm·bəʳ, $ˈsɑːm·bɚ/ *adj* serious, sad and without humour or amusement • *a sombre atmosphere/voice/face* • *sombre parents waiting for news of their children* • Colours or things which have colour, such as clothes, can be described as sombre if they are dark and plain: *His coat was a sombre brown.* ○ *sombre clouds* ○ *a sombre black hat*

som·bre·ly, *Am usually* **som·ber·ly** /£ˈsɒm·bə·li, $ˈsɑːm·bɚ-/ *adv*

som·bre·ness, *Am usually* **som·ber·ness** /£ˈsɒm·bə·nəs, $ˈsɑːm·bɚ-/ *n* [U]

som·bre·ro /£sɒmˈbreə·rəʊ, $sɑːmˈbrer·oʊ/ *n* [C] *pl* **sombreros** a hat with a wide BRIM (=part which sticks out all round), worn esp. by men in Mexico • PIC› **Hats**

some [UNKNOWN AMOUNT] /sʌm/ *determiner* an amount or number of (something) which is not stated or not known; a part of (something) • *There's some cake in the kitchen if you'd like it.* • *Here's some news you might be interested in.* • *We've been having some problems with our TV over the last few weeks.* • *Could you give me some idea of when the building work will finish?* • *Clearly the treatment has had some effect – we'll have to wait and see how much.* • *To some* **extent** *the experiment was a success.* • *I've got to do some* **more** *work before I can go out.* • LP› **Quantity words**

some /sʌm/ *pronoun* • *If you need more paper then just take some.* • *"Would you like to eat dinner with us?" "No thanks, I've already had some."* • *"Have you got any drawing pins?" "If you'll wait a moment, I'll get you some."* • *Some* **of** *you here have already met Imran.* • *Have some* **of** *this champagne – it's very good.* • The word some can also be used to mean some people: *Some have compared his work to Picasso's.* • *(esp. Am infml)* The phrase **and then some** means an amount or number more: *It looked like 20 000 people and then some at the demonstration Saturday.* • In negative sentences, you use *any* or *no* instead of *some*. In questions, you usually use *any* instead of *some*.

some [LARGE AMOUNT] /sʌm/ *determiner* a large amount or number of (something) • *It'll be some time before we go back to that awful place!* • *It was some years later when they next met.* • *We discussed the problem at some length.* • *They had to go some distance further than they had planned before they could find somewhere to stay.*

some /sʌm/ *adv* [not gradable] *Am* • *We were really* **going** *some* (=travelling fast) *when we got out of the city.*

some [PARTICULAR THING] /sʌm/ *determiner* used to refer to a particular person or thing without stating exactly which one • *Some lucky person will win more than $1 000 000 in the competition.* • *Some idiot's locked the door!* • *There must be some way you can relieve the pain.* • The expression **some thing or (an)other** refers to one of several or many possibilities but the exact one is not known or not stated : *They found the painting in some antique shop or other.* ○ *Someday or (an)other we'll meet again.*

some [ANNOYANCE] /sʌm/ *determiner infml* used before a noun, esp. at the beginning of a sentence to show annoyance or disapproval, often by repeating a word which was not accurately used • *Some people just don't know when to shut up.* • *Some hotel that turned out to be – it was dreadful!* • *"Someone who I thought was a friend sold me a radio that doesn't work." "Some friend!"* • *"Perhaps there'll still be some left for us." "Some* **hopes** (=That is unlikely)*!"*

some [EXCELLENT] /sʌm/ *determiner infml* an excellent; an enjoyable • *Wow, that was some dinner!* • *It would be some achievement if a person could make the journey to Mars and back.*

some [APPROXIMATELY] /sʌm/ *adv* [not gradable] (used in front of a number) approximately; about • *Some fifty tons of stone are taken from the quarry every day.* • *The water is some twenty to thirty metres beneath the ground.* • LP› **Approximate numbers**

some [SMALL AMOUNT] /sʌm/ *adv* [not gradable] *Am infml* by a small amount or degree; a little • *She says she's feeling some better.* • *We could turn down the heat some if that would make you more comfortable.*

some·bo·dy /ˈsʌm·bə·di, £-ˌbɒd·i, $-ˌbɑː·di/ *pronoun* SOMEONE

some·day /ˈsʌm·deɪ/ *adv* [not gradable] at some time in the future which is not yet known or not stated • *Maybe someday you'll both meet again.* • *Someday it will be possible to fly between Australia and Europe in a couple of hours.*

some·how /ˈsʌm·haʊ/, *Am infml also* **some·way**, **some·ways** *adv* [not gradable] in a way which is not known or not stated • *Somehow the dogs had escaped.* • *It won't be easy, but we'll get across the river somehow.* • Somehow also means 'for a reason which is not clear': *I know what we're doing is legal, but somehow it doesn't feel right.*

some·one /ˈsʌm·wʌn/, **some·bo·dy** *pronoun* a single person • *There's someone outside the house.* • *Someone must have seen what happened.* • *Surely someone knows where the documents are.* • *Eventually someone in the audience spoke.* • *(infml) We'll need a software engineer* **or someone** (=a person with skill of or like the stated type) *on the project team.* • *"Someone to Watch Over Me"* (title of a song written by George and Ira Gershwin, 1926) • 'Anyone' is usually used instead of 'someone' in negative sentences and questions. • LP› **Quantity words**

some·place /ˈsʌm·pleɪs/ *adv* [not gradable] *Am for* SOMEWHERE [PLACE] • *On his first visit there, he sensed it was someplace special.*

som·er·sault /£ˈsʌm·ə·sɒlt, $-ɚ·sɑːlt/ *n* [C] a rolling movement or jump, either forwards or backwards, in which you turn over completely, with your body above your head, and finish with your head on top again • *She was so happy she* **turned** *three somersaults on the lawn.*

som·er·sault /£ˈsʌm·ə·sɒlt, $-ɚ·sɑːlt/ *v* [I] • *The bus plunged down the embankment, somersaulted twice and finally landed on its side.*

some·thing /ˈsʌmp·θɪŋ/ *pronoun* an object, situation, quality or action which is not exactly known or stated • *There's something sharp in my shoe.* • *Something in the cupboard smells odd.* • *Would you like some coffee or perhaps there's something* **else** *you'd like?* • *We thought there must be something* **wrong** *because we hadn't heard from you.* • *There's something wrong with the engine – it's making strange noises.* • *Something's happened to upset him but we don't know what it is.* • *I heard something rather worrying at work this morning.* • *The meaning of life is something which a great many people have wondered about.* • *Is there something you'd like to say?* • *Don't just stand there,* **do** *something – can't you see he's hurt.* • *She could sense there was something unpleasant, something nasty lurking in the shadows.* • *A radio failure is not something you want when you're alone on the pack ice.* • *Yes,* **there is** *something* **about** *her which many men find appealing.* • Something also means a situation or an event for which you are grateful, esp. because an unpleasant thing has also happened: *The carpets were ruined by the flood but we saved the furniture – that's something isn't it?* • *(infml approving)* If a person or thing **has (really) got something** or **is (really) something** or *(Br)* **is quite something** then they are special, often in a stated way, but for reasons which it is difficult to explain: *As a violinist she's really got something/ she's really something.* • *It was quite something for her to remember us after so many years.* • If you say that a person **has got something there** you mean they have said, discovered or done an important or interesting thing. • If you **have something going with** someone, you are involved in a close, esp. sexual, relationship with them. • *(infml)* You can use **or something** to show that you are not certain about what you have just said: *She works for a bank or something.* ○ *His main interest is moths or something.* • *(infml slightly dated)* If you describe an object, event or situation as **something else** you mean it is either extremely good or extremely bad: *What fantastic food – her cooking is something else!* ○ *The emotional hammering we endured was something else.* • If a person gets **something for nothing** they get something they want such as money without doing anything such as working: *He's just a scrounger – he always* **wants** *something for nothing.* • *There probably is* **something in** (= some truth in) *the rumours of a conspiracy.* • **Something like** means similar to but not exactly like: *He sounds something like his father when he speaks on the phone.* • Also **something like/***(infml)* **around** used about an amount or a number means approximately: *Something like 25% of the local population can neither read nor write.* • *(humorous)* **Something a little stronger** means a drink containing alcohol: *We have fruit juice but perhaps you'd like something a little stronger?* • *(slightly infml)* The phrase **something of** means to a degree but not completely: *She has something of her mother's facial features.* ○ *He always was something of* **a** *moaner.* ○ *It was something of* **a** *surprise when we met so unexpectedly.* • *The building materials cost* **something over/under** (= more/less than) *$4500.* • *(slightly infml)* The expression **something to do with** means in some way connected with or about: *Didn't she have something to do with that scandal which nearly caused the president to resign?* • If **there is something in** a story, explanation description etc., there is some truth in it: *It seems there's something in his alibi after all.* • Also if **there is something in** a suggestion or an idea then it is worth considering: *There's something in catching the earlier train, it means we'd have more time to find somewhere to stay when we get there.* • *"Time for a little something* (= food)*"* (A.A.Milne in the children's book *Winnie-the-Pooh*, 1926) • 'Anything' is usually used instead of 'something' in negative sentences and questions. • LP **Quantity words**

–some·thing /-ˌsʌmp·θɪŋ, '--/ *combining form infml* • You can use -something after a number like 20, 30 etc. to refer to the age of a person who is between 20 and 29, 30 and 39 years old etc., or to a person who is of this age: *I don't know for sure, but I'd guess she's sixty-something.* ○ *Most people in the hotel were forty-somethings.*

some·time UNKNOWN TIME /'sʌm·taɪm/ *adv* [not gradable] at a time in the future or the past which is not known or not stated • *We really should meet sometime soon to discuss the details.* • *They usually go to Rome sometime* **in** *the autumn.* • *Clothes like that went out of fashion sometime last decade.* • *I last saw him sometime last year.*

some·time NO LONGER /'sʌm·taɪm/ *adj* [before n; not gradable] *fml* (esp. of a job or position) in the past but not any longer • *The enquiry will be headed by Lord Jones, sometime editor of the 'Daily News'.*

some·times /'sʌm·taɪmz/ *adv* [not gradable] at particular occasions but not all the time • *Sometimes we take food with us and sometimes we buy food when we're there.* • *Sometimes it's best not to say anything.*

some·way /'sʌm·weɪ/, **some·ways** /'sʌm·weɪz/ *adv* [not gradable] *Am infml for* SOMEHOW

some·what /£'sʌm·wɒt, $-wɑːt/ *adv* [not gradable] *slightly fml* to some degree • *The resort has changed somewhat over the last few years.* • *She's somewhat more confident than she used to be.* • *We were somewhat tired after our long walk.* • The expression **somewhat of** means to some degree: *She was well known as being somewhat of a strange character.* • Somewhat is usually not used in negative phrases or sentences.

some·where PLACE /£'sʌm·weəʳ, $-wer/, *Am also* **some·place** *adv* [not gradable] in or at a place having a position which is not stated or not known • *He was last heard of living somewhere on the south coast.* • *You must have put their letter somewhere!* • *Can we go somewhere* **else** *to talk – it's very noisy here.* • *(fig.) I seem to have got lost somewhere* (= at some point) *in what you were saying – could you just repeat the last part?* • If a person or something **gets somewhere** it has results or advances towards achieving something: *The treatment is really getting somewhere – she can walk now.* • *(infml) Wouldn't you like to go to Disneyland* **or somewhere** (= a place similar to that stated)*?* • 'Anywhere' is usually used instead of 'somewhere' in negative sentences and questions.

some·where APPROXIMATELY /£'sʌm·weəʳ, $-wer/ *adv* [not gradable] (used in front of a number) approximately; about • *Somewhere* **between** *900 and 1100 minor crimes are reported in this city every week.* • *The company's annual turnover is somewhere* **around** *£70·7 million.*

som·nam·bu·lism /£sɒm'næm·bjʊ·lɪ·zᵊm, $sɑːm-/ *n* [U] *specialized* the action, sometimes habitual, of a person walking around while they are sleeping

som·nam·bu·list /£sɒm'næm·bjʊ·lɪst, $sɑːm-/ *n* [C] *specialized*

som·no·lent /£'sɒm·nəl·ənt, $'sɑːm-/ *adj* almost sleeping, or causing sleep • *a somnolent cat/village/weekend* • *Because of his somnolent voice students find it difficult to concentrate in his classes.*

som·no·lence /£'sɒm·nəl·ənts, $'sɑːm-/ *n* [U] • *She began to feel weighed down by a heavy somnolence.* • *"The lake of my mind, unbroken by oars, heaves placidly and soon sinks into an oily somnolence"* (Virginia Woolf *The Waves*, 1931)

son /sʌn/ *n* [C] a male child of a person • *This is our son Raja.* • *We have two sons and three* **daughters.** • *Our* **eldest/oldest** *son lives in Australia and the* **youngest** *in New Zealand.* • Son is used as an informal form of address by a man to a boy or to another man who is much younger than him: *Well, son, you seem to have caused a bit of trouble.* • A son of a place is a man who was born in that place: *that notable son of Württemberg, Martin Brecht.* • If a system or an idea is a son of another then it has been obtained by changing the original system or idea into a new form: *The latest tax scheme is proving to be an unpopular son of the old system which it replaces.* • *"Dombey and Son"* (title of a book by Charles Dickens, 1846-48) • LP **Relationships, Titles and forms of address** PIC **Family tree**

son–in–law /£'sʌn·ɪn·lɔː, $-lɑː/ *n* [C] *pl* **sons-in-law** or *Br also* **son-in-laws** • A person's **son-in-law** is the husband of any of their daughters.

son of a bitch, son-of-a-bitch, *abbreviation* **S.O.B** *n* [C] *pl* **sons of bitches** *esp. Am taboo slang* • **Son of a bitch** is an offensive way of referring to someone who is thought to be unpleasant or who has done something nasty: *What low-down son of a bitch took my clothes?*

son of a gun *n* [C] *pl* **sons of guns** *Am infml* • **Son of a gun** is used to avoid saying 'son of a bitch'.

so·nar /£'səʊ·nɑːʳ, $'soʊ·nɑːr/ *n* [U] equipment, esp. on a ship, which uses sound waves to discover how deep the water is or the position of an object in the water, such as a group of fish • *(fig.) Bats have a sort of built-in sonar to help them find their way in the dark.*

so·na·ta /£sə'nɑː·tə, $-t̬ə/ *n* [C] a piece of music in three or four parts, either for a piano or for another instrument, such as a VIOLIN, sometimes also with a piano

son et lu·mi·ère /£ˌsɒn·eɪˌluː·mi'eəʳ, $ˌsɑːn·eɪˌluː·mi'er/ *n* [U] an outside entertainment which uses sounds, lights and often a spoken story to tell the history of a place

song /£sɒŋ, $sɑːŋ/ *n* a usually short piece of music with words which are sung • *In the street below a child was* **singing** *a song.* [C] • *Don't miss this chance to buy twenty great* **love** *songs together on one album.* [C] • Song is also the act of singing, or singing when considered generally: *He was so happy he wanted to* **burst/break into** *song* (= start singing). [U] ○ *In those days the house was always full of laughter and song.* [U] • The song of a bird or an insect is the musical sound it makes: *We were woken at dawn by the song of birds.* [U] ○ *A thrush's song was the only sound to break the silence.* [C] • *(infml)* If something is bought or offered for sale **for a song** it is very cheap: *She bought the bed for a song at an auction.* ○ *Because the shop's closing down, most of the stock is* **going** *for a song* (= being sold or offered for sale very cheaply). • *(Br infml disapproving)* A **song and dance** is an act of showing anger and annoyance about something, esp. in an unnecessary way: *He always* **makes** *such a song and dance* **about** *visiting his relatives.* • *(esp. Am infml)* A **song and dance** is a long and often repeated story or explanation, esp. one which is not true: *I suppose she gave you that* **whole** *song and dance about being orphaned at the age of three and growing up on the streets.* • A **song thrush** is a type of THRUSH BIRD. • See also SWANSONG.

song·bird /£'sɒŋ·bɜːd, $'sɑːŋ·bɜːrd/ *n* [C] any of many different types of bird that make musical sounds

song·book /£'sɒŋ·bʊk, $'sɑːŋ-/ *n* [C] a book containing a collection of songs showing both their words and their music

song·fest /£'sɒŋ·fest, $'sɑːŋ-/ *n* [C] *Am for* SINGSONG SINGING

song·writ·er /£'sɒŋˌraɪ·təʳ, $'sɑːŋˌraɪ·t̬ɚ/ *n* [C] a person who writes the music and words of songs • *a country-music songwriter* • *Bob Dylan is probably the most famous* singer-*songwriter* (=someone who writes and performs their own songs) *of the twentieth century.*

song·writ·ing /£ˈsɒŋˌraɪ·tɪŋ, $ˈsɑːŋˌraɪ·t̬ɪŋ/ *n* [U]

son·ic /£ˈsɒn·ɪk, $ˈsɑː·nɪk/ *adj* [not gradable] *specialized* of sound or the speed at which sound travels in air • *Sonic waves travel at approximately 332 metres per second in air at sea level.* • A **sonic boom** is an explosive sound made by an aircraft, bullet etc. travelling faster than the speed at which sound travels. • See also SUPERSONIC.

son·net /£ˈsɒn·ɪt, $ˈsɑː·nɪt/ *n* [C] a poem that has 14 lines and a particular pattern of RHYME and word arrangement

son·ny /ˈsʌn·i/ *n* [U] *infml* a form of address used by an older person to a boy or a young man • *Now then sonny, what's the matter with you?* • The word sonny (*Br also* **sonny Jim**) can also be used in an offensive way as a form of address: *Listen sonny, you should get your facts right before making accusations like that!* • LP **Titles and forms of address**

son-of-a-bitch /ˌsʌn·əv·əˈbɪtʃ/ *n* [C] *pl* **sonsofbitches** /ˌsʌnz·əvˈbɪtʃ·ɪz/ *esp. Am taboo slang* **son of a bitch**, see at SON • *I'm going to beat that sonofabitch if it kills me!*

son·o·gram /£ˈsɒn·ə·græm, $ˈsɑː·nə-/ *n* [C] *specialized* an image, esp. of a baby that is still inside the womb, which is produced by ULTRASOUND (=sound waves) • *The sonogram showed that she was carrying twins.*

so·nor·ous /£ˈsɒn·ᵊr·əs, $ˈsɑː·nɚ-/ *adj* having a deep pleasant sound • *a sonorous voice*

so·nor·ous·ly /£ˈsɒn·ᵊr·ə·sli, £ˈsɑː·nɚ-/ *adv* • *The newsreader read sonorously and slowly.*

sook /sʊk/ *n* [C] *Aus* a shy or cowardly child or person

soon /suːn/ *adv* **-er, -est** in or within a short time; before long; quickly • *It'll soon get dark/It'll get dark soon.* • *Don't panic – the ambulance will be here soon.* • *It will soon be impossible for foreigners to enter the country.* • *The sooner we leave, the sooner we'll get there.* • *Soon* **after** *agreeing to go, she realised she'd made a mistake.* • **How** *soon* (=When) *can we sign the contract?* • *"When would you like to meet?"* **"The sooner the better."** • *Wednesday of next week is the soonest we can deliver the chairs.* • *I couldn't get out of that place soon enough.* • If something happens **as soon as** another thing then it happens immediately after the other thing has happened: *As soon as her car arrived, the crowd started cheering.* • If a person does something **as soon as possible** or **as soon as** they **can** they do it as quickly as they are able to: *We need you to do the repairs as soon as possible.* ○ *Please let us know your decision as soon as you can.* • If **no sooner** had one thing happened **than** a second thing happens, the second thing happens immediately after the first: *No sooner* **had** *I started mowing the lawn than it started raining.* • The expression **no sooner said than done** means that if something is suggested it will be done immediately: *"Can you fix the phone?" "Don't worry – no sooner said than done."* • Something which will happen **sooner or later** will certainly happen in the future, although it is not known exactly when: *Don't worry, sooner or later he'll come home.* • If you **would (just) as soon/would sooner** do something, you would prefer to do it rather than something else which is possible: *"Would you like to go out for dinner?" "I'd just as soon/I'd sooner stay home – I'm not feeling very well."* ○ *I'd just as soon/I'd sooner* **not** *speak to him.*

soot /sʊt/ *n* [U] a black powder made mainly of carbon which is produced when coal, wood, etc. is burnt • *It can be dangerous to let too much soot accumulate inside a chimney.*

soot·y /£ˈsʊt·i, $ˈsʊt̬-/ *adj* **-ier, -iest** • *a haze of sooty smoke* • *The chimney is very sooty – it needs a clean.*

soothe *obj* REDUCE ANGER /suːð/ *v* [T] to calm (a person who is angry or anxious) • *It was difficult to soothe her because she was very frightened after the attack.* • *I've managed to soothe him* **down** *a bit, but he's still pretty annoyed.* [M] • *"Music has charms to soothe the savage breast"* (William Congreve in the play *The Mourning Bride*, 1697)

sooth·ing /ˈsuː·ðɪŋ/ *adj* • *soothing comments* • *a soothing smile*

sooth·ing·ly /ˈsuː·ðɪŋ·li/ *adv*

soothe *obj* REDUCE PAIN /suːð/ *v* [T] to make (an injury) less painful • *Put your hand under cold running water – doing that will soothe the burn.*

sooth·ing /ˈsuː·ðɪŋ/ *adj* • *a soothing ointment*

sooth·say·er /£ˈsuːθˌseɪ·əʳ, $-ɚ/ *n* [C] *old use* a person who has the ability to know and tell what will happen in the future

sop /£sɒp, $sɑːp/ *n* [C] *disapproving* something unimportant or of little value which is offered to stop complaints or unhappiness • *Critics see the increase in defence spending as a sop* **to** *the armed forces rather than an improvement of national security.*

sop up *obj*, **sop** *obj* **up** /£sɒp, $sɑːp/ *v adv* [M] *slightly infml* to absorb (a liquid) into a piece of solid matter • *It's surprising how much milk the bread sops up.* • *He was trying to sop the oil up with newspaper.*

so·phis·ti·cat·ed /£səˈfɪs·tɪ·keɪ·tɪd, $-t̬ɪd/ *adj approving* having a good understanding of the way people behave and/or a good knowledge of culture and fashion • *Sophisticated readers understood the book's hidden meaning.* • *Her witty conversation showed her to be very sophisticated.* • *What are sophisticated young people wearing nowadays?* • If a way of thinking, a system or a machine is sophisticated, it is complicated or made with great skill: *I think a more sophisticated approach is needed to solve this problem.* ○ *The advanced technology which is incorporated into this missile makes it one of the most sophisticated weapons in the world.*

so·phis·ti·ca·tion /səˌfɪs·tɪˈkeɪ·ʃᵊn/ *n* [U] *approving* • *Her sophistication is evident from the way she dresses.* • *The sophistication of computers is increasing as their size decreases.*

so·phis·ti·cate /səˈfɪs·tɪ·kət/ *n* [C] *fml esp. approving* • A sophisticate is a person who is sophisticated: *a restaurant that is popular with sophisticates*

soph·ist·ry /£ˈsɒf·ɪ·stri, $ˈsɑː·fɪ-/ *n* [U] *fml disapproving or specialized* the clever use of arguments which seem true but are really false, and are used in this way to deceive people

soph·i·sm /£ˈsəʊ·fɪ·zᵊm, $ˈsɑː·fɪ-/ *n* [C] *fml disapproving or specialized* • A sophism is an argument which seems true but is really false and is used to deceive people.

soph·ist /£ˈsəʊ·fɪst, $ˈsɑː-/ *n* [C] *fml disapproving or specialized* • *It was basically a selfish act, though no doubt a sophist would argue that it was done for the general good.*

soph·o·more /£ˈsɒf·ə·mɔːʳ, $ˈsɑː·fə·mɔːr/ *n* [C] *Am* a student studying in the second year of a course at a US college or **high school** (=a school for students aged 15 to 18)

sop·o·rif·ic /£ˌsɒp·ᵊrˈɪf·ɪk, $ˌsɑː·pəˈrɪf-/ *adj* causing sleep or making a person feel sleepy • *Her soporific voice made it difficult to stay awake in the lecture.*

sop·o·ri·fi·cally /£ˌsɒp·ᵊrˈɪf·ɪ·kli, $ˌsɑː·pəˈrɪf-/ *adv*

sop·ping /£ˈsɒp·ɪŋ, $ˈsɑː·pɪŋ/ *adj, adv* [not gradable] *infml* extremely (wet) • *The tent split, and everything we had was sopping after the storm.* • *You're sopping* **wet** *– go and dry yourself and put some dry clothes on.*

sop·py /£ˈsɒp·i, $ˈsɑː·pi/ *adj* **-ier, -iest** *infml* showing or feeling too much of emotions such as love or sympathy, rather than being reasonable or practical • *Films with soppy endings are often successful.* • *That's one of the soppiest stories I've ever heard!* • *Some people are really soppy* **about** *their pets.*

sop·pi·ly /£ˈsɒp·ɪ·li, $ˈsɑː·pɪ-/ *adv infml*

sop·pi·ness /£ˈsɒp·ɪ·nəs, $ˈsɑː·pɪ-/ *n* [U] *infml*

so·pran·o /£səˈprɑː·nəʊ, $-noʊ/ *n* [C] *pl* **sopranos** a woman or girl with a voice which can sing the highest notes

so·pran·o /£səˈprɑː·nəʊ, $-noʊ/ *adj, adv* [not gradable] • *a soprano aria* • *I used to sing soprano when I was younger, but now I'm an alto.*

sor·bet /£ˈsɔː·beɪ, $sɔːrˈbeɪ/, *Am also* **sher·bet, ice**, *Br dated* **wa·ter ice** *n* a food made from frozen fruit juice and water and sometimes sugar and/or the transparent part of eggs • *(a) lemon sorbet* [C/U]

sor·cery /£ˈsɔː·sᵊr·i, $ˈsɔːr·sɚ-/ *n* [U] *esp. literary* a type of magic in which spirits, esp. evil ones, are used to make things happen • *Even in modern-day Britain it seems some people still believe in sorcery and black magic.*

sor·cer·er *male*, *female* **sor·cer·ess** /£ˈsɔː·sᵊr·əʳ, $ˈsɔːr·sɚ·ɚ, -əs/ *n* [C] *esp. literary* • *The sorcerer cast an evil spell on her.*

sor·did DIRTY /£ˈsɔː·dɪd, $ˈsɔːr-/ *adj* unpleasant because dirty or in bad condition; SQUALID • *There are lots of really sordid apartments in the city's poorer areas.*

sor·did·ness /£ˈsɔː·dɪd·nəs, $ˈsɔːr-/ *n* [U]

sor·did DISHONEST /£'sɔː·dɪd, $'sɔːr-/ *adj* (of behaviour) dishonest or not deserving respect • *All the sordid* **details** *of the company's deception were published.*

sor·did·ly /£'sɔː·dɪd·li, $'sɔːr-/ *adv*

sor·did·ness /£'sɔː·dɪd·nəs, $'sɔːr-/ *n* [U] • *The sordidness of the blackmail attempt shocked many members of the public.*

sore PAINFUL /£sɔːʳ, $sɔːr/ *adj* **-r, -st** painful and uncomfortable either (of a body part) because of an injury or infection or (of a muscle) because of too much use • *All the dust has made my eyes sore.* • *She says her feet are sore because the new shoes rub.* • *I've got a sore* **throat**. • *If you're not used to skiing, it can make you sore in places which you never knew existed.* • Something which is a **sore point** with someone makes them angry or embarrassed: *Don't say anything about the football match – it's a sore point* **with** *him because they lost rather badly.* • *(infml)* If something **stands/sticks out like a sore thumb** it is very noticeable, esp. because it looks foolishly different from the other things around it: *You'll stick out like a sore thumb if you don't wear the same uniform as everybody else.* • LP› **Feelings and pains**

sore /£sɔːʳ, $sɔːr/ *n* [C] • A sore is a painful area on the surface of a body, esp. an infected area: *The poor dog's back was covered with sores.* • See also **cold sore** at COLD ILLNESS.

sore·ness /£'sɔː·nəs, $'sɔːr-/ *n* [U] • *"Do you feel any soreness when I press your arm here?" the doctor asked.* • *There's still some soreness in my ankle from when I sprained it last month.*

sore ANGRY /£sɔːʳ, $sɔːr/ *adj* **-r, -st** *Am infml* (of a person) angry, esp. because they feel they have been unfairly treated • *Honey, don't* **get** *sore* **with** *the kids – they didn't mean what they said.* • *It was all a mistake, it's nothing to be sore about.* • *Walter always wants to win the game, but he's not a sore* **loser** (=someone who does not accept defeat well).

sore·head /£'sɔː·hed, $'sɔːr-/ *n* [C] *Am infml* a person who is easily made angry • *Don't be such a sorehead – it was only meant to be a joke.*

sore·ly /£'sɔː·li, $'sɔːr-/ *adv fml* extremely; very much • *I was sorely* **tempted** *to say exactly what I thought of his offer.* • *You'll be sorely missed by everyone here, and we wish you success in your new job.*

sor·ghum /£'sɔː·gəm, $'sɔːr-/ *n* [U] a type of grain grown in hot countries

so·ror·i·ty /£sə'rɒr·ɪ·ti, $-'rɔːr·ə·t̬i/ *n* [C] *Am* a social organization for female students at some US colleges • Compare FRATERNITY.

sor·rel /£'sɒr·ᵊl, $'sɔːr-/ *n* [U] a plant with acidic-tasting leaves which are used in cooking and salads

sor·row /£'sɒr·əʊ, $'sɔːr·oʊ/ *n* (a cause of) a feeling of great sadness or regret • *The sorrow she felt* **over/at** *the death of her husband was almost too much to bear.* [U] • **It** *was a great sorrow* **to** *his parents* **that** *he dropped out of college.* [U + *that* clause] • *The sorrows of her earlier years gave way to joy in later life.* [C] • *"More in sorrow than in anger"* (Shakespeare, Hamlet 1.2)

sor·row /£'sɒr·əʊ, $'sɔːr·oʊ/ *v* [I always + adv/prep] *literary* • *For years she sorrowed* (=felt great sadness) **over/for** *her missing son.*

sor·row·ful /£'sɒr·əʊ·fᵊl, $'sɔːr·ə-/ *adj slightly literary* • *With a sorrowful sigh she folded the letter and put it away.*

sor·row·ful·ly /£'sɒr·əʊ·fᵊl·i, $'sɔːr·ə-/ *adv slightly literary*

sor·row·ing /£'sɒr·əʊ·ɪŋ, $'sɔːr·oʊ-/ *adj* [before n] *literary* • *Sorrowing friends stood by the graveside.*

sor·ry SAD /£'sɒr·i, $'sɔːr-/ *adj* [after v] **-ier, -iest** feeling sadness, sympathy, or disappointment, esp. because something unpleasant has happened or been done • *They've caused great disruption, and they don't seem at all sorry* **about** *it.* • *It's difficult not to* **feel** *sorry when you hear of such sad events.* • *It's no use just* **feeling** *sorry* **for** *them – do something about the problem.* • *I'm sorry* **(that)** *you had such a difficult journey.* [+ (*that*) clause] • *We were both sorry* **to** *hear you've been ill again.* [+ *to* infinitive] • *(esp. disapproving)* If you are sorry **for yourself**, you are (unreasonably) unhappy because of something bad that has happened to you: *He sounded very sorry* **for** *himself on the telephone.* • The expression **I'm sorry to say** is used to show that something which must be said causes sadness or disappointment: *I'm sorry to say* **that** *the project's funding has been cancelled.* ○ *Most people who start the course do, I'm sorry to say, give up within the first two weeks.* • *"Who's Sorry Now?"* (title of a song written by Bert Kalmar, Harry Ruby and Ted Snyder, 1923)

sor·ry REGRET /£'sɒr·i, $'sɔːr-/ *adj* [after v] **-ier, -iest** used to say that you wish you had not done what you have done, esp. when you want to be polite to someone you have done something bad to • *Say you're sorry and give the lady her hat back.* • *Sorry* **about/for** *the inconvenience.* • *Don't say you're sorry* **about** *what happened if you don't mean it.* • *I'm sorry* **(that)** *I agreed to go to the meeting.* [+ (*that*) clause] • LP› **Phrases and customs**

sor·ry /£'sɒr·i, $'sɔːr-/ *exclamation* • *"That's my foot you're treading on." "Sorry!"*

sor·ry REFUSAL OR DISAGREEMENT /£'sɒr·i, $'sɔːr-/ *adj* [after v] used to show politeness when expressing refusal or disagreement • *I'm sorry but I think you've made a mistake.*

sor·ry /£'sɒr·i, $'sɔːr-/ *exclamation* • *Sorry, you can't go in there.* • *(esp. Br and Aus)* Sorry can also be used when politely asking someone to repeat something or when politely interrupting someone: *Sorry, could you just say that last sentence again please?* ○ *"He's late." "Sorry?" "I said he's late."* ○ *Sorry, but before continuing could you give a little more detail about what you just suggested?*

sor·ry BAD CONDITION /£'sɒr·i, $'sɔːr-/ *adj* [before n] **-ier, -iest** deserving sympathy or causing worry; in a bad or weak condition • *It's a sorry* **state of affairs** *when there isn't any food in the cupboard.* • *They were a sorry* **sight** *when they came in covered with mud.* • *We're in a sorry mess.*

sort TYPE /£sɔːt, $sɔːrt/ *n* [C] a group of things which are of the same type or which share similar qualities • *What sort* **of** *shoes will I need?* • *Is there any sort* **of** *food which you particularly like?* • *"Would you like some strawberry ice cream?" "Yes, that's my favourite sort."* • *We saw* **all** *sorts* (= many types) **of** *animals in the park.* • *Many sorts of bacteria are resistant to penicillin.* • *This sort* **of** *camera is/(not standard) These sort* **of** *cameras are very expensive.* • *Plants* **of** *this sort need shady conditions.* • If someone or something is described as someone's sort, it means that they are of the type which that person likes: *Hmm, this is my sort* **of** *wine!* ○ *I never thought he was her sort* (=was the type of man she would really like). • You can say **of sorts** or **of a sort** to express uncertainty about something and usually to suggest that it is of low quality: *It was food of sorts, but it had no taste at all.* • *(slightly dated)* If a person is **out of sorts** they feel ill, unhappy or annoyed: *She says she's* **feeling** *out of sorts and she won't be able to come this afternoon.* • *(infml)* You can use **(a) sort of** to express uncertainty or lack of exact knowledge or understanding about something: *You said you had a sort of feeling she'd be late.* ○ *The walls were painted sort of pink.* • *(infml)* **Sort of** also means in some way or to some degree: *It's sort of silly, but I'd like a copy of the photograph.* ○ *She was sort of hoping to leave early today.* • *(saying)* 'It takes all sorts (to make a world)' means people vary very much from each other in character, opinion and ability, and you should accept this. • Ⓟ

sort *(obj)* ORDER /£sɔːt, $sɔːrt/ *v* to put (things) in an order or separate them into groups • *Paper, plastic and cans are sorted for recycling.* [T] • *I'm going to sort these old books* **into** *those to be kept and those to be thrown away.* [T] • *She found the ring while sorting* **(through)** *some clothes.* [T; I + *through*] • *Sort* **out** (=Separate from the others) *any clothes you want to throw away and give them to me.* [M] • A **sorting code** is a number used to refer to a particular bank in financial dealings. LP› **Money** • *(Br infml)* If you have a **sort-out** you put things in order or in their correct place: *These cupboards need* **a** *sort-out – I can't find anything!* • A **sorting office** is a building where letters, parcels, etc. are taken after they have been posted and where they are then put into groups according to their addresses before being delivered. • Ⓟ

sort·er /£'sɔː·təʳ, $'sɔːr·t̬ɚ/ *n* [C] • *(Am)* A **mail** sorter is someone who puts letters and parcels into groups for delivery. • A **grain** sorter is a machine which separates the wheat or other grains from any waste or unwanted material mixed in with it.

sort *obj* REPAIR /£sɔːt, $sɔːrt/ *v* [T usually passive] *Br infml* to repair (something) or put it in good order • *Can you sort the car by tomorrow?* • *We must* **get** *the phone sorted soon.* • *I must* **get** *this paperwork sorted before I go on holiday next week.* • Ⓟ

sort PERSON /£sɔːt, $sɔːrt/ *n* [C usually sing] *slightly dated* a person having the stated or suggested character • *She's a very generous sort really.* • *He seemed like a decent sort to me.* • Ⓟ

sort out *obj* DEAL WITH, **sort** *obj* **out** *v adv* [M] to deal satisfactorily or successfully with (a problem, a situation or a person who is having difficulties) • *We've sorted out the computer system's initial problems.* • *It'll be difficult to sort out* **how** *much each person owes.* [+ *wh-* word] • *Most of the job involves sorting customers out who have queries.*

sort out *obj* PUNISH, **sort** *obj* **out** *v adv* [M] *Br infml* to punish or attack (someone), esp. in order to make them understand that they have behaved badly • *Has he been bothering you again – do you want me to sort him out?*

sor·tie /£ˈsɔː·ti, $ˈsɔːr·t̬i/ *n* [C] a brief attack by a military force, such as a small group of soldiers or an aircraft, made against an enemy position • *A series of sorties was carried out at night by specially equipped aircraft.* • *(fig. infml or humorous) From our quiet home in the country we would go into town* **on a** *sortie* (= a brief journey to an unfriendly place) *for shopping once a week.* • *(fig. infml) After several sorties* **into** (= attempts to be successful in) *word processing, the company changed to writing games software.*

SOS /£ˌes·əʊˈes, $ˌ-oʊˈ-/ *n* [C] a request for help, esp. because of danger • *In Morse code, an SOS consists of three short sounds or flashes followed by three long ones and then three more short ones.* • *Within an hour of the ship transmitting an SOS* **(message/call)**, *six boats had arrived and started a rescue operation.* • *The hospital sent out an SOS* **for** *extra blood supplies.*

so–so /ˌsəʊˈsəʊ, ˈsoʊ·soʊ/ *adj, adv* [not gradable] *infml* between average quality and low quality; not good or well • *It was a so-so performance from a team which usually plays excitingly.* • *"How are you getting on with your new boss?" "So-so."*

sot·to voce /£ˌsɒt·əʊˈvəʊ·tʃi, $ˌsɑː·t̬oʊˈvoʊ-/ *adj, adv fml* said in a quiet voice so that only people near can hear • *a sotto voce comment* • *He pointed out, sotto voce, that my trousers were undone.*

sou /suː/ *n* [U usually in negatives] *Br* a very small amount of money • *I* **don't have a** *sou – could you lend me some money for the taxi?*

sou·bri·quet /ˈsuː·brɪ·keɪ/ *n* [C] *fml* a SOBRIQUET

souf·flé /£ˈsuː·fleɪ, $suˈfleɪ/ *n* a light food which has a lot of air in it, is made mainly from eggs, and can be either sweet or savoury • *a cheese/chocolate soufflé* [C] • *You can have fruit salad, lemon soufflé or strawberry tart for dessert.* [U]

sought /£sɔːt, $sɑːt/ *past simple and past participle of* SEEK • If something is **sought-after** it is wanted by many people, usually because it is rare or of high quality: *The very best football players are much sought-after and can command very high salaries.* ○ *At the age of seventeen she is already one of Hollywood's most sought-after actresses.*

soul SPIRIT /£səʊl, $soʊl/ *n* [C] the part of a person which some people believe is spiritual and continues to exist in some form after their body has died, or the part of a person which is not physical and experiences deep feelings and emotions • *She suffered greatly while she was alive, so let us hope her soul is now at peace.* • *His soul was often tormented by memories of what he had seen in the prison.* • *(esp. Br disapproving)* Something, such as a job, which is **soul-destroying** is unpleasant and destroys a person's confidence or happiness: *Repetitive work can become soul-destroying after a while.* ○ *It's soul-destroying for any team to lose most of their games.* • **Soul-searching** is deep and careful consideration of inner thoughts, esp. about a moral problem: *After much soul-searching, he decided it was wrong to vote in the elections.*

soul DEEP FEELINGS /£səʊl, $soʊl/ *n* [U] the quality of a person or work of art which shows or produces deep good feelings • *Only a person with* **no** *soul would be unmoved by her account of what happened in the prison camps.* • *Although some people think her paintings lack soul, they are very popular.* • A **soul mate** is someone who shares your way of thinking about the world and is usually someone for whom you feel a large amount of affection or love: *They realized immediately that they were soul mates on the issue of ecology.* ○ *He's spent the whole of his adult life searching for a soul mate* (= perfect lover).

soul·ful /£ˈsəʊl·fᵊl, $ˈsoʊl-/ *adj* • *a soulful performance/ballad* • *The dog looked at me with its big soulful brown eyes.*

soul·ful·ly /£ˈsəʊl·fᵊl·i, $ˈsoʊl-/ *adv*

soul·ful·ness /£ˈsəʊl·fᵊl·nəs, $ˈsoʊl-/ *n* [U]

soul·less /£ˈsəʊl·ləs, $ˈsoʊl-/ *adj disapproving* • If something is soulless it lacks any human influence or qualities: *a soulless building of grey concrete*

soul·less·ly /£ˈsəʊl·lə·sli, $ˈsoʊl-/ *adv*

soul·less·ness /£ˈsəʊl·lə·snəs, $ˈsoʊl-/ *n* [U]

soul PERSON /£səʊl, $soʊl/ *n* [C] a person of a stated type • *She was such a happy soul when she was a child.* • *Some unfortunate soul will have to tell him what's happened.* • Soul can also mean any person, and is usually used in negative statements: *There* **wasn't a** *soul around when we arrived at the beach.*

soul BLACK CULTURE /£səʊl, $soʊl/ *n* [U] *Am* a deep understanding of and pride in the culture of black people • *I like her – she's* **got** *soul.* • **Soul (music)** is a type of popular music which shows strong feelings and emotions: *Soul music is often an affirmation of, and a manifesto for, black dignity.*

soul /£səʊl, $soʊl/ *adj* [before n; not gradable] *Am* • *soul food*

soul·ful /£ˈsəʊl·fᵊl, $ˈsoʊl-/ *adj Am* • *The soulful brothers and sisters will appreciate what I'm saying.*

sound NOISE /saʊnd/ *n* (what is heard because of) quick changes of pressure in air, water etc. • *They could hear the sound of a bell tolling in the distance.* [C] • *Don't* **make** *a sound and stay absolutely still.* [C] • *Suddenly we heard a loud knocking sound from the engine.* [C] • *Sound can* **travel** *over very large distances in water.* [U] • *The sounds in some languages can be difficult for learners to pronounce.* [C] • Sound is also the activity of recording and broadcasting sound such as from a performance of music or for a film: *a sound engineer/recording* • The sound of a television or film is the volume or quality of its sound: *Could you* **turn** *the sound down on the TV – it's very loud.* [U] • The sound of a musician or group of musicians is the particular quality of the music which they produce: *The band's sound is a distinctive mixture of funk and rap.* [C] • **The sound barrier** is a large increase in the force opposing a moving object as its speed approaches the speed at which sound travels. *There is usually a sonic boom when an aircraft* **breaks** *the sound barrier.* • If someone performs a **sound check** at a music show they test the musical instruments and recording equipment, esp. before the players come on stage to see that everything is working and that the sound quality is good. • In a radio or television programme or a film the **sound effects** are the sounds other than speech or music which are added to make it seem more exciting or real. • A **sound system** is a piece or several pieces of electronic equipment which can be used to play music from recordings, radio broadcasts etc. • A **sound wave** is a wave caused by changes of pressure in air, water etc.: *In air sound waves travel at approximately 330 metres per second.* • *"Full of sound and fury, signifying nothing"* (Shakespeare, Macbeth 5.5.) • *"The Sound of Music"* (title of a musical, 1959) • LP Sound

sound *(obj)* /saʊnd/ *v* • *The factory bell sounds* (= makes a noise) *every day at five o'clock to tell people they can go.* [I] • *Sounding the car's horn, she drove at high speed through the crowded streets.* [T] • If someone sounds a warning, they cause a noise to be made or say or shout a message to warn people about something: *Quick, sound* **the alarm** *– there's a fire in the machine room!* • *We heard the trumpeter* **sound the retreat** (= play the military musical signal to move back). • See **sound the death knell** at DEATH.

sound·less /ˈsaʊnd·ləs/ *adj* • *Above the mountain, eagles circled in soundless flight.*

sound·less·ly /ˈsaʊnd·lə·sli/ *adv* • *Soundlessly she left the room, leaving her child to sleep.*

sound SEEM /saʊnd/ *v* to suggest a particular feeling, state or thing by the way something is said or the noise made • *He sounded very depressed when we spoke on the telephone yesterday.* [L only + adj] • *All the usual city noises sounded strange in the fog.* [L only + adj] • *I know* **it** *sounds silly, but I'll miss him when he's gone.* [L only + adj] • *At the press conference, he was sounding at his most relaxed.* [I always + adv/prep] • *You sound* **as though** *you have a sore throat.* [I always + adv/prep] • *He sounds just* **like** *someone I used to work with.* [I always + adv/prep] • **It** *sounds* **to** *me from the rumours* **that** *we might have some problems.* [+ *that* clause] • *Judging by what they said,* **it** *sounds* **like/as if/as though** *they had a good holiday.* [I always + adv/prep] • *Some parts of the desert sound* **like** (= seem to be) *dangerous places.* [I always + adv/prep] • *You're going to Delhi? That* **sounds fun** (= seems likely to be enjoyable). • If you use a person or group of people as a **sounding board** you test something such as a new idea or suggestion on them to see if they will accept it or if they think it will

SOUNDS AND HEARING

- Your ability to hear is called your **hearing**; it is one of the senses.
  Someone who is unable to hear is **deaf**: *Desmond* **went deaf** *years ago.*
  Turn that damned music down, you'll **deafen** *me* (= make me unable to hear)*!*

- In general when you pay attention to a person or thing that you can hear, you **listen to** them. However, you **hear** events such as concerts or talks which happen in public.
  Be quiet, I'm **listening to** *the news/your mother/some music.*
  We're going to **hear** *a heavy metal rock group at the National Exhibition Centre.*

- What you hear is a **sound**. A **noise** is an unpleasant, unwanted or loud sound.
  Strange **noises** *of tapping and rustling came from behind the wall.*
  The builders next door are **making** *a lot of* **noise**.

- The following adjectives describe the loudness of a sound:
  All day long there was a **deafening** *noise of low-flying aircraft.*
  Our neighbour's **noisy** *dogs were barking all night.*
  Gary likes playing **loud** *rock music in the evening.*

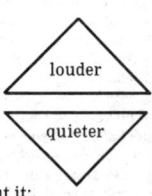

  The **faint** *sound of bells came from the end of the valley.*
  I can only get to sleep in a **quiet** *room.*
  The empty house was completely **silent**.

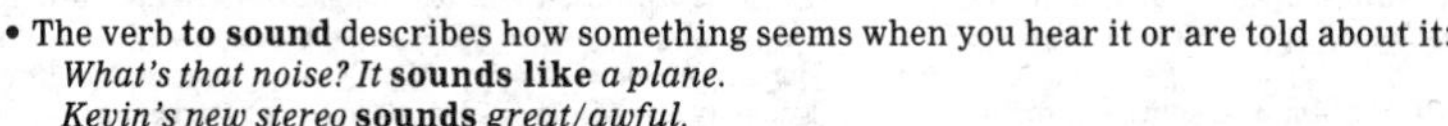

- The verb **to sound** describes how something seems when you hear it or are told about it:
  What's that noise? It **sounds like** *a plane.*
  Kevin's new stereo **sounds** *great/awful.*
  From what she says the film **sounds** *interesting.*

work: *She would often use her family as a sounding board* **for** *new recipes before trying them in her restaurant.* • LP⟩ **It**

sound /saʊnd/ *n* [U] • *I don't like* **the** *sound* **of** *the symptoms you describe* (= they seem to be bad) *– we'd better get you to a doctor.* • **By/From the** *sound* **of it** (= According to what has been said and the way it was said) *she seems to be serious about leaving.*

sound GOOD CONDITION /saʊnd/ *adj* **-er, -est** not broken or damaged; healthy; in good condition • *His body is very sound considering his age.* • *Engineers decided that the bridge was sound, but they said only one lorry should be allowed on it at any one time.* • *Was she* **of** *sound* **mind** (= not mentally ill) *at the time of the incident?* • *(infml)* If something is **(as) sound as a bell** it is in perfect condition.

sound·ness /'saʊnd·nəs/ *n* [U]

sound GOOD JUDGMENT /saʊnd/ *adj* **-er, -est** showing good judgment; able to be trusted • *She seems to have given you some very sound* **advice** *about the choice of study courses.* • *He supported his proposal with sound* **arguments**. • *Are these pesticides environmentally sound* (= will they not damage the environment)*?* • *Government bonds are a sound* **investment** *because they combine good profits and high security.* • *We've decided to appoint Browne to the post. He's very sound.*

sound·ness /'saʊnd·nəs/ *n* [U] • *The soundness of her judgment in business matters is widely respected.*

sound COMPLETE /saʊnd/ *adj* **-er, -est** complete • *How sound is her knowledge of archaeology?* • *The home team played badly and suffered a sound* (= severe) *defeat.*

sound·ly /'saʊnd·li/ *adv* • *The committee soundly rejected all of the proposed changes.* • *Anyone caught stealing will be soundly punished.*

sound SLEEP /saʊnd/ *adj, adv* **-er, -est** (of sleep) deep and peaceful • *Her sleep was very sound – the thunder didn't wake her up.* • *He was sound* **asleep** *within moments of getting into bed.*

sound·ly /'saʊnd·li/ *adv* • *I slept very soundly, thank you – the bed was really comfortable.*

sound WATER PASSAGE /saʊnd/ *n* [C] a passage of sea connecting two larger areas of sea, or an area of sea mostly surrounded by land • *the Kalmar Sound* • *Plymouth Sound*

sound *obj* WATER DEPTH /saʊnd/ *v* [T] to measure the depth of (a mass of water, such as the sea), usually by SONAR • *A piece of line with a weight at one end is sometimes used to sound a lake or river.* • See **echo sounder** at ECHO.

sound·ings /'saʊn·dɪŋz/ *pl n* • *They* **took** *soundings* (= measured the depth of water) *and found that the water was 120 feet deep.* • *(fig.) Can you* **make/take** *some discreet soundings* (= ask questions) *to see what her future plans are?*

sound off *v adv* [I] *infml* to express opinions forcefully, esp. without being asked for them • *He's always sounding off* **about** *how he thinks the country should be run.*

sound out *obj*, **sound** *obj* **out** *v adv* [M] to discover the opinions or intentions of (a person) • *Perhaps you could sound the chairwoman out before the meeting, to see which way she's going to vote?* • *We're sounding Jones out* **about** *joining our group* (= asking him if he would like to join it).

sound·bite /'saʊnd·baɪt/ *n* [C] a short sentence or phrase that is easy to remember, often included in a speech made by a politician and repeated in newspapers and on television and radio • *Most politicians want to master the art of the soundbite.*

sound·board /£'saʊnd·bɔːd, $-bɔːrd/ *n* [C] a thin sheet of wood on a musical instrument such as a guitar which the strings go over and which helps to produce the sound

sound·proof /'saʊnd·pruːf/ *adj* (of a building or part of a building) not allowing sound to go through • *a soundproof room/wall/studio/cubicle* • *The walls of our house were so soundproof that we very rarely heard the neighbours.*

sound·proof *obj* /'saʊnd·pruːf/ *v* [T] • *They soundproofed the room so it could be used for music practice.* • *It was a well soundproofed building, so we didn't hear the traffic outside.*

sound·proof·ing /'saʊnd,pruː·fɪŋ/ *n* [U] • *What's the soundproofing like in the hotel?*

sound·track /'saʊnd·træk/ *n* [C] the sounds, esp. music, of a film, or a separate recording of this • *The quality of the soundtrack on that old film is really poor.* • *I've just bought the soundtrack* (= recorded music) **from/to/of** *"Chariots of Fire."*

soup /suːp/ *n* liquid food, usually made by cooking vegetables and sometimes also meat or fish in water • *vegetable/chicken/oxtail/fish/tomato soup* [U] • *hot/cold soup* [U] • *clear/thick soup* [U] • *home-made soup* [U] • *(Br and Aus) packet/(Am) instant soup* [U] • *(Br and Aus) tinned/(Am) canned soup* [U] • *The steaming hot soup was very comforting after our long walk through the snow.* [U] • *Would you like* **some soup/a bowl of** *soup?* [U] • *There were three different soups on the menu that evening – tomato, chicken and lentil – but Rachel didn't like any of them.* [C] • *(fig.) Many scientists think that life began from molecules synthesized within a primordial cosmic soup* (= liquid substance that existed on the Earth before there were any plants, animals or humans). [U] • *(infml slightly dated)* If you are **in the soup**, you are in an unpleasant or difficult situation. • A **soup kitchen** is a place where free soup or other food is given to people with no money or no homes. • A **soup spoon** is a large spoon, often rounded, used for eating soup. • *"Soup of the evening, beautiful Soup!"* (Lewis Carroll in *Alice in Wonderland*, 1865) • PIC⟩ **Containers, Cutlery**

soup up *obj*, **soup** *obj* **up** /suːp/ *v adv* [M often passive] *infml* to make (esp. something old) more powerful or more attractive by making changes to it • *Cars and motorbikes are sometimes souped up by modifying the engine to make* *them go faster.* • *They've souped up the play by leaving out all the slow-moving and dated parts.*

souped–up /ˈsuːpt·ʌp/ *adj* [before n] • *a souped-up Mini* • *(disapproving) This so-called new textbook just looks like a souped-up* **version** *of the old one.*

soup·çon /£ˈsuːp·sɒ̃, $·sɑ̃ː/ *n* [U] *esp. humorous* a very small amount; a TRACE [SLIGHT AMOUNT] • *"Shall I add some garlic?" "Just* **a** *soupçon."* • *Only* **a** *soupçon* **of** *milk in my tea, please.* • *Do I detect* **a** *soupçon* **of** *sarcasm in what you just said?*

sour /£saʊəʳ, $saʊr/ *adj* **-er, -est** (of food) having a sharp taste, or *(fig.)* unfriendly, bad-tempered or unpleasant • *sour plums/rhubarb/gooseberries* • *Lemons always taste sour, even when they are ripe because of the acid in them.* • *If you add lemon juice to milk, it will* **go/turn** *sour.* • *(fig.) Things* **went/turned** *sour* (=The situation became unpleasant) *when David said he was leaving Joanna and moving in with Louisa.* • *(fig.) She was a sour* (=bad-tempered) *old lady who never had a good word for anybody.* • *(fig.) He gave her a sour* (=unfriendly) *look.* • **Sour grapes** is said when someone cannot have something which they really want and so they pretend that it is of no value to them: *After Claire failed to get into drama school she said she never wanted to be an actress anyway, but we think that's just sour grapes.* • **Sour cream** (*Br* also **soured cream**) is cream which is made sour by adding special bacteria, and which is used in cooking.

sour /£saʊəʳ, $saʊr/ *n* [C] *esp. Am* • A sour is a drink made from strong alcohol, lemon or LIME juice, sugar and ice: *a whisky sour*

sour *(obj)* /£saʊəʳ, $saʊr/ *v* • *Hot weather sours milk.* [T] • *Milk sours in hot weather.* [I] • *(fig.) The awful experience soured her whole attitude to life.* [T] • *(fig.) Her whole attitude to life soured as a result of the awful experience.* [I]

sour·ly /£ˈsaʊə·li, $ˈsaʊr-/ *adv* • Sourly means in a bad-tempered way: *"What have I got to be happy about?" he said sourly.*

sour·ness /£ˈsaʊə·nəs, $ˈsaʊr-/ *n* [U] • *The sourness of a fruit depends on how ripe it is.* • *(fig.) "I didn't get the job – they gave it to a young chap with no experience" he said with great sourness.*

source /£sɔːs, $sɔːrs/ *n* [C] the place something comes from or starts at, or the cause of something • *a source* **of** *heat/energy/light* • *a heat/energy/light source* • *Oranges are a good source* **of** *vitamin C.* • *The mine is the source* **of** *much of the world's uranium.* • *The journalist refused to* **disclose/reveal/identify** *her sources* (=to say who had given the information to her). • *We have it from a* **good/reliable** *source that one hostage will soon be freed.* • *According to Government sources* (=people in the Government) *many MPs are worried about this issue.* • *Students must* **list/acknowledge** *their sources* (=say which books they have used) *at the end of their essays.* • *Where did the writer get her source* **material** *from?* • *Experts are trying to* **trace/track down/locate/find** *the source of the contamination in the water supply.* • *We walked up the river to its source in the hills.* • *The tradition* **has** *its source* **in** *an ancient fertility rite.* • Something or someone can be a source **of** comfort/pride/ disappointment/embarrassment **to/for/in** someone else: *Clara Wieck was a source of inspiration for Schumann.* ○ *Money is often a source of tension and disagreements in young married couples.* • *The rumour must be stopped* **at source** (=before it starts to spread). • *(Br and Aus) Tax is deducted from my income* **at source** (=by my employer). • If you are changing something into a different language, the **source language** is the original language. Compare **target language** at TARGET.

source *obj* /£sɔːs, $sɔːrs/ *v* [often passive] • *The story in the paper wasn't sourced* (=they didn't state where it came from), *so we couldn't check it.* • *All the produce used in our restaurant is very carefully sourced* (=we are careful about where we get it from).

sour·dough /£ˈsaʊə·dəʊ, $ˈsaʊr·doʊ/ *n* [U] a mixture of flour and water which is left to FERMENT (=change chemically) and then used to make bread rise • *sourdough bread* • *Sourdough is sometimes used in addition to yeast in bread-making.*

sour·puss /£ˈsaʊə·pʊs, $ˈsaʊr-/ *n* [C] *infml slightly dated* someone who always looks unhappy and bad-tempered • *She's an old sourpuss – I've never seen her smile!*

sou·sa·phone /£ˈsuː·zə·fəʊn, $-foʊn/ *n* [C] a large TUBA (=metal musical instrument played by blowing) with tubing which goes round the player's body, sometimes used in marching musical groups

souse *obj* /saʊs/ *v* [T] to put (something, esp. fish) into salted water or vinegar and leave there for some time in order to preserve it, or to make completely wet • *She soused the fish in vinegar and spices to produce a very tasty dish.*

soused /saʊst/ *adj* [not gradable] • *soused herring/ mackerel* • *(fig. dated slang) He was so soused* (=drunk) *he could hardly stand up.* • *I got caught in a thunderstorm and got completely soused* (=wet).

south /saʊθ/ (*abbreviation* **S**, *Br also* **Sth**, *esp. Am* **So**) *n* [U] the direction which goes towards the part of the Earth below the equator, opposite to the north, or the part of an area or country which is in this direction • *The points of the compass are North, South, East and West.* • *The best beaches are* **in the** *south* **(of** *the island).* • *We usually spend our holidays* **in the** *South* **of** *France.* • *Canberra* **is/lies to the** *south* **of** *Sydney.* • *These plants grow well on a south-***facing** *wall.* • **The South** can be used to refer to the developing countries of the world, which are mainly below the equator: *Many people hope that dialogue between the North and the South will help towards a sharing of the world's resources.* See also **Third World** at THIRD. • **The South** can also mean the southeastern STATES of the US: *The American Civil War was fought between the North and the South partly over the issue of slavery.* • *"South of the Border – Down Mexico Way"* (song written by Jimmy Kennedy and Michael Carr, 1939) • [LP] **Directions**

south /saʊθ/ (*abbreviation* **S**, *Br also* **Sth**, *esp. Am* **So**) *adj, adv* • *South Africa* • *the South China Sea* • *She lives* **on the** *south coast.* • *The leisure centre is* **on the** *south side of town.* • A south **wind** is a wind coming from the south. • *They drove/travelled south towards the rain forest.* • *He rode* **due** (=directly) *south, towards the desert.* • *My room* **faces** *south, so it gets a lot of sun.* • *(Br infml) I've moved/ got a job* **down** *south* (=to/in the south of the country). • The **South Pole** is the point on the Earth's surface which is furthest south.

south·bound /ˈsaʊθ·baʊnd/ *adj* [not gradable] • Southbound means going or leading towards the south: *southbound passengers/traffic* ○ *All southbound trains leave from platform one.* ○ *An accident has blocked the southbound lanes of the motorway.*

south·er·ly /£ˈsʌð·əl·i, $-ə·li/ *adj* • *a southerly* (= towards the south) *direction* • *Los Cristianos is the most southerly* (=nearest the south) *resort in Tenerife.* • *A southerly wind/breeze/airstream* (=wind from the south) *is common at this time of year.*

south·ern /£ˈsʌð·ən, $-ərn/ (*abbreviation* **S**, *esp. Am* **So**) *adj* [not gradable] • *a southern route/bypass* • *the Southern Hemisphere* • *There will be rain in southern England during the afternoon.* • The **Southern Cross** is the group of stars which points towards the South Pole and appears on the flags of Australia and New Zealand.

south·ern·er /£ˈsʌð·ə·nəʳ, $-ər·nər/ *n* [C] • A southerner is a person who comes from the south of a country.

south·ern·most /£ˈsʌð·ən·məʊst, $-ərn·moʊst/ *adj* [not gradable] • *The nature reserve is at the southernmost* (= furthest towards the south) *tip of the lake.*

south·ward /£ˈsaʊθ·wəd, $-wərd/ *adj* [not gradable] • *We walked in a southward* (=towards the south) *direction.*

south·wards /£ˈsaʊθ·wədz, $-wərdz/, **south·ward** *adv* [not gradable] • *They cycled southwards* (=towards the south) *towards the sea.*

south·east /ˌsaʊθˈiːst/ (*abbreviation* **SE**) *n* [U] the direction which is between south and east • *Southeast is over there, towards the mountains.* • *We live in* **the** *southeast.* • **The Southeast** is an area of Britain around London which is considered to be wealthier than other parts of the country. • [LP] **Directions**

south·east /ˌsaʊθˈiːst/ (*abbreviation* **SE**) *adj, adv* [not gradable] • *Southeast Asia/South East Asia* • *There's a southeast wind today.* • *We drove southeast towards the hills.* • *The mountains* **are/lie** *southeast* **of** *the city.*

south·east·er·ly /£ˌsaʊθˈiː·stə·li, $-stər-/ *adj* [not gradable] • *The plane was flying in a southeasterly* (= towards the southeast) *direction.*

south·eas·tern /£ˌsaʊθˈiː·stᵊn, $-stərn/ (*abbreviation* **SE**) *adj* [not gradable] • *The southeastern part of Britain is the most populated.*

south·east·ward /£ˌsaʊθˈiːs·twəd, $-twərd/ *adj* [not gradable] • *If we sail in a southeastward* (=towards the southeast) *direction we'll reach land.*

south·east·wards /£ˌsaʊθ'iːs·twədz, $-twə˞dz/, **south·east·ward** *adv* [not gradable] • *Looking southeastwards* (=towards the southeast), *they could see the distant mountains.*

south·paw /£'saʊθ·pɔː, $-pɑː/ *n* [C] *(Br)* a left-handed boxer, or *(Am)* a left-handed person, esp. a left-handed PITCHER (=person who throws the ball) in the sport of baseball

south·west /ˌsaʊθ'west/ (*abbreviation* **SW**) *n* [U] the direction which is between south and west • *Southwest is the opposite direction to northeast.* • *There will be rain in* **the** *Southwest.* • LP> **Directions**

south·west /ˌsaʊθ'west/ (*abbreviation* **SW**) *adj, adv* [not gradable] • *I come from the southwest part of the island.* • *They moved southwest in an attempt to find better land.*

south·west·er·ly /£ˌsaʊθ'wes·tə·li, $-tə˞-/ *adj* [not gradable] • *They were travelling in a southwesterly direction.*

south·wes·tern /£ˌsaʊθ'wes·tən, $-tə˞n/ (*abbreviation* **SW**) *adj* [not gradable] • *The southwestern corner of Britain is the warmest.*

south·west·ward /£ˌsaʊθ'wes·twəd, $-twə˞d/ *adj* [not gradable] • *There was a southwestward* (=towards the southwest) *movement of people towards the safety of the mountains.*

south·west·wards /£ˌsaʊθ'wes·twədz, $-twə˞dz/, **south·west·ward** *adv* [not gradable] • *They sailed southwestwards* (=towards the southwest) *until they reached land.*

sou·ve·nir /£ˌsuː·vᵊn'ɪəʳ, $-və'nɪr/ *n* [C] something you buy, give or receive to help you remember a visit or an event • *He bought a model of a red London bus as a souvenir* **of** *his trip to London.* • *We found the old mug which my mother bought as a souvenir* **of** *the Coronation.* • *It is the best place to shop for souvenirs such as linen tablecloths or crystal.* • *The seafront is full of tacky souvenir shops and amusement arcades.* • (F)

sou'west·er /£ˌsaʊ'wes·təʳ, $-tə˞/ *n* [C] a waterproof hat with a wide piece at the back to protect the neck, worn esp. by sailors • Sou'wester is also another word for SOUTHWESTER. • PIC> **Hats**

sove·reign RULER /£'sɒv·ᵊr·ɪn, $'sɑːv·rən/ *n* [C] a king or queen, or the person with the highest power in a country • *The sovereign has the power to dismiss the Government in Britain.*

sove·reign /£'sɒv·ᵊr·ɪn, $'sɑːv·rən/ *adj* [before n; not gradable] • *Sovereign* (=The highest) *power is said to lie with the people in some countries, and with a ruler in others.* • *We must respect the rights of sovereign* (= completely independent) **states/nations** *to conduct their own affairs.* • *(fig.) Love is a sovereign* **remedy** *for* (=an excellent way of curing) *unhappiness!*

sove·reign·ty /£'sɒv·rɪn·ti, $'sɑːv·rᵊn·ti/ *n* [U] • *Talks are being held about who should* **have** *sovereignty* **over** (=govern) *the island.* • *The action was seen* **as a threat to national** *sovereignty* (=to independent rule).

sove·reign COIN /£'sɒv·ᵊr·ɪn, $'sɑːv·rən/ *n* [C] a British gold coin which was in use in Britain from 1817 to 1914 and was worth £1

So·vi·et NATIONALITY /£'səʊ·vi·ət, $'soʊ-/ *adj* [not gradable] (in the past) of the USSR (or Soviet Union) • *the Soviet people* • *the Soviet space programme* • *Soviet leaders/law* • *The US and Soviet governments are dismantling thousands of long-range nuclear weapons.* • The Soviet **bloc** was the countries under Communist government which grouped together with the USSR from the late 1940s to the late 1980s. • LP> **Nations and nationalities**

So·vi·et /£'səʊ·vi·ət, $'soʊ-/ *n* [C] • The Soviets were the people or the leaders of the USSR.

so·vi·et ORGANIZATION /£'səʊ·vi·ət, $'soʊ-/ *n* [C] an elected group at any of several levels in Communist countries, esp. (in the past) the USSR • *The Supreme Soviet was the highest decision-making body in the former USSR.*

sow *(obj)* PLANT /£səʊ, $soʊ/ *v past simple* **sowed**, *past part* **sown** /£səʊn, $soʊn/ or **sowed** to put (seeds) in or on the ground so that plants will grow • *Sow the seeds* **in** *pots or* **in/on** *the open ground.* [T] • *"When is the best time to sow?""I always sow early!"* [I] • *We'll sow this field* **with** *barley.* [T] • *(fig.) Now that you've sown* (=introduced) **doubts** *in my mind, I'll never again be sure I can trust him.* [T] • *He's* **sown the seeds of** (=done something which is very likely to lead to) *his own downfall.* • *He had plenty of time to* **sow** *his* **wild oats** (=have an exciting time with lots of, usually sexual, relationships) *before he got married – now he should start to behave responsibly!* • *(saying)* "As ye sow, so shall ye reap" means the way you behave in life will determine the kind of treatment you will receive from others. *(The Bible, Galatians 6:7)*

sow ANIMAL /saʊ/ *n* [C] an adult female pig • Compare BOAR; HOG ANIMAL.

soy·a bean /'sɔɪ·ə/, *esp. Am* **soy·bean** /'sɔɪ·biːn/ *n* [C] a type of bean grown esp. in Asia and the USA, which is used as a food for people and animals • *Soya beans are very rich in protein and are often used as a substitute for meat.*

soy·a /'sɔɪ·ə/, *Am* **soy** /sɔɪ/ *n* [U] • Soya is another word for soya beans: *This year the country is set for a record harvest – the crop of corn, rice and soya is expected to top 62m tonnes.* • **Soy(a) sauce** is a strong-tasting dark brown liquid made from FERMENTED soya beans and used esp. in Chinese and Japanese cooking. • **Soya oil, soya flour, soya curd** and **soya milk** are all products made from soya beans.

soz·zled /£'sɒz·l̩d, $'sɑː·zl̩d/ *adj* [after v] *Br and Aus infml slightly dated* very drunk • *Jane* **got** *absolutely sozzled at the New Year's Eve party!*

spa /spɑː/ *n* [C] an often fashionable town where water comes out of the ground and people come to drink or lie in it because they think it will improve their health, or *(esp. Am)* a place where people go in order to become more healthy, by doing exercises, eating special food, etc. • *Baden Baden in Germany, and Bath in Britain, are two of Europe's famous spa* **towns.** • *Spa* **water** *is thought to be very good for you because of the minerals it contains, but it often tastes unpleasant.* • (I)

space EMPTY PLACE /speɪs/ *n* an empty place (for something) • *That big table* **takes up** *too much space in my small kitchen.* [U] • *Is there any space* **for** *my clothes in that cupboard?* [U] • *The agency was running out of* **storage** *space, and every nook and cranny was filled.* [U] • *When the roads are wet, you must leave plenty of space* **between** *you and the car in front.* [U] • *Where shall I put these plates? – there's no* **empty** *space on the shelves.* [U] • *There isn't much* **parking** *space for the shop customers.* [U] • *They found a* **parking** *space close to the museum.* [C] • *We must remember to* **leave/save** *space* **for** *the tulips in the flowerbed.* [U] • *There were only two spaces* (=seats) **left for** *the concert.* [C] • *The* **(blank)** *space at the end of the form is* **for** *your name.* [C] • **Prime office** *space is very expensive in this part of town.* [U] • Space is also that which is around everything that exists and which is continuous in all directions: *He was absent-mindedly* **staring/gazing into** *space* (=looking, but seeing nothing). [U] ○ *Virtual Reality aims to give us artificial worlds to explore, outside normal space and time.* [U] • **Open** space is land, esp. in a town, which has no buildings on it: *What I like about Cambridge is that there's so much open space – there are parks and commons everywhere.* [U] ○ *About half the land, including the golf course, would be left as open space.* [U] • **Wide open** spaces are large areas of open countryside: *I love the wide open spaces of central Australia!* [C] • **In/Within a short space of time** (=Very quickly) *you could be speaking perfect English!* • **In/Within/During the space of** (=After) *four hours, most of the town had been destroyed.* • A **space-bar** on a computer keyboard or a TYPEWRITER is the long bar below the letter keys which you press in order to make a space between words. • A **space heater** is a movable machine for heating a room: *The hospital said that most fires were started by space heaters.* • A **space-saving** device, piece of furniture etc. is something that doesn't take up much room, for example a folding bed. • *(specialized)* **Space-time** is a part of Einstein's Theory of Relativity, which adds the idea of time to those of height, depth and length. • See also AIRSPACE. SPACE. See also AIRSPACE. • LP> **Measurements** PIC> **Office**

space *(obj)* /speɪs/ *v* • *That page looks badly spaced* (= there is too much/too little distance between the lines or words). [T] • *They've spaced* **(out)** *their family well – they have children aged 2,4,6 and 8.* [T/M] • *The flowers were spaced* **(out)** *evenly* (=planted at equal distances) *beside the path.* [T] • *We're spacing* **(out)** *our visits to the hospital so that Dad doesn't have his visitors all at once.* [T/M] • *If you're in financial difficulty, we're happy to let you space* **(out)** *your payments* (=pay in smaller amounts over a longer period of time) **over** *two years.* [T/M] • *Space* **out** (= Move so that there is more distance between you), *children, so that you've got room to dance!* [I]

spac·ing /ˈspeɪ·sɪŋ/ *n* [U] • Spacing is the amount of distance between lines or words, esp. on a printed page: *single/double/triple spacing*

spa·cious /ˈspeɪ·ʃəs/ *adj approving* • Things, esp. things with walls or edges, that are spacious have a lot of space: *a spacious house/living room/park* ○ *They have more spacious accommodation here than they had in Tokyo where their flat was very small.*

spa·cious·ly /ˈspeɪ·ʃə·sli/ *adv approving*

spa·cious·ness /ˈspeɪ·ʃə·snəs/ *n* [U] *approving* • *What I like about that house is its spaciousness – all the rooms are so big and airy.*

spa·tial /ˈspeɪ·ʃəl/ *adj* [not gradable] • *I'm really bad at parking – my spatial* **judgment** (= my ability to judge distances) *isn't good enough!* • *This task is designed to test the child's spatial* **awareness** (= understanding of where things are in relation to other things).

space [BEYOND EARTH] /speɪs/ *n* [U] the empty area outside the Earth's ATMOSPHERE, where the planets and the stars are • *space exploration/travel* • *(a) space flight* • *a space rocket* • *Who was the first human being* **in** *space/the first to go* **into** *space?* • *In the early 1970s, the winding down of the Apollo space* **programme** *(also* **space-flight programme***) resulted in a severe recession in the aerospace industry.* • **Space-age** things are very modern, esp. because of a connection with space travel: *space-age technology* • *space-age materials* • *space-age fashions.* • A **space platform** is a spacecraft with no people on it which is used for collecting scientific information. • A **space probe** is a small spacecraft, with no one travelling in it, sent into space to make measurements and send back information to scientists on Earth. • The **space race** was the competition between esp. the USA and the USSR to be the first to land on the moon or the planets, etc. • A **space shuttle** is a vehicle in which people travel into space and back again, sometimes carrying a SATELLITE or other equipment into ORBIT (= a curved path through space). • A **space station** is a vehicle in which people can travel round the Earth, outside its ATMOSPHERE, doing scientific tests.

space·craft /£ˈspeɪs·krɑːft, $-kræft/ *n* [C] *pl* **spacecraft** a vehicle used for travel in space • *a manned/unmanned spacecraft* (= with/without people inside)

spaced out /speɪst/ *adj slang* (of a person) not completely aware of what is happening around you, esp. as a result of taking drugs; HIGH [MENTAL STATE] • *She was usually spaced out* **on** *drugs.* • *He looks totally spaced out.*

space·man (*pl* **-men**), **space·wo·man** (*pl* **-women**) /ˈspeɪs·mæn, -ˌwʊm·ən/ *n* [C] a person who travels in space or (esp. in stories) a creature from another planet

space·ship /ˈspeɪs·ʃɪp/ *n* [C] (esp. in stories) a vehicle used for travel in space • *"Spaceship Earth"* (term used by R. Buckminster Fuller to describe the global ecology, 1969)

space·suit /£ˈspeɪs·sjuːt, $-suːt/ *n* [C] a piece of clothing worn by a person who travels in space to protect the body when outside the spacecraft

space·walk /£ˈspeɪs·wɔːk, $-wɑːk/ *n* [C] an act of moving around in space outside a spacecraft but connected to it • *The crew are planning a four-hour spacewalk to carry out necessary repair work on the shuttle.*

spac·ing /ˈspeɪ·sɪŋ/ *n* [U] See at SPACE [EMPTY PLACE]

spa·cious /ˈspeɪ·ʃəs/ *adj* See at SPACE [EMPTY PLACE]

spade [TOOL] /speɪd/ *n* [C] a tool used for digging esp. earth or sand, with a long handle and a flat blade • *a garden spade* • A **bucket and** spade (*Am usually* **pail and shovel**) are taken to the beach by children on holiday to use for carrying sand and water and digging. • [PIC] **Garden**

spade·ful /ˈspeɪd·fʊl/ *n* [C] • *Put a spadeful* (= the amount held by a spade) *of compost into the hole.*

spade [CARD] /speɪd/ *n* [C] a playing card with one or more black shapes like pointed leaves with short stems printed on it • *I've got four cards left – one spade and three hearts.* • [LP] **Cards** [PIC] **Spade**

spades /speɪdz/ *pl n* • Spades are one of the four SUITS (= groups) in a PACK (= set) of playing cards: *the ace/seven/queen* **of** *spades* • *(Am infml)* If you have something **in spades** you have it to a very great degree: *I don't get colds very often but when I do I get them in spades.*

spade [PERSON] /speɪd/ *n* [C] *dated taboo* a black person • *I heard that police officer call black people niggers and spades – I hope he loses his job!*

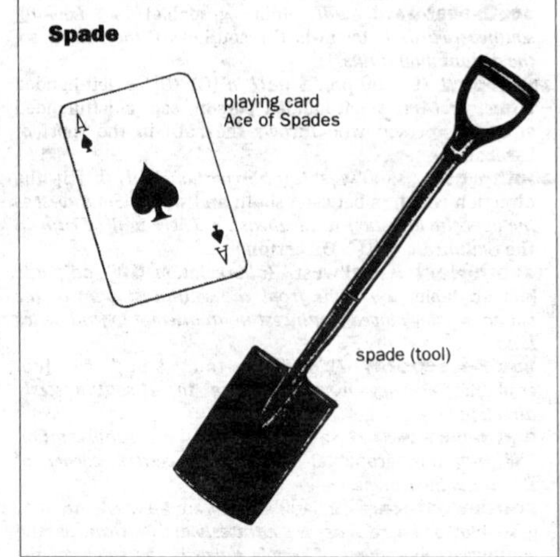

spade·work /£ˈspeɪd·wɜːk, $-wɜːrk/ *n* [U] hard, sometimes uninteresting work done in preparation for something • *Now that the spadework's all been* **done**, *we can start to write the report itself.*

spa·ghet·ti /£spəˈget·i, $-ˈgeṭ-/ *n* [U] pasta made in long, very thin round shapes, cooked in water • *Is the spaghetti ready yet, Dad?* • **Spaghetti bolognese** (*Br infml* **spag bol**) is a dish made from spaghetti and a meat sauce. • **Spaghetti Junction** is the name of a place near Birmingham, England where many roads cross each other, or *(infml)* any place where many roads cross in a complicated way. • A **spaghetti western** is a film made by Italians about COWBOYS (= workers in charge of cows esp. in the past in the US).

spake *old use or humorous* /speɪk/ *past simple of* SPEAK [SAY WORDS] • *"Thus spake the expert!" he said, ironically.*

spam /spæm/ *n* [U] *trademark* a type of meat sold in metal containers, made mostly from PORK (= pig meat) • *spam and chips* • *spam fritters* • *spam and salad* • *spam sandwiches*

span [SPACE] /spæn/ *n* [C usually sing] the length or period between two points, esp. of time • **Over a (time)** *span* **of** *only two years, the new government has transformed the country's economic prospects.* • *That child's* **concentration/attention** *span is poor – he only listens to the teacher for a few seconds at a time.* • *It's useful for a piano player to have a* **broad** *span* (= distance between the thumb and the little finger when the hand is spread). • *She has a wide/enormous span* **of** *responsibility in her new job* (= She is responsible for a lot of different things). • *The bridge crosses the river* **in a single** *span* (= there are no supports in the middle). • *"The world's a bubble; and the life of man/ Less than a span"* (Francis Bacon in the book *The World*, 1629) • See also LIFESPAN; WINGSPAN.

span *obj* /spæn/ *v* [T] **-nn-** • *Tennis has a history spanning several centuries.* • *He is now coaching football after a playing career spanning five clubs and more than 500 league games.* • *An old bridge spans* (= crosses) *the river just outside the town.* • *Her knowledge spans* (= includes) *the whole political history of Senegal.*

span [SPIN] /spæn/ *past simple of* SPIN

span [CLEAN] /spæn/ *adj* [not gradable] **spick and span**, see at SPICK [CLEAN]

span·dex /ˈspæn·deks/ *n* [U] a stretchy material used esp. for making brightly-coloured shiny clothes which fit very tightly • *She was wearing a pink and lime-green spandex jogging-suit.*

span·gle /ˈspæŋ·gl̩/ *n* [C] a small piece of shiny metal or plastic, used esp. in large amounts to decorate clothes; a SEQUIN

span·gled /ˈspæŋ·gl̩d/ *adj* • *(fig.) The hillside was spangled* (= covered and sparkling, as if with spangles) **with** *tiny white flowers.*

span·iel /ˈspæn·jəl/ *n* [C] a type of dog, with long hair and long ears that hang down • [PIC] **Dogs**

spank *obj* /spæŋk/ *v* [T] to hit (esp. a child) with the hand, usually several times on the bottom as a punishment, or to hit (an adult) on the bottom, usually with a stick etc., in order to get or give sexual pleasure • *If you haven't tidied your room by suppertime, Jamie, I'll spank you.* • (I)

spank·ing /ˈspæŋ·kɪŋ/ *n* [C] • *She gave her son a* **good/sound** *spanking when she found out that he had taken the money.*

spank·ing [FAST] /ˈspæŋ·kɪŋ/ *adj infml approving* very quick • *The first cyclists raced by at a spanking* **pace**.

spank·ing [VERY] /ˈspæŋ·kɪŋ/ *adv* [not gradable] *infml dated* (used only with particular usually positive words) very, completely • *a spanking new suit* • *spanking white sheets* • *a spanking good yarn* (= a good story) • If something is **brand** spanking **new**, it is completely new.

span·ner *Br and Aus* /£ˈspæn·əʳ, $-ɚ/, *Am* **wrench** *n* [C] a metal tool with a shaped end, used to turn NUTS and BOLTS (= fasteners that screw together) • *(Br and Aus) an open ended/adjustable/ring spanner* • *(Am) an open-end/adjustable/box wrench* • *(Br and Aus)* To **put/throw a spanner in the works** (*Am* **throw a (monkey) wrench in** something) is to be the cause of spoiling a plan: *The train strike has really thrown a spanner in the works – we'll never be able to deliver the goods on time now.* • PIC **Tools** (D)

spar [FIGHT] /£spɑːʳ, $spɑːr/ *v* [I] **-rr-** (in boxing) to hit without hitting hard, esp. when practising • *(fig.) Frank and Jill always spar* (= argue) **with** *each other at meetings, but they're good friends really.* • A **sparring partner** is a person you practise boxing with, or *(fig.)* someone you have friendly arguments with.

spar [POLE] /£spɑːʳ, $spɑːr/ *n* [C] *specialized* a strong pole, esp. one used as a MAST to hold the sail on a ship

spare *obj* [SAVE] /£speəʳ, $sper/ *v* [T] not to hurt or destroy (something or someone) • *The enemy killed all the men, but spared the women and children.* • *Spare my feelings and stop talking about people failing exams!*

spare *obj* [AVOID] /£speəʳ, $sper/ *v* [+ two objects] to cause or allow to avoid • *So far in the present crisis, the government troops have been spared loss of life, while many of the rebels have been killed.* • *It will spare him embarrassment/trouble/worry if you speak to him about it in private.* • *It was a nasty accident – but I'll spare you* (= I won't make you listen to) *the gruesome details.* • *Spare us the suspense* (= Don't make us wait) *and tell us who won the first prize!* • *(Br)* To **spare** *your* **blushes** (= To avoid making you feel embarrassed in public), *I won't tell them how brave you've been.*

spare *obj* [NOT USE] /£speəʳ, $sper/ *v* [T] not to use • *The company appears to have spared no* **expense** *in designing and building the new shoe store.* See also **no expense spared** at EXPENSE. • *The police promised to spare* **no effort(s)** *in their search/in searching for the missing child.* • *(fml)* If you do **not spare** yourself, it means you put as much effort as you can into something: *She never spared herself in the pursuit of excellence.* • *(saying)* 'Spare the rod and spoil the child' means if you don't punish a child when it does something wrong, it will not learn what is right.

spar·ing /£ˈspeə·rɪŋ, $ˈsper·ɪŋ/ *adj* • *He is sparing* **with/in** *his praise* (= doesn't praise people much). • *I admire the composer's sparing* (= no more than necessary) **use** *of the brass section.*

spar·ing·ly /£ˈspeə·rɪŋ·li, $ˈsper·ɪŋ-/ *adv* • *There wasn't enough coal during the war, so we had to use it sparingly.*

spare [EXTRA] /£speəʳ, $sper/ *adj* [not gradable] not being used, or extra to what is usually needed • *a spare key* • *a spare tyre* • *spare sheets and blankets* • *Have you got a spare pen? I've left all mine at home.* • *All children should bring a spare set of clothes in case they get wet.* • *Is this seat spare, or is it already taken?* • *What do you do in your spare* **time** (= when you are not working or doing necessary things)? • *Have you got any spare-***time** *hobbies?* • *We've got a spare* **room**, *so you can stay overnight with us.* • *Have you got a spare* **moment/minute**? *I need a bit of advice.* • *(Br infml) "Do you want this piece of cake?" "Yes, if it's* **going** *spare* (= if no one else wants it)." • *(humorous)* If you've got a **spare tyre** (*Am* **spare tire**), you have extra unwanted fat around your waist. • **Spare parts** (**spares**) are pieces that can be used to replace other similar pieces in a car or other device: *The purchase of spare parts to keep an engine going can add up to more than the engine cost originally.* • *(Br)* In **spare-part surgery** (*Am and Aus* **organ transplant surgery**), a healthy organ such as a heart or lung is taken from a person who has just died and put into a living person to replace the part which is no longer working correctly.

spare /£speəʳ, $sper/ *n* [C] • *I seem to have lost my key, but luckily I always carry a spare* (= another one which can be used if necessary). • Spares are **spare parts**.

spare [THIN] /£speəʳ, $sper/ *adj* **-r, -st** *literary* (of people) thin with no extra fat on the body, or (of food) not very good or not in large amounts • *a spare* **meal** *of bread, beans and water* • *He had the spare* **build/form** *of a runner.*

spare [NOT DECORATED] /£speəʳ, $sper/ *adj* **-r, -st** *literary, usually approving* plain and not decorated • *Boulez gave a spare, unadorned performance of the symphony.*

spare *obj* [GIVE] /£speəʳ, $sper/ *v* [T] to (be able to) give (esp. time, money or space) to (someone) esp. when it is difficult for you • *Can you spare one of those apples?* • *I'm sorry, I can't spare my secretary – you'll have to do your own typing!* • *Could you spare me £10?/Can you spare £10* **for** *me* [+ two objects] • *We can't spare room in the suitcase* **for** *all those bottles.* • *I'd love to come, but I'm afraid I can't spare (the) time* **for** *a visit.* • *Spare* **a thought for** (= Think about) *me tomorrow, when you're lying on a beach, and I'm still here in the office!* • **To spare** means left over or more than you need: *If you've got any wool to spare when you've finished the pullover, can you make me some gloves?* ○ *I caught the plane with only two minutes to spare.* ○ *There's no time/We've got no time to spare if we want to get the article written on time.* • *"Brother (sometimes 'Buddy') can you spare a dime?"* (title of a song written by Yip Harburg, 1932)

spare [ANNOYED] /£speəʳ, $sper/ *adj* [not gradable] **go spare** *Br slang* to get very upset or angry • *Mum went spare when Joel told her he'd bought a pet snake!*

spare·ribs /£ˈspeə·rɪbz, $ˈsper-/ *pl n* pig's RIBS (= chest bones) with most of the meat cut off them, which are cooked and eaten • *barbecued spareribs*

spark /£spɑːk, $spɑːrk/ *n* [C] a very small bit of fire which flies out from something that is burning or which is made by rubbing two hard things together, or a flash of light made by electricity • *Sparks were flying out of the bonfire and blowing everywhere.* • *You can start a fire by rubbing two dry pieces of wood together until you produce a spark.* • *(fig.) That small incident was the spark that set off* (= was the first small problem that caused) *the street riots.* • A spark is also a very small amount of a particular quality in a person: *There wasn't a spark* **of** *interest/hope/sympathy in the children's faces.* • *Those two hate each other – just wait till they get together, then you'll see* **the sparks fly** (= angry fighting). • A **spark plug** (also *Br dated* **sparking plug**) is a device in an engine which produces an electrical spark which lights the fuel and makes the engine start. • *(Am)* A **spark plug** is also a person who gives energy to an activity involving others: *She's the spark plug of the team – the one who gets everyone else to give their all.*

spark *obj* /£spɑːk, $spɑːrk/ *v* [T] • *The speaker's aim was to spark the reformers* **into** *action* (= cause them to act). • *This proposal will almost certainly spark another countywide debate about how to organize the school system.* • *The recent interest rises have sparked* (= caused) *new problems for the Government.* • *The visit of the all-white rugby team sparked* **off** (= caused the start of) *mass demonstrations.*

spark·le /£ˈspɑː·kl̩, $ˈspɑːr-/ *v* [I] to shine brightly with a lot of small points of light • *The snow/sea sparkled in the sunlight.* • If a person or performance sparkles they are energetic, interesting and exciting: *Alice is shy and quiet at parties, but her sister really sparkles!*

spark·le /£ˈspɑː·kl̩, $ˈspɑːr-/ *n* [U] • *The radiant smile and the sparkle in her blue eyes were the clear signs of a woman still deeply in love.* • *We need someone* **with a bit of** *sparkle to introduce the show.* • *The sparkle* **went out of/left** *her after her husband died.* • *Their latest performance of My Fair Lady really* **lacked** *sparkle.*

spark·ling /£ˈspɑː·klɪŋ, $ˈspɑːr-/ *adj* • *sparkling white teeth* • *sparkling conversation/wit* • *a sparkling performance* • A sparkling drink is one which is fizzy: *sparkling mineral water* ○ *Champagne is a sparkling wine.* Compare STILL [NOT MOVING].

spark·ler /£ˈspɑː·kləʳ, $ˈspɑːr·klɚ/ *n* [C] a FIREWORK (= coloured explosive) which children can hold in their hands, and which produces a lot of SPARKS as it burns, or *(slang)* a jewel, esp. a DIAMOND • PIC **Fires and space heaters**

spark·y /£ˈspɑː·ki, $ˈspɑːr-/ *adj* **-ier, -iest** *infml* (of a person) energetic and enjoyable to be with

spar·row /£ˈspær·əʊ, $ˈsper·oʊ/ *n* [C] a small grey-brown bird esp. common in towns • PIC **Birds**

spar·row·hawk /£ˈspær·əʊ·hɔːk, $ˈsper·oʊ·hɑːk/ *n* [C] a small HAWK (= bird which eats smaller birds) • *The sparrowhawk is a bird of prey which is found in Europe, Asia and N Africa.*

sparse /£spɑːs, $spɑːrs/ *adj* **-r, -st** small in numbers or amount and scattered over a large area • *a sparse* *population/ crowd/audience* • *sparse vegetation/woodland* • *a sparse beard* • *Information coming out of the disaster area is sparse.* • ⓘ

sparse·ly /£ˈspɑː·sli, $ˈspɑːr-/ *adv* • *a sparsely furnished house* • *The area is sparsely inhabited because the land is poor.*

sparse·ness /£ˈspɑː·snəs, $ˈspɑːr-/, **spar·si·ty** /£ˈspɑː·sɪ·ti, $ˈspɑːr·sə·t̬i/ *n* [U] • *The sparseness of the population makes this a good area for wildlife.*

spar·tan /£ˈspɑː·tən, $ˈspɑːr·t̬ən/ *adj* simple and severe with no comfort • *a spartan diet/meal* • *spartan living conditions* • *They lead a rather spartan life, with no comforts or luxuries.*

spa·sm /ˈspæz·ᵊm/ *n* a sudden uncontrollable tightening of a muscle, or a short period of activity • *a muscle/muscular spasm* [C] ○ *a spasm* **of** *pain/anger/coughing* [C] ○ *spasms* **of** *brisk trade* [C] • *(esp. Br and Aus) If your leg* **goes into** *spasm, take one of these pills immediately.* [U]

spas·mod·ic /£spæzˈmɒd·ɪk, $-ˈmɑː·dɪk/ *adj* lasting only for short periods of time; irregular • *He made spasmodic attempts to clean up the house.* • *(disapproving) The teacher says his interest in the subject is rather spasmodic.*

spas·tic /ˈspæs·tɪk/ *n* [C], *adj* [not gradable] *taboo* (a person who is) suffering from **cerebral palsy** (= a condition of the body which makes it difficult to control the muscles) • *(dated) My sister is (a) spastic.* • *The Spastics Society in Britain changed their name to SCOPE in 1994.* • *Children sometimes describe other children as spastic, to mean that they are foolish or not very skilful.*

spat [SPIT] /spæt/ *past simple and past participle of* SPIT [FORCE OUT]

spat [ARGUMENT] /spæt/ *n* [C] *infml* a short argument, usually about something unimportant • *She's just* **having a** *spat* **with** *her brother* **about** *who should do the washing up.*

spat /spæt/ *v* [I] **-tt-** *Am and Aus* • *Tom's always spatting* **with** *his little brother.*

spat [SHOE] /spæt/ *n* [C usually pl] a piece of cloth or leather covering the ANKLE (= the joint which connects the foot to the leg) and part of the shoe and fastening on the side, worn in the past by men • *a pair of spats*

spate /speɪt/ *n* [U] an unusually large number of events, esp. unwanted ones, happening at about the same time • *Police are investigating a spate* **of** *burglaries in the Kingsland Road area.* • *(Br)* If a river is **in (full) spate** it has more water in it and is flowing faster than it usually does: *After the storms the River Ganges was in full spate and thousands feared the possibility of flooding.*

spa·tial /ˈspeɪ·ʃᵊl/ *adj* [not gradable] See at SPACE [EMPTY PLACE]

spat·ter *(obj)* /£ˈspæt·əʳ, $ˈspæt̬·ɚ/ *v* to scatter (drops of liquid etc.) on a surface, or (of liquid) to fall, esp. noisily, in small drops • *The bikes raced by and spattered mud* **over** *our clothes/***in** *our faces.* [T] • *The bikes spattered them* **with** *mud.* [T] • *They could hear raindrops spattering* **on** *the roof of the caravan.* [I]

spat·ter /£ˈspæt·əʳ, $ˈspæt̬·ɚ/ *n* • *At the first spatter* **of** *rain on the tent roof, they decided they didn't like camping.*

spat·tered /£ˈspæt·əd, $ˈspæt̬·ɚd/ *adj* • *a paint-/mud-/blood-/ink- spattered shirt* • *"Why are your clothes spattered* **with** *blood?" asked the detective.*

spat·u·la /ˈspæt·jʊ·lə/ *n* [C] a cooking utensil with a wide flat blade which isn't sharp, used esp. for lifting, spreading and mixing foods • *Use a spatula to lift the steaks out of the frying pan.* • A spatula is also a small piece of wood used by a doctor to hold someone's tongue down in order to examine their mouth or throat. • *(Am)* A **(slotted)** spatula is also a **fish-slice**. See at FISH [ANIMAL].

spawn [EGGS] /£spɔːn, $spɑːn/ *n* [U] the eggs of fish, FROGS etc. • See also FROGSPAWN.

spawn *(obj)* /£spɔːn, $spɑːn/ *v* • *The frogs haven't spawned* (= produced eggs) *yet.* [I] • *(fig.) The new economic freedom has spawned hundreds of new small businesses* (= caused them to be started suddenly). [T] • *Salmon and sea trout use the upper river as a* **spawning ground**.

spawn [YOUNG] /£spɔːn, $spɑːn/ *n* [C] *pl* **spawn** *literary or disapproving* a young animal or child • *She started screaming that I was a spawn* **of** *Satan because I was smoking a cigarette.*

spay *obj* /speɪ/ *v* [T] to remove the OVARIES (= organs that produce eggs) of a (female animal) • *We're having the cat spayed – she's had enough kittens!*

speak *(obj)* [SAY WORDS] /spiːk/ *v past simple* **spoke** /£spəʊk, $spoʊk/, *past part* **spoken** /£ˈspəʊ·kᵊn, $ˈspoʊ-/ to say words, to use the voice, or to have a conversation with someone • *Would you mind speaking more slowly, please? I can't understand!* [I] • *She can't speak – she's just had six teeth out.* [I] • *"Will you please speak, not shout!" said the teacher.* [I] • *Hello, I'm Roger. We spoke* (= talked to each other) *on the phone last week.* [I] • *I spoke* **to**/*(esp. Am)* **with** *Jo yesterday* **about** *your problem.* [I] • At the beginning of a telephone conversation *"Can I speak* **to**/*(esp. Am)* **with** *Ian please?" "Speaking!"* (= This is Ian!) [I] • *"If you tell my dad what I've done, I'll never speak* **to** *you again!" he said angrily.* [I] • *The teacher should* **speak to** *those stupid boys* (= talk to them in order to explain that they have done something wrong). • *(fml) He didn't speak* **of** (= mention) *his father all evening.* [I] • *(fml) It's not good manners to speak* **of** (= discuss) *certain things in polite company!* [I] • *(fml) At the church service the Reverend David Morson spoke* **of** (= talked about) *people's sadness over the tragedy.* [I] • *She speaks very* **highly of** (= says good things about) *the new director.* [U] • *I'm sure I'm speaking* **on behalf of**/*speaking* **for** *everyone* (= representing the opinions of everyone) *when I say that this was a very enjoyable occasion.* [I] • *I can help on Saturday but I can't speak* **for** *my wife* (= I can't tell you whether she can or not). [I] • *(fml) Who is going to speak* **for** (= represent in a court of law) *the accused?* [I] • *Please don't interrupt your son, Mr Jones – he's old enough to speak* **for himself** (= to say what he thinks)*!* [I] • *I went to a film with her last week – speaking* **of** (= on the subject of) *films, have you seen Clint Eastwood's latest one?* [I] • *We've been invited to Rachel and Jamie's wedding – speaking* **of which**, *did you know that they're moving to Ealing?* [I] • *Speaking* **as** (= With my experience as) *a mother of four, I can tell you that children are exhausting!* [I] • *If no one has the courage to speak* **out** (= to give their opinion honestly and bravely) *against what is wrong, things will never improve.* [I] • *Speak* **up** (= Speak more loudly)*! We can't hear a thing at the back of the room!* [I] • *Sue speaks* **with an** *American* **accent**. [I] • *Why are you speaking* **in a whisper** (= very quietly)*? No one can hear what we're saying!* [I] • *For five whole minutes, neither of them spoke* **a word** (= they both said nothing). [T] • *Do you think he's speaking* **the truth**? [T] • Speaking is used with adverbs ending in *-ly* to show that you are talking from a particular point of view: *Scientifically/Historically speaking, the island is of great interest.* [I] ○ **Generally/Broadly** *speaking* (= In general) *the local school's quite good.* [I] ○ **Strictly** *speaking* (= If I behave according to the rules), *I should report you to the police – but I'll be kind to you this time!* [I] • If something **speaks for itself**, it is clear and needs no further explanation: *The school's good results this year speak for themselves.* • *(infml, humorous or disapproving) "We had a really boring trip."* **"Speak for yourself!** (= That's your opinion, not mine!) *I had a wonderful time!"* • If you **speak** your **mind** you say what you think about something very, and sometimes too, directly: *Some of the people at work don't like him because he's the sort of person who speaks his mind.* • *"Did you get much rain while you were in Singapore?"* "**None to speak of/No** *rain* **to speak of** (= So little that it's not important enough to mention)*."* • *We had rain, wind, snow,* **not to speak of** (= and worst of all) *the storms at the end of the week!* • **So to speak** is used to explain that what you are saying is not to be understood exactly as stated: *In their house it's Lorna who wears the trousers, so to speak* (= Lorna makes all the important decisions). • If you are **on speaking terms with** someone, or **know** someone **to speak to**, you know them well enough to talk to. • If you are **not on speaking terms (with** someone) you refuse to speak to them because you are angry with them: *They had a quarrel last night and now they're not on speaking terms (with each other).* • If you **speak too soon** you say something which is quickly shown not to be true: *"Today's the first day for weeks it hasn't rained." "Don't speak too soon – there are black clouds on the horizon."* ○ *He won't be home for ages yet.....Oh, I spoke too soon – here he is now!* • To **speak up for** someone or something is to support them by saying good things about them: *He spoke up for me when I was in trouble, and in doing so, risked his own life.* ○ *The new candidate will be Mr Eduardo Angeloz, who spoke up for democracy early in the crisis.* • If you say to someone, esp. a child, **"Speak when you're spoken to!"**, you are telling them rudely not to speak if no one speaks to them first. • See also OUTSPOKEN; SPEECH [SAY WORDS]; SPEECH [FORMAL TALK]; -SPOKEN; SPOKEN FOR. • [LP] **Say**

speak *obj* [KNOW A LANGUAGE] /spiːk/ *v* [T] *past simple* **spoke** /£spəʊk, $spoʊk/, *past part* **spoken**

/£ˈspəʊ· kᵊn, $ˈspoʊ-/ to (be able to) talk in (a language) • *What language do they speak in your country?* • *Can you hear what language that girl over there is speaking?* • *How many (foreign) languages can/do you speak?* • *Preference will be given to those who speak English* **fluently** *and are well educated.* • *I* **couldn't/didn't speak a word of** *English* (=I didn't know any English) *when I first arrived in Australia.*

speak·er /£ˈspiː·kəʳ, $-kɚ/ *n* [C] • A speaker is someone who speaks a particular language: *a French speaker* • *a* **fluent** *Russian speaker* • *non-English speakers* • *a speaker* **of** *many languages*

–speak·ing /-ˈspiː·kɪŋ, ˌ--/ *combining form* • *a Spanish-speaking country*

speak FORMAL TALK /spiːk/ *v* [I] *past simple* **spoke** /£spəʊk, $spoʊk/, *past part* **spoken** /£ˈspəʊ·kᵊn, $ˈspoʊ-/ to give a formal talk (to a group of people) • *Who is speaking in the debate tonight?* • *The Queen speaks* **to** *the nation on television every Christmas.* • *The Director will speak* **to** *the whole college* **on/about** *careers in business.* • *Janet is speaking* **for** *the motion* (=trying to persuade the people listening that the idea is good) *and Peter is speaking* **against** *(it)* (=trying to persuade them that it is bad). • *The President should speak* **from notes** (=make speeches from a written text) – *when he speaks* **from memory** (=without a written text) *he always makes so many mistakes!* • *He knows a lot about the history of this area, so he* **has** *many* **speaking engagements** (=occasions when he has been asked to give a talk) *at local clubs and societies.*

speak·er /£ˈspiː·kəʳ, $-kɚ/ *n* [C] • A speaker is a person who gives a speech at a public event: *He's a rather dull* **public** *speaker.* ○ *Please join with me in thanking our* **guest** *speaker tonight.* ○ *The Democrats have chosen the Texas state treasurer as the* **keynote** *speaker at their convention.* • The Speaker is also the person who controls the way in which business is done in an organization which makes laws, such as a parliament: *Betty Boothroyd was the first woman to be appointed Speaker in the House of Commons.* ○ *He served for eight years as Speaker of the House (of Representatives).* ○ *Mr Speaker, my honourable friend has failed to consider the consequences of his proposal.* [as form of address]

speak *(obj)* SUGGEST /spiːk/ *v past simple* **spoke** /£spəʊk, $spoʊk/, *past part* **spoken** /£ˈspəʊ·kᵊn, $ˈspoʊ-/ to show or express (something) without using words • *She was silent, but her eyes spoke her real feelings for him.* [T] • *The whole robbery spoke* **of** (=made it seem that there had been) *inside knowledge on the part of the criminals.* [I always + adv/prep] • *She said she was pleased, but her unhappy face* **spoke volumes** *(Br* **for***/Am* **about** *her unhappiness)* (=showed clearly what she really thought). • *Her report* **speaks well for** *her understanding of the problem* (=shows she understands it very well).

speak SPECIAL LANGUAGE /spiːk/ *combining form infml esp. disapproving* used to form nouns, to mean the special language used in a particular subject area or business • *computerspeak* • *advertiserspeak* • *marketingspeak* • *George Orwell used the word 'Newspeak' to describe the invented language spoken by people in his book about an imaginary future, '1984'.*

speak·eas·y /ˈspiːkˌiː·zi/ *n* [C] a place where alcohol was illegally sold and drunk, esp. in the US in the 1920s and 1930s

speak·er /£ˈspiː·kəʳ, $-kɚ/ *n* [C] the part of a radio or television, or of a piece of electrical equipment for playing recorded sound, through which the sound is played. A speaker can be part of the radio etc. or be separate from it. • *Our CD player has two speakers, one on each side.* • *There's no sound coming out of the right-hand speaker.* • *You want a good system with big speakers where you can hear every instrument to its fullest.* • See also **speaker** at SPEAK KNOW A LANGUAGE, SPEAK FORMAL TALK. • (DK) (PL)

speak·er·phone /£ˈspiː·kə·fəʊn, $-kɚ·foʊn/ *n* [C] a telephone which you can use without having to hold any part of it in your hand

spear /£spɪəʳ, $spɪr/ *n* [C] a weapon consisting of a pole with a sharp, usually metal, point at one end, which is either thrown or held in the hand • *The San people of the Kalahari desert hunt with spears.* • *Roman soldiers carried spears.* • *We went spear-***fishing** *when we were on holiday.* • A spear is also a thin pointed stem or leaf: *asparagus spears* ○ *The crocus spears are already poking their way through the ground.* • In the theatre etc. a **spear carrier** is someone who has a small part, usually without any words to say. If a person is described as a spear carrier, it means that what they do is of little or no importance, or of less importance than what someone else does: *I've had enough of being a spear carrier for my boss – I want a job where I can actually have some responsibility.*

spear *obj* /£spɪəʳ, $spɪr/ *v* [T] • *The hunters speared the antelope* (=threw or put a spear into it) *through its neck.* • *They catch the fish by spearing them.* • *(fig.) She speared a piece of cake with her fork* (=put her fork into a piece of cake in order to lift it).

spear·head *obj* /£ˈspɪə·hed, $ˈspɪr-/ *v* [T] to lead, esp. some type of attack or course of action • *British troops spearheaded the invasion.* • *A group of former soldiers is spearheading the peace movement.* • *Joe has been chosen to spearhead our new marketing initiative/effort.* • *The television company has announced a number of new documentaries to spearhead its challenge to its competitors.*

spear·head /£ˈspɪə·hed, $ˈspɪr-/ *n* [C] • *American troops formed the spearhead* (=were the leaders) **of** *the attack.* • *The publication of these leaflets is intended to act as a spearhead* **for** (=the first or main activity of) *the campaign.*

spear·mint /£ˈspɪə·mɪnt, $ˈspɪr-/ *n* [U] a strong sweet flavouring, or the plant from which this flavouring comes • *spearmint chewing-gum* • *spearmint toothpaste* • *spearmint mouthwash* • *Spearmint does not taste as strong as peppermint.* • *Spearmint is the most common form of mint grown in gardens.*

spec CHANCE /spek/ *n* [U] **on spec** *infml* taking a chance, without any certainty that you will get what you want • *They turned up at the airport on spec, hoping to be able to get tickets.* • *I just called round on spec, to see if you'd like to come out for a drink.* • *We wrote the proposal on spec in the hope that we'd be given a contract to carry it out.*

spec /spek/ *adj infml* • *(esp. Aus)* A **spec builder** is a person or company that builds houses to sell to anyone who will buy them rather than for a particular customer.

spec PLAN /spek/ *n* [C] *infml for* **specification**, see at SPECIFY • *We've had a spec* **drawn up** *for a new bathroom.*

spe·cial NOT USUAL /ˈspeʃ·ᵊl/ *adj* not ordinary or usual • *The car has a number of special safety features.* • *Is there anything special that you'd like to do today?* • *More training and resources are required to meet the special needs of dying patients.* • *Passengers should tell the airline in advance if they have any special dietary needs.* • *It was clear that both these prisoners were in need of special attention which they did not get.* • *I don't expect special treatment – I just want to be treated fairly.* • *I don't think you should attach any special significance to what he said.* • *The school doesn't usually take pupils who don't live near it, but Lucy was a special* **case** *because her father teaches there.* • *Full details of the election results will be published in a special* **edition** *of tomorrow's newspaper.* • *I only wear this suit on special* **occasions**. • *There's a 50p-off special* **offer** *on cornflakes/ (Br also) Cornflakes are* **on** *special* **offer** (=They are being sold at a reduced price) *this week.* • Special can also have the meaning unusually great or important, or having an extra quality: *Could I ask you a special favour?* ○ *Marie is my special friend.* ○ *You're very special* **to** *me.* • *I'd like this parcel sent (by)* **special delivery** (=by a delivery which is faster than the usual one, for which you have to pay extra). • A **special effect** is an unusual piece of action in a film, or an entertainment on a stage, created by using particular equipment: *Many of Steven Spielberg's films have splendid special effects.* • *(Am) Much of the money for the president's election campaign is coming from* **special interests** (= groups of people who want to have political influence in order to get advantages for their organizations). • *Much of the pressure for changing the law has come from* **special interest groups** (=groups of people who want to advance a particular principle). • *(Br)* Children with **special (educational) needs** are children whose physical or mental abilities are outside the range considered usual, and who therefore need to be taught in a different way. **Special (educational) needs** *(abbreviation* **SEN**, *Am* also **special education**) can also be used to refer to the type of teaching needed by such children. It can be used to refer to children who are unusually clever, but usually refers to children who have difficulty in learning: *She teaches children with special needs.* ○ *She teaches special needs children.* ○ *He is a special needs teacher.* ○ *(Am) She teaches a special education class.* ○ *(Am) He runs a special education program.* • The **Special Olympics** are a set of international sports competitions for people who have lower than usual mental or physical abilities. • **Special**

pleading is arguing from a particular case in order to get an unfair advantage in a more general situation: *Because she has been so successful herself, she has no time for special pleading for women.*

spe·cial /ˈspeʃ·ᵊl/ *n* [C] • *There's a two-hour special* (= a programme which is not regularly shown) *on the Olympics on television tonight.* • *(esp. Am and Aus)* A special in a restaurant is a meal that is available on a particular day which is not usually available: *Our specials today are pasta and tuna fish, and chicken with rice.* ○ *What do you have* **on** *special today?* • *(esp. Am)* Specials can also be goods sold at a reduced price: *Today's specials include a six-pack of Blotto Beer for only $2.99.*

spec·i·al·i·ty *Br and Aus* /£ˌspeʃ·iˈæl·ɪ·ti, $-ə·t̬i/, *Aus also and Am usually* **spe·cial·ty** /£ˈspeʃ·ᵊl·ti, $-t̬i/ *n* [C] • A speciality is a product that is unusually good in a particular place: *Oysters are a* **local** *speciality/a speciality* **of** *the area.* ○ *Paella is a speciality* **of the house** (= a food that is unusually good in a particular restaurant). ○ *The sign outside the hotel said 'Weddings our speciality'* (= we can provide an unusually good service for arranging parties for marriages).

spe·cial·ly /ˈspeʃ·ᵊl·i/, **es·pe·cial·ly** *adv* • *This is a specially good wine.* • *"Is there anything you want to do this evening?" "Not specially."* • *The children really enjoyed seeing the things in the museum, specially the dinosaurs.*

spe·cial PARTICULAR /ˈspeʃ·ᵊl/ *adj* [before n; not gradable] having a particular purpose • *Firefighters use special breathing equipment in smoky buildings.* • *You need special tyres on your car when you're driving in snowy conditions.* • *A special train has been laid on to take supporters to the football match.* • *He is a special correspondent for the Washington Post.* • *The President's special envoy visited several countries to discuss the plan.* • *She works as a special adviser/assistant to the President.* • *He's a special agent for the Federal Bureau of Investigation/the Inland Revenue Service.* • *We only make these curtains* **to** *special* **order** (= if a customer asks us to do so). • (The) **Special Branch** is the department of the British police which deals with crimes or other activities against the UK: *This is a job for Special Branch.* • *For the last few years, Kevin has been going to a* **special school** (= a school for children whose physical or mental abilities are outside the usual range).

spe·cial /ˈspeʃ·ᵊl/ *n* [C] • A special is a transport service provided for a particular purpose: *The train involved in the accident was a football special* (= one which was taking people to a football match). ○ *This flight is a holiday special* (= one which is taking people on holiday).

spec·ial·i·sm /ˈspeʃ·ᵊl·ɪ·zᵊm/ *n* • *His specialism (also* **speciality***)* (= the particular subject he studies or works on) *is tax law.* [C] • *I don't think too much specialism* (= limiting study or work to a few subjects) *in schools is a good idea.* [U]

spec·ial·ist /ˈspeʃ·ᵊl·ɪst/ *n* [C] • A specialist is someone who limits their studying or work to a particular area of knowledge, and who knows a lot about that area: *She's a specialist* **in** *cleaning old paintings.* ○ *He's a specialist* **on** *modern French literature.* ○ *They can't afford to pay for the advice of a specialist lawyer.* ○ *I didn't get the job because I didn't have the necessary specialist skills* (= detailed knowledge). ○ *I bought all my golf equipment from a specialist shop* (= one which sells goods connected with one particular area of activity or interest). • A specialist (also **consultant**) is also a doctor who works in and knows a lot about one particular area of medicine: *I've asked to be referred to a specialist about my bad back.* ○ *He is being treated by a leading eye specialist.* • *"The definition of a specialist as one who 'knows more and more about less and less' is good and true"* (Charles H. Mayo in *Modern Hospital*, 1938)

spec·i·al·i·ty *Br and Aus* /£ˌspeʃ·iˈæl·ɪ·ti, $-ə·t̬i/, *Aus also and Am usually* **spe·cial·ty** /£ˈspeʃ·ᵊl·ti, $-t̬i/ *n* [C] • *Her speciality (also* **specialism***)* (= the subject of her studying or work) *is heart surgery.* • *The company's speciality* (= best skill) *is the manufacture of high-performance cars.* • *(fig.) Unkind remarks are one of his specialities* (= he often makes them).

spe·cial·ize, *Br and Aus usually* **-ise** /£ˈspeʃ·ᵊl·aɪz, $-ə·laɪz/ *v* [I] • *She's hired a lawyer who specializes* **in** (= limits her studying or work to) *divorce cases.* • *We went to a restaurant that specializes* **in** *Italian food.* • *The shop specializes* **in** *(selling) antique furniture.* • *I enjoy working in general medicine, but I hope to be able to specialize in the future.*

spec·ial·i·za·tion, *Br and Aus usually* **-i·sa·tion** /ˌspeʃ·ᵊl·aɪˈzeɪ·ʃᵊn/ *n* • *In the course I'm taking, there's no opportunity for specialization* (= limiting my studying or work to one particular area) *until the final year.* [U] • *The lawyer said that he was unable to help us because our case fell outside his specialization* (= his particular area of knowledge). [C]

spe·cial·ized, *Br and Aus usually* **-ised** /£ˈspeʃ·ᵊl·aɪzd, $-ə·laɪzd/ *adj* • *Her job is very specialized* (= involves only one limited area). • *As a computer programmer, you have to have very specialized skills.* • *The hospital is unable to provide the highly specialized care needed by very sick babies.*

spe·cial·ly /ˈspeʃ·ᵊl·i/, **es·pe·cial·ly** *adv* [not gradable] • *I came here specially to see* (= with the particular purpose of seeing) *you.* • *She has a wheelchair that was specially designed/built/made for her.* • *Macmillan nurses are specially trained to help people suffering from cancer.* • *The opera 'Aida' was specially written/commissioned for the opening of the Cairo opera house in 1871.* • *A specially invited/selected audience attended the first night of the play.*

spe·cies /ˈspiː·ʃiːz/ *n* [C] *pl* **species** a set of animals or plants, members of which have similar characteristics to each other and which can breed with each other • *Biologists have estimated that there are around one million animal and plant species living in the rainforests.* • *The rhinoceros is one of the oldest surviving mammalian species.* • *Mountain gorillas are an* **endangered** *species.* • *Dinosaurs are an* **extinct** *species.* • *Dolphins are a* **protected** *species.* • *We found a* **rare** *species* **of** *orchid.* • *Over a hundred species* **of** *insect are found in this area.* • *(fig. infml humorous)* Species is sometimes also used to refer to people or things: *Women film directors in Hollywood are a rare species.* ○ *Now that so many people use computers, the typewriter has become almost an extinct species.* ○ *He was wearing a strange species* **of** *hat – like a large helmet with ear flaps.* • See also SUBSPECIES.

spe·cif·ic /spəˈsɪf·ɪk/ *adj* relating to one thing and not others; particular • *The virus attacks specific cells in the body.* • *The money is intended to be used for specific purposes.* • *I asked you a specific question – please give me a specific answer.* • *The disease seems to be specific* **to** (= only found in) *certain types of plant.* • *Are you doing anything specific this weekend?* • Specific is also used for emphasis to mean particular or special: *I'm trying to find a course that will meet my specific needs.* ○ *They seem to have no specific plans/proposals/ideas for dealing with the problem.* ○ *They haven't fixed a specific date for their wedding yet but it will be this summer.* • *(specialized)* **Specific gravity** is the density of a substance (a solid or liquid) compared to that of water under standard conditions. A more modern term is **relative density**, see at RELATIVE. • See also **specific** at SPECIFY.

spe·cif·i·cal·ly /spəˈsɪf·ɪ·kli/ *adv* • *These jeans are designed specifically for women.* • *We are aiming our campaign specifically at young people.* • *We went to London specifically to visit the British Museum.* • *The film was made with a specifically political aim.* • *Can you give us a few more details about the holiday? Specifically, we'd like to know exactly what the price includes.* • *The programme is intended for children, specifically those aged 7-11.* • *We don't know who specifically was to blame for what happened, but we know which group of boys was involved.*

spec·i·fy *(obj)* /ˈspes·ɪ·faɪ/ *v* to state or describe clearly and exactly • *It is against federal law to specify skin colour in a newspaper ad for roommates.* [T] • *She did not specify reasons for resigning.* [T] • *The peace treaty clearly/exactly/precisely specifies the terms/conditions for the withdrawal of troops.* [T] • *He would not specify* **which** *new evidence the police would be examining.* [+ *wh*-word] • *The newspaper report did not specify* **how** *the men were killed.* [+ *wh*-word] • *My contract specifies* **that** *I must give a month's notice if I leave my job.* [+ *that* clause] • *The loan must be repaid within a specified period/by a specified date.*

spe·cif·ic /spəˈsɪf·ɪk/ *adj* • Specific means clear and exact: *The report makes some specific recommendations.* • *She was unable to give a specific description of the man who attacked her.* • *Police have so far released no specific details/information about the accident.* • *No specific allegations have yet been made about the prison officers' behaviour.* • *Can you be more specific* **about** *where your back hurts?*

spe·cif·i·cal·ly /spəˈsɪf·ɪ·kli/ *adv* • Specifically means clearly: *I specifically asked you not to be late.* • *The law* *specifically prohibits acts of this kind.* • *She specifically mentioned how helpful you'd been to her.* • *It specifically said/stated on the label that the jacket should be dry-cleaned only.*

spec·i·fi·ca·tion /ˌspes·ɪ·fɪˈkeɪ·ʃᵊn/ *n* • A specification (also *infml* **spec**) is a clear detailed plan: *A specification has been* **drawn up** *for the new military aircraft.* [C] ○ *It is the builder's job to make sure that the house* **conforms to/ meets/matches** *the architect's specification in every way.* [C] • *These two computer programs seem almost identical in specification* (= seem to do the same things). [U] • *When I started work, there was no exact specification* (= clear detailed description) **of** *what my job would entail.* [U] • *The cars have been built* **to a high** *specification* (= a high standard). [C]

spec·i·fi·ca·tions /ˌspes·ɪ·fɪˈkeɪ·ʃᵊnz/ *pl n* • *We have asked to see the specifications* (= plan) *by next week.* • Specifications are also details, esp. of the size, shape, etc. of something to be made: *If you give the shop the specifications, they'll make the curtains for you.* [C]

spe·ci·fics /spəˈsɪf·ɪks/ *pl n* • Specifics are exact details: *The President's speech was lacking in specifics.* • *The specifics* **of** *the plan still have to be worked out.* • *Can you give me some specifics* **on/about** *what we'll be discussing in the meeting.*

spec·i·fic·i·ty /£ˌspes·ɪˈfɪs·ɪ·ti, $-ə·t̬i/ *n* [U] • *The machines must operate to a high* **level of** *specificity, or the cars they produce will not perform well.*

spec·i·men /ˈspes·ə·mɪn/ *n* [C] something shown or examined as an example; a typical example • *He has a collection of rare insect specimens.* • *Museums will pay large amounts of money for good dinosaur fossil specimens.* • *The astronauts brought back specimens* **of** *moon rock.* • *We have a splendid specimen* **of** *a maple in our garden.* • *This plant is a rather weedy specimen.* • A specimen (**of** urine or blood) is a small amount of urine or blood used for testing: *He was charged with failing to* **provide** *a specimen for analysis after he had been stopped by the police for drunk driving.* ○ *The doctor* **took** *a specimen of blood from the patient's arm.* ○ *I was sent away with a specimen jar and told to bring in a urine sample the following day.* • *(infml) Matt is a fine specimen* **of** *a man.* • *(infml) He was such a miserable specimen* (= type of person), *the children said.* • *We were given a specimen* **copy** (= an example) *of the form to look at before we had to fill it in.* • *When I opened my bank account, I was asked to provide a specimen* **signature**.

spe·cious /ˈspiː·ʃəs/ *adj fml disapproving* seeming to be right or true, but really wrong or false • *a specious argument* • *a specious claim* • *specious promises* • *specious allegations*

spe·cious·ly /ˈspiː·ʃə·sli/ *adv fml disapproving*

spe·cious·ness /ˈspiː·ʃə·snəs/ *n* [U] *fml disapproving*

speck /spek/ *n* [C] a very small mark, piece or amount • *Could you rub that speck off the window?* • *These islands are so small, they're just specks on the map.* • *After I'd painted the door, I found specks* **of** *paint all over the floor.* • *There's not a speck* **of** (= not any) **dust/dirt** *in their house.* • *There wasn't a speck* **of** (= any) *truth in what he told us.* • *We could see a speck* (= a small amount) **of** *light at the end of the tunnel.*

speck·le /ˈspek·l̩/ *n* [C] a very small mark of a different colour from the surface on which it is found, and which is usually found with a large number of other marks of the same type • *She wore a grey jumper with black speckles all over it.* • *A blackbird's egg is blue with brown speckles* **on** *it.*

speck·led /ˈspek·l̩d/ *adj* • *Some birds, especially thrushes, have speckled breasts* (= their fronts are pale with many small darker-coloured marks). • *The yellow fields of wheat and barley were speckled* **with** *red poppies.*

spec·ta·cle [UNUSUAL EVENT] /ˈspek·tɪ·kl̩/ *n* [C] an unusual or unexpected event or situation which attracts attention, interest or disapproval • *It was a strange spectacle to see the two former enemies shaking hands and hugging each other.* • *We witnessed the extraordinary spectacle* **of** *an old lady climbing a tree to rescue her cat.* • *The early evening news broadcast was criticized for exposing young viewers to the appalling spectacle* **of** *children being killed by soldiers.* • *(disapproving) The trial has become a* **public** *spectacle.* • *She* **made a** *real* **spectacle of herself** (= behaved in a way which attracted other people's attention and made her look ridiculous), *shouting at the waiter in the middle of a crowded restaurant.* • Ⓕ Ⓢ

spec·tac·u·lar /£spekˈtæk·jʊ·ləʳ, $-lɚ/ *adj* • *The most spectacular goal of the match was scored by Harris.* • Spectacular also means unusually great: *He turned out to be a spectacular success/failure in his job.*

spec·tac·u·lar·ly /£spekˈtæk·jʊ·lə·li, $-lɚ-/ *adv* • Spectacularly means most extremely: *She has a spectacularly well-paid job.* ○ *The players are spectacularly fit.* ○ *House prices have risen spectacularly.* ○ *You were spectacularly wrong in your judgement.*

spec·ta·cle [PUBLIC EVENT] /ˈspek·tɪ·kl̩/ *n* a splendid public event or show; a splendid appearance • *The carnival was a magnificent spectacle.* [C] • *In some parts of the world, football has developed into the most popular spectacle on television.* [C] • *The open-air production of the opera was advertised as being the greatest spectacle of the century.* [C] • *The television show was pure spectacle* (= had a splendid appearance)/*was mere spectacle* (= had a splendid appearance, but little value). [U] • Ⓕ Ⓢ

spec·tac·u·lar /£spekˈtæk·jʊ·ləʳ, $-lɚ/ *adj* • *She's a spectacular* (= splendid) *dancer.* • *There was a spectacular sunset last night.* • *The scenery in the Alps is spectacular.* • *That was one of the most spectacular exhibitions I've ever been to.*

spec·tac·u·lar /£spekˈtæk·jʊ·ləʳ, $-lɚ/ *n* [C] • *Many well-known performers are appearing in a television spectacular* (= a performance which is designed to appear very splendid) *on New Year's Eve.*

spec·tac·u·lar·ly /£spekˈtæk·jʊ·lə·li, $-lɚ-/ *adv* • *At night, the city is spectacularly* (= splendidly) *lit.*

spec·ta·cles /ˈspek·tɪ·kl̩z/, *infml* **specs** /speks/, **glas·ses** *pl n slightly fml or slightly dated* two small pieces of shaped glass (LENSES), in a frame worn in front of the eyes to improve sight • *horn-rimmed spectacles* • *steel-rimmed spectacles* • *thick spectacles* • *He put on his spectacles and examined the pictures.* • *Mrs Ramsay looked up over her spectacles and laughed.* • See also BESPECTACLED. • [LP] **Eye and seeing**

spec·ta·cle /ˈspek·tɪ·kl̩/ [before n] • *a spectacle case* • *spectacle frames*

spec·tat·or /£spekˈteɪ·təʳ, $-t̬ɚ/ *n* [C] a person who watches an activity, esp. a sporting event, without taking part • *The stadium was packed with thousands of cheering spectators.* • *Several spectators* **at** *the air show were killed when a plane crashed.* • *After she had given evidence at the trial, she returned to the courtroom as a spectator.* • *"We cannot become participants in the war," said the Prime Minister, "but nor must we be mere spectators."* • A **spectator sport** is one which people go to watch: *Football is probably the biggest spectator sport.* • [LP] **Sports**

spec·tate /spekˈteɪt/ *v* [I] • *Because of injury, he'll just be spectating* (= watching) **at** *today's game instead of playing.*

spec·tre, *Am usually* **spec·ter** /£ˈspek·təʳ, $-tɚ/ *n* [C] *literary* the influence of a person who is not present, or the expectation of something unpleasant happening which causes fear, or *(literary or old use)* a GHOST • *The spectre* **of** *his predecessor* **haunted** *the new Prime Minister's first few months in office.* • *the spectre of unemployment/bankruptcy* • *The* **awful** *spectre* **of** *civil war hangs/looms/hovers over the country.* • *Drought and war have* **raised** *the spectre* **of** *food shortages for up to 24 million African people.* • *"A spectre is haunting Europe – the spectre of Communism"* (Karl Marx and Friedrich Engels in *The Communist Manifesto*, 1848)

spec·tral /ˈspek·trᵊl/ *adj* • Spectral means coming from or seeming to be the spirit of a dead person: *a spectral figure* ○ *a spectral sound* ○ *spectral music* • See also **spectral** at SPECTRUM.

spec·trum /ˈspek·trəm/ *n* [C] *pl* **spectra** /ˈspek·trə/ or **spectrums** the set of colours into which a beam of light can be separated, or a range of waves, such as light waves or radio waves, or *(fig.)* a range of opinions, feelings, etc. • *The colours of the* **(visible)** *spectrum – red, orange, yellow, green, blue, indigo and violet – can be seen in a rainbow.* • *The radio spectrum* (= range of radio waves) *has been opened up for the use of mobile phones.* • *(fig.) The proposal has been supported by people right across the* **political** *spectrum/people on all sides of the* **political** *spectrum* (= range of political opinion). • *(fig.) Our class includes students from both ends of the* **social** *spectrum* (= range of social classes). • *(fig.) A wide spectrum* (= range) **of** *opinion was represented at the meeting.* • *(fig.) At one end of the spectrum* (= range of opinions) *are the conservatives, and at the other end are the radicals.*

spec·tral /ˈspek·trᵊl/ *adj* [not gradable] *specialized* • Spectral means of the set of colours into which a beam of light can be separated: *spectral light* • See also **spectral** at SPECTRE.

spec·u·late GUESS /ˈspek·jʊ·leɪt/ *v* to form opinions about something without having the necessary information or facts; to make guesses • *I don't really know what happened – I'm just speculating.* [I] • *So far, the police can only speculate* **on** *the possible motives for the killing.* [I] • *A spokesperson declined to speculate* **on** *the cause of the train crash.* [I] • *Journalists are speculating* **about** *whether interest rates will be cut.* [I] • *I wouldn't like to speculate* **how** *much that car must have cost him.* [+ *wh-* word] • *It would be wrong to speculate* **why** *she resigned.* [+ *wh-* word] • **It** *has been speculated* **that** *dinosaurs became extinct because the Earth's climate changed.* [+ *that* clause] • (RUS)

spec·u·la·tion /ˌspek·jʊˈleɪ·ʃᵊn/ *n* • *The rumours that they are about to marry have been dismissed as* **pure** *speculation.* [U] • *After he was dropped from the team, speculation* **about** *his future plans was rife.* [U] • *The Prime Minister's speech* **fuelled/prompted** *speculation* **that** *an election will be held later in the year.* [U + *that* clause] • *I want to* **dampen** *speculation* **that** *the school is going to close.* [U + *that* clause] • *There is intense/widespread speculation* **that** *the company is about to collapse.* [U + *that* clause] • *These theories are really no more than speculations* (= guesses). [C] • *There have been speculations* **that** *he's looking for a new job.* [C + *that* clause]

spec·u·la·tive /£ˈspek·jʊ·lə·tɪv, $-t̬ɪv/ *adj* • *Our forecast of demand for next year can only be speculative* (= based on a guess). • *There was a highly speculative story in the newspaper today about the possibility of tax increases.* • *The rumours that she's pregnant are purely/entirely speculative.*

spec·u·la·tive·ly /£ˈspek·jʊ·lə·tɪv·li, $-t̬ɪv-/ *adv*

spec·u·late TRADE /ˈspek·jʊ·leɪt/ *v* [I] to buy and sell in the hope that the value of what you buy will increase and that it can then be sold at a higher price in order to make a profit • *People who speculate have to be prepared to take the risk of losing money.* • *He made his money speculating* **on** *the London gold and silver markets.* • *The banks have plenty of clients eager to speculate* **in** *the foreign-exchange markets.* • *The company has been speculating* **in** *property for years.* • (RUS)

spec·u·la·tion /ˌspek·jʊˈleɪ·ʃᵊn/ *n* • *The government has raised interest rates in an attempt to protect its currency from speculation.* [U] • *They made a fortune from speculation* **in** *the property market.* [U] • *He has lost money on all his recent speculations.* [C]

spec·u·la·tive /£ˈspek·jʊ·lə·tɪv, $-t̬ɪv/ *adj* • *The bank has said that it intends to limit the amount of money it will lend for speculative property development* (= that based on buying in the hope of selling at a profit). • *The office block was built as a speculative venture.* • *The company has lost a large amount of money in speculative deals/activities.*

spec·u·la·tive·ly /£ˈspek·jʊ·lə·tɪv·li, $-t̬ɪv-/ *adv*

spec·u·lat·or /£ˈspek·jʊ·leɪ·təʳ, $-t̬ɚ/ *n* [C] • A speculator is a person who buys goods, property, money, etc. in the hope of selling them at a profit: *Currency speculators have driven down the value of the French franc.* ○ *These houses were built by property speculators.*

speech SAY WORDS /spiːtʃ/ *n* the ability to talk, the activity of talking, or a piece of spoken language • *Children usually develop speech in the second year of life.* [U] • *People who suffer a stroke may experience a loss of speech.* [U] • Your speech is also your way of talking: *After he'd had a few drinks, his speech became slurred and indistinct.* [U] • Speech can also mean the language used when talking: *Expressions like 'you know' are used more* **in** *speech than in writing.* [U] • A speech is a set of words spoken in a play: *Hamlet's speech at the beginning of Act III starts "To be or not to be".* [C] • **Speech bubble** (also **balloon**) is an approximately circular line drawn near the head of a character in a CARTOON (= amusing drawing) inside which the character's words or thoughts are written. • A **speech impediment** is a difficulty in speaking clearly, such as a LISP or STAMMER. • **Speech therapy** (also *Am* **speech**) is the treatment of people who have difficulty in talking. A person who gives this treatment is called a **speech therapist**: *After suffering head injuries in an accident, she was given speech therapy to help her learn to talk again.* ○ *A speech therapist helped him overcome his stammer.* ○ *John goes to speech* (= speaking classes) *three times a week.* • See also SPEAK SAY WORDS.

speech·less /ˈspiːtʃ·ləs/ *adj* [not gradable] • *Her injuries* **left** *her speechless* (= unable to talk). • Speechless also means temporarily unable to talk or to know what to say, esp. because of having strong feelings: *Everyone who has worked with John will be speechless when they find out what has happened to him.* ○ *The news* **left/rendered** *us speechless.* ○ *She was speechless* **with** *indignation.*

speech·less·ly /ˈspiːtʃ·lə·sli/ *adv*

speech·less·ness /ˈspiːtʃ·lə·snəs/ *n* [U]

speech FORMAL TALK /spiːtʃ/ *n* [C] a formal talk given usually to a large number of people on a special occasion • *I'm nervous about having to* **make** *a speech at my friend's wedding.* • *The Governor of New York* **delivered** *an eloquent/rousing* **keynote** *speech to the national convention.* • *He* **gave** *a long, rambling* **after-dinner** *speech* (= a talk given after a formal evening meal at which a large number of people are present). • *In her* **acceptance** *speech at the Oscar ceremony, the actress receiving the award thanked all the other people involved in making the film.* • **Speech day** is a day each year in some British schools when prizes are presented and formal talks are given. • *He worked as a* **speech writer** (= a person who writes formal talks for someone else, esp. a politician) *for the president.* • See also SPEAK FORMAL TALK.

speech·i·fy /ˈspiː·tʃɪ·faɪ/ *v* [I] *esp. disapproving* • *My uncle's always speechifying* (= talking as if giving a formal talk) **about** *what's wrong with the world today.*

speed RATE OF MOVEMENT /spiːd/ *n* (a) rate at which something moves or happens • *The average traffic speed in London is only 4 mph faster than 100 years ago when there were horses and carriages.* [C] • *The pilot said that our* **cruising** *speed would be around 550 miles per hour.* [C] • *The car has a* **top** *speed* **of** *155 miles per hour.* [C] • *You should lower/reduce your speed as you approach a junction.* [U] • *The orchestra played the symphony* **at** *a slower speed than usual.* [C] • *We drove at a* **steady** *speed all the way.* [C] • *He came off the road while driving his car round a bend at* **high/breakneck** *speed* (= very fast). [U] • *We are heading (at)* **full** *speed* (= fast) *for a horrific war.* [U] • *The fire spread at* **lightning** *speed* (= very fast). [U] • *Concorde was the first passenger aircraft to fly at* **supersonic** *speed.* [U] • *The rocket will travel to Mars* **at** *a speed* **of** *over 25 000 miles per hour.* [C] • The speed **of light/sound** is the rate at which light/sound travels: *The speed of light is 300 million metres per second.* [U] ○ *(fig.) The news travelled at the speed of light.* [U] ○ *These planes travel at twice the speed of sound.* [U] • *This electric drill has two speeds* (= rates at which it turns). [C] • A speed is also a GEAR (= a part of a vehicle which controls the rate at which it moves): *My bicycle has ten speeds.* [C] ○ *I have a ten-speed bicycle.* • The speed **of** a photographic film is the rate at which the film receives light: *What speed film do I need for taking photographs indoors?* [C] • The speed of a camera is the rate at which part of it opens to allow light to reach the film when a photograph is being taken: *a high/low* **shutter** *speed.* • If you get or bring something **up to speed** you make it move as fast as it can: *This kind of race requires a different set-up and we've not got the car up to speed.* • You can also say something or someone is **up to speed** if they are fully informed about what they need to do or are completely able to do it: *The BBC needed to be brought up to speed* **with** *commercial broadcasters in the areas of efficiency, savings and producer choice.* ○ *Carrington was at his country home, getting up to speed* **with** *developments down on the farm.* ○ *In any strike there are difficulties getting the company back up to speed.* • LP **Measurements**

speed *(obj)* GO FAST /spiːd/ *v past* **sped** /sped/ or **speeded** to (cause to) move, go or happen fast • *The train sped* **along** *at over 120 miles per hour.* [I] • *After the match, the two tennis players sped* **away/off** *in waiting cars.* [I] • *We sped* **down** *the ski slopes.* [I] • *This year seems to be simply speeding* **by/past.** [I] • *Ambulances sped the injured people* (= moved them quickly) *away from the scene.* [T] • *The best thing you can do to speed* (= make quicker) *your recovery is to rest.* [T] • *Doing some of the legal work ourselves speeded* **(up)** *the process of selling our house.* [T/M] • *We have succeeded in speeding* **up** *our production rates in the last few months.* [M] • *This drug may have the effect of speeding* **up** *your heart rate.* [M] • *Can the job be speeded* **up**? [T] • *The tape speeded* **up** *towards the end.* [I] • *I think you need to speed* **up** *a bit* (= drive faster) *– we're going to be late.* [I] • *The economy shows signs of speeding* **up** (= increasing activity). [I] • *We'll come to the station with you to* **speed** *you* **on** *your* **way** (= be with you to say goodbye as you leave on your journey). • *Measures should be taken to halt the* **speed-up in** (= fast rate of increase of) *population growth.* • When *speed* is used with *up*, its past form is *speeded*. Otherwise, when it is INTRANSITIVE [I] its past form is *sped* and when it is TRANSITIVE [T] its past form is usually *speeded*. • PIC> **Road**

speed /spiːd/ *n* [U] • *He's one of those people who gets a thrill from speed* (= very fast movement). • *Everyone has been struck by the speed with which* (= how fast) *the new head has made changes in the school.* • *We were surprised at the speed* **of** (= how fast we received) *the response to our enquiry.* • *(Br) Both cars were travelling* **at** *speed* (= very fast) *when the accident happened.* • *She got through her work* **with** *speed* (= quickly) *and efficiency.* • *The train* **picked up/gathered/gained** *speed* (= moved faster) *as it went down the hill.* • *(fig.) The economy has* **picked up** *speed* (= improved its performance) *recently.* • *(infml) Tony is a real speed* **freak/merchant** (= a person who enjoys driving (too) fast). • *There are speed* **restrictions** (= controls on how fast traffic is allowed to move) *on this part of the road.* • A **speed bump** (*Br also* **speed hump**, **ramp**, **rumble strip** or **sleeping policeman**) is a small raised area built across a road in order to make traffic move less fast: *Local residents are asking for speed bumps to be installed in their street.* • A **speed limit** is the fastest rate at which you are allowed to drive in a particular area: *There is a speed limit* **of** *30 miles per hour on this road.* ○ *Slow down – you're* **breaking**/*you're* **over** *the speed limit.* • A **speed trap** is special hidden equipment used by police to see whether drivers are going faster than is allowed in a particular area. • **Speed skating** is the sport of people racing on ice, usually around an oval track. • PIC> **Winter sports**

speed·ing /ˈspiː·dɪŋ/ *n* [U] • Speeding is driving faster than is allowed in a particular area: *I wasn't aware that I was speeding when I was stopped by the police.* ○ *He was* **caught** *speeding.* ○ *Susan was* **fined for** *speeding.* ○ *I got a speeding* **ticket** (= official punishment for driving too fast). ○ *There were lots of speeding* **cars/drivers**. • LP> **Crimes and criminals**

speed·y /ˈspiː·di/ *adj* **-ier, -iest** • Speedy means quick or fast: *Graham is a very speedy worker.* ○ *Delivery must be efficient, reliable and speedy.* ○ *We need to take speedy action/make a speedy decision.* ○ *Everyone is hoping for a speedy* **end** *to the conflict* (= hoping that an end to it will happen quickly). ○ *We wished her a speedy* **recovery** *from her illness* (= that she would get better quickly).

speed·i·ly /ˈspiː·dɪ·li/ *adv* • *The problem was speedily solved.*

speed·i·ness /ˈspiː·dɪ·nəs/ *n* [U]

speed DRUG /spiːd/ *n* [U] *slang for* an AMPHETAMINE • *She looks like she's* **on** *speed.*

speed·boat /£ˈspiːd·bəʊt, $-boʊt/ *n* [C] a small boat which has a powerful engine and which travels very fast • PIC> **Ships and boats**

speed·o·me·ter /£spiːˈdɒm·ɪ·təʳ, $spɪˈdɑː·mə·t̬ɚ/, *Br infml* **speed·o** /£ˈspiː·dəʊ, $-doʊ/ *n* [C] a device in a vehicle which shows how fast the vehicle is moving • *The speedometer showed that we were doing 50 miles per hour/80 kilometers per hour.* • PIC> **Meters and gauges**

speed·way /ˈspiːd·weɪ/ *n* (a special racing track used for) the sport of racing special cars, or light motorcycles without BRAKES (= devices to slow the vehicle's speed) • *the local speedway* [C] • *I enjoy going to speedway.* [U] • *The Indianapolis Motor Speedway is the venue of the Indianapolis 500.* [C]

spel·e·ol·o·gy /£ˌspiː·liˈɒl·ə·dʒi, $-ˈɑː·lə-/ *n* [U] the scientific study of caves, or (*Am usually* **spelunking**, *Br usually* **caving** or **potholing**) the sport of walking or climbing in caves

spel·e·o·log·i·cal /£ˌspiː·li·əˈlɒdʒ·ɪ·kəl, $-lɑː·dʒɪ-/ *adj* [not gradable]

spel·e·ol·o·gist /£ˌspiː·liˈɒl·ə·dʒɪst, $-ˈɑː·lə-/ *n* [C]

spell *(obj)* FORM WORDS /spel/ *v past* **spelled** /spelt, speld/ or *Br and Aus also* **spelt** /spelt/ to form (a word or words) with the letters in the correct order • *"How do you spell 'receive'?" "R E C E I V E".* [T] • *British people spell 'colour'* **with** *a 'u', but Americans don't.* [T] • *Shakespeare did not always spell his own name the same way.* [T] • *I think it's important that children should be taught to spell* (= how to form words with the letters in the correct order). [I] • *It has been suggested that students should be penalized in examinations if they spell incorrectly.* [I] • *Our address is 1520 Main Street, Albuquerque – shall I spell that* **(out)** (= say in the correct order the letters that form the word) *for you?* [T/M] • If you **spell** something **out**, you explain it in detail: *Let me spell out what I have in mind.* ○ *The government has so far refused to spell out its plans/policies.* ○ *(infml) What do you mean you don't understand – do I have to spell* **it out for you?** • To **spell-check** is to use a **spell-checker**, which is a computer program which does a **spell-check** to make sure that words in a document have the letters in the correct order: *Don't forget to spell-check the report.* ○ *After you've finished each chapter,* **run** *the spell-checker/a spell-check.* • *(saying)* 'N O spells no' is used as a reply to a request, to emphasize that when you said no previously you really meant it. • LP> **American spelling, Consonant doubling, Forms of words (spelling), 'ie' or 'ei' spelling** ⓘ

spell·er /£ˈspel·əʳ, $-ɚ/ *n* [C] • A **good/excellent** speller is someone who is good at forming words with the letters in the correct order. A **bad/poor/weak** speller is someone who is not good at forming words in the correct order.

spell·ing /ˈspel·ɪŋ/ *n* • *He's hopeless at spelling* (= forming words with the letters in the correct order). [U] • *I think that children should be taught spelling* (= how to form words correctly) *and punctuation.* [U] • *My computer has a program which corrects my spelling* (= the way I form words). [U] • *Your essay is full of spelling* **mistakes/errors**. [U] • *This dictionary includes both British and American spellings* **of** (= correct ordering of letters in) *words.* [C] • *(Am and Aus)* A **spelling bee** is a competition in which the winner is the person or group who is able to form correctly the highest number of the words they are asked to form.

spell *obj* RESULT /spel/ *v* [T] *past* **spelled** /spelt, speld/ or *Br also* **spelt** /spelt/ *infml* to have (usually something unpleasant) as a result • *This cold weather could spell trouble for gardeners.* • *The recent fall in house prices has spelt disaster for many people wanting to sell their houses.* • *Last night's defeat has spelt doom for the team's hopes of winning the competition.* • ⓘ

spell PERIOD /spel/ *n* [C] a period of time for which an activity or condition lasts continuously • *I lived in London* **for** *a spell.* • *She* **had** *a brief spell* **as** *captain of the team.* • *He* **had** *an unhappy spell working as an engineer.* • *After a long spell* **of** *unemployment, Geoff finally found a job.* • *She's had several spells* **of** *sickness this winter.* • *I keep having/getting* **dizzy** *spells* (= periods of feeling as if I'm spinning around), *doctor.* • A spell is a short period of a particular type of weather: *In 1963 there was one of the longest cold spells ever recorded in the British Isles.* ○ *The weather forecast is for dry, sunny spells.* • ⓘ

spell MAGIC /spel/ *n* [C] spoken words which are thought to have magical power, or (the condition of being under) the influence or control of such words • *In 'Macbeth', the witches' spell includes the words "Eye of newt, and toe of frog, wool of bat, and tongue of dog."* • *When the beautiful girl kissed the ugly frog, the spell* (= the condition of being controlled by magic words) *was* **broken**, *and he turned into a handsome prince.* • *In the story of 'Beauty and the Beast', the old woman* **casts/puts** *a spell* **on** *the prince* (= puts him in the condition of being controlled by magic words), *turning him into a beast.* • *Sleeping Beauty lay* **under** *the wicked fairy's spell* (= influence caused by magic words having been spoken) *until the prince woke her with a kiss.* • *(fig.) He's completely* **under** *her spell* (= is strongly attracted to and interested by her). • ⓘ

spell *obj* DO INSTEAD /spel/ *v* [T] *past* **spelled** /spelt, speld/ *esp. Am and Aus* to do something instead of (someone), esp. in order to allow them to rest • *You've been driving for a while – do you want me to spell you?* • ⓘ

spell /spel/ *n* [C] *Am and Aus* • *If we take spells* **(with)** *doing the painting, it won't seem like such hard work.*

spell·bound /ˈspel·baʊnd/ *adj* having your attention completely held by something, so that you cannot think about anything else • *The children* **listened** *to the story spellbound.* • *We were spellbound by her performance.* • *The spellbound audience watched in amazement.*

spell·bind·er /£ˈspelˌbaɪn·dəʳ, $-dɚ/ *n* [C] *infml* • A spellbinder is an event or a person that attracts people's complete attention: *The final game of the tennis match was a real spellbinder.* ○ *As an actress, she's a complete spellbinder.*

spell·bind·ing /ˈspelˌbaɪn·dɪŋ/ *adj* • *They gave a spellbinding performance* (= one which attracted people's complete attention). • *Martin Luther King began his spellbinding speech with the words "I have a dream".* • *The contest between the two former champions was spellbinding.*

spe·lunk·ing *Am* /spəˈlʌŋ·kɪŋ/ *n* [U] *Am for* **caving** or **potholing**, see at CAVE or POTHOLE UNDERGROUND • *We did some* *spelunking on our vacation.* • *Shall we* **go spelunking** *at the weekend?*

spe·lunk·er /£spə'lʌŋ·kəʳ, $-kɚ/ *n* [C] *Am for* **caver** or **potholer**, see at CAVE or POTHOLE UNDERGROUND

spend *(obj)* MONEY /spend/ *v past* **spent** /spent/ to give (money) as a payment for something • *The car salesperson asked us how much we were prepared to spend.* [I] • *If you carry on spending like this, you'll soon get into debt.* [I] • *I don't know how I managed to spend so much in the pub last night.* [T] • *We spent* **a fortune** *when we were in New York.* [T] • *They're only able to spend money* **on** *basic necessities.* [T] • *I've just spent a lot of money* **on** *four new tyres for my car.* [T] • *He spends all his money* **on** *his girlfriend.* [T] • *We went on a spending* **spree** (= We bought a lot of things) *on Saturday.* [I] • *(esp. Br dated infml)* To **spend a penny** is sometimes used to avoid saying urinate: *I just want to spend a penny before we go out.* • *(esp. Br)* People sometimes say **spend, spend, spend** to refer to people buying a lot of things: *The 1980s have been described as being years of spend, spend, spend.* • **Spending money** is another word for **pocket money**. See at POCKET BAG. • (D)

spend /spend/ *n Br* • *The total spend* **on** (= the amount paid for) *the project was almost a million pounds.*

spend·er /£'spen·dəʳ, $-dɚ/ *n* [C] • *Young people tend to be spenders* (= they buy things) *rather than savers.* • *Tourists are often* **big** *spenders* (= they buy a lot of things). • *The local council has been criticized for being a* **low** *spender* **on** (= not giving much money to pay for) *education.* • *"A man of distinction, a real big spender"* (Shirley Bassey in the song *Big Spender*, 1966) • (D)

spend·ing /'spen·dɪŋ/ *n* [U] • *We need to rein in/control/limit our spending* (= giving money for goods and services), *or we're going to find ourselves in financial difficulties.* • *The government's plans to reduce/slash defence spending have been strongly criticized.* • *Consumer spending has more than doubled in the last ten years.* • *Scientists have appealed for spending* **on** *scientific research to be increased.*

spend *obj* TIME /spend/ *v* [+ obj + adv/prep/v-*ing*] *past* **spent** /spent/ to use (time); to allow (time) to go past • *The injured boy's parents are spending all their time at his bedside.* • *Following his resignation, the minister said he was looking forward to 'spending more time with his family'.* • *It doesn't look as if you spent very long on your homework.* • *My sister always spends ages in the bathroom.* • *I've spent many years build***ing** *up my collection.* • *He's spent most of his life work***ing** *for the same company.* • *I spent an hour at the station wait***ing** *for the train.* • *We spent the weekend in London.* • *You can spend the night here if you like.* • **Spend the night** is also sometimes used to avoid saying have sex: *Did you spend the night* **with** *him?* ○ *She suggested to me that we spend the night* **together**. • (D)

spend *obj* FORCE /spend/ *v* [T] *past* **spent** /spent/ to use (energy, effort, force, etc.), esp. until there is no more left • *For the past month he's been spending all his energy trying to find a job.* • *They continued firing until all their ammunition was spent* (= there was none of it left). • *The hurricane will probably have spent most of its force* (= most of its force will have gone) *by the time it reaches northern parts of the country.* • *Her anger soon spent* **itself** (= stopped). • (D)

spent /spent/ *adj* • Something that is spent has been used so that it no longer has any power or effectiveness: *I wish you wouldn't keep putting spent matches back into the box.* ○ *Several spent bullets were found near to the scene of the crime.* ○ *After several defeats in a row, people are starting to say that the team is a spent* **force**. • *(esp. literary)* Spent also means extremely tired: *We arrived home spent after our long journey.*

spend·thrift /'spend·θrɪft/ *adj* [/C], *n infml disapproving* (of or like) a person who spends money in a wasteful way, or who spends more money than necessary • *He accused the council of being spendthrift.* • *After a brief pause, shoppers have resumed their spendthrift ways.* • *My mother always told me not to be a spendthrift.*

sperm /£spɜːm, $spɜːrm/ *n pl* **sperm** or **sperms** a reproductive cell produced by a male animal • *In human reproduction, one female egg is usually fertilized by one sperm.* [C] • *(infml)* Sperm is also used for SEMEN (= the liquid containing the reproductive cells of male animals). [U] • A **sperm bank** is a place in which sperm is stored in order to be used by doctors to try and make women pregnant. • A **sperm count** is the number of live male reproductive cells in a particular amount of the liquid in which they are contained: *He has a* **low/high** *sperm count.*

sper·ma·to·zo·on /£ˌspɜː·mə·tə'zəʊ·ɒn, $ˌspɜːr·mə·ţə'zoʊ·ɑːn/ *n* [C] *pl* **spermatozoa** /£ˌspɜː·mə·tə'zəʊ·ə, $ˌspɜːr·mə·ţə'zoʊ-/ *specialized for* SPERM

sper·mi·cide /£'spɜː·mɪ·saɪd, $'spɜːr-/ *n* [C/U] (a) substance that kills sperm, esp. used by a woman before she has sex in order to stop herself becoming pregnant or on CONDOMS

sper·mi·cid·al /£ˌspɜː·mɪ'saɪ·dᵊl, $ˌspɜːr-/ *adj* [not gradable] • *spermicidal jelly* • *spermicidal cream*

sperm whale *n* [C] a large WHALE with a very large long head

spew *(obj)* /spjuː/ *v* to vomit, to flow or come out, esp. in large amounts • *The volcano has spewed a giant cloud of ash, dust and gases* **into** *the air.* [T] • *Nearby drains spew* **(out)** *millions of gallons of raw sewage* **into** *the river.* [T/M] • *The car spewed* **out** *exhaust fumes.* [M] • *When the pipe burst, gallons of water spewed* **out**. [I] • *Paper came spewing from the computer printer.* [I] • *(slang)* To spew **(up)** is also to vomit: *I was spewing (up) all night after eating those mussels.* [I] ○ *I've got this stomach infection which is making me spew my food up.* [M]

SPF /ˌes·piː'ef/ *n* [C] *abbreviation for* sun protection factor; see at SUN

sphere ROUND OBJECT /£sfɪəʳ, $sfɪr/ *n* [C] an object shaped like a round ball • *Every point on the surface of a sphere is at an equal distance from its centre.* • *Doctors have replaced the top of his hip bone with a metal sphere.* • PIC **Shapes**

spher·i·cal /£'sfer·ɪ·kᵊl, $'sfer-/ *adj* • *The Earth is not perfectly spherical* (= round like a ball).

spher·oid /£'sfɪə·rɔɪd, $'sfɪr·ɔɪd/ *n* [C] *specialized* • A spheroid is a solid object that is almost spherical: *The Earth is a spheroid.*

sphere AREA /£sfɪəʳ, $sfɪr/ *n* [C] a range or area of activity • *It is sometimes difficult for film stars to keep the public and private spheres of their lives separate.* • *The minister said that the government planned to develop exchanges with other countries, particularly in cultural, scientific and economic spheres.* • *Most of our friends come from the same social sphere as we do.* • *He likes to work by himself within a clearly defined sphere* **of** *authority/responsibility.* • *In his speech, the President said that his goal was to give all citizens full rights in every sphere* **of life**. • *This part of the world has for many years come under America's sphere* **of influence**.

sphinc·ter /£'sfɪŋk·təʳ, $-tɚ/ *n* [C] *medical* a muscle that surrounds an opening in the body and can tighten to close it • *the anal sphincter* • *a sphincter muscle*

sphinx /sfɪŋks/ *n* [C] *pl* **sphinx** or **sphinxes** an ancient imaginary creature with a lion's body and a woman's head • *According to ancient Greek legend, the sphinx set a riddle which no one before Oedipus was able to answer.* • *She's as inscrutable as a sphinx* (= it is difficult to tell what she is thinking). • The sphinx are also huge stone statues, each with a lion's body and a person's head, found in the desert near Cairo in Egypt. • *The cat just sat there,* **sphinx-like** *and mysterious.*

spic, **spick**, **spik** /spɪk/ *n* [C] *Am and Aus taboo disapproving slang* a person from a community that speaks Spanish, or *(Aus)* any European language other than English • This is considered offensive.

spice /spaɪs/ *n* (a) powder or seeds from a plant used to flavour food. There are various types of spice. • *Cinnamon, ginger and cloves are all spices.* [C] • *Spices are widely used in Indian cooking.* [C] • *The aroma of herbs and spices came from the kitchen.* [C] • *She seasoned the mulled wine with spices.* [C] • *This curry needs a bit more spice.* [U] • *He* **added** *spice* **to** *the stew.* [U] • Spice can also mean excitement or interest: *The performance was rather lacking in spice.* [U] ○ *The team's new striker has certainly* **added** *spice* **to** *their play.* [U] ○ *He* **added** *spice* **to** *the story by making up a few things that weren't true.* [U] ○ *She complained that the spice had gone from her marriage.* [U]

spice *obj* /spaɪs/ *v* • To spice food or drink is to add flavour to it with spice: *I often spice my coffee* **with** *cinnamon.* [T] ○ *You can spice* **up** *tuna fish by adding curry powder to it.* [T] • To spice **(up)** a speech, story, etc. is to add excitement or interest: *The best man at Neil's wedding spiced* **(up)** *his speech* **with** *some rude jokes.* [T/M]

spiced /spaɪst/ *adj* • Spiced food or drink is that which has had spice added to it: *spiced pears* ○ *spiced buns* ○ *spiced wine* ○ **highly** *spiced curry*

spic·y /'spaɪ·si/ *adj* **-ier, -iest** • *Do you like spicy food* (= food that is strongly flavoured with spices, esp. hot-tasting ones)? • Spicy can also mean exciting and interesting, esp. because shocking or dealing with sexual matters: *a spicy novel* ○ *a spicy documentary* ○ *spicy details*

spic·i·ness /ˈspaɪ·sɪ·nəs/ *n* [U]

spick CLEAN /spɪk/ *adj* **spick and span** *infml* (esp. of a place) very clean and tidy • *Their house is always spick and span.* • *The council spends a lot of money keeping the town spick and span.* • *The soldiers looked spick and span in their uniforms.* • *We stayed at a spick-and-span little hotel.*

spick PERSON /spɪk/ *n* [C] a SPIC

spi·der /£ˈspaɪ·dər, $-dɚ/ *n* [C] a small insect-like creature with eight thin legs • *a spider's web* • *Spiders produce fine threads which they make into webs in order to trap insects for food.* • *A lot of people are frightened of spiders.* • A **spider monkey** is a small thin S American monkey which uses its long tail to help it to move around in the branches of trees. • A **spider plant** is a plant commonly found in houses and offices and which has long flat thin green leaves with white stripes. • *"Will you walk into my parlour?" said a spider to a fly* (Mary Howitt in the poem *The Spider and the Fly*, 1834) • PIC› **Apes and monkeys**

spi·der·y /£ˈspaɪ·dər·i, $-dɚ-/ *adj* • Spidery means consisting of thin dark bending lines, like a spider's legs: *spidery handwriting* ○ *spidery drawings* ○ *a spidery pattern*

spi·der·web /£ˈspaɪ·də·web, $-dɚ-/ *n* [C] *Am and Aus for* COBWEB

spiel /ʃpiːl/ *n infml disapproving* (a) speech, esp. one which is long and spoken quickly and is intended to persuade the listener about something • *a sales spiel* • *a marketing spiel* [C] • *They gave us a long spiel* **about** *why we needed to install double glazing in our house.* [C] • *He launched into some spiel* **about** *how his wife didn't understand him.* [U]

spif·fy /ˈspɪf·i/ *adj* **-ier, -iest** *Am infml* stylish, attractive or pleasing • *a spiffy dresser* • *"Do you want to come to Tahiti with me?" "That would be spiffy."*

spiff up *obj*, **spiff** *obj* **up** /spɪf/ *v adv* [M] *Am infml* • *He's really spiffed up his wardrobe since he started that new job.*

spi·got /ˈspɪg·ət/ *n* [C] a device used to control the flow of liquid from esp. a BARREL, or *(Am)* a TAP, esp. on the outside of a building

spik /spɪk/ *n* [C] a SPIC

spike POINT /spaɪk/ *n* [C] a narrow thin shape with a sharp point at one end, or something, esp. a piece of metal, with this shape • *There were large spikes on top of the railings around the embassy to stop people climbing over them.* • *She injured her leg on a rusty spike.* • *Some types of dinosaur had sharp spikes on their tails.* • A spike is also one of a set of short pointed pieces of metal or plastic fixed to the bottom of shoes worn for particular sports, and which stop the person wearing the shoes from sliding on the ground. Shoes with these pointed pieces are also sometimes called spikes: *These running shoes have a special combination of metal and plastic spikes.* ○ *Just before the race, he discovered that his spikes were missing.* • **Spike heels** (*Am* **spikes**) are **stiletto heels**. See at STILETTO.

spike *obj* /spaɪk/ *v* [T] • *She got badly spiked* (= sharp points were forced into her) *when one of the other runners trod on her heel.*

spiked /spaɪkt/ *adj* • *German soldiers in World War I wore spiked helmets* (= those with a sharp point on them).

spik·y /ˈspaɪ·ki/ *adj* **-ier, -iest** • Spiky means having sharp points: *a spiky cactus* ○ *spiky leaves* ○ *spiky hair* • *(fig.) From being a happy child, she turned into a spiky* (= easily annoyed) *teenager.*

spike *obj* STOP /spaɪk/ *v* [T] *infml* to stop (something) from happening • *The editor said that she would have to spike the story because there wasn't enough evidence for it.* • *We wanted to build an extra room onto the side of our house, but our neighbours* **spiked** *our* **guns** (= stopped us doing what we wanted to do).

spike *obj* MAKE STRONGER /spaɪk/ *v* [T] to make (esp. a drink) stronger by adding alcohol, or to add flavour or interest • *She claimed that someone had spiked her* **drink** *at the party.* • *The pasta was served in a cream sauce spiked* **with** *black pepper.* • *His writing is spiked* **with** *humour.*

spike *obj* HIT /spaɪk/ *v* [T] (in the sport of VOLLEYBALL) to hit (the ball) so that it goes almost straight down on the other side of the net

spill *(obj)* /spɪl/ *v past Br and Aus* **spilt** /spɪlt/ or *esp. Am, Aus also* **spilled** to (cause to) flow, move, fall or spread over the edge or beyond the limits of something • *I spilt coffee* **on** *my silk shirt.* [T] • *You've spilt something* **down** *your tie.* [T] • *Make sure you pour the juice into the glass without spilling it.* [T] • *He dropped a bag of sugar and it spilt all* **over** *the floor.* [I] • *I knocked a jug of cream over, but luckily it didn't spill* (= its contents did not fall out). [I] • *All her shopping spilled* **out of** *her bag when she dropped it.* [I] • *The conflict threatens to spill* **(over) into** *neighbouring regions.* [I] • *I try not to let my work spill* **over into** (= have an effect on) *my life outside the office.* [I] • *The talks between the two leaders look likely to spill* **over** (= to continue) **into** *the weekend.* [I] • *Crowds of football fans spilled* **onto** *the field at the end of the game.* [I] • *People were spilling* **out of** *the wine bar* (= spreading out from it because it was full) **onto** *the street.* [I] • *(fig.) I listened quietly as she spilled* **out** (= talked in an emotional way about) *all her anger and despair.* [M] • *(fig.) All his resentment spilled* **out** (= he talked emotionally about it). [I] • *So who* **spilt the beans** (= told the secret) *about her affair with David?* • *(esp. literary) The government has urged the rebels not to* **spill** *any more* **blood** (= to injure or kill any more people). • (I)

spill /spɪl/ *n* [C] • A spill is an amount of something which has come out of a container: *Could you wipe up that spill, please?* ○ *The road is closed because of a fuel spill.* ○ *In 1989, there was a massive oil spill in Alaska.* • *(infml)* A spill is also a fall: *Rachel had/***took** *a spill from her bike.*

spil·lage /ˈspɪl·ɪdʒ/ *n* • *Any spillage* (= spilling) *of fuel could be very dangerous.* [U] • *There's been another oil spillage.* [C]

spill·o·ver /£ˈspɪl,əʊ·vər, $-,oʊ·vɚ/ *n* [C] *esp. Am* an amount of liquid which has become too much for the object that contains it and flows or spreads out, or *(fig.)* the effects of an activity which have spread beyond what was originally intended • *The spillover from the adjacent river flooded the lower fields.* • *(fig.) It's important to avoid a spillover of the war into neighboring regions.* • *(fig.) The bad weather in February and March could have a spillover* **effect** *on farmers in April.*

spin *(obj)* TURN /spɪn/ *v* **spinning**, *past simple* **spun** /spʌn/ or *Br also* **span** /spæn/, *past part* **spun** /spʌn/ to (cause to) turn around and around, esp. fast • *The Earth spins on its axis.* [I] • *The roulette players silently watched the wheel spin* **around/round.** [I] • *He was killed when his car hit a tree and spun off the road.* [I] • *She heard footsteps behind her, and spun* **around/round** (= turned quickly) *to see who was there.* [I] • *Spin the ball* (= Make it turn around and around as you throw it) *and it will change direction when it hits the ground.* [T] • *Our washing machine spins the clothes* (= makes them go around in order to get water out of them) *quite fast.* [T] • *(fig.) I feel faint and my head is spinning* **(around/round)***/the room is spinning* **(around/round)** (= I feel as if my head/the room is going around and around very fast and I cannot balance). [I] • *(fig.) The country's economy seems to be spinning* **out of control** (= experiencing fast change in an uncontrolled way). [I] • *Let's* **spin a coin** (= make it turn around and around on its edge and one of us will guess which side will land facing upwards) *to decide who'll have the first turn.* Compare TOSS. • A **spin bowler** is a cricket player who BOWLS (= throws) the ball in such a way that it turns around and around and changes direction when it hits the ground. The act of doing this is called **spin-bowling**. • A **spin-dryer** (also **spin-drier**) is a machine into which you put wet clothes etc. and which turns them around and around very fast in order to get most of the water out of them. If you get water out of clothes in this way, you spin or **spin-dry** them: *It said on the label inside the skirt 'Do not spin-dry'.* ○ Compare **tumble dryer** at TUMBLE FALL. • A **spinning top** is a toy with rounded sides, a flattened top, a vertical handle, and a point at the bottom, which turns round and round on the point when the handle is pushed and pulled up and down, or twisted. • PIC› **Top**

spin /spɪn/ *n* • *I hit something on the road, which sent the car into a spin* (= a movement of turning around and around very fast). [C] • *She* **put** *a lot of spin on the ball* (= threw or hit it so that it turned around and around very fast). [U] • *These clothes need another spin* (= to be put into a machine that turns them around and around to get water out of them) – *they're still very wet.* [C] • *Suddenly, the plane went* **into a** *(Br and Aus also* **into a flat***) spin* (= a fall in which it turned around and around very fast). [C] • *(infml) The news threw them* **into a** *(Br* **flat***) spin* (= made them anxious and unable to act reasonably). • *We made the decision on the basis of a* **spin of the coin** (= by making a coin turn on its edge to see which side will fall facing up).

spin·ner /£ˈspɪn·ər, $-ɚ/ *n* [C] • In cricket, a spinner is a BOWLER who makes the ball turn around and around as he or she throws it, or a ball that is BOWLED in that way: *a left-arm spinner* ○ *a slow spinner*

spin *obj* MAKE THREAD /spɪn/ *v* [T] **spinning**, *past simple* **spun** /spʌn/ or *Br also* **span** /spæn/, *past part* **spun** /spʌn/ to make (thread) by twisting fibres, or to produce (something) using thread • *Wool is made by spinning the hair from sheep.* • *The final stage of the production of cotton is when it is spun* **into** *thread.* • *In the story of Sleeping Beauty, when the princess went into the room in the tower, she found an old woman spinning.* • *Spiders spin webs.* • *Silk is made from cocoons* (= structures made of thin threads) *spun by silkworms.* • To spin a **story/tale/yarn** is to tell a story, either for entertainment, or as an explanation or excuse: *After supper, we sat listening to Grandfather spinning yarns.* ○ *He spun some tale about needing to take time off work because his mother was ill.* ○ *They spun us a story about being in desperate need of money.* [+ two objects] • A **spinning wheel** is a small machine used, esp. in the past, at home for producing thread from fibres by turning them on a wheel operated by foot.

spin·ner /£ˈspɪn·əʳ, $-ɚ/ *n* [C] • A spinner is a person who makes thread by twisting fibres.

spin WAY OF CONSIDERING /spɪn/ *n* [U] *infml* a particular way, esp. one which is to your advantage, of considering a situation • *Salespeople always tend to* **put** *the best possible spin* **on** *a situation* (= try and make it be seen in the best possible way). • *They have tried to* **put** *a positive spin* **on** *racial conflict within the country.* • *She has been criticized for attempting to* **put** *a political spin* **on** *what has been for many people a personal tragedy.* • *We need to exercise some* **spin control** *on this situation* (= control or change the way in which it is considered) *before we find ourselves in serious trouble.* • *News coverage of the campaign can be influenced to a candidate's advantage by* **spin doctors** (= people whose job is to persuade others to consider a situation, esp. a political one, in a particular way, esp. one that is to the advantage of the people for whom they work).

spin DRIVE /spɪn/ *v* [I always + adv/prep] **spinning**, *past simple* **spun** /spʌn/ or *Br also* **span** /spæn/, *past part* **spun** /spʌn/ *infml* (of a vehicle) to move quickly, or to move quickly in a vehicle • *We were spinning* **along**, *when suddenly one of our tyres burst.*

spin /spɪn/ *n* [C] *infml dated* • *We went for a spin* (= a short journey taken for pleasure) *in Bill's new car/on Gail's new motorbike.*

spin off *obj*, **spin** *obj* **off** *v adv* [M] to produce (something unexpected or additional to that which is intended to be produced) • *The American space program has spun off new commercial technologies.* • *Every new job that is created spins off three or four more in related fields.* • *(esp. Am and Aus)* To spin off something is also to form a separate company from parts of an existing company: *The company is trying to spin off part of its business.*

spin–off /£ˈspɪn·ɒf, $-ɑːf/ *n* [C] • *The research has spin-offs* (= useful products produced in addition to the main products of a process) *in the development of medical equipment.* • *Developing the country's air-transport system could have useful spin-offs for other service industries.* • *The stage show is a spin-off* **from** *a television programme.* • *(esp. Am and Aus) The company is planning to create several spin-off* (= separate new) *businesses.*

spin out *obj*, **spin** *obj* **out** *v adv* [M] to cause to last longer than usual or necessary, or as long as possible • *Can we spin our holiday out for a few more days?* • *Somehow, she managed to spin her story out so that it took her the whole train journey to tell it.* • *The government seems to be spinning out the withdrawal of troops from the war zone.* • *We must try and spin out our money if we can.*

spi·na bi·fi·da /ˌspaɪ·nəˈbɪf·ɪ·də/ *n* [U] *specialized* a serious condition in which some of the vertical row of bones in the centre of the back are not correctly developed at birth, leaving the nerves in the back without any protection • *Spina bifida may cause physical and mental handicaps.*

spi·nach /ˈspɪn·ɪtʃ/ *n* [U] a vegetable which has wide dark green leaves which are eaten cooked or raw • *spinach salad* • *spinach lasagne* • *Eating spinach is supposed to make you strong.* • PIC> **Vegetables**

spin·dle /ˈspɪn·dl̩/ *n* [C] a part of a machine around which something turns, or a rod onto which thread is twisted when it is spun

spin·dly /ˈspɪnd·li/ *adj* **-ler, -lest** long or tall and thin, and looking weak • *a foal with long spindly legs* • *a plant with a spindly stem*

spine BONE /spaɪn/, **back·bone**, *medical* **spin·al col·umn** *n* [C] the line of bones down the centre of the back that provides support for the body and protects the **spinal cord** • *She seriously injured her spine in a riding accident.* • *These patients will benefit from a new operation to replace hopelessly damaged discs in the spine.* • *She needs an operation to correct* **curvature** *of the spine.* • *(fig.) The Apennine mountains form the spine* (= central row of mountains) *of Italy.* • You can refer to fear and excitement as physical feelings on the spine: *The sound of footsteps coming closer* **sent shivers up/down** *her spine* (= frightened her). ○ *The film/story/information was* **spine-chilling** (= very frightening). ○ *The thought of the meeting* **sent** *little* **tingles** *of anticipation* **up and down** *his spine* (= excited him). ○ *Watching Christie win the Olympic hundred metres was one of those* **spine-tingling** (= very special and exciting) *moments.* • PIC> **Spine**

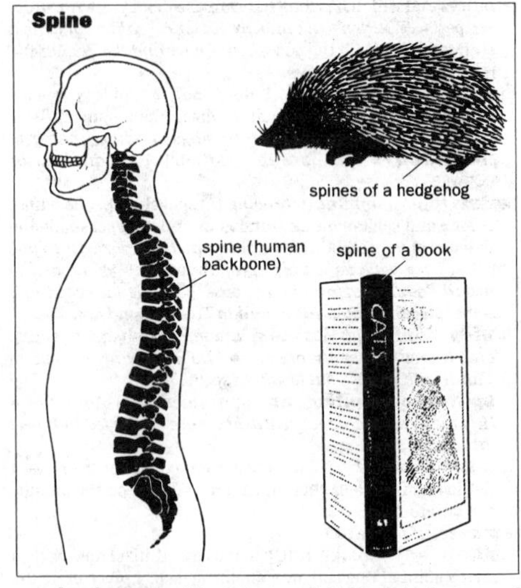

spin·al /ˈspaɪ·nəl/ *adj* [not gradable] • Spinal means of the spine: *spinal fluid* ○ *a spinal injury* ○ *a spinal disorder* • **Spinal column** is a medical word for spine. • *He suffered an accident in which his* **spinal cord** (= the set of nerves inside the spine which connect the brain to other nerves in the body) *was damaged.*

spine·less /ˈspaɪn·ləs/ *adj disapproving* • Someone who is spineless lacks determination and the willingness to take risks: *After the eighth refusal letter, she decided that American publishers were a spineless lot.*

spine·less·ly /ˈspaɪn·lə·sli/ *adv disapproving* • *"I agree with Margaret," he replied spinelessly.*

spine·less·ness /ˈspaɪn·lə·snəs/ *n* [U] *disapproving*

spine POINT /spaɪn/ *n* [C] a long sharp needle-like point growing out of an animal or plant • *Hedgehogs and cacti have spines.*

spin·y /ˈspaɪ·ni/ *adj* **-ier, -iest** • *The stems of the plant are spiny* (= covered with long sharp points). • *Some small animals have a spiny covering to protect them.*

spine BOOK PART /spaɪn/ *n* [C] the narrow strip where the cover of a book is joined to the pages, usually with the title and writer's name printed on it • *It was an old book in bad condition and when she tried to open it fully, she* **broke** *the spine.* • PIC> **Spine**

spin·i·fex /ˈspɪn·ɪ·feks/ *n* [U] a grass with SPINES (= sharp points) which grows esp. on sand hills in Australia

spin·ney /ˈspɪn·i/ *n* [C] *esp. Br* a small wood; a COPSE

spin·ster /£ˈspɪnt·stəʳ, $-stɚ/ *n* [C] a woman who is not married, esp. a woman who is no longer young and seems unlikely ever to marry • *A spinster who played the stock market from her tiny terrace home has left almost £2 million to charity.* • *Early on she had come to accept that as a career woman scientist she was virtually committed to being a spinster.* • *(disapproving) She's become a typical spinster – can't understand why with four children my house is always untidy!* • *He left his Montana ranch to his spinster sister.*

spi·ral /£ˈspaɪə·rəl, $ˈspaɪr·əl/ *n* [C] a shape made up of curves, each one above or wider than the one before • *Our galaxy, the Milky Way, is a spiral.* • *A corkscrew is spiral-***shaped**. • *The bird rose in the air in a slow, ascending* *spiral.* • *(fig.) The recent* **downward** *spiral of home prices has depressed the market.* • *(fig.) We must avoid the* **downward** *spiral in which unemployment leads to homelessness and then to crime.* • A **spiral-bound** book has a spiral-shaped piece of metal or plastic holding its pages together.

spi•ral /£'spaɪə·rᵊl, $'spaɪr·əl/ *adj* [before n; not gradable] • *a spiral staircase* • *a spiral galaxy*

spi•ral /£'spaɪə·rᵊl, $'spaɪr·əl/ *v* [I always + adv/prep] **-ll-** or *Am usually* **-l-** • *With one wing damaged, the model airplane spiralled downwards.* • If costs, prices, etc. spiral, they increase faster and faster: *Spiralling costs have squeezed profits.* • If costs, prices, etc. spiral **downwards**, they get less, at a faster and faster rate.

spire /£spaɪəʳ, $spaɪr/ *n* [C] a tall pointed structure on top of a building, esp. a church tower • *The church spire was struck by lightning.* • Ⓘ

spi•rit WAY OF FEELING /'spɪr·ɪt/ *n* [U] a particular way of thinking, feeling or behaving, esp. a way that is typical of a particular group of people, an activity, a time or a place • *After she read the letter I could see she was* **in fighting** *spirit and determined to have the decision changed.* • *It's very important to play the game* **in the right** *spirit, and not make trouble for anyone.* • *The players have a very strong* **team** *spirit* (= loyalty to each other). • *A group of Russian musicians and actors brought the spirit* **of** *their homeland to Boston last night.* • *As rock musicians in the 1960s, they were very much part of the spirit* **of the age/times.** • *We acted* **in** *a spirit* **of co-operation.** • *They went to the tennis club a few times but never really* **entered/got into the spirit of** *it* (= did not show much enthusiasm or enjoyment). • The spirit **of** a law, rule, etc. is the principle that you believe it was created to strengthen rather than the particular things it says you must or must not do: *They followed neither the spirit nor the letter of the law.* • *"Come on, we can win this game."* **"That's the spirit** (= That's the best way to think and act)."

spi•rits /'spɪr·ɪts/ *pl n* • *I've been* **in high/low** *spirits* (= feeling happy/sad) *lately.* • *Her spirits* **rose** (= She felt happier) *as she read the letter.* • *The negative reply* **dashed** *his spirits* (= made him unhappy).

-spi•rit•ed /£-'spɪr·ɪ·tɪd, $-t̬ɪd/ *combining form* • *The children are rather* **high**-*spirited*/**low**-*spirited* (= happy/ sad). • *This morning, some very* **public**-*spirited citizens are organizing a clean-up of the market area.*

spi•rit NOT MATTER /'spɪr·ɪt/ *n* the characteristics of a person that are considered as being separate from the body, and which many religions believe continue to exist after the body dies • *He is a man with great strength of spirit and purpose, a man of great courage.* [U] • *All her long life she remained young* **in** *spirit, bubbling with interests and ideas.* [U] • *Although he's now living in America, I feel he's with me* **in** *spirit* (= I feel he is present and is influencing me, in a way that is not physical). [U] • *The torture failed to* **break** *their spirit* (= destroy their confidence, strength of mind, loyalty, etc.). [U] • *It's impossible to predict what he'll do – he just acts* **as/when the spirit moves** *him* (= in a completely unplanned way). • *(humorous saying)* 'The spirit is willing but the flesh is weak' means you would like to do something, but do not have the time, skills, energy etc. to do it. [C] • A spirit is also the form of a dead person, similar to a GHOST, or the presence of a dead person which you can feel but not see: *The spirits of long-dead warriors seemed to haunt the area.* [C] ○ *The shaman claimed to have cast out many* **evil** *spirits.* [C] ○ *She communicates with the spirit* **world.**

spi•rit•ual /'spɪr·ɪ·tju·əl/ *adj* • *Traditional ways of life provided economic security and spiritual fulfilment* (= that is not physical). • *The Dalai Lama is the spiritual* (= religious) *and temporal leader of Tibet.* • A **spiritual home** is a place where you feel you belong, even though you were not born there, because you have a lot in common with the people, the culture and the way of life: *I feel that America is my true spiritual home.* • **Spiritual healing** is the activity of making a person healthy without using medicines or other physical methods, sometimes as part of a religious ceremony: *Spiritual healing has an ancient pedigree, with much evidence of success.* ○ *He was a well-known* **spiritual healer.**

spi•rit•ual•ly /'spɪr·ɪ·tju·ə·li/ *adv*

spi•rit•u•al•i•ty /£,spɪr·ɪ·tju'æl·ɪ·ti, $-ə·t̬i/ *n* [U] *approving* • *He brought wide scholarship and deep spirituality* (= understanding of the religious and not material parts of life) *to his post as Bishop of Bath.*

spi•rit•ual•i•sm /'spɪr·ɪ·tju·ᵊl·ɪ·zᵊm/ *n* [U] • Spiritualism is the belief that living people can communicate with people who have died.

spi•rit•ual•ist /'spɪr·ɪ·tju·ᵊl·ɪst/ *n* [C] • *A spiritualist had told her he could give her a message from her dead husband.*

spi•rit ENTHUSIASM /'spɪr·ɪt/ *n* [U] *approving* enthusiasm and energy • *The orchestra performed the Rite of Spring* **with** *great spirit.*

spi•rit•ed /£'spɪr·ɪ·tɪd, $-t̬ɪd/ *adj approving* • *The home team's spirited playing ensured them a comfortable victory.* • *She made a spirited reply to a question from the opposition spokesperson.*

spi•rit•less /'spɪr·ɪt·ləs/ *adj disapproving* • *It was rather a spiritless performance* (= lacking energy and enthusiasm).

spi•rit DRINK /'spɪr·ɪt/ *n* a strong alcoholic drink • *Vodka is a type of spirit.* [U] • *Spirits are more expensive than beer, but they get you drunk faster.* [C] • Some types of spirit are alcoholic liquids used esp. for cleaning, mixing with paint, etc.: *white spirit* [U]

spi•rit *(obj)* MOVE /'spɪr·ɪt/ *T always + adv/prep* to move (someone or something) into, out of or away from a place secretly • *I left my bike outside and someone spirited it* **away** *during the night.* • *Somehow the prisoners managed to spirit news* **out** *to the world outside.*

spi•rit–lev•el /£'spɪr·ɪt,lev·l̩/ *n* [C] a tool containing a tube of liquid with an air bubble in it, which shows whether a surface is level by the position of the bubble • PIC **Building and construction**

spi•rit•ual /'spɪr·ɪ·tju·əl/, **ne•gro spi•rit•ual** *n* [C] a type of religious song, originally developed by African Americans in the US • Ⓢ

spit *(obj)* FORCE OUT /spɪt/ *v* **spitting**, *past* **spat** /spæt/ or *Am also* **spit** to force out the contents of the mouth, esp. SALIVA (= a liquid produced in the mouth) • *The boys were competing to see how far they could spit.* [I] • *She spat contemptuously right* **in** *his* **face** (= forced out SALIVA onto his face to show her angry feelings). [I] • *They bought watermelons and ate them as they walked, spitting* **out** *the seeds.* [M] • *(fig.) He spat* **out** (= said quickly and angrily) *an insult in some foreign language.* [M] • If something hot, such as a fire, spits it produces short sharp noises and throws out little bits: *There was bacon already spitting in the frying pan.* [I] • If you **spit blood/venom/***(Am also)* **nails/***(Aus also)* **tacks** you speak in an angry way, or to show anger: *I thought he was going to split blood when he saw what had happened.* • *(infml)* If you say **spit it out** to someone, you are suggesting that they tell you something which they are not very willing or are taking a long time to say: *Come on, spit it out, who told you about this?* • *(infml)* If something is **in/within spitting distance**, it is very close: *The house is within spitting distance* **of the sea.** • If someone or something is **the spitting image of** someone or something else, they look extremely similar to them: *Josie is the spitting image of her granny at the same age.* See also **the spit (and image)** at SPIT *n.*

spit /spɪt/, *fml* **spit•tle** /£'spɪt·l̩, $'spɪt̬-/, *Aus infml* **slag** *n* [U] • Spit is an informal word for SALIVA (= water-like liquid produced in the mouth), esp. when it is outside the mouth: *She used a little spit on a tissue to wipe the mirror clean.* • *(infml)* If someone is **the spit (and image) of** someone else, they look extremely similar to them: *The old man was the* **(dead)** *spit of Winston Churchill.* See also **spitting image** at SPIT *v.* • *(infml) The car needs some* **spit and polish** (= careful cleaning and shining).

spit RAIN /spɪt/ *v* [I] **spitting** *infml* to rain very slightly • *If* **it's** *only spitting* **(with rain)**, *perhaps we don't need waterproofs.* • *I think* **it's** *starting to spit* **(with rain).**

spit ROD /spɪt/ *n* [C] a long thin rod put through a piece of food, esp. meat, so that it can be cooked above a fire • *spit-roasted lamb*

spit LAND /spɪt/ *n* [C] a long, thin, flat beach which goes out into the sea • *Spits often shelter river mouths.*

spit•ball /£'spɪt·bɔːl, $-bɑːl/ *n* [C] *Am* a piece of paper that has been chewed and then rolled into a ball to be thrown or shot at someone

spite HURT /spaɪt/ *n* [U] the desire to annoy, upset or hurt someone, esp. in a small way • *He's the sort of man who would let down the tyres on your car just* **from** *spite/* **out of** *spite.*

spite *obj* /spaɪt/ *v* [T] • *I almost think he died without making a will just to spite his family.*

spite•ful /'spaɪt·fᵊl/ *adj disapproving* • *One of the characters in the film is a spiteful eleven-year-old who* *punches and slaps the other children and frightens them with horror stories.* • *They say such spiteful things about their sister.*

spite·ful·ly /ˈspaɪt·fᵊl·i/ *adv disapproving*

spite·ful·ness /ˈspaɪt·fᵊl·nəs/ *n* [U] *disapproving*

spite DESPITE /spaɪt/ *n* [U] **in spite of** (used before one fact that makes another fact surprising) despite • *In spite of his* (= Although he has an) *injury, Ricardo will play in Saturday's match.* • *She was, in spite of* (= Although she has) *fame and fortune, basically an unhappy woman.* • *Well, it was a good holiday, in spite of* **everything** (= although there were problems and things that went wrong). • *She started to laugh, in spite of her***self** (= although she was trying not to).

spit·toon /spɪˈtuːn/, *Am also* **cus·pi·dor** *n* [C] a container, used esp. in the past, placed on the floor in a public place for SPITTING into

spiv /spɪv/ *n* [C] *Br dated infml disapproving* a man, esp. well-dressed in a way that attracts attention, who makes money dishonestly

splash *(obj)* /splæʃ/, *esp. Br infml also* **splosh** *v* to cause (an amount of liquid) to move through the air, usually with a loud noise, by hitting it, moving through it, or throwing it • *She splashed her face with cold water.* [T] • *He splashed water* **in** *her face to try and waken her.* [T] • *She poured a large gin and splashed soda* **into** *it from a siphon.* [T] • *The kids were splashing* **(about)** *in the shallow end of the swimming pool.* [I always + adv/prep] • If liquid splashes or if it splashes something, it hits something and scatters small drops over it: *Water was splashing from a hole in the roof.* [I always + adv/prep] ○ *Unfortunately some paint splashed* **(onto)** *the rug.* [T; I + prep] ○ *A stream of coffee splashed* **(over)** *the counter.* [T; I + prep] • *(fig.) Several newspapers splashed* (= printed in a very noticeable way) *colour pictures of Princess Di* **across** *their front pages.* [T] • **Splash-down** *is estimated to be at 1900 hours.*

splash /splæʃ/ *n* [C] • *We heard a splash* (= noise of something hitting water) *and then saw that Toni had fallen in the river.* • **A** *splash* (= small amount) **of** *fruit juice over a fruit sorbet makes a simple refreshing dessert.* • *The little girl in her flowery dress provides the only splash* **of colour** (= bright object) *in the picture.* • *(fig.)* If you **make a splash**, you are or you become suddenly very successful or well known: *Jodie Foster made quite a splash in 'Taxi Driver'.* • **Splash guard** is *esp. Am for* MUDFLAP.

splash /splæʃ/ *adv* [not gradable] • *The ball fell splash into the river.*

splash out *(obj) v adv Br and Aus* to spend (a lot of money) on buying things, esp. luxury goods; SPLURGE • *In a recession people are reluctant to splash out* **on** *consumer goods like TVs, dishwashers, etc.* [I] • *They splashed out £2000* **on** *their wedding.* [T]

splash·y /ˈsplæʃ·i/ *adj* **-ier, -iest** *Am* unnecessarily expensive, exciting, etc. • *Hollywood tends to make splashy films with lots of star actors.*

splat /splæt/ *n* [U] *infml* the sound of something wet hitting a surface or of something hitting the surface of a liquid

splat /splæt/ *adv* [not gradable] *infml* • *She fell, splat, into the water.*

splat·ter *(obj)* /£ˈsplæt·əʳ, $ˈsplæṭ·ɚ/ *v* (esp. of a thick liquid) to hit and cover (a surface) in small drops, or to cause this to happen • *The bike was splattered* **with** *mud.* [T] • *Turn the heat down, or hot fat will splatter everywhere.* [I] • *(fig.) The photographs of carnage splattered across the pages of the newspapers shocked us terribly.*

splay *(obj)* /spleɪ/ *v* to spread wide apart • *At one point the dancers flipped onto their backs and splayed their legs.* [T] • *The petals splay* **out** *from the middle of the flower.* [I]

spleen ORGAN /spliːn/ *n* [C] an organ near the stomach which produces blood before birth • (CS) (RUS)

spleen ANGER /spliːn/ *n* [U] *fml* a feeling of anger and dissatisfaction • *(esp. Br and Aus) She threatened, in a* **fit/burst of** *spleen, to resign.* • *Shareholders used the conference as an opportunity to* **vent** *their spleen* **on** (= get angry with) *the Board of Directors.* • (CS) (RUS)

splen·did /ˈsplen·dɪd/ *adj* extremely good, or (esp. of a house, work of art, or special occasion) attracting admiration and attention • *We had splendid food/a splendid holiday/splendid weather.* • *Amsterdam has some splendid eighteenth-century houses.* • *The coronation of a new king or queen is a splendid* **affair**, *with much elaborate and brilliant ceremony.* • See also RESPLENDENT.

splen·did·ly /ˈsplen·dɪd·li/ *adv* • *She had arranged a formal dinner, which went off splendidly* (= was very successful).

splen·di·fe·rous /£splenˈdɪf·ᵊr·əs, $ˈ-ɚ-/ *adj infml humorous* • *They paid £2 million for a splendiferous* (= very splendid) *apartment in the heart of London.*

splen·dour *Br and Aus, Am and Aus* **splen·dor** /£ˈsplen·dəʳ, $-dɚ/ *n* [U] great beauty which attracts admiration and attention • *They bought a decaying 16th-century manor house and restored it to its original splendour.*

splen·dours *Br and Aus, esp. Am* **splen·dors** /£ˈsplen·dəz, $-dɚz/ *pl n* • *So many writers have described the splendours* (= beautiful features) **of** *Venice.*

splice *obj* /splaɪs/ *v* [T] to join (two pieces of rope, film, etc.) together at their ends in order to form one long piece • *The machine allows segments of the film to be viewed repeatedly and at a number of speeds, so the editor can cut and splice the film.* • *Montage is splicing* **together** *different shots to create an effect not present in the shots alone.* • *Scientists have discovered how to splice pieces of DNA.* • *(infml dated)* To **get** spliced means to get married.

splice /splaɪs/ *n* [C] • *The sound engineer was joining the two bits of tape with a splice.*

spliff /splɪf/ *n* [C] *slang* a hand-rolled cigarette containing the drug MARIJUANA

splint /splɪnt/ *n* [C] a long flat object used as a support for a broken bone so that the bone stays in a particular position while it heals • *The doctor put a splint on the arm and bandaged it up.*

splint·er /£ˈsplɪn·təʳ, $-ṭɚ/ *n* [C] a small sharp broken piece of wood, glass, plastic or similar material • *The girl had got a splinter* **(of** *wood)* *in her toe.* • *The soldier suffered brain damage from shrapnel splinters.* • A **splinter group** is a group of people who have left a political party or other organization and formed a new separate organization: *The Socialist Workers' Party seemed to split into several splinter groups.*

splint·er /£ˈsplɪn·təʳ, $-ṭɚ/ *v* [I] • *The edges of the plastic cover had cracked and splintered.* • *(fig.) Will the party manage to reform itself without changing its basic structure, or will it splinter* **into** *several smaller political parties?*

split *(obj)* DIVIDE /splɪt/ *v* **splitting**, *past* **split** to (cause to) divide into two or more parts, esp. along a particular line • *The prize was split* **between** *Susan and Kate.* [T] • *Split the aubergines* **in** *half and cover with breadcrumbs.* [T] • *The teacher split the children* **(up) into** *three groups.* [T] • *I suggest we split the profits six ways/split the profits* **between** *the six of us.* [T] • *(infml) I'll split* (= share) *this croissant* **with** *you.* [T] • *Was it a good day for mankind when scientists discovered how to split* **the atom** (= break up atoms into their separate parts, so as to release energy)*?* [T] • *The woman had split her head* **open** (= got a long deep wound in her head) *when she was thrown off the horse.* [T + obj + adj] • *The wooden floor had cracked and split* (= formed cracks) *in the heat.* [I] • *His trousers split when he tried to jump the fence.* [I] • If an organization or group splits or is split, some members disagree with the other members about something: *The childcare issue has split the employers' group.* [T] ○ *The union executive has split* **down the middle** (= into two equal-sized groups who disagree with each other) *on what to do next.* [I] ○ *A group of extremists split* **(off) from** *the Labour Party to form a new "Workers' Communist Party".* [I] • *(dated infml)* To split is also to leave a place: *Let's split – but we'll meet you again at lunchtime tomorrow, okay?* [I] • *(disapproving)* If you **split hairs**, you argue about the correctness of unimportant details: *The European governments are worried about the exact figures agreed for grain imports – but they are just splitting hairs, to avoid signing the agreement.* • If you **split your sides**, you laugh a lot at something: *We nearly split our sides* **laughing/with laughter** *watching Paul trying to get the dog to go in the bicycle basket.* • If you **split the difference** you agree on a number or amount that is exactly in the middle of the difference between two other numbers or amounts: *The official price is £5000 and the black-market price would be over £15 000, so let's split the difference and call it £10 000.* • *My parents* **split up** (= ended their marriage) *when I was six.* • *I hear she's* **split up** (= ended her relationship) **with** *her boyfriend.* • A **split end** is a hair that has divided into several parts at its end: *Dry, brittle hair and split ends were the unfortunate consequence of years of dyeing it peroxide blond.* • *(specialized)* A **split infinitive** is a phrase in which an adverb or other word is put between "to" and an INFINITIVE. Some people consider split infinitives to be bad grammar, but they are becoming more acceptable: *'To quickly decide' is an example of a split infinitive.* • A **split-level** building or room has floors at different heights: *My parents have a split-level house – the living room is a few steps up from the kitchen, and a few steps down from the bedrooms.* PIC› **Accommodation** • A **split pea** is a dried PEA that has been separated into its two halves, used esp. in soups. • A **split pin** is a thin metal rod divided into two parts which open out in order to fasten parts of a machine or to stop them becoming loose. PIC› **Tools** • Someone with a **split personality** behaves so differently at different times that they seem to have more than one character. • A **split second** is a very short moment of time: *They brought out guns and for a split second nobody moved.* ○ *When the incoming missile is detected the computer starts to make split- second* (= very quick) *decisions as to its course and when to intercept it.* • A **split-up** between two people is when they end their relationship.

split /splɪt/ *n* [C] • *Rain was getting in through a split* (= crack) **in** *the plastic sheeting.* • *There is a widening split* (= division) **between** *senior managers and the rest of the workforce.* • *The tax issue has caused a split* (= division into groups who disagree with each other) **in/within** *the government.* • *There was a 55%, 25%, 20% split* **in** *the voting.* • *There was a three-***way** *split in the voting.* • A split is *Am for* **the splits**: *Carly* **did** *a split.*

splits *Br* /splɪts/ *pl n, Am* **split** *n* [C] • **The splits** is the action of sitting on the floor with your legs straight out and flat along the floor in opposite directions: *Can you* **do** *the splits?*

split·ting /£'splɪt·ɪŋ, $'splɪt̬-/ *adj* [not gradable] • A splitting **headache** is a very severe pain that you feel in your head: *Hilary arrived home from work with a splitting headache.*

split TELL /splɪt/ *v* [I] **splitting**, *past* **split** *Br and Aus dated infml* to tell other people secret and damaging information about someone • *They knew Josie wouldn't split* **on** *them* **to** *the teacher.*

splodge *esp. Br* /£splɒdʒ, $splɑːdʒ/, *Am and Aus usually* **splotch** /£splɒtʃ, $splɑːtʃ/ *n* [C] *infml* an irregularly shaped mark or spot • *He put his hand on the bed, and left a splodge of blood on the bedspread.*

splosh /£splɒʃ, $splɑːʃ/ *v* [I] *infml, esp. Br* to SPLASH • *The children sploshed* **about** *happily in the water.*

splosh /£splɒʃ, $splɑːʃ/ *n* [C] *infml, esp. Br* • A splosh is a SPLASH.

splurge *(obj)* /£splɜːdʒ, $splɜːrdʒ/ *v infml* to spend (a lot of money) on buying esp. luxury goods; SPLASH OUT • *The choice is saving the money or splurging it* **on** *a new car.* [T] • *I feel like splurging* **(out) on** *a new dress.* [I]

splurge /£splɜːdʒ, $splɜːrdʒ/ *n* [C] *infml* • *I* **had** *a splurge* **on** *cosmetics recently – I just needed a new image!*

splut·ter *(obj)* /£'splʌt·əʳ, $'splʌt̬·ɚ/ *v* (of a person) to speak in a quick and confused way, producing short unclear noises because of surprise, anger, etc., or (of a person or thing) to make a series of noises similar to this • *The old gentleman in the corner of the carriage was spluttering* **with** *indignation at something he was reading in his newspaper.* [I] • *"But...er...when...um...how?" he spluttered.* [+ clause] • *She took too big a gulp of whisky and started to cough and splutter.* [I] • *The bacon in the frying pan was spluttering and spitting fat.* [I]

splut·ter /£'splʌt·əʳ, $'splʌt̬·ɚ/ *n* [C] • *The candle* **gave** *a splutter or two and went out.*

spoil *(obj)* DESTROY /spɔɪl/ *v past Br and Aus* **spoilt** /spɔɪlt/ or *Am usually* **spoiled** /spɔɪlt, spɔɪld/ to destroy or reduce the pleasure, interest or beauty of (something) • *He tried not to let the bad news spoil his evening.* [T] • *I haven't seen the film, so don't spoil it for me by telling me what happens.* [T] • *Oil companies that spoil beautiful coastlines face billions of dollars in fines and clean-up costs.* [T] • *You'll spoil your* **appetite** *for dinner if you have a cake now.* [T] • When food spoils or is spoilt it is no longer good enough to eat: *The dessert will spoil if you don't keep it in the fridge.* [I] ○ *The dinner was spoilt because he put the oven on too high.* [T] • *(Br specialized)* To spoil a **(ballot) paper** is to make it so that it cannot be officially counted as a vote, esp. by making a mark on it that is not officially allowed: *Since she supported none of the candidates and disagreed with the electoral system anyway, she spoiled her ballot paper.* [T] • To **spoil** someone's **party** or to **spoil the party for** someone is to cause trouble for them at a moment when they are enjoying a success: *Scotland spoiled England's party by scoring an equalizing goal in the last minute of the match.*

spoil·er /£'spɔɪ·ləʳ, $-lɚ/ *n* [C] • A spoiler is a newspaper or magazine, an article in a newspaper or magazine, a television or radio programme, etc. that is produced just before or at the same time as another similar one in order to take attention away from it. • See also SPOILER.

spoil *obj* TREAT WELL /spɔɪl/ *v* [T] *past Br and Aus* **spoilt** /spɔɪlt/ or *Am usually* **spoiled** /spɔɪlt, spɔɪld/ to treat (someone) very or too well, esp. by being extremely generous • *When I'm feeling miserable I go shopping and spoil my***self** *– a couple of new dresses always make me feel better.* • *"I have tickets for the opera", he said. "Oh, you're spoiling me", she replied, laughingly.* • *There's so much good theatre and cinema in London, really one is spoilt* **for choice** (= it is difficult to choose one particular one). • To spoil a child is to allow it to behave exactly as it wants to and to give it too much praise and attention, so that it becomes selfish and lacking in care and respect for other people: *Her parents spoilt and indulged her with toys and treats of every kind.* ○ *Peters, unable for once to do exactly as he wanted, sulked just like a spoilt* **child**.

spoil RUBBISH /spɔɪl/ *n* [U] earth, stones, etc. dug out from a hole in the ground • *a spoil heap* • *Digging the tunnel produced millions of tonnes of spoil.*

spoil for *obj v prep* [T] **spoiling for a fight** very eager to fight or argue • *Local councillors are spoiling for a fight over plans to close two village schools.*

spoil·er /£'spɔɪ·ləʳ, $-lɚ/ *n* [C] a device on a car or aircraft which is positioned so that it stops the air from flowing very smoothly around the vehicle • *The spoiler on a sports car helps to keep its wheels on the ground.* • See also **spoiler** at SPOIL DESTROY. • PIC› **Car**

spoils /spɔɪlz/ *pl n fml* goods, advantages, profits, etc. obtained by your actions or because of your position or situation • *The spoils* **of victory/war** *included mounds of treasure and armour.* • *After the coalition victory, the difficulty was to* **divide** *the spoils equally among the victorious ministers.*

spoil·sport /£'spɔɪl·spɔːt, $-spɔːrt/ *n* [C] *infml disapproving* a person who stops other people from enjoying themselves • *She did ask her Dad if she could have a big party, but the old spoilsport refused.*

spoke SPEAK /£spəuk, $spouk/ *past simple of* SPEAK

spoke WHEEL PART /£spəuk, $spouk/ *n* [C] any of the rods that join the edge of a wheel to its centre, so giving the wheel its strength • *a bicycle spoke* • *(infml)* To **put a spoke in** (someone's **wheel**) is to make it difficult for them to achieve something they had planned to do: *Well, the rise in interest rates will put a spoke in the government's wheel as far as their plan for economic recovery goes.* ○ *His letter really put a spoke in our plans.* • PIC› **Bicycles**

spok·en SPEAK /£'spəu·kᵊn, $'spou-/ *past participle of* SPEAK

–spok·en MANNER OF SPEECH /£-'spəu·kᵊn, $-'spou-/ *combining form* speaking in a particular way • *a softly spoken young man* • *a well-spoken lady*

spok·en for *adj* [after v; not gradable] (of a thing) already sold to or kept for the use of someone or (*dated* of a person) already having a relationship with another person • *Most of the best paintings in the exhibition were spoken for.* • *(dated) Both girls were spoken for.*

spokes·per·son *(pl* **-people***)*, **spokes·man** *(pl* **-men***)*, **spokes·wo·man** *(pl* **-women***)* /£'spəuks,pɜː·sᵊn, $'spouks,pɜːr-/ *n* [C] a person chosen by a group or organization to give their opinions in public and to speak officially for them • *a government spokesperson* • *a spokeswoman* **for** *the environmental group Greenpeace*

spon·du·licks, spon·du·lix /£spɒn'duː·lɪks, $spɑːn-/ *pl n dated infml humorous* MONEY • *He couldn't come up with the spondulicks.*

sponge SUBSTANCE /spʌndʒ/ *n* a soft substance that is full of small holes and can absorb a lot of liquid, and is used for washing and cleaning • *Sponge is either artificial or it is the soft skeleton of a simple sea creature of the same name.* [U] • *He rubbed her back with a soapy sponge.* [C] • *Give it* **a** *sponge* (= Rub it) **with** *a damp cloth – that will remove the blood stains.* [U] • *(Br and Aus)* A **sponge bag** is a small waterproof bag used for carrying your TOOTHBRUSH, FACECLOTH, soap, etc. when you are travelling. • **Sponge rubber** is *Am for* **foam rubber**. See at FOAM.

sponge *obj* /spʌndʒ/ *v* [T] • To sponge something or someone **(down/off)** is to clean them by rubbing with a wet cloth or sponge: *Most food stains will come off if you sponge the material (down) with a little detergent.*

spong·y /ˈspʌn·dʒi/ *adj* **-ier, -iest** • *After all that rain the pitch was very spongy* (=like a sponge), *and the ball ran slowly over it.*

sponge *(obj)* GET MONEY /spʌndʒ/ *v disapproving* to get (money, food, etc.) from other people, esp. in order to live without working • *There must be a growing realization among younger people that sponging* **off** *the state is no longer possible.* [I] • *Could I sponge a cigarette* (**off** *you)?* [T]

spong·er /£ˈspʌn·dʒəʳ, $-dʒɚ/ *n* [C] *disapproving* • *Vinny, the ultimate sponger, managed to live for three years off the generosity of various soft-hearted friends.*

sponge (cake) /spʌndʒ/ *n* a soft cake made with eggs, sugar and flour but usually no fat • *He'd made a chocolate sponge.* [C] • *Trifle consists of a layer of sponge together with fruit, custard and cream.* [U] • PIC〉 **Bread and cakes**

spon·sor *obj* /£ˈspɒnt·səʳ, $ˈspɑːnt·sɚ/ *v* [T] to support (a person, organization or activity) by giving money, encouragement or other help • *The team is sponsored by JVC, so the players wear the letters JVC on their shirts.* • *Eva said she was doing a ten-mile walk for charity and asked if I'd sponsor her* **for** *£1 a mile.* • *Before you can get a visa to live in Britain, you need to find someone who will officially sponsor you.* • *(specialized) The Environment Bill is being sponsored by a Liberal Democrat MP.*

spon·sor /£ˈspɒnt·səʳ, $ˈspɑːnt·sɚ/ *n* [C] • *All the major theatres now have sponsors, especially* **for** *particular high-cost productions.* • *She got a family friend in Bristol to agree to be her sponsor.*

spon·sor·ship /£ˈspɒnt·sə·ʃɪp, $ˈspɑːnt·sɚ-/ *n* [U] • *The orchestra receives £2 million a year* **in** *sponsorship.* • *It's becoming harder to* **get** *sponsorship these days.*

spon·ta·ne·ous /£spɒnˈteɪ·ni·əs, $spɑːn-/ *adj* happening or done in a natural, often sudden way, without any planning or without being forced • *When people saw pictures of the atrocities on TV, there was a spontaneous reaction against the war.* • *Her witticisms seemed spontaneous, but were in fact carefully prepared beforehand.* • *(approving) The Italians are generally so much more spontaneous, open and friendly than the British.* • *There have been a few cases reported of people dying by* **spontaneous combustion** (=by starting to burn without any obvious cause).

spon·ta·ne·ous·ly /£spɒnˈteɪ·ni·ə·sli, $spɑːn-/ *adv* • *She spontaneously offered us a bed for the night.* • *The liquid spontaneously ignited.*

spon·ta·ne·i·ty /£ˌspɒn·təˈneɪ·ɪ·ti, $ˌspɑːn·t̬əˈneɪ·ə·t̬i/ *n* [U] *approving* • *The script has a refreshing spontaneity and sparkle.*

spoof COPY /spuːf/ *n* [C] an amusing and ridiculous piece of writing, music, theatre, etc. that copies the style of an original work • *They did a spoof* **on/of** *the Nine O'Clock News.* • *It was a spoof cowboy film.*

spoof *(obj)* DECEIVE /spuːf/ *v* [I/T] *Am infml* to try to make (someone) believe in something that is not true, as a joke • *He wondered if the others were spoofing (him), or if it could really be true.*

spook SPIRIT /spuːk/ *n* [C] *infml for* GHOST • *The film was dreadful – all spooks and vampires.* • *a spook story* • *the spook world*

spook *obj* /spuːk/ *v* [T] *esp. Am* • To spook a person or animal is to frighten them: *Seeing the police car outside the house really spooked them.*

spook·y /ˈspuː·ki/ *adj* **-ier, -iest** *infml* • *It was a spooky* (=strange and frightening) *coincidence.*

spook PERSON /spuːk/ *n* [C] *Am for* SPY SECRET PERSON

spool /spuːl/ *n* [C] a tube-shaped object with top and bottom edges that stick out and around which a length of thread, wire, film, etc. is wrapped in order to store it • *a spool* **of** *cotton* • *spools* **of** *film*

spoon /spuːn/ *n* [C] an object consisting of a round hollow part with a handle, used for mixing, serving and eating food • *Could I have a clean spoon, please?* • *Use a wooden spoon for stirring and mixing ingredients while cooking.* • Spoon is also used as a combining form: *a soup spoon* ○ *a teaspoon* ○ *a tablespoon* • A spoon (also **spoonful**) is also an amount held on a particular spoon: *a couple of spoons* **of** *sauce* • To **spoon-feed** a baby or other person is to feed them using a spoon because they cannot feed themselves. • *(disapproving)* To **spoon-feed** someone is to present information to them in a very simple and complete way, so that they do not need to think about it: *By giving out printed sheets of facts and theories, the teachers spoon-fed us* **with** *what we needed for the exam.* • See also DESSERTSPOON; TABLESPOON; TEASPOON. • PIC〉 **Cutlery**

spoon /spuːn/ *v* [T always + adv/prep] • *He spooned the mush* **into** *the baby's ever-open mouth.* • *Spoon a little sauce* **over** *the fish.*

spoon·ful /ˈspuːn·fʊl/ *n* [C] *pl* **spoonfuls** or **spoonsful** /ˈspuːnz·fʊl/ • *a spoonful of mustard* • *"A spoonful of sugar helps the medicine go down"* (song from the film *Mary Poppins,* 1964)

spoon·er·i·sm /£ˈspuː·nᵊr·ɪ·zᵊm, $-nɚ-/ *n* [C] a mistake made when speaking in which the first sounds of two words are exchanged with each other to produce a not intended and esp. amusing meaning • *The Reverend William Spooner used to produce spoonerisms such as 'a scoop of boy trouts', instead of what he had meant to say – 'a troop of boy scouts'.*

spoor /£spɔːʳ, $spʊr/ *n* [C] *specialized* the marks left by a wild animal as it travels

spo·rad·ic /spəˈræd·ɪk/ *adj* happening irregularly; not regular or continuous • *sporadic gunfire* • *a sporadic drug-taking habit* • *a sporadic electricity supply* • *More than 100 people have been killed this year in sporadic outbursts of ethnic violence.*

spo·rad·i·cal·ly /spəˈræd·ɪ·kli/ *adv* • *The volcanoes have been erupting sporadically over the last ten years.*

spore /£spɔːʳ, $spɔːr/ *n* [C] a seed-like part of a simple organism • *This group of bacteria have the ability to change into a dormant form called a spore if the cell starts to run out of food.* • *In dry weather mosses suddenly scatter their spores.* • *Other allergens are house dust, spores of fungi, and animal hairs.*

spor·ran /£ˈspɒr·ᵊn, $ˈspɔːr·ən/ *n* [C] a small bag usually made of fur worn hanging from a belt, in front of the KILT (= type of skirt), by a person wearing traditional Scottish clothes

sport GAME /£spɔːt, $spɔːrt/ *n* a game, competition or activity needing physical effort and skill that is played or done according to rules, for enjoyment and/or as a job • *Rugby and American football are* **contact** *sports in which players receive a lot of injuries.* [C] • **Indoor** *sports include fencing and squash.* [C] • *Football, cricket and hockey are all* **team** *sports.* [C] • *I enjoy* **winter** *sports like skiing and skating.* [C] • *(Br and Aus) She used to* **do/play** *a lot of sport when she was younger.* [U] • *Hunting* **for** *sport* (=as an enjoyable activity) *rather than because of the need to find food is something many British people think is wrong.* [U] • *(fig.) As kids they used to shoplift just* **for** *sport/for the sport of it* (=for amusement). [U] • LP〉 **Sports** Ⓣ

sport·ing /£ˈspɔː·tɪŋ, $ˈspɔːr·t̬ɪŋ/ *adj* • Sporting means relating to sports: *The Olympics is the biggest sporting event in the world.* ○ *We have to face the fact that we're no longer the great sporting nation that we once were.* • *(dated approving)* If someone who is playing sport behaves in a sporting way he or she shows fairness, respect and generosity towards the opposing team or player: *Distracting your opponent when he's serving mightn't be against the rules, but it certainly isn't very sporting.* • If there is a **sporting chance** that something good will happen it is possible that it will happen: *It's not definite that they'll accept our offer, but there's a sporting chance.*

sports /£spɔːts, $spɔːrts/ *adj* [before n; not gradable] • Sports means relating to sport: *He only reads the sports pages of the newspaper.* ○ *They mainly sell sports equipment.* ○ *It's the school sports day on Monday.* • A **sports car** is a fast low car, often for two people only: *She drives a flashy black sports car.* • A **sports jacket** is a man's jacket made of TWEED (=thick woollen cloth). • PIC〉 **Vehicles**

sports·per·son (*pl* **-people**), **sports·man** (*pl* **-men**), **sports·wo·man** (*pl* **-women**) /£ˈspɔːts,pɜː·sᵊn, $ˈspɔːrts,pɜːr-/ *n* [C] • A sportsperson is someone who plays sport, esp. one who is good at it. • A sportsman is also a man who play sports in a way that shows respect, fairness and generosity towards the opposing player or team: *He'll be remembered both as a brilliant footballer and as a true sportsman.*

sports·man·like /£ˈspɔːts·mən·laɪk, $ˈspɔːrts-/ *adj* • *It was very sportsmanlike* (=fair) *of you to admit your shot had gone out after the umpire had said it was in.*

sports·man·ship /£ˈspɔːts·mən·ʃɪp, $ˈspɔːrts-/ *n* [U] • Sportsmanship is the quality of showing fairness, respect and generosity towards the opposing team or player when playing sport.

sport·y /£ˈspɔː·ti, $ˈspɔːr·t̬i/ *adj* **-ier, -iest** • A person who is sporty enjoys sport and is good at it: *He's not really*

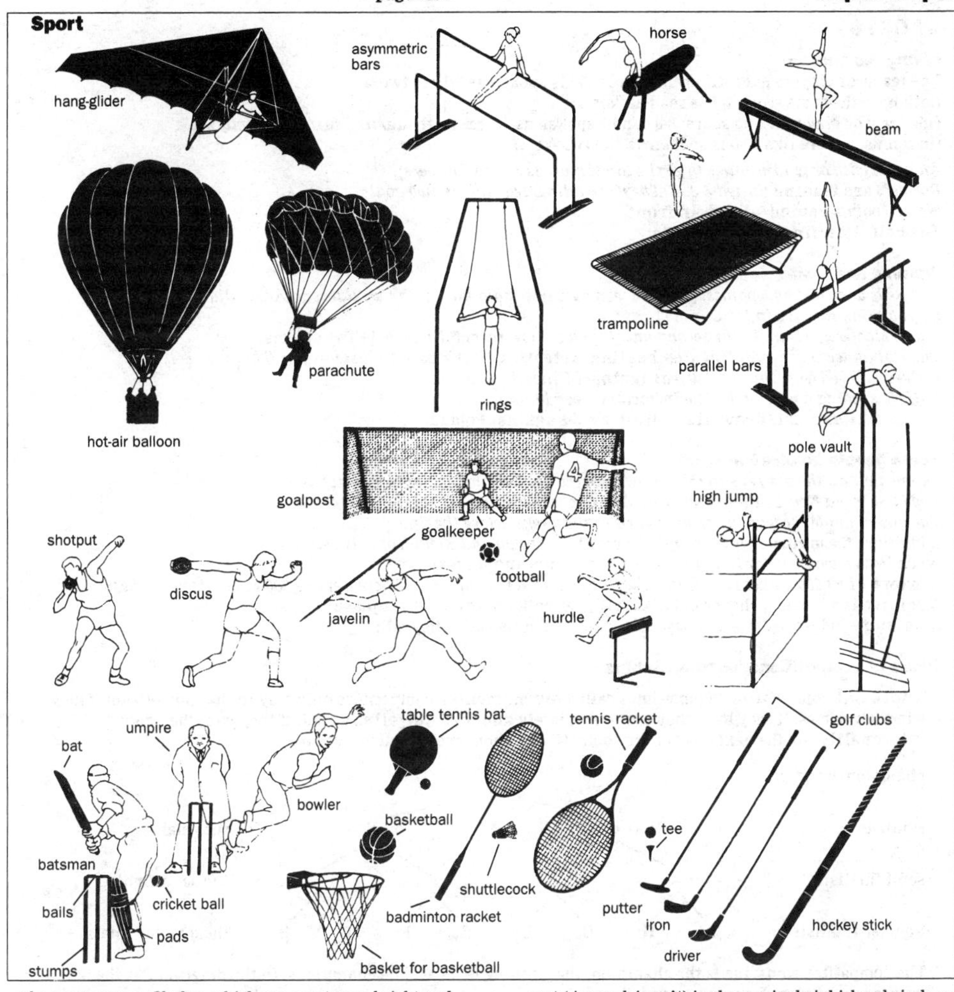

the sporty type. • Clothes which are sporty are bright and informal, often looking like the type of clothes that you could wear for sports: *I thought I'd go for the sporty look in my long blue shorts and sweatshirt.* • A sporty car is a fast low car, often for two people only: *She turned up in a sporty red two-seater.*

sport PERSON /£spɔːt, $spɔːrt/ *n* [C] *infml* a pleasant, positive, generous person who does not complain about things they are asked to do or about games that they lose • *(dated) Oh, Douglas – be a* **(good)** *sport and give me a lift to the station.* • *(Aus)* Sport is also used as a friendly way of addressing someone: *Hallo sport – how are you?* [as form of address] • See also SPOILSPORT. • (T)

sport *obj* WEAR /£spɔːt, $spɔːrt/ *v* [T] to wear or be decorated with (something) • *Back in the 1960s he sported bell-bottom trousers, platform heels and hair down past his shoulders.* • *The front of the car sported a German flag.* • (T)

sports·cast·er /£'spɔːts,kaː·stəʳ, $'spɔːrts,kæs·tɚ/ *n* [C] *esp. Am* someone who appears on television or radio, giving information and news about sporting events • *Channel 5 sportscaster Steve Bucken will present a new sports show in the Summer, concentrating on the 1994 Soccer World Cup.*

sports·wear /£'spɔːts·weəʳ, $'spɔːrts·wer/ *n* [U] (used esp. in shops) clothes that are worn for sports or other physical activities • *You'll find tennis shoes in the sportswear department.* • LP› **Shopping goods**

spot CIRCLE /£spɒt, $spaːt/ *n* [C] a small round or roundish area of colour which is differently coloured, lighter or darker than the background • Spots can form a pattern: *I wore that skirt with the green spots.* ○ *Spots and stripes are fashionable this year.* • Spots might exist singly or in small numbers: *I saw some spots of blood on the floor.* ○ *There are usually a few spots of grease on his tie.* • *(Br)* A spot (*Am and Aus* **zit**) is also a raised pinkish red circle on the skin which is temporary: *Teenagers suffer a lot from spots.* ○ *Stop* **picking** *your spots!* • *(esp. Br)* A spot **of** something can also mean a small amount or drop of it: *Shall we stop for a spot of lunch?* ○ *I'm having a spot of* **bother** (= some trouble) *with one of my back teeth.* ○ *I think I just felt a spot of rain.* ○ *"Cream in your coffee?" "Just a spot, please."* • **Spot-welding** is a way of joining together two pieces of wire or two flat pieces of metal by sending an electric current through small areas of them. • (D) (F)

spot /£spɒt, $spaːt/ *v* [I] **-tt-** *Br* • If someone says **it's** spotting **(with rain)** they mean that a few drops of rain are falling.

spot·ted /£'spɒt·ɪd, $'spaː·t̬ɪd/ *adj* [not gradable] • *She was wearing a black and white spotted dress.* • *The pavement was spotted with rain.* • *(Br)* **Spotted dick** is an old-fashioned, heavy sweet dish, often boiled in a pan, which contains dried fruit such as CURRANTS. • *(Aus)* A **spotted gum** is a tree that has a trunk that is pale with small darker areas.

spot·ty /£'spɒt·i, $'spaː·t̬i/ *adj* **-ier, -iest** • *(Br and Aus)* If someone is spotty they have spots on their skin: *I knew him when he was just a spotty youth.* ○ *I get spotty if I eat too much chocolate.* ○ *She's got such a spotty skin.* • *(Am and Aus)* Spotty (*Br and Aus* **patchy**) is used to mean bad in some parts: *She has a fairly spotty work record.* ○ *Sales have picked up a little but they're still spotty.*

spot *obj* SEE /£spɒt, $spaːt/ *v* [T] **-tt-** to see or notice (someone or something) usually when it involves looking hard • *A group of sharks were spotted off the coast earlier this month.* • *I've just spotted Malcolm – he's over there, near the entrance.* • *If you spot any mistakes in the article just mark them with a pencil.* • *I've spotted a linen jacket that I think I might buy.* • *The police spotted him driving a stolen*

SPORTS

Giving the score

The teams or players have different scores: 3-2 is spoken as "three two".
Both have the same score: 6-6 is read as "six **all**".
One team or player has no score: 3-0 can be spoken as "three **nothing**/*(Br)* **nil**/*(Am infml)* **zip**".
(In tennis, a score like 40-0 is spoken as "forty **love**".)

And now with only 10 minutes to go the latest score is 5-3 (**to** *Rangers*).
Rangers **are leading** *United 5-3.* • *They're leading/trailing* **by** *two goals.*
We're 6 points **behind/ahead/in front**.
The **half-time/final** *score was 16-14.*

Winning and losing

The Reds won/lost **by** *8 points.* [I] • *We won* **against** *India but I think we'll lose* **to** *Australia.* [I]
Do you think they'll win the Cup? [T]
It was MacGregor's try in the second half that won/lost them the match. [+ two objects]
The Italian team are confident after **beating/defeating** *their rivals 4-1 last week.* • *They won 6-4.*
Wolves suffered a crushing 4-0 defeat **against** *Millwall.*
Buffalo's scored a narrow 15-14 win/victory **over** *Miami.*
The match was a 12-12 **draw/tie**. • *We* **drew** *3-3* **against** Poland.

Some people involved in sport

I know that all the **players** *in the* **team/side** *realize how important this match is.*
The 36 year old New Zealand **captain/skipper** *was leading his side for the last time.*
The **coach** *made the team work very hard in the weeks before the final.*
Ron Fuller the **manager** *has dropped* (= omitted) *Brown and Klein from his team.*
When United won with only a minute left, their **fans/supporters** *went wild.*
A **crowd of** *63,000 gathered to watch the final game of the season.* • *There were 40,000* **spectators** *at the match.*
A **referee** is a judge in charge of basketball, football, hockey, rugby, squash.
An **umpire** judges badminton, baseball, cricket, tennis and volleyball.

Types of competitions/championships

- **Knock-out competitions** (sometimes called **tournaments**): competitors only stay in the competition if they win their games. If they lose, they are immediately **knocked out/eliminated**. If they win, they **go into/qualify for** the next level of the competition. Each level is called a **round**.

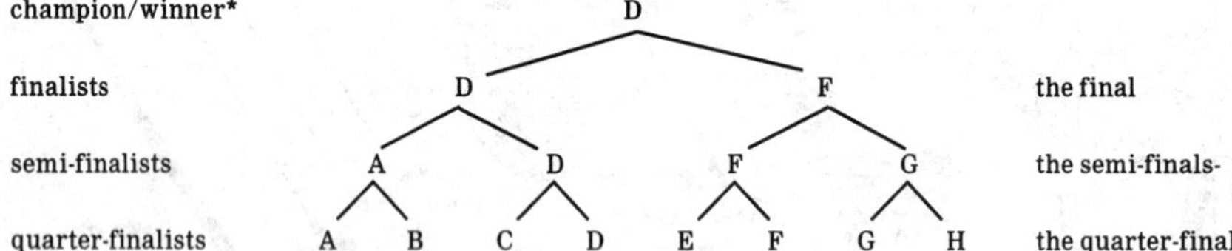

* The competitor who wins is the champion; the winning team are the champions. In the diagram F is the **runner-up** or team F are **runners-up**.

- **League competitions**: each team plays *twice* against every other team, once **at home** and once **away**. Teams get points for winning games, and these points are shown in the **league table**. When there are large numbers of teams, they are put into **divisions** depending on their abilities.

car. [+ obj + v-*ing*] • *I soon spotted* **why** *you couldn't get the printer to work – it wasn't switched on at the back.* [+ *wh*-word] • *The policeman spotted* **that** *I hadn't got my seat belt on and signalled me to stop.* [+ *that* clause] • *(Br) "I've just seen your glasses – they're under the table." "Ah,* **well spotted**!*"* • Ⓓ Ⓕ

-spot·ter /£-ˌspɒt·əʳ, $-ˌspɑː·t̬ɚ/ *combining form* • *a talent-spotter* ○ *(Br) a train-spotter*

spot·ting /£ˈspɒt·ɪŋ, $ˈspɑː·t̬ɪŋ/ *combining form* • *talent-spotting* • *(Br) Can you believe he actually goes train-spotting at the weekends!*

spot PLACE /£spɒt, $spɑːt/ *n* [C] a particular place • *This looks like a nice spot for a picnic.* • *I'll show you the exact spot where I fell off my bike.* • *I've got the best spot next to the window where I can watch everything going on.* • **On the spot** means at the place where an event is happening or has recently happened: *The police were called and they were on the spot within three minutes.* ○ *She won awards for her on-the-spot reporting during the last war.* • **On the spot** also means immediately: *She was caught without a ticket and fined thirty pounds on the spot.* ○ *You can be sacked on the spot for stealing.* • If you **put** someone **on the spot** you cause them embarrassment or difficulty by forcing them at that moment to answer a difficult question or make an important decision: *Mira rather put him on the spot by asking him when he was going to give us a pay-rise.* • A **spot check** is a quick examination of a few members of a group instead of the whole group: *The police are doing spot checks* **on** *motorists to test alcohol levels.* • A **spot fine** is a FINE (= money you have to pay as a punishment) that is given to you at the time of breaking the law: *He* **got** *a spot fine of a hundred pounds for speeding.* • *(Br and Aus)* **Spot-on** means exact: *"How old do I reckon she is? – I'd say 38." "Spot-on".* ○ *Her imitation of John was spot-on.* • Ⓓ Ⓕ

spot PART OF A SHOW /£spɒt, $spɑːt/ *n* [C] a short length of time in a show which is given to a particular performer • *She's* **got/doing** *a regular five-minute spot on his show.* • *Every Saturday they have a different entertainer on the* **guest** *spot.* • Ⓓ Ⓕ

spot·less /£ˈspɒt·ləs, $ˈspɑːt-/ *adj* extremely clean • *Her home is spotless.* • *(fig.) She seemed the perfect match for the prince – young and pretty with a spotless* (= very good) *reputation.*

spot·less·ly /£ˈspɒt·lə·sli, $ˈspɑːt-/ *adv* • *The kitchen is spotlessly clean.*

spot·light /£ˈspɒt·laɪt, $ˈspɑːt-/, *infml* **spot** *n* [C] (a circle of strong light which is sent from) a LAMP whose beam can be directed • *He delivers the whole of the speech at the front of the stage, illuminated by a spotlight.* • *When we redecorated the kitchen we put spotlights above the worktops.* • You say that someone is **in the** spotlight if he or she is receiving a lot of public attention at that moment: *The Senator has been in the spotlight recently since the revelation of his tax frauds.* • PIC **Lights**

spot·light *obj* /£ˈspɒt·laɪt, $ˈspɑːt-/ *v* [T] *past* **spotlighted** or **spotlit** /£ˈspɒt·lɪt, $ˈspɑːt-/ • *The* *paintings in the alcove were spotlit from below.* • If something spotlights a particular situation, it directs public attention to it: *The death of so many celebrities from AIDS has effectively spotlighted the disease.*

spouse /spaʊs/ *n* [C] *fml or law* a person's husband or wife • *In 60% of the households surveyed both spouses went out to work.* • [LP]› **Relationships**

spout *(obj)* [SPEAK] /spaʊt/ *v disapproving* to say or repeat (esp. stupid or meaningless things) continuously, often in a way that is boring or annoying for other people • *He spouts a load of pretentious nonsense and people are stupid enough to believe him!* [T] • *A child should learn to think for herself and not merely spout facts and figures.* [T] • *I really don't want to listen to Mike spouting over lunch.* [I] • Ⓙ

spout [OPENING] /spaʊt/ *n* [C] a tube-shaped opening which allows liquids to be poured out of a container • *This teapot has a chipped spout.* • *(Br slang)* If a woman is **up the spout** she is pregnant. • *(Br and Aus slang)* **Up the spout** also means wasted or spoiled: *We'd had the car mended just before he crashed it so that was a few hundred pounds up the spout.* ○ *Peter lost his job so that was our holiday plans up the spout.* • Ⓙ

spout *(obj)* [FLOW] /spaʊt/ *v* to flow or send out (liquid or flames) quickly and with force, in a straight line • *Flames spouted* **(out)** *from the oil wells.* [I] • *A statue of an open-mouthed young boy spouts a jet of water into the air.* [T] • *(fig.) She started to cry and soon the tears were spouting from her eyes.* [I] • Ⓙ

spout /spaʊt/ *n* [C] • *A spout of water shot out of the ground.*

sprain *obj* /spreɪn/ *v* [T] to cause an injury to (a joint in the body) by a sudden movement • *She sprained her ankle playing squash.* • *When an ankle or a wrist is sprained it means that the ligament in the joint has been stretched or torn.*

sprain /spreɪn/ *n* [C] • *He hasn't broken anything – it's just a bad sprain.*

sprang /spræŋ/ *past simple of* SPRING

sprat /spræt/ *n* [C] a small edible fish which lives in the sea

sprawl [BODY] /£sprɔːl, $sprɑːl/ *v* [I] *disapproving* to spread the arms and legs out carelessly and untidily while sitting or lying down • *Don't sprawl* **on** *your chair – sit up straight!* • *I knocked into her in the corridor and* **sent** *her sprawling* (= knocked her over).

sprawl /£sprɔːl, $sprɑːl/ *n* [U] *disapproving* • *She lay in a sprawl on the sofa.*

sprawled /£sprɔːld, $sprɑːld/ *adj* [after v] • *He lay sprawled* **across/on** *a sofa.* • *(esp. Am) He was sprawled* **out** *on the floor.*

sprawl [CITY] /£sprɔːl, $sprɑːl/ *v* [I always + adv/prep] *disapproving* (esp. of a city) to cover a large area of land with buildings which have been added at different times so that it looks untidy • *Nowadays the city sprawls messily away from its old centre.* • *The family farm sprawls over thousands of acres.* • *The refugee camps sprawl across the bush.*

sprawl /£sprɔːl, $sprɑːl/ *n* [C usually sing] *disapproving* • *The storm caused most damage in the highly populated* **urban** *sprawl of South Florida.*

sprawl·ing /£ˈsprɔː·lɪŋ, $ˈsprɑː-/ *adj disapproving* • *The firm's latest development is a sprawling complex of office buildings.* • *From the plane we looked down on miles of sprawling suburbs.* • *He's got large sprawling handwriting.*

spray [LIQUID] /spreɪ/ *n* a mass of very small drops of liquid carried in the air • *Can you feel the spray from the sea/waterfall?* [U] • Spray can refer to liquid which is forced out of a special container under pressure so that it becomes a cloud-like mass of small liquid drops: *a quick spray of perfume/polish* [C] • A spray can also be a mass of small drops of liquid scattered onto plants and crops etc. from a special piece of equipment, or the piece of equipment itself: *Farmers use a lot of* **chemical** *sprays on crops.* ○ *There are sprays in the fields, watering the crops.* [C] • *(fig.) There was a sudden spray* **of bullets.** • A **spray gun** is a device which is held in the hand and used for sending out liquid such as paint in very small drops.

spray *(obj)* /spreɪ/ *v* • *A car went past and sprayed me* **with** *water!* [T] • *She sprayed herself* **with** *perfume.* [T] • *Vandals had sprayed a graffiti* **on** *the wall.* [T] • *He opened a bottle of champagne and it sprayed all* **over** *my dress.* [I always + adv/prep] • *The pipe burst and water was spraying everywhere.* [I always + adv/prep] • *(fig.) The car was sprayed* **with bullets.** [T]

spray·er /£ˈspreɪ·əʳ, $-ɚ/ *n* [C] • A sprayer is a device for sending out small drops of liquid, esp. garden chemicals.

spray [FLOWERS] /spreɪ/ *n* [C] a single small branch or stem with leaves and flowers on it • *a spray of chrysanthemums*

spread *(obj)* /spred/ *v past* **spread** to (cause to) cover, reach or have an effect on a wider or increasing area • *The fire spread very rapidly because of the strong wind.* [I] • *It started off as cancer of the liver but it spread* **to** *other areas of the body.* [I] • *The redundancies are spread* **across** *the clothing, banking and building industries.* [T] • *We spread the picnic rug* **out** *on the ground and sat down to eat.* [T] • *The AIDS virus is spread* (= given to other people) *through contact with blood and other body fluids.* [T] • *For this exercise you need to spread your arms* **out** *above your head.* [T] • *She spread her toast* **with** *a thick layer of butter./She spread a thick layer of butter* **on** *her toast.* [T] • *It's a special sort of butter that spreads easily even when cold.* [I] • *The suburbs spread out for miles to either side of the city.* [I] • *Slowly a smile spread across her face.* [I] • *The votes were fairly* **evenly** *spread between the candidates.* [T] • *Are you spreading* (= telling a lot of people) **gossip/rumours** *again?* [T] • *She's got family spread* **(out)** *all over the world.* [T] • *If we spread* (= share) *the work out between us it won't seem so bad.* [T] • If something is spread **over** a period it happens during that time, often in stages: *I prefer to spread the cost of bills over a few months.* [T] ○ *The course is spread over two years.* [T] ○ *The repayments on the loan can be spread* **out** *over three years.* [T] • If something spreads **like wildfire**, it spreads extremely quickly: *As soon as one child has contracted the disease it spreads like wildfire throughout the school.* [I] • If you **spread** your **wings** you use your abilities for the first time in your life to do new and exciting things: *She'd been working for the same company for fifteen years and it was time to spread her wings.* • To **spread the word** is to communicate a message to a lot of people: *A lot of companies regard television advertising as the most effective way of spreading the word.* ○ *We've arranged a meeting for next Thursday so if you see anyone do spread the word.* • If someone is **spread-eagled** they are lying with their arms and legs stretched out: *She was lying spread-eagled on the grass.*

spread /spred/ *n* • *The spread of AIDS in the last few years has been alarming.* [U] • The spread of something is the area or range covered by it: *The survey found* **a wide** *spread of opinion over the proposed new building.* [U] • In a newspaper or magazine, a spread is a large article or advertisement covering one or more pages: *There's a double-page spread on the latest fashions.* [C] • A spread is a soft food for putting on bread and biscuits: *cheese/chocolate/fish spread* [U] ○ *There's bread and various spreads for tea.* [C] • Spread is also *Am for* RANCH (= a large farm on which cattle and horses are kept). [C] • *(Br and Aus dated)* A spread is also a meal, esp. one for a special occasion with a lot of different dishes arranged on a table: *Sheila* **laid on**/*(Br also)* **put on** (= made) *a lovely spread for us.* [C]

spread·sheet /ˈspred·ʃiːt/ *n* [C] a computer program, used esp. in business, which allows you to do financial calculations and plans

spree /spriː/ *n* [C] a short period of doing a particular, often enjoyable, activity much more than is usual • *I* **went on** *a drinking/***shopping***/spending spree on Saturday.* • *Twenty people were shot dead in the city making it the worst killing spree since the riots.*

sprig /sprɪg/ *n* [C] a single small plant stem with leaves on it • *Garnish the dish with sprigs of parsley.*

spright·ly /ˈspraɪt·li/ *adj* **-ier, -iest** (esp. of old people) energetic and in good health • *He's a sprightly old man of seventy-five.*

spright·li·ness /ˈspraɪt·lɪ·nəs/ *n* [U]

spring [SEASON] /sprɪŋ/ *n* the season of the year between winter and summer, lasting from March to June north of the equator, and from September to December south of the equator, when the weather becomes warmer, leaves and plants start to grow again and flowers appear • *spring flowers/rains/weather* [U] • *It really feels like spring now that the evenings are getting lighter.* [U] • *Many bulbs bloom* **in the** *spring.* [U] • *Janet's coming over for a couple of weeks next Spring.* [C] • *(Am)* A **spring chicken** (also **springer**) is a young chicken whose meat is soft. • *(infml)* If you refer to a person as a **spring chicken**, you mean that they are not young: *I thought she was a very attractive lady – I mean considering she's* **no** *spring chicken.* • If you **spring-clean** a house or give it a **spring-cleaning**, you clean it very well, cleaning all the parts that you do not usually clean, such as cupboards and drawers: *Traditionally, spring-cleaning was done at the end of winter.* • *(Br)* **Spring greens** are the leaves of young CABBAGE plants, eaten as vegetables. • *(Br and Aus)* A **spring onion** (*esp. Am* **scallion**) is a long thin green and white onion that is often eaten raw. • A **spring roll** (also *Br* **pancake roll**, *Am* **egg roll**) is a savoury Chinese PANCAKE (=flat cake) which is rolled up, filled with small pieces of vegetables and sometimes meat and fried. • *"In the spring a young man's fancy lightly turns to thoughts of love"* (Alfred, Lord Tennyson in the poem *Locksley Hall*, 1842) • PIC **Vegetables**

spring CURVED METAL /sprɪŋ/ *n* a piece of curved or bent metal that can be pressed into a smaller space but then returns to its usual shape • *I think the springs have gone* (= broken) *in the sofa – it feels very soft.* [C] • *The children have jumped on their mattresses so much that they've ruined the springs.* [C] • The spring of something is its ability to return to its usual shape after it has been pressed: *Over the years the mattress has lost its spring.* [U] • If you walk with or have a **spring in** your **step** you walk energetically in a way that shows you are feeling happy and confident: *There's been a definite spring in his step ever since he met Joanna.* • PIC **Beds and bedroom**

spring·y /ˈsprɪŋ·i/ *adj* **-ier, -iest** • *You need a running shoe with a springy sole.* • *The turf feels very springy under foot.*

sprung *Br* /sprʌŋ/, *Am* **spring** *adj* [not gradable] • A sprung floor or piece of furniture is one that is supported by springs.

spring MOVE QUICKLY /sprɪŋ/ *v past simple* **sprang** /spræŋ/ or *Aus, Am also* **sprung** /sprʌŋ/, *past part* **sprung** /sprʌŋ/ to move quickly and suddenly towards a particular place • *I sprang out of bed to answer the door.* [I always + adv/prep] • *Thinking it might be her, he sprang to the telephone.* [I always + adv/prep] • *He always springs* **to** *his* **feet** *when she walks in the room.* [I always + adv/prep] • *The organization is ready to spring* **into action** *the moment it receives its funding.* [I always + adv/prep] • *(fig.) I noticed the way you sprang* **to** *his* **defence** (=immediately started to defend him) *when Caroline started joking about his clothes.* [I always + adv/prep] • *The lid of the box sprang shut.* [L] • *Say the word 'Australia' and a vision of beaches and blue seas immediately* **springs to mind** (=comes quickly into the mind).

spring APPEAR SUDDENLY /sprɪŋ/ *v past simple* **sprang** /spræŋ/ or *Am and Aus also* **sprung** /sprʌŋ/, *past part* **sprung** /sprʌŋ/ to appear or exist suddenly • *Thousands of new businesses have sprung* **up** *in the past couple of years.* [I always + adv/prep] • *(infml) "Where did you spring* **from***? – I didn't see you come in!"* [I always + adv/prep] • *I hope he's not going to spring any nasty surprises on us at the meeting this morning.* [T]

spring BE CAUSED BY /sprɪŋ/ *v* [I] *past simple* **sprang** or *Am and Aus also* **sprung**, *past part* **sprung** to be caused by or to be a result of • *His need to be liked obviously springs* **from** *a deep-rooted insecurity.* • *Taking this course in interior design sprang* **out of** *her desire to change careers.*

spring WATER /sprɪŋ/, **springs** /sprɪŋz/ *n* [C] a place where water flows out from the ground • *bubbling/hot springs* • *bottled spring water*

spring·board /£ˈsprɪŋ·bɔːd, $-bɔːrd/ *n* [C] a FLEXIBLE (= able to bend) board which helps you to jump higher when jumping or DIVING (=jumping head first) into a swimming pool or when doing GYMNASTICS • *He dived off the springboard and swam down to the shallow end.* • A springboard is also something which provides you either with the opportunity to follow a particular plan of action, or the encouragement that is needed to make it successful: *The firm's director is confident that the new project will act as a springboard* **for/to** *further contracts.*

spring·bok /£ˈsprɪŋ·bɒk, $-bɑːk/ *n* [C] *pl* **springboks** or **springbok** an animal like a small deer that lives in S Africa, is reddish brown with a white back end and can jump very high

spring·er /£ˈsprɪŋ·əʳ, $-ɚ/ *n* [C] *Am for* **spring chicken**, see at SPRING SEASON

spring·time /ˈsprɪŋ·taɪm/ *n* [U] the season of spring • **In (the)** *springtime the woods are full of bluebells.*

sprin·kle *obj* /ˈsprɪŋ·kl̩/ *v* [T] to scatter (a few drops or bits of something), usually over a large area of (something) • *Sprinkle a few herbs* **on** *the pizza./Sprinkle the pizza* **with** *a few herbs.* • *The priest sprinkled water on the baby's head.* • *(fig.) The speech was* **liberally** *sprinkled with jokes about the incident.*

sprin·kle /ˈsprɪŋ·kl̩/, *Am also* **sprin·kling** *n* [C usually sing] • A sprinkle of rain or snow is a very light fall of it which lasts only a short time.

sprin·kler /£ˈsprɪŋ·kl̩·əʳ, $-ɚ/ *n* [C] • A sprinkler is a piece of equipment for scattering water to put out fires: *There was no sprinkler system* (=sprinklers, fitted in a building, which automatically operate if there is a fire) *in the supermarket so the fire took a hold very quickly.* • A sprinkler is also a device with a lot of small holes which you put on the end of a HOSE (=long bendable pipe used to direct water) in order to water plants, grass, etc. • PIC **Garden**

sprin·kling /ˈsprɪŋ·kl̩·ɪŋ/ *n* [C usually sing] • *Top each bowl with* **a** *generous sprinkling* **of** *fresh mint.* • *(fig.) The audience were mainly women with* **a** *sprinkling* (=a small number) **of** *earnest-looking men.* • *(fig.) Looking young for his forty years, he has just* **a** *sprinkling* (=a small number) **of** *grey hairs at the temples.*

sprint /sprɪnt/ *v* [I] to run as fast as you can over a short distance, either in a race or because you are in a great hurry to get somewhere • *Wait until the last two hundred metres of the race and then sprint.* • *We had to sprint to catch the bus.*

sprint /sprɪnt/ *n* [C] • A sprint can be a short and very fast race, such as the 100-metre race, or the last part of a longer running race which is run as fast as possible: *the 100-metre sprint* ○ *(Br and Aus) She* **put on** *a marvellous sprint down the last two hundred metres.* ○ *a sprint champion/relay* • A sprint is also a very fast run that someone does when they are in a great hurry to get somewhere: *He suddenly* **broke into** (=started) *a sprint.* ○ *(esp. Br) I had to* **put on** *a sprint to catch my train.*

sprint·er /£ˈsprɪn·təʳ, $-t̬ɚ/ *n* [C] • *Five years later and she's now a world-class sprinter.*

sprite /spraɪt/ *n* [C] *literary* a FAIRY (=small imaginary person with wings), esp. one connected with water • *a sea/water sprite*

spritz /sprɪts/ *v Am* to force a mass of very small drops of liquid out of a container, usually by pressing a part of the container; to SPRAY • *After you've applied your powder, spritz with a little mineral water.* [I]

spritz /sprɪts/ *n* [C] • *A quick spritz of scent and I'm ready.*

sprit·zer /£ˈsprɪt·səʳ, $-sɚ/ *n* [C] a drink made with white wine and esp. SODA WATER (=fizzy water)

sprit·zig /ˈsprɪt·sɪg, ˈʃprɪt-/ *adj Aus* (of a wine) slightly fizzy

sprock·et (wheel) /£ˈsprɒk·ɪt, $ˈsprɑː·kɪt/ *n* [C] a device like a wheel with one or more rows of teeth-like parts sticking out which keeps a chain moving on a bicycle or pulls film, paper etc. through a machine

sprog /£sprɒg, $sprɑːg/ *n* [C] *Br and Aus slang* a baby or small child • *She's got a couple of sprogs now.*

sprog /£sprɒg, $sprɑːg/ *v* [I] **-gg-** *Br and Aus slang* • *Has she sprogged* (=given birth) *yet?*

sprout *(obj)* /spraʊt/ *v* to produce leaves, hair and other new developing parts, or (of leaves, hair and other developing parts) to begin to grow • *It takes about three days for the seeds to sprout.* [I] • *The potatoes had been left for so long in the cupboard that they had begun to sprout.* [I] • *Hair seemed to sprout* **from** *under his shirt collar.* [I] • *Your hair is sticking up – it looks like you're sprouting horns!* [T] • *(fig.) New factories have sprouted* **up** (=are appearing) *everywhere.* [I]

sprout /spraʊt/ *n* [C] • A sprout is a newly grown part of a plant. • *(esp. Br)* A sprout is also a BRUSSELS SPROUT. • See also BEANSPROUT.

spruce TREE /spruːs/ *n* [C; U] an evergreen tree with needle-like leaves, or the pale-coloured wood of this tree

spruce TIDY /spruːs/ *adj approving* (of a person) tidy and clean in appearance • *He looked spruce and clean-shaven in a clean white shirt.*

spruce up *obj*, **spruce** *obj* **up** /spruːs/ *v adv* [M] • *I thought I'd have a shave and generally spruce myself up for the interview.* • *They've employed an advertising agency to spruce up* (=improve) *the company image.*

sprung /sprʌŋ/ *past participle and (Am) past simple of* SPRING

spry /spraɪ/ *adj* (esp. of older people) active and able to move quickly and energetically, • *He was amazingly spry for a man of almost 80.* • *Karen's spry footwork helped her win the match against a slow opponent.*

spud /spʌd/ *n* [C] *infml* a potato • *Are the spuds ready yet?*

spun /spʌn/ *past simple and past participle of* SPIN

spunk BRAVERY /spʌŋk/ *n* [U] *dated infml* bravery and determination • *For God's sake, man, where's your spunk!*

spunk·y /ˈspʌŋ·ki/ *adj* **-ier, -iest** *infml* • *She plays the part of the spunky daughter who saves her little sister from drowning.*

spunk SEXUAL LIQUID /spʌŋk/ *n* [U] *taboo slang* SEMEN (= liquid sent out through the penis during sexual activity)

spunk ATTRACTIVE MAN /spʌŋk/ *n* [C] *Aus infml* a sexually attractive man • *Have you met Malcolm yet – he's a real spunk!*

spunk·y /ˈspʌŋ·ki/ *adj* **-ier, -iest** *Aus infml* • *There were a few spunky visitors to the club*

spur *obj* ENCOURAGE /£spɜːʳ, $spɜːr/ *v* [T] **-rr-** to encourage (an activity or development) or make it happen faster • *Rising consumer sales have the effect of spurring the economy to faster growth.* • *Many shops cut prices just before Christmas in an attempt to spur sales.* • *Once I'd lost the first couple of kilos it spurred me* **(on)** *to lose some more.* • *Spurred* **(on)** *by her early success, she went on to write four more novels in rapid succession.* • Ⓙ

spur /£spɜːʳ, $spɜːr/ *n* [C] • *The manager said that the team's win on Saturday would be a spur to even greater effort this season.*

spur SHARP OBJECT /£spɜːʳ, $spɜːr/ *n* [C] a sharp metal wheel-shaped object which is fixed to the heel of boots worn by people riding horses and is used to encourage the horse to go faster • If you **win/gain** your **spurs** doing something you achieve something which proves that you are skilled in a particular type of activity and therefore win the respect of other people: *He won his political spurs fighting hospital closures during his time as a local councillor in Bristol.* • *(infml)* **Spur of the moment** means sudden and done without any planning: *We hadn't planned to go away – it was one of those spur-of-the-moment* **decisions**. ○ *We just jumped in a car* **on the** *spur of the moment* (= suddenly and without planning it). • Ⓙ

spur *obj* /£spɜːʳ, $spɜːr/ *v* [T] **-rr-** • *He spurred his horse* **on** *and shouted "Faster! Faster!".*

spur LAND /£spɜːʳ, $spɜːr/ *n* [C] a high piece of land which sticks out from a mountain or a group of mountains • Ⓙ

spu·ri·ous /£ˈspjʊə·ri·əs, $ˈspjʊr·i-/ *adj* false and not what it appears to be, or (of reasons and judgments) based on something that has not been correctly understood and therefore false • *She rejected the prime minister's claims that the economy was getting stronger as spurious.* • *Some of the arguments in favour of shutting the factory are questionable and others downright spurious.*

spurn *obj* /£spɜːn, $spɜːrn/ *v* [T] *slightly fml* to refuse to accept (something), feeling that it is not worth having • *She spurned my offers of help.* • *I think he was rather outraged that I'd spurned his advances.* • *Ellis plays the part of the spurned lover.*

spurt *(obj)* /£spɜːt, $spɜːrt/ *v* (to cause) to flow out suddenly and with force, in a fast stream • *Blood was spurting out all over the place.* [I] • *His arm was spurting blood where the vein had been severed.* [T] • *(fig. esp. Am) Shares of the jewellery-store chain spurted* (= increased by) *$6.* [I]

spurt /£spɜːt, $spɜːrt/ *n* [C] • *The water came out* **in** *spurts.* • A spurt is also a sudden and brief period of increased activity, effort or speed: *There was a sudden spurt* **of** *activity in the housing market.* ○ *He tends to work* **in** *spurts.* ○ *He had a* **growth** *spurt when he was fourteen and seemed to grow a foot overnight.* ○ *He* **put on** *a spurt in the last two-hundred metres.*

sput·ter *(obj)* /£ˈspʌt·əʳ, $ˈspʌţ·ɚ/ *v* to make repeated explosive sounds • *The car sputtered once or twice and then stopped.* [I] • *I could hear the fat sputtering in the pan.* [I] • *He was so furious he could only sputter his reply.* [T] • *The candle sputtered a little and then went out.* [I] • *(fig.) With a sputtering economy* (= With extremely brief periods of growth which may not continue) *and the dollar at an all-time low, the president's task will not be an easy one.* [I]

sput·ter /£ˈspʌt·əʳ, $ˈspʌţ·ɚ/ *n* [C] • *The engine wouldn't start – it* **gave** *one or two sputters but that was all.*

spu·tum /£ˈspjuː·təm, $-ţəm/ *n* [U] *specialized* liquid from the passages in your body which go to the lungs; PHLEGM

spy SECRET PERSON /spaɪ/ *n* [C] a person who secretly gathers and reports information about the activities of another country or organization • *She was arrested in 1949 on charges of being a spy.* • *He reads a lot of spy stories.* • *"Spies Like Us"* (title of a song by Paul McCartney, 1985) • *"The Spy Who Loved Me"* (title of a James Bond film, 1977) • *"The Spy Who Came in from the Cold"* (title of a book by John le Carré, 1963) • LP› **Crimes and criminals**

spy /spaɪ/ *v* [I] • To spy is to secretly gather and report information about the activities of another country or organization: *He's been held in prison for three years for alleged spying.* ○ *He was arrested for spying* **on** *missile sites.* • To spy **on** someone is also to watch them in secret: *I can spy on my neighbours through this window without being seen.* • *(infml) I generally like to spy* **out** (= obtain knowledge of) *restaurants before I go to eat in them.* [M] • If you **spy out the land** you try to obtain knowledge of something in advance: *We drove around the area where our new house is to spy out the land.*

spy *obj* SEE /spaɪ/ *v* [T] to see or notice (someone or something) usually when it involves looking hard • *I think I've just spied Andrew in the crowd.* • *If you spy a phone box will you let me know.*

spy·hole /£ˈspaɪ·həʊl, $-hoʊl/ *n* [C] *Br and Aus for* **peephole**, see at PEEP LOOK

sq *abbreviation for* SQUARE, see at SQUARE SHAPE • *There are plans to extend the shopping centre by a further 44 000 sq ft.* • *Her address is 5 Grosvenor Sq., London W1.*

squab /£skwɒb, $skwɑːb/ *n esp. Am* a young PIGEON (= large grey bird often seen in towns) eaten as food • *roasted squab* [U] • *I had a delicious squab pie for my lunch.*

squab·ble /£ˈskwɒb·ļ, $ˈskwɑː·bļ/ *n* [C] a silly argument over an unimportant matter • *Polly and Susie were* **having** *a squabble about who was going to hold the dog's lead.* • *Petty internal squabbles are doing nothing to help the party's image.*

squab·ble /£ˈskwɒb·ļ, $ˈskwɑː·bļ/ *v* [I] • *The kids, as usual, were squabbling in the back of the car.* • *Stop squabbling, you two!*

squad /£skwɒd, $skwɑːd/ *n* [C + sing/pl v] a small group of people trained to work together as a unit • *Two firebomb attacks in the City yesterday are being investigated by Scotland Yard's anti-terrorist squad.* • *The station was evacuated and the army bomb squad experts called.* • In sports a squad is a team from which the players for a match are chosen: *Eight of Ranger's 24-man squad are injured.* • In the army a squad is a small group of soldiers, esp. one gathered together for DRILL (= marching, etc.). • *(Br dated or Am)* A **squad car** (also **patrol car**) is a car used by police officers.

squad·die /£ˈskwɒd·i, $ˈskwɑː·di/ *Br slang* • A squaddie is a soldier: *You look like a squaddie with that haircut!*

squad·ron /£ˈskwɒd·rᵊn, $ˈskwɑː·drən/ *n* [C + sing/pl v] a unit of one of the armed forces, esp. (in Britain) the air force • *Both of the dead men were identified as from no 15 squadron.* • A **squadron leader** is an officer in the air force of Britain and of other countries.

squa·lid DIRTY /£ˈskwɒl·ɪd, $ˈskwɑː·lɪd/ *adj disapproving* (of places) extremely dirty and unpleasant, often because of lack of money • *Many prisons, even today, are overcrowded and squalid places.*

squal·or /£ˈskwɒl·əʳ, $ˈskwɑː·lɚ/ *n* [U] • *It was a dirty, damp, smelly flat – the usual student squalor.*

squa·lid IMMORAL /£ˈskwɒl·ɪd, $ˈskwɑː·lɪd/ *adj* (of situations and activities) immoral; involving sex and drugs etc. in an unpleasant way • *It's the usual squalid rock star tale of drugs, sex and overdoses.*

squal·or /£ˈskwɒl·əʳ, $ˈskwɑː·lɚ/ *n* [U]

squall STRONG WIND /£skwɔːl, $skwɑːl/ *n* [C] a sudden strong wind or brief storm • *Violent squalls signalled the approach of the hurricane.* • *Over the south-east of the country winds will be high with the occasional squall* **of** *rain or even hail.*

squall·y /£ˈskwɔː·li, $ˈskwɑː-/ *adj* • *The rest of the country will have winds of up to 60 mph with heavy squally rain.*

squall SHOUT /£skwɔːl, $skwɑːl/ *v* [I] to make a loud sharp noise • *I could hear next door's baby squalling in the middle of the night.*

squall /£skwɔːl, $skwɑːl/ *n* [C] • *With a loud squall the cat jumped off the roof.*

squan·der *obj* /£ˈskwɒn·dəʳ, $ˈskwɑːn·dɚ/ *v* [T] to spend or use (money or supplies) wastefully, often all at the same time, or to waste (opportunities) by not using them to your advantage • *They'll quite happily squander a whole year's savings on two weeks in the sun.* • *Ireland squandered several chances, including a penalty that cost them the game.*

square SHAPE /£skweəʳ, $skwer/ *n* [C] a flat shape with four sides of equal length and four angles of 90° • *First draw* *a square.* • *It's a square-shaped room.* • A square can be any square-shaped object: *I've got a large square of material that I'd like to make a dress out of.* ○ *When cooled, cut the chocolate brownies into squares.* • A square is also an area of approximately square-shaped land in a city or a village, often including the buildings that surround it: *Are they still living at 6 Eaton Square?* ○ *A band were playing on the village square.* ○ *They have a market in the town square.* • A square can also be a marked space on a board used for playing games: *Move forward three squares.* • *(infml)* If you go back to or start again from **square one**, you have to start working on a plan from the beginning because the plan of action that you first tried failed: *The deal with the house fell through so I'm afraid we're* **back to** *square one.* • *(Am and Aus)* A square is also a tool for drawing or testing **right angles** (=angles of 90 degrees).

square /£skweəʳ, $skwer/ *adj* **-r, -st** • *The recipe recommends that you use a square cake-tin.* • *He's got that square-jawed masculinity that a lot of women seem to find attractive.* • Square (*abbreviation* **sq** or *specialized* [2]) is used with units of measurement of length to express the total size of an area: *The floor is 3 metres wide by 5 metres long so its total area is 15 sq metres.* ○ *The city itself covers thirteen square miles.* ○ *(specialized) Ensure that the exposed area is less than* $2cm^2$. • Square is used immediately after measurements of length when expressing the length of the four sides of a square-shaped area: *So you want carpet for a room that's eight metres square* (=8 metres long and 8 metres wide). • *(Br)* **The Square Mile** refers to **the City**. See at CITY [FINANCIAL CENTRE]. • *(infml)* If you say that someone is a **square peg (in a round hole)**, you mean that their character makes them unsuitable for the place in which they work or live: *He never quite fitted in when he was working here – he was always a bit of a square peg.* • A **square bracket** is one of a pair of BRACKETS (=marks put around words, sentences etc.) that is shaped like half a square. • A **square dance** is a dance in which the way the four pairs of dancers stand forms squares. • *(Br and Aus infml)* Someone who is **square-eyed** watches a lot of television: *You'll* **go** *square-eyed if you sit in front of the box any more!* • **Square knot** is *Am for* **reef knot**. See at REEF [SAILS]. • A **square meal** is a satisfying meal that fills you and provides you with all the different types of food that your body needs in order to stay healthy: *If you're only eating a chocolate bar for lunch, you need a good square meal in the evening.*

square *obj* /£skweəʳ, $skwer/ *v* [T] • *He squared his shoulders* (=pulled his shoulders up and back) *and took a deep breath.* • If you try to **square the circle** you try to do something which is very difficult: *They attempted to square the circle by writing a novel in one weekend.*

squared /£skweəd, $skwerd/ *adj* [not gradable] • *Squared paper* (=paper with squares printed on it) *is better for drawing graphs on.*

square [EQUAL] /£skweəʳ, $skwer/ *adj* **-r, -st** *infml* equal or level • *Could you stand back from these shelves and tell me if they're square* (=level)*?* • If two people are **(all)** square one of them has paid off a debt to the other and neither now owes or is owed any money: *So if you pay for tonight's tickets we're all square, is that right?* • If two teams or players are **(all)** square they have an equal number of goals or points: *They're all square at thirty points each.* • A **square deal** is a fair agreement: *I reckon we got a square deal on that car.*

square *(obj)* /£skweəʳ, $skwer/ *v infml* • *I'll get this on my card and we can* **square up** (=pay each other what we owe) *later.* • *We always try to* **square the accounts/books** (=pay what is owed) *before term ends.*

square [BORING PERSON] /£skweəʳ, $skwer/ *n* [C] *dated infml* a boring person who does not like new and exciting ideas • *He's a bit of a square.*

square /£skweəʳ, $skwer/ *adj* **-r, -st** *dated infml* • *Do you think my new haircut makes me look a bit square?*

square *obj* [MULTIPLY] /£skweəʳ, $skwer/ *v* [T usually passive] to multiply (a number) by itself • *10 squared equals a hundred.* • 4^2 *means four squared and equals 16.* • [LP⟩] **Mathematics**

square /£skweəʳ, $skwer/ *n* [C] • *The square of 7 is 49.*

square [STRAIGHT] /£skweəʳ, $skwer/ *adj* **-r, -st** in a straight line • *For this exercise you need to keep your hips square.*

square·ly /£'skweə·li, $'skwer-/ *adv* • *She stood squarely, with her feet apart.*

square off *esp. Am, Br and Aus usually* **square up** *v adv* [I] to prepare to fight or compete • *A host of talented players squared off yesterday.* • *The two giants in the fast-food industry are squaring off this month with the most aggressive advertising campaigns yet.*

square up to *obj Br, Am and Aus* **face up to** *v adv prep* [T] to deal with (a problem or difficult person) bravely and with determination • *I thought she squared up to the situation admirably.*

square *(obj)* **with** *obj v prep* [T] to match or accept as able to exist together • *The problem is that his story doesn't square with the evidence.* • *These latest revelations don't quite square with the image of him that is promoted in the press.* • *I wonder how she squares her socialism with the luxury of her surroundings.* • *I don't think I could spend that much money on a jacket – I couldn't square it with my conscience* (=I would feel too guilty).

square·ly /£'skweə·li, $'skwer/, **square** *adv* [not gradable] directly and with certainty • *She refused to come down squarely on either side of the argument.* • *The government is squarely to blame.* • *She punched him square on the jaw.*

squash *obj* [CRUSH] /£skwɒʃ, $skwɑːʃ/ *v* [T] to press down or crush (something) into a flat shape, often with great force • *He accidentally sat on her hat and squashed it.* • *She squashed the cans before putting them in the recycling bin.* • *Hundreds of small animals are squashed on our roads every day.* • *The strawberries were at the bottom of the bag and had all got squashed.* • *(fig.)* **Rumours** *of a possible take-over of the company were soon squashed* (=ended) *by the management.* • If you squash a person with a critical remark, you make them feel that they are wrong or stupid: *When she asked if she could go to the meeting, he squashed her, saying it was for senior members of staff only.* ○ *He felt completely squashed when he was told his article wasn't good enough to be included in the magazine.*

squash·y /£'skwɒʃ·i, $'skwɑː·ʃi/ *adj* **-ier, -iest** • If something is squashy, it is soft and easy to crush: *I've bought some squashy pillows for the couch.* ○ *These plums must be quite old because they've gone all squashy.*

squash *(obj)* [PUSH] /£skwɒʃ, $skwɑːʃ/ *v* [always + adv/prep] to push (a person or thing) into a small space • *My car's a bit small but I think we can all squash* **in**. [I] • *The room was so full you couldn't squash another person* **in**. [M] • *If you all squashed* **up** (=moved closer together)*, we could fit an extra person in the car.* [I] • *We squashed ourselves* **up** *on the sofa so that Hannah could get in.* [T] • *Four of us squashed* **into** *the back seat of his car.* [I] • *He tried to squash his ripped jeans* **into** *the suitcase while his mother wasn't looking.* [T]

squash /£skwɒʃ, $skwɑːʃ/ *n* [U] • *There are over two hundred people coming to the party so it might be a bit of* **a** *squash.*

squash [SPORT] /£skwɒʃ, $skwɑːʃ/, *Br fml* **squash rack·ets**, *Am and Aus fml* **squash rac·quets** *n* [U] a game played between two or four people on a specially marked enclosed playing area which involves hitting a small rubber ball against a wall • *Squash is a very tiring game which requires players to be extremely fit.* • *I've just joined the college squash* **club** *so I'll need to buy a new racket.* • *I can book the squash* **court** *from 12 to 1 if you want to have a game in your lunch hour.*

squash [VEGETABLE] /£skwɒʃ, $skwɑːʃ/ *n esp. Am* a type of large vegetable with a hard skin and a lot of seeds at its centre which is very common in America • *We had roast turkey, potatoes and baked squash for Sunday dinner.* [U] • **Winter** *squashes are eaten when ripe whereas* **summer** *squashes are eaten before they are ripe.* [C]

squash [DRINK] /£skwɒʃ, $skwɑːʃ/ *n* [U] *Br and Aus* a drink which is made from water and sweetened fruit juice • *Squash is usually sold in a concentrated form and water has to be added before it is drunk.* • *"What would you like to drink?" "Some* **orange** *squash, please."*

squat [SIT] /£skwɒt, $skwɑːt/ *v* [I] **-tt-** to position yourself close to the ground balancing on the front part of your feet with your legs bent under your body • *She squatted on the ground and warmed her hands by the fire.* • *The team arranged itself in two rows for the photograph, with six players standing at the back and five squatting in front of them.* • *He squatted* **down** *and examined the front wheel of his bike.*

squat /£skwɒt, $skwɑːt/ *n* [C] • *For this exercise you need to get into* **a** *squat and then raise yourself slowly.* • A squat or **squat-thrust** is a type of physical exercise in which your hands are kept on the floor while your legs move from a position in which they are bent under the body to one in which they are straight out behind you: *She does fifty squat-thrusts and a hundred sit-ups each morning.*

squat LIVE /£skwɒt, $skwɑːt/ *v* [I] **-tt-** to live in an empty building or area of land without the permission of the owner • *When he moved to Sydney, had to squat because he had no money and nowhere to live.* • *They've been squatting* **in** *an apartment in the north of town for the past two years.* • *Work on the new offices has come to a halt because homeless families are squatting* **on** *the site.* • *The government is planning to tighten up legislation against squatting.*

squat /£skwɒt, $skwɑːt/ *n* [C] • A squat is the place that you live in when you are squatting: *They're living in a damp squat with no electricity.*

squat·ter /£'skwɒt·əʳ, $'skwɑː·t̬ɚ/ *n* [C] • *The council has begun a programme of* **evicting** *squatters from its properties at 48 hours' notice.* • *Squatter* **camps** *have sprung up all across the capital in the past few years.* • *(Aus)* In the past squatters were people who took land which did not officially belong to them in order to use it for farming.

squat SHORT /£skwɒt, $skwɑːt/ *adj* **squatter, squattest** short and wide • *Number 53 was in the middle of a row of ugly squat houses.* • *She was shown around the sports club by a heavily-built squat man.*

squat·to·cra·cy /£ˌskwɒt'ɒk·rə·si, $ˌskwɑː't̬ɑː·krə-/ *n* [C/U] *Aus* the established and wealthy owners of large properties in the countryside

squaw /£skwɔː, $skwɑː/ *n* [C] *dated* a Native American woman, esp. a wife. This word is considered offensive by many people

squawk /£skwɔːk, $skwɑːk/ *v* [I] to make an unpleasantly loud sharp cry • *As the fox came into the yard, the chickens began squawking in alarm.* • *(infml)* If someone squawks about something, they complain about it noisily: *Environmental groups have been squawking* **about** *the decision to build the motorway through a forest.*

squawk /£skwɔːk, $skwɑːk/ *n* [C] • *The only sound as we strolled along the beach was the squawks of seagulls as they circled above us.* • *(infml) The proposal to put VAT on books was greeted with squawks of protest from publishers.*

squeak *(obj)* CRY /skwiːk/ *v* to make a short very high cry or sound • *The door squeaked as it swung back and forth on its rusty hinges.* [I] • *There's something squeaking in the engine.* [I] • *As he went down into the basement, he thought he could hear the sound of mice squeaking.* [I] • *"Is anybody there?" she squeaked in a frightened voice, as she heard footsteps coming up the stairs.* [+ clause]

squeak /skwiːk/ *n* [C] • *She let out a squeak of fright as she saw a large spider crawl up the wall.* • *If I hear one more squeak out of you* (= if you say anything else), *there'll be trouble!*

squeak·er /£'skwiː·kəʳ, $-kɚ/ *n* [C] • A squeaker is a small device used inside children's toys which makes a short high sound when it is pressed.

squeak·y /'skwiː·ki/ *adj* **-ier, -iest** • *I wish someone would oil that squeaky door.* • *Her voice gets a lot squeakier when she's nervous.* • *(infml)* If something is described as being **squeaky-clean**, it is so clean that it squeaks when you rub it: *I love the squeaky-clean feel of my hair after I've washed it.* • *(infml)* If someone is described as being **squeaky-clean**, their behaviour cannot be criticized in any way: *Journalists have been trying to discover if the senator really is as squeaky-clean as he claims to be.* • *(Am saying)* 'The squeaky wheel gets the grease' means that attention is paid to those problems which are made most noticeable: *According to the squeaky wheel analysis, the policy remains unchanged because there hasn't been enough pressure put on leaders to change it.*

squeak *(obj)* SUCCEED /skwiːk/ *v* [always + adv/prep] *Am* to only just succeed (in something such as a test or competition) • *He squeaked* **through** *the exam.* [T] • *The American tennis player barely squeaked* **by** *with a 4-6, 6-3, 8-6 victory in the semi-final.* [I]

squeak·er /£'skwiː·kəʳ, $-kɚ/ *n* [C] *Am* • A squeaker is a competition or race which you only just win or lose: *The Democratic candidate won a squeaker in last month's election for state governor.* ○ *The Buffalo Bills lost a squeaker to the Dallas Cowboys in the Super Bowl.*

squeak·y /'skwiː·ki/ *adj* **-ier, -iest** *Am* • *The President had a squeaky six-vote win* (= he won by only six votes) *in Congress.*

squeal /skwiːl/ *v* to make a long very high sound or cry • *"Look out!" he squealed, as the boy ran in front of the car.* [+ clause] • *We could hear the piglets squealing as we entered the farmyard.* [I] • *The brakes squealed as the van rounded the corner.* [I] • *The police car squealed* **to a halt** *in front of the bank.* [I] • *The two children squealed* **with** *joy when they were told they were going to Disneyland.* [I] • *The group has a devoted teenage audience and regularly plays to stadiums filled with squealing fans.* • *(infml)* If you squeal about something, you complain about it loudly: *The threat of further changes in the education system is making teachers squeal.* [I] • *(slang)* If you squeal to the police, you give them information about people you know who have committed a crime: *When he finds out who squealed* **on** *him, he's going to make them very sorry.* [I]

squeal /skwiːl/ *n* [C] • *She let out a squeal of fright as she saw her brother being bundled into the car.* • *She collapsed into giggles and squeals as he began tickling her.* • *The train ground to a halt with a squeal* **of brakes**.

squea·mish /'skwiː·mɪʃ/ *adj* easily upset or shocked by things which you find unpleasant or which you do not approve of • *She's really squeamish and can't stand the sight of blood.* • *Many cooks are squeamish about putting live shellfish into boiling water.* • *'The Silence of the Lambs' is an entertaining but violent movie and is not for* **the** *squeamish.* • *A campaign to inform people about AIDS has been attacked by pressure groups made up of* **the** *morally squeamish.*

squea·mish·ly /'skwiː·mɪʃ·li/ *adv* • *She squeamishly refused to touch the dead mouse.*

squea·mish·ness /'skwiː·mɪʃ·nəs/ *n* [U] • *You'll have to overcome your squeamishness if you want to become a nurse.*

squee·gee /'skwiː·dʒiː/ *n* [C] a tool with a rubber blade and a short handle which is used for removing water from a surface such as a window or mirror after it has been washed • *He hosed down the car and then wiped the windscreen dry with a squeegee.* • A **squeegee mop** is a tool with a long handle and a square piece of SPONGE (= soft absorbent material) at the end which is used for cleaning floors.

squee·gee *obj* /'skwiː·dʒiː/ *v* [T] • *She squeegeed the windows after washing them so that no soapy marks would be left on the glass.*

squeeze *obj* PRESS TOGETHER /skwiːz/ *v* [T] to press (something) firmly from all sides in order to change its shape, reduce its size or remove liquid from it • *She unscrewed the top of the tube and squeezed some paint onto the brush.* • *As she waited to go into the exam, he squeezed her hand* (= pressed it affectionately with his hand) *and wished her good luck.* • *Cut the lemon in half and squeeze the juice into the bowl.* • *I'd like a glass of* **freshly** *squeezed orange juice, please.* • *Once he had finished cleaning the floor, he emptied the bucket of dirty water and squeezed the cloth* **out**. [M] • *He reloaded the gun, took aim and then squeezed* (= pulled back) *the* **trigger**. • *(fig.) The studio is using all sorts of marketing tricks to squeeze as much profit* **from** *the movie as they can.* • *(fig.) By reducing its cover price, the newspaper is trying to squeeze* (= force) *rival papers* **out of** *the market.* • If you are squeezed by financial demands, they cause you financial problems: *Small businesses are being squeezed by heavy taxation.* ○ *The government's high interest rate is squeezing* (= reducing) *all areas of consumer spending.* • If you **squeeze** something, esp. money or information **out of** or **from** someone, you obtain it from them using persuasion or force: *After several hours of questioning, the police finally squeezed a confession out of the suspect.* ○ *During the negotiations, the union managed to squeeze several concessions from the management.* • If you **squeeze** someone **dry/squeeze** someone **until the pips squeak** (*Am* **bleed** someone **dry**), you obtain as much from them as possible: *When they got divorced, his wife squeezed him dry and took everything.* ○ *The latest tax increase will squeeze small businesses until the pips squeak.*

squeeze /skwiːz/ *n* [C] • *She gave the present a quick squeeze and tried to guess what was inside.* • *Garnish the fish with some fresh parsley and a squeeze of lemon.* • *(fig.) The squeeze* (= The limit put) **on** *local spending means that many public services will have to be cut.* • *(fig.) The massive squeeze* (= reduction) **on** *jobs within the oil industry has resulted in thousands of people being out of work.* • A squeeze is also a period in which the supply of money is limited by the government because of economic difficulties: *The government has imposed a sharp* **credit** *squeeze in an attempt to hold down inflation.* • *(Am)* A

squeeze bottle is a plastic container whose contents can be forced out through a narrow hole at the top by pressing the sides of the bottle together: *Liquids for washing dishes are often sold in squeeze bottles.*

squeez·er /£'skwiː·zəʳ, $-zɚ/ *n* [C] • A squeezer is a device which removes the juice from fruit by pressing it: *Squeezers are normally used to extract the juice from citrus fruit such as oranges, lemons and limes.* ○ *If you want to make your own lemonade, you'll need to buy a* **lemon** *squeezer.*

squeeze *(obj)* FORCE /skwiːz/ *v* [always + adv/prep] to force (someone or something) into a small space or a short period of time • *The car's quite full but we could manage to squeeze another couple of people* **in**. [M] • *While we're in Australia, we're hoping to squeeze* **in** *a trip to the Barrier Reef.* [M] • *I'm very busy this week but I could squeeze you* **in** (=see you briefly) *at 2.30 on Tuesday.* [T] • To squeeze in, through, under, etc. is to get in, through, under, etc. with difficulty: *The doors were shutting but we just managed to squeeze* **in**. [I] ○ *I must have put on a lot of weight over Christmas because I can only just squeeze* **into** *my jeans.* [I] ○ *She squeezed* **through** *the crowd and found a seat at the front.* [I] ○ *They managed to squeeze* **under** *the fence and get into the festival without paying.* [I]

squeeze /skwiːz/ *n* • *I can give you a lift but it'll be a* **tight** *squeeze as I'm taking four other people as well.*

squeeze-box /£'skwiːz·bɒks, $-bɑːks/ *n* [C] *dated infml* an ACCORDION

squelch *(obj)* /skweltʃ/ *v* to make a sucking sound like the one produced when you are walking on soft wet ground • *He got out of the car and squelched through the mud to open the gate.* [I always + adv/prep] • *They squelched back and forth across the wet carpet carrying things out of the flooded bathroom.* [I always + adv/prep] • *(Am)* If you squelch something that is causing you problems, you end it quickly: *A spokeswoman at the White House has squelched* **rumors** *about the president's ill-health.* [T] • *(Am)* If you squelch someone, you silence them with a critical remark: *The senator thoroughly squelched the journalist who tried to interrupt him during his speech.* [T]

squelch /skweltʃ/ *n* [C usually sing] • *As the hikers walked down the path by the house, she could hear the squelch of their boots in the mud.*

squel·chy /'skwel·tʃi/ *adj* **-ier, -iest** • *His shoes had been left out in the rain and made a squelchy sound when he put them on.*

squib EXPLOSIVE /skwɪb/ *n* [C] *esp. Am* a small explosive consisting of a tube filled with powder which makes a HISSING noise when it is lit • *The boys spent the afternoon setting off squibs and firecrackers.*

squib WRITING /skwɪb/ *n* [C] a short piece of writing • A squib attacks someone or something in a humorous way: *Her latest collection of poems includes a number of squibs aimed at other writers.* • *(Am)* A squib is also used in a newspaper or magazine to introduce a longer article or to fill space: *Each section of the newspaper has an index with short squibs describing stories which appear in the section.*

squid /skwɪd/ *n pl* **squid** or **squids** a sea creature with a long body and ten arms situated around the mouth • *The squid uses its two long arms to catch its prey and the eight shorter arms to hold the creature while eating it.* [C] • *Over 200 kinds of squid are available in Japan where it is a very popular food.* [C] • *He ordered a seafood salad and ate all the prawns but left the squid.* [U] • PIC› **Mollusc**

squidg·y /'skwɪdʒ·i/ *adj* **-ier, -iest** *Br infml* soft and wet and changing shape easily when pressed • *The modelling clay was soft and squidgy to the touch.* • *Bread which has just come out of the oven is often still squidgy in the middle.*

squif·fy (**-ier, -iest**) /'skwɪf·i/, *Am also* **squiffed** /skwɪft/ *adj infml* slightly drunk • *"I've only had one glass of sherry and I feel squiffy already," she said.*

squig·gle /'skwɪg·l̩/ *n* [C] a short line that has been written or drawn which curves and twists in an irregular way • *His signature was an illegible squiggle at the bottom of the page.* • *That's not art, that's just a few squiggles on a piece of paper!*

squig·gly /'skwɪg·l̩.i/ *adj* **-ier, -iest** • *She got out her crayons and drew a few squiggly* **lines** *on the paper.* • *What are the squiggly bits meant to represent in the picture?*

squinch *obj* /skwɪntʃ/ *v* [T] *Am* to squeeze together (the features of the face or the muscles of the body) • *He squinched* **up** *his face in a look that left no doubt about his displeasure.*

squint WAY OF LOOKING /skwɪnt/ *v* [I] to close your eyes partly in order to see more clearly • *The sun was shining straight in her eyes which made her squint.* • *He squinted* **at** *the departure board at the other end of the station to see which platform his train was leaving from.*

squint /skwɪnt/ *n* [C] • *(infml)* If you **have** or **take a squint at** something, you have a quick look at it: *"The back wheel of my bike doesn't seem straight." "I'll have a squint at it if you like."*

squint EYE CONDITION /skwɪnt/ *n* [C] a condition caused by a weakness of the eye muscles which makes the eyes look in different directions from each other • *A squint can often be corrected by eye exercises or by a simple operation.* • *As a child she wore thick glasses and had a bad squint.*

squire /£skwaɪəʳ, $skwaɪr/ *n* [C] *old use* (in the past in England) a man who owned most of the land around a village • *On Christmas Eve, the squire would give a party for all the people who worked on his estate.* • *(Br infml dated)* Squire is sometimes used as a friendly greeting by one man to another who might be of a higher social class: *"I don't know if all my luggage is going to fit in the back of the taxi." "Don't worry, squire, I'll get it in."* • LP› **Titles and forms of address**

squirm /£skwɜːm, $skwɜːrm/ *v* [I] to move from side to side in an awkward way because of nervousness, embarrassment or pain • *The thought of having to speak in front of 500 people made him squirm.* • *Nobody spoke for at least five minutes and Rachel squirmed in her chair* **with** *embarrassment.* • *The fish squirmed on the ground for a few moments and then lay still.*

squirm /£skwɜːm, $skwɜːrm/ *n* [C] • *She went red and* **gave** *a squirm of embarrassment when she saw the photos of the party.*

squir·rel /£'skwɪr·ᵊl, $'skwɜːr-/ *n* [C] a small furry animal with a long tail which climbs trees and feeds on nuts and seeds • *In the winter, the squirrel relies on food that it has collected and stored during the summer.* • *The most common types of squirrel are* **red** *squirrels and* **grey** *squirrels.* • PIC› **Wild animals in Britain**

squir·rel a·way *obj*, **squir·rel** *obj* **a·way** /£'skwɪr·ᵊl, $'skwɜːr-/ *v adv* [M] *Am and Aus infml* to hide or store (something, esp. money) • *As soon as they get paid they squirrel their money away so they won't be tempted to touch it.*

squirt *(obj)* /£skwɜːt, $skwɜːrt/ *v* (to force a liquid) to flow out through a narrow opening in a fast stream • *He squirted some tomato sauce* **on** *his burger.* [T] • *She picked up the water pistol and squirted water everywhere.* [T] • *There was a leak in one of the pipes and water was squirting* **out** *all over the kitchen floor.* [I always + adv/prep] • If you squirt someone **with** a liquid, you cover them in a stream of it: *She squirted her brother with soapy water as he came out of the house.* [T] ○ *She put on some lipstick, squirted herself with perfume and then put on her coat.* [T]

squirt /£skwɜːt, $skwɜːrt/ *n* [C] • *The door should stop squeaking once I've given it a few squirts of oil.* • *(dated disapproving)* A squirt is also a young or small person whom you consider to be unimportant and who has behaved rudely towards you: *I caught my neighbour's son writing graffiti on our wall, the little squirt.* • **Squirt gun** is *Am for* **water pistol**. See at WATER.

squish *obj* /skwɪʃ/ *v* [T] *infml* to crush (something which is soft) • *Don't sit on that bag – you'll squish the sandwiches.* • *She found a squished hedgehog in the middle of the road.*

squish /skwɪʃ/ *n* [C] *infml* • *As he walked along the path through the field, he could hear the squish of the damp ground beneath his boots.*

squish·y /'skwɪʃ·i/ *adj* **-ier, -iest** *infml* • *To make the fruit tart, you need a pound of pears which are ripe but not too squishy.*

Sr *esp. Am, Br and Aus usually* **Snr** *adj* [after n; not gradable] *abbreviation for* SENIOR OLDER. Used after a man's name to refer to the older of two people in the same family who have the same name.

SS /'es·es/ *n* [before n] *abbreviation for* STEAMSHIP • *The SS Great Britain was the first steamship to cross the Atlantic.*

ssh /ʃʊʃ/ *exclamation* SH

St HOLY PERSON *n* [before n] *abbreviation for* SAINT (=a person honoured by the Christian Church for being holy and good). It is used only before personal names. • *St Andrew is the patron saint of Scotland.* • *We went to a service at St Paul's Cathedral when we were in London.*

St [ROAD] *n abbreviation for* STREET (= a road in a town or village). It is used in writing after the name of a street. • *My new address in New York is 19 East 17th St.*

st [WEIGHT] *n* [C] *pl* **st** *Br abbreviation for* STONE (= a unit of weight equal to 6.35 kilograms) • *He weighs 12st 3lbs.*

stab *obj* /stæb/ *v* [T] **-bb-** to injure (someone) with a sharp pointed object such as a knife • *The tennis player was stabbed during a tournament in Hamburg.* • *He was jailed for fifteen years for stabbing his wife* **to death**. • *(fig.) While he was speaking, he stabbed the air* **with** *his cigarette to enforce the point he was making.* • If you stab **at** something with your finger or with an object that you are holding in your hand, you make forceful pushing movements at it: *She stabbed at the switch on the cassette recorder trying to make it work.* • If someone who you know **stabs** you **in the back**, they harm you or your reputation when you thought that you could trust them: *She was stabbed in the back by her brother, who had told the newspaper about her private life.* See also **back-stabber** at BACK [BODY PART].

stab /stæb/ *n* [C] • *He was admitted to St. Vincent's hospital with stab* **wounds**. • A stab is sometimes a sudden feeling, esp. an unpleasant one such as pain: *She felt a stab* **of** *envy when she saw all the expensive presents her friend had been given for Christmas.* • A stab can also be an action or remark that attacks someone's reputation: *Her criticism of the company's plans was a stab at the chairman himself.* • *(infml)* If you **have** or **make a stab at** something, you attempt to do it although you are not likely to be very successful: *I'd never tried water skiing before but I had a stab at it while I was in Greece.* ○ *He made a decent stab at writing his essay even though he didn't have much time to do it.*

stab·bing /ˈstæb·ɪŋ/ *n* [C] • *There have been several stabbings in our neighbourhood recently.* • A stabbing **pain** is a sudden pain: *She was awoken by a* **sharp** *stabbing pain in her chest.*

sta·ble [FIXED] /ˈsteɪ·bl̩/ *adj* **-r, -st** firmly fixed or not likely to move or change • *Heavier boats are more stable than lighter boats.* • *After several part-time jobs, he's now got a stable job in a bank.* • *Their marriage was in danger of breaking up last year but it seems quite stable now.* • *She was said to be in a stable* **condition** *following the heart transplant operation.* • *People who have been abused as children often find it difficult to establish stable, loving* **relationships** *as adults.* • If someone is described as being a stable person, they are calm and not easily upset: *Her last husband was rather moody and aggressive but she's now married to a very stable, caring man.* • *(specialized)* If a substance is described as stable, it keeps the same chemical or atomic state: *Diamonds make very strong cutting tools because of their stable structure and strong bonds.*

sta·bil·i·ty /£stəˈbɪl·ɪ·ti, \$-ə·ṭi/ *n* [U] • *The country has enjoyed a period of* **political** *stability during the past ten years.* • *This relationship gives him the sort of* **emotional** *stability which he needs so badly.*

sta·bi·lize *(obj), Br and Aus usually* **–ise** /ˈsteɪ·bɪ·laɪz/ *v* • If something stabilizes, it becomes fixed or stops changing: *He suffered a second heart attack two days ago but his condition has now stabilized.* [I] ○ *Since the early 1970s, the proportion of high school graduates going to college has stabilized* **at** *50%.* [I] • If you stabilize something, you cause it to become fixed or to stop changing: *In China, the policy of one child per family was introduced to stabilize the country's population at 1·6 billion.* [T] ○ *Many people hoped that the arrival of democracy in Russia would act as a stabilizing* **force**.

sta·bi·liz·er, *Br and Aus usually* **–iser** /£ˈsteɪ·bɪ·laɪ·zəʳ, \$-zɚ/ *n* [C] • A stabilizer is a device which helps an aircraft, ship or vehicle to balance: *(Br) When you first learn to ride a bike, you often need stabilisers (Am and Aus* **training wheels***)* (= small wheels fixed on each side of the back wheel) *to help you keep your balance.* • *(specialized)* A stabilizer is also a chemical which is added to something so that it stays in the same state: *Stabilizers are often added to food so that the texture remains the same during storage.* • *(Br)* A stabiliser is also a method used to limit sudden changes in prices or to limit the level of production: *Stabilisers agreed by the EU mean that prices paid to farmers will be cut if they produce more than 160 million tonnes of cereal a year.* • [PIC] **Bicycles**

sta·bi·li·za·tion, *Br and Aus usually* **–i·sa·tion** /ˌsteɪ·bɪ·laɪˈzeɪ·ʃᵊn/ *n* [U] • *European finance ministers are hoping to achieve currency stabilization by agreeing on a programme to keep exchange rates at their present levels.*

sta·ble [BUILDING] /ˈsteɪ·bl̩/ *n* [C] a building in which horses are kept • *He scattered some hay on the stable floor and led the horse inside.* • A stable is also a group of race horses that are owned or trained by one person: *The racehorse has returned to David Smith's stable to prepare for its last racing season.* • A stable is also a group of people who perform a similar activity and who are trained by the same person or employed by the same organization: *During the 1950s, Sun Records' stable* **of** *singers included Elvis Presley, Johnny Cash and Jerry Lee Lewis.* • A **stable boy** (*Br also* **stable lad**) or a **stable girl** is a young man or woman who works in a stable and cares for the horses: *She loved horses and managed to get a job as a stable girl over the summer.* • [PIC] **Farming**

sta·ble *obj* /ˈsteɪ·bl̩/ *v* [T] • *She lives in the city so she has to stable* (= keep) *her horse at a farm in the country.*

sta·bling /ˈsteɪ·bl̩·ɪŋ, ˈ-blɪŋ/ *n* [U] • *The only alteration we've made to the house is to add stabling for five horses.*

stac·ca·to /£stəˈkɑː·təʊ, \$-ṭoʊ/ *adj, adv, n* (musical notes which are) shortened and separate when played • *The music suddenly changed from a smooth melody to a staccato rhythm.* • *She played the whole piece staccato to improve her technique.* • *He practised his staccato so it was always crisp and clean.* • If a noise is described as being staccato, it consists of a series of short and separate sounds: *She gave brief staccato replies to every question.* ○ *As the plane passed overhead, we heard the staccato burst of anti-aircraft fire.* ○ *(fig.) The sharp staccato style he used in his last book was very popular with the critics.*

stack [PILE] /stæk/ *n* [C] an ordered pile of things arranged one on top of another • *I eventually found the letter I was looking for under a stack of papers.* • *He chose a cartoon from the stack of videos on the shelf.* • *(infml)* A stack is also a large amount: *I'm sorry I can't come out tonight but I've got a stack of things to do.* ○ *"Are we going to catch this train?" "Don't worry, we've got stacks of time."* • In a LIBRARY (= a building with a collection of books that can be borrowed), **the stacks** are the shelves which are positioned close together so that a lot of books can be stored on them: *In large libraries, the stacks are often closed to the public and if you want a book that is stored there, you have to order it.* • A **stack system** is a set of electronic equipment to play recorded sound, the parts of which are put on top of each other: *A stack system usually includes a radio, amplifier, cassette deck and CD player.*

stack *obj* /stæk/ *v* [T] • *Stack the washing up by the sink and I'll do it later.* • *Once the last few people had left the hall, the caretaker began stacking* **(up)** *the chairs.* • *I've just been shopping so the fridge is stacked* (= filled) **with** *food.* • *She's got a part-time job stacking* (= filling with goods) *shelves at the local supermarket.* • If aircraft are stacked **(up)** over an airport, they circle over the airport at different heights waiting to be told they can land: *At peak times, planes are often stacked over Gatwick airport for more than an hour.* [I] • *(esp. Am)* If you **stack up** one thing against another, you compare one thing with another: *The new model of this car just doesn't stack up* **against** *previous models.* • If you **stack the cards**/*(Am)* **stack the deck**, you arrange something in a dishonest way in order to achieve the result you want: *He should have got the promotion but they stacked the deck* **against** *him.* • If **the odds/cards are stacked against** you, it is very unlikely that you will succeed because you are not in an advantageous position: *She has so many enemies in the town that the odds are heavily stacked against her being elected to the council.*

stack [ACCIDENT] /stæk/ *n* [C] *Aus infml* a car accident, esp. one that causes damage • *(infml)* A **stack-up** is a road accident involving a row of cars.

stacked /stækt/ *adj Am and Aus slang* (of a woman) having large breasts. This word is considered offensive by many women.

sta·di·um /ˈsteɪ·di·əm/ *n* [C] *pl* **stadiums** or **stadia** /ˈsteɪ·di·ə/ a large enclosed area of land with rows of seats around the sides and often with no roof which is used for sporting events and musical performances • *Thousands of football fans packed into the stadium to watch the cup final.* • *The rock group U2 performed to an audience of 100 000 at Wembley Stadium.*

staff [PEOPLE] /£stɑːf, \$stæf/ *n* [C + sing/pl v] the group of people who work for an organization • *There is a good relationship between staff and pupils at the school.* • *The staff has been cut by a quarter over the past year.* • *The staff are not very happy about the latest pay increase.* • *Our company employs seventy* **members of staff**. • *He is* **on** (= a member of) *the editorial staff of the New York Times.* • *The maths teacher is in a staff* **meeting** *and won't be able to see you until this afternoon.* • *(Br)* A **staff nurse** is a person who works in a hospital taking care of the ill and injured and whose rank is below that of a SISTER (= the person in charge of each large room into which the hospital is divided). • A **staff officer** is an army officer who helps the officer in charge to plan military activities.

staff *obj* /£stɑːf, $stæf/ *v* [T often passive] • *Many charity shops in Britain are staffed* **with** *volunteers.* • *The restaurant is staffed* **by** *a friendly team of waiters and waitresses.* • *The new director claims the company is* **over-***staffed and that many jobs will have to be cut.*

staff [STICK] /£stɑːf, $stæf/ *n* [C] *fml* a strong stick held in the hand which is used as a support when walking • *He set off towards the top of the hill with a staff in his hand.* • A staff (or **flagstaff**) is a FLAGPOLE. • A staff is also a stick which is a symbol of office or authority: *She was presented with the staff of office at the inauguration ceremony.* • Bread is sometimes described as **the staff of life** because it is considered to be one of the most important foods we eat.

staff [MUSIC] /£stɑːf, $stæf/ *n* [C] *Am for* STAVE

staff·room /£ˈstɑːf·rʊm, -ruːm, $ˈstæf-/ *n* [C] a room in a school which is for the use of the teachers when they are not teaching • *She knocked on the staffroom door and asked to see Mr Shaw, the drama teacher.* • *(fig.) The government proposal to test 14-year-olds has been causing controversy in the staffroom* (= among teachers).

stag [ANIMAL] /stæg/ *n* [C] *pl* **stags** or **stag** an adult male deer • *Stag have large branch-like horns which are called antlers.* • *Many people support the campaign to ban fox and stag* **hunting**. • *(esp. Am)* If you **go stag** to an event, you go without a partner: *The two men were going to the party stag.* • *(Br)* A **stag party/stag night** (*Am* **bachelor party**, *Aus* **bucks party**) is a party for a man who is going to get married, to which only his male friends are invited: *Stag parties are traditionally organized by the bridegroom's best man.* ○ *On his stag night, he and his friends visited every single pub in the town centre.* Compare **hen night/party** at HEN.

stag [PERSON] /stæg/ *n* [C] *Br and Aus* a person who buys shares in a company which is being sold to the public with the intention of selling them immediately for profit • *A new computer system has been developed to find stags who have made illegal applications for shares.*

stag *(obj)* /stæg/ *v* **-gg-** *Br* • *In order to prevent people from stagging, investors are being offered a bonus if they keep their shares for longer than two years.* [I] • *More and more private investors are trying to stag* **shares**, *a practice which used to be common only among professional investors.* [T]

stage [PART] /steɪdʒ/ *n* [C] a part of an activity or a period of development • *The project is in its final stages and should be completed by August.* • *They did the last stage of their journey on foot.* • *The French cyclist is in the lead in the first stage of the race.* • *The talks in Geneva mark a crucial stage in the negotiations between the two countries.* • *The manual shows you how to change the oil in three easy stages.* • *Our relationship is going through a difficult stage at the moment.* • *A lot of the text will have to be revised at the editing stage.* • *Scientists have developed a test to show the presence of cancer in the body* **at** *an early stage.* • *I've been looking for a job for so long that I've* **reached** *the stage* **where** *I don't care what I do.* • *"Has Sarah started to talk yet?" "She's* **at** *the stage* **where** *she can say individual words but not full sentences."* • *I'm not tired at the moment but I will need a rest* **at some** *stage* (= at some time) *during the walk.* • *Andrew spends all his spare time playing with his computer but it's probably* **just** *a stage he's* **going through** (= a period of development that will end soon). • If you do something **in stages**, you divide the activity into parts and complete each part separately: *"Have you finished decorating your house yet?" "We're doing it in stages so it won't be ready for another couple of months."* • A stage is also one of the separate parts of a ROCKET (= a vehicle for travelling into space), each stage having its own engine: *Once its fuel supply runs out, each stage separates from the main part of the rocket and falls back to Earth.* ○ *Most spacecraft are launched into space on top of a* **three-***stage rocket.*

stage [THEATRE] /steɪdʒ/ *n* [C] the area in a theatre which is often raised above ground level and on which actors or entertainers perform • *He stood in the middle of the stage and looked out at the audience.* • *The orchestra spent ten minutes tuning up before going* **on** *stage.* • *In Scene 2, she is left alone* **on** *stage to reveal her feelings to the audience.* • *He began his stage* **career** *at the age of 17 in a performance of 'Romeo and Juliet'.* • *The play is a stage* **adaptation** *of William Golding's novel.* • *The opera singer returns to the London stage* (= will perform again in London) *this summer.* • A stage is a particular area of public life: *The issue of nuclear power has come to the centre of the* **political** *stage.* ○ *The president was extremely popular on the* **world** *stage but was disliked in his own country.* • *The concert was meant to begin at 9p.m. but the band didn't* **take the stage** (= start to perform) *until after 11.* • *Her daughter is an artist and her son is* **on the stage** (= is an actor). • *At the age of ten, he decided that he wanted to* **go on the stage** (= become an actor). • *She always likes to* **take centre stage** (= be at the centre of attention) *in whatever she does.* • A **stage direction** is a description or instruction in the text of a play which explains how the play should be performed: *In the stage directions it says that the servant enters from the right carrying a tray of drinks.* • The **stage door** is the door which is used by the actors and theatre workers when entering and leaving the theatre: *We stood by the stage door waiting to get the actors' autographs.* • Actors or performers who have **stage fright** are nervous because they are about to perform: *She suffered so badly from stage fright on her first night that she couldn't remember any of her lines.* • **Stage left** or **stage right** is the part of the stage to the left or right of the actors when they are facing the people watching the performance: *The two women exit stage left.* • A **stage manager** is the person who is responsible for the equipment and the use of the stage during a play or performance. • A **stage name** is the name by which an actor or entertainer is publicly known and which is different from their real name: *David Bowie is the stage name of the singer David Jones.* • If you are **stage-struck**, you are interested in the theatre and want to become an actor or actress: *I had been stage-struck since childhood and used to spend my all my time at the local theatre.* • If an actor says something in a **stage whisper**, it is intended to be heard by the people watching the play but it is pretended the other actors on the stage can not hear it: *The king announces to the audience in a stage whisper that he is planning to kill his son.* • If you say something in a **stage whisper**, you intend it to be heard by people other than the ones you are talking to: *"Isn't he gorgeous," she said in a stage whisper and he looked round and smiled at her.* • *"Don't put your daughter on the stage, Mrs Worthington"* (from the song *Mrs Worthington* by Noel Coward, 1935)

stage *obj* /steɪdʒ/ *v* [T] • If you stage a play or show, you arrange and perform it: *The local drama group is staging a production of the musical 'Grease'.* ○ *The farmer has withdrawn permission for the pop group to stage an open-air concert on his land.* • If you stage an event, you organize it: *Barcelona staged the Olympic Games in 1992.* ○ *Nurses are planning to stage a 24-hour* **strike** *in protest at the closure of three major London hospitals.* • If you stage-manage an event, you arrange and control it carefully in order to achieve the result you want: *The concert was stage-managed to give the singer maximum publicity.* ○ *Many people have become cynical at the stage-managed debates between politicians which regularly appear on television.*

stag·ing /ˈsteɪ·dʒɪŋ/ *n* [C] • The staging of a play or show is the performance of it: *The production is a modern staging of the fairytale Cinderella.* ○ *The play has not been performed since its disastrous first staging in 1951.* • A **staging area** is a place where soldiers and equipment are gathered together and prepared before military activity. • *(Br)* A **staging post** is a place where stops are regularly made on long journeys: *Hong Kong is often used as a staging post on flights from Melbourne to London.* ○ *The town became a staging post for trucks carrying supplies from the ports to the centre of the war zone.* ○ *(fig.) For people who have spent a long time in mental hospital, a hostel acts as an important staging post between hospital and a home of their own.*

stag·y, **stage·y** /ˈsteɪ·dʒi/ *adj disapproving* • If someone does something in stagy manner, they do it in a way that is very theatrical and not very natural: *His last television show was little more than a stagy farewell in front of millions of viewers.*

stage·coach /£ˈsteɪdʒ·kəʊtʃ, $-koʊtʃ/ *n* [C] (in the past) a covered vehicle pulled by horses that carried passengers and goods on regular routes • *Stagecoaches were easy targets for robbers because they travelled along certain routes at regular times.* • *By 1840, all the principal cities in the US were connected by several stagecoach* **lines**.

stage·hand /ˈsteɪdʒ·hænd/ *n* [C] a person who is employed in a theatre to move the equipment on the stage

stag·fla·tion /stægˈfleɪ·ʃᵊn/ *n* [U] an economic condition in which rising prices, high unemployment and little or no economic growth are present • *The rise in oil prices in 1973 led to a* **period** *of stagflation in the late 1970s.*

stag·ger MOVE /£ˈstæg·əʳ, $-ɚ/ *v* [I] to walk or move in a way that shows a lack of balance as if you are going to fall • *After he was attacked, he managed to stagger* **to** *the phone and call for help.* • *As we went into the bar, a drunken man staggered* **out of** *the door.* • *Every morning she would wake up at 7a.m. and stagger half-awake* **into** *the bathroom to get washed.* • *(fig.) The company is staggering* **under** *a $15 million debt and will almost certainly collapse by the end of the year.*

stag·ger /£ˈstæg·əʳ, $-ɚ/ *n* [C usually sing] • *He left the pub with a drunken stagger.*

stag·ger *obj* SHOCK /£ˈstæg·əʳ, $-ɚ/ *v* [T] to cause (someone) to feel shocked or surprised because of something unexpected or very unusual happening • *They'd only known each other for two weeks so I was staggered to hear that they'd decided to get married.* • *He staggered all his colleagues by suddenly announcing that he was leaving the company at the end of the month.*

stag·ger·ing /£ˈstæg·ᵊr·ɪŋ, $ˈ-ɚ-/ *adj* • *She won the race by a staggering seven seconds.* • *It costs a staggering $50 000 per week to keep the museum open to the public.*

stag·ger·ing·ly /£ˈstæg·ᵊr·ɪŋ·li, $ˈ-ɚ-/ *adv* • *The bank charged me a staggeringly high rate of interest on my £5000 loan.* • *She gave a staggeringly good performance in the TV programme as a police officer investigating a murder.*

stag·ger *obj* ARRANGE /£ˈstæg·əʳ, $-ɚ/ *v* [T] to arrange, esp. hours of work, holidays or events, so that they begin at different times from those of other people • *Lunch breaks for shop workers are often staggered so that shops can stay open over lunchtime.* • *Travellers are being advised to stagger their journeys this weekend as long delays are expected on main roads.* • *Many countries have introduced a system of staggered holidays in schools so that roads and holiday resorts do not become overcrowded.* • If a race has a staggered **start** the competitors start at different times or in different positions: *The official starter's gun set the seven all-women teams off on a staggered start.* • *(Br) A* **staggered junction** *is a place where several roads meet a main road at a slight distance apart so that they do not all come together at the same point.*

stag·ing /ˈsteɪ·dʒɪŋ/ *n* [C] See at STAGE THEATRE

stag·nant NOT FLOWING /ˈstæg·nənt/ *adj* not flowing or moving and smelling unpleasant • *There is a stagnant* **pool** *at the bottom of the garden.* • *Disease is a serious threat in the region because food is in short supply and the water is stagnant.* • *People who live in crowded cities often experience breathing problems during the summer when high temperatures combine with stagnant polluted air.*

stag·nant NOT BUSY /ˈstæg·nənt/ *adj* not growing or developing • *The stagnant property* **market** *is making it very difficult for many people to sell their houses.* • *In 1991, while the* **economies** *of industrialized countries were stagnant, the economies of many developing countries were growing rapidly.*

stag·nate /£stægˈneɪt, $ˈstæg·neɪt/ *v* [I] • *The electronics industry is showing signs of stagnating after 15 years of tremendous growth.*

stag·na·tion /stægˈneɪ·ʃᵊn/ *n* [U] • *A fear of unemployment is one of the main factors behind the current stagnation in the property market.* • *If the* **economic** *stagnation in many countries is to be overcome, trade needs to be increased between industrial and developing nations.*

stag·y /ˈsteɪ·dʒi/ *adj* See at STAGE THEATRE

staid /steɪd/ *adj* serious, boring and slightly old-fashioned • *He has a steady job, a house in a respectable neighbourhood and leads a very staid life.* • *In an attempt to change its staid image, the newspaper has created a new section aimed at younger readers.*

stain *(obj)* /steɪn/ *v* to leave a mark on (something) which is difficult to remove • *Mind how you eat those blackcurrants – they'll stain your shirt.* [T] • *Tomato sauce stains terribly – it's really difficult to get it out.* [I] • *He had smoked for so many years that his teeth were permanently stained yellow.* [T] • *While she was changing the wheel on her car, her coat had become stained* **with** *oil.* [T] • *(fig.) The country's history is stained* **with** *the blood of* (= The country is guilty of killing) *millions of innocent men and women.* [T] • *(fig.) Several important politicians have had their* **reputations** *stained* (= public opinion of their character spoiled) **by** *this scandal.* [T] • To stain something is also to change its colour using a chemical: *Stain the cell tissues before putting them under the microscope so that they can be seen clearly.* [T] ○ *She stripped the floorboards in the living room and stained them dark brown.* [T] • If a material stains, it absorbs substances easily causing it to become marked or coloured by a chemical: *This carpet is ideal for the kitchen because it doesn't stain easily.* [I] ○ *Pine stains better than oak.* [I] • **Stained glass** is glass which has been coloured and cut into various shapes to form pictures or patterns: *Stained glass is most commonly used in the decoration of church windows.* ○ *The Rose Window is the most famous stained-glass* **window** *in York Minster.*

-stained /-steɪnd/ *combining form* • *Two women with* **tear**-*stained faces told us how the fire had destroyed their village.* • *A* **blood**-*stained blanket was found near the victim's body.*

stain /steɪn/ *n* [C] • *You can remove a red wine stain from a carpet by sprinkling salt over it.* • *You'll need some stain* **remover** *to get rid of that ink on your trousers.* • *We've just had a new stain-***resistant** *carpet* (= one which does not show marks) *put in the living room.* • A stain is also a chemical for changing the colour of something: *Use a dark oak stain on the shelves before you varnish them.*

stain·less /ˈsteɪn·ləs/ *adj* • *(fig.) Before the recent political scandal, her* **reputation** *had been stainless* (= people thought she had never done anything wrong). • **Stainless steel** is a type of steel containing CHROMIUM which does not chemically react with air or water and does not change its colour: *Stainless steel is commonly used to make kitchen equipment such as cutlery and saucepans.*

stair /£steəʳ, $ster/ *n* [C] one of the steps in a set of steps which lead from one level of a building to another • *The top stair creaked as she went upstairs and the noise woke up her mother.* • *He tripped on the stair* **carpet** *and fell down the stairs.* • *(old use or literary)* A stair can also mean a set of stairs: *He climbed the wooden stair and knocked on his grandfather's door.* ○ *I thought I could hear footsteps on the stair.*

stairs /£steəz, $sterz/ *pl n* • Stairs are a set of steps which lead from one level of a building to another: *Go up the stairs and her office is on the right.* ○ *My apartment is at the top of a steep* **flight** (= set) *of stairs.* ○ *He stood at the* **foot** (= bottom) *of the stairs and called out "Breakfast's ready!"* ○ *She fixed a rail at the* **top** *of the stairs to prevent her young daughter from falling down them.* • *(Br old use)* In a large house, **below stairs** was the part of the house in which the servants worked and lived, and **above stairs** was the part where the owner lived: *As a young girl, she found life below stairs* (= as a servant) *hard and tiring.* ○ *Having worked as a butler for 25 years, he had witnessed life both above and below stairs.*

stair·case /£ˈsteə·keɪs, $ˈster-/ *n* [C] a set of stairs inside a building which usually has a bar fixed on the wall or onto vertical poles at the side for you to hold on to • *The staircase was lined with paintings of his ancestors.* • *She descended the* **sweeping** (= long and wide) *staircase into the crowd of photographers and journalists.* • *The apartment is on two floors and has a* **spiral** *staircase* (= stairs curved around a central point) *linking both levels.*

stair·way /£ˈsteə·weɪ, $ˈster-/ *n* [C] a passage in a public place with a set of steps that leads from one level to another • *We walked round the old city exploring the narrow streets with their dark stairways.* • *The safety officer checked that the stairways in the hotel weren't blocked and that the exit doors could be opened easily.* • *"Stairway to Heaven"* (title of a song by Led Zeppelin, 1971)

stair·well /£ˈsteə·wel, $ˈster-/ *n* [C] a long vertical passage through a building around which a set of stairs has been built • *A large sculpture has been erected in the main stairwell of the museum.*

stake STICK /steɪk/ *n* [C] a thick strong stick or metal bar with a pointed end • *Stakes are pushed or hammered into the ground and can be used to mark an area, support a plant or form part of a fence.* • *The area of land on which the house was to be built was marked out with thick wooden stakes.* • *When planting a young tree, fasten it to a short stake to support it.* • *According to popular legend, a vampire can be killed by driving a stake through its heart.* • In the past, **the stake** was the wooden post to which people were tied before being burned to death as a punishment: *In medieval Europe, many women were accused of being witches and were* **burnt at** *the stake.* ○ *The priest* **went to** *the stake* **for**

his heretical beliefs. ○ *(fig.) She passionately believed that the company was being mismanaged and was prepared to* **go to** *the stake* **for** (= defend despite the risks) *her views.*

stake *obj* /steɪk/ *v* [T] • *Tomato plants should be staked* (= fastened to a wooden stick) *when they are planted to stop the fruit from ripening on the ground and rotting.* • *They staked their* **tent** *on the riverbank.* • If you **stake a claim** to something, you state that you have a right to it and that it should belong to you: *He marked the spot on his map where he had seen the gold and returned later that month to stake his claim.*

stake SHARE /steɪk/ *n* [C] a share or a financial involvement in something such as a business • *The government is encouraging employees to own a stake in the company they work for.* • *He* **holds** *a 40% stake in the company.* • *She has just sold her* **minority** *stake in the television company.* • *Foreign investors control a* **majority** *stake in the firm.* • If you **have a stake in** something which is important to you, you have a personal interest or involvement in it: *The government wants parents to have a bigger stake in their children's education.* ○ *Employers have a stake in the training of their staff.*

stake·hold·er /£'steɪkˌhəʊl·dəʳ, $-ˌhoʊl·dɚ/ *n* [C] • A stakeholder is a person or group of people who have a share or a personal or financial involvement in a business: *Due to the losses the bank has made, almost all of its stakeholders will suffer – some staff will lose their jobs, customers will have higher charges and shareholders will see the price of their shares fall.*

stake RISK /steɪk/ *n* [C] the amount of money which you risk on the result of something such as a game or competition • *He loved gambling and each time he lost he would double his stakes.* • *She spent two weeks in Las Vegas playing* **high**-*stakes blackjack at the casinos.* • In an activity or competition, the stakes are the reward for the person who wins or succeeds in it: *The team is playing for enormous stakes – the chance to play in the final.* • If you **raise/up the stakes** in an activity or competition, you increase the prize or reward for which you are competing: *As soon as I looked at my cards, I thought I'd better up the stakes.* ○ *(fig.) The UN deadline for the withdrawal of troops has raised the stakes* (= made the situation more urgent) *in the conflict.* ○ *(fig.) They are trying to raise the stakes* (= make people take notice of the situation) *by refusing to let the boat dock until they are given money and aid.* • If something that is valuable is **at stake**, it is in a situation where it might be lost: *Thousands of lives will be at stake if emergency aid does not arrive in the city soon.* ○ *This race was her last chance to win a place on the national team so* **everything** *was at stake.* ○ *The real issue at stake* (= to be discussed) *is not how much the painting should be sold for but whether it should be sold at all.* • The Stakes is/are a horse race in which the prize money is provided by all the owners of the horses which are competing in the race: *The horse will be running in* **the** *International Stakes at York.* ○ *The stakes-***winning** *horse will be retiring from racing at the end of this season.* • The stakes also refers to a competitive activity when you consider how well or badly a person does in it: *The prime minister is not very high in* **the** *popularity stakes* (= he is not very popular) *at the moment.* ○ *Her years spent as an editor in the firm give her a definite advantage in* **the** *management stakes.*

stake *obj* /steɪk/ *v* [T] • *At the roulette table, he staked $10 000 on number 21.* • *The company was taking a huge gamble by staking* (= risking) *its future on expensive new technology.* • *She'll be head of this company in five year's time – I'd stake* (= risk) *my reputation on it.* • *(Am)* If you **stake** someone **to** something, you provide them with it or with what they need to obtain it: *The governor has promised to stake the city's homeless to what they need for a fresh start.* ○ *George Bush's father staked him to a start in the oil business by providing him with several oil wells.*

stake·hold·er /£'steɪkˌhəʊl·dəʳ, $-ˌhoʊl·dɚ/ *n* [C] • A stakeholder is a person who is in charge of the prize money of people risking money on the result of a game or competition and who gives it to the winner.

stake out *obj*, **stake** *obj* **out** *v prep* [M] to mark the limits of (an area or a piece of land) in order to claim ownership of it • *Each gang in the city has staked out its territory and defends it ruthlessly from other gangs.* • *They arrived several hours early for the concert and staked out a place at the front.* • If you stake out an opinion or position, you establish it or make it clear: *Two of the president's chief advisors have staked out opposite positions on this issue.* ○ *The software company is going to find it hard staking out a position in an already crowded market.* • *(esp. Am infml)* If the police stake out a building or area, they watch it continuously in secret: *The police staked out the hotel where the two terrorists were reported to be staying.*

stake-out /'steɪk·aʊt/ *n* [C] *esp. Am infml* • A stakeout is the continuous watching of a building or area, esp. by the police: *While police officers were on a stakeout of the suspect's house, they heard gunshots from inside the building.* ○ *The film star has been the victim of a media stakeout due to a recent scandal in her private life.*

stal·ac·tite /'stæl·ək·taɪt/ *n* [C] a column of rock that hangs from the roof of a cave and which is formed over a very long period of time by drops of water containing chemicals, esp. LIME, falling from the roof of the cave

stal·ag·mite /'stæl·əg·maɪt/ *n* [C] a column of rock which rises from the floor of a cave which is formed over a very long period of time by drops of water containing LIME falling from the roof of the cave • *Stalagmites and stalactites can sometimes meet to form a continuous column.*

stale /steɪl/ *adj* **-r, -st** no longer new or fresh, usually as a result of being kept for too long • *She threw the pieces of stale* **bread** *into the garden for the birds to eat.* • *Coffee* **goes** *stale within a couple of weeks so it is best to buy it in small quantities.* • *The morning after the party, their apartment smelled of stale cigarette* **smoke**. • *(fig.) She felt their relationship had lost its initial excitement and had become stale and predictable.* • *(fig.) He gave a boring speech full of stale* **jokes**. • *(fig.) By the time he finally agreed to give an interview, the story was already stale* **news**. • *(fig.)* If a person is described as being stale, they have lost interest in what they are doing because they are bored or are working too hard: *They had been working together for over five years and they had both become a little stale.* ○ *People who work under a lot of pressure tend to* **get** *stale quickly.*

stale·ness /'steɪl·nəs/ *n* [U] • *She tried to disguise the staleness of the bread by toasting it.* • *The repetitive nature of the work resulted in boredom and staleness among many of the staff.*

stale·mate /'steɪl·meɪt/ *n* a situation in which neither group involved in an argument can win or get an advantage and no action can be taken • *The situation remains a stalemate with neither side prepared to risk the lives of their soldiers in another battle.* [C] • *Tomorrow's meeting between the two leaders is expected to* **break** *a* **diplomatic** *stalemate that has lasted for ten years.* [C] • *Neither side was willing to compromise and the negotiations* **ended in** *stalemate.* [U] • *Despite long discussions, the workers and the management remain* **locked in** *stalemate.* [U] • In CHESS, stalemate is a position in which one player is unable to move, but their king is not being attacked, which means that neither of the two players wins. Compare CHECKMATE.

stalk PLANT PART /£stɔːk, $stɑːk/ *n* [C] the main stem of a plant, or the narrow stem that joins leaves, flowers or fruit to the main stem of a plant • *She trimmed the stalks of the tulips before putting them in a vase.* • *The base and stalks of fennel can be eaten raw in salad or cooked and eaten as a vegetable.* • *For this recipe you will need some minced beef, two stalks of celery and a tin of tomatoes.* • *Wash the redcurrants, remove the stalks and then add them to the mixture.* • A stalk is also a narrow structure that supports a part of the body in some animals: *The eyes of shrimps are on movable stalks.* • *(Br and Aus)* If your **eyes** are **out on stalks**, they are wide open with surprise: *His eyes were out on stalks as he watched his neighbour drive past in a brand new Porsche.* • PIC **Fruit**

stalk *obj* FOLLOW /£stɔːk, $stɑːk/ *v* [T] to follow (an animal or person) as closely as possible without being seen or heard • *He spent the weekend stalking deer in the Scottish highlands.* • *The detective followed the suspect wherever he went, like a wild animal stalking its prey.* • *The police had been stalking the woman for three weeks before they arrested her.* • *(literary)* If something unpleasant stalks a place, it appears there in a threatening way: *When night falls, danger stalks the streets of the city.* ○ *Famine and disease began to stalk the region after the flood.* • If a group of politicians use someone as a **stalking horse**, they make that person compete for a position in order to divide the opposition or to take attention away from another person who is competing, although that person has no chance of winning: *He was used as a stalking horse in the election to steal votes from the opposition candidate.*

stalk·er /£ˈstɔː·kəʳ, $ˈstɑː·kɚ/ *n* [C] • *Stalkers pay large sums of money to hunt deer in the region.* • *The north east area of the city has been terrorized by a stalker with a shotgun who has killed six people.*

stalk [WALK] /£stɔːk, $stɑːk/ *v* [I always + adv/prep] to walk in an angry or proud way • *She refused to accept that she was wrong and stalked furiously* **out of** *the room.*

stall [SHOP] /£stɔːl, $stɑːl/ *n* [C] a large table or a small shop with an open front from which goods are sold in a public place • *In the village market, the stalls are piled high with local vegetables.* • *Their family has* **run** *a* **market** *stall for fifty years.* • *I bought some old postcards of Paris from one of the* **book***stalls on the banks of the Seine.* • *(esp. Br)* A **stall holder** is a person who rents or owns a stall in a market. • ⓘ

stall [ENCLOSURE] /£stɔːl, $stɑːl/ *n* [C] an enclosure in which an animal is kept • *He spent the holidays cleaning out the pig stalls and feeding the chickens on his parents' farm.* • *The cowshed consists of a set of stalls in which the cows are fed and milked by machine.* • A stall is also a small area of a room which is separated from the main part of the room by walls or curtains: *There was one tiny bathroom between four of us with a single washbasin and a* **shower** *stall in the corner.* • ⓘ

stall *(obj)* [ENGINE] /£stɔːl, $stɑːl/ *v* (to cause a vehicle or its engine) to stop suddenly and unintentionally • *A car may stall due to the driver braking too suddenly or using the choke incorrectly or because of mechanical failure.* [I] • *The car stalled at the junction and he had problems starting it again.* [I] • *I stalled the car twice during my driving test but still managed to pass.* [T] • LP> **Driving** ⓘ

stall *(obj)* [DELAY] /£stɔːl, $stɑːl/ *v* to delay taking action or avoid giving an answer in order to have more time to make a decision or obtain an advantage • *Stop stalling and give me a decision.* [I] • *She says she'll give me the money next week but I think she's just stalling* **for time**. [I] • If you stall a person, you delay them or prevent them from doing something for a period of time: *I managed to stall him for a few days until I'd got enough money to pay back the loan.* [T] ○ *(esp. Am) The thief broke into the office while his accomplice stalled* **off** *the security guard.* [T] • If you stall an event, you delay it or prevent it from happening for a period of time: *The commander was confident his troops would be able to stall an enemy attack by destroying bridges and blocking roads.* [T] ○ *Fears are growing that a tax increase may stall economic recovery.* [T] • ⓘ

stal·li·on /ˈstæl·jən/ *n* [C] an adult male horse which is used for breeding • *A male horse is called a stallion when it is over four years old.* • Compare MARE.

stalls [CHURCH] /£stɔːlz, $stɑːlz/ *pl n* rows of fixed seats in a church which often have their sides and backs enclosed • *The stalls are normally reserved for the choir and members of the clergy.* • *There was no room in the main part of the church so we had to sit in the* **choir** *stalls.*

stalls [THEATRE] *Br and Aus* /£stɔːlz, $stɑːlz/, *Am* **or·che·stra** *pl n* **the stalls** the seats on the main floor of a theatre or cinema, not at a higher level • *There are some seats left in the stalls but they're quite expensive.* • Compare CIRCLE [UPPER FLOOR]; GALLERY [RAISED AREA].

stal·wart [LOYAL] /£ˈstɔːl·wət, $ˈstɑːl·wɚt/ *adj* loyal, esp. for a long time; able to be trusted • *She has been a stalwart supporter of the party for many years.*

stal·wart /£ˈstɔːl·wət, $ˈstɑːl·wɚt/ *n* [C] • *Let me introduce Bob, one of the club's stalwarts* (=he has belonged to it loyally for a long time).

stal·wart·ly /£ˈstɔːl·wət·li, $ˈstɑːl·wɚt-/ *adv*

stal·wart [STRONG] /£ˈstɔːl·wət, $ˈstɑːl·wɚt/ *adj fml* (esp. of a person) physically strong • *Stalwart policemen stood guard outside.*

sta·men /ˈsteɪ·mən/ *n* [C] *pl* **stamens** or **stamina** /ˈstæm·ɪ·nə/ *specialized* the male reproductive part of a flower, consisting of a thin stem which holds an ANTHER • PIC> **Flowers and plants**

stam·i·na /ˈstæm·ɪ·nə/ *n* [U] the physical and/or mental strength to do something which might be difficult and which will take a long time • *The triathlon is a great* **test** *of stamina.* • *It takes stamina more than anything to read all the books.*

stam·mer *(obj)* /£ˈstæm·əʳ, $-ɚ/ *v* to speak or say (something) with unusual pauses or repeated sounds, either because of speech problems or because of fear and anxiety • *He usually stammers when he meets someone for the first time because it makes him nervous.* [I] • *"Wh-when can we g-go?" she stammered.* [+ clause] • *She'll stammer her words if you upset her.* [T] • Compare STUTTER [SPEAK].

stam·mer /£ˈstæm·əʳ, $-ɚ/ *n* [U] • *Robert has a bit of a stammer but it was much more noticeable when he was younger.*

stam·mer·er /£ˈstæm·əʳ·əʳ, $-ɚ·ɚ/ *n* [C] • *We need to listen and give stammerers time to finish what they are saying.*

stam·mer·ing·ly /£ˈstæm·əʳ·ɪŋ·li, $ˈ-ɚ-/ *adv*

stamp [LETTER] /stæmp/, *fml* **post·age stamp** *n* [C] a small piece of paper with a picture or pattern on it which is stuck onto a letter or parcel before it is posted to show that postage has been paid for • *I'll take these postcards please – and do you sell stamps as well?* • *When you've* **stuck** *the stamps on your letter you can put it in the postbox outside.* • *Miss Baltimore's hobbies include scuba diving and stamp collecting.* • *(Br)* A stamp is also a small piece of paper you can buy which then represents the value of the money it cost. Buying such stamps regularly allows something to be paid for over a period: *vehicle-licence stamps*

stamp *obj* /stæmp/ *v* [T] • *Are you sure you remembered to stamp the letter – Moira says she hasn't received it.* • *Please send a* **stamped addressed envelope** *(abbreviation* **sae**, *Am also* **self-addressed stamped envelope***)* (=an envelope with a stamp on it and the address of the person it is to be sent to) *if you would like to receive the free fact sheet which accompanies this programme.*

stamp *(obj)* [FOOT] /stæmp/, *Am also* **stomp** *v* to put (a foot) down on the ground hard and quickly usually making a loud noise, often to show anger • *It's no good you stamping your feet – you're going to take this medicine and that's that.* [T] • *They were stamping their feet and clapping their hands and screaming for an encore.* [T] • *She stood by the road, stamping her feet to stay warm.* [T] • *I wish those people upstairs would stop stamping* **(about/around)**. [I] • *Furious, she stamped* **out** *of the room.* [I] • *Why did you stamp* **on** *that insect – it wasn't hurting you?* [I] • *(fig.) Any opposition to the new government was immediately stamped* **on** (=stopped or prevented) *by the army.* [I] • If someone **stamps out** something/**stamps** something **out** they stop it or destroy it: *Terrorism will be ruthlessly stamped out.* ○ *Stamping tax fraud out is the main objective of this bureau.* • *(infml)* A **stamping ground** is a place or area which someone is very familiar with and which they like to go to: *Do you go back to any of our old stamping grounds any more?* • Compare STOMP.

stamp /stæmp/ *n* [C] • *With a stamp of her foot she stormed out.*

stamp [MARK] /stæmp/ *n* [C] a tool for putting a mark on an object either by printing on it or pushing into it, or the mark made • *We can make up a stamp of your company name within two hours.* • *A date stamp inside the front cover of the book shows when it should be returned.*

stamp *obj* /stæmp/ *v* [T] • *It is necessary to stamp your passport.* • *All washing machines are stamped* **with** *the inspector's name after they have been checked for quality.* • *You'll find the country of origin stamped* **on** *the base of each crate.* • *(fig.) That awful sound will be stamped* **on** *her memory for ever* (=she will always remember it).

stamp [QUALITY] /stæmp/ *n* [U] a particular quality in something or someone, or a quality in something which shows it was done by a particular person or group of people • *Although this painting clearly bears the stamp* **of** *genius, we don't know who painted it.* • *Each manager has* **left** *his or her own stamp* **on** *the way the company has evolved.* • *Her account of what happened just doesn't seem, to me, to bear the stamp* **of truth**.

stamp *obj* /stæmp/ *v* [T] • *Wittgenstein's influence stamps him* **as** *one of the most important philosophers of the twentieth century.* • *Glaze of this colour and thickness would stamp the pot* **as** *being from the Sung dynasty.* • *Our new administrator seems to be trying to stamp her authority* **on** *every aspect of the department.* • *It would be too early to stamp the changes* **with** *approval.*

stamp·ede /stæmˈpiːd/ *n* [C] a group of large animals which suddenly all move quickly in the same direction at the same time, esp. because of fear • *(fig.) Several people were injured in what was a virtual stampede outside the stadium.* • *(fig.) Motorists created a stampede to the petrol stations to avoid price rises which come into effect at midnight.*

stamp·ede *(obj)* /stæmˈpiːd/ *v* • *A loud clap of thunder made the herd stampede/stampeded the herd.* [I/T] • *(fig.*

disapproving) No amount of pressure will stampede this committee **into** *making hasty decisions.* [T]

stance OPINION /£stɑːnts, $stænts/ *n* [C] a way of thinking about something, esp. expressed in a publicly stated opinion • *He found that a tough negotiating stance paid off.* • *The doctor's stance* **on** *the issue of abortion is well known.*

stance WAY OF STANDING /£stɑːnts, $stænts/ *n* [C] a particular way of standing • *Jenny took up a stance with her feet slightly apart, ready to catch the ball.*

stanch *obj* /stɑːntʃ/ *v* [T] *Am for* STAUNCH STOP

stan·chion /£'stɑːn·tʃən, $'stæn-/ *n* [C] a strong vertical bar or pole used as a support

stand *(obj)* VERTICAL /stænd/ *v past* **stood** /stʊd/ to be in, move to be in or put into a vertical state, esp. (of a person or animal) by straightening the legs • *Stand in front of the house and I'll take a picture of you.* [I] • *Granny says if she stands for a long time her ankles hurt.* [I] • *Rick stood motionless, listening to the whispers from inside the room.* [I] • *Stand* **against** *the wall while I measure how tall you are.* [I] • *We stood* **around** *in the cold for about an hour.* [I] • *It's good to sit down, we've been standing* **(up)** *all afternoon.* [I] • *As a sign of politeness you should stand* **(up)** *when she comes in.* [I] • *Stand the bottles* **on** *the table over there.* [T always + adv/prep] • *Stand* **in** *a straight line and shut up!* [I] • *Stand* **aside** (= Move sideways) *so the doctor can get through.* [I] • *Please stand* **back** (= move further away) – *then all of you will be able to see what I'm doing.* [I] • *I'll make sure everybody is standing* **clear**, *then you can drive up to the gates.* [I] • *Stand* **still** *and be quiet!* [I] • *After the earthquake not a single building was left standing in the village.* [I] • In the past the expression **Stand and deliver!** was used by HIGHWAYMEN when they stopped a carriage on a road to demand items of value from the travellers. • If you **stand by** something, such as an agreement, you keep to it: *We shall stand by the decision/agreement/promise we made on reforms.* ○ *His wife stood by* (= stayed loyal to) *him despite all of the rumours in the press.* • People who are **standing by** are waiting ready to take action: *Cabin crew, please stand by* **for** *takeoff.* ○ *All fire fighters stand by.* ○ *Armed police are standing by if the demonstration gets out of control.* See also STANDBY. • To **stand by** is also to allow something to happen without trying to stop it: *You can't just stand by and let those trees be chopped down when they don't need to be.* See also BYSTANDER. • If someone or something **stands** their **ground** either they refuse to be pushed backwards or they maintain their beliefs in an argument. • *Two soldiers permanently* **stand guard** *outside these barracks* (= guard them). • To **stand on ceremony** is to behave in a formal way: *Please sit down and make yourself comfortable, we don't stand on ceremony here.* • *(usually disapproving)* If a person **stands on** their **dignity** they demand to be shown the respect which they think they deserve: *The Director didn't stand on her dignity, she helped us clear up.* • If someone **stands on** their **hands/head** they support themself on their hands/on their head and hands with their feet up as high as possible. • *(infml)* If someone can do something **standing on** their **head** they can do it very easily: *It's the sort of program he could write standing on his head.* • Also, if something new **stands** something established **on** its **head**, then the truth of the established thing or the beliefs on which it is based are doubted: *New data has stood the established explanation of the island's origin on its head.* ○ *Her latest play stands many conventions of theatrical performance on their head.* • *(infml)* When a person **stands on** their **own (two) feet** they can provide all of the things they need for living without help from anyone else: *She'll have to get a job and learn to stand on her own two feet sooner or later.* • To **stand or fall by** something is to completely depend on it for success. • To **stand (up) and be counted** is to make your opinions known even if doing so might cause you harm or difficulty: *Those who did have the courage to stand up and be counted were arrested and imprisoned.* • If COMEDY (= something which is amusing) is described as **stand-up**, it is performed by a single person telling jokes: *a stand-up comedian* ○ *a stand-up routine* • *"Stand by your Man"* (title of a song by Tammy Wynette, 1968)

stand·ing /'stæn·dɪŋ/ *adj* [before n; not gradable] • *Her performance received a* **standing ovation** *(Am also* **standing O**) *from an ecstatic audience* (= they stood up to clap). • *This car can reach 60mph from a* **standing start** (= from not moving) *in less than six seconds.* • **Standing room** is space in a sports ground, theatre, bus etc. where people can stand, esp. if all of the seats have people sitting in them: *All seats are taken, so now there's standing room* **only**. ○ *At the Genesis concert it's bound to be* **standing room only** (= lots of people will be there). • See also STANDING PERMANENT.

stand STATE /stænd/ *v past* **stood** /stʊd/ to be in, cause to be in or get into a particular state or situation • *With the situation as it stands* (= is) *right now it's impossible to say who will win.* [I] • *How do you think your chances stand* (= are) *of being offered the job?* [I] • *The national debt stands* **at** *fifty-five billion dollars.* [I] • *Martina is currently standing second in the world listings.* [L only + adj] • *Our firm stands* **to** *lose* (= will lose) *a lot of money if the deal is unsuccessful.* [+ *to* infinitive] • *We stand* **to** *gain/win a lot if our plans are approved.* [+ *to* infinitive] • *The danger of flooding stands* (= continues to exist) *while this heavy rain continues.* [I] • *We really can't allow the current situation to stand* (= exist unchanged). [I] • *Newtonian mechanics stood* (= was thought to be completely true) *for over two hundred years.* [I] • *Mix one sachet of paste into two litres of water, then leave the mixture to stand* (= do not touch it) *for at least fifteen minutes before use.* [I] • *It would be difficult for her to stand much lower/higher* **in my opinion** (= for me to have a worse/better opinion of her) *after the way she behaved at the party.* [I] • *(fml) You stand* **accused of** *murder, how do you plead?* [L only + adj] • *(fig.) Stand* **fast/firm** (= Be determined) *on your decision and you're more likely to get the result you want.* [L only + adj] • *(fig.) Don't stand* **over** (= watch) *me all the time – it makes me nervous.* [I] • *(fig.) We all stand* **together** (= agree) *on the issue of improving working conditions.* [I] • *Many houses built toward the end of the boom have stood* **empty** *throughout this recession.* [L only + adj] • *The old sawmill has been standing* **idle** *for a couple of years.* [L only + adj] • *She can't be released from police custody until someone* **stands bail** *for her* (= pays for her to be free). • When a person says that they **stand corrected**, they admit that a particular thing they have said or done was wrong: *I stand corrected – the date of foundation was 1411, and not 1412 as I had written.* • If an experience **stands** a person **in good stead** it is or will be of great use to them: *Even if you're not accepted, going to the interviews will stand you in good stead* **for** *applying to other colleges.* • *(slightly infml)* **It stands to reason** means it is obvious or clear from the facts: *If 20% of the Earth's population has 80% of its resources, then it stands to reason* **that** *80% of the population has only 20% of the resources.* • If a person **stands trial** they are put on trial in a court of law: *Two other men are to stand trial next month* **for** *their part in the bombing.* • Something, such as a computer or a business, which is **stand-alone** can work on its own without needing help from another similar thing.

stand *(obj)* PLACE /stænd/ *v* [always + adv/prep] *past* **stood** /stʊd/ to be in, cause to be in or put into a particular place • *The room was empty except for a desk which stood in the middle.* [I] • *An old hut covered with moss and ivy stood by the river.* [I] • *Stand the paintings against the wall while we decide where to hang them.* [T] • *The photograph shows them standing beside a banana tree.* [I] • *We've got a lot of new washing machines just standing in the showroom waiting to be bought.* [I] • Vehicles that are standing are waiting: *The train now standing* **at** *platform 8 is the 15.17 for Oxford.* [I] ○ *(Am and Aus) 'No Standing'* (= sign forbidding drivers from waiting or loading their vehicles) • *(fig.) You know I won't stand* **in** *your* **way/path** (= try to stop you) *if you want to apply for a job abroad.* [I] • *(fig.) Now that their parents have agreed to the marriage, nothing will stand* **in the way of** (= stop or prevent) *their future happiness.* [I]

stand *obj* ACCEPT /stænd/ *v* [in negatives or questions; not *be standing*] *past* **stood** /stʊd/ to successfully accept or bear (something which is unpleasant or difficult) • *I can't stand any more of her stupid questions.* • *Our tent won't stand another storm like the last one.* • *He thinks he became ill because he couldn't stand the pressure of his job.* • *I can't stand hearing her cry.* [+ v-*ing*] • *She can't stand anyone touching her.* [+ obj + v-*ing*] • *Which songs from the last year will* **stand the test of time** (= still be thought of as good in the future)? • *Aunt Gloria can't* **stand the sight of** (= hates) *cats because she was attacked by one when she was a child.* • *"If you can't stand the heat, get out of the kitchen"* (said by Harry Vaughan, but often used by US President Harry S Truman, 1884-1972)

stand SPORT /stænd/ *n* [C] *Br and Aus* a large structure at a sports ground, usually with a sloping floor and sometimes a roof, where people either stand or sit to watch a sports event • *We've got tickets for the North Stand.* • Compare GRANDSTAND.

stands /stændz/ *pl n* • *Fighting broke out in the stands* (= stand) *five minutes before the end of the match.*

stand [OPINION] /stænd/ *n* [C] an opinion, esp. one which is public • *What's her stand* **on** *sexual equality?*

stand /stænd/ *v* [I always + adv/prep] *past* **stood** /stʊd/ • *How/Where does he stand* (= What are his opinions) **on** *the issue of foreign policy?* • **From where** someone **stands** means the beliefs and ideas from which they form opinions and decisions: *You can see why they refused her demand for a pay rise, but from where she stands it probably seemed perfectly reasonable to ask.*

stand [POLITICS] *Br and Aus* /stænd/, *esp. Am* **run** *v* [I] *past* **stood** /stʊd/ to compete, esp. in an election, for an official position • *The president has announced she does not intend to stand* **for** *re-election.*

stand *obj* [SUCCEED] /stænd/ *v* [T] *past* **stood** /stʊd/ **stand a chance** to have a chance of success • *She stands a good chance* **of** *passing her exam if she works hard.*

stand [COURT] /stænd/ *n* [C] *Am for* **witness box**, see at WITNESS [LAW] • *The witness* **took** (= went to stand in) *the stand.*

stand [SHOP] /stænd/ *n* [C] a small shop or STALL or an area where products can be shown, usually outside or in a large public building, at which people can buy things or obtain information • *a candyfloss stand* • *a hot-dog stand* • *Over three thousand companies will have stands at this year's microelectronics exhibition.* • See also NEWSSTAND.

stand [FRAME] /stænd/ *n* [C] a frame or piece of furniture for supporting or putting things on • *a music stand* • *a retort stand* • *a hatstand* • *Put the dictionary back on its stand when you've finished with it.* • [PIC] **Laboratory**

stand [HEIGHT] /stænd/ *v* [L only + n] *past* **stood** /stʊd/ to be a stated height • *Even without his shoes he stood over seven feet.*

stand [OPPOSITION] /stænd/ *n* [C usually sing] an act of opposition, esp. in defence • *Environmental groups have joined to* **make a** *stand* **against** *the proposals for a road through the valley.* • *The press say she's going to* **take a** *strong stand* **on** *increasing taxation.*

stand /stænd/ *v* [I always + adv/prep] *past* **stood** /stʊd/ • *More and more people are standing* **against**/*(Br and Aus also) standing* **out against** *what is a very unpopular piece of legislation.*

stand *obj* [BUY] /stænd/ *v* [+ two objects] *past* **stood** /stʊd/ to buy (something, esp. a meal or a drink) for (someone) • *I couldn't get to the bank, can you stand me lunch?* • *They have agreed to stand* (= pay) **bail** *(***for** *their son).*

stand [PERFORMANCES] /stænd/ *n* [C usually sing] *Am* a particular number or period of performances • *The Orioles will be in town for a three-game stand against the Tigers.* • *Liza's doing a two-week stand at Radio City Music Hall next spring.*

stand down *v adv* [I] to give up one's official position • *He's decided to stand down after fifteen years as managing director.*

stand for *obj* [ACCEPT] *v prep* [usually in negatives or questions] to accept, esp. without complaining • *You don't have to stand for that sort of behaviour from him – he's not your boss.*

stand for *obj* [REPRESENT] *v prep* [T] to represent, esp. by being a shortened form • *'GMT' stands for Greenwich Mean Time.* • *(fig.) All of you know what this party stands for* (= what its principles are and what it supports).

stand in, *Am usually* **fill in** *v adv* [I] to do the usual activities of someone else • *Can we find someone to stand in* **for** *Jane at the office while she's on holiday?*

stand-in /'stænd·ɪn/ *n* [C] • A stand-in is a person who takes the place or does the job of another person for a short time, for example because the other person is ill or on holiday: *a stand-in teacher* ○ *The lecturer didn't turn up, so we had to find a stand-in.*

stand out *v adv* [I] to be very noticeable • *The black lettering really stands out on that orange background.* • *We had lots of good applicants for the job, but one stood out* **from** (= was much better than) *the rest.* • See also OUTSTANDING [EXCELLENT].

stand up *obj*, **stand** *obj* **up** *v adv* [M] *infml* to intentionally fail to meet (someone you have arranged to meet for social or sexual purposes) • *I don't know if I've been stood up or if she's just late – I'll wait another half hour.*

stand up for *obj v adv prep* [T] to defend and fight for • *Don't be bullied, learn to stand up for your***self** *and what you believe in.*

stand up to *obj v adv prep* [T] to not be changed or damaged by • *Will the lorries stand up to the journey over rough roads?* • *Their argument won't stand up to* (= appear to be true after) *detailed criticism.* • *She stood up to* (= refused to be unfairly treated by) *Phelps in the meeting.*

stand·ard [USUAL] /£'stæn·dəd, $-dɚd/ *adj* usual rather than special, esp. when thought of as being correct or acceptable • *White is the standard colour for this model of refrigerator.* • *Gloss finish is standard, but we can supply it in matt.* • *These are standard* **procedures** *for handling radioactive waste.* • *It's still a standard text in archaeology, even though it was written more than twenty years ago.* • *The metre is the standard unit for measuring length in the SI system.* • Language described as standard is the form of that language which is considered acceptable and correct by most educated users of it: *Most announcers on the BBC speak standard* **English**. ○ *In Standard* **American**, *'gotten' is used as a past participle of 'get'.* • *(esp. Br) Your new TV comes with a two year guarantee* **as** *standard.* • *(Am)* If a way of doing something is **standard operating procedure** (*abbreviation* **SOP**), it is the usual way of doing it: *Checking references before we lend money is standard operating procedure.* • In a country or a part of it, **standard time** is the time which is officially used. Compare GREENWICH MEAN TIME. • See also SUBSTANDARD.

stand·ard /£'stæn·dəd, $-dɚd/ *n* [C] • A standard is a song or other piece of music which has been regularly played over a long period of time. • *(Am)* A standard is also a car with GEARS that are changed by hand.

stand·ard·ize *obj*, *Br and Aus usually* **-ise** /£'stæn·də·daɪz, $-dɚ-/ *v* [T] • *We standardize parts such as rear-view mirrors, so that one type will fit any model of car we make.* • *School officials this year will also be scrutinizing achievement scores on standardized tests.*

stand·ard·i·za·tion, *Br and Aus usually* **-i·sa·tion** /£,stæn·də·daɪ'zeɪ·ʃᵊn, $-dɚ-/ *n* [U]

stand·ard [QUALITY] /£'stæn·dəd, $-dɚd/ *n* a level of quality • *This essay is not of an acceptable standard – do it again.* [C] • *This piece of work is well* **below** *standard/is not* **up to** *standard.* [U] • *We have very high safety standards in this laboratory.* [C] • *The food is of the standard you'd expect for the price you pay.* [C] • *It's not surprising the crops are below the minimum standard, the weather has been so bad.* [C] • *Not everyone judges success by the same standards – some people think happiness is more important than money.* [C] • *Her technique became a standard against which all future methods were compared.* [C] • A standard is also a moral rule which should be obeyed: *Most people agree that there are standards* **(of behaviour)** *which need to be upheld, but agreeing on them is rather more difficult.* [C] • A **standard of living** (also **living standard**) is the amount of wealth and comfort people have in a particular society: *The standard of living in many developing countries is low.* Compare **cost of living** at COST [MONEY].

stand·ard [FLAG] /£'stæn·dəd, $-dɚd/ *n* [C] a flag, esp. a long narrow one ending with two long points • *the royal standard* • A **standard-bearer** is the person or thing who seems to lead a group of people having similar ideas or moral opinions: *Mr Everhart wants Caltech to be the standard-bearer for excellence in scientific research of all kinds.*

stand·ard lamp *Br and Aus*, *Am* **floor lamp** *n* [C] an electric light supported by a tall pole which is fixed to a base that stays on the floor of a room • [PIC] **Lights**

stand·by /'stænd·baɪ/ *n* [C] *pl* **standbys** something which is always ready for use, esp. if a regular one fails • *Board games are a good standby to keep the children amused if the weather is bad.* • *There are standby generators but these usually only have to work for a few hours a year during power cuts.* • When a person or a thing is **on standby** they are ready to be used if necessary: *Hospitals are on standby ready to deal with casualties being flown in from the crash site.* • A **standby (ticket)** for a flight or a theatre is a cheap ticket sold just before the flight or the performance if there is a seat available: *I'm sorry, there are no standbys left.* • See also **stand by** at STAND [VERTICAL].

stand·ing [PERMANENT] /'stæn·dɪŋ/ *adj* [before n; not gradable] permanent, rather than formed or created when necessary • *a standing committee* • *You know you have a standing* **invitation** *to come and stay anytime you're in town.* • *(Br)* A **standing order** is an instruction to a bank to pay a particular amount of money at regular times from a person's bank account to another bank account. Compare **direct debit** at DIRECT STRAIGHT. • A **standing joke** is something which a particular group of people are familiar with and laugh about often, esp. in an unkind way: *The fact that Debbie is always late has become a standing joke among her friends.* ○ *After losing the court case the company became something of a standing joke in the business world.* • See also **standing** at STAND VERTICAL. • Ⓕ

stand·ing REPUTATION /ˈstæn·dɪŋ/ *n* [U] reputation, rank or position in an area of activity, system or organization • *As a pathologist of considerable standing, his opinion will have a lot of influence.* • *She may be of high social standing, but if she's committed a crime, she will be subject to the law like everyone else.* • *A financial scandal would shake the Institute's standing in the international academic community.* • Ⓕ

stand·ing TIME /ˈstæn·dɪŋ/ *n* [U] *slightly fml* the time for which something has existed • *One member,* **of** *twelve years' standing on the committee, resigned because of the changes.* • *This decision settles a squabble* **of long** *standing* (= which has existed for a long time). • See also **long-standing** at LONG TIME. • Ⓕ

stand-off /£ˈstænd·ɒf, $-ɑːf/ *n* [C] a situation in which agreement in an argument does not seem possible; STALEMATE • *Diplomats said yesterday that the renewed standoff represented a setback for the Helsinki process.*

stand-off-ish /£ˌstændˈɒf·ɪʃ, $-ˈɑː·fɪʃ/ *adj infml disapproving* slightly unfriendly; behaving in a formal way

stand-off-ish-ly /£ˌstændˈɒf·ɪʃ·li, $-ˈɑː·fɪʃ-/ *adv infml disapproving*

stand-off-ish-ness /£ˌstændˈɒf·ɪʃ·nəs, $-ˈɑː·fɪʃ-/ *n* [U] *infml disapproving*

stand-out /ˈstænd·aʊt/ *n* [C] *Am* an excellent or the best example of something • *While all the desserts are pretty good, the clear standout is the lemon pie.* • *The participants in the festival were all so good, it's difficult to pick a standout.* • *The team's standout goalie made four spectacular saves within the first 40 minutes of play.*

stand-pipe /ˈstænd·paɪp/ *n* [C] a vertical pipe which is connected to a water supply and provides water to a public place such as a road

stand-point /ˈstænd·pɔɪnt/ *n* [C] a set of beliefs and ideas from which opinions and decisions are formed • *"I have to put aside my emotions," he says, "and take it from a professional standpoint."* • *Depending on your standpoint, the play was either innovative and forward-looking or just plain drivel.*

stand-still /ˈstænd·stɪl/ *n* [U] a condition in which all movement or activity has stopped • *The runaway bus eventually* **came to a** *standstill when it rolled into a muddy field.* • *Fighting and shortages have* **brought** *normal life* **to** *a virtual standstill in the city.*

stank /stæŋk/ *past simple of* STINK

Stan-ley knife *Br and Aus* /ˈstæn·li/, *Am* **raz-or knife** *n* [C] *trademark* a sharp knife with a short blade which can be pulled back into the handle when not being used to make it safe • PIC **Tools**

stan-za /ˈstæn·zə/ *n* [C] a group of lines of poetry forming a unit; a VERSE

sta-ple WIRE /ˈsteɪ·pl̩/ *n* [C] a short thin piece of wire used to fasten sheets of paper together. It has bent ends which are pushed through the paper and then flattened by a special device • A staple is also a U-shaped piece of metal with sharp ends which is hammered into a surface to hold something, such as a wire fence, in a particular position. • A **staple-gun** is a tool which you hold in your hand and use to push staples into a surface. • PIC **Stationery**

sta-ple *obj* /ˈsteɪ·pl̩/ *v* [T] • *Would you mind stapling the reports* **together***?*

sta-pler /£ˈsteɪ·pləʳ, $-plɚ/ *n* [C] • A stapler is a small device which you can hold in your hand or use on a table to push staples through pieces of paper. • PIC **Stationery**

sta-ple BASIC /ˈsteɪ·pl̩/ *adj* [before n; not gradable] basic or main; standard or regular • *The staple* **diet** *here is mutton, fish and boiled potatoes.* • *Prices of staple* **foods** *such as wheat and vegetables have also been increasing.* • *Tourism is the staple source of income in the coastal villages.* • *Her latest film is the staple offering of action and comedy which we have come to expect.*

sta-ple /ˈsteɪ·pl̩/ *n* [C] • *Shortages mean that even staples* (= basic foods) *like bread are difficult to find.* • *Phosphate has been a staple* (= main product) *of this area for many years.* • *Romantic fiction and reference books are a staple of many public libraries.*

star OBJECT IN SPACE /£stɑːʳ, $stɑːr/ *n* [C] a very large ball of burning gas in space which is usually seen from Earth as a point of light in the sky at night, because of its great distance away • *It can take millions of years for light from a distant star to reach the Earth.* • *The star at the middle of our solar system is the Sun.* • *Stars* **twinkled** *above them as they lay on the hill.* • **Star wars** is informal for SDI. • *"Star Wars"* (title of a film by George Lucas, 1977) • *"My God, it's full of stars"* (Arthur C. Clarke *2001: A Space Odyssey*, 1968)

star-ry /£ˈstɑː·ri, $ˈstɑːr·i/ *adj* **-ier, -iest** • *a starry night/sky* • If a person is **starry-eyed** they have lots of thoughts and opinions which are unreasonably positive, so they do not understand things as they really are: *It's easy to be starry-eyed about a place you've never been to.*

star SYMBOL /£stɑːʳ, $stɑːr/ *n* [C] a symbol with four or more points • *star-shaped* • *The children were cutting stars out of paper to make decorations.* • *How many stars* (= symbols showing quality) *has this restaurant got?* See also -STAR RANK. • A star made from metal is worn by particular officials to show their rank: *a sheriff's star* • A star is also an ASTERISK (= a mark like *). LP **Asterisk** • Small gold or silver paper stars are often glued onto a young child's school work by the teacher to show that it has been done well. • *(esp. Br, often disapproving)* A **star chamber** is a court or other group which meets privately and makes judgments which can be severe. • The **Star of David** is a star with six points which symbolizes Judaism. • The **Stars and Stripes** (*Am infml* **Stars and Bars**) is the name of the US flag. • The **Star-Spangled Banner** is the national ANTHEM (= song) of the US.

starred /£stɑːd, $stɑːrd/ *adj* [not gradable] • *The starred items* (= those marked with one or more ASTERISKS) *on the agenda are the most important.*

star PERFORMER /£stɑːʳ, $stɑːr/ *n* [C] a very famous, successful and important person, esp. a performer such as a musician, actor or sports player • *a rock/movie/football star* • *Kids wanting to be stars come to Hollywood from all over America.* • *(infml)* If a group of people, a film or a show is **star-studded** there are lots of famous people in it. • See also CO-STAR; SUPERSTAR.

star /£stɑːʳ, $stɑːr/ *adj* [before n; not gradable] • *star quality* • *(fig.) Natalie is, without a doubt, the star* (= very best) *student in this year's ballet class.* • *(fig.) This afternoon the prosecution will call its star* (= most important) *witness.* • A **star turn** is either the main performer in a film, play or other show, or an extremely good performance by someone.

star *(obj)* /£stɑːʳ, $stɑːr/ *v* **-rr-** • *John Travolta starred with a baby* **in** *the film 'Look Who's Talking'.* [always + prep] • *Fowles's novel 'The French Lieutenant's Woman' was turned into a film starring Meryl Streep.* [T no passive]

star-dom /£ˈstɑː·dᵊm, $ˈstɑːr-/ *n* [U] • *Boris Becker seemed destined for stardom after he won Wimbledon at the age of 17.*

star-let /£ˈstɑː·lət, $ˈstɑːr-/ *n* [C] *often disapproving* • A starlet is a young actress who hopes to be or is thought likely to be famous in the future.

star LUCK /£stɑːʳ, $stɑːr/ *n* [C] *infml* any planet or other object in the sky thought of in ASTROLOGY as influencing a person's luck • *She was born under a lucky/an unlucky star* (= is influenced to be lucky/unlucky in life). • *(literary)* If someone or something is **star-crossed** they are unlucky: *star-crossed lovers* • A person's **star sign** is the **sign of the zodiac** which the sun was in when they were born; see at SIGN MARK: *"What star sign are you?" "I'm a Leo."* • *"The fault, dear Brutus, is not in our stars,/ But in ourselves"* (Shakespeare, Julius Caesar 1.2)

stars /£stɑːz, $stɑːrz/ *pl n* • **The stars** is informal for a HOROSCOPE: *I always like to see what the stars say in the newspaper.*

-star RANK /£-stɑːʳ, $-stɑːr/ *combining form* a ranking of quality, usually in numbers from one to five with one being the lowest • *A three-star hotel is better than a two-star.*

starred /£stɑːd, $stɑːrd/ *adj* • *a starred restaurant* (= one good enough to be ranked)

star-board /£ˈstɑː·bəd, $ˈstɑːr·bɚd/ *n* [U] *specialized* the right side of a ship or aircraft as you are facing forward • *The vessel was listing severely* **to** *starboard by the time it reached harbour.* • *Our starboard engine seems to be losing power.*

starch FOOD /£stɑːtʃ, $stɑːrtʃ/ *n* [U] a chemical which exists in large amounts in particular foods such as potatoes and rice • *Corn starch is used as a thickener in stews.* • Compare CARBOHYDRATE.

starch·y /£'stɑː·tʃi, $'stɑːr-/ *adj* **-ier, -iest** • *starchy foods*

starch [CLOTH] /£stɑːtʃ, $stɑːrtʃ/ *n* [U] a white chemical obtained from potatoes and particular grains which is used to make cloth stiff

starch *obj* /£stɑːtʃ, $stɑːrtʃ/ *v* [T] • *She wore a starched white apron over her black dress.*

starch·y /£'stɑː·tʃi, $'stɑːr-/ *adj* **-ier, -iest** *infml disapproving* behaving in a formal way and without humour • *Science museums have tried to shake off their somewhat starchy image by mounting exhibitions designed to draw in the crowds.*

starch·i·ly /£'stɑː·tʃɪ·li, $'stɑːr-/ *adv infml disapproving*

star·dust /£'stɑː·dʌst, $'stɑːr-/ *n* [U] *literary* (something which causes) a pleasant dreamy or romantic feeling

stare *(obj)* /£steəʳ, $ster/ *v* to look for a long time with the eyes wide open, esp. when surprised, frightened or thinking deeply • *Don't stare* **at** *people like that, you might upset them.* [I] • *She stared* **at** *the open wound in horror.* [I] • *Chuck sat quietly for hours staring into the distance, thinking of what might have been.* [I] • *(fig.) By half-time United were staring* **at** (=had the problem of) *a seven-goal deficit and almost certain defeat.* [I] • *During the press conference, each fighter tried to stare the other* **down**/*(Br and Aus also)* **out** (=force the other to look away by continual staring). [M] • *(infml)* If something **stares** someone **in the face** it is very easy to see or obvious: *The answer has been staring us in the face all along – we'll swop shifts.* ○ *Without water, death would be staring them in the face.*

stare /£steəʳ, $ster/ *n* [C] • *She gave him a long stare but didn't answer his question.* • *Lew turned to meet the concentrated stares of Reg and Alfie.*

star·ing /£'steə·rɪŋ, $'ster·ɪŋ/ *adj* • *In the darkness we could just make out the blank staring eyes of a child.*

star·fish /£'stɑː·fɪʃ, $'stɑːr-/ *n* [C] *pl* **starfish** or **starfishes** a flat animal that lives in the sea and has five arms which grow from its body

star·gaz·er /£'stɑːˌgeɪ·zəʳ, $'stɑːrˌgeɪ·zɚ/ *n* [C] *infml or humorous* a person who is involved in the activity of ASTRONOMY or ASTROLOGY

star·gaz·ing /£'stɑːˌgeɪ·zɪŋ, $'stɑːr-/ *n* [U] *infml or humorous*

stark [BARE] /£stɑːk, $stɑːrk/ *adj* **-er, -est** bare, simple or obvious, esp. without decoration or anything which is not necessary; severe or extreme • *It was a stark room with its white walls, and a bed and chair as the only furniture.* • *The lunar landscape is starker than any known on Earth.* • *The stark* **reality** *is that we are operating at a huge loss.* • *Casualty figures act as a stark* **reminder** *that we can still make huge improvements.* • *In the suburbs the spacious houses stand in stark* **contrast** *to the slums of the city's poor.* • Ⓢ

stark·ly /£'stɑː·kli, $'stɑːr-/ *adv* • *Her later sensual works contrast starkly with the harsh earlier paintings.* • *Jenny made it starkly obvious that she would not change her mind.*

stark·ness /£'stɑːk·nəs, $'stɑːrk-/ *n* [U]

stark [COMPLETELY] /£stɑːk, $stɑːrk/ *adv* [not gradable] completely or extremely • *The children were splashing in the river, stark* **naked** *(Am also* **buck naked** *Am also* **butt naked**). See also STARKERS. • *I think he's stark* **raving** *(Br also* **staring**) **mad** (=extremely foolish) *to want to spend his holiday watching trains!* • Ⓢ

stark·ers /£'stɑː·kəz, $'stɑːr·kɚz/ *adj* [after v; not gradable] *Br and Aus infml, often humorous* naked

star·let /£'stɑː·lət, $'stɑːr-/ *n* [C] See at STAR [PERFORMER]

star·light /£'stɑː·laɪt, $'stɑːr-/ *n* [U] the light produced by stars

star·lit /£'stɑː·lɪt, $'stɑːr-/ *adj* [not gradable] • *a starlit night*

star·ling /£'stɑː·lɪŋ, $'stɑːr-/ *n* [C] a common bird with blackish feathers which lives with others in large groups in many parts of the world

star·ry /£'stɑː·ri, $'stɑːr·i/ *adj* See at STAR [OBJECT IN SPACE]

star·struck /£'stɑː·strʌk, $'stɑːr-/ *adj often disapproving* feeling great or too much respect for famous or important people, esp. famous actors or performers • *It's the story of a starstruck young girl who goes to Hollywood to make her fortune.*

start *(obj)* [BEGIN] /£stɑːt, $stɑːrt/ *v* to begin (to do) (something) • *When do you start your course/your new job?* [T] • *We want to start (the discussion session) at six o'clock.* [I/T] • *Let's start – I want to finish this by lunchtime.* [I] • *Can you start* (= begin a new job or begin to work for a new employer) *on Monday?* [I] • *They started* **building** *the house in January.* [+ v-ing] • *I was starting* **to** *write a letter when the phone rang.* [+ *to* infinitive] • *The class start* **(on)** *their exam course next week.* [I/T] • *(infml)* To start **(on)** is to begin to complain or be annoying in some way: *He started on* **about** *the state of the roads.* [I] ○ *Don't start – I've already told you why it's not possible.* [I] • If you start **afresh/(all over) again**/*(Am)* **over** you stop doing something esp. before it is finished and begin to do it again, often in a different way: *The agreement allows old expectations to be forgotten and everyone can start afresh.* [I] ○ *We decided to abandon the first draft of the report and start all over again.* [I] • *When can we* **get started** (= begin)*?* • *He* **started work** (= began being employed) *at 16.* • **To start with** means at the beginning, or as the first of several things: *We only knew two people in London to start with, but we soon made some friends.* ○ *I can't come – to start with my car is being repaired, but I've also got another meeting that day.* See also **for starters** below. • *"I've started so I'll finish"* (phrase from the British television quiz show *Mastermind* said by Magnus Magnusson, 1972-)

start /£stɑːt, $stɑːrt/ *n* • *We were doubtful about the product's usefulness* **from the** *start.* [U] • *They announced the start* **of** *a new commercial venture.* [U] • *The publicity leaflet claimed that the centre was the start* **of something** *new in leisure facilities.* [U] • *The weather was good at the start* (= in the first part) *of the week.* [U] • *We need to* **make a** *start* **on** *(preparing) the brochure next week.* [U] • *Apparently the new manager has* **made** *a good/promising/slow start.* [C] • *The event* **got off to** *a shaky/poor start with the stage lights failing in the first few minutes.* [C] • *After several* **false** *starts* (= failures to begin satisfactorily) *we finally got the project under way.* [C] • *The novel was dreadful* **from start to finish** (= all of it was bad). • **For a start** means first or as the first in a set of things: *We'll take names and phone numbers for a start, then later on we can get more details.* See also **for starters** below.

start·er /£'stɑː·təʳ, $'stɑːr·t̬ɚ/ *n* [C] • A starter is a person, animal or organization that is involved at the beginning of an activity, esp. a race: *Of the ten starters* (= horses which started in the race), *two fell at the first fence.* • A starter is also the person who gives the signal for a race to begin: *They're* **under starter's orders** (= ready for the signal to begin the race). • A starter can also be a small savoury dish served as the first part of a meal: *We had soup/pâté/pasta as a starter.* • *(infml)* **For starters** means 'to begin with' or 'as the first, with other things to follow': *The country imports up to half its food and most of its energy, and that's just for starters* (= there are other problems too). ○ *"Why did you decide not to go to the concert?" "Well, for starters the tickets were ridiculously expensive."* See also **to start with** and **for a start** above. • *"Your starter for ten"* (phrase used in the British television quiz programme *University Challenge*, 1962-) • See also SELF-STARTER. • Ⓕ

start·ing /£'stɑː·tɪŋ, $'stɑːr·t̬ɪŋ/ *adj* [before n; not gradable] • *a starting pistol* • *a starting salary* • A **starting line** is a line drawn on the ground behind which competitors wait for a signal to begin a race. • A **starting date** (also **start date**), a **starting point** (also **start point**) or a **starting time** (also **start time**) is the day, place or time at which something begins: *The starting date is 23 June.* ○ *The starting point for the guided tour of the town is in the market square.* ○ *The committee emphasised that its report was only meant as a starting point for discussion.* ○ *Is a starting time of 6.30 p.m. too early for anyone?* • The **starting price** (*abbreviation* **SP**) is the amount of money offered just at the start of a race by a BOOKMAKER for a win. • A **starting salary** is the amount of money received when starting a particular type of job for the first time: *The average starting salary for a teacher is less than that for an accountant.*

start *(obj)* [MOVE] /£stɑːt, $stɑːrt/ *v* to begin at one point and then move to another, in distance or range • *The bus starts* **from** *the main square/***at** *the station.* [I always + adv/prep] • *We'll need to start* **(off/out)** *early because the journey takes six hours.* [I always + adv/prep] • *I'm getting* *tired – I think it's time to start back* (= begin to go back). [I always + adv/prep] • *Tell me slowly what happened – start* **at the beginning**. [I always + adv/prep] • *Ticket prices start* **at/from** *£20 and go up to £100.* [I always + adv/prep] • *There are performances all day on the hour starting* **at/from** *10 o'clock.* [I always + adv/prep] • If you start **(off/out) with** something/someone or start **(off/out) by** doing something you begin a set of activities with the thing or person mentioned: *She started with a description of her journey.* ○ *Give me your answers one by one starting off with Lucy.* ○ *You could start by weeding the flowerbeds.* • *He started (his working life)/He started* **(off) as** *an engineer but later became a teacher.* [I]

start /£stɑːt, $stɑːrt/ *n* • *They're going to* **make an early** *start* (= begin doing something early). [C] • *The other group* **had** *an hour's start/a two-hour start* **on us** (= left/began an hour/two hours before we did). [U] • *We* **gave** *the children ten minutes start* (= let them leave/begin ten minutes before we did) *but we soon caught up with them.* [U]

start *(obj)* HAPPEN /£stɑːt, $stɑːrt/ *v* to (cause something to) happen • *The advert said the relaxation class was starting* **(up)** *next month.* [I] • *A new series of wildlife programmes has started on Monday evenings.* [I] • *We want to start* **(up)** *another chess club for the children who are better players.* [T] • *A new group for single people has been started in Chesterford.* [T] • *His mother started* **(off/up)** *the craft market to sell her own goods but other people soon joined in.* [T/M] • *"You've been trying to start* **trouble** (= cause other people to do things which they shouldn't) *all morning," he said to the boy.* [T] • If you are thinking of **starting a family** you are considering having your first child. • *(infml)* If you **start something** you cause trouble: *He really started something when he wrote that letter to the paper.*

start MOVE SUDDENLY /£stɑːt, $stɑːrt/ *v* [I] to move your body suddenly because something has surprised you • *He started* **at** *the sound of the phone.* • *She started away from the cupboard when she saw someone come into the room.*

start /£stɑːt, $stɑːrt/ *n* [U] • *He woke* **with a** *start when the smoke alarm went off.* • *The child* **gave a** *start but didn't wake when his father went into the bedroom.*

start *(obj)* WORK /£stɑːt, $stɑːrt/ *v* to (cause to) work or operate in the correct way • *My friend was still having trouble starting his car.* [T] • *I heard a lawnmower start in the garden next door.* [I] • LP **Switching on and off**

start·er (mo·tor) /£'stɑː·təʳ, $'stɑːr·tɚ/ *n* [C] • A starter (motor) is an electrical device which causes an engine to begin to operate.

start·le *obj* /£'stɑː·tl̩, $'stɑːr·t̬l̩/ *v* [T] to do something, esp. unexpected which surprises and sometimes worries a person or animal • *She was concentrating on her book and his voice startled her.* • *The noise of the car startled the birds and the whole group flew up into the air.* • *Her article on diet startled many people* **into** *changing their eating habits.*

start·ling /£'stɑː·tlɪŋ, $'stɑːr·t̬lɪŋ/ *adj* • *a startling* (= very surprising) *admission/achievement* • *startling results* • *The news from the famine area was startling.*

start·ling·ly /£'stɑː·tl̩·ɪŋ·li, $'stɑːr·t̬l̩-/ *adv* • *startlingly* (= surprisingly) *poor results* • *Even though none of the witnesses had met they all gave startlingly similar stories of what had happened.*

starve *(obj)* /£stɑːv, $stɑːrv/ *v* to (cause to) become very weak or die because there is not enough food to eat • *Whole communities starved* **to death** *during the long drought.* [I] • *From looking at and talking to former prisoners in the camps, an obvious conclusion is that they have been starved.* [T] • *(fig.) People starved* **of** (= not receiving enough) *sleep start to lose their concentration and may hallucinate.* [T]

starv·ing /£'stɑː·vɪŋ, $'stɑːr-/ *adj* • *The cats were neglected and starving.* • *(infml)* Starving can also mean very hungry: *Isn't lunch ready yet – I'm starving.* • *(Br regional)* Starving also means very cold: *Could you put the heating on – I'm starving!*

star·va·tion /£stɑː'veɪ·ʃᵊn, $stɑːr-/ *n* [U] • *The animals had died* **of** *starvation.* • *If the famine continues, there is a real danger of mass starvation.* • A **starvation diet** is the very small amount of food eaten by a person who wishes to lose weight quickly.

stash *obj* /stæʃ/ *v* [T] *infml* to store or hide something, esp. a large amount • *Instead of putting money into new plant and machinery, the businessmen had stashed their earnings abroad.* • *The stolen pictures were stashed* **away** *in a London warehouse.*

stash /stæʃ/ *n* [C] • *The stash* **of** *money was discovered in a leather folder by a sorter at the recycling center.*

sta·sis /'steɪ·sɪs, 'stæs·ɪs/ *n* [U] *slightly fml* a state which does not change • *She was bored – her life was in stasis.*

state CONDITION /steɪt/ *n* [C] a condition or way of being that exists at a particular time • *They complained about the untidy state that the house had been left in.* • *It was another radio discussion about the bad economic state that the country was in.* • *The kitchen was in its original state, with a 1920s sink and stove.* • *There were things he knew when hypnotized that he couldn't remember in his conscious state.* • *She was* **in a** *(terrible)* **state** (= nervous and upset) *before the interview.* • *Her mother is in a poor state* **of** *health.* • *After the accident we were worried by his depressed state* **of** *mind.* • *I assured him that the car was in a good state* **of** *repair.* • *I came home to an unhappy* **state of affairs** (= situation). • A **state of emergency** is a temporary system of rules to deal with an extremely dangerous or difficult situation: *After the floods the government* **declared** *a state of emergency.* • If a particular activity is **state of the art** it is in its most recent stage of development: *The state of the art in car safety features means that fewer people die in car crashes now than twenty years ago.* • If something is described as **state-of-the-art** it is very modern and uses the most recent ideas and methods: *They are using state-of-the-art graphics in the film's special effects.*

state COUNTRY /steɪt/ *n* [C] a country or its government • *Some theatres receive a small amount of funding from the state/state funding.* • *The drought is worst in the central African states.* • *Britain is one of the* **member** *states of the European Union.* • *After independence the country became a* **one-party** *state* (= only the ruling political party was officially allowed). • *The government was determined to reduce the number of state-owned industries.* • *(fml) His diary included comments on* **affairs/matters of** *state* (= information about government activities). • *In Britain, the position of Home Secretary is one of the three most important* **offices of** *state* (= positions in the government). • A state is also a part of a large country with its own government, as in Germany, Australia or the US: *The speed limit in America varies from state to state.* ○ *Elections in the states will precede the national election by a month.* • *(infml)* **The States** is used to refer to the United States of America. • See also STATESMAN. • LP **Nations and nationalities, World regions**

state /steɪt/ *adj* [before n; not gradable] • *state education/schools/industries* • *state legislature/law* • *state control* • *state funding/pensions/subsidies* • The **State Department** is the part of the American government which deals with foreign matters. • **State's evidence** is *Am for* **Queen's/King's evidence**. See at EVIDENCE. • State also means formal, official and ceremonial when referring to activities involving a representative of the government or leader of the country: *the state opening of Parliament* ○ *a state funeral* • A **state occasion** is an official formal occasion, which has traditional ceremonies connected with it, and at which important members of the government or the royal family are present. • A **state premier** is the leader of an Australian state government. • A **state visit** is an official formal visit by the leader of one country to another. • When the leader of a country does something **in state** they do it officially and formally as part of their job: *The Queen rode in state to open Parliament.*

state·craft /£'steɪt·krɑːft, $-kræft/ *n* [U] • Statecraft is the skill of governing a country.

state·hood /'steɪt·hʊd/ *n* [U] • Statehood is the condition of being a country or a part of a large country that has its own government: *The US-Mexican War of 1846-48 was sparked by a dispute over impending Texas statehood.*

state·less /'steɪt·ləs/ *adj* [not gradable] • A stateless person has no country that they officially belong to.

state·side /'steɪt·saɪd/ *adj, adv* [not gradable] *Am* • *Some girls dream of finding an American husband to transport them stateside* (= to the United States).

state·wide /'steɪt·waɪd, ˌ-'-/ *adj* [not gradable] • *statewide* (= in every part of a state) *elections*

state *(obj)* EXPRESS /steɪt/ *v slightly fml* to express, esp. clearly and carefully • *The problem is so simple that it can be stated in one short sentence.* [T] • *On October 6th the government stated formally* **that** *they were opposing the pact.* [+ *that* clause] • *Officials clearly stated they felt unhappy with the limits that continue to be imposed on imports.* [+ *(that)* clause] • *Theo Mathew left a will stating*

that *his estate should be split among his four younger brothers.* [+ *that* clause] • *Send recipes, stating the source if not original, to Emily Green.* [T] • *Please state* **why** *you wish to apply for this grant.* [+ *wh-* word] • *Children in the stated* (=named) *areas were at risk from a lack of food, the report said.*

state·ment /ˈsteɪt·mənt/ *n* • If you **make a** statement you express something formally, publicly and officially, usually as an explanation of something which has happened, or you do something which makes it clear what your opinion is. What you express is your statement: *The police made a statement about their investigation* **to** *the press.* [C] ○ *After the prisoner had made his statement the police officer asked him to sign it.* [C] ○ *He threw paint over the fur coats because he wanted to make a statement about cruelty to animals.* [C] ○ *She said that their statements were false and that she had not been involved.* [C] ○ *We were not surprised by their statement* **that** *the train services would be reduced.* [C + *that* clause] • *I think your story is a fair statement* (=description) *of what happened.* [C] • A **(bank)** statement is a piece of paper which gives a list of the amounts of money paid into and taken out of your bank account during a particular period of time and the total amount that is left. [C] • *(fml) The facts of the case need honest statement* (=need to be expressed honestly). [U]

state·ly /ˈsteɪt·li/ *adj slightly fml* formal and splendid in style and appearance • *The procession moved through the mountain village at a stately* **pace.** • *He always walked with a stately* **bearing.** • *(Br)* A **stately home** is a large old house which usually has beautiful furniture, decorations and gardens. Many of these places in Britain are now owned by the government or by a preservation organization. • *"The stately homes of England, / How beautiful they stand"* (from the poem *The Homes of England* by Felicia Hemans, 1849)

state·li·ness /ˈsteɪt·lɪ·nəs/ *n* [U]

state·room /ˈsteɪt·rʊm, -ruːm/ *n* [C] a large room esp. in a PALACE (=large house owned by a royal person) which is used for formal or important occasions • *the staterooms at Windsor Castle*

states·man (*pl* **-men**), **states·wo·man** (*pl* **-women**) /ˈsteɪt·smən, -ˌswʊm·ən/ *n* [C] an experienced politician, esp. one who is respected for making good judgments • *There are still plenty of candidates eager to fill the President's post and some among them may yet turn out to be great statesmen.* • An **elder** statesman is a respected leader, often one who no longer has an active job, who is thought of as having good advice to give: *A well-known European elder statesman, a former Foreign Minister, was asked to chair the environmental commission.* ○ *Unlike many of the medical profession's elder statesmen, the members of this group prefer not to give interviews on TV.*

states·man·like /ˈsteɪts·mən·laɪk/ *adj* • *a statesmanlike speech*

states·man·ship /ˈsteɪts·mən·ʃɪp/ *n* [U]

stat·ic /£ˈstæt·ɪk, $ˈstæţ-/ *adj* staying in one place without moving, or not changing for a long time • *He pointed out that a play is not a static object like a picture.* • *The national birth rate has* **remained** *static for the last few years.* • *Oil prices were fairly static worldwide at that time.*

stat·ic (e·lec·tri·ci·ty) *n* [U] an electrical charge which collects esp. on the surface of objects made from some types of material when they are rubbed. Its presence in the air can interrupt radio and television signals. • *There's so much static on this radio I can't hear what they're saying.*

sta·tion [BUILDING] /ˈsteɪ·ʃᵊn/ *n* [C] a building or buildings and the surrounding area where trains stop for people to get on or off • *I'll meet you at the station (also* **rail station**/ *Br and Aus* **railway station**/*Am* **train station**). • *There's a taxi rank just outside the station.* • *We couldn't find a space to park near the station.* • *(Br) We decided to sit and wait in the station* **buffet.** • *The explosion occurred at one of the big* **mainline** *stations* (=a station from which trains go directly to big towns and cities). • *We looked on our map to find the nearest (Br)* **underground**/*(Br)* **tube**/*(Am)* **subway/metro** *station.* • A station is also a building or buildings and the surrounding area where a stated service can be obtained or an activity takes place: *a biological research station* ○ *a government experimental station* ○ *a ski station* • In Australia and New Zealand a station is a large farm with animals: *a sheep station* • **Station house** is *Am for* **police station.** See at POLICE. • **Station wagon** is *Am and Aus for* ESTATE (CAR). • See also STATIONMASTER; WORKSTATION. • [PIC]› **Vehicles**

sta·tion [BROADCASTING] /ˈsteɪ·ʃᵊn/ *n* [C] a company which sends out radio or television broadcasts • *a radio/television station* • *a commercial/foreign station* • *a pirate* (=illegal) *station* • *The reception is not very good – try to* **tune in to** *another station.* • *(Am and Aus)* A **station break** is a pause in a television or radio broadcast for the broadcasting station to give its name.

sta·tion *obj* [POSITION] /ˈsteɪ·ʃᵊn/ *v* [T always + adv/prep; usually passive] to cause (esp. soldiers) to be in a particular place to do a job • *I hear your son's in the army – where's he stationed?* • *The regiment was stationed* **in** *Singapore for several years.* • *Armed guards were stationed around the airport.*

sta·tion /ˈsteɪ·ʃᵊn/ *n* • *The police* **took up** *their stations at the edge of the road, holding back the crowd.* [C] • *(specialized)* If the navy or one of its boats is **on** station it is in the place to which it has been ordered: *Several destroyers are on station off the coast of Norway* [U] • **The Stations of the Cross** are 14 pictures showing different things which happened on the last days of the life of Jesus Christ which are put on the walls inside many Roman Catholic churches.

sta·tion·a·ry /£ˈsteɪ·ʃᵊn·ᵊr·i, $-ʃə·ner-/ *adj* not moving, or not changing • *By using radar, infra-red sensors and lasers, crews can pick out either moving or stationary targets.* • *We were stationary at a set of traffic lights when a 30-ton truck failed to stop and hit us from behind.* • *House prices have been stationary for several months.*

sta·tion·e·ry /£ˈsteɪ·ʃᵊn·ᵊr·i, $-ʃə·ner-/ *n* [U] the items needed for writing, such as paper, pens, pencils and envelopes • *Don't miss our summer sale of stationery and office equipment.* • *She works in the stationery department of a big store.* • Stationery is sometimes used only for items made from paper: *John Bishop founded a company that makes stationery products from recycled materials.* • Stationery sometimes means good quality paper for writing letters on and matching envelopes: *I chose pale blue stationery with our business logo embossed in dark blue.* • [LP]› **Shopping goods**

sta·tion·er /£ˈsteɪ·ʃᵊn·əʳ, $-ɚ/ *n* [C] • A stationer is a company or person who owns a business which sells stationery: *Office Supplies and General Stationer* ○ *Jones & Son Legal Stationer* • *You'll be able to get a tube of glue at the stationer's* (=shop which sells stationery) *down the road.*

sta·tion·ma·ster /£ˈsteɪ·ʃᵊnˌmɑː·stəʳ, $-ˌmæs·tɚ/ *n* [C] the person who is in charge of a railway station

sta·tis·tics /stəˈtɪs·tɪks/, *infml* **stats** /stæts/ *pl n* information based on a study of the number of times something happens or is present, or other NUMERICAL facts • *The statistics* **show/suggest** *that, in general, women live longer than men and both groups live longer than they did 100 years ago.* • *The government will* **publish** *the employment statistics* (=numbers about how many people have jobs) *at the end of the week.* • *Universities* **collect** *statistics on what jobs their students go into.* • *According to* **official** *statistics, the Japanese work longer hours than workers in many other industrialised countries.* • *The* **latest** *statistics show an increase in average pay.* • *"There are three kinds of lies: lies, damned lies, and statistics"* (believed to have been said by Benjamin Disraeli, 1804-1881)

sta·tis·tics /stəˈtɪs·tɪks/ *n* [U] • Statistics is also the science of using information discovered from studying numbers: *a degree in statistics*

sta·tis·tic /stəˈtɪs·tɪk/ *n* [C] • A statistic is a single number in a range of statistics, esp. one which shows something which might happen or be expected in a group of people: *The city's most shocking statistic is its infant mortality rate.* • *The statistic which most health professionals watch – the proportion of total calories eaten as fats – shows little improvement.* • *She died under general anaesthetic to become* **(just) another** *statistic* (=something considered unimportant) *in a 'national scandal' over safety standards.*

sta·tis·ti·cal /stəˈtɪs·tɪ·kᵊl/ *adj* • *a statistical correlation* • *detailed statistical analysis* • *statistical errors/evidence*

sta·tis·ti·cal·ly /stəˈtɪs·tɪ·kli/ *adv*

stat·is·ti·cian /ˌstæt·ɪˈstɪʃ·ᵊn/ *n* [C] • *She is a statistician by training and a former adviser to a major bank.*

stat·ue /ˈstætʃ·uː/ *n* [C] an object made from a hard material, esp. stone or metal, to look like a person or animal • *a statue* **of** *a boy and his dog* • *They planned to* **put up/erect** *a statue* **to** *the President.* • [PIC]› **Sculpture**

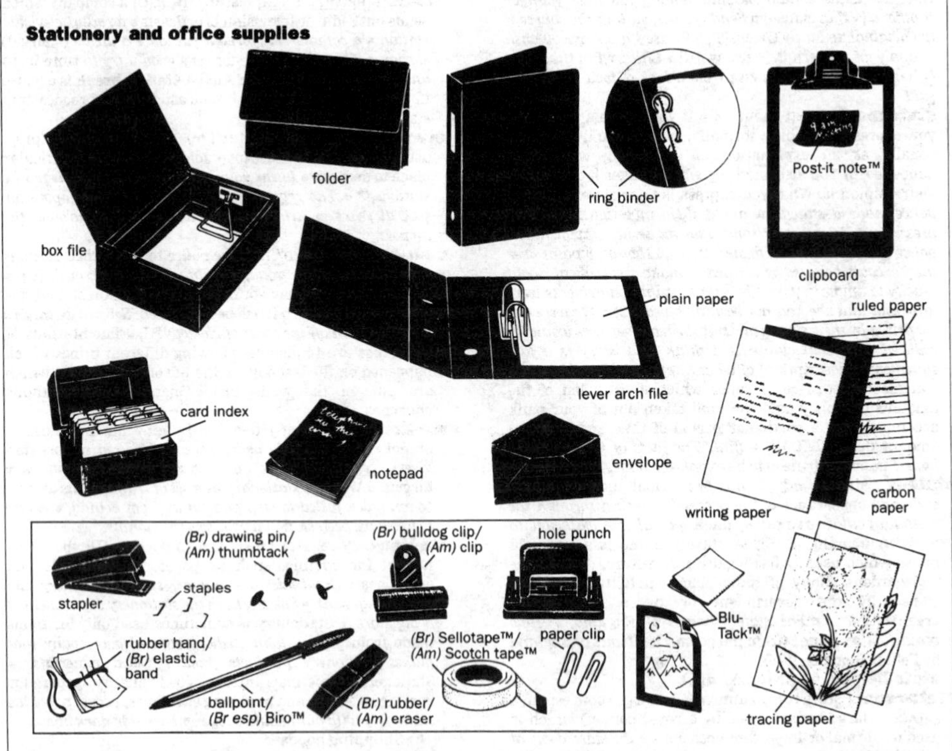

stat·u·ette /ˌstætʃ·u'et/ *n* [C] • A statuette is a statue which is small enough to stand on a table or shelf: *a bronze statuette of a ballet dancer*

stat·u·a·ry /£'stætʃ·u·ᵊr·i, $-er·/ *n* [U] *fml* • *a display of garden statuary* (= statues)

stat·u·esque /ˌstætʃ·u'esk/ *adj* (of people) large, graceful and splendid in appearance

stat·ure REPUTATION /£'stætʃ·ər, $-ɚ/ *n* [U] the good reputation a person or organization has, based on their behaviour and ability • *an artist* **of** *great stature* • *She was the sole scientist* **of (any)** *stature advising the company.* • *During his lifetime this man's stature* **as** *an art critic and social theorist was tremendous.* • *Fulton had immense stature and popularity in the black community.* • *The team have shown their growing stature in recent matches.* • *If the school continues to* **gain in** *stature then it will attract the necessary resources and support.*

stat·ure HEIGHT /£'stætʃ·ər, $-ɚ/ *n* [C usually sing] *slightly fml* (esp. of people) height • *Large stature and great physical strength do not guarantee protection from attack.* • *His red hair and short stature made him easy to recognise.* • *He was taller than his father when he reached his* **full** *stature* (= grew to his adult height).

sta·tus OFFICIAL POSITION /£'steɪ·təs, $-ṭəs/ *n* an official position, esp. in a social group • *Their chief concern is that their status as skilled specialists should be recognised and respected.* [C] • *The association works to promote the status of retired people as active and useful members of the community.* [U] • *There has been an increase in applications for refugee status.* [U] • *The success of her book has given her unexpected celebrity status.* [U] • *Applicants should have a degree or a recognized qualification of equal status.* [U] • *What's the status of these green parking permits – are they still valid?* [C] • **The status quo** is the present situation: *These people hate change – they always want to* **maintain** *the status quo.*

sta·tus RESPECT /£'steɪ·təs, $-ṭəs/ *n* [U] the amount of respect, admiration or importance given to a person, organization or object • *She described the difficulties of a society where differences of wealth and status were vast and blatant.* • *The leaders often seemed to be more concerned with status and privilege than with the problems of the people.* • A **status symbol** is a thing which some people want to have because they think other people will admire them if they have it: *Private swimming pool, fast cars, designer clothes – pick your status symbol, she has them all.*

stat·ute /'stætʃ·uːt/ *n* a law which has been formally approved and written down • *The statute is tough because it was originally designed to prevent organised crime from operating behind legitimate business fronts.* [C] • *The salaries of most federal workers are set* **by** *statute.* [U] • When a law **is on/reaches the statute book** it has been formally approved and written down and can be used in a law court: *It will be at least Easter next year before the legislation and regulations are on/reach the statute book.*

stat·u·to·ry /£'stæt·jʊ·tᵊr·i, $-tɔːr-/ *adj* [not gradable] • *statutory obligations*

staunch LOYAL /£stɔːntʃ, $stɑːntʃ/ *adj* **-er, -est** always loyal in supporting a person, organization or set of beliefs or opinions • *a staunch friend and ally* • *a staunch refusal* • *He gained a reputation as being a staunch* **defender/supporter** *of individual's rights.* • *Politically, she is a staunch* **opponent** *of reform.*

staunch·ly /£'stɔːntʃ·li, $stɑːntʃ-/ *adv* • *staunchly loyal/independent*

staunch·ness /£'stɔːntʃ·nəs, $'stɑːntʃ-/ *n* [U]

staunch *obj* STOP /£stɔːntʃ, $stɑːntʃ/, *Am also* **stanch** *v* [T] to stop something happening, or to stop liquid, esp. blood, from flowing out • *The country's asylum laws were amended to staunch the* **flow/flood** *of economic migrants.* • *To staunch the financial losses, the Glasgow factory was closed.* • *Mike pressed hard on the wound and staunched the* **flow** *of blood.*

stave /steɪv/, *Am usually* **staff** *n* [C] the five lines and four space between them on which musical notes are written

stave in *(obj)*, **stave** *(obj)* **in** /steɪv/ *v adv* to push or fall inwards causing damage; to break by pushing inwards • *The boys tried to stave in the shed door/stave the shed door in but ran off when someone disturbed them.* [M] • *The front of the car was staved in where it had hit the post.* [I]

stave off *obj*, **stave** *obj* **off** /steɪv/ *v adv* [M] to keep (something or someone) away or stop something happening, esp. for a short time • *We were hoping to stave off these difficult decisions until September.* • *They are planning to cut full-time staff in an effort to stave the crisis off.*

staves /steɪvz/ *pl of* STAFF STICK and STAVE

stay [NOT LEAVE] /steɪ/ *v* [I] to not move away from or leave • *They need an assistant who is willing to stay* **for** *six months.* • *I just wanted to bring back your book – I'm meeting Charlie at six so I can't stay.* • *Stay* **until** *the rain has stopped.* • *Can you stay after work to play tennis?* • *If you stay* **put** (= here) *with the cases I'll go and find a taxi.* • *Because of the snow, schools have been closed and children told to stay* **at home**/*(esp. Am) stay* **home**. • If something **is here to stay** or **has come to stay** it has stopped being unusual and has become generally used or accepted: *Fax machines are here to stay.* See also **come to stay** at STAY [LIVE]. • If you **stay in** you do not leave the house: *I'm going to stay in this morning because I've got some letters to write.* • *(infml)* A **stay-at-home** is someone who does not like to go to parties or events outside the home and is considered uninteresting. • (D)

stay [CONTINUE] /steɪ/ *v* to continue doing something or continue to be in a particular state • *Stay still then the wasp won't sting you!* [I always + adv/prep] • *Stay away from the edge of the cliff.* [I always + adv/prep] • *How can we get this post to stay upright?* [I always + adv/prep] • *He's decided not to stay* **in** *teaching/medicine/the army.* [I always + adv/prep] • *The final figures showed that most departments had stayed within budget.* [I always + adv/prep] • *Gill decided to stay* **(on)** *at university to do further research.* [I always + adv/prep] • *We asked him to stay* **(on)** *as a youth leader for another year.* [I always + adv/prep] • *It was so warm we stayed* **(out)** *in the garden until ten that night.* [I always + adv/prep] • If you stay **out** you go out of the house and do not come back in for a long time: *Our cat usually stays out at night.* [I always + adv/prep] • *We stayed* **up** (= went to bed late) *to watch a film.* [I always + adv/prep] • *Put a lid on the pan so the food will stay hot.* [L] • *The shops stay open until 9 p.m.* [L] • *It looks as though he's going to stay* **single** (= will not get married). [L] • *Stay awake/healthy.* [L] • *(infml) Stay* **cool** (= Do not get upset or excited). [L] • *Stay* **tuned** (= Do not switch off the radio/television or do not change it to another programme). [L] • *They stayed friends after their divorce.* [L] • *Despite all the advertising the shoppers stayed* **away (in droves/in their droves)** (= many people did not come to shop). [L] • If you **stay on the sidelines** you are not an important part of what is happening. • To **stay the course** is to continue doing something until it is finished or until you achieve something you have planned to do: *She interviewed slimmers who had failed to stay the course to find out why they had given up.* • If someone has **staying power** they continue doing what they have to do until it is finished. • *"Stayin' Alive"* (song from the musical *Saturday Night Fever*, 1978) • (D)

stay·er /£ˈsteɪ·əʳ, $-ɚ/ *n* [C] • *The horse isn't very fast but it's a stayer and always finishes even the longest races.*

stay [LIVE] /steɪ/ *v* [I] to live or be in a place for a short time as a visitor • *I stayed* **in** *Montreal for two weeks then flew down to Washington.* • *They said they'd stay* **at** *a motel.* • *The children usually stay* **with** *their grandparents for a week in the summer.* • *We arranged to* **stay overnight/stay the night** (= sleep for one night) *at my sister's house.* • *His aunt has* **come to** *stay* **with** *him for a month.* See also **come to stay** at STAY [NOT LEAVE]. • (D)

stay /steɪ/ *n* [C] • *She planned a short stay* **at** *a hotel to celebrate their anniversary.* • *The operation will only involve an overnight stay* **in** *New York Hospital.* • *A stay* **with** *your family is always interesting.* • *His stays in Finland became longer and more frequent until, finally, he decided to move there permanently.*

stay·er /£ˈsteɪ·əʳ, $-ɚ/ *n* [C] • *The longest stayers are the British, who visit Australia to see friends and relatives.*

stay [STOP PUNISHMENT] /steɪ/ *n* [C] **stay of execution** *law* an order by a judge which stops a judgment being performed until new information can be considered • (D)

St Ber·nard /£ˌseɪntˈbɜː·nəd, £ˌsənt-, $ˌseɪnt·bɚˈnɑːrd/ *n* [C] a very large strong dog which was used esp. in the past to find people who were lost in the mountains of esp. Switzerland

STD [DISEASE] /ˌes·tiːˈdiː/ *n* [C] *abbreviation for* **sexually transmitted disease**, see at SEX [ACTIVITY]

std [LEVEL] *adj abbreviation for* STANDARD

STD [TELEPHONE] /ˌes·tiːˈdiː/ *n* [U] subscriber trunk dialling (= the system in Britain and Australia by which people make telephone calls over long distances)

stead [IN PLACE OF] /sted/ *n* [U] **in** *someone's* **stead** *fml* in place of someone • *The marketing manager was ill and her deputy ran the meeting in her stead.* • *The National Ballet sacked its director and appointed someone unknown in his stead.*

stead [STATE] /sted/ *n* [U] **stand** *someone* **in good stead**, see at STAND [STATE]

stead·fast /£ˈsted·fɑːst, -fəst, $-fæst/ *adj approving* staying the same for a long time; not changing quickly or unexpectedly • *a steadfast critic/opponent* • *a steadfast friend/ally* • *steadfast loyalty* • *She commended the steadfast courage of families caring for handicapped children.* • *The group* **remained** *steadfast* **in** *its support for the new system, even when it was criticized in the newspapers.*

stead·fast·ly /£ˈsted·fɑːst·li, -fəst-, $-fæst-/ *adv*

stead·fast·ness /£ˈsted·fɑːst·nəs, -fəst-, $-fæst-/ *n* [U]

stead·y [GRADUAL] /ˈsted·i/ *adj* **-ier, -iest** happening in a smooth, gradual and regular way, not suddenly or unexpectedly • *The article was complaining about the steady erosion of civil liberties in recent times.* • *Orders for new ships are rising, after several years of steady decline.* • *Senior officials said they needed to show a steady improvement in the company's financial condition to reassure the public.* • *Over the last 10 years he has produced a steady* **flow/stream/trickle** *of stories and historical novels.* • *In the steady drizzle/rain, a little crowd waited for a bus.* • *The report concluded that, after years of steady growth, the demand for graduates has levelled off.* • *Progress has been* **slow but** *steady.* • *The procession moved through the streets at a steady pace.*

stead·i·ly /ˈsted·ɪ·li/ *adv* • *Prices have risen steadily.*

stead·i·ness /ˈsted·ɪ·nəs/ *n* [U]

stead·y [FIRM] /ˈsted·i/ *adj* **-ier, -iest** not moving or changing suddenly; STABLE [FIXED] • *I'll* **hold** *the boat steady while you climb in.* • *His lead over his rivals has* **held** *steady throughout the past 12 months of campaigning.* • *Most rental prices have* **held** *steady this year.* • *Young people assume that if you are in a steady* **relationship**, *you don't have to worry about HIV.* • *His parents were relieved when he got a steady* **job.** • **Steady as a rock** means firm and not moving.

stead·y *(obj)* /ˈsted·i/ *v* • *He wobbled about on the bike and then steadied himself.* [T] • Steady **(on)** can be said to someone who is about to fall or hit or damage something or themselves, in order to tell them to be careful: *Steady on, Jacob, look where you're going!* [I]

stead·y /ˈsted·i/ *adv* [not gradable] • *(dated)* To **go steady** is to have a romantic relationship with one person for a long period: *Sheila's been going steady* **with** *Mike for six months.*

stead·y [CONTROLLED] /ˈsted·i/ *adj* **-ier, -iest** calm and under control • *a steady voice/look* • *You need steady* **nerves** *to drive in city traffic.* • *Painting these small details needs a steady* **hand.** • A steady person is someone who can be trusted to show good judgment and act in a reasonable way. • *(Br)* **Go** *steady* **on** *(Am and Aus* **Go easy on***)* (= Do not use too much of) *the ice/whisky/spices.*

stead·y *obj* /ˈsted·i/ *v* [T] • *Some people say that a drink will steady your nerves.*

stead·i·ly /ˈsted·ɪ·li/ *adv* • *She returned his gaze steadily.*

stead·i·ness /ˈsted·ɪ·nəs/ *n* [U]

steak /steɪk/ *n* meat, esp. from cattle, usually sold as a thick slice, which can be cooked quite quickly • *Shall we have steak for dinner?* [U] • *We ordered* **rump/T-bone/sirloin** *steaks.* [C] • If you are asked in a restaurant "How would you like your steak?" you are being asked how long you would like it cooked for: *"How would you like your steak, madam?" "Rare/medium/well-done, please."* [C] • Steaks are usually BEEF (= meat from cattle) but can also be from other stated animals or fish: *turkey/gammon/salmon steaks* [C] • A **steak house** is a restaurant that specializes in serving steak. • **Steak and kidney pie/pudding** is a dish made from small pieces of meat in a sauce with pastry on top. • A **steak knife** is a sharp knife with small teeth-like parts along one edge which cuts meat easily. • **Steak tartare** is steak cut into very small pieces which is mixed with egg and spices and then eaten without being cooked. • *(Br and Aus)* **Stewing/braising steak** is meat from cattle which is usually cut into small pieces and cooked slowly in liquid. • [PIC] **Cutlery**

steal *(obj)* [TAKE AWAY] /stiːl/ *v past simple* **stole** /£stəʊl, $stoʊl/, *past part* **stolen** /£ˈstəʊ·lən, $ˈstoʊ-/ to take (something) without the permission or knowledge of the owner and keep it • *The boys were charged with stealing bikes* **from** *a house in Summerhill Rd.* [T] • *The number of cars which are stolen every year has risen considerably.* [T] • *She came home to find she'd* **had** *her TV and video stolen* (=

someone had stolen them). [T] • *When the book was published we found that the author had stolen several of our* **ideas**. [T] • *The firm is now accusing a small band of its former employees of stealing trade secrets.* [T] • *They were so hungry they had to steal in order to eat.* [I] • *He has been convicted of stealing.* [I] • Steal can also mean to do something quickly but trying not to be seen doing it: *She stole* **a glance** *at her watch.* [T] ○ *He stole* **out** *of the room while no-one was looking.* [I] • If someone or something **steals attention/ steals the limelight** they get a lot of attention and other people or things do not get any: *The experimental car certainly stole the limelight at the motor show.* • If you **steal a march on** someone you get an advantage over someone by acting before they do: *Our rival company managed to steal a march on us by bringing out their software three months ahead of ours.* • If someone or something **steals the show/scene** they are the most popular or the best part of what happened: *The child with the dog stole the show.* • To **steal** someone's **thunder** is to do what someone else was going to do before they do it, esp. if this takes success or praise away from them: *I was going to introduce my talk by giving a brief history of our group but the previous speaker stole my thunder by doing just that.* • LP› **Crimes and criminals**

steal CHEAP /stiːl/ *n* [U] **a steal** *esp. Am infml* very cheap • *I picked up a new iron at the sale – it was a steal.*

stealth /stelθ/ *n* [U] movement which is quiet and careful in order not to be seen or heard, or secret or indirect action • *These thieves operate* **with** *terrifying stealth – they can easily steal from the pockets of unsuspecting travellers.* • *It would seem that some politicians would prefer to* **use** *financial stealth rather than legislation to produce change.* • *The weapons had been acquired* **by** *stealth.* • The **Stealth bomber/fighter** is an aircraft which cannot be seen on RADAR (=equipment usually used for watching aircraft when they cannot be seen with the eyes). • *"Do good by stealth, and blush to find it fame"* (Alexander Pope *Imitations of Horace* Epilogue to the Satires, 1738)

stealth·y /ˈstel·θi/ *adj* **-ier, -iest** • *stealthy footsteps*

stealth·i·ly /ˈstel·θɪ·li/ *adv*

steam /stiːm/ *n* [U] the hot gas that is produced when water boils • *We put the bowl of water on the fire and soon it was producing lots of steam.* • Steam can be used to provide power: *steam turbines* ○ *a steam engine/locomotive* ○ *the age of steam* (=the period when steam provided power for railways and factories) ○ *The pump is driven* **by** *steam.* • To **get/pick up steam** is to start working much more effectively: *After the first three months, the fundraising project really started to get up steam.* • If you do something **under** your **own steam**, you do it without help: *When the fitness class closed, we decided to do some training under our own steam.* • A **steam iron** is an electrical IRON that has water inside and produces steam to help make clothes smooth. • **Steam shovel** is *Am for* **excavator**. See at EXCAVATE. • See also STEAMBOAT; STEAMER BOAT; STEAMROLLER VEHICLE; STEAMSHIP. • Ⓙ

steam *(obj)* /stiːm/ *v* • *The train/ship steamed* (=moved by steam power) *out of the station/harbour.* [I] • If food is steamed, it is cooked by steam: *The vegetables should be gently steamed for 15 minutes.* [T] • If you steam **open** a letter or an envelope, or you steam a stamp **off** an envelope, you use steam to soften the glue. [T] • If esp. a glass surface **steams up** or you **steam it up**, it becomes covered with a thin layer of water: *The bathroom mirror steamed up when I ran the hot water.* ○ *I can't see out – the windows are steamed up.* ○ *Going into the warm room steamed my glasses up.* • If a person is **steamed up**, they show their anger, esp. about something that other people do not think is important: *She* **got** *all steamed up about the books being left on the tables instead of being put back on the shelves.* • PIC› **Cooking**

steam·y /ˈstiː·mi/ *adj* **-ier, -iest** • Steamy means hot and HUMID (=with water in the air) like steam: *steamy summer weather* • *(infml)* Steamy also means sexually exciting or including a lot of sexual activity: *Some of the love scenes in the film are on the steamy side.* ○ *The perfume commercial was so steamy that the TV company decided to ban it.* ○ *His new novel is advertised as his steamiest yet.*

steam·ing /ˈstiː·mɪŋ/ *adj* [not gradable] • *a steaming* (=producing steam) *bowl of soup*

steam·boat /£ˈstiːm·bəʊt, $-boʊt/ *n* [C] a boat which moves by steam power • *a river steamboat*

steam·er BOAT /£ˈstiː·məʳ, $-mɚ/ *n* [C] a boat or ship which moves by steam power

steam·er CONTAINER /£ˈstiː·məʳ, $-mɚ/ *n* [C] a container with holes in the bottom which is put over boiling water in order to cook food in steam

steam·rol·ler VEHICLE /£ˈstiːmˌrəʊ·ləʳ, $-ˌroʊ·lɚ/ *n* [C] a vehicle which moves forward on a large heavy wheel in order to make the road surface flat

steam·rol·ler *obj* FORCE /£ˈstiːmˌrəʊ·ləʳ, $-ˌroʊ·lɚ/ *v* [T] *infml* to use great force either to make (someone) do something or on (something) to make it happen or be successful • *They announced what they were going to do and it was clear that they would steamroller anybody who didn't like it.* • *He steamrollered the plan through the committee.* • *I hate being steamrollered into doing something I don't want to.*

steam·rol·ler /£ˈstiːmˌrəʊ·ləʳ, $-ˌroʊ·lɚ/ *n* [C] *infml* • A steamroller is a person who forces other people to agree with them and prevents any opposition.

steam·ship /ˈstiːm·ʃɪp/ *n* [C] a ship which moves by steam power

steam·y /ˈstiː·mi/ *adj* See at STEAM

steed /stiːd/ *n* [C] *literary* a horse which is ridden • *a war steed* ○ *a fine white steed*

steel METAL /stiːl/ *n* [U] a strong metal which is made by processing iron to remove some of the carbon. It is sometimes mixed with other metals, and is used for making things which need a strong structure, esp. vehicles and buildings • *security gates made of steel* ○ *steel girders/ rods/struts* ○ *a steel helmet* ○ *a steel-plated army truck* • **Steel drums** are large oil containers which have been made into musical instruments and are played like drums by a group of musicians who form a **steel band**. • **Steel grey** is a grey colour: *a steel grey suit* • A **steel mill** is a factory where steel is made. • **Steel wool** (*Br also* **wire wool**) is a thick layer of thin steel threads twisted together, small pieces of which can be used to rub a surface smooth. • See also STEELWORKS. • PIC› **Drum, Mill**

steel·y /ˈstiː·li/ *adj* **-ier, -iest** • *steely grey* • When used about a person's behaviour or character, steely means hard and strong, not kind or comfortable: *a steely look/ stare* ○ *steely eyes/nerves* ○ *steely determination*

steel *obj* PREPARE /stiːl/ *v* [T] to force yourself to get ready to do something unpleasant or difficult • *She steeled* **herself to** *jump out of the plane.* [+ obj + *to* infinitive]

steel·works /£ˈstiːl·wɜːks, $-wɜːrks/ *n* [C + sing/pl v] *pl* **steelworks** a factory where steel is made • *The steelworks is/are closing at the end of the month.* • *The steelworks is/are* (=The people who work there are) *on strike.*

steel·work·er /£ˈstiːlˌwɜː·kəʳ, $-ˌwɜːr·kɚ/ *n* [C] • A steelworker is a person who works in a factory making steel.

steep NOT GRADUAL /stiːp/ *adj* **-er, -est** (of a slope) rising or falling at a sharp angle • *Some of the streets in San Francisco are rather steep.* • *It's a steep* **climb** *to the top of the mountain, but the view is worth it.* • *The castle is set on a steep* **hill/hillside**. • *The train slowed as it went up a steep* **incline**. • *It's dangerous to try and ski down these steep* **slopes**. • A steep rise or fall is one which goes very quickly from low to high or from high to low: *Yesterday's steep* **decline/fall/slide** *in the value of the dollar was unexpected.* ○ *There has been a steep* **increase/rise** *in prices.*

steep·en *(obj)* /ˈstiː·pᵊn/ *v* • If a slope steepens, it becomes a sharper angle: *As we got nearer to the mountains, the road began to steepen.* [I] • *If we steepened the steps* (=made them have a sharper angle) *down to the cellar, they'd take up less space.* [T] • If something such as a cost steepens, it increases: *Our costs have steepened since we began this project.* [I]

steep·ly /ˈstiː·pli/ *adv* • *The beach* **slopes** *steeply down to the sea.* • *The incidence of the disease has* **declined/ fallen** *steeply in the last few years.* • *The value of the land has* **risen** *steeply.*

steep·ness /ˈstiːp·nəs/ *n* [U] • *Rescuers had trouble reaching the injured climber due to bad weather and the steepness of the mountainside.* • *The value of shares plunged with dizzying steepness following yesterday's announcement by the Chancellor.*

steep TOO MUCH /stiːp/ *adj* **-er, -est** *infml* (esp. of prices) too much; more than is reasonable • *They are having to face very steep taxes.* • *Their demands are rather steep.* • *We enjoyed our meal at the restaurant, but the bill was* **a bit** *steep.* • *The membership fees at the golf club are* **pretty**

steep. • *"She expects me to take her children to school for her every day." "That's* **a bit** *steep* (= unreasonable)."

steep MAKE WET /stiːp/ *v* to (cause to) stay in a liquid, esp. in order to become soft or clean or to improve flavour • *The stains in this towel will come out if you let it steep for a while.* [I] • *Leave the cloth to steep in the dye overnight.* [I] • *We had pears steeped in red wine for dinner.* [T] • *(fig. fml or literary) His hands are steeped in* **blood** (= He has been responsible for the deaths of a lot of people). [T] • To be steeped **in** something is to seem to be completely surrounded by it, or involved in it, or to have a lot of knowledge of it: *The college is steeped in* **history/tradition**. [T] ○ *Part of the company's problem is that most of the managers are steeped in the old ways of doing things.* [T] ○ *In eighth-century China, society was guided by scholars, steeped in poetry and painting, as well as by the principles of good government.* [T]

stee·ple /ˈstiː·pl̩/ *n* [C] a pointed structure on the top of a church tower, or the tower and the pointed structure considered as one unit • *a church steeple*

stee·ple·chase /ˈstiː·pl̩·tʃeɪs/ *n* [C] a long race in which horses or people have to jump over fences, bushes, etc., either across the countryside or, more usually, on a track • *The Grand National is a famous steeplechase, run every year in Aintree.* • *He's a former Olympic steeplechase champion.* • *a steeplechase jockey/rider* • *a steeplechase runner*

stee·ple·jack /ˈstiː·pl̩·dʒæk/ *n* [C] a person whose job is to climb high buildings in order to repair, paint, clean them etc.

steer *(obj)* DIRECT /£stɪəʳ, $stɪr/ *v* to control the direction of (a vehicle) • *Our garage door isn't very wide and it's quite difficult to steer the car through it.* [T] • *Jenny is learning to ride a bike, but she isn't very good at steering it.* [T] • *When their grandfather took the children out in a boat, they were thrilled at being allowed to steer.* [I] • *My car isn't steering very well* (= the part that controls the steering is not working properly) *on bends at the moment.* [I] • *Make sure you steer* **clear of** (= control the direction taken so that you do not hit) *the rocks.* [I] • *(fig.) They warned their children to steer* **clear of** (= keep away from) *drugs.* [I] • *(fig.) Her speech steered* **clear of** (= avoided) *controversial issues.* [I] • If a vehicle steers, it follows a particular route or direction: *The ship passed Land's End, then steered towards southern Ireland.* [I] ○ *Racing yachts steer a difficult course to make the most of wind and water currents.* [T] ○ *(fig.) It will be difficult to steer* (= follow) *a middle course between the competing claims of the two sides in the conflict.* [T] • To steer someone or something is also to take them or cause them to go in a particular direction: *She steered her guests into the dining room.* [T] ○ *He successfully steered the company onto a new course.* [T] ○ *The most important piece of legislation that the new government will have to steer through parliament is tax reform.* [T] ○ *The police are constantly searching for new ways of steering young people* **away from** *a life of crime.* [T] ○ *I'd like to steer our discussion* **back to** *our original topic.* [T] ○ *The main task of the new government will be to steer the country* **towards** *democracy.* [T] • The **steering column** in a vehicle is the part to which the wheel is fixed that you turn in order to make the vehicle go in a particular direction: *My car has an adjustable steering column.* • A **steering committee** is a group of people chosen to direct the way an activity is carried out: *The steering committee is/are meeting tomorrow.* [+ sing/pl v] ○ *The ambassador will serve as the US representative on the steering committee for peace talks.* • A **steering wheel** is a wheel in a vehicle which the driver turns in order to make the vehicle go in a particular direction. • LP› **Driving**

steer MALE COW /£stɪəʳ, $stɪr/ *n* [C] a young male of the cattle family that has had its sex organs removed, and which is usually kept for meat • *a herd of steers*

stein /staɪn/ *n* [C] a very large cup, usually made of clay and often decorated, which has a handle and a lid, and is used for drinking beer • Stein is also *Am for* TANKARD.

stel·lar /£ˈstel·əʳ, $-ɚ/ *adj* [not gradable] of a star or stars • *a stellar explosion* • *stellar light* • *(infml)* When used of people or their activities, stellar means of an extremely high standard: *a stellar performance/player/team* ○ *the stellar duo, Simon and Garfunkel* ○ *Her career so far has been stellar.*

stem CENTRAL PART /stem/ *n* [C] a central part (of something) from which other parts can develop or grow, or which forms a support • The stem of a plant is the stick-like central part of it which grows above the ground and from which leaves and flowers grow, or a smaller thin part which grows from the central part and which supports the leaves and flowers: *Some types of daffodil have a single flower* **on** *a stem, while others have several.* ○ *A lot of the stems* **of** *the flowers in the garden were broken by the strong wind.* ○ *Cut two centimetres off the bottom of the stems before you put the roses in water.* • The stem of a glass or similar container is the vertical part which supports the part into which you put liquid: *Champagne glasses usually have long stems.* • The stem of a word is what is left when you take off the part which changes in order to show a different tense or a plural form etc.: *From the stem 'sav-' you get 'saves', 'saved', 'saving' and 'saver'.* • The stem in a ship is the main supporting structure at the front of the ship: *When the ship berthed at New York, a team of officials from the American public health service checked it* **from stem to stern** (= from the front to the back). • *(Am)* The stem of a watch is the small part on the side of the watch which you turn to change the position of the pointers on the watch, or to make the watch operate. • PIC› **Clocks and watches**

-stemmed /-stemd/ *combining form* • -stemmed means having the stated type of stem: *a thick-stemmed plant* ○ *a narrow-stemmed wine glass* ○ *a low-stemmed rose bowl*

stem ORIGIN /stem/ *v* [I always + adv/prep] **-mm-** to originate; to develop or grow (from) • *Her problems stem* **from** *her difficult childhood.* • *Their disagreement stemmed* **from** *a misunderstanding.* • *He said that children's bad behaviour often stems* **from** *boredom.* • *These practices stem* **from** *traditional Chinese medicine.* • *This law stems* **back to** *a royal decree of 1552.*

stem *obj* STOP /stem/ *v* [T] **-mm-** to stop (something unwanted that is spreading or increasing) • *These measures are designed to stem the rise of violent crime in the country.* • *They argued that it was time the government did something to stem rising unemployment/illegal immigration.* • *She tied a handkerchief round her son's arm to stem the* **flow** *of blood from his wrist.* • *They are looking for ways of stemming the* **flow** *of drugs into the country.* • *The manager said that he had no doubt that the team would soon stem the* **tide** *of defeat.*

stench /stentʃ/ *n* [U] a strong unpleasant smell • *the stench* **of** *rotting fish/burning rubber/cigarette smoke* • *There was* **a strong/powerful/unbearable** *stench* **of** *dead bodies.* • *(fig.) For a long time after the minister's resignation, the stench* **of** *scandal hung over the government* (= the event which caused public disapproval continued to have a bad effect on the government). • LP› **Smells**

sten·cil /ˈstent·sᵊl/ *n* [C] a piece of card, plastic, metal, etc. in which shapes have been cut out • *The children made a farmyard picture using stencils.* • A stencil is also a picture made by drawing or painting through the holes in such a piece of card, etc. onto paper: *We bought some tiles with a stencil pattern.* ○ *She did a stencil* **of** *a rainbow on her daughter's bedroom wall.* • PIC› **Handicraft**

sten·cil *obj* /ˈstent·sᵊl/ *v* [T] **-ll-** or *Am usually* **-l-** • *Air force pilots sometimes stencil* (= form using a stencil) *slogans on the sides of their aircraft.*

Sten gun /sten/ *n* [C] a small gun which can fire bullets continuously

ste·nog·raph·er /£stəˈnɒg·rə·fəʳ, $-ˈnɑː·grə·fɚ/, *infml* **sten·o** /£ˈsten·əʊ, $-oʊ/ *n* [C] *Am or Br dated for* **shorthand typist**, see at SHORTHAND

sten·tor·i·an /£stenˈtɔː·ri·ən, $-ˈtɔːr·i-/ *adj fml* using a very loud voice, or (of a voice) very loud • *a stentorian preacher* • *Suddenly a stentorian* **voice** *boomed across the room.*

step FOOT MOVEMENT /step/ *n* [C] the act of lifting one foot and putting it down on a different part of the ground, such as when you walk or run • *Sophie* **took** *her first steps when she was eleven months old.* • *He rose to his feet and* **took** *a couple of steps* **towards** *her.* • *(fig.) The country is* **taking** *its first* **faltering/tentative** *steps* **towards** (= It has started to move towards) *democracy.* • *(fig.) I'm pleased to say that Chris has now* **taken** *a few steps* **on the road to** *recovery* (= she has begun to get well again). • *They walked to the bus stop* **with** *hurried steps.* • **With** *every step, her shoes hurt her more and more.* • *I* **retraced** *my steps, looking for my lost keys.* • *I thought I heard some steps* (= sounds made by someone's feet when they are walking or running) *outside.* See also FOOTSTEP. • A step is also the distance you cover when you take a step: *I'd only gone a few steps down the road when I realized I'd forgotten to lock the door.* ○ *(fig.) Our house is just a* **step** (= a short distance) *from the station.* • Your step is also the way in which you move your feet when you are walking or running. It can sometimes show

how you are feeling: *His face was stained with tears and his step was slow and heavy.* [U] ○ *She walked out of the office with* **a spring in** *her step* (= in a way that showed she was happy). [U] ○ *The driver told us to* **mind/watch** *our step* (= walk carefully) *as we got off the bus.* [U] • *You need to* **mind/watch your step** (= be careful about how you behave, or you will get into trouble), *young lady.* • A step is also a particular movement that you make with your feet when you dance: *She's teaching me some basic* **dance** *steps.* ○ *"Shall we dance the waltz?" "I'm sorry, I don't know the steps."* • To move or be **in step** is to walk or march or dance with other people so that you lift the same foot off the ground and put it down again at the same time as all the other people. To move or be **out of step** is not to lift the same foot and put it down again at the same time as the other people: *The soldiers marched in step.* ○ *I'm no good at dancing – I always get hopelessly out of step.* ○ *One of the children in the parade was walking out of step* **with** *all the others.* ○ *We had only walked a short distance when we realized that we had all* **fallen into/got in/come into** *step with each other* (= were walking so that we were lifting the same foot at the same time). • If your opinions, ideas or way of living are **in step**, they are the same as those of other people. If they are **out of step**, they are different from those of other people: *The Republicans are out of step* **with** *the country, Williams said.* ○ *Television companies need to* **keep** *in step* **with** *public opinion.* ○ *He thinks that everyone is out of step except him* (= He thinks that although everyone else disagrees with him, he is right and they are wrong). • **Step aerobics** (also **step**) is a type of exercise in which you repeatedly and quickly lift one foot, then the other, onto a slightly raised surface, then put them back down on the ground again: *I do step three times a week.* ○ *Do you want to come to a step aerobics class with me tonight?*

step /step/ *v* [I always + adv/prep] **-pp-** • *Be careful not to step in the mud.* • *Ow, you stepped on my foot!* • *They stepped carefully onto the ice.* • *He stepped over a puddle.* • *(fml) Would you care to step* (= come) *this way please, sir?* • *Step* (= Move) **aside**, *please – this lady needs a doctor.* • *A man appeared at the window, then stepped* **back** *into the shadows.* • *(fig.) Visiting her house was like stepping* **back** *in time/stepping* **back** *50 years* (= going back into the past). • *She stepped* **backwards** *and fell over a chair.* • *(fig.) No one has yet stepped* **forward** *to claim the first prize in the competition* (= has announced that they are the person who has won.) • *(fig.) He just stepped* **into** *a job* (= got a job very easily) *as soon as he left college.* • *(fig. infml) He wants to get to the top, and he doesn't care who he steps* **on** (= treats unfairly or unkindly) *to get there.* • *They stepped* **out** *onto the balcony.* • *(esp. Am and Aus) I'm afraid Mr Taylor has just stepped* (= gone) **out** *(of the office) for a few minutes, but I'll tell him you called.* • *Members of the audience were invited to step* **up** *onto the stage.* • If you **step into the breach**, you do someone else's work when they are unable to do it: *Gill had to take two months off work because she broke her leg, but luckily Kathy was able to step into the breach.* • If you tell the driver of a car to **step on it** (*esp. Am also* **step on the gas**), you are telling them to drive faster. **Step on it** can also be used to mean hurry up. • If you **step out of line**, you behave in a way that is unacceptable or that is not what is expected: *I was told not to step out of line again, otherwise I would be in trouble.* • *(Am infml)* If you **step out on** someone, you have sexual relationships with people other than that person: *I don't know why she puts up with him, he's all the time stepping out on her.* • A **stepping stone** is one of a row of large flat stones on which you can walk in order to cross a stream or river that is not deep: *To cross the stream, we had to walk across some stepping stones.* ○ *(fig.) I see this job just as a stepping stone* (= a way of helping me advance) **to** *better things.*

step STAGE /step/ *n* [C] a stage in a process • *What is the next step in the programme?* • *Evans has moved a step nearer victory in the world championship.* • *We must try and stay one step* **ahead** *of our competitors.* • *I think we need to* **go** *a step* **further** (= to a more advanced position or stage in a process) *and make a formal complaint.* • *Most people believe that the decision to cut interest rates was a step* **in the right direction.** • *Following the success of our products in Europe, our logical* **next** *step is to move into the American market.* • *This job is a real step* **up** (= is an advance) *for me.* • A step is also an action in a series of actions taken for a particular purpose: *We need to* **take urgent/drastic** *steps* **to** *reduce pollution.* ○ *The government has been urged to* **take decisive/concrete** *steps* **to** *end terrorism.* ○ *The President* **took** *the* **unusual/unprecedented/rare** *step* **of** *altering his prepared speech in order to condemn the terrorist attack.* • *No one is sure whether this plan will work, but it's* **a step forward** (= an improvement or development). • *This discovery is* **a great/major/important/significant step forward** *in our understanding of the disease.* • *The changes that have been introduced are being seen as* **a step backwards/a backward step** (= going back to a worse or less advanced stage). • If you take **one step forward, two steps back**, you advance but then experience events which cause you to be further behind than you were when you made the advance. • *Let's take things* **a step/one step at a time** (= slowly). • *The model car came with* **step by step** *instructions* (= instructions about what to do at each stage of the process) *about how to put it together.* • **Step by step** also means gradually: *These changes need to be made step by step.*

step SURFACE /step/ *n* [C] a flat surface, often forming one of a series of such surfaces in which each is higher or lower than the one before, on which you put your feet in order to move up or down from one level to another • *There are some* **stone/wooden** *steps leading down into the basement.* • *We'll meet you by the cathedral steps/the steps* **of** *the cathedral.* • *We had to* **climb** *some* **rickety** *old steps.* • *There's a* **flight of** *steps leading up to the courtroom entrance.* • *If I'm not in when you deliver the parcel, just leave it on the* **(front)** *step* (= outside the door to the house). See also DOORSTEP. • *(Br)* **Mind the** *step (Am usually* **watch your** *step) as you leave the train.* • *It's difficult for people in wheelchairs to* **negotiate** (= move up and down) *steps.* • *One of the steps* **on** *the ladder is broken.* • *(fig.) We've just moved onto the first step* **on** *the property ladder* (= We have bought a house for the first time).

steps /steps/ *pl n Br* • Steps is another word for STEPLADDER: *kitchen steps* ○ *library steps*

step MUSIC /step/ *n* [C] *Am for* TONE DIFFERENCE IN SOUND

step– RELATIONSHIP /step-/ *combining form* being of the stated relationship to someone through the previous marriage of their husband or wife, or through their mother or father marrying again • *stepfather* • *stepmother* • *stepchildren* • LP **Relationships**

step back *v adv* [I] to temporarily stop being involved (in an activity or situation) in order to think about it in a new way • *Let's just step back from the problem and think about what we could do.* • *I'm sure that if you were to step back and think about the effects of your smoking, you'd give it up.* • *She says that she wants to step back* **from** *the committee's activities for a few months.*

step down/a·side *v adv* [I] to leave your job or position, esp. so that someone else can take your place • *She has said that she will be stepping down at the next election.* • *He has decided to step down* **as** *captain/***from** *the captaincy.* • *He is unwilling to step aside* **in favour of** *a younger person.*

step down *obj*, **step** *obj* **down** *v adv* [M] to reduce • *Production of this model of car is being stepped down.* • *The doctor has said that I can start stepping my medication down in a few days' time.* • *This device is used for stepping down* **voltage.**

step in *v adv* [I] to become involved in a difficult situation or argument in order to help find a solution • *The government has stepped in to stop the pound from falling any lower.* • *An outside buyer has stepped in to save the company from going out of business.* • *When the leading actress in the play broke her leg, Diana stepped in and took over.* • *I try not to step in and sort out the children's arguments, but sometimes I just have to.*

step up *obj*, **step** *obj* **up** *v adv* [M] to increase (something) in size, amount or speed • *The police are stepping up their efforts to fight crime.* • *It's time we stepped our campaign up.* • *Following the bomb explosion, security has been stepped up at the airport.* • *The pace of the reforms is being stepped up.* • *If you want to use a piece of American electrical equipment in Britain, you may need to use a transformer to step up the* **voltage.**

step·bro·ther /£ˈstepˌbrʌ·ðəʳ, $-ðɚ/ *n* [C] the son, by a previous marriage, of the person who is married to someone's father or mother • Compare **half-brother** at HALF. • LP **Relationships**

step·child /ˈstep·tʃaɪld/ *n* [C] *pl* **stepchildren** /ˈstep ˌtʃɪl·drən/ a child that someone's husband or wife had during a previous marriage • LP **Relationships**

step·daugh·ter /£ˈstepˌdɔː·təʳ, $-ˌdɑː·t̬ɚ/ *n* [C] a daughter that someone's husband or wife had during a previous marriage • *He has been married twice and has helped to bring up two daughters and two stepdaughters.* • LP› **Relationships**

step·fa·ther /£'step,fɑː·ðəʳ, $-ðɚ/ *n* [C] the man who is married to someone's mother but is not their real father • *When his mother married again, he went to live with her and his new stepfather.* • LP› **Relationships**

step·lad·der /£'step,læd·əʳ, $-ɚ/ *n* [C], *Br also* **steps** *pl n* a structure consisting of two vertical rectangular frames, one of which has steps built into it, which are joined at the top and can be separated at the bottom to allow the structure to stand, or be folded together for storing • *A stepladder is used for reaching high places.* • *I can't reach the top shelf of my bookshelves unless I use a stepladder.* • *He fell off the stepladder when he was painting the ceiling.* • *She climbed up the stepladder to pick the apples from the tree.*

step·mo·ther /£'step,mʌð·əʳ, $-ɚ/ *n* [C] the woman who is married to someone's father but is not their real mother • *When she married Tom, she became stepmother to his three children.* • LP› **Relationships**

step·pa·rent /£'step,peə·rᵊnt, $-,per·ᵊnt/ *n* [C] the man or woman who is married to someone's mother or father but is not their real father or mother • *In America, one child in five lives with a stepparent.* • LP› **Relationships**

steppe /step/ *n* (a large area of) land with grass but no trees • *China is a country surrounded by desert, sea, steppe and mountain.* [U] • *Kazakhstan covers vast territories of steppe and desert between Siberia, China and Iran.* [U] • *Wheat is grown on* **the** *steppes in Ukraine.* [C] • *These people have lived for centuries on* **the** *Russian steppes.* [C]

step·si·ster /£'step,sɪs·təʳ, $-tɚ/ *n* [C] the daughter, by a previous marriage, of the person who is married to someone's mother or father • Compare **half-sister** at HALF. • LP› **Relationships**

step·son /'step·sʌn/ *n* [C] a son that someone's husband or wife had during a previous marriage • *She had a very close relationship with her stepson, whom she had looked after since he was a young boy.*

ster·e·o /£'ster·i·əʊ, $-oʊ/ *n pl* **stereos** a way of recording or playing sound so that it is separated into two signals and produces more natural sound • *The concert will be broadcast* **in** *stereo.* [U] • *This recording was made* **in** *stereo.* [U] • A stereo is a piece of electrical equipment on which sound like this can be played: *Turn that stereo down, Mike!* [C] ○ *We could hear music blaring from their car stereo.* [C]

ster·e·o /£'ster·i·əʊ, $-oʊ/, *fml* **ster·e·o·phon·ic** /£,ster·i·əʊ'fɒn·ɪk, $-ə'fɑː·nɪk/ *adj* [not gradable] • *a stereo broadcast* • *a stereo film soundtrack* • *a stereo system* • *stereo headphones* • Compare MONO SOUND; QUADRAPHONIC.

ster·e·o·type /'ster·i·ə·taɪp/ *n* [C] *disapproving* (a person or thing that represents) a fixed set of ideas that is generally held about the characteristics of a particular type of person or thing, which are (wrongly) believed to be shared by all the people and things of that type • *Many teachers and parents are concerned that racist stereotypes are being passed on to children through toys and books.* • *She was surprised at how her children's behaviour seemed to follow sexual stereotypes.* • *There are still advertisements which draw on the old stereotypes* **of** *women obsessed about the cleanliness of their washing.* • *He doesn't* **conform to/ fit/fill** *the national stereotype* **of** *a Frenchman.* • *The characters in the book are just stereotypes* (= They represent fixed ideas about what people of that particular type are like).

ster·e·o·type *obj* /'ster·i·ə·taɪp/ *v* [T] *disapproving* • *The study claims that British advertising stereotypes women* (= presents false fixed ideas about what they are like). • *The police have been accused of having stereotyped images of black people.* • *We tried not to give the children sexually stereotyped toys.*

ster·e·o·typ·i·cal /,ster·i·ə'tɪp·ɪ·kᵊl/ *adj disapproving* • *The stereotypical family of husband, wife and two children is becoming less common.* • *He came out with some stereotypical male response to my question.* • *Customers are tired of the stereotypical, fast-talking salesperson.*

ster·e·o·typ·i·cally /,ster·i·ə'tɪp·ɪ·kli/ *adv disapproving* • *In 'Oliver Twist', Charles Dickens angered Jewish readers by making the character Fagin a Jew with stereotypically offensive characteristics.*

ster·ile UNABLE TO PRODUCE /£'ster·aɪl, $-ᵊl/ *adj* [not gradable] (of a living being) unable to produce young, or (of land) unable to produce plants or crops • *A mule is a sterile animal.* • *It is thought that one of the side effects of the drug could be to make men sterile.* • *The loss of the rain forests would upset the climates of tropical countries, bringing droughts and floods and sterile soil.* • Sterile can also mean lacking in imagination or new ideas or energy: *They are still continuing with the sterile argument about capitalism versus socialism.* ○ *We need some new ideas to liven up this sterile campaign.* ○ *This sterile conflict has been going on for years.*

ste·ril·i·ty /£stə'rɪl·ɪ·ti, $-ə·ṭi/ *n* [U] • *This chemical is known to have caused sterility* **in** *monkeys.* • *We are trying to find ways of counteracting the sterility* **of** *the land.* • *(fig.) He wrote a highly critical article about the current sterility* (= lack of imagination or new ideas) **of** *the British theatre.* • *(fig.) Over a bottle of wine, we shared our despair over the emotional sterility* (= lack of energy or interest) **of** *our marriages.*

ster·il·ize *obj*, *Br and Aus usually* **-ise** /'ster·ɪ·laɪz/ *v* [T] • A person or animal that is sterilized has had a medical operation that makes it impossible for them to produce any more young: *After having five children, she decided to be sterilized.*

ster·i·liz·a·tion, *Br and Aus usually* **-i·sa·tion** /,ster·ɪ·laɪ'zeɪ·ʃᵊn/ *n* [U] • *My wife and I have discussed sterilization* (= having a medical operation to make it impossible for us to have children), *but we haven't made a decision about it yet.*

ster·ile CLEAN /£'ster·aɪl, $-ᵊl/ *adj* [not gradable] completely clean and free from bacteria • *Sterile needles are being given to drug users to help stop the spread of infection.* • *Children with this disease need to be kept in a sterile environment.* • *The operation must be carried out under sterile conditions.* • *The label on the bottle said 'sterile until opened'.*

ster·il·ize *obj*, *Br and Aus usually* **-ise** /'ster·ɪ·laɪz/ *v* [T] • If you sterilize something, you make it completely clean and free from bacteria: *All equipment must be sterilized before use.* ○ *Has this milk been sterilized?*

ste·ril·iz·ing, *Br and Aus usually* **-ise** /'ster·ɪ·laɪ·zɪŋ/ *adj* [not gradable] • *I put my contact lenses in sterilizing* **solution** *every night.* • *When we went on holiday, we took some sterilizing* **tablets** *with us which we put in the water to make it safe to drink.*

ster·i·liz·a·tion, *Br and Aus usually* **-i·sa·tion** /,ster·ɪ·laɪ'zeɪ·ʃᵊn/ *n* [U] • *The needles have been sent off for sterilization.*

ster·il·iz·er, *Br and Aus usually* **-iser** /£'ster·ɪ·laɪ·zəʳ, $-zɚ/ *n* [C] • A sterilizer is a machine for making things completely clean and free from bacteria.

ster·ling MONEY /£'stɜː·lɪŋ, $'stɜːr-/ *n* [U] British money • *Sterling rose/fell* (= became worth more/less) *overnight.* • *The value of sterling increased against other European currencies yesterday.* • *If you buy things on the plane, you can either pay for them in* **pounds** *sterling* (= British POUNDS) *or in US dollars.*

ster·ling METAL /£'stɜː·lɪŋ, $'stɜːr-/ *adj* [not gradable] (of precious metal, esp. silver) of a fixed standard of purity • *a sterling silver candlestick* • *sterling cutlery* • *a bracelet made of sterling* (= sterling silver)

ster·ling ADMIRABLE /£'stɜː·lɪŋ, $'stɜːr-/ *adj approving* of a very high standard; admirable • *He has many sterling qualities.* • *You've done a sterling job.* • *Everyone has made a sterling effort.* • *This old television has done sterling service, but it doesn't work very well any more.*

stern SEVERE /£stɜːn, $stɜːrn/ *adj* **-er, -est** severe, or showing disapproval • *She is her own sternest critic.* • *The Bank of England has introduced sterner measures to control public borrowing.* • *Journalists received a stern warning not to go anywhere near the battlefield without proper authorization.* • *"Don't let me ever catch you doing that again," he said in a stern voice.* • If something, such as a job, is stern, it is difficult: *The President is facing the sternest test of his authority since he came to power five years ago.* • If someone is described as being **made of sterner stuff**, they are very strong and determined: *I was ready to give up the fight, but Nicky was made of sterner stuff and wanted us to carry on.*

stern·ly /£'stɜːn·li, $'stɜːrn-/ *adv* • If you say something sternly, you say it in a way that shows disapproval: *"This kind of behaviour is not acceptable," said the teacher sternly.* ○ *The newspaper editor was sternly rebuked for allowing the story to be printed.*

stern·ness /£'stɜːn·nəs, $'stɜːrn-/ *n* [U] • *He noticed an uncharacteristic sternness in her voice as she told her children not to stay out late at night.*

stern SHIP PART /£stɜːn, $stɜːrn/ *n* [C] the back part of a ship or boat • *Our cabin was at the stern* **of** *the ship.* • Compare BOW FRONT PART. • PIC› **Ships and boats**

ster·num /£'stɜː·nəm, $'stɜːr-/ *n* [C] *pl* **sternums** or **sterna** /£'stɜː·nə, $'stɜːr-/ *medical* BREASTBONE

ste·roid /£'stɪə·rɔɪd, 'ster·ɔɪd, $'stɪr·ɔɪd/ *n* [C] a type of chemical substance naturally produced in the body. There are various types of steroid. • *Steroids are responsible for maintaining many of the workings of the body.* • A steroid is also an artificial form of the natural chemical substance which is used for treating particular medical conditions. There are various types of these steroids: *I'm taking steroids/I'm* **on** *steroids for my asthma.* ○ *Steroid creams are used for treating some types of skin condition.* • A steroid is also a drug which increases the development of your muscles. These drugs are sometimes taken illegally by people taking part in sports competitions: *Ben Johnson was stripped of his Olympic gold medal and banned from athletics for taking* **anabolic** *steroids.* ○ *The swimmer has tested positive for* (= has been shown to have taken) *steroids.*

steth·o·scope /£'steθ·ə·skəʊp, $-skoʊp/ *n* [C] a piece of medical equipment which has two tubes, which doctors put into their ears, fixed to a small disc which is put on your chest or back so that they can listen to your heart or lungs • PIC› **Medical equipment**

Stet·son /'stet·sᵊn/ *n* [C] *trademark* a hat with a wide, curving lower edge, esp. worn by COWBOYS (= people who take care of cattle) • PIC› **Hats**

stew /£stjuː, $stuː/ *n* (a type of) food consisting usually of meat or fish and vegetables cooked slowly in a small amount of liquid • *lamb/bean/fish stew* [U] • *Would you like some more stew?* [U] • *She prepared a* **hearty** *stew for dinner.* [C] • If someone is **in a stew**, they are in a difficult situation which causes them to feel anxious or upset: *William is in a stew about/over the demand he received from the tax office.* ○ *The minister's remarks have* **got** *the government* **into** *a real stew.* ○ *Carol is in a stew* (= is angry) *because I forgot to do the shopping she asked me to do.*

stew *(obj)* /£stjuː, $stuː/ *v* • To stew meat, fish, vegetables or fruit is to cook them slowly and gently in a little liquid: *Stew the pears gently in red wine for a couple of hours.* [T] ○ *We had stewed beef/clams/apples/prunes for dinner.* • If a person stews, they are angry: *You're not still stewing about what happened yesterday, are you?* [I] • To stew is also to do nothing productive: *With jobs so scarce, many young people spend long hours with little to do but drink and stew.* [I] • *(infml)* To **stew (in** your **own juice)** is to think about or suffer the results of your own foolish actions, without anyone giving you any help: *I'm not going to help Thomas sort out that mistake he made – he can stew in his own juice for a bit.* ○ *Jean will calm down soon – just* **leave** *her* **to** *stew/***let** *her stew for a while.*

stewed /£stjuːd, $stuːd/ *adj* • *(Br and Aus)* Tea that is stewed has been kept too long before it is poured, and is therefore strong and bitter. • *(esp. Am infml)* If you are stewed, you are drunk: *By the end of the party most of us were really stewed.*

stew·ard /£'stjuː·əd, $'stuː·ɚd/ *n* [C] a person whose job it is to organize a particular event, or to provide services to particular people, or to take care of a particular place • *Stewards will be inspecting the race track at 9.00 a.m.* • *The organizers of the demonstration said that 500 stewards would ensure that it was peaceful.* • *If you need help at any time during the conference, one of the stewards will be pleased to help you.* • *The winning rider was disqualified after a stewards'* **enquiry**. • A steward (*female also* **stewardess**) is a person who serves passengers on a ship, train or aircraft: *We pressed the buzzer in our cabin and a steward arrived instantly.* On an aircraft, such a person is now more usually called a **flight attendant**. See at FLIGHT FLYING. • A steward is also a person who organizes the supply and serving of food at a CLUB: *He's the steward* **of** *the City of Wakefield's Working Men's Club.*

stew·ard·ship /£'stjuː·əd·ʃɪp, $'stuː·ɚd-/ *n* [U] • Someone's stewardship of something is the way in which that person controls or organizes it: *There is increasing concern about the president's stewardship* **of** *the economy.* ○ *The company has been very successful while it has been* **under** *the stewardship* **of** *Mr White.*

stick THIN PIECE /stɪk/ *n* [C] a thin piece of wood • *We dropped two sticks into the river and watched to see which one came out on the other side of the bridge first.* • *The rioters threw sticks and stones at the police.* • *Blind people sometimes carry white sticks which they use to help them find their way around.* • *Police said that the child had been beaten with a stick.* • *(fig.) The party has a number of sticks with which to beat* (= It has several ways of forcing) *the prime minister into submission.* • *A lollipop is a sweet on a stick* (= a short thin piece of wood, plastic or paper). • *The boys were chased out of the field by an angry farmer* **brandishing/wielding** *a stick.* • *They served sausages on* **(cocktail)** *sticks* (= short thin pieces of wood with a point at each end) *at the party.* • *He's still quite active, although he's now 84 and walks with the aid of a* **(walking)** *stick* (= a long thin piece of wood which you can use as a support when you are walking). • A stick is also a long thin piece of wood with a curved end used in playing HOCKEY, or a long thin piece of wood with a triangular shaped net at one end used for playing LACROSSE, or a long thin piece of wood with a solid tube-shaped piece fixed horizontally to one end of it used for playing POLO: *a hockey/lacrosse/polo stick* • A stick **of** something is a long thin piece of it: *a stick of* **celery/rhubarb/chewing-gum/chalk/dynamite** ○ *(Br) When we went to Blackpool, we bought several sticks* **of rock** (= a type of hard sweet). • A stick can also mean a piece of furniture: *When they got married, they didn't have a stick* **of furniture**. ○ *These few sticks are all she has.* • *He said that when he was a boy, his father used to* **take a stick to** *him* (= hit him with a long thin piece of wood) *to punish him.* • *(Br infml)* If you **up sticks** (*Am* **pull up stakes**), you take your belongings and go and live in a different place: *This is the fourth time in five years that we've had to up sticks.* • A **stick figure** (also **matchstick figure**) is a simple picture of a person in which the head is drawn as a circle and the body, arms and legs are drawn as lines. • A **stick insect** is a large insect with a long thin body and legs: *She's as thin as a stick insect.* • **Stick shift** is *Am for* **gear lever**. See at GEAR ENGINE PART. • *(saying)* 'Sticks and stones may break my bones, but words can never hurt me' means that I cannot be hurt by unpleasant things that are said to me. This is sometimes shortened to 'Sticks and stones'. • See also BROOMSTICK; CANDLESTICK; CHOPSTICK; JOSS STICK; POGO STICK. Compare STICKS. • PIC› **Bicycles, Sports, Stick**

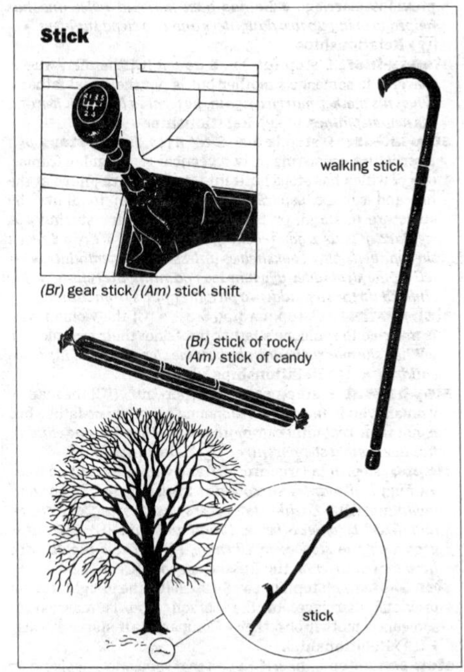

stick SEVERE TREATMENT /stɪk/ *n* [U] *Br infml* severe punishment or criticism • *Steve's dad really* **gave** *him stick when he crashed his car.* • *I really* **got/took** *stick from my boss about being late for work again.* • *The government has been* **getting**/*has* **come in for** *a lot of stick about its handling of the crisis.* • *(Br)* To **give** someone stick, or to **come in for/get/take** stick is also to laugh at someone or to be laughed at in a kind way: *Bob was given terrible stick about the tie he was wearing.*

stick *(obj)* PUSH INTO /stɪk/ *v* [always + adv/prep] *past* **stuck** /stʌk/ to push (a pointed object) into or through something, or (of a pointed object) to be pushed into or through something and stay there • *The killer stuck a knife* **into** *his victim's back.* [T] • *You can tell if the meat is cooked by sticking a fork* **into** *it.* [T] • *It really hurt when the nurse stuck the needle* **into** *my arm.* [T] • *We decided where to go for our holiday by closing our eyes and sticking a pin* **in** *the map.* [T] • *A thorn stuck* **in** *her finger.* [I] • *There's something sticking* **into** *my side.* [I] • *When I broke my leg, you could see the bone sticking* **through** *the skin.* [I]

stick *(obj)* FIX /stɪk/ *v past* **stuck** /stʌk/ to (cause to) become fixed (as if) with glue or another similar substance • *I spent the evening sticking photographs in the album.* [T] • *I forgot to stick a stamp on the envelope.* [T] • *I put a plastic cover on my book, but I didn't stick it* **down** *properly and it came off.* [M] • *He stuck* **up** *a notice on the board* **with** *pins.* [M] • *This glue won't stick.* [I] • *Can you do anything to stop this window from sticking* (= becoming fixed in a position)*?* [I] • *My car stuck* **in** *the mud.* [I] • *(fig.) For some reason, what she said stuck* **in** *my mind/head/memory* (= I remembered it). [I] • *Sugary food can stick* **to** *your teeth and cause decay.* [I] • *Stir the sauce continuously, so that it doesn't stick* **to** *the pan.* [I] • *It was so hot that my clothes were sticking* **to** *me.* [I] • *(fig.) Ellie stuck* **to** (= stayed close to) *her mother like a leech.* [I] • *My book got wet and all the pages have stuck* **together**. [I] • *(fig.) The two brothers always stick* **together** (= stay close to each other) *at school.* [I] • *They'll never make these* **charges/accusations** *stick* (= show that they are true). [I] • If a **name** sticks, it continues to be used: *Although her name is Clare, her little sister called her Lali, and somehow the name stuck/it stuck.* [I] • *(esp. Am) The group found themselves* **stuck in the muck** (= unable to move out of a difficult situation) **of** *frustration and blame.* • *It really* **sticks in** *my* **throat/craw** (= makes me angry) *that I did all the work, and she's getting all the credit.* • *This pudding will really* **stick to** *your* **ribs** (= make you feel as if you have eaten a lot because it is so heavy). • *(Br)* **Sticking plaster** (*Am and Aus* **Band-Aid**) is a material that you can put over a small cut in the skin in order to protect it and keep it clean: *I've cut my finger – could you get me some sticking plaster?* ○ *Timmy had sticking plasters on both knees.* ○ *(fig.) All the government is doing is putting a sticking plaster on the problem* (= taking temporary action which fails to solve it). • A **sticking point** in a discussion is a point on which it is not possible to reach an agreement: *Exactly how the land is to be divided up is the main sticking point of the peace talks.* • *(infml disapproving)* A **stick-in-the-mud** is someone who is not willing to change or accept new ideas: *My dad's a real stick-in-the-mud.* ○ *They have a stick-in-the-mud attitude to new ideas.* • Something that is **stick-on** has glue or other similar substance on one side of it, so that it can fix to a surface: *The plates I bought had stick-on labels on them and they were very difficult to remove.* ○ *I got some stick-on soles for my shoes, but they keep coming off.* • Compare **non-stick** at NON-; STUCK FIXED.

stick·er /£ˈstɪk·əʳ, $-ɚ/ *n* [C] • A sticker is a small piece of paper or plastic with a picture or writing on one side and glue or other similar substance on the other side, so that it will fasten to a surface: *a bumper/window/windscreen sticker* ○ *The doctor gave the child a sticker saying 'I was very brave at the doctor's today'.* ○ *The sticker on the back window of her car said 'My other car's a Porsche'.* ○ *She has a disabled sticker* (= one which shows that she finds it difficult to walk) *in her car.* ○ *There were two different* **price** *stickers on the shoes I wanted to buy, so I didn't know how much they actually cost.* • *(Am)* The **sticker price** of something, esp. a car, is the official price given by its maker: *I got my BMW for $2000 less than the sticker price.*

stick·y /ˈstɪk·i/ *adj* **-ier, -iest** • Sticky means being, made of, or covered with a substance that stays fixed to any surface it touches: *Don't touch the wet paint – it's sticky.* ○ *You shouldn't eat so many sticky sweets.* ○ *We had sticky buns for tea.* ○ *The children's faces were sticky* **with** *chocolate.* ○ *Come here, and I'll wipe your sticky* **fingers**. • *(infml)* If someone **has sticky fingers**, they are likely to steal: *Brian got a job in a shop, but he turned out to have sticky fingers and was forced to leave.* • If the weather is sticky, it is very hot and the air feels wet: *It's very sticky in New York in August.* See also HUMID. • Sticky also means difficult: *We've got a sticky problem to deal with.* ○ *There were a few sticky moments during the meeting, but everything turned out all right in the end.* ○ *The company is going through a sticky patch at the moment.* • Sticky can also mean unwilling to agree: *My dad was rather sticky* **about** *letting me go to the party.* ○ *Their bank manager was sticky* **about** *lending them the money they wanted to borrow.* • If someone **comes to/meets a sticky end**, they are killed or something unpleasant happens to them: *You'll come to a sticky end if you carry on behaving like this.* ○ *In the final scene of the film, the lovers meet a sticky end.* • **Sticky tape** is *Br and Aus for* SELLOTAPE. • A **sticky wicket** is a difficult situation: *This is something of a sticky wicket you've got us into.* ○ *I know I'm* **batting on** *a sticky wicket* (= I will get into a difficult situation) *by saying this, but I think you're wrong.*

stick·i·ness /ˈstɪk·ɪ·nəs/ *n* [U] • *If you leave the top off the glue, it will go hard and lose its stickiness.*

stick STAY /stɪk/ *v* [I always + adv/prep] *past* **stuck** /stʌk/ to stay or continue (with something) • *(infml) You go – I'll stick* **around** (= stay) *here a bit longer and wait for Jane.* • *(infml) No one stuck* **around** (= stayed) *after the game.* • *You'll never learn to play the piano if you're not prepared to stick* **at** *it* (= continue to work hard at it). • To stick **by** something or someone is to continue to support it or them: *I stick by what I said.* ○ *We must stick by our decision/policy.* ○ *Everyone has to stick by the rules.* ○ *She has stuck by him through thick and thin.* • *(Br and Aus) The unions have said that they are going to stick* **out for** (= continue to demand) *a 10% rise.* • To stick **to** something is to limit yourself to it and not change to something else: *Do we have to stick rigidly to the rules?* ○ *If you make a promise, you should stick to it.* ○ *We must try and stick to our budget.* ○ *Could you stick to the point, please?* ○ *He should stick to what he's good at, and not try and do something he knows nothing about.* ○ *We'd better stick to the main road, because the other roads are blocked with snow.* • To **stick to** your **guns** is to continue to have your beliefs or continue with a plan of action, even if other people disagree with you: *I know no one else thinks my suggestion is a good idea, but I'm sticking to my guns.* • If two or more people stick **together**, they support each other: *The country's Foreign Minister said that it was important for small nations to stick together.* • To stick **with** something is to continue to follow it and not change it: *He said that he was going to stick with the traditions established by his grandfather.* ○ *I'd rather stick with a way of doing things that I know will work.* ○ *Let's just make a decision, and then stick with it.* ○ *I'm not really enjoying the book I'm reading, but I'll stick with it* (= continue to read it) *it for a few more chapters to see if it gets any better.* ○ *Things are difficult at the moment, but if we* **stick with it** (= continue despite difficulties), *they are bound to get better.* • In some card games, if you stick, you say that you do not want to be given any more cards: *Do you want to play or are you sticking?* ○ *(fig.) "Would you like another drink?" "No thanks, I think I'd better stick* (= stop) *at this one."* • *(Am infml) You've got to admire her* **stick-to-it-iveness** (= her ability to continue working at something, despite difficulties).

stick *obj* PUT /stɪk/ *v* [T always + adv/prep] *past* **stuck** /stʌk/ *infml* to put (something), esp. in a not very careful way • *"Where shall I put these books?" "Oh, just stick them on the table for now."* • *Lisa stuck her head round the door and said, "Bye, I'm off now."* • *She stuck her fingers in her ears so that she couldn't hear the noise.* • *We'd almost signed the contract to buy the house we wanted when the sellers stuck* (= added) *another £1000 on the price.* • *I'll pay for lunch – I can stick it on my expenses.* • *Don't stick your tongue* **out** *– it's rude.* [M] • *He stuck his arm* **out** *in front of his daughter to stop her from running into the road.* [M] • *She pointed a gun at me and said "Stick your hands* **up**!/ *Stick* **'em up**!" • *(slang)* If you tell someone to stick something or where they can stick something, it means that you do not want to keep that thing: *She said that she had no intention of marrying him, and told him where he could stick his ring.* ○ *"I've had enough of working here," she said, "You can stick your job!"* • If you **stick** your **neck out**, you take a risk: *We could lose a lot of money on this deal, but even so I'm prepared to stick my neck out and accept it.*

stick *obj* BEAR /stɪk/ *v* [T often in negatives, not *be sticking*] *past* **stuck** /stʌk/ *Br and Aus infml* to bear or accept (something or someone unpleasant) • *I don't think I can stick this job a day longer.* • *I can't stick much more of this.* • *I know you like Janet, but I can't stick her.* • *I don't* *know how you can stick living in this place.* [+ v-ing] • *I've stuck this bad treatment for long enough – I'm leaving!*

stick out [GO BEYOND] *v adv* [I] to go beyond the surface or edge of something • *The way in which that nail is sticking out is rather dangerous.* • *I wish my stomach didn't stick out so much.* • *There was a handkerchief sticking out of his jacket pocket.* • *I could see Bill's legs sticking out from underneath his car as he lay there repairing it.* • *She has her hair long in order to hide her sticking-out ears.*

stick out *obj* [CONTINUE], **stick** *obj* **out** *v adv* [M] *infml* to continue to the end of (a difficult or unpleasant situation) • *I'm not sure if I'm going to be able to stick my job out for very much longer.* • *I know things are difficult at the moment, but if we just stick* **it** *out, I'm sure everything will be OK in the end.* • *I wasn't enjoying the film very much, but I stuck it out* **till the end.**

stick up [GO UP] *v adv* [I] to go up above the surface of something • *When I get up in the morning, my hair is always sticking up.* • *A few pale green shoots are sticking up* **out of** *the ground.* • *There were some large rocks sticking up* **out of** *the water.* • *The cathedral spire can be seen from miles away, sticking up into the sky.*

stick up *obj* [STEAL], **stick** *obj* **up** *v adv* [M] *infml* to steal (something) from or threaten (someone) using a gun • *Did you hear that someone stuck up the post office last night?*

stick-up /ˈstɪk·ʌp/ *n* [C] *dated infml* • *Two men ran into the bank, shouting "This is a stick-up!"* • Compare STUCK-UP.

stick up for *obj v adv prep* [T] *infml* to support or defend • *I can stick up for myself.* • *Who will you be sticking up for in the final?* • *He made sure that he stuck up for his rights.*

stick·er /£ˈstɪk·əʳ, $-ɚ/ *n* [C] See at STICK [FIX]

stick·le·back /ˈstɪk·l̩.bæk/ *n* [C] a small fish which is found in rivers, lakes, streams and parts of the sea which are not deep, and which has sharp points along its back • [PIC] **Fish**

stick·ler /£ˈstɪk·ləʳ, $-lɚ/ *n* [C] *infml* a person who thinks that a particular type of behaviour is very important, and always follows it or tries to make other people follow it • *He's a stickler* **for** *detail/accuracy/efficiency.* • *Mum's a real stickler* **about** *what time we get home when we go out for the evening.*

sticks /stɪks/ *pl n* **the sticks** *infml disapproving* an area in the countryside which is a long way from the activities that are found in a town or city • *I'm fed up with living* **in** *the sticks.* • *They live* **out in** *the sticks somewhere.*

stiff [FIRM] /stɪf/ *adj* **-er, -est** firm or hard • *stiff cardboard* • *a stiff collar/leather belt* • *His clothes were stiff with dried mud.* • *This hair spray has made my hair go all stiff.* • *Mix the powder and water into a stiff paste.* • *She swept the yard with a stiff brush* (=one with hard lengths of hair, wire, plastic, etc. in it). • If something is stiff, it cannot be easily bent or moved: *The handle on this door is rather stiff.* ○ *I can't get the lid off this jar – it's too stiff.* ○ *The man's body was* **(as)** *stiff* **as a board/poker** (=would not bend) *when it was found in the snow.* • If you are stiff or part of your body is stiff, your muscles hurt when they are moved: *We went for a long walk yesterday and I'm rather stiff today.* ○ *Sitting still at a computer terminal all day can give you a stiff neck.* [LP] **Feelings and pains** • Someone who has a **stiff upper lip** does not show their feelings when they are upset: *He was taught at school to* **keep** *a stiff upper lip, whatever happens.* ○ *The British are thought to have a stiff-upper-lip attitude.* ○ *Come on, Richard, stiff upper lip* (=do not show that you are upset).

stiff /stɪf/ *n* [C] *slang* • A stiff is a dead body: *They found a stiff in the river.*

stiff·en *(obj)* /ˈstɪf·ən/ *v* • *Beat the cream until it begins to stiffen* (=become firm). [I] • *She stiffened* (=tightened her muscles) *as he touched her.* [I] • *His body stiffened in fear.* [I] • *(fig.) These measures are intended to stiffen the spine/backbone of British industry* (=make British industry stronger and more powerful). [T]

stiff·ly /ˈstɪf·li/ *adv* • *The soldiers stood stiffly* (=very straight and without moving) *to attention.* • *I'm walking a bit stiffly* (=with difficulty in moving) *because I've hurt my back.*

stiff·ness /ˈstɪf·nəs/ *n* [U] • *A good way to ease stiffness in your muscles is by massaging them.* • *I asked the garage if they could do anything to reduce the stiffness* **of** *my car's brakes.*

stiff·y /ˈstɪf·i/ *n* [C] *Br taboo slang* • A stiffy is an ERECTION (=when a man's penis is harder and bigger than usual and points up): *to get/have a stiffy*

stiff [NOT RELAXED] /stɪf/ *adj* **-er, -est** not relaxed or friendly; formal • *We received a rather stiff and formal letter, thanking us for our invitation.* • *The general is a tall man with steel spectacles and a stiff, rather pompous* **manner.** • *She gave a stiff little* **smile.**

stiff·en /ˈstɪf·ən/ *v* [I] • *She stiffened* (=became not relaxed) *when her former husband walked into the room.*

stiff·ly /ˈstɪf·li/ *adv* • *"I don't think that it's anything to do with you," he said stiffly.* • *The wedding was a stiffly formal event.*

stiff·ness /ˈstɪf·nəs/ *n* [U] • *Her initial stiffness began to wear off as we got to know her.*

stiff [SEVERE] /stɪf/ *adj* **-er, -est** severe; difficult to deal with or do • *I think that rapists should be given a stiff prison sentence.* • *The athlete was give a stiff punishment for using drugs.* • *They are campaigning for stiffer penalties for people who drink and drive.* • *He has come in for some stiff criticism.* • *Some stiff cuts in public spending have been proposed.* • *There has been stiff* **opposition/resistance** *to the proposed tax increases.* • *They've got a stiff task ahead of them.* • *The prime minister is facing a stiff test of his authority.* • *It's a stiff climb to the top of the hill.* • *Some college courses have stiffer entry requirements than others.* • *We face a stiff challenge in the next round of the competition.* • *Both companies are worried about losing business in the face of stiff* **competition.** • A stiff **wind/breeze** is a strong one: *A stiff wind blew sand in our faces as we walked along the beach.* • A stiff **drink** is a strong alcoholic drink: *I had such a bad day that as soon as I got home I poured myself a stiff drink.* ○ *I need a stiff gin/whisky/brandy.* • A stiff price is a very or unacceptably expensive price: *The main reason this model of car has not sold well is because of its stiff price.* ○ *We had to pay a stiff membership fee to join the health club.*

stiff·en *(obj)* /ˈstɪf·ən/ *v* • *These events have stiffened* (=made stronger) *our resolve to succeed.* [T] • *Penalties for selling illegal drugs have been stiffened.* [T] • *Wilson has been brought in to stiffen the team's defence.* [T] • *She said that the experience of hardship can help stiffen a person's moral fibre* (=make their character stronger). [T] • *Resistance to the proposals has been stiffening* (=becoming stronger). [I] • *Stiffening competition in the market has led to a reduction in the company's profits this year.* [I]

stiff·ly /ˈstɪf·li/ *adv* • *I wrote a stiffly-worded* (=using strong words) *letter of complaint to the council.*

stiff·ness /ˈstɪf·nəs/ *n* [U] • *Everyone was surprised at the stiffness* **of** *the sentence/punishment/penalty/sanctions.*

stiff [VERY MUCH] /stɪf/ *adv* [not gradable] very much; to a great degree • *That book* **bored** *me stiff.* • *I got* **frozen** *stiff* (=very cold) *waiting at the bus stop.* • *I was* **scared** *stiff when I heard someone moving around upstairs.* • *Why didn't you call to say you'd be late – I've been* **worried** *stiff.*

stiff [PERSON] /stɪf/ *n* [C] *Am infml* a person of the type described • *a working stiff* • *you lucky stiff*

sti·fle *(obj)* [NO AIR] /ˈstaɪ·fl̩/ *v* to (cause to) be unable to breathe because of a lack of air • *We stifled in the heat of the city.* [I] • *They were stifled by the smoke.* [T] • *He is said to have stifled his victim with a pillow.* [T] • *He threw a blanket over the burning frying pan to stifle the flames* (=to stop the fire burning by preventing a supply of air from reaching it). [T]

sti·fling /ˈstaɪ·fl̩·ɪŋ/ *adj* • *It was hot and stifling in the train.* • *I can't bear this stifling humidity.* • *Several hundred people were crammed into the stifling room.*

sti·fling·ly /ˈstaɪ·fl̩·ɪŋ·li, -flɪŋ-/ *adv* • *It's stiflingly hot in here.*

sti·fle *obj* [PREVENT HAPPENING] /ˈstaɪ·fl̩/ *v* [T] to prevent (something) from happening, being expressed or continuing • *She stifled a cough/yawn/scream/cry.* • *I don't know how I managed to stifle my anger.* • *We should be encouraging imagination, creativity and new ideas, not stifling them.* • *The government has stifled all opposition to its plans.* • *These measures will have the effect of stifling competition.* • *He has been accused of attempting to stifle political debate.*

sti·fling /ˈstaɪ·fl̩·ɪŋ/ *adj* • *We had to deal with a lot of stifling bureaucracy.*

stig·ma [FEELING] /ˈstɪg·mə/ *n* [C usually sing] a deep feeling that other people do not respect you or have a good opinion of you • *He found it hard to bear the stigma* **of** *being unemployed.* • *There is no longer any stigma* **to** *being divorced.* • *She said that she thought there should be no stigma* **attached to** *mental illness.* • *Being an unmarried mother no longer* **carries** *the* **social** *stigma that it used to.*

stig·ma·tize *obj, Br and Aus usually* **-ise** /ˈstɪg·mə·taɪz/ *v* [T] • If someone is stigmatized, they are made to feel that they are not respected: *AIDS is a terrible disease, but I don't think that people who suffer from it should be stigmatized.* ○ *People should not be stigmatized on the basis of race.* ○ *He said that it doesn't help young offenders for them to be stigmatized* **as** *delinquents.*

stig·ma [FLOWER PART] /ˈstɪg·mə/ *n* [C] the top of the central female part of a flower, where POLLEN (=a powder produced by the male parts of flowers) is received

stig·ma·ta /ˈstɪg·mə·tə, £ˌstɪgˈmɑː-, $ˌstɪgˈmɑː·t̬ə/ *pl n* marks that appear on a person's body in the same places as those caused on Jesus Christ's body when he was nailed to a cross • *Christ's stigmata were said to be imprinted on the body of St Catherine of Siena.* • *He claims he* **received** *the stigmata after seeing a vision of Christ.*

stile /staɪl/ *n* [C] a set of usually two steps which you climb over in order to cross a fence or a wall, esp. between fields • (I)

sti·let·to /£stɪˈlet·əʊ, $-ˈlet̬·oʊ/ *n* [C] *pl* **stilettos** (a woman's shoe with) a narrow high heel • *She was wearing a tight short skirt and stilettos.* • *Wearing stiletto* **heels** *can make your legs look longer.* • PIC> **Shoes**

still [CONTINUING] /stɪl/ *adv* [not gradable] continuing until this or that time • *I'm still hungry.* • *"Have you got your exam results yet?" "No, I'm still waiting."* • *There is still no news from the hospital about how Kevin is.* • *Do you still work for Unilever?* • *It's past ten o'clock and the 9.30 train still hasn't arrived.* • *Hope is fading that the missing child is still alive.* • *We've still got some wine left over from the party.* • *There's still time for us to get to the cinema before the film starts.* • *"Will you still need me, will you still feed me, / When I'm sixty-four"* (from the song *When I'm sixty-four* by the Beatles, 1967) • *"Still crazy after all these years"* (title of a record by Paul Simon, 1975) • (D)

still [DESPITE] /stɪl/ *adv* [not gradable] despite that • *You may not approve of what he did, but he's still your brother.* • *I know you don't like her, but you still don't have to be so rude to her.* • *Even though she hasn't really got the time, she still offered to help.* • *I did the best I could, but I still didn't get the job finished in time.* • *You're very late. Still (Am also* **Still and all**), *I'm glad you're here now.* • (D)

still [GREATER DEGREE] /stɪl/ *adv* [not gradable] to an even greater degree or in an even greater amount • *The number of people killed in the explosion is likely to rise still higher.* • *The company is hoping to extend its market still further.* • *However much the children are given, they always seem to want still more.* • *Still more snow fell overnight.* • *It takes us a long time to get to my parents' house from here, and still longer to get to my sister's.* • *The bracelet was expensive, but the necklace was more expensive still.* • *I'll meet you at the theatre. No,* **better** *still, let's meet in a pub and have a drink first.* • *I'm worried that his car has broken down, or* **worse** *still, that he's had an accident.* • *Why do you have to tell me still* (=even) *more lies?* • *I don't want you to make still* (=even) *more excuses.* • (D)

still [NOT MOVING] /stɪl/ *adj* **-er, -est** not moving; staying in the same position • *Children find it difficult to* **sit/stand** *still for very long.* • *I can't brush your hair if you don't* **keep** *still.* • *I want you to* **stay** *as still as a statue.* • *She lay absolutely/completely/perfectly still on her bed.* • *The* **air** *was so still* (=There was so little wind) *that not even the leaves on the trees were moving.* • *It was a still* (=quiet and with no wind), *cloudless night.* • *She dived into the still* (=calm and not flowing) **water** *of the lake.* • A still drink is one that is not fizzy: *still cider* ○ *Would you like still or sparkling water?* • A **still life** is a (type of) painting or drawing of an arrangement of objects that do not move, such as flowers, fruit, bowls, etc.: *We went to an exhibition of 17th century Dutch still lifes.* [C] ○ *I find still life rather uninteresting.* [U] ○ *He's an expert still life painter.* • *(saying)* 'Still waters run deep' means that a person who says little might in fact know a lot. • *"...the still point of a turning world"* (T.S. Eliot in the poem *Burnt Norton*, 1936) • PIC> **Drawing and painting** (D)

still *obj* /stɪl/ *v* [T] • *He tried to still* (=stop) *the swaying of the rope bridge as he walked across it.* • *(literary) She cuddled her baby to still* (=make quiet) *its cries.* • *The minister's speech did little to still* (=end) *public anxiety about tax increases.*

still /stɪl/ *n* • A still is a photograph of a piece of action in a film: *A German photographer has been asked to take the stills for the movie.* [C] • *(esp. literary)* Still is also quietness and calmness: *In the still* **of the night**, *nothing moved.* [U]

still [EQUIPMENT] /stɪl/ *n* [C] a piece of equipment used for making alcohol • (D)

still·birth /£ˈstɪl·bɜːθ, $-bɜːrθ/ *n* [C] the birth of a baby who has already died inside the mother • *For months she had been recovering from the emotional pain of a stillbirth.* • *Research has shown that older women are no more likely than younger women to* **have** *stillbirths.* • Compare **abortion** at ABORT; MISCARRIAGE.

still·born /£ˌstɪlˈbɔːn, $-ˈbɔːrn, ˈ--/ *adj* [not gradable] • *After eight months of pregnancy, she gave birth to a stillborn baby.* • If an idea or event is stillborn, it is unsuccessful or does not happen: *Several activities planned for the festival were stillborn after one of the companies sponsoring the event pulled out.*

stilt·ed /£ˈstɪl·tɪd, $-t̬ɪd/ *adj disapproving* (of a person's behaviour or way of speaking or writing) too formal and not smooth or natural • *He writes in a formal and rather stilted style.* • *The dialogue sounded stilted and unnatural, perhaps because of the translation from the original Russian.*

stilt·ed·ly /£ˈstɪl·tɪd·li, $-t̬ɪd-/ *adv disapproving* • *She moved to England five years ago and still speaks English rather stiltedly.*

Stil·ton /ˈstɪl·tᵊn/ *n* [U] a white and blue English cheese with a strong flavour

stilts /stɪlts/ *pl n* long pieces of wood or metal used to support a building so that it is above the ground or above water • *In some Pacific countries, the houses are built* **on** *stilts several metres above the water level.* • Stilts are also two long pieces of wood with supports for the feet which allow you to stand and walk high above the ground: *I gave my niece a pair of stilts for her eighth birthday.* ○ *I can walk ten steps* **on** *stilts.*

sti·mu·late *(obj)* /ˈstɪm·jʊ·leɪt/ *v* to encourage (something) to grow, develop or become active • *The government plans to cut taxes in order to stimulate the economy.* [T] • *The book was an attempt to stimulate discussion of the problem of global warming.* [T] • If you stimulate someone, you make them full of ideas and enthusiasm: *The film was intended to stimulate and amuse.* [I] ○ *Good teachers should ask questions that stimulate the children* **to** *think.* [T + obj + *to* infinitive] • *(specialized)* If something stimulates part of the body, it causes it to move or react: *These drugs stimulate the body's own defences.* [T] ○ *The drugs stimulate the damaged tissue* **into** *repairing itself.* [T]

sti·mul·ant /ˈstɪm·jʊ·lənt/ *n* [C] • *Tourism has acted as a stimulant* **to** *the country's economy* (=It has made the economy grow). • A stimulant is also a substance, such as a drug, which makes the mind or body more active: *Caffeine, which is found in coffee and tea, is a mild stimulant.* ○ *An American athlete has been disqualified from the championship for the use of a banned stimulant.* ○ *She was found to have taken strychnine, a substance which acts as a stimulant* **to** *the central nervous system.*

sti·mu·lat·ing /£ˈstɪm·jʊ·leɪ·tɪŋ, $-t̬ɪŋ/ *adj* • If something is stimulating, it encourages new ideas: *We had a stimulating discussion about using sources of natural power, such as the sun and wind.* ○ *Universities have been asked to make their courses more attractive and stimulating.* • If someone is stimulating, they make you feel enthusiastic and full of ideas: *She is a really stimulating teacher.* • If an activity is stimulating, it causes your body to be active: *Aerobics is one of the most stimulating forms of exercise.*

sti·mu·la·tion /ˌstɪm·jʊˈleɪ·ʃᵊn/ *n* [U] • *Economists have advised the government to reduce interest rates in order to give some kind of stimulation to the economy* (=make it grow). • *Foreign travel can act as a great stimulation for the mind* (=It encourages new ideas). • *While she was at home looking after her children, she felt deprived of* **intellectual** *stimulation* (=new ideas and mental activity). • *(specialized) Electric stimulation* (=Using electricity to cause a reaction in the body) *causes the regrowth of bones and has* [illegible] *used to heal fractured bones.*

sti·mu·lus /ˈstɪm·jʊ·ləs/ *n* [C] *pl* **stimuli** /ˈstɪm·jʊ·laɪ, -liː/ • A stimulus is something that causes growth or activity: *Foreign investment has been a stimulus* **to** *the industry.* ○ *The book will provide a stimulus* **to** *research in this very important area.* • *(specialized)* A stimulus is something which causes part of the body to react: *The tip of the tongue is sensitive to salt and sweet stimuli and the back of the tongue is sensitive to bitter stimuli.*

sting *(obj)* HURT /stɪŋ/ *v past* **stung** /stʌŋ/ (of particular insects, plants and animals) to produce a small but painful injury, usually with a poison, by brushing against the skin or making a very small hole under the skin • *Do all types of bee sting?* [I] • *She wore gloves when she was gardening to prevent the nettles from stinging her.* [T] • If something stings, it causes you sharp but usually temporary pain: *The disinfectant stung as he poured it over the cut.* [I] ○ *The mixture of industrial pollution and dust stung her* **eyes**. [T] • If someone's hurtful remarks sting you, they make you feel upset and annoyed: *He was stung by her criticisms.* [T] ○ *She managed to give a stinging reply* (=an angry answer intended to upset), *before slamming down the phone.* ○ *(Br and Aus) The negative comments stung me* **into** *action* (= made me act because they were upsetting). [T] • A **stinging nettle** is a wild plant which has leaves with very short hairs that sting. • LP› **Feelings and pains**

sting *Br and Aus* /stɪŋ/, *Am and Aus also* **sting·er** /£ˈstɪŋ·əʳ, $-ɚ/ *n* [C] • A sting is a usually pointed part of an insect, plant or animal that can be used to touch or go through a person's or animal's skin and leave behind some poison if the insect or plant feels that it is in danger: *The honeybee leaves its sting in the wound, and then dies.* • If something, such as a story or joke, **has a sting in the/its tail** (*Am infml* **has a stinger in it**), it has a surprising or unpleasant part which only becomes clear at the end: *It's a humorous short story with a sting in its tail.* ○ *The 10% pay increase does have a sting in the tail because the increase will depend on how much work you do.* • If something **takes the sting out of** an unpleasant situation, it makes it less unpleasant: *The new policy of shorter working hours will serve to take the sting out of the pay cut.*

sting *obj* CHARGE /stɪŋ/ *v* [T] *past* **stung** /stʌŋ/ *infml* to charge (someone) a surprisingly large amount of money for something • *The bank stung me* **for** *£50 in charges when I went overdrawn.*

sting /stɪŋ/ *n* [C] *esp. Am slang* • A sting is a clever and complicated act of stealing: *A bank employee was involved in the sting in which $5 million was stolen.* • A sting is also a police action to catch criminals in which the police pretend to be criminals: *The sting went badly wrong and the undercover agents were forced to flee.*

sting·ray /ˈstɪŋ·reɪ/ *n* [C] a large flat round fish with a long tail that has poisonous points on it

sting·y /ˈstɪn·dʒi/ *adj* **-ier, -iest** *infml disapproving* unwilling to spend money • *He's really stingy and never buys the drinks when we go out.* • *The owners are so stingy – they've refused to pay for new carpets or even a bit of paint to brighten up the house.*

stin·gi·ly /ˈstɪn·dʒɪ·li/ *adv infml disapproving* • *The industry has been accused of spending stingily on research and development.*

stin·gi·ness /ˈstɪn·dʒɪ·nəs/ *n* [U] *infml disapproving* • *He blames government stinginess for the lack of money available to spend on new text books in schools.*

stink *(obj)* SMELL /stɪŋk/ *v* [not *be stinking*] *past simple* **stank** /stæŋk/ or *Am and Aus also* **stunk** /stʌŋk/, *past part* **stunk** /stʌŋk/ to smell very unpleasant • *Your feet stink!* [I] • *The morning after the party, the whole house stank* **of** *beer and cigarettes.* [I] • *He hadn't washed for over a week and stank* **to high heaven** (= greatly). [I] • *The woman next to me sprayed on some perfume and (Br and Aus) stank* **out**/*(Am) stunk* **up** *the whole shop* (=filled it with an unpleasant smell). [M] • LP› **Smells**

stink /stɪŋk/ *n* [C] • A stink is a strong unpleasant smell: *The stink* **of** *rotting seaweed was strong along the seashore.* • A **stink bomb** is a small container of a chemical substance that gives off an extremely bad smell when the container is broken: *The two boys were caught letting off stink bombs in the school toilets.*

stink·ing /ˈstɪŋ·kɪŋ/ *adj* [not gradable] • *a pile of stinking rotten food* • *The report criticized the stinking conditions in the prison.*

stink BE BAD /stɪŋk/ *v* [I not *be stinking*] *past simple* **stank** /stæŋk/ or *Am and Aus also* **stunk** /stʌŋk/, *past part* **stunk** /stʌŋk/ *infml disapproving* to be extremely bad or unpleasant • *I think her whole attitude stinks.* • *His acting stinks, but he looks good, so he's offered lots of movie roles.*

stink /stɪŋk/ *n* [U] *infml* • If something **causes a stink**, it causes trouble and makes people angry: *The article about political corruption caused a real stink.* • If someone **creates/kicks up/raises a stink**, they make a strong public complaint: *She created a stink* **about** *the lack of recycling facilities in the town.* ○ *When it was announced that the plane had been delayed yet again, he went to the airport authorities and kicked up an* **almighty** (=a great) *stink.* • *(slang)* If someone works **like stink**, they work extremely hard: *He works like stink just to earn enough money to feed his family.*

stink·er /£ˈstɪŋ·kəʳ, $-kɚ/ *n* [C] *infml dated disapproving* • Someone or something that is a stinker is very unpleasant: *What a stinker that man is!* ○ *She'd had a real stinker* **of a** *day at work.*

stink·ing /ˈstɪŋ·kɪŋ/ *adj infml disapproving* • Something which is stinking is very unpleasant or bad: *I hate this stinking job!* ○ *She had a stinking* **cold** *and felt very sorry for herself.* • If someone is **stinking rich**, they are extremely rich.

stint PERIOD /stɪnt/ *n* [C] a fixed or limited period of time spent doing a particular job or activity • *He has just finished a stint of compulsory military service.* • *Perhaps her most productive period was her five-year stint as a foreign correspondent in New York.*

stint *(obj)* LIMIT /stɪnt/ *v* [usually in negatives] to take or use only a small amount of (something) • *Don't stint yourself – take another slice of cake.* [T] • *The company has been accused of stinting money on safety measures in the factory.* [T] • *The bride's parents did not stint* **on** *the champagne and there was over a bottle for each guest.* [I] • See also UNSTINTING.

sti·pend /ˈstaɪ·pend/ *n* [C] a fixed regular income • *As deputy chairman of the company, he will receive an annual stipend of $220 000.* • In Britain, a stipend is usually the income paid to a priest. • CS PL RUS

sti·pen·di·a·ry /£staɪˈpen·di·ᵊr·i, $-er·/ *adj* [not gradable] • *He was appointed as a stipendiary* **priest** *in the diocese of York.* • In England and Wales, a stipendiary **magistrate** is one who receives a fixed income and who has legal qualifications.

stip·ple *obj* /ˈstɪp·l̩/ *v* [T] *specialized* to draw or paint (something) in small spots or marks • *She tried to create the impression of strong sunlight by stippling the canvas in yellow and white.* • *(fig.) The evening sky was stippled with a few wisps of low-lying clouds.*

stip·pled /ˈstɪp·l̩d/ *adj specialized* • *She painted her bedroom a beautiful stippled blue.* • *The divers saw tropical fish stippled in gold and black.*

stip·pling /ˈstɪp·l̩.ɪŋ, ˈstɪp·lɪŋ/ *n* [U] *specialized* • *He uses stippling in the painting to give the effect of light shining on the water.*

sti·pu·late *obj* /ˈstɪp·jʊ·leɪt/ *v* [T] *fml* to state exactly how (something) must be or must be done • *She agreed to buy the car, but stipulated racing tyres and a turbo-powered engine.* • *The law stipulates* **that** *new cars must have seat belts for the driver and every passenger.* [+ *that* clause] • *We have signed a contract which stipulates* **when** *the project must be completed.* [+ *wh-* word]

sti·pu·la·tion /ˌstɪp·jʊˈleɪ·ʃᵊn/ *n fml* • *Is there any stipulation as regards qualifications?* [U] • *The only stipulation is* **that** *candidates must be over the age of 35.* [C + *that* clause] • *In the contract, there was a stipulation* **that** *she could not keep a pet in the apartment.* [C + *that* clause]

stir *(obj)* MIX /£stɜːʳ, $stɜːr/ *v* **-rr-** to move an object such as a spoon in a circular movement in (a liquid or other substance) in order to mix it • *Use a wooden spoon to stir the sauce.* [T] • *Stir* (= Mix) *the egg yolks* **into** *the mixture.* [T] • *Slowly add the flour, stirring until completely blended.* [I] • If you **stir-fry** meat, fish or vegetables, you cook thin pieces of them quickly in very hot oil, moving them around all the time: *You should use a wok or large frying pan to stir-fry.* [I] ○ *Stir-fry the pieces of chicken for one minute, then add the vegetables.* [T]

stir /£stɜːʳ, $stɜːr/ *n* [C] • *Could you* **give** *the onions a quick stir?*

stir–fry /£ˈstɜː·fraɪ, $ˈstɜːr-/ *n* [C] • *We're having a vegetable stir-fry for supper tonight.* • *At home, I mainly cook pasta, stir-fries and rice dishes.*

stir *(obj)* MOVE /£stɜːʳ, $stɜːr/ *v* **-rr-** to (cause to) move slightly • *A light breeze stirred the leaves lying on the path.* [T] • *The air was still and not a leaf or a blade of grass stirred.* [I] • *He stirred in his sleep as I looked at him.* [I] • *We went out for a walk at five in the morning, when not a soul was stirring* (=when no one else was awake or moving about). [I] • To stir or stir **yourself** is to wake up or begin to move or take action: *Come on, stir yourselves, or you'll be late!* [T] ○ *The alarm clock went off, but she didn't stir.* [I] ○ *After three years of recession, the property market is* *beginning to stir again.* [I] ○ *All winter the hedgehog never stirs* **from** (=leaves) *its warm hiding place.* [I] • If something stirs you, it makes you feel a strong emotion: *I was deeply stirred by her moving performance.* [T] ○ *The speech stirred the crowd* **to** *take action.* [T + obj + *to* infinitive] • *(literary)* If an emotion stirs within you, you begin to feel it: *Hope stirred within her breast.* [I] • To stir **up** something, such as earth or dust, is to cause it to move and rise up: *The explosion stirred up clouds of mud from the sea bed.* [M] • *(literary)* If something **stirs** your **blood**, it excites you: *His adventure stories never fail to stir the blood.*

stir /£stɜːʳ, $stɜːr/ *n* [U] • *(infml)* If something **causes/creates a stir**, it causes a lot of interest or excitement: *The scandal created quite a stir at the time.* ○ *The news caused a stir* **of** *interest on the Stock Exchange.*

stir·ring /£ˈstɜː·rɪŋ, $ˈstɜːr·ɪŋ/ *n* [C] • A stirring of something, such as an emotion or thought, is the beginning of it: *She felt a faint stirring* **of** *envy when she heard that one of her colleagues had been promoted.* ○ *Several journalists have noticed stirrings* **of** *interest among foreign buyers.* ○ *As the band began to play 'God Bless America', he felt the stirring of national pride within him.*

stir·ring /£ˈstɜː·rɪŋ, $ˈstɜːr·ɪŋ/ *adj approving* • A stirring speech or song is one which produces strong positive emotions: *The band played a stirring patriotic song.* ○ *She gave a stirring speech about the importance of European unity.*

stir·ring·ly /£ˈstɜː·rɪŋ·li, $ˈstɜːr·ɪŋ-/ *adv approving* • *During the war, the newspapers printed patriotic and stirringly heroic pictures of soldiers marching off to fight.*

stir *(obj)* CAUSE TROUBLE /£stɜːʳ, $stɜːr/ *v* **-rr-** *infml disapproving* to cause trouble intentionally between other people, esp. by telling false or secret information • *(Br and Aus) There's a lot of gossip about me going around. Have you been stirring?* [I] • *(Am) Ignore her, she's just stirring* **trouble.** [T] • If a person or thing **stirs up** an unpleasant emotion, they cause it to begin or become stronger: *A child's professional success can stir up rivalry between child and parent.* ○ *They have been accused of stirring up racial hatred against Asian immigrants.* ○ *The teacher told him to stop stirring up* **trouble**.

stir·rer /£ˈstɜː·rəʳ, $ˈstɜːr·ɚ/ *n* [C] *infml disapproving* • A stirrer is a person who causes trouble intentionally between other people: *He's such a stirrer!*

stir PRISON /£stɜːʳ, $stɜːr/ *n* [U] *Am slang* prison • *He's* **in** *stir for pushing drugs.*

stir–cra·zy /£ˈstɜːˌkreɪ·zi, $ˈstɜːr-, ˌ-ˈ--/ *adj esp. Am slang* upset, angry and disappointed because you have been prevented from going somewhere or doing something for a long time • *It's been raining here for two weeks and I'm* **going** *stir-crazy.*

stir·rup /ˈstɪr·əp/ *n* [C] one of a pair of D-shaped pieces of metal that hangs from the side of a horse's SADDLE (=seat) and which is used for resting your foot in when you are riding • *You're quite small/tall, so you might need to* **shorten/lengthen** *the stirrups.*

stitch THREAD /stɪtʃ/ *n* [C] a piece of thread sewn in cloth, or the single movement of a needle and thread into and out of the cloth which produces this • *Secure the two pieces together with a couple of stitches.* • *She had sewn the wrong bits of material together and so had to unpick* (=take out) *the stitches and start again.* • A stitch is also a turn of wool made around a **knitting needle** or **crochet-hook**: *He* **cast on/off** *a stitch* (=added/removed a length of thread from the needle). ○ *I've* **dropped** *a stitch* (=lost a length of thread from the needle). • A stitch is also a particular type of stitch made in sewing or KNITTING, or the pattern which this produces: *The bedspread was embroidered with cross-stitch.* ○ *The most common sewing machines use a stitch called a lock stitch.* • A stitch is also a length of special thread used to join the edges of a deep cut in the flesh: *Her head wounds needed 50 stitches.* ○ *He's gone to the doctor's to have his stitches taken out.* ○ *He got hit with a broken bottle and needed five stitches* **in** *his cheek.* • *(infml usually in negatives)* A stitch is also a piece of clothing: *I haven't got a stitch to wear* (=I have not got anything to wear) *for this party tonight.* ○ *She ran down the corridor to the bathroom without a stitch on* (=naked). • *(saying)* 'A stitch in time (saves nine)' means that it is better to act or deal with problems immediately, because if action is delayed until later, things will get worse and the problems will take longer to deal with.

stitch *(obj)* /stɪtʃ/ *v* • *Her new dress needed altering, so she spent most of the evening stitching.* [I] • *This button needs to be stitched back* **onto** *my shirt.* [T] • *Stitch the sheets* **together** *with a needle and thread along the fold.* [T] • *(fig.) Britain is likely to stitch* **together** (=form quickly) *some sort of political deal to avoid a confrontation.* [T] • *(fig.) Attempts are being made to stitch* **up** *the political fabric* (=solve the political problems) *in the Middle East.* [T] • If someone is stitched **up**, they have a deep cut closed with stitches: *After giving birth, she was stitched up by a junior doctor.* [T]

stitch·ing /ˈstɪtʃ·ɪŋ/ *n* [U] • *The stitching along my coat hem is coming undone.*

stitch PAIN /stɪtʃ/ *n* [C] a sharp pain in the side of your stomach or chest, often caused by not breathing enough when running or laughing • *If you are prone to stitches, don't eat or drink anything before you exercise.* • *I* **got** *a stitch after I had been running for about half an hour.* • *(infml)* If a joke or an amusing story **has/keeps** you **in stitches**, it makes you laugh uncontrollably: *That story she told had me in stitches!*

stitch up *obj v adv* [M] *Br slang* to make (someone) seem guilty when they are not • *He claims he was stitched up by the police.*

stitch–up /ˈstɪtʃ·ʌp/ *n* [C] *Br slang* • A stitch-up is when someone has done something bad or illegal and has attempted to hide the truth about it: *Journalists claim that there has been a government stitch-up over the question of arms supplies.*

stoat /£stəʊt, $stoʊt/ *n* [C] a small thin furry animal which has brown fur in summer and white fur, except for the end of its tail, in winter • *A stoat is very similar to a weasel, but slightly larger.* • *The white fur trimming on the cloak is ermine – the name given to the white winter fur of the stoat.* • PIC› **Wild animals in Britain**

stock SUPPLY /£stɒk, $stɑːk/ *n* a supply of something for use or sale • *It is now halfway through winter and food stocks are already low.* [C] • *The local shop has a stock* **of** *postcards and guidebooks.* [C] • *Much of the city's* **housing** *stock* (=the number of houses in the city) *is over 100 years old.* [U] • Stock is also the total amount of goods or the amount of a particular type of goods available in a shop: *The jeans shop is selling off old stock.* [U] ○ *We don't have any green jackets* **in** *stock at present.* [U] ○ *The new edition is* **in/out of** *stock* (=available/not available) *in major bookshops.* [U] • If you **put stock in** something that someone says or does, you have a high opinion of it: *He's been wrong several times before, so I don't put much stock in what he says anymore.* • To **take stock (of** something) is to think carefully about a situation or event and form an opinion about it, so that you can decide what to do: *After two years spent teaching abroad, she returned home for a month to take stock of her life.* • In a company or shop, **stock control** is the system of making certain that new supplies are ordered and that goods have not been stolen: *Many supermarkets have computer systems to improve stock control and give quick and accurate information on sales.* • Ⓙ

stock *obj* /£stɒk, $stɑːk/ *v* [T] • If a shop or factory stocks something, it keeps a supply of it: *Most supermarkets stock a wide range of wines.* • *The college has a* **well-stocked** *wine cellar* (=It keeps a lot of different types of wine). • If you stock **(up)** something, such as a cupboard or shelves, you fill it with food or goods: *He has a Saturday job stocking shelves in the local supermarket.* ○ *I always stock up the fridge before my sister comes to stay.* • If you **stock up on/up with** something, you buy a large quantity of it: *During the emergency, people stocked up on essential items like candles, medicines and tins of food.*

stock·ist /£ˈstɒk·ɪst, $ˈstɑː·kɪst/ *n* [C] *Br and Aus* • A stockist of a particular type of goods is a shop that sells it: *She tried to discover where her nearest health food stockist was.*

stocks /£stɒks, $stɑːks/ *pl n* • *Many countries are now beginning to take more care of their stocks* (=supply) **of** *timber.* • See also STOCKS.

stock·tak·ing /£ˈstɒkˌteɪ·kɪŋ, $ˈstɑːk-/ *n* [U] *Br also* **stocktake** /£ˈstɒk·teɪk, $ˈstɑːk-/ • Stocktaking is the counting of all the goods, materials, etc. kept in a place such as a shop: *The warehouse staff were all busy with the annual stocktaking.*

stock MONEY /£stɒk, $stɑːk/ *n* the amount of money which a company has through selling shares to people, or *(Am)* part of the ownership of a company which people buy as an investment • *They own 20% of the company's stock.* [U] • *She buys and sells stocks* **and shares**. [C] • *(Am) Stock* prices *(Br and Aus* **share prices***) fell yesterday in heavy trading.* • *(Br)* Stock is also money which people invest in the government and which produces a fixed rate of INTEREST: *British Government stocks pay a fixed amount of income each year and, like shares, their value can fluctuate.* [C] ○ *There was a steady rise in the value of government stock in the early part of the year.* [U] • A **stock exchange** or **stock market** is a place where parts of the ownership of companies are bought and sold, or the organization of people whose job is to do this buying or selling: *They bought some shares* **on** *the London stock exchange.* ○ *The company is being floated* (= sold to the public) **on** *the stock exchange.* ○ *One of the busiest day's trading* **on** *the stock market saw more than £8.6 billion added to share values.* ○ *The stock market* **crash** (= The sudden fall in the prices of stocks and shares) *in October 1987 resulted in many investors going bankrupt.* • Ⓙ

stock·brok·er /£ˈstɒkˌbrəʊ·kəʳ, $ˈstɑːkˌbroʊ·kɚ/ *n* [C] • A stockbroker is a person or company that buys and sells stocks and shares for other people: *The main business of stockbrokers who look after private clients is buying and selling individual shares.* • *(Br infml slightly disapproving)* The **stockbroker belt** is the area near London where many rich people live in large houses and from where they travel to work in the City (= the financial area of London): *They've bought a house in a small stockbroker belt village near Redhill in Surrey.*

stock·brok·ing /£ˈstɒkˌbrəʊ·kɪŋ, $ˈstɑːkˌbroʊ·kɪŋ/ *n* [U] • *Stockbroking used to be a popular career for recently graduated students.*

stock·hold·er /£ˈstɒkˌhəʊl·dəʳ, $ˈstɑːkˌhoʊl·dɚ/ *n* [C] • Stockholder is *Am for* SHAREHOLDER.

stock [FLAVOUR] /£stɒk, $stɑːk/ *n* [U] a liquid made by boiling meat or fish bones or vegetables in water, which is used to add flavour to soups and other food • *vegetable/beef/chicken stock* • *Add a pint of chicken stock to the recipe and stir.* • A **stock cube** *(Am usually* **bouillon cube***)* is a small block of dried stock which you dissolve in hot water before using it. • Ⓙ

stock [ANIMALS] /£stɒk, $stɑːk/ *n* [U] animals, such as cows or sheep, kept on a farm • *(Aus)* A **stock route** is a road on which traffic must stop so that cattle and sheep which are being moved from one place to another can go past. • Ⓙ

stock [POPULARITY] /£stɒk, $stɑːk/ *n* [U] *fml* the degree to which a person or organization is popular and respected • *At present, the Prime Minister's stock is* **high/low**. • Ⓙ

stock [ORIGIN] /£stɒk, $stɑːk/ *n* [U] *slightly fml* the family or group from which a person or animal originates • *He's an American* **of** *Irish stock.* • *She's* **of** *peasant/noble stock.* • *The animals are all* **of** *very good stock.* • Ⓙ

stock [HANDLE] /£stɒk, $stɑːk/ *n* [C] the support or handle of a tool, esp. the triangular part of a gun that rests against your shoulder • *The gun has a detachable metal stock.* • Ⓙ

stock [PLANT] /£stɒk, $stɑːk/ *n* [C] a garden plant with small pleasant-smelling, brightly-coloured flowers • Ⓙ

stock [USUAL] /£stɒk, $stɑːk/ *adj* [not gradable] (of an idea, expression or action) usual or typical, and used or done so many times that it is no longer original • *a stock phrase/response* • *"Don't worry – worse things happen at sea" is her stock expression for whenever anything goes wrong.* • The **stock-in-trade** of a person or thing is their typical way of behaving, or a job or skill that is usual for them: *The song was perfect for the soft vocals that are her stock-in-trade.* ○ *Even today, many playwrights rely too much on irony – that stock-in-trade of English drama.* • Ⓙ

stock·ade /£stɒkˈeɪd, $stɑːˈkeɪd/ *n* [C] a strong wooden fence built around an area to defend it against attack • *After the first attack, the settlers put up a stockade around the village.*

stock·car /£ˈstɒk·kɑːʳ, $ˈstɑːk·kɑːr/ *n* [C] an ordinary car that has been made stronger and faster so that it can be driven in special races • *He spends every Saturday watching stockcar* **racing**.

stock·i·ly /£ˈstɒk·ɪ·li, $ˈstɑː·kɪ-/ *adv* See at STOCKY

stock·i·ness /£ˈstɒk·ɪ·nəs, $ˈstɑː·kɪ-/ *n* [U]

stock·ing /£ˈstɒk·ɪŋ, $ˈstɑː·kɪŋ/ *n* [C] one of a pair of tight-fitting coverings for the feet and legs made of light, usually artificial, material and worn by women • *Stockings come up to the mid-thigh and are usually held in place with suspenders.* • *I've got a ladder* (= a long vertical hole) *in one of my stockings.* • *She's just spent $15 on a pair of* **silk** *stockings.* • *Jerome stands 1m 75* **in** *his* **stocking/stockinged feet** (= when he is not wearing shoes). • **Stocking cap** is *Am for* **bobble hat**. See at BOBBLE. • A **stocking-filler** *(Am also* **stocking-stuffer***)* is a small cheap Christmas present: *We usually buy the children one big present and lots of stocking-fillers.* • A **stocking mask** is a stocking which thieves pull over their heads to hide their faces: *The men were filmed as they robbed the bank, but they were all wearing stocking masks and couldn't be identified.* • Compare **nylons** at NYLON; TIGHTS. • [PIC] **Hats**

stock·pile /£ˈstɒk·paɪl, $ˈstɑːk-/ *n* [C] a large amount of food, goods or weapons which are kept ready for future use • *a wheat and barley stockpile* • *They have a stockpile of weapons and ammunition that will last several months.*

stock·pile *obj* /£ˈstɒk·paɪl, $ˈstɑːk-/ *v* [T] • If you stockpile something, you store a large supply of it for future use: *The country's government has been accused of secretly stockpiling chemical weapons.*

stock·room /£ˈstɒk·rʊm, -ruːm, $ˈstɑːk-/ *n* [C] a room in a shop, factory or office which is used for storing a supply of goods or materials • *"I'll just go to the stockroom and see if we have those shoes in your size," said the shop assistant.*

stocks /£stɒks, $stɑːks/ *pl n* (in the Middle Ages) a wooden frame which was locked around someone's feet, hands and sometimes head, so that they were forced to sit or stand for a long time in public as a punishment • *He was* **put in the** *stocks for a day.* • See also **stocks** at STOCK [SUPPLY].

stock–still /£ˌstɒkˈstɪl, $ˌstɑːk-/ *adv* [not gradable] without moving; completely still • *On seeing us, the deer* **stood** *stock-still for a moment, then turned and retreated into the forest.*

stock·tak·ing /£ˈstɒkˌteɪ·kɪŋ, $ˈstɑːk-/ *n* [U] See at STOCK [SUPPLY]

stock·y /£ˈstɒk·i, $ˈstɑː·ki/ *adj* **-ier, -iest** (of a person, esp. a man) having wide shoulders and chest, and often short in height • *The man was described as short and stocky and very strong.* • Compare STURDY.

stock·i·ly /£ˈstɒk·ɪ·li, $ˈstɑː·kɪ-/ *adv* • *He is a stockily-built man with short dark hair.*

stock·i·ness /£ˈstɒk·ɪ·nəs, $ˈstɑː·kɪ-/ *n* [U] • *He was a short man, but had a stockiness of build that made him look taller than he actually was.*

stock·yard /£ˈstɒk·jɑːd, $ˈstɑːk·jɑːrd/ *n* [C] a set of enclosures where farm animals are kept before being sold or killed

stodge /£stɒdʒ, $stɑːdʒ/ *n* [U] *Br and Aus infml disapproving* heavy food, such as potatoes and rice, which contains too much STARCH and makes you feel very full • *The food in the school canteen is just stodge – lots of potatoes, bread and pies.*

stodg·y /£ˈstɒdʒ·i, $ˈstɑː·dʒi/ *adj* **-ier, -iest** *Br and Aus infml disapproving* • *She ate a stodgy meal of meat pie and chips.* • *His doctor told him to avoid stodgy food like bread and potatoes.* • If a person or company is stodgy, they are serious, boring and lack new ideas: *New ownership can often bring a fresh outlook to stodgy companies.* • An activity which is stodgy is slow and boring: *The game was dull and stodgy.* • A product which is stodgy is rather unattractive and old-fashioned: *The firm's business declined as it continued to sell stodgy men's clothing.*

stodg·i·ness /£ˈstɒdʒ·ɪ·nəs, $ˈstɑː·dʒɪ-/ *n* [U] *Br and Aus infml disapproving* • *She doesn't like the stodginess of traditional British food and so eats a lot of fresh fruit and salads.* • *(fig.) The design company has lost its previous stodginess* (= boring and old-fashioned reputation) *and taken on a new team of lively, talented designers.*

sto·ic /£ˈstəʊ·ɪk, $ˈstoʊ-/, **sto·i·cal** /£ˈstəʊ·ɪ·kəl, $ˈstoʊ-/ *adj slightly fml* determined not to show any sign of the emotion you are feeling • *We knew she must be in pain, despite her stoic attitude.* • *He showed a stoic resignation towards his fate.* • *Her father died aged 58 after a stoic struggle against cancer.* • *Although she was desperate to win the contest, she pretended to be stoical* **about** *the outcome.* • *Local people were stoical* **about** (= did not complain about) *the damage caused by the hurricane.*

sto·ic /£ˈstəʊ·ɪk, $ˈstoʊ-/ *n* [C] *slightly fml* • A stoic is someone who does not show their emotions: *My father is a stoic by nature and found it hard to express his grief when my mother died.*

sto·i·cal·ly /£ˈstəʊ·ɪ·kli, $ˈstoʊ-/ *adv slightly fml* • *She listened stoically as the guilty verdict was read out.* • *Stoically, and with great determination, the people set about rebuilding the village.*

sto·i·ci·sm /£ˈstəʊ·ɪ·sɪ·zəm, $ˈstoʊ-/ *n* [U] *slightly fml* • *He endured the pain of his wounds with great stoicism.*

stoke *obj* /£stəʊk, $stoʊk/ *v* [T] to add fuel to (a large enclosed fire) and move the fuel around with a stick so that it burns well and produces a lot of heat • *The furnaces in old steamships needed continual stoking.* • *She was responsible for the daily household chores, such as stoking the fire and making the beds.* • *(fig.) He has been publicly accused of stoking the fires of nationalism* (=encouraging it to develop). • *When the fire had been stoked* **up**, *the house began to get warm.* • If someone **stokes (up)** an emotion or idea, they encourage it to develop: *It seems some unscrupulous politicians have been stoking up racial hatred.* ○ *Rumours of an emergency meeting of the finance ministers stoked the atmosphere of crisis.* • *(infml)* If you **stoke up on/ up with** food, you eat a lot to avoid feeling hungry or weak later: *As it was a cold morning, she stoked up on bacon, eggs and beans on toast.*

stok·er /£'stəʊ·kəʳ, $'stoʊ·kɚ/ *n* [C] • A stoker is a person whose job it is to add fuel to a large enclosed fire: *The locomotive had a narrow platform on the back with barely enough room for a driver and stoker.*

stole CLOTHING /£stəʊl, $stoʊl/ *n* [C] *fml* a long narrow piece of cloth or fur which is worn around the shoulders by women, usually on special occasions • *She wore a white satin evening gown and an ermine stole.* • *(specialized)* A stole is also a long narrow piece of cloth, esp. silk, which is worn by some priests in the Christian Church during religious ceremonies. It is worn over the shoulders and hangs down the front of the body to the knees.

stole TOOK /£stəʊl, $stoʊl/ *past simple of* STEAL

stol·en /£'stəʊ·lᵊn, $'stoʊ-/ *past participle of* STEAL

stol·id /£'stɒl·ɪd, $'stɑː·lɪd/ *adj slightly disapproving* (of a person) feeling and showing little emotion or interest in anything, or (of a thing) not interesting or attractive • *He's a very stolid, serious man.* • *The stolid, rather old-fashioned look of the new car has discouraged some potential buyers.* • *The college is a stolid-looking building with no campus and no lawn.*

sto·mach /'stʌm·ək/ *n* [C] *pl* **stomachs** an organ in the body where food is digested, or the front part of your body below the waist • *Our dog died of cancer of the stomach.* • *She was kept alive by a feeding tube through her nose which pumped food into her stomach.* • *These trousers are too tight around the stomach.* • *The doctor asked him to lie down* **on** *his stomach.* • *A couple of hours after eating, James got a terrible stomach* **ache** (=a pain in his stomach). LP› **Feelings and pains** • *She's been in bed for the past few days with a stomach* **bug** (=a slight illness caused by infection). • *The sight of blood always* **churns/turns** *his stomach* (= makes him feel as if he is going to vomit). • *We had a stomach-***churning** *ferry crossing from Newhaven to Dieppe.* • *She can't eat spicy food because she's got a very* **delicate** *stomach* (=some types of food make her feel ill easily). • *I must be hungry because my stomach's started* **growling/ rumbling** (=making noises). • *She missed the game because of stomach* **pains**. • *He felt a knot of nervousness in the* **pit** (= bottom) *of his stomach.* • *I suggested that a cup of tea might* **settle** (=calm) *her stomach.* • *Last night's meal has given me an* **upset** *stomach* (=slight illness of the stomach). • If you have a **strong** stomach, you are able to smell, taste or see something unpleasant without feeling ill or upset. • If you have a **weak** stomach, you feel ill or upset easily when you smell, taste or see something unpleasant. • *I don't like to drink anything alcoholic* **on an empty stomach** (=when I have not eaten recently). • *You shouldn't exercise* **on a full stomach** (=when you have eaten recently). • If you **have no stomach for/do not have the stomach for** a type of food, you do not want to eat it: *I've got no stomach for this heavy food.* • If you **have no stomach for/do not have the stomach for** an unpleasant activity, you do not want to do it: *They wrongly believed that the United States would not have the stomach for a long and difficult war.* • If someone has their stomach **pumped**, a doctor uses a **stomach pump** (=a device with a long tube which is pushed down the throat) to remove the contents of the stomach: *She was rushed to hospital to have her stomach pumped after she took an overdose of sleeping pills.* • *"He that hath no stomach* (= courage) *for this fight"* (Shakespeare, Henry V 4.3)

sto·mach *obj* /'stʌm·ək/ *v* [T usually in negatives] • If you cannot stomach something, you find it very difficult or unpleasant to accept: *He can't stomach the idea that Peter might be the next chairman.* ○ *She found the violence in the film* **hard to** *stomach.*

stomp /£stɒmp, $stɑːmp/ *v* [I] to walk with intentionally heavy steps, esp. as a way of showing annoyance • *She stomped up the stairs and slammed her bedroom door.* • *He woke up in a bad mood and stomped off to the bathroom.* • Stomp is also *Am for* STAMP FOOT. • *(esp. Am)* To stomp **on** someone is to kick them, or *(fig.)* to defeat or treat them badly: *The fighting left the teenager with serious injuries to his head and chest which had been stomped on.* ○ *(fig.) This is just another example of the big companies joining together to stomp on small businesses.* • Compare STAMP FOOT.

stone ROCK /£stəʊn, $stoʊn/ *n* (a small piece of) the hard solid substance found in the ground which is often used for building • *a stone wall/floor* • *a flight of stone steps* • *a primitive stone axe* • *They cut enormous blocks of stone out of the hillside.* [U] • *Some demonstrators were arrested for throwing stones at the police.* [C] • *Stonehenge is composed of about 80 massive standing stones, each weighing 20 to 50 tonnes.* [C] • A stone is also a piece of hard material which can form in some organs in the body and cause severe pain: *He had an operation to have his* **kidney** *stones removed.* [C] • *Witnesses say that there was an explosion and then the plane* **fell/dropped like a** *stone* (=fell very quickly in a straight line) *to earth.* [C] • *The box fell into the water and* **sank like a** *stone* (=moved very quickly down in a straight line). [C] • If a place is **a stone's throw (away)**, it is very close: *"Is your house far from here?" "No, it's only a stone's throw away."* ○ *The cottage is just a stone's throw away* **from** *the sea.* • If something is **set/carved in (tablets of) stone**, it is very difficult to change. • The **Stone Age** is the earliest period known in human history when people made tools and weapons only out of stone: *The Stone Age has been divided into two periods – the Old Stone Age (Palaeolithic) and the New Stone Age (Neolithic).* ○ *Excavations have uncovered evidence of a stone age settlement/site.* ○ *(fig. disapproving) Knowledge of how these enzymes work is still at a stone age* (=very limited and not satisfactory) *level.* Compare **Bronze Age** at BRONZE; **Iron Age** at IRON METAL. • Something or someone that is **stone-cold** is very or completely cold: *The boiler was stone-cold and obviously hadn't been used for a while.* ○ *Your dinner's been on the table for over an hour and it's stone-cold.* • If someone is **stone-cold sober**, they have not drunk any alcohol. • Someone or something that is **stone-dead** is completely dead: *The frost* **killed** *the young plants stone-dead.* ○ *(fig.) Renewed fighting has* **killed** *the peace talks stone-dead* (= stopped them completely). ○ *(fig.) One bad review can* **kill** *a film stone-dead* (=cause it to be unpopular). • If someone is **stone-deaf**, they are completely unable to hear anything: *She has been stone-deaf since birth.* • Flour that is **stone-ground** has been made by crushing grain between two large stones: *She bakes delicious bread using stone-ground flour.*

stone *obj* /£stəʊn, $stoʊn/ *v* [T] • To stone something or someone is to throw stones at it or them: *Rioters set up barricades and stoned police cars.* • If someone is **stoned to death**, they are punished by having stones thrown at them until they are dead: *Those found guilty were stoned to death.* • *(Br and Aus dated infml)* **Stone the crows**/*(Br also)* **Stone me** is an expression of surprise: *Well, stone the crows – it's five o'clock already!*

ston·y /£'stəʊ·ni, $'stoʊ-/ *adj* **-ier, -iest** • Ground which is stony contains a lot of stones: *The ground is too dry and stony to be farmed successfully.* ○ *The island has several small stony beaches which are usually deserted.* ○ *(fig.) The country has long been stony* **ground for** *anti-nuclear movements* (=They are not popular or successful there). ○ *(fig.) Her speech about the need for a peaceful solution to the crisis* **fell on** *stony* **ground** (=was not popular among the people listening). • A stony expression or attitude is one which shows no sympathy or kindness: *He listened to her story with a stony expression.* ○ *She gave me a stony glare as I walked into the room.* ○ *He is well known for being a stony-***faced** *and stony-***hearted** *politician.* ○ *Most of her comments were met with a stony* **silence**. • *(Br and Aus infml)* If you are **stony broke** (*Am infml* **stone-broke**), you are completely without money.

stone WEIGHT /£stəʊn, $stoʊn/ (*abbreviation* **st**) *n* [C] *pl* **stone** or **stones** *Br* a unit of weight equal to 6·35 kilograms or 14 POUNDS, used esp. when talking about a person's weight • *I weigh ten and a half stone.* • *She has* **put on/lost** *a stone* (=is a stone heavier/lighter). • *"I was a seven stone weakling"* (from an advertisement for the Charles Atlas body-building course, 1922-) • LP› **Units**

stone JEWEL /£stəʊn, $stoʊn/ *n* [C] a small piece of a hard valuable substance, such as a diamond, which is found in the ground and used in jewellery • *The stones, including* *several huge diamonds, now form part of the famous Albertville necklace.*

stone [SEED] /£stəʊn, $stoʊn/, *Am usually* **pit** *n* [C] a large hard seed inside some types of fruit and vegetables • *Peaches, plums, dates, avocados and olives all contain stones.* • *She spat out a cherry stone.* • Compare PIP [SEED]. • [PIC]> **Fruit**

stone *obj* /£stəʊn, $stoʊn/, *Am usually* **pit** *v* [T] • *Could you stone* (=remove the stones from) *the cherries before putting them in the fruit salad?*

stoned /£stəʊnd, $stoʊnd/, *Am usually* **pit·ted** *adj* [not gradable] • *For this recipe, you need 15 stoned green olives* (= from which the stones have been removed). • See also STONED.

stoned /£stəʊnd, $stoʊnd/ *adj slang* experiencing the effects of a drug, such as MARIJUANA • *They spent the evening* **getting** *stoned* **on** *hash.* • See also **stoned** at STONE [SEED].

stone·fish /£ˈstəʊn·fɪʃ, $ˈstoʊn-/ *n* [C] *pl* **stonefish** or **stonefishes** a tropical fish with a very poisonous bite which looks like a piece of rock on the bottom of the sea • *Stonefish often hide in coral reefs.*

stone·ma·son /£ˈstəʊnˌmeɪ·sᵊn, $ˈstoʊn-/, **ma·son** *n* [C] a person whose job it is to cut, prepare and use stone for building

stone·wall *(obj)* /£ˈstəʊn·wɔːl, $ˈstoʊn·wɑːl/ *v* to stop a discussion from developing by refusing to answer questions or by talking in such a way that you prevent other people from giving their opinions • *The interviewer accused the minister of stonewalling on the issue of tax increases.* [I] • *Queries about civilian casualties during the bombing raid were stonewalled by government officials.* [T]

stone·ware /£ˈstəʊn·weəʳ, $ˈstoʊn·wer/ *n* [U] plates, dishes, cups etc. which are made from a special clay baked at a very high temperature • *Stoneware is tough and cannot be scratched, although it can sometimes crack.* • *She established a pottery at St Ives, where she made earthenware and stoneware.*

stone·washed /£ˈstəʊn·wɒʃt, $ˈstoʊn·wɑːʃt/ *adj* [not gradable] (of a new piece of clothing, esp. DENIM) washed together with small pieces of stone in order to make it lose some of its colour and look older • *He wore a pair of stonewashed* **jeans.**

stone·work /£ˈstəʊn·wɜːk, $ˈstoʊn·wɜːrk/ *n* [U] the parts of a building made of stone • *The front of the church has some beautifully carved 17th century stonework.*

stonk·ered /£ˈstɒŋ·kəd, $ˈstɑːŋ·kɚd/ *adj Br and Aus slang* defeated or extremely tired • *I was completely stonkered after that game of squash.*

stonk·ing /£ˈstɒŋ·kɪŋ, $ˈstɑːŋ-/ *adj* [not gradable] *Br slang* used to emphasize how good something is • *We had a stonking good time at the party last night.*

ston·y /£ˈstəʊ·ni, $ˈstoʊ-/ *adj* See at STONE [ROCK]

stood /stʊd/ *past simple and past participle of* STAND

stooge /stuːdʒ/ *n* [C] *disapproving* a person forced or paid by someone in authority to do an unpleasant or secret job for them • *The newly appointed mayor is widely regarded as a government stooge.* • In an amusing show in the theatre or on television, a stooge is an actor whose job it is to let the main actor make him or her look foolish. • Stooge is also *Am for* STOOL PIGEON.

stool [SEAT] /stuːl/ *n* [C] a seat without any support for the back or arms • *a bar/kitchen/piano stool* • *a three-legged stool* • *He perched on a tall stool by the bar and ordered a drink.* • See also FOOTSTOOL. • [PIC]> **Chair** Ⓓ (RUS)

stool [EXCRETION] /stuːl/ *n* [C] *fml or specialized* a piece of excrement • *He told the doctor he had been* **passing** *bloody stools.* • Ⓓ (RUS)

stool pi·geon, *Am also* **stooge** *n* [C] *slang disapproving* a person, often a criminal, who gives information in secret to the police and helps them to catch other criminals

stoop [BEND] /stuːp/ *v* [I] to bend the top half of the body forward and down • *The doorway was so low that we had to stoop to go through it.* • *Something fell out of her coat pocket and she stooped* **down** *and picked it up.* • If someone stoops, their head and shoulders are always bent forwards and down: *He's over six feet tall, but the way he stoops makes him look shorter.* • *(disapproving)* If someone **stoops to** something, they lower their moral standards by doing something which is unpleasant, dishonest or unfair: *I don't believe that our senator would ever stoop to bribery or blackmail.* ○ *"These scare tactics just prove what level the opposition party is prepared to stoop to," said the prime minister.* ○ *He was amazed that a reputable firm would stoop to selling the names of their clients to other companies.* [+ v-ing] ○ *I didn't think she would stoop* **so low** *as to sell the story to the newspapers.*

stoop /stuːp/ *n* [U] • *She walks with* **a** *pronounced stoop.* • *He is a tall man with* **a** *slight stoop.*

stooped /stuːpt/ *adj* • *She is small and slightly stooped.*

stoop [STEPS] /stuːp/ *n* [C] *Am* a raised flat area in front of the door of a house, with steps leading up to it • *She got home to find the kids sitting on the stoop waiting for her.*

stop *(obj)* [FINISH] /£stɒp, $stɑːp/ *v* **-pp-** to (cause to) finish moving or doing (something), or to (cause to) end • *I heard someone call my name so I stopped and looked round.* [I] • *Once I start eating chocolate, I can't stop.* [I] • *We had to keep stopping so that John could get out of the car and be sick.* [I] • *What time do you normally stop work?* [T] • *Something must be done to stop the fighting.* [T] • *Stop shouting – you're giving me a headache!* [+ v-ing] • *I couldn't stop laughing.* [+ v-ing] • *After we've been driving for a couple of hours, we'll stop* (= stay for a short time) *at a pub for some lunch.* [I] • *Does this train stop* (= stay without moving, briefly, to allow passengers to get on or off) **at** *Finsbury Park?* [I] • *My watch must have stopped* (= is no longer working). [I] • *If I was really naughty when I was little, my pocket money was stopped* (= was no longer given to me). [T] • To stop can mean to finish doing something that you do regularly or as a habit: *Apparently she's stopped drinking.* [+ v-ing] ○ *I stopped seeing him last year* [+ v-ing] ○ *I wish you'd stop telling me what to do!* [+ v-ing] • If you stop **to** do something, you finish what you are doing for a moment in order to do something else: *I stopped to pick up a letter that I had dropped.* [+ to infinitive] ○ *If you have to keep stopping to answer the telephone, you never get any work done.* [+ to infinitive] • If you **stop at nothing** to achieve something, you are willing to do anything in order to achieve it, even if it involves danger, great effort or harming other people: *He's one of those people who sets himself a goal and he'll stop at nothing in order to achieve it.* • If you **stop short of** doing or saying something, you decide not to do or say it although you almost do: *I stopped short of telling him the brutal truth but only just.* • *(Am)* A **stop-and-go** activity is one in which there are short periods of movement regularly interrupted by a lack of movement: *stop-and-go traffic on city streets* • *(Br and Aus)* A **stop-go** situation is one in which there are periods of development and activity quickly followed by periods without activity, especially in the country's economy: *The UK cannot afford another stop-go* **cycle** *of the kind that brought ruin in the last decade.* • *(Br and Aus)* **Stop press** refers to a particular space on the front or back page of a newspaper which contains very recent news items which were added to the newspaper after the printing process had started. • A **stop sign** is a sign on the road which tells drivers of vehicles to stop for other vehicles to go past before continuing. • [LP]> **Switching on and off** (CS)

stop /£stɒp, $stɑːp/ *n* [C] • *It was a five-hour walk including a thirty-minute stop for lunch.* • *We had a few problems at the beginning of the project so there were a lot of stops* **and starts.** • *The car slowed down and gradually* **came to a** *stop* (= stopped). • If you **put a stop to** something, esp. an unpleasant or unwanted activity or habit, you stop it from continuing: *He used to smoke in bed when I first got to know him – I soon put a stop to that!* • A stop is a place where vehicles, esp. buses, stop in order to allow passengers to get off and on: *I'm getting off at the next stop.* ○ *Is this our stop* (= where we must get off?) ○ *There's a* **(bus-)***stop outside the shops.* • Stop is also *Br for* **full stop**. See at FULL [COMPLETE]. • See also DOORSTOP.

stop·page /£ˈstɒp·ɪdʒ, $ˈstɑː·pɪdʒ/ *n* [C] • A stoppage is a time when work is stopped because of a disagreement between workers and employers: *All these stoppages are very damaging to the economy.* • *(Br)* A stoppage (*Am and Aus* **deduction**) is also an amount which is already subtracted from the money that you are paid before you officially receive it: *Stoppages include things like tax, pension contributions and national insurance.* • *(Br)* In a game of football, **stoppage time** is **injury time**. See at INJURY.

-stop·per /£-ˌstɒp·əʳ, $-ˌstɑː·pɚ/ *combining form* • *a conversation stopper* • *a crowd-stopper* • *a heart stopper* • See also SHOWSTOPPER.

stop *obj* [PREVENT] /£stɒp, $stɑːp/ *v* [T] **-pp-** to prevent (someone) from doing something • *If she really wants to leave, I don't understand what's stopping her.* • *They've put barriers up to stop people* **(from)** *getting through.* [+ obj + v-ing] • *Some people smoke because they think it stops them*

(from) *putting on weight.* [+ obj + v-*ing*] • *The only thing that stops me* **(from)** *travelling more is money.* [+ obj + v-*ing*] • If you stop a CHEQUE (= printed piece of paper for making payments)/*(Am also)* stop payment on a check, you prevent the money from being paid from your bank account. • (CS)

stop [STAY] /£stɒp, $stɑːp/ *v* [I] **-pp-** to stay in a place • *Are you coming with me or are you stopping here?* • *I can't stop – Malcolm's waiting for me outside.* • *(Br) Now that you're here, why don't you stop for some tea?* • *(Br) I've been out every night this week, so I thought I'd stop* **in** (= stay at home) *tonight.* • *(Br) We stopped* **up** (= did not go to bed) *until two o'clock last night watching the late film.* • To stop **by** is to visit someone briefly, usually on the way to somewhere else: *I was passing your house, so I thought I'd stop by for a coffee.* • To stop **off** is to visit or stay at a place briefly on the way to somewhere else: *I'll stop off* **(at** *the shops) on my way home and get some wine.* ○ *We're going to stop off* **in** *Paris for a couple of days before heading south.* • To stop **over** is to stay at a place for one night or a few nights on the way to somewhere else or before returning home: *They're stopping over in Malaysia for a couple of nights on the way to Australia.* ○ *(Br) Come round for dinner one night and you can stop over (Am* **stay over***).* • *(esp. Am)* To stop **around/round** is to visit someone briefly, esp. at their home: *Why don't you stop round some time?* • (CS)

stop *obj* [BLOCK] /£stɒp, $stɑːp/ *v* [T] **-pp-** to block (a hole) • *I found a mouse hole and stopped it* **(up)** *with plaster.* • *We stopped* **(up)** *the gap with some rags.* • (CS)

stop·per /£ˈstɒp·əʳ, $ˈstɑː·pɚ/ *n* [C] • A stopper is an object which fits into the top of a bottle. • Stopper is also *Am for* BUNG [CLOSING DEVICE]. • (PIC) **Bottles and flasks, Laboratory**

stop·cock /£ˈstɒp·kɒk, $ˈstɑːp·kɑːk/ *n* [C] a VALVE (= opening and closing device) in a pipe which controls the flow of liquid through it

stop·gap /£ˈstɒp·gæp, $ˈstɑːp-/ *n* [C] something intended for temporary use until something better or more suitable can be obtained • *Hostels are usually provided* **as a** *stopgap until the families can be housed in permanent accommodation.* • *We might have to employ someone temporarily as a stopgap* **measure** *until we can fill the post.*

stop·light /£ˈstɒp·laɪt, $ˈstɑːp-/ *n* [C/U] *Am for* **traffic lights**, see at TRAFFIC [VEHICLES]

stop·o·ver /£ˈstɒpˌəʊ·vəʳ, $ˈstɑːpˌoʊ·vɚ/ *n* [C] a brief stay in a place that you make while you are on a longer journey to somewhere else • *Our tickets to Australia include a stopover for two nights in Singapore.* • See also **stop over** at STOP [FINISH].

stop·per /£ˈstɒp·əʳ, $ˈstɑː·pɚ/ *n* [C] See at STOP [BLOCK]

stop·watch /£ˈstɒp·wɒtʃ, $ˈstɑːp·wɑːtʃ/ *n* [C] a watch that can be started and stopped in order to measure the exact time of an event, esp. a sports event • *I timed him running four hundred metres with a stopwatch.* • (PIC) **Clocks and watches**

store [SHOP] /£stɔːʳ, $stɔːr/ *n* [C] a place where you can buy goods or services; a shop. In Britain, the word 'store' is only used of a **department store** or a very large shop which sells only one type of goods • *(Am and Aus) a clothing/health-food/liquor store* • *a DIY/furniture store* • *People like shopping in the larger stores because they can get everything under one roof.* • *(Am infml)* If something is **store-bought** (*Br usually* **shop-bought**), it has been obtained in a shop and not made at home: *It's foolish to use store-bought pastry when it's so easy to make your own.* • A **store-card** is a small plastic card which can be used as a method of payment at a particular shop, the money being taken from you at a later date. • A **store detective** is a person who works in a large shop, esp. a **department store**, watching the customers so that they do not steal goods. • (LP) **Shopping goods**

stores /£stɔːz, $stɔːrz/ *n* [C + sing/pl v] • A stores is a shop which serves the needs of a small area, selling food and basic goods needed in the home: *We have a local village stores.*

store *obj* [KEEP] /£stɔːʳ, $stɔːr/ *v* [T] to put or keep (things) in a special place for use in the future • *I stored various possessions* **in** *my mother's house while I was living in Spain.* • *I've stored my thick sweaters and jackets* **(away)** *at the back of the wardrobe until next summer.* [T/M] • *My grandmother always keeps a few bags of sugar stored* **away** *in case there's a shortage.* [M] • *He keeps his money stored safely* **(away)** *in the bank.* [T/M] • *The data is stored on a hard disk and backed up on a floppy disk.* • *Squirrels store* **(up)** *nuts for the winter.* [T/M] • *(fig.) If you don't deal with the problem now, you'll be storing up* **trouble** *for yourself* (= the problem will be much worse) *in the future.*

stor·age /£ˈstɔː·rɪdʒ, $ˈstɔːr·ɪdʒ/ *n* [U] • Storage is the putting and keeping of things in a special place for use in the future: *We've had to build some cupboards to give us more storage* **space**. ○ *If you're looking for some basic storage* **drawers**, *madam, this is the range that we do.* • If items such as furniture are **in** storage, they are being kept safe in a special building while they are not needed. • A **storage device** is a piece of computer equipment in which information and instructions can be kept. • *(Br)* A **storage heater** is an electric device for heating rooms which uses electricity during the hours when it is cheapest in order to store warmth for later use. • (PIC) **Beds and bedroom**

store /£stɔːʳ, $stɔːr/ *n* [C] • A store is an amount of something which is being kept for future use: *He's got an impressively large store* **of** *wine in his cellar.* ○ *Food stores are reported to be running dangerously low in the capital.* ○ *(fig.) I'm afraid my great store of wit is rather depleted* (= I'm not able to be very amusing) *this evening.* • A store is also a building in which things are kept until they are needed: *a grain/weapons store* • *(esp. Br and Aus)* If items such as furniture are **in store**, they are being kept safe in a special building while they are not needed: *Melissa's furniture is in store until she buys a house.* • **In store** also means going to happen soon: *You never know what's in store* **for** *you.* ○ *There's a bit of a shock in store* **for** *him when he gets home tonight!*

stores /£stɔːz, $stɔːrz/ *pl n* • *I had to ask my secretary to get some more stationery from (the) stores* (= the place in an office, factory, etc. where equipment is kept until needed).

store [IMPORTANCE] /£stɔːʳ, $stɔːr/ *n* [U] value or importance • If you **put** or **set** great/little **store by** or **on** something, you consider it to be of great/little importance or value: *She's setting a lot of store by this job interview – I only hope she gets it.* ○ *What would happen if this relationship that she has set so much store by ended?*

store·front /£ˈstɔː·frʌnt, $ˈstɔːr-/ *n* [C] *Am* the part of a shop which faces the road • *A number of storefronts were damaged in the riots.* • *(Am) He started his career preaching in a storefront* **church** (= a shop that a religious group use as a church). • *(Am) She set up a number of storefront legal* **clinics** (= law offices in shops) *in poor neighborhoods throughout the city.*

store·house /£ˈstɔː·haʊs, $ˈstɔːr-/ *n* [C] *pl* **storehouses** /£ˈstɔːˌhaʊ·zɪz, $ˈstɔːr-/ *Am for* WAREHOUSE • *Two large storehouses belonging to relief agencies were robbed and food and clothing supplies stolen.* • *(fig. fml) The importance of books – those storehouses of culture and knowledge – cannot be overstated.*

store·keep·er /£ˈstɔːˌkiː·pəʳ, $ˈstɔːrˌkiː·pɚ/ *n* [C] *Am for* SHOPKEEPER

store·room /£ˈstɔː·rʊm, -ruːm, $ˈstɔːr-/ *n* [C] a room for keeping items in while they are not being used • *We're using the third bedroom as a storeroom for all the junk that Edward refuses to throw out.*

sto·rey *Br and Aus, Am* **sto·ry** /£ˈstɔː·ri, $ˈstɔːr·i/ *n* [C] a level of a building • *a three-storey house* • *Their new house has four storeys including the attic.*

sto·reyed *Br and Aus, Am* **sto·ried** /£ˈstɔː·rid, $ˈstɔːr·id/ *adj* [not gradable] • *It's a normal two-storeyed house.*

sto·ried /£ˈstɔː·rid, $ˈstɔːr·id/ *adj* [before n] *esp. Am* often spoken of or written about; famous • *Theirs was the most storied romance in Hollywood.*

stork /£stɔːk, $stɔːrk/ *n* [C] a large mostly white bird with very long legs which walks around in water to find its food • *Storks are often depicted bringing new-born babies to their parents.*

storm [VIOLENT WEATHER] /£stɔːm, $stɔːrm/ *n* [C] an extreme weather condition with very strong wind, heavy rain and often thunder and lightning • *A lot of trees were blown down in the recent storms.* • *They're still clearing up the storm damage.* • A storm is also a very angry reaction by a lot of people: *The announcement was met with a storm* **of** *angry cries in parliament.* ○ *The* **political** *storm* **raging** *over the factory closures looks set to continue.* • *(fig.) There was a storm* **of protest** (= a great deal of strong criticism and disagreement from a lot of people) *after the announcement about the new tax.* • *(Br and Aus)* **A storm in a teacup** (*Am* **A tempest in a teapot**) is a lot of unnecessary anger and anxiety about an unimportant matter. • **Storm clouds** are large dark clouds which bring rain or come before a storm: *Do you think those are storm clouds on the horizon?* ○ *(fig. literary) The storm clouds* **of**

war *seem to be* **gathering** *over the east.* (= It seems there is going to be a war there.) ○ *(fig.) Economic storm clouds are* **gathering** *over India.* ● *(Am)* A **storm door/window** is an extra door/window which is fitted to the usual door/ window for protection in bad weather.

-storm /£-stɔːm, $-stɔːrm/ *combining form* ● *a rainstorm/a sandstorm/a snowstorm/a thunderstorm/a windstorm*

storm /£stɔːm, $stɔːrm/ *v* [I] ● *(esp. Am) It was storming again last night.* ● *(literary)* To storm is to express anger in a loud and often uncontrolled way: *I could hear her storming in the kitchen.* ● To storm **into** or **out of** a place is to enter or leave it angrily, often in a way that shows your anger: *He stormed out of the house, slamming the door as he went.* ○ *She stormed into my office this morning and demanded to know why she hadn't been told.*

storm·y /£'stɔː·mi, $'stɔːr-/ *adj* **-ier, -iest** ● *The ship was beached in the Shetlands in stormy* **weather**. ● *The sky was dark and stormy.* ● Stormy can be used to mean involving a lot of fierce argument and shouting: *The issue has provoked a stormy debate between the left and the right of the party.* ○ *They had a passionate and often stormy relationship.*

storm *obj* ATTACK /£stɔːm, $stɔːrm/ *v* [T] to attack (a place or building) by entering suddenly in great numbers ● *The presidential palace was stormed by hundreds of people in the early hours of Saturday morning.* ● *(fig. infml) He had stormed* (= been extremely successful at) *the 1966 Olympiad in Havana, winning three games in brilliant style.* ● *(fig. infml) They did a storming* (= exciting and extremely successful) *gig at Wembley last month.*

storm /£stɔːm, $stɔːrm/ *n* [U] ● If you **take** a place or people **by storm**, you are suddenly extremely successful in that place or with those people: *Today we interview the 20-year-old woman from Newcastle whose performance on the West End stage has taken the critics by storm.* ● A **storm trooper** was a soldier in the private army of the Nazi political party in Germany before and during World War Two: *storm trooper tactics*

sto·ry DESCRIPTION /£'stɔː·ri, $'stɔːr·i/ *n* [C] a description, either true or imagined, of a connected series of events and, often, the characters involved in them ● *Will you* **read/tell** *me a story, daddy?* ● *She chose her favourite book of* **bedtime** *stories.* ● *He writes* **children's** *stories.* ● *She told me a story about a man who found a rat in his fried chicken.* ● *I don't know if it's true but it's a good story* (= entertaining to listen to although probably not true). ● *I've heard a story* **that** *you may be retiring next year – is it true?* [+ *that* clause] ● *She gave me her version of what had happened, but it would be interesting to hear his* **half/side of the** *story* (= the events as described by him). ● *Apparently his first words to her were "Will you marry me?"* **or so** *the story* **goes** (= that is what people say happened). ● In a newspaper or on a news broadcast, a story is a report of something that has happened: *The main story in the papers today is the bomb-blast in the City.* ○ *Now, with a look at today's main stories, here's Isobel Smart.* ● A story can also be a lie: *He* **made up** *some story about having to be at his aunt's wedding anniversary.* ○ *If you've been* **telling** *stories again, Ruth, I'll be very cross with you!* ● *(infml) Honestly,* **it's the story of** *my* **life** (= this type of thing always happens to me) – *I meet a totally gorgeous bloke and he's leaving for Australia the next day!* ● *(humorous) Anyway, I'm not overweight – my bones are just heavier than most people's –* **that's my story and I'm sticking to it** (= that is my explanation even if it is not true)*!* ● A **story line** in a book, film or play is its PLOT (= the series of events which happen in it).

sto·ry LEVEL /£'stɔː·ri, $'stɔːr·i/ *n* [C] *Am for* STOREY

sto·ry·board /£'stɔː·ri·bɔːd, $'stɔːr·i·bɔːrd/ *n* [C] (in films and television) a series of drawings or images showing the order of images planned for a film ● *The show's plot and script is edited at the storyboard stage.*

sto·ry·book /£'stɔː·ri·bʊk, $'stɔːr·i-/ *adj* [before n] (of real life situations) happy and pleasant in the way that situations in children's stories usually are ● *If you're looking for a storybook romance, you're always going to be disappointed.*

sto·ry·tel·ler /£'stɔː·riˌtel·əʳ, $'stɔːr·iˌtel·ɚ/ *n* [C] a person who writes, tells or reads stories ● *My father was a great storyteller.*

stout FAT /staʊt/ *adj* **-er, -est** (esp. of older people) quite fat and solid-looking, esp. around the waist, or *(approving)* (of things) thick and strong-looking ● *Mrs Blower was the rather stout lady with the glasses and the sensible shoes.* ● *(approving) I've bought myself a pair of good stout boots for hiking.* ● *(fig.) A stout* (= strong and determined) *defender of women's rights, she has campaigned repeatedly for abortion on demand.* ● Someone who is **stout-hearted** has courage.

stout·ly /'staʊt·li/ *adv* ● *stoutly-made boots* ● *(fig.) They have stoutly* (= firmly and determinedly) *denied the recent rumours that there are problems with their marriage.* ● *(fig.) He spoke passionately about animal rights, a cause in which he stoutly* (= firmly) *believed.*

stout ALCOHOLIC DRINK /staʊt/ *n* [U] a dark bitter and slightly creamy type of beer ● *A pint of stout, please.*

stout·heart·ed /£ˌstaʊt'hɑː·tɪd, $-'hɑːr·t̬ɪd/ *adj dated literary* brave and determined ● *Even the most stouthearted of climbers have had to turn back half way up this mountain.*

stove /£stəʊv, $stoʊv/ *n* [C] a piece of equipment which burns fuel or uses electricity in order to heat a place, or *(esp. Am and Aus)* a cooker ● PIC **Kitchen** Ⓙ

stove·top /£'stəʊv·tɒp, $'stoʊv·tɑːp/ *n* [C] *Am and Aus for* HOB ● PIC **Kitchen**

stow *(obj)* /£stəʊ, $stoʊ/ *v* to store (something) ● *There's a big cupboard under the stairs for stowing toys.* [T] ● *I think I'll stow the camping equipment* **(away)** *in the loft until next summer.* [T/M] ● *It's advertised as 'a free-standing barbecue which neatly stows* **away** *in its own case for easy storage'.* [I] ● If a person stows **away**, he or she hides on a ship, aircraft or other vehicle in order to escape from a place or to travel without paying. [I] See also STOWAWAY.

stow·age /£'stəʊ·ɪdʒ, $'stoʊ-/ *n* [U] ● *The problem with a two-seater sports car is that it lacks any stowage space.*

stow·a·way /£'stəʊ·əˌweɪ, $'stoʊ-/ *n* [C] a person who hides on a ship, aircraft or other vehicle in order to escape or travel without paying

strad·dle *obj* /'stræd·l̩/ *v* [T] to sit or stand with your legs on either side of (something) ● *He watched as she straddled her 10-year-old moped.* ● *In the past, ladies used to ride with both their legs on one side rather than straddle the horse.* ● *(fig.) The National Park straddles* (= is on each side of) *the Tennessee – North Carolina border.* ● *(fig.) It's described as a new kind of dance music which straddles* (= combines) *both jazz and soul styles.* ● *(esp. Am disapproving)* If someone straddles an **issue**, they do not state clearly what their opinion is in an argument: *It's not the first time this year that the president has been accused of straddling an issue.*

strafe *obj* /streɪf/ *v* [T] to attack (an enemy) by shooting from aircraft which are flying low in the sky ● *Nine of the dead were strafed by US aircraft.* ● *Each vehicle had been strafed or bombed.*

strag·gle /'stræg·l̩/ *v* [I] to move or spread untidily and in small numbers or amounts ● *The refugees straggled wearily down the hillside, many of them injured and limping.* ● *I tie my hair up because I don't like it straggling down my back.* ● *A whole year after the bombing, tourists are beginning to straggle* (= come in small numbers) *back to this beautiful country.*

strag·gle /'stræg·l̩/ *n* [C] ● *A straggle of crumbling buildings is all that remains of this hill-side village.*

strag·gler /£'stræg·ləʳ, $-lɚ/ *n* [C] ● In a group of people who are walking or running, the stragglers are the few at the back who are moving much more slowly than the others, often separated from each other or in small groups: *We watched the last of the stragglers come in, three hours after the first runner.*

strag·gly /'stræg·li/ *adj* **-ier, -iest** ● *I wish she'd have that straggly grey hair cut!* ● *Fed up with straggly eyebrows? In our beauty feature this week we show you how to pluck them into shape.*

straight NOT CURVING /streɪt/ *adj, adv* **-er, -est** continuing in one direction without bending or curving ● *Have you got a ruler or something I can draw straight lines with?* ● *She's got straight blonde hair.* ● *She has the straight back of a dancer.* ● *Skirts this summer are long and straight.* ● *You've got a perfect, straight nose.* ● *Can't you see it? – it's straight* **ahead** *(of you)!* ● *The dog seemed to be coming straight* **at/for** *me.* ● *Go straight along this road and turn left at the traffic lights.* ● *After a couple of Granny's gins, I was having difficulty walking straight!* ● *The road runs (Br and Aus)* **(as) straight as a die**/*(Am)* **straight as a pin** (= very straight) *for fifty or so miles.* See also **straight as a die** at STRAIGHT HONEST. ● *"Second to the right, and straight on till morning"* (J.M.Barrie *Peter Pan*, 1904) ● PIC **Clothes** Ⓘ

straight·en *(obj)* /£'streɪ·tᵊn, $-t̬ᵊn/ *v* ● *He looked in the mirror and straightened his tie.* [T] ● *Her hair is naturally* *curly but she always straightens it.* [T] • *The road straightens* **out** *after a few miles.* [I] • *For this next exercise, straighten* **up** (=make your body straight and vertical after bending) *and lift your hands above your head.* [I] • *(fig.) Once we get these few problems straightened* **out** (= solved), *we should be all right.* [M] • *(fig. dated infml) I thought that once he got a girlfriend that would straighten him* **out** (=make him behave in a more moral and acceptable way). [T]

straight LEVEL /streɪt/ *adj* **-er, -est** not sloping to either side; level • *Before I bang the nails in, could you tell me if this mirror is straight.* • *She hasn't cut my fringe straight – it slopes to one side.* • Ⓘ

straight·en *obj* /£ˈstreɪ·tᵊn, $-t̬ᵊn/ *v* [T] • *I think I'll ask my hairdresser to straighten* **(up)** *the ends of my hair.* [T/M]

straight IMMEDIATELY /streɪt/ *adv* [always + adv/prep; not gradable] without pausing or delaying; immediately • *I got home and went straight to bed.* • *Shall we go straight to the party or stop off at a pub first?* • *We'll leave straight after we've eaten.* • *He ate four helpings of cake, one straight after another.* • *Time is short so I'll get straight* **to the point** (=explain the matter immediately). • If you do something straight **off**, you do it immediately: *We don't need to go straight off – we've got ten minutes for a coffee.* • See also STRAIGHTAWAY. • Ⓘ

straight TIDY /streɪt/ *adj* [after v] **-er, -est** tidy; arranged in order • *It only took an hour to get the flat straight after the party.* • *Have you got a mirror? – I'll just put my* **hair** *straight.* • Ⓘ

straight·en *obj* /£ˈstreɪ·tᵊn, $-t̬ᵊn/ *v* [T] • *She stood up and straightened her clothes.* • *Could you just straighten* **(up)** *the front room before people start to arrive.* [T/M]

straight PLAIN /streɪt/ *adj* [not gradable] plain and basic; without anything added • *It's a straight sponge cake recipe with a few almonds added at the end.* • *No tonic for me, please, I like my vodka straight.* • *Straight pasta, of course, is very bland – it's the sauces that you add to it that make it interesting.* • *You won't find straight reporting in any of the papers because it's all biased in some way.* • *Having written fiction all your life, wasn't it difficult writing straight biography?* • Ⓘ

straight HONEST /streɪt/ *adj, adv* **-er, -est** truthful; honest • *Just be straight with her and tell her how you feel.* • *Now, Elaine, I want a straight answer – Do I look fat in these trousers?* • *(infml)* **Tell** *me straight, would you rather we didn't go tonight?* • *(infml) I* **told** *him straight – I said "Look, I've got a boyfriend already and I'm not interested, all right!"* • *(infml)* If you tell someone something straight **out**, you tell them directly and honestly, without trying to make what you are saying more pleasant: *I told her straight out that there was no possibility of a pay increase.* ○ *(esp. Am) He wants to know the truth, so just give him a* **straight-out** (=honest) *answer.* • *(dated slang) "You're a really attractive woman,* **straight up** (=that's the truth)*!"* • *(dated slang) "You're not telling me she's sixty! –* **Straight up** (=really)*?"* • *She's* **as straight as a die** (=completely honest), *I can trust her to tell me what she's really thinking.* See also **straight as a die** at STRAIGHT NOT CURVING. • Compare BENT DISHONEST. See also STRAIGHTFORWARD HONEST. • Ⓘ

straight SERIOUS /streɪt/ *adj* **-er, -est** (of the face) not laughing; serious • *I can never play jokes on people because I can't keep a straight* **face**. • *He told the story so* **straight-faced** (=He had such a serious expression when he told it), *I just presumed it was true.* • In a COMEDY (=humorous) act between two men, the **straight man** is the more serious of the two who is often made to look ridiculous by his partner. • Ⓘ

straight CLEAR /streɪt/ *adj, adv* [not gradable] simple or clear; not complicated • *It's a straight choice – either you leave him or you stay.* • *There isn't a straight answer to the problem because it just isn't that simple.* • *We both liked each other's houses so we did a straight swap.* • See also STRAIGHTFORWARD SIMPLE. • Ⓘ

straight /streɪt/ *adv* [not gradable] • *You know you've had too much to drink when you can't* **see** *straight* (= clearly). • *I'm so tired I can't* **think** *straight any more.* • *Let's* **get this** *straight* (=make certain we understand correctly), *we're exchanging contracts on the Thursday and moving in on the Saturday.* • If you **put/set** someone straight about a matter that has not been understood, you make certain that they understand the real facts: *Now, let me set you straight* **(on this matter)**, *I arranged with you that the computers would arrive on March 11th.*

straight FOLLOWING EACH OTHER /streɪt/ *adj* [before n; not gradable] following one after another without an interruption; CONSECUTIVE • *They're the only team to have won ten straight games this season.* • Ⓘ

straight TRADITIONAL /streɪt/ *adj* **-er, -est** *infml* traditional or serious • *(disapproving) He was a nice enough bloke, but he was so straight – I always felt I had to be on my best behaviour with him.* • *There's a lot of straight theatre at the festival as well as the newer, more experimental stuff.* • Ⓘ

straight SEXUALITY /streɪt/ *adj* [not gradable] *infml* not homosexual • *AIDS will attack anyone, whether gay or straight.* • Ⓘ

straight /streɪt/ *n* [C] *infml* • *Both nightclubs are attended mainly by gays and lesbians but a few straights go there too.*

straight NO DRUGS /streɪt/ *adj* **-er, -est** *infml* not using illegal drugs or alcohol • *She thinks straight people are much less interesting than druggies.* • Ⓘ

straight SPORTS TRACK /streɪt/, *Am usually* **straight·a·way** *n* [C] the straight part of a RACETRACK (= the track on which competitors race) • *And the runners are just coming up to the* **finishing** *straight.* • Ⓘ

straight NOT OWING MONEY /streɪt/ *adj* [after v; not gradable] *infml* neither owing nor owed any money • *You bought the tickets, so if I pay for the taxi, we'll be straight.* • Ⓘ

straight·a·way /£ˌstreɪt·əˈweɪ, $ˌstreɪt̬-/ *adv* [not gradable] immediately • *We don't have to go straightaway, do we?* • *I saw his face across the room and straightaway I knew something was wrong.* • Straightaway is also *Am for* STRAIGHT SPORTS TRACK.

straight·for·ward SIMPLE /£ˌstreɪtˈfɔː·wəd, $-ˈfɔːr·wɚd/ *adj* easy to understand; simple • *Just follow the signs to Bradford – it's very straightforward.* • *There isn't a straightforward solution to the problem because the situation is so very complex.*

straight·for·ward HONEST /£ˌstreɪtˈfɔː·wəd, $-ˈfɔːr·wɚd/ *adj* (of a person) not tending to hide their opinions or deceive anyone; honest • *At least Roz is straightforward and you know what she's thinking.*

straight·for·ward·ly /£ˌstreɪtˈfɔː·wəd·li, $-ˈfɔːr·wɚd-/ *adv* • *He explained quite straightforwardly that there was no longer the money to keep all the staff and that some of us would have to go.*

straight·jack·et /ˈstreɪtˌdʒæk·ɪt/ *n* [C] a STRAITJACKET

strain PRESSURE /streɪn/ *n* a force or influence that stretches, pulls or puts pressure on something, sometimes causing damage, or *(fig.)* something which pushes someone or something to its outer limits, often causing problems, anxiety or pain • *The hurricane* **put** *such* **a strain on** *the bridge that it collapsed.* [U] • *Wires are put in to reduce the strain on the protruding beam.* [U] • *If you bend your legs when you're lifting heavy things, it lessens the risk of back strain.* [U] • *As you get older, excess weight* **puts** *a lot of* **strain on** *the heart.* [U] • A strain is an injury to a part of the body: *He was taken off the field suffering from a groin/hamstring strain.* [C] • *The recent decline in the dollar has* **put a** *bigger* **strain on** *the economic system.* [U] • *Migration into the cities is putting* **a** *strain* **on** *already stretched resources.* [U] • *(fig.) With his divorce and his problems at work, he's been* **under** *a lot of strain recently.* [U] • *(fig.) The strain of being polite all day to someone I detest is unbearable.* [U] • *(fig.) We have rather an uneasy relationship and I* **found it** *quite* **a** *strain having her to stay with us.* [U] • *(fig.) She's a lot better than she was but she's still not ready to face the* **stresses and** *strains of a job.* [C] • See also EYESTRAIN.

strain *(obj)* /streɪn/ *v* • *I've put on such a lot of weight recently – this dress is straining* (=being pulled tightly) *at the seams.* [I] • *Every time Shem sees another dog, you can feel him straining* **at the leash** (=eager to escape). [I] • *I strained a muscle in my back playing squash.* [T] • *Don't read in this light or you'll strain your* **eyes**! [T] • *Waste matter should pass through the body easily without the need for straining.* [I] • *I really had to strain* (=try very hard) **to** *reach those top notes.* [+ to infinitive] • *I was straining* **(my ears)** (=listening hard) *to hear what they were saying.* [I/T] • *She's* **straining every nerve** (=making the greatest possible effort) *to get the work finished on time.* • *I find his style of writing so artificial – he always seems to be* **straining for effect**/*(Br also)* **straining after effect** (= trying so hard to be entertaining that it seems false). • *I agree she's lost weight, but I think it's* **straining the truth** *a* *little* (= not really true) *to describe her as slim.* • Compare RESTRAIN.

strained /streɪnd/ *adj* • *Relations between the two countries have become a little strained* (= difficult) *recently.* • *Her eyes were anxious and her smile strained* (= she was smiling with difficulty). • *She was looking strained* (= anxious and tired) *and had dark circles beneath her eyes.*

strain *obj* SEPARATE /streɪn/ *v* [T] to separate (liquid food) from (solid food), esp. by pouring it through a utensil with small holes in it • *Could you strain the vegetables, please.* • *I usually strain the juice* **off** *the pineapple and use it in another recipe.* [T/M]

strain·er /£ˈstreɪ·nəʳ, $-nɚ/ *n* [C] • A strainer is a kitchen utensil with a lot of holes in it for separating liquid from solid: *a* **tea** *strainer* ○ *Strain the purée through a fine mesh strainer.* • PIC〉 **Kitchen**

strain TYPE /streɪn/ *n* [C] a particular type or quality • *There's a strain* **of** *eccentricity in that family.* • *A strain* **of** *puritanism runs through all her work.* • A strain is also an animal or plant from a particular group whose characteristics are different in some way from others of the same group: *Scientists have discovered a new strain* **of** *virus which may be responsible for the disease.*

strains /streɪnz/ *pl n literary* the sound of music being played or performed • *I could hear the strains* **of** *Mozart in the background.*

strait /streɪt/ *n* [C often pl] a narrow area of sea which connects two larger areas of sea • *The Straits of Gibraltar* • *The Bering Strait separates Asia and America.* • See also STRAITS.

strait·ened /£ˈstreɪ·tᵊnd, $-t̬ᵊnd/ *adj fml* (of a person's situation) difficult because there is much less money than there was in the past • *With job losses and high interest rates a lot of people are finding themselves in very straitened* **circumstances.**

strait·jack·et, straight·jack·et /ˈstreɪtˌdʒæk·ɪt/ *n* [C usually sing] a strong item of special clothing which ties the arms to the body and is used for limiting the movements of dangerous prisoners and mentally ill patients whose behaviour is violent • *(disapproving)* A straitjacket is also anything that severely limits development or activity in a way that is damaging: *The police are concerned that the new regulation will act as a straitjacket in combating crime.* ○ *He refused to be fitted into any ideological straitjacket.*

strait-laced /£ˌstreɪtˈleɪst, $ˈ--/ *adj disapproving* having old-fashioned and fixed morals, esp. relating to sexual matters • *I didn't dare tell her I lived with my boyfriend – she's so straitlaced.*

straits /streɪts/ *pl n* a difficult and troubled situation, esp. because of financial problems • *So many companies are* **in** *such* **dire/difficult** *straits that their prices have come right down.* • *According to the paper's literary editor, the British novel is in* **dire** *straits.* • See also STRAIT.

strand THREAD /strænd/ *n* [C] a thin thread of something, often one of a few twisted around each other to make a cord or rope • *She tucked a loose strand of hair behind her ears.* • *She pulled a strand of cotton that was hanging from his shirt.* • *I had a delicious soup with vegetables and thin strands of pasta in it.* • *(Am and Aus) She was wearing a strand* (= single connected row) *of pearls.* • *(fig.) You have your work and your home and rarely do those two strands* (= parts) *of your life come together.* • *(fig.) There are so many different strands* (= parts) *to the plot that it's actually quite hard to follow.* • Ⓓ DK Ⓢ

strand COAST /strænd/ *n* [C] *literary* a SHORE • Ⓓ DK Ⓢ

strand·ed /ˈstræn·dɪd/ *adj* unable to leave somewhere because of an inconvenience such as lack of transport or money • *A French air-traffic-control strike has* **left** *hundreds of tourists stranded at airports.* • *He* **left** *me stranded in town with no car and no money for a bus.* • *If the tide comes in, we'll be stranded on these rocks.* • *(fig.) You walked off,* **leaving** *me stranded in the kitchen with the most boring man I've ever met!*

strange UNUSUAL /streɪndʒ/ *adj* **-r, -st** unusual and unexpected or difficult to understand • *He's got some very strange ideas about women!* • *You say the strangest things sometimes.* • *It was a strange film and I'm not entirely sure that I understood it.* • *She had a strange accent and I couldn't work out where she was from.* • *I had a strange feeling that we'd met before.* • **It's** *strange* **that** *tourists almost never visit this village.* [+ *that* clause] • *She's got a very strange-***looking** *boyfriend.* • *I hope that fish was all right – my stomach feels a bit strange* (= uncomfortable and not as it should feel). • **That**'s *strange – I'm sure I put my glasses in my bag and yet they're not there.* • *"You don't think Katie and Darryl are falling in love, do you?" "Well,* **stranger things have happened***"* (= it's possible). • Ⓘ

strange·ness /ˈstreɪndʒ·nəs/ *n* [U]

strange·ly /ˈstreɪndʒ·li/ *adv* • *I've never seen a man walk so strangely!* • *She was strangely calm – I found it quite disturbing.* • **Strangely enough** (= This is surprising), *when it came to the exam I actually felt quite relaxed.*

strange NOT FAMILIAR /streɪndʒ/ *adj* **-r, -st** not known or familiar • *I must say, I don't usually accept lifts from strange men.* • *With so many strange faces around her, the baby started to cry.* • *I've never been here before either so it's all strange* **to** *me too.* • *It was my first time abroad and the language, the food, everything was so strange.* • Ⓘ

strange·ness /ˈstreɪndʒ·nəs/ *n* [U] • *She was struck by the strangeness of her surroundings.*

strang·er /£ˈstreɪn·dʒəʳ, $-dʒɚ/ *n* [C] • A stranger is someone whom you do not know: *Children have to be taught not to speak to strangers.* ○ *I'd never met anyone at the party before – they were* **complete** *strangers.* ○ Do not confuse with FOREIGNER (= a person from another country). • A stranger in a particular place is someone who has never been there before: *Do you know the way to St Peter's church or are you a stranger here too?* • *(humorous)* Someone might say **'hello stranger'** to a person that they know but have not seen for a long time: *Hello stranger, I haven't seen you for weeks!* • *(fml)* **No stranger to** (= Familiar with) *success, she has four times been the winner of this much coveted award.* • Ⓔ Ⓘ Ⓟ

stran·gle *obj* /ˈstræŋ·gl̩/ *v* [T] to kill (someone) by pressing their throat so that they cannot breathe • *She had been strangled with her own scarf and her body dumped in the woods.* • *(fig.) He spoke with great difficulty and there was a strangled tone to his voice.* • *(infml) He's the sort of bigoted fascist who should have been* **strangled at birth.** • *(fig.) It's perfectly natural that she should try to strangle the opposition to her plans at birth* (= stop it at an early stage).

stran·gler /£ˈstræŋ·gləʳ, $-glɚ/ *n* [C] • A strangler is a person who kills people by pressing their throats so that they cannot breathe: *The newspapers dubbed him 'the Boston Strangler'.*

stran·gu·lat·ed /£ˈstræŋ·gjʊ·leɪ·tɪd, $-t̬ɪd/, *Am and Aus also* **stran·gled** /ˈstræŋ·gl̩d/ *adj* [not gradable] *specialized* • An organ or other part inside the body which is strangulated has become tightly pressed, blocking the flow of blood or air through it: *a strangulated hernia* • *(fig.) His voice is a strangulated growl.*

stran·gu·la·tion /ˌstræŋ·gjʊˈleɪ·ʃᵊn/ *n* [U] • Strangulation is the action of killing someone by pressing their throat so that they cannot breathe, or the act of dying in this way: *The post-mortem showed that the boy had died from strangulation.*

stran·gle·hold /£ˈstræŋ·gl̩·həʊld, $-hoʊld/ *n* [U] *disapproving* complete control • *The two major companies have been tightening their stranglehold* **on** *the beer market.*

strap /stræp/ *n* [C] a narrow piece of leather or other strong material used for fastening something or giving support • *Could you help me fasten the strap around my suitcase?* • Strap is also used as a combining form: *I need a new* **watch** *strap.* ○ *I got the shoes with the* **ankle** *straps.* • A strap is also a strong strip of material hanging from the roof of a bus, train or other public vehicle which passengers who are standing can hold onto.

strap *obj* /stræp/ *v* [T always + adv/prep] **-pp-** • If you strap something somewhere, you fasten it in position by fixing a narrow piece of leather or other strong material around it: *Are the kids strapped into their car seats?* ○ *He had a gun strapped to his middle.* ○ *We strapped the surfboard to the car roof.* • In a car, aircraft or other vehicle, if you are strapped **in**, you have a seat belt fastened around you for safety purposes. • *(Br and Aus)* If a leg, arm or other part of the body is strapped **up** (*Am* **taped up**), it has a BANDAGE (= strip of material for wrapping around injuries) on it: *He'd just injured himself playing football and his arm was strapped up.*

strap·less /ˈstræp·ləs/ *adj* [not gradable] • A strapless dress, BRA or other piece of woman's clothing for the top half of the body is one which does not have pieces of material going over the shoulders: *She was wearing a strapless taffeta evening gown.*

strap·py /ˈstræp·i/ *adj* [not gradable] *infml* • *I bought myself a pair of strappy* **sandals** (= open shoes with straps) *for the summer.*

strapped /stræpt/ *adj infml* not having enough money • *I'd love to come to Malaysia with you but I'm afraid I'm a bit strapped* **(for cash)** *at the moment.* • *Financially strapped companies are having to cut down on staff.*

strap·ping /ˈstræp·ɪŋ/ *adj* [before n] *infml often humorous* (esp. of a person) tall and strong-looking • *A big strapping lad like you shouldn't have much difficulty lifting that!*

strat·a·gem /£ˈstræt·ə·dʒəm, $ˈstræt̬-/ *n* a carefully planned way of achieving or dealing with something, often involving a trick • *Her stratagem for dealing with her husband's infidelities was to ignore them.* [C] • *He was a master of stratagem.* [U]

strat·e·gy /£ˈstræt·ə·dʒi, $ˈstræt̬-/ *n* a detailed plan for achieving success in situations such as war, politics, business, industry or sport, or the skill of planning for such situations • *The president held an emergency meeting to discuss military strategy with his defence commanders yesterday.* [U] • *She accused the government of lacking any coherent industrial strategy.* [U] • *The company will spend $6 million on the development of new products and sales strategies.* [C] • *Their marketing strategy* **for** *the product involves obtaining as much free publicity as possible.* [C] • *We're working on new strategies* **to** *improve our share of the market.* [C + *to* infinitive]

stra·te·gic /strəˈtiː·dʒɪk/ *adj* • *strategic planning* • *a strategic withdrawal/advance* • *The company has appointed a new marketing director to broaden its strategic expertise.* • *Their bombs are always placed in strategic positions to cause as much chaos as possible.* • Strategic can be used to refer to weapons, war or places that provide military forces with an advantage: *There are plans to modernize the US strategic forces.* ○ *Both countries want control of this strategic oil-producing city.* ○ *strategic arms reduction talks* ○ *strategic nuclear weapons*

stra·te·gi·cal·ly /strəˈtiː·dʒɪ·kli/ *adv* • *Her scarf was strategically* **placed** *to hide a tear in her shirt.* • *The government has decided to set up a small stockpile of strategically* **important** *materials for use by industry.*

strat·e·gist /£ˈstræt·ə·dʒɪst, $ˈstræt̬-/ *n* [C] • A strategist is someone with a lot of skill and experience in planning, esp. in military, political or business matters: *Few* **military** *strategists consider the use of chemical weapons to be a desirable option.* ○ *He's the president's chief* **political** *strategist.*

strat·i·fy *obj* /£ˈstræt·ɪ·faɪ, $ˈstræt̬-/ *v* [T usually passive] to arrange the different parts of (something) in separate layers or groups • *The sample of people questioned was drawn from the university's student register and stratified* **by** *age and gender.* • *A society that is highly stratified has clear divisions between different social groups.*

strat·i·fi·ca·tion /£ˌstræt·ɪ·fɪˈkeɪ·ʃən, $ˌstræt̬-/ *n* [U] • *The Prime Minister wants to reduce social stratification and make the country a classless society.*

stra·tum /£ˈstrɑː·təm, $ˈstræt̬·əm/ *n* [C] *pl* **strata** /£ˈstrɑː·tə, $ˈstræt̬·ə/ • A stratum is one of the clear divisions into which something is separated: *The report shows that drugs have penetrated every stratum* **of** *American society.* ○ *Motorists from the higher social classes are slightly more likely to be involved in crashes than those in the lower strata of society.* ○ *(specialized) An aquifer is a water-bearing rock stratum* (= layer) *such as sandstone or chalk.*

strat·o·sphere /£ˈstræt·ə·sfɪəʳ, $ˈstræt̬·ə·sfɪr/ *n* [U] **the stratosphere** the layer of gases surrounding the Earth at a height of between 15 and 50 kilometres. The weather has no effect on it and its temperature increases with greater height. • *The stratosphere is part of the Earth's atmosphere and its temperature ranges from -50°C to zero.* • *During the 1980s, the amount of ozone in the stratosphere above Europe decreased by about 8%.* • *(fig.) She made her fortune when property prices* **went into** *the stratosphere* (= increased a lot). • Compare IONOSPHERE.

straw [DRIED STEMS] /£strɔː, $strɑː/ *n* [U] the dried yellow stems of crops such as wheat or rice which are used as bedding or food for animals and for making traditional objects used in the home • *It's thirsty work stacking* **bales** *of straw!* • *Martha bought a lovely straw basket at the craft fair.* • *Gareth had long straw-***coloured** *hair and piercing blue eyes.* • *Frank took off his broad straw* **hat** *and nodded to Alexandra.* • You **clutch** or **grasp at straws** when you are willing to try anything to improve a difficult or disadvantageous situation, even if it has little chance of success: *She offered to take a pay cut to keep her job, but she was just grasping at straws.* ○ *"I'll do all the housework and gardening if you promise not to leave me," said her boyfriend, clutching at straws.* • A **straw boater** is a stiff hat with a flat top and wide straight BRIM which is traditionally worn when travelling along a river in a boat to protect the wearer from the sun: *The rowing crew looked very smart in their blazers and straw boaters.* • A **straw man** or **man of straw** is someone, often an imaginary person, who is used to hide an illegal or secret activity: *The fraud depended on hundreds of bank accounts being opened on behalf of straw men.* • In a discussion, a **straw man** or **man of straw** is also an invented argument which one side accuses the opposing side of supporting in order to defeat that argument completely and so help defeat the opposing side: *Both sides in the dispute felt obliged to attack the other, with the result that straw men were often set up in order to be demolished.* ○ *The idea that national identity will be lost as a result of European integration is just a man of straw which he is wasting his time fighting.* • A **straw poll** is an unofficial vote which is taken to discover what people think about an idea or problem or how they intend to vote in an election: *A straw poll of local inhabitants in Mediterranean resorts concluded that British tourists were the worst dressed and Italians the most stylish.* ○ *She overhauled her election campaign when she was placed third in a straw poll.* • The **final straw** or the **last straw** or the **straw that breaks the camel's back** is a problem which can be dealt with on its own, but which makes a situation very difficult or impossible when it is added to existing problems: *Losing my job was bad enough, but being evicted from my house was* **the** *straw that broke the camel's back.* ○ *She's always been rude to me, but it was* **the** *last straw when she started insulting my mother.* • A **straw in the wind** is something that suggests what might happen: *There were a few straws in the wind yesterday which indicated that an air attack was imminent.*

straw [TUBE] /£strɔː, $strɑː/ *n* [C] a thin tube made of plastic or waterproof paper through which a drink can be sucked into the mouth • *Why don't you drink your cocktail* **through** *a straw?*

straw·ber·ry /£ˈstrɔː·bər·i, $ˈstrɑːˌber·i/ *n* [C] a small juicy red fruit which has small brown seeds on its surface, or the plant with white flowers on which this fruit grows • *Strawberries grow at ground level.* • *He made a delicious fruit salad with loads of strawberries and raspberries.* • *I thought we'd have strawberries* **and cream** *for dessert.* • *Would you like marmalade or strawberry* **jam** *on your toast?* • *The strawberry* **season** *is almost over, thanks to the recent hot weather that ripened the fruit a little early.* • *You should put some nets over your strawberry* **beds** *to keep off the birds.* • *The* **wild** *strawberry has fruits that are 2 cm long.* • A **strawberry blonde** is a woman or girl who has hair which is a pale yellow colour but also slightly red: *Who was that strawberry blonde I saw you talking to at Mark's party?* ○ *Do you think her* **strawberry-blonde** *hair is natural or dyed?* • A **strawberry mark** is a permanent dark red mark on a person's skin which has existed since birth: *Mikhail Gorbachev, the former Soviet president, had a strawberry mark on his forehead.* • *"Strawberry Fields Forever"* (title of a song by The Beatles, 1967) • [PIC] **Berries**

stray /streɪ/ *v* [I] to travel along a route that was not originally intended, or to move beyond a limited area • *The accident was caused by a herd of cattle that had strayed into the road.* • *They got lost when they strayed* **too far from** *the footpath.* • *(fig.) I think we've strayed* **too far from** *our original plan.* • *The ship capsized after straying off course in a heavy storm.* • *After the murder, many children were kept indoors or warned not to stray beyond the garden gate.* • *Most visitors to America's national parks rarely stray more than a few yards from their cars or tour buses.* • *What can be done about the straying hands of unwanted admirers in the office?*

stray /streɪ/ *n* [C] • A stray is a pet that no longer has a home or cannot find its home: *"Who owns that cat?" "I don't know. I think it must be a stray."* ○ *A lot of stray* **dogs** *are pets that have been given as Christmas presents and then abandoned.*

stray /streɪ/ *adj* [before n; not gradable] • Stray things have moved apart from similar things and are not in their expected or intended place: *There are still a few stray spots of paint on the window pane.* ○ *Throughout our meal, stray sentences from the conversation of the women at the table next to us wafted in our direction.* ○ *His drawers are full of stray socks* (= single socks that are no longer part of a pair).

◦ *Several journalists have been killed or injured by stray* **bullets** *while reporting on the civil war.*

streak MARK /striːk/ *n* [C] a long thin mark which is easily noticed because it is very different from the area surrounding it • *Whenever he washes the windows he always leaves dirty streaks behind.* • *I've been dyeing my hair for years to hide my grey streaks.* • *You can tell from the yellow streaks on the leaves that the plant has been infected.* • *Meteors produce streaks* **of** *light as they burn up in the Earth's atmosphere.* • *Can you explain why that streak* **of** *blood is on your face?* • *(fig.) There's a streak* (= small amount) *of German blood in him – his great-grandmother came from Berlin.* • *(fig.) Suddenly she grabbed the money and ran out of the shop* **like a streak of lightning** (= extremely quickly).

streak *obj* /striːk/ *v* [T] • If a surface has been streaked, there are streaks on it: *Doesn't Chris look good with her hair streaked?* ◦ *When she stood up, her clothes were streaked* **with** *mud.* ◦ *By the time he'd finished explaining how his daughter had died, his cheeks were streaked* **with** *tears.* ◦ *White marble is frequently streaked* **with** *grey, black or green.*

streak·y /ˈstriː·ki/ *adj* **-ier, -iest** • *We'll have to give this door another coat of paint – it's still looking rather streaky.* • *Streaky* **bacon** *has strips of fat between the meat.*

streak CHARACTERISTIC /striːk/ *n* [C] an often unpleasant characteristic which is very different from other characteristics • *There's an aggressive streak* **in** *him that I don't like very much.* • *Her* **stubborn** *streak makes her very difficult to work with sometimes.* • *There's a* **nasty** *streak* **of** *misogyny* **running through** *his latest novel.* • *You need to have a* **competitive** *streak when you're working in marketing.* • *Her* **mischievous** *streak makes her great fun to be with.*

streak SHORT PERIOD /striːk/ *n* [C] a short period of good or bad luck • *Obviously I'm delighted with my recent success, and I just hope my* **lucky** *streak continues until the world championships.* • *With yesterday's victory, they extended their* **unbeaten** (= successful) *streak to six games.* • *Her* **winning** *streak of six races is the highest so far this season.* • *Their longest* **losing** *streak has been three games.* • *The team was understandably relieved to have ended its three-***game** *losing streak.* • *After winning a couple of bets, he thought he was* **on** *a winning streak and gambled away all his savings.*

streak MOVE FAST /striːk/ *v* [I always + adv/prep] to move somewhere extremely quickly, usually in a straight line • *Concorde, the supersonic airliner, can streak* **through** *the sky at over 2100 kilometres per hour.* • *She suddenly grabbed my bag and streaked* **down** *the street on her motorbike.* • *Did you see that bird streak* **past** *the window?* • *An asteroid streaked* **within** *90 000 miles of Earth last month.* • *(fig.) After a disappointing performance last year, the company has streaked* **ahead** *of* (= been much more successful than) *the competition recently.*

streak RUN NAKED /striːk/ *v* [I] to run naked through a public place in order to attract attention or to express strong disapproval of something • *He was arrested after streaking across a cricket pitch to protest against an increase in ticket prices.*

streak·er /£ˈstriː·kəʳ, $-kɚ/ *n* [C] • *The match was interrupted briefly when two streakers ran onto the field with a banner pleading for world peace.*

stream SMALL RIVER /striːm/ *n* [C] water that flows naturally along a fixed route formed by a channel cut into rock or earth, usually at ground level, but sometimes underground • *Rivers are wider, deeper and longer than streams.* • *His body was found in a* **mountain** *stream two days after he disappeared.* • *There's a lovely stream that* **flows** *through their garden.* • Sometimes a stream is any current of water or liquid: *The coastal waters of the British Isles do not freeze because the Gulf Stream* (= water from the Gulf of Mexico which flows across the Atlantic Ocean) *keeps the temperature relatively warm.* ◦ *The pregnancy test is easy to use and requires you to hold a special stick in your stream of urine.* ◦ *There is conflicting evidence about whether the level of cholesterol in the* **blood** *stream is related to the amount of fat that we eat.* • A stream is also the direction in which water is moving: *After a while she stopped rowing and let the boat float with the stream.* ◦ *(fig.) It's easier to go* **with** *the stream than* **against** *it* (= to agree with people rather than to disagree). • Ⓓ

stream CONTINUOUS FLOW /striːm/ *n* [C] a continuous flow of things or people • *The mountains were once the hiding place for local villagers escaping the* **endless** *stream of foreign invaders.* • *There has been a* **steady** *stream of phone calls from worried customers about the safety of the product.* • *I had a* **constant** *stream of visitors while I was ill, so I was never bored.* • *When she complained to her neighbour about the noise, she received a stream of* **abuse** *and was told to mind her own business.* • Something in industry or business that is **on stream** is being produced or is available for use: *When the new terminal is on stream, the airport's capacity will be 20% greater.* ◦ *The company's increased sales were primarily a result of new stores* **coming** *on stream.* • *(specialized)* **Stream of consciousness** is a literary style that is used to represent a character's feelings and thoughts in long continuous pieces of text that have little obvious organization or structure: *James Joyce and Dorothy Richardson were notable early exponents of the stream-of-consciousness technique.* • Ⓓ

stream /striːm/ *v* [I] • When something streams somewhere, it flows there quickly in large amounts without stopping: *"How could they do this to my children?" cried one man with* **tears** *streaming* **down** *his* **face**. ◦ *One woman was carried from the scene of the accident with* **blood** *streaming* **from** *her head.* ◦ *We were all very excited as we streamed* **out of** *our final exam.* ◦ *Red Cross officials estimate that 20 000 refugees streamed* **into** *the city last week.* ◦ *It was a beautiful Saturday afternoon in the forest, with the sun streaming* **through** *the leaves.* ◦ *His hair streamed* **out** *behind him* (= It was blown into an almost horizontal position), *as he rode away on his motorbike.* ◦ *I've got a terrible cold and my nose has been streaming* (= producing a lot of liquid) *all week.*

stream STUDENTS *Br and Aus* /striːm/, *Am usually* **track** *n* [C] a group of school students with similar intelligence who are approximately the same age and are taught together • *I'm in the A stream for maths, and the B stream for English.* • Ⓓ

stream *obj Br and Aus* /striːm/, *Am usually* **track** *v* [T] • *We start to stream the children in the third form.* • *Some people object to streaming because it gives an unfair advantage to intelligent children.*

stream·er /£ˈstriː·məʳ, $-mɚ/ *n* [C] a long narrow strip of brightly coloured paper that is used as a decoration for special occasions such as parties • *I got some streamers and balloons to decorate the office for Paul's leaving party.*

stream·line *obj* SHAPE /ˈstriːm·laɪn/ *v* [T] to shape (something) so that it can move as effectively and quickly as possible through a liquid or gas • *Streamlining cars increases their fuel efficiency.* • *The bodies of dolphins are more streamlined than those of porpoises.* • *Birds' bodies are streamlined with a smooth covering of short overlapping feathers.*

stream·line *obj* IMPROVE /ˈstriːm·laɪn/ *v* [T] to improve the effectiveness of (an organization such as a business or government), often by simplifying the way activities are performed • *The cost-cutting measures include streamlining administrative* **procedures** *in the company.* • *Her proposals will control the costs of health care and streamline the* **bureaucracy** *that contributes to those costs.* • *150 staff have been sacked as part of the company's streamlining* **efforts**. • *The government recently announced details of its* **plan** *to streamline the taxation system.* • *We need to find ways of streamlining the decision-making* **process**. • *Streamlining* **management** *could save at least 10 percent in costs.*

street /striːt/ *n* [C] a road in a city, town or village which has buildings that are usually close together along one or both sides • *The streets were strewn with rubbish after the carnival.* • *The streets are quiet at the moment, but renewed fighting could erupt at any time.* • *Our daughter lives just* **across** *the street from us.* • *It really upsets me when I see people begging* **in the** *street.* • *The recent violence has led to armed police* **on** *the streets.* • *Despite being a qualified teacher, her basic salary is less than street* **cleaners** *earn.* • *My grandmother can remember when there were still horse-drawn cabs and* **cobbled** *streets in London.* • *Be sure to look both ways when you* **cross** *the street.* • *It is hoped that the curfew will bring the street* **demonstrations** *under control.* • *The town was still busy at eight, but the streets were* **deserted** *by nine.* • *More than 120 people have been killed in four days of vicious street* **fighting**. • *I wish you'd do something constructive at the weekends instead of* **hanging about on** *street* **corners** *with your friends.* • *Inadequate street* **lighting** *makes many people afraid to go out at night.* • *If you want to try the best local cuisine, you'll need to avoid the streets* **lined** *with tourist restaurants.* • *Despite being* *away for several years, he felt he could still handle the* **mean** (=dangerous and dirty) *streets of Washington.* • *The church is surrounded by a maze of* **narrow** *streets.* • *Riot police were* **patrolling** *the streets of South London last night after violence erupted at an anti-racist march.* • *Even at five in the morning, there were still crowds of people* **roaming** *the streets, singing and shouting.* • *Few visitors to the town stray from the main* **shopping** *streets.* • *Builders jeer at us even when we're just* **walking down the** *street.* • *Keep your voice down, we don't want the* **whole** *street* (=everyone living along this road) *to hear us!* • *(fig.) Few people will be* **dancing in the** *streets* (=very happy) *about a two per cent pay rise.* • *(fig.) Many asylum seekers appear to be economic migrants, convinced that the streets of Europe are* **paved with gold** (=that they can become rich in Europe). • *There have been several street* **protests** *against the tax increases.* • *Go and wash your face, Molly! You look like a street* **urchin**. • *I bought these sunglasses from a street* **vendor** *when I was in Florence.* • *(Br and Aus)* Something that is **streets ahead of** something else is much better or much more advanced than it: *The latest sales figures show that we're streets ahead of the competition.* ○ *Don't worry about them. We're streets ahead.* • Someone who is **on the streets** or **walking the streets** has no home: *Some of these people have been on the streets for years.* ○ *He's terrified of losing his home and having to walk the streets.* • Sometimes a woman or girl who is **on the streets** or **walking the streets** is someone whom men pay to have sex with them: *I needed money to buy drugs and I ended up walking the streets.* See also STREETWALKER. • When people **take to the streets**, they express their opposition to something publicly and often violently: *Thousands of people have taken to the streets to protest against the military coup.* • If something is **up** your **street** (*esp. Am* **up** your **alley**), you are interested in it or you enjoy doing it: *Carpentry isn't really up my street. I'd rather pay someone else to do it.* ○ *I've got a little job for you which is right up your alley.* • *(Br and Aus)* If you have **street-credibility** (also **street-cred**), you are likely to be accepted by ordinary young people who live in towns and cities because you have the same fashions, styles, interests, culture or opinions: *That jacket won't do much for your street cred. It looks awful!* ○ *Many celebrities develop a working class accent to increase their street credibility.* ○ *The store is trying to attract more teenage customers by developing a more* **street-credible** *image.* • **Street furniture** is equipment such as lights, road signs and telephone boxes that is positioned at the side of a road for use by the public. • *(Am)* **Street people** are people who do not have a home and who often sleep outside in cities: *About one-third of the country's street people are drug or alcohol abusers.* • *(Am)* **Street smarts** is the ability to manage or succeed in difficult or dangerous situations, esp. in big towns or cities: *You haven't got the street smarts to last ten minutes in New York without getting ripped off.* • **Street theatre** is free theatrical entertainment that is performed outside in public places, particularly near shops, restaurants and bars: *We spent many evenings sitting in cafés watching the street theatre.* • The **street value** of an illegal drug is the price that is paid for it by the person who uses it: *Customs officers discovered heroin with a street value of £6 million at Felixstowe docks earlier today.* • The **man/woman in the street** is an ordinary, average person whose opinions are considered to be representative of most people: *To win the election he needs to appeal to the typical man and woman in the street.* • *"Street Fighting Man"* (title of a song by the Rolling Stones, 1968) • LP〉 **Capital letters**

street·car /£'striːt·kɑːʳ, $-kɑːr/ *n* [C] *Am for* TRAM • *The cheapest way of doing a tour of the city is to* **take** *a streetcar.* • *"A Streetcar Named Desire"* (title of a play by Tenessee Williams, made into a film in 1951 starring Marlon Brando, 1947)

street·light /'striːt·laɪt/, **street·lamp** /'striːt·læmp/ *n* [C] a light in or at the side of a road or public area which is usually supported on a tall post • *He was killed when he crashed his car into a streetlight.* • PIC〉 **Lights**

street·walk·er /£'striːtˌwɔː·kəʳ, $-ˌwɑː·kɚ/ *n* [C] *dated* a woman or girl who is paid by men for having sex with them and who finds her customers outside in public places • *He resigned after he was caught talking to a streetwalker at Kings Cross station.*

street·wise /'striːt·waɪz/, *Am also* **street–smart** /£'striːt·smɑːt, $-smɑːrt/ *adj* able to manage or succeed in dangerous or difficult situations in big towns or cities where poor people live or where there is a lot of crime • *Soon after arriving from Russia, he learned the streetwise ways of the multi-ethnic culture that was developing in New York.* • *McDonald was as streetwise as any of the criminals he had investigated.* • *She recently adopted a streetwise Washington youngster from a crime-ridden neighborhood whose father was in jail.* • *Training shoes are an important streetwise status symbol for many teenagers.*

strength EFFORT /streŋkθ/ *n* the ability to do things that demand a lot of physical or mental effort, or the degree to which something is strong or powerful • *She had the strength and stamina to take the lead and win the gold medal by 0·39 seconds.* [U] • *Admitting you've made a mistake is a sign of strength, not weakness.* [U] • *Modern surgical techniques require dexterity, not* **brute** *strength.* [U] • *He showed great strength* **of character** *when he refused to accept the bribes.* [U] • *The latest opinion polls put the* **combined** *strength of the two ecology parties at 15% nationwide.* [U] • *We shall struggle on,* **drawing** *our strength from the courage of others.* [U] • *If she's going to get through this ordeal, she's going to have to* **draw** *on her* **inner** *strength.* [U] • *He has lost a lot of weight after the operation, but he should be back to* **full** *strength in a couple of months.* [U] • *She's* **gaining** *strength, but it will be several weeks before she's fully recovered from the illness.* [U] • *There are still few definite signs that the economic recovery is* **gathering** *strength.* [U] • *You can* **gauge** (=measure) *the strength of a democracy by the way it treats its minorities.* [U] • *Much of the country's military strength* **lies in** *its missile force.* [U] • **Physical** *strength is unnecessary for an increasing number of jobs.* [U] • *She has been preparing for the strength-***sapping** *humidity of the rainforest by training in her parents' greenhouse.* • *The economy's* **underlying** *strength is evident from the rise in manufacturing production.* [U] • *The strengths of our beers range from 3% alcohol to 6%.* [C] • *(esp. Br)* **Give me strength!** is an exclamation which expresses surprise or amused annoyance about someone else's stupidity or inability to do something: *Oh, give me strength! Do you want me to do it for you?* • Something that **goes from strength to strength** gradually becomes increasingly successful: *The firm's gone from strength to strength since the new factory was built.* • If you do something **on the strength of** something such as advice, you do it because you have been influenced by it or believe it: *I invested in the company on the strength of my brother's advice.*

strength·en *(obj)* /'streŋk·θᵊn/ *v* • When something strengthens or is strengthened, it becomes stronger or more effective: *They have been strengthening their border* **defences** *in preparation for war.* [T] ○ *Pregnant women can make childbirth easier by doing exercises that help the abdominal* **muscles** *to strengthen.* [I] ○ *The police want tougher laws to strengthen their* **hand** (=give them more power) *against drug traffickers.* [T] ○ *She really ought to strengthen her* **grip** *on* (=take more control of) *the department.* [T] ○ *His battle against cancer has strengthened his* **belief** *in God.* [T] ○ *The accident strengthens the* **case** *for better safety measures at fairgrounds.* [T] ○ *The devolution of power from central government would help to strengthen local* **democracy**. [T] ○ *The bank loan has* **greatly** *strengthened our financial* **position**. [T] ○ *The economy has been strengthened* **immeasurably** *by Japanese investment.* [T] ○ *More should be done to strengthen industry's* **links** *with universities.* [T] ○ *The organization's aim is to strengthen the cultural* **ties** *between Britain and Germany.* [T] ○ *The new constitution will further strengthen the* **powers** *of the president.* [T] ○ *The violence is self-defeating as it only strengthens the* **resolve** *of ordinary people against their campaign.* [T] ○ *The rise in US interest rates caused the dollar to strengthen* (=increase in value) **against** *all the European currencies.* [I] ○ *Most financial experts expect the stock market to strengthen* **further** *over the coming months.* [I]

strength GOOD FEATURE /streŋkθ/ *n* [C] a good characteristic • *She's well aware of her strengths and weaknesses as an artist.* • *His greatest strengths are his determination and resilience.* • *Her great strength as a manager is that she is very well organized.* • *Could you summarise the strengths* **of** *your proposal for us?*

strength NUMBER /streŋkθ/ *n* [U] the number of people in a group • *What's the current strength of the Cambridgeshire police force?* • *Demonstrators arrived* **in strength** (=A lot of them arrived) *to protest against the closure of the factory.* • *(esp. Br and Aus) The office will be* **below strength** (=There will be fewer people than usual in the office) *in August* *when a lot of people will be away.* • *The staff cuts have meant that we haven't been working* **at full strength** (= with the usual number of people) *for over a year.*

stren·u·ous /ˈstren·ju·əs/ *adj* demanding or using a lot of physical or mental effort or energy • *He rarely does anything more strenuous than changing the channels on the television.* • *She has been a strenuous campaigner for animal rights for more than twenty years.* • *His doctor advised him not to take any strenuous* **exercise** *until he had completely recovered.* • *Strenuous* **efforts** *were made throughout the war to disguise the scale of civilian casualties.* • **Despite** *strenuous* **efforts** *to revive him, he was dead before the ambulance arrived.* • *Surprisingly, the most strenuous* **opposition** *to the tax changes has come from the people who will benefit most from them.*

stren·u·ous·ly /ˈstren·ju·ə·sli/ *adv* • *He strenuously* **denies** *all the allegations against him.* • *Most of the villagers strenuously* **object** *to the proposals for the new road.* • *They have strenuously* **resisted** *all attempts to investigate their financial affairs.* • *The aircraft's safety record has been strenuously* **defended** *by both the manufacturer and the airlines using it.* • *The closure of the railway station is being strenuously* **opposed** *by local residents.*

strep /strep/ *n* [C] *esp. Am infml for* STREPTOCOCCUS • **Strep throat** is a severe bacterial infection of the throat.

strep·to·coc·cus /£ˌstrep·təˈkɒk·əs, $-ˈkɑː·kəs/, *esp. Am infml* **strep** *n* [C] *pl* **streptococci** /£ˌstrep·təˈkɒk·saɪ, $-ˈkɑːk-/ *specialized* a bacterium, many types of which cause disease • *The streptococcus is spherical and usually occurs in twisted chains.* • *Tonsillitis is normally caused by infection with streptococci.*

strep·to·coc·cal /£ˌstrep·təˈkɒk·l̩, $-ˈkɑː·kᵊl/ *adj* [not gradable] *specialized* • *Pneumonia tends to be caused by streptococcal or viral infection.*

stress [WORRY] /stres/ *n* great worry caused by a difficult situation, or something which causes this condition • *Financial hardship places severe stress* **on** *married couples, but it does not usually cause divorce by itself.* [U] • *People* **under** *a lot of stress may experience headaches, minor pains and sleeping difficulties.* [U] • *Yoga is a very effective technique for* **combating** *stress.* [U] • *In* **moments of** *severe stress, he would close his eyes and start humming.* [U] • *Employers should do more to reduce the number of working days lost through stress-***related** *illness.* • *Working unsocial hours is just one of the stresses* **and strains** *of the job.* [C] • **Stress management** is the limitation of stress and its effects by learning special types of behaviour and ways of thinking which reduce it: *The treatment for people addicted to tranquillizers includes training in stress management and relaxation techniques.*

stressed /strest/ *adj* [after v] • *She's been* **feeling** *very stressed* (= worried and anxious) *since she started her new job.*

stress·ful /ˈstres·fᵊl/ *adj* • *Be nice to Dad, Tyler. He's had an extremely stressful day at the office.* • *At best, police work is physically demanding and stressful, and at worst, it's downright dangerous.* • *Teaching can be a tiring and stressful job.* • *She's very good at coping in stressful* **situations**. • *Many commuters* **find** *travelling to work stressful.*

stress out *obj*, **stress** *obj* **out** *v adv* [M] • When something stresses out a person, it makes them feel very nervous and worried: *Interviews always stress me out.* ○ *I was really stressed out after the exam.*

stress *obj* [EMPHASIZE] /stres/ *v* [T] to give emphasis or special importance to (something) • *She has repeatedly stressed* **(that)** *she has no intention of standing as a candidate for the leadership of the party.* [+ *(that)* clause] • *He is careful to stress* **(that)** *the laboratory's safety standards are the best in the country.* [+ *(that)* clause] • *The president stressed* **the need for** *calm in TV and radio broadcasts throughout the day.* • *I'd just like to stress* **the importance of** *neatness and politeness in this job.* • *She was* **at pains to** (= anxious to) *stress* **(that)** *she had no intention of resigning over the issue.* [+ *(that)* clause]

stress /stres/ *n* [U] • *During his speech, he* **laid** *particular stress on the freedom of the press.*

stress *obj* [PRONOUNCE] /stres/ *v* [T] to pronounce (a word or syllable) with greater force than other words in the same sentence or other syllables in the same word • *The interpretation of a sentence can change according to which word is stressed.* • *In the word 'engine', you should stress the first syllable.* • [LP] **Stress in pronunciation**

stress /stres/ *n* • *The meaning of a sentence often depends on stress and intonation.* [U] • *When 'insert' is a verb, the stress is* **on** *the second syllable, but when it is a noun, the stress is* **on** *the first syllable.* [C] • When the pronunciation of a word is being shown, a **stress mark** is a short vertical line which is printed before the syllable that receives the most stress or the second most stress in the word: *Stress marks above the line indicate* **primary** *stress, while those below the line show* **secondary** *stress.*

stress [FORCE] /stres/ *n specialized* a force that acts in a way which tends to change the shape of an object • *Metal fatigue is a weakness which develops in a metal structure that has been subjected to many repeated stresses.* [C] • *Many joggers are plagued by knee stress and foot strains caused by unsuitable footwear.* [U] • *He needs to have an operation for a stress* **fracture** *in his back.*

stretch *(obj)* [LENGTHEN] /stretʃ/ *v* to (cause an elastic material to) become longer or wider than usual as a result of pulling at the edges • *These exercises are designed to stretch and lengthen the muscles around your stomach and the lower part of your back.* [T] • *That elastic band will snap if you stretch it too far.* [T] • *This substance is very flexible and stretches* **to** *any shape you want.* [I] • *My T-shirt's stretched in the wash.* [I] • *Stretch* **fabrics** *are ideal for pregnant women.* • *These stretch* **velvet** *trousers are very popular with our customers.* • If a material stretches, it is elastic: *Rubber stretches when you pull it.* [I] • A **stretch limousine** or *(infml)* **stretch limo** is a large luxurious car that has been specially lengthened to provide extra space or seats and is used by very rich, famous or important people: *The crowd cheered as the president stepped out of the stretch limo.*

stretch /stretʃ/ *n* [U] • The stretch of an elastic material is the degree to which it is able to be lengthened or widened by pulling: *This fabric doesn't have much stretch in it, does it?*

stretch·y /ˈstretʃ·i/ *adj* **-ier**, **-iest** • *I don't like all these synthetic stretchy fabrics, I prefer natural ones like cotton and silk.*

stretch *obj* [GO BEYOND] /stretʃ/ *v* [T] to go as far as or beyond the usual limit of (something) • *You shouldn't stretch yourself* **beyond** *your means and get yourself into debt.* • *Many families'* **budgets** *are already stretched* **to breaking point** *and these tax rises will make their situation worse.* • *I think that shouting at people until they agree with you is stretching the* **definition** *of negotiation.* • *We can't work any harder, Paul. We're already* **fully** *stretched.* • *Southend beat Mansfield by two goals to one, stretching* (= increasing) *their* **lead** *to six points at the top of the Third Division.* • *With this computer, we're stretching the* **limits** *of the available technology.* • *This movie really stretches the credulity of the audience* **to the limit**. • *We don't normally allow in people under 18, but I suppose we could stretch the* **rules** *for you as it's your birthday tomorrow.* • *Their army is stretched too* **thin** *to hold on to the territory for long.* • *She's very clever, but it's* **stretching it** *a bit* (= going beyond the truth) *to call her a genius.* • *"How much money do you want to borrow?" "Could you* **stretch to** (= manage as much as) *£50?"* • If you **stretch a point**, you make a claim which is not completely true, or you do something which goes beyond what is considered to be reasonable: *They claim to be the biggest company in the world, which is stretching a point, but it's true if you include their subsidiaries.* ○ *She was right to ask for a pay increase, but she was stretching the point when she asked for an extra week off as well.*

stretch /stretʃ/ *n* [U] • If you do something **at full stretch**, you use all your available skill, energy and ability to do it: *It's impossible to increase output – we're already working at full stretch.* • **By no stretch/Not by any stretch of the imagination** is used to describe things that are impossible to believe, even with a lot of effort: *By no stretch of the imagination could he be seriously described as an artist.* ○ *Not by any stretch of the imagination does she look like a rector's wife.*

stretch *(obj)* [REACH] /stretʃ/ *v* to cause (something) to reach as far as possible • *A woman has died after being knocked from her motorcycle by a wire that had been stretched across the road between two lampposts.* [T] • *He removed his hat and stretched* **out** *his arms to embrace her.* [M] • *She strode briskly down the street, ignoring the beggars who were stretching* **out** *their hands for money.* [M] • *He collapsed into the armchair and stretched his long legs* **out** *in front of him.* [M] • *She stretched out her* **hand** *and helped him from his chair.* [M] • *(fig.) I'd like to stretch* **out**

STRESS IN ENGLISH PRONUNCIATION

In every English word of two or more syllables (= spoken parts), one syllable is given particular emphasis compared to the others; this is called **primary stress**. Vowels in the unstressed syllables are often pronounced /ə/ as in 'convenient' /kən'viː·ni·ənt/, or /ɪ/ as in 'resulting' /rɪ'zʌl·tɪŋ/. Although it is often not possible to know where to place the stress in an unfamiliar word, it can be helpful to remember the following approximate rules:

- **Many common nouns and adjectives are stressed on the first syllable**, especially those words that have two syllables: 'daugh·ter • 'hob·by • 'e·vil • 'ea·ger

  Compound words, particularly nouns, are usually stressed on the first part :
  'coun·try·side • a 'fol·low-through (but to ˌfol.low 'through) • 'fam·i·ly man

  but when the words do not form a compound they are usually stressed independently:
  The '**White House** *is in Washington.* • *She lives in the* '**white** '**house** *on the corner.*

- **Generally, combining forms do not receive primary stress**
  'cri·ti·**cize** • 'mean·ing·**ful** • **im**·'prove • **un**·'like·ly

  But the following word endings are usually stressed:

-ee	ref·er·'ee	**-ese**	Chi·'nese	**-ique**	mys·'tique
-eer	vol·un·'teer	**-esque**	gro·'tesque	**-ette**	dis·'kette

- In some words the first syllable is stressed when the word is a noun or adjective, but is not stressed when it is a verb: *The child's* '**con·duct** *disturbed the teacher.* • *She wasn't able* **to con·'duct** *herself appropriately.*

  The following are the important words where this happens. Notice that in American English the first syllable is often stressed even in the verb form. These words are marked *

attribute	contrast*	frequent*	produce	reject
combat*	convert	import*	progress	subject
compound*	convict	insult*	project	survey*
conduct	decrease*	object	protest*	suspect
construct	exploit	perfect	rebel	transfer*
contest	export*	permit	recall*	transport*
contract*	extract	present	record	upset

- The following word endings do not usually cause the primary stress to move:

-age	'pa·rent	'pa·rent·age
-en	a'wake	a'wa·ken
-ful	'tea·spoon	'tea·spoon·ful
-ing	'broad·cast	'broad·cast·ing
-less	di'rec·tion	di'rec·tion·less
-ly	'reg·u·lar	'reg·u·lar·ly
-ment	de'vel·op	de'vel·op·ment
-ness	'youth·ful	'youth·ful·ness
-y	'com·for·ta·ble	'com·for·ta·bly

- But the following endings cause the stress to move to the syllable immediately before the suffix:

-graphy	'pho·to·graph	pho·'tog·ra·phy
-eous	ad·'van·tage	ad·van·'ta·geous
-ious	'in·ju·ry	in·'ju·ri·ous
-ial	'com·merce	com·'mer·cial
-ian	'co·me·dy	co·'me·di·an
-ion	'gen·er·ate	ˌgen·e'ra·tion
-ic	e·'con·o·my	ˌe·co·'nom·ic
-ical	phi·'los·o·phy	ˌphil·o'soph·ic·al
-ity	e'lec·tric	ˌel·ec'tric·i·ty

my mortgage payments over a longer period if possible. [M] • *(fig.) My present job doesn't stretch me* (=need me to learn new things which use my skill and experience) *as much as I would like, so I'm looking for something more demanding.* [T] • If you stretch your body or your arms or legs, you straighten them so that they are as long as possible in order to exercise the joints after you have been in the same place or position for a long time: *"I'm so tired," she said, yawning and stretching.* [I] ○ *It's a good idea to stretch before you take vigorous exercise.* [I] ○ *I try to do ten minutes of stretching* **exercises** *every morning.* ○ *I'd quite like to stay at home tonight and stretch* **out** *on the sofa in front of the TV.* [I] • If you **stretch** your **legs**, you go for a walk after sitting in the same position for a long time: *We drove there in three hours, including a couple of stops to stretch our legs.*

stretch /stretʃ/ *n* [C usually sing] • *The first thing I do when I get out of bed in the morning is* **have** *a good stretch.*

stretch SPREAD /stretʃ/ *v* [I always + adv/prep] to spread over a large area or distance • *On the horizon, a huge cloud of dense smoke from the burning oil well stretched* **across** *the sky.* • *The market stretches all the way* **along** *the street.* • *The Andes stretch* **for** *7250 km along the west coast of South America.* • *If all the roads on the island of Jersey were laid end to end, they would stretch* **from** *London* **to** *Amsterdam and back.* • *In the 14th century, Barcelona was the capital of a Mediterranean empire that stretched* **to** *Naples and even Athens.* • *The refugee camps stretch* **as far as the eye can see.** • If something **stretches the length of** something very long, it is the same length as it: *The underground chambers stretch the length of a football pitch.* ○ *The mountains stretch the entire length of the country.*

stretch /stretʃ/ *n* [C usually sing] • A stretch is a continuous area of land or water: *Local residents are campaigning for a 20 mph speed limit on the stretch* **of** *road near the school.* ○ *It is easy to see what has attracted so many retired Britons to this particular stretch of* **coast**. ○ *There is little chance of protecting the long stretches of* **coastline** *where birds, turtles and fish are threatened by pollution.* ○ *The accident means that traffic is at a standstill* **along** *a* **five-mile** *stretch of the M11 just south of Cambridge.* ○ *Some very* *rare birds inhabit our stretch of the* **river**. ○ *The Whitby line is a very* **scenic** *stretch of railway.* ○ *There are* **vast** *stretches of derelict wasteland in the old industrial area of the city.* ○ *The Dead Sea is the largest landlocked stretch of* **water** *in the Middle East.* • A stretch can also be a stage in a race, or a part of a race track: *She looked certain to win as she entered the* **final** *stretch.* ○ *He fell from his horse as he was galloping down the* **home** *stretch* (= towards the finish). ○ *(fig.) As the election campaign hits the* **home** *stretch* (= goes into the final stage), *voters still have little idea about what to expect from him.* ○ *(Am) They need a player who can score points* **down the** *stretch* (= towards the end of a game or sporting season).

stretch LONG TIME /stretʃ/ *v* [I always + adv/prep] to spread over a long period of time • *The dispute stretches* **back** *over many years.* • *He has a series of drug convictions stretching* **back to** *1981.* • *This ancient* **tradition** *stretches* **back** *hundreds of years.* • *The restoration work could stretch* **from** *months into years.* • *Although we were supposed to finish this month, it looks like the work will stretch well* **into** *next year.* • *You're too young to be pessimistic. You've got your whole life stretching* **out** *in front of you.*

stretch /stretʃ/ *n* [C usually sing] • A stretch is a continuous period of time: *The longest unbroken stretch of sub-zero temperatures in London was 14 days in February 1947.* ○ *Babies can sleep for 20 hours a day, while the elderly may need far less rest and tend to sleep in several short stretches.* • If you do something **at a stretch**, you do it continuously or without any interruptions: *There's no way I could work for ten hours at a stretch.* ○ *A lion can lie in the same spot without moving for 12 hours at a stretch.* • A stretch is also a period of time that a criminal spends in prison: *Her brother's doing a ten-year stretch behind bars for an armed robbery.*

stretch·er /£ˈstretʃ·əʳ, $-ɚ/ *n* [C] a light frame which is made of poles and covered by a soft material and is used for carrying people who are ill, injured or dead • *She was clearly in tremendous pain as she was carried off the track on a stretcher.* • A **stretcher-bearer** is someone who carries a stretcher, with one person at either end of it, particularly in a war or emergency: *Stretcher-bearers ran in and out of the building as firefighters struggled to put out the blaze.* • PIC **Emergency services**

stretch·marks /£ˈstretʃ·mɑːks, $-mɑːrks/ *pl n* [C] thin silvery lines or marks on the front or sides of the body of a woman who has given birth • *Stretchmarks are caused by the skin being stretched during pregnancy.* • *She's worried about having children because she doesn't want to get stretchmarks or lose her figure.* • *People who used to be very fat can also have stretchmarks.*

streus·el /ˈstruː·zəl, £ˈstrɔɪ-/ *n* [U] *esp. Am* a topping for cakes and breads made with butter, sugar, flour, spices and sometimes nuts, or a cake made with fruit and this topping • *apple streusel* • *Be sure to cover the fruit with plenty of streusel.* • *I'd like a piece of streusel and a cup of coffee, please.*

strew *obj* /struː/ *v* [T] *past simple* **strewed**, *past part* **strewn** /struːn/ or **strewed** to scatter (things) untidily over a surface, or to be scattered untidily over (a surface) • *The bomb was very large and had strewn wreckage over a wide area.* • *They marked the end of the war by strewing flowers over the graves of 18 000 soldiers.* • *Wine bottles and dirty dishes were strewn across the lawn.* • *Villagers are still clearing away the glass strewn over the streets and trying to assess the cost of the damage.* • *The burglar had been through all her drawers looking for jewellery, and her clothes lay strewn on the floor.* • *The path from the church to their waiting car was strewn* **with** *flowers.* • *(fig.) The path to a lasting peace settlement is strewn* **with** *difficulties.* • *Local residents complained that the park was strewn* **with** *litter after the concert.* • *Television has made us all too familiar with the* **rubble**-*strewn streets of the numerous war zones around the world.* • *One of the first things I noticed about New York was its* **trash**-*strewn streets.*

strewth, struth /struːθ/ *exclamation infml Aus and dated Br* used to express surprise or disappointment • *Strewth, look at the size of that steak!* • *Struth! You could have told me sooner that you didn't want to go to the party.*

stri·at·ed /£straɪˈeɪ·tɪd, $-t̬ɪd/ *adj* [not gradable] *specialized* having long thin lines, marks or strips of colour • *The town perches dizzily on the striated cliffs.* • *(fig.) The novel is not a solid block of agony, but is striated with all kinds of emotion.*

stri·a·tion /straɪˈeɪ·ʃən/ *n* [C usually pl] *specialized* • Striations are long thin lines, marks or strips of colour: *What has caused the striations in this rock?*

strict /strɪkt/ *adj* **-er, -est** greatly limiting someone's freedom to behave as they wish, and likely to cause them to be severely punished if disobeyed • *My parents were very strict* **with** *me when I was young.* • *Strict* **adherence** *to the safety regulations is expected at all times.* • *There was strict* **censorship** *of the media throughout the war.* • *In Pakistan, women must conform to a strict Islamic dress* **code** (= it is very important that they obey Islamic rules about the types of clothing they are allowed to wear). • *Stricter* **controls** *on air pollution would help to reduce acid rain.* • *We have strict* **criteria** *for the selection of new recruits.* • *A strict* **curfew** *has been imposed from dusk till dawn.* • *The school is an old-fashioned institution where strict* **discipline** *is still the norm.* • *We follow very strict* **guidelines** *on the use and storage of personal details on computers.* • *He would be found guilty under a strict* (= exact) **interpretation** *of the law.* • *Do you think stricter gun* **laws** *would reduce the murder rate in the United States?* • *There's a strict time* **limit** *for claiming the prize.* • *Sweden maintained a policy of strict* **neutrality** *throughout the war.* • *During the Islamic Revolution, Iran returned to strict* **observance** *of Muslim principles and traditions.* • *Opponents of the conservationists argue that stricter* **regulations** *would hinder economic growth.* • *Strict testing* **requirements** *mean that it can take several years for a new drug to become generally available.* • *Strict* **rules** *govern the export of high-tech equipment such as computers.* • *The drug should only be administered under strict medical* **supervision**. • *He blames his strict religious* **upbringing** *for his sexual problems.* • *In its strict* **sense** (= In its most limited meaning), *frost refers simply to a temperature of zero degrees Celsius or less.* • *The negotiations have taken place in strict* (= total) **secrecy**. • *I'm telling you this* **in the strictest confidence** (= expecting that you will not tell anyone else). • Strict can also describe someone who follows the rules and principles of a belief or way of living very carefully and exactly: *His parents were strict Catholics.* ○ *She's a strict* **vegetarian** *and refuses to eat any poultry or fish.* • See also RESTRICT.

strict·ly /ˈstrɪkt·li/ *adv* • *I have acted strictly* **in accordance with** *the regulations at all times.* • *It is essential that the safety procedures are strictly* **adhered to**. • *Their salaries are not strictly* **comparable** (= cannot be directly compared) *because of the differences in UK and US tax rates.* • *Should I mark this letter to your accountant 'strictly* **confidential**'? • *Broadcasting was strictly* **controlled** *throughout the war.* • *The proposed change in the law would make abortion illegal except for strictly* **defined** *medical reasons.* • *The speed limit is strictly* **enforced** *on urban roads.* • *The use of cameras in this museum is strictly* **forbidden**. • *This unrepeatable half-price offer is only available for a strictly* **limited** *period.* • *Are all these questions strictly* (= really) **necessary**? • *Political donations made by trade unions are more strictly* **regulated** *than those made by companies.* • **Strictly speaking** (= Being completely accurate), *Great Britain consists of Scotland, Wales and England, and the United Kingdom consists of Great Britain and Northern Ireland.*

strict·ness /ˈstrɪkt·nəs/ *n* [U] • *The increased strictness of the immigration rules will make it harder than ever to settle in this country.*

stric·ture CRITICISM /£ˈstrɪk·tʃəʳ, $-tʃɚ/ *n* [C] *fml* a statement of severe criticism or disapproval • *The strictures of the United Nations have failed to have any effect on the warring factions.* • *The government remains unmoved by the strictures* **on** *its handling of the crisis.*

stric·ture LIMITATION /£ˈstrɪk·tʃəʳ, $-tʃɚ/ *n* [C] *fml* a severe moral or physical limitation • *He defended the strictures* **on** *freedom of expression as a necessary evil during a period of tremendous political instability.*

stride WALK /straɪd/ *v* [I always + adv/prep] *past simple* **strode** /£strəʊd, $stroʊd/, *past part* **stridden** /ˈstrɪd·ən/ or **strode** /£strəʊd, $stroʊd/ to walk somewhere quickly with long steps • *She strode* **purposefully** *up to the desk and demanded to speak to the manager.* • *The soldiers strode* **across** *the street with bazookas on their shoulders.* • *(fig.) After several difficult years, the company is now striding* **forward** (= advancing) *into the future.* • **Stride piano** is a style of jazz piano playing in which the right hand plays the tune while the left hand repeatedly plays a single note and then a CHORD (= group of notes).

stride /straɪd/ *n* [C] • A stride is a long step when walking or running: *She attributes her record-breaking speed to the length of her stride.* ○ *She approached the last hurdle too fast and had to take 17 strides instead of the 16 she had planned.* • *"We will appeal," the attorney announced without* **breaking** *his stride* (= stopping walking). • *(esp. Br and Aus)* If you **get into** your **stride** (*Am usually* **hit** your **stride**), you become familiar with something you have recently started doing: *We ought to wait until she's got into her stride before we ask her to negotiate that contract.* • *(esp. Br)* Someone or something that **puts** you **off** your **stride** briefly takes your attention away from something you are doing, making it more difficult to do: *The slightest noise puts him off his stride when he's performing.* • If you **take** a problem or difficulty **in** your **stride** (*Am also* **take** something **in stride**), you deal with it calmly and do not let it have an effect on what you are doing: *When you become a politician, you soon learn to take criticism in your stride.* ○ *(Am) She has taken the scandal in stride and continued to work normally.*

stride [DEVELOPMENT] /straɪd/ *n* [C] an important positive development • *The West* **made** *impressive strides in improving energy efficiency after the huge rises in oil prices during the seventies.* • *The detective leading the murder investigation expects to have made significant strides* **forward** *within the next couple of weeks.* • *She made a giant stride* **towards** *power in last year's elections.*

stri·dent [LOUD] /ˈstraɪ·dᵊnt/ *adj* sounding loud, unpleasant and rough • *Although he has some very good ideas, people are put off by his strident voice.*

stri·dent·ly /ˈstraɪ·dᵊnt·li/ *adv* • *She shouted stridently across the room at him.*

strid·en·cy /ˈstraɪ·dᵊnt·si/ *n* [U] • *He found the harsh stridency of Pat's voice very annoying at times.*

stri·dent [FORCEFUL] /ˈstraɪ·dᵊnt/ *adj* expressing or expressed in forceful language which does not try to avoid upsetting other people • *He recently expressed his opposition to changing the law in a strident newspaper article.* • *She told her side of the story in typically strident language during a television interview.* • *They are becoming increasingly strident in their criticism of government economic policy.*

stri·dent·ly /ˈstraɪ·dᵊnt·li/ *adv* • *She was arrested in 1984 on suspicion of being a spy, an accusation she has always stridently denied.* • *He is stridently opposed to abortion.* • *Many English residents in Scotland are much more stridently in favour of independence than the Scots.*

strid·en·cy /ˈstraɪ·dᵊnt·si/ *n* [U] • *As the situation becomes more desperate, there is a growing stridency in the appeals for aid.*

strides /straɪdz/ *pl n* [C] *Aus infml* TROUSERS • *That's a smart* **pair of** *strides you're wearing, Bruce.*

strife /straɪf/ *n* [U] violent or angry disagreement • *What are the prospects for overcoming the strife* **between** *the Christian minority and Muslim majority?* • *Twenty years of* **civil** *strife have left the country's economy in ruins.* • *He is accused of attempting to destabilise the country and provoke* **ethnic** *strife.* • *The company has managed to reduce the workforce with little* **industrial** *strife.* • *We do not intend to be drawn into the* **internal** *strife of another country.*

strike *(obj)* [HIT] /straɪk/ *v past* **struck** /strʌk/ to hit or attack forcefully or violently • *She died when her car went out of control and struck an oncoming vehicle.* [T] • *The leading yacht was forced to abandon the race after it struck an iceberg.* [T] • *The police have warned the public that the killer is highly dangerous and could strike again.* [I] • *The autopsy revealed that his murderer had struck him* **on** *the head with an iron bar.* [T] • *The murder victim had been struck repeatedly* **about** *the head with a blunt instrument.* [T] • *Have you ever been struck* **by lightning**? [T] • *It's a myth that lightning never strikes twice in the same place.* [I] • *The president intends to introduce the death penalty for terrorists who strike* **at** *civilians.* [I] • *We were only teasing her about her spots when she suddenly struck* **out** *in all directions* (= started hitting people uncontrollably). [I] • *The objective in a game of croquet is to strike your* **ball** *through a set of hoops in a particular order before finally hitting the central peg.* [T] • *The two foreign ministers have agreed to remove* **missiles** *that can strike at targets in each other's countries.* [I] • When a clock strikes, its bells ring to show what the time is: *The clock was striking ten as we went into the church.* [T] • *Is it 10.30 already? I never heard the clock strike.* [I] • When a time strikes, a clock's bells ring to show what time it is: *Midnight had just struck when I went upstairs to bed.* [I] • If you **strike a blow against** or **at** something, you harm it severely: *Her resignation has struck a blow against the company's plans for expansion.* • If you **strike a blow for** something, you do something which supports it: *The judge's ruling that she was unfairly dismissed has struck a blow for racial equality.* ○ *The council's decision not to build the road has struck a blow for common sense.* • When people **strike camp**, they take down their tents in preparation for leaving the place where they have been staying: *We woke up late and it was ten o'clock before we struck camp.* • If someone is **struck down**, they die suddenly or start to suffer from a serious illness: *It's a tragedy that these young people were struck down in their prime.* ○ *He was struck down by polio when he was a teenager.* • If you are **struck dumb** by something, it surprises you so much that you cannot say anything: *We were struck dumb when she announced she was pregnant.* • If something **strikes fear** or **terror** into you, it makes you extremely frightened: *The brutal military regime has struck terror into the whole population.* ○ *Even the mere mention of his name would strike fear into his enemies.* • If you **strike at the heart of** something, you damage it severely by attacking the most important part of it: *Victory depends on our being able to strike at the heart of the enemy's military command.* ○ *The increase in income tax strikes at the heart of the government's declared intention to reduce taxation.* • If something **strikes home**, it hits the intended place or has the intended effect: *The laser guidance system dramatically increases the likelihood that the missile will strike home.* ○ *The government's message about the dangers of smoking seems to have struck home.* • If you **strike while the iron is hot**, you take advantage of an opportunity as soon as it exists, in case the opportunity goes away and does not return: *"I can't decide whether or not to take the job." "You should strike while the iron is hot – you may not get another chance as good as this one."* • If you **strike a match**, you cause it to burn by rubbing it against a hard rough surface: *She struck a match and lit another cigarette.* ○ *He lent down and struck a match* **on** *the sole of his boot.* • If a place is **within striking distance**, it is near: *We live within striking distance of both Baltimore and Washington.* • If something is **within striking distance**, you are very near to obtaining or achieving it: *Both sides believe they are within striking distance* **of** *a lasting peace agreement.* ○ *His victory in the Brazilian Grand Prix puts him within striking distance* **of** *the world championship.*

strike /straɪk/ *n* [C] • *A lightning conductor is a means of protecting buildings and tall structures from* **lightning** *strikes.* • *(esp. Am and Aus) What is needed is a multinational paramilitary strike* **force** *to combat the drug traffickers.* • A strike is often a sudden brief military attack, particularly one by aircraft or MISSILES: *The United Nations has authorised the use of* **air** *strikes if the siege has not been lifted by the end of the month.* ○ *The violence is unlikely to stop without* **military** *strikes* **against** *terrorist bases.* ○ *The oil refineries are the most likely targets of any* **missile** *strike.* ○ *Would you support a* **nuclear** *strike to bring an end to a war?* ○ *We have no intention of* **launching** *a* **pre-emptive** *strike, but we will retaliate if provoked.* ○ *(fig.) Their takeover of the company is a* **pre-emptive** *strike to avoid being taken over themselves.* ○ **Surgical** (= Extremely accurate) *strikes have kept civilian casualties to a minimum.* ○ *If a* **retaliatory** *strike is launched, helicopters and ground troops will be at the forefront.*

strik·er /£ˈstraɪ·kəʳ, $-kɚ/ *n* [C] • A striker is a player in a game such as football whose main purpose is to try to score goals rather than to prevent the opposing team from scoring: *The club's new manager is a former England striker.* ○ *The 24-year-old striker* **scored 35 goals** *for Hartlepool last season.* ○ *Millwall have* **signed** *striker Mark Falco from Queen's Park Rangers for £175 000.*

strike *(obj)* [CAUSE SUFFERING] /straɪk/ *v past* **struck** /strʌk/, *past part esp. Am* **stricken** /ˈstrɪk·ᵊn/ to cause (a person or place) to suffer severely from the effects of something very unpleasant that happens suddenly • *You never know when serious illness will strike you abroad, so it's a good idea to take out travel insurance.* [T] • *I've got a life insurance policy that will look after my family if* **disaster** *strikes.* [I] • *The disease has stricken the whole community, sometimes wiping out whole families.* [T] • *Many seismologists expect that a large* **earthquake** *will strike the east coast before the end of the decade.* [T]

strick·en /ˈstrɪk·ᵊn/ *adj* • Someone or something that is stricken is suffering severely from the effects of something

All the oil All the oil from the stricken tanker has now leaked into the sea. ○ *My country has been stricken* **by** *war for the past five years.* ○ *At the age of seven, he was stricken* **with** *polio and paralysed in his right leg.* ○ *He has been stricken with* **grief** *since the death of his wife.* ○ *The civil war has prevented humanitarian aid reaching the millions of people in the* **drought**-*stricken north of the country.* ○ *We ought to be increasing emergency aid for* **famine**-*stricken countries, not reducing it.* ○ *Five people were trampled to death as the* **panic**-*stricken crowd tried to escape the flames.* ○ *He lives in one of the most* **poverty**-*stricken areas of the country.*

strike [STOP WORK] /straɪk/ *v* [I] *past* **struck** /strʌk/ to refuse to continue working because of an argument with an employer about working conditions, pay levels or job losses • *Democratisation has brought workers* **the right to** *strike and join a trade union.* • *6500 striking steel* **workers** *have voted to return to work after they were offered a 15% pay increase.* • *We're striking* **for** *a reduction in the working week and an improvement in safety standards.*

strike /straɪk/ *n* [C] • *After the hardship caused by last year's long and bitter strike, few people are in the mood for further industrial action.* • *The result of the strike* **ballot** *will not be known until tomorrow morning.* • *Most of the workers have ignored their union's* **call** *for strike* **action**. • *He* **called** *the strike to protest against what he described as the murder of democracy.* • *Some miners are* **calling for** *a nationwide strike in support of their sacked colleagues.* • *The strike* **disrupted** *holiday travel and freight traffic throughout France.* • *They have voted to stage* **lightning** (= sudden and brief) *strikes in pursuit of their demands.* • *Travelling has become a nightmare because of frequent half-day strikes which have* **paralysed** *public transport.* • *We've voted to* **stage** *a series of* **one-day** *strikes to express our opposition to the job losses.* • *A* **wave of** *strikes has swept across the country over the past few months.* • *(esp. Am) The petroleum industry has been afflicted by a series of* **wildcat** *strikes recently.* • When workers are **(out) on strike**, they are taking part in a strike: *What will we do for money when you're out on strike?* ○ *All 2500 employees have* **gone** *on strike* (= started to strike) *in protest at the decision to close the factory.* ○ *(Am) They've been on strike* **against** *the company for three weeks.* • **Strike pay** is money that is paid to people involved in a strike by their union from a sum of money saved specially for this purpose: *The union cannot afford to provide strike pay indefinitely.*

strike·bound /ˈstraɪk·baʊnd/ *adj* [not gradable] • If a place is **strikebound**, it is closed or unable to operate because the people employed there are refusing to work: *The factory has been strikebound for two months because of a pay dispute.*

strike·break·er /£ˈstraɪkˌbreɪ·kəʳ, $-kɚ/ *n* [C] • A strikebreaker is someone who continues working during a strike or who takes the job of a worker who is involved in a strike: *Many of the strikebreakers have been subjected to verbal and physical attacks.*

strike·break·ing /ˈstraɪkˌbreɪ·kɪŋ/ *n* [U] • *The firm hopes that strikebreaking will enable it to maintain production.*

strik·er /£ˈstraɪ·kəʳ, $-kɚ/ *n* [C] • A striker is someone who is involved in a strike: *The company recently* **sacked** *320 strikers who were fighting compulsory redundancy.*

strike *obj* [REMOVE] /straɪk/ *v* [T always + adv/prep] *past* **struck** /strʌk/, *past part Am also* **stricken** /ˈstrɪk·ᵊn/ *fml* to remove (something) officially from a document • *I would be grateful if you would strike my name* **from** *your mailing list immediately.* • *Several unreliable dealers have been struck* **off** *our list of authorised suppliers.* • *The investigation has revealed that some patients are simply being struck* **off** *long waiting lists.* • *(Am) The courts* **struck down** *local segregation laws* (= ruled they were illegal and should not be obeyed) *because they violated the federal constitution.* • *(Br and Aus)* If someone with a responsible job such as a doctor or lawyer is **struck off**, they are prevented from continuing to do their job because they have done something seriously wrong: *A dentist from Essex has been struck off* **the register** *for failing to provide adequate sterilization facilities.* ○ *A solicitor who insulted two officials from the Law Society has been struck off for abusive behaviour.* • If you **strike out** or **through** text in a document, you draw a line through it to show that it does not relate to you: *Please strike out whichever option does not apply to you.*

strike *obj* [DISCOVER] /straɪk/ *v* [T] *past* **struck** /strʌk/ to discover (oil, gas or gold) underground • *The first person to strike* **oil** *in the US was Edwin Laurentine Drake, who discovered it in Pennsylvania in 1859.* • *They have to invest a lot of money in drilling but they can make huge profits if they strike* **oil** *or* **gas**. • *We're rich! We've struck* **gold**! • *(fig.) A few lucky people have struck* **gold** (= made large profits) *by investing in this company.* • *(fig.) She is the favourite to strike* **gold** (= win a gold MEDAL) *in the 400 metres hurdles.* • If you **strike it lucky**/*(Br and Aus also)* **strike lucky**, you suddenly have a lot of unexpected luck: *What would you do if you struck it lucky in the national lottery?* • If you **strike it rich**, you become rich suddenly and unexpectedly: *His father struck it rich in the diamond business, but then he gambled away his millions in the casinos.* • If you **strike on** or **upon** something, you discover it or think of it: *She struck on the idea for her novel while she was travelling in Russia.*

strike /straɪk/ *n* [C] • *The Middle East's petro-chemical industry began in 1908 with an* **oil** *strike in Persia.* • *The population and settlement of Colorado expanded after the* **gold** *strike of 1858.*

strike *obj* [AGREE] /straɪk/ *v* [T] *past* **struck** /strʌk/ to reach or make (an agreement) • *Do you think the government should try to strike a* **deal** *with the terrorists?* • *He struck a* **bargain** *with his mother which meant that she would pay for his training on the condition that he passed all his exams.* • If you **strike a balance** between two things, you accept parts of both things in order to satisfy some of the demands of both sides in an argument, rather than all the demands of just one side: *How can we strike a balance* **between** *economic growth and environmental protection?* ○ *It's a question of striking the* **right** *balance between quality and productivity.* ○ *We need to strike a* **fair** *balance* **between** *the rights of the individual and the safety of the public.* • If something **strikes a chord**, it causes people to approve of or agree with it: *The party's policy on childcare facilities has struck a* **responsive** *chord* **with** *women voters.* ○ *Her speech struck a* **sympathetic** *chord* **among** *business leaders who are frustrated by over-regulation.*

strike *obj* [CAUSE A FEELING] /straɪk/ *v* [T] *past* **struck** /strʌk/, *past part Am also* **stricken** /ˈstrɪk·ᵊn/ to cause (someone) to have a feeling or idea about something • *My report may strike some people* **as** *pessimistic, but at least it's realistic about the problems we face.* • *I was immediately struck* **by** *the similarities between the two murders.* • *We were both struck* **by how** *unaffected she was by her husband's death.* • *So how does my proposition strike you* (= What do you think of it)? • *From what you've said, it strikes me* **(that)** *you'd be better off working for someone else.* [+ obj + *(that)* clause] • *Almost everything he said struck me as* **absurd**. • *We'd only just met, but I was already struck quite* **forcibly** *by the fact that she was extremely intelligent.* • *Doesn't it strike you as rather* **odd** *that he never talks about his family?* • If something **strikes a chord**, it causes people to remember something else because it is similar to it. • If you **strike a note**, you express an idea about something: *I find it really difficult to strike the right note when I'm writing job applications.* ○ *The president struck a sombre note in his New Year address to the country.* ○ *At the end of her speech, she struck a note* **of** *warning about the risks involved in the project.* ○ *The latest statistics strike an* **upbeat** *note about the economy.*

strik·ing /ˈstraɪ·kɪŋ/ *adj* • A person or thing that is striking attracts a lot of attention by being very unusual or easily noticed: *Perhaps the most striking* **aspect** *of this computer is that it is so easy to use.* ○ *She* **bears** *a striking* **resemblance** *to her mother.* ○ *There's a striking* **contrast** *between what he does and what he says he does.* ○ *There are striking* **differences** *between the north and south of the country.* ○ *The most striking* **example** *of the dangers of nationalism is the violence that engulfed the former Yugoslavia.* ○ *The cathedral is the most striking* **feature** *of the city.* ○ *There are striking* **parallels** *between the experiences of the two women.* ○ *There are striking* **similarities** *between the two cases.* ○ *Their production of Macbeth was the most* **visually** *striking performance I've ever seen.* • A person who is striking is unusually attractive: *He's quite good-looking, but he's not as striking as his brother.*

strik·ing·ly /ˈstraɪ·kɪŋ·li/ *adv* • *Japanese has a strikingly* **different** *structure and writing system from any European language.* • *They gave a strikingly* **original** *performance of the play.* • *The problems we face are strikingly* **similar**. • *Her husband is strikingly* **handsome**, *isn't he?*

strike *obj* [CAUSE TO THINK] /straɪk/ *v* [T not *be striking*] *past* **struck** /strʌk/ to cause (someone) to think about something suddenly • *She was suddenly struck by the thought that she'd left her book on the train.* • *It's just struck me* **that** *I still owe you for the concert tickets.* [+ *that* clause]

strike *obj* [MOVE BODY] /straɪk/ *v* [T] *past* **struck** /strʌk/ to move your body into (a position) • *She struck the agitated* **pose** *of her boss negotiating a deal on the telephone.* • *I thought she'd become an actress because she was always striking* **poses** *in the classroom and imitating the teachers.* • *(fig.) Until now they have struck a* **pose** *of resistance to* (= they have been against) *government interference.* • If people or things **strike attitudes**, they make very noticeable what they want others to think they believe or support: *Some politicians prefer to strike attitudes on the world stage rather than deal with problems in their own countries.* • If you **strike out** somewhere, you start to go on a difficult journey: *It was just starting to rain as we struck out across the field.* • To **strike out** also means to start doing something new, independently of other people: *After working for her father for ten years, she felt it was time to strike out* **on her own**.

strike *obj* [MAKE COINS] /straɪk/ *v* [T] *past* **struck** /strʌk/ to make (a metal disc-shaped object such as a coin) with a machine that quickly presses a picture into a piece of metal • *When was the first pound* **coin** *struck?* • *A special medal has been struck to celebrate the end of the war.*

strike [BASEBALL] /straɪk/ *n* [C] a ball that has been thrown by the PITCHER and not been hit successfully when it should have been • *A batter is out after three strikes.* • *Baylor has a count of three balls and two strikes* **on** *him.* • *(fig.) If you're poor and you've been to prison, you've got two strikes* (= important disadvantages) **against** *you.* • *(fig.) The president suggested that from now on criminals with three strikes* (= occasions when they have been found guilty of crimes) *would be jailed for life.*

strike out *(obj)*, **strike** *(obj)* **out** *v adv* • If you strike out in baseball, you fail three times to hit the ball successfully and you therefore lose one of your team's chances to score: *Winfield struck out with the bases loaded in the sixth inning.* [I] ○ *The pitcher struck out both batters* (= made them both fail three times to hit the ball) *in the ninth inning and saved the game.* [M] • *(fig. Am) I really struck out* (= failed to succeed) *with her – she wouldn't even kiss me goodnight.* [I]

strike·out /ˈstraɪk·aʊt/ *n* [C] • A strikeout is the act of failing three times to hit the ball, or of making a hitter do this: *He averaged 14 strikeouts per game last season, which was the best rate for any starting pitcher in the league.*

strike up *(obj)* [START PLAYING] *v adv* to start to play or sing • *A lot of the seats were still empty when the orchestra struck up.* [I] • *There was a short round of applause when he finished his speech, then a regimental band struck up the national anthem.* [T]

strike up *obj* [CREATE] *v prep* [T] to create or establish (a relationship or conversation) with someone • *He doesn't find it easy to strike up a* **conversation** *with a complete stranger.* • *He gets really jealous if his girlfriend strikes up a* **friendship** *with another man.* • *We struck up a good* **rapport** *with each other as soon as we met.* • *She struck up a* **relationship** *with an artist soon after she arrived in Paris.*

strim·mer *Br trademark* /£ˈstrɪm·əʳ, $-ɚ/, **edge trim·mer**, *Am trademark* **weed whack·er** /£ˈwiːdˌwæk·əʳ, $-ɚ/ *n* [C] an electric tool that is held in the hand and is used for cutting grass in places that are difficult to reach with a larger machine • *I'll use the strimmer on the grass around the trees while you're mowing the lawn.* • [PIC] **Garden**

strine /straɪn/ *n* [U] *Aus infml* Australian English, esp. the Australian accent

string [CORD] /strɪŋ/ *n* (a piece of) strong thin cord which is made by twisting very thin fibres together and which is used for fastening and tying things • *The parcel had been damaged in the mail and was held together with string.* [U] • *Do you think it'll be okay to hang this picture on the wall with* **a piece of** *string?* [U] • *For my birthday I want a puppet with strings that you* **pull** *to move its arms and legs.* [C] • *(Br) A string* **vest** *keeps you warm by trapping air between your skin and your clothes.* • If there are **strings attached** to something such as an agreement, there are special demands or limitations involved: *Most of these so-called special offers come with strings attached.* ○ *The bank's agreed to lend me £1000 with* **no** *strings attached.* • A **string bag** is a shopping bag which is made of pieces of string tied together and has large spaces between each piece: *I don't know how he manages to get all his shopping into one string bag.* • **String bean** is *Am and Aus for* **runner bean**. See at RUNNER [STEM]. • *(specialized)* **String theory** is a theory in physics about **elementary particles** in which the most basic items (strings) are considered to be extremely small lines or circles rather than points. • [PIC] **Bags**

string up *obj*, **string** *obj* **up** *v adv* [M] • If you string up something that is long and thin, you fasten the ends of it to two points that are high up, allowing the rest of it to hang freely: *I think we should string up a banner in the garden to welcome him home.* • *(infml)* When a person strings someone up, they kill them by hanging them by the neck from a rope, usually as a punishment for a crime: *Well, I reckon they're too soft on mass murderers – they ought to string them up instead of putting them in prison.* ○ *(fig.) He ought to be strung up* (= punished) *for what he said about his mother.* • Compare STRUNG UP.

string·y /ˈstrɪŋ·i/ *adj* **-ier**, **-iest** • Something that is stringy has a characteristic that is similar to string: *These beans are rather stringy* (= hard and difficult to chew). ○ *His body is very stringy* (= so thin that his muscles can be seen). • *(Aus)* A **stringy-bark** is any of various types of EUCALYPTUS tree that have a hard fibrous outer covering.

string [MUSIC] /strɪŋ/ *n* [C] a thin wire or cord which is stretched across a musical instrument and is used to produce a range of notes which depend on its thickness, length and tightness • *A violin has four strings.* • **Guitar** *strings are made from steel or nylon, but they used to be made from the dried intestines of animals such as sheep.* • *Pizzicato is the technique of* **plucking** *the strings of a musical instrument, such as a violin or cello, with your fingers.* • *You can* **pluck** *the strings on a guitar with your fingers or a plectrum.* • *Is a twelve-string guitar harder to play than a six-string one?* • The strings or string **section** in an ORCHESTRA are a group of instruments which produce sound with strings: *Violins and cellos are part of the strings, but guitars and pianos are not.* ○ *He's one of the strings* (= players of instruments with strings) *in the school orchestra.* ○ *I play the violin in a nine-***piece** (= nine musicians) *string* **orchestra**. ○ *Is it easy for string* **players** *to learn to play wind instruments?* • A **string instrument** is a **stringed instrument.** • A **string quartet** is a group of four instruments with strings that play together, or a piece of music written for such a group: *A string quartet consists of two violins, a viola and a cello.* ○ *Joseph Haydn's works include 104 symphonies and 84 string quartets.* • If you have **another string/a second string/two strings to** your **bow**, you have an additional interest or skill which you can use if your main one cannot be used: *I enjoy my work, but I'd like to have another string to my bow in case I lose my job.* • [PIC] **Musical instruments**

string *obj* /strɪŋ/ *v* [T] *past* **strung** /strʌŋ/ • *First you need to learn how to string* (= put strings on) *and tune your guitar.*

stringed /strɪŋd/ *adj* [before n] • A **stringed instrument** (also **string instrument**) is a musical instrument with strings which produce sound by moving very quickly from side to side as a result of being pulled, hit or rubbed: *Guitars, pianos and cellos are different types of stringed instrument.*

string [SPORT] /strɪŋ/ *n* [C] one of the thin plastic cords which are stretched between the sides of the frame of a RACKET (= an object used for hitting the ball in some sports) • *She hit the ball so hard that she broke a couple of strings.*

string *obj* /strɪŋ/ *v* [T] *past* **strung** • *You ought to have your racket re-strung* (= have new strings put on it) *before the competition.*

string [SET] /strɪŋ/ *n* [C] a set of objects joined together in a row on a single cord or thread • *In the seat opposite, a boy sat playing with a string of wooden* **beads**. • *She was wearing a linen suit and a string of* **pearls**.

string *obj* /strɪŋ/ *v* [T] *past* **strung** /strʌŋ/ • *Would you help me string these beads* (= put them on a string)*?* • *(fig.) People tend to be very impressed if you can string* **together** (= say) *a couple of sentences in Japanese.*

string out *obj*, **string** *obj* **out** *v adv* [M] • If a set of things are strung out, they are arranged in a long line or row with spaces between each of them: *Most of Canada's population is strung out along its 5525-mile border with the United States.* ○ *The geese were strung out in a long line along the river bank.* • If you string out an activity, you make it last longer than necessary: *We strung out the tennis match so that we could use the court all afternoon.*

string SERIES /strɪŋ/ *n* [C] a series of related things or events • *Business confidence has been undermined by the recent string* **of** *political* **scandals.** • *Her new novel is just the latest in a string of* **successes.** • *He had a string of top-twenty* **hits** *during the eighties.* • *Her life has been one long string of* **disappointments.**

string COMPUTING /strɪŋ/ *n* [C] *specialized* a usually short piece of text consisting of letters, numbers or symbols which is used in computer processes such as searching through large amounts of information • *If you type in the* **search** *string 'ing', the computer will find all the words containing 'ing', such as 'thing', 'ring' and 'laughing'.*

string a·long *obj*, **string** *obj* **a·long** *v adv* [M] to deceive (someone) by seeming to agree with them or do what they want and delaying the time when they discover your true intentions • *She's been promising to pay back the money for six months, but I reckon she's just stringing me along.* • *We're not prepared to bargain with them, and we won't be strung along by them.*

strin·gent SEVERE /ˈstrɪn·dʒənt/ *adj* having a very severe effect, or being extremely limiting • *Some of the* **conditions** *in the contract are too stringent.* • *The government is to* **impose** *stringent* **restrictions** *on the number of immigrants to be allowed into the country.* • *The most stringent* **laws** *in the world are useless unless there is the will to enforce them.* • *Security will be improved with the introduction of more stringent* **measures** *such as identity cards.* • *Stringent safety* **regulations** *were introduced after the accident.* • *Our training* **requirements** *are the most stringent in the industry.* • *Car manufacturers argue that the more stringent pollution* **standards** *will increase prices.* • *The preparation of food in restaurants and cafés is* **subject to** *stringent safety* **rules.**

strin·gent·ly /ˈstrɪn·dʒənt·li/ *adv* • *Fire regulations are stringently enforced in all our factories.* • *Parliament should give the courts extra powers to deal stringently with those who commit these terrible offences.*

strin·gen·cy /ˈstrɪn·dʒᵊnt·si/ *n* [U] • *The stringency of the safety regulations threatens to put many manufacturers out of business.*

strin·gent LIMITING MONEY /ˈstrɪn·dʒənt/ *adj* [not gradable] *specialized* involving a lack of money that is available for borrowing which results from firm controls on the amount of money in an economy • *Already low living standards have been worsened by stringent economic reforms.*

strin·gen·cy /ˈstrɪn·dʒᵊnt·si/ *n* [U] *specialized* • *Greater* **financial** *stringency is needed to eradicate inflation from the economy.*

strip *obj* REMOVE COVER /strɪp/ *v* [T] **-pp-** to remove, pull or tear (the covering or outer layer) from something • *Because of the pollution, the trees are almost completely stripped* **of** *bark.* • *The paintwork was so bad that we decided to strip* **off** *all the paint and start again.* • *She asked us to strip the sheets* **off** *the bed and bring them downstairs when we leave.* • *During the summer months the sheep strip the mountains* **bare.** [+ obj + adj] • *Their house is full of stripped* **pine** *furniture.* • *(fig.) Since the military coup, human rights have been stripped* **away** (= gradually reduced) *to the absolute minimum.* • If you **strip** someone or something **of** a title, you remove it from them: *He was fined £3 million and stripped* **of** *his knighthood after he was convicted of stealing from the company.* ○ *When the athlete was found to have taken drugs before the race, she was stripped of her gold medal.*

strip·per /£ˈstrɪp·əʳ, $-ɚ/ *n* • A stripper is a liquid chemical or an electric tool that is used for removing things such as paint: *I'll need another can of* **paint** *stripper to finish that door.* [U] ○ *My new* **wallpaper** *stripper works by producing a lot of steam at high pressure.* [C]

strip *(obj)* REMOVE CLOTHING /strɪp/ *v* **-pp-** to remove your clothing, or to remove all the clothing of (someone else) • *Suddenly he (Br and Aus) stripped* **off**/*(Am and Aus) stripped* (= removed all his clothes) *and ran into the sea.* [I] • *It was so hot that we stripped* **off** *our shirts.* [T] • *After he was interrogated, he was stripped* **naked** *and beaten with an electric cable.* [T + obj + adj] • *I thought he was working hard in the garden, but I found him stripped* **to the waist** (= with no clothes on the top part of his body), *lying in the middle of the lawn.* • If you **strip (down) to** some clothing, you remove everything except for that clothing: *I had to strip down to my underwear for my medical examination.* • A **strip-search** is the removal of the clothes of a prisoner or someone thought to have committed a crime by a police officer or government official in order to find any illegal items, such as drugs, hidden in their clothing or on their body: *The police said she was found to be in possession of a substantial quantity of heroin during a strip-search.* ○ *We were stopped by customs officers at the airport and* **strip-searched** *for no apparent reason.*

strip /strɪp/ *n* [C] • A strip is an entertainment in which the performer removes all his or her clothing: *When his song came on the jukebox, he jumped up on the table and started to do a strip.* • A **strip club** or **strip joint** is a bar where the main entertainment is performers removing their clothes while dancing to music: *The city is notorious for its red light district and strip clubs.* ○ *She worked in a strip joint before she became a model.* • **Strip poker** is a card game in which players remove an item of clothing each time they lose.

strip·per /£ˈstrɪp·əʳ, $-ɚ/ *n* [C] • A stripper is someone whose job is removing all their clothing to entertain other people: *Our boss was really cross when we organised a male stripper for her 50th birthday party.*

strip·per·gram, **strip·pa·gram** /£ˈstrɪp·ə·græm, $ˈ-ɚ-/ *n* [C] • A strippergram is a surprise visit on a special occasion from a person who is paid to remove most or all of their clothes before giving someone a message from their friends or relatives: *Why don't we organize a strippergram for Pat's retirement party?*

strip *obj* REMOVE PARTS /strɪp/ *v* [T] **-pp-** to remove parts of (a machine, vehicle or engine) in order to clean or repair it • *I've decided to strip* **down** *my motorbike and rebuild it.* • Something that is **stripped-down** has been reduced to its most simple form: *I think the stripped-down version of your proposal has more chance of being accepted.* • *(Am and Aus)* If you strip a **car**, you remove its parts in order to sell them: *Hugh never thought his car was worth stealing, but someone took it and stripped it.*

strip PIECE /strɪp/ *n* [C] a long flat narrow piece • *He didn't have a bandage, so he ripped up his shirt into* **thin** *strips.* • *We lost thousands of soldiers in the war and all we got was this* **narrow** *strip* **of** *land in return.* • *To prolong the working life of your credit card, keep the* **magnetic** *strip protected from scratches, heat, damp or other damage.* • *About 30 million people live along the Californian* **coastal** *strip.* • **Strip cartoon** is *Br for* **comic strip**. See at COMIC MAGAZINE. • **Strip lighting** is a type of electric lighting that uses long glass tubes, often with a protective plastic cover: *Strip lighting is very effective in offices, but it's too bright for the home.* • *(Am)* **Strip mining** is a method of removing substances such as coal from the ground, which involves removing the top layer of earth instead of digging deep holes underground. • PIC› **Lights**

strip CLOTHING /strɪp/ *n* [C] *Br and Aus* clothing worn by a football team which has the team's colours on it • *The team will be wearing its new strip at next Saturday's match.*

stripe COLOURED STRIP /straɪp/ *n* [C] a strip on the surface of something which is a different colour from the surrounding surface • *The zebra is a wild African horse with black and white stripes.* • *Do you think he'd prefer a tie with spots or stripes?* • *Governments* **of every stripe** (= of all political opinions) *have a bad habit of interfering in state broadcasting.* • PIC› **Patterns**

strip·y, **stripe·y** /ˈstraɪ·pi/ *adj* **stripier**, **stripiest** • If something is stripy it has a lot of stripes on it: *He always wears stripy shirts with white collars.*

striped /straɪpt/ *adj* [not gradable] • Something that is striped has stripes on it: *Do you prefer plain or striped* **shirts?** ○ *He looked ravishing in his green and white striped* **pyjamas.**

stripe MATERIAL /straɪp/, *Am also* **bars** *n* [C] a strip of material that is sewn onto the arm of a military uniform to show the rank of the person wearing it • *By the age of 25 he'd already got his third stripe and become a sergeant.* • PIC› **Bar**

strip·tease /ˈstrɪp·tiːz, ˌ-ˈ-/ *n* (a performance of) the activity in which a performer, usually a woman, takes off their clothes in a way which is sexually exciting to the people who are watching • *I'm not the sort of person who'd* **do** *a striptease.* [C] • *Striptease, whether you like it or not, is big business in this country.* [U] • *At night the bars, restaurants and striptease* **clubs** *are empty.*

strive /straɪv/ *v* [I] *past simple* **strove** /£strəʊv, $stroʊv/ or **strived**, *past part* **striven** /ˈstrɪv·ᵊn/ or **strived** to try very hard to do something or make something happen, esp. for a long time or against difficulties • *All of us will continue striving* **to** *meet the very highest standards.* [+ to infinitive] • *Mr Roh has kindled expectations that he must now strive* **to** *live up to.* [+ to infinitive] • *In her writing she strove* **for** *a balance between innovation and familiar prose forms.* • *Many researchers have striven* **for** *a greater understanding of the processes which occur inside stars.*

strobe light, *infml* **strobe** /£strəʊb, $stroʊb/ *n* [C] a light which quickly flashes on and off • *The strobes and loud music in the club made her want to dance.*

strode /£strəʊd, $stroʊd/ *past simple of* STRIDE WALK

stroke *obj* TOUCH /£strəʊk, $stroʊk/ *v* [T] to move a hand, another part of the body or an object gently over (something), usually repeatedly and for pleasure • *Stroke the dog if you like, it won't bite.* • *She lovingly stroked Chris's face with the tips of her fingers.*

stroke /£strəʊk, $stroʊk/ *n* [C] • *Don't be frightened, just give the horse a stroke.*

stroke ILLNESS /£strəʊk, $stroʊk/ *n* [C] a sudden change in the blood supply to a part of the brain, which can cause a loss of the ability to move particular parts of the body • *She* **suffered/had** *a stroke which left her unable to speak.* • See also SUNSTROKE.

stroke MARK /£strəʊk, $stroʊk/ *n* [C] (a line or mark made by) a movement of a pen or pencil when writing or a brush when painting • *a brush stroke* • *With a few* **bold** *strokes, she signed her name.* • If something is done with **the stroke of a pen**, it is done quickly and easily by someone, as if they were writing their name on a piece of paper: *Politicians know they cannot create a lawful society simply* **at** *the stroke of a pen.*

stroke HIT /£strəʊk, $stroʊk/ *n* [C] an act of hitting a ball when playing a sport, or *(slightly dated)* of hitting someone with a weapon • *She returned the volley with a powerful stroke of her racket to win the game.* • *(slightly dated) The punishment was twenty strokes of the lash.*

stroke *obj* /£strəʊk, $stroʊk/ *v* [T] • *The batsman stroked the ball effortlessly to the boundary.*

stroke SWIMMING ACTION /£strəʊk, $stroʊk/ *n* [C] (a particular movement which is usually repeated in) a method of swimming • *With powerful strokes she set out across the lake.* • *What's your best stroke when you're swimming?* • See also BACKSTROKE; BREASTSTROKE; SIDESTROKE.

stroke PIECE /£strəʊk, $stroʊk/ *n* [C] a piece or act of something • *By a stroke* **of luck**, *someone else was walking along the path and heard my shouts.* • *Without doubt, it was a stroke* **of genius** *to try the experiment in a vacuum.*

stroke WORK /£strəʊk, $stroʊk/ *n* [U usually in negatives] *infml* a small amount (of work) • *She's been gossiping and hasn't* **done a** *stroke* **(of work)** *all morning.*

stroke ACTION /£strəʊk, $stroʊk/ *n* [C] a quick forceful action • *Ending negotiations was seen as a* **bold** *stroke by many commentators.* • *By computerizing we could,* **at a (single)/in one** *stroke, improve efficiency and reduce costs.*

stroke CLOCK SOUND /£strəʊk, $stroʊk/ *n* [C] one of the sounds which some clocks make at particular times, esp. by ringing a bell once for each number of the hour • *How many strokes did you count?* • *Fireworks started* **at/on the** *stroke* **of** *ten* (= exactly at 10 o'clock).

stroke SLOPING LINE /£strəʊk, $stroʊk/ *n* [C] *Br* (esp. used in spoken English) an OBLIQUE DIAGONAL • *Please complete form D7/8 (read as 'D seven stroke eight').* • *"Every child is responsible for his stroke* (= or) *her own sports equipment."* • LP **Slash**

stroll /£strəʊl, $stroʊl/ *v* [I] to walk in a slow relaxed manner, esp. for pleasure • *We could stroll into town if you like.*

stroll /£strəʊl, $stroʊl/ *n* [C] • *The whole family was enjoying a* **leisurely** *stroll in the sunshine.*

strol·ler /£'strəʊ·ləʳ, $'stroʊ·lɚ/ *n* [C] • *On the promenade strollers* (= people who stroll) *were taking the evening air.* • Stroller is also *esp. Am and Aus* for PUSHCHAIR. • PIC **Chair**

strong NOT WEAK /£strɒŋ, $strɑːŋ/ *adj* **-er, -est** powerful; having great force or control and able to use it; very able • *She must be very strong to carry such a weight on her back.* • *After the accident he had to get around in a wheelchair, which made his arms and the top part of his body much stronger.* • *It is surely the duty of the stronger members in a society to help those who are weak.* • *Melanie said in the strongest of terms* (= very forcefully) *she wasn't interested in his suggestion.* • *It would be true to say that my grandmother had a strong* **influence/effect** *on my early childhood.* • *We will need strong policies if our economic problems are to be solved.* • *The stronger economies of the world have profound effects on many of the others.* • *Strong winds are forecast in the area for the next few days.* • *Danger! Strong currents – do not swim here!* • *It's surprising what strong memories a photograph can produce.* • *Our managing director has made the marketing department stronger over the past five years.* • *What a strong likeness there is between the brothers.* • *They had such strong accents – it was difficult to understand them.* • *Suddenly a very strong light shone straight in her eyes.* • *He needs strong lenses in his glasses because his eyesight is so bad.* • *Strong trading links exist between us and many South American countries.* • *Without a doubt, she's the strongest* (= most able) *candidate we've interviewed for the post.* • *As a guitarist, he's strong* **on** (= good at) *technique but perhaps lacks feeling in some pieces.* • *There's a really strong smell of bleach in the corridor.* • *I don't like coffee/tea if it's too strong* (= has a too powerful flavour). • *We can give you stronger* (= more effective) *pain-killing drugs if these aren't strong enough.* • *Not everybody likes a room to be decorated in strong* (= bright) *colours.* • *(disapproving)* If a method is **strong-arm**, it uses force and threats to make people do what is demanded: *The curfew is seen as an unnecessary strong-arm* **tactic/method** *imposed to subdue the local population.* • **Strong language** is speech which states ideas forcefully and might contain swearing. • A *(esp. Br and Aus)* **strong point**/*(esp. Am and Aus)* **strong suit** is a particular skill or ability which a person has: *You could safely say that tact is* **not** *her strong point, judging by the way she behaved.* • See also STRENGTH EFFORT.

strong /£strɒŋ, $strɑːŋ/ *adv* **-er, -est** *infml* • If someone **comes on strong**, either they behave in a way which makes it clear they are sexually interested in a particular person, or they behave towards another person in a way which many people think is too severe: *He's always coming on strong to me – I wish he'd stop.* ○ *You came on too strong then – she didn't do it deliberately.* • Something which is **(still) going strong** has existed for a long period and is still successful or working well: *After two hundred years, the town's theatre is still going strong and is as popular as it ever was.* ○ *His father is still going strong* (= alive and well) *at 94.*

strong·ly /£'strɒŋ·li, $'strɑːŋ-/ *adv* • *They strongly believe their children should make choices for themselves.* • *The captain was* **criticized** *strongly for her part in the team's defeat.* • *Many locals are strongly* **opposed** *to the development.* • LP **Very, completely**

strong DIFFICULT TO BREAK /£strɒŋ, $strɑːŋ/ *adj* **-er, -est** difficult to break, destroy or make ill • *The window is made from very strong glass – it won't shatter.* • *Is the container strong enough to survive an impact with a train?* • *He's never been very strong, and I'm afraid all the excitement was too much for him.* • *I've never seen anyone with such a strong will to live – he simply refused to die.* • *You need* **strong nerves/a strong stomach** (= the ability to not be upset by unpleasant things) *to work in the accident department.* • A **strong-box** is a specially made lockable box which is very difficult to break. Valuable items are put in it to keep them safe. • See also STRENGTH EFFORT.

strong·ly /£'strɒŋ·li, $'strɑːŋ-/ *adv* • *Equipment will have to be strongly made to endure weather conditions on the ice cap.*

strong DETERMINED /£strɒŋ, $strɑːŋ/ *adj* **-er, -est** difficult to argue with; firm and determined • *There are strong* **arguments** *to support cancelling the whole project.* • *She has strong* **opinions** *about religion.* • *He has a strong* **personality**, *but don't let him bully you.* • *Most of the group have strong* **views** *on the subject of divorce.* • If someone is **strong-minded**, they are determined and unwilling to change their opinions and beliefs: *You'll have to be strong-minded if you're going to push the changes through.* • A person who is **strong-willed** is determined to behave in a particular way although there might be good reasons for them not doing so: *She's very strong-willed and if she's decided to leave school, nothing will stop her.*

strong LIKELY /£strɒŋ, $strɑːŋ/ *adj* **-er, -est** having a large probability of the stated type • *There's a strong* **possibility/likelihood** *of finding the child within the next few hours.* • *The treatment's* **chances** *of success are stronger* (= better) *if you can start it as soon as the disease has been diagnosed.*

strong IN NUMBER /£strɒŋ, $strɑːŋ/ *adj* [after n; not gradable] having the stated number of esp. people • *Our social club is currently about eighty strong, but it's not as* *popular as it used to be.* • *With a 185 000-strong membership, the union is a force to be reckoned with.* • See also STRENGTH [NUMBER].

strong·hold /£ˈstrɒŋ·həʊld, $ˈstrɑːŋ·hoʊld/ *n* [C] a building or position which is strongly defended, or a place or area where a particular belief or activity is common • *a rebel stronghold* • *They captured the airbase, last stronghold* **of** *the presidential guard.* • *Rural areas have been traditionally thought of as a stronghold* **of** *old-fashioned attitudes.*

strong·man /£ˈstrɒŋ·mæn, $ˈstrɑːŋ-/ *n* [C] *pl* **-men** a person who is very powerful and able to cause change, esp. of a political type, or a man who is employed for his great physical strength • *Haitian strongman Duvalier could feel his power slipping away.* • *If she talks to the police, Joey's strongmen will be paying her a visit.*

strong·room /£ˈstrɒŋ·rʊm, -ruːm, $ˈstrɑːŋ-/ *n* [C] a special room with strong walls and a strong lockable door where valuable items can be kept safe • *the bank's strongroom*

strop /£strɒp, $strɑːp/ *n* [C] *Br and Aus infml* a bad mood, esp. one in which a person will not do what they are asked and is unpleasant to other people • *Don't go in unless you have to – she's* **in a (real)** *strop.* • *And why have you* **got (such) a** *strop* **on** (=why are you in such a bad mood), *what's happened?*

strop·py /£ˈstrɒp·i, $ˈstrɑː·pi/ *adj* **-ier, -iest** *Br and Aus infml* • *It's no use* **getting** *stroppy – I said no and I meant it!*

strop·pi·ly /£ˈstrɒp·ɪ·li, $ˈstrɑː·pɪ-/ *adv Br and Aus infml*

strop·pi·ness /£ˈstrɒp·ɪ·nəs, $ˈstrɑː·pɪ-/ *n* [U] *Br and Aus infml*

strove /£strəʊv, $stroʊv/ *past simple of* STRIVE

struck /strʌk/ *past simple and past participle of* STRIKE

struc·ture [ARRANGEMENT] /£ˈstrʌk·tʃəʳ, $-tʃɚ/ *n* the way in which the parts of a system or object are arranged or organized, or the system arranged in this way • *Anthropologists have not studied the structure* **of** *these ancient societies.* [C] • *This protein's structure is particularly complex.* [C] • *With such an old-fashioned management structure, it's not surprising they're having problems.* [C] • *Modernism as a structure* (=system of ideas) *was very influential, although it had its critics.* [C] • *Some people like the sense of structure that a military lifestyle imposes.* [U]

struc·ture *obj* /£ˈstrʌk·tʃəʳ, $-tʃɚ/ *v* [T] • *We must carefully structure and rehearse each scene.* • *It would be wise to structure each proposal to take into account the individual customer's needs.* • *It was a very well-structured argument.*

struc·tur·al /£ˈstrʌk·tʃəʳr·əl, $-tʃɚ-/ *adj* [not gradable] • *The political reforms have led to major structural changes in the economy.*

struc·tur·al·ly /£ˈstrʌk·tʃəʳr·əl·i, $-tʃɚ-/ *adv* [not gradable]

struc·tur·al·i·sm /£ˈstrʌk·tʃəʳr·əl·ɪ·zəm, $-tʃɚ-/ *n* [U] *specialized* • Structuralism is a system of ideas used in the study of esp. language, literature, art, ANTHROPOLOGY and SOCIOLOGY, which emphasizes the importance of the basic structures and relationships that lie underneath these subjects as we ordinarily see them.

struc·tur·al·ist /£ˈstrʌk·tʃəʳr·əl·ɪst, $-tʃɚ-/ *adj* [not gradable], *n specialized* • *The leading structuralist Lévi-Strauss claimed that there are similar underlying patterns of social life in all human cultures.* [C]

struc·ture [BUILDING] /£ˈstrʌk·tʃəʳ, $-tʃɚ/ *n* [C] something which has been made or built from parts, esp. a large building • *It is proposed that the new office tower will be a steel and glass structure some 43 storeys high.*

struc·tur·al /£ˈstrʌk·tʃəʳr·əl, $-tʃɚ-/ *adj* [not gradable] • *Hundreds of houses in the typhoon's path suffered structural* **damage**.

struc·tur·al·ly /£ˈstrʌk·tʃəʳr·əli, $-tʃɚ-/ *adv* [not gradable] • *Few buildings were left structurally safe after the earthquake.*

stru·del /ˈstruː·dəl/ *n* a type of cake made from fruit which is wrapped in a thin layer of pastry and then baked • *(an) apple strudel* [C/U]

strug·gle [EFFORT] /ˈstrʌg·l̩/ *v* [I] to experience difficulty and make a very great effort in order to do something • *You can clearly see marks on the dog's leg caused while it was struggling* **to** *get free of the wire noose.* [+ *to* infinitive] • *I've been struggling* **to** *understand this article all afternoon.* [+ *to* infinitive] • *Hospital staff struggled* **to** *provide an emergency service throughout last night's power cut.* [+ *to* infinitive] • *Fish struggle* **for** *survival when the water level drops in the lake.* • *He struggled* (=made his way with great effort) *along the rough road holding his son.* • *If Bobbie leaves, we'll have to struggle* **on** (=continue despite difficulties) *until we find a replacement.* • *After the first half United were really struggling* (=in danger of defeat) *at 1-3 down, but in the end they managed a draw.*

strug·gle /ˈstrʌg·l̩/ *n* [C] • *Trying to accept her death was a terrible struggle for him.* • *At last, her struggle* **for** *recognition as a painter was over.* • *The people of this country will continue in their struggle* **for** *independence.* • *She never* **gave up** *the struggle to have her son freed from prison.* [+ *to* infinitive] • *The company is successful now, but at first it was a real struggle* **to** *keep going.* [+ *to* infinitive] • *It's going to be an* **uphill** *struggle* (=very difficult) *to get your ideas accepted.*

strug·gling /ˈstrʌg·lɪŋ/ *adj* • *It's the story of a struggling* (=unsuccessful but trying hard to succeed) *artist who marries a rich woman.*

strug·gle [FIGHT] /ˈstrʌg·l̩/ *v* [I] to fight, esp. with the hands and arms • *They struggled desperately* (**with** *each other) for a few seconds, both of them trying to grab the case.* • *He struggled* **with** *his attacker who then ran off.* • *(fig.) For years she struggled* **with/against** *the establishment to get her theories accepted.*

strug·gle /ˈstrʌg·l̩/ *n* [C] • *After a struggle* (=fight) **with** *the armed robber, the two police officers managed to arrest him.* • *Clearly there will be a* **power** *struggle within the party.* • *This painting is an allegory of the struggle* **between** *good and evil.* • *(fig.) We did finish the race, but not without a struggle* **against** *appalling weather conditions.*

strum *(obj)* /strʌm/ *v* **-mm-** to play (a stringed instrument, such as a guitar) by hitting all of the strings together with a part of the hand rather than playing them singly • *She was sitting on a cushion strumming (a guitar) gently.* [I/T]

strum·pet /ˈstrʌm·pɪt/ *n* [C] *old use* a female PROSTITUTE (=person who has sex for money), or *(humorous or disapproving)* a woman who wears clothes that are intended to be very sexy and who might behave in a sexually immoral way

strung /strʌŋ/ *past simple and past participle of* STRING

strung out *adj* [after v] *slang* experiencing the strong effects of drugs such as COCAINE or HEROIN • *For most of her teenage years, she was strung out* **on** *crack.*

strung up *adj* [after v] *Br infml* nervous or anxious • *She always gets strung up before a performance.* • Compare **string up** at STRING [CORD].

strut [WALK] /strʌt/ *v* [I] **-tt-** to walk in a proud way trying to look important • *The boys strutted around trying to get the attention of a group of girls who were nearby.* • *(infml, esp. humorous)* If someone **struts** their **stuff**, they dance in a confident and usually sexually exciting way, esp. trying to be noticed by other people: *Hey baby, why don't you get out on the floor and strut your stuff?* • *(infml)* To **strut** your **stuff** can also be to show your abilities: *Wimbledon is the opportunity for all the world's best tennis players to strut their stuff.*

strut [ROD] /strʌt/ *n* [C] a strong rod, usually made from metal or wood, which helps to hold something such as a vehicle or building together

struth /struːθ/ *exclamation* STREWTH

strych·nine /ˈstrɪk·niːn/ *n* [U] a very poisonous chemical sometimes given in very small amounts as a medicine

stub [SHORT END] /stʌb/ *n* [C] the short part of something which is left after the main part has been used, such as a cigarette after it has been smoked or a small piece of paper left in a book after a CHEQUE or ticket has been torn out of it • [LP]〉 **Money**

stub·by /ˈstʌb·i/ *adj* **-ier, -iest** • *His fat body was supported by two stubby* (=short and thick) *legs.* • See also STUBBY.

stub out *obj*, **stub** *obj* **out** *v adv* [M] • If a person stubs out a cigarette or CIGAR, they stop it burning by pressing the hot end against something.

stub *obj* [HURT] /stʌb/ *v* [T] **-bb-** to hurt (your toe) by accidentally hitting it against a hard object

stub·ble /ˈstʌb·l̩/ *n* [U] the short hair which grows on a man's face if he has not cut the hair for a few days, or the short stems left after a crop such as wheat has been cut • *With the back of his hand, he rubbed the stubble sprouting on his chin.* • *In the distance, a wisp of smoke rose from burning stubble.*

stub·bly /ˈstʌb·li/ *adj* • *a stubbly chin*

stub·born /£ˈstʌb·ən, $-ɚn/ *adj esp. disapproving* (of a person) determined to do what they want and refusing to do anything else, or (of an object) difficult to move, change or deal with • *I don't know who's more stubborn, you or your grandmother – neither of you will compromise.* • *As a table-tennis player, he was famed for his stubborn resistance and his refusal to accept defeat.* • *Stubborn* **stains** *can be removed using a small amount of detergent.* • *Unemployment is a stubborn problem which won't just disappear overnight.*

stub·born·ly /£ˈstʌb·ən·li, $-ɚn-/ *adv esp. disapproving* • *She stubbornly refused to sign the document.*

stub·born·ness /£ˈstʌb·ən·nəs, $-ɚn-/ *n* [U] *esp. disapproving* • *His stubbornness was well known to all the nurses.*

stub·by /ˈstʌb·i/ *n* [C] *Aus* a small beer bottle, which contains 375 ml • See also **stubby** at STUB [SHORT END].

stuc·co /£ˈstʌk·əʊ, $-oʊ/ *n* [U] a type of PLASTER used for covering walls and ceilings, esp. one which can be formed into decorative patterns

stuc·coed /£ˈstʌk·əʊd, $-oʊd/ *adj* [not gradable]

stuck [STICK] /stʌk/ *past simple and past participle of* STICK

stuck [FIXED] /stʌk/ *adj* fixed in a particular position, place, situation or way of thinking; unable to move, leave or change a situation • *This door seems to be stuck – can you help me push it open?* • *Our lorry got stuck* **in** *the sand and we had to abandon it.* • *Seven of us were stuck* **in** *the lift for over an hour.* • *I'm really stuck* (= cannot go any further with what I'm doing) – *have you got any ideas how to answer these questions?* • *We'd be stuck* (= in a difficult situation) *if your sister hadn't offered to come round and look after the children tonight.* • *I hate being stuck* (= having to be) *behind a desk, I'd rather work outside.* • *We were stuck* **with** (= unable to get away from) *him for the entire train journey!* • *(infml dated)* If someone is **stuck on** another person or an idea, they have a very strong liking for the person or the idea: *Nick's really stuck on Mitzie – he doesn't talk about anything else.* • *(Br and Aus infml)* To **get stuck in(to** something) is to start and usually continue doing it enthusiastically: *We showed them where the crates had to be moved to, and they got stuck in straightaway.* ○ *You really got stuck into your food* (= ate your food quickly) – *you must have been hungry.* • See also STICK [FIX].

stuck–up /ˌstʌkˈʌp, $ˈ--/ *adj infml disapproving* (of a person) too proud and considering yourself to be very important

stud [HORSE] /stʌd/ *n* [C] a group of animals, esp. high quality horses, kept for breeding • *The Derby winner Generous will be* **put to** *stud in Britain at the end of the season.* • *David Grenfell runs a 170-acre stud farm in Co. Wexford, Ireland.*

stud [MAN] /stʌd/ *n* [C] *slang* a man who is thought to have sex a lot and be good at it • *In the film he plays a young stud whose extreme success with women is matched only by his extreme lack of brains.* • *(Am)* A **stud-muffin** is a very sexy attractive young man: *She met her latest stud-muffin in the gym.*

stud [DECORATION] /stʌd/ *n* [C] a small specially shaped piece of metal, many of which are fixed to a surface for decoration, esp. on leather clothing, or a nail with a large round top, many of which are hammered into a surface to make a pattern • *'Suzy' was emblazoned across the back of his motorcycle jacket in chrome-plated studs.*

stud·ded /ˈstʌd·ɪd/ *adj* • *a studded dog-collar* • *Her jacket was studded* **with** *precious stones.* • *(fig.) Behind the house stretched a large park studded* **with** (= decorated with many) *sculptures.*

stud [JEWELLERY] /stʌd/ *n* [C] a small piece of jewellery worn esp. in the ear made from a short thin piece of metal which goes through a hole in the skin and has a small jewel or piece of metal on the outside end • *Quite a lot of young people have studs in their noses these days.* • [PIC] **Jewellery**

stud [BOOT] *Br and Aus* /stʌd/, *Am* **cleat** *n* [C] any of the small pointed objects which stick out from the bottom of some boots and shoes used in particular sports, esp. football • [PIC] **Shoes**

stud [FASTENER] /stʌd/ *n* [C] a fastener used for clothing, esp. shirts, which is made from two small flat parts joined together by a short bar • [LP] **Dressing and undressing**

stud [TYRE] /stʌd/ *n* [C] *Am* a small piece of metal, many of which are fixed to special tyres used for driving in the snow

stu·dent /£ˈstjuː·dᵊnt, $ˈstuː-/ *n* [C] a person who is learning at a college or university, or sometimes at a school • *a chemistry student* (= someone learning about chemistry) • *a postgraduate student* • *a student teacher* (= a person training to become a teacher) • *student politics* (= political activity at colleges and universities) • *He was a student* **at** *the University of Chicago in the 1970's.* • If someone is a student **of** a stated subject, they are interested in it, but have not necessarily studied it in a formal way: *She is an accomplished student of Mayan culture.* ○ *When you're a nurse, you get to be a bit of a student of* (= to know about) *human nature.* • A **student loan** is an agreement by which a student at a college or university borrows money from a bank to pay for their education and then pays the money back after they finish their studying and start a job. • A **students' union** (also **student union**) is an organization of students in a college or university which arranges social events and sometimes helps to provide health services and places to live. It is also the building or part of a building specially used by students to meet socially, which typically has a shop, a bar and a large meeting room. • [LP] **Schools and colleges**

stu·di·o [ARTIST'S ROOM] /£ˈstjuː·di·əʊ, $ˈstuː·di·oʊ/ *n* [C] *pl* **studios** a room in which an artist, esp. a painter or photographer, works, or a company making artistic or photographic products • *The studio where she painted was at the very top of the house.* • *The firm grew to be one of Europe's foremost graphics studios within ten years.* • A studio (*Br also* **studio flat**, *esp. Am* **studio apartment**) can also be a small apartment designed to be lived in by one or two people. It usually has one large room for sleeping and living in, a bathroom and possibly a separate kitchen.

stu·di·o [RECORDING AREA] /£ˈstjuː·di·əʊ, $ˈstuː·di·oʊ/ *n* [C] *pl* **studios** a specially equipped room where television or radio programmes or music recordings are made • *After three months in the studio working on her latest album, she returns to live performance with her show here tonight.* • *If you would like to be a member of our studio* **audience** (= people who watch or listen to a programme while it is being made in the studio), *please write in.* • A studio is also a building or place where films are made for the cinema, or the company which makes them: *Ealing Studios made some famous British comedies in the 40s and 50s.* • A studio can also be a room or building where dancing is taught or practised: *a dance studio*

stud·y *(obj)* [LEARN] /ˈstʌd·i/ *v* to learn about (a particular subject or subjects), esp. in an educational course or by reading books • *Next term we shall study plants and how they grow.* [T] • *She's been studying* **for** *her doctorate for three years already.* [I] • *I can't come out tonight, I've got to study – there's a test in the morning.* [I] • *As a young painter, he studied* **under** (= was taught by) *Picasso.* [I]

stud·y /ˈstʌd·i/ *n* [U] • *Find somewhere quiet for study* (= studying) – *a place where you won't be disturbed.*

stud·y /ˈstʌd·i/ *n* [C] • A study is a room, esp. in a house, used for quiet work such as reading or writing.

stud·ies /ˈstʌd·iz/ *pl n* • *Of course her studies* (= studying) *will suffer if she's worried about money.* • *The college is going to set up a new department for business studies.*

stu·di·ous /£ˈstjuː·di·əs, $ˈstuː-/ *adj* • *She was a studious child* (= liked to study), *happiest when reading.*

stu·di·ous·ly /£ˈstjuː·di·ə·sli, $ˈstuː-/ *adv*

stu·di·ous·ness /£ˈstjuː·di·ə·snəs, $ˈstuː-/ *n* [U]

stud·y *obj* [EXAMINE] /ˈstʌd·i/ *v* [T] to examine (something) very carefully • *I want time to study this contract thoroughly before signing it.* • *Researchers have been studying* **how** *people under stress make decisions.* [+ *wh*-word]

stud·y /ˈstʌd·i/ *n* [C] • *A congressional budget-office study puts the total cost of the war to the US at $42 billion.* • *Some studies have suggested a link between certain types of artificial sweetener and cancer.* • A study is also a drawing which an artist makes so they can test ideas before starting a painting of the same subject.

stud·ied /ˈstʌd·id/ *adj* • Something that is studied is very carefully done, made or considered, and so might not be completely honest or sincere: *After a pause he gave a studied answer.* ○ *She listened to his remarks with studied indifference.*

stu·di·ous /£ˈstjuː·di·əs, $ˈstuː-/ *adj* [before n] • *The report was obviously prepared with studious* (= very great) *care and attention.*

stu·di·ous·ly /£ˈstjuː·di·ə·sli, $ˈstuː-/ *adv* • *They studiously* **avoided/ignored** *each other.*

stu·di·ous·ness /£ˈstjuː·di·ə·snəs, $ˈstuː-/ *n* [U]

stuff SUBSTANCE /stʌf/ *n* [U] *infml* substance, matter or objects, esp. of a stated type or having the stated quality • *There's sticky stuff all over the chair.* • *I won't offer you any cheese, I know you detest the stuff!* • *Do you want any help bringing your stuff* (=possessions) *in from the van?* • *We'll have to carry all our camping stuff when we walk, so only pack essentials.* • *We've heard all of this stuff* (=these things) *before – haven't you got anything new to offer?* • *Their presentation was just the same old stuff.* • *Her appetite for shopping became* **the stuff of legend** (=famous). • *(Am)* In baseball, a PITCHER's stuff is the quality and variety of their PITCHES (=throws): *Avery had* **great** *stuff, total command of all three of his pitches.* • *(infml)* If someone **does** their **stuff**, they do what they should do or what is expected of them: *If all the members of the team do their stuff, we should win easily.* • *(dated)* The expression **stuff and nonsense** is used by a person to show that they think something is not true and/or is silly: *Her accusations are all stuff and nonsense.* • *"We are such stuff as dreams are made on (often '...made of')"* (Shakespeare, Tempest 4.1)

stuff *obj* EAT /stʌf/ *v* [T] *infml* to (make yourself or another person) eat a very large amount of (food) • *They'd been stuffing* **themselves** *with snacks all afternoon, so they didn't want any dinner.* • *Stop stuffing* **your face** (=eating enthusiastically) *and help me put the decorations up.* • *I suppose I could stuff* **down** *another sandwich.* [M]

stuff NECESSARY /stʌf/ *n* [U] **the stuff of** *literary or fml* the most necessary or most important part of (something) • *A good story and good characterization are the* **(very)** *stuff of fiction.*

stuff *obj* HAVE SEX /stʌf/ *v* [T] *esp. Br and Aus taboo slang* (of a man) to have sex with (a woman) • *(esp. Br and Aus slang)* If a person says stuff a situation, person or thing, they are showing anger, disapproval or a lack of obedience: *He's expecting us to work late, well stuff that/him!* ○ *"Shall we tidy up now?" "No, stuff it!"* • *(esp. Br and Aus slang)* The expression **get stuffed!** is thought to be quite offensive by some people and extremely offensive by others and is used to show annoyance, anger or disagreement: *"I'll give you ten quid for the car." "Get stuffed!"*

stuff·ing MATERIAL /ˈstʌf·ɪŋ/ *n* [U] material which is pushed inside something to make it firm • *The stuffing is made from small pieces of foam rubber.* • *(infml) The muggers really* **beat/kicked/knocked the stuffing out of** *him* (=hit or kicked him very severely). • To **knock/take the stuffing out of** someone is also to weaken them: *Her illness has really knocked the stuffing out of her.*

stuff *obj* /stʌf/ *v* [T] • *Stuff the cushion* (=Fill it with soft material) *and then sew up the final seam.* • *Under her bed they found a bag stuffed* (=filled) **with** *money.* • *This case is absolutely full – I can't stuff* (=push) *another thing* **into** *it.* • If a dead animal is stuffed, its skin is treated with special chemicals and then filled with material so that it looks as if it is still alive.

stuffed /stʌft/ *adj* [not gradable] • *a stuffed furry toy* • *There is an important collection of stuffed birds in the museum.* • *(infml disapproving)* Someone who is described as a **stuffed shirt** behaves in a very formal and old-fashioned way and thinks that they are very important. • When someone is **stuffed-up**, their nose is blocked with MUCUS (=thick liquid), usually because they have a COLD (=slight infection of the nose): *He sounds all stuffed-up – is he all right?*

stuff·ing FOOD /ˈstʌf·ɪŋ/ *n* [U] a mixture of food, such as bread, onions and herbs, which is put inside something which is going to be eaten, such as a chicken or a vegetable, before they are cooked together • *sage-and-onion stuffing*

stuff *obj* /stʌf/ *v* [T] • *Stuff the turkey* (=Fill it with stuffing), *then put it into a pre-heated oven.*

stuffed /stʌft/ *adj* [not gradable] • *stuffed peppers*

stuf·fy FORMAL /ˈstʌf·i/ *adj* **-ier, -iest** *disapproving* (of people or organizations) old-fashioned, formal and boring • *Service in the restaurant is not at all stuffy, and the food is excellent.* • *It would be difficult to find a stuffier, stupider, more arrogant man.* • Ⓘ

stuf·fi·ly /ˈstʌf·ɪ·li/ *adv disapproving*

stuf·fi·ness /ˈstʌf·ɪ·nəs/ *n* [U] *disapproving*

stuf·fy WITHOUT AIR /ˈstʌf·i/ *adj* **-ier, -iest** *disapproving* (of a room or building) unpleasant because of a lack of fresh air • *a stuffy office* • *It's really hot and stuffy in here – open the window and let some of the smoke out.* • Ⓘ

stuf·fi·ness /ˈstʌf·ɪ·nəs/ *n* [U] *disapproving*

stul·ti·fy *obj* /£ˈstʌl·tɪ·faɪ, $-t̬ə-/ *v* [T] *disapproving fml* to prevent (something) from developing into its best possible state • *While personal attention is important, do not be overly impressed by tiny classes – a year in a group of five or fewer can be stultifying.* • *She felt the repetitive exercises stultified her musical technique so she stopped doing them.*

stul·ti·fy·ing /£ˈstʌl·tɪˌfaɪ·ɪŋ, $-t̬ə-/ *adj disapproving fml* • *These countries are trying to shake off the stultifying effects of several decades of state control.*

stum·ble FALL /ˈstʌm·bl̩/ *v* [I] to put a foot down awkwardly while walking or running, and because of this to fall or begin to fall • *Running along the beach, she stumbled* **on** *a log and fell on the sand.* • *In the final straight Meyers stumbled, and although he didn't fall it was enough to lose him first place.* • A **stumbling block** is something which prevents action or agreement: *Lack of willingness to compromise on both sides is the* **main/major** *stumbling block* **to** *reaching a settlement.*

stum·ble NOT CONTROLLED /ˈstʌm·bl̩/ *v* [I always + adv/prep] to walk in a way which does not seem controlled • *We could hear her stumbling* **about/around** *the bedroom in the dark.*

stum·ble PAUSE /ˈstʌm·bl̩/ *v* [I] to make a mistake, such as repeating something or pausing for too long, while speaking or playing a piece of music • *Just relax and be confident, and you won't stumble when you give your speech.* • *When the poet stumbled* **over** *a line in the middle of a poem, someone in the audience corrected him.*

stum·ble a·cross/on/u·pon/on·to *obj v prep* [T] to discover or find (something or someone) by chance • *Workmen stumbled upon the mosaic while digging foundations for a new building.*

stump PART LEFT /stʌmp/ *n* [C] the part of something such as tree, tooth, arm or leg which is left after most of it has been removed • *After the storm only stumps were standing in many areas of the forest.* • *Her smile broadened to reveal two rows of brown stumps, which were all that was left of her teeth.*

stump·y /ˈstʌm·pi/ *adj* **-ier, -iest** *infml, sometimes disapproving* • *There was a large ring on each of her stumpy* (=short and thick) *fingers.*

stump *obj* NO ANSWER /stʌmp/ *v* [T] *slightly infml* to be too difficult for (someone) to answer or solve • *You've stumped me – what is the total mass of the moon?* • *We're all completely stumped – we can't work out how she escaped.*

stump WALK /stʌmp/ *v* [I always + adv/prep] to walk awkwardly and noisily • *She stumped* **out** *of the room, deeply offended by his reaction.* • PIC> **Sports**

stump *obj* POLITICS /stʌmp/ *v* [T] *Am* to travel around (an area) giving speeches and trying to get political support • *She likes to tell stories about the time her dad ran for governor and stumped the north of the state.*

stump /stʌmp/ *n Am* • *The premier's wife may not have an easy time out* **on the stump** (=travelling around trying to get political support). • *He squeezed his usual 30-minute stump* **speech** *down to five minutes.*

stump up *(obj) v adv Br infml* to pay (money) for something, esp. unwillingly • *Large corporations regard legal fees as annoying but necessary, and just stump up (the cash).* [I/T]

stumps /stʌmps/ *pl n* (in cricket) the three vertical wooden poles at which the ball is thrown

stun *obj* SHOCK /stʌn/ *v* [T] **-nn-** to shock or surprise (someone) very much • *News of the disaster stunned people throughout the world.* • *She was stunned by the amount of support she received from well-wishers.* • *They stood in stunned* **silence** *beside the bodies.*

stun·ning /ˈstʌn·ɪŋ/ *adj* • *All the ideas have a stunning simplicity.*

stun·ning·ly /ˈstʌn·ɪŋ·li/ *adv* • *He's stunningly naive for a person of his age.*

stun *obj* MAKE UNCONSCIOUS /stʌn/ *v* [T] **-nn-** to make (a person or animal) unconscious or cause them to lose the usual control of their mind, esp. by hitting their head hard • *Stunned by the impact, he lay on the ground wondering what had happened.* • *This injection stuns the rhinoceros, so we can examine it.* • A **stun gun** is a device which is used to stop an animal or human temporarily from moving but does not permanently harm them.

stung /stʌŋ/ *past simple and past participle of* STING

stunk /stʌŋk/ *past simple and past participle of* STINK

stun·ning /ˈstʌn·ɪŋ/ *adj* extremely beautiful or attractive • *a stunning dress* • *From the bedroom there is a stunning view over the bay of Saint Tropez.*

stun·ning·ly /ˈstʌn·ɪŋ·li/ *adv* • *She really is stunningly* (=extremely) *attractive.*

stun·ner /£ˈstʌn·əʳ, $-ɚ/ *n* [C] *infml dated* • A stunner is a person or thing which is very beautiful, esp. a woman: *The new administrator in accounts is a real stunner.*

stunt [EXCITING ACTION] /stʌnt/ *n* [C] an exciting action which is often done in a way which makes it look dangerous and is usually performed by a skilful person, esp. for use in a cinema film • *It's a typical action film with plenty of* **spectacular** *stunts and a very thin story line.* • *The stunt flying was incredible.* • A **stunt man/woman** is a man/woman who performs stunts, esp. instead of an actor in a film or television programme.

stunt [GET ATTENTION] /stʌnt/ *n* [C] *esp. disapproving* an action which is intended to get attention for the person or people responsible for it • *an advertising stunt* • *He agreed to a* **publicity** *stunt in which he would be locked in a glass cage for seven days to write a novel.* • *(fig. infml) What did you want to* **pull** *a (stupid) stunt* (=do something silly and risky) *like that for?*

stunt *obj* [PREVENT GROWTH] /stʌnt/ *v* [T] to prevent (the growth or development of) something from reaching its limit • *Drought has stunted (the* **growth** *of) this year's cereal crop.* • *A lack of teaching resources early on will almost certainly stunt the learning potential of all the children here.*

stunt·ed /£ˈstʌn·tɪd, $-t̬ɪd/ *adj* • *A few stunted trees were the only vegetation visible.*

stu·pe·fy *obj* [TIRE] /£ˈstjuː·pɪ·faɪ, $ˈstuː-/ *v* [T usually passive] to make (someone) tired and unable to think clearly • *Stupefied by tiredness and having eaten so much, she just sat in front of the fire.*

stu·pe·fac·tion /£ˌstjuː·pɪˈfæk·ʃən, $ˌstuː-/ *n* [U] *fml* • *Because of the drugs he was in a state of stupefaction by the time we found him.*

stu·pe·fy·ing·ly /£ˈstjuː·pɪ·faɪ·ɪŋ·li, $ˈstuː-/ *adv* • *That was the most stupefyingly* **dull/boring** *play I've ever seen.*

stu·pe·fy *obj* [SURPRISE] /£ˈstjuː·pɪ·faɪ, $ˈstuː-/ *v* [T usually passive] to surprise or shock (someone) very much • *We were so stupefied by the news that we all sat in silence for a long time.*

stu·pe·fac·tion /£ˌstjuː·pɪˈfæk·ʃən, $ˌstuː-/ *n* [U] *fml* • *To her parents' stupefaction, she announced her intention to leave the next day.*

stu·pen·dous /£stjuːˈpen·dəs, $stuː-/ *adj* very surprising, usually in a pleasing way, esp. by being large in amount or size • *The main character is a young woman of stupendous beauty with a liking for fast cars.* • *Over the following year he ran up stupendous debts through his extravagant lifestyle.* • *Stupendous news! We've won £500 000!*

stu·pen·dous·ly /£stjuːˈpen·də·sli, $stuː-/ *adv* • *Our charity appeal has been stupendously successful.*

stu·pid /£ˈstjuː·pɪd, $ˈstuː-/ *adj* **-er, -est** foolish or unwise; lacking judgment or intelligence • *She was really stupid to quit her job like that.* • *Whose stupid idea was it to travel at night?* • *One more stupid* **mistake** *like that and the whole deal could fall apart.* • *You've said that retiring early was a stupid* **thing** *to do. Why did you do it?* • *It would be stupid not to take the threats seriously.* • *(infml)* A person might also say a thing is stupid because it annoys them or has in some way caused them a problem: *Have your stupid book back if it's so important to you.* ○ *I hate doing this stupid exercise, I just can't get it right.*

stu·pid /£ˈstjuː·pɪd, $ˈstuː-/ *n* [as form of address] *infml* • *Don't lock it, stupid!*

stu·pid·i·ty /£stjuːˈpɪd·ɪ·ti, $stuːˈpɪd·ə·t̬i/ *n* [U] • *Her stupidity is beyond belief sometimes.* • *It was sheer stupidity to refuse at the price they were offering.*

stu·pid·ly /£ˈstjuː·pɪd·li, $ˈstuː-/ *adv* • *Sorry, I stupidly forgot to bring my copy of the report – could I look at yours?*

stu·por /£ˈstjuː·pəʳ, $ˈstuː·pɚ/ *n* [C usually sing] a state in which a person is almost unconscious and their thoughts are very unclear • *While in a* **drunken** *stupor he became abusive and violent and had to be restrained by hotel staff.*

stur·dy /£ˈstɜː·di, $ˈstɜːr-/ *adj* **-ier, -iest** physically strong, esp. because of being thick, and therefore unlikely to break or be hurt • *It's a sturdy truck and just what we need for the rough roads.* • *Of course she'll finish the climb, she's very sturdy.* • *(fig.) They put up a sturdy* (=strong and determined) *defence of their proposal, and it was finally accepted.*

stur·di·ly /£ˈstɜː·dɪ·li, $ˈstɜːr-/ *adv* • *We could see the boat was sturdily built/constructed, which made us feel more confident.* • *Our expedition leader strode sturdily on and we followed as best we could.*

stur·di·ness /£ˈstɜː·dɪ·nəs, $ˈstɜːr-/ *n* [U]

stur·geon /£ˈstɜː·dʒən, $ˈstɜːr-/ *n* [C] a type of fish which lives in northern parts of the world and is usually caught for its eggs, which are eaten as CAVIAR

stut·ter *(obj)* [SPEAK] /£ˈstʌt·əʳ, $ˈstʌt̬·ɚ/ *v* to speak or say something, esp. the first part of a word, with difficulty, for example pausing before it or repeating it several times • *She stutters a bit, so let her finish what she's saying.* [I] • *"C-c-can we g-go now?" stuttered Jenkins.* [+ clause] • Compare STAMMER.

stut·ter /£ˈstʌt·əʳ, $ˈstʌt̬·ɚ/ *n* [C] • *Toni's developed a slight stutter over the last few months.*

stut·ter·er /£ˈstʌt·ər·əʳ, $ˈstʌt̬·ɚ·ɚ/ *n* [C]

stut·ter·ing·ly /£ˈstʌt·ər·ɪŋ·li, $ˈstʌt̬·ɚ-/ *adv*

stut·ter [WORK UNEVENLY] /£ˈstʌt·əʳ, $ˈstʌt̬·ɚ/ *v* [I] to work or happen unevenly • *Suddenly the engine stuttered and then it stopped completely.*

stut·ter·ing /£ˈstʌt·ər·ɪŋ, $ˈstʌt̬·ɚ-/ *adj* • *Stuttering* (= Sometimes good and sometimes bad) *productivity figures over the last two years have made the industry unattractive to investors.*

stut·ter·ing·ly /£ˈstʌt·ər·ɪŋ·li, $ˈstʌt̬·ɚ-/ *adv* • *The recession is coming to an end stutteringly.*

sty [STRUCTURE] /staɪ/ *n* [C] a PIGSTY

sty [SWELLING], **stye** /staɪ/ *n* [C] a small sore swelling on the edge of an EYELID (=a piece of skin which protects an eye)

Sty·gi·an /ˈstɪdʒ·i·ən/ *adj literary* extremely and unpleasantly dark • *Stygian* **gloom**

style [WAY] /staɪl/ *n* a way of doing something, esp. one which is typical of a person, group of people, place or period • *Jones favours a dynamic, hands-on style of management.* [C] • *His office is very utilitarian* **in** *style, with no decoration.* [U] • *The painting's certainly* **in** *the style of Rembrandt, but I don't think it's actually by him.* [C] • *It's difficult to distinguish between the two artists by style since their works are so similar.* [U] • *One local style* **for** *houses is to have a flat roof and white-washed walls.* [C] • *(fig. infml) He wouldn't try to mislead you – it's not his style* (=not the type of thing he would do). [U] • A **company/house style** is a set of rules a company follows for such things as spelling and design in all the things it produces: *To project a strong corporate image, we apply our house style to all the sales literature.* • See also LIFESTYLE. • Ⓙ

-style /-staɪl/ *combining form* • *Japanese-style management* ○ *an executive-style office* ○ *antique-style furniture*

styl·is·tic /staɪˈlɪs·tɪk/ *adj* • *The variety of schemes submitted provides an indication of the stylistic range of current architecture.* • *All three sculptors explore the same subject matter, and their works have stylistic similarities.*

styl·is·ti·cal·ly /staɪˈlɪs·tɪ·kli/ *adv*

style·less /ˈstaɪl·ləs/ *adj* • *The production is deliberately styleless* (=without a particular style), *and this takes the play out of its historical context.*

styl·ized /ˈstaɪə·laɪzd/, *Br and Aus usually* **-ised** *adj* • If something is stylized, it is represented with an emphasis on a particular style, esp. one which simplifies details rather than trying to show it as it really is: *The Japanese actors brought vivid emotion to the stylized parts of the play.*

style [HIGH QUALITY] /staɪl/ *n* [U] *approving* high quality in appearance, design or behaviour • *That car's* **got real** *style, which is no surprise considering how much it cost.* • *If she decides to do something you can be sure she'll do it* **in/with** *great style.* • *It* **takes** *style to make a mistake like that and still go on to win.* • *You can't deny she's successful and rich, but she has no style.* • Ⓙ

styl·ish /ˈstaɪ·lɪʃ/ *adj approving* • *The film's direction is subtle and stylish but the story is absurd.*

styl·ish·ly /ˈstaɪ·lɪʃ·li/ *adv approving* • *stylishly dressed*

styl·ish·ness /ˈstaɪ·lɪʃ·nəs/ *n* [U] *approving*

style *obj* [DESIGN] /staɪl/ *v* [T usually passive] to shape or design (something such as a person's hair or an object like a piece of clothing or furniture), esp. so that it looks attractive • *You've had your hair styled – it really suits you.* • *This range of jackets is styled to look good whatever the occasion.* • *The car was styled by European designers.* • The word styling is often used in the name of products or devices which are used for shaping a person's hair: *styling mousse* • *styling gel* • *a styling comb* • ⓙ

style /staɪl/ *n* [C] • *They had hundreds of styles* (= types) *of light bulb in stock.* • See also HAIRSTYLE.

styl·ist /'staɪ·lɪst/ *n* [C] • *I've been going to the same* **(hair)** *stylist for years.* • *Our team of stylists have designed an exciting new car which should be popular for many years.* • A stylist is also someone who is very careful about the way they write and tries to make it good: *She's no stylist, but she writes very exciting stories.*

style [FASHION] /staɪl/ *n* fashion, esp. in clothing • *a style consultant* • *I always read the fashion pages in the newspapers to keep up with the latest styles.* [C] • *The classic black dress is always* **in** *style.* [U] • *(fig. infml) She was gulping down sandwiches and cakes as if they were* **going out of** *style* (= she was eating a lot of them). [U] • LP **Shopping goods** ⓙ

style *obj* [TITLE] /staɪl/ *v* [T] to give a title to (a person or group) • *The group, styling itself* **as** *the 'People's Freedom Army', was responsible for at least three murders.* • *She styles herself 'Doctor' but she doesn't have a degree.* [+ obj + n] • See also SELF-STYLED. • ⓙ

sty·lus /'staɪ·ləs/ *n* [C] a small pointed device like a needle which picks up the sound signals stored on a record • ⒼⓇ

sty·mie *obj* /'staɪ·mi/ *v* [T] **stymieing** *infml* to prevent (something) from happening or (someone) from achieving a purpose, so causing annoyance and discouragement • *Because of the holiday period, their attempts to get a quick reply were stymied.* • *In our search for evidence, we were stymied by the absence of any recent documents.*

Sty·ro·foam /£'staɪ·rə·fəʊm, $-foʊm/ *n* [U] *Am trademark for* POLYSTYRENE

suave /swɑːv/ *adj* (esp. of men) having a pleasant and charming manner, which is sometimes considered to be false • *He is suave, sophisticated, well-educated and extremely well-spoken.*

suave·ly /'swɑːv·li/ *adv*

suav·i·ty /£'swɑː·vɪ·ti, $-və·t̬i/ *n* [U] • *She was highly impressed by his elegance and suavity.*

sub [MONEY] /sʌb/ *n* [C] *Br and Aus infml for* **subscription**, see at SUBSCRIBE • *Have you paid your tennis-club sub yet?*

sub [CHANGE] /sʌb/ *n* [C] *Br and Am infml for* SUBSTITUTE • *One of the players was injured during the match, so a sub was brought on.* • *Our class had a sub today because our teacher is ill.*

sub /sʌb/ *v* [I] **-bb-** • *Diane was scheduled to sub* **for** *Ted* (= to do his job temporarily) *as anchor of the late-night news show.*

sub [SHIP] /sʌb/ *n* [C] *infml for* SUBMARINE • *a nuclear sub*

sub [BREAD] /sʌb/ *n* [C] *Am infml for* SUBMARINE SANDWICH

sub– [BELOW] /sʌb-/ *combining form* under or below • *Winter weather brought sub-zero* (= less than 0 degrees) *temperatures to much of the country.*

sub– [NOT QUITE] /sʌb-/ *combining form* almost or nearly • *subhuman* • *subtropical*

sub– [NOT EQUAL] /sʌb-/ *combining form* less important or lower in rank • *a sublieutenant* • *a subordinate*

sub– [SMALLER] /sʌb-/ *combining form* a smaller part of a larger whole • *a subcontinent* • *a subcommittee meeting* • *to subdivide*

sub·al·tern /£'sʌb·əl·tən, $səb'ɔːl·tɚn/ *n* [C] *Br* an army officer whose rank is lower than CAPTAIN

sub·a·qua /sʌb'æk·wə/ *adj* [before n; not gradable] *Br* relating to sports that involve swimming under water • *She belongs to a subaqua club.*

sub·ar·id /£ˌsʌb'ær·ɪd, $-'er-/ *adj specialized* (of land or weather) quite dry; having little rain

sub·a·tom·ic /£ˌsʌb·ə'tɒm·ɪk, $-'tɑː·mɪk/ *adj* [not gradable] *specialized* smaller than or within an atom • *a subatomic particle*

sub·com·mit·tee /£'sʌb·kəˌmɪt·i, $-ˌmɪt̬-/ *n* [C] a number of people chosen from a COMMITTEE (= a small group of people who represent a larger organization and make decisions for it) to study and report on a particular subject • *Several subcommittees will be* **set up** *to deal with specific environmental issues.*

sub·com·pact /£ˌsʌb'kɒm·pækt, $-'kɑːm-/ *n* [C] *Am* a very small car • *I rent a subcompact when I'm travelling alone.* • *A subcompact is smaller than a compact.*

sub·con·scious /£sʌb'kɒn·ʃəs, $-'kɑːn-/ *n* [U] the part of your mind which notices and remembers information when you are not actively trying to do so, and which influences your behaviour even though you are not aware of it • *Freud's theory of the subconscious had a profound influence on the Surrealist movement.* • *By freeing memories that were lodged in her subconscious, she succeeded in piecing together the trauma that had affected her as a child.*

sub·con·scious /£sʌb'kɒn·ʃəs, $-'kɑːn-/ *adj* [before n; not gradable] • *subconscious thoughts* • *Nail biting is often a subconscious reaction to tension.* • *Such memories exist only* **on/at** *the subconscious level.* • *Our subconscious* **mind** *registers things which our conscious mind is not aware of.* • Compare CONSCIOUS [THINKING].

sub·con·scious·ly /£ˌsʌb'kɒn·tʃə·sli, $-'kɑːn-/ *adv* [not gradable] • *The colours used in the painting are meant to subconsciously remind you of the Miro painting nearby* (= make you think of the painting without being aware that you are doing so).

sub·con·ti·nent /£sʌb'kɒn·tɪ·nənt, $'sʌbˌkɑːn·t̬ən·ənt/ *n* [C] a large area of land which is part of a continent. The word 'subcontinent' is often used to refer to India, Pakistan and Bangladesh • *the Indian subcontinent* • *He has written a book about the history of railways in* **the** *subcontinent.* • LP **World regions**

sub·con·tract *obj* /ˌsʌb·kən'trækt/ *v* [T] to pay someone else to do part of (a job that you have agreed to do) • *The car parts are designed here but are subcontracted* **to** *another manufacturer to be produced.* • *Most of the bricklaying has been subcontracted* **(out) to** *a local builder.*

sub·con·trac·tor /£ˌsʌb·kən'træk·təʳ, $-t̬ɚ/ *n* [C] • A subcontractor is a person or company that does part of a job which another person or company is responsible for: *The latest model of computer was designed in our Luton office and produced by a subcontractor in Asia.*

sub·cul·ture /£'sʌbˌkʌl·tʃəʳ, $-tʃɚ/ *n* [C] the way of life, customs and ideas of a particular group of people within a society, which are different from the rest of that society • *youth subcultures* • *the gay subculture*

sub·cu·ta·ne·ous /ˌsʌb·kjʊ'teɪ·ni·əs/ *adj* [not gradable] *medical* existing under the skin • *subcutaneous fat/muscle*

sub·di·vide *obj* /ˌsʌb·dɪ'vaɪd/ *v* [T] to divide (something) into smaller parts • *Each chapter is subdivided* **into** *smaller sections.* • *In the past, when farmers died, their land was often subdivided* **among** *their children* **into** *tiny holdings.*

sub·di·vi·sion /'sʌb·dɪˌvɪʒ·ən, ˌ--'--/ *n* • *Each category has several subdivisions.* [C] • *They agreed that subdivision of the house* **into** *apartments would be a good idea.* [U] • Subdivision is also *Am and Aus for* **housing estate**. See at HOUSE [HOME]. [C]

sub·due *obj* /£səb'djuː, $-'duː/ *v* [T] to reduce the force of (something), or to prevent (something) from existing or developing • *The fire burned for eight hours before the fire crews began to subdue it.* • *He criticized the school for trying to subdue individual expression.*

sub·dued /£səb'djuːd, $-'duːd/ *adj* • If a colour or light is subdued, it is not very bright: *subdued lighting* • If a noise is subdued, it is not loud: *subdued laughter* ○ *subdued cheers* • If a person is subdued, they are not as happy as usual or they are unusually quiet: *Tense, nervous and subdued, he sat in the corner of the room and refused to talk to anyone.*

sub·head·ing /'sʌbˌhed·ɪŋ/ *n* [C] a word, phrase or sentence which is used to introduce part of a text • *The subheadings are numbered within each chapter.*

sub·hu·man /sʌb'hjuː·mən/ *adj* [not gradable] *disapproving* having or showing behaviour or characteristics which are much worse than those expected of ordinary people • *Their treatment of prisoners is subhuman.*

sub·ject [AREA OF STUDY] /'sʌb·dʒekt/ *n* [C] the thing which is being discussed, considered or studied • *Our subject for discussion is homelessness.* • *She has made a series of documentaries* **on the** *subject* **of** *family relationships.* • *While we're* **on the** *subject* **of** (= talking about) *the party, do you know how many people are coming to it?* • *The number of planes flying over the town has been* **the** *subject* **of** (= has caused) *concern since last summer.* • *He was willing to be* **the** *subject* **of** (= to be the person involved in) *an experiment to test allergic reactions.* • *I'd tried to explain the situation, but he just* **changed** *the subject* (= he started talking about something else). • *The guest lecturer* **took as** *her subject* (= decided to speak about) *'punishment and imprisonment in modern society'.* • *I didn't think the subject* **matter** (= the subject) *was suitable for children.* • A subject is also an area of knowledge which is studied in school, college or university: *My favourite subjects at school were history and geography.* ○ *(esp. Br) Her subject* (= special area of study) *is low-temperature physics.*

sub·ject PERSON /ˈsʌb·dʒekt/ *n* [C] a person who lives or who has the right to live in a particular country, esp. a country with a king or queen • *He is a British subject.* • Compare CITIZEN.

sub·ject *obj* GOVERN /səbˈdʒekt/ *v* [T] to defeat (people or a country) and then control them against their wishes and limit their freedom • *The invaders quickly subjected the local tribes.*

sub·ject /ˈsʌb·dʒekt/ *adj* [before n; not gradable] • *The country tried to protect its security by collecting an empire of subject peoples within the borders of its state.*

sub·jec·tion /səbˈdʒek·ʃᵊn/ *n* [U] • *The book discusses the political subjection* (= control) *of the island by its larger neighbour.* • *It had been a great and splendid city, with several towns* **in** *subjection* **to** *it* (= being controlled by it).

sub·ject HAVING /ˈsʌb·dʒekt/ *adj* [after v; not gradable] **subject to** having or experiencing the stated thing, esp. something unpleasant • *Cars are subject to a high domestic tax.* • *You could be subject to many dangers by travelling alone in that area.* • *In recent years, she has been subject to attacks of depression.* • *The structure of all parts of the department was continually subject to reappraisal.*

sub·ject DEPEND /ˈsʌb·dʒekt/ *adj* [after v; not gradable] **subject to** depending on the stated thing happening • *We plan to go on Wednesday, subject to your approval.* • *Any such settlement is subject to the court's permission.* • *Moving all the books should not take long, subject to there being* (= if there are) *enough helpers.*

sub·ject GRAMMAR /ˈsʌb·dʒekt/ *n* [C] *specialized* (in grammar) the person or thing which performs the action of a verb, or which is joined to a description by a verb • *'Bob' is the subject of the sentence 'Bob threw the ball'.* • *'The book' is the subject of the sentence 'The book feels heavy'.* • Compare OBJECT GRAMMAR. • LP› **Verbs**

sub·ject *obj* **to** /səbˈdʒekt/ *v prep* [T] to cause (someone or something) to experience something, esp. something unpleasant • *Everyone interviewed had been subjected to unfair treatment.* • *"I didn't want to subject him to the long journey," she said.* • *The company's accounts were subjected to close scrutiny.*

sub·jec·tive /£səbˈdʒek·tɪv, $-t̬ɪv/ *adj* influenced by or based on personal beliefs or feelings, rather than based on facts • *I think my husband is the most handsome man in the world, but I realize my judgment is rather subjective.* • *More specific and less subjective criteria should be used in selecting people for promotion.* • Compare OBJECTIVE FAIR OR REAL.

sub·jec·tive·ly /£səbˈdʒek·tɪv·li, $-t̬ɪv-/ *adv* • *Most people tend to look at things subjectively rather than objectively.*

sub·jec·ti·vi·ty /£ˌsʌb·dʒekˈtɪv·ɪ·ti, $-t̬ɪv·ə·t̬i/ *n* [U] • *Although the film is based on real events, the director admits to a certain amount of subjectivity during the making of it.*

sub ju·dice /ˌsʌbˈdʒuː·dɪ·si/ *adj* [after v; not gradable] *law* being studied or decided in a law court at the present time • *In Britain, cases which are sub judice cannot be publicly discussed on television or radio, or in the newspapers.*

sub·ju·gate *obj* DEFEAT /ˈsʌb·dʒʊ·geɪt/ *v* [T] *fml* to defeat (people or a country) and rule them in a way which allows them no freedom

sub·ju·ga·tion /ˌsʌb·dʒʊˈgeɪ·ʃᵊn/ *n* [U] *fml* • *They are bravely resisting subjugation by their more powerful neighbours.*

sub·ju·gate *obj* CONTROL /ˈsʌb·dʒʊ·geɪt/ *v* [T] *fml* to treat (yourself, your wishes or your beliefs) as being less important than other people or their wishes or beliefs • *She subjugated herself unwillingly* **to** *her mother's needs.* • *Journalists must subjugate personal political convictions* **to** *their professional commitment to fairness and balance.*

sub·junc·tive /səbˈdʒʌŋk·tɪv/ *n* [U] *specialized* (in some languages) a set of forms of a verb that refer to actions which are possibilities rather than facts • *In the sentence 'I wish I were rich', the verb 'were' is* **in the** *subjunctive.*

sub·let *obj* /sʌbˈlet, $ˈ--/ *v* [T] **subletting**, *past* **sublet** to allow someone to rent all or part of (a house or other building which you are renting from someone else) • *Our rental contract states that we are not allowed to sublet the house.*

sub·lieu·ten·ant /£ˌsʌb·lefˈten·ᵊnt, $-luː-/ *n* [C] an officer of low rank in the British navy

sub·li·mate *obj* /ˈsʌb·lɪ·meɪt/ *v* [T] *fml or specialized* to express (strong emotions) or use (energy) by doing an activity, esp. an activity which is considered socially acceptable • *Hostile feelings and violent responses often seem to be sublimated* **into** *sporting activities.*

sub·li·ma·tion /ˌsʌb·lɪˈmeɪ·ʃᵊn/ *n* [U] *fml or specialized* • *He told her that emotional repression and sublimation was preventing her from understanding her own behaviour.*

sub·lime /səˈblaɪm/ *adj slightly literary* extremely good, beautiful or enjoyable • *Mozart had the ability to transform the popular musical styles of his day into something sublime.* • *The book contains sublime descriptive passages.* • Sublime also means very great: *He possesses sublime self-confidence.*

sub·lime /səˈblaɪm/ *n* [U] *slightly literary* • If something goes **from the sublime to the ridiculous**, it starts with something good but becomes foolish: *The dresses in the fashion show went from the sublime to the ridiculous.* • *"From the sublime to the ridiculous is just one step"* (believed to have been said by Napoleon, 1769-1821)

sub·lime·ly /səˈblaɪm·li/ *adv* • Sublimely means extremely: *The play is sublimely funny.*

sub·li·mi·ty /£səˈblɪm·ɪ·ti, $-ə·t̬i/ *n* [U] *slightly literary* • *No one could fail to be moved by the sublimity and beauty of the painting.*

sub·li·mi·nal /ˌsʌbˈlɪm·ɪ·nəl/ *adj* not recognized or understood by the conscious mind, but still having an influence on it • *The interview was carried out in front of a factory to give voters the subliminal* **message** *that the Prime Minister was a man of the people.* • Subliminal **advertising** uses indirect ways of influencing people to be attracted to a product, such as using a picture of a farm to advertise food to suggest that it is fresh.

sub·ma·chine gun /ˌsʌb·məˈʃiːŋ·gʌn/ *n* [C] a type of automatic gun which is light enough to be carried easily

sub·ma·rine /ˌsʌb·məˈriːn/, *infml* **sub** *n* [C] a ship which can travel under water • *a nuclear submarine* • *a submarine base/fleet/commander* • *"We all live in a Yellow Submarine"* (in the song *Yellow Submarine* by The Beatles, 1966) • PIC› **Ships and boats**

sub·ma·rine /ˌsʌb·məˈriːn/ *adj* [not gradable] *specialized* • Submarine means existing below the surface of the sea: *submarine telephone cables* ○ *a submarine tunnel*

sub·ma·rine (sand·wich), *infml* **sub** *n* [C] *Am* a long thin loaf of bread filled with salad and cold meat or cheese

sub·merge *(obj)* /£səbˈmɜːdʒ, $-ˈmɜːrdʒ/ *v* to go below the surface of the sea or a river or lake • *The submarine submerged when enemy planes were sighted.* [I] • *She was taken to hospital after being submerged* **in** *an icy river for 45 minutes.* [T] • To submerge something also means to cover or hide it: *They decided to submerge their different interests and unite in pursuit of a common goal.* [T] • If you submerge **yourself** in an activity, you put all your effort into doing that activity: *She is an actress who always tries to submerge herself completely in a role.* [T]

sub·mer·sion /£səbˈmɜː·ʒᵊn, $-ˈmɜːr-/ *n* [U] • *The fruit was preserved by submersion* **in** *alcohol.*

sub·mer·si·ble /£səbˈmɜː·sɪ·bl̩, $-ˈmɜːr-/ *n* [C] *specialized* a type of ship which can travel under water, esp. one which operates without people being in it • *The inventor of the submersible says the machine is capable of reaching a depth of 600 metres.*

sub·mit *(obj)* ALLOW /səbˈmɪt/ *v* **-tt-** to allow another person or group to have power or authority over (you), or to accept (something) unwillingly • *We protested about the changes for a long time, but in the end we had to submit.* [I] • *She decided to resign from the party rather than submit* **herself to** *the new rules.* [T]

sub·mis·sion /səbˈmɪʃ·ᵊn/ *n* [U] • Submission is the state in which someone has complete control over you: *He was fooled into thinking her calm and docile manner was submission.* ○ *They thought the country could be bombed* **into** *submission.* ○ *The teachers agreed to a special meeting,* **in** *submission* **to** (= because they accepted) *parents' demands.*

sub·mis·sive /səbˈmɪs·ɪv/ *adj* • If a person is submissive, they allow themselves to be controlled by other people: *He was looking for a quiet submissive wife who would obey his every wish.*

sub·mis·sive·ly /səbˈmɪs·ɪv·li/ *adv*

sub·mis·sive·ness /səbˈmɪs·ɪv·nəs/ *n* [U]

sub·mit *obj* GIVE /səbˈmɪt/ *v* [T] **-tt-** to give or offer (something) for a decision to be made by others • *You must submit your application before January 1st.* • *Applicants for the job are asked to submit samples of their handwriting for analysis.* • *The developers submitted building plans* **to** *the council for approval.* • *Journalists were required to submit all stories that covered political circumstances* **to** *the* *military censors.* • *(fml) In conclusion, I submit* (= suggest) **that** *the proposal will not work without some major changes.* [+ *that* clause]

sub·mis·sion /səbˈmɪʃ·ᵊn/ *n* • *No date has yet been set for the submission of applications.* [U] • *The final deadline for submissions is February 21st.* [C] • *(fml) The judge will hear the defence's submission* (= suggestion) **that** *the case be dismissed.* [C + *that* clause] • *(fml)* **In** *my* **submission** (= I think that) *the government is completely mistaken.* [U]

sub·nor·mal /£sʌbˈnɔː·mᵊl, $-ˈnɔːr-/ *adj* below an average or expected standard, esp. of intelligence • *mentally/educationally subnormal* • *This winter has seen subnormal temperatures in the region.*

sub·or·di·nate /£səˈbɔː·dɪ·nət, $-ˈbɔːr-/ *adj* having a lower or less important position • *a subordinate role* • *subordinate status* • *The individual's needs are subordinate* **to** *those of the group.* • *(specialized)* In grammar, subordinate refers to a clause which cannot form a separate sentence but which can form a sentence when joined with a main clause.

sub·or·di·nate /£səˈbɔː·dɪ·nət, $-ˈbɔːr-/ *n* [C] • Your subordinate is a person who has a less important position than you in an organization: *He left the routine checks to one of his subordinates.*

sub·or·di·nate *obj* /£səˈbɔː·dɪ·neɪt, $-ˈbɔːr-/ *v* [T] • *Her personal life has been subordinated* **to** (= treated by her as less important than) *her career.*

sub·or·di·na·tion /£səˌbɔː·dɪˈneɪ·ʃᵊn, $-ˌbɔːr-/ *n* [U] • *She claims that society is still characterized by male domination and female subordination.* • *They complained that there was constant subordination of high standards* **to** *quick results* (= quick results were treated as more important than high standards).

sub·plot /£ˈsʌb·plɒt, $-plɑːt/ *n* [C] a part of the story of a book or play which develops separately from the main story

sub·poe·na *obj* /səˈpiː·nə/ *v* [T] *law* to order (someone) to go to a court of law to answer questions or to order that (documents) must be produced in a court of law • *A friend of the victim was subpoenaed* **as** *a witness by lawyers representing the accused.* • *They were subpoenaed* **to** *testify before the judge.* [+ obj + *to* infinitive] • *They subpoenaed documents from the firm to look for evidence of wrongdoings.*

sub·poe·na /səˈpiː·nə/ *n* [C] *law* • A subpoena is a legal document ordering someone to appear in a court of law: *Subpoenas were issued to several government employees.*

sub·scribe *(obj)* /səbˈskraɪb/ *v* to pay (money) to an organization in order to receive a product, use a service regularly or support the organization • *She subscribes* **to** *women's magazines and the local newspaper.* [I] • *About 60 percent of television viewers subscribe* **to** *cable television.* [I] • *I subscribe £10 a month* **to** *the charity.* [T] • *(specialized)* In business matters, to subscribe means to offer to buy something: *Existing shareholders subscribed* **to** *only 49% of the new share issue.* [I] ○ *The investment company will subscribe £25 million* **for** *40% of the shares.* [T]

sub·scrib·er /£səbˈskraɪ·bəʳ, $-bɚ/ *n* [C] • *The typical subscriber* **to** *the magazine is retired.* • Subscribers to a service are people who pay to use that service: *Cable television companies have launched major campaigns to increase their number of subscribers.*

sub·scrip·tion /səbˈskrɪp·ʃᵊn/, *infml* **sub** *n* [C] • *(Br) We bought our niece an* **annual** *subscription* **to** *the tennis club as a gift.* • *I decided to* **take out** (= pay for) *a subscription* **to** *a gardening magazine.* • *She* **cancelled/renewed** *her subscription* **to** *the charity.*

sub·scribe to *obj v prep* [T] to agree with or support (an opinion, belief or theory) • *Frank subscribed firmly to the belief that human kindness would overcome evil.* • *Only a political settlement to which all the key parties subscribe will halt the violence.*

sub·sec·tion /ˈsʌbˌsek·ʃᵊn/ *n* [C] one of the smaller parts into which the main parts of a document or organization are divided • *Further details can be found in section 7 subsection 4 of the report.*

sub·se·quent /ˈsʌb·sɪ·kwənt/ *adj* [not gradable] happening after something else • *The book discusses his illness and subsequent resignation from the government.* • *There were pictures on the news of the crashed vehicles and subsequent traffic problems.* • *He is starting the first school himself, but subsequent ones will also use his methods.* • *Those explosions must have been subsequent* **to** (= must have happened after) *our departure, because we didn't hear anything.*

sub·se·quent·ly /ˈsʌb·sɪ·kwənt·li/ *adv* [not gradable] • *The old school was bought and subsequently turned into a private house.*

sub·ser·vi·ent /səbˈsɜː·vi·ənt, $-ˈsɜːr-/ *adj disapproving* willing to do what other people want, or considering your wishes as less important than those of other people • *The attempt to look for a consensus of opinion was regarded as weak and subservient.* • *The government was accused of being subservient* **to** *the interests of the pro-Europe campaigners.*

sub·ser·vi·ent·ly /£səbˈsɜː·vi·ənt·li, $-ˈsɜːr-/ *adv disapproving*

sub·ser·vi·ence /£səbˈsɜː·vi·ənts, $-ˈsɜːr-/ *n* [U] *disapproving* • *Independence came to the country after centuries of subservience* **to** *powerful neighbours.*

sub·side /səbˈsaɪd/ *v* [I] (of a condition) to become less strong, or (of a building, area of land or level of water) to go down to a lower level • *The police are hoping that the violence will soon subside.* • *As the pain in my foot subsided, I was able to walk the short distance to the car.* • *The ground was in danger of subsiding near the edge of the cliff.* • *Homeowners are worried that their homes will subside* (= go lower into the ground) *because of the drought.* • *The worst flooding for over 100 years has begun to subside.*

sub·sid·ence /səbˈsaɪ·dᵊnts/ *n* [U] • Subsidence is the sinking of land or buildings to a lower level: *Household insurance premiums have been increased by 90% to reflect the high cost of subsidence in the area.*

sub·si·di·ar·i·ty /£ˌsʌb·sɪd·iˈær·ɪ·ti, $-er·ə·ṭi/ *n* [U] *specialized* the principle that decisions should always be taken at the lowest possible level or closest to where they will have their effect, for example locally rather than nationally • *MPs argued for subsidiarity in European Union decision-making.*

sub·si·di·a·ry /£səbˈsɪd·i·ᵊr·i, $-er-/ *adj* less important than something else with which it is connected • *Their main reason for not buying the car was that it was too big – subsidiary reasons were the style and quality.*

sub·si·di·a·ry /£səbˈsɪd·i·ᵊr·i, $-er-/ *n* [C] • A subsidiary is a company which is owned by a larger company.

sub·si·dy /ˈsʌb·sɪ·di/ *n* [C] money given as part of the cost of something, to help or encourage it to happen • *The company was given a substantial subsidy by the government.* • *The government is planning to abolish subsidies* **to** *farmers.*

sub·si·dize *obj*, *Br and Aus usually* **-ise** /ˈsʌb·sɪ·daɪz/ *v* [T] • To subsidize something is to pay part of the cost of it: *£50 would help to subsidize the training of an unemployed teenager.* ○ *The refugee families live in subsidized housing that the authorities had found for them.*

sub·si·di·za·tion, *Br and Aus usually* **-i·sa·tion** /ˌsʌb·sɪ·daɪˈzeɪ·ʃᵊn/ *n* [U]

sub·si·diz·er, *Br and Aus usually* **-iser** /£ˈsʌb·sɪ·daɪ·zəʳ, $-zɚ/ *n* [C] • *European countries are quite aggressive subsidizers of grain exports.*

sub·sist /səbˈsɪst/ *v* [I] *fml* to obtain enough food or money to stay alive • *According to a recent study, at least 2 000 people subsist* **by** *picking through the city's garbage.* • *The prisoners were subsisting* **on** *a diet of bread and water.*

sub·sis·tence /səbˈsɪs·tᵊnts/ *n* [U] *fml* • Subsistence is what a person needs in order to stay alive: *The money is intended to provide a basic subsistence and should not be paid to someone who receives other income.* ○ *Most people lived on communal land, producing food only for their own subsistence.* • Subsistence also means producing enough food or earning enough money to keep yourself alive: *subsistence farming* ○ *subsistence wages* ○ *The family were living* **at** *subsistence* **level**.

sub·soil /ˈsʌb·sɔɪl/ *n* [U] the layer of earth which is under the surface level • Compare TOPSOIL.

sub·son·ic /£sʌbˈsɒn·ɪk, $-ˈsɑː·nɪk/ *adj* [not gradable] slower than the speed of sound

sub·spe·cies /ˈsʌbˌspiː·ʃiːz/ *n* [C] *pl* **subspecies** *specialized* a division of a SPECIES (= a set of animals or plants), the members of which are different in some clear ways from those of other divisions of the species

sub·stance MATERIAL /ˈsʌb·stᵊnts/ *n* material with particular physical characteristics • *Peat is an organic substance which is formed when plants partially decompose.* [C] • *Celery contains a valuable chemical substance that helps lower blood pressure.* [C] • *Polluting substances are found in many rivers.* [C] • *What sort of substance could withstand those temperatures?* [U] • *(fml)* **Illegal** substances are illegal drugs. [C] • *(fml)* **Substance abuse** is the use of drugs for pleasure. • *(fml)* A **substance abuser** is a person who uses drugs for pleasure.

sub·stance IMPORTANCE /ˈsʌb·stᵊnts/ *n* [U] *fml* importance, seriousness or relationship to real facts • *There is no substance* **in/to** *the allegation that he was bribed* (=It is not true). • *There appears to be little substance* **to** *the new plans.* • *This information is important and* **gives** *substance* **to** *the stories we have heard.* • See also SUBSTANTIVE.

sub·stan·dard /£sʌbˈstæn·dəd, $-dərd/ *adj* below a satisfactory standard • *substandard housing/buildings/accommodation* • *substandard work/goods*

sub·stan·tial LARGE /səbˈstæn·ʃᵊl/ *adj* large in size, value or importance • *The findings show a substantial difference between the opinions of men and women.* • *She inherited a substantial fortune from her grandmother.* • *The first draft of his novel needed a substantial amount of rewriting.* • *We need substantial improvements in public transport.* • *After a substantial lunch, he decided to have a rest.*

sub·stan·tial·ly /səbˈstæn·ʃᵊl·i/ *adv* • *The new rules will substantially* (=to a large degree) *change how we do things.*

sub·stan·tial GENERAL /səbˈstæn·ʃᵊl/ *adj* [before n] relating to the main or most important things being considered • *At the end of the meeting, we were in substantial agreement* (=we agreed about most things that we had discussed).

sub·stan·tial·ly /səbˈstæn·ʃᵊl·i/ *adv* • *This model has a few extra fittings, but the two cars are substantially* (=generally) *the same.* • *What she is saying is substantially* (=generally) *true.*

sub·stan·ti·ate *obj* /səbˈstæn·ʃi·eɪt/ *v* [T] *fml* to show (something) to be true, or to support (a claim) with facts • *We have evidence to substantiate* **allegations** *that corruption took place.* • *Reports that children had been hurt have not been substantiated.*

sub·stan·ti·a·tion /səbˌstæn·ʃiˈeɪ·ʃᵊn/ *n* [U] *fml* • *The lawyer found no substantiation for the accusation against his client* (=no facts to support the accusation). • *The company produced receipts* **in** *substantiation* **of** (=to support) *its claim.*

sub·stan·tive /£səbˈstæn·t̬ɪv, $-t̬ɪv/ *adj fml* important, serious or related to real facts • *Substantive research on the subject needs to be carried out.* • *The documents are the first substantive information obtained by the investigators.* • *The lack of substantive discussion of serious issues is slowing down the project.* • See also SUBSTANCE IMPORTANCE.

sub·sta·tion /ˌsʌbˈsteɪ·ʃᵊn/ *n* [C] a division of an organization which works under the general control of a larger office • *(Am) a police substation* • An **electricity** substation is a place which allows electricity to go from one part of the production system to another.

sub·sti·tute *(obj)* /£ˈsʌb·stɪ·tjuːt, $-tuːt/ *v* to use (someone or something) instead of another person or thing • *You can substitute oil* **for** *butter in this recipe.* [T] • *The company illegally substituted cheap bolts and screws* **for** *more expensive materials.* [T] • *He tries to avoid using sexist language wherever possible, such as substituting the term 'humankind'* **for** *'mankind'.* [T] • *Dayton was substituted* **for** *Williams in the second half of the match.* [T] • If something substitutes **for** something else, it performs the same job as the other thing or takes its place: *Gas-fired power stations will substitute for less efficient coal-fired equipment.* [I]

sub·sti·tute /£ˈsʌb·stɪ·tjuːt, $-tuːt/ *n* [C] • *Tofu can be used as a meat substitute in vegetarian recipes.* • *Vitamins should not be used as a substitute* **for** *a healthy diet.* • *You can work from plans of a garden, but* **there's no** *substitute* **for** (=nothing is as good as) *going to visit the site yourself.* • In sports, a substitute (*infml* **sub**) is a player who is used for part of a game instead of another player: *Johnson* **came on** *as a substitute towards the end of the match.* ○ *The manager decided to* **bring on** *(Am also* **send in***) another substitute in the last ten minutes of the game.* • **Substitute (teacher)** (*infml* **sub**) is *Am for* **supply teacher**: *We had a substitute for two weeks when Mr Brady had the flu.*

sub·sti·tu·tion /£ˌsʌb·stɪˈtjuː·ʃᵊn, $-ˈtuː-/ *n* • *Scientists believe that substitution* **of** *metals* **by** *new composite materials still has a long way to go.* [U] • *It looks as though the coach is going to make a substitution* (=change one player for another in the game). [C]

sub·struc·ture /£ˈsʌbˌstrʌk·tʃəʳ, $-tʃər/ *n* [C] a firm structure which supports something built on top of it • *The explosion damaged the bridge, but the substructure remained intact.* • *(fig.) If centralized power is placed on an incomplete political substructure, it may lead to instability rather than control.*

sub·sume *obj* /£səbˈsjuːm, $-ˈsuːm/ *v* [T usually passive] *fml* to include (something or someone) as part of a larger group • *It has been suggested that all housing subsidies should be subsumed* **into** *a single housing allowance.* • *Soldiers from many different countries have been subsumed* **into** *the United Nations peace-keeping force.* • *All the statistics have been subsumed* **under** *the general heading 'Facts and Figures'.*

sub·ten·ant /ˌsʌbˈten·ᵊnt/ *n* [C] a person who rents a building from someone who is renting it from the owner

sub·ter·fuge /£ˈsʌb·tə·fjuːdʒ, $-tər-/ *n* an action taken to hide something from someone • *It was clear that they must have obtained the information by subterfuge.* [U] • *Consumers complain that varieties of products which are advertised as 'new' or 'improved' are merely introduced as a subterfuge for raising the price.* [C]

sub·ter·ra·ne·an /£ˌsʌb·tᵊrˈeɪ·ni·ən, $-təˈreɪ-/ *adj* [not gradable] under the ground • *subterranean passages* • *a subterranean river*

sub·text /ˈsʌb·tekst/ *n* [C] a hidden or less obvious meaning • *The political subtext of her novel is a criticism of government interference in individual lives.*

sub·ti·tle /£ˈsʌbˌtaɪ·tl̩, $-t̬l̩/ *n* [C] a word, phrase or sentence which is used as the second part of a book title and is printed under the main title at the front of the book

sub·ti·tled /£ˈsʌbˌtaɪ·tl̩d, $-t̬l̩d/ *adj* [not gradable] • *The novel, subtitled 'A Fable', follows a young actor's attempt to become a film-star.*

sub·tit·les /£ˈsʌbˌtaɪ·tl̩z, $-t̬l̩z/ *pl n* words shown at the bottom of a film or television picture to explain what is being said • *The Chinese film was shown with English subtitles.* • *The evening news has subtitles for deaf people.*

sub·ti·tled /£ˈsʌbˌtaɪ·tl̩d, $-t̬l̩d/ *adj* [not gradable] • *Is the film dubbed* (=are the voices of the actors changed into a different language) *or is it subtitled?*

sub·tle /£ˈsʌt·l̩, $ˈsʌt̬-/ *adj* **-r, -st** *approving* not loud, bright, noticeable or obvious in any way • *The room was painted a subtle shade of pink.* • *The play's message is perhaps too subtle to be understood easily by the youngest children in the audience.* • *A subtle approach is necessary, because Philip does not like being criticized.* • Subtle can also mean small but important: *There is a subtle difference between these two plans.* • Subtle can also mean achieved in a quiet way which does not attract attention to itself and which is therefore good or clever: *a subtle plan/suggestion* ○ *subtle questions*

subt·ly /£ˈsʌt·l̩.i, $ˈsʌt̬-/ *adv approving* • *She subtly suggested that she was willing to help if needed, but she didn't press the point.*

sub·tle·ty /£ˈsʌt·l̩.ti, $ˈsʌt̬·l̩.t̬i/ *n approving* • *Listening to the interview, I was impressed by the subtlety of the questions.* [U] • A subtlety is a small but important detail: *All the subtleties of the music are conveyed in this new recording.* [C] ○ *He prides himself on his sensitivity to the subtleties of language.* [C] ○ *In this painting, she manages to capture on canvas all the subtleties of light and atmosphere.* [C]

sub·to·tal /£ˈsʌbˌtəʊ·tᵊl, $-ˌtoʊ·t̬ᵊl/ *n* [C] the total of one set of numbers to which other numbers will be added • *You have to add the cost of postage to the subtotal.*

sub·tract *obj* /səbˈtrækt/ *v* [T] to remove (a number) from another number • *Four subtracted* **from** *ten equals six.* • *You have to subtract 25% tax* **from** *the sum you receive.* • Compare ADD; DIVIDE; MULTIPLY. • LP **Mathematics**

sub·trac·tion /səbˈtræk·ʃᵊn/ *n* [U] • *The test involves simple calculations, such as addition and subtraction.*

sub·trop·i·cal /£sʌbˈtrɒp·ɪ·kᵊl, $-ˈtrɑː·pɪ-/ *adj* [not gradable] belonging to or relating to parts of the world that have very hot weather • *a subtropical climate* • *subtropical plants* • *Subtropical regions are cooler than equatorial regions.*

sub·urb /£ˈsʌb·ɜːb, $-ɜːrb/ *n* [C] an area on the edge of a large town or city where people who work in the town or city often live • *Box Hill is a suburb of Melbourne.* • *They live in the Parisian suburb of Bobigny.* • *We drove from middle-class suburbs to a very poor area of the inner city.* • (E)

sub·urbs /£ˈsʌb·ɜːbz, $-ɜːrbz/ *pl n* • The suburbs is the outer area of a town, rather than the shopping and business centre in the middle: *The company decided to relocate to the suburbs because the rent was much cheaper.*

sub·ur·ban /£sə'bɜː·bən, $-'bɜːr-/ *adj* • *suburban schools/housing* • *They live in suburban Washington.* • *(disapproving)* Suburban is sometimes used to suggest that something is boring and lacks excitement: *suburban life*

sub·ur·ban·ite /£sə'bɜː·bə·naɪt, $-'bɜːr-/ *n* [C] *Am and Aus* • A suburbanite is a person who lives in the suburbs of a large town or city: *The farm holds workshops in which modern suburbanites can learn how to milk a cow or make butter.*

sub·ur·bi·a /£sə'bɜː·bi·ə, $-'bɜːr-/ *n* [U] *esp. disapproving* • Suburbia is the outer parts of a town, where there are houses, but no large shops, places of work or places of entertainment: *They live in a two-bedroomed house in the heart of suburbia.* • Suburbia also refers to the people who live in the outer parts of a town or to their way of life: *He has written a book about middle-class suburbia.*

sub·vert *obj* /£səb'vɜːt, $-'vɜːrt/ *v* [T] *fml* to try to destroy or weaken (something, esp. an established political system) • *The rebel army is attempting to subvert the government.* • *Our best intentions are sometimes subverted by our natural tendency to selfishness.*

sub·ver·sive /£səb'vɜː·sɪv, $-'vɜːr-/ *adj fml* • *subversive elements/groups in society* • *a subversive activity* • *subversive ideas/influences*

sub·ver·sive·ly /£səb'vɜː·sɪv·li, $-'vɜːr-/ *adv fml*

sub·ver·sive·ness /£səb'vɜː·sɪv·nəs, $-'vɜːr-/ *n* [U] *fml*

sub·ver·sion /£səb'vɜː·ʃən, $-'vɜːr-/ *n* [U] *fml* • Subversion is the attempt to destroy or weaken an established system or government: *He was found guilty of subversion and imprisoned.*

sub·way [UNDERGROUND PASSAGE] /'sʌb·weɪ/ *n* [C] *Br and Aus* an underground passage which allows people on foot to cross a busy road • *I walked through a graffiti-covered subway that stank of urine.*

sub·way [UNDERGROUND RAILWAY] /'sʌb·weɪ/ *n* [C] *esp. Am* an underground electric railway; METRO; TUBE [RAILWAY] • *We took the subway uptown to Yankee Stadium.*

suc·ceed [ACHIEVE SOMETHING] /sək'siːd/ *v* [I] to achieve something that you have been aiming for, or (of a plan or piece of work) to have the desired results • *She's been trying to pass her driving test for six years and she's finally succeeded.* • *You need to be pretty tough to succeed* **in** *the property world.* • *There's a certain type of character that succeeds no matter what the circumstances.* • *If the business succeeds, she'll be a very wealthy woman.* • *The campaign has certainly succeeded* **in** *raising public awareness of the issue.* • *(humorous) Well done, Richard, with a single remark you've succeeded* **in** *offending* (= managed to offend) *just about everybody in the room!* • *(saying)* 'If at first you don't succeed, try, try again' means you should attempt to do something again if you fail the first time. • *"How to succeed in business without really trying"* (title of a book by Shepherd Mead, 1952) • *"Nothing succeeds like excess"* (Oscar Wilde in the play *A Woman of No Importance*, 1893)

suc·cess /sək'ses/ *n* • Success is the achieving of desired results: *To what do you owe the tremendous success of your business?* [U] ○ *The success of almost any project depends largely on its manager.* [U] ○ *I've been trying to persuade her to take on more staff but so far without much success.* [U] ○ *She* **enjoyed** *great success with all three records in the States.* [U] ○ *I'm not* **having** *much success* **in** *getting through to* (= communicating with) *him at the moment.* [U] ○ *The success* **rate** *for the operation is very low.* [U] • A success is something that achieves positive results: *It's too early to say yet whether the operation has been a success.* [C] ○ *Both films have been a big box-office success in this country.* [C] ○ *It won't be an easy project to get off the ground, but she seems determined to make a success of it.* [C] ○ *That salmon dish was a success, wasn't it?* [C] • A **success story** is something or someone that achieves great success, often by making a lot of money: *Angela Black's biscuit company is a rare success story in these times of recession.* • Ⓟ

suc·cess·ful /sək'ses·fəl/ *adj* • *Fortunately, my second attempt at making flaky pastry was more successful than my first.* • *It was one of those irritating articles that tells you how to combine a successful career with raising a family.* • *Tonight he'll be interviewing Bill Davies, author of several* **hugely** *successful children's books* (= books which have been bought by a lot of people). • *The Birmingham Royal Ballet has had a highly successful season* (= A lot of people have paid to see them dance). • *She runs a very successful* (= profitable) *computer business.* • *This year's harvest was one of the most successful since the record crop of 1985.* • *Lloyd Webber and Rice have perhaps been the most commercially successful partnership in British musical theatre since Gilbert and Sullivan.*

suc·cess·ful·ly /sək'ses·fəl·i/ *adv* • *A number of patients have been successfully treated with the new drug.* • *You get a certificate to show that you've successfully completed the course.* • *The nineteen-year-old Brazilian successfully defended the 500-metre title he won in Rome.*

suc·ceed *(obj)* [FOLLOW] /sək'siːd/ *v* to come after (another person or thing) in time • *Kamen was named company chairman, succeeding Robert Schwartz, who is retiring after 44 years.* [T] • *In 1946 he succeeded his father* **as** *editor and became co-publisher with his brother, Robert Hardman.* [T] • *When the queen dies, her eldest son will succeed* **to** *the throne.* [I] • *Almost from its beginnings, New York has produced succeeding generations of intellectuals.* • *In the succeeding weeks, five more patients showed similar symptoms.*

suc·ces·sion /sək'seʃ·ən/ *n* [U] • *Manchester scored three goals* **in quick** *succession* (= one after another). • *She had her first three children* **in rapid** *succession.* • *This is the seventh year* **in** *succession that they've won the cup.* • *A succession* **of** *scandals and revelations has undermined the government over the past year.* • *A succession* **of** *short-lived rulers did nothing to increase the country's stability.* • *Life was just* **an** *endless succession* **of** *parties and dinners.* • *There is increasing speculation about the succession to the throne* (= about who will be queen or king next).

suc·ces·sive /sək'ses·ɪv/ *adj* [before n; not gradable] • *It was the team's third successive defeat and their fourth defeat in five matches.* • *Last month the Democrats won their third successive election victory.*

suc·ces·sive·ly /sək'ses·ɪv·li/ *adv* [not gradable] • *Since the championship began in 1987, they have finished successively in ninth, seventh and fifth position.*

suc·ces·sor /£sək'ses·ər, $-ɚ/ *n* [C] • A successor is a person or thing that follows another person or thing in time: *There is growing speculation surrounding the appointment of a successor* **to** *Flanagan, the executive director.* ○ *This range of computers is very fast, but their successors will be even faster.* • A **successor state** is a new smaller country formed after a larger country has been divided up: *Russia, Georgia and Ukraine are three of the successor states to the Soviet Union.*

suc·cinct /sək'sɪŋkt/ *adj approving* (of writing or speech) clear and short; expressing what needs to be said without unnecessary words • *Her writing is confident and succinct.* • *Keep your letter succinct and to the point.*

suc·cinct·ly /sək'sɪŋkt·li/ *adv approving* • *I thought she expressed her feelings most succinctly in the meeting.* • *Three words succinctly evoked the Kennedy era and what it meant at the time: "Everything seemed possible".*

suc·cinct·ness /sək'sɪŋkt·nəs/ *n* [U] *approving*

suc·cour *Br and Aus, Am and Aus* **suc·cor** /£'sʌk·ər, $-ɚ/ *n* [U] *fml* help given to someone who is suffering • *She crossed the enemy lines, disguised as a civilian, to bring medical succour to the Resistance fighters.* • *Now, amongst the queues of unemployed, the Church is rediscovering its role of comfort and succour.*

suc·cour *obj Br and Aus, Am and Aus* **suc·cor** /£'sʌk·ər, $-ɚ/ *v* [T] *fml* • *Students of all kinds should be encouraged, supported and succoured.*

suc·cu·lent [JUICY] /'sʌk·jʊ·lənt/ *adj approving* (of food) pleasantly juicy • *These are wonderfully succulent peaches.* • *I like nothing better than to sink my teeth into a big piece of succulent steak.*

suc·cu·lence /'sʌk·jʊ·lənts/ *n* [U] *approving* • *If the grilling is done right, the chicken has a wonderful flavour and succulence.*

suc·cu·lent [PLANT] /'sʌk·jʊ·lənt/ *n* [C] *specialized* a plant such as a CACTUS in which the leaves and stem are thick and fleshy and can store a lot of water • *Succulents often have thick waxy cuticles to minimize water loss.*

suc·cumb /sə'kʌm/ *v* [I] *fml* to lose the determination to oppose something; to accept defeat • *The town finally succumbed last week after being pounded with heavy artillery for more than two months.* • *I'm afraid I succumbed* **to** *temptation and had a piece of cheesecake.* • *I felt sure it would only be a matter of time before he succumbed* **to** *my charms.* • *He wanted to be an actor but succumbed* **to** *parental pressure to be respectable and trained as a lawyer.*

• If you succumb **to** an illness, you start to suffer from it: *Thousands of cows have succumbed to the disease in the past few months.*

such SO GREAT /sʌtʃ/ *predeterminer, determiner* used before a noun or noun phrase to add emphasis • *That's such a good film.* • *I've never in my life had such delicious food.* • *It seems like such a long way to drive for just one day.* • *Oh Richard, you're such an idiot!* • *It was such a dreadful thing to do.* • *Have you ever seen anyone with such long legs?* • *I've never known such kindness.* • *There, that wasn't such an ordeal after all, was it?* • *Such cruelty really is beyond my comprehension.* • *I'd put on such a lot of weight* **that** *I couldn't get into my trousers.* [+ *that* clause] • *It was such nice weather* **that** *we were able to have lunch in the garden.* [+ *that* clause]

such OF THAT TYPE /sʌtʃ/ *predeterminer, determiner, pronoun* of that or a similar type • *Small companies such* **as** *ours are very vulnerable in a recession.* • *I'm looking for a cloth for cleaning silver. Do you have such a thing?* • *Present on this grand occasion were Andrew Davies, Melissa Peters and other such stars.* • *Sometimes the child doesn't want to go back to the parent. In such cases the situation is almost impossible to resolve.* • *"She's just bought a brand new leather coat." "I'm surprised she's got the money to spend on such things when her husband is unemployed!"* • *People such* **as** *Derek and your mother only ever travel first class.* • *It's one of those gourmet shops that sells such things* **as** *smoked salmon, coffee beans and expensive biscuits.* • *I tried to tell her in such a way* **that** *she wouldn't be offended.* • *That sum of money is to cover costs* **such as** *travel and accommodation.* • *Darling, Mummy's told you before,* **there's no such thing as** *ghosts* (= they do not exist)*!* • *He said she had a cold, superior manner or* **some** *such remark – I don't remember his exact words.* • *(dated infml) I just bought one or two things – bread and milk* **and** *such (also* **suchlike***).* • *(dated infml) We talked about the kids and the weather* **and** *such (also* **suchlike***).* • *(fml) Our lunch was such* (= of a type) *that we don't really need an evening meal.* • *So here I am, without a girlfriend again. Oh well,* **such is life** (= this is what happens and is to be expected in life). • **Such as it is** can be used to suggest that something you have referred to is of low quality, not enough or not good enough: *You're welcome to borrow my tennis racket, such as it is.* ○ *Breakfast, such as it was, consisted of a couple of croissants and a cup of coffee.*

such EXACTLY /sʌtʃ/ *n* [U] **as such** in the true or exact meaning of the word or phrase • *There wasn't much vegetarian food as such, although there were several different types of cheese.* • *We don't have a secretary as such, but we do have a student who comes in to do a bit of filing and typing.*

such and such *predeterminer infml* used to refer to something which you do not want to name or say exactly • *If they tell you to arrive at such and such a time, just get there a couple of minutes early.*

such·like /ˈsʌtʃ·laɪk, ˌ-ˈ-/ *determiner, pronoun* things of that type • *There's a shop in the hospital where they sell flowers and chocolates and suchlike.* • *So why do ducks and ships and suchlike float?*

suck *(obj)* PULL IN /sʌk/ *v* to pull in (esp. liquid) through your mouth without using your teeth, or to move the tongue and muscles of the mouth around (something inside your mouth), often in order to dissolve it • *She was sitting on the grass sucking lemonade through a straw.* [T] • *As a child, I used to bite the end off the cone and suck the ice-cream through it.* [T] • *Only the female mosquito can suck blood and transmit malaria.* [T] • *I sucked my* **thumb** *until I was seven.* [T] • *Sometimes a baby will hold the nipple in her mouth without really sucking* **on** *(Br also* **at***) it.* [I] • *I tried sucking* **(on)** *a mint to stop myself coughing.* [T; I + *on*] • *They always give you sweets to suck* **on** *(Br also* **at***) in aeroplanes to stop your ears from going pop.* [I] • *If you think it will comfort your baby, give him a dummy to suck* **(on)**. [T; I + *on*] • *I can't bear it when my grandma sucks* **(at)** *her teeth after a meal.* [T; I + *at*] • A place or organization that has been sucked **dry** has lost all its useful or valuable qualities or possessions: *The city has been sucked dry* **of** *local talent.* [T + obj + adj] • *(taboo slang)* To **suck** someone **off** is to use the tongue, lips and mouth to excite someone's sexual organs to give pleasure. • *(infml disapproving)* If you **suck up to** someone in a position of authority, you do and say things in order to make them like and approve of you: *"Why do you think he offered to take all that work home?" "Ah, he's just sucking up to the boss."* • Something which sucks a liquid or an object in a particular direction pulls it with great force: *The waves came crashing over my head and I could feel myself being sucked under by the currents.* [T] • *(fig.) I really don't want any part in this whole argument but I can feel myself being sucked* **into** *it* (= forced to be involved). [T] • *(fig.) Continued rapid growth in consumer spending will suck* **in** *more imports.* [M] • *(Br and Aus infml saying)* 'Suck it and see' means try it and see if it is successful.

suck /sʌk/ *n* [C usually sing] • *Can I have a suck of your lolly please?*

suck BE BAD /sʌk/ *v* [I] *esp. Am slang* to be without value or interest • *Man, this job sucks!*

suck·er FOOLISH PERSON /£ˈsʌk·əʳ, $-ɚ/ *n* [C] *infml disapproving* a person who believes everything they are told and is therefore easy to deceive • *You didn't actually believe him when he said he had a yacht, did you? Oh, Annie, you sucker!* • *"There's a sucker born every minute"* (believed to have been said by the American showman Phineas T. Barnum, 1810-1891) • *"Never give a sucker an even break"* (phrase often used by the comedian W.C.Fields, 1923-)

suck·er *obj* /£ˈsʌk·əʳ, $-ɚ/ *v* [T] *Am* • If you sucker someone **into** something, you persuade them to do it by deceiving them: *We were suckered into doing the job for free.*

suck·er LIKING /£ˈsʌk·əʳ, $-ɚ/ *n* [C] *infml* a person who finds the stated thing so persuasive or attractive that they cannot refuse it or judge its real value • *I'm a real sucker* **for** *this style of architecture – I just love it.* • *I have to confess I'm a bit of a sucker* **for** *musicals.*

suck·er THING OR PERSON /£ˈsʌk·əʳ, $-ɚ/ *n* [C] *Am infml* used to refer to a thing or person that is unpleasant or that needs effort • *I've been working on that paper for weeks and almost have the sucker finished.* • *He's a nasty little sucker, isn't he?*

suck·er STICKING DEVICE /£ˈsʌk·əʳ, $-ɚ/ *n* [C] a part of an animal's body which allows it to stick to a surface • *The leech has a sucker at each end of its body.* • Sucker is also *Br infml for* **suction cup**. See at SUCTION.

suck·er SWEET /£ˈsʌk·əʳ, $-ɚ/ *n* [C] *Am and Aus infml for* LOLLIPOP • *We got Tyler one of those* **all-day** (= very big) *suckers, but she dropped it in the sand.*

suck·er PLANT PART /£ˈsʌk·əʳ, $-ɚ/ *n* [C] *specialized* a new growth on an existing plant that develops under the ground from the root or the main stem, or from the stem below a GRAFT (= part where a new plant has been joined on)

suck·le *(obj)* /ˈsʌk·l̩/ *v* to feed (a baby, esp. a baby animal) with milk from the organ in the mother that produces milk, or (of a baby, esp. a baby animal) to drink milk from the mother • *We watched the cow suckling her calves.* [T] • *The puppies went back to their mother to suckle.* [I]

suck·ling /ˈsʌk·lɪŋ, ˈ-l̩·ɪŋ/ *n* [C] • A suckling is an animal that is still young enough to be drinking milk from its mother: *The practice of rearing suckling calves in dark crates for veal was banned.*

su·crose /£ˈsuː·krəʊz, $-kroʊs/ *n* [U] *specialized* the type of sugar that exists naturally in most plants that grow on land • *Sucrose passes into the bloodstream within fifteen minutes.*

suc·tion /ˈsʌk·ʃᵊn/ *n* [U] the process by which the removal of air from a space results in a lower pressure in that space, causing liquid, gases or other substances to enter that space or causing two surfaces to stick together • *Cylinder vacuum cleaners work entirely* **by** *suction.* • *In the hospital, a suction machine was used to clear the child's airways.* • *Once the oil spill has been contained, it can be sucked up into tankers using suction* **pumps**. • A **suction cup** *(Br and Aus also* **sucker***)* is a circular piece of rubber which sticks to surfaces when pressed against them: *You can stick it on your car window by pushing these suction cups against the glass.*

sud·den /ˈsʌd·ᵊn/ *adj* happening or done quickly and without warning • *So why the sudden change?* • *Drop the gun, put your hands in the air, and don't make any sudden movements.* • *It was so sudden – the cancer was diagnosed in June and three months later she was dead.* • *There were just two weeks to go until the wedding and I had a sudden change of heart.* • *He had a sudden heart attack while he was on holiday.* • *She gets these sudden mood swings and you never know when it's going to happen.* • *First they announce their engagement and then they tell me Angie's pregnant – it's all a bit sudden really.* • *(infml) It seemed to happen* **all of a sudden** (= very quickly) – *I felt dizzy, then my legs went weak and I just collapsed.* • *"Sudden Impact"* (title of a film, 1983)

sud·den·ly /ˈsʌd·ᵊn·li/ *adv* • *I was relaxing in the bath when I suddenly remembered I'd promised to pick Marco up from the airport.* • *"Do you remember much about the accident?" "No, it all happened so suddenly."* • *I was just dozing off to sleep when I suddenly heard a scream from outside.* • *She just suddenly decided that she'd had enough and she left him.* • *He hadn't been well for years, but he suddenly got a lot worse.* • *She caught sight of Johnny in the bar and suddenly her whole expression changed.* • *I suddenly realised what I'd said, but it was too late.*

sud·den·ness /ˈsʌd·ᵊn·nəs/ *n* [U] • *It was the suddenness of his illness that came as such a shock.*

suds /sʌdz/, **soap·suds** *pl n* the mass of small bubbles that form on the surface of soapy water • *(Am)* Suds can also be a mass of small bubbles that forms on the surface of any liquid. • Suds is also *Am dated infml for* BEER: *I'll buy one more round of suds, then we've got to go.*

suds·y /ˈsʌd·zi/ *adj* **-ier, -iest** *esp. Am* • *You're not rinsing the dishes properly, honey – look, they're all sudsy!*

sue *(obj)* /suː/ *v* to take legal action against (a person or organization), esp. by making a legal claim for money because of some harm that they have caused you • *He was so furious about the accusations in the letter that he threatened to sue.* [I] • *She's sued the paper* **for** (= in order to obtain) *damages after they wrongly described her as a prostitute.* [T] • *She is suing her husband* **for** (= in order to obtain a) *divorce.* [T] • *My father sued his dentist* **for** (= because of) *some treatment which he'd had that had gone wrong.* [T] • LP **Crimes and criminals**

suede /sweɪd/ *n* [U] a soft leather which is slightly rough to touch and is not shiny • *a suede belt/jacket* • *suede shoes* • *Do these shoes come in normal leather or just suede?*

su·et /ˈsuː·ɪt/ *n* [U] a hard waxy fat used in cooking which is taken from around the KIDNEYS of such animals as sheep and cows • *Suet is used to make baked or steamed puddings and heavy cakes.* • *Have you ever eaten suet* **pudding**?

suf·fer FEEL PAIN /£ˈsʌf·əʳ, $-ɚ/ *v* [I] to experience physical or mental pain • *It's terrible to see someone you love suffer so much.* • *I think he suffered quite a lot when his wife left him.* • *I don't want to cause my mother any more anguish – I think she's suffered enough already.* • *Jack was really suffering this morning – he stayed up drinking all night!* • *She suffers terribly in the winter when it's cold and her joints get stiff.* • *He doesn't often get colds, but when he does he really suffers.* • *The rock-star is said to be suffering* **from** *acute exhaustion.* • *She's been suffering* **from** (= been ill with) *cancer for two years.* • *Johnny suffers* **from** (= is often ill with) *asthma.* • *If you're not happy with it, you should complain. Don't just suffer* **in silence** (= without saying anything).

suf·fer·er /£ˈsʌf·ᵊr·əʳ, $-ɚ·ɚ/ *n* [C] • A sufferer is a person who has or frequently gets a particular illness: *A drug currently being tested may give new hope to thousands of hay-fever sufferers.* ○ *He does a lot of work with AIDS sufferers.* ○ *Almost 50 per cent of cancer sufferers are treated successfully and have a normal life span.*

suf·fer·ing /£ˈsʌf·ᵊr·ɪŋ, $ˈ-ɚ-/ *n* • *There is no doubt that the war will cause widespread devastation and human suffering.* [U] • *The lines around her eyes told of years of suffering.* [U] • *Even when he was very ill he continued with his work, his manner betraying no hint of his sufferings.* [C]

suf·fer *(obj)* EXPERIENCE /£ˈsʌf·əʳ, $-ɚ/ *v* to experience or show the effects of (something bad) • *The government have suffered one of their worst setbacks since they came to power.* [T] • *The Democrats suffered a crushing defeat in the last election.* [T] • *The industry has suffered severe job losses this year.* [T] • *Twenty-five policemen suffered minor injuries during the protest.* [T] • *Both sides suffered considerable casualties.* [T] • *The city suffered another blow last month with the closure of the local car factory.* [T] • *If you will insist on eating three helpings of dessert, I'm afraid you'll have to suffer* **the consequences**! [T] • *I had to suffer her father moaning for half an hour on the phone last night!* [T + obj + v-*ing*] • *When you're working such long hours, it's inevitable that your marriage will start to suffer.* [I] • *My work is beginning to suffer because I just can't concentrate.* [I] • *Like a lot of his films, it suffers* **from** *being a bit too long.* [I] • *The people who will suffer if the road is built are those who live locally.* [I] • If you do not **suffer fools gladly**, you have very little patience with people whom you think are foolish or have stupid ideas.

suf·fer·ance /£ˈsʌf·ᵊr·ᵊnts, $ˈ-ɚ-/ *n* [U] **on sufferance** *slightly fml* with unwilling permission • *Eventually she granted permission for the project, but it was obvious that it was on sufferance.* • If a person stays in a particular place **on** sufferance, they are allowed but not wanted there: *He gave me a bed for a couple of nights but I felt I was there on sufferance.* • *(dated)* If someone does something **under** sufferance, they do it very unwillingly: *He only visits his parents under sufferance.*

suf·fi·cient /səˈfɪʃ·ᵊnt/ *adj* [not gradable] enough for a particular purpose • *Temperatures in the mountains can drop suddenly and it is important to make sure you are wearing sufficient clothing.* • *This recipe should be sufficient* **for** *five people.* • *It was thought that he'd committed the crime but there wasn't sufficient evidence* **to** *convict him.* [+ *to* infinitive] • *(slightly fml) "Would you like some more stew?" "No thanks, I've* **had sufficient** (= eaten enough)."

suf·fi·cient·ly /səˈfɪʃ·ᵊnt·li/ *adv* • *McGeechan hopes to have recovered sufficiently from his knee injury to play in the semi-finals next week.* • *The food was fairly good and the portions were sufficiently large to please the men.* • *Even the calmest person will get angry if sufficiently provoked.* • *The case was sufficiently serious to warrant investigation by the police.*

suf·fi·cien·cy /səˈfɪʃ·ᵊnt·si/ *n* [U] *fml or humorous* • *"More ham, Mr Fletcher?" "No thank you – it was delicious, but I've had* **a** *sufficiency* (= I have eaten enough)."

suf·fice /səˈfaɪs/ *v* [I not *be sufficing*] • *I'm taking four hundred pounds' worth of travellers' cheques – I think that should suffice* (= be enough). • **Suffice (it) to say**, (= It is enough to say that) *Mike won't be going to Tina's birthday party after what he said about her to her boss.*

suf·fix /ˈsʌf·ɪks/ *n* [C] a letter or group of letters added at the end of a word to make a new word • *The suffix '-ness' added to the end of the word 'sweet' forms the word 'sweetness', thereby changing an adjective into a noun.* • LP **Combining forms**

suf·fo·cate *(obj)* /ˈsʌf·ə·keɪt/ *v* to (cause someone to) die because of a lack of oxygen • *The report said that the victims had suffocated in the fumes.* [I] • *She suffocated him by holding a pillow over his head until he stopped moving.* [T] • *(fig. infml) I've got to open the window – it's suffocating* (= uncomfortably hot and lacking fresh air) *in here!* [I] • To suffocate something is to prevent its advancement and positive development: *The democratic press, he said, was suffocated by the Communist Party.* [T] ○ *It remains to this day a land of antiquated social rules and suffocating traditions.* [I]

suf·fo·ca·tion /ˌsʌf·əˈkeɪ·ʃᵊn/ *n* [U] • *According to the doctor, her death resulted from suffocation.*

suf·frage /ˈsʌf·rɪdʒ/ *n* [U] the right to vote in an election, esp. for representatives in a parliament or similar organization • *There have only been Labour administrations for 20 out of the 72 years since* **universal** *male suffrage was introduced.* • *Female suffrage was introduced in South Australia in 1894.*

suf·frag·ette /ˌsʌf·rəˈdʒet/ *n* [C] • A suffragette was a woman in Britain, Australia and the United States in the early 20th century who was a member of a group that demanded the right of women to vote and that increased awareness of the matter with a series of public PROTESTS: *The suffragette Emily Davidson threw herself under the King's horse at the Derby in 1913 in order to draw attention to the campaign.*

suf·frag·ist /ˈsʌf·rə·dʒɪst/ *n* [C] • A suffragist is someone who supports suffrage, esp. a supporter of the right of women to vote in the early 20th century.

suf·fuse *obj* /səˈfjuːz/ *v* [T usually passive] *literary* to spread through or over (something) completely • *Her eyes were shining brightly and her face was suffused* **with** *colour.* • *Each fragrant dish was suffused* **with** *a different herb.* • *His voice was low and suffused* **with** *passion.*

Su·fi /ˈsuː·fi/ *n* [C] a member of an Islamic religious group which tries to achieve unity with God by living a simple life and by praying and MEDITATING

Su·fic /ˈsuː·fɪk/, **Su·fi** *adj* [not gradable] • *He's a member of a Sufic order.*

Su·fi·sm /ˈsuː·fɪ·zᵊm/ *n* [U]

su·gar /£ˈʃʊg·əʳ, $-ɚ/ *n* a sweet substance which is obtained esp. from the plants **sugar cane** and **sugar beet** and used to sweeten food and drinks • *brown/white sugar* [U] • *caster/granulated sugar* [U] • *icing sugar* [U] • *a lump of sugar* [U] • *Do you take sugar in your coffee?* [U] • *How many sugars* (= spoonfuls or lumps of sugar) *do you take in your tea?* [C] • *Beat together the butter and sugar until the mixture is light and fluffy.* [U] • *The western diet is generally thought to contain too much fat and sugar.* [U] • *Sugar is* *bad for the teeth.* [U] • *Most big supermarkets now sell a range of reduced-sugar products such as jams and fizzy drinks.* • *(specialized)* A sugar is any of several types of simple CARBOHYDRATE that dissolves in water: *Glucose and lactose are sugars.* [C] • *(esp. Am)* Sugar is also used as an affectionate way of addressing someone that you know: *Hi, sugar, did you have a good day at school?* [as form of address] LP **Titles and forms of address** • *(infml)* People say 'Oh sugar' when something annoying happens, often as a humorous way to avoid saying the slang word 'shit': *Oh sugar, I've just spilt coffee all down my jacket!* • If you describe someone as being **sugar and spice**, you mean that they are behaving in a kind and friendly way: *She could be all sugar and spice when she wanted to be.* • **Sugar beet** is a plant from whose white root sugar can be obtained. • **Sugar cane** is a tropical plant from whose tall thick stems sugar can be obtained. • **Sugar-coated** foods or pills are covered with a thin layer of sugar: *I like any of those sugar-coated breakfast cereals that they make for kids.* • *(disapproving)* An announcement or promise that is **sugar-coated** is intended to seem positive or pleasant, although in fact it will result in something unpleasant or unacceptable. • *(infml)* A **sugar daddy** is a rich and usually older man who buys presents for or gives money to a young person, esp. a woman, usually in order to spend time with them or have a sexual relationship with them. • **Sugar-free** foods do not contain any sugar and are usually artificially sweetened: *sugar-free chewing-gum* • *(Br)* **Sugar (snap) peas** (*Am and Aus* **snow peas**, *Am* **snap peas**) are small round sweet green vegetables in an outer covering which can be eaten. • *"Brown Sugar, you make me feel so good."* (from the song *Brown Sugar* by The Rolling Stones, 1971)

su·gar *obj* /£ˈʃʊg·əʳ, $-ɚ/ *v* [T] • *Oh, I forgot to sugar* (= put sugar in) *your coffee.*

su·gar·y /£ˈʃʊg·ər·i, $ˈ-ɚ-/ *adj* • *It's all the sugary snacks that kids eat between meals that ruin their teeth.* • *(disapproving)* Sugary is also used to mean too good or kind or expressing feelings of love in a way that is not sincere: *It's that sugary smile of his that I can't bear – it makes me want to hit him!*

sug·gest *(obj)* MENTION /səˈdʒest/ *v* to mention (an idea, possible plan or action) for other people to consider • *They were wondering where to hold the office party and I suggested the Italian restaurant near the station.* [T] • *(fml) Might I suggest a white wine with your salmon, sir?* [T] • *I suggest* **(that)** *we wait a while before we make any firm decisions.* [+ (*that*) clause] • *Liz suggested* **(that)** *I try the shop on Mill Road.* [+ (*that*) clause] • *What do you suggest* **(that)** *we do with them in the afternoon?* [+ (*that*) clause] • *I'm afraid he's out of the office – I suggest* **(that)** *you try again after lunch.* [+ (*that*) clause] • *I suggested putting the matter to the committee to hear what they've got to say.* [+ v-*ing*] • *Can you suggest* **where** *I might find a chemist's?* [+ *wh*-word]

sug·ges·tion /səˈdʒes·tʃən/ *n* • *I don't know what to wear tonight – have you got any suggestions?* [C] • *She* **made** *some very helpful suggestions but her boss* **rejected** *them all.* [C] • *They didn't like my suggestion* **that** *we should all share the cost.* [C + *that* clause] • *I have a few favourite restaurants that I tend to go back to, but I'm always* **open to** *new suggestions* (= willing to try new restaurants that people suggest). [C] • *I have a very good manager who is always* **open to** *suggestion* (= who is always willing to listen to other people's suggestions). [U] • *I went to the Park Street dentist's* **at** *Ann's suggestion* (= as a result of Ann suggesting it) *and I was really impressed.* [U]

sug·gest·i·ble /£səˈdʒes·tɪ·bl̩, $-t̬ɪ-/ *adj fml disapproving* • Someone who is suggestible is easily influenced by other people's opinions: *The success of advertising proves that we are all* **highly** *suggestible.*

sug·gest *obj* SHOW/EXPRESS /səˈdʒest/ *v* [T] to communicate or show (an idea or feeling) without stating it directly or giving proof • *Recent polls seem to suggest* **that** *the government's popularity is at an all time low.* [+ *that* clause] • *Evidence suggests* **that** *exposure to lead may cause mental damage in children before they show any adverse physical symptoms.* [+ *that* clause] • *She's applied for a lot of jobs recently, which suggests* **that** *she's not altogether happy with her present position.* [+ *that* clause] • *She made one or two remarks which suggested* **that** *the company was in financial trouble.* [+ *that* clause] • *Now, I'm not suggesting* **that** *you were flirting with Adrian, but you were certainly paying a lot of attention to him.* [+ *that* clause] • *Are you suggesting* **(that)** *I look fat in these trousers?* [+ (*that*) clause] • *Something about his manner suggested a lack of interest in what we were doing.*

sug·ges·tive /£səˈdʒes·tɪv, $-t̬ɪv/ *adj* • Suggestive is often used to describe something that makes people think about sex: *Some of his lyrics are rather suggestive.* ○ *He's always making sexually suggestive jokes.* • *(fml)* If something is suggestive **of** something else, it makes you think about it: *The amplified sounds are suggestive of dolphins chatting under the sea.*

sug·gest *obj* PRODUCE AN IDEA /səˈdʒest/ *v* [T] *slightly fml* to produce (an idea) in the mind • *He told me a story which suggested a plot for a novel.* • *Does anything suggest* **itself** (= Have you got any ideas about what we should do)*?*

su·i·cide /ˈsuː·ɪ·saɪd/ *n* the act of killing yourself intentionally, or a person who has done this • *After several years of mental illness, she* **committed** *suicide last month.* [U] • *He'd* **attempted** *suicide three times before he actually succeeded.* [U] • *The suicide rate among men between the ages of 16 and 25 has risen alarmingly in the past five years.* • *She regarded suicide as the ultimate act of escapism.* [U] • *His suicide left us all deeply shocked.* [U] • *There is growing concern over the number of suicides that happen in prisons.* [C] • Suicide might also refer to any act which has the effect of causing your own defeat: *As a leader he knows that it is* **political** *suicide to be seen to be weak and indecisive.* [U] ○ *It would be suicide* **to** *take the best player off the field at this stage in the game.* [U + *to* infinitive] • A **suicide pact** is an agreement between two or more people to kill themselves together at the same time: *The leader of the religious sect and thirty of his followers killed themselves in a suicide pact last year.* • Compare MANSLAUGHTER; MURDER.

su·i·cid·al /ˌsuː·ɪˈsaɪ·dəl/ *adj* • People who are suicidal want to kill themselves or are in a mental state in which it is likely that they will try to do so: *Pete was so depressed after she left him that I actually thought he was suicidal.* ○ *Prisoners with suicidal* **tendencies** *are closely observed throughout their stay.* • Suicidal behaviour is likely to result in death: *He took a suicidal leap from one roof to the next.* ○ *(fig.) It would be suicidal for the Prime Minister to call an election at a time when he's so unpopular* (= It would cause his own defeat).

suit *obj* BE CONVENIENT /£sjuːt, $suːt/ *v* [T] to be convenient and cause the least difficulty for (someone) • *What time suits you best?* • *We could go now or this afternoon – whatever suits you.* • *"How about eight o'clock outside the cinema?" "That suits me* **fine**.*"* • *She remembers her manners when it suits her – like when she wants something from you!* • *The great thing about working at home is that you can suit yourself about when you work.* • *Part-time work would* **suit me right down to the ground** (= suit me very well). • *(infml)* The expression **suit yourself** is used either humorously or angrily to mean do what you want to do: *"I don't think I'll come to the party tonight." "All right, suit yourself!"*

suit *obj* BE RIGHT /£sjuːt, $suːt/ *v* [T] to be right for (a particular person, situation or occasion) • *That type of crop is grown a lot in this area – the soil seems to suit it very well.* • *The lifestyle seems to suit her – she's certainly looking very well.*

suit·ed /£ˈsjuː·tɪd, $ˈsuː·t̬ɪd/ *adj* • *With her qualifications and experience, she would seem to be ideally suited* **to** *the job.* • *Rodriguez, being an older and more experienced singer, is better suited* **to** *the more mature roles.* • *I'm not really suited* **to** *this sort of work.* • If two people who have a relationship are suited (**to** each other), they have a good relationship which will probably last, often because they share a lot of interests: *They were never suited from the start – they've got nothing in common.*

suit·a·ble /£ˈsjuː·tə·bl̩, $ˈsuː·t̬ə-/ *adj* • *We think we've found a suitable site for the factory.* • *What's a suitable present for a couple celebrating their twenty-fifth wedding anniversary?* • *My mother doesn't like me wearing short skirts to church – she doesn't think they're suitable.*

suit·a·bly /£ˈsjuː·tə·bli, $ˈsuː·t̬ə-/ *adv* • *I think I'll wear my green suit for the wedding – it's suitably smart.*

suit·a·bil·i·ty /£ˌsjuː·təˈbɪl·ɪ·ti, $ˌsuː·t̬əˈbɪl·ə·t̬i/ *n* [U] • *Her suitability* **for** *the post has been questioned.*

suit *obj* LOOK ATTRACTIVE /£sjuːt, $suːt/ *v* [T] (usually of a colour or style of clothes) to increase (someone's) attractiveness • *You should wear more black – it suits you with your blonde hair.* • *Short skirts don't really suit me – I haven't got the legs for them.* • *He looks good in casual clothes – they suit him.*

suit [SET OF CLOTHES] /£sjuːt, $suːt/ *n* [C] a set of clothes made of the same material which are intended to be worn together • A man's suit usually consists of a matching jacket and trousers, and sometimes a WAISTCOAT: *a pin-stripe/three-piece suit.* • A woman's suit is usually a matching skirt and jacket: *a skirt suit* ○ *She looked very smart in a pale grey suit.* • A suit is also a set of clothes or a piece of clothing to be worn in a particular situation or while doing a particular activity: *a bathing/diving/protective/ski suit* ○ *a swimsuit* ○ *a spacesuit* ○ *a suit of armour* • *(Br)* A **suit bag** (*Am* **garment bag**) is a long flat bag which is carried folded in half in which a suit can be kept while travelling. • [PIC>] **Clothes, Luggage**

suit [LEGAL PROBLEM] /£sjuːt, $suːt/, **law·suit** *n* [C] a problem taken to a court of law, by an ordinary person or an organization rather than the police, for a legal decision • *He* **brought**/*(esp. Am)* **filed** *a $12 million libel suit against the newspaper, claiming his professional reputation had been damaged by the paper's stories.* • *a malpractice/negligence/paternity suit*

suit [PLAYING CARDS] /£sjuːt, $suːt/ *n* [C] any of the four types of card in a set of playing cards, each having a different shape printed on it • *The four suits in a pack of cards are hearts, spades, clubs and diamonds.* • *You have to put down a card of the same suit or the same number.* • [LP>] **Cards**

suit·case /£'sjuːt·keɪs, $'suːt-/, *esp. Br also* **case** *n* [C] a large, often box-shaped, container with a handle for carrying clothes and possessions while travelling • *a leather suitcase* • *Have you* **packed/unpacked** *your suitcase yet?* • [PIC>] **Luggage**

suite [SET OF ROOMS] /swiːt/ *n* [C] a set of connected rooms, esp. in a hotel • *The singer was interviewed in his £1500 a night* **hotel** *suite.* • *At around midnight we waved the happy couple off to their* **bridal** *suite.* • *Guests were invited to the president's hospitality suite for a celebratory drink.* • *They've got a whole suite* **of** *offices on the second floor.*

suite [SET OF FURNITURE] /swiːt/ *n* [C] a set of furniture for one room, of matching design and colour • *We're having a new bathroom suite fitted at the weekend.* • *You should see Chris's new bedroom suite – it's gorgeous.* • *I've just ordered a new suite for the living-room.*

suite [MUSIC] /swiːt/ *n* [C] a piece of instrumental music with several parts, usually all in the same KEY (=set of musical notes based on one particular note) • *Stravinsky's 'Firebird Suite'* • *Tchaikovsky's 'Nutcracker Suite'*

suit·or /£'sjuː·tər, $'suː·t̬ɚ/ *n* [C] *literary* a man who wants to marry a particular woman • *It's the story of a young woman who can't make up her mind which of her many suitors she should marry.* • *(specialized)* A person or company who wants to take control of another company can also be called a suitor: *PJH Corporation said it had been approached by two possible suitors who had submitted bids to buy the company.*

sul·fur /£'sʌl·fər, $-fɚ/ *n* [U] *Am and Aus for* SULPHUR

sulk /sʌlk/ *v* [I] *disapproving* to be silent and childishly refuse to smile or be pleasant to people in order to let them know that you are angry about something that they have done • *He's sulking in a corner somewhere because I wouldn't let him have a second bar of chocolate.* • *I can't stand it when she sulks.*

sulk /sʌlk/ *n* [C] *disapproving* • *If she doesn't get what she wants she* **goes into a** *sulk just like a child.* • *Jim's in one of his sulks again – just ignore him.* • *Don't tell me she's got* **the** *sulks* (= that she's sulking) *again!*

sulk·y /'sʌlk·i/ *adj* **-ier, -iest** • *She brought along a couple of sulky looking kids who didn't say a word all evening.*

sulk·i·ness /'sʌlk·ɪ·nəs/ *n* [U]

sul·len /'sʌl·ən/ *adj* bad-tempered and unwilling to smile or be pleasant to people • *I was served by a sullen-faced youth.* • *They stared at him with a blank expression of sullen resentment.* • *(literary) She looked up at the sullen* (= dark and unpleasant) *sky and shuddered.*

sul·len·ly /'sʌl·ən·li/ *adv* • *She turned her back to him and stared sullenly out of the window.*

sul·len·ness /'sʌl·ən·nəs/ *n* [U]

sul·ly *obj* /'sʌl·i/ *v* [T] *fml* to spoil (something or someone's perfect reputation, purity or cleanliness) • *His reputation, he said, had been unfairly sullied by allegations, half-truths and innuendos.* • *The record company fears its association with the discredited rock star might sully its image.* • *My mother didn't want me to associate with the rough boys down the road in case they sullied my mind.* • *No speck of dirt had ever sullied his hands.*

sul·phate, *esp. Am* **sul·fate** /'sʌl·feɪt/ *n* a chemical formed from SULPHUR, oxygen and another element • *The problem of acid rain is caused mainly by sulphates and nitrates released into the environment by humans.* [C] • *Adding sulphate to the solution will give a precipitate.* [U]

sul·phide, *esp. Am* **sul·fide** /'sʌl·faɪd/ *n* a chemical formed from SULPHUR and another element • *hydrogen sulphide* [U] • *Most metal sulphides will not dissolve in water.* [C]

sul·phur, *esp. Am* **sul·fur** /£'sʌl·fər, $-fɚ/ *n* [U] a pale yellow element which exists in various physical forms • *Sulphur, which burns with a blue flame and a pungent smell, is used in making matches and gunpowder.* • **Sulphur dioxide** is a colourless gas which has a strong unpleasant smell and dissolves in water. It is used in various industrial processes and for preserving food, and it is also a serious air pollutant: *The European Union is reviewing controls for sulphur dioxide* **emissions** *from coal-fired power stations.* • The **sulphur-crested cockatoo** is a large white PARROT from Australia which is often kept as a pet in other countries.

sul·phur·ous, *esp. Am* **sul·fur·ous** /£'sʌl·fᵊr·əs, $-fɚ-/ *adj* • *The sulphurous fumes and smoke from the mines were overpowering.*

sul·phur·ic ac·id, *esp. Am* **sul·fur·ic ac·id** /£sʌl'fjʊə·rɪk, $-fjʊr·ɪk/ *n* [U] a strong colourless acid • *Experts say that continued use of sulphuric acid could further deplete the ozone layer.*

sul·tan /'sʌl·tᵊn/ *n* [C] a ruler, esp. in the past, of some Muslim countries • *the Sultan* **of** *Brunei*

sul·tan·ate /'sʌl·tə·nət/ *n* [C] • A sultanate is a country ruled by a sultan: *the Sultanate of Oman*

sul·tan·a /sʌl'tɑː·nə/ *n* [C] a dried seedless white GRAPE (= small fruit) used esp. in cakes • *Sultanas are paler in colour than currants and raisins.* • *I've bought some delicious new cereal with sultanas and nuts in it.*

sul·try [WARM] /'sʌl·tri/ *adj* **-ier, -iest** (of weather) uncomfortably warm and with air that is slightly wet • *It was a sultry July afternoon in upstate New York.*

sul·tri·ness /'sʌl·trɪ·nəs/ *n* [U]

sul·try [SEXY] /'sʌl·tri/ *adj* **-ier, -iest** (esp. of a woman's face or voice) sexually attractive in a way that suggests sexual desire • *She's the sultry blonde in that new chocolate commercial.* • *Who's the sultry-voiced woman who answers the phone in your office?*

sul·tri·ness /'sʌl·trɪ·nəs/ *n* [U]

sum [AMOUNT OF MONEY] /sʌm/ *n* [C] an amount of money • *Huge sums of money are spent on national defence.* • *Nobody knows exactly how much compensation she received but it was certainly a* **substantial** *five-figure sum.* • *The American show-business magazine is being bought by the publishing giant for an* **undisclosed** *sum.* • *He'll get £50 000 from the company when he retires which is a* **tidy** (= large) *sum.* • *(humorous) I worked for three whole weeks for which I received the* **princely** (= very low) *sum of $100.*

sum [CALCULATION] /sʌm/ *n* [C] a calculation, esp. a simple one, using such processes as adding, subtracting, multiplying or dividing • *I remember how much I hated* **doing** *sums when I was at school.* • *Well, if I've got my sums right, we should have £800 left over even after we've paid for the holiday.* • *(esp. Br) I must confess that I* **got** *my* **sums wrong** (= I calculated the cost wrongly) *– the house extension is costing a lot more than I expected.* • [LP>] **Mathematics**

sum [TOTAL] /sʌm/ *n* [U] the whole number or amount when two or more numbers or amounts have been added together • **The** *sum* **of** *thirteen and eight is twenty-one.* • *So what's* **the** *grand sum – how much money have we collected altogether?* • *(fig.) So is that the entire sum* **of** *three day's work?* (= Is there no more?) • *(fml) The meeting was,* **in sum** (= considered as a whole), *a disaster.* • The **sum total** of something is the whole of it, or everything: *It's the sum total of what you eat over a long period that matters and not what you consume in a day.* ○ *It's wrong to judge someone on the basis of one part of their life rather than the sum total of it.* • *"The whole is more than the sum of its parts"* (from the *Metaphysics* of Aristotle, 384-322 B.C.)

sum up *(obj)*, **sum** *(obj)* **up** *v adv* to express all the most important facts or characteristics about (something) in a brief way • *The purpose of a conclusion is to sum up the main points of the essay.* [M] • *The best way of summing* **the situation** *up in our office is 'absolute chaos'.* [M] • *The government's policy under the present leader is easy to sum up – there isn't any.* [M] • *He's a small man with a big ego –*

that about sums him up, doesn't it. [M] • *I'd just like to sum up by saying that it's been a tremendous pleasure to work with you.* [I] • *Some people you can sum up* (= know what they are like) *at a glance.* [M] • A judge sums up towards the end of a trial when he or she makes a speech to the JURY (= a group of people who decide whether a person is guilty or not in court) telling them again of the main matters to consider in a case: *The judge, summing up at the trial of some of the rioters, made it quite clear where the duties of the jury lay.* [I]

sum·ming–up /ˌsʌm·ɪŋˈʌp/ *n* [C] • *It was alleged that the trial judge had misrepresented the defence case and had given more weight to the prosecution in his summing-up.*

sum·mar·ize *(obj), Br and Aus usually* **–ise** /£ˈsʌm·ᵊr·aɪz, $-ə·raɪz/ *v* to express the most important facts or characteristics about (something) in a short and clear form • *Could you summarize the plot so far because I haven't seen any of the episodes?* [T] • *I think I managed to summarize the basic aims of the project in the allotted time.* [T] • *I'll just summarize the main points if I may.* [T] • *The editorial summarized the President as 'a center-right traditionalist'.* [T] • *I know you weren't there but, to summarize, the party was a huge success.* [I]

sum·ma·ry /£ˈsʌm·ᵊr·i, $ˈ-ɚ-/, *fml* **sum·ma·tion** /səˈmeɪ·ʃᵊn/ *n* [C] • *I'd read the plot summary before I saw the play.* • *At the end of the news, they often give you a summary of the main headlines.* • *No brief summary can possibly do justice to the depth of this report.* • *(fml) The commission's final report gave a summation of evidence gathered during the two-year investigation.*

sum·ma·ry /£ˈsʌm·ᵊr·i, $ˈ-ɚ-/ *adj* done suddenly, without delay and sometimes unreasonably • *Witnesses presented accounts of summary executions and torture by the secret police.* • *Curtis has said that he plans to appeal against his summary dismissal.* • *The new law gives the police summary powers to expel suspected terrorists from the country.*

sum·mar·i·ly /ˌsʌmˈer·ɪ·li/ *adv* • *He claims he was summarily dismissed by the club chairman Derrick Richardson last month.* • *When workers at the brewery went on strike, 120 were summarily fired.* • *The regime routinely arrests thousands without warrants and summarily executes hundreds.*

sum·mat /ˈsʌm·ət/ *pronoun Br not standard* something • *There's summat wrong with this machine.*

sum·mer /£ˈsʌm·əʳ, $-ɚ/ *n* the season of the year between spring and autumn when the weather is warmest, lasting from June to September north of the equator and from December to March south of the equator • *We have breakfast on the balcony* **in (the)** *summer.* [U] • *Last summer they went to Australia, and two summers ago they went to Brazil.* [C] • *The worst outbreak of riots occurred in the summer of '68.* [C] • *It was a long hot summer.* [C] • *I love these warm summer nights.* • *During the summer season the town tends to get very crowded.* • *It was a perfect summer's day.* [U] • A **summer school** is an educational course that happens during the summer when other courses have finished: *She's running a summer school during August.* • *(Am)* A **summer school** is also one or more educational courses taken during the summer which replaces courses that were missed or failed during the autumn, winter or spring, or which makes it possible for students to advance more quickly toward a degree or GRADUATION. • *(Br)* **Summer pudding** is a cold sweet dish consisting of several soft red and purple fruits, such as RASPBERRIES and BLACKBERRIES, enclosed in bread. • *"Summer Loving"* (from the song *Summer Nights* in the film *Grease*, 1978) • *"Summer in the City"* (title of a song by The Lovin' Spoonful, 1966) • See also INDIAN SUMMER.

sum·mer /£ˈsʌm·əʳ, $-ɚ/ *v* [I always + adv/prep] • *If your cactus has summered* (= spent the summer) *outdoors, move it into the garage or house when overnight temperatures drop below 65°F.*

sum·mer·y /£ˈsʌm·ᵊr·i, $ˈ-ɚ-/ *adj* • Summery means typical of or suitable for summer: *Clare just walked by looking very summery in a pale blue sundress.*

sum·mer·house /£ˈsʌm·ə·haʊs, $ˈ-ɚ-/ *n* [C] *pl* **summerhouses** /£ˈsʌm·əˌhaʊ·zɪz, $ˈ-ɚ-/ a small building in a garden used for sitting in during the summer • *They sat in her summerhouse and drank tea out of small blue cups.* • *(Am)* A summerhouse is also a house at the beach or in the mountains that you live in for part or all of the summer: *We try to get to the summerhouse in Lake Hewitt every year, even if it's only for a week or two.*

sum·mer·time /£ˈsʌm·ə·taɪm, $ˈ-ɚ-/ *n* [U] the season of summer • *You should see the garden in the summertime – it's beautiful.* • *We get quite a few tourists here in summertime.*

sum·mit HIGHEST POINT /ˈsʌm·ɪt/ *n* [C] the highest point of a mountain • *On this day in 1784, Dr Michel Paccard and Jacques Balmat reached the summit of Mont Blanc.* • *(fig.) I certainly haven't reached the summit* (= highest point) *of my career.*

sum·mit MEETING /ˈsʌm·ɪt/ *n* [C] an important formal meeting between leaders of governments from two or more countries • *On June 8th, the leaders of the world's seven main industrial countries will meet in Venice for their annual economic summit.* • *A special summit* **meeting** *of European heads of government has been arranged to discuss the matter.*

sum·mon *obj* ORDER /ˈsʌm·ən/ *v* [T] to order (someone) to go to or be present at a particular place, or to officially arrange (a meeting of people) • *On July 20th, the council was summoned* **to** *hear an emergency report on its finances.* [+ obj + *to* infinitive] • *I'm afraid I'll have to go – I'm being summoned by my wife.* • *In late October the prime minister summoned an emergency meeting.*

sum·mons /ˈsʌm·ənz/ *n* [C] • *I sat outside the boss's office awaiting my summons.* • *(law)* A summons is an official demand to appear in a court of law: *Mr Clarke's insurance company had* **issued** *a summons for unpaid mortgage repayments.*

sum·mon *obj* GATHER STRENGTH /ˈsʌm·ᵊn/ *v* [T] to gather (your bravery or strength), esp. with effort • *It took me six months to summon* **(up)** *the* **courage** *to ask him out for a drink.* [T/M]

su·mo wres·tling /£ˈsuː·məʊ, $-moʊ/ *n* [U] a style of WRESTLING (= a fighting sport), originally from Japan, in which each man tries to defeat the other either by pushing him outside of a marked ring or by forcing him to touch the ground with a part of his body other than the bottom part of the foot

su·mo wres·tler /£ˈsuː·məʊ, $-moʊ/ *n* [C]

sump /sʌmp/ *n* [C] a hole or container, esp. in the lower part of an engine, into which a liquid that is not needed can flow • *They claim that the lack of collection sumps into which rain and spilt liquids can drain could contaminate the surrounding land.*

sump·tu·ous /ˈsʌmp·tju·əs/ *adj* luxurious and showing wealth • *The guests turned up dressed in sumptuous evening gowns.* • *Dinner at the hotel was a sumptuous affair – steaming platters of meat, rich desserts and countless bottles of wine.*

sump·tu·ous·ly /ˈsʌmp·tju·ə·sli/ *adv* • *They live in a sumptuously furnished flat in Mayfair.*

sun STAR /sʌn/ *n* [U] the star that the Earth spins around, which provides light and heat for the Earth, or the light or heat that the Earth receives from this star • *The sun is the centre of our solar system.* • *The sun* **rises** *in the east and* **sets** *in the west.* • *I can feel the sun on my back.* • *The sun's rays are at their most powerful at midday.* • *You've been in the sun, haven't you? Look how brown you are!* • *I think I've had a bit too much sun today – I've got a headache.* • *Shall we go and sit out* **in the sun?** • *We thought we'd go out for a walk while the sun was* **shining.** • *I've tried everything* **under the sun** (= everything possible) *on this stain, but I just can't get rid of it.* • An area of land or a place that is **sun-baked** is very dry and shows that it has received a lot of sun: *Judging by the cracks in the sun-baked earth, it had not rained for weeks.* ○ *We strolled along the sun-baked streets of Naples.* • A place that is **sun-drenched** frequently receives a lot of sun: *We spent the entire holiday lying on the sun-drenched beaches at the south end of the island.* • **Sun-dried** vegetables have been dried by leaving them in the sun so that their flavour becomes much stronger: *The sauce is made from onions, wine and sun-dried* **tomatoes.** • A **sun-god** is the sun worshipped as a god in some ancient religions. • *Remember to pack your* **sun-hat** (= hat to protect your head from the sun). • *(esp. humorous)* **Sun-kissed** might describe a place that receives a lot of sun or a person whose appearance is attractive because they have recently been in the sun: *When I last saw them, they were heading for the sun-kissed shores of Spain.* ○ *Her hair had gone blonder and she had that sun-kissed look about her.* • **Sun-up** is *Am for* SUNRISE. • A **sun visor** is a flat piece at the top of the front window of a vehicle which protects the driver's eyes from strong sun. • *"Here Comes the Sun"* (title of a song by the Beatles, and later Steve Harley and

Cockney Rebel, 1969) • *"The Sun Also Rises"* (title of a book by Ernest Hemingway, 1926)

sun *obj* /sʌn/ *v* [T] **-nn-** • If you sun yourself, you lie or sit somewhere where there is a lot of sun, esp. in order to make your skin darker: *I sat on the balcony sunning myself.*

sun·ny /ˈsʌn·i/ *adj* **-ier, -iest** • *We're having the party in the garden, so I'm praying it'll be sunny.* • *The weather forecast said it would be dry with a few sunny spells/intervals.* • *The sunny weather is likely to continue until the weekend, when thunderstorms are expected.* • A person who is sunny or who has a sunny character is usually happy and relaxed and does not tend to get anxious or angry: *She has a very sunny disposition.* • *"Grab your coat, and get your hat, / Leave your worry on the doorstep,/ Just direct your feet / To the sunny side of the street"* (from the song *On the Sunny Side of the Street* written by Dorothy Fields, 1930)

sun·less /ˈsʌn·ləs/ *adj literary* • *It was a grey and sunless* (= lacking sun) *day and our spirits were low.*

Sun DAY OF THE WEEK *n abbreviation for* Sunday

sun·bathe /£ˈsʌm·beɪð, $ˈsʌn-/ *v* [I] to sit or lie in the sun in order to make your skin darker • *I like to sunbathe in the morning when the sun is not so hot.*

sun·bath·ing /£ˈsʌmˌbeɪ·ðɪŋ, $ˈsʌn-/ *n* [U] • *Have you been sunbathing? You're lovely and brown.* • *The government has issued a report on the links between sunbathing and skin cancer.*

sun·beam *Br and Aus* /ˈsʌn·biːm/, *Am and Aus* **sun·ray** *n* [C] a beam of light from the sun

sun·bed *Br* /ˈsʌn·bed/, *Am* **tan·ning bed** *n* [C] a bed-like frame containing a device for producing light which you lie on in order to make the skin go darker • *She'd either been on holiday or she'd been on a sunbed – she was very brown.* • *They're having some sunbeds fitted at the health club that I go to.*

sun·belt /ˈsʌn·belt/ *n* [U] **the Sunbelt** the southern part of the US • *The Sunbelt stretches from Florida to southern California.*

sun·block /£ˈsʌn·blɒk, $-blɑːk/ *n* [U] SUNSCREEN

sun·burn /£ˈsʌm·bɜːn, $ˈsʌn·bɜːrn/ *n* [U] (the condition of someone who has) sore swollen reddened skin caused by spending too long in the strong heat of the sun • *She applied calamine lotion to her sunburn.* • *When it's hot, children should always wear hats outside, in order to prevent sunburn.* • *The seas are so clear you wonder why the fish don't get sunburn.* • Compare SUNTAN.

sun·burnt, sun·burned /£ˈsʌm·bɜːnt, $ˈsʌn·bɜːrnt/ *adj* • Sunburnt can be used either to describe the condition of skin being reddened and sore because of having been in the strong heat of the sun for too long, or to mean very SUNTANNED: *When you go out in the hot sun, you should always put cream on your skin to avoid getting sunburnt.* ○ *Fishermen with sunburnt faces sat on the beach mending their nets.*

sun·dae /ˈsʌn·deɪ/ *n* [C] a food made from ice cream, with pieces of fruit, nuts, cream, sweet sauce etc. on top of it • *a chocolate sundae* • *a hot fudge sundae* • *a banana sundae*

Sun·day /ˈsʌn·deɪ/ (*abbreviation* **Sun**) *n* the day of the week after Saturday and before Monday, when most people in Western countries do not go to work • *Sunday is the day when members of Christian religions go to church.* [U] • *We're going to visit my aunt and uncle* **on** *Sunday* (= the next Sunday that there is). [U] • *(Br infml and Am) What are you doing Sunday* (= next Sunday)*?* [U] • *Would you like to come to tea* **on** *Sunday afternoon?* • *Do you think shops should be allowed to open* **on** *Sundays/***on** *a Sunday* (= every Sunday that there is)*?* [C] • *Do you think that Sunday* **trading** (= shops being open on every Sunday that there is) *should be allowed?* • *I'm playing cricket* **this/next** *Sunday.* [U] • *I played cricket* **last** *Sunday.* [U] • *I play cricket* **every** *Sunday.* [U] • *It's Emily's birthday* **the** *Sunday* **after next/** *It was Emily's birthday* **the** *Sunday* **before last**. [C] • *We arrive in Paris on* **the** (= a particular) *Sunday, and leave the following Wednesday.* [C] • *In Britain, the traditional Sunday* **lunch** *consists of the Sunday* **joint/roast** (= meat), *potatoes and other vegetables.* • The Sunday **papers** (*Br* also **Sundays**) are newspapers which are sold on Sundays. They are usually bigger than newspapers sold on other days of the week, and often have several different parts. • *(dated) Everyone turned up to the school concert wearing their* **Sunday best** (= their best clothes which they wear on special occasions). • *(disapproving)* If someone is described as a **Sunday driver**, it means that they drive unnecessarily slowly, often annoying other drivers. • **Sunday school** is a class held on Sundays in which esp. Christian children are given religious teaching: *They sent all their children* **to** *Sunday school.* ○ *She has been a Sunday-school teacher for years.* • LP **Calendar**

sun·deck /ˈsʌn·dek/ *n* [C] a part of a ship or a flat area beside or on the roof of a house where you can sit in order to enjoy the sun

sun·dial /ˈsʌn·daɪl/ *n* [C] a device used outside, esp. in the past, which consists of a thin piece of metal fixed to a flat surface marked with numbers, which shows the time by the metal making a dark line on the surface as the sun moves across the sky above it • *English churchyards often have sundials in them – sometimes there is one on the church itself.* • *"I am a sundial, and I make a botch/ Of what is done much better by a watch"* (in the poem *On a sundial* by Hilaire Belloc, 1938) • PIC **Clocks and watches**

sun·down /ˈsʌn·daʊn/ *n* [C] *esp. Am and Aus for* SUNSET

sun·dress /ˈsʌn·dres/ *n* [C] a informal dress without sleeves that is worn in hot weather

sun·dry /ˈsʌn·dri/ *adj* [before n; not gradable] several different; various • *This cream can be used to treat cuts and bruises and sundry other minor injuries.* • *Sundry distant relatives, most of whom I hardly recognized, turned up for my brother's wedding.* • *(infml) I don't want* **all and sundry** (= everyone, including people who are not specially important to me) *knowing about our problems.*

sun·dries /ˈsʌn·driz/ *pl n* • Sundries are various different small items which are considered together, usually because they are not important enough to be considered separately: *There's an item on the hotel bill for sundries.*

sun·flow·er /£ˈsʌnˌflaʊəʳ, $-ˌflaʊr/ *n* [C] a plant usually having a very tall stem and a single large round flat yellow flower, with many long thin narrow petals close together • *Sunflowers are sometimes grown commercially for their seeds which can be eaten or used for making cooking oil.* • *I tend to cook with sunflower* **oil**. • PIC **Flowers and plants**

sung /sʌŋ/ *past participle of* SING

sun·glas·ses /£ˈsʌŋˌglɑː·sɪz, $ˈsʌnˌglæs·ɪz/, **dark glas·ses**, *infml* **shades** *pl n* dark glasses which you wear to protect your eyes from bright light from the sun • *a* **pair of** *sunglasses* • *I always* **wear** *sunglasses when I'm driving on a sunny day.* • *He looked very fashionable in his designer sunglasses.*

sunk /sʌŋk/ *past participle of* SINK

sunk·en /ˈsʌŋ·kən/ *adj* having (been) sunk, or (been) moved into a position below the surrounding level • *Thousands of people watched as the sunken sixteenth-century* **ship** *was raised from the bottom of the harbour.* • *They're diving for sunken* **treasure**. • *We're putting a sunken* **bath** *in our bathroom.* • If someone's **eyes** or **cheeks** are sunken, they look as if they have fallen inwards into their face, esp. because they are tired, or have been ill, or are old: *Pictures of people in the prison camps showed them with protruding ribs and sunken eyes.* ○ *She looked old and thin with sunken cheeks and hollow eyes.*

sun·lamp /ˈsʌn·læmp/ *n* [C] a device which produces light which has similar effects to that of light from the sun, and which is used esp. for making the skin brown • *She spends several hours a week* **under** *a sunlamp to keep her skin looking tanned.* • *Sunlamps can also be used to help treat injured muscles.*

sun·less /ˈsʌn·ləs/ *adj* See at SUN STAR

sun·light /ˈsʌn·laɪt/ *n* [U] the light that comes from the sun • *Tall buildings block out the sunlight in many New York streets.* • *The early morning/afternoon/evening sunlight shone through the curtains.* • *The lake sparkled in the* **bright/brilliant** *sunlight.* • *I always try not to leave my car parked in* **direct/strong** *sunlight.* • **Dappled** *sunlight shone through the leaves of the trees.*

sun·lit /ˈsʌn·lɪt/ *adj* [not gradable] • *a sunlit room/courtyard/patio* (= one which receives a lot of light from the sun)

Sun·ni /ˈsʊn·i/ *adj* [not gradable], *n* [C] (a member) of the largest Islamic religious group, which follows the teachings only of Mohammed, not those of any of the religious leaders who came after him • *a Sunni Muslim* • *a Sunni sect* • *Saudi Arabia is a mainly Sunni country.* • *Muslims in Saudi Arabia are mainly Sunnis.*

sun·ny /ˈsʌn·i/ *adj* **-ier, -iest** See at SUN STAR

sun·ray /ˈsʌn·reɪ/ *adj* [before n; not gradable] *Br and Aus* using ULTRAVIOLET light • *a sunray lamp* • *He's having sunray treatment for his bad back.*

sun·ray /ˈsʌn·reɪ/ *n* [C] • Sunray is *Am and Aus for* SUNBEAM.

sun·rise /ˈsʌn·raɪz/ *n* the time in the morning when the sun first comes into the sky, or the appearance of the sky at that time • *We have to leave before sunrise (also esp. Am* **sun·up***) tomorrow.* [U] • *They went out* **at** *sunrise in order to go bird-watching.* [U] • *There was a beautiful sunrise this morning.* [C]

sun·roof /ˈsʌn·ruːf/ *n* [C] part of a roof of a car which can be opened to let in air and light from the sun • *an electric/sliding sunroof* • *a removable sunroof* • PIC Car

sun·screen /ˈsʌn·skriːn/, **sun·block** *n* [U] a substance which you put on your skin to prevent it from being burnt by the sun • *People with fair skin should always use a sunscreen when they're out in the sun.* [C] • *Have you put any sunscreen on the children?* [U]

sun·set /ˈsʌn·set/ *n* the time in the evening when you last see the sun in the sky, or the appearance of the sky at that time • *The fishermen set out* **at** *sunset (also esp. Am* **sundown***) for a night's fishing.* [U] • *We sat on the beach watching the sunset.* [C] • *Some of the most spectacular sunsets I've seen have been in the Caribbean.* [C] • *It was one of those films where at the end, they* **rode/drove/walked** *off into the* sunset (= the film ended happily, with the main characters riding etc. away at sunset). [U] • *(fig.) So do you think Matthew and Caroline are going to be* **riding/driving/walking** *off into the* sunset together (= that their relationship will last and that they will be happy)? [U]

sun·shade /ˈsʌn·ʃeɪd/ *n* [C] an object similar to an UMBRELLA (= round cloth-covered frame on a stick) which you carry to protect yourself from light from the sun • *The baby's chair had a sunshade fixed to it.* • A sunshade (*Am and Aus usually* **umbrella**) is also a larger folding frame of this type, which you put into the ground to form an area which is sheltered from the light of the sun: *Our garden table has a hole in the centre of it through which you can put a sunshade.* • Sunshade is also *Am for* AWNING.

sun·shine /ˈsʌn·ʃaɪn/ *n* [U] the light and heat that come from the sun • *The children were out playing* **in the** *sunshine.* • *After the early morning mist has lifted, most areas should have some sunshine today.* • *The beach was packed with people basking in the* **blazing/brilliant** *sunshine.* • *I can't remember when we last had a day of* **unbroken** (= continuous) *sunshine.* • *(fig.) Their grandchildren have brought sunshine into their lives* (= made them very happy). • *(esp. Br infml)* Sunshine can also be used as a form of address, either in a friendly way, or to express unwillingness to accept another person's delays, weaknesses etc.: *Hello, sunshine!* ○ *Come on, sunshine, get a move on.* • *"You are the sunshine of my life* (= You are the thing in my life that makes me the most happy)*"* (title of a song by Stevie Wonder, 1973)

sun·spot /£ˈsʌn·spɒt, $-spɑːt/ *n* [C] a dark spot on the surface of the sun which appears for a few days or weeks then disappears

sun·stroke /£ˈsʌn·strəʊk, $-stroʊk/ *n* [U] a serious illness caused by spending too much time in strong heat and light from the sun • *Someone who is suffering from sunstroke feels dizzy and has a high temperature, but does not sweat.*

sun·tan /ˈsʌn·tæn/, **tan** *n* [C] the state of white skin having turned brown or brown skin turning darker brown, because of having been in the light and heat from the sun • *She wore a white T-shirt to show off her suntan.* • *They came back from their holiday in the Mediterranean with* **deep** *suntans.* • *The only thing he wants to do when he's in Malta is* **get** *a suntan.* • *What sort of suntan* **cream/lotion/oil** (= cream or oil used to help skin become darker in the light and heat from the sun) *do you use?* • Compare SUNBURN.

sun·tanned /ˈsʌn·tænd/, **tanned** /tænd/ *adj* • *They looked healthy and suntanned after their week in Jamaica.* • *She crossed her long, suntanned legs.*

sun·trap /ˈsʌn·træp/ *n* [C] *Br and Aus* a sheltered place that receives a lot of light and heat from the sun • *The house is built round a small courtyard, which is a* **real** *suntrap.*

sup *(obj)* /sʌp/ *v* **-pp-** *esp. Br* to drink or to eat • *(regional or humorous) He spends most of his evenings in the pub, supping* (= drinking) *beer.* [T] • *(regional or humorous) Sup* **up** *and have another!* [I always + adv/prep] • *He had used his home as a hotel for foreign visitors, charging £1800 a week with promises of being able to "sup or dine* (= eat an evening meal)*" with a lord.* [I always + adv/prep] • *(dated) They supped* **on/off** *cold meat.* [I always + adv/prep] • *(saying)* 'If you sup with the devil you need a long spoon' means it is best not to become involved in risky or bad dealings with others.

su·per EXCELLENT /£ˈsuː·pəʳ, $-pɚ/ *adj infml slightly dated or humorous* excellent; extremely good • *Thank you for a super evening.* • *That's a super dress you're wearing.* • *The Natural History Museum is a super place for kids.* • *"Did you enjoy the film?" "Yes, I thought it was super."* • In the US, the **Super Bowl** is a game of American football, played in January, in which the winner of one of the two football divisions plays the winner of the other, and the one which wins is considered the leading team in the country. • Ⓙ ⓀⓄⓇ Ⓣ

su·per PERSON /£ˈsuː·pəʳ, $-pɚ/ *n* [C] *Br infml for* **superintendent**, see at SUPERINTEND

su·per- MORE THAN USUAL /£ˈsuː·pəʳ-, $-pɚ-/ *combining form* larger, or more effective, or more powerful, or more successful than usual; very or more than usually • *a supercomputer* • *a superstate* • *a supermodel* • *a superhero* • *the super-rich* • *a superfast car* • *superfine stockings* • *super-soft toilet paper* • *super-absorbent paper towels* • *superconcentrated detergent*

su·per- OVER /£ˈsuː·pəʳ-, $-pɚ-/ *combining form* over; above • *superscript* • *a superstructure* • *to superimpose*

su·per·a·bun·dant /£ˌsuː·pəʳ·əˈbʌn·dənt, $-pɚ-/ *adj* [not gradable] existing in very large amounts • *Grapes and olives are superabundant in this part of France.* • *We've had such a superabundant crop of apples this year, I don't know what to do with them all.*

su·per·a·bun·dance /£ˌsuː·pəʳ·əˈbʌn·dənts, $-pɚ-/ *n* [U] • *There's* **a** *superabundance* **of** *films being shown at this year's film festival.*

su·per·an·nu·at·ed /£ˌsuː·pəʳˈæn·ju·eɪ·tɪd, $-pɚˈæn·ju·eɪ·t̬ɪd/ *adj humorous* old, and almost no longer suitable for work or use • *Why do you want to go and see that superannuated rock band?* • *No one supports these superannuated* (= old-fashioned) *policies.*

su·per·an·nu·a·tion *Br and Aus* /£ˌsuː·pəʳˌæn·juˈeɪ·ʃən, $-pɚ-/, *Aus infml* **su·per** *n* [U] money which people pay while they are working, so that they will receive payment when they stop working when they are old, or the payment they receive when they stop working • *I'm paying superannuation/I'm paying into a superannuation scheme.* • *What happens to your superannuation if you retire early?*

su·perb /£suːˈpɜːb, $-ˈpɜːrb/ *adj* of excellent quality; very great • *She is a superb teacher/dancer/musician/tennis player.* • *The museum has a superb collection of twentieth-century art.* • *Taylor scored a superb goal at the end of the first half.* • *This chocolate cake is superb.*

su·perb·ly /£suːˈpɜː·bli, $-ˈpɜːr-/ *adv* • *a superbly written book* • *The orchestra played superbly.* • *I thought you handled that problem superbly.*

su·per·charge *obj* /£ˈsuː·pə·tʃɑːdʒ, $-pɚ·tʃɑːrdʒ/ *v* [T usually passive] to make (an engine) more powerful by forcing in more air and fuel than usual • *a supercharged Mercedes* • *(fig.) The economy has expanded at a supercharged pace* (= very quickly). • *(fig.) There was a supercharged atmosphere* (= very strong feelings were expressed) *during the debate in the House of Commons last night.*

su·per·charg·er /£ˈsuː·pəˌtʃɑː·dʒəʳ, $-pɚˌtʃɑːr·dʒɚ/ *n* [C] • A supercharger is a device which produces more power in an engine by forcing more air into the part of it in which fuel burns.

su·per·cil·i·ous /£ˌsuː·pəˈsɪl·i·əs, $-pɚ-/ *adj disapproving* behaving as if or showing that you think that you are better than other people, and that their opinions etc. are not important • *I don't like going in that shop because the assistants are always so supercilious.* • *She has a very supercilious manner.* • *He spoke in a haughty, supercilious voice.*

su·per·cil·i·ous·ly /£ˌsuː·pəˈsɪl·i·ə·sli, $-pɚ-/ *adv disapproving* • *"How nice," she said superciliously when I told her where I'd been for my holiday.*

su·per·cil·i·ous·ness /£ˌsuː·pəˈsɪl·i·ə·snəs, $-pɚ-/ *n* [U] *disapproving*

su·per·con·duc·ti·vi·ty /£ˌsuː·pəˌkɒn·dʌkˈtɪv·ɪ·ti, $-pɚˌkɑːn·dʌkˈtɪv·ə·t̬i/ *n* [U] the ability of some substances, esp. metals, to allow an electrical current to move freely through them at very low temperatures

su·per·con·duc·tor /£ˈsuː·pə·kənˌdʌk·təʳ, $-pɚ·kənˌdʌk·tɚ/ *n* [C] • A superconductor is a substance, esp. a metal, that allows an electrical current to move freely through it at a very low temperature.

su·per·e·go /£ˌsuː·pəˈriː·gəʊ, $-pɚˈiː·goʊ/ *n* [C] *pl* **superegos** *specialized* (in PSYCHOANALYSIS) the part of your mind which knows what is right and wrong according to the rules of the society in which you live, and which causes you to feel guilty when you do something wrong • Compare EGO; ID.

su·per·fi·cial /£ˌsuː·pəˈfɪʃ·ᵊl, $-pɚ-/ *adj* on the surface only • *I thought that article was written at a very superficial level* (= it only dealt with the obvious parts of its subject, not with all the parts). • *The documentary's treatment/analysis of the issues was very superficial* (= was not detailed). • *The interviewer asked rather superficial questions.* • *I only have a superficial* (= slight) *knowledge of French.* • *(disapproving)* A person who is superficial does not care very much or think very seriously about anything, esp. important matters: *He's fun to be with, but he's very superficial.* ○ *She has a certain superficial charm, but no real depth.* • Damage that is superficial is caused only to the surface of something: *The car was completely wrecked in the accident, but the driver only received superficial injuries/cuts/wounds* (= only the surface of his or her body was hurt). • Superficial can also be used to describe the appearance that something has the first time you look at it, esp. when this is not what it is really like: *There are superficial similarities between the two cars, but actually they're quite different.*

su·per·fi·ci·al·i·ty /£ˌsuː·pəˌfɪʃ·iˈæl·ɪ·ti, $-pɚˌfɪʃ·iˈæl·ə·t̬i/ *n* [U] • *Despite a certain superficiality* **of** *analysis* (= its only dealing with the obvious parts of its subject), *the book contains some interesting new ideas.* • *It was impossible for him to conceal the superficiality* **of** *his knowledge* (= how slight it was). • *We were struck by her superficiality* (= her lack of serious thinking and caring very much). • *The doctor says that because of the superficiality* **of** *the wound* (= because it is only the surface of the body that has been damaged), *it will heal quickly.*

su·per·fi·cial·ly /£ˌsuː·pəˈfɪʃ·ᵊl·i, $-pɚ-/ *adv* • *Religious education is poorly and superficially taught* (= not taught in a detailed way) *in 60 per cent of all schools.* • *Superficially, the company's financial results look good this year* (= They look good if they are not examined in a detailed way). • *The job I've been offered is superficially* (= seems to be) *attractive/appealing, but I think I might find it boring after a while.* • *Superficially, the twins are* (= They seem to be) *very similar/alike, but there are actually a lot of differences between them.*

su·per·flu·ous /£suːˈpɜː·flu·əs, $-ˈpɜːr-/ *adj* more than is needed or wanted • *Whenever I go travelling, I always make sure that I don't take any superfluous luggage with me.* • *There was an article in the magazine about ways of removing superfluous hair.* • *In the circumstances, his comments were rather superfluous* (= unnecessary because they did not add anything). • *Their eyes met across the room, and words were superfluous.* • **It** *seems almost superfluous* **to** *say how grateful I am to you.* [+ to infinitive] • *As children become older and start to lead their own lives, their parents can sometimes begin to feel that they are superfluous* (= no longer needed or wanted).

su·per·flu·i·ty /£ˌsuː·pəˈfluː·ɪ·ti, $-pɚˈfluː·ə·t̬i/ *n* [U] *fml* • *The new director has said that there is* **a** *superfluity* **of** *staff* (= more than are needed) *in the organization, and that cuts must be made.*

su·per·flu·ous·ly /£suːˈpɜː·flu·ə·sli, $-ˈpɜːr-/ *adv* • *"It's broken," he said, somewhat superfluously, surveying the wreckage of the chair.*

su·per·flu·ous·ness /£suːˈpɜː·flu·ə·snəs, $-ˈpɜːr-/ *n* [U]

su·per·glue /£ˈsuː·pə·gluː, $-pɚ-/ *n* [U] *trademark* a very strong glue

su·per·grass /£ˈsuː·pə·grɑːs, $-pɚ·græs/ *n* [C] *Br* a person, esp. a criminal, who gives the police a lot of information about the activities of criminals, esp. serious ones

su·per·high·way /£ˈsuː·pəˌhaɪ·weɪ, $-pɚ-/ *n* [C] *Am* a road with two or more LANES (= parallel divisions) in each direction on which traffic travels at high speed

su·per·hu·man /£ˌsuː·pəˈhjuː·mən, $-pɚ-/ *adj* having more powers than, or seeming beyond the powers of, a human • *I'll never get all this work done in a week – I'm not superhuman!* • *He seems to have almost superhuman strength.* • *Thanks to the superhuman efforts of the volunteers, some aid is now getting through to those areas worst affected by the fighting.*

su·per·im·pose *obj* /£ˌsuː·pə·rɪmˈpəʊz, $-pɚ·ɪmˈpoʊz/ *v* [T] to put (esp. a picture, words etc.) on top of something else, esp. another picture, words etc., so that what is in the lower position can still be seen, heard etc. • *She said that the picture showed her body, but with someone else's head superimposed* (**on** *it*). • *Outlines of national boundaries in the eighteenth century were superimposed* **over** *a map of modern Europe.*

su·per·in·tend *obj* /£ˌsuː·pə·rɪnˈtend, $-pɚ·ɪn-/ *v* [T] to be in charge of • *I've been asked to superintend the department in Mr Clark's absence.* • *Her job is to superintend the production process.*

su·per·in·ten·dent /£ˌsuː·pə·rɪnˈten·dənt, $-pɚ·ɪn-/ *n* [C] • A superintendent is a person who is in charge of work done in a particular department, office, etc., or is responsible for keeping a building or place in good condition: *In the US, a superintendent of schools is in charge of the schools in a particular area.* ○ *The park superintendent has agreed to put up a fence around the children's play area to keep dogs out.* ○ *We asked the superintendent (also Am infml* **super**) (= the person responsible for keeping a building in good condition) *to have the broken window in our apartment repaired.* • *(Br)* A superintendent (*infml* **super**) is also a police officer of high rank: *She recently became a superintendent.* ○ *The officer in charge of the case is Superintendent Lewis.*

su·pe·ri·or BETTER /£suːˈpɪə·ri·əʳ, $-ˈpɪr·i·ɚ/ *adj* [not gradable] better than average or better than other people or things of the same type • *This is clearly the work of a superior artist.* • *They are people of superior taste.* • *We chose her for the job because she was the superior candidate.* • *The rebels were no match for the government troops with their vastly superior weapons.* • *Manufacturing companies spend millions of pounds trying to convince customers that their products are superior* **to** *those of other companies.* • *For all babies, breastfeeding is far superior* **to** *bottlefeeding.* • *It makes her very angry when he says that men are intrinsically superior* **to** *women.* • *(disapproving)* Someone who is superior or who behaves in a superior way is also someone who believes that they are better than other people: *I can't bear Louise – she's so superior.* ○ *Leonard's superior manner offended people almost immediately.* ○ *She gave a superior smile.* • *The demonstrators were superior* **in** *numbers* (= There were more of them), *but the police were superior* **in** *strength* (= they had greater strength). • Compare INFERIOR.

su·pe·ri·or·i·ty /£suːˌpɪə·riˈɒr·ɪ·ti, $-ˌpɪr·iˈɔːr·ə·t̬i/ *n* [U] • *The Australians demonstrated their superiority* (= that they were better than the other team) *early in the match.* • *The compact disc's technological superiority* **over** *records lies in the fact that it stores music in the same way as computers store information.* • *(disapproving) Her sense of superiority* (= that she is better than other people) *makes her very unpopular.* • *The allied troops were victorious because of their superiority* **in** *numbers* (= there were more of them). • *(infml)* If you have a **superiority complex**, you believe that you are better, cleverer or more important than other people. • Compare **inferiority** at INFERIOR.

su·pe·ri·or HIGHER /£suːˈpɪə·ri·əʳ, $-ˈpɪr·i·ɚ/ *n, adj* [not gradable] (a person or group of people who are) higher in rank or social position than others • *I will pass your complaint on to my superiors.* [C] • *The soldier was reported to his superior officer for failing in his duties.* • *It used to be common practice for men to remove their hats when they were in the presence of a social superior.* [C] • *She is socially superior* **to** *her husband.* • *In the Indian caste system, marrying someone from a superior caste is not allowed.*

su·pe·ri·or·i·ty /£suːˌpɪə·riˈɒr·ɪ·ti, $-ˌpɪr·iˈɔːr·ə·t̬i/ *n* [U] • *racial superiority*

su·per·la·tive GRAMMAR /£suːˈpɜː·lə·tɪv, $-ˈpɜːr·lə·t̬ɪv/ *n* [C] the form of an adjective or adverb which expresses that the thing or person being described has more of the particular quality than anything or anyone else of the same type • *'Richest'* **is the** *superlative* **of** *'rich'.* • *'Most' is* **the** *superlative* **of** *'many'.* • *The magazine article contained so many superlatives that I found it hard to believe that what it was saying was true.* • LP **Comparing and grading**

su·per·la·tive /£suːˈpɜː·lə·tɪv, $-ˈpɜːr·lə·t̬ɪv/ *adj* [not gradable] • *'Slowest' is the superlative form of 'slow'.* • *'Best' is the superlative form of 'good'.*

su·per·la·tive BEST /£suːˈpɜː·lə·tɪv, $-ˈpɜːr·lə·t̬ɪv/ *adj* [not gradable] of the highest quality; the best • *We went to a superlative restaurant.* • *The performance was superlative.*

su·per·la·tive·ly /£suː'pɜː·lə·tɪv·li, $-'pɜːr·lə·t̬ɪv-/ *adv* [not gradable] • *The company has been superlatively successful* (= successful to the highest degree) *this year.* • *The Australian team played superlatively.*

su·per·man (*pl* **-men**), **su·per·wo·man** (*pl* **-women**) /£'suː·pə·mæn, $-pɚ-, -ˌwʊm·ən/ *n* [C] a person who has greater strength, ability, intelligence, etc. than other humans • *The film portrays Gandhi as a kind of superman.* • *It would take a superman to get the company out of its present financial difficulties.* • Superwoman is often used to refer to a woman who combines a successful job with having children and taking care of a home: *She said that she was tired of being expected to be a superwoman.*

su·per·mar·ket /£'suː·pəˌmɑː·kɪt, $-pɚˌmɑːr-/ *n* [C] a large shop which sells most types of food and other goods needed in the home, in which people take from shelves the items they want to buy and pay for them as they leave • *You get a much bigger choice of things at a supermarket than you do at the local corner shop.* • *The major supermarket* **chains** (= companies which own a lot of different supermarkets in different parts of the country) *are involved in a price war.* • *(Br and Aus) Why is it that supermarket* **trolleys** *(Am* **carts***) always have one wheel which goes in the opposite direction to the other three?* • *(Am)* A **supermarket tabloid** is a newspaper sold in supermarkets which contains reports about famous people's private lives, or other things that have happened which are often hard to believe: *He had a copy of one of the supermarket tabloids, those weekly newspapers that offer readers a feast of gossip, scandal and believe-it-or-not phenomena.* • PIC **Supermarket**

su·per·mo·del /£'suː·pəˌmɒd·əl, $-pɚˌmɑː·dəl/ *n* [C] any of a small group of the most famous and highly paid MODELS (= people, esp. women, who wear clothes to show them to possible buyers) in the world

su·per·na·tur·al /£ˌsuː·pə'nætʃ·ər·əl, $-pɚ'nætʃ·ɚ-/ *adj* caused by forces that are not able to be explained by science • *Ghosts and evil spirits are supernatural.* • *She is said to have supernatural* **powers** *and to be able to communicate with the dead.* • *Strange supernatural* **beings** *were painted on the walls of the caves.*

su·per·na·tur·al /£ˌsuː·pə'nætʃ·ər·əl, $-pɚ'nætʃ·ɚ-/ *n* [U] • *I don't believe in* **the** *supernatural* (= matters and experiences connected with forces that cannot be explained by science).

su·per·na·tur·al·ly /£ˌsuː·pə'nætʃ·ər·əl·i, $-pɚ'nætʃ·ɚ-/ *adv*

su·per·no·va /£ˌsuː·pə'nəʊ·və, $-pɚ'noʊ-/ *n* [C] *pl* **supernovas** or **supernovae** /£ˌsuː·pə'nəʊ·viː, $-pɚ'noʊ-/ a star which has exploded, greatly increasing its brightness for a few months • *A supernova is about ten thousand million times brighter than the Sun.*

su·per·po·wer /£'suː·pəˌpaʊər, $-pɚˌpaʊr/ *n* [C] a country which has very great political and military power • *Before the break-up of the Soviet Union, it and the USA were considered to be the main superpowers in the late twentieth century.*

su·per·sa·ver /£'suː·pəˌseɪ·vər, $-pɚˌseɪ·vɚ/ *n* [C] a ticket for travel by aircraft, train, etc. for which you pay less, either by buying it in advance or because you make your journey during a less busy period; or *(Br)* any item which you buy at specially reduced price • *a supersaver fare* • *a supersaver ticket* • *a New York-London supersaver* • *(Br) The supersavers on offer this week are baked beans, chocolate biscuits, cornflakes and bananas.*

su·per·script /£'suː·pə·skrɪpt, $-pɚ-/ *n, adj* [not gradable] (a word, letter, number, or symbol) written or printed just above a word, letter, number or symbol, usually in a smaller size • *References to the notes are given* **in** *superscript.* [U] • *The number 2 written* **in** *superscript after another number means that the number is to be multiplied by itself.* [U] • *The superscript numbers in the text refer to the bibliography.*

su·per·sede *obj* /£ˌsuː·pə'siːd, $-pɚ-/ *v* [T] to replace (esp. something older or more old-fashioned) • *Most of the old road – which stretched from Chicago to Los Angeles – has been superseded by the great Interstate highways.* • *No sooner do you buy a computer than they bring out a new one which supersedes it.* • *Odell is within one match of superseding White* **as** *the youngest English amateur champion.*

su·per·son·ic /£ˌsuː·pə'sɒn·ɪk, $-pɚ'sɑː·nɪk/ *adj* [not gradable] (which can fly) at or faster than the speed of sound • *a supersonic fighter aircraft* • *a supersonic missile* • *The supersonic travel age began on May 24, 1976 when Concorde first flew from London to Washington.*

su·per·star /£'suː·pə·stɑːr, $-pɚ·stɑːr/ *n* [C] an extremely famous actor, singer, musician, sports player etc. • *a football superstar* • *a rock superstar* • *a superstar quarterback* • *All the Hollywood superstars are gathering for tonight's Oscar ceremony.*

su·per·star·dom /£'suː·pəˌstɑː·dəm, $-pɚˌstɑːr-/ *n* [U] • *She shot to superstardom almost overnight.*

su·per·sti·tion /£ˌsuː·pə'stɪʃ·ən, $-pɚ-/ *n* (a) belief which is not based on human reason or scientific knowledge, but is connected with old ideas about magic etc. • *According to superstition, if you walk under a ladder it brings you bad luck.* [U] • *Out of superstition, she never has 13 people sitting at the table to eat together.* [U] • *I don't believe that four-leaved clovers are lucky – that's just a superstition.* [C] • *Even in modern times, people cling to superstitions handed down through the centuries.* [C] • *There's a superstition* **that** *if you break a mirror, you'll have seven years' bad luck.* [C + that clause]

su·per·sti·tious /£ˌsuː·pə'stɪʃ·əs, $-pɚ-/ *adj* • *Some people are superstitious* **about** *spilling salt on the table.* • *I think it's just superstitious nonsense that 13 is an unlucky number.*

su·per·sti·tious·ly /£ˌsuː·pə'stɪʃ·ə·sli, $-pɚ-/ *adv*

su·per·store /£'suː·pə·stɔːr, $-pɚ·stɔːr/ *n* [C] an extremely large shop which sells food and/or other goods usually for use in the home at cheaper prices than most other shops • *a food superstore* • *a furniture superstore* • *a DIY superstore* • *a giant superstore* • *an out-of-town superstore* • *a discount superstore*

su·per·struc·ture /£'suː·pəˌstrʌk·tʃər, $-pɚˌstrʌk·tʃɚ/ *n* [C] a structure built on top of something else • The superstructure **of** a building is the part of a building which is above the ground: *The foundations are finished and work has now begun on building the superstructure of the new library.* • The superstructure **of** a ship is the part of it above the main DECK: *The battleship was hit by a missile which damaged its superstructure.* • A superstructure is also the ideas and systems of a society or organization which develop from more basic ideas and systems: *According to Marxist theory, a society's superstructure is its legal, social, cultural and political institutions, which are based on its economic systems.*

su·per·tank·er /£'suː·pəˌtæŋ·kər, $-pɚˌtæŋ·kɚ/ *n* [C] a very large ship, which transports esp. oil • *Thousands of gallons of oil were spilled when the supertanker ran aground.*

su·per·ti·tle /£'suː·pəˌtaɪ·tl̩, $-pɚˌtaɪ·t̬l̩/ *n* [C] *Am for* SURTITLE

su·per·vise *obj* /£'suː·pə·vaɪz, $-pɚ-/ *v* [T] to watch over (an activity or job) to make certain that it is done correctly, or to watch over (someone) to make certain that they are behaving correctly or are safe • *The UN is supervising the distribution of aid to those areas worst affected by the fighting.* • *Each group of construction workers who are working on the building is supervised by its own foreman.* • *Her new job involves supervising the company's operations in Japan.* • *The teachers take it in turn to supervise the children* (= make certain that they behave correctly and are safe) *at playtime.*

su·per·vi·sion /£ˌsuː·pəˈvɪʒ·ᵊn, $-pɚ-/ *n* [U] • *Small children should not be left alone without supervision* (= being watched to make certain that they behave correctly and are safe). • *Students are not allowed to handle these chemicals unless they are* **under** *the supervision* **of** *a teacher* (= watched by a teacher to make certain that they act correctly).

su·per·vis·or /£ˈsuː·pə·vaɪ·zəʳ, $-pɚ·vaɪ·zɚ/ *n* [C] • *The shop assistant said that he needed to get his supervisor* (= the person who was in charge of him) *to authorize my refund.* • In some colleges, a supervisor is also a teacher with responsibility for a particular student: *My supervisor wants my essay in by Friday.* • *(Am)* A **town** or **county** supervisor is an elected official who manages local government services.

su·per·vis·o·ry /£ˌsuː·pəˈvaɪ·zᵊr·i, $-pɚˈvaɪ·zɚ-/ *adj* [not gradable] • *A supervisory body* (= one which watches over activities to see that they are done correctly) *has been set up to monitor the activities of the press.* • *We need to employ more supervisory staff.*

su·per·wo·man /£ˈsuː·pəˌwʊm·ən, $-pɚ-/ *n* [C] *pl* **-women** See at SUPERMAN

su·pine /ˈsuː·paɪn, £ˈsjuː-/ *adj, adv* [not gradable] *fml* (lying) flat on your back, looking up • *We walked along the beach, past the rows of supine bodies soaking up the sun.* • *When he injured his back, he had to lie supine for several weeks.* • *(fig. disapproving)* If you are supine, you are weak and willingly accept the control of others: *The new director has introduced a series of changes against little opposition from the supine staff.* • Compare PRONE [LYING DOWN].

su·pine·ly /ˈsuː·paɪn·li, £ˈsjuː-/ *adv* [not gradable] *fml* • *(fig. disapproving) The public seem willing supinely* (= weakly and willingly) *to accept all that the government says.*

sup·per /£ˈsʌp·əʳ, $-ɚ/ *n* a small meal eaten in the late evening, or a main meal eaten in the evening • *We usually have tea at about 5.30 p.m., then supper before we go to bed.* [U] • *Do you want some supper?* [U] • *Would you like to come to supper tonight?* [U] • *We're having pasta for supper.* [U] • *They had a late supper after they'd been to the theatre.* [C]

sup·plant *obj* /£səˈplɑːnt, $-ˈplænt/ *v* [T] *slightly fml* to replace • *In most offices, the typewriter has now been supplanted by the computer.* • *The state of the economy has supplanted all other issues as the major item of current public concern.* • *Small children can often feel supplanted (in their parents' affections)* (= that their parents no longer like them as much) *when a new brother or sister is born.*

sup·ple /ˈsʌp·l̩/ *adj* **-r, -st** bending or able to be bent easily; not stiff • *I'm not supple enough* (= My body doesn't bend easily enough) *to be able to touch the floor with my hands while I'm standing up.* • *You need to have supple* **limbs** *to be a dancer.* • *His shoes were made of supple leather.* • *Using a moisturizing cream can help keep your skin supple.* • *(fig.) She has shown that she has a supple mind* (= that she is able to think quickly and clearly, and can produce and deal with new ideas).

sup·ple·ness /ˈsʌp·l̩.nəs/ *n* [U] • *We were amazed at the suppleness* **of** *the gymnasts.* • *Regular polishing will improve the suppleness* **of** *the leather.*

sup·ple·ment /ˈsʌp·lɪ·mənt/ *n* [C] something which is added to something else in order to improve it or complete it; something extra • *The money I get from teaching evening classes provides a supplement* **to** *my income from my job.* • *We paid a supplement* (= an extra amount of money) *so that we could have a cabin on board the ship.* • *Perhaps you should take a vitamin supplement.* • A supplement is also a part of a magazine or newspaper, either produced separately or as part of the magazine or newspaper: *The Times Higher Education Supplement* • *the Sunday supplements* ○ *The newspaper publishes a sports supplement every Monday.* ○ *The magazine this month is running a special supplement, its 'A-Z of Safe Food'.* • A supplement **to** a book is an additional part of it, either produced separately or included at the end of the book, which contains information that was not available when the book was first produced: *The dictionary has a supplement containing new words at the end of it.*

sup·ple·ment *obj* /ˈsʌp·lɪ·ment, ˌ-ˈ-/ *v* [T] • *He supplements* (= adds to) *his income by working in a bar in the evening.* • *Some vegetarians like to supplement their diets* **with** *iron tablets.* • *In the busy holiday season, extra buses are provided to supplement the existing service.*

sup·ple·men·ta·ry /£ˌsʌp·lɪˈmen·tᵊr·i, $-t̬ɚ-/, *Am also* **sup·ple·men·tal** /£ˌsʌp·lɪˈmen·tᵊl, $-t̬ᵊl/ *adj* [not gradable] • *Although the book does not represent a thorough course in astrophysics, it will make excellent supplementary reading.* • *The farmer has a supplementary income from letting part of his land to campers.* • *The money he makes from selling the vegetables he grows in his garden is supplementary* **to** *his main income.* • *(specialized)* If an angle is supplementary **to** another angle, it forms 180° when combined with it: *An angle of 80° is supplementary to an angle of 100° – they are* **supplementary angles**.

sup·pli·cate *(obj)* /ˈsʌp·lɪ·keɪt/ *v fml or literary* to ask (esp. a god or a person who is in a position of power) for (something) in an anxious way that shows that you do not think that you are very important • *It is humiliating to be forced to supplicate assistance* **from** *your former enemy/ supplicate your former enemy* **for** *assistance.* [T] • *The members of the congregation bowed their heads, silently supplicating.* [I]

sup·pli·cant /ˈsʌp·lɪ·kənt/ *n* [C] *fml or literary* • A supplicant is a person who asks esp. a god or someone who is in a position of power for something in an anxious way that shows that they do not think that they are very important: *In the otherwise empty church, a solitary supplicant knelt before the altar.* ○ *Supplicants* **for** *mercy were brought before the king.*

sup·pli·ca·tion /ˌsʌp·lɪˈkeɪ·ʃᵊn/ *n fml or literary* • *Inside the temple, worshippers were kneeling in supplication.* [U] • *They have made a supplication* **for** *help.* [C]

sup·ply *obj* /səˈplaɪ/ *v* [T] to provide (something that is needed), or to provide something that is needed to (someone) • *Electrical power is supplied by underground cables.* • *He's been accused of supplying drugs.* • *The tourist office can supply information about accommodation and activities in the area.* • *I'm afraid I can't supply the answer to your question.* • *Three people have been arrested for supplying arms* **to** *the terrorists.* • *The company has supplied the royal family* (= provided them with something they need) *for years.* • *At the beginning of term, students are supplied* **with** *a list of books that they are expected to read.* • *The car comes supplied* **with** *stereo equipment, sunroof, electric windows, and more.*

sup·ply /səˈplaɪ/ *n* • *These birds generally nest within 20 minutes' flying time of a steady food supply* (= an amount of food available for use). [C] • *Whenever she goes out with her baby, she always takes a large supply* **of** *baby food with her.* [C] • *There was an unlimited supply* **of** *drink at the party.* [C] • *His doctor prescribed him a month's supply* **of** *the tablets* (= enough to last for a month). [C] • *There is a possibility that using chemical fertilizers might pollute the region's water supply* (= the water available for use). [C] • *In London, demand for cheap housing far outstrips supply* (= what is provided). [U] • *We need a reliable source of supply* **of** *cheap raw materials.* [U] • *Strawberries are in* **plentiful/short** *supply* (= there are many/not many of them available) *at the moment.* [U] • *A supply* **ship** (= one carrying goods, needed esp. by armed forces) *has been sunk.* • *The army's supply* **line** (= the route it used for providing goods needed by the soldiers) *has been cut by the enemy.* • *Prices have been allowed to be determined by the forces of* **supply and demand** (= the balance between the amount of goods available and the amount that people want to buy). • *(Br and Aus)* A **supply teacher** (*Am* **substitute (teacher)**) is a teacher who replaces other teachers at different schools when they are absent from work: *Does Ann Woodford still work as a supply teacher?*

sup·plies /səˈplaɪz/ *pl n* • Supplies are food and other ordinary goods needed by people every day: *The place where we're going camping is a long way from any shops, so we'll need to make sure we take sufficient supplies with us.* ○ *The refugees are urgently in need of food and medical supplies.* • Supplies are also an amount of something available: *Extensive mining has reduced the supplies* **of** *coal in the area.*

sup·pli·er /£səˈplaɪ·əʳ, $-ɚ/ *n* [C] • *The Soviet Union used to be the country's main supplier* **of** (= used to provide the country with most of its) *fuel and military equipment.* •

Paperworks Ltd is a leading stationery supplier (= a company which sells paper and other items used for writing), *with over 100 000 customers.* • *He said that he had got the drugs from his usual supplier* (= a person who sells drugs illegally).

sup·pli·ers /£sə'plaɪ·əz, $-ɚz/ *pl n* • Suppliers are a company which sells something: *I'll contact the suppliers and see if I can get the paint you want by Friday.*

sup·port *obj* ENCOURAGE /£sə'pɔːt, $-'pɔːrt/ *v* [T] to give encouragement and approval to (someone or something) because you want them to succeed • *My father supported the Labour Party all his life.* • *The majority of people in the town strongly support the plans to build a by-pass.* • *The motion was supported by 221 votes to 79.* • *I think it's important to support local businesses* (= to buy things from them). • *(esp. Br)* If you support (*Am usually* **root for**, *Aus* **barrack for**) a sports team or a sports player, you want them to win, and might show it by going to watch them play: *Which team do you support?* ○ *Who will you be supporting in the final?*

sup·port /£sə'pɔːt, $-'pɔːrt/ *n* [U] • *The victorious candidate in the election thanked everyone for their support.* • *Environmental groups are fast gaining support among young people.* • *Union leaders have not succeeded in winning grass-roots support* **for** *the strike.* • *Initially, public support* **for** *the war was overwhelming, but now it has become lukewarm.* • *We've succeeded in* **drumming up** *a lot of support* **for** *our attempt to stop the hospital being closed.* • *The British Prime Minister* **pledged** *support* **for** *the UN sanctions.* • *His organization has also tried to enlist the support of Members of Parliament.* • *The miners have come out on strike* **in** *support* **of** *their pay claim.* • *I signed a petition* **in** *support* **of** *the campaign to end the marketing of baby milk in developing countries.*

sup·port·er /£sə'pɔː·tə^r, $-'pɔːr·t̬ɚ/ *n* [C] • *He is one of the Prime Minister's strongest supporters* (= He strongly approves of him/her and agrees with what he/she is doing). • *Police think that the break-in at the laboratory was carried out by supporters* **of** *the animal rights campaign* (= people who want it to succeed). • *(esp. Br) Thousands of supporters (Am usually* **fans***)* (= people who want a particular team to win and might show it by going to watch them play) *are expected to travel to London this weekend for the cup final.* • LP **Sports**

sup·por·tive /£sə'pɔː·tɪv, $-'pɔːr·t̬ɪv/ *adj* • *Doubts about the government's policies are being expressed even by people who have been supportive* (= have approved) **of** *the government in the past.*

sup·port *obj* HELP /£sə'pɔːt, $-'pɔːrt/ *v* [T] to help (someone) emotionally or practically • *We all tried to support Joe when his wife died.* • *Alcoholics Anonymous is a group which supports people who are trying to stop drinking too much alcohol.* • *My family has always supported me* **in** *whatever I've wanted to do.* • *The union is supporting Linda* **in** *her claim that she was unfairly dismissed.*

sup·port /£sə'pɔːt, $-'pɔːrt/ *n* • *Liz gave me a lot of support when I lost my job.* [U] • *She said that she'd been very encouraged by all the letters/messages of support she'd received when she was hurt in the accident.* [U] • *You've been a great support* **to** *me.* [C] • *After their baby died, they joined a local* **support group** (= a group of people who have had similar experiences, esp. difficult ones, and who provide help to each other). • *It's almost impossible for battered women to start their lives again without a good* **support system/network** (= many people who provide emotional and practical help).

sup·por·tive /£sə'pɔː·tɪv, $-'pɔːr·t̬ɪv/ *adj approving* • *Children with supportive parents often do better at school than those without.* • *Thank you for being so supportive.* • *My boss has never been very supportive* **of** *me.* • *Her family was generally supportive* **of** *her decision.*

sup·por·tive·ly /£sə'pɔː·tɪv·li, $-pɔːr·t̬ɪv-/ *adv*

sup·por·tive·ness /£sə'pɔː·tɪv·nəs, $-'pɔːr·t̬ɪv-/ *n* [U]

sup·port *obj* STOP FROM FALLING /£sə'pɔːt, $-'pɔːrt/ *v* [T] to hold (something) firmly or bear its weight, esp. from below, to stop it from falling • *Two large timber beams support the roof.* • *The church dome is supported by/***on** *marble pillars.* • *Do you think the ice on the lake is thick enough to support our weight?* • *When babies first learn to stand, they hold on to something to support themselves* (= to stop themselves from falling). • *My ankle is rather weak, so I always put a bandage on it to support it when I play tennis.* • *(fig.) The Bank of England has taken measures to support the pound* (= to stop it from being reduced in value).

sup·port /£sə'pɔːt, $-'pɔːrt/ *n* • *The floor is held up by wooden supports* (= pieces of wood which bear its weight). [C] • *I've hurt my wrist, so I've got it bandaged to give it some support* (= to hold it firmly). [U] • *That bridge seems to have no* **(visible) means of** *support* (= no way of being held up). [U] • A support is also a device worn to hold part of the body, esp. a weak part, firmly in position: *Jim always wears a knee support when he goes running.* [C] ○ *She often wears support tights/stockings/(Am) hose to stop her legs getting tired.*

sup·port *obj* PROVIDE /£sə'pɔːt, $-'pɔːrt/ *v* [T] to provide (someone or something) with money or physical things that they need, esp. in order to continue to exist • If you support a person, you give them the money they need in order to buy food and clothes and pay for somewhere to live: *My parents supported me while I was at college.* ○ *He has a wife and four children to support.* ○ *She has no children to support her in her old age.* • *The land is so poor here that it cannot support* (= provide enough food and water for) *any crops.* • If you support an activity or a habit, you provide the money needed to pay for it: *The drug company is supporting cancer research.* ○ *I don't know how they manage to support their expensive lifestyle.* ○ *Some drug addicts turn to crime in order to support their habit.*

sup·port /£sə'pɔːt, $-'pɔːrt/ *n* [U] • *He is dependent on his father for support* (= for paying for food, a place to live, etc.). • *The government has decided to withdraw support from* (= stop giving money to) *the ballet company.* • *The BBC's 'Children in Need' Appeal attracted a lot of support from the public* (= they gave a lot of money to it). • *Since her husband has been in prison, she has had no* **(visible) means of** *support.*

sup·port *obj* ARGUE FOR /£sə'pɔːt, $-'pɔːrt/ *v* [T] to help to show (something) to be true • *There is insufficient evidence to support the theory.* • *These figures support my argument.* • *You can't make a statement like that without any supporting documentation.* • *The television replay supported the player's claim that the ball was out.*

sup·port /£sə'pɔːt, $-'pɔːrt/ *n* [U] • *This new evidence lends support to the theory that she was murdered.* • **In** *support* **of** *the idea, he produced some very complicated figures.* • *We had to send a doctor's report* **in** *support* **of** *our claim to the insurance company.*

sup·port·a·ble /£sə'pɔː·tə·bl̩, $-'pɔːr·t̬ə-/ *adj fml* • *a supportable proposition* (= one which can be shown to be true)

sup·port *obj* BEAR /£sə'pɔːt, $-'pɔːrt/ *v* [T usually in negatives] *fml* to bear; to allow to happen • *I can no longer support this stifling heat, day after day.* • *The headteacher told the boys that he would not support that kind of behaviour.*

sup·port·ing /£sə'pɔː·tɪŋ, $-'pɔːr·t̬ɪŋ/ *adj* [before n; not gradable] (in entertainment) not the most important • *She had a small supporting* **part/role** *in the play.* • *He has twice won an Oscar for best supporting actor.* • *(Br) A short supporting film was shown in advance of the main feature.* • *(Br) The main film starts at 2.30 p.m., but there's a supporting programme which starts at 1.45 p.m.* • *They first performed as a supporting act (Am usually* **opening act***) to a leading band five years ago.*

sup·pose THINK LIKELY /£sə'pəʊz, $-'poʊz/ *v* [+ (*that*) clause] to consider something to be likely; to expect • *What time do you suppose he'll be arriving?* • *I couldn't get any reply when I called Dan, so I suppose he's gone out.* • *He found it a lot more difficult to get a job than he supposed it would be.* • *I suppose I'll get the blame as usual.* • *I don't suppose Ann will let me borrow her car.* • *"That's not a very good idea." "No, I suppose* **not***."* [+ *not/so*] • *"Will they have arrived by now?" "I don't suppose* **so***."* [+ *not/so*] • *Do you suppose Gillian will marry him?* • **It** *is widely supposed* **that** *the minister will be forced to resign.* • Suppose is used in making polite requests: *I don't suppose you could/I suppose you couldn't lend me £5 till tomorrow, could you?* • Suppose can be used to show that you think something is so, although you wish that it were not: *I suppose all the tickets will be sold by now.* • Suppose can also be used to express annoyance: *I suppose you're going to be late again.* ○ *I suppose you think that's funny. Well, I certainly don't.* ○ *I suppose he's relying on me to take him there as usual.* • Suppose can also be used to show unwillingness to agree: *"Can I go out tonight?" "Oh, I suppose* **so***."* [+ *so*] ○ *"We'd better not take it without asking." "No, I suppose* **not***."* [+ *not*] ○ *Well, it was for the best, I suppose.* • Suppose can also be used to introduce a statement that you think is an explanation for something: *I suppose the reason we haven't heard from Carol lately is because she's been busy.* ○ *I suppose he's feeling a bit resentful about not having been promoted.* ○ *You don't suppose they could have had an accident, do you?* • Suppose can also be used to show that you are making a guess about something: *I suppose it's been about six months since I last saw Jim.* ○ *I suppose she would have been about 70 when she died.* ○ *Who do you suppose I met in town today?*

sup·po·si·tion /ˌsʌp·əˈzɪʃ·ən/ *n* • *That article was based on pure supposition* (=on what the writer considered likely to be true, rather than on what was certainly true). [U] • *You can't accuse someone on the basis of a supposition* (=something that is likely but not proved to be the truth). [C] • *There is no evidence or reason to think that the supposition* **that** *the phone call was made by the defendant is correct.* [C + *that* clause]

sup·pose *obj* BELIEVE /£səˈpəʊz, $-ˈpoʊz/ *v* [T usually passive] to believe that something is true • *(fml) I had always supposed* **that** *he was honest.* [+ *that* clause] • *(fml) We all supposed him* **to** *be German, but in fact he was from Switzerland.* [+ obj + *to* infinitive] • *Her new book is supposed* **to** *be* (=Generally people think it is) *very good.* [+ obj + *to* infinitive] • *Her parents were supposed* **to** *have died when she was very young.* [+ obj + *to* infinitive] • *Eating too much fat is commonly supposed* **to** *cause heart disease.* [+ obj + *to* infinitive]

sup·posed /£səˈpəʊzd, $-ˈpoʊzd/ *adj* [before n; not gradable] • *This new evidence shows that the supposed killer* (=the person who was thought to be the killer) *could not have been guilty.* • *The cost of the scheme far outweighs its supposed benefits/advantages.*

sup·po·sed·ly /£səˈpəʊ·zɪd·li, $-ˈpoʊ-/ *adv* [not gradable] • *The tickets are supposedly in the mail.* • *There is a supposedly simple explanation for what happened.* • *Asthma is supposedly becoming more common in children* (=People say or believe that this is so, although it is not a proved fact).

sup·pose *obj* NEED /£səˈpəʊz, $-ˈpoʊz/ *v* [T] *fml* to have (something) as necessary for being or happening; to need • *An expansion of this kind supposes* (=would not be possible without) *an increase in the company's profits this year.* • *He tried unconvincingly to argue that a belief did not necessarily suppose* (=could exist without) *a believer.* • See also PRESUPPOSE.

sup·pose /£səˈpəʊz, $-ˈpoʊz/, **sup·pos·ing** /£səˈpəʊ·zɪŋ, $-ˈpoʊ-/ *conjunction* • Suppose is used at the beginning of a sentence or clause to mean what would happen if: *Suppose we miss the train – what will we do then?* ○ *You should always wear a helmet when you're riding your bike – supposing you fell off?* • *We'd love to come and see you on Saturday, supposing* (=if) *I don't have to work that day,* • Suppose can also be used to introduce a suggestion: *"Do you think Dad will let me go to the party?" "I don't know – suppose/supposing* (=I suggest that) *you ask her?"* • LP> **Conditionals**

sup·posed DUTY /£səˈpəʊzd, $-ˈpoʊzd/ *adj* [not gradable] **be supposed to** to have to; to have a duty or a responsibility to • *The children are supposed to be at school by 8.45 a.m.* • *What are you doing out of bed – you're supposed to be asleep.* • *You're not supposed* (=allowed) *to park here.*

sup·posed INTENDED /£səˈpəʊzd, $-ˈpoʊzd/ *adj* [not gradable] **be supposed to** to be intended to • *These batteries are supposed to last for a year.* • *I thought these plates were supposed to be unbreakable.* • *Using this cream is supposed to stop you getting sunburnt.* • *The meeting was supposed to end at 4.00 p.m.* • *We were supposed to have gone away this week, but Debbie's ill so we couldn't go.* • *How am I supposed to* (=How can I) *find that much money by the end of the week?*

sup·pos·i·to·ry /£səˈpɒz·ɪ·tri, $-ˈpɑː·zə·tɔːr·i/ *n* [C] a small solid piece of a medicinal substance which is put inside the RECTUM or vagina, where it dissolves easily

sup·press *obj* END BY FORCE /səˈpres/ *v* [T] to end (something) by force • *The Hungarian uprising in 1956 was suppressed by the Soviet Union.* • *The Chinese leaders suppressed the student protest in Tiananmen Square.* • *He has succeeded in suppressing all the opposition to his plans.*

sup·pres·sion /səˈpreʃ·ən/ *n* [U] • *There has been widespread condemnation of the police's brutal suppression* **of** *the riots.* • *One of the government's main aims has been the suppression* **of** *terrorism.*

sup·press *obj* PREVENT /səˈpres/ *v* [T] to prevent (something) from being seen or expressed or from operating • *She could barely suppress her anger/annoyance/delight.* • *It's very difficult to suppress a sneeze.* • *I suppressed the urge to say what I really thought.* • *His feelings of resentment have been suppressed for years.* • *He denied that he had suppressed any evidence.* • *The government tried to suppress the book because of the information it contained about the security services.* • *This country has long suppressed human rights.* • *The virus suppresses the body's immune system.*

sup·pres·sion /səˈpreʃ·ən/ *n* [U] • *I think it's her suppression* **of** *her anger that has made her so bitter and resentful.* • *One of the effects of the school's rigid system is the suppression* **of** *all individuality among its pupils.* • *The police chief said that he had not been aware of any suppression* **of** *evidence.*

sup·pres·sor /£səˈpres·əʳ, $-ɚ/ *n* [C] • *The brakes on the truck have been fitted with a noise suppressor* (=a device which stops noise being heard). • *Plastic is a good weed suppressor* (=a substance which stops them from growing). • A suppressor is also a device which prevents an electrical machine from having a bad effect on the picture or sound of a television or radio which is near to the machine.

sup·pu·rate /ˈsʌp·jʊ·reɪt/ *v* [I] *specialized* (of an injury etc.) to form or give out a thick yellow liquid because of infection • *The bodies of the plague victims were covered in suppurating sores.* • *Soldiers with suppurating wounds were left untreated because there were no medical supplies.*

su·pra·na·tional /ˌsuː·prəˈnæʃ·ən·əl/ *adj* [not gradable] involving more than one country; having power or authority which is greater than that of single countries • *The World Bank is a supranational institution.* • *NATO is a supranational organization.*

su·preme /suːˈpriːm/ *adj* [not gradable] at the highest level • *the supreme commander of the armed forces* • *The former Emperor of China was the supreme ruler of his country.* • *The present constitution gives supreme authority to the presidency.* • Supreme is used in a title to show that someone or a group of people is at the highest level in an organization: *the Supreme Court* • *the Supreme Soviet* • *She was awarded a medal for showing supreme courage/bravery.* • *For me, dieting requires a supreme effort of will.* • *This invention is one of the supreme achievements of the present century.* • *The supreme irony is that this was all Tom's idea in the first place.* • *There is a supreme moment* (= one which causes great pleasure) *at the end of the opera.* • *(literary)* (The) **Supreme Being** is God.

su·preme /suːˈpriːm/ *adv* • *From 1960 to 1970, Ayatollah Mohsen al-Hakim* **reigned** *supreme among the Shi'ites of Iraq, Lebanon, Iran, Pakistan and elsewhere.* • *(fig.) In the nurseries of Britain, the teddy bear still* **reigns** *supreme* (= has the most importance).

su·preme·ly /suːˈpriːm·li/ *adv* • *She thought Sandy was opinionated and supremely* (=extremely) *selfish.* • *Wales are supremely confident of winning the match.* • *James plays the violin supremely well.*

su·prem·a·cy /suːˈprem·ə·si/ *n* [U] • *This victory clearly proves the supremacy* **of** *the West Indies* (=the fact that they are the best) *in world cricket.* • *The company has begun to challenge the supremacy* (=leading position) **of** *the current leading manufacturers in the textiles industry.* • *Henry Ford II's greatest ambition was always to recapture the supremacy* (=leading position) **over** *General Motors which Ford had lost during the 1920s.* • *The allies have established* **air** *supremacy* (=military control of the sky).

su·prem·a·cist /suːˈprem·ə·sɪst/ *n* [C] *esp. disapproving* • A supremacist is someone who believes that a particular type or group of people is better than other types or groups of people: *a male supremacist* (=someone who believes that men are better than women) ○ *He has a supremacist attitude towards members of other racial groups.*

su·prem·o /£suːˈpriː·məʊ, $-moʊ/ *n* [C] *pl* **supremos** *Br and Aus infml* a person who is considered to have a lot of, or the most, power, authority, skill, importance etc. in a particular activity, organization etc. • *the entertainment supremo, Alan Partridge* • *former BBC supremo, Lord Reith* • *a tennis supremo* • *the supremos* **of** *the computer company*

Supt *n* [before n] *abbreviation for* SUPERINTENDENT • *Chief Supt. Young*

sur·charge /£ˈsɜː·tʃɑːdʒ, $ˈsɜːr·tʃɑːrdʒ/ *n* [C] a charge in addition to the usual amount paid for something, or the amount already paid • *There is a surcharge* **for** *a single room.* • *Surcharges may be made* **for** *deliveries outside* *normal hours.* • *Residents are protesting about the 5% surcharge* **on** *their local tax bills.*

sur·charge *(obj)* /£'sɜː·tʃɑːdʒ, $'sɜːr·tʃɑːrdʒ, ,-'-/ *v* • *We were surcharged* (= charged extra) **on** *our extra luggage.* [T] • *The airlines have been given permission to surcharge because of increased fuel costs.* [I]

sure /£ʃɔːʳ, $ʃʊr/ *adj* **-r, -st** certain; without any doubt • *"No more dessert for me, thank you." "Are you sure?"* • *"What's wrong with him?" "I'm not really sure."* • *I'm sure* **(that)** *I left my keys on the table.* [+ (*that*) clause] • *I'm sure* **(that)** *you're right.* [+ (*that*) clause] • *Are you sure* **(that)** *the film is on tonight?* [+ (*that*) clause] • *I'm not sure* **(that)** *this colour really suits me.* [+ (*that*) clause] • *Is she* **absolutely** *sure* **(that)** *she wants to marry him?* [+ (*that*) clause] • *I* **feel** *sure* **(that)** *you've made the right decision.* [+ (*that*) clause] • **Make** *sure* **(that)** *you lock the door behind you when you go out.* [+ (*that*) clause] • *It now* **seems** *sure* **(that)** *the election will result in another victory for the government.* [+ *that* clause] • *Simon isn't sure* **whether** *he'll be able to come to the party or not.* [+ *wh-* word] • *I'm not sure* **where** *they live.* [+ *wh-* word] • *I'm not quite sure* **how** *this works.* [+ *wh-* word] • *It is difficult to be sure* **which** *parts of the former Chancellor's speech will prove most damaging to the Government.* [+ *wh-* word] • *She's not sure* **if** *she'll be able to meet us for a drink tonight.* [+ *wh-* word] • *I'm not entirely sure* **about** *what to do for the best.* • *Is there anything you're not sure* **of/about?** • If you are sure **about/of** a person, you have confidence in them and trust them: *Henry has only been working for us for a short while, and we're not really sure about him yet.* ○ *You can always be sure of Kay.* • If you are sure **of yourself**, you are very or too confident: *She's become much more sure of herself since she started work.* ○ *(disapproving) What makes you so sure of yourself?* • *He said that he wasn't completely sure* **of** *his facts* (= not certain that his information was correct). • *Sophie is sure* **of** (= certain to have) *good exam results.* • *We arrived early, to be sure* **of getting** *a good seat.* • *A majority of Congress members wanted to put off an election until they could be sure* **of winning** *it.* • *She's sure* **to** *win.* [+ *to* infinitive] • *I want to go somewhere where we're sure* **to** *have good weather.* [+ *to* infinitive] • *We're sure* **to** *see you again before you leave.* [+ *to* infinitive] • *There is only one sure way* (= one way that can be trusted) *of finding out the truth.* • *Those patches on the wallpaper are a sure* **sign** *of damp.* • If you have a sure knowledge or understanding of something, you know or understand it very well: *I don't think he has a very sure understanding of the situation.* • *(esp. Am) "Could you give me a lift home tonight?"* **"Sure thing** (= Yes, certainly)*!"* • *(fml) This is not his best book,* **to be sure** (= certainly), *but it is still worth reading.* • See also COCKSURE.

sure /£ʃɔːʳ, $ʃʊr/ *adv* **-r, -st** *infml* • *"Do you want to come swimming with us?" "Sure* (= Yes, certainly)*."* • *(esp. Am) "Will you help me with this?" "Sure I will."* • *(Am) I sure* (= certainly) *don't want to be around when Gene finds out what's happened to his car.* • *(Am) I sure am* (= I am very) *hungry.* • *(Br dated) One day he'll realize that I was right,* **(as) sure as eggs is eggs** (= very certainly). • *(slang) I'm* **(as) sure as hell** (= very certainly) *not climbing up all those steps.* • **For sure** means certain or certainly: *You'll never get Jane to agree to that, and that's for sure.* ○ *I know for sure that I won't be able to go to the party.* ○ *The shop said that they'd deliver the table on Friday for sure.* ○ *One thing's for sure – once the baby's born, your lives will never be the same again.* • *He said he'd left the book on the desk, and* **sure enough** (= as expected), *there it was.*

sure·ly /£'ʃɔː·li, $'ʃʊr-/ *adv* [not gradable] • Surely can be used to express that you are certain or almost certain about something, or that you are surprised about something: *That surely can't be a good idea.* ○ *The fault surely lies in the design of the equipment.* ○ *These children surely deserve something better than a life on the streets.* ○ *Surely you don't expect me to believe that.* ○ *Surely there must be some mistake.* ○ *You must agree, surely?* ○ *It must surely be possible for you to get this finished today.* ○ *"He said he couldn't come." "Oh, surely not."* • *(Am) "May I sit here?" "Surely* (= Yes, certainly)*."* • *Things are* **slowly but** *surely* (= certainly) *improving.* • *Without more food and medical supplies, these people will surely not survive.* • If you do something surely, you do it confidently: *Katie has now learnt to ride a bike quite surely.* ○ *He seemed to speak very surely.* • *(dated Br infml)* **Surely to God/goodness** (= You must admit that) *you could have called to say you'd be late – I've been worried sick!*

sure·ness /£'ʃɔː·nəs, $'ʃʊr-/ *n* [U] • Sureness is confidence and control: *The child sang with sureness and clarity.* ○ *We admired the sureness* **of** *the orchestra's playing.* ○ *She has an enviable sureness* **of touch** (= She deals with things confidently and well).

sure·fire /£'ʃɔː·faɪəʳ, $'ʃʊr·faɪr/ *adj* [before n] *infml* certain or likely, esp. to succeed • *The film looks a surefire Oscar winner.* • *There's no surefire remedy for the common cold.*

sure·foot·ed /£'ʃɔː,fʊt·ɪd, $'ʃʊr,fʊt̬-/ *adj* able easily to walk on rough ground, without falling • *a surefooted goat/llama/mule* • *I don't think I'm surefooted enough to walk over these slippery rocks.* • *(fig.) The minister handled the journalist's questions in a very surefooted way* (= a way showing the ability to make good judgments in a difficult situation).

sure·foot·ed·ly /£,ʃɔː'fʊt·ɪd·li, $,ʃʊr'fʊt̬-/ *adv* • *At the inn, we said goodbye to our guides and the mules that had carried us so surefootedly through the Sierra Mazatec.* • *(fig.) They dealt with the complaints against them very surefootedly* (= in a way that showed their ability to make good judgments).

sure·foot·ed·ness /£,ʃɔː'fʊt·ɪd·nəs, $,ʃʊr'fʊt̬-/ *n* [U]

su·re·ty /£'ʃɔː·rə·ti, $'ʃʊr·ə·t̬i/ *n law* a person who accepts legal responsibility for another person's debt or behaviour, or (money given as) a promise that you will do something that you have said you will do, such as pay a debt or appear in court • *Her brothers are acting as sureties* **for** *her.* [C] • *No one has yet been found who is willing to* **stand** (= act as a) *surety* **for** *Mr Naylor.* [U] • *What are you able to provide as a surety* (= promise) *that you will repay the loan?* [C] • *He was released on bail of £5000 surety* (= money given as a promise that he would appear in court). [U]

surf /£sɜːf, $sɜːrf/ *n* [U] the waves on the sea when they approach the coast or hit against rocks • *They threw off their clothes and ran into the surf.* • *We were almost deafened by the crash/roar of the surf.*

surf /£sɜːf, $sɜːrf/ *v* [I] • To surf is to ride on a wave as it comes in towards land, while standing or lying on a special board: *It's not safe to surf here.* ○ *They* **go** *surfing every weekend.* • See also BODYSURF; **windsurf** at WINDSURFER.

surf·er /£'sɜː·fəʳ, $'sɜːr·fɚ/ *n* [C] • *This beach is very popular with surfers* (= people who ride on waves on special boards). • See also WINDSURFER.

surf·ing /£'sɜː·fɪŋ, $'sɜːr-/ *n* [U] • *Surfing* (= The sport of riding on waves on special boards) *is very popular in California.* • *"Surfing USA"* (song by The Beach Boys, 1963) • See also **windsurfing** at WINDSURFER.

sur·face /£'sɜː·fɪs, $'sɜːr-/ *n* [C] the outer or top part or layer of something • *Tropical rain forests used to cover 10% of the Earth's surface.* • *Marble has a smooth, shiny surface.* • *All the pots she makes have glazed surfaces.* • *Neil Armstrong was the first person to set foot* **on** *the surface* **of** *the moon.* • *A thin film of oil was floating* **on** *the surface* (= top part) **of** *the sea.* • *The body was clearly visible just* **beneath** *the surface* **of** *the water.* • *He believes that it isn't dangerous for a baby to be born underwater, provided that it is brought* **to** *the surface* (= brought above the top part of the water) *within seconds of being born.* • *The trapped miners were eventually brought* **to** *the surface* (= top part of the land). • *The world's deepest mine is South Africa's Western Deeps, where gold is mined 2·4 miles* **below** *the surface.* • *It was so hot that the surface* (= top layer) **of** *the road melted.* • *This frying-pan has a non-stick surface.* • *A lot of head injuries to children are caused by their falling onto hard surfaces* (= top layers of the ground) *in playgrounds.* • A surface is also the top layer of a field or track on which particular types of sports are played: *The match will be played on an artificial/all-weather surface.* ○ *She's a very talented tennis player and can win on any surface.* • A surface is also the flat top part of a table, cupboard, etc.: *Roll the pastry out* **on** *a lightly floured surface.* ○ *Don't put anything wet* **on** *a polished surface, or it will leave a mark.* • **The** surface of a situation or person is what is obvious about them or the qualities they have which are not hidden or difficult to see: *The television documentary we watched examined no more than the surface* **of** *the issues it was supposed to be dealing with.* ○ **On** *the surface, this seems like a difficult problem, but in fact there's an easy solution to it.* ○ *He's like a swan – so calm* **on** *the surface, but paddling away like mad underneath* (= but very anxious in reality). ○ **Beneath** *the surface of contemporary West Indian life lurk memories of slavery.* ○ *He seems relaxed, but actually he has a lot of tension simmering just* **below** *the surface.* ○

Suddenly, all her anger **came (bubbling) to** *the surface* (= became obvious). ○ *Their resentment is beginning to* **rise to** *the surface* (= beginning to become obvious). • To **scratch/scrape the surface** is to deal with only a very small part of a subject or a problem: *There's far more to be said – I've only had time to scratch the surface in this talk.* ○ *The amount of aid which has been offered is hardly going to scratch the surface of the suffering.* • **Surface tension** is the natural force existing in a liquid which holds its surface together: *Some types of small insect can walk on the surface of water because its surface tension will support their weight.* • A MISSILE (= type of flying weapon) that is **surface-to-air** is fired from land or the sea towards aircraft or other missiles: *a surface-to-air missile (abbreviation* **SAM***)* • A MISSILE (= type of flying weapon) that is **surface-to-surface** is fired from land or the sea towards a place on land or a ship.

sur·face *(obj)* /£'sɜː·fɪs, $'sɜːr-/ *v* • *The submarine surfaced* (= came to the top of the sea) *a few miles off the coast.* [I] • *The new road just needs to be surfaced* (= have a layer put on top of it), *and then it will be ready for use.* [T] • If a feeling or information surfaces, it becomes known: *Doubts are beginning to surface* **about** *whether the right decision has been made.* [I] ○ *A rumour has surfaced that the company is about to go out of business.* [I] • *(fig. infml) He never surfaces* (= gets out of bed) *until at least 11.00 a.m. on a Sunday.* [I]

sur·face /£'sɜː·fɪs, $'sɜːr-/ *adj* [not gradable] • *There are indications that the surface* **temperature** (= the temperature on the outer part) *of the Earth is increasing.* • *Luckily, the accident caused only surface damage to my car.* • Surface also means working or operating on the top of the land or sea, rather than under the land or sea, or by air: *After he was injured in an explosion in the mine, Joe became a surface* **worker**. ○ *The government is proposing to reduce the country's surface* **fleet**. ○ *Would you like this parcel sent by air or surface* **mail** (= a way of sending letters and parcels so that they travel by land or sea)? • *Our surface impressions* (= those obtained quickly, without careful thought) *of the proposal are that it seems worth considering further.*

surf·board /£'sɜːf·bɔːd, $'sɜːrf·bɔːrd/ *n* [C] a long narrow board made of wood or plastic which is used for riding on waves as they come in towards the beach • PIC› **Water sports**

sur·feit /£'sɜː·fɪt, $'sɜːr-/ *n* [U] *fml* an amount which is too large, or is more than is needed • *It's wrong that some people have* **a** *surfeit* **of** *food, while others don't have any.* • *The country has* **a** *surfeit* **of** *cheap labour.* • *I think we've had* **a** *surfeit* **of** *this sort of violent film on TV recently.*

surge /£sɜːdʒ, $sɜːrdʒ/ *n* [C] a sudden and great increase, or a sudden and great movement forward • *An unexpected surge* **in** *electrical power caused the computer fault.* • *There has been a surge* **in** *house prices recently.* • *The company has found it difficult to cope with the surge* **in** *demand for their products.* • *A sudden surge* **of** *imports can threaten a domestic industry.* • *She was overwhelmed by a surge* **of** *remorse.* • *I felt a sudden surge* **of** *sympathy for him.* • *At the end of the game, there was a surge* (= a sudden and great movement forward) **of** *fans onto the field.* • **A tidal** *surge* (= sudden and great rise in the level of the sea which causes water to flow where it usually does not) *caused severe flooding to the area by the sea.* • See also RESURGENCE.

surge /£sɜːdʒ, $sɜːrdʒ/ *v* [I] • *The company's profits have surged* (= increased suddenly and strongly). • *An angry crowd surged through the gates of the president's palace.* • *He had been in the ocean for 10 hours with waves surging 13 feet or more.* • *A few metres before the end of the race, Jenkins surged* (= suddenly moved powerfully) **into the lead.** • *She felt a wave of resentment surging* **(up)** (= developing strongly) *inside her.* • *We struggled against the surging* **tide** *to keep the boat from sinking.*

sur·geon /£'sɜː·dʒᵊn, $'sɜːr-/ *n* [C] a doctor who is specially trained to perform medical operations • *The surgeon who carried out the operation said that it had been a success.* • *He has an appointment to see a brain/eye/heart surgeon* (= a doctor who does medical operations on the brain/eyes/heart) *next week.* • In the US, the **Surgeon General** is the person who is in charge of the public health service: *The Surgeon General has determined that smoking cigarettes is bad for your health.*

sur·ge·ry MEDICAL OPERATION /£'sɜː·dʒᵊr·i, $'sɜːr·dʒɚ-/ *n* [U] the treatment of injuries or diseases in people or animals by cutting open the body and removing or repairing the damaged part • *open-heart surgery* • *hip-replacement surgery* • *eye surgery* • *He has an injury which can only be cured by surgery.* • *The doctor who* **performed** *the surgery gave Aikman an 85% chance of full recovery by September.* • *The patient* **underwent** *eight hours of surgery* **on** *his heart.* • *He* **had** *surgery* **on** *his left knee six weeks ago.* • *She needs* **major/minor** *surgery* **on** *her leg.* • *Mrs Nuttall made a good recovery after surgery* **to** *remove a brain tumour.*

sur·gi·cal /£'sɜː·dʒɪ·kᵊl, $'sɜːr-/ *adj* [not gradable] • Surgical **equipment** is that which is used for medical operations: *surgical supplies/instruments/gloves* • Surgical also means involved in performing medical operations: *surgical procedures/techniques/intervention* ○ *surgical staff* • A surgical piece of clothing is worn in order to treat a particular medical condition: *a surgical shoe/collar/corset* • Surgical can also be used to refer to a type of military attack which is done in an exact way on a particular place: *A surgical* **strike/attack** *was carried out on the enemy's military headquarters.* • *(Br)* **Surgical spirit** *(Am and Aus* **rubbing alcohol***)* is a type of liquid used for cleaning the skin or cleaning medical equipment so that it is free from bacteria.

sur·gi·cal·ly /£'sɜː·dʒɪ·kli, $'sɜːr-/ *adv* [not gradable] • *The tumour can be surgically* **removed.**

sur·ge·ry ADVICE /£'sɜː·dʒᵊr·i, $'sɜːr·dʒɚ-/ *n Br and Aus* (the fixed period of opening of) a place where you can go to ask advice from or receive treatment from a doctor or DENTIST • *If you come to the surgery (Am* **office***) at 10.30, the doctor will see you then.* [C] • *What time does the surgery (Am* **doctor's office***) open?* [C] • *On Saturday mornings, surgery* (= the fixed period of opening of the place where you can go to see your doctor) *is (Am* **office hours** *are) from 9.00 to 12.00.* [U] • *(Br)* A surgery is also the regular period of time when a person can visit their **Member of Parliament** (= the person who represents them in parliament) to ask advice: *Our MP* **holds** *a weekly surgery on Friday mornings.* [C]

surl·y /£'sɜː·li, $'sɜːr-/ *adj* **-ier, -iest** bad-tempered, unfriendly and not polite • *We were served by a very surly waiter.* • *He gave me a surly look.* • *The ticket collector at the station was very surly when I couldn't find my ticket.*

sur·li·ness /£'sɜː·lɪ·nəs, $'sɜːr-/ *n* [U]

sur·mise *obj* /£'sə·maɪz, $sɚ-/ *v* [T] *fml* to guess (something), without having much or any proof • **As** *we surmised, Duncan had not been telling the truth.* [+ clause] • *There must be another explanation, he surmised.* [+ clause] • *The police surmise* **that** *the robbers have fled the country.* [+ *that* clause] • *Archaeologists are only able to surmise* **what** *these strange symbols might mean.* [+ *wh-* word]

sur·mise /£'sə·maɪz, $sɚ-/ *n fml* • *My surmise* (= guess) *turned out to be right.* [C] • *That article is all just* **wild** *surmise and innuendo.* [U] • **It** *is my surmise* **that** *William is involved in some illegal activity.* [C + *that* clause]

sur·mount *obj* DEAL WITH /£sə'maʊnt, $sɚ-/ *v* [T] *fml* to deal successfully with (a difficulty or problem) • *She has had to surmount the* **problem/difficulty/challenge** *of bringing up six children on her own.* • *They managed to surmount all the* **opposition/objections** *to their plans.* • *There are still a few technical* **obstacles/hurdles** *to be surmounted before the product can be put on sale to the public.*

sur·mount·a·ble /£sə'maʊn·tə·bḷ, $sɚ'maʊn·t̬ə-/ *adj fml* • *These difficulties will not be easily surmountable.*

sur·mount *obj* BE ON TOP /£sə'maʊnt, $sɚ-/ *v* [T] *fml* to be on top of (esp. something tall) • *The central 12-foot column is surmounted by a bronze angel with outspread wings.* • *A statue representing justice surmounts the law court.*

sur·name /£'sɜː·neɪm, $'sɜːr-/, **fam·i·ly name**, *Am also* **last name**, *Br and Aus also* **sec·ond name** *n* [C] the name that you share with other members of your family • *Her first name is Sheila and her surname is Kane.* • *An increasing number of women no longer take their husband's surname when they get married.* • LP› **Capital letters**

sur·pass *obj* /£sə'pɑːs, $sɚ'pæs/ *v* [T] *fml* to do or be better than • *His time for the 100 metres surpassed the previous world record* **by** *one hundredth of a second.* • *Our students' educational achievements equal, and in many cases surpass, those of students in previous years.* • *The book's success has surpassed everyone's expectations.* • *The director has really surpassed* **himself** (= done better than he has done before) *with this new film.*

sur·pass·ing /£sə'pɑː·sɪŋ, $sɚ'pæs·ɪŋ/ *adj* [before n] *fml or literary* • Surpassing means extremely great: *a girl of surpassing loveliness* ○ *a restaurant of surpassing excellence*

sur·plice /£'sɜː·plɪs, $'sɜːr-/ *n* [C] *specialized* a white, loose piece of clothing, which is worn over other clothing during religious ceremonies by some Christian priests and members of groups who sing in churches

sur·plus /£'sɜː·pləs, $'sɜːr-/ *n, adj* [not gradable] (an amount which is) more than is needed • *The world is now producing large food surpluses.* [C] • *There is a surplus* **of** *staff in some departments of the company.* [C] • *We are unlikely to produce any surplus this year.* [U] • *Every country has a pool of surplus labour.* • *Farmers are feeding all their surplus wheat to pigs.* • *The government has authorized the army to sell its surplus weapons.* • *(Br) The store is selling off stock that is surplus* **to requirements** (= goods which are more than they need to have). • *(Br) He was told that he had become surplus* **to requirements** (= that he was no longer needed in his job). • A surplus is also the amount of money you have left when you sell more than you buy, or spend less than you have: *There has been a sharp increase in the country's* **trade** *surplus.* [C] ○ *The government is forecasting a* **budget** *surplus this year.* [C] ○ *The school's bank account is currently* **in** *surplus.* [U]

sur·prise /£sə'praɪz, $sɚ-/ *n* an unexpected event, or the feeling caused by something unexpected happening • *Don't tell Ann that we've arranged a party for her – I want it to be a surprise.* [C] • *Your letter was a nice/pleasant surprise.* [C] • *I didn't expect to see you here, Nick – what a lovely surprise!* [C] • *It was a nasty surprise to get home and find that someone had broken into our house.* [C] • *Last night's heavy snow* **came as** *a complete surprise.* [C] • *It* **came as** *a total surprise* **to** *her when he told her he loved her.* [C] • *You're always* **full of** *surprises* (= doing unexpected things). [C] • *I wish you wouldn't keep* **springing** *surprises* **on** *me* (= telling me unexpected things or causing unexpected things to happen). [C] • *They* **expressed** *surprise* **at** *the result.* [U] • *He looked at her* **in/with** *surprise* (= with the feeling caused by something unexpected happening). [U] • **To** *my great surprise, they agreed to all our demands.* [U] • *If you want to attack the enemy, it's important to retain an* **element of** *surprise.* [U] • *The Soviet air force was almost destroyed by the German surprise* (= unexpected) *attack on 21 June 1941.* • *Clark was the surprise winner of the race.* • *My uncle paid us a surprise visit yesterday.* • *"I've forgotten my keys again." "***Surprise, surprise** (= That is not unusual)*!"* • Compare SHOCK.

sur·prise *obj* /£sə'praɪz, $sɚ-/ *v* [T] • *The news surprised* (= was unexpected by) *everyone.* • *It doesn't surprise me* **that** *their parents don't want them to get married.* [+ obj + *that* clause] • *It will not surprise anyone* **to** *learn that the offer has been rejected.* [+ obj + *to* infinitive] • *Janet was surprised* **how** *quickly the time passed.* [+ obj + *wh-* word] • To surprise someone is also to find, catch or attack them when they are not expecting it: *The robbers had just opened the safe when they were surprised by the police.* ○ *His mother surprised him help***ing** *himself to her gin.* [+ obj + v-*ing*] • *"Surprised by Joy"* (title of a poem by William Wordsworth, 1885)

sur·prised /£sə'praɪzd, $sɚ-/ *adj* • *She looked at him with a surprised expression* (= one showing that something unexpected had happened) *on her face.* • *"Charlie's resigned." "I'm not surprised* (= That is what I expected)*."* • *We were very surprised* **at** *the result.* • *It's not like you to behave like this, Alice – I'm surprised* **at** *you* (= it disappoints me that you have done so)*!* • *I'm not surprised* **(that)** *he didn't keep his promise.* [+ (*that*) clause] • *I'm surprised* **to** *see you here.* [+ *to* infinitive] • *We were pleasantly surprised* **to** *find that the hotel was much more comfortable than we were expecting it would be.* [+ *to* infinitive] • *I've managed to fix your car for now, but* **don't be** *surprised* **if** *it breaks down again* (= it probably will stop working again).

sur·pris·ing /£sə'praɪ·zɪŋ, $sɚ-/ *adj* • *He gave a rather surprising* (= unexpected) *answer.* • **It's hardly** *surprising* **(that)** *you're putting on weight, considering how much you're eating.* [+ (*that*) clause] • **It** *would be surprising* **if** *there were no opposition to the proposals.* [+ *wh-* word] • *I must say that* **it's** *surprising* **to** *find you agreeing with me for once.* [+ *to* infinitive]

sur·pris·ing·ly /£sə'praɪ·zɪŋ·li, $sɚ-/ *adv* • *These chairs are surprisingly* (= unexpectedly) *comfortable.* • *The restaurant turned out to be surprisingly cheap.* • *Surprisingly, they agreed to all our demands.* • *Not surprisingly, the jury found them guilty.*

sur·real /sə'rɪəl/ *adj* strange; not like reality; like a dream • *Driving through the total darkness was a slightly surreal experience.* • *Buñuel's films have a surreal quality.* • *He has a surreal sense of humour.* • *I find it rather surreal, seeing live pictures of the war on television.*

Sur·real·i·sm /sə'rɪə·lɪ·zᵊm/ *n* [U] *specialized* • Surrealism is a type of 20th century art and literature in which unusual or impossible things are shown happening: *One of the main aims of Surrealism was to go beyond ordinary processes of thought and logic into the world of dreams and the subconscious.*

Sur·real·ist /sə'rɪə·lɪst/ *n, adj* [not gradable] *specialized* • *Dali and Magritte are well-known Surrealists.* [C] • *The poem is full of Surrealist imagery.*

sur·real·is·tic /səˌrɪə'lɪs·tɪk/ *adj* • *The play is a surrealistic comedy* (= one in which things happen in an unusual or seemingly impossible way). • *The desert landscape is surrealistic* (= not like reality)*, with its strange-shaped rocks and unusual colours.*

sur·rend·er [ACCEPT DEFEAT] /£sᵊr'en·dəʳ, $sə'ren·dɚ/ *v* [I] to stop fighting and admit defeat • *They would rather die than surrender.* • *President Noriega surrendered* **to** *US troops after the invasion of Panama.* • *(fig.) I finally surrendered* **to** (= stopped trying to fight) *temptation, and ate the last remaining chocolate.*

sur·rend·er /£sᵊr'en·dəʳ, $sə'ren·dɚ/ *n* • *The rebels are on the point of surrender.* (= They will very soon stop fighting and admit defeat.) [U] • *The terms have finally been agreed for a surrender* (= an act of stopping fighting and admitting defeat). [C]

sur·rend·er *obj* [GIVE] /£sə'ren·dəʳ, $-dɚ/ *v* [T] *slightly fml* to give (something that is yours) to someone else because you have been forced to do so or because it is necessary to do so • *The police demanded that the gang surrender* (= give up) *their weapons/arms/guns.* • *Neither side is willing to surrender any territory/any of their claims.* • *The High Court has ordered his passport to be surrendered.* • *They have surrendered their share of the company.*

sur·rend·er *n* [U] *slightly fml* • *They are not willing to agree to any surrender* (= giving up) **of** *sovereignty.* • *The army has set a deadline for the surrender* (= the giving up) **of** *illegally held weapons.*

sur·rep·ti·tious /£ˌsʌr·əp'tɪʃ·əs, $ˌsɜːr-/ *adj* done secretly, without anyone seeing or knowing • *She seemed to be listening to what I was saying, but I couldn't help noticing her surreptitious glances at the clock.* • *Through a series of surreptitious meetings with an informer, the journalists Woodward and Bernstein found out about Watergate.* • *He'd been so surreptitious* **about** *his drinking that no one realized he'd become an alcoholic.*

sur·rep·ti·tious·ly /£ˌsʌr·əp'tɪʃ·ə·sli, $ˌsɜːr-/ *adv* • *She surreptitiously searched through her husband's desk.*

sur·rep·ti·tious·ness /£ˌsʌr·əp'tɪʃ·ə·snəs, $ˌsɜːr-/ *n* [U]

sur·ro·gate /£'sʌr·ə·gət, $'sɜːr-/ *n, adj* [before n; not gradable] (someone or something) replacing someone else or used instead of something else • *She seems to regard him as a surrogate* **for** *her dead father.* [C] • *For some people, reading travel books is a surrogate* **for** *actual travel.* [C] • *He regards football as a kind of surrogate warfare.* • *Because she had no children of her own, her friend's sons became surrogate children to her.* • Surrogate is also used to refer to a woman having a baby for another woman who is unable to become pregnant or have a baby herself: *She has agreed to act as a surrogate* **mother** *for her sister.* ○ *There are strict regulations surrounding surrogate* **motherhood**. ○ *The number of surrogate* **births** *is increasing.*

sur·ro·ga·cy /£'sʌr·ə·gə·si, $'sɜːr-/ *n* [U] • Surrogacy is the action of a woman having a baby for another woman who is unable to do so herself: *Many people think that surrogacy is acceptable so long as nobody is paid.*

sur·round *obj* /sə'raʊnd/ *v* [T] to be everywhere around (something) • *Snow-capped mountains surround the city.* • *The house is surrounded by a large garden.* • *Gwen sat at her desk, surrounded by books and papers.* • *He said that he would not get a fair trial because of the publicity surrounding the case.* • *Mystery still surrounds the exact circumstances of Stalin's death.* • *He has failed to surround himself with a staff of real quality or experience* (= failed to get a team of such people to work for him). • *She said that she wanted to die surrounded by the people she loves* (= with them all present). • *Early this morning, armed police were* *surrounding* (=moving into a position so that they were everywhere around) *a house which they thought contained an escaped prisoner.*

sur·round /sə'raʊnd/ *n* [C] • *The mirror has a decorative brass surround* (=border). • *Our bath has a tiled surround* (=area around the bath).

sur·round·ing /sə'raʊn·dɪŋ/ *adj* [before n; not gradable] • *A lot of the children at the school do not live in the town, but come in from the surrounding countryside.* • *Hundreds of people have fled from the fighting in the city and are now living in the surrounding hills.*

sur·round·ings /sə'raʊn·dɪŋz/ *pl n* • *Some butterflies* **blend in with** *their surroundings* (=the area around them) *so that it's difficult to see them.* • *It's important that buildings should fit in with their surroundings* (=the other buildings, countryside, etc. around them). • Your surroundings are the place where you live and the conditions you live in: *They live in very comfortable/pleasant/drab/bleak surroundings.*

sur·rounds /sə'raʊndz/ *pl n Am* • *I don't think there are any video stores in the immediate surrounds* (=the area near here).

sur·tax /£'sɜː·tæks, $'sɜːr-/ *n* [U] an additional tax which is paid by people who earn more than a particular large amount, or an additional tax which is added to something which is already taxed • *a surtax on company profits*

sur·ti·tle /£'sɜːˌtaɪ·tḷ, $'sɜːrˌtaɪ·ṭḷ/, *Am usually* **su·per·ti·tle** *n* [C] a written form in the listener's own language of the words that are being sung in an opera, which are shown above the stage during a performance • *I like having surtitles at the opera, because it makes it easier to understand.*

sur·veil·lance /£sə'veɪ·lənts, $sɚ-/ *n* [U] the careful watching of someone who is thought likely to do something wrong, or of somewhere where it is thought likely that something wrong might be done • *She claimed that her telephone had been tapped and that she was* **under** *surveillance.* • *The police have* **kept** *the nightclub* **under** *surveillance because of suspected illegal drug activity.* • *Farmers are calling for more surveillance* **of** *the nation's food supply.* • *The police are using an* **electronic** *surveillance system to catch drivers who commit motoring offences.* • *A close watch is being kept on the area by surveillance* **aircraft/satellites**. • *More banks are now installing surveillance* **cameras**.

sur·vey QUESTIONS /£'sɜː·veɪ, $'sɜːr-/ *n* [C] an examination of opinions, behaviour etc., made by asking people questions • *Smoking among 16- to 19-year-olds in Britain has dropped by some 15%, according to a new survey.* • *A recent survey* **found** *that 58% of people did not know where their heart is.* • *A* **public opinion** *survey has* **shown** *that the prime minister has become very unpopular.* • *A survey* **of** *the country's eating habits* **revealed** *that people are eating too much fatty food.* • *A survey* **of** *modern marriage* **carried out** *by a magazine found that over 50% of marriages end in divorce.* • **In a nationwide** *survey* **conducted** *by the Washington Post, 85% of respondents had 'a great deal' or 'quite a lot' of confidence in the US military.*

sur·vey *obj* /£'sɜː·veɪ, $'sɜːr-/ *v* [T usually passive] • *Many of the listeners surveyed* (=questioned) *said that they were not satisfied with the programmes that the radio station was broadcasting.* • *The researchers surveyed* (=did a survey of) *the attitudes of 2000 college students.*

sur·vey *obj* LOOK AT /£sə'veɪ, $'sɜːr·veɪ/ *v* [T] *slightly fml* to look at or examine (something), esp. carefully • *After we'd finished painting the kitchen, we stood back and surveyed our work.* • *They climbed to the top of a nearby rock and surveyed the* **scene** *around them.* • *She has written a book which surveys* (=describes in detail) *the history of feminism.* • *(Br)* If a building is surveyed (*Aus* **inspected**), it is examined carefully by a specially trained person, in order to discover whether there is anything wrong with its structure: *I would never buy a house without having it surveyed first.* • To survey an area of land is to measure it and record the details of it, esp. on a map: *The schoolchildren surveyed 100 square kilometres for a botanical atlas.* ○ *Before the new railway was built, its route was carefully surveyed.* • *(humorous)* If you are **lord/master/mistress/king/queen of all** you **survey**, you own or control the place in which you live or work.

sur·vey /£'sɜː·veɪ, $'sɜːr-/ *n* [C] • *His new book is a survey* (=description) **of** *the theatre in the nineteenth century.* • *A comprehensive survey* (=examination) **of** *the country's historic buildings is being carried out.* • *(Br)* A survey (*Aus* **inspection**) is an examination of the structure of a building by a specially trained person: *The bank will not lend you any money to buy a house unless you have a survey done* **on** *it.* • A survey is also the measuring and recording of the details of an area of land: *A* **geological** *survey has shown that this area of land may contain oil.*

sur·vey·or /£sə'veɪ·əʳ, $sɚ'veɪ·ɚ/ *n* [C] • A surveyor is a person whose job is to measure and record the details of areas of land. • *(Br)* A surveyor (*Am* **structural engineer**) is also a person who is specially trained to examine buildings and discover whether there are any problems with their structure.

sur·vive *(obj)* /£sə'vaɪv, $sɚ-/ *v* to continue to live or exist, esp. after coming close to dying or being destroyed or after being in a difficult or threatening situation • *The baby was born with a problem with its heart and only survived for a few hours.* [I] • *These plants cannot survive in very cold conditions.* [I] • *Animals that have been reared in captivity can find it difficult to survive in the wild.* [I] • *None of Shakespeare's plays survives in its original manuscript form.* [I] • *This is one of the few water mills in the area to have survived* **intact** (=without great changes to it). [I] • *They are struggling to survive* **on** *very little money.* [I] • *They were very lucky to survive the accident.* [T] • *The prime minister succeeded in surviving the challenge to his leadership/authority.* [T] • *Few buildings survived the earthquake* **unscathed**. [T] • If you survive someone, esp. a member of your family, you continue to live after they have died: *He is survived by his wife and four children.* [T] ○ *Most parents expect that their children will survive them.* [T] • *(infml) "Oh, you've cut your finger!" "Don't worry,* **I'll** *survive* (=it's not serious)." [I] • *(infml) "How are you?" "Oh, (I'm) surviving* (=things are satisfactory, but not particularly good)." [I]

sur·viv·a·ble /£sə'vaɪ·və·bḷ, $sɚ-/ *adj fml* • *Head injuries of the kind she has received are not usually survivable.* (=It is not usually possible to continue to live after suffering them.)

sur·vi·val /£sə'vaɪ·vᵊl, $sɚ-/ *n* • *The doctors told my wife I had a 50/50 chance of survival* (=continuing to live). [U] • *He is fighting for survival after his operation.* [U] • *The majority of the world's poorest people depend on the natural environment for their survival.* [U] • *His main concern is to ensure his own political survival.* [U] • *Her chances of survival* **as** *prime minister now look slim.* [U] • *They are fighting for the survival* **of** *their country.* [U] • *England are fighting for survival* (=trying not to be defeated) *in the match.* [U] • A survival is something that has continued to exist from a previous time: *Most of these traditions are survivals from earlier times.* [C] • *We all have a strong survival* **instinct**. • *The survival* **rate** *for people who have this form of cancer is now more than 90%.* • A **survival kit** is a small box containing items that you need in order to stay alive if you are in a difficult or dangerous situation in which you are unable to get help. • **Survival of the fittest** is the principle that animals and plants suited to the conditions they live in are more likely to stay alive and produce other animals and plants than those which are not: *Some scientists have suggested that the extinction of many animals may have been partly due to chance, not just to the survival of the fittest.*

sur·viv·ing /£sə'vaɪ·vɪŋ, $sɚ-/ *adj* [before n; not gradable] • *The rhinoceros is one of the oldest surviving species* (=those which continue to exist). • *This is one of the few surviving photographs of my grandfather as a child.* • *He is the longest surviving* (=still working) *national newspaper editor in the country.* • *Her estate was divided between her three surviving children* (=those who continued to live after her death).

sur·viv·or /£sə'vaɪ·vəʳ, $sɚ'vaɪ·vɚ/ *n* [C] • A survivor is a person who continues to live, despite nearly dying: *After the boat sank, 63 survivors were picked up from the sea.* ○ *He was the* **sole** *survivor* **of** *the plane crash.* ○ *She's a cancer survivor/a survivor* **of** *cancer.* • A survivor is also a person who is able to continue living their life successfully despite experiencing difficulties: *He's one of life's survivors.* ○ *Many people have been calling for the minister to resign because of what she said, but she's a great survivor.* • *(Am)* A person's survivors are the members of his or her family who continue to live after he or she has died: *His survivors include his wife, two children and five grandchildren.*

sus·cep·ti·ble INFLUENCED /sə'sep·tɪ·bḷ/ *adj* easily influenced or harmed by something • *She isn't very susceptible* **to** *persuasion/pressure.* • *Some people are more* *susceptible* **to** *alcohol than others.* • *These plants are particularly susceptible* **to** *frost.* • *Among particularly susceptible children, the disease can develop at a very young age.* • A person who is susceptible is easily emotionally influenced: *He took advantage of the susceptible young girl.*

sus·cep·ti·bil·i·ty /£sə,sep·tɪ'bɪl·ɪ·ti, $-ə·ṭi/ *n* [U] • *Some people have a great susceptibility* **to** (=are easily influenced by) *advertising.* • *People vary in their susceptibility* **to** (=in how easily they catch) *infectious diseases.*

sus·cep·ti·bil·i·ties /£sə,sep·tɪ'bɪl·ɪ·tiz, $-ə·ṭiz/ *pl n* • Your susceptibilities are the feelings you have which are likely to be hurt: *I didn't mean to offend/upset/hurt your susceptibilities.*

sus·cep·ti·ble [PROVIDED WITH] /sə'sep·tɪ·bl̩/ *adj* [after v] *fml* (esp. of an idea or statement) able to be provided with something • *Shakespeare's plays are susceptible* **to** (=can have) *various interpretations.* • *Theories about history are not susceptible* **to** *being proved in the same way that scientific theories are.* • *(Br) The facts are susceptible* **of** *other explanations.*

su·shi /'suː·ʃi/ *n* [U] a type of Japanese food consisting of squares or balls of cold boiled rice, with small pieces of food, esp. raw fish on top • *a sushi bar* (=a place where this type of food is served)

su·spect *(obj)* [THINK LIKELY] /sə'spekt/ *v* [not *be suspecting*] to think or believe (something) to be true or probable • *So far, the police do not suspect foul play.* [T] • *We had no reason to suspect* **(that)** *he might try to kill himself.* [+ *(that)* clause] • *I* **half** *suspected* **(that)** *he was lying.* [+ *(that)* clause] • *Doctors* **strongly** *suspect* **(that)** *the child's injuries were not accidental.* [+ *(that)* clause] • *"Do you think she'll have told them?" "I suspect* **not/so.**" [+ *not/so*] • *"I think we should tell the truth about what happened." "Yes, I suspect* **(that)** *you're right* (=you're probably right)." [+ *(that)* clause]

su·spec·ted /£sə'spek·tɪd, $-ṭɪd/ *adj* [not gradable] • *He has a suspected broken leg.*

su·spic·ion /sə'spɪʃ·ᵊn/ *n* [C] • *I* **have** *a suspicion* (=belief or idea) **that** *he only asked me out because my brother persuaded him to.* [+ *that* clause] • *There is a growing suspicion* **that** *the men who were jailed for the bombing were in fact innocent.* [+ *that* clause] • *Despite the findings of the investigation, strong suspicions remain* **that** *the government knew that the weapons were being sold illegally.* [+ *that* clause] • *She* **had** *a* **lurking/nagging/sneaking** *suspicion* **that** *she might have sent the letter to the wrong address.* [+ *that* clause] • *What he did has* **confirmed** *all my worst suspicions* **about** *him.*

su·spi·cious·ly /sə'spɪʃ·ə·sli/ *adv* • *She brushed away what looked suspiciously like* (=looked as if it probably was) *a tear.*

su·spect *obj* [THINK GUILTY] /sə'spekt/ *v* [T not *be suspecting*] to think or believe (someone) to be guilty of a crime or to have done something wrong • *No one knows who killed her, but the police suspect her husband.* • *She is suspected* **of** *murder.* • *The police suspect him* **of** *carrying out two bomb attacks.* • *Three suspected terrorists have been arrested.*

su·spect /'sʌs·pekt/ *n* [C] • *A suspect* (=person believed to have committed a crime) *is considered to be innocent until proved guilty.* • *Police have issued a photograph of the suspect.* • *The* **prime** *suspect* **in** *the murder of the president has committed suicide.* • *No one knows what caused the outbreak of food poisoning, but shellfish are the main suspect* (=are thought to have caused it). • *"Major Stasser has been shot. Round up the usual suspects"* (said by Claude Rains in the film *Casablanca*, 1942)

su·spic·ion /sə'spɪʃ·ᵊn/ *n* • *"I'm arresting you* **on** *suspicion* **of** (=in the belief that you are guilty of) *illegally possessing drugs," said the police officer.* [U] • *(esp. Br) She is* **under** *suspicion* (=believed to be guilty) **of** *murder.* [U] • *In this particular case, they are* **above/beyond** *suspicion* (=cannot be thought to be guilty). [U] • *(fig.)* **The finger of** *suspicion for the unauthorized publication of the report points to two members of the committee* (=they are thought to be guilty). [U] • *His strange behaviour aroused/raised his neighbours' suspicions* (=beliefs or feelings that he was doing something wrong). [C]

su·spi·cious /sə'spɪʃ·əs/ *adj* • *The fire at the bank is being treated as suspicious* (=as if it was caused by someone doing something wrong). • **It's** *a bit suspicious* **that** (=It seems as if there is something wrong because) *no one knows where he was at the time of the murder.* [+ *that* clause] • *Her behaviour was very suspicious (Aus infml* **suss**). • *Police said that there were no suspicious circumstances* (=those involving behaviour that is wrong) *surrounding her death.* • *Motorists were asked if they might have spotted the boy or noticed any suspicious activity on the afternoon that he disappeared.* • *There were some suspicious characters* (=people who looked as if they might do wrong) *hanging around outside.* • *Shopkeepers have been advised not to accept any suspicious-***looking** *bank notes.* • *There's a suspicious-***looking** *van parked at the end of the road.* • *His new book bears suspicious resemblance to a book written by someone else* (=His book is so similar to the other book that it seems as if he has copied it).

su·spi·cious·ly /sə'spɪʃ·ə·sli/ *adv* • *The officers noticed two men acting suspiciously* (=as if they were doing something wrong) *in a car.*

su·spect *obj* [DOUBT] /sə'spekt/ *v* [T not *be suspecting*] to not trust; to doubt • *I have no reason to suspect her honesty/loyalty.* • *We suspected his motives in making his offer.*

su·spect /'sʌs·pekt/ *adj* • *The study was carried out with such a small sample that its results are suspect* (=cannot be trusted). • *His book is yet another load of nonsense from someone with highly suspect ideas about women.* • *A suspect* (=possibly dangerous) *parcel was found at the station.* • *These tomatoes look a bit suspect* (=their freshness is doubtful).

su·spic·ion /sə'spɪʃ·ᵊn/ *n* • *The proposals are being viewed with suspicion* (=doubt). [U] • *Since they discovered the truth about his background, his colleagues have regarded him with suspicion* (=lack of trust). [U] • *He* **has** *a profound suspicion* **of** *anyone in authority.* [U] • *They feel that she* **harbours** (=has) *suspicions* **of** *their politics.* [C]

su·spi·cious /sə'spɪʃ·əs/ *adj* • *She told her lover that she thought her husband was starting to get suspicious* (=to think that something was wrong). • *His colleagues became suspicious* (=thought that there was something wrong) *when he did not appear at work, since he was always punctual.* • *Her parents have become suspicious* **about** *her behaviour.* • *They are* **deeply** *suspicious* **of** *one another/***of** *each other's motives.* • *I'm* **highly** *suspicious* **of** *the findings of this survey.* • *My mother has a very suspicious nature* (=does not trust people).

su·spi·cious·ly /sə'spɪʃ·ə·sli/ *adv* • *He looked at her suspiciously* (=in a way that showed he did not trust her). • *Donna eyed the food on her plate suspiciously* (=doubtfully). • *The children are suspiciously quiet* (=are so quiet that they are probably doing something wrong). • *His hair is suspiciously black* (=looks darker than it should be, and is therefore probably not natural) *for a man of his age.*

su·spend *obj* [STOP] /sə'spend/ *v* [T] to stop or to cause to be not active, either temporarily or permanently • *The ferry service has been suspended because of bad weather.* • *The company's share price fell so low that trading had to be suspended.* • *The President has suspended the constitution and assumed total power.* • *Both sides in the conflict have agreed* **temporarily** *to suspend hostilities.* • *The talks have been suspended* **indefinitely.** • *When you go to the theatre, you have to be willing to suspend* **disbelief** (=to act as if you believe that what you are seeing is real or true, although you know that it is not). • *I'm suspending* **judgment** (=not forming an opinion) *on the book I'm reading until I've got a bit further through it.* • *(law) Mr Young was given a six-month jail* **sentence** *suspended for two years.* (=If he commits another crime within two years, he will have to go to prison for six months for his original crime.) • If someone is suspended, they are temporarily not allowed to work, go to school or take part in an activity because they have done something wrong: *The doctors were suspended for three months after being found guilty of misconduct.* ○ *She was suspended* **from** *school for fighting.* ○ *He was suspended* **from** *playing football for four matches after arguing with the referee.* • **Suspended animation** is a state in which life in a body is temporarily slowed down or stopped: *Some animals, such as hedgehogs, exist in a state of suspended animation during the winter.* ○ *(fig.) A cut in interest rates would lift the economy out of its current state of suspended animation.*

su·spen·sion /sə'spen·ʃᵊn/ *n* • *The suspension* **of** *fighting is to take effect at 6 am on Monday.* [U] • *There have been calls for the drug's immediate suspension, following reports that it has dangerous side effects.* [U] • *The union is protesting about the suspension* **of** *a restaurant worker* (=the worker not being allowed to work). [U] • *The manager of the department is* **under** *suspension pending an internal* *investigation.* [U] • *The footballer is likely to receive either a fine or a suspension* (= a punishment of not being allowed to play for a period of time) *following an incident in yesterday's game.* [C] • *"That willing suspension of disbelief for the moment, which constitutes poetic faith"* (Coleridge in the book *Biographia Literaria*, 1817) • See also SUSPENSION.

su·spend *obj* HANG /sə'spend/ *v* [T always + adv/prep; often passive] to hang • *A bare light bulb was suspended* **from** *the ceiling.* • *The builders worked from wooden platforms, suspended by ropes* **from** *the roof of the house.* • *She suspended the hammock* **between** *two trees.* • *It was very uncomfortable lying on the hospital bed with my legs suspended* **in the air**. • *One of Magritte's paintings is of a man with his hat suspended* **in mid-air** *above his head.* • If small bits of solid material are suspended in a gas or a liquid, they hang or float in the gas or liquid: *The drug is suspended* **in** *a saline solution.* ○ *A cloud of smoke was suspended* **in** *the air.*

su·spen·sion /sə'spen·ʃən/ *n* [C] • A suspension is a liquid in which small pieces of solid are contained, but not dissolved: *a suspension of fine cornflour in corn oil* • A **suspension bridge** is a bridge which is supported by strong steel ropes hung from a tower at each end of the bridge: *When the Golden Gate bridge in San Francisco was built, it was the world's longest suspension bridge.* • See also SUSPENSION. • PIC **Bridge**

su·spend·er *Br and Aus* /£sə'spen·dəʳ, $-dɚ/, *Am* **gar·ter** *n* [C] a fastener which is fixed by a short elastic strap to a type of belt which women wear round their waists under their clothes, and which is used for holding up STOCKINGS by their tops • *(Br and Aus)* A **suspender belt** (*Am* **garter belt**) is a piece of women's underwear worn round the waist, which has fasteners fixed to it for holding up STOCKINGS by their tops.

su·spend·ers /£sə'spen·dəz, $-dɚz/ *pl n Am for* **braces**, see at BRACE SUPPORT

su·spense /sə'spents/ *n* [U] the feeling of excitement or anxiety which you have when you are waiting for something to happen and are uncertain about what it is going to be • *They are waiting* **in** *suspense to hear what the jury's verdict will be.* • *She* **kept** *him* **in** *suspense for several days before she said that she would marry him.* • *Come on,* **put** *me* **out of** *my suspense – tell me what happened.* • *The suspense* **is killing** *me* (= I am extremely eager to know what is going to happen or to know what I am going to be told). • *The play is full of intrigue and suspense* (= causes feelings of excitement because it is not certain what is going to happen). • *There is a gradual* **build-up of** *suspense throughout the film, until it comes to an unexpected ending.*

su·spen·sion /sə'spen·ʃən/ *n* [U] the part of a vehicle which is fixed to the wheels in order to reduce the uncomfortable effects of going over uneven road surfaces • *At higher speeds, the car's suspension doesn't cope very well with potholes and bumps.* • See also **suspension** at SUSPEND.

su·spic·ion /sə'spɪʃ·ən/ *n* [U] a small amount • *He gave just* **a** *suspicion* **of** *a smile.* • *I have* **a** *suspicion* **of** *doubt about whether I should accept his invitation or not.* • See also **suspicion** at SUSPECT.

suss *(obj)* DISCOVER /sʌs/ *v Br and Aus infml* to discover (about); to understand • *He never sussed* **(out) that** *they'd tricked him.* [+ *that* clause] • *It took us some time to suss* **(out) wh***at was going on.* [+ *wh-* word] • *She thinks she's got me sussed* **(out)** (= She thinks she understands me), *but she's wrong.* [T/M] • *I had this odd feeling he was sussing me* **out** (= discovering things about me) *in some way.* [M] • *I want to suss* **out** (= discover things about) *the college before I decide whether I want to go there or not.* [M]

suss UNABLE TO BE TRUSTED /sʌs/ *adj Aus infml for* **suspicious**, see at SUSPECT THINK GUILTY • *Her explanation seemed suss to me.*

sus·tain *obj* MAINTAIN /sə'steɪn/ *v* [T] to keep (something) in existence • *The economy looks set to sustain its growth into next year.* • *We do not have sufficient resources to sustain our campaign for long.* • *He seems to find it difficult to sustain relationships with women.* • *(Am) There is not sufficient evidence to sustain a* **case** *against them.* • *(Am) The judge sustained* (= accepted) *the lawyer's objection.* • To sustain is also to keep alive: *The baby's lungs were unable to sustain her, and she died in her parents' arms.* ○ *The soil in this part of the world is not rich enough to sustain a large population.* • If you sustain a note when you are playing a piece of music or singing, you play or sing it for a slightly longer time than usual.

sus·tain·a·ble /sə'steɪ·nə·bl̩/ *adj* • If something is sustainable, it is able to be continued in its present form: *I don't believe that they have a sustainable argument.* ○ *The myth about a woman's place being in the home is no longer sustainable.* • Sustainable is also used to refer to a way of using natural products so that no damage is caused to the environment: *A large international meeting was held with the aim of promoting sustainable* **development** *in all countries.*

sus·tain·a·bil·i·ty /£sə͵steɪ·nə'bɪl·ɪ·ti, $-ə·t̬i/ *n* [U] • *The sustainability* (= ability to be continued) *of the government's financial policies has been brought into question.* • *A report on the sustainability of the world's tropical forests* (= the using of them in a way that does not cause environmental damage) *says that less than 1% of rainforests are being managed in a way that allows the timber to replace itself.*

sus·tained /sə'steɪnd/ *adj* • Sustained means continuing for a long time: *The president's speech was greeted by sustained applause.* ○ *He said that he considered low inflation to be the key to sustained economic growth.* • Sustained also means determined: *We must make a sustained effort to get this task finished this week.*

sus·tain *obj* SUFFER /sə'steɪn/ *v* [T] *fml* to suffer or experience (esp. damage or loss) • *She sustained multiple injuries in the accident.* • *Many buildings sustained serious/severe damage in the earthquake.* • *The company has sustained heavy losses this year.*

sus·tain *obj* SUPPORT /sə'steɪn/ *v* [T] to support emotionally • *She was sustained by the strength of her religious faith.* • *He prayed for strength to sustain him at this difficult time.* • *The love of my family and friends sustained me through my ordeal.*

sus·te·nance FOOD /'sʌs·tɪ·nənts/ *n* [U] *fml* food • *Children need a lot of sustenance.* • *During this cold weather, the food put out by householders is the only form of sustenance that the birds have.* • Sustenance is also the ability of food to provide people and animals with what they need to make them strong and healthy: *A stick of celery does not provide much sustenance.*

sus·te·nance SUPPORT /'sʌs·tɪ·nənts/ *n* [U] *fml* emotional or mental support • *I rely on my family for emotional sustenance.* • *When her husband died, she* **drew** *sustenance* **from**/*she* **found** *sustenance* **in** *her religious beliefs.*

sut·tee /'sʌt·iː/ *n* [U] SATI

su·ture /£'suː·tʃəʳ, $-tʃɚ/ *n* [C] *medical* a stitch used to sew up a cut in a person's body • *The doctor put six sutures in the wound on his face.*

su·ture *obj* /£'suː·tʃəʳ, $-tʃɚ/ *v* [T] *medical* • To suture a cut in a person's body is to sew it together: *After the operation, the incision was carefully sutured.*

svelte /svelt, sfelt/ *adj* attractively thin, graceful and stylish • *She claimed that she lost her job in the restaurant when she was pregnant because her boss wanted svelte waitresses, and a pregnant woman is not svelte.* • *Tony drove up in his svelte new sports car.*

SW SOUTHWEST *n* [U], *adj abbreviation for* SOUTHWEST or SOUTHWESTERN

SW RADIO *n* [U] *abbreviation for* **short wave**, see at WAVE ENERGY

swab MEDICINE /£swɒb, $swɑːb/ *n* [C] a small piece of soft material used for cleaning a cut or for taking a small amount of substance from a body, or the substance itself which can then be tested • *The nurse cleaned the cut on my leg with a swab.* • *"I'm just going to take a swab* **of** *your ear," said the doctor.*

swab *obj* /£swɒb, $swɑːb/ *v* [T] **-bb-** • *The nurse swabbed my arm* (= cleaned it with a small piece of soft material) *before giving me an injection.* • *This wound will need to be carefully swabbed* **out**, *then stitched.* [M]

swab *obj* WASH /£swɒb, $swɑːb/ *v* [T] **-bb-** to wash (esp. the open flat areas of a ship) with a wet cloth or MOP • *On our sailing holiday, we all took it in turns to swab* **(down)** *the deck of the boat.* [T/M]

swad·dle *obj* /£'swɒd·l̩, $'swɑː·dl̩/ *v* [T] *dated* to wrap (a baby) tightly in cloth • *Some people think that swaddling a baby tightly* **in** *a blanket is a good way to stop it crying.*

swag STEAL /swæg/ *n* [U] *dated slang* stolen goods • *The cartoon showed a picture of a robber carrying a bag with 'swag' written on it.*

swag POSSESSIONS /swæg/ *n* [U] *Aus dated* possessions wrapped in a cloth and carried by a person who does not have a home or a job, but walks around from place to place

swag·ger /£'swæg·əʳ, $-ɚ/ *v* [I] to walk, esp. with a swinging movement, in a way that shows that you are very confident and think that you are important, or to act in that way • *They swaggered into the room.* • *A group of young men swaggered* **about** *outside the bar.* • *His swaggering self-confidence irritates many people.*

swag·ger /£'swæg·əʳ, $-ɚ/ *n* [U] • *He walked out of the room with* **a** *self-confident swagger.* • *Underneath all his swagger* (=way of acting that shows he is very confident and thinks that he is important), *he's actually quite nervous.*

swag·ger·ing·ly /£'swæg·ᵊr·ɪŋ·li, $'-ɚ-/ *adv*

swal·low *(obj)* THROAT /£'swɒl·əʊ, $'swɑː·loʊ/ *v* to cause (esp. food and drink) to move from your mouth into your stomach by using the muscles of your throat, or to use the muscles of your throat as if doing this • *My throat is so sore that it really hurts when I swallow.* [I] • *If you don't chew your food properly, it's difficult to swallow it.* [T] • *He put a grape into his mouth and swallowed it* **whole**. [T] • *The baby died after accidentally swallowing some pills.* [T] • To swallow is also to use the muscles of your throat, as if moving something from your mouth into your stomach, because you are nervous or frightened, or are about to say something: *She swallowed as she turned over the examination paper and looked at the first question.* [I] ○ *He swallowed* **hard** *and said, "Dad, I've got something to tell you."* [I] • If something swallows something or someone **(up)**, it takes them into itself, so that they no longer exist separately or can no longer be seen, or it uses them completely: *An increasing amount of the countryside is being swallowed up by the town.* [M] ○ *Many small businesses have been swallowed up by large companies.* [M] ○ *Most of the company's profits have been swallowed* (=completely used) *by higher wages.* [T] ○ *Taxes have swallowed up nearly half of my pay increase.* [M] • If you **swallow the bait**, you completely accept something, esp. an offer of some type: *I told Dad that if he let me borrow the car for the weekend, I'd clean it for him, but he didn't swallow the bait.*

swal·low /£'swɒl·əʊ, $'swɑː·loʊ/ *n* [C] • A swallow is an act of using the muscles of your throat, or the amount of something you move into your stomach from your mouth by using the muscles of your throat: *He gave a swallow, then began speaking.* ○ *Just let me have a couple more swallows of my coffee, and I'll be ready.*

swal·low *obj* ACCEPT /£'swɒl·əʊ, $'swɑː·loʊ/ *v* [T] *infml* to accept (something) without question or without expressing disagreement • *I found his explanation rather hard to swallow.* • *Not surprisingly, this excuse was too much for them to swallow.* • *He swallowed her story* **whole**. • *She swallowed his sales pitch line* **hook, line and sinker** (=believed it completely). • *I found it hard to swallow his insults.* • *They eventually* **swallowed** *their* **pride** (=accepted that they had to change their opinion) *and signed a transport deal with the neighbouring country.*

swal·low *obj* NOT EXPRESS /£'swɒl·əʊ, $'swɑː·loʊ/ *v* [T] not to express or show (something) • *She swallowed her disappointment, saying, "That's OK, it doesn't matter."* • *I don't know how I managed to swallow my anger.* • *He was forced to swallow his* **pride** *and ask if he could have his old job back.* • *I was made to* **swallow** *my* **words** (=admit that I was wrong) *when the scheme turned out to be a great success.*

swal·low BIRD /£'swɒl·əʊ, $'swɑː·loʊ/ *n* [C] a small bird with pointed wings and a tail with two points, which flies quickly and catches insects to eat as it flies. There are various types of swallow. • *Swallows come to northern countries when it's summer there, and fly south in the northern winter.* • *(saying)* 'One swallow doesn't make a summer' means that just because one good thing has happened, it is not therefore the case that the situation you are in is going to improve. • *(Br and Aus)* A **swallow dive** (*Am* **swan dive**) is a DIVE (=an act of jumping into water so that your head enters the water before your feet) which you do with your arms held out from your side until you are close to the water. • *"Swallows and Amazons"* (title of a children's book by Arthur Ransome, 1930) • PIC› **Birds**

swam /swæm/ *past simple of* SWIM

swa·mi /'swɑː·mi/ *n* [C] (the title of) a Hindu religious teacher

swamp WET LAND /£swɒmp, $swɑːmp/ *n* (an area of) very wet soft land • *a peat swamp* [C] • *a mangrove swamp* [C] • *an alligator-infested swamp* [C] • *The Everglades are an area of swamp in southern Florida.* [U] • *Most coal-fields began life as swamps about 300 million years ago.* [C] • *The ground is like a swamp after all that rain.* [C]

swamp·y /£'swɒm·pi, $'swɑːm-/ *adj* **-ier, -iest** • Swampy land is land that is soft and very wet: *swampy ground* ○ *a swampy area*

swamp *obj* COVER /£swɒmp, $swɑːmp/ *v* [T] to cover (a place or thing) with a large amount of water • *High tides have swamped the coast.* • *The boat was swamped* **by** *an enormous wave.* • If something swamps a person or thing, it comes to them in a larger amount than they can easily deal with: *Foreign cars have swamped the UK market.* ○ *I'm swamped* **with** *work* (=have more work than I can easily deal with) *at the moment.* ○ *On her 100th birthday she was swamped* **with** (=received a lot of) *cards and messages of congratulations.* • To swamp someone or something also means to cause them no longer to be able to operate: *In many parts of the world, the rate of population growth already swamps the ability of society to cope.* • *(fig.) I bought a new dress for my daughter, but it absolutely swamped her* (=was much too big for her).

swan BIRD /£swʌn, $swɑːn/ *n* [C] a large usually white bird with a long neck that lives on rivers and lakes. There are various types of swan. • *The children went to feed the ducks and swans on the river.* • **Swan dive** is *Am for* **swallow dive**. See at SWALLOW BIRD. • PIC› **Birds**

swan GO /£swʌn, $swɑːn/ *v* [I always + adv/prep] **-nn-** *Br and Aus infml disapproving* to go or travel somewhere for pleasure rather than as work, and without having a clear purpose • *She swanned into the room, carrying a glass of wine, taking no notice of the fact that she'd kept us all waiting for hours.* • *He's been swanning* **around** (=not doing any work) *all morning.* • *I suppose they've swanned* **off** *somewhere warm for the winter as usual.*

swank /swæŋk/ *v* [I] *infml disapproving* to behave or speak in a way that shows that you think that you are important, in order to attract other people's attention and admiration • *Just because you won, there's no need to swank.* • *People around here don't swank* **about** *their money.*

swank /swæŋk/ *n* [U] *infml disapproving* • *In spite of all his swank* (=behaviour that shows that he thinks he is important), *he's never really achieved very much.* • *I think these threats are just swank – they haven't got the strength to carry them out.*

swank·y /'swæŋ·ki/ *adj* **-ier, -iest** *infml* • Swanky means very expensive and fashionable, in a way that is intended to attract people's attention and admiration: *They live in a swanky house, drive a swanky car, and their children go to a swanky school.* ○ *We stayed in a swanky hotel.* • *(disapproving)* Swanky also means behaving in a way that shows that you think you are important: *I'm sick of his swanky talk.*

swan·song /£'swʌn·sɒŋ, $'swɑːn·sɑːŋ/ *n* [C] a person's last piece of work, achievement, or performance • *The opera 'Death in Venice' turned out to be Benjamin Britten's swansong.* • *This weekend's match was his swansong as the team's captain.*

swap *(obj)*, *Br also* **swop** /£swɒp, $swɑːp/ *v* **-pp-** to give (something) and be given something else instead; to exchange • *When you've finished reading your book, and I've finished mine, shall we swap?* [I] • *The children have decided that they want to swap bedrooms.* [T] • *The two computer manufacturers plan to build a series of products that will enable their machines to swap data.* [T] • *We swapped addresses* **with** *the people we met on holiday.* [T] • *Would you swap one packet of the new brand of washing powder* **for** *two packets of your old one?* [T] • *When he got a job in a bank, he had to swap his jeans and T-shirt* **for** *a suit* (=he had to wear formal clothes instead of informal ones). [T] • *They've decided to swap their life in the city* **for** *one in the country* (=to live in the countryside instead of the city). [T] • *I'll swap you my chocolate bar* **for** *your peanuts.* [+ two objects] • *We spent the evening in the pub, swapping* (=telling each other) *stories/jokes.* [T] • *The purpose of this meeting is just to swap ideas.* [T] • *After the first course of the meal, we all (Br)* **swapped over/round/** *(Am)* **swapped seats/** *(Br also and Aus)* **swapped places** (=exchanged seats) *so that we were sitting next to somebody different.*

swap, *Br also* **swop** /£swɒp, $swɑːp/ *n* [C] • *I thought the meal Simon ordered in the restaurant looked nicer than mine, and he thought mine looked better, so we* **did a swap** (=exchanged them). • *Do you want to look through my swaps* (=things I have that I am willing to exchange) *and* *see if there are any stamps that you'd like?* • *This comic was a swap* (=something that was exchanged) *that I got from Nick.* • **Swap meet** is *Am for* **car-boot sale**. See at CAR.

swarm /£swɔːm, $swɔːrm/ *n* [C] a large group of insects, or *(fig.)* of people, moving all together • *a swarm* **of** *bees/ wasps/ants/locusts* • *The dead sheep was covered with swarms* **of** *flies.* • *(fig.) A swarm* **of**/*Swarms* **of** *journalists followed the film star's car.* • PIC› **Wasps and bees**

swarm /£swɔːm, $swɔːrm/ *v* [I] • When insects swarm, they come together in a large group: *In the summer, male midges start to swarm at dusk.* • When people swarm, they move in a large group or in large numbers: *After the game, thousands of football fans swarmed onto the ground.* ○ *Angry crowds swarmed through the gates of the embassy.* ○ *Children swarmed round the ice cream stand.* • *The garden is swarming* **with** *wasps* (=There are a lot of them in the garden). • *The Lake District is swarming* **with** *tourists for much of the year.*

swar·thy /£'swɔː·ði, $'swɔːr-/ *adj* **-ier, -iest** (of a person or their skin) dark-coloured • *a swarthy face* • *a swarthy complexion* • *a swarthy fisherman*

swash·buck·ling /£'swɒʃˌbʌk·lɪŋ, $'swɑːʃ-/ *adj* [before n; not gradable] behaving in a brave and exciting way, esp. like a fighter in the past • *a swashbuckling hero* ○ *a swashbuckling pirate* • *The players displayed a swashbuckling confidence.* • *He has a swashbuckling approach to running a company.*

swas·ti·ka /£'swɒs·tɪ·kə, $'swɑː·stɪ-/ *n* [C] a symbol in the form of a cross with each of its arms bent at a 90 degree angle half way along • *The swastika was the symbol used by the Nazi party in Germany.* • *Fascists painted swastikas on the walls in immigrant neighbourhoods.*

swat *obj* /£swɒt, $swɑːt/ *v* [T] **-tt-** to hit (esp. an insect) with a wide or flat object or your hand • *I swatted the fly with a rolled-up newspaper.* • *He tried to swat the ball too hard, and missed it entirely.* • *(fig.) These missiles are capable of swatting* (=hitting) *enemy planes with deadly accuracy.*

swat /£swɒt, $swɑːt/ *n* [C] • *He gave the mosquito a swat.*

swatch /£swɒtʃ, $swɑːtʃ/ *n* [C] a small piece of cloth used as an example of the colour and type of the cloth • *a fabric swatch* • *When I went to choose the wallpaper for my bedroom, I took a swatch* **of** *the curtain material with me to match the colour.*

swathe AREA, **swath** /sweɪð/ *n* [C] a long strip of a crop or grass that has been cut by a machine, or, more generally, a large area or part • *The long grass was cut in swathes.* • **Huge** *swathes* (=areas) **of** *rain forest are being cleared for farming and mining.* • *The fire reduced* **vast** *swathes* **of** *the city to ruins.* • *A thousand years ago, pandas could be found over a* **wide** *swathe* **of** *China.* • *The film spreads over a large swathe* **of** *time, but concentrates mainly on the late 1940s.* • *(fig.) These people represent a wide swathe* (=range) **of** *opinion.*

swathe *obj* CLOTH /sweɪð/ *v* [T often passive] to wrap round or cover with cloth • *He came out of the hospital swathed* **in** *bandages.* • *Her head was swathed* **in** *a scarf.* • *I love to swathe* (=dress) *myself* **in** *silk.*

swathe, swath /sweɪð/ *n* [C] • *His head was wrapped in swathes* (=long strips) **of** *bandages.*

sway MOVE /sweɪ/ *v* [I] to move slowly from side to side • *The trees were swaying in the wind.* • *The movement of the ship caused the masts to sway* **(from side to side/ backwards and forwards)**. • *A drunk was standing in the middle of the street, swaying uncertainly and trying hard to stay upright.* • *We lay on the sand, beneath the swaying palm trees.* • *She walked with her hips swaying.*

sway *obj* PERSUADE /sweɪ/ *v* [T usually passive] to persuade (someone) to believe or do one thing rather than another • *Were you swayed by her arguments?* • *Her speech failed to sway her colleagues* **into** *supporting the plan.* • *(fig.) Recent developments have swayed* (=changed) *the balance of power in the region.*

sway CONTROL /sweɪ/ *n* [U] *esp. fml or literary* control or influence • *In the 1980s, the organization came* **under the** *sway* **of** (=became strongly influenced by) *Christian fundamentalism.* • *Her parents no longer seem to have much sway* **over** *her.* • *The US is extending its strategic sway in many parts of the world.*

swear USE RUDE WORDS /£sweəʳ, $swer/ *v* [I] *past simple* **swore** /£swɔːʳ, $swɔːr/, *past part* **sworn** /£swɔːn, $swɔːrn/ to use words that are rude or offensive as a way of emphasizing what you mean or as a way of insulting someone or something • *It was a real shock, the first time I heard my mother swear.* • *When the taxi driver started to swear* **at** *him, he walked off.* • A **swear word** is a rude or offensive word: *All swear words, even mild ones such as 'damn', were deleted from the text.* LP› **Labels**

swear *(obj)* PROMISE /£sweəʳ, $swer/ *v past simple* **swore** /£swɔːʳ, $swɔːr/, *past part* **sworn** /£swɔːn, $swɔːrn/ to state or promise that you are telling the truth or that you will do something or behave in a particular way • *I don't know anything about what happened, I swear.* [I] • *You might find it difficult to believe, but I swear* **(that)** *the guy just came up to me and gave me the money.* [+ (that) clause] • *New gang members must swear* **to** *obey the gang leaders at all times.* [+ to infinitive] • *In some countries, witnesses in court have to swear* **on the Bible.** [I] • *I swore an* **oath** *to tell the truth, the whole truth and nothing but the truth.* [T] • When someone is sworn **in**, they make a formal promise to be honest or loyal, either because they are in a law court or because they are starting a new official job: *The next witness was sworn in.* [M] ○ *William Jefferson Clinton was sworn in as the 42nd President of the United States of America.* [M] • *A few of us knew what was going to happen, but we were sworn* **to** *secrecy* (=we were forced to promise that we would keep it a secret). [T] • *(infml) I think his birthday is on the 5th, but I wouldn't/couldn't swear* **to** *it* (=I am not completely certain about it). [I] • *(esp. Br infml) She* **swore blind** (=emphasized that it was true) **(that)** *she didn't know what had happened to the money.* • *(infml) My dad* **swears by** (=believes in the effectiveness of) *these vitamin pills.*

swear off *obj v prep* [T] to make a decision not to do (something) or not take harmful drugs, alcohol etc. • *After those months of treatment, he swore off drugs completely.*

sweat /swet/, *fml* **per·spire** *v* [I] to excrete a salty colourless liquid through the skin because you are hot, ill or afraid • *It was so hot when we arrived in Tripoli that we started to sweat as soon as we got off the plane.* • *The prisoners were sweating* **with** *fear.* • *(infml) I was so afraid, I was sweating* **like a pig** (=sweating a lot). • *(fig. infml) It seemed that the authorities had delayed the news just to make us sweat* (=keep us waiting in a state of anxiety). • If something sweats, it has drops of liquid on the outside: *Don't put the cheese in a plastic bag – it'll sweat.* ○ *The walls in older houses sometimes sweat* **with** *damp.* • *(infml)* To **sweat blood** or **sweat** your **guts out** is to make a great effort: *We sweated blood to get the work finished on time.* • *(Am infml)* If you **sweat bullets**, you sweat a lot: *The combination of hard physical work and high temperatures soon had us sweating bullets.* • If you **sweat it out**, you are involved in hard physical exercise: *I like to sweat it out in the gym for a couple of hours every day.* • To **sweat it out** is also to suffer while you wait for an unpleasant situation to end: *My exams finish next week then I'll be sweating it out for a month waiting for the results.* • To **sweat over a hot** piece of equipment is to work hard using it: *I've been sweating over a hot* **stove** *all morning.* ○ *I spent all day sweating over a hot computer.*

sweat /swet/, *fml* **per·spir·a·tion** *n* [U] • *The dancers were* **dripping/pouring with** *sweat* (=the salty colourless liquid that you excrete through your skin) *after a morning's rehearsal.* • *By the time we'd climbed to the top of the hill, we were* **covered in** *sweat.* • *She wiped the* **beads** (=drops) *of sweat from her forehead.* • *(fig. infml) He tends to get* **in a** *sweat* (=to worry) *about flying.* • *The cathedral was built by human toil and sweat* (=effort). • *(infml)* If you say that something is **no sweat**, you mean that it will not be difficult or cause problems: *"Can you fix my car for me?" "No sweat!"* • A **sweat band** is a thin strip of material that someone doing sport or exercise wears round their head to stop sweat going into their eyes or wears round their wrists to stop sweat going onto their hands. • The **sweat glands** are the small organs under the skin which produce sweat. • **Sweat suit** is a TRACKSUIT.

sweat·y /£'swet·i, $'sweţ-/ *adj* **-ier, -iest** • *a sweaty face* (=one covered in sweat) • *sweaty clothes* (=those full of and smelling of sweat) • *We spent the evening in a sweaty* (=that causes you to sweat) *pub.*

sweat·ed /£'swet·ɪd, $'sweţ-/ *adj* [before n; not gradable] *disapproving* involving workers who are paid very little and who work many hours in very bad conditions • *a sweated workshop* • *The textile industry still relies to some extent on sweated* **labour**.

sweat·er /£'swet·əʳ, $'sweţ·ɚ/, *Br and Aus also* **jump·er**, **pull·over** *n* [C] a usually woollen piece of clothing with long sleeves which is worn on the upper part of the body and which does not open at the front • *Put a sweater on if you're cold.* • *He was wearing a V-necked sweater.* • Compare CARDIGAN. • [PIC] **Clothes**

sweat·shirt /£'swet·ʃɜːt, $-ʃɜːrt/ *n* [C] a piece of informal clothing with long sleeves, usually made of thick cotton, worn on the upper part of the body • *She was dressed casually in jeans and a sweatshirt.* • [PIC] **Clothes**

sweat·shop /£'swet·ʃɒp, $-ʃɑːp/ *n* [C] *disapproving* a small factory where workers are paid very little and work many hours in very bad conditions • *sweatshop conditions*

swede *Br and Aus* /swiːd/, *Am usually* **rut·a·ba·ga** *n* [C/U] a round vegetable with dark yellow flesh and a brown or purple skin • [PIC] **Vegetables**

sweep *obj* [CLEAN] /swiːp/ *v* [T] *past* **swept** /swept/ to clean (esp. a floor) by using a brush to collect the dirt into one place from which it can be removed • *I found a broom to sweep the floor with.* • *The chimney needs sweeping.* • *Sweep the dust* **into** *the dustpan.* • *Shall I sweep* **out** *the garden shed* (= clear the dirt from its floor)*?* [M] • *The boys said they would sweep* **up** *the leaves* (= collect and remove them). [M] • To **sweep** a difficult or unpleasant situation **under the carpet/***(Am also)* **under the rug/***(Aus also)* **under the mat** is to hide it and try to keep it secret: *The committee is being accused of sweeping financial problems under the carpet to avoid embarrassment and a possibly damaging scandal.*

sweep /swiːp/ *n* • *I've given the kitchen floor* **a** *sweep* (= I have swept it). [U] • Sweep is also *infml dated for* CHIMNEYSWEEP. [C]

sweep·er /£'swiː·pəʳ, $-pɚ/ *n* [C] • *a carpet sweeper* (= a machine for cleaning them) • *a road sweeper* (= a person whose job is cleaning the roads) • In football, a sweeper is a player whose position is behind the other defenders.

sweep *obj* [REMOVE] /swiːp/ *v* [T always + adv/prep] *past* **swept** /swept/ to remove and/or take in a particular direction, esp. in a fast and powerful way • *A large wave swept* **away** *half the sandcastle.* [M] • *He swept* **back** *his long hair.* [M] • *Smiling, he swept me* **into** *his arms.* • *She swept the pile of papers and books* **into** *her bag.* • *She swept* **up** (= picked up) *her things and walked out of the room.* [M] • *The boat was swept* **out to sea** (= away from land) *by the tide.* • *Government troops swept* **aside** *the rebel forces* (= caused them to move away from the area in which they were). [M] • *(fig.) They swept his doubts and objections* **aside** (= They refused to consider them as important). [M] • *(fig.) We were swept* **away/along** (= made to feel very enthusiastic and positive) *by her eloquence and the force of her personality.* • To **sweep** someone **off** their **feet** is to cause them to become suddenly and completely in love with you: *The first time he met her, he was completely swept off his feet.* • See also **sweeping** at SWEEP [MOVE].

sweep *(obj)* [MOVE] /swiːp/ *v past* **swept** /swept/ to move, esp. quickly and powerfully • *The train swept* **along**. [I always + adv/prep] • *The army swept* **over** *the border, eliminating all resistance.* [I always + adv/prep] • *Everyone looked up as she swept* **into** *the room.* [I always + adv/prep] • *The fire swept* (= spread quickly) **through** *the house.* [I always + adv/prep] • *A new virus is sweeping* (= spreading quickly) **through** *the dairy cattle herds.* [I always + adv/prep] • *(fig.) A 1970s fashion revival is sweeping* (= spreading through and influencing) *Europe.* [T] • *Her gaze swept* (= looked round) *across the assembled crowd.* [I always + adv/prep] • *The National Party swept* **into power** (= easily won the election) *with a majority of almost 200.* [I always + adv/prep] • To sweep an area is also to travel across all of it, esp. when looking for something: *American minesweepers are sweeping the Arabian sea.* [T] • If a road, river or range of mountains, houses, steps etc. sweeps in a particular direction, they follow a particular path: *The road sweeps down to the coast.* [I always + adv/prep]

sweep /swiːp/ *n* [C] • *With a sweep* (= horizontal movement) **of** *its tail, the alligator knocked her under the water.* • *A broad sweep* (= area) **of** *flat countryside stretched to the horizon in all directions.* • *The film showed the breadth of Arab culture and the sweep* (= range) **of** *its history.* • *In a sweep* (= search) **of** *houses within the neighbourhood, police discovered hidden weapons and ammunition.*

sweep·ing /'swiː·pɪŋ/ *adj* • *It is obvious that sweeping* (= large and having a wide effect) **changes** *are needed in the legal system.* • *We need to make sweeping* (= large) *cuts to our budget.* • *(disapproving) Sweeping* (= Not carefully enough considered) **generalizations** *about such a complex and difficult situation are not helpful.* • *Her latest novel has a sweeping historical narrative* (= one which moves quickly through a lot of time).

sweep *obj* [WIN] /swiːp/ *v* [T] *past* **swept** /swept/ *Am infml* to win all the parts of (a competition), or to win very easily • *The Yankees swept a four-game series* **from** *the Blue Jays.* • *The radicals swept all the seats on the committee.* • To **sweep the board** is to win everything that is available: *Australia swept the board in the swimming, with gold medals in every race.*

sweep /swiːp/ *n* [C] • *Romania* **made a (clean)** *sweep of the medals* (= won all of them).

sweep·ing /'swiː·pɪŋ/ *adj* • *The party have failed to win the sweeping* (= complete) *victory they expected.*

sweeps /swiːps/ *pl n Am* a period of time when measurements of the number of people watching different television stations are made so that the cost of advertising on each station can be set • *Stations often broadcast their most popular shows during the sweeps in order to boost their ratings.*

sweep·stake /'swiːp·steɪk/, *infml* **sweep** *n* [C] a type of GAMBLING, usually on a horse race, in which people pay a small amount of money and choose a particular horse. The person who chooses the winning horse receives all the money paid by everyone else.

sweet /swiːt/ *adj* **-er, -est** (esp. of food or drink) having a taste similar to that of sugar; not bitter or salty • *Do you want your pancakes sweet or savoury?* • *The pineapple was very ripe – sweet and juicy.* • *It's quite a sweet-smelling perfume.* • *(Am)* Sweet **butter** has had no salt added to it. • If an emotion or event is sweet, it is very pleasant and satisfying: *For her,* **revenge** *was sweet.* ○ *She was enjoying the sweet* **smell of success.** • If a sound is sweet, it is pleasant and easy to like: *She has a sweet singing voice.* • Sweet can be used, esp. of something or someone small, to mean charming and attractive: *The little baby elephant looked so sweet.* ○ *They live in a sweet little house.* ○ *What a sweet baby!* • Sweet can also mean kind, generous and likeable: *I think Alex is really sweet.* ○ **It** *was sweet* **of** *you to help me.* ○ *They were very sweet* **to** *us when we stayed with them.* • To **keep** someone **sweet** is to try to keep them satisfied and pleased with you: *We're allowing the French engineers to use our computers, to keep them sweet in case we need their help later on.* • *(dated infml)* If you are **sweet on** someone, you like them very much or you are in love with them: *She's still sweet on him after all this time!* • **Sweet-and-sour** food has a flavour that is both sweet and sour: *sweet-and-sour chicken* ○ *Sweet-and-sour dishes and sauces are typical of Chinese cooking.* • *(Br)* A **sweet chestnut** (*Am* **chestnut**) is a large tree with leaves divided into five parts and large round nuts that are cooked and eaten hot. • *(slang)* **Sweet Fanny Adams** (*abbreviation* **sweet F A**) means nothing: *I know sweet Fanny Adams about it.* • *(humorous)* **Sweet nothings** are romantic and loving talk: *They're the couple in the corner,* **whispering/murmuring** *sweet nothings to each other.* • A **sweet pea** is a climbing plant with pale-coloured sweet-smelling flowers. • A **sweet pepper** is a PEPPER [VEGETABLE]. • A **sweet potato** (*esp. Am also* **yam**) is a pinkish brown or orange-coloured vegetable with yellow flesh. • *(infml)* To **sweet-talk** someone is to talk to them in a pleasing and/or clever way in order to persuade them to do or believe something: *At election time, the politicians arrive and sweet-talk us but they never keep their promises.* ○ *The salesman tried to sweet-talk me* **into** *buying a bigger car.* ○ *Don't let the* **sweet talk** *fool you!* • If you have a **sweet tooth**, you like eating sweet foods, esp. sweets and chocolate. • *"Ah! Sweet Mystery of Life, at last I've found thee"* (title of a song written by Rida Johnson Young and Victor Herbert, 1910) • *"A sweet disorder in the dress"* (Robert Herrick in the poem *Delight in Disorder*, 1648) • *"Sweet Dreams are Made of This"* (title of a song by The Eurythmics, 1983)

sweet /swiːt/ *n* • *(Br and Aus)* A sweet (*Br infml also* **sweetie**, *Am* **candy**, *Aus also* **lolly**) is a small piece of sweet food, made of sugar: *I ate a lot of sweets and chocolate as a child, especially* **boiled** (= hard) *sweets and toffees.* [C] • *(Am)* A sweet is also any food with a lot of sugar in it: *Don't fill up on sweets, we'll be having dinner soon.* [C] • *(Br and Aus)* A sweet is also sweet food eaten at the end of a meal: *He had cooked a delicious sweet – apple pie.* [C] ○ *I don't want any sweet, thanks.* [U] • *(infml)* People sometimes say **my** sweet to a person they love: *"Are you all right, my sweet?"* [as form of address] • *(Br and Aus)* A **sweet shop** (*Am* **candy store**) is a shop which sells sweets, cigarettes and often newspapers.

sweet·en *obj* /£'swiː·tᵊn, $-t̬ᵊn/ *v* [T] • *The apple mixture can be sweetened* **with** *honey.* • *(fig.) I think you should try to sweeten him* **(up)** (= put him in a good mood) *before you ask him for the loan.* [M] • *(fig.) The management sweetened the deal* (= made it more attractive) *by offering an extra 2% to staff on the lowest end of the pay scale.*

sweet·en·er /£'swiːt·nəʳ, $-nɚ/ *n* • *I don't need sugar – I've got a/some sweetener* (= an artificial substance that produces a similar taste to sugar) *for my coffee.* [C/U] • *(fig.) The government has been accused of offering sweeteners to various companies* (= offering money or presents in order to persuade them to do something). [C]

sweet·ie /£'swiː·ti, $-t̬i/ *n* [C] *infml* • *(Br)* (used esp. by or to children) *The children bought sweeties* (= sweets) *and some ice creams.* • A sweetie (also **sweetie-pie**) is also a very pleasant or kind person: *What a sweetie you are!* • People sometimes say sweetie to a person they love: *Hey sweetie, isn't it time to go?* [as form of address] • LP› **Titles and forms of address**

sweet·ly /'swiːt·li/ *adv* • *She sang so sweetly.* • *He smiled sweetly at her.*

sweet·ness /'swiːt·nəs/ *n* [U] • *the sweetness of honey* • *(fig.) a sweetness of character* • *(fig.) The two of them got into a big argument yesterday, but by this morning it was all* **sweetness and light** (= peaceful and friendly) *once more.*

sweet·bread /'swiːt·bred/ *n* [C usually pl] the PANCREAS (= organ near the stomach) of a young sheep or cow, used as food

sweet·corn /£'swiːt·kɔːn, $-kɔːrn/, *esp. Am* **corn** *n* [U] the yellow seeds of a particular type of the MAIZE plant, which is eaten as a vegetable

sweet·heart /£'swiːt·hɑːt, $-hɑːrt/ *n* [C] a person you love, esp. a person with whom you have a romantic or sexual relationship • *She eventually married her* **childhood** *sweetheart.* • *"Happy birthday, sweetheart," he said.* [as form of address] • Sweetheart can also mean a kind and generous person: *"Oh, you're a sweetheart," she said, when I placed the breakfast tray on her lap.* • A **sweetheart deal/sweetheart agreement** is an agreement that you make in which you get something that is to your advantage, esp. by agreeing to give up something else. • LP› **Titles and forms of address**

sweet·meat /'swiːt·miːt/ *n* [C] *dated* a small piece of sweet food, made of or covered in sugar

swell *(obj)* INCREASE /swel/ *v past simple* **swelled**, *past part* **swollen** /£'swəʊ·lən, $'swoʊ-/ or **swelled** to become larger and rounder than usual; to (cause to) increase in size or amount • *It was obvious she had broken her toe, because it immediately started to swell* **(up).** [I] • *The grains of rice swell* **(up)** *as they absorb water.* [I] • *Sun and rain ripen and swell the fruit* (= make it grow). [T] • *The extra sales in the US will swell* (= cause to increase) *this year's profits* **to** *£78 million.* [T] • *Twenty-five employees have joined the union in this month alone, swelling its* **ranks** (= increasing its size) *to 110.* [T] • *(literary) His heart/breast swelled* **with pride** (= He felt very proud) *as he stood watching his son graduate.* [I] • *Heavy rain in the last few weeks has swelled the rivers and lakes* (= caused the amount of water in them to increase). [T] • If music swells, it becomes louder. [I]

swell /swel/ *n* [U] • Swell means an increase in sound produced by a musical instrument or instruments: *the swell of the orchestra*

swell·ing /'swel·ɪŋ/ *n* • *She had swellings on her face where she'd been bitten by a mosquito.* [C] • *Put your foot into cold water to help the swelling go down.* [U]

swell WAVE MOVEMENT /swel/ *n* [U] the slow up and down movement of the sea with large but smooth waves • *The* **heavy** *swell made things difficult for the boats.* • See also GROUNDSWELL.

swell EXCELLENT /swel/ *adj* **-er, -est** *esp. Am slightly dated infml* very good or pleasant • *That's a swell idea!* • *The trip out there was swell, but the hotel was a bit crummy.* • *"How's everything?" "Swell, thanks."*

swell /swel/ *adv* **-er, -est** *esp. Am slightly dated infml* • *Everything's going real swell* (= very well).

swel·ter /£'swel·təʳ, $-t̬ɚ/ *v* [I] (of a person) to feel very hot • *The soldiers were sweltering in their best uniforms.*

swel·ter·ing /£'swel·tᵊr·ɪŋ, $-t̬ɚ-/ *adj* • *In the summer,* **it's** *sweltering* (= extremely and uncomfortably hot) *in the smaller classrooms.*

swept /swept/ *past simple and past participle of* SWEEP

swept-back /'swept·bæk, ˌ-'-/ *adj* having a front edge which faces backwards at an angle • *a swept-back hairstyle* • *an aircraft with swept-back wings*

swerve /£swɜːv, $swɜːrv/ *v* [I] to change direction, esp. suddenly • *The bus driver swerved to avoid hitting the cyclists.* • *Shorrock took the penalty kick, making the ball swerve* (= move in a curve) **into** *the top right-hand corner of the net.* • *(fig.) She is one of those rare politicians whom one can trust not to swerve* **from** *policy and principle.* • Compare UNSWERVING. • PIC› **Driving**

swerve /£swɜːv, $swɜːrv/ *n* [C] • *He's famous in Italian football for his brilliant sudden swerves around and between opposition defenders.*

swift QUICK /swɪft/ *adj* **-er, -est** *slightly literary* moving or happening at great speed or within a short time, esp. in a smooth and easy way; fast or quick • *The gazelle is one of the swiftest and most graceful of animals.* • *The country seems to have made a swift and successful transition to a capitalist economy.* • *The local police took swift action against the squatters.* • *Thank you for your swift reply.* • *She gave him a swift kick in the groin.*

swift·ly /'swɪft·li/ *adv slightly literary* • *Walking swiftly, he was at the station within ten minutes.*

swift·ness /'swɪft·nəs/ *n* [U] *slightly literary* • *As magicians say, the swiftness of the hand deceives the eye.*

swift BIRD /swɪft/ *n* [C] a small bird with curved pointed wings that can fly very fast

swig *obj* /swɪg/ *v* [T] **-gg-** *infml* to drink, esp. by swallowing large amounts in a series of single actions • *Since there were no glasses, we swigged the beer straight from the bottle.* • *Hey, don't swig it all!*

swig /swɪg/ *n* [C] *infml* • *She* **took** *a swig of whisky, straight from the bottle.*

swill *obj* MOVE LIQUID /swɪl/ *v* [T always + adv/prep] to cause (a liquid) to flow around or over something, often in order to clean it • *The dentist handed me a glass of water to swill my mouth* **out** *with.* [M] • *She swilled the brandy gently* **round and round** *in the glass.*

swill /swɪl/ *n* [U] • *Give it* **a** *quick swill* (= act of moving liquid over or around it) *to get it clean.*

swill *obj* DRINK /swɪl/ *v* [T] *infml often disapproving* to drink (esp. alcohol) quickly and in large amounts • *He's one of those people who swill their beer* **(down)**, *without even noticing what it tastes like.* [T/M]

swill PIG FOOD /swɪl/ *n* [U] PIGSWILL

swim *(obj)* MOVE IN WATER /swɪm/ *v* **swimming**, *past simple* **swam** /swæm/ or *Aus also* **swum** /swʌm/, *past part* **swum** /swʌm/ to move through water by moving the body or parts of the body • *There were dolphins swimming in front of the boat.* [I] • *We spent the day on the beach but it was too cold to* **go** *swimming.* [I] • *Her ambition is to swim* **(across)** *the English Channel.* [T; I + across] • *Emily has just been given a badge for swimming 5 metres.* [I] • *(disapproving)* If food swims **in/with** a liquid, it has too much of that liquid in it or on it: *The salad is swimming in oil.*

swim /swɪm/ *n* [C] • *Shall we* **go for/have** *a swim this afternoon?*

swim·mer /£'swɪm·əʳ, $-ɚ/ *n* [C] • *Are you a good swimmer?* • *Oliver is a very* **strong** *swimmer.*

swim·mers /£'swɪm·əz, $-ɚz/ *pl n* • Swimmers is *Aus infml for* **swimming costume** or **swimming trunks.**

swim·ming /'swɪm·ɪŋ/ *n* [U] • *The doctor recommended swimming as the best all-round exercise.* • *(Br and Aus)* A **swimming costume** (*esp. Am* **swimsuit**, *Br and Aus also* **bathing costume**, *Br and Aus also* **bathing suit**, *Br and Aus infml* **cossie**, *Aus infml* **swimmers**, *esp. Aus infml* **togs**) is a piece of clothing, or sometimes two pieces of clothing, which is worn by women for swimming. • A **swimming pool**/*(Br fml dated)* **swimming bath(s)** (also **pool**) is an artificially maintained area of water for swimming, or a building containing this: *There's an* **indoor/outdoor** *swimming pool near the town.* ○ *Having a swimming pool in your back garden is quite a status symbol.* • **Swimming trunks** (also **bathing trunks**, *Aus also* **board shorts**, *Aus infml* **swimmers**, *esp. Aus infml* **togs**) are a piece of clothing worn by men on the lower part of the body for swimming. • PIC› **Trunk**

swim SEEM TO MOVE /swɪm/ *v* [I] **swimming**, *past simple* **swam** /swæm/, *past part* **swum** /swʌm/ (of an object) to seem to move in circles or backwards and forwards, or (of a person's mind) to feel confused and unable to see, act or think clearly • *Getting up too suddenly made the room swim before her eyes.* • *After the second or* *third drink, my* **head** *began to swim.* • *Just the thought of all this work makes my head/brain swim.*

swim·ming·ly /ˈswɪm·ɪŋ·li/ *adv infml* successfully and without any problems • *Everything* **went** *swimmingly until Peter started talking about money.*

swim·suit /£ˈswɪm·sjuːt, $-suːt/ *n* [C] *esp. Am for* **swimming costume**, see at SWIM [MOVE IN WATER]

swim·wear /£ˈswɪm·weəʳ, $-wer/ *n* [U] clothes worn for swimming • [LP]> **Shopping goods**

swin·dle *obj* /ˈswɪn·dl̩/ *v* [T] to obtain (money) dishonestly from (someone) by deceiving or cheating them • *You won't get away with trying to swindle the tax authorities.* • *They swindled local businesses* **out of** *thousands of pounds/swindled thousands of pounds* **from** *local businesses.*

swin·dle /ˈswɪn·dl̩/ *n* [C] • *Fraud-squad officers are investigating a £5·6 million swindle.*

swin·dler /£ˈswɪnd·ləʳ, $-lɚ/ *n* [C] • *He was very successful as a financial swindler because he was able to persuade people to believe in him.*

swine [PERSON] /swaɪn/ *n* [C] *pl* **swine** or **swines** *dated infml disapproving* a person whom you consider to be extremely unpleasant and unkind • *You* **filthy** *swine!* [as form of address] • *Her ex-husband sounds like an absolute swine.*

swin·ish /ˈswaɪ·nɪʃ/ *adj dated infml disapproving* • *swinish behaviour* • *a swinish* (= extremely unpleasant) *person*

swine [ANIMAL] /swaɪn/ *n* [C] *pl* **swine** *old use or specialized* a pig • **Swine fever** is a serious disease of pigs.

swing *(obj)* [MOVE SIDEWAYS] /swɪŋ/ *v past* **swung** /swʌŋ/ to (cause to) move, esp. smoothly backwards and forwards or from one side to the other and esp. from a fixed point • *A large pendulum swung back and forth inside the grandfather clock.* [I] • *He walked briskly along the path swinging his rolled-up umbrella.* [T] • *The door swung open.* [I] • *The truck driver swung himself* (= moved himself through the air while holding on to a fixed point) **up** *into the driver's seat.* [T] • *She swung her tennis racket* (= moved it smoothly through the air) *to hit the ball.* [T] • To swing is also to turn (something) round quickly: *Jack swung the car* **round** *so that it was facing the other way.* [M] ○ *She heard a sudden noise behind her, and swung* **round** *to look behind her.* [I] • If you swing **at** someone, you try to hit them. [I] • To swing is also to change: *His* **mood** *swings* **between** *elation and despair.* [I] ○ *As the election results come in, it looks as though the country is swinging* **to** (= is changing so that it is supporting) *the Democrats.* [I] • To **swing into action** is to quickly start working: *The emergency services swung into action as soon as the news of the bomb explosion reached them.* • If something **swings the balance**, it is the thing which causes a particular situation to happen or a particular decision to be made when other situations or decisions are possible: *This latest election promise might just swing the balance in the government's favour.* • A **swing bridge** is a bridge that can be turned to a position that is at 90° to its usual position, so that ships can go through. • *(Br and Aus)* A **swing door** (*Am* **swinging door**) is a door that can swing open in both directions. • [PIC]> **Doors**

swing /swɪŋ/ *n* [C] • *With a swing of his axe, he chopped the wood in half.* • A swing can be an attempt to hit someone, esp. with your hand: *The drunk* **took** *a wild swing* **at** *Harry.* • A swing is also a seat joined by two ropes or chains to a metal bar or a tree, on which esp. a child can sit and move backwards and forwards: *Can we* **go on** *the swings?* • A swing is also a change: *He experiences severe* **mood** *swings* (= sudden changes from one extreme mood to another). ○ *The Democrats only need a 5% swing* (= need 5% of voters to change to supporting them) *to win this election.* • *(esp. Am)* A swing can also be a fast journey: *Next week the President's campaign team is* **going on/taking** *a swing* **through** *the southern states.* • *(Br saying)* 'What you lose on the swings, you gain on the roundabouts' or 'It's swings and roundabouts' means that the positive and negative results of a situation or action balance each other: *"The route through town would be shorter, but there'll be more traffic." "Well, it's just swings and roundabouts."* • [PIC]> **Playground**

swing [BE EXCITING] /swɪŋ/ *v* [I] *past* **swung** /swʌŋ/ *infml* to be exciting and enjoyable; involving a lot of activity • *You need music to make a* **party** *swing.*

swing /swɪŋ/ *n* [U] *infml* • *(Br) The Festival always* **goes with a** *swing* (= is exciting, enjoyable and successful, and involves a lot of activity). • *(infml)* If you **get into the swing of it/things**, you start to understand, enjoy and be active in something: *I hadn't worked in an office for several years, so it took me a while to get back into the swing of it.*

swing·er /£ˈswɪŋ·əʳ, $-ɚ/ *n* [C] *dated infml* • A swinger is either a person who dresses and acts fashionably, or someone who is willing to have sex often with many different people: *Back in the 1960s, Sam was a real swinger.*

swing·ing /ˈswɪŋ·ɪŋ/ *adj dated infml* • *It's a nostalgia trip back into the youth culture of the swinging* (= exciting and fashionable) *60s.*

swing *(obj)* [MUSIC] /swɪŋ/ *v past* **swung** /swʌŋ/ (of music, esp. jazz) to have a strong exciting rhythm with notes of uneven length, or (of musicians) to play (esp. jazz) in this way • *The jazz you hear these days just doesn't swing as much as the big bands of the 1930s and 40s.* [I] • *Louis Armstrong? Now there's a man who could really swing (a tune).* [I/T]

swing /swɪŋ/ *n* [U] • Swing was a popular dance music of the 1930s and 1940s.

swing *obj* [ARRANGE] /swɪŋ/ *v* [T] *past* **swung** /swʌŋ/ *infml* to arrange for (something) to happen, by persuading people and often by acting slightly dishonestly • *If you want an interview with Pedro, I could probably swing* **it** **(for** *you).*

swing [DIE] /swɪŋ/ *v* [I] *past* **swung** /swʌŋ/ *old use infml* to be killed as a legal punishment by being dropped from a height with a rope tied around the neck; to HANG [KILL] • *(fig.) If there's an error in the calculations, you know who'll swing* **for** *it* (= be punished because of it)!

swinge·ing /ˈswɪn·dʒɪŋ/ *adj Br fml* having a serious and unpleasant effect; causing harm or difficulty • *We are going to have to make swingeing* **cuts** *in the budget.* • *There are swingeing sanctions and penalties for failing to pay your taxes.*

swin·ish /ˈswaɪ·nɪʃ/ *adj* See at SWINE [PERSON]

swipe *(obj)* [HIT] /swaɪp/ *v* to hit or try to hit (something), esp. with a sideways movement • *She opened the window and swiped* **at** *the flies with a rolled-up newspaper to make them go out.* [I always + adv/prep] • *She swiped him* **round** *the head.* [T] • *(esp. Am) The car swiped the garage door as he pulled out.* [T] • See also SIDESWIPE [HIT].

swipe /swaɪp/ *n* [C] • *Edwin* **took** *a swipe* **at** *the ball and missed.* • *(fig.) In a recent interview, she* **takes** *a swipe* **at** (= criticizes) *the theatre management.*

swipe *obj* [STEAL] /swaɪp/ *v* [T] *infml esp. humorous* to steal • *Okay, who's swiped my keys?*

swipe *obj* [MOVE] /swaɪp/ *v* [T] to move (a card containing information stored on a magnetic strip) through a device that reads this information • *The woman at the check-out swiped my credit card through the machine.*

swirl *(obj)* /£swɜːl, $swɜːrl/ *v* [always + adv/prep] to (cause to) move quickly with a twisting circular movement • *Swirl a little oil* **around** *the pan before putting it on the heat.* [T] • *A flood of water swirled* **across** *the deck and* **around** *the mast.* [I] • *He lost his footing on the bridge and fell into the swirling water below.* • *It was difficult to see where we were going because of the swirling fog/mist.*

swirl /£swɜːl, $swɜːrl/ *n* [C] • *The truck went by in a swirl of dust.*

swish *(obj)* [MOVE] /swɪʃ/ *v* to (cause to) move quickly through the air making a high soft sound • *I heard the rope swish through the air.* [I] • *The horses swished their tails to get rid of the flies hovering around them.* [T]

swish /swɪʃ/ *n* [C] • *With a swish of the curtains, the stage was revealed for Act One of the opera.*

swish [FASHIONABLE] /swɪʃ/ *adj* **-er, -est** *infml* fashionable or luxurious • *a swish hotel* • *a very swish dress* • Swish also be used disapprovingly when something is considered too luxurious or expensive: *"And he's had the sofa reupholstered in black leather." "Oh, very swish!"*

swish [LIKE A WOMAN] /swɪʃ/ *n* [C] *Am slang disapproving* a man who behaves or appears in a way that is generally considered more suited to a woman, and who lacks manly qualities

swish·y /ˈswɪʃ·i/ *adj* **-ier, -iest** *Am slang disapproving*

Swiss ar·my knife *n* [C] a small folding knife with many small folding tools built in to it • [PIC]> **Knife**

Swiss roll *esp. Br, Am* **jel·ly roll**, *Aus* **jam roll** *n* [C] a cake spread with cream, JAM or chocolate and then rolled into a cylindrical shape • [PIC]> **Bread and cakes**

switch [DEVICE] /swɪtʃ/ *n* [C] a small device, usually pushed up or down with your finger, that controls and turns on or off an electric current • *a light switch* • *an on/off switch* • *He* **flicked** *the switch to turn off the light.* • [LP]> **Switching on and off** [PIC]> **Lights, Plugs**

SWITCHING ON AND OFF

	lights	television, radio etc.	machines with motors	cars etc.	gas, water
turn on/off	•	•	•		•
switch on/off	•	•	•		
put on	•	•			
start/			•	•	
stop			•		

You can turn/switch/put lights **out**.
You usually **start** a car, but **turn off** the engine. This is done by switching on/off the IGNITION.
Notice that **open, shut** and **close** are used for windows and doors but not for lights, radios, etc.

You can use devices such as switches and buttons to control machines. Here are the common verbs connected with them:

	SWITCH	
	press	*He* **pressed** *a switch but nothing happened.*
	push	**Push** *the middle switch to turn on the lights.*
	BUTTON	
	press	*Which button do I* **press** *to rewind the tape?*
	push	*She* **pushed** *the button on the door and waited.*
	hit	*Quick,* **hit** *the stop button!*
	KEY	
	press	**Press** *the grey + key on the right of the keyboard.*
	hit	*In order to continue,* **hit** *the PageDown key.*
	hold down	**Hold down** *the shift key and press Q.* [M]
	PLUG	
	push in	**Push in** *the plug before turning on the power.* [M]
	plug in	**Plug in** *the answer machine to a phone socket.* [M]
	pull out	*Do not* **pull** *the plug* **out** *if the machine is on.* [M]
	unplug	*I* **unplug** *my phone whenever I have a bath.*
	KNOB, DIAL, CONTROL*	
	turn	**Turn** *this knob to increase the volume.*
	turn to	**Turn** *the dial* **to** *maximum.*
	turn up/down	*I'm cold –* **turn** *the fire* **up** *a bit.* [M]
	set to/at	**Set** *the temperature control* **to** *25°C.*
	HANDLE, KNOB	
	turn	*I* **turned** *the handle but the door was locked.*
		Suddenly someone **turned** *the door knob.*
	(Br) TAP/*(Am)* FAUCET	
	turn	*I can't* **turn** *the tap, it's too stiff.*
	turn on/off	**Turn** *the tap* **off**, *the bath's full.* [M]

* All the buttons, knobs etc. of a machine, considered together, are called its controls: *The car's controls are conveniently positioned and easy to use.*

switch *(obj)* /swɪtʃ/ *v* [always + adv/prep] • *Switch* (= Change or move by using a switch) *the heater* **to** *maximum.* [T] • *Oh, switch that TV* **off/on**. [M] • *Don't forget to switch* **off/on** *before you leave.* [I] • *Shall I switch* **over** *to another channel?* [I] • If someone **switches off**, they stop giving something their attention: *If he gets bored, he just switches off and looks out the window.* • *(usually disapproving)* If someone **switches on** a particular emotion or behaviour, they suddenly start to feel or behave in that way, but usually not sincerely: *When a customer walks in, she switches on the charm.* • *(dated slang)* If someone is **switched on**, they know about or are involved with the most recent fashions and ideas.

switch·es /ˈswɪtʃ·ɪz/ *pl n* • Switches is *Am for* POINTS.

switch *(obj)* CHANGE /swɪtʃ/ *v* to change suddenly or completely, esp. from one thing to another, or to exchange by replacing one person or thing with another • *Above 10 000 feet, the vegetation switches* **to** *high altitude forest.* [I always + adv/prep] • *She started studying English at college, but switched* **to** *Business Studies in her second year.* [I always + adv/prep] • *The country seemed to switch almost overnight* **from** *dictatorship* **to** *democracy.* [I always + adv/prep] • *In the 1980s, several companies switched their* *attention* **to** *the US market.* [T] • *In 1971, Britain switched* **over** (=changed completely) **to** *a decimal currency.* [I always + adv/prep] • *After the bank robbery, the gang switched cars* (=left one car and got into another). [T] • *Martin didn't want to do the Sunday shift but I didn't mind, so he switched* (=exchanged) **with** *me.* [I always + adv/prep] • *If the painting in the gallery is a forgery, somebody must have switched* (=exchanged) *it* **for** *the original since the gallery bought it.* [T] • LP› **Switching on and off**

switch /swɪtʃ/ *n* [C] • *Halfway through the game the manager made a switch* (=change), *taking Smith off and putting Daley on instead.* • *There has been a switch* **in** *emphasis – we are aiming now more for the student market.*

switch·back /'swɪtʃ·bæk/ *n* [C] a path, road or railway which bends sharply from one direction to almost the opposite direction as it goes up and down steep slopes • *a switchback trail over the mountains*

switch·blade /'swɪtʃ·bleɪd/ *n Am for* **flick knife**, see at FLICK • PIC› **Knife**

switch·board /£'swɪtʃ·bɔːd, $-bɔːrd/ *n* [C] a piece of equipment which is used to direct all the telephone calls made to and from a particular building or area • *All the calls into the building go through the switchboard.* • *Ring the hotel switchboard and they* (=the person operating this equipment) *will connect you to Mr Tremin.* • *Tearful fans* **jammed** *the radio station's switchboard after the singer's death* (=so many people rang that all the telephones were busy). • A **switchboard operator** is a person whose job is to receive telephone calls and connect them to other numbers: *I asked the switchboard operator to transfer any calls for me to your office.* • LP› **Telephone**

swi·vel *(obj)* /'swɪv·ᵊl/ *v* **-ll-** or *Am usually* **-l-** to turn (something) round in order to face in another direction • *She swivelled* **round** *to look out of the window.* [I] • *He swivelled his chair* **round**. [T] • *The ostrich swivelled its head in our direction.* [T]

swi·vel /'swɪv·ᵊl/ *adj* [before n; not gradable] • *a swivel chair* • *a swivel lamp* • *a swivel gun* • PIC› **Chair**

swiz /swɪz/, **swizz**, **swiz·zle** /'swɪz·l̩/ *n* [U] *Br slang* (used esp. by children) something that is disappointing or unfair • *"There's only half as much in the new packets." "What a swiz!"*

swiz·zle stick /'swɪz·l̩/ *n* [C] a small glass or plastic rod for mixing drinks

swol·len INCREASE /£'swəʊ·lən, $'swoʊ-/ *past participle of* SWELL INCREASE

swol·len LARGER /£'swəʊ·lən, $'swoʊ-/ *adj* larger than usual • *a bruised and swollen face* • *The doctor says I've got swollen glands.* • *The stream is swollen because of the heavy rain.* • *(infml disapproving)* If you say that someone has a **swollen head** (*Am usually and Aus also* **swelled head**), you mean that they think they are more intelligent and more important than they really are: *Don't compliment him any more, or he'll* **get** *a swollen head.* Compare **big-head** at BIG IMPORTANT. ○ *She's become very* **swollen-headed** (=thinks that she is more intelligent or more important than she really is) *since she got that new job.* Compare **big-headed** at BIG IMPORTANT.

swoon /swuːn/ *v* [I] to feel a lot of pleasure, love, etc. because of something or someone, or *(dated literary)* to FAINT (=lose consciousness) • *British audiences swoon* **with** *delight* **over** *films like this.* • *(dated literary) On hearing the news of D'Arcy's death, she swooned to the floor.*

swoon /swuːn/ *n* [C] *dated literary* • *It was one of those plays where the ladies were always* **falling down in** *swoons* (=losing consciousness and therefore falling to the ground).

swoop /swuːp/ *v* [I] to move very quickly but smoothly through the air, esp. down from a height in order to attack, or *(infml)* to make a sudden attack on a place or group of people in order to surround and catch them • *You can see the bats begin to swoop and dart at nightfall.* • *The eagle swooped* **down** *to snatch a young rabbit.* • *(infml) Undercover police swooped* **on** *three houses in Bristol at 5 a.m. this morning.*

swoop /swuːp/ *n* [C] • *The owl made a sudden swoop* (=movement) **down** *and caught the mouse.* • *(infml) Several sub-machine guns with ammunition were captured in a dawn swoop* (=attack).

swoosh /swʊʃ/ *n, v infml* (to make) a sound like that of fast-moving air • *The basketball swooshed through the net.* [I] • *The air rushed out with a swoosh.* [C]

swop *(obj)* /£swɒp, $swɑːp/ *v* [I/T] **-pp-** *esp. Br for* SWAP

sword /£sɔːd, $sɔːrd/ *n* [C] a weapon with a long sharp metal blade and a handle, used esp. in the past • *Sir Lancelot* **drew** (=took out of its cover) *his sword.* • *(literary) Thousands of people were* **put to the sword** (=killed). • If you have a **sword of Damocles hanging over** you/your **head**, something bad seems very likely to happen to you: *Government threats to cut the budget by 50% are hanging over the Opera House like a sword of Damocles.* • *(literary)* To **beat/turn swords into ploughshares** is to change to a peaceful way of life and spend money on peaceful things rather than weapons. • PIC› **Blade, Knife**

swords·man (*pl* **-men**), **swords·wo·man** (*pl* **-women**) /£'sɔːdz·mən, $'sɔːrdz-, -ˌwʊm·ən/ *n* [C] • A swordsman or swordswoman is a person skilled in fighting with a sword.

swords·man·ship /£'sɔːdz·mən·ʃɪp, $'sɔːrdz-/ *n* [U] • *He is known for his expert swordsmanship* (=skill at fighting with a sword)

sword·fish /£'sɔːd·fɪʃ, $'sɔːrd-/ *n* [C/U] *pl* **swordfish** or **swordfishes** a large long fish with a very long pointed beak-like part at the front of its head, often eaten as food

swore /£swɔːʳ, $swɔːr/ *past simple of* SWEAR

sworn SWEAR /£swɔːn, $swɔːrn/ *past participle of* SWEAR

sworn OFFICIALLY STATED /£swɔːn, $swɔːrn/ *adj* [before n; not gradable] formally and officially stated as being true • *a sworn testimony* • *sworn evidence* • *She made a sworn* **statement**. • *They signed a sworn* **affidavit**. • **Sworn enemies** are people who are completely opposed to each other.

swot *(obj) Br and Aus* /£swɒt, $swɑːt/, *Am* **grind** *v* **-tt-** *infml* (used esp. by children) to study hard, usually by reading about or learning something, esp. before taking an exam • *She's at home, swotting* **for** *her maths exam/ swotting* **up on** *her maths.* [I] • *I'm swotting* **up** *my geometry theorems.* [M]

swot /£swɒt, $swɑːt/ *n* [C] *infml disapproving* • *The rest of the class called him a swot* (=a person, esp. a child, considered to work too hard and/or be too clever).

swum /swʌm/ *past participle and Aus past simple of* SWIM

swung /swʌŋ/ *past simple and past participle of* SWING

sy·ba·rite /£'sɪb·ᵊr·aɪt, $-ə·raɪt/ *n* [C] *fml* a person who loves luxury and pleasure • Compare **hedonist** at HEDONISM.

sy·ba·ri·tic /£ˌsɪb·ᵊr'ɪt·ɪk, $-ə'rɪt̬-/ *adj fml* • *a sybaritic lifestyle* • *He has a sybaritic taste in clothes – everything has to be silk or satin.*

sy·ca·more /£'sɪk·ə·mɔːʳ, $-mɔːr/ *n* [C] a tree with leaves divided into five parts and seeds that spin slowly to the ground when they fall

sy·co·phan·tic /£ˌsɪk·ə'fæn·tɪk, $-t̬ɪk/ *adj fml disapproving* (of a person or of behaviour) praising people in authority in a way that is not sincere, usually in order to get some advantage from them • *a sycophantic biographer* • *a sycophantic courtier* • *There was sycophantic laughter from the audience at every one of his terrible jokes.* • GR

sy·co·phant /'sɪk·ə·fænt/ *n* [C] *fml disapproving* • *The Prime Minister is surrounded by sycophants.* • GR

syl·la·ble /'sɪl·ə·bl̩/ *n* [C] a single unit of speech, either a whole word or one of the parts into which a word is separated when it is spoken or divided when it is printed. It usually contains a vowel. • *There are two syllables in the word 'silver' and three in 'appetite'.* • *In the word 'particular', the stress falls on the second syllable.* • *(fig.) "It's three months since the argument and you still haven't spoken to each other?" "Not one syllable!* (=No, we haven't said anything to each other!)*"* • See also DISYLLABIC; MONOSYLLABIC; POLYSYLLABIC. • LP› **Pronunciation, Stress in pronunciation**

syl·la·bic /sɪ'læb·ɪk/ *adj* [not gradable] *specialized*

syl·la·bub /'sɪl·ə·bʌb/ *n* [U] a sweet cold dish consisting of thickened cream mixed with sugar, white wine and sometimes the colourless part of an egg

syl·la·bus /'sɪl·ə·bəs/ *n* [C] *pl* **syllabuses** or *fml* **syllabi** /'sɪl·ə·baɪ/ (a plan showing) the subjects or books to be studied in a particular course, esp. a course which leads to an examination • *Which modern novels are* **on** *the syllabus this year?* • *Have you got (a copy of) next year's syllabus?* • Compare CURRICULUM.

syl·lo·gi·sm /'sɪl·ə·dʒɪ·zᵊm/ *n* [C] *specialized* (in PHILOSOPHY) a process of LOGIC in which two general statements lead to a more particular statement • *'All birds lay eggs, an ostrich is a bird, therefore an ostrich lays eggs' is an example of a syllogism.*

syl·lo·gis·tic /ˌsɪl·ə'dʒɪs·tɪk/ *adj specialized* • *syllogistic logic* (= producing a particular statement from two general statements)

sylph·like /'sɪlf·laɪk/ *adj usually humorous* (of a woman or girl) attractively thin and delicate • *You really need to be sylphlike to wear clothes like that.*

sym·bi·o·sis /£ˌsɪm·baɪ'əʊ·sɪs, $-'oʊ-/ *n* [U] *specialized* a relationship of dependence between two animals or plants in which each provides for the other the conditions necessary for its continued existence • *(fig.) New England's wealth was created by a symbiosis* **between** *the region's universities, its financiers and its high-tech manufacturers.*

sym·bi·ot·ic /£ˌsɪm·baɪ'ɒt·ɪk, $-'ɑː·t̬ɪk/ *adj specialized* • *The relationship between the ant and the tree is symbiotic – the tree provides food for the ant, and the ant protects the tree from harmful insects.* • *(fig.) For some time, the two countries had enjoyed a symbiotic existence, one providing the oil and the other the grain.*

sym·bi·ot·i·cal·ly /£ˌsɪm·baɪ'ɒt·ɪ·kli, $-ɑː·t̬ɪ-/ *adv specialized*

sym·bol /'sɪm·bᵊl/ *n* [C] a sign, shape or object which is used to represent something else • A symbol can be used to represent a quality or idea: *The wheel in the Indian flag is a symbol* **of** *peace.* ○ *The heart shape is a symbol* **of** *love.* ○ *Water, a symbol* **of** *life, recurs as an image throughout her poems.* • Symbols are used in mathematics, music and science and also have various practical uses: *The symbol* **for** *oxygen is O_2.* ○ *You see the symbol on this label – does that mean I have to dry-clean this shirt?* • An object can be described as a symbol **of** something else if it seems to represent it because it is connected with it in a lot of people's minds: *The private jet is a symbol* **of** *wealth.* ○ *The car is a symbol* **of** *freedom.* • Compare EMBLEM. • [LP] **Symbols**

sym·bol·ic /£sɪm'bɒl·ɪk, $-'bɑː·lɪk/, **sym·bol·i·cal** /£sɪm'bɒl·ɪ·kᵊl, $-'bɑː·lɪ-/ *adj* • *The skull at the bottom of the picture is symbolic* **of** *death.* • An action can be described as symbolic if it expresses or seems to express an intention or feeling, although it has little practical influence on a situation: *Five hundred troops were sent in, more as a symbolic* **gesture** *than as a real threat.* ○ *The symbolic importance of the release of the first two hostages cannot be overestimated.*

sym·bol·i·cal·ly /£sɪm'bɒl·ɪ·kli, $-'bɑː·lɪ-/ *adv* • *Capturing the capital city wasn't difficult from a military point of view, but symbolically it was very important.*

sym·bol·i·sm /'sɪm·bᵊl·ɪ·zᵊm/ *n* [U] • Symbolism is the use of symbols in art, literature, films etc. to represent ideas: *Religious symbolism is very characteristic of the paintings of this period.* • *(specialized)* Symbolism also refers to a type of art and literature that originated in France and Belgium in the late 19th century. It attempted to express states of mind rather than represent reality, using the power of words and images to produce ideas in the imagination: *Symbolism has been described as a reaction against naturalism and realism.* Compare **Naturalism** at NATURE [LIFE]; **realism** at REAL [NOT IMAGINARY] • **Expressionism** at EXPRESS [SHOW].

Sym·bol·ist /'sɪm·bᵊl·ɪst/ *n, adj* [not gradable] *specialized* • *the Symbolist movement* • *Symbolist poets* • A Symbolist is a writer or an artist connected with Symbolism: *Leading Symbolists included Mallarmé, Verlaine and Rimbaud.* [C]

sym·bol·ize *obj, Br and Aus usually* **-ise** /£'sɪm·bᵊl·aɪz, $-bə·laɪz/ *v* [T] • *The lighting of the Olympic torch symbolizes* (= represents) *peace and friendship among the nations of the world.*

sym·met·ry /'sɪm·ə·tri/ *n* [U] the quality of having parts that match each other, esp. in a way that is attractive, or similarity of shape or contents • *The design of the house had a* **pleasing** *symmetry, its oblong shape being picked up in its elongated windows.* • *The symmetry* **between** *the graph for recorded burglaries and the graph of unemployment is too striking to be coincidental.* • *(specialized)* In mathematics, symmetry is the quality of having two parts that match exactly, either as if one half is a reflection of the other in a mirror, or when one part can take the place of another if it is turned through 90° or 180°. • Compare **asymmetry** at ASYMMETRIC.

sym·met·ri·cal /sɪ'met·rɪ·kᵊl/ *adj* • *Do you want the paintings hung either side of the fireplace so that they are symmetrical?*

sym·met·ri·cal·ly /sɪ'met·rɪ·kli/ *adv* • *The gardens were laid out symmetrically, in the 18th-century manner.*

sym·pa·thy [UNDERSTANDING] /'sɪm·pə·θi/ *n* [U] (an expression of) understanding and care for someone else's suffering • *The president has sent a message of sympathy to the relatives of the dead soldiers.* • *I don't really have much sympathy* **for** *people who've brought their troubles on themselves.* • *He kept going on and on about his problems – I suppose he was just looking for a bit of sympathy.* • *On the days when I have to walk with my stick, I get looks of sympathy from complete strangers.* • *(Br and Aus infml)* A **sympathy vote** is an occasion when a lot of people vote for or support a particular person because he or she has suffered recently: *A sympathy vote for his recent illness won Andrew Davies an award for his latest novel.* • Compare EMPATHY. • (CS) (D) (E) (F) (GR) (N) (NL) (P) (PL) (RUS) (S)

sym·pa·thet·ic /£ˌsɪm·pə'θet·ɪk, $-'θet̬-/ *adj* • If you are sympathetic, you show, esp. by what you say, that you understand and care about someone's suffering: *He suffers from back trouble too, so he was very sympathetic* **about** *my problem.* ○ *She just needed someone who would lend a sympathetic ear to her* (= listen to her in a kind and understanding way) *once in a while.* ○ *She's very sympathetic, which is unusual in a doctor.* • If a character in a book or film is sympathetic, they are described or shown in such a way that you are able to understand their feelings and the reasons for their actions, and so you like them: *She comes across as a more sympathetic character in the film.*

sym·pa·thet·i·cal·ly /£ˌsɪm·pə'θet·ɪ·kli, $-'θet̬-/ *adv* • *She listened sympathetically, nodding her head now and again.*

sym·pa·thies /'sɪm·pə·θiz/ *pl n fml* • If you **offer** or **send** someone your sympathies, you express your sadness that a relative or friend of theirs has recently died: *I went along to the funeral in order to offer my sympathies.*

sym·pa·thize, *Br and Aus usually* **-ise** /'sɪm·pə·θaɪz/ *v* [I] • If you sympathize **with** someone who has a problem, you listen to them and show them that you understand and you care: *I was just sympathizing with Susie* **over** *her mother-in-law troubles.* ○ *I know what it's like to have migraines, so I do sympathize (with you).*

sym·pa·thy [SUPPORT] /'sɪm·pə·θi/ *n* [U] support and agreement • *I must confess I have some sympathy* **with** *his views.* • *Her views tend to be* **in sympathy with** *the left of the party.* • *The government are concerned that other unions may stage sympathy* **strikes** *in support of the nurses.* • *The railway workers* **came out in sympathy with** (= stopped work to show their support for) *the miners.* • (CS) (D) (E) (F) (GR) (N) (NL) (P) (PL) (RUS) (S)

sym·pa·thet·ic /£ˌsɪm·pə'θet·ɪk, $-'θet̬-/ *adj* • Sympathetic means agreeing or supporting: *The Labour party are supposed to be sympathetic* **to/towards** *the unions.* ○ *Did he give your proposal/complaints a sympathetic* **hearing**?

sym·pa·thies /'sɪm·pə·θiz/ *pl n* • *Of those people questioned, 93% said their sympathies were* **with** (= they supported) *the teachers.* • *He is known to have right-wing sympathies.*

sym·pa·thize, *Br and Aus usually* **-ise** /'sɪm·pə·θaɪz/ *v* [I] • *I sympathize* **with** (= support) *the general aims of the party, but on this particular issue I'm afraid I disagree.*

sym·pa·thiz·er, *Br and Aus usually* **-iser** /£'sɪm·pə·θaɪ·zəʳ, $-zɚ/ *n* [C] • A sympathizer is a person who supports a political organization or believes in a set of ideas: *Suspected Communist sympathizers were refused influential positions.* ○ *He had been a known IRA sympathizer.*

sym·pho·ny /'sɪmp·fə·ni/ *n* [C] a long piece of music for an ORCHESTRA (= large group playing different instruments), usually with four MOVEMENTS (= parts) • *They played Mahler's 9th symphony.* • *the Sydney Symphony Orchestra*

sym·phon·ic /£sɪm'fɒn·ɪk, $-'fɑː·nɪk/ *adj* [not gradable] • *symphonic music*

sym·po·si·um /£sɪm'pəʊ·zi·əm, $-'poʊ-/ *n* [C] *pl* **symposiums** or **symposia** /£sɪm'pəʊ·zi·ə, $-'poʊ-/ *fml* an occasion at which people who have great knowledge of a particular subject meet in order to discuss a matter of interest • *They're holding a symposium* **on** *the European cinema.* • *She was speaking at an energy-efficiency symposium.*

symp·tom /'sɪmp·təm/ *n* [C] any feeling of illness or physical or mental change which is caused by a particular disease • *He's complaining of all the usual symptoms of flu – a high temperature, headache and so on.* • *He's been HIV-positive for six years, but just recently he's started to* **develop** *the symptoms of AIDS.* • *(fig.)* A symptom is also any single problem which is caused by and shows a more

COMMON SYMBOLS, SIGNS AND MARKS

The following table gives the common symbols that you might need to recognize or read out. The names of certain accents are also included, although these are generally used only when spelling out foreign words and names.

Punctuation marks

,	comma
.	full stop/*(Am)* period
:	colon
;	semicolon
( )	brackets/*(esp. Am)* parentheses
'	apostrophe
' '	quotation marks
" "	quotation marks
–	dash
-	hyphen
?	question mark
!	exclamation mark/*(Am)* exclamation point
...	dots/ellipsis
/	slash/stroke

Other common marks and symbols

&	ampersand (read as 'and')
*	asterisk/star
"	ditto
©	copyright symbol
™	trademark symbol
®	registered trademark symbol
✓	*(Br)* tick/*(Am)* check
✗	cross
•	bullet

Different forms of print

normal text
italic text
underlined text
bold text

Common signs and symbols used with numbers and quantities

(the list shows how the signs are read out)

+	plus
–	minus
=	equals
×	times (used with numbers)
×	by (used with lengths)
· or .	point
%	per cent
@	at (used before prices)
′	feet
″	inches
°	degrees

Accents

Examples of letters with accents:

é	e acute
è	e grave
ô	o circumflex
ä	a umlaut
ñ	n tilde
ç	c cedilla

Only the most common mathematical symbols are given here: LP **Mathematics**. Each punctuation mark is explained in a Language Portrait: look in the dictionary at the name of the mark.

serious and general problem: *It's her feeling that the recent outbreaks of violence are a symptom of the dissatisfaction that is currently affecting our society.* ○ *By putting homeless people into temporary accommodation, the government is treating the symptoms and not the cause.*

symp·to·mat·ic /£ˌsɪmp·tə'mæt·ɪk, $-'mæṭ-/ *adj* • If something bad is symptomatic **of** something else, it is caused by the other thing and is proof that it exists: *Jealousy within a relationship is usually symptomatic of low self-esteem in one of the partners.*

sy·na·gogue /£'sɪn·ə·gɒg, $-gɑːg/ *n* [C] a building in which Jewish people worship and study their religion

sy·napse /'saɪ·næps/ *n* [C] *specialized* the point at which electrical signals move from one nerve cell to another

sy·nap·tic /£saɪ'næp·tɪk, $-ṭɪk/ *adj* [not gradable] *specialized*

sync, **synch** /sɪŋk/ *n* [U] *infml for* **synchronization**, see at SYNCHRONIZE • *He's putting himself forward as a president whose ideas are* **in** *sync* **with** (=are suited to and show an understanding of) *a nation demanding change.* • *He's got to improve his game – he's* **out of** *sync* **with** (=he does not play well with) *the rest of the players.*

syn·chro·ni·ci·ty /£ˌsɪŋ·krə'nɪs·ɪ·ti, $-ə·ṭi/ *n* [U] *specialized* the happening by chance of two or more related or similar events at the same time • *The twins died, with eerie synchronicity, on the same day in different countries.*

syn·chro·nize *(obj), Br and Aus usually* **-ise** /'sɪŋ·krə·naɪz/ *v* to (cause to) happen at the same time • *The show was designed so that the lights synchronized* **with** *the music.* [I] • *If you're also going home at some point this month, why don't we synchronize our weekends and meet up?* [T] • If you synchronize clocks or watches, you change them so that they all show the same time: *We'd better synchronize our watches if we all want to be there at the same time.* • **Synchronized swimming** is a sport in which a group of people make graceful dance-like movements in the water at the same time.

syn·chro·ni·za·tion, *Br and Aus usually* **-i·sa·tion** /ˌsɪŋ·krə·naɪ'zeɪ·ʃᵊn/ *n* [U] • *The entire roomful of dancers moved* **in** *perfect synchronization* (=at exactly the same time), *just like in the movies.*

syn·co·pa·ted /£'sɪŋ·kə·peɪ·tɪd, $-ṭɪd/ *adj* (of a tune) having a rhythm in which strong notes are not on the beat • *syncopated jazz rhythms*

syn·co·pa·tion /ˌsɪŋ·kə'peɪ·ʃᵊn/ *n* [U]

syn·di·cate /'sɪn·dɪ·kət/ *n* [C + sing/pl v] a group of people or companies who join together in order to share the cost of a particular business operation for which a large amount of money is needed • *A syndicate* **of** *banks is/are financing the deal.* • *A lot of race-horses are owned by syndicates.* • *The president has announced new measures for fighting organized crime and drug syndicates.* • See also **syndicate** at SYNDICATED. • GR

syn·di·cate *obj* /'sɪn·dɪ·keɪt/ *v* [T] • *The loan was so large it had to be syndicated* (=shared between several banks).

syn·di·ca·tion /ˌsɪn·dɪ'keɪ·ʃᵊn/ *n* [U]

syn·di·cat·ed /£'sɪn·dɪ·keɪ·tɪd, $-ṭɪd/ *adj* [not gradable] (of articles and photographs) sold to several different newspapers and magazines for publishing, or *(esp. Am)* (of television or radio programmes) sold to several different broadcasting organizations • *He continues to write a syndicated newspaper column.*

syn·di·cate *obj* /'sɪn·dɪ·keɪt/ *v* [T] • *Her weekly column is syndicated in 200 newspapers throughout North America.*

syn·di·cate /'sɪn·dɪ·kət/ *n* [C] • A syndicate is an organization that supplies articles and photographs to different newspapers and magazines for publishing.

syn·di·ca·tion /ˌsɪn·dɪ'keɪ·ʃᵊn/ *n* [U]

syn·drome /£'sɪn·drəʊm, $-droʊm/ *n* a combination of medical problems that commonly go together, which may show the existence of a particular disease or mental condition • *There is a lack of research on risk factors for fatigue and fatigue syndromes.* [C] • Syndrome is used in the names of various illnesses: *acquired immune deficiency syndrome (AIDS)* [U] ○ *irritable bowel syndrome* [U] ○ *premenstrual syndrome* [U] ○ *post-traumatic stress syndrome* [U] ○ *toxic shock syndrome* [U] ○ *The AIDS syndrome is a group of specific infections and cancer which occur as a result of a compromised immune system.* [U] • A syndrome is also a type of negative behaviour or mental state that is typical of a person in a particular situation: *It's a classic case of the bored-housewife syndrome – she's* *got nothing to do all day except drink and go shopping.* [C] • See also DOWN'S SYNDROME.

syn·er·gy /£'sɪn·ə·dʒi, $'-ɚ-/, **syn·er·gism** /£'sɪn·ə·dʒɪ·zᵊm, $'-ɚ-/ *n* [U] *specialized* the combined power of a group of things when they are working together which is is greater than the total power achieved by each working separately • *Team work at its best results in a synergy that can be very productive.* • *The potential synergy* **between** *the two companies makes them ideal candidates for a merger.*

sy·nod /'sɪn·əd, £-ɒd/ *n* [C] *specialized* a regular meeting of church members for the discussion of religious matters • *The report on homosexuality in the clergy is to be discussed by the Church of England's General Synod next week.*

sy·no·nym /'sɪn·ə·nɪm/ *n* [C] a word or phrase which has the same or nearly the same meaning as another word or phrase in the same language • *The words 'small' and 'little' are synonyms.* • *It is sometimes said that there are no true synonyms in the English language, and that all words have a slightly different meaning.* • Compare ANTONYM.

sy·non·y·mous /£sɪ'nɒn·ɪ·məs, $-'nɑː·nə-/ *adj* • *The words 'annoyed' and 'irritated' are more or less synonymous.* • *The word 'annoyed' is more or less synonymous* **with** *'irritated'.* • If you say that one thing is synonymous **with** another, you mean that the two things are so closely connected in most people's minds that one suggests the other: *'Chanel' is for most people synonymous with style.* ○ *Oscar Wilde's name is synonymous with wit.*

syn·op·sis /£sɪ'nɒp·sɪs, $-'nɑːp-/ *n* [C] *pl* **synopses** /£sɪ'nɒp·siːz, $-'nɑːp-/ a brief description of the contents of something such as a film or book • *I haven't seen any of the previous episodes, so you'll have give me a brief synopsis.*

syn·tax /'sɪn·tæks/ *n* [U] *specialized* the grammatical arrangement of words in a sentence

syn·tac·tic /sɪn'tæk·tɪk/ *adj* [not gradable] *specialized* • *Syntactic differences between languages often present the learner with difficulties.*

syn·tac·ti·cal·ly /sɪn'tæk·tɪ·kli/ *adv* [not gradable] *specialized*

syn·the·sis /'sɪn·θə·sɪs/ *n pl* **syntheses** /'sɪn·θə·siːz/ *fml* the mixing of different ideas, influences or things to make a whole which is different or new • *He describes his latest record as 'a synthesis of African and Latin rhythms'.* [C] • *(specialized)* The synthesis of a substance is its production from simpler materials after a chemical reaction: *Plants need sunlight for the synthesis of their food* **from** *carbon dioxide and water.* [U] • See also PHOTOSYNTHESIS.

syn·the·size *obj, Br and Aus usually* **-ise** /'sɪn·θə·saɪz/ *v* [T] *specialized* • *There are many vitamins that the body cannot synthesize* (= produce) *itself.*

syn·the·siz·er, *Br and Aus usually* **-iser** /£'sɪn·θə·saɪ·zəʳ, $-zɚ/ *n* [C] • A synthesizer is an electronic keyboard instrument which can reproduce and combine a large range of recorded sounds, often in order to copy other musical instruments or voices. • PIC **Musical instruments**

syn·thet·ic /£sɪn'θet·ɪk, $-'θet̬-/ *adj* • Synthetic products are made from artificial substances, often copying a natural product: *synthetic flavourings/sweeteners* ○ *a synthetic fur coat* ○ *synthetic rubber* • *(fig. disapproving) She criticized the synthetic* (= false or artificial) *charm of television presenters.*

syn·thet·i·cal·ly /£sɪn'θet·ɪ·kli, $-'θet̬-/ *adv* • *This fabric is produced synthetically.*

sy·phi·lis /'sɪf·ɪ·lɪs/ *n* [U] a **venereal disease** (= disease caught during sexual activity with an infected person) which spreads slowly from the sex organs to all parts of the body

sy·phon /'saɪ·fᵊn/ *n* [C] a SIPHON

sy·ringe /sɪ'rɪndʒ, srɪnʒ/ *n* [C] a hollow cylindrical piece of equipment which is used for sucking liquid out of or pushing liquid into something, esp. one with a needle which can be put under the skin and used to INJECT drugs, remove small amounts of blood etc. • *AIDS can be spread among drug users through the use of shared syringes.* • PIC **Medical equipment**

sy·ringe *obj* /sɪ'rɪndʒ, srɪnʒ/ *v* [T] • If your **ears** are syringed, their inside is cleaned by having water pushed into and sucked out of them using a syringe.

sy·rup /'sɪr·əp/ *n* [U] a very sweet, sometimes thick, light-coloured liquid made by dissolving sugar in water • *She always has prunes in syrup for breakfast.* • *I like syrup on my pancakes.* • Syrup can also be a type of sweet liquid medicine: *cough syrup* • Compare TREACLE.

sy·rup·y /'sɪr·əp·i/ *adj* • *This wine is a bit syrupy for my liking.* • *(disapproving)* Syrupy is also used to mean too good or kind or expressing feelings of love in a way which is not sincere: *He specializes in love songs with dreadful syrupy lyrics.*

sys·tem SET /'sɪs·təm/ *n* [C] a set of connected items or devices which operate together • *We're having a new central-heating system installed.* • *The gym that I go to has a really good* **music/sound** *system* (= set of electronic devices for playing recorded music). • *The country has a very inefficient* **rail/road/transport** *system.* • A system is also a set of computer equipment and programs used together for a particular purpose: *The system keeps* **crashing** *and no one is able to figure out why.* • In the body, a system is a set of organs or structures which have a particular job to do: *the digestive system* ○ *the immune system* ○ *the nervous system* • System can also refer to the way that the body works, esp. in the way that it digests and excretes: *A run in the morning is good for* **the** *system – it wakes the body up and gets everything going.* ○ *Long-haul flights disrupt your system.* • *(infml)* If you **get** something **out of** your **system**, you get rid of a desire or emotion, esp. a negative one, by allowing yourself to express it: *I had a really good shout at him this morning and got it out of my system.* ○ *I figured that if she really wanted to travel the world, it was better for her to do it and get it out of her system.*

sys·tem·ic /sɪ'stem·ɪk/ *adj specialized* • A systemic drug, disease or poison reaches and has an effect on the whole of a body or a plant and not just one part of it: *systemic drugs* ○ *systemic fungicides* • *(fml)* A systemic problem or change is a basic one, experienced by the whole of an organization or a country and not just particular parts of it: *The current recession is the result of a systemic change within the structure of the country's economy.*

sys·tem METHOD /'sɪs·təm/ *n* a way of doing things; a method • *We'll have to work out a proper filing system.* [C] • **Under** *our education system, you're supposed to be able to choose the type of schooling that your child receives.* [C] • *The legal system* **operates** *very differently in the US and Britain.* [C] • *Like a lot of companies, they have a system whereby people are generally promoted from within.* [C] • *When we were students, we had a system in which the person who finished the milk had to buy the next carton.* [C] • A system is also a particular method of counting, measuring or weighing things: *the binary system of counting* ○ *the metric system of measuring and weighing* • *(approving)* System can also be used to mean the intentional and organized use of a system: *There doesn't seem to be any system to the books on these shelves – they're certainly not in alphabetical order.* [U] • *(disapproving)* **The system** can also refer to the unfair laws and rules that prevent people from being able to improve their situation: *I'd do a second job, but the amount I'd be taxed on it wouldn't make it worth my while – that's the system for you, isn't it!* ○ *He has his own ways of* **beating** *the system, making sure that he has good relationships with influential people.* • A **systems analyst** is a person who examines complicated industrial and business operations in order to find ways of improving them, esp. by the introduction of computer programs and equipment.

sys·tem·at·ic /£ˌsɪs·tə'mæt·ɪk, $-'mæt̬-/ *adj* • Systematic means using a fixed and organized plan: *(approving) We've got to be a bit more systematic in the way that we approach this task.* ○ *(disapproving) We're hearing reports of the systematic rape and torture of prisoners.*

sys·tem·at·i·cal·ly /£ˌsɪs·tə'mæt·ɪ·kli, $-'mæt̬-/ *adv* • *(approving) I systematically worked my way through a whole list of potential employers, and wrote or telephoned each one.* • *(disapproving) This government is engaged in systematically dismantling the country's health service.*

sys·tem·a·tize *obj, Br and Aus usually* **-ise** /'sɪs·tə·mə·taɪz/ *v* [T] *specialized* • To systematize something is to plan a system for it: *Thinking has been discussed by philosophers and systematized by logicians ever since the Ancient Greeks.*

sys·tem·a·ti·za·tion, *Br and Aus usually* **-i·sa·tion** /ˌsɪs·tə·mə·taɪ'zeɪ·ʃᵊn/ *n* [U] *specialized*

T t

T, t /tiː/ *n* [C] *pl* **T's** or **Ts** or **t's** or **ts** the 20th letter of the English alphabet • LP> **Silent letters** (KOR)

T–bone (steak) /£'tiː·bəʊn, $-boʊn/ *n* [C] a piece of meat (from a cow) cut thinly and which has a T-shaped bone in it

T–junc·tion *Br* /'tiːˌdʒʌŋk·ʃᵊn/, *Am* **in·ter·sec·tion** *n* [C] a place where one road meets another without crossing it, forming the shape of a letter T • PIC> **Road**

T–shirt /£'tiː·ʃɜːt, $-ʃɜːrt/, **tee shirt** *n* [C] a simple piece of clothing which covers the top part of the body and which has no collar and usually short sleeves • *I have to wear smart clothes for work all week, so at the weekend I like to wear comfortable things like jeans and a T-shirt.* • PIC> **Clothes**

T–square /£'tiː·skweəʳ, $-skwer/ *n* [C] a long flat T-shaped piece of wood, metal or plastic, which is used to draw parallel lines • Compare SETSQUARE. • LP> **Mathematics**

ta /tɑː/ *exclamation Br infml* thank you

tab /tæb/ *n* [C] a small strap connected to something for hanging, pulling, or fastening, or a small piece of paper, plastic or metal, esp. one giving information and sticking out from something larger • *Make a file for these documents and write 'finance' on the tab.* • *On audio and video tapes a tab can be used to lock the tape and prevent further recording.* • *(Am)* A tab (*Br and Aus* **ringpull**) is also the small piece of metal, often joined to a ring, which is pulled off or pushed into the top of a can to open it. • *(esp. Am and Aus infml)* The tab is also the total money charged in a restaurant or hotel for food, drinks etc.: *He kindly offered to* **pick up** *the tab* (= pay). ○ *Just* **put it on** *the tab please* (= add it to the total charge). • *(Br regional)* A tab is also a cigarette: *I'd like a packet of tabs, please.* • A tab **of acid** is a small piece of paper containing the drug LSD. • To **keep tabs on** something is to watch it carefully: *I like to keep tabs on my bank account so that I don't overdraw.*

ta·bas·co (sauce) /£tə'bæs·kəʊ, $-koʊ/ *n* [U] *trademark* a red sauce with a hot taste which is used on food for flavouring

tab·by /'tæb·i/ *n* [C], *adj* [not gradable] (a cat) having dark coloured marks on grey or brown fur • PIC> **Cats**

ta·ber·na·cle /£'tæb·əˌnæk·l̩, $-ɚˌ-/ *n* [C] *fml old use* a place of worship • For the Jews in ancient times, a tabernacle was a type of tent moved from place to place and used for worship. • Tabernacle is also used by some Christian groups to mean a church and, by Roman Catholics, to mean the box in a church in which the holy bread and wine is kept.

ta·ble FURNITURE /'teɪ·bl̩/ *n* [C] a flat surface, usually supported by four legs, used for putting things on • *In the kitchen we have a large table and four chairs.* • *(fig.) The (whole) table* (= all the people sitting at the table) *was looking at the speaker.* • If a plan or suggestion has been put/laid **on the table** it has been presented for people to talk about it. • If something is done **under the table**, it is a secret, hidden action: *He voted for their side since they offered him money under the table.* • *(Br) My aunt always* **kept a good table** *(Am* **set a good table***)* (= provided a lot of good food). • **Lay/set the** *dining/kitchen* **table** (= put a cloth, knives and forks, etc. on the table) *and we'll have lunch.* • **Table forks** and **table knives** are large knives and forks used for eating the main dish of a meal. • A **table lamp** is a small light which is used on a table. • **Table linen** is the cloths and NAPKINS that are put on a table for a meal. • **Table mats** are small covers which protect a table against heat damage from food containers. • *The children were so hungry they grabbed the food without remembering their* **table manners** (= socially acceptable behaviour when eating a meal with others). • In **table tennis**, which is played on a large table, two or four players hit a ball over a low net: *a table tennis bat* • A **table wine** is a wine which is not very expensive and of average quality. • PIC> **Cutlery, Lights, Sports, Table**

ta·ble *obj* DISCUSS /'teɪ·bl̩/ *v* [T] *(Br and Aus)* to suggest (something) for discussion or *(Am)* to leave discussion to a later time • *(Br and Aus) An amendment to the proposal was tabled* (= suggested for consideration) *by Mrs James.* • *(Am) The suggestion was tabled* (= left) *for discussion at a later date.*

ta·ble INFORMATION /'teɪ·bl̩/ *n* [C] an arrangement of facts and numbers in rows or blocks, esp. in printed material • *The table shows, in four columns, the names of our members

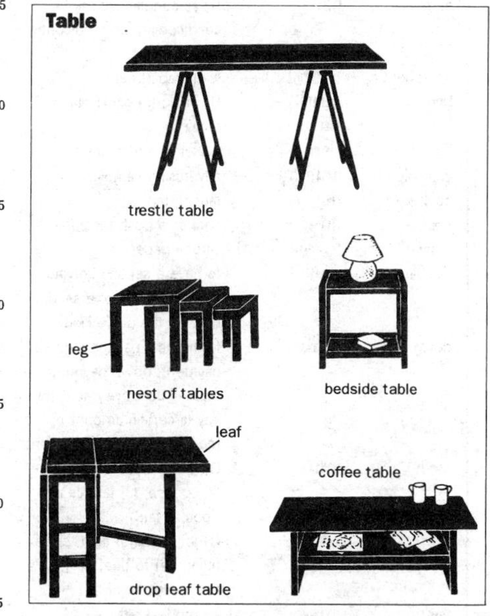

of staff, how many years they have been with us, what department they work in and how much they are paid.* • A table **of contents** is a list of the information that is contained in a book. • A table is also a **multiplication table**. See at MULTIPLY.

tab·u·lar /£'tæb·jʊ·ləʳ, $-lɚ/ *adj* [before n; not gradable] *fml* • *We presented the results of the survey in tabular form* (= in the form of a table).

tab·u·late *obj* /'tæb·jʊ·leɪt/ *v* [T] *fml* • *We are going to tabulate the findings of our survey.*

tab·leau /£'tæb·ləʊ, $-loʊ/ *n* [C] *pl* **tableaux** /£'tæb·ləʊ, £-ləʊz, $-loʊ, $-loʊz/ or **tableaus** the representation, esp. on a stage, of a scene by people who do not move or speak

ta·ble·cloth /£'teɪ·bl̩·klɒθ, $-klɑːθ/ *n* [C] a piece of material which is used to cover a table, esp. during a meal • PIC> **Cutlery**

ta·ble d'hôte /£ˌtɑː·blə'dəʊt, $-bl̩'doʊt/ *adj, adv* [not gradable] (of food in a restaurant) consisting of a complete meal at a fixed price but with little choice of dishes • Compare A LA CARTE.

ta·ble·spoon /'teɪ·bl̩·spuːn/ (*abbreviation* **tbsp**) *n* [C] (the amount held by) a large spoon used for measuring or serving food • *a silver tablespoon* • *3 tablespoons of sugar* • *As a standard cook's measure for liquids, one tablespoon = 15ml.* • Compare DESSERTSPOON; TEASPOON. • PIC> **Cutlery**

ta·ble·spoon·ful /'teɪ·bl̩ˌspuːn·fʊl/ (*abbreviation* **tbsp**) *n* [C] *pl* **tablespoonsful** /'teɪ·bl̩ˌspuːnz·fʊl/ or **tablespoonfuls** • *Sprinkle a tablespoonful* (= the amount a tablespoon can hold) *of grated cheese over the pasta.*

tab·let MEDICINE /'tæb·lət/ *n* [C] a small round solid object made of substances taken esp. to improve health; a PILL • *a sleeping tablet* • *a vitamin tablet* • *I've taken two tablets but my headache still hasn't gone.* • (D)

tab·let BLOCK /'tæb·lət/ *n* [C] a thin flat often square piece esp. of a hard material such as wood, stone or metal • *The oldest map in existence was made on a clay tablet around 4500 years ago.* • *A tablet engraved with his favourite poem was put on the wall of the building erected in his memory.* • *(Br) There was a tablet* **of soap** *on the edge of the sink.* • *(esp. Scot Eng)* Tablet is also a sweet similar to FUDGE. • (D)

ta·ble·ware /£'teɪ·bl̩·weəʳ, $-wer/ *n* [U] *fml* the knives, forks, spoons, plates, glasses, etc. used for meals • *That new shop stocks a large selection of unusual tableware.*

tab·loid /'tæb·lɔɪd/ *n* [C], *adj* [not gradable] a type of popular newspaper with small pages which has many pictures and short simple reports • *the tabloid press* • *a*

THAI FALSE FRIENDS

agent *n*	เอเย่นต์	authorized dealer
air *n*	แอร์	(1) air-conditioned; air-conditioning; air-conditioner; (2) air hostess
apartment *n*	อพาร์ตเมนต์	luxury apartment
bank *n*	แบงก์	(1) bank; (2) banknote
bill *n*	บิล	receipt
boy *n*	บ๋อย	waiter in a restaurant
campaign *n*	แคมเปญ	advertising campaign
cock *n*	ก๊อก	faucet; tap
cook *n*	กุ๊ก	cook in a posh restaurant
copy *n*	กระดาษก๊อบปี้	carbon paper
double *v*	เบิ้ล	to have a second serving of the same food or a second drink of the same kind
down *adv*	ดาวน์	(of money) paid as a down payment; down payment; to make a down payment for; to pay (a certain amount of money) as a down payment
fan *n*	แฟน	(1) girlfriend or boyfriend; (2) spouse; (3) fan (as in 'football fan')
fit *v*	ฟิต	(1) (of clothing) tight; close-fitting; (2) to beef up (one's knowledge or skill)
flat *n*	แฟลต	(1) modest flat; (2) tenement
high/low *adj*	ไฮโล	a type of dice game
knot *n*	นอต	knot ('unit of speed')
knot *n*	นอต	nut (for screwing onto a bolt)
mail *n*	เมล์	(of buses or boats) operated along a particular route as a means of public transport
motel *n*	โมเต็ล	motel, especially where a couple meet for sex and where sex services can be found
(T)		
number *n*	เบอร์	(1) number used to show the position of something in an ordered set or list; (2) underground lottery
over- *prefix*	เว่อร์	to exaggerate; overdo
partner *n*	พาร์ตเนอร์	paid female dancing or drinking partner at a nightclub
pipe *n*	แป๊ป	(1) water pipe; (2) exhaust pipe
pump *n*	ปั๊ม, ปั๊มน้ำมัน	petrol station
racing *v*	ซิ่ง	to drive recklessly at a very high speed
re-examine *v*	รีเอ็กแซม, แซม	to take another examination as a result of failure in a previous one
repeat *v*	รีพีท, พีท	to repeat a year in college or university
restaurant *n*	เรสโตรอง	luxurious Western-style restaurant
retire *v*	รีไทร์, ไทร์	(of students) to be dismissed from a college or university
sanction *v*	แซงก์ชั่น	to impose sanctions upon
shipping *n*	ชิปปิ้ง	person hired to help with customs clearance of goods
smart *adj*	สมาร์ต	neat or elegant in dress or appearance
sport *n*	สปอร์ต	generous
super *adj*	ซุปเปอร์	(1) high-octane leaded petrol; (2) the supermarket section of a department store
turn *v*	เทอร์น	to trade in (especially a used car)
tutor *v*	ติว	to tutor (especially a small group of students) for a test or examination
van *n*	แวน	station wagon
view *n*	วิว	scenery
zigzag *v*	ซิกแซ็ก	to achieve or obtain something wrongfully or dishonestly

tabloid newspaper • *a tabloid format* • *Information on the personal life of a film star is just the sort of story the tabloids love.*

ta·boo /tə'buː/ *n* [C], *adj pl* **taboos** the avoidance, among a particular group of people, of particular actions or words for religious or social reasons • *Death is a taboo subject.* • LP **Labels**

tach·o·graph /£'tæk·əʊ·grɑːf, £-græf, $-ə·græf/ *n* [C] a machine inside a vehicle such as a truck which records speed, distance travelled and stopping periods, and which is used to control the driver's legal hours of work

tach·o·met·er /£tæk'ɒm·ɪ·təʳ, $-'ɑː·mɪ·t̬ɚ/ *n* [C] a device for measuring the rate at which something turns • *The engine speed is indicated on the tachometer which is to the left of the speedometer.*

tac·it /'tæs·ɪt/ *adj* understood without being expressed directly • *tacit agreement/approval/support*

tac·it·ly /'tæs·ɪt·li/ *adv*

tac·i·turn /£'tæs·ɪ·tɜːn, $-ə·tɜːrn/ *adj* saying little, esp. habitually • *He was a reserved, taciturn person when I first knew him.* • *'Did you enjoy your holiday?' 'Yes', came the taciturn reply.*

tack NAIL /tæk/ *v*, *n* (to fix with) a small sharp nail with a flat end • *a box of tacks* [C] • *Tack the carpet* **to** *the floorboards./Tack the carpet* **down**. [T] • See also THUMBTACK. • PIC **Tools**

tack SAIL /tæk/ *v*, *n* (to change) the direction in which a boat moves to receive the wind on its sails • *He took the dinghy along the coast in a series of long tacks.* [C] • *We tacked slowly back to harbour.* [I always + adv/prep] • *In mid-sentence she suddenly* **set/went/started off on a different tack** (= began to talk about something else).

tack SEW /tæk/, *Am and Aus also* **baste** *v*, *n* (to sew with) a long, loose stitch which holds two pieces of material together until they are stitched more effectively • *Unpick the tacks after machining the seam.* [C] • *I've just tacked the hem of this dress to check the length.* [T] • *I've only tacked on the collar of this dress.* [I always + adv/prep] • *(infml) At the last minute, they* **tacked on** (= added) *a couple of extra visits* **to** *my schedule.*

tack·ing /'tæk·ɪŋ/ *n* [U] • *A row of tacking held the pleat in place.*

tack RIDING EQUIPMENT /tæk/ *n* [U] all the objects which the rider of a horse needs, including SADDLES and BRIDLES • *One of my jobs was to clean the tack in the* **tack room** *every morning.*

tack·le *obj* SPORT /'tæk·l̩/ *v* [T] (esp. in football or **field hockey**) to try to take the ball from a player in the other team, or (in RUGBY or **American football**) to do this by taking hold of the player and causing them to fall

tack·le /'tæk·l̩/ *n* [C] • *Brilliantly avoiding a series of tackles he reached the box and scored a goal.*

tack·le *obj* DEAL WITH /'tæk·l̩/ *v* [T] to try to deal with (something or someone) • *There are many ways of tackling this problem.* • *I don't think I can tackle this job until next week.* • *I tackled him* **about** *his careless work and frequent absences.*

tack·le EQUIPMENT /'tæk·l̩/ *n* [U] all the objects needed for a particular activity • *fishing tackle* • *shaving tackle* • *We'll need heavy lifting tackle* (= ropes, etc.) *to move that block of stone.*

tack·y STICKY /'tæk·i/ *adj* **-ier**, **-iest** sticky, (esp. of paint or glue) not completely dry • *Be careful, the paint's still tacky on that door.* • *The horse did not run well on the tacky ground.*

tack·i·ness /ˈtæk·ɪ·nəs/ *n* [U]

tack·y [LOW QUALITY] /ˈtæk·i/ *adj* **-ier, -iest** *infml disapproving* clearly of cheap quality or in bad style • *The shop sold tacky souvenirs and ornaments.* • *That was such a tacky comment to make even if she did not like my decorating.*

tack·i·ness /ˈtæk·ɪ·nəs/ *n* [U] • *The opening ceremony had all the glitz and tackiness of a Las Vegas floor show.*

tac·o /£ˈtæk·əʊ, $ˈtɑː·koʊ/ *n* [C] *pl* **tacos** a hard folded TORTILLA (=thin flat bread) filled with meat, cheese, particular raw vegetables and hot spicy sauce

tact /tækt/ *n* [U] the ability to say or do the right thing without making anyone unhappy or angry • *The young nurse showed great tact in dealing with worried parents.* • *He's never had much tact and people don't like his blunt manner.*

tact·ful /ˈtækt·fᵊl/ *adj* • *Mentioning his baldness wasn't very tactful.*

tact·ful·ly /ˈtækt·fᵊl·i/ *adv* • *We must explain, as tactfully as possible, that she has made a mistake.*

tact·less /ˈtækt·ləs/ *adj* • *It was rather tactless of you to invite his ex-girlfriend.*

tact·less·ly /ˈtækt·lə·sli/ *adv*

tact·less·ness /ˈtækt·lə·snəs/ *n* [U]

tac·tic /£ˈtæk·tɪk, $-t̬ɪk/ *n* [C usually pl] a planned way of doing something • *It's not a tactic I've used before and it may not be the best one, but it seems to get results.* • *I don't like his tactics, he sets one person against another.* • A military official who is skilled in **tactics** is good at planning the arrangement and use of his soldiers and equipment in war.

tac·ti·cal /£ˈtæk·tɪ·kᵊl, $-t̬ɪ-/ *adj* • *There can be a lot of tactical* **voting** *in some elections, when people vote for a party they do not normally support to try to beat a third party.* • Tactical **weapons** are for use over short distances and, especially in the case of nuclear weapons, have a local effect only.

tac·ti·cal·ly /£ˈtæk·tɪ·kli, $-t̬ɪ-/ *adv* • *We* **voted** *tactically in the last three elections.*

tac·ti·cian /£tækˈtɪʃ·ᵊn, $-ˈt̬ɪʃ-/ *n* [C] • *a brilliant tactician*

tac·tile /£ˈtæk·taɪl, $-tᵊl/ *adj fml* related to touch • *The right hemisphere of the brain is specialized for the perception of complex patterns, both visual and tactile.* • If something is tactile, it has a surface which is pleasant or attractive to touch: *The theatre has been refurbished with the tactile materials of carved wood, iron and copper.* ○ *Her paintings have a very tactile quality.* • A tactile person touches other people a lot.

tad /tæd/ *n* [U] **a tad** *infml* a little, slightly • *just a tad more sugar* • *The fish was OK, but the chips were a tad greasy.*

tad·pole /£ˈtæd·pəʊl, $-poʊl/ *n* [C] a small black creature with a large head and long tail which lives in water and develops into a FROG or TOAD

taf·fe·ta /£ˈtæf·ə·tə, $-ɪ·t̬ə/ *n* [U] a stiff, shiny cloth made from silk or artificial material, used esp. for dresses to be worn at special events • *a taffeta skirt/ball gown*

Taf·fy /ˈtæf·i/, **Taff** /tæf/ *n* [C] *Br infml or disapproving* a Welshman • *I think the Taffs will win this rugby match.*

tag [SMALL PART] /tæg/ *n* [C] a small piece of paper, cloth or metal, on which there is information, fixed onto something larger • *Whose coat is this? Look at the* **name** *tag.* • *This skirt hasn't got a* **price** *tag, how much is it?* • *(fig.)* *This house has a price tag of* (=costs) *half a million pounds.*

tag *obj* /tæg/ *v* [T] **-gg-** • *I've tagged the pages I want you to read.* • *We know from the records kept of tagged birds that they return to the same place year after year.* • *(specialized)* If you tag computer information, you mark it so that you can process it later: *Eighty records in the database have been tagged* **for** *deletion.*

tag [GAME] /tæg/ *n* [U] a game played by two or more children in which one child chases the others and tries to touch one of them. This child then becomes the one who does the chasing.

tag [WORDS] /tæg/ *n* [C] a well known, often used phrase (esp. in a foreign language), or a phrase added on to a sentence for emphasis, to get agreement or to make it into a question • *'C'est la vie' is a French tag which means 'that's life'.* • *In the following sentences 'he is', 'aren't we' and 'isn't it' are tags – He's clever, he is./We're going home now, aren't we?/It's Thursday, isn't it?* • [LP]› **Short forms**

tag a·long *v adv* [I] *infml* to go somewhere with a person or group but to stay slightly separate • *I don't know her, she just tagged along* **with/after/behind** *our group.* • *It's hard to shop with two children tagging along.*

tag on *obj*, **tag** *obj* **on** *v adv* [M] to add something extra, at a later time • *Just tag your news on* **to/at** *the end of my letter.* • *Tag on a couple of paragraphs about recent events.* • *Tag yourself on* **to** *that party of visitors for now.*

tag·li·a·tel·le /£ˌtæl·li·əˈtel·i, $ˌtɑːl·jəˈ-/ *n* [U] a type of pasta shaped into long thin flat pieces

t'ai chi /ˌtaɪˈtʃiː/ *n* [U] a form of exercise involving slow movements of muscles, originally practised in China

tail [ANIMAL] /teɪl/ *n* [C] a part of an animal's body, sticking out from the base of the back, or something similar in shape or position • *a peacock's tail* • *a lizard's tail* • *a fish's tail* • *a rabbit's tail* • *A dog wags its tail, but a horse swishes its tail.* • *The airline's symbol was painted on the aircraft's tail/tail of the aircraft.* • *She was late and had to go to the tail (end)* (=back) **of** *the queue.* • *I only saw the* **tail end of** (=final part of) *the TV news.* • A **tail coat** (also **tails**) is an old-fashioned type of man's coat, waist-length at the front and with the lower half of the back divided into two pieces, now only worn on very formal occasions: *wearing white tie and tails* • **Tail lights** (also **tail-lamps**) are the (usually) red lights on the back of a vehicle. • A **tail wind** is a wind blowing from behind a vehicle: *Planes travelling from America to Europe usually have a tail wind rather than a head wind.* • To be **on** someone's **tail** is to follow them closely: *The policemen were on the robber's tail from the scene of the crime.* ○ *That driver's been/kept on my tail* (=following very closely behind my vehicle) *for miles.* • If a large group has to do something to satisfy a small group that can be **(a case of) the tail wagging the dog.** • *They* **went off/away with** *their* **tails between** *their* **legs** (=showing they were defeated and unhappy) *after losing the match.* • [PIC]› **Car**

tail /teɪl/ *v* [I] • *(Br)The traffic* **tailed back** *(Am was* **backed up**) (=formed a long, slow line) *along the road for ten miles because of road repairs.* • Something that **tails off** or **tails away** becomes gradually smaller or quieter: *His voice tailed off as he drifted into sleep.* ○ *The profits tailed off after a few years.*

–tailed /-teɪld/ *combining form* • *a furry-tailed animal*

tail *obj* [FOLLOW] /teɪl/ *v* [T] to follow and watch someone very closely, esp. in order to get information secretly • *That car has been tailing me for the last 10 minutes.* • *It's not safe to meet, the police are tailing me.*

tail /teɪl/ *n* [C] *infml* • A tail is someone who follows another person to discover where the other person goes to, who they speak to, what they do, etc.: *They* **put** *a tail* **on** (=told a tail to follow) *the spy as he left the airport.*

tail·back /ˈteɪl·bæk/ *n* [C] *esp. Br* a line of vehicles that have stopped or are moving only very slowly, because of an accident or other problem on the road in front of them • *Yesterday there was a four-mile tailback on the main road into the city after a crash involving a truck and a car.* • [PIC]› **Motorway**

tail·board /£ˈteɪl·bɔːd, $-bɔːrd/, *Am and Aus* **tail·gate** /ˈteɪl·geɪt/ *n* [C] the door or board at the back of a vehicle which can be lowered for loading

tail·gate *obj* /ˈteɪl·geɪt/ *v* [I/T] *esp. Am* to drive too closely behind the vehicle in front

tail·or [CLOTHES MAKER] /£ˈteɪ·ləʳ, $-lɚ/ *n* [C] someone whose job is to adjust, repair and make clothes, esp. someone who makes jackets, trousers, coats, etc. for particular customers, usually men • *My father used the same tailor for his suits for twenty years.*

tail·ored /£ˈteɪ·ləd, $-lɚd/, **tail·or–made** *adj* [not gradable] • *a hand-tailored/well-tailored jacket* • *a tailor-made suit* • *She wore a tailored suit* (=one that fits well or closely) *to her interview.*

tail·or *obj* [MAKE SPECIALLY] /£ˈteɪ·ləʳ, $-lɚ/, **tail·or–make** (*past* **tailor-made**) /£ˌteɪ·ləˈmeɪk, $-lɚ-/ *v* [T] to make or prepare (something) following particular instructions • *We can tailor a large order* **for** *you/***to** *your individual* **requirements.**

tail·or–made /£ˌteɪ·ləˈmeɪd, $-lɚ-/ *adj* [not gradable] • *(fig.) It sounds as though you're tailor-made* (=have all the right skills and abilities) *for the job.*

tail·pipe /ˈteɪl·paɪp/ *n* [C] *Am for* **exhaust pipe**, see at EXHAUST [GAS] • [PIC]› **Car**

tails [COIN SIDE] /teɪlz/ *n* [U] the side of a coin which does not have a person's head on it • *We tossed a coin and it came down tails* (=with this side highest). • *I'll toss the coin and you call* **heads or** *tails.*

tails [JACKET] /teɪlz/ *pl n* a **tail coat**, see at TAIL [ANIMAL]

taint *obj* /teɪnt/ *v* [T] to damage (something), esp. by causing a reduction or change in quality, taste, etc. •

Onions will taint cheese if they are stored next to each other. • *This meat is tainted* (=tastes bad). • *In the middle of this century in London tainted brown air obscured the winter sun.* • *His reputation was permanently tainted by the financial scandal.* • *"Tainted Love"* (title of a song by Soft Cell, 1981)

taint /teɪnt/ *n* [U] • *The enquiry cleared him of any taint* **of** *suspicion/dishonesty.*

take *obj* [REMOVE] /teɪk/ *v* [T] *past simple* **took** /tʊk/, *past part* **taken** /ˈteɪ·kᵊn/ to move (something) away, esp. without permission, or to remove (esp. clothes) • *Who's taken my notes?* • *Has anything been taken* (=stolen)? • *Here's your pen, I took it by mistake.* • *Take these chairs* **away** *– we don't need them.* [M] • *Four take* **away** *two is* (=If you subtract two from four, the answer is) *two.* [M] • *If you take* (=subtract) *4* **(away) from** *12 you get 8.* [T/M] • *All possessions had been taken* **from** *her.* • *(fig.) The plot is not original, it's taken* **from** (=based on) *Shakespeare.* • *He took* **off** *his clothes and got into the bath.* [M] • *These covers can be taken* **off** *for cleaning.* • *After the poisoning scare, the product was taken* **off** *the shelves/the market* (=removed from sale). • *It's difficult for me to take time* **off** *(work) during the summer.* • *He took* **off** *two weeks in September.* [M] • *Some people are always taking days* **off** *sick.* • *Take* **out** *the seeds before you slice up the fruit.* [M] • *Digging in the garden certainly* **takes it out of/takes a lot out of** *me* (=makes me very tired) *these days.* • *(Br)* If you **take** someone **out of** themselves, you try to change their mood and stop them from thinking about what was making them unhappy. • [LP] **Dressing and undressing**

take /teɪk/ *n* [U] *Am* • *I honestly don't trust him – he always seems to be* **on the take** (=in search of personal profit).

take *obj* [ACCEPT] /teɪk/ *v* [T not *be taking*] *past simple* **took** /tʊk/, *past part* **taken** /ˈteɪ·kᵊn/ to accept; to receive willingly • *We'd like you to take a gift of your choice.* • *I tried to telephone him, but he refused to take my call.* • *This restaurant takes credit cards.* • *Do you take sugar and milk in your tea* (=Do you drink tea with sugar and milk in it)? • *Take this medicine* (=Put it into your body by swallowing) *three times a day.* • *Keep taking the tablets.* • *This container will take* (=has room for) *six litres.* • *My car takes five people, but I only have four seat belts.* • *This camera takes* (=has room for and uses) *two small batteries.* • *My camera takes 35 mm films.* • *It's a girls' school which has started taking boys as well.* • *My roses took* (=received) *first prize at the flower show.* • *We've stopped taking* (=regularly buying) *a newspaper.* • *(Br) We took* (=rented) *a cottage in France last summer.* • *If you'd taken my* **advice**, *you wouldn't have lost so much money.* • *I refuse to take any* **responsibility** *for what's happened.* • *She can't take* **criticism**. • *"How did he take the news of the accident?" "He took it badly."* • *We're taking the bomb threats very* **seriously**. • *I just can't take being insulted like that.* [+ v-*ing*] • *He continually abuses her, and she just sits there and takes it.* • *She can't take him teasing her.* [+ obj + v-*ing*] • *If you think I'm going to take that* **lying down** (=accept it without complaining), *you're very much mistaken.* • *I can't* **take it** (=deal with anything bad) *any more. I've had enough.* • *"How do you like your tea?" "I'll take it* **as it comes** (=accept it whatever it is like)." • *He can't take* **a joke** (=doesn't like people joking about him). • *I take* **the/your point** (=accept the argument), *but I still don't think you should have gone.* • If you say **point** taken, it means that you accept what someone has said. • You can use take when you want to mention something as a particular example of what you are talking about: *I've been very busy recently. Take last week, I had meetings on four evenings.* • If you take someone or something **to** be something, or you take them **for** something, you accept or believe that they are that thing: *I took him to be more intelligent than he turned out to be.* [+ obj + *to* infinitive] ○ *(fml) I take the situation to require* (=I believe that it requires) *prompt action.* [+ obj + *to* infinitive] ○ *These creatures are generally taken to be descended from primitive fishes.* [+ obj + *to* infinitive] ○ *In the dark I could have taken him for* (=mistakenly believed that he was) *your brother.* ○ *I'm not going to forge his signature for you! What do* **you** *take* **me** *for?* (=You should not believe I could do a thing like that.) • *If the dress is too small the shop will take it* **back** *and refund your money* [M] • *His wife took him* **back** *when he left his girlfriend.* [M] • *All right, I'll* **take it** *(all)* **back** (=admit that what I said was wrong). • *(Br)* You can say **if you take my meaning** (*Am and Aus* **if you catch my drift**) to suggest that there is more information than can be given openly: *Let's just say we had 'problems', if you take my meaning.* • *His aunt* **took** *him* **in** (=took care of him in her home) *when his mother died.* • *Several families* **take in** (=take care of for payment) *foreign students.* • If someone says 'I **take it**', they think that what they say is likely to be true, even though it is not proved: *You'll be staying the night,* **I** *take it.* ○ **I** *take it* **(that)** *you'll be staying the night.* ○ *So we can take it you've resigned?* • *It won't work,* **take it from me/take my word for it** (=accept what I say). • *That's my final offer – you can* **take it or leave it** (=accept it as it is or refuse it completely). • **Take that!** is said as someone hits someone else, esp. in humorous films or CARTOONS (=picture stories). • If you **won't/don't take no for an answer**, you will not allow someone to refuse what you have offered: *I've told Steve I'm not interested, but he keeps asking me out – he won't take no for an answer.*

tak·er /£ˈteɪ·kəʳ, $-kɚ/ *n* [C] • *I put an advert in the paper to sell my bike but I haven't had any takers* (=no one was willing to accept my offer to sell).

take *obj* [HOLD] /teɪk/ *v* [T] *past simple* **took** /tʊk/, *past part* **taken** /ˈteɪ·kᵊn/ to move in order to hold (something) in the hand(s) • *I held out my hand and she took it.* • *He took my arm and led me to the door.* • *Take an egg and break it into the bowl.* • *Can you take this bag while I open the door?* • *She took* **(up)** *her pen and started to write.* [T/M] • To **take hold** of something is the same as to take it: *He took hold of my arm and led me to the door.* ○ *Can you take hold of this bag while I open the door?*

take *obj* [CATCH] /teɪk/ *v* [T] *past simple* **took** /tʊk/, *past part* **taken** /ˈteɪ·kᵊn/ to catch or get possession of • *Rebels ambushed the train and took several prisoners.* • *Government forces expect to have taken the city by the end of the week.* • *In chess, if your opponent takes your queen you're usually in trouble.* • *There was a report of a baby taken by a wolf.* • *The Liberals needed just 200 more votes to take the seat from Labour.* • *The terrorists took him prisoner.* [+ obj + n] • *The rebels have taken* **power**. • *The new director* **took (up) office** (=started their job) *in December.*

take *obj* [MOVE] /teɪk/ *v* [T] *past simple* **took** /tʊk/, *past part* **taken** /ˈteɪ·kᵊn/ to move (something or someone) from one place to another • *Rain is forecast, so take your umbrella when you go out.* • *The suitcases were taken* **to** *Madrid by mistake.* • *I forgot to take my report* **to** *the meeting.* • *Take the book over/down* **to** *Mary.* • *John's taking me* **to** *a concert this evening.* • *Take these biscuits* **with** *you – I don't want them.* • *If the dress is too small, you can take it* **back** *to the shop and get a refund.* [M] • *I'll take the curtains* **down** *tomorrow to wash them.* [M] • *As he took* **down** *his trousers, I could see his legs were badly scarred.* [M] • *This skirt is too short/long, I'll have to take* **down/up** *the hem.* [M] • *Take the book* **up** *to the third floor of the library.* [M] • *I suggested that he should take her some chocolates/take some chocolates* **to** *her* (=bring them to her as a present). [+ two objects] • *We took him* **to** *look at some new houses.* [+ obj + *to* infinitive] • *Will you take me swimming/house-hunting tomorrow?* [+ obj + v-*ing*] • If you take someone **out**, you do an activity with them and usually pay for it: *The first time she took me out we went to the cinema.* [M] ○ *Our boss took us out* **for** *a meal.* [M] • Something that **takes** you **back** makes you remember: *That piece of music really took me back* **(to** *my schooldays).* • *The sudden noise* **took** *her* **unawares/by surprise** (=surprised her). • *I'll have to* **take** *this dress* **in** (=make it smaller) *at the waist – it's too big.* • A person's **take-home pay** is the amount of earnings that they have left after tax and any other payments they have to make have been paid.

take *(obj)* [NEED] /teɪk/ *v past simple* **took** /tʊk/, *past part* **taken** /ˈteɪ·kᵊn/ to have as a necessary condition; to need • *Parachuting takes (a lot of) nerve/courage.* [T] • *I take size 5 shoes/a size five.* [T] • *Transitive verbs take a direct object.* [T] • *His story took* **some** *believing* (=was difficult to believe). [+ v-*ing*] • *She didn't take* **much** *persuading* (=was easy to persuade). [+ v-*ing*] • If something takes a particular time, that period is needed in order to complete it: *The cooking process only takes ten minutes.* [L only + n] ○ *"How long does this paint take* **to** *dry?" "It takes three hours."* [L only + n] ○ *The journey should have taken us twenty minutes.* [L (+obj) + n] ○ **It** *took all day* **for** *us* **to** *drive home.* [L only + n] ○ **It** *took us all day* **to** *drive home.* [L (+obj) +n] • If someone does not **take long**, they act quickly: *I'm just going to the shops – I won't take long.* • *Broken bones always* **take time** (=a long time) *to mend.* • *She didn't even* **take the time** *to wish me good morning.* • If you are told to **take** your **time** it means that you can spend as much time as you need in doing something, or that you should slow down. • *That painter really* **takes** *his* **time** (= does things slowly). • [LP]> **It**

take *obj* [ACT] /teɪk/ *v* [T] *past simple* **took** /tʊk/, *past part* **taken** /ˈteɪ·kᵊn/ to do the actions connected with (something); to perform • *The Archbishop took our service of thanksgiving.* • *Shelley is taking* (= studying) *economics at university.* • *(Br) My older daughter took* (= obtained) *a first* (= the best possible qualification in a college degree) *in maths last year.* • *(Br and Aus) Mr Marshall takes* (= teaches) *physics/takes us* **for** *physics.* • *Will you take* (= have your) *lunch now, madam?* • Take is used with many nouns to make a verb phrase that is equal in meaning to the related verb: *I think we'll take a break* (= we'll break) *there.* ◦ *If you're tired you should take a rest* (= you should rest). ◦ *I always like to take a walk* (= to walk) *after lunch.* • *There are many problems, but let's* **take one (thing) at a time** (= do one thing before starting another). • [LP]> **Do: verbs meaning 'perform'**

take *obj* [REACTION] /teɪk/ *v* [T] *past simple* **took** /tʊk/, *past part* **taken** /ˈteɪ·kᵊn/ to have or come to have (a particular feeling or opinion) • *He doesn't take any* **interest in** *his children.* • *Don't take any* **notice of** *the cameras.* • *She takes* **offence** *too easily.* • *They took* **pity on** *the stray cat and fed it.* • *I take a less critical* **view of** *the incident.* • *I take* **the view that** *fuel should be heavily taxed to reduce road use.*

take *obj* [RECEIVE] /teɪk/ *v* [T] *past simple* **took** /tʊk/, *past part* **taken** /ˈteɪ·kᵊn/ to receive (money) from sales or as payment for entrance to an event • *The show took $100 000 in its first week.*

take /teɪk/ *n* [U] • *The box office take* (= money received from payments) *was huge for the new show.*

tak·ings /ˈteɪ·kɪŋz/ *pl n* • *Our takings were down this week because the weather was so bad.*

take *obj* [SEPARATE] /teɪk/ *v* [always + adv/prep] *past simple* **took** /tʊk/, *past part* **taken** /ˈteɪ·kᵊn/ to separate the individual parts of (something) • *We took the bike/watch/engine* **apart/to pieces** *and replaced all the worn parts.* [T] • *The bed takes* **apart/to pieces** (= its parts can be separated), *so it's easy to carry about.* [I] • *(fig.) Our football team really took the visiting team* **apart** (= defeated them severely) *– we won 7-0.* [T]

take *obj* [WRITE] /teɪk/ *v* [T] *past simple* **took** /tʊk/, *past part* **taken** /ˈteɪ·kᵊn/ to write • *I hope you're all taking notes.* • *She asked her secretary to take a letter* (= to write one from the words she said). • *Journalists were taking* **down** *every word I said.* [M]

take *obj* [PHOTOGRAPH] /teɪk/ *v* [T] *past simple* **took** /tʊk/, *past part* **taken** /ˈteɪ·kᵊn/ to make (a photograph) of (someone or something) • *Photographers were crowding round him taking photos/pictures.* • *She doesn't like having her photo taken.* • *The photographer had taken her performing in the opera.* [+ obj + v-*ing*]

take *obj* [TRANSPORT] /teɪk/ *v* [T] *past simple* **took** /tʊk/, *past part* **taken** /ˈteɪ·kᵊn/ to use as one way of getting from one place to another • *I always take the train – it's less hassle than a car.* • *She took the 10.30 flight to Edinburgh.* • *If you take the road on the left, you'll come to the post office.* • *He took that last bend too fast and crashed into the hedge.*

take [PERFORM WELL] /teɪk/ *v* [I] *past simple* **took** /tʊk/, *past part* **taken** /ˈteɪ·kᵊn/ to work or perform as expected • *These new plants haven't taken – they don't like this dry soil.* • *Unfortunately the skin graft didn't take.* • *The dye took, and now the white dress is green.*

take [FILM] /teɪk/ *n* [C] the filming of a SCENE (= small part of a film) • *This scene of the film needed ten takes before we felt it was right.*

take af·ter *obj v prep* [T no passive] to be like or look like (a family member or group) • *He takes after his mother/his mother's side of the family.*

take a·gainst *obj v prep* [T] *Br* to come to dislike (someone) • *The children have really taken against the boy next door.*

take in *obj* [UNDERSTAND], **take** *obj* **in** *v adv* [M] to understand completely the meaning or importance of (something) • *I had to read the letter twice before I could take it all in.* • *He was so surprised he just couldn't take in what I was trying to tell him.* • *It was an interesting exhibition, but there was too much to take in all at one time.*

take in *obj* [INCLUDE], **take** *obj* **in** *v adv* [M] to include • *The new town takes in three former villages.*

take in *obj* [WATCH], **take** *obj* **in** *v adv* [T] *Am and Aus* to go to watch (a performance) • *After dinner, let's take in a film/show/play/cabaret.*

take in *obj* [DECEIVE], **take** *obj* **in** *v adv* [M] to cause (someone) to believe something which isn't true; to trick or deceive (someone) • *The teacher was completely taken in by my excuse.* • *My disguise really took him in!*

take off [LEAVE] *v adv* [I] to leave suddenly, esp. to leave the ground and fly; to DEPART • *The plane took off at 8.30 a.m.* • *(infml) When he saw me, he took off in the other direction.* • *(infml) We're going to take off with the tent and tour France and Italy.* • *(fig.) The project/idea/plan/scheme really took off* (= rose suddenly in success or popularity) *amongst young mothers.*

take–off /£ˈteɪk·ɒf, $-ɑːf/ *n* [C] • *The plane is cleared for take-off.* • *Night take-offs and landings are banned at this airport.*

take off *obj* [COPY], **take** *obj* **off** *v adv* [M] *Br and Aus* to copy the way (a particular person) usually speaks, moves, etc., or the way (something) is usually done, in order to amuse; to MIMIC • *All the children tried to take off their favourite pop stars.* • Compare IMPERSONATE.

take–off /£ˈteɪk·ɒf, $-ɑːf/ *n* [C] • *It was the best take-off* **of** *the Prime Minister that I have ever seen.* • *The article was an amusing take-off* **of** *a Jane Austen novel.*

take on *obj* [BEGIN], **take** *obj* **on** /teɪk/ *v adv* [M] to begin to have, use or do (something) • *A chameleon takes on the colour of its surroundings.* • *Her voice took on a troubled tone.* • *She took too much on* (= tried to do to much) *and made herself ill.* • *The plane has two scheduled stops to take on passengers and fuel.* • *I usually take some students on* (= employ them) *for fruit-picking in the summer.* • *She was taken on* **as** *a laboratory assistant.*

take on *obj* [FIGHT], **take** *obj* **on** *v adv* [M] to compete against or fight (someone) • *I'll take you on in a game of tennis next week.* • *The Government took on the unions and won.* • *Take on someone your own size!*

take on [UPSET] *v adv* [I] *dated* to get upset • *Don't take on so!*

take out *obj*, **take** *obj* **out** *v adv* [M] to kill or destroy (someone or something) • *We need that command post taken out.* • *The soldiers said that they were trying to take the snipers out.*

take *obj* **out on** *obj v adv prep* [T] to cause (someone) to suffer because of (your own feelings) rather than because of what the other person has done • *Don't take your anger out on me, I wasn't even there!* • *She only took it out on me because she was tired and disappointed.*

take o·ver *obj*, **take** *obj* **o·ver** *v adv* to do (something) instead of or to obtain (something) from someone else • *Do you want me to take over the digging if you're tired?* [M] • *He's taken over the bedroom for his model railway.* [M] • *You've let this job take you over completely.* [M] • *This firm has taken over* (= obtained control of) *three companies this year.* [M] • *He took over* **from** *the headmaster in February.* [I] • *I've asked my assistant to take over preparing the reports.* [+ v-*ing*]

take·o·ver /£ˈteɪkˌəʊ·vəʳ, $-ˌoʊ·vɚ/ *n* [C] • *My organization was involved in a takeover last year.* • *The company* **made a takeover bid** *for* (= tried to obtain control of) *a rival firm.* • *(fig.) Are you trying to make a takeover bid for my job/wife/bookshelf?*

take to *obj* [LIKE] *v prep* [T] to start to like (something or someone) • *His wife took to Cambridge/her new neighbours/his plan at once.* • *I'm rather concerned about how he will take to his new school* (= whether he will like it or not). • *She's taken to tennis* **like a duck to water** (= she likes it and is good at it).

take to *obj* [START A HABIT] *v prep* to start doing something habitually • *She was so depressed she took to drink/drugs.* [T] • *He's taken to staying out very late.* [+ v-*ing*]

take to *obj* [ESCAPE] *v prep* [T] to go or escape into • *The refugees took to the hills/forest/countryside for safety.* • *We'll have to take to the streets to get our protest noticed.* • *Every time she has a headache, she takes to her bed.*

take up *obj* [START], **take** *obj* **up** *v adv* to start doing (something), esp. either with other people or after someone or something else has stopped • *He's taken up skiing/a new job.* [M] • *She's just taken up cycling to work.* [+ v-*ing*] • *We're not very good at French, we only took it up recently.* [M] • *The children took up the song when the singer asked them to join in.* [M] • *I paused and my friend took the story up for a while.* [M] • *The clarinet took up the tune.* [M]

take up *obj* DISCUSS, **take** *obj* **up** *v adv* [M] to ask for (something) to receive more attention • *The school took the matter up* **with** *the police.* • *(Br and Aus) I'd like to take you up* **on** *your sales figures for June.*

take up *obj* FILL, **take** *obj* **up** *v adv* [M] to fill (space or time) • *This desk takes up too much room.* • *Too much of this report is taken up* **with** *out-of-date figures.* • *I can't see you, my day is completely taken up* **with** *meetings.*

take *obj* **up on** *obj v adv prep* [T] to accept (an offer) made by (someone) • *He's offered me a free ticket. Should I take him up on it?*

take up with *obj v adv prep* [T] to become friendly with or to spend time with (someone) • *She's taken up with a strange crowd of people.*

take·a·way *Br and Aus* /ˈteɪk·ə·weɪ/, *Am* **take·out** /ˈteɪk·aʊt/, *Am and Scot Eng* **car·ry·out** *n* [C] a meal cooked and bought at a shop or restaurant but taken somewhere else, often home, to be eaten, or the shop or restaurant itself • *Let's have Chinese takeaway for dinner tonight.* • *Let's go to the Indian takeaway and get something to eat.*

tak·en TAKE /ˈteɪ·kən/ *past participle of* TAKE

tak·en GIVING RESPECT /ˈteɪ·kən/ *adj* [after v] **taken with/by** believing (something) to be deserving of respect or admiration • *The committee was very taken with/by your proposals.* • *A lot of people have been taken with/by her abilities as a singer.*

tal·cum pow·der /£ˈtæl·kəm,paʊ·dər, $-dɚ/, **talc** *n* [U] a powder, usually having a pleasant smell, put on the skin to make it feel smooth or to help it stay dry

tale /teɪl/ *n* [C] a story or report, esp. one which might be invented or difficult to believe • *The children love his tales about pirates and smugglers.* • *He* **told** *some fascinating tales about his life in India.* • *She told me/invented/concocted a tale about missing the bus to explain her lateness.* • *I asked how he was and he gave me a real* **tale of woe** (= report of bad things which had happened to him). • *"Tales from the Riverbank"* (title of a children's television series, 1960-71) • *"A Tale of Two Cities"* (title of a book by Charles Dickens, 1859)

tal·ent /ˈtæl·ənt/ *n* (someone who has) a natural ability to be good at something, esp. without being taught • *Her talent* **for** *music showed at an early age.* [U] • *She is a young dancer of great talent.* [U] • *His artistic talents were wasted in his boring job.* [C] • *(humorous) Sewing isn't among my many talents.* [C] • *Nobody with real talent applied for the job.* [U] • *We are looking for new/fresh/young/local talent* (= new/fresh/young/local people with talent). [U] • *Promising talent is hard to find.* [U] • *(Br and Aus slang esp. humorous)* Talent can also mean people who are sexually attractive: *There was plenty of talent at the party last night.* ○ *He's always eyeing up the talent.* • A **talent contest** is an event in which people compete to show who is the most skilled, esp. at being entertaining. • A **talent scout** or **talent spotter** is someone who looks for people who have the skills they want, especially in entertainment or sport. • (J) (KOR)

tal·ent·ed /£ˈtæl·ən·tɪd, $-t̬ɪd/ *adj* • *a talented footballer/pianist*

tal·is·man /ˈtæl·ɪz·mən, -ɪs-/ *n* [C] *pl* **talismans** an object believed to bring good luck or to keep its owner safe from harm • *She has worn the ring as a talisman ever since she survived the plane crash.*

talk *(obj)* /£tɔːk, $tɑːk/ *v* to say words aloud to give information; to speak to one or more people • *If you want to talk, go in the other room, I'm trying to work.* [I] • *He talked very quietly, never raising his voice.* [I] • *We talked and talked but couldn't make a decision.* [I] • *She talked* **to** *her mother on the phone every week.* [I] • *When no one else is around, she tends to talk* **to** *herself.* [I] • *(fig.) The teacher uses sign language to talk* **to** (= communicate with) *the deaf children.* [I] • *(fig.) That parrot talks* (= makes sounds as if talking) *all day long.* [I] • *She talks English at work and French at home.* [T] • *He spent a lot of time talking* **about** *his hobbies.* [I] • *(infml) I don't understand what he's talking* **about** (= understand what he's saying) *a lot of the time.* [I] • *(infml)* The expression **talk about** is used before something to emphasize that it is very noticeable in the stated way: *What a film – talk about boring!* • *The psychiatrist encouraged her to talk* **over** (= discuss completely) *her problems.* [M] • *If we talk* **up** (= speak with enthusiasm about) *the event, people will surely come.* [I] • **Can we talk?** (= Can we can talk privately?) • *(infml)* To talk something such as business, money or a serious subject means to talk about it or discuss arrangements about it: *Are we talking big money here?* [T] ○ *Whenever they're together, they talk politics.* [T] • *(Am) He* **talked a blue streak** (= He talked quickly and without stopping) *all through breakfast.* • Someone who **talks dirty** describes sexual acts to another person using basic or rude words. • *She* **talked** *her/my* **head off** (= She talked for a long time). • *(Br infml)* If someone can **talk the hind leg(s) off a donkey** they can talk without stopping for a long time. • The expression **talking nonsense**/*(esp. Br)* **rubbish** is used to show that something doesn't make sense or is not believed. It is offensive to say this to the person who is being doubted: *Is it just me or was she talking nonsense in the meeting?* • *(Br)* **Talking of** *(esp. Am* **speaking of***) John* (= while we are talking about John), *I saw a friend of his last week.* • *Why don't you* **talk sense**! (= say something reasonable!) • **Talking shop** means talking about your job with those you work with when not at work: *Even at a party they have to talk shop!* • infml *If you say that someone is* **talking through** *their* **hat**/*(Br also)* **neck** *you mean that they do not understand what they are talking about. It is offensive to say this to the person being doubted:* Nothing of what he said made sense – he was talking through his hat. • *(esp. Am infml)* **Talk turkey** means to discuss something honestly and directly: *Let's talk turkey!* • *(infml)* **Look who's talking/You're a fine one to talk/You can (can't) talk**/*(Am also)* **You should talk** all mean that you have blamed someone else for doing something you do yourself: *I'm lazy? You're a fine one to talk!* • *Our new car will* **give** *the neighbours* **something to talk about**/*(Br)* **set** *the neighbours* **talking** (= give them something to discuss). • A **talking book** is a spoken recording of a book, used esp. by blind people. • A **talking point** is something which encourages discussion: *That painting is a good talking point.* • A **talking-to** is a severe talk with someone who has done something wrong: *I gave her a good talking-to* **about** *doing her homework on time.* • *"There is only one thing in the world worse than being talked about, and that is not being talked about"* (from the story *The Picture of Dorian Gray* by Oscar Wilde, 1891) • *"Talking 'bout my generation"* (from the song *My Generation* by the Who, 1965) • LP **Say**

talk /£tɔːk, $tɑːk/ *n* • *I've had many talks* **with** *Wilson over the last few months.* [C] • *I asked him to* **have** *a* **talk with** (= talk to) *his mother* **about** *his plan.* [C] • *He* **gave** *a talk* (= spoke to a group of people) **about/on** *his visit to America.* [C] • *Her talks are always very interesting.* [C] • *Talk won't get us anywhere.* [U] • **The** *talk*/*Her talk* (= everything that was said) *was all about the wedding.* [U] • *Her behaviour is* **the talk of** (= what is being discussed in) *the neighbourhood/office.* • *The new statue in the park is* **the talk of the town** (= what everyone is talking about). • He's **all talk (and no action)**/It's **just talk** means that someone talks about doing something, but never does it: *She's all talk when it comes to doing something about the problem.* • *(Br)* A **talk show** is a radio or television programme on which ordinary people appear to discuss matters which are of interest or some part of their lives: *Radio talk shows have been besieged with callers expressing outrage on this subject.* Compare **chat show** at CHAT. • *(Am and Aus)* A **talk show** is a radio or television programme on which famous guests are asked questions about themselves, or members of the public appear to discuss a particular subject: *TV talk shows such as the 'Oprah Winfrey Show' have become much more popular than comedies and soap operas.* • *(Br dated saying)* 'Careless talk costs lives' means you shouldn't talk about private or secret things in front of people you don't know very well.

talk·er /£ˈtɔː·kər, $ˈtɑː·kɚ/ *n* [C]

talks /£tɔːks, $tɑːks/ *pl n* • Talks are serious and formal discussions on an important subject usually intended to produce decisions or agreements: *We were involved in talks* **about** *buying another company.* ○ *Talks were* **held** *in Madrid* **about** *the fuel crisis.* ○ *Salary talks have* **broken down**.

talk at *obj v prep* [T] to speak to (someone) without listening to what they say • *I don't like the way he talks at me.*

talk back *v adv* [I] to answer someone in a rude way, esp. someone in authority such as a teacher • *Children who talk back are regarded as cheeky and disrespectful.*

talk down *obj* PREVENT, **talk** *obj* **down** *v adv* [M] to speak loudly or without stopping to prevent someone else from speaking • *I tried to explain, but he just talked me down.*

talk down *obj* [GIVE ADVICE], **talk** *obj* **down** *v adv* [M] to speak with someone to help them come down from a high place • *The policeman talked the girl down after she had been on the roof for two hours.*

talk down to *obj v adv prep* [T] to speak to (someone) with words or ideas that are too simple, as if they cannot understand • *I wish politicians wouldn't talk down to us as though we couldn't see where their policies will lead.*

talk *obj* **into** *obj v prep* [T] to persuade (someone) to do (something) • *Try to talk them into a game of tennis on Friday.* • *I've talked her into coming camping with us.* [+ v-ing]

talk out *obj*, **talk** *obj* **out** *v adv* [M] to discuss (something such as a problem) completely in order to find agreement or a solution • *If you two don't talk out the differences between you it'll be very difficult for you to continue working together.*

talk *obj* **out of** *obj v adv prep* [T] to persuade (someone) not to do (something) • *You've talked me out of it, I won't go.* • *How did you talk the manager out of complaining?* [+ v-ing] • *With some difficulty, he was able to talk his way out of paying the fine.*

talk o·ver *obj*, **talk** *obj* **o·ver** *v adv* [M] to discuss (something) • *We'll talk it over when I've got some more details.* • *Let's talk over the arrangements* **with** *the others before we make a decision.*

talk *obj* **round** [PERSUADE] *v adv* [T] *Br* to persuade (someone) to agree • *She didn't want to help but we talked her round.* • *Do you think you can talk your mother round* **to** *lending us some money?*

talk round *obj* [SPEAK INDIRECTLY] *Br*, *Am* **talk a·round** *v prep* [T] to avoid speaking directly about something • *We talked round the whole area of family problems until I had some idea what was causing his unhappiness.*

talk·a·tive /£ˈtɔː·kə·tɪv, $ˈtɑː·kə·t̬ɪv/ *adj* talking a lot • *She's a lively, talkative person.*

talk·back /£ˈtɔːk·bæk, $ˈtɑːk-/ *n* [C] *Aus* a radio programme in which listeners use telephone to take part

talk·ie /£ˈtɔː·ki, $ˈtɑː-/ *n* [C] *old use* a cinema film with speech and sound made during the period when most films were silent • Compare **silent film** at SILENCE [NO SPEAKING].

tall /£tɔːl, $tɑːl/ *adj* **-er, -est** of more than average height, or of a particular height • *a tall girl* • *a tall tree* • *a tall building* • *He's tall, in fact he's exactly six feet tall.* • *She's much taller* **than** *me.* • *Imran's one of the tallest boys in the class.* • *You'd have more chance of success if you'd* **stand/walk tall** (= behave as if you were tall and confident). • *Getting the essay done on time will be a* **tall order** (= something which is difficult to do). • *After dinner she told me a* **tall story** (= a story or fact which is difficult to believe) *about her pet.* • [LP] **Measurements**

tal·lish /£ˈtɔː·lɪʃ, $ˈtɑː-/ *adj* [not gradable] • *He's tallish* (= quite tall) *with fair hair and glasses.*

tall·ness /£ˈtɔːl·nəs, $ˈtɑːl-/ *n* [U]

tal·low /£ˈtæl·əʊ, $-oʊ/ *n* [U] fat from animals which is used for making soap and, esp. in the past, candles

tal·ly [AGREE] /ˈtæl·i/ *v* [I] to match or agree with something else • *Our numbers/figures don't tally – you've made it twenty pounds more than me.* • *Your plans don't tally* **with** *mine.*

tal·ly [COUNT] /ˈtæl·i/ *n* [C usually sing] *slightly dated* a record or count of a number of items • *His tally today is three fish but yesterday he caught five.* • *Will you* **keep a tally of** *the number of customers going in and out?* • *I'll* **keep the** *tally* **(of** *points scored in the game).* • *Have you* **kept a** *tally* **of** *what I owe you/what you spent?* • *(Aus)* A **tally-room** is a room in which votes are collected after an election.

tal·ly *(obj)* /ˈtæl·i/ *v slightly dated* • *If the game's over I'll tally* **up**. [I] • *Will you tally* **(up)** *what I owe you?* [T]

tal·ly–ho /£ˌtæl·iˈhəʊ, $-ˈhoʊ/ *exclamation* a shout made by a hunter who sees a FOX, or *(dated or humorous)* a shout given when starting any exciting physical action

Tal·mud /£ˈtæl·mʊd, $ˈtɑːl-/ *n* [U] **the Talmud** the collection of ancient Jewish laws and tradition for religious and social matters

Tal·mud·ic /£tælˈmʊd·ɪk, $tɑːl-/ *adj* [not gradable]

tal·on /ˈtæl·ən/ *n* [C] a sharp nail on the foot of a bird which it uses when hunting animals • *The eagle sank its talons into the rabbit.* • *(fig.) She pointed to the photo with a long talon* (= long finger nail). • ⓘ

tam·a·rind /£ˈtæm·ᵊr·ɪnd, $-ɚ·ɪnd/ *n* [C/U] (fruit of) a type of tropical tree

tam·bour·ine /£ˌtæm·bᵊrˈiːn, $-bəˈriːn/ *n* [C] a small musical instrument, consisting of a circular wooden frame with metal discs loosely fixed to it and sometimes having plastic stretched across one side of it, which is shaken or hit with the hand • *"Mr Tambourine Man"* (title of a song by Bob Dylan, 1965) • [PIC] **Musical instruments**

tame /teɪm/ *adj* **-r, -st** (esp. of animals) not wild or fierce, either naturally or because of training or long involvement with humans • *The birds in the park are quite tame and will take food from your hand.* • *Tame rabbits are good as children's pets.* • *(fig.) It was a tame* (= not interesting or exciting) *film in comparison to some that she's made.*

tame *obj* /teɪm/ *v* [T] • *It's hard to tame a tiger.* • *(fig.) He'll need to tame* (= control) *his temper if he wants to succeed.*

tame·a·ble /ˈteɪ·mə·bl̩/ *adj*

tam·er /£ˈteɪ·məʳ, $-mɚ/ *n* [C] • A tamer is someone who tames something that is wild, esp. an animal: *a lion-tamer*

tamp *obj* /tæmp/ *v* [T] to press (esp. earth) down firmly • *Tamp* **(down)** *the soil around the post.*

tamped /tæmpt/ *adj* [not gradable] • *a floor of tamped earth*

tamp·er with *obj* /£ˈtæm·pəʳ, $-pɚ/ *v prep* [T] to touch or change (something) without permission or without enough knowledge of how it works • *I could see at once that my desk drawers had been tampered with.* • *You shouldn't tamper with electric wiring.*

tam·pon /£ˈtæm·pɒn, $-pɑːn/ *n* [C] a small cylinder of cotton or other material which a woman puts in her vagina to absorb her MENSTRUAL blood

tan [COLOUR] /tæn/ *v* **-nn-** to change the colour of a person's skin to brown or a darker brown, esp. because of being in the sun • *Her skin tans very quickly in the summer, but mine burns.* [I] • *The blazing sun quickly tanned their limbs.* [T] • *Tanned workmen were sitting around the dock.* • *I use a tanning lotion if I'm going to lie under the sun for long.*

tan /tæn/, **sun·tan** *n* [C] • *We came back from our holiday with deep/light/nice tans.*

tan /tæn/ *adj* [not gradable] • *I need a pair of tan* (= pale yellowish brown) *shoes.*

tan *obj* [LEATHER] /tæn/ *v* [T] **-nn-** to change (animal skin) into leather using special chemicals such as TANNIN • *I'll* **tan** *his* **hide** *(Br also* **tan the hide off** *him)* (= beat him) *if I catch him.*

tan·ner /£ˈtæn·əʳ, $-ɚ/ *n* [C] • A tanner is a person who tans leather.

tan·ner·y /£ˈtæn·ᵊr·i, $-ɚ-/ *n* [C] • A tannery is the place where leather is made.

tan [TRIANGLE] /tæn/ *n* [C] *abbreviation for* TANGENT

tan·dem /ˈtæn·dəm/ *n* [C] a bicycle made for two people who sit one behind the other • If two pieces of equipment, people, etc. are working **in tandem** they are working together, esp. well or closely: *I want these two groups to work/operate in tandem on this project.* • Also **in tandem** means at the same time: *In tandem* **with** *our Tokyo office we'll be updating our software.* • [PIC] **Bicycles**

tan·dem /ˈtæn·dəm/ *adv* [not gradable] • *riding tandem*

tan·doo·ri /£tænˈdʊə·ri, $tɑːnˈdʊr·i/ *n* [U] a particular Indian method of cooking food in a clay cooker • *tandoori chicken*

tang /tæŋ/ *n* [C] a strong sharp taste or smell • *What's in this drink? It's got a tang of lemon.* • *There was the tang of the sea in the air.*

tang·y /ˈtæŋ·i/ *adj* **-ier, -iest** • A tangy flavour is pleasantly strong and sharp: *For dessert I had the most delicious tangy lemon tart.*

tan·gent [CIRCLE] /ˈtæn·dʒᵊnt/ *n* [C] a straight line which touches but does not cut into a curve • If someone *(esp. Br)* **goes off at a tangent**/*(Am and Aus)* **goes off on a tangent**/*(Br and Aus)* **flies off at a tangent** they suddenly change what they were talking or thinking about: *It's hard to get a firm decision out of him – he's always going off at a tangent.*

tan·gen·tial /tænˈdʒen·tʃᵊl/ *adj* • *(slightly fml) I agree it's an important subject, but it's tangential* (= only indirectly related) **to** *the problem under discussion.*

tan·gent [TRIANGLE] /ˈtæn·dʒᵊnt/ *(abbreviation* **tan**) *n* [C] *specialized* (in a triangle that has one angle of 90°) the RATIO of the length of the side opposite an angle less than 90° divided by the length of the shorter of the two sides that are next to the angle • Compare COSINE; SINE.

tan·ge·rine /£ˌtæn·dʒᵊrˈiːn, ˈ---, $ˌtæn·dʒəˈriːn/ *n* [C] a fruit like a small orange, usually with few or no seeds and a thin skin

tan·ge·rine /£ˌtæn·dʒəˈriːn, ˈ---, $ˌtæn·dʒəˈriːn/ *adj* [not gradable] • *a tangerine* (=dark or reddish orange colour) *dress*

tan·gi·ble /ˈtæn·dʒə·bl̩/ *adj* real or not imaginary; able to be shown or touched • *We need tangible* **evidence** *if we're going to take legal action.* • *Other tangible* **benefits** *include an increase in salary and shorter working hours.*

tan·gi·bly /ˈtæn·dʒə·bli/ *adv*

tan·gle /ˈtæŋ·gl̩/ *n* [C] an untidy mass of things that are not in a state of order, or a state of confusion or difficulty • *Be careful as you brush the tangles out of my hair.* • *When I opened the box all I could see was* **a** *tangle* **of** *wires.* • *My knitting/hair is* **in a** *tangle.* • *I'm* **in an** *awful tangle* **with** *my work, can you help?*

tan·gle *(obj)* /ˈtæŋ·gl̩/ *v* • *The cat has tangled* **(up)** *my wool.* [T] • *These wires have become tangled* **(up)**. [I] • *Don't* **tangle with** (=become involved, esp. by arguing or fighting with) *drunks.* • See also ENTANGLE.

tang·led /ˈtæŋ·gl̩d/ *adj* • *tangled string* • *The floor of the forest was covered with tangled undergrowth.* • *"O what a tangled web we weave, / When first we practise to deceive!"* (Sir Walter Scott in *Marmion*, 1808)

tan·go /£ˈtæŋ·gəʊ, $-goʊ/ *n* [C] *pl* **tangos** an energetic dance of S American origin for two people, or the music for this dance • *I watched them* **do** *the tango.*

tan·go /£ˈtæŋ·gəʊ, $-goʊ/ *v* [I] *past* **tangoed** • *We waltzed and tangoed.*

tang·y /ˈtæŋ·i/ *adj* See at TANG

tank CONTAINER /tæŋk/ *n* [C] a container which holds liquid or gas • *a fuel/petrol/propane tank* • *Oil leaking from the storage tank had reached the beach.* • *My* **fish** *tank is only big enough for two goldfish.*

tank·ful /ˈtæŋk·fʊl/ *n* [C] • *We did so much driving – we used three tankfuls of fuel in as many days.*

tank VEHICLE /tæŋk/ *n* [C] a large military fighting vehicle built to protect those inside it from attack which is driven by wheels which turn inside moving metal belts • *The troops in their tanks and armoured cars gave no warning.* • *The soldiers started firing into the air and the tanks* **rolled** *over cars and bikes in their way, crushing them.* • *Advisers proposed the development of new conventional weapons, such as better tank armour.*

tank·ard /£ˈtæŋ·kəd, $-kɚd/ *n* [C] a large usually metal drinking cup with sloping sides, which has a handle and sometimes a lid, mainly used for drinking beer • *a pewter tankard*

tanked up /tæŋkt/ *adj* drunk; showing or feeling the effects of having drunk a lot of alcohol • *By the time I got to the party Patrick and Delia were completely tanked up.*

tank·er /£ˈtæŋ·kəʳ, $-kɚ/ *n* [C] a ship, aircraft, road or railway vehicle which is built to carry liquid or gas • *More than 2000 people are believed to have died when the ferry sank after colliding with an* **oil** *tanker.* • *Tanker spills now average one a day.* • *Smaller quantities of gas are delivered as liquids by tanker-trucks.* • PIC **Ships and boats, Vehicles**

tank top *n* [C] a piece of clothing, often made of wool, that covers the upper part of the body but not the arms, and usually has a V-shaped opening at the neck • *Tank tops were very fashionable in the 70s.*

tan·ner·y /£ˈtæn·ᵊr·i, $-ɚ·i/ *n* [C] See at TAN LEATHER

tan·nin /ˈtæn·ɪn/, **tan·nic ac·id** /ˌtæn·ɪk/ *n* (one of) a group of chemicals which are found in plant cells, esp. in leaves, BARK (=the outer covering of a tree), and fruit which is not ripe • *Tannin is used in making leather and ink.* [U] • *Tea and red wine have a high level of tannins.* [C]

Tan·noy /ˈtæn·ɔɪ/ *n* [C] *Br trademark* a system of equipment which is used for making speech loud enough for a large number of people to hear, esp. in order to give information • *I missed my train because I couldn't hear what was given out* **over** *the Tannoy.* • *We couldn't hear the announcement that was made on the tannoy system.* • *Vans with tannoys fixed to them were driving around the streets, urging people to go and vote.*

tan·ta·lize *obj*, *Br and Aus usually* **-ise** /£ˈtæn·tᵊl·aɪz, $-t̬ə·laɪz/ *v* [T usually passive] to excite or attract (someone) by an offer or a suggestion of something which is, in fact, unlikely to happen • *Tantalized* **by** *the prospect of two weeks in the Bahamas, she bought ten lottery tickets.*

tan·ta·liz·ing, *Br and Aus usually* **tan·ta·lis·ing** /£ˈtæn·tᵊl·aɪ·zɪŋ, $-t̬ə·laɪ-/ *adj* • Something that is tantalizing causes desire and excitement in you although sometimes it is unlikely that it will provide a way of satisfying that desire: *She gave me one of her tantalizing smiles and walked off.* ○ *I'd had a tantalizing glimpse of the sparkling blue sea as we drove along the coast.* ○ *From the kitchen came the tantalizing smell of garlic.*

tan·ta·liz·ing·ly, *Br and Aus usually* **tan·ta·lis·ing·ly** /£ˈtæn·tᵊl·aɪ·zɪŋ·li, $-t̬ə·laɪ-/ *adv* • *The sea looked tantalizingly close but it was an hour's walk away.*

tan·ta·mount /£ˈtæn·tə·maʊnt, $-t̬ə-/ *adj* [not gradable] **tantamount to** *slightly fml* being almost the same or having the same effect as (usually something bad) • *The bank wouldn't lend any more money, which was tantamount to making the business close down.* • *Her refusal to answer was tantamount to an admission of guilt.*

tan·trum /ˈtæn·trəm/ *n* [C] a sudden period of uncontrolled childish anger • *Johnny* **had/threw** *a tantrum in the shop because I wouldn't buy him any sweets.* • *If she doesn't get her own way she has* **temper** *tantrums just like a child.*

Taoi·seach /ˈtiː·ʃək/ *n* [C] the leader of the government of the Republic of Ireland

Ta·o·i·sm, **Dao·i·sm** /£ˈtaʊ·ɪ·zᵊm, $ˈdaʊ·ɪ-/ *n* [U] a religion developed originally in ancient China which emphasizes a simple and natural life

tap DEVICE /tæp/, *Am* **fau·cet** *n* [C] a device which controls the flow of liquid, esp. water (*Am* faucet), or gas • *bath taps* • *the hot/cold tap* • *a gas tap* • *Could you* **turn the** *tap* **on/off**, *please.* • *From the bathroom I could hear the sound of a* **dripping** *tap.* • Beer which is **on tap** is served from a BARREL (=large container) through a tap: *The local pub has over twenty different beers on tap.* • *(fig.) Working in a library as I do, I have all this information* **on tap** (=available to be used at any time). • **Tap water** is the water which comes out of the taps in a building, which are usually connected to the main supply of the local water system. • LP **Switching on and off** PIC **Bathroom, Laboratory**

tap *(obj)* HIT /tæp/ *v* **-pp-** to hit (something) gently, and often repeatedly, esp. making short sharp noises • *The branches tapped* **against** *the window.* [I] • *I could hear him tapping his fingers on the desk.* [T] • *Turn the tin over and tap the bottom gently till the cake comes out.* [T] • *I was tapping my feet* (=hitting the floor gently with my feet) *to the music.* [T] • *I felt someone tap me* **on the shoulder**. [T] • *I could hear her tapping* **away** (=repeatedly) *on her computer next door.* [I]

tap /tæp/ *n* [C] • *There was a sudden tap* **at/on** *the door.* • *I felt a tap* **on the shoulder** *and turned around to see Ellis.*

tap *obj* OBTAIN /tæp/ *v* [T] **-pp-** to obtain or make use of (something) • *For more than a century, Eastern cities have expanded their water supplies by tapping ever more remote sources.* • *The potential for tapping* **(into)** *the* **market** *further is huge.* • *There is a rich vein of literary talent here just waiting to be tapped* **(into)** *by publishers.* • *Pain has the effect of helping you tap* **(into)** *unexplored sources of aggression and strength.* • *(fig. infml dated) Sandra tried to tap me* **for** *her train fare/ information on the project* (=tried to force/persuade me to give it to her).

tap *obj* TELEPHONE /tæp/ *v* [T] **-pp-** to use a small device fixed to a telephone in order to listen secretly to what people are saying • *In December of last year he complained that his* **telephone** *had been tapped.* • *His name was mentioned in connection with the drugs deal in one of the tapped telephone conversations.* • *He resigned as prime minister in 1992 after a* **phone**-*tapping scandal.*

tap /tæp/ *n* [C] • *He claims that he knew nothing of government* **phone** *taps on journalists during those years.* • *On July 28 a tap was placed on her phone by Hadfield, following an order signed by Brinkworth.*

tap (danc·ing) /tæp/ *n* [U] a type of dance in which the rhythm is marked by the noise of the dancer's shoes on the floor. Special shoes are worn which have pieces of metal fixed under them. • *I did tap classes as well as ballet.* • *Are you going to do a tap* **dance** *for us, Susie?* • *Caroline was quite a good tap* **dancer** *in her youth.*

tap·as /ˈtæp·əz/ *pl n* small amounts of Spanish food that are served, esp. with alcoholic drinks, in Spanish bars and restaurants • *a tapas bar*

tape STRIP /teɪp/ *n* a long narrow strip of material which is sometimes sticky on one side • *adhesive tape* • *insulating tape* • *masking tape* • *(Br and Aus) sticky tape* • *(Am) Scotch tape* • *There are tapes attached to the life jacket which you tie at the side.* [T] • When competitors in a race cross **the (finishing) tape** they complete the race by going past a tape stretched across the finishing line. • A **tape measure** is a strip of cloth, plastic or bendable metal with measurements marked on it which is used for measuring.

Compare **ruler** at RULE DRAW. • See also TICKER-TAPE PARADE.

tape *obj* /teɪp/ *v* [T] • To tape something is to use strips of sticky material, esp. to fix two things together or to fasten a parcel: *She taped a note* **to/on/onto** *the door.* • *I've taped* **(up)** *the box securely so it won't burst open.* [T/M] • *Tape* **(up)** *the ends of the wires.* [T/M]

tape RECORD /teɪp/ *n* thin plastic in a long narrow strip with a magnetic covering which allows sounds or sounds and pictures to be recorded and played again, or a CASSETTE, esp. one on which sound is (to be) recorded • *audio tape* • *magnetic tape* • *recording tape* • *a half-hour/three-hour tape* • *If you give me a* **blank** *tape I'll record it for you.* [C] • *I've got that film* **on tape** *(also* **on video***)* (=recorded as pictures and sound) *if you want to borrow it.* • *I only managed to get the last few minutes of conversation* **on tape**. • *She bought me some tapes of ballet music for my birthday.* [C] • *Did you tape-***record/make** *a tape (recording) of* (=record on tape) *the conversation?* [C] • A **tape deck** is a machine which is used for playing and recording sound, often as a part of a set of electronic equipment on which music is played. • A **tape recorder** is a machine which is used for playing and recording sound, usually one which is light and small enough to be carried.

tape *obj* /teɪp/ *v* [T] • If you tape something you record it on tape: *My mother wanted me to tape the documentary on pandas for her.* ○ *I've asked Alexander to tape a couple of records for me.* • *(Br and Aus infml)* If someone says that they have **got** someone **taped** it means that they are aware of the faults in that person's character.

tap·er *(obj)* BECOME NARROW /£'teɪ·pəʳ, $-pɚ/ *v* to (cause to) become narrower or reduced in some way • *The river soon tapers into a stream as you follow it up the mountain.* [I] • *The stick was tapered* **to** *a point.* [T] • *You'll have to taper it to make it fit.* [T] • *Turn left where the road tapers* **(off)** *into a track.* [I] • *Her voice tapered* **off** *as she realised everyone was listening.* [I] • *We had a lot of interest in the book, but it has tapered* **off** *recently.* [I] • *She had long tapering fingers*

tap·er CANDLE /£'teɪ·pəʳ, $-pɚ/ *n* [C] a very thin candle or a long thin piece of waxed string, twisted paper or very thin wood used for lighting candles, fires, etc.

tap·e·stry /'tæp·ɪ·stri/ *n* [C] a piece of cloth whose pattern or picture is created by sewing or weaving different coloured threads onto a special type of strong cloth • *a tapestry cushion* • *a tapestry chair seat* • *a tapestry bag* • *I hung the tapestry my mother did in the hall.* • *(fig.) Why Jim, your garden is a veritable tapestry of* (=has a lot of different) *colours!*

tape·worm /£'teɪp·wɜːm, $-wɜːrm/ *n* [C] a long flat-bodied PARASITE (=an organism which lives in another from which is obtains its food) which lives inside the bowels of humans and other animals

tap·i·o·ca /£ˌtæp·i'əʊ·kə, $-'oʊ-/ *n* [U] small hard pieces of the dried and crushed root of the CASSAVA plant, usually cooked with milk and sugar to make a sweet food • *tapioca pudding*

tap·pet /'tæp·ɪt/ *n* [C] a part of a machine which causes another part to move by hitting it

tar /£tɑːʳ, $tɑːr/ *n* [U] a black substance, sticky when hot, used esp. for making roads • *It was so hot the tar on the road melted.* • Tar also refers to one of the poisonous substances that is found in tobacco: *If you must smoke, choose a cigarette with a low tar and nicotine content.* • *(Am infml) The boxer* **beat/knocked/whaled the tar out of** (=hit forcefully and repeatedly) *his opponent.*

tar *obj* /£tɑːʳ, $tɑːr/ *v* [T] **-rr-** • *They've been tarring the roads this week.* • Someone who is tarred **and feathered** is covered in tar and feathers as a punishment. • *Because they were so close John was* **tarred with the same brush** *as* (=thought to have similar faults to) *Tim.*

tar·a·ma·sa·la·ta /£ˌtær·ə·mə·sə'lɑː·tə, $ˌtɑːr·ɑː·mɑː·sɑː'lɑː·tɑː/ *n* [U] a pale pink food, originally from Greece, which is made mainly from a mixture of fish eggs, bread and oil

ta·ran·tu·la /tə'ræn·tjʊ·lə/ *n* [C] any of various large hairy SPIDERS (=insect-like creatures with eight legs), some of which have a poisonous bite

tard·y /£'tɑː·di, $'tɑːr-/ *adj* **-ier**, **-iest** *fml* slow or late in happening or arriving • *Dinner was somewhat delayed on account of David's rather tardy arrival*

tar·di·ness /£'tɑː·dɪ·nəs, $'tɑːr-/ *n* [U] *fml*

tar·get OBJECT FIRED AT /£'tɑː·gɪt, $'tɑːr-/ *n* [C] an object fired at during shooting practice, often a circle with a pattern of rings, or any object or place at which bullets, bombs etc. are aimed • *I had four shots but I didn't even* **hit** *the target.* • *The target* **of** *the attack was a train station in the centre of the city.* • *Any major airport or station is potentially a* **terrorist** *target.* • *(fig.) Recently she has been the target* **for** (=has experienced) *a series of obscene phone calls.* • *(fig.) His outspoken views have in the past made him an* **easy** *target* **for** *mockery* (=able to be easily criticized and laughed at). • *(fig.) The target audience* **for** *the TV series are* (=It is directed at and intended for) *young people aged 13 to 18.* • If you are **on target** with a piece of work, you are advancing well and likely to achieve what you planned.

tar·get *obj* /£'tɑː·gɪt, $'tɑːr-/ *v* [T] • *During the Cold War American missiles were targeted* **at/on** (=aimed at) *Russian cities.* • *It is hoped that civilians will not be targeted during the war.* • *(fig.) The paper is targeted specifically* **at** (=directed at and intended for) *young people.* • *(fig.) Campaigns to stop the spread of AIDS must continue to be targeted* (=directed) **at** *the whole population, said Fussell.* • *(fig.) Most ads target* (=are directed at) *a specific area of the market.*

tar·get AIM /£'tɑː·gɪt, $'tɑːr-/ *n* [C] a level or situation which you intend to achieve • *The government's target of 3·5% annual growth seems easily attainable.* • *The target we need to* **reach/meet** *in order to rebuild the church is £250 000.* • *I've* **set** *myself a target weight which I hope to reach by Christmas.* • *Further slippage would delay the target* (=intended) *opening date for the new airport.* • *(specialized)* A **target language** is a language into which you are TRANSLATING.

tar·iff /'tær·ɪf/ *n* [C] a charge or list of charges for services, or on goods entering a country • *The tariff* **for** *rooms and meals was pinned to the door of the hotel.* • **Import** *tariffs* **on** *electrical goods are to be increased.*

tar·mac /£'tɑː·mæk, $'tɑːr-/, **tar·mac·ad·am** /£ˌtɑː·mə'kæd·əm, $ˌtɑːr-/ *n* [U] *trademark* (an area of) black material used for surfacing roads, etc., which consists of TAR mixed with small stones • *We'll surface the path with tarmac.* • *Three planes were standing on* **the** *tarmac* (=area outside the airport buildings).

tar·mac *obj* /£'tɑː·mæk, $'tɑːr-/ *v* [T] **tarmacking**, *past* **tarmacked** *Br* • *Our neighbours are having their drive tarmacked.*

tarn, Tarn /£tɑːn, $tɑːrn/ *n* [C] a small mountain lake • *There's a tarn marked on the map.*

tar·nish *(obj)* /£'tɑː·nɪʃ, $'tɑːr-/ *v* to make or (esp. of metal) become less bright or a different colour • *Silver tarnishes easily and turns black if not polished regularly.* [I] • *(fig.) By this time a series of scandals had effectively tarnished* (=spoiled) *the leader's* **image/reputation.** [T]

tar·nished /£'tɑː·nɪʃt, $'tɑːr-/ *adj* • *The silver was looking a bit tarnished so I thought I'd polish it.* • *(fig.) The singer has recently been involved in a lot of charity work, some say in an attempt to restore his tarnished* (=spoilt) *reputation.*

ta·ro /£'tær·əʊ, $-oʊ/ *n* [C] *pl* **taros** a tropical plant of which the root is cooked and eaten

tar·pau·lin /£tɑː'pɔː·lɪn, $tɑːr'pɑː-/ *n* (a large piece of) heavy cloth coated with a waterproof substance which is used as a covering • *We'll need a sheet of tarpaulin to cover the machine.* [U] • *Put a tarpaulin over those tools if you're going to leave them outside.* [C]

tar·ra·gon /£'tær·ə·gən, $-gɑːn/ *n* [U] a plant with whitish flowers whose narrow leaves are used in cooking as a herb, having a taste which is similar to LIQUORICE • *Tarragon is often used in chicken dishes.* • PIC **Herbs and spices**

tar·ry /£'tær·i/ *v* [I] *old use* to stay somewhere for longer than expected and delay leaving • *Tarry awhile, I pray you.*

tart FOOD /£tɑːt, $tɑːrt/ *n* an open pastry case with a filling, usually of something sweet such as fruit • *apple/strawberry/custard tart* • *Ann brought in a plate of jam tarts.* [C] • *Help yourself to a* **slice of** *apple tart.* [U] • PIC **Bread and cakes**

tart SOUR /£tɑːt, $tɑːrt/ *adj* **-er, -est** (esp. of fruit) tasting sour or acidic • *Gooseberries are too tart for my taste.* • *You might need some sugar on the rhubarb – it's a bit tart.*

tart·ness /£'tɑːt·nəs, $'tɑːrt-/ *n* [U]

tart BEHAVIOUR /£tɑːt, $tɑːrt/ *adj* **-er, -est** (esp. of a way of speaking) quick or sharp and unpleasant • *a tart remark/comment/reply*

tart·ly /£'tɑːt·li, $'tɑːrt-/ *adv* • *'You don't seem to appreciate the situation,' she said tartly.*

tart·ness /£'tɑːt·nəs, $'tɑːrt-/ *n* [U]

tart WOMAN /£tɑːt, $tɑːrt/ *n* [C] *disapproving infml* an esp. young woman who intentionally wears the type of clothes and make-up that attract sexual attention in a way that is too obvious • *You should have seen the tart that Paul brought along to Guy's party!* • *(dated)* A tart is also a PROSTITUTE.

tart·y /£'tɑː·ti, $'tɑːr·t̬i/ *adj* **-ier, -iest** *disapproving* • Tarty means intentionally attracting sexual attention: *I always think short skirts and high heels look a bit tarty.*

tart up *obj*, **tart** *obj* **up** *v adv* [M] *esp. Br infml* to make (yourself) or (something) look more attractive or decorative, usually by making very quick or very obvious changes • *I was in the bathroom tarting* **myself** *up to go out with Peter when it happened.* • *I thought I'd get a couple of pizzas out of the freezer and tart them up with a few olives and anchovies.*

tar·tan /£'tɑː·tᵊn, $'tɑːr·t̬ᵊn/ *n* a pattern of different coloured straight lines crossing each other at 90 degree angles, or a cloth with this pattern • *a tartan kilt* • *Tartan is mainly associated with Scotland.* [U] • *The MacDonald and Stewart tartans are famous tartan patterns associated with different Scottish family groups or clans.* [C] • PIC› **Patterns**

tar·tar SUBSTANCE /£'tɑː·təʳ, $'tɑːr·t̬ɚ/ *n* [U] a hard substance which forms on the teeth • *You should brush your teeth regularly to stop tartar building up.*

tar·tar·ic /£tɑː'tær·ɪk, $tɑːr-/ *adj* [before n; not gradable] • **Tartaric acid** is an acidic substance found in many plants and fruits and is used to make **cream of tartar**.

tar·tar PERSON /£'tɑː·təʳ, $'tɑːr·t̬ɚ/, **Tar·tar** *n* [C] *dated disapproving* a person with a fierce, severe manner • *The new boss is a bit of a tartar, he won't even let us stop for a coffee!*

tar·tar sauce /£ˌtɑː·tə, £-tɑː, $ˌtɑːr·t̬ɚ/, **tar·tare sauce** *n* [U] a cold white sauce containing small pieces of herbs and hot-tasting vegetables, usually eaten with fish.

task WORK /£tɑːsk, $tæsk/ *n* [C] a piece of work to be done, esp. one done regularly, unwillingly or with difficulty • *Many nurses complain that they are given menial tasks which make little use of their skills.* • *Getting the children ready for school on time is no easy task.* • *We usually ask interviewees to* **perform** *a few simple tasks on the computer just to test their aptitude.* • *The government now faces the* **daunting** *task of restructuring the entire health service.* • *I had the* **unenviable** *task of entertaining a houseful of bored kids.* • *I've* **set/given** *them/myself* **the task of** *finding out how many countries we have contacts in.* • A **task force** is a group of people, often a military group, who are brought together to do a particular job: *Retired teachers have formed a task force to help schools in Poland.* ○ *Last month doctors set up a national task force to investigate each asthma death.* • A **(hard) task master** is someone who gives others a lot of work to do and/or expects to work very hard.

task *obj* /£tɑːsk, $tæsk/ *v* [T usually passive] *specialized* • *We have been tasked* **with** (=given the task of) *setting up camps for refugees.*

task SPEAK ANGRILY /£tɑːsk, $tæsk/ *n* [U] **take** *someone* **to task** to criticize or speak angrily to (someone) for something that they have done wrong • *She took her assistant to task* **for/over** *her carelessness.*

tas·sel /'tæs·ᵊl/ *n* [C] a group of short threads or cords held together at one end, which is used as a hanging decoration on hats, curtains, furniture etc. • *She was wearing one of those hippy skirts with tassels around the hem.* • PIC› **Hats**

tas·selled, *Am usually* **tas·seled** /'tæs·ᵊld/ *adj* [not gradable] • *tasselled curtains/lampshades*

taste FLAVOUR /teɪst/ *n* the flavour of something, or the ability of a person or animal to recognize different flavours • *Sugar has a sweet taste and lemons have a sour taste.* [U] • *I love the taste* **of** *garlic.* [U] • *I had a sandwich over an hour ago and I've still got the taste* **of** *onions in my mouth.* [U] • *Do you think this sauce lacks a bit of taste?* [U] • *I lose my* **sense of** (=ability to) *taste when I've got a cold.* [U] • *I didn't like red wine before but I* **acquired** *a taste* **for** *it* (=started to like it as I became familiar with it) *while I was living in France.* [U] • *Olives are perhaps an* **acquired** *taste* (=you only like them after you have become familiar with their taste). [C] • *You can* **lose** *your taste* **for** (=stop enjoying the taste of) *sweet things as you get older.* [U] • A taste of food is a small amount of it: *Just a taste of cake for me, please, I'm supposed to be dieting!* [C] ○ *(fig.) I* **had** *a taste of* (=I briefly experienced) *office work during the summer and that was quite enough.* [C] • **Taste buds** are a group of cells, found esp. on the tongue, which allow different tastes to be recognized. • See also AFTERTASTE. • Ⓓ

taste *(obj)* /teɪst/ *v* • *I've burnt my tongue and I can't taste my food* (=cannot recognize or enjoy different flavours). [T] • *Taste* (=try a little of) *this sauce and tell me if I add need to add some more salt.* [T] • *Whatever's this food? I've never tasted* (=eaten) *anything like it.* [T] • You might say that a food or drink tastes in a particular way meaning that it has that flavour: *Sugar tastes sweet.* [L only + adj] ○ *Oh, this tastes delicious!* [L only + adj] ○ *What's in this bread – it tastes* **of** *onions.* [I always + adv/prep] ○ *This coffee tastes more* **like** *hot water!* [I always + adv/prep] • *(fig.) Once you've tasted* (=experienced briefly) *luxury it's very hard to settle for anything else.* [T]

taste·less /'teɪst·ləs/ *adj* • *Unfortunately my soup was cold and rather tasteless* (=without taste).

tast·er /£'teɪ·stəʳ, $-stɚ/ *n* [C] • A taster is a person who tastes food or drink as a job: *He works as* **wine-taster**. • A taster is also a small amount or brief experience of something which is intended either to make you understand what it is like or to make you want more of it: *I'm giving you a page from the book just as a taster, there'll be more to follow.*

-tast·ing /-ˌteɪ·stɪŋ/ *combining form* • *sweet/bitter/sour-tasting* • *hot-tasting* • *foul-tasting*

tast·y /'teɪ·sti/ *adj approving* • Tasty is usually used of savoury food and describes food which has a strong and very pleasant flavour: *Helen, this soup is so tasty.* • *(infml)* Tasty is also used of people and means very sexually attractive: *If you're coming to the party you can bring that tasty Canadian friend of yours!*

taste JUDGMENT /teɪst/ *n* a person's appreciation of and liking for particular things • *His taste* **in** *clothes leaves a little to be desired.* [C] • *I've never understood Liz's taste* **in** *men.* [C] • *Some people like older buildings and others prefer bold new architecture – it's really just a question of taste.* [U] • *I've never really cared much for flash new cars – old vintage cars are more* **to my taste** (=what I like). [U] • *(approving)* Taste is also a person's ability to judge and appreciate what is good or suitable, esp. relating to such matters as art, style, beauty and manners: *She* **has** *taste, I'll give her that.* [U] ○ *Every present I've ever received from Camille has been* **in** *perfect taste.* [U] ○ *He* **has** *the most awful taste so you can probably imagine what his house looks like.* [U] ○ *He told a joke about death that I thought was* **in** *rather* **poor** *taste considering that Steve's father had just died.* [U] ○ *I'm having a* **bad** *taste party on Saturday so you've got to come along in the worst clothes you can find.* [U] ○ *(humorous) I'm not sure that it's* **in the best possible** *taste to tell jokes about divorce at a wedding!* • Ⓓ

tastes /teɪsts/ *pl n* • A person's tastes are what they like: *I'm afraid I have expensive tastes* (=I like expensive things). ○ *We* **have** *very different tastes, Ben and myself, so we argue constantly about how we're going to decorate the house.*

taste·ful /'teɪst·fᵊl/ *adj approving* • *It's very tasteful, their house, but I can't help thinking it lacks a little character.*

taste·ful·ly /'teɪst·fᵊl·i/ *adv* • *Tastefully decorated throughout, the hotel offers comfortable lounges, a beautiful restaurant and a stylish piano bar.*

taste·less /'teɪst·ləs/ *adj* • *He was wearing a rather tasteless* (=unattractive) *pink and yellow shirt.* • *He told one or two rather tasteless* (=rude or offensive) *jokes which my mother didn't particularly enjoy.*

taste·less·ly /'teɪst·lə·sli/ *adv* • *She dresses fairly tastelessly considering she's got so much money.*

tat /tæt/ *n* [U] *infml* anything which looks cheap, is of low quality or in bad condition • *Like most souvenir shops it sells a lot of old tat.*

tat·ty /£'tæt·i, $'tæt̬-/ *adj* **-ier, -iest** • Tatty means old and in bad condition: *You are going to change out of those tatty* **old** *jeans, aren't you.* ○ *I'm sure I have a copy of the book but it'll be very old and tatty.*

ta-ta /£tə'tɑː, £tæt'ɑː, $tɑː'tɑː/ *exclamation Br infml* goodbye • *Ta-ta, then.*

tat·ters /£'tæt·əz, $'tæt̬·ɚz/ *pl n* **in tatters** (esp. of cloth) badly torn • *Her clothes were old and in tatters.* • *(fig.) After the newspaper story appeared his reputation was in tatters* (=badly damaged).

tat·tered /£'tæt·əd, $'tæt̬·ɚd/ *adj* • *A tattered flag fluttered in the breeze.* • *(fig.) He did everything he could to restore his tattered* (=badly damaged) *reputation but to little avail.*

tat·tle /£'tæt·l̩, $'tæt̬-/ *n* See TITTLE-TATTLE • **Tattle-tale** is *Am for* **tell-tale**. See at TELL [SPEAK].

tat·too [DECORATION] /tæt'uː/ *n* [C] *pl* **tattoos** /tətuːz/ a permanent image, pattern or word on the skin which is created by using needles to put colours under the skin • *The previous week she'd brought home a greasy-haired biker with tattoos all over his arms.* • *Karen has a tattoo of a swallow on her shoulder.*

tat·too *obj* /tə'tuː/ *v* [T] **tattooed** • *Susan had a dragon tattooed* **on** *her back while she was in Amsterdam.*

tat·tooed /tæt'uːd/ *adj* [not gradable] • *He rolled up his sleeve, revealing a heavily tattooed arm.*

tat·too·ist /tæt'uː·ɪst/ *n* [C] • A tattooist or **tattoo artist** is someone whose job is to put tattoos on people.

tat·too [MILITARY SHOW] /tæt'uː/ *n* [C] *pl* **tattoos** an outside show, with several military performances esp. of marching and music

tat·ty /£'tæt·i, $'tæt̬-/ *adj* See at TAT

taught /£tɔːt, $tɑːt/ *past simple and past participle of* TEACH

taunt *obj* /£tɔːnt, $tɑːnt/ *v* [T] to intentionally annoy and upset (someone) by making unkind remarks to them, laughing at them etc. • *The other children used to taunt him in the playground because he was fat and wore glasses.*

taunt /£tɔːnt, $tɑːnt/ *n* [C] • *The protesters shouted taunts at the police.*

Tau·rus /£'tɔː·rəs, $'tɔːr·əs/ *n* [not after *the*] the second sign of the ZODIAC relating to the period 21 April to 22 May, represented by a BULL (= a male cow), or a person born during this period • *My mother was born* **under** *Taurus* (= during this period). [U] • *She's a typical Taurus.* [C]

taut /£tɔːt, $tɑːt/ *adj* **-er, -est** tight or completely stretched • *Washing my face with soap makes my skin feel taut and dry.* • *She tightened the strings of the guitar until they were taut.* • *He kept his eyes on the road ahead, his face taut with concentration.* • *(fig.) His latest film was described in today's paper as a taut* (= exciting with fast action) *thriller.* • Compare SLACK [NOT TIGHT].

taut·en *(obj)* /£'tɔː·tᵊn, $'tɑː·t̬ᵊn/ *v* • *The muscles in his face suddenly tautened.* [I] • *He tautened the ropes that were holding the tent down.* [T]

taut·ly /£'tɔːt·li, $'tɑːt-/ *adv* • *(fig.) He specializes in tautly written detective stories* (= ones which are exciting with fast action).

taut·ness /£'tɔːt·nəs, $'tɑːt-/ *n* [U]

taut·ol·o·gy /£tɔː'tɒl·ə·dʒi, $tɑː'tɑː·lə-/ *n* the unnecessary and usually unintentional use of two words to express one meaning • *"Nothing was covered up and no information was concealed," said the minister, producing his second tautology of the interview.* [C] • *The president's weakness for repetition sometimes results in tautology.* [U]

taut·o·log·i·cal /£ˌtɔː·tə'lɒdʒ·ɪ·kᵊl, $ˌtɑː·t̬ə'lɑː·dʒɪ-/ *adj* • *It is tautological to talk about 'little droplets' since droplets are by their very nature small.*

taut·o·log·i·cal·ly /£ˌtɔː·tə'lɒdʒ·ɪ·kli, $ˌtɑː·t̬ə'lɑː·dʒɪ-/ *adv*

tav·ern /£'tæv·ᵊn, $-ɚn/ *n* [C] *old use* a place where alcohol is sold and drunk; a PUB • Ⓖⓡ

taw·dry /£'tɔː·dri, $'tɑː-/ *adj* **-ier, -iest** looking bright and attractive but in fact cheap and of low quality • *The clothes that had looked so beautiful on stage looked tawdry hanging in the dressing room.*

taw·dri·ness /£'tɔː·drɪ·nəs, $'tɑː-/ *n* [U]

taw·ny /£'tɔː·ni, $'tɑː-/ *adj* **-ier, -iest** of a light yellowish brown colour, like that of a lion • *a tawny mane* • *tawny fur*

tax [MONEY] /tæks/ *n* (an amount of) money paid to the government, usually a percentage of personal income or of the cost of goods or services bought • *They're putting up the tax* **on** *cigarettes.* [C] • *I'm entitled to a decent level of health-care from the state – I* **pay** *my taxes, don't I?* [C] • *Tax will be deducted automatically from your salary.* [U] • *Tax* **cuts** (= reductions in taxes) *are always popular.* • *In Britain, if you are a foreign visitor you can buy goods tax-***free** (= without paying tax) *to take back to your own country.* • *Tax* **evasion** (= not paying tax) *is unlawful.* • A tax-**evader** is someone who tries not to pay those taxes which legally they should. • Tax **deducted**/*(Br and Aus also)* **paid at source** refers to tax taken from your pay before you receive it. • *What do you earn* **before tax/after tax** (= before/after you have paid tax on the money you earn)? • *The company, based in Lancashire, last year made* **pre-tax** *profits of 6·3 million.* • Your **tax allowance** is the amount of income on which you do not have to pay tax. • *Your* **tax assessment/bill** *shows how much* **income** *tax you will have to pay in this* **tax year**. • *(Am and Aus) Is it tax-***deductible** (= Can tax on it be avoided)? • A **tax disc** is a small round sign which you put in the corner of the front window of your car or other vehicle to show that you have paid the tax to use it: *I had to pay a hefty fine because my tax disc had run out.* • A **tax exile** is a rich person who has moved to a **tax haven** (= a foreign country where taxes are lower than at home) in order to pay less tax. • **Tax relief** is the system of allowing someone not to pay tax on a part of their income. • A self-employed person must fill in a **tax return** (= give information about what they earn) every year: *Have you* **done** *your tax return yet?* • A **tax shelter** is a financial arrangement by which investments can be made without paying tax: *He was responsible for the elimination of a host of tax shelters for the rich.* • *(fig.) Looking after my handicapped mother has been a severe* **tax on** *my resources* (= has been very expensive). [U] • *"Tax without representation is tyranny"* (James Otis, 1725-1783) • Ⓢ

tax *obj* /tæks/ *v* [T] • *Husbands and wives may be taxed independently/together.* • *This group of people have in the past been very* **heavily/lightly** *taxed.*

tax·a·ble /'tæk·sə·bl̩/ *adj* [not gradable] • *taxable income/profits*

tax·a·tion /tæk'seɪ·ʃᵊn/ *n* [U] • Taxation is money obtained from the act of taxing people: *The government raised* **indirect** *taxation (Am hidden taxes)* (= taxes on goods and services) *so that they could reduce* **direct** *taxation* (= taxes on income).

tax *obj* [NEED EFFORT] /tæks/ *v* [T] to need a lot of effort, either physical or mental • *He only has to read a short report – it shouldn't tax him unduly.* • Ⓢ

tax·ing /'tæk·sɪŋ/ *adj* • *I like a bit of light reading when I'm on holiday – nothing too taxing* (= needing too much effort).

tax·i [VEHICLE] /'tæk·si/, **tax·i·cab**, *infml* **cab** *n* [C] a car with a driver whom you pay to take you somewhere • *I* **took** (= was driven in) *a taxi from the station to the hotel.* • *Tell me when you're ready and I'll* **call** (= telephone for) *a taxi.* • *The hotel doorman* **hailed** *a taxi* (= waved to a taxi to make it stop). • *I'll go* **by taxi**. • *Her husband is a taxi-***driver**. • *It's just a short taxi* **ride** *from the station to Mira's house.* • *There's a taxi* **rank** *outside the station.*

tax·i [MOVE] /'tæk·si/ *v* [I] **taxis, taxiing**, *past* **taxied** (of an aircraft) to move slowly on the ground • *The plane taxied across to the terminal building.*

tax·i·der·my /£'tæk·sɪ·dɜː·mi, $-dɜːr-/ *n* [U] the activity of cleaning, preserving and filling the skins of dead animals with special material to make them look as if they are still alive

tax·i·der·mist /£'tæk·sɪ·dɜː·mɪst, $-dɜːr-/ *n* [C] • *My grandfather was a taxidermist.*

tax·i·way /'tæk·si·weɪ/ *n* [C] a long path which aircraft travel along in order to get to or return from a RUNWAY (= place where aircraft take off and land)

tax·man /'tæks·mæn/ *n* [U] **the taxman** the government department that is responsible for collecting taxes • *The study at the time reckoned that the richest 5% were handing over 32·5% of their income to the taxman.* • *The new system means that it is more difficult to conceal these figures from the taxman.*

tax·on·o·my /£tæk'sɒn·ə·mi, $-'sɑː·nə-/ *n* [C/U] *specialized* a system for naming and organizing things, esp. plants and animals, into groups which share similar qualities

tax·pay·er /£'tæksˌpeɪ·ər, $-ɚ/ *n* [C] a person who pays tax • *$130 million of taxpayers' money will be needed to build the new stadium.* • *The result of the restructuring would be a net saving of several billion pounds of taxpayers'* **money** *a year.* • **The taxpayer** refers to all the people in one country who pay tax to the government: *If implemented, the new reforms could cost the taxpayer and the economy billions.*

TB /ˌtiː'biː/ *n* [U] *abbreviation for* TUBERCULOSIS

tbsp *n* [C] *pl* **tbsp** *abbreviation for* **tablespoonful**, see at TABLESPOON

tea /tiː/ *n* (a drink made by pouring hot water onto) dried and cut leaves and sometimes flowers, esp. the leaves of the tea plant • *China/Indian tea* [U] • *jasmine/herbal tea* [U] • *iced/lemon tea* [U] • *I'd love a* **cup of** *tea, please.* [U] • *Tea* **and biscuits** *will be provided at 11 o'clock.* [U] • *Two teas* (= cups of tea), *please.* [C] • *How do you like your tea –* **strong** *or* **weak**? [U] • *I'm not much of a tea* **drinker**. • *We sat in the shade of a tree,* **sipping** *tea and eating scones.* [U] • *(esp. Br)* Tea or **afternoon tea** is a small meal eaten in the late afternoon, usually including cake and a cup of tea:

Afternoon tea is served in the dining room from 3 to 5 p.m. every day. [U] • *(Br regional and Aus)* Tea also refers to a meal which is eaten early in the evening and which is usually cooked. [U] • *(dated) I wouldn't take that job* **for all the tea in China** (= nothing would persuade me to do it). • *(dated) It's time for action, not just* **tea and sympathy** (= words and behaviour which are comforting but useless). • A **tea bag** is a small paper bag filled with enough tea leaves to make tea for one person. • *(Br and Aus) We have a morning and an afternoon* **tea break** *every day when we stop work for about ten minutes and have a drink.* • *(esp. Am)* A **tea ball** is a small wire ball which is filled with tea leaves to make usually a pot of tea. • *A friend brought me a beautifully decorated* **tea caddy** (= container to keep tea leaves in) *from Japan.* • A **tea chest** is a large wooden box used first for storing tea and after that for other things, esp. when someone is moving from one house to another: *The removal men will pack the china into tea chests.* • A **tea cosy** is a thick covering, like a hat, which is put on a TEAPOT to keep the tea warm. • A **tea garden** is either an outside restaurant where drinks and small meals are served, or a tea PLANTATION (= large area of land where tea plants are grown). • In China and Japan, **tea-houses** are small buildings in which tea is served. • A **tea party** is an occasion when people meet in the afternoon to drink tea and eat a small amount of food. • A **tea room/shop** is a small restaurant where drinks and small meals, such as tea and cakes, are served. • A **tea service/set** is a set of small plates, cups, etc., with a matching pattern, for serving tea and small amounts of food such as cakes and SANDWICHES. • A **tea strainer** is used to collect the tea leaves when the tea is poured through it into a cup. • A **tea towel**/ *(Br also)* **tea cloth** (*Am* **dish towel/kitchen towel**) is a small cloth used for drying washed plates, knives, forks, etc. • A **tea tray** is a small TRAY (= flat surface for carrying esp. food and drink). • *(Br and Aus)* A **tea trolley**/ *(esp. Am)* **tea wagon/ tea cart** is a small table on wheels, sometimes with an upper and a lower shelf, for serving drinks and food. • PIC〉 **Kitchen**

tea·cake /ˈtiː·keɪk/ *n* [C] *Br* a small round sweet cake containing dried fruit, which is often cut open, heated and eaten with butter • *We had* **toasted** *teacakes and tea.*

teach *(obj)* /tiːtʃ/ *v past* **taught** /£tɔːt, $tɑːt/ to give (someone) knowledge or to instruct or train (someone) • *She works in a bank and he teaches.* [I] • *We have a shortage of people who can teach physics.* [T] • *She taught English* **to** *foreign students.* [T] • *He taught his children English/taught English* **to** *his children.* [+ two objects] • *She was taught at home by her parents.* [T] • *I could teach you* **what** *you need to know.* [T + obj + *wh-* word] • *I can't sew – I wish someone would teach me* **(how)**. [T/T + obj + *wh-* word] • *Who taught you* **to** *cook?* [T + obj + *to* infinitive] • *Failing the test taught me* **to** *work harder.* [T + obj + *to* infinitive] • *Failing the test taught me* **that** *I needed to work harder.* [T + obj + *(that)* clause] • *(Am) Ever since she was a child her dream has been to* **teach school** (= to be a teacher in a school). • A person or experience that **teaches** you **a lesson** improves your future behaviour by making you experience the bad effects of your actions: *Having my unlocked car stolen really taught me a lesson – I'll never do it again.* ○ *He's always leaving his food out in the kitchen so I thought I'd teach him a lesson and I let the cat eat it.* • If someone says that they or an unpleasant experience **will teach you (not) to** do something, they mean that they will stop you from doing it in future by making you experience the bad effects of your action: *So Roger spent the night in a freezing garage, did he? That'll teach him* **to** (= show him that he should not) *go out without his house keys!* • To **teach** your **grandmother to suck eggs** is to try to teach someone how to do something that they already know more about than you. • *(dated)* A **teach-in** is a meeting for discussion on a subject of public interest, often held among college students.

teach·er /£ˈtiː·tʃəʳ, $-tʃɚ/ *n* [C] • *My father was a history teacher.* • A *(Br)* **teacher-training college**/ *(Am)* **teacher's college**/ *(Aus)* **teachers college** is a college which trains teachers. • *(disapproving)* A **teacher's pet** is a student in a class who is liked best by the teacher and therefore treated better than the other students. • LP〉 **Schools and colleges**

teach·ing /ˈtiː·tʃɪŋ/ *n* [U] • *He's always wanted to go into teaching* (= have a job as a teacher). • *Our teaching* **in** *science was fairly poor.* • *The teaching profession is very undervalued.* • *She works in a teaching hospital* (= hospital where medicine is taught). • See also TEACHINGS.

teach·ings /ˈtiː·tʃɪŋz/ *pl n* moral, religious or political opinions, esp. of a famous leader • *Christ's teachings* • *the teachings of St Francis* • *the teachings of Chairman Mao*

tea·cup /ˈtiː·kʌp/ *n* [C] a cup with a handle from which tea is drunk • *a teacup and saucer* • *Mark went and smashed one of my best china teacups.*

teak /tiːk/ *n* [U] (the wood of) a type of large tropical tree • *Is this table teak?* • *a teak tree* • *a teak forest* • *teak furniture* • *teak oil* • *teak veneer* • *a teak-panelled room*

tea·ket·tle /£ˈtiːˌket·l̩, $-ˌket̬-/ *n* **ass over teakettle**, see at ARSE

teal /tiːl/ *n* [C] a small wild DUCK (= a short-legged water bird)

team /tiːm/ *n* [C + sing/pl v] a number of people or animals who do something, esp. sport, together as a group • *a basketball/hockey/netball team* • *a team* **of** *investigators* • *a team* **of** *circus horses* • *Which* **football** *team do you support?* • *Our cricket/swimming team is/are the best.* • *Football is a team* **game**. • *The cart was pulled by a team* (= group) **of** *oxen/huskies.* • *He kicked the ball to his* **team-mate** (= a player on the same team) *who then scored the goal.* • Team is used in a number of phrases which refer to people working together as a group in order to achieve something: *It was a real team* **effort** *– everyone contributed something to the success of the project.* ○ *All the players perform well individually but they seem to lack a little team* **spirit** (= the desire to work as a team). ○ *Only good team* **work** (= everyone working together as a team) *will enable us to get the job done on time.* • LP〉 **Sports**

team up *v adv* [I] • To team up is to join a person or group of people in order to do something, esp. work, together: *They teamed up for a charity performance in July.* ○ *The 82-year-old director teamed up* **with** *scriptwriter Steve Jackim for the $44 million dollar project based on Conrad's novel.* ○ *The banks have teamed up* **with** *the various card protection services to help those who lose their cards or have them stolen.*

team·ster /£ˈtiːmp·stəʳ, $-stɚ/ *n* [C] *Am* someone who drives a TRUCK as a job

tea·pot /£ˈtiː·pɒt, $-pɑːt/ *n* [C] a container with a handle and a SPOUT (= tube-shaped opening through which the tea is poured) in which you make tea and from which tea is served • PIC〉 **Kitchen**

tear CRY /£tɪəʳ, $tɪr/ *n* [C usually pl] a drop of salty liquid which flows from the eye, as a result of strong emotion, esp. unhappiness, or pain • *tears* **of** *remorse/regret/happiness/ joy/laughter* • *Did you notice the tears* **in** *his* **eyes** *when he talked about Diane?* • *We laughed until the tears* **ran/rolled down** *our cheeks.* • *I felt a tear* **trickle down** *my nose.* • *She* **burst into** *tears* (= suddenly started to cry). • *Her* **eyes filled with** *tears as she told me about her son.* • *Why do arguments with you always* **reduce** *me* **to** *tears* (= make me cry)? • *I* **won't shed (any)** *tears* (= I will not be unhappy) *when he goes, I can tell you!* • *I found him* **in tears** (= crying) *in his bedroom.* • **Tear gas** is a gas used by some police and armed forces to control crowds of people. It hurts the eyes and makes them produce tears. • *(infml)* A **tear jerker** is a book, film, play etc. which has a sad story that is intended to make people cry or be sad: *I'd recommend that you take a pile of tissues with you when you see that film – it's a* **real** *tear jerker!* • *"The Tears of a Clown"* (title of a song by Smokey Robinson, 1970) • See also TEARDROP.

tear·ful /£ˈtɪə·fəl, $ˈtɪr-/ *adj* • *Waving Peter off at the airport had made me feel a bit tearful* (= sad and wanting to cry). • *After a tearful farewell at the station, we went our separate ways.* • *Katy's always a bit tearful* (= She tends to cry) *when it's time to go back to school.*

tear·ful·ly /£ˈtɪə·fəl·i, $ˈtɪr-/ *adv* • *We said goodbye tearfully and then he went to board his plane.*

tear·ful·ness /£ˈtɪə·fəl·nəs, $ˈtɪr-/ *n* [U]

tear *(obj)* SEPARATE /£teəʳ, $ter/ *v past simple* **tore** /£tɔːʳ, $tɔːr/, *past part* **torn** /£tɔːn, $tɔːrn/ to pull or be pulled apart, or to pull pieces off • *You have to be very careful with books this old because the paper tends to tear very easily.* [I] • *The pastry tore as I was putting it into the dish.* [I] • *I tore my skirt on the chair as I stood up.* [T] • *A couple of pages had been torn* **out** *of/***from** *the book.* [T] • *He tore the letter* **up** (= tore it into small pieces). [M] • *(fig.) The employer just tore* **up** (= treated as totally unimportant) *the agreement with the union without consultation.* [M] • *She tore his cheque* **into shreds** (= small pieces) *and threw them in the bin.* [T] • *(fig. infml) The examiner just tore my thesis/me* **to shreds** (= severely criticized my work/me). [T] • *The dogs tore the rabbit* **apart/to pieces**. [T] • *(fig.) Our department* *was torn* **apart/to pieces** (= destroyed) *by silly quarrels.* [T] • *(fig.) She tore the room* **apart** (= moved everything, opened all drawers, cupboards, etc.) *looking for her ring.* [M] • *You've torn* **a hole** *in the knee of your trousers.* [T] • *She tore* **(off)** *a strip of material to make a bandage.* [T/M] • If you tear **off** your clothes you remove them quickly and carelessly: *I tore my sweaty clothes off and jumped into the shower.* [M] • *(Br and Aus)* If you **tear a strip off** someone/**tear** them **off a strip** you criticize them severely. • If you tear someone **away from** somewhere, you make them leave there: *They had to tear the little boy away from his dead cat.* [T] ○ *I had to tear my***self** *away from the party at 10 o'clock, but I didn't want to go.* [T] • *(esp. disapproving)* To tear **down** something, esp. a vertical structure, is to destroy it: *They tore down the most beautiful old buildings to put up those monstrosities.* [M] ○ *My fence was torn down in the storm.* [M] • If you are **tearing** your **hair out over** a problem, you are feeling a lot of anxiety over it: *She's been tearing her hair out over the final chapter of her novel for the last month.* • *The pictures of hungry children* **tore at** *my* **heart/tore** *my* **heart out** (= made me very sad). • *Unfortunately, if he doesn't agree with you, he tends to* **tear into** *you* (= attack you with words).

tear /£teəʳ, $ter/ *n* [C] • *Have you seen you've got a tear in the sleeve of your shirt.*

tear [HURRY] /£teəʳ, $ter/ *v* [I always + adv/prep] *past simple* **tore** /£tɔːʳ, $tɔːr/, *past part* **torn** /£tɔːn, $tɔːrn/ *infml* to move hurriedly; to RUSH • *He went tearing along the road after the bus.* • *They tore out of town on their motorbikes.* • *(Br and Aus dated) I can't stop to talk, I'm* **in a tearing hurry** (= in a great hurry).

tear·a·way /£'teə·rə·weɪ, $'ter·ə-/ *n* [C] *Br and Aus infml* a young person, usually male, who behaves in an uncontrolled way and is often causing trouble • *He was a real tearaway at school – he was always in trouble with teachers or with the police.*

tear·drop /£'tɪə·drɒp, $'tɪr·drɑːp/ *n* [C] a single tear • *She was wearing teardrop-shaped earrings.*

tease *(obj)* /tiːz/ *v* to laugh at, joke about or intentionally annoy (another person or animal) • *I used to hate being teased* **about** *my red hair when I was at school.* [T] • *Don't tease the dog by waving that stick if you aren't going to throw it.* [T] • *I was only teasing* (= joking), *I didn't mean to upset you.* [I]

tease /tiːz/ *n* [C] • A tease is someone who is always teasing people: *Johnny, don't be such a tease – leave your sister alone!* • *(slang disapproving)* A tease is also someone who enjoys causing sexual excitement and interest in people with whom she or he does not intend to have sex.

teas·er /£'tiː·zəʳ, $-zɚ/, **brain·teas·er** *n* [C] • A teaser is a problem or difficult question that makes you think for a long while.

tease out *obj*, **tease** *obj* **out** *v adv* [M] to use the fingers to gradually pull apart or straighten the separate threads of a twisted mass of something • *While it was still wet, I gently teased out the tangled knots in Rosie's hair.* • *(fig.) It sometimes takes time to tease the truth out of him.*

teas·el /'tiː·zᵊl/, **tea·zel**, **tea·zle** *n* [C] a tall, branched plant with light blue flowers or its large seed case covered in sharp points, which is popular for dried flower arrangements

tea·spoon /'tiː·spuːn/ *n* [C] a small spoon used to STIR (= mix) tea and coffee in a cup • Compare DESSERTSPOON; TABLESPOON. • [PIC] **Cutlery**

tea·spoon·ful /'tiː·spuːn·fʊl/ *n* [C] • A teaspoonful is the amount a teaspoon can hold but as a standard cook's measure for liquids, one teaspoon (*abbreviation* **tsp**) = 5 ml: *Add a teaspoonful* (= the amount a teaspoon can hold) *of sugar to the sauce.*

teat /tiːt/ *n* [C] an animal's NIPPLE (= one of several raised parts of the chest through which an animal takes its mother's milk) or an artificial one which allows a human baby or an animal to take milk from a bottle

tea·time /'tiː·taɪm/ *n* [C usually sing] the time in the afternoon when some people eat a small meal

tech /tek/ *adj*, *n* [U] *abbreviation for* TECHNICAL or TECHNOLOGY

tech·ni·cal /'tek·nɪ·kᵊl/ *adj* having or needing special, usually learned, skills or knowledge, esp. in science or ENGINEERING • *There have been a number of technical* **problems** *with the production.* • *Despite the array of technical* **wizardry**, *some traditional problems still trouble air crews, such as bad weather conditions.* • *Personally, I found some parts of the book a little too technical to follow.* • *She knows more about the technical aspects of the business* (= the details of how the business works) *than I do.* • See also **technical** at TECHNIQUE. • (GR)

tech·ni·cal·ly /'tek·nɪ·kli/ *adv* • *Technically, it is a very complex process.* • *Technically* **speaking** (= to be completely correct), *"England" only means the country of England, not the whole of the British Isles.*

tech·ni·cal·i·ty /£ˌtek·nɪ'kæl·ə·ti, $-nə'kæl·ə·ti/ *n* [C] a detail or small matter • *He was disqualified from the competition* **on a** *technicality.* • *She lost her case* **on a** *technicality, but feels she won a moral victory.* • *(disapproving) Don't confuse me with technicalities, all I need to know is how to turn the machine on and off.*

tech·ni·cian /tek'nɪʃ·ᵊn/ *n* [C] a worker trained with special skills, esp. in science or ENGINEERING • *a laboratory technician* • *an aircraft technician*

Tech·ni·col·or *trademark*, *Br and Aus also* **tech·ni·col·our** /£'tek·nɪˌkʌl·əʳ, $-ɚ/ *n* [before n], *adj* (from a method of producing cinema films in colour) having many colours or brightly coloured • *a technicolour sunset* • *(disapproving) Her room was painted* **in glorious technicolour.** [U] • *"Joseph and the Amazing Technicolor Dreamcoat"* (title of a musical by Tim Rice and Andrew Lloyd-Webber, 1968)

tech·nique /tek'niːk/ *n* (a) way of doing an activity requiring skill, in the arts, sport, science, etc. • *We have developed a new technique* **for** *detecting errors in the manufacturing process.* [C] • *If you're looking for a new job you'd better brush up your interview technique.* [U] • *The skating duo got full marks for technique but were marked down on artistic expression.* [U] • *She's a wonderfully creative dancer but she doesn't have the technique of a truly great performer.* [U] • (CS) (DK) (N) (PL) (RUS) (S)

tech·ni·cal /'tek·nɪ·kᵊl/ *adj* • Technical means showing technique: *You might not like her style but you cannot deny her technical brilliance/virtuosity as a dancer.* ○ *Kanchelskis is a player of real technical* **skill**. ○ *He's a very technical skier* (= His skills and method are good). • See also TECHNICAL.

tech·ni·cal·ly /'tek·nɪ·kli/ *adv* • *Technically she's the most accomplished dancer in the company but she's not the most exciting to watch.*

tech·ni·cian /tek'nɪʃ·ᵊn/ *n* [C] • A technician is a person whose technique is very good: *A brilliant technician, Palmer was probably the most accomplished pianist of her generation.*

tech·nol·o·gy /£tek'nɒl·ə·dʒi, $-'nɑː·lə-/ *n* (the study and knowledge of) the practical, esp. industrial, use of scientific discoveries • *nuclear technology* • *space-age technology* • *manufacturing technology* • *computer technology* • *What we have here is a new generation of* **advanced/high**-*technology weapons.* [U] • **Modern** *technology is amazing, isn't it.* [U] • *What this country needs is a long-term policy for investment in* **science and** *technology.* [U] • *They're part of a consortium of US companies formed to advance computer technologies.* [C] • *Dairy producers are experimenting with new technologies that aim to make dairy products healthier without spoiling their taste.* [C] • See also BIOTECHNOLOGY.

tech·no·log·i·cal /£ˌtek·nə'lɒdʒ·ɪ·kᵊl, $-'lɑː·dʒɪ-/ *adj* • *We are living in an era of rapid technological change.* • *Technological* **advances** *in computing and telecommunication will reduce the need for many people to travel to work.* • *The company, insisted its president, was about technological* **innovation**, *not gimmicks.*

tech·no·log·i·cal·ly /£'tek·nə'lɒdʒ·ɪ·kli, $-'lɑː·dʒɪ-/ *adv* • *As a company they now have some of the most technologically advanced design and manufacturing systems in Europe.*

tech·nol·o·gist /£tek'nɒl·ə·dʒɪst, $-'nɑː·lə-/ *n* [C] • *a medical/food/computer technologist* • *Worldwide there are still comparatively few female scientists and technologists.*

ted·dy (bear) /'ted·i/ *n* [C] a soft toy bear • *She's kept all her teddy bears from her childhood.* • *They held an exhibition of teddies which had been owned by famous people.* • *Children, parents and teddies are invited to a* **Teddy Bears' picnic** (= a light meal outside to which people bring their toy bears). • [PIC] **Toy**

ted·dy /'ted·i/ *n* [C] a piece of women's underwear for the upper body, without legs or sleeves, worn next to the skin

ted·dy boy, *infml* **ted** /ted/ *n* [C] a young British man, esp. in the 1950s, who typically dressed in narrow trousers, a long, loose jacket and shoes with thick SOLES (= bottoms)

te·di·ous /'tiː·di·əs/ *adj* uninteresting and tiring, esp. because too slow or long; boring • *I spent a tedious hour in a* *traffic jam.* • *Filing papers at the office is a tedious job.* • *The trouble is I find most forms of exercise so tedious.* • *I had an argument with a tedious* (=annoying) *little man who wouldn't accept my card because the signature on it was my husband's.*

te·di·ous·ly /ˈtiː·di·ə·sli/ *adj* • *Second-rate acting and a tediously familiar plot contrive to make this one of the dullest film releases this year.*

te·di·ous·ness /ˈtiː·di·ə·snəs/ *n* [U]

te·di·um /ˈtiː·di·əm/ *n* [U] • Tedium is boredom: *Soldiers often say that the worst thing about fighting is not the moments of terror, but all the hours of tedium in between.* ○ *She had to wait in a room for three hours without so much as a magazine to relieve the tedium.*

tee /tiː/ *n* [C] a short plastic stick with a cup-shaped top on which a golf ball is put to be hit. A tee is also the area where this is used to start the play for each hole. • PIC› Sports

tee off /tiː/ *v adv* [I] • To tee off is to hit a golf ball off the tee, or to begin a game of golf by doing this: *We'll tee off at 10 o'clock.* • See also TEE OFF.

tee up *(obj)* /tiː/ *v adv* [I/M] • To tee up is to put a golf ball on the tee in preparation for playing.

tee off *obj*, **tee** *obj* **off** *v adv* [M] *Am infml* to make (someone) angry • *It really tees me off when she doesn't listen to me.* • *If my children talk back to me, I get teed off.*

teem /tiːm/ *v* [I] to rain heavily • *It's been teeming* **(down)** *all day.* • *It's teeming* **with** *rain.* • *The rain teemed* **down** *all through lunch.*

teem with *obj v prep* [T] to contain large numbers of (esp. animals or humans) • *The river teemed with fish.* • *The jungles are teeming with life.* • *The mall was teeming with shoppers that Saturday.*

teem·ing /ˈtiː·mɪŋ/ *adj* [not gradable] • *the teeming metropolis*

teen·ag·er /£ˈtiːnˌeɪ·dʒəʳ, $-dʒɚ/ *n* [C] a young person between 13 and 19 years old • *There was the usual gang of teenagers outside the cinema.* • *The magazine is aimed at teenagers and young adults.* • LP› Age

teen·age /ˈtiːn·eɪdʒ/, **teen·aged** /ˈtiːn·eɪdʒd/, **teen** /tiːn/ *adj* [before n; not gradable] • *teenage fashions* • *teenage problems* • *a teenaged nephew*

teens /tiːnz/ *pl n* **in** *your* **teens** aged between 13 and 19 • *Both my daughters are in their teens.* • *He's in his* **early/mid/late** *teens.*

teen·y (ween·y) (**-er, -est**) /ˈtiː·ni/, **teen·sy (ween·sy)** /ˈtiːn·zi/ *adj infml* very small • *Just look at those teensy weensy mice!* • *Just a teeny weeny slice of cake for me, please – I'm supposed to be on a diet.* • *(humorous) Isn't that a teeny* **bit** (= very) *exaggerated?*

teen·y·bop·per /£ˈtiː·niˌbɒp·əʳ, $-ˌbɑː·pɚ/ *n* [C] *infml* a TEENAGER (=a person between 13 and 19 years old), esp. a girl, who eagerly follows the most recent fashion, music, and other interests of her age group

tee·pee /ˈtiː·piː/ *n* [C] a TEPEE

tee shirt /tiː/ *n* [C] a T-SHIRT

tee·ter /£ˈtiː·təʳ, $-t̬ɚ/ *v* [I always + adv/prep] to appear to be about to fall while moving or standing • *Delia was teetering around in five-inch heels.* • *The ladder teetered dangerously and I nearly fell off.* • *The old couple teetered down the road.* • *What we are seeing now is a country* **teetering on the brink/edge of** (=dangerously close to) *civil war.*

tee·ter–tot·ter /£ˌtiː·təˈtɒt·əʳ, $-t̬ɚˈtɑː·t̬ɚ/ *n* [C] *Am for* SEESAW • PIC› **Playground**

teeth TOOTH /tiːθ/ *pl of* TOOTH

teeth POWER /tiːθ/ *pl n* effective force or power • *This committee can make recommendations but it has no real teeth.*

teeth AGAINST /tiːθ/ *pl n* **in the teeth of** against, because of, or despite • *The plan collapsed/survived in the teeth of fierce opposition from the public.*

teethe /tiːð/ *v* [I] (of a baby or small child) to grow teeth • *My sister was up most of the night with her baby who's teething.* • *I think Joe's teething – look at the red patches on his cheeks.* • *(Br and Aus)* **Teething troubles/problems** are problems which happen in the early stages of doing something new: *There were the usual teething troubles at the start of the project, but that's to be expected.*

tee·to·tal /£ˌtiːˈtəʊ·tᵊl, $-ˈtoʊ·t̬ᵊl/ *adj* [not gradable] never drinking alcohol or opposed to the drinking of alcohol • *Three-quarters of the 672 doctors interviewed claimed to have fewer than four drinks a week and 12% said they were teetotal.*

tee·to·tal·ler *Br and Aus, Am usually* **tee·to·tal·er** /£ˌtiːˈtəʊ·tᵊl·əʳ, $-ˈtoʊ·t̬ᵊl·ɚ/ *n* [C] • *A confirmed teetotaller, he is said to be the driving force behind the campaign against alcoholism.*

tel, **tel no** *n abbreviation for* telephone number • LP› Letters

tel·e– /£ˌtel·ɪ-, $ˌtel·ə-/ *combining form* over a long distance, done by telephone, or on or for television • *telecommunications* • *telemarketing*

tel·e·com·mu·ni·ca·tions /£ˌtel·ɪ·kəˌmjuː·nɪˈkeɪ·ʃᵊnz, $ˌ-ə-/ *pl n* the sending and receiving of messages over distance, esp. by telephone, radio and television • *a telecommunications satellite* • *the telecommunications industry* • *The company specializes in telecommunications.*

tel·e·gen·ic /£ˌtel·ɪˈdʒen·ɪk, $-əˈ-/ *adj approving* (esp. of a person) appearing attractive on television • *With their new youthful and telegenic leader, the Labour party looks set to woo the voters.*

tel·e·gram /ˈtel·ɪ·græm/, *Am also* **wire** *n* [C] (esp. in the past) a piece of paper with a message sent by TELEGRAPH • *It was while I was in Italy that I got a telegram telling me that my brother had collapsed and was seriously ill.* • *We sent them a message of congratulations* **by** *telegram.* • *In Britain the telegram has been replaced by the Telemessage.*

tel·e·gram·ese /£ˌtel·ɪ·græmˈiːz, $ˌ-ə-/, **tel·e·graph·ese** /£ˌtel·ɪ·grɑːˈfiːz, £-græfˈiːz, $ˌ-ə-/ *n* [U] • Telegramese is a style of writing which ignores unimportant words: *'Can do. Discuss Wednesday p.m.' is telegramese for 'I can do it. We'll discuss it on Wednesday afternoon.'*

tel·e·gram·mat·ic /£tel·ɪ·grəˈmæt·ɪk, $-ə·grəˈmæt̬-/ *adj* • *His writing has an abrupt, telegrammatic style.*

tel·e·graph /£ˈtel·ɪ·grɑːf, £-græf, $ˈ-ə-/ *n* [U] (esp. in the past) a method of sending and receiving messages by electrical or radio signals, or the special equipment for this purpose • *The news came* **by** *telegraph.* • *(Br and Aus)* A **telegraph pole** (*Am* **telephone pole**) is a tall wooden pole to which telephone wires are fixed.

tel·e·graph *obj* /£ˈtel·ɪ·grɑːf, £-græf, $ˈ-ə-/ *v* [T] • *He telegraphed his proposal of marriage* **to** *her from Burma.* • *The story was immediately telegraphed* **to** *New York.* • *They telegraphed me the bad news.* [+ two objects]

tel·e·mar·ket·ing /£ˌtel·ɪˈmɑː·kɪ·tɪŋ, $-əˈmɑːr·kə·t̬ɪŋ/ *n* [U] *esp. Am for* TELESALES

Tel·e·mes·sage *Br* /ˈtel·ɪˌmes·ɪdʒ/, *Am* **Mail·gram** *n* [C] *trademark* a message sent by telephone or TELEX and delivered in printed form • *Telemessages have replaced telegrams in Britain.*

tel·e·ol·o·gy /£ˌtiː·liˈɒl·ə·dʒi, $-ˈɑː·lə-/ *n* [U] *specialized* (in PHILOSOPHY) the belief that everything has a special purpose or use

tel·e·o·log·i·cal /£ˌtiː·li·əˈlɒdʒ·ɪ·kᵊl, $-ˈlɑː·dʒɪ-/ *adj specialized* • *a teleological argument*

te·le·path·y /təˈlep·ə·θi/ *n* [U] the ability to know what is in someone else's mind or communicate with them mentally, without using words or other physical signals • *There existed between them a sort of telepathy which made words sometimes unnecessary.*

tel·e·path·ic /£ˌtel·ɪˈpæθ·ɪk, $-əˈ-/ *adj* • *How did you know what I was thinking? You must be telepathic.*

tel·e·phone /£ˈtel·ɪ·fəʊn, $-ə·foʊn/ *v, n* (to use) a PHONE • *You can telephone from your hotel room.* [I] • *Thousands of cancer sufferers had telephoned the institute in the hope of receiving the new therapy.* [T] • *The telephone's* **ringing** *– will you answer it, please?* [C] • *I tried to contact her* **by** *telephone.* [U] • A **telephone directory** (*infml* **phone book**) contains all the telephone numbers for a particular area, organization, etc. • A **telephone exchange** is the building which contains the equipment for connecting telephone calls. • LP› **Telephone** PIC› **Box**

te·le·pho·nist /təˈlef·ᵊn·ɪst/ *n* [C] *Br* • A telephonist is a **switchboard operator**, see at SWITCHBOARD.

tel·e·pho·to lens /£ˈtel·ɪˌfəʊ·təʊ, $-əˌfoʊ·toʊ/ *n* [C] a camera LENS (= specially shaped glass) that makes distant objects look nearer and larger when they are photographed

tel·e·print·er /£ˈtel·ɪˌprɪn·təʳ, $-t̬ɚ/, *esp. Am* **tel·e·type·writ·er** /£ˌtel·ɪˈtaɪp·raɪ·təʳ, $-t̬ɚ/ *n* [C] a type of electric printer for sending and receiving messages down a telephone line • See also TELEX.

Tel·e·Prompt·er /£ˈtel·ɪˌprɒmp·təʳ, $-ˌprɑːmp·t̬ɚ/ *n* [C] *Am trademark for* AUTOCUE

tel·e·sales /ˈtel·ɪ·seɪls/, *Am and Aus* **tel·e·mar·ket·ing** *n* [U] the advertising or selling of goods or services by telephone

TELEPHONE

A **public/pay** telephone might be **coin operated** or could be a **card phone**.

lift the receiver

insert (= put in) coins or a phone card into the slot

dial the number by pressing the buttons

Finding a telephone number

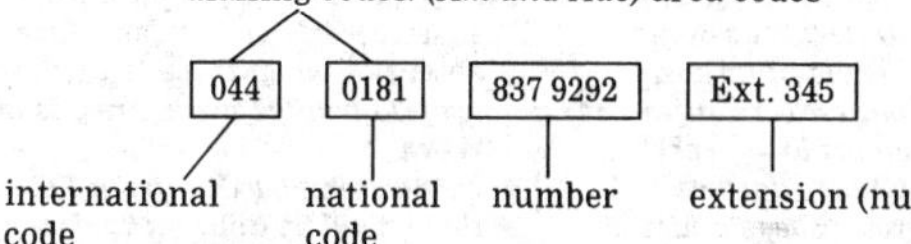

The numbers are usually pronounced separately. For example 90233 is said "nine oh two double three". Someone working in an office has an **extension number** which is used by people within the office. Callers from outside must first telephone the **switchboard** of the company to be connected.

I'm **on** *309 2194. • If you can't* **reach/get** *me at home,* **try** *my work number. I'm on extension 433. • If you don't know the number,* **look** *it* **up** *in the phone book/telephone directory, or dial (Br) directory enquiries / (Am) directory assistance and ask the operator.*

Making a telephone call

- Common phrases meaning to telephone:
  She said she'd **phone/telephone/call/ring** *(you) tomorrow.*
  I'll **give** *you a* **ring/call/phone call**.
  I need to **make** *a* **call/phone call (to** *Brazil***)**.
  Why don't you **ring** *your mother* **up** *and see if she's okay?*
  Mr Richards isn't in this morning. Shall I ask him to **ring/call/phone** *(you)* **back**?
- A **reverse charge call**/*(Am)* **collect call** is paid for by the person who receives it.
- Notice the following uses of *through:*
  Can I call Japan **direct** *from here, or do I have to* **go through** *the operator?*
  The lines were really busy and I couldn't **get through (to** *the airport***)**.
  Can you **put** *me* **through to** *Miss Shaw on extension 345, please?*
- Some people have an *(esp. Br)* **answerphone**/*(esp. Am)* **answering machine** which plays a recorded message to callers if they are not at home. This message usually ends with a 'bleep' sound: *Sorry I'm not at home at the moment. Please leave a message after the bleep/beep.*

Problems

I've been trying to get Sonia all morning but her line/she is always **engaged**/*(Am usually)* **busy**.
"Is that Mike Fraser?" "No. I think you've got **a wrong number** *– this is 456678."*
"Customer accounts, please." "The line's busy – do you want to **hold the line/hold on?**"
It's a **bad/terrible line**, *I can hardly hear you. Can you speak a bit louder?*
Hello, can you connect me to Katie Moore again – we were **cut off** *in the middle of our call.*
The phone is **out of order** *– there's a coin stuck in the slot, I think.*

tel·e·scope DEVICE /£'tel·ɪ·skəʊp, $-ə·skoʊp/ *n* [C] a cylindrical device for making distant objects look nearer and larger, using a combination of LENSES (=specially shaped pieces of glass) or lenses and curved mirrors • *In 1609, Galileo improved the telescope and used it to study the stars and planets.*

tel·e·scop·ic /£ˌtel·ɪ'skɒp·ɪk, $-ə'skɑː·pɪk/ *adj* • *You will see the bird more clearly through the telescopic lens.*

tel·e·scope *(obj)* SHORTEN /£'tel·ɪ·skəʊp, $-ə·skoʊp/ *v* to make or become shorter by reducing the length of the parts • *We had to telescope five visits into two days.* [T] • *When the train crashed, several coaches telescoped into the back of the engine.* [I]

Tel·e·text /£'tel·ɪ·tekst, $'-ə-/ *n* [U] *trademark* a system for giving written information on many subjects (such as news and sports results) by television

tel·e·thon /£'tel·ɪ·θɒn, $-ə·θɑːn/ *n* [C usually sing] a television show, usually several hours long, whose purpose is to make money for CHARITY (=organizations which help people)

tel·e·van·gel·i·sm /ˌtel·ɪ'væn·dʒə·lɪ·zᵊm/ *n* [U] (esp. in the US) the activity of PREACHING (=giving religious speeches) on television in order to persuade people to become Christians and give their money to religious organizations

tel·e·van·gel·ist /ˌtel·ɪ'væn·dʒə·lɪst/ *n* [C] • *The flow of money, for many televangelists, is central to their message as well as their needs.*

tel·e·vise *obj* /£'tel·ɪ·vaɪz, $'-ə-/ *v* [T] to show or broadcast on television • *The leader is now letting the political parties he once banned televise their views for 15 minutes every evening.* • *The match will be televised* **live** (=shown as it is being played) *on BBC Scotland.*

te·le·vised /£'tel·ɪ·vaɪzd, $'-ə-/ *adj* • *Neither issue was the subject of the president's televised address on Friday night.*

tel·e·vi·sion /£'tel·ɪ·vɪʒ·ᵊn, £ˌ-'--, $'tel·ə·vɪʒ-/, **TV**, *Br and Aus infml* **tel·ly** *n* a box-like device with a screen which receives electrical signals and changes them into moving images and sound, or the method or business of sending images and sound by electrical signals • *a colour/black-and-white television* • *television news* • *a television commercial* • *a television show* • *television coverage* • *a television newscaster/producer/reporter* • *Could you turn the television down.* [C] • *Television was first introduced in Britain in the 1930s.* [U] • *It's one of the few television* **programmes** *that I always make a point of watching.* • *Is there anything interesting* **on** *television tonight?*

[U] • *Clare has worked* **in** *television since she left college.* [U] • *Your problem is that you* **watch** *too much television.* [U] • PIC> **Room**

tel·ex /ˈtel·eks/ *n* a method of sending written messages down a telephone line from one TELEPRINTER to another, the machine which does this, or the message itself • *The details were sent* **by** *telex.* [U] • *The telex (machine) is on the third floor.* [C] • *Two telexes came while you were away.* [C]

tel·ex *(obj)* /ˈtel·eks/ *v* • *We telexed him the news at once.* [+ two objects] • *They telexed us* **that** *they needed more time.* [+ obj + *that* clause] • *Telex him* **to** *stay another week.* [T + obj + *to* infinitive] • *I don't write letters anymore, I just telex instead.* [I]

tell *(obj)* SPEAK /tel/ *v past* **told** /£təuld, $tould/ to give information or instructions, esp. by using speech; to say (something) to (someone) • *He told his problems* **to** *his wife.* [T] • *Can you tell me the way to the station?* [+ two objects] • *Tell me* **about** *your holiday then.* [T] • *(fml) He told us* **of** *his extraordinary childhood.* [T] • *(literary) He told* **of** *faraway lands, beautiful maidens and mysterious one-eyed creatures.* [I] • *Did you tell anyone* **(that)** *you were coming to see me?* [T + obj + (*that*) clause] • *The book told him* **what** *to do*/**how** *to do it.* [T + obj + *wh-* word] • *"I'm leaving you," she told him.* [+ obj + clause] • *I told* (= ordered) *her* **to** *go home.* [T + obj + *to* infinitive] • *Do* **what** *you are told* (= ordered to do). [T + obj + *wh-* word] • *I was told not* **to** *trust what I read in the newspapers.* [T + obj + *to* infinitive] • *She's always* **telling lies** (= saying things which are not true). • *How do you know she's* **telling the truth** (= being honest)*?* • **To tell (you) the truth** (= To be honest), *I didn't understand a word of what he was saying.* • **I told you so** means I warned you that something bad would happen and now it has. • *My daughter has just learned to* **tell the time** (= understand a clock). • *Who's been* **telling tales (out of school)** (= talking about other people's secrets)*?* • *(infml)* If you **tell on** someone, you are giving information about something, usually bad, that they have said or done, to someone else, esp. a person in authority. • *At the fair, there was a lady who* **told** *your* **fortune**/**told fortunes** (= told you what would happen to you in the future). • *(Br and Aus)* **Tell me another**/*(Am and Aus)* **Tell me another one** means I don't believe what you've told me: *"I worked all day yesterday." "Oh yeah, tell me another!"* • *(infml)* **You're telling me** means I strongly agree with what you have just said: *"Stephen's in such a bad mood today." "You're telling me."* • *(infml)* If you **tell it like it is**, you tell the facts without hiding anything. • A **tell-tale** (*Am usually* **tattletale**, *Aus* **dobber**) is a person, esp. a child, who secretly tells someone in authority, esp. a teacher, that someone else has done something bad in order to cause trouble. • See also TELLTALE. • LP> **Say**

tell *(obj)* KNOW /tel/ *v past* **told** /£təuld, $tould/ to know, recognize or be certain • *"He's Dutch." "How can you tell?"* [I] • *It's too dark for me to tell* **what** *it says on the sign.* [+ *wh-* word] • *I could tell* **(that)** *you were unhappy.* [+ (*that*) clause] • *It's easy to tell a blackbird* **by/from** *its song.* [T] • *As babies, the twins were so similar that I just couldn't* **tell** *them* **apart** (= didn't know which was which). • *This coffee is about half the price of that one and yet you really can't* **tell the difference** (= notice any difference in quality). • **There is no telling** (= there is no way of knowing) *what the future will hold for them.* • **You never can tell/You can never tell** means you can never know or be certain: *Who knows what will happen to Peter and me in the future – you can never tell.*

tell HAVE AN EFFECT /tel/ *v* [I] *past* **told** /£təuld, $tould/ to make a noticeable difference; to have an effect • *She's been under a lot of stress recently and it's starting to tell.* • *(Br fml)* To tell **against** someone is to have a negative or damaging effect on them: *His reputation as a troublemaker told against him when he tried to change his job.* • To tell **on** means to have a bad effect on someone's health or behaviour: *A succession of late nights had begun to tell on him and his work was suffering.* ○ *You might not feel it now but these exercises will really begin to tell on you tomorrow.*

tell·ing /ˈtel·ɪŋ/ *adj* • *He didn't turn up for the meeting and I found that very telling* (= It showed his hidden intentions). • *(fml) The most telling* (= most effective) *argument for wearing seat belts is the number of lives they save.*

tell off *obj*, **tell** *obj* **off** *v adv* [M] to speak severely to and criticize (someone who has done something wrong) • *The teacher told me off* **for** *swearing.* • *I'll have to tell him off* **about** *leaving that door unlocked.*

tell·ing–off /£tel·ɪŋˈɒf, $-ˈɑːf/ *n* [C] *pl* **tellings-off** • *He* **gave** *me a good telling-off* **for** *forgetting the meeting.*

tel·ler /£ˈtel·əʳ, $-ɚ/ *n* [C] a person who counts votes at an election or *(Am and Aus)* a person employed in a bank to receive and pay out money

tell·tale /ˈtel·teɪl/ *adj* [before n] allowing a secret to become known • *She found lipstick all over his shirts – the telltale* **sign** *that Katherine had been around again.*

tel·ly /ˈtel·i/ *n Br and Aus infml for* TELEVISION • *What's on telly tonight?* [U] • *We've just bought a new telly.* [C]

te·mer·i·ty /£təˈmer·ɪ·ti, $-ə·t̬i/ *n* [U] *fml disapproving* a willingness to do or say something that shocks, angers or upsets other people • *She* **had the** *temerity* **to** *call me a liar.* [+ *to* infinitive] • *He had the temerity to tell me that smoking was bad for me when I know that he smokes himself.* [+ *to* infinitive]

temp /temp/ *n* [C] *infml* a person employed to work for a short period, esp. in an office while another person is absent or when there is extra work • *We'll have to get a temp to help us while Anne is on maternity leave.* • LP> **Work**

temp /temp/ *v* [I] *infml* • *I decided to temp for a while so that I could try different kinds of jobs.*

tem·per BEHAVIOUR /£ˈtem·pəʳ, $-pɚ/ *n* the usual state of your feelings which makes you become angry easily or stay calm • *John has* **a** *bad/foul temper* (= He becomes angry easily). [C] • *I admire people with* **an** *even temper* (= who are naturally calm). [C] • *She has* **a** *very sweet temper* (= She is naturally very pleasant). [C] • *I found it hard to* **keep** *my temper* (= not become angry) *with so many things going wrong.* [C] • *The children behaved so badly that I* **lost** *my temper* (= I became angry). [C] • Your temper is also the way you are feeling at a particular time: *He is* **in a** *bad/good temper* (= He is angry/happy at the moment). [C] • *Ask her when she's* **in a** *better temper.* [C] • Temper is also a tendency to become angry easily: *You should learn how to control your temper.* [C] ○ *He has a very quick temper* (= He becomes angry easily). [C] ○ *She had a sudden fit of temper and through a glass vase at him.* [U] • If you say that **tempers were getting (rather) frayed/short**, you mean that people were getting angry with each other.

–tem·pered /£-ˌtem·pəd, $-pɚd, ˈ--/ *combining form* • -tempered means having or showing the stated type of temper: *even-tempered* ○ *sweet-tempered* ○ *bad-tempered* ○ *ill-tempered* ○ *short-tempered*

tem·per *obj* REDUCE /£ˈtem·pəʳ, $-pɚ/ *v* [T] *fml* to reduce the pleasant or unpleasant effects of (something) • *His joy that she was alive was tempered by the knowledge that she would never walk again.* • *Breaking both his legs hasn't tempered his enthusiasm for rock climbing.* • *He tried to temper the bad news* **with** *some hope of better things in the future.*

tem·per *obj* METAL /£ˈtem·pəʳ, $-pɚ/ *v* [T] to heat and then cool (a metal) in order to bring it to the correct degree of hardness or elasticity

tem·pe·ra /£ˈtem·pᵊr·ə, $-pɚ·ə/ *n* [U] a method of painting with colours which are mixed with egg and water

tem·per·a·ment /£ˈtem·pᵊr·ə·mənt, £-prə·mənt, $-pɚ·ə-/ *n* the usual state of mind of a person or animal which is shown in the way that they behave • *He's got a fiery/excitable temperament.* [C] • *She is quiet* **by** *temperament.* [U] • *Judges are usually people* **of** *conservative temperament.* [U] • *Labradors make good guide dogs because of their calm temperament.* [U] • *The degree to which different people cope with stress depends on their temperament.* [U]

tem·per·a·men·tal /£ˌtem·pᵊr·əˈmen·tᵊl, £-prəˈ-, $-pɚ·əˈmen·t̬ᵊl/ *adj* • Temperamental means caused by your own character or feelings: *I have a temperamental dislike of crowds and large meetings.* • If someone is temperamental, their mood tends to change very suddenly: *She's very temperamental.* ○ *They're a very temperamental couple.* • *(infml)* If a machine is temperamental, it sometimes works and sometimes does not: *You have to treat our video recorder very carefully – it's rather temperamental.*

tem·per·a·men·tal·ly /£ˌtem·pᵊr·əˈmen·tᵊl·i, £-prəˈ-, $-pɚ·əˈmen·t̬ᵊl-/ *adv* • *He's temperamentally unsuited to taking responsibility of any kind.*

tem·per·ance /£ˈtem·pᵊr·ᵊnts, £ˈ-prənts, $-pɚ·ᵊnts/ *n* [U] *fml* control of your own behaviour, such as not drinking or eating too much • *As a Methodist, he was a fervent advocate of temperance.* • Temperance is also the habit of not drinking alcohol because you believe it is dangerous or wrong: *Temperance societies were set up in the 18th and 19th centuries to persuade people to stop drinking alcohol.*

tem·per·ate /£'tem·pər·ət, £'-prət, $-pɚ·ət/ *adj fml* • If someone's behaviour is temperate, it is calm and controlled: *He is a sensible and temperate man who managed to negotiate an agreement between the two sides.* ○ *Temperate criticism can encourage people to make improvements.*

tem·per·ate /£'tem·pər·ət, £'-prət, $-pɚ·ət/ *adj* (of weather conditions) neither very hot nor very cold • *Britain's climate is temperate – it is neither tropical nor arctic.* • Plants that are temperate grow naturally in places where the weather is not extreme.

tem·per·a·ture /£'tem·prə·tʃər, $-pɚ·ə·tʃɚ/ *n* the measured amount of heat in a place or in the body • *What are the average summer temperatures in the north and south of the country?* [C] • *Preheat the oven to a temperature of 200 degrees Celsius.* [C] • *The normal body temperature of an adult is about 37°C.* [C] • *There has been a sudden rise in temperature over the past few days* (=The weather has become warmer). [U] • If you say that the temperature in a particular situation is rising, you mean that it is likely to become violent because people have become angry: *The temperature of the discussion started to rise as each side added its own arguments.* [U] • If you **are running/have a temperature**, you have a high temperature and are ill. • You **take** your **temperature** with a THERMOMETER (=an instrument for measuring heat in the body) to discover how high it is. • LP **Measurements, Units**

tem·pest /'tem·pɪst/ *n* [C] *literary* a violent storm • *The ship was blown 200 miles off-course by the tempest.*

tem·pes·tu·ous /tem'pes·tju·əs/ *adj* • *(literary) We set sail in tempestuous* (=stormy) *conditions.* • If something such as a relationship or performance is tempestuous, it is full of strong emotions: *They got divorced in 1992 after a tempestuous marriage.* • If someone's life is tempestuous, it is full of successes and failures: *He had a tempestuous career, becoming the youngest world champion at the age of 23 and retiring at the age of 29.* • A discussion or argument which is tempestuous is one in which people disagree strongly with one another.

tem·pes·tu·ous·ly /tem'pes·tju·ə·sli/ *adv* • To do something tempestuously is to do it in a way which expresses the strong emotions you are feeling: *He picked up the vase and hurled it tempestuously at the wall.*

tem·plate /'tem·pleɪt/ *n* [C] a pattern made of metal, plastic or paper, which is used for making many copies of a shape or to help cut material accurately • *Make a circle out of cardboard and use it as a template to cut 12 circles of cloth.*

tem·ple BUILDING /'tem·pl̩/ *n* [C] a building used for the worship of a god or gods in some religions • *a Sikh temple* • *a Roman/Greek temple* • *The temple was built in the 12th century and is filled with ornate carvings.* • Ⓕ

tem·ple BODY PART /'tem·pl̩/ *n* [C] the flat area at each side of the top part of the head • *He had a large bruise on his left temple.* • Ⓕ

tem·po /£'tem·pəʊ, $-poʊ/ *n pl* **tempos** or *specialized* **tempi** /'tem·piː/ *fml* the speed at which an event happens, or *(specialized)* the speed at which a piece of music is played • *The tempo* **of** *change has increased this year.* [C] • *We're going to have to* **up** *the tempo* (=work faster) *if we're to finish on time.* [C] • *(specialized) Which of these tempi do you think is the most appropriate for this piece?* [C] • *(specialized) Did you notice the change* **in** *tempo in the middle of the piece?* [U] • Ⓝⓛ

tem·po·ral /£'tem·pər·əl, $-pɚ·əl/ *adj fml* relating to practical matters or material things • *Temporal power and wealth are more important to many people than a spiritual promise of life after death.*

tem·po·ra·ry /£'tem·pər·ər·i, £-prər-, $-pə·rer·i/ *adj* not lasting or needed for very long • *The ceasefire will only provide a temporary solution to the crisis.* • *The council is using mobile homes as temporary housing for homeless families.* • *The company has a large workforce of permanent and temporary staff.* • Compare PERMANENT. • LP **Work**

tem·po·rar·i·ly /£'tem·pər·er·ɪ·li, $-pə·rer-/ *adv* • *This office is closed temporarily for redecoration.*

tem·po·rize, *Br and Aus usually* **-ise** /£'tem·pər·aɪz, $-pə·raɪz/ *v* [I] *fml disapproving* to delay making a decision or stating your opinion in order to obtain an advantage • *The government temporized for months, waiting for the economy to pick up before calling an election.*

tempt *obj* /tempt/ *v* [T] to persuade (someone) to do something, esp. an action which seems unwise • *The offer of a free TV tempted her* **into** *buying the car.* • *They tempted him to join the company* **by** *offering him a large salary and a company car.* • If you are tempted to do something, you want to do it: *"Did you apply for that job?" "Well, I was very tempted but in the end I decided not to."* ○ *I was* **sorely** (=very) *tempted* **to** *resign after my boss was so rude to me.* [+ obj + *to* infinitive] • If something tempts you, it attracts you and makes you want it: *"Would you like any dessert?" "I'm very tempted by that apple tart."* ○ *The sunny day tempted me* **into** (=made me want to wear) *shorts and a T-shirt.* • If you **tempt fate/providence** by doing something, you take a foolish risk by doing it and depend too much on your good luck: *You're tempting fate by riding your bike without wearing a cycle helmet.*

temp·ta·tion /temp'teɪ·ʃən/ *n* • *Advertising relies heavily on temptation* (=trying to attract people). [U] • Temptation is also the desire to do or have something which you know you should not do or have: *I know I shouldn't eat chocolate cake when I'm dieting, but I find it hard to* **resist** *temptation.* [U] ○ *As a young actress, she managed to* **resist** *the temptation* **to** *move to Hollywood and become a film star.* [C + *to* infinitive] • A temptation is something that you want to do or have: *After living in Manhattan for five years, they succumbed to the temptations of life in the country.* [C] • *"I can resist everything except temptation"* (Oscar Wilde in the play *Lady Windermere's fan*, 1891) • *"Lead us not into temptation"* (Bible *The Lord's Prayer*, St Matthew 6.9)

tempt·ing /'temp·tɪŋ/ *adj* • *The display of fresh fruit looked tempting* (=attractive). • If something is tempting to do, you want to do it: *It's tempting* **to** *blame television for the increase in crime.* [+ *to* infinitive]

tempt·ing·ly /£'temp·tɪŋ·li, $-t̬ɪŋ-/ *adv* • *Unfortunately, war is sometimes temptingly simpler than diplomacy.*

tempt·ress /'temp·trɪs/ *n* [C] *literary or humorous* a woman who tries to sexually attract men

ten /ten/ *determiner, pronoun, n* (the number) 10 • *nine, ten, eleven* • *a ten-seater bus* • *a ten-volume dictionary* • *There were ten people on the bus.* • *"How many apples are there?" "Ten."* • *The teacher wrote a big red ten at the bottom of my test, to show that I'd got all the answers right.* [C] • If you say **ten to one** that something will or will not happen, you mean it is very likely that it will or will not happen: *Ten to one he won't be there tonight.* • **The Ten Commandments** are the rules of behaviour which God gave to Israel through Moses on Mount Sinai, according to the Old Testament of the Bible. • *(esp. Am)* If you say **ten-four** (also **10-4**), you mean that a message has been received.

tenth /tentθ/ *determiner, pronoun, adj, adv* [not gradable], *n* • *This is his tenth year of working for the company.* • *My birthday is on the tenth of May.* • *He was tenth in the batting order/He batted tenth.* • A tenth is one of the ten equal parts into which something is divided: *As one of the ten partners in the firm, he receives a tenth of the profits.*

ten·a·ble /'ten·ə·bl̩/ *adj* (of an opinion or position) that is able to be defended successfully or held for a particular period of time • *His theory is no longer tenable now that new facts have appeared.* • *The university fellowship is tenable* **for** (=lasts for) *three years.*

te·na·cious /tə'neɪ·ʃəs/ *adj* holding tightly onto something, or keeping an opinion in a determined way • *The baby took my finger in its tenacious little fist.* • *The conservation group was tenacious* **in** *its opposition to the new airport.*

te·na·cious·ly /tə'neɪ·ʃə·sli/ *adv* • *She has fought tenaciously* (=in a determined way) *to maintain her authority in the city.*

te·nac·i·ty /£tə'næs·ə·ti, $-t̬i/ *n* [U] • Tenacity is the determination to continue what you are doing: *In their campaign, the women proved their ability to unite behind a political cause and pursue it with tenacity.*

ten·ant /'ten·ənt/ *n* [C] a person who pays rent for the use of land or a building • *The building has trouble attracting tenants willing to pay its relatively high rents.* • *The landlord threatened to evict the tenants if they didn't pay the rent they owed.* • *(Br) The government has made it possible for* **council** *tenants to buy the houses and flats that they have been renting.*

ten·an·cy /'ten·ənt·si/ *n* • Tenancy is the right to use land or live in a building on payment of rent: *She has sole tenancy of the apartment.* [U] ○ *He went to court to evict the family from the tenancy of his London home.* [C] ○ *We have a 12-month tenancy agreement.* • A tenancy is the period of time for which you have the right to use a building or piece of land: *I have a two-year tenancy on the house.* [C]

tend BE LIKELY /tend/ *v* [I] to be likely to behave in a particular way or have a particular characteristic • *She tends not* **to** *go away in the summer.* [+ *to* infinitive] • *We tend* **to** *get cold winters and warm, dry summers in this part of the country.* [+ *to* infinitive] • *I am tending* **towards** (= I am likely to choose) *Sue's plan rather than David's.*

ten·den·cy /ˈten·dənt·si/ *n* [C] • If you have a particular tendency, you are likely to behave in that way or like that particular thing: *His tendency* **to** *exaggerate is well known.* [+ *to* infinitive] ○ *She showed musical tendencies from an early age.* ○ *He's always had a tendency* **towards** (= He has always liked) *fast cars.* ○ *How do we know if we have a hereditary tendency* **towards** (= if we are likely to suffer from) *a particular disease?* • If there is a tendency for something to happen, it is likely to happen or it often happens: *There is a tendency* **for** *unemployment to rise in the summer.* • If there is a tendency to do something, it starts to happen more often or starts to increase: *There is a growing tendency* **to** (= More and more people are starting to) *regard money more highly than quality of life.* [+ *to* infinitive]

tend *obj* CARE /tend/ *v* [T] to care for (something or someone) • *He carefully tended his sunflower plants all summer.* • *The nurse gently tended the patient's cuts and bruises.* • *The shepherds were tending their sheep on the hillside.* • If you tend **to** someone or something, you deal with their problems or needs: *Would you mind waiting? I'm tending to another customer at the moment.*

ten·den·tious /tenˈden·tʃəs/ *adj fml disapproving* (of speech or writing) expressing or supporting a particular opinion which many other people disagree with • *He claims that the article gives a distorted and highly tendentious view of the political situation in the country.*

ten·den·tious·ly /tenˈden·tʃə·sli/ *adv fml disapproving*

ten·den·tious·ness /tenˈden·tʃə·snəs/ *n* [U] *fml disapproving*

ten·der GENTLE /£ˈten·dəʳ, $-dɚ/ *adj* **-er, -est** gentle, caring or sympathetic • *She gave him a tender look/smile.* • *What you need is some tender loving care.* • *He resolved to be more tender and considerate towards his family.* • *The film is a moving, tender love story.* • If someone is **tender-hearted**, they are very kind and sympathetic: *She is so tender-hearted that everyone tells her their problems.*

ten·der·ly /£ˈten·dᵊl·i, $-dɚ·li/ *adv* • *She stroked the cat tenderly behind the ears.* • *He talked tenderly of his wife and daughter who were living in New Zealand.*

ten·der·ness /£ˈten·də·nəs, $-dɚ-/ *n* [U] • *She nursed her father with devotion and great tenderness during his long illness.* • *"Try a Little Tenderness"* (title of a song written by Harry Woods, James Campbell and Reginald Connelly, 1933)

ten·der PAINFUL /£ˈten·dəʳ, $-dɚ/ *adj* **-er, -est** (of part of the body) painful, sore or uncomfortable when touched • *My arm was very tender after the injection.* • *Babies' skin is very tender, so you need to use mild soap.* • *(fig.) Be careful what you say to him about his weight because it's a tender subject* (= he gets upset about it easily).

ten·der·ness /£ˈten·də·nəs, $-dɚ-/ *n* [U] • *There was an area of tenderness and swelling on her lower leg.*

ten·der SOFT /£ˈten·dəʳ, $-dɚ/ *adj* **-er, -est** (of meat or vegetables) easy to cut or chew • *My steak was juicy and beautifully tender.* • *For this recipe, you need 500g of tender young spinach.* • Tender plants are those which are easily damaged by cold weather. • *(literary)* Tender is also used to mean young: *He was a child* **of** *tender* **years**. ○ *She was married* **at** *a tender* **age**. ○ *He was sent off to boarding school* **at** *the tender* **age of** *seven.*

ten·der·ize *obj, Br and Aus usually* **-ise** /£ˈten·dᵊr·aɪz, $-də·raɪz/ *v* [T] • To tenderize meat is to make it tender by beating it or preparing it in a particular way: *Leave the beef to soak overnight in a marinade to tenderize it.*

ten·der OFFER /£ˈten·dəʳ, $-dɚ/ *n* [C] a written or formal offer to supply goods or do a job for an agreed price • *Three builders put in/submitted tenders* **for** *our new garage.* • *The council has* **invited** *tenders for the building contract.* • *Our company has* **won** *the tender for the new sports complex.* • *(specialized)* A tender is also a written offer to buy or sell shares in a company: *He acquired Fairchild Industries in a $400 million tender offer last week.* • *(Br)* If you **put** work **out for tender**, you ask people to make offers to do it: *Education departments in all the prisons are being put out to tender.*

ten·der /£ˈten·dəʳ, $-dɚ/ *v* • If you tender for a job, you make a formal offer to do it for a stated price: *Five companies have tendered* **for** *the hospital contract.* [I] • *(specialized)* If you tender for something such as shares, you make a formal offer to buy them for a stated price. [I] • *(fml)* To tender also means to give or offer something: *Please tender the exact fare.* [T] ○ *The health minister has tendered her* **resignation** (= has offered to leave her job). [T]

ten·der CONTAINER /£ˈten·dəʳ, $-dɚ/ *n* [C] *specialized* a vehicle used for transporting water, wood or coal, esp. one which is pulled behind a railway engine or used by the fire service, or a small boat used for transporting people or goods between a larger boat and the coast

ten·der·loin /£ˈten·dᵊl·ɔɪn, $-dɚ·lɔɪn/ *n* [U] a strip of meat taken from the lower back of cows or pigs, which is not fatty and is easy to cut or chew

ten·don /ˈten·dən/ *n* [C] *specialized for* SINEW

ten·dril /ˈten·drᵊl/ *n* [C] a thin, stem-like part of a climbing plant which holds on to walls or other plants for support

ten·e·ment /ˈten·ə·mənt/ *n* [C] a large building divided into apartments, usually in a poor area of a city • *Although every tenement has its own balcony, none of them is painted and the overall impression is one of drabness.* • *They live in a grim tenement* **block** *on the edge of the city.*

ten·et /ˈten·ɪt/ *n* [C] *fml* one of the principles on which a belief or theory is based • *It is a tenet of contemporary psychology that an individual's mental health is supported by having good social networks.*

ten·ner /£ˈten·əʳ, $-ɚ/ *n* [C] *infml (Br)* a £10 note, or *(Am and Aus)* a $10 note • *She said she'd give me a tenner for my bike.* • *Have you got change for a tenner?* • See also FIVER. • LP› **Money**

ten·nis /ˈten·ɪs/ *n* [U] a game played between two or four people on a specially marked playing area which involves hitting a small ball across a central net • *I play a lot of tennis in the summer.* • *She has beaten me in every tennis* **match** *we've played.* • *He's just bought an expensive new tennis* **racket**. • **Tennis elbow** is a painful swelling near the ELBOW (= a joint in the arm) which is caused by frequent twisting of the hand and arm. • A **tennis shoe** is a sports shoe with a rubber bottom and a top made of leather or strong cotton. • LP› **Sports**

ten·on /ˈten·ən/ *n* [C] *specialized* the end of a piece of wood which is shaped to fit into a MORTISE (= an opening) in another piece of wood to form a joint • A **tenon saw** (*Am* **back saw**) is a small tool with a sharp thin blade and a strong metal back. • PIC› **Tools**

ten·or MUSIC /£ˈten·əʳ, $-ɚ/ *n* [C] a male singer with a high voice, or (esp. in combinations) a musical instrument which has the same range of notes as the tenor singing voice • *Our choir is short of tenors.* • *She plays the tenor recorder in the school orchestra.* • *He plays the tenor saxophone in a jazz band.*

ten·or CHARACTER /£ˈten·əʳ, $-ɚ/ *n* [U] *fml* the general meaning, character or pattern of something • *I followed the tenor* **of** *his speech, but I found the details hard to understand.* • *The* **even** *tenor* **of** *their lives was shattered by the arrival of a new baby.* • *I think we should* **raise** *the tenor* **of** (= improve the quality of) *the proceedings.*

ten·pin bowl·ing /ˈten·pɪn/, *Am* **ten·pins** /ˈten·pɪnz/ *n* [U] **bowling**, see at BOWL ROLL

tense STRETCHED /tents/ *adj* **-r, -st** (of your body or part of the body) stretched tight and stiff • *His biceps were hard and tense.* • *You cannot play the piano properly if your fingers are too tense.*

tense *(obj)* /tents/ *v* • If you or your muscles tense **(up)**, your muscles stiffen and become stretched tight because you are frightened or are preparing yourself to do something: *She tensed up as the car swerved.* [I] ○ *He tensed his body, waiting for the blow to fall.* [T] ○ *The muscles in his arms tensed visibly.* [T]

tense·ly /ˈtent·sli/ *adv* • *His clenched fists were tensely tightening and relaxing in time with every word he spoke.*

tense·ness /ˈtent·snəs/ *n* [U] • *You should always warm up before a race to lose any tenseness you may have.*

ten·sile /£ˈtent·saɪl, $-sɪl/ *adj fml* • If a material is tensile, it can be stretched: *Cotton is a relatively tensile material and is easier to stretch than wool.* • *(specialized)* The **tensile strength** of a material such as wire, rope or stone is its ability to support a load without breaking: *White marble is often used for stonecarving because it combines the right level of hardness with tensile strength.*

ten·sion /ˈtent·ʃᵊn/ *n* [U] • The tension of a wire or rope is the degree to which it is stretched: *There is not enough tension in the wires – pull them tighter.* • See also **tension** at TENSE NERVOUS.

tense NERVOUS /tents/ *adj* **-r, -st** nervous and anxious and unable to relax • *She was very tense as she waited for the interview.* • If a situation is tense, it causes feelings of anxiety: *The family was facing a very tense financial situation.*

tensed up /tentst/ *adj* • If someone is tensed up, they are very nervous and worried and are unable to relax because of something that is going to happen: *You seem very tensed up. Are you still waiting for that phone call?*

tense·ly /'tent·sli/ *adv* • *He tensely ran his fingers through his hair as he sat in the dentist's waiting room.*

ten·sion /'tent·ʃᵊn/ *n* [U] • Tension is a feeling of nervousness before an important or difficult event: *You could feel the tension in the room as we waited for our exam results.* • See also **tension** at TENSE STRETCHED.

tense VERB FORM /tents/ *n* [C] any of the forms of a verb which show the time at which an action happened • *"I sing" is present tense and "I will sing" is future tense.* • LP **Tenses**

tent /tent/ *n* [C] a movable shelter usually made of strong cotton, which is supported by poles and held in position by ropes fixed into the ground with hooked nails • *When I went camping with my brother, we slept in a two-man tent.* • *The first thing to do when you set up camp is to pitch/put up/erect your tent.* • *As soon as we got to the festival, he headed straight for the* **beer tent** (=the large tent where beer is served). • *Refreshments are being served in the* **tea tent**.

ten·ta·cle /£'ten·tə·kl̩, $-t̬ə-/ *n* [C] one of the long thin arm-like parts of particular sea creatures, which are used for feeling and holding things, catching food and moving • *An octopus has eight long tentacles.*

ten·ta·tive /£'ten·tə·tɪv, $-t̬ə·t̬ɪv/ *adj* (of a plan or idea) not certain or agreed, or (of a suggestion or action) said or done in a careful but uncertain way because you are not sure if you are right • *I have made tentative plans to take a trip to Seattle in July.* • *I think we're moving to a bigger house in June, but it's only tentative.* • *After looking at all the applications, we reached the tentative conclusion that three or four people might be worth interviewing.*

ten·ta·tive·ly /£'ten·tə·tɪv·li, $-t̬ə·t̬ɪv-/ *adv* • If you do or say something tentatively, you do or say it in an uncertain way: *She spoke tentatively, scared that someone might interrupt her or criticize her ideas.*

ten·ta·tive·ness /£'ten·tə·tɪv·nəs, $-t̬ə·t̬ɪv-/ *n* [U] • *The tentativeness of his answer made me suspect his honesty.*

ten·ter·hooks /£'ten·tə·hʊks, $-t̬ɚ-/ *pl n* **on tenterhooks** worried or anxious about something that is going to happen • *I was on tenterhooks* **to** *find out who had won.* [+ *to* infinitive] • *We were* **kept** *on tenterhooks all morning until the telephone rang.*

tenth /tentθ/ *pronoun, n, determiner, adv* [not gradable] See at TEN

ten·u·ous /'ten·ju·əs/ *adj* weak; easily damaged or proved false • *I found an excuse to phone her, but it was rather tenuous.* • *We were only able to make a tenuous connection between the two robberies.*

ten·ure /£'ten·jəʳ, £-jʊəʳ, $-jɚ, $-jʊr/ *n* [U] *fml* the legal possession of land, a job or an official public position, or the period of time during which you possess it • *They have bought the house with a 999-year lease which gives them security of tenure.* • *During his tenure as dean, he had a real influence on the students.* • If you **have** tenure in your job, your job is permanent: *She is one of the few lecturers in this department who have tenure.*

te·pee, tee·pee /'tiː·piː/ *n* [C] a type of round tent made from animal skins which is the typical shelter of some Native Americans

tep·id /'tep·ɪd/ *adj* (of liquid) not very warm • *A baby's bath water should be tepid.* • A tepid reaction is one which is not enthusiastic: *I got a tepid response to my suggestion that we should start work earlier.*

te·qui·la /tə'kiː·lə/ *n* a strong alcoholic drink originally from Mexico • *Tequila is used in a lot of cocktails.* [U] • *I'd like a tequila and lemonade, please.* [C] • A **tequila slammer** is a drink consisting of tequila mixed with a sweet fizzy drink, which is shaken and then drunk very quickly.

ter·cen·ten·a·ry *esp. Br* /£,tɜː·sen'tiː·nᵊr·i, £-'ten·ᵊr-, $tɚ'sen·t̬ə·ner-/, *esp. Am* **ter·cen·ten·ni·al** /£,tɜː·sen'ten·i·əl, $,tɜːr-/ *n* [C] the day or year which is 300 years after an important event • *This year is the tercentenary* **of** *the poet's birth.* • *Tecentenary celebrations are being held next year to mark the founding of the college.*

term TIME /£tɜːm, $tɜːrm/ *n* [C] the fixed period of time which something lasts for • *He received a prison term/a term of imprisonment* **for** *drunk driving.* [C] • *The Government's* **term of office** (=The period in which they have power) *expires at the end of the year.* [C] • A term (*esp. Am and Aus* **semester**) is one of the two or three periods into which a year is divided at school, college or university: *This is Stephen's first term at university.* [C] ○ *In Britain, the spring term starts in January and ends just before Easter.* [C] ○ *We're going skiing in the February* **half- term** (=the holiday which happens in the middle of the term). [C] ○ *We're very busy in* **term-time** (=during the term). • *(Am)* A **term-paper** is the main report written by a student for a particular class or subject in the middle of each school term. [C] • *(fml)* A term is also the period of time which a legal agreement lasts for: *The lease on our house is near the end of its term.* [C] • *(fml)* A pregnant woman's term is the end of her pregnancy when her baby is expected to be born: *She is near her term.* [U] ○ *Her last pregnancy went to term* (=The baby was born after the expected number of weeks). [U] • **In the long/medium/short term** means for a long, medium or short period of time in the future: *Taking this decision will cost us more in the short term, but will be beneficial in the long term.* ○ *The project will have long-term benefits.* • **Term insurance** is an **insurance policy** (=a written agreement to pay money to a person in the case of particular conditions, such as death, accident, or illness) which lasts for a limited time period. Compare **life insurance** at LIFE. • See also TERMS. • Ⓟ

term DESCRIPTION /£tɜːm, $tɜːrm/ *n* [C] a word or expression used in relation to a particular subject, such as to describe an official or technical word • *The term used to describe the Treasury Minister in Great Britain is 'the Chancellor'.* • *'Etiolated' is a specialized term used for plants which have grown tall and pale by being kept in the dark.* • *'Without let or hindrance' is a legal term which means 'freely'.* • *'Dear' is a term* **of endearment** (=a kind or friendly name to call someone). • *'You idiot' is a term* **of abuse** (=an unkind or unpleasant way of speaking to someone). • If you talk about something **in** particular terms, you express it using language which clearly shows your feelings: *He complained in strong/the strongest terms* (=complained strongly). ○ *She spoke of his achievements in* **glowing** *terms* (=in a very approving way). ○ *She told him what she thought of his contribution* **in no uncertain terms** (=She made her disapproval clear). • See also TERMINOLOGY; TERMS. • Ⓟ

term *obj* /£tɜːm, $tɜːrm/ *v* [T + obj + (*as*) n/adj] • To term something is to give it a name or describe it with a particular expression: *Technically, a horse which is smaller than 1·5 metres at the shoulder is termed a pony.* ○ *A White House spokeswoman has termed the treaty 'an amicable agreement'.* ○ *I would term his behaviour unacceptable.* ○ *Foreigners or,* **as** *we term them in Scotland, 'sassenachs' are always welcome.*

ter·ma·gant /£'tɜː·mə·gᵊnt, $'tɜːr-/ *n* [C] *disapproving* a woman who argues noisily to obtain or achieve what she wants

ter·mi·nal DEATH /£'tɜː·mɪ·nəl, $'tɜːr-/ *adj* [not gradable] (of a disease or illness) leading gradually to death • *She has terminal cancer.* • A terminal patient is one who is seriously ill and will die soon. • *(infml)* Terminal is also used to mean extreme when it refers to something unpleasant or negative: *He has nothing to do all day and is suffering from terminal* **boredom**. ○ *She claims that the shipbuilding industry is in terminal* **decline**.

ter·mi·nal·ly /£'tɜː·mɪ·nə·li, $'tɜːr-/ *adv* • *He is a terminally ill child.*

ter·mi·nal BUILDING /£'tɜː·mɪ·nəl, $'tɜːr-/ *n* [C] the area or building at a station, airport or port which is used by passengers leaving or arriving by train, aircraft or ship • *The new air/rail/ferry terminal is very large and well-designed.* • *Please do not leave any of your luggage unattended in the terminal building.* • *Your flight to Perth will leave from Terminal 4.*

ter·mi·nal COMPUTER /£'tɜː·mɪ·nəl, $'tɜːr-/ *n* [C] a piece of equipment consisting of a keyboard and screen, which is used for communicating with the main processor in a computing system

ter·mi·nal ELECTRICITY /£'tɜː·mɪ·nəl, $'tɜːr-/ *n* [C] the point at which a connection can be made in an electric CIRCUIT (=an electric system) • *Connect one wire to the positive terminal and one to the negative terminal on the battery.*

TENSES

PRESENT SIMPLE

Main idea: Events with no particular time, for example: general truths, complete events and unchanging situations in present time.

- *Water boils at 100°C.* — Expressing general or scientific truth. No specific time.
- *Her sister works in Chicago.* — A situation which does not change.
- *We visit my parents every Christmas.* — Habit.
- *The flight for Miami leaves at 2 o'clock.* — Information about fixed arrangements (which might be in the future).
- *I agree. I think you're right. Who doesn't want to be rich?* — States of mind, beliefs and opinions; emotions and desires.
- *As soon as I arrive, I'll phone you.* — Future time, after some conjunctions: *after, before, as soon as, until, when.*
- *Earthquake kills 500* — Sometimes when describing past events, for example in newspaper headlines.

THE CONTINUOUS FORM (PROGRESSIVE FORM)

Main idea: Actions or events that are (or were, or will be) **happening** at a particular point in time—they have reached a stage somewhere **between their beginning and their end.**

- Verbs such as *seem* or *wish,* which refer to states rather than to events that happen, are rarely used in a continuous form: LP **Verbs rarely used in a continuous form** at CONTINUE.
- When the continuous form is used with verbs referring to very brief events, it shows that the event is repeated: *Your bag is hitting my leg, can you move it?*

PRESENT CONTINUOUS

Main idea: Actions or events happening now or developing.

- *He's watching TV.* • *It's raining hard.* — Action or event happening now.
- *The weather's getting colder.* — Event or change now developing.

Present continuous + time phrase:

- *The latest Spielberg film is coming soon.* — Events in the near future.
- *I'm flying to Paris tomorrow.* — Future plans.
- *She's finishing college next summer.* — Future fixed events.
- *They're staying with me for a few days.* — Temporary situation.

Present continuous with 'always':

- *The children are always arguing.* — Events that tend to happen often.
- *She's always smiling.* — Series of events that do not stop.

being + adjective describing behaviour or character:

- *You're not being very helpful, are you?* — Temporary behaviour or quality.

PAST SIMPLE

Main idea: Completed actions and events in past time.

- *Serious floods occurred yesterday.* — Reporting completed events in the past.
- *The bridge was built ten years ago.* — Used with 'ago'.
- *I wanted to see the manager. Is he free?* — Polite expressions of desires.
- *The model T Ford was produced for 19 years.* — Completed periods in the past.
- *She recorded six songs with CBS before she made her first hit single in 1990.* — Completed events or actions following each other in past time.

PAST CONTINUOUS

Main idea: Incomplete or interrupted past actions or events.

- *"What were you doing at 6 p.m.?" "I think we were walking home."* — Event incomplete at a point in the past.
- *The aircraft was approaching the airport when an engine failed.* — Past action or event interrupted by another.
- *While I was crossing the road I noticed a crowd in the distance.* — Past action or event that occurred during another one.
- *People were running down the road and the area was being cleared. Just then there was an explosion...* — Reporting what events were happening when a series of complete events began.
- *I was reading a good cook book last night. I couldn't put it down.* — Past action seen as not complete.

PRESENT PERFECT

Main idea: Connects the past with the present: completed or unchanging actions or events. Notice that this tense cannot generally be used when a reference to a particular point or period (*last week, in January, at 3 a.m.*) is given or is possible.

- *He's been all over the world. Sorry, I don't know you. Have we met?* — Completed actions or events at some time before now (no particular time given).
- *That's twice I've made that mistake today! – I didn't make it once yesterday.* — Actions or events in periods of time not yet finished.
- *He's won!* — Achievements.
- *"Have you ever flown?" "No. I've never even been on a ship."* — With 'ever' and 'never', referring to any time up to now.
- *"How long have you lived here?" "I've been here a year now."* — Unchanging situations in periods of time up to now.

• *He's had at least six serious accidents and still has a driver's licence.* *She's visited S Korea three times since 1983.*	Series of completed actions up to now.
• *We won't leave until I've checked all the doors are locked.*	Future time, after some conjunctions: *after, before, as soon as, until, when.*

PRESENT PERFECT CONTINUOUS

Main idea: Connects the past with the present: incomplete actions or events.

• *Who's been drinking my coffee? It's nearly all gone!*	Effects of past action which are noticeable now.
• *They've been repairing that house for ages.*	Events over periods of time up to now.
• *He's been getting to work late recently.*	Situation up to now, seen as temporary.

PAST PERFECT

Main idea: Complete actions or events that happened before another point in the past.

• *When Paul returned to the car park his car had been stolen.*	Connects a point in the past to a still earlier event (no particular time given).
• *The police found his car at midnight. Paul had reported the theft at 8 p.m.*	Action or event at a particular time before the main time the writer is referring to.
• *He had been with the company for 25 years when he retired.*	Period of time up to a point in the past.

PAST PERFECT CONTINUOUS

Main idea: Actions or events happening before a point in the past.

• *The afternoon was fine but it had been raining earlier in the day.*	Effects of a still earlier event or action noticeable at a point in the past.
• *He had been playing tennis for an hour when he was taken ill.*	How long something was happening for up to a point in the past.

EXPRESSING THE IDEA OF THE FUTURE

(1) Future with WILL

Main idea: Suggests certainty; stating what you know will happen.

• *It will rain tomorrow.*	Predicting a complete future event.
• *I'll write and complain!*	Stating a decision.
• *It will be raining in the morning.*	Predicting a continuing future event.
• *I'll be standing under the station clock when you arrive.*	Future event happening when another occurs.

(2) Future with GOING TO

Main idea: Connects the present with the future.

• *Look at those black clouds: it's going to rain soon*	There is a reason now to believe that an event will happen in the future.
• *My sister's going to have a baby.*	The process has now started.

(3) Future with BE + to-infinitive

Main idea: Future fixed arrangements. Implies the arrangements were made by someone else.

• *He's to go into hospital tomorrow.* *You're to collect the keys at 9.30.*	Arrangements have been made for this to happen.

(4) Present Continuous + time phrase (see examples above at Present Continuous)

(5) Present Simple + time phrase (see examples above at Present Simple)

(6) Future Perfect

Main idea: Used to say that something will already have happened before a certain time in the future.

• *I'm late. The meeting will have started by the time I get to the office.*

Further information is given in the following Language Portraits: **Conditionals**; **Forms of Words** at FORM and **Verbs rarely used in a continuous form** at CONTINUE

ter·mi·nate *(obj)* /£'tɜː·mɪ·neɪt, $'tɜːr-/ *v fml* to (cause something to) end or stop • *They terminated my contract in October.* [T] • *This train will terminate at the next stop – passengers who wish to continue should change trains.* [I] • *(fml or specialized)* If you terminate a pregnancy, you end it intentionally, usually by having a medical operation. [T]

ter·mi·na·tion /£ˌtɜː·mɪ'neɪ·ʃᵊn, $ˌtɜːr-/ *n* • *I asked for an early termination of my contract.* [U] • *(fml or specialized)* A termination is the intentional ending of a pregnancy, usually by a medical operation: *Although her pregnancy was not planned, she was very happy about it and turned down the possibility of a termination when it was suggested by her doctor.* [C]

ter·mi·nol·o·gy /£ˌtɜː·mɪ'nɒl·ə·dʒi, $ˌtɜːr·mɪ'nɑː·lə-/ *n* special words or expressions used in relation to a particular subject or activity • *I find scientific terminology hard to understand.* [C] • *The document will have to be written again as there are difficulties in the terminology.* [U] • Compare JARGON.

ter·mi·no·log·i·cal /£ˌtɜː·mɪ·nə'lɒdʒ·ɪ·kᵊl, $ˌtɜːr·mɪ·nə'lɑː·dʒɪ-/ *adj* • *She shows great concern for terminological accuracy in her book.*

ter·mi·no·log·i·cal·ly /£ˌtɜː·mɪ·nə'lɒdʒ·ɪ·kli, $ˌtɜːr·mɪ·nə'lɑː·dʒɪ-/ *adv*

ter·mi·nus /£'tɜː·mɪ·nəs, $'tɜːr-/ *n* [C] *pl* **terminuses** or **termini** /£'tɜː·mɪ·naɪ, $'tɜːr-/ the last stop or the station at the end of a bus or railway route

ter·mite /£'tɜː·maɪt, $'tɜːr-/, **white ant** *n* [C] a small white tropical insect which lives in nests of piled earth and which eats through wood

terms /£tɜːmz, $tɜːrmz/ *pl n* the conditions which control an agreement, arrangement or activity • *We will have to discuss your terms of employment.* • *The terms of the contract are not negotiable.* • *I bought this dishwasher* **on** *favourable/reasonable terms* (= I paid a reasonable price for it.) • *Consider it* **in terms of** (= as) *an investment.* • If you **bring** someone **to terms**, you force them to accept particular conditions: *The United Nations tried to bring the warring sides to terms to put an end to the war.* • If you **come to terms with** someone, you agree with them about something: *We will have to come to terms with him about how many hours a week he is going to work for us.* • If you **come to terms with** something unpleasant or difficult, you learn to accept it and deal with it: *He has come to terms with his wife's illness and says he will nurse her at home.* • If you talk about something **in particular terms** or **in terms of** something, you use it to make clear which particular area of a subject you are discussing: *A 200-year-old building* *is very old in American terms/in terms of American history.* • If you are **thinking/talking in terms of** doing something, you are considering doing it: *I'm thinking in terms of retiring next year and travelling overseas.* • If you buy something **on easy terms**, you pay for it over a period of time. • If you do something **on** your **own terms**, you decide the conditions under which you will do it, because you are in a position of power. • If two people are treated **on equal/on the same terms**, they are treated in the same way: *We can't work on equal terms unless we speak a common language.* • If two people are **on good/bad terms**, they have a good/bad relationship with one another: *I've always been on good terms with my neighbours.* • *(fml)* **Terms of reference** are the matters to which a study or report is limited: *Working hours were within our terms of reference, whereas rates of pay were outside our terms of reference.* • *(Am)* **Terms of reference** are ideas or experiences which people use to make decisions: *He is always concerned about money – finance is his only term of reference.*

tern /£tɜːn, $tɜːrn/ *n* [C] a small black and white sea bird with long pointed wings and a divided tail

ter·race GROUND /ˈter·əs/ *n* [C] a flat raised area • A terrace is a flat area of stone or grass outside a house, where people sit and sometimes eat: *We ate lunch on the terrace.* • A terrace is also one of several narrow strips of land which are built like steps on the slope of a hill and which are used for growing crops on. *(Br)* A **spectators'/viewing** terrace is an area in an airport where people can watch aircraft landing and taking off.

ter·race *obj* /ˈter·əs/ *v* [T] • If you terrace a slope, you build narrow strips of land on it so that people can plant crops there: *The hillsides had been terraced and planted with lemon trees.*

ter·rac·es /ˈter·ə·sɪz/ *pl n Br specialized* • The terraces are the wide steps on which people stand to watch a football match.

ter·race HOUSE /ˈter·əs/ *n* [C] *Br and Aus* a row of small houses joined together along their side walls • *Our new house is an* **end-of-terrace** (= the end house in a row). • PIC> **Accommodation**

ter·raced /ˈter·ɪst/, **ter·race** *adj* [not gradable] *Br and Aus* • A **terraced/terraced** house (*Am* **row house**) is a house joined to others in a row: *She has just bought a Victorian terraced house in Islington.* • Terraced roads are roads which contain only terraced houses.

ter·ra·cot·ta /£ˌter·əˈkɒt·ə, $-ˈkɑː·t̬ə/ *n* [U] hard, baked reddish-brown clay • *Our kitchen tiles are made from terracotta.* • *The courtyard was full of exotic plants in terracotta pots.* • Terracotta is also a reddish-brown colour: *I've painted my bedroom terracotta.*

ter·ra fir·ma /£ˌter·əˈfɜː·mə, $-ˈfɜːr-/ *n* [U] dry land, when compared with the sea or air • *It was good to get back on terra firma again after that awful sea crossing.*

ter·ra·form·ing /£ter·əˌfɔː·mɪŋ, $-ˌfɔːr-/ *n* [U] *specialized* changing the environmental conditions of a planet other than Earth so that it would be possible for humans to live there • *Most scientists believe that terraforming is only a very distant possibility.*

ter·rain /təˈreɪn/ *n* [U] an area of land, when considering its natural features • *The car handles particularly well on rough terrain.* • *The resort is one of the most popular Swiss destinations for skiers who demand extensive and challenging ski terrain.*

ter·ra·pin /ˈter·ə·pɪn/ *n* [C] *pl* **terrapin** or **terrapins** a type of small N American TURTLE (= an animal with a thick shell covering its body) which lives in warm rivers and lakes

ter·re·stri·al /təˈres·tri·əl/ *adj* [not gradable] *fml* relating to the planet Earth, or *(specialized)* (of animals) living on the land rather than in the sea or air • *The plant is found in the Antarctic and grows in the harshest terrestrial conditions on our planet.* • *(specialized) Crustaceans live mostly in marine but also in freshwater and terrestrial habitats.* • Terrestrial television channels are ones which broadcast from stations on the ground and do not use SATELLITES (= communication devices in space). • Compare EXTRATERRESTRIAL.

ter·ri·ble UNPLEASANT /ˈter·ə·bl̩/ *adj* very unpleasant or serious • *I've had a terrible night – I just couldn't sleep.* • *Reports have just come in of a terrible crash on the freeway.* • *We have just received some terrible news.* • *"How was your trip?" "Terrible – it rained all week."* • *It was terrible to see her suffer so much.* [+ *to* infinitive] • *It is terrible* **that** *he spent ten years in prison for a crime that he did not commit.* [+ *that* clause] • *(Br infml)* **Terrible twins** are two people who behave in a way which attracts attention. • *"Changed, changed utterly:/ A terrible beauty is born."* (W.B.Yeats in the poem *Easter, 1916*, 1920) • Ⓕ

ter·ri·bly /ˈter·ə·bli/ *adv* • Terribly means very badly: *I slept terribly last night.* ○ *He did terribly in the race.*

ter·ri·ble VERY GREAT /ˈter·ə·bl̩/ *adj infml* used to emphasize the great degree of something • *This project is a terrible waste of money.* • *She's a terrible nuisance.* • Ⓕ

ter·ri·bly /ˈter·ə·bli/ *adv infml* • Terribly is used to mean very or extremely: *I'm terribly pleased to hear that you've got a job.* ○ *She was terribly sorry not to have seen you last Saturday.* • LP> **Very, completely**

ter·ri·er /£ˈter·i·əʳ, $-ɚ/ *n* [C] a breed of small active dog, originally used for hunting and chasing animals into or out of their underground holes • *They own a Scotch terrier called Macdonald.* • PIC> **Dogs**

ter·ri·fic VERY GOOD /təˈrɪf·ɪk/ *adj infml* very good or enjoyable • *We had a terrific time at the zoo.* • *He gave a terrific speech about saving the forests.*

ter·ri·fi·cal·ly /təˈrɪf·ɪ·kli/ *adv* [not gradable] *infml* • *We get on with each other terrifically* (= We have a very good relationship).

ter·ri·fic VERY GREAT /təˈrɪf·ɪk/ *adj infml* used to emphasize the great amount or degree of something • *The police car drove past at a terrific speed.* • *These plants quickly grow to a terrific height.*

ter·ri·fi·cal·ly /təˈrɪf·ɪ·kli/ *adv infml* • *My tooth is terrifically* (= extremely) *painful.*

ter·ri·fy *obj* /ˈter·ə·faɪ/ *v* [T] to frighten (someone) severely • *We terrified the girls* **with** *spooky stories.* • *He terrified her* **by** *jumping out at her from a dark alley.*

ter·ri·fied /ˈter·ə·faɪd/ *adj* • If someone is terrified, they are very frightened: *He huddled in the corner like a terrified child.* ○ *I'm terrified* **of** *the dark.* ○ *They're terrified* **of being** *robbed.* ○ *He's terrified* **at the** *prospect* **of** *losing his job.* ○ *She's terrified* **(that)** *her mother might find out her secret.* [+ *(that)* clause] ○ *He was too terrified* **to** *look over the edge of the cliff.* [+ *to* infinitive]

ter·ri·fy·ing /ˈter·ə·faɪ·ɪŋ/ *adj* • If something is terrifying, it is very frightening: *a terrifying experience/ordeal*

ter·ri·fy·ing·ly /ˈter·ə·faɪ·ɪŋ·li/ *adv*

ter·rine /terˈiːn/ *n* a savoury dish made of small pieces of cooked meat, fish or vegetables which have been pressed into a rectangular shape, and which is eaten cold • *She made a duck terrine for dinner.* [C] • *We started our meal with terrine of salmon and dill.* [U] • A terrine is also the type of cooking dish in which this food is made. [C]

ter·ri·tory /£ˈter·ɪ·tᵊr·i, £-tri, $-tɔːr·i/ *n* (an area of) esp. land or sea, which is considered as belonging to or connected with a particular country or person • *He was shot down in enemy/unknown/uncharted territory.* [U] • *The UN is sending aid to the* **occupied** *territories.* [C] • *My sister's bedroom is* **forbidden** *territory to the rest of us.* [U] • *The robin keeps other birds off that part of the garden – that's his territory* (= the area he tries to control). [U] • *Children's books are a new territory* (= area of activity) *for the publisher.* [C] • *Medieval literature is not my territory* (= not a subject that I know about). [U] • *The director is back* **on** *familiar territory* (= a familiar subject) *with his latest film.* [U] • If you say something **goes/comes with the territory**, you mean it is an expected fact or result of a particular situation or position: *The public attention that famous people get just goes with the territory.*

ter·ri·tor·i·al /£ˌter·ɪˈtɔː·ri·əl, $-ˈtɔːr·i-/ *adj* [not gradable] *fml* • *The country suffered heavy territorial losses in the war.* • *His territorial ambitions* (= his desire to take land for his own) *included most of Europe.* • *Some animals and birds are territorial* (= they mark out areas which they defend against others). • **Territorial waters** are the area of sea near a country's coast and under its legal control. • *(Br)* **The Territorial Army** is a group of men and women who, without payment and during the time when they are not working, are trained as soldiers.

ter·ri·tor·i·al /£ˌter·ɪˈtɔː·ri·əl, $-ˈtɔːr·i-/ *n* [C] • A territorial is a member of the **Territorial Army**.

ter·ror /£ˈter·əʳ, $-ɚ/ *n* (violent action which causes) extreme fear • *They fled from the city* **in** *terror.* [U] • *There was* **sheer/abject** *terror in her eyes when he came back into the room.* [U] • *Lots of people have a terror* **of** *spiders/drowning.* [U] • *What he said* **struck** *terror* **in** *my* **heart** (= made me very frightened). [U] • *The separatists started a* *campaign of terror* (=violent action causing fear) *to get independence.* [U] • *Each change of regime has been accompanied by bloodshed, culminating in the permanent* **(reign of)** *terror* (=violent action causing fear) *of the present government.* [U] • *Heights* **have/hold** *no terrors for me* (=do not frighten me). [C] • *The terrors* (=frightening experiences) *of their months in captivity left their mark.* [C] • A terror is also someone, esp. a child, who behaves badly and is difficult to control: *My brother is a* **real** *little terror.* [C] • If you **are/go/live in terror of** your **life**, you are frightened that you will be killed. • If someone or something is **the terror of** people, it causes them extreme fear: *The tiger was the terror of the villagers for several months.* ○ *(infml) That boy is the terror of* (=causes trouble in) *the neighbourhood.* • **Terror-stricken/Terror-struck** means extremely frightened: *They were terror-stricken when they heard someone moving around downstairs in their house at night.*

ter·ror·ize *obj, Br and Aus usually* **–ise** /ˈter·ə·raɪz/ *v* [T] • *Street gangs have been terrorizing the neighbourhood* (=causing fear to people by the threat or acts of violence) – *smashing windows and burning cars.* • *Old people have been terrorized* (=forced by threats or acts of violence) *into staying at home after dark.*

ter·ror·i·sm /£ˈter·ə·rɪ·zᵊm, $-ɚ·ɪ-/ *n* [U] (threats of) violent action for political purposes • *Governments must cooperate if they are to fight/combat international terrorism.* • *The bomb explosion was one of the worst* **acts of** *terrorism that Italy has experienced in recent years.* • LP〉 **Crimes and criminals**

ter·ror·ist /£ˈter·ə·rɪst, $-ɚ·ɪst/ *n* [C] • *Several terrorists have been killed by their own bombs.* • *There has been an increase in terrorist attacks.* • *The government has said that it will not be intimidated by terrorist threats.*

ter·ry /ˈter·i/, **ter·ry to·well·ing**, **ter·ry cloth** *n* [U] a type of thick cotton cloth with short threads on each side, used esp. for making TOWELS (=cloths used for drying yourself) • *a terry bathrobe* • *Do you agree that it's better for the environment if parents use terry* **nappies** *for their babies, rather than disposables?*

terse /£tɜːs, $tɜːrs/ *adj* **-r, -st** using few words, sometimes in a way that seems rude or unfriendly • *Her newspaper articles are terse and to the point.* • *"Are you feeling any better?" "No," was the terse* **reply.** • *In a terse* **statement** *yesterday, the company announced that it was closing three of its factories.*

terse·ly /£ˈtɜː·sli, $ˈtɜːr-/ *adv* • *When I asked what had happened, he replied rather tersely that he had no idea.*

terse·ness /£ˈtɜː·snəs, $ˈtɜːr-/ *n* [U]

ter·tia·ry /£ˈtɜː·ʃᵊr·i, $ˈtɜːr·ʃi·er·/ *adj* [not gradable] *fml or specialized* for or in a third level or stage • *(Br and Aus)* Tertiary is often used to mean connected with education in colleges or universities: *tertiary* **education** *(Am* **higher education***)* ○ *tertiary students* ○ *a tertiary college* • When used of an industry, tertiary means providing a service, rather than being involved with obtaining the materials with which goods are made, or with the making of goods.

Ter·y·lene *Br and Aus* /ˈter·ə·liːn/, *Am* **Dac·ron** /£ˈdæk·rɒn, £ˈdeɪ·krɒn, $ˈdeɪ·krɑːn, $ˈdæk·rɑːn/ *n* [U] *trademark* (cloth made from) an artificial fibre • *Terylene does not crease.* • *He was wearing a Terylene shirt.*

TESL /ˈtes·l̩/ *n* [U] *abbreviation for* teaching English as a second language

TESOL /£ˈtiː·sɒl, $-sɑːl/ *n* [U] *abbreviation for* teaching English to speakers of other languages

TESSA /ˈtes·ə/ *n* [C] *abbreviation for* Tax Exempt Special Savings Account (=in Britain, an account into which you can pay money which is allowed to earn profit of up to a particular amount without any tax being charged on the profit, if you leave the money in the account for a particular period of time)

tes·sel·late, *Am also* **tes·se·late** /ˈtes·ᵊl·eɪt/ *v* [I] *specialized* (of shapes) to fit together in a pattern with no spaces in between • *Hexagons tessellate, circles do not.*

tes·sel·lat·ed, *Am also* **tes·se·lat·ed** /£ˈtes·ᵊl·eɪ·tɪd, $-t̬ɪd/ *adj* [not gradable] *specialized* • A tessellated floor is one made from small pieces of coloured stone fitted together to make a pattern or picture.

tes·sel·la·tion, *Am also* **tes·sel·a·tion** /ˌtes·ᵊlˈeɪ·ʃᵊn/ *n* [C/U] *specialized*

test /test/ *n* [C] a way of discovering, by questions or practical activities, what someone knows, or what someone or something can do or is like • *a spelling test* • *an IQ test* • *an aptitude test* • *A new driver has to* **take** *a* **(driving)** *test before being able to drive alone.* • A test is also a medical examination of part of your body in order to find out how healthy it is or what is wrong with it: *a blood/urine test* ○ *an eye test* ○ *a pregnancy test* ○ *The doctors have done some tests to try and find out what's wrong with her.* • A test is also an act of using something to find out whether it is working correctly or how effective it is: *a safety test* ○ *The new missiles are currently* **undergoing** *tests.* ○ *Tests have* **shown/proved** *that new Brita really does wash clothes cleaner!* • A test can also be a situation which shows how good something is: *Driving on that icy road was a real test* **of** *my skill.* ○ *Her constant questions were a real test* **of** *my patience.* • To **put** something **to the test** is to find out how good it is: *Those icy roads certainly put my driving to the test.* ○ *Her constant questions really put my patience to the test!* • A **test ban** is an agreement between countries to stop examining the effectiveness of nuclear weapons: *a test ban treaty* • *(Br)* A **test card**/*(Am and Aus)* **test pattern** is a picture or pattern broadcast so that the quality of the television picture received can be examined and improved if necessary by adjusting the controls on the equipment. • A **test case** is a case in a court of law which establishes principles in relation to which other similar cases are considered in the future. • A **test drive** is an act of driving a car that you are considering buying, in order to see if you like it. • A **test (match)** is a game of cricket or RUGBY played by the national teams of two countries. • A **test pilot** is someone whose job is to fly new aircraft in order to make sure that they are effective. • A **test tube** is a small glass tube, with one closed, rounded end, which is used in scientific experiments. • A **test tube baby** is a baby which developed from egg and sperm which were joined outside the body and then replaced in the mother to grow. • PIC〉 **Laboratory** ⓘ

test *(obj)* /test/ *v* • *Will you test me* **on** (=ask me questions to see if I know) *the chemical formulae I've been learning?* [T] • *This machine is designed for testing people's hearing* (=finding out if there is anything wrong with it). [T] • *We test the equipment* **for** *accuracy* (=make sure that it is working correctly) *every Friday morning.* [T] • *The manufacturers are currently testing the new engine* (=making sure that it is working effectively). [T] • *They started testing* (=searching) **for** *oil.* [I] • To test someone or something can also be to present them with a situation which show how good they are at dealing with difficulties: *That lecture really tested my powers of endurance, it was so boring.* [T] • To test something, esp. a theory or an idea, **out** is to find out how it works in a practical situation or how people react to it: *The students tested out their cost-cutting ideas in several companies.* [M] ○ *I find it valuable to test my writing out on someone else before it is published.* [M] • **To test the water(s)** is to find out what people's opinions of something are before you ask them to do something or try and sell them something: *We put an advertisement about a nursery school in the paper to test the water.*

test·er /£ˈtes·təʳ, $-tɚ/ *n* [C] • A tester is a person or a machine which tests something. • A tester is also a small container of a product which you can buy in order to see if you like it.

test·ing /ˈtes·tɪŋ/ *n* [before n] *esp. Br* • Testing means difficult to deal with: *a testing situation* ○ *These are very testing* **times** *for our family.*

tes·ta·ment /ˈtes·tə·mənt/ *n fml* proof • *The detail of her wildlife paintings is (a) testament* **to** (=proof of) *her powers of observation.* [C/U]

tes·tate /ˈtes·teɪt/ *adj* [not gradable] *fml* (of a person) having left a WILL (=written instructions about what should happen to your possessions after your death)

tes·ti·cle /ˈtes·tɪ·kl̩/, *fml* **tes·tis** /ˈtes·tɪs/, *slang* **balls**, *Br and Aus slang* **bol·locks**, *esp. Am slightly taboo slang* **nuts** /nʌts / nʌts/ *n* [C] either of the two round male sex organs which produce sperm and are enclosed in the SCROTUM (=bag of skin) behind and below the penis

tes·ti·fy /ˈtes·tɪ·faɪ/ *v* to speak seriously about something, esp. in a court of law; to give or provide EVIDENCE (=proof or facts) • *She testified* **for/on behalf of** *her family.* [I] • *They testified* **for** *the prosecution.* [I] • *No one expected him to testify* **against** *his former employer.* [I] • *He testified* **to having** *seen the man leaving the building around the time of the murder.* [I] • *He testified* **that** *he had seen the man leaving the building around the time of the murder.* [+ *that* clause] • *(fml) The open door testified* **to** (=showed or proved) *the fact that she had left in a hurry.* [I] • *(fml) The* *open door testified* (= showed or proved) **that** *she had left in a hurry.* [+ *that* clause]

tes·ti·mo·ni·al /£ˌtes·tɪˈməʊ·ni·əl, $-ˈmoʊ-/ *n* [C] a statement about the character or qualities of someone or something, esp. *(fml or dated)* a formal written description of someone's character and qualities given by a previous employer • *(fml or dated) Two of the candidates for the job come with excellent testimonials.* • *After hearing his testimonial* **to** *the treatment's effectiveness, I decided to try it myself.* • A **testimonial (match/game)** is one played to honour a famous player who will receive a sum of money after it.

tes·ti·mo·ny /£ˈtes·tɪ·mᵊn·i, $-moʊ·ni/ *n fml* (an example of) spoken or written statements that something is true, esp. those given in a court of law • *Some doubt has been expressed about whether their testimony was really true.* [U] • *The dead man's family's testimonies helped to win the case.* [C] • *(fig.) The reports are testimony* **to** (= clearly show) *the many hours of research completed by this committee.* [U] • *(fig.) Your success is a testimony* **of** (= clearly shows) *all your hard work.* [C]

tes·tis /ˈtes·tɪs/ *n* [C] *pl* **testes** /ˈtes·tiːz/ *specialized* TESTICLE

tes·tos·te·rone /£ˌtesˈtɒs·tᵊr·əʊn, $-ˈtɑː·stɚ·oʊn/ *n* [U] a male HORMONE (= chemical substance produced in the body) that causes a stage of growth in older boys and change in their reproductive organs

test·y /ˈtes·ti/ *adj* **-ier, -iest** bad-tempered and lacking patience • *a testy old man* • *testy comments* • *Her reply was rather testy.*

tes·ti·ly /ˈtes·tɪ·li/ *adv*

tes·ti·ness /ˈtes·tɪ·nəs/ *n* [U]

tet·a·nus /ˈtet·ᵊn·əs/, *infml dated* **lock·jaw** *n* [U] an infectious disease caused by bacteria from earth entering the human body through small cuts, and in which the muscles esp. around the mouth stiffen

tetch·y /ˈtetʃ·i/ *adj* **-ier, -iest** easily made angry, unhappy or upset • *You're very tetchy today – has something upset you?* • *Be careful what you say to Anna – she's in a rather tetchy mood.*

tetch·i·ly /ˈtetʃ·ɪ·li/ *adv*

tetch·i·ness /ˈtetʃ·ɪ·nəs/ *n* [U]

tête-à-tête /ˌteɪt·əˈteɪt/ *adv* [after v; not gradable] *fml or humorous* (of an activity) including two people who are together in private • *We dined tête-à-tête.*

tête-à-tête /ˌteɪt·əˈteɪt/ *n* [C] • A tête-à-tête is an informal private conversation between two people, esp. friends: *We must have a tête à tête sometime.*

teth·er /£ˈteð·əʳ, $-ɚ/ *n* [C] a rope or chain used to tie esp. an animal to a post or other fixed place, usually so that it can move freely within a small area • *We keep the goat on a tether when it is grazing.* • *The hot-air balloon broke free of its tether and floated away.* • **At the end of** your **tether** means having no strength or patience left: *By 6 o'clock after a busy day I'm at the end of my tether.*

teth·er *obj* /£ˈteð·əʳ, $-ɚ/ *v* [T] • *He tethered his horse* **to** *a fence.* • *(fig.) I've been tethered* **to** (= unable to get away from) *my desk all day.*

teth·ered /£ˈteð·əd, $-ɚd/ *adj* [not gradable] • *tethered animals*

Teu·ton·ic /£tjuːˈtɒn·ɪk, $tuːˈtɑː·nɪk/ *adj* [not gradable] of, or thought to be typical of, the groups of people in north-western Europe of German origin • *a Teutonic language* • *Teutonic features* • *Teutonic efficiency*

Tex–Mex /ˌteksˈmeks/ *adj* [not gradable] referring to the Mexican-American culture existing in Texas and the SW United States • *Tex-Mex cooking* • *Tex-Mex music*

text /tekst/ *n* written or printed material • *The book has 100 pages of closely printed text.* [U] • *We need to break up the text with some drawings.* [U] • *The references have been taken out of the main text* (= the main part) *of the book and listed at the end of each chapter.* [U] • *Can we see the text* (= the exact words) **of** *his speech before Tuesday?* [U] • Text can be used to mean a book or various different forms of a book, etc.: *Several early texts are being auctioned next week.* [C] ○ *'Ulysses' was a* **set** *text for* (= a book which must be studied by students taking) *the Cambridge exam this year.* [C] • A text can also be a sentence or reference from the Bible which a priest reads aloud in church and talks about: *"My text today is 'Love one another' John 13:34-35," said the vicar.* [C] • Ⓙ

tex·tu·al /£ˈteks·tju·əl, $-tʃu-/ *adj* [not gradable] • Textual means relating to written or printed material: *textual errors* • *textual differences* • Textual can also mean relating to the style in which something has been written: *textual criticism* ○ *textual analysis*

text·book BOOK /ˈtekst·bʊk/ *n* [C] a book that contains detailed information about a subject for people who are studying that subject • *a science textbook* • *a history textbook* • *a textbook on chemistry* • Ⓓ

text·book TYPICAL /ˈtekst·bʊk/ *adj* [before n; not gradable] (of an example of something) extremely good, or thought to be usual or typical • *That was a textbook goal from Taylor.* • *She gave a textbook performance in the leading role.* • *The company is adopting textbook* (= usual) *methods of developing its market.* • *To all my questions, she just gave the standard* (= usual) *textbook answer.* • *This is a textbook* (= typical) **example** *of how to deal with the problem.*

tex·tile /ˈtek·staɪl/ *n* [C] a cloth which is either woven by hand or machine • *woollen/cotton textiles* • *a textile mill/factory* • *The textile* **industry** *is the state's top producer of income and jobs.*

tex·ture /£ˈteks·tʃəʳ, $-tʃɚ/ *n* the quality of something that can be decided by touch; the degree to which something is rough or smooth, or soft or hard • *a smooth/rough/coarse texture* [C] • *a soft/hard texture* [C] • *Different types of fabric have different textures.* [C] • *This artificial fabric has the texture of* (= feels like) *silk.* [U] • *The manufacturers say that using this cream will help improve your skin texture* (= the appearance of your skin). [U] • *This cheese has a firm but crumbly texture* (= structure). [C] • The texture of a piece of writing or music is its character: *The play has a rich and complex dramatic texture.* [U] ○ *The surface texture of the writing is so dense that we are prevented from seeing clearly below it.* [U]

tex·tured /£ˈteks·tʃəd, $-tʃɚd/ *adj* • Textured means having a surface that is not smooth but has a raised pattern on it: *textured wallpaper* ○ *a textured fabric*

-tex·tured /£-ˈteks·tʃəd, $-tʃɚd/ *combining form* • -textured means having a texture of the stated kind: *coarse-textured/fine-textured sand* ○ *a crisp-textured apple* ○ *an even-textured paste* ○ *a rich-textured play/poem*

tha·li·do·mide /θəˈlɪd·ə·maɪd/ *n* [U] a drug which was once used to help people relax or sleep, and which was found to cause damage to babies inside the womb, esp. by stopping the development of their arms and legs, when it was taken by their mothers • *a thalidomide victim*

than /ðæn/ *prep, conjunction* used to join two parts of a comparison • *My son is taller than my daughter.* • *Susannah's car is bigger than mine.* • *You always walk faster than I do!* • *My brother's older than I am/than me.* • *You're earlier than usual/than you usually are.* • *She's friendlier than before/than she used to be.* • Than is used with **more** or **less** to compare numbers or amounts: *I spent more than I intended to.* ○ *She invited more than 30 people to her party.* ○ *It cost less than I expected.* ○ *The time available is less than we had hoped for.*

thank *obj* /θæŋk/ *v* [T] to express to (someone) that you are pleased about or appreciate something that they have done • *Don't thank me, thank everyone who helped.* • *He thanked me* **for** *taking him home.* • If you thank someone **for** something, you can also mean that they are responsible or to blame for it: *You can thank John* **for** *this problem.* • If you **have** someone **to thank for** something, they are responsible or to blame for it: *You have John to thank for this problem.* ○ *He's only got him***self** *to thank* **for** *losing his job.* • **I'll thank you (not) to** can be used to give an order: *I'll thank you to be quiet* (= Be quiet). ○ *I'll thank you not to* (= Don't) *touch that.* • You can say **thank God/goodness/heaven(s)** to express happiness that something bad has been avoided or has finished: *Thank goodness you found the key I lost.* ○ *I caught the train, thank goodness.* • **Thank you** (also **Thanks**) is the usual way of expressing gratitude to someone: *That was a delicious lunch, thank you.* ○ *"Here's your coffee." "Thank you* **very much (indeed)**." ○ *Thank you* **for** *my birthday present/***for** *coming to see me.* • You also say **thank you** (also **thanks**) when you are replying to a polite question or remark: *"How are you?" "I'm fine, thank you."* ○ *"You look very nice in that dress." "Thank you* **very much**." • You also use **thank you** (also **thanks**) to politely accept or refuse something that has been offered to you: *"Would you like some more cake?" "Yes, I will have a small piece, thank you."* ○ *"Do you need any help?" "No, thank you."* • You can also say **thank you** in order to express your disapproval of something: *I don't want to hear that kind of language, thank you* **(very much)**. • A **thank you** is something that you say or do in order to express your gratitude for something: *I'd like to say a* **big** *thank you* **to** *everyone for all their help.* ○ *I helped her move her furniture, but I never received so much as a thank you.* ○ *He wrote a thank-you* **note/letter** *to his granny to thank her for the birthday present she sent him.* • To **thank** your **lucky stars** is to be grateful or feel pleased: *She thanked her lucky stars that she had taken out insurance when she was involved in an accident on holiday.* • If someone **won't thank** you **for** doing something, they will not be pleased if you do it: *She won't thank you for telling everyone how old she is.* • *"Thank Heavens for Little Girls"* (title of a song written by Alan Jay Lerner, 1956) • LP **Phrases and customs**

thank·ful /ˈθæŋk·fᵊl/ *adj* • *I was thankful* (=pleased or grateful) **that** *the meeting didn't last long, because I had a train to catch.* [+ *that* clause] • *She was thankful* **to** *receive a good report.* [+ *to* infinitive] • *After a long cold walk I was thankful* **for** *a hot drink.*

thank·ful·ly /ˈθæŋk·fᵊl·i/ *adv* • *It's been hard work, but thankfully* (=I am pleased) *the worst is over now.*

thank·ful·ness /ˈθæŋk·fᵊl·nəs/ *n* [U]

thank·less /ˈθæŋ·kləs/ *adj* • *Keeping the children's rooms tidy is a thankless* **task/job** (=one that is unlikely to be successful or appreciated).

thanks /θæŋks/ *pl n* • Thanks are feelings of appreciation and gratitude: *They expressed their thanks to the organisers.* ○ *He wrote a letter of thanks to the hospital.* ○ *(fml) Her campaign for road safety earned her the thanks of her community.* ○ *Let us* **give** *thanks to God.* • Thanks is also an informal way of saying **thank you**: *"Here's a cup of coffee for you." "Thanks/***Many** *thanks/Thanks* **a lot***/ Thanks* **very much (indeed).***"* ○ *"Shall I do that for you?" "No, thanks."* • If someone says 'Thanks **a lot**'/'Thanks **for nothing**'/'Thanks **a bunch**', they sometimes mean they are not grateful for what you have done and that you have not helped them: *"I told Dad you'd love to wash his car." "Thanks a lot."* ○ *Thanks a lot for supporting me* (=You did not help me). • **Thanks to** means because of: *It's thanks to Sandy that I heard about the job.* ○ *(disapproving) The baby is awake thanks to your shouting.* • **No thanks to** means despite: *It's no thanks to you that I arrived on time.*

thanks·giv·ing /ˌθæŋksˈgɪv·ɪŋ/ *n* an expression of gratitude, esp. to God • *a service of thanksgiving* [U] • **Thanksgiving (Day)** is a public holiday and celebration, held on the fourth Thursday of November in the US and on the second Monday of October in Canada, to remember the thanks that the people who first came from Europe gave to God when they gathered crops for the first time in their new country: *We always go to my parents' house for Thanksgiving.* [U] ○ *I've had to spend the last two Thanksgivings away from home.* [C] • LP **Holidays**

that SOMETHING NOT HERE /ðæt/ *determiner, pronoun pl* **those** /£ðəuz, $ðouz/ used to refer to a person, object, idea etc. which is separated from the speaker by space or time • *I don't like this dress (here), I prefer that one (over there).* • *Put that box down before you drop it.* • *I've never liked that cousin of hers.* • *Who's that? Is that the girl you told me about?* • *Is that you making all the noise, John?* • *"Hello. Is that Jean?" she said when she heard a voice answer the phone.* • *That was a good suggestion of yours.* • *That was a difficult problem to resolve.* • *The coldest hours are those just before dawn.* • *These peaches aren't ripe enough to eat, try those on the table.* • *Those who want to can come back by a later train.* • *If you hold it like that* (=in the way in which you are doing) *it will break.* • *(fml) His handwriting is like that* (=the writing) **of** *a much younger child.* • *(fml) We are often afraid of that which* (=of what) *we cannot understand.* • That/Those are also used to make a connection with an earlier statement: *My usual train was cancelled. That's why I'm so late.* ○ *No smoking and modern equipment. Those are two of the things I like about working here.* ○ *The garage still isn't finished. That's builders* **for you** (=Such behaviour is typical of builders). • That can also be used to express a reaction to something: *I didn't know she'd been so ill. That's terrible.* ○ *You mean you can't come to the party? That's a pity.* ○ *Turn the engine on, then put the car in gear. That's* **right** (=you are doing it correctly). ○ *Smile for the camera. That's* **more like it** (=that smile is better than before). • That/Those are often used to refer to something which has been mentioned or was involved earlier, or to something with which the listener will be familiar: *That guy* (=The man I told you about whom) *I met at the party gave me the idea.* ○ *Where's that pen* (=the one I was using earlier) *gone?* ○ *She lives in that house by the bus station* (=you know which one I mean). • **That's it** means that something is correct: *You switch the computer on at the back. That's it.* • **That's it** can also mean that something has ended: *Well, that's it, we've finished – we can go home now.* ○ *That's* **(absolutely)** *it! I'm not putting up with any more of her rudeness.* • **That's/That was that** means that something has ended: *She left the room and that was that, I never saw her again.* ○ *I won't agree to it and that's that* (=I won't discuss it any longer). • You say **that is (to say)** when you want to give further details or be more exact about something: *I'll meet you in the city, that is, I will if the trains are running.* • **That will do** means that you do not want any more of something: *"Shall I put some more peas on your plate?" "No, that'll do, thank you."* ○ *That will do, Charles. I don't want to see any more of that kind of behaviour.* • *(slightly literary)* **With that** means after something as been said or done, or then: *"I still think you're wrong," he said and with that he drove off.* • *(saying)* 'That's life/That's how it is/Life's like that means that you have to accept what happens. • LP **Determiners**

that INTRODUCING A CLAUSE /ðæt/ *conjunction* used to introduce a clause which reports something or gives further information, although it can often be omitted • *She said (that) she'd collect it for me after work.* • *I knew (that) he'd never get here in time.* • *It's possible (that) there'll be a vacancy.* • *Is it true (that) she's gone back to teaching?* • *My advice is (that) you should sell.* • **Given** *(that) you haven't had much time to do this, I think you've done it very well.* • *We'll be there at about 7.30,* **provided/providing** *(that) there's a suitable train.* • *It was* **so** *dark (that) I couldn't see anything.* • LP **Clauses**

that USED TO REFER /ðæt/ *pronoun* used to show what particular thing or things is or are being referred to, but can sometimes be omitted • *There's the car (that) John wants to buy.* • *I can't find the books (that) I got from the library.* • *Is this the train that stops at Cambridge?* • *Have you been to the new restaurant that's just opened in town?* • 'That' can sometimes be omitted in informal or spoken English when the noun it comes after is the object of the following clause.

that AS MUCH /ðæt/ *adv* [not gradable] as much as suggested • *It was at least that tall.* • *She's too young to walk that far.* • *It wasn't* **(all)** *that* (=very) *good.* • *I haven't seen* **(all)** *that* (=very) *much of her since the summer.* • *It hasn't been* **(all)** *that* (=very) *cold recently.* • *(Br and Aus not standard) It hurt me that much* (=so much) *that I cried.*

thatch /θætʃ/ *v, n* (to put on a building) a roof covering of dry grass, REEDS, etc. • *They're thatching a* **cottage** *in the village this week.* [T] • *They live in a thatched* **cottage***/a* **cottage** *with a thatched roof.* • *Some of the thatch on the barn needs replacing.* [U] • *There's a bird nesting in the thatch* (=the roof made of this). [U] • A **thatch of hair** is a mass of thick or untidy hair. • PIC **Accommodation**

thatch·er /£ˈθætʃ·əʳ, $-ɚ/ *n* [C] • A thatcher is a person whose job is thatching roofs.

thaw *(obj)* /£θɔː, $θɑː/ *v* to (cause to) change from a solid, frozen state to become liquid or soft, because of an increase in temperature • *The lake is thawing fast.* [I] • *The pipes are starting to thaw* **(out)** (=The water which had frozen in the pipes is starting to melt). [I] • *It is sometimes recommended that frozen meat should be thawed* **(out)** (=caused to become not frozen) *in the fridge.* [T] • *You need to thaw a frozen turkey for at least 24 hours.* • **It's** *beginning to thaw* (=The weather is warm enough for snow and ice to melt). [I] • **It** *won't thaw* (=snow and ice will not melt) *for another three months.* [I] • *(fig.) I came in from the cold half an hour ago, but I'm only just beginning to thaw* **out** (=get warm). [I] • *(fig.) She was rather unfriendly to me at first, but she soon began to thaw (out)* (=become friendlier). [I] • Compare FREEZE.

thaw /£θɔː, $θɑː/ *n* • *The thaw* (=period of warmer whether when snow and ice begin to melt) *has* **set in** *early this year.* [C] • *(fig.) There are signs of a thaw* (=an increase in friendliness) *in relations between the two countries.* [U]

the PARTICULAR /ðiː, ðə/ *determiner* used before nouns to refer to things or people when a listener or reader knows which particular things or people are being referred to, esp. because they have already been mentioned or because what is happening makes it clear • *I just bought a new shirt and some new shoes. The shirt was quite expensive, but the shoes weren't.* • *There's someone at the door.* • *Please would you pass the salt.* • *I'll pick you up at the station.* • *Alex was sent to the headteacher for behaving badly in class.* • 'The' is used before some nouns that refer to place when you want to mention that type of place, without showing exactly which example of the place you mean: *Where are the toilets?* ○ *We spent all day at the beach.* ○ *Shall we go to the movies this evening?* ○ *I must go to the bank and change some money.* ○ *You should go to the dentist's at least twice a year.* • You use 'the' before noun phrases in which the range of meaning of the noun is limited in some way: *I really enjoyed the book I've just finished reading.* ○ *Do you like the other students in your class?* • 'The' is used to refer to things or people when only one exists at any one time: *The sky was full of stars.* ○ *It's impossible to tell what will happen in the future.* ○ *After I leave college, I want to travel round the world.* ○ *They live in the north of Spain.* ○ *Let's get together later in the week.* ○ *What's the name of that new restaurant in Merton Street?* ○ *Ed Koch was for many years the mayor of New York.* ○ *When we went to Paris, we went up the Eiffel Tower.* • 'The' is also used before superlatives and other words, such as 'first' or 'only' or numbers showing something's position in a list, which refer to only one thing or person: *That was one of the best films I've ever seen.* ○ *What's the highest mountain in Europe?* ○ *I shall never forget the first time we met.* ○ *This is the only smart dress I've got.* ○ *Every time we come to this restaurant, you always have the same thing.* ○ *You're the fifth person to ask me that question.* ○ *Today is the 24th of May/(esp. Br) May the 24th.* This is used mainly in spoken English. • 'The' can be used to express that the particular person or thing being mentioned is the best, greatest, most famous, etc. In this use, 'the' is usually given strong pronunciation: *Harry's Bar is the place to go.* ○ *You don't mean you met the Richard Gere, do you?* • 'The' can be used before some adjectives to turn the adjective into nouns which refer to one particular person or thing described by the adjective: *It seems that the deceased* (=this particular dead person) *had no living relatives.* ○ *I suppose we'll just have to wait for the inevitable* (=the particular thing that is certain to happen). • 'The' can also be used before some adjectives to turn the adjectives into nouns which refer to people or things in general that can be described by the adjective: *She lives in a special home for the elderly.* ○ *More needs to be done to help the unemployed to find work.* ○ *The French were defeated at Waterloo in 1815.* • You can use 'the' before a singular noun to refer to all the things or people represented by that noun: *The panda is becoming an increasingly rare animal.* ○ *The car is responsible for causing a lot of damage to our environment.* ○ *Exercise is good for the circulation.* • If you use 'the' before a particular family name, you are referring to two people who are married or to a family: *The Schmidts are coming to lunch on Saturday.* • 'The' can be used before some nouns referring to musical instruments or dances, to mean the type of instrument or dance in general: *Nico is learning to play the piano.* ○ *Can you do the waltz?* • 'The' is sometimes used before a noun to represent the activity connected with that noun: *I've got to go under the surgeon's knife* (=have a medical operation) *next week.* ○ *It's not a good idea to spend more that three hours at the wheel* (=driving a vehicle) *without a break.* • You use 'the' before the numbers that are used to refer to periods of 10 years: *the 1930s* ○ *the sixties* • 'The' is used before each of two comparative adjectives or adverbs when you want to show how one amount gets bigger or smaller in relation to the other: *The sooner I get this piece of work finished, the sooner I can go home.* ○ *The longer we live here, the more we like it.* • 'The' is also used before comparative adjectives or adverbs when you want to show that someone or something has become more or less of a particular state: *She doesn't seem to be any the worse* **for** *her bad experience.* ○ *I'm glad I decided to take a year off to travel, but I'm much the poorer* **for** *it!* • You can use 'the' for emphasis when you are expressing a strong opinion about someone or something: *That dog's been digging in my flowerbed again, the wretched thing!* ○ *André's got a new job, the lucky devil.* • LP **Articles**

the [YOUR] /ðiː, ðə/ *determiner* used instead of 'your', 'my', 'his', 'her', etc. • *An apple fell out of the tree and hit me on the head!* • *He held his daughter tightly by the arm.* • *"How's the leg today, Mrs Steel?" "Not too bad, thank you, doctor."* • *The patient is complaining of pain in the chest.* • *I can't remember where I parked the* (=my) *car.* • *It would be nice to see you and the* (=your) *family sometime soon.*

the [ENOUGH] /ðiː, ðə/ *determiner* [usually in negatives and questions] enough • *I'd like to go out this evening, but I don't think I've got the energy.* • *I don't think he has the experience* **for** *this kind of work.* • *I haven't got the time* **to** *talk to you now.* [+ *to* infinitive]

the [EACH] /ðiː, ðə/ *determiner* each; every • *How much does your car do to the litre?* • *These potatoes are sold by the kilo* (=are measured in that unit to calculate their price).

the·a·tre [BUILDING], *Am usually* **the·a·ter** /£ˈθɪə·təʳ, £θi ˈet·əʳ, $ˈθiː·ə·tɚ/ *n* [C] a building, room or outside structure with rows of seats, each row usually higher than the one in front, from which people can watch a performance or other activity • *the Lyceum Theatre* • *an open-air theatre* • *a lecture theatre* • *a theatre ticket/seat* • *When we're in town we always go to the theatre* (=go to see a play). • Theatre is also *Am and Aus for* CINEMA: *a movie theatre* • Theatre is *Br for* **operating theatre**: *a theatre nurse/sister* See at OPERATE [MEDICAL PROCESS]. • A **theatre in the round** is a theatre where people sit on all sides of the performers, not just in front of them. It is also a type of performance which tries to involve the people watching.

the·a·tre [PERFORMING ARTS], *Am usually* **the·a·ter** /£ˈθɪə·təʳ, £θiˈet·əʳ, $ˈθiː·ə·tɚ/ *n* [U] (the writing or performance of) plays, musicals or opera, written to be performed in public • *Greek theatre* • *modern theatre* • *the Theatre of the Absurd* • *theatre studies* • *His latest play has delighted theatre* **audiences** *and theatre* **critics** *alike.* • *The musical was wonderful theatre* (=The material was performed in a way that kept the attention or interest of the people watching). • *(fig.) Her tears were* **pure** *theatre* (=were produced in order to achieve a particular effect, but were not sincere). • *He's a member of the National/Youth Theatre* (=that company which performs plays). • *She made her career* **in the** *theatre* (=Her job was to produce or perform plays etc.).

the·at·ri·cal /θiˈæt·rɪ·kᵊl/ *adj* • *theatrical make-up* • *a theatrical agent* (=a performer's business manager) • *theatrical digs* (=places where performers live when they are travelling) • *(fig.) He made a very theatrical* (=intended to attract attention, but not sincere) *display of being apologetic.* • *(fig.) She's always making theatrical* (=intended to attract attention) *gestures.*

the·a·tri·cal·i·ty /£θiˌæt·rɪˈkæl·ɪ·ti, $-ə·ṭi/ *n* [U] • *The play had a vibrant theatricality* (=the material in it held the attention and interest of the people watching it). • *(fig.) Her speech was full of theatricality* (=behaviour intended to attract attention, but often not sincere) *but said little of importance.*

the·at·ri·cal·ly /θiˈæt·rɪ·kli/ *adv*

the·a·tri·cals /θiˈæt·rɪ·kᵊlz/ *pl n* • Theatricals are stage performances by people who are not trained or paid to act, but who practise and perform in the time when they are not working: *amateur theatricals*

the·a·tre [MILITARY] /£ˈθɪə·təʳ, £θiˈet·əʳ, $ˈθi·ə·tɚ/ *n* [C] an area or place in which important military events take place • *a theatre of war* • *a theatre of operations*

the·a·tre·go·er /£ˈθɪə·təˌgəʊ·əʳ, £θiˈet·ə-, $ˈθiː·ə·ṭɚˌgoʊ·ɚ/, *Am usually* **the·a·ter·go·er** *n* [C] someone who regularly goes to the theatre

thee /ðiː/ *pronoun old use* object form of thou (=*old use for* you), used when speaking to one person • *With this ring, I thee wed.*

theft /θeft/ *n* (the act of) dishonestly taking something which belongs to someone else and keeping it; stealing • *Unfortunately, we have had several thefts in the building recently.* [C] • *Shoplifting is theft.* [U] • See also THIEF. • LP **Crimes and criminals**

their /£ðeəʳ, $ðer/ *determiner* of or belonging to them • *He gave them their coats.* • *Children should always brush their teeth before going to bed.* • *They asked him to take their picture.* • *She was touched by their concern for her.* • *They seem to be wasting their time on this project.* • Their can also be used to refer to one person in order to avoid saying 'his or her': *Has everyone got their passport?* ○ *One of the students has left their book behind.* ○ *Why don't you see a doctor and get their advice?* • LP **Determiners**

theirs /£ðeəz, $ðerz/ *pronoun* of or belonging to them • *Here's my car. Where's theirs?* • *Theirs are the ones in blue envelopes.* • *I think she's a relation of theirs.*

the·ism /ˈθiː·ɪ·zᵊm/ *n* [U] the belief that there is only one God, who is completely separate from those things (the Earth, people, etc.) he has created, rather than being part of them • Compare **atheism** at ATHEIST; DEISM.

them [THOSE PEOPLE/THINGS] /ðem/ *pronoun* object form of 'they' used after a verb or preposition • *I've lost my keys. I can't find them anywhere.* • *I told them I was leaving next week.* • *We went fishing with them last year.* • *It's them.*

They've arrived early. • *Who? Oh, them. No, I've never met them.* • Them can be used to refer to a single person in order to avoid saying 'him or her': *When each passenger arrives, we ask them to fill in a form.* • *(infml)* **Them and us** is used when describing disagreements esp. between different social groups: *If parents are encouraged to be involved in school, there is less chance of a them-and-us situation developing.* ○ *The senior staff have their own restaurant. – It's definitely a case of them and us.*

them THOSE /ðem/ *determiner not standard for* THOSE • *Who gave you them sweets?*

theme /θiːm/ *n* [C] the main subject of a talk, book, film, etc. or a short, simple tune on which a piece of music is based • *He has written several stories on the theme* **of** *lost happiness.* • *Does the conference* **have a central** *theme this year?* • *Most of the articles she writes are* **on a** *religious theme,* • *Her books are all* **variations on the same/a** *theme.* • *The plays he has written all have a* **recurrent/ recurring/common** *theme.* • A theme is also a song or tune which is played several times in a film, etc. and which is therefore remembered as belonging to that film: *a theme song/tune* ○ *theme music* • A **theme park** (*Am also and Aus* **amusement park**) is a large permanent area for public entertainment, with amusements such as big machines to ride on or play games on, restaurants, etc., all connected with a single subject: *Disney is famous for its fantastic theme parks, like Disneyworld in Florida.* • Ⓙ

them·at·ic /£θɪˈmæt·ɪk, $θiːˈmæṭ-/ *adj* [not gradable] • *In her study, the author has adopted a thematic* (= one based on different subjects) *rather than a chronological approach to the French Revolution.*

them·selves /ðəmˈselvz/ *pronoun* reflexive form of 'they', sometimes used for emphasis • *Did they enjoy themselves at the theatre?* • *They asked themselves where they had gone wrong.* • *I think they gave themselves a bad fright.* • *They made themselves a fortune selling sports clothes.* ○ *They made a fortune for themselves selling sports clothes.* • *(fml) They themselves had no knowledge of what was happening.* • *They collected the evidence* **(all by) themselves** (= without help). • *I wish people would just* **be themselves** (= act in their usual manner) *instead of trying to be important.* • *They* **had** *the whole campsite* **to themselves** (= They were alone and did not have to share it with anyone). • *These facts are unimportant* **in themselves** (= when considered alone), *but if you put them together, they may mean more.* • *They* **keep (themselves) to themselves** (= do not want to socialize with other people). • LP› **Reflexive pronouns and verbs**

then TIME /ðen/ *adv, adj* [before n; not gradable] (at) that time (in the past or in the future) • *I was working in the city then.* • *Mrs Johnson, or Miss Clark as she was then, is in the back row in the photo.* • *Give me the report tomorrow – I'll have time to read it then.* • *(fml) The police questioned the then chairman about the missing money.* • *(fml) I wanted to live in the city, but my then husband* (= the man who was my husband at that time) *preferred the country.* • *I won't have time to read it* **before/until then.** • *I'll phone you tomorrow – I should have the details* **by then.** • *She had a car accident a year ago and has suffered from back pain* **from then on** (= since that time). • *She sewed the button on* **then and there** *(also* **there and then***)* (= immediately).

then NEXT /ðen/ *adv* [not gradable] next or after that • *Let me finish this job, then we'll go.* • *He smiled, then turned to me and nodded.* • *The boy began to cheer, then another joined in.* • *Give her the letter to read, then she'll understand.* • *If it's not on the table, then look in the cupboard.*

then ADDITIONALLY /ðen/ *adv* [not gradable] in addition • *This is the standard model, then there's the de luxe version which costs more.* • *I agree she types accurately,* **but then (again)** (= but when you give more thought to the matter), *she's very slow.* • *(esp. Am) He gave it his best effort* **and then some** (= and much more).

then RESULT /ðen/ *adv* [not gradable] as a result; in that case; also used as a way of joining a statement to an earlier piece of conversation • *Stop for a rest now – then you won't have to go to bed early.* • *Then I suppose you'll want to leave quite soon?* • *You'll be selling your house, then?* • *Have you heard the news, then?* • **If** *I haven't heard from you by Friday,* **then** *I'll assume you're not coming.* • LP› **Conditionals**

thence /ðents/ *adv* [not gradable] *dated or fml* from there; from that place • *We travelled to my parents' home and thence to my sister's.*

thence·forth /£ˌðentsˈfɔːθ, $-ˈfɔːrθ/, **thence·for·ward** /£ˌðentsˈfɔː·wəd, $-ˈfɔːr·wɚd/ *adv* [not gradable] *dated or fml* after that; from that time forward • *He left home when he was 18 and thenceforth travelled the world.*

the·ol·o·gy /£θiˈɒl·ə·dʒi, $-ˈɑː·lə-/ *n* the study of religion and religious belief, or a set of beliefs about a particular religion • *These new books on theology might interest you.* [U] • *Our theologies differ in several respects.* [C]

the·o·lo·gian /£ˌθiː·əˈləʊ·dʒən, $-ˈloʊ-/ *n* [C]

the·o·log·i·cal /£ˌθiː·əˈlɒdʒ·ɪ·kəl, $-ˈlɑː·dʒɪ-/ *adj* • *After graduating from Toronto University, he went to theological* **college**, *and in 1936 was ordained as a minister with the United Church of Canada.*

the·o·log·i·cal·ly /£ˌθiː·əˈlɒdʒ·ɪ·kli, $-ˈlɑː·dʒɪ-/ *adv*

the·or·em /£ˈθɪə·rəm, $ˈθiː·ɚ·əm/ *n* [C] *specialized* (esp. in mathematics) a formal statement that can be shown to be true by reasoning • *a mathematical theorem*

the·ory /£ˈθɪə·ri, $ˈθɪr·i/ *n* a formal statement of the rules on which a subject of study is based or of ideas which are suggested to explain a fact or event or, more generally, an opinion or explanation • *economic theory* [U] • *scientific theory* [U] • *music theory* [U] • *Einstein's theory* **of** *relativity* [C] • *Darwin's theory* **of** *evolution* [C] • *His theory is that the hole was caused by a meteorite.* [C + *that* clause] • **In theory** (= According to the facts), *the journey ought to take three hours, but in practice* (= when it happens) *it usually takes four because of roadworks.*

the·or·et·i·cal /£θɪəˈret·ɪ·kəl, $ˌθiː·əˈreṭ-/ *adj* • *theoretical and applied genetics* • *theoretical and practical studies* • A **theoretical possibility** is something which could, but is unlikely to, happen or be true according to the known facts.

the·or·et·i·cal·ly /£θɪəˈret·ɪ·kli, $ˌθiː·əˈreṭ-/ *adv* • *Theoretically* (= According to the facts), *women have the same opportunities as men, but the reality is very different.*

the·or·ist /£ˈθɪə·rɪst, $ˈθiː·ɚ·ɪst/ *n* [C] • *a well-known economic theorist*

the·or·ize, *Br and Aus usually* **-ise** /£ˈθɪə·raɪz, $ˈθɪr·aɪz/ *v* [I] • *It's easy to theorize* (= create theories) **about** *what might have happened.*

ther·a·peu·tic /£ˌθer·əˈpjuː·tɪk, $-ṭɪk/ *adj* causing someone to feel happier and more relaxed or to be more healthy • *I find gardening very therapeutic.* • *the therapeutic effects of a high-fibre diet*

ther·a·py /ˈθer·ə·pi/ *n* [U] treatment which helps someone feel better, grow stronger, etc., esp. after an illness • *occupational therapy* • *speech therapy* • *group therapy* • *Joining a club can be* **a** *therapy* **for** *loneliness.*

ther·a·pist /ˈθer·ə·pɪst/ *n* [C] • *a speech therapist* • *I'm seeing my therapist on Friday morning.*

there PLACE /£ðeəʳ, $ðer/ *adv* [not gradable] (to, at or in) that place • *Put the chair there.* • *The museum was closed today. We'll go there tomorrow.* • *There's that book you were looking for.* • *Read out the rest of the letter, don't stop there!* • *I'll have to stop you there, we've run out of time.* • *I've left the boxes over/out/under there.* • *We'll never* **get there** (= arrive) *in time.* • *(fig.) Try again, you'll* **get there** (= succeed) *in the end.* • *(fig.) You'll* **get there** (= understand) *if you think about it hard enough.* • *It was 20 miles* **there and back** (= the total distance to and from the place). • **There and then** (also **then and there**) means immediately, in the past or future: *I suggested he phone his mother and he did it there and then.* ○ *Tell me which day you want to go and I'll book the tickets there and then.* • *Best friends are* **(always) there for** *each other* (= available to provide help or support) *in times of trouble.* • *"Because it is there"* (George Mallory when asked why he wanted to climb Mount Everest, 1923)

there INTRODUCING A SENTENCE /£ðeəʳ, $ðer/ *pronoun* used to introduce sentences, esp. before the verbs *be, seem* and *appear* • *There's someone on the phone for you.* • *There's no doubt who is the best candidate.* • *(not standard) There's* (= There are) *lives at stake and we can't afford to take any risks.* • *Plan it carefully – I don't want there to be any problems.* • *There appeared/seemed to be some difficulty in fixing a date for the meeting.* • *Never has there been such a terrible disaster.* • *(fml) There may come a time when you'll regret that decision.* • *(literary)* Some children's stories written in a traditional style begin with 'there': *There once was/lived a poor widow who had a beautiful daughter.* • **There's a good boy/girl/dog** is used to show approval or encouragement: *Tie your shoelaces, there's a good girl.* • **There you are**, or more informally, **there you go** is a phrase used when giving something to someone, usually

THERE

Uses with 'be'

'There' is often used to refer to something for the first time. It is possible to say *A cat is in the kitchen* but it is much more common to use 'there' to introduce the sentence:

A cat is in the kitchen. — *There's a cat in the kitchen.*
Lots of people are outside. — *There are lots of people outside.*
Ice was all over the road. — *There was ice all over the road.*

- **followed by words of number or quantity**:
There are **no** *seats left.* • *There's* **somebody** *at the door.* • *Is there* **anything** *I can do?* • *There have been* **seven** *phone calls for you.* • *There was* **a pint of** *water in the bottle.*
Words for distances take 'there' when they refer to a quantity of something: *There are* **2 yards of** *cloth on the shelf.* But notice: *It's a mile to the station.*
- **followed by a noun and a present participle, *to*- infinitive or *that* clause:**
There was a man **drawing** *pictures on the ground.*
There are some letters **to** *write* (= that should be written).
There's no doubt (**that**) *he's dying.*

Uses with other intransitive verbs

- **to describe states** (this use is more common in formal English):
There **appeared/seemed** *to be some difficulty in fixing a date for the meeting.* • *There* **remained** *very little to do.* • *There will now* **follow** *a short talk.*
- **with modal verbs** *There* **must** *be an answer.* • *There* **should** *be more support for local business.* • *There* **may** *come a time when you'll regret that decision.* • *There* **might** *seem nothing more to say.*

In some of these uses, 'there' might be confused with 'it'. LP› **It**

after a request for the item, such as giving someone goods that they have bought. • **There you go** can express acceptance of something unlucky: *We didn't win the competition, but there you go – we can always try again next year.* • **There you are** is also used to mean 'I told you so': *There you are, I knew you'd forget if you didn't write it down.* • **There** you **go again** is a way of emphasizing that an action is repeated often: *There they go again, making trouble/complaining.* ○ *There she goes again – she never knows when to give up.* • LP› **There**

there SYMPATHY/SATISFACTION /£ðeəʳ, $ðer/ *exclamation* used to express sympathy or satisfaction • **There, there/ There now**, *don't cry, it won't hurt for long.* • *There, I've made it work at last.*

there·a·bouts /£'ðeəʳ·ə·bauts, ,–'-s, $'ðer·ə·bauts/ *adv* approximately • *He's lived in Norwich for 40 years, or thereabouts.*

there·aft·er /£,ðeəʳ'ɑːf·təʳ, $,ðer'æf·tɚ/ *adv fml* continuing on from a particular point in time, esp. after something else has stopped happening • *For the first month you will be working in teams of four, but thereafter you will be working in pairs.* • *He left the priesthood in 1970 and settled in the Washington area* **shortly** *thereafter* (= soon after that).

there·by /£,ðeə'baɪ, $,ðer-/ *adv fml or dated* because of this; as a result of this action • *She said the musicians' and actors' unions had failed to agree pay levels and that these unions had thereby deprived over 250 people of work.* • *Diets that are high in saturated fat and cholesterol tend to clog up our arteries, thereby reducing the blood flow to our hearts and brains.* [+ v-ing] • *(humorous) "Why are you limping?" "Ah,* **thereby hangs a tale** (= there's a long explanation involved)."

there·fore /£'ðeə·fɔːʳ, $'ðer·fɔːr/ *adv* [not gradable] as a result; because of that; for that reason • *I missed the last flight, and therefore decided/(fml) decided therefore to stay the night at the airport.* • *We were unable to get funding and therefore had to abandon the project.*

there·in /£,ðeə'rɪn, $,ðer'ɪn/ *adv fml* in or into a particular place, thing etc. • *(dated) Susan opened the box to find a key and a faded, dusty map therein.* • *(fig.) Suzy's a socialist but her boyfriend votes Conservative – therein* **lies** (= this is) *the reason why they argue.*

ther·mal /£'θɜː·məl, $'θɜːr-/ *adj* [before n] *specialized* connected with heat • *At room temperature, the thermal* **conductivity** *of a diamond* (= its ability to carry heat) *is about six times higher than that of a piece of copper.* • *Triple glazing consists of three layers of glass separated by air spaces to give improved thermal or acoustic* **insulation**. • *It was the Romans who first recognised the medicinal benefits of Hungary's thermal* **springs** (= ones which produce hot water). • **Thermal imaging** is the use of special electronic equipment, in conditions in which it is difficult to see, to create a picture based on the heat produced by a person or object: *Firefighters use thermal imaging to search for people in buildings filled with smoke.* • **Thermal underwear** is underwear that has been specially designed to keep you warm.

ther·mal /£'θɜː·məl, $'θɜːr-/ *n* [C] • *(specialized)* A thermal is a large column of hot air rising from the ground: *Birds and gliders circle in thermals to gain height.* • *(infml)* Thermals are also **thermal underwear**: *It's very wintry now, isn't it? I'll have to put my thermals on.*

therm·al·ly /£'θɜː·mə·li, $'θɜːr-/ *adv*

therm·o– /£'θɜː·məʊ-, $'θɜːr·moʊ-, ,–-/ *combining form* connected with heat or temperature • *thermo-electric* • *thermo-nuclear*

ther·mo·dy·nam·ics /£,θɜː·məʊ·daɪ'næm·ɪks, $,θɜːr·moʊ-/ *n* [U] *specialized* the area of physics concerned with the mechanical action of heat and other types of energy, and the relationship between them • *The First Law of Thermodynamics states that in any process energy can change from one form to another, but it cannot be destroyed or created.*

ther·mo·dy·nam·ic /£,θɜː·məʊ·daɪ'næm·ɪk, $,θɜːr·moʊ-/ *adj* [before n· not gradable] *specialized* • *thermodynamic equilibrium/properties* • *the thermodynamic behaviour of a gas*

ther·mo·me·ter /£θə'mɒm·ɪ·təʳ, $θɚ'mɑː·mə·ţɚ/ *n* [C] a device used for measuring temperature, esp. of the air or in a person's body • *A thermometer is usually a small glass cylinder containing a line of mercury that moves up or down as the temperature rises or falls.* • *Last night the thermometer fell below freezing.* • *(fig.) The official thermometer* (= recorded level) *of inflation will rise above 5% in August.* • PIC› **Medical equipment, Meters and gauges**

Therm·os (flask) /£'θɜː·məs, $'θɜːr-/ *n* [C] *trademark* a **vacuum flask**, see at VACUUM • PIC› **Bottles and flasks**

therm·o·stat /£'θɜː·mə·stæt, $'θɜːr-/ *n* [C] a device which keeps a system within a usually limited temperature range by automatically switching the supply of heat on and off • *a central heating thermostat* • *an oven thermostat*

therm·o·stat·i·cally /£,θɜː·məʊ'stæt·ɪ·kli, $,θɜːr·moʊ'stæţ-/ *adv* • *A thermostatically-***controlled** *heating element maintains the water temperature.*

the·sau·rus /£θɪ'sɔː·rəs, $-'sɔːr·əs/ *n* [C] *pl* **thesauruses** or *fml* **thesauri** /£θɪ'sɔː·raɪ, $-'sɔːr·aɪ/ a type of dictionary in which words with similar meanings are grouped together • *At the entry for 'kill', my thesaurus lists 'murder', 'assassinate' and 'waste'.* • GR

these /ðiːz/ *pl of* THIS

the·sis /'θiː·sɪs/ *n* [C] *pl* **theses** /'θiː·siːz/ a long piece of writing on a particular subject, esp. one that is done for a higher college or university degree • *She is writing her thesis* **on** *black holes.* • *a doctoral thesis* (= for a PHD) • *(fml)*

A thesis is also the main idea, opinion or theory of a person or group, or in a piece of writing or a talk: *Their main thesis was that war was inevitable.* • LP› **Schools and colleges**

thes·pi·an /ˈθes·pi·ən/ *adj* [not gradable] *slightly fml* connected with acting and the theatre • *The biography covers a thespian career which spanned four decades.* • *There is a great deal of unused thespian talent/skill in this country.*

thes·pi·an *slightly fml* /ˈθes·pi·ən/, *infml or disapproving* **thesp** /θesp/ *n* [C] • A thespian is an actor: *She describes Tony Hopkins as the greatest British thespian since Olivier.* ○ *Most of the people at Caroline's party were thesps and artists.*

they /ðeɪ/ *pronoun* used as the subject of a verb to refer to people, animals or things already mentioned or, more generally, to a group of people not clearly described • *I've known the Browns for a long time. They're very pleasant people.* • *Where are my glasses? They were on the table just now.* • *They* (= People who know) *say things will be better in the new year.* • *They've* (= The people in control) *decided to change the bus route into town.* • *(infml)* They can be used to avoid saying 'he or she': *"There's someone on the phone for you." "What do they want?"* • LP› **Sexist language**

thick NOT THIN /θɪk/ *adj* **-er, -est** having a large distance between two sides, or having a large DIAMETER (= measurement through the centre) • *a thick rope* • *thick eyebrows* • *a thick layer of dust* • *She picked up a thick volume and began to read out loud.* • *What I'd really like to eat is a thick juicy steak.* • *The walls are two metres thick.* [after n] • *He pulled on a thick* (= made of thick material) *sweater/coat before stepping out into the darkness.* • Someone who is **thick-skinned** does not appear to be easily hurt by criticism.

thick·ly /ˈθɪk·li/ *adv* • *Spread the mixture thickly across the baking tray, before popping it into a pre-heated oven.*

thick·ness /ˈθɪk·nəs/ *n* • *The thickness of the mulch will prevent weeds growing around the shrubs.* [U] • *Put several thicknesses* (= layers) **of** *newspaper on the table before you start to paint your model aircraft.* [C]

thick CLOSE TOGETHER /θɪk/ *adj* **-er, -est** close together, and often difficult to see through • *thick cloud* • *thick forest* • *(fig.) thick* (= very great) *darkness* • *(infml)* If people are **as thick as thieves** they are very friendly. • *(esp. Br infml)* Things which are **thick on the ground** exist in large numbers: *Female engineers are not too thick on the ground.*

thick·en /ˈθɪk·ən/ *v* [I] • *The smoke thickened rapidly.*

thick NOT FLOWING /θɪk/ *adj* **-er, -est** (of a liquid) not flowing easily • *thick syrup* • *thick paint* • Compare THIN WEAK.

thick·en *obj* /ˈθɪk·ən/ *v* [T] • *Thicken the sauce with a little flour.*

thick·en·er /£ˈθɪk·ən·əʳ, $-ɚ/, **thick·en·ing** /ˈθɪk·ən·ɪŋ, ˈθɪk·nɪŋ/ *n* [C; U] • A thickener is a substance which is used to make something else thick: *gravy thickening* ○ *Cornflour can be used as a thickener in sauces.*

thick STUPID /θɪk/ *adj* **-er, -est** *slang* mentally slow or stupid • *I told you not to touch that – are you deaf or just thick?* • If you say that someone is **as thick as two short planks**, you are calling them very stupid: *There's no point asking Harold – he's as thick as two short planks!*

thick·o /£ˈθɪk·əʊ, $-oʊ/ *n* [C] *pl* **thickos** *slang* • *Don't be such a thicko* (= stupid person).

thick·et /ˈθɪk·ɪt/ *n* [C] an area of trees and bushes growing closely together

thick·set /ˌθɪkˈset/ *adj* (esp. of the male human body) wide and short; STOCKY • *A thickset young man appeared in the doorway.*

thief /θiːf/ *n* [C] *pl* **thieves** /θiːvz/ a person who steals • *Shoplifters are thieves and will be prosecuted.* • *A post office was broken into last night, and the thieves got away with £120 000.* • *(saying)* 'Like a thief in the night' means secretly or unexpectedly and without being seen. • *(saying)* 'It takes a thief to catch a thief' or 'Set a thief to catch a thief' means that one dishonest person can guess what another dishonest person might do. • *"Procrastination is the thief of Time"* (Edward Young in the poem *Night Thoughts*, 1742) • See also THEFT. • LP› **Crimes and criminals**

thiev·ing /ˈθiː·vɪŋ/ *n* [U] *slightly literary or fml* • *His was a life of thieving* (= stealing) *and cheating.*

thiev·ing /ˈθiː·vɪŋ/ *adj* [before n; not gradable] • *(humorous) Take your thieving* **hands off** *my cake!* (= Don't touch it!) • *Those thieving kids tried to steal my car.*

thigh /θaɪ/ *n* [C] the part of a person's leg above the knee • *His fall left him with a nasty bruise on his thigh.* • *She broke her thigh* **bone** *in the accident.* • *He went off the field limping from a thigh* **injury** *that may take some time to heal.*

thim·ble /ˈθɪm·bl̩/ *n* [C] a small cover, made of metal, plastic or PORCELAIN, worn to protect the finger which pushes the needle when sewing

thim·ble·ful /ˈθɪm·bl̩·fʊl/ *n* [C] • A thimbleful is a humorous expression for a very small amount: *He poured* **a** *thimbleful* **of** *whisky into the glass.* ○ *I'll just have a thimbleful, thank you.*

thin NOT THICK /θɪn/ *adj* **thinner, thinnest** having a small distance between two sides or a small DIAMETER (= measurement through the centre) • *a thin book* • *a thin layer of dust* • *thin black lines* • *a thin cable/wire* • *a thin jacket* (= made from thin material) • *I like beef sliced really thin.* • *(Br)* It's **the thin end of the wedge** means that something bad can be started by something quite small: *Identity cards for football supporters could be the thin end of the wedge – soon everyone might have to carry identification.* • Someone who is **thin-skinned** is easily hurt by criticism or is easily made unhappy.

thin·ly /ˈθɪn·li/ *adv* • *thinly-***sliced** *ham*

thin NOT FAT /θɪn/ *adj* **thinner, thinnest** (of the body) with little flesh on the bones • *Did you notice how thin her wrists were?* • *His face was pale and thin.* • *Thin, hungry dogs roamed the streets.*

thin down *v adv* [I] • *He's thinned down a lot* (= become much less fat) *since I last saw him.*

thin TRANSPARENT /θɪn/ *adj* **thinner, thinnest** not difficult to see through • *thin mist/cloud*

thin·ly /ˈθɪn·li/ *adv* • *The mist swirled thinly round the tombstones.*

thin FEW /θɪn/ *adj* **thinner, thinnest** having only a few items in a large area • *The attendance at the meeting was rather thin.* • *(Br and Aus) Shops which will deliver goods are* **thin on the ground** (= not common) *these days.* • *He's* **thin on top**. (= He's lost a lot of his hair.) • To **disappear/vanish into thin air** is to disappear suddenly and completely. • *I can't come up with £10 000* **out of thin air** (= from nothing) *– it'll take a while to find that kind of money.*

thin *(obj)* /θɪn/ *v* **-nn-** • *Thin* **(out)** (= remove some of) *the plants to give them room to grow.* [T/M] • *The traffic will thin out* (= There will be less of it) *after the rush hour.* [I]

thin·ly /ˈθɪn·li/ *adv* • *Sprinkle the seeds thinly in rows and cover lightly with soil.*

thin FLOWING EASILY /θɪn/ *adj* (of a liquid) flowing easily • *a thin soup*

thin *obj* /θɪn/ *v* [T] **-nn-** • *Thin* **(down)** *the sauce with a little stock.*

thin·ner /£ˈθɪn·əʳ, $-ɚ/ *n* [U] • Thinner is a substance added esp. to paint to make it flow more easily: *paint thinner*

thin WEAK /θɪn/ *adj* **thinner, thinnest** weak or of poor quality • *a thin excuse* • *thin humour* • *a thin disguise* • *a thin nervous voice* • *a thin smile* • To have **a thin time (of it)** is to have bad or unhappy experiences: *He's been having a thin time (of it) since his accident.*

thine /ðaɪn/ *determiner old use* THY (before a vowel sound); your • *thine eyes* • *thine honour*

thine /ðaɪn/ *pronoun old use* • Thine means 'yours'. • *"For thine is the kingdom, the power and the glory"* (Bible *The Lord's Prayer*, Matthew 6.9)

thing OBJECT /θɪŋ/ *n* [C] used to refer in an approximate way to an object or to avoid naming it • *What's that thing over there?* • *There are several things on the table which belong to you.* • *She makes a lot of things herself.* • *There are some nice things in the shops this summer.* • *I don't eat sweet things* (= sweet food). • *How does this damn thing work?* • *(infml) She's just bought a new word processor thing* (= I'm not sure exactly what it is). • Your **things** are either your possessions or a particular set of your possessions: *All their things were destroyed in the fire.* ○ *Bring your swimming things if the weather's nice.* • **Things** are also a particular set of objects: *Let me help you clear away the tea things* (= cups, plates, etc. that are used for having tea). • *"A wandering minstrel I /A thing of shreds and patches"* (W.S.Gilbert in the opera *The Mikado*, 1885) • *"A thing of beauty is a joy for ever"* (Keats in the poem *Endymion*, 1818) • *"What is this thing called love?"* (title of a song written by Cole Porter, 1929)

thing IDEA/EVENT /θɪŋ/ *n* [C] used to refer in an approximate way to an idea, subject, event, action, etc. • *One of the things I want to talk about is buying books – another thing is ordering stationery.* • *That was an unkind/*

a helpful thing to say. • *I've got so many things to do I don't know where to start.* • *Your information is correct but you left out one thing.* • **First thing** and **last thing** refers to activities done or events that take place earliest and latest in the day: *I'll phone him first thing tomorrow.* ○ *I usually have a bath last thing before I go to bed.* • **What with one thing and another** (= Because I was so busy) *I forgot to phone you yesterday.* • *I've been so busy today. It's been* **one thing after another** (= Many things have been happening in a short time). • **It's a** good/difficult/lucky **thing** means something is good/difficult/lucky: *It's a good thing* **(that)** *we booked our tickets early.* ○ *Learning to ride a bike was a difficult/easy thing* (= was difficult/easy) *for me to do.* • *(Br)* **A close/near thing** (*Am and Aus* **close call**) is something which almost happened: *The car just missed the child but it was a very close thing.* ○ *We gave the job to Michael in the end, but it was a close thing* (= difficult to decide) *as all the applicants were good.* • *(infml)* To be **on to a good thing** is to have an easy and pleasant life or job in which it is not necessary to work hard: *He's on to a good thing, he has free accommodation in return for answering the phone when the family are out.* • *(infml)* To **do** your **own thing** is to do what you want without caring what anyone else thinks of you. • *(infml)* To **have a thing about** something means you strongly like or dislike something: *She's got a thing about fast cars.* • *(infml)* To **make a (big) thing (out) of** something means to give something too much importance: *He always makes a big thing out of helping me cook.* ○ *I want a party, but I don't want to make a big thing of it.* • *At first, we were just dancing together, but* **one thing led to another** (= there was a series of events in which each event was caused by the previous one), *and I ended up in bed with him.* • **The thing is** is used to introduce a subject for discussion, a problem or a question: *The thing is, my parents like me to be home by 10 o'clock. Can we get home in time?* ○ *I liked the dress, but the thing was, it didn't fit me very well.* • You can also use **the thing is** to emphasize the importance of what you are saying: *The thing is to be watchful even when you think your child is safe.* • **It's (just) one of those things** means that there was no way of planning to avoid something: *The road was blocked, so we missed the meeting – I'm afraid it was just one of those things.* • If someone is **hearing/imagining/seeing things** they think they are experiencing something which is not really happening: *I'm sure I saw/left my glasses on this table, but they're not here now. I must have been seeing/imagining things.* • *(humorous)* **Things that go bump in the night** is used to describe anything unknown which might be frightening, esp. a noise. • **Things** is often used to refer to the general situation: *Things have been going very well (for us) recently.* • Someone might say that something is good **all things considered** to mean it was generally good although the situation was not perfect: *I think the party was great, all things considered – I mean we didn't have much time to prepare and no help, but it still went well.* • *(infml)* **How are things (with you)?** (= How are you?) • *(infml)* **What are things like** (= What is happening/What are you doing) *in Cambridge/at work these days?* • **The way things are/As things stand** (= In the present situation), *I'll never have this ready by June.* • *(saying)* 'Things ain't (= aren't) what they used to be' means the situation is not as good as it was in the past. • **The shape of things to come**, the title of a book by H.G. Wells, is now a phrase which refers to how a situation will develop: *Ever-increasing computerization is the shape of things to come.* • *My doctor's told me to* **take things easy** (= relax and not work too hard) *for a while.*

thing PERSON/ANIMAL /θɪŋ/ *n* [C always after adj] used to refer affectionately or sympathetically to a person or animal • *He's had a bad time recently, poor thing.* • *The poor things were kept in small cages without room to move.* • *She's a dear little thing.* • *You lucky thing winning a car.* [as form of address] • *What a lazy/noisy/stupid thing you are!* • *"Wild Thing, I think I love you"* (from a song by The Troggs, 1966) • *"Where the Wild Things are"* (title of a children's book by Maurice Sedak, 1963)

thing·y /ˈθɪŋ·i/ *n* [U] *infml* • Thingy is sometimes used if you can't remember someone's name: *Ask thingy over there, he'll know.*

thing ANYTHING /θɪŋ/ *n* [U] used instead of anything, everything, something or nothing for emphasis • *After the guests had gone,* **there wasn't a (single) thing** (= anything) *left to eat.* • *Don't worry about* **a thing** (= anything). *I'll take care of it all.* • *(humorous)* I **haven't got a thing** (= anything) **to wear** means I have no clothes that are suitable for the occasion. • *He broke his promise and* **there wasn't a thing** *we* **could do about it** (= and we couldn't do anything about it). • **All things considered** (= Taking everything into consideration) I think he did a good job. • **All/Other things being equal** (= If everything happens as expected), *I'll be at home on Tuesday.* • If you try to be **all things to all men/people** you try to do things which will please everyone. • *Be true to yourself* **in all things** (= in everything). • *I value my freedom* **above all things** (= more than everything else). • **If there's one thing** (= something) *I want to know, it's where he goes on Thursday afternoons.* • **One thing** (= Something)/**Another thing** (= Something else) *you'll have to agree to is working in the evenings.* • *I went by plane,* **a thing** (= something) *I hardly ever do.* • *I'm having trouble paying attention – I have* **a thing or two** (= some matters) *on my mind.* • *Why don't you ask Andrew about it? He knows* **a thing or two** *about* (= has some knowledge of) *computers.* • *She thinks she knows everything about raising children, but I'll show/tell her* **a thing or two** (= some action/information she was not expecting or aware of). • Something or someone that **does things to** you has a strong, usually pleasurable, effect on you: *That music really does things to me.* • **For one thing** is used to introduce a reason for something: *"Why won't you come to New York with me?" "For one thing, I don't like flying, and for another, I can't afford it."* • **And another thing** is used to introduce one more in a series of arguments or complaints: *And another thing, why didn't you tell me you were going out?* • **It's one thing to** *buy a train ticket, quite another to get a seat.* (= You cannot be certain of finding a seat, even if you have a ticket.) • **A thing of the past** is something which no longer happens: *Giving up your seat to an older person seems to be a thing of the past.* • *(saying)* 'If it's not one thing it's another/the other' means that whatever you do, there are always difficulties.

thing NOUN PHRASES /θɪŋ/ *n* [U; always after adj/adv] **the thing** used to make noun phrases with particular adjectives and adverbs • *(esp. Br)* **The done thing** (*Am usually* **the thing to do**) is what you are expected to do in a social situation: *Don't forget to shake hands – it's the done thing, you know.* • *(esp. Br)* If something is **not the done thing** (*Am usually* **not the thing to do**), it is not socially acceptable to do it: *Smoking during a meal is not the done thing.* • **The first/next thing** *(to do) is to write your name at the top of the page.* • *Go home? That's* **the last thing** *I want to do!* (= I'm certain that I don't want to!) • **The (latest) thing** is something which is very new and fashionable: *It's become the thing among young people in the city to wear T-shirts in the middle of winter.* ○ *Biodegradable plastic is the latest thing.* • *Training isn't* **the same thing** (= the same) *as education.* • **The real thing** is something which is not false or a copy: *The fire alarm goes off accidentally so often that when it's the real thing nobody will take any notice.* • *A week's rest would be* **the very thing/just the thing** *for her* (= just what she needs). • *Let's call* **the whole thing** *off.* ○ *I want to forget* **the whole thing** (= everything planned/discussed). • *Your letter has told me precisely* **the thing** (= exactly what) *I needed to know.*

thing·a·ma·bob /£ˈθɪŋ·ə·mə·bɒb, $-bɑːb/, **thing·u·ma·bob**, *Br* **thing·um·my** /ˈθɪŋ·ə·mi/, **thing·a·ma·jig** /ˈθɪŋ·ə·mə·dʒɪg/ *n* [C] *infml* a word used, esp. in spoken English, when the name of an object has been forgotten • *Put those thingamabobs/thingummies down, please, and come over here.* • See also **thingy** at THING PERSON/ANIMAL.

think *(obj)* CONSIDER /θɪŋk/ *v past* **thought** /£θɔːt, $θɑːt/ to believe, consider, have as an opinion or idea • *I think* **(that)** *I've met you before.* [+ *(that)* clause] • *He thought* **(that)** *they'd be going away in June.* [+ *(that)* clause] • *"Do you think* **(that)** *you could get me some stamps while you're in town?"* [+ *(that)* clause] • *I think* **(that)** *I'll go swimming after lunch.* [+ *(that)* clause] • *"Do you think this is the right house?" "Yes, I think* **so**./*No, I don't think* **so**.*"* [+ *so*] • *Arnold was happy to work in the evenings – or* **so** *I thought.* [after *so*] • *I missed the bus. It left earlier* **than** *I thought* (= I expected that it would leave later than it did). [I] • *I always thought him a rather annoying child.* [T + obj + n/adj] • *Salmon used to be thought expensive/thought a luxury.* [T + obj + n/adj] • *He was thought* **to** *have boarded the plane in New York.* [+ obj + *to* infinitive] • *What do you think* **about/of** (= what is your opinion of) *my new dress.* [I] • *I'm thinking* **about/of** (= considering) **buying** *a new car.*

[I] • *I think* **of** *him* (= consider him) **as** *someone who will always help me.* [I] • *(esp. disapproving) "Rupert's left without paying us back that money."* **"I thought as much"** (= I am not surprised). • *So, Adrian is seeing Emma, is he?* **Who would have thought** *it* (= That is surprising)? • **I can't think** (= I don't know) **why** *she hasn't phoned*/**how** *I lost my keys.* • *She* **couldn't think** (= didn't know) **wh***at to do next*/**how** *to do it.* • *(fml)* **Think not** is a formal way of disagreeing or saying no: *"Will you be going tonight James?" "I think not."* ○ *I asked him if he was likely to get the job and he said he thought not.* • *It's no good asking me all the time, Anna – you're going to have to learn to* **think for yourself** (= make your own decisions)! • *When the children are misbehaving, it makes me* **think again about** (= reconsider) *having a large family.* • *Originally we were going to buy John's old car but we* **thought better of it** (= decided it wasn't a good idea). • If you **think highly of/a lot of/well of/the world of** someone or something, you have a good opinion of that person or thing. • To **not think much of** someone or something means you have a low opinion of that person or thing: *I don't think much of my new accommodation/of hav***ing** *to work on Saturdays.* • To **think nothing of** something means to consider it easy or simple: *When I was younger, I thought nothing of cycling 50 miles in a day.* ○ *"Thank you for helping."* **"Think nothing of it."** • *I know she will always do well because she* **thinks big** (= has big plans). • *"Just when you thought it was safe to go back in the water"* (advertisement for the film *Jaws II*, 1978)

think·ing /ˈθɪŋ·kɪŋ/ *n* [U] • *What's the thinking* **behind** *the decision to combine the two departments* (= Why have they been combined)? • *I don't agree with his thinking* (= opinion) *on that point.* • **To my way of thinking** (= In my opinion) *the plan should never have been approved.*

think REASON /θɪŋk/ *v past* **thought** /£θɔːt, $θɑːt/ to use the brain to plan something, solve a problem, make a decision, etc. • *What are you thinking, Peter?* [I] • *She didn't join in the talk and was obviously thinking.* [I] • *He just does these things without thinking and he gets himself into such a mess.* [I] • *You think too much – that's your problem.* [I] • *Which language do you think in?* [I] • *He thought* **to himself** (= he thought) *why didn't she phone me?* [+ clause] • *I'm sorry I forgot to mention your name. I just* **wasn't** *think***ing**. [I] • *We'll have to think* **of/up** (= create) *a pretty good excuse for being late.* [I/M] • To **think long and hard** or **think twice** about something means to think carefully or deeply about it: *I should think long and hard before you make any important decisions.* ○ *I'd just do it if I were you and I wouldn't think twice.* • To **think** something **over/through** means to think carefully about something: *I need some time to think it through – I don't want to make any sudden decisions.* • *"What did you say?" "Oh, nothing, I was just* **thinking aloud** (= saying what I was thinking). • *I'd never heard about the firm before so I had to* **think on** *my* **feet** (= make a quick decision/give an answer quickly). • *Whoever did this can't have been* **thinking straight** (= not using good judgment). • *(humorous) You're very quiet. I can see you're* **thinking great/beautiful/interesting thoughts**. • *(saying)* 'Think before you act' means consider the effects of an action before you do it. • *"I think therefore I am"* (Descartes *La Discours de la méthode*, 1637) • *"Don't think twice, it's all right"* (title of a song by Bob Dylan, 1963)

think /θɪŋk/ *n* [U] • To **Have a think** about something is to consider it for some time: *I'll need to/I'd better/Let me have a think* **about** *it before I decide.* ○ *Have a think over the weekend and tell me what you've decided.* • A **think tank** is a group of specialists, brought together usually by a government, to develop ideas on a particular subject and to make suggestions for action.

think·er /£ˈθɪŋ·kəʳ, $-kɚ/ *n* [C] • *She was one of the most progressive thinkers on women's rights of her generation.* • *He was know for being an original/unorthodox thinker.* • *The industry, he said, needed more strategic thinkers.*

think·ing /ˈθɪŋ·kɪŋ/ *n* [U] • *I'll have to* **do** *some thinking about how best to arrange the books.* • To **put** your **thinking cap on** is to think seriously about something: *I'm in need of some interesting suggestions so if you can put your thinking cap on I'd be grateful.* • *"There is nothing either good or bad but thinking makes it so"* (Shakespeare, Hamlet 2.2)

think·ing /ˈθɪŋ·kɪŋ/ *adj* [before n; not gradable] • *All thinking people realise that we must stop wasting our natural resources.* • *(Br humorous)* **The thinking woman's/man's crumpet** is a way of describing a man or a woman who is popular with the opposite sex because they are intelligent as well as being physically attractive: *Paxman is surely the ultimate thinking woman's crumpet.*

think REMEMBER /θɪŋk/ *v* [I always + adv/prep] *past* **thought** /£θɔːt, $θɑːt/ to remember or imagine • *I just want you to know that we may be 4500 miles apart but I'm thinking* **about/of** *you.* • *I always think* **about/of** *her when it snows.* • *I'm sorry I can't be at your wedding, but I'll be thinking* **about/of** *you.* • *I thought* **about/of** *you immediately when they said they wanted someone who could speak English.* • *I always think* **of** *Roz in that long pink coat.* • *I was just thinking* **about/of** *you when you phoned.* • *He was thinking* **about/of** *the time he spent in the army.* • *It might help you to understand if you think* **back to** *when you were her age.*

third /£θɜːd, $θɜːrd/ *pronoun, n, determiner, adv* [not gradable] 3rd; related to 3 • *the third option* • *the third road on the right* • *the third time* • *the third of September* • *He's had four wives and Sarah was the third.* • **Third class/rate** means of low quality: *I don't want to work for some third rate company.* • *(infml)* **The third degree** is serious questioning and/or rough treatment to get information: *They* **gave** *him the third degree to find out who his contacts were.* ○ *I* **got** *the third degree when I got home last night.* • A **third-degree burn** is a very serious burn. • *(law)* A **third party** is a third person or organization less directly involved in a matter than the main people, etc. that are involved. • **Third-party insurance** will pay money to a person or group damaged in some way by the person or group who have it. • **The Third World** is a group word for the countries of Africa, Latin America and Asia which have less developed industries: *a third-world country/economy* • *"The Third Man"* (title of a book by Graham Greene, 1950)

thirst /£θɜːst, $θɜːrst/ *n* [U] a need for something to drink, or *(fig.)* a great desire for something • *The animals died of thirst.* • *Hundreds more refugees collapsed from thirst and hunger.* • *I've got* **a** *terrible thirst after all that running.* • *In order to* **quench/slake** (= satisfy) *my thirst I was drinking three or four bottles of water a day.* • *I woke up with a thumping headache and a* **raging** (= extreme) *thirst.* • *(fig.) He's always had* **a thirst for** *adventure/excitement/power/knowledge.*

thirst af·ter/for *obj* /£θɜːst, $θɜːrst/ *v prep* [T] • *(fig. literary) A taste of power had left him thirsting for* (= desiring) *more power.*

thirst·i·ly /£ˈθɜː·stɪ·li, $ˈθɜːr-/ *adv* • *He picked up the bottle and drank thirstily.*

thirst·y /£ˈθɜː·sti, $ˈθɜːr-/ *adj* **-ier, -iest** • *I feel hot and thirsty after my game of squash.* • *Sawing wood is* **thirsty work** (= makes you thirsty). • *(fig.)* Someone who is thirsty **for** power or knowledge wants to have it very much.

thir·teen /£θɜːˈtiːn, $θɜːr-/ *determiner, pronoun, n* (the number) 13 • *eleven, twelve, thirteen, fourteen* • *All in all there were thirteen (people) round the table.* • *Thirteen is thought by some people to be an unlucky number.* [U] • *Is the number on that bus a thirteen?* [C]

thir·teenth /£θɜːˈtiːntθ, $θɜːr-/ *determiner, pronoun, adj, adv, n* • *It's Sarah-Jane's thirteenth birthday on Monday.* • *"What's the date today?" "The thirteenth."* • **Friday the** thirteenth is thought by some people to be an unlucky day. • *Catrin was/came thirteenth in her race.* • A thirteenth is one of thirteen equal parts of something. [C]

thir·ty /£ˈθɜː·ti, $ˈθɜːr·t̬i/ *determiner, pronoun, n* (the number) 30 • *twenty-nine, thirty, thirty-one* • *I'm going to be thirty on my next birthday.* • *I think there'll be about thirty (people) at the evening reception.* • *Is that number a thirty or a fifty?* [C] • *(saying)* 'Thirty days has September, April, June and November (all the rest have thirty-one, except for February which stands alone)' is used to help remember the number of days in each month of the year. • *"Thirty-nine Steps"* (title of a book by John Buchan, 1915)

thir·ties /£ˈθɜː·tiz, $ˈθɜːr·t̬iz/ *pl n* • **The** thirties is the range of temperature between 30° and 39°: *The temperature is expected to be* **in** *the thirties tomorrow.* • **The** thirties is also the period of years between 30 and 39 in any century: *These dresses were fashionable* **in** *the thirties* (= between 1930 and 1939). • A person's thirties are the period in which they are aged between 30 and 39: *My brother is* **in** *his thirties.*

thir·ti·eth /£ˈθɜː·ti·əθ, $ˈθɜːr·t̬i-/ *determiner, pronoun, adj, adv* [not gradable], *n* • *Sarah's having a party to celebrate her thirtieth birthday.* • *The last day in September is the thirtieth.* • *Oh dear, you mean you were/came thirtieth* *out of thirty.* • A thirtieth is one of thirty equal parts of something.

this THING REFERRED TO /ðɪs/ *determiner, pronoun pl* **these** /ðiːz/ used for a person, object, idea, etc. to show which one is referred to • *Can you sign this form* **(here)** *for me?* • *Which bowl do you want to use – this glass one* **(here)** *or that blue one over there?* • *These books are too heavy for me to carry.* • *(infml) We met this girl* (= the girl I am going to tell you about) *in the hotel.* • *I did it/I'll do it this morning/afternoon/evening* (= at the time mentioned). • *I did it/I'll do it this Monday/week/month/year* (= in the present week/month/year). • *Stop fighting* **this minute** (= now). • *I thought you'd have finished* **by this time/ before this** (= already). • **These days** (= now) *she doesn't get home till six.* • *I've been given some new medicine and a diet and I'm hoping this* (= what has been mentioned) *will help.* • *The cat has always liked this old chair of* **mine/of** *my mother's. This is Andrew (here). That's Paul (over there).* • *This is the one I wanted.* • *Listen to this. 'Election date set for November.'* • *What's this? Is this what you're looking for?* • *What's all this (about)* (= what's the problem?/what is happening)*?* • *What's this I hear about your moving to Scotland?* • *If you hold it* **like** *this* (= in this way) *it will feel more comfortable.* • *"What were you talking about?" "Oh,* **this and that/this, that and the other** (= various things)*."* • LP› **Determiners**

this AS MUCH /ðɪs/ *adv* [not gradable] as much as shown or to a particular degree • *It was only about this high off the ground.* • *Will this much be enough for you?* • *She has never been this late for school before.*

thi·stle /ˈθɪs·l̩/ *n* [C] a wild plant with sharp points on the leaves and, typically, purple flowers • *The thistle is the national emblem of Scotland.* • PIC› **Flowers and plants**

thi·stle·down /ˈθɪs·l̩.daʊn/ *n* [U] the mass of thin soft white threads which are joined to THISTLE seeds and which help them to be blown through the air • *as light as thistledown*

thi·ther /£ˈðɪð·əʳ, $-ɚ/ *adv* [not gradable] *old use* to that place, in that direction

thong /£θɒŋ, $θɑːŋ/ *n* [C] a narrow piece of esp. leather used to fasten something or as part of a whip • *She was wearing a leather thong around her neck.* • A thong is also is a narrow piece of cloth worn between a person's legs to cover their sexual organs that is held in place by a piece of string around their waist: *She emerged from the sea wearing only a thong.* • Thong is also *Am and Aus for* FLIP-FLOP. • PIC› **Shoes**

tho·rax /£ˈθɔː·ræks, $ˈθɔːr·æks/ *n* [C] *pl* **thoraces** /£ˈθɔː·rə·siz, $ˈθɔːr·ə-/ or **thoraxes** *specialized* the middle part of the body, (in humans and animals) below the head and above the ABDOMEN; the chest • PIC› **Insects**

tho·rac·ic /£θɔːˈræs·ɪk, $θoʊˈræs-/ *adj specialized* • *thoracic cavity*

thorn /£θɔːn, $θɔːrn/ *n* [C] a small sharp pointed growth on the stem of a plant • *rose thorns* • *thorn bushes* • **A thorn in the flesh/side** is something which continually annoys you or causes you pain: *A relentless campaigner, he was a thorn in the government's side for a number of years.*

thorn·y /£ˈθɔː·ni, $ˈθɔːr-/ *adj* **-ier, -iest** • *a thorny shrub/tree* • *(fig.) It's a thorny* **issue/matter/problem/question** (= one that is difficult to deal with).

thor·ough CAREFUL /£ˈθʌr·ə, $ˈθɜːr-/ *adj* [not gradable] detailed, careful • *a thorough revision of the manuscript* • *thorough plans* • *She's very thorough in her preparation for her lessons.* • *They did a thorough search of the area but found nothing.* • LP› **'-ough' pronunciation**

thor·ough·ly /£ˈθʌr·ə·li, $ˈθɜːr-/ *adv* [not gradable] • *We went through the report thoroughly but the information we wanted wasn't given anywhere.*

thor·ough·ness /£ˈθʌr·ə·nəs, $ˈθɜːr-/ *n* [U] • *I was impressed by his thoroughness.*

thor·ough COMPLETE /£ˈθʌr·ə, $ˈθɜːr-/ *adj* complete, very great, very much • *It was a thorough waste of time.*

thor·ough·ly /£ˈθʌr·ə·li, $ˈθɜːr-/ *adv* • *I was thoroughly exhausted after walking ten miles.* • *I went to the opera for the first time and I thoroughly enjoyed it.* • LP› **Very, completely**

thor·ough·bred /£ˈθʌr·ə·bred, $ˈθɜːr-/ *n* [C], *adj* [not gradable] (a horse) with parents which are of the same breed and have good qualities • *a thoroughbred racehorse*

thor·ough·fare /£ˈθʌr·ə·feəʳ, $ˈθɜːr·ə·fer/ *n* [C] *fml* a main road for public use or a passage through somewhere • *a busy thoroughfare* • *one of the main city thoroughfares* • On road signs, **no thoroughfare** means no entry.

thor·ough·go·ing /£ˌθʌr·əˈgəʊ·ɪŋ, £ˈ--ˌ--, $ˌθɜːr·əˈgoʊ-/ *adj fml* complete, detailed, careful • *We can't get thoroughgoing economic reform in our country until we have political reform.*

those /£ðəʊz, $ðoʊz/ *determiner, pronoun, pl of* THAT • *Those (people) who would like to go on the trip should put their names on the list.*

thou YOU /ðaʊ/ *pronoun old use* (used, with old verb forms, when speaking to one person) you • *Thou art sad, fair Rosalind.* • *"Stand by thyself, come not near to me; for I am holier than thou."* (Bible, Isaiah 65.5)

thou THOUSAND /θaʊ/ *n* [C] *pl* **thou** *infml* thousand, esp. when referring to an amount of money • *"How much do you reckon it cost him?" "About thirty thou."*

though /£ðəʊ, $ðoʊ/ *conjunction* despite the fact that; although • *She hasn't phoned,* **(even)** *though she said she would.* • *Strange though it may seem* (= Although it might seem strange)*, I still enjoy parachuting even after my accident.* • *The report was critical though fair.* • Though can also mean 'but': *His English has not improved greatly, though he should continue to attend classes.* • **As though** means as if: *You look as though you've had a bad time!* • LP› **'-ough' pronunciation**

though /£ðəʊ, $ðoʊ/ *adv* [not gradable] • Though means 'despite this': *We were at school together. I haven't seen her for years though.* • *"This wine's very sweet." "It's nice, though, isn't it."*

thought THINK /£θɔːt, $θɑːt/ *past simple and past participle of* THINK

thought THINKING /£θɔːt, $θɑːt/ *n* the act of thinking about or considering something or the matters which are thought about • *Give yourself plenty of time for thought before you decide.* [U] • *Have you* **given** *the arrangements any thought yet?* [U] • *Ask me again tomorrow. I'll have to* **give** *it some thought.* [U] • *She* **doesn't give any** *thought* **to** *her appearance.* [U] • *Let me have your thoughts* (= ideas) **on/about** *that report by Friday.* [C] • *I'm worried by/at the thought* **of** (= I'm worried when I think about) *the interview.* [U] • **Spare a** *thought* **for** (= Think about) *all those without shelter on a cold night like this.* • *He's the author of a book on the history of European thought* (= matters thought about). [U] • **The thought had crossed** *my* **mind** (= I had already thought) *that I would need some help with this project before you suggested working together.* • **That's a thought** means that's a good idea or that's possible: *"Shall we go on Thursday instead of Friday?" "That's a thought."* • *When Beth is writing a letter, she looks* **deep in/lost in** *thought* (= thinking without attention to anything else). [U] • **With no thought for** (= not thinking about) *his own safety, he rushed towards the burning car.* • *To me the whole scheme seemed to be badly* **thought-out** (= planned). • *"Thoughts that do often lie too deep for tears"* (William Wordsworth in the poem *Intimations of Immortality*, 1807)

thought·ful /£ˈθɔːt·fəl, $ˈθɑːt-/ *adj* • Thoughtful means carefully considering the effect of your actions or caring towards other people: *He has a thoughtful approach to his work.* ○ *The doctor looked thoughtful for a moment and then started to write a prescription.* ○ *Thank you for phoning to see if I was feeling better – it was very thoughtful of you.* ○ *She's a very thoughtful person.*

thought·ful·ly /£ˈθɔːt·fəl·i, $ˈθɑːt-/ *adv* • *I had with me one or two sandwiches, thoughtfully* **provided** *by my colleague.* • *He gazed thoughtfully into the distance.* • *Ingrid eyed him thoughtfully.*

thought·ful·ness /£ˈθɔːt·fəl·nəs, $ˈθɑːt-/ *n* [U] • *It's her thoughtfulness that impresses me.*

thought·less /£ˈθɔːt·ləs, $ˈθɑːt-/ *adj* • Thoughtless means not carefully considering the effect of your actions: *It was thoughtless not to phone and say you'd be late.* ○ *I'm sorry I said that about his mother – it was very thoughtless of me.* ○ *She's not intentionally unkind – she's just a little thoughtless sometimes.*

thought·less·ly /£ˈθɔːt·lə·sli, $ˈθɑːt-/ *adv*

thought·less·ness /£ˈθɔːt·lə·snəs, $ˈθɑːt-/ *n* [U]

thou·sand /ˈθaʊ·zənd/ *determiner, pronoun, n pl* **thousand** or **thousands** (the number) 1000 • *a thousand pounds* • *five thousand men* • *two thousand sheets of paper* • *A crowd of thousands watched the children's procession.* • *It costs thousands* **of** *pounds to have a kid privately educated.* • *"Two Thousand and One – A Space Odyssey"* (title of a book and a film by Arthur C.Clarke, 1968) • LP› **Hundred**

thou·sandth /ˈθaʊ·zᵊndθ/ *n* [C], *adj* [not gradable] • *a thousandth of an inch* • *the thousandth time* • *It was the thousandth business to go bust.*

thrash *(obj)* /θræʃ/ *v* to hit hard or make a series of violent and uncontrolled movements • *He thrashed the horse with his whip.* [T] • *He slept badly, thrashing* **about**/*thrashing from side to side all night.* [I] • *(fig.) We thrashed* (= defeated) *the visiting team 6-0.* [T]

thrash out *obj*, **thrash** *obj* **out** *v adv* [M] *infml* to discuss (a problem) energetically and in detail until you find a solution • *If we've got an important decision to make we sometimes spend a whole day thrashing it out in a meeting.*

thread [FIBRE] /θred/ *n* (a length of) a very thin fibre • *cotton/nylon thread* • *needle and thread* [U] • *loose threads* • *gold threads* • *woollen threads* [C] • *(fig.) A thin thread* **of** *light made its way through the curtains.* [C] • The **thread of** a book, discussion, speech etc. is its story or the way that it develops, one part connecting with another: *One of the main threads of the film is the development of the relationship between the boy and his uncle.* ○ *Unfortunately my attention wandered for a moment and I* **lost** *the thread of* (= forgot) *what I was saying.*

thread *obj* [PUT THROUGH] /θred/ *v* [T] to put something thin through a hole or into a small space. • *I always find threading a* **needle** *difficult.* • *Thread the rope slowly through the gap.* • *Thread the beads onto a shorter string.* • *The sari had gold strands threaded through the material at the hem. (fig.) She threaded her* **way through** (= walked with many changes of direction) *the crowd/the narrow streets.* [T]

thread [SCREW] /θred/ *n* [C] a continuous raised line, such as the one which goes around the outside of a screw or BOLT or the inside of a hole • *The handle won't screw in properly, the thread in the socket is damaged.*

thread·bare /£ˈθred·beəʳ, $-ber/ *adj* (of material) become thin or damaged because of being used a lot • *He wore a threadbare coat and old shoes.* • *(fig.) She produced the old threadbare* (= too often used) *excuses – the alarm didn't go off, the train was late etc.*

threat /θret/ *n* [C] a suggestion that something unpleasant will happen, esp. unless a particular action or order is followed • *She* **carried out** *her threat* **to** *throw away any clothes that were left on the floor.* [+ *to* infinitive] • *I'm not taking any notice of his threats – he can't do anything.* • *The threat* **of** *jail is a strong deterrent to people reluctant to pay the tax, new figures suggest.* • *Drunken drivers are/***pose** *a (serious/grave/major) threat* (= cause a lot of harm) *to road users.* • *She left the country* **under threat of** *arrest if she returned.* • *He says he'll stop supplies getting in but it's just an* **empty** *threat* (= it will not happen) *because there are many other routes.*

threat·en *(obj)* /ˈθret·ᵊn/ *v* • *The man threatened revenge on the police.* [T] • *They threatened the shopkeeper* **with** *violence/a gun.* [T] • *They threatened* **to** *kill him unless he did as they asked.* [+ *to* infinitive] • *Look at those clouds! There's a storm threatening.* [I] • *The weather threatens* **to** *change by the end of the week.* [+ *to* infinitive] • *Changing patterns of agriculture are threatening* (= causing damage to) *the countryside.* [T]

threat·en·ing·ly /ˈθret·ᵊn·ɪŋ·li, ˈ-nɪŋ-/ *adv*

three /θriː/ *determiner, pronoun, n* (the number) 3 • *three cats/trees/houses* • *a house with three bedrooms* • *a three-bedroom house* • *"How many children have you got?" "Three (daughters)."* • *Is that number a five or a three?* [C] • **Three-D** or **three-dimensional** means having or appearing to have three DIMENSIONS (= height, length and width) and therefore looking real: *The picture had a three-D* **effect**/*3-D* **effect**. • In a **three-legged race** the right leg of one person is tied to the left leg of another person and then the two people run together as if they had three legs. PIC⟩ **Outdoor games for children** • In Britain, a **three-line whip** is an instruction given to Members of Parliament by the leaders of their party telling them they must vote in the way that the party wants them to on a particular subject. • A **three-piece suit** is a matching jacket, trousers and WAISTCOAT (*Am* **vest**) esp. for men. PIC⟩ **Clothing** • *(Br)* A **three-piece suite** (*Am* **living room suite**) is a SOFA with two matching chairs. PIC⟩ **Room** • A **three-point turn** is a method of turning a car round to face the other direction by moving forwards across the road, then backwards in the opposite direction across the road and then forwards again. • **Three-ply** wool has three threads woven together to make one. • **Three-ply** wood has three layers joined together. • **Three quarters** of something is three fourths of it: *Three quarters of the book is about the sea voyage.* • A **three-quarter length** coat is between the length of a jacket and a coat. • *(infml)* **The three Rs** means basic education: reading, writing and mathematics. • A **three-star** service/hotel is one of good quality. • A **three-wheeler** is a vehicle with three wheels. • *"Three Men and a Baby"* (title of a film, 1987) • *"When shall we three meet again / In thunder, lightning, or in rain?"* (Shakespeare, the witches in Macbeth 1.1) • *"Three Men in a Boat"* (title of a book by Jerome K. Jerome, 1889) • *"Yes sir, yes sir, three bags full"* (from the traditional children's song *Baa, Baa, Black Sheep*)

three·some /ˈθriː·səm/ *n* [C] *infml* three people as a group • *You can come with us and we'll go* **in a/as a** *threesome.*

thresh *obj* /θreʃ/, **thrash** *v* [T] to remove the seeds of (crop plants) by hitting, using either a machine or a hand tool

thresh·old /£ˈθreʃ·həʊld, $-hoʊld/ *n* [C] the entrance to a building or room, the floor in this entrance or *(fig.)* a point or level at which something begins or starts to take effect • *She stopped on the threshold, looking to see who was in the room.* • *It's an old tradition for a man to carry his wife over the threshold when they first enter their new home after getting married.* • *(fig.) Are you over the* **higher** *tax threshold?* (= Do you earn enough money to start paying a higher rate of tax?) • *(fig.) I have a* **low boredom/pain** *threshold* (= I feel boredom/pain easily). • *We are* **on the threshold of** (= very soon to start) *a new era of European relations.*

threw /θruː/ *past simple and past participle of* THROW

thrice /θraɪs/ *adv* [not gradable] *old use* three times

thrift [AVOIDING WASTE] /θrɪft/ *n* [U] the careful use of money, esp. by avoiding waste • *The concept of thrift is foreign to me.* • *(Am)* A **thrift shop** is a shop which sells clothes and other goods that people no longer want, in order to raise money for people who are ill or have no food, homes, etc.

thrift·y /ˈθrɪf·ti/ *adj* **-ier**, **-iest** • *They have plenty of money now, but they still tend to be thrifty.*

thrift·i·ly /ˈθrɪf·tɪ·li/ *adv*

thrift·i·ness /ˈθrɪf·tɪ·nəs/ *n* [U]

thrift [PLANT] /θrɪft/ *n* [U] a small plant with, typically, pink flowers on long stems which often grows wild on cliffs by the sea

thrill /θrɪl/ *n* [C] a feeling of extreme excitement, usually caused by something pleasant • *So why do people still go hunting – is it the thrill of the chase?* • *It* **gave** *me a real thrill to see her again after so many years.* • *Lewis himself can recall the thrill of his first taste of violence.* • *A thrill* **of** *fear ran through her at the sound of thunder.* • *I'm no thrill-***seeker** *but I do like a bit of excitement in my life.* • *The video shows the* **thrills and spills** (= the excitement and the accidents) *of motor racing.*

thrill *(obj)* /θrɪl/ *v* • *Just standing next to him thrilled her.* [T] • *(fml) She thrilled* (= reacted with pleasure) **to** *his voice.* [I]

thrilled /θrɪld/ *adj* • Thrilled means extremely pleased: *She was thrilled* **to** *find that the bouquet was for her.* [+ *to* infinitive] • *I was thrilled* **that** *so many people turned up to the party.* [+ *that* clause] • *"Did she like the gift?" "She was* **thrilled to bits** (= extremely pleased) *with it."*

thril·ler /£ˈθrɪl·əʳ, $-ɚ/ *n* [C] • A thriller is a book, play or film which has an exciting story often about solving a crime: *His latest film falls into the category of spy/courtroom thriller.* ○ *It's described here as a taut psychological thriller.* ○ *He's a thriller writer.*

thrill·ing /ˈθrɪl·ɪŋ/ *adj* • *It says on the back of the book that it's a thrilling adventure story.* • *It was thrilling to see so many countries represented.* [+ *to* infinitive]

thrive /θraɪv/ *v* [I] *past simple* **thrived** or *Am also* **throve** /£θrəʊv, $θroʊv/, *past part* **thrived** or *Am also* **thriven** /ˈθrɪv·ᵊn/ to grow, develop or be successful • *My garden is too dry and shady – not many plants thrive in those conditions.* • *His business thrived in the years before the war.* • *She seems to thrive* **on** *stress/hard work.*

thriv·ing /ˈθraɪ·vɪŋ/ *adj* • *It's a thriving* (= very successful) *business/community/economy/industry.* • *Business is thriving.* • *"So how are the children?" "Thriving* (= very healthy and happy)."

throat /£θrəʊt, $θroʊt/ *n* [C] the front of the neck, or the space inside the neck down which food and air can go • *He was later found dead, with his throat* **cut/slit**. • *I swallowed a fish bone and it got* **stuck in** *my throat.* • *My colds always start with a* **sore** *throat.* • *He* **cleared** *his throat and started speaking.* • *Around her pale creamy throat she wore a black* choker. • *Those two are always* **at each other's throats** (= arguing). • If you **force/thrust/ram** something **down** someone's **throat** you try to force them to accept it: *I can't bear it when someone starts ramming their views down your throat.*

-throat·ed /£-ˌθrəʊ·tɪd, £-ˈ--, $-ˌθroʊ·t̬ɪd, $-ˈ--/ *combining form* • *a red/brown-throated bird* (= a bird with a red/brown throat) • *He gave a* **full**-*throated* (= loud) *roar.*

throat·y /£ˈθrəʊ·ti, $ˈθroʊ·t̬i/ *adj* **-ier**, **-iest** • Throaty means sounding low and rough: *a throaty voice/chuckle/ cough /Outside she heard the throaty roar of a motorbike engine.* ○ *I'm afraid I'm rather throaty today because of my cold.*

throat·i·ly /£ˈθrəʊ·tɪ·li, $ˈθroʊ·t̬ɪ-/ *adv*

throat·i·ness /£ˈθrəʊ·tɪ·nəs, $ˈθroʊ·t̬ɪ-/ *n* [U]

throb /£θrɒb, $θrɑːb/ *v* [I], *n* [C] **-bb-** (to produce) a regular beat or one that is fast and forceful • *A pulse started throbbing in my right temple.* • *His* **head** *throbbed, and his body ached as if he had been beaten up.* • *I hit my toe against the door this morning and it's starting to throb.* • *Both records have a good throbbing bass which is great to dance to.* • *The throbbing (pain) in his leg was becoming unbearable.* • *He felt the throb of her heart.* • See also HEARTTHROB. • LP> **Feelings and pains**

throes /£θrəʊz, $θroʊz/ *pl n* **in the throes of** in the process of doing something which is difficult, unpleasant or painful • *The country is once again in the throes of famine.* • *We're in the final throes of selling our house.* • *The country is presently in the throes of the worst recession since the second world war.* • *My brother is in the throes of a mid-life crisis which makes him rather difficult to live with.* • *(humorous) It is difficult to imagine this man in the throes* **of passion**.

throm·bo·sis /£θrɒmˈbəʊ·sɪs, $θrɑːmˈboʊ-/ *n* [C] *pl* **thromboses** /£θrɒmˈbəʊ·siːz, $θrɑːmˈboʊ-/ a blockage preventing the flow of blood in the body caused by a CLOT (= half solid lump) of blood • *a cerebral thrombosis* • *a coronary thrombosis*

throne /£θrəʊn, $θroʊn/ *n* [C] the special chair used by a ruler, esp. a king or queen, or a decorated chair of this type • *The carnival queen sat on a magnificent gold and white throne.* • **The throne** is used to mean the state of being a ruler: *Elizabeth II* **ascended/came to** *the throne* (= became queen of Britain) *when her father died.*

throng /£θrɒŋ, $θrɑːŋ/ *n* [C] a crowd or large group of people • *A huge throng had gathered round the speaker.* • *A throng* **of** *children was/were surrounding the ice-cream van.* [+ sing/pl v] • *Throngs* of (= Very many) people were milling about the airport waiting for delayed planes.

throng *(obj)* /£θrɒŋ, $θrɑːŋ/ *v* • *Summer visitors thronged the narrow streets.* [T] • *The narrow streets were thronged with summer visitors.* [T] • *The demonstrators thronged over the bridge towards the government buildings.* [I always + adv/prep] • *The public is thronging* **to** *see* (= A lot of people are going to) *the new musical.* [+ *to* infinitive]

throt·tle [CONTROL] /£ˈθrɒt·l̩, $ˈθrɑː·t̬l̩/ *n* [C] a VALVE (= control device) which allows more or less fuel to go into an engine and so changes the power with which the engine operates • *The operator* **opened/closed** *the throttle a little and the machine ran faster/slower.* • *It's running* **at half/ full** *throttle* (= speed). • *(fig.) He's working* **at full** *throttle* (= as much as he can) *to get the job finished.* • *(fig.) He's only working* **at half** *throttle* (= He's not working as much as he can) *because he's been ill.* • *She took her foot off the throttle* (= speed control in a car) *and the car slowed down.*

throt·tle back/down *(obj)*, **throt·tle** *(obj)* **back/ down** *v adv* • *The pilot throttled back (the engines)* (= reduced speed) *as he came in to land.* [I/M]

throt·tle *obj* [THROAT] /£ˈθrɒt·l̩, $ˈθrɑː·t̬l̩/ *v* [T] to try to kill (someone) by pressing their throat so that they cannot breathe • *She had been throttled and left for dead.* • *(infml) Sometimes he gets me so annoyed I could throttle him.* • *(fig.) The reduction in funds is throttling* (= preventing) *the development of new programmes.*

through [PLACE] /θruː/ *prep, adv* [not gradable] among or between (a number or amount of something), or from one side of a hole to the other • *They walked slowly through the woods/fields/streets.* • *The boy waded through the water to reach his boat.* • *He struggled through (the crowd) till he reached the front.* • *I couldn't see the girl through the smoke.* • *We could hear cries through the noise of the machines.* • *How long the journey takes will depend on how long it takes to* **get** *through the traffic.* • *Her words kept running through my mind/head* (= I kept hearing her words in my imagination). • *Don't let that cat through (the door).* • *Thread the cotton through (the needle).* • *He pushed the ball through (the gap in the fence).* • *We drove through (the tunnel).* • *Can we drive through (the square)?* • *Go right/ straight through – I'll be with you in a minute.* • *"Have you read the report* **(all/right)** *through?" "No, I just looked/ glanced/thumbed/flicked through (it)* (= read bits of it quickly). • *I saw him drive through* **a red light** (= he did not stop at the red traffic light). • *You should* **think it** *through very carefully before you make any decisions.* • *Think through how it might affect your job and so on.* • *I'll put you through* (= connect you by telephone) *(***to** *the sales department).* • *My mother is Irish* **through and through** (= completely). • LP> **Telephone, '-ough' pronunciation** PIC> **Prepositions of movement**

through [FINISHED] /θruː/ *adj, adv* [not gradable] finished or completed • *Are you through* **with** *that atlas?* • *I've got some work to do but I should be through in an hour if you can wait.* • *I'll never* **get** *through this report by Friday.* • *I* **got** *through so much work this morning.*

through [TIME] /θruː/ *prep, adv* [not gradable] during a period of time, esp. from the beginning to the end • *We do checks at different times through the night/year.* • *I was grateful for her support* **(all)** *through my illness.* • *It rained* **(all/right)** *through June and into the first half of July.* • *We sat through two lectures and then left.* • *She had just enough energy to* **get** *through the day.* • *Paul saw/took the project through to its completion* (= directed or managed it until finished). • *We were cut off* **halfway through** *(our telephone conversation).* • *(Am) She works Monday through Thursday* (= from Monday to Thursday) *most weeks.*

through [RESULT] /θruː/ *prep* as a result of • *The company lost the order through production delays.* • *He's had a lot of days off through illness this year.*

through [USING] /θruː/ *prep* by; using • *I got my car through my brother who works in a garage.* • *We found the address through a process of elimination.* • *We sold the bike through advertising in the local paper.*

through [IN EVERY PART] /θruː/ *adv* [not gradable] **wet through**, see at WET [NOT DRY]

through [DIRECT] /θruː/ *adj* [not gradable] going directly from one place to another • If you travel on a **through train**, you stay on the same train for the whole journey. • **No through** *(Br)* **road/***(Br and Aus)* **way** *(Am* **No through traffic/No thoroughfare)** means that one end of the road or path is blocked so that you cannot get through. • A **through route** is a road which avoids a town centre. • **Through traffic** is traffic which does not want to stop in a town.

through [SUCCESSFUL] /θruː/ *adj* [after v], *adv* having achieved success in an exam • *"Has she heard about her entrance exams yet?" "Yes, she's through."* • *She's through* **to** *the next round of interviews.* • *If I ever* **get** *through* (= pass) *these exams I'm going to have such a massive party.*

through·out /θruˈaʊt/ *prep, adv* [not gradable] in every part, or during the whole period of time • *People throughout the country are out of work.* • *He yawned throughout the performance.* • *The school has been repainted throughout.* • *If you wish to come you'll have to stand throughout.*

through·put /ˈθruː·pʊt/ *n* [U] an amount (of work, etc.) done in a particular period of time • *We need to improve our throughput because demand is high at present.*

throve /£θrəʊv, $θroʊv/ *past simple and past participle of* THRIVE

throw *(obj)* [SEND THROUGH AIR] /£θrəʊ, $θroʊ/ *v past simple* **threw** /θruː/, *past part* **thrown** /£θrəʊn, $θroʊn/ to send (something) through the air with force, esp. by a sudden movement of the arm • *You can throw next.* [I] • *My friend threw the* **ball** *back over the fence.* [T] • *The coat was thrown over the back of the chair.* [T] • *She threw herself into a chair exhausted.* [T] • *The builders have thrown all this dirt* **about**. [T] • *Would you like me to throw the rope down/ up/over?* [M] • *Throw me the keys./Throw the keys* **to** *me.* [+ two objects] • *The rider was thrown as the horse jumped the fence.* [T] • *I shook the dice and threw two fours.* [T] • *He threw* **a punch** *at* (= hit) *his attacker.* [T] • If you **throw out the baby with the bath-water**, you lose valuable ideas or things in your attempt to get rid of what is unwanted. • *She* **threw** *all his failures* **back in** *his* **face** (= said unkind things during an argument about past events). • *(infml) After the accident, the safety inspector* **threw the book at** (= very severely criticized) *the company's practices.* • *He doesn't earn much, but still seems to have enough money to*

throw around (=spend obviously or without concern about amount spent). • To **throw caution to the wind(s)** is to do something which might have a bad result intentionally: *She threw caution to the winds and bought the most expensive one.* • *You're always* **throwing cold water on** (=being discouraging about) *my suggestions.* • When someone **throws in the sponge**, they admit defeat. • *The boy* **threw a** *frightened* **glance/look** (=looked in a frightened way) *in the direction of the house.* • *Having that old car you bought repainted would just be* **throwing good money after bad** (=wasting money by trying to improve something that has already cost money and is no good). • *(infml) We won't solve this problem by* **throwing money at it** (=spending a lot of money). • *(infml)* To **throw** your**self at** someone is to make it very obvious to that person that you want a sexual relationship with them. • To **throw** your**self into** something means to do it actively and enthusiastically: *She's thrown herself into this new job.* • If you **throw** your **voice**, you make something which is not real, such as a toy, seem to be speaking. • *The other players did not appreciate how he* **threw** *his* **weight around/about** (=told them what to do as if in authority) *in practice.*

throw *obj* MOVE QUICKLY /£θrəʊ, $θroʊ/ *v* [T] *past simple* **threw** /θruː/, *past part* **thrown** /£θrəʊn, $θroʊn/ to (cause to) move/act quickly or carelessly • *He threw the switch and the lights came on.* • *The horse threw* **back** *its head and snorted.* • *She threw* **back** *her hair and tucked it behind her ears.* • *David threw* **open** *the window to get some air.* • *(fig.) The competition has been thrown* **open** (=opened) *to the public.* • *When his parents died the boy was* **thrown back on** *his* **own resources** (=had to take care of himself). • *When I bought this car the stereo was* **thrown in** (=included in the price). • *They* **threw off** (=quickly removed) *their clothes and jumped in the sea.* • *They* **threw off** (=escaped) *the police car by turning off into a car park.* • *I can't seem to* **throw off** (=get rid of) *this cold.* • *(infml) I just* **threw** *the cake* **together** (=made it quickly) *at the last minute.* • *We were* **thrown together** (=We met) *by chance at a conference.* • *They threw up their hands to protect their heads.* • *They* **threw up** *their* **hands in horror/despair at** (=were shocked by) *his reply.* • *(infml) He's* **thrown up** (=given up/left) *his job and gone off to Africa.* • *(infml) She* **threw** *him* **over for** *a richer man* (=she finished her relationship with him and started one with a richer man).

throw *obj* CONFUSE /£θrəʊ, $θroʊ/ *v* [T often passive] *past simple* **threw** /θruː/, *past part* **thrown** /£θrəʊn, $θroʊn/ to confuse or cause difficulty • *I wasn't expecting a visitor. I was really thrown.* • *The news of the coup threw them into confusion/into a state of panic.* • *The question* **threw** *him* **(off balance)** *for a moment.*

throw *obj* PARTY /£θrəʊ, $θroʊ/ *v* [T] *past simple* **threw** /θruː/, *past part* **thrown** /£θrəʊn, $θroʊn/ **throw a party** to have a party • *Janet threw a party for Jack's fiftieth birthday.*

throw *obj* ANGER /£θrəʊ, $θroʊ/ *v* [T] *past simple* **threw** /θruː/, *past part* **thrown** /£θrəʊn, $θroʊn/ to experience and show (a strong feeling of anger), esp. suddenly • *My mother threw a* **fit**/*(Br infml)* **wobbly** *when she saw what a mess we'd made of her kitchen.* • *Alexander throws a* **tantrum** *when he doesn't get his own way.*

throw *obj* MAKE /£θrəʊ, $θroʊ/ *v* [T] *past simple* **threw** /θruː/, *past part* **thrown** /£θrəʊn, $θroʊn/ *specialized* to shape (clay) on a special wheel • *They were selling* **hand-thrown** *pottery.*

throw EACH ITEM /£θrəʊ, $θroʊ/ *n* [U] **a throw** *infml* for each item or each time • *We could get a coffee in there but they charge two quid a throw which is a real rip-off.*

throw a·way/out *obj*, **throw** *obj* **a·way/out** *v adv* [M] get rid of (something) because it is no longer wanted • *So when are you going to throw away those old magazines of yours?* • *I threw those trousers out years ago.*

throw up *(obj)*, **throw** *(obj)* **up** *v adv infml* to vomit • *He threw up all over his shoes.* [I] • *I spent the night throwing up.* [I] • *She threw her meal up all over the carpet.* [M]

throw·a·way /£ˈθrəʊ·ə·weɪ, $ˈθroʊ-/ *adj* [before n; not gradable] made to be destroyed after use • *throwaway cups and plates* • *the throwaway society* • *Sadly ours is a throwaway culture* (=a way of life which gives little value to people and things). • A **throwaway line/remark** is something which is said in a way which suggests the speaker considers it completely unimportant.

thrush BIRD /θrʌʃ/, **song thrush** *n* [C] a brown bird with a pale, spotted breast which is known for its singing

thrush DISEASE /θrʌʃ/ *n* [U] an infection which can be given by one person to another, usually causing white areas in the mouth and throat in children and in the vagina in women

thrust *(obj)* /θrʌst/ *v* [always + adv/prep] *past* **thrust** to push suddenly and strongly • *She thrust the money into his hand.* [T] • *They thrust the boy into the car and drove off.* [T] • *He thrust his hands deep into his dressing gown pockets and said nothing.* [T] • *They thrust a microphone in front of me and made me speak.* [T] • *She thrust the papers* **at** *me* (=towards me). [T] • *He thrust* **at** (=moved suddenly towards) *me* **with** *a knife.* [I] • *He thrust back the chair and rushed out of the room.* [M] • *"Some men are born great, some achieve greatness, and some have greatness thrust upon them"* (Shakespeare, Twelfth Night 2.5)

thrust /θrʌst/ *n* • *a sword thrust* [C] • *(fig.) The main thrust* (=the main subject) *of her argument was that women are compromised by the demands of childcare.* [C] • *(specialized)* Thrust is the driving force produced by, for example, an aircraft engine. [U]

thud /θʌd/ *v* [I always + adv/prep], *n* [C] **-dd-** (to make) the sound of something heavy hitting a hard surface • *The bag thudded to the floor.* • *He thudded angrily on the table with his fist.* • *The boy fell down the stairs with a series of thuds.* • *I could hear the thud* **of** *horses' hooves down the track.*

thug /θʌg/ *n* [C] a man who acts violently, esp. to commit a crime • *Some thugs smashed his windows.*

thug·gish /ˈθʌg·ɪʃ/ *adj infml* • *She brought along a thuggish looking youth to the party with a shaven head and tattoos on his arms.*

thumb /θʌm/ *n* [C] the short finger which is at an angle to the other fingers, making it possible to hold and pick things up easily • *How did you cut your thumb?* • *The thumb of a glove is the part which covers a person's thumb.* • **Thumbs down** means disapproval and **thumbs up** means approval: *They've* **given** *our plan* **the** *thumbs up/down* (=They have agreed to/disagreed with our plan). • *(infml)* To be **all (fingers and) thumbs** means to be very awkward with your hands: *Can you untangle this thread for me, I'm all thumbs today.* • If you are **under** someone's **thumb** you are under their control or power: *He's got the committee firmly under his thumb – they agree to whatever he asks.*

thumb *(obj)* /θʌm/ *v infml* • You thumb by standing near the edge of a road and holding out your hand with the thumb raised as a signal for a vehicle to stop and take you on its journey: *We thumbed* **(a lift) to** *London for the weekend.* [I/T] • To **thumb** your **nose at** someone is to show a lack of respect towards them: *He has thumbed his nose at authority all his life.* • You **thumb through** a book or some papers by turning the pages quickly and only reading small parts: *"Have you read the report?" "Well I thumbed through (it) quickly on the train."* • A **well-thumbed** book/copy/magazine is one whose slightly damaged appearance shows that it has been used many times.

thumb·nail /ˈθʌm·neɪl/ *n* [C] the nail on the thumb • *I've broken my thumbnail.* • A **thumbnail sketch** is a short description mentioning only the most important features: *He gave a thumbnail sketch of life in Moscow in the 1960s.*

thumb·screw /ˈθʌm·skruː/ *n* [C], **screws** *pl n* device used esp. in the past to TORTURE people (=cause them great pain) by crushing their thumbs

thumb·tack /ˈθʌm·tæk/ *n* [C] *Am and Aus for* **drawing pin**, see at DRAW PICTURE • PIC **Pins and needles, Stationery**

thump *(obj)* /θʌmp/ *v* to hit once or many times, often making making a soft, heavy noise • *He thumped him in the face.* [T] • *The rabbit was always thumping its paw against the cage.* [T] • *He thumped* **on** *the door but nobody came.* [I] • *She thumped the heavy bag down* (=put the bag down quickly and hard) *on the floor.* [T] • If your **heart** thumps it beats more strongly and quickly than usual, because of exercise, fear or excitement: [I] • If your **head** is thumping you are in pain because you can feel the beating in your head: *When I woke up my mouth was dry and my head was thumping.* [I] ○ *I've got a* **thumping headache**.

thump /θʌmp/ *n* [C] • *If he does that again I'm going to* **give** *him a thump.*

thump·ing /ˈθʌm·pɪŋ/ *adj, adv* [not gradable] *infml* very (big) • *I'm not carrying these thumping great books around with me all day.* • *The prime minister was re-elected only a year ago with a thumping parliamentary majority.*

thun·der /£'θʌn·dəʳ, $-dɚ/ *v, n* [U] (to make a noise like) the sudden loud noise which comes after a flash of lightning esp. during a storm • *a clap/crash/rumble of thunder* • *We had thunder* **and lightning** *last night.* • *There's thunder in the air, I wouldn't be surprised if we had a storm.* • *(fig.) I couldn't hear what he said over the thunder* (=loud noise) *of the waterfall/guns/passing train.* • *The sky grew dark and it started to thunder.* [I] • *The train/horses thundered along/by/past* (=moved making a lot of noise), *shaking the house.* [I] • *"I never want to see you here again," he thundered* (=shouted loudly and angrily) **at** *the boy.* [+ clause]

thun·der·ing /£'θʌn·dᵊr·ɪŋ, $-dɚ·ɪŋ/ *n* [U] • *We could hear the thundering* (=continuous loud noise) *of the guns all night.* • *To the back of the mill is a thundering* (=loud) *waterfall.*

thun·der·ous /£'θʌn·dᵊr·əs, $-dɚ·əs/ *adj* [before n] • Thunderous means very loud: *thunderous applause* • *a thunderous reception*

thun·de·ry /£'θʌn·dᵊr·i, $-dɚ·i/ *adj* • *thundery weather* • *The weather has been thundery all week.*

thun·der·bolt /£'θʌn·də·bəʊlt, $-dɚ·boʊlt/ *n* [C] a flash of lightning and the sound of thunder together • *(fig.) He dropped a thunderbolt on us* (=made a shocking announcement) *this morning when he told us that we were closing down.*

thun·der·clap /£'θʌn·də·klæp, $-dɚ-/ *n* [C] a single loud sound of thunder

thun·der·cloud /£'θʌn·də·klaʊd, $-dɚ-/ *n* [C often pl] a large dark cloud which produces thunder and lightning

thun·der·storm /£'θʌn·də·stɔːm, $-dɚ·stɔːrm/ *n* [C] a storm with thunder and lightning and usually heavy rain

thun·der·struck /£'θʌn·də·strʌk, $-dɚ-/ *adj* [after v] very surprised • *Ruth was thunderstruck when he presented her with an engagement ring.*

thun·de·ry /£'θʌn·dᵊr·i, $-dɚ·i/ *adj* **-ier, -iest** See at THUNDER

Thurs·day /£'θɜːz·deɪ, $'θɜːrz-/ (*abbreviation* **Thur, Thurs**) *n* the day of the week after Wednesday and before Friday • *Can you come to dinner next Thursday?* [U] • *The shop is closed* **on** *Thursday.* [U] • *My birthday is* **on** *a Thursday this year.* [C] • *We go swimming on Thursdays.* [C] • LP› **Calendar** Ⓓⓚ Ⓝ

thus /ðʌs/ *adv* [not gradable] *fml* in this way, with this result • *Bend from the waist, thus.* • *They shook hands and the contract was thus agreed.* • *They planned to reduce waste and thus to cut costs.* • *He is retiring in March and is thus not able to take on the project.* • **Thus far** means as far as this or until now: *We haven't had any problems thus far.*

thwack /θwæk/ *v* [T], *n* [C] (to make, esp. with a stick) a hard, noisy hitting sound • *I heard the thwack of the whip against the horse's side.* • *She thwacked the hedge with her stick in a bad-tempered way.*

thwart *obj* /£θwɔːt, $θwɔːrt/ *v* [T] to stop (something) from happening or (someone) from doing something • *My holiday plans have been thwarted by the strike.* • *She is constantly trying to thwart my efforts to make new friends.*

thy /ðaɪ/ *determiner old use* your, used when speaking to one person • *"Thy will be done"* (Bible *The Lord's Prayer*, Matthew 6.9.)

thyme /taɪm/ *n* [U] a type of small bush with sweet smelling leaves which are sometimes used as a herb in cooking

thy·roid (gland) /£'θaɪə·rɔɪd, $'θaɪ-/ *n* [C] a GLAND (=an organ) in the front of the neck which is involved in controlling the way the body develops and works

thy·self /ðaɪ'self/ *pronoun old use* reflexive form or strong form of THOU; yourself, used when speaking to one person

ti·a·ra /£ti'ɑː·rə, $-'er·ə/ *n* [C] a piece of metal in the shape of half a circle decorated with jewels which is worn on the head by a woman, esp. a queen, etc., at very formal social occasions • PIC› **Hats**

ti·bi·a /'tɪb·i·ə/ *n* [C] *pl* **tibiae** /'tɪb·i·aɪ/ or **tibias** *medical* a SHINBONE (=the bone which can be felt at the front of the lower leg)

tic /tɪk/ *n* [C] a sudden and uncontrolled small movement, esp. of the face, esp. because of a nervous illness • *He developed a nasty tic when he was depressed.*

tick SOUND /tɪk/ *v, n* (to make) a quiet short regularly repeated sound like that made by a clock • *The ticks seem to be coming from that bag over there.* [C] • *All the clocks in the shop were ticking.* [I] • *The hand of the timer ticked* **round** *(Am* **around***)* (=moved with a ticking sound) *to twelve.* [I] • *Time was ticking* **away/by** (=going past) *and she still hadn't arrived.* [I] • *There was no sound except the clock ticking/ the ticking of the clock.* [I] • *(infml) The clock went 'tick tock'.* • *I've left the car with the engine* **ticking over** (=running at its slowest speed). LP› **Driving** • *(Br infml)* **Hold/Hang on (just) a tick/two ticks** (=a very short period of time). ○ *I'll* **be with you in a couple of ticks/in two ticks.** • *(fig.) I'll be able to* **keep** *things* **ticking over** (=maintain basic activities) *in the office until you get back.* • *I've never been able to decide* **what makes** *him* **tick** (=what are his reasons for acting as he does).

tick·er /£'tɪk·əʳ, $-ɚ/ *n* [C] *dated infml* • A ticker is a heart: *He's got a weak ticker.*

tick MARK *esp. Br and Aus* /tɪk/, *Am usually* **check** *n* [C] a mark (✓), against an item, esp. on a piece of paper, to show that it has been examined in some way and, in the case of answers to questions, is correct • **Put** *a tick* **by/against** *the names of the people who have accepted the invitation.* • *I was pleased to see a page of ticks* (=correct answers marked with a tick). • LP› **Symbols**

tick *obj esp. Br and Aus* /tɪk/, *Am usually* **check** *v* [T] • *Tick* **(off)** *each item on the list as you complete it.* [T/M] • *He took them through the schedule slowly,* **ticking** *each item* **off on** *his fingers* (=touching the fingers of one hand with the first finger of the other).

tick PAYING LATER /tɪk/ *n* [U] **on tick** *Br infml dated* buying something and paying for it later; CREDIT PAYMENT • *Can you let me have this on tick until Thursday?*

tick ANIMAL /tɪk/ *n* [C] a very small creature like an insect which lives on and sucks the blood of other animals

tick off *obj* SPEAK SEVERELY, **tick** *obj* **off** *v prep* [M] *Br and Aus infml* to speak severely to someone • *I had to tick him off for being late again.*

tick·ing off /ˌtɪk·ɪŋ/ *n* [C] *pl* **tickings off** *esp. Br* • *I gave her a real ticking off yesterday.*

tick off *obj* MAKE ANGRY, **tick** *obj* **off** *v adv* [M] *Am infml* to make someone angry • *It really ticks me off when she doesn't keep her promises.* • *Poor service in a restaurant ticks him off more than anything else.*

tick·er–tape pa·rade /'tɪk·ə·teɪp/ *n* [C] *Am* a ceremony in which a person or people being honoured walks or drives along streets in a large city and small pieces of paper are thrown over them from the windows of tall buildings • *Atlanta threw a ticker-tape parade for the team after they won the World Series.*

tick·et PROOF OF PAYMENT /'tɪk·ɪt/ *n* [C] a small piece of paper or card given to someone, usually to show that they have paid for an item or activity • *a concert/cinema ticket* • *a train/bus/plane ticket* • *a lottery/raffle ticket* • *a cloakroom ticket* • *a season ticket* • *ticket office* • *a (railway) ticket collector* • *a ticket agent* • *It says on the door entrance* **by** *ticket* **only.** • *(slightly dated)* If you say that something is **just the ticket**, you mean that it is very suitable and exactly what you needed.

tick·et PRICE CARD /'tɪk·ɪt/ *n* [C] a piece of card or paper which is put on an item to show its size or price • *I can't find a* **price** *ticket on it anywhere.* • *It says it's a medium on the ticket and yet it looks very small.* • A ticket is also an amount of money that has to be paid as a punishment for not obeying a rule or law: *I got another speeding ticket at the weekend.* LP› **Crimes and criminals** ○ *Don't leave your car here – you'll only get a ticket.* • *(Br)* The ticket that someone stands for election on is the range of ideas and plans that they support: *She's standing on an education ticket.* • *(Am and Aus)* A ticket is the group of people representing a particular political party in an election: *the Republican/ Democratic ticket*

tick·le *(obj)* /'tɪk·l̩/ *v, n* (to cause, esp. by touching lightly) a slightly uncomfortable physical feeling, sometimes causing laughter • *I've got a tickle in the middle of my back.* [C] • A tickle in your throat is an unpleasant feeling which might make you cough. [C] • If you **give** someone a tickle, you tickle them. [C] • *She tickled his feet until he couldn't stop laughing.* [T] • *I don't like woollen trousers because they tickle.* [I] • *My nose is tickling, I think I'm going to sneeze.* [I] • *(infml) Can you see anything that tickles you/***tickles** *your* **fancy** (=that you like and want to have). • *(infml) I was* **tickled pink/tickled to death** (=pleased) **to** *receive the invitation to her wedding.* • *She was very tickled* (=pleased) *that her father and I went to school together.* • LP› **Feelings and pains**

tick·lish /'tɪk·l̩·ɪʃ, '-lɪʃ/ *adj* • *Are you ticklish* (=Do you laugh if someone tickles you)*?* • A ticklish situation is one that needs to be dealt with carefully.

tick–tack–toe /£ˌtɪk·tæk'təʊ, $-toʊ/ *n Am for* **noughts and crosses**, see at NOUGHT ZERO

tid·bit /ˈtɪd·bɪt/ *n* [C] *Am for* TITBIT

tid·dler /£ˈtɪd·l̩.əʳ, £ˈ-ləʳ, $ˈ-l̩·ɚ, $ˈ-lɚ/ *n* [C] something very small, esp. a fish or *(infml)* a child

tid·dly /ˈtɪd·l̩.i, ˈ-li/ *adj* **-ier, -iest** *infml* • *All you ate was a tiddly little* (= very small) *piece of cake.*

tid·dly /ˈtɪd·l̩.i, ˈ-li/ *adj* **-ier, -iest** *Br and Aus dated infml* slightly drunk • *Are you feeling a bit tiddly, Elaine?* • See also **tiddly** at TIDDLER.

tid·dly·winks /ˈtɪd·l̩.i·wɪŋks, ˈ-li-/ *n* [U] a game in which players try to get small plastic discs into a cup by pressing one piece against another to make it fly through the air

tid·dly·wink /ˈtɪd·l̩.i·wɪŋk, ˈ-li-/ *n* [C] • A tiddlywink is one of the pieces used in the game of tiddlywinks.

tide SEA /taɪd/ *n* [C] the rise and fall of the sea that happens twice every day • *high/low tide* • *a flood tide* • *The tide* **turns** (= starts to go in the opposite direction) *at 10 o'clock today.* • *We can/can't play on the sand because the tide is* **out/in**. • *The ebb and flow of the tide leaves many strange things on the beach.* • *We sail* **with/on the** *tide* (= when the tide is high). • *Beware of strong tides* (= flows of water) *in the channel.* • *(fig.) The tide of public opinion is turning against smoking/in favour of banning smoking.* • *(fig.) We must look for ways of* **stemming** (= stopping) *the rising tide of protest.* • To **go/swim with the tide** to follow what everyone else is doing. To **go/swim against the tide** is not to follow what everyone else is doing. • A **tide-table** is a list of the times at which the tide in a particular place is high for each day. • *"There is a tide in the affairs of men / Which taken at the flood, leads on to fortune"* (Shakespeare, Julius Caesar 4.3)

ti·dal /ˈtaɪ·dᵊl/ *adj* • *This part of the river is tidal.* • *a tidal river* • *There is increasing interest in tidal power/energy* (= electricity produced by using the rise and fall of the tide). • A **tidal wave** is an extremely large wave caused by movement of the earth under the sea when there is an EARTHQUAKE or a **volcanic eruption**, or *(fig.)* a sudden large increase: *(fig.) There was a tidal wave* **of** *complaints about aircraft noise.*

-tide TIME /-taɪd/ *combining form old use* a period of time • *Christmastide/Yuletide/Eastertide/Whitsuntide*

tide *obj* **o·ver** *v adv* [T] to help (someone) during a short period of difficulty • *Can you lend me some money to tide me over till the weekend?* • *Have another piece of cake. It'll tide you over till supper.*

tide·mark /£ˈtaɪd·mɑːk, $-mɑːrk/ *n* [C] a line of waste left on a beach which marks the highest point the sea reaches, more usually called the **high water mark** • *(fig. Br) Who didn't clean the tidemark* (= dirty mark left by the water) *off the bath?*

ti·dings /ˈtaɪ·dɪŋz/ *pl n old use* news • *tidings of great joy* • *glad/sad tidings* (= good/bad news)

ti·dy ORDERED /ˈtaɪ·di/ *adj* **-ier, -iest** (of appearance or behaviour) looking well ordered and cared for • *a tidy house/garden* • *a tidy person* • *neat and tidy* • *a tidy solution*

ti·dy *(obj)* /ˈtaɪ·di/ *v* • *Tidy* **(up)** *these papers/Tidy these papers* **(up)** *before you leave, please.* [M] • *I'm tired of asking you to tidy* **(up)** *your room/tidy your room* **up**. [M] • *The children were expected to tidy* **away** *their toys/to tidy their toys* **away** (= put them in the correct place) *before bedtime.* [M] • *(Br) Next week I'm going to tidy* **out** *my drawers/tidy my drawers* **out** (= tidy them by removing unwanted things). [M] • *Have you tidied up yet, kids?* [I]

ti·dy /ˈtaɪ·di/ *n* [C] • A tidy is a small container for a few items: *a desk/sink/car tidy*

ti·di·ly /ˈtaɪ·dɪ·li/ *adv* • *Put your clothes away tidily.*

ti·di·ness /ˈtaɪ·dɪ·nəs/ *n* [U]

ti·dy–up /ˈtaɪ·di·ʌp/ *n* [U] • *It's amazing how* **a** *quick tidy-up can transform your home.*

ti·dy LARGE /ˈtaɪ·di/ *adj* [before n] **-ier, -iest** *infml* (of amounts of money) large • *His business deals make him a tidy sum/profit/fortune/penny.*

tie *(obj)* FASTEN /taɪ/ *v* **tying**, *past* **tied** to fasten together two ends of (a piece of string or other long thin material), or to (cause to) hold together with a long, thin piece of string, material, etc. • *Could you help me tie this piece of string?* [T] • *This sleeping bag ties at the neck.* [I] • *She tied the ribbon tightly* **in** *a bow/knot.* [T] • *I'll tie the flowers* **into** *a bunch for you.* [T] • *I tie* **back** *my hair/I tie my hair* **back** *when it's hot.* [M] • *Make sure you tie* **down** *anything which might blow away in the storm.* [M] • *Tie it down.* [M] • *(fig. infml) He's tied* **down** (= limited in what he can do) *by having to work every Saturday.* [T] • *(fig. infml) I'll try to tie her* **down** (= get a firm decision from her) **on** *her plans.* [T] • *(fig.) I can't tie* **in** *what he said today* (= connect it or make it agree) **with** *what he told me last week.* [T] • *(fig.) We're trying to tie* **in** *our holiday/tie our holiday* **in with** *the lecture tour* (= to do these things at the same time). [M] • *(fig.) Is the allergy tied* **to** (= connected with) *dairy products, for example?* [T] • *(fig. infml) I'm tied* **to** (= have a special reason not to leave) *the house today because I'm expecting a new bed to be delivered.* [T] • *Tie* **(up)** *your shoelaces, or you'll trip over.* [T] • *Could you tie* **up** *the parcel for me.* [T] • *Sorry I'm late – I was tied* **up by** (= held back by) *an accident on the way home.* [T] • *(fig. infml) My money is tied* **up (in** *property/a trust fund)* (= the use of it is limited in some way). [T] • *(fig. infml) I'm not free till Wednesday – I'm tied* **up** (= am busy or have an arranged meeting) *on Monday and Tuesday.* [T] • *(fig. Br) Can you tie the allergy* **up** (= connect it) **with** *anything you've eaten?* [M] • *(disapproving)* If you say that someone, esp. a man, is **tied to** his mother's/wife's **apron strings**, it means that he is strongly influenced and controlled by that person: *George never comes out with the rest of us – he's tied to Martha's/his wife's apron strings.* • *So when are you two going to* **tie the knot** (= get married)? • *He* **tied** *me* **(up) in knots** (= confused me) *by asking difficult questions.* • *(Br)* A **tied cottage/tied house** is a house owned by your employer that you can live in for as long as you are employed in a particular job. • *(Br and Aus)* A **tied house** is also a PUB (= a place where alcohol is served) which is owned by a particular beer company and which only sells that company's products. Compare **free house** at FREE NOT LIMITED. • LP **Dressing and undressing**

tie /taɪ/ *n* [C] • A tie (also *esp. Am* **necktie**) is a long thin piece of material that is worn under a shirt collar, esp. by men, and tied in a knot at the front: *I was given a silk tie as a gift.* • A tie is also any piece of string, plastic, metal, etc. which is used to fasten or hold together something: *Can you see the ties for the rubbish bags in the cupboard?* • PIC **Clothes**

ties /taɪz/ *pl n* • Ties are the friendly feelings that people have for other people, or special connections with places: *I no longer feel any ties with my home town.* ○ *He urged governments worldwide to break* **diplomatic** *ties with the existing regime.* ○ *The themes that run throughout his work are friendship,* **family** *ties and first love.* ○ *Of all the political parties they are the most in favour of forging* **closer** *ties with Europe.*

tie FINISH EQUAL /taɪ/ *v* [I] **tying**, *past* **tied** to finish at the same time or score the same number of points etc. in a competition as someone or something else • *Jane and I tied* **(for** *first place) in the spelling test.* • *We tied* **with** *a team from the south in the championships.* • LP **Sports**

tie /taɪ/ *n* [C] • *It's a tie* **for** *first place* (= two people finished at the same time). • *They have changed the scoring system because there have been too many ties.* • A **tie-breaker** (*Br also* **tie-break**) in a game where players or teams have equal points, is extra play at the end of a regular game to decide who is the winner.

tie–dye *obj* /ˈtaɪ·daɪ, ˌ-ˈ-/ *v* [T] **tie-dyeing** to colour (cloth) by tying it in knots so that when it is put in a DYE (= liquid substance for changing the colour of things) the tied areas absorb less colour and produce circular patterns when unfastened • *There are pictures of us in the sixties wearing flares and tie-dyed T-shirts.*

tie·pin /ˈtaɪ·pɪn/ *n* [C] a small thin often decorative piece of metal used to hold the two parts of a tie together

tier /£tɪəʳ, $tɪr/ *n* [C] one of several layers or levels • *We sat in one of the upper tiers of the football stands.* • *My wedding cake had four tiers, each supported by small pillars.* • *I don't understand why you think we need yet another tier of management.*

tier *obj* /£tɪəʳ, $tɪr/ *v* [T] • *We could tier it more steeply to get more rows in.* • *The seats in the theatre were steeply tiered.*

-tiered /£-tɪəd, $-tɪrd/ *combining form* • *a two-tiered structure* • *a three-tiered cake*

tiff /tɪf/ *n* [C] *infml* a slight argument • *We* **had** *a slight tiff over whose turn it was to clean the floor.* • *Have you* **had** *a* **lovers'** *tiff?*

ti·ger, *female also* **ti·gress** /£ˈtaɪ·gəʳ, $-gɚ, -grəs/ *n* [C] a large wild cat which has yellowish orange fur with black stripes • PIC **Cats**

tight FIRMLY TOGETHER /taɪt/ *adj, adv* **-er, -est** (held or kept together) firmly or closely • *I can't untie the knot – it's too tight.* • *This lid is on very tight.* • *He took a tight hold of her arm.* • *The people stood talking in tight groups.* • *The aircraft flew past in tight formation.* • Clothes or shoes that are tight or **a tight fit** fit the body too closely and are uncomfortable: *That jacket's too tight – you want a bigger size.* • If you have a tight feeling in your chest you have an uncomfortable feeling of pressure, caused by illness, fear, etc. • Tight controls or rules are ones which limit what can happen. • If time or money is tight there isn't enough of it: *I can't stop, I'm tight for time.* ○ *They're raising three kids on one small salary so money is very tight.* • *(infml disapproving)* Someone who is tight with money, or **tight-fisted**, is unwilling to spend it: *You won't get a drink out of Gillian – she's too tight-fisted.* • If someone is **tight-lipped** they are pressing their lips together to avoid showing anger or they are refusing to speak about something: *He's been very tight-lipped about what happened at the meeting.* • A **tight situation/corner/spot** is a difficult situation: *When they both asked me to help I found myself in a tight corner.* • A **tight turn** or a **tight bend** is a sudden sharp turn. • *The plastic cover was stretched tight* (= stretched as much as it could be) *across the tank.* • *The child clung/held on tight to its mother when it was time to leave.* • *Check that windows and doors are shut tight* (= completely shut) *before you leave.* • See also AIRTIGHT; WATERTIGHT.

tight·ly /ˈtaɪt·li/ *adv*

tight·ness /ˈtaɪt·nəs/ *n* [U]

tight·en *(obj)* /£ˈtaɪ·tᵊn, $-t̬ᵊn/ *v* • *Tighten the straps so they don't rub.* [T] • *As he struggled, the ropes tightened even more.* [I] • *The police are* **tightening the net** (= coming closer to catching) *around the smugglers.* • *Are there any plans to tighten* **(up/up on)** *control of advertising?* [I/T] • *It's time we tightened* **up** *round here* (= we must improve the way we do things). [I] • If you **tighten** your **belt** you spend or use less because of lack of money: *We're all going to have to tighten our belts until your mother finds another job.*

tight [DRUNK] /taɪt/ *adj dated infml* having had too much alcohol; drunk • *Jim, you're tight!*

tight·rope /£ˈtaɪt·rəʊp, $-roʊp/ *n* [C] a tightly stretched wire or rope fixed high above the ground, which skilled people walk across, esp. in order to entertain others • *Charles Blondin crossed Niagara Falls on a tightrope in 1859.* • *One of the acrobats who* **walked** *the tightrope at the circus did it blindfolded.* • *Tightrope* **walkers** *often carry long poles to help themselves balance.* • If you **walk/tread a tightrope**, you have to deal with a difficult situation, esp. one involving making a decision between two opposing plans of action: *Many manufacturers have to walk a tightrope* **between** *pricing their goods too high and not selling them, and pricing them low and losing money.*

tights *Br* /taɪts/, *Am and Aus* **pan·ty·hose** *pl n* a piece of clothing made of thin stretchy material which covers the legs and lower part of the body below the waist, and which is worn by women and girls • *Tights are often made of nylon.* • *She bought a new* **pair of** *tights.* • *Oh no, I've got a ladder/run/hole in my tights.* • In the US and Australia, tights are the same type of clothing made from thicker material and worn by dancers and people doing physical exercises for health.

tight·wad /£ˈtaɪt·wɒd, $-wɑːd/ *n* [C] *Am and Aus slang disapproving* a person who is not willing to spend money • *There's no point in asking Joe to lend you the money – he's a real tightwad.*

ti·gress /ˈtaɪ·gres/ *n* [C] a female TIGER • *She fought like a tigress* (= very fiercely) *not to have her children taken from her.* • *(fig.) She can be a real tigress* (= can be very fierce) *sometimes.*

tike /taɪk/ *n* [C] TYKE

tilde /ˈtɪl·də/ *n* [C] (used when writing some languages) a mark made above a letter, esp. n, to show that the letter has a special sound • LP> **Symbols**

tile /taɪl/ *n* [C], *v* [T] (to cover with) a thin, usually square or rectangular, piece of baked clay, plastic, etc. used for covering roofs, floors, walls, etc. • *roof tiles* • *floor tiles* • *ceramic tiles* • *carpet tiles* • *Several tiles fell off the roof during the storm.* • *I was* **(out) on the tiles**/*had a* **night out on the tiles** *last night* (= I was enjoying myself in an uncontrolled way, esp. by drinking a lot of alcohol), *and I've got a dreadful headache this morning.* • *We're going to tile the bathroom* (= put tiles on the walls/floor of it) *ourselves.* • PIC> **Accommodation, Bathroom**

tiled /taɪld/ *adj* [not gradable] • *The kitchen has a tiled floor* (= a floor covered with tiles).

til·er /£ˈtaɪ·ləʳ, $-lɚ/ *n* [C] • *Can you recommend a good tiler* (= a person who fixes tiles to a surface)*?*

till [UNTIL] /tɪl/ *prep, conjunction* up to (the time that); until • *We waited till half past six for you.* • **Up** *till 1918, women in Britain were not allowed to vote.* • *How long is it till your baby is due?*

till [MONEY DRAWER] /tɪl/, *Am usually* **reg·is·ter** *n* [C] the drawer in a **cash register** (= a machine in a shop which records sales, and in which money is kept), or *(esp. Br infml)* a **cash register** • *Next time you have the till open, could you give me some change?* • *I'm afraid this till is closed* (= is not available to receive money) – *could you take your purchases to the one over there?* • *I think these items have been rung up wrongly on the till.* • *I'll be with you in a minute, I just have to change the* **till roll** (= paper on which amounts of money are recorded). • PIC> **Supermarket**

till *obj* [PREPARE LAND] /tɪl/ *v* [T] to prepare and use (land) for growing crops • *This piece of land has been tilled for hundreds of years.*

til·ler /£ˈtɪl·əʳ, $-ɚ/ *n* [C] a long handle fixed to and used to turn a RUDDER (= blade at the back of a boat used to control the boat's direction) • PIC> **Ships and boats**

tilt *(obj)* [SLOPE] /tɪlt/ *v* to (cause to) move into a sloping position • *She tilted the sunshade so that it shaded her chair.* [T] • *He tilted his chair backwards and put his feet up on his desk while he was talking on the phone.* [T] • *Anna looked up at him with her head tilted to one side.* [T] • *Tom wore his baseball cap tilted at an angle on his head.* [T] • *The front seats of the car tilt.* [I] • *(fig.) Many voters who haven't yet made up their minds are tilting* **away from/towards** (= are beginning to support/not to support) *the Democrats.* [I] • *(fig.) In the first half of the match, Liverpool had control, but in the second half, the balance tilted* **towards** *Sheffield* (= Sheffield started to get control). [I] • *(fig.) The local election results have tilted the balance of power* **in favour of** *the opposition* (= has put them in a stronger or controlling position). [T] • If something **tilts the balance/scales**, it is the thing which causes a particular situation to happen or a particular decision to be made when other situations or decisions are possible: *This latest election promise might just tilt the balance in the government's favour.*

tilt /tɪlt/ *n* [C usually sing] • *She wore her hat* **at a tilt**. • *(fig.) There has been a tilt* **to/towards/away from** *the right among some groups of young people.*

tilt [FIGHT] /tɪlt/ *v* [I] **tilt at windmills** *infml* to fight enemies who do not really exist

tim·ber /£ˈtɪm·bəʳ, $-bɚ/ *n* trees that are grown so that the wood from them can be used for building, or (*Am also* **lumber**) wood used for building • *a timber forest* [U] • *a timber merchant* [U] • *These trees are being grown for timber.* [U] • A timber is a long piece of wood used for building, esp. houses and ships: *roof timbers* [C] ○ *a timber-framed building* [C]

tim·ber /£ˈtɪm·bəʳ, $-bɚ/ *exclamation* • *People shout "timber!" to show that a tree that has been cut is about to fall.*

tim·ber·line /£ˈtɪm·bə·laɪn, $-bɚ-/ *n* [U] *Am for* TREELINE

time [MINUTES/DAYS/YEARS] /taɪm/ *n* [U] that part of existence which is measured in seconds, minutes, hours, days, weeks, months, years, etc., or this process considered as a whole • *All things exist in space and time.* • *As time* **passed**, *he slowly recovered from his injuries.* • *She grew more and more fascinated by the subject as time* **went on/by**. • *People may have done that when you were young, Dad, but time has* **moved/marched on** *since then* (= things have changed as years have gone past). • *(fig.) I saw the car coming straight towards me, and for a moment time* **stood still** (= it seemed as if the process of movement from one second to the next had stopped). • *The curtains have faded* **over/with** *time* (= as years have gone past). • *You'll forget her* **in time** (= in the future). • **Over the course of** *time* (= as years have gone past), *holes have formed in the rock.* • *The doctor says that* **in the course of** *time* (= after weeks, months, etc. have gone past), *the scars will fade.* • *I only worked there for a short* **period of** *time.* • *In his resignation statement, the minister said that he wanted to be able to* **spend** *more time with his family.* • *(fig.) I'm not doing much at the moment, just* **killing** *time* (= doing very little while I wait for something, esp. a planned activity, to happen) *till the next school term begins.* • *He said that he would love her* **for all time** (= always). • *If you carry on driving like that, it'll only be a* **matter/question of time** *before you have an accident* (= you will have an accident at some point in the future). • *She's been called the greatest opera singer* **of all time** (= ever to have lived). • If you say that **time is on** your **side**, or that you **have time on** your **side**, you mean that you do not have to do quickly whatever it is that you want or have to do: *We don't have to make a final decision till next* *week, so we've got time on our side.* • **(Only) time will/can tell** (= We will discover in the future) *whether we made the right decision.* • *On her wedding day, she followed the* **time-honoured** (= valued and respected because of having existed for many years) *custom/tradition/practice of wearing something old, something new, something borrowed and something blue.* • (esp. in stories and films) A **time machine** is a machine in which people can travel into the past or the future. • *The school uses the old,* **time-tested** *approaches to/methods of* (= those which have been in use for a long period, and have been proved to work well for) *teaching children to read.* • *"Dr Who" is a popular British television programme about* **time travel** (= the theoretical process of travelling into the past or the future). • A **time warp** is a theoretical change in the measurement of time in which people and events from one part of history are imagined as existing in another part: *(fig.) He's living in a time warp* (= He is old-fashioned). • *(saying)* 'Time and tide wait for no man/no one' means people cannot stop hours, weeks, etc. going past, therefore you should not delay doing things. • *(saying)* 'Time heals (all wounds)/Time's a (great) healer' means that a painful or difficult situation gets better after a number of days, months, etc. have gone past. • *(saying)* 'Time flies/Doesn't time fly?' means that hours, weeks, years, etc. go past quickly. Often used to express surprise that so many weeks, etc. have gone past since you saw someone or while you have been doing something. People also sometimes say 'Time flies when you're having fun.' • *(saying)* 'Time passes/Time moves on' is also used to express surprise that so many weeks, etc. have gone past since they saw someone or something happened. • *(saying)* 'Time is money' means that you should not do nothing, or do something for which you do not get paid, when you could be working and earning money. • *(saying)* 'Time is of the essence' means that it is important to do the particular activity you are doing quickly. • *(saying)* 'Time hangs heavy' means that minutes, hours, weeks etc. seem to go past very slowly: *Time hangs heavy when you have nothing to do.* • *"Time, time, time is on our side, yes it is"* (The Rolling Stones in the song *Time is on my side*, 1982) • *"Time, like an ever-rolling stream, bears all its sons away"* (from the hymn *Our God, Our Help in Ages Past* by Isaac Watts, 1719) • *"As time goes by"* (title of a song written by Herman Hupfeld, sung in the film *Casablanca*, 1931) • *"But at my back I always hear/ Time's wingèd Chariot hurrying near"* (Andrew Marvell in the poem *To his Coy Mistress*, 1681) • [LP]> **Tenses, Time**

time·less /ˈtaɪm·ləs/ *adj* • Something that is timeless does not change as the years go past: *the timeless English countryside*

time·less·ly /ˈtaɪm·lə·sli/ *adv*

time·less·ness /ˈtaɪm·lə·snəs/ *n* [U]

time [PERIOD] /taɪm/ *n* a particular period of seconds, minutes, hours, days, weeks, months, years, etc. for which something has been happening, or which is needed for something, or which is available for something • *I enjoyed my course at first, but* **after a** *time I got bored with it.* [U] • *They only stayed* **for a short** *time* (= a short period). [U] • *That was the best restaurant I've been to* **for/in a long** *time* (= a long period has gone past since I went to such a good restaurant). [U] • *I used to live in New York, but that's* **a** *long time* **ago** *now* (= a long period of months, years, etc. has gone past since then). [U] • *It was* **some** *time* **ago** *that I last heard from her.* [U] • *We're going on holiday* **in** *two weeks' time* (= after two weeks have gone past). [U] • **During** *her time* (= While she was) *in office, the Prime Minister introduced a large number of changes.* [U] • *"Where did you go for your holiday?" "We spent some time/some of the time/ part of the time* (= the period for which the holiday lasted) *in Florence, and part of the time in Rome."* [U] • *"Do your children get on well together?" "Yes, most of the time* (= the period during which they are together)*."* [U] • *When Paula was ill, I took her some magazines to help her* **pass** *the time* (= to give her something to do so that it did not seem as if the hours, etc. were going past slowly). [U] • *If you'd* **taken** *more time* **with/over** (= spent more hours doing) *this essay, you could have done it much better.* [U] • *It* **takes** *a long time* (= many hours are needed) *to get from London to Sydney.* [U] • *We'd* **save** *time on our journey* (= It would be quicker) *if we went by train.* [U] • If you have **got** time, you have enough time to do something: *We haven't got much time before the train leaves.* [U] ○ *Have you got time* **for** *a quick drink after work?* [U] ○ *I'd like to learn to sail, but I haven't got* **the** *time* (= I am too busy). [U] ○ *I haven't got time* **to** *go to the shops today.* [U + *to* infinitive] • If you **find (the)** time, you arrange to have enough time to do something: *I don't know how you find time* **to** *do all the things you do.* [U + *to* infinitive] ○ *I'd like to help you, but I don't think I'll be able to find the time today.* [U] • If you **give** someone time, you allow them a number of hours, weeks, etc. in which to do something: *Can you give me some more time to pay back the money I owe you?* [U] ○ *You'll forget her,* **given** *time* (= in the future). [U] • If you **have** time **to kill**, you have nothing to do for that particular period: *We've got some time to kill before our train arrives – shall we have a drink?* [U] • *I'd love to stop and chat but I'm rather* **pressed for** *time* (= am in a hurry). [U] • *She didn't finish her exam paper because she* **ran out of** *time* (= there were not enough hours, etc. available for her to finish). [U] • *If you'd got on with your work instead of* **wasting** *time* (= not making good use of the hours, etc. that you have available) *chatting, you'd be finished by now.* [U] • *Stop* **wasting** *my time* (= causing me not to make good use of the hours, etc. that I have available for doing things) *with your stupid questions.* [U] • If you **have** or **take** time **off**, you stop what you are doing, esp. working, in order to do something else: *I asked my boss if I could have some time off to go to the dentist.* [U] ○ *He's taken some time off* **from** *his job in order to travel round the world.* [U] • *What do you like doing in your* **spare/free** *time* (= when you're not working)*?* [U] • Your time in a race is the number of minutes, hours, etc. you take to complete it: *Her time* **for** *the marathon was just under three hours.* [C] ○ *They're trying to improve their times.* [C] ○ *That result was the fastest time in the world so far this year.* [C] ○ *He won the 100 metres in* **record** *time.* [U] ○ *(fig.) We got here in* **record** *time* (= very quickly). [U] • *I wish you'd stop criticizing me* **all the time** (= continuously). • *The doctor made me feel as if she had* **all the time in the world** (= a large number of hours, etc. available) *to listen to my problems.* • To **do/ serve time** is to spend a period of weeks, months, years, etc. in prison: *It's not always easy to find a job after you've done time. / She's serving time for murder, though she claims she is innocent.* • If you do something **for a time**, you do it for a short period: *For a time, we all thought that Sheila and Frank would get married.* ○ *You lived in London for a time, didn't you?* • *Leave the ironing* **for the time being** (= for a limited period) *– I'll do it later.* • If you say that you **have a lot of time for** someone, it means that you like them and have a good opinion of them. If you **have no time for** them, you do not like them and do not want to be involved with them: *I have a lot of time for people who help with charity work.* ○ *She has no time/She doesn't have much time for her son-in-law.* • *Now that her children are all at school, Mary has found that she has* **time on** *her* **hands** (= has nothing to do)*, so she is taking a college course.* • If you do something **in no time (at all)/in less than no time (at all)/in next to no time (at all)**, you do it quickly or soon: *The children ate their dinner in no time.* ○ *We'll be home in next to no time.* • If you say there is or that you have **no time to lose**, it means that you must do quickly whatever it is that you want to do: *Come on, there's no time to lose, we must get home before John finds out where we've been.* • If you **take** your **time**, you do something slowly: *Take your time, there's no hurry.* ○ *He's certainly taken his time* **in** *answering my letter.* ○ *The council have taken their time* **to** *repair the road.* [+ *to* infinitive] • *(infml) OK everyone,* **time's up** (= there are no more minutes, etc. available) *for this week – see you all again at next week's class.* • *(Am and Aus infml) "Sorry, folks, we're* **(all) out of** *time now* (= there are no more minutes, etc. available)*. See you next week," said the host of the television game show.* [U] • If you are paid **time and a half** for a job, you are paid what you are usually paid for it with half the usual rate added on to it. • A **time-and-motion study** is a study of work methods, esp. in industry or business, in order to find the most effective way of operating. • *Producing a dictionary is a very* **time-consuming** *job* (= a large number of hours, months, years, etc. is needed for it). • A **time frame** is a period of days, weeks, months, etc. within which an activity is intended to happen: *Have you* **set** *a time frame* **for** *completing the job?* ○ *The government plans to introduce these changes* **in/within** *a fairly long/short time frame.* • A **time lag** (also **lag**) is a period between two related events: *There'll be a time lag of about a week* **between** *the blood test being done and the results being known.* • **Time-lapse** filming/photography is a method of filming very slow actions by taking a series of single pictures over a period of time, then putting them together to show the action happening very quickly. •

We've set a **time limit (of** *ten minutes)* **on** *each child's turn on the trampoline* (=each turn must be completed in ten minutes). • A **time-out** is a short period during a game in some sports when the players stop playing in order to rest, plan what they are going to do next, etc.: *The coach* **called** *a time-out to discuss strategy.* • *(Am)* People say **time-out** when they want other people to stop what they are doing, esp. when they are having an argument or disagreement: *OK, time-out, everyone, let's all quiet down and talk about this calmly.* • The **time scale** of something is the period of time over which it happens: *We're doing this job on a short/long time scale.* ○ *Police officers are trying to construct the time scale* **of** *events leading up to the murder.* ○ *What's the time scale* **for** *this* (=how long will it take)*?* • A **time share** is a holiday house or apartment which is owned by several different people, each of whom is able to use it for a particular period of the year. A time share (also **time-sharing**) is also the activity of doing this: *We've bought a time share in Spain.* • **Time-sharing** is also the use of a central computer by several other smaller computers connected to it. • A **time sheet** (*Am also* **time card**) is a piece of paper on which an employee records the number of hours they have worked. • *"I am just going outside, and may be some time"* (final words of Captain Oates before leaving the tent in which the others died, recorded in Scott's diary of his expedition to the South Pole, 1912) • *"A week is a long time in politics"* (Remark by Harold Wilson, c.1964) • LP **Periods of time**

time *obj* /taɪm/ *v* [T] • *Will you time me to see how long* (=measure the number of minutes) *it takes me to swim a length?* • *The winning team was timed* **at** *5 minutes 26 seconds.*

-time /-taɪm/ *combining form* • *springtime* (=the spring period) • *summertime* (=the summer period) • *Christmas-time* • *daytime* • *night-time*

time·less /ˈtaɪm·ləs/ *adj* • Something that is timeless has a value that is not limited to a particular period but will last forever: *a timeless book/play/film/classic* • *a timeless jacket* • *timeless values/questions/quality*

time·less·ly /ˈtaɪm·lə·sli/ *adv*

time·less·ness /ˈtaɪm·lə·snəs/ *n* [U]

tim·er /£ˈtaɪ·məʳ, $-mɚ/ *n* [C] • A timer is a device which records when a particular number of minutes, hours, etc. have gone past: *He* **set** *the timer on the oven to/for 20 minutes* (=to record when 20 minutes had gone past). ○ *The timer has* **gone off** (=has made a noise to show that the period it was set to record has gone past), *so the cakes must be cooked.* • Compare **timer** at TIME [PARTICULAR POINT].

time [PARTICULAR POINT] /taɪm/ *n* a particular point in the day, as expressed in hours and minutes or shown on a clock, or a particular point in the day, week, month or year, etc. • *"What's* **the** *time?" "It's ten o'clock."* [U] • *What time is it?* [U] • *What time do you finish work?* [U] • *Have you got* **the** *time* **(on** *you)* (=the particular point in the day it is, expressed in hours and minutes)*?* [U] • *He's teaching his daughter to* **tell** *the time* (=to recognize what particular point in the day it is by looking at a clock). [U] • *Did you find out the times* **of** *the trains to London* (=the particular points in the day at which they leave)*?* [C] • *The estimated time* **of** *arrival/departure of this flight is 11.15.* [C] • *Oh dear, is that the* **(right)** *time* (=Is the particular point in the day I've been told it is or seen on a clock correct)*? I'm late for work.* [U] • *We arrived at the cinema at the* **wrong** *time* (=the wrong point in the day), *and the film had already started.* [U] • *The kitchen clock is* **gaining/losing** *time* (=is showing a particular point in the day that is increasingly later or earlier than the real one). [U] • *My watch has never* **kept** *very good time* (=been correct in showing what particular point in the day it is). [U] • *She's always busy doing something, from* **the** *time* (=particular point in the day at which) *she gets up in the morning till* **the** *time she goes to bed.* [U] • *We always have dinner* **at the same** *time every day.* [C] • *The programme was being shown* **at a different** *time from usual.* [C] • *I was exhausted* **by the** *time I got home.* [U] • *"What would be the best time* **of day** *for us to deliver the table?" "Oh, any time will be OK."* [C] • *Today's temperatures will be normal* **for the** *time* **of** *year* (=will be as they are expected to be at this particular point in the year). [C] • *Just think,* **this** *time* (=at the same particular point during) *next week we'll be in Mauritius.* [U] • *We regret that* **at the present** *time (Am also* **at this time***)* (=for now, although it is hoped not in the future) *we are unable to supply the goods you ordered.* [U] • *The time is fast* **drawing near/approaching** *when* (=it will soon be the particular point at which) *we'll have to make a decision one way or the other.* [U] • Time is also used to refer to the system of recording hours used in different parts of the world: *Greenwich Mean Time* [U] ○ *daylight saving time* [U] • *(esp. Am) Let's meet for lunch. I'll call you* **ahead of time** (=in advance) *to fix a time and a place.* • *When you're at the airport, you should make sure you have your luggage with you* **at all times** (=continuously). • *Parking is not allowed here* **at any time** (=ever). • *When we visited the Tower of London we had to wait outside because only a certain number of people were allowed in* **at (any) one time/at any given time** (=at any particular point in the day). • **At** *Grandad's* **time of life** (=Now that he is his present age), *he ought to be taking things easy.* • *It seemed like a good idea* **at the time** (=at the particular point at which it was thought of). • If someone will **not give** you **the time of day**, they are unfriendly and refuse to speak to you: *We had an argument with our neighbours, and now they won't even give us the time of day.* • A **time bomb** is a bomb which contains a device that makes it explode at a particular point in the day. • A **time bomb** is also a situation which is likely to become difficult to deal with or control: *By ignoring the wishes of their employees, the managers are* **setting/creating** *a time bomb for themselves.* ○ *The prison governors are* **sitting on** *a time bomb* (=are having to deal with a bad situation that is likely to become difficult to deal with or control). • A **time clock** is a clock which employees use to record the particular point in the day at which they arrive at and leave work. • *Some medicines exist in the form of* **time(d)-release capsules** (=as pills which release their contents gradually during the day). • *I always set my watch by the* **time signal** (=a signal which is broadcast on the radio every hour, for example at one o'clock, two o'clock, three o'clock, etc. to show exactly what particular point in the day it is). • *(Br and Aus)* A **time switch** is a **timer**: *Our heating system is controlled by a time switch.* • A **time zone** is one of 24 equal parts into which the world is divided. In any place within each part, the particular point in the day is the same, and is an hour in front of or behind that in the parts on either side: *If you go from New York to London, you cross five time zones.*

time *obj* /taɪm/ *v* [T] • *The meeting has been timed* **for** (=has been arranged so that it is at) *2 o'clock.* • *We timed our trip* **to** (=arranged it so that it would) *coincide with my cousin's wedding.* [+ *to* infinitive] • A **timed ticket** is one which allows you to go into a place, such as a famous building which the public is able to visit, at a particular time. • *The bomb contained a* **timing device** (=a device that caused it to start operating at a particular point in the day) *which was set so that it would go off when the station was very busy.*

tim·er /£ˈtaɪ·məʳ, $-mɚ/, *Br and Aus also* **time switch** *n* [C] • A timer is a device on a machine which causes the machine to start or stop working at a particular point in the day: *Most video recorders have a timer which you can set to record a programme if you're going to be out at the time it is being shown.* • Compare **timer** at TIME [PERIOD].

time [SUITABLE POINT] /taɪm/ *n, combining form* a particular point of the day, week, month, year, etc. that is suitable for a particular activity, or at which something is expected to happen • *holiday time* [U] • *party time* [U] • *Put your toys away now, it's time* **for** *bed/bedtime.* [U] • *It's time* **(that)** *I was leaving.* [U] • *Is it time* **to** *go home yet?* [U + *to* infinitive] • *When would be* **a good time** *for me to call you?* [C] • *This is not the time* (=not a suitable moment) *to be thinking about buying a house.* [U] • *This is no time* (=not a suitable moment) *to change your mind.* [U] • *I feel that the time has* **come** (=now is a suitable moment) *for me to move on.* [U] • *The repairs to the road were finished two weeks* **ahead of** *time* (=sooner than was expected). [U] • *Why is it that the trains never run* **on** *time* (=make their journeys in the expected number of hours, etc.)*?* [U] • *She's grown old* **before** *her time* (=sooner than she might have been expected to have done). [U] • *(saying)* 'There's a time and a place for everything' means every activity has a particular point in the day which is suitable for it. Often used to suggest that a particular point is not suitable for a particular activity which is happening. Sometimes shortened to 'There's a time and a place'. • *(saying)* 'There's no time like the present' means that now is a suitable moment to start doing something. Often used to suggest that a particular activity should be started immediately. • *(infml)* If it is **about time/high time** that someone did something, it should have been done sooner or a long time

THE TIME

COMMON WAYS OF GIVING THE TIME

When giving the time in full, 'minutes' is often omitted when the number of minutes is 5, 10, 20 and so on. The hour may also be droppped if it is clear what hour is meant. In American English you can say 'after' instead of 'past', and 'of' or 'before' instead of 'to'. The abbreviations 'a.m.' and 'p.m.' are used after the time when it is important to be clear whether the time is in the morning or evening.

a.m. = before noon	**7.00**	seven/seven o'clock
	8.05	eight o five/five past eight/five minutes past eight *(Am also)* five after eight/five minutes after eight
	9.17	nine seventeen/seventeen minutes past nine
	10.30	ten thirty/half past ten/*(Br infml)* half ten/*(Am infml)* half after ten
	11.40	eleven forty/twenty to twelve/twenty minutes to twelve *(Am also)* twenty of twelve/twenty before twelve
	12.00	twelve/twelve o'clock/midday/noon/twelve noon
p.m. = after noon	**2.01**	two o one/a minute past two/one minute past two
	3.15	three fifteen/quarter past three/a quarter past three
	8.45	eight forty-five/quarter to nine/a quarter to nine
	12.00	twelve/midnight/twelve o'clock/twelve midnight

The 24-hour clock is generally used for railway and air timetables, though less often in America. Times are read simply as numbers *13.15 – thirteen fifteen* and the exact hours are read using 'hundred' *16.00 – sixteen hundred (hours).*

OTHER WAYS OF REFERRING TO A TIME

- **Referring to a period in the day**

in the morning, this morning, yesterday/tomorrow morning, early/mid/late morning (also: afternoon, evening) • **at** night, tonight, last night, tomorrow night • **at** lunchtime, **at** teatime

- **Giving approximate times**

around four,
about four
(infml) four-ish

nearly four,
coming up to four
just before four

just after four,
(Br) just gone four

ago: *It's about time* **(that)** *the school improved its meals service.* ○ *It's high time* **(that)** *we had the car serviced.* ○ *It is high time* **for** *Europe to take responsibility for its own defence and stop depending on the United States.* • *(infml) "So Ben's finally found a job." "Yes, and* **about time (too)/** **(***Br and Aus also***) not before time** (= he should have done so before now)."• If someone is **ahead of/**(*Br also*) **before their time**, they have new ideas or opinions or ways of living long before most other people do. • If you are **in time**, you are early enough: *I got home just in time – it's starting to rain.* ○ *If we don't hurry up, we won't be in time* **to** *catch the train.* [+ *to* infinitive] ○ *We arrived in* **good** *time* (= We arrived early) **for** *the start of the match.* • *The bus arrived* **exactly/dead/right on time** (= at the particular point at which it was expected). • **Time** is the particular point in the day at which people who are drinking in a bar in Britain have to finish their drinks and leave: *"Time, please," called the landlord.* ○ *Is it time already?* • If you say that **the time is ripe**, you mean that it is a suitable point for a particular activity: *I'm waiting till the time is ripe before I tell my parents that I failed my exams.* • *"The time has come, the Walrus said, to talk of many things"* (Lewis Carroll in his book *Alice Through the Looking Glass*, 1872)

time *obj* /taɪm/ *v* [T] • *If you time your departure* (= arrange it so that it happens at a suitable point) *carefully, you should be able to miss the worst of the traffic.* • *She won the game with a brilliantly timed shot* (= one played at exactly the right moment).

time·ly /ˈtaɪm·li/ *adj* **-ier, -iest** • Something that is timely happens at a suitable moment: *Your letter came as a timely reminder that we need to arrange a meeting.* ○ *The timely arrival of their guests prevented Helen and Jim's disagreement from turning into a fight.* ○ *The change in the exchange rate provided a timely boost to the company's falling profits.* • *(esp. Br fml)* If something happens in a timely **manner/fashion**, it happens quickly: *I hope we'll be able to deal with the business of the meeting in a timely manner.*

time·li·ness /ˈtaɪm·lɪ·nəs/ *n* [U]

ti·ming /ˈtaɪ·mɪŋ/ *n* [U] • *"Have we arrived too early?" "No, your timing is perfect* (= you have arrived at exactly the right moment) *– dinner is almost ready."* • *It was unfortunate timing that my mother called just as we were about to go out.* • *To be a good tennis player, you have to have good timing* (= to be able to hit the ball at the right moment).

time OCCASION /taɪm/ *n* [C] an occasion or period, or the experience connected with it • *The last time we went to Paris, it rained every day.* • *I'll know better next time.* • *Every time/Each time I ask you to do something, you always say you're too busy.* • *Do you remember the time that Alistair fell in the river.* • *They go swimming three or four times a week.* • *I've seen "Casablanca" lots of times.* • *How many times do I have to tell you not to do that?* • *There are times* **when** *I wish I didn't live where I do.* • *The (Br and Aus) four-times/(Am) four-time champion* (= the person who had been the winner on four occasions in the past) *was unexpectedly defeated in the second round of the competition.* • *If I'd known* **at** *the time* (= then) *that she was his former wife, I'd never have said what I did.* • *Sometimes I enjoy my English lessons, but* **at** *other times* (= on other occasions) *I find them really boring.* • **For** *the* **umpteenth/hundredth/thousandth** *time,* (= I've told you on many occasions to) *stop hitting your sister.* • *Did you* **have** *a* **good** *time* (= an enjoyable experience) *at the beach?* • *I'm sorry to hear you've been* **having** *such a* **bad/hard/difficult** *time.* • *She had an* **easy/hard** *time* **of it** (= a comfortable/uncomfortable experience) *with the birth of her second baby.* • *You can be really annoying* **at times** (= sometimes), *you know.* • **From time to time** (= Occasionally) *I still think of her.* • *(infml)* If you **give** someone **a hard time**, you make things difficult or unpleasant for them: *Her kids always give her a hard time when she takes them shopping.* ○ *My mother gave me a really hard time* (= was angry with me) *about staying out late.* • **Time after time** (= again and again) *she gets herself involved in relationships with unsuitable men.* • *I've told you* **time and (time) again** (= very often) *– make sure you look before you cross the road.*

• *We had* **the time of** *our* **lives** (= an extremely enjoyable experience) *at Ali's party.* • *(Br)* **The times** *I've told you* (= I've told you on many occasions to do something and you are still not doing it), *ask before you borrow my clothes.* • *"The first time ever I saw your face, I thought the sun rose in your eyes"* (Roberta Flack in the song *The first time ever I saw your face*, 1972) • *"This could be the last time, maybe the last time, I don't know"* (The Rolling Stones in the song *The Last Time*, 1965)

time HISTORICAL PERIOD /taɪm/ *n* [C], **times** *pl n* a period in history • *Charles Dickens' novel "A Tale of Two Cities" is set at the time* **of** *the French Revolution.* • **In/During** *medieval times, women thought to be witches were burnt at the stake.* • **In** *times gone by, all crops were harvested by hand.* • *Times were hard* (= The conditions of life were uncomfortable) *when I was a boy.* • *He is widely regarded as one of the best writers of* **modern/our** *times* (= the present or very recent past). • *I never thought it would happen in my time* (= before I died). • *Were things really so different in our great grandparents' time* (= when they were alive)? • *We sat and talked about* **old** *times* (= things that had happened to us in the past.) • **At one time** (= In the past), *George Eliot lived here.* • If something or someone is **before** your **time**, they happened or existed before you were born, or were old enough to remember them: *I don't remember The Beatles – they were before my time.* • If something or someone is **behind the times**, they are old-fashioned. • *My family has lived in this village* **from/since time immemorial/time out of mind** (= since long ago in the past). • If you **keep up/ move/***(Am)* **change with the times**, you change your ideas, opinions or way of living or working to make them modern: *I don't really like working on a computer, but you have to move with the times, I suppose.* • **Time was** (= there was a period in the past) **when** *you could buy a loaf of bread for sixpence.* • A **time capsule** is a container which is filled with objects considered to be typical of the present period in history and then buried, so that it can be dug up and studied in a future period. • *(saying)* 'Times are changing' means society is very different from the way it was in the past: *You used to be able to call the mother of a child called John Smith Mrs Smith automatically, but times are changing and now mothers, fathers and children often have different surnames.* • *"The Times They Are A-Changing"* (title of a song by Bob Dylan, 1964) • LP› **Periods of time**

time MUSIC /taɪm/ *n* [U] the number of beats in a BAR (= very small part of a piece) of music, or the speed at which a piece of music is intended to be played • *This piece is written in 4/4 time.* • *Small children often have difficulty singing* **in** *time* **with** *the music* (= at the same speed at which the music is being played). • *It seemed to me as if the violins were playing* **out of** *time* (= at a different speed from the other instruments playing the same piece of music). • To **beat** time is to make a regular series of sounds at the same speed as a piece of music is intended to be played. • *Watching the conductor will help you to* **keep** *time* (= to play the music at the speed at which it is intended to be played). • A **time signature** is a symbol, usually in the form of two numbers, one above the other, written at the beginning of a piece of music to show how many beats there are in each BAR.

ti·ming /ˈtaɪ·mɪŋ/ *n* [U] • *My singing teacher says I must try and improve my timing* (= try to sing at the same speed as the music).

time·keep·er /£ˈtaɪmˌkiː·pəʳ, $-pɚ/ *n* [C] an object or person that records (an amount of) time • *There's no point in having a clock which looks attractive if it isn't a good timekeeper* (= if it doesn't record the time correctly). • A timekeeper is a person who records the amount of time that people taking part in a race or competition take to finish the race or competition, or the amount of time that people at work spend working on their jobs. • If you say that someone is a good timekeeper, you mean that they regularly arrive, esp. at work, at the time at which they are expected. A bad timekeeper is regularly late.

time·keep·ing /ˈtaɪmˌkiː·pɪŋ/ *n* [U]

time·piece /ˈtaɪm·piːs/ *n* [C] *dated or fml for* a clock or watch

tim·er /£ˈtaɪ·məʳ, $-mɚ/ *n* [C] See at TIME PERIOD, TIME PARTICULAR POINT

times HISTORY /taɪmz/ *pl n* another word for TIME HISTORICAL PERIOD

times MULTIPLIED /taɪmz/ *prep* multiplied by • *Two times two equals four (2 x 2 = 4).* • *The area of a rectangle is its height times its width.* • LP› **Mathematics**

times AMOUNT /taɪmz/ *predeterminer, adv* (used to show the difference in amount of two things, by multiplying one of them by the stated number) • *She earns five times* **as much as** *I do./She earns five times* **more than** *I do.* • *My foot swelled up to three times the normal size when it was stung by a wasp.* • *(fig.) This piece of work is ten times better* (= much better) *than the last piece you did.*

time·sav·ing /ˈtaɪmˌseɪ·vɪŋ/ *adj* reducing the amount of time needed for doing something • *Washing machines and vacuum cleaners are timesaving devices.*

time·ser·ver /£ˈtaɪmˌsɜː·vəʳ, $-ˌsɜːr·vɚ/ *n* [C] *disapproving* a person who does not work very hard at their job, but who is waiting until they reach the age at which they can stop work • A timeserver is also someone who changes their ideas and opinions in order to make them more like those that are fashionable or are held by people in power, esp. because they believe it will be to their advantage.

time·serv·ing /£ˈtaɪmˌsɜː·vɪŋ, $-ˌsɜːr-/ *n* [U] • *timeserving politicians*

time·ta·ble /ˈtaɪmˌteɪ·bl̩/, *Am usually* **sched·ule** *n* [C] a list of times at which particular activities or events, esp. the arrival and leaving times of buses, trains etc., or *(Br and Aus)* classes in a school, are planned to happen • *Do you have a Birmingham to London train timetable that I could borrow?* • *The first lesson* **on** *the timetable* **for** *Monday morning is history.* • *The timetable* **for** *our trip to Paris includes visits to Notre Dame, the Eiffel Tower and the Louvre.* • *Here is the timetable* **of** *events* **for** *the day.* • *I've got a very busy timetable next week* (= I have a lot of activities planned).

time·ta·ble *obj* /ˈtaɪmˌteɪ·bl̩/ *v* [T often passive] • *The lecture is timetabled* **for** (= planned to start at) *5.00 p.m.* • *We are timetabled* **to** *go to the British Museum on Thursday and the Tower of London on Friday.* [+ obj + *to* infinitive]

time·worn /£ˈtaɪm·wɔːn, $-wɔːrn/ *adj* (no longer of interest or value because of) having been used a lot over a long period of time • *a timeworn expression/excuse* • *a timeworn path*

ti·mid /ˈtɪm·ɪd/ *adj* **-er, -est** shy and nervous; lacking confidence; easily frightened • *Lucy is a rather timid child.* • *My horse is a bit timid and is easily frightened by traffic.*

ti·mid·ly /ˈtɪm·ɪd·li/ *adv* • *"Um, excuse me," he said timidly.*

ti·mid·i·ty /£tɪˈmɪd·ɪ·ti, $-ə·t̬i/ *n* [U]

ti·ming /ˈtaɪ·mɪŋ/ *n* [U] See at TIME SUITABLE POINT, TIME MUSIC

ti·mor·ous /£ˈtɪm·ᵊr·əs, $-ɚ·əs/ *adj fml or literary* nervous; lacking confidence; easily frightened; TIMID • *"Wee, sleekit, cow'rin' tim'rous beastie* (= sly, cowering, timorous little beast)*"* (Robert Burns *To a Mouse*, 1785)

ti·mor·ous·ly /£ˈtɪm·ᵊr·ə·sli, $ˈ-ɚ-/ *adv*

ti·mor·ous·ness /£ˈtɪm·ᵊr·ə·snəs, $ˈ-ɚ-/ *n* [U]

tim·pa·ni /ˈtɪm·pə·ni/ *pl n* a set of KETTLEDRUMS (= large metal drums with round bottoms) played in an ORCHESTRA

tim·pa·nist /ˈtɪm·pə·nɪst/ *n* [C] • A timpanist is a person who plays the timpani.

tin /tɪn/ *n* (a container made from) a silvery-coloured metal • *a tin tray* • *tin-plated steel* • *If you go to Cornwall, you can visit the old tin mines.* • *(Br and Aus)* A tin (also **tin can, can**) is a small closed metal container, usually cylindrical, in which food or other substances are sold: *a tin* **of** *soup* [C] ○ *a tin* **of** *paint* [C] ○ *Do you want pineapple juice in a tin or a carton?* [C] ○ *When you pack the shopping, don't put all the tins in one bag or it'll make it too heavy.* [C] • A tin is also a metal container, usually with a lid, esp. used for storing food, or a metal container without a lid *(esp. Am* **pan***)* used for cooking: *a biscuit/cake tin* (= containers used for storing biscuits/cakes) [C] ○ *a loaf/ cake tin* (= containers used for cooking bread/cakes). [C] • *(Br and Aus)* A tin *(esp. Am* **can***)* is also the contents of a tin or the amount of something a tin contains: *The children ate two tins* **of** *beans.* [C] ○ *We used four tins* **of** *paint when we painted the ceiling.* [C] • **Tin foil** is shiny metallic material, as thin as paper, which is used esp. for wrapping food in order to store it or cook it: *He wrapped his sandwiches in tin foil.* ○ *If you cover the meat with tin foil before you put it in the oven, that will help seal in the juices.* • *(infml disapproving)* A **(little) tin god** is a person who is considered to be, or behaves as if they are, more important than they really are. • *(infml)* A **tin hat** is a protective metal hat worn by soldiers. • *(Br and Aus) I can't get this* **tin-opener** *(also esp. Am* **can-opener***)* (= a device for opening tins of food) *to work.* • *(infml)* **Tin Pan Alley** is sometimes used to refer to the people who write, perform and produce popular music, esp. in the first half of the 20th century. • *(infml) He works for some* **tin-pot** *little organization* (= one which is not important and has little worth). • A **tin whistle** is a small musical instrument consisting of a thin metal tube which the player blows down. The tube has holes in it, which are covered or left open in order to play different notes. • PIC **Containers** DK

tinned *esp. Br and Aus* /tɪnd/, *Am and Aus also* **canned** *adj* [not gradable] • Something, esp. food, which is tinned is put in a tin in order to preserve it: *I don't like tinned tomatoes/spaghetti/milk.*

tin·ny /ˈtɪn·i/ *adj* **-ier, -iest** • If a sound is tinny, it is of low quality and sounds like metal being hit: *a tinny piano* ○ *a tinny recording of a piece of music* • *(infml disapproving)* If something made of metal is tinny, it is not strong and not of good quality: *a tinny toy* ○ *a cheap tinny car*

tinc·ture /£ˈtɪŋk·tʃəʳ, $-tʃɚ/ *n* a medicine which consists of a mixture of alcohol and a small amount of a drug • *a/some tincture* **of** *iodine/myrrh* [C/U]

tin·der /£ˈtɪn·dəʳ, $-dɚ/ *n* [U] small pieces of something dry that burns easily and which can be used for lighting fires • *We used some dry grass and dead twigs as tinder to light the camp fire.* • *The grass is tinder-***dry** (= so dry that it will burn easily), *so there's a risk of fire.*

tin·der·box /£ˈtɪn·də·bɒks, $-dɚ·bɑːks/ *n* [C] a dangerous and uncontrolled situation in which violence is likely to happen • *The racial tension in the area is a tinderbox ready to ignite.*

ting /tɪŋ/ *adv* [not gradable], *n* (with) a clear high ringing sound • *The bell on the hotel receptionist's desk went ting when I pressed it.* • *Some timers give a ting when the amount of time they have been set to measure has passed.* [C] • *(infml) Small children often call* **"ting-a-ling"** *(esp. Am and Aus* **ding-a-ling***) to represent the sound of a bell when they are riding on bicycles or tricycles.*

tinge /tɪndʒ/ *n* [C] a very slight amount of a colour or of a feeling • *After a day in the sun, their skin had a slightly pink tinge.* • *His hair is starting to show tinges* **of** *grey.* • *I have a tinge* **of** *regret that I didn't accept her offer.* • *There was a tinge* **of** *bitterness in what she said.*

tinge *obj* /tɪndʒ/ *v* [T usually passive] • *Her joy at the birth of her son was tinged* **with** (= contained a slight amount of) *sadness that her father had not lived to see him.* • *Their disapproval of his behaviour was tinged* **with** *admiration of his courage.* • *The Grand Canyon is often tinged pink and purple* (= made slightly pink and purple) *by the early morning sun.*

tin·gle /ˈtɪŋ·gl̩/ *v* [I] to have a feeling as if a lot of sharp points are being put quickly and lightly into your body • *Her face tingled where he had slapped her.* • *My toes and fingers are tingling* **with** *cold.* • *(fig.) She tingled* **with** *fear* (= felt frightened) *as she walked down the dark alleyway.* • *(fig.) The children are tingling* **with** *excitement/anticipation as it gets closer to the holidays.* • If your **spine** tingles, or something **makes** your **spine** tingle, you feel excited or frightened: *His spine tingled as he was handed the keys to his new sports car.* ○ *Reading that ghost story made my spine tingle.*

tin·gle /ˈtɪŋ·gl̩/ *n* [U] • *She felt* **a** *tingle* **of** *embarrassment* (= felt embarrassed) *when she realized her mistake.*

tin·gling /ˈtɪŋ·gl̩·ɪŋ, ˈ-glɪŋ/ *n* [C usually sing] • *I've got this tingling* (= a feeling as if a lot of sharp points are being put quickly and lightly into my body) *in my chest, doctor.*

tin·gly /ˈtɪŋ·gl̩·i, ˈ-gli/ *adj* **-ier, -iest** • If you **feel** tingly or have a tingly **feeling**, you feel slightly excited or frightened: *Her kiss gave him a tingly feeling.* ○ *The film was so scary, it made me feel tingly all over.*

tink·er MAKE CHANGES /£ˈtɪŋ·kəʳ, $-kɚ/ *v* [I always + adv/prep] to make small changes to something in a way that is not decisive or directed, esp. in an attempt to repair or improve it • *He spends every weekend tinkering* **(about) with** *his car.* • *I don't think you'd better tinker* **with** *the washing machine – let's get someone to come and fix it.* • *There's no need to keep tinkering* **with** *your essay – it's fine as it is.* • *"What have you been doing today?" "Not much – just tinkering* **about** *in the garden."* • *I wish the government would stop tinkering* **with** *the health service.* • Compare FIDDLE MOVE ABOUT.

tink·er /£ˈtɪŋ·kəʳ, $-kɚ/ *n* • *(Br) I'll just have* **a** *tinker* **with** *the television* (= make some changes to it to try to repair it) *and see if I can get it to work.* [U] • A tinker is also a person who travels from place to place, esp. in the past, repairing pans or other metal containers. [C] • If you say that you don't **give a tinker's (cuss/damn)** about something, you mean that it isn't important to you: *I couldn't give a tinker's damn* **about** *what they think.* ○ *He's been punished many times, but he never gives a tinker's.*

tink·er CHILD /£ˈtɪŋ·kəʳ, $-kɚ/ *n* [C] *Br infml, slightly dated* a child who behaves badly • *You tinker, Nicky, you shouldn't have done that.* [as form of address] • *Don't be such a tinker.*

tin·kle /ˈtɪŋ·kl̩/ *v, n* (to make) a light ringing sound • *Some small old-fashioned shops still have a bell which tinkles when you push the door open.* [I] • *The wind-chimes made a tinkling sound in the breeze.* [I] • *In the distance we heard the* **silvery** *tinkle of a stream.* [C] • *I thought I heard the faint tinkle of a telephone.* [C] • *(dated infml) I'll* **give** *you* **a tinkle** (= will make a telephone call to you) *some time next week.* • *(infml)* A tinkle is also used to avoid saying an act of urinating: *Do you need a tinkle before we go out?* ○ *I'll just* **have/go for** *a tinkle.*

tinned /tɪnd/ *adj* [not gradable] See at TIN

tin·ni·tus /£ˈtɪn·ɪ·təs, £tɪˈnaɪ-, $-t̬əs/ *n* [U] *medical* a condition of the ear in which the person suffering from it hears noises such as ringing

tin·ny /ˈtɪn·i/ *adj* **-ier, -iest** See at TIN

tin·plate /£ˈtɪm·pleɪt, $ˌtɪnˈpleɪt/ *n* [U] thin sheets of iron or steel covered with a thin layer of TIN

tin·plat·ed /£tɪmˈpleɪ·tɪd, $ˌtɪnˈpleɪ·t̬ɪd/ *adj* [not gradable]

tin·sel /ˈtɪnt·səl/ *n* [U] short pieces of thin shiny material used as decoration, esp. at Christmas • *a Christmas tree decorated with tinsel* • *The children were dressed as fairies, with silver wands and costumes covered in tinsel.* • If something, esp. the entertainment business or someone's way of living, is referred to as tinsel, it means that although it might seem exciting and attractive, it is really of low quality or value: *The show was all tinsel and glitter.*

tin·sel·ly /ˈtɪnt·səl·i/ *adj*

tint /tɪnt/ *n* [C] a small amount of a colour • *The paint we're using for the bathroom is white with a yellow tint.* • *The evening sky was deep pink, with tints* **of** *purple and red in it.* • A tint is also a small amount of DYE (= a substance used for changing the colour of something), esp. used on the hair, or the act of using such a substance: *She's had blonde tints put in her hair.* ○ *I'm going to the hairdresser's for a tint.* ○ *I'm thinking about having an eyelash tint.*

tint *obj* /tɪnt/ *v* [T] • *Do you think he tints his hair* (= slightly changes its colour)*?*

tint·ed /£ˈtɪn·tɪd, $-t̬ɪd/ *adj* • *The church windows are made of tinted* **glass** (= glass to which a small amount of colour has been added). • *Wearing tinted* **glasses**/*glasses with tinted* **lenses** (= those made with glass that has been made slightly dark) *can help make bright lights less glaring.* • *The President arrived at the airport in a car with tinted* **windows** (= windows made of glass that has been made dark so that people cannot see into the car).

ti·ny /ˈtaɪ·ni/ *adj* **-ier, -iest** extremely small • *a tiny flower* • *a tiny helping of food* • *a tiny scratch* • *An increasing number of women are now choosing to go back to work while their children are still tiny.* • *"Would you like some more cake?" "Yes, please, just a tiny piece."* • *I don't know why you're so cross – we're only a tiny* **bit** *late.*

-tion /-ʃən/ *combining form* See at -ION ACTION

tip END /tɪp/ *n* [C] the usually pointed end of something, esp. something which is long and thin • *We had asparagus tips for dinner.* • *If I stand on the tips* **of** *my toes, I can just reach the top of the cupboard.* • *He cut the tip* **of** *his finger when he was chopping an onion.* • *The Keys are coral islands off the southern tip* **of** *Florida.* • *The snowy owl is all white, apart from some brown on the tips* **of** *its wings and in its tail.* • *There was a tiny smudge where the tip* **of** *her nose had touched the window pane.* • A tip is also a small part fitted to the end of something, esp. something which is long and thin: *a walking cane with a metal tip* ○ *the filter tip* **of** *a cigarette* • *Her name is* **on the tip of** *my* **tongue** (= I can almost but not quite remember it). • *It was on the tip of my tongue to say* (= I almost said) *what I thought, but I managed to stop myself.* • *These small local protests are just the* **tip of the iceberg** (= the small part that can be seen of something which is really much larger than it seems). • *She's a professional* **to the tips of** *her* **fingers** (= completely). • PIC **Body**

tip *obj* /tɪp/ *v* [T usually passive] **-pp-** • *The giraffe was killed with a spear that had been tipped* **with** *poison* (= which had had poison put on its end).

-tipped /-tɪpt/ *combining form*

tip INFORMATION /tɪp/ *n* [C] a useful piece of information, esp. about how to do something or about the likely winner of a race or competition • *gardening/cooking/sewing tips* • *travel tips* • *She* **gave** *me a useful/helpful/valuable/practical tip* **about/for** *growing tomatoes.* • *Our racing correspondent has the following tips* **for** *the 3.15 and the 3.45 at Newmarket* (= thinks that they will be the winners in those races). • *I've got a* **hot** *tip* **for** *you* (= I can tell you about a particular winner of a race or competition, or give you a valuable piece of information). • *(saying)* 'Take a tip from an old timer' means take advice from someone who is experienced.

tip *obj* /tɪp/ *v* [T] **-pp-** *esp. Br* • *(Br and Aus) He is being tipped* **as** (= is thought likely to be) *the next Prime Minister.* • *Josie is tipped* **for** *success* (= is thought likely to be successful). • *Davis is being tipped* **to** *win the championship.* [+ obj + *to* infinitive] • *(Br)* If you **tip** someone **the wink** or **tip the wink to** someone, you give them a piece of secret or private information that might be of benefit to them: *Thanks for tipping me the wink* **about** *those cheap tickets, Bill.* ○ *We were tipped the wink* **that** *we'd get a better deal somewhere else.* [+ *that* clause] ○ *They don't know who tipped the wink to the police.* • *(Am)* If you **tip** your **hand** you say what you are going to do or what you believe, esp. when you didn't intend to: *For weeks there was speculation in the newspapers, but the government wouldn't tip its hand by saying who the new legislation would cover.*

tip off *obj*, **tip** *obj* **off** *v adv* [M] • *The prison governor was tipped off* (= given secret information) **about** *the prisoner's escape plans.* • *Somebody must have tipped the burglars off* **that** *the house would be empty.* [+ *that* clause]

tip-off /£'tɪp·ɒf, $-ɑːf/ *n* [C] *infml* • *Acting on a tip-off* (= a warning or piece of secret information), *the police arrested the drug dealers.* • *Following a tip-off from a friend, we sold all our shares in the company.* • *The newspapers received an anonymous tip-off* **about** *where the bomb had been left.*

tip RUBBISH *Br and Aus* /tɪp/, *esp. Am* **dump** *n* [C] a place where rubbish can be taken and left • *a rubbish/waste tip* • *We need to take this old carpet to the tip.* • *(Br infml) This room is a complete/absolute/real tip* (= is very untidy) – *tidy it up at once.*

tip *(obj) Br and Aus* /tɪp/, *Am and Aus also* **dump** *v* **-pp-** • *A lot of waste is being tipped into the sea* (= put into the sea and left there). [T always + adv/prep] • *"Shall we keep these left-overs?" "No, just tip them in the bin."* [T always + adv/prep] • *The sign by the side of the road said "No tipping".* [I]

tip *obj* POUR /tɪp/ *v* [T always + adv/prep] **-pp-** *Br and Aus* to pour (a substance) from one container into another or onto a surface • *He tipped his breakfast cereal into a bowl.* • *The child picked up the box and tipped the toys* **out** *all over the floor.* [M] • *(Br infml) We won't be able to go to the beach today* – **it's tipping (it) down** (= it's raining very hard).

tip·per /£'tɪp·əʳ, $-ɚ/ *n* [C] • *(Br)* A **tipper truck/lorry** (*Am* **dump truck**, *Aus* **tip truck**) is a large truck for transporting heavy loads, part of the back of which can be raised so that its contents fall out. • PIC **Vehicles**

tip *(obj)* NOT STRAIGHT /tɪp/ *v* **-pp-** to (cause to) become not straight, or to (cause to) turn or fall • *Don't tip your chair back like that, you'll fall.* [T] • *If you put too many books on one end of the shelf, it'll tip* **up**. [I] • *Children should always be strapped into their buggies, otherwise they might tip* **out**. [I] • *Be careful not to tip that cup of coffee* **over**. [T] • *The boat tipped* **over** *when he leant over the side.* [I] • If something **tips over (from** something**) into** something else, it stops being the first thing, and becomes the second: At various points in the play, the action tips over (from comedy) into farce (= stops being amusing and becomes ridiculous). [I] • If something **tips the scales/balance** it is the thing which causes a particular situation to happen or a particular decision to be made, when other situations or decisions are possible: *The teams were evenly matched until two quick goals from Robson tipped the balance* **in favour of** *England.* ○ *Jackie was a good candidate for the job, but her lack of computer skills tipped the scales* **against** *her, and it was given to someone else.* • *The baby* **tipped the scales at** (= weighed) *3·75 kgs.*

tip PAYMENT /tɪp/ *n* [C] a small amount of money given to someone who has provided you with a service, in addition to the official payment and for their personal use • *a 15% tip* • *He gave the porter a tip.* • *We don't need to leave a tip* **for** *the waiter, because there's a service charge included in the bill.*

tip *(obj)* /tɪp/ *v* **-pp-** • *The taxi driver was so rude to her that she didn't tip him.* [T] • *They tipped the waiter £5.* [+ two objects] • *I object to being expected to tip at the hairdresser's.* [I]

tip·per /£'tɪp·əʳ, $-ɚ/ *n* [C] • *Waiters often say that they can always tell if a customer is going to be a* **good** *tipper* (= going to leave a large additional amount of money for them) *or not.*

Tipp-Ex *Br trademark* /'tɪp·eks/, *esp. Am and Aus trademark* **Liq·uid Pa·per**, *Am and Aus* **white-out** *n* [U] a white liquid used for painting over mistakes in a piece of writing • *You have to let the Tipp-Ex dry before you write over it.*

tip·ple /'tɪp·l̩/ *n* [C] *infml* an alcoholic drink • *What's your tipple* (= What alcoholic drink do you usually drink)? • *Gin is her* **favourite** *tipple.*

tip·pler /£'tɪp·l̩·əʳ, £'-ləʳ, $'-l̩·ɚ, $'-lɚ/ *n* [C] • A tippler is someone who often drinks alcohol.

tip·ster /£'tɪp·stəʳ, $-stɚ/ *n* [C] a person who gives information to people, usually in exchange for money, esp. about the likely winner of a race or competition, or who gives information to an official organization esp. about someone who has done something wrong • *All the tipsters were wrong about the gold medal winner.* • *An anonymous tipster has leaked confidential government information to the press.*

tip·sy /'tɪp·si/ *adj* **-ier**, **-iest** *infml* slightly drunk • *Drinking sherry always makes me tipsy.* • *Auntie Pat is getting a little tipsy again.* • *We were kept awake by a crowd of tipsy students celebrating the end of their exams.*

tip·si·ly /'tɪp·sɪ·li/ *adv*

tip·si·ness /'tɪp·sɪ·nəs/ *n* [U]

tip·toe /£'tɪp·təʊ, $-toʊ/ *n* [C] **on tiptoe(s)** on your toes with the heel of your foot lifted off the ground • *The children stood on tiptoe in order to pick the apples from the tree. They walked on tiptoes across the hot sand.*

tip·toe /£'tɪp·təʊ, $-toʊ/ *v* [I always + adv/prep] • *He waited until his daughter was asleep, then tiptoed quietly out of the room.* • *(fig.) We keep tiptoeing* **(a)round** (= avoiding dealing with) *the problem, instead of confronting it.* • *"Tiptoe through the Tulips"* (title of a song written by Al Dubin, 1929)

tip-top /£'tɪp·tɒp, $-tɑːp/ *adj infml* excellent; perfect • *I try and keep in tip-top* **shape** *by exercising every day.* • *Even though our house is in tip-top* **condition**, *we're having problems selling it.* • *The hotel we stayed in was absolutely tip-top.*

ti·rade /£taɪ'reɪd, £tɪ-, $'taɪ·reɪd/ *n* [C] a long angry speech expressing strong disapproval • *He* **delivered** *a long tirade* **against** *the government.* • *She launched into an* **angry** *tirade* **about** *how she had been unfairly treated.* • *In a furious tirade* **of** *abuse, the opposition spokesperson demanded the minister's resignation.*

tire *(obj)* LOSE ENERGY /£taɪəʳ, $taɪr/ *v* to (cause to) feel as if you have no energy and want to rest or go to sleep • *She's been leading throughout the race, but it now looks as if she's tiring.* [I] • *You'll need to take it easy for a few days after your operation because you'll tire very easily.* [I] • *Let the children run around in the garden for a while before bedtime – that'll soon tire them.* [T] • *Digging the garden has tired me* **out** (= caused me to feel very much in need of rest or sleep). [T] • *(fig.) This is the kind of toy that children will soon tire* **of** (= become bored with). [I] • *(fig.) He never tires* **of** (= He enjoys) *pointing out my mistakes.* [I]

tired /£taɪəd, $taɪrd/ *adj* **-er**, **-est** • *I was so tired* (= in need of rest or sleep) *when I got home from work last night.* • *Are you getting tired? Shall we stop for a while?* • *You'll have to excuse Joanna – she's feeling rather tired and emotional at the moment.* • *(Br humorous)* **Tired and emotional** is also sometimes used to avoid saying drunk. • *My legs are tired.* • *She spoke in a tired voice.* • *We were all really tired* **out** (= very much in need of rest or sleep) *after our long journey.* • *(fig.) I'm* **(sick and)** *tired* **of** (= bored with) *doing the same job, day after day.* • *(fig.) I'm* **(sick and)** *tired* **of** (= have lost patience with) *you telling me what to do all the time.* • *(fig. disapproving) He's always coming out with the same tired excuses/clichés/ideas* (= saying things which are not original). • *(fig. disapproving) It's always the same tired* **old** *faces/people* (= people who are uninteresting because they are very familiar) *at these meetings.* • *"When a man is tired of London, he is tired of life"* (Samuel Johnson in Boswell's *Life of Johnson*, 1777)

tired·ly /£'taɪəd·li, $'taɪrd-/ *adv* • *He spoke tiredly of his ordeal.*

tired·ness /£ˈtaɪəd·nəs, $taɪrd-/ *n* [U] • *He said that it was tiredness* (= the feeling of needing to rest or sleep) *that led him to make the mistake.* • *I was overtaken by a sudden wave of tiredness.*

tire·less /£ˈtaɪə·ləs, $ˈtaɪr-/ *adj* • *Tony is a tireless worker* (= he works energetically and continuously). • *The prisoner's family is conducting a tireless campaign for his release.* • *Her enthusiasm is tireless* (= does not stop). • *The police have been tireless* **in** *their search for the child's killer.* • *They have been tireless* **in** *raising money for guide dogs for the blind.*

tire·less·ly /£ˈtaɪə·lə·sli, $ˈtaɪr-/ *adv* • *He has worked tirelessly to achieve his goal.* • *Sylvia Pankhurst campaigned tirelessly for votes for women in Britain in the early twentieth century.*

tir·ing /£ˈtaɪə·rɪŋ, $ˈtaɪ-/ *adj* • *I've had a very tiring day.* • *Looking after the kids is extremely tiring.*

tire [WHEEL] /£taɪəʳ, $taɪɚ/ *n* [C] *Am for* a TYRE

tire·some /£ˈtaɪə·səm, $ˈtaɪr-/ *adj* boring or annoying; causing a lack of patience • *I find it very tiresome doing the same job day after day.* • *Don't be so tiresome, Oliver – do as you're told.* • *He has the tiresome habit of finishing your sentences for you.*

tire·some·ly /£ˈtaɪə·səm·li, $ˈtaɪr-/ *adv* • *a tiresomely repetitive speech* • *a tiresomely long wait*

ti·sane /tɪˈzæn/, **herb·al tea** *n* (a) drink made by pouring boiling water onto particular types of dried or fresh flowers or leaves • *a camomile tisane* [C] • *a tisane* **of** *peppermint* [C] • *Would you like some tisane?* [U]

tis·sue [PAPER] /ˈtɪʃ·uː, ˈtɪs·juː/ *n* thin light paper used esp. for wrapping things, or (a small rectangular piece of) soft paper which is used for cleaning, esp. your nose, and is thrown away after use • *The shop assistant wrapped the glasses carefully in tissue (also* **tissue paper***) in order to protect them.* [U] • *She wiped her eyes and blew her nose on a tissue.* [C] • *I always keep a box of tissues in the car.* [C] • *He used a piece of tissue to clean his sunglasses.* [U] • **Bathroom/toilet tissue** are other words for **toilet paper**. See at TOILET [CONTAINER]. • Compare HANDKERCHIEF. • [PIC] **Containers**

tis·sue [CELLS] /ˈtɪʃ·uː, ˈtɪs·juː/ *n* [U] a group of connected cells in an animal or plant that are similar to each other, have the same purpose and form the stated part of the animal or plant • *human tissue* • *plant tissue* • *brain/lung/muscle/fat tissue* • *His face is covered with scar tissue where he was badly burned.* • *Many people disapprove of the use of fetal tissue for the treatment of people with certain illnesses.* • Tissue **culture** is the process of growing a group of cells in a scientifically controlled way outside the plant or animal they come from, or the group of cells produced in this way.

tit [BIRD] /tɪt/ *n* [C] a common small bird found in the northern half of the world. There are many different types of tit. • *a blue tit* • *a great tit* • *We get a lot of tits and finches in our garden in winter because we put nuts out for them.*

tit [BREAST] /tɪt/ *n* [C] *infml* a woman's breast. This word is considered offensive by some people • *He says he likes women with big tits.* • *(Br slang) Stop it, Joe, you're really* **getting on** *my* **tits** (= annoying me).

tit [PERSON] /tɪt/ *n* [C] *Br slang* a stupid person. This word is considered offensive by some people • *Why did you do that, you stupid great tit?*

ti·tan /£ˈtaɪ·tᵊn, $-t̬ᵊn/ *n* [C] *fml or literary* a person who is very important, powerful, strong, big, clever, etc. • *a financial titan* • *an intellectual titan* • *The final will be a* **clash of (the)** *titans.* • *The soft drink titans* (= big companies who produce these drinks) *are* **struggling** *for control of the market.*

ti·tan·ic /taɪˈtæn·ɪk, tɪ-/ *adj* • Something that is titanic is extremely powerful, strong, important or large: *a titanic actor* ○ *titanic mountains* ○ *a titanic battle/struggle*

ti·ta·ni·um /£tɪˈteɪ·ni·əm, taɪ-, $tɪ-/ *n* [U] a light strong white metallic element • *Titanium is often used for making parts of aircraft.*

tit·bit, *Am usually* **tid·bit** /ˈtɪt·bɪt, ˈtɪp-/ *n* [C] a small piece of interesting information, or a small item of pleasant-tasting food • *I've only been able to pick up a few titbits* **of** *information about what happened.* • *Our guide gave us some interesting titbits* **about** *the history of the castle.* • *This magazine is full of* **juicy** *titbits* (= small pieces of interesting information, esp. about other people's private lives). • *Grandma always has a few titbits* (= small items of pleasant-tasting food) *for the children when they go to visit her.*

titch·y /ˈtɪtʃ·i/ *adj* **-ier, -iest** *Br infml* extremely small; used esp. by children • *We've got a great big car, and you've only got a titchy little one.*

titch /tɪtʃ/ *n* [C] *Br* • *I don't need to take any notice of a titch* (= a small person, esp. a child) *like you.* • *Come on, titch.* [as form of address]

tit for tat /tɪt/ *adj* [not gradable] (of an action) done intentionally as a punishment as a reaction to something unpleasant done to you • *I noticed she didn't send me a card – I think it was tit for tat because I forgot her birthday last year.* • *Recent months have seen a pattern of tit-for-tat killings between the two sides.* • *(disapproving) The government shouldn't resort to this sort of tit-for-tat reprisal as if they were silly children in a playground.*

tit–for–tat /£ˌtɪt·fəˈtæt, $-fɚ-/ *n* [U] • *(disapproving) There seems to be a strong element of tit-for-tat in her criticisms of the Prime Minister.*

ti·tian /ˈtɪʃ·ᵊn/ *adj* [not gradable] *literary* (of hair) reddish gold • *the titian-haired princess*

ti·til·late *(obj)* /£ˈtɪt·ɪ·leɪt, $ˈtɪt̬-/ *v* to excite intentionally but only a little, usually with sexual images or descriptions • *So many adverts nowadays are designed to titillate.* [I] • *(humorous) Carter's biography is only spoiled by the fact that he refuses to titillate* (= interest) *his readers with any gossip.* [T]

ti·til·lat·ing /£ˈtɪt·ɪ·leɪ·tɪŋ, $ˈtɪt̬·ɪ·leɪ·t̬ɪŋ/ *adj* • *The photos, which include some mildly titillating semi-nude shots of the actress, will be on display for a week.* • *The game shows are a curious mix of titillating soft porn and family entertainment.* • *(humorous) It seems that people can't resist titillating* (= interesting and shocking) *headlines, especially if they concern the Royal family.*

ti·til·la·tion /£ˌtɪt·ɪˈleɪ·ʃᵊn, $ˌtɪt̬-/ *n* [U] • *Some men can't get through breakfast without titillation* (= being sexually excited), *judging by the number of bare-breasted women in the daily papers.*

ti·ti·vate *(obj)* /£ˈtɪt·ɪ·veɪt, $ˈtɪt̬·ə-/ *v* to improve small details of the appearance of (someone) by arranging the hair, putting on make-up, etc. • *Camille is in the bathroom titivating.* [I] • *She titivated the art display before the guests arrived.* [T]

ti·tle [NAME] /£ˈtaɪ·tl̩, $-t̬l̩/ *n* [C] the name of a film, book, painting, piece of music, etc. • *I can never remember film titles.* • *The title of Evelyn Waugh's first novel was 'Decline and Fall'.* • *And this next record is the title* **track** *on the album 'The Red Shoes'* (= the piece of music and the record are both called 'The Red Shoes'). • Title is also used, esp. by publishers, to mean book: *Last year we published over a hundred new titles.* • A **title page** is a page at the front of a book on which you find the name of the book, the writer and the publisher. • A **title role** in a play or film is the character referred to in its name, usually the main part: *She is currently to be seen at the National Theatre playing the title role in Pam Gems' play 'Queen Christina'.* • See also SUBTITLE; SURTITLE. • [LP] **Capital letters, Italics, Quotation marks**

ti·tled /£ˈtaɪ·tl̩d, $-t̬l̩d/ *adj* [after v; not gradable] • *Reed wrote a novel about de Sade titled* (= with the title of) *'When the Whip Comes Down'.* • *His second film, a box-office disaster, was aptly titled 'The Loser'.* • *We're currently planning a programme titled 'TV Hell'.*

ti·tle [PERSON] /£ˈtaɪ·tl̩, $-t̬l̩/ *n* [C] a word which is used before someone's name, stating their social rank, qualifications, position in an organization, sex, etc. • *What's her title – is she Professor or just Doctor?* • *Princess Royal is a title sometimes bestowed on the eldest or only daughter of a sovereign.* • *He's got some title – the ninth Earl of Marlborough, or something.* • *He will retain the honorary title of non-executive chairman.* • *What's your* **job** *title now – are you managing director?* • *Her title changes when she qualifies – she becomes Staff Nurse Phillipa Duggan.* • [LP] **Capital letters, Titles and forms of address**

ti·tled /£ˈtaɪ·tl̩d, $-t̬l̩d/ *adj* [not gradable] • A person who is titled has a special word, such as SIR or LADY, before their own name, showing that they have a high social rank: *one of his titled friends*

ti·tle [SPORTS PRIZE] /£ˈtaɪ·tl̩, $-t̬l̩/ *n* [C] the position you get by beating all other competitors in a sports competition • *Moorhouse defends his 100-metres breaststroke title tonight.* • *Hendry won the world snooker title after a tense 35-frame final.* • *Guy Forget netted his third singles title of the year by beating Sampras, the US Open champion.* • *Andries won his sixth world title fight on points after 12 rounds.*

TITLES AND FORMS OF ADDRESS

English has a number of titles and ways of addressing people but these are used much less often than in many other languages. These words are generally *not* used in a normal situation of talking to people you do not know. When you want to attract their attention or show you are talking to them, you use phrases like 'excuse me': *Excuse me, can you tell me the way to Fleet Street?* (LP **Meeting people** at MEET.)

PEOPLE WHO DO NOT KNOW EACH OTHER

In particular situations you might hear the following forms of address used in conversation:

sir **madam** *(Am also)* **ma'am**	*Can I get you the menu, sir?* *Excuse me, madam, can you help me?*	Polite. *(Br fml)* used e.g. to customers in shops. *(Am)* used typically with older people.
love/luv **dear/deary**	*That'll be 50 pence, love.* *Is that your bag, dear?*	*(Br infml)* friendly; not used between men.
lady	*Sorry, lady, we're closed.*	*(Am infml not polite)* used to a woman.
mate	*Have you got a light, mate?*	*(Br infml)* used between men.
buddy	*Thanks, buddy.*	*(Am infml)* used between men.
man	*That's real bad news, man.*	*(Am infml dated)*
bub, buster **mister, mac**	*Listen, buster, you'd better shut up!* *Watch where you're going, mister.*	*(Am not polite)* used to a man, esp. to a man who is annoying you.
guv, chief, **squire**	*Can you spare me a pound, guv?* *That's a nice car you've got, chief.*	*(Br infml often humorous)* used to speak to a man.
lad, **son, sonnie**	*Be careful in that tree, lad.*	Used to a boy or young man.
folks **everybody**	*See you next week, folks.* *Hello, everybody.*	*(infml)* used to a group of men or women.
chaps, lads	*Come on, lads, let's go!*	*(Br)* used to a group of men.
guys	*Can you believe it, guys?* *Where are you guys going?*	Used to a group of *(Am)* people or *(Br)* men.
girls *	*Bye, girls, see you tomorrow.*	Used to a group of girls or women.
ladies *	*What would you like, ladies?*	Used to a group of women.
Ladies and Gentlemen	*Ladies and Gentlemen, it is a great honour to be speaking to you today.*	*(fml)* used to a group, esp. at the beginning of a speech.

*Some people consider these offensive if used by men to a group of women.

PEOPLE WHO KNOW EACH OTHER'S NAMES

• **Informal situations** In general, you use somebody's first name, even at work: *See you tomorrow, Jane.* • *David, have you sent that payment yet?*

People often use short forms of their names with friends and family:
Phil (Phillip), Chris (Christopher or Christine), Gill (Gillian), Sue (Susan), Bob (Robert), Dick (Richard)

• **Formal situations** It is common to use the first name with the family name: *Phillip Brent, Mary McCall.*
It is more formal to put a title before the full name or family name:

Mrs	*Do you have a moment, Mrs Kent?* *This week's winner is Mrs Sue Burton.*	Used for married women. The family name is that of the husband.
Miss	*Miss Preston is in a meeting right now.* *You can leave your car here, miss.* *Please, Miss, can I leave the room?* *the famous actress, Miss Maggie Smith*	Used for • women or girls who are not married • female teachers by their students • some married women, esp. famous ones, who keep their original name.
Ms	*Ms P. Jones will interview the applicants.*	Can be used for both married and unmarried women.
Mr	*Can I speak to Mr James Burton?* *Nice to have met you, Mr Grant.*	Used for men, also *(Br)* for male surgeons and dentists.
Dr	*Dr Forster will see you this morning.* *Dr Lake will start her lectures tomorrow.*	Used for male and female medical doctors, and for people who have a PhD degree.

Sometimes people are addressed or referred to by their family name on its own:

Have you done your homework, Jones?	school
I was talking to that idiot Gregson in Accounts.	work
Kitson has not played for three games due to injury.	news reports, sport
One is impressed by Goehr's intellectual power.	articles about books, music

Names of jobs are not often used as forms of address, except for doctors, nurses and the police: *I can't sleep very well, doctor.* • *Can you help me, nurse?* • *Excuse me, officer.*

TALKING TO YOUR FAMILY

Mother **Mom, Mommy** *(Br)* **Mum, Mummy** **Ma, Mama, Mammy**	*Will you read me a story, Mum?* *Mom, where are my trainers?*	In Br *Mother* is rather formal, but not in the US. *Mommy* and *Mummy* are used by children.
Father **Dad, Daddy** **Pa, Pop, Papa**	*Are you alright, Father?* *Daddy, my bike's broken.*	In Br *Father* is rather formal, but not in the US. *Daddy* is used by children.
darling, dear, **sweetheart,** *(Am)* **honey**	*What's the matter, darling?* *Just a minute, sweetheart.*	Used by parents to their children, and by a couple to each other.

There are many forms of address used by couples to show affection. Some of these are commonly used in songs. Examples are: sweetie, sugar, babe, baby, angel, love, lovie, (*Am* to a woman) doll.

ti·tle LEGAL RIGHT /£ˈtaɪ·tl̩, $-t̬l̩/ *n* [U] *specialized* the legal right to own a piece of land or a building • *If you wish to sell the property, you will first have to prove your title* **to** *it.* • A **title deed** is a document which states and proves a person's legal right to own a piece of land or a building.

tit·le·hold·er /£ˈtaɪ·tl̩ˌhəʊl·dəʳ, $-ˌhoʊl·dɚ/ *n* [C] a person who is in the position of having beaten all other competitors in a sports competition • *The field includes Portugal's Rosa Mota, the Olympic, world and European titleholder.*

tit·les /£ˈtaɪ·tl̩z, $-t̬l̩z/, **film cred·its** *pl n* the information given at the end or beginning of a film or television programme, stating the names of the people who acted in it or were involved in its production

tit·ter /£ˈtɪt·əʳ, $ˈtɪt̬·ɚ/ *v* [I] to laugh nervously, often at something that you feel you should not be laughing at • *In the silence that followed, the audience tittered nervously.*

tit·ter /£ˈtɪt·əʳ, $ˈtɪt̬·ɚ/ *n* [C] • *The love scene raised a few titters from a party of schoolboys.*

tit·tle–tat·tle /£ˈtɪt·l̩ˌtæt·l̩, $ˈtɪt̬·l̩ˌtæt̬-/ *n* [U] *infml dated* talk about other people's lives that is usually unkind, disapproving or not true; GOSSIP • *There has even been talk of resignations within the party which the Prime Minister has dismissed as 'idle tittle-tattle'.* • *It seems the love of tittle-tattle about royal families is universal.*

tit·ty /£ˈtɪt·i, $ˈtɪt̬-/ *n* [C] *infml* a TIT BREAST

tit·u·lar /£ˈtɪt·jʊ·ləʳ, $ˈtɪtʃ·ə·lɚ/ *adj* [before n; not gradable] having the title of a position but not the responsibilities, duties or power; in name only • *It is already agreed that Mr Alfonso Escamez will be the titular head of the new bank.* • *Australia is a commonwealth of states with the Queen as its titular head of state.*

tiz·zy /ˈtɪz·i/, *Br also* **tizz** /tɪz/ *n* [U] *infml* a temporary state of anxiety and confusion • *She got herself* **in a** *real* **tizzy** *because she couldn't find her car keys and she thought they'd been stolen.*

TNT /ˌtiː·enˈtiː/ *n* [U] a powerful yellow explosive substance • *In her apartment, police found a number of guns, some silencers and a quantity of TNT.*

to INFINITIVE /tuː/ *prep* used before a verb to show that it is in the infinitive • To is used after some verbs, especially when the action referred to in the infinitive is to happen later: *She agreed to help.* ○ *I'll have to tell him.* ○ *You promised not to say anything!* ○ *I asked her to have the report finished by Friday.* ○ *I don't expect to be finishing any later than seven.* ○ *Sadly she didn't live to see her grandchildren.* • Many verbs of agreeing, needing and wanting are followed by 'to' + infinitive: *I need to eat something first.* ○ *I'd love to live in New York.* ○ *Would you like to dance?* ○ *That child ought to be in bed.* ○ *I want to go now.* • Instead of repeating a verb clause you can simply say 'to': *"Are you going tonight?" "I'm certainly hoping to."* ○ *"Would you like to go and see the Russian clowns?" "Yes, I'd love to."* ○ *"Did you get in touch with Liz?" "Well, I've tried to on several occasions but she's never in."* • To is used in phrases where there are reported orders and requests: *He told me to wait.* ○ *I told him to keep his mouth shut.* ○ *I asked her to give me a call.* ○ *Did anyone ask Daniel to book the room?* • To is used after some adjectives: *It's not likely to happen.* ○ *I was afraid to tell her.* ○ *She'd be delighted to hear from you, I'm sure.* ○ *Three months is* **too** *long to wait.* ○ *She's not strong* **enough** *to go walking up mountains.* • To is used after some nouns: *He has this enviable ability to ignore everything that's unpleasant in life.* ○ *This will be my second attempt to make flaky pastry.* • A clause containing 'to' + infinitive can be used as a subject of a sentence: *To go overseas on your own is very brave.* ○ *My plan was to get it all arranged before I told anyone.* ○ *To have accomplished all that by the age of thirty is quite remarkable.* ○ *To do it yourself would be cheaper.* ○ *Just to sleep in on a Saturday morning would be wonderful.* ○ *To tell her was fairly stupid in the first place.* • To is also used after *wh-* words: *I don't know what to do.* ○ *I don't know where to begin.* ○ *She was wondering whether to ask David about it.* ○ *Can you tell me how to get there?* • 'To' + infinitive can also be used to express purpose: *I'm going there to see my sister.* ○ *She's gone to pick Jean up.* ○ *I stopped at the shop to buy some wine.* ○ *I just called to say hello really.* ○ *This tool is used to make holes in leather.* ○ *To make this cake, you'll need 2 eggs, 175 g sugar and 175 g flour.* ○ *This is just a brief note to thank you for the meal last night.* ○ *He works to get paid, not because he enjoys it.* • You can introduce a clause with a phrase containing 'to' + infinitive: *To be honest* (=Speaking honestly), *Elaine, I prefer you in the grey shirt.* ○ *To be quite truthful with you, Dave, I never really liked the man.* • 'To' + infinitive can follow the pattern 'there is' + noun: *There's an awful lot of work to be done.* ○ *Of course there are the children to consider too.* ○ *"Why can't we go out?" "Well, there's the washing to be done for one thing."* • *(Br and Aus)* **To be going on with** means in order to continue with the present activity or situation: *Do we have enough paint to be going on with, or should I get some more while I'm out?*

to FUTURE /tuː/ *prep* used before an infinitive, usually with *be*, to form the future tense • *The government is to cut funding for the arts.* • 'To' is often used in this pattern to say what someone should do or to give an order: *You're not to* (=You must not) *bite your nails like that.* • *What celebrations there were on that* **never-to-be-forgotten** *day* (=that day which will never be forgotten)*!* • Newspapers often use 'to' + infinitive without 'be' in their HEADLINES (=titles of articles) when reporting planned future events: *US to send troops in* • See also TO-BE. • LP **Tenses**

to SHOWING DIRECTION /tuː/ *prep* in the direction of • *We're going to town.* • *We went to Prague last year.* • *I've got to go to the bank.* • *I asked someone the way to the town centre.* • *You can walk from here to the station in under ten minutes.* • *She pointed to a distant spot on the horizon.* • *We're going to Anthony's on Saturday.* • *This is a road to nowhere!* • *I've asked Helen and Ben to dinner* (=invited them to come and eat dinner with me) *next week.* • *We received another invitation to a wedding this morning.* • *I had my back to them, so I couldn't see what they were doing.* • *She walked* **over** *to the window.* • *He went* **up** *to a complete stranger and started talking.* • *You've got your sweater on back to front.*

to AGAINST /tuː/ *prep* against or very near • *Stand back to back.* • *They were dancing cheek to cheek.* • *She put her hand to his breast and felt the pounding of his heart.* • *She clasped the letter to her bosom.* • *Can't you tie the dog's lead to the fence?*

to RECEIVING /tuː/ *prep* used for showing who receives something or who experiences an action • *I lent my bike to my brother.* • *I told that to Glyn and he was horrified.* • *Who's the letter addressed to?* • *You should show that rash to the doctor and see what he says.* • *What have they done to you, love?* • With many verbs that have two objects, to can be used before the **indirect object**: *Give me that gun./Give that gun to me.*

to IN CONNECTION WITH /tuː/ *prep* in connection with • *What was their response to that?* • *And what did you say to that?* • *She was so rude to me.* • *There's a funny side to everything.*

to [COMPARED WITH] /tuː/ *prep* compared with • *It's a tough prison sentence, but it's* **nothing** *to the pain he's caused that family.* • *She's earning a reasonable wage, but* **nothing** *to what she could if she was in the private sector.* • *It's still a bit painful, but it's* **nothing** *to what it was a week ago.* • *Paul beat me by three games to two.* (=He won three and I won two.) • *He was old enough to be her father – she looked about thirty to his sixty.* • To can be used to show the position of something or someone in comparison with something or someone else: *He's standing to the left of Adrian in the photo.* ○ *Twenty miles to the north of the city lie the Dales.*

to [UNTIL] /tuː/ *prep* until (a particular time, state or level) is reached • *It's only two weeks to your birthday.* • *We're open daily from 2 to 6 p.m.* • *Unemployment has risen to almost eight million.* • *You can read the whole thing from beginning to end in under three hours.* • *He drank himself to death.* • *She nursed me back to health.* • To is used when saying the time, to mean before the stated hour: *It's twenty to six.* • To can be used to suggest an extreme state: *Look at your shirt – it's torn to shreds!* ○ *She was thrilled to bits.* ○ *I was bored to tears.* • [LP] **Time**

to [CAUSING] /tuː/ *prep* causing (a particular feeling) in a particular person • *To my immense relief she's decided against telling him.* • *That's when I learned, to my horror, that she was coming here.* • *He just drops his dirty clothes on the floor, much to my annoyance.*

to [CONSIDERED BY] /tuː/ *prep* considered by • *Does this make any sense to you?* • *I realize it may sound strange to you.* • *To me it sounds like he's ending the relationship.* • *I mean, fifty pounds is nothing to him* (=he would not consider it a large amount). • *(infml) "I hear you've been going out with Sally." "Well,* **what's it** *to you?* (=it should not interest you, and you have no right to ask about it.)*"*

to [SERVING] /tuː/ *prep* serving • *As a personal trainer to the rich and famous, he earns over a million dollars a year.* • *It says that they are hat makers to Her Majesty the Queen, no less.* • *She was Ophelia to Olivier's Hamlet in the televised production.* (=She acted the part of Ophelia, and Olivier acted the more important part of Hamlet.)

to [MATCHING] /tuː/ *prep* matching or belonging to • *He's given me the keys to his car – the fool!* • *I've lost the trousers to this jacket.* • *Have you seen the top to this pen?* • To also means having as a characteristic feature: *She has a mean side to her.* ○ *There is a very moral tone to this book.*

to [IN HONOUR OF] /tuː/ *prep* in honour or memory of • *I proposed a toast to the bride and the groom.* • *The record is dedicated to her mother, who died recently.* • *And the next record goes out to Angie Black from her boyfriend Johnny.*

to [FOR EACH] /tuː/ *prep* for each; PER • *How many francs are there to the pound?* • *This car does about fifty miles to the gallon.* • *If we go swimming together I do six lengths to her twelve.*

to [AT THE SAME TIME AS] /tuː/ *prep* at the same time as (music or other sound) • *I like exercising to music.* • *I can't dance to this sort of music.* • *He left the stage to the sound of booing.* • *The band walked on stage to rapturous applause.*

to [BETWEEN] /tuː/ *prep* used in phrases which show a range • *There must have been thirty to thirty-five* (=a number between 30 and 35) *people there.* • *We've got two to three inches of snow where we are.* • *I'd say she was about twenty to twenty-five.*

to [ENCOURAGING] /tuː/ *prep* encouraging a positive reaction or result • *Is the room to your* **liking**, *madam?* • *I think being present at the meeting would be to your* **advantage**.

to [CLOSED] /tuː/ *adv* [not gradable] into a closed position • *I'll just push the door to.*

toad /£təʊd, $toʊd/ *n* [C] a small brownish green animal, similar to a FROG, which has big eyes and long back legs for swimming and jumping • *Toads have dryer, lumpier skins than frogs and spend less time in the water.* • *(infml)* A toad is also an extremely unpleasant man, esp. one who is physically very unattractive: *Are you talking about the education minister? Oh, he's a toad, isn't he!* ○ *You lying toad!* [as form of address] • *(Br)* **Toad-in-the-hole** is a savoury food, consisting of SAUSAGES (=tubes of meat) cooked in a mixture of eggs, milk and flour.

toad·stool /£'təʊd·stuːl, $'toʊd-/ *n* [C] a poisonous FUNGUS with a round top and a narrow stem • *With their scarlet* **caps** *and white spots, these are the typical toadstools of fairy-tale illustrations.* • *I wouldn't dare pick wild mushrooms in case I got a toadstool by mistake.* • Compare MUSHROOM.

toad·y /£'təʊ·di, $'toʊ-/ *n* [C] *disapproving* a person who praises and is artificially pleasant to people in authority, usually in order to get some advantage from them • *He was a dictatorial prime minister with a cabinet of weaklings and toadies.*

toad·y /£'təʊ·di, $'toʊ-/ *v* [I] *disapproving* • *She was always toadying* (=being artificially pleasant) **to** *the boss, but she didn't get a promotion out of it!*

to and fro /£ˌtuː·ənd'frəʊ, $-'froʊ/ *adv, adj* [not gradable] in one direction and then in the opposite direction, a repeated number of times • *I was disturbed by all the people walking to and fro outside the office.* • *She was gazing out the window, rocking rhythmically to and fro.* • *The to-and-fro movement of the boat made me feel ill.*

to-ing and fro-ing /£ˌtuː·ɪŋ·ənd'frəʊ·ɪŋ, $-'froʊ-/ *n* [U] • *Inevitably, when both parents have custody of the child, there's a lot of to-ing and fro-ing* (=moving from one place to another) *between them.* • *(fig.) After months of bureaucratic to-ing and fro-ing* (=changing activities), *Marhoul's plan looks set to go ahead.*

to-ings and fro-ings /£ˌtuː·ɪŋz·ənd'frəʊ·ɪŋz, $-'froʊ-/ *pl n* • *(fig.) The legal to-ings and fro-ings* (=to-ing and fro-ing) *could delay the start of the trial for up to six months.*

toast [BREAD] /£təʊst, $toʊst/ *n* [U] sliced bread made warm, CRISP (=hard and dry) and brown by being put near a high heat • *Just one* **slice of** *toast for me, please.* • *I've ordered buttered toast and coffee.* • *I have toast and marmalade for breakfast.* • *Can I smell burnt toast?* • *I'm having beans* **on** *toast for supper.* • A **toast rack** is a device for serving pieces of toast which supports them vertically. • [PIC] **Rack**

toast *obj* /£təʊst, $toʊst/ *v* [T] • If you toast bread or other food you make it warm, CRISP and brown by putting it near a high heat: *Do you want this bread toasted?* ○ *I like my bread lightly toasted.* ○ *I've ordered toasted scones.* ○ *Can I have a toasted* **sandwich***?* • *(fig.) He's just toasting* (=warming) *his feet by the fire.* • A **toasting fork** is a fork with a long handle used for holding slices of bread near a fire to make toast.

toast·er /£'təʊ·stəʳ, $'toʊ·stɚ/ *n* [C] • A toaster is an electric device for making toast. • *(Am)* A toaster **oven** is an electric device that can be used to toast or bake food. • [PIC] **Kitchen**

toast·y /£'təʊ·sti, $'toʊ-/ *adj* **-ier, -iest** • *a white wine with a toasty* (=like toast), *oaky flavour* • *(fig. esp. Am) There's nothing better on a cold winter night than curling up with a good book in front of a nice toasty* (=comfortably and pleasantly warm) *fire.*

toast·y, toast·ie /£'təʊ·sti, $'toʊ-/ *n* [C] *esp. Br* • A toasty is a SANDWICH (=two slices of bread with food spread between them) that has been toasted: *a cheese/ham/tuna toasty*

toast [DRINK] /£təʊst, $toʊst/ *n* [C] an expression of good wishes or respect for someone which involves holding up and then drinking from a glass of alcohol, esp. wine, after a short speech • *Now, if you'd all please raise your glasses, I'd like to* **propose** *a toast* **to** *the bride and groom.* • *Champagne corks popped as the guests* **drank** *a toast* **to** *the happy couple.* • *You're meant to save your champagne for the toast.* • The toast might be the person who is being honoured in this way. • *(dated)* **The toast of** a particular place is a person who is very much admired there for something they have recently done: *Not so long ago Viviana was a little-known actress playing in a provincial theatre – these days she's the toast of* **the town**.

toast *obj* /£təʊst, $toʊst/ *v* [T] • *We toasted the bridesmaids and the bride's parents and all the usual people.* • *We toasted him* **with** *champagne at his leaving party.*

to·bac·co /£tə'bæk·əʊ, $-oʊ/ *n* [U] a substance which is smoked in cigarettes, pipes, etc., or which is sometimes chewed, which is prepared from the dried leaves of a particular plant • *Total cigarette consumption is declining – yet tobacco-industry profits are booming.* • *Twenty-eight per cent of people asked thought that the advertising of tobacco* (=tobacco and products made from it, such as cigarettes) *and alcohol should be banned.* • *Cancer of the tongue develops most often in heavy users of alcohol and tobacco.* • *Pollution, tobacco smoke and sun rays are all potentially harmful to our skin.* • *My grandfather used to chew tobacco.* • (J)

to·bac·co·nist /tə'bæk·ən·ɪst/ *n* [C] • A tobacconist is a person who is in charge of a shop where tobacco, cigarettes, etc. are sold.

to-be /tə'biː/ *adj* [after n; usually in combinations; not gradable] in the near future • *a bride-to-be* • *mothers-to-be*

to·bog·gan /£tə'bɒg·ᵊn, $-'bɑː·gᵊn/ *n* [C] an object used for sliding over snow and ice which consists of a low frame on which a person or people sit

to·bog·gan /£tə'bɒg·ᵊn, $-'bɑː·gᵊn/ *v* [I] • *We spent New Year's Day tobogganing in the Dales.* • *We could* **go** *tobogganing on Primrose Hill.* • *It was the British who organized the first European tobogganing race in 1833 at Davos, Switzerland.*

to·by jug /£'təʊ·bi, $'toʊ-/, *Am also* **to·by** *n* [C] a drinking container shaped like a fat old man wearing a hat with three corners and smoking a pipe • PIC› **Jug**

tod /£tɒd, $tɑːd/ *n* [U] **on** *your* **tod** *Br dated infml* alone • *Are you on your tod?*

to·day /tə'deɪ/ *adv* [not gradable], *n* (on) the present day • *What's the date today?* • *He's going to call at some point today.* • *I'm feeling a lot better today.* • *We could go today or tomorrow.* • *A report published today suggests that more than half of Britain's prisons are understaffed.* • *The government will today announce a scheme to set up hostels for homeless youngsters in London.* • *I was expecting to have received your report before today.* [U] • *Today's even hotter than yesterday!* [U] • *Is that today's paper?* [U] • *He left today, which is a Tuesday, so he should be back today* **week**/*a* **week** *today* (= on the Tuesday of next week). • Today can also be used more generally to mean the present time: *Today, people are much more concerned about their health than they were in the past.* ○ *With today's technology almost anything seems possible.* [U] ○ *The youth of today don't know how lucky they are.* [U] • *"We've just about cornered the market in North America." "Well,* **today** *North America,* **tomorrow the world** (= we hope to control this everywhere)." • *"Today is the first day of the rest of your life"* (Charles Dederich, c1969) • LP› **Calendar**

tod·dle /£'tɒd·l̩, $'tɑːd·l̩/ *v* [I] (esp. of a young child) to walk with short steps, trying to keep the body balanced • *I spent the afternoon in the garden, watching my nephew toddling around after his puppy.* • *(infml)* Toddle can also be used to mean walk, esp. in sentences which state the place that you are going to: *I'm just toddling* **off** *to the shops.* ○ *I thought we might toddle across the road for a pre-dinner drink.*

tod·dler /£'tɒd·ləʳ, $'tɑːd·lɚ/ *n* [C] a young child, esp. one who is learning or has recently learned to walk • *She watched a group of toddlers running around in the back garden.* • *It's a good idea for parents of toddlers to put a gate at the top of their staircase to prevent them from falling down the stairs.* • *Delia takes Carlo to a mothers' and toddlers' group on Tuesday mornings.* • LP› **Age**

to–do /tə'duː/ *n* [C usually sing] *infml* difficulty or trouble, usually which is more than the situation deserves • *What a to-do that was, getting my passport renewed at the consulate!*

toe [BODY PART] /£təʊ, $toʊ/ *n* [C] any of the five movable jointed parts at the end of the foot • *It looks like you've broken your toe.* • *Your toe is peeping out the end of your sock!* • *Look how she points her toes when she walks.* • *You've got to stay* **on** *your toes when you're playing squash so that you're ready to move anywhere.* • *I* **stubbed** (= knocked) *my toe on the edge of a bed.* • *If you can feel your toes at the end of the boot you probably need the next size up.* • *The whole show is full of the sort of rhythmic numbers that have you* **tapping** *your toes* (= moving them up and down). • Toe can also refer to the part of a sock, shoe or other foot covering that goes over the toes: *I don't think those shoes would be very comfortable – they've got very pointed toes.* • Someone or something that keeps you **on your toes** forces you to continue directing all your attention and energy to what you are doing: *I work with people who are half my age so that keeps me on my toes.* • If you **tread/step on** someone's **toes** you say or do something that upsets or annoys them, esp. by making remarks about or involving yourself in matters that are their responsibility. • A **toe cap** is a hard protective covering for the toe end of a shoe or boot: *metal toe caps* • *(Br infml)* If an experience is **toe-curling** or makes your **toes curl**, it makes you feel extremely embarrassed and ashamed for someone else: *I saw the worst comedy act I've ever seen last night – it was absolutely toe-curling!*

–toed /£-təʊd, $-toʊd/ *combining form* • *Never, on any account, wear open-toed sandals with socks.* • A two-/three-/four-toed animal has two/three/four toes on each foot: *the two-toed sloth*

toe *obj* [OBEY] /£təʊ, $toʊ/ *v* [T] **toe the line** to do what you are ordered or expected to do • *Ministers who wouldn't toe the* **party** *line were swiftly got rid of.*

toe·hold /£'təʊ·həʊld, $'toʊ·hoʊld/ *n* [C] a small place on a rock which provides a climber with just enough surface to put the end of his or her foot down • *I searched desperately for a toehold in the rockface.* • A toehold can also be a strong first position from which further advances can be made: *Insurance is a very difficult market to* **get** *a toehold* **in**.

toe·nail /£'təʊ·neɪl, $'toʊ-/ *n* [C] the hard slightly curved part that covers and protects the end of a toe • *She was cutting/painting her toenails.* • PIC› **Nail**

toe·rag /£'təʊ·ræg, $'toʊ-/ *n* [C] *Br slang* an extremely unpleasant person • *The man's an absolute toerag, really!* • *Look what you've done to my book, you toerag.* [as form of address]

toff /£tɒf, $tɑːf/ *n* [C] *Br and Aus dated* a rich person from a high social class • *Gone are the days when champagne-drinking was just for toffs.*

tof·fee /£'tɒf·i, $'tɑː·fi/ *n* a hard, chewy, often brown sweet that is made from sugar boiled with butter • *a lump of sticky toffee* [U] • *liquorice/mint/treacle/chocolate-covered toffees* [C] • *(Br infml)* If you say that someone cannot do something **for toffee** you mean that they are extremely bad at it: *He can't paint for toffee!* • A **toffee apple** is an apple covered with a sticky layer of toffee and held on a stick: *Daddy, can I have a toffee-apple?* • *(Br infml disapproving)* People who are **toffee-nosed** consider themselves to be better than other people, esp. other people of a lower social class: *He's a toffee-nosed git – take no notice of him!*

to·fu /£'təʊ·fuː, $'toʊ-/, **bean curd** *n* [U] a soft pale cheese-like food with very little flavour, but high in PROTEIN, which is made from the seed of the Asian SOYA bean plant • *tofu burgers* • *Tofu is a dietary staple in most east Asian countries.*

tog /£tɒg, $tɑːg/ *n* [C] *Br* a unit of measurement showing the degree of warmth of a bed cover, esp. a DUVET • *The higher the tog, the warmer the duvet.* • *Do you know anything about tog* **ratings**, *Guy – I want to buy a duvet.*

tog *obj* **up/out** /£tɒg, $tɑːg/ *v adv* [T usually passive] *infml* to dress (yourself) in clothes that are specially for a particular occasion or activity • *We'd all got* **ourselves** *togged up in walking gear for the hike.* • *They were obviously off to a party somewhere because they were all togged out* **in** *dinner jackets and ball-gowns.*

togs /£tɒgz, $tɑːgz/ *pl n infml* • Togs are clothes: *Get your togs on, love, then we can go.* ○ *They do a range of colourful togs for children.* • Togs is also *esp. Aus infml for* **swimming costume** or **swimming trunks**. See at SWIM [MOVE IN WATER].

to·ga /£'təʊ·gə, $'toʊ-/ *n* [C] a piece of clothing worn by people in ancient Rome, consisting of a long piece of cloth hanging loosely from the shoulders

to·geth·er [WITH EACH OTHER] /£tə'geð·əʳ, $-ɚ/ *adv* [not gradable] with each other • *Shall we go together or separately?* • *We used to go to aerobics together.* • *I thought we sang rather well together.* • *We worked together on a project a couple of years back.* • *Could you add these figures together for me?* • *You mix all the dry ingredients together before you add the milk.* • *I like both flavours separately but I don't like them together.* • *You could stick that back together* (= join the separate parts to each other) *with a bit of glue.* • *Never trust a man whose eyes are so* **close** *together!* • *The waiter asked if we were* **all** *together so I explained that we were two separate parties.* • *They left the party together, which started a few rumours.* • *Together we walked along the bank of the canal.* • *Sara and I were at college together – that's where we met.* • *We should* **get** *together* (= meet each other socially) *some time and have a drink.* • If two people are described as together, it means that they have a close romantic and often sexual relationship with each other: *Mira and Ellis have been together now for almost five years.* ○ *I was pleased to hear that Chris and Pat are* **back** *together again.* ○ *We went out with each other for four years, but we never* **lived** *together* (= shared a home as if we were married). ○ *(infml) Do you think they're* **sleeping** *together* (= having a sexual relationship)? • *(infml)* If two people **get it together** they start a sexual relationship with each other: *We'd seen each other once or twice in a group, but we didn't really get it together till Rachel's party.* See also **get it together** at TOGETHER [ORGANIZED]. • If two things **go** together they exist or are able to be combined with each other: *Unfortunately, brains and good looks don't always go together.* ○ *Both garments are fine worn separately but they don't go together.* ○ *Do you think this jacket and these trousers go well together?* • See also ALTOGETHER.

to·geth·er·ness /£tə'geð·ə·nəs, $'-ɚ-/ *n* [U] • Togetherness is the pleasant feeling of being united with other people in friendship and understanding: *War had given to the community a greater sense of togetherness.*

to·geth·er AT THE SAME TIME /£tə'geð·əʳ, $-ɚ/ *adv* [not gradable] at the same time • *Everyone seemed to arrive together.* • *We can deal with the next two items on the list together.* • *These two factors are of course related and must be considered together.*

to·geth·er COMBINED /£tə'geð·əʳ, $-ɚ/ *adv* [not gradable] combined • *Together they must earn over eighty thousand dollars a year.* • *She's got more sense than the rest of you* **put** *together.*

to·geth·er IN ONE PLACE /£tə'geð·əʳ, $-ɚ/ *adv* [not gradable] in one place • *I'll just gather my things together and then we'll be off.*

to·geth·er AND ALSO /£tə'geð·əʳ, $-ɚ/ *adv* [not gradable] **together with** in addition to; and also • *That bottle of champagne together with those chocolates will make a nice present.* • *The money that I owe you for the telephone together with the rent equals £300.*

to·geth·er ORGANIZED /£tə'geð·əʳ, $-ɚ/ *adj* [not gradable] *infml approving* organized, confident of your abilities and able to use them to achieve what you want • *He's strikes me as a fairly together sort of a guy.* • To **get it together** is to get something organized: *We were going to do something more ambitious over Christmas this year but we never got it together.* See also **get it together** as TOGETHER WITH EACH OTHER.

tog·gle COMPUTER SWITCH /£'tɒg·l̩, $'tɑː·gl̩/ *n* [C] a key or button on a computer which is pressed to turn a feature on and then off • *Select the function you require by pointing to the toggle* (= image of a button on the screen) *with the mouse and then clicking.*

tog·gle *(obj)* /£'tɒg·l̩, $'tɑː·gl̩/ *v* • To toggle is to switch a feature on a computer on and off by pressing the same button or key: *Use this key to toggle* **between** *the two typefaces.* [I] ○ *By toggling this key, you can switch the italics on and off.* [T]

tog·gle FASTENER /£'tɒg·l̩, $'tɑː·gl̩/ *n* [C] a small bar of wood or plastic which acts as a fastener by being put through a hole or LOOP

toil /tɔɪl/ *n* [U] hard work, esp. that which is physically tiring • *An illegal worker will earn more here in a week than he would in a month of toil back home.* • *Lindi has achieved her comfortable life only after years of* **hard** *toil.* • *Prison rarely persuades a criminal of the advantages of* **honest** *toil over theft.* • *(humorous) Well, after a day's toil in the office I like to relax a little.* • *"Double, double, toil and trouble; / Fire burn and cauldron bubble"* (Shakespeare, the witches in Macbeth 4.1)

toil /tɔɪl/ *v* [I] • *England's cricketers have been toiling in the 100-degree heat over the past week.* • *I was relaxing in the bath, having toiled* **away** *in the garden all afternoon.* • If you toil in a particular direction, you move there, slowly and with great effort: *I was toiling up the hill with four heavy bags when he took pity on me.* • *(literary) For the toiling* **masses** (= people in general) *these higher food prices are very bad news.*

toi·let CONTAINER /'tɔɪ·lət/ *n* [C] a bowl-shaped device with a seat which you sit on or stand near when emptying the body of urine or excrement, or another device used for this purpose • *I was* **on** (= using) *the toilet when the phone rang.* • *Don't forget to* **flush** *the toilet.* • *I think the toilet's blocked again.* • *If you're going to serve food you need some sort of toilet facilities.* • *The toilet* **seat** *was cracked and there was no paper.* • A toilet (*Am usually* **bathroom**) is also a room with a toilet in it: *If you want the toilet, it's the second door on the left.* ○ *Someone's in the toilet.* ○ *I spent half the night in the toilet being violently ill.* • *Our neighbour's cat uses our garden as a toilet* (= it excretes there). • To **go to the toilet** is to empty the body of urine or excrement, using a toilet to do so: *It's going to be a long journey, kids, so if you want to go to the toilet do so now.* • A **toilet brush** is a plastic or wooden brush that has a long handle and is used to clean the inside of a toilet. • **Toilet paper** is soft, absorbent paper, usually in a long roll, that people use to clean themselves when they have emptied their body of urine or excrement: *We've run out of toilet paper again.* • *(Br and Aus)* A **toilet roll** is a long, narrow length of toilet paper, rolled around a cardboard cylinder: *a toilet-roll holder* • **Toilet-trained** means **potty-trained**. See at POTTY TOILET. • LP› **Phrases and customs** PIC› **Bathroom**

toi·lets /'tɔɪ·ləts/ *pl n, Am usually* **bath·room** *n* [C], *Am also* **la·dies'/men's room** *n* [C] • Toilets refers to a room or small building in a public place in which there are several toilets: *It really puts me off a place when the toilets are dirty.* ○ *Do you know where the ladies' toilets are?* ○ *(Am) Could you direct me to the ladies' room, please?* ○ *Where are the nearest* **public** *toilets?*

toi·let WASHING /'tɔɪ·lət/ *n* [U] *dated fml* the process of washing and dressing yourself • *Virginia had spent longer than usual* **over** *her toilet that evening, with pleasing results.* • *Mr Tolley called while you were* **at** *your toilet, my lady. He asked me to give you this letter.* • A **toilet bag** (*Am also* **dopp kit**) is a bag that you put such items as soap and brushes in, esp. when you are travelling. • **Toilet soap** is sweet-smelling soap that is intended for washing the body. • **Toilet water** is a weak PERFUME (= liquid with a pleasant smell).

toi·let·ries /'tɔɪ·lə·triz/ *pl n* • Toiletries are items and substances that you use in washing yourself and preventing the body from smelling unpleasant: *Women's toiletries are at the other end of the shop, madam.* • LP› **Shopping goods**

to·ken SYMBOL /£'təʊ·kᵊn, $'toʊ-/ *n* a thing that you give or an action that you take which expresses your feelings or intentions, although it might have little practical effect • **As a** *token of our gratitude for all that you have done, we would like you to accept this small gift.* [C] • *Traditionally a man will buy his woman jewellery as a token* **of** *his love for her.* [C] • *In her will, she left all her friends some little token* **of** *her* **affection**, *whether it was a piece of jewellery or an ornament.* [C] • *It doesn't have to be a big present – it's just a token really.* [C] • *(fml) They bowed their heads* **in token of** (= to show) *respect for him.* [U]

to·ken /£'təʊ·kᵊn, $'toʊ-/ *adj* [before n; not gradable] • Token can be used to describe actions which although small or limited in their practical effect, have a symbolic importance: *The release of two out of the twenty hostages is being seen as token* **gesture** *of goodwill.* ○ *He said he hoped the president would agree to at least a token U.S. troop presence in the area.* ○ *The forces in front of us either surrendered or offered token* **resistance**. ○ *At the time they were the only country to argue for even token recognition of the Baltic states' independence.* • *(disapproving)* Token also describes something which is done to prevent other people complaining, although it is not sincerely meant and has no real effect: *The truth is that they appoint no more than a token number of women to managerial jobs.* ○ *As a token* **effort** *he may wash the occasional plate, but the rest of the housework is left entirely to me.* ○ *Women at this time had only a token representation on the committee.* ○ *He retired from acting in 1956, tired of being the token black in a white-dominated industry.*

to·ken·i·sm /£'təʊ·kᵊn·ɪ·zᵊm, $'toʊ-/ *n* [U] *disapproving* • Tokenism describes actions which are the result of pretending to give advantage to those groups in society who are often treated unfairly, in order to give the appearance of fairness: *Even at the risk of tokenism, we would like to see the post go to a woman.*

to·ken PAPER WORTH MONEY *Br and Aus* /£'təʊ·kᵊn, $'toʊ-/, *Am* **gift cer·ti·fi·cate** *n* [C] a piece of paper with a particular amount of money printed on it which can be exchanged in a shop for goods of that value • *a book/gift/record token* • *I bought him a £20 book token for his birthday.*

to·ken DISC /£'təʊ·kᵊn, $'toʊ-/ *n* [C] a round metal or plastic disc which is used instead of money in some machines • *You have to get a token from reception if you want to use the washing machine.*

told /£təʊld, $toʊld/ *past simple and past participle of* TELL • *There were 550 people there* **all told** (= as a complete total).

tol·e·ra·ble /£'tɒl·ᵊr·ə·bl̩, $'tɑː·lɚ-/ *adj* of a quality that is acceptable, although certainly not good • *The food was just about tolerable, but the service was appalling.* • *At their best the conditions in these prisons are scarcely tolerable.* • *A lot of the summer jobs available here are only tolerable if you're young and don't mind working hard.* • *For me it's friendships that make this life tolerable.*

tol·e·ra·bly /£'tɒl·ᵊr·ə·bli, $'tɑː·lɚ-/ *adv slightly fml* • Tolerably means to a limited degree or quite: *I play the piano tolerably* **well**, *though I have no particular talent for it.* ○ *Hubert's translation reads tolerably* **well**, *though it lacks the excitement of the original.* ○ *The meal was tolerably* **good**, *but I wouldn't eat there again.* ○ *The play is tolerably amusing, but it is let down by the actors' weak performances.*

tol·e·rance [ACCEPTANCE] /£'tɒl·ər·ənts, $'tɑː·lɚ-/, *fml* **tol·e·ra·tion** /£ˌtɒl·ər'eɪ·ʃən, $ˌtɑː·lə'reɪ-/ *n* [U] willingness to accept behaviour and beliefs which are different from your own, although you might not agree with or approve of them • *This period in history is not noted for its* **religious** *tolerance.* • *A social reformer and advocate of racial tolerance, he was in many ways a progressive thinker.* • *It's a culture in which there is absolutely no tolerance* **of** *dissent.* • *Some members of the party would like to see it develop a greater tolerance* **towards** *contrary points of view.* • *The tolerance* **of** *eccentricity is almost a tradition in Britain.* • *Later in life, his affairs were conducted in England, where sexual tolerance was greater than in Ireland.*

tol·e·rant /£'tɒl·ər·ənt, $'tɑː·lɚ-/ *adj* • *The present government is even less tolerant* **of** *dissent.* • *There's a general feeling that the president has been too tolerant* **of** *corruption.* • *Georgia is historically a remarkably tolerant country.* • *On the continent people are more tolerant* **of** *children in public places.*

tol·e·rant·ly /£'tɒl·ər·ənt·li, $'tɑː·lɚ-/ *adv* • *I would tell my grandmother about all the crazy things I'd been doing and she would just smile tolerantly.*

tol·e·rate *(obj)* /£'tɒl·ər·eɪt, $'tɑː·lə·reɪt/ *v* [usually in negatives] • *I'm afraid I can't tolerate that sort of behaviour in my class.* [T] • *People in this country are not prepared to tolerate a racist state in Europe.* [T] • *I won't tolerate lying.* [+ v-*ing*]

tol·e·rance [ABILITY TO BEAR] /£'tɒl·ər·ənts, $'tɑː·lɚ-/ *n* [U] the ability to bear something unpleasant or annoying, or to continue existing despite disadvantageous conditions • *My tolerance* **of** *heat is considerably greater after having lived in the Far East for a couple of years.* • *I think I must have a very low pain-tolerance* **threshold**. • *(specialized)* Tolerance is also an animal or plant's ability not to be harmed by a drug or poison over a long period of time: *It was said that Holmes had a greater tolerance* **to** *the drug than most people.*

tol·e·rant /£'tɒl·ər·ənt, $'tɑː·lɚ-/ *adj* • *I think I grow less tolerant* **of** *fools the older I get.* • *I think on average men are less tolerant* **of** *stress than women.* • *(specialized) Compared to other plants, rye is less susceptible to disease and reasonably tolerant* **of** *drought.*

tol·e·rate *obj* /£'tɒl·ər·eɪt, $'tɑː·lə·reɪt/ *v* [T] • *I can't tolerate excessive heat.* • *It seems these ants can tolerate temperatures which would kill other species.* • *She can't tolerate noise of any sort when she's trying to write.* • *(specialized) It's an alternative treatment for people who cannot tolerate the medicine because of heart problems or other medical conditions.*

tol·e·rance [VARIATION] /£'tɒl·ər·ənts, $'tɑː·lɚ-/ *n* [U] *specialized* the amount by which a measurement or calculation might vary and still be acceptable

toll [CHARGE] /£təʊl, $toʊl/ *n* [C] a small amount of money that you have to pay to use a road, cross a bridge etc. • *There's a two-pound toll to cross the bridge.* • *He's just got a job collecting tolls at the start of the motorway.* • *The advantage of toll* **roads** *is that they raise money from car users instead of general tax-payers.* • *(Am)* Toll can also refer to the money a long-distance telephone call costs: *Is Bayonne a toll* **call** (= a more expensive telephone call) *from New York?* ○ *There are plans to establish a national toll-***free** *hotline* (= one for which the caller does not have to pay anything).

tolled /£təʊld, $toʊld/ *adj* [not gradable] *esp. Br* • *There are plans to build a tolled motorway* (= one which you pay to use) *around the perimeter of the city.*

toll [SUFFERING] /£təʊl, $toʊl/ *n* [U] suffering, deaths or damage • *Independent sources say that the civilian* **death** *toll runs into thousands.* • If something **takes** its **toll/takes a toll/exacts a toll**, it causes suffering, deaths or damage: *The problems of the past few months have taken their toll* **on** *her health and there are shadows beneath her eyes.* ○ *The deepening recession has also taken its toll in the south of the country, where unemployment is rife.* ○ *Any lengthy period of separation inevitably takes its toll* **on** *a relationship.* ○ *Malaria exacts a* **heavy** *toll of illness and death in this region, especially among children.*

toll *(obj)* [RING] /£təʊl, $toʊl/ *v* to (cause a large bell to) ring slowly and repeatedly • *At the news of victory, church bells were tolled across the land.* [T] • *At Cathedral Square, the bell of the medieval tower tolled.* [I] • *In the distance, a church bell tolled the hour* (= announced the time by ringing). [T] • *"The curfew tolls the knell of parting day"* (Thomas Gray in the poem *Elegy Written in a Country Churchyard*, 1751)

toll·gate /£'təʊl·geɪt, $'toʊl-/, *Am usually* **toll·booth** /£'təʊl·buːð, $'toʊl-/ *n* [C] a gate at the start of a road or bridge at which you pay an amount of money in order to be allowed to use the road or bridge • *Tollgates now stand on every road into Oslo, about seven kilometres from the centre.*

toll·house /£'təʊl·haʊs, $'toʊl-/ *n* [C] *pl* **tollhouses** /£'təʊlˌhaʊ·zɪz, $'toʊl-/ esp. in the past, a small house at a TOLLGATE, in which the person who collects the money lives • (S)

Tom, Dick and/or Har·ry /£ˌtɒmˌdɪk·ən*d*'hær·i, $ˌtɑːmˌdɪk·ən*d*'her-/, **Tom, Dick and/or Har·ri·et** /£ˌtɒmˌdɪk·ən*d*'hær·i·ət, $ˌtɑːmˌdɪk·ən*d*'her-/ *n* [U] *disapproving* any ordinary person • *You'd better get a qualified electrician to sort this out – you don't want* **any** *Tom, Dick or Harry messing around with your electrics.* • *Draw your curtains, Pat, or you'll have* **every** *Tom, Dick and Harriet who walks past peering in at you!*

tom·a·hawk /£'tɒm·ə·hɔːk, $'tɑː·mə·hɑːk/ *n* [C] a small fighting AXE (= tool with a blade) used by Native Americans • PIC› **Axe**

to·ma·to /£tə'mɑː·təʊ, $-'meɪ·t̬oʊ/ *n pl* **tomatoes** a small red sharp-tasting fruit with a lot of seeds which is eaten cooked or raw as a savoury food • *tomato puree/ sauce/soup* • *I've ordered a tomato and basil salad.* • *Most people think of a tomato as a kind of vegetable.* [C] • *There's too much tomato in this casserole.* [U] • **Tomato ketchup** is a sweet red tomato sauce, eaten cold and usually poured from a bottle: *No, I can't eat chips without tomato ketchup.* • PIC› **Vegetables**

tomb /tuːm/ *n* [C] a large stone structure or underground room where someone, esp. an important person, is buried • *A few red roses were scattered on Karl Marx's tomb.* • *In 1922 the magnificent tomb of Tutankhamen was discovered intact near Luxor.* • *There was one tomb more lordly than all the rest, and on it was but one word, Dracula.*

tom·bo·la /£tɒm'bəʊ·lə, $tɑːm'boʊ-/ *n* [C] *Br and Aus* a game in which numbered tickets are bought from a spinning cylindrical container and small prizes are won when the numbers on the tickets are the same as the numbers on the prizes • *I won a bottle of port* **on** *the tombola at the fair.* • *We're planning to hold a raffle and a tombola at the Christmas party.*

tom·boy /£'tɒm·bɔɪ, $'tɑːm-/ *n* [C] a girl who acts and dresses like a boy, traditionally liking noisy, physical activities • *I grew up with four older brothers so I was a bit of a tomboy when I was at school.*

tomb·stone /£'tuːm·stəʊn, $-stoʊn/ *n* [C] a GRAVESTONE

tom·cat /£'tɒm·kæt, $'tɑːm-/ *n* [C] a male cat

tome /£təʊm, $toʊm/ *n* [C] *usually humorous* a large heavy book • *She's written several* **weighty** *tomes on the subject.* • *His new biography of Jane Austen is far better than most of the other tomes about her.*

tom·fool·e·ry /£ˌtɒm'fuː·lər·i, $ˌtɑːm'fuː·lɚ-/ *n* [U] *dated* foolish, often playful, behaviour • *That's enough tomfoolery, class – now let's get on with some work, shall we!* • *Sergeant Lander described the incident involving two eight-year-old boys as "a piece of tomfoolery that went horribly wrong."*

tom·my gun /£'tɒm·i, $'tɑː·mi/ *n* [C] a light **machine gun** (= quick firing gun) held in the hand

to·mor·row /£tə'mɒr·əʊ, $-'mɔːr·oʊ/ *adv* [not gradable], *n* (on) the day after today • *I'll be at home tomorrow.* • *He said he'll call in tomorrow after work.* • *I've arranged to see Rachel tomorrow night.* • *Oh, leave it till tomorrow.* [U] • *Tomorrow's Friday, thank goodness.* [U] • *Is John coming to tomorrow's meeting?* [U] • *He left today, that's Tuesday, and he'll be back tomorrow* **week** (= the Wednesday of next week). • Tomorrow can also be used more generally to mean the future: *Today's problem child may be tomorrow's criminal.* [U] ○ *We make sacrifices now to give our children a better tomorrow.* [C] • *(infml)* If someone does something **like/as if there were/as if there was no tomorrow**, they do it very fast, in large amounts and without thinking carefully: *After his win on the football pools, he began spending money like there was no tomorrow.* • LP› **Calendar**

tom–tom /£'tɒm·tɒm, $'tɑːm·tɑːm/ *n* [C] a drum which is usually beaten with the hands

ton [WEIGHT] /tʌn/ *n* [C] *pl* **tons** or **ton** a unit of weight for measuring large amounts • A ton is equal to 1016 kg (*specialized* **long ton**), 907 kg (*specialized* **short ton**), or 1000 kg (*specialized* **metric ton**, TONNE). • *a five-ton truck* •

Steel production fell last week by 4·7% to 1 689 000 tons. • *(fig. infml) What on earth have you got in this bag, Elaine? It* **weighs a** *ton!* (=It is very heavy!) • **Like a ton of bricks** means very strongly or forcefully: *If father finds out what you've been doing, he'll* **come down on** (=punish) *you like a ton of bricks!* ○ *The Serious Fraud Office will now come down on these solicitors like a ton of bricks.* • LP› **Units**

tons /tʌnz/ *pl n infml* • Tons **of** means an extremely large amount of: *We'd better eat some of this cheese up – we've got tons of the stuff!*

ton SPEED /tʌn/ *n* [U] **do a ton** *infml dated* to drive at 100 miles per hour • *We were doing at least a ton when I noticed we were being followed by the police.*

tone VOICE EXPRESSION /£təʊn, $toʊn/ *n* [U] a quality in the voice which expresses the speaker's feelings or thoughts, often towards the person being addressed • *I tried to use a sympathetic tone* **of voice**. • *It's that patronising tone* **of voice** *that I can't bear.* • *Don't speak to me in that tone* **of voice** (=angrily), *young lady!* • *It wasn't so much what she said that annoyed me – it was her tone.* • *When finally he spoke, his tone was conciliatory.* • (DK)

tones /£təʊnz, $toʊnz/ *pl n literary* • *She recounted the story to me* **in** *shocked tones* (=in a shocked tone). • *For more than half a century, the reassuring tones of BBC newscasters have informed British television viewers about world events.* • *"Mr Mellors," she said* **in** *suitably reverent tones, "is the church organist."* • *Mother had one of her headaches and was only to be addressed* **in** *hushed tones.*

-toned /£-təʊnd, $-toʊnd/ *combining form* • *Low-toned mutterings could be heard in the next room.*

tone·less /£'təʊn·ləs, $'toʊn-/ *adj literary* • A voice which is toneless does not express any emotion: *"So is that what you bought me for my birthday?" says my eight-year-old son in a toneless voice, plainly unimpressed.*

tone GENERAL MOOD /£təʊn, $toʊn/ *n* [U] the general mood or main qualities of something, esp. a speech or piece of writing • *I didn't like the jokey tone of the article – I thought it inappropriate.* • *Underneath the humour, there is a very moral tone* **to** *this book.* • *The same elegiac and lonely tone continues to haunt the later poems.* • *The tone of the party was surprisingly restrained, considering it was supposed to be a celebration.* • *He was in a very bad mood when he arrived, and that* **set** *the tone* **for** *the whole meeting* (=that established what the whole meeting would be like). • (DK)

-toned /£-təʊnd, $-toʊnd/ *combining form* • *a high-toned discussion*

tone STANDARD /£təʊn, $toʊn/ *n* [U] the standard of something • *A stunning goal from Brinkworth just before half-time* **set** *the tone* (=established the standard) **for** *a much improved second-half performance from the Manchester team.* • *I don't think they like students living next to them because it* **lowers** *the tone of the neighbourhood.* • *Trust you to* **lower** *the tone of the evening by telling vulgar jokes, Martin!* • *Well, I thought it might* **raise** *the moral tone of the evening if I invited a vicar to the party.* • (DK)

tone COLOUR VARIETY /£təʊn, $toʊn/ *n* [C] a variety or different form or degree of a colour • *She doesn't wear bright colours, preferring the neutral tones of beige and cream.* • (DK)

tone in *v adv* [I] • If one colour tones in **with** another it matches and looks pleasant with it: *The green of your scarf tones in with your shoes.*

tone FIRMNESS OF BODY /£təʊn, $toʊn/ *n* [U] the healthy firmness of the body, esp. the muscles • *After you've had a baby you lose the* **muscle** *tone in your stomach.* • *It is claimed that massage helps to improve skin tone.* • (DK)

toned /£təʊnd, $toʊnd/ *adj* • *If you want a nicely toned* (=firm and strong) *body you have to work at it.*

tone *obj* /£təʊn, $toʊn/ *v* [T] • If you tone **(up)** a part of the body you make it firmer and stronger, usually by taking physical exercise: *Aerobics is good for generally toning up the body.* [M]

ton·er *n* • *I always use (a) toner* (=(a) substance that you put on your face after you have cleaned it, in order to make the skin feel firm) *on my face.* [C/U]

tone DIFFERENCE IN SOUND /£təʊn, $toʊn/, *Am also* **step** *n* [C] the largest difference in sound between two notes which are next to each other in the western musical SCALE • *The interval from G to A is a* **whole** *tone.* • *In the fourth bar you go up a* **half** *tone.* • Someone who is **tone-deaf** is not able to recognize different notes or sing tunes accurately: *Don't ask me to sing – I'm tone-deaf!* • *(specialized)* A **tone language** is one in which the same series of sounds can represent different meanings, depending on how high or low they are spoken: *Chinese is a tone language.* • (DK)

ton·al /£'təʊ·nəl, $'toʊ-/ *adj specialized* • Tonal music is music that is based on MAJOR and MINOR KEYS (=sets of notes): *Schoenberg's early works were tonal, but his later works were atonal.*

tone MUSICAL QUALITY /£təʊn, $toʊn/ *n* the quality of sound of a musical instrument or singing voice • *To listen to the beautiful rich tones of his tenor voice, you'd think he'd been singing for years.* [C] • *I think the tone of that piano could be improved.* [U] • (DK)

ton·al /£'təʊ·nəl, $'toʊ-/ *adj specialized* • *There is plenty of tonal variety in his singing.*

tone TELEPHONE NOISE /£təʊn, $toʊn/ *n* [C] one of the sounds that a telephone makes when you pick up the RECEIVER (=the part that you hold to the ear) • *I don't think the telephone is working – it's making this strange bleeping tone.* • *I've called him several times but I keep getting the engaged tone.* • *Please wait until you hear the (Br)* **dialling**/*(Am)* **dial** *tone* (=the sound that a telephone makes when it is ready to be used) *before inserting your money.* • (DK)

tone down *obj*, **tone** *obj* **down** *v adv* [M] to make (something) less forceful or offensive • *Some of the language in the original play has been toned down for the television version.* • *The president has been advised to tone down the rhetoric of his campaign.* • *They have toned down certain parts of last year's show considerably in order to make it suitable for a family audience.*

tongs /£tɒŋz, $tɑːŋz/ *pl n* a device used for picking up objects, consisting of two long pieces of metal or wood which are joined at one end and are pressed together in order to hold an object between them • *coal tongs* • *sugar tongs* • *You're supposed to use the tongs for putting ice in the drinks – not your fingers!* • PIC› **Fires and space heaters**

tongue MOUTH PART /tʌŋ/ *n* the movable fleshy part in the mouth that is used in tasting, crushing and swallowing food and, in people, in the production of speech • *Ow, I just bit my tongue!* [C] • *I burnt my tongue on some hot soup last night.* [C] • *He was staring at me so I stuck my tongue out at him.* [C] • *A great dog lay at her heels, its tongue lolling out of its mouth.* [C] • *The snake darted out its long thin tongue.* [C] • *She ran her tongue over her lips in anticipation.* [C] • *A few whiskies should* **loosen** *his tongue* (=make him speak openly). [C] • Tongue can refer to the tongue of an animal, used as food: *cold tongue and salad* [U] • A tongue can also be a part of an object which is tongue-shaped, esp. the piece of material which is under the LACES (=cord used to fasten openings) in a shoe. [C] • To **get** your **tongue round/around** a difficult word or phrase is to pronounce it: *Try getting your tongue round some of those names after a couple bottles of wine!* ○ *It's one language that I have real difficulty getting my tongue round.* • *(infml)* If something that someone says or does **sets/starts tongues wagging** it causes other people to start talking and guessing things about their private lives: *Do you think if we leave the party together it will set tongues wagging?* ○ *I think it was their dancing together that really started tongues wagging.* • If you say something **tongue in cheek** or **with** your **tongue in** your **cheek**, you intend it to be understood as a joke, although you might appear to be serious: *He's reported as having said that he was America's greatest lover, although I suspect it was tongue in cheek.* ○ *Her latest play is a* **firmly** *tongue-in-cheek look at the world of advertising.* • If you give someone a **tongue-lashing**, you speak angrily to them about something that they have done wrong: *After a tongue-lashing from their manager the team returned, shame-faced, to the field.* • If you get **tongue-tied**, you find it difficult to express yourself, usually because you are nervous: *Why is it that when you're with someone that you really want to impress, you find yourself completely tongue-tied!* • A **tongue twister** is a sentence or phrase that is intended to be difficult to say, esp. when repeated quickly and often: *'She sells seashells on the seashore' is a well-known tongue twister.* • PIC› **Shoes**

tongue LANGUAGE /tʌŋ/ *n* [C] *literary or fml* a language • *With the immigrants struggling to learn a strange tongue he was unfailingly patient.* • *This ancient tongue is spoken by one in six of the nation's inhabitants.* • *He lets fall a casual phrase to display his effortless mastery of a foreign tongue.*

tongue STYLE OF EXPRESSION /tʌŋ/ *n* [U] a person's way of expressing their ideas and feelings • *She is a prolific writer with critical views and a* **sharp** (=severe and critical) *tongue.* • *An outspoken republican, he is known for his razor-sharp tongue.*

-tongued /-tʌŋd/ *combining form* • *Coleman plays the part of the* **sharp-tongued** (= severe and critical) *lawyer.* • *He was younger than her, in his forties, and had a* **silver-tongued** *charm* (= said charming things).

ton·ic /£ˈtɒn·ɪk, $ˈtɑː·nɪk/ *n* [C] a liquid medicine which has the general effect of making you feel better rather than treating a particular health problem that you might have • *He'd been feeling low after his illness, and the doctor prescribed a tonic.* • *Caffeine became a familiar component of all kinds of tonics and 'health drinks' once it had been isolated from the coffee bean.* • *(fig.) The magazine is lively and interesting – the pictures alone are* **a** *tonic* (= make you feel happy). • *(fig.) Their new player has proved* **just the** *tonic* (= exactly what was needed) *to raise the standard of the team's game.*

ton·ic (wa·ter) /£ˈtɒn·ɪk, $ˈtɑː·nɪk/ *n* fizzy water with a bitter taste which can be drunk on its own or added to alcoholic drinks • *Do you like vodka and tonic?* [U] • *Two gin and tonics, please.* [C]

to·night /təˈnaɪt/ *adv* [not gradable], *n* (during) the night of the present day • *I knew that tonight I had a great chance of winning and breaking the record.* • *Tonight the charity believes up to 5000 people will be sleeping on the streets.* • *Tonight will be my first opportunity to meet her.* [U] • *Tonight's meeting will take place in the main school hall.* [U] • *"Not tonight, Josephine"* (phrase made famous by the film *I Cover the Waterfront*, 1933)

ton·nage /ˈtʌn·ɪdʒ/ *n* [U] the weight of goods that esp. a ship is able to carry, or the total amount of ships • *Britain's merchant tonnage* (= its number of ships carrying goods) *has decreased significantly in recent years.*

tonne /tʌn/, **met·ric ton** *n* [C] *pl* **tonnes** or **tonne** 1000 kilograms • *Oil deliveries will fall 2·5 million tonnes short of demand this year.* • *The 7554-tonne liner had been chartered by a millionaire to celebrate his daughter's marriage.* • LP **Units**

ton·sils /£ˈtɒnt·səlz, $ˈtɑːnt-/ *pl n* the two small soft organs at the back of the mouth

ton·sil·li·tis /£ˌtɒnt·sɪˈlaɪ·təs, $ˌtɑːnt·sɪˈlaɪ·t̬əs/ *n* [U] • *He had bad tonsillitis* (= a painful infection of the tonsils) *as a child, and had to have his tonsils out.*

ton·sure /£ˈtɒn·tʃəʳ, $ˈtɑːnt·ʃɚ/ *n* [C] the top back part of the head from which a circle of hair has been removed • *Some monks have tonsures as one way of showing that they have a particular type of religious life.*

too MORE /tuː/ *adv* [not gradable] more than is needed or wanted; more than is suitable or enough • *You're too fat.* • *I can't reach the shelf – it's* **(a bit)** *too high.* • *There were* **(far)** *too many people for such a small room.* • *You're* **(much)** *too late – the meeting has finished.* • *This picture's too big* **to** *put on that wall.* [+ *to* infinitive] • *It's too difficult* **(for** *me)* **to** *explain.* [+ *to* infinitive] • *It was too hot* **(for** *them)* **to** *want to go sightseeing.* [+ *to* infinitive] • *(fml) It was too expensive a desk for a child's room.* • **All/Only too** can be used to emphasize an adjective: *"Would you like to make a donation?" "I'd be only too* (= extremely) *pleased."* ○ *The holidays flew by all too* (= regrettably very) *quickly.* ○ *It's all too* (= very) *easy* **to** *say yes because your friends encourage you.* • *It's* **(all)** *too much* (= more than I can deal with) *– I can't bear it.* • *(infml)* If you say something is **too bad** you can mean that you are sympathetic about someone else's problem, or that you are not. The difference is in what is being talked about and the way that you say it: *It's too bad that you can't come to see Mark in his school play.* ○ *"I can't come on Friday." "That's too bad – I've already bought the tickets so you'll still have to pay."* • To be **in too deep** is to be too involved in a difficult situation. • *We thought it was* **too good** *an opportunity* **to miss** (= we should take the opportunity). • **Too good to be true** means so good that it is not believable: *Her new job sounds too good to be true.* • If an action is **too little (and) too late** it has not happened early enough or in a strong enough way to stop a bad situation getting worse: *Officials admit that the replanting of the hillsides only started five years ago and seems to be* **a** *classic* **case of** *too little and too late.* ○ *The organization claimed that the food aid given was too little, too late.* • *You can have* **too much of a good thing** (= become bored of something even if it is good). • *I don't like gardening – it's* **too much like hard work** (= although it is done for enjoyment it needs a lot of effort). • *"Too Much Too Young"* (Song by The Specials, 1980) • Do not confuse with VERY.

too VERY /tuː/ *adv* [usually in negatives; not gradable] very, or completely • *He wasn't too* **pleased/happy** *when I told him about the mistake.* • *My mother hasn't been too* **well** *recently.* • *I'm not too* **sure** *if I can come to the party.* • *We wouldn't be too* **surprised** *if they decided to stay longer.* • *(fml) Thank you, you're too* **kind**.

too ALSO /tuː/ *adv* [not gradable] (esp. at the end of a sentence) in addition, also • *I'd like to come too.* • *You'll need dictionaries – and bring a notebook too.* • *"I love Thornton's chocolates." "I like them too./(infml) Me too."* • Too is sometimes used to show surprise: *It's a wonderful picture of light shining through trees – and by a child too!* Compare **as well** at WELL IN ADDITION; MOREOVER • **what's more** at WHAT THAT WHICH.

too CERTAINLY /tuː/ *adv* [not gradable] *Am infml* used to emphasize a positive answer to a negative statement • *"I'm not going to school today." "You are too!"*

took /tʊk/ *past simple of* TAKE

tool EQUIPMENT /tuːl/ *n* [C] a piece of equipment which you use to help you do a job, esp. something which you use with your hands to make or repair something • *power tools* • *machine tools* • *The only tool you really need for this job, apart from a drill and a knife, is a saw to cut the plywood to size.* • *This special tool, a diamond file, is set in a durable plastic handle for ease of use.* • *The cutting tool works by moving the metal under a fixed laser.* • *A free low-interest credit card can be a* **useful** *budgeting tool.* • *We will continue to investigate written tests as one of several assessment tools for children of different ages.* • *(fig. disapproving) The President was regarded as the tool* **of** *the military* (= he did what they wanted him to do because they had control over him). • A **tool of** the **trade** is something you need to use to do your job: *For the modern sales executive, a car phone is one of the tools of the trade.* ○ *As a broadcaster, his mastery of words and his naturally beautiful speaking voice are the tools of his trade.* • A **tool box** is a container in which you keep and carry small tools, esp. those used in the house or for repairing a car: *Is there another screwdriver in your tool box?* • A **tool kit** is a set of tools. • A **tool shed** is a small building, esp. in a garden, in which tools and garden equipment are kept. • *(saying)* 'Give us the tools and we'll finish the job' means that you are willing to do something but you need money or some other type of help to be able to do it. • *"Give us the tools and we will finish the job"* (speech on the radio by Sir Winston Churchill, 1941)

tooled /tuːld/ *adj* [not gradable] • Something, esp. a piece of leather, which is tooled is marked with decorative patterns using a special tool: *a tooled leather belt* ○ *a book with a hand-tooled leather binding*

tool PENIS /tuːl/ *n* [C] *taboo slang* a penis

tooled up /tuːld/ *adj* [after v] *slang* carrying a weapon, esp. a gun

toot SOUND /tuːt/ *v, n* (to make) a short sound or series of short sounds, esp. with the HORN of a car as a warning • *The driver tooted (her horn).* [I/T] • *I tooted the cyclist to make sure he knew I was behind him.* [T] • *The waiting taxi* **gave** *a toot* **on** *its horn.* [C]

toot TOILET /tuːt/ *n* [C] *Aus infml for* TOILET

tooth MOUTH /tuːθ/ *n* [C] *pl* **teeth** /tiːθ/ any of the hard white objects in the mouth, which are used for biting and chewing • *a broken tooth* • *a missing tooth* • *front/back teeth* • *false teeth* • **Brush** *your teeth thoroughly morning and night.* • *(Br and Aus) I had to have a tooth* **out** *(Am* **pulled***)* (= removed). • *Sugar is believed to be the major cause of tooth* **decay**. • *The dentist said he would be able* **fill** *the tooth rather than take it out.* • To **get** your **teeth into** something is to deal with it or become involved in it with great energy and enthusiasm: *I'm so bored at work, I wish they'd give me something I could really get my teeth into.* • If something **sets** your **teeth on edge** it annoys you very much: *That DJ's voice really sets my teeth on edge.* • If you fight **tooth and nail** you try very hard to get something you want: *We* **fought** *tooth and nail to get the route of the new road changed.* ○ *They opposed the legislation tooth and nail.* • The **tooth fairy** is an imaginary being whom children believe takes away a **baby tooth** which has come out and leaves them money instead. • See also EYETOOTH.

-toothed /-tuːθt/ *combining form* • *black-toothed* • *gap-toothed* (= with a space between the top two front teeth)

tooth·less /ˈtuːθ·ləs/ *adj* [not gradable] • *an ugly toothless hag* • *(fig.)* An organization or a set of rules which is toothless has no power: *This well-intentioned but toothless law will do nothing to improve the situation.*

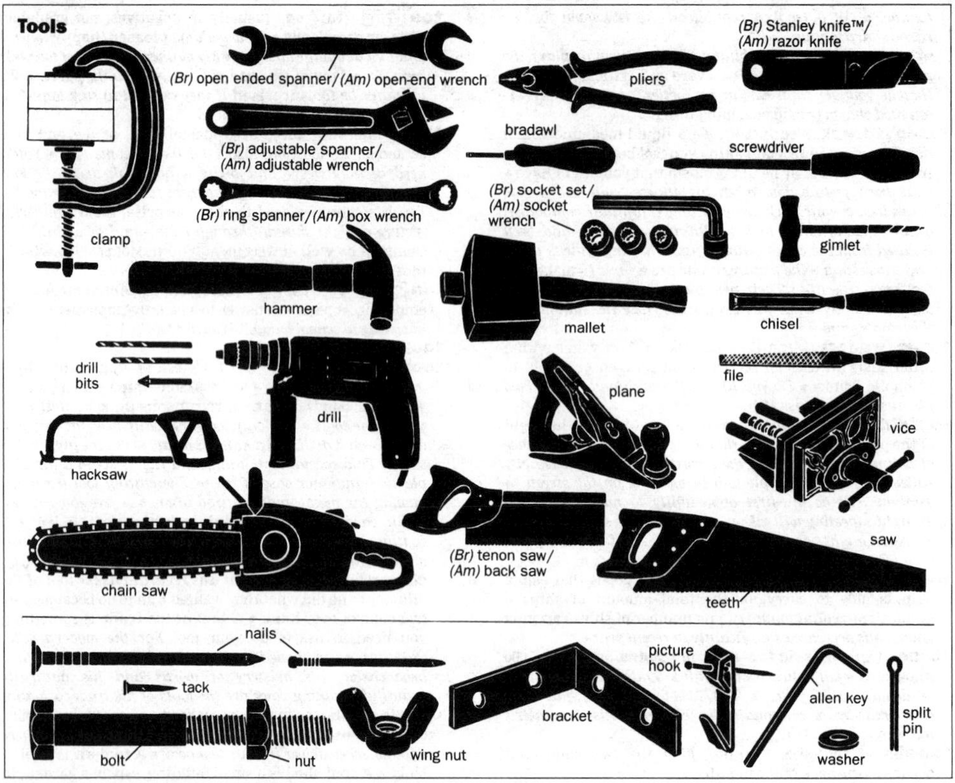

Tools

clamp
(Br) open ended spanner/(Am) open-end wrench
(Br) adjustable spanner/(Am) adjustable wrench
(Br) ring spanner/(Am) box wrench
hammer
drill bits
drill
hacksaw
chain saw
(Br) Stanley knife™/(Am) razor knife
pliers
bradawl
screwdriver
(Br) socket set/(Am) socket wrench
gimlet
mallet
chisel
file
plane
vice
(Br) tenon saw/(Am) back saw
saw
teeth
nails
tack
bolt
nut
wing nut
bracket
picture hook
allen key
washer
split pin

tooth·y /ˈtuː·θi/ *adj* **-ier, -iest** • If you give or have a toothy **grin**, you show a lot of your teeth when you smile.

tooth POINT /tuːθ/ *n* [C usually pl] *pl* **teeth** /tiːθ/ any of the row of metal or plastic points which stick out from the edge of a tool or piece of equipment, such as a COMB, SAW or ZIP • PIC› **Tools**

tooth·ache /ˈtuːθ·eɪk/ *n* (a) pain caused by something being wrong with one of your teeth • *I've got a terrible toothache.* [C] • *The broken tooth kept her awake all night with toothache.* [U] • LP› **Feelings and pains**

tooth·brush /ˈtuːθ·brʌʃ/ *n* [C] a small brush with a long handle which you use to clean your teeth • PIC› **Brush**

tooth·comb /£ˈtuːθ·kəʊm, $-koʊm/ *n* See **with a fine-tooth comb** at FINE THIN

tooth·paste /ˈtuːθ·peɪst/ *n* [U] a thick creamy substance which you put onto a TOOTHBRUSH to clean your teeth • *a tube of toothpaste* • *spearmint-flavoured toothpaste* • *The child squeezed too much toothpaste onto her brush.*

tooth·pick /ˈtuːθ·pɪk/ *n* [C] a small thin pointed stick of wood, plastic or metal which can be used for removing pieces of food from between the teeth, esp. after a meal • PIC› **Pick**

tooth·some /ˈtuːθ·səm/ *adj* (esp. of food) attractive or pleasant • *Lamb casserole makes an excellent family dish, toothsome in flavour and robust in texture.*

tooth·y /ˈtuː·θi/ *adj* See at TOOTH MOUTH

toot·le /£ˈtuː·tl̩, $-t̬l̩/ *v* [I always + adv/prep] *infml* to go, esp. to drive, slowly • *The car in front was just tootling along admiring the scenery.*

toot·sie FOOT, **toot·sy** /ˈtʊt·si/ *n* [C] *infml* (used by or to children) a toe or a foot • *Don't get your tootsies cold.*

toot·sie WOMAN /ˈtʊt·si/, **toots** /tʊts/ *n* [C] *esp. Am infml* a woman • *That might have worked for you once, tootsie, but not any more.* [as form of address] • *See you later, toots. I'll be home around eight.* [as form of address] • *She was a good-looking tootsie.* • LP› **Titles and forms of address**

top HIGHEST PART /£tɒp, $tɑːp/ *n* [C] the highest place or part • *There was a picture of the climbers reaching the top* **of** *the mountain.* • *She waited for me* **at the top of** *the stairs.* • *The bird sat* **on the top of** *the tree.* • *There were flags* **on** *the* **tops of** *many of the buildings.* • *The top* (= flat surface) *of the table/desk was badly scratched.* • *There was a pile of books* **on top of** (= on) *the table.* • *Put the letter* **on top of** *that pile of books, where it can be seen easily.* • *(fig.) They've finally*

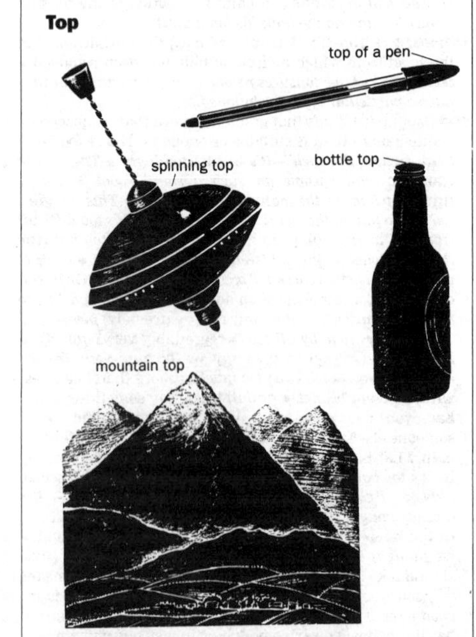

got **on top of** *the situation* (= they have control of it). • *They cleaned the house* **from top to bottom** (= completely). • *A woman came into the room dressed in red* **from top to toe.** • *She was feeling* **on top of the world** (= very happy). See also **on top of** at TOP ALSO. • *(Br infml disapproving)* Someone who is **off** their **top** is not reasonable or acting with good judgment. • *(infml) "What's the capital of Mauritania?" "I couldn't tell you* **off the top of** *my* **head** (= from the knowledge I have), *but I could go and look it up."* • *(Br and Aus infml)* If something is or someone goes

over the top (*abbreviation* **OTT**) too much attention or effort is given to something, esp. in an uncontrolled way: *I thought the decorations were* **way** (=very) *over the top.* ○ *The speech was a bit OTT.* ○ *I thought his comments were rather OTT.* ○ *He made a dreadful fuss about the seating arrangements, but afterwards I think he realised he'd* **gone** *over the top.* ● *She shouted his name* **at the top of** *her* **voice** (=very loudly). ● A **top-down approach/strategy** is one in which decisions are made by a few people in authority rather than by the people who are influenced by the decision. ● See also CLIFFTOP; HILLTOP; MOUNTAINTOP; ROOFTOP; TREETOPS. Compare BOTTOM [LOWEST PART]; SUMMIT [HIGHEST POINT]. ● [PIC]〉 **Top**

top /£tɒp, $tɑːp/ *adj* [before n; not gradable] ● *There's a dirty mark on the top left-hand corner of the photo.* ● *The offices are on the top floor of the building.* ● *We live in the top apartment.* ● *As deputy leader, she was in sight of* **the top rung of the ladder** (= the highest position)

top *obj* /£tɒp, $tɑːp/ *v* [T] **-pp-** ● *The record topped the charts* (=sold the largest number of recordings) *for five weeks.* ● *She topped the bill* (=was the most important act in the show). ● *The dessert was topped* **(off) with** (=had on its surface, esp. as a decoration) *cream and pieces of fruit.* See also TOPPING. ● *(fig., esp. Am and Aus) She topped* **off** *her performance* **with** *a dazzling encore.* [M] ● If you top **and tail** esp. beans or GOOSEBERRIES you cut the hard parts at each end off when you prepare them for cooking. ● To **top** something **up** is to add something to it until a limit is reached, esp. to add liquid in order to fill to the top a container which is already partly full: *I'll just top up the water in the vases.* ○ *Students are able to take out loans to top up their grants.* ○ *Shall I top up your drink?* ○ *(infml) Can I top you up* (=put more drink into your glass or cup)*?* ○ *Have you finished your coffee – would you like a* **top-up***?* ○ *The bank agreed to £500 as a* **top-up** *loan.*

top·most /£'tɒp·məust, $'tɑːp·moust/ *adj* [before n; not gradable] ● *We couldn't reach the apples on the topmost* (=highest) *branches.*

top·ping /£'tɒp·ɪŋ, $'tɑː·pɪŋ/ *n* ● A topping is a substance, esp. a sauce, cream or pieces of food, which is put on top of other food to give extra flavour and to make it look attractive: *pizza topping* ○ *chocolate cream topping* [U] ○ *a topping of toasted almonds* [C]

top [UPPER PART] /£tɒp, $tɑːp/ *adj* [before n; not gradable] in the part nearest to the highest part; in the upper part ● *Her name came in the top half of the list.* ● *The top few steps were damaged and broken.* ● *As a chess player he's among the top 10% in the country.* ● *Top* **management** (=the people in charge of a company) *don't appreciate how the ordinary employees feel.* ● If something is **top-heavy**, it has more weight in the higher part than in the lower part and will not balance correctly: *(fig.) a top-heavy organizational structure*

top /£tɒp, $tɑːp/ *n* [C] ● A top is any piece of light clothing worn by women on the part of the body above the waist: *a skimpy/summer/silk top* ○ *cotton skirts with matching/coordinating tops* ○ *an evening top* ● [PIC]〉 **Top**

top·less /£'tɒp·ləs, $'tɑː·pləs/ *adj, adv* [not gradable] ● Topless means wearing nothing on the upper part of your body from the waist to the neck: *a topless dancer* ● *Many women now* **go** *topless on European beaches.*

tops /£tɒps, $tɑːps/ *pl n* ● The parts of a plant which grow above the ground are the tops: *We fed the rabbit some beetroot tops.* ○ *If you put carrot tops in water they start to grow.*

top [BEST] /£tɒp, $tɑːp/ *adj, adv* [not gradable] (in the position of being) most important or successful; best ● *England is my top choice for a holiday.* ● If you **are**/*(Br)* **come** top (of the class), you are the student who got the best results: *Her parents were pleased that she'd come top of the class.* ○ *Sam was top* **at/in** *Science and Lynn got top marks* **in** *Technology.* ● Top people, organizations or activities are the most important or successful ones: *top athletes/executives/earners/fashion designers* ○ *top jobs* ○ *top universities* ● Top is used with many different words to mean best: *top-class* ● *top-ranking* ● *The train thundered through the station* **at top speed** (=as fast as it could go). ● *(Br) Paul's back* **on top form**/*(Am and Aus)* **in top form** (=feeling or doing things as well as possible) *after his illness.* ● The **top brass** are the people with the highest positions of authority, esp. in the armed forces. ● *infml* Someone who is **top dog** has achieved a position of authority or SUPERIORITY over other people. ● *He's one of out* **top-flight** (=best) *engineers.* ● A **top-level** activity is one in which the most important people in an organization or country take part: *top-level talks/negotiations/discussions* ● *infml That restaurant's really* **top-notch** (=very good). ● If you give something **top priority** you treat it as very urgent and deal with it immediately: *Give this report top priority.* ○ *This case has top priority.* ○ *a top-priority decision* ● Something which is **top secret** or **top security** is very secret and must not be told or shown to anyone outside a particular group of people: *a top-secret military research project* ○ *These papers are top secret.* ○ *a top-security briefing* ○ *top-security information channels* ● A **top-security** prison or hospital is one which is extremely well guarded because it has dangerous people inside it. ● The **top ten** is the set of ten recordings which has sold the most copies in the previous week, or *(fig.)* a set of most popular things: *Their record has been in the Top Ten for three weeks.* ○ *(fig.) 'Casablanca' is in my top ten films./'Casablanca' is one of my top ten films.* ● *(Br infml) I'd say she earns about £12 000 a year* **top whack** (=at the most). ● *"Top Cat"* (title of a cartoon, 1961-) ● *"Top of the Pops"* (title of a British television popular music show, 1964-)

top /£tɒp, $tɑːp/ *n* [U] ● *At forty he was* **at** *the top* (=most important point) **of** *his profession.* ● *Life* **at** *the top* (=in an important position) *is exciting but stressful.*

top *obj* /£tɒp, $tɑːp/ *v* [T] **-pp-** ● *"They've offered me £1000." "I'm afraid we can't top* (=offer more or better than) *that."* ● *She topped my suggestion* **with** *an even better one of her own.*

tops /£tɒps, $tɑːps/ *n* [U] *dated* ● **The tops** is the best: *You're the tops.*

top [LID] /£tɒp, $tɑːp/ *n* [C] the cover or lid used to close a container ● *a screw-on top* ● *a plastic/metal top* ● *a bottle top* ● *I had to prise the top off the paint tin.* ● *The top of the jar had been screwed on too tightly.* ● *Who's left the top off the toothpaste tube again?* ● *I can't find the top* (=cover for the point) *of my pen.* ● [PIC]〉 **Top**

top [TOY] /£tɒp, $tɑːp/ *n* [C] a **spinning top,** see at SPIN [TURN] ● *(dated infml)* Someone who is sleeping **like a top** is sleeping very deeply. ● [PIC]〉 **Top**

top [ALSO] /£tɒp, $tɑːp/ *n* [U] **on top of** in addition to (esp. something unpleasant) ● *We missed the train, and on top of that we had to wait for two hours for the next one.*

top *obj* [KILL] /£tɒp, $tɑːp/ *v* [T] **-pp-** *Br slang* to kill (esp. yourself) ● *I heard she'd topped herself.*

to·paz /£'təu·pæz, $'tou-/ *n* a transparent yellow precious stone which is often used in jewellery ● *a necklace of topaz* [U] ● *a casket full of diamonds, emeralds and topazes* [C] ● *a topaz ring*

top·coat /£'tɒp·kəut, $'tɑːp·kout/ *n* a layer of paint put onto a surface over another layer, or the type of paint used to do this ● *a gallon of topcoat* [U] ● *I usually give the doors one undercoat and two topcoats.* [C] ● Compare UNDERCOAT.

to·pee /£'təu·piː, $'tou-/, **to·pi** /£'təu·piː, $'tou-/ *n* [C] a PITH HELMET

top hat, *infml* **top·per** *n* [C] a tall black or grey hat worn by men on some formal occasions ● *"I'm puttin' on my top hat,/ Tyin' up my white tie,/ Brushin' off my tails"* (from the song *Top Hat, White Tie and Tails* written by Irving Berlin, 1935) ● [PIC]〉 **Hats**

to·pi·a·ry /£'təu·pjᵊr·i, $'tou·pi·er-/ *n* [U] *specialized* the art of cutting bushes into attractive shapes, esp. of animals and birds ● [PIC]〉 **Garden**

top·ic /£'tɒp·ɪk, $'tɑː·pɪk/ *n* [C] a subject which is discussed, written about or studied ● *Our discussion ranged over various topics, such as acid rain and the hole in the ozone layer.* ● Ⓔ

top·i·cal /£'tɒp·ɪ·kᵊl, $'tɑː·pɪ-/ *adj* of interest at the present time; relating to things which are happening at present ● *The discussion focused on topical issues in medicine, including the question of being able to choose the sex of a child.* ● *The material had clearly been chosen some time ago, and it was disappointing to find no up-to-date or topical content.* ● *The book contains much of topical interest and has an extensive bibliography.* ● ⒼⓇ

top·i·cal·i·ty /£ˌtɒp·ɪ'kæl·ə·ti, $ˌtɑː·pɪ'kæl·ə·ṭi/ *n* [U] ● *Tuesday's news report of an another baby mix-up case sadly lent topicality to last night's TV drama on a similar subject.*

top·i·cal·ly /£'tɒp·ɪ·kli, $'tɑː·pɪ-/ *adv* ● *She began her speech, topically enough, with a reference to the recent fighting.*

top·knot /£'tɒp·nɒt, $'tɑːp·nɑːt/ *n* [C] long hair tied into a small lump on the top part of the back of the head

top·less /£'tɒp·ləs, $'tɑː·pləs/ *adj, adv* See at TOP [UPPER PART]

top·most /£'tɒp·məust, $'tɑːp·moust/ *adj* [before n] See at TOP [HIGHEST PART]

to·pog·raph·y /£təʊ'pɒg·rə·fi, $tə'pɑː·grə-/ *n* [U] *specialized* the physical appearance of the natural features of an area of land, esp. the shape of its surface

to·po·graph·i·cal /£,tɒp·əʊ'græf·ɪ·kᵊl, $,tɑː·pə-/ *adj* [not gradable] *specialized*

to·po·graph·i·cally /£,tɒp·əʊ'græf·ɪ·kli, $,tɑː·pə-/ *adv* [not gradable] *specialized*

to·po·graph·er /£təʊ'pɒg·rə·fəʳ, $tə'pɑː·grə·fɚ/ *n* [C] *specialized*

top·per /£'tɒp·əʳ, $'tɑː·pɚ/ *n infml for* a TOP HAT

top·ple /£'tɒp·l̩, $'tɑː·pl̩/ *v* to (cause to) lose balance and fall down • *The statue of the dictator was toppled* **(over)** *by the crowds.* [T] • *The tree toppled* **over**/*toppled and fell.* [I] • *(fig.) The church was prominently involved in the struggle that toppled the dictatorship.* [T]

top·soil /£'tɒp·sɔɪl, $'tɑːp-/ *n* [U] (the earth which forms) the top layer of ground in which plants grow • *It takes centuries to build up a centimetre or two of topsoil.* • Compare SUBSOIL.

top·spin /£'tɒp·spɪn, $'tɑːp-/ *n* [U] a forward turning movement of a ball as it travels through the air

top·sy–tur·vy /£,tɒp·si'tɜː·vi, $,tɑːp·si'tɜːr-/ *adj, adv infml* (in a state of being) confused, not well organized or giving importance to unexpected things; upside down • *The government's topsy-turvy priorities mean that spending on education remains low.* • *For a few weeks after the accident her world was* **turned** *topsy-turvy.*

To·rah /£'tɔː·rə, $'toʊ·rə/ *n* [U] **the Torah** the holy book of the Jews

torch *Br and Aus* /£tɔːtʃ, $tɔːrtʃ/, *esp. Am* **flash·light** *n* [C] a small light which is held in the hand and which receives its power from stored electricity, esp. a BATTERY • *She* **shone** *the torch through the window and the beam of light picked out a small box in the middle of the dark empty room.* • *People had been buying up torches, torch batteries and candles because of the predicted strike by electricity workers.* • A torch is also a thick stick with material which burns tied to the top of it in order to give light: *a flaming/blazing torch* ○ *The runner carried the* **Olympic** *torch into the cheering stadium.* ○ *The crowd brandished torches.* ○ *It took a year to restore order in the city, by which time many buildings had been* **put to the** *torch* (=burned intentionally). • *(fig.) The torch illuminating* (=good situation influencing) *Latin America at the moment is that of liberty and democracy.* • *(fig.) Like so many black fathers of his era, he was dedicated to* **passing** *the torch* **of** (=giving the advantages of) *education to his children through hard work and sacrifice.* • Torch is also *Am for* BLOWLAMP. • [PIC] Lights

torch *obj* /£tɔːtʃ, $tɔːrtʃ/ *v* [T] *infml* • To torch a building or other large thing is to burn it intentionally and usually illegally: *They smashed a side door to get in and then torched the warehouse when they had taken what they wanted.* ○ *The kids torched the stacks of paper.*

torch·light /£'tɔːtʃ·laɪt, $'tɔːrtʃ-/ *n* [U] the light of a TORCH • *Staff evacuated passengers from the underground train* **by** *torchlight through the tunnel to the station.* • *I saw the blade of an open knife shine in his hand in the torchlight.*

torch·light /£'tɔːtʃ·laɪt, $'tɔːrtʃ-/, **torch·lit** /£'tɔːtʃ·lɪt, $'tɔːrtʃ-/ *adj* [before n; not gradable] • A torchlight event is lit by burning torches: *a torchlight/torchlit procession*

tore /£tɔːʳ, $tɔːr/ *past simple of* TEAR

tor·e·a·dor /£'tɒr·i·ə·dɔːʳ, $'tɔːr·i·ə·dɔːr/ *n* [C] a person, usually a man, who takes part in a BULLFIGHT riding a horse • Compare MATADOR; PICADOR.

tor·ment /£'tɔː·ment, $'tɔːr-/ *n* great mental suffering and unhappiness, or great physical pain • *The family said they had* **endured** *years of torment and abuse from neighbours.* [U] • *After five years of imprisonment in appalling conditions he still had no idea when his lonely torment would end.* [U] • *At the question she started to sob, clearly revealing her* **inner** *torment.* [U] • *There's no greater torment than waiting for the result of medical tests.* [U] • *He spent the night* **in** *torment, trying to decide what was the best thing to do.* [U] • *After three days* **in** *torment, she decided it was time to visit the dentist.* [U] • A torment is something or someone that causes great suffering or annoyance: *The tax forms were an annual torment* **to** *him.* [C]

tor·ments /£'tɔː·ments, $'tɔːr-/ *pl n* • *mental torments* (=torment) • *Nothing can describe the torments* (=torment) *we* **went through** *while we were waiting for news.*

tor·ment *obj* /£tɔː'ment, $tɔːr-/ *v* [T] • *The animals are tormented* (=caused to suffer) *mercilessly by flies, mosquitoes and other insects.* • *The camera turned to focus on a group of women whose faces were tormented* **by/with** (=showing that they were suffering) *grief.* • *The question tormented me* (=caused me to worry) *all day – did I remember to lock the door when I left the house?*

tor·men·tor /£tɔː'men·təʳ, $tɔːr'men·tɚ/ *n* [C] • *A day came when she couldn't tolerate his cruelty anymore – she took a knife and stabbed her tormentor.*

torn /£tɔːn, $tɔːrn/ *past participle of* TEAR • If you are **torn between** two possibilities, you find it very difficult to choose between them: *I don't know what to do tonight – I'm torn between staying in and watching a video and going to Erika's party.*

tor·na·do /£tɔː'neɪ·dəʊ, $tɔːr'neɪ·doʊ/, *Am infml also* **twist·er** *n* [C] *pl* **tornados** or **tornadoes** a strong dangerous wind which forms itself into an upside-down spinning cone and is able to destroy buildings as it moves across the ground

tor·pe·do /£tɔː'piː·dəʊ, $tɔːr'piː·doʊ/ *n pl* **torpedoes** a long thin bomb which travels under water in order to destroy the ship at which it is aimed • *The Navy's latest submarine entered service three years late and virtually unable to* **fire** *its torpedoes.* [C] • *Both ships were sunk* **by** *torpedo.* [U]

tor·pe·do *obj* /£tɔː'piː·dəʊ, $tɔːr'piː·doʊ/ *v* [T] he/she/it **torpedoes**, **torpedoing**, *past* **torpedoed** • *After being torpedoed and badly damaged by* (=hit and damaged by a torpedo fired from) *a submarine, the ship made its way slowly into the nearest port.* • *(fig. infml) Efforts to reduce the budget deficit have been torpedoed* (=destroyed) *by a refusal to face the political consequences of raising taxes.*

tor·pid /£'tɔː·pɪd, $'tɔːr-/ *adj fml* not active; moving or thinking slowly, esp. as a result of feeling sleepy or being lazy • *The meeting developed a torpid character as the afternoon wore on – people stopped asking questions and stifled yawns.* • *If you have a sudden loss of cabin pressure at 20 000 feet, people become torpid, experience increased stupor and lose consciousness in 10 minutes.*

tor·pid·ly /£'tɔː·pɪd·li, $'tɔːr-/ *adv fml*

tor·por /£'tɔː·pəʳ, $'tɔːr·pɚ/, **tor·pid·i·ty** /£tɔː'pɪd·ɪ·ti, $tɔːr'pɪd·ɪ·t̬i/ *n* [U] *fml* • *The campaign recently has shown new energy after being widely criticized for summer-long torpor* (=lack of activity). • *(specialized)* Torpor is the state of reduced activity that some animals experience during the winter.

torque /£tɔːk, $tɔːrk/ *n* [U] *specialized* a force which causes ROTATION (=a turning movement) • *In a car engine, more torque means better acceleration.* • *The mechanism can withstand 1200 inch lb of torque.*

tor·rent /£'tɒr·ᵊnt, $'tɔːr-/ *n* a (too) large amount, esp. one which seems to be uncontrollable • *He let out* **a** *torrent* **of** *abuse/angry words* [U] • *They are worried that the flow/trickle/stream of tourists could swell into* **an** *unmanageable torrent if there are no controls.* [U] • A torrent is also a large amount of fast-moving water: *Intense storms in the mountains of the Massif Central can turn the river into a* **rushing** *torrent.* [C] ○ *Street by street, they've been improving the drainage so that rainstorms don't turn the roads into* **raging** *torrents.* [C]

tor·rents /£'tɒr·ᵊnts, $'tɔːr-/ *pl n* • *torrents* (=a torrent) *of letters/requests* • *torrents of rain* • *Applications for tickets came in* **in** *torrents after the commercial appeared on TV.* • *The rain came down/fell* **in** *torrents.*

tor·ren·tial /£tə'ren·tʃᵊl, $tɔː'rent·ʃᵊl/ *adj* • Torrential is used to refer to very heavy rain: *torrential rain/rains* • *a torrential downpour/storm*

tor·rid [WEATHER] /£'tɒr·ɪd, $'tɔːr·ɪd/ *adj fml* extremely hot and dry • *In the torrid heat of May, no-one felt the need to walk far or indulge in strenuous exercise.* • *His most recent book is set at the turn of the century in a torrid port on Colombia's Caribbean coast.*

tor·rid [EMOTIONS] /£'tɒr·ɪd, $'tɔːr·ɪd/ *adj* involving strong feelings • *His weekly column has covered such torrid topics as rape, child molestation, drug abuse and serial killers.* • Torrid is often used of strong sexual feelings: *The film ends with a torrid love scene.* • *(Br and Aus)* If you **have/give** someone **a torrid time**, you (cause someone to) experience a period of very difficult conditions: *The company's building services division is having a torrid time in the* *depressed construction market.* ◦ *The Oldham team gave Liverpool a torrid time early on in the game.*

tor·sion /£ˈtɔː·ʃᵊn, $ˈtɔːr-/ *n* [U] *specialized* the act of twisting, the force which causes twisting or the state of being twisted • *Excessive torsion on the coupling will cause metal fatigue.* • *Some organs in the body, especially the testicles, may develop torsion.*

tor·so /£ˈtɔː·səʊ, $ˈtɔːr·soʊ/ *n* [C] *pl* **torsos** the human body without head, arms or legs, or a statue representing this • *The air bag mounted in the steering wheel inflates on impact, and provides a cushion for the head and torso.* • *We bought a postcard of the famous marble torso in the museum shop.* • [PIC]› **Sculpture**

tor·til·la /£tɔːˈtiː·ə, $tɔːrˈtiː·jə/ *n* [C] a type of thin round Mexican bread made from MAIZE flour and eggs • *Rolled and filled tortillas can be covered with sauce and cheese then baked until melted or deep fried into crisp parcels.* • **Tortilla chips** are small fried pieces of tortilla, often eaten with a spicy sauce.

tor·toise /£ˈtɔː·təs, $ˈtɔːr·t̬əs/ *n* [C] an animal with a thick shell into which it can move its head and legs for protection. It eats plants, moves very slowly and sleeps during the winter. • [PIC]› **Reptiles and amphibians**

tor·toise·shell /£ˈtɔː·təʃ·ʃel, $ˈtɔːr·t̬əs-/ *n* [U] the hard shell of a TURTLE which is yellow, orange and brown and which is used to make decorative items, or an artificial substance made to look like this • *a tortoiseshell comb* • *glasses with tortoiseshell frames* • A **tortoiseshell butterfly** has yellow, orange and brown marks on its wings and a **tortoiseshell cat** has similar marks on its fur.

tor·tu·ous /£ˈtɔː·tʃu·əs, $ˈtɔːr-/ *adj* with many turns and changes of direction; not direct or simple • *He claims the tortuous* **route** *through back streets avoids the worst of the traffic.* • *The path to peace seems at last to be clear, although it may be a long and tortuous one.* • *For many adopted children finding their natural mother can be a particularly tortuous process.* • *The plot of the play is so tortuous it is hard to remember just who is related to whom.*

tor·tu·ous·ly /£ˈtɔː·tʃu·ə·sli, $ˈtɔːr-/ *adv*

tor·tu·ous·ness /£ˈtɔː·tʃu·ə·snəs, $ˈtɔːr-/ *n* [U]

tor·ture /£ˈtɔː·tʃəʳ, $ˈtɔːr·tʃɚ/ *n* (the act of causing) great physical pain in order to persuade someone to do something or to give information, or as an act of cruelty to a person or animal • *About half of the prisoners were murdered or died after torture or starvation.* [U] • *In a number of cases, senior army officers had carried out the torture.* [U] • *The book suggests that women are more used to pain than men, as so are not as likely to divulge secrets* **under** *torture.* [U] • *The report describes deprivation of sleep, threats about family members and various forms of* **mental** *torture.* [U] • *In the castle is a medieval torture* **chamber** *still furnished with the original* **instruments of** *torture, such as racks and thumbscrews.* [U] • *(fig.) The rush-hour traffic was* **sheer** *torture as usual.* [U] • *(fig.) We suffered the twin tortures of heat and boredom as we waited in a long line for our turn to come.* [C]

tor·ture *obj* /£ˈtɔː·tʃəʳ, $ˈtɔːr·tʃɚ/ *v* [T] • *Smith was accused of kidnapping and torturing two men and attempting to kidnap another.* • *It is claimed that the officers tortured a man* **to death** *in 1983 in a city police station.* • *(fig.) She was tortured by the memory of their last conversation.* • *(fig.) He tortured* **himself** *for years* **with** *the thought that he could have stopped the boy from running into the road.*

tor·tured /£ˈtɔː·tʃəd, $ˈtɔːr·tʃɚd/ *adj* • Tortured means involving suffering and difficulty: *the country's tortured past* • *the tortured history of race relations*

tor·tur·er /£ˈtɔː·tʃᵊr·əʳ, $ˈtɔːr·tʃɚ·ɚ/ *n* [C]

To·ry /£ˈtɔː·ri, $ˈtɔːr·i/ *n, adj* [not gradable] (a member) of the British Conservative Party • *a lifelong Tory* • *local Tories* [C] • **The** *Tories* (= the Tory party) *have dropped in the opinion poll ratings.* • *Tory voters/supporters* • *a Tory MP*

To·ry·i·sm /£ˈtɔː·ri·ɪ·zᵊm, $ˈtɔːr·i-/ *n* [U] • *The contrast between the Toryism of the post-war years and the attitudes of today's Conservatives is striking.*

tosh /£tɒʃ, $tɑːʃ/ *n* [U] *infml dated* nonsense • *That's all tosh.* • *It's just a lot of tosh.*

toss *(obj)* /£tɒs, $tɑːs/ *v* to throw (esp. something light) carelessly • *He had carelessly tossed the clothes into the machine without checking the pockets.* [T] • *His horse was startled by something and tossed him onto the ground.* [T] • *He tossed the paper away over his shoulder.* [T] • *Andrew tossed the ball quickly* **to** *his brother.* ◦ *Andrew tossed him the ball.* [+ two objects] • *Within minutes, the hurricane ripped up greenhouses, tossed a 63-foot trailer 50 yards and destroyed homes.* [T] • *(fig.) He saw Florida as a frontier state where all the rules had been tossed* **aside** (= got rid of) *in the scramble to settle, to build, to prosper.* [M] • *(fig.) That much money is not to be tossed* **away** (= spent or lost) *lightly.* [M] • *(fig.) One thought being tossed* **around** (= considered by many people) *is that a larger programme of saving might be stretched over a couple of years.* [M] • If you toss your hair or a part of your body you move it up and back suddenly: *The girl tossed back her hair.* [M] ◦ *The horse tossed its head/mane.* [T] • When you toss food you shake or mix small pieces of it together with a sauce or DRESSING: *Any leftover sauce can be tossed* **with** *plain cooked cubed chicken and water chestnuts for a tasty salad.* [T] ◦ *a tossed salad* ◦ *carrots tossed* **in** *butter* • You toss a **pancake** by moving the pan in which it is cooking quickly into the air so that the pancake comes out and turns over before falling back into the pan. [T] • If you **toss and turn** you move about from side to side or turn a lot in bed, esp. because you cannot sleep: *I was tossing and turning all night.* • When you toss **(up)** or **toss a coin** you throw the coin up into the air and guess which side will land facing up as a way of deciding which of two things you will do: *"I'll toss you* **(for** *it) – heads or tails?" "Tails!" "It's heads, so I win!"* [T] ◦ *They tossed* **(up) for** *the last ticket.* [I] ◦ *Let's toss a coin to see who'll go first.* • *(infml)* If you describe a situation as a **toss-up** you mean that either of two possibilities are equally likely: *It was* **a** *toss-up which company would get the contract.* ◦ *It's* **a** *toss-up* **between** *Angela and Moira for the editor's job.*

toss /£tɒs, $tɑːs/ *n* [C] • *"I don't care," she replied with a toss of her head.* • *If a coin is tossed only twice, then there is a one-in-two chance that the tosses will be either both heads or both tails.* • If you **win/lose the toss** you guess correctly/wrongly which side of a coin will be facing up when it lands on the ground after being thrown. • *(Br infml)* If you don't **give/care a toss** about something, you have no interest in it: *She doesn't give a toss what other people think about her clothes.* • [PIC]› **Food preparation**

toss off *obj* [DO QUICKLY], **toss** *obj* **off** *v adv* [M] *infml* to do (something) quickly, esp. in a careless way or with little effort • *She tossed off a reply to the letter before she left for the meeting.* [T]

toss *(obj)* **off** [SEXUALLY EXCITE] *v adv* [T/I] *Br and Aus taboo slang* to excite the sexual organs of (yourself or someone else) using your hands; to MASTURBATE

toss·er /£ˈtɒs·əʳ, $ˈtɑː·sɚ/ *n* [C] *Br slang* • A tosser is a stupid or unpleasant person: *Barry's such a tosser.*

tot [CHILD] /£tɒt, $tɑːt/ *n* [C] *infml* a small child • *These are good strong toys for* **tiny** *tots.* • [LP]› **Age**

tot [DRINK] /£tɒt, $tɑːt/ *n* [C] a small drink of alcohol • *a tot* **of** *whisky/rum* • *He poured them each a generous tot.*

tot up *(obj)*, **tot** *(obj)* **up** /£tɒt, $tɑːt/ *v adv infml* to add up (numbers, amounts etc.), or to have a particular total when added up • *She quickly totted up our bill and added an amount for the waiter.* [M] • *That tots up* **to** *£20.* [I]

to·tal [AMOUNT] /£ˈtəʊ·tᵊl, $ˈtoʊ·t̬ᵊl/ *n* [C] the amount obtained when several smaller amounts are added together • *She got 40 000 votes, more than the combined totals of her two popular rivals.* • *Another 17 airlines are now operating from the airport, increasing the total to 87.* • *At that time of day, cars with only one occupant accounted for almost 80% of the total.* • **A** *total* **of** *21 horses was entered for the race.* • *Last week forty people* **in total** *came to the advice centre, but Thursday was the busiest day with eighteen attending.*

to·tal /£ˈtəʊ·tᵊl, $ˈtoʊ·t̬ᵊl/ *adj* [before n; not gradable] • *Total losses after all charges were $800.* • *At a total cost of only £300, we thought the estimate for the work was good value.* • *Australia's total wine exports were half that amount only five years ago.*

to·tal *(obj)* /£ˈtəʊ·tᵊl, $ˈtoʊ·t̬ᵊl/ *v* **-ll-** or *Am usually* **-l-** • *This is the eighth volume in the series, which totals* (= has as its complete amount) *21 volumes in all.* [L only + n] • *We totalled* **(up)** *the money we had each earned* (= added the amounts together), *and then shared it equally among the three of us.* [T]

to·tal·i·ty /£təʊˈtæl·ə·ti, $toʊˈtæl·ə·t̬i/ *n* [U] • *It isn't the individual amounts that count, it's the totality of what's spent that we need to consider.* • *It's a large collection* **in its** *totality* (= considered all together).

to·tal [VERY GREAT] /£ˈtəʊ·tᵊl, $ˈtoʊ·t̬ᵊl/ *adj* [not gradable] very great or to the largest degree possible • *total secrecy* • *a total disregard for their feelings* • *total silence* • *It was a total surprise.* • *The organization of the event was a total* *shambles* (= very bad). • *The collapse, when it came, was total.*

to·tal·ly /£'təʊ·təl·i, $'toʊ·t̬əl-/ *adv* [not gradable] • *Her second husband is totally different from Mark.* • *I totally agree with you.* • *We oppose these proposals totally.* • LP> **Very, completely**

to·tal·i·ty /£təʊ'tæl·ə·ti, $toʊ'tæl·ə·t̬i/ *n* [U] *fml* • *He lives for his work – it's the totality of his life.* • *We need to consider the situation* **in its** *totality* (= as a complete whole).

to·tal·i·ta·ri·an /£təʊˌtæl·ɪ'teə·ri·ən, $toʊˌtæl·ə'ter·i-/ *adj disapproving* of or being a political system in which those in power have complete control and do not allow people freely to oppose them • *a totalitarian regime/state* • *In totalitarian systems, everyone tends to suspect everyone else, even members of their own circle of family and friends.*

to·tal·i·ta·ri·an·i·sm /£təʊˌtæl·ɪ'teə·ri·ə·nɪ·zəm, $toʊˌtæl·ə'ter·i-/ *n* [U] *disapproving* • *World War II destroyed the fascist regimes of Germany, Italy and Japan, but of course it did not eliminate totalitarianism from the world.*

tote *obj* CARRY /£təʊt, $toʊt/ *v* [T] *infml* to carry (esp. something heavy or awkward) • *Wherever you go these days, there is someone toting a mobile phone.* • *Two fathers toted* **along** *video cameras to record their children's first day at school.* [M] • *She usually toted the baby* **around** *in a backpack.* • *The building was surrounded with bodyguards toting sub-machine* **guns**. • **Gun**-*toting security men were posted at all the entrances.* • A **tote bag** is a large strong bag.

tote RACING /£təʊt, $toʊt/ *n* [U] **the tote** *specialized* a system of putting BETS on horses or dogs in a race

to·tem /£'təʊ·təm, $'toʊ·t̬əm/ *n* [C] an object which is respected by a group of people, esp. for religious reasons • *Television is sometimes seen as a totem of modern society.* • A **totem pole** is a tall wooden pole with symbols cut or painted on it, which is part of the tradition of the Native Americans of the west coast of Canada and the northern USA.

to·tem·ic /£təʊ'tem·ɪk, $toʊ-/ *adj* • *The religion of ancient Egypt emerged from the worship of tribal deities represented as totemic animals.*

to·to /£'təʊ·təʊ, $'toʊ·t̬oʊ/ *n* [U] See IN TOTO

tot·ter /£'tɒt·əʳ, $'tɑː·t̬ɚ/ *v* [I] to move or walk in a way that is not well controlled, is shaking or is making small movements from side to side as if about to fall • *I could see the pile of books tottering but couldn't reach them before they fell.* • *She tottered unsteadily down the stairs in her high-heeled shoes.* • *(fig.) The industry has tottered from crisis to crisis now for two decades.* • *(fig.) This major change is occurring just as old family support systems are tottering towards extinction.* • Compare STAGGER MOVE; TEETER.

tot·ter·ing /£'tɒt·ər·ɪŋ, $'tɑː·t̬ɚ-/ *adj* [not gradable] • *She walked slowly with tottering steps.* • *(fig.) It was the last major decision of a tottering government.*

tot·ter·y /£'tɒt·ər·i, $'tɑː·t̬ɚ-/ *adj* • *a tottery chair* • *a tottery old man*

tou·can /£'tuː·kən, $-kæn/ *n* [C] a S American bird that has a brightly coloured beak

touch *(obj)* USE FINGERS /tʌtʃ/ *v* to move esp. the fingers or the whole hand quickly and lightly onto and off (something) • *That paint is wet – don't touch (it).* [I/T] • *He touched the girl* **on** *the arm to get her attention.* [T] • *The child touched the worm* **with** *a twig.* [T] • *The driver just touched the brake* (= put his foot on it lightly) *and the car swerved.* [T] • *(fig.) The setting sun touched the trees* **with** *red* (= made them appear red for a short time). [T] • *(fig.) Tragedy touched their lives* (= they experienced it) *when their son was 16.* • *(infml)* If you say you do not touch a food or drink, you mean that you never eat or drink it: *No thanks, I never touch chocolate/alcohol.* [T] ○ *Honestly, I haven't touched* **a drop** (= drunk any alcohol) *all night.* [T] • *(Br) I wouldn't* **touch it with a barge pole**/*(Am also)* **touch it with a ten-foot pole** (= I wouldn't buy it or be involved with it in any way). • If a situation is **touch-and-go**, it is uncertain: *The doctor says that it is touch-and-go* **whether** *the patient will survive.* • Something which **touches a (raw) nerve** makes you remember something which makes you feel unhappy or uncomfortable: *The newspaper article touched a raw nerve – people still resent the closure of the local school.* • *The talk was about educational opportunities for adults, and the speaker also* **touched on/upon** (= spoke briefly about) *sources of finance.* • *(Br infml) She claimed that he had tried to* **touch her up** *(Am* **feel** *her* **up***)* (= touch her in a sexual way without her wanting him to). See also TOUCH UP. • *(infml)* If you say **touch wood** you are hoping for a good result or good luck: *The deal will be agreed on Wednesday, touch wood.* • *(Am and Aus)* **Touch football** is an informal type of football in which play stops if a player puts their hand onto the person who has the ball. • *(trademark)* A **Touch-Tone phone** is a telephone which produces different sounds when the different buttons with numbers on them are pressed. Touch-Tone telephones can be used for exchanging information electronically by telephone: *You can call your bank and perform a transaction using a Touch-Tone phone.* • *I'm learning to* **touch-type** (= to use a keyboard without looking at the keys).

touch /tʌtʃ/ *n* • Touch is the ability to know what something is like by feeling it with the fingers: *the sense of touch* [U] ○ *I found the right coin in the dark by touch.* [U] ○ *The material was soft* **to the/my touch** (= it felt soft). [U] • A touch is a quick light movement of one thing, esp. a hand, onto and off another thing: *I felt a cold touch on my arm.* [C] ○ *At a/the touch* **of** *the button, the door opened.* [C] ○ *With a/the touch* **of** *the button, the door opened.* [C]

touch·y–feel·y /ˌtʌtʃ·i'fiː·li/ *adj infml* • Someone who is touchy-feely likes frequently to put their hands on other people: *She's one of those touchy-feely people who are always putting their hands on your arm while they're talking to you.*

touch *(obj)* CLOSE TOGETHER /tʌtʃ/ *v* (of two or more things) to be so close together that there is no space between; to be in CONTACT • *He fell asleep as soon as his head touched the pillow.* [T] • *The edge of the town touches the forest.* [T] • *She pushed the two bookcases together until they touched/were touching.* [I] • To touch also means to reach the standard of. It is usually used in negative sentences: *Her novels* **can't** *touch* (= are not as good as) *those of her sister.* [T] ○ **There's no one to** *touch him* **as** *an illustrator of children's books.* [T] • When an aircraft **touches down**, it lands. See also TOUCHDOWN. • LP> **Each other**

touch /tʌtʃ/ *n* [U] • If you are **in touch** with someone, you see them or are involved with them in some other way regularly: *Are you and your American cousins in touch at all?* ○ *Are you still in touch* **with** *your school friends?* ○ *No, we haven't* **kept** *in touch.* ○ *We're in* **daily/weekly/close** *touch with our office in Spain.* ○ Compare **lose touch** at LOSE NOT HAVE. • If you are **in touch/out of touch with** a subject, activity or situation your knowledge about it is recent/not recent: *He's not really in touch* **with** *what young people are interested in.* ○ *I didn't look at a newspaper all the time I was on holiday – I'm really out of touch* **with** *what's been happening.*

touch *obj* INFLUENCE /tʌtʃ/ *v* [T] to influence emotionally or cause feelings of sympathy in (someone) • *The TV report about the children's work for charity really touched us.*

touched /tʌtʃt/ *adj* [after v] • If you are touched, you are grateful for something kind that someone has done: *I was very touched by all the cards my friends sent me when I was in hospital.* ○ *He was touched* **that** *you remembered his birthday.* [+ *that* clause] • See also TOUCHED.

touch·ing /'tʌtʃ·ɪŋ/ *adj* • *a touching story* • *The way she looked after her little sister was really touching.*

touch·ing·ly /'tʌtʃ·ɪŋ·li/ *adv* • *He spoke touchingly about the courage of the people he had worked with.*

touch ABILITY /tʌtʃ/ *n* [U] an ability to do things in the stated way • *a deft touch* • *her own special touch* • *I admire her lightness/sureness of touch as a cook.* • *He used to be a good writer but I think he's* **losing** *his touch.*

touch SMALL AMOUNT /tʌtʃ/ *n* [C] a small amount • *"Would you like milk?" "Just* **a touch.***"* • **A** *touch less red would have made the picture more attractive.* • *We're expecting a touch* **of** *frost.* • *There was a touch* **of** *irony/humour in her voice.* • *(infml)* To show that an illness is not too serious you can say you have had a touch of it: *I've had a touch of flu/hayfever.* ○ *The child was suffering from a touch of the sun* (= being too long in hot sun). • A touch is also a small addition or detail which makes something better: *The speech had several comic touches.* ○ *Using a sailing ship as the company badge was a touch* **of genius** (= a good/clever idea or action), *offering as it did a romantic past to a modern office complex in the docklands development.* ○ *The flowers on the table provided the* **finishing** *touch.* • *The weather has turned* **a touch** (= quite) *nasty.*

touch SPORT /tʌtʃ/ *n* [U] the area outside either of the long edges of the space on which football and similar games are played • *Playing for safety, he kicked the ball* **into** *touch.* • See also TOUCHLINE.

touch *obj* **for** *v prep* [T] *infml disapproving* to ask if (someone) will give or lend (money) • *Only last week he touched me for £10/for his train fare home.*

touch in *obj*, **touch** *obj* **in** *v adv* [M] to draw or paint with quick light marks

touch off *obj*, **touch** *obj* **off** *v adv* [M] to start (something) in a sudden or violent way • *The argument/fight/disagreement was touched off by a passing remark about her family.* • *The plans for a new airport have touched off a storm of protest.*

touch up *obj*, **touch** *obj* **up** *v adv* [M] to improve by making small changes or additions • *She touched up her lipstick and brushed her hair.* • *We thought the picture had probably been touched up, because he looked so much younger in it.* • See also **touch up** at TOUCH [USE FINGERS].

touch·down [LANDING] /ˈtʌtʃ·daʊn/ *n* [C] the landing of an aircraft or of some spacecraft • *One of the plane's tyres burst on touchdown.* • *A few hours before touchdown, the base where the space shuttle was due to land was engulfed in fog.* • See also **touch down** at TOUCH [CLOSE TOGETHER].

touch·down [FOOTBALL] /ˈtʌtʃ·daʊn/ *n* [C] (in American football) the act of carrying the ball across the other team's goal line or throwing the ball across the other team's goal line so that it is caught by a member of your own team behind that line • *He scored three touchdowns.* • *Taylor dropped a touchdown pass.*

tou·ché /tuːˈʃeɪ/ *exclamation* used to admit that someone has made a good point against you in an argument or discussion • *"You say we should support British industries, but you always drink French wines." "Touché."*

touched /tʌtʃt/ *adj* [after v] *dated infml* behaving in an unusual and strange way; CRAZY • *Our friends think we're completely touched to be going camping in Scotland in the middle of winter.* • See also **touched** at TOUCH [INFLUENCE].

touch·ing /ˈtʌtʃ·ɪŋ/ *adj* See at TOUCH [INFLUENCE].

touch·line *Br* /ˈtʌtʃ·laɪn/, *Am and Aus* **side·line** /ˈsaɪd·laɪn/ *n* [C] one of the two lines marking the long edges of the area in which particular games, such as football, are played • *The linesman runs up and down the touchline.* • *She spends her Saturday afternoons standing on the touchline, watching her boyfriend play rugby.*

touch·pa·per /£ˈtʌtʃˌpeɪ·pəʳ, $-pɚ/ *n* [C] a small piece of paper on one end of a FIREWORK (= decorative explosive), which you light in order to start the firework burning • *The instructions on the fireworks said "Light the blue touchpaper, and stand well clear."*

touch·stone /£ˈtʌtʃ·stəʊn, $-stoʊn/ *n* [C] an established standard or principle by which something is judged • *In business, having a large share of the market is often assumed to be the touchstone for success.*

touch·y /ˈtʌtʃ·i/ *adj* **-ier, -iest** *slightly infml* easily offended or upset; needing to be dealt with carefully • *You have to be careful what you say to Kevin – he's rather touchy.* • *She's very touchy about the fact that her husband has been married before.* • *This is a touchy* **subject/issue/point**, *so we'd better avoid it.*

touch·i·ly /ˈtʌtʃ·ɪ·li/ *adv slightly infml* • *"I wish you wouldn't keep making remarks about my clothes," she said touchily.*

touch·i·ness /ˈtʌtʃ·ɪ·nəs/ *n* [U] *slightly infml* • *Everyone is aware of the touchiness* **of** *the situation* (= that it needs to be dealt with carefully).

tough [STRONG] /tʌf/ *adj* **-er, -est** strong; not easily broken or weakened or defeated • *These toys are made from tough plastic.* • *Children's shoes need to be tough.* • *These plants are not tough enough to survive outside in winter.* • *You have to be tough to be successful in politics.* • *He has a reputation for being a tough* **guy**. • *(infml) Their lawyer is a real tough* **customer/nut** (= person). • *(infml) One minute she looks like one tough* **cookie**, *and the next minute she seems utterly vulnerable.* • *We need to take a tough-***minded** (= strong and determined) *approach to these problems.* • *She's a tough-***talking** *businesswoman* (= one who uses strong and determined language). • Action that is tough is strong and determined: *Tough measures need to be taken to protect the environment.* ○ *Tough new safety standards have been introduced for cars.* ○ *The government is continuing to take a tough* **stance/line** *on terrorism.* ○ *There have been calls for tougher controls/restrictions on what newspapers are allowed to print.* ○ *After some tough bargaining, we finally agreed on a deal.* • *I think it's time the police* **got** *tougher* **on/with** (= treated more severely) *people who drink and drive.* • Food that is tough is difficult to cut or eat: *This steak is very tough.* ○ *These apples have tough skins.* • **Tough as old boots/ Tough as nails** means very strong, and not easily weakened: *The doctor said that the old man was as tough as old boots and would quickly recover from his illness.* ○ *"Do you think Eva was offended by my criticisms of her?" "No, she's as tough as nails."* • **Tough as old boots** (*Am also* **tough as shoe leather**) can also be used to refer to food that is difficult to cut or eat. • [LP]› **'-ough' pronunciation**

tough·en *obj* /ˈtʌf·ən/ *v* [T] • *The UN has announced its intentions to toughen sanctions still further.* • *The government wants to toughen* **(up)** *existing drug laws/controls/restrictions.* • *Car windows are usually made from toughened glass* (= glass that has been made stronger). • *The time he spent in the army certainly toughened him* **up** (= made him stronger and better able to deal with difficult situations). [M] • *Be careful not to toughen* (= make difficult to cut and eat) *the chicken by overcooking it.*

tough·ly /ˈtʌf·li/ *adv* • *These boots are very toughly* (= strongly) *made.* • *The newspaper published a toughly worded article about racist behaviour.* • *The law needs to be more toughly enforced.* • *His firm is toughly run, with good cost control.*

tough·ness /ˈtʌf·nəs/ *n* [U] • *She has a reputation for toughness* (= being strong and determined). • *He seems to lack the inner toughness and singleness of purpose needed in a president.* • *I'm sorry about the toughness* **of** *the meat* (= its being difficult to cut and eat).

tough out *obj*, **tough** *obj* **out** /tʌf/ *v adv* [M] *infml* • *The prime minister toughed out* (= defeated) *all the opposition to her proposals.* • *We're in a difficult situation at the moment, but if we can just tough* **it** *out* (= continue to exist during it), *things are bound to get better soon.*

tough [DIFFICULT] /tʌf/ *adj* **-er, -est** difficult (to do or deal with) • *The process of adjusting to life with a baby can be pretty tough.* • *They've had an exceptionally tough life.* • *They will be a tough team* **to** *beat.* [+ to infinitive] • *It's one of the best colleges and it's very tough* **to** *get into.* [+ to infinitive] • *The last six years have been increasingly tough* **for** *the country's economy.* • *The company is going through a tough* **time** *at the moment.* • *Many small shops are finding it difficult to cope with tough* **competition** *from large stores.* • *We've had to make some very tough* **decisions**. • *My boss has given me a tough* **job/assignment**. • *Many homeless people are facing a tough* **winter**. • *The climate in most of Africa is too tough* **for** *rice and wheat.* • *(humorous saying)* 'It's tough at the top' means that people who are in important positions have a lot of advantages and get a lot of benefits.

tough·en /ˈtʌf·ən/ *v* [I] • *Amid toughening* **competition** (= competition which is becoming difficult to deal with) *in the market, many firms are going out of business.*

tough·ie, tough·y /ˈtʌf·i/ *n* [C] *infml* • *She turned and asked me a real toughie* (= a difficult question). • See also **toughie** at TOUGH [VIOLENT].

tough·ly /ˈtʌf·li/ *adv* • *We live in a toughly* **competitive** *world.*

tough·ness /ˈtʌf·nəs/ *n* [U] • *They can't face the toughness* **of the competition**.

tough [VIOLENT] /tʌf/ *adj* **-er, -est** likely to be violent or to contain violence; not kind or pleasant • *They live in a very tough neighbourhood.* • *Some of the kids at this school are really tough.* • *Many of the country's toughest criminals are held in this prison.*

tough /tʌf/, **tough·ie** /ˈtʌf·i/ *n* [C] *esp. Am infml* • *His friend was shot dead last year by a group of toughs* (= violent people). • *Bands of armed toughs roamed the city.* • See also **toughie** at TOUGH [DIFFICULT].

tough [UNLUCKY] /tʌf/ *adj* **-er, -est** *infml* unlucky • *"I've been told I've got to work late today because I'm very behind on my work." "Oh, tough* **luck**!*"/(Br) "Oh, that's a bit tough!"* • *It's tough* **on** *Geoff that he's going to miss the party.* • Tough can also be said in a way that shows that you do not have any sympathy for someone's problems or difficulties: *"I haven't got any money left." "Tough* **(luck)**/ *That's tough – you shouldn't have spent it all on cigarettes."* ○ *If you get cold because you're not wearing a coat, that'll be your tough* **luck**. • *(taboo slang) "They lost a lot of money on their investment."* '**Tough shit** (= I have no sympathy for them) *– they should have been more careful."*

tou·pée /£ˈtuː·peɪ, $-ˈ-/ *n* [C] a small specially shaped piece of artificial hair which is worn by a man to cover an area of his head on which he does not have any hair • *I was introduced to an accountant named Colin who was wearing a nasty green suit and a rather obvious toupée.*

tour /£tʊəʳ, £tɔːʳ, $tʊr/ *n* [C] a visit to a place or area, esp. one during which you look round the place or area and learn about it • *We* **went on** *a* **guided** *tour* **of**/*(Br also)* **round** *the cathedral/museum/castle/factory.* • *A bus took us* **on** *a* **sightseeing** *tour* **of** *the city.* • *They've just come back from a tour* **of**/*(Br also)* **round** (= a journey made for pleasure, esp. as a holiday, visiting several different places in) *Devon and Cornwall.* • *This summer, we're going on a* **walking** *tour* **of** *the Swiss Alps/a* **cycling** *tour* **of** *Provence.* • *When we went to France, we were accompanied by an English-speaking tour* **guide**. • *Tour* **operators** (= companies which arrange holidays for people) *report that many people are booking their holidays early this year.* • A tour is also a planned visit to several places in a country or area which is made for a special purpose, such as by a politician or a sports team or a group of musicians or dancers or actors: *The Queen is* **making** *a two-week tour* **of** *Australia.* ○ *The England cricket team is currently* **on** *tour in Pakistan.* [U] ○ *The band is about to begin a* **world/ nationwide** *tour.* ○ *She is performing in Birmingham tonight, on the third* **leg of** (= stage of) *her national* **concert** *tour.* ○ *He had to cancel a* **lecture** *tour in the US because of ill-health.*

tour *(obj)* /£tʊəʳ, £tɔːʳ, $tʊr/ *v* • *We spent a month touring* **(around/round/in)** (= travelling for pleasure and visiting places in) *Kenya.* [T; I + prep] • *The New Zealand team will be touring* (= playing sports games in different places) **(in)** *Europe this winter.* [T; I + prep] • *The President toured* (= made an official visit to) *US military bases yesterday.* [T] • *The play will be performed first in London, and will then tour* (= be performed in) *the rest of the country.* [T] • *When she first started singing, she once toured* (= performed in several different places) **with** *the Beatles.* [I] • *The band are currently touring to promote their new album.* [I] • See also TOURISM.

tour·ing /£'tʊə·rɪŋ, £'tɔː·rɪŋ, $'tʊr·ɪŋ/ *adj* [before n; not gradable] • *She sings with a small touring opera* **company**. • *He was captain of the touring* **side/team** *which played in India last summer.*

tour (of du·ty) /£tʊəʳ, £tɔːʳ, $tʊr/ *n* [C] a period of time which someone, esp. a soldier or an official, spends working in a foreign country • *The soldiers have just completed a six-month tour* **in** *the Philippines.* • *He served two tours of duty* **in** *Vietnam.* • *The French ambassador left Moscow at the end of his tour of duty last week.*

tour de force /£ˌtʊə·də'fɔːs, $ˌtʊr·də'fɔːrs/ *n* an achievement or performance which shows great skill and attracts admiration • *The painting is* **a** *tour de force.* • *It was* **a** *tour de force to achieve a peace agreement under such difficult conditions.* • *Her performance was* **a** *stunning/ brilliant tour de force.* • *When it was first produced, the car was* **a** *technical tour de force.*

Tour·ette's syn·drome /£tʊə'rets, $tʊ-/ *n* [U] a rare illness of the brain in which the sufferer swears, makes noises and moves in a way that they cannot control • *There is a theory that Mozart may have suffered from Tourette's syndrome.*

tour·i·sm /£'tʊə·rɪ·zᵊm, £'tɔː-, $'tʊr·ɪ-/ *n* [U] the business of providing services, such as transport, places to stay or entertainment, for people who are on holiday • *Tourism is Venice's main industry.* • *These beautiful old towns have remained relatively untouched by tourism.* • **Mass** *tourism has caused serious damage to the environment in some areas of the Mediterranean.*

tour·ist /£'tʊə·rɪst, £'tɔː-, $'tʊr·ɪst/ *n* [C] • *Millions of tourists* (= people who visit places for pleasure and interest, usually while they are on holiday) *visit Rome every year.* • *Unusual wildlife and nice beaches attract plenty of* **foreign** *tourists to the area.* • **Hordes** *of tourists* **flock to** *the Mediterranean each year.* • *Disneyworld is one of Florida's major tourist* **attractions**. • *Stratford-upon-Avon is a popular tourist* **destination**. • *The local tourist* **(information) office** *will provide a free map of the region.* • *The summer months are the height of the area's tourist* **season**. • *We stayed in a small hotel, well off the tourist* **track** (= away from the places that tourists usually go to). • *Many people travel to the country on tourist* **visas**, *then stay and work there illegally.* • *(Br and Aus)* A tourist is also a member of a sports team who is travelling from place to place in a foreign country, playing games: *The West Indies easily defeated the tourists.* • **Tourist class** (also **tourist**) on an aircraft or a ship is the ordinary travelling conditions that you get when you buy the cheapest tickets, which are less comfortable than those you get if you buy more expensive tickets: *The airline was only able to offer us seats in (the) tourist class at the back of the aircraft.* ○ *I always travel tourist.* • *(disapproving) This used to be a very pretty little village, but now it's become a real* **tourist trap** (= a crowded place which provides entertainment and things to buy for tourists, often at high prices).

tour·ist·y /£'tʊə·rɪ·sti, £'tɔː-, $'tʊr·ɪ-/ *adj disapproving* • *This used to be an attractive seaside town, but now it's become very touristy* (= unattractive because a lot of tourists visit it as it has many things for them to see and do and buy).

tour·na·ment /£'tʊə·nə·mənt, £'tɔː-, $'tɜːr-/, *Am also* **tour·ney** /£'tʊə·ni, £'tɔː-, $'tɜːr-/ *n* [C] a competition in which there are several parts, which happen one after the other. The winner of one part continues to play in the next part, until all the parts have been completed, and one winner is left. • *a tennis tournament* • *a chess tournament* • *a golf tournament* • *They were defeated in the first* **round of** *the tournament.* • *They've got through to the finals of the tournament.* • LP **Sports**

tour·ni·quet /£'tʊə·nɪ·keɪ, £'tɔː-, $'tɜːr·nɪ·kɪt/ *n* [C] a strip of cloth which is tied tightly round an injured arm or leg to stop it bleeding • *It is sometimes better to try and stop bleeding by pressing on a limb, rather than by* **applying** *a tourniquet* **to** *it.*

tou·sled /'taʊ·zḷd/ *adj* (esp. of hair) looking untidy, as if having been rubbed • *Naomi stood in front of them, her face flushed, her* **hair** *tousled.* • *He comes down to breakfast, bleary and tousled, in last night's clothes.*

tout *(obj)* MAKE KNOWN /taʊt/ *v* to advertise or make known or praise (something or someone) repeatedly, esp. as a way of encouraging their sale, popularity or development • *The car manufacturers have produced a series of television advertisements touting their cars' safety features.* [T] • *Several insurance companies are now touting their services/wares on local radio.* [T] • *As an education minister, she has been touting these ideas for some time.* [T] • *This cream is being touted* **as** *a way of making your skin look younger.* [T] • *He is being widely touted* **as** *the new leader of the Social Democratic party.* [T] • *She is being touted* **for** *an Oscar.* [T] • To tout is also repeatedly to try to persuade people to buy your goods or services: *There were hundreds of taxis at the airport, all touting* **for** *business/custom.* [I always + prep/adv]

tout *obj* SELL UNOFFICIALLY *Br* /taʊt/, *Am* **scalp** *v* [T] *disapproving* to sell (esp. a ticket for a sports game or theatre performance) unofficially, usually at a much higher price than the official price • *£30 seats for the tennis match were being touted* **for** *£500.*

tout *Br* /taʊt/, *Am* **scal·per** *n* [C] *disapproving* • *The only way to get a ticket for the show is to buy one from a tout* (= a person who sells tickets for a popular sporting event or theatre performance, for which it is hard to get tickets, at a price higher than the official price). • *Britain's best-known* **ticket** *tout, or "ticket broker" as he prefers to be called, once boasted that he could get you tickets for anything.*

tow *obj* /£təʊ, $toʊ/ *v* [T] (esp. of a vehicle) to pull (esp. another vehicle) along, using a rope or a chain • *You shouldn't drive fast when your car is towing a caravan.* • *The boat was towing a water-skier.* • *The road was closed while the vehicles that had been involved in the accident were towed* **away/off**. [M] • *You're not allowed to park here – your car will be towed* **away** (= lifted onto an an official truck and taken to a place from which you have to pay to collect it). [M] • *The damaged boat was towed to safety.* • A **tow-away** is an act of a car being officially removed from a place where it has been illegally left: *I was late for work, and couldn't find a parking meter, so I decided to park illegally and risk a tow-away.* ○ *This part of town is a tow-away area/zone* (= Your car will be removed if you leave it here). • A **tow bar** is a bar fixed to the back of a car which is used for pulling a CARAVAN or TRAILER. • **Tow truck** is *Am and Aus for* **breakdown truck**. See at BREAKDOWN FAILURE. • PIC **Car, Vehicles**

tow /£təʊ, $toʊ/ *n* • *When my car broke down, a police car gave me a tow* (= pulled my car using a rope or chain) *to the nearest garage.* [C] • *The car in front of us is (Br)* **on**/*(Am)* **in**/*(Aus also)* **under** *tow* (= being pulled along) – *that's why we're going so slowly.* [U] • *The damaged boat drifted for days before it was finally* **taken in** *tow.* [U] • *(fig. infml) She arrived at the party, with a tall, silver-haired man* **in tow** (= with her).

to·wards MOVEMENT *Br and Aus* /£tə'wɔːdz, $tʊ'wɔːrdz/, *esp. Am* **to·ward** /£tə'wɔːd, $tʊ'wɔːrd/ *prep* in the direction of; closer to • *She stood up and walked towards him.* • *He leaned towards his wife and whispered, "Can we* *go home soon?"* • *They turned towards where they thought the noise was coming from.* • *"Whatever is that?" he asked, pointing towards the sky.* • *She kept glancing towards the telephone, as if by doing so she could make it ring.* • *All their energies are directed towards helping homeless people.* • *The country seems to be drifting towards war.* • *The talks are being seen as a step towards ending the conflict.* • *This is an important moment in the history of the country's move towards independence.* • *There has been little progress towards finding a cure for the disease.* • *There is a trend towards healthier eating among all sectors of the population.* • PIC› **Prepositions of movement**

to·wards RELATION *Br and Aus* /£tə'wɔːdz, $tʊ'wɔːrdz/, *esp. Am* **to·ward** /£tə'wɔːd, $tʊ'wɔːrd/ *prep* in relation to • *They've always been very friendly towards me.* • *There has been a change in government policy towards energy efficiency.* • *My parents finally changed their attitude towards my not wanting to go to college.* • *He feels a lot of anger/hostility/antagonism/animosity towards his father.* • *Eighty-five per cent of people questioned thought that most newspapers are biased towards one particular political party.* • *The work that students do during the term counts towards their final grade.*

to·wards POSITION *Br and Aus* /£tə'wɔːdz, $tʊ'wɔːrdz/, *esp. Am* **to·ward** /£tə'wɔːd, $tʊ'wɔːrd/ *prep* near to; just before or around • *Our seats were towards the back of the theatre, and we couldn't see very well.* • *We're well towards the front of the queue, so we shouldn't have any difficulty in getting tickets.* • *My steak was rather burnt towards the edges.* • *The book will be published towards the end of the year.* • *Towards the end of his life he was so ill that he didn't even recognize his family.* • *I often get hungry towards the middle of the morning.* • *It's beginning to turn colder now that we're getting towards winter.*

to·wards PURPOSE *Br and Aus* /£tə'wɔːdz, $tʊ'wɔːrdz/, *esp. Am* **to·ward** /£tə'wɔːd, $tʊ'wɔːrd/ *prep* for the purpose of (buying or achieving) • *I'm saving up to buy a car, and Dad has given me some money towards it.* • *Would you like to make a contribution* (=give some money) *towards a present for Linda?* • *Parents have raised several thousand pounds towards the cost of a swimming pool for the school.* • *A little kindness can go a long way towards making the world a happier place.*

to·wel /taʊəl/ *n* [C] a usually rectangular piece of cloth or paper used for drying someone or something that is wet • *Many public toilets no longer provide towels, but have machines which dry your hands.* • *She came downstairs after her shower, wrapped in a towel.* • *The school provides* **paper** *towels for the children to dry their hands on.* • *We have a heated towel (Br and Aus)* **rail**/*(Am)* **rack** *in our bathroom.* • To **throw/chuck in the towel** is to stop trying to do something because you have become aware that you cannot succeed: *Three of the original five candidates for the Democratic presidential nomination have now thrown in the towel.* • See also TERRY. • PIC› **Bathroom, Rail**

to·wel *obj* /taʊəl/ *v* [T] **-ll-** or *Am usually* **-l-** • *She towelled her hair dry* (=rubbed it with a towel to dry it). [+ obj + adj] • *After we'd been for a swim, we quickly towelled ourselves* **down**, *then went off to play tennis.*

to·wel·ling, *Am usually* **to·wel·ing** /£'taʊə·lɪŋ, $'taʊə-/ *n* [U] • Towelling is a soft thick cloth used esp. for making TOWELS or clothing: *a towelling bath robe* • *towelling socks* • *towelling nappies*

to·wel·ette /£ˌtaʊə'let, $ˌtaʊə-/ *n* [C] a small square of wet paper, used esp. for cleaning your face and hands when there is no water available • *After we'd finished our dinner on the plane, we wiped our hands on the towelette that the flight attendant had brought for us.*

to·wer /£taʊəʳ, $taʊə/ *n* [C] a tall narrow structure, often square or circular, which either forms part of a building or stands alone • *the Eiffel tower* • *the leaning tower of Pisa* • *the twin towers of the World Trade Center* • *There is a tower at each corner of the castle walls.* • *There's a clock on the* **church** *tower.* • *He works in an* **office** *tower in downtown San Francisco.* • A tower is also a tall usually metal structure used for broadcasting: *a radio tower* • *a transmission tower* • *(Br)* A **tower block** *(Am* **high-rise**) is a tall building divided into apartments or offices: *A large number of tower blocks were built in the 1960s and 1970s.* ○ *They live in a crumbling concrete tower block.* • **A tower of strength** is a person who gives you help and support when you are in a difficult situation: *Polly was a tower of strength* **to** *me when I was ill.* • See also WATCHTOWER.

to·wer /£taʊəʳ, $taʊə/ *v* [I always + adv/prep] • *Canary Wharf towers* **over/above** (=is very tall in comparison with) *the Dockland area of London.* • *Although he's only 12, David towers* **over/above** (=is taller than) *his mother.* • *We turned the corner, and there was the cathedral, towering* (=seeming very large) *in front of us.* • *(fig.) One computer manufacturer towers* **above** (=is bigger and more successful than) *all the rest.*

to·wer·ing /£'taʊə·rɪŋ, $'taʊə·ɪŋ/ *adj* • *We wandered under the towering* (=very high) *walls of the Acropolis/the towering redwood trees of Yosemite/the towering ceiling of the cathedral.* • Towering also means very great: *Laurence Olivier's Othello was a towering performance.* ○ *He is a towering figure in the British art world.* ○ *I have rarely seen a man in such a towering* (=very great) *temper.*

town /taʊn/ *n* a place where there are a lot of houses, shops, places of work, places of entertainment, places of worship, etc. in which people live and work. A town is usually larger than a village, but smaller than a city. • *a seaside/coastal/resort town* • *an industrial town* • *a fishing town* • *a mining town* • *a border/frontier town* [C] • *They live in a sleepy provincial town.* [C] • *He was born in the small town* **of** *Castleford, in Yorkshire.* [C] • *She was buried in her* **home** *town* (=the town in which she was born). [C] • *Mr Dunn has been a member of the town* **council**/*a town* **councillor** *for many years.* • *We stayed in the best hotel* **in** *town.* [U] • *The swimming pool is a couple of miles* **out of** *town.* [U] • *There was a lot of traffic on the main road* **into/out of** *town.* [U] • *Many people like to do their shopping at an* **out-of-town** *shopping centre.* • *(esp. Am)* Town can also mean the place where you live or work: *I'm leaving town for a few days tomorrow.* [U] ○ *I'll be* **in** *town on Monday and Tuesday, then away for the rest of the week.* [U] ○ *Barbara is* **out of** *town on business this week.* [U] • **(The)** town *(Br also* **town centre**) is also the part of a town where the main shops are: *I'm going* **into/to** *town at lunch-time to do some shopping.* [U] ○ *I met Charles while I was* **in** *town.* [U] ○ *The town was very busy.* [U] ○ *It's very difficult to find anywhere to park your car in the town centre.* • Town is also used to refer to the most important city or town in a country or area: *We went* **up to** *town to see a play.* [U] ○ *Many people go* **into** *town* (=New York) *from New Jersey on weekends.* [U] • Town can also be used to refer to the people who live in the town: *The* **whole** *town is/are hoping that their football team will win the final tomorrow.* [C + sing/pl v] • *I've always lived in* **the** *town* (=in a town or city rather than in the countryside). [U] • If you **go to town (on** something), you do it in a detailed and enthusiastic way, esp. by spending a lot of money: *They've really gone to town on their wedding.* ○ *All the newspapers have gone to town on* (=printed a lot of details about) *this unusual murder trial.* • **On the town** means enjoying yourself by going to places of entertainment in a town or city: *I was* **out** *on the town/I had* **a night** *on the town last night, and I feel really tired today.* • If you are a **man-about-town/woman-about-town**, you are someone who spends a lot of time in fashionable places and doing fashionable things. • In Britain, a **town clerk** is an official who is responsible for acting on the decisions made by a town COUNCIL. • A **town hall** is a building in which local government officials and employees work and have meetings. • *They live in a beautiful four-storey* **town house** (=a house in a town or city, esp. one that is comfortable and expensive, and in a fashionable area, and, esp. in the US, often one which is joined to other similar houses). • *(Am)* A **town meeting** is a gathering of the people who live or pay taxes in a town, for the purpose of governing the town. • **Town planning** is the planning of the way in which towns and cities are built in order to make them pleasant to live in: *He studied town planning at college.* ○ *Her husband is a* **town planner**. • See also DOWNTOWN; HOMETOWN; UPTOWN.

town·ie, **town·y**, *Br also* **town·ee** /'taʊ·ni/ *n* [C] *infml disapproving* • A townie is a person who lives in a town where there is a college but who is not involved with the college: *The students made fun of him because he was a townie.* • *(Br)* A townie *(Aus infml* **city slicker**) is also a person who lives in a town, and has no experience of or knowledge about living in the countryside: *A couple of townies walked into the village pub, looking very out of place in their smart suits.*

town·ship /'taʊn·ʃɪp/ *n* [C] (in S Africa) a town in which only black people are allowed to live, (or in the US and Canada) a unit of local government consisting of a town and the area surrounding it • *a black township* • *the* *township* **of** *Soweto* • *township music* • *the township* **of** *Dulce, New Mexico* • *Princeton Township*

towns·peo·ple /'taʊnz,piː·pl̩/, **towns·folk** /£'taʊnz·fəʊk, $-foʊk/ *pl n* people who live in a particular town, considered as a group, or people who live in towns rather than in the countryside • *The townspeople have raised $9 million for a new museum.* • *Increasing numbers of townspeople are moving to live in the countryside.*

tow·path /£'təʊ·pɑːθ, $'toʊ·pæθ/ *n* [C] a path which goes along the side of a river or a CANAL, and which was used in the past by horses pulling boats • *We went for a walk* **along** *the towpath.* • PIC› **Canal**

tow·rope /£'təʊ·rəʊp, $'toʊ·roʊp/ *n* [C] a rope or chain which a vehicle uses to pull another vehicle

tox·ae·mi·a, *esp. Am* **tox·e·mi·a** /£tɒk'siː·mi·ə, $tɑːk-/ *n* [U] *specialized* the condition of having a poisonous substance or substances in your blood

tox·in /£'tɒk·sɪn, $'tɑːk-/ *n* [C] a poisonous substance, esp. one which is produced by bacteria and which causes disease • *Some types of bean contain a toxin which must be destroyed by cooking them at high temperature before eating them.*

tox·ic /£'tɒk·sɪk, $'tɑːk-/ *adj* • *toxic waste/chemicals/effluent*

tox·i·ci·ty /£tɒk'sɪs·ɪ·ti, $tɑːk'sɪs·ə·t̬i/ *n* [U] • *Tests of the chemical have shown that it has a high level of toxicity* (= degree of being poisonous). • *The toxicity* (= quality of being poisonous) **of** *the drug severely limits its use.*

tox·i·col·o·gy /£,tɒk·sɪ'kɒl·ə·dʒi, $,tɑːk·sɪ'kɑː·lə-/ *n* [U] • Toxicology is the scientific study of the characteristics and effects of poisons.

tox·i·col·o·gist /£,tɒk·sɪ'kɒl·ə·dʒɪst, $,tɑːk·sɪ'kɑː·lə-/ *n* [C] • A toxicologist is a person who studies or knows a lot about poisons.

toy GAME /tɔɪ/ *n* [C] an object that children play with • *a cuddly/soft/stuffed toy* • *a wooden toy* • *a clockwork/wind-up toy* • *a toy train* • *a toy farm* • *a toy soldier* • *(Br) toy bricks (Am and Aus blocks)* • *Put your toys away now – it's time for bed.* • *Leave daddy's camera alone – it isn't a toy!* • *Jayne is so pleased with her new car, she's like a child with a new toy.* • Toy is also used to refer to an object which is used by an adult for amusement rather than for serious use: *His latest toy is a mobile phone.* ○ *She has several* **executive** *toys on her desk.* • *(infml)* A **toy boy** is a young man who is an older woman's lover or partner: *Pam turned up at the Hampsons' party with her new toy boy.* • PIC› **Toy**

toy SMALL /tɔɪ/ *adj* [before n; not gradable] (of a breed of dog) very small and kept as a pet • *a toy poodle/spaniel*

toy with *obj* CONSIDER *v prep* [T] to consider or think about (something) in a not very serious way, and without making a decision • *We're toying with* **the idea** *of going to Peru next year.* • *They toyed with my suggestion for a while, then rejected it.*

toy with *obj* HANDLE CARELESSLY *v prep* [T] to handle or move (something) around without any clear purpose or without thinking carefully about it • *She just toyed with her salad.* • *He toyed nervously with a button on his jacket as he was speaking.* • *(fig.) I don't think he's really serious about our relationship, he's just toying with me/with my affections.*

trace *obj* FIND /treɪs/ *v* [T] to find or discover about (something or someone) by examining the direction in which they have gone or the way in which they have developed • *The police are trying to trace the mother of a new-born baby found abandoned outside a hospital.* • *Attempts to trace* **the whereabouts of** *a man seen leaving the scene of the crime have so far been unsuccessful.* • *Their missing daughter was finally traced* **to** (= found in) *Manchester.* • *The phone company were unable to trace the call* (= discover where it had come from). • *No one has yet been able to trace* (= discover) *the source of the rumour.* • *The cause of the fire was traced* **to** (= discovered to have been) *an electrical fault.* • *The American Democratic party traces its origins* **to** (= has its origins in) *the Democratic-Republican party, which came into being in the 1790s.* • To trace something is also to discover its cause or origin by examining the way in which it has developed: *The outbreak of food poisoning was traced* **to** *some contaminated shellfish.* ○ *The practice of giving eggs at Easter can be traced* **back to** *festivals in ancient China.* ○ *Rivalries between the gangs can be traced* **back to** (= first happened in) *the 1950s in some black and Hispanic neighbourhoods.* ○ *Alex Haley's book 'Roots' is about a black American who traces his* **ancestry** *back to an African slave.* • To trace something is also to describe the way in which it has developed: *The film traces the events leading up to the Russian Revolution in 1917.* ○ *Her book traces the history of girls' education in Britain.*

trace /treɪs/ *n* • A trace is a sign that something has happened or existed: *He attempted to cover up all the traces* **of** *his crimes.* [C] ○ *The child's body bore/showed the traces* **of** *having been beaten.* [C] ○ *She stayed in the house for a few weeks, but when she went, she* **left** *no trace* **of** *having been there.* [C] ○ *I've been looking for my missing wallet for several days, but I can't find any trace* **of** *it.* [C] ○ *The Bermuda Triangle is an area of the Pacific Ocean where ships are said to have disappeared* **without** *trace.* [U] ○ *He seems to have vanished* **without** *a trace* (= No one knows where he is). [C] ○ *(fig.) Her last book sank* **without** *trace* (= did not attract any attention or interest.) [U] • A trace is an act of finding information about something electronically. Trace can also refer to the record of the information found in this way: *The phone company* **put** *a trace* **on** *the call.* [C] ○ *She fell downstairs while she was pregnant, but a trace showed that the baby was all right.* [C]

trace·a·ble /'treɪ·sə·bl̩/ *adj* • *In theory, most telephone calls should be traceable* (= it should be possible to discover where they have come from). • *His medical problems were shown to be traceable* **to** (= to have been caused by) *his having been exposed to dangerous chemicals.*

trace *obj* DRAW /treɪs/ *v* [T] to copy (a drawing, pattern, etc.) by drawing over its lines through a thin piece of transparent paper • *Did you draw this picture yourself, or did you trace it?* • *She learnt to write her name by tracing* **out** *the letters.* [M] • To trace something is also to draw the outer lines of it: *The child was tracing patterns in the sand with a stick.*

trac·ing /'treɪ·sɪŋ/ *n* [C] • A tracing is a copy of a drawing or pattern made by drawing over it through a piece of thin transparent paper: *He made a tracing* **of** *the picture.* • *The children copied the map using* **tracing paper** (= thin transparent paper which you use for copying a picture by drawing over its lines through the paper). • PIC› **Stationery**

trace SLIGHT AMOUNT /treɪs/ *n* [C] a very slight amount • *After he died, traces* **of** *drugs were found in his blood.* • *Traces* **of** *dangerous chemicals have been found in the river.* • *There is just a trace* **of** *grey in his hair.* • *She speaks English without the slightest trace* **of** *an accent.* • *There was the faintest trace* **of** *a smile on her lips.* • *His face showed no trace* **of** *emotion as the judge passed sentence on him.* • *"How wonderful!" she said, without any trace* **of** *sarcasm.* • A **trace element** is a simple chemical substance that is necessary for healthy growth and development, and which exists in animals and plants in small amounts. There are various types of trace element: *Seaweed is a good source of minerals and trace elements.*

trac·er /£'treɪ·səʳ, $-sɚ/ *n* [C] a bullet which leaves a line of flame or smoke behind it when it is fired, so that you can see the direction it has taken • *Tracer bullets streaked through the sky.* • *The sky was bright with tracer fire.*

trach·e·a /trə'kiː·ə/ *n* [C] *medical for* WINDPIPE

track PATH /træk/ *n* a path or rough road which is made of earth rather than having a surface covered with stone or other material • *We walked along a muddy track at the side of the field.* [C] • *The house is at the end of a dirt/unmade track.* [C] • (A) track is also a pair of metal bars fixed on the ground at an equal distance from each other, along which trains travel: *Passengers are requested not to walk across the tracks.* [C] ○ *The accident happened on a stretch of track with a 30mph speed limit.* [U] • Track is also *Am for* PLATFORM: *The Chattanooga train is on Track 29.* [C] • Track is also sometimes used to refer to the direction in which someone's job or education develops: *Her first job was as a lawyer, but then she changed track completely and became a doctor.* [U] ○ *He took the academic track through high school.* [C] • *I think we're getting* **off the track** *here* (= talking about something that is not part of what we should be talking about) – *we're supposed to be discussing our advertising campaign.* • If something is **on track**, it is developing as it is expected to develop: *The company is on track* **to** *make record profits.* ○ *We were rather behind on our schedule for finishing this job, but we've managed to get back on track now.*

track·less /'træk·ləs/ *adj* [not gradable] *esp. literary* • Trackless means having no paths or roads: *a trackless waste/wilderness/desert*

track MARKS /træk/ *n* [C usually pl] a mark or line of marks left on a surface, esp. the ground, by an animal, person or vehicle which has moved over the surface, and

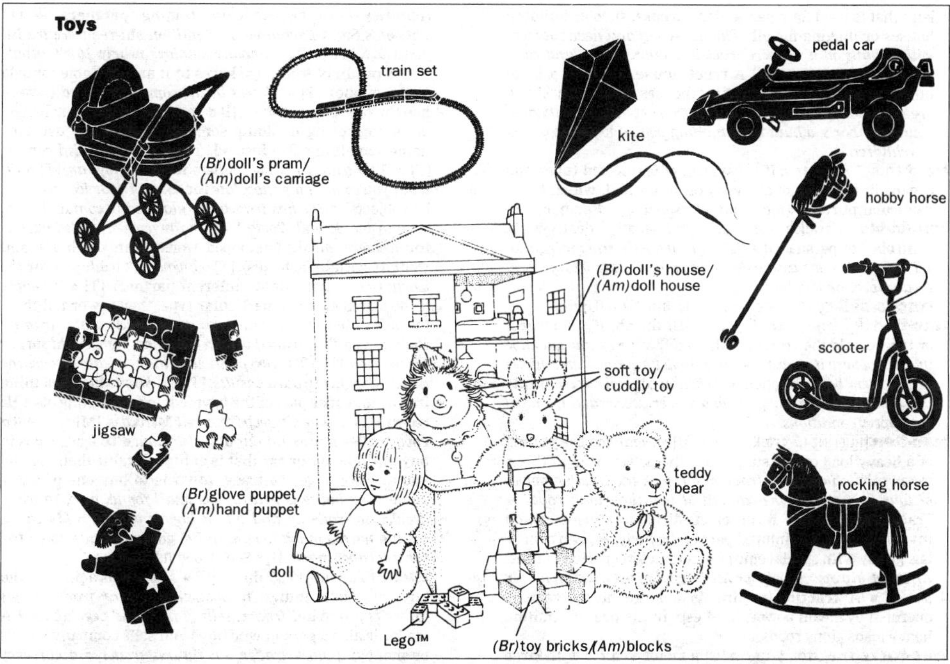

which shows which direction the animal, etc. has taken • *There were tracks in the snow where our cat had walked across it.* • *Police found tyre tracks in the mud.* • *I think these are badger tracks.* • *The hunters followed the tracks* **of** *the deer for hours.* • *The burglars were careful not to* **leave** *any tracks behind them.* • *(fig.) The police are* **on the** *track* **of** *the killer* (=are following the signs which show where the killer has gone). • A track is also the direction which something has taken or will take through the air: *People living in the track* **of** *the hurricane have been advised to leave their homes until it has passed.* ○ *Air traffic controllers use radar to control the tracks* **of** *aircraft.* • Track can also be used to refer to the way in which a thought or idea has developed or might develop: *I found it difficult to follow the track* **of** *his argument.* • **In** your **tracks** means in the exact place where you are standing: *He fell dead in his tracks.* ○ *A sudden loud scream* **stopped** *me* **(dead)** *in my tracks* (=caused me suddenly to stop what I was doing because I was so surprised). • If you **keep track**, you make certain that you know what is happening or has happened to someone or something: *My sister has had so many different jobs, I find it hard to keep track.* ○ *I always make sure I keep track* **of** *all the money I spend.* ○ Compare **lose track** at LOSE [NOT HAVE]. • If you **make tracks** you leave somewhere to go home: *It's getting late, Jim – I think we should make tracks.*

track *(obj)* /træk/ *v* • *It's difficult to track an animal* (=find where it is by following the marks it has made on the ground) *over stony ground.* [T] • *The military use radar satellites to track targets* (=follow the direction they take) *through clouds and at night.* [T] • *The study tracked* (=followed) *the careers of 1226 doctors who trained at the University of Michigan Medical School.* [T] • *The terrorists were tracked* **to** (=found in) *Amsterdam.* [T] • *I'm trying to track* **down** (=find) *one of my old school friends.* [M] • *He finally managed to track* **down** *the book he wanted.* [M] • If a television or film camera tracks, it moves along while it is filming: *The film ends with a long tracking shot around the deserted house.* [I] • *(specialized)* If a moving part of a recording machine tracks, it gets into the correct position for operating: *Our VCR tracks automatically.* [I] • A **tracking station** is a place where electrical waves are used to follow the direction of objects, such as spacecraft, in space. • See also BACKTRACK; SIDETRACK.

track·er /£'træk·əʳ, $-ɚ/ *n* [C] • A tracker is a person who is able to find animals or people by following the marks they leave on the ground after they have moved over it: *An Aboriginal tracker led them to the place where the plane had crashed.* • *The bodies of the two men were found after an extensive search by police using* **tracker dogs** (=dogs specially trained to help the police find people they are looking for).

track [SPORT] /træk/ *n* a type of path or road, often in the shape of a ring, which has been specially prepared for sporting events, particularly racing • *a cinder track* • *an all-weather track* • *a dog track* [C] • *The runners are now on their final lap of the track.* [C] • *(Am)* Track is also a sport in which people compete with each other by running a race on a specially prepared circular path: *She's a member of her college track team.* ○ *The Americans have so far won four track gold medals in the competition.* • **Track and field** (also **track**) is *esp. Am for* **athletics**. See at ATHLETE. • A **track event** is a sporting event in which people compete with each other by running a race on a specially prepared circular path. See also **field event** at FIELD [SPORT]. • *(Am) The two college teams are taking part in a* **track meet** (=a sporting competition between two or more teams, involving running races as well as jumping and throwing competitions) *next week.* • Your **track record** is all your achievements or failures in the past: *The school has an impressive/strong track record in getting its students through examinations.* ○ *The team's track record has been poor/dismal so far this year.* • A **track shoe** is a shoe with short pointed pieces of metal or plastic fixed to the bottom, worn by people who compete in running races: *a pair of track shoes.* • See also RACETRACK.

track [MUSIC] /træk/ *n* [C] one of several songs or pieces of music on a CD or other musical recording • *The album includes four previously unreleased tracks.* • *The band ended their concert with the title track from their latest album.* • A track is also a part of a magnetic strip onto which sound can be recorded. There are several tracks on one magnetic strip: *When a piece of music is recorded, each instrument is recorded separately on a 24- or 48-track tape.* ○ *Singers on television often mime to pre-recorded backing tracks.* • See also SOUNDTRACK.

track·suit /£'træk·sjuːt, $-suːt/ *n* [C] a loose top and trousers, worn either by people who are training for a sport or exercising, or as informal clothing

track·suit·ed /£'træk·sjuː·tɪd, $-suː·t̬ɪd/ *adj* [not gradable] • *a tracksuited runner* (=one wearing a tracksuit)

tract [WRITING] /trækt/ *n* [C] a short piece of writing, esp. on a religious or political subject, which is intended to influence other people's opinions • *a moral/religious/socialist tract* • *Have you read John Milton's tracts* **on** *divorce?* • *He wrote a tract* **against** *feminism.*

tract [LAND] /trækt/ *n* [C] a large area of land • *The house is surrounded by vast tracts* **of** *woodland.* • *London has large tracts* **of** *common* **land** *such as Hampstead Heath and Richmond Park.* • *(Am)* A tract is also a measured area of land that is used for a particular purpose, such as building houses or digging for oil: *The new company headquarters will be built on a 132-acre tract in Irving.* ○ *The land costs $154 000 per tract.* • *(Am)* A **tract house** is one of a large number of very similar-looking houses built on a single area of land: *The suburban ideal is a tract house identical to your neighbor's, a built-in swimming pool, a wife, a dog and 2·3 children.*

tract [TUBE] /trækt/ *n* [C] a system of connected tubes and organs in the body of a person or an animal, which has a particular purpose • *the urinary/respiratory/digestive tract*

trac·ta·ble /ˈtræk·tə·bl̩/ *adj fml* easily dealt with, controlled or persuaded • *He's quite a docile, tractable child.* • *This problem is turning out to be rather less tractable than I was expecting it to be.*

trac·ta·bil·i·ty /£ˌtræk·təˈbɪl·ɪ·ti, $-ə·t̬i/ *n* [U] *fml*

trac·tion [HOLDING] /ˈtræk·ʃən/ *n* [U] the ability of a wheel or tyre to hold the ground without sliding • *People who live in areas where it snows a lot use snow tyres on their vehicles to give them better traction.* • *Traction control electronically prevents wheels spinning when a driver accelerates too hard in slippery conditions.*

trac·tion [PULLING] /ˈtræk·ʃən/ *n* [U] *specialized* the pulling of a heavy load over a surface, or the power used in this • *steam traction* • *electric traction* • *It took the traction power of four men to pull the car out of the ditch with ropes.* • Traction is also a form of medical treatment which involves pulling an injured part of the body, esp. an arm or leg, gently with special equipment for a long period of time: *After her hip operation poor Mira was* **in/on** *traction for six weeks.* • A **traction engine** is a large heavy vehicle, operated by steam power, used esp. in the past for pulling heavy loads along roads.

trac·tor /£ˈtræk·təʳ, $-tɚ/ *n* [C] a motor vehicle with large back wheels and thick tyres, which is used on farms for pulling machinery • **Tractor-trailer** is *Am for* JUGGERNAUT. See at JUGGERNAUT [VEHICLE]. • [PIC] **Farming, Vehicles**

trad (jazz) *Br* /træd/, *Am* **dix·ie·land** *n* [U] a type of jazz, which was first played in the 1920s, in which the players invent the music as they play it

trad /træd/ *adj Br and Aus infml for* **traditional**, see at TRADITION • *a trad detective story* • *His style of dressing is very trad.*

trade [BUYING AND SELLING] /treɪd/ *n* [U] the activity of buying and selling, or exchanging, goods and/or services between people or countries • *The country's trade* **in** *manufactured goods has expanded in the last ten years.* • *An international agreement has been signed to control the trade* **in** *ivory.* • *Seventy per cent of the country's trade is* **with** *Europe.* • *There has been a sharp increase in the volume of trade* **between** *the two countries.* • *The two countries have signed a trade* **agreement** *for one year only.* • *The government has introduced trade* **barriers** *as a way of controlling imports.* • *The UK trade* **deficit/gap** *widened/narrowed last month.* • *The chemical industry has a large and growing trade* **surplus**. • Trade can also be used to mean amount of business activity: *Since the supermarket opened, many of the small local shops have lost up to 50% of their trade.* ○ *It's been so hot today that shops have been doing a* **roaring/brisk** *trade* **in** (=selling a lot of) *cold drinks and ice creams.* • A country's **trade balance** is its **balance of trade**. See at BALANCE [EQUALITY]. • *The Frankfurt book fair is an important international* **trade fair** *(Am also* **trade show***)* (=a large gathering at which companies show and sell their products and try to increase their business) *for people working in book publishing.* • A country's **trade figures** are a record of how much the country has paid for goods which it has bought from other countries, compared with how much it has been paid for goods which it has sold to other countries: *The last set of trade figures showed exceptionally strong export growth.* • A **trade name** is a **brand name**. See at BRAND [PRODUCT]. • *(Br) I bought my coat direct from the factory at* **trade price** *(Am and Aus* **wholesale***)* (=the price at which goods are sold to shops by the people who produce them, rather than the price which the customer usually pays in the shop). • A **trade route** is a route, often covering a long distance, that people buying and selling goods habitually used in the past: *Merchants carried diamonds from India along trade routes through the Middle East.*

trade *(obj)* /treɪd/ *v* • *For centuries, Native Americans traded* (=bought and sold or exchanged goods) **with** *European settlers.* [I] • *The company has been trading* **in** (=buying and selling) *oil for many years.* [I] • *The two countries have become close trading* **partners**. • *On London's Stock Exchange, 18·5 million* **shares** *were traded yesterday.* [T] • *The company employs nearly 10 000 people and is* **publicly** *traded* (=shares in it are available for sale to the public). [T] • *Shares in the company traded* (=were bought and sold) **actively**. [I] • To trade is also to exchange, or to stop using or doing something and start using or doing something else instead: *The children traded comics.* [T] ○ *Billy traded his toy soldiers* **for** *Joe's toy car.* [T] ○ *I'll trade you some of my chocolate* **for** *some of your ice cream.* [+ two objects] ○ *She has traded her glasses* **for** *contact lenses.* [T] ○ *In the Second World War, many women traded aprons* **for** *welders' masks* (=stopped working in the home and went to work in factories). [T] ○ *I wouldn't trade you* **for** *the world* (=I do not want a different partner). [T] • If people trade statements of a particular type, they say or tell them to each other: *We sat around the dinner table, trading stories.* [T] ○ *They traded bets on how long Tom would stay in his new job.* [T] ○ *The two politicians didn't really discuss the issues, they just traded insults.* [T] • If you trade something **in**, you give it as part of the payment for something else: *He recently traded in his Jeep* **for** *a red Mercedes.* [M] ○ *We got a good* **trade-in** *price for our old television.* • To trade **up** is to buy esp. a house or car that is of higher value than the one you already have. To trade **down** is to buy one of lower value: *Our house is getting too small for us now, so we've decided to trade up and buy a bigger one.* [I] ○ *My car is costing me too much to run, so I'm going to trade down* **to/for** *a cheaper model.* [I] • See also HORSETRADE.

trad·er /£ˈtreɪ·dəʳ, $-dɚ/ *n* [C] • A trader is a person who buys and sells things: *a wool/grain/sugar trader* ○ *His father is a* **market** *trader, selling fruit and vegetables.* • A trader is also a person who buys and sells company shares or money: *a stock trader* • *a futures trader* • *a currency trader* ○ *He is a well-known trader on the floor of the New York Stock Exchange.*

trad·ing /ˈtreɪ·dɪŋ/ *n* [U] • *Many shops have reported a fall in trading* (=buying and selling) *in the last few months.* • *She said that she didn't approve of Sunday trading* (=shops being open on Sunday). • Trading is also the buying and selling of shares and money: *The stock market moved ahead slightly in active trading today.* ○ *They have been accused of* **insider** *trading* (=using their special knowledge which they have from working for the company to make a profit from buying or selling its shares). • *(Br)* A **trading estate** is an **industrial estate**. See at INDUSTRY [PRODUCTION]. • A **trading post** is a small place, esp. in the past, which is a long way from other places in which people live, where goods can be bought and sold or exchanged: *New York was originally a Dutch trading post.*

trade [BUSINESS] /treɪd/ *n* a particular business or industry • **the** *building/catering/tourist trade* • **the** *book/car/fur trade* [C] • *He worked* **in** *the same trade all his life.* [C] • *The company supplies its goods only to* **the** *trade* (=people who work in a particular business or industry), *not direct to the public.* [U] • *People who work* **in** *the trade* (=the same business or industry) *can buy their books at a discount.* [U] • A trade **publication/journal/magazine/paper** is a newspaper produced for people working in a particular business or industry: *the trade publication, 'Automotive World'* • *a steel industry trade journal* • A trade is also a job, esp. one which needs special skill and which involves working with your hands: *After she left school, she went to college to learn a trade.* [C] ○ *He's a carpenter* **by** *trade.* [U] • *(Am)* A **trade school** *(Aus* **technical** *school) is a school where students learn skills which involve working with your hands:* After junior high school he went to a trade school, where he learned to be an auto mechanic. • A **trade secret** is a piece of information about a product that is known only to the particular company that makes it: *The exact ingredients of Coca Cola are a trade secret.* ○ *(fig.) My aunt says that it's a trade secret* (=that she is not willing to tell anyone) *how old she is.* • A **trade union** (also **trades union**, **union**, *Am* **labor union**) is an organization of workers in a particular industry, which represents them and aims to improve their pay and working conditions. This system of representation and its principles are known as **trade unionism**. A person who is an active member of such an organization is a **trade unionist**: *The government's proposals have been strongly criticized by the trade unions.* ○ *The rally was organized by local trade union officials.* ○ *He was a member of the Conservative trade union* **movement**, *and in 1960 he became the first trade unionist to chair the Conservative party conference.* ○ *In many* *industrial countries, trade unionism has declined.* See also TUC.

trade on *obj*, **trade u·pon** *obj v prep* [T] to use (something, esp. a characteristic) for your own advantage, esp. unfairly • *People are always trading on his generosity.* • *She said that she wanted to be successful as an actress in her own right, not just to trade on her famous father's name.* • *This kind of advertising trades on people's fears.* • *He trades on his good looks.*

trade·mark /£ˈtreɪd·mɑːk, $-mɑːrk/ *n* [C] a name or a symbol which is put on a product to show that it is made by a particular producer. The product cannot be legally made by any other producer, and the name or symbol cannot be legally used by any other producer. • *Velcro is a* **registered** *trademark.* • *(fig.) He was wearing one of the brightly coloured ties that are his trademark* (= typical of him). • *(fig.) She gave one of her trademark* (= typical) *smiles.* • LP› **Symbols**

trade–off /£ˈtreɪd·ɒf, $-ɑːf/ *n* [C] a balancing of two opposing situations or qualities, both of which are desired • *There is a trade-off* **between** *doing the job accurately and doing it quickly.* • *She said that she'd had to make a trade-off* **between** *her job and her family.* • A trade-off is also something that you do not really want but that you accept in order to have something else that you do want: *For some car buyers, lack of space is an acceptable trade-off* **for** *a sporty design.*

trades·man /ˈtreɪdz·mən/ *n* [C] *pl* **-men** a man who buys and sells goods, esp. someone who owns a shop • *Local tradesmen have objected to the plans to build a big new shopping centre on the edge of the town.* • *(Br, often humorous)* The **tradesmen's entrance** is the side or back door of a house, as used, esp. in the past, by people delivering goods to large private houses, who were not allowed to use the door at the front of the house: *I've forgotten my front-door key, so we'll have to use the tradesmen's entrance.*

trades·peo·ple /ˈtreɪdzˌpiː·pl̩/ *pl n* people who buy and sell goods, esp. people who own a shop • *Local tradespeople have generously contributed to the appeal to raise money for the hospital.*

tra·di·tion /trəˈdɪʃ·ᵊn/ *n* a belief, principle or way of acting which people in a particular society or group have continued to follow for a long time, or all of these in a particular group or society considered as a whole • *Fireworks have long been an American tradition on the Fourth of July.* [C] • *Switzerland has a* **long** *tradition* **of** *neutrality.* [C] • *The villagers still follow the* **old/ancient** *tradition* **of** *women and children sitting on one side of the church and men on the other.* [C] • *"My great-great-grandmother began brewing in 1795 and there has been a* **family** *tradition* **of** *brewing ever since," he said.* [C] • *I think children should learn about* **religious** *traditions other than their own.* [C] • *There's a tradition in our office* **that** *when it's somebody's birthday, they bring in a cake for us all to share.* [C + *that* clause] • *It was* **breaking (with)** (= ending) *a 600-year-old tradition when the university started taking women students.* [C] • *There is a great tradition* **of** *dance* (= a lot of dances have been created and performed) *in St Petersburg.* [C] • *His paintings are* **in the** *tradition* **of** (= have features similar to) *those of Bacon and Spencer.* [C] • *Her poetry is deeply rooted in Irish tradition.* [U] • *According to tradition, a headless ghost walks through the corridors of the house at night.* [U] • *The Dinka people of north Africa are cattle-farmers* **by** *tradition.* [U] • LP› **Holidays**

tra·di·tion·al /trəˈdɪʃ·ᵊn·ᵊl, -ˈdɪʃ·nᵊl/ *adj* • *The villagers retain a strong attachment to their traditional values/customs/beliefs* (= those that have been believed or followed by a particular society or group of people for a long time without changing). • *He said that sex discrimination laws had not really succeeded in changing traditional views about the roles of men and women in society.* • *The school uses a combination of modern and traditional methods for teaching reading.* • *Recent polls suggest that voters are still faithful to their traditional party loyalties.* • *The dancers were wearing traditional Hungarian dress/costume.* • *Traffic jams, train cancellations, and crowded airports marked a traditional start to the Easter holiday.* • *She's very traditional* (= Her opinions and ways of behaving are like those that have existed for a long time, rather than being modern).

tra·di·tion·al·i·sm /trəˈdɪʃ·ᵊn·ᵊl·ɪ·zᵊm, ˈ-nᵊl-/ *n* [U] • Traditionalism is the belief in, or act of following, ideas and ways of doing things that have been believed or followed by a particular society or group of people for a long time: *He argued that the country's training and education systems were still dominated by traditionalism.* ○ *The building's design is an interesting blend of traditionalism and modernism.*

tra·di·tion·al·ist /trəˈdɪʃ·ᵊn·ᵊl·ɪst, ˈ-nᵊl-/ *n* [C] • *Religious traditionalists* (= people who believe in and follow ideas and ways of behaving that have been followed by a particular society or group for a long time) *objected to theories of evolution being taught in schools.* • *In his early career as a jazz musician, he was regarded as a bit too modern for the traditionalists, and a bit too traditional for the modernists.* • *She holds traditionalist Muslim views.* • *This production of 'Swan Lake' is in traditionalist style.*

tra·di·tion·al·ly /trəˈdɪʃ·ᵊn·ᵊl·i, -ˈdɪʃ·nᵊl-/ *adv* • *The fast of Ramadan is traditionally broken with a few dates.* • *Quaker meetings are traditionally held in silence.* • *In Spain, rice is traditionally the symbol of plenty.* • *Traditionally, the company's main markets have been Britain and the US.*

tra·duce *obj* /£trəˈdjuːs, £-ˈdʒuːs, $-ˈduːs/ *v* [T] *fml* to criticize (someone or something) very negatively • *Clark claimed that he had been traduced by the press.*

traf·fic VEHICLES /ˈtræf·ɪk/ *n* [U] the amount of vehicles moving along roads, or the amount of aircraft, trains or ships moving along a route • *Was there a lot of traffic on your journey?* • *There was* **heavy** *traffic on the roads this morning.* • *We got* **stuck in** *traffic for several hours.* • *I try to avoid the* **commuter/rush-hour** *traffic.* • *Traffic* **jams/clogs/chokes** *the roads leading into London.* • *New measures have been introduced to try and ease traffic* **congestion** *in the city.* • *Five people were injured in a traffic* **accident** (= one involving vehicles). • *The runway at the airport is not long enough to take transatlantic traffic* (= aircraft). • **Air** *traffic has increased 30% in the last decade.* • **Rail** *traffic was disrupted after last night's heavy snow.* • Traffic is also people or goods transported by road, air, train or ship, as a business: *The airline has cut its overseas service by half because of a sharp reduction in traffic.* ○ *Environmental groups argue that more* **passenger** *and* **freight** *traffic should be moved off the roads and onto trains.* • *(Br)* If a road is **traffic calmed**, or **traffic calming** is added to it, raised areas are built across it, or small ROUNDABOUTS or other similar structures are built onto it, so that vehicles are forced to move more slowly along it: *Local residents are demanding that traffic calming* **measures** *are introduced to reduce the number of accidents on the road.* • **Traffic circle** is *Am for* ROUNDABOUT CIRCULAR OBJECT. • A **traffic cone** is a cone-shaped object, usually red and white or yellow, which is used to mark an area of a road on which cars are temporarily not allowed to go, usually because repairs are being done: *One lane of the road was closed off by traffic cones.* PIC› **Cone** • A **traffic island** (also **island**) is a raised area in the middle of a road where people who are crossing the road can wait safely for traffic to go past. • **Traffic island** is also *Am for* **central reservation**. See at CENTRAL NEAR THE MIDDLE. • A **traffic jam** is a large number of vehicles close together moving very slowly or unable to move at all: *Roadworks have caused traffic jams throughout the city centre.* ○ *I was* **stuck in** *a traffic jam for an hour yesterday.* • **Traffic lights** (also **lights**, *Am also* **stoplight**) are a set of red, yellow and green lights which control the movement of vehicles at a point where two or more roads join. A **traffic light** is also any one of this set of lights: *Turn left at the traffic lights, and Hinton Road is the second on your right.* ○ *The traffic lights turned green as we approached the junction.* ○ *She shot across just as the lights were changing.* ○ *He was stopped by the police for failing to stop at a red traffic light.* • The **traffic police** (*Am also* **traffic cops**) are police officers whose job is to direct the movement of vehicles on a road, or to stop drivers who are breaking the law and give them an official notice that they have done so. • *(Br)* A **traffic warden** (*Aus* **parking policeman**) is a person whose job is to make certain that people do not leave their cars in places where they are not allowed to leave them, or for longer than they are allowed to leave them: *A traffic warden gave me a ticket for parking on a double yellow line.* • PIC› **Motorway, Road** Ⓕ

traf·fic TRADE /ˈtræf·ɪk/ *n* [U] illegal trade • *The two governments are working together to try and cut down the traffic* **in drugs**/*the* **drug** *traffic across their borders.* • *Police are looking for ways of curbing the traffic* **in guns**. • LP› **Crimes and criminals** Ⓕ

traf·fic /ˈtræf·ɪk/ *v* [I] **trafficking**, *past* **trafficked** • *They were arrested for trafficking* **in** *the eggs of protected species of birds.* • *It has been said that the government knew that the arms trafficking had been going on.*

traf·fick·er /£ˈtræf·ɪ·kəʳ, $-kɚ/ *n* • A trafficker is a person who trades in illegal goods, particularly drugs: *a drug trafficker* • *an international arms trafficker*

trag·e·dy /ˈtrædʒ·ə·di/ *n* a very sad event or situation, esp. one involving death or suffering, or a play or literature about death or suffering • *The Holocaust is one of the greatest tragedies the world has ever known.* [C] • *The pilot averted a tragedy when he succeeded in preventing the plane from crashing.* [C] • *Hitler's invasion of Poland led to the tragedy* **of** *the Second World War.* [C] • *Seeing so many disasters on television makes us less sensitive to* **human** *tragedy and suffering.* [U] • *His life was touched by hardship and* **personal** *tragedy.* [U] • *They had only recently arrived in London when tragedy* **struck** *in the form of their son being killed in an accident.* [U] • *It's a tragedy* **(that)** *so many young people are unable to find jobs.* [C + (*that*) clause] • *Shakespeare's tragedies* (= plays about suffering that end sadly) *include 'Hamlet', 'King Lear' and 'Othello'.* [C] • *In Greek tragedy* (= plays about death or suffering), *the role of the chorus is to express the audience's reactions to what is happening in the play.* [U] • *The play is a combination of tragedy and farce/comedy.* [U]

trag·ic /ˈtrædʒ·ɪk/ *adj* • *His friends were deeply shocked and saddened by the tragic* (= very sad because involving death or suffering) *news of his death.* • *The bomb explosion resulted in a tragic loss of life.* • *The war has had tragic consequences for thousands of families.* • *Hospital authorities admitted that a tragic mistake/error had been made in giving the patient the wrong drug.* • **It** *is tragic* (= very sad) *that the theatre has had to close.* [+ *that* clause] • Tragic can also be used to refer to literature about death or suffering: *In his career as an actor, he has played all Shakespeare's great tragic heroes.*

trag·i·cal·ly /ˈtrædʒ·ɪ·kli/ *adv* • *Both his parents were tragically killed when he was a baby.* • *She died tragically young.* • *Tragically, the side-effects of the drug were not discovered until many people had been seriously damaged by it.*

trag·i·com·e·dy /£ˌtrædʒ·ɪˈkɒm·ə·di, $-ˈkɑː·mə-/ *n* [C/U] a (type of) play or story which is both sad and amusing

trag·i·com·ic /£ˌtrædʒ·ɪˈkɒm·ɪk, $-ˈkɑː·mɪk/ *adj*

trail PATH /treɪl/ *n* [C] a path through the countryside, often made or used for a particular purpose • *a forest/mountain trail* • A trail is also the smell or series of marks left by a person, animal or thing as it moves along: *The dogs are specially trained to* **follow** *the trail left by the fox.* ○ *The trail was still* **warm** (= was clear and easy to follow)/*had gone* **cold** (= was not clear and easy to follow, or had disappeared). ○ *He went inside,* **leaving a** *trail* **of** *muddy footprints behind him.* ○ *(fig.) The police admit that the thieves have* **left** *no trail* (= things that would show where they went) *for them to follow up.* ○ *The three men went to the Bahamas,* **on the** *trail* **of** (= searching for) *a sunken 17th-century galleon full of treasure.* • A **trail blazer** is the first person to do something or go somewhere, who shows that it is also possible for other people: *Orville and Wilbur Wright were aviation trail blazers.* • Compare TRACK PATH.

trail *obj* /treɪl/ *v* [T] • *Hunters can trail* (= follow the marks left by) *wild animals through the forest.*

trail *(obj)* COME AFTER /treɪl/ *v* to (allow to) move slowly along the ground or through the air or water, after someone or something • *Katherine, your skirt's trailing* **in** *the mud!* [I always + adv/prep] • *As the boat moved slowly forward, he trailed his hand* **in** *the water.* [T] • If a person or group is trailing, the competitor is winning: *The Swiss team are trailing* **by** *6 points.* [I always + adv/prep] ○ *The election is only two weeks away, and still the Nationalist Party is trailing* **(behind)** *the Liberals.* [T; I + *behind*] • Trail can also mean to move slowly and without energy: *The delegates trailed back into the conference room for the afternoon session.* [I always + adv/prep] ○ *After a mile or two the youngest children were trailing* **behind**. [I always + adv/prep]

trail·ing /ˈtreɪ·lɪŋ/ *adj* [before n; not gradable] • Trailing plants grow along the ground or over the surface of something: *a trailing rose*

trail a·way/off *v adv* [I] (esp. of a person's voice) to become less loud and/or confident and then stop completely • *His voice trailed off hesitantly, as he saw the look on her face.*

trail·er VEHICLE /£ˈtreɪ·ləʳ, $-lɚ/ *n* [C] a vehicle without an engine, often in the form of a flat frame or a container, which is pulled by another vehicle • *The car was* **pulling** *a trailer, which carried a racing motorcycle.* • A trailer is also the separate back part of a large truck. • Trailer is *Am for* CARAVAN. • PIC **Farming**

trail·er ADVERTISEMENT /£ˈtreɪ·ləʳ, $-lɚ/ *n* [C] an advertisement for a (new) film, television or radio programme, consisting of brief SCENES (= parts) from it • *I saw a trailer* **for** *the latest Spielberg film and thought it looked quite interesting.*

train VEHICLE /treɪn/ *n* [C] a railway engine connected to carriages for carrying people or wheeled containers for carrying goods • *a fast/slow train* • *a goods/freight/passenger train* • *the train to/from Bristol* • *a train journey* • *a train station* • *Did you come* **by** *train?* • *She* **caught/took** *the train to Edinburgh.* • *Hurry up, or we'll* **miss** (= arrive too late for) *the train.* • *He asked her to marry him while they were* **on** *the train from Calais to Paris.* • A **train set** is a toy train, together with the equipment, toy houses etc. that go with it. • *(Br)* A **train spotter** is a person whose hobby is collecting the numbers that each railway engine has, by writing them down when they see them. • *"Let the train take the strain"* (advertisement for trains, 1970-) • PIC **Toy**

train *(obj)* PREPARE /treɪn/ *v* to prepare or be prepared for a job, activity or sport, by learning skills and/or by mental or physical exercise • *She trained* **as** *a pilot.* [I] • *Isn't Michael training* **to** *be a lawyer?* [+ *to* infinitive] • *She spent a few years training teachers* **to** *use new technology.* [+ obj + *to* infinitive] • *They still teach Latin because they believe it trains the mind/brain.* [T] • *I've had to train* **myself to** *be more assertive at work.* [+ obj + *to* infinitive] • *She trained hard* **for** *the race, sometimes running as much as 60 miles a week.* [I] • *(humorous) I'm trying to train my boyfriend* **to** *do the occasional bit of housework.* [+ obj + *to* infinitive] • *(specialized) The computer comes with scanning software that can be trained* **to** *recognize and read different sorts of text.* [+ obj + *to* infinitive]

trained /treɪnd/ *adj* • *I didn't realize Philippa was a trained nurse.* • *Are you trained* **in** *the use of this equipment?* • *(humorous) "Did I hear you say your children cleared up after the party?" "Oh yes, I've got them* **well**-*trained!"*

train·ee /ˌtreɪˈniː/ *n* [C] • A trainee is a person who is learning and practising the skills of a particular job: *a trainee dentist/electrician/monk* ○ *a graduate trainee*

train·er /£ˈtreɪ·nəʳ, $-nɚ/ *n* [C] • A trainer is a person who teaches skills to people or animals and prepares them for a job, activity or sport: *They showed pictures of the horse and its trainer* (= the person who prepared it for its races). ○ *A lot of wealthy people have their own* **personal** *trainer* (= a person they employ to help them exercise). • See also TRAINER.

train·ing /ˈtreɪ·nɪŋ/ *n* [U] • *a training course* • *a teacher-training college* • *in-house/on-the-job training* • *New staff* **have/receive** *a week's training* **in** *how to use the computers.* • *The players have to turn up for training* (= an occasion of practising skills and doing exercise) *three times a week.* • When you are **in** training **for** a competition, you exercise a lot and eat particular food in order to prepare yourself. • If you say that something is **good** training, you mean that it is useful experience and will be helpful when doing other similar things in the future: *His experience as a teacher was good training* **for** *parenthood.* • KOR

train *obj* AIM /treɪn/ *v* [T always + adv/prep] *fml or specialized* to aim or point (a gun, camera, light, etc.) at something or someone • *With five guns suddenly trained* **on** *him, he was understandably nervous.*

train *obj* DIRECT GROWTH /treɪn/ *v* [T] to direct the growth of (a plant) in a particular direction by cutting it and tying it • *The vines were trained* **over** *an arch, providing shade as well as fruit.*

train SERIES /treɪn/ *n* [C] a series of connected thoughts or events, or a line of animals, people or things moving along together • *What amazing train* **of thought** *led you from Napoleon to global warming?* • *The book describes the train* **of events** *that led up to the assassination.* • *(fig.) The reform process was* **put/set in train** (= started) *in 1985, by the Liberal government.* • *a wagon train* • *a baggage train* • *a mule/camel train*

train PART OF DRESS /treɪn/ *n* [C] the part of a long dress that spreads out onto the floor behind • *Veronica had a very elaborate wedding dress with a long train.*

train·er *Br* /£'treɪ·nəʳ, $-nɚ/, *Br also* **train·ing shoe**, *Am* **run·ning shoe** *n* [C] a shoe made specially for doing sport, that gives extra support to the foot • PIC› Shoes

traipse /treɪps/ *v* [I always + adv/prep] *disapproving* to walk or go, esp. tiredly or unwillingly from one place to another • *She spent the day traipsing* **round** *the shops, but found nothing suitable to buy.* • *It was awful having the builders traipsing* **through** *our home every day.*

trait /treɪt/ *n* [C] a particular characteristic that can produce a particular type of behaviour • *His sense of humour is one of his better traits.* • *Arrogance is a very unattractive* **character** *trait.* • *It's a* **genetic** *trait that causes deafness at an early age.*

trait·or /£'treɪ·təʳ, $-t̬ɚ/ *n* [C] *disapproving* a person who is not or stops being loyal to their own country, social class, beliefs etc. • *The leaders of the rebellion were hanged as traitors.* • *The Chinese Communist Party* **branded** (= called) *Mr Gorbachev 'a traitor* **to** *socialism'.* • *You've betrayed us, you traitor!* [as form of address]

trait·or·ous /£'treɪ·tᵊr·əs, $-t̬ɚ-/ *adj fml disapproving*

tra·jec·to·ry /£trə'dʒek·tᵊr·i, £'-tri, $-tɚ·i/ *n* [C] *specialized* the curved path that an object follows after it has been thrown or fired into the air • *the trajectory of a bullet/missile* • *If you throw a heavy object its natural trajectory tends to be a parabola.* • *(fig.) The Government is now claiming that inflation is on a downward trajectory* (= is getting lower).

tram *Br and Aus* /træm/, *Am usually* **street·car**, *Am also* **trol·ley** *n* [C] an electric vehicle that transports people, usually in cities, and goes along metal tracks in the road

tram·lines TRACK /'træm·laɪnz/ *pl n* two metal tracks set in the road, along which a TRAM (= vehicle) goes

tram·lines SPORT /'træm·laɪnz/ *pl n Br* two parallel painted lines along the edge of the playing area used in tennis and BADMINTON. Players lose a point if they hit the ball so that it lands between them, except if it is a game when four people are playing.

tramp *(obj)* WALK /træmp/ *v* to walk esp. long distances, or with heavy steps • *We spent a week tramping the streets of Rome, looking for movie locations.* [T] • *Maddy tramped upstairs and started shouting angrily.* [I always + adv/prep] • Ⓓ

tramp /træmp/ *n* [U] • *The streets echoed with the tramp* **of** *soldiers' feet* (= the sound they made, all walking together). • *The girls* **went for** *a tramp* (= a long walk) **through** *the countryside.*

tramp POOR PERSON /træmp/ *n* [C] *dated* a person with no home, job or money who travels around and asks for money from other people • Ⓓ

tramp WOMAN /træmp/ *n* [C] *esp. Am disapproving* a woman who has sex often with a lot of different partners • *She'll sleep with anyone – she's a real tramp!* • *"That's why the lady is a tramp"* (from the song *The Lady is a Tramp* written by Lorenz Hart, 1940) • Ⓓ

tram·ple *(obj)* /'træm·pl̩/ *v* to step heavily on (something or someone) causing damage or injury • *Somebody trampled* **all over** *my flowerbeds in the night!* [always + prep] • *A herd of stampeding cattle had trampled* **(down)** *the crops.* [T/M] • *Eight people were trampled* **to death** (= killed) *when the stadium collapsed and the crowd rushed out onto the football pitch.* [T] • *Several people were trampled* **underfoot** *and seriously injured in the rush to get out of the building.* [T] • *(fig.) The government she described as 'a bunch of careless vandals, trampling* **on** (= acting without any respect for) *the needs and rights of the ordinary citizen.'* [always + prep]

tram·po·line /£'træm·pᵊl·iːn, £,--'-, $'---/ *n* [C] a piece of sports equipment which you use for jumping on, consisting of a piece of stretchy material joined by springs to a frame • PIC› Sports

tram·po·lin·ist /£'træm·pᵊl·iː·nɪst, £,-'--, $'----/ *n* [C] • *She was a very good trampolinist when she was at school.*

trance /£trɑːnts, $trænts/ *n* [C] a temporary mental condition in which someone is not completely aware of and/or not in control of themselves and of what is happening to them • *First she* **goes/falls into** *a deep trance and then the spirit voices start to speak through her.* • *When a hypnotist* **puts** *you* **in(to)** *a trance, you no longer have conscious control of yourself and you do whatever the hypnotist says.* • *He sat staring out of the window as if* **in** *a trance, dazed and unaware.*

tran·quil /£'træŋ·kwɪl, $'træn-/ *adj slightly literary* calm and peaceful and without noise, violence, anxiety, etc. • *She stared at the tranquil surface of the water.* • *It's a beautiful, civilized hotel in a tranquil rural setting.* • *The murders occurred in what is, at first glance, a tranquil neighbourhood.* • *A spasm of pain crossed his normally tranquil features.*

tran·quil·ly /£'træŋ·kwɪ·li, $'træn-/ *adv slightly literary*

tran·quil·li·ty, *Am usually* **tran·quil·i·ty** /£træŋ'kwɪl·ɪ·ti, $træn'kwɪl·ə·t̬i/ *n* [U] *slightly literary* • *The first priority for a government is to enable its citizens to live in* **peace and** *tranquillity.* • *I love the tranquillity of the countryside.*

tran·quil·lize *obj*, *Am usually* **tran·quil·ize**, *Br and Aus usually* **–ise** /£'træŋ·kwɪ·laɪz, $'træn-/ *v* [T] • To tranquillize an animal or person is to give them a drug that makes them become unconscious or calm: *The leopard died when zoo officials tried to tranquillize it.* ○ *Sales of tranquillizing medicines began to drop as doctors became more aware of the risks associated with them.*

tran·quil·liz·er, *Am usually* **tran·quil·i·zer**, *Br and Aus usually* **–iser** /£'træŋ·kwɪ·laɪ·zəʳ, $'træn·kwɪ·laɪ·zɚ/ *n* [C] • A tranquillizer is a drug used to make a person or animal calmer: *She was* **on** *tranquillizers for a long time after her son died.*

trans– ACROSS /trænts-, trɑːnts-, trænz-, trɑːnz-/ *combining form* across • *Several major carriers admit their trans-Atlantic flights are now on schedule less than half the time.* • *The trans-Alaskan pipeline carries oil right across Alaska.*

trans– CHANGED /trænts-, trɑːnts-, trænz-, trɑːnz-/ *combining form* having changed from one thing to another • *Kate has transformed* (= completely changed) *that house since she moved in.* • *She is a transsexual* (= She has changed from being a man to a woman).

trans·act *obj* /£træn'zækt, £trɑːn-, $træn-/ *v* [T] *fml* to do and complete (a business activity) • *My guides vanished into the village to transact their mysterious* **business**. • *The sale was transacted in conditions of the greatest secrecy.*

trans·ac·tion /£træn'zæk·ʃᵊn, £trɑːn-, $træn-/ *n* [C] • *a business transaction* • *Each transaction at the foreign exchange counter seems to take forever.*

trans·at·lan·tic /£,træn·zət'læn·tɪk, £,trɑːn-, $,træn·zæt-/ *adj* [not gradable] crossing the Atlantic ocean, or relating to countries on both sides of the Atlantic Ocean • *transatlantic flights/routes/traffic* • *a transatlantic telephone call*

trans·cend *obj* /£træn'send, £trɑːn-, $træn-/ *v* [T] *fml* to go beyond, rise above or be more important or better than (something, esp. a limit) • *The best films are those which transcend national or cultural barriers.* • *Fortunately the acting and photography are so good that they somehow manage to transcend the limitations of the film's plot.* • *The underlying message of the film is that love transcends everything else.* • *One factor transcends* (= is more important than) *all the rest.*

trans·cen·dence /£træn'sen·dənts, £trɑːn-, $træn-/ *n* [U] *fml*

trans·cen·dent /£træn'sen·dənt, £trɑːn-, $træn-/ *adj fml* • *Freud banished for many people the belief that a transcendent* (= greater than all others) *authority exists to which mankind is accountable for its actions.*

trans·cen·den·tal /£,trænt·sen'den·tᵊl, £,trɑːnt-, $,trænt·sen'den·t̬ᵊl/ *adj fml or specialized* • An experience, event, object or idea that is transcendental is extremely special and unusual and cannot be understood in ordinary ways: *a transcendental vision of the nature of God* • **Transcendental meditation** (*abbreviation* **TM**) is a method of calming the mind and becoming relaxed by silently repeating a special word or series of words many times.

trans·con·ti·nen·tal /£,trænz,kɒn·tɪ'nen·tᵊl, £,trɑːnz-, $,trænz,kɑːn·t̬ə-/ *adj* [not gradable] crossing a continent • *The transcontinental railway goes from New York in the east to San Francisco in the west.*

tran·scribe *obj* RECORD /£træn'skraɪb, £trɑːn-, $træn-/ *v* [T] to record (something written, spoken or played) by writing it down • *Tape recordings of conversations are transcribed by typists and entered into the database.*

tran·script /£'trænt·skrɪpt, £'trɑːnt-, $'trænt-/ *n* [C] • *Mysteriously, the transcript* (= exact written copy) **of** *what was said at the trial went missing.*

tran·scrip·tion /£træn'skrɪp·ʃᵊn, £trɑːn-, $træn-/ *n* [U] • *I think it is probably just an error in transcription* (= the process of making an exact written copy of something).

tran·scribe *obj* CHANGE /£træn'skraɪb, £trɑːn-, $træn-/ *v* [T] to change esp. (one writing system) into another or (music for one group of instruments) into music for others • *Transcribing the Ethiopian text* **into** *the English alphabet was their first task.* • *The quintet had been transcribed* **for** *clarinet and piano.*

tran·scrip·tion /£træn'skrɪp·ʃᵊn, £trɑːn-, $træn-/ *n* [C] • *This is a* **phonetic** *transcription* (= written representation of sounds) **of** *the conversations that were recorded on tape.*

tran·sept /£'trænt·sept, £'trɑːnt-, $'trænt-/ *n* [C] either of the two side parts of a cross-shaped church that are at an angle of 90 degrees to the main part

trans·fer *(obj)* MOVE /£trænts'fɜːʳ, £trɑːnts-, $'trænts·fɜːr/ *v* **-rr-** to (cause to) move from one place, position, job, vehicle, person or group to another • *He has been transferred* **to** *a psychiatric hospital.* [T] • *She transferred her gun* **from** *its shoulder holster* **to** *her handbag.* [T] • *I'll be upstairs, so could you transfer my phone calls* (= arrange that I can receive them) **up** *there please?* [T] • *All passengers were transferred* **out of** *one bus and* **into** *another.* [T] • *Police are investigating how £20 million was illegally transferred* **out of** *the Trust's bank account.* [T] • *The oil company tried to transfer the blame for the disaster* **to** *the ship's crew and captain.* [T] • *The aim is to transfer* **power/control/responsibility to** *self-governing regional councils.* [T] • *Angela didn't respond to Gavin's charms so he transferred his* **affections to** *her best friend* (= started to love the friend instead). [T] • If you transfer property **to** someone, you make them the legal owners of it: *She transferred the house* **to** *her daughter before she died.* [T] • If a football CLUB transfer a player they sell him to another team: *He threatened to give up football if his club didn't transfer him.* [T] ○ *Some very high-profile British players have transferred* **to** *clubs abroad.* [I always + adv/prep]

trans·fer /£'trænts·fɜːʳ, £'trɑːnts-, $'trænts·fɜːr/ *n* • Transfer might refer to the process of moving from one place, position, etc. to another: *Black's transfer* **to** *an Italian football club came as a shock to Coventry supporters.* [C] ○ *The official transfer* **of** *ownership will take a few days to complete.* [U] ○ *New technology will speed up the transfer* **of** *information.* [U] • A transfer may also be a person or thing that has moved: *They've a new transfer* **from** *Tottenham playing for them.* [C] • *(Am)* A transfer is also a ticket which allows a passenger to change routes or to change from one bus or train to another. [C] • *(Br)* A **transfer fee** is the amount of money a sports team pays in order to buy a new player from another team: *The transfer fee for Brinkworth was £500 000.* • *(Br) The club's top goalkeeper is on the* **transfer list** (= they are offering to sell him to another team). • *(Br) McLoughlin, Southampton's latest buy from Swindon last December, has been* **transfer-listed** (= offered for sale) *at his own request.*

trans·fer·ence /£trænts'fɜː·rənts, £trɑːnts-, $'trænts·fɚ·ənts/ *n* [U] *fml* • *UN observers were there to ensure the smooth transference of power.* • *(specialized)* In PSYCHOLOGY, transference happens when a person who is receiving treatment transfers the thoughts and emotions they have been having about one person on to someone else, esp. the person who is trying to treat them: *Therapists should always be on the lookout for transference from their clients.*

trans·fer·a·ble /£trænts'fɜː·rə·bl̩, £trɑːnts-, $trænts'fɜːr·ə-/ *adj* [not gradable] • *The tickets were marked 'Not Transferable', so if you bought one you weren't allowed to sell it to anyone else.*

trans·fer PATTERN /£'trænts·fɜːʳ, £'trɑːnts-, $'trænts·fɜːr/ *n* [C] a picture or pattern made so that when it is rubbed or heated while it is pressed against a surface, it becomes fixed to that surface • *The kids bought transfers and ironed them onto their T-shirts.* • Compare DECAL.

trans·fi·gure *obj* /£trænts'fɪg·əʳ, £trɑːnts-, $trænts'fɪg·jɚ/ *v* [T usually passive] *fml* to change (the appearance of a person or thing) very noticeably, usually in a very positive and often spiritual way • *Her face, as she stared down at the baby, was transfigured* **with** *tenderness.* • *The assassination somehow transfigured Kennedy* **into** *a modern American saint.*

trans·fi·gu·ra·tion /£ˌtrænts·fɪ·gᵊr'eɪ·ʃᵊn, £ˌtrɑːnts-, $ˌtrænts·fɪg·jə'reɪ-/ *n* [U] *fml*

trans·fix *obj* /£trænts'fɪks, £trɑːnts-, $trænts-/ *v* [T usually passive] *literary* to cause (a person or animal) to feel unable to move, usually because their interest in or fear of something is so strong • *The conference delegates were transfixed by her speech.* • *Rabbits transfixed in the glare of car headlights are common victims on the roads.* • *(fml)* To transfix someone or something also means to push a long pointed object through them: *A body lay in the corner, transfixed by a spear.*

trans·form *obj* /£trænts'fɔːm, £trɑːnts-, $trænts'fɔːrm/ *v* [T] to change completely the appearance or character of (something or someone), esp. so that they are improved • *The reorganization will transform the British entertainment industry.* • *A few mirrors can transform a dark room, making it look larger and lighter instantly.* • *Whenever a camera was pointed at her, Marilyn would instantly transform her***self into** *a radiant star.*

trans·for·ma·tion /£ˌtrænts·fə'meɪ·ʃᵊn, £ˌtrɑːnts-, $ˌtrænts·fɚ-/ *n* • *Local people have mixed feelings about the planned transformation of their town* **into** *a regional capital.* [U] • *I'd never seen Carlo in smart evening clothes before – it was quite a transformation.* [C]

trans·form·er /£trænts'fɔː·məʳ, £trɑːnts-, $trænts'fɔːr·mɚ/ *n* [C] *specialized* a device which changes the VOLTAGE or other characteristic of electrical energy as it moves from one CIRCUIT (= system of wires) to another • *You may need a transformer if you want to run a personal stereo off mains electricity.*

trans·fu·sion /£trænts'fjuː·ʒᵊn, £trɑːnts-, $trænts-/ *n* the process of adding an amount of blood to a person's or animal's body, or the amount of blood itself • *She was infected with AIDS as a result of a contaminated* **blood** *transfusion.* [C] • *When a patient has lost a lot of blood transfusion is the only answer.* [U] • *(fig.) The World Bank is being asked to arrange a large scale transfusion* **of** *funds* **into** *the project.* [C]

trans·gress *(obj)* /£trænz'gres, £trɑːnz-, $trænz-/ *v fml* to break (a law or moral rule) • *The military court decided he had transgressed the standing orders.* [T] • *Those are the rules, and anyone who transgresses will be severely punished.* [I]

trans·gres·sion /£trænz'greʃ·ᵊn, £trɑːnz-, $trænz-/ *n fml* • *Transgression* **of** *the rules was met with severe punishment.* [U] • *Who is supposed to have* **committed** *these transgressions?* [C]

trans·gres·sor /£trænz'gres·əʳ, £trɑːnz-, $trænz'gres·ɚ/ *n* [C] • *The system seems to be designed to punish the transgressor* (= the person breaking the rules) *rather than help his victim.*

tran·si·ent /£'træn·zi·ənt, £'trɑːn-, $'trænt·ʃᵊnt/, **tran·si·to·ry** /£'træn·zɪ·tᵊr·i, £'trɑːn-, $'træn·zə·tɔːr·i/ *adj fml* lasting for only a short time; temporary • *A glass of whisky has only a transient warming effect.* • *The city has a large transient population* (= many people who are living in it only temporarily).

tran·si·ent /£'træn·zi·ənt, £'trɑːn-, $'trænt·ʃᵊnt/ *n* [C] *fml* • *It's an organization set up to provide money and help for transients* (= people living temporarily in a place).

tran·si·ence /£'træn·zi·ənts, £'trɑːn-, $'trænt·ʃᵊnts/ *n* [U] *fml* • *the transience of fame*

tran·sis·tor /£træn'zɪs·təʳ, £trɑːn-, $træn'zɪs·tɚ/ *n* [C] a small electrical device containing a SEMICONDUCTOR, used in televisions, radios, etc. to control or increase an electric current, or *(dated)* a small radio containing these

tran·sis·tor·ized, *Br and Aus usually* **–ised** /£træn'zɪs·tᵊr·aɪzd, £trɑːn-, $træn'zɪs·tə·raɪzd/ *adj* [not gradable] • Transistorized devices use transistors rather than VALVES: *transistorized amplifiers*

tran·sit /£'træn·zɪt, £'trɑːn-, $'træn-/ *n* [U] the movement of goods or people from one place to another • *The question is whether road transit is cheaper than rail.* • *Britain imports over 100 000 birds each year, but 20 000 die* **in** *transit.* • *It is possible to make an insurance claim for any goods lost or damaged* **in** *transit.* • *We went on one of those new* **rapid-transit** *trains.* • *(esp. Br) The refugees were in a* **transit camp** *in Austria, on their way from Iraq to Germany.*

tran·si·tion /£træn'zɪʃ·ᵊn, £trɑːn-, $træn-/ *n* a change from one form or type to another, or the process by which this happens • *The health-care system is* **in** *transition at the moment.* [U] • *There will be an interim government to oversee the transition* **to** *democracy.* [C] • *Last summer I* **made** *the transition* **from** *an ordinary long-board windsurfer* **to** *a more dynamic short board.* [U]

tran·si·tion·al /£træn'zɪʃ·ᵊn·əl, £trɑːn-, $træn-/ *adj* [not gradable] • *a transitional government* • *a transitional* **period** *of two or three months*

tran·si·tive /£'trænt·sə·tɪv, £'trɑːnt-, $'trænt·sə·t̬ɪv/ *adj* [not gradable] *specialized* (of a verb) having or needing an object • *In this dictionary, transitive verbs, such as 'put', are marked* [T] • Compare DITRANSITIVE; INTRANSITIVE. • LP⟩ **Verbs**

tran·si·tive /£'trænt·sə·tɪv, £'trɑːnt-, $'trænt·sə·t̬ɪv/ *n* [C] *specialized* • *Can 'cry' be a transitive* (=a transitive verb)*?*

tran·si·tive·ly /£'trænt·sə·tɪv·li, £'trɑːnt-, $'trænt·sə·t̬ɪv-/ *adv* [not gradable] *specialized* • *Can 'cry' be used transitively?*

tran·si·ti·vi·ty /£ˌtrænt·sə'tɪv·ɪ·ti, £ˌtrɑːnt-, $ˌtrænt·sə'tɪv·ə·t̬i/ *n* [U] *specialized*

trans·late *(obj)* /£trænt'sleɪt, £trɑːnt-, $træn-/ *v* to change (words) into a different language, or *(fig.)* to change (something) into a new form, esp. to turn (a plan) into reality • *The instructions had been translated* **from** *the Japanese.* [T] • *She works for the EU, translating* **from** *English* **into** *French and Italian.* [I] • *I don't speak French – is there anyone here who could translate* **(for** *me)?* [I] • *(fig.) The Tourist Board do not have the money to enable them to translate these grand ideas* **into** *reality.* [T] • *(fig.) The ways of working that he had learnt at college did not translate* **well** (=were not suitable) **to** *the world of business.* [I] • *(fig.) He mumbled something which I translated* **as** (=decided it meant) *agreement.* [T] • Compare INTERPRET [BETWEEN LANGUAGES].

trans·la·tion /£trænt'sleɪ·ʃᵊn, £trɑːnt-, $træn-/ *n* • *The children do one French translation a week.* [C] • *A literal translation* **of** *'euthanasia' would be 'good death'.* [C] • *She reads Proust* **in** *translation* (=changed into her own language, not in the original language). [U] • *The English version is boring – perhaps it has* **lost** *something* **in** *translation* (=is not as good as the original). [U]

trans·lat·or /£trænt'sleɪ·təʳ, £trɑːn-, $træn'sleɪ·t̬ɚ/ *n* [C] • A translator is a person whose job is changing esp. written words (but also sometimes spoken words) into a different language. • Compare **interpreter** at INTERPRET [BETWEEN LANGUAGES].

trans·li·te·rate *obj* /£trænz'lɪt·ᵊr·eɪt, £trɑːnz-, $træn'slɪt̬·ə·reɪt/ *v* [T] *specialized* to write (a word or letter) in a different alphabet • *On the road signs, the Greek place names have been transliterated into the Latin alphabet, sometimes in several different ways.*

trans·li·te·ra·tion /£ˌtrænz·lɪ·tᵊr'eɪ·ʃᵊn, £ˌtrɑːnz-, $trænˌslɪt̬·ə'reɪ-/ *n specialized* • *The Wade-Giles transliteration of Chinese characters* **into** *the Roman alphabet has been replaced by Pinyin.* [C] • *The texts await transliteration.* [U]

trans·lu·cent /£trænz'luː·sᵊnt, £trɑːnz-, $trænz-/ *adj often approving* (of glass, plastic, etc.) almost transparent, allowing some light through so that objects can be seen through it but not very clearly • *This china is so fine and delicate that if you hold it up to the light it's translucent.* • *Delia's skin has a translucent quality so that you can almost see the veins under it.* • Compare OPAQUE; TRANSPARENT.

trans·lu·cence /£trænz'luː·sᵊnts, £trɑːnz-, $trænz-/ *n* [U]

trans·mit *(obj)* /£trænz'mɪt, £trɑːnz-, $trænz-/ *v* **-tt-** to send or give (something) in ways that cannot be seen • *Radio Seven transmits* **on** *201 medium wave* (=uses those particular radio waves to broadcast on). [I] • *Fibre-optic cables will transmit* (=carry) *the electronic signals.* [T] • *Cholera is transmitted* **through** *contaminated water.* [T] • *He got a sexually transmitted disease.* [T] • *Some diseases are transmitted* **from** *one generation* **to** *the next.* [T] • *Somehow your panic and fear transmits* **itself to** *the horse that you're riding.* [T]

trans·mis·sion /£trænz'mɪʃ·ᵊn, £trɑːnz-, $trænz-/ *n* • *These crowded cities are the perfect environment for the transmission* **of** *infection.* [U] • *We apologize for the interruption to our transmissions* (=broadcasts) *this afternoon, caused by an electrical fault.* [C] • A vehicle's transmission is the machinery that brings the power produced by the engine to the wheels: *automatic transmission* [U] ○ *The car had a faulty transmission, so I took it in to the garage.* [C]

trans·mit·ter /£trænz'mɪt·əʳ, £trɑːnz-, $træn'smɪt̬·ɚ/ *n* [C] • *National Radio have set up transmitters* (=equipment for broadcasting radio or television signals) *on two hills in the middle of the city.*

trans·mog·ri·fy *obj* /£trænz'mɒg·rɪ·faɪ, £trɑːnz-, $træn'smɑː·grə-/ *v* [T often passive] *fml or humorous* to change (something or someone) completely • *These parts of the East End of London, formerly so Jewish, have gradually been transmogrified* **into** *an Asian area.* • *Alf Haigh, now transmogrified* **into** *Lord Haigh, will be an unusual addition to the House of Lords.*

trans·mog·ri·fi·ca·tion /£ˌtrænz·mɒg·rɪ·fɪ'keɪ·ʃᵊn, £ˌtrɑːnz-, $trænˌsmɑː·grə-/ *n* [U] *fml or humorous*

trans·mute *(obj)* /£trænz'mjuːt, £trɑːnz-, $trænz-/ *v* [always + adv/prep] *fml* to change (something) completely, esp. into something different and better • *A shaft of sunlight had suddenly transmuted the room* **into** *a bright and welcoming place.* [T] • *(fig.) I still can't believe that the obnoxious youth that I knew actually transmuted* **into** *a nice man.* [I] • *(specialized) Plutonium transmutes* **into/to** *uranium when it is processed in a nuclear reactor.* [I] • *A few centuries ago alchemists thought they could transmute lead* **into** *gold.* [T]

trans·mu·ta·tion /£ˌtrænz·mjuː'teɪ·ʃᵊn, £ˌtrɑːnz-, $ˌtrænz-/ *n* [C/U] *fml*

tran·som (win·dow) /'trænt·səm/ *n* [C] *Am for* FANLIGHT • [PIC] **Doors**

trans·par·ent /£trænt'spær·ᵊnt, £trɑːnt-, $træn'sper-/ *adj* able to be seen through; that allows light through, so that objects on the other side can be seen clearly • *The plants are in a transparent plastic box, so the children can see the roots growing.* • *You couldn't wear this blouse with nothing underneath – it's practically transparent!* • *(fig. disapproving) How can politicians stand there and come out with such transparent* (=obvious) *nonsense!* • *(fig.) I think we should try to make the instructions more transparent* (=clear and easy to understand). • Compare OPAQUE; TRANSLUCENT. • (CS) (RUS)

trans·par·en·cy /£træn'spær·ᵊnt·si, £trɑːn-, $træn'sper-/ *n* • *The old-fashioned type of plastic lacked transparency* (=the characteristic of being easy to see through). [U] • *(specialized)* A transparency is a SLIDE (=photograph you can shine light through to show it on a screen). [C]

trans·pire [BECOME KNOWN] /£træn'spaɪəʳ, £trɑːn-, $træn'spaɪɚ/ *v* [+ *that* clause] (of a fact which was secret or not known) to become known • **It** *may yet transpire* **that** *ministers knew more than they are admitting.* [+ *that* clause] • **It** *transpired* **that** *Mr Keller and I had both been to the same school.* [+ *that* clause] • **As it** *later transpired, she had known him at school.* • (F)

trans·pire [HAPPEN] /£træn'spaɪəʳ, £trɑːn-, $træn'spaɪɚ/ *v* to happen • *No one is willing to predict what may transpire at the peace conference.* [I] • (F)

trans·pire *(obj)* [LOSE WATER] /£træn'spaɪəʳ, £trɑːn-, $træn'spaɪɚ/ *v* [I/T] *specialized* (of a body or plant) to lose water through its surface • (F)

trans·pi·ra·tion /£ˌtrænt·spɪ'reɪ·ʃᵊn, £ˌtrɑːnt-, $ˌtrænt-/ *n* [U] *specialized*

trans·plant *(obj)* /£træn'splɑːnt, £trɑːn-, $træn'splænt/ *v* to move (something) or be moved from one place or person to another • *The plants should be grown indoors until spring, when they can be transplanted outside* (=put in the ground outside). [T] • *Beetroot doesn't transplant well.* [I always + adv/prep] • *Doctors transplanted a monkey's heart* **into/in** *a two-year old child* (=Doctors removed the child's faulty heart and put in a monkey's). [T] • *(fig.) Management has a crazy plan to close the London office and transplant the staff* **to** *the regions.* [T] • Compare IMPLANT.

trans·plant /£'trænt·splɑːnt, £'trɑːn-, $'trænt·splænt/ *n* [C] • *a heart/kidney transplant* • *transplant surgery* • *a transplant operation/patient* • *He* **had** *a heart transplant* (=Doctors took out his heart and put in a different, healthier one). • *The transplant* (=new organ) *was accepted/rejected by the body.* • Compare IMPLANT.

trans·plan·ta·tion /£ˌtrænt·splɑːn'teɪ·ʃᵊn, £ˌtrɑːnt-, $ˌtrænt·splæn-/ *n* [U] • *Transplantation of organs from living donors raises ethical issues.*

trans·pon·der /£træn'spɒn·dəʳ, £trɑːn-, $træn'spɑːn·dɚ/ *n* [C] an electronic device that gives out a radio signal when it receives a similar signal telling it to • *Aircraft are required by law to carry transponders, so that they can be identified.*

trans·port *obj* /£træn'spɔːt, £trɑːn-, $'træn·spɔːrt/ *v* [T] to take (goods or people) from one place to another • *The pipeline was constructed to transport oil* **across** *Alaska* **to** *ports on the coast.* • *Such heavy items are expensive to transport* **(by** *plane).* • *(fig.) The film transported us* **back to** (=made us feel as if we were in) *the New York of the 1950s.* • In the past, when criminals were transported, they were sent to live in a country far away, as a punishment: *Thousands were transported* **to** *Australia.*

trans·port /£'trænt·spɔːt, £'trɑːnt-, $'trænt·spɔːrt/ *n* • *the Department of Transport* • *investment in* **public** *transport* (=buses, trains, etc. available for everyone to use) • *transport costs* • *For short distances, the bicycle is surely the best* **means of** *transport.* [U] • *Do you have your own transport* (=vehicle)*?* [U] • *The company will arrange transport from the airport.* [U] • *The transport* (=transporting) *of live animals should be forbidden.* [U] • A transport (also **transport plane** or **transport ship**) is an aircraft or ship for taking esp. soldiers or military supplies from one place to another: *a troop transport* [C] • *(literary)* If you are **in transports (of delight/joy)** or **in a transport of delight/joy** you are extremely pleased or happy. • *(Br)* A **transport café** (*Am and Aus* **truck stop**) is a cheap restaurant next to a main road, used mainly by truck drivers. • PIC〉 **Aircraft**

trans·por·ta·tion /£ˌtræn*t*·spɔːˈteɪ·ʃᵊn, £ˌtrɑːn*t*-, $ˌtræn*t*·spɚ-/ *n* [U] • *The transportation* (=transporting) *of live animals is forbidden.* • *(esp. Am and Aus) In Los Angeles many companies encourage their employees to use alternative means of transportation* (=transport)*, rather than the car.* • *In the past, British convicts could be sentenced to transportation (***to** *Australia).*

trans·port·er /£trænˈspɔː·tɚ, £trɑːn-, $trænˈspɔːr·t̬ɚ/ *n* [C] • A transporter is a long vehicle used for moving several large objects such as cars from one place to another: *a car transporter* • PIC〉 **Vehicles**

trans·pose *obj* /£trænˈspəʊz, £trɑːn-, $trænˈspoʊz/ *v* [T] *fml specialized* to change (something) from one position to another, or to exchange the positions of (two things) • *In their latest production they have reworked 'King Lear', transposing it* **to** *pre-colonial Africa.* • *The confusion was caused when two numbers were accidentally transposed by a Social Security clerk.* • *(specialized)* To transpose a piece of music is to play it in a different KEY (=set of musical notes based on a particular note): *The pianist transposed the song* **into** *C.*

trans·po·si·tion /£ˌtræn*t*·spəˈzɪʃ·ᵊn, £ˌtrɑːn*t*-, $ˌtræn*t*-/ *n* [C/U]

trans·sex·u·al /£trænzˈsek·sjʊəl, £trɑːnz-, £-sju·əl, $trænzˈsek·ʃu·əl/ *n* [C] a person, esp. a man, who feels that they should have been the opposite sex, and therefore behaves and dresses like a member of that sex, or a person who has had a medical operation to change their sex

tran·sub·stan·ti·a·tion /£ˌtræn*t*·səbˌstæn·*t*ʃiˈeɪ·ʃᵊn, £ˌtrɑːn*t*-, $ˌtræn*t*-/ *n* [U] *specialized* the esp. Roman Catholic belief that during MASS (=a religious ceremony) bread and wine are changed into the body and blood of Jesus Christ

trans·verse /£trænzˈvɜːs, £trɑːnz-, $træn*t*sˈvɜːrs/ *adj* [not gradable] *specialized* in a position or direction that is at an angle of 90° to something else • *The main roof beams are given extra support by the smaller transverse beams.*

trans·ves·tite /£trænzˈves·taɪt, £trɑːnz-, $trænz-/ *n* [C] a person, esp. a man, who wears the clothes of the opposite sex, often for sexual pleasure • Compare TRANSSEXUAL.

trans·ves·ti·sm /£trænzˈves·tɪ·zᵊm, £trɑːnz-, $trænz-/ *n* [U] *fml*

trap CATCHING DEVICE /træp/ *n* [C] a device or hole for catching animals or people and preventing their escape • *The farmer* **sets** *traps to catch rats in his barns.* • *The fox got its foot* **caught in** *a trap.* • A trap is also a dangerous or unpleasant situation which you have got into and from which it is difficult or impossible to escape: *When the undercover agents went to the rendezvous, they did so knowing it might be a trap.* ○ *She's too clever to* **fall into** *the trap of doing any unpaid work.* • Ⓙ

trap *obj* /træp/ *v* [T] **-pp-** • *She survived in the forest by eating berries and trapping small animals and birds.* • *The two men died when they were trapped* **in** (=unable to escape from) *a burning building.* • *Fire officers had to use cutting equipment to free his legs, which were trapped under* (=unable to be removed from) *a steel beam.* • *(fig.) Jack left the job after ten years because he was beginning to* **feel** *trapped.* • If you are trapped **into** (doing) something you are forced to do it although you do not want to: *Trapped into marriage and early motherhood, Martha used drink as a means of escaping domestic pressure.* [T] ○ *I hope you don't feel that you've been trapped into taking her.* [T] • To trap something such as heat or water is to keep it in one place, esp. because it is useful: *The greenhouse stays warm because the glass traps the heat of the sun.*

trap·per /£ˈtræp·əʳ, $-ɚ/ *n* [C] • A trapper is a person who traps wild animals, esp. in order to sell their fur: *a fur trapper*

trap MOUTH /træp/ *n* [C] *slang* a mouth • *Oh,* **shut** *your trap* (=stop talking) *– I'm bored of listening to you!* • *I've told him it's a secret and he's to* **keep** *his* **trap shut** (=not say anything about it). • Ⓙ

trap VEHICLE /træp/ *n* [C] (esp. in the past) a light carriage with two wheels pulled by a horse • Ⓙ

trap·door /£træpˈdɔːʳ, $-ˈdɔːr/ *n* [C] a small door in a ceiling or floor • *There's a trapdoor* **into** *the attic.* • PIC〉 **Doors**

tra·peze /trəˈpiːz/ *n* [C] a short bar hanging high up in the air from two ropes, that is used by ACROBATS when performing special swinging movements • *A man and woman performed* **on the flying** *trapeze.* • *The best thing about the circus is the trapeze* **artists**, *I think.*

tra·pe·zi·um *Br and Aus* /trəˈpiː·zi·əm/, *Am* **tra·pe·zoid** /ˈtræp·ɪ·zɔɪd/ *n* [C] *pl* **trapeziums** or **trapezia** /trəˈpiː·zi·ə/ *specialized* a flat four-sided shape, where two of the sides are parallel

trap·pings /ˈtræp·ɪŋz/ *pl n* all the things that are part of or are typical of a particular job, situation or event • *He enjoyed the trappings* **of power**, *such as a chauffeur-driven car and bodyguards.* • *They have rejected capitalism and the trappings* **of** *a 'corrupt' Western-style economy.* • *The demonstration had* **all the** *trappings* **of** *a typical 1960s peace demo.*

Trap·pist (monk) /ˈtræp·ɪst/ *n* [C] a member of a Roman Catholic organization with very extreme rules, such as no talking • *Being married to him must be like living with a Trappist monk – he hardly ever says anything.*

trap·shoot·ing /£ˈtræpˌʃuː·tɪŋ, $-t̬ɪŋ/ *n* [U] the sport of shooting at **clay pigeons** (=round flat breakable clay objects that are thrown into the air)

trash /træʃ/ *n* [U] *infml disapproving* something that is worthless and of low quality, or *(esp. Am)* waste items or rubbish • *(disapproving) I can't believe that someone of his intelligence can read such trash!* • *Saturday night television is such trash!* • *(esp. Am) The trash really stinks – why don't you take it out?* • **Trash bag** is *Am for* **dustbin bag**. See at DUSTBIN. • **Trash can** is *Am for* DUSTBIN. • **Trash can liner** is *Am for* **dustbin bag/liner**. See at DUSTBIN. • *(Am infml disapproving)* If you describe a group of people as trash, you mean that they are worthless: *We don't have anything to do with the people in the apartment below us – they're trash.* • *(Am infml)* If you **talk** trash, you say things that do not have a lot of meaning: *There are too many radio shows featuring idiots who call in and talk trash all day.* • *(Am infml)* You can also **talk** trash by criticizing others, esp. unfairly or cruelly.

trash *obj* /træʃ/ *v* [T] *infml* • *The guys got angry and trashed* (=severely damaged) *the bar.* • *She was annoyed because her work had been trashed* (=severely criticized).

trash·y /ˈtræʃ·i/ *adj* **-ier, -iest** *infml disapproving* • *Why do so many people watch such ridiculous trashy* (=worthless and of low quality) *programmes?*

trash·can /ˈtræʃ·kæn/ *n* [C] *Am for* DUSTBIN

trau·ma /£ˈtrɔː·mə, ˈtraʊ-, $ˈtrɑː-/ *n* severe emotional shock and pain caused by an extremely upsetting experience • *Five years of psychotherapy helped him to deal with his childhood traumas.* [C] • *These people are experiencing the trauma* **of** *military defeat and foreign occupation.* [U] • *(medical)* (A) trauma is also a severe injury, esp. caused by violence or in an accident. [C/U]

trau·ma·tic /£trɔːˈmæt·ɪk, traʊ-, $trɑːˈmæt̬-/ *adj* • *Some of the most disturbed children had witnessed really traumatic things, such as rape and murder.* • *Don't you find exams traumatic* (=frightening and difficult to be calm about)*?*

trau·ma·tize *obj* /£ˈtrɔː·mə·taɪz, $ˈtrɑː-/, *Br and Aus usually* **-ise** *v* [T usually passive] • *She was completely traumatized by the death of her mother.* • *The whole experience left him traumatized.*

tra·vails /ˈtræv·eɪlz, trəˈveɪlz/ *pl n esp. literary* the difficulties that are experienced as part of a particular situation • *Tonight's documentary looks at the life of a struggling young actor, with all its travails, its despair and its joy.* • *The travails of the British car industry are seldom out of the news.*

trav·el *(obj)* /ˈtræv·ᵊl/ *v* **-ll-** or *Am usually* **-l-** to make a journey, usually over a long distance • *To travel* **across** *the Sahara desert on camels would be the adventure of a lifetime.* [I] • *She spent a year travelling, mostly in Africa and Asia, after leaving school.* [I] • *I travel* **to** *work* **by** *train and it normally takes about an hour.* [I] • *It's a good idea to travel* **light** (=without taking a lot of heavy things with you). [I] • *If you travel 20 miles a day, you should be in Paris by the end of the month.* [I] • *As a young man he had travelled* (=been to many parts of) **the world**. [T] • Travel can also mean to move or go from one place to another: *Supersonic planes can travel faster than the speed of sound.* [I] ○ *Air pollution can travel great distances.* [I] • If something such as food travels **well/badly**, it does/does not stay in good condition if it is moved long distances: *They say that real Yorkshire beers don't travel well.* [I] • *(infml)* If you say that a vehicle is **really** travelling, you mean that it is going very fast: *We were doing 90mph, so that other car that passed us must have been really travelling!* [I] • *(humorous saying)* If you say '**have** something, **will travel**', you mean that you want to go on a journey and use a particular skill: *The ad in the newspaper read 'Have English language skills, will travel.'* • *"To travel hopefully is a better thing than to arrive"* (Robert Louis Stevenson in the book *Virginibus Puerisque*, 1881) • *"He travels the fastest who travels alone"* (from *The Story of the Gadsbys* by Rudyard Kipling, 1890) • (I)

trav·el /'træv·ᵊl/ *n* [U] • *air travel* • *space travel* • *business travel* • *We share a love of literature, food and travel.* • *Since 90% of the country is jungle, travel is not easy.* • *It said on the travel* **news** *that there'd been an accident on this stretch of the road.* • A **travel agent** is a person or (also **travel agency**) a company that arranges tickets, hotel rooms, etc. for people going on holiday or making a journey. • **Travel expenses** are money that your employer pays you because you are spending that amount on travel which is necessary for your work. • A **travel plug** is one that connects a piece of electrical equipment brought from one country to the electricity supply in another when they cannot be connected directly, used esp. when travelling. • **Travel sickness** (also **motion sickness**) is a feeling of illness, esp. of needing to vomit, which some people get in a moving vehicle. • PIC> **Plugs**

trav·elled, *Am usually* **trav·eled** /'træv·ᵊld/ *adj* • *It's a well-/much-/little-travelled route* (= many/few people have travelled along it). • *They're a well-travelled/widely travelled couple* (= they have visited many countries).

trav·el·ler, *Am usually* **trav·el·er** /£'træv·ᵊl·əʳ, £'-ləʳ, $-ᵊl·ɚ/ *n* [C] • *This hotel is for serious travellers, rather than tourists on two-week package holidays.* • *(Br)* Traveller is another word for GYPSY. • *(Br)* **New Age** *travellers* (= people living in vehicles, without a permanent home or job) *were on the road again today, looking for a place to hold their midsummer festival.* • *(Br)* A **traveller's cheque**/ *(Am)* **traveler's check** is a piece of paper that you buy from a bank or a travel company and that you can use as money or exchange for the local money of the country you visit. It is safer than ordinary money because it needs your signature before it can be used. • *"I met a traveller from an antique land"* (from the poem *Ozymandias* by Percy Bysshe Shelley, 1819)

trav·ell·ing, *Am usually* **trav·el·ing** /'træv·ᵊl·ɪŋ, '-lɪŋ/ *n* [U] • *Do you like travelling?* • *I love the work but I hate the travelling that's involved.* • *He belongs to a travelling opera company/travelling circus.* • *(dated)* A **travelling salesman** is a **sales representative**. See at SALE.

trav·els /'træv·ᵊlz/ *pl n* • *The book is the record of her travels* (= journeys) *around the Far East.* • *"Gulliver's Travels"* (title of a book by Jonathan Swift, 1726) • *"Travels with a Donkey"* (title of a book by R.L.Stevenson, 1879)

trav·el·ogue, *Am also* **trav·el·og** /£'træv·ᵊl·ɒg, $-ə·lɑːg/ *n* [C] a film or book about travelling to or in a particular place • *Peter Jackson's latest book 'Africa' is part travelogue, part memoir.*

trav·erse *obj* /£trə'vɜːs, $-'vɜːrs/ *v* [T] *fml* to move or travel through (an area) • *She was an experienced traveller who'd traversed both Africa and Europe in her twenties.* • *(fig.) The film traverses the history of an American family in the 1930s and 1940s.*

trav·e·sty /'træv·ə·sti/ *n* [C] *slightly fml* something which fails to represent the values and qualities that it is intended to represent, in a way that is shocking or offensive • *Their production of 'Macbeth' was quite the worst I've ever seen – it was a travesty.* • *Langdale described the court ruling as a travesty* **of justice**. • Compare PARODY.

trawl *(obj)* /£trɔːl, $trɑːl/ *v* to pull a large cone-shaped net through the sea at a deep level behind a special boat in order to catch fish • *They trawl these waters* **for** *cod.* [T] • If you trawl **for** people or information you search among a large number or a great variety of places in order to find what you want: *The newspaper had trawled its files for photos of the new minister.* [T] ○ *You need to trawl* **through** *a lot of data to get results that are valid.* [I always + adv/prep]

trawl /£trɔːl, $trɑːl/ *n* [C] • A trawl or **trawl net** is a large cone-shaped net pulled through the sea at a deep level behind a special boat in order to catch fish. • *(fig.) We* **did** *a wide trawl* (= searched among a lot of people) *to find the right person to play the part.*

trawl·er /£'trɔː·ləʳ, $'trɑː·lɚ/ *n* [C] • A trawler is a large boat that uses a wide cone-shaped net to catch fish. • PIC> **Ships and boats**

tray /treɪ/ *n* [C] a flat object, usually with raised edges, used for carrying food and drinks, or *(esp. Br)* a similar but deeper object used in offices etc. for keeping papers in • *She was carrying a tray* **of** *drinks.* • *I don't know where I put that article – it must be in the bottom of my tray.* • See also ASHTRAY.

treach·er·ous [DANGEROUS] /£'tretʃ·ᵊr·əs, $'-ɚ-/ *adj* (of the ground or the sea) extremely dangerous, esp. because of bad weather conditions • *Snow and ice in the South-East has left many roads treacherous, and motorists are warned to drive slowly.*

treach·er·ous [NOT LOYAL] /£'tretʃ·ᵊr·əs, $'-ɚ-/ *adj esp. old use* (of a person) guilty of deceiving and lacking loyalty • *Vargas plays the part of treacherous aristocrat who betrays his king and country.* • *I get a nagging sense of being treacherous* **to** *my own sex if I ever make general criticisms of women.*

treach·e·ry /£'tretʃ·ᵊr·i, $'-ɚ-/ *n* [U] *esp. old use* • *Corley said she was standing down as leader because of the treachery of her own colleagues.* • *Such treachery – and from his own son!*

trea·cle /'triː·kl̩/, **black trea·cle** *n* [U] *Br* a sweet dark thick liquid which is used in cooking sweet dishes and sweets • *treacle tart/toffee* • Treacle is also another word for **golden syrup**. See at GOLD [COLOUR]. • Compare SYRUP.

trea·cly /'triː·kl̩·i, '-kli/ *adj* **-ier**, **-iest** • *He'd coated the shelves with a thick treacly* (= dark and sticky) *varnish.* • *(disapproving)* Treacly is also used to mean too pleasant or kind, or expressing feelings of love in a false way: *The film is spoilt by a slightly treacly sentimentality.*

tread *(obj)* [STEP] /tred/ *v past simple* **trod** /£trɒd, $trɑːd/ or *Am also* **treaded**, *past part* **trodden** /£'trɒd·ᵊn, $'trɑː·dᵊn/ or *Am and Aus also* **trod** /£trɒd, $trɑːd/ to put the foot down; step • *I kept treading* **on** *his toes when we were dancing.* [I always + adv/prep] • *Mind you don't tread in the oil when you get out of the car.* [I always + adv/prep] • *He trod all over my nice clean floor in his filthy boots!* [I always + adv/prep] • *He trod* (= walked) *heavily and reluctantly up the stairs.* [I always + adv/prep] • *Some of the grass is trodden* **down** *where people have been playing football.* [T] • *Yuck! Look what I've just trodden* **in**! [I always + adv/prep] • *A load of food had been trodden* (= crushed by the feet) **into** *the carpet.* [T] • *Before the days of automation, they used to tread* **grapes** *to make wine.* [T] • *(literary) I sometimes see him flash past in his sports car as I tread my weary way* (= walk in a tired way) *to work.* [T] • To tread **carefully** is to speak or behave carefully to avoid upsetting or causing offence to anyone: *The government know they have to tread carefully on this issue.* [I always + adv] • *(fig.) Well, that's how you get to the top – you tread* **on** *other people* (= treat them badly). [I always + adv/prep] • *(humorous)* To **tread the boards** is to act in plays: *It's three years now since you've trodden the boards, Ken – how does it feel to be back?* • To **tread water** is to float vertically in the water by moving the legs and the arms up and down: *(fig.) I think she feels that she's just treading water in that job* (= not advancing in any way). • *"I have spread my dreams under your feet; / Tread softly because you tread on my dreams"* (W.B.Yeats in the poem *Aedh Wishes for the Cloths of Heaven*, 1929)

tread /tred/ *n* • Your tread is the sound that your feet make on the ground as you walk: *Then I heard someone's tread on the stairs.* • A tread is also the horizontal part of a step on which you put your foot.

tread [PATTERN ON TYRE] /tred/ *n* [C/U] the pattern of raised lines on a tyre which prevents a vehicle from sliding on the road • *The tread on your tyres is very worn.*

trea·dle /'tred·l̩/ *n* [C] a part of a machine which, when operated by the foot, gives the power to turn a wheel in the machine • *My grandmother still uses her old treadle sewing machine.*

tread·mill /'tred·mɪl/ *n* [C] a wide wheel turned by the weight of people climbing on steps around its edge, used in the past to provide power for machines or, more usually, as a punishment for prisoners • *The treadmill was introduced as a punishment in prisons in 1817.* • A treadmill is also an exercise machine which consists of a moving strip or two step-like parts on which you walk without moving forward. • A treadmill is also any type of repeated work which is boring and tiring and seems to have no positive effect and no end: *There were days when child-rearing seemed like an endless treadmill of feeding, washing and nappy-changing.*

trea·son /ˈtriː·zᵊn/ *n* [U] (the crime of) lack of loyalty to your country, esp. by helping its enemies or attempting to defeat its government • *In the seventeenth century a man called Guy Fawkes was executed for treason after he took part in a plot to blow up the British Parliament building.*

trea·son·a·ble /ˈtriː·zᵊn·ə·bl̩/, **trea·son·ous** /ˈtriː·zᵊn·əs/ *adj* [not gradable] *fml* • *He denied that he had had 'treasonable communications' with the enemy.*

treas·ure /£ˈtreʒ·əʳ, $-ɚ/ *n* wealth, usually in the form of a store of precious metals, precious stones or money • *Stories about pirates often include a search for* **buried** *treasure.* [U] • *When they opened up the tomb they found treasure beyond their wildest dreams.* [U] • *(infml)* You might describe someone as a treasure if you like them and they are very helpful in some way: *I don't know what I'd have done without Lizzie when I was ill – she was an absolute treasure.* [C] • *(infml, esp. Br)* Treasure is also an affectionate way of addressing someone, esp. a child: *Come on, treasure, let's go and see Granny.* • A **treasure hunt** is a game in which the players are given a series of CLUES (= pieces of information) to direct them to a hidden prize. • (A) **treasure trove** is a large amount of money or a large number of valuable metals, stones or other objects found hidden somewhere and seeming to belong to no one: *(fig.) Though small, this museum is a veritable treasure trove* **of** (= is full of) *history.* • *"Treasure Island"* (title of a story by Robert Louis Stevenson, 1883)

treas·ure *obj* /£ˈtreʒ·əʳ, $-ɚ/ *v* [T] • If you treasure something you take great care of it because you love it or consider it very valuable: *If I give you grandma's watch you'll promise me that you'll treasure it.* ○ *I shall always treasure those* **memories** *of her.* ○ *This pen that my grandfather gave me is one of my most treasured* **possessions**.

treas·ures /£ˈtreʒ·əz, $-ɚz/ *pl n* • Treasures are very valuable things, esp. pieces of art: *The museum houses some of the most priceless* **art** *treasures in the world.*

treas·ur·er /£ˈtreʒ·ᵊr·əʳ, $-ɚ·ɚ/ *n* [C] a person who is responsible for an organization's money • *Anthony Fletcher is the committee's/society's/Conservative party treasurer.*

treas·u·ry /£ˈtreʒ·ᵊr·i, $ˈ-ɚ-/ *n* [U] **the treasury** (in various countries) the government department responsible for financial matters such as spending and tax • *A Treasury spokesperson refused to comment on the rumours of tax increases.* • A US **Treasury bond** is an official document showing that someone has lent money to the US government which will be paid back after 10 years and on which INTEREST (= money) will be paid twice a year. • Compare EXCHEQUER.

treat *obj* DEAL WITH /triːt/ *v* [T always + adv/prep] to behave towards (someone) or deal with (something) in a particular way • *My parents treated us all the same when we were kids.* • *He treated his wife very badly.* • *They treated my suggestion* **as** *a joke* (= behaved as if it was not serious). • *It's wrong to treat animals* **as if** *they had no feelings.* • *(infml) They were treated* **like dirt** (= extremely badly)*!* • *The staff in the hotel treated us* **like royalty** (= very well). • *I treat remarks like that* **with** *the contempt that they deserve.* • *You know what I always say about men – treat them mean, keep them keen.* • See also **ill-treat** at ILL BAD; MALTREAT; MISTREAT.

treat·ment /ˈtriːt·mənt/ *n* • *They got some fairly rough treatment from the policemen in the local station.* [U] • *Peter gets* **special** *treatment because he knows the boss.* [U] • *The same subject matter gets a very different treatment* (= is considered and examined differently) *by Chris Wilson in his latest novel.* [C]

treat *obj* GIVE MEDICAL CARE /triːt/ *v* [T] to use drugs, exercises, etc. in order to cure a person of a disease or heal an injury • *It said in the papers that he was being treated* **for** *a rare skin disease.* • *Doctors recommend that this condition should be treated* **with** *bed-rest.* • *Western medicine tends to treat* **the symptoms** *and not the cause.*

treat·ment /ˈtriːt·mənt/ *n* • *Heat treatment certainly helped my knee.* [U] • *In the UK you get free dental treatment while you're pregnant.* [U] • *Perhaps it's time to try a new course of treatment.* [U] • *The problem with this disease is that it doesn't generally* **respond to** (= improve as a result of) *treatment.* [U] • *There are various treatments* **for** *this complaint.* [C]

treat SPECIAL EXPERIENCE /triːt/ *n* [C] a special and enjoyable occasion or experience • *We're going to Italy for the weekend – it's my* **birthday** *treat.* • *As a* **special** *treat I'll take you to my favourite tea-shop.* • *I had a real treat this morning – my husband took the kids out while I had a good long sleep.*

treat *obj* PAY FOR /triːt/ *v* [T] to buy or pay for something for (someone else) • *Put your money away – I'm going to treat you* (**to** *this*). • *He's hardly got any clothes, so I thought I'd treat him* **to** *a new sweater.* • *I'm going to treat my***self to** (= buy for myself) *a new pair of sandals.*

treat /triːt/ *n* [U] • *No, you paid for dinner last time – this is my treat* (= I will pay).

treat *obj* PUT ON /triːt/ *v* [often passive] to put a special substance on (material such as wood, cloth, metal, etc.) or do a special process to it, in order to give it a particular quality • *The material has been treated* **with** *resin to make it waterproof.*

treat VERY WELL /triːt/ *n* [U] **a treat** *Br infml* very well; with good results • *If you've spilt a drop of red wine on something and you don't want it to stain, put some salt on it – it* **works** *a treat.* • *That soup was lovely – it went down a treat* (= tasted very good)*!* • *I polished that old desk of grandma's and it came up a treat* (= its appearance improved).

trea·tise /£ˈtriː·tɪs, $-t̬ɪs/ *n* [C] a formal piece of writing that considers and examines a particular subject • *He's the author of a six-volume treatise* **on** *trademark law.*

trea·ty /£ˈtriː·ti, $-t̬i/ *n* [C] a written agreement between two or more countries formally approved and signed by their leaders • *a* **peace** *treaty* • *The treaty* **on** *European union calls for the creation of a single currency by 1999.* • *We've* **signed/concluded** *a treaty* **with** *neighbouring states* **to** *limit emissions of harmful gases.* [+ *to* infinitive] • *The treaty must be* **ratified** (= approved and signed) *by all member governments before it can take effect.*

treb·le THREE TIMES /ˈtreb·l̩/ *predeterminer* three times greater in amount, number or size • *He earns almost treble the amount that I do.*

treb·le *(obj)* /ˈtreb·l̩/ *v* • *The price of property has almost trebled* (= become three times greater) *in the last ten years.* [I] • *That recipe is only enough for two, so treble the quantities* (= make them three times greater) *for six of you.* [T]

treb·le MUSIC /ˈtreb·l̩/ *adj* [before n], *adv* [not gradable] (of a boy's voice) singing the highest notes, or (of an instrument) playing the highest notes • *songs for the treble voice* • *He sings treble.* • A **treble clef** (also **G clef**) is a sign on a STAVE (= the five lines on which music is written) which shows that the notes are above **middle C** (= the C near the middle of a PIANO keyboard).

treb·le /ˈtreb·l̩/ *n* [C] • *This part is for a* **boy** *treble* (= a boy with a high voice).

tree /triː/ *n* [C] a tall plant which has a wooden trunk and branches that grow from its upper part • *They've got some wonderful plum trees in the back garden.* • *We sat under a tree for shade.* • *This area used to be a massive forest, but all the trees have been cut down to make paper.* • *I* **climbed (up)** *that tree once when I was a kid.* • Other tall plants which do not have wooden trunks are also often referred to as trees: *palm trees* • A **tree fern** is a large tropical FERN (= plant with feathery leaves) with a trunk-like stem. • *When we were kids we had a* **tree house** (= small building among the branches of a tree) *where we used to play for hours.* • A **tree-lined** road is one that has trees on both sides of it. • A **tree ring** (also **annual ring, growth ring**) is one of the rings that you can see in a tree trunk if you cut through it, which shows one year's growth. • See also SHOETREE. Compare BUSH; SHRUB. • PIC **Tree** DK S

tree·line /ˈtriː·laɪn/, **tim·ber·line** *n* [U] the height above sea level or the distance south or north of the equator beyond which trees do not grow

tree·tops /£ˈtriː·tɒpz, $-tɑːpz/ *pl n* **the treetops** the upper branches of a group of trees • *Monkeys were playing in the treetops.*

trek /trek/ *v* [I always + adv/prep] **-kk-** to walk a long distance, usually over land such as hills, mountains or forests • *We spent the day trekking through forests and over mountains.* • *He's* **going** *trekking in Peru this summer.* • *(infml) I trekked* (= walked a long and tiring distance) *all the way into town to meet him and he didn't even turn up.*

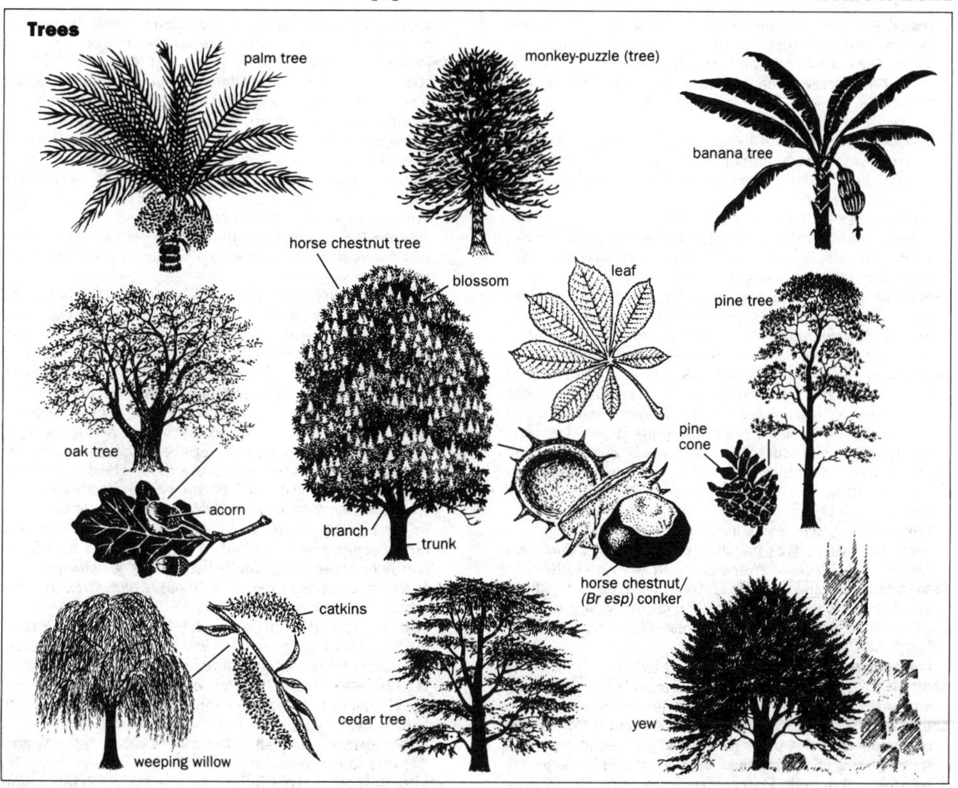

trek /trek/ *n* [C] • *We did an eight hour trek between the two villages yesterday.* • *(infml) You can walk to town from here but it's a bit of a trek* (=it's a long distance to walk).

trel·lis /ˈtrel·ɪs/ *n* [C] a light frame made of bars of wood or metal crossed over each other which, fastened to a wall, supports plants as they grow up it • PIC› **Garden**

trem·ble /ˈtrem·bl̩/ *v* [I] to shake slightly, usually because you are cold, frightened, or very emotional • *He hasn't got enough clothes on – look, he's trembling* **with** *cold.* • *He remembered her as a small child, bright red and trembling* **with** *rage if she was refused something.* • *Her* **bottom lip** *trembled and tears welled up in her eyes.* • *His* **voice** *started to tremble and I thought he was going to cry.* • If you say that you **tremble to think** about or **tremble at the prospect of** a possible future event, you are worried or frightened about it: *I tremble to think what will happen when he finds out.*

trem·ble /ˈtrem·bl̩/ *n* [U] • *There was a slight tremble in her voice as she recalled her husband.*

tre·men·dous /trɪˈmen·dəs/ *adj* very great in amount or level, or extremely good • *They were making the most tremendous amount of noise last night.* • *She's spent a tremendous amount of money on that house.* • *She's been a tremendous* (=very great) *help to me over the last few months.* • *I liked the whole play but the singing especially I thought was tremendous.* • *You won? That's tremendous!* • LP› **Very, completely** Ⓔ Ⓘ Ⓟ

tre·men·dous·ly /trɪˈmen·də·sli/ *adv* • *He's produced some tremendously successful films.* • *We all enjoyed ourselves tremendously.*

trem·o·lo /£ˈtrem·əl·əʊ, $-ə·loʊ/ *n* [C] *pl* **tremolos** (in music) a shaking sound which is achieved, when singing or playing an instrument, by repeating the same note extremely quickly or by playing two notes very quickly, one after the other • Compare VIBRATO.

trem·or /£ˈtrem·əʳ, $-ɚ/ *n* [C] a slight shaking movement in a person's body, esp. because of nervousness or excitement, or a slight EARTHQUAKE (=sudden violent movement of the Earth's surface) • *The disease mostly affects people over 50, causing paralysis and uncontrollable tremors.* • *There was a slight tremor in her voice.* • *The tremor was centered just south of San Francisco and it was felt as far as 200 miles away.* • *(fig.) A tremor* **of** *excitement went through the audience as he came on stage.* • *(fig.) Stock-market tremors again shook bond prices.*

trem·ul·ous /ˈtrem·jʊ·ləs/ *adj literary* • If a person's voice or a part of their body is tremulous it is shaking slightly: *He watched her tremulous hand reach for the teacup.* ○ *She scarcely recognised the tremulous voice on the end of the phone.*

trem·ul·ous·ly /ˈtrem·jʊ·lə·sli/ *adv*

trench /trentʃ/ *n* [C] a narrow channel which is dug into the ground • *One of the workmen was killed when the sides of the trench they were working in collapsed.* • A trench is also a deep channel used by soldiers as a place from which they can attack the enemy while being hidden: *the trenches of World War I* • *trench warfare.* Compare FOXHOLE. • A **trench coat** is a long loose coat with a belt, usually made from waterproof material and similar in style to a military coat. • PIC› **Coats and jackets**

trench·ant /ˈtren·tʃənt/ *adj slightly fml* (esp. of criticism, remarks, etc.) severe and expressed with force • *His most trenchant criticism is reserved for the party leader, whom he describes as 'the most incompetent and ineffectual the party has known.'* • *He wrote a series of trenchant articles on the state of the British theatre.* • *Dorothy Parker's writing is characterized by a trenchant wit and sophistication.*

trench·ant·ly /ˈtren·tʃənt·li/ *adv slightly fml* • *A woman of firm views, trenchantly expressed, Denys could be sharply critical.*

trench·an·cy /ˈtren·tʃənt·si/ *n* [U] *slightly fml*

trench·er /£ˈtrent·ʃəʳ, $-ʃɚ/ *n* [C] *Aus for* MORTARBOARD

trend /trend/ *n* [C] a general development or change in a situation or in the way that people are behaving • *Surveys of housing show a trend* **away from** *home-ownership and towards rented accommodation.* • *Sales were 20% lower than last year, continuing the* **downward** *trend of the last few years.* • *Certainly among the middle-classes, there's a trend* **towards** *having children in the early or mid-thirties.* • *I can't keep up with all the latest music trends – they come and go so rapidly.* • A trend is often a new development in clothing, make-up, etc.: *Whatever the latest* **fashion** *trend you can be sure Nicki will be wearing it.* ○ *I don't want people to see me with this haircut – perhaps I could* **set** (=start) *a new trend for wearing paper bags over the head.* ○ *The trend at the moment is* **towards** *a more natural and less made-up look.* • LP› **Shopping goods**

trend·y /ˈtren·di/ *adj* **-ier, -iest** • Trendy means modern and influenced by the most recent fashions or ideas: *She's always in very trendy clothes.* ○ *It's one of those ultra trendy nightclubs where they won't let you in if you're not dressed right.* ○ *He writes for some trendy magazine for the under 30's.*

trend·y /ˈtren·di/ *n* [C] *esp. disapproving* • A trendy is a person who is very influenced by the most recent ideas and fashions: *This is where all the North London trendies go for a night out.*

trend·set·ter /£ˈtrendˌset·əʳ, $-ˌset̬·ɚ/ *n* [C] a person, organization, etc. that starts new fashions, esp. in clothes • *They are not only the world's biggest fast-food chain but also the industry's trendsetter.*

trep·i·da·tion /ˌtrep·ɪˈdeɪ·ʃᵊn/ *n* [U] *fml* fear or anxiety about what is going to happen • *There's always a certain amount of trepidation when you're starting any new job.* • *We view future developments* **with** *some trepidation.*

tres·pass BREAK LAW /£ˈtres·pəs, $-pæs/ *v* [I] to go onto someone's land or enter their building without permission • *I hope this is a public footpath and we're not trespassing* **on** *someone's land.* • *(fml)* If you **trespass on/upon** a good quality in someone's character, you take unfair advantage of it: *They said we should stay another night, but I didn't want to trespass on their hospitality.* • Ⓕ Ⓘ

tres·pass /£ˈtres·pəs, $-pæs/ *n* [U/C]

tres·pass·er /£ˈtres·pə·səʳ, $-pæs·ɚ/ *n* [C] • *Can't you read the sign? It says 'Trespassers will be prosecuted!'*

tres·pass IMMORAL ACTION /£ˈtres·pəs, $-pæs/ *n* [C] *old use* a SIN • *"Forgive us our trespasses as we forgive those who trespass against us"* (Bible *The Lord's prayer,* Matthew 6.9) • Ⓕ Ⓘ

tres·pass /£ˈtres·pəs, $-pæs/ *v* [I] *old use*

tres·ses /ˈtres·ɪz/ *pl n literary* a woman's hair, esp. long hair • *Her black tresses lay around her on the pillow.*

tres·tle /ˈtres·l̩/ *n* [C] a supporting structure for a table, consisting of a flat piece of wood supported at each end by two pairs of sloping legs, or a set of sloping supports holding a horizontal structure, used esp. for railway bridges • A **trestle table** is a table which consists of a board supported by a trestle. • PIC〉 **Table**

trews /truːz/ *pl n dated humorous* trousers • *I can't find my trews anywhere.*

tri·ad /ˈtraɪ·æd/ *n* [C] a secret Chinese organization involved in illegal activities such as selling drugs

trial LEGAL PROCESS /traɪl/ *n* the hearing of statements and showing of objects etc. in a court of law for the purpose of judging whether a person is guilty of a crime or for deciding a case or a legal matter • *trial proceedings* • *a trial judge* • *Trial* **by jury** *is a fundamental right.* [U] • *It was a very complicated trial that went on for months.* [C] • *She's* **going on/standing** *trial* **for** *fraud.* [U] • *He's currently awaiting trial* **for** *rape.* [U] • *I can't remember whether the case* **went to** *trial.* [U] • See also TRY LAW. • LP〉 **Crimes and criminals, Law**

trial TEST /traɪl/ *n* a test, usually over a limited period of time, to discover how effective or suitable something or someone is • *They're doing* **clinical** *trials on a drug in America which they hope might control the symptoms.* [C] • *She's having a six-month trial* **(period)** *and if they think she's good enough they'll give her a permanent job.* [C] • *They're not going to get a divorce yet, but they're having a trial* **separation**. • *(esp. Br) The shop offers you any of their garden equipment* **on** *trial/(Am and Aus usually)* **on** *a trial* **basis**, *and if you don't like it you can give it back.* [U] • **Trial and error** is a way of achieving an aim or solving a problem by trying a number of different methods and learning from the mistakes that you make: *There's no instant way of finding a cure – it's just a* **process of** *trial and error.* • A **trial run** is a practical test of something new or unknown to discover its effectiveness: *We're holding a tournament in the new ice-hockey stadium, as a trial run for next year's Winter Olympics.*

trial *obj* /traɪl/ *v* [T] **-ll-** or **-l-** • *We're trialing* (= testing) *the new drug in several hospitals.*

trial PROBLEM /traɪl/ *n* [C] a person or thing that is annoying and causes a lot of problems • *She was a real trial* **to** *her parents when she was younger.* • *The book's main theme is youth and the trials of growing up.* • *It's been a real trial having my mother staying with us these past few days.* • When people refer to **trials and tribulations** they mean troubles and events that cause suffering: *the trials and tribulations of marriage*

tri·an·gle /ˈtraɪ·æŋ·gl̩/ *n* [C] a flat shape with three straight sides • *an equilateral triangle* • *an isosceles triangle* • A triangle is also anything which has three straight sides: *Which ear-rings did you buy in the end – the triangles or the circles?* • A triangle is also a musical instrument consisting of a thin metal bar bent into a triangle shape which is hit with a metal bar to make a sound. • Triangle is also *Am for* SETSQUARE. • PIC〉 **Musical instruments, Shapes**

tri·an·gu·lar /£traɪˈæŋ·gjʊ·ləʳ, $-lɚ/ *adj* • *It's a more or less triangular plot of land.* • *The play is performed on a triangular stage.*

tri·an·gu·la·tion /traɪˌæŋ·gjʊˈleɪ·ʃᵊn/ *n* [U] *specialized* • Triangulation is the division of a map or plan into triangles for measurement purposes, or the calculation of positions and distances using this method.

tri·ath·lon /£traɪˈæθ·lɒn, $-lɑːn/ *n* [C] a competition in which the people competing must swim, ride a bicycle and run particular distances without stopping between events

tribe /traɪb/ *n* [C + sing/pl v] a group of people, often of related families, who live together, sharing the same language, culture and history, esp. those who do not live in towns or cities and do not have industry or writing • *a tribe of Amazonian Indians* • *the Masai tribe* • *Many tribes which in the past governed themselves are nowadays part of a larger country.* • *(fig. infml)* A tribe can also be a large family or other group you belong to: *We've invited Carol's sisters and brothers and their spouses and children – the whole Cassidy tribe.*

trib·al /ˈtraɪ·bᵊl/ *adj* [not gradable] • *tribal dress/leaders* • *(fig. infml) The fierce tribal* **loyalty** *among soccer supporters leads to violence between opposing fans.*

trib·al·i·sm /ˈtraɪ·bᵊl·ɪ·zᵊm/ *n* [U] • Tribalism is the state of existing as a tribe, or a very strong feeling of loyalty to your tribe.

tribes·man *(pl* **-men**), **tribes·wo·man** *(pl* **-women**) /ˈtraɪbz·mən, -ˌwʊm·ən/ *n* [C]

tri·bu·la·tion /ˌtrɪb·jʊˈleɪ·ʃᵊn/ *n* See **trials and tribulations** at TRIAL PROBLEM.

tri·bun·al /traɪˈbjuː·nəl/ *n* [C] a special court or group of people who are officially chosen, esp. by the government, to examine (legal) problems of a particular type • *A war-crimes tribunal is to be set up in order to investigate the alleged atrocities.* • *She took her case to an immigration appeals tribunal.*

tri·bu·ta·ry /£ˈtrɪb·jʊ·tᵊr·i, £-tri, $-ter·i/ *n* [C] a river or stream that flows into a larger river or a lake • *I planned a series of walks along the Indre, a lesser tributary of the Loire.*

tri·bute RESPECTFUL ACTION /ˈtrɪb·juːt/ *n* [C] something that you say, write or give which shows your respect and admiration for someone, esp. on a formal occasion • *Tributes have been pouring in from all over the world for the famous actor who died yesterday.* • *The minister* **paid** *tribute* **to** (= praised) *the men who had fought the blaze, saying their bravery had saved countless lives.* • *For wedding bouquets,* **floral** *tributes* (= flowers sent to someone's funeral) *and all your flower needs, call Mandy's Florists.*

tri·bute BENEFICIAL EFFECT /ˈtrɪb·juːt/ *n* [U] something which shows very clearly the benefit or positive effect of something else • *I've never known a 5-year-old as well-behaved as your son – he's a tribute* **to** *you!* • *No one is willing to predict the result of the England-Germany game, which is a tribute* **to** *the recent improvement in England's play.*

trice /traɪs/ *n* [U] **in a trice** *dated infml* in a very short time • *Jim, of course, had the wheel mended in a trice.*

tri·ceps /ˈtraɪ·seps/ *n* [C] *pl* **triceps** or **tricepses** the large muscle at the back of the upper arm • Compare BICEPS.

trick ACT OF DECEIVING /trɪk/ *n* [C] an action which is intended to deceive, either as a way of cheating someone, or as a joke or form of entertainment • *She* **played** *a really nasty trick* **on** *me – she put syrup in my shampoo bottle!* • *In Britain it's traditional to* **play** *tricks* **on** *people on the morning of April Fool's Day (April 1st).* • *My Uncle Andrew used to* **do** *tricks for us with playing cards when we were kids.* • *My niece was showing me all the tricks that she's learned to* **do** *with her new magic set.* • *It's a bit of trick* **photography** *– she's meant to look like she's walking on water.* • *For a moment I thought you had a patch of grey hairs, but it's just a* **trick of the light** (= the light made it appear differently). • A **trick question** is one in which the real question being asked is hidden within a different question. • **Trick or treat** is a Halloween (=31st October) tradition, esp. in America and Canada, in which a small group of children dressed to look frightening or strange visit different houses demanding that the people living there give them sweets or a small amount of money. If the people don't do this, the children play a trick on them: *'Trick or treat' is now discouraged by a lot of parents because they consider it dangerous.* • LP **Holidays**

trick *obj* /trɪk/ *v* [T] • If you trick someone you deceive them, often as a part of a plan: *The court heard how Dean had tricked the old lady* **into** *giving him eight hundred pounds, claiming that he would invest it for her.* ○ *Her lawyer claimed that she'd been tricked* **into** *making a false confession.*

trick·e·ry /£ˈtrɪk·ər·i, $ˈ-ɚ-/ *n* [U] *disapproving* • *The government, he said, had resorted to political trickery in their attempts to retain power.*

trick·ster /£ˈtrɪk·stər, $-stɚ/ *n* [C] *disapproving* • A trickster is a person who deceives people: *a confidence trickster*

trick·y /ˈtrɪk·i/ *adj* **-ier, -iest** • *Be careful if you do business with him – he's a tricky* (=deceiving) *fellow.* • See also TRICKY.

trick METHOD /trɪk/ *n* [C] an effective or quick way of doing something • *What's the trick* **of** *getting this to chair to fold up?* • *On page 21, twenty tricks to speed up your beauty routine.* • *(infml)* If you say that something will **do the trick** you mean that it will achieve the necessary or desired effect: *I need something to give this sauce a bit of flavour – ah, a lemon should do the trick.* • *I've tried* **every trick in the book** (=every possible way) *to seduce him and still no luck!* • *Newspapers often improve photographs before they print them – it's one of the* **tricks of the trade**.

trick WEAK /trɪk/ *adj* [before n; not gradable] *Am* (of a part of the body, esp. a joint) weak • *I've got a trick ankle which gives me problems if I do much running.*

tri·ckle /ˈtrɪk·l̩/ *v* [I] (of liquid) to flow slowly and without force in a thin line • *Blood trickled out of the corner of his mouth.* • *Oil was trickling from a tiny hole in the tank.* • *She felt a tear escape and trickle warmly down her cheek.* • *(fig.) Gradually people trickled back* (=returned slowly) *into the theatre for the second half.* • **Trickle-down** is when something that starts in the high parts of a system spreads to the whole of the system: *The supposed trickle-down* **effect** *of lower taxes for the rich has not yet resulted in greater prosperity for society as a whole.*

tri·ckle /ˈtrɪk·l̩/ *n* [C] • *A trickle of melted butter made its way down his chin.* • *(fig.) We usually only get a trickle* (=a very small number) *of customers in the shop in the mornings.*

tricks /trɪks/ *pl n* **How's tricks?** *infml slightly dated* How are you? • *"Hi, how's tricks?" "Oh, fine, how are you doing?"*

trick·y /ˈtrɪk·i/ *adj* **-ier, -iest** (of a piece of work or a problem) difficult to deal with and needing careful attention or skill • *Now comes the tricky bit – getting the cake out of the tin in one piece.* • *Those bird models are quite tricky* **to** *make, aren't they?* [+ *to* infinitive] • *I'm in a bit of a tricky situation really – whatever I do I'll offend someone.* • See also **tricky** at TRICK ACT OF DECEIVING.

tri·co·lour *Br and Aus, Am and Aus* **tri·co·lor** /£ˈtrɪk·əl·ər, $ˈtraɪˌkʌl·ɚ/ *n* [C] a flag which is divided into three equal parts of different colour • *the French tricolour* • *The coffins were draped in the white-blue-red tricolour of old Imperial Russia.*

tri·cy·cle /ˈtraɪ·sɪ·kl̩/, **trike** *n* [C] a CYCLE (=vehicle powered by the rider's legs) with two wheels at the back and one at the front, used esp. by young children • PIC **Bicycles**

tri·dent LARGE FORK /ˈtraɪ·dənt/ *n* [C] a weapon used in the past consisting of a pole with three sharp metal points on the end

Tri·dent EXPLOSIVE WEAPON /ˈtraɪ·dənt/ *n* [C not after the] a type of **ballistic missile** (=explosive weapon for sending over long distances) which is sent from under the sea, whose explosive front ends can be aimed separately • *a Trident missile/programme/submarine*

tried /traɪd/ *past simple and past participle of* TRY

tri·en·ni·al /traɪˈen·i·əl/ *adj* [not gradable] happening every three years • *The party's triennial congress will be taking place next week.*

tri·er /£ˈtraɪ·ər, $-ɚ/ *n* [C] See at TRY ATTEMPT

tri·fle SWEET DISH /ˈtraɪ·fl̩/ *n* a sweet cold dish consisting of a layer of fruit and SPONGE (=cake), a layer of CUSTARD (=sweet yellow milky sauce) and a top layer of cream • *(a) sherry trifle* [U/C] • PIC **Bread and cakes**

tri·fle UNIMPORTANT THING /ˈtraɪ·fl̩/ *n* [C] *fml* a matter or item of little value or importance • *I brought a few trifles back from India – bits of jewellery and material mainly.* • *We couldn't decide whether to order blue pens or black – such are the trifles of office life.* • **A** trifle means slightly: *I'm a trifle confused about the arrangements for tonight.* • *"A snapper-up of unconsidered trifles"* (Autolycus the thief in Shakespeare's Winter's Tale 4.2) • *"Trifles, light as air, / Are to the jealous confirmations strong"* (Shakespeare, Othello 3.3)

tri·fle with *obj v prep* [T] *fml* • If you trifle with someone you treat them carelessly or without respect: *As you know, Caroline O'Neill is not a woman to be trifled with.*

tri·fling /ˈtraɪ·fl̩·ɪŋ, ˈ-flɪŋ/ *adj fml* • A trifling matter or amount of money is a small or unimportant one: *It was such a trifling sum of money to argue about!* ○ *As usual the committee were discussing some trifling matter at great length.*

trig·ger GUN PART /£ˈtrɪg·ər, $-ɚ/ *n* [C] a part of a gun which causes the gun to fire when pressed • *It's not clear who actually* **pulled** *the trigger.* • *(infml)* Someone who is **trigger-happy** tends to use his or her gun a lot, shooting with very little reason: *Their police are worryingly trigger-happy.* ○ *(fig.) The US seemed intent on assuring Security Council members that it was not trigger-happy* (=willing to use force without careful consideration).

trig·ger *obj* START /£ˈtrɪg·ər, $-ɚ/ *v* [T] to cause (something bad) to start • *Some people find that certain foods trigger their headaches.* • *The racial killings at the weekend have triggered* **off** *a wave of protests throughout the country.*

trig·ger /£ˈtrɪg·ər, $-ɚ/ *n* [C usually sing] • *There are fears that the incident may act as a trigger for* (=cause) *further violence in the capital.*

tri·go·nom·e·try /£ˌtrɪg·əˈnɒm·ə·tri, $-ˈnɑː·mə-/, *infml* **trig** /trɪg/ *n* [U] a type of mathematics that deals with the relationship between the angles and sides of triangles. Practical uses are the measurement of the height of buildings, mountains etc. • *Trigonometry concerns the functions of angles, such as sine, cosine and tangent.*

trike /traɪk/ *n* [C] a TRICYCLE • PIC **Bicycles**

tril·by /ˈtrɪl·bi/ *n* [C] *esp. Br* a man's FELT (=thick firm cloth) hat with a deep fold along its top • PIC **Hats**

tri·lin·gual /ˌtraɪˈlɪŋ·gwəl/ *adj* [not gradable] able to speak three languages • Compare BILINGUAL.

trill BIRD SONG /trɪl/ *v* [I] (of birds) to sing a series of quickly repeated high notes • *The larks were trilling.* • *(literary) "Tea is ready," trilled Daphne* (=she said in a very high voice). [+ clause]

trill /trɪl/ *n* [C] • *We heard the familiar trill of the lark.*

trill MUSICAL EFFECT /trɪl/ *n* [C] *specialized* (the effect achieved by) the fast playing of a note and the note above or below it, one after the other

tril·li·on /ˈtrɪl·jən/ *determiner, n* [C], *pronoun pl* **trillion** or **trillions** 1 000 000 000 000 • *(infml)* Trillions can be used to mean an extremely large number: *I've never seen so many birds – there were trillions of them!* • LP **Hundred**

tril·li·onth /ˈtrɪl·jənθ/ *determiner, n* [C], *pronoun*

tril·o·gy /ˈtrɪl·ə·dʒi/ *n* [C] a series of three books or plays written about the same situation or characters, forming a continuous story • *A film was made out of the first and second parts of the trilogy.*

trim *obj* CUT /trɪm/ *v* [T] **-mm-** to make (something) tidier or more level by cutting a small amount off it • *My hair needs trimming.* • *She's busy trimming the garden hedge.* • *Trim* **off** *the leafy ends of the vegetable before cooking.* [M] • *(fig.) They're trying to trim* (=reduce) *their costs, so staff who leave are not being replaced.*

trim /trɪm/ *n* [U] • *It only costs me £10 at my local hairdressers for* **a** *trim.* • *Just* **give** *the ends* **a** *trim, please.*

trim /trɪm/ *adj* **trimmer, trimmest** • Something can be described as trim if it is tidy and well-ordered: *trim lawns and neat flower beds*

trim·mer /£ˈtrɪm·ər, $-ɚ/ *n* [C] • A trimmer is a device used for making something tidier or more level by cutting a small amount off it: *a hedge trimmer* • PIC **Garden**

trim·mings /ˈtrɪm·ɪŋz/ *pl n* • Trimmings are small pieces that have been cut from something larger to make it tidier: *Don't throw away your pastry trimmings, because we'll be using them later to decorate the tart.* ○ *I always save the* **hedge** *trimmings for the compost heap.*

trim THIN /trɪm/ *adj* **trimmer, trimmest** *approving* attractively and healthily thin • *You're looking very trim – have you lost weight?*

trim /trɪm/, **trim·ming** *n* [C] • *I wore my red jacket with the black trim.*

trim PREPARED /trɪm/ *n* [U] **in trim** *infml* physically prepared and ready • *Are you in trim* **for** *the run on Sunday?*

tri·ma·ran /'traɪ·mə·ræn/ *n* [C] a small fast sailing boat which has a central HULL (=floating part) that is joined to two other smaller hulls, one at each side

tri·mes·ter /£trɪ'mes·tər, $-t̬ɚ/ *n* [C] a three-month period • A trimester is any of the three three-month periods that a human pregnancy is divided into: *Many women find the second trimester to be the easiest part of their pregnancy.* • *(Am)* A trimester is any of the three-month periods into which the school or college year is sometimes divided: *Many students arrange internships or work-study placements during the second trimester.* Compare SEMESTER.

trimmed /trɪmd/ *adj* [after v; not gradable] (of clothes and other cloth items) decorated, esp. around the edges • *She was wearing a black suit trimmed* **with** *white.*

trim /trɪm/ *n* [U] • *I wore my red jacket with the black trim.*

trim·mings /'trɪm·ɪŋz/ *pl n* • *I want a plain black jumper with no fancy trimmings.* • *(fig.) In spite of the democratic trimmings* (=additional things which look good) *of an elected national assembly, one man still runs the country.* • *(fig.) I've always dreamt of having a big wedding celebration* **with all the** *trimmings.* • *(fig.) I'll have the turkey* **with all the** *trimmings* (=with the vegetables and other things that are eaten with it), *please.*

tri·ni·ty /'trɪn·ɪ·ti/ *n* [C usually sing] *literary* a group of three things or people • *The inclusion of the trinity* **of** *Richards, Thompson and Cole in the team offers England the best chance of victory.* • In Christianity, **the (Holy)** Trinity is the existence of God in three forms (the 'Father', the 'Son' and the 'Holy Spirit') that are part of a single being. • *British culture now appears to revolve around the* **unholy** *trinity of sport, shopping and sex.*

trin·ket /'trɪŋ·kɪt/ *n* [C] a small decorative object, or an item of jewellery that is cheap or of low quality • *She always returns from vacation with a few souvenirs, even if they're only* **cheap** *trinkets.* • *Lovers have exchanged trinkets on St Valentine's Day since medieval times.*

tri·o /£'triː·əʊ, $-oʊ/ *n* [C] *pl* **trios** three people or things in a group • *There was disappointment for our trio* **of** *200 metre runners, all of whom failed to reach the final.* • *The first trio* **of** *missiles hit the city shortly after midnight.* • Sometimes a trio is a group of three musicians or singers who perform together: *Many* **jazz** *trios consist of a piano, guitar and double bass.* ○ *A* **string** *trio is normally composed of a violin, viola, and cello, while in a* **piano** *trio, a piano replaces the viola.* • A trio can also be a piece of music that has been written to be performed by three people: *Are there any trios we can play together?* ○ *The final item in today's programme is Beethoven's Trio in B flat, Opus 11.*

trip *(obj)* LOSE BALANCE /trɪp/ *v* **-pp-** to lose your balance after knocking your foot against something when you are walking or running, or to cause (someone) to do this • *Unfortunately he tripped and fell over, tearing a hole in his trousers and grazing his knee.* [I] • *A 72-year-old woman is suing a supermarket after she tripped* **over** *a cardboard box and broke her leg.* [I] • *That cable looks rather dangerous. Someone might trip* **over** *it.* [I] • *Look at this bruise I got when I tripped* **on** *the stairs.* [I] • *I'm terribly sorry. I didn't mean to trip you* **up**. [T] • *He was sent off for deliberately tripping Robson when he was about to score a goal.* [T] • *(fig.) It would be a tremendous pity if the plans for the new hospital are tripped* **up** (=delayed) *by bureaucracy.* [T] • If you trip **up** or are tripped **up**, you make a mistake: *The interview was really stressful. They were trying to trip me up all the way through.* [T] ○ *I think the exam went quite well, except at the end when I tripped up* **on** *the final question.* [I]

trip /trɪp/ *n* [C] • *She broke her ankle when she had a nasty trip on the stairs.*

trip JOURNEY /trɪp/ *n* [C] a journey in which someone goes to a place and returns from it and which usually takes a short time or involves travelling a short distance • *The trip* **from** *York* **to** *Newcastle takes about an hour by train.* • *Do you want to go* **on** *the school trip to France this year?* • *I thought we might hire a motorboat this afternoon and take a trip* **round/around** *the bay.* • *(esp. Br) I don't think we can afford another trip* **abroad** *this year.* • *On a warm sunny day there are few things more pleasant than a gentle boat trip down the Thames.* • *I'm afraid she's away on a* **business** *trip and won't be back until next week.* • *She has had to cancel her trip because of illness.* • *He disappeared during a* **fishing** *trip in Scotland.* • *We hoped she'd be with us for Christmas, but she was too weak to* **make** *the trip.* • *It's a 10-mile trip from the airport to the city centre.* • *His visit to Rome will be his first trip* **overseas** *since he became prime minister.* • *I was thinking we might go on a* **shopping** *trip to Oxford on Saturday.*

trip·per /£'trɪp·ər, $-ɚ/ *n* [C] *esp. Br* • A tripper is someone who visits a place briefly, often with a large group of other people: *It's very peaceful around here and we don't get many trippers.* ○ *I'd avoid cafés that are full of* **coach** *trippers if I were you.*

trip MOVE /trɪp/ *v* [I always + adv/prep] **-pp-** to move with quick gentle steps • *She looked stunning as she tripped* **down** *the stairs in her ball gown.* • Something that **trips off the tongue** is easy to say or pronounce: *The new company will need to have a name that trips off the tongue and is easy to remember.*

trip *obj* SWITCH /trɪp/ *v* [T] **-pp-** to move (a switch that operates an electrical system), or to cause (such a system) to start or stop working by moving a switch • *A special system prevents the circuitry being tripped accidentally by a power surge or lightning strike.* • A **trip switch** is a safety switch which automatically stops electricity flowing to a machine if a dangerously large current is created by the machine failing to operate as it should.

trip EXPERIENCE /trɪp/ *v* [I] **-pp-** *infml* to experience the effects of taking an illegal drug which causes the user to see, hear or feel things that do not exist • *You can't get much sense out of him when he's tripping.* • *When I was a student I spent a lot of time tripping* **out on** *LSD.*

trip /trɪp/ *n* [C] • *If you take this stuff when you're depressed, you'll have a really bad trip* (=experience). • *(fig.) She's been* **on** *a real* **power** *trip* (=greatly enjoying having power) *since she became the office manager.*

tri·par·tite /£ˌtraɪ'pɑː·taɪt, $-pɑːr·t̬aɪt/ *adj* [not gradable] *fml or specialized* involving three people or organizations, or existing in three parts • *The minister is to hold tripartite meetings with the oil and car industries to discuss ways of reducing pollution.* • *A tripartite agreement brought together government, industry and trade unions in an effort to reduce unemployment.* • *The poem has a tripartite structure.*

tripe FOOD /traɪp/ *n* [U] the covering of the inside of the stomach of an animal such as a cow or sheep used for food • *The traditional British recipe for tripe involves stewing it with onions, vegetables and herbs.*

tripe STUPID IDEAS /traɪp/ *n* [U] *infml* ideas, suggestions or writing that are stupid, silly or have little value • *She said my last essay was complete tripe.* • *People* **talk a lot of** *tripe about fashion.*

trip·y /'traɪ·pi/ *adj* **-ier, -iest** *infml* • *He spends all day watching tripy videos on TV.*

tri·ple /'trɪp·l̩/ *adj* [not gradable] consisting of three parts, or being repeated twice • *Her trainer is a triple Olympic* **champion.** • *There's a triple* **bill** *of Hitchcock films* (=three films) *on at the cinema next Sunday.* • *The number of one-parent U.S. households reached 10·1 million in 1991,* **nearly** *triple* (=three times as large as) *that of 1971.* • **Triple glazing** is three layers of glass in a door or window that are separated by air spaces to prevent heat escaping from a room or to reduce the amount of noise coming in from outside: *The insulation from triple glazing is significantly greater than that from double glazing.* • The **triple jump** is a sporting event in which the competitor jumps from one foot and lands on it, then jumps from one foot and lands on the other, and finally jumps with both feet: *She's the European triple jump champion.* ○ *He is Britain's leading* **triple jumper** *and is expected to win a medal in the European championships.*

tri·ple *(obj)* /'trɪp·l̩/ *v* • *The firm expects the number of vacancies to double or triple* (=become three times larger) *next year.* [I] • *We have tripled our output over the past two years.* [T] • *The workforce has tripled* **in size** *since the new factory opened.* [I]

tri·plet /'trɪp·lət/ *n* [C] one of three children born to the same mother at the same time • *I was amazed when my doctor told me I was going to have triplets.*

tri·pli·cate /'trɪp·lɪ·kət/ *adj* [before n; not gradable] *specialized or fml* existing in three parts that are exactly the same • *Triplicate samples were prepared for each blood test.* • If a form is **in triplicate**, two exact copies have been made of it: *The application has to be completed in triplicate, with the original being kept by the bank and the copies going to the customer and the tax office.*

tri·pod /£ˈtraɪ·pɒd, $-pɑːd/ *n* [C] a support with three adjustable legs for a piece of equipment such as a camera • *For photographs requiring long exposure times, your camera should be* **mounted on** *a tripod.* • PIC Laboratory

trip·tych /ˈtrɪp·tɪtʃ, -tɪk/ *n* [C] *specialized* a set of three paintings that are often joined in a way that allows the two outer ones to fold in towards the larger central one • *A medieval triptych hung above the altar.*

trip·wire /£ˈtrɪp·waɪəʳ, $-waɪr/ *n* [C] a wire which is stretched low above the ground and operates an explosive device, a gun or a device for catching animals when it is touched by the foot of a person or animal • *The border fence is fortified with tripwires, anti-tank ditches, spotlights and watchtowers.*

trip·y /ˈtraɪ·pi/ *adj* See at TRIPE STUPID IDEAS

trite /traɪt/ *adj disapproving* expressed too frequently to be interesting or seem sincere • *The sentiments about love and peace in the lyrics of his songs are too trite for me to take them seriously.* • *My speech seemed lively and interesting as I was writing it, but it came out trite, dull and ridiculous.* • *It can be very hard to tell someone you love them without* **sounding** *trite.*

trite·ly /ˈtraɪt·li/ *adv disapproving* • *"I don't love you, but I really value you as a friend," she said tritely.*

trite·ness /ˈtraɪt·nəs/ *n* [U] *disapproving* • *Many literary critics have sneered at the triteness of her latest novel.*

tri·umph /ˈtraɪ·əmpf/ *n* a very great success, achievement or victory, or a feeling of great satisfaction or pleasure caused by this • *Samuel Johnson described marrying for a second time as a triumph of hope* **over** *experience.* [C] • *The book celebrates the hostages' remarkable triumph* **over** *appalling adversity.* [C] • *His visit will be seen as a major* **diplomatic** *triumph* **for** *the military regime.* [C] • *It was a day full of triumphs and* **disasters**. [C] • *1992 was the year of the Republican Party's third* **election** *triumph in a row.* [C] • *The eradication of smallpox by vaccination was one of medicine's greatest triumphs.* [C] • *The constitutional changes have been* **hailed as** *a triumph* **for** *democracy.* [C] • *The signing of the agreement was a* **personal** *triumph* **for** *the Prime Minister.* [C] • *There's little doubt that a* **sporting** *triumph is good for national morale.* [C] • *I got a tremendous feeling of triumph from winning that argument with Robin.* [U] • *The match ended in triumph for the French team.* [U] • *The winning team's supporters leapt up* **in** *triumph as the final whistle blew.* [U] • *He* **returned in** *triumph from the sales with stereo system he'd got for half price.* [U]

tri·umph /ˈtraɪ·əmpf/ *v* [I] • *The movie tells the story of a woman from a working-class ghetto who triumphs* **against the odds** *to win a place at a top university.* • *I believe that sooner or later good must triumph* **over** *evil.*

tri·um·phal /traɪˈʌmp·fᵊl/ *adj* • Triumphal things celebrate a great victory or success: *The Arc de Triomphe is a triumphal* **arch** *in Paris which commemorates Napoleon's military victories.* ○ *Shortly after his triumphal* **entry** *into Havana in January 1959, Castro spoke on television for seven hours without a break.* ○ *Her popularity has declined since her triumphal* **return** *from exile two years ago.*

tri·um·phal·i·sm /traɪˈʌmp·fᵊl·ɪ·zᵊm/ *n* [U] *disapproving* • Triumphalism is obtaining pleasure and satisfaction from the defeat of someone else: *There wasn't a hint of triumphalism in her acceptance speech at the awards ceremony.* ○ *The country needs to pull together, and whoever wins the election should avoid indulging in triumphalism.*

tri·um·phal·ist /traɪˈʌmp·fᵊl·ɪst/ *adj* [not gradable], *n* [C] *disapproving* • *Many people would be offended by a triumphalist victory parade to celebrate the end of the war.* • *She is no triumphalist and looks forward to working with her former rivals.*

tri·um·phant /traɪˈʌmp·fənt/ *adj* • Someone who is triumphant has achieved a great victory or success, or is very happy and proud because of such an achievement: *It seemed as though the whole city had turned out for their team's triumphant homecoming.* ○ *She* **emerged** *triumphant from the court after all the charges against her were dropped because of a lack of evidence.* ○ *She made a triumphant* **return** *to the stage after several years working in television.* ○ *The success of the missile system is being interpreted as a triumphant* **vindication** *of the government's policies.*

tri·um·phant·ly /traɪˈʌmp·fənt·li/ *adv* • *She looked so cross when Frank triumphantly announced his promotion.*

tri·um·vir·ate /traɪˈʌm·vɪ·rət/ *n* [C] a group of three people who are in control of an activity or organization • *The shape of post-war Europe was decided in Potsdam in 1945 by the Allied triumvirate of Churchill, Truman and Stalin.* • *She was a member of the triumvirate that ordered the assassination of the President.*

tri·vet /ˈtrɪv·ɪt/ *n* [C] *specialized* a metal stand that protects the surface of a table from hot dishes or pans, which are put on it rather than directly on the table

tri·vi·a /ˈtrɪv·i·ə/ *pl n* unimportant details or information • *He accused the newspapers of directing public attention away from important political issues towards sex scandals and show-business trivia.* • *She has an encyclopedic knowledge of pop trivia.* • *I'm fascinated by the trivia of everyday life.* • *(esp. Br) Would you like to join my team for the trivia* **quiz**?

tri·vi·al /ˈtrɪv·i·əl/ *adj* • Things that are trivial have little value or importance: *A man who was involved in an apparently trivial dispute in a pub was later hacked to death by a gang of ten men.* ○ *I don't know why he gets so upset about something that is* **utterly** *trivial.* ○ *It is* **seemingly** *trivial things like effective communication that enable an office to operate efficiently.* ○ *Sexual harassment in the workplace is not a trivial* **matter**. ○ *She just* **dismissed** *my problem* **as** *too trivial to be worth discussing.* • A trivial problem is one that is easy to solve: *Getting computers to understand human language is not a trivial problem.* ○ *The discovery of penicillin made curing infections suddenly seem trivial.* • (I) (N) (RUS)

tri·vi·al·i·ty /£ˌtrɪv·iˈæl·ə·ti, $-t̬i/ *n* • A triviality is something that is unimportant: *I'm a busy man – don't bother me with trivialities.* [C] • The triviality of something is its lack of importance: *The prison sentence seemed rather harsh, considering the triviality of the offence.* [U]

tri·vi·al·ize *obj, Br and Aus usually* **-ise** /ˈtrɪv·i·ə·laɪz/ *v* [T] *disapproving* • When you trivialize something, you make it seem less important than it really is: *Television trivializes almost everything it touches and make us less sensitive to human tragedy and suffering.* ○ *I don't want to trivialise the problem, but I do think there are more important matters to discuss.*

trod /trɒd/ *past simple and past participle of* TREAD • *It really hurt when Mark trod* **on** *my foot.* • *One of the victims was a child who had trod* **on** *a mine while walking to school.*

trod·den /£ˈtrɒd·ᵊn, $ˈtrɑː·dᵊn/ *past participle of* TREAD • *The manufacturers claim the truck is strong enough to survive being trodden* **on** *by an elephant.*

trog /£trɒg, $trɑːg/ *v* [I always + adv/prep] **-gg-** *Br infml* to go somewhere in an informal way, usually by walking • *If you've got nothing better to do, why don't you trog* **along** *with us to the cinema?*

trog·lo·dyte /£ˈtrɒg·lə·daɪt, $ˈtrɑː·glə-/ *n* [C] *specialized* a person who lives in a cave • *Most people associate troglodytes with prehistoric times, but troglodyte communities still exist in Tunisia and China.* • *(fig.) Computer programmers are often thought of as troglodytes who work alone with their machines and have little contact with other people.*

troi·ka /ˈtrɔɪ·kə/ *n* [C] a group of three people, esp. government officials • *She is a member of the president's troika of close advisers.* • *The troika of European Union foreign ministers has so far failed to persuade the warring factions to accept a ceasefire.*

Tro·jan horse /£ˌtrəʊ·dʒən, $ˌtroʊ-/ *n* [C] a person or thing that enters something secretly in order to attack it • *Older supporters have accused the new leadership of being a Trojan horse that will try to destroy the party from the inside.* • *Some French politicians suspect the United States of using Britain as a Trojan Horse to undermine the long-term aims of the European Union.*

troll /£trɒl, $troːl/ *n* [C] an imaginary creature in traditional Scandinavian stories with magical powers which lives in mountains or caves and is either very large or very small • *Originally trolls were thought of as giant ogres, but later trolls were mischievous dwarfs that guarded treasure and were skilled with their hands.*

trol·ley CARRIER *esp. Br and Aus* /£ˈtrɒl·i, $ˈtrɑː·li/, *Am usually* **cart** *n* [C] *pl* **trolleys** *or* **trollies** a small vehicle with two or four wheels that is used for transporting large or heavy objects and is pushed or pulled by a person • *The hospital is so overcrowded that some patients are being treated on trolleys in the corridors.* • *I'd go by bus more often* *if there was room for my* **shopping** *trolley.* • *Why will* **supermarket** *trolleys never move in the direction that you push them in?* • *I'll look for a* **luggage** *trolley for our cases.* • Sometimes a trolley is a table on four small wheels with one or more shelves beneath it which is used when serving food or drinks in unusual places: *Betty almost ran me over with her* **tea** *trolley as I was walking into the office!* ○ *The service was excellent, and every thirty minutes or so the flight attendant would* **wheel** *the* **drinks** *trolley down the aisle.* • *(infml)* Someone who is **off** their **trolley** is behaving in an extremely unusual way or doing something very silly: *Anyone who saw us doing this would think we were off our trolleys.* ○ *Have you* **gone** *completely off your trolley? You'll never get away with it!*

trol·ley [VEHICLE] /£'trɒl·i, $'trɑː·li/, **trol·ley·car** /£'trɒl·i·kɑːʳ, $'trɑː·li·kɑːr/ *n* [C] *Am for* TRAM • *You can take a trolley from the rail station to the city center.*

trol·ley·bus /£'trɒl·i·bʌs, $'trɑː·li-/ *n* [C] a public transport vehicle which travels along ordinary roads in towns and is powered by electricity that is collected from a wire above the road • *The trolleybus's major advantages are that it is quiet and pollution-free.* • *The trolley bus differs from the tram by having rubber tyres and not running on tracks.*

trol·lop /£'trɒl·əp, $'trɑː·ləp/ *n* [C] *disapproving* a woman or girl who has had a lot of sexual relationships without any emotional involvement • *That woman's a real trollop. Every time I see her she's with a different man.*

trom·bone /£trɒm'bəʊn, $trɑːm'boʊn/ *n* [C] a large metal musical instrument which is played by blowing air through it and has a U-shaped tube that is slid backwards and forwards to change its effective length and produce different notes • *Trombones are made of brass.* • *There are some wonderful trumpet and trombone solos in the piece.* • [PIC] **Musical instruments**

trom·bon·ist /£trɒm'bəʊ·nɪst, $trɑːm'boʊ-/ *n* [C] • A trombonist is someone who plays a trombone: *My cousin is a jazz trombonist.*

trompe l'oeil /£trɒ̃mp'lɜi, $trɑ̃ːmp-/ *n* [C] a painting which is cleverly designed to trick people into thinking that the objects represented in it are really there • *He is said to have painted a trompe l'oeil of grapes which was so realistic that birds tried to peck at them.*

troop [GROUP] /truːp/ *n* [C] a group of soldiers, esp. ones who fight in strong military vehicles or on horses • *the King's Troop of the Royal Horse Artillery* • *A troop of former border guards is being employed to dismantle the fortifications.* • A troop is also an organized group of young people who are SCOUTS: *We've got a troop of scouts camping in one of our fields this weekend.* ○ *They belonged to the same scout troop.*

troop·er /£'truː·pəʳ, $-pɚ/ *n* [C] • A trooper is a soldier who belongs to the lowest rank in the part of an army that fights in strong military vehicles or on horses: *Troopers in the American First Infantry Division boast that they have led the US army since the American Civil War.* • *(Am)* A trooper is a police officer in one of the forces of the 50 political areas of the United States: *Troopers are called out in emergencies or dangerous situations.* ○ *Everyone had to walk through a metal detector and a dozen* **state** *troopers were deployed around the courtroom.* • Someone who swears **like a trooper** swears a lot: *He was extremely drunk and* **swearing** *like a trooper by the time he'd finished the whisky.*

troop [WALK] /truːp/ *v* [I always + adv/prep] to walk somewhere in a large group, usually with one person behind another • *The little boys trooped* **after** *him across the playing fields.* • *The Norwich fans gave their team a loud cheer as they trooped* **off** *the field.* • *Hundreds of thousands of visitors troop* **through** *the museum every year.* • *None of us knew what to expect as we trooped* **into** *her office.* • *(fig.) I suppose head office expects us all to troop* **down** (= travel) *to London for this meeting.* • *(Br)* **Trooping the colour** is a ceremony in which a military flag is carried in public with the soldiers that it represents marching behind it: *The original purpose of trooping the colour was to teach soldiers to recognize their unit's flag in the middle of a battle.*

troops /truːps/ *pl n* soldiers on duty in a large group • *The general is credited with preventing* **airborne** *troops being used to support the coup.* • *Traditionally, United Nations troops have been* **deployed** *only in a peace-keeping role.* • *Experts believe the air war might be over within days, paving the way for an early attack by* **ground** *troops* (= soldiers who fight on land). • *If the violence gets any worse they'll have to* **send in** *the troops.* • *In 1988, about 220 000 American troops were* **stationed** *in Western Europe.* • *All troops will be* **withdrawn** *by the end of the year.*

troop /truːp/ *adj* [before n; not gradable] • *Satellite photographs provide us with a lot of information about their troop* **movements.** • *The troop* **withdrawal** *is scheduled to begin the day after the ceasefire.* • A **troop carrier** is a vehicle, ship or aircraft that has been designed for transporting a lot of soldiers: *The allies claim to have destroyed more than two-thirds of the enemy's* **armoured** *troop carriers.*

troop·ship /'truːp·ʃɪp/ *n* [C] a ship that is used for transporting large numbers of soldiers, esp. one that was previously used for trading rather than military purposes

tro·phy /£'trəʊ·fi, $troʊ-/ *n* [C] a prize, such as a gold or silver cup, which is given to the winner of a competition or race and which sometimes has to be returned after a year so that it can be given to the winner of the competition in the following year • *He's an excellent snooker player, but he's never* **won** *a* **major** *trophy.* • *The Duchess of Kent will be* **presenting** *the trophies.* • *The first prize is £20 000, and the winner will also* **receive** *a trophy and a certificate.* • A **trophy wife** or **girlfriend** is a young attractive woman who is the partner of a rich and successful older man and acts as a symbol of his social position: *I suppose having a trophy girlfriend makes him feel younger.* • A trophy is also something used as a symbol of success from hunting or war: *That stuffed pike above the fireplace is Pat's trophy from a fishing holiday in Scotland.*

trop·ic /£'trɒp·ɪk, $'trɑː·pɪk/ *n* [C] one of the two imaginary lines around the Earth at approximately 23·5 degrees north and 23·5 degrees south of the Equator • The **Tropic of Cancer** is the northern tropic, and the **Tropic of Capricorn** is the southern one. • *"Tropic of Cancer/ Tropic of Capricorn"* (titles of books by Henry Miller, 1934 & 1938)

trop·ics /£'trɒp·ɪks, $'trɑː·pɪks/ *pl n* • The tropics is the hottest area of the Earth, between the Tropic of Cancer and the Tropic of Capricorn: *She's a botanist and spent several years researching in* **the** *tropics.* • *The toucan is a largish brightly-coloured bird with an enormous bill which is native to the New World tropics.*

trop·i·cal /£'trɒp·ɪ·kəl, $'trɑː·pɪ-/ *adj* [not gradable] • Something that is tropical is from or relates to the area between the two tropics: *Leprosy is one of the few tropical* **diseases** *which could be eradicated early in the 21st century.* ○ *She's decided to specialise in tropical* **medicine** (= the treatment of diseases from the tropical areas of the world). ○ *I'd love to live somewhere with a tropical* **climate.** ○ *The organization has campaigned vigorously against imports of tropical* **hardwoods.** ○ *Tropical* **forests** *contain around half of all the world's species of animals and plants.* ○ *The Amazon river basin contains the world's largest tropical* **rainforest** . ○ *The hurricane was downgraded to a tropical* **storm** *when its speed dropped to 70mph.* • *(fig.) The weather was tropical* (= extremely hot) *last summer.* • See also SUBTROPICAL.

trop·po /£'trɒp·əʊ, $'trɑː·poʊ/ *adj Aus infml* mentally ill

trot /£trɒt, $trɑːt/ *n* a way in which a four-legged animal moves which is faster than walking and which involves a front leg and the back leg on the opposite side moving together • *He climbed onto his horse and set off* **at** *a* **relaxed** *trot down the lane.* [U] • *Have we got time for another trot* (= ride) *down the road before lunch?* [C] • *(fig.) It was clear from a quick trot through* (= examination of) *the sales figures that the company was not doing as well as it claimed.* [C] • A trot is also a slow run by a human: *The team warmed up for the match with a trot around the pitch.* [C] • If you do things **on the trot** you do them directly after each other without pausing: *She worked 30 hours on the trot to get the job finished on time.* • If you have been **on the trot** you have been very busy for a long time: *I've been on the trot all day and I'm absolutely exhausted!*

trot /£trɒt, $trɑːt/ *v* [I always + adv/prep] **-tt-** • *We were trotting* **along** *the lane when a car suddenly appeared from nowhere and almost made me fall off my pony.* • *The dog trotted* **down** *the path to greet me.* • *It was delightful to watch the deer trotting* **through** *the heather.* • *(infml)* When people trot somewhere, they go there quickly, hurriedly or busily: *She just expects me to trot* **along** *to meetings at a moment's notice.* ○ *She left her purse on the counter so I had to trot* **down** *the street after her.* ○ *Mike's just trotted* **off** *to the supermarket, but he should be back soon.* ○ *"I'm in a bit of a rush. I'll give you a ring," said James, and* **off** *he trotted.* ○ *Although she retired from politics five years ago, she still* *trots* **around the globe** (= travels around the world), *giving speeches and meeting world leaders.* See also GLOBETROTTER. ○ *(fig.) She was rather nervous and trotted* **through** *her speech a bit too quickly.* • Compare CANTER; GALLOP.

trots /£trɒts, $trɑːts/ *pl n infml* • Someone who has **the trots** is suffering from DIARRHOEA (= a condition in which the contents of the bowels are emptied too often): *I think it must have been that prawn curry which gave me the trots.*

trot out *obj*, **trot** *obj* **out** *v adv* [M] **-tt-** *disapproving* to state (an idea, opinion or fact, esp. one that has been stated often before or is foolish) • *You trot out that argument whenever I try to discuss this matter with you.* • *Whenever I ask him why his essay's late he just trots out the same* **old** *excuses.* • When a person is trotted out they are sent to appear in public in order to represent or defend an idea or opinion: *Whenever the President is in difficulties, her spokesman is trotted out to face the press.* ○ *Cigarette companies are always trotting out their experts to try and prove that smoking isn't dangerous.*

troth /£trəʊθ, £troʊθ/ *n* [U] **plight** your **troth**, see at PLIGHT [MARRY]

trot·ter /£'trɒt·əʳ, $'trɑː·t̬ɚ/ *n* [C usually pl] a pig's foot used for food • *Yum! It's trotters and tripe for supper!*

trou·ba·dour /£'truː·bə·dɔːʳ, $-dɔːr/ *n* [C] a male poet and singer who travelled around S France and N Italy between the 11th and 13th centuries entertaining wealthy people • *Troubadours mainly wrote love poems.*

troub·le [DIFFICULTIES] /'trʌb·l̩/ *n* problems or difficulties • *The form was terribly complicated and I* **had** *a lot of trouble* **with** *it.* [U] • *She* **had** *a lot of trouble* **trying** *to explain to her husband where the money had gone.* [U + v-*ing*] • *Their problems seem to be over for the moment, but there could be more trouble* **ahead**. [U] • *Giving him such a powerful car when he's only just learned to drive is* **asking for** (= likely to cause) *trouble.* [U] • *The trouble* **began when** *my father came to live with us.* [U] • *Trouble had been* **brewing** (= developing gradually) *for several months, so we weren't surprised when she got the sack.* [U] • *Parents often* **have** *trouble* **finding** *restaurants that welcome young children.* [U + v-*ing*] • *I* **had** *a lot of trouble* **getting** *pregnant the second time.* [U + v-*ing*] • *Did you* **have** *any trouble* **getting** *a work permit?* [U + v-*ing*] • *She hasn't started studying for her exams and she's* **heading for** *real trouble.* [U] • *I think you'll* **have** *trouble* **persuading** *him that it's a good idea.* [U + v-*ing*] • *The latest opinion polls* **spell** (= suggest that there will be) *trouble* **for** *the government.* [U] • *You'll only be* **storing up** *trouble* **for** *the future if you don't go to the dentist now.* [U] • *I should get it finished over the weekend without* **too much** *trouble.* [U] • *She thought her troubles would be over once she'd got divorced.* [C] • *A lack of money seems to be the cause of all his troubles.* [C] • *My Christmas shopping is* **the least of** *my troubles at the moment. I haven't even got enough money to pay the rent.* [C] • *My troubles* **started** *the day I decided to buy a house.* [C] • *Most of the current troubles* **stem from** *our new computer system.* [C] • A person or thing's trouble is a characteristic that is considered a disadvantage or problem: *Ron's trouble is that he's too impatient.* [U] ○ **The** *trouble* **with** *Pat's new girlfriend is that she drinks too much.* [U] ○ **The** *trouble* **with** *this carpet is that it gets dirty very easily.* [U] ○ *It's a brilliant idea.* **The only** *trouble* **is that** *we don't know how much it will cost.* [U] • Sometimes trouble is problems or difficulties caused by something failing to operate as it should: *I haven't* **had** *much trouble* **with** *the car recently.* [U] ○ *The smoke was so thick that I was* **having** *trouble* **breathing**. [U + v-*ing*] ○ *The plane developed* **engine** *trouble shortly after takeoff.* [U] ○ *They have a good reputation for building reliable trouble-***free** *cars.* ○ *Her* **knee** *trouble is expected to keep her out of the game for the rest of the season.* [U] • Trouble can also be problems in the form of arguments, fighting or violence: *Listen, I don't want any trouble in here, so please just finish your drink and leave.* [U] ○ *You can only go to the match if you promise to leave* **at the first sign of** *trouble.* [U] ○ *There have been riots in the capital, and trouble has also* **flared up** *in other parts of the country.* [U] ○ *He says he doesn't go* **looking for** *trouble, but he still manages to get into a fight most Saturday nights.* [U] ○ *My little brother's always trying to* **stir up** (= create) *trouble* **between** *me and my boyfriend.* [U] • Trouble is also a situation in which you experience problems, usually because of something you have done wrong or badly: *I didn't think he was* **in** *trouble at first – I thought he was just pretending to be drowning.* [U] ○ *He's never been* **in** *trouble* **with** *his teachers before.* [U] ○ *She'll be in* **big** *trouble if she crashes Sam's car.* [U] ○ *You'll get into* **deep** *trouble if you continue being late for work.* [U] ○ *The country is in tremendous* **economic** *trouble.* [U] ○ *He got into* **financial** *trouble after his divorce.* [U] ○ *I hope you won't* **get into** *trouble because of what I said to your dad.* [U] ○ *She was always* **getting into** *trouble* **with** *the police when she was a teenager.* [U] ○ *The camp is a great way of getting kids off the street and* **keeping** *them* **out of** *trouble.* [U] ○ *I hope I haven't* **landed** *you* **in** *trouble with your boss.* [U] ○ *The marriage* **ran into** *trouble because of her husband's heavy drinking.* [U] ○ *I would have been in* **real** (= a large amount of) *trouble if I'd been caught.* [U] ○ *The company will be in very* **serious** *trouble if we lose this contract.* [U] ○ *He's* **stayed out of** *trouble since he was released from jail last year.* [U] ○ *He usually tries to lie his* **way out of** *trouble.* [U] • *(dated)* If a man **gets** a woman or girl who is not married **into trouble**, he makes her pregnant: *When he got his girlfriend into trouble they had to choose between marriage and an abortion.* • A **trouble spot** is a place where there is regularly political violence: *There is increasing demand for the United Nations to intervene in trouble spots throughout the world.* • A **trouble spot** is also a part of a road where traffic is moving unusually slowly because there is a lot of it or because of an accident: *Thousands of holidaymakers have been caught up in trouble spots throughout the country.*

troub·le *obj* /'trʌb·l̩/ *v* [T] • *He has been troubled by* (= suffering from) *a knee injury for most of the season.*

troub·led /'trʌb·l̩d/ *adj* • *The survival package involves selling off the unprofitable parts of the troubled* **company**. • *The exhibition covers the key moments of the city's troubled* **history**. • *This troubled* **region** *has had more than its fair share of wars over the the centuries.* • *They had two children during their long and troubled* **relationship**. • *In these troubled* **times** *of war and famine it makes a change to hear some good news.*

Troub·les /'trʌb·l̩z/ *pl n* • **The Troubles** means the political violence in N Ireland that began in the late 1960s.

troub·le·some /'trʌb·l̩.səm/ *adj* • A person or thing that is troublesome causes a lot of problems or worries for someone: *Her hip has been troublesome for quite a while, and she'll probably need surgery on it.* ○ *Many people regard the scandal as* **potentially** *troublesome for the President.* ○ *The negotiations have* **proven** *more troublesome than any of us expected.*

troub·le [INCONVENIENCE] /'trʌb·l̩/ *n* [U] inconvenience or effort • *She was very kind and generous, and nothing was ever too much trouble* **for** *her* (= she didn't mind doing anything at all). • *I didn't mean to* **cause** *you any trouble.* • *It's annoying, but I can't be bothered to* **go to the** *trouble* **of making** *an official complaint.* • *"I'd love some more tea, if it isn't too much trouble." "Oh, it's* **no** *trouble* **at all.**" • *I don't want to* **put** *you* **to** *any trouble* (= create any work for you). • *I thought I'd* **save** *you the trouble* **of** *picking up these books and by bringing them round myself.* • *You really ought to have* **taken the** *trouble* **to** *thank her for the present.* [+ *to* infinitive] • *If you* **took the** *trouble* **to** *listen to what I was saying, you'd know what I was talking about.* [+ *to* infinitive] • *He always takes* **so much** *trouble* **with** *his work.* • *They* **went to a lot of** *trouble* (= made a lot of effort) **for** *their dinner party, but half the guests didn't bother to turn up.* • *It's not* **worth the** *trouble* **(of)** *applying for that job. You've no chance of getting it.* • **It's more trouble than it's worth** (= It's not worth making the effort) **to** *take it back to the shop and ask for a replacement.*

troub·le *(obj)* /'trʌb·l̩/ *v slightly fml* • If you trouble someone, you cause them a small amount of inconvenience or effort: *May I trouble you* **for** (= Please give me) *some more wine, please?* [T] ○ *Could I trouble you* **to** *open that window? I'm afraid I can't reach it.* [T + obj + *to* infinitive] ○ *For the moment we don't need to trouble* **ourselves** (= make the effort to think) **about** *the precise details.* [T] • *He went off to France* **without** *troubling* **to** *tell me where he was going.* [+ *to* infinitive; in negatives]

troub·le *obj* [WORRY] /'trʌb·l̩/ *v* [T] to cause (someone) to be worried or anxious • *What's troubling you, dear? You look ever so worried.* • *Many of us are deeply troubled* **by** *the chairman's decision.* • *She doesn't seem to be* **unduly** (= greatly) *troubled by her financial problems.* • *I must say* **it** *troubles me* **(that)** *you didn't discuss your problems with me earlier.* [+ obj + (*that*) clause]

trou·bling /'trʌb·l̩ɪŋ, 'trʌb·lɪŋ/ *adj* • *Some troubling* **questions** *remain about the legal status of frozen embryos.* • *The increasing violence is troubling* **to** *many people.*

trou·bling·ly /ˈtrʌb·lɪŋ·li/ *adv* • *We've rung him several times but, troublingly, there's never been any reply.*

troub·le·ma·ker /£ˈtrʌb·l̩ˌmeɪ·kəʳ, $-kɚ/ *n* [C] someone who intentionally causes problems for other people, esp. people who are in a position of power or authority • *I was worried that I would be regarded as a troublemaker if I complained about the safety standards in the factory.* • *The régime has a policy of imprisoning people it considers to be* **potential** *troublemakers.*

troub·le·shoot·er /£ˈtrʌb·l̩ˌʃuː·təʳ, $-t̬ɚ/ *n* [C] someone whose job involves discovering why something does not work effectively and making suggestions about how to improve it • *A troubleshooter is being appointed to make the prison service more efficient.*

trouble·shoot *(obj)* /ˈtrʌb·l̩.ʃuːt/ *v past* **troubleshot** /£ˈtrʌb·l̩.ʃɒt, $-ʃɑːt/ • *I've been brought in to troubleshoot – to go in, sort out the problem, and get out again.* [I] • *A top German engineer has been appointed to troubleshoot the cause of the accident.* [T]

troub·le·shoot·ing /£ˈtrʌb·l̩ˌʃuː·tɪŋ, $-t̬ɪŋ/ *n* [U] • *The instruction manual includes a section on troubleshooting to help you with any simple problems you might have with the television.*

trough CONTAINER /£trɒf, $trɑːf/ *n* [C] a long narrow container without a lid that usually holds water or food for farm animals • *The cows at the feeding trough were surprised to see us.* • The word trough is sometimes used to mean a supply of money or other advantage which people eagerly and perhaps dishonestly take a share of: *The council had been handing out grants indiscriminately, and people were hurrying to get their* **snouts in the** *trough.* ○ *(Am) He accused leading senators of* **feeding at the public** *trough* (=taking government money and using it dishonestly for their own advantage). • LP› **'-ough' pronunciation**

trough LOW POINT /£trɒf, $trɑːf/ *n* [C] a low point in a regular series of high and low points • *His career was a series of spectacular peaks and dismal troughs that spanned thirty years.* • *Investing small amounts regularly is a good way of smoothing out the* **peaks and** *troughs of the stock market.* • *Some economists believe the trough of the* **recession** *has already been reached.* • *(specialized)* In the study of weather patterns, a trough is a long area of low air pressure between two areas of high air pressure: *A trough of low pressure over hilly areas will bring heavy thunderstorms and possibly some flooding overnight.*

trounce *obj* /traʊnts/ *v* [T] *infml* to defeat (a competitor) by a large amount • *France trounced Germany by five goals to one in the qualifying match.* • *She trounced her* **rivals** *in the election.*

trounc·ing /ˈtraʊnt·sɪŋ/ *n* [C usually sing] *infml* • *The party's recent trouncing* (=serious defeat) *in the local elections is likely to result in a re-organisation of its campaigning activities.* • *Major changes are expected in the England team following their 3-0 trouncing last Saturday.* • *Bannockburn is the site of the Scots' trouncing of the English in 1314.*

troupe /truːp/ *n* [C + sing/pl v] a group of performers such as singers or dancers who work and travel together • *When she was eighteen she joined a* **dance** *troupe and travelled all over Europe.* • *A troupe of* **dancers** *from Beijing is one of the leading attractions in the festival.*

troup·er /£ˈtruː·pəʳ, $-pɚ/ *n* [C] a successful entertainer who has had a lot of experience • *He often surprises his audiences by inviting an* **old** *trouper to make a guest appearance on stage.* • *(approving)* A trouper can also be anyone with a lot of experience who can be depended on and does not complain: *Good old Edna – she's a real trouper to do the washing-up without even being asked!* ○ *He took his disappointment* **like a** *trouper.*

trou·sers /£ˈtraʊ·zəz, $-zɚz/, *Am usually and Aus also* **pants** /pænts/ *pl n* a piece of clothing that covers the lower part of the body from the waist to the feet, consisting of two cylindrical parts, one for each leg, which are joined at the top • *I need a new* **pair of** *trousers to go with this jacket.* • *Why aren't you* **wearing** *any trousers, David?* • *I'd rather wear* **baggy** *trousers than a skirt.* • *He prefers wearing corduroy trousers to jeans.* • *Are flared trousers in fashion or out of fashion at the moment?* • PIC› **Clothes**

trou·ser /£ˈtraʊ·zəʳ, $-zɚ/, *Am usually, Aus also* **pants** /pænts/ *adj* [before n; not gradable] • *"Just look at this scar," said Brian proudly, rolling up his trouser* **leg**. • A **trouser press** is a device for making or keeping trousers smooth by pressing them between two boards. • *(Br)* A **trouser suit** (*Am and Aus* **pantsuit**) is a matching jacket and pair of trousers that is worn by women on formal occasions: *She's bought a very smart trouser suit for her job interviews.*

trous·seau /£ˈtruː·səʊ, $-soʊ/ *n* [C] *dated* a collection of personal possessions, such as clothes, that a woman takes to her new home when she gets married

trout FISH /traʊt/ *n pl* **trout** or **trouts** a fish that is a popular food and exists in two main forms, a brown one that lives in rivers and lakes, and a silver one that lives in the sea but returns to rivers to reproduce • *Trout are similar to salmon, but they are smaller and spotted.* [C] • *Thousands of young salmon and trout have been killed by the pollution.* [C] • *Have you ever eaten smoked trout?* [U] • *Loch Leven is famous for its trout* **fishing**. • PIC› **Fish**

trout PERSON /traʊt/ *n* [C] *pl* **trouts** *Br infml* an old unattractive person, esp. a woman • *Don't take any notice of her – she's just a miserable* **old** *trout who complains about everything.*

tro·wel BUILDING TOOL /traʊəl/ *n* [C] a small tool consisting of a flat metal blade joined to a handle which is used for spreading building materials such as CEMENT • PIC› **Building and construction, Garden**

tro·wel GARDENING TOOL /traʊəl/ *n* [C] a small tool with a curved pointed metal blade which is used in the garden for digging small holes and removing small plants from the earth

tru·ant /ˈtruː·ənt/ *n* [C] a child who is regularly absent from school without permission • *There are too many truants hanging around on street corners instead of going to school.* • *(dated)* A **truant officer** is an official who searches for truants and returns them to school.

tru·ant *esp. Br and Aus* /ˈtruː·ənt/ *v* [I] • Children who truant or **play truant** (*Am usually and Aus also* **play hooky**) are regularly absent from school, usually while pretending to their parents that they have gone to school: *You'll fail all your exams if you carry on truanting.* ○ *Most parents are horrified when they discover their children have been playing truant* **from school**.

tru·an·cy /ˈtruː·ənt·si/, **tru·ant·ing** /ˈtruː·ən·tɪŋ/ *n* [U] • *My daughter's school has very good exam results and hardly any truancy.* • *Truanting was a serious problem in a fifth of the schools surveyed.*

truce /truːs/ *n* [C] a brief interruption in a war or argument, or a usually temporary agreement to stop fighting or arguing • *After years of rivalry, the two companies have (Br)* **agreed**/*(Am and Aus)* **agreed to** *a truce.* • *We've got to spend the weekend together, so we might as well* **call** (= have) *a truce.* • *Following last month's riots, the two big gangs in Los Angeles have finally* **declared** *a truce, ending years of bloodshed.* • *The officer arrived under* **a flag of** *truce to negotiate the withdrawal of the tanks.* • *The* **fragile** *truce* **between** *the two sides is not expected to last long.* • *The week-old truce appears to be* **holding** *throughout the war zone.* • *A United Nations peace-keeping force will* **monitor** *the truce.* • *Few people expected the truce to last when it was* **signed** (= agreed to) *last week.* • *She's managed to negotiate an* **uneasy** *truce* **with** *her former husband which will enable her to see their children.*

truck VEHICLE /trʌk/, *Br also* **lor·ry** *n* [C] a big road vehicle which is used for transporting large amounts of goods and has a separate part for the driver • *The road is completely blocked by an overturned truck.* • *She says she wants to be a truck* **driver** *when she grows up.* • *(Br)* A truck (*Am* **car**) can also be a part of a train that is used for carrying goods or animals: *Hundreds of refugees were herded into* **cattle** *trucks for the gruelling ten-hour journey.* • *(Am)* A **truck farm** is a small farm where fruit and vegetables are grown for selling to the public: *We buy as much as possible from the local truck farm.* ○ *The floods have had a severe effect on the livelihoods of* **truck farmers** *in the area.* • *(Am and Aus)* A **truck stop** is an area next to an important road with a restaurant, fuel and repair services, where the main customers are truck drivers wanting to eat and drink cheaply. • See also DUMPER (TRUCK). • LP› **Driving** Ⓙ Ⓝ

truck *obj* /trʌk/ *v* [T always + adv/prep] *esp. Am* • When goods are trucked somewhere, they are transported there in trucks: *Most of the aid is being trucked into the city, although some is arriving by boat.* • *(infml)* If you **keep on trucking** you continue to do something that tends to be ordinary and uninteresting: *"How's work going?" "It's okay, thanks. I just keep on trucking."*

truck·er *Br and Am* /£ˈtrʌk·əʳ, $-ɚ/, *Aus* **truck·ie** /ˈtrʌk·i/ *n* [C] • A trucker is someone whose job is driving trucks.

truck·ing *Am and Aus* /ˈtrʌk·ɪŋ/, *Br* **road haul·age** *n* [U] • *The railroads have lost a lot of business to trucking* **companies**. • *The trucking* **industry** *is reluctant to pay an unfair share of the costs of highway construction and maintenance.*

truck·load /£ˈtrʌk·ləud, $-loud/ *n* [C] • A truckload of something is the amount of it that can be carried by a truck: *Truckloads* **of** *rice have been brought in to the areas affected by drought.* ○ *Donations of food and medicines have been arriving* **by** *the truckload all week.*

truck [INVOLVEMENT] /trʌk/ *n* [U] **have no truck with** *infml* to refuse to have any involvement or connection with (someone or something) • *I have no truck with people who refuse to listen to the opinions of others.* • Ⓙ Ⓝ

truc·u·lent /ˈtrʌk·jʊ·lənt/ *adj* bad-tempered and tending to argue a lot • *She's been very truculent since she heard she wasn't going to be promoted.* • *He was in a very truculent mood throughout the meeting.*

truc·u·lent·ly /ˈtrʌk·jʊ·lənt·li/ *adv* • *"I'm not coming with you, and that's final," said Chris, truculently.*

truc·u·lence /ˈtrʌk·jʊ·lənts/ *n* [U] • *His truculence can make him very difficult to work with sometimes.*

trudge /trʌdʒ/ *v* [I always + adv/prep] to walk slowly with a lot of effort, esp. over a difficult surface or while carrying something heavy • *You must be exhausted after trudging all that way with your backpack!* • *I find trudging around the supermarket really exhausting.* • *"Oh well, I suppose I'd better get back to work," he said, and trudged off down the corridor.* • *We trudged* **along** *the muddy track to the top of the hill.* • *Martha and Jamie had great fun trudging* **through** *the snow.* • *(fig.) I spent the whole weekend trudging* **through** (= slowly reading) *this report, and I still haven't finished reading it.*

trudge /trʌdʒ/ *n* [C] • *We came back from our trudge across the moor wet and tired.* • *(fig.) Her long trudge* (= difficult rise) *to the top of the company began forty years ago when she joined as a secretary.*

true [NOT FALSE] /truː/ *adj* [not gradable] (esp. of facts or statements) right and not wrong; correct • *"Dad, Mary's stolen ten pounds from me." "Is this true, Mary?"* • *"You could have rung to tell me you would be late." "True, but I wasn't near a phone."* • **It is certainly** *true* **that** *the risks associated with pregnancy increase with age.* [+ *that* clause] • *You were in the restaurant on the night of the murder – true* **or false**? • *The allegations,* **if** *true, could lead to her resignation.* • *Her story is only* **partly** *true.* • *Now that's not* **quite** *true, is it?* • *I'm afraid your story doesn't quite* **ring** *true* (= is not completely believable). • *Would* **it** *be true* **to** *say that you've never liked Jim?* [+ *to* infinitive] • **It's simply not** *true* **to** *say that we can do the same amount of work with fewer staff.* [+ *to* infinitive] • *The witness failed to give a true* **picture** (= accurate description) *of what had happened.* • *I don't believe these exam results are a true* **reflection** *of your abilities.* • *The movie is based on the true* **story** *of a London gangster.* • *She has since admitted that her earlier statement was not* **strictly** (= completely) *true.* • *What do you think will happen to him if these rumours* **turn out to be** *true?* • *He used to be the hardest working person in the department, but that's no longer true* (= that situation does not exist any more). • Something that is true of a group of people relates to all the people in that group: *Alcohol should be consumed in moderation, and this is particularly true* **for** *pregnant women.* ○ *Parents of young children often become depressed, and* **this is** *especially true* **of** *single parents.* ○ *The survey was carried out in Sweden, but the results are* **equally** *true of this country.* ○ *I'm very sorry that you've decided to leave, and I'm sure that* **holds** *true* **for** *everyone else here.* ○ *She was a great expert on sport, and this was* **particularly** *true* **when it came to** *tennis.* ○ *On average women earn less than men, and as long as that* **remains** *true there cannot be genuine equality.* ○ *She would be very good for the job, but* **the same is** *true* **of** *several other candidates.* • See also TRUTH.

tru·ism /ˈtruː·ɪ·zᵊm/ *n* [C] • A truism is a statement which is so obviously true that it is almost not worth mentioning: *As far as your health is concerned,* **it**'*s a truism* **that** *prevention is better than cure.* [+ *that* clause]

tru·ly /ˈtruː·li/ *adv* [not gradable] • *I like him, but I can't truly say I love him.*

true [REAL] /truː/ *adj* [before n] **-r, -st** being what exists, rather than what was thought, intended or claimed; ACTUAL • *She discovered Matt's true* **colours** (= real intentions) *when he spent the night with another woman.* • *There cannot be true* **democracy** *without reform of the electoral system.* • *It wasn't until daylight that the true* **extent** *of the catastrophe was revealed.* • *The true* **heir** *to the fortune was eventually identified with genetic tests.* • *The true* **horror** *of the accident did not become clear until the following morning.* • *She claims to know the true* **identity** *of the bombers.* • *Mark's new girlfriend seems really nice. Do you think it's true* **love** *this time?* • *She earned a living teaching the piano, but her true* **love** *was the guitar.* • *During the London blitz it was felt that civilian morale would be at risk if the true* **nature** *of the devastation were revealed.* • *They've gone on a weekend meditation course to try and find their true* **selves** (= discover what sort of people they really are). • If a hope, wish or desire **comes true**, it happens even though it was unlikely that it would: *I'd always dreamt of owning my own house, but I never thought it would come true.* ○ *After all the problems I'd had getting pregnant, the birth of Jennifer was a* **dream** *come true* (= was a wonderfully pleasing event). ○ *When my house burnt down it was my* **worst nightmare** *come true.* • *(esp. Br) Julie's brother's* **so** *handsome* **it's not true** (= is extremely and surprisingly attractive). • A **true-life story** is one that is based on real rather than imaginary events: *The film is based on the true-life story of a cancer sufferer.* • *The novel's plot was quite interesting but the characters weren't very* **true-to-life** (= realistic). • **True north** is the direction towards the top of the Earth along an imaginary line at an angle of 90° to the Equator: *True north runs parallel to the earth's axis.* • *"The course of true love never did run smooth"* (Shakespeare, Midsummer Night's Dream 1.1)

tru·ly /ˈtruː·li/ *adv* • *These will be the first truly* **democratic** *elections in the country's history.* • *It's hard to obtain truly* **independent** *financial advice.* • *This is a desperate situation which requires a truly* **radical** *solution.* • *Without a change in the voting system, the prospects for truly* **representative** *government are extremely bleak.* • Truly is sometimes used to emphasize the truth of something: *The river is truly a beautiful sight at this time of year.* ○ *The truly* **astonishing** *thing is that nobody thought of it before.* ○ *She is a truly* **great** *actress.* ○ *The takeovers would turn the company into the world's* **only** *truly* **international** *brewer.* ○ *The Channel Tunnel is a truly* **remarkable** *achievement.* ○ *The play climaxes with a truly* **shocking** *outburst of cruelty and violence.* ○ *It's a mystery to me why anyone who has ever suffered from a truly* **terrible** *hangover ever has another one.* ○ *It must have been a truly* **terrifying** *experience.* • *"Truly, Madly, Deeply"* (title of a film, 1990)

true [SINCERE] /truː/ *adj* **-r, -st** sincere or loyal, and likely to continue to be so in difficult situations • *There are few true* **believers** *in communism left in the party.* • *She has vowed to remain true* **to** *the president whatever happens.* • *She is one of the few politicians who remains true* **to** *her* **principles**, *even when it makes her unpopular with the voters.* • *He said he'd repay the money the next day, and true* **to** *his* **word** (= as he had promised), *he gave it all back to me the following morning.* • Someone who is **true-blue** is completely loyal to a person or belief: *Although many multinational US companies have foreign managers, there is a feeling that real control should be kept in true-blue American hands.* • If you are **true to** your**self** you behave according to your beliefs and do what you think is right: *You only live once, so you have to be true to yourself, and not worry about what other people think of you.* • Someone who does something **true to form** or **type**, behaves as other people would have expected from previous experience: *True to form, when it came to his turn to buy the drinks, he said he'd left his wallet at home.*

tru·ly /ˈtruː·li/ *adv fml* • *I'm truly sorry about the accident.* • *She truly cares for her patients.* • *I didn't mean to break it, truly!* • *He truly* **believes** *he can cure himself by willpower alone.* • *(esp. Am)* **Yours truly** is sometimes used to end a letter: *I look forward to hearing from you. Yours truly, Taylor Champinski.* • *(infml)* Sometimes **yours truly** is the person who is speaking or writing, often when they are talking about something they have done unwillingly: *She didn't have any money, so yours truly ended up having to lend her some.*

true [HAVING NECESSARY QUALITIES] /truː/ *adj* [before n] **-r, -st** possessing all the characteristics necessary to be accurately described as something • *Only true deer have antlers.* • *Ecologists are radicals in the true* **sense of the word**, *as they go to the roots of the problems that affect the planet.* • *(slightly dated) This portrait is a very true* **likeness** *of her* (= looks very much like her). • *In true*

Hollywood **style** (=In a way that is typical of Hollywood), *she's had five marriages and three facelifts.*

tru·ly /ˈtruː·li/ *adv* • *Mushrooms aren't truly vegetables, but many people think they are.*

true [ACCURATE] /truː/ *adj* [after v] fitted or positioned accurately • *The carpenters left a lot of rough edges and none of the drawers were true.*

true /truː/ *adv* **-r, -st** • *Make sure you hit the nails in true* (=straight and without moving to either side), *otherwise you'll have to pull them out and start again.*

true /truː/ *n* [U] • If an object is **out of true** it is not in the correct position or is slightly bent out of the correct shape: *This door won't shut properly. I think the frame must be out of true.*

true·love /ˈtruː·lʌv/ *n* [C] *literary* a person who is loved by someone more than anyone else in the world

truf·fle [RARE FOOD] /ˈtrʌf·l̩/ *n* [C] an edible type of FUNGUS which grows underground and is expensive because it is very rare • *The Dordogne region's gastronomic specialities include truffles and foie gras.* • *The traditional recipe uses truffles, but you can economise by substituting mushrooms.*

truf·fle [CHOCOLATE] /ˈtrʌf·l̩/ *n* [C] a small round chocolate which is soft and creamy • *Truffles are often flavoured with rum.*

trumps /trʌmps/ *pl n* [C] one of the four groups in a set of playing cards which has been chosen to have the highest value during a particular game or part of a game • *Which suit do you want to have trumps? Hearts, diamonds, spades or clubs?* • *(Br)* If you **turn up/come up trumps**, you complete an activity successfully or produce a good result, esp. when you were not expected to: *England really came up trumps when they beat the West Indies at cricket.*

trump /trʌmp/ *n* [C] • A trump is a card that belongs to the group of cards that has been chosen to have the highest value in a particular game: *My partner thought I should have played a trump.* ○ *Luckily, I* **drew** *a trump.* • *Diamonds are the trump* **suit**. • A **trump card** is an advantage over others or the most effective thing available to obtain an advantage: *The unions* **held** *all the trump cards in their pay negotiations.* ○ *She has one trump card still to* **play** *– without her agreement, they can't get the money to go ahead with the project.* • Ⓙ

trump *obj* /trʌmp/ *v* [T] • If you trump another player's card, you beat it with a card that belongs to the group of cards that has been chosen to have the highest value in the game you are playing: *(fig.) Their million-pound bid for the company was trumped at the last moment by an offer for almost twice as much from their main competitor.*

trump up *obj*, **trump** *obj* **up** *v adv* [M] to create (a false accusation) against someone in order to have an excuse for punishing them • *He claims his employers trumped up the accusations against him so that they had a reason to sack him.* • *She was imprisoned on trumped up corruption* **charges.**

trum·pet [INSTRUMENT] /ˈtrʌm·pɪt/ *n* [C] a BRASS musical instrument consisting of a metal tube with one narrow end, into which the player blows, and one wide end. Three buttons are used to change notes. • *The main orchestral brass instruments are the horn, trumpet, trombone and tuba.* • *The prince's arrival was heralded by a trumpet* **fanfare**. • *I was a trumpet* **player** *in the jazz band at school.* • PIC› **Musical instruments**

trum·pet·er /ˈtrʌm·pɪtəʳ/ *n* [C] • A trumpeter is a musician who plays a trumpet: *I started off as a classical musician but I always wanted to be a* **jazz** *trumpeter.*

trum·pet [ANIMAL CALL] /ˈtrʌm·pɪt/ *v* [I] (of a large animal, esp. an ELEPHANT) to produce a loud call • *We could hear the elephants trumpeting in the distance.*

trum·pet *obj* [ANNOUNCE] /ˈtrʌm·pɪt/ *v* [T] *esp. disapproving* to announce or state (something) proudly to a lot of people • *The judgement is being trumpeted by campaigners as a victory for human rights.* • *The museum has been* **loudly** *trumpeting its reputation as one of the finest in the world.* • *Their* **much-***trumpeted price cuts affect only 5% of the goods that they sell.*

trun·cate *obj* /trʌŋˈkeɪt/ *v* [T] to make (something) shorter or briefer, esp. by removing the end of it • *Television coverage of the match was truncated by a technical fault.* • *There simply isn't enough time to teach everything, so we've had to truncate the syllabus.*

trun·cat·ed /£trʌŋˈkeɪ·tɪd, $-t̬ɪd/ *adj* • *The new production is a truncated version of the ballet, and lasts for only two hours including the interval.* • *This article appeared in a truncated form in late editions of yesterday's paper.*

trun·ca·tion /trʌŋˈkeɪ·ʃən/ *n* [U] • *The proposed truncation of the railway line would force more traffic onto roads which are already congested.*

trun·cheon *Br and Aus* /ˈtrʌnt·ʃən/, *Am usually* **night·stick**, **bat·on**, *Am also* **bil·ly (club)** *n* [C] a short thick stick which police officers use in dangerous or threatening situations to hit other people • *The police broke up the demonstration with tear gas and truncheons.* • *Most British police officers are only armed with truncheons.*

trun·dle *(obj)* /ˈtrʌn·dl̩/ *v* [always + adv/prep] (to cause something) to move slowly and unevenly on wheels • *She trundled the wheelbarrow down the garden.* [T] • *Hundreds of trucks full of fruit and vegetables trundle across the border each day.* [I] • *There were a lot of delays and we were trundling* **along** *very slowly for most of the journey.* [I] • *(fig.) The property market has been trundling along* (=been only slightly active) *for several months and there is no sign yet of a significant recovery.* [I] • *(fig. disapproving) The negotiations have been trundling* **on** (=developing slowly) *for months and there's still no end in sight.* [I] • *(fig. disapproving) They seem to trundle* **out** *the same old films* (=they broadcast them) *every Christmas.* [M] • *(Am and Aus)* A **trundle bed** is a low bed on wheels which is stored under an ordinary bed ready for use by visitors. • PIC› **Beds and bedroom**

trunk [MAIN PART] /trʌŋk/ *n* [C] the thick main stem of a tree, from which its branches grow • *Bark protects the trunks and branches of trees from extremes of temperature.* • *His dog strangled itself when it ran off and got its lead tangled around a* **tree** *trunk.* • The trunk of a person is the main part of their body, not including the head, legs or arms: *These exercises are designed to develop the muscles in your trunk.* • *(Br)* A **trunk road** is an important road for travelling long distances at high speed, which is suitable for large vehicles and a lot of traffic: *Plans to upgrade the trunk road into a motorway have met considerable opposition.* • PIC› **Tree, Trunk**

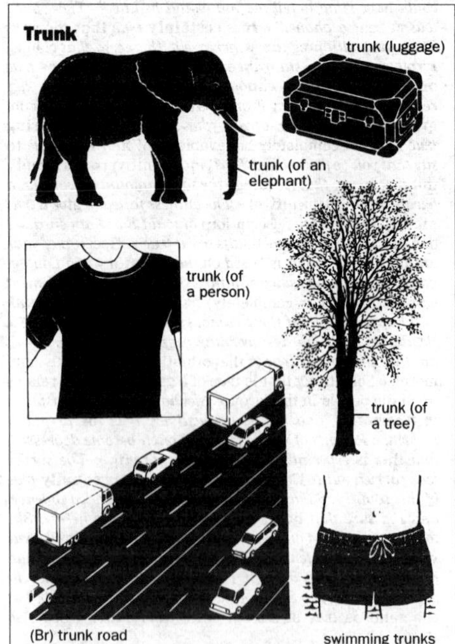

trunk [NOSE] /trʌŋk/ *n* [C] a ELEPHANT'S nose which is long and tubular and can bend easily • *Elephants can use their trunks for grasping or lifting things.* • PIC› **Trunk**

trunk [CASE] /trʌŋk/ *n* [C] a large strong case that is used for storing clothes and personal possessions, often when travelling or going to live in a new place • *We packed all our equipment into a couple of tin trunks and started out for Calcutta by train.* • Trunk is also *Am for* BOOT [CAR]: *She was arrested when her husband's body was discovered in the trunk of her car.* • PIC› **Car, Trunk**

trunks /trʌŋks/ *pl n* [C] short tight trousers worn by men when swimming or relaxing on a beach • *How could you come to the beach and forget to bring your trunks?* • *He walked into the restaurant wearing nothing but a pair of* **swimming** *trunks.* • *Have you seen my* **bathing** *trunks anywhere?* • PIC› **Trunk**

truss *obj* TIE /trʌs/ *v* [T] to tie the arms and legs of (someone) together tightly and roughly with rope to prevent them from moving or escaping • *Police said the couple had been trussed* **up** *and robbed before being shot.* [M] • *I arrived home to discover him gagged and trussed on the bathroom floor.* • If you truss a bird that you are going to eat, you prepare it for cooking by tying its wings and legs to its body: *Stuff two dried apricots into each quail, then truss them with butcher's twine.*

truss DEVICE /trʌs/ *n* [C] a device for holding an organ of the body, esp. part of the INTESTINE, in its correct position after it has moved because of an injury • *He was wearing a truss for several months after the operation on his hernia.*

truss SUPPORT /trʌs/ *n* [C] *specialized* a support for a roof or bridge that is usually made of stone or brick

trust *(obj)* BELIEVE /trʌst/ *v* to have belief or confidence in the honesty, goodness, skill or safety of (a person, organization or thing) • *Trust me – have I ever lied to you in the past?* [T] • *It's not surprising she doesn't trust him any more considering what he did.* [T] • *You must trust your own feelings and decide for yourself.* [T] • *Grandma doesn't trust air travel – she says it's unnatural.* [T] • *Of course you can trust him* **to** *look after the money – he's completely honest.* [T + obj + *to* infinitive] • *If anyone should be trusted* **to** *solve the problem, it's Mortimer.* [T + obj + *to* infinitive] • *That man is* **not to be** *trusted.* [T] • *He can't be trusted* **with** *much responsibility yet – he's still very inexperienced.* [T] • *(slightly fml) Sometimes you simply have to trust* **in** *the goodness of human nature.* [I always + prep] • *However much you plan an expedition like this, you still have to trust* **to** (= rely on) **luck** *to a certain extent.* [I] • *(infml)* **Trust** *you* **to** (= It is typical of you to) *upset her by talking about the accident.* • If you can **not trust** someone **as far as** you **can/could throw** them/*(esp. Br and Aus also)* **not trust** someone **an inch**, it is not possible to ever trust them: *From what I've heard about Sam, I wouldn't trust him as far as I could throw him.* • *"Put your trust in God, and keep your powder* (= gunpowder) *dry"* (believed to have been said by Oliver Cromwell) • *"In God we trust"* (words written on most American coins, 1865-) • *"Never trust a man over 30"* (Jerry Rubin, 1960s)

trust /trʌst/ *n* [U] • *Their relationship is based on trust and understanding.* • *It can be difficult to* **gain** *a child's trust if people have treated her or him badly.* • *We were obviously wrong to* **put/place** *our trust* **in** *her.* • *Surely it's wrong for someone in* **a position of** *trust* (= a position with responsibilities, esp. to the public) *to speak so openly to the press.* • *Why should I* **take** *what you're saying* **on trust** (= believe what you're saying without doubting it)*?*

trust·ed /£ˈtrʌs·tɪd, $-t̬ɪd/ *adj* • *You've always been a trusted* **friend** *– now tell me honestly what you think.*

trust·ing /£ˈtrʌs·tɪŋ, $-t̬ɪŋ/, **trust·ful** /ˈtrʌst·fəl/ *adj* • *The child gave a trusting smile.* • *You shouldn't be so trusting – people take unfair advantage of you.*

trust·ful·ly /ˈtrʌst·fəl·i/ *adv*

trust·ful·ness /ˈtrʌst·fəl·nəs/ *n* [U]

trust·y /£ˈtrʌs·ti, $-t̬i/ *adj* [before n] **-ier, -iest** *humorous or dated* • *He took his trusty* (= reliable, esp. because of having been owned and used for a long time) *bike with him on his expedition into the Himalayas.*

trust ARRANGEMENT /trʌst/ *n* [C] a legal arrangement in which a person or organization controls property and/or money for the benefit of another person or organization • *Under the terms of the trust he receives interest on the money, but he cannot get at the money itself.* • A trust is also the controlling organization, which might be a group of people, or the property and/or money controlled: *He works for a charitable trust.* ○ *Housing trusts help to provide houses for people who are not well off.* ○ *Camden and Islington Health Trust is responsible for providing health services for people in its area.* ○ *Our local hospital is a self-governing trust.* ○ *We've put some money into an investment trust.* • *(Am)* Trust is also used in the name of some banks: *Morgan Guaranty Trust* ○ *Bankers Trust* • *The large amounts of money which her father made are being kept* **in trust** (= being controlled) *for her until she's 30.* • A **trust fund** is an amount of money which is being controlled for the benefit of a person or organization by another person or organization: *There are some tax advantages in setting up a trust fund for each of your children.*

trus·tee /ˌtrʌsˈtiː/ *n* [C] • A trustee is a person, often one of a group, who controls property and/or money for the benefit of another person or an organization: *the museum's board of trustees*

trus·tee·ship /ˌtrʌsˈtiː·ʃɪp/ *n* [C/U] • (A) trusteeship is the position or responsibility of a trustee.

trust HOPE /trʌst/ *v* [+ (*that*) clause] *fml* to hope and expect that something is true • *I trust* **(that)** *you slept well?* • *The meeting went well, I trust.*

trust·wor·thy /£ˈtrʌstˌwɜː·ði, $-ˌwɜːr-/ *adj* able or deserving to be trusted • *Television should be a trustworthy source of information from which the public can find out what's going on.* • *I wouldn't tell any secrets to Rachel if I were you – she's not very trustworthy.*

trust·wor·thi·ness /£ˈtrʌstˌwɜː·ðɪ·nəs, $-ˌwɜːr-/ *n* [U]

truth /truːθ/ *n* [U] the quality of being true • *There would seem to be some truth* **in** *what she says.* • *There is no truth* **in** *the reports of his resignation.* • *You cannot question the truth* **of** *his alibi.* • *The suggestion that the gun was fired accidentally seems to contain at least* **a grain of** (= a small amount of) *truth.* • **The** truth is the real facts about a situation, event or person: *I don't think you're* **telling** *us the* **whole** *truth.* ○ *Will we ever know the truth* **about/of** *what happened on that day?* ○ *It might be difficult to discover the truth* **about** *your parents' identities.* ○ *I told her it didn't matter that she couldn't come to the meeting, but to* **tell (you)** *the truth/(fml slightly dated) truth* **to tell** (= really) *I was really very annoyed.* • *(fml)* The expression **in truth** is used to show or emphasize that something is true: *In truth we feared for her safety although we didn't let it be known.* • *(saying)* 'Truth is stranger than fiction' means that strange things often happen in real life. • *(saying)* 'Truth will out' means that the truth will always be discovered. • *"The truth is rarely pure and never simple"* (Oscar Wilde in the play *The Importance of Being Earnest*, 1895) • *"The truth, the whole truth, and nothing but the truth"* (said by witnesses in court) • See also TRUE.

truth /truːθ/ *n* [C] *pl* **truths** /truːðz, truːθs/ • A truth is a fact or principle which is thought to be true by most people: *It would seem to be a general truth that nothing is as straightforward as it at first seems.* ○ *The entire system of belief is based on a few simple truths.*

truth·ful /ˈtruːθ·fəl/ *adj* • *The public has a right to expect truthful* (= true) *answers from politicians.* • *Are you being quite truthful* **with** *me* (= Is what you say true)*?*

truth·ful·ly /ˈtruːθ·fəl·i/ *adv* • *You must answer the questions truthfully* (= by saying what is true). • *Truthfully* (= What I am saying is true), *I don't know what happened.*

truth·ful·ness /ˈtruːθ·fəl·nəs/ *n* [U]

try *(obj)* ATTEMPT /traɪ/ *v* to attempt (to do something) • *It might take a while, but if you keep trying you'll find a job eventually.* [I] • *Even if you don't get into the academy this year, you can try* **again** *next year.* [I] • *You'll have to try* **hard** *if you want to get into the football team.* [I] • *I'm trying my* **best/hardest**, *but I just can't do it.* [I] • *Of course the exercises are difficult, but you must try* **to** *do them.* [+ (*to*) infinitive] • *Please try* **to** *be home by eleven o'clock.* [+ (*to*) infinitive] • *Try putting the aerial over there – it might work better.* [+ v-*ing*] • *Perhaps you should try getting* **up** (= You should get up) *earlier in the mornings.* [+ v-*ing*] • *Try using* (= You should use) *a bit of tact – you might find you're more successful.* [+ v-*ing*] • *(Br and Aus) He's working long hours at the moment because he's trying* **for** (= attempting to get) *promotion.* [I] • To try **for** something is to attempt to get it: *Are you going to try for that job in the sales department?* • *(Am and Aus)* To try **out for** a sports team or play is to compete for a position in the team or part in the play: *Luke's trying out for the college football team.* [I] • *(Br and Aus infml) Please* **try and** (= try to) *keep clean.* [I] • *(infml) I've never been hang-gliding, but I'd like to* **try** *my* **hand** *(at it)* (= attempt it).

try /traɪ/ *n* [C] • *It's difficult to finish the test in the allotted time, but just* **have** *a try and see how much you get done.* • *This will be her third try* **at** *jumping the bar.* • *Send in your entry for the competition – it's* **worth** *a try.*

tri·er /£ˈtraɪ·əʳ, $-ɚ/ *n* [C] *approving* • *Lindy's a* **real** *trier – she'll always keep working at something until she can do it.*

try *obj* TEST /traɪ/ *v* [T] to test (something) to see if it is suitable or useful or if it works • *Have you tried that new breakfast cereal which has been advertised on TV?* • *I'm afraid we don't sell newspapers, but have you tried the shop on the corner?* • *Would you like to try parachuting?* [+ v-*ing*]

• *Perhaps we should try seeing each other less often for a while.* [+ v-*ing*] • *We should try* **out** *all the equipment before setting up the experiment.* [M] • *Try* **on** (=put on) *the shoes to see if they fit.* [M] • *What a lovely dress – why don't you try it* **on for size** (=put it on to discover whether it fits)? [M] LP> **Dressing and undressing** • *(Br and Aus infml)* If you **try** something **for size** (*Am and Aus* **try** something **on for size**), you use it or think about it for a short time to see if it would be useful or suitable. • *I've forgotten my door-keys – we'd better try the window* (=test it to see if it is open). • *(Br and Aus infml)* When a person **tries it on** they deceive someone or behave badly, esp. in order to discover how much of their bad behaviour will be permitted: *He's not really ill, he's just trying it on.* • *(Br and Aus infml)* A **try-on** is an attempt to deceive someone, or to behave badly, esp. in order to discover how much of their bad behaviour will be permitted: *She's not sick – it's just a try-on.* • If someone **tries** their **luck**, they attempt to succeed, esp. at something they have not done before or in a place they have not been before: *Why don't you try your luck in another job – it couldn't be worse than the one you've got.* • *(infml)* A **try-out** is a test to see how useful or effective something or someone is: *After a try-out in Bath, the play is due to open in Edinburgh next month.* ○ *The try-outs* **for** *the team will be next weekend.*

tried /traɪd/ *adj* [not gradable] • Something which is tried has worked well so frequently in the past that it can be depended on to work well in the future: *I'll give you my mother's tried* **and tested/trusted** *recipe for wholemeal bread.*

try *obj* LAW /traɪ/ *v* [T] to examine (a person accused of committing a crime) in a court of law by asking them questions and considering known facts, and then decide if they are guilty • *Because of security implications the officers were tried in secret.* • *They are being tried* **for** *murder.* • See also TRIAL LEGAL PROCESS. • LP> **Law**

try *obj* WORRY /traɪ/ *v* [T] to worry or annoy (someone) or upset (a person's patience) with many, often slight, difficulties • *The demands of the job have tried him* **sorely**. • *You've been trying my* **patience** *all morning with your silly questions.* • *Her endless demands would try* **the patience of a saint** (=are very annoying).

try·ing /ˈtraɪ·ɪŋ/ *adj* • *Most people find him very trying, he just won't stop chatting.* • *Julie's had a very trying* **time** *lately with her husband being ill and all of the problems at work.*

try SPORT /traɪ/ *n* [C] (in the game of RUGBY) the act of a player putting the ball on the ground behind the opposing team's goal line, which scores points for the player's team

tryst /trɪst/ *n* [C] *old use or humorous* a meeting between two lovers, esp. a secret one

tsar *Br and Aus* /£zɑːʳ, $zɑːr/, **tzar**, *Am and Aus* **czar** *n* [C] (before 1917) the male Russian ruler • *Tsar Nicholas I*

tsar·i·na *Br and Aus* /£zɑːˈriː·nə, $zɑːˈriː-/, **tzar·i·na**, *Am and Aus* **czar·i·na** *n* [C] • A tsarina was (before 1917) the wife of a tsar or the female Russian ruler.

tsar·ist *Br and Aus* /£ˈzɑː·rɪst, $ˈzɑːr·ɪst/, **tzar·ist**, *Am and Aus* **czar·ist** *adj* [not gradable], *n* • *the tsarist empire* • *Tsarist Russia* • A tsarist was a person who supported the tsar. [C]

tset·se fly /ˈtet·si/ *n* [C] an African FLY (=a flying insect) which feeds on blood and can give serious diseases to the person or animal it bites. There are various types of tsetse fly. • *The scheme is intended to eradicate all tsetse flies, the carriers of sleeping sickness, in the area.*

tsk /tʌt/, **tsk tsk** *exclamation dated* TUT

tsp *n* [C] *pl* **tsp** *abbreviation for* **teaspoonful**, see at TEASPOON • *2 tsp pepper* • *Add one tsp each of ground cumin and ground coriander.*

tub CONTAINER /tʌb/ *n* [C] a container, esp. a large round one for various purposes, or a small usually round one for storing food in • *We've got a tub for compost at the bottom of our garden.* • *On the patio were roses and camellias planted in tubs.* • *Do you want your ice-cream in a tub or a cone?* • *When you go to the shop, please could you get a tub* **of** *margarine?* • PIC> **Containers, Garden**

tub BATH /tʌb/ *n* [C] *Br infml or Am and Aus for* BATH • *It's good to sink into a hot tub at the end of a hard day's work.*

tu·ba /ˈtjuː·bə/ *n* [C] a BRASS musical instrument consisting of a long bent metal tube which the player blows into, producing low notes

tub·by /ˈtʌb·i/ *adj* **-ier, -iest** *infml* (of a person) fat • *Our chef was a genial, slightly tubby man.*

tube PIPE /tjuːb/ *n* [C] a long hollow cylinder made from plastic, metal, rubber or glass, esp. used for moving or containing liquids or gases • *Gases produced in the reaction pass through this tube and can then be collected.* • In biology, a tube is any hollow cylindrical structure in the body that carries air or liquid: *the bronchial tubes* • *(infml)* If a woman **has** her **tubes tied**, she has a medical operation in which her FALLOPIAN TUBES are closed to stop her eggs being released so that she cannot become pregnant. • *(Aus infml)* A tube is also a CAN (=small metal container) or bottle of beer: *a tube of lager* • *(infml)* If something **goes down the tubes**, it fails completely: *If business doesn't pick up soon, the company will go down the tubes.*

tube·less /ˈtjuː·bləs/ *adj* [not gradable] • A tubeless tyre is one that fits tightly to the wheel around its edges so that air does not escape, and therefore it does not need an inside tube.

tub·ing /ˈtjuː·bɪŋ/ *n* [U] • Tubing is material in the form of a tube: *a length of plastic tubing* ○ *Rubber tubing* (=Rubber tubes) *can perish after a few years.*

tub·u·lar /£ˈtjuː·bjʊ·ləʳ, $-bjə·lɚ/ *adj* • Tubular means made in or having the shape of a tube: *tubular steel* • *"Tubular Bells"* (title of a record by Mike Oldfield, 1973)

tube CONTAINER /tjuːb/ *n* [C] a long thin container made of soft metal or plastic, which is closed at one end and has a small hole at the other, usually with a cover, and which is used for storing thick liquids • *a tube of toothpaste* • *Squeeze the base of the tube gently and apply an even coat of glue to both surfaces.*

tube RAILWAY /tjuːb/ *n* [U] **the tube** *Br infml* London's underground train system • *a tube station* • *We can go* **on the/by** *tube or we can catch a bus.*

tube TELEVISION /tjuːb/ *n* [U] **the tube** *esp. Am* the television • *What's on the tube this weekend?*

tu·ber /£ˈtjuː·bəʳ, $-bɚ/ *n* [C] a swollen underground stem or root of a plant from which new plants can grow, as in the potato

tu·ber·ous /£ˈtjuː·bə·rəs, $-bɚ·əs/ *adj*

tu·ber·cul·o·sis /£tjuːˌbɜː·kjʊˈləʊ·sɪs, $-ˌbɜːr·kjəˈloʊ-/ (*abbreviation* **TB**, *dated* **con·sump·tion**) *n* [U] a serious disease which is infectious and can attack many parts of a person's body, esp. their lungs

tu·ber·cul·ar /£tjuːˈbɜː·kjʊ·ləʳ, $-ˈbɜːr·kjə·lɚ/ *adj* [not gradable]

tub–thump·ing /ˈtʌbˌθʌm·pɪŋ/ *adj* [before n] *infml disapproving* (esp. of a person's style of speaking) strong, emphatic or violent • *a tub-thumping speech/campaigner*

TUC /ˌtiː·juːˈsiː/ *n* [U] **the TUC** *abbreviation for* the Trades Union Congress (=the British organization of the larger **trade unions**)

tuck *obj* TIDY /tʌk/ *v* [T always + adv/prep] to push a loose end of (a piece of clothing or material) into a particular place or position, esp. to make it tidy or comfortable • *Tuck your blouse* **into** *your skirt before you go out!* • *She had a napkin tucked* **in** *the neck of her blouse.* • *Richard came towards us tucking* **in** *his Hawaiian shirt as he walked.* [M] • *He tucked the bottom of the sheet* **under** *the mattress.*

tuck *obj* STORE SAFELY /tʌk/ *v* [T always + adv/prep] to put (something) into a safe or convenient place • *Tuck your gloves* **in** *your pocket so that you don't lose them.* • *She tucked her favourite doll* **under** *her arm and went upstairs to bed.* • *Eventually I found the certificate tucked* **under** *a pile of old letters.* • *Grandma always keeps a bit of money tucked* **away** (=keeps some money in a place which is safe and she can get to easily) *in case there's an emergency.* [M] • *Tuck your chair* **in** (=put it so that the seat of it is under the table) *so that no one trips over it.* • Something that is tucked in a particular place is in a place which is hidden or where few people go: *Tucked* **along/down** *this alley are some beautiful timber-framed houses* ○ *A group of tiny brick houses is tucked* **away** *behind the factory.* • If you tuck part of your body, you hold it in a particular position: *Stand up straight, tuck your tummy* **in** *and tuck your bottom* **under**. ○ *She sat with her legs tucked* **under** *her.*

tuck FOLD /tʌk/ *n* [C] a narrow fold sewn into esp. a piece of material, either for decoration or to change its shape • *This skirt doesn't fit properly so I'm going to* **put** *a tuck in at the waist.* • A tuck is also an operation to remove unwanted fat from a part of the body: *She had a* **tummy** *tuck.*

tuck in EAT *v adv* [I] *infml* to eat enthusiastically or eagerly • *There's plenty of food so please tuck in.*

tuck into *obj v prep* [T] *infml* • *Judging by the way they tucked into their dinner, they must have been very hungry.*

tuck /tʌk/ *n* [U] *Br dated* • (used esp. by and to children at school) Tuck is food, esp. sweets and cakes: *a tuck shop* • See also TUCKER.

tuck in *obj* [PUT TO BED], **tuck** *obj* **in**, *Br also* **tuck up** *obj*, **tuck** *obj* **up** *v adv* [M] to make (someone, esp. a child) comfortable in their bed for example by straightening the sheets • *Daddy, if I go to bed now will you tuck me in?* • *The children are safely tucked up in bed.*

tuck·er /£ˈtʌk·əʳ, $-ɚ/ *n* [U] *Aus infml* food • *a tucker bag*

Tue *n* [C/U] *abbreviation for* Tuesday

Tues·day /£ˈtjuːz·deɪ, $ˈtuːz-/ (*abbreviation* **Tue**, **Tues**) *n* the day of the week after Monday and before Wednesday • *We'll meet at eight* **on** *Tuesday.* [U] • *Every Tuesday she goes to art class.* [U] • *They should arrive Tuesday afternoon.* • *The twenty-ninth is a Tuesday isn't it?* [C] • *Tuesdays are my busiest day because I teach all day without a break.* [C] • [LP>] **Calendar**

tuft /tʌft/ *n* [C] a number of short pieces of esp. hair or grass which closely grow together or are held together near the base • *He had a few tufts* **of** *hair on his chin, but you could hardly call it a beard.*

tuft·ed /£ˈtʌf·tɪd, $-t̬ɪd/ *adj* • *the tufted duck*

tug *(obj)* [PULL] /tʌg/ *v* **-gg-** to pull (something) quickly and usually with a lot of force • *"You'd better move on" said the bodyguard, tugging her elbow.* [T] • *Her children were tugging* **at** *her hair.* [I]

tug /tʌg/ *n* [C] • *Feeling a tug at his sleeve, he turned to see Joe beside him.* • *(Br infml)* **Tug-of-love** is used, esp. in newspapers, to describe a situation in which one of the separated parents of a child takes care of the child but the other parent claims that right, or a situation in which a child is being looked after by people other than the child's parents but the parents claim that right: *a tug-of-love story* • A **tug-of-war** is a type of sport in which two teams show their strength by pulling against each other at the opposite ends of a rope, and each team tries to pull the other over a line on the ground: *(fig.) Prices have been caught in a tug-of-war, pulled in one direction by strong demand and in the opposite direction by high output.*

tug [BOAT] /tʌg/, **tug·boat** /£ˈtʌg·bəʊt, $-boʊt/ *n* [C] a boat with a powerful engine which can change direction easily and is used to pull large ships into and out of port • [PIC>] **Ships and boats**

tu·i·tion /tjuːˈɪʃ·ᵊn/ *n* [U] *(esp. Br)* teaching, esp. when given to a small group or a single person, such as in a college or university, or *(esp. Am)* the money paid for this • *(esp. Br) All students receive tuition* **in** *logic and metaphysics.* • *(esp. Br) Some bursaries and scholarships towards tuition* **fees** *are available.* • *(esp. Am) Few can afford the tuition of $12 000 a term.*

tu·lip /ˈtjuː·lɪp/ *n* [C] a plant which has a large brightly coloured bell-shaped flower on a stem and which grows from a BULB, or the flower itself • [PIC>] **Flowers and plants**

tulle /tjuːl/ *n* [U] a light net-like cloth of silk or similar material which is used on dresses, or to decorate hats, or for particular types of VEIL

tum·ble [FALL] /ˈtʌm·bl̩/ *v* [I] to fall quickly and without control • *They jumped out just before their car tumbled* **down** *the mountainside.* • *At any moment the whole building could tumble* **down**. See also TUMBLEDOWN. • *Tumbling* **over** *rocks, the river makes its way through the canyon.* • *He lost his balance and tumbled* **over**, *landing in the mud.* • *(fig.) An excited group of children tumbled* (=moved in an uncontrolled way, as if likely to fall) **out** *of school.* • *(fig.) Share prices tumbled* (=quickly lost a lot of value) *yesterday.* • A **tumble dryer** (also **tumble drier**, *Am usually* **dryer** or **drier**) is a machine which dries wet clothes by turning them in hot air. Compare **spin dryer** at SPIN [TURN]. • [PIC>] **Cleaning**

tum·ble /ˈtʌm·bl̩/ *n* [C] • *She* **had** *a nasty tumble on her way to work and grazed her arm badly.* • *(fig.) Company profits* **took** *a tumble* (=were lower) *last year, a spokesperson said, because of investment in new machinery.*

tum·ble [UNDERSTAND] /ˈtʌm·bl̩/ *v dated infml* to understand (something), esp. suddenly • *I think he's tumbled* **(to our plan)** *– we'll have to try something else.* [I] • *She quickly tumbled* **that** *something was wrong.* [+ *that* clause]

tum·ble·down /ˈtʊm·bl̩·daʊn/ *adj* [before n] (of a building) in a very bad condition, esp. in a state of decay • *a tumbledown cottage*

tum·bler /£ˈtʌm·bləʳ, $-blɚ/ *n* [C] a drinking container which does not have a handle or a stem • *a tumbler* **of** *orange juice*

tum·ble·weed /ˈtʌm·bl̩·wiːd/ *n* [U] a bush-like plant of N America and Australia which breaks near the ground when it dies and is then rolled about in large balls by the wind

tu·mes·cent /£tjuːˈmes·ᵊnt, $tuː-/ *adj specialized* (esp. of parts of the body) swollen or becoming swollen • *a tumescent penis*

tu·mes·cence /£tjuːˈmes·ᵊnts, $tuː-/ *n* [U] *specialized*

tum·my /ˈtʌm·i/ *n* [C] *infml* (used esp. by or to children) the stomach, or the lower front part of the body • *a tummy ache* • *Was that your tummy rumbling?* • *Samantha hit me in the tummy.* • *(Br infml)* A **tummy button** (*Am and Aus infml* **belly button**) is a NAVEL.

tu·mour *Br and Aus*, *Am and Aus* **tu·mor** /£ˈtjuː·məʳ, $ˈtuː·mɚ/ *n* [C] a mass of diseased cells which might become a lump or cause illness • *She has a* **malignant/benign** *tumour in her breast.* • *They were shattered by the news that their child had been diagnosed as having an inoperable brain tumour.*

tu·mult /£ˈtjuː·mʌlt, $ˈtuː-/ *n fml* a loud noise, esp. that produced by an excited crowd, or a state of confusion, change or uncertainty • *You couldn't hear her speak over the tumult from the screaming fans.* [C] • *From every direction, people were running and shouting and falling over each other in a tumult* **of** *confusion.* [C] • *We are living in a time of tumult.* [U] • *The financial markets are* **in** *tumult.* [U]

tu·mul·tu·ous /£tjuːˈmʌl·tjʊəs, $tuː-/ *adj* • *Dame Joan appeared to tumultuous* **applause** *and a standing ovation.* • *After the tumultuous events of 1990, Eastern Europe was completely transformed.*

tu·mul·tu·ous·ly /£tjuːˈmʌl·tjʊə·sli, $tuː-/ *adv*

tu·na /£ˈtjuː·nə, $ˈtuː-/ *n pl* **tuna** or **tunas** a large fish which lives in warm seas, or its flesh eaten as food • *shoals of tuna* [C] • *a can of tuna (fish)* [U]

tun·dra /ˈtʌn·drə/ *n* [U] (part of) the very large area of land in N Asia, N America and N Europe where, because it is cold, trees do not grow and earth below the surface is permanently frozen • *Reindeer roam the tundra in large herds.* • *Few plants grow in tundra regions.*

tune [MUSICAL NOTES] /£tjuːn, $tuːn/ *n* [C] a series of musical notes, esp. one which is pleasant and easy to remember; a MELODY • *a signature tune* • *a theme tune* • *That's a very* **catchy** (=easy to remember) *tune.*

tune·ful /£ˈtjuːn·fᵊl, $ˈtuːn-/ *adj* • *The first track on their album is surprisingly tuneful* (=has a pleasant tune).

tune·ful·ly /£ˈtjuːn·fᵊl·i, $ˈtuːn-/ *adv*

tune·ful·ness /£ˈtjuːn·fᵊl·nəs, $ˈtuːn-/ *n* [U]

tune·less /£ˈtjuːn·ləs, $ˈtuːn-/ *adj* • *That's not music – it's just a tuneless* (=having no tune, esp. sounding unpleasant) *noise!*

tune·less·ly /£ˈtjuːn·lə·sli, $ˈtuːn-/ *adv* • *She sang rather tunelessly.*

tune *obj* [INSTRUMENT] /£tjuːn, $tuːn/ *v* [T] to change a part of (a musical instrument) so that the instrument produces sounds at the correct PITCH (=degree to which the sound is high or low) when played • *Get into the habit of tuning your guitar every day before you practise.* • *She tuned* **(up)** *her violin before the concert.* [M] • A **tuning fork** is a metal object in the form of a small bar which is divided into two for about half of its length, and which, when hit gently, produces a note of a particular PITCH. It is used when tuning musical instruments. • A **tuning peg** (also **tuning pin**) is a short wooden or metal stick with a flat rounded end, that is turned to make the strings on a musical instrument tighter or looser. • [PIC>] **Fork, Musical instruments, Peg**

tune /£tjuːn, $tuːn/ *n* [U] • *This piano is* **in tune/out of** *tune* (=the notes are at the correct/wrong PITCH). • *(fig.) Much of his success comes from being* **in tune with** (=knowing) *what his customers want.* • *(fig.) Her theories were* **out of** *tune* (=in disagreement) **with** *the scientific thinking of the time.*

tune up *v adv* [I] • *After the orchestra had tuned up* (=made changes to their instruments so that they produced the correct note), *the conductor walked on to the stage.*

tun·er /£ˈtjuː·nəʳ, $ˈtuː·nɚ/ *n* [C] • *We need to get the* **piano** *tuner to tune our piano.*

tun·ing /£ˈtjuː·nɪŋ, $ˈtuː-/ *n* [U] • Tuning is the way an instrument is tuned: *The tuning on this piano is awful.*

tune *(obj)* [RADIO] /£tjuːn, $tuːn/ *v* to move the controls on (a radio, television etc.) so that it receives programmes broadcast from a particular station • *Press this button and the video will automatically tune itself* **to** *the next channel.* [T] • *Tune* **in** *(***to** *this station)* (= Make your radio receive programmes from it) *next week to hear the latest charts.* [I] • *We always tune* **in to** (= listen to or watch) *the nature programmes.* [I] • *(Am and Aus) Millions of viewers tune* **in** (= listen to or watch) *'News at Night' every weekday.* [T] • Someone who is **tuned in** to something is aware of it: *She's very tuned in* **to** *her students' worries.* • *(Am infml) She* **tuned out** (= gave no attention to) *her parents' advice because she had already made her own decision.*

tun·er /£'tjuː·nəʳ, $'tuː·nɚ/ *n* [C] • A tuner is the part of a radio or television which allows you to choose the broadcasting station you want to listen to or watch. • A tuner is also a radio which is part of a **music system**. See at MUSIC.

tune *obj* [ENGINE] /£tjuːn, $tuːn/ *v* [T] to change the setting of particular parts of (an engine), esp. slightly, so that it works as well as possible • *The* **engine** *certainly needs tuning but there's nothing wrong with the car.* • *Could you tune* **(up)** *the* **engine** *for me, please?* [T/M]

tune–up /£'tjuːn·ʌp, $'tuːn-/, *Br also* **tune** /tjuːn/ *n* [C] • *The engine needs a tune-up, and can you give the car a good service as well?*

tune [AMOUNT] /£tjuːn, $tuːn/ *n* [U] **to the tune of** to the stated amount • *The City Council had financed the new building to the tune of over 4 million pounds.*

tung·sten /'tʌŋ·stən/ *n* [U] a hard metallic element • *tungsten steel* • *The filaments of light bulbs are made from tungsten wire.*

tu·nic /'tjuː·nɪk/ *n* [C] a piece of clothing which fits loosely over a person's body, reaches to the waist or knees and often has no sleeves • *a soldier's tunic*

tun·nel /'tʌn·ᵊl/ *n* [C] a long passage under or through the earth, esp. one made by people • *If you drive on the mountain road, you'll go through a lot of tunnels.* • *The tunnel under the Channel is for rail transport only.* • If someone has **tunnel vision**, they can only see things which are directly in front of them. • *(disapproving)* To have **tunnel vision** is also to consider only one part of a problem or situation, or to hold a single opinion rather than having a more general understanding.

tun·nel *(obj)* /'tʌn·ᵊl/ *v* **-ll-** or *Am usually* **-l-** • *The decision has not yet been made whether to tunnel* **under** *the river or build a bridge over it.* [I] • *The alternative is to tunnel a route through the mountain if the road can't be built around it.* [T] • *The people trapped in the collapsed building had to tunnel their* **way** *out.* [T]

tun·nel·ler *Br and Aus, Am* **tun·nel·er** /£'tʌn·ᵊl·əʳ, $-ɚ/ *n* [C]

tup·pence /£'tʌp·ᵊnts/, **two·pence** *n* [U] *infml* two old or new British PENCE • *You can't buy much for tuppence.* • *(Br infml)* If someone **doesn't care/give tuppence** about something, they do not care about it in any way: *I don't care tuppence* **about** *what she says – I'm not going!* • *(Br infml)* If something **doesn't matter tuppence**, it is not important: *It doesn't matter tuppence what you think.* • *(Br infml)* If a person says they **wouldn't give tuppence for** something happening, they mean that they do not think it will succeed: *I wouldn't give tuppence for their chances of winning the match.*

tup·pen·ny /'tʌp·ᵊn·i, '-ni/, **two·pen·ny** *adj* [before n; not gradable] *dated infml* • *a tuppenny stamp*

Tup·per·ware /£'tʌp·ə·weəʳ, $-ɚ·wer/ *n* [U] *trademark* plastic containers, usually for storing food, and usually having a lid which fits tightly

tuque /tuːk/ *n* [C] *Canadian Eng for* a **bobble hat**, see at BOBBLE

tur·ban /£'tɜː·bən, $'tɜːr-/ *n* [C] a head covering for a man, worn esp. by Sikhs, Muslims and Hindus, and made from a long piece of cloth which is wrapped around the top of the head many times • PIC **Hats**

tur·baned /£'tɜː·bənd, $'tɜːr-/ *adj* [not gradable] • *a turbaned man*

tur·bid /£'tɜː·bɪd, $'tɜːr-/ *adj literary or specialized* (of a liquid) not transparent because a lot of small pieces of matter are held in it • *Several different species of fish inhabit these turbid shallow waters.* • *The once-clear waters of the lake have become turbid with microscopic algae.*

tur·bid·i·ty /£tɜː'bɪd·ɪ·ti, $tɜːr'bɪd·ə·t̬i/ *n* [U] *specialized or literary* • *The stream's turbidity is caused by the sewage which is emptied into it.*

tur·bine /£'tɜː·baɪn, $'tɜːr-/ *n* [C] a type of machine through which liquid or gas flows and turns a special wheel with blades in order to produce power • *a steam turbine* • *a gas turbine* • *a turbine engine* • (I)

tur·bo·charg·er /£'tɜː·bəʊˌtʃɑː·dʒəʳ, $'tɜːr·boʊˌtʃɑːr·dʒɚ/ *n* [C] a small TURBINE turned by the waste gases from an engine which pushes the fuel and air mixture into the engine at a higher pressure, so increasing the power produced by the engine

tur·bo·charged /£'tɜː·bəʊ·tʃɑːdʒd, $'tɜːr·boʊ·tʃɑːrdʒd/ *adj* [not gradable] • *a turbocharged engine* • *(approving slang)* If something is turbocharged, it is very strong or powerful: *The little singer with the turbocharged voice gave a stunning performance.*

tur·bo·fan /£'tɜː·bəʊ·fæn, $'tɜː·boʊ-/ *n* [C] a TURBINE used as an engine, esp. for an aircraft, which provides some force for movement from the gas that it pushes out, and some by turning a large special wheel with blades which also pushes air out, or an aircraft powered by this type of engine

tur·bo·jet /£'tɜː·bəʊ·dʒet, $'tɜːr·boʊ-/ *n* [C] a TURBINE used as an engine, esp. for an aircraft, which provides a forward force for movement from the gas it pushes out, or an aircraft powered by this type of engine

tur·bo·prop /£'tɜː·bəʊ·prɒp, $'tɜːr·boʊ·prɑːp/ *n* [C] a TURBINE used as an aircraft engine which provides most force for movement by turning a PROPELLER (= a set of spinning blades), or an aircraft powered by this type of engine

tur·bot /£'tɜː·bət, $'tɜːr-/ *n* [C/U] *pl* **turbot** or **turbots** a fish with a flat body which lives near to the coast in European seas, or its flesh eaten as food

tur·bul·ence /£'tɜː·bjʊ·lənts, $'tɜːr·bjə-/ *n* [U] a state of confusion and lack of order, or strong uneven movements within air or water • *The era was characterized by political and cultural turbulence.* • *There are signs of turbulence ahead for the economy.* • *We'll be flying through some turbulence* (= uneven movements)*, so it might get bumpy.*

tur·bul·ent /£'tɜː·bjʊ·lənt, $'tɜːr·bjə-/ *adj* • *He has had three turbulent marriages.* • *This has been a turbulent week for the government.* • *The sea was too turbulent for us to be able to take the boat out.*

turd /£tɜːd, $tɜːrd/ *n* [C] *taboo slang* a piece of solid excrement • To call someone a turd is a very rude and offensive way of expressing that you think they are unpleasant: *I don't know how you can do business with a turd like him.* ○ *When are you going to pay me the money you owe me, you little turd?*

tu·reen /tjʊ'riːn/ *n* [C] a large bowl, usually with a lid, from which esp. soup is served • PIC **Cutlery**

turf [GRASS] /£tɜːf, $tɜːrf/ *n pl* **turfs** or *esp. Br* **turves** /£tɜːvz, $tɜːrvz/ the surface layer of land on which grass is growing, consisting of the grass and the earth in which its roots grow, or a piece of this which is cut from the ground and is usually rectangular • *Lush turf lined the river's banks.* [U] • *We're going to* **lay** *turfs behind our house to make a lawn.* [C] • **The turf** is the sport of horse racing. • *(Br fml)* A **turf accountant** is a BOOKMAKER.

turf *obj* /£tɜːf, $tɜːrf/ *v* [T] • *It would cost too much to turf the whole garden.*

turf [AREA] /£tɜːf, $tɜːrf/ *n* [U] *esp. Am infml* the subject in which a person or group has a lot of knowledge or influence • *Antiques are very much her turf.* • A group's turf is also the area which it considers its own: *The gang defended its turf against the newcomers in the neighbourhood.* ○ *The gymnastics team won the championship on home turf.*

turf out *obj*, **turf** *obj* **out** *v adv* [M] *esp. Br infml* to force (someone or something) to leave a place or an organization • *Did you see the bouncers turfing that guy out for starting a fight?* • *She'll be turfed out* **of** *the study group if she carries on being disruptive.*

tur·gid [TOO SERIOUS] /£'tɜː·dʒɪd, $'tɜːr-/ *adj fml disapproving* (of speech, writing, style etc.) too serious about its subject matter; boring • *The articles she writes are very turgid which makes them difficult to read.* • *His books are always full of turgid prose.*

tur·gid·i·ty /£tɜː'dʒɪd·ɪ·ti, $tɜːr'dʒɪd·ə·t̬i/ *n* [U] *fml disapproving*

tur·gid·ly /£'tɜː·dʒɪd·li, $'tɜːr-/ *adv disapproving, slightly fml*

tur·gid [NOT FLOWING] /£'tɜː·dʒɪd, $'tɜːr-/ *adj fml* (of water) not flowing easily • *The stream that came down from the valley was turgid, dark, and flowed silently.*

tur·gid [SWOLLEN] /£'tɜː·dʒɪd, $'tɜːr-/ *adj specialized* (of an organ or living tissue) swollen

tur·gid·i·ty /£tɜːˈdʒɪd·ɪ·ti, $tɜːr·dʒɪd·ə·ti/ *n* [U] *specialized*

tur·key BIRD /£ˈtɜː·ki, $ˈtɜːr-/ *n* a large bird grown for its meat on farms and eaten in Britain esp. at Christmas and in the US esp. at Thanksgiving, or its flesh used as food • *(a) roast turkey* [C/U] • LP› **Holidays** PIC› **Birds**

tur·key FAILURE /£ˈtɜː·ki, $ˈtɜːr-/ *n* [C] *esp. Am and Aus infml* something that fails badly • *Critics are suggesting his latest film will be a turkey even before it's been released.* • *(Am and Aus infml)* A turkey can also be a stupid or silly person: *Now what did you go and do that for, you turkey.* [as a form of address]

Tur·kish bath /£ˌtɜː·kɪʃ, $ˌtɜːr-/ *n* [C] (the place where you get) a special way of cleaning the body by sitting in a room full of steam, then being washed and MASSAGED (=rubbed) by someone before jumping into or standing under cold water • *Shall we have/go to a Turkish bath?* • Compare SAUNAS.

Tur·kish de·light /£ˌtɜː·kɪʃ, $ˌtɜːr-/ *n* [U] a soft type of sweet, usually in the form of square pink pieces covered with powdered sugar

tur·me·ric /£ˈtɜː·mᵊr·ɪk, $ˈtɜːr·mɚ·ɪk/ *n* [U] a yellow powder which is used as a spice to flavour particular foods, esp. CURRY, and give them a yellow colour. It is made from the root of an Asian plant.

tur·moil /£ˈtɜː·mɔɪl, $ˈtɜːr-/ *n* a state of confusion, uncertainty or lack of order • *The country is in a state of political turmoil.* [U] • *The Stock Exchange is* **in** *turmoil following a huge wave of selling.* [U] • *Although her mind was* **in** *a turmoil, she tried to stay calm for the sake of her children.* [C] • *The company's management was* **thrown into** *a turmoil by the take-over bid.* [C] • *The entire region has been devastated by the turmoils of war.* [C]

turn *(obj)* GO ROUND /£tɜːn, $tɜːrn/ *v* to (cause to) move in a circle round a fixed point or line • *The earth turns* **on** *its axis once every 24 hours.* [I] • *The little girl turned* **on** *her toes, holding out her skirt.* [I] • *The wheels started to turn* **(round).** [I] • *The dog turned* **round and round,** *flattening the grass to make its bed.* [I] • *She turned the door knob and opened the door quietly.* [T] • *He turned the dial/knob/control on the oven.* [T] • *(specialized)* If you turn a piece of wood, you shape it while a machine keeps making it go round: *a turned bowl* • If you are able to **turn a phrase**, you are good at saying things in a clever way: *Tony is a master of the* **well**-*turned phrase.* • If something **turns on** something else, it depends on it or is decided by it: *The success of the talks turns on whether both sides are willing to make some concessions.* ○ *The plot of the film turns on making you believe that the child would not recognize her mother.* • A **turning circle** (*Am usually* **turning radius**) is the amount of space a vehicle needs in order to go round in a complete circle: *The car has an excellent turning circle, which makes city parking straightforward.* • See also TURN AROUND. • Ⓣ

turn /£tɜːn, $tɜːrn/ *n* [C] • *Give the screw a couple of turns to make sure it's tight.* • If something is described as another **turn of the screw**, it is something which makes a situation worse: *The trade embargo was another turn of the screw in the attempt to change the country's policy.* • *He has a good/nice* **turn of phrase** (=He expresses himself well). • *"The Turn of the Screw"* (title of a ghost story by Henry James, 1898)

turn *(obj)* CHANGE DIRECTION /£tɜːn, $tɜːrn/ *v* to (cause to) change the direction in which you are facing or moving • *She told me to turn right and then left until I came to a grocer's shop.* [I] • *The path* **twists and** *turns so much that it's hard to tell which direction it's going in.* [I] • *We have to turn down/into/up the next road on the right.* [I] • *It's just along here that we have to turn* **off** (=move off this road onto another). [I] • *After four kilometres, we turned onto a smaller road.* [I] • *The plants turned towards the source of light.* [I] • *She turned to face her father.* [I] • *The children turned* **round** *at the top of the stairs and waved to us.* [I] • *(Am) Cheetahs are legendary for being able to turn* **on a dime** (=in a very small space). [I] • *He angrily turned* **on his heel** (=turned quickly to face the opposite direction) *and left the room.* [I] • *The person on my left turned* **to** *me and whispered "Not another speech!".* [I] • *We're lost – we'll have to turn* **back** (=go back). [I] • *They turned us* **away/back** *at the entrance* (=did not allow us to enter) *because we hadn't got tickets.* [M] • *He turned his head at the sound of her voice.* [T] • *The driver turned the limousine* **round** *outside the hotel and drove back the way he had come.* [M] • *His wife tried to speak to him, but he turned his back* **(on her)/** *turned away (from her)* (=moved himself round and away from her to show his anger). [I] • *Now the children are older, they've* **turned** *their* **back on/turned away from** (=are not interested in) *toys and want computers instead.* • *Surely you won't* **turn** *your* **back on** (=refuse to help) *them.* • *We watched until the car had turned* (=gone round) *the corner.* [T] • If you **turn the corner**, a bad situation starts to improve: *After three months of poor sales we started to turn the corner in December.* • *She put out the light, turned* **over** (=rolled in order to face in another direction) *and went to sleep.* [I] • If you turn something **(over)**, you place the surface which was on top on the bottom: *She turned over the book to look for the price.* [M] ○ *He turned (over) two or three pages.* [T/M] • *His father had been turning the idea* **over** *(in his mind)* (=thinking about it) *for some time.* [M] • *Now turn* **to** (=open the book at) *page 23 and look at the first paragraph.* [I] • *The army turned their guns* **on** (=pointed them at and started to shoot at) *the protesters.* [T] • To turn an emotion or your attention **on/to** something or someone is to start to feel or do it: *The child turned her anger* **onto** (=became angry with) *her sister.* [T] ○ *The judge turned his gaze* **on** (=turned to look at) *the defendant.* [T] ○ *After a few minutes of general chat, she turned (the conversation)* **to** (=started to talk about) *more serious matters.* [I/T] ○ *We turned our attention* **to** (=started to consider) *next year's budget.* [T] ○ *As soon as the trip was over, they started to turn their* **minds to** (=to consider) *where they would go next year.* [T] • *Some of the children could turn* (=perform) **somersaults.** [T] • *At about three o'clock,* **the tide** *started to turn* (=the sea started to come closer to or move away from the beach). [I] • You **turn a blind eye** by ignoring something that you know is wrong: *He parked in a 'disabled' space, hoping that the carpark attendant would turn a blind eye* **(to** *what he'd done).* • If you **turn a deaf ear**, you ignore what someone is asking you: *His mother turned a deaf ear* **to** *his request for more money.* • *He did***n't turn a hair** (=did not seem surprised/worried) *when we said it would cost £1 000.* • *The caretaker can* **turn** *his* **hand to anything** (=is able to do many useful things). • If something **turns** someone's **head**, it has an influence on how they behave, esp. by making them too proud: *Her success has never turned her head – she's still the same simple unaffected girl she always was.* • To **turn** something **on its head** is to cause it to be the opposite of what it was before: *These new findings turn the accepted theories on their head.* • *John would* **turn in** *his* **grave** (=John, who is dead, would be upset) *if he could see the way the new owner looks after the garden.* • If someone **turns on** you, they attack you suddenly and unexpectedly: *The mutinying soldiers turned on their officers and shot them all.* • If you **turn the other cheek**, you do not do anything to hurt someone who has hurt you. • *She decided to* **turn over a new leaf** (=start a new and better way of behaving) *and give up smoking.* • To **turn the spotlight on** someone or something is to attract attention to them, usually to give information about something bad: *The documentary turned the spotlight on the low wages paid to manual workers.* • When you **turn the tables** on someone, you are able to change from being in a weaker position to being in a stronger position in relation to someone else: *He turned the tables* **on** *his opponents by publishing letters which showed they had criminal connections.* • *As soon as they saw we had guns, they* **turned tail** (=turned round) *and ran away.* • To **turn to** someone or something is to ask them for or use them as help or support: *Without someone to turn to* **for** *advice/help/guidance, making the most appropriate choice can be difficult.* ○ *Her family lived a long way away, and she had no one to turn to.* ○ *In stressful situations, he tended to turn to drink.* • If you **turn** somewhere **upside down**, you search everywhere for something, sometimes leaving the place very untidy: *The burglars turned the house upside down but they didn't take much.* ○ *I couldn't find those photos, although I turned the place upside down.* • A **turning point** is the time at which a situation starts to change in an important way: *ASH, the anti-smoking group, called the new regulations a turning point in the campaign against smoking.* ○ *The turning point in her political career came when she was chosen to fight a crucial by-election.* • A **turn-off** is a road which leaves another road to go in a different direction: *It's 4 km to the turn-off* **for** *Norwich/the Norwich turn-off.* See also **turn-off** at TURN SWITCH. • **Turn signal** is *Am for* **indicator**. See at INDICATE SIGNAL. • See also TURN AROUND; TURN DOWN; TURN OUT; TURN OVER; TURN UP. • PIC› **Car** Ⓣ

turn /£tɜːn, $tɜːrn/ *n* [C] • *We got as far as the school, and there we had to* **make** *a right turn.* • *The path was full of* **twists and** *turns.* • *One aircraft had gone into a sharp low-level turn.* • *(fig.) Her television career* **took** *a new turn when she became presenter of a children's show.* • *(fig.) The situation* **took** *a nasty turn and the police were called.* • **At every turn** means in all ways or all the time, and is often used in a negative way: *The campus at Heslington shows signs of his influence at every turn, from the lay-out of the colleges to the choice of lettering for the signs.* ◦ *They do their best to frustrate my efforts at every turn.* • **The** turn **of** something is the point at which it changes or moves in a different direction: *the turn of the tide* ◦ *She was born around the turn of the century* (= around 1900). • A **turn of mind** is a characteristic tendency or way of thinking: *His natural supporters are the urban poor, the young, and educated people of a liberal turn of mind.* ◦ *The independent turn of mind of the youngsters first showed itself when they were invited to choose from a range of jobs.* • Something which is **on the turn** is about to change direction: *The tide is on the turn.* ◦ *Young people's opinion on smoking seems to be on the turn.* • *This is a dangerous* **turn of events** (= change of situation). • See also U-TURN.

turn·ing /£'tɜː·nɪŋ, $'tɜːr-/ *n* [C] • A turning is a place, esp. a road, track or path, where you can leave the road you are on: **Take** *the third turning on the left after the traffic lights.* • See also **turn-off** at TURN [CHANGE DIRECTION].

turn *(obj)* [BECOME] /£tɜːn, $tɜːrn/ *v* to (cause to) become, change into or come to be (something) • *The weather has suddenly turned cold.* [L] • *When I refused to pay, the man turned nasty.* [L] • *The girl turned pale and started to shiver.* [L] • *The mood of the meeting turned solemn when the extent of the problem became known.* [L] • *The companies worked well together for a time, but eventually the relationship turned sour* (= became bad). [L] • *Sykes had turned* **informer** *and told the police where to find his fellow gang members.* [L] • *I would never have believed you'd turn* **traitor**. [L] • *Keele, pop star turned business tycoon, has launched a new range of cosmetics.* [L] • *The dry weather turned the soil* **into/to** *concrete.* [T always + adv/prep] • *The council was hoping to turn a children's home* **into** *a residence for adolescent girls.* [T always + adv/prep] • *Her attitude turned* **from** *politely interested* **to** *enthusiastic during the course of our conversation.* [I] • *The town turned* **from** *a small seaside resort* **into** *a major commercial centre when oil was discovered.* [I] • *The witch cast a spell on the prince and turned him* **into** *a frog/and he turned* **into** *a frog.* [always + adv/prep] • *(humorous) It's too late for me – I* **turn into a pumpkin** (= need to go home or to bed) *at eleven.* • Turn is used with times and ages to show that a particular point has been reached or gone past: *It's just turned* (= It's a little later than) *10 o'clock.* [L] ◦ *She turned* (= became) *18 last year.* [L] ◦ *He still hasn't retired although he's turned* (= is now a little older than) *60.* [L] • *By the end of September, the leaves have started to turn* (= become brown). [I] • If something **turns out** in a particular way, it becomes that way in the end, or it finally becomes known: *As events turned out, we were right to have decided to leave early.* ◦ *How did the recipe turn out?* ◦ *Did your visit to your parents turn out all right?* ◦ **It** *turns* **out** (= It is now known, although it was not before) **that** *she had known him when they were children.* [+ *that* clause] ◦ *The truth turned out* **to** *be stranger than we had expected.* [+ *to* infinitive] ◦ *He turned out* **to** *have a younger brother.* [+ *to* infinitive] • (T)

turn /£tɜːn, $tɜːrn/ *n* [U] • If a person, esp. one who is ill, or a situation **takes a turn for the worse**, they become worse: *Her son has taken a turn for the worse.* ◦ *Their relationship took a turn for the worse when he lost his job.*

turn *(obj)* [SWITCH] /£tɜːn, $tɜːrn/ *v* [always + adv/prep] to use a control to switch (a piece of equipment) on or off or to increase or reduce what it is producing • *Turn* **off/out** *the light.* [M] • *Who turned the telly* **on**? [M] • *I asked him to turn* **down** *the heating.* [M] • *Turn the sound* **up** *– I can't hear what they're saying.* [M] • *This programme's boring – shall I turn* **over** (= change the station) *to BBC?* [I] • *This sort of heater turns* **off** (= can be switched off) *at the mains.* [I] • *(infml)* If something **turns** you **on**, it interests or excites you, esp. sexually. If something **turns** you **off**, it does not interest you or excite you: *Short men really turn me on.* ◦ *"In my spare time I make models out of matchsticks." "Oh well,* **anything that/whatever turns you on**, *I suppose* (= That would not interest or excite me)." ◦ *The smell of her breath would turn any man off.* • *(infml)* A **turn-off** is something which you dislike or which you do not find interesting or sexually exciting: *This system may provide a powerful tool for adults who find computers a turn-off yet need to learn to use them.* ◦ *A carefully worded questionnaire (excluding turn-off words such as 'arts' and 'culture') found that more than 90% of the people wanted good theatres and museums to be available.* • *(infml)* A **turn-on** is something which you find exciting, esp. sexually: *To the advertisers who created the image she is a successful businesswoman but also a turn-on* **to** *men.* • If you try to **turn the clock back**, you want things to be the way they were in the past. • *"Turn on, tune in, and drop out"* (Dr Timothy Leary, quoted in his *The Politics of Ecstasy*, 1968) • [LP] **Switching on and off** (T)

turn [OPPORTUNITY] /£tɜːn, $tɜːrn/ *n* [C] an opportunity or a duty to do something at a particular time or in a particular order, before or after other people • *Is it my turn yet?* • *I waited so long for my turn* **to** *see the careers adviser that I missed my train.* [+ *to* infinitive] • *It's your turn* **to** *do the washing up!* [+ *to* infinitive] • *In this game if you give the wrong answer you have to* **miss** *a turn.* • *I'm bored with this – do you want to* **have/take** *a turn?* • If you **take turns** (*esp. Br also* **take it in turns**), a number of people do the same thing one after the other: *We take turns* **to** *answer the phone.* [+ *to* infinitive] • *Each of us collects the mail* **in turn/by turns**/*(Br also)* **turn and turn about** (= one after the other in an agreed order). • If you **speak/talk out of turn** you say something which you should not have said: *I'm sorry if I've spoken out of turn, but I thought everyone had already been told.* • Compare GO [OPPORTUNITY]. • (T)

turn *obj* [TWIST] /£tɜːn, $tɜːrn/ *v* [T] to damage the muscles in (the foot) by suddenly bending it too strongly • *She turned her ankle on the rocks and had to hobble back to camp.* • (T)

turn [ACTION] /£tɜːn, $tɜːrn/ *n* [C] **good/bad turn** an action which is helpful/not helpful • *You* **did** *me a good turn by warning me about the new plans.* • *(saying)* 'One good turn deserves another' means that if someone helps you, you should help them. • (T)

turn [PERFORMANCE] /£tɜːn, $tɜːrn/ *n* [C] a stage act or performance • *The first couple of turns were children singing and dancing.* • *The writer reduced the main character to a kind of comic turn.* • (T)

turn [ILLNESS] /£tɜːn, $tɜːrn/ *n* [C] *infml* a slight illness, a strange feeling or a nervous shock • *After the accident I started having funny turns.* • *It* **gave** *me quite* **a** *turn to see him after all these years.* • (T)

turn *(obj)* /£tɜːn, $tɜːrn/ *v infml* • If your **stomach** turns or something turns your stomach, you feel as if you are going to vomit: *That smell makes my stomach turn.* [I] ◦ *The pictures of the victims turned my stomach.* [T]

turn [COOKED] /£tɜːn, $tɜːrn/ *n* [U] **cooked/done to a turn** cooked for exactly the right amount of time • *The beef was done to a turn.* • (T)

turn *obj* **a·round**, *Br also* **turn** *obj* **round** *v adv* [T] to cause (a situation or organization) to improve • *The new management team turned the ailing company around in under six months.*

turn·a·round /£'tɜːn·ə·raʊnd, $'tɜːrn-/, *Br also* **turn·round** *n* [U] • *The chairman, Tony Bramall, was responsible for the turnround* (= improvement) *in the company's fortunes.* • A turnaround can also be any change from one thing to its opposite: *What a turnaround – at halftime they were losing 3-0, but in the end they won 4-3.* • See also TURNAROUND.

turn down *obj*, **turn** *obj* **down** *v adv* [M] to refuse to accept • *He offered her a trip to Australia but she turned it/him down.* • *She offered to help but he turned her down* **flat** (= completely refused her offer). • *The company turned down a request for reduced prices for pensioners.* • *He turned down the job because it involved too much travelling.*

turn in *obj* [GIVE], **turn** *obj* **in** *v adv* [M] to give or return (something) to or produce (something) for esp. an official • *Please turn your old parking permits in at the end of the week.* • *The group turned in an interesting report on young people's responses to advertising.* • *We were pleased that the company turned in good results again this year.* • *The hit-and-run driver turned himself in* **to** *the police the day after the accident.* • See also TURN OVER [GIVE].

turn in [BED] *v adv* [I] *infml* to go to bed • *I usually turn in at about midnight.*

turn out *obj* [EMPTY], **turn** *obj* **out** *v adv* [M] to take everything out of • *We turned out all the cupboards and drawers and found things we hadn't seen for years.* • *The* *boy turned out his pockets and produced a few coins, some string and a sticky sweet.*

turn out *obj* [REMOVE], **turn** *obj* **out** *v adv* [M] to force to leave • *They said the landlord had turned them out (***of** *their home) when they couldn't pay the increased rent.*

turn out [COME] *v adv* [I] to come, appear or be present • *The whole family turned out for the match.* • *Not many people were prepared to turn out so early.* • *Twenty people turned out to help us.* • Compare TURN UP [COME].

turn·out /£'tɜːn·aʊt, $'tɜːrn-/ *n* [C] • A turnout is the number of people who are present at an event, esp. the number who go to vote at an election: *There was a disappointingly poor turnout to hear such a well-known speaker.* ○ *Good weather on polling day should ensure a good turnout.*

turn out *obj* [PRODUCE], **turn** *obj* **out** *v adv* [M] to produce or make, usually quickly or in large amounts • *The company turns out new computer games at a great rate.* • *(fig.) He's always well turned out* (= well and tidily dressed).

turn o·ver *obj* [GIVE], **turn** *obj* **o·ver** *v adv* [M] to give, esp. to an official • *They turned the man/the videos over* **to** *the police.* • See also TURN IN [GIVE].

turn o·ver *obj* [PRODUCE] *v adv* [T] to produce or make (esp. money) from business activities • *The profits are not high, but the company turns over a large sum every year.*

turn·o·ver /£'tɜːnˌəʊ·vəʳ, $'tɜːrnˌoʊ·vɚ/ *n* • A company's turnover is the amount of business done in a period of time: *Large supermarkets have high turnovers* (= their goods sell very quickly). [C] ○ *The business has an annual turnover of £50 000.* [C] • *The engineering group announced it had made a pre-tax loss and turnover had fallen.* [C] • The turnover of **staff** is the rate at which employees leave a company and are replaced by new people: *They've had a high turnover of staff in recent years.* [C] ○ *(Am) They've had a lot of turnover at the factory recently.* [U] • See also TURNOVER.

turn o·ver *obj* [STEAL], **turn** *obj* **o·ver** *v adv* [M] *infml* to steal from (a place), esp. leaving it untidy • *Did you hear Paul's flat got turned over last week?* • A person who is turned over is attacked and has something stolen from them: *Frank was turned over by some muggers in the park.* • *(fig.) England got turned over* (= badly defeated) *by Germany 4-0.*

turn up *(obj)* [COME], **turn** *(obj)* **up** *v adv* to (cause to) come or appear, esp. unexpectedly • *Do you think many people will turn up?* [I] • *She turned up at my house very late.* [I] • *The missing letter eventually turned up inside a book.* [I] • *Don't worry about it – something might/will turn up* (= something might happen to improve the situation). [I] • *See what you can turn up* (= discover) *about the family in the files.* [M] • If someone **turns up like a bad penny** they are always appearing at events where they are not wanted.

turn–up /£'tɜːn·ʌp, $'tɜːrn-/ *n* • *(Br)* A **turn-up for the book(s)** (*Am* **one for the books**) is a surprising or unexpected event: *Well, there's a turn-up for the book – I never thought he'd get the job.*

turn up *obj* [FOLD], **turn** *obj* **up** *v adv* [M] to make (a piece of clothing or part of a piece of clothing) shorter by folding material and esp. sewing it into position • *I had to turn up her skirt because it was far too long.* • *You could always turn the sleeves up.* • If you **turn** your **nose up** at something you do not like it or want it, esp. because you do not think it is special enough: *They turned their noses up* **at** *the only hotel that was available.* ○ *When I suggested a new tie he turned up his nose.*

turn–up *esp. Br* /£'tɜːn·ʌp, $'tɜːrn-/, *Am and Aus usually* **cuff** *n* [C] • A turn-up is a piece of material at the bottom of a trouser leg which is folded back: *trouser turn-ups* • PIC› **Clothes**

turn·a·bout /£'tɜːn·ə·baʊt, $'tɜːrn-/ *n* [C] a complete change from one situation or condition to its opposite • *What accounts for the dramatic turnabout* **in** *Britain's international trading performance?*

turn·a·round /£'tɜːn·ə·raʊnd, $'tɜːrn-/, *Br usually* **turn·round** /£'tɜːn·raʊnd, $'tɜːrn-/ *n* [U] the amount of time taken for something to happen after esp. a vehicle, an instruction or an order for goods arrives at a place • *We'll have to improve the turnround – 3 days is too long.* • *Turnround* **time** *for the information is some four days and the average cost £12.* • *An aircraft's turnaround* **time** *is the time it takes after it has landed to prepare it for taking off again.* • See also TURN AROUND.

turn·coat /£'tɜːŋ·kəʊt, $'tɜːrn-/ *n* [C] *disapproving* a person who changes from one opinion to an opposite one in a way which shows they are not loyal to people who share the original opinion

tur·nip /£'tɜː·nɪp, $'tɜːr-/ *n* [C] a rounded white root which is eaten cooked as a vegetable, or the plant which produces it • PIC› **Vegetables**

turn·key /£'tɜːŋ·kiː, $'tɜːrn-/ *adj* [before n; not gradable] (of a piece of equipment) ready for immediate use by the person who is buying or renting it • *More and more manufacturers are offering to tailor-make a turnkey system from their own components.*

turn·out /£'tɜːn·aʊt, $'tɜːrn-/ *n* [C] See at TURN OUT [COME]

turn·o·ver /£'tɜːnˌəʊ·vəʳ, $'tɜːrnˌoʊ·vɚ/ *n* [C] a small cake made from a folded piece of pastry with fruit inside • *an apple turnover* • See also TURN OVER.

turn·pike /£'tɜːm·paɪk, $'tɜːrn-/, *infml* **pike** *n* [C] *Am* a main road which you usually have to pay to use; a MOTORWAY • *the New Jersey Turnpike*

turn·stile /£'tɜːn·staɪl, $'tɜːrn-/ *n* [C] a device which controls the way into or out of a building, room or area of land, esp. one which you have to pay to enter. It is a post with a number of short poles sticking out from it which have to be pushed round as each person walks through the entrance. • *The number of spectators going through the turnstiles is up on last season.*

turn·ta·ble /£'tɜːnˌteɪ·bl̩, $'tɜːrn-/ *n* [C] a flat round piece of equipment which allows something put on top of it to turn in a circle • *Put another record on the turntable.* • *There was a major problem when trains had to change tracks and instead of points the railway had a turntable.* • *The cutter puts one of the discs on the turntable, where it is held in place by a vacuum.* • *Fire fighters with turntable* **ladders** *yesterday rescued six people from the fifth floor of an office building.*

tur·pen·tine /£'tɜː·pᵊm·taɪn, $'tɜːr-/, *infml* **turps** /£tɜːps, $tɜːrps/ *n* [U] a colourless liquid with a strong smell which burns easily. It is sometimes used in products for removing paint from brushes.

tur·pi·tude /£'tɜː·pɪ·tjuːd, $'tɜːr·pɪ·tuːd/ *n* [U] *fml* behaviour which is not morally or socially acceptable • *Filling in a false tax return is not in itself a crime of gross* **moral** *turpitude like lying in court would be.*

tur·quoise /£'tɜː·kwɔɪz, $'tɜːr-/ *n* a bluish green precious stone which is often used in jewellery • *The handle was inlaid with turquoise.* [U] • *The ring is set with a magnificent turquoise.* [C] • *turquoise earrings*

tur·quoise /£'tɜː·kwɔɪz, $'tɜːr-/ *adj* • Things that are bluish green in colour can be called turquoise: *a turquoise sweater* • *the clear turquoise water of the bay*

tur·ret [TOWER] /'tʌr·ət/ *n* [C] a small circular tower which is part of a castle or a large building

tur·ret·ed /£'tʌr·ɪ·tɪd, $-ə·t̬ɪd/ *adj* • *The medieval town with its turreted walls stands on a little hill eight kilometers from the coast.* • *The hotel is not unlike one of those sinister, turreted houses in old-fashioned horror films.*

tur·ret [GUN PART] /'tʌr·ət/ *n* [C] a part of a military vehicle which contains a large gun or guns and which can move to face any direction

tur·tle /£'tɜː·tl̩, $'tɜːr·t̬l̩/ *n* [C] *pl* **turtles** or **turtle** an animal which lives in or near water, which has a thick shell covering its body into which it can move its head and legs for protection • PIC› **Reptiles and amphibians**

tur·tle·dove /£ˌtɜː·tl̩'dʌv, $ˌtɜːr·t̬l̩-/ *n* [C] a small pale brown bird which makes a soft pleasant sound

tur·tle·neck *Br* /£'tɜː·tl̩·nek, $'tɜːr·t̬l̩-/, *Am* **mock tur·tle·neck** *n* [C] a piece of clothing for the upper part of the body, or the tight part at the neck of such a top which does not fold over itself • *I bought a new turtleneck.* • *The sweater has a turtleneck.* • *a turtleneck sweater* • Turtleneck is also *Am for* **polo neck**. See at POLO. • PIC› **Clothes**

turves /£tɜːvz, $tɜːrvz/ *pl of* TURF [GRASS]

tush /tʊʃ/ *n* [C] *Am slang for* BOTTOM [BODY PART]

tusk /tʌsk/ *n* [C] either of the two long pointed teeth which stick out from the mouth of some animals, esp. ELEPHANTS, WALRUSES and WARTHOGS

tus·sle /'tʌs·l̩/ *v* [I] to argue strongly with someone else • *The residents are still tussling* **over** *the ever-scarcer street parking.* • *During his twelve years in Congress he has tussled* **with** *the chemical, drug and power companies on behalf of the ordinary person's right to breathe clean air.* • *(fig.) It is an idea that Mr Wolfe has been tussling* **with** (= trying hard to understand or develop) *for a while.* • To tussle is also to fight with another person using your arms and body: *The boys started to tussle in the corridor.*

tus·sle /ˈtʌs·l̩/ *n* [C] • *a bureaucratic tussle* • *a boardroom tussle* • *a legal tussle* • *There followed a long tussle* **for** *custody of the children.* • *From the state of his clothes and hair he had been* **in a** *tussle.*

tut /tʌt/, **tut tut** *exclamation* a written representation of the sound made to show you disapprove of something, or a word said twice in a humorous way to suggest disapproval • *Tut, it's raining – I'm going to get soaked.* • *You're late again – tut tut!*

tut /tʌt/ *v* **-tt-** • *He walked off, tutting to himself.* [I] • *"Still not out of bed?" she tutted* (= said disapprovingly). [+ clause]

tu·tel·age /£ˈtjuː·tɪ·lɪdʒ, $ˈtuː·t̬əl·ɪdʒ/ *n fml* help, advice or teaching about how to do something • *The focus of the seminar will be on dance in all its exuberant, expressive and multicultural forms,* **under the** *tutelage* **of** *a master in movement.* • **Under the** *tutelage* **of** *Professor Roberts, the 900 delegates assessed and discussed the social market economy.*

tu·tor /£ˈtjuː·təʳ, $ˈtuː·t̬ɚ/ *n* [C] a teacher who works with one student or a small group, either at a British college or university or in the home of a child • *His tutor encouraged him to read widely in philosophy.* • *During her illness she continued her school work with* **home** *tutors and returned in June to take her exams.* • LP〉 **Schools and colleges** Ⓣ

tu·tor *obj* /£ˈtjuː·təʳ, $ˈtuː·t̬ɚ/ *v* [T] • *Children are routinely tutored for hours after school.* • *The Literacy Council will begin workshops for volunteers who will tutor foreign-born people* **in** *English as a Second Language.*

tu·tor·i·al /£tjuːˈtɔː·ri·əl, $tuːˈtɔːr·i-/ *n* [C] • A tutorial is a period of study with a tutor involving one student or a small group: *I've got a tutorial this afternoon.*

tu·tu /ˈtuː·tuː/ *n* [C] a very short skirt made of many layers of very thin stiff material, which is worn by female BALLET dancers

tu–whit tu–whoo /tʊˌwɪt·tʊˈwuː/ *exclamation* a written representation of the sound made by an OWL (= type of bird)

tux·e·do /£tʌkˈsiː·dəʊ, $-doʊ/, *infml* **tux** /tʌks/ *n* [C] *pl* **tuxedos** *Am for* **dinner jacket**, see at DINNER

TV /ˌtiːˈviː/ *n abbreviation for* TELEVISION • *We're getting a new TV.* [C] • *What's* **on** *TV tonight?* [U] • *"I think you* **watch** *too much TV."* [U] • *They had their meal* **in front of** (= while they were watching) *the TV.* [C] • *The prizes were given out by TV personalities.* • A **TV dinner** is a meal which you buy ready prepared from a shop and which only needs to be heated before being eaten, esp. while watching TV.

twad·dle /£ˈtwɒd·l̩, $ˈtwɑː·dl̩/ *n* [U] *infml* speech or writing which is foolish or not true; nonsense • *She dismissed the findings as* **utter** *twaddle*/**a load of old** *twaddle.*

twain /tweɪn/ *n old use* two

twang SOUND /twæŋ/ *n, v* (to make) a noise like that of a tight string being sharply pulled and released • *He twanged the guitar string/his braces.* [T] • *The springs twanged.* [I] • *(fig.) A stressful meeting didn't help to soothe his twanged nerves.* [T] • *We heard a twang as the cable broke.* [C]

twang VOICE /twæŋ/ *n* [C usually sing] a quality of the human voice, produced by air passing out through the nose as you speak • *a nasal/southern twang*

twat VAGINA /twæt/ *n* [C] *Am taboo* the outer female sex organ; the vagina

twat PERSON /twæt/ *n* [C] *Br and Aus taboo slang* a stupid person

tweak *obj* /twiːk/ *v* [T] to pull and twist with a small sudden movement, or *(fig.)* to change slightly, esp. in order to make more correct, effective, or suitable • *The player tweaked a back muscle during Saturday's semi-final.* • *Standing in front of the mirror she tweaked a strand of hair into place.* • *Horrified, he tweaked* **out** *a grey hair.* [M] • *(fig.) The aircrew debated whether tweaking a control would fool the autothrottle into revving up one engine.* • *(fig.) Once the computer system is in place, the software needs only to be tweaked a little to meet your requirement.* • *(fig.) This proposal still needs some tweaking.*

tweak /twiːk/ *n* [C] • *She allowed the horse to move freely with just the odd tweak on the reins.*

twee /twiː/ *adj esp. Br infml disapproving* artificially attractive or too perfect • *The village has escaped all modern developments, yet without becoming twee or 'preserved'.*

tweed /twiːd/ *n* a thick material woven from wool of several different colours • *a length of tweed* [U] • *suits in check or plain tweeds* [C] • *a tweed jacket/skirt*

tweeds /twiːdz/ *pl n* • Tweeds are clothes made from tweed, esp. a jacket and matching trousers/skirt: *He was a heavily built man with a penchant for thick tweeds and British country style.*

tweed·y /ˈtwiː·di/ *adj* **-ier, -iest** • *a tweedy* (= of or like tweed) *sports jacket* • Tweedy also refers to the life of wealthy people with homes in the countryside and an interest in sports like hunting: *We met a tweedy man walking a couple of dogs.* ○ *Paintings of a hunting dog and a bay mare, velvet drapery, antique globes and leather-bound books bestowed a tweedy elegance on the room.*

tweet /twiːt/ *v* [I], *n* [C] *infml* (to make) a short weak sound like that made by a young bird • *We could hear the baby birds tweeting.* • *"Tweet, tweet" went the little chicks.*

twee·zers /£ˈtwiː·zəz, $-zɚz/, *Am also* **twee·zer** /£ˈtwiː·zəʳ, $-zɚ/ *pl n* a small piece of equipment made of two narrow strips of metal joined at one end. It is used to pull out hairs or to pick up small objects by pressing the two strips of metal together with the fingers. • *a pair of tweezers* • *eyebrow tweezers* • *Carr removed the bean from the child's ear with tweezers.* • *Customs officials used tweezers to extricate one-tenth of a gram of marijuana from the lining of her handbag.* • PIC〉 **Cosmetics, Medical equipment**

twelve /twelv/ *determiner, pronoun, n* (the number) 12 • *ten, eleven, twelve, thirteen* • *a twelve-seater minibus* • *"How many seats are left?" "Twelve (seats)."* • *Jones is in the England twelve* (= the 12 players from which the team of 11 will be chosen) *for Wednesday's match.* [C] • See also DOZEN.

twelfth /twelfθ, twelθ/ *determiner, pronoun, adj, adv* [not gradable], *n* • *the twelfth volume* • *the twelfth floor* • *December is the twelfth month.* • *I'll see you on the twelfth (of June).* • *He was/came twelfth in his class.* • *Six twelfths are a half.* [C] • *(Br and Aus)* The **twelfth man** in a CRICKET team is a RESERVE (= extra player). • **Twelfth Night** is the sixth of January, twelve days after Christmas.

twen·ty /£ˈtwen·ti, $-t̬i/ *determiner, pronoun, n* (the number) 20 • *nineteen, twenty, twenty-one* • *space for twenty people* • *a twenty-metre separation* • *"How many minutes have we got till we have to leave?" "Oh, about twenty."* • *Have you ever scored a treble twenty at darts?* [C] • *Some people have a big party for their* **twenty-first** *(birthday)* (= when people in Western societies are traditionally said to become adults). • The **twenty-four-hour clock** is the system of using 24 instead of 12 numbers to refer to each hour of the day: *The video uses the twenty-four-hour clock – so you'll have to programme it for 21.00 hours instead of 9 p.m.* • If someone has **twenty-twenty vision** they have *(infml)* extremely good sight or *(specialized)* perfect sight as measured by a standard test. • See also SCORE TWENTY.

twen·ties /£ˈtwen·tiz, $-t̬iz/ *pl n* • **The** twenties is the range of temperature between 20° and 29°: *The temperature is expected to be* **in** *the twenties tomorrow.* • **The** twenties is also the period of years between 20 and 29 in any century: *My grandparents were born* **in** *the twenties* (= between 1920 and 1929). • A person's twenties are the period in which they are aged between 20 and 29: *I'm enjoying being* **in** *my twenties.*

twen·ti·eth /£ˈtwen·ti·əθ, $-t̬i-/ *determiner, pronoun, adj, adv* [not gradable], *n* • *the twentieth century* • *The meeting is on the twentieth (of November).* • *The school was/came twentieth in the district for its exam results.* • *Divide it into twentieths.* [C]

twerp, twirp /£twɜːp, $twɜːrp/ *n* [C] *dated slang* a stupid person • *You silly twerp! Why did you do that?* [as form of address]

twice /twaɪs/ *predeterminer, adv* [not gradable] two times • *I've already asked him twice.* • *She has visited India twice.* • *(fml) She has twice visited India.* • *He has to empty the bucket twice daily* (= two times every day). • *There are twice as many houses in this area as there used to be.* • *She gave me twice the number of cards I asked for.* • *The state is at least twice as big as England.* • *The boy was twice her size/twice Jill's size* (= much bigger than she was). • LP〉 **Two**

twid·dle *(obj)* /ˈtwɪd·l̩/ *v* to move (something) repeatedly between your fingers, esp. without any purpose • *She was twiddling* **(with)** *the pencil/her hair.* [T; I + *with*] • *Twiddle* **a dial/knob** *on a radio in Britain and you may hear more voices speaking crackly French or German than English.* • If you **twiddle** your **thumbs** you do nothing for a period of time, usually while you are waiting for something to happen: *He arrived early for the meeting so he had to twiddle his thumbs for half an hour.*

twid·dle /ˈtwɪd·l̩/ *n* [C] • *At the twiddle of a knob the operators can focus on a tiny amount of airspace or scan the whole area.*

twid·dly /ˈtwɪd·l̩.i, ˈ-li/ *adj* **-ier, -iest** *infml* curly or decorative, esp. in an unnecessary way • *The frame had twiddly bits at the corners which got very dusty.*

twig BRANCH /twɪg/ *n* a small thin branch of a tree or bush, esp. one removed from the tree or bush and without any leaves • *We collected dry twigs to start the fire.* [C] • *Chimpanzees use tools to obtain food in the wild – they use twigs to fish termites out of holes.* [C] • *The birds carried little bits of straw and twig to the higher branches of the trees for their nests.* [U]

twig·gy /ˈtwɪg·i/ *adj* **-ier, -iest** • *Prop up the young pea plants with twiggy sticks.* • *Cut off all those twiggy old branches and leave the straight, young shoots.*

twig *(obj)* UNDERSTAND /twɪg/ *v* [not *be twigging*] **-gg-** *infml* to suddenly understand or know (something); to REALIZE • *She still hasn't twigged* **how** *to do it.* [+ *wh*-word] • *Suddenly twigging* **what** *I meant, he ran to the phone.* [+ *wh*- word] • *Ann's expecting a baby – had you twigged?* [I] • *(esp. Am) When she mentioned Monte Carlo, I twigged* **to** *what was going on.* [T; I + *to*]

twi·light /ˈtwaɪ·laɪt/ *n* [U] the period just before it becomes completely dark in the evening • *I could make out a dark figure in* **the** *twilight.* • *They descended the stairs and went out into a thickening twilight.* • *The streets became increasingly eerie in a fake twilight created by a smog of mist and smoke.* • *(fig.) Keith is only one of several players in* **the** *twilight* **of** (= in the last years of/at the end of) *his career.* • Twilight is used to describe a way of life characterized by uncertainty and difficult or slightly illegal situations, which is on the edge of normal society: *The remaining inhabitants of this once-prosperous market town have got used to a twilight* **existence.** ○ *He said that leaving a secure job for 'the twilight* **world** *of pop music' was a mistake.* • *I'm not just talking about people well into their* **twilight years** (= the last years of their lives). • The **twilight zone** is an area where two different ways of life or states of existence meet: *the twilight zone between life and death* ○ *There are hundreds of thousands of old people living in that long twilight zone of extreme debilitation and touched by senility.* • *"The Twilight Zone"* (title of a television series of horror stories, 1950s-)

twi·lit /ˈtwaɪ·lɪt/ *adj* [not gradable] • *a twilit street/room* • *(fig.) the twilit state between waking and sleeping*

twill /twɪl/ *n* [U] a strong cotton cloth which has raised diagonal lines on the surface

twin /twɪn/ *n* [C] either of two children born to the same mother on the same occasion • *They are the parents of four-year-old twins.* • *My sister has twin sons.* • Twin is also used of things which are very similar to each other, are one of two similar things or are one of two things which are connected in some way: *The two countries are often regarded as economic twins.* ○ *The car has twin exhausts.* ○ *The twin hubs of the world art market are London and New York.* ○ *Handing over the land to peasants could quickly solve the twin problems of food shortages and distribution.* • A **twin bed** is one of a set of two beds which are each big enough for one person. A **twin-bedded room** (also **twin room** or **twin**) is a room with two such beds. • *(Br and Aus)* A **twin set** is a woman's SWEATER and CARDIGAN which have the same colour or pattern and are worn together: *My aunt is the sort of elderly woman who always wears a twin set* **and pearls.** • *(Br)* A **twin town** (*Am* **sister city**) is a town or city which shares planned activities and visits with a similar town in another country: *Cambridge and Heidelberg are twin towns.* • LP **Two** PIC **Beds and bedroom, Clothes**

twin *obj* /twɪn/ *v* [T] **-nn-** • *Cambridge is twinned* **with** *Heidelberg.* • *There's talk of twinning the two parishes* (= joining them together in some way). • *Under the scheme, industrialists are twinned* **with** *teachers and spend three days with them.* • *The two problems are twinned – you can't really separate them.*

twine *(obj)* WRAP /twaɪn/ *v* [always + adv/prep] to wrap round an object several times • *The vine twines* **round/up** *the pole.* [I] • *Twine the different coloured threads* **together.** [T] • See also ENTWINE; INTERTWINE.

twin·ing /ˈtwaɪ·nɪŋ/ *adj* [not gradable] • *a twining plant*

twine STRING /twaɪn/ *n* [U] strong string made of two or more lengths of string twisted together • *a ball of twine* • *garden twine*

twinge /twɪndʒ/ *n* [C] a sudden short feeling of physical or mental pain • *He was feeling twinges from a calf injury after 20 minutes of the game.* • *My left knee has been giving me a few twinges in this cold weather.* • *This rheumatism gives me twinges* **in** *the back.* • *I felt a sudden twinge* **of** *toothache.* • *When she saw him she experienced a twinge* **of** *anxiety/conscience/fear/guilt/regret/shame.*

twin·kle /ˈtwɪŋ·kl̩/ *v* [I] (of light or a shiny surface) to shine repeatedly strongly then weakly, as if flashing on and off very quickly • *The lights of the bay twinkled below the restaurant terrace.* • *The stars twinkled in the clear sky.* • *It is a very rare marble, with special crystals in it that make it twinkle at night.* • *His brown eyes twinkled behind the gold-rimmed glasses.* • *Their eyes were caught by the twinkling of the diamonds.* • *"Twinkle, twinkle, little star, How I wonder what you are"* (from a nursery rhyme by Jane Taylor, 1783-1824)

twin·kle /ˈtwɪŋ·kl̩/ *n* • *the twinkle of the stars/lights/diamonds* • *"There couldn't have been a better result," he added with a knowing twinkle* (= smiling and with his eyes shining). • *He was holding the phone with a mischievous twinkle* **in** *his* **eye.** • *(saying)* 'When you were (just/no more than) a twinkle in your father's eye' means before you were born: *(fig.) The economic arguments for building the nuclear reactor are much weaker now than when the project was first a twinkle in the government's eye* (= when they first had the idea).

twin·kling /ˈtwɪŋ·kl̩·ɪŋ, ˈ-klɪŋ/ *adj* • *the twinkling stars/lights/gold* • *(fig.) the dancer's twinkling* (= moving very fast) *feet*

twin·kling /ˈtwɪŋ·kl̩·ɪŋ, ˈ-klɪŋ/ *n* a very short time • *In the four-billion-year history of life, 100 000 years is a twinkling.* • *The peace ended in Yugoslavia and elsewhere in Europe when communist rule vanished* **in** *a twinkling.* • *Microprocessors do the calculations* **in the twinkling of an eye** (= very quickly).

twirl *(obj)* /£twɜːl, $twɜːrl/ *v* to (cause to) give a sudden quick turn or set of turns in a circle • *She danced and twirled across the room.* [I always + adv/prep] • *The skirt twirled and flared around her ankles.* [I always + adv/prep] • *He twirled the ribbon round the stick.* [T] • *He twirled his* **umbrella** *as he walked.* [T] • *I was always fascinated at the way he twirled the ends of his* **moustache.** [T] • *(Am)* If a girl twirls (a BATON) she is part of a group of girls who wear a uniform and march while spinning batons in the air: *She twirled her baton high in the air as she led the parade.*

twirl /£twɜːl, $twɜːrl/ *n* [C] • *We asked dance teacher Derek Hartley to give Andrea some expert advice on the moves, twirls and etiquette of the waltz.*

twirl·er /£ˈtwɜː·ləʳ, $ˈtwɜːr·lɚ/, **ma·jor·ette** *n* [C] *Am* • A twirler is a girl who marches as part of a group while spinning a BATON (= short metal stick) or throwing it in the air and then catching it.

twirl·ing /£ˈtwɜː·lɪŋ, $twɜːr-/ *n* [U] *Am* • Twirling is the action or skill of spinning a BATON: *Twirling practice will be held on Thursday at 3.30.*

twirl·y /£ˈtwɜː·li, $ˈtwɜːr-/ *adj* **-ier, -iest** *infml* • Twirly means with turns or curls: *a twirly moustache* • *twirly writing*

twirp /£twɜːp, $twɜːrp/ *n* [C] a TWERP

twist *(obj)* TURN /twɪst/ *v* to turn (something), esp. repeatedly, or to turn or wrap (one thing) around another • *The road twists through several villages.* [I] • *Although it looks direct on the map the path twists* **and turns** *a lot.* [I] • *In the double helix of DNA, two strands of DNA are twisted around each other.* [T] • *The visitor twisted* **round**/*twisted his* **neck** *to look at the photograph on the wall behind him.* [I/T] • *Twist the rope tightly round that post over there.* [T] • *The man twisted the wire quickly into a circle.* [T] • *Can you twist this lid* **off** (= remove it by turning) *for me?* [M] • If you twist a part of your body you hurt a muscle in that place: *He twisted his* **ankle/back/knee/neck** *in the match on Saturday.* [T] • *His face then twisted* **with** *grief/***in** *agony* (= showed extreme pain/unhappiness) *and he began sobbing.* [I] • *The policeman grabbed the rioter and twisted* (= bent and tightly held) *his* **arm** *behind his back.* [T] • If you **twist** someone's **arm** you make it very difficult for them to refuse to do something: *I didn't want to go to the exhibition but Linda twisted my arm.* ○ *"I'm surprised to see you here." "I had my arm twisted."* • To **twist yourself into knots** is to became confused and make what you are trying to say more difficult to understand: *He twisted himself into knots trying to explain what employees could and could not say to the press.* • If someone can **twist** you **round** their

little finger they are able to persuade you easily to do what they want: *I knew we'd be allowed to go to the concert because Ellen can twist Dad round her little finger.* • *(esp. Am and Aus)* A **twist-tie** is a short piece of wire covered in plastic or paper which is used to fasten a plastic bag.

twist /twɪst/ *n* [C] • *Give the cap another twist – make sure it's tight.* • *She punctuated her song with a little Elvis-style twist* **of** *the pelvis.* • A twist can be the shape of or a piece of something which has been twisted: *a twist* **of** *hair* ○ *a twist* **of** *lemon* • A twist is also a tight bend, or *(fig.)* a complicated situation or plan of action: *a path with many twists* **and turns** ○ *(fig.) the twists* **and turns** *of fate* ○ *(fig.) It has proved very difficult to unravel the twists* **and turns** *and contradictions of the evidence.* • **The** twist is a dance in which people stay in one place and twist their bodies from side to side to music. • *(dated)* To **be/go round the twist** or **send** someone **round the twist** is to be, become or make someone else become angry or unable to behave in a reasonable way: *If I'd had to stay there any longer, I'd have gone round the twist.* • *I'm* **in a twist** (=confused or worried) *about these figures.*

twist·ed /£'twɪs·tɪd, $-t̬ɪd/ *adj* • *a twisted tree trunk* • *a twisted ankle* • *twisted metal* • *Negotiations have followed a twisted course in recent months.* • See also TWISTED.

twist·ing /£'twɪs·tɪŋ, $-t̬ɪŋ/ *adj* • *a twisting country road* • *twisting vines*

twist·y /£'twɪs·ti, $-t̬i/ *adj* **-ier, -iest** *infml* • *The car allows the driver to select an intermediate gear when driving on hilly or twisty roads.*

twist *obj* CHANGE /twɪst/ *v* [T] *disapproving* to change (information) so that it gives the message you want it to give, esp. in a way that is dishonest • *He twisted the facts of his early life to give the appearance of extreme poverty.* • *This report shows how she twisted the truth to claim successes where none, in fact, existed.* • *You're twisting my words – that's not what I said at all.*

twist /twɪst/ *n* [C] • A twist is a change in the way in which something happens: *It's really only a slight twist of the rules to allow her to take part in the competition.* ○ *The story* **took** *a new/surprise twist today with media reports that the doctor had resigned.* ○ *The incident was the* **latest** *twist in the continuing saga of fraud and high scandal in banks and stockbroking firms.* ○ *But for a cruel twist* **of fate/fortune**, *he could now be running his own business.* ○ *I won't spoil the end of the book by telling you what happens – there's an unexpected twist* **in/to** *the plot.*

twist·er /£'twɪs·təʳ, $-t̬ɚ/ *n* [C] *infml disapproving* • *That man's a real twister* (=he cheats people).

twist·ed /£'twɪs·tɪd, $-t̬ɪd/ *adj* being unpleasantly strange • *The letter was clearly the product of a twisted* **mind**. • *(Br and Aus) In those days I was* **bitter and** *twisted – I hated everybody.* • See also **twisted** at TWIST TURN.

twist·er /£'twɪs·təʳ, $-t̬ɚ/ *n* [C] a TORNADO or a WHIRLWIND

twit /twɪt/ *n* [C] *infml* a stupid person • *He's such a twit!* • *You stupid twit!*

twitch *(obj)* UNCONTROLLED MOVEMENT /twɪtʃ/ *v* (to cause) to make a sudden small movement with (a part of the body), usually unintentionally • *He tried to suppress a smile but felt the corner of his mouth twitch.* [I] • *She twitched her nose like a rabbit.* [T]

twitch /twɪtʃ/ *n* [C] • *I've got a twitch at the corner of my eye – can you see it?*

twitch·y /'twɪtʃ·i/ *adj* **-ier, -iest** • If you are twitchy you are nervous and anxious, sometimes showing this through sudden movements or movements which do not appear smooth or relaxed: *On camera he appears twitchy and ill at ease.* ○ *The president is reportedly getting twitchy about the recent fall in his popularity.*

twitch *obj* PULL /twɪtʃ/ *v* [T] to give (something) a sudden light pull • *You'll feel something twitch the line when you get a fish.*

twitch /twɪtʃ/ *n* [C]

twit·ter /£'twɪt·əʳ, $'twɪt̬·ɚ/ *v* [I] (of a bird) to make a series of short high sounds • *I was woken up in the early hours by a bird twittering just outside my window.* • If a person twitters they talk quickly and nervously in a high voice, saying very little of importance or interest: *She comes in here when I'm trying to work and just twitters on about nothing.*

twit·ter /£'twɪt·əʳ, $'twɪt̬·ɚ/ *n* [C]

twixt /twɪkst/ *prep old use or poetic* between

two /tuː/ *determiner, pronoun, n pl* **twos** (the number) 2 • *They've got two houses.* • *He's got two leather jackets already.* • *I spent two years in Ethiopia.* • *It's two o'clock.* •

WORDS WITH THE MEANING 'TWO'

counting two things or people

She had her **second** child in 1983.
I met a **couple** of friends in town.
The Adamsons are a newly married **couple**.
You two are a **pair** of idiots!
A **pair** of trousers/shoes/gloves/scissors/glasses LP **Pair**
Karen and Dee are so alike they could be **twins**.

counting two events

I've been to Singapore **twice**.
This is only my **second** time on a horse.
She read the letter a **second** time.
(She **re**-read the letter/read the letter **once more** = She read the letter **again**)

choosing between two events

Hurry up and choose **one or the other**.
These are no good – I don't like **either** of them.
Jim **neither** smokes **nor** drinks.
Trish has two cats and she loves both of them/them **both**.
I want to close **both** of my bank accounts.

adjectives and compounds

We booked a **double** room at the Royal Hotel.
I sold the ring for **double/twice** the price I paid for it.
She drives a powerful **two**-seater sports car.
This **dual** purpose machine is both a fax and a photocopier.
The two oil companies signed a **bilateral** agreement.
bi-weekly (= every two weeks)

making two things

Double your money in less than 10 years!
Don't **duplicate** the work you have already done.
Send a **duplicate** of this letter to Saunders and Co.

two parts

The Wimbledon **semi-finals** are held this weekend.
The bank is about **half-way** along the High Street.
We divided the chocolate **in two** and each took **half**.
The number of elephants has been **halved** since 1986.
The equator divides the world into two **hemispheres**.

There are two ways of interpreting what you just said. • *There's a special offer on at the moment – you can get two T-shirts* **for the price of one**. • *He'll be two (years old) in February.* • *"How many children have you got?" "Just the two."* • *Are you coming over to the bar, you two?* • *"I can't eat all of that!" "Well, cut it* **in** *two and we'll have half each."* • *Three twos are six.* [C] • If you say there are **no two ways about it** you mean that something is a firm decision or situation and there can be no doubts or different decisions: *We'll have to go, there are no two ways about it.* • *(Am and Aus infml)* Your **two cents worth** is your spoken opinion on a particular matter: *I thought I'd just* **throw in** (=add) *my two cents worth.* • *(infml)* If you do not for certain know the facts about a particular situation but you form a judgment from what you consider to be obvious proof you might say that you **put two and two together**: *"How did you know they were having an affair?" "Well, I'd seen them out together a couple of times so I just put two and two together."* • *(infml humorous)* If you **put two and two together and make five** you understand a particular situation wrongly, often in a way which is more shocking or exciting than the truth: *"Why ever did she think you were pregnant?" "I was sick once or twice and I suppose she just put two and two together and made five."* • *(Br)* If you are **in two minds** (*Am and Aus* **of two minds**) about a decision

VERBS WITH TWO OBJECTS

- Some verbs such as 'give', 'buy' and 'offer' can have two objects. These verbs are marked [+ two objects] in this dictionary. In the sentence *I gave Sally a present* the present is what I gave, and Sally is the person I gave it to. The main object (the present) is called the **direct object**. The other object (Sally) is called the **indirect object**.
- Most verbs like this can be used to say exactly the same thing in a different way by putting a preposition in front of one of the objects (usually the indirect object): *I gave a present* **to** *Sally*. The prepositions most commonly used are 'to' and 'for'. In the lists below, verbs marked * can also use another preposition.
- The commonest passive form has the indirect object first (usually the person who has received something), as in *Sally was given a present,* but it is also possible to say *A present was given to Sally.*

USED WITH *to*

Verbs with this pattern often express the idea of giving or exchanging something: *Please send me your new catalogue. / Please send your new catalogue* **to** *me.*

give, award, grant	*The government awarded the firm a $250 000 contract.*
sell, lease, rent	*Leeds have sold fans 4,500 tickets for the game next week.*
lend, loan, offer, owe	*Can you lend me twenty pounds?* • *Don't forget you owe me $100.*
pay, repay, refund	*They only pay me £4 an hour.*
hand, throw, serve*	*Throw me that blue towel, will you?* • *She served us a delicious lunch.*
bring*, send, take	*Cheryl brought us news from home.*
post, mail, fax, telex, wire	*I'll fax you the order.*
tell, show, teach	*Mother taught me the piano when I was three.*
write, read, sing	*Will you read me another story?*
promise, recommend	*I promised Jamie a surprise for his birthday.* • *Can you recommend us a good hotel?*
deny	*They denied him any freedom.*

USED WITH *for*

Often these verbs express the idea of doing something that another person wants: *Could you get me a coffee? / Could you get a coffee* **for** *me?*

buy	*She bought us lunch.*
change, spare	*Can you change me this £20 note?* • *Can you spare me a couple of pounds?*
earn, win, gain	*Callcott's goal won us the match.*
keep, save, reserve	*Please save me a seat on the train.*
order, book	*I'll book us a table for dinner tonight.*
fetch, get, bring*, find	*Fetch me a newspaper, will you?* • *He's trying to find us a room.*
cook, make	*Shall I cook you spaghetti for dinner?*
cut, slice, pour	*She cut everyone a big slice of cake.*
make, build, design	*He built the children a play house.*

Notice that 'envy', 'excuse' and 'forgive' are used with 'for' in front of the **direct** object: *I envy you your success. / I envy you for your success.*

USED WITH OTHER PREPOSITIONS

ask	*I asked him a question. / I asked a question* **of** *him.*

Notice that 'serve' and 'pay' are used with 'to' but can also be used with a different preposition before their **direct** object:

serve	*Serve them the steak. / Serve them* **with** *the steak.*
pay	*He paid me cash for the job. / He paid me* **with** *cash for the job.*

NOT USED WITH A PREPOSITION

With some verbs, neither of the objects can be expressed with a preposition. You can say *They charged me £40* but you would not say 'They charged £40 to me'.

bet	*I bet you £10 Doris gets the job.*
cost, charge, fine	*It cost me $40.* [no passive] • *She was fined $500 for possessing drugs.*
allow	*The police only allowed me 10 minutes to talk to him.*
refuse	*Officials refused him entry into the US.*

VERBS FOLLOWED BY AN OBJECT AND A NOUN OR ADJECTIVE

With some verbs the object can be followed by a noun or noun phrase that does not refer to a separate person or thing and is therefore not a second object. Compare *We made him dinner* (= we made dinner for him) and *We made him chairman* (he <u>is</u> now chairman). These verbs are marked [+ obj + n] in the dictionary. They usually name or describe someone or give them a title, and the noun refers to the name or title:

I **named** *my dog Hamlet.* • *Never* **call** *me a fool again.*
He was **elected** *president of the society.* • *He was* **crowned** *world champion.*
But notice the special use of *take*: *Armed police* **took** *nine terrorists* **prisoner**.

Sometimes the object can be followed by an adjective or an adjective-like phrase. This grammar pattern is marked [+ obj + adj]:

I would **call** *your action selfish.* • *Things like that* **make** *me so angry.*

With some verbs, 'to be' or 'as' can be placed before the noun or adjective:

We **consider** *you* **to be** *well qualified for the job.* [+ obj + *to be* adj]
Everyone **regarded** *her* **as** *a perfect student.* [+ obj + *as* n]

you can not decide which of two different plans of action you should take: *I don't know whether to go to this conference or not – I'm in two minds about it.* • *"Patrick and Glyn got on really well, didn't they." "Yes, well they're* **two of a kind** (=similar characters) *really, aren't they.'"* • *"I have absolutely no idea what's going on."* **"That makes two of us** (=I'm in the same, esp. bad, situation)". • *Well, when I found out that my husband had been having an affair I thought* **two can play at that game** (=if someone does something selfish that causes you to suffer, you can do the same thing yourself)! • *(saying)* 'It takes two to tango' means an activity needs two people willing to take part for it to happen: *She may want to argue, but it takes two to tango and I won't stoop to her level.* • *(saying)* You can say 'two's company, three's a crowd' if two people are relaxed and enjoying each other's company but another person would make them feel less comfortable. • If you **put/stick two fingers in the air/up** or **give** someone **two fingers** you hold your first and second fingers up in a V shape with the back of your hand towards someone, which is a rude sign in Britain, to show that you are angry or have no respect for them. • *(Am infml disapproving)* Something or someone that is **two-bit** is worth very little or is very unimportant: *He plays a two-bit Chicago gangster in the play.* • A **two-by-four** is a standard size of finished wood used for building which measures slightly less than two INCHES wide and four inches deep and can be cut to various lengths: *You'll need four eight-foot two-by-fours to frame out that wall.* • **Two-dimensional** means flat, having width and length but not depth. • *(disapproving)* A person or story which is **two-dimensional** is too simple, showing a lack of deep, serious thought and understanding: *I didn't believe in any of the characters in the book – they were somehow two-dimensional.* • A knife or other cutting device which is **two-edged** has two sharp edges for cutting with: *a two-edged sword* • A **two-edged** remark can be understood in two very different ways, one of them positive and one of them negative: *"That was amazingly generous of you!" "Well, that was a two-edged comment – are you saying I'm usually very mean?"* • *(disapproving)* Someone who is **two-faced** is not sincere, saying unpleasant things about you to other people while seeming to be pleasant when they are with you: *I wouldn't trust her if I were you – she can be really two-faced.* • Something which is **two-handed** needs or involves the use of both hands at the same time: *a two-handed saw* ○ *My tennis is really improving – I've got a formidable two-handed backhand.* • *(Br)* A **two-hander** is a play written for two actors. • A **two-piece** is a set of clothes which consists of two separate but matching parts, esp. a woman's clothes for swimming or (also **two-piece suit**) a man's matching jacket and trousers. • **Two-ply** material, wood or wool consists of two layers or two sets of thread for added thickness or strength. • A **two-seater** is a car which has seats for only two people. • *(infml)* To **two-time** someone that you are having a relationship with is to deceive them by having a secret sexual relationship with someone else at the same time: *I finished with him when I found out he was two-timing me.* • *(infml)* A **two-timer** is a person who deceives their partner by having a secret sexual relationship with someone else. • Clothes or shoes that are **two-tone** are two different colours or are a lighter and a darker variety of the same colour. • **Two-way** means in both directions: *a two-way street* • **Two-way** radios can both send out and receive signals. • The phrase **two-way** is also used of situations that involve two people or two groups of people working together to achieve a shared aim: *Negotiations are a two-way thing – both sides have to come to a compromise.* ○ *Remember, friendships are a* **two-way street** (=both people have to make an effort). • A **two-way mirror** is a mirror that can be used in the usual way from one side but is transparent from the other side and can therefore be used to watch people without them knowing. • [LP]› **Two**

two·pence /ˈtʌp·ᵊnts/ *n* TUPPENCE

two·pen·ny /ˈtʌp·ᵊn·i, ˈ-ni/ *adj* [before n; not gradable]

two·some /ˈtuː·səm/ *n* [C] two people considered together • *Zoe and I were inseparable as kids – my mother used to call us the terrible twosome.*

ty·coon /taɪˈkuːn/ *n* [C] a person who has succeeded in business or industry and has become very wealthy and powerful • *a business/shipping tycoon* • *There were rumours that a Hong Kong property tycoon was going to withdraw his millions from the bank.*

tyke, tike /taɪk/ *n* [C] *infml (Br and Aus)* a child who is badly behaved in a playful way, or *(Am)* a small child • *(Br) Come here, you cheeky little tyke!* • *(Am) After the triplets were born, David and Linda's house seemed like it was wall-to-wall tykes.*

type [GROUP] /taɪp/ *n* [C] a particular group of people or things which shares similar characteristics and forms a smaller division of a larger set • *There were so many different types* **of** *bread that I didn't know which to buy.* • *What type* **of** *clothes does she wear?* • *It was dark so I didn't notice what type* **of** *car it was.* • *He's the type* **of** *man you could take home to your mother.* • *He's very attractive, if you like the blond athletic type.* • *They sell dried flowers and baskets and that type* **of** *thing.* • *We have a range of moisturizers for all different skin types.* • *She was young and she was wearing student-type clothes so I assumed she was studying here.* • *He took me to a dreadful pub in Soho full of actor types speaking at the tops of their voices.* • *(infml) I mean he's a nice enough guy – he's just* **not** *my* **type** (=not what I find interesting or attractive). • *(fml)* Type can be used to mean a person who seems to represent a particular group of people, having all the qualities that you usually connect with that group: *He doesn't use fully rounded characters in his plays – he uses types.* • A **type A** person is frequently excitable and full of nervous anxiety and is more likely to have a **heart attack**. • A **type B** person is usually relaxed and calm and less likely to have a **heart attack**.

ty·pi·cal /ˈtɪp·ɪ·kᵊl/ *adj* • If something is typical it shows all the characteristics that you would usually expect from that particular group of things: *I must look like the typical tourist with my shorts and my camera.* ○ *This sort of hot and spicy food is very typical* **of** *the food in the south of the country.* ○ *Typical symptoms would include severe headaches, vomiting, dizziness – that sort of thing.* • *(disapproving)* Something which is typical might also show all the bad characteristics that you expect from someone or something, often in a way that is annoying: *It's just typical* **of** *Ian to spend all that money on the equipment and then lose interest half way through the course.* ○ *"He phoned in at the last minute to say he wasn't coming." "Typical! You can't rely on Dave for anything!"* • (GR)

ty·pi·cally /ˈtɪp·ɪ·kli/ *adv* • Typically means showing all the characteristics that you would expect from the stated person, thing or group: *She has that reserve and slight coldness of manner which is typically English.* ○ *Paul, in typically rude fashion, told him he was talking a load of rubbish.* • You can also say typically if you are giving an average or usual example of a particular thing: *Typically, a doctor will see about thirty patients a day.* ○ *Tickets for such events will typically cost around thirty dollars.*

ty·pi·fy *obj* /ˈtɪp·ɪ·faɪ/ *v* [not *be typifying*] • Something which typifies a particular group of things shows all the characteristics that you would usually expect from it: *With her cropped hair and and her mannish clothes, she typifies the sort of feminist often feared by men.* • Something might also typify something else by being characteristic of it: *His latest book reflects the old preocccupations with sex and religion that typify much of his work.*

type *(obj)* [WRITE] /taɪp/ *v* to write using a machine, either a TYPEWRITER or a computer keyboard • *She asked me to type a couple of letters.* [T] • *I can't type properly – I just use two fingers.* [I] • *I was typing* **away** *into the early hours of the morning just to get the thing finished.* [I] • If you type **up** a piece of writing you make a typed copy of something written by hand: *Could you type* **up** *the minutes from the meeting, please?* [M] • If you type an instruction or piece of information **in** a computer you press the necessary letters, numbers or other key on the computer's keyboard: *Type in your password.* [M]

typ·ing /ˈtaɪ·pɪŋ/ *n* [U] • *a typing error* • *It's the usual boring secretarial job – a bit of typing and some filing.* • *What's your typing speed?*

typ·ist /ˈtaɪ·pɪst/ *n* [C] • A typist is a person who is employed to type letters, reports and other documents.

type [PRINTED LETTERS] /taɪp/, *specialized* **type·face** /ˈtaɪp·feɪs/ *n* [U] the style and size of printed letters used in a piece of printed writing such as in a newspaper, book or article • *Use bold type for your headings.* • *You can choose from over twenty sorts of typeface with this new software package.*

type·cast *obj* /£ˈtaɪp·kɑːst, $-kæst/ *v* [T usually passive] *past* **typecast** to always give (an actor) the same type of character to play, usually because he or she is physically suited to that type of part • *With her blonde good looks she has tended to be typecast as the young bimbo.*

type·script /ˈtaɪp·skrɪpt/ *n* [C] a TYPED copy of a piece of writing such as a book • *She's just sent in a typescript of the first chapter of her novel to the publishers.*

type·writ·er /£ˈtaɪpˌraɪ·təʳ, $-t̬ɚ/ *n* [C] a machine for producing writing that looks like printed text. It has a set of keys which when hit with the fingers, produce on paper the letters, numbers and other symbols shown on them • *an electric typewriter* • PIC› **Office**

type·writ·ten /£ˈtaɪpˌrɪt·ən, $-ˌrɪt̬-/ *adj* [not gradable] • *a typewritten memo*

ty·phoid (fe·ver) /ˈtaɪ·fɔɪd/ *n* [U] an infectious disease spread by dirty water and food, causing a high body temperature, red spots on the upper body, severe pains in the bowels and sometimes death

ty·phoon /taɪˈfuːn/ *n* [C] a violent wind which has a circular movement, found in the W Pacific Ocean • *The 169 000-ton vessel went down during a typhoon in the South China Sea.*

ty·phus /ˈtaɪ·fəs/ *n* [U] an infectious disease spread by LICE (= small insects which live on the body), causing a high body temperature, severe pains in the head and purple spots on the body

ty·pi·cal /ˈtɪp·ɪ·kəl/ *adj* See at TYPE GROUP

ty·pi·fy /ˈtɪp·ɪ·faɪ/ *v* [not *be typifying*] See at TYPE GROUP

typ·ist /ˈtaɪ·pɪst/ *n* [C] See at TYPE WRITE

ty·pog·raph·y /£taɪˈpɒg·rə·fi, $-ˈpɑː·grə-/ *n* [U] the style, size and arrangement of the letters in a piece of printing

ty·po·graph·i·cal /£ˌtaɪ·pəʊˈgræf·ɪ·kəl, $-poʊ-/, **typ·o·graph·ic** /£ˌtaɪ·pəʊˈgræf·ɪk, $-poʊ-/ *adj* [not gradable] • *Both magazines are well-known for their typographical* **errors.**

ty·ran·no·saur·us /£tɪˌræn·əˈsɔː·rəs, $-ˈsɔːr·əs/, **ty·ran·no·saur** /£tɪˈræn·ə·sɔːʳ, $-sɔːr/ *n* [C] a fierce DINOSAUR with large, powerful back legs, small front legs and a long tail • *The children's favourite dinosaur is Tyrannosaurus* **Rex.**

ty·ran·ny /ˈtɪr·ən·i/ *n* [U] government by a ruler or small group of people who have unlimited power over the people in their country or state and use it unfairly and cruelly • *This, the president promised us, was a war against tyranny.* • *(fig.) Women, the play seems to suggest, must resist the tyranny* (= unfair power over their lives) *of domesticity.*

ty·ran·ni·cal /tɪˈræn·ɪ·kəl/ *adj* • *a tyrannical leader/regime/political system* • *In the end she left home just to escape the tyrannical rule of her mother.*

ty·ran·ni·cal·ly /tɪˈræn·ɪ·kli/ *adv*

ty·ran·nize *obj, Br and Aus usually* **-ise** /ˈtɪr·ən·aɪz/ *v* [T] • *He was one of those school bullies who tyrannized the whole playground.*

ty·rant /£ˈtaɪə·rənt, $ˈtaɪ-/ *n* [C] • A tyrant is a ruler who has unlimited power over other people, and uses it unfairly and cruelly: *Tamir, one of several sons of the exiled ruler, vowed he would liberate his country from the tyrant.* ○ *(fig. humorous) Overnight my boss seems to have turned into a tyrant.*

tyre *Br and Aus, Am* **tire** /£taɪəʳ, $taɪr/ *n* [C] a thick rubber ring, often filled with air, which is fitted around the outer edge of the wheel of a vehicle, allowing the vehicle to stick to the road surface and improving the smoothness of the journey • *Your tyres are very worn – I think you should get them changed.* • *There's an instrument at the garage that measures the tread on your tyres.* • *He was driving along a motorway when his tyre burst.* • *Have you got a bicycle repair kit? I've got another puncture in my back tyre.* • *I keep a* **spare** *tyre in the back of the car.* • When you measure the **tyre pressure** of your car tyres, you see how much air is in them: *There's a chart over there which shows the recommended tyre pressures for every make of car.* • PIC› **Bicycles, Car**

tzar /£zɑːʳ, $zɑːr/ *n* [C] a TSAR

tze·tze fly /ˈtet·si/ *n* [C] a TSETSE FLY

U u

U LETTER (*pl* **U's**), **u** (*pl* **u's**) /juː/ *n* [C] the 21st letter of the English alphabet • A **U-bend** is a U-shaped piece of piping, esp. one fixed under a toilet or BASIN, which holds water in its lower part and prevents unpleasant gases from getting out: *There was a blockage in the U-bend which caused the kitchen to flood.* • PIC› **Bathroom**

U FILM *Br* /juː/, *Am and Aus* **G** *n, adj* [not gradable] (a film) considered suitable for children of any age • *The film is (classified as) a U.* [C] ○ *The film is rated U.*

U COLLEGE /juː/ *n* [U] *Am and Aus abbreviation for* UNIVERSITY • *She goes to Kansas U/Sydney U.*

U SOCIAL BEHAVIOUR /juː/ *adj* [not gradable] *Br and Aus dated* (of behaviour or ways of speaking) acceptable to or expected to be used by people of high social class • Compare **non-U** at NON-.

U–boat /£ˈjuː·bəʊt, $-boʊt/ *n* [C] a German SUBMARINE (= ship which can travel under water), used esp. in World Wars 1 and 2

U–turn /£ˈjuː·tɜːn, $-tɜːrn/, *Aus infml* **U–ie** *n* [C] a turn made by a car in order to go back in the direction from which it has come, or *(fig. esp. disapproving)* a complete change from one opinion or plan of action to an opposite one • *It is illegal to* **make** *a U-turn on a motorway.* • *(fig.) Whether it was always her intention to make these changes, or she just* **did** *a quick U-turn in response to adverse publicity, we will never know.* • *(fig.) The dramatic series of U-turns in policy in the past few months has lost the government credibility.*

UAE /ˌjuː·eɪˈiː/ *n* [U] **the UAE** *abbreviation for* United Arab Emirates

u·biq·ui·tous /£juːˈbɪk·wɪ·təs, $-wə·t̬əs/ *adj* existing or found everywhere • *Leather is very much in fashion this season, as of course is* **the** *ubiquitous denim.* • *The Swedes are not alone in finding their language under pressure from* **the** *ubiquitous spread of English.* • *The radio, that most ubiquitous of consumer-electronic appliances, is about to enter a new age.*

u·biq·ui·tous·ly /£juːˈbɪk·wɪ·tə·sli, $-wə·t̬ə-/ *adv*

u·biq·ui·ty /£juːˈbɪk·wɪ·ti, $-wə·t̬i/ *n* [U] *fml* • *These days it's possible to travel in any developed country without ever tasting the native cuisine, thanks to the ubiquity of fast-food outlets* (= the fact that they are found everywhere).

ud·der /£ˈʌd·əʳ, $-ɚ/ *n* [C] the milk-producing organ of a cow, sheep or other animal that hangs like a bag between the legs

UFO /£ˌjuː·efˈəʊ, $-ˈoʊ/ *n* [C] *pl* **UFO's** or **UFOs** /£ˈjuː·fəʊz, $-foʊz/ *abbreviation for* an unidentified flying object (= an object seen in the sky which is thought to be a spacecraft sent from another planet) • *Several UFO sightings have been reported in the Pennine foothills.* • *There's a woman in Manchester who claims her husband was abducted by aliens on board a UFO.*

ugh /ʌg, ɜː/ *exclamation* used to express a strong feeling of disgust at something very unpleasant • *Ugh, I've got something horrible on the bottom of my shoe!* • *Ugh, I'm not eating that!*

ug·ly VERY UNATTRACTIVE /ˈʌg·li/ *adj* **-ier, -iest** (of people, animals or things) extremely unattractive • *I find a lot of modern architecture very ugly.* • *Their house is full of ugly 1950's furniture.* • *Yesterday in town I saw the ugliest baby I've ever seen in my life.* • *The first thing that struck her when she came home was how ugly everyone looked in the street.* • *She's got one of those really ugly dogs with a squashed face.* • *I feel really fat and ugly at the moment.* • *(Am)* An **ugly American** is an American visiting a foreign country who behaves in a way that offends people who live in that country. • *You haven't met her husband have you? He's a dreadful man and he's* **as ugly as sin** (= very ugly)*!* • An **ugly duckling** is someone who is not very attractive or popular as a very young person but who is likely to become so as he or she grows older. • *"The Ugly Duckling"* (title of a Hans Christian Andersen story, 1846)

ug·li·ness /ˈʌg·lɪ·nəs/ *n* [U] • *What struck me about the city was its ugliness.*

ug·ly THREATENING /ˈʌg·li/ *adj* **-ier, -iest** unpleasant and threatening or violent • *Unfortunately the match was spoiled by an ugly incident between rival groups of fans.* • *Our refusal to pay what the taxi driver demanded resulted in a rather ugly scene.* • *The demonstration turned ugly when a group of protesters started to throw bottles at the* *police.* • *An ugly mood is developing in Congress over the dispute.*

ug·li·ness /'ʌg·lɪ·nəs/ *n* [U]

UHF /ˌjuː·eɪtʃ'ef/ *n* [U] *abbreviation for* ultrahigh frequency (= radio waves between 300 MHz and 3000 MHz) • Compare VHF.

uh–huh /ʌ̃'hʌ/ *exclamation infml* a written representation of the sound that people sometimes make in order to give certainty to, agree with or show understanding of something that has just been said • *"Did you hear what I just said?" "Uh-huh."* • *"You know that strange guy we saw yesterday?" "Uh-huh." "Well, he was outside the house again this morning."* • *"Does he like his new job?" "Uh-huh, he seems to."*

uh–oh /£ˌə'əʊ, $-'oʊ/ *exclamation infml* a written representation of the sound that people make when they discover that they have made a mistake or done something wrong • *Uh-oh, I think I just locked my keys in the car.*

UHT /ˌjuː·eɪtʃ'tiː/ *adj* [not gradable] *abbreviation for* (of milk) ultra-heat-treated (= previously treated at a very high temperature so that it will last longer while it is in a container that has not been opened) • *UHT milk*

UHT /ˌjuː·eɪtʃ'tiː/ *n* [U] *infml* • *a pint of UHT*

uh–uh /'ʌ̃ˌʌ̃/ *exclamation esp. Am and Aus infml* a written representation of the sound that people sometimes make to give a negative answer • *"You didn't have time to go to the store?" "Uh-uh, no chance."*

UK /ˌjuː'keɪ/ *n* [U] **the UK** *abbreviation for* the United Kingdom; the country of Great Britain and Northern Ireland • *I'll be over in the UK in June. Can we fix a meeting then?* • LP **Britain**

UK /ˌjuː'keɪ/ *adj* [before n] • *the UK ambassador to Sweden*

u·ke·le·le, u·ku·le·le /ˌjuː·kə'leɪ·li/ *n* [C] a small guitar or BANJO with four strings • *George Formby made the ukelele famous in his films in the 1940s.*

ul·cer /£'ʌl·sə^r, $-sɚ/ *n* [C] a break in the skin or on the surface of an organ inside the body, which does not heal naturally • *She gets a lot of* **mouth** *ulcers.* • *He's got a duodenal/peptic/stomach ulcer so he has to watch his diet.*

ul·cer·at·ed /£'ʌl·sə^r·eɪ·tɪd, $-sɚ·eɪ·t̬ɪd/ *adj* • A surface of the skin which is ulcerated is covered in ulcers: *She had lain in bed for so long that her shoulder blades had become ulcerated.*

ul·cer·a·tion /£ˌʌl·sə^r'eɪ·ʃ^ən, $-sə'reɪ-/ *n* [U]

ul·cer·ous /£'ʌl·sə^r·əs, $-sɚ-/ *adj*

ul·te·ri·or /£ʌl'tɪə·ri·ə^r, $-'tɪr·i-/ *adj* (esp. of a reason for a particular action) secret, often bad, and usually different from the claimed reason • *He claims that his attempts to depose the leader were only for the good of the party, but I suspect he may have some ulterior* **motive**.

ul·ti·mate /£'ʌl·tɪ·mət, $-t̬ə-/ *adj* [not gradable] most extreme or important because either the original or final, or the best or worst • *Of course the ultimate responsibility for the present conflict without doubt lies with the aggressor.* • *Although other people can advise him, the ultimate decision about who to employ lies with Andrew.* • *Your ultimate goal as an athlete is to represent your country.* • *In theory capital punishment is the ultimate deterrent.* • *Infidelity is the ultimate betrayal.* • *The 21-year-old painter is about to receive the ultimate accolade of a one-man exhibition at New York's Museum of Contemporary Art.* • *The yacht is owned by the world's seventh-richest man, and is the ultimate luxury cruiser.*

ul·ti·mate /£'ʌl·tɪ·mət, $-t̬ə-/ *n* [U] • *He drives a gold Rolls Royce Corniche –* **the** *ultimate* **in** *luxury.* • *Chocolate really is* **the** *ultimate* **in** *indulgence.* • *You mean he actually tried to tackle six men single-handedly! Well, that really is* **the** *ultimate* **in** *stupidity!*

ul·ti·mate·ly /£'ʌl·tɪ·mət·li, $-t̬ə-/ *adv* [not gradable] • Ultimately means finally: *Everything will ultimately depend on what is said at the meeting with the directors next week.* ○ *Ultimately, of course, he'd like to have his own business but that won't be for some time.* • Ⓓ Ⓟ

ul·ti·mat·um /£ˌʌl·tɪ'meɪ·təm, $-t̬ə'meɪ·t̬əm/ *n* [C] *pl* **ultimatums** or **ultimata** /£ˌʌl·tɪ'meɪ·tə, $-t̬ə'meɪ·t̬ə/ a threat in which a person or group of people are warned that if they do not do a particular thing, something unpleasant will happen to them. It is usually the last and most extreme in a series of actions taken to bring about a particular result • *He* **gave** *her an ultimatum – she could either stop seeing her other man and come back to him or it was divorce.* • *On Wednesday night the UN* **issued** *its toughest ultimatum to date, demanding that all troops withdraw from the city.*

ul·tra– /ˌʌl·trə-/ *combining form* extreme or extremely • *ultra-expensive* • *ultra-modern architecture* • *ultra-rich* • *ultra-sensitive* • *an ultra-short haircut* • *ultra-trendy*

ul·tra·ma·rine /ˌʌl·trə·mə'riːn/ *adj* bright blue

ul·tra·son·ic /£ˌʌl·trə'sɒn·ɪk, $-'sɑː·nɪk/ *adj* [not gradable] (of sound waves) of a FREQUENCY (= rate of sound waves each second) which is too high for people to hear • *Bats use ultrasonic waves to locate flying insects at night, and engineers use them to detect flaws in metals.*

ul·tra·sound /'ʌl·trə·saʊnd/ *n* [U] sound waves at very high FREQUENCIES used in such processes as examining organs inside the body and directing the path of SUBMARINES (= ships which can travel under water) • *The ultrasound scan helps to determine the age of the foetus as well as check for hereditary abnormalities.*

ul·tra·vi·o·let /ˌʌl·trə'vaɪə·lət/ (*abbreviation* **UV** /ˌjuː'viː/) *adj* [not gradable] (of light) having a WAVELENGTH which is beyond the VIOLET (= light purple) end of the range of colours that can be seen by human beings. Light of this type causes the skin to become darker in the sun. • *Ultraviolet radiation from the sun can cause skin cancer.* • *The doctor recommended that she use an ultraviolet lamp to improve her skin.*

um /əm/ *exclamation* a written representation of a sound that people make when they are pausing or deciding what to say next • *"What do you think of this jacket?" "I'm not sure – um, I don't know if I like the colour."* • *"So what did you talk about?" "Um, I don't remember, I suppose work mainly."* • *Um, I can't seem to get this machine to work.*

um·bi·li·cal cord /ʌm'bɪl·ɪ·k^əl/ *n* [C] the long tube-like structure which connects a baby which has not yet been born to its mother's PLACENTA (= the organ which provides it with food and oxygen) • *He asked the nurse if he could cut his son's umbilical cord.*

um·brage /'ʌm·brɪdʒ/ *n* [U] **take umbrage** *slightly fml* to feel upset or annoyed, usually because you feel that someone has been rude or shown a lack of respect to you • *You don't think she'll take umbrage if she isn't invited to the wedding, do you?*

um·brel·la /ʌm'brel·ə/ *n* [C] a device for protection against the rain which consists of a stick with a folding, material-covered frame at one end and usually a handle at the other, or a similar, often larger, device used for protection against the sun • *I felt a few spots of rain so I put my umbrella up.* • *You can take your umbrella down now – the rain's finished.* • *I left another umbrella on the bus yesterday.* • *I bought a folding umbrella to take with me.* • *If you've had enough of the sun come and lie under the umbrella for a while.* • Umbrella also refers to something which includes or represents a range of similar things: *Donations should be sent to the Disaster Emergency Committee, an umbrella* **organization** *for UK based aid agencies.* ○ *Existentialism was really an umbrella term to lump together the works of several philosophers and writers.* • *"The rain, it raineth on the just / And also on the unjust fella: / But chiefly on the just, because / The unjust steals the just's umbrella."* (Lord Bowen, 1835-94)

um·laut /'ʊm·laʊt/ *n* [C] a mark put over a vowel in some languages, such as German, to show that the pronunciation of the vowel is changed • *The German word 'Gebäude', which means 'building', has an umlaut over the a.* • LP **Symbols**

um·pire /£'ʌm·paɪə^r, $-paɪr/ *n* [C] a person who is present at a sports competition in order to make certain that the rules of that particular game are obeyed and to make judgments about whether particular actions are acceptable • *He's the umpire for the local cricket club.* • *In 14 years as an umpire in the major leagues, Kobel had never seen two baseball teams fight like this.* • LP **Sports**

um·pire *obj* /£'ʌm·paɪə^r, $-paɪr/ *v* [T] • *Starmers has been chosen to umpire the next cricket test match.*

ump·teen /ʌmp'tiːn, '–/ *determiner, pronoun infml* very many; a lot (of) • *We've eaten at that restaurant umpteen times and she still can't remember how to get there!*

ump·teenth /ʌmp'tiːnθ, '–/ *n, determiner infml* • *For the umpteenth time, Anthony, knives and forks go in the middle drawer!*

un– /ʌn-/ *combining form* used to add the meaning 'not', 'lacking' or 'the opposite of' before adjectives, adverbs, verbs and nouns • *unrealistic* • *unhappily* • *unscrew* • *unfairness* • LP **Opposites**

'un /ən/ *pronoun not standard* one • *Mira'll fit in the back of the car – she's only a little 'un!*

UN /ˌjuːˈen/ *n* [U] **the UN** *abbreviation for* the United Nations (= an international organization that was established in 1945 to maintain world peace) • *The UN has decided to impose sanctions.*

UN /ˌjuːˈen/ *adj* [before n] • *the UN Security Council* • *UN troops*

un·a·bashed /ˌʌn·əˈbæʃt/ *adj* without any worry about possible criticism or embarrassment • *Despite everything, he is an unabashed communist.* • *They were completely unabashed in praising themselves.* • *Unabashed by her critics, she continued writing simple optimistic romances.* • Compare ABASHED.

un·a·bat·ed /£ˌʌn·əˈbeɪ·tɪd, $-t̬ɪd/ *adj, adv fml* without weakening in strength or force • *The fighting has continued unabated throughout the last week.* • *Meanwhile the recession continues unabated.* • Compare ABATE.

un·a·ble /ʌnˈeɪ·bl̩/ *adj* [not gradable] not ABLE CAN DO

un·a·bridged /ˌʌn·əˈbrɪdʒd/ *adj* [not gradable] (of a book, speech or article) complete; not made shorter

un·ac·cep·ta·ble /ˌʌn·əkˈsep·tə·bl̩/ *adj* too bad to be accepted, approved of or allowed to continue • *The unions have described the latest pay offer as unacceptable.* • *The fact that millions of people are living in poverty in one of the richest nations in the world is totally unacceptable.* • *The taking of hostages, said the minister, was totally unacceptable under any circumstances.* • *The report found what it described as 'unacceptable levels of air pollution' in several major cities.* • *(Br and Aus)* **The unacceptable face of** a particular system or set of beliefs is the bad side to it: *The paper showed a picture of homeless people sleeping on the streets with the caption underneath 'the unacceptable face of capitalism'.*

un·ac·cep·ta·bly /ˌʌn·əkˈsep·tə·bli/ *adv* • *The investigation found unacceptably high levels of lead in several areas of the city.* • *The disparity between rich and poor has become unacceptably high.*

un·ac·com·pan·ied /ˌʌn·əˈkʌm·pᵊn·id/ *adj* [not gradable] (of a person) going somewhere alone, or (of a voice or musical instrument) sung or played alone with no ACCOMPANIMENT (= music played at the same time) • *To everyone's great surprise, the princess arrived at the ball unaccompanied.* • *She sang the first three verses with a piano and the last verse unaccompanied.*

un·ac·count·a·ble NOT RESPONSIBLE /£ˌʌn·əˈkaʊn·tə·bl̩, $-t̬ə-/ *adj* [not gradable] not expected to explain or provide a reason for your actions • *When Knight became leader, the council was run by a clique of officers largely unaccountable* **to** *the elected members.*

un·ac·count·a·ble SURPRISING /£ˌʌn·əˈkaʊn·tə·bl̩, $-t̬ə-/ *adj* not able to be explained or understood • *For some unaccountable reason he keeps his wallet in his underwear drawer.*

un·ac·count·a·bly /£ˌʌn·əˈkaʊn·tə·bli, $-t̬ə-/ *adv* • *I felt unaccountably happy this morning as I left the house.* • *I'm looking for my pen which unaccountably vanished from my desk overnight.*

un·ac·cus·tomed /ˌʌn·əˈkʌs·təmd/ *adj* not ACCUSTOMED

un·a·dul·te·ra·ted /£ˌʌn·əˈdʌl·tᵊr·eɪ·tɪd, $-t̬ə·reɪ·t̬ɪd/ *adj* not spoilt or made weaker by the addition of other substances; pure • *Of course people injecting drugs can never be sure that they're using unadulterated substances.* • *(fig.) As far as his speech was concerned, I've never heard such unadulterated* (= complete) *nonsense in my life!*

un·af·fect·ed NOT CHANGED /£ˌʌn·əˈfek·tɪd, $-t̬ɪd/ *adj* not influenced, harmed or interrupted in any way • *The west of the city was largely unaffected* **by** *the bombing.* • *The funeral industry remains unaffected* **by** *the recession.* • *It is hoped that train services on the main lines will be unaffected* **by** *today's industrial action.*

un·af·fect·ed SINCERE /£ˌʌn·əˈfek·tɪd, $-t̬ɪd/ *adj approving* (of a person) natural and sincere • *For someone who has spent forty years in show business she remains remarkably unaffected.*

un·af·fect·ed·ly /£ˌʌn·əˈfek·tɪd·li, $-t̬ɪd-/ *adv*

un·aid·ed /ˌʌnˈeɪ·dɪd/ *adj* [not gradable] without any help from anyone else; independently • *After his accident, he was barely able dress or go to the toilet unaided.* • *The two explorers attempted an unaided walk across the South Pole.*

un·al·loyed /ˌʌn·əˈlɔɪd/ *adj literary* (esp. of a positive feeling) not spoilt by any amount of negative feeling; pure • *Spending time with one's family is never an unalloyed pleasure* (= There are bad things about it too). • *We had the perfect holiday – two weeks of unalloyed bliss.*

un·am·big·u·ous /ˌʌn·æmˈbɪg·ju·əs/ *adj* expressed in a way which makes it completely clear what is meant • *The minister said she would give a clear and unambiguous* **statement** *on the future of the coal industry at the earliest possible opportunity.*

un·am·big·u·ous·ly /ˌʌn·æmˈbɪg·ju·ə·sli/ *adv* [not gradable] • *Smith stated that the Labour Party should reject unambiguously the low moral standards of the present government.*

un–A·mer·i·can /ˌʌn·əˈmer·ɪ·kən/ *adj Am disapproving* guilty of activities, behaviour or beliefs that show opposition or a lack of loyalty to the US and its political system • *From 1940 to 1943, he was general counsel of the House committee investigating un-American* **activities.** • *To be small is not beautiful. Worse, it is un-American.*

un·an·i·mous /juːˈnæn·ɪ·məs/ *adj* [not gradable] (of a group of people) all agreeing about one particular matter or voting the same way, or (of a decision or judgment) formed or supported by everyone in a group • *The jury returned a unanimous* **verdict** *of guilty after a short deliberation.* • *After a lengthy discussion we reached a unanimous* **decision** *on the proposal.* • *The unanimous vote ended a two-day hearing into the plan.* • *The new format has unanimous support and could be introduced next season.*

un·an·i·mous·ly /juːˈnæn·ɪ·mə·sli/ *adv* [not gradable] • *The UN General Assembly unanimously adopted a treaty making hostage-taking an international crime.* • *All four proposals to the committee were unanimously approved.* • *The motion was carried unanimously.*

un·a·nim·i·ty /£ˌjuː·nəˈnɪm·ɪ·ti, $-ə·t̬i/ *n* [U] *fml* • *The new legislation allows the members to make most decisions by majority vote, rather than by unanimity.*

un·an·nounced UNEXPECTED /ˌʌn·əˈnaʊntst/ *adj, adv* (esp. of a person's arrival somewhere) sudden and unexpected • *His evening was rather spoiled by the unannounced arrival of his ex-wife.* • *She appeared unannounced and took control of the meeting.*

un·an·nounced NOT PUBLICLY KNOWN /ˌʌn·əˈnaʊntst/ *adj* [not gradable] not made publicly known • *The Texan singer will be supported by two other bands, as yet unannounced.*

un·an·swer·a·ble CLEARLY TRUE /£ʌnˈɑːnt·sᵊr·ə·bl̩, $-ˈænt·sɚ-/ *adj fml* (esp. of an argument or claim) impossible to be disagreed with because it is so clearly true • *In economic terms the need to reduce inflation is unanswerable.* • *The case for military intervention, said the minister, was now unanswerable.*

un·an·swer·a·ble WITHOUT AN ANSWER /£ʌnˈɑːnt·sᵊr·ə·bl̩, $-ˈænt·sɚ-/ *adj* (of a question) without an answer • *The unanswerable question is how long this war is going to last.*

un·an·swered /£ʌnˈɑːnt·səd, $-ˈænt·sɚd/ *adj* [not gradable] not answered or explained • *Suspicions were first aroused after questions from local residents remained unanswered.*

un·ap·prec·i·a·tive /£ˌʌn·əˈpriː·ʃi·ə·tɪv, $-t̬ɪv/ *adj* not appreciative

un·ap·proach·a·ble /£ˌʌn·əˈprəʊ·tʃə·bl̩, $-ˈproʊ-/ *adj* (of a person) having an unfriendly and slightly frightening manner which tends to discourage other people from speaking to them • *His father was an authoritarian, a rather unapproachable man of whom both sons were afraid.*

un·ar·gu·a·ble /£ʌnˈɑːg·ju·ə·bl̩, $-ˈɑːrg-/ *adj* not arguable

un·armed /£ʌnˈɑːmd, $-ˈɑːrmd/ *adj* [not gradable] not armed

un·a·shamed /ˌʌn·əˈʃeɪmd/ *adj* not ashamed; without hiding behaviour or opinions that other people might consider unacceptable • *Greg is an unashamed fan of Kylie Minogue.* • *She is unashamed* **of** *her rather extreme views, even though many people find them offensive.*

un·a·sham·ed·ly /ˌʌn·əˈʃeɪ·mɪd·li/ *adv* • *The school's headmistress is unashamedly traditional and refuses to allow the girls to wear trousers.* • *The Government is openly and unashamedly putting party before country.*

un·as·sum·ing /£ˌʌn·əˈsjuː·mɪŋ, $-ˈsuː-/ *adj approving* (of a person) quiet and showing no desire for attention or admiration • *He was shy and unassuming and not at all how you expect an actor to be.*

un·at·tached NOT MARRIED /ˌʌn·əˈtætʃt/ *adj* [not gradable] not married or not having a relationship with anyone; single • *He's thirty-two, he's gorgeous, he's got his own house and, what's more, he's unattached.*

un·at·tached NOT CONNECTED /ˌʌn·əˈtætʃt/ *adj* [not gradable] not connected • *Please enclose your signed cheque and payment slip unattached and unfolded.*

un·at·tain·a·ble /ʌn·əˈteɪ·nə·bl̩/ *adj* [not gradable] not achievable • *an unattainable ideal* • *Some economists think that full employment in Europe is an unattainable* **goal**.

un·at·tend·ed /ˌʌn·əˈten·dɪd/ *adj* [not gradable] not being watched or taken care of • *Please do not leave your luggage unattended.* • *According to the report, most accidents occur when young children are left unattended in the home.*

un·at·trac·tive /£ˌʌn·əˈtræk·tɪv, $-t̬ɪv/ *adj* plain to look at or slightly ugly, or slightly unpleasant • *He was an unattractive man with staring eyes and an oddly pale skin.* • *The table had a shiny finish which she found unattractive.* • *The options were decidedly unattractive.*

un·at·trac·tive·ly /£ˌʌn·əˈtræk·tɪv·li, $-t̬ɪv-/ *adv*

un·auth·o·rized /£ʌnˈɔː·θə·raɪzd, $-ˈɑː-/ *adj* [before n; not gradable] without someone's official permission • *I managed to obtain an unauthorized* **version** *of the play/book/record.* • *This unauthorized* **biography** *of the Princess has sold over 10 000 copies in its first week in print.* • *The Minister complained that there had been too many unauthorized* **leaks** *of information to the press from civil servants.*

un·avail·ing /ˌʌn·əˈveɪ·lɪŋ/ *adj literary* (esp. of an attempt to do something) unsuccessful; having no positive effect • *Diplomatic efforts at peace-making have so far proved unavailing.*

un·a·void·a·ble /ˌʌn·əˈvɔɪ·də·bl̩/ *adj* not avoidable

un·a·ware /£ˌʌn·əˈweəʳ, $-ˈwer/ *adj* [after v] not aware • *He was unaware* **that** *the police were watching him.* [+ *that* clause] • *She remained quite unaware* **of** *the illegal activities of her husband.*

un·a·wares /£ˌʌn·əˈweəz, $-ˈwerz/ *adv* suddenly and unexpectedly without any warning • *The overnight invasion* **took** *the military experts unawares.* • *The prime minster seemed to have been* **caught** *unawares by* (= was not expecting) *this sudden attack of criticism.*

un·bal·ance *obj* /ʌmˈbæl·ənts/ *v* [T] to cause not to balance

un·bal·anced /ʌmˈbæl·əntst/ *adj* • A person who is unbalanced is mentally ill.

un·bear·a·ble /£ʌmˈbeə·rə·bl̩, $-ˈber·ə-/ *adj* so unpleasant or painful that you cannot or do not want to experience or deal with it; INTOLERABLE • *All I remember of childbirth was the unbearable pain and the relief when it was all over.* • *Can you imagine how proud of herself she'll be if she gets this job – she'll be unbearable!* • *The atmosphere at work at the moment is quite unbearable.* • *I'm afraid I can't listen to any more reports about the war – the whole thing is just unbearable.* • *It was a very beautiful country but I found the heat unbearable.*

un·bear·a·bly /£ʌmˈbeə·rə·bli, $-ˈber·ə-/ *adv* • *The sun was almost unbearably hot today and I spent most of the day in the water.* • *It's a very good film but it's unbearably sad.* • *I found him condescending and almost unbearably smug.*

un·beat·a·ble /£ʌmˈbiː·tə·bl̩, $-t̬ə-/ *adj* [not gradable] *approving* unable to be defeated or improved because of excellent quality • *The 23-year-old US tennis star looks unbeatable this season.* • *For good pizzas at a reasonable price they're unbeatable.*

un·be·known /£ˌʌm·bɪˈnəʊn, $-ˈnoʊn/, **un·be·knownst** /£ˌʌm·bɪˈnəʊnst, $-ˈnoʊnst/ *adv* [not gradable] *fml* without the knowledge of • *Unbeknown* **to** *me* (= without me knowing), *he'd gone and rented out the apartment in my absence.*

un·be·liev·a·ble SURPRISING /ˌʌm·bɪˈliː·və·bl̩/ *adj* extremely surprising • *She eats an unbelievable amount of food and yet she's really thin.* • *I've never known anyone with such an ego – he's unbelievable.* • *So Robert's blaming me for everything now, is he? It's unbelievable!* • *You've had such bad luck it's unbelievable.* • *You should see her wardrobe – it's unbelievable – she's got about fifty pairs of shoes.*

un·be·liev·a·bly /ˌʌm·bɪˈliː·və·bli/ *adv* • *He works unbelievably hard.* • *It was an unbelievably stupid thing to do.*

un·be·liev·a·ble UNLIKELY /ˌʌm·bɪˈliː·və·bl̩/ *adj* unable to be believed because unlikely • *I found most of the characters in the play totally unbelievable.*

un·be·liev·er /£ˌʌm·bɪˈliː·vəʳ, $-vɚ/ *n* [C] a person who does not have any religious beliefs • *Most church schools are nevertheless open to unbelievers, whom they do not attempt to convert.*

un·bend /ʌmˈbend/ *v* [I] *past* **unbent** /ʌmˈbent/ to relax and become less formal and serious in your manner • *I'd hoped that after a glass or two of wine she might unbend a little*

un·bend·ing /ʌmˈben·dɪŋ/ *adj fml* (of a person) tending to make fixed judgments and decisions which he or she is unwilling to change • *He has earned a reputation as a stern and unbending politician.*

un·bi·ased /ʌmˈbaɪəst/ *adj* not **biased**, see at BIAS

un·bid·den /ʌmˈbɪd·ᵊn/ *adj, adv literary* not invited or wanted • *During the day he left her alone but at night his image would come unbidden into her mind.*

un·bind *obj* /ʌmˈbaɪnd/ *v* [T] *past* **unbound** /ʌmˈbaʊnd/ to release (someone or something) from a rope, string, etc. that has been tying them up • *My hands were unbound and my blindfold removed.*

un·bleached /ʌmˈbliːtʃt/ *adj* [not gradable] (esp. of flour or material) not made white artificially by the use of chemicals • *We bought an unbleached cotton duvet.* • *I buy unbleached flour from the local health food store.*

un·blem·ished /ʌmˈblem·ɪʃt/ *adj* (esp. of a reputation, character etc.) not spoiled in any way; faultless • *For six years his championship record was unblemished.* • *He has given 38 years to the prison service and has an unblemished career.*

un·born /£ʌmˈbɔːn, $-ˈbɔːrn/ *adj* [not gradable] not yet born; in the mother's womb • *The opponents of abortion see the operation as a crime – they say nobody has the right to murder an unborn child.* • LP **Age**

un·bound·ed /ʌmˈbaʊn·dɪd/ *adj* (esp. of positive feelings) very great; seeming to have no limits • *The president's unbounded optimism about the new British leader has been worrying close advisers.*

un·bri·dled /ʌmˈbraɪ·dl̩d/ *adj esp. literary or fml* not controlled or limited • *unbridled passion/lust/ambition/enthusiasm/optimism* • *We need to campaign against the unbridled use of the motor car.*

un·buck·le *obj* /ʌmˈbʌk·l̩/ *v* [T] to unfasten (a shoe, belt, etc.) by releasing its BUCKLE (= metal fastener)

un·bur·den *obj* /£ʌmˈbɜː·dᵊn, $-ˈbɜːr-/ *v* [T] to free (yourself) of something that is worrying you, by talking about it to someone • *Talking to a psychotherapist was a way of unburdening himself* **of** *a lot of worries and buried anger.* • *He's happy to unburden himself* **to** *anyone who'll listen.*

un·called for /£ʌŋˈkɔːld, $-kɑːld/ *adj disapproving* (esp. of a criticism or insult) unfair and/or unkind and therefore considered to be unnecessary • *an uncalled-for remark* • *How could she have made such a cruel joke about his lame leg – I think it was totally uncalled for.*

un·can·ny /ʌŋˈkæn·i/ *adj* **-ier, -iest** strange or mysterious; difficult or impossible to explain • *It's uncanny how much you and Elizabeth look like sisters.* • *The old guy has an uncanny ability to pick the winning horse.*

un·can·ni·ly /ʌŋˈkæn·ɪ·li/ *adv* • *The fortune-teller's predictions turned out to be uncannily accurate.*

un·cared for /£ʌŋˈkeəd, $-ˈkerd/ *adj* not taken care of well enough • *She was left alone and uncared for in her old age.* • *The old house had an uncared-for look.*

un·car·ing /£ʌŋˈkeə·rɪŋ, $-ˈker·ɪŋ/ *adj disapproving* not worrying about other people's troubles or doing anything to help them • *The bishop criticized the government for its "callous, uncaring attitude" to the homeless and the unemployed.*

un·ceas·ing /ʌnˈsiː·sɪŋ/ *adj fml* continuing and unlikely to stop or become less • *Unceasing efforts have been made to solve these problems.* • *The authors are grateful for the unceasing support of the editors in London and New York.*

un·ceas·ing·ly /ʌnˈsiː·sɪŋ·li/ *adv*

un·cer·e·mon·i·ous /£ʌnˌser·ɪˈməʊ·ni·əs, $-ˈmoʊ-/ *adj fml* done in a rude, sudden or informal way • *an unceremonious refusal* • *an unceremonious dismissal note* • *Meeting Lord Portish and his wife, I was pleasantly surprised by their unceremonious, relaxed attitude to life.*

un·cer·e·mon·i·ous·ly /£ʌnˌser·ɪˈməʊ·ni·ə·sli, $-ˈmoʊ-/ *adv fml* • *He was unceremoniously removed from the list of members, for gross misconduct.*

un·cer·tain /£ʌnˈsɜː·tᵊn, $-ˈsɜːr-/ *adj* (of a person) not knowing what to do or believe, or (of a situation) not fixed or able to be completely known • *She's uncertain* **whether** *to go to New Zealand or not.* [+ *wh-* word] • *Ever since we heard the rumour that the factory might be closing, we've been uncertain* **of** *our position.* • *New arrivals face an uncertain* **future**. • *The political outlook is* **still** *uncertain.* • *The weather is rather uncertain at the moment.* • *I'm afraid he does have a bit of an uncertain temper* (= his moods can change suddenly). • LP **Question mark**

un·cer·tain·ly /£ʌn'sɜː·tᵊn·li, $-'sɜːr-/ *adv* • *He greeted me uncertainly and asked if he was in the right place.*

un·cer·tain·ty /£ʌn'sɜː·tᵊn·ti, $-'sɜːr·t̬ᵊn·t̬i/ *n* • *Nothing is ever decided, and all the uncertainty is very bad for staff morale.* [U] • *The only thing I'm sure of is that life is full of uncertainties.* [C]

un·chal·lenged /ʌn'tʃæl·ɪndʒd/ *adj* accepted without being questioned or criticized • *We can't allow her comments to* go *unchallenged.*

un·char·i·ta·ble /£ʌn'tʃær·ɪ·tə·bl̩, $-'tʃer·ə·t̬ə-/ *adj* unkind and unfair • *It was uncharitable to call him stupid – he was just exhausted from jetlag.*

un·char·i·ta·bly /£ʌn'tʃær·ɪ·tə·bli, $-'ter·ə·t̬ə-/ *adv* • *He felt that she judged him uncharitably.*

un·chart·ed /£ʌn'tʃɑː·tɪd, $-'tʃɑːr·t̬ɪd/ *adj literary* (of a situation) completely new and therefore never before described • *Nuclear fusion has taken physicists into uncharted* **seas/territory/waters** (= a new and unknown area).

un·checked /ʌn'tʃekt/ *adj* (esp. of something harmful) continuing or increasing without or despite any limits or attempts to prevent it • *If present trends* **go/continue** *unchecked there will be a major epidemic of heart disease in the next five years.* • *There was an unchecked frenzy of share buying that ended in disaster.* • *The war raged on, unchecked* **by** *the UN's efforts to stop it.*

un·christ·ian /ʌŋ'krɪs·tjən/ *adj* not good, kind or caring about other people; not showing the qualities expected of a Christian • *We quarrelled with unchristian ferocity.* • *The motives that led her parents to forbid their friendship were so unreasonable, so unchristian, that it was hard to understand them.*

un·ci·vil /ʌn'sɪv·ᵊl/ *adj fml* not polite • *He was most uncivil* **to** *your father – called him an old fool.* • See also INCIVILITY.

un·civ·i·lly /ʌn'sɪv·ɪ·li/ *adv*

un·civ·i·lized, *Br and Aus usually* **-ised** /ʌn'sɪv·ɪ·laɪzd/ *adj* not CIVILIZED, esp. below the usual standards of Western society • *Conditions in these inner-city housing estates can be pretty uncivilized.* • *(infml) Sorry to phone you at such an uncivilized* (= very early or very late) *hour.*

un·cle /'ʌŋ·kl̩/ *n* [C] the brother of someone's mother or father, or the husband of someone's aunt • *I've got several uncles and aunts.* • *He's my Uncle George.* • *Did you bring me a present, Uncle Jack?* [as form of address] • *Hello, uncle.* [as form of address] • A man who is not a relative but who is a close friend of the family is also sometimes called uncle by children: *One of our neighbours became such a good family friend that when I was a child I called him Uncle Bruno.* • If you are male and your brother or sister has a child, you become an uncle yourself: *How strange to be 15 years old and yet have two little nieces who call me Uncle Ali.* • *(dated infml) "Who was at the reception?" "Oh,* **(old) Uncle Tom Cobleigh and all** (= everyone, including the least important or famous)*."* • *"Uncle Tom's Cabin"* (title of a book by Harriet Beecher Stowe, 1852) • PIC **Family tree**

un·clean /ʌŋ'kliːn/ *adj* not clean and therefore likely to cause disease • *The health risk from drinking unclean water is considerable.* • *(fml) Jews and Muslims consider pigs unclean* (= They do not eat pigs because their religions say they are not clean or pure).

un·clear /£ʌŋ'klɪəʳ, $-'klɪr/ *adj* not obvious or easy to see or know • *The ownership of the painting remains unclear.* • *It's unclear* **wh**at *actually happened that night.* [+ *wh-* word] • *It's unclear* **wh**ether *he arrived before or after the shot was fired.* [+ *wh-* word] • If you are unclear **about** something, you are not certain about it: *I'm unclear about a couple of points in your proposal – could you go over them again?* • *I'm unclear* **(as to) wh**ether *we're meant to stay here or not.* [+ *wh-* word]

un·clear·ly /£ʌn'klɪə·li, $-'klɪr-/ *adv*

Un·cle Sam /ˌʌŋ·kl̩'sæm/ *n* [U] *infml* the United States of America, or its government • *Who is in control of this war – the UN or Uncle Sam?* • Uncle Sam is also an image of a tall thin man with a white beard and a tall hat that is used to represent the US, esp. in political CARTOONS (= drawings).

Un·cle Tom /£ˌʌŋ·kl̩'tɒm, $-'tɑːm/ *n* [C] *disapproving* a black person who is considered to be too eager to help or agree with white people or too willing to accept being treated in a way that is not equal to white people • *Those who have taken courses in Afro-American studies have surely come across the work of Henry Louis Gates and know that he is no Uncle Tom.*

un·com·fort·a·ble /£ʌŋ'kʌmpf·tə·bl̩, $'kʌmp·fɚ·t̬ə-/ *adj* not comfortable or not relaxed or calm • *an uncomfortable chair* • *sitting in an uncomfortable position* • *She felt slightly uncomfortable, meeting him for the first time.*

un·com·fort·a·bly /£ʌŋ'kʌmpf·tə·bli, $-'kʌmp·fɚ·t̬ə-/ *adv* • *The chair was uncomfortably low.* • *They were uncomfortably aware of being in the wrong.*

un·com·mit·ted /£ˌʌŋ·kə'mɪt·ɪd, $-'mɪt̬-/ *adj* having made no promise to support any particular group, plan, belief or action • *Such vague proposals are not going to persuade the average uncommitted voter.* • *Twenty-five senators have admitted they are still uncommitted* **on** *the taxation question.*

uncommon NOT FREQUENT /£ʌŋ'kɒm·ən, $ʌn'kɑː·mən/ *adj* not seen, happening or experienced often • *That type of bird is very uncommon in this part of the world.* • *Accidents due to failure of safety equipment are uncommon nowadays.* • *It's not uncommon for people who have had an experience like that to become very depressed.*

uncommon UNUSUALLY LARGE /£ʌŋ'kɒm·ən, $ʌn'kɑː·mən/ *adj dated fml esp. approving* (esp. of a human quality) unusually large in amount or degree • *She's a woman of uncommon kindness and gentleness.*

un·com·mon·ly /£ʌŋ'kɒm·ən·li, $ʌn'kɑː·mən-/ *adv dated fml* • *"Have a cigar." "That's uncommonly* (= very) *good of you, my dear fellow."*

un·com·mun·i·ca·tive /£ˌʌn·kə'mjuː·nɪ·kə·tɪv, $-t̬ɪv/ *adj* not willing to talk • *Oh, you'll never get him to tell you what happened – he's been so uncommunicative recently.*

un·com·plain·ing /ˌʌŋ·kəm'pleɪ·nɪŋ/ *adj approving* willing to do boring or difficult work patiently and without complaining • *His job is boring, but he is cheerful and uncomplaining, and grateful to have any work at all.*

un·com·plain·ing·ly /ˌʌŋ·kəm'pleɪ·nɪŋ·li/ *adv approving* • *Uncomplainingly, Pat cleared the table and washed the dishes while the others played cards.*

un·com·pli·men·ta·ry /£ʌŋˌkɒm·plɪ'men·tᵊr·i, $-ˌkɑːm·plə'men·t̬ɚ-/ *adj* rudely critical • *She had some very uncomplimentary things to say about you.*

un·com·pro·mis·ing /£ʌŋ'kɒm·prə·maɪ·zɪŋ, $-'kɑːm-/ *adj* (of a person or their beliefs) fixed and not changing, esp. when faced with opposition • *The city council has taken an uncompromising stand against the proposals for the new building.* • *Every note in this performance is played with an uncompromising clarity.*

un·com·pro·mis·ing·ly /£ʌŋ'kɒm·prə·maɪ·zɪŋ·li, $-'kɑːm-/ *adv*

un·con·cerned /£ˌʌŋ·kən'sɜːnd, $-'sɜːrnd/ *adj* not worried or not interested, esp. when you should be worried or interested • *He was strolling around with an unconcerned air.* • *Are you as unconcerned* **about** *the situation as you appear?* • *She seems unconcerned* **by** *the danger of going over budget.* • *Unfortunately, they seem unconcerned* **with** *anything except their own welfare.* • *They're unconcerned* **that** *their action may provoke a war in the region.* [+ *that* clause]

un·con·cern·ed·ly /£ˌʌŋ·kən'sɜː·nɪd·li, $-'sɜːr-/ *adv*

un·con·di·tion·al /ˌʌŋ·kən'dɪʃ·ᵊn·ᵊl/ *adj* complete and not limited in any way • *unconditional surrender* • *the immediate and unconditional release of all political prisoners* • *an unconditional love*

un·con·di·tion·al·ly /ˌʌŋ·kən'dɪʃ·ᵊn·ᵊl·i/ *adv*

un·con·nect·ed /£ˌʌŋ·kə'nek·tɪd, $-t̬ɪd/ *adj* [not gradable] not connected; not related • *It's no longer possible to argue that crime is unconnected* **with** *unemployment.* • *A series of apparently unconnected events led to his resignation.*

un·con·scion·a·ble /£ʌŋ'kɒn·tʃᵊn·ə·bl̩, $-'kɑːn-/ *adj fml disapproving* (of a size, amount, length of time, etc.) too great • *They took an unconscionable time to reply to my letter.* • *Why is the British economy in such an unconscionable mess?*

un·con·scion·a·bly /£ʌŋ'kɒn·tʃᵊn·ə·bli, $-'kɑːn-/ *adv fml disapproving*

un·con·scious /£ʌŋ'kɒn·tʃəs, $-'kɑːn-/ *adj* in the state of having lost consciousness, esp. as the result of a head injury, or (of actions) done without conscious thought • *A stone hit him on the head and knocked him unconscious.* • *That holiday had touched an unconscious desire in me to be free again, and soon afterwards I gave up my job in the big city.* • *I'm not sure whether these things she does are conscious or unconscious* (= whether she knows she is doing them or not).

un·con·scious /£ʌŋ'kɒn·tʃəs, $-'kɑːn-/ *n* [U] • *(specialized)* In PSYCHOANALYSIS, **the unconscious** is the part of the mind which holds the deepest and most hidden thoughts and feelings.

un·con·scious·ly /£ʌŋˈkɒn·tʃə·sli, $-ˈkɑːn-/ *adv*

un·con·scious·ness /£ʌŋˈkɒn·tʃə·snəs, $-ˈkɑːn-/ *n* [U]

un·con·sid·ered /£ˌʌŋ·kənˈsɪd·əd, $-ɚd/ *adj fml* (of an action) not carefully thought about • *He takes unconsidered decisions which tend to land him in trouble.*

un·con·sti·tu·tion·al /£ʌŋˌkɒn·stɪˈtjuː·ʃən·əl, $-ˌkɑːn·stɪˈtuː-/ *adj* not allowed by the CONSTITUTION (= set of rules for government) of a country or organization • *Such a change in the law would be unconstitutional.*

un·con·sti·tu·tion·al·ly /£ʌŋˌkɒn·stɪˈtjuː·ʃən·əl·i, $-ˌkɑːn·stɪˈtuː-/ *adv*

un·con·trol·la·ble /£ˌʌŋ·kənˈtrəʊ·lə·bl̩, $-ˈtroʊ-/ *adj* too strong or violent to be controlled • *I was suddenly overcome with an uncontrollable desire to hit him.*

un·con·trol·la·bly /£ˌʌŋ·kənˈtrəʊ·lə·bli, $-ˈtroʊ-/ *adv* • *I arrived home to find him* **sobbing** *uncontrollably on the doorstep.*

un·con·trolled /£ˌʌŋ·kənˈtrəʊld, $-ˈtroʊld/ *adj* • *uncontrolled aggression* • *the uncontrolled spread of dangerous drugs*

un·con·ven·tion·al /ˌʌŋ·kənˈven·tʃən·əl/ *adj* different from what is usual or from the way most people do things • *He has an unconventional golf technique.* • *They have an unconventional attitude to marriage and lead quite separate lives.*

un·con·ven·tion·al·ly /ˌʌŋ·kənˈven·tʃən·əl·i/ *adv*

un·con·vinc·ing /ˌʌŋ·kənˈvɪnt·sɪŋ/ *adj* (esp. of an explanation or story) that does not sound or seem true or real • *They produced some rather unconvincing explanations for the system failure.* • *The dialogue was unconvincing, partly because it was American actors trying to speak London English.*

un·con·vinc·ing·ly /ˌʌŋ·kənˈvɪnt·sɪŋ·li/ *adv* • *He spoke unconvincingly about the need for caution.*

un·co·op·er·a·tive /£ˌʌŋ·kəʊˈɒp·ər·ə·tɪv, $-koʊˈɑː·pɚ·ə·t̬ɪv/ *adj* not willing to work with or be helpful to other people • *I will never try to work with anyone so rude and uncooperative again.*

un·co·op·er·a·tive·ly /£ˌʌŋ·kəʊˈɒp·ər·ə·tɪv·li, $-koʊˈɑː·pɚ·ə·t̬ɪv·li/ *adv*

un·co·op·er·a·tive·ness /£ˌʌŋ·kəʊˈɒp·ər·ə·tɪv·nəs, $-koʊˈɑː·pɚ·ə·t̬ɪv-/ *n* [U]

un·co·or·din·at·ed /£ˌʌŋ·kəʊˈɔː·dɪn·eɪ·tɪd, $-koʊˈɔːr·dɪ·neɪ·t̬ɪd/ *adj* with different parts failing to work or move well together • *The marketing campaign was an uncoordinated effort by several different departments.* • *She was clumsy and uncoordinated as a girl.*

un·cork *obj* /£ʌŋˈkɔːk, $-ˈkɔːrk/ *v* [T] to open (a bottle) by pulling out its CORK (= cylindrical piece of soft wood used to close it) • *"Who's for some more wine?" asked Polly, uncorking another bottle.*

un·count·a·ble /£ʌŋˈkaʊn·tə·bl̩, $-t̬ə-/ *adj* [not gradable] *specialized* (of a noun) naming something that you can have more or less of but that you cannot count or have many of • *Words like 'electricity', 'blood' and 'happiness' are uncountable – you cannot say 'two electricities', 'a lot of bloods' or 'many happinesses' – and they are marked* [U] *in this dictionary.* • Compare **countable** at COUNT [NUMBER].

un·coup·le *obj* /ʌŋˈkʌp·l̩/ *v* [T] to separate (two things joined together) • *The engine had been uncoupled* **from** *the rest of the train.* • *Uncoupling the Labour Party* **from** *the unions was always going to be a difficult, painful process.*

un·couth /ʌŋˈkuːθ/ *adj disapproving* (of a person or their behaviour) lacking grace, politeness and a pleasant appearance; rude and/or unpleasant • *All these punk bands were aggressive and uncouth.*

un·cov·er *obj* /£ʌŋˈkʌv·əʳ, $-ɚ/ *v* [T] to discover (something secret or hidden) or remove (something covering something else) • *The investigation uncovered evidence of a large-scale illegal trade in wild birds.* • *In her biography of Taylor, she attempts to uncover the inner man.* • *He pulled back the sheet, to uncover a beautiful 18th-century armchair.* • If you uncover something buried under the ground, you find it by removing the earth on top of it: *Digging in her garden, she uncovered a hoard of gold dating back to the 9th century.*

un·cri·ti·cal /£ʌŋˈkrɪt·ɪ·kəl, $-ˈkrɪt̬-/ *adj often disapproving* accepting something too easily, because of being unwilling or unable to criticize • *He naturally prefers an adoring, uncritical audience.* • *The Daily News' uncritical acceptance of the official statistics is most surprising.*

un·cri·ti·cal·ly /£ʌŋˈkrɪt·ɪ·kli, $-ˈkrɪt̬-/ *adv often disapproving*

un·crowned king *male, female* **un·crowned queen** /ˌʌnˈkraʊnd, ˌʌŋ-/ *n* [C] a person who is considered to be the best, the most famous or the most powerful in a particular area of life, esp. when they do not have an official rank or title • *Django Reinhardt, the uncrowned king* **of** *jazz guitarists*

un·crush·a·ble /ˌʌŋˈkrʌʃ·ə·bl̩/ *adj* [not gradable] (of cloth) made of an artificial fibre and designed to stay free of unwanted folds • *an uncrushable hat*

unc·tu·ous /ˈʌŋk·tju·əs/ *adj fml disapproving* (of a person or their manner) full of praise, interest, friendliness, etc. that is unpleasant because it is false • *He came up to me, oozing unctuous sympathy, hoping that I would buy him a drink.*

un·cut /ʌŋˈkʌt/ *adj* [not gradable] complete and in its original form • *In the original uncut version of the film, there was a long and bloody death scene.* • *Uncut diamonds are worth less than those that have been cut and shaped.*

un·dat·ed /£ʌnˈdeɪ·tɪd, $-t̬ɪd/ *adj* [not gradable] (of something such as a letter) without a DATE • *The cheque was undated.*

un·daunt·ed /£ʌnˈdɔːn·tɪd, $-ˈdɑːn·t̬ɪd/ *adj* [after v] *slightly literary* still determined and enthusiastic, despite problems or lack of success • *Undaunted* **by** *the cold and the rain, people danced until 2 am.* • *The team* **remain** *undaunted, despite three defeats in a row.*

un·de·cid·ed /ˌʌn·dɪˈsaɪ·dɪd/ *adj* (of a person) not having made a decision or judgment about something, or (of something) not decided or finished • *Are you still undecided* **about** *the job in Brussels?* • *54% of voters were in favour, 30% against, and the rest were undecided.* • *The whole question is still undecided.*

un·de·fin·a·ble /ˌʌn·dɪˈfaɪ·nə·bl̩/ *adj Am and Aus for* INDEFINABLE

un·de·ni·a·ble /ˌʌn·dɪˈnaɪ·ə·bl̩/ *adj* so obviously true that it cannot be doubted • *Mr Jones' good intentions are undeniable.* • *She's a woman of undeniable brilliance.*

un·de·ni·a·bly /ˌʌn·dɪˈnaɪ·ə·bli/ *adv* • *She is undeniably brilliant.*

un·der [LOWER POSITION] /£ˈʌn·dəʳ, $-dɚ/ *prep* in or to a position below or lower than (something else), often so that one thing covers the other • *He hid under the bed.* • *I'll leave the key under the mat for you, okay?* • *In AD 79 the city of Pompei was buried under a layer of ash seven metres deep.* • *She put the thermometer under my tongue.* • *She was holding a file under her arm* (= between her upper arm and the side of her chest). • *If I don't get at least seven hours sleep, I get bags under my eyes* (= dark marks develop on my face below my eyes). • *If you've burnt your finger, put it under the cold tap* (= hold it so that the water flows over it). • *In 1913, a woman called Emily Wilding Davidson threw herself under the hooves of the King's horse during a race, to protest about not being able to vote.* • *They stood under a tree* (= below its branches) *to avoid getting wet.* • *The pedestrian subway runs under the main road* (= it goes from one side of the road to the other, below the ground). • *People born under* (= during the period of) *the star sign Pisces are supposed to be dreamy and artistic.* • *Under* (= When looked at with) *a microscope, a human hair seems to be the size of a piece of string.* • *(fig.) The company's accounts were put under the microscope* (= examined very carefully) *by the tax investigators.* • *(specialized)* If a piece of land is under a particular type of plant, that plant is growing on the whole of that area: *The main fields are under wheat.* ○ *What percentage of the land is under cultivation* (= planted with crops)*?* • *(fig.) I wonder what Britain was like under the Romans* (= during the time when the Romans controlled Britain). • *(fig.) He's a Colonel, with hundreds of soldiers under him* (= obeying his orders). • *(fig.) She* **fell** *under his influence/spell* (= He had a strong and probably negative effect on her) *when he was her tutor at university.* • *(fig. Br usually humorous) "Are you ill?" "Yes, I've got a virus and I've been under the doctor* (= been treated by a doctor)*."* • If a book, article, or piece of information is under a particular title, you can find it there: *Books on Cecil Beaton will probably be under Art or Photography, not under Drama.* ○ *Trifle? That* **comes** *under Puddings and Desserts.* • Compare OVER [HIGHER POSITION]. • [PIC] **Prepositions of movement** Ⓝ Ⓢ

un·der /£ˈʌn·dəʳ, $-dɚ/ *adv* [not gradable] • *Because I'm a bad swimmer, I often go under* (= go below the surface of the water) *and swallow a lot of water.* • *(fig.) Thousands of* *companies went under* (= were unsuccessful and had to stop doing business) *during the recession.*

un·der– /£ˈʌn·dəʳ-, $-dɚ-/ *combining form* • *Remember to put an under-blanket on the bed before you put the sheet on.* • An **under-secretary** is a person who works for and has a slightly lower rank than the SECRETARY (= person in charge) of a government department: *She's Under-Secretary of State for Foreign Affairs.* • Compare **over-** at OVER [HIGHER POSITION].

un·der [LESS THAN] /£ˈʌn·dəʳ, $-dɚ/ *prep* less than • *All items cost/are under a pound.* • *The discount applies only to children under* **(the age of)** *ten* (= younger than ten). • *If you get under 50%, you've failed the exam.* • Ⓝ Ⓢ

un·der /£ˈʌn·dəʳ, $-dɚ/ *adv* [not gradable] • *These toys would be suitable for kids of five and under.*

un·der– /£ˈʌn·dəʳ-, $-dɚ-/ *combining form* • Under- means not enough, or not done as well or as much as is necessary: *Five minutes isn't long enough to boil potatoes – these are undercooked.* ○ *We're all overworked and underpaid.* ○ *His boss says he's under-performing* (= not doing as well as he should) *at work.* • Compare **over-** at OVER [MORE THAN].

un·der [EXPERIENCING] /£ˈʌn·dəʳ, $-dɚ/ *prep* happening during, as a result of or according to (a particular situation, event, rule, etc.) • *The work was completed under very difficult conditions.* • *I hate being/going under anaesthetic.* • *Now that the deadline is approaching we all feel under pressure.* • *The chair broke under his weight* (= because he was too heavy for it). • *The global ecosystem is breaking down under the demands imposed on it by human beings.* • *Peace talks began last year under the auspices/aegis* (= with the official support) *of the United Nations.* • *Under the present rules, you can buy ten litres of wine.* • Someone or something that is under attack, discussion, etc. is in the process of being attacked, discussed, etc.: *The town is under fire* (= is being attacked) *from the air.* ○ *The proposals are now under consideration by the Board of Governors.* ○ *The police deny it, but I'm sure she's under suspicion.* ○ *The situation is still not under control.* • To be under an **impression/belief** is to have it: *He was under the mistaken belief* (= He believed wrongly) *that I was in charge.* • *(specialized)* If you are under **oath**, you have promised to tell the truth, usually in a law court: *Once in the courthouse, they were too frightened to lie under oath, so the whole story came out.* • If you are under **orders** to do something, you have been ordered to do it: *They are under strict orders not to talk about their salaries or working conditions.* ○ *He's under* **doctor's** *orders* (= been told by a doctor) *to cut down on fatty food.* • If you do something, write something or live somewhere under a particular name, you use that name while you are doing it or living there: *He writes under the name* **(of)** *John le Carré.* ○ *For his own safety, he has to operate under a false name/an alias.* • If something is **under way** it is happening now: *Economic recovery is* **already** *under way.* ○ *The film festival* **gets** *under way* (= begins) *on 11th July.* • Ⓝ Ⓢ

un·der /£ˈʌn·dəʳ, $-dɚ/ *adj* [after v; not gradable] • *In major operations, a patient can be under* (= unconscious because of a medical drug) *for six hours or more.*

un·der·a·chieve /£ˌʌn·də·rəˈtʃiːv, $-dɚ·ə-/ *v* [I] to do less well than you could or should • *The teacher said Paul was underachieving, because he was getting Bs and Cs when he should be getting As.*

un·der·a·chiev·er /£ˌʌn·də·rəˈtʃiː·vəʳ, $-dɚ·əˈtʃiː·vɚ/ *n* [C]

un·der·age /£ˌʌn·dəˈreɪdʒ, $-dɚˈeɪdʒ/ *adj* [not gradable] younger than the lowest age at which a particular activity is legally or usually allowed • *There are laws against underage sex and underage drinking.* • *What's that kid doing in the bar? He's clearly underage.*

un·der·arm [TOP OF ARM] /£ˈʌn·də·rɑːm, $-dɚ·ɑːrm/ *adj* [before n], *adv* [not gradable] used to avoid saying ARMPIT (= hollow place under the top of your arm) • *underarm deodorants/odours* • *(Br) Do you shave underarm?*

un·der·arm /£ˈʌn·də·rɑːm, $-dɚ·ɑːrm/ *n* [C] • *Do you shave your underarms?*

un·der·arm [THROW] /£ˈʌn·də·rɑːm, $-dɚ·ɑːrm/, *Am also* **un·der·hand** *adj, adv* [not gradable] (done by) moving the arm below shoulder level • *underarm bowling* • *He bowled underarm for the younger children.*

un·der·bel·ly /£ˈʌn·dəˌbel·i, $-dɚ-/ *n* [U] *literary* the weakest or most unpleasant part of something which is most likely to fail or be easily defeated • *The film* **exposes** *the sordid underbelly of modern urban society.* • *Small businesses are the* **soft** *underbelly* (= weakest parts) *of the British economy, and they need as much government support as possible.*

un·der·car·riage /£ˈʌn·dəˌkær·ɪdʒ, $-dɚˌker-/ *n* [C usually sing] *Br for* **landing gear**, see at LAND [ARRIVE]

un·der·charge *(obj)* /£ˌʌn·dəˈtʃɑːdʒ, $-dɚˈtʃɑːrdʒ/ *v* to charge (someone) less than the correct price for something • *It's a pleasant surprise when you find a shop that undercharges* **(for** *its goods).* [I] • *The sales assistant made a mistake and undercharged me* **by** *£2.* [T]

un·der·class /£ˈʌn·də·klɑːs, $-dɚ·klæs/ *n* [C] a group of people with a lower social and economic position than any of the other classes of society • *The long-term unemployed now constitute a sort of underclass.*

un·der·clothes /£ˈʌn·də·kləʊðz, $-dɚ·kloʊðz/ *pl n*, **un·der·cloth·ing** /£ˈʌn·dəˌkləʊ·ðɪŋ, $-dɚˌkloʊ-/ *n* [U] *fml for* UNDERWEAR

un·der·coat /£ˈʌn·də·kəʊt, $-dɚ·koʊt/ *n* a first layer of paint that is put on a surface in order to improve the appearance of the final one, or the paint used for this • *a tin of undercoat* [U] • *Those red walls will probably need two undercoats.* [U] • *Undercoats come in various colours.* [C] • Compare TOPCOAT.

un·der·cov·er /£ˌʌn·dəˈkʌv·əʳ, $-dɚˈkʌv·ɚ/ *adj* [before n; not gradable] (esp. of the police) using a false appearance in order to work secretly • *an undercover police operation* • *an undercover detective*

un·der·cov·er /£ˌʌn·dəˈkʌv·əʳ, $-dɚˈkʌv·ɚ/ *adv* [not gradable] • *He was working undercover at the time – gathering evidence on a London-based drugs ring.*

un·der·cur·rent /£ˈʌn·dəˌkʌr·ᵊnt, $-dɚˌkɜːr-/ *n* [C] an emotion, belief, or characteristic of a situation that is hidden and usually negative or dangerous but that has an indirect effect • *undercurrents of racism/anxiety/violence* • *Beneath the smooth surface of day-to-day political life, one senses powerful and dangerous undercurrents.*

un·der·cut *obj* [CHARGE LESS THAN] /£ˌʌn·dəˈkʌt, $-dɚ-/ *v* [T] **undercutting**, *past* **undercut** to charge less than (a competitor) • *Big supermarkets can undercut all rivals, especially small high-street shops.* • *They claim to undercut their competitors* **by** *at least 5%.*

un·der·cut *obj* [WEAKEN] /£ˌʌn·dəˈkʌt, $-dɚ-/ *v* [T] **undercutting**, *past* **undercut** to weaken, damage or cause to fail; UNDERMINE • *The Americans don't like the proposed agreement, and are clearly intent on undercutting it.*

un·der·de·vel·oped /£ˈʌn·də·dɪˈvel·əpt, $-dɚ-/ *adj* (esp. of a country) without modern industry or modern services that provide transport, health care etc. • *an underdeveloped country* • *the underdeveloped world* • *It's in the poorer, underdeveloped eastern region of the country that the biggest problems exist.*

un·der·dog /£ˈʌn·də·dɒg, $-dɚ·dɑːg/ *n* [C] a person or group of people who have less power, money, etc. than the rest of society, or (in a competition) the person or team considered to be the weakest and the least likely to win • *As a politician, her sympathy was always for* **the** *underdog in society/society's underdogs.* • *The Australian team have been cast in the role of underdogs for this match.*

un·der·done /£ˌʌn·dəˈdʌn, $-dɚ-/ *adj* (esp. of meat) cooked for only a short time, or cooked for less time than is necessary • *I like my steak underdone.* • *These potatoes are underdone – I'll put them back in the oven.*

un·der·dressed /£ˈʌn·dəˈdrest, $-dɚ-/ *adj* wearing clothes that are not attractive enough or formal enough for a particular occasion • *Without a jacket or tie, I felt rather underdressed at their wedding.*

un·der·es·ti·mate *(obj)* /£ˌʌn·dəˈres·tɪ·meɪt, $-dɚˈes-/ *v* to fail to guess or understand the real cost, size, difficulty, etc. of (something), or to fail to understand how strong, skilful, intelligent or determined (someone, esp. a competitor) is • *Originally the builders gave me a price of £2000, but now they say they underestimated and it's going to be at least £3000.* [I] • *One shouldn't underestimate the difficulties of getting all the political parties to the conference table.* [T] • *Never underestimate your enemy!* [T] • *"No man ...has ever lost money by underestimating the intelligence of the great masses of the plain people"* (H.L.Mencken in the *Chicago Tribune*, 1926)

un·der·es·ti·mate /£ˌʌn·dəˈres·tɪ·mət, $-dɚˈes-/ *n* [C] • *Clearly £25 was a serious underestimate.*

un·der·ex·pose *obj* /£ˈʌn·də·rɪkˈspəʊz, $-dɚ·ɪkˈspoʊz/ *v* [T] to give too little light to (a piece of photographic film) when taking a photograph

un·der·floor /£ˌʌn·də'flɔːʳ, $-dɚ'flɔːr/ *adj* [not gradable] *esp. Br* (esp. of a heating system) under the surface of a floor

un·der·foot /£ˌʌn·də'fʊt, $-dɚ-/ *adv* [not gradable] under your feet as you walk; on the ground • *The grass was cool and pleasant underfoot.* • *Many people were* **trampled/crushed** *underfoot when the police tried to break up the demonstration.* • *(fig.) These reactionaries want to* **trample** *underfoot* (= destroy) *everything we have achieved in the last ten years.*

un·der·fund·ed /£ˌʌn·də'fʌn·dɪd, $-dɚ-/ *adj* (of an organization) not supplied with a large enough income • *The government does not admit that the Hospital Service is underfunded.*

un·der·gar·ment /£'ʌn·dəˌgɑː·mənt, $-dɚˌgɑːr-/ *n* [C] *very fml* an item of underwear

un·der·go *obj* /£ˌʌn·də'gəʊ, $-dɚ'goʊ/ *v* [T] he/she/it **undergoes, undergoing,** *past simple* **underwent** /£ˌʌn·də'went, $-dɚ-/, *past part* **undergone** /£ˌʌn·də'gɒn, $-dɚ'gɑːn/ to experience (something which is unpleasant or involves a change) • *She underwent an operation on a tumour in her left lung last year.* • *Cinema in Britain is undergoing a revival of popularity.*

un·der·grad·u·ate /£ˌʌn·də'græd·ju·ət, $-dɚ-/ *n* [C] a student who is studying for their first degree at college or university • Compare GRADUATE [PERSON]. • [LP] **Schools and colleges**

un·der·ground /£ˌʌn·də'graʊnd, $-dɚ-/ *adj, adv* [not gradable] below the surface of the earth; below ground • *an underground cave/passage/cable* • *an underground shopping centre* • *an underground nuclear test site* • *Moles live underground.* • *You can park underground below the cinema.* • Something that happens underground is secret and usually illegal: *an underground newspaper* • *an underground movement* ○ *The Communist Party was forced (to* **go***) underground, and its leaders went into hiding.* ○ *The ban on all other political parties has* **driven** *opposition underground.*

un·der·ground /£'ʌn·də·graʊnd, $-dɚ-/ *n* [U] • *(esp. Br)* **The** underground (*Br also* **tube,** *Am* **subway**) is a railway system in which electric trains travel along passages below ground: *the London Underground system* ○ *They went* **on the/by** *Underground.* • **The** underground is also a group of people who secretly fight against the government: *a member of the underground* ○ *The role the underground played was to harass the occupying forces with a campaign of bombings and assassinations.* • **The** underground is also those people in a society who are trying new and often shocking or illegal ways of living or forms of art: *In Britain and the USA in the 1970s the underground was a powerful subversive force.* ○ *She began her career working in underground films.*

un·der·growth /£'ʌn·də·grəʊθ, $-dɚ·groʊθ/ *n* [U] a mass of bushes, small trees and plants growing under the trees of a wood or forest • *I dreamt of grizzly bears crashing through the undergrowth.* • *Police discovered the body hidden in thick undergrowth.*

un·der·hand [SECRETIVE] /£ˌʌn·də'hænd, $-dɚ-/, *Am usually* **un·der·hand·ed** /£ˌʌn·də'hæn·dɪd, $-dɚ-/ *adj disapproving* done secretly, and sometimes dishonestly, in order to achieve an advantage • *What really angered her was the dirty underhand way they had tricked her.* • *It was an underhanded attempt to win the contract for himself.*

un·der·hand [THROW] /£ˌʌn·də'hænd, $-dɚ-/ *adj, adv* [not gradable] *Am for* UNDERARM

un·der·lay /£'ʌn·dᵊl·eɪ, $-dɚ·leɪ/ *n* [U] *Br and Aus* thick material put between a CARPET and the floor for extra comfort and to protect the carpet and keep the room warm. It can also be used to make an uneven floor seem level. • *felt/foam underlay* • *a piece of underlay*

un·der·lie *obj* /£ˌʌn·də'laɪ, $-dɚ-/ *v* [T] **underlying,** *past simple* **underlay** /£ˌʌn·də'leɪ, $-dɚ-/, *past part* **underlain** /£ˌʌn·də'leɪn, $-dɚ-/ to be an esp. hidden cause of or strong influence on (something) • *The key events which underlie many of the present government's troubles took place in 1918-22.* • *Psychological problems very often underlie apparently physical disorders.* • *Professor Hill reveals the principles which underlay the political ideology and actions of the party during the 1920s.*

un·der·ly·ing /£ˌʌn·də'laɪ·ɪŋ, $-dɚ-/ *adj* [before n; not gradable] • *And what might be the underlying* (= real but not immediately obvious) *significance of these supposedly random acts of violence?*

un·der·line *obj* /£ˌʌn·də'laɪn, $-dɚ-/, **un·der·score** *v* [T] to draw a line under (a word), esp. in order to show its importance • *All the technical words have been underlined* **in** *red.* • Underline also means to emphasize: *She put the figures up on the board to underline the seriousness of the situation.* ○ *To underline their disgust, the crowd started throwing bottles at the stage.* ○ *This series of victories will underline their claim to be a top class team.* ○ *Management are underlining* **that** *no one will lose their job.* [+ *that* clause]

un·der·ling /£'ʌn·dᵊl·ɪŋ, $-dɚ·lɪŋ/ *n* [C] *disapproving* a person of low rank and little authority who works for someone more important • *She surrounded herself with underlings who were too afraid of her to ever answer back.*

un·der·manned /£ˌʌn·də'mænd, $-dɚ-/ *adj dated for* UNDERSTAFFED

un·der·men·tioned /£ˌʌn·də'men·tʃᵊnd, $-dɚ-/ *adj* [before noun; not gradable] *fml* that can be found in a later part of the same text • *the undermentioned figures* • *The undermentioned staff all wish to join the union.* • Compare **above-mentioned** at ABOVE.

un·der·mine *obj* /£ˌʌn·də'maɪn, $-dɚ-/ *v* [T] to weaken (esp. someone's power or chances of success), often gradually • *The President has accused two cabinet ministers of working secretly to undermine his position/him.* • *The killings have undermined* **hopes** *for a peaceful solution.* • *Every mistake that she makes further undermines her authority/her.* • *Criticism undermines their confidence.* • *A fall in interest rates might undermine sterling.*

un·der·neath /£ˌʌn·də'niːθ, $-dɚ-/ *prep, adv* [not gradable] under or below • *The tunnel goes right underneath the city.* • *They found a bomb underneath the car.* • *Underneath that shy exterior, she's actually a very warm person.* • *He was wearing a garish T-shirt underneath his shirt.* • *When the painting was restored, a much older picture was discovered underneath.*

un·der·neath /£ˌʌn·də'niːθ, $-dɚ-/ *n* [U] • **The** underneath is the lower part or surface: *Bake it in the oven for half an hour – the top should be brown and crisp, and the underneath moist and succulent.*

un·der·nour·ished /£ˌʌn·də'nʌr·ɪʃt, $-dɚ'nɜːr-/ *adj* not eating enough food to maintain good health • *Many of the children are undernourished and suffering from serious diseases.*

un·der·pants /£'ʌn·də·pænts, $-dɚ-/, *Br also* **pants** *pl n* a piece of underwear covering the area between the waist and the tops of the legs • *a pair of underpants* • 'Underpants' usually refers to men's and boy's underwear. Compare PANTIES; KNICKERS.

un·der·pass /£'ʌn·də·pɑːs, $-dɚ·pæs/, *Br and Aus* **sub·way** *n* [C] a road or path that goes under something such as a busy road, allowing vehicles or people to go from one side to the other • *You can risk the traffic or you can use the underpass, smelly and horrible though it is.*

un·der·pay *obj* /£ˌʌn·də'peɪ, $-dɚ-/ *v* [T usually passive] *past* **underpaid** /£ˌʌn·də'peɪd, $-dɚ-/ to pay (someone) too little for the work they do • *She reckons her employer has been underpaying her by £50 per week.*

un·der·paid /£ˌʌn·də'peɪd, $-dɚ-/ *adj* • *underpaid staff/teachers/workers* • *They're ridiculously underpaid, especially as the work is so dangerous.*

un·der·pin *obj* /£ˌʌn·də'pɪn, $-dɚ-/ *v* [T] **-nn-** to give support, strength or a basic structure to (something) • *He presented very few facts to underpin his argument.* • *It's a fast-moving film, underpinned by an exciting soundtrack.* • *Gradually the laws that underpinned* (= formed part of the basic structure of) *apartheid were abolished.* • *Better trade figures are underpinning the dollar* (= keeping it at a higher level). • *When restoring the building, the first priority was to underpin the exterior walls by adding wooden supports along the foundations.*

un·der·pin·ning /£ˌʌn·də'pɪn·ɪŋ, $-dɚ-/ *n* [C] • *Such behaviour attacks the moral underpinning of* (= structure that supports) *society.* • *After a while, we found ourselves questioning the spiritual and philosophical underpinnings of the American way of life.*

un·der·play *obj* /£ˌʌn·də'pleɪ, $-dɚ-/ *v* [T] to make (something such as a dangerous situation) seem less important or dangerous than it really is • *While not wanting to underplay the seriousness of the situation, I have to say that it is not as bad as people seem to think.*

un·der·pri·vi·leged /£ˌʌn·də'prɪv·ɪ·lɪdʒd, $-dɚ-/ *adj* lacking the money, possessions, education, opportunities, etc. that the average person has • *Children from an underprivileged family background are statistically more* *likely to become involved in crime.* • *The charity raises money for holidays for* **the underprivileged** (=poor people).

un·der·rate *obj* /ˌʌn·dəˈreɪt/ *v* [T] to fail to understand how skilful, important, etc. (someone or something) is • *The company has consistently underrated the importance of a well-trained workforce.*

un·der·rat·ed /£ˌʌn·dəˈreɪ·tɪd, $-t̬ɪd/ *adj* • *In my opinion, fennel is a really underrated vegetable – few people here seem to realize how delicious it is.*

un·der·score *obj* /£ˌʌn·dəˈskɔːʳ, $-dɚˈskɔːr/ *v* [T] to UNDERLINE

un·der·sea /£ˌʌn·dəˈsiː, $-dɚ-/ *adj* [before n; not gradable] below the surface of the sea • *undersea exploration* • *an undersea experimental station*

un·der·sell *obj* LOW PRICE /£ˌʌn·dəˈsel, $-dɚ-/ *v* [T] *past* **undersold** /£ˌʌn·dəˈsəʊld, $-dɚˈsoʊld/ to sell goods at a price lower than (a competitor) • *A big supermarket can usually undersell a small local store.*

un·der·sell *obj* BE MODEST /£ˌʌn·dəˈsel, $-dɚ-/ *v* [T] *past* **undersold** /£ˌʌn·dəˈsəʊld, $-dɚˈsoʊld/ to not give (someone, esp. yourself, or something) the praise they deserve • *She's a great sportswoman, but she tends to undersell her***self** *to the media and give too much credit to her teammates.* • *I feel that the book undersells Washington's cultural scene.*

un·der·shirt /£ˈʌn·də·ʃɜːt, $-dɚ·ʃɜːrt/ *n* [C] *Am for* VEST

un·der·side /£ˈʌn·də·saɪd, $-dɚ-/ *n* [C usually sing] the side of something that is usually nearest the ground • *The car had turned over in the ditch, and its underside was covered in oil and mud.*

un·der·signed /£ˌʌn·dəˈsaɪnd, $-dɚ-/ *pl n* **the undersigned** *fml* the people whose signatures appear below in the text, usually at the end of a formal letter • *We, the undersigned, strongly object to the closure of St. Mary's Hospital: Jack James (Dr), Philippa Curry (Dr), Hugh Edwards.*

un·der·sized /£ˌʌn·dəˈsaɪzd, $-dɚ-/, **un·der·size** /£ˌʌn·dəˈsaɪz, $-dɚ-/ *adj* smaller than average, or smaller than it should be • *an undersized, malnourished boy*

un·der·staffed /£ˌʌn·dəˈstɑːft, $-dɚˈstæft/, **un·der·manned** *adj* (of a shop, business or organization) not having enough employees • *The school was overcrowded and desperately understaffed.*

un·der·stand *(obj)* KNOW /£ˌʌn·dəˈstænd, $-dɚ-/ *v* [not *be understanding*] *past* **understood** /£ˌʌn·dəˈstʊd, $-dɚ-/ to know the meaning of (something), or to know how or why (a person or thing) behaves or operates in the way that they do • *He writes using lots of long words that I don't understand.* [T] • *She explained again what the computer was doing, but I still didn't understand.* [I] • *I need to make sure that we understand* **one another/each other** (=that we both know what the other means and wants and that we have an agreement). [T] • *Is there anyone here who understands Arabic?* [T] • *I think he was phoning from a pub – it was so noisy I couldn't understand* (=recognize) *a word he said.* [T] • *Understanding advanced maths was more than I could manage.* [T] • *You don't understand* **what** *it's like/***how** *it feels to have to beg on the streets.* [+ *wh-* word] • *I couldn't understand* (= didn't know the reason) **why** *I felt so guilty.* [+ *wh-* word] • *I can understand your feeling upset about what has happened.* [T] • *Ade's dad never understood* **about** *how important her singing was to her.* [I] • *When he said 3 o'clock, I understood him* **to** *mean* (=I thought he meant) *in the afternoon.* [T + obj + *to* infinitive] • *She sat in a corner and cried, moaning that no one understood her* (= that no one had any sympathy for her or knew what she was feeling). [T] • *(approving) Jack really understands horses* (=knows how and why they behave as they do and has a sympathetic way of working with them). [T] • *Since they spoke only Swahili, we used signs and gestures to* **make** *ourselves* **understood** (=to communicate).

un·der·stand·a·ble /£ˌʌn·dəˈstæn·də·bl̩, $-dɚ-/ *adj* • *You've got to put the facts into a form that's understandable* **to** *everyone.* • **It**'*s understandable* **that** *she should feel upset – no one talked to her the whole evening.* [+ *that* clause] • If you feel that something, such as the way a person has behaved, is understandable, you feel that it is usual and not strange or difficult to understand: *Their refusal to cooperate is perfectly/completely understandable, considering the circumstances.* ○ *The contradictory explanations caused understandable confusion.*

un·der·stand·a·bly /£ˌʌn·dəˈstæn·də·bli, $-dɚ-/ *adv* • *His parents were understandably angry.* • *Everton players, understandably enough, seemed to have lost hope.*

un·der·stand·ing /£ˌʌn·dəˈstæn·dɪŋ, $-dɚ-/ *n* [U] • *She doesn't have any understanding* **of** *politics/human nature/what it takes to be a good manager.* • *My understanding* **of** *the agreement* (= What I think it means) *is that they will pay £50 000 over two years.* • Understanding is also a positive, truthful relationship between two people: *How can there be peace in the region until there is* **(a)** *much improved understanding* **between** *all groups?* • See also UNDERSTANDING.

un·der·stand·ing /£ˌʌn·dəˈstæn·dɪŋ, $-dɚ-/ *adj approving* • An understanding person is good at knowing how someone else is feeling or what their situation is, and can forgive them if they do something wrong: *He had expected her to be horrified, but she was actually very understanding.* ○ *He gave me an understanding smile.*

un·der·stand *(obj)* BE AWARE /£ˌʌn·dəˈstænd, $-dɚ-/ *v past* **understood** /£ˌʌn·dəˈstʊd, $-dɚ-/ *fml* to know or become aware of (something) because you have been told it • *She had understood* **(that)** *she would soon be promoted.* [+ (*that*) clause] • *I understand* **(that)** *you are interested in borrowing some money from us.* [+ (*that*) clause] • *The Director had* **given** *her* **to** *understand* (=told her) **that** *she would be promoted.* [+ *that* clause] • *"I've been promoted." "***So** *I understand."* [after *so*] • *A secret buyer is understood* **to** *have paid £1 million for the three pictures* (=there is unofficial news that this has happened). [T + obj + *to* infinitive] • *Am I to understand* **from** *this letter* **that** *you are resigning?* [+ *that* clause] • *You must understand* **that** *a person in my position in the company can't afford any bad publicity.* [+ *that* clause] • *In the library* **it is understood that** (=everyone knows and accepts that) *loud talking is not permissible.* • *When Alan invites you to dinner, what's understood* (=known although not said) *is* **that** *it'll be more of an alcohol than a food experience.* [+ *that* clause] • Sometimes understand is used when making certain that someone knows what you mean and that they will do as you want: *I don't want you to see that boy again. Understand?/Do you understand?/Is that understood?* [I/T]

un·der·stand·ing /£ˌʌn·dəˈstæn·dɪŋ, $-dɚ-/ *n* [C] an informal agreement between people • *It took several hours of discussion before they could* **come to/reach** *an understanding.* • If you do something **on the understanding that** something else can or will happen, you do it because someone else has promised that it can or will: *They bought the cupboard on the understanding that they could return it if it didn't fit their living room.* • See also **understanding** at UNDERSTAND KNOW.

un·der·state *obj* /£ˌʌn·dəˈsteɪt, $-dɚ-/ *v* [T] to state or describe (something) in a way that makes it seem less important, serious, bad, etc. than it really is • *She believes the research understates the amount of discrimination women suffer.*

un·der·stat·ed /£ˌʌn·dəˈsteɪ·tɪd, $-dɚˈsteɪ·t̬ɪd/ *adj* • *She said that we were facing a few difficulties, which was a fairly understated way of putting it!* • *(approving) He's very elegant, in an understated* (=not too obvious) *way.*

un·der·state·ment /£ˌʌn·dəˈsteɪt·mənt, $-dɚ-/ *n* • *To say that her resignation was a shock would be an understatement – it caused panic.* [C] • *That New York City is not a peaceful place to live is* **the** *understatement* **of the** *year/month/century.* [C] • *He's a master of understatement.* [U]

un·der·stu·dy /£ˈʌn·dəˌstʌd·i, $-dɚ-/ *n* [C] an actor who learns the parts of other actors in a play, so that he or she can replace them if necessary, for example because of illness • *She's the understudy* **for** *Lady Macbeth at the Adelaide Theatre.* • *I can't sing tonight – my understudy will have to go on.*

un·der·stu·dy *obj* /£ˈʌn·dəˌstʌd·i, $-dɚ-/ *v* [T] • *She's understudying (the actress playing) Lady Macbeth.*

un·der·take *(obj)* /£ˌʌn·dəˈteɪk, $-dɚ-/ *v past simple* **undertook** /£ˌʌn·dəˈtʊk, $-dɚ-/, *past part* **undertaken** /£ˌʌn·dəˈteɪ·kᵊn, $-dɚ-/ *slightly fml* to do or begin to do (something), or *(fml)* to promise that you will do something • *Students are required to undertake simple experiments.* [T] • *It's the largest survey ever undertaken.* [T] • *A local business undertook the work, but went bankrupt before they finished.* [T] • *The United Nations was supposed to undertake* (=take responsibility for) *the role of global peace-keeper.* [T] • *(fml) She undertook not* **to** *publish the names of the people involved.* [+ *to* infinitive] •

(fml) The government undertook **that** *the buildings would not be redeveloped.* [+ *that* clause]

un·der·tak·ing /£ˌʌn·dəˈteɪ·kɪŋ, $-dɚ-/ *n* [C] • *The construction of the tunnel is a large and complex undertaking* (=job, business or piece of work). • *(fml) The manager* **gave** *a written undertaking* (=made a formal promise) **that** *no one would lose their job.* [+ *that* clause] • *(fml) The airline failed in its undertaking* (=formal promise) **to** *ensure the safety of its passengers.* [+ *to* infinitive]

un·der·tak·er /£ˈʌn·dəˌteɪ·kəʳ, $-dɚˌteɪ·kɚ/, *Am* **mor·ti·cian** *n* [C] a person whose job is to prepare dead bodies that are going to be buried or CREMATED (=burned) and to organize funerals

un·der·tone CHARACTERISTIC /£ˈʌn·də·təʊn, $-dɚ·toʊn/ *n* [C] a particular but not obvious characteristic that a piece of writing or speech, an event or a situation has • *I thought her speech had slightly sinister undertones.* • *It was a comedy act with an undertone* **of** *cruelty and spite.*

un·der·tone QUIET VOICE /£ˈʌn·də·təʊn, $-dɚ·toʊn/ *n* [U] a very quiet way of speaking • *Freddie muttered something to me* **in an** *undertone.*

un·der·tow /£ˈʌn·də·təʊ, $-dɚ·toʊ/ *n* [U] a strong current flowing under water in a different direction to the way the water on the surface is moving, esp. the strong current that flows under water away from the land at the same time as a wave hits the beach • *On some beaches the undertow is dangerous because it can pull swimmers out into deep water.*

un·der·used /£ˌʌn·dəˈjuːzd, $-dɚ-/ *adj* not used as much as it could or should be • *Since the main hospital was built, the local clinics have been rather underused.*

un·der·va·lue *obj* /£ˌʌn·dəˈvæl·juː, $-dɚ-/ *v* [T] to consider (someone or something) as less valuable or important than they really are • *The company had undervalued the building* **by** *£20 000.* • *He felt undervalued and underpaid.*

un·der·wa·ter /£ˌʌn·dəˈwɔː·təʳ, $-dɚˈwɑː·t̬ɚ/ *adj, adv* [not gradable] under the surface of the water, esp. under the surface of the sea • *an underwater camera* (=a camera that you can use under water) • *underwater currents* • *underwater photography* • *Some species of turtle can remain underwater for 24 hours.* • *She pushed his head underwater.*

un·der·wear /£ˈʌn·də·weəʳ, $-dɚ·wer/ *n* [U], *fml* **un·der·clothes** *pl n*, **un·der·cloth·ing** /£ˈʌn·dəˌkləʊ·ðɪŋ, $-dɚˌkloʊ-/ *n* [U] clothes worn next to the skin, under other clothes • *Underpants, panties, bras and tights are all underwear.* • LP **Shopping goods**

un·der·weight /£ˌʌn·dəˈweɪt, $-dɚ-/ *adj* (of people) too light and thin • *By the time she was admitted to hospital she was seriously underweight.* • *According to the chart he's four kilos underweight.* [after n] • Compare OVERWEIGHT.

un·der·went /£ˌʌn·dəˈwent, $-dɚ-/ *past simple of* UNDERGO

un·der·whelmed /£ˌʌn·dəˈwelmd, $-dɚ-/ *adj humorous* feeling no excitement about or admiration for something or someone • *I get the feeling that the staff are distinctly underwhelmed by John's latest proposal.*

un·der·wired /£ˌʌn·dəˈwaɪəd, $-dɚˈwaɪrd/ *adj* [not gradable] (of a BRA) having a length of wire under the breasts for additional support

un·der·world CRIME /£ˈʌn·də·wɜːld, $-dɚ·wɜːrld/ *n* [U] the part of society consisting of criminal organizations and activities • *These latest measures are part of the president's attempt to rid the country of its mafia-style criminal underworld.* • *It was always rumoured of the singer that he had underworld* **connections.** • *The central character of the novel is a sort of underworld figure.*

un·der·world SPIRITS /£ˈʌn·də·wɜːld, $-dɚ·wɜːrld/ *n* [U] **the underworld** (in Greek MYTHOLOGY) a place under the earth where the spirits of the dead go; HADES

un·der·write *obj* /£ˌʌn·dᵊrˈaɪt, $ˈʌn·də·raɪt/ *v* [T] *past simple* **underwrote** /£ˌʌn·dᵊrˈəʊt, $·də·roʊt/, *past part* **underwritten** /£ˌʌn·dᵊrˈɪt·ᵊn, $ˈʌn·dəˌrɪt̬·ən/ (of a bank or other organization) to support (an event or other activity) by giving or promising money to those who are responsible for it and in so doing protect them against the possibility of failure or loss of money • *The race-track owners have so far failed to find anyone who will underwrite the event.* • *(specialized)* If a company underwrites an **insurance policy**, someone's property, etc., they have an agreement to pay out money in cases of damage or loss: *Insurance underwriting losses were heavy last year due to a number of natural disasters.*

un·der·writ·er /£ˈʌn·dᵊrˌaɪ·təʳ, $-də·raɪ·t̬ɚ/ *n* [C] • *He works for Lloyds the underwriters.*

un·de·sir·a·ble /£ˌʌn·dɪˈzaɪə·rə·bl̩, $-ˈzaɪr·ə-/ *adj disapproving* not wanted, approved of or popular • *Houses near industrial sites often do not sell so quickly because they are regarded as undesirable.* • *(humorous) I tried to avoid the back room where the undesirable* **elements** (=people whose behaviour or appearance was unacceptable) *of the party were gathered.* • *She expressed concern over the procedure for the arrest and expulsion of undesirable* **aliens** (=people that the government do not want in the country).

un·de·sir·a·ble /£ˌʌn·dɪˈzaɪə·rə·bl̩, $-ˈzaɪr·ə-/ *n* [C] *humorous* • Undesirables are people whose behaviour or appearance makes them unacceptable in society or at a particular occasion: *There are guards on the door to keep out the undesirables.* ○ *Mad people and other social undesirables were generally locked up in the past.*

un·de·vel·oped /ˌʌn·dɪˈvel·əpt/ *adj* (of a place or land) not built on or used for farming • *The real estate for sale includes 2000 acres of undeveloped land.*

un·dies /ˈʌn·diz/ *pl n infml sometimes humorous* UNDERWEAR • *I don't seem to have any clean undies.*

un·dis·guised /ˌʌn·dɪsˈgaɪzd/ *adj* (of feelings that are usually hidden) clearly shown or expressed • *There was a note of undisguised irritation in his voice when he spoke.* • *She looked at him with undisguised lust.*

un·di·vid·ed /ˌʌn·dɪˈvaɪ·dɪd/ *adj* existing as a whole, not in separate parts • *1989 saw the fall of the Berlin Wall and the rebirth of an undivided Germany.* • Undivided **attention** is complete attention: *If you just wait till I've finished this bit of work you will* **have/***I will* **give** *you my undivided attention.*

un·do *obj* UNFASTEN /ʌnˈduː/ *v* [T] **undoing**, *past simple* **undid** /ʌnˈdɪd/, *past part* **undone** /ʌnˈdʌn/ to unfasten (something that is fastened or tied) • *Can someone help me to undo my seat belt?* • *I'd eaten so much that I had to undo my belt by a couple of holes.* • LP **Dressing and undressing**

undone /ʌnˈdʌn/ *adj* [not gradable] • *Why didn't you tell me my zip was undone!* • *Damn, my shoe-laces have* **come** *undone again.* • See also UNDONE.

un·do *obj* REMOVE EFFECTS /ʌnˈduː/ *v* [T] **undoing**, *past simple* **undid** /ʌnˈdɪd/, *past part* **undone** /ʌnˈdʌn/ to remove the good or bad effects of (an action or several actions) • *I did a really tough aerobics class and then went out for a meal and undid all* **the good work!** • *It's very difficult to undo* **the damage** *that's caused by inadequate parenting in a child's early years.* • *"What's done cannot be undone"* (Shakespeare, Macbeth 5.1)

un·done /ʌnˈdʌn/ *adj* [after v] *old use* (of a person) without hope for the future, having experienced great disappointment, loss of money, etc. • *I am undone and my spirit broken.* • See also **undone** at UNDO UNFASTEN.

un·do·ing /ʌnˈduː·ɪŋ/ *n* [U] *fml* • The undoing of someone or something is the cause of their failure, loss of power or loss of wealth: *He had a great fondness for women – some say it was his undoing.* ○ *Greed has been* **the** *undoing* **of** *many a businessman.*

un·doubt·ed /£ʌnˈdaʊ·tɪd, $-t̬ɪd/ *adj* not questioned or doubted; accepted as the truth • *She is the undoubted star of British ballet.*

un·doubt·ed·ly /£ʌnˈdaʊ·tɪd·li, $-t̬ɪd-/ *adv* [not gradable] • *It is undoubtedly the best French film this year.* • *Of course she's good at her job – that is undoubtedly true.*

un·dreamed of, **un·dreamt of** /ʌnˈdrempt, -ˈdriːmd-/ *adj* (esp. of wealth, success or advancement) better or greater than anyone would think possible • *These two lads from a remote village in Norway have enjoyed undreamed of success with their first album.* • *We in the west enjoy a standard of living undreamed of by the majority of people in the world.*

un·dress *(obj)* /ʌnˈdres/ *v* to remove your clothes or remove the clothes from (someone else) • *Could you undress the kids, Steve.* [T] • *She watched him as he undressed.* [I] • *(infml)* If someone **undresses** you **with** their **eyes** they look at your body with strong, and often unpleasant, sexual desire. • LP **Dressing and undressing**

un·dress /ʌnˈdres/ *n* [U] *humorous* • If a person is **in a state of** undress he or she is not wearing many or any clothes: *He came to the door in a state of undress.*

un·dressed /ʌnˈdrest/ *adj* [not gradable] • *I remember the first time I saw him undressed and I couldn't believe how hairy he was.* • *You* **get** *undressed, Alice, and I'll run the bath water.*

un·due /£ʌn'djuː, $-'duː/ *adj fml* to a level which is more than is necessary, acceptable or reasonable • *It's difficult to find a way of spreading information about the disease without causing undue alarm.* • *The councillor promised that the new system would not impose undue burdens on the local tax payer.*

un·du·ly /£ʌn'djuː·li, $-'duː-/ *adv* • *There's no need to be unduly* **pessimistic** *about the situation.* • *He didn't seem unduly concerned about his wife's health.*

un·du·lat·ing /£'ʌn·djʊ·leɪ·tɪŋ, $-t̬ɪŋ/ *adj fml* (esp. of land) having small hills and slopes that look like waves, or, less commonly, (of something which can move) moving gently up and down • *I prefer the gently undulating hills of the Dales to the more dramatic landscape of the Moors.* • *He watched, hypnotized, the undulating stomach of the belly-dancer.*

un·du·late /'ʌn·djʊ·leɪt/ *v* [I]

un·dy·ing /ʌn'daɪ·ɪŋ/ *adj* [before n] *literary* (of a feeling or a belief) permanent; without ending • *He would be remembered, said the leader, for his undying loyalty and commitment to the party.* • *She recalled the wedding ceremony at which they had pledged their undying love for each other.*

un·earned /£ʌn'ɜːnd, $-'ɜːrnd/ *adj* earned or obtained without having been worked for • **Unearned income** is obtained as a result of investments and property owned instead of being earned by working: *Any unearned income has to be declared as well as salary.*

un·earth *obj* /£ʌn'ɜːθ, $-'ɜːrθ/ *v* [T] to discover (something) in the ground, or *(fig.)* to discover (proof or some other information), esp. after careful searching • *Building at the site was halted after human remains were unearthed earlier this month.* • *(fig.) Fresh evidence has been unearthed suggesting that he did not in fact commit the crime.*

un·earth·ly [INCONVENIENT] /£ʌn'ɜːθ·li, $-'ɜːrθ-/ *adj* **-ier, -iest** *infml* (of a time) very inconvenient because it is too early in the morning or too late at night • *I was woken up* **at some** *unearthly* **hour** *of the morning by someone knocking on my door.*

un·earth·ly [STRANGE] /£ʌn'ɜːθ·li, $-'ɜːrθ-/ *adj* **-ier, -iest** strange in a mysterious and sometimes frightening way • *The silence half way up the mountain was quite unearthly.* • *Cats' cries have an unearthly quality.* • *Early photographs taken of the actress capture a pale, almost unearthly beauty.*

un·eas·y /ʌn'iː·zi/ *adj* **-ier, -iest** (of people) slightly anxious or uncomfortable about a particular situation, or (of situations) causing slight anxiety • *I feel a bit uneasy* **about** *asking her to do me such a big favour.* • *Few are willing to predict how long this uneasy peace between the two countries will last.* • *She has a rather uneasy relationship with her mother-in-law.* • *"Uneasy lies the head that wears a crown"* (Shakespeare, Henry IV, part 2 3.1)

un·eas·i·ly /ʌn'iː·zɪ·li/ *adv* • *At each question she shifted uneasily in her seat.* • *Responsibility of any sort sits very uneasily on her shoulders.*

un·eas·i·ness /ʌn'iː·zɪ·nəs/, **un·ease** /ʌn'iːz/ *n* [U] • *There is some uneasiness* **over** *what the president will say when he addresses the conference next Tuesday.* • **Growing** *unease* **at** *the prospect of an election is causing fierce arguments within the party.*

un·ec·o·nom·ic /£ʌn,iː·kə'nɒm·ɪk, £-,ek·ə-, $-'nɑː·mɪk/, **un·ec·o·nom·i·cal** /£ʌn,iː·kə'nɒm·ɪ·kᵊl, £-,ek·ə-, $-'nɑː·mɪ-/ *adj* (of businesses and industries) not making enough profit, or losing money • *The minister maintained that the coal-mines were uneconomic and would have to be closed.* • Uneconomical processes or activities are wasteful and tend to result in loss of money: *Many of the alternatives to coal, oil and nuclear power are quite simply uneconomical.*

un·ed·i·fy·ing /ʌn'ed·ɪ·faɪ·ɪŋ/ *adj fml* unpleasant, unattractive and offensive, causing people to feel no respect • *We were treated to the unedifying spectacle of two cabinet ministers fighting over a seat.*

un·ed·u·cat·ed /£ʌn'ed·jʊ·keɪ·tɪd, $-t̬ɪd/ *adj* having received little or no education

un·em·ployed /,ʌn·ɪm'plɔɪd/ *adj* [not gradable] not having a job that provides money • *He's been unemployed for over a year.* • [LP] **Work**

un·em·ployed /,ʌn·ɪm'plɔɪd/ *pl n* • *There are now over four million unemployed* (=people without jobs) *in this country.* • *Tickets are £10 to get in or £5 for* **the unemployed.**

un·em·ploy·ment /,ʌn·ɪm'plɔɪ·mənt/ *n* [U] • Unemployment refers to the number of people who do not have a job which provides them with money: *Unemployment has* **risen** *again for the third consecutive month.* ◦ *Italy's unemployment* **rate** *rose to twelve per cent of the labour force in July.* • Unemployment is also the state of being unemployed: *Fear of unemployment nowadays causes more people to stay in jobs that they hate.* • *(Br and Aus)* **Unemployment benefit** (also *infml* **dole**) is an amount of money that is regularly paid by the government to people who do not have a job: *She* **claimed** (=received) *unemployment benefit for six months.* • **Unemployment (compensation), unemployment insurance** and **dole** are all *Am for* unemployment benefit.

un·end·ing /ʌn'en·dɪŋ/ *adj slightly fml* (esp. of something unpleasant) seeming to have no end • *The weekend's bomb explosion was just the latest in an unending series of terrorist attacks.* • *Motherhood seemed to her an unending cycle of cooking, washing and cleaning.*

un·en·dur·a·ble /£,ʌn·ɪn'djʊə·rə·bl̩, $-'dʊr·ə-/ *adj fml* (of a situation or experience) so unpleasant or painful that it is almost impossible to bear • *The suspense of not knowing if or when he was going to be released was quite unendurable.* • *In the last few months of his illness he suffered unendurable pain.*

un·en·force·a·ble /£,ʌn·ɪn'fɔː·sə·bl̩, $-'fɔːr-/ *adj* (of a rule or law) that is impossible to force people to obey

un·en·light·ened /£,ʌn·ɪn'laɪ·tᵊnd, $-t̬ᵊnd/ *adj* not **enlightened**, see at ENLIGHTEN

un·en·vi·a·ble /ʌn'en·vi·ə·bl̩/ *adj* (esp. of a duty or other action that has to be done) unpleasant or difficult • *I had the unenviable* **task** *of taking a car-load of kids ice-skating.*

un·e·qual [NOT THE SAME] /ʌn'iː·kwᵊl/ *adj fml* not the same • *She cut two slices of noticeably unequal size.*

un·e·qual·ly /ʌn'iː·kwᵊl·i/ *adv*

un·e·qual [UNFAIR] /ʌn'iː·kwᵊl/ *adj* not treating everyone the same; unfair • *Common themes in her writing are sexism and the unequal treatment of blacks and whites.* • *Until women are paid as much as men they will be competing on unequal terms.* • *They have a rather unequal relationship.*

un·e·qual·ly /ʌn'iː·kwᵊl·i/ *adv*

un·e·qualled, *Am usually* **un·e·qualed** /ʌn'iː·kwᵊld/ *adj slightly fml* better or more extreme than any other • *Though small, this restaurant offers a range of fish dishes unequalled anywhere else in London.* • *During these years the country enjoyed a period of unequalled prosperity.*

un·e·qual to /ʌn'iː·kwᵊl/ *adj* [after v; not gradable] *fml* lacking the necessary ability, power or qualities to achieve something • *He tried to cheer her up but found himself unequal to* **the task.**

un·e·qui·vo·cal /,ʌn·ɪ'kwɪv·ə·kᵊl/ *adj* total or (expressed) without any doubt • *The Prime Minister, he said, had the party's unequivocal support.* • *The church has been unequivocal in its condemnation of the violence.* • *The union's unequivocal rejection of the latest pay offer will almost certainly lead to further strikes.*

un·e·qui·vo·cal·ly /,ʌn·ɪ'kwɪv·ə·kli/ *adv* • *I wouldn't unequivocally state that I love all children.*

un·err·ing /£ʌn'ɜː·rɪŋ, $-'er·ɪŋ/ *adj* never failing in your aiming of a ball or other object, or *(fig.)* in your judgment or ability • *Shots like this have earned Brinkworth his reputation as an unerring goal scorer.* • *He has an unerring talent for writing catchy melodies.* • *The author's scholarship is unerring and her scope wide.*

un·err·ing·ly /£ʌn'ɜː·rɪŋ·li, $-'er·ɪŋ-/ *adv*

UNESCO, Unes·co /£juː'nes·kəʊ, $-koʊ/ *n* [U not after the] *abbreviation for* United Nations Educational, Scientific and Cultural Organization (=a department of the United Nations through which richer nations can help poorer nations)

un·eth·i·cal /,ʌn'eθ·ɪ·kᵊl/ *adj* not **ethical**, see at ETHIC

un·e·ven [NOT EVEN] /ʌn'iː·vᵊn/ *adj* not EVEN, see EVEN [EQUAL], EVEN [FLAT], EVEN [CONTINUOUS] • *Take care when you walk on that path – the paving stones are rather uneven.* • *Distribution is uneven as between different parts of the country.* • *The contest was very uneven – the other team was far stronger than us.*

un·e·ven·ly /ʌn'iː·vᵊn·li/ *adv* • *The two boxers were unevenly matched.*

un·e·ven·ness /ʌn'iː·vᵊn·nəs/ *n* [U]

un·e·ven [NOT GOOD] /,ʌn'iː·vᵊn/ *adj* varying in quality; often used to avoid saying bad • *Your work has been rather uneven this term, Matthew.*

un·e·ven·ly /,ʌn'iː·vᵊn·li/ *adv*

un·e·ven·ness /,ʌn'iː·vᵊn·nəs/ *n* [U]

un·e·vent·ful /,ʌn·ɪ'vent·fᵊl/ *adj* not **eventful**, see at EVENT

un·e·vent·ful·ly /ˌʌn·ɪˈvent·fᵊl·i/ *adv*

un·ex·cep·tion·a·ble /ˌʌn·ɪkˈsep·ʃᵊn·ə·bl̩/ *adj fml* which could not be criticized or disapproved of • *Her speech was unexceptionable though she didn't say much that we don't already know.*

un·ex·cep·tion·al /ˌʌn·ɪkˈsep·ʃᵊn·ᵊl/ *adj* ordinary, not EXCEPTIONAL • *He was a hard-working, if unexceptional, student.*

un·ex·pect·ed /£ˌʌn·ɪkˈspek·tɪd, $-t̬ɪd/ *adj* not expected • *Well, fancy seeing you here! This was an unexpected* **pleasure***!*

un·ex·pect·ed·ly /£ˌʌn·ɪkˈspek·tɪd·li, $-t̬ɪd-/ *adv* • *Around the world, limited supplies of both cotton and wool and unexpectedly high demand have sent prices rocketing.*

un·ex·pur·gat·ed /£ʌnˈek·spə·geɪ·tɪd, $-spɚ·geɪ·t̬ɪd/ *adj* (of a book, article, film, etc.) complete; containing everything, including parts considered likely to cause offence • *I only read the complete unexpurgated version of the novel after I left school.*

un·fail·ing /ʌnˈfeɪ·lɪŋ/ *adj* (of a positive quality of someone's character) showing itself at all times • *One of the good things about Amanda is that you can always rely on her unfailing enthusiasm.*

un·fail·ing·ly /ʌnˈfeɪ·lɪŋ·li/ *adv* • *She's unfailingly cheerful no matter what the circumstances.* • *The thing I noticed about the people was how unfailingly polite they were.*

un·fair /£ʌnˈfeəʳ, $-ˈfer/ *adj* **-er, -est** not FAIR [RIGHT]

un·fair·ly /£ʌnˈfeə·li, $-ˈfer-/ *adv*

un·fair·ness /£ʌnˈfeə·nəs, $-ˈfer-/ *n* [U]

un·faith·ful /ʌnˈfeɪθ·fᵊl/ *adj* having (had) a sexual relationship or experience with a person who is not your husband, wife or usual sexual partner • *If a man was unfaithful* **to** *me I'd leave him no matter what the circumstances.* • *She's been unfaithful on more than one occasion.*

un·faith·ful·ness /ʌnˈfeɪθ·fᵊl·nəs/ *n* [U]

un·fal·ter·ing /£ʌnˈfɒl·tᵊr·ɪŋ, $-ˈfɑːl·t̬ɚ-/ *adj* not **faltering**, see at FALTER

un·fas·ten *(obj)* /£ʌnˈfɑː·sᵊn, $-ˈfæs-/ *v* to take (a fastening) apart, or to take apart the fastenings on (something) • *I can't unfasten this button.* [T] • *He unfastened his belt and dropped his trousers.* [T] • *This blouse unfastens* (= can be unfastened) *at the back.* [I] • [LP] **Dressing and undressing**

un·fa·thom·a·ble /ʌnˈfæð·ə·mə·bl̩/ *adj slightly fml* impossible to understand • *For some unfathomable reason they built the toilet next to the kitchen.*

un·fa·thom·a·bly /ʌnˈfæð·ə·mə·bli/ *adv fml* • *He writes in unfathomably long and complex sentences.*

un·fa·vour·a·ble *Br and Aus, Am and Aus* **unfavorable** /£ʌnˈfeɪ·vᵊr·ə·bl̩, $-vɚ-/ *adj* not **favourable**, see at FAVOUR [SUPPORT]

un·fa·vour·a·bly /£ʌnˈfeɪ·vᵊr·ə·bli, $-vɚ-/ *adv*

un·fazed /ʌnˈfeɪzd/ *adj infml* not surprised or worried • *Fame has happened almost overnight for the 27-year old actress, but she seems unfazed by all the recent media attention.*

un·fea·si·ble /ʌnˈfiː·zɪ·bl̩/ *adj* not FEASIBLE

un·fea·si·bly /ʌnˈfiː·zɪ·bli/ *adv*

un·feel·ing /ʌnˈfiː·lɪŋ/ *adj disapproving* not feeling sympathy for other people's suffering • *She accused me of being unfeeling because I didn't cry at the end of the film.*

un·fet·tered /£ʌnˈfet·əd, $-ˈfet̬·ɚd/ *adj fml* not limited by rules or any other controlling influence • *In writing poetry one is unfettered by the normal rules of sentence structure.*

un·fit /ʌnˈfɪt/ *adj* **unfitter, unfittest** not FIT, see FIT [HEALTHY], FIT [SUIT]

un·flag·ging /ʌnˈflæg·ɪŋ/ *adj* (of qualities such as energy, interest and enthusiasm) never weakening • *He thanked Tony for the 'unflagging energy and* **enthusiasm***' with which he had worked on the project.*

un·flap·pa·ble /ʌnˈflæp·ə·bl̩/ *adj* not tending to get anxious, nervous or angry even in difficult situations • *She's totally unflappable – you have to be when working in such a highly-pressured environment.*

un·flinch·ing /ʌnˈflɪn·tʃɪŋ/ *adj* not frightened of or trying to avoid danger or unpleasantness • *It is a brave and unflinching account of prison life.* • *She had the fearless, unflinching gaze of a child.*

un·fold *(obj)* [DEVELOP] /£ʌnˈfəʊld, $-ˈfoʊld/ *v* (of a situation or story) to develop or become clear to other people, or *(fml)* to explain (your plans) to someone • *Like a lot of people I've watched the* **events** *of the last few days unfold on TV.* [I] • *The scandals about women have never ceased unfolding since the president's death.* [I] • *As the plot unfolds you gradually realise that all your initial assumptions were wrong.* [I] • *(fml) I've arranged a lunch with him next Thursday at which I intend to unfold my proposal.* [T]

un·fold *obj* [OPEN] /£ʌnˈfəʊld, $-ˈfoʊld/ *v* [T] to open or spread out (something that has been folded) • *If we unfold the table we can fit eight people around it.* • *He watched her expression as she unfolded the letter.*

un·fore·seen /£ˌʌn·fəˈsiːn, $-fɚ-/ *adj* unexpected • *Due to unforeseen* **circumstances** *the cost of the improvements has risen by twenty per cent.* • *Unless there are any unforeseen problems the whole project should be finished by the spring.*

un·for·get·ta·ble /£ˌʌn·fəˈget·ə·bl̩, $-fɚˈget̬-/ *adj* (of an experience) having such a strong effect or influence on you that you cannot forget it • *Rarely does one eat a meal in a restaurant that can truly be described as unforgettable.* • *"Unforgettable, that's what you are"* (from the song *Unforgettable* sung by Nat King Cole, 1951)

un·for·get·ta·bly /£ˌʌn·fəˈget·ə·bli, $-fɚˈget̬-/ *adv* • *John Wood plays unforgettably the part of the tyrant king in the Belgrade theatre's new production.*

un·for·tun·ate [UNLUCKY] /£ʌnˈfɔː·tʃᵊn·ət, $-ˈfɔːr-/ *adj* unlucky or having bad effects • *She's inherited her father's nose, which is very unfortunate.* • *The report warned that the lack of staff in the hospital could have very unfortunate consequences.* • **It** *was just unfortunate* (**that**) *he phoned exactly as our guests were arriving.* [+ (*that*) clause]

un·for·tun·ate /£ʌnˈfɔː·tʃᵊn·ət, $-ˈfɔːr-/ *n* [C] *fml or humorous* • An unfortunate is an unlucky person who is in a bad situation: *Mendez plays an unfortunate who suddenly finds himself homeless and without money in a big city.* ○ *He was one of the poor unfortunates who invested in the company and now finds himself a few thousand pounds poorer.*

un·for·tun·ate·ly /£ʌnˈfɔː·tʃᵊn·ət·li, $-ˈfɔːr-/ *adv* • *Unfortunately, by the time we got there most of the food had gone.* • *Unfortunately I didn't have my credit card with me or I'd certainly have bought it.*

un·for·tun·ate [UNSUITABLE] /£ʌnˈfɔː·tʃᵊn·ət, $-ˈfɔːr-/ *adj fml* (of remarks or behaviour) unsuitable in a way which could cause offence • *The housing director's remark that 'the homeless could do more to help themselves' was unfortunate to say the least.* • *He has an unfortunate manner.*

un·found·ed /ʌnˈfaʊn·dɪd/ *adj* (of a claim or piece of news) not based on fact; UNTRUE • *The Palace has dismissed rumours of a marriage break-up as 'totally unfounded'.* • *I'm pleased to see that our fears about the weather* **proved** *unfounded.*

un·friend·ly /ʌnˈfrend·li/ *adj* **-ier, -iest** showing dislike and lack of sympathy; not friendly • *I hope she didn't think I was being unfriendly – I just wasn't in a mood for talking.*

un·friend·li·ness /ʌnˈfrend·lɪ·nəs/ *n* [U]

un·furl *(obj)* /£ʌnˈfɜːl, $-ˈfɜːrl/ *v* (of a flag, sail or BANNER) to become open from a rolled position, or to cause (a flag, etc.) to do this • *The demonstrators unfurled a banner which said 'Liberty will die with us.'* [T] • *The flags unfurled in the breeze.* [I] • *(fig. literary) She could see in his baby features an adult face waiting to unfurl* (= develop). [I]

un·gain·ly /ʌŋˈgeɪn·li/ *adj* **-ier, -iest** awkward and graceless in movement • *She walks heavily with both feet turned out at an ungainly angle.* • *Though graceful and fluid while swimming, ducks are somehow ungainly on land.*

un·glued /ʌŋˈgluːd/ *adj* **come unglued** *Am infml* to experience difficulties and fail • *When the secret arrangements came unglued, the president was revealed to have ordered the burglary.*

un·god·ly /£ʌŋˈgɒd·li, $-ˈgɑːd-/ *adj* [before n] **-ier, -iest** *infml* extreme or unacceptable • *I had to get up at some ungodly* **hour** *to take her to the airport.* • *The kids were making such an ungodly noise that I couldn't hear myself think!*

un·gov·ern·a·ble /£ʌŋˈgʌv·ᵊn·ə·bl̩, $-ɚ·nə-/ *adj* unable to be governed or controlled • *The radio later reported that the country had become ungovernable.* • *Poor Liz is working on a summer school, trying to teach English to a bunch of ungovernable adolescents.*

un·gram·mat·i·cal /£ˌʌŋ·grəˈmæt·ɪ·kᵊl, $-ˈmæt̬-/ *adj* not **grammatical**; see at GRAMMAR

un·grate·ful /ʌŋˈgreɪt·fᵊl/ *adj* not GRATEFUL

un·guard·ed /£ʌŋ'gɑː·dɪd, $-'gɑːr-/ *adj* not guarded or protected • *With Norway's goalkeeper half way up the field, Green was able to head the ball into an unguarded goal.* • *I shouldn't leave your bag unguarded in a pub like this.* • If you make an unguarded remark or say something in an unguarded **moment** you tell someone something, possibly unwisely, that you would usually keep secret: *In an unguarded moment I said that I thought Carlo was quite attractive.*

un·guent /£'ʌŋ·gju·ənt, $-gwənt/ *n* [C] *literary* a thick oily substance for the skin, usually having a pleasant smell • *He smelled powerfully of long immersion in bath salts and shaving unguents.*

un·hand *obj* /ʌn'hænd/ *v* [T] *old use or humorous* to take your hands off (someone) • *Unhand me, sir, for shame!*

un·hap·py /ʌn'hæp·i/ *adj* **-ier, -iest** not HAPPY PLEASED

un·hap·pi·ly /ʌn'hæp·ɪ·li/ *adv*

un·hap·pi·ness /ʌn'hæp·ɪ·nəs/ *n* [U]

un·heal·thy /ʌn'hel·θi/ *adj* **-ier, -iest** not **healthy**, see at HEALTH

un·heal·thi·ly /ʌn'hel·θɪ·li/ *adv*

un·heard /£ʌn'hɜːd, $-'hɜːrd/ *adj* **go unheard** to not be listened to or considered • *We complained but as usual our voices went unheard.*

un·heard–of /£ʌn'hɜːd·ɒv, $-'hɜːrd·ɑːv/ *adj* surprising or shocking because not known about or previously experienced • *It was not all that long ago that it was almost unheard-of for an unmarried couple to live together.*

un·hinged /ʌn'hɪndʒd/ *adj esp. humorous* mentally ill; INSANE • *I sometimes think that your mother is a little unhinged.*

un·hinge *obj* /ʌn'hɪndʒ/ *v* [T] *esp. humorous* • *Do you think he was a little unhinged by the experience?*

un·ho·ly CAUSING HARM /£ʌn'həʊ·li, $-'hoʊ-/ *adj* (of combinations) bad and causing harm • *Religious fanatics have formed an unholy* **alliance** *with right wing groups.* • *There was a smell emanating from the fridge – an unholy combination of over-ripe cheese and unwrapped fish.*

un·ho·ly EXTREME /£ʌn'həʊ·li, $-'hoʊ-/ *adj* [before n] *infml* extreme and unacceptable • *I don't know what they were arguing about but there was an unholy noise coming from the bedroom.* • *The proposed restructuring of the company has provoked an unholy row among senior directors.* • *She has to get up at some unholy hour to get her train.*

u·ni– ONE /'juː·nɪ-/ *combining form* having or consisting of only one • *unilateral* • *unisex*

u·ni COLLEGE /'juː·ni/ *n* [C] *Br and Aus infml for* UNIVERSITY • *Which uni was she at?*

UNICEF /'juː·nɪ·sef/ *n* [U not after *the*] *abbreviation for* United Nations International Children's Fund (=a department of the United Nations that deals with the problems of illness, hunger, etc. in children from all countries) • *He works for UNICEF.*

u·ni·corn /£'juː·nɪ·kɔːn, $-kɔːrn/ *n* [C] an imaginary horse-like creature with a single horn growing from the front of its head • PIC **Imaginary creatures**

u·ni·cy·cle /'juː·nɪˌsaɪ·kl̩/ *n* [C] a bicycle with one wheel, used esp. in a CIRCUS (=a form of entertainment, usually in a tent) • PIC **Bicycles**

un·i·den·ti·fied /£ˌʌn·aɪ'den·tɪ·faɪd, $-t̬ə-/ *adj* [not gradable] whose name is not known or is being kept secret • *Police are investigating the death of an unidentified man whose body was found in Crackley Woods yesterday.* • *Bermudez was shot dead by an unidentified assailant in the car park of a hotel in the city on Saturday night.* • *The airline is currently having talks with an unidentified partner about the possible takeover of the company.* • See also UFO.

u·ni·form CLOTHES /£'juː·nɪ·fɔːm, $-fɔːrm/ *n* [C] a particular set of clothes which has to be worn by the members of the same organization or group of people • *military/school uniform* • *a police officer's uniform* • *a nurse's uniform* • *I love a man* **in uniform**! • A uniform can also be a type of clothes that are connected with any group of people: *Photographs show him wearing the scruffy T-shirt and jeans that were the student's uniform of the time.*

u·ni·formed /£'juː·nɪ·fɔːmd, $-fɔːrmd/ *adj* [not gradable] • *uniformed officers/police/soldiers* • Compare MUFTI.

u·ni·form SAME /£'juː·nɪ·fɔːm, $-fɔːrm/ *adj* the same; not varying or different in any way • *As in so many offices that you see, the walls and furniture are a uniform grey.* • *Small businesses are demanding that they receive uniform treatment from the banks.*

u·ni·form·ly /£'juː·nɪ·fɔːm·li, $-fɔːrm-/ *adv* • *Critics were uniformly enthusiastic about the production.* • *Her friends are uniformly dull.*

u·ni·for·mi·ty /£ˌjuː·nɪ'fɔː·mɪ·ti, $-'fɔːr·mə·t̬i/ *n* [U] • *There's a depressing uniformity about the architecture of this part of town.*

u·ni·fy *obj* /'juː·nɪ·faɪ/ *v* [T] to bring together; combine • *If the new leader does manage to unify his warring party it will be quite an achievement.* • LP **One**

u·ni·fied /'juː·nɪ·faɪd/ *adj* • *Once again there were calls for a unified European currency.*

u·ni·fi·ca·tion /ˌjuː·nɪ·fɪ'keɪ·ʃən/ *n* [U] • *the unification of East and West Germany*

u·ni·lat·e·ral /£ˌjuː·nɪ'læt·ər·əl, $-'læt̬·ɚ-/ *adj* [not gradable] involving only one group or country • *The party leader has actually declared her support for unilateral nuclear* **disarmament** (=giving up her country's nuclear weapons without first waiting for other countries to do the same). • *The rebel movement declared a unilateral and indefinite ceasefire from the beginning of the year.* • *The event was cancelled when the main sponsors took the unilateral decision to pull out.* • Compare BILATERAL; MULTILATERAL.

u·ni·lat·e·ral·ly /£ˌjuː·nɪ'læt·ər·əl·i, $-'læt̬·ɚ-/ *adv* [not gradable] • *The Justice Department says the president does not have the authority to act unilaterally.*

u·ni·lat·e·ral·i·sm /£ˌjuː·nɪ'læt·ər·əl·ɪ·zəm, $-'læt̬·ɚ-/ *n* [U]

u·ni·lat·e·ral·ist /£ˌjuː·nɪ'læt·ər·əl·ɪst, $-'læt̬·ə-/ *n* [C]

un·i·mag·in·a·tive /£ˌʌn·ɪ'mædʒ·ɪ·nə·tɪv, $-t̬ɪv/ *adj* not **imaginative**, see at IMAGINE

un·im·peach·a·ble /ˌʌn·ɪm'piː·tʃə·bl̩/ *adj fml approving* (of a person's character) completely honest and moral so that there is no cause for doubt or criticism • *Lord Fletcher, said the Bishop, was a man of unimpeachable integrity and character.*

un·im·por·tant /£ˌʌn·ɪm'pɔː·tənt, $-'pɔːr·t̬ənt/ *adj* not IMPORTANT • *Staffing is still a* **relatively** *unimportant issue compared to the other problems that we're encountering.*

un·im·pressed /ˌʌn·ɪm'prest/ *adj* [after v] not **impressed**, see at IMPRESS • *They looked the house over, but they seemed unimpressed* (**by** *it*).

un·im·pres·sive /ˌʌn·ɪm'pres·ɪv/ *adj*

un·in·formed /£ˌʌn·ɪn'fɔːmd, $-'fɔːrmd/ *adj* not **informed**, see at INFORM

un·in·hab·i·ta·ble /£ˌʌn·ɪn'hæb·ɪ·tə·bl̩, $-t̬ə-/ *adj* not HABITABLE • *There's no water or electricity, the floor is rotting, the roof leaks – in short, the house is uninhabitable.*

un·in·hab·it·ed /£ˌʌn·ɪn'hæb·ɪ·tɪd, $-t̬ɪd/ *adj* • *an uninhabited island*

un·in·hi·bit·ed /£ˌʌn·ɪn'hɪb·ɪ·tɪd, $-t̬ɪd/ *adj approving* free and natural, without embarrassment or too much control • *The students we spoke to were surprisingly uninhibited in talking about sex.* • *We watched two hours of glorious, uninhibited football.* • *She gave a loud uninhibited laugh.*

un·in·i·ti·at·ed /£ˌʌn·ɪ'nɪʃ·i·eɪ·tɪd, $-t̬ɪd/ *pl n* **the uninitiated** *esp. humorous* people who are without knowledge or experience of a particular subject or activity • *Michelle, for the uninitiated, is the central female character in ITV's latest comedy series.*

un·in·i·ti·at·ed /£ˌʌn·ɪ'nɪʃ·i·eɪ·tɪd, $-t̬ɪd/ *adj esp. humorous* • *To the uninitiated spectator, rugby can look just like a lot of overweight men wrestling in mud.*

un·in·spired /£ˌʌn·ɪn'spaɪəd, $-'spaɪrd/ *adj* not **inspired**, see at INSPIRE

un·in·spir·ing /£ˌʌn·ɪn'spaɪə·rɪŋ, $-'spaɪr·ɪŋ/ *adj*

un·in·tel·li·gi·ble /ˌʌn·ɪn'tel·ɪ·dʒə·bl̩/ *adj* not INTELLIGIBLE

un·in·ten·tion·al /ˌʌn·ɪn'ten·tʃən·əl/ *adj* not **intentional**, see at INTEND

un·in·ten·tion·al·ly /ˌʌn·ɪn'ten·tʃən·əl·i/ *adv* [not gradable]

un·in·te·rest·ed /£ʌn'ɪn·tər·es·tɪd, $-tɚ·es·t̬ɪd/ *adj* not **interested**, see at INTEREST INVOLVEMENT

un·in·ter·rupt·ed /£ʌnˌɪn·tər'ʌp·tɪd, $-t̬ə'rʌp-/ *adj* [not gradable] (esp. of a period of time) not broken by anything • *The weakness of the opposition has allowed the present government eight uninterrupted years in office.*

un·in·ter·rupt·ed·ly /£ʌnˌɪn·tər'ʌp·tɪd·li $-t̬ə'rʌp-/ *adv* [not gradable]

u·ni·on, U·ni·on /'juː·ni·ən/ *n* See at UNITE

u·ni·que /jʊ'niːk/ *adj* [not gradable] being the only existing one of its type or, more generally, unusual or special in some way • *Each person's genetic code is unique except in the case of identical twins.* • *I'd recognise your handwriting anywhere – it's unique.* • *Do not miss this unique opportunity to buy all six pans at half the recommended price.* • *As many as 100 species of fish, some unique* **to** (= only found in) *these waters, may have been affected by the pollution.* • LP› **One**

u·ni·que·ly /jʊ'niː·kli/ *adv* [not gradable] • *The son of the president, he would seem uniquely qualified to play the role of a politician.*

u·nique·ness /jʊ'niːk·nəs/ *n* [U] • *It is the uniqueness of her painting style for which she will be remembered.*

u·ni·sex /'juː·nɪ·seks/ *adj* intended for use by both males and females • *unisex clothes* • *unisex clothes sizes* • *a unisex hairdresser's* • *a unisex public toilet*

u·ni·son /'juː·nɪ·sᵊn/ *n* [U] **in unison** together; at the same time • *Try to sing in unison if you can.* • *We all stood up in unison.* • *The international community must act in unison if we are to find a lasting resolution to this problem.*

u·nit PEOPLE /'juː·nɪt/ *n* [C + sing/pl v] a group of people living or working together, esp. for a particular purpose • *Do you think it's true that the traditional family unit is becoming more and more a thing of the past?* • *He's now head of the Prime Minister's policy unit.* • *Dr Nussbaum is director of the Civil Liberties Research Unit at King's College, London.* • *A new national anti-terrorist unit has been established.* • *Both soldiers spent two weeks in training before being allowed to rejoin their unit* (= the particular part of the army to which they belonged).

u·nit MEASUREMENT /'juː·nɪt/ *n* [C] a standard measure which is used to express amounts • *A centimetre is a unit of length.* • *A calorie is a unit of energy.* • *The standard unit* **of currency** *in the US is the dollar.* • *That little dial on the meter shows you how many units of electricity you've used.* • *(Br)* A unit is also a standard measure of alcohol: *Experts say that women should not drink more than 14 units of alcohol a week compared with 19 for men.* • LP› **Units**

u·nit SEPARATE PART /'juː·nɪt/ *n* [C] a single item or a separate part of something larger • *The first year of the course is divided into four units.* • *Each unit of the course book focuses on a different grammar point.* • A unit is a piece of furniture or equipment which is intended to be fitted as a part of a set of similar or matching pieces: *kitchen/shelf/sink units* • A unit is also a small machine or part of a machine which has a particular purpose: *the central processing unit of a computer* • *a waste-disposal unit* • *a video display unit* • *(specialized)* Especially in business, a unit is a single complete item of the type that you are selling. • *(Am and Aus)* A unit can also be a single apartment in a bigger building: *a multiple-unit dwelling* ○ *The city is planning to sell public housing units to low-income families.* • *(Br)* A **unit trust** (*Am* **mutual fund**) is an organization which sells shares to the public and invests the money obtained in a range of different businesses.

u·nit HOSPITAL DEPARTMENT /'juː·nɪt/ *n* [C] a department in a hospital for the treatment of people with similar illnesses or conditions • *She's in the burns/paediatric/psychiatric unit.*

u·nit SINGLE NUMBER /'juː·nɪt/ *n* [C] any whole number less than ten, or *(specialized)* the number 1 • *Tens go in the left-hand column and units in the right.*

U·nit·a·rian /£ˌjuː·nɪ'teə·ri·ən, $-'ter·i-/ *n, adj* [not gradable] (a member of) a division of the Christian church which does not believe in the Trinity • *a Unitarian church/minister*

un·it·ar·y /£'juː·nɪ·tri, $-ter·i/ *adj Br* of a system of local government in the UK in which official power is given to one organization which deals with all matters in a local area instead of to several organizations which deal with only a few • *Wales will be divided into 21 unitary* **authorities** *instead of eight counties and 37 districts.*

u·nite *(obj)* /jʊ'naɪt/ *v* to bring or come together; combine • *If the opposition manages to unite, it may command over 55% of the vote.* [I] • *If ever a dance company could unite the differing worlds of rock and ballet, the Joffrey Ballet is it.* [T] • *"By uniting we stand, by dividing we fall (often found in the form 'United we stand, divided we fall')"* (John Dickinson *The Liberty Song*, 1768) • See also REUNITE. • LP› **One**

u·nit·ed /£jʊ'naɪ·tɪd, $-t̬ɪd/ *adj* • *Factions previously at war with one another are now united* **against** *the common enemy.* • *A whole village, united* **in** *their grief, comfort each other at the funeral of six-year-old Kylie Smith.* • *On that issue we're united* (= we agree). • *This year has seen the first film festival to take place in a united Germany.* • *The party's main failing has been their inability to present a united* **front** (= the appearance of being together and a whole) *to the people.* • **The United Nations** (also **UN**) is an international organization that was established in 1945 to maintain world peace: *The United Nations peacekeeping force has been sent to the region.* • **The United Kingdom** (also **UK**) is Britain and Northern Ireland. • See also UK. • LP› **Britain**

u·ni·ty /£'juː·nɪ·ti, $-nə·t̬i/ *n* [U] • Unity is the state of being joined together or in agreement: *Western European leaders remain sceptical about European political and economic unity.* ○ *It is feared that calls for national unity will go unheard in the present climate of fighting*

u·ni·on /'juː·ni·ən/ *n* • Union refers either to the act or the state of being joined together: *Meanwhile the debate on European political and monetary union continues.* [U] ○ *(fml or old use) She believes that the union* (= marriage) *of man and woman in holy matrimony is for ever.* [U] • A **(trade) union** is an organization of workers from a particular PROFESSION (= type of work) or trade which represents and protects the rights of workers within that profession and has discussions with employers over such matters as pay and working conditions: *the electricians'/machinists' union* [C + sing/pl v] • The **Union Flag** is the red, white and blue flag of Great Britain. • The **Union Jack** is *(fml)* the Union Flag when it is shown on a ship, or *(infml)* the flag of Great Britain.

u·nion·ize *obj, Br and Aus usually* **-ise** /'juː·ni·ᵊn·aɪz/ *v* [T] • To unionize is to organize workers into (trade) unions: *They're about to launch a campaign to unionize workers at all major discount supermarkets in the area.* ○ *unionized employees/labour/workers*

u·nion·i·za·tion, *Br and Aus usually* **-i·sa·tion** /ˌjuː·ni·ᵊn·aɪ'zeɪ·ʃᵊn/ *n* [U]

u·ni·ver·sal /£ˌjuː·nɪ'vɜː·sᵊl, $-'vɜːr-/ *adj* existing everywhere or involving everyone • *Food, like sex, is a subject of almost universal interest.* • *Charlie Chaplin is a comic actor of universal appeal.* • *The new reforms have not met with universal approval within the government.* • *Among other things, the group are demanding universal suffrage.* • *The latest bomb attacks serve as a reminder of the universal truth that wars are conducted for political purposes.* • A **universal joint** is a joint in a machine or engine which connects two parts and allows movement in all directions.

u·ni·ver·sal·ly /£ˌjuː·nɪ'vɜː·sᵊl·i, $-'vɜːr-/ *adv* • *The basic certificate is a universally recognised qualification.* • *"It is a truth universally acknowledged, that a single man in possession of a good fortune, must be in want of a wife"* (the beginning of *Pride and Prejudice* by Jane Austen, 1813)

u·ni·ver·sal·i·ty /£ˌjuː·nɪ·vɜː'sæl·ɪ·ti, $-vɜːr'sæl·ə·t̬i/ *n* [U] *fml*

u·ni·verse /£'juː·nɪ·vɜːs, $-vɜːrs/ *n* everything that exists, esp. all physical matter, including all the stars, planets, GALAXIES, etc. in space • *the big bang theory of the origin of* **the universe** [U] • *Is there intelligent life elsewhere in* **the** *universe?* [U] • *Scientists have speculated about the possibility of parallel universes.* [C] • *(fig.) The characters in his novels inhabit a bleak and hopeless universe.* [C] • You can also talk about a universe meaning the world, or the world that you are familiar with: *His family is his whole universe* (= everything that is important to him). [U]

u·ni·ver·si·ty /£ˌjuː·nɪ'vɜː·sɪ·ti, $-'vɜːr·sə·t̬i/ *n* [C] a college or collection of colleges at which people study for a degree • *Which university did you* **go to**/*were you* **at** (= did you study at)? • *She's teaches at the University of Connecticut.* • *a university campus/course/lecturer* • LP› **Schools and colleges**

un·just /ʌn'dʒʌst/ *adj disapproving* not JUST FAIR • *an unjust decision* • *The selection procedure is felt to be unjust be many people.*

unjustly /ʌn'dʒʌst·li/ *adv disapproving* • *Her complaint was unjustly dealt with.*

unjustifiable /ʌnˌdʒʌs·tɪ'faɪ·ə·bl/ *adj disapproving* • *The cost to the taxpayers of such a celebration would be unjustifiable* (= impossible to show to be fair or reasonable).

unjustifiably /ʌn'dʒʌs·tɪ·faɪ·ə·bli/ *adv disapproving* • *unjustifiably dangerous*

unjustified /ʌn'dʒʌs·tɪ·faɪd/ *adj disapproving* • *He said the proceedings were unfair and that any punishment would*

UNITS OF MEASUREMENT

The international system of metric units of measurement is not used in the US. It is now used in Britain but many people, especially older people, still use the older system of **imperial** units such as pounds, feet and gallons. Below are some of these common terms with their approximate values in the metric system. Please notice that some of the units have the same names but mean different quantities in Britain and the US. (For information on the use units of measurement, LP **Measurement** at MEASURE)

APPROXIMATE VALUES OF NON-METRIC UNITS

• units of length and distance

1 inch (in)	2.5 cm
1 foot (ft)	30 cm
1 yard (yd)	90 cm
5 miles (m)	8 km

1 foot - 30 cm

1 inch - 2.5 cm

UPTON 5miles

5 miles - 8 km

• units of area

11 square feet	1 m²
5 acres	2 hectares
1 square mile	2.6 square km

• units of weight and volume

1 ounce (oz)	28 g
1 pound (lb)	450 g
14 pounds	= *(Br)* 1 stone
	= 6.4 kg
1 ton	= *(Br)* 1 tonne
	= *(Am)* 0.9 tonnes

170 cm
73 kg

(Br)
5½ feet /
5 foot 6

11½ stone /
11 stone 7

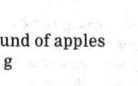

(Am)
5½ feet /
5 foot 6

160 pounds

There are 8 pints in a gallon:

	(Br)	*(Am)*
1 pint	0.6 litres	0.5 litres
1 gallon	4.5 litres	3.8 litres

• units of temperature

temperatures are given in degrees Fahrenheit, rather than Celsius.

	°F	°C
ice	32	0
warm room	70	20
hot day	85	30
body temperature	98	37
boiling water	212	100

a pound of apples
450 g

a pint of milk
(Br) 0.6 litres
(Am) 0.5 litres

be unjustified (=wrong and/or not deserved). • *His abounding, and as it turns out unjustified, confidence in his own judgment is not out of character.*

un·kempt /ʌŋ'kempt/ *adj disapproving* untidy; not cared for • *He always looks unkempt, as if he's only just got out of bed.* • *Theirs is the only garden in the neighbourhood with an unkempt lawn.* • *"Unkempt about those hedges blows/ An English unofficial rose"* (Rupert Brooke in the poem *The Old Vicarage at Grantchester,* 1915)

un·kind /ʌŋ'kaɪnd/ *adj* **-er, -est** not KIND GOOD • *an unkind remark* • *It was unkind* **of** *you* **to** *take his rattle away.* [+ *to* infinitive]

un·kind·ly /ʌŋ'kaɪnd·li/ *adv*

un·kind·ness /ʌŋ'kaɪnd·nəs/ *n* [U]

un·know·ing /£ʌn'nəʊ·ɪŋ, $-'noʊ-/ *adj literary* not aware of a particular situation or problem • *Having concealed himself in a nearby apartment he was then free to take pictures of his unknowing subjects.* • *She was dragged unknowing into the whole business.*

un·know·ing·ly /£ʌn'nəʊ·ɪŋ·li, $-'noʊ-/ *adv* • *A great number of people unknowingly* (=without knowing it) *carry the AIDS virus.*

un·known /£ʌn'nəʊn, $-'noʊn/ *adj, adv* not known or familiar • *The exact number of people carrying the virus is unknown.* • *As recently as six months ago her name was almost unknown in Britain.* • *His precise whereabouts is unknown.* • *Unknown to me, she'd gone and organized a party for my birthday in the evening.* • An **unknown quantity** is a person or a thing whose abilities, powers or effects are not yet known: *The third candidate for the party leadership is a relatively unknown quantity.*

un·known /£ʌn'nəʊn, $-'noʊn/ *n* • *Racism is in some ways just a fear of* **the** *unknown* (=what is not familiar or known to you). [U] • An unknown is a person, esp. a performer or sports player, who is not famous: *For her latest film she deliberately chose a cast of unknowns.* [C] • *(esp. Am and Aus)* An unknown is also something that cannot be guessed at or calculated because so little is known about it: *It's the big unknowns that make insurance companies uneasy.* [C]

un·law·ful /£ʌn'lɔː·fəl, $-'lɑː-/ *adj* not **lawful**, see at LAW RULE

un·law·ful·ly /£ʌn'lɔː·fəl·i, $-'lɑː-/ *adv*

un·lead·ed /ʌn'led·ɪd/ *adj* [not gradable] (of PETROL (=a fuel)) not containing LEAD (=a metallic element) • *Does your car use unleaded (petrol)?*

un·learn *obj* /£ʌn'lɜːn, $-'lɜːrn/ *v* [T] to make an effort to forget your usual way of doing something so that you can learn a new and sometimes better way • *I've had to unlearn the way I played guitar since I started taking formal lessons.*

un·leash *obj* /ʌn'liːʃ/ *v* [T] to release suddenly (a strong, uncontrollable and usually destructive force) • *At worst, nuclear war could be unleashed.* • *Rachel's arrival on the scene had unleashed passions in him that he could scarcely control.*

un·leav·ened /ʌn'lev·ənd/ *adj* [not gradable] (esp. of bread) made without YEAST and therefore flat • *A lot of the bread eaten in India is unleavened.*

un·less /ən'les/ *conjunction* except if • *You can't get a job unless you've got experience* (=you can only get a job if you've got experience). • *Unless you call me to say you're not coming I'll see you at the theatre* (=I will see you there if you do not call to say you're not coming). • *Don't promise* *anything unless you're 100 per cent sure* (=only promise things that you're 100 per cent certain of). • LP› **Conditionals**

un·like DIFFERENT FROM /ʌn'laɪk/ *prep* different from • *Dan's actually quite nice, unlike his father.* • *Unlike you, I'm not a great dancer.* • *Julia's a sociable sort of person – she's very unlike her sister in that respect.*

un·like NOT TYPICAL /ʌn'laɪk/ *prep* not typical or characteristic of • *It's unlike you to be quiet – is something wrong?*

un·like·ly /ʌn'laɪ·kli/ *adj* **-ier**, **-iest** not LIKELY • *"Do you think she'll get the work done on time?" "Seems unlikely."* • *It's pretty unlikely* **(that)** *they'll turn up now – it's nearly ten o'clock.* [+ (*that*) clause] • *He seems an unlikely-looking policeman* (=He is not what I expect a policemen to look like).

un·li·mit·ed /£ʌn'lɪm·ɪ·tɪd, $-ṭɪd/ *adj* not limited; not having a maximum possible amount, number or level • *Passes are available for one month's unlimited travel within Europe.* • *Demand for health care appears virtually unlimited*

un·list·ed /£ʌn'lɪs·tɪd, $-ṭɪd/ *adj* [not gradable] not included on a list of **stock exchange** company prices, or (*Am and Aus*) telephone numbers • *The company have just opened for business on the unlisted* **investments market**.

un·load (*obj*) /£ʌn'ləʊd, $-'loʊd/ *v* to remove the contents of (something), esp. a load of goods from a vehicle, the bullets from a gun or the film from a camera • *They showed pictures of the army unloading truck-loads of food aid in some of the worst hit areas.* [T] • *We watched a ship unloading.* [I] • *I'm just unloading my camera.* [T] • *(fig.) I'm afraid I've been unloading my worries* **on** *poor Ann here* (= telling her about them).

un·lock *obj* /£ʌn'lɒk, $-'lɑːk/ *v* [T] to open (something, esp. a door which is locked) using a key or an electronic device • *Could you unlock the door for me – my hands are full.* • *I keep worrying that I've left the garage door unlocked.* • *(fig.) A chemical has been discovered that may be the key to unlocking* (= solving) *the mysteries of Parkinson's disease.* • *(fig.) One of poetry's functions is to somehow unlock the imagination.*

un·looked–for /£ʌn'lʊkt·fɔːʳ, $-fɔːr/ *adj* [before n] unexpected; UNFORESEEN • *Of course there were one or two unlooked-for problems along the way but eventually we got the project finished.*

un·luck·y /ʌn'lʌk·i/ *adj* **-ier**, **-iest** not **lucky**, see at LUCK • *The couple were unlucky* **enough to** *be in the hotel when the terrorist group struck.* [+ *to* infinitive] • *If you are unlucky* **enough to** *get a cold, it can take months for catarrh and blocked sinuses to clear.* [+ *to* infinitive]

un·luck·i·ly /ʌn'lʌk·ɪ·li/ *adv*

un·made /ʌn'meɪd/ *adj* [not gradable] (of a bed) having sheets and covers that are still untidy from having been slept in • *An unmade bed was strewn with dirty clothes and beer cans leaned against one wall.*

un·make *obj* /ʌn'meɪk/ *v* [T usually passive] *past* **unmade** /ʌn'meɪd/ to destroy (a reputation or a CAREER) • *Actors' reputations have been made and unmade on this London stage.*

un·manned /ʌn'mænd/ *adj* [not gradable] (of a spacecraft or a place where military guards work) having no people present to operate or be in charge of it • *The unmanned spacecraft carries an infrared telescope.* • *An unmanned mission to the planet Mars is planned for next year.* • *Bombs had caused enemy troops to desert in such numbers that some defensive lines were left virtually unmanned.*

un·mar·ried /£ʌn'mær·ɪd, $-'mer-/ *adj* [not gradable] not **married**, see at MARRY • *In the borough of Lambeth, two births in five are to unmarried* **mothers**. • *The survey shows that more and more unmarried couples are choosing to live together.* • *Their youngest son is still unmarried.* • LP› **Relationships**

un·mask *obj* /£ʌn'mɑːsk, $-'mæsk/ *v* [T] to show the bad, and previously hidden, truth about (someone or something) • *You spend the whole film believing that she's the innocent victim and when she's finally unmasked it's quite a shock.* • *The alleged conspirators were unmasked and summarily shot.* • *The investigation led to the unmasking of his fraud.*

un·matched /ʌn'mætʃt/ *adj* [not gradable] *fml* having no equal; better than any other of the same type • *For years they have enjoyed a standard of living unmatched* **by** *anyone else in Europe.* • *She has an intellectual capacity unmatched in the rest of the group.*

un·men·tion·a·ble /ʌn'men·tʃᵊn·ə·bl̩/ *adj* shocking and embarrassing and therefore forbidden or disapproved of as a subject of conversation • *In the past pregnancy was considered to be something unmentionable.* • *What's the matter with him – or is it some unmentionable* **disease** *that he doesn't like people to know about?*

un·mind·ful /ʌn'maɪnd·fᵊl/ *adj fml* not **mindful**, see at MIND BE CAREFUL

un·miss·a·ble /ʌn'mɪs·ə·bl̩/ *adj* [not gradable] *infml* (esp. of a film, play, etc.) so good that it must be seen • *It's fairly entertaining as films go but I wouldn't describe it as unmissable.*

un·mis·tak·a·ble /ˌʌn·mɪ'steɪ·kə·bl̩/ *adj* not likely to be confused with something else; clearly recognizable • *There was an unmistakable smell of incense in the air.* • *The rash of reddish spots are an unmistakable symptom of the disease.*

un·mi·ti·gat·ed /£ʌn'mɪt·ɪ·geɪ·tɪd, $-'mɪṭ·ɪ·geɪ·ṭɪd/ *adj* (esp. of something bad or unsuccessful) total, esp. lacking any good or positive points • *For the people living near it, the new road has been an unmitigated* **disaster**. • *She described the film as 'ninety minutes of gloom, unmitigated by* (= lacking) *the slightest hint of humour'.*

un·moved /ʌn'muːvd/ *adj* [after v] not feeling any emotion • *Both men appeared unmoved as the judge read out their sentence.* • *It was an emotional speech and few people in the audience remained unmoved.*

un·nat·u·ral /£ʌn'nætʃ·ᵊr·ᵊl, $'-ɚ-/ *adj* not **natural**, see at NATURE LIFE

un·nat·u·ral·ly /£ʌn'nætʃ·ᵊr·ᵊl·i, $'-ɚ-/ *adv*

un·nec·es·sa·ry /ʌn'nes·ə·ser·i/ *adj* not needed or wanted, or more than is needed or wanted • *I found a lot of the violence in the film totally unnecessary.* • *The idea is to kill the animal as quickly as possible without causing unnecessary suffering.* • *Obviously we don't want to incur any unnecessary expenses.* • *It's claimed that the police used unnecessary force to control the crowds at last Saturday's demonstration.* • A remark or action that is rude or offensive might be described as unnecessary: *He just humiliated her in front of everyone – it was so unnecessary.*

un·nec·es·sar·i·ly /ʌn'nes·ə·ser·ɪ·li/ *adv* • *Many heart attack victims are dying unnecessarily, it is claimed in a report out this week.* • *Of course we don't want to alarm people unnecessarily but they should be alerted to potential dangers.* • *I thought his explanation was unnecessarily complex.*

un·nerve *obj* /£ʌn'nɜːv, $-'nɜːrv/ *v* [T] to make (someone) feel less confident and slightly frightened • *I think it unnerved me to be interviewed by so many people.* • *He's quite a sociable baby but I think it unnerves him to have so many strangers in the room.* • *The long silence unnerved him.*

un·nerv·ing /£ʌn'nɜː·vɪŋ, $-'nɜːr-/ *adj* • *Meeting a twin brother I didn't know I had was an unnerving experience.* • *It's the way that he stares that I find so unnerving.* • *Even for the toughest child, the first day at school is bound to be an unnerving occasion.* • *I don't study the opposition very hard before a race – I find it too unnerving.*

un·nerv·ing·ly /£ʌn'nɜː·vɪŋ·li, $-'nɜːr-/ *adv*

un·ob·tru·sive /ˌʌn·əb'truː·sɪv/ *adj approving* not noticeable; seeming to fit in well with the background • *In the north of the city the army's presence is unobtrusive.* • *He was the perfect waiter, being efficient, unobtrusive and yet attentive.* • *I've replaced that orange flowery wallpaper with a more unobtrusive beige and white print.* • *Make-up this season is unobtrusive and natural-looking.*

un·ob·trus·ive·ly /ˌʌn·əb'truː·sɪv·li/ *adv approving* • *We slipped into the back of the hall as unobtrusively as possible.*

un·ob·trus·ive·ness /ˌʌn·əb'truː·sɪv·nəs/ *n* [U] *approving*

un·of·fi·cial /ˌʌn·ə'fɪʃ·ᵊl/ *adj* [not gradable] not **official**, see at OFFICE RESPONSIBILITY • *Unofficial* **estimates** *claim Japanese men work a staggering 2 700-3 000 hours a year on average, or around 55 hours a week.* • *There has, according to unofficial* **figures**, *been a 51% increase in the numbers of men convicted of minor offences in the last four years.* • *Unofficial* **reports** *said the death toll could be much higher.* • *Many newspapers gave evidence of the difficulty in assessing the validity of rumours and the need to rely on unofficial* **sources**.

un·of·fi·cial·ly /ˌʌn·ə'fɪʃ·ᵊl·i/ *adv* • *Unemployment has been unofficially* **estimated** *at 70%.*

un·or·tho·dox /£ʌn'ɔː·θə·dɒks, $-'ɔːr·θə·dɑːks/ *adj* (of behaviour, ideas, methods, etc.) different from what is usual or expected • *Steiner was recognized as an original if unorthodox thinker.* • *He was an unorthodox choice to be director of a mild family film.*

un·pack *(obj)* /ʌm'pæk/ *v* to remove (things) from (a SUITCASE, bag or box) • *I haven't even had time to unpack yet.* [I] • *I'll make us some supper while you're unpacking your* **bags**. [T] • *It won't take long to unpack my clothes.* [T] • *She's in the kitchen unpacking the shopping.* [T] • To unpack also means to explain or to make a meaning clearer: *He read the agreed statement to the group and then began to unpack it for them.* [T] ○ *The new procedures manual will take some unpacking!*

un·pal·a·ta·ble /£ʌn'pæl·ə·tə·bl̩, $-t̬ə-/ *adj fml* (esp. of a fact or idea) unpleasant or shocking and therefore difficult to accept • *The truth is unpalatable – before war broke out these murderers, rapists and torturers were ordinary men.* • *But facts must be faced, unpalatable as they are, and there simply isn't enough work for that number of staff.* • *Which ever way you look at it unpalatable decisions will have to be made and factories will close.* • Food which is unpalatable is unpleasant to taste or eat: *I find raw fish completely unpalatable!*

un·par·al·leled /£ʌn'pær·əl·eld, $-'per-/ *adj fml* having no equal; better or greater than any other • *They enjoyed success on a scale unparalleled by any previous pop group.* • *As executive editor of the Times, he held a position of almost unparalleled power in American journalism.*

un·pick *obj* /ʌm'pɪk/ *v* [T] to cut or remove (the stitches) from (a line of sewing) • *You can try unpicking the seams and letting out some of the material.* • *(fig.) The former leader now has to watch his successor unpicking* (= destroying) *much of what he strived so hard to achieve.*

un·placed /ʌm'pleɪst/ *adj* [not gradable] (in horse racing) not one of the first three horses to finish a race • *The sole British runner, White Knight, was unplaced.*

un·play·a·ble WELL HIT /ʌn'pleɪ·ə·bl̩/ *adj* (of a ball) hit or thrown so hard or skilfully that it is impossible to hit • *And that's Mendoza's serve at its best – quite unplayable.*

un·play·a·ble NOT USABLE /ʌn'pleɪ·ə·bl̩/ *adj* (of an area of ground used for sports) not able to be played on, esp. because of bad weather conditions • *After last night's heavy frosts the course was this morning declared unplayable.*

un·play·a·ble DIFFICULT MUSIC /ʌn'pleɪ·ə·bl̩/ *adj* (of a piece of music) too difficult to perform • *When Schoenberg completed his Violin Concerto, in California in 1936, it was declared unplayable.*

un·pleas·ant /ʌm'plez·ənt/ *adj* not PLEASANT • *an unpleasant surprise* • *the unpleasant truth*

un·pleas·ant·ly /ʌm'plez·ənt·li/ *adv*

un·pleas·ant·ness /ʌm'plez·ənt·nəs/ *n* [C/U]

un·pop·u·lar /£ʌm'pɒp·jʊ·lər, $-'pɑː·pjə·lɚ/ *adj* not POPULAR LIKED • *Night flights from the airport are extremely/***deeply** *unpopular.* • *The government is becoming* **increasingly** *unpopular.*

un·pop·u·lar·i·ty /£ˌʌn·pɒp·jʊ'lær·ɪ·ti, $-pɑː·pjʊ'ler·ə·t̬i/ *n* [U]

un·prec·e·dent·ed /£ʌn'pres·ɪ·den·tɪd, $-t̬ɪd/ *adj* never having happened or existed in the past • *Rivalry in recruiting students, and hence for funds, is set to reach unprecedented* **heights**. • *This century has witnessed environmental destruction on an unprecedented* **scale**. • *In an unprecedented* **step**, *Walt Disney have had the scene cut from the film.*

un·pre·dic·ta·ble /ˌʌn·prɪ'dɪk·tə·bl̩/ *adj* tending to change suddenly and seemingly without reason and therefore not able to be PREDICTED (= judged in advance) or depended on • *Changes in the market are, of course, largely unpredictable.* • *The weather there can be a bit unpredictable – one minute it's blue skies and the next minute it's pouring down.* • *Six months before a presidential election, French politics have never looked so unpredictable.* • *The hours in this job are very unpredictable – you sometimes have to work late at very short notice.* • *He was totally unpredictable – you never really knew what he would be like from one day to the next.*

un·pre·dic·ta·bly /ˌʌn·prɪ'dɪk·tə·bli/ *adv* • *Fashions change quite unpredictably.* • *His peculiar bursts of laughter, which would erupt quite unpredictably, had begun to worry his wife.* • *New infectious diseases, such as AIDS and herpes, have unpredictably appeared.*

un·pre·dic·ta·bil·i·ty /£ˌʌn·prɪ·dɪk·tə'bɪl·ɪ·ti, $-ə·t̬i/ *n* [U] • *Africa is the world's driest continent, but the unpredictability of the rains is as much of a problem as the lack of them.*

un·pre·pared /£ˌʌn·prɪ'peəd, $-'perd/ *adj* not prepared; not ready • *He was completely/totally/wholly unprepared* **for** *what he saw.* • *The extreme cold weather* **caught** *them unprepared.*

un·pre·ten·tious /ˌʌn·prɪ'ten·ʃəs/ *adj* not PRETENTIOUS

un·prin·ci·pled /ʌn'prɪnt·sɪ·pl̩d/ *adj* having or showing no moral rules or standards of good behaviour • *Ford, he said, was one of the most unpleasant men he had ever met – an unprincipled and egotistical philanderer.*

un·print·a·ble /£ʌn'prɪn·tə·bl̩, $-t̬ə-/ *adj* containing swear words or other offensive language and therefore not acceptable in printed form, for example in a newspaper • *The taxi driver entertained us with unprintable* **observations/remarks/views** *about government ministers all the way to the airport.* • *His response to the journalist's enquiry was unprintable.*

un·pro·fes·sion·al /ˌʌn·prə'feʃ·ən·əl/ *adj* not showing the standard of behaviour or skills that are expected of a person in a skilled job • *Doctor Rivers was charged with gross negligence, unprofessional conduct and improper use of dangerous drugs.* • *I'd rather not be discussing one of my colleagues behind her back – it's a bit unprofessional.*

un·pro·fes·sion·al·ly /ˌʌn·prə'feʃ·ən·əl·i/ *adv*

un·prom·is·ing /£ʌn'prɒm·ɪ·sɪŋ, $-'prɑː·mɪ-/ *adj* not **promising**, see at PROMISE

un·prompt·ed /£ʌn'prɒmp·tɪd, $-'prɑːmp·t̬ɪd/ *adj* without being told to say or do something • *It's nice if children can remember to say thank you for things unprompted.* • *Jim was remarkably charming this evening – he even said, unprompted, how nice Margot looked in her dress.*

un·pro·nounce·a·ble /ˌʌn·prə'naʊnt·sə·bl̩/ *adj* difficult to say or (of something written) difficult to know how to say • *She's got some unpronounceable name which seems to be all consonants.*

un·pro·voked /£ˌʌn·prə'vəʊkt, $-'voʊkt/ *adj* (esp. of an unpleasant action or remark) not caused by anything and therefore unfair • *Police claimed they were forced to fire after coming under unprovoked* **attack**. • *This, said the judge, was a cold-blooded murder, an act of unprovoked aggression for which there was no justification.*

un·pun·ished /ʌn'pʌn·ɪʃt/ *adj* [after v; not gradable] not punished • *If a referee allows a foul like that to* **go** *unpunished he's asking for trouble.* • *It might be his first offence but if people like him* **go** *unpunished it sets a bad example to others.*

un·put·down·a·ble /ˌʌn·pʊt'daʊ·nə·bl̩/ *adj infml* (of a book) so exciting that you do not want to stop reading it • *"Was it a good read?" "Oh, totally unputdownable – I read it solidly for two whole days."*

un·qual·i·fied WITHOUT QUALIFICATIONS /£ʌŋ'kwɒl·ɪ·faɪd, $-'kwɑː·lɪ-/ *adj* lacking the qualifications needed for a particular job • *Schools that find it hard to recruit qualified teachers often have to employ on unqualified ones.*

un·qual·i·fied TOTAL /£ʌŋ'kwɒl·ɪ·faɪd, $'kwɑː·lɪ-/ *adj* not limited in any way; total • *We achieved most of the project's initial aims though I wouldn't say that it's been an unqualified* **success**. • *The proposal has the unqualified* **support** *of the entire committee.* • *He was an exceptional man who will be remembered with unqualified love.*

un·ques·tion·a·ble /ʌŋ'kwes·tʃə·nə·bl̩/ *adj* not **questionable**, see at QUESTION ASKING

un·ques·tion·a·bly /ʌŋ'kwes·tʃə·nə·bli/ *adv*

un·ques·tion·ing /ʌŋ'kwes·tʃə·nɪŋ/ *adj esp. disapproving* (esp. of obedience or acceptance) total; given without consideration, opposition or doubt • *Like all tyrannical leaders, he demanded unquestioning obedience from his followers.* • *What amazes me is her unquestioning acceptance of everything he says.*

un·ques·tion·ing·ly /ʌŋ'kwes·tʃə·nɪŋ·li/ *adv* • *He supports the administration on foreign policy, but not unquestioningly.*

un·qui·et /ʌŋ'kwaɪət/ *adj literary* troubled and anxious; not peaceful or calm • *One can only hope that his unquiet spirit found some peace in the grave.*

un·quote /£ʌŋ'kwəʊt, $-'kwoʊt, '--/ *adv* [not gradable] See **quote unquote** at QUOTE SAY.

un·rav·el *(obj)* /ʌn'ræv·əl/ *v* **-ll-** or *Am usually* **-l-** (of a piece of woollen or woven cloth) to separate into threads, or to separate the single threads of (a piece of cloth, a knot or a mass of threads) • *You'd better mend that hole before the whole sweater starts to unravel.* [I] • *I had to unravel one of the sleeves because I realised I'd knitted it too small.* [T] • *(fig.) No-one has yet satisfactorily unravelled* (= solved) *the* *mystery of Johnson's death.* [T] • *(fig.) We've got a long way to go before we unravel* (= discover) *the secrets of genetics.* [T] • *(fig.) As talks between the leaders broke down, several months of careful diplomacy were unravelled* (= destroyed). [T]

un·read·a·ble /ʌn'riː·də·bl̩/ *adj* too boring, complicated or badly written to be worth reading, or ILLEGIBLE (= impossible to read because unclear or untidy) • *I know a lot of people who've really enjoyed James Joyce's 'Ulysses' but I found it totally unreadable.* • *His views were controversial – Keats he considered overrated, Henry James unreadable.* • *The page had so many corrections and comments on it that the original text was virtually unreadable.*

un·real [IMAGINARY] /£ʌn'rɪəl, $-'riːl/ *adj* as if imagined; strange and dream-like • *The funeral passed like some awful dream – it all seemed completely unreal somehow.* • *The whole evening had a sort of bizarre, unreal quality to it.*

un·re·al·i·ty /£ˌʌn·ri'æl·ɪ·ti, $-ə·t̬i/ *n* [U] • *There was an air of unreality about the visit, as if I'd stepped into another world for two weeks.*

un·real [SURPRISING] /£ʌn'rɪəl, $-'riːl/ *adj slang* extremely or surprisingly good • *He gave you how much? Man, that's unreal!* • *It was unreal, no kidding it was the best film I've ever seen!*

un·rea·son·a·ble /ʌn'riː·zᵊn·ə·bl̩/ *adj* not REASONABLE

un·rea·son·a·bly /ʌn'riː·zᵊn·ə·bli/ *adv*

un·rea·son·ing /ʌn'riː·zᵊn·ɪŋ/ *adj fml* (esp. of feelings or beliefs) not based on reason or judgment • *There exists between these two ethnic groups an unreasoning hatred of one another.* • *Clarke has dismissed the report as unreasoning nonsense.*

un·re·con·struct·ed /£ˌʌn·riː·kᵊn'strʌk·tɪd, $-t̬ɪd/ *adj often humorous* having opinions or behaving in a way which is not considered to be modern or politically acceptable in modern times • *An unreconstructed socialist, he is passionately against all forms of privatization.* • *She describes herself as an unreconstructed feminist.*

un·re·fined /ˌʌn·rɪ'faɪnd/ *adj* not **refined**, see at REFINE

un·re·lent·ing /£ˌʌn·rɪ'len·tɪŋ, $-t̬ɪŋ/ *adj fml* extremely determined; never weakening in effort or admitting defeat • *She will be remembered as an unrelenting opponent of racial discrimination.* • *The government's efforts to solve the conflict would be unrelenting, said the president.*

un·re·lent·ing·ly /£ˌʌn·rɪ'len·tɪŋ·li, $-t̬ɪŋ-/ *adv fml*

un·re·li·a·ble /ˌʌn·rɪ'laɪə·bl̩/ *adj* not RELIABLE

un·re·lieved /ˌʌn·rɪ'liːvd/ *adj fml* (esp. of something bad) continuous; never improved, not even for a short period • *She held the family together through years of unrelieved poverty.* • *Bringing up a child would mean whole days and weeks of unrelieved tedium.* • *So the economic outlook is not one of unrelieved gloom – there is a faint glimmer of hope.*

un·re·liev·ed·ly /ˌʌn·rɪ'liː·vɪd·li/ *adv* • *The tone of all this is unrelievedly smug and supercilious, and thus makes for very unpleasant reading.*

un·re·mit·ting /£ˌʌn·rɪ'mɪt·ɪŋ, $-'mɪt̬-/ *adj fml* never stopping, weakening in effort or failing • *Our thanks are due to Bob Lawrence whose unremitting labours have ensured the success of the whole scheme.* • *She fought valiantly against the government whose hostility towards reform was unremitting.*

un·re·mit·ting·ly /£ˌʌn·rɪ'mɪt·ɪŋ·li, $-'mɪt̬-/ *adv* • *Some viewers complain about the unremittingly pro-government press and television.*

un·re·pen·tant /£ˌʌn·rɪ'pen·tənt, $-t̬ənt/ *adj* not **repentant**, see at REPENT

un·rep·re·sen·ta·tive /£ˌʌn·rep·rɪ'zen·tə·tɪv, $-t̬ə·t̬ɪv/ *adj* not **representative**, see at REPRESENT [ACT FOR], REPRESENT [DESCRIBE]

un·re·quit·ed /£ˌʌn·rɪ'kwaɪ·tɪd, $-t̬ɪd/ *adj fml or humorous* (of love) not returned • *It's just another poem on the pain of unrequited* **love**. • *But, alas, Miss Twining's* **love** *for the parson was unrequited.*

un·re·served /£ˌʌn·rɪ'zɜːvd, £-'zɜː·vɪd, $-'zɜːrvd, $-'zɜːr·vɪd/ *adj fml* without any doubts or feeling uncertain; total • *He was a good strong leader, she said, who deserved his party's unreserved support.* • *The scheme was accepted, though it certainly didn't meet with unreserved approval.*

un·re·serv·ed·ly /£ˌʌn·rɪ'zɜː·vɪd·li, $-'zɜːr-/ *adv fml* • *The paper's editor has admitted that the accusations were unfounded and apologized unreservedly to the senator.* • *It was a fairly entertaining film, though I wouldn't recommend it unreservedly.*

un·re·solved /£ˌʌn·rɪ'zɑlvd, $-'zɑːlvd/ *adj* [not gradable] *fml* (esp. of a problem or difficulty) not solved or ended • *The question of contracts* **remains** *unresolved.* • *The unresolved tension is the key to the play's fascination.*

un·re·spon·sive /£ˌʌn·rɪ'spɒnt·sɪv, $-'spɑːnt-/ *adj* not **responsive**, see at RESPOND

un·rest /ʌn'rest/ *n* [U] disagreements or fighting between different groups of people • *It is feared that the civil unrest we are now witnessing in this country could lead to full-scale civil war.* • *The whole of this region seems to be in the grip of nationalist and ethnic unrest.* • *More unemployment could stir new industrial unrest in a country already beset by social problems.*

un·re·strained /ˌʌn·rɪ'streɪnd/ *adj* not limited in any way; free • *His speech earned him unrestrained* **criticism** *from the opposition parties.* • *He's very critical of the sort of unrestrained consumerism that we see in the West.* • *I expected a little sympathy from you and what do I get – unrestrained laughter!*

un·ri·valled, *Am usually* **un·ri·valed** /ʌn'raɪ·vᵊld/ *adj* having no equal; better than any other of the same type • *Among other things, the museum boasts an unrivalled collection of French porcelain.* • *The misfortunes of others are, of course, an unrivalled source of amusement.*

un·roll *(obj)* /£ʌn'rəʊl, $-'roʊl/ *v* to (cause to) open and become flat from a rolled position • *I always fix the toilet paper so that it unrolls over the top.* [I] • *She unrolled the most beautiful silken embroidery for us to look at.* [T]

un·ruf·fled /ʌn'rʌf·l̩d/ *adj* calm; not nervous or worried, usually despite a difficult situation • *For a man in imminent danger of losing his job, he appeared quite unruffled.*

un·ru·ly /ʌn'ruː·li/ *adj* **-ier, -iest** (of people) difficult to control and not tending to obey rules, or (of hair) difficult to keep tidy, tending to stick up or out • *I had an unruly class of adolescents on Thursday that I used to dread teaching.* • *An unruly crowd of demonstrators suddenly turned riotous as the police appeared.* • *With an unruly mop of black hair and one of his front teeth missing, he's quite an alarming sight.*

un·ru·li·ness /ʌn'ruː·lɪ·nəs/ *n* [U] • *The police visited the nightclub on two occasions after complaints of unruliness by nearby residents.*

un·sad·dle *obj* /ʌn'sæd·l̩/ *v* [T] to take the SADDLE (= seat for a horse's back) off (a horse) or to cause (someone riding a horse) to fall off

un·safe [IN DANGER] /ˌʌn'seɪf/ *adj* not SAFE

un·safe [LAW] /ʌn'seɪf/ *adj Br law* (of a decision that someone is guilty) able to be APPEALED against (= considered again) in court • *an unsafe conviction/verdict*

un·said /ʌn'sed/ *adj* [after v; not gradable] not said, although thought of or felt • *I know she's put on weight, Michael, but some things are* **better left** *unsaid!* • *We're close friends – there should be nothing* **left** *unsaid between us.* • See also UNSPOKEN.

un·sat·is·fac·to·ry /£ʌnˌsæt·ɪs'fæk·tᵊr·i, $-ˌsæt̬·ɪs'fæk·tɚ-/ *adj* not SATISFACTORY

un·sa·vou·ry *Br and Aus, Am and Aus* **un·sa·vo·ry** /£ʌn'seɪ·vᵊr·i, $-vɚ-/ *adj* unpleasant or morally offensive • *A great deal is written in the book about the ageing rock-star's unsavoury sexual practices.* • *He kept talking about his operation over dinner – it was most unsavoury.* • *Some sort of Mafia connection in the 60s earned him a rather unsavoury reputation.*

un·scathed /ʌn'skeɪðd/ *adj* [after v] without injuries or damage being caused • *Her husband died in the accident and she, amazingly, escaped unscathed.* • *According to recent polls, the government appears to be emerging relatively unscathed from the recent crisis.*

un·sci·en·ti·fic /ˌʌn·saɪən'tɪf·ɪk/ *adj disapproving* not obeying scientific methods or principles • *The industry's claim that its products are tested to meet indoor air quality standards is misleading and unscientific.* • *The newspaper printed a rather unscientific account of how you inherit characteristics from your parents.*

un·scram·ble *obj* /ʌn'skræm·bl̩/ *v* [T] to discover the meaning of (information given in a secret or complicated way); to DECODE • *You need a decoding device to unscramble some of the signals sent out by satellite and cable TV.* • *(fig.) The author has spent 12 years unscrambling a continent's history.*

un·screw *obj* [REMOVE LID] /ʌn'skruː/ *v* [T] to take (the lid or top) off (something) by twisting it round • *I can't unscrew the top – it's really tight.* • *Can you unscrew this jar for me?* •

He unscrewed the top off his favourite silver fountain pen and began to write.

un·screw *obj* [REMOVE SCREWS] /ʌnˈskruː/ *v* [T] to remove (something) by taking the screws out of it • *You'll need to unscrew the back of the box to get to the faulty circuit.*

un·script·ed /£ʌnˈskrɪp·tɪd, $-t̬ɪd/ *adj* [not gradable] not **scripted**, see at SCRIPT [TEXT]

un·scru·pu·lous /ʌnˈskruː·pjʊ·ləs/ *adj disapproving* not SCRUPULOUS

un·sea·son·a·ble /ʌnˈsiː·zᵊn·ə·bl̩/ *adj fml* (of weather) not suitable for the time of year • *When you're used to snow in January, warm sunny weather feels unseasonable.*

un·sea·son·a·bly /ʌnˈsiː·zᵊn·ə·bli/ *adv fml* • *Unseasonably low temperatures have left the beaches deserted in what are usually the busiest two weeks of summer.*

un·seat *obj* [REMOVE FROM POWER] /ʌnˈsiːt/ *v* [T] to remove (someone) from power, esp. as a result of an election • *The opposition candidate failed by only 39 votes to unseat the cabinet minister.*

un·seat *obj* [REMOVE FROM SEAT] /ʌnˈsiːt/ *v* [T] (of a horse) to throw (a person) from its back • *Only twenty horses completed the course – eight fell, six were pulled-up and four unseated their riders.*

un·seed·ed /ʌnˈsiː·dɪd/ *adj* [not gradable] not SEEDED in a tennis competition • *Connors, in 1991, was unseeded for the first time since 1973.*

un·see·ing /ʌnˈsiː·ɪŋ/ *adj literary* (esp. of eyes) not seeing or noticing anything, although able to see • *Bored out of its mind, the monkey stares out of the cage with unseeing eyes.*

un·seem·ly /ʌnˈsiːm·li/ *adj* not SEEMLY

un·seem·li·ness /ʌnˈsiːm·lɪ·nəs/ *n* [U]

un·seen /ʌnˈsiːn/ *adj* [not gradable] not seen or not able to be seen • *She found the side-door open and slipped into the house unseen.* • *Unseen birds sang in the trees above us.* • *"Full many a flower is born to blush unseen"* (Thomas Gray in the poem *Elegy Written in a Country Churchyard*, 1751)

un·self·ish /ʌnˈsel·fɪʃ/ *adj* not **selfish**, see at SELF [PERSONAL ADVANTAGE]

un·self·ish·ly /ˌʌnˈsel·fɪʃ·li/ *adv*

un·self·ish·ness /ʌnˈsel·fɪʃ·nəs/ *n* [U]

un·set·tled [CHANGEABLE] /£ʌnˈset·l̩d, $-ˈset̬-/ *adj* tending to change suddenly; not calm or having a regular pattern • *The 5-day Alpine forecast is for continuing unsettled* **weather**, *with even more snow to come.* • *Such an unsettled political climate inevitably discourages foreign investment.* • *This unsettled period saw a succession of governments in office.*

un·set·tling /£ʌnˈset·l̩ɪŋ, $-ˈset̬-/ *adj* • Unsettling means causing change: *The sudden drop in crude oil prices has had an unsettling effect on the oil sector, dramatically lowering share prices.*

un·set·tle *obj* /£ʌnˈset·l̩, $-ˈset̬-/ *v* [T] • *There are fears that the airline's decision to cut air fares will unsettle the market.*

un·set·tled [ANXIOUS] /£ʌnˈset·l̩d, $-ˈset̬-/ *adj* anxious and worried; unable to relax • *Any child will become unsettled if the care it receives continually changes.*

un·set·tling /£ʌnˈset·l̩ɪŋ, $-ˈset̬-/ *adj* • Unsettling means causing anxiety: *I received the rather unsettling news that the funding for my research may finish at the end of the year.* ○ *It's very unsettling to have to keep moving every couple of years.* ○ *One of the film's many unsettling images is of a child playing with her father's gun.*

un·set·tle *obj* /£ʌnˈset·l̩, $-ˈset̬-/ *v* [T] • *Rumours of a company takeover have unsettled shareholders.* • *Even the most experienced of West Indian batsmen was unsettled by the sheer speed of this bowler.*

un·shake·a·ble, **un·shak·a·ble** /ʌnˈʃeɪ·kə·bl̩/ *adj* (esp. of trust or a belief) firm and not able to be weakened or destroyed • *I have unshakeable faith in my eldest daughter's common sense.* • *What keeps me going, I suppose, is my unshakeable conviction that it will all be all right in the end.* • *She was blessed with an unshakeable belief in her own abilities.*

un·shav·en /ʌnˈʃeɪ·vᵊn/ *adj* not having had the hair removed • *a unshaven chin/man*

un·sight·ly /ʌnˈsaɪt·li/ *adj* **-ier, -iest** *slightly fml* unattractive; ugly • *He had undone the buttons of his shirt, exposing an unsightly expanse of white flesh.* • *Dog muck on the pavements is not only unsightly, it's also a health hazard.*

un·skilled /ʌnˈskɪld/ *adj* (of people) without any particular work skills, or (of work) not needing any particular skills • *In the mid-1940's the introduction of mechanical cotton pickers greatly reduced the demand for unskilled* **labour**. • *He had a succession of unskilled* **jobs** *in restaurants and on building sites.* • *The report shows that wage rates for unskilled* **workers** *have risen relative to those for skilled workers.*

un·sliced /ʌnˈslaɪst/ *adj* [not gradable] not **sliced**, see at SLICE [PIECE] • *unsliced bread* • [PIC] **Bread and cakes**

un·so·cia·ble /£ʌnˈsəʊ·ʃə·bl̩, $-ˈsoʊ-/ *adj* not **sociable**, see at SOCIAL

un·so·cial /£ʌnˈsəʊ·ʃᵊl, $-ˈsoʊ-/ *adj* (of hours that are worked) during the weekend, the night or at other times outside the usual working day • *Nurses' pay is low even though the job is demanding and often unpleasant and the hours are unsocial.* • *I don't want to work unsocial* **hours**.

un·so·li·cit·ed /£ˌʌn·səˈlɪs·ɪ·tɪd, $-t̬ɪd/ *adj* not requested • *He rarely offers unsolicited advice.* • *I get so much unsolicited mail – it really annoys me.* • *So what distinguishes one novel from the 5000 or so unsolicited manuscripts that a publisher receives annually?*

un·so·phis·ti·cat·ed /£ˌʌn·səˈfɪs·tɪ·keɪ·tɪd, $-t̬ɪd/ *adj* not SOPHISTICATED

un·sound [NOT ACCEPTABLE] /ʌnˈsaʊnd/ *adj* (esp. of a person's activities) not good enough, acceptable or able to be trusted • *Kilmer, who is serving a life sentence, claims he was convicted on the basis of unsound police evidence.* • *There have been allegations that he approved unsound practices as director of the now-defunct bank.* • *I've always been convinced that the judgement of most film critics is unsound.*

un·sound [WEAK] /ʌnˈsaʊnd/ *adj* (esp. of a building) in bad condition and likely to fall down or fail • *The bridge is one of several said to be structurally unsound in some degree.*

un·spar·ing [HIDING NOTHING] /£ʌnˈspeə·rɪŋ, $-ˈsper·ɪŋ/ *adj* showing no kindness or no desire to hide the unpleasant truth • *An experienced commentator on political affairs, he was unsparing* **in** *his criticism of the government.* • *The documentary went through all the graphic details of the operation in unsparing detail.* • *What impressed me about this biography is its unsparing honesty.*

un·spar·ing [GENEROUS] /£ʌnˈspeə·rɪŋ, $-ˈsper·ɪŋ/ *adj fml* extremely generous with money, time, help, etc. • *Last of all, our thanks go to the caterers who have been unsparing* **in** *their efforts to make this afternoon such a success.*

un·speak·a·ble /ʌnˈspiː·kə·bl̩/ *adj* too bad or shocking to be expressed in words • *The prosecutor called the young man's crimes the most unspeakable acts he had ever heard of.* • *There is no adequate explanation for the unspeakable atrocities that have been committed in this war.* • *No report can convey the unspeakable suffering that this war has caused.* • *The stench coming from the toilets was quite unspeakable.* • *"The English country gentleman galloping after a fox – the unspeakable in full pursuit of the uneatable"* (from the play *A Woman of No Importance* by Oscar Wilde)

un·speak·a·bly /ʌnˈspiː·kə·bli/ *adv* • *He's been unspeakably vile all week.*

un·spo·ken /£ʌnˈspəʊ·kᵊn, $-ˈspoʊ-/ *adj* [not gradable] not spoken, although thought of or felt • *unspoken doubts/fears* • *There's an unspoken assumption in the department that Sue will take over the post when Ian leaves.* • *We have an unspoken agreement that neither of us talks about our previous lovers.*

un·sport·ing /£ʌnˈspɔː·tɪŋ, $-ˈspɔːr·t̬ɪŋ/ *adj* not **sporting**, see at SPORT [GAME]

un·sta·ble /ʌnˈsteɪ·bl̩/ *adj* not solid and firm and therefore not strong, safe or likely to last • *I don't think you ought to let anybody sit in that chair – it looks a bit unstable to me.* • *It is a poor and politically unstable society in which warlords wield more power than the government.* • *The future of the world's second largest auctioneer looks increasingly unstable this week.* • A person might be described as unstable if they suffer from sudden and extreme changes in their mental and emotional state: *I would describe her as emotionally unstable.*

un·stead·y /ʌnˈsted·i/ *adj* **-ier, -iest** not STEADY [FIRM] • *She's been in bed with the flu and she's still a bit unsteady on her feet.*

un·stead·i·ly /ʌnˈsted·ɪ·li/ *adv*

un·stint·ing /£ʌnˈstɪn·tɪŋ, $-t̬ɪŋ/ *adj fml* extremely generous with time, money, praise, help, etc. • *A distinguished figure on the London musical scene, she gave unstinting support to young artists and composers.* • *Where the family were concerned she was quite unstinting* **in** *her* generosity. • *The new leader has earned unstinting admiration for his political courage.*

un·stop·pa·ble /£ʌnˈstɒp·ə·bl̩, $-ˈstɑː·pə-/ *adj* unable to be stopped or prevented from developing • *It is hoped that the peace talks bring about some sort of resolution before the unstoppable momentum of war takes over.* • *The band has enjoyed a seemingly unstoppable rise in popularity.* • *Once she has decided on a particular course of action, she's like an unstoppable juggernaut.*

un·stuck NOT STUCK /ʌnˈstʌk/ *adj* [after v; not gradable] no longer stuck • *The sticky tape on the parcel* **came** *unstuck and the whole thing came undone.*

un·stuck FAIL /ʌnˈstʌk/ *adj* **come unstuck** to experience difficulties and fail • *It was in the third round of the championships that they came unstuck.* • *I came unstuck at the stage when you fold the egg whites into the mixture.*

un·suc·cess·ful /ˌʌn·səkˈses·fᵊl/ *adj* not **successful**, see at SUCCEED ACHIEVE SOMETHING

un·suc·cess·ful·ly /ˌʌn·səkˈses·fᵊl·i/ *adv*

un·suit·a·ble /£ʌnˈsjuː·tə·bl̩, $-ˈsuː·t̬ə-/ *adj* not **suitable**, see at SUIT BE RIGHT

un·suit·a·bly /£ˌʌnˈsjuː·tə·bli, $-ˈsuː·t̬ə-/ *adv*

un·sung /ʌnˈsʌŋ/ *adj* [not gradable] not noticed or praised for hard work, bravery or great achievements • *The whole article is devoted to the goalkeeper, that* **unsung hero** *of the football pitch.* • *So much of the real heroism of this war* **went** *unsung.*

un·su·spect·ing /£ˌʌn·səˈspek·tɪŋ, $-t̬ɪŋ/ *adj* trusting; not aware of any danger or harm • *The killer lured his unsuspecting victims back to his apartment.* • *(fig.) He plans to spend two years at drama school before unleashing his talents on an unsuspecting world.*

un·swerv·ing /£ʌnˈswɜː·vɪŋ, $-ˈswɜːr-/ *adj* (esp. of trust or a belief) always strong; never weakening • *It was this unswerving* **loyalty** *to her boss that would eventually be her downfall.* • *She commanded unswerving devotion both from her family and from her friends.*

un·sym·pa·thet·ic /£ˌʌn·sɪm·pəˈθet·ɪk, $-ˈθet̬-/ *adj* not SYMPATHETIC • *When I told him about leaving my suitcase on the train, he was unsympathetic and just said I should have been insured.* • Ⓓ

un·tan·gle *obj* /ʌnˈtæŋ·gl̩/ *v* [T] to remove the knots from an untidy mass of string, wire, etc. and separate the different threads • *I spent ages trying to untangle the knots in Rosie's hair.* • *Are you any good at untangling wires, Steve?* • *(fig.) It took years to untangle* (=make clear and understandable) *the legal complexities of the case.*

un·tapped /ʌnˈtæpt/ *adj* (of a supply of something valuable) not yet used or taken advantage of • *Scotland has an untapped national asset in its wealth of renewable energy resources.* • *The firm has managed to penetrate the biggest untapped telecommunications market in the world.* • *By overlooking racial minorities, these companies are missing out on a wealth of untapped talent and skills.*

un·ten·a·ble /ʌnˈten·ə·bl̩/ *adj fml* (esp. of a theory or argument) not able to be supported or defended against criticism, or (of a situation) no longer able to continue • *The government's science budget has forced deep cuts in research and is politically untenable.* • *The cliffs are collapsing into the sea and living in the cottages at the cliff edge is now untenable.* • *If three people in four no longer support the government, isn't this an untenable situation?*

un·think·a·ble /ʌnˈθɪŋ·kə·bl̩/ *adj* too shocking or unlikely to be imagined as possible • *For most people in this country, the prospect of war is unthinkable.* • *You can't imagine what it would be like to have your child die – it's quite unthinkable.* • *Nowadays wines are being produced in areas that would have been unthinkable even ten years ago.* • **The unthinkable** *had happened – his secret activities had been discovered by the press.*

un·think·ing /ʌnˈθɪŋ·kɪŋ/ *adj fml esp. disapproving* not based on serious thought or an examination of the information • *What annoys me about these people is their unthinking hostility to anything foreign or unfamiliar.*

un·think·ing·ly /ʌnˈθɪŋ·kɪŋ·li/ *adv* • *I really didn't mean to offend her – I just said it unthinkingly.*

un·ti·dy /ʌnˈtaɪ·di/ *adj* **-ier, -iest** not TIDY ORDERED

un·ti·di·ly /ʌnˈtaɪ·dɪ·li/ *adv*

un·ti·di·ness /ʌnˈtaɪ·dɪ·nəs/ *n* [U]

un·tie *obj* /ʌnˈtaɪ/ *v* [T] **untying**, *past* **untied** to unfasten (a knot or something tied) • *Could someone help Joe untie his shoelaces, please?* • LP **Dressing and undressing**

un·til TIME /ᵊnˈtɪl, ˈʌn·tɪl/, **till** *prep, conjunction* up to (the time that) • *I was up until three o'clock trying to get it finished!* • *Wait till you see what Rachel's wearing!* • *Hadn't we better wait until Antony's here?* • **Not** until means not before a particular time or event: *We didn't eat till past midnight.* ○ *Once he starts a job he won't stop until it's finished.* ○ *He didn't have a girlfriend until he was thirty.* ○ *Don't move until I tell you.*

un·til DISTANCE /ᵊnˈtɪl, ˈʌn·tɪl/, **till** *prep, conjunction* as far as • *You should stay on the train until Manchester and then change.*

un·time·ly /ʌnˈtaɪm·li/ *adj* **-ier, -iest** *fml* (of something bad) happening unexpectedly early or at a time which is not suitable • *It was this passion for fast cars that led to his untimely* **death** *at the age of 43.* • *The evening was brought to an untimely* **end** *by a police raid and a string of arrests.* • *Holden's untimely injury comes just three days before he's due to play in the European Cup semi-finals.*

un·tir·ing /£ʌnˈtaɪə·rɪŋ, $-ˈtaɪr·ɪŋ/ *adj* (of qualities such as energy, interest and enthusiasm) never weakening • *And of course we must mention Tony Richardson, without whose untiring enthusiasm this campaign would not have succeeded.*

un·to /ˈʌn·tʊ, -tə/ *prep old use or biblical* to • *And the Lord spake unto him.*

un·told /£ʌnˈtəʊld, $-ˈtoʊld, ˈ--/ *adj* (esp. of something bad) so great in amount or level that it can not be measured or expressed in words • *Words alone do not convey the untold misery endured by people in these refugee camps.* • *The explosion ripped through the church and did untold damage to several neighbouring buildings.* • *Question number four caused untold havoc for a number of you, so perhaps we'd better look over it.*

un·touch·a·ble SOCIAL CLASS /ʌnˈtʌtʃ·ə·bl̩/ *n* [C] a member of the lowest social group in Indian society

un·touch·a·ble PROTECTED /ʌnˈtʌtʃ·ə·bl̩/ *adj* not able to be punished, criticized or changed in any way • *We've got to change the present system in which high court judges are regarded as somehow untouchable.* • *But the defence budget which accounts for some 20% of total government expenditure is virtually untouchable.*

un·touch·a·ble NOT DEFEATED /ʌnˈtʌtʃ·ə·bl̩/ *adj* not able to be defeated or equalled • *Coventry City have proved untouchable this season – they've just won their sixth consecutive game.* • *Now that the competition is catching up, Honda no longer seems quite so untouchable.*

un·touched /ʌnˈtʌtʃt/ *adj* not changed or spoilt in any way • *Brugge was untouched by the industrial revolution that ravaged other European cities in the last century.* • *Most of the east coast remains mercifully untouched by tourism.* • If food is untouched it has not been eaten: *She took a few spoonfuls of soup but left her main course untouched.*

un·to·ward /£ˌʌn·tʊˈwɔːd, $-ˈtə·wɔːrd/ *adj* unexpected and inconvenient or unpleasant • *Unless anything untoward happens we should be there just before midday.* • *I managed to drink water from the tap for three weeks without any untoward side effects.*

un·tram·melled, *Am usually* **un·tram·meled** /ʌnˈtræm·ᵊld/ *adj fml* not limited by rules or any other controlling influence • *Self-governing schools, untrammelled by local education authorities, have the freedom to manage their own budgets.* • *He's very sceptical about the notion of untrammelled free enterprise.*

un·true /ʌnˈtruː/ *adj* not true; false • *The director claimed that his remarks were irresponsible and untrue.*

un·truth /ʌnˈtruːθ/ *n* a statement that is not true, or the state of not being true • *It's not the first time that the paper has been in trouble for printing untruths about people's private lives.* [C] • *The untruth of this statement was immediately clear to me.* [U]

un·tu·tored /£ʌnˈtjuː·təd, $-ˈtuː·t̬ərd/ *adj fml* having no knowledge of or education in a particular subject • *You see, to my untutored* **eye** *that just looks like a load of random brush strokes and yet it's a very valuable painting.*

un·used /ʌnˈjuːzd/ *adj* [not gradable] not being used at present, or never having been used • *You might as well take your father's car – there's no point in having it sit there unused in the garage.* • *It's a plan to convert unused property into accommodation for the homeless.*

un·used to /ˌʌnˈjuːst/ *adj* not familiar with (a particular habit or experience) • *If you're unused to exercise you'll find your joints ache the next day.* • *I'm unused to getting up so early so it's a bit of a shock to me.* [+ v-ing]

un·u·su·al /ʌnˈjuː·ʒu·əl/ *adj* different from others of the same type in a way that is surprising, interesting or attractive • **It**'*s unusual* **to** *have adult conversation like that* *with such a young child.* [+ *to* infinitive] • *I was actually on time, which is unusual for me.* • *She was wearing a very unusual necklace – I had to remark on it.* • *"Do you like the new settee?" "Very much, it's most unusual."*

un·u·su·al·ly /ʌn'juː·ʒu·ə·li/ *adv* • *Unusually for me, I couldn't actually finish the meal.* • *He was unusually polite* (= more polite than usual).

un·ut·ter·a·ble /£ʌn'ʌt·ᵊr·ə·bḷ, $-'ʌṭ·ɚ-/ *adj fml* too bad to be expressed in words • *After an afternoon of unutterable boredom I was finally allowed to leave.*

un·ut·ter·a·bly /£ʌn'ʌt·ᵊr·ə·bli, $-'ʌṭ·ɚ-/ *adv fml* • *The talk was long and unutterably dull.* • *She was wearing an unutterably* (= extremely) *tasteless outfit.*

un·var·nished /£ʌn'vɑː·nɪʃt, $-'vɑːr-/ *adj* [before n] (of a statement) expressed plainly and truthfully • *It's a bit optimistic to expect a politician to tell you the unvarnished truth!*

un·veil *obj* /ʌn'veɪl/ *v* [T] to remove a curtain-like covering from (a new statue, etc.) at a formal ceremony in order to show the opening or completion of a new building or work of art • *The memorial to those who had died in the war was unveiled in 1948.* • *(fig.) Ten top designers will this week unveil* (= show for the first time) *their autumn/winter collections at the fashion fair.* • *(fig.) A new government policy on forests is due to be unveiled* (= made known) *in April.*

un·versed /£ʌn'vɜːst, $-'vɜːrst/ *adj* not VERSED

un·waged /ʌn'weɪdʒd/ *pl n* **the unwaged** *Br* unemployed people • *It's six pounds entrance fee, four pounds for the unwaged.*

un·waged /ʌn'weɪdʒd/ *adj* [not gradable] *Br*

un·want·ed /£ʌn'wʌn·tɪd, $-'wɑːn·ṭɪd/ *adj* not **wanted**, see at WANT [DESIRE]

un·war·rant·ed /£ʌn'wɒr·ᵊn·tɪd, $-'wɔːr·ᵊn·ṭɪd/ *adj fml* lacking a good reason; unnecessary • *A right-to-privacy bill has been proposed which would protect people against unwarranted intrusion into their private lives.* • *Richardson, the company director, claimed the criticism was unwarranted and unjust.* • *Opposition MPs are demanding an investigation to see if there has been unwarranted waste of public money.*

un·well /ʌn'wel/ *adj* [after v] not well; ill • *I hear you've been unwell.*

un·wield·y [DIFFICULT TO MOVE] /ʌn'wiːl·di/ *adj* (of an object) difficult to move or handle because it is heavy, large or a strange shape • *The problem with pushchairs is that they're so unwieldy to take on public transport and get in and out of shops.* • *A piano is a very unwieldy item to get down a flight of stairs.*

un·wield·y [NOT EFFECTIVE] /ʌn'wiːl·di/ *adj* (of a system) slow and not effective, usually because it is too big, badly organized or involves too many different organizations or people • *The irony is that the whole unwieldy criminal justice system is costing £8 billion annually to produce criminals instead of justice.* • *One disadvantage for the bank is that its huge size – 15 000 staff, 5000 of them abroad – makes it unwieldy and slow-moving.*

un·will·ing /ʌn'wɪl·ɪŋ/ *adj* not WILLING

un·will·ing·ly /ʌn'wɪl·ɪŋ·li/ *adv*

un·will·ing·ness /ʌn'wɪl·ɪŋ·nəs/ *n* [U]

un·wind *obj* [UNFASTEN] /ʌn'waɪnd/ *v* [T] *past* **unwound** /ʌn'waʊnd/ to unfasten (something) that is wrapped around an object • *In a nearby medical tent, a US Army doctor gently unwinds Metruk's bandage.*

un·wind [RELAX] /ʌn'waɪnd/, **wind down** *v* [I] *past* **unwound** /ʌn'waʊnd/ to relax and let your mind be free from anxiety after a period of work or some other activity that has made you anxious • *A glass of wine in the evening helps me to unwind.* • *I think he finds it quite difficult to unwind after work.*

un·wise /ʌn'waɪz/ *adj* **-r, -st** not WISE [CLEVER]

un·wise·ly /ʌn'waɪz·li/ *adv*

un·wit·ting /£ʌn'wɪt·ɪŋ, $-'wɪṭ-/ *adj* [before n] *fml* without knowing or planning • *The two women claimed they were the unwitting victims of a drugs dealer who planted a large quantity of heroin in their luggage.*

un·wit·ting·ly /£ʌn'wɪt·ɪŋ·li, $-'wɪṭ-/ *adv fml* • *I regret any anxiety or concern which I may, unwittingly, have caused.*

un·wont·ed /£ʌn'wəʊn·tɪd, $-'wɑːn·ṭɪd/ *adj* [before n] *fml* unusual; rarely experienced or shown • *He sprang to the telephone with unwonted vigour.*

un·writ·ten /£ʌn'rɪt·ᵊn, $-'rɪṭ-/ *adj* not **written**, see at WRITE. • An unwritten law/rule is one which does not exist officially but which people generally accept and obey: *Strictly speaking, you can wear want you like to work, but there's an unwritten rule that you don't wear jeans.*

un·zip *obj* /ʌn'zɪp/ *v* [T] **-pp-** to open (something) by using a ZIP (= a fastener consisting of two rows of metal or plastic teeth) • *He unzipped his suitcase.* • [LP] **Dressing and undressing**

up [HIGHER] /ʌp/ *adv* [not gradable] towards a higher position; towards a higher value, number or level • *Pick your clothes up and put them away.* • *Put those books up on the top shelf.* • *They flew up through the clouds into sunshine above.* • *A gravel road leads through the jungle and up into the Andes.* • *Above the dust we could see a rocket climbing up into a blue sky.* • *Pushing the number of unit sales up every quarter can't be continued indefinitely.* • *(fig.) He spent the afternoon digging carrots up* (= out of the ground). • If a person or thing moves **up and down**, they move, usually repeatedly, higher and then lower: *Our daughter started jumping up and down with rage when she heard she couldn't go.* • *The water was up* **to**/*had come up* **to** *the level of the windows.* • You can use **up to** to say that something is less than or equal to but not more than a stated value, number or level: *Research suggests that up to half of those who were prescribed the drug have suffered side effects.* ○ *Up to two hundred people were on board the ship.* ○ *We can teach dancers up to intermediate level here.* See also UP TO. • **Up to** (also **Up until, Up till**) also means until: *Up to yesterday, we had no idea where the child was.* ○ *It's an old house but it has all of the* **up-to-date** (= modern) *conveniences you could want.* See also UPDATE. ○ *Great trouble is taken to keep our database* **up-to-date** (= corrected with the most recent information). See also UPDATE. ○ *Now we're going live to our reporter in Moscow for* **up-to-the-minute** (= containing the latest information) *news on the situation there.* • If a person or a thing is **up to** their **ears/eyeballs/eyes/neck** in something, it is causing them a lot of problems: *The business has been up to its eyes in problems ever since their managing director resigned.* • *(infml dated)* The phrase **up (with)** is shouted or written on notices to show support: *Up with freedom, down with repression!* • *(esp. Br)* If a door is an **up-and-over** type, it opens by being lifted and it then slides into a horizontal position as it rises higher. [PIC] **Accommodation** • *"Be nice to people on your way up because you'll meet them on your way down"* (believed to have been said by Wilson Mizner, 1876-1933) • Compare DOWN [LOWER POSITION].

up /ʌp/ *prep* • *We followed her up the stairs to a large meeting room.* • *Suddenly, a lizard ran up the wall.* • *It's hard work climbing* **up and down** *a ladder* (= moving to a higher and then a lower position, esp. repeatedly) *when you're carrying bricks.* • *(taboo slang)* Someone might say **Up yours!** to a person as an insulting way of showing that they very much dislike the person or what that person has just said or done. This is a very offensive expression. • [PIC] **Prepositions of movement**

up /ʌp/ *adj* [not gradable] • *an up escalator* • *The cost of car insurance is up* (= has increased), *but not very much.* • *Latest figures suggest the crime rate will be up.* • *Last year the company's turnover was $240 billion, up 3%* **on** (= compared with) *the previous year.* • *You look nice with your hair up* (= styled to be on the top or back of the head). • See also UPPER [HIGHER].

up /ʌp/ *n* [U] *esp. Am infml* • A person who is **on the up and up** is honest and can be trusted. Compare **on the up and up** at UP [IMPROVE].

up *obj* /ʌp/ *v* [T] **-pp-** *infml* • *We won't be able to make a profit on the deal without upping* (= increasing) *the sale price.* • *It looks like tax rates are going to be upped again.*

up [VERTICAL] /ʌp/ *adv* [not gradable] in or into a vertical position • *Would you stand up for a moment, I want to see how tall you are.* • *Was she standing up or sitting down?* • *As soon as the suspect was brought in, the victim's mother jumped up and started screaming.* • *They put up* (= build) *new houses in no time nowadays.* • A person or thing which is **up-and-coming** is likely to achieve success soon or in the near future: *Playing the role of Tanya is Sylvia Roberts, one of our up-and-coming young actresses.* • Compare DOWN [LOWER POSITION].

up /ʌp/ *v* [I] **-pp-** *infml* • You can use **up and** to emphasize that someone did something in a sudden and possibly unexpected way: *After dinner they just upped and went without saying goodbye.* ○ *She couldn't take the pressure of her job any more so she upped and left.*

up [TOP] /ʌp/ *adv* [not gradable] in a high position; at the top • *In the winter most locals move to houses up in the hills.* • *Our boardroom is up on the twenty-third floor.* • *You can tell which* **way** *up the crates have to be because they all have 'TOP' stencilled on the lid.* • *The boxes had been stored bottom up.* • Compare DOWN [LOWER LEVEL].

up /ʌp/ *prep* • *You'll find a dusty attic up* (= at the top of) *these stairs.* • *If you want to talk to Fred, he's up that ladder.*

up [ALONG] /ʌp/ *prep* (further) along • *The car shot off up the road at high speed.* • *There's a newsagent's just up the road – they probably sell cigarettes.* • *He was running* **up and down** *the path* (= moving along the path in one direction and then in the opposite direction, esp. repeatedly) *in a state of panic, shouting for help.* • *(fig.) Cinemas* **up and down** (= everywhere in) *the country are reporting huge audiences for the film.*

up [INCREASE] /ʌp/ *adv* [not gradable] to a greater degree; in order to increase • *When the dust hits the Earth's atmosphere and heats up* (= becomes hotter), *it glows – producing the brief fiery trails of shooting stars.* • *Can you* **speak** *up* (= speak louder), *there's a lot of interference on the line.* • *Grandma always* **turns** *the TV up really loud because she can't hear very well.* • *Try not to get* **worked** *up* (= increasingly excited or angry), *I'm sure we can sort the problem out.*

up [OUT OF BED] /ʌp/ *adv* [not gradable] not in bed • *What time did you* **get** *up?* • *"It's time to* **get** *up now – you've got school in fifteen minutes!"*

up /ʌp/ *adj* [after v; not gradable] • *They're not up yet – they were working until late last night.* • *(infml)* If someone is **up and about/around** their health has improved enough after a period of illness for them to be able to get out of bed and move around as they did in the past.

up [EXIST] /ʌp/ *adv* [not gradable] into existence, view or consideration • *Would this be a good time to* **bring** *up the issue of salary?* • *Sorry darling, something unexpected has* **come** *up* (= has happened) *at the office, I'll be home late.* • **Coming** *up* (= Happening next) *after the break, we have a man who claims he can communicate with fish.* • *Originally the charity was* **set** *up to help orphans in urban areas.*

up /ʌp/ *adj* [after v; not gradable] • *Everyone was talking in whispers, and I could tell something was up* (= something unusual was happening). • **What's** *up* (= What is happening or what is wrong)?

up [EQUAL] /ʌp/ *adv* [not gradable] so as to be equal in quality or achievement • *She couldn't go to school for a few weeks because of illness, but she'll be able to* **catch** *up* (**with** *her lessons) quickly.* • *So much scientific research is being performed that it's virtually impossible to* **keep** *up* (**with** *all the new developments).* • *(Am infml) Kate and I were both playing well, and after ten minutes the score was 6-up* (= 6 points each). • *(infml)* If you are **up there with** someone else you match them in ability or a particular skill: *As a pianist he wasn't very talented, but as a composer he was up there with the best.* • *He wants to compete at international level, but frankly I don't think he's* **up to** (= good enough for) *it.* • *It was a serious fall – it'll be a while before you feel* **up to** (= strong enough for) *walking again.* [+ v-ing] • *At the halfway stage, they're* **up with the clock** (= have not used more time than they should).

up [NEAR] /ʌp/ *adv* [not gradable] very near • *She sidled up* (= moved very near) *and spoke to me.* • *Carrying a gun, he walked up* **to** *the cashier and demanded money.* • *A limousine* **drew** *up* **to** *us where we were standing.*

up [TOGETHER] /ʌp/ *adv* [not gradable] in a state of being together with other similar things • *You've got half an hour to gather up anything you'll need for the journey.* • **Add** *up the column of figures in your head and then tell me what the sum is.*

up [TIGHTLY] /ʌp/ *adv* [not gradable] tightly or firmly in order to keep something safe or in position • *Can you* **do** *my shoelaces up for me?* • **Tie** *up the top of the bag so the rubbish doesn't fall out.* • *You'd better* **wrap** *up* (= wear warm clothes) *– it's cold outside.* • [LP]› **Dressing and undressing**

up [IN OPERATION] /ʌp/ *adj* [after v; not gradable] (of a system or machine, esp. a computer) operating, esp. in its usual way • *Andy, do you know when the network will be up again?* • If something, esp. a system or a machine, is **up and running** it is operating: *It'll be a couple of days before the air-conditioning is up and running because we need to get some spare parts.* • Compare DOWN [NOT IN OPERATION].

up [SMALLER] /ʌp/ *adv* [not gradable] broken or cut into smaller pieces; made smaller in area • *The car* **blew** *up* (= exploded) • **Cut** *the magazines up if there are any pictures you want out of them.* • *Write your suggestion on a piece of paper and then* **fold** *it up so no one can read it.*

up [AGE] /ʌp/ *adv* [not gradable] to a greater age • *No one said that* **growing** *up would be easy or painless.* • *Many single parents struggle to* **bring** *their children up on a low income.*

up [FINISHED] /ʌp/ *adj* [after v; not gradable] (of a time period) finished • *When the two hours were up nobody had answered all of the questions.* • *Your time is up – it's someone else's turn on the training equipment now.*

up [INTENDED] /ʌp/ *adj* [after v; always + *for*; not gradable] intended, suggested or being considered • *The terms for release of the hostages are not up* **for** *negotiation.* • *That house at the end of our road is up* **for** *sale again.* • *Are you really up* **for** *promotion?* • *(infml) I'm up* **for** *organizing* (= willing to organize) *the meeting if nobody else wants to.*

up /ʌp/ *adv* [not gradable] • *How many candidates will your party be* **putting** *up* (= offering for election) *at the elections next week?*

up [IMPROVE] /ʌp/ *adv* [not gradable] into an improved position or state • *By lap 26 Senna had* **moved** *up into second position.* • *Her piano playing is very good – she'll be* **moving** *up to the advanced class soon.* • *Stein had a bad start to the race, but by the ninth lap she was up* **with** *the leaders.* • *She's been very* **up and down** (= sometimes happy and sometimes sad) *since her husband's death.* • *After an* **up-and-down** (= sometimes successful and sometimes unsuccessful) *career in marketing he decided to quit his job and travel round the world.* • Compare DOWN [LOWER LEVEL].

up /ʌp/ *n infml* • *(Br and Aus)* If someone or something is **on the up (and up)** they are continually improving: *Her career has been on the up and up since she moved into sales.* Compare **on the up and up** at UP [HIGHER]. • If someone or something experiences **ups and downs**, a mixture of good and bad things happens to them: *Like most married couples we've had our ups and downs, but life's like that.*

up [ROAD] /ʌp/ *adj* [after v; not gradable] *Br and Aus* (of a road) being repaired and so not suitable for use • *The council has got the road up because of a broken sewer.*

up [TRIAL] /ʌp/ *adj* [after v; not gradable] on trial in a court • *If he doesn't pay the fine soon he'll be up* **before** *the magistrate.* • *Max is up* **for** *armed robbery.*

up [END] /ʌp/ *adv* [not gradable] to an end, finish or state of completion • **Finish** *up the old packet of biscuits before you open a new one.* • *Crime won't help – you'll* **end** *up in prison.* • *They were poor and* **used** *up all their money on food.* • *When are you going to* **pay** *up the money you owe me?* • *I'd like to* **round** *up the meeting by thanking all those who were able to attend at such short notice.*

up [NORTH] /ʌp/ *adv* [not gradable] towards the north or towards a more important place, esp. a city • *On Tuesday she'll be travelling up* **to** *Newcastle from Birmingham.* • *She comes up* **from** *Washington about once a month on the train.*

up /ʌp/ *adj* [before n; not gradable] *Br dated* • *What time does the next up train* (= train going to an important place such as a capital city) *leave?*

up [ORIGIN] /ʌp/ *prep* towards the starting point of (esp. a river or stream) • *Rowing up the river against its current was very hard work.* • If you say you are going **up-country** you are going to the parts of a country further from the coast, esp. where there are few towns and people: *We'll travel up-country by horse tomorrow.* ○ *Some people find up-country customs strange.* • See also UPRIVER; UPSTREAM.

up [TO] /ʌp/ *prep Br and Aus infml not standard* to or at • *Are you* **going** *up the club tonight?* • *I'll* **see** *you up the pub later.* • Compare DOWN [TO].

up– [COMBINING FORM] /ʌp-/ *combining form* higher or improved • *uphill* • *uplift* • **Up-market** (also *esp. Am* **upscale**) goods and products are of specially high quality and are intended to be bought by people who are quite rich: *an up-market brand name* ○ *Many garment exporters want to move up-market.* Compare DOWNMARKET. • **Up-tempo** music is music that is played at a fast beat.

up·beat /ʌp'biːt, '--/ *adj infml* full of hope, happiness and good feelings • *Live music and a parade set an upbeat mood for the official opening.* • *We're aiming to deliver an upbeat message in our advertising campaign.* • Compare DOWNBEAT.

up·braid *obj* /ʌp'breɪd/ *v* [T] *fml* to forcefully or angrily tell (someone) they should not have done a particular thing and criticize them for having done it • *In newspaper articles she consistently upbraided those in authority who overstepped their limits.*

up·bring·ing /ˈʌpˌbrɪŋ·ɪŋ/ *n* [C usually sing] the way in which someone is treated and educated when they are young, esp. by their parents, particularly in relation to the effect which this has on how they behave and make moral decisions • *Clary had a conventional upbringing in an ordinary suburb.* • *Is it right to say all the crimes he committed were simply the result of his upbringing?* • See also BRING UP.

up·com·ing *esp. Am* /ˈʌpˌkʌm·ɪŋ/, *Br usually* **forth·com·ing** *adj* [before n; not gradable] happening soon • *Tickets are selling well for the group's upcoming concert tour.*

up·date *obj* /ʌpˈdeɪt/ *v* [T] to make (something) more modern or suitable for use now by adding new information or changing its design • *An updated version of the software will be available within six months.* • To update someone is to give them the most recent information: *Will you quickly update me* **on** *what's been happening?* ○ *We'll update you* **on** *this news story throughout the day.*

up·date /ˈʌp·deɪt/ *n* [C] • *When was the last update performed on the mailing list?*

up·end *obj* /ʌpˈend/ *v* [T] *infml* to push or move (something) so that the part which usually touches the ground does so no longer • *She upended the chessboard halfway through the game because she was losing.* • *A hard tackle upended him just as he was about to score.*

up·front /ʌpˈfrʌnt/ *adj* [after v] *infml* speaking or behaving in a way which makes intentions and beliefs clear • *She's very upfront* **about** *why she wants the job – she'd earn a lot more money.* • See also **up front** at FRONT [PLACE].

up·grade *obj* /ʌpˈgreɪd/ *v* [T] to improve the quality or usefulness of (something, such as a machine or a computer program), or give (a person) a more important job or state that (their job) is more important than it was in the past • *It's quite simple to upgrade the indexing software.* • *Congratulations, I hear you've been upgraded* **to** *divisional manager.* • *He's been trying to get his job upgraded for years, but management won't because they'd have to pay him more.* • Compare DOWNGRADE.

up·grade /ˈʌp·greɪd/ *n* [C] • *a hardware upgrade* • *an upgrade kit* • *The upgrade to version 5·0 costs $395.*

up·heav·al /ʌpˈhiː·vᵊl/ *n* (a) great change, esp. causing or involving much difficulty, activity or trouble • *Yesterday's coup brought further upheaval to a country already struggling with famine.* [U] • *It would cause a tremendous upheaval to install a different computer system.* [C]

up·hill /ʌpˈhɪl, ˈ--/ *adj, adv* leading to a higher place on a slope, or *(fig.)* needing a large amount of effort • *an uphill climb* • *running uphill* • *(fig.) It'll be an uphill* **struggle/battle/fight** *to get the new proposals accepted.* • Compare DOWNHILL.

up·hold *obj* /£ʌpˈhəʊld, $-ˈhoʊld/ *v* [T] *past* **upheld** /ʌpˈheld/ to defend or maintain (a principle or law), or to state that (a decision which has already been made, esp. a legal one) is correct • *As a police officer you are expected to uphold the law whether you agree with it or not.* • *Judge Davis upheld the county court's decision that the guns had been obtained illegally.*

up·hold·er /£ʌpˈhəʊl·dəʳ, $-ˈhoʊl·dɚ/ *n* [C] • *Nancy is the great upholder* **of** *tradition within our family.*

up·hol·ster *obj* /£ʌpˈhəʊl·stəʳ, $-ˈhoʊl·stɚ/ *v* [T] to cover (an object for sitting on, such as a chair) with suitable cloth and fill it with suitable substance

up·hol·stered /£ʌpˈhəʊl·stəd, $-ˈhoʊl·stɚd/ *adj* [not gradable] • *a nicely upholstered sofa*

up·hol·ster·er /£ʌpˈhəʊl·stᵊr·əʳ, £-ˈhoʊl·stɚ·ɚ/ *n* [C] • *an experienced upholsterer*

up·hol·ster·y /£ʌpˈhəʊl·stᵊr·i, $-ˈhoʊl·stɚ-/ *n* [U] • Upholstery is the cloth used for covering a seat and the substance used for filling it: *an old sofa with faded green upholstery* • Upholstery is also the activity of upholstering objects: *She's taking evening classes in upholstery.*

up·keep /ˈʌp·kiːp/ *n* [U] the cost or process of keeping something, such as a building, in good and usable condition • *The upkeep* **of** *larger old properties tends to be more than many people can afford.* • *Council employees are responsible for the upkeep of the gardens.*

up·land /ˈʌp·lənd/ *adj* [not gradable] (of a land area) situated high up, such as on a hill or mountain • *The whole plateau comprises one vast upland plain.*

up·lands /ˈʌp·ləndz/ *pl n* • *Soil quality is poor in the uplands* (= high areas of land).

up·lift [IMPROVEMENT] /ˈʌp·lɪft/ *n* [U] *slightly fml* improvement of a person's moral or spiritual condition • *We are counting on your speech, bishop, to give some moral uplift to the delegates.*

up·lift·ing /£ʌpˈlɪf·tɪŋ, $-ṱɪŋ/ *adj slightly fml* • *an uplifting performance/experience*

up·lift *obj* [RAISE] /ʌpˈlɪft/ *v* [T] *esp. specialized* to raise to a higher position • *Large areas of paving were uplifted by the earthquake.*

up·lift·ed /£ʌpˈlɪf·tɪd, $-ṱɪd/ *adj slightly fml* • *With uplifted* (= stretching up) *arms he ran towards them.*

u·pon /£əˈpɒn, $-ˈpɑːn/ *prep slightly fml* on • *There was nothing upon the table but a few old plates.* • *Upon her head she wore a black velvet hat.* • *You can never place enough emphasis upon the importance of safety.* • *Upon your arrival* (= As soon as you arrive), *please report to the reception desk.* • Upon can also be used to show that something is going to happen soon: *Another couple of weeks and the holidays will be upon us.*

up·per [HIGHER] /£ˈʌp·əʳ, $-ɚ/ *adj* [before n; not gradable] at a higher position or level (than something else), or being the top part of something • *The office block's upper floors were engulfed with flames.* • *If the infection is not checked it will probably spread to the upper body.* • *The upper reaches of the river* (= the part nearest to the origin) *are quiet and flow through gentle countryside.* • *(specialized)* If letters are in **upper case**, they are written as capitals. Compare **lower case** at LOWER. • The **upper class** (also **upper classes** or *infml* **upper crust**) is the group of people who have the highest rank in society and are usually rich: *upper-class attitudes* ○ *an upper-class buffoon* ○ *The upper class traditionally enjoys itself/enjoy themselves by watching horse racing.* ○ *The upper classes usually send their children to expensive private schools.* Compare **lower class** at LOWER; **middle class** at MIDDLE • **working class** at WORK [ACTIVITY]. • If you have **the upper hand**, you have more power than anyone else and so have control: *After hours of fierce negotiations, the president* **gained/got/had** *the upper hand.* • In a parliament which has two main groups, one is usually called **the upper house** (also **the upper chamber**): *In Britain, the upper house is also called the House of Lords, and it does not have as much power as the House of Commons.* ○ *The upper house of the US Congress is the Senate.* Compare **lower house** at LOWER. • [PIC] **Writing**

up·per /£ˈʌp·əʳ, $-ɚ/ *n* [C] • An upper is the top part of a shoe which covers a person's foot and to which the heel and the SOLE are fixed: *These shoes have leather uppers and synthetic soles.* • *(infml dated)* If someone is **on their uppers** they are very poor.

up·per·most /£ˈʌp·ə·məʊst, $-ɚ·moʊst/ *adj, adv* [not gradable] • *The office block's uppermost floors* (= those in the highest position) *were engulfed with flames.* • *Store the canisters with their lids uppermost* (= in the highest position). • *If environmental considerations are uppermost* (= most important), *then energy efficiency measures must take priority over profitability.* • *What's uppermost* **in your mind** (= the most important thing you are thinking about) *just before a race when you're waiting for the starter's signal?*

up·per [DRUG] /£ˈʌp·əʳ, $-ɚ/ *n* [C] *infml* a drug which causes a person taking it to feel very active and excited

up·pi·ty /£ˈʌp·ɪ·ti, $-ə·ṱi/ *adj infml disapproving* (of a person) behaving in an unpleasant way because they think that they are more important than they really are • *He* **got/became** *very uppity when his fashion designs were criticized.*

up·right [STRAIGHT] /ˈʌp·raɪt/ *adj, adv* (standing or being) vertical and as straight as possible • *Stand upright when you're being spoken to!* • *The sound of breaking glass made her sit* **bolt** *upright* (= sit with her back very straight). • Upright can also be used to refer to something which is is taller than it is wide: *an upright freezer* • An **upright piano** (also **upright**) is a PIANO (= type of musical instrument) in which the strings are vertical. Compare **grand piano** at GRAND [SPLENDID].

up·right /ˈʌp·raɪt/ *n* [C] • An upright is a vertical part of something and it supports other things: *Firmly secure the two uprights to opposite walls in the alcove and then slot the shelves in between them.* • An upright is also a GOALPOST: *Shearer slotted the ball between the uprights for his second goal of the afternoon.*

up·right [MORAL] /ˈʌp·raɪt/ *adj approving* honest, responsible and moral • *She behaved as any upright* **citizen** *would have under the circumstances.*

up·right·ly /'ʌp·raɪt·li/ *adv approving*

up·right·ness /'ʌp·raɪt·nəs/ *n* [U] *approving*

up·ris·ing /'ʌpˌraɪ·zɪŋ/, **ri·sing** *n* [C] an act of opposition, sometimes using violence, by many people in one area of a country against those who are in power • *Following a determined resistance in the east, there was eventually a* **popular** *uprising in the capital.*

up·ri·ver /£ˌʌp'rɪv·əʳ, $-ɚ/ *adv* towards the place where a river starts • *We paddled upriver for a couple of hours.*

up·roar /£'ʌp·rɔːʳ, $-rɔːr/ *n* [U] a noisy state of confusion, esp. caused by angry people • *Uproar followed the announcement of further job cuts.* • *The uproar over her dismissal will no doubt continue.* • (NL) (S)

up·roar·i·ous /£ʌp'rɔː·ri·əs, $-'rɔːr·i-/ *adj* • *an uproarious debate* • Uproarious also means extremely amusing: *an uproarious farce* ○ *It's a very amusing play with an uproarious final act.*

up·roar·i·ous·ly /£ʌp'rɔː·ri·ə·sli, $-'rɔːr·i-/ *adv* • *an uproariously funny comedian*

up·root *obj* [PLANT] /ʌp'ruːt/ *v* [T] to pull (a plant including its roots) out of the ground • *Hundreds of mature trees were uprooted in the storm.*

up·root *obj* [PERSON] /ʌp'ruːt/ *v* [T] to remove (a person) from their home or usual surroundings • *The war has uprooted nearly two-thirds of the country's population.*

up·scale /'ʌp·skeɪl/ *adj esp. Am for* **up-market**, see at UP- [COMBINING FORM]

up·set *obj* [WORRY] /ʌp'set/ *v* [T] **upsetting**, *past* **upset** to make (someone) worried, unhappy or angry • *It still upsets Mark when he thinks about the accident.* • *Don't upset yourself by thinking about what might have been.*

up·set /ʌp'set/ *adj* [after v] • *Don't get upset* **about** *the dress – there's only a little stain on it.* • *She was very upset* **to** *hear that the holiday had been cancelled.* [+ to infinitive] • *He was very upset* **that** *you didn't reply to his letters.* [+ that clause]

up·set·ting /£ʌp'set·ɪŋ, $-'seṭ-/ *adj* • *Seeing her again would be an upsetting experience after so many years.*

up·set *obj* [CHANGE] /ʌp'set/ *v* [T] **upsetting**, *past* **upset** to change the usual or expected state or order of (something), esp. in a way which stops it from happening or working • *Any mechanical problems would upset our plans of driving across the desert.* • *It would be a shame to upset the good working relationships which have developed.*

up·set /'ʌp·set/ *n* • *How much upset will the new monitoring procedures cause?* [U] • *The knee injury was a serious upset* **to** *her chances of being selected for the team.* [C] • *It would be quite an upset if the favourite didn't win.* [C]

up·set *obj* [KNOCK] /ʌp'set/ *v* [T] **upsetting**, *past* **upset** to push or knock (something) out of its usual position, usually accidentally, esp. causing it to fall • *Our dog upset the table, spilling food over the floor.* • *(infml)* If someone or something **upsets the apple cart** they cause a plan, system or event to not happen as it should.

up·set [ILLNESS] /'ʌp·set/ *n* [C] *infml* a slight illness, esp. of the stomach • *Melanie's got a* **stomach/tummy** *upset so she won't be going to school today.*

up·set /ʌp'set/ *adj* [not gradable] *infml* • *I've got an upset* **stomach/tummy** *– serves me right for eating so much.*

up·set *obj* /ʌp'set/ *v* [T] **upsetting**, *past* **upset** • *He can't eat grapes – they upset him/his stomach.*

up·shot /£'ʌp·ʃɒt, $-ʃɑːt/ *n* [U] something which happens as a result of other actions, events or decisions • *The upshot* **of** *the discussions is that there will be no redundancies.*

up·side /'ʌp·saɪd/ *n* [U] (esp. in business) the good, advantageous or pleasant part of something • *It's annoying that we can't travel until Thursday, but the upside is that the fare's cheaper then.* • Compare DOWNSIDE.

up·side down /ˌʌp·saɪd'daʊn/ *adj, adv* [not gradable] having the part which is usually at the top turned to be at the bottom • *Put the lid on tightly,* **turn** *the honey jar upside down and see how slowly the air bubbles rise.* • *The most exciting part of the display was when the plane was flying upside down at high speed.* • *One car flipped over in the crash and came to rest upside down in the middle of the road.* • *(fig.) Another poor harvest could* **turn** *the country's economy upside down* (= completely change it in a bad way). • *(fig.) He lived in an upside-down world after she left him, in which nothing seemed to make sense.*

up·stage *obj* [STEAL ATTENTION] /ʌp'steɪdʒ/ *v* [T] to take people's attention away from (someone) and make them listen to or look at you instead • *Most bands who tour as the support act tend to be just starting out on their career, and rarely upstage the star.*

up·stage [THEATRE AREA] /ʌp'steɪdʒ, '--/ *adv, adj* towards or at the part of a theatre stage that is furthest from the people watching the performance • *He looks upstage to where the body is lying.* • Compare DOWNSTAGE.

up·stairs /£ʌp'steəz, $-'sterz/ *adv, adj* [not gradable] towards or on the highest floor or floors of a building • *an upstairs landing/window* • *He heard glass breaking and ran upstairs to see what had caused it.* • *The people who live upstairs are very noisy.* • Compare DOWNSTAIRS.

up·stairs /£ʌp'steəz, $-'sterz/ *n* [U] • *Sadly,* **the** *upstairs of the house was gutted by fire.*

up·stand·ing /ʌp'stæn·dɪŋ/ *adj slightly fml* behaving in a good and moral way • *She is regarded as an upstanding* **citizen** *in the local community.*

up·start /£'ʌp·stɑːt, $-stɑːrt/ *n* [C] *disapproving* a person, esp. a young one, who has suddenly got power or an important position and takes advantage of this in an unpleasant way • *People in the office think he's an upstart because he was so young when he was promoted.* • *Small upstart entrepreneurial companies have repeatedly produced quality software quicker than their larger competitors.*

up·state /'ʌp·steɪt/ *adj, adv Am* towards or of the northern parts of a STATE (= area of the US), esp. those which are far from cities where a lot of people live • *upstate New York* • *We're going upstate for our vacation.*

up·stream /ʌp'striːm/ *adj, adv* (moving) on a river or stream towards its origin • *Salmon swim upstream against very strong currents to reach the breeding areas.* • *The upstream part of the river flows gently through meadows.* • Compare DOWNSTREAM.

up·surge /£'ʌp·sɜːdʒ, $-sɜːrdʒ/ *n* [C] a sudden and usually large increase of something • *Over the last few years there has been an upsurge* **in** *students wanting to take ecology-related courses.* • *An upsurge* **of** *violence in the district has been linked to increased unemployment.*

up·swing /'ʌp·swɪŋ/ *n* [C] an increase or improvement • *Many analysts are predicting an upswing* **in** *the economy.*

up·take /'ʌp·teɪk/ *n* [U] *specialized* the rate or act of taking something in • *Plants in their growth stage generally exhibit an increased uptake* **of** *nutrients.* • *(Br and Aus)* Uptake can also be the rate or act of accepting something: *Uptake* **of** *places on the training course has been disappointing.* • *(infml)* If someone is **quick/slow on the uptake** they understand things easily/with difficulty: *She's very quick on the uptake, so you won't have to explain much.* ○ *He's a bit slow on the uptake, so you may have to repeat the instructions a few times.*

up·tight /ʌp'taɪt/ *adj infml* nervous, anxious or worried, esp. about something • *There's no need to be so uptight all the time, try to be more relaxed.* • *Don't get uptight* **about** *the exam – just do your best.*

up to [RESPONSIBILITY] *prep* being the responsibility of (someone) • *It's up to the manager to sort out the problems and make sure things are done on time.* • *It's up to you to make the final decision about which course you want to take.* • See also **up to** at UP [HIGHER].

up to [DOING] *prep infml* doing (something which might be bad or illegal), often secretly • *What's he up to with all those crates in his garage?* • *She's up to* **no good**/*up to* **something** *– you can always tell because she stays in her room.*

up·town /ʌp'taʊn, '--/ *adj, adv* [not gradable] *Am* in or towards the northern part of a city or town, esp. if there is not much business or industry there • *Dey plays the part of an uptown Manhattan restaurateur.* • *We could walk uptown or we could take the train.* • *I can get lunch in Chinatown for half of what it costs uptown.* • Compare DOWNTOWN.

up·turn /£'ʌp·tɜːn, $-tɜːrn/ *n* [C] (esp. in economics) an improvement or advantageous change to a higher level or value • *Investors should not expect a sharp upturn* **in** *the economy.* • Compare DOWNTURN.

up·turned /£'ʌp·tɜːnd, $-tɜːrnd/ *adj* pointing or looking up, or having the part which is usually at the bottom turned to be at the top • *An upturned boat on the beach provided shelter.* • *If you do encounter an extraterrestrial, smile, put out your hands with upturned palms and walk slowly towards them.*

up·ward /£'ʌp·wəd, $-wɚd/ *adj* [not gradable] moving towards a higher position, level or value • *With an upward trend in inflation, you might expect prices to rise.* • **Upward mobility** is the possibility of moving to a higher social class or group: *Social service jobs were an important source of African American upward mobility.* • Compare **downward** at DOWNWARDS.

up·wards /£'ʌp·wədz, $-wɚdz/, *Am usually* **up·ward** *adv* [not gradable] • *She turned her face upwards to the midday sun.* • *The cost of completion has been revised upwards again due to further delays.* • *Flying upward they broke through the cloud into sunlight.* • If you say something is **upward(s) of** a number or value, you mean it is at least the stated amount and probably more: *Upwards of fifty thousand people assembled in the main square.* ○ *A designer dress like this costs upward of $5000.* • Compare DOWNWARDS.

up·ward·ly /£'ʌp·wəd·li, $-wɚd-/ *adv* [not gradable] • If someone is **upwardly mobile**, they are moving or able to move to a higher social class, for example by becoming more wealthy: *The meeting attracted upwardly mobile professional and political women.*

up·wind /ʌp'wɪnd/ *adj, adv* in the direction from which the wind is blowing • *On the upwind side of the fire, flames advanced only slowly into the bush.* • *Stay upwind* **of** *the fumes if you can.* • Compare DOWNWIND.

u·ra·ni·um /£ jə'reɪ·ni·əm, $ juː-/ *n* [U] a heavy metal which is RADIOACTIVE and is used in the production of nuclear power and in some types of nuclear weapon

U·ra·nus /£'jʊə·rᵊn·əs, £ jə'reɪ·nəs, $'jʊr·ᵊn·əs/ *n* [U not after *the*] the planet seventh in order of distance from the Sun, after Saturn and before Neptune

ur·ban /£'ɜː·bᵊn, $'ɜːr-/ *adj* [before n] of or in a city or town • *urban regeneration/renewal* • *urban development* • *urban decay* • *In urban* **areas** *of industrialising nations, millions of people have no secure shelter.* • *(disapproving)* The **urban jungle** is city life, esp. the unpleasant parts of it: *Traffic noise, pollution, huge concrete buildings – how can people survive in the urban jungle?* • Compare RURAL.

ur·ba·nize *obj, Br and Aus usually* **-ise** /£'ɜː·bᵊn·aɪz, $'ɜːr-/ *v* [T] • *Spain urbanized* (= changed from countryside into town) *much of its natural coastline during the tourist boom of the Sixties and Seventies.*

ur·ba·ni·za·tion, *Br and Aus usually* **-i·sa·tion** /£ˌɜː·bᵊn·aɪ'zeɪ·ʃᵊn, $ˌɜːr-/ *n* [U] • Urbanization is the process by which more and more people live in cities: *Large-scale urbanization occurred with the industrial revolution, as families moved from the country into the cities to find work in factories.*

ur·bane /£ɜː'beɪn, $ɜːr-/ *adj approving* (esp. of a man) confident, comfortable and polite in social situations • *John Herschel was an urbane, kindly and generous man.*

ur·bane·ly /£ɜː'beɪn·li, $ɜːr-/ *adv approving* • *"My dear, please don't apologize. It was nothing," he said urbanely.*

ur·ban·i·ty /£ɜː'bæn·ɪ·ti, $ɜːr'bæn·ə·t̬i/ *n* [U] *approving*

ur·chin /£'ɜː·tʃɪn, $'ɜːr-/ *n* [C] *dated or humorous* a small child, esp. one who behaves badly and is dirty or untidily dressed • *a street urchin*

u·re·thra /£jʊə'riː·θrə, $juː-/ *n* [C] *pl* **urethras** or *specialized* **urethrae** /£jʊə'riː·θriː, $juː-/ *specialized* the tube in most mammals which carries urine from the BLADDER out of the body. In males it also carries sperm.

urge [DESIRE] /£ɜːdʒ, $ɜːrdʒ/ *n* [C] a strong desire, esp. one which is difficult or impossible to control • *These people seem unable to control their sexual urges.* • *What drives him on is the urge* **for** *power.* • *He had a powerful urge* **to** *compete and succeed.* [+ *to* infinitive] • *The urge* **to** *steal is very strong in many of the young men we look after here.* [+ *to* infinitive] • Ⓟ

urge *(obj)* [ADVISE] /£ɜːdʒ, $ɜːrdʒ/ *v* to strongly advise or ask (someone) to do a particular thing or for (something) to happen • *The dogs are urged* **into** *fighting more fiercely by loud shouts from the crowd.* [T] • *I urge you all* **to** *take the time to read at least three novels on the list.* [T + obj + *to* infinitive] • *Lawyers will urge the parents* **to** *take further legal action if necessary.* [T + obj + *to* infinitive] • *Investigators urged* **that** *safety procedures at the site should be improved.* [+ *that* clause] • *Police urged continued vigilance in the fight against crime.* [T] • *From the beginning of their training our coach urges* **on** *players the importance of physical fitness.* [T] • *We shall continue to urge* **for** *leniency to be shown to these prisoners.* [I] • Ⓟ

ur·ging /£'ɜː·dʒɪŋ, $'ɜːr-/ *n* • *He was happy to comply without any further urging from me.* [U] • *It was only because of Alison's urgings that he sold the house.* [C]

ur·gent [IMPORTANT] /£'ɜː·dʒᵊnt, $'ɜːr-/ *adj* needing attention very soon, esp. before anything else, because important • *There are a lot of papers to sign, but the only urgent one is this contract.* • *The most urgent thing is to make sure everyone is out of the building.* • *Many people are in urgent* **need** *of food and water.*

ur·gen·cy /£'ɜː·dʒᵊnt·si, $'ɜːr-/ *n* [U] • *It now is a matter of urgency that aid reaches the famine area.*

ur·gent·ly /£'ɜː·dʒᵊnt·li, $'ɜːr-/ *adv* • *Help is urgently needed to complete the building before bad weather starts.*

ur·gent [CONTINUALLY TRYING] /£'ɜː·dʒᵊnt, $'ɜːr-/ *adj fml* (esp. of a person's actions) continual and determined in trying to get or do something • *His urgent pleas of innocence made no difference to the judge's decision.*

ur·gent·ly /£'ɜː·dʒᵊnt·li, $'ɜːr-/ *adv*

u·ric /£'jʊə·rɪk, $'jʊr·ɪk/ *adj* [before n; not gradable] *specialized* of urine • *uric acid*

u·rine /£'jʊə·rɪn, $'jʊr·ɪn/ *n* [U] the liquid waste material which is stored in the BLADDER until it is excreted from the body

u·ri·nate /£'jʊə·rɪ·neɪt, $'jʊr·ɪ-/ *v* [I] • *This type of infection of the bladder will make the patient want to urinate* (= excrete urine) *frequently.*

u·ri·na·tion /£ˌjʊə·rɪ'neɪ·ʃᵊn, $ˌjʊr·ɪ-/ *n* [U] • *The disease is characterized by painful urination.*

u·ri·na·ry /£'jʊə·rɪ·nᵊr·i, $'jʊr·ɪ·ner-/ *adj* [not gradable] • Urinary refers to urine or to the structures in a body which produce and carry urine: *urinary excretion* ○ *urinary tract infections*

u·ri·nal /£jʊ'raɪ·nᵊl, $'jʊr·ᵊn·ᵊl/ *n* [C] • A urinal is a device, usually fitted to a wall, into which men or boys can urinate, or a building which contains one or more of these devices.

urn /£ɜːn, $ɜːrn/ *n* [C] a container, esp. a large round one on a stem, which is used for decorative purposes in a garden, or one which has a lid and is used for holding the ASHES of a dead person's body which has been CREMATED (= burnt) • An urn is also a large cylindrical metal container with a lid which is used for holding a large amount of drink such as tea or coffee and keeping it hot. • (RUS)

us [GROUP] /ʌs, əs/ *pronoun* (used as the object of a verb or a preposition) me and at least one other person • *Thank you for driving us to the station.* • *It would be rude for us to leave so early.* • *Many of us disagree with the changes that are happening.* • *How much longer are you going to keep us waiting?*

us [ME] /ʌs, əs/ *pronoun Br and Aus infml not standard* (esp. used in spoken English) me • *Give us a light, mate.* • *Give us it here and I'll see if I can mend it.*

US [AMERICA] /ˌjuː'es/ *n* [U] **the US** *abbreviation for* the United States • *A new study of attitudes to censorship in the US has just been published.*

US /ˌjuː'es/ *adj* [before n] • *a US citizen*

USA /ˌjuː·es'eɪ/ *n* [U] **the USA** *abbreviation for* the United States of America

USAF /ˌjuː·es·eɪ'ef/ *n* [U] **the USAF** *abbreviation for* the United States Air Force

use *obj* [PURPOSE] /juːz/ *v* [T] *past* **used** to put (something such as a tool, skill or building) to a particular purpose • *Are you using this knife or can I borrow it?* • *Computers should be designed for the people who are supposed to use them.* • *Going on the expedition gives me a chance to use all the training I've had.* • *The old hospital isn't used anymore.* • *This glass has been used – please fetch me a clean one.* • *Use scissors* **to** *cut the shapes out.* [+ obj + *to* infinitive] • *You can use the palette knife* **to** *apply paint directly to the canvas.* [+ obj + *to* infinitive] • *This device is used* **to** *clear blocked sinks.* [+ obj + *to* infinitive] • *These lights are used* **for** *illuminating the playing area.* • *To use military force* **against** *the protesters would be unacceptable.* • *It was a dull speech, full of* **much**-*used expressions and clichés.* • *(infml) I could use* (= I would like) *some help putting these decorations up if you're not too busy.* • If you tell someone to **use** their **head**/*(infml)* **use** their **loaf**, you are saying to them that they should think carefully about what they are doing or are planning to do: *Why didn't you use your loaf and cover the furniture before you started decorating?* • *"Any thing you say may be taken down and used in evidence"* (warning given by the police to people they are arresting) • Ⓟ

use /juːs/ *n* • *A food processor* **has** *a variety of uses in the kitchen.* [C] • *Don't throw that cloth away, you'll find a use* **for** *it one day.* [C] • *She hurt her arm in the fall and lost the use* **of** (= the ability to use) *her fingers temporarily.* [U] • *They said we could* **have the** *use* **of** (= stay in) *their flat at the coast whenever they weren't there.* [U] • *Do you have any use* **for** *these old notes or have you finished with them?* [U] • *Perhaps his advice will be* **of** *use to you when you're older.* [U] • *We might as well* **make** *use* **of** (= use) *the hotel's facilities.* [U] • *You should be able to* **put** *your experience in electronics* **to (good)** *use in your new job.* [U] • *No, I don't want to buy a* *boat – I* **have no use for** (= do not need) *one!* [U] • *The radio was an excellent gift, it's been* **in** *use ever since she received it.* [U] • *Sorry but the escalator is* **out of** *(Am and Aus usually* **not in**) *use* (= not operating). [U] • *Traditional farming methods are* **going out of/coming into** *use* (= used less and less/more and more) *in many areas.* [U] • *His advice turned out to be* **no use** *at all* (= was not effective or helpful). [U] • *Oh, you're* **no use**, *James – just go back to sleep!* [U] • *There's* **no use** *arguing any more.* [U + v-*ing*] • **It's no use** *trying* (= There is no purpose in trying) *to escape – no one has ever got away before.* • **It's no use** (= I cannot succeed) *– I just can't get this lid off.* • **It's no use** (= Despite what you say) *– I simply can't stand the man.* • *Try not to get depressed – after all,* **what's the use of/what use is** *worrying?* (= worrying will not help)

us·a·ble /ˈjuː·zə·bl̩/ *adj* [not gradable] • *The specific software is also usable* (= can be used) *in other areas of research.* • *A lot of our original ideas will be usable in the final product.*

u·sage /ˈjuː·sɪdʒ/ *n* • Usage is the way in which particular words in a language, or a language in general, is really used: *a guide to common English usage* [U] ○ *The earliest recorded usage of the word is in the twelfth century.* [C] • The usage which something receives is the way it is treated or used: *Sports equipment is designed to withstand hard usage.* [U] • LP **Labels**

use·ful /ˈjuː·sfᵊl/ *adj* • *A good knife is probably one of the most useful* (= effective when used) *things you can have in a kitchen.* • *Interesting and useful bits of information are often heard in informal conversation.* • *Do the exercises serve any useful purpose?* • *Now you're here you might as well* **make** *yourself* **useful** (= do something to help).

use·ful·ly /ˈjuː·sfᵊl·i/ *adv* • *We could usefully spend the free time sightseeing.*

use·ful·ness /ˈjuː·sfᵊl·nəs/ *n* [U] • *The usefulness of lavender essence for treating burns is well known.* • *Some people think this system of education has* **outlived** *its usefulness* (= is no longer useful).

use·less /ˈjuː·sləs/ *adj* • *Without fuel, the vehicles will become useless* (= of no use) **for** *moving supplies.* • *When he's in one of his moods, it's useless* **trying** *to discuss anything with him* (= discussion will not be successful, so you shouldn't try). [+ v-*ing*] • *It's useless* **to** *speculate without more information.* [+ *to* infinitive] • *She's very good at methodical work, but useless when there's a lot of pressure.* • *(infml) You're absolutely useless* (= not able to act effectively) *– can't you even go to the shops without getting lost!*

use·less·ly /ˈjuː·slə·sli/ *adv*

use·less·ness /ˈjuː·slə·snəs/ *n* [U] • *Too ill to get out of bed, feelings of uselessness haunted her.*

us·er /£ˈjuː·zəʳ, $-zɚ/ *n* [C] • *Unemployed people are the main users of this advice centre.* • *Telephone users will be facing higher bills next quarter.* • If something, esp. something related to a computer, is **user-friendly** it is simple for people to use: *a user-friendly printer* ○ *We have gone to a lot of trouble to make the questionnaire as user-friendly as possible.* ○ *The* **user-friendliness** *of the software has made it very popular.*

use *obj* REDUCE /juːz/ *v* [T] *past* **used** to reduce the amount of or finish (something), such as by eating it, burning it, writing on it or changing it chemically; to CONSUME • *We've used nearly all of the bread – will you buy some more if you go out?* • *Industrialised countries are using the earth's resources at a terrifying rate.* • *Does she still use drugs?* • *There's no more paper after this is used* **(up)** (= finished). • *Don't worry if you use* **up** (= finish) *the polish – I'm going shopping tomorrow.* [M] • Ⓟ

use /juːs/ *n* • *Building a dam would be a use* **of** *financial resources which this country cannot afford.* [C] • *There has been some increase in* **the** *use* **of** *casual labour over recent years.* [U]

us·er /£ˈjuː·zəʳ, $-zɚ/ *n* [C] • *The gas industry has said it will improve its service to domestic users.* • *Intravenous drug users are particularly prone to a range of medical problems.*

use *obj* TAKE ADVANTAGE /juːz/ *v* [T] *past* **used** *usually disapproving* to take advantage of (a person or situation); to EXPLOIT USE UNFAIRLY • *He's just using you – he'll steal your ideas and then take the credit for them himself.* • *It might be possible to use their mistake to help us get what we want.* • Ⓟ

use *obj* BEHAVE /juːz/ *v* [T always + adv] *past* **used** *fml* to behave towards or treat (someone) in the stated way • *Within the relationship he feels ill* (= badly) *used most of the time.* • *He's used her despicably, and I wouldn't blame her if she left.* • Ⓟ

u·sage /ˈjuː·sɪdʒ/ *n* [U] *fml* • *Many had complained about the usage they'd received at his hands.*

used IN THE PAST /juːst/ *v* [+ *to* infinitive] used to show that a particular thing always happened or was true in the past, esp. if it no longer happens or is no longer true • *Aunt Betty used* **to** *live in Australia.* • *You used* **to** *be able to walk around the town at night without fear of being mugged.* • *She used* **to** *like cats but one attacked her and she doesn't anymore.* • *You don't come and see me like you used* **(to)**. • *(not standard) He did used* **to** *work there, didn't he?* • 'Used to' can form negatives and questions in the same way as modal auxiliary verbs: *When we were younger we used* **not to** *be allowed to drink coffee.* ○ *Used he/Didn't he use* **to** *read the news on television?* ○ *(fml) Used you* **to** *work in banking?* • Used to only has the past simple tense. • LP **Auxiliary verbs**

use /juːs/ *v* [+ *to* infinitive] • 'Use to' can be used instead of 'used to' after 'did' in negatives and questions: *You didn't use* **to**/*(slightly fml) You usen't* **to** *like cream.* ○ *Didn't he use* **to** *be the doctor in 'Star Trek'?*

used NOT NEW /juːzd/ *adj* [not gradable] that has been put to the purpose it was intended for; not new • *a used airline ticket* • *The blackmailers demanded to be paid in used £20 notes.* • A used car is one that has already been owned by at least one person, and is being sold again: *a used-car salesman*

used to /juːst/ *adj* [after v] familiar with (something or someone) • *We're used to tourists here.* • *She was not used to speaking Cantonese.* [+ v-*ing*] • *Eventually you'll* **get** *used to the smells in the laboratory.* • *There are some things you never* **get** *used to.* • *It'll take a while for people to* **become** *used to the new building.*

ush·er /£ˈʌʃ·əʳ, $-ɚ/ *n* [C] a person who shows people where they should sit, esp. at a formal event such as a ceremony where people are married

ush·er *obj* /£ˈʌʃ·əʳ, $-ɚ/ *v* [T always + adv/prep] • *The mayor's guests were ushered* **to** *their seats before the conductor walked onto the stage.* • *(fig.) She ushered* (= brought) *us* **into** *her office without giving us a chance to think about what we wanted to say.* • *(fig.) The legislation should usher* **in** (= make available) *a host of new opportunities for school-leavers.* [M]

ush·er·ette *female, male* **ush·er** /ˌʌʃ·əˈret, £ˈʌʃ·əʳ, $-ɚ/ *n* [C] a person who works in a cinema or theatre where they show people to their seats and sell sweets and drinks

USN /ˌjuː·esˈen/ *n* [U] **the USN** *abbreviation for* the United States Navy

USS /ˌjuː·esˈes/ *n* [before n] *abbreviation for* United States ship (= a ship of the US navy) • *the USS Forrestal*

USSR /£ˌjuː·es·esˈɑːʳ, $-ˈɑːr/ *n* [U] **the USSR** *abbreviation for* the Union of Soviet Socialist Republics • *The USSR was dissolved in December 1991.* • *"Back in the USSR"* (title of a song by The Beatles, 1968)

u·sual /ˈjuː·ʒu·əl/ *adj* happening, done or used most often • *There was more rainfall than usual this summer in the mountain areas.* • *The film is full of Allen's usual deadpan humour.* • *You'll find the cutlery in its usual place.* • *Bill was,* **as usual**, *slow to respond.* • *This shop is open for business* **as usual** *despite the shortages.* • **As** *usual for this time of year, all of the restaurants are closed.* • *Is it usual* **for** *a child* **to** *be so interested in money?* [+ *to* infinitive]

u·sual /ˈjuː·ʒu·əl/ *n* [C usually sing] *infml* • Someone's usual is the drink, esp. an alcoholic one, which they most often have, for example when they are in a bar.

u·sual·ly /ˈjuː·ʒu·ə·li/ *adv* • *Is your friend usually so rude?* • *It's not usually possible to see inside the castle, so we're very lucky.* • *We usually go to France in August.* • *Usually I get home about 6 o'clock.* • *"Does this shop open on Sundays?" "Usually."*

u·surp *obj* /£juːˈzɜːp, £-ˈsɜːp, $-ˈzɜːrp, $-ˈsɜːrp/ *v* [T] *slightly fml* to take (control or a position of power), esp. without having the right to • *The powers of local councils are being usurped by central government.*

u·surp·er /£juːˈzɜː·pəʳ, £-ˈsɜː-, $-ˈzɜːr·pɚ, $-ˈsɜːr-/ *n* [C] *slightly fml*

u·su·ry /£ˈjuː·ʒjʊ·ri, $-ʒɚ·i/ *n* [U] *specialized or disapproving* the activity of lending someone money with the agreement that they will pay much larger sums later

u·sur·er /£ˈjuː·ʒjʊ·rəʳ, $-ʒɚ·ɚ/ *n* [C] *disapproving*

u·sur·i·ous /£juːˈzjʊə·ri·əs, $juːˈʒʊr·i-/ *adj disapproving* • *usurious interest rates*

u·ten·sil /jʊˈten·sɪl/ *n* [C] a tool or container with a particular use, esp. in a kitchen or house • *wooden utensils* • *In the drawer was a selection of* **kitchen** *utensils – spoons, spatulas, knives and whisks.*

u·ter·us /£ˈjuː·tᵊr·əs, $-t̬ɚ-/ *n* [C] *pl* **uteri** /£ˈjuː·tᵊr·aɪ, $-t̬ə·raɪ/ or **uteruses** *specialized* a womb

u·ter·ine /£ˈjuː·tᵊr·aɪn, $-t̬ə·raɪn/ *adj* [not gradable] • *the uterine wall* • See also IUD.

u·til·i·tar·i·an·i·sm /£ˌjuː·tɪ·lɪˈteə·ri·ə·nɪ·zᵊm, $-ter·i-/ *n* [U] the system of thought which states that the best action or decision in a particular situation is the one which most benefits the most people

u·til·i·ty /£juːˈtɪl·ɪ·ti, $-ə·t̬i/ *n slightly fml* the usefulness of something, esp. in a practical way • *The utility of the rescue equipment has still to be assessed in a real emergency.* [U] • A utility is a service which is used by the public, such as an electricity or gas supply or a train service: *Different tax arrangements apply to* **public** *utilities.* [C] ○ *high utility bills* • A **utility room** is a room, esp. in a house, where useful equipment such as a washing machine is used and where things can be stored.

u·til·i·tar·i·an /£ˌjuː·tɪ·lɪˈteə·ri·ən, $-ˈter·i-/ *adj* • *Like many factories it's a very utilitarian* (= designed to be useful rather than decorative) *building.*

u·til·ize *obj, Br and Aus usually* **-ise** /£ˈjuː·tɪ·laɪz, $-t̬ᵊl·aɪz/ *v* [T] *fml* • *At the development phase it was possible to utilize* (= use) *earlier research which had been performed in rocket propulsion.*

u·til·iz·a·ble, *Br and Aus usually* **-is·a·ble** /£ˈjuː·tɪ·laɪ·zə·bl̩, $-t̬ᵊl·aɪ-/ *adj* [not gradable] *fml*

u·til·i·za·tion, *Br and Aus usually* **-i·sa·tion** /£ˌjuː·tɪ·laɪˈzeɪ·ʃᵊn, $-t̬ᵊl·ɪ-/ *n* [U] *fml* • *Sensible utilization of the world's resources must be given priority.*

ut·most /£ˈʌt·məʊst, $-moʊst/, **ut·ter·most** /£ˈʌt·ə·məʊst, $ˈʌt̬·ɚ·moʊst/ *adj* [before n; not gradable] (the) greatest; (the) most possible • *I need to speak to you on a matter of utmost importance.* • *Their campaign of violence and subversion was put down with* **the** *utmost ferocity.* • *His resignation has put us in a position of* **the** *utmost difficulty.* • *(literary) He searched to* **the** *utmost* **ends of the earth.**

ut·most /£ˈʌt·məʊst, £-məst, $-moʊst/, **ut·ter·most** /£ˈʌt·ə·məʊst, $ˈʌt̬·ɚ·moʊst/ *n* [U] • *The children's endless demands tried her patience to* **the** *utmost.* • *The new model of the car offers* **the** *utmost* **in** *power and performance.* • To **do/try** your **utmost** is to do something as well as you can by making a big effort: *Each area felt it must do its utmost* **to** *make its part of the festival a success.* ○ *She tried her utmost* **to** *finish in time.*

u·to·pi·a /£juːˈtəʊ·pi·ə, $-ˈtoʊ-/ *n* (the idea of) a perfect society in which everyone works well with each other and is happy • *He said that people are too obsessed with a utopia that will never come, instead of thinking of the quality of life now.* [C] • *The people who built this city had wanted it to be a Utopia which would be a shining example to all nations.* [C] • *She left her home and travelled across the sea in search of utopia, but she never found it.* [U]

u·to·pi·an /£juːˈtəʊ·pi·ən, $-ˈtoʊ-/ *adj* • *a utopian vision* • *Utopian goals*

ut·ter [COMPLETE] /£ˈʌt·əʳ, $ˈʌt̬·ɚ/ *adj* [before n; not gradable] complete or extreme • *utter confusion/misery/chaos* • *utter nonsense/rubbish/drivel* • *The meeting was an utter* **waste** *of time.* • *The organization of the project was an utter shambles.* • *Their children are an utter delight.* • *Lying back in the hot bath was utter bliss.*

ut·ter·ly /£ˈʌt·ᵊl·i, $ˈʌt̬·ɚ·li/ *adv* [not gradable] • *What an utterly stupid thing to do!* • *Are you utterly convinced that he is guilty?* • *The smell was utterly irresistible.* • [LP] **Very, completely**

ut·ter *obj* [SPEAK] /£ˈʌt·əʳ, $ˈʌt̬·ɚ/ *v* [T] *slightly fml* to say (something) or to make (a sound) with your voice • *Before he announced the names of the winners, he uttered a firm 'Thank you!' to the crowd to quieten them.* • *Everyone ignored the warnings that he uttered.* • *She sat through the whole meeting without uttering a word.* • *For several minutes after he left, no one was able to utter a sound.*

ut·ter·ance /£ˈʌt·ᵊr·ᵊnts, $ˈʌt̬·ɚ-/ *n* • *The senator's weekend utterances* (= things that he said) *were promptly rebutted by three of his colleagues on Monday.* [C] • *(fml) He has adopted a rather pompous style of utterance* (= way of speaking). [U] • *(literary) She has one great fear* **to** *which she will never* **give utterance** (= which she will never express).

V v

V [LETTER] (*pl* **V's** or **Vs**), **v** (*pl* **v's** or **vs**) /viː/ *n* [C] the 22nd letter of the English alphabet • A **V-neck** is a piece of clothing with an opening at the neck which looks like a V: *I wore that black dress of mine with the V-neck.* ○ *I bought a V-neck (also* **V-necked***) sweater/T shirt.* • If something is **V-shaped** it looks like a V. • A **V-sign** (also **vee sign**), which is used to express victory or the hope of victory, is made by holding up the first two fingers of one hand in the shape of a V, while the thumb and other fingers are folded down and face out. In the US, a V-sign is also used to express a desire for peace, and is usually called a 'peace sign'. In Britain, a similar sign (also called **two fingers**), which is made with the back of the hand facing out, is used for expressing dislike or anger and is very offensive: *The driver shouted rudely at the cyclist and* **gave** *her a/the V-sign.* • [PIC] **Clothes**

V [NUMBER], **v** /viː/ *n* [C] the sign used in the Roman system for the number 5 and as part of the numbers 4 (iv), 6 (vi), 7 (vii) and 8 (viii)

v [AGAINST] /viː/, **vs** *prep abbreviation for* VERSUS • *I need to consider the advantages and disadvantages of full-time v part-time employment at this stage in my life.* • In sport 'v' is used to show who the competitors are in a game: *Carlsberg Championship – Quarter-final play-offs: Kingston v Hemel* • *Sunderland v Worthing* • *Thames Valley v Manchester* • *Leicester v Derby.* • In law 'v' is used to show the two sides involved in a court case: *The 1973 Supreme Court decision, Roe v Wade, recognized a constitutional right to abortion in the US.*

v [VERY] /viː/ *adv* (used esp. in writing notes) *abbreviation for* VERY [EXTREMELY] • *The teacher wrote 'v. good' on my essay.*

v [VERB] *n* [C] *abbreviation for* VERB

vac [PERIOD] /væk/ *n* [C] *Br infml for* VACATION [PERIOD] • *I'm going home for the vac tomorrow.* • *Have you managed to get a job for the* **long** (= summer) *vac?*

vac [EQUIPMENT] /væk/ *n infml for* **vacuum cleaner**, see at VACUUM • *I'll just get the vac out and clear up these crumbs.* [C] • A vac is an act of cleaning something with a **vacuum cleaner**: *Could you give the bedrooms a vac?* [U]

vac *(obj)* /væk/ *v* **-cc-** *infml* • *I've nearly finished the cleaning, I just need to vac* (= clean with a **vacuum cleaner**). [I] • *Have you vacced the carpet?* [T]

va·cant [EMPTY] /ˈveɪ·kᵊnt/ *adj* [not gradable] not filled or OCCUPIED; available to be used • *The hospital has no vacant beds.* • *There are several vacant plots in the area available for building on.* • *The sign on the toilet door said 'vacant'.* Compare ENGAGED [IN USE]. • *Today there are thought to be about 100 full-time posts vacant.* • *Five out of six posts* **falling** *vacant are being kept empty.* • *Where possible, the middle seat in a row on an aircraft is* **left** *vacant to give passengers more room.* • *Dennis Bass was appointed to* **fill** *the vacant seat on the Board.* • *(Br and Aus specialized) The people selling the house could either sell it to the sitting tenant or, with* **vacant possession** (= with no one living in it) *to a third party.*

va·can·cy /ˈveɪ·kᵊnt·si/ *n* [C] • A vacancy is a space or place which is available to be used: *We wanted to book a hotel room in July but there were no vacancies.* ○ *The dentist can't see you today but she has a vacancy tomorrow morning.* ○ *There is a vacancy* (= job) *for a shop assistant on Saturdays.* ○ *There are still some vacancies* **for** *students in science and engineering courses, but those in the arts and humanities have been* **filled**.

va·cant [NOT INTERESTED] /ˈveɪ·kᵊnt/ *adj* showing no interest or activity • *She had a vacant* **look/expression** *on her face.*

va·cant·ly /ˈveɪ·kᵊnt·li/ *adv* • *He spent some time* **staring** *vacantly at the pad in front of him.* • *She* **gazed** *vacantly into space/ahead.*

va·cate *obj* /vəˈkeɪt, £veɪ-/ *v* [T] *fml* to leave, esp. in order to make available for other people • *Hotel guests are* *requested to vacate their rooms by twelve noon.* • *Passengers are offered money to vacate their seats when planes are overbooked.* • *Jack Clarke takes the place in the team vacated by Hooks.* • *Denis vacates his post/job at the end of the week.* • *Firms are vacating offices in the city and moving out of town.*

va·ca·tion HOLIDAY /veɪˈkeɪ·ʃᵊn/ *v, n Am* (to go on) holiday • *Remember that time we were vacationing* **in** *Vermont?* [I] • *We're taking a vacation in June.* [C] • *They went to Europe* **on** *vacation.* [U] • *I've still got some vacation left before the end of the year.* [U] • LP› **Work**

va·ca·tion·er /£veɪˈkeɪ·ʃᵊn·əʳ, $-ɚ/ *n* [C] • Vacationer is *Am for* HOLIDAYMAKER.

va·ca·tion PERIOD /veɪˈkeɪ·ʃᵊn/, *Br infml* **vac** *n* [C] a period during the year when students do not study at college or university or *(Am and Aus)* at school, or when law courts do not operate • *the Christmas/Easter/summer/long vacation*

vac·cine /ˈvæk·siːn/ *n* a substance which contains part of, or a harmless form of, a virus or a bacterium, and which is given to a person or animal to prevent them from getting the disease which the virus or bacterium causes • *This vaccine protects against some kinds of the bacteria which cause meningitis.* [C] • *Relief workers in the area reported that many children have the disease, and that supplies of vaccine were short.* [U]

vac·cin·ate *obj* /ˈvæk·sɪ·neɪt/ *v* [T] • *The children were vaccinated* **against** *the major childhood diseases.* • See also INOCULATE; **immunize** at IMMUNE.

vac·cin·a·tion /ˌvæk·sɪˈneɪ·ʃᵊn/ *n* • *When we went to the tropics, we had to have several different vaccinations.* [C] • *Children entering kindergarten must have received two vaccinations* **against** *measles and one mumps vaccination.* [C] • *Vaccination by mouth – on a lump of sugar – is the most common way of administering the polio vaccine, though others are usually given by injection.* [U]

vac·il·late /ˈvæs·ɪ·leɪt/ *v* [I] *disapproving* to be uncertain what to do or to change frequently between two opinions • *He vacillated for too long and the opportunity to accept was lost.* • *Her mood vacillated* **between** *hope and despair.*

vac·il·la·tion /ˌvæs·ɪˈleɪ·ʃᵊn/ *n* [C/U]

vac·u·ous /ˈvæk·ju·əs/ *adj fml* not expressing or showing intelligent thought or purpose • *a vacuous remark/question*

vac·u·ous·ly /ˈvæk·ju·ə·sli/ *adv*

vac·u·ous·ness /ˈvæk·ju·ə·snəs/, **va·cu·i·ty** /£ˌvæk·juː·ɪ·ti, $-ə·t̬i/ *n* [U]

vac·uum /ˈvæk·juːm/ *n* a space from which most or all of the air, gas or other material has been removed or is not present • *Sound waves cannot travel through a vacuum.* [C] • *The main limitation on the life of a light bulb is not the thickness of the filament but the degree of vacuum.* [U] • A vacuum can also be a lack of something: *The withdrawal of troops from the area has* **created** *a security vacuum which will need to be* **filled**. [C] ○ *His resignation has* **left** *a power/political vacuum* (= lack of powerful/political leadership) *at the head of the party.* [C] ○ *"Composers are often too afraid of being influenced," Simpson says, "but you can't compose* **in** *a vacuum* (= kept separate from other people and activities)." [U] • A **vacuum (cleaner)** (*Br trademark also* **hoover** or *infml* **vac**) is a piece of electrical equipment which sucks dirt from floors and other surfaces. An **upright** vacuum cleaner is one in which the dirt is collected in a vertical part, and a *(Br)* **cylinder**/*(Am)* **canister** vacuum cleaner is one in which the dirt is collected through a long tube into a horizontal cylinder. • *(Br)* A **vacuum flask** (also **thermos flask**, *Br also* **flask**) is a container which keeps hot liquids hot or cold liquids cold and which usually has a lid which can be used as a cup. • Something, esp. food, which is **vacuum-packed** is in a soft container from which the air has been removed in order to make it possible for the contents to be stored for longer. • A **vacuum pump** is a piece of equipment for removing air or gas from a container, creating a vacuum inside. • PIC› **Bottles and flasks, Cleaning**

vac·uum *obj* /ˈvæk·juːm/, *Br and Aus* **hoo·ver** *v* [T] • To vacuum is to use a vacuum cleaner to collect dust, dirt, etc.: *Vacuum* **(up)** *the cake crumbs.* [T/M] • PIC› **Cleaning**

vag·a·bond /£ˈvæg·ə·bɒnd, $-bɑːnd/ *n* [C] *esp. old use or literary* a person who has no home and usually no job, and who travels from place to place, esp., in the past, one who was thought to be of low worth • *A series of laws in 16th century England specified how idle vagabonds were to be dealt with.* • *They live a vagabond life/existence, travelling around in a caravan.* • *Vagabond children live on the streets of the city.* • Compare VAGRANT.

va·ga·ries /£ˈveɪ·gᵊr·iz, $-gɚ-/ *pl n* unexpected and uncontrollable happenings or changes which have an influence on a situation • *She has her own style and is not influenced by* **the** *vagaries* **of fashion.** • *The success of the event will be determined by* **the** *vagaries* **of the weather.** • *The statistics on near-misses between aircraft depend too much on* **the** *vagaries* **of** *reporting to be reliable.* • *If seasonal vagaries are taken into account, the figures show no significant decline.*

va·gi·na /vəˈdʒaɪ·nə/ *n* [C] the tube which connects a female mammal's womb to an opening between her legs

va·gin·al /vəˈdʒaɪ·nᵊl/ *adj* [not gradable] • *vaginal intercourse* • *a vaginal examination*

va·gin·al·ly /vəˈdʒaɪ·nᵊl·i/ *adv* [not gradable] • *The baby was not delivered vaginally but by Caesarean section.*

va·grant /ˈveɪ·grᵊnt/ *n* [C] *slightly dated or law* a person who is poor and does not have a home or job; a TRAMP POOR PERSON • *Vagrants and drunks hang around the bars at the end of the street.* • *The town has shelters and food handouts for vagrants.*

va·gran·cy /ˈveɪ·grᵊnt·si/ *n* [U] • *He got deported for vagrancy.* • *The economic situation has led to rising unemployment and increased vagrancy.* • *Most European countries have abandoned laws that make vagrancy a crime.*

vague /veɪg/ *adj* **-r, -st** not clearly expressed, known, described or decided • *The patient had complained of vague pains and backache.* • *Next morning the discussion was a vague memory.* • *The remedies proposed for dealing with the situation are only vague promises for action for the future.* • *They agreed to attend the session with a vague sense of uneasiness.* • *Legal norms and definitions often remain vague.* • *Unfortunately, our information on this is even more vague.* • *The two countries have argued fiercely over their vague frontier.* • *We agreed to meet on Thursday but we left the time vague* (= we did not decide what time of day). • Vague also means not clear in shape, or not clearly seen: *Through the mist I could just make out a vague figure.* • If a person is vague, they are not able to think clearly, or, sometimes as a way of hiding what they really think, they do not express their opinions clearly: *My aunt is incredibly vague – she can never remember where she's left things.* ○ *On important details, Mr Baker was vague.* ○ *Their report is* **studiously** *vague* (= intentionally not exact) *on future economic prospects.* ○ *She was* **suitably** *vague* (= intentionally not exact in a way that is approved of) *about just what this cash would be spent on.* ○ *I asked him what the plans were, but he only replied in vague terms.* • Ⓟ

vague·ly /ˈveɪ·gli/ *adv* • *I vaguely* **remembered** *having met her before.*

vague·ness /ˈveɪg·nəs/ *n* [U]

vain UNSUCCESSFUL /veɪn/ *adj* **-er, -est** unsuccessful or useless; of no value • *The community leaders called the attacks 'vain and futile'.* • *She made a vain* **attempt** *to persuade him to lend her the money.* • *The doctors are giving him more powerful drugs in the vain* **hope** *that he might recover.* • *(fml)* **It** *was vain* **to** *pretend to himself that he was not disappointed.* [+ *to* infinitive] • If something is **in vain**, it is unsuccessful: *We put tables and chairs out in the garden but it started to rain and all our efforts were in vain.* • If you do something **in vain**, you do it unsuccessfully or uselessly: *They tried in vain to take the gun away from him.* ○ *The police looked for him in vain.* ○ *If this fighting finally brings peace to the area, the soldiers will not have died in vain.*

vain·ly /ˈveɪn·li/ *adv* • *He tried vainly to make them listen.*

vain SELFISH /veɪn/ *adj* **-er, -est** too interested in your own appearance or achievements • *He was very vain* **about** *his clothes.* • *She's one of those vain people who can't pass a mirror without looking into it.*

van·i·ty /£ˈvæn·ɪ·ti, $-ə·t̬i/ *n* [U] *disapproving* • *You have to have a certain amount of vanity to be a model, don't you?* • *He wants the job purely for reasons of vanity and ambition, without regard for how it might affect his family.* • A **vanity press** is a publishing company where writers pay to have their books produced. • *(Am)* **Vanity plates** are **number plates** on a vehicle which have particular numbers or letters on them that the vehicle's owner has specially chosen and paid to have. • A **vanity unit** is a VANITORY UNIT. • A **vanity** is *Am for* a VANITORY UNIT.

val·ance /ˈvæl·ənts/ *n* [C] a short piece of gathered material which hangs down esp. around the base of a bed, or *(Am)* a PELMET • PIC› **Beds and bedroom**

vale /veɪl/ *n* [C] used in the name of some valleys • *the Vale of Evesham* • *the Vale of York* • *(literary)* **This vale of tears** is the the world we live in, seen as sad and difficult.

val·e·dic·to·ri·an /£ˌvæl·ɪ·dɪk'tɔː·ri·ən, $-'tɔːr·i-/ *n* [C] *Am* a student, usually one who has been the most successful in a particular class, who makes a speech at a special ceremony at the end of a school year

val·en·tine /'væl·ən·taɪn/ *n* [C] someone you love or would like to have a romantic relationship with, to whom you send a **valentine card** • *The message on the card said 'Be my Valentine'.* • A **valentine (card)** is a decorative card which is sent, often without your name on it, on 14 February (St Valentine's Day) to someone you admire or love. *Did you get any valentines?* ○ *Most of the valentine cards either had hearts on them or were very rude.* • LP **Holidays** PIC **Heart**

val·et /'væl·eɪ, $væ'leɪ/ *n* [C] (esp. in the past) the personal male servant of a wealthy man, or (in the present) someone in a hotel who cleans clothes or someone at a hotel or restaurant who puts your car in a parking space for you • *"No man is a hero to his valet"* (believed to have been said by various people including Anne Bigot de Cornuel, 1605-1694)

val·et /'væl·eɪ, $væ'leɪ/ *adj* [not gradable] • *(Am and Aus)* **Valet parking** is the service offered by a restaurant, hotel, etc. of putting your car in a parking space. • **Valet service** is the service of cleaning clothes offered by a hotel to people staying there.

val·et *obj* /'væl·eɪ, £-ɪt, $væ'leɪ/ *v* [T] *Br* • *There's a service which will valet* (= clean, esp. the inside of) *your* **car** *for you while it is parked at the airport.*

val·i·ant /'væl·i·ənt/ *adj* very brave or bravely determined, esp. when things are difficult or the situation gives no cause for hope • *Venice's valiant crusade against unsuitably dressed tourists is being closely watched elsewhere in Europe.* • *The company has made a valiant* **effort/attempt** *in the last two years to make itself more efficient.* • *"He who would valiant be / 'Gainst all disasters / Let him in constancy / Follow the Master."* (Hymn based on John Bunyan's *Pilgrim's Progress*, 1684)

val·i·ant·ly /'væl·i·ənt·li/ *adv*

val·id /'væl·ɪd/ *adj* based on truth or reason; able to be accepted • *What valid deductions can be drawn from this evidence?* • *We were not satisfied that a valid reason had been given for granting extra time.* • *There is still no valid* **research/evidence/data** *that supports your theory.* • *My way of thinking might be different from yours, but it's equally valid.* • *I don't think your criticisms are really valid.* • *There are two prizes to be won and in the event of there being three or more valid claims, the winners will be decided by a draw.* • A ticket or other document is valid if it is based on or used according to a set of official conditions which often include a time limit: *My passport is valid for another two years.* ○ *The ticket is valid for off-peak travel only.* ○ *The documents are not valid without a signature.* ○ *Are these qualifications valid throughout Europe?* • Valid can also mean having legal force: *Is this* **contract/agreement** *valid?* • Compare INVALID NOT CORRECT. • Ⓕ

val·i·date *obj* /'væl·ɪ·deɪt/ *v* [T] • To validate something is to make it officially acceptable or approved, esp. after having checked it first: *It is a one-year course validated by London's City University.* ○ *The data is entered on to a computer which validates it.* ○ *Some toothpaste tubes carry a logo indicating that the manufacturers' claims have been validated by a medical association.* ○ *By quoting only opponents of the survey, Mr. Kenworthy appeared to validate their criticisms when in fact legitimate differences of opinion exist.*

val·i·da·tion /ˌvæl·ɪ'deɪ·ʃᵊn/ *n* [U] • *External validation of the teachers' assessments is recommended.* • *The investigators have focused on the company's validation procedures for its drugs, the spokesman said.* • *Visitors may park free for three hours with ticket validation from businesses in the Food Court.*

va·lid·i·ty /£və'lɪd·ɪ·ti, $və'lɪd·ə·ti/ *n* [U] • *The way the study was designed brings into doubt the validity* **of** *its conclusions.* • *The tests have been shown to be of dubious validity.* • *This research seems to* **give/lend** *some validity to the theory that the drug might cause cancer.*

val·id·ly /'væl·ɪd·li/ *adv* • *These tests must be extensively checked before they can be validly applied.* • *If a man is already validly married, a second 'marriage' would be simply invalid.*

Val·i·um /'væl·i·əm/ *n* [U] *trademark* a drug which makes you calm and helps you to stop worrying • *She was* **on** (= using) *Valium for a while several years ago.*

val·ley /'væl·i/ *n* [C] an area of low land between hills or mountains, often with a river running through it • *the Nile Valley* • *the Thames valley* • *There was snow on the hill tops but not in the valley.* • *"Valley of the Dolls"* (title of a book by Jacqueline Susann, 1966) • Compare CANYON; GORGE VALLEY; RAVINE.

val·our *Br and Aus, Am and Aus* **val·or** /£'væl·əʳ, $-ɚ/ *n* [U] *fml* great bravery • *He served the rebel cause with conspicuous valour for many years.* • *In the course of the battle he was promoted to the rank of general in recognition of his valour.* • Ⓕ Ⓟ

val·ue IMPORTANCE /'væl·juː/ *n* [U] the importance or worth of something for someone • *For them, the house's main value lay in its quiet country location.* • *They are known to* **place/put/set a** *high value* **on** *good presentation.* • If something is **of** a stated value or **has** a stated value, it has that quality or type of importance: *The show had poor entertainment value for children.* ○ *The photos are of immense* **historical** *value.* ○ *His contribution was of little or no* **practical** *value.* ○ *The necklace had great* **sentimental** *value.* • A **value judgment** is a statement of how good or bad you think an idea or action is: *He's always making value judgments about his co-workers' personalities when he really should only worry about the quality of their work.* ○ *There was an attempt to replace value judgments by objective, scientific evaluation.*

val·u·a·ble /'væl·jʊ·bl̩/ *adj* • *Parents gave the school valuable* (= helpful and important) *support in its case for getting its facilities improved.* • *He was able to provide the police with some valuable information.* • *These players have gained valuable experience in the last year.* • *Opposition is valuable* (= important) *in a democracy.*

val·ue·less /'væl·jʊ·ləs/ *adj* • *His comments were so general as to be nearly valueless.*

val·ue *obj* /'væl·juː/ *v* [T] • *I valued* (= considered as important) *your comments on the report.*

val·ued /'væl·juːd/ *adj fml* • *a valued member of staff*

val·ues /'væl·juːz/ *pl n* • Your values are the principles you have which control your behaviour: • *family/moral/traditional/Victorian values* • *She believes strongly in* **basic** *values like courage, loyalty and honesty.*

val·ue MONEY /'væl·juː/ *n* the amount of money which can be received for something; the worth of something in money • *She had already sold everything* **of** *value that she possessed.* [U] • *They had to sell their farm at below* **market** *value.* [U] • *The value of the award is £1000 a year for three years.* [U] • *The value of the pound* **fell** *against other European currencies yesterday.* [U] • *Property values have fallen since the plans for the airport were published.* [C] • *I thought the offer was* **good** *value* **(for money)**/*(Am also)* **a good** *value* (= a lot was offered for the amount of money paid). [U] • See also VAT. • LP **Expensive**

val·u·a·ble /'væl·jʊ·bl̩/ *adj* • *The museum's most valuable possessions* (= those with great financial worth) *are two series of pictures by William Hogarth, an 18th century painter.* • *The company sells all types of gem diamonds, including the most valuable ones.* • *He argues that restrictions on exports lose national companies valuable business.*

val·u·a·bles /'væl·jʊ·bl̩z/ *pl n* • Valuables are small objects, esp. jewellery, which might be sold for a lot of money: *Five men boarded the train and threatened passengers, asking them to hand over any valuables.*

val·ue·less /'væl·jʊ·ləs/ *adj* • *We thought the chair was an antique worth a lot of money, but it turned out to be a valueless replica.*

val·ue *obj* /'væl·juː/ *v* [T] • If you value something, you say how much money it might be sold for: *He valued the painting* **at** *$2000.* ○ *The insurance company said I should have my jewellery valued.* ○ *The bank valued the house* **at** *$100 000/***at** *less than the price the seller was asking.*

val·u·er /£'væl·juː·əʳ, $-ɚ/ *n* [C] *Br* • *This statement includes the valuer's* (= a person who says how much money something might be sold for) *estimate of what the property was worth at the end of last year.* • *Problems arise when building society valuers undervalue houses – in some cases not even close to the price agreed between buyer and seller.*

val·u·a·tion /ˌvæl·ju'eɪ·ʃᵊn/ *n* • Valuation is the act of deciding how much money something might be sold for or the amount of money decided on: *You can receive a home loan of up to 95% of the official valuation of the property.* [C]

○ *For the purpose of valuation, expected capital gains can be ignored.* [U] ○ *The company is offering a 50% discount on valuation* **fees** *to all new borrowers.*

valve /vælv/ *n* [C] a device which allows air or liquid to enter, or be prevented from entering, a container, or a similar structure in the human body, esp. the heart and the VEINS, that controls the flow of liquid, esp. blood • *The nuclear reactor was briefly shut down after an escape of non-radioactive steam from a faulty valve.* • *The valve failed to* **open/close.** • *On-shore oil fields are often built with emergency valves below ground level, to shut off the supply if a well gets out of control.* • *If the No. 3 hydraulic line became ruptured, a* **shut-down/shut-off** *valve would automatically close.* • *It was a weak* **heart** *valve that caused her death.* • A valve is also part of a musical instrument such as a TRUMPET which changes the sound by controlling the flow of air. • PIC› **Bicycles**

vamp /væmp/ *n* [C] a woman who is conscious of and makes use of her attractiveness to men in order to get what she wants • Compare FEMME FATALE; SIREN WOMAN. • Ⓘ

vam·pish /ˈvæm·pɪʃ/ *adj* • *vampish behaviour*

vamp *obj* /væmp/ *v* [T] • *The dress is simple and elegant, but you could vamp it* **up** (= make it more exciting) *for evening wear with some stunning jewellery.* [M]

vam·pire /£ˈvæm·paɪəʳ, $-paɪr/ *n* [C] (in stories) an imaginary human-like creature which is said to be a dead person come back to life who will suck blood from other people at night • *The most famous vampire is Count Dracula of Transylvania in the stories of Bram Stoker.* • A **vampire bat** is a small Central and S American flying animal which sucks blood from other animals: *Scientists have found that the saliva of the vampire bat prevents congealing of the blood and is effective in dissolving blood clots in humans.*

van VEHICLE /væn/ *n* [C] a medium-sized road vehicle used esp. for carrying goods and which often has no windows in the sides of the back half, or *(Am)* a similarly sized vehicle with windows all round, used for carrying more people than an ordinary car • *a delivery van* • *a Transit van* • *a van driver* • *A plumber's/builder's/electrician's van was parked outside the house opposite when I got home.* • *In the commercial vehicle sector, exports of vans and trucks were both higher this year.* • Compare LORRY; TRUCK VEHICLE. • LP› **Driving** Ⓣ

van FRONT /væn/ *n* [U] **in the van** at the front; in the most advanced position • *The United States is in the van* **of** *the quest to establish contact with beings from the beyond.* • See also VANGUARD. • Ⓣ

van·dal /ˈvæn·dəl/ *n* [C] a person, often in a group, who, esp. when they are drunk or out of control, damages property belonging to other people • *Vandals daubed the building with slogans in thick yellow paint.* • *Vandals looted stores, smashed windows, hurled bottles, overturned cars and uprooted trees in the downtown shopping district.* • LP› **Crimes and criminals**

van·dal·i·sm /ˈvæn·dəl·ɪ·zəm/ *n* [U] • *Beset by drug problems, prostitution, violence and vandalism, this is one of the most unpleasant areas in the city.* • *These schools are known to be vulnerable to vandalism.* • Vandalism is also any activity that is considered to be damaging or destroying something that was good: *Cutting down the hedges was* **an act of** *vandalism.* ○ *They established a city conservation area in an effort to preserve what buildings were left after the vandalism of the seventies.* [U] ○ *The advertising industry's use of classic songs is vandalism of popular culture, he said.*

van·dal·ize *obj, Br and Aus usually* **-ise** /ˈvæn·dəl·aɪz/ *v* [T] • *When I got back, my car had been vandalized.* • *They are the type of teenagers likely to vandalize phone boxes.* • *Theresa needed a police escort when she returned to salvage what remained in her vandalized house.*

vane /veɪn/ *n* [C] a flat narrow part of a FAN, PROPELLER, etc. which turns because of the pressure of air or liquid against it

van·guard /£ˈvæŋ·gɑːd, $ˈvæn·gɑːrd/ *n* [U] *fml* the front part of a group of people who are moving forward esp. an army, or *(fig.)* who are making changes or developments • *A UN peace-keeping vanguard arrived in the area this week.* • *The families who arrived this week were only the vanguard* **of** *what turned into a flood of refugees.* • *(fig.) He sees himself as being* **in** *the vanguard* **of** *economic reform.* • See also FOREFRONT. Compare REARGUARD.

va·nil·la /vəˈnɪl·ə/ *n* [U] a substance made from the seeds of a tropical plant, which is used to give flavour to sweet foods • *vanilla essence/extract* • *vanilla ice-cream/yoghurt* • *a vanilla milk-shake* • *Add two teaspoons of vanilla and stir.* • *Keeping a vanilla (Br)* **pod**/*(Am and Aus)* **bean** (= seed container) *in your sugar jar will add a delicate flavour.*

van·ish /ˈvæn·ɪʃ/ *v* [I] to disappear or stop being present or existing, esp. in a sudden, surprising way • *The child vanished while on her way home after a game of tennis.* • *We rushed out of the shop in hot pursuit, but the thief had vanished* **into thin air** (= had completely disappeared). • *At least 5000 jobs a week are vanishing in the catering and leisure industries and tourism.* • *Cheap rural housing is vanishing in the south of the country.* • *He entertained the rich and famous in a fashion which recalled an era that has vanished – lavish dinners served by white-gloved servants.* • *They expressed worry about the district's current budget crisis and its vanishing middle-class work force.* • *The old Ottoman building on the Hebron road is a distant reminder of a vanished empire.*

van·i·to·ry u·nit *Br* /£ˈvæn·ɪ·tri, $-tɔː·ri/, *Br also* **van·i·ty u·nit**, *Am and Aus* **van·i·ty** *n* [C] a small cupboard which stands on the floor in a bathroom and has a WASHBASIN (= fixed bowl-shaped container for water) in the top

van·i·ty /£ˈvæn·ɪ·ti, $-ə·t̬i/ *n* See at VAIN SELFISH

van·quish *obj* /ˈvæŋ·kwɪʃ/ *v* [T] *esp. literary* to defeat, esp. in war • *Napoleon was vanquished at the battle of Waterloo in 1815.* • *The vanquished army surrendered their weapons.* • *The team unexpectedly vanquished their old rivals.* • *Many of the diseases that afflicted society 50 years ago have now been vanquished.*

van·tage point /£ˈvɑːn·tɪdʒ, $ˈvæn·t̬ɪdʒ/ *n* [C] a place, often a high place, which provides a good clear view of an area or *(fig.)* a way of thinking or a set of opinions • **From** *our lofty vantage point, we could see the city spread out below us.* • *(fig.) The documentary contains a first-hand description of political life in Havana* **from** *the vantage point* **of** *a senior bureaucrat.* • *(fig.) He is writing his account of the war* **from** *the unique vantage point* **of** *an outsider who was an insider when the campaign was started.*

vap·id /ˈvæp·ɪd/ *adj fml* boring; having no imagination or excitement • *American television is full of programmes which, however vapid their content, look spectacular.* • *Few clients today would put up with a report containing vapid generalizations based on a largely academic study of business.*

va·pid·i·ty /£væpˈɪd·ɪ·ti, $-ə·t̬i/ *n* [U] • *the spiritual vapidity of Western materialism*

va·pour *Br and Aus, Am and Aus* **va·por** /£ˈveɪ·pəʳ, $-pɚ/ *n* gas which results from the heating of a liquid or solid • *The hollow glass tank contains hot mercury vapour.* [U] • *Poisonous vapours burst out of the factory during the accident.* [C] • *Warmer air is able to hold more water vapour than cold air and so has a higher humidity.* [U] • *The biggest greenhouse gas by far is water vapour.* [U] • A **vapour trail** is water vapour seen as a line of white 'smoke' behind an aircraft as it flies: *High in the sky, we could see the vapour trails of the bombers moving northwards.*

va·por·ize *(obj), Br and Aus usually* **-ise** /£ˈveɪ·pər·aɪz, $-pɚ·aɪz/ *v* • To vaporize is to (cause to) turn from a solid or liquid state into gas: *Shortsightedness can be corrected by using a laser beam to vaporize microscopic layers of the eye's surface in order to reshape the eye.* [T] • *Carburettors control engine air flow, mix air and fuel for engine operation, and help vaporize that mixture for combustion.* [T] • *Meteorites striking land usually vaporize instantly.* [I]

va·pours *Br, Am* **va·pors** /£ˈveɪ·pəz, $-pɚz/ *pl n* **the vapours** *old use or humorous* a state of feeling suddenly ill, often as the result of an unpleasant situation or bad news, esp. in women • *The letter gave her (an* **attack**/*a* **fit** *of) the vapours.*

va·ri·a·ble /£ˈveə·ri·ə·bl̩, $ˈver·i-/ *adj, n* See at VARY

va·ri·ance /£ˈveə·ri·ənts, $ˈver·i-/ *n*

va·ri·ant /£ˈveə·ri·ənt, $ˈver·i-/ *n*

va·ri·a·tion /£ˌveə·riˈeɪ·ʃən, $ˌver·i-/ *n*

var·i·cose veins /£ˈvær·ɪ·kəʊs, $ˈver·ɪ·koʊs/ *pl n* a condition in which the tubes which carry blood, esp. those in the legs, are swollen and can be seen on the skin • *Pregnant women often* **get/suffer from** *varicose veins.*

va·ried /£ˈveə·rɪd, $ˈver·ɪd/ *adj* See at VARY

va·ri·e·ga·tion /£ˌveə·rɪˈgeɪ·ʃən, $ˌver·i·ə-/ *n* [U] a pattern of different colours, esp. yellow, white or red, on the leaves of a plant • *Many hollies have delightful yellow-and-white variegation.*

va·ri·e·gat·ed /£ˈveə·rɪ·geɪ·tɪd, $ˈver·i·ə·geɪ·t̬ɪd/ *adj* • *variegated leaves* • *variegated ivy*

va·ri·e·ty [DIFFERENCE] /£və'raɪə·ti, $-t̬i/ *n* [U] the characteristic of frequently changing and being different • *When preparing meals, you need to think about variety and taste as well as nutritional value.* • *Sexual reproduction serves to create genetic variety.* • *Work on the production line is monotonous and lacks variety.* • **A** variety **of** things means several different things: *She does a variety of fitness activities.* ○ *The variety* **of** *plans submitted for the new gallery indicates the range of current architecture.* ○ *The company has hired dozens of academics as consultants on a variety of matters.* ○ *The equipment could be used for a variety of educational purposes.* ○ *Manufacturers need large sales to justify offering a big variety in export markets.* • *(Am)* A **variety store** is a shop which sells many different things. • *(saying)* 'Variety is the spice of life' means that what makes life interesting is doing different things.

va·ri·e·ty [TYPE] /£və'raɪə·ti, $-t̬i/ *n* [C] a type, esp. a group of things which are of the same type and are different to other similar types • *The article was about the different varieties* **of** *Spanish spoken in South America.* • *The seed catalogue featured a new variety* **of** *sweetcorn and a disease-resistant potato variety.* • *"57 Varieties"* (advertisement for Heinz foods, 1896-)

va·ri·e·ty [ENTERTAINMENT] *Br* /£və'raɪə·ti, $-t̬i/, *Am* **vau·de·ville**, *Br dated* **mu·sic hall** *n* [U] a type of entertainment, popular in the past, which includes several separate short performances, such as singing, dancing, magic tricks and telling jokes • *a variety show*

va·ri·ous /£'veə·ri·əs, $'ver·i-/ *adj* [not gradable] several (things or people) which are different • *The company, which has been exploring various means of expansion, has decided to open 10 more restaurants.* • *We had various problems on our journey, including a puncture.* • *The author gave various reasons for having written the book.* • *These three diseases are caused by various species of Asian river worm.* • *Bidermann sells clothes under various labels, including Yves Saint Laurent for men and Ralph Lauren for women.* • *Girardo was out of action with various injuries for most of last season.* • *Various people whom we weren't expecting turned up at the meeting.*

va·ri·ous·ly /£'veə·ri·ə·sli, $'ver·i-/ *adv* [not gradable] • Variously means in several different ways, at several different times, or by several different people: *It is one of a new class of electronic products variously called 'personal communicators' or 'personal digital assistants'.* • *Called variously Empire, classical or neoclassical, the architectural style at its best is exquisite, at its worst exceptionally unattractive.* • *The number of cases this year of salmonella poisoning linked to eggs has been variously put at 26, 46, 49 or 51.*

var·nish /£'vɑː·nɪʃ, $'vɑːr-/ *n* a liquid which is painted onto wood or paintings to protect the surface, or the hard shiny surface it produces when it dries • *Polyurethane varnish provides a tough water, heat and scratch resistant finish.* [U] • *Dyes and stains offer no surface protection for the wood, which requires a final* **coat of (clear)** *varnish.* [U] • *Plywood comes in a variety of facings and can be stained to any colour, and then* **sealed with** *a* **clear** *varnish.* [C] • **The** *varnish* (= layer of varnish on top of something) *had been deliberately scratched.* [U]

var·nish *obj* /£'vɑː·nɪʃ, $'vɑːr-/ *v* [T] • *They decided to spend the weekend varnishing their boat.* • To varnish is also to use **nail varnish**.

var·nished /£'vɑː·nɪʃt, $'vɑːr-/ *adj* • *a varnished surface* • *varnished wood*

var·si·ty *Am* /£'vɑː·sɪ·ti, $'vɑːr·sə·t̬i/ *adj* [before n, not gradable] (of sports teams at schools or colleges) of the most skilled level of play • *He was the manager of the varsity baseball team.* • *This season was the first for girls' lacrosse as a varsity sport in the region.*

va·ry /£'veə·ri, $'ver·i-/ *v* to (cause to) change or be different , esp. from one occasion to another or from one item to another within a group • *Attitudes to wasteland vary* **greatly/widely**, *but the official view is that it is unsightly and depressing.* [I] • *Salary scales vary* **between** *states/***from** *state* **to** *state/***according to** *state.* [I] • *The samples varied* **in** *quality but were generally acceptable.* [I] • *Some people give a regular monthly donation to charity while others vary the amount they give from time to time.* [T]

va·ried /£'veə·rɪd, $'ver·ɪd/ *adj* • If something is varied, it contains many different types or changes often: *a varied group of people* ○ *a lengthy and varied career* ○ *He said that, with its varied climate, the country can grow anything from drought-resistant cotton to tropical and temperate fruits.*

va·ri·a·ble /£'veə·ri·ə·bl̩, $'ver·i-/ *adj, n* • If something is variable, it is likely to change frequently: *The variable performance of the laboratories doing the testing means that the results cannot be relied on.* ○ *Increasingly more companies are establishing variable pay programmes to reward top performers on their staff.* ○ *British weather is perhaps at its most variable in the spring.* • *(specialized)* A variable is something which can change: *The data was analysed according to neighbourhoods, but other key variables like credit rating, job history, savings and marital status were ignored altogether.* [C]

va·ri·ance /£'veə·ri·ənts, $'ver·i-/ *n* [U] • *There has been some unusual variance in temperature this month.* [U] • *(Am) We had to get* **a (zoning)** *variance* (= approval from the local government to do something that is not usually allowed) *before we could build the extension on our house.* [C] • To be **at variance with** someone or something is to be in disagreement with them or different from them: *Young people's reactions to world events are often at variance with those of their parents.* ○ *She said that the approaches of some teachers are at variance with the real needs of schools.* ○ *Most heavy metal fans are under 20 – this is at variance with the age of the bands themselves, who are often on the wrong side of 40.*

va·ri·ant /£'veə·ri·ənt, $'ver·i-/ *n* [C] • A variant is something which differs a little from other similar things: *Many of the temple complexes built in Thai cities are variants* **on** *Burmese and Indian originals.* ○ *There are many colas on the market now, all variants* **on** *the original drink.* ○ *There are four variants* **of** *malaria, all transmitted to humans by a particular family of mosquitoes.* ○ *Words spelt with 'ae', such as 'encyclopaedia', have a variant spelling with 'e', as in 'encyclopedia'.*

va·ri·a·tion /£ˌveə·ri'eɪ·ʃən, $ˌver·i-/ *n* • Variation is change in amount or level: *Unemployment rates among white-collar workers show much less regional variation than corresponding rates among blue-collar workers.* [U] • *The medical tests showed some variation* **in** *the baby's heart rate.* [U] • A variation is a difference: *There are* **wide** *variations in the way pensioners have benefited from the system.* [C] ○ *The research team has a very good record of day-to-day variation* **in** *pollution in the atmosphere.* [C] ○ *A group of scientists studied global temperature variations over the last 140 years.* [C] ○ *The films she makes are all variations* **on** *the same* **theme**. [C] • In music, a variation is one of the several short tunes which are based on the same simple tune, but are different from it and from the others. *Symphonic variations* [C] ○ *He composed his first piece for the band, Variations* **on** *Annie Laurie, at the age of 12.* [C]

vas·cu·lar /£'væs·kjʊ·lər, $-lɚ/ *adj* [not gradable] *specialized* of the tubes which carry blood or liquids in animals and plants • *Clinical studies show that aspirin can reduce the incidence of death from heart attack or stroke in people who have already suffered from vascular* **disease**. • *The poison affected the victim's vascular* **system**.

vase /£vɑːz, $veɪs/ *n* [C] container for holding flowers or for decoration. Vases range from very small to very large, can be many different shapes and are made from different materials including glass or clay. • *a vase of flowers* • [PIC] **Room**

va·sec·to·my /və'sek·tə·mi/ *n* [C/U] the medical operation of cutting the tubes through which a man's sperm move, in order to make him unable to make a woman pregnant

Vas·e·line /'væs·ə·liːn/ *n* [U] *trademark* a soft yellow or white oily substance which is used esp. on the skin to protect it or on surfaces to LUBRICATE them (= stop them sticking together)

vast /£vɑːst, $væst/ *adj* **-er, -est** extremely big • *In 1918 the Bolsheviks used radio to help spread revolution across a vast country.* • *A vast audience watched the broadcast.* • *The amount of detail the book contains is vast.* • *The people who have taken our advice have saved themselves a vast amount of money.* • *The vast* **majority** *of pupils attend state schools.*

vast·ly /£'vɑːst·li, $'væst·li/ *adv* • *vastly different* • *vastly superior* • *vastly improved*

vat /væt/ *n* [C] a large container used for mixing or storing liquid substances esp. in a factory • *The wines used to be made in deep wooden vats.*

VAT, Vat /ˌviː·eɪ'tiː, væt/ *n* [U] value-added tax (= a type of tax in European countries which is paid by the person who buys the goods and services)

VAT·a·ble /£'væt·ə·bl̩, $'væt̬-/ *adj* [not gradable] • VATable goods are those on which VAT has to be paid: *The*

VARIETIES OF ENGLISH

Labels in the dictionary give information about three important varieties of English:

Am	North American English
Aus	Australian English
Br	British English

These labels refer to the standard type of English used by speakers from the country mentioned. Items that are used in all these varieties of English are not labelled. Within British and North American English there are additional varieties. The following are labelled:

Canadian Eng	Canadian English
Irish Eng	Irish English
Scot Eng	Scottish English
regional	used mostly by people from other areas of Britain or the US

Some words, such as 'dunno' (=do not know) or 'gimme' (= give me), are often used in informal speech but are not considered correct English by most speakers. These are labelled *not standard.*

• Differences in words and phrases

Differences between varieties of English are especially common in some areas of language, for example transport, food and clothing. American words are frequently taken into British English, but it is less common for American speakers to use new British words. Australian English uses words from both British and American English. For examples of differences between American, Australian and British English, LP **Australian English**.

- A word or phrase with a single label is only used in the variety of English mentioned. It is almost never used by speakers of other varieties of English, and might not be understood by them. Examples are:

panhandle *(Am)*	the verb 'panhandle' is used only in American English. It is not used in British or Australian English.
(Br and Aus) maths/ *(Am)* math	'maths' and 'math' mean the same. 'Maths' is used only in British and Australian English and 'math' is used only in American English.

- Usually the differences between the varieties of English are less fixed and exact. For example, American, Australian and British speakers all understand and use both 'pack' and 'deck' to refer to a set of playing cards, but they are different in which word they more frequently use. The dictionary gives this type of information in the following ways:

biscuit/ *(esp. Am)* cookie	'Biscuit' is the usual word in British and Australian English but is rarely used in American English. 'Cookie' is the usual word in American English and is sometimes also used in British and Australian English.
flat/ *(Am usually)* apartment	'Flat' is the usual word in British and Australian English and is sometimes used in American English. 'Apartment' is the usual word in American English and is sometimes used in British and Australian English.
car/ *(Am also)* auto	'Car' is used in all varieties of English. American English also uses 'auto' but this is rare in British and Australian English.

• Differences in spelling

In American English, words tend to be spelled more simply or more like the way they are pronounced. Compare the following American spellings (on the right) with their usual British spellings:

litre	*liter*	*equalled*	*equaled*
tyre (of a wheel)	*tire*	*equalise*	*equalize*
plough	*plow*	*honour*	*honor*

When there is a difference in spelling between American and British English, there is usually a spelling that is acceptable in both varieties (for example 'likeable') and a spelling that is acceptable only in American writing (for example 'likable'). For more examples, LP **Spelling differences between American and British English** at AMERICAN. Australian English usually follows British spellings: American spellings are rarer but generally are also acceptable.

• Differences in stress

Generally in English many nouns and adjectives are stressed on the first syllable. When a noun can also be used as a verb, for example 'conduct', the stress usually moves to the second syllable in the verb: *his 'con·duct, to con'duct.* In American English the verb is often stressed on the first syllable as with 'decrease': *£ de'crease, $ 'de·crease.* LP **Stress**

• Differences in grammar

American, Australian and British English do not have many differences in grammar. Here are some important ways in which American English differs from British (and Australian) English:

the past forms of some verbs can be different
In American English some irregular verbs can have an additional form of the past simple or past participle that is not used in British English. Examples are: *He* **dived**/*(Am also)***dove** *into the pool.* • *Jake has* **got**/*(Am usually)***gotten** *really fat.* • *Corrie (Br and Aus)***spelt**/*(Am)***spelled** *the word correctly.*

the past simple is used more widely
In many situations where British English uses the present perfect form of the verb, American English can also use the past simple: *I think I've lost my camera. / (Am also)I think I lost my camera.* • *Thanks, but I've already eaten. / (Am also)Thanks, but I already ate.* • *Have you opened my letter yet? / (Am also)Did you open my letter yet?*

different prepositions are sometimes used
Sometimes British and American English prefer different prepositions: *The shop is open (Br)* **from** *Monday* **to** *Saturday. / (Am)Monday* **through** *Saturday* • *We should leave by ten* **to** *eight/(Am also)ten* **of** *eight.* • *It's a quarter* **past** *seven/(Am also)quarter* **after** *seven.* • *She's always leaving her clothes (esp. Br)***about**/*(Am usually)***around**.

nouns referring to groups are usually followed by a singular verb
In British English, words for some groups such as 'government', 'public' or 'company' can be followed by a plural or singular verb: *The group have/has shown little interest in this project.* (Nouns like this are labelled [+ sing/pl v] in the dictionary.) American English uses the singular form of the verb.

• Differences in pronunciation

The dictionary gives pronunciations for two standard English accents, BBC pronunciation (the standard British accent, labelled £) and General American (labelled $). For more details, LP **Pronunciation** at PRONOUNCE. There are important differences in the pronunciation of some vowels and diphthongs (= two vowels together), and in the pronunciation of 'r' and 't'.

Br	Am		Br	Am	
ɑː	æ	fast plant	fɑːst plɑːnt	fæst plænt	Where Br has /ɑː/, Am usually has /æ/, except before 'r'.
ɔː	ɑː	ought laundry	ɔːt 'lɔːn·dri	ɑːt 'lɑːn–	Where Br has /ɔː/, Am usually has /ɑː/, except before 'r'.
ɒ	ɑː ɔː	cloth loss foreign	klɒθ lɒs 'fɒr·ɪn	klɑːθ lɑːs 'fɔːr–	The vowel /ɒ/ is not found in Am and is replaced by /ɑː/ or /ɔː/.
əʊ	oʊ	nose rose	nəʊz rəʊz	noʊz roʊz	The diphthong /əʊ/ is not found in Am and is always replaced by /oʊ/.
ɪə eə ʊə	ɪ e ʊ	ear steer hair fare wear pure	ɪəʳ stɪəʳ heəʳ feəʳ weəʳ pjʊəʳ	ɪr stɪr her fer wer pjʊr	The diphthongs /ɪə/, /eə/ and /ʊə/ are not found in Am and are replaced by the vowels shown.
juː	uː	due knew resume tube	djuː njuː ri'zjuːm tjuːb	duː nuː –'zuːm tuːb	Where Br has /juː/ after d, n, r, or t Am speakers say /uː/.
t	t̬	metal fatten	'met·əl 'fæt·ən	'met̬– 'fæt̬–	't' and 'tt' in the middle of a word are pronounced more like 'd' in Am.
əʳ	ɚ	other actor	'ʌð·əʳ 'æk·təʳ	–ɚ –tɚ	The 'r' in the endings '-er' and '-or' is always pronounced in Am.
	r	farm horse bird car	fɑːm hɔːs bɜːd kɑːʳ	fɑːrm hɔːrs bɜːrd kɑːr	Am pronounces the 'r' in a word. In Br 'r' is not pronounced before a consonant or at the end of a word.*

* For more exact rules and an explanation of the symbols used, LP **Pronunciation of 'r' in British and American English** at R

rich spend more than the poor on VATable goods. ○ *Those who spend more on VATable items will pay more.*

Vat·i·can /£'væt·ɪ·kən, $'væt̬-/ *n* [U] **the Vatican** the main offices of the Catholic Church in Rome, which includes the building where the Pope lives, or the Pope or the officials who represent the Pope • *The joint declaration was issued as the Archbishop of Canterbury ended a four-day visit to the Vatican/the Vatican City.* • *The information was given by a Vatican official.* • *In 1980 the Vatican* (= the Pope or the Pope's representatives) *ordered all priests and nuns to give up elected offices.* • *The Cardinal said yesterday he had not consulted the Vatican before writing the article.*

vau·de·ville /£'vɔː·də·vɪl, $'voʊd·vɪl/ *n* [U] *Am for* VARIETY ENTERTAINMENT

vau·de·vil·li·an /£vɔː·də'vɪl·i·ən, $voʊd'vɪl-/ *n* [C] *Am*

vault ARCH /£vɒlt, $vɑːlt/ *n* [C] a type of arch which supports a roof or ceiling, esp. in a church or public building, or a ceiling or roof supported by several of these arches

vault·ed /£'vɒl·tɪd, $'vɑːl·t̬ɪd/ *adj* • *a vaulted ceiling* • *a vaulted room*

vault·ing /£'vɒl·tɪŋ, $'vɑːl·t̬ɪŋ/ *n* [U] • *After the explosion nothing of the walls or vaulting* (= arches supporting the roof) *remained intact.*

vault ROOM /£vɒlt, $vɑːlt/ *n* [C] a room, esp. in or under the ground floor of a large building, which is used to store things in safe conditions • *Museums usually keep original transparencies and negatives of photographs in temperature-controlled, dark storage vaults.* • In a bank, a vault is where money, jewellery, important documents, etc. are locked for protection: *In the robbery, the bank vaults were completely emptied and they lost most of their files, deeds and records.* ○ *The steel and concrete vaults hold 800 000 gold bars.* • A vault is also a room under a church or is a small building in a CEMETERY (= area of ground used for burying dead bodies) where dead bodies are kept: *His coffin was placed in what was to be a temporary vault.* ○ *She was buried in the* **family** *vault.* • Compare CELLAR.

vault *(obj)* JUMP /£vɒlt, $vɑːlt/ *v* to (cause to) jump over (something) • *He vaulted* **over** *the gate.* [I always + adv/prep] • *She vaulted the wall and kept running.* [T] • *(specialized) He has vaulted 6·02 m in indoor competition, but still trails by 10 cm outdoors.* See also **pole vault** at POLE STICK. [T] • *(fig.) Last week's changes vaulted* (= suddenly moved to a more important position) *the general to the top, over the heads of several of his seniors.* [T] • PIC **Sports**

vault·ing /£'vɒl·tɪŋ, $'vɑːl·t̬ɪŋ/ *adj disapproving* • Someone who has **vaulting ambition** has a desire to achieve important and powerful positions and thinks this is more important than anything else: *He sacrificed his marriage to his vaulting political ambition.*

vaunt·ed /£'vɔːn·tɪd, $'vɑːn·t̬ɪd/ *adj* praised frequently in a way that is considered to be more than acceptable or reasonable • *His* **(much)** *vaunted new scheme has been shown to have serious weaknesses.*

vaunt *obj* /£vɔːnt, $vɑːnt/ *v* [T] *fml* • *Planning, patience, and discipline were vaunted as virtues in the army.*

VC /ˌviː'siː/ *n* [C] *abbreviation for* Victoria Cross (= a MEDAL which is the highest honour for bravery which can be given to a British soldier, or the person who receives the medal) • *He was awarded the VC.* • *He's a VC.*

VCR /£ˌviː·siː'ɑːʳ, $-'ɑːr/ *n* [C] *Am abbreviation for* **video cassette recorder**, see at VIDEO

VD /ˌviː'diː/ *n* [U] *abbreviation for* **venereal disease**, see at VENEREAL

VDT /ˌviː·diː'tiː/ *n* [C] *Am abbreviation for* video display terminal (= a piece of equipment with a screen on which information from a computer can be shown)

VDU /ˌviː·diː'juː/ *n* [C] *abbreviation for* visual display unit (= a piece of equipment with a screen on which information from a computer can be shown) • [PIC] **Office**

've /v/ *short form of* have • *I've been waiting for ages.* • *We've decided to go home early.* • *They've agreed to our request.*

veal /viːl/ *n* [U] meat from a very young cow • *I don't cook veal very often because it's quite expensive.* • *I chose breaded veal escalopes from the menu.*

vec·tor [CALCULATION] /£'vek·təʳ, $-t̬ɚ/ *n* [C] *specialized* something physical such as a force which has size and direction

vec·tor [ANIMAL] /£'vek·təʳ, $-t̬ɚ/ *n* [C] an insect or animal which carries a disease from one animal or plant to another • *Mosquitoes are the vectors* **of** *malaria.*

Ve·dan·ta /vɪ'dæn·tə/ *n* [U] one of the main systems of Hindu thought

Ve·da /'veɪ·də/ *n* [C] one or all of the holy books of writings of Hinduism

Ved·ic /'veɪ·dɪk/ *adj*

veep /viːp/ *n* [C] *Am infml* a **vice president**, see at VICE [TITLE]

veer /£vɪəʳ, $vɪr/ *v* [I always + adv/prep] to change direction • *There was a sudden flash of light, making the driver veer sharply.* • *The officer said he saw the car veer* **off** *the side of the road.* • *The jet was taking off on the north-east runway when it veered* **to** *the north.* • *The walking is flat and easy, with tracks frequently veering* **off to** *isolated farms.* • *Three men were feared dead last night after a helicopter veered* **off course** *into an oil platform and ditched into the North Sea.* • *The story never veers* **off course.** • *Our talk soon veered* **onto** *the subject of football.* • *The wind veered round* **to** *the north.* • *Manic depressives may veer* **back and forth** *between periods of destructive behavior and the appearance of normality.*

veg /vedʒ/ *n pl* **veg** *esp. Br infml* a VEGETABLE • *a fruit and veg stall* • *meat and two veg* [C] • *Do you have a favourite veg?* [C] • *Would you like some veg?* [U]

veg out /vedʒ/ *v adv* [I] *infml for* VEGETATE • *She told me she couldn't find a job and couldn't afford to go out, so she just tended to veg out all day in front of the TV.*

ve·gan /'viː·gən/ *n* [C] a person who does not eat or use any animal products, such as meat, fish, eggs, cheese or leather • *Vegans get all the protein they need from nuts, seeds, beans and cereals.* • Compare VEGETARIAN.

ve·gan /'viː·gən/ *adj* [not gradable] • *a vegan diet* • *She decided to* **turn** *vegan after watching a documentary about how poultry is raised.*

veg·e·bur·ger /£'vedʒ·ɪˌbɜː·gəʳ, $-ˌbɜːr·gɚ/ *n* [C] *Br for* VEGGIEBURGER

veg·e·ta·ble /'vedʒ·tə·bl̩/, *esp. Br infml* **veg**, *esp. Am and Aus infml* **veg·gie** *n* [C] (a part of) a plant that is used as food, particularly in savoury dishes • *The potato is the most popular vegetable in Britain.* • *The current trend for healthy eating has led to a rise in demand for fresh* **green** *vegetables.* • *His diet consisted mainly of meat and white bread and included very little* **fresh fruit and** *vegetables.* • *In the winter we tend to eat more* **root** *vegetables, such as carrots and parsnips.* • **Raw** *vegetables contain more potassium than* **cooked** *ones.* • *Each main dish is served with an assortment of* **seasonal** *vegetables.* • *We had vegetable soup/curry for dinner.* • *California produces almost half the US fruit and vegetable* **crop**. • *Barbara and Tom created a vegetable* **garden** *at the back of the house and sold their produce at the local market.* • *A vegetable* **knife** *is a small sharp knife used for cutting vegetables.* • Vegetable can also sometimes mean any plant, especially in the question 'animal, vegetable or mineral?', asked in a guessing game. • *(fig.) The driver was killed in the car crash and his passenger was left a vegetable* (= unable to think or move correctly because of severe brain damage). This usage can be considered offensive. • *(fig.) Sitting at home all day in front of the TV slowly turned her into a vegetable* (= a person who does not or cannot do anything). • **Vegetable oil** is cooking oil made from plants. • Compare FRUIT [PLANT PART]. • [PIC] **Kitchen, Knife**

veg·e·tar·i·an /£ˌvedʒ·ɪ'teə·ri·ən, $-'ter·i-/, *infml* **veg·gie, veg·gy** *n* [C] a person who does not eat meat for health or religious reasons or because they want to avoid cruelty to animals • *Of the four million people who have become vegetarians in Britain, nearly two-thirds are women.* • *He stopped eating meat at the age of sixteen but gave up fish and became a* **strict** *vegetarian two years later.* • Compare VEGAN.

veg·e·tar·i·an /£ˌvedʒ·ɪ'teə·ri·ən, $-'ter·i-/, *infml* **veg·gie, veg·gy** *adj* [not gradable] • *vegetarian cooking/food* • *a vegetarian dish/meal/restaurant* • *A well-balanced vegetarian* **diet** *can be a lot healthier for you than the average meat-eater's diet because it contains less fat and more fibre.* • *She's* **gone**/*become vegetarian.*

veg·e·tar·i·an·ism /£ˌvedʒ·ɪ'teə·ri·ə·nɪ·zᵊm, $-'ter·i-/ *n* [U] • *Vegetarianism is becoming increasingly popular among young people in Britain, especially among teenage girls.*

veg·e·tate /'vedʒ·ɪ·teɪt/, *infml* **veg out** *v* [I] to live in a way that lacks physical and mental activity • *A report has shown that children spend too much time vegetating in front of the TV when they come home from school.*

veg·e·ta·tion /ˌvedʒ·ɪ'teɪ·ʃᵊn/ *n* [U] plants in general or plants which are found in a particular area • *The railway track will have to be cleared of vegetation if it is to be used again.* • *Much of the region's native vegetation has been damaged by developers who are building hotels along the coast.*

veg·gie /'vedʒ·i/, **veg·gy** *n* [C] a VEGETARIAN or *(esp. Am and Aus)* a VEGETABLE • *People in Britain are becoming veggies at the rate of 28 000 every week.* • *The restaurant's menu is heavily veggie, and those dishes that contain meat can be made vegetarian.* • *(esp. Am and Aus) I often buy a prepared pizza base and let the kids put their favourite veggies and cheese on top of it.* • *Linda made us a delicious veggie lasagne.*

veg·gie·bur·ger, *Br also* **veg·e·bur·ger** /£'vedʒ·iˌbɜː·gəʳ, $-ˌbɜːr·gɚ/ *n* [C] a type of savoury food made by pressing together small pieces of vegetables, seeds, nuts and grains into a flat round shape • *Veggieburgers can be fried or grilled and are often eaten as a vegetarian alternative to hamburgers.*

ve·he·ment /'viː·ɪ·mənt, £'vɪə-/ *adj* expressing strong feelings, or characterized by strong feelings or great energy or force • *a vehement critic/denial/objection/reaction* • *They launched a vehement* **attack** *on the government's handling of environmental issues.* • *She was overcome by a vehement* **desire** *to punch him.* • *Despite the vehement* **opposition** *from his family, he married a woman who was 15 years his senior.*

ve·he·ment·ly /'viː·ɪ·mənt·li, £'vɪə-/ *adv* • *The president vehemently* **denied** *having an extra-marital affair.* • *She vehemently* **defended** *her right to a fair trial.*

ve·he·mence /'viː·ɪ·mənts, £'vɪə-/ *n* [U] • *She argued* **with** *such vehemence against the proposal that they decided to abandon it.*

ve·hi·cle /'viː·ɪ·kl̩/ *n* [C] *fml* a machine usually with wheels and an engine which is used for transporting people or goods on land, particularly on roads • *A truck driver died last night when his vehicle overturned.* • **Road** *vehicles include cars, buses and trucks.* • *Tractors are* **farm** *vehicles.* • *The number of thefts of* **motor** *vehicles rose by a third last year.* • *Two soldiers travelling in the* **armoured** *vehicle were injured when the mine exploded.* • *Environmentalists have been campaigning for a substantial reduction in vehicle* **emissions** (= gases produced by vehicles) *over the next few years.* • *(fig.) The conference was seen as an ideal vehicle* **for** (= way of achieving) *increased cooperation between the member states.* • *(fig.) The film seems to be little more than a vehicle* (= way of obtaining public attention) **for** *its director and star.* • [LP] **Driving**

ve·hi·cu·lar /£vɪ'hɪk·jʊ·ləʳ, $viː'hɪk·jʊ·lɚ/ *adj* [not gradable] *fml* • *The cottage has no vehicular access but can be reached by a short walk across the moor.*

veil /veɪl/ *n* [C] a piece of thin material worn to protect or hide the face or head • *After the ceremony, the bride lifted up her veil to kiss her husband.* • *She chose a pink hat with a veil to wear at the mayor's garden party.* • *The Muslim women were dressed in black veils that covered everything but their eyes.* • *(fig.) The view over the lake was obscured by a veil* (= thin covering through which you can see) **of mist** *that hung in the air.* • *(fig.) The government has been urged to lift the veil* (= something that prevents you from knowing what is happening) **of secrecy** *surrounding the minister's*

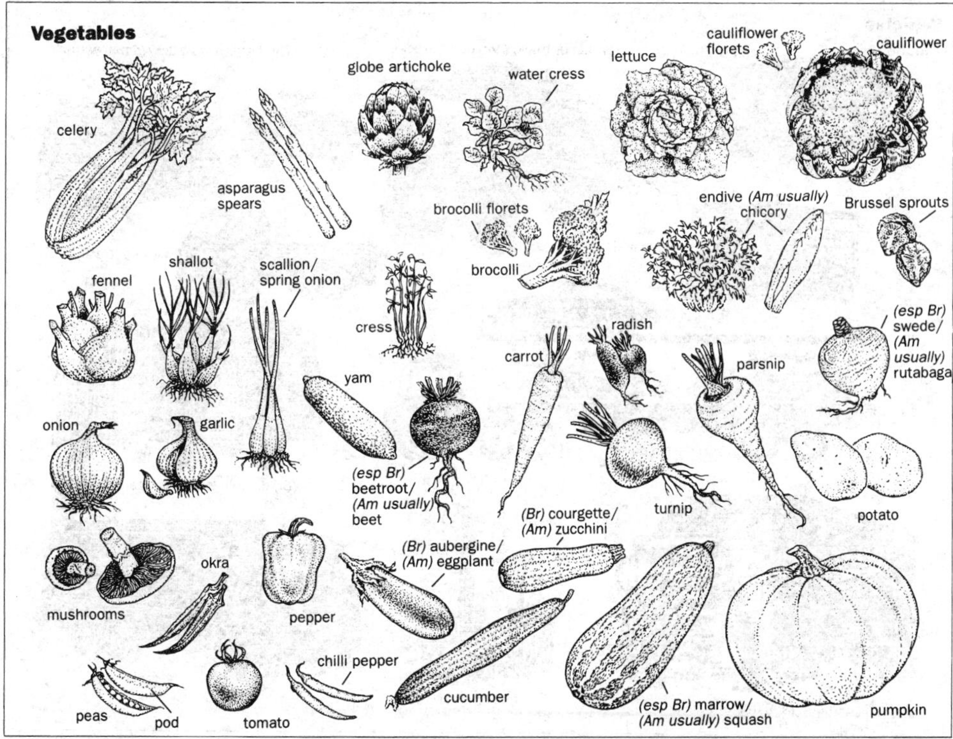

unexpected resignation. • A Christian woman who **takes the veil** becomes a NUN (= a member of a female religious group): *Shortly after taking the veil, Sister Catherina moved to India to set up a school for orphans.* • A Muslim woman who **takes** or **adopts the veil** decides to wear traditional Muslim clothing: *Many women who take the veil say that it liberates them, because men no longer chat them up.* • PIC› **Wasps and bees**

veil *obj* /veɪl/ *v* [T] • *In some societies, women are expected to be veiled when they go out in public.* • *(fig.) Thick fog veiled* (= covered) *the city.* • *(fig.) Veiled* (= Hidden) *in shadow, he managed to slip unnoticed through the gateway.*

veiled /veɪld/ *adj* • A veiled statement, remark, etc. is one which is not direct or expressed clearly: *a veiled hint/ reference/suggestion/threat/warning* ○ *veiled contempt/ criticism/language* ○ *They launched a* **thinly** *veiled* **attack** *on his abilities as a leader.*

vein TUBE /veɪn/ *n* [C] a tube that carries blood to the heart from the other parts of the body • *The pulmonary vein is the only vein in the human body which carries oxygenated blood.* • *Some drugs have to be injected directly into patients' veins.* • A vein also forms the frame of a leaf or an insect's wing: *Leaf veins distribute food and water throughout the leaf.*

veined /veɪnd/ *adj* • *These plants have pale pink flowers and deeply veined leaves.* • *(fig.) Her hands were veined* **with** (= marked with the lines of) *tiny scars.*

-veined /-veɪnd/ *combining form* • *The dragonfly slowly flapped its red-veined wings.*

vein LAYER /veɪn/ *n* [C] a narrow layer of a substance which forms in or fills a crack in rock • *A* **rich** *vein* **of** *iron ore was found in the hillside.* • A vein is also a particular quality or characteristic: *A vein* **of** *satirical anger runs through all his work.* ○ *In its bid to be elected, the party is attempting to* **tap** *an underlying vein* **of** *nationalism in the country.*

vein MOOD /veɪn/ *n* [U] a style or a temporary mood • *The opening scene is very violent, and the rest of the film continues* **in (a) similar** *vein.* • *His latest book is written* **in** *the vein* **of** *the 19th century romantic novelists.* • *After laughing over the photo, they began to talk* **in (a)** *more serious vein* (= mood) *about the damaging effect it could have on her career.*

Vel•cro /£ˈvel·krəʊ, $-kroʊ/ *n* [U] *trademark* a fastener for clothing that consists of two strips of NYLON, one rough and one with very small hooks, which stick together when pressed • LP› **Dressing and undressing**

veld, veldt /felt, velt/ *n* flat open country with few trees, which is characteristic of parts of southern Africa

vel•lum /ˈvel·əm/ *n* [U] a thick, cream-coloured, very high-quality writing paper or, esp. in the past, a material for writing on, or a covering for a book, made from the skins of young animals, esp. cows or sheep • *The writing set contains 20 vellum sheets and 10 envelopes.* • *She always carried a small vellum notebook around with her to jot down ideas for her latest novel.*

ve•loc•i•ty /£vəˈlɒs·ɪ·ti, $-ˈlɑː·sə·t̬i/ *n fml* the speed at which an object is travelling • *Light travels at the highest achievable velocity in the universe.* [C] • *The footballer scored with such velocity that the goalkeeper didn't stand a chance of saving the goal.* [U] • *He always used* **high** *velocity lead bullets in his rifle.*

ve•lour, ve•lours /£vəˈlʊəʳ, $-ˈlʊr/ *n* [U] a material similar to VELVET that has a soft surface and which is used for clothes and for covering furniture • *Emma was wearing a pair of slim velour trousers and an embroidered jacket.* • *They've just bought a new green velour couch and curtains to match.*

Ve•lux /ˈviː·lʌks/ *n* [C] *Br trademark* a window which is built into a roof

vel•vet /ˈvel·vɪt/ *n* [U] a cloth usually woven from silk or cotton with a thick soft furry surface • *She kept the necklace in a mahogany box lined with crimson velvet.* • *Her skin was* **as soft as** *velvet.* • *(fig.) They strolled hand in hand along the river bank under the velvet* (= dark and soft) **sky.** • *(fig.) Michael crooned the lyrics in a velvet* (= deep and soft) **voice** *to the group of female fans sitting in the front row.*

vel•vet•y /£ˈvel·vɪ·ti, $-və·t̬i/ *adj* • *(fig.) His velvety* (= soft and deep-looking) **brown** *eyes had been his passport to fame.* • *(fig.) This is a very velvety* (= smooth) *beer.*

ve•nal /ˈviː·nᵊl/ *adj fml* (of a person) willing to behave in a dishonest or immoral way in exchange for money, or (of an activity) done in order to obtain money • *a venal magistrate/regime/ruler* • *He was renowned in the business world for being a venal character.* • *They are accused of being involved in venal practices.*

ve•nal•i•ty /£viːˈnæl·ɪ·ti, $vɪˈnæl·ə·t̬i/ *n* [U] *fml* • *There has never been any hint of corruption or venality in the company.*

vend•ing /ˈven·dɪŋ/ *n* [U] *fml* the selling of goods • *They were arrested at the football game for illegal vending.* • *He*

had his street vending licence taken away because he was caught selling illegal drugs. • A **vending machine** (*Br and Aus also* **slot machine**) is a machine from which you can buy small items such as cigarettes, drinks and sweets by putting coins into it: *The vending machine in the office* **dispenses** *really tasteless coffee.*

ven·dor /£ˈven·dəʳ, $-dɚ/ *n* [C] • *For the past few months she's been working as a* **street** *vendor* (= seller) *selling fruit and veg.* • *(fml) The vendor of the house wants the contracts exchanged before the end of the month.*

ven·det·ta /£venˈdet·ə, $-ˈdet̬-/ *n* [C] a long and violent argument between people or families in which one group tries to harm the other in order to punish them for things that have happened in the past • *The families have been engaged in a brutal vendetta which so far has claimed five lives.* • *He saw himself as the victim of a* **personal** *vendetta being* **waged** *by his political enemies.*

ve·neer /£vəˈnɪəʳ, $-ˈnɪr/ *n* a thin layer of decorative wood or plastic used to cover a cheaper material • *The wardrobe is made of chipboard with a pine veneer.* [C] • *The Japanese cover their television sets in artificial wood veneers especially for the British market.* [C] • A veneer is also something which hides something unpleasant or unwanted: *A veneer* **of** *self-confidence thinly concealed his nervousness.* [U] ○ *She managed to hide her corrupt dealings under a veneer* **of respectability**. [U]

ve·neered /£vəˈnɪəd, $-ˈnɪrd/ *adj* • *veneered wood* • *a veneered bookcase/surface/table*

ven·e·ra·ble /ˈven·ər·ə·bl̩/ *adj* deserving respect because of age, high position or religious or historical importance • *(fml) a venerable tradition/company/family* • *(fml) the venerable ruins of the abbey* • *(infml, esp. humorous)* Venerable can also be used to describe something that has been in use, or someone who has been involved in something, for a long time: *I see you still have your venerable old car!* ○ *In recent years there has been a noticeable decline in such venerable British* **institutions** *as afternoon tea and the Sunday roast.* ○ *The venerable rock star received a special award today for his 20 years in the music business.* • An ARCHDEACON in the Church of England is given the title Venerable: **the** *Venerable John Brown* • A person who is considered holy by the Roman Catholic Church but who has not yet been made a SAINT is also called Venerable: *The Pope took the first step towards canonizing* *the priest yesterday by announcing that he was entitled to be called Venerable.* • Venerable is also a title given to a MONK in Buddhism: *Venerable Amaro lit a candle and sat cross-legged on the floor.*

ven·e·rate *obj* /£ˈven·ᵊr·eɪt, $-ə·eɪt/ *v* [T] *fml* to honour or greatly respect (a person or thing) • *Robert Burns is perhaps Scotland's most venerated poet.*

ven·e·ra·tion /£ˌven·ᵊrˈeɪ·ʃᵊn, $-əˈeɪ-/ *n* [U] • *Mother Theresa has become an object of widespread veneration because of her unceasing work for the poor.*

ve·ne·re·al /£vəˈnɪə·ri·əl, $-ˈnɪr·i-/ *adj* [not gradable] caused or spread by sexual activity with another person • *a venereal infection* • *(dated)* **Venereal disease** (*abbreviation* **VD**) is a disease that is spread through sexual activity with an infected person: *Syphilis and gonorrhoea are both venereal diseases.* • *Venereal disease is an older term for sexually transmitted disease or STD.*

ve·ne·tian blind /vəˈniː·ʃᵊn/ *n* [C] a cover for a window made of thin horizontal pieces of wood, plastic or metal, which can be raised or lowered or set at an angle with strings in order to vary the amount of light that is let in

venge·ance /ˈven·dʒᵊnts/ *n* [U] the punishing of someone for harming you or your friends or family, or the desire for such punishment to happen • *On the day after the terrorist attack, the overall mood in the town was one of vengeance.* • *(literary) As she cradled her daughter's lifeless body in her arms, she swore that vengeance* **would be** *hers.* • **With a vengeance** means with great force or extreme energy: *He's been working with a vengeance over the past few weeks to make up for lost time.* ○ *Flared trousers are* **back** *with a vengeance* (= very popular again) *this summer.*

venge·ful /ˈvendʒ·fᵊl/ *adj fml* expressing a strong desire to punish someone who has harmed you or your family or friends • *She sprayed her name in red paint all over his car in one last vengeful act before leaving him for good.*

venge·ful·ly /ˈvendʒ·fᵊl·i/ *adv fml* • *The child vengefully smashed her brother's toy because he wouldn't let her play with it.*

venge·ful·ness /ˈvendʒ·fᵊl·nəs/ *n* [U] *fml* • *Strains of vengefulness run through his autobiography.*

ve·ni·al /ˈviː·ni·əl/ *adj fml* not serious and therefore easily forgivable • *a venial sin/error*

ven·i·son /ˈven·ɪ·sᵊn/ *n* [U] meat that comes from a deer • *She cooked venison in red wine sauce for dinner.* • *The* **haunch of** *venison was hung in the larder to mature.*

Venn di·a·gram /ven/ *n* [C] a mathematical plan which shows how items that belong to mathematical sets relate to each other, which is represented by circles that OVERLAP (= partly cover each other) within a particular area

ven·om /ˈven·əm/ *n* [U] a poisonous liquid which some snakes, insects, etc. produce when biting or stinging • *A vaccine has been created for people who are allergic to bee stings, which uses the venom extracted from bees.* • *He was shocked at the* **sheer** *venom* (= expression of feelings of hatred or extreme anger) *of her reply.*

ven·om·ous /ˈven·ə·məs/ *adj* • *He was bitten by a large venomous snake.* • *(fig.) The prisoner gave the judge a venomous* (= hateful) **look** *as she read out the verdict.* • *(fig.) Ms Brown has launched a venomous* (= angry) **attack** *against the newspaper for printing allegations about her private life.*

ven·om·ous·ly /ˈven·ə·mə·sli/ *adv* • *(fig.) She spoke venomously* (= in a way expressing hatred and anger) *about her ex-husband who had run off with another woman.*

ve·nous /ˈviː·nəs/ *adj* [not gradable] *medical* of or relating to the VEINS (= tubes that carry blood to the heart) • *venous blood* • *the venous system* • See also INTRAVENOUS.

vent OPENING /vent/ *n* [C] a small opening which allows air, smoke or gas to enter or escape from an enclosed space • *If you have a gas fire in a room, you should have some kind of outside vent.* • *Have you seen that photo of Marilyn Monroe standing over an* **air** *vent with her skirt blowing up around her?* • A vent is also a cut in the bottom of a piece of clothing to allow the person wearing it to move more easily: *The skirt is long and straight with two side vents.*

vent *obj* EXPRESS FEELINGS /vent/ *v* [T] to express (an emotion) forcefully • *Strong emotions were vented during the negotiations as one side accused the other of lying.* • *Teenagers have scrawled graffiti on the walls of the job centre to vent their* **frustration** *at the lack of work.* • *There's no need to vent your* **anger/rage/spleen on** *me.*

vent /vent/ *n* [U] • To **give vent to** a feeling is to express it forcefully: *The meeting will be an opportunity for everyone to give vent to their feelings.*

ven·ti·late *obj* PROVIDE AIR /£ˈven·tɪ·leɪt, $-t̬ᵊl·eɪt/ *v* [T] to cause fresh air to enter and move around an enclosed space • *She opened the window to ventilate the room.* • *I work in a very well-/poorly-ventilated building.* • *After the fire broke out in the mine, they realized there was no ventilated escape route they could use.*

ven·ti·la·tion /£ˌven·tɪˈleɪ·ʃᵊn, $-t̬ᵊlˈeɪ-/ *n* [U] • *Her tiny attic room had* **poor** *ventilation and in summer it became unbearably stuffy.* • *The office has recently been refurbished and the ventilation* **system** *improved.*

ven·ti·lat·or /£ˈven·tɪ·leɪ·təʳ, $-t̬ᵊl·eɪ·t̬ə/ *n* [C] • *Once the ventilator* **shaft** *became blocked, the warehouse quickly filled with fumes.* • A ventilator is also a machine that helps people breathe correctly by allowing air to flow in and out of their lungs: *He was brought into intensive care shortly after the crash and immediately* **put on a** *ventilator.*

ven·ti·late *obj* MAKE KNOWN /£ˈven·tɪ·leɪt, $-t̬ᵊl·eɪt/ *v* [T] *fml* to state an opinion or mention a subject so that it can be discussed by others • *She used the meeting to ventilate all her* **grievances.**

ven·tri·cle /ˈven·trɪ·kl̩/ *n* [C] *medical* either of two small hollow spaces, one in each side of the heart, which force blood into the tubes leading from the heart to the other parts of the body • *After a massive heart attack, he underwent an operation to replace his two ventricles with an artificial heart.*

ven·tri·lo·qui·sm /venˈtrɪl·ə·kwɪ·zᵊm/ *n* [U] the ability to speak without moving your lips so that your voice seems to be coming from someone or something else, usually as a way of entertaining people

ven·tri·lo·quist /venˈtrɪl·ə·kwɪst/ *n* [C] • A **ventriloquist's dummy** is a puppet that ventriloquists operate and project their voice onto, to make it seem as if it were alive.

ven·ture BUSINESS /£ˈven·tʃəʳ, $-tʃə/ *n* [C] a plan of action, usually in business, which involves risk or uncertainty • *She advised us to look abroad for more lucrative* **business** *ventures.* • *He thought the venture far too* **risky** *and didn't want to become involved.* • *There are many* **joint** *ventures* **between** *American and Japanese companies.* • *The company's overseas turnover is expanding with* **joint** *ventures being* **launched** *in the Far East.* • **Venture capital** is money that is invested or is available for investment in a new company, esp. a risky one: *They'll need to raise £1 million in venture capital if they're to get the business off the ground.* ○ *Increasing competition in local markets is forcing* **venture capitalists** *to look farther afield for companies to back.* ○ *Simon is a manager of a venture capital company/firm/group/fund.*

ven·ture *(obj)* RISK /£ˈven·tʃəʳ, $-tʃə/ *v fml* to risk going somewhere or doing something that might be dangerous or unpleasant, or to risk saying something that might be criticized • *Those people who ventured* **to** *the lakes on the weekend were rewarded with three days of glorious weather.* [I always + adv/prep] • *She rarely ventured* **outside**, *except when she went to stock up on groceries at the corner shop.* [I always + adv/prep] • *As we set off into the forest, we felt as though we were venturing* **forth into** *the unknown.* [I always + adv/prep] • *"He has much more talent than anyone else we've interviewed so far," I ventured* (= said riskily). [+ clause] • *She tentatively ventured* (= said riskily) **the opinion** *that the project would be too expensive to complete.* [T] • If you venture a thing that is valuable **on** something, you take the risk of losing it in order to achieve the second thing: *He ventured the company's reputation* **on** *his new invention.* [T] • *(Br)* A **Venture Scout** (*Am* **Explorer Scout**, *Aus* **Venturer**) is a young person aged 15 to 20 years old who is a member of the international youth organization called the Scouts. • *(saying)* 'Nothing ventured, nothing gained' means that you will never achieve anything if you never take a risk or make an effort: *"There's no point even applying for the job because I'm not going to get it." "I think you really ought to try – after all, nothing ventured, nothing gained."*

Ven·tur·er *Aus* /£ˈven·tʃə·rəʳ, $-tʃə·ə/ *n* [C] a **Venture Scout**, see at VENTURE

ven·ture·some /£ˈven·tʃə·səm, $-tʃə-/ *adj fml* (of a person) willing to take risks, or (of an action or behaviour) risky • *They set out on a venturesome journey across the mountains.* • *He has become more venturesome this season with dress designs that incorporate a variety of ethnic influences.*

ven·ue /ˈven·juː/ *n* [C] the place where a public event or meeting happens • *The band's recent American tour played* *to full houses at every venue.* • *The hotel is an ideal venue* **for** *conferences and business meetings.* • *The stadium has been specifically designed as a venue* **for** *European Cup matches.* • *(Am specialized)* A venue is also the city or COUNTY in which a trial happens: *Defense lawyers requested a* **change of** *venue, claiming that they wouldn't be able to find unbiased jurors in the town where the crime took place.*

Ve·nus /'viː·nəs/ *n* [U not after *the*] the planet second in order of distance from the Sun, after Mercury and before the Earth. It is the nearest planet to the Earth. • *Venus is sometimes called the morning or evening star because it is the most brilliant of all the objects in the night sky.* • A **Venus flytrap** is a plant which feeds on insects and catches them by quickly closing its leaves when their surface is touched so that the insects cannot escape.

ve·rac·i·ty /£və'ræs·ɪ·ti, $və'æs·ə·ṭi/ *n* [U] *fml* the quality of being true, honest or accurate • *Doubts were cast on the veracity of her alibi after three people claimed to have seen her at the scene of the robbery.*

ve·ran·da, ve·ran·dah /və'ræn·də/, *Am also* **porch** *n* [C] a raised, covered and sometimes partly enclosed area, often made of wood, on the front or side of a building • *Every evening she would sit in her rocking chair on the wooden veranda watching the sun go down.* • *They had a couple of drinks and watched the cricket match from the sports club veranda.*

verb /£vɜːb, $vɜːrb/ *n* [C] a word or phrase that describes an action, condition or experience • *The words 'run', 'keep' and 'feel' are all verbs.* • *'Kick' is a* **transitive** *verb and 'die' is an* **intransitive** *verb.* • *New verbs are sometimes* **coined** *from nouns, such as 'to privilege', or 'to test-tube'.* • *I spent most of my time in French lessons* **conjugating** (= listing the different grammatical forms of) *irregular verbs.* • LP **Forms of words (spelling), Stress in pronunciation, Verbs**

ver·bal SPOKEN /£'vɜː·bəl, $'vɜːr-/ *adj* [not gradable] spoken rather than written • *a verbal agreement/description/explanation* • *Airport officials received a stream of verbal* **abuse** *from angry passengers whose flights had been delayed.* • *You have to admire her verbal* **dexterity** (= ability to use language). • *Several people were reported to have suffered verbal and physical attacks.* • *(infml)* If you have **verbal diarrhoea**, you talk too much.

ver·bal·ly /£'vɜː·bəl·i, $'vɜːr-/ *adv* [not gradable] • *At what age do children start to communicate verbally?* • *Schools are starting to crack down on students who are verbally* **abusive** *towards their classmates.*

ver·bal WORDS /£'vɜː·bəl, $'vɜːr-/ *adj* [not gradable] relating to words • *It can sometimes be difficult to give a verbal description of things like colours and sounds.* • *The study investigated differences in verbal ability/skills between girls and boys.* • *The children are required to take a verbal reasoning test at the age of 11.*

ver·bal·ize *(obj), Br and Aus usually* **-ise** /£'vɜː·bəl·aɪz, $'vɜːr·bə·laɪz/ *v* to express (ideas, opinions or emotions) in words • *Some concepts are difficult to verbalize.* [T] • *He found it hard to verbalize his* **feelings** *towards his son.* [T] • *Children may start to verbalize* (= talk) *at an earlier age if they are brought up in a friendly, talkative environment.* [I]

ver·ba·tim /£vɜː'beɪ·tɪm, $vɜːr'beɪ·ṭəm/ *adj, adv* [not gradable] using exactly the same words as were originally used • *He kept verbatim transcripts of discussions with his friends so he could use them in his next novel.* • *She had an amazing memory and could recall verbatim quite complex conversations.*

ver·bi·age /£'vɜː·bi·ɪdʒ, $'vɜːr-/ *n* [U] *fml* language which is very complicated and which contains a lot of unnecessary words • *His explanation was wrapped up in so much technical verbiage that I simply couldn't understand it.*

ver·bose /£vɜː'bəʊs, £və-, $vəˈbous/ *adj fml* using or containing more words than are necessary • *a verbose explanation/report/speech/style* • *He was renowned for being a verbose and rather tedious after-dinner speaker.*

ver·bose·ly /£vɜː'bəʊ·sli, £və-, $vəˈbous-/ *adv fml*

ver·bos·i·ty /£vɜː'bɒs·ɪ·ti, $vəˈbɑː·sə·ṭi/ *n* [U] *fml* • *She's just spent two hours telling us all about her future plans with her usual verbosity.*

ver·dant /£'vɜː·dənt, $'vɜːr-/ *adj literary* covered with healthy green plants or grass • *Much of the region's verdant* **countryside** *has been destroyed in the hurricane.* • *The colleges all have well-kept verdant* **lawns**.

ver·dict /£'vɜː·dɪkt, $'vɜːr-/ *n* [C] an opinion or decision made after judging the facts that are given, esp. one made at the end of a trial • *The jury* **returned** *a* **unanimous** *verdict of* **(not) guilty**. • *(Br and Aus) After deliberating for seven hours, the jury* **reached** *a* **majority** *verdict* **of** *10 to 2 in favour of the defendant.* • *The judge directed the jury to* **deliver** *a verdict* **of** *unlawful killing.* • *She took her case to the court of appeal but the guilty verdict was* **upheld**. • *(Br and Aus) There wasn't enough evidence to establish the exact cause of the man's death and so the coroner* **recorded** *an* **open** *verdict* (= a verdict that the cause was not known). • *Voters gave their verdict* **on** *the government's economic record last night by voting overwhelmingly for the opposition.* • *"What's your verdict* **on** *her work so far?" "Oh, fairly positive."* • *The studio is anxiously awaiting the box-office verdict* **on** *the movie* (= the public reaction to it, in relation to the number of people who pay to see it).

ver·di·gris /£'vɜː·dɪ·grɪs, $'vɜːr-/ *n* [U] a greenish blue substance that forms on the surface of some metals in wet conditions • *Copper, brass and bronze are all affected by verdigris if they are exposed to moist air for a long period of time.*

ver·dure /£'vɜː·djər, $'vɜːr·dʒə/ *n* [U] *literary* (the green colour of) fresh healthy plants

verge /£vɜːdʒ, $vɜːrdʒ/ *n* [C] the edge or border of something • *They set up camp on the verge of the desert before embarking upon their long trek the following day.* • *(Br)* A verge *(Am* **shoulder**) is also the strip of land which borders a road or path: *She left her car by the side of the road and walked along the* **grass** *verge to the emergency phone.* • If you are **on the verge of** something or come **to the verge of** something, you are very near to experiencing it: *on the verge of collapse/success/death/disaster* ○ *The country is on the verge of civil war.* ○ *He was on the verge of* **tears** *at several points during the trial.* ○ *She's been on the verge of having a nervous breakdown ever since she lost the baby.* • *Her husband's violent and abusive behaviour* **drove** *her to the verge of despair.*

verge on *(obj)* /£vɜːdʒ, $vɜːrdʒ/ *v prep* to be very near to doing or experiencing (something) • *At times, his performance verged on brilliance, but at others it was only ordinary.* [T] • *UN reports clearly show that the country is verging on having the capability to produce nuclear weapons.* [+ v-*ing*]

verg·er /£'vɜː·dʒər, $'vɜːr·dʒə/ *n* [C] an official in some Christian churches who takes care of the inside of a church and performs some simple duties during church ceremonies

ver·i·fy *(obj)* /'ver·ɪ·faɪ/ *v* [T] to make certain of or prove the truth or accuracy of (something) • *Are you able to verify your account/allegation/report/theory?* [T] • *Rape is a crime which results in relatively few convictions as it is often difficult to verify.* [T] • *Every athlete competing in this year's games must undergo a physical examination to verify their gender.* [T] • *These figures are surprisingly high and they'll have to be verified.* [T] • *Under interrogation, she verified* **(that)** *the tapes were authentic.* [+ (*that*) clause]

ver·i·fi·a·ble /'ver·ɪ·faɪ·ə·bl̩/ *adj* • *Throughout the trial, he didn't produce a single verifiable fact to prove that the alleged incident had ever taken place.*

ver·i·fi·ca·tion /ˌver·ɪ·fɪ'keɪ·ʃən/ *n* [U] • *The report was forwarded to a committee for* **independent** *verification.* • *After following various verification* **procedures**, *he declared the manuscript to be genuine.*

ver·i·ly /'ver·ɪ·li/ *adv* [not gradable] *old use* really or truly

ver·i·si·mil·i·tude /£ˌver·ɪ·sɪ'mɪl·ɪ·tjuːd, $-tuːd/ *n* [U] *fml* the quality of seeming true or of having the appearance of reality • *She has included photographs and reproductions of letters in the book to lend verisimilitude to her story-telling.* • *His sculptures are famous for their verisimilitude.*

ver·i·ta·ble /£'ver·ɪ·tə·bl̩, $-ə·ṭə-/ *adj* [before n; not gradable] (used to describe something as something else more exciting, interesting, unusual, etc. as a way of emphasizing what it is like) almost a; exactly like • *My garden had become a veritable jungle by the time I came back from holiday.* • *The normally sober menswear department is set to become a veritable kaleidoscope of colour this season.*

ver·i·ta·bly /£'ver·ɪ·tə·bli, $-ə·ṭə-/ *adv* [not gradable]

ver·i·ty /£'ver·ɪ·ti, $-ə·ṭi/ *n fml* truthfulness, or a belief, idea or principle that is generally accepted as being true • *In the film, he plays a spy whose mission is to confirm the verity of a secret military document.* [U] • *The country has finally abandoned the outmoded verities* (= beliefs or principles) *of the past and adopted a more open outlook.* [C]

• *She has spent her life in a search for eternal/scientific/universal verities* (= truth). [C]

ver·mi·cel·li /£ˌvɜː·mɪˈtʃel·i, $ˌvɜːr-/ *n* [U] a type of Italian food in the form of long thin threads made of a mixture of flour, eggs and water, which is cooked in boiling water • *Vermicelli is a type of pasta which is similar to spaghetti but thinner.* • *Minestrone is a thick vegetable soup which includes either rice or vermicelli.* • *(Br)* Vermicelli is also extremely small pieces of chocolate used for decorating cakes.

ver·mil·i·on, ver·mil·li·on /£vəˈmɪl·i·ən, $vəˈmɪl·jən/ *adj* [not gradable], *n* (of) a bright red orange colour • *His new sports car is bright vermilion.* • *He bought her a dozen vermilion roses for her birthday.* • *She was wearing a jacket of bright vermilion.* [U] • *The morning sky was full of vermilions and reds.* [C]

ver·min /£ˈvɜː·mɪn, $ˈvɜːr-/ *pl n* small animals and insects that can be harmful and which are difficult to control when they appear in large numbers • *Flies, lice, rats, foxes and cockroaches can all be described as vermin.* • *Farmers are involved in a constant battle to* **control** *vermin which ruin their crops and damage their livestock.* • People who are unpleasant and harmful to society can also be described as vermin: *He thought all terrorists were vermin and that prison was too good for them.*

ver·min·ous /£ˈvɜː·mɪ·nəs, $ˈvɜːr-/ *adj* • *She would beg during the day and spend the night on a park bench wrapped in an old verminous* (= covered with insects) *blanket.*

ver·mouth /£vəˈmuːθ, $vɚ-/ *n* [U] a strongly alcoholic red or white wine flavoured with herbs and spices • **Dry** *vermouth is often used as an ingredient in cocktails, such as a dry martini in which it is mixed with gin.* • *The recipe calls for a splash of* **sweet** *vermouth.*

ver·nac·u·lar /£vəˈnæk·jʊ·ləʳ, $vɚˈnæk·jə·lɚ/ *n, adj* (in) the form of a language that a regional (or other) group of speakers use naturally, esp. in informal situations • *The French I learned at school is very different from the local vernacular of the village where I'm now living.* [C] • *More and more computer terms are now* **entering the** *vernacular.* [U] • *Many Roman Catholics regret the replacing of the Latin mass by* **the** *vernacular.* [U] • *His lively vernacular* **style** *goes down well with younger viewers.* • *Some technical language eventually becomes vernacular.* • Vernacular can also be used to refer to dance, music, art, etc. that are in a style liked or performed by ordinary people: *Jazz dance is a form of vernacular dancing.* • Vernacular can also mean (in) a local style of architecture in which ordinary houses are built.

ver·nal /£ˈvɜː·nəl, $ˈvɜːr-/ *adj* [before n] relating to or happening in the spring • *vernal celebrations/flowers* • *the vernal season* • The **vernal equinox** is the time in the spring when the sun crosses the equator, and when night and day are of equal length: *In the northern hemisphere, the vernal equinox occurs on about March 21 – in the southern hemisphere it is on about September 23.*

ver·ru·ca /£vəˈruː·kə, $vəˈruː-/ *n* [C] *pl* **verrucas** or **verrucae** /£vəˈruː·kiː, $vəˈruː-/ a small hard infectious growth on the skin, usually on the bottom of the foot • *Verrucas can be painful, but they aren't serious.* • *If you have a verruca you must be careful not to walk around barefoot otherwise you might infect other people.*

ver·sa·tile /£ˈvɜː·sə·taɪl, $ˈvɜːr·sə·t̬əl/ *adj* able to change easily from one activity to another or able to be used for many different purposes • *A leather jacket is a timeless and versatile garment that can be worn in all seasons and with all kinds of outfits.* • *He's a very versatile young actor who's as happy in horror films as he is in TV comedies.*

verse /£vɜːs, $vɜːrs/ *n* writing which is arranged in short lines with a rhythmic pattern, or one of the parts into which a poem or song is divided • *comic/light/satirical verse* [U] • *A lot of verse is written in rhyme which means that the endings of certain words at the end of a line sound the same.* [U] • *His publications include a book of short stories and several volumes of verse.* [U] • *Shakespeare wrote* **in** *verse.* [U] • *Each verse* (= part of the song) *was sung as a solo and then everyone joined in on the chorus.* [C] • *Most British people have trouble remembering any more than the first verse* (= part) *of the national anthem.* [C] • A verse can also be one of the series of short parts into which the writing of a holy book is divided: *She* **recited** *a verse from the Bible/the Koran.* [C] • Compare CHORUS [SONG PART]; PROSE.

versed /£vɜːst, $vɜːrst/ *adj* **versed in** *fml* knowing a lot about (a subject) or experienced in (a skill) • *She is deeply versed in the classics.* • *I'm not sufficiently versed in computers to understand what you're saying.* • *As a former MP, he is* **well** *versed in parliamentary procedure.*

ver·sion /£ˈvɜː·ʃən, -ʒən, $ˈvɜːr-/ *n* [C] a particular form of something which varies slightly from other forms of the same thing • *"So what happened?" "Well, do you want my version or Sandra's version?"* • *The two witnesses gave* **contradictory** *versions* **of** *what had happened that night.* • *The* **official** *version* **of** *events is that the police were attacked and were just trying to defend themselves.* • *You can make a reduced fat version* **of** *the cheesecake by using cottage cheese instead of cream cheese.* • *She was reading an* **abridged** *version* **of** *'War and Peace'.* • *Two* **different** *versions* **of** *'Frankenstein' are currently being made in Hollywood.* • *An English-language version* **of** *the book is planned for the autumn.* • *The TV series is a* **watered-down** *version* **of** *the movie, especially designed for family viewing.* • A version can also be a TRANSLATION: *the English version of Goethe's 'Faust'* • (KOR)

ver·sus /£ˈvɜː·səs, $ˈvɜːr-/ (*abbreviation* **v, vs**) *prep* against • *"Who are we playing today?" "It's us versus the older kids."* • *The debate about whether to build the shopping centre has turned into the politically sensitive issue of jobs versus the environment.* • Versus is also used in legal cases to show who a person is fighting against: *Abortion was legalized nationally in the United States following the Roe versus Wade case.*

ver·te·bra /£ˈvɜː·tɪ·brə, $ˈvɜːr·t̬ə-/ *n* [C] *pl* **vertebrae** /£ˈvɜː·tɪ·briː, $ˈvɜːr·t̬ə-/ one of the small bones that form the SPINE (= the line of bones down the middle of the back) • *She suffered facial bruising and a* **fractured** *vertebra in the attack.*

ver·te·bral /£ˈvɜː·tɪ·brəl, $ˈvɜːr·t̬ə-/ *adj* [not gradable] *specialized* • *The vertebral* **column** *surrounds and protects the spinal cord.*

ver·te·brate /£ˈvɜː·tɪ·brət, $ˈvɜːr·t̬ə-/ *n* [C], *adj* [not gradable] *specialized* (an animal) having a SPINE (= the line of bones down the middle of the back) • *Birds, fish, mammals, amphibians and reptiles are all vertebrates.* • *Giant tortoises can live for up to 150 years and are the longest living vertebrate animals.* • Compare INVERTEBRATE.

ver·tex /£ˈvɜː·teks, $ˈvɜːr·t̬eks/ *n* [C] *pl* **vertexes** or **vertices** /£ˈvɜː·tɪ·siːz, $ˈvɜːr·t̬ɪ-/ *specialized* (in mathematics) the point where two lines meet to form an angle, or the point that is opposite the base of a shape • *the vertex of a triangle/cone/pyramid* • A vertex is also the highest point of something.

ver·ti·cal /£ˈvɜː·tɪ·kəl, $ˈvɜːr·t̬ə-/ *adj* standing or pointing straight up or at an angle of 90° to a horizontal surface or line • *By the time the lifeboat arrived, the ship was almost vertical in the water.* • *His shirt was a brightly coloured pattern of vertical and horizontal* **lines**. • *She looked over the cliff and found she was standing at the edge of a vertical* **drop**. • A **vertical blind** is a cover for a window made of vertical strips of stiff cloth which can be pulled to one side or set at an angle with strings in order to vary the amount of light that is let in. • **Vertical integration** is a process in business where a company buys its suppliers or its customers in order to control all the processes of production: *For a computer company, vertical integration might mean doing everything from manufacturing chips to running computer shops.* • A **vertical take-off** aircraft is one that rises straight up off the ground: *a vertical take-off* **jet** • Compare HORIZONTAL.

ver·ti·cal·ly /£ˈvɜː·tɪ·kli, $ˈvɜːr·t̬ə-/ *adv* • *Walls of rock towered vertically on either side of them as they edged their way along the narrow mountain path.*

ver·ti·go /£ˈvɜː·tɪ·gəʊ, $ˈvɜːr·t̬ə·goʊ/ *n* [U] a feeling of spinning round and being unable to balance caused by looking down from a height • *She can't stand heights and has always* **suffered from** *vertigo.*

ver·ti·gi·nous /£vɜːˈtɪdʒ·ɪ·nəs, $vɚ-/ *adj fml* • Vertiginous means causing or having a feeling of spinning round, because of being very high: *The two skyscrapers were connected by a vertiginous walkway.* ○ *Thousands of refugees are walking over the vertiginous mountains in search of food.* ○ *Just looking down from the top of a bus makes me feel vertiginous.*

verve /£vɜːv, $vɜːrv/ *n* [U] great energy and enthusiasm • *She delivered her speech* **with** *tremendous wit and verve.* • *He managed to conceal the pain he was suffering and greeted his friends* **with** *his old verve.* • *(fig.) A vividly coloured jacket or some striking accessories can give a plain outfit added verve.*

VERBS: TRANSITIVE AND INTRANSITIVE GRAMMAR PATTERNS

- The **subject** of a sentence is the thing or person which is being discussed: *Nora packed her bags.* • *My friend laughed.* • *The roads are quiet.* • *You must come.*
- Transitive verbs have an **object**. What the subject does has a direct effect on someone or something – the object: *Nora packed her bags.*
- Intransitive verbs refer to an action which does not directly affect anything, and so they do not have an object: *My friend laughed.*
- There are other types of verbs which have no object and do not refer to an action: linking verbs (*The roads are quiet*), auxiliary verbs (*Do you like it?*) and modal auxiliary verbs (*You must come*). LP **Linking verbs** at LINK and **Auxiliary verbs**.
- Many verbs can be followed by a clause or by another verb: *I expect* **that** *you are hungry.* • *I enjoy sing***ing**. • *Do you want* **to** *leave?* These patterns are not described as transitive or intransitive in this dictionary. LP **Clauses** and ***-ing* form of verbs** at -ING.

Sometimes all uses of a verb follow a particular grammar pattern. In these cases the grammar code is given before the definition. Often a verb has additional grammar patterns which are found only in some uses. These are shown in example sentences followed by the grammar code.

TRANSITIVE VERB PATTERNS

blame *obj*	*I blame them.*	[T]	A verb which always has an object is followed by *'obj'* in the dictionary and has [T] immediately before its definition.
give	*I gave Vera a newspaper./I gave a newspaper* **to** *Vera.*	[+ two objects]	Verb that takes a direct object and an indirect object. In the examples 'Vera' is the indirect object and 'a newspaper' is the direct object. LP **Verbs with two objects** at TWO
buy	*I bought Vera a newspaper./I bought a newspaper* **for** *Vera.*		

• Patterns where the object is followed by another verb or by a clause

For more information, see the Language Portraits on **Clauses** and ***-ing* form of verbs** at -ING.

tell	*He told us* **(that)** *he could come.*	[+ obj + (*that*) clause]	The object is followed by a *that* clause.
want	*I want her* **to** *write a letter.*	[+ obj + *to* infinitive]	The object is followed by an infinitive with *to*.
see	*I saw a man get into the car.*	[+ obj + infinitive without *to*]	The object is followed by an infinitive but *to* must be omitted.
get	*I'll get the work finish***ed** *today.*	[+ obj + v-*ed*]	The object is followed by a past participle. LP **Get**
watch	*I watched him clean***ing** *the car.*	[+ obj + v-*ing*]	The object is followed by the -*ing* form of another verb.
ask	*She asked us* **where** *to go*	[+ obj + *wh*- word]	The object is followed by a clause with *when, where, why, whether, if* or *how.*
consider	*I consider him* **to be** *an adult.* *I consider this* **to be** *critical.*	[+ obj + *to be* n/adj]	The object is followed by *to be* and a noun or adjective.

• Other grammatical patterns

put	*Put your bags* **down**. *Put your bags* **in** *the corner.*	[T always + adv/prep]	The object must be followed by an adverb, or by a phrase beginning with a preposition. The verb cannot be used with the object on its own. For example, you cannot say simply 'Put your bags' but must say something like *Put your bags* **on** *the table.*
call	*Don't call me lazy.*	[+ obj + adj]	The object is followed by an adjective or noun which describes or names the object. LP **Verbs with two objects** at TWO
elect	*They elected him president.*	[+ obj + n]	
consider	*We consider them dangerous/a danger.*	[+ obj + n/adj]	
regard	*Do you regard him* **as** *a friend?*	[+ obj + *as* n]	

INTRANSITIVE VERB PATTERNS

exist	*Only two copies of the book exist.*	[I]	A verb which never has an object is not followed by '*obj*' or '(*obj*)' in the dictionary, and has [I] before its definition.
live	*She lives* **upstairs**. *She lives* **on** *the first floor.*	[I always + adv/prep]	The verb cannot be used alone but must be followed by an adverb, or a by a phrase beginning with a preposition.

VERBS THAT HAVE BOTH TRANSITIVE AND INTRANSITIVE USES

- A verb which can be used either with or without an object is followed by '(*obj*)' in the dictionary. It does not have [T] or [I] before the definition but examples showing transitive and intransitive uses are marked [T] or [I]:

eat (*obj*)	*He ate two cheeseburgers.*	[T]	Transitive use.
	Shall we eat soon?	[I]	Intransitive use.
	We were eating (dinner).	[I/T]	This example shows both a transitive and an intransitive use.

Verbs of this type might follow any of the transitive or intransitive patterns given above. In order to make clear whether the verb has an object in that pattern, some of the codes are given with 'T' or 'I' first, for example [T always + adv/prep] or [I always + adv/prep].

- A few verbs have a transitive form and an intransitive form with a preposition, and these can be used in the same sentence patterns with the same or similar meaning. An example is *conceive:*

conceive	*I conceive the universe as a vast ball.*	(transitive)
	I conceive **of** *the universe as a vast ball.*	(intransitive + preposition)

This pattern is shown as: *I conceive* **(of)** *the universe as a vast ball* [T; I + *of*]. When several prepositions are possible the pattern is marked [T; I + prep].

- In the two sentences *They shouted the news* [T] and *They were shouting* [I] the transitive and intransitive uses of the verb take the same subject, *they*. This is the usual pattern. But some verbs follow a different pattern:

break	*Linda broke my chair.* [T]	
	My chair broke. [I]	(but not 'Linda broke.')
change	*People have changed their diets.* [T]	
	People's diets have changed. [I]	(but not 'People have changed.')

Here the **object** of the transitive verb becomes the subject of the intransitive verb. Other verbs that can be used in this way include: *start, stop, open, close, move, shake; cook, bake, boil, fry.* In the dictionary verbs like this are often defined in one of the following ways (notice the underlined phrases):

break (*obj*) (DAMAGE)	to (cause to) stop working by being damaged
change (*obj*) (BECOME DIFFERENT)	to make or become different

ve·ry [EXTREMELY] /ˈver·i/ *adv* [not gradable] (used to add emphasis to an adjective or adverb) to a great degree or extremely • *The situation is very serious.* • *I'm very pleased with your progress.* • *We're very sorry about what's happened.* • *It's been a very difficult time for them.* • *Think about it very carefully before deciding.* • *It was very kind of her to give us a lift to the airport.* • *He's always been very good at making friends.* • *I haven't heard from her all day and I'm very worried.* • *His selfish behaviour makes me very, very cross.* • *How very childish of her to refuse to speak to me!* • *You'll have to wash this in very hot water to get the stain out.* • *"Are you tired?" "No, not very."* • *Thank you very much.* • *She doesn't like her new school very much.* • *He felt very much at home in the south of France.* • *We couldn't do very much* (= There was not much we could do) *to help them.* • *"Did you enjoy the play?" "Very much so* (= Yes).*"* • *There's nothing very interesting* (= There's not much of interest) *on TV tonight.* • *"How are you?" "Very well, thanks."* • *"Can't I stay for five minutes longer?" "Oh, very well* (= I agree).*"* • *She couldn't very well* (= It would not be right to) *say sorry when she didn't think she had done anything wrong.* • Very can also be used to add force to a superlative adjective or with the adjectives 'own' or 'same': *This is* **the very best** *chocolate cake I've ever tasted.* ○ *They're* **the very best** *of friends.* ○ *Don't worry if you don't pass, just do* **the very best** *you can.* ○ *You should give him a birthday card at* **the very least**. ○ *She always leaves her homework to* **the very last** *moment.* ○ *We now have our very* **own** *post office in the village.* ○ *This is* **the very same** (= exactly the same) *place we sat in as the last time we came.* • If you say that something is **all very well/fine/good** you mean that you think it may not be a good idea: *It's all very well to want to get rich quickly,* **but** *don't expect any sympathy from me if things go wrong.* • **Very Reverend** is a title of respect given to particular Church officials: *The Dean of Lincoln Cathedral, the Very Reverend David Smith, will be the speaker at today's meeting.* • [LP]> **Very, completely**

ve·ry [EXACT] /ˈver·i/ *adj* [before n; not gradable] (used to add emphasis to a noun) exact or particular • *This is the very book I've been looking for all month.* • *You're the very person we need for the job.* • *Although they're sisters, they're the very opposite of one another.* • *The letter was sent on Monday from Munich and arrived in London the very* **next day**. • *The very* **fact** *that he didn't show up should have warned them that something was wrong.* • *The very* **thought** *of having her friends to stay fills me with dread.* • *Why not take garlic to stop you getting colds – it's the very* **thing** (= it is exactly what is needed). • Very can also be used to show an extreme: *He found the piece of paper he had lost at the very bottom of the pile.* ○ *We were at the very end of the queue and so didn't manage to get any tickets.*

ves·pers /£ˈves·pəz, $-pɚz/ *pl n* the evening ceremony in some Christian churches • *In Catholic places of worship, vespers are sung daily between 3.00 and 6.00 p.m.*

ves·sel [SHIP] /ˈves·ᵊl/ *n* [C] *fml* a large boat or ship • *a cargo/fishing/patrol/sailing/supply vessel* • *Two minesweepers are being sent to join the six other* **naval** *vessels which are patrolling the coast.* • *At the height of his shipping career, he owned about 60* **oceangoing** *vessels.*

ves·sel [CONTAINER] /ˈves·ᵊl/ *n* [C] *fml* a curved container which is used to hold liquid • *The remains of some Roman earthenware vessels were found during the dig.* • *They filled a large* **cooking** *vessel with vegetables and let it simmer over the campfire.* • *(literary)* A vessel can also be a person who possesses a particular quality or who is used for a particular purpose: *As a young and spirited politician, he seems a worthy vessel for the nation's hopes.*

ves·sel [TUBE] /ˈves·ᵊl/ *n* [C] a tube that carries liquids such as blood through the body • *A heart attack is caused by the* **blood** *vessels that supply the blood to the heart muscle getting blocked.*

vest [CLOTHING] *Br* /vest/, *Am* **un·der·shirt**, *Aus* **sin·glet** *n* [C] a type of underwear, often with no sleeves, which covers the upper part of the body and which is worn for extra warmth • *a cotton/woollen/string vest* • *She always wore a long-sleeved* **thermal** *vest in winter.* • Vest is also *Am and Aus for* WAISTCOAT. • A **bullet-proof** vest is a piece of clothing worn under other clothes, which is made from a very strong material and which can stop a bullet from entering someone's body: *Her bullet-proof vest had saved her life more than once while she was reporting from the war zone.* • *(Br)* A **vest (top)** is also a piece of sleeveless clothing, usually made out of cotton, which is worn in the summer or for sport: *He wore a vest and a pair of luminous shorts to the beach party.* [C] ○ *The cyclists were all dressed in tight lycra shorts and* **the** *official team vest.* • [PIC]> **Clothes** (CS) (D) (F) (N) (P)

vest *obj* [PLACE] /vest/ *v* [T always + prep] *fml* to give or place (rights, power, authority, etc.) • *He has been vested* **with** *the* **power/authority** *to implement whatever changes he sees fit.* • **Control** *has been vested* **in** *local authorities.* • *The war-torn country has vested* (= placed) *all its hopes* **in** *the peace negotiators.* • If you have a **vested interest** in something, you have a strong personal interest in it because you could benefit from it: *As both a teacher and parent, she* **had** *a vested interest* **in** *seeing the school remain*

'VERY', COMPLETELY' AND OTHER INTENSIFIERS

Intensifiers are adverbs or adjectives which increase the strength of other words. They can be used with most parts of speech:

WITH ADJECTIVES

Certain adverbs can be used before adjectives and past participles to give them a more powerful meaning. Often an adverb is used especially with particular adjectives. For example, a film can be *enormously popular*, while a government is *deeply unpopular*. I might be *totally unprepared* for some bad news, but I will be *absolutely delighted* by a surprise. Words which are connected like this are called word partners. LP **Words used together** at WORD

- **Adverbs meaning 'very'**

  Very and **extremely** are used with most adjectives. Other intensifying adverbs connect with positive and negative adjectives as follows:

WITH POSITIVE ADJECTIVES		WITH NEGATIVE ADJECTIVES
	awfully	
(esp infml) glad/nice/good	•	sorry/dull/hard/difficult/late
	bitterly	
	•	disappointed/divided/opposed/cold
	deeply	
grateful/rooted/concerned/involved/affected	•	unpopular/divided/suspicious/offensive
	enormously	
popular/impressed/beneficial/important	•	complex
	especially	
important/true/useful/strong/valuable	•	difficult
	extraordinarily	
amusing/generous/lucky/powerful	•	difficult/complex
	highly	
regarded/skilled/educated/respected	•	critical/competitive/unlikely/undesirable
	hugely	
popular/successful/talented	•	expensive
	immensely	
popular/wealthy/valuable/powerful	•	difficult
	intensely	
personal/dramatic/moving/political	•	competitive/irritated
	seriously	
(humorous) rich	•	injured/ill/weakened/damaged/hurt/wrong
	severely	
	•	disabled/damaged/restricted/limited
	terribly	
important/excited/funny	•	wrong/sad/upset/hard
	wonderfully	
refreshing/funny/well	•	

- **Adverbs meaning 'completely'**

  All these adverbs occur often with the adjectives 'different' and 'dependent'; other common uses are:

	absolutely	
right/clear/sure/necessary/certain	•	awful/ridiculous/appalling/crazy
	entirely	
predictable/devoted/separate/due to/clear	•	mistaken/selfish/wrong
	fully	
appreciated/aware/recovered/justified	•	
	perfectly	
normal/acceptable/reasonable/clear/good	•	ridiculous
	quite*	
sure/happy/capable/right	•	wrong/absurd
	thoroughly	
modern/professional/satisfactory	•	spoilt/unpleasant
	totally	
satisfying/secure/free	•	opposed/unacceptable/lacking
	utterly	
persuasive/charming	•	wrong/evil/mistaken/false
	wholly	
convincing	•	unexpected/unacceptable/inadequate

***Quite** followed by 'enough' is often used in negative sentences: *I'm sorry, but your work is not* **quite** *good* **enough**. In British English 'quite' sometimes means 'rather': *I'm* **quite** *cold.*

Much, considerably and *far* are common intensifiers used when making comparisons: *Our new house is* **much** *bigger.* • *She was* **considerably** *older than her husband.* • *It's* **far** *more difficult than I expected.*

WITH VERBS

- The adverb can go before or after the verb but cannot be placed immediately before the object of the verb:
  I **really** *admire what she's doing.*
  Our political views differ **greatly**.
  Her death affected him **deeply**.
- Common intensifiers are: **greatly**, **very much**, **completely** (these can occur before or after the verb), **quite**, **absolutely** (usually before the verb).
- Strong intensifiers are often used with verbs which have a powerful meaning:
  It's absolutely pouring (= raining very much)
  I **utterly** *despise them* (= very much dislike them).

work/succeed/*sports verbs like* play/catch/save **brilliantly** (after verb)
vary/strengthen **considerably** (after verb)
vary/benefit/enjoy/help **enormously** (after verb)
entirely depend on/rely on/consist of
greatly improve/increase/reduce/help/benefit/change/vary
contrast/fall/rise/criticize/improve/differ/increase/drop **sharply** (usually after verb)
strongly oppose/criticize/support/feel/believe/deny

WITH NOUNS

The following adjectives are commonly used as intensifiers in front of nouns :

absolute certainty/minimum/nonsense/disgrace
complete disaster/confidence/failure/contrast/mess
deep breath/depression/sleep/trouble/mistrust/concern/regret
great difficulty/success/pity/surprise/skill/care/danger/joy/sadness/importance
heavy rain/losses/traffic/responsibility/smoker/drinker
high proportion/quality/standards/priority/hopes/degree/expectations

perfect happiness/harmony/timing/example/opportunity/conditions
profound implications/effect/silence/change
strong wind/support for/opposition to/criticism of/sense of (fun etc.)/feelings
tremendous amount/pressure/opportunity/achievement/excitement/speed
utter confusion/rubbish/nonsense/lack of

WITH ADVERBS AND PRONOUNS

- Some adverbs can be given a stronger meaning by putting another adverb in front:
  Quite clearly *you don't understand* .
  You know **perfectly well** *what I mean.*
  His plan went **horribly wrong**.
  Quite, **very** and **extremely** are often used in this way.
- Intensifiers are rarely used with pronouns, but notice: *He sat around doing* **absolutely nothing**.

open. • **Vested interests** are those people or organizations who have a financial or personal interest in a business, company or an existing system: *A compromise has to be reached between all the powerful vested interests before any restoration work in the city can take place.* • (CS)(D)(F)(N)(P)

ves·ti·bule /ˈves·tɪ·bjuːl/ *n* [C] *fml* a room just inside the outer door of a public building, which you go through in order to reach the other rooms of the building; FOYER • *Visitors are asked to leave their umbrellas in the vestibule.* • *I'll wait for you in the vestibule.* • *(Am)* A vestibule is also a small enclosed area on the front of a house; a porch.

ves·tige /ˈves·tɪdʒ/ *n* [C] a still existing small part or amount of something larger, stronger or more important that existed in the past but does not exist now • *The old city still shows vestiges* **of** *a colonial past.* • *There are few vestiges* **of** *the original plan remaining.* • *His win removed the* **last** *vestige* **of** *doubt about his abilities.* • *There is now no vestige* **of** *hope that the missing children will be found alive.*

ves·ti·gial /vesˈtɪdʒ·i·əl/ *adj* [not gradable] • *Although the central government has some vestigial* (= a small amount of) *authority, power has largely passed to the individual states.* • *(specialized)* Vestigial can also be used to refer to something, esp. a part of the body, that has not developed completely, or has stopped being used and has almost disappeared: *a vestigial organ* ○ *a vestigial limb* ○ *a vestigial tail* ○ *a vestigial language* ○ *An ostrich has vestigial wings.*

ves·ti·gi·al·ly /vesˈtɪdʒ·i·əl/ *adv* [not gradable]

vest·ments /ˈvest·mənts/ *pl n* the special clothes worn by priests during church ceremonies

ves·try /ˈves·tri/, **sac·ri·sty** *n* [C] a room in a church, esp. one in which priests and the group of people who sing in church put on the special clothes they wear for church ceremonies, and in which items used in church ceremonies are sometimes kept

vet [ANIMAL DOCTOR] /vet/, *Br and Aus fml* **vet·e·ri·na·ry sur·geon**, *Am fml* **vet·e·ri·nar·i·an** *n* [C] a person trained to take care of the health of animals • *The farmer called the vet out to treat a sick cow.*

vet's /vets/ *n* [C] *pl* **vets** or **vets'** • A vet's is the office where a vet works: *We took our cat to the vet's for its annual cat flu injection.*

vet *obj* [EXAMINE] /vet/ *v* [T] **-tt-** to examine (something or someone) carefully to make certain that they are acceptable or suitable • *During the war, the government vetted all newspaper, television and radio reports before they were published.* • *The bank vets everyone who applies for an account.* • *Prospective tenants are carefully vetted before they are allowed to move into the apartment building.*

vet [ARMED FORCES] /vet/ *n* [C] *Am infml for* VETERAN (= a person who has served in the armed forces) • *a Vietnam vet*

vet·e·ran /£ˈvet·ər·ən, $ˈveṭ·ə-/ *n* [C] a person who has had a lot of experience of a particular activity in the past • *He's a 20-year veteran* **of** *the New York Police Department.* • *Francis is a veteran* **of** *15 international matches.* • *The new national security adviser is a veteran* **of** *the former president's staff.* • *She's a veteran campaigner for human rights.* • *The after-dinner speaker was a veteran actor.* • A veteran (*Am infml* **vet**) is also someone who has been in the armed forces, *(Br)* esp. an old person: *Everyone sat in silence as a young Vietnam veteran spoke about his experiences during the war.* ○ *The ceremony was attended by veterans* **of** *World War II.* • *(Br)* Veteran also means old: *He collects veteran* **cars** (= cars made before 1905). Compare VINTAGE [HIGH QUALITY]. ○ *(humorous) She rides around on a veteran bicycle.* • **Veterans Day** in the US and Canada is a legal holiday on November 11th, when people honour members of their countries' armed forces who have fought in wars. • (J)

vet·e·ri·na·ry /£ˈvet·ᵊr·ɪ·nᵊr·i, $-ner-/ *adj* [before n; not gradable] connected with taking care of the health of animals • *veterinary medicine* • *veterinary science* • *Following the outbreak of the disease, several sheep and lambs were destroyed on veterinary advice.* • **Veterinary surgeon** is *Br and Aus fml for* VET [ANIMAL DOCTOR].

ve·to /£ˈviː·təʊ, $-t̬oʊ/ *n pl* **vetoes** (a) refusal to allow something to be done • *The proposal was removed by Congress under threat of presidential veto.* [U] • *The Ministry of Defence has the power of veto over all British arms exports.* [U] • *In theory the British government could use its veto to block this proposal.* [C] • *The Senate voted to override the President's veto* **of** *the proposed measures.* [C] • *(esp. Br) Mum has* **put** *a veto* **on** *our watching television for more than two hours an evening.* [C] • *(esp. Br) The author has insisted on having a veto* **over** *the film version of her book.* [C]

ve·to *(obj)* /£ˈviː·təʊ, $-t̬oʊ/ *v* he/she/it **vetoes**, **vetoing**, *past* **vetoed** • *In 1961, President De Gaulle vetoed* (= refused to allow) *Britain's entry into the Common Market.* [T] • *The President has threatened to veto the legislation/education bill.* [T] • *I was surprised when the committee vetoed my proposal.* [T] • *My boss vetoed my tak***ing** *any more time off this year.* [+ v-*ing*]

vex *obj* /veks/ *v* [T] *dated* to cause difficulty to (someone), or to cause (someone) to feel angry, annoyed or upset • *This issue looks likely to continue to vex the government.* • *I've been vexed by this problem for weeks.* • *I was vexed by the things that people were always telling me that I must do.* • *If they find out what I've done, they'll be extremely vexed* (= angry or annoyed) **with** *me.*

vex·a·tion /vekˈseɪ·ʃᵊn/ *n dated* • *Their defeat caused them considerable vexation.* [U] • *After several unsuccessful attempts to start his car, he swore in vexation.* [U] • *It was a great vexation* **to** *her that no one seemed to believe what she said.* [C]

vex·a·tious /vekˈseɪ·ʃəs/ *adj dated* • *a vexatious child* • *These continuing problems with my computer are extremely vexatious.* • *This settlement will resolve one of the most vexatious* (= difficult) *problems in the field of industrial relations.*

vex·a·tious·ly /vekˈseɪ·ʃə·sli/ *adv dated*

vexed /vekst/ *adj* • Vexed means difficult to deal with and causing a lot of disagreement and argument: *The government has to deal with the vexed* **question** *of how to reduce its spending.* ○ *The* **question** *of how wars end is a vexed one.* ○ *His views about language acquisition have changed people's ideas about that vexed* **issue/subject**. ○ *He had a vexed* **relationship** *with his mother-in-law.*

vgc /ˌviː·dʒiːˈsiː/ *Br abbreviation for* very good condition (used in advertisements for second-hand goods) • *Bike for sale, vgc, £50.*

VHF /ˌviː·eɪtʃˈef/ *n* [U] *abbreviation for* very high frequency (= radio waves between 30 to 300 MHz) • *a VHF radio* • *a VHF band* • *a VHF transmitter* • *The new radio station, which is on a VHF* **frequency**, *will provide a mixture of music and talk.* • *Specialized radio stations often broadcast* **on** *VHF.* • Compare UHF.

VHS /ˌviː·eɪtʃˈes/ *n* [U] *trademark abbreviation for* Video Home System (= a system for recording moving pictures and sound onto the magnetic strip in a VIDEO)

vi·a /vaɪə, ˈviː·ə/ *prep* through; using • *The flight goes via Frankfurt.* • *We came via the ring road.* • *Reports are coming in via satellite.* • *It is thought that he was paid via a Swiss bank account.* • *I only found out about it via my sister.* • *The virus is transmitted via physical contact.* • *The baby is currently being fed via a tube.*

vi·a·ble /ˈvaɪ·ə·bl̩/ *adj* able to work as intended or to succeed, or *(specialized)* able to continue to exist as or develop into a living being • *In order to make the company viable, it will unfortunately be necessary to reduce staffing levels.* • *The government has agreed to allow the mines to stay in operation, as long as they can show that they can become viable.* • *Do you think solar power is really a viable* **alternative** *as a way of providing heat?* • *Many are doubtful that this technology will ever be* **commercially/economically/financially** *viable.* • *In the present economic climate, building a luxury hotel hardly seems a viable* **plan/proposition/proposal**. • *(specialized) There is a continuing debate about the age at which a human fetus can be considered viable.* • *(specialized) A mule is not a viable animal* (= it cannot produce young). • ⓘ

vi·a·bil·i·ty /£ˌvaɪ·əˈbɪl·ɪ·ti, $-ə·t̬i/ *n* [U] • *Rising costs are threatening the viability* **of** *many businesses.* • *The main priority for the company is to establish* **commercial/economic/financial** *viability.* • *(specialized) As the world population of Hawaiian geese has shrunk to very small numbers, the bird's continuing viability is in doubt.*

vi·a·bly /ˈvaɪ·ə·bli/ *adv*

vi·a·duct /ˈvaɪə·dʌkt/ *n* [C] a long high bridge, usually held up by many arches, which carries a railway or a road over a valley or other similar area at a lower level • *a railway viaduct* • *It will cost £6 million to repair the viaduct over the Ribblehead valley.* • *He was killed when he drove his car over the edge of the viaduct.* • PIC **Bridge**

vi·al /vaɪəl/ *n* [C] a PHIAL

vibes [INSTRUMENT] /vaɪbz/ *pl n infml for* VIBRAPHONE

vibes [FEELING] /vaɪbz/, *fml* **vi·bra·tions** *pl n infml* the general feeling of a place, esp. the good or bad feeling experienced as coming from other people • *He decided to leave the job because, he said, he didn't like the vibes.* • *There are really* **good/bad** *vibes in the club.*

vi·brant /ˈvaɪ·brᵊnt/ *adj* energetic, exciting and full of enthusiasm • *She came across as a vibrant, enthusiastic person.* • *As a saxophonist, he was known for his vibrant playing.* • *Belinda gave a vibrant performance in the leading role in the school play.* • *She spoke in a voice vibrant* **with** *emotion.* • *The hope is that this area will develop into a vibrant commercial centre.* • *Our main aim is to build a strong, vibrant economy.* • A vibrant colour or vibrant light is bright and strong: *He always uses vibrant colours in his paintings.* ○ *The leaves on this plant remain a deep vibrant green all year.*

vi·brant·ly /ˈvaɪ·brᵊnt·li/ *adv* • *a vibrantly coloured image* • *a vibrantly catchy tune*

vi·bran·cy /ˈvaɪ·brᵊnt·si/ *n* [U] • *She* **has** *a vibrancy about her that draws people to her.* • *No one can fail to be struck by the vibrancy* **of** *New York.* • *The economy at present* **has** *little remaining vibrancy.* • *The colours in these paintings* **have** *a rich vibrancy.*

vi·bra·phone /£ˈvaɪ·brə·fəʊn, $-foʊn/, *infml* **vibes**, *Am also* **vi·bra·harp** /£ˈvaɪ·brə·hɑːp, $-hɑːrp/ *n* [C] a musical instrument consisting of a set of metal bars in a frame which have electrical devices fixed to them so that when they are hit they produce notes which shake slightly • *The Modern Jazz Quartet includes a vibraphone player.*

vi·brate *(obj)* /vaɪˈbreɪt/ *v* to (cause to) shake slightly and quickly, in a way that is felt rather than seen or heard • *The whole station seemed to vibrate as the express train rushed through.* [I] • *If I drive my car too fast, the engine starts to vibrate.* [I] • *The atoms in diamonds vibrate at very high frequencies.* [I] • *His voice vibrated* **with** *anger.* [I] • *(fig.) She seems to vibrate* **with** *enthusiasm.* [I] • *In musical instruments like the clarinet, notes are produced by the player's breath vibrating a thin piece of wood called a reed.* [T]

vi·bra·tion /vaɪˈbreɪ·ʃᵊn/ *n* • *Vibrations were felt hundreds of miles from the centre of the earthquake.* [C] • *Aircraft manufacturers want to reduce noise and vibration for the sake of both comfort and safety.* [U] • *When you speak, the vibration* **of** *your vocal chords causes small changes in air pressure in your mouth.* [U]

vi·bra·tor /£vaɪˈbreɪ·təʳ, $-t̬ɚ/ *n* [C] • A vibrator is a device which shakes slightly and quickly and which is held against the body in order to reduce pain or to give sexual pleasure.

vi·bra·to /£vɪˈbrɑː·təʊ, $-t̬oʊ/ *n* [C/U] *pl* **vibratos** *specialized* (a) repeated slight shaking in a musical note, either when played on an instrument or sung, which gives a fuller sound to the note • Compare TREMOLO.

vi·car /£ˈvɪk·əʳ, $-ɚ/ *n* [C] (in the Church of England) a priest who is in charge of a church and the religious needs of people in a particular area • *We were married by our local vicar.* • **Vicar of Christ** is the title sometimes given to the Pope.

vi·car·age /£ˈvɪk·ᵊr·ɪdʒ, $ˈ-ɚ-/ *n* [C] • A vicarage is the house in which a VICAR lives: *Vicarages are usually situated close to the church.* ○ *That film was so scary, it made the last thriller I saw look* **like** *a vicarage* **tea-party** (= seem calm, and not exciting).

vi·car·i·ous /£vɪˈkeə·ri·əs, $-ˈker·i-/ *adj* experienced by watching, listening to or reading about the activities of other people, or *(fml)* experienced for someone else • *There's a certain vicarious pleasure in reading books about travel.* • *They get a vicarious thrill from watching motor racing.* • *Parents who haven't succeeded themselves hope for vicarious satisfaction through their children.*

vi·car·i·ous·ly /£vɪˈkeə·ri·ə·sli, $-ˈker·i-/ *adv* • *As the novel progresses, it becomes clear that Harriet lives vicariously through Tessa and Imogen.* • *If I couldn't afford a vacation, I could at least experience one vicariously, by reading fellow travellers' accounts of their adventures.*

vi·car·i·ous·ness /£vɪˈkeə·ri·ə·snəs, $-ˈker·i-/ *n* [U]

vice [MORAL FAULT] /vaɪs/ *n* (a) moral fault or weakness in someone's character, or immoral activity, esp. involving illegal sex, drugs, etc. • *Greed, pride, envy, dishonesty, and lust are considered to be vices.* [C] • *All the candidates have their virtues and vices* (= their strengths and weaknesses). [C] • *(esp. humorous) My one real vice* (= bad habit) *is chocolate.* • *The chief of police said that he was committed to wiping out vice* (= illegal immoral activities) *in the area.* [U] • *The drug dealers have been picked up by the* **vice squad** (= police officers whose job it is to stop criminal immoral activities). • *It is believed that the pornographic films are being distributed by a* **vice ring** (= a group of people involved in criminal immoral activities). • *"Extremism in the defense of liberty is no vice"* (Barry Goldwater in a speech, 1964)

vice [TOOL] *esp. Br and Aus, Am usually* **vise** /vaɪs/ *n* [C] a tool with two parts which can be moved together by tightening a screw so that an object can be held firmly between them while it is being worked on • *Vices are often used to hold pieces of wood that are being cut or smoothed.* • *Her hand tightened like a vice around his arm.* • Something that is **vice-like** is very tight: *He holds his tennis racket with a vice-like* **grip**. ○ *She maintains vice-like control over her staff.* ○ *A heart attack produces a vice-like pain* (= a pain which feels like something is tightening round your chest). • [PIC] **Tools**

vice [TITLE] /vaɪs/ *combining form* used as part of the title of particular positions. The person who holds one of these positions is next below in authority to the person who holds the full position and can act for them • *the vice captain of the team* • *a vice admiral* • In a British college or university, the **vice-chancellor** is the person responsible for controlling the business and teaching. • The **Vice President** (*Am abbreviation* **VP**, *Am infml* **veep**) is the person who has the position below that of President: *Geraldine Ferraro tried to become the first woman Vice President of the US, but did not succeed.* ○ *Vice President Humphrey* ○ *Excuse me, Mr Vice President!* [as form of address]

vice·roy /ˈvaɪs·rɔɪ/ *n* [C] a representative of a king or queen who rules for them in another country • *Earl Mountbatten was the last viceroy of India.*

vice ver·sa /£ˌvaɪsˈvɜː·sə, $ˌvaɪ·səˈvɜːr-/ *adv* [not gradable] used to state that what you have just said is also true in the opposite order • *He doesn't trust her, and vice versa* (= she doesn't trust him). • *Aristarchus of Samos reasoned that the Earth went round the sun, not vice versa, though nobody believed him for centuries.* • *It seemed as if the teacher was learning more from the student than vice versa.* • *Never use indoor lights outdoors or vice versa.*

vi·cin·i·ty /£vɪˈsɪn·ɪ·ti, $vəˈsɪn·ə·t̬i/ *n* the immediately surrounding area • *No one was seen* **in** *the vicinity at the time of the murder.* • *The people who were hurt in the accident were taken to the only hospital* **in** *the* **immediate** *vicinity.* • *There are several hotels* **in** *the vicinity* **of** *the station.* • *(fig.) The football team is believed to have paid* **in** *the vicinity* **of** (= about) *£3 million for their latest new player.*

vi·cious /ˈvɪʃ·əs/ *adj* having or showing an intention or desire to hurt very badly • *a vicious criminal* • *a vicious thug* • *a vicious dog* • *Many people were injured in the vicious fighting that broke out between the demonstrators and the police.* • *The police said that this was one of the most vicious attacks they'd ever seen.* • *Small children can be very vicious.* • *I thought that what she said was unnecessarily vicious.* • *He gave her a vicious look.* • An object which is vicious is one which can be used to cause great pain or harm: *The museum has a large collection of vicious medieval torture instruments.* • *I've got a vicious* (= extremely painful) *headache.* • *Make sure you wrap up warmly – there's a vicious* (= extremely strong) *wind out there.* • A **vicious circle** is a difficult situation in which something that happens causes something else unpleasant to happen: *The long-term unemployed are* **trapped in** *a vicious circle – the longer somebody has been out of work, the harder it is to get a job.* ○ *Many people get* **caught in** *a vicious circle of dieting and weight gain.*

vi·cious·ly /ˈvɪʃ·ə·sli/ *adv* • *She was viciously attacked/assaulted/beaten.* • *That was one of the most viciously written articles I've ever read.* • *It was viciously* (= extremely) *cold last night.*

vi·cious·ness /ˈvɪʃ·ə·snəs/ *n* [U] • *Everyone was horrified by the viciousness* **of** *the killings.* • *I was surprised at the viciousness with which he spoke about his father.*

vi·cis·si·tudes /£vɪˈsɪs·ɪ·tjuːdz, $-tuːdz/ *pl n fml* changes which happen at different times during the life or development of someone or something, esp. those which result in conditions being worse • *The President's followers have continued to support him through all his vicissitudes.* • *You could say that losing your job is just one of the vicissitudes* **of** *life.* • *Whether we are able to hold the party outside or not depends on the vicissitudes* **of** *the weather.*

vic·tim /ˈvɪk·tɪm/ *n* [C] someone or something which has been hurt, damaged or killed or has suffered, either because of the actions of someone or something else, or because of illness or chance • *The chances of being the victim* **of** *a* **crime** *are still much lower in Britain than they are in America.* • *The children are the innocent/helpless victims* **of** *the fighting.* • *The law prevents newspapers and television from naming victims* **of** *rape/rape victims.* • *A new drug has been developed which might help save the lives of cancer/AIDS/heart-attack victims.* • *Congress has agreed to provide financial aid to the hurricane/flood victims.* • *We appear to have been the victims* **of** *a cruel hoax.* • *Our local hospital has become the latest victim* **of** *the cuts in government spending.* • *The school has become a victim* **of its own success** (= its success is causing it to have problems) *– it's in danger of becoming overcrowded.* • If you **fall** victim **to** someone or something, you are hurt, damaged, killed or suffer because of them: *In 1948, Gandhi fell victim to a member of a Hindu gang.* ○ *The company has fallen victim to increased competition.*

vic·tim·ize *obj, Br and Aus usually* **-ise** /ˈvɪk·tɪ·maɪz/ *v* [often passive] • If someone is victimized, they are intentionally unfairly treated, esp. because their race, sex or beliefs are not liked: *The young blacks believed that they had been victimized.* ○ *Mary Jo set out to show that women are victimized by the law.* ○ *Nixon felt that he was being victimized by the media.*

vic·tim·i·za·tion, *Br and Aus usually* **-i·sa·tion** /ˌvɪk·tɪ·maɪˈzeɪ·ʃᵊn/ *n* [U] • *He claimed that there had been systematic victimization* **of** *black people by the police.*

vic·tim·less /ˈvɪk·tɪm·ləs/ *adj* [not gradable] • A victimless **crime** is one in which no one suffers, usually because the people on whom the crime has an effect have agreed to take part in it: *Stock market fraud is sometimes regarded as a victimless crime.*

Vic·tor·i·an /£vɪkˈtɔː·ri·ən, $-ˈtɔːr·i-/ *adj* of, made in or living in the time when Queen Victoria was queen of Britain (1837-1901) • *Our house was originally Victorian, but it has had a lot of alterations made to it.* • *Charles Dickens is one of the best-known Victorian novelists.* • *Lillie Langtry was a star of the Victorian stage.* • Victorian morals, opinions, ways of living etc. are those which are thought to have been common when Queen Victoria was queen of Britain. They include an emphasis on self-control, hard work, loyalty and strong religious beliefs: *While she was Prime Minister, Margaret Thatcher was said to want to see a return to Victorian* **values**. • *(Aus)* Victorian means of or from the state of Victoria.

Vic·tor·i·an /£vɪkˈtɔː·ri·ən, $-ˈtɔːr·i-/ *n* [C] • *the eminent Victorian, Benjamin Disraeli* • *The Victorians believed that children should be seen and not heard.*

Vic·tor·i·an·a /£vɪkˌtɔː·riˈɑː·nə, $-ˌtɔːr·iˈæn·ə/ *n* [U] • *Her living room is cluttered with Victoriana* (= objects, esp. decorative items, pictures and toys, which were made while Queen Victoria was queen of Britain).

vic·tory /£ˈvɪk·tᵊr·i, $-tɚ-/ *n* (an example of) success in a game, competition, election, war, etc. • *a three-stroke victory (in golf)* • *a five-wicket victory (in cricket)* • *a straight-sets victory (in tennis)* [C] • *The Redskins opened the season with a* **resounding/stunning/impressive** *25-3 victory* **over** *Detroit.* [C] • *King is expected to* **achieve/gain** *a* **comfortable/easy** *victory* **against** *Cooper in tomorrow's match.* [C] • *The England team* **clinched** *a* **clear-cut/convincing/decisive** *victory* **over** *Sri Lanka yesterday.* [C] • *Bobby Fischer* **won** *a* **historic** *victory* **in** *the 1972 world chess championship.* [C] • *The socialists* **won** *a* **landslide** *victory* **in** *the election.* [C] • *This result is a victory* **for** *democracy.* [C] • *There is no doubt that the court's decision is a victory* **for common sense** (= is very reasonable). [C] • *No one wants to see the terrorists* **score** *a* **propaganda** *victory.* [C] • *When the votes were counted, the result was so close that* *neither candidate could claim victory.* [U] • *Napoleon led his troops to victory in the Battle of Austerlitz.* [U] • *They did not expect to* **secure** *victory so easily.* [U] • *Plans have been made for an enormous victory parade in Washington when the troops start returning home.* • *"Victory at all costs, victory in spite of all terror; victory, however long and hard the road may be; for without victory, there is no survival"* (Sir Winston Churchill in a speech, 1940) • See also PYRRHIC VICTORY. • LP› **Sports**

vic·tor /£'vɪk·tər, $-tɚ/ *n* [C] • *The victor* (=winner) **in** *the 1960 US Presidential election was John F. Kennedy.* • *Lord Nelson was the victor* **of** *the Battle of Trafalgar in 1805.* • *Scotland were the victors* **over** *Ireland in last night's football game.* • *It seems likely that the Conservative candidate will* **emerge (as)** *the clear victor.* • *"To the victor belongs the spoils"* (William Learned Marcy in a speech to the American Senate, 1832)

vic·tor·i·ous /£vɪk'tɔː·ri·əs, $-'tɔːr·i-/ *adj* • *The victorious team* (=The team who won) *were loudly cheered by their fans.* • *She was partly responsible for organizing the victorious president's election campaign.* • *The state of Prussia was abolished by the victorious wartime allies.* • *The German player* **emerged** *victorious after a long five-hour match.*

vic·tor·i·ous·ly /£vɪk'tɔː·ri·ə·sli, $-'tɔːr·i-/ *adv*

vict·uals /£'vɪt·əlz, $'vɪṭ-/ *pl n dated or humorous* food and drink • *"I can't bear to see good victuals wasted," said Martha.* • *I'm starving – did we bring any victuals with us?*

vi·de·o /£'vɪd·i·əʊ, $-oʊ/, **vi·de·o·tape** /£'vɪd·i·əʊ·teɪp, $-oʊ-/ *n pl* **videos** (a) recording of moving pictures and sound that has been made on a long narrow strip of magnetic material inside a rectangular plastic container, and which can be played on a special machine so that it can be watched on television, or this container with the magnetic strip inside it • *I bought the video* **of** *'Jurassic Park' for the children.* [C] • *Ed came over last night to watch the video* **of** *the football match that I'd* **recorded**. [C] • *We had a video made* **of** *our wedding.* [C] • *If I go to the (Br and Aus) video* **shop/***(Am) video* **store** (=a shop which sells or esp. rents videos) *on the way home, what video would you like me to get?* [C] • *I want to record this television programme, but I can't find any* **blank** *videos* (=those on which nothing has yet been recorded). [C] • *A lot of films now come out* **on** *video* (=in the form of a video) *very soon after they've been shown at the cinema.* [U] • *I wish we'd got some video* (=some recordings in the form of videos) *of the children when they were little.* [U] • A video (*also* **music video**) is also a short film made to advertize a popular song: *One of the first videos to be made was for Queen's 'Bohemian Rhapsody'.* • *These kids spend too much of their time playing games in the* **video arcade** (=a place where there are machines on which video games can be played when money is put into the machines). • A **video camera** is a camera which records moving pictures and sound onto a video: *Many shops have video cameras fixed to their walls or ceilings for security reasons.* ○ *They bought a video camera when their first child was born so that they could record her growing up.* Compare CAMCORDER. • A **video cassette** is a video: *Finding a video cassette* **of** *a good opera isn't easy.* • A **video disc** is a large disc, on which moving pictures and sound have been recorded and which can be played on a television: *a video disc system* ○ *a video disc player* • A **video game** is a game in which the player controls moving pictures on a screen by pressing buttons: *a hand-held video game.* ○ *A lot of video games seem to me to be very violent.* • *(Am and Aus)* A **video monitor** is a device with a screen on which moving pictures can be shown: *The officers' vans are equipped with video monitors which can receive pictures from police helicopters.* • *(Br)* A **video nasty** is a video of a film containing extremely unpleasant violence and/or sex. • A **video recorder** (also **video cassette recorder**, *Am usually* **VCR**, **videotape recorder** or *Br infml* **video**) is a machine on which pictures and sounds can be recorded from a television or a camera onto a video and on which a video can be played: *Don't forget to set the video (recorder) before you go out.* • See also TAPE. • PIC› **Room**

vi·de·o *obj* /£'vɪd·i·əʊ, $-oʊ/, **tape** *v* [T] he/she/it **videos**, **videoing**, *past* **videoed** • *There's a play on television tonight that I'd like to video* (=record from television onto a video). • *Mark wasn't able to go to see his daughter performing in the school concert, so Alan videoed it* (=recorded it using a video camera) *for him.*

vi·de·o /£'vɪd·i·əʊ, $-oʊ/ *adj* [not gradable] • *a video recording* • *a video film* (=those recorded onto a video) • *(specialized)* Video also means connected with or used in the showing of moving pictures by television: *a video signal* ○ *video frequencies* ○ *a video link between two places* ○ *video conferencing* (=the activity of two or more people who are far apart being able to talk to each other and see each other on a television screen)

vi·de·o·fit /£'vɪd·i·əʊ·fɪt, $-oʊ-/ *n* [C] *Br* a picture of the face of a person whom police think might have committed a particular crime, which is produced electronically by combining pictures of different eyes, noses, mouths, etc. and is based on descriptions of the person given by people who saw the crime happen. • *The police have* **issued** *a videofit* **of** *the suspect.*

vie /vaɪ/ *v* [I] **vying**, *past* **vied** to compete • *Six candidates are currently vying* **for** *the Democratic presidential nomination.* • *The children tend to vie* **for** *their mother's attention.* • *The streets were full of cars vying* **with** *each other* **for** *parking spaces.* • *Car dealers are vying* **with** *each other* **to** *attract customers by offering discounts.* [+ *to* infinitive] • *The two groups of scientists are vying* **to** *get funding for their research projects.* [+ *to* infinitive]

view OPINION /vjuː/ *n* [C] (an) opinion or belief or idea, or a way of thinking (about something) • *Do you have a view* **about/on** *what we should do now?* • **In** *my view, her criticisms were completely justified.* • *It's my view* **that** *the price is much too high.* [+ *that* clause] • *What are your views* **about/on** *this idea, Jim?* • *There is a* **prevailing/ widespread** *view* **that** *the convicted men are innocent.* [+ *that* clause] • *Some people* **hold/take** *the view* **that** *children should not be smacked.* [+ *that* clause] • *My father and I* **have** *sharply conflicting/contrasting/differing/opposing views on politics.* • *She* **holds** *strong/traditional/ conservative/radical/unconventional views* **about** *how children should be taught.* • *Everyone will have a chance to* **make** *their views* **known**. • *You've* **expressed** *your views very clearly.* • *This view is not widely* **shared**. • *The German Chancellor* **echoed/endorsed** *the French President's view.* • *We had a friendly* **exchange of** *views.* • **The** *view* **from** *the White House* (=The opinion of the American President) *is that the invasion by US troops was entirely justified.* • *He seems to have no clear view* **of** (=idea about) *what he wants to do with his life.* • *The official view* (=way of thinking) *is that there are signs of improvement in the economy.* • *Our* **world** *view* (=way of thinking about the world) *is quite different from that of writers in the fourth century BC.* • *We need to* **take an overall** *view* **of** *the problem* (=to think about all parts of it). • *He* **takes/has** *a cynical/optimistic/ pessimistic view* **of** *our chances of winning* (=He thinks about our chances in those ways). • *He seems to* **have/take** *a very* **jaundiced** *view* **of** (=thinks in a negative way about) *life.* • *We* **take** *a very serious view* **of** *the situation* (=think that the situation is serious). • *I* **take** *a very* **dim/poor** *view* **of** *this kind of behaviour* (=think that this type of behaviour is unacceptable). • *In making this investment, we need to* **take** *a* **long/long-term** *view* (=think about what the future results of the decision will be, not the immediate ones). • **In view of** (=Because of) *what you've said, I think we should reconsider our proposed course of action.* • *These measures have been taken* **with a view to** (=with the aim of) *increasing the company's profits.* • (T)

view *obj* /vjuː/ *v* [T] • *How do you view your prospects/ chances* (=What do you consider your chances to be) *in tomorrow's race?* • *The journalist asked the minister how he viewed* (=what he thought about) *recent events.* • *She is viewed* (=considered) **as** *a strong candidate for the job.* • *He is being viewed by Amnesty* **as** *a prisoner of conscience.* • *We view the situation* **with** *concern/satisfaction.* • *The plans have been viewed* **with** *suspicion.* • *If we view the problem* **from** *a different* **angle**, *a solution may become more obvious.*

view SIGHT /vjuː/ *n* what you can see from a particular place, or the ability to see from a particular place • *The view* **from** *the top of the mountain is breathtaking/ magnificent/spectacular/stunning.* [C] • *The rooftop restaurant* **affords** *a panoramic view* (=allows you to see a wide area) *across the bay.* [C] • *Don't stand in front of me – you're* **blocking/obstructing** *my view.* [U] • *He lifted his daughter up so that she could get a good/better view* **of** *the clowns.* • *We have a clear view* **of** *the ocean from our bedroom window.* [C] • If you have a **grandstand** view **of** something, you can see all of it very easily: *From where we stood, we had a grandstand view of the parade.* [C] • A view is also a picture of a particular place: *She sent us a postcard showing a local view.* [C] ○ *He paints rural views* (=pictures of the countryside). [C] • *(Br)* A view (*Br also and Am and Aus* **viewing**) is also an occasion for a special look at an EXHIBITION, film, etc.: *We've been invited to a* **private** *view, before the exhibition opens.* [C] • *I always make sure I keep the children* **in** *view* (= am able to see them) *whenever we're in a public place.* [U] • *The cloud lifted, and the tops of the mountains suddenly* **came into** *view* (= could be seen). [U] • *She turned a corner, and disappeared* **from** *view/out of view.* [U] • *The house is hidden/shielded* **from** *view behind a high hedge.* [U] • If you have something **in view**, you have planned it: *Have you anything in view for when you leave college?* • If something is **on view**, it is arranged so that it can be seen by the public: *Local artists' paintings are on view in the library this week.* ○ *The plans for the new road will soon be on view* **to the public**. • *"A Room with a View"* (title of a book by E.M.Forster, 1908) • Ⓣ

view *(obj)* /vjuː/ *v* • To view is to watch or look at: *The censors felt that the movie was too disturbing for general viewing.* [I] ○ *There's a special area at the airport where you can view aircraft taking off and landing.* [T] ○ *The extent of the flooding can only be fully appreciated when viewed from the air.* [T] ○ *Studies have shown that viewing too much television causes strange behaviour in children.* [T] ○ *The site where the Viking ship was found has been preserved for public viewing.* [I] ○ *The controllers of the television station are looking for new ways of boosting its viewing* **figures** (= the number of people who watch broadcasts). [I] • To view is also to look at carefully: *When we put our house up for sale, a few people came to view it, but no one was interested in buying it.* [T] ○ *Has everyone had a chance to view the figures?* [T]

view·er /£'vjuː·ə^r, $-ɚ/ *n* [C] • A viewer is a person who watches something, esp. television: *The average viewer watches television for about two hours a day.* ○ *Millions of viewers will be glued to their sets for this match.* ○ *Many outraged viewers* **of** *the news last night called to complain about the violent scenes that were shown.* • A viewer is also a device for looking at SLIDES (= transparent colour photographs).

view·find·er /£'vjuːˌfaɪn·də^r, $-dɚ/ *n* [C] the part of a camera that you look through to see what it is that you are taking a photograph of

view·point [VIEW] *Br* /'vjuː·pɔɪnt/, *Am* **o·ver·look**, *Aus* **look·out** *n* [C] a place where people can look down or out, esp. at an area of natural beauty • *The viewpoint gave us a stunning panorama of the whole valley.* • *The viewpoint and carpark were marked on the map.*

view·point [OPINION] /'vjuː·pɔɪnt/ *n* [C] **point of view**, see at POINT [TIME OR PLACE]

vi·gil /'vɪdʒ·ɪl/ *n* (an act of) staying awake, esp. at night, in order to be with an ill person, or to express esp. political disagreement, or to pray • *His parents* **kept** *vigil beside his bed for weeks before he finally died.* [U] • *Supporters of the peace movement* **held** *an all-night candlelit* **prayer** *vigil outside the cathedral.* [C] • *Her friends plan to* **hold/ maintain/stage** *a daily vigil outside the prison to protest about her unfair conviction.* [C]

vi·gil·ant /'vɪdʒ·ɪ·lənt/ *adj* always being careful to notice things, esp. possible danger • *Following the bomb scare at the airport, the staff have been warned to be extra vigilant.* • *Teachers have been told to be more vigilant in spotting signs of drug abuse among their students.* • *The break-in was discovered by a vigilant police officer.* • *Somehow, the children managed to escape the vigilant* **eye** *of their mother, and run off.*

vi·gil·ant·ly /'vɪdʒ·ɪ·lənt·li/ *adv* • *Passengers are advised to watch their belongings vigilantly at all times.*

vi·gil·ance /'vɪdʒ·ɪ·lənts/ *n* [U] • *Increased vigilance* (= more careful attention) *among doctors has led to the disease being more frequently diagnosed in its early stages.* • *The police said that it was thanks to the vigilance* **of** *a neighbour that the fire was discovered before it could spread.* • *The minister warned that vigilance* **against** *terrorism must not be* **relaxed**.

vi·gil·an·te /£ˌvɪdʒ·ɪ'læn·ti, $-'læn·t̬i/ *n* [C] a person who tries in an unofficial way to prevent crime, or to catch and punish someone who has committed a crime, esp. because they do not think that official organizations, such as the police, are controlling crime effectively. Vigilantes usually join together to form groups. • *Support for vigilantes is a reflection of the apparent breakdown of law and order.* • *The Guardian Angels are a group of vigilantes who try to prevent crime on the New York subway.* • *The area is patrolled by members of a vigilante* **group/force/patrol/squad**. • *(fig.) Feminist groups proposed that vigilantes* (= people who make sure that something is acceptable) *should examine all the books on the students' reading list.*

vi·gil·an·ti·sm /£ˌvɪdʒ·ɪ'læn·tɪ·z^{ə}m, $-t̬ɪ-/ *n* [U] • *The police are concerned about the recent rapid growth of vigilantism on the streets.*

vign·ette /vɪ'njet/ *n* [C] a short piece of writing, music, acting, etc. which clearly expresses the typical characteristics of something or someone • *a vignette* **of** *small-town life* • *The history of the community is told through photographs and vignettes from conversations with residents.* • *The play tells its story in a series of courtroom vignettes.*

vi·gour *Br and Aus, Am and Aus* **vi·gor** /£'vɪg·ə^r, $-ɚ/ *n* [U] strength, energy or enthusiasm • *We must pursue our aims* **with** *vigour.* • *They set about their work* **with** *youthful vigour and enthusiasm.* • *They expressed their opinions* **with** *great vigour.* • *The head teacher said that she hoped the children would return to school after the summer holidays* **with renewed** *vigour.* • *We were impressed by the vigour* **of** *the orchestra's playing.* • *Excellent ticket sales reflect the new-found vigour* **of** *the local theatre.* • Vigour can also mean forcefulness of thought, opinion, expression, etc.: *His book is written* **with** *considerable vigour.*

vi·gor·ous /£'vɪg·^{ə}r·əs, $'-ɚ-/ *adj* • *There has been vigorous* (= very strong) *opposition to the proposals for a new road.* • *Despite his vigorous election campaign, he is a shy man.* • *She launched into a vigorous defence of her son's actions.* • *The debate about the star's involvement with the failed business continues to be as vigorous as ever.* • *Cutting the bush back in the autumn will help promote vigorous growth in the spring.*

vi·gor·ous·ly /£'vɪg·^{ə}r·ə·sli, $'-ɚ-/ *adv* • *The family vigorously defended their decision.* • *For years they have campaigned vigorously against nuclear weapons.* • *The people who have been arrested have vigorously denied the charges.* • *Local people are vigorously opposing plans to build a new supermarket.* • *Don't exercise too vigorously at first.*

Vi·king /'vaɪ·kɪŋ/ *n* [C] a person belonging to a race of Scandinavian people who travelled by sea and attacked parts of northern and southern Europe between the 8th and the 11th centuries, often staying to live in places they travelled to • *a Viking ship* • *a Viking helmet* • *a Viking axe* • *In late Anglo-Saxon times, England was under constant attack from the Vikings.*

vile /vaɪl/ *adj* **-r, -st** evil or disgusting, or *(infml)* very bad or unpleasant • *Vile racial abuse has been painted on elevators, hospitals, homes and houses of worship.* • *Who could have carried out such a vile attack?* • *This vile policy of ethnic cleansing must be stopped.* • *(infml) We had a terrible holiday – the hotel was vile, the food was vile and the weather was vile.* • *(infml) This cheese smells vile.* • *(infml) Why are you being so vile to me?* • *(infml) Pat's in a vile mood/temper today.*

vile·ly /'vaɪl·li/ *adv* • *a vilely ruthless act* • *(infml) a vilely behaved child*

vile·ness /'vaɪl·nəs/ *n* [U]

vi·li·fy *obj* /'vɪl·ɪ·faɪ/ *v* [T] *fml* to say or write unpleasant things about (someone or something), in order to cause other people to have a bad opinion of them • *Lindy Chamberlain was vilified by society after being convicted of murdering her baby daughter.* • *He said that the press had been vilifying homosexuals for years.* • *When it was discovered that he had been operating as a spy, he was vilified* **as** *a traitor.*

vi·li·fi·ca·tion /ˌvɪl·ɪ·fɪ'keɪ·ʃ^{ə}n/ *n* [U] *fml* • *The family said that they had been subjected to a vilification campaign by their neighbours.* • *Their first aim, the vilification* **of** *nuclear weaponry as a concept in warfare, has been won.*

vil·la /'vɪl·ə/ *n* [C] a house usually in the countryside or near the sea, particularly in southern Europe, and often one which people can rent for a holiday • *a villa in Spain/ on the Algarve/in the south of France* • *a Tuscan villa* • Ⓔ Ⓚⓞⓡ Ⓢ

vil·lage /'vɪl·ɪdʒ/ *n* [C] a group of houses and other buildings, such as a church, a school and some shops, which is smaller than a town, usually in the countryside • *a fishing village* • *a mining village* • *a farming village* • *a mountain village* • *a seaside village* • *a village shop* • *a village school* • *a village pub* • *a village green* • *a village hall* • *Many towns and villages have been affected by the flooding.* • *The terrorists are hiding out in a remote village.* • *Many people come from the outlying/surrounding villages to* *work in the town.* • *My sister and I live in neighbouring villages.* • *We really enjoy village life.* • *He was born in the Yorkshire village* **of** *Great Ayton.* • Village can also be used to refer to all the people who live in a village: *The village is/are campaigning for a by-pass to be built.* [+ sing/pl v] • *"Some village-Hampden, that with dauntless breast / The little tyrant of his fields withstood"* (Thomas Gray *Elegy Written in a Country Churchyard*, 1751)

vil·lag·er /£'vɪl·ɪ·dʒəʳ, $-dʒɚ/ *n* [C] • A villager is a person who lives in a village: *The villagers are angry about the plans to close their local school.*

vil·lain /'vɪl·ən/ *n* [C] a bad person who harms other people or breaks the law • *Some people believe that Richard III did not murder his nephews and was not the villain he is generally thought to have been.* • *He's either a hero or a villain, depending on your point of view.* • *The union has been* **cast as** *a villain standing in the way of progress.* • *Bert's just a small-time villain* (= criminal) *– he'd never get involved in a major crime of this type.* • *(fig.) The major villain* (= thing that causes harm) *in causing lung cancer is smoking.* • A villain is also a character in a book, play, film, etc. who harms other people: *He made his reputation as an actor playing villains.* ○ *Again, Superman overpowered the villain, Lex Luthor.* • *(infml)* The **villain of the piece** is someone or something which is seen as being the cause of trouble on a particular occasion: *When the minister was forced to resign, the press was generally seen as the villain of the piece.*

vil·lain·ous /'vɪl·ə·nəs/ *adj* • Villainous means evil: *a villainous dictator* ○ *a villainous regime* ○ *villainous behaviour* ○ *a villainous character* ○ *a villainous role* ○ *In Shakespeare's 'Othello', Othello is deceived by the villainous Iago.*

vil·lain·y /'vɪl·ə·ni/ *n* [U] • *I wouldn't have thought she was capable of such villainy.* • *Charlie strongly denied the acts of villainy of which he was accused, such as forcing people to watch while he smashed up their homes.*

vim /vɪm/ *n* [U] *dated* energy and enthusiasm

vin·ai·grette /ˌvɪn·ɪ'gret/, **French dress·ing** *n* [U] a sauce made from oil and vinegar, and sometimes other flavourings, which is used esp. on salad

vin·di·cate *obj* /'vɪn·dɪ·keɪt/ *v* [T] to show to have been right or true or to show to be free from guilt or blame • *The police said that their policy of community liaison had been fully vindicated.* • *The decision to include Morris in the team was completely vindicated when he scored three goals.* • *Their scepticism was vindicated by events.* • *The investigation vindicated her complaint about the newspaper.* • *These findings vindicate my theory.* • *They said they welcomed the trial as a chance to vindicate themselves* (= show themselves to be free from guilt or blame).

vin·di·ca·tion /ˌvɪn·dɪ'keɪ·ʃᵊn/ *n* • *The army's victory is being seen as a vindication* **of** *their tactics.* [C] • *They are hoping for vindication in court.* [U]

vin·dic·tive /vɪn'dɪk·tɪv/ *adj* having or showing a desire to harm someone because you think that they have harmed you; unwilling to forgive • *Don't take any notice of what Sarah says – she's just being vindictive.* • *In the film 'Cape Fear', a lawyer's family is threatened by a vindictive former prisoner.*

vin·dic·tive·ly /vɪn'dɪk·tɪv·li/ *adv* • *"I'll get you back for what you've done," he thought vindictively.*

vin·dic·tive·ness /vɪn'dɪk·tɪv·nəs/ *n* [U] • *No one expected that he would behave with such vindictiveness.* • *I was surprised by the vindictiveness* **of** *her remarks.*

vine /vaɪn/, **grape·vine** *n* [C] the climbing plant which produces GRAPES as its fruit • *Vines produce better grapes as they age.* • A vine is also any type of plant which climbs or grows along the ground and which has woody twisting stems: *Ivy is a type of vine.* ○ *Monkeys swing between the trees on vines.* • See also VINEYARD.

vi·ne·gar /£'vɪn·ɪ·gəʳ, $-gɚ/ *n* [U] a sharp-tasting liquid, made esp. from sour wine, MALT or CIDER, which is used for flavouring or preserving food • *wine vinegar* • *malt vinegar* • *raspberry vinegar* • *tarragon vinegar* • *Would you like* **oil and** *vinegar on your salad?* • *Do you want* **salt and** *vinegar on your chips?* • *This wine tastes like vinegar.*

vi·ne·gary /£'vɪn·ɪ·gᵊr·i, $-gɚ·/ *adj* • *a vinegary sauce* (= one which tastes of vinegar) • *This salad dressing is rather vinegary* (= has a lot of vinegar in it). • *(fig.) He writes extremely vinegary* (= bad-tempered, unkind or very critical) *articles in the local newspaper.*

vine·yard /£'vɪn·jɑːd, $-jɚd/ *n* [C] a piece of land on which VINES, plants which produce GRAPES, are grown • These wines come from the great French vineyards of Bordeaux and Burgundy. • *A May frost could cost the vineyards some 10% of their production.*

vi·no /£'viː·nəʊ, $-noʊ/ *n* [U] *infml for* WINE • *Would you like a drop more vino?* • *Is there any vino left?*

vin·tage [WINE] /£'vɪn·tɪdʒ, $-t̬ɪdʒ/ *n* [C] the wine made in a particular year, or a particular year in which wine has been made • *The 1983 vintage was one of the best.* • *It is impossible to predict how good this year's vintage will be.* • *I recommend that you look for the younger, fresher vintages* (= wines which have been made recently). • *What vintage is this wine* (= In what year was it made)*?* • *1989 was not the greatest of vintages in California.* • *(fig.) He is undoubtedly England's best captain of recent vintage* (= in recent years). • *(fig.) My car is of 1960s vintage* (= was made between 1960 and 1969).

vin·tage /£'vɪn·tɪdʒ, $-t̬ɪdʒ/ *adj* [not gradable] • Vintage **wine** is wine of high quality that was made in a particular year, and which can be kept for several years in order to improve it: *vintage champagne* ○ *vintage port* ○ *vintage claret* ○ *Is this wine vintage or not?*

vin·tage [HIGH QUALITY] /£'vɪn·tɪdʒ, $-t̬ɪdʒ/ *adj* [not gradable] (esp. of something old) of high quality and lasting value, or showing the best characteristics of its type • *a vintage pistol* • *a vintage aircraft* • *a vintage joke* • *a vintage comic book* • *a vintage recording* • *a vintage Hollywood movie* • *vintage television comedy* • *(Br and Aus)* A vintage **car** is one which was made between 1919 and 1930: *a vintage BMW* ○ *a vintage Rolls Royce* ○ *a vintage model* ○ *We went to a vintage car rally.* • *This film is vintage* (= has the best characteristics typical of films made by) *Disney.* • *Johnstone was on/in vintage form* (= played extremely well) *in last night's championship game.* • *The film dates from the vintage years of the British film industry* (= years in which many extremely successful films were made).

vint·ner /£'vɪnt·nəʳ, $-nɚ/ *n* [C] a person whose job it is to buy and sell wine

vi·nyl /'vaɪ·nᵊl/ *n* [U] strong plastic which can be bent, and which is used for making floor coverings, furniture, clothing, records, etc. • *vinyl flooring* • *vinyl upholstery* • *a vinyl raincoat* • *a vinyl tablecloth* • *a vinyl record* • *Customers have been so impressed by the superior quality of compact discs that they have given up old-fashioned vinyl* (= records). • (J)

vi·ol·a /£vaɪ'əʊ·lə, $-'oʊ-/ *n* [C] a wooden musical instrument with four strings which is held against the neck and played by moving a BOW (= stick with hairs fixed to it) across the strings. It is larger than the VIOLIN. • *William Walton's viola concerto* • [PIC] **Musical instruments**

vi·o·late *obj* /'vaɪə·leɪt/ *v* [T] to break or act against (esp. a law, agreement, principle, etc., or something that should be treated with respect) • *They were charged with violating federal law.* • *The construction of the building violated fire rules/regulations.* • *The companies protest that the amendment violates the state constitution.* • *It seems that the planes deliberately violated the cease-fire agreement.* • *All countries have agreed not to violate the UN sanctions/the international treaty.* • *The doctor has been accused of violating professional ethics.* • To violate is also to go, esp. forcefully, into a place or situation which should be treated with respect and in which you are not wanted or not expected to be: *The fishermen claimed that ships from another country had violated their territorial waters.* ○ *It was said that the curse of Tutankhamen would fall on anyone who violated his tomb.* ○ *Questions of this kind violate my privacy and I am not willing to answer them.* • *(fml)* Violate can also be used to avoid saying RAPE (= have sex with someone, esp. a woman by force): *The little girl seems not to have been violated by her kidnappers.* • *She said that she had been treated so roughly by the hospital staff that she felt violated.*

vi·o·la·tion /ˌvaɪə'leɪ·ʃᵊn/ *n* • *Human rights violations* (= Acts against human rights) *were overlooked in a country where even children were tortured.* [C] • *He claimed that the way he'd been treated was a gross violation* **of** *his civil/constitutional rights.* [C] • *The takeover of the embassy constitutes a flagrant/blatant violation* **of** *international law.* [C] • *The truck was stopped for a minor traffic violation.* [C] • *It was decided that there had been no violation* **of** *the rules.* [U] • *It was clear that they had not acted* **in** *violation* **of** *the rules.* [U]

vi·o·lat·or /£ˈvaɪə·leɪ·tər, $-t̬ɚ/ *n* [C] • *If the council adopts the law, violators could be fined up to $250.* • *Violators* **of** *the curfew will be shot.*

vi·o·lence /ˈvaɪə·lənts/ *n* [U] actions or words which are intended to hurt people; extreme force • *The prime minister has refused to talk to the terrorists unless they renounce violence.* • *The incidence of violence* **against** *women is staggering.* • *It seems that the attack was a gratuitous/random/mindless* **act of** *violence.* • *The recent* **outbreak** *of* **racial/ethnic** *violence in the area is very troubling.* • *The report documents cases of* **domestic** *violence.* • *There has been an* **escalation/upsurge** *of gang violence in the city.* • *Violence* **erupted** *in the crowd during the second half of the match.* • *Some new research is being done on the effects that* **sex and** *violence on television might have on viewers.* • *The storm turned out to be one of unexpected violence* (=force). • *We were all surprised at the violence* (=force) **of** *his anger/rage.* • LP **Crimes and criminals**

vi·o·lent /ˈvaɪə·lənt/ *adj* • Violent means using force to hurt or attack: *A woman jailed for life for murdering her violent husband has appealed against the conviction.* ○ *Don't be so violent towards your brother.* ○ *Edward has a violent nature.* ○ *A violent crime is committed in the United States every 17 seconds.* • Violent also refers to a situation in which people are hurt: *There was a violent clash/confrontation between rival supporters after the match.* ○ *There has been a series of violent incidents in the prison in the last few weeks.* ○ *These figures show that we are becoming an increasingly violent society.* ○ *The more violent scenes in the film were cut when it was shown on television.* ○ *Her family are still trying to come to terms with her violent death* (=death caused suddenly and unexpectedly by the use of physical force, esp. murder). • Violent can mean very strong in effect: *Mary has a violent temper.* ○ *A violent thunderstorm caused severe flooding.* ○ *There was a violent explosion when the gas pipe burst.* ○ *The speaker launched into a violent attack* (=spoke forcefully against) *the government's policies.* • *(fig. slightly disapproving) She was wearing a violent* (=extremely bright) *pink sweater.*

vi·o·lent·ly /ˈvaɪə·lənt·li/ *adv* • Violently means in a forceful way that causes people to be hurt: *The fans violently attacked their rival supporters.* ○ *He claimed to have been violently assaulted/beaten while he was in detention.* ○ *The demonstration was violently suppressed.* • Violently can mean strongly or extremely: *I violently disagree with what you say.* ○ *They are violently opposed to the plans.* ○ *Alice is violently jealous of her new baby sister.* ○ *I was violently sick last night.*

vi·o·let COLOUR /ˈvaɪə·lət/ *adj, n* [C/U] (having) a bluish purple colour • See also ULTRAVIOLET.

vi·o·let PLANT /ˈvaɪə·lət/ *n* [C] a small plant with pleasant-smelling purple, blue or white flowers

vi·o·lin /ˌvaɪəˈlɪn/ *n* [C] a wooden musical instrument with four strings which is held against the neck and played by moving a BOW (=stick with hairs fixed to it) across the strings • *The violin is the highest-sounding instrument in the violin family, the others being the cello and the viola.* • *She plays the violin in an orchestra.* • PIC **Musical instruments**

vi·o·lin·ist /ˌvaɪəˈlɪn·ɪst/ *n* [C] • *He's a violinist* (=plays a violin).

vi·o·lin·cel·lo /£ˌvaɪə·lənˈtʃel·əʊ, $-oʊ/ *n* [C] *pl* **cellos** *fml for* CELLO

vi·o·lon·cel·lo /£ˌvaɪə·lənˈtʃel·əʊ, $-oʊ/ *n pl* **violoncellos** *fml* a CELLO

VIP /ˌviː·aɪˈpiː/ *n* [C] a very important person; a person who is treated better than ordinary people because they are famous or influential in some way • *They were in the VIP* **lounge** *at the airport.* • *We were given the full VIP* **treatment**.

vi·per /£ˈvaɪ·pər, $-pɚ/ *n* [C] a small poisonous snake, or *(fig. literary)* a very unpleasant person whom you can not trust • *Vipers are found all over the world except in Australia.* • *(fig.) When I started my new job, I didn't realize that I was walking into a nest of vipers.*

vi·ra·go /£vɪˈrɑː·gəʊ, $-ˈreɪ·goʊ/ *n* [C] *pl* **viragos** or **viragoes** *dated disapproving* a fierce, unpleasant woman who shouts a lot • *When you say to people that you're a feminist, they expect you to be some sort of virago.* • *The poor man has a virago of a wife.*

vi·ral /ˈvaɪ·rəl/ *adj* [not gradable] See at VIRUS SMALL ORGANISM

vir·gin /£ˈvɜː·dʒɪn, $ˈvɜːr-/ *n* [C] someone who has never had sex • *She remained a virgin till she was over thirty.* • *D'you think he's still a virgin?* • *"Like a Virgin"* (title of a song by Madonna, 1984)

vir·gin /£ˈvɜː·dʒɪn, $ˈvɜːr-/ *adj* [not gradable] • *a virgin bride* • Virgin can be used of forests and areas of land which have not yet been cultivated or used by people: *The railway is being extended into areas of virgin* **forest**. ○ *Antarctica is virgin* **territory**, *waiting to be exploited.* ○ *(fig.) The television company is moving into virgin* **territory** (=a new area of activity) *by producing programmes of this type.* • *(literary)* Virgin can also be used to mean pure and not spoilt, esp. when referring to something white: *a virgin sheet of paper* (=one with nothing written on it) ○ *the virgin* (=pure white) *snow* ○ *She was dressed in virgin-white.* • Virgin is also used to refer to oil, esp. **olive oil**, which is obtained directly from pressing the fruit, rather than by using heat: **extra** *virgin olive oil*

vir·gin·al /£ˈvɜː·dʒɪ·nəl, $ˈvɜːr-/ *adj* • *virginal innocence/modesty/purity* • *a virginal blush*

vir·gi·ni·ty /£vəˈdʒɪn·ɪ·ti, $vɚˈdʒɪn·ə·t̬i/ *n* [U] • *She* **lost** *her virginity at the age of sixteen.* • *Here in the West, virginity is no longer as highly valued as it once was.* • *The white of the bride's dress is meant to symbolize virginity.*

vir·gi·ni·a creep·er /£vəˈdʒɪn·jə, $vɚ-/, *Am also* **wood·bine** *n* [U] a VINE (=climbing plant) often grown on walls, the leaves of which become dark red in autumn

Vir·go /£ˈvɜː·gəʊ, $ˈvɜːr·goʊ/ *n* [not after *the*] *pl* **Virgos** the sixth sign of the ZODIAC, relating to the period 23 August to 22 September, represented by a young woman, or a person born during this period • *People born* **under** *Virgo* (=during this period) *are supposed to be highly critical.* [U] • *My mother and sister are Virgos.* [C]

Vir·go·an /£vɜːˈgəʊ·ən, $vɜːrˈgoʊ-/ *n, adj* [not gradable] • *Several of my friends are Virgoans.* [C] • *Perfectionism is a Virgoan trait.*

vir·ile /£ˈvɪr·aɪl, $-əl/ *adj approving* (of a man, esp. a young man) full of sexual strength and energy in a way that is manly and attractive, or *(fig.)* powerful and energetic • *She likes her men young and virile.* • *He is tall, weather-beaten, short-haired and virile, not remotely effeminate.* • *(fig.) In this role, Durante is able to give full expression to that wonderfully virile* **voice**.

vi·ril·i·ty /£vɪˈrɪl·ɪ·ti, $vəˈrɪl·ə·t̬i/ *n* [U] *approving* • *He dismissed Tate as 'just another middle-aged poet obsessed by the virility of youth'.* • *In the American memory, John F. Kennedy is forever young, the image of the virility of power.* • *(fig.) If a country's foreign trade is a measure of its economic virility* (=strength), *this country looks sadly impotent.*

vir·ol·o·gy /£vaɪəˈrɒl·ə·dʒi, $vaɪˈrɑː·lə-/ *n* [U] the scientific study of viruses and the diseases that they cause

vir·tu·al /£ˈvɜː·tju·əl, $ˈvɜːr-/ *adj* [not gradable] almost, even if not exactly or in every way • *Ten years of incompetent government had brought about the virtual collapse of the country's economy.* • *Now that the talks have broken down, war in the region looks like a virtual certainty.* • *She was a virtual unknown when she was chosen for the part.* • *Nowadays, television has a virtual* **monopoly** *over cultural life.* • *Snow brought the whole of Guernsey to a virtual* **standstill** *yesterday.* • **Virtual reality** is a set of images and sounds produced by a computer which seem to represent a place or a situation in which a person experiencing it can take part. • Ⓔ

vir·tu·al·ly /£ˈvɜː·tju·ə·li, $ˈvɜːr-/ *adv* [not gradable] • *Their twins are virtually* (=almost) *identical.* • *It used to be virtually impossible to find vegetarian restaurants outside the major cities, but it's much easier now.* • *That wine stain on my shirt has virtually disappeared.* • *Unemployment in this part of the country is virtually non-existent.* • *On the carton, the milk is described as 'virtually fat-free'.*

vir·tue GOODNESS /£ˈvɜː·tjuː, $ˈvɜːr-/ *n* a good moral quality in a person, or the general quality of goodness in a person • *Patience is a virtue.* [C] • *Modesty seems to me to be a very overrated virtue.* [C] • *(fml) In fairy tales, virtue is always* **rewarded** *whereas in real life it very often isn't.* [U] • *"Virtue is its own reward"* (the Roman poet Ovid in *Ex Ponto*, 43 BC - c.AD17) • Compare vice.

vir·tu·ous /£ˈvɜː·tju·əs, $ˈvɜːr-/ *adj* • Virtuous means possessing good moral qualities: *I've been up working since 6 o'clock this morning so I'm feeling very virtuous.* ○ *He described them as a virtuous and hard-working people.* ○ *Who wants to read about virtuous people – they're boring.* • *(disapproving)* Virtuous can also describe a person who thinks himself or herself morally better than other people: *I'm convinced he only does that charity work so that he can* *feel virtuous.* ○ *He disliked intensely what he called 'the virtuous tendency' in the socialist party.* • (RUS)

vir·tu·ous·ly /£'vɜː·tju·ə·sli, $'vɜːr-/ *adv*

vir·tue [ADVANTAGE] /£'vɜː·tjuː, $'vɜːr-/ *n* (an) advantage or benefit • *The virtue* **of** *having such a small car is that you can park it easily.* [C] • *It always looks odd to see an actress on TV* **extolling** (=praising) *the virtues* **of** *washing-up liquid.* [C] • *Would there be any virtue in taking an earlier train?* [U] • To **make a virtue (out) of** something, esp. a bad situation, is to use it to your advantage, knowing that you can not change the situation: *I had a couple of months to spare between jobs so I thought I'd make a virtue of* **necessity** *by acquiring a few new skills.*

vir·tue [BECAUSE OF] /£'vɜː·tjuː, $'vɜːr-/ *n* [U] **by virtue of** *fml* because of; as a result of • *She succeeded by virtue of her tenacity rather than her talent.* • *Unique by virtue of its location, charm and quality of service, this is one of Paris's most exclusive hotels.* • *He believes that it's wrong that some people should enjoy wealth, privilege, influence and power solely by virtue of an accident of birth.*

vir·tu·o·so /£,vɜː·tju'əʊ·səʊ, £-zəʊ, $,vɜːr·tʃu'oʊ·soʊ/ *n* [C] *pl* **virtuosos** or **virtuosi** /£,vɜː·tju'əʊ·si, £-zi, $,vɜːr·tʃu'oʊ·si/ a person who is extremely skilled at something, especially at playing an instrument or performing • *Famous mainly for his wonderful voice, Cole was also a virtuoso* **on** *the piano/a virtuoso pianist.* • *The Times critic described her dancing as 'a virtuoso* **performance** *of quite dazzling accomplishment'.* • *The world's greatest tenor treated us to a virtuoso* **display** *of his abundant talent.* • *Clay was a virtuoso* **of** *politics.*

vir·tu·os·i·ty /£,vɜː·tju'ɒs·ɪ·ti, $,vɜːr·tʃu'ɑː·sə·ṭi/ *n* [U] *fml* • *He is a violinist of quite remarkable technical virtuosity.* • *Dancing once again with the Royal Ballet, she gave a performance of exquisite virtuosity.*

vir·u·lent /'vɪr·jʊ·lᵊnt/ *adj* (of a disease or poison) dangerous and spreading or having an effect very quickly • *A particularly virulent* **strain** *of flu has recently claimed a number of lives in the US.* • *(fml)* Virulent can also mean full of hate and fierce opposition: *Several virulent* **attacks** *have been made on ethnic minorities in the area.* ○ *A virulent* **critic** *of US foreign policy, he has made himself very unpopular in certain circles.* ○ *She is very virulent* **about** *her former employer.*

vir·u·lence /'vɪr·jʊ·lᵊnts/ *n* [U] • *The severity and virulence* (=danger and speed of spreading) *of the disease are causing great concern in medical circles.* • *(fml) We are witnessing racism of a virulence* (=strength of hatred and opposition) *that we haven't seen in Europe since the 1940s.*

vi·rus [SMALL ORGANISM] /'vaɪ·rəs/ *n* [C] a very small organism, smaller than a bacterium, which causes disease in humans, animals and plants • *a chicken pox/flu/herpes/mumps virus* • *In humans, viruses cause such illnesses as the common cold, flu and measles.* • *Evidence suggested that the AIDS virus (HIV) was* **spreading** *very quickly among the heterosexual community.* • *Most people who get liver cancer are afflicted with the hepatitis B virus.* • Virus also means a disease caused by a virus: *I don't know exactly what's wrong with her – I think it's some sort of virus.*

vi·ral /'vaɪ·rᵊl/ *adj* [not gradable] • *The continuing search for drugs to combat viral* **infections** *presents modern medicine with one of its greatest challenges.* • *It is extremely difficult to make effective anti-viral drugs.* • *Genetic engineering will eventually produce plants resistant both to pests and viral disease.*

vi·rus [COMPUTER PROBLEM] /'vaɪ·rəs/ *n* [C] a hidden instruction in a computer program which is intended to introduce faults into a computer system and in so doing destroy information stored in it

vi·sa /'viː·zə/ *n* [C] an official mark made in a PASSPORT which allows you to enter or leave a particular country • *Do British people need a visa to visit Australia?* • *Under the old rules, she needed an* **exit** *visa every time she left the country.* • *He was refused an* **entry** *visa when invited to give a lecture in the United States 25 years ago.* • *I have to leave in June because my visa* **runs out/expires** *in June.* • *Visa restrictions in these countries have largely been lifted.*

vi·sage /'vɪz·ɪdʒ/ *n* [C] *literary* the face • *(fig.) Veiled beneath a cloud was the moon's pale visage.*

–vi·saged /-'vɪz·ɪdʒd/ *combining form literary* • *He emerged,* **grim**-*visaged, from the meeting.*

vis–a–vis /,viz·ə'viː/ *prep fml* in relation to, or in comparison with • *Vis-a-vis the meeting with Eves and Co, could we schedule it for the week after the conference?* • *I've got to speak to James Lewis vis-a-vis the arrangements for Thursday.* • *The decline in the power of local vis-a-vis* (= in comparison with) *central government does not disturb them unduly.*

vis·ce·ra /£'vɪs·ᵊr·ə, $'-ɚ-/ *pl n specialized* the large organs inside the body, including the heart, stomach, lungs and INTESTINES

vis·ce·ral /£'vɪs·ᵊr·ᵊl, $'-ɚ-/ *adj* [not gradable] *specialized*

vis·ce·ral /£'vɪs·ᵊr·ᵊl, $'-ɚ-/ *adj literary* based on deep feeling and emotional reactions rather than on reason or thought • *His approach to acting is visceral rather than intellectual.* • *She has nothing of the cool detachment of the critic – her responses to the paintings are passionate and visceral.* • *Between these two ethnic groups there exists a visceral hatred of one another.* • *The film fails to convey the visceral excitement of the book.*

vis·cose /£'vɪs·kəʊs, $-koʊs/ *n* [U] a smooth material similar to silk but made from plant substances

vis·count *male, female* **vis·coun·tess** /'vaɪ·kaʊnt, ˌvaɪ·kaʊn'tes/ *n* [C] (the title of) a person of high social rank • *The viscount, now aged 63, inherited his title at 15 while at Eton.* • *Viscount Linley was present at the ball, as was his wife.* • A viscountess is a woman who has the rank of viscount, or a woman who is married to a viscount.

vis·cous /'vɪs·kəs/ *adj* (of a liquid) thick and sticky; not flowing easily • *The oil in its thick and viscous form can kill birds and animals by poisoning them.*

vis·cos·i·ty /£vɪ'skɒs·ɪ·ti, $-'skɑː·sə·ṭi/ *n* [U] • *The viscosity* (=thickness) *of a liquid generally decreases when you heat it.*

vise /vaɪs/ *n* [C] *Am for* VICE [TOOL]

vi·si·ble /'vɪz·ɪ·bḷ/ *adj* able to be seen • *You should wear something light when you're cycling at night so that you're more visible.* • *The writing on the tombstone was* **barely** *visible.* • *Even from Britain the Milky Way is* **clearly** *visible if you can get away from artificial lights.* • *There are few visible* **signs** *of the illness that kept her in hospital for so long.* • *The bullet holes in the wall are a visible* **reminder** *of the bloody massacre that took place here a month ago.* • *Be honest now – do I have a visible panty line in these trousers?* • *The comet should be visible* **to the naked eye** *as a fuzzy patch three times the size of the Moon.* • Visible also means able or tending to attract public attention and be noticed: *In a very short period of time, she has become a* **highly** *visible national leader.* ○ *A* **highly** *visible public-transport strike put the government in a difficult position.*

vi·si·bly /'vɪz·ɪ·bli/ *adv* • *It's described as a moisturising treatment which leaves the skin visibly* (=able to be seen as being) *fresher.* • *The Princess, visibly* (=obviously) *moved, kept her head bowed during the ceremony.*

vi·si·bil·i·ty /£,vɪz·ɪ'bɪl·ɪ·ti, $-ə·ṭi/ *n* [U] • Visibility refers to the clearness with which objects can be seen outside, as influenced by the weather conditions: *The ski report for Andorra was for heavy snow and* **poor** *visibility.* ○ *Fog is still causing problems, and visibility in some areas is down to two metres.* • Visibility also refers to the degree to which something is seen by the public: *The increasing visibility of the nation's poor and homeless has forced the government into taking action.*

vi·sion [SIGHT] /'vɪʒ·ᵊn/ *n* [U] the ability to see • *She has very little vision in her left eye.* • *Since the accident, he has suffered from memory loss and impaired vision.* • *Some drugs cause drowsiness, others a dry mouth and blurred vision.* • *(fig.) To all his writing Gibson brought a* **breadth of** *vision* (=he considered many different subjects in many different ways) *and a depth of historical understanding.* • [LP] **Eye and seeing**

vi·sion [MENTAL IMAGE] /'vɪʒ·ᵊn/ *n* [C] an imagined mental image of something • *We see in his novels his sinister, almost apocalyptic, vision* **of** *the dark, destructive forces at work in human nature.* • *These young people reject the past without having a vision* **of** *the future.* • *For me, the smell of coconut oil* **conjures up** *visions* **of** *palm trees waving in the breeze.* • *Johnny was late home and, as usual, I had visions* **of** *him* (= anxiously imagined him) *lying dead in some alley.* • A vision can be a religious experience or it can be caused by mental illness or by taking drugs: *A sixteenth century nun living in this valley had visions in which the angel Gabriel appeared to her.* ○ *People suffering from schizophrenia sometimes report having visions.*

vi·sion·a·ry /£'vɪʒ·ᵊn·ri, $-er·i/ *n* [C] • A visionary is a person who has a religious or spiritual experience in which they see a holy person who is not living or they see a holy event that cannot be explained scientifically: *Maria* *was regarded as a visionary in the village after she repeatedly saw the statue of the Virgin Mary weeping.* ○ *The question remains though – was he a visionary or a madman?*

vi•sion•a•ry /£ˈvɪʒ·ᵊn·ri, $-er·i/ *adj* • *He described the visionary experiences that he had had on LSD.* • *Other persons taking this drug discover a world of visionary* (= imagined) *beauty.*

vi•sion VIEW OF THE FUTURE /ˈvɪʒ·ᵊn/ *n* [U] the ability to imagine how a country, society, industry, etc. will develop in the future and to plan in a suitable way • *He didn't have the mental agility or vision required for a senior politician.* • *The new theatre company director is a person of great artistic vision.* • *As a prime minister, he lacked the strategic vision of, say, someone like Churchill.*

vi•sion•a•ry /£ˈvɪʒ·ᵊn·ri, $-er·i/ *n* [C] • A visionary is a person who possesses the ability to imagine how a country, society, industry, etc. will develop in the future and to plan in a suitable way: *She was a social reformer and a great visionary.*

vi•sion•a•ry /£ˈvɪʒ·ᵊn·ri, $-er·i/ *adj* • *The current administration shows few signs of any visionary thinking.*

vi•sion BEAUTIFUL SIGHT /ˈvɪʒ·ᵊn/ *n esp. humorous* (used when referring to a person) a beautiful and splendid sight • *And that vision* **of loveliness** *over there is his wife.* • *She emerged from the bedroom, a vision* **in** *cream silk.*

vi•sit *(obj)* /ˈvɪz·ɪt/ *v* to go to a place in order to look at it, or to a person in order to spend time with them • *We visited a few galleries while we were in Prague.* [T] • *I thought we'd better go and visit my aunt while we were in Belgium.* [T] • *My grandma is always complaining that we don't go to visit her enough.* [T] • *Are you going to come and visit me when I'm in hospital?* [T] • *When did you last visit the dentist?* [T] • *We're not staying here – we're just visiting for the afternoon.* [I] • *(Am) I was hoping to visit* **with** (= spend some time talking socially with) *Katie while I was in town.* [I] • *(Am) My parents are visiting* **with** (= staying with) *us this weekend.* [I] • **Visiting hours** are the times that you are allowed to go and spend time with someone who is in a hospital, prison, etc.: *Visiting hours are between 6.00 and 9.00 p.m.*

vi•sit /ˈvɪz·ɪt/ *n* [C] • *Do you think we'll have time to fit in a visit* **to** *the space museum when we're in Washington?* • *I think I'll* **pay** *a visit* **to** *the hairdresser's while I'm in town.* • *I may have to cut short my visit if Peter rings.* • *We're expecting a visit from the doctor at around midday.* • *We had a visit from the school inspector last week.* • *I can't stop for a cup of tea – this is just a* **flying** (= very short) *visit.*

vi•sit•a•tion /ˌvɪz·ɪˈteɪ·ʃᵊn/ *n* • *He explained that the hospital had strict policies about visitation* (= the act of visiting). [U] • *On May 13, 1917 three young shepherd children reported a visitation* (= a visit) **from** *the Virgin Mary.* [C] • *(esp. humorous)* A visitation is an official visit from someone important: *We're awaiting a visitation from the inspector.* [C] • *(Am)* Visitation is the act of a DIVORCED (= previously but no longer married) parent spending time with the child(ren) he or she no longer lives with, at agreed times and under agreed conditions: *The court ordered that she only be allowed* **supervised** *visitation.* [U] ○ *The mother had earlier agreed to visitation* **rights**, *but then began restricting the father's time with the child.*

vi•sit•or /£ˈvɪz·ɪ·təʳ, $-t̬ɚ/ *n* [C] • *Ben, you've got some visitors.* • *My grandma is always complaining she doesn't get enough visitors.* • *The family settled in a quiet street near rue Mouffetard, where Paul Celan was a frequent visitor.* • *Every year Bolton Abbey receives over 100 000 visitors.* • *Visitors are asked to sign in at reception.* • *No, he doesn't work here – he's got a visitor's badge on his jacket.* • A **visitors' book** is a book sometimes found in a hotel or a place of interest in which people are asked to write their name, address and anything they would like to say about the quality of what they have experienced.

vi•sit *obj* **on/u•pon** *obj v prep* [T usually passive] *old use or fml* to force (something unpleasant) on someone or something • *He left in 1983, horrified by the devastation that warfare and famine had visited on his homeland.* • *You seem to think that all the evils visited on this society are caused by television.*

vi•sit•a•tion /ˌvɪz·ɪˈteɪ·ʃᵊn/ *n* [C] *fml* • A visitation is an event which is considered to be a message or a punishment from God: *The poor harvest was seen as a visitation* **of** *God.*

vi•sor /£ˈvaɪ·zəʳ, $-zɚ/ *n* [C] a movable part of a HELMET (= hard protective head cover) which can be lowered to cover the face, or a curved piece of stiff material which is worn above the eyes to give protection from strong light from the sun

vi•sta /ˈvɪs·tə/ *n* [C] a view, esp. a splendid view from a high position • *After a hard climb, we were rewarded by a picture-postcard vista* **of** *rolling hills under a deep blue summer sky.* • *Wherever you stand in the 100-hectare grounds of Versailles, you get a breathtaking vista.* • *(fig.) As leader, he* **opened up** *exciting vistas of* (= new possibilities for) *global co-operation.* • *(fig.) In an already troubled region, fresh conflict like this raises frightening vistas.*

vi•sual /ˈvɪʒ·u·əl/ *adj* relating to seeing • *These animals have excellent visual ability/acuity.* • *The tests examined the speed with which a visual stimulus was transmitted along nerves to the visual cortex of the brain.* • *Unfortunately the play is stronger on visual impact and theatrical effect than it is on acting.* • *The film has some very powerful visual imagery.* • A **visual aid** is something that you are shown, such as a picture, film or map, in order to help you understand or remember information: *Visual aids can often help you understand something better than just being told about it.* • The **visual arts** are the arts of painting and SCULPTURE, rather than literature and music: *I think that schools often put too little emphasis on learning about the visual and performing arts.* • See also VDU.

vi•sual•ly /ˈvɪʒ·u·ə·li/ *adv* • *Guide dogs open up the lives of the blind or visually* **impaired**. • *There are now several mainstream schools where visually handicapped children follow an ordinary curriculum.* • *Mitchell's production, though highly polished and visually striking, lacks depth.* • *Books for children have to be visually very exciting.*

vi•sual•ize *obj, Br and Aus usually* **-ise** /ˈvɪʒ·u·ᵊl·aɪz/ *v* [T] • To visualize something or someone is to imagine or remember them by forming a picture in your mind: *Describe the sort of jacket you're looking for again – I'm having problems visualizing it.* ○ *I know it's somewhere off Silver Street but I just can't visualize where it is.* ○ *I was so surprised when he turned up – I'd visualized someone much older.*

vi•sual•i•za•tion, *Br and Aus usually* **-i•sa•tion** /ˌvɪʒ·u·ᵊl·aɪˈzeɪ·ʃᵊn/ *n* [U] • *He believed that real art was about the visualization of fantasy and dream.*

vi•ta /£ˈviː·tə, $-t̬ə/ *n* [C] *pl* **vitas** *Am infml for* CV

vi•tal /£ˈvaɪ·tᵊl, $-t̬ᵊl/ *adj* necessary for the success or continued existence of something; extremely important • *Most people view the existence of a strong opposition as vital* **to** *a healthy democracy.* • *"Was anything interesting said at the meeting?" "Nothing of vital* **importance**.*"* • *"The United States must be prepared to deal with hostile actions against our citizens or our vital* **interests**,*" Carter added.* • *Trust is a vital* **element/component** *in any close relationship.* • *I was going to make a lemon tart until I realised I was missing one of the vital* **ingredients**. • *The kidney plays a vital* **role/part** *in the removal of waste products from the blood.* • **It's** *absolutely vital* **that** *you get that form sent off by the twenty-third of this month.* [+ *that* clause] • **It** *is vital* **to** *get medical supplies to the area as soon as possible.* [+ *to* infinitive] • See also **vital** at VITALITY.

vi•tal•ly /£ˈvaɪ·tᵊl·i, $-t̬ᵊl-/ *adv* • *It's not vitally* **important** *that we get extra funding for the project but it would help.* • *Will it matter vitally if I get to the meeting half an hour late?*

vi•tal•i•ty /£vaɪˈtæl·ɪ·ti, $-ə·t̬i/ *n* [U] *approving* energy and strength • *According to the packet, these vitamin pills will restore lost vitality.* • *The election of a 38-year-old leader will doubtless help the Democrats to project an image of youth and vitality.* • *It is hoped that the opening of two new factories will add to the economic vitality of the region.*

vi•tal /£ˈvaɪ·tᵊl, $-t̬ᵊl/ *adj fml approving* • *He had never felt so vital* (= energetic) *and full of life.* • Vital also means relating to life: *This system of Taoist physical and breathing exercises has the object of increasing a person's vital* **energy**. • The **vital organs** are the main organs inside the body, such as the heart, lungs and brain, which are necessary for existence. • *(specialized)* **Vital signs** are such things as a person's body temperature and the rate at which they are breathing and their heart is beating: *The babies in this unit have various devices attached to them which* **monitor** *the vital signs.* • **Vital statistics** are a group of official facts which show such things as the number of births, deaths and marriages in a particular country, area etc. and the length of time that people live. • *(humorous dated)* A woman's **vital statistics** are the measurements of her breasts, waist and hips.

vi·ta·min /£'vɪt·ə·mɪn, $'vaɪ·t̬ə-/ *n* any of a group of natural substances which are necessary in small amounts for growth and good health and which must be obtained from food or pills as they cannot usually be produced by the body • The various different vitamins are named by a letter from the alphabet: *Vitamins A,B,C,D,E,G,H,K,P* ○ *Vitamin A is found in such foods as carrots, butter and egg-yolk.* [U] ○ *Vitamin B refers to a group of vitamins, all of which assist in the working of various enzymes.* [U] ○ *Vitamin K is needed to help the blood clot.* [U] • *I don't like liver, but it's full of vitamins.* [C] • *Pregnant women often take a vitamin supplement.* • *Vitamin* **deficiencies** *can lead to various diseases.* • *My mother takes a whole handful of vitamin* **pills** *at breakfast.*

vi·ti·ate *obj* /'vɪʃ·i·eɪt/ *v* [T usually passive] *fml* to destroy or weaken (something) • *He said that American military power should never again be vitiated by political concerns.*

vi·ti·cul·ture /£'vɪt·ɪˌkʌl·tʃəʳ, $-t̬ɪˌkʌl·tʃɚ/ *n* [U] *specialized* the growing of GRAPES, or the science or study of this

vi·tre·ous /'vɪt·ri·əs/ *adj* made of or similar to glass • *vitreous china/enamel*

vi·tri·ol /'vɪt·ri·əl/ *n* [U] fierce hate and anger expressed through severe criticism • *He is a writer who has often been criticized by the press but never before with such vitriol.* • *While his administration has been attacked, the President has been spared the personal vitriol regularly directed at his predecessor.* • *She came out with a stream of vitriol about her former husband.*

vi·tri·ol·ic /£ˌvɪt·ri'ɒl·ɪk, $-'ɑː·lɪk/ *adj* • *He launched a vitriolic* **attack** *on the prime minister, accusing him of shielding corrupt friends.* • *As a newspaper columnist, she was widely feared for her vitriolic pen.*

vi·tri·ol·i·cal·ly /£ˌvɪt·ri'ɒl·ɪ·kli, $-'ɑː·lɪ-/ *adv*

vi·tro /£'viː·trəʊ, $-troʊ/ *n* See IN VITRO

vi·tu·pe·ra·tive /£vaɪ'tjuː·pᵊr·ə·tɪv, $-'tuː·pə·reɪ·t̬ɪv/ *adj fml* (of a spoken or written attack) full of angry accusations • *Miss Snowden yesterday launched a vituperative attack on her ex-boss and former lover.* • *His most vituperative criticism is reserved for the party leader, whom he clearly despises.*

vi·tu·pe·ra·tion /£vaɪˌtjuː·pᵊr'eɪ·ʃᵊn, $-ˌtuː·pə'reɪ-/ *n* [U] *fml* • *Her speech was one long stream of vituperation.*

vi·va EXAMINATION /'vaɪ·və/, **vi·va vo·ce** /£ˌvaɪ·və'vəʊ·tʃi, $-'voʊ-/ *n* [C] a spoken examination for a college qualification

vi·va APPROVAL /'viː·və/ *exclamation esp. Am* used to express approval or good wishes • *Throngs of his supporters were shouting "Viva, Ollie, viva!"*

vi·va·cious /vɪ'veɪ·ʃəs/ *adj approving* (esp. of a woman or girl) attractively full of energy and enthusiasm • *He brought along his wife, a vivacious blonde, some twenty years his junior.* • *She had a wonderfully vivacious manner.* • *The vivacious and colourful street life of Bangkok was a tourist attraction in itself.*

vi·va·cious·ly /vɪ'veɪ·ʃə·sli/ *adv approving* • *The role was vivaciously acted by Ms Collins.*

vi·vac·i·ty /£vɪ'væs·ɪ·ti, $-ə·t̬i/ *n* [U] *approving* • *It was for her wit and vivacity that she was celebrated rather than her beauty.*

vi·vid /'vɪv·ɪd/ *adj* very brightly coloured or (of descriptions, memories, etc.) producing very clear, powerful and detailed images in the mind • *She was wearing a vivid pink shirt.* • *Parts of my childhood are so vivid* (=producing clear images) **to** *me that they could be memories of yesterday.* • *He gave a very vivid and often shocking account/description of his time in prison.* • *I don't have very vivid memories of that period – it's all a bit vague.* • *She's one of those people with a very vivid* **imagination** *– every time she hears a noise she's convinced it's someone breaking in.*

vi·vid·ly /'vɪv·ɪd·li/ *adv* • *I vividly remember my first day at school.* • *His third novel depicts very vividly the horrors of modern warfare.*

vi·vid·ness /'vɪv·ɪd·nəs/ *n* [U] • *It was the vividness of the dream that was so extraordinary.*

vi·vi·pa·rous /£vɪ'vɪp·ᵊr·əs, $'-ɚ-/ *adj* [not gradable] *specialized* giving birth to young that have already developed inside the mother's body rather than producing eggs

vi·vi·sec·tion /ˌvɪv·ɪ'sek·ʃᵊn/ *n* [U] the cutting up or other use of living animals in tests which are intended to increase our knowledge of human diseases and the effects of using particular drugs • *I buy this make-up because I know that vivisection hasn't been used in testing it.* • *But what are the alternatives to vivisection?*

vi·vi·sec·tion·ist /ˌvɪv·ɪ'sek·ʃᵊn·ɪst/ *n* [C] • A vivisectionist is a person who is involved in the activity of, or believes in the use of, vivisection: *The scientific establishment says being a scientist and an* **anti-***vivisectionist are incompatible positions.*

vi·xen /'vɪk·sᵊn/ *n* [C] a female FOX, or *(dated)* an unpleasant woman

viz /vɪz/ *adv* [not gradable] *dated* used, esp. in written English, when you want to give more detail or be more exact about something you have just written • *We both shared the same ambition, viz, to make a lot of money and to retire at 40.*

vo·cab /£'vəʊ·kæb, $'voʊ-/ *n* [U] *infml* VOCABULARY • *Did you manage to pick up much Italian vocab when you were in Rome?*

vo·cab·u·la·ry /£və'kæb·jʊ·lᵊr·i, $voʊ'kæb·jə·ler-/ *n* all the words used by a particular person or all the words which exist in a particular language or subject • *By the age of two a child will have a vocabulary of about two hundred words.* [C] • *Reading certainly helps to* **widen** *your vocabulary.* [C] • *You do know that swearing is a sign of a limited vocabulary, don't you?* [C] • *New words are coming into the vocabulary* (=all the words used in a particular language) *all the time.* [C] • *It is said that English has one of the largest vocabularies* (=total number of words) *of any language.* [C] • *Every week our French teacher gives us a list of vocabulary* (=words) *to learn.* [U] • *Computing, like any subject, has its own vocabulary* (=set of words that it used). [C] • *(fig. humorous) Did you say 'tact'? The word isn't in his vocabulary* (=He has none of this quality)*!* [C]

vo·cal OF THE VOICE /£'vəʊ·kᵊl, $'voʊ-/ *adj* [not gradable] relating to or produced by the voice, either in singing or speaking • *The six principal roles in this opera have an average vocal* **range** *of two octaves.* • *As a singer, he is now at the height of his vocal powers.* • *Haydn's works include 104 symphonies, about 50 concertos, 12 masses and various vocal pieces.* • *The vocal sounds made by young babies are very similar to those used in early speech.* • The **vocal cords/vocal chords** are a pair of folds at the upper end of the throat whose edges move quickly backwards and forwards and produce sound when air from the lungs moves over them.

vo·cal /£'vəʊ·kᵊl, $'voʊ-/ *n* [C often pl] • A vocal is the singing in a piece of popular music: *The vocals are shared by two members of the band.* ○ *Is that Tamsin Palmer* **on** *vocals* (=singing)*?* ○ *She usually sings backing vocals, but tonight she's the lead vocal* (=singer).

vo·cal·ly /£'vəʊ·kᵊl·i, $'voʊ-/ *adv* [not gradable] • *It really is the most impressive performance, both vocally and theatrically.*

vo·cal·ist /£'vəʊ·kᵊl·ɪst, $'voʊ-/ *n* [C] • A vocalist is a person who sings esp. with a group who play popular music: *a lead/backing vocalist* ○ *She won the Grammy Award for Best Female Vocalist in 1976.*

vo·cal·ize /£'vəʊ·kᵊl·aɪz, $'voʊ·kə·laɪz/ *v*

vo·cal OFTEN HEARD /£'vəʊ·kᵊl, $'voʊ-/ *adj* often expressing opinions and complaints in speech • *During these years, suffrage demands by women became increasingly vocal and difficult to ignore.* • *The Independence Party is a small but vocal* **minority**. • *He had always been a very vocal* **critic** *of the president.*

vo·cal·ly /£'vəʊ·kᵊl·i, $'voʊ-/ *adv* • *Yeats vocally opposed censorship.*

vo·ca·tion /£vəʊ'keɪ·ʃᵊn, $voʊ-/ *n* a type of work that you feel you are suited to doing and to which you should give all your time and energy, or the feeling of suitability itself • *"We need teachers who regard their profession as a vocation, not just a job," said the Minister.* [C] • *It was only when he turned to politics that he felt he'd* **found** *his vocation.* [C] • *You've* **missed** *your vocation, Liz, you should have been a nurse!* [C] • *He began to feel that the church was his* **true** *vocation and at the age of 30 joined a seminary.* [C] • *To work in medicine, you should* **have** *a vocation* (=feeling of suitability) **for** *it.* [C] • *She's a doctor by vocation* (=feeling of suitability). [U] • *They don't work with any sense of vocation* (=feeling of suitability), *merely for financial reward.* [U]

vo·ca·tion·al /£vəʊ'keɪ·ʃᵊn·ᵊl, $voʊ-/ *adj* providing skills and education that prepare you for a job • *The Swedes regard vocational* **training** *as a part of a youngster's education.* • *Most of my friends who went to* *college did vocational* **courses**, *like nursing.* • *The school I went to valued academic study above vocational education.*

vo·ca·tion·al·ly /£vəʊ'keɪ·ʃᵊn·ᵊl·i, $voʊ-/ *adv* • *He said that parents should be able to opt for either an academic or a vocationally oriented education for their children.*

vo·cif·er·ous /£və'sɪf·ᵊr·əs, $'-ɚ-/ *adj* (of people) repeatedly expressing opinions and complaints in speech, or (of demands, etc.) repeatedly and loudly made • *Local activist groups have become increasingly vociferous as the volume of traffic passing through the village has grown.* • *A vociferous* **opponent** *of gay rights, he is well-known for his right-wing views.* • *Vociferous* **objections** *have been raised to the plan.*

vo·cif·er·ous·ly /£və'sɪf·ᵊr·ə·sli, $'-ɚ-/ *adv* • *The Republican party has vociferously opposed any clemency for convicted terrorists.*

vod·ka /£'vɒd·kə, $'vɑːd-/ *n* a colourless strong alcoholic drink made from a variety of substances including grain and potatoes • *Vodka was originally made in Russia and Poland.* [U] • *"What would you like to drink?" "Some vodka and tonic please."* [U] • *This is my third vodka* (= glass of vodka). [C]

vogue /£vəʊg, $voʊg/ *n* a fashion or general liking, esp. one which is temporary • *In the 1920s, short hair for women became* **the** *vogue.* [U] • *I really don't understand the current vogue* **for** *buying all these ready-prepared meals – food tastes much better if you cook it yourself.* [C] • *The film created a vogue* **for** *1950s-style rock 'n roll.* [C] • *The postwar vogue* **for** *tearing down buildings virtually destroyed the city's architecture.* [C] • *She is a writer who has lately* **had**/*enjoyed (a) considerable vogue* (= been fashionable) *in France, though she is less well-known in Britain.* [C/U] • *The short hemline is very much* **in** *vogue* (= fashionable) *this spring.* [U] • *Platform heels are* **back in** *vogue* (= fashionable again). [U] • *The treatment that used to be given for this illness is now* **out of** *vogue* (= no longer fashionable). [U]

voice SOUNDS /vɔɪs/ *n* the sounds that are made when people speak or sing • *a loud/soft voice* [C] • *a low-pitched/high-pitched voice* [C] • *a booming/breathy/clear/deep/fruity/gravelly/husky/squeaky voice* [C] • *a baritone/soprano voice* [C] • *I could hear some hushed/muffled voices from inside the room.* [C] • *You could tell from her voice that she wasn't pleased.* [C] • *I didn't recognise his voice – he sounded different on the telephone.* [C] • *He has a wonderfully throaty voice – I could listen to him talk for hours.* [C] • *She's got one of those very harsh/rasping voices that goes right through your head.* [C] • *I thought I detected an irritable edge to your voice.* [C] • *I remember at school she had a lovely singing voice.* [C] • *"I don't know what you mean," said Fran* **in** *a quavering voice.* [C] • *Her voice* **lowered** *to a whisper.* [C] • *His voice* **trailed off/away**, *uncertain what Lucas would think of him.* [C] • *You'll have to* **raise** *your voice* (= speak louder) *if you want to be heard in here.* [C] • *I've got a cold and I think I'm* **losing** *my voice* (= becoming unable to speak). [C] • *He's at that age when his voice is* **breaking** (= changing from a boy's to a man's). [C] • *She's done a lot of work with voice-***activated** *computers.* • *Some day, voice-***recognition** *technology could make some telephone operator services obsolete.* • *(fig.) I wouldn't work for Peter if I were you – this is the voice* **of experience** *talking* (= I know because I have experienced it myself)*!* [U] • *(fig.) She just won't listen to the voice* **of reason** (= wise advice). [U] • If someone is **in** a particular type of voice, they sing in that way: *Well, choir, I trust we're all in* **good** *voice today!* [U] • To **give voice to** your thoughts, feelings, fears, etc. is to express them in words: *I always had doubts about the relationship, but I never gave voice to them.* • *(fml)* If a group of people express an opinion or decide something **with one voice** they all agree: *The committee decided with one voice to accept the proposal.* • A **voice box** is a LARYNX. • **Voice mail/Voice messaging** is an electronic telephone answering system used by businesses. • A **voice-over** on a television programme or film is the spoken words of a person that you cannot see: *Famous actors often provide voice-overs for wild-life documentaries.*

-voiced /-vɔɪst/ *combining form* • *I took my loud-voiced friend, Roz, with me to the party.* • *The gravel(ly)-voiced actor died today at the age of 89, at his home in Los Angeles.*

voice OPINION /vɔɪs/ *n* (the right to) an expression of opinion • *Unfortunately a strike was the only way of making our voices heard.* [C] • *There was only one dissenting voice.* [C] • *The committee represents the voice* **of** *the students.* [C] • *"We are strong at the local level, but lack* **a** *strong voice* (= way of expressing our opinions) *at the national level," said one member.* [U] • *Developing countries are demanding a stronger voice* (= right to express opinions) *in the debate.* [U] • *The community group was launched last August to give local people a voice.* [U] • *Her documentaries* **give** *voice* **to** (= express) *multiple points of view probably because she herself has seen life from many different angles.* [U] • A voice **within** you is your CONSCIENCE (= the part of you which tells you when you are doing something immoral): *A voice within him said he shouldn't be driving so fast.* [C] ○ *Suddenly this voice within her told her to stop being so stupid.* [C] • *"The voice of the people is the voice of God"* (from a letter to the Emperor Charlemagne from Alcuin, 735-804)

voice *obj* /vɔɪs/ *v* [T] • If you voice an opinion, idea or emotion, you say what you are thinking or feeling, usually with force: *The opposition leader has repeatedly voiced 'grave doubts' about the wisdom of the attack.* ○ *Leading educationalists have voiced their concern over the new proposals.* ○ *I have on several occasions voiced my objections to the plan but I have consistently been ignored.*

voice·less /'vɔɪ·sləs/ *adj* [not gradable] *literary* • A group of people who are voiceless lack the power or the legal right to express their opinions: *A committed socialist, he upheld the rights of the voiceless and the underprivileged.*

void EMPTY SPACE /vɔɪd/ *n* [C] a large hole or empty space, or *(fig.)* a feeling of unhappiness because someone or something is missing • *She stood at the edge of the chasm and stared into the void.* • *At the end of the opera, Tosca throws herself into the void by jumping off the castle walls.* • *Before Einstein, space was regarded as a formless void.* • *(fig.) They tried to describe their attempts to* **fill** *the void* **left** *by their son's death.* • *(fig.) She sensed the black void of despair inside him.*

void UNACCEPTABLE /vɔɪd/ *adj* [not gradable] having no legal authority and therefore unacceptable • *The country's constitution had been* **declared** *void by the UN Security Council many years before.* • *The race was* **declared** *void after it started too early.* • See also NULL AND VOID.

void *obj* /vɔɪd/ *v* [T] • *They claimed that the actions of the other party to the contract had voided* (= removed the legal force from) *the agreement.*

void WITHOUT /vɔɪd/ *adj* **void of** *literary* without; lacking in • *He's completely void of charm so far as I can see.*

voi·la /ˌvwɑː'lɑː/ *exclamation* used when showing to other people something that you have just made or obtained and are pleased with • *Corn tortillas can be cut into strips, fried until golden, and sprinkled with salt – voila! tortilla chips.*

vol /£vɒl, $vɑːl/ *n* [C] *abbreviation for* VOLUME

vol·a·tile /£'vɒl·ə·taɪl, $'vɑː·lə·t̬ᵊl/ *adj* likely to change suddenly and unexpectedly or suddenly become violent or angry • *Food and fuel prices are very volatile.* • *The volatile ethnic and religious mix in this region has led to a lot of conflict over the years.* • *The situation was made more volatile by the fact that people had been drinking a lot of alcohol.* • *Like many actors, he had a rather volatile temper and can't have been easy to live with.* • *She's a rather volatile tennis player.* • A liquid or solid substance that is volatile will change easily into a gas.

vol·a·til·i·ty /£ˌvɒl·ə'tɪl·ɪ·ti, $ˌvɑː·lə'tɪl·ə·t̬i/ *n* [U] • *There was little sign of serious volatility in financial markets yesterday.* • *The volatility of recent opinion polls means that no-one can really predict the results of next month's election.*

vol–au–vent /£'vɒl·ə·vɑ̃ː, $ˌvɔː·loʊ'vɑ̃ː/ *n* [C] a small, light, cup-shaped pastry case with a savoury sauce filling • *chicken/mushroom/prawn vol-au-vents*

vol·ca·no /£vɒl'keɪ·nəʊ, $vɑːl'keɪ·noʊ/ *n* [C] *pl* **volcanoes** or **volcanos** a mountain with a large circular hole at the top through which LAVA (= hot liquid rock), gases, steam and dust are or have been forced out • *an extinct/dormant volcano* • *an active volcano* • *Volcanoes discharge massive quantities of dust into the stratosphere.* • *Ash from the* **erupting** *Mount Pinatubo volcano in the Philippines reached Australian skies.*

vol·can·ic /£vɒl'kæn·ɪk, $vɑːl-/ *adj* [not gradable] • *volcanic ash/activity/rock* • *a volcanic island* • *That spring, El Chichon in Mexico produced one of the biggest volcanic* **eruptions** *of the century.*

vole /£vəʊl, $voʊl/ *n* [C] a small mouse-like animal with a thick body, short tail and small ears • *Voles usually live in fields or woods or near rivers.*

vo·li·tion /və'lɪʃ·ᵊn/ *n* [U] *fml* the power to make your own decisions • *The Minister wished it to be known that he had left the cabinet* **of** *his* **own** *volition* (= it was his decision). •

Of course I'll visit her, but **(out) of** *my* **own** *volition and not because I've been forced.*

vol·ley [BULLETS] /£'vɒl·i, $'vɑː·li/ *n* [C] a large number of bullets (seeming to be) fired at the same time • *Even as the funeral took place, guerrillas hidden nearby* **fired/let off** *a fresh volley* **of** *machine-gun fire.* • *(fig.) A volley* **of** (= a lot of quickly produced) *enquiries greeted the prime minister at this morning's question time.* • *(fig.) I'm afraid my proposal was met with a volley* (= a lot) **of** *criticisms.*

vol·ley [SPORTS SHOT] /£'vɒl·i, $'vɑː·li/ *n* [C] (in sports) a kick or hit in which a player returns a moving ball before it touches the ground • *Roberts scored with a stunning volley with his right foot.* • *That was a marvellous backhand volley.*

vol·ley *(obj)* /£'vɒl·i, $'vɑː·li/ *v* • *His timing when he volleys is so good.* [I] • *She volleyed the ball from the back of the court.* [T]

vol·ley·ball /£'vɒl·i·bɔːl, $'vɑː·li·bɑːl/ *n* [U] a game in which two teams use their hands to hit a large ball backwards and forwards over a high net without allowing the ball to touch the ground

volt /£vɒlt, $voʊlt/ *n* [C] the standard unit used to measure how strongly an electrical current is sent around an electrical system • *Electricity in Britain is 240 volts, AC.*

volt·age /£'vɒl·tɪdʒ, $'voʊl·t̬ɪdʒ/ *n* • *At* **high** *voltages, cables need to be properly insulated.* [C] • *Transistors are safe to use because they only need* **low** *voltage.* [U] • *The voltage regulator on my car is broken.* • *(fig.) Sara Hughes gives a high-voltage* (= very exciting) *performance in one of the most exciting plays to hit London this year.* [U]

volte–face /£ˌvɒlt'fæs, $ˌvoʊlt-/ *n* [C usually sing] *pl* **volte-face** *literary* a sudden change to an opposing set of beliefs or plan of action • *In 1986 he* **made/did** *a very public and dramatic political volte-face from Left to Right.* • *She seems to have compromised her earlier views somewhat by going along with her party's volte-face* **on** *defence.*

vol·u·ble /£'vɒl·jʊ·bl̩, $'vɑːl-/ *adj fml* (of a person) speaking a lot, with confidence and enthusiasm, or (of speech) expressed in many words • *Many see Parker as the obvious leader, whose voluble style works well on TV.* • *A straight and voluble talker, he approached each subject with unfailing enthusiasm.* • *It's not often that one hears such voluble praise for this government.*

vol·u·bly /£'vɒl·jʊ·bli, $'vɑːl-/ *adv fml* • *It was an excellent performance for which the audience expressed their appreciation volubly.* • *I'd never heard her speak so volubly before.*

vol·ume [AMOUNT] /£'vɒl·juːm, $'vɑːl-/ *n* [U] the amount of space that is enclosed within an object or solid shape • *Which of these bottles do you think has the greater volume?* • *The symbol for volume is V.* • Volume can also be used more generally to mean the number or amount of something: *The main difficulty with teaching was the* **sheer** *volume of work.* ○ *The volume of retail sales increased by 6·4% in Britain in the year to October.* ○ *It's the sheer volume of traffic in the city that is causing the problems.* • [LP] **Measurements, Units**

vol·ume [SOUND LEVEL] /£'vɒl·juːm, $'vɑːl-/ *n* the level of sound produced by a television, radio, etc., or the switch or other device controlling this • *Could you turn the volume down, please, I'm trying to sleep.* • *I'll turn it up if you tell me which is the volume* (= switch).

vol·ume [BOOK] /£'vɒl·juːm, $'vɑːl-/ *n* [C] one in a set of related books, or *(fml)* any type of book • *I have an edition of Proust's 'Remembrance of Things Past', in three volumes.* • *Now 'Realms Of Strife', his second volume* **of** *memoirs, is available too.* • *(fml) While still an undergraduate, his first slim volume 'Fighting Terms' enjoyed a considerable success.*

vo·lu·mi·nous /və'luː·mɪ·nəs/ *adj fml* (of a piece of clothing) large and consisting of a lot of cloth, or (of a piece of writing) long and detailed • *Her voluminous silk dress billowed out behind her.* • *She was wearing a very voluminous shirt so I didn't realize how plump she'd become.* • *Have you read McClelland's voluminous account of his life and work?* • *A record of their relationship exists in a voluminous correspondence that lasted over 20 years.*

vol·un·ta·ry /£'vɒl·ən·tri, $'vɑː·lᵊn·ter·i/ *adj* [not gradable] done, made or given willingly, without being forced or paid to do it • *Is it voluntary, or do we have to go?* • *They chose to take voluntary redundancy.* • *It's a charitable organization, depending for its income upon voluntary contributions from the public.* • *She does voluntary work for the Red Cross two days a week.* • A voluntary organization is one that is controlled and supported by people who give their time and money to it without being paid and that exists to help other people: *The hospital has asked various voluntary organizations to help raise money for the new operating theatre.* • Ⓕ Ⓘ

vol·un·tar·i·ly /£'vɒl·ən·trᵊl·i, $'vɑː·lᵊn·ter·ᵊl-/ *adv* • *If they will not leave the city voluntarily, the government will use force to get them to return to their villages.*

vol·un·teer /£ˌvɒl·ən'tɪəʳ, $ˌvɑː·lən'tɪr/ *n* [C] a person who does something, esp. helps other people, willingly and without being forced or paid to do it • *The Health clinic is relying on volunteers to run the office and answer the telephones.* • *Since it would be a highly dangerous mission, the Lieutenant asked for volunteers.* • *It's a volunteer army with no paid professionals.* • Compare CONSCRIPT.

vol·un·teer *(obj)* /£ˌvɒl·ən'tɪəʳ, $ˌvɑː·lən'tɪr/ *v* • To volunteer is to offer to do something that you do not have to do, often without having been asked to do it and/or without expecting payment: *During the emergency many staff volunteered* **to** *work through the weekend.* [+ *to* infinitive] ○ *I volunteered myself* **for** *the post of Health and Safety Representative.* [T] ○ *He volunteered* **for** *the army* (= He was not forced by law to join the army). • To volunteer information is to give it without being asked: *If I were you, I wouldn't volunteer any details of what happened.* [T] ○ *"I saw her going out of the main entrance at about half past two," he volunteered.* [+ clause]

vo·lup·tu·ous /və'lʌp·tju·əs/ *adj approving* (esp. of women's bodies) sexually attractive, esp. by having large breasts, hips or lips • *a voluptuous body* ○ *voluptuous lips* ○ *a voluptuous woman* • *(literary approving)* If you describe something as voluptuous you mean that it gives you a lot of pleasure because it feels extremely soft and comfortable or it sounds or looks extremely beautiful: *such voluptuous pleasure* ○ *I sank into the bed's voluptuous warmth.* ○ *It was a voluptuous, richly decorated masterpiece of 17th century art.*

vo·lup·tu·ous·ly /və'lʌp·tju·ə·sli/ *adv literary* • *He allowed himself to settle voluptuously down into the bed.*

vo·lup·tu·ous·ness /və'lʌp·tju·ə·snəs/ *n* [U]

vom·it *(obj)* /£'vɒm·ɪt, $'vɑː·mɪt/ *v* to empty the contents of the stomach through the mouth • *He came home drunk and vomited all over the kitchen floor.* [I] • *I almost vomited at the thought of eating liver.* [I] • *She was vomiting blood.* [T] • *(slang) It makes me want to vomit* (= I find it extremely unpleasant), *thinking of her having got the job I really wanted.* [I] • *"The fish ...vomited out Jonah upon the dry land"* (Bible, Jonah 2.10)

vom·it /£'vɒm·ɪt, $'vɑː·mɪt/ *n* [U]

voo·doo /'vuː·duː/ *n* [U] a type of religion involving magic and the worship of spirits, esp. common in Haiti • *(infml)* Voodoo is also used to mean bad luck: *They felt as if there was some sort of voodoo on the band, because everything just went wrong.*

vo·ra·cious /və'reɪ·ʃəs/ *adj slightly literary* very eager (for something, esp. a lot of food) • *He has a voracious* **appetite** (= he eats a lot). • *Locusts are voracious predators and can devour whole forests.* • *The fashion business has a voracious appetite for constant novelty.* • *He's a voracious reader of historical novels* (= He reads a lot of them eagerly and quickly).

vo·ra·cious·ly /və'reɪ·ʃə·sli/ *adv*

vo·ra·cious·ness /və'reɪ·ʃə·snəs/ *n* [U]

vor·tex /£'vɔː·teks, $'vɔːr·t̬eks/ *n* [C] *pl* **vortexes** or **vortices** /£'vɔː·tɪ·siːz, $'vɔːr·t̬ɪ-/ *specialized* a mass of air or water that spins around very fast and pulls objects into its empty centre • *The corn circles are believed to have been created by a vortex – a sort of small whirlwind.* • A vortex is also a dangerous or destructive situation in which you become more and more involved without being able to escape: *The play is about love, sex and betrayal – a vortex* **of** *intense emotion which* **drags/draws** *the trio inevitably towards tragedy.* ○ *They were* **sucked into** *a vortex* **of** *despair.*

vote *(obj)* /£vəʊt, $voʊt/ *v* to express your choice or opinion, esp. by officially marking a paper or by raising your hand or speaking in a meeting • *In a democracy, all adult citizens have* **the right to** *vote – the people choose the government.* [I] • *She was too young to vote* **in** *the national election.* [I] • *The committee voted* **on** *the proposal, and accepted it unanimously.* [I] • *Over 55% voted Liberal.* [I] • *A woman with a megaphone was shouting "Vote* **for** *Kennedy! Vote Kennedy!"* [I] • *A majority of staff voted* **to** *accept the offer of an 8% pay rise.* [+ *to* infinitive] • *I vote* **(that)** *we* (= It is my opinion that we should) *go to the cinema first and eat* *afterwards.* [+ (*that*) clause] • *The evening was voted a tremendous success* (= This was most people's opinion). [T + obj + n] • *She was voted Best Director at the Cannes Film Festival.* [T + obj + n] • *It was the younger members who voted Smith* **onto** *the committee* (= Smith joined because he was the choice of the younger members). [T] • *The Republican Party was voted* **into office** (= was chosen in an election to become the government). [T] • To vote something **for** (*Br also* **to**/*Am also* **towards**) someone or something means to decide to give it to them: *The Board of Directors voted $1 million funding for the project./The Board of Directors voted the project $1 million funding.* [+ two objects] ○ *They voted a generous pension* **to** *his widow./They voted his widow a generous pension.* [+ two objects] • *(specialized)* To **vote** something **down** is to decide as a group not to accept it or do it: *The proposal to build a new road through the forest was voted down by the local council.* ○ *The Bill was voted down.* • *(specialized)* To **vote** something **through** is to decide as a group to accept or do something: *The committee voted through a proposal to cut the defence budget.* • If you **vote with** your **feet**, you leave an organization or stop supporting, using or buying something, and change to a new organization, service, or product: *When the price of skiing in the mountain resorts doubled, tourists voted with their feet and just stopped going.* • *(esp. Am)* A **voting machine** is a machine used to automatically record and count votes in an election.

vote /£vəʊt, $voʊt/ *n* • *The suggestion was approved, with 25 votes in favour, and 7 against.* [C] • *She* **cast** *her vote* (= voted) *for the Communist Party.* [C] • *We called a meeting in order to* **take/hold** *a vote* **on** *the issue.* [C] • *The proposal was read out and then* **put to the/a vote** (= voted on). • *The green Party got/took 10% of the total vote* (= 10% of the total number of votes). [U] • *They are trying to capture the working-class vote* (= to persuade those people to vote for them). [U] • *In some countries women still don't* **have** *the vote* (= are not allowed to vote in elections). [U] • In a **vote of confidence**, in some parliamentary systems, the members of a group are asked to say that they support the people in authority and agree with their actions: *The government* **held** *a vote of confidence and lost it because 30 MPs voted with the opposition.* ○ *(fig.) I think the fact that so many of you are here tonight is a vote of confidence in* (= means that you are pleased with) *the quality of our local performers.* • In a **vote of no confidence** the members of a group are asked to say that they do not support the people in authority and disagree with their actions: *Union members today passed a vote of no confidence* **in** *their national leadership.* • *(Am and Aus)* A **vote-getter** is something that will win votes because it is popular with the voters: *Her stance on taxation could be a big vote-getter in this election.* • In a **vote of thanks** someone formally and publicly thanks a person or organization for something they have done: *At the end of the meeting the new Chairperson stood up and* **proposed** (= said) *a vote of thanks to the retiring Chair and Committee for all their hard work.*

vot·er /£ˈvəʊ·təʳ, $ˈvoʊ·t̬ɚ/ *n* [C] • *Of course, tax cuts are usually popular with (the) voters* (= the people who have the legal right to vote in elections). • *Are you a Labour voter?*

vo·tive /£ˈvəʊ·tɪv, $ˈvoʊ·t̬ɪv/ *adj* [not gradable] *specialized* given or done to honour and esp. to thank a god • *Votive* **candles** *flickered in the church.*

vouch *(obj)* /vaʊtʃ/ *v* to be able from your knowledge or experience to prove the truth of something or the honesty and good character of someone • *Patricia has checked the reports and vouches* **for** *the accuracy of the information.* [I] • *As a medical examiner I* **can** *vouch from experience* **that** *his death was accidental.* [+ *that* clause] • *He brought along a couple of friends to vouch* **for** *him* (= to say that he had a good character). [I]

vouch·er /£ˈvaʊ·tʃəʳ, $-tʃɚ/ *n* [C] *Br and Aus* a piece of paper that is a record of money paid or one that can be used to pay for particular goods or services or that allows you to pay less than the usual price for them • *The voucher is valid between July and December and entitles you to 10% off all overseas flights.* • *The government should run a voucher* **system** *to help people pay for training and so learn new skills.*

vouch·safe *obj* /ˌvaʊtʃˈseɪf, ˈ--/ *v* [T] *fml* to tell or give (something) esp. to someone considered to be less important • *He vouchsafed the information that the meeting had been postponed.*

vow *obj* /vaʊ/ *v* [T] to make (a determined decision or promise) to do something • *The guerillas vowed* **(that)** *they would overthrow the government.* [+ (*that*) clause] • *After the meals we had last year I vowed* **to** *do more of the cooking myself.* [+ *to* infinitive] • *"I vow to thee , my country – all earthly things above – / Entire and whole and perfect, the service of my love"* (Cecil Arthur Spring-Rice *Last Poem*, 1920)

vow /vaʊ/ *n* [C] • *She* **took** *a vow* (= decided) *never to lend money to anyone again.*

vo·wel /vaʊəl/ *n* [C] a speech sound produced by human beings when the breath flows out through the mouth without being blocked by the teeth, tongue or lips • *A* **short** *vowel is a short sound as in the word 'cup'.* • *A* **long** *vowel is a long sound as in the word 'shoe'.* • A vowel is also a letter that represents a sound produced in this way: *The vowels in English are a, e, i, o and u, but in some other languages y, h, r and w are also considered to be vowels.* • Compare CONSONANT.

vox pop /£ˌvɒksˈpɒp, $ˌvɑːksˈpɑːp/ *n* [U] *Br and Aus infml* the opinions of people recorded talking informally in public places • *The documentary included some vox pop from the streets of Birmingham.*

voy·age /ˈvɔɪ·ɪdʒ/ *n* [C] a long journey, esp. by ship • *We crossed the Equator* **on** *the voyage.* • *He was a young sailor on his first sea voyage.* • *(fig.) The first year of a loving relationship is a voyage* (= period) **of** *discovery.*

voy·age /ˈvɔɪ·ɪdʒ/ *v* [I] *old use or literary* • *In their little boat they planned to voyage* **to** *distant lands.*

voy·ag·er /£ˈvɔɪ·ɪ·dʒəʳ, $-dʒɚ/ *n* [C] • A voyager is a person who goes on a long and sometimes dangerous voyage: *Those voyagers who first ventured into space certainly showed courage.*

voy·eur /£vwɑːˈjɜːʳ, $-ˈjɜːr/ *n* [C] *disapproving* a person who gets sexual pleasure from esp. secretly watching other people in sexual situations, or (more generally) a person who watches other people's private lives • *I felt like a voyeur visiting the war zone and seeing badly injured people being dragged from their bomb-shattered homes.*

voy·eur·i·sm /£ˈvwɑː·jɜː·rɪ·zᵊm, $-jɜːr-/ *n* [U] *disapproving*

voy·eur·is·tic /£ˌvwɑː·jɜːˈrɪ·stɪk, $-jəˈrɪs·t̬ɪk/ *adj disapproving* • *The film was criticized for its voyeuristic photography, showing the prostitutes in a flattering and shadowy light.*

VP *n* [C] *Am abbreviation for* **Vice President**, see at VICE [TITLE]

vroom /vruːm, vrʊm/ *exclamation infml* a written representation of the sound of a car engine at high speed • *"Vroom, vroom" went Jamie, as he pushed his toy car along on the floor.*

vs *prep abbreviation for* VERSUS

vul·can·ized, *Br and Aus usually* **-ised** /ˈvʌl·kə·naɪzd/ *adj* [not gradable] (esp. of rubber) made stronger by a chemical process • *Vulcanized rubber is used to make products such as tyres and raincoats.*

vul·gar [NOT SUITABLE] /£ˈvʌl·gəʳ, $-gɚ/ *adj disapproving* (esp. of objects) not suitable, simple, graceful or beautiful; common or not in the style preferred by the upper classes of society • *Only someone with no sense of taste would own a car as vulgar as that!* • *They thought his accent was terribly vulgar.* • *It's rather vulgar to talk about how much money you earn.*

vul·gar·i·ty /£vʌlˈgær·ɪ·ti, $-ə·t̬i/ *n* [U] • *The unashamed vulgarity of the house was quite unexpected.*

vul·gar·ly /£ˈvʌl·gᵊl·i, $-gɚ·li/ *adv* • *The walls were vulgarly decorated in gold and black.*

vul·gar [RUDE] /£ˈvʌl·gəʳ, $-gɚ/ *adj disapproving* rude, because referring to sex, excretion etc. • *He is a vulgar man to make such gestures.* • *It was an extremely vulgar joke.*

vul·gar·i·ty /£vʌlˈgær·ɪ·ti, $-ə·t̬i/ *n* [U] • *Her vulgarity shocked the rest of the guests.*

vul·gar·ly /£ˈvʌl·gᵊl·i, $-gɚ·li/ *adv*

vul·ne·ra·ble /£ˈvʌl·nᵊr·ə·bl̩, £ˈvʌn·rə-, $ˈvʌl·nɚ·ə-/ *adj* able to be easily physically, emotionally, or mentally hurt, influenced or attacked • *I felt very vulnerable, standing there without any clothes on.* • *His parents divorced when he was at a very vulnerable age.* • *It is on economic policy that the government is most vulnerable.* • *Tourists are more vulnerable* **to** *attack, because they do not know which areas of the city to avoid.* • *The troops were in a vulnerable position, completely exposed to attack from the air.*

vul·ne·ra·bil·i·ty /£ˌvʌl·nᵊr·əˈbɪl·ɪ·ti, £ˌvʌn·rə-, $ˌvʌl·nɚ·əˈbɪl·ə·t̬i/ *n* [U] • *Perhaps his arrogance is a cover for an underlying vulnerability.* • *The vulnerability of the economy* **to** *recession is only too obvious.*

vul·ture /£'vʌl·tʃəʳ, $-tʃɚ/ *n* [C] a large bird with almost no feathers on its head or neck that eats the flesh of dead animals • *(fig.) In a crisis, the vultures are always hovering* (= there are people eager to get some advantage from other people's difficulties or weaknesses). • PIC› **Birds**

vul·va /'vʌl·və/ *n* [C] *pl* **vulvas** or **vulvae** /'vʌl·viː/ the parts of a woman's sex organs which are outside the body between the legs

vy·ing /'vaɪ·ɪŋ/ *pres part of* VIE

W w

W LETTER (*pl* **W's** or **Ws**), **w** (*pl* **w's** or **ws**) /'dʌb·l̩.juː/ *n* [C] the 23rd letter of the English alphabet • LP› **Silent letters**

W WEST *n* [U], *adj* [not gradable] *abbreviation for* WEST or WESTERN • *W Australia*

W ELECTRICITY *n* [C] *abbreviation for* WATT • *a 100W light bulb*

wack·o *esp. Am* /£'wæk·əʊ, $-oʊ/ *n* [C] *pl* **wackos** *infml* a person whose behaviour is strange and different from that of most people; an ECCENTRIC

wack·y /'wæk·i/ *adj* **-ier, -iest** *infml* unusual in a pleasing and exciting or silly way • *He decided to become a clown to join the wacky world of the circus.* • *I love his wonderfully wacky illustrations.* • *She's a bit wacky – she has some strange ideas.*

wack·i·ness /'wæk·ɪ·nəs/ *n* [U]

wad /£wɒd, $wɑːd/ *n* [C] a number of esp. flat and/or small objects pressed tightly together • *a wad of banknotes* • *a wad of gum* • *She used a wad* (= a mass) *of tissues to wipe away the blood.*

wad·ding /£'wɒd·ɪŋ, $'wɑː·dɪŋ/ *n* [U] any soft material used for filling a space, esp. in order to protect something or to give something shape • *The chandelier arrived in a big box, tightly packed around in wadding.* • *The sofa had split underneath and the wadding was coming out.*

wad·dle /£'wɒd·l̩, $'wɑː·dl̩/ *v* [I always + adv/prep] (usually of a person or animal with short legs and a fat body) to walk with short steps, swinging the body from one side to the other • *A duck waddled quickly across the road.*

wad·dle /£'wɒd·l̩, $'wɑː·dl̩/ *n* [C] • *She walks with a peculiar waddle.*

wad·dy /£'wɒd·i, $'wɑː·di/ *n* [C] *Aus* a heavy stick

wade *(obj)* /weɪd/ *v* to walk through (water) esp. with difficulty because of the pressure of the water against your legs • *The river was full but we managed to wade* **across**. [I always + adv/prep] • *We can wade shallow rivers, but deeper ones we'll have to swim.* [T] • *There was no choice but to wade* **through** *the muddy water.* [I always + adv/prep] • Wade is *Am for* PADDLE WALK. • **Wading pool** is *Am for* **paddling pool**. See at PADDLE WALK. • PIC› **Playground**

wad·er /£'weɪ·dəʳ, $-dɚ/, **wad·ing bird** /'weɪ·dɪŋ/ *n* [C] • A wader is a bird with long legs and a long neck that lives near water and eats fish.

wad·ers /£'weɪ·dəz, $-dɚz/ *pl n* • Waders are rubber boots that cover the whole leg to keep a person dry in water: *The fishermen put on their waders.*

wade in *v adv* [I] *infml* to start to do or say something in a forceful and determined way • *Whenever she sees a problem, she wades in immediately and works until it's solved.* • *Doctors sometimes wade in too soon, when it would be better to give the body a chance to heal itself.* • *Even when she knows nothing about it, she wades in with her opinion.*

wade into *obj v prep* [T] *infml* to attack or begin to deal with (someone or something) • *And then for no good reason the boss waded into me as well.*

wade through *obj v prep* [T] *infml* to spend a lot of time and effort doing and finishing (something boring or difficult) • *She spends her days wading through* (= reading) *books in another language.* • *There was a mound of ironing to wade through.*

wadge /£wɒdʒ, $wɑːdʒ/ *n* [C] *Br infml* a WODGE

wa·di /£'wɒd·i, $'wɑː·di/ *n* [C] *specialized* a usually steep-sided valley, with a river which flows only when it has rained, common in desert areas of N Africa and S W Asia

wa·fer /£'weɪ·fəʳ, $-fɚ/ *n* [C] a very thin dry biscuit which is often sweet and flavoured • *(specialized)* A wafer is also a very thin round piece of dry bread which the priest gives to people to eat during **Holy Communion** (= a Christian religious ceremony). • Something that is **wafer-thin** is extremely thin: *The rooms were divided only by a wafer-thin partition.* • A **wafer biscuit** is a light sweet biscuit slightly thicker than a wafer with a creamy filling. • PIC› **Bread and cakes**

waf·fle TALK /£'wɒf·l̩, $'wɑː·fl̩/ *v* [I] *disapproving* to talk or write a lot without giving any useful information or any clear answers • *If you don't know the answer, it's no good just waffling* **(on)** *for pages and pages.* • *The President has been waffling* **on** *this issue, probably because he is still uncertain about what to do.*

waf·fle /£'wɒf·l̩, $'wɑː·fl̩/ *n* [U] *disapproving* • *When asked a difficult question on TV or radio, she gives herself time to think with some preliminary waffle.* • *"What did he say?" "Oh, it was a load of waffle – nothing important at all."*

waf·fle CAKE /£'wɒf·l̩, $'wɑː·fl̩/ *n* [C] a thin light cake, the surface of which is formed into a pattern of raised squares • *Waffles are more common in the US and Canada than in Britain, and are typically eaten with syrup poured over them.*

waft *(obj)* /£wɒft, $wɑːft/ *v* [always + adv/prep] *literary* (to cause) to move gently through the air • *A gentle breeze wafted the scent of roses in through the open window.* [T] • *The sound of a flute wafted* **down** *the stairs.* [I] • *Birdsong wafted* **through** *the trees.*

wag *(obj)* MOVE /wæg/ *v* **-gg-** (esp. of a tail or finger) to move from side to side or up and down, esp. quickly and repeatedly, or to cause this to happen • *The little dog's tail wagged in delight.* [I] • *Wagging his finger sternly, he told them never to go into the attic again.* [T] • *(fig.) They tried to keep their affair secret, but it wasn't long before* **tongues** *began to wag* (= people began to notice and talk about it). [I]

wag /wæg/ *n* [C usually sing] • *With a single wag of her finger she managed to convey her total disapproval.*

wag HUMOROUS PERSON /wæg/ *n* [C] *infml dated* a humorous person who likes to make jokes • *David's such a wag, but I wish he'd find some new jokes.*

wag·gish /'wæg·ɪʃ/ *adj infml dated* • *He has a very waggish approach to song writing.*

wage MONEY /weɪdʒ/ *n* [U] a fixed amount of money that is paid, usually every week, to an employee, esp. one who does work that needs physical skills or strength, rather than a job needing a college education • *a very low/high wage* • *an hourly/daily/weekly/annual wage* • *a wage demand/limit/settlement* • *He gets/earns/is paid a good wage, because he works for a fair employer.* • *Some countries have a* **minimum** *wage, set by law.* • *They went on strike, demanding a* **living** *wage* (= an income large enough for a family). • *For skilled and unskilled workers, wage* **differentials** (= the difference between high wages and low wages) *have increased.* • A **wage earner** is a person who works at a job for money. • A **wage freeze** is when a company or government fixes wages and will not allow any increases. • *(Br and Aus) Once you take out rent, food and bills from your* **wage packet** *(Am* **paycheck***)* (= income, often contained in an envelope) *you are not left with much.* • Compare INCOME; SALARY. • LP› **Money**

wa·ges /'weɪ·dʒɪz/ *pl n* • *The smaller shops pay very low wages* (= a very low wage). • *As inflation has increased,* **real wages** (= the amount you can buy with your income) *have declined.*

wage *obj* FIGHT /weɪdʒ/ *v* [T] *slightly fml* to fight (a war) • *Surely the President needs Congress' permission to wage war?* • *(fig.) The police don't have the resources to wage (a) war* **on/against** *crime.*

wa·ger /£ˈweɪ·dʒəʳ, $-dʒɚ/ *n* [C] an amount of money that you risk in the hope of winning more, by trying to guess something uncertain, or the agreement that you make to take this risk; a BET • *She put a* **cash** *wager of £20 on some horse race.* • *He tried to eat 50 hard-boiled eggs,* **for** *a wager.*

wa·ger *(obj)* /£ˈweɪ·dʒəʳ, $-dʒɚ/ *v* • *I'd wager* **(that)** (= I believe that) *she's interested in you.* [+ *(that)* clause] • *I'll wager you £5* **that** *they'll get there first.* [+ two objects + *that* clause]

wag·gle *(obj)* /ˈwæg·l̩/ *v* (to cause) to move quickly up and down or from side to side • *One of his party tricks is to waggle his* **ears**. [T] • *A woman suddenly jumped out and started waggling a gun in my direction.* [T] • *All I could see was two feet sticking out from under the blanket with toes waggling.* [I]

wag·on, *Br and Aus* **wag·gon** /ˈwæg·ən/ *n* [C] a vehicle with four wheels, which must be pulled or pushed and can vary in size and use • *In America, children often pull around toy wagons.* • *The first white settlers journeyed across America in* **covered wagons** *pulled by horses, often long lines of them forming* **wagon trains**. • *(Br and Aus)* A wagon (*Am* **freight car**) is also a large wheeled container for transporting goods, that is pulled by a train: *an open wagon* ○ *The locomotive was pulling a line of* **goods** *wagons.* • *(infml)* If you are **on the wagon**, you have decided not to drink any alcohol for a period of time: *He was on the wagon for ten years, when he was living in Connecticut.* ○ *When her husband died, she* **fell off the wagon** (= started drinking alcohol, after a period when she had drunk none). • *(Br)* A **wagon-lit** is a **sleeping car**. See at SLEEP [RESTING STATE]. • See also BANDWAGON. • (CS) (PL) (RUS)

waif /weɪf/ *n* [C] *literary* a child or animal without a home or enough care • *She's like a waif out of a Dickens novel.* • *(Br) The hostel is designed to give a bed for the night to homeless people and other* **waifs and strays** (= people without anywhere to stay for various reasons).

wail /weɪl/ *v esp. disapproving* (to make) a long, high cry, usually because of pain or sadness • *The women gathered around the coffin and began to wail, as was the custom in the region.* [I] • *"My finger hurts," wailed the child.* [+ clause] • *She had that passionate wailing voice, so typical of country music singers.* • *(fig.) Business people wailed* (= complained) **that** *their trade would be ruined.* [+ *that* clause]

wail /weɪl/ *n* [C] • *a wail of anguish* • *the wail of the police sirens*

waist /weɪst/ *n* [C] the part of the body above and slightly narrower than the hips • *a small/narrow/tiny/large/thick waist* • *The trousers are a bit tight around my waist.* • The waist of a piece of clothing is the part that goes around or covers this area of the body: *The skirt had an elasticated waist.* • **Waist pack** is *Am for* BUMBAG. • [PIC] **Bags** (J)

waist·ed /£ˈweɪs·tɪd, $-t̬ɪd/ *adj* [not gradable] • *This particular jacket is rather waisted* (= narrow at the waist)

-waist·ed /£-ˈweɪs·tɪd, $-t̬ɪd/ *combining form* • *a slim-waisted boy* • *a* **high**-*waisted pair of trousers*

waist·band /ˈweɪst·bænd/ *n* [C] a strip of material that forms the waist of a pair of trousers or a skirt • *He had a gun tucked into the waistband of his trousers.*

waist·coat *Br* /£ˈweɪst·kəʊt, $-koʊt, ˈwes·kət/, *Am and Aus* **vest** *n* [C] a piece of clothing that covers the upper body but not the arms and usually has buttons down the front • *Waistcoats were mainly worn in the past under a jacket, as part of a three-piece suit.* • [PIC] **Clothes**

waist·line /ˈweɪst·laɪn/ *n* [C] an imaginary line going round the narrowest part of your waist • *a bulging/expanding waistline* • *She started jogging twice a week to try to reduce her waistline.*

wait *(obj)* /weɪt/ *v* to allow time to go by, esp. while staying in one place without doing very much, until someone comes, until something that you are expecting happens or until you can do something • *I waited in the corridor while she went in to see the doctor.* [I] • *Wait here* **for** *me – I'll be back in a minute.* [I] • *I'm sorry for the delay, but I'm still waiting* **for** *the letter to arrive.* [I] • *The dentist kept me waiting* **for** *ages.* [I] • *There were a lot of people waiting* **to** *use the telephone.* [+ to infinitive] • *Can you wait* **until** *tomorrow?* [I] • *Wait* **till** *you see what I've got for you* (= I've got something special for you)*!* [I] • *We spent the whole day waiting* **around** *(Br also* **about***) for something exciting to happen, but nothing did.* [I] • *When the thieves left the building, the police were waiting* **for** *them* (= were expecting them and ready to deal with them). [I] • You can also use wait when you are referring to a situation, job or object, rather than a person: *An envelope was waiting* **for** *me when I got home.* [I] ○ *The meeting will have to wait* (= be delayed) *until tomorrow, because I'm too busy now.* [I] ○ *The paperwork* **can't** *wait until tomorrow* (= is urgent and must be done now). [I] • *(Am)* To wait a meal **for** someone is to delay serving it until they arrive: *Don't wait dinner for me – I'll be home late.* [T] • **I can't wait to** *see you* (= I am very eager to see you). • **I can hardly wait to** *be in France* (= I am very eager to be there). • You can also use wait as a way of threatening someone: **Just you wait**, *Maria, till I get my hands on you!* ○ **You wait**, *Ted! You're going to be in big trouble!* • *(Br) The sign by the side of the road said* **No Waiting** *(Am and Aus* **No Standing***)* (= vehicles are not allowed to park even for short periods). • You say **wait a minute/moment/second** in order to interrupt someone, or to get their attention or when you have suddenly thought of something important: *Now, wait a moment – I don't agree with that.* ○ *Wait a minute – I've just had an idea.* • *No decision will be made until next year, so you'll just have to* **wait and see** (= be patient until then, when the situation will become clear). • To **wait behind** is to stay in a place after all the other people have left: *The teacher asked her to wait behind after the class.* • *(infml)* **Wait for it!** (= Don't start until the correct moment!) *I haven't said 'go' yet.* • *(infml)* You say **wait for it** to show that you are about to say something surprising, amusing or difficult to believe: *The new soap opera will be screened, wait for it, five times each day.* • *(Br)* To **wait in** is to stay at home because you are expecting someone or something to arrive: *I waited in all day, but of course the gas repair people never turned up.* • If someone or something is **waiting in the wings**, they are not yet active or important, but are ready or likely to be so soon: *The team has several talented young players waiting in the wings.* ○ *There are further problems waiting in the wings.* • *(fml)* To **wait on** someone or something is to delay doing something until they take action or until something happens: *The lawyers were waiting on the jury's verdict.* • To **wait on** someone is to serve them: *(Am) She waited on shoppers all day at the department store.* ○ *His mother waited on him as long as he lived at home.* ○ *While she was pregnant, her husband waited on her* **hand and foot** (= did everything for her). • To *(Br and Aus fml)* **wait at table(s)**/*(Am)* **wait (on) table(s)** is to serve meals to people in a restaurant, as your job. • *(Am and Aus) It would be better to* **wait out** *the storm* (= wait until the end of it) *before we start out on our trip.* • *If people were more polite, they would* **wait** *their* **turn** (= wait until it was really their turn). • If you **wait up**, you stay awake because you are expecting someone to arrive: *Don't wait up for me – I've got my key.* • To play a **waiting game** is to delay taking any action, so that you can watch how a situation develops and see what it is best for you to do: *In a contest like this, the stronger side can afford to* **play** *a waiting game.* • A **waiting list** is a list of people who have asked for something which is not immediately available but which they will or might be able to receive in the future: *The hospital has a 2-year waiting list for minor operations.* ○ *I'm afraid the course is full, but I can put you* **on** *the waiting list, in case someone else cancels.* • A **waiting room** is a room in a place where people can sit and rest while waiting, as in a railway station or a doctor's office.

wait /weɪt/ *n* [U] • *We* **had** *a three-hour wait before we could see the doctor.* • *The long wait* **for** *the doctor/***to** *see the doctor really made me anxious.* • *The gunmen were* **lying in wait** (= hiding, ready to attack) *when Mr Predit came out of the hotel.*

wait·er *male, female* **wait·ress** /£ˈweɪ·təʳ, $-t̬ɚ, -trəs/ *n* [C] a person whose job is to serve meals to people in a restaurant • *the head waiter* • *a wine waiter* • *A waiter came to the table to take our order.*

waive *obj* /weɪv/ *v* [T] *fml* to not demand (something you have a right to) or not cause (a rule) to be obeyed • *The bank manager waived the charge* (= said we didn't have to pay)*, as we were old and valued customers.* • *If the government waives* (= removes) *the time limit, many more applications will come in.* • *He persuaded the delegates to waive* (= give up) *their objections.*

waiv·er /£ˈweɪ·vəʳ, $-vɚ/ *n* [C] • *We had to sign a waiver, giving up any rights to the land in the future.* • *They are asking for a waiver of* (= an agreement so that they do not have to pay) *the $24 million debt that they owe.*

wake *(obj)* [STOP SLEEPING] /weɪk/ *v past simple* **woke** /£wəʊk, $woʊk/ or **waked**, *past part* **woken** /£ˈwəʊ·kən, $ˈwoʊ-/ or **waked** or *Am also* **woke** /£wəʊk, $woʊk/ to (cause someone to) become awake and conscious after sleeping • *Did you wake at all during the night?* [I] • *Please wake me early tomorrow.* [T] • *If we talk quietly, we won't wake the baby.* [T] • *I woke* **up** *with a headache.* [I] • *The noise of the storm woke me* **(up)**. [T/M] • *He woke himself* **up** *with his own snoring!* [T] • *Jane's hand on my shoulder woke me* **out of/from** *a bad dream.* [T] • *(fig.) Wake* **up** (= Give attention) *Daniel! It's your turn.* [I] • *(fig.) Governments are finally waking* **up to** (= becoming aware of) *the fact that the environment should be cleaned up.* [I]

wake·ful /ˈweɪk·fəl/ *adj fml* • *We spent a wakeful night* (= We did not sleep very much) *worrying about where he was.* • *I felt wakeful* (= awake and aware) *and alert.*

wake·ful·ness /ˈweɪk·fəl·nəs/ *n* [U]

wak·en *(obj)* /ˈweɪ·kən/ *v fml* • *I shook him but he didn't waken.* [I]

wak·ey wak·ey /ˌweɪ·kiˈweɪ·ki/ *exclamation humorous* • *Gloria knocked on the door and shouted "Wakey wakey!"* (= Wake up!)

wak·ing /ˈweɪ·kɪŋ/ *adj* [before noun; not gradable] • *She seems to spend every* **waking hour** (= all her available time) *at the piano.*

wake WATER /weɪk/ *n* [C] an area of water whose movement has been changed by a boat or ship moving through it • *The wake spread out in a v-shape behind the ship.* • *The little boats were left bobbing about in the cruise ship's wake.* • *The demonstrators rampaged through the town centre,* **leaving** *chaos* **in** *their* **wake** (= behind them). • If something happens **in the wake of** something else, it happens after and often because of it: *Airport security was extra tight in the wake of yesterday's bomb attacks.*

wake FUNERAL /weɪk/ *n* [C] a gathering of the family and friends of a dead person in order to look at the dead body the night before it is buried, or a gathering held after a dead person has been buried, at which their family and friends drink and talk about the person's life • *The Irish are famous for* **holding** *wakes that go on for days and involve lots of drinking.*

walk *(obj)* /£wɔːk, $wɑːk/ *v* to move along by putting one foot in front of the other, allowing each foot to touch the ground before lifting the next • *It takes half an hour to walk to the office, or 10 minutes to cycle.* [I] • *He walks the two kilometres for exercise every morning.* [T] • *It's only two miles – you can walk* **it** *in half an hour.* [T] • *I walked home.* [I] • *She walked away laughing.* [I] • *A cat was walking along the top of the fence.* [I] • To walk someone **to** a particular place is to walk with them until they have reached it usually because you are being friendly or polite, wish to protect them from danger, or show them the way: *He offered to walk her home/to the station.* [T] • To walk an animal, esp. a dog, is to take it for a walk: *She walks the dog for an hour every afternoon.* [T] • *(Br infml)* To walk something such as an examination or game is to pass or win it easily: *She'll walk the interview – the job is practically hers already.* [T] • If you describe someone as a walking **disaster, encyclopedia** etc., you mean that they are a human form of that thing: *You've sat on another pair of glasses? – Oh, you're a walking disaster!* ○ *Bruce is a walking encyclopedia – is there anything he doesn't know about?* • To **walk all over** someone is to treat them very badly or defeat them very easily: *If you don't want to work at the weekend, say so – don't let the boss walk all over you.* • *(disapproving)* To **walk away from** a difficult or dangerous situation is to end your involvement in it and stop trying to improve it: *It's no good walking away from the problem – it'll only be worse by next year.* • If you **walk away from** an accident, you escape from it without being badly hurt: *She overturned the car, but walked away from it* **(without a scratch)**. • If a person or team **walks away from** their competitors, they win easily: *Regis walked away from the rest of the players.* • To **walk away/off with** a prize is to win it easily: *German teams walked away with gold medals in three events.* • To **walk in on** someone or something is to go into a room and see or interrupt what is happening there: *Thinking there was no one at home, I went upstairs and walked in on Peter wrapping my birthday present.* • If you **walk (right) into** something, you are caught or tricked by it because you did not know what was happening: *We set a trap and they walked right into it.* • To **walk into** a job is to be given it without any delay or difficulty: *With her brains and personality, she just walks into good jobs.* • To **walk off** a negative emotion or a pain is to go for a walk as a way of getting rid of it: *He walked off his depression.* • To **walk off with** something is to take it without asking if you can: *Who's walked off with my cup?* • To **walk on air** is to feel extremely excited or happy: *After the delivery of her baby, she was walking on air.* • If you are **walking on eggs/eggshells**, you are being very careful not to offend someone or do anything wrong: *When my mother is staying at our house, I feel like I'm walking on eggshells.* • To **walk out (of** something) is to leave it before it is finished because you are not enjoying it or because you do not agree with it: *It was such a violent play that several people walked out in the first few minutes.* ○ *All of the parents walked out of the meeting in protest.* • To **walk out** also means to go on STRIKE (= to stop working in order to express complaint): *Workers are threatening to walk out.* ○ See also WALKOUT. • To **walk out on** someone is to end your relationship or involvement with them suddenly: *You can't walk out on me like this – just when things are getting busy!* ○ *He walked out on his wife and two kids.* • *(Am and Aus)* To **walk (someone) through** something is to practise it or to show someone else how to do it from beginning to end: *The actors walked through the play during rehearsal.* ○ *During her training, the instructor walked her through the steps on the computer.* • If storage space is described as **walk-in**, it is large enough for a person to enter and walk around in: *a walk-in wardrobe* ○ *(Am) a walk-in closet* ○ *(Aus) a walk-in cupboard* • *(esp. Am)* A **walk-in clinic** or other centre is one which you can go to without having already made an arrangement: *It's a walk-in dental clinic – the sign outside said 'Walk-in patients welcome'.* • **Walking papers** is *Am for* **marching orders**. See at MARCH WALK. • A **walk-on (part)** in a play is a very small part in which the actor is on the stage very briefly and speaks very few or no words. • *(Am)* A **walk-up** is a building with several floors and no LIFT (= a device for going from one floor to another), or an apartment or office in such a building. • *"Walk, Don't Run"* (title of a song and a film, 1960) • *"Walkin' Back to Happiness"* (title of song by Helen Shapiro, 1961) • See also JAYWALK; **sleepwalk** at SLEEPWALKER.

walk /£wɔːk, $wɑːk/ *n* • *He* **went for/took** *a walk around the block, to clear his head.* [C] • *They went on a ten-mile walk to raise money for charity.* [C] • *Every afternoon she takes her Grandad out for a walk.* [C] • *The station is only a five minute walk away.* [U] • *He's got a strange walk* (= way of walking). [U] • *She slowed the horses to a walk* (= walking speed). [U] • *Do you know any nice walks* (= places or paths suitable for walking) *around here?* [C] • When people talk about **walk(s) of life** they are referring to different types of jobs and different levels of society: *We've got lawyers in this club, and builders and hairdressers, and there's even an actor – people from all* **(different)** *walks of life.* ○ *In my job I see people from* **every** *walk of life.* • *"A Walk on the Wild Side"* (title of a song by Lou Reed, 1973) • See also BOARDWALK; CATWALK; CROSSWALK; SIDEWALK; SPACEWALK.

walk·er /£ˈwɔː·kər, $ˈwɑː·kɚ/ *n* [C] • *She's a very fast/slow walker.* • A walker is also a person who walks as a hobby: *They've been keen walkers ever since they read about the benefits of exercise.* • Walker is *Am for* ZIMMER FRAME. • PIC› **Frame**

walk·ing /£ˈwɔː·kɪŋ, $ˈwɑː-/ *n* [U] • *walking (Am and Aus also* **hiking***) boots* ○ *a walking stick* ○ *a walking tour* • *Walking is one of the most popular forms of recreation.* • *(Br also)* A **walking frame** is a ZIMMER FRAME. • PIC› **Frame, Medical equipment, Shoes**

walk·a·bout /£ˈwɔː·kə·baʊt, $ˈwɑː-/ *n* [C] *esp. Br infml* an occasion when an important person walks around a public place, meeting and talking to members of the public • *The princess* **went on** *a walkabout in the town centre.* • *(infml humorous)* If you say that an object has **gone** walkabout you mean that it is missing, often because someone has taken it: *My pen was here this morning but it seems to have gone walkabout.*

walk·ies /£ˈwɔː·kiz, $ˈwɑː-/ *exclamation, pl n Br infml* said to a dog to tell it that it is time for a walk • *Walkies, Shem, come on, walkies!* • *Come on, Shem, let's* **go** *walkies!*

walk·ie–talk·ie /£ˌwɔː·kiˈtɔː·ki, $ˌwɑː·kiˈtɑː-/ *n* [C] a small radio held in the hand which is used for both sending and receiving messages • *The policeman was speaking to HQ* **on** *his walkie-talkie.*

Walk·man /£ˈwɔːk·mən, $ˈwɑːk-/, **per·son·al ster·e·o** *n* [C] *pl* **Walkmans** *trademark* a small **cassette player**, sometimes with radio, with small HEADPHONES, which people use for listening to music when they are walking around, sitting on public transport, etc. • *I'd like to see Walkmans banned on public transport.*

walk·out /£'wɔː·kaʊt, $'wɑː-/ *n* [C] the act of leaving an official meeting as a group in order to show disapproval, or of leaving a place of work to start a STRIKE (= a stopping of work following a disagreement between workers and employers) • *Senior union workers* **staged** (= had) *a walkout this afternoon at the annual conference over the proposed changes in funding.* • *Rail-workers are to* **stage** (= have) *a twenty-four-hour walkout next Monday unless an agreement is reached at today's meeting.* • See also **walk out** at WALK.

walk·o·ver EASILY WON GAME /£'wɔːk,əʊ·vəʳ, $'wɑːk,oʊ·vɚ/, *Am and Aus also* **walk·a·way** /£'wɔː·kə·weɪ, $'wɑː-/ *n* [C] *infml* a game or sporting event that is won very easily by one side or one person • *Norway won't have any problems beating France in the semi-final tomorrow – it should be a walkover.* • See also **walk all over** at WALK.

walk·o·ver WIN WITHOUT PLAYING /£'wɔːk,əʊ·vəʳ, $'wɑːk,oʊ·vɚ/ *n* [C] the act of winning one stage of a competition without having to compete in it because the person that you should be playing against is no longer taking part • *Travis won a walkover in the second round because Watson still hadn't recovered from his earlier fight and had to back out.*

walk·way /£'wɔː·kweɪ, $'wɑː-/ *n* [C] a passage or path, esp. one which is covered or raised above the ground • *When you leave the station, walk along the covered walkway that takes you across the main road.*

wall /£wɔːl, $wɑːl/ *n* [C] a vertical structure, often made of stone or brick, that divides or encloses something • *The walls in this apartment are so thin you can hear just about every word the neighbours say.* • *The walls look a bit bare – can't we put some pictures up?* • *We had to climb over a ten-foot wall.* • *There's a wall around the old part of the town.* • *The Berlin Wall came down in 1989.* • *I bought a couple of beautiful wall* **hangings** *for the living room.* • In the body a wall is any outer part of a hollow structure: *the wall of the womb/stomach* ○ *an artery wall* • A wall **of** people or things can also be a mass of them formed in such a way that you cannot get through or past them: *The demonstrators formed a solid wall to stop the police from getting past them.* ○ *I had to make my way through a wall* **of** *men to get to the bar!* • *(fig.) A wall* **of silence** *surrounded the Defence Ministry prior to the attack* (= they refused to say anything). • If a company **goes to the wall** it is destroyed financially: *After nine months of massive losses the company finally went to the wall.* • Something which is **off the wall** is surprising and unusual: *an off-the-wall joke* ○ *off-the-wall leisure pursuits.* • **Up the wall** means extremely angry: *My flatmate is* **driving** *me up the wall at the moment.* ○ *"What did David say about your bumping his car?" "He* **went** *up the wall!"* • *It's a typically suburban house with a three-piece suite and* **wall-to-wall carpets** (= ones which cover the whole floor). • Something might also be described as **wall-to-wall** if it is continuous or if it is happening everywhere around you: *I went away to college thinking it would be wall-to-wall parties and all the freedom I wanted.* ○ *Not all our viewers are happy with the wall-to-wall coverage of this world-famous tennis tournament.* • **Wall Street** is a street in New York which represents the financial centre of the US: *On Wall Street today the Dow Jones rose ten points following good economic figures.* • *(saying)* 'Walls have ears' means it is not safe to speak now because other people might be listening.

wall *obj* /£wɔːl, $wɑːl/ *v* [T always + adv/prep] • *They've walled* **off** (= built a wall around) *the electric sub-station for safety reasons.* • *In those days people walled* **up** (= filled in with brick or stone) *their windows in order to avoid the window tax.*

walled /£wɔːld, $wɑːld/ *adj* [not gradable] • Walled means surrounded by a wall: *Why not visit the beautiful walled city of York?* ○ *They have a beautiful walled herb-garden that you can wander around.*

wal·la·by /£'wɒl·ə·bi, $'wɑː·lə-/ *n* [C] an animal found in Australia and New Guinea which is like a small KANGAROO, having strong back legs for jumping with and a long tail

wal·lah, wal·la /£'wɒl·ə, $'wɑː·lə/ *n* [C] *infml humorous* a person who has a particular duty • *I made the tea yesterday so it's Mira's turn to be tea wallah this afternoon.*

wall·board /£'wɔːl·bɔːd, $'wɑːl·bɔːrd/ *n* [U] PLASTERBOARD

wal·let /£'wɒl·ɪt, $'wɑː·lɪt/, *Am also* **bill·fold** *n* [C] a small folding case for carrying paper money, **credit cards** and other flat objects, used esp. by men • *a leather wallet* • *He had his wallet stolen from the hotel room.* • *He got out a big fat wallet stuffed with bank notes.* • A wallet can also be a larger flat case used for holding pieces of paper such as documents . • Compare PURSE BAG. • PIC> **Bags**

wall·flower PLANT /£'wɔːl,flaʊəʳ, $'wɑːl,flaʊr/ *n* [C] a pleasant smelling garden plant that has yellow, orange or brown flowers which grow in groups

wall·flower SHY PERSON /£'wɔːl,flaʊəʳ, $'wɑːl,flaʊr/ *n* [C] *infml* a shy person, esp. a girl or woman, who is frightened to involve herself in social activities and does not attract much interest or attention • *Sooner or later someone would take pity on the poor wallflower and ask her to dance.*

wal·lop *obj* /£'wɒl·əp, $'wɑː·ləp/ *v* [T] *infml* to hit (someone) hard with the hand or with something held in the hand, or *(fig.)* to defeat (someone) easily, esp. in sports • *She walloped him across the back of the head.* • *(fig.) "How did your tennis match go last night?" "Oh, I was walloped again."*

wal·lop /£'wɒl·əp, $'wɑː·ləp/ *n* [C] *infml* • *My mother* **gave** *me such a wallop when she eventually found me.*

wal·lop·ing /£'wɒl·ə·pɪŋ, $'wɑː·lə-/ *n* [C usually sing] *infml* • If you give someone, esp. a child, a walloping you hit them hard as a punishment: *I* **got** *such a walloping from my father when he came home.* ○ *I was* **given** *such a walloping by my father.*

wal·lop·ing /£'wɒl·ə·pɪŋ, $'wɑː·lə-/ *adj* [before n; not gradable] *infml humorous* very big or great • *You've cut me a walloping* **(great)** *slice of cake – I don't know if I'll be able to manage it.* • *(Am)* Walloping can also mean very good: *We had a walloping* **(good)** *time at Daryl's wedding party.*

wal·low /£'wɒl·əʊ, $'wɑː·loʊ/ *v* [I] (esp. of particular animals) to lie or roll about slowly in deep wet earth, sand or water • *Watching her husband relaxing in the shallow waters she was reminded of a hippopotamus wallowing* **in** *mud.* • *(disapproving)* To wallow **in** a negative emotion or situation is to intentionally stay in that state without doing anything positive to help yourself get out of it: *I wish she'd do something to help herself instead of just wallowing in self-pity!* • You can also wallow **in** something pleasurable by allowing yourself to enjoy it very much: *My idea of a holiday is to book myself into a five-star hotel and just wallow in the luxury for a week.*

wal·low /£'wɒl·əʊ, $'wɑː·loʊ/ *n* [C usually sing] *infml* • *He likes a good wallow in the bath.*

wall·pa·per /£'wɔːl,peɪ·pəʳ, $'wɑːl,peɪ·pɚ/ *n* a thick, often decorative, paper used for covering the walls and sometimes ceilings of a room • *We'll need eight* **rolls of** *wallpaper for the big bedroom.* [U] • *We thought we'd* **put up/hang** *some wallpaper in the children's bedroom to make it brighter.* [U] • *I saw a wallpaper today that would be just right for the bathroom.* [C] • *We'll need some wallpaper* **paste** *and a big brush.* • *(Br infml disapproving)* **Wallpaper music** *(Am* **Elevator music**, *trademark* **muzak**) is music which is very boring, having no particular qualities or characteristics, and can be played without you noticing it: *It sounds to me like the sort of wallpaper music that they play in hotel receptions.*

wall·pa·per *obj* /£'wɔːl,peɪ·pəʳ, $'wɑːl,peɪ·pɚ/ *v* [T] • *We've wallpapered the bedrooms but we've decided to paint the living room.*

wal·ly /£'wɒl·i, $'wɑː·li/ *n* [C] *Br infml* a silly or useless person • *You fell off your bike again? – you wally!* • *I'll look a right wally in these shorts!*

wal·nut /£'wɔːl·nʌt, $'wɑːl-/ *n* a slightly bitter-tasting nut with a series of folds in it and a hard shell, or (the expensive light brown wood from) the tree that produces these nuts • *coffee and walnut cake* • *Are there walnuts in this sauce?* [C] • *a walnut cabinet* • *a cabinet made of walnut* [U] • PIC> **Nut**

wal·rus /£'wɔːl·rəs, $'wɑːl-/ *n* [C] *pl* **walruses** or **walrus** a mammal which lives in the sea and on beaches in the Arctic. It is similar to a SEAL but larger with two TUSKS (= very long teeth which stick out from the mouth) and long hairs. growing near its mouth • *The walrus is unusual in that the female seems to be free to choose her partner.* • A **walrus moustache** is a MOUSTACHE (= line of hair growing above the upper lip) which is long and hangs down at both sides of the mouth.

waltz DANCE /£wɒlts, $wɑːlts/ *n* [C] a formal dance in which two people holding each other move around a large room, turning as they go and repeating a movement of three steps, or a piece of music with three beats in a BAR written for this style of dancing • *The first dance that I* *learned at my ballroom dancing classes was the waltz.* • *I bought a record of Strauss waltzes.*

waltz /£wɒlts, $wɑːlts/ *v* [I] • *The film opens with a succession of elderly couples waltzing* **round** *a church hall.* • *"Waltzing Matilda"* (title of a song by Andrew Paterson, 1903)

waltz WALK /£wɒlts, $wɑːlts/ *v* [I always + adv/prep] *infml* to walk somewhere quickly and confidently • *I find it difficult to just waltz* **up to** *complete strangers and start talking.* • *A whole hour later than we'd arranged, Glyn* **waltzed** *into the bar as if nothing was wrong!* • *My idiot wife has gone and waltzed* **off with** *my car keys and left me without any means of transport!* • *(fig.) He waltzed* **through** (=got through easily) *the first two rounds of the competition.*

wan /£wɒn, $wɑːn/ *adj* **wanner, wannest** *literary* (of a person's face) paler than usual and tired-looking • *He would remember the child's wan face at the window.*

wan·ly /£ˈwɒn·li, $ˈwɑːn-/ *adv literary* • *She smiled wanly* (=weakly).

wand /£wɒnd, $wɑːnd/ *n* [C] a thin stick waved by a person who is performing magic tricks or by an imaginary creature who is doing magic • *The magician held his wand over the handkerchief and out hopped a rabbit.* • *The fairy godmother waved her magic wand over the cabbages and they immediately turned into horses.*

wan·der *(obj)* /£ˈwɒn·dəʳ, $ˈwɑːn·dɚ/ *v* to walk around slowly in a relaxed way or without any clear purpose or direction • *We spent the morning wandering* **around** *the old part of the city.* [I] • *She was found several hours later, wandering the streets, lost.* [T] • *He was here a moment ago but he's wandered* **off** *somewhere.* [I] • *(fig.) We've wandered off the point somewhat* (=started talking about a different subject). [I] • If your **mind** or your **thoughts** wander, you stop thinking about the subject that you should be giving your attention to and start thinking about other matters: *Halfway through the meeting my mind started to wander.* [I] • If you say that an old person's mind is beginning to wander, you mean that they are starting to get very confused because of their age: *Her mind is beginning to wander and she doesn't always know who I am.* [I] • ⓓⓚ

wan·der /£ˈwɒn·dəʳ, $ˈwɑːn·dɚ/ *n* [C usually sing] *infml* • *While you're in your meeting I can* **go for/have/take** *a wander around the city.*

wan·der·ings /£ˈwɒn·dᵊr·ɪŋz, $ˈwɑːn·dɚ-/ *pl n* • You might refer to your time spent travelling in a variety of different foreign countries as your wanderings: *After all her wanderings she had come back home to stay.* • *(humorous infml) If you see Alan* **on your** *wanderings* (=while you are walking around between various places) *will you tell him he's wanted in the office.*

wan·der·lust /£ˈwɒn·də·lʌst, $ˈwɑːn·dɚ-/ *n* [U] the desire to travel far away and to many different places • *Hearing Roz's tales of India has given me wanderlust.* • *In July wanderlust takes over the whole nation.*

wane /weɪn/ *v* [I] to weaken in strength or influence • *By the late seventies the band's popularity was beginning to wane.* • *Public interest in environmental issues tends to wane during a recession.* • The moon wanes when it gradually appears less and less round, after the **full moon**. • Compare WAX APPEAR LARGER.

wane /weɪn/ *n* [U] • *There are signs that support for the party is* **on the wane** (=getting less strong).

wan·gle *obj* /ˈwæŋ·gl̩/ *v* [T] *infml* to succeed in obtaining or doing something by persuading someone or by being clever in some way • *I'll be so jealous if you manage to wangle an invitation to his house.* • *He's only been here two months and already he's managed to wangle his way* **into** *the biggest property company in London.* • *If I can think of some excuse to wangle my way* **out of** *going tonight I will do!*

wank /wæŋk/ *v* [I] *Br and Aus taboo slang* to MASTURBATE (=excite your own or someone else's sex organs by hand)

wank /wæŋk/ *n* [C] *Br and Aus taboo slang* • *to* **have** *a wank*

wank·er /£ˈwæŋ·kəʳ, $-kɚ/ *n* [C] *Br and Aus taboo slang* • *(disapproving)* A wanker is a very stupid, unpleasant or useless person, usually a man: *They're a bunch of wankers, seriously!* • Less commonly, a wanker is a person who MASTURBATES.

wank·y /ˈwæŋ·ki/ *adj* **-ier, -iest** *Br and Aus taboo slang disapproving* • *Dave's got some wanky* (=very stupid) *notion that you're only respectable if you own a piece of property.*

wan·ly /£ˈwɒn·li, $ˈwɑːn-/ *adv* See at WAN

wan·na /£ˈwɒn·ə, $ˈwɑː·nə/ *v not standard* want to or want a • *D'you wanna go now?* [+ infinitive without *to*] • *I wanna hamburger, Mom.* [T]

wan·na·be, wan·na·bee /£ˈwɒn·ə·bi, $ˈwɑː·nə-/ *n* [C] *esp. Am infml disapproving* a person who is trying to achieve success or fame, usually unsuccessfully • *The bar is frequented by wannabe actresses and film directors.*

want *(obj)* DESIRE /£wɒnt, $wɑːnt/ *v* to desire (a particular thing or plan of action). Want is not used in polite requests in British English. • *I want some chocolate.* [T] • *She wants a word with you.* [T] • *He's everything you'd ever want in a man – bright, funny and attractive.* [T] • *What do you want out of life?* [T] • *What do you want* **to** *eat?* [+ *to* infinitive] • *What do you want* **to** *be when you grow up?* [+ *to* infinitive] • *I want* **to** *be picked up at the airport at about nine o'clock.* [+ *to* infinitive] • *Do you want me* **to** *take you to the station?* [T + obj + *to* infinitive] • *This letter – do you want it sent first class?* [T + obj + v-*ed*] • *Do you want this pie hot?* [T + obj + adj] • *I don't want a load of traffic going past my house all night, waking me up.* [T + obj + v-*ing*] • To want someone is also to wish them to be present: *Johnny, your mother wants you on the phone.* [T] ○ *Am I wanted at the meeting tomorrow?* [T] ○ *He is wanted by the police* (=The police are searching for him) *in connection with the murder of teenager Peter Lewis.* [T] • Want is not used in the present continuous tense although the continuous form of the verb is sometimes used in other tenses: *I've been wanting to see that film for months!* [+ *to* infinitive] ○ *You wait – she'll be wanting her own horse next!* [T] • *(infml)* Someone who wants **out of/in** an activity or plan of action wants to stop or start being involved in it: *I want out of the whole venture before it's too late.* [I] • **Want ad** is *Am for* **classified ad**. See at CLASSIFY. • *"I want to be alone"* (Greta Garbo in the film *Grand Hotel*, 1932) • Compare LIKE WANT.

want·ed /£ˈwɒn·tɪd, $ˈwɑːn·t̬ɪd/ *adj* • *She was a much wanted baby* (=her parents wanted to have her). • *He's a wanted man* (=the police are searching for him).

want *obj* NEED /£wɒnt, $wɑːnt/ *v* [T] to have need of (something) • *Do you think this soup wants a bit of salt?* • *The wine is in the fridge – it just wants cooling for a couple of minutes.* [+ v-*ing*] • *It wants a coat of paint but otherwise it's in good condition.* • *If you ask me that child wants a good slap!* • *You'll want a coat on – it's cold outside!* • Want **to** is sometimes used in giving advice, meaning 'should': *You want* **to** *tell him before it's too late.* [+ *to* infinitive] ○ *You don't want to go to bed so late if you're tired all the time!* [+ *to* infinitive]

want /£wɒnt, $wɑːnt/ *n* • *He appeared tired and* **in want of** (=needing) *a shave.* [U] • *(fml) Our wants* (=needs) *are few.* [C]

want for *obj v prep* [T] *fml* • Someone who doesn't want for anything has all the basic things that are needed to lead a satisfactory life: *As children we never wanted for anything – my grandmother made sure of that.*

want LACK /£wɒnt, $wɑːnt/ *n* a lack of something • **For want of** *anything better to do I watched television for a while.* [U] • *If we fail it won't be* **for want of trying** (=we have tried even if we fail). [U]

want·ing /£ˈwɒn·tɪŋ, $ˈwɑːn·t̬ɪŋ/ *adj fml* • *I think she's perhaps a little wanting* **in** *charm.* • *This government's policies, said the speaker, have been* **tried and found wanting** (=discovered to be not effective).

wan·ton WITHOUT CARE /£ˈwɒn·tən, $ˈwɑːn·tᵊn/ *adj fml* (of something bad, such as damage, cruelty, waste) extreme and showing complete lack of care • *Never before had we in the West experienced such wanton destruction of human life.* • *Taylor's driving, said the judge, had shown a wanton disregard for the safety of his passengers.* • *Shall I buy all three dresses or would that just be wanton extravagance?*

wan·ton·ly /£ˈwɒn·tən·li, $ˈwɑːn·tᵊn-/ *adv fml* • *It seemed to her that he had wantonly destroyed their relationship.*

wan·ton SEXUAL /£ˈwɒn·tən, $ˈwɑːn·tᵊn/ *adj old use or humorous* (of a woman) behaving or appearing in a very sexual way • *She advanced to him with outstretched hands and a wanton smile.*

wan·ton·ly /£ˈwɒn·tən·li, $ˈwɑːn·tᵊn-/ *adv old use or humorous* • *"Jonathan, come into my arms," she murmured, wantonly.*

wan·ton·ness /£ˈwɒn·tən·nəs, $ˈwɑːn·tᵊn-/ *n* [U] *old use or humorous*

war /£wɔːʳ, $wɔːr/ *n* armed fighting between two or more countries or groups, or a particular example of this •

nuclear war [U] • *a war film/grave/hero/poet* • *If this country* **goes to** (=starts to fight in a) *war we will have to face the fact that many people will die.* [U] • *Britain and France* **declared** *war* **on** *Germany in 1939 as a result of the invasion of Poland.* [U] • *War* **broke out** *between the two countries after a border dispute.* [U] • *They've been* **at** *war for the last five years.* [U] • *He died in World War 1/the Vietnam war.* [C] • A war **of attrition** is a war which is fought over a long period and only ends when one side has neither the soldiers and equipment nor the determination left to continue fighting. [C] • A war **of nerves** is a situation, often before a competition or BATTLE, in which two opposing sides attempt to frighten or discourage each other by making threats or by showing how strong or clever they are: *The lead-up to tonight's boxing match has seen the usual war of nerves in the press.* [C] • A war is also any situation in which there is fierce competition between opposing sides or a great fight against something harmful: *The new import tax could provoke a trade war between the two nations.* [C] ○ *The past few months have witnessed a* **price** *war between leading supermarkets.* ○ *The government are to step up their attempt to* **wage** *war* **against/on** *drugs.* [U] • A **war bride** is a girl or woman who, during a war, marries a member of the armed forces from a different country. • If someone says that **war clouds** are gathering over a particular country they mean that a war seems increasingly likely there: *It was the 1930s, unemployment was around three million and war clouds were already on the horizon in Europe.* • A **war crime** is a crime which is committed during a war which breaks the accepted international rules of war: *Genocide is a war crime.* • *He was a Nazi* **war criminal** (=someone who committed war crimes). • A **war cry** (also **battle cry**) is a phrase or word shouted by people as they start to fight, which is intended to give them the strength and courage to fight harder: *(fig.) The phrase 'burn your bra!' was the feminists' war cry of the 1970s.* • A **war dance** is a ceremonial dance, performed by some TRIBAL people, either before they fight or after a victory: *You quite often see footballers doing a sort of war dance just after they've scored a goal these days.* • A **war game** is a pretend military BATTLE which is performed only for the purpose of training officers. • A **war memorial** is a large structure, made esp. of stone, which is built in honour of those people who died in a particular war. • **War paint** is a paint used by some TRIBAL people to decorate the face and body before fighting. • *(humorous)* **War paint** is also make-up. • *"Sometime they'll give a war and nobody will come"* (Carl Sandburg in the poem *The People, Yes,* 1936) • *"The war to end all wars"* (used to describe World War I)

war·ring /£ˈwɔː·rɪŋ, $ˈwɔːr·ɪŋ/ *adj* [before n; not gradable] • Warring countries or groups of people are at war with or fighting each other: *A peace mediator has been appointed to try to bring together the warring parties in the south of the country.* ○ *The Labour Party, he said, had disintegrated into warring* **factions**.

war·like /£ˈwɔː·laɪk, $ˈwɔːr-/ *adj fml* • people who are warlike are often involved in and eager to start wars: *It has often been said, perhaps unfairly, that they are a warlike* **nation/people**. ○ *The atmosphere in the football stadium was positively warlike.* ○ *Crowds of men were shouting warlike chants at the top of their voices.*

war·ble /£ˈwɔː·bl̩, $ˈwɔːr-/ *v* [I] (of a bird) to sing pleasantly, or *(humorous)* (of a woman) to sing in a high voice • *(humorous) Was that you I heard warbling in the bathroom this morning?*

war·bler /£ˈwɔː·bləʳ, $ˈwɔːr·blɚ/ *n* [C] • A warbler is a small bird that lives in trees and sings.

ward HOSPITAL /£wɔːd, $wɔːrd/ *n* [C] one of the parts or large rooms into which a hospital is divided, for treating people with a similar type of condition • *a geriatric/maternity/psychiatric ward* • *(Am)* A ward is also one of the parts into which a prison is divided. • PIC› **Medical equipment**

ward CITY AREA /£wɔːd, $wɔːrd/ *n* [C] (in many countries) one of the areas into which a city, town or village is divided, having its own elected political representative or its own organizations for managing services • *Jackson has campaigned these past two years to bring attention to one of the poorest wards in the city.*

-ward TOWARDS /£-wəd, $-wɚd/ *combining form* towards the stated place or direction • *At least we're walking in a homeward direction.* • *The living room has seaward facing windows.* • *Take the northward road.* • *At last, to our great joy we were sailing landward.* • *Move onward three squares.* • LP› **Combining forms, Directions**

-wards /£-wədz, $-wɚdz/ *combining form* • *Take a couple of steps backwards/forwards.* • *Keep looking upwards as you climb – if you look downwards you'll feel dizzy.* • *Stand in a circle all facing inwards.* • *We continued walking southwards for another three or four kilometres.* • Generally, adjectives are formed using -ward and adverbs are formed using -wards: *an eastward journey; moving backwards.* The -ward form of the adverb is also possible, esp. in American and Australian English.

ward (of court) /£wɔːd, $wɔːrd/ *n* [C] a person, esp. a child, who is legally put under the protection of a court of law • *The child was* **made** *a ward of court to stop her father taking her out of the country.* • *His ward, Mary Lennox, had been orphaned in India and was now living with him.*

ward off *obj,* **ward** *obj* **off** /£wɔːd, $wɔːrd/ *v adv* [M] to prevent (something unpleasant) from harming or approaching you • *She was given a magic charm to ward off evil spirits.* • *She tends to wear a rather threatening expression in public to ward off unwanted approaches.* • *In the winter I take vitamin C – it helps to ward colds off.*

war·den MANAGER OF BUILDING /£ˈwɔː·dᵊn, $ˈwɔːr-/ *n* [C] a person who is in charge of (the people in) a particular building • *She's the warden of a home for mentally handicapped people.* • *(Br and Aus)* The head of a college is sometimes called a warden: *He's the warden of Wadham College, Oxford.* • *(Am)* A warden is also a prison governor (=a person who is in charge of a prison): *a prison warden*

war·den OFFICIAL /£ˈwɔː·dᵊn, $ˈwɔːr-/ *n* [C] a person whose job is to make certain that members of the public obey particular rules • *an animal warden* • *a dog/game/park/traffic warden*

war·der *male, female dated also* **ward·ress** /£ˈwɔː·dəʳ, $ˈwɔːr·dɚ, -drəs/ *n* [C] *Br and Aus* a person who is in charge of people in prison

ward·robe /£ˈwɔː·drəʊb, $ˈwɔːr·droʊb/ *n* a tall cupboard in which you hang your clothes, or all of the clothes that a person owns • *She was showing me her new* **built-in**/*(Br)* **fitted** *wardrobes.* [C] • *I sometimes feel that my summer wardrobe is rather lacking* (=I don't have many clothes for summer). [U] • In the theatre the wardrobe is the group of people who are in charge of the clothes that the actors wear on stage, making certain that they are clean, repairing them and sometimes making them: *He's in charge of wardrobe at the local amateur theatre.* [U] ○ *She's the wardrobe mistress at the theatre.* • PIC› **Beds and bedroom**

-ware /£weəʳ, $wer/ *combining form* used, often in shops, to refer to items of the same material or type, esp. items used in cooking and serving food • *tableware* ○ *earthenware* ○ *silverware* • *the kitchenware department* • LP› **Shopping goods**

ware·house *Br and Aus* /£ˈweə·haʊs, $ˈwer-/, *Am* **store·house** *n* [C] *pl* **-houses** /-ˌhaʊ·zɪz/ a large building for storing items before they are sold, used or sent out to shops, or a large shop selling a large number of a particular items at a cheap rate • *The goods have been sitting in a warehouse for months because a strike has prevented distribution.* • *We bought both sofas from a big furniture warehouse that's just off the motorway.* • *They'd organized a party in a derelict warehouse somewhere just outside London.* • Ⓓ Ⓝⓛ

wares /£weəz, $werz/ *pl n* small items for selling, in a market or on the street but not usually in a shop, or *(infml)* a company's products • *Some displayed their wares on stalls, while others had just spread them out on the pavement.* • *(infml) The company must do more to promote their wares overseas.*

war·fare /£ˈwɔː·feəʳ, $ˈwɔːr·fer/ *n* [U] the activity of fighting a war, often including the weapons and methods that are used • *guerrilla/naval/nuclear/trench warfare* • *He wrote of the horrors of modern warfare.*

war·fa·rin /£ˈwɔː·fᵊr·ɪn, $ˈwɔːr·fɚ-/ *n* [U] *trademark* a substance which is used to kill RATS and is also used in a slightly different form as a medical treatment in order to prevent blood from CLOTTING (=becoming solid)

war·head /£ˈwɔː·hed, $ˈwɔːr-/ *n* [C] the front end of a bomb or MISSILE that contains explosives • *The Scud missile which hit a block of flats carried a conventional, high-explosive warhead.*

war·horse PERSON /£ˈwɔː·hɔːs, $ˈwɔːr·hɔːrs/ *n* [C] *infml* an old and experienced politician, soldier or sportsperson, esp. one who is still active • *An old civil rights warhorse,* *she has returned to the political arena to fight another battle.* • *Manchester City football club's old warhorse, still fighting fit at 36, was sent off for fouling after half an hour.*

war·horse ESTABLISHED SHOW /£'wɔː·hɔːs, $'wɔːr·hɔːrs/ *n* [C usually sing] *often disapproving* a piece of music, television show, play or other performed piece of work which has often been performed or shown and is very famous • *I don't understand why a ballet company can't perform fresh new material instead of just bringing out the same* **old** *warhorses year after year.*

wa·ri·ly /£'weə·rɪ·li, $'wer·ɪ-/ *adv* See at WARY

war·lord /£'wɔː·lɔːd, $'wɔːr·lɔːrd/ *n* [C] *esp. disapproving* a military leader who controls a country or, more frequently, an area within a country • *a brutal warlord* • *a regional warlord* • *There is a great fear that the country will break up into a series of unstable cantons, each with its own warlord.*

warm HIGH TEMPERATURE /£wɔːm, $wɔːrm/ *adj* **-er, -est** having or producing a comfortably high temperature, although not hot • *Are you warm enough or do you want the fire on?* • *It was so* **nice and** *warm in bed.* • *I've got my hands in my pockets to keep them warm.* • *This beer's warm – I can't drink it!* • Items such as clothes and covers that are warm are made of a material that keeps the body warm: *I don't have a warm winter coat.* ○ *Those gloves look nice and warm.* • A warm **colour** is one which is based on or contains a colour such as red, pink or orange which suggests warmth. • A **warm-blooded** animal has a body temperature which stays the same and does not change with the temperature of its surroundings: *Birds and mammals are warm-blooded.* ○ Compare **cold-blooded** at COLD LOW TEMPERATURE. • A **warm up** is a short period of gentle exercise and stretching that people do before they do more active exercise: *A warm-up is important before a run so as not to strain any muscles.*

warm *(obj)* /£wɔːm, $wɔːrm/ *v* • *You're so cold – come and warm your hands by the fire.* [T] • *She warmed her cold feet against his.* [T] • *Warm the sauce over a low heat but don't let it boil.* [T] • *Your supper's just warming* **through** *in the oven.* [I] • *The August sun warmed the fields.* [T] • *It doesn't take long for the room to warm* **up** *once you've put the heating on.* [I] • *We can warm the room* **(up)** *quite quickly with this electric fire.* [T/M] • *It always takes a couple of minutes for the car engine to warm* **up** (=become warm enough to start working well). [I] • *I'll just warm* **up** *the engine while you're getting your coats on.* [M] • *(fig. infml) The party was only just starting to warm* **up** (=start to be interesting and active) *as I left.* [I] • If you warm food **up/** *(Am also)* **over**, you heat food that you have already cooked again: *I might just warm up the left-overs from yesterday's meal in the microwave.* [M] • If you warm **up** before doing physical exercise, you do a few gentle exercises and stretches in order to prepare the body: *If you don't warm up before taking exercise, you risk injuring yourself.* [I] • *(Am disapproving)* If something such as an idea or performance is **warmed over**, it is boring and not imaginative: *These commercials are just warmed-over imitations of earlier TV ads.* • If you **warm to/towards** someone, you start to like them: *I wasn't sure about Sarah at first, but I warmed to her after we'd been out together a few times.* • If you **warm to** an idea, you start to become interested in or enthusiastic about it: *He didn't want to move overseas at first, but I think he's warming to the idea.* ○ *Unfortunately, I had to leave just as the speaker was warming to his theme.* Something that is said to **warm the heart** or *(humorous)* **warm the cockles of** your **heart**, makes you happy and makes you feel positive towards people in general: *It's nice to see a good love story once in a while – it warms the heart.*

warm /£wɔːm, $wɔːrm/ *n* [U] *Br* • **The warm** refers to any warm place: *It's cold standing out here – come into the warm.*

warm·ing /£'wɔː·mɪŋ, $'wɔːr-/ *adj approving* • Food or drink which is warming makes you feel warm: *Have a nice warming bowl of soup.*

warm·ly /£'wɔːm·li, $'wɔːrm-/ *adv* • *You're not dressed warmly enough – put a sweater on.*

warmth /£wɔːmpθ, $wɔːrmpθ/ *n* [U] • *A baby's needs are quite basic – food, warmth and love.* • *I've put a T-shirt on under my sweater for extra warmth.*

warm FRIENDLY /£wɔːm, $wɔːrm/ *adj* **-er, -est** friendly and affectionate • *They're a very warm family.* • *He has a lovely warm smile.* • *I'd like to give a warm* **welcome** *to our guests this evening.* • A **warm-hearted** person is kind and affectionate: *She's a good warm-hearted woman.*

warm·ly /£'wɔːm·li, $'wɔːrm-/ *adv* • *He shook my hand warmly.*

warmth /£wɔːmpθ, $wɔːrmpθ/ *n* [U] • *His manner lacks a certain warmth.*

warm NEAR /£wɔːm, $wɔːrm/ *adj* [after v] **-er, -est** *infml* (esp. in children's games) near to guessing a correct answer or to discovering a hidden object • *You're* **getting** *warmer!*

war·mon·ger /£'wɔːˌmʌŋ·gəʳ, $'wɔːrˌmʌŋ·gɚ/ *n* [C] *disapproving* a politician or other leader who is often encouraging a country to go to war • *He was no warmonger but he did believe in nuclear weapons.*

war·mon·ger·ing /£'wɔːˌmʌŋ·gəʳr·ɪŋ, $'wɔːr·mʌŋ·gɚ-/ *n* [U] *disapproving* • *The president was accused of warmongering.*

warn *(obj)* /£wɔːn, $wɔːrn/ *v* to make (someone) aware of a possible danger or problem, esp. one in the future • *Scientists have warned* **that** *further extremely high winds are likely.* [+ *that* clause] • *We were warned not* **to** *eat the fish which might give us a slight stomach upset.* [T + obj + *to* infinitive] • *Have you warned them* **(that)** *there will be an extra person for dinner?* [T + obj + *(that)* clause] • *I was warned* **against/off** *going to the east coast because it was so full of tourists.* [T] • *There were signs warning* **of** *fog as soon as we got onto the motorway.* [I] • *This particular curry is extremely hot – you have been warned!* [T] • *"Has anyone told you about Paul?" "Yes, I have been warned."* [T] • *Put that ball down and come over here, Laura – I'm warning you* (=I will punish you if you do not!) [T]

warn·ing /£'wɔː·nɪŋ, $'wɔːr-/ *n* • *Completely without warning he turned up on my doorstep with all four children!* [U] • *There's a warning on the cigarette packet that says 'tobacco seriously damages health'.* [C] • *He gave a warning* **that** *he would not put up with any more bad behaviour.* [+ *that* clause] • *That's what happens when you won't let yourself grow old and you start dyeing your hair and starving yourself –* **let it be a** *warning to you!* [C] • *Just a* **word of** *warning – restaurants in this area can be very expensive.* [U] • *(fml) The government have today* **issued** *a warning about the dangers of sunbathing.* [C] • *They can't dismiss you just like that – they have to* **give** *you a* **written** *warning first.* [C] • *The police fired warning* **shots** *but the protesters took no notice.* • People sometimes say that they **hear warning bells** or that **warning bells start to ring/ sound** to mean that they see signs that something bad has started or is going to happen: *For me, the warning bells started to ring when she stopped eating properly and lost all that weight.* • A **warning sign** is something that tells you of a particular danger: *There were several warning signs because of the fog.* ○ *In some bars there are* **warning signs** (=notices) *telling women of the dangers of drinking alcohol during pregnancy.* ○ *The* **warning signs** (=The physical signs that show the presence) *of the illness are respiratory problems and dizziness.*

warp *(obj)* BEND /£wɔːp, $wɔːrp/ *v* (esp. of wood) to become damaged by bending or twisting, usually as a result of the presence of water or heat, or (of water or heat) to damage (esp. wood) by bending or twisting it • *Left in the garage where it was damp, the wooden frame had warped.* [I] • *If I put the shelves near the radiator, the heat might warp them.* [T] • *(fig.) Peter was brought up by a mother who was completely mad, and unfortunately it had warped his mind* (=made him strange and unpleasant). [T]

warped /£wɔːpt, $wɔːrpt/ *adj disapproving* or *humorous* • *Have you noticed how warped these shelves are?* • *(fig.) I suppose I shouldn't be laughing about death – perhaps I've got a warped* (=strange and unpleasant) **mind/sense of humour**!

warp THREADS /£wɔːp, $wɔːrp/ *n* [U] **the warp** *specialized* the threads that go along the length of a piece of cloth or a LOOM (=a device for weaving) • Compare WEFT.

war·path /£'wɔː·pɑːθ, $'wɔːr·pæθ/ *n* [U] **on the warpath** *infml usually humorous* angry and likely to argue or punish • *If there was one thing she couldn't face in the morning it was her mother on the warpath.*

war·rant *obj* MAKE NECESSARY /£'wɒr·ənt, $'wɔːr-/ *v* [T] to make (a particular activity) necessary • *Obviously what she did was wrong, but I don't think it warranted quite such severe punishment.* • *It's a relatively simple task that really doesn't warrant a great deal of time being spent on it.* • See also UNWARRANTED.

war·rant /£'wɒr·ənt, $'wɔːr-/ *n* [U] *dated* • *There's no warrant for that sort of behaviour!*

war·rant DOCUMENT /£'wɒr·ᵊnt, $'wɔːr-/ *n* [C] an official document, signed by a judge or other person in authority, which gives the police permission to search someone's home, ARREST a person or take some other action • *a search warrant* • *Judge La Riva had issued an arrest warrant/a warrant* **for** *his arrest.* • *(esp. Am fml) Several officers* **executed** *a warrant* (= did what the warrant allowed them to do) *at the suspect's home.* • A **warrant officer** is a rank in the armed forces, between a **commissioned officer** and a **non-commissioned officer**.

war·rant *obj* PROMISE /£'wɒr·ᵊnt, $'wɔːr-/ *v* [T] *fml* to promise that (something) will be done or will happen • *The retailer warranted* **that** *he would take back any faulty goods.*

war·ran·ty /£'wɒr·ᵊn·ti, $'wɔːr·ᵊn·ṭi/ *n* [C] • A warranty is a written promise by a company to repair or replace a product that develops a fault within a fixed period of time or do again a piece of work that is not satisfactory: *The warranty* **covers** *the car mechanically for a year with unlimited mileage.*

war·ren /£'wɒr·ᵊn, $'wɔːr-/, **rab·bit war·ren** *n* [C] a series of connecting underground passages and holes in which rabbits live • *(esp. disapproving)* A warren can also be a very crowded and confusing building or part of a city in which it is easy to get lost: *They live on a great concrete warren of a housing estate.*

war·ri·or /£'wɒr·i·əʳ, $'wɔːr·i·ɚ/ *n* [C] a soldier, usually one who has both experience and skill in fighting, esp. in the past • *a Samurai/Kamikaze warrior* ○ *a warrior king/nation*

wars /£wɔːz, $wɔːrz/ *pl n* **in the wars** *Br infml* having injuries to many different parts of the body • *You've got a cut on your arm as well, you poor thing, you are in the wars!*

war·ship /£'wɔː·ʃɪp, $'wɔːr-/ *n* [C] a ship equipped with guns, for use in war

wart /£wɔːt, $wɔːrt/ *n* [C] a small hard lump which grows on the skin, often on the face and hands • *She had a big wart on the end of her nose.* • *(infml)* A **warts and all** description or representation of a person is one that includes all the faults in that person's character and makes no attempt to hide them: *He tried to portray the president as he really was, warts and all.*

wart·y /£'wɔː·ti, $'wɔːr·ṭi/ *adj* **-ier, -iest** • *warty hands*

wart·hog /£'wɔːt·hɒg, $'wɔːrt·hɑːg/ *n* [C] an African wild pig with a large head, TUSKS (= long teeth which stick out from the mouth) and little lumps on the male's face that look like WARTS

war·time /£'wɔː·taɪm, $'wɔːr-/ *n* [U] a period of time during which a war is being fought • **In** *wartime food is often scarce.* • *The film is set in wartime England.* • Compare PEACETIME.

wa·ry /£'weə·ri, $'wer·i/ *adj* **-ier, -iest** not completely trusting or certain about something or someone • *I'm a bit wary* **of/about** *giving people my address when I don't know them very well.* • *She's been a bit wary* **of** *dogs ever since one bit her as a child.*

wa·ri·ly /£'weə·rɪ·li, $'wer·ɪ-/ *adv* • *The two children stood behind their mothers, eyeing each other warily.*

was /£wɒz, $wɑːz, £wəz/ *past simple of* BE • *I was aged three at the time.* • *He was here a moment ago.*

wa·sa·bi /'wæs·æb·i/ *n* [U] Japanese MUSTARD (= spicy sauce)

wash *(obj)* CLEAN /£wɒʃ, $wɑːʃ/ *v* to clean with water • *wash your car/clothes/hair/hands* [T] • *These sheets need washing.* [T] • *Do you think these stains will wash* **out** (= be removed by washing)*?* [I] • *I'll wash the bottle* **out** (= clean its inside) *and use it again.* [M] • To wash (*Am also* **wash up**) is to clean yourself, or a part of yourself, with water and usually soap: *I'd like to wash before dinner* [I] • *(Br and Aus)* To **wash up** (*Am* **do the dishes**) is to clean the plates, pans, knives and forks, etc. that you have used in cooking and/or in eating. • A particular material or piece of clothing is said to wash well if it is not damaged by repeated washing. [I] • *(disapproving)* People who **wash** their **dirty linen in public** discuss or allow to be discussed in public, matters which should be kept private. • If you **wash** your **hands of** something that you were previously responsible for, you intentionally stop being involved in it or connected with it in any way: *She couldn't wait to wash her hands of the whole project.* • Someone who has used a swear word might be told, humorously, to **wash** their **mouth out (with soapy water)**. • Material that looks **washed-out** has become less bright as a result of frequent washing: *She was wearing a washed-out old T-shirt and jeans.* • Someone who feels or looks **washed-out** feels or looks very tired: *I have to wear a bit of make-up in the winter or I look completely washed-out.* • See also BRAINWASH; EYEWASH; WASHOUT. • LP Reflexive pronouns and verbs

wash /£wɒʃ, $wɑːʃ/ *n* [U] • *Those curtains need* **a** *good wash* (= need to be washed). • To **have a** wash is to wash your body or a part of it: *I haven't had a wash for days.* • To **do a** wash is to clean clothes, sheets, etc., esp. in a washing machine: *Are you doing a wash tonight?* • **The** wash refers to all the clothes that are washed together, esp. in a washing machine: *Can I put this shirt in with the white wash?* ○ *"Where's my pink shirt?" "It's* **in** *the wash"* (= being washed or in a pile of clothes that is going to be washed). • **The** wash is also *Am for* **the washing**.

wash·a·ble /£'wɒʃ·ə·bl̩, $'wɑː·ʃə-/ *adj* [not gradable] • *Are these trousers washable* (= Can you wash them without causing damage), *do you know?* • *I never buy clothes that aren't* **machine***-washable.*

wash·er /£'wɒʃ·əʳ, $'wɑː·ʃɚ/ *n* [C] • Washer is *Am for* **washing machine**. • A **washer-drier** is a machine which both washes and dries clothes, sheets, etc.

wash·ing /£'wɒʃ·ɪŋ, $'wɑː·ʃɪŋ/ *n* [U] • **The** washing (*Am also* **The wash**) is the act of washing clothes: **Doing** *the washing is such a bore!* ○ *I'd hate to have twins – imagine all that washing!* • Washing (*Am also* **Wash**) also refers to clothes, sheets, etc. that need to be or have just been washed: *Would you believe he still takes all his washing home for his mother to do!* ○ *I'm just going to* **hang/peg out** *the washing.* • A **washing machine** is a machine for washing clothes, sheets and other cloth items: *a front/top loading washing machine* ○ *Could you empty/load the washing machine, please?* • *(Br and Aus)* **Washing-up** (*Am* **Dishes**) refers either to the act of cleaning plates, pans, knives and forks, etc., or to the items needing to be washed: *You* **do** *the washing-up and I'll do the drying.* ○ *There's an enormous pile of washing-up in the sink.* • *(Br and Aus)* **Washing-up liquid** (*Am* **Dish liquid**) is a thick liquid DETERGENT which is added to hot water when washing pans, knives and forks, etc. • *(Br and Aus)* **Washing powder/liquid** (*Am and Aus* **laundry detergent**) is a DETERGENT in the form of a powder or liquid which is used for washing clothes and other cloth items: *biological washing powder* • PIC Cleaning

wash *(obj)* FLOW /£wɒʃ, $wɑːʃ/ *v* [always + adv/prep] (of liquid, esp. water) to flow in a particular direction • *(literary)* If water washes somewhere it flows there, usually repeatedly: *She stood on the shore and let the water wash* **over** *her tired feet.* [I] ○ *The water washed gently* **against** *the boat.* [I] • If something is washed **away**, it is removed or carried away by a flow of water or by rain: *Floods have washed away several villages in India.* [M] ○ *The blood on the pavement had been washed away by the rain overnight.* [M] ○ *A storm had washed away some of the earth and revealed the rocks beneath.* [M] • If the sea washes something **up** or washes it **ashore**, it leaves it on the beach: *Overnight the sea had washed up a lot of rubbish.* [M] ○ *More than 400 dolphins had been washed ashore, dead or dying from internal injuries.* [M] • *A Spanish crew member had been washed overboard* (= carried off a ship into the sea by the force of the water) *in the storm.* [T] • *(infml) Supper was lemon soup, followed by fresh salmon and vegetables, and all washed* **down with** (= eaten with) *a couple of bottles of white wine.* [T] • If an occasion is washed **out**, it is prevented from happening or stopped early because of heavy rain: *The men's semi-finals in the tennis were washed out this morning.* [T] • *(infml)* If an excuse or argument **won't wash (with** someone), they are unlikely to believe or accept it. • If you are **washed-up**, the job for which you are trained is finished and you have no further chances of success in the future: *The tragedy of being a dancer is that you're* **all** *washed-up by the time you're thirty-five.*

wash /£wɒʃ, $wɑːʃ/ *n* [U] *literary* • *Outside the flat, she could hear the gentle wash of the waves on the beach.*

wash THIN LAYER /£wɒʃ, $wɑːʃ/ *n* [C] a thin layer of water or watery paint, esp. one which is brushed lightly over a painting to make the lines softer • *a blue wash* • *a wash painting* • *Just before the paint dries, I give it a light wash.*

wash EVEN SITUATION /£wɒʃ, $wɑːʃ/ *n* [C usually sing] *Am* an event or situation in which positive and negative things balance each other • *If pollution controls are enforced here, the factories will move to where they're allowed to pollute, so it'll be a wash as far as clear air goes.*

wash·ba·sin *Br and Aus* /£'wɒʃˌbeɪ·sᵊn, $'wɑːʃ-/, *Am* **sink** *n* [C] an open container in a bathroom or near a toilet which holds water for washing the hands and face, and which has pipes to supply and carry away water • *I keep finding her hairs in the washbasin.* • PIC> **Bathroom**

wash·cloth /£'wɒʃ·klɒθ, $'wɑːʃ·klɑːθ/ *n* [C] *Am for* FACECLOTH • PIC> **Bathroom**

wash·er /£'wɒʃ·əʳ, $'wɑː·ʃɚ/ *n* [C] a flat ring of metal, rubber or plastic which is put esp. between a screw or BOLT and a surface in order to improve the connection between them • *Washers can also be used between joined pipes to seal their connection or between moving parts to prevent damage from rubbing.* • PIC> **Tools**

wash·out /£'wɒʃ·aʊt, $'wɑː·ʃaʊt/ *n* [C usually sing] *infml* a complete failure • *The last party was a bit of a washout – hardly anyone turned up and those who did left by midnight!*

wash·room /£'wɒʃ·rʊm, -ruːm, $'wɑːʃ-/ *n* [C] *Am dated for* TOILET

wash·stand /£'wɒʃ·stænd, $'wɑːʃ-/ *n* [C] a small table for holding a BASIN (= container for water), used esp. in the past • *a marble-topped washstand*

was·n't /£'wɒz·ᵊnt, $'wɑː·zᵊnt/ *short form of* was not • *I wasn't very old at the time.* • *Wasn't it ridiculous?* • *It was you who told me that, wasn't it?*

wasp INSECT /£wɒsp, $wɑːsp/ *n* [C] a black and yellow flying insect which can sting you • *Keep still – there's a wasp near your head.* • *There's a wasps' nest in that old tree.* • *Wasp* **stings** *are incredibly painful.* • A piece of clothing which is **wasp-waisted** is noticeably narrow at the waist: *a wasp-waisted jacket* • PIC> **Wasps and bees**

WASP PERSON, **Wasp** /£wɒsp, $wɑːsp/ *n* [C] *esp. Am disapproving* White Anglo-Saxon Protestant (= a white American whose family originally came from northern Europe, and is therefore part of a group often considered the most influential and wealthy in American society) • *My mother comes from an old WASP family which has been in this country for 350 years.* • *The dominance of the WASP is far from over and newer Americans often tend to adopt the manners of the old.*

WASP·y /£'wɒs·pi, $'wɑː·spi/, **WASP·ish** /£'wɒs·pɪʃ, $'wɑː·spɪʃ/, **Wasp·ish** *adj* [not gradable] *esp. Am disapproving* • *Carter plays the respectable WASPy lawyer who finds himself irresistibly attracted to a New York hooker.*

wasp·ish /£'wɒs·pɪʃ, $'wɑː·spɪʃ/ *adj disapproving* likely to make sharp, slightly cruel remarks; having a slightly angry and unpleasant manner • *She had a waspish tongue which could hurt.* • *He had a sharp, sometimes waspish, wit which made people rather wary of him.*

waste BAD USE /weɪst/ *n* [U] an unnecessary or wrong use of money, substances, time, energy, abilities, etc. • *That meeting achieved absolutely nothing – it was a complete waste* **of time**. • *She's been unemployed for two years and it's such* **a** *waste* **of** *her talents.* • *It's such a waste of energy to have these constant arguments!* • *I can't believe that beautiful building is still empty – it's* **such a** *waste.* • *It's* **such a** *waste giving good food to Dave – he really doesn't appreciate it.* [+ v-ing] • *My mother couldn't bear waste – she always made us eat everything on our plates.* • *He's so handsome and yet he's not interested in women –* **what a** *waste!* • *Don't feed that to the dog – it's* **a** *waste* **of** *a good piece of meat.* • Waste **ground** or **land** refers to an area of ground in or near a city which is not built on, cultivated or used in any way: *The waste ground opposite us is being redeveloped.* ○ *His body had been dumped in an area of waste land just outside the city.* • *"Go on, finish off this tart, Paul." "Well, it seems a shame to let it* **go to waste** (= not be eaten/ used)*."* • *(infml) He's a total* **waste of space** (= useless person), *that man.* • *"What a waste"* (title of a song by Ian Dury, 1978)

waste *obj* /weɪst/ *v* [T] • *You waste a lot of water washing vegetables under running water at the sink.* • *She never wastes anything – every bit of packaging is re-used in some way.* • *Come on, let's get started – we've wasted enough* **time** *already.* • *Don't waste your* **money** *on me, love, keep it for yourself.* • *When I think of all those wasted years I spent with him!* • *He wasn't in when I got there, so it was a completely wasted journey.* • *You mean he was standing on his own at the party, and I wasn't there? Damn, another wasted* **opportunity**! • *(Am slang)* To waste someone means to kill them: *"Waste them", he instructed and turned away as the bullets were fired.* • If you say that something is **wasted on** someone, you mean that it is too clever or its quality is too high for them and they will not understand its true value: *No, I'm afraid your wit was wasted on them, darling.* ○ *I'm not going to serve that good coffee to Chris and Melanie – it would be wasted on them.* • If you **waste** your **breath**, you spend time and energy trying to give advice which is ignored: *Honestly, you're wasting your breath – he doesn't want to hear what anyone else has got to say.* • If someone does **not waste words**, they talk only about what is important using as few words as possible: *He explained the whole system in about 30 seconds – he doesn't waste words, does he?* • *(saying)* 'Waste not, want not' means if you do not waste anything you will not lack it in the future.

wast·age /'weɪ·stɪdʒ/ *n* [U] • *Water companies have got to cut down on wastage.* • *One of the big arguments in favour of public transport is that is cuts down on fuel wastage.* • Wastage is *Br and Aus for* **natural wastage**. See at NATURE LIFE. • *(Br)* Wastage (*Am and Aus* **attrition**) can also refer to the people who leave an educational or training course before it has finished: *The wastage rates on the degree courses are a cause for concern.*

waste·ful /'weɪst·fᵊl/ *adj disapproving* • *It's wasteful the way you throw so much food away!* • *All this excessive packaging – it's so wasteful.* • *He is particularly critical of what he sees as wasteful public spending.* • *It's very wasteful* **of** *electricity to have so many lights on at once.*

waste·ful·ly /'weɪst·fᵊl·i/ *adv disapproving* • *I'm afraid I rather wastefully tipped the rest of the wine down the sink.*

wast·er /£'weɪ·stəʳ, $-stɚ/ *n* [C] *infml disapproving* • *a time waster* ○ *a money waster* ○ *a waster of precious resources* • *(Br and Aus)* A waster (*Am and Aus* **bum**) is a person who does nothing positive with their life, making no use of their abilities or the opportunities that are offered them: *There were the usual bunch of wasters hanging round the bar.* ○ *He'll never do anything with his life – he's a complete waster.*

waste UNWANTED MATTER /weɪst/ *n* unwanted matter or material of any type, often that which is left after useful substances or parts have been removed • *Modern packaging is often excessive, and produces a lot of waste.* [U] • *Britain produces 20 million tonnes of* **household** *waste each year.* [U] • *He opposes any kind of* **nuclear** *waste being dumped at sea.* [U] • *The commission lays down strict guidelines for the disposal of* **hazardous** *waste.* [U] • *It is much cheaper to recycle aluminium from waste than to extract it from bauxite.* [U] • *Substantial energy savings are made by* **recycling** *waste materials.* • *Every day, 30 million gallons of untreated human waste* (= excrement) *flow from Ciudad Juarez into the Rio Grande.* [U] • *Now they are set to tackle one of their most ambitious clean-up jobs yet – radioactive waste.* [U] • *Without a licensed waste* **disposal** *site, toxic wastes now must be shipped out of state or stored.* [C] • *Oil spills are common, as is the dumping of toxic industrial wastes.* [C] • *The Japanese recycle more than half of their waste* **paper**. • *The waste* **pipes** *from the bath and washbasin go through this wall.* • A **waste product** is a substance of no value or use which is made during a process in which something useful is produced: *Faeces and urine are two of the body's waste products.* ○ *The disease affects the body's ability to break down some of the body's toxic waste products.* ○ *Up to 0·2 kg of toxic cadmium, a waste product from the electronics industry, enters the sea from the Thames every day.*

waste a·way *v adv* [I] to gradually get thinner and weaker, in a way that is unhealthy • *It is not death he fears, but wasting away, becoming dependent.* • *You get thinner every time I see you, Sara – you're wasting away!*

wast·ed /£'weɪs·tɪd, $-t̬ɪd/ *adj* • *He had the wasted body of a drug-addict.* • *Underneath the hospital blankets I could see the outline of her poor wasted body.* • See also WASTED.

wast·ing /£'weɪ·stɪŋ, $-t̬ɪŋ/ *adj* [not gradable] *before n* • The word 'wasting' when referring to a disease means that the disease causes you to become very thin and weak: *She suffers from a little-known muscle-wasting disease.*

wast·ed /£'weɪ·stɪd, $-t̬ɪd/ *adj esp. Am slang* extremely tired, or very drunk or ill from drugs • *Man, I'm wasted! I've been on duty for 36 hours!* • *We'll take a cab – I'll be wasted after a few drinks.* • See also **wasted** at WASTE AWAY.

waste·land /'weɪst·lænd/ *n* an empty area of land in or near a city which is not cultivated or built on, or used in any way • *The car was dumped in a stretch of wasteland in the south of the city.* [U] • *A survey in 1976 suggested that there were then 104 670 hectares of urban wasteland in Great Britain.* [U] • *The wastelands are awaiting transformation into neat farms or parks.* [C] • Wasteland can be used to refer to a place, time or situation which lacks anything positive or productive: *In his later work, Britain's inner*

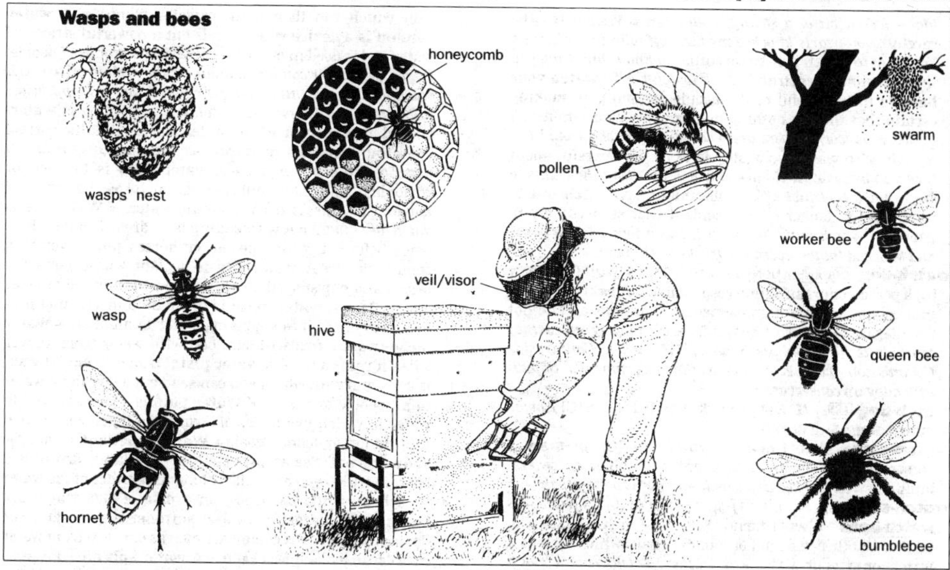

cities are depicted as a **cultural** *wasteland.* ○ *Their relationship had become an* **emotional** *wasteland.* ○ *This new surge of interest in religion is perhaps a reaction to the the* **spiritual** *wasteland of the 1980s.*

waste·pa·per bas·ket /£ˌweɪstˈpeɪ·pəʳ, $-pɚ/, *Br and Aus also* **(waste·pa·per) bin**, *esp. Aus infml* **WPB** /ˌdʌb·l̩.juː·piːˈbiː/, *esp. Am* **waste·bas·ket** /£ˈweɪstˌbɑː·skɪt, $-ˌbæs·kɪt/ *n* [C] an open container which stands on the floor inside buildings and is used for putting rubbish in, esp. paper • *Nine-tenths of the letters they receive end up in the wastepaper basket.* • PIC⟩ **Basket**

wastes /weɪsts/ *pl n* large areas of land that are not cultivated and have few living animals or plants • *The missiles could be pointed north to fall harmlessly on the Arctic wastes of northern Siberia.*

wast·rel /ˈweɪ·strəl/ *n* [C] *literary* a person who does nothing positive with their life, making no use of their abilities or the opportunities that are offered them • *His son turned to be a bit of a wastrel who drank and gambled away the family fortune.*

watch SMALL CLOCK /£wɒtʃ, $wɑːtʃ/ *n* [C] a small clock which is worn on a strap around the wrist or, sometimes, connected to a piece of clothing by a chain • *a digital/analogue watch* • *Ian bought Elaine a gold watch for Christmas.* • *My watch seems to have stopped – it says 10:15 but I'm sure it must be later.* • *He glanced nervously at his watch.* • LP⟩ **Time**

watch *(obj)* LOOK AT /£wɒtʃ, $wɑːtʃ/ *v* to look at (something) for a period of time, esp. something that is changing or moving • *I had dinner and watched TV for a couple of hours.* [T] • *He spent the entire afternoon watching cricket videos.* [T] • *Do you mind if I watch the news?* [T] • *I watch my teacher do the exercise first before I attempt it myself.* [T + obj + infinitive without *to*] • *She watched the rain as it trickled down the window.* [T] • *I watched him get into a taxi.* [T + obj + infinitive without *to*] • *Uncle Johnny, come and watch me do a headstand.* [T + obj + infinitive without *to*] • *He's one of those bosses that watches everything you do.* [T + obj + infinitive without *to*] • *I got the feeling I was being watched.* [T] • *I prefer watching sports to taking part in them.* [T] • *I've never seen anyone run so fast – just watch him go!* [T + obj + infinitive without *to*] • *I sit by the window and watch people walking past.* [T + obj + v-*ing*] • *It's fascinating watching children grow up.* [T + obj + infinitive without *to*] • *Just watch* **how** *he slides that ball in past the goal-keeper.* [+ *wh-* word] • *Bonner watched helplessly as the ball sneaked in at the near post.* [I] • *You don't believe me that I can drink all this in one gulp? Watch me!* [T] • *She'll pretend that she hasn't seen us – you watch.* [I] • *If you want me to watch the kids* (= watch them and make certain that they're safe) *for a bit while you go out let me know.* [T] • *I've had one of those incredibly boring days at work when you seem to spend the whole day* **watching the clock** (= seeing what the time is and wishing it were later). • *I love sitting in outdoor cafes* **watching the world go by** (= looking at people as they go past). • If someone says **watch this space** they mean that there will very soon be more exciting developments in their situation. • If you **watch out for** someone or something you look for them or you keep remembering to look for them: *Tony Pritchard should be running in this race so remember to watch out for him.* • To **watch over** someone is to protect them and make certain that they are safe: *The princes' bodyguard was by the pool, watching over them as they played* • *(infml humorous) "So you don't want to watch the football?" "To be honest I'd rather* **watch paint dry** (= I would be extremely bored)*".* • LP⟩ **Eye and seeing**

watch /£wɒtʃ, $wɑːtʃ/ *n* • *Once your name has been linked with a drug offence, the police* **keep a close** *watch* **on** *you.* [U] • *I'm just going to use his telephone – could you* **keep** *watch and warn me if he comes.* [U] • *The soldiers slept at night, except for one who stayed awake* **on** *watch.* [U] • *He was in the hospital wing of the prison* **under** *close watch, after trying to kill himself.* [U] • A watch is also a group of soldiers or guards whose duty is to protect a person, place or thing from danger or attack. [C] • **Keep a watch out** (= Look for) *for Nicki and Steve – they should be here somewhere.*

watch·a·ble /£ˈwɒtʃ·ə·bl̩, $ˈwɑː·tʃə-/ *adj infml* • A television programme or film that is watchable is entertaining: *It's not the most profound series I've ever seen but it's very watchable.*

watch·ful /£ˈwɒtʃ·fəl, $ˈwɑːtʃ-/ *adj* • *He lay in front of the fire like any domestic beast, his green eyes open and watchful.* • *She remembered him as a tall serious boy with dark watchful* **eyes**. • *Under the* **watchful eye** *of* (= watched carefully by) *their mother, the two boys played on the shore.* • *She keeps a fairly* **watchful eye** *on* (= watches carefully) *her husband to see that he behaves himself.*

watch·ful·ly /£ˈwɒtʃ·fəl·i, $ˈwɑːtʃ-/ *adv* • *Slowly and watchfully they walked around the perimeter of the clearing.*

watch·ful·ness /£ˈwɒtʃ·fəl·nəs, $ˈwɑːtʃ-/ *n* [U]

–watch·er /£-ˈwɒtʃ·əʳ, $-ˈwɑː·tʃɚ/ *combining form* • Watcher, used after another noun, means a person who is interested in and enjoys watching the stated thing: *He's a keen bird-watcher.* ○ *Royal-watchers have once again been speculating on the health of the princess.*

watch·er /£ˈwɒtʃ·əʳ, $ˈwɑː·tʃɚ/ *n* [C] • *The new channel is certainly good news for the movie watcher.* • *What this sort of film does very well is to immerse the watcher in its own fantastic world.*

watch *obj* BE CAREFUL /£wɒtʃ, $wɑːtʃ/ *v* [T] to be careful of (something) • *I have to watch my* **weight** (= be careful not to become too heavy) *now I'm not doing so much sport.* • *Watch your language* (= Do not use rude words) *in front of ladies, young man!* • *Watch* **(that)** *you don't get glue on your fingers, won't you.* [+ (*that*) clause] • *Watch* **what** *you're doing with that knife, Jim, it's sharp.* [+ *wh-* word] • *You have to really watch* **what** *you say to her – she takes offence so easily.* [+ *wh-* word] • *You want to* (= You should) *watch* *him – he's a bit of a strange character.* • **Watch it** (= be careful), *you nearly knocked my head off with that plank!* • *You want to* **watch it** (= be careful), *you know, anything you say to Stefanie goes straight back to John.* • To **watch** your **back** is to be careful of the people around you, making certain that they do nothing to harm you: *I have to watch my back at work – there are a lot of people who would like my job.* • To **watch** your **step** is to be very careful about how you behave: *He'll have to watch his step if he wants to keep that job of his!* • Someone might say **watch out** to warn you of danger or an accident that seems likely to happen: *"Watch out!" he shouted, but it was too late – she had knocked the whole tray of drinks on the floor.*

watch·dog [ORGANIZATION] /£ˈwɒtʃ·dɒg, $ˈwɑːtʃ·dɑːg/ *n* [C] a person or organization responsible for making certain that companies maintain particular standards and do not act illegally • *The rail passenger watchdog revealed that complaints increased last year by 54%.* • *The Countryside Commission was set up as a the government's official watchdog* **on** *conservation.*

watch·dog [DOG] /£ˈwɒtʃ·dɒg, $ˈwɑːtʃ·dɑːg/ *n* [C] *Am for* **guard dog**, see at GUARD

watch·man /£ˈwɒtʃ·mən, $ˈwɑːtʃ-/ *n* [C] *pl* **-men** a person who is employed to guard a building or several buildings • *He worked as a watchman for a roofing firm.*

watch·strap *esp. Br* /£ˈwɒtʃ·stræp, $ˈwɑːtʃ-/, *Am and Aus* **watch·band** /£ˈwɒtʃ·bænd, $ˈwɑːtʃ-/ *n* [C] a strip of leather or other material or a metal chain which fastens a watch onto your wrist • *a leather watchstrap* • [PIC]> **Clocks and watches**

watch·to·wer /£ˈwɒtʃˌtaʊəʳ, $ˈwɑːtʃˌtaʊr/ *n* [C] a high tower, the top of which provides a good position from which to see anyone who is approaching • *A security fence, with watchtowers, protects the base against attack by ground forces.*

watch·word /£ˈwɒtʃ·wɜːd, $ˈwɑːtʃ·wɜːrd/ *n* [C usually sing] (a word or phrase which represents) the main ideas or principles directing the way that someone behaves or the way that something is done • *Simplicity would seem to be the watchword of this designer.* • *For the property world the watchword for this decade is buy, not build.* • *And remember, let caution be your watchword.*

wa·ter /£ˈwɔː·təʳ, $ˈwɑː·t̬ɚ/ *n* [U] a clear liquid, without colour or taste, which falls from the sky as rain and is necessary for animal and plant life • *a bottle/drink/glass of water* • *bottled/mineral/tap water* • *hot/cold water* • *Cook the pasta in plenty of salted water.* • *Bring the water to the boil.* • *You're supposed to drink about two and a half litres of water a day.* • *Can I have a* **drop** *of water in my whiskey, please.* • *Is the water hot enough for a bath?* • *The human body is about 50% water.* • Water often refers to an area of water, such as the sea, a lake or a swimming pool: *The water's much warmer today – are you coming for a swim?* ○ *How deep is the water at the far end of the pool?* ○ *I like swimming but I don't like getting my head* **under** (= in) *water.* ○ *Dad, I swam a whole length of the pool* **under** *water* (= with the whole head and body below the surface of the water) *!* • Water can also refer to the level of an area of water: **Low** *water levels on the Mississippi are causing problems.* ○ *In Vienna, the Danube topped the* **high**-*water mark at 30 feet.* ○ *High water this morning at Portsmouth is at 11.17 a.m.* • Water is sometimes used as a combining form: *rainwater* ○ *freshwater* ○ *saltwater* • *(esp. disapproving)* Criticisms of or warnings to a particular person that are **(like) water off a duck's back** have no effect on that person: *I've told him that he's heading for trouble, but he doesn't listen – it's just water off a duck's back.* • If someone refers to problems that they had in the past as **water under the bridge**, they mean that they do not worry about them because they happened a long time ago and can not now be changed: *Yes, we did have our disagreements but that's water under the bridge now.* • A **water bed** is a bed which is filled with water. • A **water bill** is a regular charge which is made to people for the use of their local water supply. • A **water bird** is any bird that lives in or near water: *Typical examples of water birds are swans and herons.* • A **water biscuit** is a thin hard biscuit, which is often eaten with cheese. • A **water bottle** is a container for carrying drinking water on a journey: *He filled up the water bottle and put it back on his bike.* • A **water buffalo** is a large cow-like Asian animal with horns that curve backwards, which is often used for pulling farming tools. • *(Br and Aus)* A **water butt** (*Am* **rain barrel**, *Aus* **water tank**) is a large container for collecting rain which can then used to water plants. • A **water cannon** is a device which sends out a powerful stream of water and is used in order to scatter large groups of people: *Police used water cannon to break up the demonstration.* ○ *If you have ever been hit by a water cannon, you will appreciate that water can be used as a tool.* • If something is **water-cooled**, it is surrounded by water to keep it at the correct operating temperature: *a water-cooled nuclear reactor* ○ *a water-cooled petrol engine* • A **water filter** is a device for removing unwanted substances such as bacteria or harmful chemicals from drinking water. • **Water ice** is *dated for* SORBET. • A **water jump** is an area of water with a fence before it, which people or horses jump over in a competition. • A **water lily** is a plant whose large flat leaves and cup-shaped petals float on the surface of lakes and pools. • A **water main** is the main underground pipe in a system of pipes supplying water to an area. • **Water meadows** are fields which flood with water from a river when it rains a lot. • A **water pistol** (*Am also* **squirt gun**) is a toy gun with which you can send out a stream of water to hit people or things. • **Water polo** is a game played in water in which two teams of swimmers try to get the ball into the other team's goal. • **Water-repellant** is *Am for* **showerproof**. See at SHOWER [RAIN]. • **Water skiing** is a sport in which you are pulled along the surface of the water by a boat, while balancing on a pair of SKIS which are fastened to your feet. • A **water softener** is a substance or device that removes chemicals such as CALCIUM from water in order to make it less HARD. • A **water-soluble** substance can dissolve in water: *Are these tablets water-soluble?* • **Water sports** are sports such as swimming, SURFING and **water skiing** which you do on or in water: *Beach holidays are fine if you like water sports like surfing and wind surfing.* • A **water supply** is the water that is provided and treated for a particular area: *Fifty percent of the world's population does not have access to an adequate water supply.* • The **water table** is the level below the surface of the ground at which you start to find water. • A **water taxi** is a small boat on a river or other area of water which is operated by a person whom you pay to take you where you want to go. • A **water tower** is a device to provide water pressure by positioning a large container for water on top of a tower-like structure. • **Water vapour** is water in the form of a gas resulting from heating water or ice. • *"Water, water every where, / And not a (originally 'Nor any') drop to drink"* (Coleridge in the poem *The Ancient Mariner*, 1798) • [LP]> **Switching on and off** [PIC]> **Bicycles**

wa·ter *(obj)* /£ˈwɔː·təʳ, $ˈwɑː·t̬ɚ/ *v* • If you water plants, you pour water over the earth in which they are growing: *I've asked my neighbour to water the plants while I'm away.* [T] • To water an animal is to give it water to drink: *The horses had been fed and watered.* [T] • When your eyes water, they produce tears but not because you are unhappy: *How do you stop your eyes from watering when you're cutting up onions?* [I] ○ *That cold wind has made my eyes water.* [I] • If your mouth waters, it produces a lot of SALIVA, usually because you can see or smell some food that you would like to eat: *Ooh, the smell of that bread is making my mouth water!* [I] • If a drink is watered **down**, it is made weaker by the addition of water: *This lager is so weak it tastes as if it's been watered down.* [T] ○ *(fig.) The socialism he preached has been watered down* (= is intentionally less forceful in order to be more acceptable) *in an attempt to win American favour.* [T] ○ *(fig.) They have returned with a watered down and more acceptable version of the proposal.* • A **watering can** is a container for water with a handle and a SPOUT (= long hollow tube) used for pouring water onto garden plants. • *(humorous)* A **watering hole** is a PUB or bar where people go to drink alcohol: *I thought we might go to the local watering hole for a quick drink.* • [PIC]> **Containers**

wa·ters /£ˈwɔː·təz, $ˈwɑː·t̬ɚz/ *pl n* • A country's waters are the area of sea that is near to it and belongs to it: *St Lucia depends on clean coastal waters because fishing and tourism provide much of its income.* ○ *In the shallow waters of the Gulf of Mexico, oil rigs attract shoals of fish, and fishermen too.* ○ *(fig.) After the Wall Street crash, the American economy moved into uncharted waters* (= a situation not experienced before and where there is nothing to lead you in the right direction). ○ *(fig.) In the last two chapters of the book, she enters the murky waters of* (= complicated areas of thought about) *male sexuality.* • *(old use)* **The** waters, esp. in the past, was often used to refer to water from a spring, esp. when it was being drunk or

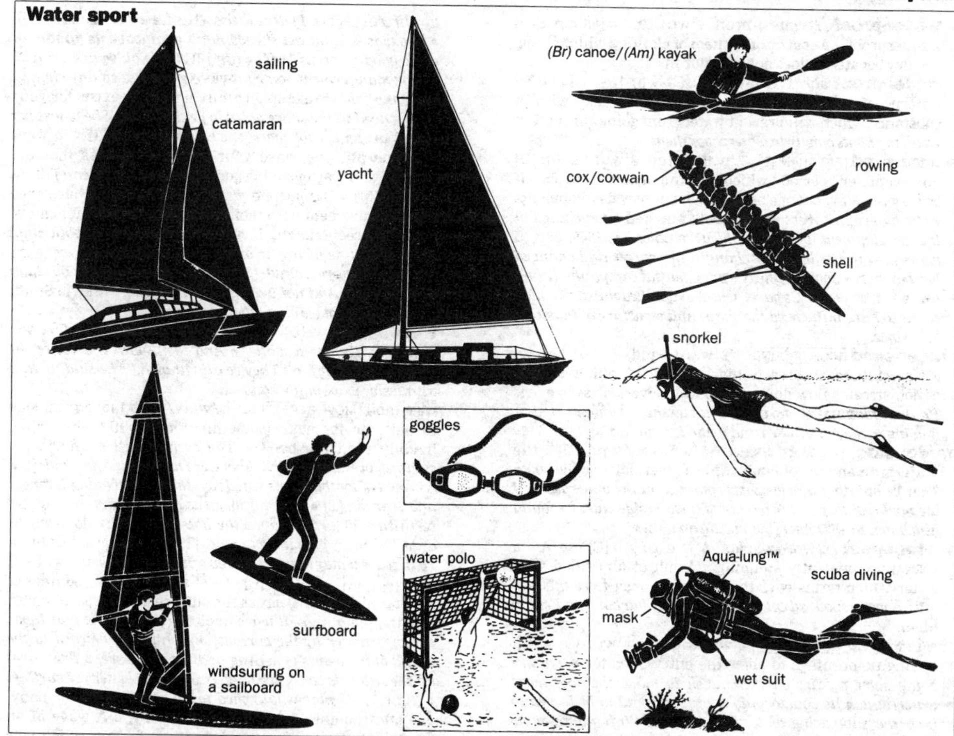

used for swimming in order to improve the health: *In those days, people used to come to this city especially to* **take** (=drink and swim in) *the waters.* • When a pregnant woman's *(Br and Aus)* waters **break**/*(Am)* water **breaks**, the liquid surrounding the baby in her womb suddenly flows out through her vagina, showing that the baby is almost ready to be born: *At around three o'clock her waters broke, so we rushed her into hospital.* • Ⓕ

wa·ter·y /£ˈwɔː·tᵊr·i, $ˈwɑː·t̬ɚ·i/ *adj* **-ier, -iest** • *(disapproving)* Food or drink that is watery contains too much water and is therefore weak in taste: *The soup was thin and watery and you could scarcely taste the mushrooms.* ○ *She drank two mouthfuls of watery brown coffee.* • Watery also means pale or weak in colour or strength: *The sun shed its thin watery* **light** *over the sea.* • *(literary)* A **watery grave** refers to death by DROWNING (=dying because you can not breathe under water): *It was off the coast of Italy that Shelley met his watery grave.*

wa·ter·borne /£ˈwɔː·tə·bɔːn, $ˈwɑː·t̬ɚ·bɔːrn/ *adj* [not gradable] carried by or through water • *The disease, causing extreme stomach upsets, is caused by a waterborne parasite.* • *The helicopter and waterborne attack will certainly be the most complicated of the offensive.*

wa·ter·col·our *Br and Aus, Am and Aus* **wa·ter·col·or** /£ˈwɔː·tə͵kʌl·əʳ, $ˈwɑː·t̬ɚ͵kʌl·ɚ/ *n* a paint which is mixed with water and used to create pictures, or a picture which has been done with this type of paint • *Graham paints with both watercolours and oils.* [C] • *Generally, I prefer oils to watercolours.* [C] • *Her best work is when she uses the simple medium of watercolour on paper.* [U] • *He's done some lovely watercolour sketches.*

wa·ter·course /£ˈwɔː·tə·kɔːs, $ˈwɑː·t̬ɚ·kɔːrs/ *n* [C] a stream of water such as a river or CANAL, or the channel along which it flows • *Some watercourses are constructed and others occur naturally.*

wa·ter·cress /£ˈwɔː·tə·kres, $ˈwɑː·t̬ɚ-/ *n* [U] a plant which grows in water whose hot-tasting green leaves are used as food, often eaten raw in salads • PIC› **Vegetables**

wa·ter·fall /£ˈwɔː·tə·fɔːl, $ˈwɑː·t̬ɚ·fɑːl/ *n* [C] water, esp. from a river or stream, dropping from a higher to a lower point, sometimes from a great height

wa·ter·fowl /£ˈwɔː·tə·faul, $ˈwɑː·t̬ɚ-/ *n* [C/U] *pl* **waterfowl** any bird that spends much of its life on or around a river or lake, esp. one which is shot for food or sport • *The park had a big lake with many different kinds of waterfowl.* [C]

wa·ter·front /£ˈwɔː·tə·frʌnt, $ˈwɑː·t̬ɚ-/ *n* [C usually sing] a part of a town which is next to an area of water such as a river or the sea • *She owns a popular tourist restaurant on the town's waterfront.* • *The plan is to turn the waterfront area into a major tourist destination.*

wa·ter·hole /£ˈwɔː·tə·həul, $ˈwɑː·t̬ɚ·houl/ *n* [C] a small pool of water in a dry area where animals go to drink

wa·ter·line /£ˈwɔː·tə·laɪn, $ˈwɑː·t̬ɚ-/ *n* [U] **the waterline** *specialized* the line marked on a ship which shows the level reached by the water when the ship is at sea • *Like an aircraft carrier, she is narrow at the waterline and much wider on the deck.*

wa·ter·logged /£ˈwɔː·tə·lɒgd, $ˈwɑː·t̬ɚ·lɑːgd/ *adj* (of land) full of water and almost covered by a layer of it, or (of a boat) full of water and therefore unable to keep moving or floating • *Unfortunately the game was cancelled because of a waterlogged (Br)* **pitch**/*(Am and Aus)* **field.**

wa·ter·mark PAPER /£ˈwɔː·tə·mɑːk, $ˈwɑː·t̬ɚ·mɑːrk/ *n* [C] a mark which is made on some types of paper during its production which can only be seen if it is held against the light • *The watermark on a bank note is virtually invisible on a flat surface.* • *The unusual watermark on this stamp makes it particularly valuable.*

wa·ter·mark RIVER/SEA /£ˈwɔː·tə·mɑːk, $ˈwɑː·t̬ɚ·mɑːrk/ *n* [C] a mark showing the highest or lowest level that a river or the sea reaches • *Recent floods/droughts caused a record* **high**/*low watermark.*

wa·ter·mel·on /£ˈwɔː·tə͵mel·ən, $ˈwɑː·t̬ɚ-/ *n* a large round or oval-shaped fruit with dark green skin, sweet watery pink flesh and a lot of black seeds • *a slice of watermelon* [U] • *I bought a watermelon and some peaches.* [C] • PIC› **Fruit**

wa·ter·mill /£ˈwɔː·tə·mɪl, $ˈwɑː·t̬ɚ-/ *n* [C] a MILL (=a machine which produces flour) whose power is provided by a large wheel which is turned by moving water, esp. a river • PIC› **Mill**

wa·ter·po·wer /£ˈwɔː·tə·pauəʳ, $ˈwɑː·t̬ɚ·paur/ *n* [U] power that is obtained from water flowing from one level to a lower level

wa·ter·proof /£ˈwɔː·tə·pruːf, $ˈwɑː·t̬ɚ-/ *adj* not allowing water to go through • *You'll need something waterproof on top of that sweater if you're going walking in the hills.* • *Canvas boots are all right but they're not as waterproof as leather.*

wa·ter·proof /£'wɔː·tə·pruːf, $'wɑː·t̬ɚ-/ *n* [C] *esp. Br* • A waterproof is a coat or other item of clothing which keeps you dry because it does not let water in.

wa·ter·proof *obj* /£'wɔː·tə·pruːf, $'wɑː·t̬ɚ-/ *v* [T] • To waterproof something is to treat its surface with a substance which will prevent water from going through it: *I wax my boots chiefly to waterproof them.*

wa·ter·shed [BIG CHANGE] /£'wɔː·tə·ʃed, $'wɑː·t̬ɚ-/ *n* [U] an event or period which is important because it represents a big change and the start of new developments • *His biographical essay on Mozart* **marked a** *watershed in the development of biographical studies.* • *1969 was a watershed in her life – she changed her career and changed her partner.* • *John Kennedy's presidential campaign in 1960 was a watershed.* • *'Cabaret' was a watershed musical which seems to have influenced the shape and structure of musicals ever since.*

wa·ter·shed [HIGH GROUND] /£'wɔː·tə·ʃed, $'wɑː·t̬ɚ-/ *n* [C] *specialized* an area of high ground on either side of which streams flow down to separate rivers or seas • *The Pindus mountains form the watershed between rivers flowing to the Aegean Sea and to the Ionian Sea.*

wa·ter·side /£'wɔː·tə·saɪd, $'wɑː·t̬ɚ-/ *n* [U] **the waterside** an area of land beside a river, lake or the sea • *They're building a new sports complex on the waterside.* • *I ate my breakfast on the terrace of a waterside cafe.* • *I found him down by the waterside, sitting on a rock.*

wa·ter·spout /£'wɔː·tə·spaut, $'wɑː·t̬ɚ-/ *n* [C] *esp. Am* a TORNADO (=violently spinning column of air) filled with water which forms over the sea • *Two men were missing after a waterspout swept through the city harbour on Friday night.*

wa·ter·tight [NO WATER] /£'wɔː·tə·taɪt, $'wɑː·t̬ɚ-/ *adj* having no openings to allow the entry of water • *They're doing some repairs on the church to make the roof more watertight.* • *Its bow torpedo doors have had to be locked to keep the submarine watertight.* • *(fig.) With nurses now involved in a lot of research work, perhaps the rigid compartments of the medical profession are not as watertight* (= separate) *as they used to be.*

wa·ter·tight [NO DOUBTS] /£'wɔː·tə·taɪt, $'wɑː·t̬ɚ-/ *adj* (of a theory, plan or agreement) formed very carefully in every detail so that there is no doubt or uncertainty • *The medical argument against this substance is, however, not watertight.* • *A lot of trouble could have been avoided if the government had made sure that the economic boycott was watertight.* • *This book is designed to be provocative rather than a watertight piece of economic analysis.*

wa·ter·way /£'wɔː·tə·weɪ, $'wɑː·t̬ɚ-/ *n* [C] a narrow area of water, such as a river or CANAL, which ships or boats can sail along • *There is no direct waterway between Sofia and the Black Sea port of Bourgas.* • *Altogether eight canals were built in the city and are the nucleus of a waterway network.*

wa·ter·wheel /£'wɔː·tə·wiːl, $'wɑː·t̬ɚ-/ *n* [C] a large wheel which is turned round by flowing water and used to provide the power for machinery • [PIC] **Mill**

wa·ter·works /£'wɔː·tə·wɜːks, $'wɑː·t̬ɚ·wɜːrks/ *pl n* a system of buildings and pipes in which a public supply of water is stored and treated and from which it is sent out • *They are now busy designing a mapping system for the city of Hiroshima's waterworks.* • *(Br)* Doctors often use the word waterworks to mean the parts of the body that deal with the removal of urine: *How are your waterworks?* • *(dated disapproving)* Waterworks can also refer to crying and is usually used of or to children who cry too often: *She's one of those irritating children who just* **turns on the** *waterworks if ever she doesn't get her own way.* ○ *You can* **turn on the** *waterworks all you like – I'm not going to change my mind!*

wa·ter·y /£'wɔː·tᵊr·i, $'wɑː·t̬ɚ·i/ *adj* See at WATER

watt /£wɒt, $wɑːt/ (*abbreviation* **W**) *n* [C] the standard measure of electrical power • *Do you want 60-watt light bulbs for this room?*

wat·tage /£'wɒt·ɪdʒ, $'wɑː·t̬ɪdʒ/ *n* [U] • *For lower wattage ovens, heating time must be increased.*

wat·tle and daub /£,wɒt·l̩-, $,wɑːt̬-/ *n* [U] a mixture of sticks, earth and clay which is used in some parts of the world as a building material • *a wattle and daub hut*

wave *(obj)* [HAND MOVEMENT] /weɪv/ *v* to move (the hand), usually in a raised position, as a way of greeting someone, telling them to do something or adding emphasis to an expression • *She waved from the window.* [I] • *I waved* **to/at** *him across the room but he didn't see me.* [I] • *We stood waving from the platform until the train was out of sight.* [I] • *I was waving my hand madly but he never once looked in my direction.* [T] • *I felt rather sad as we waved* **goodbye**. [I] • *She was so annoyed she wouldn't even wave us* **goodbye**/ *wave goodbye* **to** *us.* [I/T] • *(fig.) Well, if you've argued with senior management you can* **wave goodbye to** *any chances of promotion!* (=that opportunity no longer exists for you). • *We waved* **to** *the shore to try to get help.* [I] • *She waves her hands around a lot when she's talking.* [T] • If you wave someone **off**, you wave your hand to them as they are leaving, as a way of saying goodbye: *We waved her off at the station.* [M] • If someone waves you **away**, **on**, etc., they make a movement with their hand which tells you to move in that direction: *You'll have to wait till the policeman waves this line of traffic on.* [M] ○ *You can't just wave me away as if I were a child!* [M] • *"I was much further out than you thought/ And not waving but drowning"* (Stevie Smith in the poem *Not waving but drowning*, 1957)

wave /weɪv/ *n* [C] • **Give** *Grandpa a wave, Alice, you won't see him for a while.* • *And then, with a wave of the hand, she was off.* • *"They're all rubbish," she said, with a dismissive wave of the hand.*

wave *(obj)* [MOVE REPEATEDLY] /weɪv/ *v* to move from side to side, or to make (something) move like this while holding it in the hand • *The corn waved gently in the summer breeze.* [I] • *The flags were waving in the wind.* [I] • *A crowd of football fans ran down the street waving banners and scarves.* [T] • *She ran towards me excitedly waving her certificate.* [T] • *He waved the letter under my nose but he didn't actually give it me to read.* [T] • *He seems to just think I can wave a magic wand and everything will be all right.* [T]

wave [WATER] /weɪv/ *n* [C] one of a series of raised lines of water which moves across the surface of an area of water, esp. the sea • *A great wave* **broke** *over my head and I was dragged under by the current.* • *At night, I listened to the sound of the waves* **crashing** *against the shore.* • *The waves off the Atlantic coast are bigger so they're better for surfing.* • *(fig.) Allied planes launched wave after wave of* (=many, one after another) *air attacks on the city.* • A wave **of** an emotion or feeling is a sudden strong feeling which gets stronger as it spreads: *A wave of panic swept through the crowd and people started running.* ○ *She felt a sudden wave of* (=sudden strong) *desire for him.* • A wave **of** something can also be an unusually large number of events of a similar, often bad, type, happening within the same period: *This latest wave of redundancies comes only three months after the closure of the region's main car factory.* ○ *In the 1970s, the country came close to collapse as it was swept by massive inflation, industrial unrest and a wave of terrorism.* ○ *The recent ruling* **sparked off** (=started) *a wave of protests in the capital.* • To **make waves** is to intentionally cause trouble: *If a member of the Cabinet started making waves, the prime minister simply got rid of them.*

wave [HAIR CURVES] /weɪv/ *n* [C] a series of slight curves in a person's hair • *Your hair has a natural wave whereas mine's just straight and boring.* • See also WAVY. Compare CURL.

wave *(obj)* /weɪv/ *v* • *If she leaves her hair to dry on its own, it just waves naturally.* [I] • *She's had her hair waved – it used to be straight.* [T]

wave [ENERGY] /weɪv/ *n* [C] the pattern in which some types of energy, such as sound, light and heat are spread or carried • *radio waves* • **Long** wave refers to a range of radio waves used for broadcasting and receiving which are of 1000 metres or more in length: *Radio stations that broadcast* **on** *long wave can be received further away than any others.* • **Medium** wave refers to radio waves which have a length of between about 150 and 550 metres. • **Short** wave refers to waves of a length which is less than 60 metres. • A wave **band** is a set of radio waves of similar length which are used for broadcasting radio programmes. • See also BRAINWAVE.

wave·length /'weɪv·leŋkθ/ *n* [C] the distance between two waves of energy, or the length of the radio wave used by a particular radio station for broadcasting programmes • *I don't know which wavelength the station is* **on** *– is it on long wave?* • *I can't seem to get on with him – we're just* **not on the same wavelength** (= we think very differently and are not interested in the same things).

wa·ver /£'weɪ·vəʳ, $-vɚ/ *v* [I] to lose strength, determination or purpose, esp. temporarily • *I'm afraid my concentration began to waver as lunch approached.* • *He has never wavered* **in** *his support for the leader.* • *Her candid blue gaze never wavers for a moment.* • *Although exhausted by a rigorous round of talks and press conferences, her eyes and voice never wavered.* • If you waver **between** two possibilities, you can not decide which of them to choose or you keep choosing one way and then the other: *"What are you having?" "Er, I'm wavering* **between** *the fish soup and the mushroom tart."* ○ *The company wavered* **between** *centralized and decentralized organization.*

wa·ver·ing /£ˈweɪ·vᵊr·ɪŋ, $-vɚ-/ *adj* ● *It's the party's last attempt to persuade some of the nation's wavering voters to support them.*

wa·vy /ˈweɪ·vi/ *adj* **-ier**, **-iest** having a series of curves ● *Sarah's got lovely wavy blond hair.* ● *In the end I chose the curtains with the wavy patterns.* ● *He was wearing a blue sweater with wavy white lines.*

wax SUBSTANCE /wæks/ *n* [U] a solid fatty substance that softens and melts at a low temperature ● *She watched the wax as it dripped down the side of the candle.* ● *You should put some wax on those boots.* ● *Really you should use a good wax* **polish** *on wood like this.* ● Wax also refers to the soft yellowish substance inside your ears. ● See also BEESWAX.

wax *obj* /wæks/ *v* [T] ● To wax something is to put a thin layer of wax on its surface, either to make it waterproof or to improve its appearance: *Have you waxed your walking boots?* ○ *I waxed the floor so I'm afraid it's a bit slippery.* ○ *Martin waxes his moustache.* ○ *I bought a waxed jacket for the winter.* ● **Waxed paper** is a type of paper which has a thin layer of wax on it and is used for wrapping food.

wax·en /ˈwæk·sᵊn/ *adj literary* ● If you describe someone's face as waxen, you mean that their skin is pale and shiny and does not look healthy: *a waxen complexion*

wax·y /ˈwæk·si/ *adj* **-ier**, **-iest** ● *These apples have a slightly waxy* (= shiny and oily) *skin.* ● *Boil some large cubes of waxy potato* (= potato which stays firm when cooked). ● *The flowers of the plant have large white waxy* (= thick and looking like wax) *petals.*

wax APPEAR LARGER /wæks/ *v* [I] *fml or literary* (of the moon) to gradually appear larger and increasingly round ● *(fig.) It's in the nature of romantic love that it* **waxes and wanes** (= grows stronger and then weaker).

wax BECOME /wæks/ *v* [L only + adj] *old use or fml* to become ● *Brendan waxed eloquent on the subject of free enterprise.* ● *My mother, a Spaniard, always used to wax* **lyrical** *about the lemon trees which grew in the family garden.*

wax·head /ˈwæks·hed/ *n* [C] *Aus infml* someone who goes SURFING (= rides on the waves of the sea on a special board)

wax·work /£ˈwæks·wɜːk, $-wɜːrk/ *n* [C] a wax model of a person ● *The prime minister yesterday inspected his new waxwork at Madame Tussaud's.*

wax·works /£ˈwæks·wɜːks, $-wɜːrks/ *pl n* ● A waxworks is a place where there are a lot of wax models of famous people for the public to look at.

way ROUTE /weɪ/ *n* [C] a route, direction or path ● *Do you know the way* **to** *the train station?* ● *Which way is the train station?* ● *I've only been living in Madrid for a couple of weeks so I don't really know my way* **around** *it yet.* ● *The way* **to** *the airport is very clearly signed.* ● *We'll have to stop for fuel* **on the** *way to the airport.* ● *At first it's difficult to* **find** *your way* **(out of/into** *the building).* ● *It's getting late – we should* **make** *our way* (= go) *home soon.* ● *Because of arthritis she can only* **make** *her way* (= move) *around the house slowly.* ● *He elbowed his way* (= moved using his elbows) *to the front of the crowd.* ● *The coach stopped for us to eat lunch but within half an hour we were* **on** *our way/* **under** *way* (= travelling) *again.* ● *Will you get some bread* **on** *your way home?* ● *There's no way through the centre of town in a vehicle – it's for pedestrians only.* ● *You'll have to go* **by** *way* **of** (= travel through) *Copenhagen if you want to go to Southern Sweden from here.* ● *Many people have* **lost** *their way* (= become lost) *in the forest.* ● *Only a local person could* **find** *their way* **through** (= not become lost when going through) *the maze of narrow streets.* ● *The council plans to build several more cycle ways between the city centre and outlying districts.* ● Way is also used in road names: *Our offices are at 17, King's Way.* ● *(fig.) I'm* **(well) on the** *way* **to** *completing* (= I have nearly completed) *the report.* ● *(fig.) He started as an office junior and* **worked** *his way up* (= advanced) *through the company to become a director.* ● *(fig.) Finding a way through* (= Being able to well enough understand) *the legislation is impossible without expert advice.* ● *(fig.) The research group is* **leading the** *way in developing new types of computer memory.* ● *(fig.) I'll take my complaint* **all the** *way to the managing director if I have to.* ● *(fig.) You might be able to* **talk** *your way* **out of** (= give what seem to be good reasons for not doing) *most things but you still have to clean the dishes!* ● You can use way to talk about the direction in which something is facing: *Which way* **up** *should this box be* (= Which side should be on top)? ○ *The numbers are the wrong way round – it should be 71, not 17.* ● The phrase **by the way** is used to introduce a new subject for consideration or to give further information: *I think we've discussed everything we need to – by the way what time is it?* ○ *The second group of storms were not quite as severe as those of five years ago which, by the way, were the worst this century.* ● *(Br and Aus)* When referring to the movement of vehicles on roads, **give way** *(Am* **yield)** means permit other traffic to move first: *When you join a main road, remember to give way* **(to** *vehicles which are already on it).* ● If you **go out of** your/**the way**, you try especially hard: *They really went out of their way* **to** *make us feel welcome.* ● If you **go** your **own (sweet) way**, you do what you want to do without considering other people: *He always goes his own way, without taking any notice of what his family wants.* ● When people or groups of people choose to **go** their **own ways**, they agree or decide to live or work without continuing their previous personal or business relationship: *After a couple of years together, we realized that we were not suited to one another and decided to go our own ways.* ● If a place or a building is **out of the way**, it is a long distance from where most people live: *It's a very beautiful village where Cindy and Tony live but it's very out of the way.* ● If a person tries to discover **which way the wind blows/is blowing**, they try to discover information about a situation, esp. other people's opinions, before they take action: *I think I'll* **see** *which way the wind blows before I vote at the board meeting.* ● *(Am)* A **way station** is a place where people can stop when travelling from one place to another: *A space station in high orbit might be a convenient way station for future cosmonauts intending to visit Mars.* ● *(saying)* 'The way to a man's heart is through his stomach'. ● PIC> **Road**

way DISTANCE /weɪ/, *Am* **ways** *n* [U] distance or a period of time ● *We walked* **a long** *way yesterday.* ● *(Am) We've still got a long way to go.* ● *She stayed with him in the ambulance* **all the** *way to the hospital.* ● *The holidays seem like they're* **a long** *way* **off**, *but I've got a lot of work to do first.* ● *(Am) The plane flew for a ways above the ice before climbing into the air.* ● *(fig.) There were people of every political belief at university, ranging* **all the** *way from communists to fascists.* ● **All the way** also means completely: *If you want to take it up with the boss, I'll support you all the way.* ○ *I agree with you all the way, but I still don't think you'll change anything by protesting.* ● If someone **gives way**, they stop arguing or fighting and accept that they have been beaten by the other person or people involved: *Neither of them will give way, so they could be arguing for a very long time.* ○ *Don't give way* **to** *your fears.* ● **Give way** also means break, esp. when under the influence of strong forces: *Because of an unusually strong current, the bridge's central support gave way, tipping a coach into the river.* ● **Give way to/make way for** means to become replaced by something, esp. because it is better, cheaper, easier, etc.: *In some areas, modern intensive farming is giving way to the re-introduction of traditional methods.* ○ *She believes that older institutions should make way for improved replacements.*

way POSSIBILITY /weɪ/ *n* a particular choice, opinion, belief or action, esp. from among several possibilities ● *I like the way you've had your hair done.* [C] ● **In** *which ways does the zebra resemble a horse?* [C] ● **In some/many** *ways it would be better if we met on Monday rather than Wednesday.* [C] ● *The reports* **in no** *way suggest the existence of extraterrestrial life.* [C] ● **In a** *way* (= Partly), *I would prefer it if they didn't come because it would mean extra work.* [U] ● *He looked at me* **in** *a sinister way* (= manner). [C] ● *He might have to resign or he might be demoted, but* **either** *way, his career is effectively over.* [U] ● *You're so selfish – you just want to* **have** *everything your* **own** *way* (= do exactly want you want), *don't you!* [U] ● *If she doesn't* **get** *her* **own** *way* (= If she isn't allowed to do what she wants), *she sulks just like a four-year old.* [U] ● *If I* **had** *my way* (= If I could do what I wanted), *we'd eat fish every day.* [U] ● *Don't be alarmed – it's just his way* (= particular manner of behaving). [U] ● **The** *way he was shouting* (= He was shouting in such a manner that) *you'd have thought he was badly hurt.* [U] ● *(infml)* **It's** *amazing* **the** *way she manages to stay so calm* (= The fact that she stays calm is amazing). [U] ● *They don't write songs* **the** *way* (= as) *they used to.* [U] ● **It's always the** *way* (= This always happens) *at work – either I've got nothing to do and I'm bored or there's so much work I can't keep up with it!* [U] ● *You can go for weeks* *without even one party invitation and then you get three on the same night – isn't it* **always the** *way!* [U] • *(infml)* To **go all the way** is to have sex, esp. after a period in which there has only been kissing and touching. • **To** *my way* **of thinking** (=It is my opinion that) *they shouldn't be building so many roads.* • If you **have it both ways**, you benefit from two opposing things: *You* **can't** *have it both ways – you either work longer and get paid more or have more leisure time and get paid less.* • *(infml)* If you say **no way** about something, you mean that it is impossible: *No way will she agree to you leaving early.* ○ *I'm sorry but* **there's** *no way we can help you.* • *(infml)* **No way** can also be used to say no in a forceful way: *"Go on, lend me your bike." "No way!"* • If a person says they **wouldn't have** something **any other way**, they mean they would not change any of it, esp. despite connected difficulties: *Our marriage has not been easy at times, but even so, I wouldn't have* **it** *any other way.* • A person's **way of life** is how they live: *Sleeping in doorways, begging for food and money – it's not a very enviable way of life.* ○ *Watching football on Saturdays and cleaning the car on Sundays are all part of the British way of life.* • *"I did it my way"* (from the song *My Way* by Paul Anka, 1969)

ways /weɪz/ *pl n* • *Over the years we've got used to his funny little ways* (=types of behaviour).

way [FREE SPACE] /weɪ/ *n* [U] the space needed for a particular movement or action • *Sorry, am I* **in** *your way? I'll move.* • *I couldn't see the stage because there was a pillar* **in the** *way* (=between me and the stage). • *Rioters deliberately put concrete blocks* **in the** *way* **of** *the advancing police vans.* • *Please* **make** *way so the ambulance can get by.* • *The best thing you can do if you're near to a tornado is get* **out of** *its way.* • *Look, there's not much space in this kitchen so I'll just get* **out of** *your way and leave you to it.* • *(fig.) May nothing* **stand in the** *way* **of** (=prevent) *your future happiness together!* • *(fig.) She's determined to succeed and she won't let anything* **get/stand in** *her way* (=prevent her).

way [METHOD] /weɪ/ *n* [C] an action that can produce the result you want; a method • *There are many ways* **of** *solving the problem.* • *That's not the way* **to** *do it – let me show you.* [+ *to* infinitive] • *That method hasn't worked, so let's try your way.* • **By way of** means as a type of: *He sent me some flowers by way of an apology.* ○ *By way of an introduction to the subject, let me give you a brief history.* • The **ways and means** of achieving something are the methods and other things needed to make it happen: *With today's technology even people working on their own have the ways and means to produce professional-looking documents.*

way [CONDITION] /weɪ/ *n* [U] the bad condition or state of someone or something, esp. the state of a person's health • *He's been in a* **bad** *way* (=very ill) *ever since the operation.* • *She's in* **a** *terrible way* (=very upset) *since her husband left her.*

way [EMPHASIS] /weɪ/ *adv* [always + adv/prep; not gradable] *slightly infml* used to emphasize degree or separation, esp. in space or time • *After the third lap, she was way behind the other runners.* • *Dinosaurs became extinct way before you were born.* • *It would be way better for you to wait until it gets light.* • *Their car is way faster than yours.* • *Come on now Alexander, it's way* **past your bedtime**. • *She spends way too much money on clothes.* • *The company's way ahead of its competitors in terms of research.* • *(infml dated)* If a person or a thing is described as **way-out**, it is unusual, esp. because it is very modern: *A lot of experimental theatre is too way-out for me.*

way [PLACE] /weɪ/ *adv* [after n; not gradable] *slightly dated* in the direction of • *I think they live Birmingham way.*

way·lay *obj* /ˌweɪˈleɪ/ *v* [T] *past* **waylaid** /ˌweɪˈleɪd/ to wait for and then stop (someone), esp. either to talk to them or to attack them • *A woman on her way to deposit $120 000 in a bank was waylaid by two men who punched her and snatched her handbag yesterday.* • *I meant to leave earlier but I was waylaid on the way out of a meeting by my manager.*

ways [DISTANCE] /weɪz/ *n* [U] *Am for* WAY [DISTANCE]

-ways [MANNER] /-weɪz/ *combining form* (used in adverbs) in the stated direction or manner • *edgeways* • *lengthways* • *sideways*

way·side /ˈweɪ·saɪd/ *n* [U] **fall by the wayside** see at FALL [ACCIDENT]

way·ward /£ˈweɪ·wəd, $-wɚd/ *adj dated* (esp. of a person's behaviour) changeable, selfish and difficult to control • *In this latest dramatization the novel's wayward heroine is played by Sara Huws.*

way·ward·ness /£ˈweɪ·wəd·nəs, $-wɚd-/ *n* [U] *dated*

wa·zoo /ˈwæz·uː/ *n* [C] *pl* **wazoos** *Am slang for* ASS [BOTTOM]

WC /ˌdʌb·l̩.juˈsiː/ *n* [C] *abbreviation for* water closet (=a type of toilet which is cleaned after use by a flow of water) • WC is usually seen on notices or in advertisements, meaning toilet: *All hotel rooms have private bath/shower/wc, colour TV and telephone.* • This abbreviation is used mainly in advertisements.

we [GROUP] /wiː, wɪ/ *pronoun* (used as the subject of a verb) the speaker and at least one other person when considered together or as a group • *Can we go to the swimming pool this afternoon?* • *We have few options left.* • *We're going to Cyprus for our holidays this year.* • *If you don't hurry up we'll be late.* • We can be used by a speaker or a writer to refer to the listener(s) or reader and the person speaking or writing: *Perhaps we could move on to discuss the next item on the agenda.* ○ *As we saw in a previous chapter the proof of this theorem is not trivial.*

we [ALL PEOPLE] /wiː, wɪ/ *pronoun* (used as the subject of a verb) all people, esp. when considered as a group • *The planet on which we live should be cherished and not exploited.* • *We* **all** *know what it's like to be disappointed in love.* • *We've* **all** *experienced pain of some sort.*

we [YOU] /wiː, wɪ/ *pronoun infml dated* (used as the subject of a verb; used esp. to children) you • *Now we don't want to be late for school, do we?*

we [I] /wiː, wɪ/ *pronoun fml* (used by a queen or king when speaking officially) I • *"We are not amused"* (Queen Victoria, 1819-1901)

weak [NOT STRONG] /wiːk/ *adj* **-er**, **-est** not strong; not strong enough to work, last, succeed, persuade or be effective • *It's not surprising you feel weak if you haven't eaten properly for days.* • *You're bound to feel weak after a fever.* • *The refugees were weak and frightened when soldiers found them hiding in an old shed.* • *The electromagnetic field strength becomes weaker as you move further away from high voltage cables.* • *He was a weak ruler surrounded by corrupt advisers.* • *Our candidate shouldn't appear to be weak* **on** *controversial issues so close to an election.* • *Any evidence that exists to support the hypothesis is fairly weak.* • *The arguments in favour of building a new road across open countryside seem very weak.* • *It was a very weak attempt to justify their actions.* • *He gave the weakest of excuses when asked why he was late.* • A drink which is weak contains a lot of water compared to the amount of other substances: *I can't stand weak coffee/tea.* • If someone is **weak at the knees**, they lose their strength and feel ill, usually because something unpleasant has happened or is being discussed: *Just talking about blood makes him* **go** *weak at the knees.* • *(infml disapproving) He always was* **weak-kneed** (=lacking firmness of belief in his own opinions) *when he had to make a decision which might make him unpopular.* • A **weak link** is a weak part, esp. the weakest part of something: *They're a fairly good team – their only weak link is a relatively inexperienced goalkeeper.* ○ *A chain can only be as strong as its weakest link, so we must look at the least committed country to see if the alliance will hold.* • Someone who is **weak-minded** lacks determination, or is stupid. • A **weak spot** is a weak part in something: *Stressing the opponent's weak spots is a typical technique in politics.* ○ *The fuse is a safety device, a deliberate weak spot in the circuit.* • If a person is **weak-willed**, they lack the determination that is needed to continue with a difficult course of action: *My diets are never successful – I'm just too weak-willed.* ○ *To get addicted to heroin you have to be crazy, or weak-willed, or young and foolish.* • The expression **the weaker sex** is sometimes used to refer to women in general and is considered offensive by many people.

weak·en *(obj)* /ˈwiː·kᵊn/ *v* • *You could see the dog weakening daily as the disease spread through its body.* [I] • *Many factors weaken a body's ability to combat infection.* [T] • *Another defeat in parliament would seriously weaken the president's ability to govern.* [T] • *She's weakening – ask her some more questions and see if she confesses.* [I] • *Various indicators show that the country's economy continues to weaken.* [I] • *They were weakened by hunger and climbing became difficult.* [T] • *We know that prolonged exposure to vibration can weaken aircraft components.* [T]

weak·ly /ˈwiː·kli/ *adv* • *"The pain seems to have eased a little with these new tablets," he said weakly.* • *"Cheer up," said Peter, "I'll be back in less than three months." "Yes, you're right." she said and smiled weakly.*

weak·ness /ˈwiːk·nəs/ *n* • *Any change of policy will be interpreted as a sign of weakness.* [U] • *There are definite weaknesses in their security arrangements.* [C] • A weakness is also a fault in someone's character: *What's interesting about this film is that the hero manifests a whole range of human weaknesses.* [C] ○ *Vanity was her greatest weakness.* [C] • A weakness is also a strong liking, usually for something which might have unpleasant or unwanted effects: *My diet would be fine if only I didn't have this weakness* **for** *sweet things.* [C] ○ *Aside from a weakness* **for** *silk shirts, she's not really an extravagant woman.* [C]

weak [BELOW STANDARD] /wiːk/ *adj* **-er, -est** below standard; not good enough, esp. in ability, skill or quality • *He was always weak* **at/in** *languages but strong at/in science.* • *Our quiz team is a bit weak* **on** *sport.* • *In the end I think the film was spoilt by a weak story line.*

weak·ness /ˈwiːk·nəs/ *n* [C] • *The later novels show none of the weaknesses of his earlier work.*

weak·ling /ˈwiː·klɪŋ/ *n* [C] *disapproving* someone who is weak, either physically or in character • *It would need more than a few exercises to turn a seven-stone weakling into a heavyweight boxer.* • *She has a reputation on the committee for being a weakling when decisions have to be made.*

weal /wiːl/ *n* [C] a raised mark on the skin caused by being hit or injured in some other way • *His back was covered with weals where he had been repeatedly beaten.*

wealth [MONEY] /welθ/ *n* [U] a large amount of money and other valuable possessions • *During a successful business career, she accumulated a great amount of wealth.* • *In the future, wealth generation may depend more on the service industries and less on manufacturing.* • *Because he's inherited considerable personal wealth, he doesn't have to work.*

weal·thy /ˈwel·θi/ *adj* **-ier, -iest** • *He's a very wealthy man.* • *He was born in 1907 to a fabulously wealthy Edwardian family whose fortune had been made in mining and railways.* • *With their natural resources they are potentially a very wealthy country.*

weal·thy /ˈwel·θi/ *pl n* • **The wealthy** are rich people.

wealth [LARGE AMOUNT] /welθ/ *n* [U] a large amount or number of possibilities, skills or qualities • *Jim has a whole wealth* **of** *teaching experience.* • *Russia has a wealth* **of** *coal, timber, diamonds, gold and other minerals.*

wean *obj* /wiːn/ *v* [T] to cause (a baby or young animal) to stop feeding on its mother's milk and to start eating other food, esp. solid food, instead • *The studies were carried out on calves that had been weaned at 5 weeks of age.* • *She started to wean her baby when it was about six months old.* • *(fig.) As a child she was weaned* **on** (= grew and developed being strongly influenced by) *TV soap operas and rock music.* • To wean someone **off/from** a habit is to gradually cause them to stop it: *It's difficult to wean an addict off cocaine once they're hooked.* ○ *The whole scheme is intended to wean people off welfare dependency and to discourage the spread of single-parent welfare mothers.* ○ *I'm trying to wean myself off fatty foods.*

wean·ing /ˈwiː·nɪŋ/ *n* [U] • *A lot of mothers find early weaning from breast milk more convenient.*

weap·on /ˈwep·ən/ *n* [C] any object used in fighting or war, such as a gun or a bomb • *a lethal weapon* • *chemical/nuclear/biological weapons* • *The youths were dragged from their car and searched for weapons.*

weap·on·ry /ˈwep·ən·ri/ *n* [U] • *nuclear/conventional weaponry* (= weapons in general) • *All hi-tech weaponry demands frequent servicing to ensure accuracy and efficiency.*

wear *obj* [ON BODY] /£weəʳ, $wer/ *v* [T] *past simple* **wore** /£wɔːʳ, $wɔːr/, *past part* **worn** /£wɔːn, $wɔːrn/ to have (clothing or jewellery) on your body • *Tracey is wearing a simple black dress made from a cotton and Lycra mix.* • *What are you wearing* **to** *Caroline's wedding?* • *She was complaining that she had nothing to wear* **to** *the party.* • *Some musicians don't like to wear rings when they're playing.* • *He wears glasses for reading.* • To wear your hair in a particular style is to have it arranged that way: *When she's working she wears her hair* **in** *a pony-tail.* ○ *You should wear your hair* **up** (= so that it does not hang down) *more often – it suits you.* • *(fig.) The minister wore a confident smile throughout the interview.* • If a person **wears** their **heart on** their **sleeve** they make their feelings and emotions obvious rather than hiding them. • In a relationship, a person, esp. a woman, who **wears the trousers**/*(Am and Aus)* **wears the pants** is the one who is in control and makes decisions for both people: *Lisa may appear more pliant and easy-going than Brian but I'll tell you she wears the trousers in that relationship.* • [LP] **Dressing and undressing**

wear /£weəʳ, $wer/ *n* [U] • The word wear, often used in combination, means clothes suitable for a particular use or clothes of a stated type: *casual wear* • *evening wear* • *leisure wear* • *beachwear* • *knitwear* • [LP] **Shopping goods**

wear·a·ble /£ˈweə·rə·bl̩, $ˈwer·ə-/ *adj* • Clothes that are wearable are easy to wear because they are comfortable, acceptable in most social situations and look attractive in combination with other clothes: *Unlike a lot of women's fashion magazines, it features clothes that are both affordable and wearable.*

wear·er /£ˈweə·rəʳ, $ˈwer·ɚ/ *n* [C] • *In medieval times the sapphire was believed to offer protection to its wearer.* • *Clothes, of course, say a lot about the wearer.*

wear [WEAKEN] /£weəʳ, $wer/ *v* [I] *past simple* **wore** /£wɔːʳ, $wɔːr/, *past part* **worn** /£wɔːn, $wɔːrn/ to become weaker, damaged or thinner because of continuous use • *I'm very fond of this shirt but it's starting to wear at the collar.* • *The wheel bearings have worn over the years, which is what's causing the noise.* • *In some diseases the protective layer in a joint wears* **away** (= becomes thinner and disappears because of repeated rubbing). • *Most patients find that the numbness wears* **off** (= becomes less and finally disappears) *after about an hour.* • *Parts of an engine which move can wear* **out** (= be made increasingly weak until they become useless). • *(fig.) It's been a popular TV series, but the plot is much the same every week and it's* **all wearing** *a bit* **thin** (= becoming boring or annoying because it has been seen or used too much).

wear /£weəʳ, $wer/ *n* [U] • Wear is the amount or type of use an item has had or can be expected to have, esp. before showing damage: *The chairs have a bit more wear left in them before they have to be replaced.* ○ *I've had a lot of wear* **out of** *these boots – they've done really well.* ○ *Cutlery in the restaurant gets a lot of* **hard** *wear.* ○ *This silk shirt's very nice, but I've only worn it a couple of times and it's already showing* **signs of** *wear* (= damage). • The phrase **wear and tear** means the damage which happens to an object in ordinary use during a period: *Seat covers on trains* **take** *a lot of wear and tear so they need to be made from strong material.*

wear *obj* [MAKE A HOLE] /£weəʳ, $wer/ *v* [T always + adv/prep] *past simple* **wore** /£wɔːʳ, $wɔːr/, *past part* **worn** /£wɔːn, $wɔːrn/ to produce (something such as a hole or loss of material) by continuous use, rubbing or movement • *I always seem to wear* **a hole** *in the left elbow of my sweaters.* • *Over many years flowing water wore deep grooves* **into** *the rock.* • *Chewing food wears* **away** *a person's teeth after many years.* [M] • *Wind and water slowly wore* **down** *the mountain's jagged edges.* [M] • *Heavy traffic and variable weather can wear* **out** (= make increasingly weak until useless) *the surface of a road.* [M] • *(fig.) After years of travelling I know what sorts of things wear me* **down** (= tire me). [M] • *(fig.) Both sides are trying to wear the other* **down** (= weaken the other) *by being obstinate in the negotiations.* [M] • *(fig.) Walking around a museum all day really wears you* **out** (= makes you extremely tired). [M]

wear *obj* [PERMIT] /£weəʳ, $wer/ *v* [T usually in questions and negative sentences] *past simple* **wore** /£wɔːʳ, $wɔːr/, *past part* **worn** /£wɔːn, $wɔːrn/ *Br and Aus infml dated* to permit or accept (something) • *I'd ask my boss for some time off but I don't think she'd wear* **it**. • *He's always been rude to her but I don't think she'll wear* **it** *for much longer.*

wear on *v adv* [I] (of a period of time) to pass slowly • *Months wore on and still he heard no news of his family.*

wear·ing /£ˈweə·rɪŋ, $ˈwer·ɪŋ/ *adj* tiring • *Looking after three children all day is very wearing.* • *I find conversation with her very wearing.*

wea·ri·some /£ˈwɪə·ri·sᵊm, $ˈwɪr·i-/ *adj fml* causing a person to be tired and/or bored • *Simple repetitive tasks can be very wearisome.*

wea·ry /£ˈwɪə·ri, $ˈwɪr·i/ *adj* **-ier, -iest** very tired, esp. after working hard for a long time • *I think he's a little weary after his long journey.* • *Although weary, the riders appeared together for a photograph after the race.* • *Here, sit down and rest your weary legs.* • If you are weary **of** something, you are bored with it because you have experienced too much of it: *I've been going out with the same people to the same clubs for years and I've just* **grown** *weary of it.*

wea·ry *(obj)* /£ˈwɪə·ri, $ˈwɪr·i/ *v fml or literary* • *Children weary me with their constant inquiries and* *demands.* [T] • *Some people never seem to weary* **of** (=find boring) *eating the same type of food every day.* [I]

wea·ri·ly /£ˈwɪə·rɪ·li, $ˈwɪr·ɪ-/ *adv* • *I dragged myself wearily out of bed at five o'clock this morning.*

wea·ri·ness /£ˈwɪə·rɪ·nəs, $ˈwɪr·ɪ-/ *n* [U] • *We'd been working on the same project for months and there was a feeling of weariness about the team.*

wea·ry·ing /£ˈwɪə·ri·ɪŋ, $ˈwɪr·i-/ *adj* • *We'd had a wearying* (=tiring) *journey and we wanted to sleep rather than socialize.*

wea·sel /ˈwiː·zəl/ *n* [C] a small mammal with reddish brown fur and a long body which can kill other small animals such as mice and birds for food • *(infml)* Speech which is described as **weasel words** is speech intentionally used either to avoid answering a question clearly or to make someone believe something that is not true. • PIC› **Wild animals in Britain**

wea·sel out of *obj* /ˈwiː·zəl/ *v adv prep* [T] *esp. Am infml* to avoid doing (something that you do not want to do) • *Although they had signed the contract they tried to weasel out of the deal later.*

weath·er AIR CONDITIONS /£ˈweð·əʳ, $-ɚ/ *n* [U] the conditions in the air above the Earth such as wind, rain or temperature, esp. at a particular time over a particular area • *bad/cold/dry/hot/stormy/warm/wet weather* • *We usually have good weather here in the summer.* • *The weather in the hills can change very quickly, so take suitable clothing.* • *To combat cold weather, birds ruffle their feathers, trapping layers of warm air to insulate their bodies.* • *We're going to have a picnic, weather* **permitting** (=if the weather is good enough). • If something is done **in all weathers** it is done in every type of weather: *He's a real enthusiast – he goes fishing in all weathers.* • *(infml)* If someone is **under the weather** they feel ill: *I'm feeling a bit under the weather – I think I've caught a cold.* • Something, such as skin or building material, which is **weather-beaten** has been marked or damaged by the weather: *a weather-beaten face* (=a face which is brown and has many deep lines) ○ *weather-beaten columns* • A **weather forecast** is a statement of what the weather is likely to be for the next day or few days, usually broadcast on television or radio or printed in a newspaper. • A **weather forecaster** is someone who scientifically studies weather conditions and says what the weather is likely to be in the future. • Also a **weather forecaster** (also *male* **weatherman**, *female* **weathergirl**) is a person on a television or radio programme who gives a weather forecast. • A **weather station** is a building or place where information is gathered about local weather conditions. • A **weather vane** is a pointer with a flat blade at one end which is put on top of a high building and turns round in the wind to show which way it is blowing from. • LP› **Phrases and customs**

weath·er *(obj)* /£ˈweð·əʳ, $-ɚ/ *v* • If something weathers it changes in colour or form over a period of time because of the effects of sun, wind or other weather conditions: *The paint on the outside walls has weathered badly* (=changed a lot). [I] ○ *When rock weathers it crumbles and you can easily break it in your hands.* [I] ○ *Rock is weathered by the action of ice and changes in temperature.* [T]

weath·ered /£ˈweð·əd, $-ɚd/ *adj* • *weathered stone/tiles*

weath·er *obj* DEAL WITH /£ˈweð·əʳ, $-ɚ/ *v* [T] to deal successfully with (a difficult situation or a problem) • *As a small new company they did well to weather the recession.* • *At 34, she's weathered a disastrous marriage, a nervous breakdown and bankruptcy.* • *Few doubt that the leader will be able to weather the latest round of criticisms.* • If someone or something **weathers the storm** they successfully deal with a very difficult problem: *In the next few days we shall see if the ambassador can weather the political storm caused by his ill-advised remarks.*

weath·er·board·ing /£ˈweð·əˌbɔː·dɪŋ, $-ɚˌbɔːr-/ *n* [U] a set of boards fixed across the bottom of a door to stop water from entering a building

weath·er·cock /£ˈweð·ə·kɒk, $-ɚ·kaːk/ *n* [C] a type of **weather vane** (=device for showing which way the wind is blowing) in the form of a COCK (=male chicken)

weath·er·proof /£ˈweð·ə·pruːf, $ˈ-ɚ-/ *adj* not allowing wind or rain to go through • *a weatherproof tent/coat* • Compare WATERPROOF.

weave *(obj)* MAKE CLOTH /wiːv/ *v past simple* **wove** /£wəʊv, $woʊv/ or *Am also* **weaved**, *past part* **woven** /£ˈwəʊ·vən, $ˈwoʊ-/ or *Am also* **weaved** to make cloth by repeatedly crossing a single thread through two sets of long threads on a LOOM (=special frame) • *Workers on the islands typically weave for eight hours a day.* [I] • *How long does it take to weave three metres of cloth?* [T] • *This type of wool is woven* **into** *fabric which will make jackets.* [T] • PIC› **Handicraft**

weave /wiːv/ *n* [C] • The weave of a cloth is either the way it has been woven, for example with the threads pulled firmly together, or the pattern made on it: *a tight weave* • *a striped weave*

weav·er /£ˈwiː·vəʳ, $-vɚ/ *n* [C] • *Textile weavers receive low wages in the rural areas.*

weav·ing /ˈwiː·vɪŋ/ *n* [U] • *Aided by increasing automation of spinning and weaving, some big surviving factories have cut their workforces by a half.*

weave *obj* TWIST /wiːv/ *v* [T] *past simple* **wove** /£wəʊv, $woʊv/ or *Am also* **weaved**, *past part* **woven** /£ˈwəʊ·vən, $ˈwoʊ-/ or *Am also* **weaved** to twist (long objects) together, or to make (something) by doing this • *We were shown how to roughly weave ferns and grass* **together** *to make a temporary shelter.* [M] • *It takes great skill to weave a basket* **from** *rushes.* • *(fig.) The biography is woven* **from** (=combines) *the many accounts which exist of things she did.*

weav·er /£ˈwiː·vəʳ, $-vɚ/ *n* [C] • *basket weavers*

weav·ing /ˈwiː·vɪŋ/ *n* [U]

weave *(obj)* MOVE QUICKLY /wiːv/ *v* [always + adv/prep] *past* **weaved** to go or make (a path) by moving quickly and changing direction often, esp. to avoid hitting things • *To escape from police officers the thief weaved* **through/between** *stationary traffic on a bicycle.* [I] • *(fig.) She's a superb diplomat – she'll weave her* **way** *through the questions and persuade everyone to do what she wants.* [T] • *(Br dated infml)* If you tell someone to **get weaving** you either want them to start something or to hurry what they are doing: *We'd better get weaving – we've got a lot to do today.*

web NET /web/ *n* [C] a fixed net made by many types of SPIDER (=a small eight-legged animal) from the sticky thread that its body produces. It is used to catch insects • *a spider's web* • *We watched a spider* **spin** *a web between three tall grass stems.* • *(fig.) Those involved in the fraud created an* **intricate** *web of trading companies to hide their activities.* • *(fig.) The evidence which has been given was described as a web* **of deceit**. • See also COBWEB.

web SKIN /web/ *n* [C] the skin connecting the toes of some birds and other animals living by or on water which helps them when swimming • If an animal is **web-footed/toed** its feet have webs.

webbed /webd/ *adj* • *webbed toes* • *webbed hind feet*

web·bing /ˈweb·ɪŋ/ *n* [U] fibre woven into strong strips, used to make belts and straps and to support springs in furniture

wed *(obj)* /wed/ *v* [not *be wedding*] *past* **wedded** or **wed** *old use or slightly humorous* to marry (someone) • *The couple eventually wed after an eighteen year engagement.* [I] • *She wed her childhood sweetheart.* [T] • *The prince will wed diplomat Masako Owada.* [T] • See also NEWLYWED.

wed·ded /ˈwed·ɪd/ *adj* [before n; not gradable] • *your lawful wedded husband/wife* • *Elaine and Ian have been living in wedded* **bliss** *for almost half a year now.*

we'd /wiːd/ *short form of* we had *or* we would • *We'd better be more careful in the future.* • *It was one of the saddest stories we'd heard.* • *We'd be grateful for an answer.* • *There are certain improvements we'd all like to see.*

Wed *n abbreviation for* WEDNESDAY

wed·ded /ˈwed·ɪd/ *adj* [after v; always + *to*] believing firmly in (an idea or theory) and unwilling to change that belief • *The Social Democrats are still wedded* **to** *the concepts of high taxation and regulation.*

wed·ding /ˈwed·ɪŋ/ *n* [C] a marriage ceremony and any celebrations such as a meal or a party which follow it • *a wedding cake/dress/invitation/present/reception* • *Do you know the date of Caroline and Matthew's wedding?* • *It was their twenty-fifth wedding* **anniversary** *last week.* • A **wedding ring** (*Am also* **wedding band**) is a ring, often of gold, worn by a person to show that they are married. • PIC› **Bread and cakes**

wedge /wedʒ/ *n* [C] a piece of metal, wood, rubber etc. with a pointed edge at one end and a wide edge at the other, which is either pushed between two objects to keep them still or forced into something to break pieces off it • *Push a wedge under the door to keep it open while we're carrying the boxes in.* • *Pieces of stone can be split off by forcing wedges* **between** *the layers.* • *(fig.) Auntie Ann put a* *huge wedge* (= triangular-shaped piece) *of fruit cake on my plate.*

wedge *obj* /wedʒ/ *v* [T] • *Find something to wedge the window* **open/closed** *with.* [+ obj + adj] • *I was standing waiting for a bus, wedged* **between** (= fixed between and unable to move away from) *two old ladies and their bags of shopping.*

wed·lock /£'wed·lɒk, $-lɑːk/ *n* [U] *old use* the state of being married • The expression **out of wedlock** refers to parents who are not married or not married to each other: *In many European countries children are increasingly being born out of wedlock.*

Wed·nes·day /'wenz·deɪ, 'wed·ᵊnz-/ (*abbreviation* **Wed**) *n* the day of the week after Tuesday and before Thursday • *Did you say the meeting is* **on** *Wednesday?* [U] • *The restaurant is always closed* **on** *Wednesdays.* [C] • *Wednesday would be a good day for us to go running.* [U] • *Our anniversary falls/is on a Wednesday this year.* [C] • LP **Calendar**

wee SMALL /wiː/ *adj* [before n; not gradable] *Scot Eng or infml* small; little • *There were these beautiful wee ponies in the field.* • *There's a wee cottage inside the grounds.* • *Would you care for a wee* **bit** *more to eat?*

wee URINATE /wiː/, **wee–wee** /'wiː·wiː/ *v* [I] *infml* to urinate • *Daddy, I want to wee!*

wee /wiː/, **wee–wee** /'wiː·wiː/ *n* [C usually sing] *infml* • *Do you* **need/want** *(to do)* **a** *wee-wee* (= to urinate) *before we go?* • The word wee is especially used to and by children and wee-wee is especially used to and by very young children.

weed /wiːd/ *n* any wild plant which grows in an unwanted place, esp. in a garden or field where it prevents the cultivated plants from growing freely • *Many chemicals can be used to stop weeds growing, but most of them have side effects.* [C] • *(Br infml disapproving)* A weed is also someone who is thin and physically weak or who is weak in character: *He looks like a real weed in those shorts.* [C] • *(infml dated)* People sometimes say **the weed** to refer to tobacco: *Are you still off the weed* (= not smoking tobacco)*?* [U] • *(slang dated)* Weed also means MARIJUANA. [U] • **Weed whacker** is *Am trademark for* STRIMMER. • PIC **Garden**

weed *(obj)* /wiːd/ *v* • *I'm weeding (the vegetable garden)* (= removing weeds from it) *– would you like to help?* [I/T]

weed·ing /'wiː·dɪŋ/ *n* [U] • *There's plenty of weeding to* **do** *now that the growing season's started.*

weed·y /'wiː·di/ *adj* **-ier, -iest** • *a weedy pavement* • If a person is weedy they are thin and physically weak: *a weedy child* ○ *(fig.) The story had a weedy* (= uninteresting) *plot.*

weed out *obj*, **weed** *obj* **out** *v adv* [M] to get rid of (an unwanted thing or a person) • *A simple computer program could easily weed out the duplicate records.* • *The first round of interviews only really serves to weed out the very weakest of applicants.*

weed·kil·ler /£'wiːd,kɪl·əʳ, $-ɚ/ *n* [C/U] (a) chemical used for killing WEEDS

week /wiːk/ *n* [C] a period of seven days either from the beginning of Sunday to the end of Saturday or from the beginning of Monday to the end of Sunday • *We go to the cinema about once a week.* • *Will you be going to next week's class?* • *Last week my bicycle was stolen.* • *It usually takes about four weeks to get the forms processed.* • *Just a few weeks ago inspectors said the bridge was safe.* • *Don't do anything strenuous for a week* **or two** (= at least a week but preferably two). • *It'll be weeks* (= several weeks) *before the flood damage is cleared up.* • A week (also **working week**) can also be the amount of hours spent working during a week or the number of days on which a person works: *Many offices operate a thirty-seven-and-a-half hour week.* ○ *A lot of farm labourers* **work** *a six-day week.* • *(infml)* Also a week can be from the beginning of Monday to the end of Friday but not Saturday or Sunday: *We're usually too tired to do much socializing during the week.* • The expressions **a** week **(on)** Tuesday and Tuesday **week** both mean one week after Tuesday and can be used in the same way for any day: *The first performance of the play is a week tomorrow.* ○ *Our holiday starts a week on Saturday.* ○ *Can I just check – are we going to meet a week this Sunday or a week next Sunday?* ○ *She has to go back to see the doctor Friday week.* • The expressions **a** week **last** Tuesday and **a** week **ago (this)** Tuesday both mean one week before Tuesday and can be used for any day: *The problems with the TV started a week last Monday.* ○ *It was his birthday a week ago yesterday.* • **For weeks on end** means for a long period of time: *He would go up into the mountains alone for weeks on end.* • You can use **from week to week** or **week by week** to mean each week, esp. if there is a noticeable change in it during that period: *From week to week we could see his health deteriorate.* • A thing or person **of the Week** is one that has been chosen as the best in a particular week: *Book of the Week: Dog Breeds by A J Barker and H A Barker.* • The expressions **week after week** and **week in, week out** both mean regularly or continuously for many weeks: *I go to aerobics three times a week, week in, week out.* • LP **Calendar, Periods of time**

week·ly /'wiː·kli/ *adj, adv* [not gradable] • *a weekly magazine/report* • *a twice-weekly meeting* • *We should work out what our weekly costs are.* • *The fire alarm has a weekly test/is tested weekly.* • *Until he was eighty he went swimming weekly.*

week·ly /'wiː·kli/ *n* [C] • A weekly is a newspaper or magazine which is published once every week.

week·day /'wiːk·deɪ/ *n* [C] any day of the week except Sunday and usually Saturday • *On weekdays I'm usually in bed by ten o'clock.* • *Our office hours are from 9am to 7.30pm weekdays and 9am to 4pm on Saturdays – call us now, we can help!* • *Admission to the best enclosure at Deauville costs a mere £2 on weekdays, £3 on Sunday!*

week·end /ˌwiːk'end, '–/ *n* [C] Saturday and Sunday and sometimes also Friday evening. A time when many people living in the West do not go to work • *Have you got anything planned for* **the** *weekend?* • *They usually go windsurfing (Br and Aus)* **at***/(Am, Aus also)* **on** *weekends/the weekend/the weekends.* • *This weekend we're going to see some friends.* • Also a weekend can be a holiday or a visit taken at a weekend: *How much would a weekend for two in Amsterdam cost?* ○ *They've got a weekend cottage in Sussex.*

week·night /'wiːk·naɪt/ *n* [C] the evening or night of any day of the week except Sunday and usually Saturday

ween·y /'wiː·ni/ *adj* **-ier, -iest** *infml* extremely small • *All right, I'll have a slice of cake then – but just a weeny bit.*

weep *(obj)* CRY /wiːp/ *v past* **wept** /wept/ *slightly literary* to cry (tears) • *She wept and wept when Paul left.* [I] • *I know I'm going to weep at the airport.* [I] • *I could hear him weeping from the bedroom.* [I] • *People in the streets wept* **with** *joy when the truce was announced.* [I] • *It's not worth weeping even a single tear* **over** *him.* [T]

weep /wiːp/ *n* [U] *literary* • *It might help you to* **have a** *weep.*

weep·y /'wiː·pi/ *adj* **-ier, -iest** • *I'd just waved Peter off at the airport and was feeling a bit weepy* (= sad and likely to cry).

weep·y, weep·ie /'wiː·pi/ *n* [C] *infml* • A weepy is a film or a book which makes people want to cry because it is sad: *If I were you I'd take some tissues to the cinema – it's a real weepy.*

weep INJURY /wiːp/ *v* [I] *past* **wept** /wept/ (of an injury) to produce liquid such as PUS (= thick yellowish liquid) • *The sore is still weeping a lot so you'll have to change the dressing once a day.*

weep·ing wil·low /'wiː·pɪŋ/ *n* [C] a type of WILLOW tree having long thin branches which hang down • PIC **Tree**

wee·vil /'wiː·vᵊl/ *n* [C] any of various BEETLES (= types of insect) which destroy crops such as grains and cotton

weft /weft/ *n* [U] **the weft** *specialized* the threads that go across the length of a piece of cloth or a LOOM (= special frame for weaving) • Compare WARP THREADS.

weigh *(obj)* HEAVINESS /weɪ/ *v* to have a heaviness of a stated amount, or to measure the heaviness of an object • *Yesterday a satellite weighing 15 tonnes was successfully placed in orbit.* [L only + n] • *Improvements to the armour are heavy, and the tank weighs about 40 tons.* [L only + n] • *The baby was in perfect health and weighed 3·8 kilograms at birth.* [L only + n] • *You'll weigh more now because you've just eaten a big meal.* [L only + n] • *She weighs* **herself** *every week on the scales in the bathroom.* [T] • *Your luggage must be weighed before it is put on the aircraft.* [T] • *Will you weigh* **out** *two kilograms of flour/weigh two kilograms of flour* **out** *for me please?* [M] • If a load **weighs** someone or something **down** its heaviness causes an effect, esp. one which is unwanted: *Weighed down* **with** *supplies they found the steep path difficult to climb.* ○ *The boughs of the tree were weighed down* **with** *all the fruit.* ○ *(fig.) I thought she looked somehow older, weighed down* (= made anxious and unhappy) **by** *all her new responsibilities.* • When the competitors in a boxing competition or a horse race **weigh in** they are weighed just before or after the event. See also **weigh in** at WEIGH INFLUENCE. • LP **Measurements**

weight /weɪt/ *n* • *What weight can this lorry safely carry?* [C] • *We think the weight of snow on the roof caused it to collapse.* [U] • *There was a slight decrease* **in** *his weight after a week of dieting.* [C] • *(fig.) It's a great weight* (= worry) **off** *my mind to know that the building is finally finished.* [C] • A weight is also a piece of metal of known heaviness which can be used to measure the heaviness of other objects. [C] • Also a weight can be any object which is heavy: *If you have to lift a heavy weight keep your back straight and bend your legs at the knees.* [C] ○ *Joe's a big lad so he's quite a weight to carry round all afternoon.* [C] • If you **take the weight off** your **feet/legs** you sit down, esp. after standing or walking for a long time: *You must be exhausted after all that shopping – why don't you take the weight off your feet.* • **Weight training** is the activity of lifting heavy objects for exercise, esp. to improve the strength of muscles and the appearance of the body: *I* **do/go** *weight training in a gym during the week.* Compare **body-building** at BODY [PHYSICAL STRUCTURE]; WEIGHTLIFTING. • [LP] **Units**

weight *obj* /weɪt/ *v* [T] • *Our car was heavily weighted* **with** *luggage.* • *Paper tablecloths need to be weighted* **down** *or they tend to blow away in the wind.* [M]

weight·y /£ˈweɪ·ti, $-t̬i/ *adj* **-ier**, **-iest** • *I don't want to carry this bag around all afternoon – it's quite weighty* (= heavy).

weigh [INFLUENCE] /weɪ/ *v* [I always + adv/prep] (of something such as a fact or an event) to have an influence or be important • *Easy access to a railway network weighed heavily* **with** *us when we chose a site for the new factory.* • *Academic ability doesn't weigh much* **in** *my mind when I'm interviewing someone for a job.* • *(infml)* When a person **weighs in** to a discussion they join in, esp. by saying something important or persuasive: *Eventually the chairperson weighed in* **with** *a compromise solution.* See also **weigh in** at WEIGH [HEAVINESS].

weight /weɪt/ *n* [U] • Opinions which have weight are respected and trusted by people and therefore have influence on situations: *Her experience does give her opinions weight.* ○ *After he was voted out of power few people* **attached** *much weight* **to** *what he said.* ○ *Radical views don't* **carry** *much weight anymore.*

weight·ed /£ˈweɪ·tɪd, $-t̬ɪd/ *adj* [after v] • If a system is weighted to produce a particular effect, such as produce an advantage, it will tend to produce that effect instead of any other: *The system of benefits is weighted* **in favour of** *those who have children.*

weight·y /£ˈweɪ·ti, $-t̬i/ *adj* **-ier**, **-iest** • If something is weighty, such as a subject or a book, then it is important or serious: *weighty matters/issues* • *a weighty tome*

weigh *obj* [CONSIDER] /weɪ/ *v* [T] to carefully consider, esp. by comparing (facts or possibilities) in order to make a decision • *Only when we have weighed all the factors involved can we decide when would be the best time to start.* • *Economic benefits must be carefully weighed* **against** *the possible dangers of handling radioactive waste.* • If you **weigh** your **words/weigh each word** you carefully think about everything you're going to say before you say it: *He gave evidence to the court, weighing each word as he spoke.* • When a person **weighs up** several possibilities they carefully compare them so that they can make a decision or form an opinion: *You should weigh the potential gains and losses up if you're thinking of a career change.* • Also if you **weigh** someone **up** you form an opinion about their abilities and character by watching them and talking to them: *If you're a detective you learn to weigh people up quickly.* • Compare OUTWEIGH.

weigh *obj* [SHIP] /weɪ/ *v* [T] **weigh anchor** to lift the ANCHOR (= a heavy metal object) of a ship from under the water so that it can move freely

weigh on *obj v prep* [T] (of problems, responsibilities etc.) to cause feelings of anxiety or guilt in (someone or their mind) • *He's under huge pressure at work and it's really weighing on him.* • *She knew she had treated him badly and it weighed* **heavily** *on her mind for a long time.*

weigh·bridge /ˈweɪ·brɪdʒ/ *n* [C] a machine consisting of a large area in a road which vehicles and their loads can be driven onto to weigh them

weight·ing /£ˈweɪ·tɪŋ, $-t̬ɪŋ/ *n* [U] *Br* an increase in an amount, esp. extra money paid to someone because they work in an area where it is expensive to live • *Many city firms offer a weighting to encourage applicants who might otherwise look for jobs in areas where property prices are lower.* • A weighting is also an amount which a number is multiplied by to make it comparable with others: *When the final marks are calculated greater weighting is given to the practical tests than to the written work.*

weight·less /ˈweɪt·ləs/ *adj* having or appearing to have no weight • *There is a lot of interest in carrying out experiments in the weightless conditions which are experienced aboard space stations.*

weight·less·ly /ˈweɪt·lə·sli/ *adv*

weight·less·ness /ˈweɪt·lə·snəs/ *n* [U] • *Astronauts quite often find that weightlessness makes them feel sick.*

weight·lift·ing /£ˈweɪtˌlɪf·tɪŋ, $-t̬ɪŋ/ *n* [U] the activity of lifting heavy objects either as a sport or for exercise

weight·lift·er /£ˈweɪtˌlɪf·tər, $-t̬ɚ/ *n* [C]

weir /£wɪər, $wɪr/ *n* [C] a wall built under the water across a river, over which the water flows from one level to another in a controlled way

weird /£wɪəd, $wɪrd/ *adj* **-er**, **-est** very strange and unusual, unexpected or not natural; BIZARRE • *He was sitting alone by a window with a weird contraption on the bench in front of him.* • *The details of her childhood were the weirdest I had ever heard.* • *The man we spoke to was really weird.* • *That's weird – I thought I'd left my keys on the table but they're not there.* • *There is nothing to rival the weird* **and wonderful** *things that come out on the streets at carnival time.*

weird·ly /£ˈwɪəd·li, $ˈwɪrd-/ *adv* • *The house was weirdly quiet.* • *He was dressed really weirdly.*

weird·ness /£ˈwɪəd·nəs, $ˈwɪrd-/ *n* [U] • *What fascinates all of us is the very weirdness of these creatures from the deep ocean.*

weird·o /£ˈwɪə·dəʊ, $ˈwɪr·doʊ/ *n* [C] *pl* **weirdos** *infml disapproving* • *I wouldn't want to be left alone with him – he's a real weirdo* (= strange person).

welch /weltʃ/, **welsh** *v* [I] *disapproving* to avoid doing something you have promised to do, esp. not to pay a debt • *The companies do not wish to welch* **on** *their debts to bankers.* • *Their competitors' behaviour gave them a great opportunity to welch* **on** *their promises.*

wel·come *obj* [MEET] /ˈwel·kəm/ *v* [T] to meet or speak to (someone) in a friendly way when they come to the place where you are • *The visitors were* **warmly** *welcomed by the librarian who later showed them round the new collection.* • *As we stepped down from the bus, we were enthusiastically welcomed by a group of children holding out flowers.* • *Browning stood at the door, welcoming newcomers with a large smile and a pat on the arm.* • You can say 'Please welcome' as a polite way of greeting and introducing someone who has come to a place officially: *Please welcome our guest of honour – Charlotte King.* • *She gave everyone a welcoming smile.*

wel·come /ˈwel·kəm/ *n* • *They were given a* **warm** *welcome.* [C] • *The opposition leader returned to a* **hero's/heroine's** *welcome after seven years in exile.* [C] • *She referred to his previous visit in her* **speech of** *welcome/welcome* **speech**. [U] • If you **outstay/overstay** your welcome, you stay too long: *I left after a couple of days – and even then I had the impression I might have outstayed my welcome.* [U] ○ *(fig.) He certainly outstayed his welcome as Mayor – he should have given it up years ago.* [U] • A **welcome mat** is a small piece of strong material with the word 'welcome' written on it which is put on the floor by the door to greet people as they come in: *(fig.) A new immigration law means the US will be dusting off the welcome mat for* (= will be ready to welcome) *famous people who want to live in the country.* • To **put the welcome mat out** is to offer welcome. • *(Am trademark)* The **Welcome Wagon** is an organization which gives information about businesses and services in a town to people who have recently moved there: *(fig.) She likes to* **roll out** *the welcome wagon* (= greet and be friendly to) *everyone who moves onto the block.*

wel·come /ˈwel·kəm/ *exclamation* • People often say welcome as a greeting to someone arriving at a place: *Welcome – come in.* ○ *Welcome* **home/back** *– we've missed you!* ○ *Welcome* **to** *Cambridge.* ○ (on an aircraft) *Welcome on board.* ○ (on a ship) *Welcome aboard.* • *"Welcome to the House of Fun"* (title of a song by Madness, 1982)

wel·come /ˈwel·kəm/ *adj* • *Out in the desert the traveller is a welcome* **guest**. • If someone is welcome you are pleased when they visit you: *Come and see us whenever you're in town – you're always welcome/you'll always be welcome.* • If you **make** someone **welcome** you show them that you are pleased that they are with you: *The restaurant made the children very welcome.*

wel·come *obj* SUPPORT /ˈwel·kəm/ *v* [T] to be pleased about and encourage or support (something) • *In his speech he welcomed the announcement that the system would be reviewed.* • *The new appointment has been widely welcomed.*

wel·come /ˈwel·kəm/ *n* • *Their supporters* **gave** *the decision a guarded/cautious welcome.*

wel·come /ˈwel·kəm/ *adj* • *The holiday was a welcome* **change/break/relief**. • *The new book is a welcome* **addition** *to the series.* • *She offered him the welcome* **chance/opportunity** *to do something different.* • *That drink was* **very/most/particularly** *welcome.* • *(infml)* If someone **is welcome to** someone or something they can have it or do it, esp. because it is not valued by anyone else: *You're welcome to it – I can never get it to work properly.* ○ *They're welcome to him – he only caused trouble when he worked for us.* ○ *If they want to change the rules, they are welcome to try.* [+ *to* infinitive] • 'You're welcome' is a polite answer when someone thanks you for doing something: *"It was very kind of you to help." "You're welcome."*

weld *obj* JOIN METAL /weld/ *v* [T] to join two pieces of metal together permanently by melting the parts that touch • *Iron spikes have been welded* **to** *the railings around the embassy.* • *The cell door was sheet metal welded* **on to** *a frame of iron.*

weld /weld/ *n* [C] • *A team of eight divers repaired a cracked weld on the oil platform in almost 600 feet of water.*

weld·er /£ˈwel·dəʳ, $-dɚ/ *n* [C] • *He was employed as a welder.*

weld·ing /ˈwel·dɪŋ/ *n* [U] • Welding is the activity of joining metal parts together: *Many companies now use robots for the welding involved in car manufacture.*

weld *obj* JOIN PEOPLE /weld/ *v* [T] to make separate people into a group who can work together successfully • *He is a born leader, who welded a collection of gifted individualists* **into** *a real team.* • *The next task is to weld the players* **into** *a force capable of maintaining the record set last year.*

wel·fare HEALTH AND HAPPINESS /£ˈwel·feəʳ, $-fer/ *n* [U] physical and mental health and happiness, esp. of a person • *The police are very concerned for the welfare* **of** *the missing child.* • *These organizations have fought very hard for the rights and welfare* **of** *immigrants.* • *The working environment should have adequate facilities and arrangements for employees' welfare, the report says.* • *Many people who have adopted children from poor countries believe they are contributing to that country's long-term welfare.* • *Scientists have to consider the balance between human health and animal welfare as they push forward the frontiers of research.*

wel·fare HELP /£ˈwel·feəʳ, $-fer/ *n* [U] help given, esp. by the state or an organization, to people who need it, esp. because they do not have enough money • *This national fund pays for welfare* **benefits** *such as unemployment and sickness pay.* • *The party was urged to set up a commission to enquire into tax, income distribution and welfare* **policy**. • *Spending cuts are expected in education, transport and* **social** *welfare.* • *They interviewed workers at a welfare* **agency** *operating in the Klong Poey slums.* • *(Br) After her month's sick leave she was summoned to see the company's welfare* **officer**. • A **welfare state** is a system of taxation which allows the government of a country to provide social services such as health care, unemployment pay, etc. to people who need them. • *(Am)* If a person is **on** welfare, they are receiving financial help from the state because they are poor or have not been employed for a long time.

well HEALTHY /wel/ *adj* [usually after v] **better, best** healthy; not ill • *He hasn't been too well lately.* • *When she came home from school she didn't* **look** *at all well.* • *I'm sorry you're ill – I hope you* **get** *well soon.* • *They sent a get well* **card**. • *The health centre has set up a* **well woman/man clinic** (= a place where particular features of health important to women/men can be tested).

well·ness /ˈwel·nəs/ *n* [U] *Am* • *a wellness clinic*

well EXCLAMATION /wel/ *exclamation* used to introduce something you are going to say, often to show surprise, doubt, slight disagreement or annoyance, or to continue a story • *Well, what shall we do now?* • *Well now, how are we going to arrange things?* • *Well then, who's coming with me?* • *"Who was that?" "Well, I'm afraid I can't remember her name."* • *"He's decided to give up his job and move to the north with her." "Well, well – that's what love does for you."* • *"Will you be able to come on Tuesday?" "Well, I'm not sure – I'll have to see how busy I am."* • *Well, with all the trouble we've had, I'm not sure we'd want to do it again.* • *Well, perhaps I'd have time to collect it on my way home.* • *Well, really, how thoughtless of him!* • *Well? What did you do next?* • *Well, after that we went camping in the mountains.* • *Well/* **Oh** *well, it doesn't matter – I can always buy another one.* • **Very** *well, if you insist I'll meet him next week.*

well IN A GOOD WAY /wel/ *adv* **better, best** in a good way, to a high or satisfactory standard • *The documentary presented both sides of the problem well.* • *She organizes that kind of event very well.* • *The concert was well enough advertised but ticket sales were poor.* • *a well-made table* • *a well-cut suit* • *a well-lit room* • *a well-paid job* • *a well-trained dog* • *a well-planned project* • *The house and garden were well cared for.* • *The kitchen was well equipped.* • *We thought the book had been very well researched.* • *That was well* **put** (= expressed in a good or clever way). • *His point about the need to reduce waste was well* **taken** (= it was accepted as a good criticism). • *They took two hours to discuss the plans and considered it time well* **spent** (= it had been a useful discussion). • *I can't do it* **as** *well* **as** *Marie can.* • *"I passed my exam."* "**Well done!**" See also WELL-DONE. • *(Br and Aus) They seem to think he was* **well out of it** (= lucky not to be involved). • *"All's Well that Ends Well"* (title of a play by William Shakespeare)

well TO A GREAT DEGREE /wel/ *adv* **better, best** extremely, completely, much or to a great degree • *Knead the dough well, then divide it into four pieces.* • *He could well imagine how much his promise was going to cost him.* • *I can't catch the bus – there are no buses after midnight, as you well know.* • *(fml) I well remember the last time they visited us.* • *I knew her* **pretty** (= very) *well when I lived in Brighton.* • *He's plays the piano well enough* (= to a satisfactory standard). • *The party was* **well and truly** (= completely) *over when he arrived.* • Well is used with some prepositions for emphasis: *The results are well above/below/beyond what we expected.* ○ *The child was standing well apart from the rest of the group.* ○ *Keep well away from the edge of the cliff.* ○ *They kept the crowd well behind the white line.* ○ *Stand well clear of the doors!* ○ *It cost well over £100.* ○ *The factory complex is well north/south/east/west of here.* • Well is used with a few adjectives for emphasis: *The police are well aware of the situation.* ○ *We were well pleased/satisfied with the progress we had made.* ○ *The museum is well worth a visit.* ○ *Some machines look more like cheap, plastic toys – leave these well alone.* • *(Br and Aus)* If you **leave well alone** (*Am usually* **leave well enough alone**) you do not change something which is not causing a problem: *Is telling her the right thing to do, or should I leave well alone?* ○ *Only when they have solved this problem can surgeons be sure when it is worth operating and when it is best to leave well alone.* ○ *They think they know what's best for everybody and will not leave well alone.* • *(Br slang)* Well is used to mean very: *We were well bored at the concert.* ○ *They think they're well hard* (= they think that they are very strong). • *(Br infml)* If someone is **well away** they are completely involved in what they are doing: *He was soon well away on* (= talking a lot about) *his favourite subject of steam train conservation.* ○ *After a few moments her head started to nod and she was soon well away* (= sleeping). ○ *The noise from the pub was audible halfway down the street – they were well away* (= drunk) *already.* • *(Br infml) They're* **well in with** *(Am* **in well with***)* (= have a good relationship, to their own advantage, with) *a company that supplies catering equipment.* • **All very well** or **all well and good** is used to show that something is good up to a point but you are not completely pleased about it: *Electric heating is all very well until there's a power cut.* ○ *That's all well and good but I prefer to do things in a more organized way.*

well REASONABLY /wel/ *adv* **better, best** with good reason • *I couldn't very well refuse their kind offer.* • *You may well think it was his fault – I couldn't possibly comment.* • *It may well be finished by tomorrow.* • *She might well be the best person to ask.* • *He may well wonder why no-one was there – he forgot to confirm the date.* • You can say **just as well** (*esp. Br also* **as well**) to suggest that something will be a good thing to do or that it was lucky that something was done or happened: *"Shall I phone him to remind him?" "That would be just as well."* ○ *It's just as well you're not here – you wouldn't like the noise.* ○ *He left at three, which was just as well or he'd have missed the train.* ○ *(Br) It would be as well to check the small print.* ○ See also **as well (as)** at WELL IN ADDITION.

well HOLE /wel/ *n* [C] a deep hole in the ground from which water, oil or gas can be obtained • *Families in the area get their water from wells and boreholes.* • *The cameras are used* *for detecting leaks in oil wells and pipelines.* • *The exploration and production division is responsible for locating oil reserves,* **drilling** *wells and pumping crude oil and natural gas.* • See also STAIRWELL.

well [IN ADDITION] /wel/ *adv* [not gradable] **as well (as)** in addition (to) • *Invite Emlyn – and Simon as well.* • *I want to visit Andrew as well* **as** *Martin.* • See also **(just) as well** at WELL [REASONABLY].

well [SURFACE] /wel/ *v* [I always + adv/prep] (of liquid) to appear on the surface of something or come slowly out from somewhere • *Dirty water welled out of the damaged pipe.* • *As she read the letter tears welled up in her eyes.* • *(fig.) Conflicting emotions welled* **up** *in his heart.*

well–ad·just·ed /£ˌwel·əˈdʒʌs·tɪd, $-t̬ɪd/ *adj* (of a person) acting with good judgment and not showing difficult or strange behaviour • *His family could not understand how this quiet, well-adjusted man could have been driven to this terrible deed.* • *The children are quiet and shy at first, but they leave the school happy and well adjusted.*

well–ad·vised /ˌwel·ədˈvaɪzd/ *adj* [after v] *fml* showing good judgment • *You would be well-advised* **to** *book in advance.* [+ *to* infinitive]

well–ap·point·ed /£ˌwel·əˈpɔɪn·tɪd, $-t̬ɪd/ *adj fml* having a good supply of comfortable or necessary furniture and attractive decorations • *The hotel has spacious, well-appointed public rooms and bedrooms, and good food.*

well–ar·gued /£ˌwelˈɑː·gjuːd, $-ˈɑːr-/ *adj* described or requested in a persuasive and clever way • *She presented a well-argued case for the banning of smoking in public places.* • *It is a great pity when a well-argued thesis is spoilt by a simple error of fact.*

well–at·tend·ed /ˌwel·əˈten·dɪd/ *adj* with many people present • *The information was given at an unusually well-attended press conference yesterday.* • *The meeting was not well attended.*

well–bal·anced /ˌwelˈbæl·əntst/ *adj* containing a mixture of ideas, people, etc. with each one being represented equally or fairly • *a well-balanced article* • *a well-balanced team* • Food which is well-balanced contains a good range of the things needed to stay healthy: *a well-balanced diet/meal* • A person who is well-balanced is calm and reasonable, and acts in a way that shows good judgment: *a well-balanced individual* ○ *Do these nurseries produce the happy, well-balanced children that teachers and parents say they do?*

well–be·haved /ˌwel·bɪˈheɪvd/ *adj approving* behaving in a way that is accepted as correct • *a well-behaved child* • *Apart from a small minority, the crowd have been good humoured and well behaved.*

well–being /ˌwelˈbiː·ɪŋ/ *n* [U] the state of feeling healthy and happy • *People doing yoga benefit from the increased feeling of well-being and a feeling of being more in control which it brings.* • *Business executives believe that holidays are vital to their well-being, according to a survey commissioned by a major hotel group.*

well–bred /ˌwelˈbred/ *adj* speaking or acting in a way that is generally considered correct and polite, or *(dated)* coming from a family that has a high social position • *A television announcer with a well-bred voice was reading the news.*

well–brought–up /£ˌwel·brɔːˈtʌp, $-brɑːˈt̬ʌp/ *adj approving* (esp. of children) polite and acting in a quiet and pleasant way • *A well-brought-up person wouldn't make such threats.* • *Some children were well brought up, despite family breakdown, he admitted.*

well–built /ˌwelˈbɪlt/ *adj* (of a person) large and strong, or *(Br and Aus)* used to avoid saying fat or *(Am)* having an attractive body

well–chos·en /£ˌwelˈtʃəʊ·zən, $-ˈtʃoʊ-/ *adj* carefully chosen • *These debates have made a successful series, mostly because of well-chosen speakers and lively topics.* • *There are times during the monologue when you feel a few well-chosen* **words** *would be more effective.* • **A few well-chosen words** sometimes means a short speech: *He introduced the visitors with a few well-chosen words.*

well–con·nect·ed /£ˌwel·kəˈnek·tɪd, $-t̬ɪd/ *adj* having friends or family members who are important or powerful people • *She was born in 1940 into a well-connected family.*

well–de·fined /ˌwel·dɪˈfaɪnd/ *adj* clearly expressed, explained or described • *We were not expecting Mr Levy to give us a clear or well-defined answer.* • *To make profits we will have to have a well-defined product for a well-defined clientele.* • *Scientists follow several well-defined steps in investigating unexpected outbreaks of disease.*

well–de·vel·oped /ˌwel·dɪˈvel·əpt/ *adj* having grown or increased in a positive way • *The less well-developed areas of Europe are much less attractive as investment prospects than the major centres.* • *She is a physically well-developed teenager with the emotional and mental level of a four-year-old.* • *He's a warm and friendly man with a well-developed sense of humour.*

well–dis·posed /£ˌwel·dɪˈspəʊzd, $-ˈspoʊzd/ *adj* friendly and helpful • *If you've got a good feeling about yourself, you are more likely to feel well-disposed* **to/towards** *other people.*

well–doc·u·ment·ed /£ˌwelˈdɒk·jʊ·men·tɪd, $-ˈdɑː·kjʊ·men·t̬ɪd/ *adj* having been frequently recorded • *The medicinal values of garlic are well-documented.* • *Another well-documented scandal has been the sale of unsuitable or dangerous medicines in the Third World.*

well–done /ˌwelˈdʌn/ *adj* (of meat) cooked all the way through and not just on the outside • *"How would you like your steak?" "Well-done."* • See also **well done** at WELL [IN A GOOD WAY].

well–dressed /ˌwelˈdrest/ *adj* wearing attractive and stylish clothes

well–earned /£ˌwelˈɜːnd, $-ˈɜːrnd, ˈ--/ *adj Br and Aus* deserved because of what you have done or experienced; much or well deserved • *His second goal, a quarter of an hour from time, sealed a well-earned victory.* • *Liz won't be at work next week – she's having a well-earned break/rest/holiday.*

well–ed·u·cat·ed /£ˌwelˈed·jʊ·keɪ·tɪd, $-t̬ɪd/ *adj* having had a good education • *well-educated and highly motivated workers* • *It is an industrialised, urbanised country with well-educated people.* • *Our readers are among the most affluent, highly qualified and well-educated in Europe, according to independent research.*

well–en·dowed /ˌwel·ɪnˈdaʊd/ *adj* having a lot of something, esp. money, possessions or physical attraction • *The city is well-endowed* **with** *modern medical facilities.* • *It is one of the least well-endowed colleges.* • *She's very well-endowed* (= She has large breasts).

well–es·tab·lished /ˌwel·ɪˈstab·lɪʃt/ *adj* having a recognized position or being generally known about • *The rules, though not written down, are fairly well established.* • *World Music is now well established and popular with mass audiences and mainstream companies.* • *His new novel is built on another well-established theme, the emotional complexities of the father-and-son relationship.*

well–fed /ˌwelˈfed/ *adj* having a lot to eat • *It should be possible to be warm and well-fed, and to enjoy all the good things of life, while respecting the needs of the planet.*

well–found·ed /ˌwelˈfaʊn·dɪd/ *adj* based on facts • *He had to show that he had a well-founded fear of persecution on religious or political grounds to qualify as a refugee.* • *The traditional belief that banks do not lose customers once they have got them is not well founded, the study suggests.*

well–groomed /ˌwelˈgruːmd/ *adj* having a tidy and pleasant appearance that is produced with care • *He is the sort of well-groomed man you expect to inhabit an executive-size corporate office.*

well–ground·ed /ˌwelˈgraʊn·dɪd/ *adj* being based on or having a good knowledge of facts • *The young players all seemed very well grounded* **in** *the rich history of the music they were performing.* • *The claim must be well grounded* **in** *fact.*

well–guard·ed /£ˌwelˈgɑː·dɪd, $-ˈgɑːr-/ *adj* carefully protected • *It's been a well-guarded* **secret** *for centuries.*

well–heeled /ˌwelˈhiːld/ *adj infml* rich • *His family was very well-heeled.* • *The area has a mix of student bedsits and well-heeled family homes.*

well–heeled /ˌwelˈhiːld/ *pl n* • *The shop attracted a loyal and large following among* **the** *well-heeled with its personal service.*

well–in·formed /£ˌwel·ɪnˈfɔːmd, $-ˈfɔːrmd/ *adj* having a lot of knowledge or information about a particular subject or things in general • *He was well-informed and shrewd, with good, calm judgment.* • *How well-informed is the customer* **about** *the range, quality and cost of the products on offer?* • *We were shown round by a well-informed guide.*

wel·ling·ton (boot) /ˈwel·ɪŋ·tən/, *infml* **wel·ly, wel·lie,** *Aus* **gum·boot** *n* [C] *esp. Br* a waterproof boot • *He left his muddy wellingtons outside the back door.* • [PIC] **Shoes**

well–in·ten·tioned /ˌwel·ɪnˈten·ʃənd/ *adj* wanting to have good effects, but sometimes having bad effects which were not expected • *He described the report as well-intentioned, but misguided.* • *Well-intentioned development projects can have unintended effects on population control.* • See also WELL-MEANING.

well–kept [TIDY] /ˌwelˈkept/ *adj* clean, tidy and cared for • *Saunders said his guest was astonished to find pleasant public parks, nice streets and well-kept houses.*

well–kept [HIDDEN] /ˌwelˈkept/ *adj* (of a secret) not told or shown to anyone; kept hidden • *The details of the new car were a well-kept* **secret**.

well–known /£ˌwelˈnəʊn, $-ˈnoʊn/ *adj* known or recognized by many people • *a well-known local artist* • *a well-known face/voice* • *well-known difficulties* • *Her views on the subject are already well known.* • *It is well known* **that** *he never gives interviews.* • *The restaurant is well known* **for** *its friendly atmosphere and excellent service.*

well–liked /ˌwelˈlaɪkt/ *adj* liked by many people • *A colleague described him as well-liked and respected by all.*

well–man·nered /£ˌwelˈmæn·əd, $-ɚd/ *adj* behaving in a pleasant and polite way • *The other visitors were too well-mannered to complain.* • *Competition within the group is keen but well-mannered.*

well–matched /ˌwelˈmætʃt/ *adj* similar or equal (to something) • *At the start of the competition the three teams looked extremely well matched.* • *Her skills are well-matched* **to** *the job.* • *They are an attractive and well-matched couple.*

well–mean·ing /ˌwelˈmiː·nɪŋ/ *adj* wanting to have a good effect, but not always achieving one • *I know he's well-meaning, but I wish he'd leave us alone.*

well–meant /ˌwelˈment/ *adj* • *a well-meant suggestion* • *An irresponsible action maybe, but it was well-meant and essentially harmless.*

well·ness /ˈwel·nəs/ *n* [U] See at WELL [HEALTHY]

well–nigh /ˌwelˈnaɪ/ *adv* [not gradable] almost or very nearly • *With no help, finishing the job in a day was well-nigh* **impossible**. • *The problem is well-nigh insoluble.*

well–off [RICH] /£ˌwelˈɒf, $-ˈɑːf/ *adj* rich • *Her family was very well-off.* • *This is the best way of getting assistance to those families who are less well-off.* • *She earned a large salary and accumulated a group of privileged and well-off friends.* • If you **don't know when** you **are well off**, you don't understand that your present situation is good compared with other people's or with what it might be like: *She's always complaining about her car – she doesn't know when she's well off* (= she's lucky to have a car even if it's bad)*!*

well–off /£ˌwelˈɒf, $-ˈɑːf/ *pl n* • *It is a resort that clearly caters for* **the** *well-off.*

well off [HAVING A LOT] *adj* [after v] having a lot of or a number of • *The city is well off* **for** *parks and gardens.* • *There are plenty of books and games – we are well off there.*

well–oiled [DRUNK] /ˌwelˈɔɪld/ *adj slang* drunk

well–oiled [EFFECTIVE] /ˌwelˈɔɪld/ *adj* working smoothly and effectively • *a well-oiled political machine*

well–pre·served /£ˌwel·prɪˈzɜːvd, $-ˈzɜːrvd/ *adj* (esp. of something old) kept in good condition • *It was a pretty town with a picturesque harbour and well-preserved buildings.* • *Most female models have to retire around the age of 25, whereas a well-preserved man can go on working into his forties.*

well–qua·li·fied /£ˌwelˈkwɒl·ɪ·faɪd, $-ˈkwɑː·lɪ-/ *adj* having suitable experience or formal qualifications • *Ken has more than 10 years of experience in photography behind him, so he is well qualified* **to** *offer advice.* [+ *to* infinitive] • *He seems well qualified* **for** *the job.*

well–read [KNOWLEDGEABLE] /ˌwelˈred/ *adj* (of people) having obtained a lot of information on different subjects by reading • *She is well-read, multilingual and with extensive experience of cultures other than her own.*

well–read [MUCH READ] /ˌwelˈred/ *adj* (of books, magazines and newspapers) read a lot; read by many people • *There was a well-read copy of Hello! magazine on the table.*

well–round·ed /ˌwelˈraʊn·dɪd/ *adj* involving or having experience in a wide range of ideas or activities • *It's a well-rounded article which is fair to both sides of the dispute.* • *She describes herself as a "well-rounded person" who works hard but has a varied social life.* • *The screen characters are unreal, lacking normal well-rounded lives.*

well–spok·en /£ˌwelˈspəʊ·kᵊn, $-ˈspoʊ-/ *adj* having a pleasant and polite way of speaking which is considered socially acceptable • *The two men who called at the house were well-spoken and had a reassuring manner.*

well·spring /ˈwel·sprɪŋ/ *n*, **well·springs** /ˈwel·sprɪŋz/ *pl n literary* the place something comes from or starts at, or the cause of something; the SOURCE • *the wellsprings of the creative spirit*

well–thought–of /£ˌwelˈθɔː·tɒv, $-ˈθɑː·t̬ɑːv/ *adj* considered by other people as good; admired and approved of • *He was efficient at his job and well-thought-of.* • *It's a well-thought-of school.*

well–thought–out /£ˌwel·θɔːˈtaʊt, $-θɑːˈt̬aʊt/ *adj* planned in an effective way • *a well-thought-out scheme for traffic control*

well–timed /ˌwelˈtaɪmd/ *adj* happening or caused to happen at a suitable or effective time • *A well-timed joke stopped the disagreement developing into something more serious.*

well–to–do /ˌwel·təˈduː/ *adj infml* rich • *well-to-do families*

well–tried /ˌwelˈtraɪd/ *adj* used many times before and known to be effective • *a well-tried recipe*

well–trod·den /£ˌwelˈtrɒd·ᵊn, $-ˈtrɑː·dᵊn/ *adj* much used or visited • *We followed the well-trodden tourist route from Paris to Chartres.* • *(fig.) The survey showed that people become managers by well-trodden* **paths** (= in the same way as many other people).

well–turned /£ˌwelˈtɜːnd, $-ˈtɜːrnd/ *adj* cleverly expressed • *a well-turned phrase*

well–versed /£ˌwelˈvɜːst, $-ˈvɜːrst/ *adj* knowing a lot about (something) • *He was well-versed* **in** *modern history.*

well–wish·er /£ˈwelˌwɪʃ·əʳ, $-ɚ/ *n* [C] a person who encourages or supports you • *The syringes were donated by sponsors and well-wishers.* • *He was clutching the award he had just won for Best Newcomer, surrounded by fans and well-wishers.*

well–worn /£ˌwelˈwɔːn, $-ˈwɔːrn/ *adj* (of clothes) frequently worn and becoming old, or *(fig.)* used too often • *a well-worn sports jacket* • *(fig.) Social class is a well-worn students' topic.* • *(fig.) The subject of conservation can be approached without relying on well-worn examples such as tropical rain forests.*

wel·ly /ˈwel·i/ *n* [C] *esp. Br infml for* WELLINGTON

welsh /weltʃ/ *v* [I] to WELCH

Welsh rare·bit, Welsh rab·bit *n* [U] a piece of bread with cheese on it which is heated until the cheese melts

welt /welt/ *n* [C] a raised red area of skin caused by being hit or by cuts healing • *One young man showed me the welts and bruises on his back which he said had been administered by soldiers.*

wel·ter /£ˈwel·təʳ, $-t̬ɚ/ *n* [U] a large and esp. not well organized number (of things) • *This report raises* **a welter of** *questions.* • *We are reducing the company's welter* **of** *development projects and will streamline sales and marketing.*

wel·ter·weight /£ˈwel·tə·weɪt, $-t̬ɚ-/ *n* [C] a boxer whose body weight is between LIGHTWEIGHT and MIDDLEWEIGHT

wench /wentʃ/ *n* [C] *old use* a young woman

wend *obj* /wend/ *v* [T] **wend** *your* **way** to move slowly and indirectly • *The thieves then wended their way through the unlit back streets to the docks.*

Wen·dy house /ˈwen·di/ *n* [C] *Br* a toy house or PLAYHOUSE • [PIC]> **Playground**

went /went/ *past simple of* GO

wept /wept/ *past simple and past participle of* WEEP

were /£wɜːʳ, $wɜːr, £wəʳ, $wɚ/ *past simple of* BE

weren't /£wɜːnt, $wɜːrnt/ *short form of* were not • *Weren't we lucky with the weather?* • *You weren't supposed to know about that.*

were·wolf /£ˈwɪə·wʊlf, £ˈweə-, $ˈwɪr-, $ˈwer-/ *n* [C] *pl* **werewolves** /£ˈwɪə·wʊlvz, £ˈweə-, $ˈwɪr-, $ˈwer-/ someone who, in stories, changes into a WOLF at the time of the **full moon** (= when the moon is a complete circle)

west [DIRECTION] /west/ (*abbreviation* **W**) *n* [U] the direction in which the sun goes down in the evening, opposite to the east, or the part of an area or country which is in this direction • *The points of the compass are North, South, East and West.* • *The sun rises in* **the east** *and sets in* **the west**. • *Bristol is* **in the** *west* **of** *England.* • *America* **is/lies to the** *west of Britain.* • *She chose the west-***facing** *bedroom.* • In the US, **the West** is the part of the country west of the Mississippi river which only became developed in the late 1800s: *the Wild West* • *"How the West was Won"* (title of a film, 1962) • [LP]> **Directions**

west /west/ (*abbreviation* **W**) *adj, adv* [not gradable] • *West Africa* • *the west coast of Ireland* • *the west wing of the house* • *the west gate* • *the west side of town* • A west **wind** is a wind coming from the west. • *Ireland is west* **of** *Britain – you travel west from Britain to get there.* • *After a couple of miles, we turned west towards the forest.* • *Go* **due** (= directly) *west until you see a lake.* • *The town is* **due** (= directly) *west* **of** *here.* • *The balcony* **faces** *west.* • *(infml)* If something **goes west** it is lost, damaged or spoilt in some way: *I couldn't get a ticket – my last chance to see the show gone west.* • In the US, the **West Coast** is the area of the Pacific coast which includes California: *They moved to* **the** *West Coast.* ○ *West Coast companies* • In Britain, the **West Country** is the area in the south-west of the country: *We spent our holiday in the West Country.* ○ *a West Country accent* • In Britain, the **West End** is the part of central London where all the big shops and theatres are: *We went to a restaurant in* **the** *West End.* ○ *a West End theatre* • **West Indian** means of or from the West Indies: *West Indian music* ○ *a West Indian poet* ○ *a family of West Indians* • *"Go West, young man"* (advice from the American John L.B.Soule, 1851)

west·bound /ˈwest·baʊnd/ *adj, adv* [not gradable] • Westbound means going or leading towards the west: *The two westbound planes carried a total of almost 600 passengers.* • *In 1932 the Scottish aviator Jim Mollison made the first westbound transatlantic solo flight.* • *The accident occurred about 2:35 a.m. in the westbound lanes of Interstate 66.* • *The worst areas for traffic were westbound between the Beltway and Nutley Street and eastbound between Nutley and Route 123.* • *There is also an Off Peak Season fare which differs slightly depending on whether you fly westbound or eastbound.*

west·er·ly /£ˈwes·tᵊl·i, $-tɚ·li/ *adj* • *A westerly* (= towards the west) *direction.* • *So far, only the westerly* (= west) *part of the site has been developed or redeveloped.* • *I arrived at Lower Treginnis, the most westerly* (= nearest the west) *farm in Wales, at first light on a cold February morning.* • *westerly winds/gales* (= winds from the west)

west·ern /£ˈwes·tən, $-tɚn/ (*abbreviation* **W**) *adj* [not gradable] • *western France* • *western Europe* • *southern California and other western states* • *the western outskirts of Phoenix*

west·ern /£ˈwes·tən, $-tɚn/ *n* [C] • A western (also **cowboy film**) is a film based on invented stories about life in the west of the US in the past: *Clint Eastwood has been the hero of westerns for three decades.*

west·ern·most /£ˈwes·tən·məʊst, £-təm-, $-tɚn·moʊst/ *adj* [not gradable] • *Ouessant is the westernmost* (= furthest west) *point of France.*

west·ward /£ˈwest·wəd, $-wɚd/ *adj* [not gradable] • *The westward* (= towards the west) *advance of the road repairs is being held up by protesters.*

west·wards /£ˈwest·wədz, $-wɚdz/, **west·ward** *adv* [not gradable] • *The boat drifted westwards* (= towards the west) *in the prevailing winds.* • *The army were pushing the frontier westwards.*

West [COUNTRIES] /west/ *n* [U] **the West** North America, those countries in Europe which did not have COMMUNIST governments before the 1990s, and some other parts of the world • *East-West relations* • *There has been concern* **in/throughout** *the West about the effects of this measure.* • [LP]› **World regions**

west·ern /£ˈwes·tən, $-tɚn/ *adj* • *western opinion/culture* • *a Western-educated engineer* • *western medicine*

west·ern·er /£ˈwes·tə·nəʳ, $-tɚ·nɚ/ *n* [C] • *Some of the Buddhists came from Sri Lanka, South-East Asia and East, while others were Westerners by birth and upbringing.*

west·ern·ize *obj, Br and Aus usually* **-ise** /£ˈwes·tən·aɪz, $-tɚ·naɪz/ *v* [T] • To westernize something is to introduce the ideas and ways of doing things which are common in north America and parts of Europe to other parts of the world.

west·ern·i·za·tion, *Br and Aus usually* **-i·sa·tion** /£ˌwes·tᵊn·aɪˈzeɪ·ʃᵊn, $-tɚ·naɪ-/ *n* [U]

West·min·ster /£ˌwestˈmɪnt·stəʳ, $-stɚ/ *n* the part of London where the parliament buildings are. Westminster is often used as a way of referring to the British Parliament.

wet [NOT DRY] /wet/ *adj, n* [U] **wetter, wettest** with liquid in, on or around (something); not dry • *a wet floor* • *a wet umbrella* • *wet coats* • *wet hair* • *Be careful with that cup of coffee – I don't want my papers to* **get** (= become) *wet.* • *I had to cycle in the rain and got* **soaking** *wet.* • *You poor thing – you're* **all** *wet* (= very wet). • *Come in quickly – you're* **wet through** (= completely wet). • *Try and keep off* **the** *wet* (= the wet ground) *– it's a bit firmer on this side of the path.* • If paint, ink, etc. is wet, it has not had time to dry and become hard: *The paint's still wet.* ○ *Wet paint!* • When the weather is wet it rains: *We've had wet weather all week.* ○ *This is the first wet day for two months.* ○ *The presentation will take place indoors if it's wet.* ○ *(fig.) It was about as much fun as a* **wet weekend** (= it was not enjoyable). ○ *Don't leave those boxes out in* **the** *wet.* • Someone who is **wet behind the ears** is young and without experience. • If something is **wet-look** it is shiny: *wet-look hair gel* • A **wet blanket** is a person who says or does something that stops other people enjoying themselves. • A **wet dream** is a man's sexually exciting dream which is followed by the release of sperm during or just after sleep. • A **wet nurse** was a woman employed to give her breast milk to another woman's baby. *(disapproving)* If you **wet nurse** someone you treat them too carefully as if they are unable to do anything themselves. • A **wet suit** is a piece of clothing, made from rubber, which covers the whole body closely and is designed to keep you warm when you are swimming in esp. the sea for long periods: *divers/surfers in wet suits* • [PIC]› **Water sports** Ⓙ

wet *obj* /wet/ *v* [T] **wetting**, *past* **wet** or **wetted** • *Wet the powder thoroughly and mix to remove lumps.* • *The flood water wet all the carpets.* • *He wetted a cloth and tried to rub the mark away.* • *Some products require wetting the surface prior to application, and others are used on dry wood surfaces.* • If esp. a child wets he/she causes something to become wet by urinating: *He still wets in the night.* [I] ○ *He wet him***self**. [T] ○ *She wet* **the bed**. [T] • *(infml dated)* To **wet** your **whistle** is to have a drink.

wet·ly /ˈwet·li/ *adv*

wet·ness /ˈwet·nəs/ *n* [U] • *A lot of the wetness will evaporate before the rain reaches the plant's roots.*

wet [WEAK] /wet/ *adj, n* [C] **wetter, wettest** (of a person) having a weak character and not forceful in expressing their own opinions • *He's wet.* ○ *He's a wet.* • In Britain, a wet in the Conservative Party of the 1980s was a person without strong or extreme opinions. • Ⓙ

wet·ly /ˈwet·li/ *adv*

wet·ness /ˈwet·nəs/ *n* [U]

wet·land /ˈwet·lənd, -lænd/ *n* a large area of land covered with SWAMP or MARSH • *Tens of thousands of acres of wetland have been destroyed by the ocean.* [U] • *Ancient plants like this are now found only in the wetlands of Brazil.* [C]

whack [HIT] /hwæk/ *v* [T], *n* [U] (to make) a hard noisy hit • *He whacked the tree trunk with his stick.* • *She* **gave** *the cushions a good whack.* • *(infml)* If you **have a whack** at something you try to do it: *If you need any help, I'll have a whack* **at** *it.*

whack·ing /ˈhwæk·ɪŋ/ *n* [C] *Br and Aus dated* • A whacking is hitting esp. a child as a punishment.

whack [SHARE] /hwæk/ *n* [U] a share or part • *Low earners will pay only half the charge but high earners will have to* **pay full** *whack* (= pay the whole amount). • *That's not a* **fair** *whack.*

whack [NOT WORKING] /hwæk/ *n* **out of whack** *Am and Aus* not operating correctly or looking right • *You can use Carol's old bike – the gears are out of whack, but it still goes.*

whacked /hwækt/, **whacked out** *adj infml dated* very tired • *I'm whacked.* • *(Am)* Whacked-out means suffering the effects of drugs or alcohol: *He was whacked-out on speed, jabbering a mile a minute and making no sense at all.*

whack·ing /ˈhwæk·ɪŋ/ *adj, adv* [not gradable] very big • *a whacking (great) boulder* • *a whacking fine*

whack·y (**-ier, -iest**), *Am usually* **wack·y** (**-ier, -iest**) /ˈhwæk·i/ *adj infml* strange or unusual • *There are some very whacky, creative commercials on TV that people actually like to watch.* • *The place is stuffed with whacky memorabilia like a sculpture of the Seven Dwarfs that Walt Disney gave to Debbie Reynolds.*

whale /hweɪl/ *n* [C] a very large sea mammal • If you have **a whale of a time** you enjoy yourself very much: *We had a whale of a time on holiday.* • *(Am and Aus)* **A whale of a** means a very great amount of (something) or a very good (thing): *That's a whale of a story.* ○ *Another thousand dollars would make a whale of a difference.*

whal·er /£ˈhweɪ·ləʳ, $-lɚ/ *n* [C] • A whaler is (someone who works on) a boat which is designed for hunting whales.

whal·ing /ˈhweɪ·lɪŋ/ *n* [U] • Whaling is the activity of hunting whales.

wham SOUND /*h*wæm/ *n* [C], *exclamation infml* used to suggest the sound of a sudden hit • *The boys in the cartoon were punching each other – wham, zap!*

wham SUDDENLY /*h*wæm/ *exclamation* used to show that something you are describing happened suddenly • *Everything was fine until, wham, the wire snapped.* • *(saying, slang)* 'Wham, bam, thank you ma'am' is used to mean a very quick act of sex: *He invited me up for a drink and before I knew what was happening it was wham, bam thank you ma'am and I was on my way home. / (fig.) In this new TV series, she starts work as a secretary then after one brilliant idea it's wham, bam thank you ma'am and into the boardroom with you.*

wham·my /ˈ*h*wæm·i/ *n* [C] *Am and Aus infml* a magical spell or power that causes someone to have a difficult or unpleasant time • *He* **put the** *whammy* **on** *me.*

wharf /£*h*wɔːf, $*h*wɔːrf/ *n* [C] *pl* **wharves** /£*h*wɔːvz, $*h*wɔːrvz/ an area like a wide wall built beside the edge of the sea or a river where ships can be tied and goods unloaded • *Canary Wharf* • *Butler Wharf* • *The riverbank changes from high-rise office blocks and trendy wharf developments to neat gardens and countryside.* • *The cargo on the wharf is the first of two shipments of chemical waste.*

what QUESTION, *Br not standard* **wot** /£*h*wɒt, $*h*wɑːt/ *determiner, pronoun, exclamation* used to introduce general questions • When what is a determiner, it refers to people or things: *What time is it?* ○ *What books did you buy?* ○ *What size shoes do you take?* ○ *I don't know what (also* **which***) children she was talking about.* • When what is the subject or object of a sentence, it refers to things, not people: *What happened after I left?* ○ *What's your address?* ○ *They asked me what I needed to buy.* ○ *He asked what to say if anyone made enquiries.* ○ *I can't decide what to do.* ○ *What do you do* (= what is your job)*?* ○ *Are you going to help me –* **or what** (= or are you going to do something else)*?* • What is also used in questions which show surprise or lack of belief: *"While I was there I stayed with the President." "You did what?/What did you say?/What?"* • *What's this I hear? You're leaving?* • *(infml)* What is also used to ask someone to say something again, but it is less polite than saying 'pardon' or 'sorry': *"I think we should leave at twelve." "What?" "I said I think we should leave at twelve."* • **What about** means what do you think about (something) or what is your opinion: *What about Lalla – shall we invite her?* ○ *What about taking a few days off?* • **What for** means what is the purpose of (something) or *(infml)* why is something being done: *What are these tools for?* ○ *(infml) What is he keeping it secret for* (= Why is he keeping it secret)*?* ○ *(infml) "I think I'll go now." "What for?"* ○ *(infml) I'll* **give** *you* **what for** (= punish you) *if I catch you doing that again.* • **What if** means what will happen if: *What if the train's late?* ○ *What if not enough people want to come?* • **What of it** means why is it important: *So not many people replied to the questionnaire – what of it, there were enough.* • **What** (someone/something) **like** is a request for you to give a description: *"What's the weather like?" "It's stopped raining."* ○ *"Can you tell me what she was like?" "She was tall, dark-haired, very friendly..."* • **What does** it **matter** or **what does** someone **care** means it is not important (to someone): *What do qualifications matter? – it's experience that we're interested in.* ○ *What does he care about the problems of teenagers?* • **What's on** means what is happening. It is often used as the title of the part of a newspaper which tells you about events and entertainment happening in the next week or month. • **What (the)** is used to show anger or surprise: *What the* **devil/hell** *are you doing to my car?* ○ *What* **on earth***'s been going on in here?* ○ *What* **in God's/heaven's name** *did you think was likely to happen?* • *(infml)* **What's the matter** or **What's up** means what is wrong: *You're looking worried – what's the matter?* ○ *What's (up)* **with** *Terry this week?* • You can use **what's** his **name**, **whatsisname**, **what do you call** him, **what's** he **called**, or *(slang)* **what's** his **face** when you can't remember someone's name: *I gave it to what's her name – the new girl.* • You can use **what's** it **called**, **whatsit** or *(infml)* **whatchamacallit** when you can't remember what something is called: *It looks like a what's it called – a plunger?* • LP **Determiners, Measurements**

what THAT WHICH, *Br not standard* **wot** /£*h*wɒt, $*h*wɑːt/ *pronoun* the thing(s) which; that which • *What I wanted to find out first was how long it was going to take.* • *What really concerned her was how unhappy the child was.* • *She wouldn't tell me what he said.* • *I hadn't got much money on me but I gave them what I had.* • *The letter showed clearly what they were planning.* • *She was carrying an armful of coats and sweaters and* **what have you** (= various other things like that). • *I can't decide what* **to** *do next.* [+ *to* infinitive] • *Have you thought about what* **to** *send as a present?* [+ *to* infinitive] • You can use what to introduce something you are going to say: *You'll never* **guess** *what – Laurie won first prize!* ○ *I'll tell you what – we'll collect the parcel on our way to the station.* • **What's more** means the next thing is more important: *The decorations were beautiful and what's more, the children made them themselves.* • **What** (also **whatever) someone says goes** means you have to do what they say: *We don't like keeping this information secret, but what the director says goes.* • *(infml)* If someone **knows what's what** they have experience and know how to behave to achieve what they want. • **What with** introduces the reasons for a situation: *I'm very tired, what with travelling all day yesterday and having a disturbed night.* • LP **Clauses**

what OPINION /£*h*wɒt, $*h*wɑːt/ *predeterminer, determiner* used to introduce your opinion • *"She can't come." "What* (= I think it is) *a shame/pity."* • *What a lovely view!* • *What strange clothes he was wearing.* • *What nonsense/rubbish!*

what·ev·er NOT IMPORTANT WHAT /£*h*wɒtˈev·əʳ, $*h*wɑːˈt̬ev·ɚ/ *pronoun, determiner* it is not important what is; it makes no difference what (is) • *We'll go whatever the weather.* • *Whatever happens you know that I'll stand by you.* • *Whatever else may be said of him, Mr Meese is not scared of a fight.* • *Whatever the outcome of the war, there will be no winners.* • *Whatever the reason, more Britons are emigrating to Australia today than at any time since the 1950s.* • *"Que sera, sera, whatever will be, will be"* (title of a song written by Ray Evans and Jay Livingston, 1955) • LP **Determiners**

what·ev·er ANYTHING /£*h*wɒtˈev·əʳ, $*h*wɑːˈt̬ev·ɚ/ *pronoun, determiner* anything or everything • *I eat whatever I want and I still don't seem to put on weight.* • *"What shall we do tonight then?" "It's up to you – whatever you want."* • *Whatever I say I always seem to get it wrong.* • *Don't, whatever you do, tell Patrick or the world will know!* (= You certainly should not tell Patrick.) • *Do whatever you want – it won't affect me.* • *"So I'll bring red wine then." "Sure, whatever* (= bring that or anything else)*."* • *Apparently he discovered himself in India, whatever* **that means** (= although I don't know what that means).

what·ev·er SURPRISE /£*h*wɒtˈev·əʳ, $*h*wɑːˈt̬ev·ɚ/ *pronoun* used instead of the word *what* to add emphasis to a phrase, usually expressing surprise • *Whatever is he doing with that rod!* • *Whatever's that yellow thing on your plate?* • *Whatever has she got on her head? It looks like a small dog!* • *Whatever did you say that for!* • *Whatever does she see in him – he's revolting!* • *Whatever made him buy that awful purple jacket.* • Whatever can also be used to show that the speaker is not surprised: *"I don't think she likes me." "Whatever made you think that, Andrew?* (= That seems obvious.)*"*

what·ev·er EMPHASIS /£*h*wɒtˈev·əʳ, $*h*wɑːˈt̬ev·ɚ/ *adv* [not gradable] WHATSOEVER

what·not /£ˈ*h*wɒt·nɒt, $ˈ*h*wɑːt·nɑːt/ *n* [U] **and whatnot** *infml* and other similar things • *You can buy crisps and whatnot at the bar.* • *That'll leave you a bit of time so that you can get the table set and whatnot.*

what·sit /£ˈ*h*wɒt·sɪt, $ˈ*h*wɑːt-/ *n* [C] *infml* any object or person whose name you have temporarily forgotten or do not know or do not want to say • *Where's the whatsit that you change channels with?* • *You'd better tell whatsit – what's his name – the guy in charge of stationery.* • *She kicked him in the whatsits.*

what·so·ev·er /£ˌ*h*wɒt·səʊˈev·əʳ, $ˌ*h*wɑːt·soʊˈev·ɚ/, **what·ev·er** *adv* [after n; not gradable] used after a negative phrase to add emphasis to the idea that is being expressed • *He has no respect for authority whatsoever.* • *I can honestly say that I have no interest whatsoever in the royal family.* • *There is no evidence whatever to show that this is in fact the case.* • *"Had you any idea what was happening at the time?" "None whatsoever".*

wheat /*h*wiːt/ *n* [U] a plant whose yellowish brown grain is used for making flour, or the grain itself • *wheat fields* • *Wheat is a staple crop for millions of people across the world.* • *He's allergic to wheat flour, so he has to eat a special bread.* • *Wheat prices in Chicago have risen to $3·20 a bushel, the highest for a year.* • **Wheat germ** is the central part of a grain of wheat which is sometimes added to food, esp. bread, because it contains substances which are good for the body: *wholemeal bread with added wheat germ* •

Something which separates **the wheat from the chaff** helps to separate things or people that are of high quality or ability from those that are not: *The first round of interviews really* **separates** *the wheat from the chaff.* • See also WHOLEWHEAT. • PIC› **Cereals**

wheat·meal /ˈhwiːt·miːl/ *n* [U] *Br* a brown flour which contains some but not all of the outer covering and central part of the wheat grain • *wheatmeal digestive biscuits* • *Wheatmeal flour is halfway between wholemeal and white flour.*

whee·dle *(obj)* /ˈhwiː·dl̩/ *v disapproving* to try to persuade (someone) to do (something) or give you (something) by praising them or being intentionally charming • *She's one of those children who can wheedle you* **into** *giving her anything she wants.* [T always + adv/prep] • *I was going to stay in, but Rosie wheedled me* **into** *taking her to the cinema.* [T always + adv/prep] • *She wasn't invited, but somehow she managed to wheedle her* **way in**. [T always + adv/prep] • *He wasn't going to tell me but I managed to wheedle it out of him.* [T always + adv/prep] • *I tried all manner of different approaches – I wheedled, threatened, demanded, cajoled.* [I]

whee·dling /ˈhwiː·dl̩·ɪŋ/ *adj disapproving* • *I knew by your wheedling tone that you wanted something from me.*

wheel ROUND OBJECT /hwiːl/ *n* [C] a circular object connected at the centre to a bar, which is used for making vehicles or parts of machines move • *I got my bag caught in the wheel of my bicycle.* • *He lost control of his car when a front/rear wheel hit a stone as he approached the first bend.* • *The new model has leather upholstery, seat-heaters, anti-lock braking and alloy wheels.* • *Peering inside the engine room I could see all sorts of wheels and cogs turning round.* • Something that is **on** wheels has wheels under it so that it can be pulled or pushed along: *My suitcase is on wheels so that makes life a little easier.* ○ *My two-year-old niece has one of those little dogs that's on wheels.* • **The** wheel refers to a **steering wheel** (= a wheel inside a vehicle which the driver turns to make the vehicle go in a particular direction): *Keep your hands on the wheel, Roz!* ○ *I never feel safe with Richard* **at/behind** *the wheel* (= driving). ○ *Do you think you could* **take** *the wheel* (= drive) *for a couple of hours?* • A wheel can also be a wooden or metal wheel which is turned to make a ship go in a particular direction: *He swung the wheel to port in a desperate attempt to avoid a collision.* • To **set the wheels in motion** is to do something which will cause a series of actions to start: *I thought a phone call to the right person might set the wheels in motion.* • **Wheels within wheels** refers to hidden or unknown things that influence a particular situation, making it more complicated than it at first seems. • *(esp. Br and Aus)* A **wheel clamp** (*Am usually* **(Denver) boot**) is a metal device fixed to the wheel of an illegally parked car which will only be removed when the owner pays an amount of money: *I hope we're not going to find a wheel clamp on my car when we get back.* ○ *My car was* **wheel-clamped** *because I was parked on double-yellow lines.* • See also FERRIS WHEEL; FLYWHEEL; WATERWHEEL. • PIC› **Bicycles**

wheel *obj* /hwiːl/ *v* [T always + adv/prep] • If you wheel an object with wheels under it, you push it or pull it so that it moves in a particular direction: *I saw her last night wheeling a pram along Green Lane.* ○ *Halfway through the talk someone wheeled in a trolley laden with drinks.* ○ *Doctors put her on a respirator and wheeled her downstairs to the intensive care unit.* • *(disapproving)* If you **wheel out** something or **wheel** something **out** you use or repeat the same thing that you have done on several previous occasions: *Every time we have this argument you wheel out the same old statistics, and I'm still not convinced!* ○ *Year after year they wheel out the same third-rate celebrities to entertain us.* ○ *Every time you come for dinner I seem to wheel out the same old dishes.*

-wheeled /-hwiːld/ *combining form* • *It looks like a motorized version of a child's two-wheeled scooter.*

-wheel·er /£-ˈhwiː·lər, $-lɚ/ *combining form* • *He drives a three-wheeler* (= a car with three wheels).

wheels /hwiːlz/ *pl n infml* • Wheels can be used to refer to a car: *I've got to get some wheels – this public transport system's a joke!*

wheel FLY IN CIRCLES /hwiːl/ *v* [I] to fly repeatedly in a circular pattern • *She watched a flock of seagulls wheeling around above her.*

wheel TURN ROUND /hwiːl/ *v* [I always + adv/prep] to turn round quickly • *She wheeled* **round** *and slapped him in the face.*

wheel·bar·row /£ˈhwiːlˌbær·əʊ, $-ˌber·oʊ/, **bar·row** *n* [C] a movable container with a wheel at the front and two handles at the back, used esp. in the garden for carrying things around • *I saw the gardener pushing a wheelbarrow full of bulbs round the back of the house.* • PIC› **Garden**

wheel·base /ˈhwiːl·beɪs/ *n* [C usually sing] the distance between the front and the back wheels of a motor vehicle • *The car comes in a short wheelbase Sport form and a long wheelbase four-door version.*

wheel·chair /£ˈhwiːl·tʃeər, $-tʃer/ *n* [C] a chair on wheels which people who are unable to walk use for moving around • *He spent the last ten years of his life* **in a** *wheelchair after a fall which left him paralysed from the waist down.* • *The building isn't designed very well from the point of view of wheelchair access.* • PIC› **Chair, Medical equipment**

wheel·ie /ˈhwiː·li/ *n* [C] *infml* an act of raising the front wheel of a bicycle off the ground while seated on or riding the bicycle • *I can* **do** *great wheelies on this bike.*

wheel·ie bin /ˈhwiː·li/ *n* [C] a container for rubbish which has wheels so that it can be moved easily • *We put our wheelie bin out to be emptied every Thursday morning.*

wheel·ing and deal·ing /ˈhwiː·lɪŋ/ *n* [U] *infml* trying to make a profit or get an advantage using methods that are clever, complicated and often deceiving people or breaking the usual rules • *Over the next three days there will be secret meetings, wheeling and dealing, and many subtle forms of blackmail.* • *It's a film about all the wheeling and dealing that goes on on Wall Street.*

wheel and deal *v* [I] *infml* • To **be wheeling and dealing** is to do the activity of wheeling and dealing: *He was always wheeling and dealing, always looking for a fast buck.* ○ *He spends his time wheeling and dealing on the stock exchange.*

wheel·er–deal·er /£ˌhwiː·ləˈdiː·lər, $-lɚˈdiː·lɚ/ *n* [C] *infml* • A wheeler-dealer is a person who tries to make a profit or get an advantage using methods that are clever, complicated and often deceptive and breaking the usual rules: *In the film, Sheen plays the ambitious young Wall Street wheeler-dealer.* ○ *He worked in the property business for a number of years, acquiring a reputation as a formidable wheeler-dealer.*

wheeze BREATHE /hwiːz/ *v* [I] to make a high rough noise while breathing because of some breathing difficulty • *I could hear the old man behind me wheezing.* • *I know when I've been smoking too much because I start to wheeze when I run for a train.* • *I thought he must suffer from asthma because he was wheezing such a lot.*

wheeze /hwiːz/ *n* [C] • *The cough, wheeze and shortness of breath are things that go with smoking, not with age.*

wheez·y /ˈhwiː·zi/ *adj* **-ier, -iest** • *He's got a very wheezy chest which hasn't been helped by a recent cold.*

wheeze PLAN /hwiːz/ *n* [C] *Br infml* a clever and often imaginative idea or plan, esp. one which is intended to achieve a profit or some other advantage • *As a part of their latest marketing wheeze they've planted fifty-pound notes in a number of the crisp packets.* • *So the public actually pay to feed the animals in the zoo? That seems like a* **good** *wheeze.* • *I've* **had** *a wheeze – why don't we put both kids in the small room and that will leave the back room free.*

whelk /£welk, $hwelk/ *n* [C] a soft sea animal, similar to a SNAIL, that lives in a hard shell

when AT WHAT TIME /hwen/ *adv* [not gradable], *conjunction* at what time; at the time at which • *"I did tell you about it." "When? I don't remember."* • *When do you want to go?* • *When's the baby due?* • *When are you next seeing Ann?* • *We'll go when you're ready.* • *Tell me when* **to** *start.* [+ to infinitive] • *Do you know when he'll be back?* • *Ask him when he's next coming home.* • *When do you expect to have the project completed* **(by)**? • *She was only twenty when she had her first baby.* • *He was quite shocked when I told him.* • *I hate it when there's no one in the office.* • *I used to love that film when I was a child.* • *I think I'll do it at the weekend when I've got a bit more time.* • *I was just getting into the bath when the telephone rang.* • *I was about to ask after his wife when I suddenly remembered that they were getting a divorce.* • LP› **Clauses**

when /hwen/ *pronoun* • *Until when* (= Until what time) *do you wish to stay?* • *"Did you know Roz was back in England?" "Is she –* **since** *when?"* • *(fig.)* **Since** *when did you have the right to tell me what to do?* (= You do not have that right.)

when CONSIDERING THAT /hwen/ *conjunction* considering the fact that • *How can you say you don't like something when you've never even tried it!* • *You can't complain of* *being lonely when you don't make any effort to meet people.* • *Why is she training to be a teacher when she doesn't even like children?* • *I don't suppose I can really call myself a vegetarian when I eat fish.*

when [ALTHOUGH] /hwen/ *conjunction* despite the fact that • *He says he hasn't got any money when in fact he's got thousands of dollars in his account.* • *I don't understand how he can say that everything's fine when it's so obvious that it's not.*

whence /hwents/ *adv* [not gradable], *conjunction fml or old use* (from) where • *His last years he spent in Rome, whence he came.* • *It has been returned to the shop* **from** *whence it came.*

when·ev·er [EVERY TIME] /£hwen'ev·əʳ, $-ɚ/ *adv* [not gradable], *conjunction* every or any time • *I blush whenever I think about it.* • *Whenever I go there they seem to be in bed.* • *I try to use olive oil whenever possible.* • *If I leave it on the shelf you can just use it whenever you want.* • *"Will it be okay if I do it tomorrow?" "Sure, whenever* (= then or at any other time)*."* • *Do it in a spare moment at the weekend or whenever – it really doesn't matter.* • *I'm talking about last July or whenever it was that you got back from India.* • *Whenever I hear the word culture I start to feel queasy.*

when·ev·er [SURPRISE] /£hwen'ev·əʳ, $-ɚ/ *adv* [not gradable] used instead of the word 'when' to add emphasis to a phrase, usually expressing surprise • *Whenever do you get the time to do these things?*

where /£hweəʳ, $hwer/ *adv* [not gradable], *conjunction* to, at or in what place • *Where does he live?* • *"I put it on your desk." "Where? I can't see it?"* • *Where are we going?* • *Now where did I put my glasses?* • *Where's the party being held?* • *Could you tell me where Barker Drive is please?* • *Do you know where my black bag is?* • *Where did you put my umbrella?* • *Show me where* **to** *go.* [+ *to* infinitive] • *I've left my keys somewhere and I don't know where.* • *You've found my diary – where on earth was it?* • *I've been meaning to ask you where you get your hair cut.* • *Bradford, where Bren comes from, has a lot of good curry restaurants.* • *She lived in Rome for a couple of years, where she taught English.* • *You see where Mira is standing? Well, he's behind her.* • *I like to have him next to me where I can keep an eye on him.* • *I read it somewhere – I don't know where* (= in which book, newspaper etc.). • Where can be used to mean at what stage: *You reach a point in any project where you just want to get the thing finished.* ○ *I've reached the stage where I just don't care any more.* • Where can also be used to mean in what situation: *You're not available on the 12th and Andrew can't make the 20th – so where does that leave us?* ○ *Where do you see yourself five years from now?* • *(slightly dated) In the classical music world these days, authentic instruments are* **where it's at** (= considered fashionable). • *I see/know* **where you're coming from** (= I understand what your opinion is and why you think that way). • [LP] **Clauses**

where·a·bouts /£'hweə·rə·baʊts, $'hwer·ə-/ *n* [U + sing/pl v] the place where a person or thing is • *Moreno's whereabouts are unknown, although associates have said he was planning a trip to Guatemala.* • *Trupin is thought to be in the Caribbean, although his exact whereabouts is a mystery.* • *I don't suppose you know the whereabouts of my silver pen, do you?*

where·a·bouts /£ˌhweə·rə'baʊts, $ˌhwer·ə-/ *adv* [not gradable] • *Whereabouts in* (= In what part of) *Madrid do you live?* • *Whereabouts* (= In what area) *is your office then?*

where·as /£hweə'ræz, $hwer'æz/ *conjunction* compared with the fact that; but • *He must be about sixty, whereas his wife looks about thirty.* • *Your mother was at home while you were children, whereas mine went out to work.* • *You eat a massive plate of food for lunch, whereas I have just a sandwich.*

where·by /£hweə'baɪ, $hwer-/ *adv* [not gradable], *conjunction* by which way or method • *They've set up a plan whereby you can spread the cost over a period.* • *We need to devise some sort of system whereby people can liaise with each other.* • (not standard) Whereby is also used to mean 'in which' or 'with which': *It's put me in a position whereby I can't afford to take a job.*

where·fores /£'hweə·fɔːz, $'hwer·fɔːrz/ *pl n* See **the whys and wherefores** at WHY [REASON]

where·in /£hweə'rɪn, $hwer'ɪn/ *adv* [not gradable], *conjunction old use or fml* in which, or in which part • *He gazed once more around the room, wherein were assembled his entire family.* • *He was certainly a pleasant man but wherein lay his charms, she wondered.*

where·so·ev·er /£ˌhweə·səʊ'ev·əʳ, $ˌhwer·soʊ'ev·ɚ/ *adv* [not gradable], *conjunction fml for* WHEREVER [EVERY PLACE]

where·u·pon /£ˌhweə·rə'pɒn, $ˌhwer·ə'pɑːn/ *conjunction* immediately after which • *We went home for a coffee, whereupon Viv became violently ill with food poisoning.* • *I told her she looked fat, whereupon she threw the entire contents of a saucepan at me and burst into tears.*

wher·ev·er [EVERY PLACE] /£hweə'rev·əʳ, $hwer'ev·ɚ/ *adv* [not gradable], *conjunction* to or in any or every place • *We can go wherever you like.* • *Wherever I go I always seem to bump into him.* • *All across Europe, wherever you look, marriage is in decline and divorce rates are soaring.* • *Wherever you choose to live there are always going to be disadvantages.* • *Wherever you look there are pictures.* • Wherever can also mean 'in every case': *Wherever possible I use honey instead of sugar.*

wher·ev·er [SURPRISE] /£hweə'rev·əʳ, $hwer'ev·ɚ/ *adv* [not gradable] used instead of the word 'where' to add emphasis to a phrase, usually expressing surprise • *Wherever did you find that hat!* • *Wherever did you get that idea!* • *Wherever does he get the money from to go on all these exotic journeys?* • *Are you really going to eat that mountain of food? Wherever do you put it!*

where·with·al /£'hweə·wɪ·ðɔːl, $'hwer·wɪ·ðɑːl/ *n* [U] **the wherewithal** the money necessary for a particular purpose • *Ideally I'd like to buy a bigger house but I* **lack** *the wherewithal.* • *Poor families* **lack** *the wherewithal* **to** *hire good lawyers and the sophistication to fight the system.* [+ *to* infinitive]

whet *obj* [INTEREST] /hwet/ *v* [T] **-tt- whet** *someone's* **appetite** to increase someone's interest in and desire for something, usually by giving them a small experience of it • *I read a brief extract of his new novel on the train and it has rather whetted my appetite* **for** *it.* • *That one kiss had whetted his appetite.*

whet *obj* [SHARPEN] /hwet/ *v* [T] **-tt-** *old use* to sharpen the blade of (a knife or similar tool) • *He whetted his knife against the stone.*

wheth·er [IF] /£'hweð·əʳ, $-ɚ/ *conjunction* (used esp. in reporting questions and expressing doubts) if, or not • *I was wondering whether she'd prefer to come a little later.* • *I wasn't sure whether you'd like it.* • *She asked me whether I was interested in working for her.* • *I'm wondering whether to have the fish or the beef.* • *I doubt whether it'll work.* • *I don't know whether to be pleased or offended.* • *I was merely questioning whether we have the money to fund such a project.* • *The question is whether it would be safer to leave them here or in the car.* • Whether is often followed by **or not**: *She can't decide whether or not to tell him.* ○ *It all depends on whether or not she's got the time.* ○ *Anyway, it's a good story, whether or not it's true.* • [LP] **Clauses**

wheth·er [NOT IMPORTANT IF] /£'hweð·əʳ, $-ɚ/ *conjunction* (used to introduce two or more possibilities) it is not important if • *Whether you like it* **or** *not it's going to happen.* • *Someone's got to tell her, whether it's you* **or** *me.* • *Whether we do it now* **or** *later, it's got to be done some time.* • *Let's face it – you're going to be late whether you go by bus* **or** *train.* • *Well, I'm going to go, whether he likes it* **or** *not.*

whet·stone /£'hwet·stəʊn, $-stoʊn/ *n* [C] a stone used for sharpening the blades of knives or other cutting tools

whew /ɸhjuː/ *exclamation infml* PHEW

whey /hweɪ/ *n* [U] the watery part of milk which is separated from the solid CURDS during the process of making cheese

which [QUESTION] /hwɪtʃ/ *determiner, pronoun* (used in questions and structures in which there is a fixed or limited set of answers or possibilities) what one or ones • *Which party would you prefer to go to – Anna's or Ian's ?* • *Which doctor did you see – Sewards?* • *I didn't know which brother I was speaking to.* • *Which button do I press next?* • *Which time suits you better – 12.30 or one o'clock?* • *"Jacinta came last night with her boyfriend." "Which (one)? She's got several."* • *Which is mine? The smaller one?* • *See if you can guess which one is me in my old school photo.* • *It's either Spanish or Portuguese that she speaks, but I've forgotten which.* • Which (and never 'what') can be followed by **of**: *Which of the desserts did you have?* ○ *Which of your parents do you feel closer to?* ○ *Which of your many outfits are you wearing tonight?* ○ *Which of you* (= who) *knows where the keys are kept?* • *Those two paintings look so alike I'm surprised anyone can tell* **which is which**

(= can recognize each one separately). • [LP] **Clauses, Determiners**

which [USED TO REFER] /hwɪtʃ/ *pronoun* used to show what thing or things (not usually people) is/are being referred to • In some sentences 'which' is a slightly more formal way of saying 'that': *You know that little Italian restaurant – the one which I mentioned in my letter?* ○ *These are principles which we all believe in.* • Which (never 'that') can also follow a preposition: *Is that the film in which he kills his mother?* ○ *The death of his son was an experience from which he never fully recovered.* ○ *It isn't a subject to which I devote a great deal of thought.*

which [ADDS INFORMATION] /hwɪtʃ/ *pronoun* used to add extra information to a previous clause, in writing usually after a comma • *That bar on Milton Street, which by the way is very nice and quite cheap, is owned by Trevor's brother.* • *She says it's Anna's fault, which is rubbish, and that she blames her for it.* • *Anyway, that evening, which I'll tell you more about later, I ended up staying at Rachel's place.* • *That building, the interior of which is rather better than the outside, was designed by the same architects.* • *It's the third in a sequence of three books, the first of which I really enjoyed.* • *He showed me round the town, which was very kind of him.* • *She said it would be done by March, which personally I doubt very much.*

which /hwɪtʃ/ *determiner* • *The picking of the fruit (for which work they receive no money, incidentally) takes about a week.* • *It might be made of plastic,* **in which case** (= if that is true) *you could probably carry it.*

which·ev·er [ANY ONE] /£hwɪ'tʃev·əʳ, $-ɚ/ *determiner, pronoun* any one from a limited set • *We can go to the seven o'clock performance or the eight – whichever suits you best.* • *Either Thursday or Friday – choose whichever day is best for you.* • *"Which bar would you prefer to meet in?" "Whichever – it doesn't matter to me."* • [LP] **Determiners**

which·ev·er [NOT IMPORTANT WHICH] /£hwɪ'tʃev·əʳ, $-ɚ/ *determiner* it is not important which • *It's going to be expensive whichever way you do it.* • *Richard was partly to blame, whichever way you look at it.* • *Whichever party gets in at the next election, the economy is going to be in a mess.* • *Whichever option we choose there'll be disadvantages.*

whiff /hwɪf/ *n* [C usually sing] a brief smell, carried on a current of air • *I* **caught/got** *a* **whiff of** *perfume as she swept past me.* • *During the first few months of pregnancy the slightest whiff* **of** *food cooking made my stomach turn.* • *He leaned towards me and I caught a whiff* **of** *garlic on his breath.* • *(fig.) There's a whiff* **of** *revolution in the air once again, the distant threat of civil disobedience.* • *(fig.) A strong whiff* **of** *corruption hangs over the government.* • *"A whiff of grapeshot"* (Thomas Carlyle in his book *A History of the French Revolution*, 1837)

Whig /hwɪg/ *n* [C], *adj* [not gradable] (a member) of a British political party in the 17th, 18th and 19th centuries which supported political and social change

while [LENGTH OF TIME] /hwaɪl/ *n* [U] a length of time • *I only stayed for a short while because I had some other things to do.* • *You were there* **quite a** *while* (= a long time), *weren't you?* • *"When did that happen?" "Oh, it was* **a** *while* (= a long time) *ago."* • *I haven't seen him for a while* (= a long time). • *There was me thinking you were out and you were upstairs asleep in bed* **all the** *while!* • *I'll be fine* **in a** *while* (= soon), *so please don't look so worried.* • See also WORTHWHILE. • [LP] **Periods of time**

while [DURING] /hwaɪl/, *esp. Br fml* **whilst** /hwaɪlst/ *conjunction* during the time that, or at the same time as • *I read it while you were drying your hair.* • *I was listening to the radio while I was in the bath.* • *While you were out socialising with all your friends I was at home working!* • *While I was in Italy I went to see Alessandro.* • *I thought I heard him come in while we were having dinner.* • *I was making a cake anyway so I thought while I was doing that I might as well make some biscuits.* • *"I'm going to the post office." "While you're there can you get me some stamps?"*

while [ALTHOUGH] /hwaɪl/, *esp. Br fml* **whilst** /hwaɪlst/ *conjunction* despite the fact that; although • *While I accept that he's not perfect in many respects, I do actually quite like the man.* • *While I fully understand your point of view, I do also have some sympathy with Michael's.*

while [BUT] /hwaɪl/ *conjunction* compared with the fact that; but • *He gets thirty thousand pounds a year while I get a meagre fifteen!* • *Tom is very extrovert and confident while Katy's shy and quiet.* • *I do every single bit of housework while he just does the dishes now and again.* • *I spend two hours getting ready to go out while Roz is ready in ten minutes!*

while a·way *obj*, **while** *obj* **a·way** /hwaɪl/ *v adv* [M] to spend (time) in a relaxed or lazy way, sometimes while waiting for something else to happen • *I used to knit a lot when I was pregnant, just to while away the time.* • *If you're late I can always while away a couple of hours in a cafe.* • *That's the bar where Sara and I used to while away the hours between lectures.* • *We whiled away the afternoon playing cards in front of the fire.*

whim /hwɪm/ *n* [C] a sudden desire or idea, esp. one that cannot be reasonably explained • *"Did you have any particular reason for wanting to go there?" "No – it was just a whim."* • *When you're subject to the whims of a complete madman there's no saying what will happen.* • *And, like any other form of clothing, it is vulnerable to the whim of fashion.* • *You can add what you like to this mixture – brandy, whisky or nothing at all – as the whim takes you.* • *But, Daryl, marriage is not something to be entered into* **on a** *whim!* • *Purely* **on a** *whim I took up belly-dancing classes.* • *Oh for a husband who would indulge my* **every** *whim!*

whim·per /£'hwɪm·pəʳ, $-pɚ/ *v* [I] (esp. of an animal) to make a series of small weak sounds, expressing pain or unhappiness • *A half-starved dog sat miserably in the corner, whimpering pathetically.* • *I said she couldn't have an ice cream and she started to whimper.*

whim·per /£'hwɪm·pəʳ, $-pɚ/ *n* [C] • *She* **gave** *a little whimper as the vet inspected her paw.* • *In the end he went to school without so much as a whimper of protest.*

whim·si·cal /'hwɪm·zɪ·kəl/ *adj* unusual and strange in a way that might be amusing or annoying • *Too often, though, I found myself wondering whether the piece of whimsical, artless charm I was watching had any point at all.* • *Despite his kindly, sometimes whimsical air, he was a shrewd observer of people.*

whimsically /'hwɪm·zɪ·kli/ *adv* • *Hoffman plays the whimsically wicked Captain Hook.*

whim·si·cal·i·ty /£,hwɪm·zɪ'kæl·ɪ·ti, $-ə·t̬i/ *n* [U] *fml*

whim·sy /'hwɪm·zi/ *n* *disapproving* something that is intended to be strange and amusing but in fact has little real meaning or value • *Personally I've always considered mime to be a lot of white-faced whimsy.* [U] • *As a play I think it's a reasonably diverting piece of English whimsy but that's all.* [U] • *I was taken to see a film, but it was one of the worst Walt Disney whimsies, which I dislike.* [C]

whine /hwaɪn/ *v* [I] (esp. of an animal) to make a long, high complaining sound, or (*disapproving* esp. of a child) to complain or express dissatisfaction continually • *Leon's dog was sitting by the door whining, so I thought I'd better take it for a walk.* • *If you drive much faster than this the engine starts to whine* (= make an unpleasant continuous high sound). • *Alice, if you carry on whining like that I won't take you – do you understand!* • *It's that whining voice of hers that I can't stand.*

whine /hwaɪn/ *n* [C usually sing] • *Much of the script she delivers in a high-pitched nasal whine.* • *(fig.) From the next room came the familiar whine* (= long high sound) *of Tracey's hair dryer.*

whin·er /£'hwaɪ·nəʳ, $-nɚ/ *n* [C] *disapproving* • A whiner is a person, esp. a child, who complains or expresses dissatisfaction continually: *Nobody likes a whiner, Ben.* ○ *So have we become a nation of whiners?*

whinge /hwɪndʒ/ *v* [I] **whingeing** or **whinging** *Br and Aus infml disapproving* to complain, esp. about something which does not seem important • *She's always whingeing* **(on)** *about something – it gets very boring!* • *Oh stop whinging, for heaven's sake!* • *You phone me and all I do is whinge for half an hour – I am sorry.*

whinge /hwɪndʒ/ *n* [C usually sing] *Br and Aus infml disapproving* • *We were just* **having** *a whinge about our boss – nothing new.* • *The princess's autobiography he dismissed as "one long self-pitying whinge."*

whing·er /£'hwɪn·dʒəʳ, $-dʒɚ/ *n* [C] *Br and Aus infml disapproving* • *He hates defeatism and he hates whingers* (= people who complain a lot).

whin·ny /'hwɪn·i/ *v* [I] (of a horse) to make a soft high sound • *A horse whinnied into the cold morning.*

whip [DEVICE FOR HITTING] /hwɪp/ *n* [C] a piece of leather or rope which is fastened to a stick, used for hitting animals or people • *She lashed the horses mercilessly with her long whip.* • *The lion-tamer* **cracked** *his whip.* • *There's a shop in Camden where you can buy leather gear and whips.* • **The whip hand** is the position of most power in a situation: *During the last decade the right wing of the party has* **held** *the whip hand.*

whip *(obj)* /ˈhwɪp/ *v* **-pp-** • *I don't like the way the drivers whip their horses.* [T] • *Some of the prisoners were whipped across the soles of their feet and almost all were physically beaten.* [T] • *(fig.) The wind whipped* (=moved quickly) *across the half-frozen lake.* [I always + adv/prep] • *(fig.) A fierce, freezing wind whipped torrential rain* (=caused it to move quickly) *into their faces.* [T] • If you **whip** someone or something **into** a particular state, you quickly and effectively cause them to be in that state: *Karl Smith, the 19-year old singer, had whipped the crowd of teenage girls into* **a frenzy** *merely by removing his shirt.* ○ *The prime minister's final speech had the desired effect, whipping his party into a patriotic fervour.* • *(esp. disapproving)* If you **whip up** a particular feeling in a person, you encourage or cause them to have it: *She criticized the government of trying to whip up anti-German prejudice.* ○ *Dina was trying to whip up some enthusiasm for Sunday's coach trip to Leeds Castle.* ○ *It's only a week till the elections, so the candidates are endeavouring to whip up some support.* ○ *There have been complaints that the radio station is deliberately whipping up ethnic strife.* ○ *His critics believe he has taken the lead in whipping up nationalist tension.*

whip·ping /ˈhwɪp·ɪŋ/ *n* [C] • *They should be given a good whipping* (=punishment by being whipped)*, young louts like that!* • *(Am)* A whipping can also be a severe beating: *Your dad is going to give you a whipping when he gets home.* • A **whipping boy** is a person whose purpose is to take the blame and/or punishment for the faults and mistakes of others.

whip *obj* [ACT QUICKLY] /hwɪp/ *v* [T always + adv/prep] **-pp-** to bring or take (something) quickly • *I was going to pay but before I knew it he'd whipped* **out** *his credit card.* [M] • *She whipped a handkerchief* **out of** *her pocket and wiped his face.* • *He sat down on the seat opposite and whipped a portable phone* **out of** *his coat pocket.* • *They whipped my plate* **away** *before I'd even finished.* [M]

whip [POLITICS] /hwɪp/ *n* [C] (in many elected political systems) a member of a political party in parliament or in the LEGISLATURE whose job is to make certain that other party members are present at voting time and also to make certain that they vote in a particular way • *Hargreaves is the MP who got into trouble with his party's* **chief** *whip for opposing the tax reform.* • A whip in British politics is also a written order demanding that party members be present in parliament when there is to be an important vote or demanding that they vote in a particular way: *In 1970 Smith defied the* **three-line** (=most urgent) *whip against EC membership.*

whip *obj* [BEAT FOOD] /hwɪp/ *v* [T] **-pp-** to beat (food, esp. cream) with a special utensil in order to make it thick and firm • *Could you whip the cream for me.* • *Try whipping a little brandy or other liqueur* **into** *the cream.* • *Top with whipped* **cream** *and a sprinkle of sugar.* • *(infml)* To **whip up** food or a meal is to make it quickly: *I think I've just about got enough time to whip up an omelette.* • *Steve managed to whip up a plate of spaghetti in under twenty minutes.*

whip *obj* [STEAL] /hwɪp/ *v* [T] **-pp-** *Br dated infml* to take (something) without the permission of the owner; steal • *Someone's whipped my ruler!*

whip·lash /ˈhwɪp·læʃ/ *n* [U] a neck injury caused by a sudden forward movement of the upper body, esp. in a car accident • *(a) whiplash injury* • *Fortunately he escaped from the wreck with nothing more serious than whiplash.*

whip·per·snap·per /£ˈhwɪp·əˌsnæp·əʳ, $-ɚˌsnæp·ɚ/ *n* [C] *dated or humorous* a young person who is too confident and shows a lack of respect towards other, esp. older, people • *I'm not going to have some* **young** *whippersnapper come round here and tell me what to do!*

whip·pet /ˈhwɪp·ɪt/ *n* [C] a thin dog, like a small GREYHOUND, often used for racing

whip–round /ˈhwɪp·raʊnd/ *n* [C] *Br infml* a collection of money made by a group of people which is then given to a particular person or used to buy a present for them • *We usually* **have** *a whip-round at work* **for** *people who are leaving.*

whirl *(obj)* /£hwɜːl, $hwɜːrl/ *v* to (cause something to) spin round • *She saw a mass of bodies whirling round on the dance floor.* [I] • *He stepped out into the night and the whirling snow.* [I] • *He whirled her* **round** *until she felt quite sick.* [T] • *(fig.) Camilla had been introduced to so many young men that her head was whirling with the excitement of it all!* [I]

whirl /£hwɜːl, $hwɜːrl/ *n* [C] • *(fig.) I found myself swept up in the* **social** *whirl* (=continuous exciting activity) *of college life and scarcely had time for work.* • If your head is **in a whirl** you are confused and often excited, and cannot think clearly: *Declarations of love from three different men and now an offer of marriage! Sophie's head was in a whirl.* • If you **give** something **a whirl** you try it for the first time: *What about this new agency then – shall we give them a whirl?*

whirl·i·gig /£ˈhwɜː·lɪ·gɪg, $ˈhwɜːr-/ *n* [C] something that is full of fast activity and always changing • *The whirligig* **of** *parties and dinners had exhausted her, and she yearned for some respite.* • *By June of this year the whirligig* **of** *politics had kicked the Conservatives out and put the Liberal Democrats in.* • *"Thus the whirligig of time brings in his revenges"* (Shakespeare, Twelfth Night 5.1)

whirl·pool /£ˈhwɜːl·puːl, $ˈhwɜːrl-/ *n* [C] a small area of the sea or other water in which there is a powerful circular current of water which can pull objects down into its centre

whirl·wind /£ˈhwɜːl·wɪnd, $ˈhwɜːrl-/, *Am also* **twist·er** *n* [C] a tall column of spinning air which moves across the surface of the land or sea • *A freak whirlwind destroyed 20 vehicles and damaged roofs and windows in west Wales early yesterday.* • *(fig.) They married three months after they met – it was a real whirlwind* **romance** (=it happened very quickly and unexpectedly).

whir·ly·bird /£ˈhwɜː·lɪ·bɜːd, $ˈhwɜːr·lɪ·bɜːrd/ *n* [C] *dated Am for* HELICOPTER

whirr, *esp. Am* **whir** /£hwɜːʳ, $hwɜːr/ *v* [I] **-rr-** (esp. of machines) to make a low soft continuous sound • *I could hear the washing machine whirring in the kitchen.* • *As film cameras whirred, he bowed deeply and said he was resigning.*

whirr, *esp. Am* **whir** /£hwɜːʳ, $hwɜːr/ *n* [C usually sing] • *He heard a whirr of wings and the ducks shot up into the air.*

whisk *obj* [REMOVE] /hwɪsk/ *v* [T always + adv/prep] to take (something or someone) somewhere else suddenly and quickly • *Our coffees were whisked* **away** *before we'd even finished them.* [M] • *I went to see the doctor and was immediately whisked* **off to** *a specialist.* • *We only had half an hour to see her before she was whisked* **off to** *some exotic location.* • *Her husband whisked her* **off to** *Egypt for her birthday.*

whisk *obj* [MOVE TAIL] /hwɪsk/ *v* [T] (of an animal) to make a quick brushing movement with (its tail) • *The horse whisked its tail, irritated by the settling flies.*

whisk /hwɪsk/ *n* [C] • *A whisk of the cow's tail sent a cloud of flies buzzing into the air.*

whisk *obj* [BEAT FOOD] /hwɪsk/ *v* [T] to beat (eggs, cream, etc.) with a special utensil in order to add air and make the food light • *Whisk the egg whites until stiff.* • *Remove mixture from heat and whisk in the brandy and vanilla essence.*

whisk /hwɪsk/ *n* [C] • A whisk is a kitchen utensil which you use for beating food such as eggs and cream in order to add air and make it light: *an electric whisk* ○ *a hand-held whisk* • PIC› **Kitchen**

whisk·er /£ˈhwɪs·kəʳ, $-kɚ/ *n* [C] any of the long stiff hairs growing on the face of a cat, mouse or other mammal • *He watched the cat cleaning the milk off her whiskers.* • In the phrases **by a whisker** and **within a whisker**, whisker means the smallest amount possible: *He lost count of the number of times in his career as an army medical officer that he came within a whisker of death.* ○ *She beat the Brazilian by a whisker last time she ran.*

whisk·ers /£ˈhwɪs·kəz, $-kɚz/ *pl n* the hair growing on a man's face, esp. the sides and/or the lower part • *You've grown some whiskers!*

whisk·ered /£ˈhwɪs·kəd, $-kɚd/ *adj* [not gradable] • *Above the fireplace there was a big old oil painting, a portrait of a forbidding, grey-whiskered gentleman.*

whis·ky *esp. Br and Aus, esp. Am and Irish Eng* **whis·key** /ˈhwɪs·ki/ *n* a strong, pale brown alcoholic drink, originally from Scotland and Ireland, made from grain such as BARLEY, MAIZE or RYE • *Whisky and ginger ale is her favourite drink.* [U] • *How many whiskies have you had?* [C]

whi·sper *(obj)* /£ˈhwɪs·pəʳ, $-pɚ/ *v* to speak or say very quietly using the breath but not the voice, so that other people cannot hear you • *She leaned over and whispered something in his ear.* [T] • *What are you two girls whispering about?* [I] • *"Where are the toilets?" she whispered.* [+ clause] • *The last thing I remembered was the doctor and my parents* *whispering at the end of my bed.* [I] • *It's rude to whisper!* [I] • *(fig.) It is whispered* (=People have suggested in secret) **that** *she has another man!* [+ *that* clause] • *(disapproving)* A **whispering campaign** is the intentional damaging of an important person's reputation by saying things about them which, whether true or false, are unpleasant.

whi·sper /£'hwɪs·pəʳ, $-pɚ/ *n* [C] • *I heard whispers outside my room.* • *His usually forceful voice was lowered to a barely audible whisper.* • *She said it* **in a** *whisper so I presumed it wasn't common knowledge. "You see," she said, lowering her voice to a whisper, "he hasn't been well recently."* • *(fig.) I've heard a whisper* (=People have suggested in secret) **that** *they're heading for divorce.* [+ *that* clause] • *(fig. literary) The silence was broken only by the whisper* (=soft low noise) *of the leaves in the gentle breeze.*

whist /hwɪst/ *n* [U] a card game played between two pairs of players in which each side tries to win more cards than the other • *(Br)* A **whist drive** is a social occasion at which people play whist.

whi·stle *(obj)* /'hwɪs·l̩/ *v* to make a high sound by forcing air through a small hole or passage, esp. through the lips, or a special device held to the lips • *He whistled as he worked.* [I] • *How loud can you whistle?* [I] • *Someone was whistling Beatles tunes outside my window.* [T] • *The referee whistled and the game was over.* [I] • *She has one of those kettles that whistles when the water has boiled.* [I] • You can whistle **at** someone to attract their attention: *On the days when she wore a skirt the men on the building site would whistle at her.* [I] • You can whistle **to** a dog to tell it to do something: *She's well trained – she'll come running back to me when I whistle (to her).* [I] • Something can be said to whistle if it makes a high sound while moving quickly: *She heard the wind whistling through the trees and the howl of a distant wolf.* [I] ○ *I stepped out of the building and immediately a bullet whistled past my head.* [I] • A bird can be said to whistle if it makes a high sound. [I] • *"Whistle while you Work"* (title of a song written by Larry Morey, 1937) • *"You don't have to do anything. Not a thing. Oh, maybe just whistle. You know how to whistle, don't you, Steve? You just put your lips together and blow"* (Lauren Bacall to Humphrey Bogart in the film *To Have and to Have Not*, 1945)

whi·stle /'hwɪs·l̩/ *n* [C] • *From the bottom of the garden I recognised my father's tuneless whistle.* • *It sounded like the whistle of an old-fashioned steam train.* • *She heard the whistle of the wind through the trees and shivered.* • A whistle is also a device for making a loud high sound which you hold to your lips and blow through: *The referee* **blew** *his whistle for half-time.* ○ *The teacher blows her whistle at the end of play-time.* • A **whistle-blower** is a person who tells someone in authority about something illegal that is happening, esp. in a government department. • A **whistle-stop tour** is a series of brief visits to different places made usually by a politician.

whit /hwɪt/ *n* [U] **not a whit** *fml or old use* not any amount • *There's not a whit* **of** *sense in that head of his!* • *It's just as good and not a whit more expensive.*

white [COLOUR] /hwaɪt/ *adj*, *n* **-r, -st** (of) a colour like that of snow, milk or bone • *white linen* • *a white T-shirt* • *white walls* • *He looked like a waiter in his black trousers and white shirt.* • *The neighbour's dog is black and white.* • *As an old lady she had* **snowy** *white hair.* • *Unless your teeth are* **pearly** *white, don't wear orange-based lip colours.* • *A* **pure** *white blanket of snow lay around her.* • *The flowers have* **creamy** *white petals and dark green leaves.* • *Andrew was the white-haired bloke with the orange waistcoat.* • *In some countries it is traditional for a bride to wear white.* [U] • *The colour white for many people in the western world is seen as representing purity and goodness.* [U] • *"How do you like your coffee?" "White* (=With milk or cream) *and no sugar, please."* • White is used in the name of various food and drink products, many of which are not pure white but slightly cream, yellow, grey or transparent: *white bread/chocolate/flour/pepper/rice/rum/sugar/wine* • The white **of the eye** is the part of the eye that is white: *Don't shoot until you see the whites of their eyes* (=until the people are very close to you). [C] • A white **(of an egg)** is the transparent part of an egg which surrounds the YOLK and becomes white when cooked: *Whisk four* **egg** *whites into stiff peaks.* [C] • If you describe someone as being **(as) white as a sheet**, you mean their face is very pale, usually because of illness, shock or fear. • **Whiter than white** means never doing anything wrong: *I was never convinced by the image of the whiter than white princess depicted in the press.* • A **white ant** is a TERMITE. • A **white blood cell/white corpuscle** is a cell in the blood that has no red colouring and is involved in the fight against infection. • A **white Christmas** is a Christmas in which there is a layer of snow on the ground: *Do you think we might have a white Christmas this year?* • **White-collar** means relating to people who work in offices, doing work that needs mental rather than physical effort: *white-collar workers/unions* • *(disapproving)* A **white elephant** is something that has cost a lot of money but has no useful purpose: *That office building is a real white elephant – it's been empty ever since it was built.* • A **white flag** symbolizes the acceptance of defeat or a lack of intention to attack: *The soldiers lay down their guns and walked towards the enemy camp, carrying a white flag.* ○ *We had to raise a white flag on our bus and negotiate our crossing with the authorities on both sides.* • **White heat** is the very high temperature at which metal gives out a white light: *(fig.) In the white heat* (=strength of feeling) **of** *the moment, we both said things we regretted later.* • A **white hope** is a person or thing which people hope will be very successful in the near future: *This young Italian-born dancer is the white hope of the Royal Ballet.* ○ *This new car is seen as the* **great** *white hope of the British motor industry.* • *(Br literary)* **White horses** *(Am* **whitecaps***)* are waves which are white at the top. • Metal which is **white-hot** is so hot that it is giving out a white light. • *(specialized)* **White goods** are large electrical goods for the house, such as cookers and washing machines. • **The White House** is the official Washington home of the American President, or the American government itself: *Last Saturday 2800 people visited the White House.* ○ *The White House is set to announce health-care reforms.* • A **white knight** is a person or organization that saves a company from financial difficulties or an unwanted change of ownership by putting money into the company or by buying it: *At the last minute, a white knight came in and saved the company from takeover.* • *(humorous)* A **white-knuckle** experience is one that causes you to feel very frightened: *They've built a new theme park there, if you're into white-knuckle* **rides**. • A **white lie** is a lie that is told in order to be polite or to stop someone from being upset by the truth. • **White magic** is magic which is used only to do good things. • **White meat** is either a meat such as chicken or VEAL that is pale in colour, or the whitest flesh, usually the breast, of a cooked bird. • **White noise** is a mixture of sounds or electrical signals which consists of all sounds or signals in a large range. • *(Am and Aus)* The **White Pages** is a book that lists the names, addresses and telephone numbers of people living and businesses operating in a city or area. ○ Compare **yellow pages** at YELLOW [COLOUR]. • In various countries, including Britain and Australia, a **white paper** is a government report on a particular subject giving information and details of future planned laws: *The Home Secretary has just promised a white paper followed by legislation to reform section 2 of the Official Secrets Act.* ○ Compare **green paper** at GREEN [COLOUR]. • A **white pointer** is a large dangerous type of SHARK (=a large fish with a vertical triangular part on its back). • **White sauce** is a thick savoury sauce made from flour, butter and milk. • *(Br)* **White spirit** *(Am and Aus* **turpentine***)* is a colourless alcoholic liquid which is used for making paint thinner and removing it from brushes and clothes. • A *(esp. Br)* **white stick**/*(esp. Am)* **white cane** is a white-coloured stick that people who are blind use when walking, in order to help them find where they are going and also to show other people that they are blind. • A **white-tie** social occasion is one at which the men wear formal clothes including white **bow ties**: *His first White House party was a white-tie diplomatic reception.* • **White water** is water in a river which flows fast and strongly in an esp. narrow channel: *white-water rafting* • A **white wedding** is a traditional Christian marriage in a church, at which the woman who is getting married wears a white dress: *She wants a proper white wedding.* • *"There'll be bluebirds over the white cliffs of Dover"* (song *The White Cliffs of Dover* sung by Vera Lynne during the Second World War, 1941) • *"Whiter than white"* (advertisement for washing powder) • *"A whiter shade of pale"* (title of a song by Procol Harum, 1967) • *"The white heat of technological revolution"* (popular verison of a speech made by Harold Wilson, 1963)

whit·en *(obj)* /£'hwaɪ·tᵊn, $-t̬ᵊn/ *v* • To whiten is to make or become whiter: *She's had her nicotine-stained teeth whitened.* [T] ○ *Frost gradually crept across the ground, whitening the grass.* [T] ○ *I must whiten my tennis shoes –*

they're covered in grass stains. [T] ○ *Her hair had whitened over the years.* [I]

whit·en·ing /£'*h*waɪ·tᵊn·ɪŋ, $-t̬ᵊn-/, **whit·en·er** /£'*h*waɪ·tᵊn·əʳ, $-t̬ə·nɚ/ *n* [U] • Whitening is a substance that you put on sports shoes to make them whiter and cleaner.

whites /*h*waɪts/ *pl n* • Whites are white clothes, either worn for sports or *(infml)* put together to be washed at the same time: *There was a group of men in* **cricket** *whites in the pub.* ○ *Can I put a pale yellow shirt in with the whites?*

whit·ish /£'*h*waɪ·tɪʃ, $-t̬ɪʃ/ *adj* • *Three whitish forms could be seen in the mist.* • *Her face had gone a ghastly whitish-grey colour.*

white PEOPLE /*h*waɪt/ *adj, n* [C] **-r, -st** (of) a person of a race which has a pale skin; CAUCASIAN • *He had a black mother and a white father.* • *It's a predominantly white neighbourhood.* • *This neighbourhood mainly has whites living in it, though there are a few blacks.* • *(Am)* **White flight** is the act of white people moving out of an area because people of other races are moving in. • **White supremacy** is the belief that people with pale skin are better than people with darker skin. A **white supremacist** is someone who believes this. • *(Am disapproving slang)* **White trash** means poor, badly educated white people.

white out *obj*, **white** *obj* **out** /*h*waɪt/ *v adv* [M] to cover (a mistake in writing) with a special white liquid • *You don't have to retype the whole page, just white out the mistakes.*

white·out *Am and Aus* /£'*h*waɪ·taʊt, $-t̬aʊt/, *Br trademark* **Tipp-Ex**, *Am and Aus trademark* **Liq·uid Pa·per** *n* [U] • *I had to use three coats of whiteout to cover up the mistake I'd made.* • See also WHITEOUT.

white·bait /'*h*waɪt·beɪt/ *n* [U] small young fish of various different types, fried and eaten whole

white·board /£'*h*waɪt·bɔːd, $-bɔːrd/ *n* [C] a board with a smooth white surface, often fixed to a wall, on which you can write and draw using special pens

White·hall /'*h*waɪt·hɔːl, ˌ-'-/ *n* [U not after *the*] the British **civil service** (=officials employed to perform the work of the British government) • *Traditionally, newspaper editors seek advice from Whitehall before publishing information relating to 'national security'.* • *The Minister claimed that the government's plans were being obstructed by Whitehall.*

white·out /£'*h*waɪ·taʊt, $-t̬aʊt/ *n* [C] a weather condition in which snow and clouds change the way light is reflected so that only very dark objects can be seen • *Persistent whiteouts were only one of the hazards that the polar expedition faced.* • See also **whiteout** at WHITE OUT.

white·wash PAINT /£'*h*waɪt·wɒʃ, $-wɑːʃ/ *n* [U] a white liquid that is a mixture of LIME (=a chemical) or powdered CHALK (=a soft white rock) and water, used for making walls or ceilings white

white·wash *obj* /£'*h*waɪt·wɒʃ, $-wɑːʃ/ *v* [T] • *Make sure you cover all the furniture before you whitewash the ceiling.* • *The inside of the church had been whitewashed.*

white·wash *obj* HIDE /£'*h*waɪt·wɒʃ, $-wɑːʃ/ *v* [T] *disapproving* to make (something bad) seem acceptable by hiding the truth • *The government is trying to whitewash the incompetence of the Treasury officials.*

white·wash /£'*h*waɪt·wɒʃ, $-wɑːʃ/ *n* [C] *disapproving* • *The official report on the killings has been denounced as a whitewash.*

white·wash *obj* DEFEAT *Br* /£'waɪt·wɒʃ, $-wɑːʃ/, *Am usually* **shut out** *v* [T] *infml* to defeat (a player or team) completely, esp. while preventing them from scoring any points • *The Australians whitewashed them 6-0.*

white·wash *Br* /£'waɪt·wɒʃ, $-wɑːʃ/, *Am usually* **shut·out** *n* [C] *infml* • *The game was a 6-0 whitewash.*

white·y /£'*h*waɪ·ti, $-t̬i/ *n* [C; as form of address] (used esp. by black people) a white person. This is generally considered offensive.

whi·ther /£'*h*wɪð·əʳ, $-ɚ/ *adv* [not gradable] *old use* to where • *Whither are they going?*

whit·ing /£'*h*waɪ·tɪŋ, $-t̬ɪŋ/ *n pl* **whiting** or **whitings** a small black and silver sea fish, eaten as food • *The fishermen had caught cod and whiting.* [C] • *We're having grilled whiting for lunch.* [U]

whit·ish /£'*h*waɪ·tɪʃ, $-t̬ɪʃ/ *adj* See at WHITE COLOUR

Whit·sun /'*h*wɪt·sᵊn/ *n* [U] the seventh Sunday after Easter, and the period around it • *We're going to Scotland for a week* **at** *Whitsun.* • *They're planning a Whitsun wedding.*

whit·tle *(obj)* /£'*h*wɪt·l̩, $'*h*wɪt̬-/ *v* to make (something) out of a piece of wood by cutting off small thin pieces • *An old sailor sat on the dockside, whittling a toy boat.* • To **whittle away (at)** something or to **whittle** something **away** is to make it gradually smaller or less important or effective: *Every year, management whittles away at the number of jobs in the company.* ○ *In the second half of the race, the Italian driver began to whittle away Mansell's five-second lead.* ○ *A series of new laws has gradually whittled away basic human rights in the country.* • To **whittle down** something or **whittle** something **down** is to make it gradually smaller: *By half time Argentina had whittled the gap down to one goal.*

whizz MOVE FAST *Br, Am usually* **whiz** /*h*wɪz/ *v* [I always + adv/prep] *infml* to move very fast • *A police car whizzed* **by**, *on its way to the accident.* • *We whizzed* **through** *the rehearsal, so that we'd be finished by lunchtime.* • *Time just whizzes* **past** *when you're enjoying yourself.*

whizz EXPERT *Br, Am usually* **whiz** /*h*wɪz/ *n* [C usually sing] *infml approving* a person with a very high level of skill or knowledge in a particular area • *She's a computer whizz.* • *He's a whizz in the field of economics.* • *Steve is a whizz* **at** *poker.* • A **whizz kid** is a young person who is extremely successful because of their very high level of skill or knowledge in a particular area: *Jo was one of those whizz kids who are millionaires by the time they're 25.*

who ASKING /huː/ *pronoun* used esp. in questions as the subject or object of a verb, when asking which person or people, or when asking what someone's name is • *Who did this?* • *Who's she?* • *Who are all those people?* • *Hi, I'm Liz – who are you?* • *She asked me if I knew who had got the job.* • *Who (also fml* **whom***) do you want to talk to?* • *I don't know who (also fml* **whom***) to ask to the party.* • Who can also be used with verbs relating to knowing, when you want to say that something is not known: *"Are they going to get married?" "Who* **knows***?"* (=It is not possible to know at the moment.) ○ *Who can* **tell** *why they killed themselves?* (=No one can know the real reason.) • To know **who's who** is to know the name and position of each person, esp. in an organization. • **Who's Who** is a book containing information about the world's richest or most famous people. A **who's who** is any list of the main people in a particular group: *Who's Who states he retired in 1980.* ○ *The guest list reads like a who's who of top American businessmen.* • LP **Clauses**

who ADDING INFORMATION /huː/ *pronoun* used as the subject or object of a verb when referring to a particular person or when adding information about a person just mentioned • *I think it was your Dad who phoned.* • *Actors are usually people who love to be the centre of attention.* • *He rang Geoffrey, who was a good friend as well as the family doctor.* • *The other people who (also* **that***) live in the house are really friendly.* • *This is Frank, who (also fml* **whom***) I told you about.*

WHO /£ˌdʌb·l̩.juːˌeɪtʃ'əʊ, $-'oʊ/ *n* [U] *abbreviation for* World Health Organization (=an international organization which is involved in improving standards of health everywhere in the world)

who·a /£*h*wəʊ, $*h*woʊ/ *exclamation* used when telling esp. a horse to stop • *(fig. infml) "Whoa* (=Slow down)*," I said, "Talk slower, please."* • *(fig. infml) Whoa* (=Stop what you're doing) *there! Be careful what you're doing with that knife!*

who·dun·it, **who·dun·nit** /ˌhuː'dʌn·ɪt/ *n* [C] *infml* a story about a crime and the attempt to discover who committed it • *The book/film is one of those whodunits where you don't find out who the murderer is till the very end.*

who·ev·er PERSON /£huː'ev·əʳ, $-ɚ/ *pronoun* the person who • *Whoever uprooted that tree ought to be ashamed of themselves.* • *Could I speak to whoever is in charge of International Sales please?*

who·ev·er ANYONE /£huː'ev·əʳ, $-ɚ/ *pronoun* any person who • *They are shooting at whoever leaves the building.* • *I don't have time to talk to them, whoever they are* (=I do not have time to talk to anyone). • *He says he bought the car from Frank, whoever Frank is* (=I do not know who Frank is).

who·ev·er SURPRISE /£huː'ev·əʳ, $-ɚ/ *pronoun* used in questions as a way of expressing surprise • *Whoever can that be in the car with Max?* • *Whoever heard such an unlikely story?* • *Whoever said being rich is easy?* (=It is not easy.)

whole /£həʊl, $hoʊl/ *adj* [not gradable] complete or not divided • *We both spent the whole night unable to sleep.* • *There's still a whole month till my birthday.* • *He cooked a meal for the whole staff of the school.* • *After my exercise class, my whole body ached.* • *If you drink that whole bottle* *of vodka, you'll be ill.* • *The whole town was destroyed by the earthquake.* • *Climate change and rising sea levels threaten the whole world.* • *This whole* **thing** (=situation) *is ridiculous.* • *Chris does nothing but moan the whole* **time** (=all the time). • *You have to stand up in court and promise to tell 'the truth, the whole* **truth** *and nothing but the truth.'* • *The snake had* **swallowed** *the little animal whole* (=swallowed it in one piece, without chewing it). • *Her dance compositions added a whole* (=completely) *new dimension to the contemporary dance repertoire.* • *(infml)* Whole can also be used to emphasize something: *I've got a whole heap of work to do this afternoon.* ○ *The new computers are* **a** *whole* **lot** (=much) *faster.* • *(Br and Aus)***The whole bit**/*(Am)* **the whole enchilada** is everything related to a particular activity, idea, area or way of behaving: *He's into jogging, squash, aerobics, the whole (exercise) bit.* ○ *When we're in Paris we're going to* **do** *the whole bit – the Eiffel Tower, the Louvre, Sacré Coeur, the Bastille and especially the Left Bank.* • To **go the whole hog** is to do something as completely as possible: *Having already limited local taxation, why not go the whole hog and abolish it completely?* • **The whole (kit and) caboodle** means everything: *I covered the vegetables with sauce, sprinkled cheese on top and put the whole caboodle in the oven.* • *(Am)* **The whole shebang** means the structure or organization of something: *The wedding's next week, but my parents are taking care of the whole shebang.* • **Whole-hearted** means completely enthusiastic: *I'd like to thank Jane for her whole-hearted efforts on our behalf.* ○ *All the members are* **whole-heartedly** *in favour of the changes.* • **Whole-note** is *Am for* SEMIBREVE. • **A whole number** is a number, such as 1, 17 or 3 126, which has no FRACTIONS or **decimal places** after it. • *"Whole Lotta Shakin' Going On"* (song by Jerry Lee Lewis, 1957) • *"He's got the Whole World in his Hands"* (title of a traditional song)

whole /£həʊl, $hoʊl/ *n* • *Two halves make a whole* (=a complete thing). [C] • *You must consider each problem as an aspect of* **the** *whole* (=everything that is involved) *– the total picture.* [U] • *I'll be on holiday* **the whole of** (=all of) *next week.* [U] • **The** *whole* **of** (=all of) *his finger was sore and bruised.* [U] • **The** *whole* **of** *the village* (=Everyone in the village) *was out looking for the children during the storm.* [U] • *The new system is pretty good* **as a whole** (=most things work well most of the time). • **On the whole** (=Generally) *I prefer to listen to classical music.*

whole·ness /£ˈhəʊl·nəs, $ˈhoʊl-/ *n* [U] • *She uses Jungian psychotherapy to try and restore a sense of wholeness* (=being emotionally healthy) *to her clients.*

whol·ly /£ˈhəʊl·li, $ˈhoʊl-/ *adv* • *This motorcycle is wholly* (=completely) *British-made.* • *I wasn't wholly convinced by her explanation.* • *That's a wholly different matter.* • LP **Very, completely**

whole·food /£ˈhəʊl·fuːd, $ˈhoʊl-/ *n* [U] *Br* food that has not had any of its natural features taken away or any artificial substances added • *a wholefood shop/cookbook/diet*

whole·foods /£ˈhəʊl·fuːdz, $ˈhoʊl-/ *pl n Br* • Wholefoods are natural foods which have not been processed: *The children insist on eating only wholefoods, like beans and brown rice.*

whole·grain /£ˈhəʊl·greɪn, $ˈhoʊl-/ *adj* [not gradable] *esp. Br and Aus* (of particular types of food) containing whole seeds • *wholegrain bread* • *wholegrain mustard* • *wholegrain breakfast cereal*

whole·meal *Br* /£ˈhəʊl·miːl, $ˈhoʊl-/, *Am* **whole·wheat** *adj* [not gradable] (of flour or food made from flour) containing all the natural features of the grain, with nothing taken away • *wholemeal flour/pastry* • *Is this* **bread** *wholemeal?*

whole·sale SELLING /£ˈhəʊl·seɪl, $ˈhoʊl-/ *adj, adv* [not gradable] of or for the selling of goods in large amounts at low prices to shops and businesses, rather than the selling of goods in shops to customers • *wholesale prices* • *a wholesale supplier/business* • *We only sell wholesale, not to the public.* • *If you like, I can get that camera you want cheaper for you wholesale.* • Compare RETAIL.

whole·sal·er /£ˈhəʊlˌseɪ·ləʳ, $ˈhoʊlˌseɪ·lɚ/ *n* [C] • Wholesalers buy and sell goods in large amounts to shops and businesses: *a furniture wholesaler*

whole·sale COMPLETE /£ˈhəʊl·seɪl, $ˈhoʊl-/ *adj often disapproving* (esp. of something bad or too extreme) complete or total • *wholesale slaughter* • *a wholesale surrender* • *the wholesale destruction of towns and villages* • *What the system needs is wholesale reform.*

whole·some /£ˈhəʊl·səm, $ˈhoʊl-/ *adj approving* beneficial for you, and likely to improve your life either physically or morally or emotionally • *A healthy diet includes lots of wholesome natural* **food** *with plenty of proteins and vitamins.* • *We're going on a camping holiday to give the kids a taste of the wholesome outdoor life.* • *This film is good wholesome family entertainment.* • *Her parents want her to marry a nice wholesome young man.*

whole·some·ness /£ˈhəʊl·səm·nəs, $ˈhoʊl-/ *n* [U]

whole·wheat /£ˈhəʊl·hwiːt, $ˈhoʊl-/ *adj* [not gradable] *esp. Am for* WHOLEMEAL

whom ADDING INFORMATION /huːm/ *pronoun fml* used as the object of a verb or after a preposition when referring to a particular person or when adding information about a person just mentioned • *The women whom you mentioned are all former employees.* • *He took out a photo of his son, whom he adores.* • *There were 500 passengers, of whom 121 drowned.* • *The Kenyans have three runners in the 1500 metres, any of whom could take the gold medal.* • *To whom do you wish to speak?* • In ordinary speech, it is more usual to use 'who' rather than 'whom', except after a preposition, when you should use 'whom'.

whom ASKING /huːm/ *pronoun fml* used esp. in questions as the object of a verb or after a preposition, when asking which person or people, or when asking what someone's name is • *When you say 'various people,' whom do you mean?* • *Of whom can it truly be said that they have never done a dishonest thing?* • In ordinary speech, it is more usual to use 'who' rather than 'whom', except after a preposition, when you should use 'whom'. • See also WHO ASKING.

whom·ev·er /£huːˈmev·əʳ, $-ɚ/ *pronoun fml* WHOEVER • *Give it to whomever you please.*

whoop /hwuːp, huːp/ *v* [I] to give a loud, excited shout, esp. to show your enjoyment of or agreement with something • *The audience was whooping and clapping.* • To **whoop it up** is to enjoy yourself in a noisy and excited way. • See also WHOOPING COUGH.

whoop /hwuːp, huːp/ *n* [C] • *As she played the last winning shot, he gave a whoop of triumph.*

whoop·ee /£ˈhwʊp·i, $ˈhwuː·pi/ *exclamation* a loud excited shout of happiness, enjoyment or agreement • *"Oh, whoopee!" he shouted.*

whoop·ee /£ˈhwʊp·i, $ˈhwuː·pi/ *n* [U] *infml dated* • To **make whoopee** is to have a celebration and enjoy yourself a lot.

whoop·ing cough /ˈhuː·pɪŋ/ *n* [U] a disease caught esp. by children, which causes severe coughing

whoops /hwʊps/, **oops** *exclamation infml* said when someone has (almost) made a slight mistake or (almost) had a slight accident • *Whoops! I think I've given you the wrong change.* • *"Whoops!/Whoops* **a daisy**!*" she said, as the little boy tripped and fell over the door step.* • *Whoops! Mind you don't spill your juice.* • LP **Phrases and customs**

whoosh /hwʊʃ/ *exclamation, n* [C usually sing] *infml* a soft sound made by something moving fast through the air or like that made when air is pushed out of something • *Whoosh, the doors closed automatically behind them.* • *The train sped through the station with a whoosh.* • *(fig.) They expect* **a** *whoosh* (=a lot in a short time) **of** *money to flood into the country.* • *(fig.) No sooner had she arrived than, whoosh* (=suddenly), *she was off again.*

whoosh /hwʊʃ/ *v* [I always + adv/prep] *infml* • *A fast motorboat whooshed* (=moved quickly, making a soft sound) *past us.*

whop *obj* /£hwɒp, $hwɑːp/ *v* [T] **-pp-** *esp. Am infml* to hit or defeat • *She whopped him with her handbag.* • *The Yankees whopped the Cleveland Indians 17-2.*

whop·per /£ˈhwɒp·əʳ, $ˈhwɑː·pɚ/ *n* [C] *humorous* something that is surprising because it is so much bigger than the usual size • *What a whopper! That's an incredibly big nose he has!* • A whopper is also a big lie: *As usual he told them a whopper and everyone believed it.*

whop·ping /£ˈhwɒp·ɪŋ, $ˈhwɑː·pɪŋ/ *adj* [not gradable] *infml* • *a whopping* **(great)** *bruise* • *a whopping 35% pay rise* • *a whopping lie* • *She got a whopping 12 000 votes more than her closest opponent.*

whore /£hɔːʳ, $hɔːr/ *n* [C] *dated, or taboo slang* a female PROSTITUTE (=someone who is paid for sex) or a woman whose behaviour in her sexual relationships is considered immoral • *In this part of town, there are whores on every street corner.* • *Get out of my sight, you little whore!* [as form of address]

whore·house /£'hɔː·haʊs, $'hɔːr-/ *n* [C] *pl* **whorehouses** /£'hɔːˌhaʊ·zɪz, $'hɔːr-/ • Whorehouse is *esp. Am for* BROTHEL. • *"The Best Little Whorehouse in Texas"* (title of a film, 1982)

whorl /£hwɜːl, $hwɜːrl/ *n* [C] *specialized or literary* a circular pattern of lines, with the smallest circle in the middle, surrounded by other circles, each one wider and larger than the previous one

whose [ASKING ABOUT OWNERSHIP] /huːz/ *pronoun, determiner* used esp. in questions when asking about which person owns or is responsible for something • *Whose is this bag?* • *Whose bag is this?* • *I don't care whose fault it is.* • [LP]> **Determiners**

whose [ADDING INFORMATION] /huːz/ *determiner* used for adding information about a person or thing just mentioned • *Cohen, whose contract expires next week, is likely to move to play for a European club.* • *There was a horrid picture in the paper of a man whose leg had been blown off.* • *They meet in an old house, whose basement has been converted into a chapel.* • *Fraud detectives are investigating the company, three of whose senior executives have already been arrested.*

who·so·ev·er /£ˌhuː·səʊ'ev·əʳ, $-soʊ'ev·ɚ/ *pronoun old use for* WHOEVER

why [REASON] /hwaɪ/ *adv* [not gradable], *conjunction* for what reason • *Why do you like living in Paris?* • *"I'm going home." "Why?"* • *Why wait? Let's leave now.* • *Why should I bother to help you, if you're so ungrateful?* • *Why is it that I find chocolate so addictive?* • *The police asked me to explain why I hadn't reported the accident sooner.* • *I don't know why she isn't here.* • *Why the computer won't work is a mystery.* • *There is no* **reason** *why we shouldn't succeed.* • *Don't ask me the* **reason** *why.* • **Why not** can be used to make a suggestion or to express agreement: *If you're so unhappy, why not get a divorce?* ○ *"Shall we eat Italian tonight?" "Yes, why not."* • [LP]> **Clauses**

whys /hwaɪz/ *pl n* • The **whys and wherefores (of)** something are the reasons (for) it: *I don't want to hear all* **the** *whys and wherefores – just get it finished properly this time.* ○ *He spent ages explaining the whys and wherefores of the decision.*

why [SURPRISE] /hwaɪ/ *exclamation esp. Am or dated* used to express surprise or annoyance • *Why, if it isn't old Georgie Frazer! How are you after all these years?* • *Why, you greedy pig, you'd better not have eaten all those biscuits.*

WI /ˌdʌb·l̩.juː'aɪ/ *n* [C] *abbreviation for* **Women's Institute**, see at WOMAN

wick /wɪk/ *n* [C] a piece of string in the centre of a candle, or a similar part of a light, which supplies fuel to a flame • *(Br infml dated)* To **get on** someone's **wick** is to annoy them by your behaviour. • [PIC]> **Lights**

wi·cked [BAD] /'wɪk·ɪd/ *adj* **-er, -est** *dated* morally wrong and bad • *There's no doubt that he was a wicked, ruthless and dishonest man.* • *Of course, in the end, the wicked witch does get killed.* • *In the story, she has a wicked step-mother/wicked step-father, who makes her life a misery.* • Wicked can also mean slightly immoral or bad for you, but in an attractive way: *a wicked grin* ○ *a wicked sense of humour* ○ *What a wicked-looking chocolate cake.* • Wicked can also mean dangerous, extreme and/or likely to cause pain or harm: *She sent the car into a wicked spin.* ○ *He showed me a wicked-looking knife.* • *(saying)* 'There's no rest/peace for the wicked' means you must continue with your work or other activity that you should be doing, not rest. • Compare EVIL; NAUGHTY [BADLY BEHAVED].

wi·cked [EXCELLENT] /'wɪk·ɪd/ *adj, exclamation* **-er, -est** *infml* (used to express approval) excellent • *He's got a wicked tape collection.* • *"So do you feel like coming to the party?" "Yeah, man, wicked!"*

wi·cker /£'wɪk·əʳ, $-ɚ/ *adj* [not gradable] made of very thin pieces of wood twisted together • *a wicker basket/chair* • [PIC]> **Basket**

wick·er·work /£'wɪk·ə·wɜːk, $-ɚ·wɜːrk/ *n* [U] • *The chairs are either wickerwork* (= made of thin pieces of wood) *or pine.* • *She brought the cakes in on a wickerwork tray.*

wi·cket /'wɪk·ɪt/ *n* [C] (in cricket) a set of three vertical sticks with two small pieces of wood balanced across the top of them, at which the ball is aimed. There are two wickets on a cricket field. • *A direct throw from one of the fielding players hit the wicket.* • A wicket is also the length of ground between the two sets of wickets. • A wicket is also a turn that a player has to hit the ball: *Five wickets have* **fallen** *since tea time* (= Five players have been caused to finish their turn). ○ *As a fast bowler, he* **took** *many wickets* (= caused many players to finish their turns). • A **wicket keeper** is a cricket player who stands behind the wicket in order to catch the ball.

wide /waɪd/ *adj* **-r, -st** having a larger distance from one side to the other than is usual or expected, esp. in comparison with its length; not narrow • *a wide river/road/gap/table/nose/foot* • *His eyes were wide* (= opened much more than usual) **with** *surprise.* • *(fig.) There's a wide* (= large) *gap between her publicly stated policies and her private views.* • You use wide when describing how long the distance between the two sides of something is: *The rectangle is 5 cm long and 1·9 cm wide.* ○ *How wide are your skis?* ○ *The swimming pool is 5 metres wide.* • Wide is also used to describe something that includes many different types of thing or that covers a large range or area: *They sell a wide range of skin-care products.* ○ *She has a wide experience of teaching, in many different schools.* ○ *The Green Party no longer enjoys wide support* (= the support of many people). • *(infml)* To **give** someone or something **a wide berth** is to avoid a person or place: *He owed me money so was giving me a very wide berth.* • *They are not realistic plays, and it would not be too far* **wide of the mark** (= wrong) *to call them dreams or fantasies.* • A **wide-angle (lens)** is a camera LENS that provides a wider view than usual. • A **wide-bodied** aircraft is wider and larger than average: *Most of the planes which carry passengers across the Atlantic are wide-bodied* **jets**. • *(Br infml disapproving)* A **wide boy** is a man who is dishonest or who deceives people in the way he does business: *Some of the younger property developers are real wide boys.* • If you say that someone is **wide-eyed**, you mean that their eyes are open much wider than usual or *(fig.)* that they are too willing to believe and admire what they see or are told: *At that time I was still a wide-eyed youngster.* • See also WIDTH. • [LP]> **Measurements**

wide /waɪd/ *adv* **-r, -st** • *They moved the goal posts wider* **apart** (= so that there was a larger distance between them). • *His eyes* **opened** *wide* (= opened much more than usual) *with the pain.* • *"***Open** *wide* (= Open your mouth as far as possible)*," said the dentist.* • Wide can also mean completely: *She left the door wide* **open**. ○ *The town was wide* **open to** *attack.* ○ *At 2-2 with five minutes to go, the game is still wide* **open**. ○ *It was 3 a.m. and we were still wide* **awake**, *unable to sleep because of the noise of the rain.* • **Wide-ranging** means covering many subjects: *After the lecture, there was a wide-ranging discussion.*

wide·ly /'waɪd·li/ *adv* • *She smiled widely* (= gave a large smile) *at me.* • *His plays are still widely performed* (= performed in many places) *in the USA.* • *French used to be widely spoken* (= spoken in many places and by many people) *in Kampuchea.* • *His work on DNA was widely* **admired** (= admired by many people). • *This theory is no longer widely* **accepted/believed** (= accepted/believed) *by many people.* • *They travelled widely in Asia during their retirement.* • *She is very widely* **read** (= has read many books, on many subjects). • *The two groups have widely* **differing** *aims* (= there is a large difference between their aims). • *Reactions to the proposal have* **varied** *widely* (= by a large amount).

wid·en *(obj)* /'waɪ·dᵊn/ *v* • *As it approaches the sea, the river begins to widen* **(out)**. [I] • *They widened the room by knocking down a partition.* [T] • *His eyes/smile widened.* [I] • *Why not widen the discussion to include the Muslim and Jewish points of view?* [T]

wide·spread /ˌwaɪd'spred/ *adj* existing or happening in many places and/or among many people • *There are reports of widespread flooding in northern France.* • *Widespread rioting in the area led to 25 deaths.* • *Malnutrition in the region is widespread – affecting up to 78% of children under five years old.* • *The campaign has received widespread* **support**. • *There is widespread* **speculation** *that he is going to resign.*

wi·dow /£'wɪd·əʊ, $-oʊ/ *n* [C] a woman whose husband has died and who has not married again • *The money was paid to Mr Desai's widow.* • *She found it very hard to adjust to being a widow.* • *(infml humorous)* A fishing/football/golf/etc. widow is a woman whose husband is very often away fishing or playing football or golf, etc. • [LP]> **Relationships**

wi·dowed /£'wɪd·əʊd, $-oʊd/ *adj* [not gradable] • If you have been widowed, your husband or wife has died: *We went to stay with her widowed mother.* ○ *He was widowed at the age of 52.*

wi·dow·hood /£'wɪd·əʊ·hʊd, $-oʊ-/ *n* [U] • Widowhood is the fact or period of being a widow.

wi·dow·er /£ˈwɪd·əʊ·əʳ, $-oʊ·ɚ/ *n* [C] a man whose wife has died and who has not married again • LP› **Relationships**

width /wɪtθ, wɪdθ/ *n* the distance across something from one side to the other • *The length of the rectangle is 10 cm and the width is 6 cm.* [U] • *It is 5 metres* **in width**. [U] • *The needle is seven times smaller than the width* **of** *a human hair.* [U] • *The new back bedroom stretches the* **full width of** (= all across) *the house.* [U] • *The material is available in various widths.* [C] • Width is also the fact of being very wide: *The width* **of** *the computer screen makes the words easier to read.* [U] • Width can also be used to mean amount or size: *There is a surprising width of support for the proposal.* [U] ○ *The company is planning to extend the width of its range.* [U] • A width is also the distance across a swimming pool from one side to the other: *I managed to swim 2 widths underwater.* [C] • See also WIDE. Compare LENGTH.

wield *obj* /wiːld/ *v* [T] to have and/or use (power, authority, influence, etc.) or *(literary)* to hold and use (a weapon) • *As Executive Director she wields a lot of* **power**. • *(literary) The police were there in force, wielding batons.*

wife /waɪf/ *n* [C] *pl* **wives** /waɪvz/ the woman to whom a man is married; a married woman • *"I love you," he said. "Will you be my wife?"* • *She's his third wife* (= She is the third woman to whom he has been married). • **Wife swapping** is when two sets of married people decide to have sex with each other's partners. • LP› **Relationships**

wife·ly /ˈwaɪ·fli/ *adj fml* • *wifely duties* (= duties considered to be those of a wife)

wig /wɪg/ *n* [C] a covering of artificial hair worn on the head to hide a lack of hair or to cover your own hair • *She wears/has a blonde wig.* • *In Britain, judges wear white wigs in court.* • Compare TOUPÉE.

wig·gle *(obj)* /ˈwɪg·l̩/ *v infml* to (cause to) move up and down and/or from side to side with small quick movements • *He tried wiggling the control stick but nothing happened.* [T] • *She wiggled her toes in the water.* [T] • *Her hips wiggle as she walks.* [I]

wig·gle /ˈwɪg·l̩/ *n* [C] *infml* • *With a wiggle of his hips, he pulled up the trousers.* • A wiggle is also a line with many short curves in it.

wig·gly /ˈwɪg·l̩.i, ˈwɪg·li/ *adj infml* • *a wiggly country road* • *Is that wiggly* **line** *you've drawn supposed to be a snake?*

wig·wam /ˈwɪg·wæm/ *n* [C] a cone-shaped tent made and lived in, esp. in the past, by Native Americans in the eastern US

wild NATURAL /waɪld/ *adj, adv* **-er, -est** living or growing independently of people, in natural conditions and with natural characteristics • *wild flowers* • *wild grasses* • *a herd of wild horses* • *Lions and tigers are wild animals.* • Wild land is not cultivated, and has few people living in it: *the wilder mountain regions* • *The lions that had been living wild never really adapted to captivity.* • *(infml)* **Wild horses couldn't/wouldn't drag** *me* (= Nothing could persuade me to go) *to any party of hers.* • A **wild boar** is a large fierce hairy pig that lives wild in forests. • *"The Wilder Shores of Love"* (title of a book by Lesley Blanch, 1954)

wild /waɪld/ *n* • *The animals would produce more young* **in the wild** (= living independently of people, in natural conditions) *than they do in the zoo.* • *She lives somewhere* **in the wilds of** *Borneo* (= in a part of that country that has few towns or roads, is difficult to get to and is not considered an easy place to live).

wild·ness /ˈwaɪld·nəs/ *n* [U] • *She longed for the wildness* (= natural and extreme beauty) *of the mountains of her birthplace.*

wild NOT CONTROLLED /waɪld/ *adj* **-er, -est** uncontrolled, violent or extreme • *The school has a few wild students, one of whom came in with a knife last week.* • *As a youth, he led a wild life of drink, drugs and fast cars.* • *They went on a wild £900 shopping spree.* • *The audience burst into wild applause.* • *She felt a wave of wild fury overcome her.* • *When I told him what I'd done, he was/***went wild** (= angry). • *We were all wild/We all* **went wild with** *excitement* (= were/became extremely excited). • *The band* **drove** *the audience wild* (= made them excited and enthusiastic). • *Her eyes were wild/She had a wild look in her eyes* (= Her eyes were wide open, as if she were frightened, or mentally ill). • *His hair was wild* (= long and untidy) *and his clothes full of holes.* • *There have been wild* (= extreme) *variations in the level of spending.* • *It's just a wild* (= not based on fact or careful thought) *guess.* • *She fired a couple of wild* (= not carefully directed) *shots, none of which went anywhere near him.* • *They get some wild weather* (= many severe storms) *in the north.* • *It was a wild* (= stormy or very windy) *night, with the wind howling and the rain pouring down.* • *(slang)* Wild is also used to mean excellent, special and/or unusual: *The music they play is just wild.* • *(infml) No, I'm* **not** *wild* **about** (= I don't very much like) *Indian food.* • *(infml) Oh, Chris has always been wild* **about** *Madonna* (= has always liked Madonna's music very much). • *(specialized)* In computers, a **wild card** is a symbol that has no particular meaning of its own so that its space can be filled by any real character that is necessary: *The wild cards are represented here by asterisks.* • A **wild card** is also someone who is allowed to take part in a contest, even though they have not qualified for it in the usual way: *Phillips is hoping for a wild card entry to the Queensland tennis championships.* • A **wild card** is also someone or something whose behaviour you cannot be certain of in advance: *The wild card in this election is the Green Party – no one knows exactly how much support they will get.* • *(infml)* A **wild-goose chase** is a search which is completely unsuccessful and a waste of time because the person or thing being searched for does not exist or is somewhere else: *We* **went on***/We were* **sent on** *a wild goose chase.* • Your **wildest dreams** are your hopes or thoughts about the things, esp. very good things, that could possibly happen in the future: *They promised him he would soon be rich* **beyond** *his wildest dreams.* ○ **Never in** *my wildest dreams did I think she'd actually carry out her threat.* • The **Wild West** is the name given to the western part of the US during the time when Europeans were first beginning to live there and when there was fighting between them and the Native Americans: *(fig.) It seems the Wild West has come to this part of Europe – the rule of law has broken down and it's every one for themselves.* • *"Tales of the Wild and Woolly West"* (title of a book by Adair Welcher, 1891) • *"I'm just Wild about Harry"* (title of a song written by Noble Sissle and Eubie Blake, 1921) • *"Wild at Heart"* (film title, 1990)

wild·ly /ˈwaɪld·li/ *adv* • *He was dancing wildly.* • *Inflation figures have fluctuated wildly between 0·2% and 25%.* • *It was wildly* (= very) *expensive.* • *I must say I'm not wildly* (= very) *keen on the idea.*

wild·ness /ˈwaɪld·nəs/ *n* [U] • *His wildness made him a difficult employee.*

wild /waɪld/ *adv* **-er, -est** • *When their parents died, the kids started to* **run** *wild* (= behave in uncontrolled, extreme ways, doing only what they wanted).

wild·cat strike /ˌwaɪld·kætˈstraɪk/ *n* [C] a sudden unofficial STRIKE (= stopping of work)

wil·de·beest /ˈwɪl·dɪ·biːst/ *n* [C] *pl* **wildebeest** or **wildebeests** a GNU

wil·der·ness /£ˈwɪl·də·nəs, $-dɚ-/ *n* [C usually sing] an area of land that has not been cultivated or had towns and roads built on it, esp. because it is difficult to live in as a result of its extremely cold or hot weather or bad earth • *She said Alaska was the last great wilderness.* • *(esp. Am and Aus) It's a wilderness* **area**, *under the protection of the Parks Department.* • *(fig.) The garden was a wilderness* **of** *weeds and overgrown bushes* (= There were a lot of plants growing close together and untidily in it). • *(fig.) Unemployment, drugs and crime are the key ingredients in the wilderness* (= unpleasant and dangerous areas in which few people live) *of the inner city.* • If someone, such as a politician, is **in the wilderness**, they no longer have a position of authority and are no longer in the news: *After five years in the political wilderness, she was recalled to be foreign minister.*

wild·fire /£ˈwaɪld·faɪəʳ, $-faɪr/ *n* [C] a fire which is burning strongly and out of control on an area of grass or bushes in the countryside • *Major wildfires have destroyed thousands of acres in Idaho, Oregon and Montana.* • **Like wildfire** means very fast and often in an uncontrolled way: *This new dance craze has caught on like wildfire in the clubs of New York.* ○ *The news* **spread** *like wildfire.*

wild·fowl /ˈwaɪld·faʊl/ *pl n* birds that people shoot for sport, esp. ones such as DUCKS that live near water

wild·life /ˈwaɪld·laɪf/ *n* [U] animals and plants that grow independently of people, usually in natural conditions • *a documentary on Peruvian wildlife* • *wildlife groups/conservation* • *It is a patch of wasteland that is home to all sorts of wildlife, including wild grasses, butterflies, frogs and even a fox.*

wild·ly /ˈwaɪld·li/ *adv* See at WILD NOT CONTROLLED

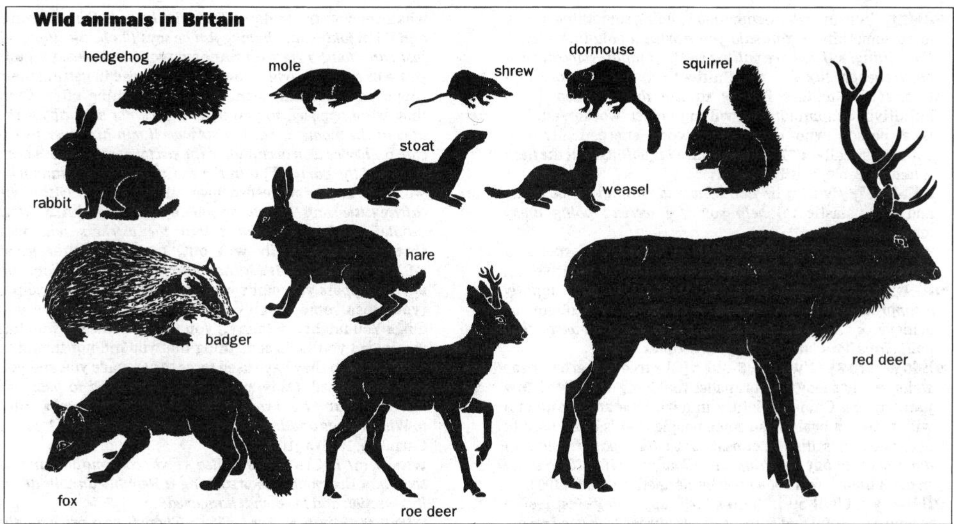

wiles /waɪlz/ *pl n fml* methods of persuasion that cleverly trick someone into doing something • *He'll have to* **use** *all his wiles on her to get her to agree.*

wil·ful, *Am usually* **will·ful** /ˈwɪl·fəl/ *adj disapproving* (of something bad) done intentionally or (of a person) determined to do exactly as you want, even if you know it is wrong • *The present crisis is the result of years of wilful neglect by the council.* • *They eat too many sweet and fried foods, in wilful disregard of their health.* • *She developed into a wilful, difficult child.*

wil·ful·ly, *Am usually* **will·ful·ly** /ˈwɪl·fəl·i/ *adv* • *Some basic safety rules were wilfully ignored.*

wil·ful·ness, *Am usually* **will·ful·ness** /ˈwɪl·fəl·nəs/ *n* [U] • *The children's sheer wilfulness made them exhausting to look after.*

will FUTURE /wɪl/ *v aux* [+ infinitive without *to*; not *be willing*], **'ll** *short form* he/she/it **will**, *past simple* **would** /wʊd/ used when referring to the future • *Clare will be five years old next month.* • *The train leaves at 8.58, so we'll be in Scotland by lunchtime.* • *I will see him tomorrow./I will be seeing him tomorrow.* • *Will it rain today, I wonder?* • *It won't be easy to find another secretary.* • *There'll be trouble, unless this is finished by tomorrow.* • **Will have** is used to refer back to the past from a point in the future: *By the time we get there, Jim will have left.* • See also SHALL WILL. • LP› **Auxiliary verbs, Tenses**

will INTENTION /wɪl/ *v aux* [+ infinitive without *to*; not *be willing*], **'ll** *short form* he/she/it **will**, *past simple* **would** /wʊd/ used to express your intentions • *I will always love you.* • *I won't have him ruining my party.* • *"Will you pick up the dry-cleaning on your way home from work?" "Yes, I will."* • *Is there anyone who will* (= is willing to) *help me?* • *I will* (= I promise to) *have it done by Friday.* • *I won't* (= I refuse to) *lend her any money – she never pays it back.*

will REQUEST /wɪl/, *v aux* [+ infinitive without *to*; not *be willing*], **'ll** *short form he/she/it* **will**, *past simple* **would** /wʊd/ used to ask or tell someone to do something • *Will you give me her address, please?* • *Will you stop that awful noise this instant!* • *You'll do it because I said so.* • 'Will' can be used as a polite way of inviting someone to do something, or of offering someone something: *Will you come in?* ○ *Will you have some cake?* • 'Won't' can be used as a more formal way of inviting someone to do something, or of offering someone something: *Won't you come in.* ○ *Won't you have some cake?*

will CAN /wɪl/ *v aux* [+ infinitive without *to*; not *be willing*], **'ll** *short form* he/she/it **will**, *past simple* **would** /wʊd/ used to refer to what is possible; to be able to do something • *But will a single open fire heat the whole house?* • *This quantity of lasagne will feed six people.* • *The car won't start.*

will ALWAYS /wɪl/ *v aux* [+ infinitive without *to*; not *be willing*], **'ll** *short form* he/she/it **will**, *past simple* **would** /wʊd/ used when referring to something that always or usually happens • *Fruit will keep longer in the fridge.* • *The product with the better-known brand name will always sell better.* • *Accidents will happen.* • *She's 85 now, but she will insist on doing all her own housework.*

will LIKELY /wɪl/ *v aux* [+ infinitive without *to*; not *be willing*], **'ll** *short form* he/she/it **will**, *past simple* **would** /wʊd/ used to refer to what is likely • *When the telephone rang she said "That'll be Scott."* • *As you will all probably already know, election day is next week.* • **Will have** is used to refer to a time by which something is likely to have happened: *They'll have got home by now, won't they?* ○ *I've decided to retire next year, but you won't have been told that yet, I suppose.*

will MENTAL POWER /wɪl/ *n* the mental power used to control and direct your thoughts and actions, or a determination to do something, despite any difficulties or opposition • *She'll need a* **strong/iron will** *in order to succeed.* [C] • *After six months in hospital she began to lose* **the will to** *live* (= the desire and determination to stay alive). [U + *to* infinitive] • **Against** *their will, they were forced to hold a meeting* (= They were forced to do it, even though they did not want to). [U] • Someone's will is also what they want to happen: *It was God's will.* [U] ○ *The Communist Party was supposed to follow the will* **of** *the people, wasn't it?* [U] ○ *The government has failed to impose its will* **upon** *regional communities* (= to make them do as it wants). [U] • If you feel **good/ill will** towards someone, you like/dislike them: *I don't* **bear** *you any ill will.* [U] ○ *She felt only good will towards them.* [U] • *As an actor, he has to be able to cry* **at will** (= any time he wants to). • *Did she sell the house* **of** *her* **own free will** (= without being forced)*?* See also **free will** at FREE NOT LIMITED. • *(dated) They worked* **with a will** (= energetically) *and had cleared a path by 10.00 a.m.* • *I try to let him do the job, but honestly,* **with the best will/all the will in the world** (= despite good intentions) *he's just not up to it.* • *(saying)* 'Where there's a will there's a way' means that if you are determined enough, you can find a way to achieve what you want, even if it is very difficult.

will *(obj)* /wɪl/ *v* • To will something to happen is to try to make it happen by your thoughts: *She willed herself* **to** *remember his name.* [T + obj + *to* infinitive] • *(fml)* To will something is also to want it: *What the Minister wills is what happens.* [T] ○ *Stay or go,* **as you** *will.* [I]

-willed /-wɪld/ *combining form* • *She's very strong-willed/weak-willed.*

will DOCUMENT /wɪl/ *n* [C] an official statement of what a person has decided should be done with their money and property after their death • *The lawyer helped him to* **draw up/make** *his will.*

will *obj* /wɪl/ *v* [T] • *She willed the house* **to** *her brother* (= arranged for it to be given to him after her death). • *He willed his grandchildren £10 000 each.* [+ two objects]

will·ful /ˈwɪl·fəl/ *adj Am for* WILFUL

wil·lie, wil·ly /ˈwɪl·i/ *n* [C] *Br infml* (used esp. by and to children) a penis

wil·lies /ˈwɪl·iz/ *pl n* **the willies** *infml* a feeling of nervousness and fear, esp. caused by something strange or threatening • *Spending a night in the house alone always* **gives** *me the willies.* • *Seeing something in the shadows, I suddenly* **got** *the willies and ran.*

will·ing /ˈwɪl·ɪŋ/ *adj* not opposed to doing something; ready to do something • *You said you needed a volunteer – well, I'm willing.* • *If you are willing* **to** *fly at night, you can get a much cheaper ticket.* [+ *to* infinitive] • *Apparently John and Gabriel are willing* **for** *us* **to** *use their garden.* [+ *to* infinitive] • *(approving)* A willing helper/worker/student is a person who does their work energetically and enthusiastically. • *"The spirit indeed is willing, but the flesh is weak"* (Bible, Matthew 26.41)

will·ing·ly /ˈwɪl·ɪŋ·li/ *adv* • *I would willingly* (= be ready and enthusiastic to) *help you if I weren't going away tomorrow.*

will·ing·ness /ˈwɪl·ɪŋ·nəs/ *n* [U] • *She shows a willingness* **to** *work on her own initiative.* [+ *to* infinitive]

will–o'–the–wisp /ˌwɪl·ə·ðəˈwɪsp/ *n* [C] *slightly disapproving* something that is impossible to obtain or achieve • *Full employment is a will-o'-the-wisp that politicians have been chasing for decades.*

wil·low (tree) /£ˈwɪl·əʊ, $-oʊ/ *n* [C] a tree that grows near water and has long thin branches that hang down • **Willow pattern** is a Chinese picture in dark blue and white of a willow tree, a bridge and some people that is often used to decorate plates, dishes, cups, etc.: *a willow-pattern plate* ○ *I don't want to buy anything in willow pattern.* • *"The Wind in the Willows"* (title of a book by Kenneth Graham, 1908)

wil·low·y /£ˈwɪl·əʊ·i, $-oʊ-/ *adj approving* (esp. of a woman) graceful and thin • *Clothes always look good on her because she's so tall and willowy.*

will·power /£ˈwɪl·paʊəʳ, $-paʊr/ *n* [U] the ability to control your own thoughts and the way in which you behave; determination • *It took a lot of willpower to stay calm and not panic.*

wil·ly, wil·lie /ˈwɪl·i/ *n* [C] *Br infml* (used esp. by and to children) a penis • See also WILLIES.

wil·ly–nil·ly /ˌwɪl·iˈnɪl·i/ *adv* [not gradable] whether you want it or not • *She found herself forced, willy-nilly, to lend him more money.* • *The neighbouring countries have become involved willy-nilly in the conflict.* • *(Am)* Willy-nilly also means without any order: *She threw her clothes willy-nilly into a drawer.*

wilt /wɪlt/ *v* [I] (of a plant) to become weak and begin to bend towards the ground, or (of a person) to become weaker, tired or less confident • *Cut flowers will soon wilt without water.* • *After only an hour's walking they were beginning to wilt in the heat.* • *He had intended to say something, but when all the hostile faces turned towards him, he wilted.*

wi·ly /ˈwaɪ·li/ *adj* **-ier, -iest** (of a person) clever, having a very good understanding of situations, possibilities and people, and often willing to use tricks to achieve an aim • *a wily politician* • *Their boss is a bit of a wily old fox.* • *With some wily forward planning, we should be able to meet our financial targets.* • See also WILES.

wimp /wɪmp/ *n* [C] *infml disapproving* a person who is not strong, brave or confident • *What a wimp that boy is!* • *"I'm afraid I'm a bit of a wimp when it comes to climbing up ladders," she said.*

wimp·ish /ˈwɪm·pɪʃ/ *adj infml disapproving* • *He's the wimpish one with no muscles to speak of.* • *They took the wimpish* (= easy) *way down the mountain.*

wimp out /wɪmp/ *v adv* [I] *disapproving* • To wimp out **of** something is to decide not to do it because you are frightened.

win *(obj)* /wɪn/ *v* **winning**, *past* **won** /£wʌn, $wɑːn/ to achieve first position and/or get a prize in a competition or competitive situation • *Which year was it that Italy won the World Cup?* [T] • *He won first prize/a bottle of gin in the raffle.* [T] • *Who's winning?* [I] • *This is the third medal she's won this season.* [T] • *Who won the men's finals in the tennis?* [T] • *She'll win easily.* [I] • *They won the war, although it cost them millions of lives.* [T] • *If this government win the next election I'm leaving the country.* [T] • *I think you won that argument, Peter.* [T] • *It was his goal that won us the match/won the match* **for** *us.* [+ two objects] • *Remember, it's not the winning that counts!* • *Her firm have just won* (= beaten other companies to get) *a cleaning contract worth £3 million.* [T] • You win something positive, such as approval, loyalty, affection or love, by receiving it because you have earned it: *He won a lot of support in the south of the country because of his agricultural policies.* [T] ○ *This is Jamie, the four-year old who won* **the hearts** *of the nation* (= made everyone love him and/or feel sympathy for him). [T] ○ *She would do anything to win his love!* [T] ○ *Winning* **back** *his trust was the hardest part.* [M] • *(infml)* Someone might say you **can't win**, meaning you can't succeed whatever you try to do: *If I'm quiet he says I'm miserable and if I'm joking and having fun he says I'm being stupid – I just can't win!* • *He* **won hands down** (= very easily.) • If you **win** someone **over/round** you succeed in getting their support or in making them agree to something, often when they were opposed to you before: *He's not sure about the idea at the moment, but I'm sure we'll win him over in the end.* ○ *They've won over a lot of the electorate since she's been leader of the party.* [T] • *In the end it was the Italians who* **won the day** (= succeeded/beat all the others) *with their catchy little song 'It's all for you'.* • *(esp. Br and Aus) Most people are fairly confident that the workers will* **win through** *(Am usually* **win out***)* (= succeed after great effort) *in the end.* • *It's a shame you didn't get the job – oh well, I suppose* **you can't win them all/(you) win some, (you) lose some** (= you can't succeed in everything you do)*!* • You might say **(okay,) you win** to someone who has persuaded you to do something that you did not intend to do, esp. when they have used force to persuade you and you are not pleased: *Okay, you win, I can't stand to hear one more complaint from you – we'll go home tomorrow!* • *"How to Win Friends and Influence People"* (title of a book by Dale Carnegie, 1936) • [LP]> **Sports**

win /wɪn/ *n* [C] • *It was United's sixth consecutive win this season.* • *Everyone was predicting a Republican win at the last election and look what happened!*

win·ner /£ˈwɪn·əʳ, $-ɚ/ *n* [C] • *There'll be a prize for the winner.* • *The winner of this match will play Violente in the semi-finals.* • *And to find out who are the lucky winners of our competition, Samantha is going to draw some names out of the bag.* • *(infml)* In sports, winner (*Am also* **game-winner**) sometimes refers to a goal or point that causes a person or a side to win a game: *Neil Eaves scored the winner in the last four minutes of the match.* • *(infml)* A winner is also something that is extremely successful and popular: *That lemon tart was a winner, wasn't it – I've never had so much praise for something I cooked!* ○ *I think they're* **onto** *a winner with this latest product* (= it will succeed). • In a competition, **winner-takes-all** means that a prize is given only to the person who wins, and not to the people who come second, third, fourth etc.. • See also BREADWINNER.

win·ning /ˈwɪn·ɪŋ/ *adj* [before n] • *Have you heard the winning entry in this year's Eurovision Song Contest?* • *It's nice to be on the winning side for a change!* • If someone has a winning **smile** or way of behaving, it is friendly and charming and tends to make people like them: *I'm sure Anna with her winning* **ways** *will be able to persuade him that it's a good idea.* • *Did you see which horse was first past the* **winning post** (= post at the point where a race ends)*?*

win·nings /ˈwɪn·ɪŋz/ *pl n* • Winnings are an amount of money that has been won: *What are you going to spend your winnings on?*

wince /wɪnts/ *v* [I] to show pain briefly and suddenly in the face, often moving the head back at the same time • *Did I hurt you? – I thought I saw you wince.* • *It makes me wince even thinking about eye operations.*

wince /wɪnts/ *n* [C usually sing] • *She* **gave** *a wince as the nurse put the needle in.*

winch /wɪntʃ/, **wind·lass** *n* [C] a machine which lifts heavy objects by turning a chain or rope around a tube-shaped device • [PIC]> **Emergency services**

winch *obj* /wɪntʃ/ *v* [T] • *Two helicopters winched the passengers to safety from the deck of the ship.*

wind [CURRENT OF AIR] /wɪnd/ *n* a current of air moving approximately horizontally, esp. one strong enough to be felt • *There isn't enough wind to fly a kite.* [U] • *The weather forecast warned of winds of up to 60-miles-an-hour today.* [C] • *There was a light wind blowing.* [C] • *Strong/High winds made the crossing very unpleasant.* [C] • *The sails flapped* **in the** *wind.* [U] • *(literary) There wasn't a* **breath of** (= even a slight amount of) *wind.* [U] • *A* **gust** *of wind suddenly caught her skirt.* [U] • *The wind is beginning to* **pick up** (= get stronger). [U] • *She ran* **like the** *wind* (= very fast) *to catch up.* [U] • To **get wind of** a piece of secret information is to hear about it: *I don't want my colleagues to get wind of the fact that I'm leaving in case they tell my boss.* • *(Br and Aus)* If something **puts/gets the wind up** someone it frightens them or causes them severe anxiety: *Tell them your father's a policeman – that'll put the wind up them!* • To **take the wind out of** someone's **sails** is to take away their confidence, anger or determination suddenly by doing or saying something that they are not expecting: *I was all ready to tell him that the relationship was over when he greeted me with a big bunch of flowers – it rather took the* *wind out of my sails.* • **Wind-chill** is the effect that wind has on how cold the air feels: *It's two degrees outside, but with the wind-chill* **factor** *it feels like minus five.* • **Wind chimes** are an arrangement of shells or small decorative shapes of metal or wood that hang from pieces of wire or string and make a gentle noise when moved by the wind. • A **wind gauge** is a device for measuring the force of the wind. • A **wind instrument** is a musical instrument whose sound is produced by blowing: *Saxophones and flutes are wind instruments.* • A **wind tunnel** is an enclosed passage or room through which currents of air of different strengths are forced in order to study the effects of moving air on aircraft and other vehicles travelling at various speeds. • A **wind turbine** is a tall structure with blades that are blown round by the wind and produce power to make electricity. • *"The wind of change is blowing through this continent* (= Africa)*, and, whether we like it or not, this growth of national consciousness is a political fact"'* (from a speech made by Harold Macmillan (Lord Stockton) at Cape Town, 1960) • *"Gone with the Wind"* (title of a book by Margaret Mitchell, 1936) • [PIC] **Energy**

wind·y /ˈwɪn·di/ *adj* **-ier, -iest** • *It was a windy night.* • *It was wet and windy for most of the week.*

wind [BREATH] /wɪnd/ *n* [U] breath or the ability to breathe • *I'd been running so I stopped to* **get my** *wind* (= let my breathing get slower and easier). • *(infml disapproving)* Wind is sometimes used to describe meaningless words and false claims: *I rarely bother to listen to politicians' speeches – it's all just wind.* [U]

wind *obj* /wɪnd/ *v* [T] • If you wind someone you make it difficult or temporarily impossible for them to breathe, usually by hitting them in the stomach.

wind·ed /ˈwɪn·dɪd/ *adj* [after v; not gradable] • If you are winded you are temporarily unable to breathe, either because you have been hit in the stomach or because you have just done some physical exercise: *Simon is so unfit – he gets winded just from walking up a flight of stairs.*

wind [DIGESTIVE PROBLEM] *Br and Aus* /wɪnd/, *Am* **gas** *n* [U] gas in the bowels or in a baby's stomach, esp. that which causes a feeling of being uncomfortable • *I like garlic but it gives me terrible wind.* • *The baby's crying a lot – do you think he's got a bit of wind?*

wind *obj Br* /wɪnd/, *Am and Aus* **burp** *v* [T] • If you wind a baby, you rub or very gently hit his or her back to allow air to come up from the stomach.

wind *(obj)* [TURN] /waɪnd/ *v past* **wound** /waʊnd/ to turn (something) or cause it to turn • *She wound the handle but nothing happened.* [T] • *Once she'd got into the car, she wound the window* **down/up** (= caused it to open/close by turning a handle). [M] • *Wind the cassette* **back/forward** *would you?* [M] • *(Br and Aus) Does this camera wind* **on** (= does the film in it move forward) *automatically?* [I always + adv/prep] • *That noise you can hear is the tape winding* **back**. [I always + adv/prep] • To wind **(up)** a clock or watch is to cause it to work by turning a key, handle or other device: *I've forgotten to wind my watch (up) again.* [T] • See also REWIND.

wind·er /£ˈwaɪn·dər, $-dɚ/ *n* [C] • *(Br)* A winder (*Am* **stem**) is a small KNOB (= round handle) on a watch, which you use for winding it. • A winder is also a key or handle for winding a clock. • [PIC] **Clocks and watches**

wind *obj* [WRAP AROUND] /waɪnd/ *v* [T always + adv/prep] *past* **wound** /waʊnd/ to wrap (something) around an object several times or twist it repeatedly around itself • *She wound a scarf* **around** *her neck.* • *He wound the string* **into** *a ball.* • *He wound a small bandage* **round** *her finger.* • *You take the hair back, wind it round and round until it's in a tight ball and then pin it.*

wind [FOLLOW BENDING ROUTE] /waɪnd/ *v* [I always + adv/prep] *past* **wound** /waʊnd/ (of a road, path or river) to follow a route which bends repeatedly in different directions • *The river winds through the valley.*

wind·ing /ˈwaɪn·dɪŋ/ *adj* • *There's a very long, winding path leading up to the house.*

wind down *(obj)* [END], **wind** *(obj)* **down** *v adv* to (cause to) end gradually or in stages • *They're winding down their operations abroad because they're losing money.* [M] • *The government intends to wind the scheme down in early spring.* [M] • *At last it seems the war is winding down.* [I] • *Unfortunately the party was just winding down as we got there.* [I]

wind down [RELAX], **un·wind** *v adv* [I] to relax and let your mind be free from anxiety after a period of work or some other activity that has made you anxious • *When he goes on holiday, it takes him the first couple of days just to wind down.* • *A lot of people find that music helps them to wind down.* • *It's one of the winding-down exercises that I do at the end of my aerobics class.*

wind up *obj* [FINISH], **wind** *obj* **up** *v adv* [M] to end (something) • *I think it's about time we wound this meeting up.* • *(Br and Aus)* To wind up a company is to close it down because it cannot pay its debts.

wind up [BECOME] *v adv infml* to come to be in an unexpected and usually unpleasant situation, esp. as a result of what you do • *If he carries on like this he's going to wind up in prison!* [I always + adv/prep] • *You don't want to wind up homeless, do you.* • *You could wind up having a huge debt to pay off if you're not careful.* [+ v-ing]

wind *obj* **up** [DECEIVE] *v adv* [T] *Br infml* to tell (someone) something that is not true as a joke or in order to annoy them • *Are you serious or are you just trying to wind me up?* • *It's really easy to wind her up because she just believes anything you tell her.*

wind–up /ˈwaɪnd·ʌp/ *n* [C usually sing] *Br infml* • *You can't be serious – is this a wind-up?*

wind *obj* **up** [ANNOY] *v adv* [T] *Br infml* to annoy or upset (someone) • *It really winds me up when he goes on about teachers having an easy life.* • *I'm able to just ignore him when he's being annoying but he gets Elaine really wound up.*

wind·bag /ˈwɪnd·bæg/ *n* [C] *infml disapproving* a person who talks too much about boring things • *The Labour leader gained an alarming reputation as a windbag.*

wind·break /ˈwɪnd·breɪk/ *n* [C] something which gives protection from the wind, such as a row of trees, a wall or (*Am also* **windscreen**) a piece of strong cloth fixed vertically in the ground • *A row of fir trees in the garden can serve as a useful windbreak.* • *We'd better take the windbreak down to the beach.*

wind·break·er /£ˈwɪndˌbreɪ·kər, $-kɚ/ *n* [C] *Am* a jacket which is made of a material which protects you from the wind • [PIC] **Coats and jackets**

wind·fall [UNEXPECTED MONEY] /£ˈwɪnd·fɔːl, $-fɑːl/ *n* [C] an amount of money that you win or receive from someone unexpectedly • *I had an unexpected windfall last week – an uncle who I'd scarcely even met died and left me a thousand pounds.*

wind·fall [FRUIT] /£ˈwɪnd·fɔːl, $-fɑːl/ *n* [C] a piece of fruit blown down from a tree • *I tend to leave the windfalls for the birds to pick at.*

wind·lass /ˈwɪnd·ləs/, **winch** *n* [C] a machine which lifts heavy objects by turning a chain or rope around a tube-shaped object

wind·mill /ˈwɪnd·mɪl/ *n* [C] a building or structure with large blades on the outside which, when turned by the force of the wind, provide the power for getting water out of the ground or crushing grain • *Gift shops in Holland are full of wooden shoes and miniature windmills.* • A windmill is also a **wind turbine**. See at WIND [CURRENT OF AIR]. • A windmill (*Am also* **pinwheel**) is also a child's toy which consists of a stick with brightly coloured pieces of plastic at one end which turn around when you blow them or hold the toy in the wind. • [PIC] **Mill**

win·dow [GLASS] /£ˈwɪn·dəʊ, $-doʊ/ *n* [C] a space usually filled with glass in the wall of a building or in a vehicle, to let light and air in and to allow people inside the building to see out • *Is it all right if I open/close the window?* • *Half the time when she's meant to be studying she's staring out of the window.* • *He was leaning out of the window.* • *I saw a child's face* **at** *the window.* • *She's got some wonderful plants* **in** *the window* (= on a surface at the bottom of the window). • *Someone had climbed in through the kitchen window in the night.* • *My son smashed the dining-room window with a cricket ball.* • *Could you give the side windows a wipe as well as the windscreen, please?* • *I particularly liked the cathedral's stained-glass windows.* • *Have you paid the window* **cleaner** (= person whose job is to clean the outside of windows)? • *The window* **frames** *are rotting.* • *(fig.) The film provides a window* **on** *the immigrant experience* (= shows other people what it is like). • *So that's another idea* **out (of) the window** (= that is useless or to be got rid of)! • In an envelope, a window is a transparent rectangle on the front through which you can read the address written on the letter inside. • In a shop, a window consists of the decorative arrangement of goods behind the window in addition to the window itself: *How much is the jacket* **in** *the window?* ○ *The shop windows are wonderful around Christmas time.* • A **window box** is a box filled with earth

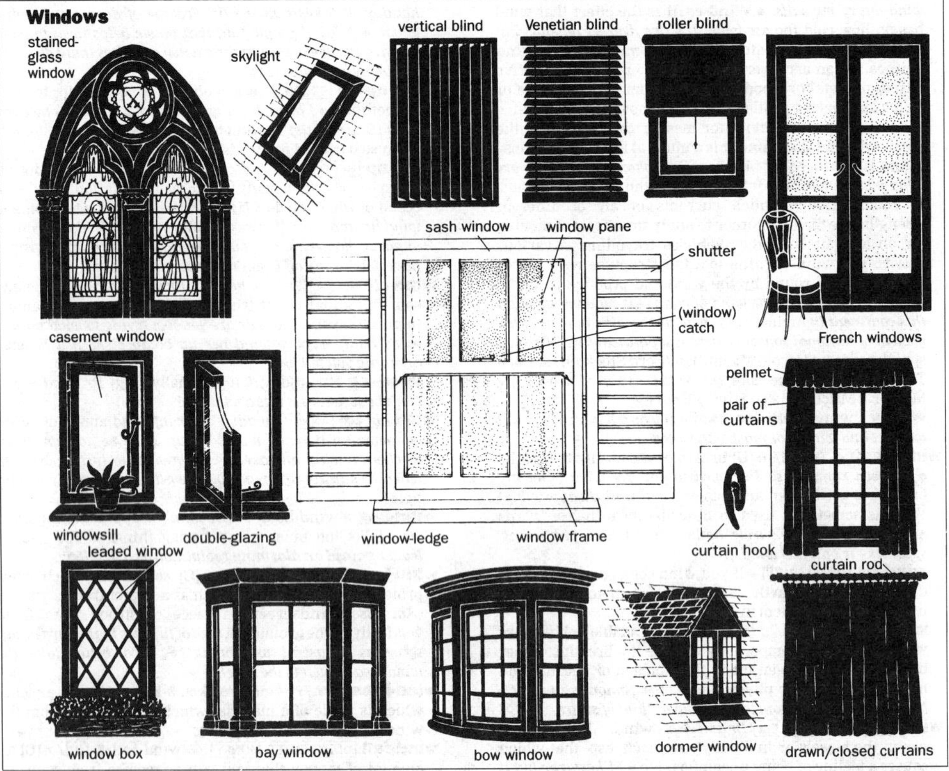

for growing decorative plants in, which is put on an outside WINDOWSILL: *window boxes full of brightly coloured geraniums* • **Window dressing** is the skill of decorating shop windows and arranging goods in them so that they look attractive to people going past. • *(disapproving)* **Window dressing** is also anything extra which is said or done in order to make an attractive effect but which is of no real importance: *Never mind the extra day's holiday, the free health care, and all the other window dressing in the company's offer – the point is, how much more money are we getting?* • A **window-ledge** is a WINDOWSILL (= a shelf below a window). • A **window seat** is a seat on a train, aircraft or other, esp. public, vehicle which is next to a window: *I always like a window seat on an aeroplane so that I can gaze out at the views.* • A **window seat** is also a seat in a building which is below a window: *It was one of those rooms with a big bay window and a window seat.* • *(Am)* A **window shade** is a BLIND (= a cover for a window). • If you go **window-shopping**, or you **window-shop**, you spend time looking at the goods on sale in shop windows without intending to buy any of them. (KOR) • PIC› **Accommodation, Window**

win·dow COMPUTER /£ˈwɪn·dəʊ, $-doʊ/ *n* [C] an area of a computer screen which shows a particular type of information

win·dow OPPORTUNITY /£ˈwɪn·dəʊ, $-doʊ/ *n* [C] a period when there is an opportunity to do something • *There might be a window in his busy schedule next Friday when he could see you.* • *There's a* **launch** *window for the space shuttle on the 14th of next month.* • *If a* **window of opportunity** (= an opportunity) *should present itself I'd be a fool not to take advantage of it.*

win·dow·pane /£ˈwɪn·dəʊ·peɪn, $-doʊ-/ *n* [C] a single piece of glass in the window of a building • *One of the windowpanes in the dining-room is broken.*

win·dow·sill /£ˈwɪn·dəʊ·sɪl, $-doʊ-/, **win·dow–ledge** /£ˈwɪn·dəʊ·ledʒ, $-doʊ-/ *n* [C] a shelf below a window, either inside or outside a building • *He's got a few plants in pots on the windowsill.*

wind·pipe /ˈwɪnd·paɪp/, *medical* **trach·e·a** *n* [C] the tube in the body which carries air that has been breathed in from the upper end of the throat to the lungs • *A bit of food went down my windpipe and gave me a coughing fit.*

wind·screen *Br and Aus* /ˈwɪnd·skriːn/, *Am* **wind·shield** /ˈwɪnd·ʃiːld/ *n* [C] the window at the front of a car or other four-wheeled vehicle • *You'd better give your windscreen a clean – it's filthy.* • Windscreen is also *Am for* WINDBREAK. • *(Br)* A **windscreen wiper** (*Am* **windshield wiper**) is a rubber-edged blade, often one of a pair, which moves repeatedly against the outside of a windscreen, clearing it of rain or snow. • PIC› **Car**

wind·sock /£ˈwɪnd·sɒk, $-sɑːk/ *n* [C] a tube of cloth fastened at one end to a pole which shows the direction of the wind at an airport

wind·surf·er /£ˈwɪnd,sɜː·fəʳ, $-,sɜːr·fɚ/, **sail·board** *n* [C] *trademark* a narrow board with a sail fixed to it which you hold, standing up, while the wind blows you along the surface of a sea or lake • A windsurfer is also someone who goes windsurfing.

wind·surf /£ˈwɪnd·sɜːf, $-sɜːrf/ *v* [I] • *Where do you windsurf?*

wind·surf·ing /£ˈwɪnd,sɜː·fɪŋ, $-,sɜːr-/ *n* [U] • *I went windsurfing most afternoons.* • Compare **surfing** at SURF. • PIC› **Water sports**

wind·swept /ˈwɪnd·swept/ *adj* (of places) open to and not protected from strong winds, or (of people) having hair that is untidy and (looks as if it has been) blown in different directions by the wind • *We drove down to the windswept Atlantic coast of Portugal.* • *The report said that football grounds were 'nasty, cold and windswept places.'* • *She had that windswept look so fashionable among young people these days.*

wind·ward /£ˈwɪnd·wəd, $-wɚd/ *adj, adv* [not gradable] *specialized* (on the side of a hill, etc.) facing the wind • *On the windward leg of the race the wind was strong.* • Compare LEEWARD.

wind·y /ˈwɪn·di/ *adj* See at WIND CURRENT OF AIR

wine /waɪn/ *n* an alcoholic drink made from GRAPES, or less commonly an alcoholic drink made in a similar way but from other fruits or flowers • *a wine cellar/connoisseur/cooler/glass* • *red/white/dry/sweet/sparkling/table wine* [U] • *Shall we have a* **bottle/glass of** *wine with dinner?* [U] • *I love Australian wines, especially the white wines.* [C] • *We've been invited to a wine-tasting evening.* [U] • *Would you like to see the wine* **list**, *sir?* [U] • *She makes her own elderberry wine.* [U] • A **wine bar** is a bar or small restaurant which serves mainly wines. • A **wine rack** is a wooden and metal frame used to store bottles of wine horizontally. • PIC〉 **Bottles and flasks, Rack**

wine /waɪn/ *v* • If you **wine and dine** someone you entertain them by giving them food and drink: *The survey concludes that most women like to be wined and dined on the first few dates.*

wing STRUCTURE FOR FLYING /wɪŋ/ *n* [C] the movable, usually flat, part of the body which a bird, insect or BAT uses for flying, or one of the flat horizontal structures that stick out from the side of an aircraft and support it when it is flying • *the delicacy of a butterfly's wings* • *I much prefer the white breast-meat of the chicken to the wing.* • *I could see the plane's wing out of my window.* • *(literary)* A bird that is **on the wing** is flying. • If you **take** someone **under** your **wing** you start to protect and take care of them: *I was a bit lonely and fed up at the time and she took me under her wing.* • A **wing chair** is a chair with a high back from which large side pieces stick out. • A **wing collar** is the strip of material which goes around the neck on a man's formal shirt and is folded down into the shape of two small triangles at the front. • A **wing nut** is a NUT (=small metal fastening device) which has two flat pieces on it that you can hold with your fingers while tightening it. • *"Comin' in on a wing and a prayer"* (title of a song written by Harold Adamson, based on the remark of an airplane pilot, 1943) • PIC〉 **Aircraft, Birds, Chair, Clothes, Tools, Wing**

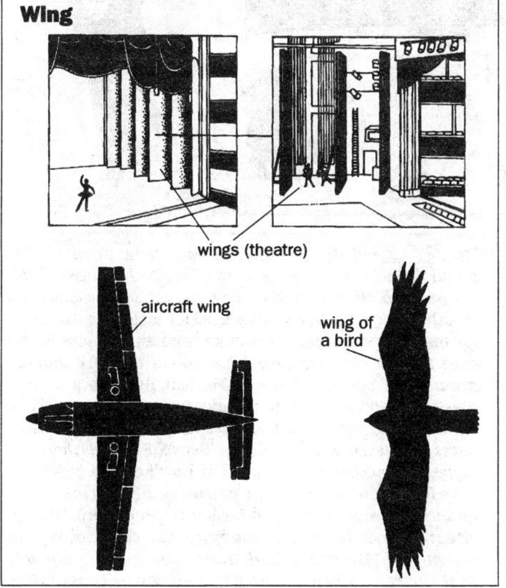

winged /wɪŋd, ˈwɪŋ·ɪd/ *adj* [before n; not gradable] • *a high-winged aeroplane* • A winged animal or form has wings: *The winged adult mosquitos emerge from the pupae.* ○ *Cupid is usually depicted as a winged boy with a bow and arrow.*

wing POLITICAL GROUP /wɪŋ/ *n* [C] a group within a political party or organization whose beliefs are in some way different from those of the main group • *The president is on the* **left/right** *wing of the Democratic party.*

wing PART OF BUILDING /wɪŋ/ *n* [C] a part of a large building which sticks out from the main part, often having been added at a later date • *The maternity ward will be in the new wing of the hospital.* • *The west wing of the house is still lived in by Lord and Lady Carlton, while the rest of the house is open to the public.*

wing PART OF CAR *Br* /wɪŋ/, *Am* **fend·er** *n* [C] one of the four parts at the side of a car which go over the wheels • *There's a dent in the left wing.* • *Look in your wing* **mirror**. • PIC〉 **Car**

wing SPORTS /wɪŋ/ *n* [C] (in various team games, such as football and HOCKEY) either of the two sides of the sports field, or a player whose position is at either of the two sides of the field • *Minelli passes the ball to Hernandez out there on the wing.* • *I used to play wing defence in the school netball team.* • *He played* **left/right** *wing for Manchester United.*

wing·er /£ˈwɪŋ·əʳ, $-ɚ/ *n* [C] • In various team games, such as football and HOCKEY, a winger is a player whose position is at either of the two sides of the field: *Liverpool have just spent £800 000 on the talented 25-year-old winger.*

wings /wɪŋz/ *pl n* **the wings** the sides of a stage which cannot be seen by the people watching the play • *I was standing* **in** *the wings waiting for my cue to come on stage.* • PIC〉 **Wing**

wing·span /ˈwɪŋ·spæn/ *n* [C] the distance between the ends of the wings of a bird, insect or aircraft • *Future versions of the Boeing 747 will have a wingspan at least 30 ft wider than today's jumbos.* • *The female bird is slightly taller and her wingspan measures a metre and a half.*

wink /wɪŋk/ *v* [I] to close one eye briefly as a way of greeting someone or showing friendliness, affection, sexual attraction etc., or of showing that you are not serious about something you have said • *She winked* **at** *me as he turned his back.* • *For a moment I thought he was being serious, but then he winked* **at** *me.* • *Ugh! That revolting old man at the bar just winked* **at** *me in a horribly suggestive way.* • *(fig.) Reflected in the water, the lights winked* (=flashed) **at** *us from the other side of the lake.* • If you **wink at** something bad that is happening, you pretend not to notice it because that is more convenient to you: *Politicians continue to criticize people who buy foreign goods while winking at the country's continuing dependence on foreign energy sources.* • Ⓢ

wink /wɪŋk/ *n* [C] • *He* **gave** *me a conspiratorial wink as they left the room.* • If you **don't sleep a wink** or you **don't get a wink of sleep** you don't manage to sleep despite trying to: *I didn't get a wink of sleep last night with that party going on next door.*

wink·le /ˈwɪŋ·kl̩/, *Am usually* **per·i·wink·le** *n* [C] a small edible sea SNAIL (=small soft animal with a shell on its back)

wink·le out *obj*, **wink·le** *obj* **out** /ˈwɪŋ·kl̩/ *v adv* [M] *esp. Br* to obtain or find (something or someone) with difficulty • *Somehow they managed to winkle out the traitor in their midst.*

win·nings /ˈwɪn·ɪŋz/ *pl n* See at WIN

win·now *obj* /£ˈwɪn·əʊ, $-oʊ/ *v* [T] to blow the CHAFF (=the outer coverings) from (grain) before it can be used as food, or *(fig.)* reduce (a large number of people or things) to a much smaller number by judging their quality • *the winnowing wind* • *We've winnowed* **down** *the bunch of people that we originally saw and come up with a short-list of eight.*

win·o /£ˈwaɪ·nəʊ, $-noʊ/ *n* [C] *pl* **winos** *infml* a person, esp. a homeless person, who drinks too much wine or other alcoholic drink • *There were the usual bunch of winos outside the station.*

win·some /ˈwɪn·səm/ *adj literary approving* (esp. of people) attractive and pleasing, esp. because of child-like qualities • *Maria brought along her oldest daughter – a winsome lass with brown eyes and a ready smile.* • *(disapproving)* You can also call someone or something winsome if you think they are too charming, esp. in pretending to be like a child: *It's that winsome smile of hers that makes me want to hit her.*

win·some·ly /ˈwɪn·səm·li/ *adv*

win·ter /£ˈwɪn·təʳ, $-t̬ɚ/ *n* the season between autumn and spring, lasting from November to March north of the equator and from May to September south of the equator, when the weather is coldest • *Last winter we went skiing.* [C] • *It's been a surprisingly mild winter.* [C] • *Winter's a depressing season.* [U] • *I think you tend to eat more* **in the** *winter.* [U] • *I find it difficult to get up on these dark winter mornings.* [U] • *I prefer winter clothes to summer clothes.* [U] • **Winter sports** are sports that are done on snow or ice: *a winter-sports holiday* ○ *Skiing and skating are winter sports.* • *"Now is the winter of our discontent / Made glorious summer by this sun of York"* (Shakespeare, Richard III 1.1.)

win·ter /£ˈwɪn·təʳ, $-t̬ɚ/ *v* [I always + adv/prep] • *Birds migrate so that they can winter* (=spend the winter) *in a warmer country.* • *Kuwait Bay is one of the world's most important wintering grounds for wading birds.*

win·try /ˈwɪn·tri/ *adj* • Wintry means typical of winter: *It looks like this wintry weather is here to stay.* ○ *This afternoon we may see some wintry* **showers** (=snow mixed with rain) *over higher ground.* ○ *Wintry conditions are making roads hazardous for drivers in the northeast of England.* ○ *Not a sound broke the silence of the wintry landscape.* ○ *(fig.) She gave a wintry* (=cold and unfriendly) *smile and said nothing.*

win·ter·time /£ˈwɪn·tə·taɪm, $-t̬ɚ-/ *n* [U] the season of winter • *Horses acquire a thicker coat* **in** *wintertime to*

keep them warm. • *Like most seaside resorts* **in the** *wintertime, it's quite deserted.*

wipe *(obj)* /waɪp/ *v* to slide something, esp. a piece of cloth, over the surface of (something else), in order to remove (dirt, food or liquid) • *Have you got a cloth that I can wipe the floor with?* [T] • *I'll just get a sponge and wipe the crumbs off the table.* [T] • *Don't wipe your nose* **on** *your sleeve – that's what your handkerchief's for!* [T] • *Someone has wiped their dirty hands* **on** *my nice clean towel!* [T] • *I was just wiping* **up** *the soup that you spilt in the kitchen.* [M] • *(Br and Aus) If you wash, I'll wipe* (=dry the washed plates, etc. with a cloth). [I] • *(Br and Aus) When you've wiped* **up** *(the dishes), don't forget to put them away.* [I/T] • If you wipe information, images or sound **off** a computer, VIDEO or CASSETTE, you remove it: *Everything was wiped off my diskette when I entered the wrong command!* [M] • *(infml)* To **wipe the floor with** a person or a team is to defeat them by a very large amount: *"I hear Italy beat France in the semi-finals last night." "Beat them? They wiped the floor with them!"* • *There are bombs so powerful that whole nations could be* **wiped off the map/wiped off the face of the earth** (=destroyed totally) *by them.* • To **wipe the slate clean** is to start a new and better way of behaving, forgetting about any bad experiences in the past: *A new relationship presents you with the opportunity to wipe the slate clean.* • *Tell him you saw Helena at the cinema with another guy – that should* **wipe the smile off** *his* **face** (=make him less satisfied with and proud of himself)*!*

wipe /waɪp/ *n* [C] • A wipe is an act of wiping: *I'd better* **give** *the floor a quick wipe before someone slips on it.* ○ **Give** *the table a wipe with this cloth, would you?* • A wipe is also a piece of cloth or soft paper that you use for wiping: *a baby wipe*

wipe out *obj* [DESTROY], **wipe** *obj* **out** *v adv* [M] to destroy totally • *Whole villages were wiped out in the fighting.* • *One bad harvest could wipe out all of a grower's profits for the previous two years.*

wipe out [LOSE CONTROL] *v adv* [I] *esp. Am* to lose control, esp. of a vehicle, and have an accident • *I was going too fast and I wiped out on the bend.* • *She wiped out skiing down the big slope and broke both her legs.*

wiped out [TIRED] /waɪpt/ *adj* [after v] *infml* extremely tired • *After that 5-mile run I was completely wiped out!*

wiped out [DRUNK] /waɪpt/ *adj* [after v] *Am slang* suffering from the effects of drinking alcohol or taking drugs

wire [METAL THREAD] /£waɪəʳ, $waɪr/ *n* (a piece of) thin metal thread which can be bent • *We fixed a (piece of) wire across the bottom of the doorway, so that anyone who comes in will touch it.* [C/U] • Wire is used for fastening things and for making particular types of strong items: *a wire basket/cage/fence* • *wire-cutters* ○ *I had to cut the wire that was around the package.* [U] • Wire, usually with a layer of plastic around it, is also used for carrying electric currents: *Someone had cut the telephone wires.* [C] ○ *Don't touch those wires whatever you do.* [C] ○ *Electrical fittings had been ripped out exposing bare wires.* [C] • **The** wire can be the wire fence round a prison or **prison camp**: *During the war he spent three years* **behind** *the wire* (= in prison). [U] • If a situation goes **(down) to the wire**, the result of it is not known until the end: *I think the election will go right down to the wire.* • When people **get** their **wires crossed** they have a different understanding of the same situation: *We got our wires crossed, she thought I said the train left at 3 o'clock in the afternoon, when in fact it leaves at 3 o'clock in the morning.* • A **wire brush** is a brush with pieces of wire fixed into it, used esp. for cleaning metal. • A dog that is **wire-haired** has stiff, rough hair: *a wire-haired dachshund* • **Wire netting** is a net made of twisted wire which is often used for fences. • **Wire-tapping** is the action of secretly listening to other people's conversations by connecting a listening device to their telephone: *If he suspected an employee of dishonesty he was not above wire-tapping.* • **Wire wool** is *Br for* **steel wool**. See at STEEL [METAL]. • See also TRIPWIRE.

wire *obj* /£waɪəʳ, $waɪr/ *v* [T] • *She had her jaws wired* **together** (=fastened together with wire) *so that she wouldn't be able to eat.* • *The stereo didn't work because he hadn't wired it* **up** *properly.* • *Nearly one home in ten across the country is wired* **(up)** *to receive TV via cable.* • *(Br)* A person or place that is **wired up** *(Am wired)* is secretly equipped with an electric device that records conversations.

wir·ing /£ˈwaɪə·rɪŋ, $ˈwaɪr·ɪŋ/ *n* [U] • The wiring in a building is the system of wires that carry electricity: *The club closed after the fire brigade declared its wiring to be unsafe.*

wir·y /£ˈwaɪə·ri, $ˈwaɪr·i/ *adj* **-ier, -iest** • Wiry **hair** is strong, thick and rough to touch. • See also WIRY.

wire *obj* [SEND MESSAGE] /£waɪəʳ, $waɪr/ *v* [T] *esp. Am* to send (a message) using an electrical communication system, esp. to send (an amount of money) to someone in this way • *The insurance company wired millions of dollars* **to** *its accounts to cover the payments.* • *Luckily my father wired me two hundred bucks.* [+ two objects] • In the past to wire someone was to send them a TELEGRAM: *Janet wired me to say she'd be here a day later than planned.*

wire /£waɪəʳ, $waɪr/ *n* [C] *esp. Am* • *I got a wire this morning telling me my grandpa had died.* • A **wire service** is an organization that supplies news to newspapers, radio and television stations, etc. using an electrical communication system.

wired ANXIOUS /£waɪəd, $waɪrd/, **wired up** *adj* [after v] *Am infml* nervous or anxious about a future event • *I was totally wired before the interview – I mean I didn't sleep for about two nights.*

wired ARRANGED /£waɪəd, $waɪrd/ *adj* [not gradable] **have** *something* **wired** *Am slang* to be certain that something is already arranged or done • *She said she'd have to advertise the job, but that I shouldn't worry, I had it wired* (= I would certainly get it).

wire·less /£ˈwaɪə·ləs, $ˈwaɪr-/ *n* [C] *Br dated* a radio • *It was one of those wartime scenes of a whole family sitting around a wireless.*

wir·y /£ˈwaɪə·ri, $ˈwaɪr·i/ *adj* **-ier, -iest** (of people and animals) thin but strong, and often able to bend easily • *Like a lot of good marathon runners he's very wiry.* • *She has a dancer's wiry frame.* • See also **wiry** at WIRE METAL THREAD.

wise CLEVER /waɪz/ *adj* **-r, -st** *approving* possessing or showing the ability to make good judgments, based on a deep understanding and experience of life • *She's a very wise woman, my aunt – it's worth listening to her views on almost anything.* • *"No more wine for me, thank you, I never have more than four glasses." "How wise of you."* • *Looking at the weather, I think we made a wise decision not to go to the coast this weekend.* • *I think it/you would be wiser* **to** *wait and see how much money you've got left before you make any decisions.* [+ to infinitive] • *Was it Thomas More who said that the wise man learns from the experience of others?* • *(infml)* If you *(Am)* **act** wise or *(esp. Am)* **get** wise **with** someone, you act or speak in a way that shows you do not respect them: *Don't get wise with me, young man – when I say no talking in class, I mean it!* ○ *She was always acting wise in high school, ridiculing her teachers and cutting classes.* • *(infml)* If you **are** wise **to** or **get** wise **to** a dishonest situation or way of doing something, you know about it or you start, because of experience, to understand it and begin to take advantage of it yourself: *When I started working for myself I used to be scrupulously honest with the tax office – then I got wise to the game!* • *I listened very hard to your explanation but I'm afraid I'm still* **no wiser/none the** *wiser* (= I still don't understand). • *I never used to save any money but now that I'm a little* **older and** *wiser I can see the sense in it.* • *(infml disapproving)* You might call someone a **wise guy** who annoys you by trying to show how much greater their knowledge is than yours: **Okay,** *wise guy, if you're so damned smart, you can tell everyone how it's done!* • *(saying, esp. Br and Aus)* 'It's easy to be wise after the event' means that it is easy to understand what you could have done to prevent something bad from happening after it has happened: *In retrospect I suppose we should have insisted on checking inside, but then it's easy to be wise after the event.* • *"It is a wise father that knows his own child"* (Shakespeare, Merchant of Venice 2.1)

wise up /waɪz/ *v adv* [I] *esp. Am infml* • If someone wises up to an unpleasant situation or a fact, they start to understand the truth, although it is difficult or unpleasant to accept: *Come on, wise up, Frank, life isn't like that and you should know it!* ○ *She hasn't yet wised up* **to** *the fact that her boyfriend is not all that he pretends to be.*

wise·ly /ˈwaɪz·li/ *adv* • *Sian had very wisely left the party before all the trouble started.* • *Invest your money wisely through Home Counties Savings Trust.*

wis·dom /ˈwɪz·dəm/ *n* [U] • *One certainly hopes to gain a little wisdom as one grows older.* • *He's got a weekly radio programme in which he* **dispenses** *wisdom* (= gives his opinions) *on a variety of subjects.* • *I tend to* **doubt** *the wisdom of separating a child from its family whatever the circumstances.* • *Did we ever stop to* **question** *the wisdom of going to war?* • *Before I went off to university my father gave me a few* **words of** *wisdom.* • *Unfortunately the council,* **in** *their* **wisdom** (= for some reason that I do not completely understand but consider stupid), *have decided I must pay back the money they lent me immediately.* • **Conventional/ Received/Popular** *wisdom* (= What most people think) *has it that women are more emotional than men, but in my experience it often just isn't the case.* • **With the wisdom of hindsight** (= Because of experience) *we now know that the old-fashioned aerosol sprays were a mistake.* • Your **wisdom teeth** are the four teeth at the back of the JAW that are the last to grow: *She's having her wisdom teeth out.*

-wise IN THIS WAY /-waɪz/ *combining form* in this way or in this direction • *As an actor he had his own peculiar way of walking crabwise across a stage.* • *Cut the fish open lengthwise.* • *That's interesting – you use the spoon clockwise to whip food and I do it in the opposite direction.*

-wise RELATING TO /-waɪz/ *combining form infml* relating to • *What shall we do foodwise – do you fancy going out to eat?* • *Moneywise, of course, I'm much better off than I used to be.* • *What do we need to take with us clothes-wise?* • *We were very lucky weather-wise yesterday.*

wise·crack /ˈwaɪz·kræk/ *n* [C] *infml* a remark which is intended as a clever joke, esp. one which criticizes someone • *He* **made** *some wisecrack about my lack of culinary ability.*

wise·crack·ing /ˈwaɪzˌkræk·ɪŋ/ *n* [U], *adj* [before n] *infml* • *Sadly, despite the crazy antics and the relentless wisecracking, there's very little plot to carry this film.* • *I sometimes wonder what's behind that wisecracking manner of his.*

wish REGRET /wɪʃ/ *v* [+ *(that)* clause; not *be wishing*] to desire some situation that is different from the one that exists in reality • Wish can be used with the past simple tense to express regret about a state or situation that exists at the moment: *I wish* **(that)** *I didn't have to go to work today.* ○ *I wish* **(that)** *I was/were a bit taller.* ○ *I wish* **(that)** *you were coming with me, Peter.* • Wish can be used with the past perfect tense to express regret about a particular action in the past: *I wish* **(that)** *I hadn't said that!* ○ *I wish* **(that)** *I hadn't eaten so much.* ○ *I bet she wishes* **(that)** *she'd never got involved in the whole affair.*

wish DESIRE /wɪʃ/ *n* [C] a desire for something • *It was grandpa's greatest wish* **that** *one of his grandchildren would become a doctor.* [+ *that* clause] • *Did he express any wish* **to** *see me?* [+ *to* infinitive] • *In accordance with his wishes* (= what he wanted), *he was buried next to his wife.* • *They've deliberately gone against my wishes and sold the apartment.* • **Wish-fulfillment** is the achievement of real desires in imaginary situations, mainly in dreams, but also in films, literature and poetry: *Men, in these dramas of female wish-fulfillment, are reduced to the status of playthings.*

wish *(obj)* /wɪʃ/ *v* • *(fml) We could go to the cinema or we could go out for dinner – whatever you wish.* [T] • *(fml) "Shall we ask Diana if she'd like to come to the theatre tonight?" "If/As you wish."* [I] • *(fml) I wish* **to** *make a complaint.* [+ *to* infinitive] • *(fml) Passengers wishing* **to** *take the Kings Cross train should go to platform 9.* [+ *to* infinitive] • *(fml) I don't wish* **to** *worry you but he did say he'd be back by midnight.* [+ *to* infinitive] • *Sometimes I was so low I wished myself dead.* [T + obj + adj] • Wish can be used to express annoyance: *I wish she'd shut up for a moment and let someone else speak.* [+ *(that)* clause] ○ *I wish you'd look at me when I'm trying to speak to you!* [+ *(that)* clause] ○ *I wish you wouldn't keep calling me 'dear'.* [+ *(that)* clause]

wish MAGIC /wɪʃ/ *n* [C] a hope that is made real with magical powers • *If I could have just one wish I suppose it would be* **that** *all the fighting in the world would stop tomorrow.* [+ *that* clause] • *Close your eyes and* **make** *a wish.* • *It's that bit in the story where the fairy* **grants** *the little girl three wishes.* • *May all your wishes come true.*

wish *(obj)* /wɪʃ/ *v* • *I remember blowing out the candles on my birthday cake and wishing* **that** *John Lee would be my boyfriend.* [+ *that* clause] • *You're not allowed to tell me what you wished* **for** *or it won't come true.* [I] • *If I could wish myself anywhere in the world* (= go anywhere as a result of making a wish) *right now it would be somewhere hot and sunny.* [T] • *He's funny, bright, handsome – everything a girl could wish* **for really.** [I] • *Being shut in a room with Dina all afternoon was like a nightmare – really I* **wouldn't wish** *it* **on anyone/on** *my* **worst enemy** (= wouldn't want anyone to suffer in that way)*!*

wish *obj* HOPE /wɪʃ/ *v* [+ two objects] to hope or express hope for another person's success or happiness or pleasure on a particular occasion • *We wish you every success in the future.* • *I didn't even see her to wish her a happy birthday/ wish a happy birthday* **to** *her.* • *I wished her a safe journey and waved her off.* • *So you've started up your own business – I* **wish** *you* **well** (= hope you will succeed).

wish·es /ˈwɪʃ·ɪz/ *pl n* • *Do* **give/send** *Patrick my* **best** *wishes* **for** *a speedy recovery.* • *He ended the letter "***Best** *wishes/***All good** *wishes, John."*

wish·bone /£ˈwɪʃ·bəun, $-boun/ *n* [C] the V-shaped bone between the neck and breast of a cooked bird which traditionally is removed from the bird and pulled apart by two people, allowing the one who gets the longer piece to make a secret wish

wish·ful think·ing /ˈwɪʃ·fᵊl/ *n* [U] the imagining or discussion of a very unlikely future event or situation as if it were possible and might one day happen • *Mike and I were talking about the sort of house that we'd like to buy – it's just wishful thinking really, since we can't even sell this one.*

wish·y–wash·y /£ˈwɪʃ·iˌwɒʃ·i, $-ˌwɑː·ʃi/ *adj infml disapproving* lacking in colour, firm ideas, principles or noticeable qualities of any type • *Politically they're neither right-wing nor left – just a bunch of wishy-washy pseudo-liberals.* • *She uses very pale colours in her paintings which are a bit wishy-washy for my taste.*

wisp /wɪsp/ *n* [C] a delicate, thin and sometimes twisting piece or line of something • *soft wisps* **of** *baby hair* • *A few wisps* **of** *hay still clung to her skirt.* • *Blue wisps* **of** *cigarette smoke curled in the air.* • *(fig.) Like most ballet dancers she was a wisp* **of a** *creature* (= very thin and delicate).

wisp·y /ˈwɪs·pi/ *adj* **-ier, -iest** • *Do you want a wispy fringe or something heavier?*

wis·te·ri·a /£wɪˈstɪə·ri·ə, $-ˈstɪr·i-/ *n* [U/C] a climbing plant with groups of small purple, blue or white flowers hanging from it

wist·ful /ˈwɪst·fᵊl/ *adj* sad and thinking about something that is impossible or past • *She cast a wistful glance at her friend's invitation and wished she had been invited to the party.* • *As his granddaughter talked about her life in the theatre, he began to* **grow** *wistful* **about** *his own days as an actor.*

wist·ful·ly /ˈwɪst·fᵊl·i/ *adv* • *She gazed wistfully at the chocolate cake in the shop window and wished she wasn't on a diet.* • *"I would love to go back to Venice," he said wistfully.*

wist·ful·ness /ˈwɪst·fᵊl·nəs/ *n* [U] • *"Congratulations on your promotion," she said, trying to keep the trace of wistfulness out of her voice.*

wit HUMOUR /wɪt/ *n* the ability to use words in a clever and humorous way • *She has an infectious smile and a* **ready/sharp** *wit.* [U] • *He is a born politician whose speeches crackle with a* **dry, biting** *wit.* [U] • *Her conversation sparkled with her own subtle blend of wit and charm.* [U] • *His caustic/cutting/savage* (= cruelly clever) *wit comes through strongly in his writing.* [U] • A person who is skilled at using words in a clever and humorous way can be called a wit: *Sydney Smith, a notable wit, once remarked that he never read a book before he reviewed it because it might prejudice his opinion of it.* [C] • See also WITS; WITTICISM.

wit·ty /£ˈwɪt·i, $ˈwɪt̬-/ *adj* **-ier, -iest** • *a witty comment/remark* • *She is well-known for being one of the wittiest people on television.* • *You may think you're very witty calling him names, but I think you're just being rude.*

wit·ti·ly /£ˈwɪt·ɪ·li, $ˈwɪt̬-/ *adv* • *"We're going to a dinner party not a fancy dress party," she wittily* **remarked** *as he walked into the room wearing a green shirt and pink tie.*

wit THAT IS /wɪt/ *v* **to wit** *fml* that is to say • To wit is used to introduce a statement, esp. in official writing such as legal documents: *Several pieces of major legislation have been introduced in the US over the past few years, to wit: the Americans With Disabilities Act, the Clean Air Act and the Civil Rights Act.*

witch /wɪtʃ/ *n* [C] a woman who is believed to have magical powers and who uses them to harm or help other people • *Witches were persecuted all over western Europe from the 15th to the 17th century as it was claimed that they had dealings with the Devil.* • *The negative image of a witch in popular culture is an evil old woman stirring a simmering cauldron and casting spells, who wears a black cloak and a tall pointed hat and carries a broomstick.* • *(infml disapproving)* A woman who is considered ugly or evil is sometimes called a witch. • *(infml) What's that* **witches' brew** (= unpleasant liquid mixture, of which you do not know the contents) *you're concocting there – surely you don't expect me to drink it?* • *(disapproving)* A **witch-hunt** is an attempt to find and punish people whose opinions are unpopular and who are said to be a danger to society: *In America in the 1950s, Senator Joseph McCarthy led a witch-hunt* **against** *people suspected of being communists.* • See also BEWITCH. Compare WIZARD. • PIC **Imaginary creatures**

witch·craft /£ˈwɪtʃ·krɑːft, $-kræft/ *n* [U] the activity of performing magic to help or harm other people • *It used to be thought that women who* **practised** *witchcraft had a pact with the Devil.* • *Witchcraft is now a recognized religion in the United States.*

witch·doc·tor /£ˈwɪtʃˌdɒk·təʳ, $-ˌdɑːk·tɚ/ *n* [C] a person in some societies who cures people using traditional magic or medicine; a SHAMAN • *In tribal S America, the witchdoctor is responsible for healing people with herbal remedies and exorcising evil spirits using magic.* • *Witchdoctors have been integrated into health teams in many African countries, so that their skills in traditional medicine can be studied.*

witch–haz·el /ˈwɪtʃˌheɪ·zᵊl/, *Br* **wych–haz·el** *n* a small flowering tree, or liquid from this tree which is used as a medicine • *Witch-hazel has cheerful yellow flowers in winter, before the leaves appear.* [C] • *She put some witch-hazel on the child's leg to help reduce the bruising.* [U]

witch·ing /ˈwɪtʃ·ɪŋ/ *adj* [not gradable] **the witching hour** the time when witches are said to appear, usually 12 o'clock at night

with COMPANY /wɪð/ *prep* in the company or presence of (a person or thing) • *She's in the kitchen with her father.* • *He lives with his grandmother.* • *He's an impossible person to work with.* • *I'm going to France with a couple of friends.* • *Ingrid Bergman starred with Humphrey Bogart in the film 'Casablanca'.* • *You can leave your coats with the cloakroom attendant.* • *Could I have some ice cream with my apple pie, please?* • *Does the vacuum cleaner have attachments with it or are they sold separately?* • *Mix the butter with the sugar and then add the beaten egg.* • *I'll be with you* (= I will give you my attention) *in a moment.* • *She's staying with her parents* (= at their house) *for a few months.* • *He's been with the department* (= working in it) *since 1982.* • *She's been with The Times* (= working for it) *for the past two years.* • *Did you know that spectacles have been with us* (= they have existed) *since the 14th century?* • *(infml, slightly dated)* Someone who is **with it** knows about present ideas and fashions: *He reads all the style magazines and thinks he's really with it.* ○ *Don't you know anything about computers? Come on, Grandma,* **get** *with it!* • *(infml dated)* Something that is **with it** is fashionable: *He was wearing a very with-it-***looking** *tie.* • See also **with it** at WITH UNDERSTANDING.

with METHOD /wɪð/ *prep* using (something) • *He was shot at close range with a pistol.* • *She wiped her lipstick off with a tissue.* • *Fix the two pieces together with glue.* • *I paid for the jacket with the vouchers I'd been given for Christmas.* • *Sylvester Stallone shot to fame with his leading role in the film, 'Rocky'.* • *Please handle this package with care.* • *They set up a business with the help of a bank loan.* • 'With' refers to the object used for doing an action, 'by' (with a passive verb) refers to the person or object that performs the action: *The car window was smashed by the thief with a baseball bat.*

with DESCRIPTION /wɪð/ *prep* having or possessing • *I'd like a double room with a sea view.* • *She left school with no qualifications.* • *He's married with three children and lives in Oxford.* • *The doctor spoke with a soft Irish accent.* • *We're an international company with offices in Paris, New York and Sydney.* • *Two coffees please, one with milk and one without.* • *The moisturizer with natural plant extracts costs $3·50.* • *You'll need to speak to the tall woman with fair hair.* • *He arrived in Los Angeles with nothing but the clothes he was wearing.* • *They found it difficult living in a cottage with no running water.* • *He woke up in the morning with a dreadful headache.* • *I was second in the race with a time of 14·2 seconds.* • *With a bit of luck, we should be back in time for dinner.* • *Both their children graduated with degrees in economics.* • *The play begins with the main character as a boy and ends with him as an old man.* • With can be used in various phrases for finishing a letter: *With best wishes from Charles.* ○ *With love from Roberta.* • With can also mean including: *With your contribution, that makes a total of £45.*

with RELATIONSHIP /wɪð/ *prep* relating to or in the case of (a person or thing) • *How are things with you?* • *Russia has just drawn up a trade agreement with Norway.* • *This hasn't got anything to do with you* (= This is not something you should be interested in). • *The government's policies have not been popular with* (= among) *the voters.* • *He's very careless with his money.* • *In an interview with the BBC, he* *talked about his relationship with his co-star.* • **The trouble/problem** *with inviting Mandy to come with us is that she gets travel sick.* • *What's* **the matter** *with her?*

with [SHOW] /wɪð/ *prep* used to show what is on or in something • *She'd laid the table with the best china and silverware.* • *Her blouse was spattered with blood.* • *The room was littered with all his possessions.* • *The side of the police car was riddled with bullets.* • *The trucks were laden with food and medicine to take to the war zone.* • *Can you fill the car's radiator up with antifreeze before you go out?*

with [CAUSE] /wɪð/ *prep* because of or caused by (someone or something) • *He winced with pain as he tried to move his foot.* • *I was trembling with fear at the thought of another injection.* • *She's been at home with a bad cold for the past week.* • *(infml) Dad's in bed again with his back* (= because his back is injured). • *I can't do any work with all that noise the builders are making.* • *Hopes were dashed in the war-torn capital with the news that no aid would be arriving that week.* • *With exams approaching, it's a good idea to review your class notes.* • **(What)** *with all the excitement and confusion, I forgot to say goodbye to her.*

with [DIRECTION] /wɪð/ *prep* in the same direction as (something) • *The current was with them on the way back and the boat was carried swiftly along.* • Compare AGAINST [IN OPPOSITION].

with [TIME] /wɪð/ *prep* at the same rate or time as (something) • *This wine will improve with age.* • *Stopping distances for cars vary with the speed they are travelling at.*

with [OPPOSITION] /wɪð/ *prep* against (something) • *She has fought a constant battle with depression throughout her career.* • *The two countries went to war with one another over oil prices.* • *I always end up arguing with my friends about where to go on Saturday night.* • *A truck had* **collided** *with a car and blocked both lanes on the freeway.*

with [SUPPORT] /wɪð/ *prep* supporting (someone or something) • *If you want to go for a promotion, I'll be with you all the way.* • *You've got to decide where you stand on this issue – you're either with me or against me.* • Compare AGAINST [IN OPPOSITION].

with [UNDERSTANDING] /wɪð/ *prep infml* used to express understanding • *Are you with me* (= Do you understand what I'm saying)? • *I'm sorry, but I'm not with you.* • *(infml)* **With it** means quick to see, understand or act: *You're really not very with it today, are you?* • See also **with it** at WITH [COMPANY].

with [SEPARATION] /wɪð/ *prep* used with words showing separation • *She found it hard to* **part** *with the baby even though she'd decided to have it adopted.* • *He decided to put his failed marriage behind him and make a (clean)* **break** *with the past.*

with [DESPITE] /wɪð/ *prep* despite (something) • *With all her faults, she's still one of the best teachers we've ever had.*

with [AND] /wɪð/ *prep* and, or followed by • *I'd like a steak and baked potato, with some chocolate gateau for dessert.* • *$200 is payable immediately with a further $100 payable on delivery.* • **With that** is used to mean 'and then' or 'having said or done that': *He gave a slight moan and with that he died.*

with [COMPARISON] /wɪð/ *prep* used in comparisons • *I've got nothing in common with my brother.* • *This cake's delicious compared with the last one you made.* • *She's replaced her old camera with a new compact model.*

with [EXPRESSIONS] /wɪð/ *prep* used to express a wish or instruction • *Away with you* (= Go away)! • *Off to bed with you* (= Go to bed)! • *On with the show* (= Let it continue)! • *Down with school* (= We don't want/like it)!

with·draw *(obj)* /£wɪð'drɔː, $-'drɑː/ *v past simple* **withdrew** /wɪð'druː/, *past part* **withdrawn** /£wɪð'drɔːn, $-'drɑːn/ to take or move out or back, or to remove • *This credit card allows you to withdraw up to £200 a day* **from** *cash dispensers.* [T] [LP› **Money**] • *There's been a lot of debate about whether the UN should withdraw its troops* **from** *the country.* [T] • *Eleven million bottles of water had to be withdrawn* **from sale** *due to a health scare.* [T] • *Once in court, he withdrew the statement he'd made to the police* (= he claimed it was false). [T] • *All charges against them were withdrawn after the prosecution's case collapsed.* [T] • *(Br) By withdrawing their* **labour** (= stopping work), *the workers showed they were unwilling to accept wage cuts.* [T] • *After lunch, we withdrew* **into** *her office to finish our discussion in private.* [I] • *(esp. Br) The team captain was forced to withdraw* **from** *the match due to injury.* [I] • *Following his nervous breakdown, he withdrew* **from public life** *and refused to give any interviews.* [I] • *Many students in the US are now tending to withdraw* **from** *college in their junior year and are applying to study abroad.* [I] • *(fig.) As a child, she frequently withdrew* **into** *her own fantasy world.* [I] • *(fig.)* If you withdraw **(into yourself)**, you become quiet and shy in the company of other people: *After the accident, he withdrew (into himself) and refused to talk to either his family or friends.* [I]

with·draw·al /£wɪð'drɔː·ᵊl, $-'drɑː-/ *n* • *The bank became suspicious after several large withdrawals* (= removals of money) *were made* **from** *his account in a single week.* [C] • *The commander-in-chief was given 36 hours to* **secure** *a withdrawal of his troops* **from** *the combat zone.* [C] • *Doctors demanded the withdrawal of the drug after several cases of dangerous side-effects were reported.* [U] • *Her sudden withdrawal* **from** *the championship caused a lot of press speculation about her health.* [U] • *Even several years after the car crash, she still suffered from disturbed sleep and withdrawal* (= lack of interest in the outside world). [U] • **Withdrawal symptoms** are the unpleasant physical and mental effects which result when you stop doing or taking something, esp. a drug, which has become a habit: *He was* **suffering from** *all the classic withdrawal symptoms associated with giving up heroin – inability to sleep, anxiety, sweating and fever.* ○ *(fig.) There was no TV where we were staying and so I* **suffered** *severe withdrawal symptoms* **from** *my daily dose of news.*

with·drawn /£wɪð'drɔːn, $-'drɑːn/ *adj* • If you are withdrawn, you are shy and quiet and would rather be alone than with other people: *Following her son's death, she became quiet and withdrawn and rarely went out.*

wi·ther *(obj)* /£'wɪð·əʳ, $-ɚ/ *v* (to cause) to become weak and dry and decay • *The region's livelihood has been completely destroyed by drought, with the crops withering and the cattle dying.* [I] • *The hot dry wind withered the plants.* [T] • *She forgot to ask someone to water her plants while she was away over the summer and they withered* **(away)** *in the heat.* [I] • *(fig.) This country is in danger of allowing its industrial base to wither* **(away)**. [I] • *(fig.) Public interest in the refugees soon withered* **(away)** *when the media no longer focused on their plight.* [I] • Something that **withers on the vine** disappears gradually rather than being destroyed suddenly: *There was some debate as to whether the benefit scheme should be withdrawn or simply allowed to wither on the vine.*

wi·thered /£'wɪð·əd, $-ɚd/ *adj* • *withered leaves/flowers* • *His hands were all withered from constant exposure to the wind and cold.* • *(esp. old use)* A withered arm or leg is one that has not grown to its correct size because of disease.

wi·ther·ing /£'wɪð·ᵊr·ɪŋ, $'-ɚ-/ *adj* • *We only managed to walk a few steps before collapsing in the withering* **heat**. • *He made a withering* **attack** (= severe and critical) *on government policy.* • *The march turned into a scene of bloody pandemonium as the protesters ran to escape the withering* (= very heavy and severe) **(gun)fire**. • *(fig.) The coach is under withering* **fire** *from* (= being severely criticized by) *the media for the team's poor performance.* • *(fig.)* A withering look/remark/etc. is one that is intended to make someone feel ashamed: *She shot him a withering* **glance** *as he made fun of her habit of falling asleep in meetings.* ○ *The committee treated his proposal with withering* **contempt/scorn**.

wi·thers /£'wɪð·əz, $-ɚz/ *pl n specialized* the highest part of the back of a horse, which is situated above its shoulders • *From the ground to the withers the horse measures 16 hands or 1·6 metres.*

with·hold *obj* /£wɪð'həuld, $-'hould/ *v* [T] *past* **withheld** /wɪð'held/ to refuse to give (something) or to keep back (something) • *to withhold information/support* • *During the trial, the prosecution was accused of withholding crucial* **evidence from** *the defence.* • *Police are withholding the dead woman's* **name** *until her relatives have been informed.* • *She withheld her rent until the landlord agreed to have her drains unblocked.* • *The government is planning to withhold benefit payments* **from** *single mothers who refuse to name the father of their child.* • *(Am and Aus)* **Withholding tax** is the sum of money taken from a person's income and paid directly to the government by their employer.

with·in /wɪ'ðɪn/ *prep, adv* [not gradable] inside or not beyond (an area or period of time) • *Two-thirds of Californians live within 15 miles of the coast.* • *In 1992 cross-border controls within the EU were dismantled.* • *For orders within the UK, please enclose £2·50 for post and packing.* • *The resort lies within* **easy reach** *of* (= not far from) *the ski slopes.* • *We recommend that this wine should be consumed* *within six months.* • *Within the past few minutes reports have come in of a major earthquake in Los Angeles.* • *Within hours of the tragedy happening, an emergency rescue team had been assembled.* • *The tickets should reach you within the week* (= before the end of this week). • *He's regarded within his profession as a highly skilled and inventive chef.* • *He couldn't believe a direct challenge to his leadership was coming from within his own party.* • *She managed to complete her last film well within budget.* • *The target was now within* **range** *and so she took aim and fired.* • *He could sense that his goal was within* **reach** (= it could be reached). • *The cathedral spire was within* **sight** (= it could be seen) *and we knew we only had another few miles to go.* • *You might think she's been dishonest but she's still been acting within* **the law** (= legally). • *He knew within himself that she wouldn't recover* (= he thought it but did not say so publicly). • *We came within five points of beating them* (= We would have beaten them if we had had five more points). • *If things are to change, the company must be reformed* **from within** (= the people involved it, and not people from outside, must plan changes). • *Suddenly our car skidded off the road and screeched to a halt* **within inches of/within an inch of** (= very close to) *an oak tree.* • *She came* **within inches of/within an inch of** *losing her job* (= almost lost her job).

with·out /wɪ'ðaʊt/ *prep, adv* [not gradable] not having or doing (something), or lacking (something) • *It's just started to rain and I've come out without my umbrella.* • *She looks much better without make-up.* • *Do you have tea with milk or without?* • *He sneaked off to the party without his parents' knowledge.* • *Thank you so much for your help – I couldn't have done it without you.* • *She's a good person to work for, forceful without being bossy.* • *I'll be another five minutes getting ready. Why don't you start without me?* • *Breakfast is not the same without a cup of coffee and the morning paper.* • *(fml) The prime minister is not without* (= he does have) *his critics.* • *The rumours circulating about me are completely without* **foundation** (= There is no truth in them). • *This is without* **(a) doubt**/*without* **question** (= certainly) *the best Chinese food I've ever had.* • *You shouldn't drive for more than three hours without taking a break.* [+ v-*ing*] • *He wondered if he could slip out of the lecture without anyone noticing.* [+ v-*ing*] • *Without wishing to be rude* (= I don't want to be rude, but), *don't you think you need a hair cut?* [+ v-*ing*] • *She walked away from the house* **without so much as a** (= with no) *backward glance.* • *He took my book* **without so much as a by-your-leave** (= without asking permission). • See also DO WITHOUT; GO WITHOUT.

with·stand *obj* /wɪð'stænd/ *v* [T] *past* **withstood** /wɪð'stʊd/ to bear or not be changed by (something) or to oppose (a person or thing) successfully • *The region needs housing which is strong enough to withstand severe wind and storms.* • *Our toys are designed to withstand the rough treatment of the average five-year-old.* • *The aircraft base is protected with specially designed shelters which are built to withstand ground and air* **attacks**. • *He managed to stay in power for over five years, withstanding all the* **criticism** *and the* **pressure** *on him to resign.* • *She is an artist whose work will undoubtedly withstand* **the test of time** (= it will still be popular in the future).

wit·less /'wɪt·ləs/ *adj disapproving* stupid or lacking intelligence • *The novel centres around a witless father who is continually being conned by his three children.* • *The film looks set for disaster, with a witless script, bad direction and poor acting.* • If you **scare/frighten** someone witless, you give them a great fright: *I wish Rachel would drive a bit more slowly – I was scared witless the last time she drove me down to London.* • See also WITS.

wit·ness [SEE] /'wɪt·nəs/ *n* a person who sees an event happening, esp. a crime or an accident • *Following the crash on the motorway last night, police have appealed for witnesses* **to** *the accident to come forward.* [C] • *According to* **(eye)** *witnesses, the robbery was carried out by two teenage boys.* [C] • If someone is witness **to** something, they see it: *She was witness to the tragic event.* [U] ○ *During the play, the audience is witness to intrigue, betrayal and murder.* [U] • If something is **(a) witness to** or **bears witness** to something, it shows or proves it: *This latest rise in sales is (a) witness to the universal appeal of our recent advertising campaign.* ○ *As last week's riots bear witness, the political situation is very unstable.* ○ *The enormous popularity of the film bears witness* **to** *the fact that people still like a simple adventure story.* • A witness is also someone who is asked to be present at a particular event and sign their name in order to prove that things have been done correctly: *He signed the treaty* **in the presence of** *two witnesses.* [C] ○ *They were married a week after they first met, with two friends* **acting as** *witnesses.* [C]

wit·ness *obj* /'wɪt·nəs/ *v* [T] • *A woman who witnessed the accident said that the car was going at more than 80 mph when it crashed.* • *We were staying in the capital at the time of the riots and witnessed several street battles.* • *He arrived home just in time to witness his brother being taken away by the police.* [+ obj + v-*ing*] • *This university has witnessed* (= experienced) *quite a few changes over the years.* • *The past few years have witnessed* (= During the past few years there have been) *momentous changes throughout Eastern Europe.* • Witness also means to show or give proof of something: *This year's charity ball was the most successful one ever,* **as** *witnessed* **by** *the number of tickets sold.* ○ *The programme aroused strong feelings – witness the number of letters received.* • If you are asked to witness an event, you are asked to be present at it and sign your name to prove that things have been done correctly: *Her will was drawn up by a solicitor and witnessed by two colleagues.*

wit·ness [LAW] /'wɪt·nəs/ *n* [C] a person in a law court who states what they know about a legal case or a particular person • *Ten witnesses are expected to testify at the trial today.* • *The* **key** *witness* **for** *the prosecution was offered police protection after she received death threats.* • *At the trial, his teacher, who was* **called** *as a* **character** *witness* (= asked to speak about his student's usual behaviour), *said he was a quiet boy who had never been in trouble before.* • An **expert** witness is a person who is allowed to give their opinion in a law court because of their knowledge or practical experience of a particular subject: *A psychiatrist was called as an expert witness for the defence.* • *(Br)* A **witness box**/*(esp. Am)* **witness stand** is the place in which a person stands in a law court when they are being questioned: *He smiled at his parents as he went into the witness box.* ○ *(esp. Am) She was asked to* **take** *the witness stand and was then cross-examined by the state attorney.* • [LP] **Law**

wit·ness to *v prep Br fml* • If you witness to something in a law court, you state that it is true or that it has happened: *The handwriting expert witnessed to the authenticity of the letter.* [T] ○ *She witnessed to having seen the robbery take place.* [+ v-*ing*]

wits /wɪts/ *pl n* practical intelligence or understanding • *She's learned to survive on her* **keen** *wits and intellect.* • *He'll need all the wits and political experience he can muster if he's going to run for president.* • *The trial became an elaborate* **game of** *wits between the two lawyers.* • *In the gameshow, each contestant has to* **pit** *their wits* **against** (= compete in a test of intelligence and knowledge with) *the celebrity guest if they want to go for the star prize.* • If you **collect/gather** your **wits** after something shocking or unexpected has happened, you try to control your feelings and think clearly again: *When he heard that the police were after him, he had just enough time to gather his wits and leave town before they arrived at his house.* ○ *She spent the five-minute break between games gathering her wits and rethinking her strategy for the second half of the match.* • To **have/keep/need (all)** your **wits about** you is to be ready to think and react quickly to something that is going to happen: *You'll have to keep your wits about you when negotiating the contract.* ○ *The Italian team are going to need all their wits about them if they want to beat the French in the final tomorrow.* • If you are **at** your **wits' end**, you are so worried by something that you do not know what to do next: *I'm at my wits' end* **with** *Lucy – she goes out every night and doesn't come home till four.* • If something scares, frightens, etc. you **out of** your **wits**, or scares **the wits out of** you, it makes you very frightened: *That loud noise scared the wits out of me.* • See also WIT; WITLESS.

wit /wɪt/ *n* [U] • *Is it really beyond the wit* (= wits) *of the council to realise they can't postpone this decision indefinitely?* • *He hadn't the wit* (= wits) *to ask for professional advice before starting the business.*

-wit·ted /£-'wɪt·ɪd, $-'wɪt̬-/ *combining form* • *She is extremely* **quick**-*witted* (= intelligent) *and can always talk her way out of difficult situations.* • *I'm a little* **slow**-*witted* (= slow to understand) *when it comes to fixing anything electrical.* • *I can't believe he's set up his own business – he always seemed rather* **dim**-*witted* (= stupid) *at school.*

wit·ter /£'wɪt·əʳ, $'wɪt̬·ə/ *v* [I] *Br infml disapproving* to talk about unimportant things for an unnecessarily long time • *Oh, do stop wittering and just tell me what you want!*

• *Your mother does tend to witter* **on a bit,** *doesn't she?* • *He spent all morning wittering* **on about** *what a mess the builders had made in his back yard.*

wit·ti·cism /£'wɪt·ɪ·sɪ·zᵊm, $'wɪt̬-/ *n* [C] a remark that is both clever and humorous • *The best man's speech contained all sorts of witticisms about the bridegroom.* • *Woody Allen has built up a reputation for films that are full of witticisms.* • See also WIT.

wit·ti·ly /£'wɪt·ɪ·li, $'wɪt̬-/ *adv* See at WIT [HUMOUR]

wit·ty /£'wɪt·i, $'wɪt̬-/ *adj*

wives /waɪvz/ *pl of* WIFE

wi·zard /£'wɪz·əd, $-ɚd/ *n* [C] a man who is believed to have magical powers and who uses them to harm or help other people • *Wizards in stories and legends usually wear long cloaks and tall pointed hats and use magic wands to perform spells.* • *(infml)* A wizard (also **wiz**) is also someone who is an expert at something or who has great ability in a particular subject: *She's a real computer/financial wizard.* ○ *Your mother's a wizard* **at** *Scrabble.* ○ *He's a wizard* **at** *raising money.* • *"The Wonderful Wizard of Oz"* (title of a book by L.Frank Baum, 1900) • Compare **magician** at MAGIC; WITCH. • [PIC] **Imaginary creatures**

wi·zard·ry /£'wɪz·ə·dri, $'-ɚ-/ *n* [U] • Wizardry is the skill of a wizard or *(fig.)* clever or surprising ways of doing things, esp. with special machines: *(fig.) Using their new* **high-tech** *wizardry, the police were able to locate the owners of the stolen property within hours of it being seized.* • *(fig.) The drama company has invested heavily in lighting, stage equipment and* **electronic/technical** *wizardry to convert the hall into a theatre.*

wi·zened /'wɪz·ᵊnd/ *adj* having a lined, dry skin, esp. because of old age • *He was a wizened old man with yellow skin and deep wrinkles.* • *The only food they could find in the house was some stale bread and a few wizened apples.*

wk *n* [C] *abbreviation for* WEEK

wob·ble *(obj)* /£'wɒb·l̩, $'wɑː·bl̩/ *v* to (cause something to) shake or move from side to side in a way that shows a lack of balance • *I wouldn't use that bookcase if I were you because it wobbles whenever you put anything on it.* [I] • *You'll spill my coffee if you wobble the table like that!* [T] • *His many fat chins wobble when he laughs.* [I] • *I wish he wouldn't try to reach high notes because his* **voice** *always wobbles when he sings them.* [I] • *(fig.) The company's shares wobbled with the news of a foreign take-over bid.* [I]

wob·ble /£'wɒb·l̩, $'wɑː·bl̩/ *n* [C] • *She can't have put the tent up very well because the whole thing collapsed when I gave the poles a slight wobble.* • *(fig.) Despite recent stock market wobbles, there was strong demand for shares in the company when it was floated on the stock exchange.*

wob·bly /£'wɒb·l̩.i, $'wɑː·bl̩-/ *adj* **-ier, -iest** • *The ladder's a bit wobbly.* • *I've just spent a week in bed with flu and so my legs are still feeling all wobbly.* • *"Look, I've got a wobbly* **tooth,***" said her little daughter proudly.*

wob·bly /£'wɒb·l̩.i, $'wɑː·bl̩-/ *n* [C] *Br infml* a state of being extremely angry and upset • *My parents* **threw** *a wobbly* (= became very angry and upset) *when they found out I'd had a party while they were away.*

wodge, wadge /£wɒdʒ, $wɑːdʒ/ *n* [C] *esp. Br and Aus infml* a thick piece or a large amount of something • *She cut herself a large wodge* **of** *chocolate* **cake.** • *He hurried towards the staffroom with a wodge* **of papers** *under his arm.*

woe /£wəʊ, $woʊ/ *n* [U] *fml* extreme sadness • *Her clothes were tattered and her face was lined and full of woe.* • *Last Saturday was a* **day of** *woe for the team because they lost the final 3-2.* • *He told me a real* **tale of** *woe about how he had lost both his job and his house in the same week.* • If you say **woe betide** someone, it means there will be trouble for them: *This is the second time he's been sent home from school this week, so woe betide him if it happens again!* • *(old use or humorous)* If you say **woe is me**, you are expressing how unhappy you are: *I'm cold and wet and I haven't even got enough money for my bus fare home. Oh woe is me!*

woe·ful /£'wəʊ·fᵊl, $'woʊ-/ *adj fml* • *She was looking very woeful* (= extremely sad) *with her eyes red and swollen and her cheeks wet with tears.* • *When I saw her woeful face, I knew she had bad news.* • See also WOEFUL.

woes /£wəʊz, $woʊz/ *pl n fml* great problems or troubles • *The new chairman spends much of his time blaming the company's woes on his predecessor.* • *The country has been beset by* **economic** *woes for the past decade.*

woe·be·gone /£'wəʊ·bɪ·gɒn, $'woʊ·bɪ·gɑːn/ *adj literary* looking very sad • *The downtown area of the city is full of beggars with woebegone faces and hands outstretched waiting for coins.* • *Our dog always sits by the door with a woebegone* **expression** *when it wants to be taken for a walk.*

woe·ful /£'wəʊ·fᵊl, $'woʊ-/ *adj* very bad or (of something very bad or unpleasant) very great or extreme • *The team's woeful* **record** *consists of six defeats in seven matches.* • *They displayed woeful* **ignorance** *of the safety rules.* • See also WOEFUL at WOE.

woe·ful·ly /£'wəʊ·fᵊl·i, $'woʊ-/ *adv* • Woefully means extremely when referring to something bad: *Our local theatre is woefully short of cash and might have to close down.* ○ *The children have to use text books that are woefully out-of-date because the school can't afford any more.* ○ *The safety precautions taken by large resort hotels are often woefully* **inadequate** *for the number of people who stay there.*

wog /£wɒg, $wɑːg/ *n* [C] *(Br and Aus taboo slang)* a black or dark-skinned person or *(Aus infml)* an IMMIGRANT who does not speak English. This word is considered very offensive.

wok /£wɒk, $wɑːk/ *n* [C] a large curved Chinese pan used for frying food quickly in hot oil • *Heat some oil in a wok, then add the vegetables and stir-fry until crisp.*

woke /£wəʊk, $woʊk/ *past simple of* WAKE [STOP SLEEPING]

wok·en /£'wəʊ·kᵊn, $'woʊ-/ *past participle of* WAKE [STOP SLEEPING]

wolf [ANIMAL] /wʊlf/ *n* [C] *pl* **wolves** /wʊlvz/ a wild animal of the dog family • *Wolves hunt in groups known as packs.* • *As we sat round the campfire, we could hear wolves* **howling** *in the distance.* • *(fig. dated) He had the reputation of being a bit of a wolf* (= a man who tries to have sex with many women). • **A wolf in sheep's clothing** is a person who hides the fact that they are evil with a pleasant and friendly appearance. • If you **keep the wolf from the door**, you have just enough money to be able to eat and live: *As a student, he took an evening job to keep the wolf from the door.* • To **wolf-whistle** or to give a **wolf-whistle** is to make a sound consisting of two long notes, one high and one low, which a person, esp. a man, makes when they see a person whom they find sexually attractive: *Builders are renowned for wolf-whistling at any woman who walks by.* ○ *The last time she went out wearing those ripped jeans she got several wolf-whistles.* • [PIC] **Dogs**

wol·fish /'wʊl·fɪʃ/ *adj* • *(fig. dated) He gave her a wolfish* **grin** (= smiled at her in a sexually interested way).

wolf *obj* [EAT] /wʊlf/ *v* [T] *infml* to eat a large amount (of food) very quickly • *My brother was wolfing biscuits while he watched TV.* • *The boys wolfed the sandwiches* **(down)** *and then started on the cakes.* [T/M]

wolf·hound /'wʊlf·haʊnd/ *n* [C] a type of very large dog • *Wolfhounds were originally bred for hunting wolves.* • *He specialises in breeding large dogs such as* **Irish** *wolfhounds.*

wo·man /'wʊm·ən/ *n pl* **women** /'wɪm·ɪn/ an adult female human being • *"What's your new boss like?" "She seems to be a very nice woman."* [C] • *A woman and two men were arrested on the day after the explosion.* [C] • *Women first got the vote in Britain in 1918.* [C] • *The women's singles final was won by Margaret Smith.* [C] • *He is writing a book on the representation of woman* (= women in general) *in medieval art.* [U] • *(infml)* A man's wife or partner is sometimes called his woman: *Have you heard? Geoff's got a new woman.* [C] • Woman also means female: *She is Ireland's first woman* (= female) *president.* ○ *The rape victim asked to see a woman police officer.* ○ *There are three women candidates for the post of company director.* ○ *Tracy Edwards led the first* **all-woman/all-women** *crew to success in the round-the-world yacht race.* • The **Women's Institute** (*abbreviation* **WI**) is an organization in Britain consisting of local groups which allow women to meet together socially and learn new skills: *She's an active member of the WI and is always organizing talks for her local group.* • **Women's liberation** (*infml* **women's lib**) is the aim of achieving equality for women in all areas of society: *As a student, I was heavily involved in women's lib and went to loads of meetings and demonstrations.* ○ *"I'm not a* **women's libber** *but I do believe women should be paid the same as men," she said.* • The **women's movement** is those people whose social and political aims are to change women's position in society and increase awareness of women's condition in society: *The early 20th century women's movement fought for the political emancipation of women.* • A *(Br and Aus)* **women's refuge**/*(Am)* **women's shelter** is a house where women whose husbands have been violent towards them can go with their children for protection. • *She has applied to do a postgraduate course in* **women's studies** (= a course of studies which deals with women in history, society and literature). • *(saying)* 'A woman's work is never done'. • *"A woman is only a woman but a good cigar is a smoke"* (Rudyard Kipling in the poem *The Betrothal*, 1888) • *"A woman without a man is like a fish without a bicycle"* (believed to have been said by the feminist Gloria Steinem, 1934-) • *"Little Women"* (title of a book by Louisa M. Alcott, 1868) • *"All women become like their mothers. That is their tragedy. No man does. That is his."* (from the play *The Importance of Being Earnest* by Oscar Wilde, 1895) • 'Woman' is the general word for an adult female human being. • See also WOMANKIND; WOMENFOLK. • LP **Age, Sexist language**

-wo·man /-ˌwʊm·ən/ *combining form pl* **-women** • *Jean's an Englishwoman who has been living in Sweden for the past 25 years.* • *"Who's chairing this meeting?" "Sally Davies will be acting as chairwoman."* • LP **Sexist language**

wo·man·hood /ˈwʊm·ən·hʊd/ *n* [U] • *The novel deals with a teenage girl's journey towards womanhood.* • *Brigitte Bardot was the dominant image of womanhood in French cinema during the 1960s.* • Compare MANHOOD at MAN MALE.

wo·man·ly /ˈwʊm·ən·li/ *adj* • Womanly means typical of a woman: *She referred to the 'traditional womanly goals of marriage and motherhood' several times in her talk.* ○ *She'd used her womanly* **wiles** *to persuade him to change his mind.* • Compare **manly** at MAN MALE.

wo·man·li·ness /ˈwʊm·ən·lɪ·nəs/ *n* [U]

wo·man·ize, *Br and Aus usually* **-ise** /ˈwʊm·ə·naɪz/ *v* [I] *disapproving* (of a man) to try to get many women to have sex with him • *He drank, womanized and wasted money.* • *Both his first and second wife divorced him on account of his womanizing.*

wo·man·iz·er, *Br and Aus usually* **-iser** /£ˈwʊm·ə·naɪ·zəʳ, $-zɚ/ *n* [C] *disapproving* • *As a young actor, he had brief affairs with many of his female co-stars and quickly gained a reputation as a womanizer.*

wo·man·kind /ˌwʊm·əŋˈkaɪnd/ *n* [U] *dated* female human beings in general • *In her latest book she discusses the menopause, which is a subject that concerns all womankind.* • Compare MANKIND; HUMANKIND.

womb /wuːm/ *n* [C] the organ in the body of a woman or other female mammal in which a baby develops before birth; UTERUS • *Babies born before 22 weeks have a very low survival rate, because their organs are not sufficiently developed to support life outside the womb.* • A womb is also a safe and enclosed place: *She spent much of her time inside the womb of her hotel room sheltering from the gunfire.*

wom·bat /£ˈwɒm·bæt, $ˈwɑːm-/ *n* [C] an Australian wild animal which is similar to a small bear

wo·men·folk /£ˈwɪm·ɪn·fəʊk, $-foʊk/ *pl n* the women in a family or society • *The communal land which surrounds the group of huts is cultivated by the womenfolk in the tribe.* • Compare MENFOLK at MAN MALE.

won /£wʌn, $wɑːn/ *past simple and past participle of* WIN

won·der *(obj)* QUESTION /£ˈwʌn·dəʳ, $-dɚ/ *v* to ask yourself questions or express a desire to know about something • *Hadn't you better phone home? Your parents will be wondering* **where** *you are.* [+ *wh-* word] • *He's starting to wonder* **whether** *he did the right thing in accepting this job.* [+ *wh-* word] • *I haven't seen Jim in years. I wonder* **what** *he looks like now?* [+ *wh-* word] • *I've been sitting in my room for the past hour wondering* **how** *I'm going to begin this letter.* [+ *wh-* word] • *His poor performance in the Olympics had many people wondering* **if** *his career as a world-class sprinter was finished.* [+ *wh-* word] • *Will this turkey be big enough for eight, I wonder?* [+ clause] • **Why**, *one wonders, is the school getting rid of more teachers when they are already short of staff?* [+ *wh-* word] • *"Have you decided where you're going next summer?" "I've been wondering* **about** (= considering) *going to Florida."* [I] • *I've been wondering* **about** (= having doubts about) *Jack's health recently.* [I] • *Many MPs have been wondering* **out loud about** (= expressing doubts in public about) *the prime minister's competence in the handling of this crisis.* [I] • You can use wonder in phrases at the beginning of a request if you want to make it more formal and polite: *I wonder* **whether** *you could pass me the butter?* [+ *wh-* word] ○ *I wonder* **if** *you could give me some information about places to visit in the area?* [+ *wh-* word] ○ *I was wondering* **if** *you were busy Friday night. If not, would you like to come to the cinema with me?* [+ *wh-* word] ○ *I wonder – could you help me carry these books?* [+ clause] • *(esp. Br infml) "Where's Mark been recently?" "Up to no good,* **I shouldn't wonder** (= probably)." • Ⓓ

won·der SURPRISE /£ˈwʌn·dəʳ, $-dɚ/ *v* to feel or express great surprise at something • *He was behaving so badly at school today, I wonder* **(that)** *he wasn't sent home straight away.* [+ (*that*) clause] • *I don't wonder* **(that)** *she burst into tears after the way you spoke to her.* [+ (*that*) clause] • *You can only wonder* **at** *her behaviour in asking for another pay increase this year.* [I] • Ⓓ

won·der /£ˈwʌn·dəʳ, $-dɚ/ *n* • Wonder is a feeling of great surprise and admiration caused by seeing or experiencing something that is strange and new: *She could barely conceal her wonder as she gazed around the richly decorated room.* [U] ○ *The sight of the Grand Canyon stretching out before them* **filled** *them* **with** *wonder.* [U] ○ *His parents shook their heads* **in** *wonder as he told them of his extraordinary journey down the Amazon.* [U] • A wonder is an object which causes a feeling of great surprise and admiration: *We spent a week in Athens visiting the wonders of Ancient Greek civilization.* [C] ○ *With the wonders* **of modern technology**, *you can fax a letter to the other side of the world in a few seconds.* [C] • *(infml)* If you describe someone as a wonder, they are extremely useful or skilful: *Our new baby-sitter's an* **absolute** *wonder – she'll come at very short notice and the children love her.* [C] • **It's a wonder (that)** (= It is surprising that) *he ever reached Paris, because he set off with only £5 in his pocket.* • *Her car's been broken for the past two months, so it's* **little/small wonder (that)** (= it is not really surprising that) *she hasn't come to visit you recently.* • **No wonder (that)** (= It is not surprising that) *the children are excited, this is the first time they've been abroad.* • *(infml)* A **wonder drug** is a very effective new medicine: *It has proved to be a wonder drug for sufferers of epilepsy, reducing seizures by up to 80%.* • *(infml)* If something **does/works wonders**, it has a very good effect: *After a hard day at the office, a long bath will work wonders.* ○ *Doctors have discovered that keeping a pet can do wonders* **for** *your health.* • *(humorous saying)* If you say 'Wonders will never cease' (also 'Will wonders never cease?'), you are expressing surprise at something that is unexpected: *Lynda has actually managed to get up before ten o'clock. Wonders will never cease!*

won·der·ment /£ˈwʌn·də·mənt, $-dɚ-/ *n* [U] *literary* • *He listened* **with** *quiet wonderment* (= great and pleasant surprise) *as his grandfather told him of his life in the circus.*

won·der·ful /£ˈwʌn·də·fᵊl, $-dɚ-/ *adj* extremely good • *He's a wonderful cook.* • *"Did you know that Daryl's getting married?" "No, I didn't. How wonderful!"* • *We had a wonderful* **time** *in Italy last summer.* • *"I thought I'd buy James a new bike for his birthday." "That's a wonderful* **idea**!*"* • *She announced her retirement last week after 20 wonderful years in the movie business.* • *"It's a Wonderful Life"* (title of a film, 1946)

won·der·ful·ly /£ˈwʌn·də·fli, $-dɚ-/ *adv* • Wonderfully means extremely (well): *I used to hate my brother when I was a child but now we get on wonderfully.* ○ *She's coped wonderfully with the stress of bringing up two children on her own.* ○ *This sauce goes wonderfully well with fish, asparagus or new potatoes.* • LP **Very, completely**

won·der·land /£ˈwʌn·dᵊl·ænd, $-dɚ·lænd/ *n* [C] a place that has unusual attractiveness or beauty • *The family emigrated to New Zealand in 1949, which seemed a wonderland in comparison with post-war England.* • *As the train sped through the snow-covered countryside, she gazed out on the* **winter** *wonderland.* • *"Alice's Adventures in Wonderland"* (title of a book by Lewis Carroll, 1865)

won·drous /ˈwʌn·drəs/ *adj fml* surprisingly good • *Our new improved face-cream has wondrous effects on tired-looking skin.* • *Her appointment as managing director of the company is a wondrous achievement for a woman who started her career as an office clerk.*

won·drous·ly /ˈwʌn·drə·sli/ *adv fml* • Wondrously means extremely when referring to something good: *Every car is sold with a wondrously sophisticated alarm system and a two-year guarantee.*

wonk /£wɒŋk, $wɑːŋk/ *n* [C] *Am infml* a person who works or studies too much • *"Why don't you ask Mike to go to the movies with you?" "He's such a wonk he probably spends Saturday night in the library."* • *The president has been given so much different advice by the Washington* **policy** *wonks that he's now incapable of dealing with the current crisis in a swift and decisive manner.*

wonk·y /£ˈwɒŋ·ki, $ˈwɑːŋ-/ *adj* **-ier, -iest** *Br and Aus infml* shaky or weak • *One of the legs on this chair is a bit wonky. Could you fix it for me?* • *I was in bed with a bad cold last week and I'm still feeling a bit wonky.* • *Their relationship is going through rather a wonky period at the moment.*

wont /£wəʊnt, $woʊnt/ *n* [after possessive] *fml* someone's habit or custom • *She arrived at the dinner party an hour late,* **as is** *her wont* (= as she usually does).

wont /£wəʊnt, $woʊnt/ *adj* [after v; always + *to* infinitive] *fml* • If you are wont **to** do something, you have the habit of doing it: *The previous city council was wont to overspend.* ○ *The two men spent much of the time at the reunion reminiscing about the war, as old soldiers are wont to (do).*

wont·ed /£ˈwəʊn·tɪd, $ˈwoʊn·t̬ɪd/ *adj* [before; not gradable] *fml* • *He replied sharply, and without his wonted* (= usual) *courtesy.*

woo *obj* /wuː/ *v* [T] he/she/it **woos, wooing,** *past* **wooed** to attempt to obtain the support of (someone) by persuasion • *The party has been trying to woo the voters* **with** *promises of electoral reform.* • *After graduating, bright students are often wooed* **away from** *science and engineering to jobs in business and finance.* • *The airline has been offering discounted tickets to woo passengers* **away from** *their competitors.* • *(dated)* If a man woos a woman, he gives her a lot of attention in an attempt to persuade her to marry him: *She decided to accept his offer of marriage after he wooed her for months* **with** *flowers and expensive presents.* ○ *The novel centers around an American heiress who is wooed by a hard-up actor who is planning to murder her for her fortune.*

woo·er /£ˈwuː·əʳ, $-ɚ/ *n* [C]

wood MATERIAL /wʊd/ *n* a hard substance which forms the branches and trunks of trees and which can be used as a building material, for making things or as a fuel • *He gathered some wood to build a fire but it was too damp to light.* [U] • *She made some simple shelves by fixing a couple of* **planks** *of wood to the wall.* [U] • *The bowls were made from polished olive wood.* [U] • *There was a small table made from cherry wood in the corner of the room.* [U] • *Mahogany is a* **hard** *wood and pine is a* **soft** *wood.* [C] • *The room was heated by a wood-***burning** *stove.* [U] • In golf, a wood is a type of specially shaped stick with a wooden end and a long handle which is used for hitting the ball over a long distance: *He likes to use a number 2 wood to tee off.* [C] • *(Br)* If a drink such as wine or beer is described as being **from the wood**, it has been stored in a wooden container. • **Wood pulp** is wood which has been changed into a soft mass which can then be used for making paper. • See also WOODCARVING; WOODCUT.

wood /wʊd/ *adj* [not gradable] • *Solid wood furniture is much more sturdy and durable than chipboard furniture.* • *We spent hours sanding and polishing the wood* **floor** *in the living room.* • *Much of the original 18th-century wood* **panelling** *in the house was destroyed in the fire.* • See also WOODBLOCK.

wood·en /ˈwʊd·ən/ *adj* • *Accommodation at the ski resort will be in wooden chalets that sleep four.* • *The house was surrounded by a tall wooden* **fence**. • *Stir the mixture with a wooden* **spoon** *and then pour into a baking tin.* • *(Br and Aus infml)* A **wooden spoon** is the imaginary prize that a person or team is given if they finish last in a race or competition: *Our college team* **took** *the wooden spoon in the inter-collegiate league this season.*

wood·y /ˈwʊd·i/ *adj* **-ier, -iest** • *The wine has been aged in oak barrels, which gives it a woody flavour.* • Plants with hard stems can also be described as woody: *When we bought the house, the garden was overgrown with woody plants such as hawthorn and bramble.*

wood GROUP OF TREES /wʊd/ *n* [C] an area of land covered with a thick growth of trees • *an oak wood* • *A wood is usually smaller than a forest.* • *The red squirrel is one of the shyest animals that live in the wood.* • If you **can't see the** *(Br and Aus)* **wood/***(Am)* **forest for the trees**, you are unable to get a general understanding of a situation because you are too worried about the details • *(infml)* If you are **out of the wood**, you are no longer in danger or difficulty: *The club has been given funding for another year but it's not out of the wood yet.* • See also WOODLAND.

wood·ed /ˈwʊd·ɪd/ *adj* • *The banks of the river are* **densely** *wooded* (= covered with trees). • *The village is surrounded by wooded hills.* • *The police found a vital clue to the girl's disappearance in a wooded* **area** *near her home.*

woods /wʊdz/ *pl n* • *We went for a walk in the woods* (= wood) *after lunch.* • *We used to play in the woods behind our house when we were children.* • *"If you go down to the woods today, you're sure of a big surprise"* (from the song *The Teddy Bear's Picnic* written by Jimmy Kennedy, 1932)

wood·y /ˈwʊd·i/ *adj* **-ier, -iest** • *They lived in a remote cottage set high on a woody hillside.*

wood·bine /ˈwʊd·baɪn/ *n* [U] a climbing plant with yellow flowers that have a pleasant smell • Woodbine is also *Am for* VIRGINIA CREEPER.

wood·block /£ˈwʊd·blɒk, $-blɑːk/ *n* [C] a piece of wood on which a pattern is cut which is used for printing • *She designs her own fabrics using woodblocks and stencils to create patterns on the material.* • *The book of children's stories is illustrated with a series of woodblock* **prints**. • *(Br)* A woodblock is also one of a set of small flat pieces of wood which are used to make a wooden floor: *The woodblocks are sold in packs of 10.* ○ *a woodblock floor* ○ See also PARQUET.

wood·carv·ing /£ˈwʊdˌkɑː·vɪŋ, $-ˌkɑːr-/ *n* the process of cutting into the surface of wood to create a decorative shape or pattern, or a piece of wood that has been decorated in this way • *Some of the finest examples of woodcarving in Europe can be found in medieval churches.* [U] • *The exteriors of many houses in the village were adorned with elaborate woodcarvings.* [C]

wood·chuck *Am* /ˈwʊd·tʃʌk/, **ground·hog** *n* [C] a small animal with short legs and rough reddish brown fur which lives in N America

wood·cut /ˈwʊd·kʌt/ *n* [C] a picture printed from a pattern which has been cut in the surface of a block of wood

wood·en WOOD /ˈwʊd·ən/ *adj* See at WOOD MATERIAL

wood·en AWKWARD /ˈwʊd·ən/ *adj disapproving* (of behaviour) stiff and awkward, or lacking in expression • *She gave a wooden* **smile** *to the camera as she posed for another publicity shot.* • *"Did you enjoy the play?" "Not really. I thought the man who played the lead gave rather a wooden* **performance**.*"*

wood·en·ly /ˈwʊd·ən·li/ *adv disapproving* • *As he was introduced to another group of guests at the party, the mayor woodenly shook their hands and murmured a greeting.* • *You can tell Debbie didn't warm up properly before she began dancing this morning because she's moving so woodenly.*

wood·land /ˈwʊd·ləndz/ *n* (an area of) land on which many trees grow • *The Forestry Commission is responsible for preserving over 2 million acres of woodland.* [U] • *Some very rare plants grow in these woodlands.* [C]

wood·louse /ˈwʊd·laʊs/ *n* [C] *pl* **woodlice** /ˈwʊd·laɪs/ a small creature which looks like an insect with a black flattened body divided into several parts, and which can curl itself into a ball

wood·peck·er /£ˈwʊdˌpek·əʳ, $-ɚ/ *n* [C] a bird with a strong beak which it uses to make holes in tree trunks so that it can find insects to eat • PIC〉 **Birds**

wood·shed BUILDING /ˈwʊd·ʃed/ *n* [C] a small building where wood for burning is stored

wood·shed PRACTICE /ˈwʊd·ʃed/ *v* [I] *Am infml* to practice a musical instrument • *Parker spent the next few months at his parents' house woodshedding, getting ready for the gig.*

wood·wind /ˈwʊd·wɪnd/ *adj* [before n; not gradable] of a type of musical instrument which is played by blowing • *The clarinet, flute, saxophone and bassoon are all woodwind* **instruments**. • Compare BRASS MUSICAL INSTRUMENTS; PERCUSSION. • PIC〉 **Musical instruments**

wood·wind /ˈwʊd·wɪnd/ *n* [U + sing/pl v] • **The woodwind** is/are the group of woodwind instruments and their players in an ORCHESTRA: *The woodwind was particularly haunting during the slow second movement.*

wood·work BUILDING /£ˈwʊd·wɜːk, $-wɜːrk/ *n* [U] the wooden parts of a building, esp. a house • *There's some rotting woodwork on the outside of the house that we need to replace.* • *(esp. disapproving)* Something or someone that **comes/crawls out of the woodwork** appears after having been hidden or not active for a long time: *After you've been in a relationship for a while all sorts of little secrets start to come out of the woodwork.* ○ *People are starting to crawl out of the woodwork to talk about fraudulent practices in the industry.*

wood·work ACTIVITY *esp. Br* /£ˈwʊd·wɜːk, $-wɜːrk/, *Am usually* **wood·work·ing** /£ˈwʊdˌwɜː·kɪŋ, $-wɜːr-/ *n* [U] the activity of making objects such as furniture from wood, esp. when this is done skilfully • *woodwork classes/lessons* • *I used to enjoy woodwork at school.*

wood·worm /£'wʊd·wɜːm, $-wɜːrm/ *n pl* **woodworm** the young form of particular types of BEETLE which make small holes in wood as they feed on it • *Woodworm are white, C-shaped and have tiny legs.* [C] • Woodworm is also the damage which woodworm do to objects made from wood when they feed on it: *The roof timbers were riddled with woodworm.* [U]

woof /wʊf/ *n* [C] (esp. in children's books) a written representation of the noise that a dog makes • *"Miaow, miaow," went the cat. "Woof, woof," went the dog.*

woof /wʊf/ *v* [I] • *Daddy, that doggy woofed* **at** *me!*

wool /wʊl/ *n* [U] hair which grows from the bodies of sheep and some other animals, or thread or cloth made from this • *The blankets are made from wool and the sheets from cotton.* • *Put on your red wool cardigan – it'll be nice and warm.* • *How many* **balls of** *wool would you need to knit that sweater?* • If you **pull the wool over** someone's **eyes** you deceive them, esp. in order to prevent them from discovering something: *You can't pull the wool over my eyes, Emilio, I know you're angling for promotion.* • PIC› Handicraft

wool·len, *Am usually* **wool·en** /'wʊl·ən/ *adj* [not gradable] • *woollen socks* • *a woollen scarf*

wool·lens, *Am usually* **wool·ens** /'wʊl·ənz/ *pl n* • Woollens are clothes made from wool or sometimes from wool mixed with artificial fibres: *I hate washing woollens – they take such a long time to dry.*

wool·ly (-ier, -iest), *Am also* **wool·y (-ier, -iest)** /'wʊl·i/ *adj* • *a woolly hat/jumper* • See also WOOLLY.

wool·ly, *Am also* **wool·y** /'wʊl·i/ *n* [C] *dated infml* • A woolly is a piece of clothing made from wool, esp. a SWEATER.

wool·ly /'wʊl·i/ *adj* (of ideas and reasoning) unclear and confused, not having been considered carefully enough • *He had some woolly notion that kids had an innate understanding of right and wrong if you let them think for themselves.* • *It's the woolly thinking behind the book that I find so infuriating.* • *If there's one thing I can't stand it's a woolly-***headed/-minded** *liberal!* • See also **woolly** at WOOL.

wool·li·ness, *Am also* **wool·i·ness** /'wʊl·ɪ·nəs/ *n* • The woolliness of an idea or suggestion is the quality of it being unclear or not accurate: *The proposals have a woolliness that make them difficult to understand.*

Woop Woop /'wuːp·wuːp/ *n* [C] *Aus infml* a small town which is far away from anywhere important

woosh /hwʊʃ/ *exclamation, n infml* WHOOSH

woo·zy /'wuː·zi/ *adj* **-ier, -iest** *infml* feeling weak or ill and unable to think clearly • *The sea was very rough and many of us felt woozy after the boat journey.*

woo·zi·ness /'wuː·zɪ·nəs/ *n* [U] *infml*

wop /£wɒp, $wɑːp/ *n* [C] *slang* a man from S Europe, esp. Italy. This word is considered offensive by most people.

Wor·cester sauce *Br* /£'wʊs·tər, $-tɚ/, *Am and Aus* **Wor·cester·shire sauce** /£'wʊs·tə·ʃər, $-ʃɚ/ *n* [U] a dark brown spicy liquid added to food to increase its flavour

word LANGUAGE UNIT /£wɜːd, $wɜːrd/ *n* [C] a single unit of language which has meaning and can be spoken or written • *Your essay should be no more than two thousand words long.* • *Some words are more difficult to spell than others.* • *What's the word* **for** *bikini in French?* • *In English the same word often has several meanings.* • *It's sometimes very difficult to* **find** *exactly* **the right** *word to express precisely what you want to say.* • *The words of the song are really beautiful.* • *Rather than using words* (= language) *many mathematical concepts are more effectively expressed in equations.* • *(infml, esp. humorous)* Word is often used after the first letter of another word to avoid saying that word: *So how's the diet going – or would you rather I didn't mention the d-word?* ○ *You're still not allowed to say the f-word on TV in the US.* • To **breathe/say a word** about something is to tell other people about it: *If you breathe a word* **of** *this to anyone, I'll be really upset.* ○ *What I just told you is top-secret so please don't breathe a word* **of** *it to anyone.* ○ *He asked her not to say a word* **about** *the accident to his mother.* • **By word of mouth** means in speech but not in writing: *All the orders were given by word of mouth to avoid leaving written evidence which might be later discovered.* • *(infml)* To **get a word in edgeways** means to have an opportunity to speak: *Roz was talking so much that nobody else could get a word in edgeways!* • **In other words** means expressing the same meaning but in another way, for example by using different words: *You think he should make a positive career move outside this organization – in other words you think he should leave.* • If a person says something **in** their **own words**, they speak without copying what someone else has said: *The court has heard accounts from several witnesses of what happened that night – now please tell us in your own words what you saw.* • **In words of one syllable** means in simple language avoiding long, difficult or specialized words: *Could you* **explain** *to me in words of one syllable how an electron microscope works?* • If you say that someone **put words in/into** your **mouth**, you mean that they suggested you meant one thing when in fact you really meant another: *Stop putting words in my mouth – I didn't say you looked fat in the red dress – I merely said you looked very slim in the black!* • If you **take the words out of** someone's **mouth**, you say something which they were just about to say or which they were thinking: *"What a rude and obnoxious man!" "You took the words* **right** *out of my mouth!"* • **Word for word** means using exactly the same words: *We want a word-for-word* **account**, *if possible, of the questions you were asked and your answers.* • If speech or writing is changed **word for word** from one language into another, it is changed one word at a time in the same order rather than in phrases or other larger units of meaning. • *(dated)* The expressions **my word!** and **upon my word!** are used to show surprise: *My word, isn't that Jenkins on the roof!* • **Word association** is a method sometimes used in PSYCHOANALYSIS (= a way of treating the mind) in which the person being treated says the first word they think of when a particular word is said. Some people believe that this method can be used to discover how parts of the mind work. • *(Br and Aus)* When a person is **word-perfect** (*Am* **letter-perfect**), they can repeat from memory all the words of a particular text without making a mistake: *He goes for long walks in the park, muttering to himself until he has the whole play or film script word perfect.* • A **word processor** is a computer used for preparing documents and letters, or the program that is used for this: *With suitable software you can use your PC as a word processor.* ○ *Which word processor do you have on your computer?* • **Word processing** is the organization of text in electronic form such as on a computer: *word processing software* ○ *a word processing program/package* • If someone says **words fail me**, they want to emphasize that they are surprised or shocked, esp. because they cannot believe what they have just seen or been told: *"Have you heard about how rude Paul was to the Belgian guy?" "Yes. Words fail me! I can't believe that man."* • *"So what did you think of Olive's pink outfit?" "Words fail me, I've never seen anything quite like it!"* • See also WORDPLAY; WORDSMITH.

word *obj* /£wɜːd, $wɜːrd/ *v* [T always + adv/prep] • *He worded* (= carefully chose the words of) *the reply in such a way that he did not admit making the original error.* • See also REWORD.

word·ed /£'wɜː·dɪd, $'wɜːr-/ *adj* [not gradable] • *In a* **carefully/strongly** *worded* **statement**, *Carlos denied all the allegations.*

word·ing /£'wɜː·dɪŋ, $'wɜːr-/ *n* [U] • *Considerable effort goes into the wording* (= exact choice and meaning of words used) **of/for** *advertisements.*

word·less /£'wɜːd·ləs, $'wɜːrd-/ *adj* [not gradable] • *The first half of the second act is largely wordless.* • *We sat in wordless contemplation of the view.*

word·less·ly /£'wɜːd·lə·sli, $'wɜːrd-/ *adv* [not gradable] • *We held each other tight and then drew apart wordlessly.*

word·y /£'wɜː·di, $'wɜːr-/ *adj* **-ier, -iest** *disapproving* • *As usual she gave a reply which was wordy* (= contained an unnecessarily large amount of words) *and didn't answer the question.*

wor·di·ness /£'wɜː·dɪ·nəs, $'wɜːr-/ *n* [U] *disapproving*

word BRIEF STATEMENT /£wɜːd, $wɜːrd/ *n* [U] a brief discussion or statement • *The manager wants* **a** *word.* • *I was hoping you might* **put in a good** *word* **for** (= say positive things about) *me with your boss.* • *Could I* **have a** *word* **(with** *you) about the sales figures?* • *I'd like* **a quick/brief** *word (with you) before the meeting.* • *Perhaps you would* **have a quiet** *word with Simon* (= gently explain to him) *about the problem.* • **A word in** someone's **ear** is a piece of secretly given advice or information: *I think I'd better* **have** *a quick word in Patrick's ear and ask him not to mention it to anyone.* • **In a word** (= Briefly and directly), *she's lying.*

words /£wɜːdz, $wɜːrdz/ *pl n* • *We* **had/exchanged** *a few words as we were coming out of the meeting.* • Words sometimes means angry words: *Both competitors*

exchanged/ had *words* (= argued) *after the match.* ○ *Words* **passed between** *both competitors* (= They argued) *after the match.* • *(disapproving)* Words also means discussion about something, esp. rather than action: *We've heard enough words about reducing crime – when is something going to be done about it!*

word NEWS /£wɜːd, $wɜːrd/ *n* [U] news or a message • *Have you* **had/heard** *word from Paul since he went to New York?* • *We* **got** *word of their plan from a former colleague.* • *Word* **of** *the discovery caused a stir among astronomers.* • *(Am) Hey, Martin, what's the* **good** *word* (= what positive news can you tell me)*?* • If someone **puts the word about/ around/out/round** they state a new piece of news: *Putting the word out that her health is failing would affect her chances of election.* ○ *So, the new manager has been appointed – should we put the word around?* • **Word gets about/around/round** means that news spreads fast within a group of people: *"I hear you were having drinks with a tall dark handsome man last night." "Wow, word certainly gets around!"* ○ *It was amazing how quickly word got round the school – within an hour of the arrest everyone knew.* • *(slightly infml)* **Word has it** is used to refer to something which is generally thought to be true although not official or known to be a fact: *Word has it* **(that)** *they may separate.* ○ *Word has it* **(that)** *the scandal about finances was kept quiet for years.* • The phrase **(the) word is** refers to something which has been reported but not officially stated: *The word is* **(that)** *more hostages will be released over the next few weeks.* • If **the word is out** then a piece of news is known, esp. if it was secret or if it will cause changes: *The word is out* **that** *superstar Candice is to marry towards the end of this year.*

word PROMISE /£wɜːd, $wɜːrd/ *n* a promise • *I shall* **keep** *my word – I said I'd visit him and that's what I'm going to do.* • *You* **have** *my word – I won't tell a soul.* • *(fml) He* **gave** *his word that he would marry her and she had no cause to doubt him.* • To **take** someone **at** their **word** or **take** someone's **word for it** means to believe what they say is true: *He said he'd give me a job and I just took him at his word.* ○ *If he says there's $500 in the envelope then I'll take his word for it.* • *(dated or humorous)* If someone's **word is** their **bond**, they always keep their promises: *"But listen, you must promise never to tell anyone." "My word is my bond."* ○ *His word is his bond.* • A **man of his word/ woman of her word** is someone who keeps their promise: *You can trust him – he's a man of his word.*

word ORDER /£wɜːd, $wɜːrd/ *n* [C usually sing] an order • *We're waiting for the word from head office before making a statement.* • *Miranda, if at any point you want to leave, just* **say the** *word* (= tell me what you want). • *If you want me to order any books for you just* **give me the** *word.* • *Don't shoot until you hear my word.* • *The troops will go into action as soon as their commander* **gives/says** *the word.* • **At** *a word from their teacher, the children started to tidy away their books.* • **From the word go** means from the start of something: *The bridge building project had problems with funding right from the word go.*

word·play /£ˈwɜːd·pleɪ, $ˈwɜːrd-/ *n* [U] joking about the meanings of words, esp. in a clever way • *Much of the play's humour derives from the witty wordplay between the lovers.*

word·smith /£ˈwɜːd·smɪθ, $ˈwɜːrd-/ *n* [C] a person who has skill with using words, esp. in writing • *In today's review section Anthony Edwards, playwright, poet, novelist and general wordsmith, talks about his glittering career.*

wore /£wɔːʳ, $wɔːr/ *past simple of* WEAR

work ACTIVITY /£wɜːk, $wɜːrk/ *n* [U] an activity, such as a job, in which a person uses their body and/or their mind to make or do something, usually for money, or the material used or what is produced • *I've got so much work to* **do**. • *Carrying heavy loads around all day is* **hard** *work.* • *What time do you* **start/finish** *work?* • *Work in the laboratory was interesting but not very well paid.* • *Adrian* **does** *most of the work around the house.* • *Johnny got the house quite cheap but he had to* **do** *a lot of work* **on** *it.* • *What sort of work do you have experience in?* • *That's odd, she's never late for work.* • *She tends to wear quite smart clothes for work.* • *Roger's work involves a lot of travelling.* • *Labourers were* **at** *work* (= working) *in the fields reaping.* • *(fig.) It seems as though forces of destruction are increasingly* **at** *work throughout* (= having a bad effect on) *society.* • *Some* **pioneering** *research work was done on this subject in the 1950s.* • *I'll have to take this work home with me and finish it there.* • *All the furniture is the work of residents here.* • *His work* **in** *leather is always of a very high standard.* • When you **get/go/set to work** on something you start doing it: *We'd better get to work* **on** *stacking this wood if we want to finish before it gets dark.* • If someone **has** their **work cut out (for** them) to do something then it will be very difficult: *She'll really have her work cut out to finish all those reports by the end of the week.* • *Increasingly, people who are* **in** *work* (= have a job) *are getting busier and those who are* **out of** *work* (= do not have a job) *are finding it harder to get a job.* • The **work ethic** is the belief that work is morally good: *The work ethic was never very strong in Simon.* • **Work experience** is either the experience that a person already has of working, or a period of time in which a student temporarily works for an employer to gain experience: *Please list your educational qualifications and work experience.* ○ *Many firms understand that giving work experience to students from colleges and schools will benefit everyone in the long term.* • A **work permit** is an official document which gives permission to someone who is foreign to work in a country. • A **work surface** is a WORKTOP. • *(saying)* 'All work and no play (makes Jack a dull boy)' means that someone who works all of the time will become boring and uninteresting. • *"Work expands so as to fill the time available for its completion"* (C. Northcote Parkinson *Parkinson's Law*, 1958) • LP **Work**

work *(obj)* /£wɜːk, $wɜːrk/ *v* • *She works incredibly* **hard**. [I] • *He works at the local hospital.* [I] • *She worked* **as** *a cleaner at the hospital for a long time.* [I] • *Both parents lived and worked abroad for many years.* [I] • *Mike works* **for** *a computer company.* [I] • *It's not unusual for a junior doctor to work a seventy or sometimes an eighty hour week.* [T] • *Have you any experience of working* **with** *children who have learning difficulties?* [I] • *His dancing technique is good but he needs to work* **on** (= make an effort to improve) *his fitness.* [I] • *Most couples would agree that for a marriage to succeed, both parties have to work* **at** *it* (= make a positive effort). [I] • *A project like this only succeeds if people work* **together** *as a team.* [I] • *Dr Lehrer has worked for years* **to** *save these very rare birds.* [+ to infinitive] • *The instructors worked us very* **hard** *on the survival course.* [T] • *(approving)* If a person *(Br)* **works like a Trojan**/*(Am and Aus)* **works like a dog**, they work very hard. • If you **work till/until** you **drop**, you work until you are so tired that you cannot work any more. • If someone **works** their **fingers to the bone** they work extremely hard, esp. for a long time: *She worked her fingers to the bone to provide a home and food for seven children.* • When people **work to rule** they carefully obey all of the rules and instructions given to them about their jobs with the intention of reducing the amount of work they do. • A **work-to-rule** is a case of people working to rule: *Most work-to-rules are done as a protest against low pay or bad working conditions.*

-work /£-wɜːk, $-wɜːrk/ *combining form* • The word -work is used to refer to work of a stated type: *homework* • *paperwork* • -Work also refers to the type of material which is used in a particular activity: *Girls and boys study woodwork and metalwork at this school.* • -Work can also be used to name things that are made of a stated material: *stonework* • *ironwork*

work·er /£ˈwɜː·kəʳ, $ˈwɜːr·kɚ/ *n* [C] • A worker is someone who works in a particular job or in a particular way: *factory/social/construction workers* • *a good/tireless/ skilled/average worker* • *(esp. dated)* A worker is also a person who is employed to work with their hands rather than organize: *Many companies still treat their management staff better than their workers.* • In bees and some other types of insects, a worker is a female which cannot produce young but collects food for other bees. • PIC **Wasps and bees**

work·ing /£ˈwɜː·kɪŋ, $ˈwɜːr-/ *adj* [before n; not gradable] • *Generally, working people don't have time to shop for food every day.* • *Changes to the taxation system will affect 90% of the working population.* • *She likes to change out of her working* **clothes** *as soon as she gets home.* • *The working* **hours** *here are variable because we operate a shift system.* • *Many car workers are employed on a 37-hour working* **week**. • *Working* **conditions/practices** *in the mill have hardly changed over the last twenty years.* • *She has a difficult working* **relationship** *with many of her staff.* • *There's a great deal to do so we'd better have a working* **lunch/ breakfast** (= a meal during which work is discussed). • The **working capital** of a company is the money it has which is immediately available for business use, rather than money in investments or property. • The **working class/classes** is the group of people in society who are paid a

WORDS USED TOGETHER

The dictionary definition of a word does not give you all the information you need in order to understand and use that word. You cannot use a word in a natural way unless you also know how it is used in sentences or groups of words. This means recognizing which words go naturally together and sound right. The example sentences and phrases in this dictionary help you in many ways to do this, as you can see in the following examples of the verb 'make':

WAYS THAT WORDS CAN BE USED TOGETHER

grammar patterns
The words are placed together for grammatical reasons. The grammar labels in square brackets [ ] tell you the grammar pattern. Words in **bold** cannot be omitted unless they are in round brackets ( ).
The prisoners were made **to** *dig holes.* [+ *to* infinitive]
I make the answer (**to be**) *105.6.* [+ obj + (*to be*) n/adj]

preposition partners
Only particular prepositions can be used. Changing the preposition changes the meaning and might be an error.
Butter is made **out of/from** *milk.* • *He made some coffee* **for** *us.*
They made the attic **into** *a spare room.*

word partners (collocations)
Words that are often placed together, although there is no strong grammatical reason for them to be together. The meaning of the word group is clear from the definitions of the words it contains. It is usually not wrong to choose different words, but these might not sound natural.
She's made a **request** *for a new car.* • *Lizzie, have you made your* **bed***?*
How do you make **a living** *as a painter?*

phrases, idioms
The word group has a special meaning or use which you cannot easily guess from the meanings of the words it contains. Generally the parts of the phrase cannot be changed for others. Idioms are very important in informal speech.
The boss has the power to **make or break** (=cause success or complete failure for) *your career.* • If you say someone is **made of money** you mean they are very rich.

compounds
The meaning is usually related to the meaning of its parts, but the combination has a particular meaning of its own and should be learned as a separate item.
make-believe • *makeweight* • *troublemaker*

sayings
Well known and wise statements. Generally we do not know who first used a particular saying (compare quotations).
You've made your bed and now you must lie in it.

quotations
Well-known sentences or phrases taken from books, songs, films etc.
Go ahead, make my day! (said by Clint Eastwood in the film "Dirty Harry").

Additional notes

• **Compound nouns**
Compound nouns are written in three ways: as one word (*landslide*), as separate words (*bank account*), or using a hyphen (-) to connect the word (*father-in-law*). There are no simple rules about this, and the same word might be written in all three ways by different people.
When spoken, compound nouns often have a main stress on the first part: compare *Her mother's bracelets were much too large for her small arms and kept falling off* with *The terrorists had been trying to smuggle small arms* (=small guns) *into the country.* The usual stress is shown in the Phrase Index.

• **Compound verbs (phrasal verbs)**
These verbs are made up of two or three words, for example: *make up* or *make off with.* They are very common in both informal and ordinary styles of English. LP **Compound verbs** at COMPOUND.

• **Word partners (collocations)**
Word partners are easy to understand, but learners in their own writing or speaking might use different partners which do not sound natural or 'right'. *My grandfather made this house* sounds strange because we usually say *built.* Some combinations are wrong: for example you cannot say 'She did a mistake', but only *She made a mistake.*
Knowledge of word partners is important for developing a richer and more interesting use of English. For example, when praising something English speakers choose from many words: *a fine poem, an impressive performance, a brilliant career, a helpful suggestion, a great success.* Learners tend to use the same basic word (for example *good*) again and again.
Example sentences in the dictionary give important word partners. Computers were used to measure how often particular words are used together, and then to calculate how important these partners are. (Partners like *the* or *some* are very common but are often not important for meaning.)

WORK

Here are some common words and expressions we use in everyday conversation to talk about the work we do, leaving work, being out of work and looking for a job.

The work we do

What do you do? • *What (sort of) work do you do?* • *What do you do for a living?*
Where do you work? asks about your employer as well as the place where you work.

I'm a nurse. • *I work* **for** *a finance company* **as** *an accountant.* • *I work* **at/in** *the supermarket.*
I've got a **part-time** *job two days a week.* (The opposite of part-time is full-time)
I got a **temporary** *job at the local garage until April.* (The opposite of temporary is permanent)
Casual work is not regular or fixed: *I do a bit of casual work as a receptionist.*

If we know a person we might ask: *How's work (going)?* • *How's your job (going)?*

Leaving a job

The words we use depend on the reason the person left their job:

- They chose to leave:
  Are you still working for Kett & Smith? No, I **left** *there months ago.*
  Jane **resigned from** *her job so she could go to college.*
  I was so angry at the way my boss treated me I **resigned/quit** *straight away.*
  You usually **give notice** that you will be leaving a job: *You need to give a month's notice.*
- Their employer no longer needed them or could no longer pay them:
  120 people **lost their jobs/were laid off** *when the factory closed.*
  (Br) The company had to **make** *another four sales reps* **redundant**.
  (Am) I'm sorry, George, but it looks like we're going to have to **let** *you* **go**.
- Their employer was not happy with their work:
  He was **dismissed/fired/asked to leave**.
  (infml) Did you hear that Rita **was sacked/got the sack** *again?*
- They left for a temporary period:
  He **took** *three month's* **leave** *and travelled around Africa.*
  I was ill last year and had to **take** *a lot of* **time off work**.
  Is Sam in today? No, he's **on leave/(Br) holiday/(Am) vacation**. • *Don't forget I'm* **off** *next week.*
  Ann is taking **maternity leave** (to have a baby). • *two weeks'* **sick leave**.
- They had reached the age when people usually stop working:
  Mr Peters **retired** *last month. He was 65.*
  I'm planning to **take** *early* **retirement** *when I'm 55.* • *I'm* **retired**: *I stopped work two years ago.*

Being out of work and looking for a job

I haven't got a job at present. • *I'm* **unemployed/out of work/between jobs** *at the moment.*
I'm **looking for** *work.* • *I'm getting quite good at* **job-hunting** (looking for work).
I **applied for** *a job with Saunders and they've invited me to an interview.*
I **tried/went for** *a job last week: I hope I get it.*

comparatively low amount of money for their work, often being paid only for the hours or days that they work, and who often use physical rather than mental skills in their jobs: *The working class usually react/reacts in a predictable way to government policies.* ○ *The working classes tend to travel more now than they did in the past.* ○ *He was born into a working-class* **family**. ○ *You and your working-class* **mentality**! Compare **lower class** at LOWER; **middle class** at MIDDLE; **upper class** at UPPER [HIGHER]. • A **working day** (*esp. Am* **workday**) is either the amount of time a person spends doing their job on a day when they work, or a day on which most people go to work: *An eight-hour working day is still typical for many people.* ○ **On** *a working day I tend to get up around seven o'clock.* ○ *Please allow three full working days for the money to be transferred.* • *(infml dated)* A **working girl** is a female PROSTITUTE (= a woman who has sex for money). • *His entire* **working life** (= the part of a person's life when they are at work) *was spent with the same firm.* • *Little provision is made for* **working mothers** (= women who have a job and care for their children) *by many large companies.* • A **working party** is a small group of people, for example one chosen by a government, which studies a particular problem or situation and then reports on what it has discovered and any suggestions it has: *An official working party is examining different voting systems for all tiers of government.* • *(Am)* **Working papers** are official documents which allow someone under 16 years old to be employed.

work *(obj)* [OPERATE] /£wɜːk, $wɜːrk/ *v* (of a machine, device, plan or suggestion) to operate or cause to operate,

• Quotations and sayings

The dictionary includes over 2,000 quotations so that you can recognize them and understand better what is being said. These are the quotations which are most commonly found in ordinary conversations, newspapers and so on. They are expressions from popular songs, television, films, books, plays and sayings by famous people. Information is also given about where each quotation comes from and when it was first used.

Quotations and sayings are often used in full, for example: *I'll make him an offer he can't refuse* (Mario Puzo, 1961). Sometimes only part of the sentence is mentioned: *My new job is better paid than my old one, but the work's not so interesting–it's swings and roundabouts, really* (referring to the *(Br)* saying *'What you lose on the swings, you gain on the roundabouts'*).

People might also change a quotation or refer to it indirectly, often in order to be humorous. These indirect, suggested quotations are especially common in newspaper and magazine headlines and advertisements. They are often difficult for a learner to recognize and understand: *He has worked on a number of Hollywood movies: the good, the bad and the very successful* (referring to the film 'The Good, the Bad and the Ugly'). • *A brave new world of international banking will be dominated by ten or 15 giant banks* (referring to the book 'Brave New World' by Aldous Huxley describing an imaginary perfect world in the future).

esp. correctly and without failure • *Our telephone isn't working.* [I] • *You need a team of about twelve people to work a furnace this size.* [T] • *We only have electricity when the generator is working.* [I] • *The pump works* **off/on** (= uses) *wind power.* [T] • *The pump is worked* **by** (= uses to operate) *wind power.* [T] • *Guy, could you help me – I can't* **make** *this washing machine work.* [I] • *I can't* **get** *the radio* **to** *work.* [I] • *Nobody really understands how the human mind works.* [I] • *These tablets will start to work* (= have an effect) *a few minutes after they have been swallowed.* [I] • *Her idea for reorganizing the department will never work* **in practice**. [I] • *Arguably, monarchy worked* **well** *for many centuries.* [I] • *(Br) This new drill works* **a treat** (= works very well) *on hard metals.* [T] • Something which **works like a charm/works like magic** is very effective possibly in a surprising way: *Flattery usually works like a charm with him.* • If something **works miracles/wonders** it produces very beneficial effects: *Often a little bit of oil works wonders if you want to stop a hinge squeaking.* ○ *You're very tired – a week off would work miracles* **for** *you.*

work·a·ble /£'wɜː·kə·bl̩, $'wɜːr-/ *adj* • A workable plan or system is one that can operate effectively: *a workable solution/compromise/proposal* ○ *The country's tragedy is that there is now no workable option: it cannot stay together, nor can it peacefully fall apart.*

work·ing /£'wɜː·kɪŋ, $'wɜːr-/ *adj* [before n; not gradable] • *It has taken about five years to restore the aircraft to* **(full)** *working* **condition/order**. • In a machine the working parts are those which move: *It is essential that all working components are properly lubricated.* • If an idea or knowledge can be described as working then it is good enough to be useful: *We have a working* **theory/hypothesis** *about what caused the crash, which we shall test over the next few days.* ○ *She's fluent in French and English and has a working* **knowledge** *of Spanish.* • The **working life** of a machine is the complete amount of time for which it can be expected to operate: *The working life of most vehicles can be increased if they are serviced regularly.*

work·ings /£'wɜː·kɪŋz, $'wɜːr-/ *pl n* • **The** workings **of** an organization, machine or organism are the way it operates: *the workings of government* ○ *I don't know anything about the workings of other departments or about the organization as a whole.* ○ *Marshall's papers provided a rare look into the workings of the contemporary court.* • See also WORKINGS.

works /£wɜːks, $wɜːrks/ *pl n* • The works of a machine are its parts, esp. those that move: *If you take the back off this clock you can see its/the works.* • See also **works** at WORK [PLACE] and WORKS.

work [PLACE] /£wɜːk, $wɜːrk/ *n* [U] a place where a person goes specially to do their job • *Do you have far to travel* **to** *work each day?* • *She'll be* **at** *work until late this afternoon.* • *Thousands of people are seriously injured* **at** *work every year.* • *When does she leave* **for** *work?* • *"Go to work on an egg"* (advertisement for eggs, 1957-)

works /£wɜːks, $wɜːrks/ *n* [C + sing/pl v] *pl* **works** • A works is an industrial building, esp. one where a lot of people are employed: *a steel/car works* • See also **works** at WORK [OPERATE] and WORKS.

work *(obj)* [ACHIEVE] /£wɜːk, $wɜːrk/ *v* [always + adv/prep] to achieve or cause (something), esp. gradually, either by making an effort or by making many small movements • *He started as a technician and worked his* **way up** *through the company over the next thirty years to become managing director.* [T] • *Vibration does tend to make nuts and screws work (*__*themselves*__*) loose.* [I/T] • *Eventually she worked her* **way through** (= read) *the huge amount of technical papers.* [T] • *We worked* **up** *a real appetite climbing in the mountains.* [M] • *It's strange but I can't work any enthusiasm* **up** *for going on this trip.* [M] • *He's very shy but he's slowly working* **himself**/*his way* **up to** *letting her know what he feels about her.* [T] • *I think they're both gradually working* **around to/round to** (= preparing themselves slowly for) *talking to each other again.* [I] • If you **work off** an unpleasant feeling you rid yourself of it: *She works off stress by running for at least half an hour every day.* ○ *Do something to work off your frustration with the job or you'll become ill.*

work [OBJECT] /£wɜːk, $wɜːrk/ *n* [C] an object produced as a result of effort, esp. an artistically pleasing object • *The museum has many works* **by** *Picasso as well as other modern painters.* • *Our group specializes in performing works* **by/the** *works* **of** *South and Central American composers.* • A **work of art** is an object made by an artist of great skill, esp. a painting, drawing or statue: *The mosque's decoration was a work of art.*

work *obj* [SHAPE] /£wɜːk, $wɜːrk/ *v* [T] to shape, change or process (a substance) • *Working iron requires higher temperatures than bronze.* • *Gently work the butter* **into** *the flour until there are no lumps left.* • *Put the flour and butter into a bowl and work the butter* **in**. [M]

work·a·ble /£'wɜː·kə·bl̩, $'wɜːr-/ *adj* • *The ground is too hard to be workable* (= dug).

work [HAVE EFFECT] /£wɜːk, $wɜːrk/ *v* [I always + adv/prep] (of a condition or fact) to have an effect, esp. one which either helps or causes difficulties • *Inexperience can work* **against** *a candidate looking for a job but if they will accept a low initial salary then that can work* **for them/in** *their* **favour**.

work *obj* [ARRANGE] /£wɜːk, $wɜːrk/ *v* [T] *infml* to arrange for (something to happen), esp. by not using official methods and/or by being clever • *I don't know how she worked* **it** *but she retired at fifty on a full salary.* • *Can we work* **things (out)** *so that there's always someone here to answer the telephone during office hours?* • *Would it be possible to work* **in** *a meeting for all those concerned some time later this week?* • *(slightly infml)* If you **work on** someone you try to persuade or influence them: *I'm working on my father to get him to take me to the airport.*

work [PHYSICS] /£wɜːk, $wɜːrk/ *n* [U] *specialized* force multiplied by distance moved

work out *obj* [REASON], **work** *obj* **out** *v adv* [M] to use reasoning or calculation either to discover or understand (an answer or an idea) or to make (a decision or a plan) • *It would take a huge amount of time to work out the solution to these equations if we didn't use a computer.* • *Investigators needed several months to work out* **that** *a fraud had been committed.* [+ *that* clause] • *There will be a full investigation to work out* **what** *caused the accident.* [+ *wh-* word] • *Can we work out* **who** *will take responsibility for organising the food?* [+ *wh-* word] • *I can't work out* **when** *we'll be away until I've spoken with the travel agent again.* [+ *wh-* word]

work out [HAPPEN] *v adv* [I] (of a situation) to happen or develop in a particular, often satisfactory or pleasing way, or (of a person) to be suitable for a particular situation • *It will be interesting to see how the new monitoring procedure works out.* • *How are* **things** *working out at home with the new baby?* • *We all hope that your new job will work out* **(well)** *for you.* • *Don't worry about anything – it'll* **all** *work out* **(for the best)** (= everything will be satisfactory), *you'll see.* • *Is your new assistant/roommate working out OK?*

work out [CALCULATE] *v adv* to calculate something to be a particular amount • *These figures work out differently each time I add them.* [I always + adv/prep] • *The safe load for a truck of this size works out* **at** *nearly twenty tonnes.* [I always + adv/prep] • *In fact the trip worked out cheaper than we'd expected.* [L only + adj]

work out [EXERCISE] *v adv* [I] to exercise in order to improve the strength or appearance of the body • *Huw works out in the gym two or three times a week.*

work·out /£'wɜː·kaʊt, $'wɜːr-/ *n* [C] • *a vigorous/light workout* • *He can lose up to four pounds in sweat in an hour's workout.*

work o·ver *obj*, **work** *obj* **o·ver** *v adv* [M] *slightly dated infml* to attack and injure (someone) • *Shopkeepers who couldn't pay the money demanded from them were often worked over by gang members.*

work *obj* **up** [MAKE UPSET] *v adv* [T] to make yourself or another person feel upset or feel strong emotions • *Try not to work* **yourself** *up about the exams.* • *By the time they arrived at the house she'd worked* **herself** *up* **into** *a real state.* • *Nationalist speeches worked the crowd up* **into a frenzy**.

worked up /£wɜːkt, $wɜːrkt/ *adj* [after v] • *It's easy to* **get** *worked up when you're tired and everything seems to be against you.* • *He was very worked up* **about** *seeing his family again after so many years apart.*

work up *obj* [IMPROVE], **work** *obj* **up** *v adv* [M] to improve (a piece of work such as a study or a piece of writing), esp. gradually • *We hope to work the data we've collected up* **into** *a series of reports.*

work·a·day /£'wɜː·kə·deɪ, $'wɜːr-/ *adj* [before n] ordinary; not unusual • *Compared to the extravagance and glamour of last winter's clothes, this season's collection look simple, almost workaday.*

work·a·hol·ic /£ˌwɜː·kə'hɒl·ɪk, $ˌwɜːr·kə'hɑː·lɪk/ *n* [C] a person who works a lot of the time and finds it difficult not to work • *A self-confessed workaholic, Tony Richardson can't remember when he last had a holiday.*

work·a·hol·i·sm /£'wɜː·kə·hɒl·ɪ·zᵊm, $'wɜːr·kə·hɑː·lɪ-/ *n* [U] • *Once workaholism sets in, it progresses through stages similar to those in alcoholism and drug addiction.*

work·bas·ket /£'wɜːkˌbɑː·skɪt, $'wɜːrkˌbæs·kɪt/, *esp. Br*
work·box /£'wɜːk·bɒks, $'wɜːrk·bɑːks/ *n* [C] a small container in which items used for sewing, such as needles, pins and thread, are kept

work·bench /£'wɜːk·bentʃ, $'wɜːrk-/ *n* [C] a strong table for working on, esp. one on which objects such as pieces of wood or metal can be firmly held so that tools can be used on them

work·book /£'wɜːk·bʊk, $'wɜːrk-/ *n* [C] a book containing instructions or a book used in school having text and questions and sometimes having spaces for a student to write answers in • *There's a workbook to accompany the course book.*

work·day /£'wɜːk·deɪ, $'wɜːrk-/ *n* [C] *esp. Am and Aus for* **working day**, see at WORK [ACTIVITY]

work·force /£'wɜːk·fɔːs, $'wɜːrk·fɔːrs/ *n* [C + sing/pl v] the group of people who work in a company, industry, country etc. • *The majority of factories in the region have a workforce* **of** *50 to 100 (people).* • *Much of the workforce in the banking sector is/are affected by the new legislation.* • *Singapore attracts foreign investors in part by advertising its educated workforce.*

work·horse /£'wɜːk·hɔːs, $'wɜːrk·hɔːrs/ *n* [C] a person who does a lot of work, esp. of a type which is necessary but uninteresting • *Graham was the sort of workhorse a local political party could rely on throughout a campaign.* • A workhorse is also a machine which operates without failing for long periods although it might not be very interesting or exciting: *The steam engine was the workhorse of the Industrial Revolution.*

work·house /£'wɜːk·haʊs, $'wɜːrk-/ *n* [C] *pl* **workhouses** /£'wɜːkˌhaʊ·zɪz, $'wɜːrk-/ (in Britain in the past) a building where very poor people worked in exchange for food and shelter • *Throughout the later 19th century, workhouses were seen as places of degradation and inhumanity.* • Compare POORHOUSE.

work·ings /£'wɜː·kɪŋz, $'wɜːr-/ *pl n* the system of holes which has been dug in the ground in order to remove metal, coal, etc. • *old mine workings* • *colliery workings* • *disused workings* • See also **workings** at WORK [OPERATE].

work·load /£'wɜːk·ləʊd, $'wɜːrk·loʊd/ *n* [C] the amount of work to be done, esp. by a particular person or machine in a period of time • *Teachers are always complaining about their* **heavy** *workloads.* • *Students do find that their workload* **increases** *throughout the course.*

work·man /£'wɜːk·mən, $'wɜːrk-/ *n* [C] *pl* **-men** a man who uses physical skill and especially his hands in his job or trade • *We'll have to get a workman in to fix the plumbing/window/roof.*

work·man·like /£'wɜːk·mən·laɪk, $'wɜːrk-/ *adj* • *(approving)* Workmanlike means skilful: *The Australian side turned in a very workmanlike and solid* **performance**. • *(disapproving)* Workmanlike also means showing an acceptable level of skill but no great ability: *I had hoped for a little more from the world's greatest tenor, whose performance was workmanlike but hardly inspired.*

work·man·ship /£'wɜːk·mən·ʃɪp, $'wɜːrk-/ *n* [U] • Workmanship is the skill with which something was made or done: *shoddy/fine workmanship* ○ *The workmanship which went into some of these pieces of furniture was truly remarkable.* ○ *The leading lady's gowns were made by Lucile and were masterpieces of intricate workmanship.*

work·mate /£'wɜːk·meɪt, $'wɜːrk-/ *n* [C] *infml* a person who works in the same place as you, esp. one with whom you are friendly • *I went out for a drink with a few workmates.*

work·out /£'wɜː·kaʊt, $'wɜːr-/ *n* [C] See at WORK OUT [EXERCISE]

work·place /£'wɜːk·pleɪs, $'wɜːrk-/ *n* a building or room where people perform their jobs, or these places generally • *The survey asks workers about facilities in their workplace.* [C] • *There is growing concern in the chemical industry about safety standards in* **the** *workplace.* [U]

work·room /£'wɜːk·rʊm, $'wɜːrk-/ *n* [C] a room in which work is done, esp. sewing

works /£wɜːks, $wɜːrks/ *pl n* **the works** *infml* everything in a particular group or situation • *The bridegroom was wearing a morning suit, gloves, top hat – the works.* • *She saw the works during the war – starving kids, dead bodies, wounded soldiers.* • *(esp. Am) And let me have two large pizzas* **with** *the works* (= with all available types of food on top). • *(dated slang)* To **give** someone **the works** means to severely attack them physically. • See also **works** at WORK [OPERATE], WORK [PLACE].

work·shop [ROOM] /£'wɜːk·ʃɒp, $'wɜːrk·ʃɑːp/ *n* [C] a room or building where things are made or repaired using machines and/or tools • *a carpentry/stone workshop* • *an engineering workshop* • *In the workshop he could see a row of lathes with a bench and set of tools behind each one.*

work·shop [MEETING] /£'wɜːk·ʃɒp, $'wɜːrk·ʃɑːp/ *n* [C] a meeting of people to discuss and/or perform practical work in a subject or activity • *a drama/training workshop* • *a weekend workshop* • *The local council* **runs** *a stress-management workshop.* • *Dancers who* **attend** *the workshops find them very helpful.* • A workshop **production** is a play which has been produced and sometimes written by a group of people in an informal way.

work·shy /£'wɜːk·ʃaɪ, $'wɜːrk-/ *adj Br disapproving* disliking work and trying to avoid it when possible • *Most of the unemployed are not workshy and genuinely do want jobs.*

work·sta·tion /£'wɜːkˌsteɪ·ʃᵊn, $'wɜːrk-/ *n* [C] a keyboard and screen with which a person can use a computer system, or an area in an office, factory etc. where a single person works

work·top *Br* /£'wɜːk·tɒp, $'wɜːrk·tɑːp/, **work sur·face**, *Am usually* **count·er**, *Aus usually* **bench (top)** /£'bentʃ·tɒp, $-tɑːp/ *n* [C] a flat surface in a kitchen, esp. on top of low furniture, on which food can be prepared • *Plastic coated worktops are easy to keep clean.* • [PIC] **Kitchen**

world [THE EARTH] /£wɜːld, $wɜːrld/ *n* [U] the planet on which human life has developed, esp. including all people and their ways of life • *The world's population is over five and a half billion.* • *Different parts of the world have very different climatic conditions.* • *Which bridge has the longest span in the world?* • *News of the disaster shocked the* **(whole/entire)** *world.* • *We live in a* **changing** *world and people must learn to adapt.* • *What kind of (a) world will we leave for our children?* • *He's very young and still has a lot to learn about* **the ways of the** *world* (= what types of behaviour are acceptable and how things are done). • *She's a world* **authority** *on foetal development.* • *How long it will be before the world chess* **champion** *is a computer is anyone's guess.* • *Merlene Ottey of Jamaica equalled her own world* **record** *in winning the 200 metres.* • If a person is in a **world of** their **own**, they consider their own thoughts and ideas and do not give much attention to what is happening around them: *When she was young, she* **lived in** *a world of her own and had very few friends.* • *(Br)* The expression **(all) the world and her husband/his wife** (*Am* **everyone and his brother**) means a great many people, esp. in a particular place at a particular time: *I'd never have gone on holiday that week if I'd known all the world and his wife were going as well.* • To be **at one with the world** means to be happy because you feel that you belong in the world and generally agree with what happens. • The expression **for all the world** means exactly: *She sounds for all the world* **like** *her mother on the telephone.* • If you say of something that it **makes the world go around/round**, you mean that it is extremely important and many ordinary events could not happen without it: **Love/Money** *makes the world go round.* • *(infml)* The phrase **out of this world** means extremely good: *What a restaurant – the food was out of this world!* ○ *The movie's special effects were out of this world.* • Someone who **has the world at** their **feet** is extremely successful and admired by a great number of people: *Five years after her debut, the diminutive star of the Royal Ballet has the world at her feet.* • The phrase **the world at large** means people generally: *Sometimes we think our job is hard, but in the world at large many people have much more unpleasant things to do.* • **If the world is** someone's **oyster**, they can do what they want to or go where they want to: *You're young and healthy and you have no commitments – the world is your oyster.* • You can use **in the world** to emphasize a question or a statement: *What in the world are you doing in the cupboard?* ○ *Who in the world could do such a thing?* ○ *She was in love and felt as though she didn't have a care in the world.* • A **man/woman of the world** has a lot of experience of life and people and can deal with most situations. • The **World Bank** is an international organization which was formed in 1945 to help economic development, esp. of poorer countries. • A **world-beater** is a person or thing that is better than any other of its type:

WORLD REGIONS

The following names are commonly used to refer to regions (= areas) of the world. They are not political units LP ➤ **Nations and nationalities.**

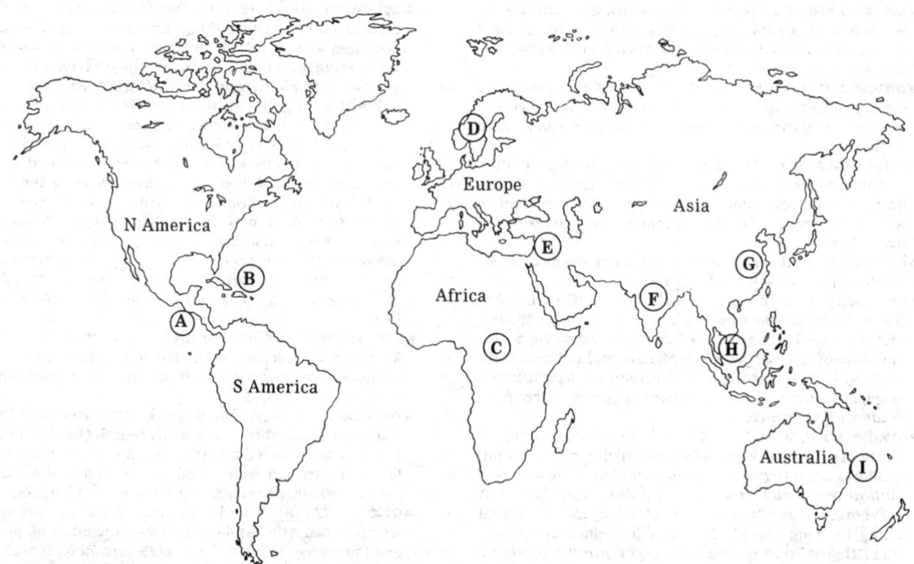

	Name of area	Some of the countries which are included
A	**Central America**	Guatemala, El Salvador, Nicaragua, Belize, Honduras, Costa Rica, Panama (**Latin America** is South America, Central America and Mexico)
B	**the Caribbean / the West Indies**	the islands of the Caribbean include Jamaica, Barbados, the Bahamas, Cuba, Puerto Rica and the Lesser Antilles
C	**Sub-Saharan Africa**	all the countries in Africa which are south of Algeria, Libya and Egypt
	Southern Africa	Namibia, Botswana, Mozambique, Zimbabwe and South Africa
D	**Scandinavia**	Norway, Sweden, Denmark, the Faroes, sometimes also Iceland and Finland
E	**the Middle East/ (*Am also*) the Mideast**	Egypt, Sudan, Iraq, Iran, Jordan, Israel, Syria, Saudi Arabia, sometimes also Turkey
	the Gulf States	Bahrain, Kuwait, Qatar, Oman, United Arab Emirates (*Am also*) the US states on the Gulf of Mexico
F	**South Asia**	Pakistan, India, Bangladesh, Sri Lanka. This area is also called the **Indian subcontinent**
G	**East Asia**	China, Japan, Taiwan, Korea, Hong Kong. This area is also called **the Far East**
H	**South East Asia/ Southeast Asia**	Thailand, the Philippines, Malaysia, Singapore, Cambodia, Vietnam, Burma, Laos, Indonesia
I	**Australasia**	Australia, New Zealand, Tasmania, Papua New Guinea
		Pacific Rim countries include Australia, Korea, Taiwan, sometimes also Japan and China

The continents are the main areas of land named on the map (Antarctica is not shown). The main part of Europe (without the islands of Britain and Ireland) is *(Br)* **the Continent**.

She has loads of natural talent as a runner and with rigorous training she could be a world-beater. • If something is **world-beating**, it is better than all the others of its type: *a world-beating partnership* • If a person or thing is **world-class**, they are among the best that there are of their type: *a world-class athlete/performance* • The **World Cup** is a football competition held every four years between teams from many countries in order to decide which is the best team: *the World Cup final* • *the Dutch World Cup squad* • A person or thing which is **world-famous** is known about by many people from most parts of the world: *a world-famous actress/hotel* • The **World Health Organization** (*abbreviation* **WHO**) is an international organization which tries to improve the health of people in all countries. • The expression **world music** refers to popular music which originates from many countries and is very different in style to ROCK (= a type of popular music). • A **world power** is a country which has enough economic or political strength to influence events in many other countries. • The **World Series** is a series of baseball games played each year in N America to decide which is the region's best team. • Something which is **world-shattering/world-shaking** is extremely surprising and important, often changing the way you think about something: *world-shattering news* • A **world war** is a war in which large forces from many countries fight, esp. **World War I** (*abbreviation* **WWI**) of 1914-1918 and **World War II** (*abbreviation* **WWII**) of 1939-1945. • Someone who is **world-weary** is not enthusiastic about anything, often because they have had too much experience of a particular way of life: *Fifteen years in the teaching profession had left him world-weary and cynical.* ○ *She spoke with the* **world-weariness** *of a star who has been under public scrutiny for too long.* • *"All the world's a stage, / And all the men and women merely players"* (Shakespeare, As You Like It 5.1) • *"The world is everything that is the case"* (Ludwig Wittgenstein in *Tractatus Logico-Philosphicus*, 1922) • LP› **World regions**

world GROUP/AREA /£wɜːld, $wɜːrld/ *n* [C usually sing] a group of things such as countries or animals, or an area of human activity or understanding • *the Muslim World* • *the industrialised world* • *the modern world* • *the animal world* • *the world of dogs* • *Many stars from the rock music world will be at the awards ceremony.* • *Bizarre and unexpected things can happen in* **the** *world* **of** *subatomic particles.* • *(Br infml)* When a person **goes up/comes down in the world** (*Am and Aus* **moves up/down in the world**) they have more/less money or a better/worse social position: *Roger and Ann have gone up in the world – these days they only ever travel first-class.*

world EVERYTHING /£wɜːld, $wɜːrld/ *n* [U] **the world** all that there is including the physical universe and all else that there is or might be • *If I took that job I'd have to leave the kids and I wouldn't do that* **for** *all the world* (=I could never do that). • *(slightly infml)* If someone **would never/would not** do something **for the world**, they would never do it whatever happens: *It's not possible – he'd never hurt his children for the world.* • If someone or something **is all the world** to you or **means (all) the world** to you then they are extremely important to you: *Her children mean all the world to her.* ○ *You mean the world to me, you know that Peter.*

world LARGE DEGREE /£wɜːld, $wɜːrld/ *n* [U] a large degree • *There's* **a** *world* **of difference** *between the service in the two hotels.*

worlds /£wɜːldz, $wɜːrldz/ *pl n* • *They are worlds* **apart** (=completely opposed) *in their political views.*

world PLANET /£wɜːld, $wɜːrld/ *n* [C] a planet or other part of the universe, esp. one where life might or does exist • *There was a man on the news last night who reckons we've been visited by beings from other worlds.*

world·ly PHYSICAL /£'wɜːld·li, $'wɜːrld-/ *adj* [before n] of physical things and ordinary life rather than spiritual things • *But your whole argument is based on worldly considerations alone and that isn't enough.* • *Her worldly success can hardly be denied.* • *For many of the refugees the clothes they are wearing are all the worldly* **goods** (=possessions) *they have.* • *"With all my worldly goods I thee endow"* (Marriage service from *The Book of Common Prayer*, 1662)

world·ly PRACTICAL /£'wɜːld·li, $'wɜːrld-/ *adj* practical and experienced, esp. rather than too moral • *She seems to be much more worldly than the other students in her class.* • If a person is **worldly-wise** they are experienced in the ways in which people behave and are able to deal with most situations: *Tyler is remarkably worldly-wise for such a young girl.*

world·li·ness /£'wɜːld·lɪ·nəs, $'wɜːrld-/ *n* [U]

world·wide /£ˌwɜːld'waɪd, $ˌwɜːrld-, '--/ *adj, adv* [not gradable] existing or happening in all parts of the world • *As we're always being told there's a worldwide recession.* • *An increase in average temperature by only a few degrees could cause environmental problems worldwide.*

worm /£wɜːm, $wɜːrm/ *n* [C] a small animal with a long narrow soft body without arms, legs or bones • *As worms move through soil they help to maintain its fertility.* • *I'm terrified of worms.* • A worm is also the young of particular types of insect: *It's distressing enough to find a worm in your apple but finding half of one is worse.* See also WOODWORM. • Some types of worm live in or on an animal's body and feed off it: *a parasitic worm* ○ *The vet says our dog* **has** *worms.* See also TAPEWORM. • *(disapproving)* If you call someone a worm, you mean that they are unpleasant and do not deserve respect: *He's just a worm, he's always nice to people when he's with them and then says horrid things about them later.* • If you say **the worm turns** you mean that a person or group of people that is usually obedient and does not cause any trouble becomes forceful when in a difficult situation: *It seems the worm has turned – after years of silence local people are beginning to protest about waste emissions from the factory.* • A **worm cast** is a small pile of earth or sand pushed up to the surface of the ground by particular types of worm, esp. EARTHWORMS. • Something such as a piece of wood which is **worm-eaten** has small holes in it which were made by the young of particular types of insect: *a worm-eaten table/beam* • PIC› **Worm**

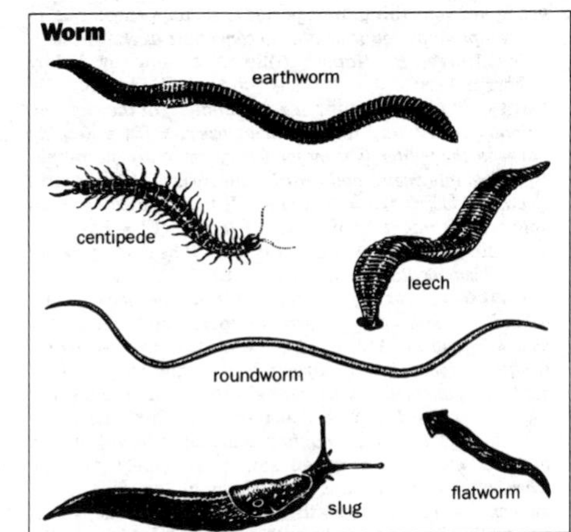

worm *obj* /£wɜːm, $wɜːrm/ *v* • If you worm an animal, esp. a pet dog or cat, you give it medicine to kill any worms which might be living inside it: *Has your dog been wormed?* [T] • If a person worms they move slowly or carefully, esp. because of difficulties: *Because he was so small he could worm (his* **way***) through the crowd.* [I/T always + adv/prep] ○ *She wormed* **herself** *under the fence.* [T always + adv/prep] • *(disapproving)* If a person worms their way or herself or himself **into** a position of trust they gradually achieve it, possibly by being dishonest: *He wormed himself into her affections without her ever suspecting he only did it for her money.* [T] • To **worm** information **out** of someone means to gradually obtain it from them, possibly dishonestly, although they are trying to keep it secret: *After repeated questioning the police wormed out of him what had actually happened.* [M]

worm·y /£'wɜː·mi, $'wɜːr-/ *adj* **-ier, -iest** • *The soil here is quite wormy* (=contains many worms). • *Look at these vegetables – they're all mottled and wormy* (=damaged by and usually still containing worms).

worm·hole /£'wɜːm·həʊl, $'wɜːrm·hoʊl/ *n* [C] a hole made by a worm such as in a piece of furniture, a piece of fruit or the ground • Also in physics a wormhole is a special type of structure which might exist connecting parts of space and time which are not usually connected.

worn /£wɔːn, $wɔːrn/ *past participle of* WEAR • If an object is **worn-out** it is no longer usable because it has had continued use which has made it too weak: *worn-out clothes/bearings* • If a person or an animal is **worn-out** they are extremely tired: *They were worn-out after their long walk.*

wor·ry *(obj)* /£'wʌr·i, $'wɜːr-/ *v* (to cause a person) to think about unpleasant things which might happen or about problems, esp. in a way which makes the person unhappy • *Try not to worry – there's nothing you can do to change the situation.* [I] • *"I'm sorry I didn't call you last night." "Don't worry, I wasn't offended."* [I] • *You worried your mother by not writing.* [T] • *The continued lack of rain is starting to worry people.* [T] • *She's worried* **(that)** *she might not be able to find another job.* [+ (*that*) clause] • *It's silly worrying* **about** *things which are outside your control.* [I] • *The leak of radioactive material has worried many people.* [T] • *"I haven't finished the designs yet." "They'll only be changed again next week –* **why worry?"** [I] • If a person or an animal worries something, they shake, pull at or touch it repeatedly: *The dog was worrying its bone.* [T] ○ *She was worrying the papers on her desk throughout the meeting.* [T] • If a dog worries another animal it chases and frightens it and might also bite it: *Any dog caught worrying sheep in these fields will be shot.* [T] • To **worry at** a problem means to keep trying to find a way of solving it: *She'll worry at those figures until she's sure they've been worked out properly.* • *(infml humorous)* The phrase **don't worry your pretty little head** is used to mean do not worry: *"What about all the work that needs doing in the kitchen?" "I'll sort that out – don't worry your pretty little head* **about** *it!"* • *(infml)* You can use the phrase **not to worry** to show that you are not worried or upset because something has gone wrong or something unexpected has happened: *Not to worry – perhaps you'll be able to come next week instead.* • *"Don't Worry, Be Happy"* (title of a song by Bobby McFerrin, 1988)

wor·ry /£ˈwʌr·i, $ˈwɜːr-/ *n* • *Fortunately, at the moment, we don't really have any financial worries.* [C] • *Keeping warm in the winter is a major worry for many old people.* [C] • *Unemployment, bad health – all sorts of things can be a cause of worry.* [U] • *Do you really not have any worries* **about** *what might happen in the future?* [C] • *But there was a* **nagging** *worry in his mind that if he'd acted sooner the problem would not have arisen.* [C]

wor·ried /£ˈwʌr·id, $ˈwɜːr-/ *adj* • *She was sitting behind her desk with a worried* **expression/look** *on her face.* • *I don't think you should be* **unduly** *worried by the swelling – you clearly haven't broken anything.* • *They don't seem particularly worried* **about** *the situation.* • *You* **had** *me worried* (=You made me feel anxious) *for a moment back there – I thought you wouldn't be able to stop in time.* • *He was* **worried sick** (=extremely worried) *when he heard that there had been an accident.* • *My mother's* **worried to death** (=extremely worried) *about my brother because she hasn't heard from him for over a month.*

wor·ried·ly /£ˈwʌr·id·li, $ˈwɜːr-/ *adv* • *He was standing with his back to the door, worriedly looking over his shoulder.*

wor·ri·er /£ˈwʌr·i·əʳ, $ˈwɜːr·i·ɚ/ *n* [C] • *I can't help being a worrier* (=a person who worries a lot) – *some people are just born that way.*

wor·ry·ing /£ˈwʌr·i·ɪŋ, $ˈwɜːr-/ *adj* • *It's a worrying situation to have a serious disease which is spreading through the population and to be unable to cure it.*

wor·ry·ing·ly /£ˈwʌr·i·ɪŋ·li, $ˈwɜːr-/ *adv* • *Worryingly, the gun was never found.* • *The last time I saw her she was looking worryingly thin.*

wor·ri·some /£ˈwʌr·ɪ·səm, $ˈwɜːr-/ *adj fml or dated* • *It is a worrisome* (=worrying) *possibility that the drugs may have side effects which were not initially recognized.* • *Alcohol and tobacco consumption by young people is especially worrisome because habits formed early are likely to persist.*

wor·ry·wart /£ˈwʌr·i·wɔːt, $ˈwɜːr·i·wɔːrt/ *n* [C] *esp. Am and Aus infml* a person who tends to worry, esp. about unimportant things • *Don't listen to him – he's just an old worrywart.*

worse /£wɜːs, $wɜːrs/ *adj* [not gradable], *comparative of* BAD; more unpleasant, difficult or severe than before or than something else • *The conditions they're living in are worse* **than** *we thought.* • *Annette may be bad at giving directions but Kate's worse.* • *Their relationship is so bad, it's difficult to see what could* **make** *it worse.* • *His manners are* **even** *worse than his sister's.* • *If the rain gets any worse we'll have to stop walking.* • *The vibration gets worse at higher speeds.* • *The heat is* **much** *worse in the daytime.* • When a person who is ill **gets** worse they become more ill: *My cold seems to be getting worse.* ○ *If his throat gets* **any** *worse I'll take him to the doctor's.* • *Don't say anything – you'll only* **make matters worse** (=make the situation even more unpleasant or difficult). • The expression **none the worse (for)** means not harmed or damaged (by): *They were trapped in the cave for a couple of days but they were none the worse for their experience.* ○ *He's lost some weight but he's none the worse* (=he's better) *for that.* • If someone is **the worse for drink** they have had too much alcohol: *By the time I got to the party Patrick was looking* **a bit** *the worse for drink.* • Someone or something which is **the worse for wear** is tired or in poor condition because of a lot of work or use: *After a month of journeying over rough roads the drivers and their trucks were looking the worse for wear.* • *(infml)* You can add **worse luck** to the end of a statement to show unhappiness or annoyance about what has been stated: *I've got to work on Saturday, worse luck.* • Compare BETTER [COMPARATIVE OF GOOD].

worse /£wɜːs, $wɜːrs/ *n* [U] • *By the third month of the expedition they had endured many hardships, but worse was to follow.* • *"What about the bride's dress – wasn't it appalling?" "I don't know, I've* **seen** *worse."* • If something changes or happens **for the worse**, the unpleasantness or difficulty increases: *It looks like the weather is* **changing** *for the worse.* ○ *"The atmosphere in this office has changed a lot recently." "For the worse or for the better?"* • Compare BETTER [IMPROVEMENT].

worse /£wɜːs, $wɜːrs/ *adv* • Worse is the comparative of badly: *He did worse than he was expecting in the exams* ○ *He drives worse now than he did when he was younger.*

wors·en *(obj)* /£ˈwɜː·sᵊn, $ˈwɜːr-/ *v* • *As the company's financial problems worsened, several directors resigned.* [I] • *Meanwhile, the president's health continues to worsen and is a source of considerable concern.* [I] • *The continued supply of arms to the region will only worsen the situation.* [T]

wors·en·ing /£ˈwɜː·sᵊn·ɪŋ, $ˈwɜːr-/ *adj* • *Many people are concerned about the country's worsening political situation.*

wors·en·ing /£ˈwɜː·sᵊn·ɪŋ, $ˈwɜːrs-/ *n* [U] • *Rather worryingly, the survey shows a worsening of child health in many areas.*

wor·ship *(obj)* /£ˈwɜː·ʃɪp, $ˈwɜːr-/ *v* **-pp-** or *Am usually* **-p-** to have or show a strong feeling of respect and admiration for God or a god • *In the various regions of India, Hindus worship different gods and observe different religious festivals.* [T] • Worship also means to go to a religious ceremony: *They work for the same company, socialise together and worship in the same mosque.* [I] ○ *According to a recent poll, 80% of Americans pray regularly and over 40% worship on a weekly basis.* [I] • To worship is also to have a strong feeling of respect and admiration for people or objects, often without being aware of their faults: *Her parents worship her.* [T] ○ *As a child, I worshipped my older brother.* [T] ○ *He was* **hero** *worshipped* (=admired greatly) *by the younger children.* [T] ○ *He worships* **the ground she walks on** (=He loves and admires her greatly). [T] ○ *(fig.) He may not worship* **at the altar of** (=He does not support) *government intervention in business, but he is in favour of limited support for industry.* [I] ○ *(fig.) She thinks that young people today are becoming increasingly selfish, and worship* **at the shrine of** (=they believe in achieving) *individual happiness and gratification.* [I]

wor·ship /£ˈwɜː·ʃɪp, $ˈwɜːr-/ *n* [U] • Worship is the strong feeling of respect and admiration for God or a god, which is often shown through praying or singing: *Hymns are a very important part of worship in the Church of England.* ○ *For Jews, the synagogue is the centre for community worship and study.* ○ *English and Welsh state schools have daily* **acts of** *worship for their pupils.* ○ *There have been several complaints from local people about improperly dressed tourists entering* **places of** *worship* (=buildings for religious ceremonies or private prayer). ○ *(fml) They regularly* **attended** *worship* (=went to a religious ceremony). • Worship is often used to suggest that something is liked too much: *In this era of fitness and health worship, people have become obsessed with exercise and dieting.* ○ *He deplores the money worship common among young people.* • *(esp. Br fml)* Worship is also a title of respect given to important officials: *His Worship the Mayor will present the awards.* ○ *Thank you, Your Worship.* [as form of address]

wor·ship·per, *Am usually* **wor·ship·er** /£ˈwɜː·ʃɪp·əʳ, $ˈwɜːr·ʃɪp·ɚ/ *n* [C] • *At 11a.m. on Sunday morning, worshippers began to stream out of the cathedral.* • *The three-hour ceremony was relayed on giant television screens to thousands of worshippers in the surrounding streets.* • Worshipper is also used in combinations: *sun worshippers* ○ *devil worshippers*

wor·ship·ping /£ˈwɜː·ʃɪp·ɪŋ, $ˈwɜːr-/ *combining form* • Worshipping is used as a combining form to suggest that something is liked or admired greatly: *We are a youth-worshipping society.*

Wor·ship·ful /£ˈwɜː·ʃɪp·fᵊl, $ˈwɜːr-/ *adj* [not gradable] *esp. Br fml* used in the title of societies of skilled workers or some important officials • *the Worshipful Company of Silversmiths*

worst [SUPERLATIVE OF BAD] /£wɜːst, $wɜːrst/ *adj* [not gradable] of the lowest quality, or the most unpleasant, difficult or severe • *That was the worst meal I've ever eaten.* • *Cleaning offices was the worst job I have ever had.* • *"It was the worst moment of my life," she admitted.* • *The news that the factory was to close confirmed everyone's worst* **fears**. • *He is my worst* **enemy**. • If someone is described as their **own worst enemy**, their faults are greater than the bad things which happen to them. • **Worst-ever** means the most unpleasant or harmful of its type that there has ever been: *2000 people were killed in this country's worst-ever shipping disaster.* • The **worst case scenario** is the most unpleasant or serious thing which could happen in a situation: *The United Nations has put forward its worst case scenario for the war: about 400 000 people could die through a* *combination of killings and starvation.* ○ *Military planners have told the authorities to prepare for a worst case scenario of 20 planeloads of casualties arriving in the US every day.*

worst /£wɜːst, $wɜːrst/ *adv* [not gradable] • *Small businesses have been worst hit by the recession.* • *The students voted him the school's worst-dressed teacher.* • *Roads in the Central and Tayside regions of Scotland were worst affected by the snow.*

worst /£wɜːst, $wɜːrst/ *n* [U] • *That was* **the** *worst I've seen him play in several years.* • *None of my friends sang very well, but I was easily* **the** *worst.* • *We arrived at the party two hours late, soaking wet and very hungry, and worst* **of all** (= the most unpleasant thing was) *there was no food when we got there.* • *We hoped that they would be found safe and uninjured, but we* **feared the** *worst* (= we thought something unpleasant might have happened to them). • *I'm not frightened of him – let him* **do** *his worst* (= do the most unpleasant or harmful thing he can). • **At worst**, *all she can do is* (= The most unpleasant thing she will do is to) *tell you off for being late.* • *She is* **at worst** (= considering it as unkindly as possible) *corrupt, and at best has been knowingly breaking the rules.* • *I'm* **at** *my* **worst** (= I am not very active or intelligent) *first thing in the morning.* • *This problem over late payment has showed him* **at** *his* **worst** (= has shown the most unpleasant side of his character). • If you say that something might happen **if the worst comes to the worst**, you mean that it might happen if the situation develops in the most serious or unpleasant way: *We should be in when you arrive, but if the worst comes to the worst, the neighbours have a spare key and will let you into our house.*

worst *obj* DEFEAT /£wɜːst, $wɜːrst/ *v* [T] *old use* to defeat (someone) in a fight or argument • *He was challenged to a fight but was severely worsted.*

worst•ed /£ˈwʊs·tɪd, $ˈwɜːr·stɪd/ *n* [U] a type of woollen cloth used to make jackets, trousers and skirts • *He worked as an independent craftsmen in the Norfolk worsted industry.* • *She wore a pale grey worsted suit.*

worth MONEY /£wɜːθ, $wɜːrθ/ *n* [U] the amount of money which something can be sold for • *The estimated worth of the plastics and petrochemical industry is about $640 billion.* • *If you are unhappy with your hotel room, we will give you another* **of** *comparable* **worth** (= which has a similar price). • *We were determined to* **get** *our* **money's worth** (= get good value) *from our day tickets and went to every museum in the city.* • A particular amount of money's worth **of** something is the amount of money that it would cost if you bought it: *$4 million worth* **of** *souvenirs and gift items have been produced for the event.* • LP› **Expensive**

worth /£wɜːθ, $wɜːrθ/ *adj* [not gradable] • Worth means having a value in money of: *Our house is worth about £200 000.* ○ *First prize in the competition was designer clothes worth several thousand pounds.* ○ *Two men and a woman were charged last night after heroin worth about $5 million was seized.* • *(infml)* If a person is worth a particular amount of money, they have that amount: *She must be worth at least half a million.* • If you say that something is worth the amount of money which you paid for it, you mean that it is good value: *Four days' car hire costs £80, which is* **well** *worth it for the places you are able to drive to.* • If you **make** something **worth** someone's **while**, you pay them some money to do it: *If you can get me the list of names I want, I'll make* **it** *worth your while.* • Someone or something that is **not worth a bean** is unimportant and does not deserve your attention: *Forget about him – he's not worth a bean.* • Something that is **not worth the paper** it **is printed on** is of very little value. • If someone is **worth** their **salt**, they are good at their job: **Any** *accountant worth their salt should be aware of the latest changes in taxation.* • If someone or something is **worth** their **weight in gold**, they are very useful or helpful to you: *This recipe book is worth its weight in gold – it tells you everything you need to know about cookery.* ○ *Boys who can sing like that are worth their weight in gold* **to** *the choir.*

worth•less /£ˈwɜːθ·ləs, $ˈwɜːrθ-/ *adj* • Worthless means having no value in money: *A £30 million fund has been created to reimburse those people whose tickets became worthless following the collapse of the airline.* ○ *Investors must be careful not to be left with worthless shares from the large number of companies that are going bankrupt.*

worth•less•ness /£ˈwɜːθ·lə·snəs, $ˈwɜːrθ-/ *n* [U] • *The main problem the new government faces is rising inflation and the worthlessness of the currency.*

worth IMPORTANCE /£wɜːθ, $wɜːrθ/ *n* [U] the importance or usefulness of something or someone • *He felt as though he had no worth.* • *She has proved her worth on numerous occasions.* • *She wants the government to recognize the worth of women who stay at home and look after sick or elderly relations.* • *Campaigns are under way in Britain and America demanding equal pay for work* **of** *comparable worth.*

worth /£wɜːθ, $wɜːrθ/ *prep* • Worth means important or useful: *Events like this will not be worth a mention* (= are not important enough to be reported) *in the national press.* • If something is worth having or doing, it is important or useful enough to have or do: *There are only two things worth read***ing** *in this newspaper – the TV listings and the sports page.* [+ v-*ing*] ○ *If you are a young, inexperienced driver, it is worth hav***ing** (= it is useful to have) *comprehensive insurance.* [+ v-*ing*] ○ **It's** *worth mention***ing** (= I should tell you) *that you will have to travel quite a lot in this job.* [+ v-*ing*] ○ **It's** *worth remember***ing** (= You should remember) *that prices go up on February 1st.* [+ v-*ing*] • Worth also means likely to give you pleasure or satisfaction: *The band's latest record is worth a listen.* ○ *The house is open to the public and is* **well** *worth a visit.* • If something for which you have to make an effort is **worth it**, it is enjoyable or beneficial despite the effort which is needed to do it: *It was a long climb to the top of the hill, but the view from the top was worth it.* ○ *They wanted me to stay the night but it wasn't worth it* (= it would not have been very useful) – *I could easily catch the last train.* • If an activity is **worth** your **while**, you will benefit from doing it: *It's worth your while taking out some travel insurance before you travel.* • If you do something **for all** you **are worth**, you put a lot of effort into it: *We pushed the car for all our worth but we still couldn't get it started.* • *(infml)* If you say **for what it's worth** when you are giving someone a piece of information, you mean you are not certain if that information is useful or important: *For what it's worth, I think he may be right.* ○ *The relevant leaflets are available from the library, for what it's worth.* • *(infml)* If someone says **what's it worth** when you have just asked them for a piece of information, they want to know what you will give them if they give you that piece of information: *"Do you know where Dave's living at the moment?" "What's it worth?"* • *(saying)* 'If a thing is worth doing, it's worth doing well.'

worth•less /£ˈwɜːθ·ləs, $ˈwɜːrθ-/ *adj* • Worthless means unimportant or useless: *She was criticised so much by her employers that she began to feel worthless.* ○ *More than 90% of the refugees are refused entry at the borders, their passports and visas forged or worthless.*

worth•less•ness /£ˈwɜːθ·lə·snəs, $ˈwɜːrθ-/ *n* [U] • *People who have been abused as children often experience feelings of worthlessness.*

worth AMOUNT /£wɜːθ, $wɜːrθ/ *n* [U] an amount of something which will last a stated period of time or which takes a stated amount of time to do • *I did a month's worth* **of** *shopping while I was at the supermarket.* • *I've done three hour's worth* **of** *work this morning.*

worth•while /£ˌwɜːθˈhwaɪl, $ˌwɜːrθ-/ *adj* useful, important or beneficial enough to be a suitable reward for the money or time spent or the effort made • *She considers teaching a worthwhile career.* • *The time and expense involved in keeping up to date with all the changes has been worthwhile.* • *For wildlife enthusiasts the journey is worthwhile – the region is renowned for its sea birds.* • *If you want him to help you with this project, you've got to make it* **financially** *worthwhile for him* (= you will have to pay him a suitable amount of money for the amount of work involved).

wor•thy DESERVING RESPECT /£ˈwɜː·ði, $ˈwɜːr-/ *adj* **-ier**, **-iest** *fml* deserving respect, admiration or support • *We need to translate these worthy principles into workable rules.* • *He is unlikely to succeed in getting his bill through Congress, however worthy it is.* • *Every year she makes a large donation to a worthy* **cause**. • *Two points in this report are especially worthy* **of** *notice* (= They are important and deserve to be noticed). • Worthy can also refer to something that should be admired for its good and beneficial qualities but which is rather uninteresting: *Educational toys and games are often more worthy than fun.* • *"I am not worthy"* (phrase from the television show and film *Wayne's World*, 1990s)

wor·thy /£ˈwɜː·ði, $ˈwɜːr-/ *n* [C] *humorous* • A worthy is a person who is important, esp. in a small town: *The front row of chairs was reserved for local worthies.*

wor·thi·ly /£ˈwɜː·ðɪ·li, $ˈwɜːr-/ *adv fml* • *After he retired, he was appointed chairman of the parish council, a post he filled worthily for several years.*

wor·thi·ness /£ˈwɜː·ðɪ·nəs, $ˈwɜːr-/ *n* [U] *fml* • *The reviews of the film were mixed, with much praise for its worthiness but criticism for its lack of historical accuracy.*

wor·thy SUITABLE /£ˈwɜː·ði, $ˈwɜːr-/ *adj* **-ier, -iest** suitable for, or characteristic of • *He threw a party worthy* **of** *a millionaire and attracted a glittering crowd of beautiful people.* • *A consultant will go to extremes worthy* **of** *a secret agent to avoid betraying the identity of his client, such as refusing to give out telephone numbers and not discussing the job outside the office.*

–wor·thy /£-ˌwɜː·ði, $-ˌwɜːr-/ *combining form* • Worthy means suitable or deserving to receive: *trustworthy* ○ *creditworthy* ○ *blameworthy* ○ *noteworthy* ○ *newsworthy* • Worthy also refers to the suitability of a boat, aircraft or vehicle to be used: *seaworthy* ○ *airworthy* ○ *roadworthy*

wor·thi·ness /£ˈwɜː·ðɪ·nəs, $ˈwɜːr-/ *n* [U] • *She persuaded the board of her worthiness* (= suitability) *to run the company.* • *One of the firm's chief businesses is to compile reports that rate the* **credit** *worthiness of millions of American companies* (= their suitability to borrow money).

wot /£wɒt, $wɑːt/ *pronoun Br not standard, esp. humorous* used in writing for *what* or *that* • *Wot? No food?* • *Things ain't wot they used to be.* • *It's him wot won it.*

wot·cher, wot·cha /£ˈwɒt·ʃəʳ, $ˈwɑː·tʃɚ/ *exclamation Br infml* used as an informal greeting, esp. between friends • *Wotcher, mate!* • *Wotcher gorgeous!*

would FUTURE /wʊd, wəd/ *v aux* [+ infinitive without *to*; not *be woulding*], **'d** /d/ *short form* he/she/it **would** used to refer to future time from the point of view of the past • *He said he would see his brother tomorrow* (= He said "I will see my brother tomorrow". • *They knew there would be trouble unless the report was finished by the next day.* • *We realised it wouldn't be easy to find another secretary.* • **Would have** is used to refer to a time in the past when someone was referring back to the past from a point of view in the future: *We thought they would have got home by five o'clock, but there was no reply when we phoned.* • LP› **Auxiliary verbs, Tenses**

would INTENTION /wʊd, wəd/ *v aux* [+ infinitive without *to*; not *be woulding*], **'d** /d/ *short form* he/she/it **would** used to refer to an intention from the point of view of the past • *He said he would always love her* (= He said "I will always love you". • *They promised that they would help.* • *They took me to see the house where I would be staying.* • *There was nobody left who would* (= was willing to) *do it.* • *I asked him to move his car but he said he wouldn't* (= he refused). • **Would-be** means wanting or trying to be: *a would-be artist/politician*

would POSSIBLE /wʊd, wəd/ *v aux* [+ infinitive without *to*; not *be woulding*], **'d** /d/ *short form* he/she/it **would** used to refer to a situation that you can imagine happening • *I would hate to miss the show.* • *Christmas wouldn't be the same without a roast turkey.* • *Don't bother to remove all the weeds – it would take too long.* • *I'd go myself but I'm too busy.* • *It would* **have** *been very boring to sit through the whole speech.* • Would is used with 'if' in CONDITIONAL sentences (= sentences which refer to what happens if something else happens): *What would you do if you lost your job?* ○ *I'd refuse to go if they asked me.* ○ *If I'd had time, I would* **have** *gone to see Graham.* • LP› **Conditionals**

would REQUEST /wʊd, wəd/ *v aux* [+ infinitive without *to*; not *be woulding*], **'d** /d/ *short form* he/she/it **would** used as a more polite form of *will* in requests and offers • *If you would just wait a moment, I'll see if I can find her.* • *Would you mind sharing a room?* • *Would you like me to come with you?* • *"Would you like some cake?" "Yes, I would."*

would ALWAYS /wʊd, wəd/ *v aux* [+ infinitive without *to*; not *be woulding*], **'d** /d/ *short form* he/she/it **would** used to suggest that something in the past happened often or always • *When we were younger we would help each other with our homework.* • *He would always turn and wave at the end of the street.* • *(disapproving)* Would is also used to suggest that what happens is expected because it is typical, esp. of a person's behaviour: *"She rang to say she can't help because she has to pick up Jenny from the station." "She would – she always has an excuse."* ○ *He would say that, wouldn't he.* ○ *The bus would be late when I'm in a hurry.* • *"He would, wouldn't he"* (Mandy Rice-Davies in court when a well-known man said he had not had a relationship with her, 1963)

would OPINION /wʊd, wəd/ *v aux* [+ infinitive without *to*; not *be woulding*], **'d** /d/ *short form* he/she/it **would** used to express an opinion in a polite way without being forceful • *I would imagine there are some people we need to speak to before we make definite arrangements.* • *It's not what we would* **have** *expected from a professional service.* • *She would* **have** *liked/preferred more information* (= but she was not able to have it) *to help her decide.* • *I wouldn't* **have** *thought you should do it like that.*

would LIKELY /wʊd, wəd/ *v aux* [+ infinitive without *to*; not *be woulding*], **'d** /d/ *short form* he/she/it **would** used to refer to what is quite likely • *"The guy on the phone had an Australian accent." "That would be Tom, I expect."*

would CHOICE /wʊd, wəd/ *v aux* [+ infinitive without *to*; not *be woulding*], **'d** /d/ *short form* he/she/it **would would rather/sooner** used in saying you prefer one thing to another • *I would rather go early and get home before it gets dark.* • *Which would you sooner do – go swimming or play tennis?* • *Wouldn't you rather finish it tomorrow?* • *They offered me this expensive wine but frankly I'd rather* **have** *had beer.* • *He'**d rather die** than* (= He certainly does not want to) *let me think he needed help.* • *"Will you make a speech?" "I'**d rather die*** (= Certainly not)."

would ADVISE /wʊd, wəd/ *v aux* [+ infinitive without *to*; not *be woulding*], **'d** /d/ *short form* he/she/it **would** SHOULD ADVISE • *I wouldn't* (= I advise you not to) *worry about it, if I were you.*

would REASON /wʊd, wəd/ *v aux* [+ infinitive without *to*; not *be woulding*], **'d** /d/ *short form* he/she/it **would** SHOULD REASON • *Why would anyone want to eat something so horrible?*

would WILL /wʊd, wəd/ *past simple of* WILL CAN • *The car wouldn't start this morning.*

would that *conjunction fml* (used to express a wish) if only • *Would that she could see her famous son now.*

woul·dn't /ˈwʊd·ᵊnt/ *short form of* would not • *Wouldn't it be nice to go to the seaside?* • *I wouldn't do that if I were you.*

wound WIND /waʊnd/ *past simple and past participle of* WIND

wound INJURY /wuːnd/ *n* [C] a damaged area of the body, such as a cut or hole in the skin or flesh made by a weapon • *Police said the victim was found lying in the alley with a* **gunshot** *wound* **in** *her chest.* • *The doctor said that death was due to multiple* **stab** *wounds* **to** *the neck and upper body.* • *The nurse carefully bandaged the* **flesh** (= not deep) *wound.* • *He received a* **leg** *wound which required seven stitches.* • *Horrified workmates saw him collapse with blood pouring from the* **open/gaping** *wound.* • A wound is also a problem or great unhappiness: *This wound will* **fester** (= The problem will get worse) *unless you try to sort things out between you.* ○ *She refuses to talk about the incident, saying it would only* **reopen** *an* **old** *wound* (= make her remember an unhappy experience).

wound *obj* /wuːnd/ *v* [T] • *During the shoot-out, a man was wounded* **in** *the leg.* • *The flying glass wounded her* **in** *the face and neck.* • *The police chief was* **badly** *wounded in the bomb explosion on the road to the state capital.* • *A young girl was* **fatally/mortally** *wounded by sniper fire* (= She had injuries which would result in death). • If you are wounded by something that someone has said or done, you are offended or upset by it: *Jackie was* **deeply** *wounded by the suggestion that she was lying.*

wound·ed /ˈwuːn·dɪd/ *adj* • *A wounded soldier was carried away from the battle zone with blood streaming from his head.* • *Estimates of the number of people wounded ranged from four to twenty-eight.* • If someone has wounded feelings, they are upset by something that someone has said or done: *Wounded national* **pride** *and economic discontent combined to form an explosive mixture that led to war.*

wound·ed /ˈwuːn·dɪd/ *pl n* • *Ambulances took* **the** *wounded to local hospitals.* • *There was a temporary ceasefire to evacuate* **the** *wounded from the area.* **The walking** *wounded* (= people who were injured but able to walk) *were made to sit in the waiting area while doctors treated the badly injured.*

wove /£wəʊv, $woʊv/ *past simple of* WEAVE MAKE CLOTH, WEAVE TWIST

wo·ven /£ˈwəʊ·vᵊn, $ˈwoʊ-/ *past participle of* WEAVE MAKE CLOTH, WEAVE TWIST

wow SURPRISE /waʊ/ *exclamation infml* used to show surprise and sometimes pleasure • *Wow! Did you make that* *cake? It looks delicious.* • *Wow, did you see that bright light over there behind the houses?* • *I showed my new bike to my friends and they all say 'wow.'* • LP Phrases and customs

wow SUCCESS /waʊ/ *n* [C] *infml* a person or thing that is very successful, attractive or pleasant • *The film may not be a wow* **with** *the public but it got great reviews.* • *He's not particularly good-looking but he's a real wow* **with** *the girls in his class.* • *I had a wow* **of a time** (=a very good time) *at the party last night.*

wow *obj* /waʊ/ *v* [T] *infml* • If a person or thing wows you, you like and admire them or it greatly: *The movie has been a surprise hit and has wowed audiences throughout the States.*

WP, wp /ˌdʌb·l̩.juːˈpiː/ *n* [C/U] *abbreviation for* **word processor** or **word processing**, see at WORD LANGUAGE UNIT

WPC /ˌdʌb·l̩.jʊˌpiːˈsiː/ *n* [C] *abbreviation for* Woman Police Constable (=a female member of the lowest rank of the British police force) • *A WPC came to interview them after their house had been burgled.* • WPC is the title used before the last name of a female police officer: *WPC Johnson*

WRAC /ræk, £ˌdʊb·l̩.juːˌɑː·reɪˈsiː, $-ˌɑːr·eɪ-/ *n* *abbreviation for* Women's Royal Army Corps • *She was a nurse and a captain in* **the** *WRAC.* [U] • *She's a WRAC* (=a member of this organization). [C]

wrack /ræk/ *n* **go to wrack/rack and ruin**, see at RACK DECAY

WRAF /£ˌdʌb·l̩.juːˌɑː·reɪˈef, $-ˌɑːr·eɪ-/ *n abbreviation for* Women's Royal Air Force • **The** *WRAF was formed in 1918.* [U] • *She had been a WRAF* (=a member of this organization) *during the war.* [C] • *She went on a WRAF training course.*

wraith /reɪθ/ *n* [C] *literary* a spirit of a dead person which is sometimes represented as a pale, transparent image of that person • *Like a wraith in the night, he was there and then he was gone.* • *She wore a pale, floating dress and looked wraith-***like** (=thin and pale) *and insubstantial.* • Wraith also refers to something which is pale or weak and without a clear shape: *He watched the misty wraiths* **of** *moisture making patterns on the window pane.* ○ *Her wraith* **of a** *voice* (=Her weak voice) *gave the songs a moving quality.*

wran·gle /ˈræŋ·gl̩/ *n* [C] an argument, esp. one which continues for a long period of time • *A deal was first suggested in January but endless wrangles followed.* • *There was a lengthy wrangle* **about/over** *the cost of the project.* • *The joint venture ended in a* **legal** *wrangle between the two companies.*

wran·gle /ˈræŋ·gl̩/ *v* [I] • *While the politicians wrangle, the economy continues its slide from bad to worse.* • *They had been wrangling* **with** *the authorities* **about/over** *parking spaces for weeks.*

wran·gling /ˈræŋ·gl̩·ɪŋ/ *n* [U] • *The two sides have been involved in ongoing political wrangling.* • *The dispute was settled in February after weeks of bitter wrangling.*

wrap *obj* /ræp/ *v* [T] **-pp-** to cover or enclose (something) with paper, cloth or other material • *She wrapped* **(up)** *the present and tied it with ribbon.* [T/M] • *Wrap the chicken* **in** *foil and cook it for two hours.* • *Wrap the glasses* **in** *plenty of tissue paper before you put them in the box.* • If you wrap a piece of clothing or material **around/round** you, you put it around you, usually to keep warm: *You can wrap the blanket round you for warmth.* ○ *It was so cold that he wrapped a scarf tightly around his face before he went out.* • If a person or animal wraps part of their body such as their fingers or arms **around/round** something, they put that part of their body around it tightly: *She sat back in her chair and wrapped her arms around her knees.* ○ *The monkey wrapped its tail round the branch and swung to and fro.* • If you can **wrap** someone **around/round** your **little finger**, you can easily persuade them to do what you want them to do: *She could wrap her father round her little finger.* • *(Br)* If you **wrap** someone **(up) in cotton wool**, you try to protect them too carefully: *You can't wrap (up) your children in cotton wool for ever.* • *(slightly disapproving)* If you **wrap** your**self in the flag/***(Br)* **Union Jack/***(Am)* **Stars and Stripes**, you show great loyalty and support for your country in a way that is not critical: *Although national pride is important to the prime minister, he does not wrap himself in the flag as his predecessor used to do.*

wrap /ræp/ *n* • A wrap (*Am also* **wrapper**) is a loose piece of clothing which is worn tied around the body: *a towelling wrap* [C] ○ *a beach wrap* [C] • *(esp. Am)* A wrap is a long piece of cloth which a woman wears around her shoulders to keep warm or for decoration: *a chiffon/silk wrap* [C] • Wrap is material which is used to cover or protect objects: *foil wrap* [U] ○ *He wrapped up all his crockery in* **bubble** *wrap and then packed it into boxes.* [U] • If you keep something **under wraps**, you keep it secret: *We are taking every precaution to make sure the plans remain under wraps.* ○ *They tried to* **keep** *the report under wraps.* • If you **take the wraps off** something, you let people know about it: *Today the company takes the wraps off the hotel, which they have spent millions of dollars restoring.*

wrapped /ræpt/ *adj* • *The chocolates were individually wrapped* **in** *foil.* • *(Aus infml)* Wrapped (also **rapt**) means extremely pleased or happy: *I'm really wrapped to see you again.* • If something such as plan is **wrapped (up) in secrecy**, the details about it are kept secret. • *(infml)* If you are **wrapped up in** someone or something, you are very interested in them and ignore other people or things: *Young people are often wrapped up in their careers.* ○ *He's completely wrapped up in her.*

wrap·per /£ˈræp·əʳ, $-ɚ/ *n* [C] • A wrapper is a piece of paper, plastic or other material which covers and protects something: *a (Br and Aus) sweet/(Am) candy wrapper* ○ *Packaging for fast food includes boxes, bags, wrappers, straws and paper cups.* ○ *Restaurants often provide plain wooden chopsticks in a paper wrapper, which are thrown away afterwards.* • Wrapper is also *Am for* **wrap**.

wrap·ping /ˈræp·ɪŋ/ *n* • Wrapping is a piece of paper or plastic which covers or protects something: *Try to choose products with as little wrapping as possible.* [U] ○ *Some of the seats still have the protective plastic wrappings on them.* [C] • **Wrapping paper** is decorated paper which is used to cover presents.

wrap up *(obj),* **wrap** *(obj)* **up** *v adv* • To wrap yourself up is to put on warm clothes: *We wrapped ourselves up* **against** *the bitter wind.* [M] ○ *Wrap up* **warmly** *and take a flask of coffee.* [I] • See also WRAP UP.

wrap up *obj,* **wrap** *obj* **up** *v adv* [M] *infml* to complete or finish (something) successfully • *She wrapped up a deal with the union just before the deadline.* • *He hit two free throws to wrap up the game for Seattle.* • *That just about wraps it up for today.*

wrap /ræp/ *n* [C] *infml* • A wrap is a film which has been completed successfully: *The director decided that was enough filming for one day and said, "It's a wrap. Thank you, everybody."*

wrap·a·round /ˈræp·ə·raʊnd/, *Br also* **wrap-round** /ˈræp·raʊnd/ *adj* [not gradable], *n* [C] (a piece of clothing that is) made so that it can be tied around the body • *She was wearing a white cotton shirt and a blue denim wraparound skirt.* • *Her favourite skirt was a black leather wraparound.* • Wraparound also refers to something which curves round in one continuous piece: *The sunglasses have gold wraparound lenses.*

wrath /£rɒθ, $rɑːθ/ *n* [U] *fml or dated* extreme anger • *He left home to escape his father's wrath.* • *The newspaper carried a large photograph of the bomb damage which fuelled popular wrath.* • *He* **incurred** (=experienced) *the wrath* **of** *many people in the acting world by saying there was a marked lack of talented young actors.*

wrath·ful /£ˈrɒθ·fəl, $ˈrɑːθ-/ *adj* • *His plight shows what can happen when a tiny company faces the full legal power of a wrathful multinational company.*

wrath·ful·ly /£ˈrɒθ·fəl·i, $ˈrɑːθ-/ *adv*

wreak *obj* /riːk/ *v* [T] *past* **wreaked** or **wrought** /£rɔːt, $rɑːt/ *fml* to cause (something) to happen in a violent and often uncontrolled way • *The recent storms have wreaked* **havoc** *on crops.* • *The oil spill wreaked* **havoc** *with wildlife and the fishing industry.* • *Changes in the climate have wrought* **havoc** *with* (=severely changed) *the city's usual weather pattern.* • *Experts say that the ecological* **damage** *wreaked by pollution is increasing rapidly.* • *She was determined to wreak* **revenge/vengeance** *on both him and his family.*

wreath /riːθ/ *n* [C] *pl* **wreaths** /riːðz, riːθs/ an arrangement of flowers and leaves in a circular shape, which is used as a decoration or as a sign of respect and remembrance for a person who has died • *Groups of children placed brightly coloured wreaths around the necks of the visitors.* • *In the week before Christmas, most of the houses in the street had wreaths/(Br also) holly wreaths/(Am also) Christmas wreaths on the doors.* • *The bride wore a veil with a wreath* **of** *silk flowers.* • *The badge shows a dove in a wreath* **of** *olive leaves.* • *The actor, wearing a Roman toga and with a* **laurel** *wreath on his head, came forward and made a speech.* • *There were two large wreaths* *on the coffin.* • *After the road accident in which a local child died, neighbours placed wreaths on the pavement where it had happened.* • *The President ended his visit by* **laying** *a wreath at the war memorial.*

wreathe *obj* /riːð/ *v* [T usually passive] *literary* to cover or surround (something) • *The peak of the mountain is perpetually wreathed* **in** *cloud.* • *On our drive through the hills, we saw villages wreathed* **in** *cherry blossom and wild flowers everywhere.* • *(fig.) The main character in the novel is wreathed* **in** *melancholy* (= She is very sad). • If someone is **wreathed in smiles**, they smile and look extremely happy: *He was wreathed in smiles as he accepted the award.*

wreck *obj* /rek/ *v* [T] to destroy or badly damage (something) • *The explosion shattered nearby windows and wrecked two cars.* • *Our greenhouse was wrecked in last night's storm.* • *Their lives have been wrecked by the death of their daughter.* • If someone wrecks a plan or idea, they spoil it: *He has been warned that his behaviour might wreck his chances of promotion.*

wreck /rek/ *n* [C] • A wreck is a vehicle or ship that has been destroyed or badly damaged: *Divers exploring the wreck managed to salvage some coins and jewellery.* ○ *The burnt-out wrecks* **of** *cars littered the road.* ○ *The wreck* **of** *the plane could be clearly seen on the hillside.* • *(infml)* If a person is described as a wreck, they are in bad physical or mental condition: *The stress she had been under at work reduced her to a* **nervous/quivering** *wreck.*

wrecked /rekt/ *adj* • *Their village was bombed during the war, and they now live in half wrecked houses with no electricity or water supply.* • *(slang)* If someone is wrecked, they are drunk: *He* **got** *completely wrecked last Saturday night.* • To be wrecked is also to be in a SHIPWRECK.

wreck·age /ˈrek·ɪdʒ/ *n* [U] • Wreckage is a badly damaged object or the separated parts of a badly damaged object: *Eighty people on the boat survived, but the rest died in the water or were trapped in the wreckage.* ○ *The wreckage, scattered over a wide area, was all that was left of a sports car which had careered out of control.* ○ *It took firemen three hours to bring out the dead and injured because they were hampered by wreckage and smoke.* • Wreckage is also what is left of something that has been spoiled or that has failed: *At last there is some hope for those left* **clinging to** *the wreckage of small businesses.*

wreck·er /£ˈrek·əʳ, $-ɚ/ *n* [C] *Am for* **breakdown truck**, see at BREAKDOWN [FAILURE]

wren [BIRD] /ren/ *n* [C] a very small brown bird

Wren [WOMAN] /ren/ *n* [C] *Br infml* a member of the British Women's Royal Naval Service • *a Wren officer* • *There are more than 1100 crew members on board the ship, including a large number of Wrens.* • See also WRNS.

wrench *obj* /rentʃ/ *v* [T] to pull and twist (something) suddenly or violently away from a fixed position • *The photographer tripped over a lead, wrenching a microphone* **from** *its stand.* • *The box was wrenched* **from/off** *the wall just inside the door.* • *The ball was wrenched* **out of** *his grasp by a player on the other team.* • *His hands had been tied behind his back, but he managed to wrench one hand* **free** *and untie himself.* • If you wrench part of your body, such as your arm or leg, you twist it badly and injure it: *He wrenched his right shoulder during a game of hockey.* ○ *She was not hurt in the car crash but her passenger suffered a wrenched neck.* • If someone is wrenched **from** people whom they like or love, they are taken away from them suddenly, which causes them great unhappiness: *At the age of eight, she was wrenched from her foster parents and sent to live with another family.* • *(fig. infml) Laura gave me a* **gut**-*wrenching* (= unpleasant and realistic) *description of the accident.* • *(fig.) Shortly after the letter arrived the* **heart**-*wrenching* (= causing suffering or unhappiness) *decisions began.*

wrench /rentʃ/ *n* [C] • A wrench is a sudden, violent twist or pull: *He freed the pole with a wrench.* • If the act of leaving someone or somewhere is a wrench, it is difficult to do because it makes you unhappy: *It was a wrench when the time came to part company with his family.* • *(esp. Am)* Wrench is another word for SPANNER, esp. one which can be made larger or smaller for holding and turning objects of different sizes: *an adjustable wrench* ○ See also MONKEY WRENCH.

wrest *obj* /rest/ *v* [T] *fml* to obtain (something) with difficulty, effort or violence • *Central government has been trying to wrest power* **(away) from** *the local councils.* • *The shareholders are planning to wrest* **control** *of the company* **(away) from** *the current directors.* • *For centuries, farmers have wrested a living* **from** *these barren hills.*

wres·tle *(obj)* /ˈres·l̩/ *v* to fight with someone (esp. as a sport) by holding them and trying to throw them to the ground • *He has wrestled professionally for five years.* [I] • *The police officer tackled the man and wrestled him* **to the ground.** [T]

wres·tler /£ˈres·ləʳ, $-lɚ/ *n* [C] • *She is a professional wrestler.* • *He is one of the most famous* **Sumo** *wrestlers in Japan.*

wres·tling /ˈres·lɪŋ/ *n* [U] • *mud wrestling* • *arm wrestling* • *Do you like watching wrestling on television?* • *He enjoys going to wrestling bouts* (= competitions).

wres·tle with *obj v prep* [T] to try very hard to deal with (something) which is difficult, such as trying to solve a problem or make a decision • *The government is wrestling with difficult economic problems.* • *He wrestled with the decision for several weeks, wondering what he should do.* • *She seemed to be wrestling with some deep inner confusion.*

wretch [UNHAPPY PERSON] /retʃ/ *n* [C] a person who experiences something unpleasant • *The tax on domestic fuel has badly affected those* **poor** *wretches who have low or no incomes.*

wretch [BAD PERSON] /retʃ/ *n* [C] an unpleasant or unkind person • *The papers described him as villain and a wretch who had stolen money from his employees' pension fund.* • *(infml) You wretch! You promised you'd give me a lift.* • *(humorous) The two children who live next door are little wretches who are always up to some mischief.*

wretch·ed /ˈretʃ·ɪd/ *adj* unhappy, unpleasant or of low quality • *She had had a wretched life as a child.* • *The house was in a wretched state.* • *The game is now improving after a wretched start.* • *They lived on a wretched diet of bread, potatoes and cabbage.* • *There can be few experiences as wretched as moving house.* • Wretched is also used to express annoyance: *It's a wretched nuisance – I've left my briefcase at home.* ○ *My wretched car's broken down again.* • If someone **feels** wretched, they feel ill or unhappy: *I think I must be coming down with flu because I've been feeling wretched all day.*

wretch·ed·ly /ˈretʃ·ɪd·li/ *adv* • Wretchedly is used to mean 'extremely' when referring to something unpleasant or of low quality: *Unemployment is still wretchedly high in some areas of the country.* ○ *Some of the samples were wretchedly inadequate.*

wretch·ed·ness /ˈretʃ·ɪd·nəs/ *n* [U] • *Everywhere they went, they were confronted by poverty and wretchedness.* • *He moved to Montreal because he could not stand the wretchedness of life at home.*

wrig·gle *(obj)* /ˈrɪg·l̩/ *v* to make small quick movements with the body, turning from side to side • *Jonathan began wriggling in his seat, unable to hide his boredom any longer.* [I] • *A large worm wriggled out of the freshly dug earth.* [I] • *There is nothing more relaxing than lying on a beach and wriggling your toes in the sand.* [T] • *She wriggled her shoulders against the cushions, making herself more comfortable.* [T] • *After twisting and turning for a while, he managed to wriggle* **free.** [I] • If a person or animal wriggles somewhere, they move to that place using short, quick twisting movements: *The tunnel was low and dark, but she managed to wriggle through to the other side.* [I] • *(infml)* If someone **wriggles out of** something they do not want to do, they manage to avoid doing it: *He appears to have wriggled out of paying back that money he owes.* • *(infml)* If someone **wriggles off the hook**, they avoid a responsibility or avoid doing something: *He's not busy today – he just doesn't want to help you and is trying to wriggle off the hook by saying that he's got other things planned.*

wrig·gle /ˈrɪg·l̩/ *n* [C] • *With a wriggle, she managed to crawl through the gap.*

wri·ly /ˈraɪ·li/ *adv* See at WRY

wring *obj* /rɪŋ/ *v* [T] *past* **wrung** /rʌŋ/ to hold (something) tightly with both hands and twist by turning your hands in opposite directions • If you wring **(out)** something that is wet such as a cloth or a piece of clothing, you remove the water by twisting with your hands: *She wrung out the shirt and hung it out to dry.* • If you wring something that you want **from/out of** someone, you force or persuade them to give it to you: *The nurses' popularity with the public enabled them to wring concessions from the government.* • If you **wring** your **hands**, you show that you are worried or unhappy: *Car dealers are wringing their hands* **over** *low sales this summer.* ○ *We must all do something to help rather* *than merely wringing our hands* **in despair** *and saying how awful the situation is.* • If someone wrings a bird's neck, they kill it by twisting and breaking its neck. • *(infml)* If you say you'll **wring** someone's **neck**, you are very angry with them: *I'll wring his neck if he does that again.*

wring·er /£ˈrɪŋ·əʳ, $-ɚ/ *n* [C] • A wringer (also **mangle**) is a machine used, esp. in the past, for pressing water out of clothes by putting the clothes between two heavy rollers which are turned by hand: *A large cast-iron clothes wringer stood in a corner of the kitchen.* • *(infml)* If you **put** someone **through the wringer**, you ask them difficult or unpleasant questions, esp. to find out whether they are doing their job satisfactorily: *The committee really put our department through the wringer – investigating our procedures and questioning students and staff.* ○ *Outside investigators will put the company's accounting practices through the wringer.*

wring·ing /ˈrɪŋ·ɪŋ/ *adj* [not gradable] • If something is wringing **(wet)**, it is extremely wet: *I left the washing out in the rain and now it's wringing wet.*

wrin·kle /ˈrɪŋ·kl̩/ *n* [C] a small line in the skin caused by old age, or a small fold in cloth • *Fine lines and wrinkles tend to appear around the eyes and mouth as you get older.* • *Do* **anti-***wrinkle creams really work?* • *There are some wrinkles in the back of your skirt where you've been sitting down.* • *(fig.) There are still a lot of wrinkles to* **iron out** (= problems to solve) *before the agreement can be signed.*

wrin·kle *(obj)* /ˈrɪŋ·kl̩/ *v* • If something such as cloth or your skin wrinkles, it gets small lines or folds in it: *The apples were beginning to wrinkle and shrivel.* [I] ○ *Put only a few garments in the drier at one time to prevent them from wrinkling.* [I] ○ *Sunbathing can prematurely age and wrinkle the skin.* [T] • If you **wrinkle** your **brow**, you make folds appear on your face above your eyes to show that you are surprised or confused: *He wrinkled his brow, clearly puzzled by the letter.* • If you **wrinkle (up)** your **nose** at something unpleasant, you show your dislike of it by tightening the muscles in your nose so that small lines appear in the skin: *She wrinkled up her nose* **at** *the strange smell coming from the kitchen.* ○ *(fig.) She knew his nose would wrinkle (up)* (= he would show he was not pleased) **at** *the mention of the restaurant where he had got food poisoning.*

wrin·kled /ˈrɪŋ·kl̩d/ *adj* • *a wrinkled face* • *wrinkled apples* • *I opened the drawer and found a very wrinkled white shirt.*

wrin·kly, wrink·lie /ˈrɪŋ·kli/ *n* [C] *Br and Aus slang* • A wrinkly is an old person: *In the winter, the resort is taken over by wrinklies who spend their time playing golf or bingo.*

wrist /rɪst/ *n* [C] the part of the body between the hand and the arm • *I sprained my wrist while playing squash.* • If someone **slashes/slits** their wrists, they try to kill themselves by making a cut in two of the main tubes that take blood to the heart: *She threatened to slit her wrists if he ever left her.* • (DK) (S)

wrist·watch /£ˈrɪst·wɒtʃ, $-wɑːtʃ/ *n* [C] a watch that is worn on the wrist • PIC **Clocks and watches**

writ DOCUMENT /rɪt/ *n* [C] *law* a legal document from a court of law which informs someone that they will be involved in a legal process and instructs them what they must do • *a civil writ* • *a libel writ* • *There have been at least seven writs* **issued against** *him for late payment of bills.* • *She has* **served** *a writ* **for** *libel* **on** *the newspaper* (= She has delivered it to them officially). • *He was not allowed to appeal against the decision and the court rejected his application for a writ* **of habeas corpus.**

writ AUTHORITY /rɪt/ *n* [U] *fml* the authority to rule or make laws • *The union's writ runs in Canada as well as in the United States.* • *It took 46 years to establish the writ* **of law** *in this country.*

writ WRITE *old use* /rɪt/ *past participle of* WRITE • *(fml)* If something is **writ large**, it is very obvious: *Her distress was writ large in her face.* • *(fml)* If one thing is another thing **writ large**, it is similar to it but larger or more obvious: *Hollywood is often said to be American society writ large.*

write *(obj)* /raɪt/ *v past simple* **wrote** /£rəʊt, $roʊt/, *past part* **written** /£ˈrɪt·ən, $ˈrɪt̬-/ or *old use* **writ** /rɪt/ to make marks which represent letters, words or numbers on a surface, such as paper or a computer screen, using a pen, pencil or keyboard, or to use this method to record thoughts, facts or messages • *The children were already learning to* **read and** *write.* [I] • *When you fill in the form, please write* **clearly/legibly** *in black ink.* [I] • *"I hope to see you next Saturday," she wrote.* [+ clause] • *I'll write the prices* **(down)** *on the back of this envelope.* [T] • *Why not write* **(down)** *your ideas on a piece of paper before you start your essay?* [T] • *The receptionist wrote the details* **(out)** *on a small card.* [T] • *Please will you write* **(out)** *your name and address* **in full**. [T] • *I wrote my sister a letter./I wrote a letter to my sister.* [+ two objects] • *When she was on holiday, she wrote her friend a postcard/she wrote a postcard* **to** *her friend.* [+ two objects] • *I wrote him a cheque* (= I put the necessary information on it and my signature) *for £50.* [+ two objects] • If you write something such as a book, poem, song or computer program, you create it and record it on paper or on a computer: *She writes recipe books.* [T] ○ *When are you going to finish writing your thesis?* [T] ○ *She has written a piece of software to check spelling.* [T] ○ *He is best known for the music he wrote* **for** *films and TV shows.* [T] ○ *The article was written* **in** *German and translated into French.* [T] ○ *He wrote me a poem./He wrote a poem* **for** *me.* [+ two objects] • To *(Br and Aus)* write **to** someone/*(Am)* write someone also means to give them information or express your thoughts or feelings in a letter: *I spent the afternoon writing* **to** *various friends and relatives.* [I] ○ *(Br and Aus) She wrote to me/(Am) She wrote me last Tuesday* **that** *her mother was very ill.* [+ obj + *that* clause] ○ *My mother wrote* **to** *give me details about the party.* [+ *to* infinitive] ○ *The travel company has written* **giving** *information about the trip.* [+ v-*ing*] ○ *When you write* **back** (= reply), *tell him that I'll try and see him next time he comes.* [I] ○ *Did you write* **(away/off) for** (= write to ask for) *tickets?* [I] ○ *Thousands of people wrote* **in** *to the BBC* (= sent letters to the organization) *asking for an information sheet.* See also WRITE IN. ○ *The performance was* **nothing to write home about** (= not exciting or special in any way). • If someone writes, their job is to create books, stories or articles that will be published: *He started to write for a living after his business failed.* ○ *She writes* **about/on** *medical matters* **for** *a national newspaper.* [I] • To write also means to state in a book, newspaper or magazine: *In the article, he writes* **that** *the problems in the refugee camps are getting worse.* [+ *that* clause] • If a particular detail or rule is written **into** something such as an agreement, it is included in it: *An agreement to produce five novels a year was written into her contract.* ○ *The scene, which opens up the possibility of a sequel, was written into the script at the request of the film studio.* • *(specialized)* If you write **to** a DISK (= a device used for storing information on a computer), you record information on it. [I] • To write someone **out of** a television programme is to change the story so that the part played by that person is removed from the story: *The actor who plays Charles wants to leave the TV series so they're going to write him out by making the*

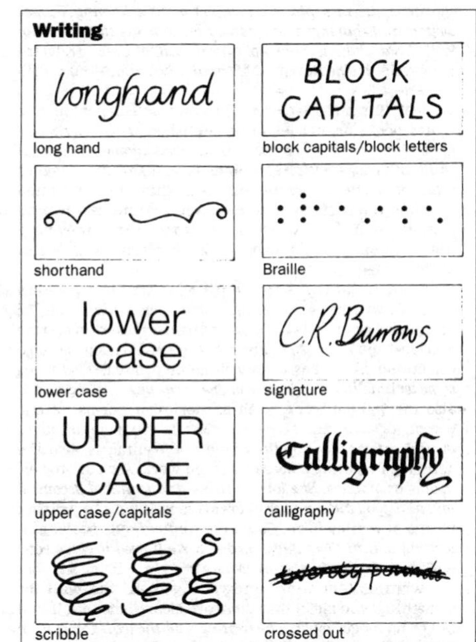

character die in a plane crash. [T] • *"The Moving Finger writes; and, having writ,/ Moves on: nor all thy Piety not Wit/ Shall lure it back to cancel half a Line"* (Edward Fitzgerald in *The Rubáiyát of Omar Khayyám*, 1859) • LP〉 Letters

writ·er /£ˈraɪ·təʳ, $-t̬ɚ/ *n* [C] • A writer is a person who writes books or articles to be published: *a travel/sports/ fiction/crime writer* ○ *She is a well-known writer of children's books.* • **Writer's block** is an inability to create a piece of written work because something in your mind prevents you from doing it. • **Writer's cramp** is a painful stiffness in the hand which people suffer from if they have been writing continuously for a long time. • See also SCRIPTWRITER.

writ·ing /£ˈraɪ·tɪŋ, $-t̬ɪŋ/ *n* [U] • Writing is a person's style of writing with a pen or paper which can be recognized as their own: *Do you recognise the writing on the envelope?* ○ *This isn't my writing.* • Writing is also something which has been written or printed: *There was some writing in the margins on one of the pages.* • Writing is also the written work, such as stories or poems, of one person or a group of people: *She is studying women's writing at the turn of the century.* • Writing is also the activity of creating pieces of written work, such as stories, poems or articles: *She loves writing and wants to become a journalist.* ○ *I did a course in* **creative** *writing.* • **In writing** means in written form: *Could you confirm your booking* **in** *writing within three days, please.* ○ *We'll need to have your agreement in writing before we can proceed.* • If you say that the **writing/***(Am also)* **handwriting is on the wall** for something, you mean that there are clear signs that it will fail or no longer exist: *The writing's on the wall* **for** *cars in cities.* ○ *She and her colleagues have* **read/seen** *the writing on the wall* **for** *the company* (= They have understood that the company will fail) *and have been making plans to find other jobs.* • A **writing desk** is a desk (= a table for working at) with drawers. • **Writing paper** (also **notepaper**) is paper of good quality which is used for writing letters. It is available in different colours and sizes, and usually has matching envelopes.

writ·ings /£ˈraɪ·tɪŋz, $-t̬ɪŋz/ *pl n* • Writings are the written works of a person, esp. when they have been published as books: *A complete edition of her writings was published in 1941.* ○ *He keeps a copy of the writings* **of** *Karl Marx in his bedroom.*

writ·ten /£ˈrɪt·ᵊn, $ˈrɪt̬-/ *adj* [not gradable] • *He left written instructions for his family, instructing them what he wanted them to do after his death.* • *She got an A grade for her written work but a C grade for her oral exam.* • If an emotion is **written all over** someone's **face**, it is clear what they are feeling: *Guilt was written all over her face.* • If you believe that something is **written in the stars**, you believe that it will be made to happen by the force that controls the future: *It was written in the stars that they would meet and fall in love.* • The **written word** refers to language in written form: *She loves to communicate her ideas to the public, both orally and through the written word.* ○ *Teachers are trying to make children interested in the written word at an early age.*

write in *obj*, **write** *obj* **in** *v adv* [M] *Am* to give (the name of someone not yet listed on an official paper) as your choice at an election • *They organized a campaign to have voters write in their candidate's name if it didn't appear on the ballot in their state.* • *a write-in candidate/campaign*

write off *obj* FINANCE, **write** *obj* **off** *v adv* [M] to accept that (a debt) will not be paid • *The bank wrote $17 million of bad debts off last year.* • *The World Bank is being urged to write off debts from developing countries.*

write off *obj* LOSE INTEREST, **write** *obj* **off** *v adv* [M] to consider that (someone or something) is not good or suitable enough or will not be successful • *When he lost three races in a row, some observers began to write him off.* • *She has been written off as a possible candidate for the presidential elections.*

write off *obj* DAMAGE, **write** *obj* **off** *v adv* [M] *Br and Aus* to damage (a vehicle) so badly that it cannot be repaired • *He wrote his car off last week in an accident.*

write–off /£ˈraɪ·tɒf, $-t̬ɑːf/ *n* [C] *Br and Aus* • *I wasn't hurt in the accident but the car's a* **complete** *write-off.*

write up *obj*, **write** *obj* **up** *v adv* [M] to record (something) on paper or on a computer in a complete or final form using notes that you have made • *He was given only six months to write up ten years of work.* • *Have you written up that report yet?* • *Most students spend two years doing research for their thesis and one year writing it up.* • To write up something such as a play or film is to write an article or report which gives an opinion or makes a judgment about it: *The play was written up in the Saturday edition of the paper.* ○ *The hotel was written up favourably in last year's holiday guide.* • *(Am)* To write up someone is to report them for not obeying a law or rule: *The cop said he'd have to write me up for not stopping at the red light.*

write–up /£ˈraɪ·tʌp, $-t̬ʌp/ *n* [C] • A write-up is a report or article which makes a judgment about something, such as a play or film: *The inspector didn't give the restaurant a very favourable write-up.* ○ *I liked the show and gave it a good write-up in the college magazine.*

writhe /raɪð/ *v* [I] to make large twisting movements with the body • *He could not tolerate the pain and writhed and screamed in agony.* • *She was writhing* **around** *in pain on the ground.* • *(fig.) He and four other senators were writhing in the glare of* (= experiencing the unpleasant effects of) *unfavorable publicity.* • *They showed the children a tub filled with writhing worms.* • *The dance floor was a mass of writhing bodies.*

writ·ten /£ˈrɪt·ᵊn, $ˈrɪt̬-/ *past participle of* WRITE

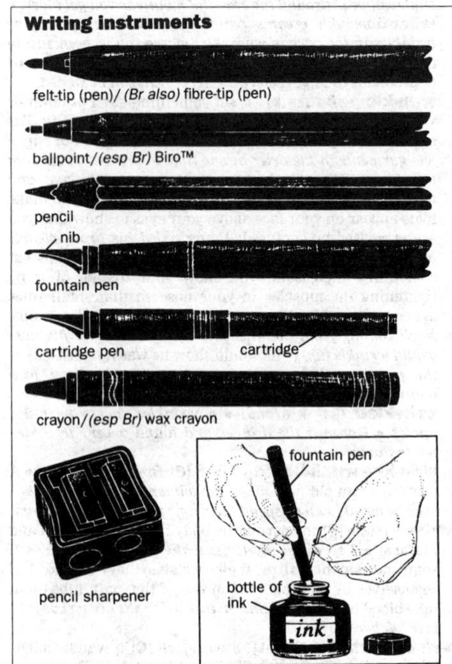

WRNS /£ˌdʌb·l̩.juːˌɑː·renˈes, $-ˌɑːr·en-/ *n* [U] **the WRNS** *abbreviation for* the Women's Royal Naval Reserve • See also WREN WOMAN.

wrong NOT CORRECT /£rɒŋ, $rɑːŋ/ *adj* [not gradable] not correct • *Three of your answers were wrong.* • *That clock is wrong – it's 12.30 not 12.15.* • *He's wrong* **in thinking** *that we will support the project financially.* • *Some of his facts are questionable, others are* **plainly** (= completely) *wrong.* • If you are wrong **about** something, you are not correct in your judgment or statement about it: *He was right about the first date but wrong about the second.* ○ *You were wrong about the time – the shop closed at 7 not 8.* • *He was* **proved** *wrong when the money was paid the next day* (= he thought it would not be paid). • *I thought she couldn't do it, but she* **proved** *me wrong* (= her actions showed that my judgment of her was not correct). • *Her friend* **got (hold of) the wrong end of the stick** (= did not understand correctly). • If food or drink **goes down the wrong way**, it goes down the wrong tube in your throat and causes you to cough or stop breathing for a short time. • *I hadn't expected the question and it* **caught** *me* **on the wrong foot** (= I was not prepared for it). • *(Br and Aus)* If you **wrong-foot** someone in a sport such as tennis or football, you hit or kick the ball in such a way that you make the other player believe the ball will go in the opposite direction to the one in which it will really go in order to make them move in the wrong direction: *The cleverly-concealed angle on her volley wrong-*

footed her opponent. ○ *The goalkeeper was wrong-footed and could only watch in despair as the ball shot past him into the goal.* ○ *(fig.) The company was completely wrong-footed by the dollar's sudden recovery* (=They were unprepared for it). • *"When people agree with me I always feel that I must be wrong"* (Oscar Wilde in *The Critic as Artist*, 1891) • Compare RIGHT [CORRECT]. • [LP]› **Opposites**

wrong /£rɒŋ, $rɑːŋ/ *adv* [not gradable] • *Bill will show you what you're doing wrong.* • *You* **got** *three questions right and two wrong.* • *I spent hours doing that calculation and I still* **got** *the answer wrong.* • If you **get** something wrong, you make a mistake about something because you did not understand correctly what someone said: *You* **got it** *wrong – it's Maria who's coming not Marina.* • *Don't* **get** *me* **wrong** (=Do not think something which is not correct) *– I'd love to come but I'm too busy next week.* • If someone **goes wrong**, they make a mistake: *These shelves are very easy to put together – you can't go wrong.* ○ See also **go wrong** at WRONG [NOT WORKING], WRONG [NOT SUITABLE]. • See also **wrongly**.

wrong·ly /£ˈrɒŋ·li, $ˈrɑːŋ-/ *adv* [not gradable] • *You wrongly stated on two occasions that the article was published in the Sydney Morning Herald.* • *Customers remain convinced that money has been wrongly taken out of their bank accounts.* • *They interviewed several people wrongly convicted of crimes.* • *He even spelled his own client's name wrongly (also* **wrong***).*

wrong /£rɒŋ, $rɑːŋ/ *n* • *He insisted that we had agreed to meet on Tuesday, but he was definitely* **in the wrong** (=he was not correct). See also **in the wrong** at WRONG [IMMORAL].

wrong [NOT SUITABLE] /£rɒŋ, $rɑːŋ/ *adj* [not gradable] not suitable or desirable, or not as it should be • *She's the wrong person for the job.* • *I think we're going the wrong way.* • *We must have taken a wrong turning.* • *She married for all the wrong reasons.* • *This is the wrong time to ask me about my travel plans – I'm far too busy to think about it.* • **It's** *wrong* **that** *you always pay when we go out for a meal.* [+ *that* clause] • **What's** *wrong* **with** *spending Saturday night in the pub* (=Why do you think it is not suitable)*?* • *The seating plan's* **all** *wrong – I wanted to sit next to Alex and James!* • *I'm sorry, you've got the wrong* **number** (=this is not the telephone number you wanted). • *"Who was on the phone?" "Oh, it was just a wrong* **number** (=a telephone call connected to my phone unintentionally)*."* • Wrong is also used to describe something that is not considered to be socially acceptable or desirable: *They live on the wrong side of town.* ○ *She got in with the wrong crowd* (=a group of people who were not considered socially acceptable) *at university.* • If you ask someone if there is something wrong, you want to know what is worrying or upsetting them: *You've been quiet all evening. Is there anything wrong?* ○ *What's wrong with you today? You've been in a dreadful mood all morning.* • If a situation or event **goes wrong**, it becomes unpleasant and is not a success: *They started rowing on their honeymoon and their marriage began to go wrong from then on.* • If someone **goes wrong**, they make a lot of bad decisions: *He found it was very easy to go wrong when he was young and inexperienced.* ○ See also **go wrong** at WRONG [NOT CORRECT], WRONG [NOT WORKING]. • *The information* **got/fell into the wrong hands** (=was obtained by people who would use it to harm others). • *If the government refuses to provide aid, it would* **send/give out (all) the wrong signals** (=give an undesirable message about the government) *to the rest of the world.* • *You've got your skirt on* **the wrong way** *(Br and Aus)* **round**/*(Am)* **around** (=The part that should be at the front is at the back). • *(disapproving)* Someone that is **wrong-headed** continues to have an unsuitable idea or follow an unsuitable course of action and often makes judgments which are not correct: *He criticized the wrong-headed town planners of the 1960s who often thought of buildings before people.* • *(disapproving)* A plan or idea that is **wrong-headed** has not been considered or planned with enough care and is not suitable for the situation: *He admitted that the party had followed policies which were now considered as wrong-headed.* • *(saying)* 'If anything can go wrong it will'. • Compare RIGHT [SUITABLE].

wrong [IMMORAL] /£rɒŋ, $rɑːŋ/ *adj, adv* [not gradable] not considered morally acceptable by most people • *The Koran teaches that violence is wrong except if it is used in defence.* • *Opinion polls showed that the public felt the decision was fundamentally wrong and immoral.* • **It** *was wrong* **of** *her to take your car without asking.* • *The department admitted publicly that it was wrong* **to** *refuse to look into Miss Wood's complaints.* [+ *to* infinitive] • *So far we have not prevented schools from raising money and I think it would be* **plainly** (=obviously) *wrong to do so.* • Compare RIGHT [MORALLY ACCEPTABLE].

wrong /£rɒŋ, $rɑːŋ/ *n* • Wrong is what is considered to be morally unacceptable: *Her work is guided by an intensely felt sense of* **right and** *wrong.* [U] ○ *"I've always been brought up to tell the truth and* **know right from** *wrong," he said.* [U] ○ *I wanted to be reassured that I had* **done** *her* **no** *wrong* (=that I had not harmed her or behaved in an unfair way towards her). [U] • Wrong is also an unfair action: *He has* **done** *us a great wrong.* [C] ○ *She tried to* **right** (=do something to make better) *the wrong which her family had done to him.* [C] • If someone **does wrong**, they do something which is illegal or not morally acceptable: *We knew we had done wrong and would have to pay the consequences.* ○ *As far as her parents are concerned, she* **can do no wrong** (=she is perfect in every way). • If you are **in the wrong**, you have done something which is bad or illegal: *The owners in that case were unquestionably in the wrong.* ○ See also **in the wrong** at WRONG [NOT CORRECT]. • *(saying)* 'Two wrongs do not make a right' means that it is not acceptable to do something bad to someone just because they did something bad to you first.

wrong *obj* /£rɒŋ, $rɑːŋ/ *v* [T often passive] *fml* • If someone is wronged, they are treated in an unfair or unacceptable way: *He regarded himself as the person who had been wronged, but everyone else blamed him for what had happened.* ○ *If the panel think that a candidate has been wronged, it can remark their papers.* • To wrong someone is to judge them unfairly and express uncertainty about their character: *I knew I had wronged her by saying she was unfit for the job.*

wrong·ful /£ˈrɒŋ·fᵊl, $ˈrɑːŋ-/ *adj* • Wrongful means unfair or illegal: *The bankruptcy was not caused by any wrongful or dishonest act.* ○ *She is claiming damages from the company for wrongful* **dismissal**. ○ *Ten demonstrators are suing the police for damages for alleged wrongful* **arrest/imprisonment**.

wrong·ful·ly /£ˈrɒŋ·fᵊl·i, $ˈrɑːŋ-/ *adv* • *He claims he was wrongfully arrested by the police.*

wrong [NOT WORKING] /£rɒŋ, $rɑːŋ/ *adj, adv* [not gradable] not working correctly • *Doctors still cannot tell what is wrong* (=what the problem is) *in 85% of cases of backache.* • *"What's wrong* **with** *you?" "I've got a headache."* • *Something's wrong* **with** *the television – the picture's gone fuzzy.* • *We'll try and* **find out** *what's wrong and call you back.* • If a machine **goes** wrong, it does not work correctly: *My car's gone wrong again.* ○ See also **go wrong** at WRONG [NOT CORRECT], WRONG [NOT SUITABLE].

wrong·do·er /£ˈrɒŋˌduː·əʳ, $ˈrɑːŋˌduː·ɚ/ *n* [C] a person who does something bad or illegal • *They were condemned as wrongdoers before anything had been proven.* • *There was a great desire to punish the wrongdoers and deter them from committing similar crimes in the future.*

wrong·do·ing /£ˈrɒŋˌduː·ɪŋ, $ˈrɑːŋ-/ *n* [U] • Wrongdoing is bad or illegal behaviour: *They have started an investigation into alleged police wrongdoing.* ○ *The managing director has been* **accused of** *wrongdoing.* ○ *She acknowledged she made a mistake but has strenuously* **denied** *any criminal wrongdoing.*

wrote /£rəʊt, $roʊt/ *past simple of* WRITE

wrought [MADE] /£rɔːt, $rɑːt/ *adj* [not gradable] *fml* made or done in a careful or decorative way • *The new album contains some* **carefully**-*wrought new songs and a number of familiar hits.* • *Her poems are* **well**-*wrought and intensely personal.* • **Wrought iron** is a type of pure iron often shaped into attractive patterns: *a wrought-iron gate/table*

wrought [CAUSED] /£rɔːt, $rɑːt/ *past simple and past participle of* WREAK • *Mr Simmonds has wrought* (=caused) *considerable changes in the company.*

wrung /rʌŋ/ *past simple and past participle of* WRING

wry /raɪ/ *adj* showing that you find a bad or difficult situation slightly amusing • *a wry smile* • *a wry comment* • *He was a kindly man with a wry sense of humour.*

wri·ly /ˈraɪ·li/ *adv* • *"I thought he wasn't meant to be in good form," the Welsh captain remarked wrily as the Scottish midfielder scored his third goal of the match.*

wt *n* [U] *abbreviation for* WEIGHT • *On the card she had written: wt 60 kg, ht 1·64 m.*

wun·der·kind /£ˈwʊn·də·kɪnd, $-dɚ·kɪnt/ *n* [C] a person who is very clever or good at something and achieves success at a young age • *With his latest offering,* *wunderkind Spielberg has once again demonstrated his gift for making movies.* • *The magazine featured an interview with the wunderkind theatre and opera director.*

wuss /wʊs/ *n* [C] *Am slang* a person who is weak or not effective • *Don't be such a wuss – you can come out with us after work.* • *Her boyfriend turned toward me and growled, "Hey, wuss!"* [as form of address]

WWF /ˌdʌb·l̩.juːˌdʌb·l̩.juːˈef/ *n* [U] **the WWF** *abbreviation for* Worldwide Fund for Nature

WWI *n* [U] *abbreviation for* World War I, see at WORLD [THE EARTH]

WWII *n* [U] *abbreviation for* World War II, see at WORLD [THE EARTH]

wych-haz·el /ˈwɪtʃˌheɪ·zᵊl/ *n* [C/U] *Br for* WITCH-HAZEL

WYSIWYG *specialized* /ˈwɪz·ɪ·wɪg/ *abbreviation for* what you see is what you get. It refers to the relationship between the picture on a computer screen and what the computer will print.

X x

X [LETTER] (*pl* **X's** or **Xs**), **x** (*pl* **x's** or **xs**) /eks/ *n* [C] the 24th letter of the English alphabet • An **X-chromosome** is a sex CHROMOSOME which exists as one of a pair in the cells of female humans and many female animals: *A female has two X-chromosomes in each cell while a male has one X- and one Y-chromosome.*

X [NUMBER], **x** /eks/ *n* [C] the sign used in the Roman system for the number 10

X [FILM] /eks/ *adj* (of a film or show, esp. in the past) not suitable for people under 16 or 18 years old, esp. because of sexual content • *an X-rated film*

x [AMOUNT NOT STATED] /eks/ *n* [U] used to represent a number, or the name of person or thing, which is not known or stated • *If 2x = 8, then x = 4.* • *So let's say you have x number of ball bearings and you want to ship them from Hong Kong to Los Angeles.* • *Witness x stated that she had seen Cooper on repeated occasions outside the murdered woman's home.*

x [KISS] *n* [C] used at the end of written notes to symbolize a kiss • *Write soon, all my love, Katy xxx*

x [WRONG] *n* [C] written on an answer to a question to show that the answer is not correct

x [VOTE] *n* [C] used when voting to mark the name of the person that you are choosing

x *obj* [REMOVE] /eks/ *v* [T] *Am* to remove (from a list) • *I xed* **out** *all the names of the people I wouldn't be sending cards to.* [M]

xen·on /£ˈzen·ɒn, $-nɑːn/ *n* [U] a type of gas which has no colour or smell and is used in special BULBS (=devices which produce light)

xen·o·pho·bi·a /£ˌzen·əˈfəʊ·bi·ə, $-ˈfoʊ-/ *n* [U] extreme dislike or fear of foreigners, their customs, their religions, etc. • *My grandparents are suspicious of foreigners to the point of xenophobia.* • *Xenophobia and racism became an increasingly strong undercurrent in the films they made at that time.* • *The twin pressures of recession and immigration have undoubtedly fueled xenophobia.*

xen·o·pho·bic /£ˌzen·əˈfəʊ·bɪk, $-ˈfoʊ-/ *adj* • *He unfortunately has a xenophobic mistrust of everything that isn't British.* • *We are supposed to be striving towards a better society for all and yet xenophobic violence has intensified.*

xen·o·phobe /£ˈzen·ə·fəʊb, $-foʊb/ *n* [C] • A xenophobe is a person who strongly dislikes or fears foreigners, their customs, their religions, etc.: *It's not true that they're a nation of bigots and xenophobes.* ○ *"We are not xenophobes," he told an audience in Bourges. "We are not racists."*

Xe·rox /£ˈzɪə·rɒks, $ˈzɪr·ɑːks/ *n* [C] *trademark* a copy of a document or other piece of paper with writing or printing on it made by a machine that uses a photographic process, or the machine itself • *I can give you a Xerox of the letter if you like.*

Xe·rox *obj*, **xe·rox** /£ˈzɪə·rɒks, $ˈzɪr·ɑːks/ *v* [T] • *Would you xerox six copies of the report, please?* • *Ferlinghetti finally sent a Xeroxed copy of the document.*

X·mas /ˈkrɪst·məs, ˈek·sməs/ *n* [U] *abbreviation for* CHRISTMAS • *Happy Xmas to all our customers.* • *In the shops Xmas trees and decorations were on sale.*

X-ray /ˈeks·reɪ/ *n* [C] a type of RADIATION that can go through many solid substances, allowing hidden objects such as bones and organs in the body to be photographed • *As well as their diagnostic uses, X-rays can also be used in the treatment of cancerous tissue.* • *The shorter the wavelength of an X-ray, the more powerful it is.* • *X-rays are used at airports to check luggage for such things as weapons and explosives.* • An X-ray is also a photograph of a part of the body made using X-rays: *The X-ray showed a slight irregularity in one of the heart's valves.* • An X-ray can also refer to an examination of a part of the body using this method: *She* **had** *an X-ray to see if any of her ribs were broken.*

x-ray *obj* /ˈeks·reɪ/ *v* [T] • *They x-rayed my nephew's hip* **to** *see if it was forming properly.* • *My arm was x-rayed at the hospital but fortunately nothing was broken.*

xy·lo·phone /£ˈzaɪ·lə·fəʊn, $-foʊn/ *n* [C] a musical instrument consisting of flat wooden bars of different lengths which you hit with a pair of sticks that have hard round ends made from wood or plastic

Y y

Y [LETTER] (*pl* **Y's** or **Ys**), **y** (*pl* **y's** or **ys**) /waɪ/ *n* [C] the 25th letter of the English alphabet • A **Y-chromosome** is a sex CHROMOSOME that exists only in male cells: *If a Y-chromosome combines with an X-chromosome during fertilization, a male baby will result.* • (*Br trademark*) **Y-fronts** are a piece of underwear for men and boys, covering the area between the waist and the tops of the legs, which have an opening at the front which is the shape of an upside-down Y.

y [AMOUNT NOT STATED] /waɪ/ *n* used to represent the second of two numbers or names which are not known or stated when the first is represented by 'x' • *If 2x = 3y and x=6, then y=4.* • *The children on trial, known as child X and child Y, were accompanied by their parents.*

-y [QUALITY] /-i/ *combining form* added to nouns to form adjectives meaning like the stated thing • *inky* • *cheesy* • [LP] **Stress in pronunciation**

yacht /£jɒt, $jɑːt/ *n* [C] a boat with sails and sometimes an engine, used for either racing or travelling on for pleasure • *Her yacht is moored in the harbour.* • *More than 800 yachts from 26 classes are racing at Cowes this year.* • *He owns a 50-acre vineyard near Bordeaux in France, a house in London and two* **luxury** *yachts.* • [PIC] **Ships and boats, Water sports**

yacht·ing /£ˈjɒt·ɪŋ, $ˈjɑː·t̬ɪŋ/ *n* [U] • *The president goes yachting a lot.* • *Roger and Anne are members of a yachting club in Sydney.*

yachts·man (*pl* **-men**), **yachts·wo·man** (*pl* **-women**) /£ˈjɒt·smən, $ˈjɑːt-, -ˌswʊm·ən/ *n* [C] • A yachtsman or yachtswoman sails or owns a yacht: *He's a very keen yachtsman – he goes racing whenever he can.*

yack /jæk/ *v* [I] *slang* to talk continuously, esp. informally • *We hadn't seen each other for years, so we were yacking* **(away/on)** *for hours.*

yah /jɑː, jʌ/ *adv* [not gradable] *Br infml* YES • *Yah, okay, I understand what you're saying.* • *Oh yah, I like that a lot.*

ya·hoo /ˈjɑː·huː/ *n* [C] *pl* **yahoos** *literary* a rude, loud and unpleasant person, usually. a man, esp. one who lacks education • *Sadly, in the summer the resort is invaded by armies of beer-drinking yahoos.* • *To see archive film of those banner-waving yahoo Conservative conferences is truly frightening.*

yak /jæk/ *n* [C] a type of cattle with long hair and long horns, found mainly in Tibet

yak·ka, yak·ker /ˈjæk·ə/ *n* [U] *Aus infml* work

Yale (lock) /jeɪl/ *n* [C] *trademark* a type of lock, esp. for doors, which is cylindrical and is operated by a flat key • *a Yale key* • PIC› **Locks and home security**

y'all /£jɔːl, $jɑːl/ *pronoun Am regional infml* used to address a group of people that you are speaking to • *Are y'all coming tonight?* • *Y'all seem very busy.*

yam /jæm/ *n* [C/U] an edible potato-like root from a tropical climbing plant, or the plant it grows from, or *(Am)* a **sweet potato** • PIC› **Vegetables**

yam·mer /£ˈjæm·əʳ, $-ɚ/ *v* [I] *esp. Am infml* to talk continuously for a long time in a way that is annoying to other people • *His sister phoned up and yammered* **on/away** *about nothing, as usual.*

yang /jæŋ/ *n* **yin and yang**, see at YIN

yank *obj* PULL /jæŋk/ *v* [T] *infml* to pull (something) forcefully with a quick movement • *My two-year-old nephew yanked the corner of the tablecloth and a bottle of red wine tipped over.* • *In the past, if you had a problem with your teeth, the dentist would just yank them* **out**. • *While you're there could you yank the plug* **out** *for me please.* • *(fig. esp. Am) I was yanked* **out of** (=removed suddenly from) *school and forced to seek work.*

yank /jæŋk/ *n* [C] *infml* • **Give** *the battery a yank and it should come out.*

Yank AMERICAN /jæŋk/, **Yank·ee** /ˈjæŋ·ki/ *n* [C] *infml* a person from the United States of America • *There are a lot of expats living out there – mainly Yanks and Brits and one or two Aussies.* • *(disapproving) The place was full of yanks.*

yank·ee /ˈjæŋ·ki/ *n* [C] *infml* a YANK, or *(Am)* an American who comes from the Northern US • *(Am) It's a sleepy little Mississippi town where folks are still a bit mistrustful of yankees.*

yap /jæp/ *v* [I] **-pp-** *disapproving* (of a small dog) to make short high sounds; to BARK • *She's got a horrible little dog that yaps around your ankles when you go and visit her.* • *(fig. infml) I've just had Ian's mother on the phone, yapping* **(away/on)** (=talking continuously) *for half an hour!*

yap /jæp/ *n* [C] • *I stood on the dog's foot and it* **(gave/made)** *a yap.*

yap·py /ˈjæp·i/ *adj* • *a yappy little dog*

yard UNIT OF MEASUREMENT /£jɑːd, $jɑːrd/ (*abbreviation* **yd**) *n* [C] a unit of measurement equal to three FEET or approximately 91·4 centimetres • *This room measures about eight yards by ten.* • *There must have been* **yards and yards** (=a lot) *of material in that dress.* • LP› **Units**

yard WORK AREA /£jɑːd, $jɑːrd/ *n* [C] an area of land in which a particular type of work is done, often one from which goods are sold • *He used to work in a wood yard, chopping and selling logs.* • *They get their materials cheap from a builders' yard.* • *A scrap yard would buy your old car off you.* • See also BOATYARD; DOCKYARD; JUNKYARD; LUMBERYARD; SHIPYARD; STOCKYARD.

yard LAND NEXT TO BUILDING /£jɑːd, $jɑːrd/ *n* [C] an area of land next to a building which is covered with concrete or other hard material • *The house has a small yard at the back but you could put some pots out there if you wanted to grow flowers.* • *When the alarm went off the prisoners were out in the yard doing their exercises.* • See also BACKYARD; BARNYARD; FARMYARD.

yard GARDEN /£jɑːd, $jɑːrd/ *n* [C] *Am* a piece of land next to a house usually used for growing flowers, grass and other plants

yard·stick /£ˈjɑːd·stɪk, $ˈjɑːrd-/ *n* [C] a fact or standard by which you can judge the success or value of something • *If the yardstick* **of** *success is popularity then he's undoubtedly done very well.* • *You can measure a car's success by a couple of yardsticks – the number built, and the length of time it has been in production.* • *Her performance of Cherubino became a yardstick by which all others have since been measured.*

yar·mul·ke /£ˈjʌm·əl·kə, $ˈjɑːr·məl-/ *n* [C] a small circular cover for the head worn by Jewish men, esp. at religious ceremonies • PIC› **Hats**

yarn THREAD /£jɑːn, $jɑːrn/ *n* [U] thread used for making cloth or for KNITTING

yarn STORY /£jɑːn, $jɑːrn/ *n* [C] a story, usually a long one with a lot of excitement or interest • *He knew how to write a* **good** *yarn that held your interest from beginning to end.* • *I like* **adventure** *yarns with action and suspense – I don't care if they're not intellectual.*

yash·mak /ˈjæʃ·mæk/ *n* [C] a piece of cloth worn by some Muslim women to cover parts of the face when they are in public

yaw /£jɔː, $jɑː/ *v* [I] *specialized* (of an aircraft or a ship) to move slightly to the side of its intended direction

yaw /£jɔː, $jɑː/ *n* [C/U] *specialized*

yawn /£jɔːn, $jɑːn/ *v* [I] to open the mouth wide and deeply breathe in and out without conscious effort, usually when tired or bored • *I can't stop yawning – I must be tired.* • *Every few minutes he stopped to yawn and stretch.* • *I think she bored him – he didn't stop yawning the whole time she was talking to him!* • *(fig.) There exists nowadays a yawning* (=very large) **gap between** *fashion and style.* • *(fig.) As Finance Minister he is going to have to find a way to decrease the yawning* (=very large) *budget deficit.*

yawn /£jɔːn, $jɑːn/ *n* [C] • *Her eyes watered as she tried to* **stifle** (=stop) *a yawn.* • *(infml)* Something that is very boring might be referred to as a yawn: *We have to go to dinner with Simon's boss on Saturday which is a bit of a yawn.*

yd *n* [C] *pl* **yd** *abbreviation for* YARD UNIT OF MEASUREMENT

ye YOU /jiː/ *pronoun old use* (used when addressing more than one person) you • *Ye cannot serve God and mammon.*

ye THE /jiː/ *determiner old use* the • *He goes to a pub in the village called Ye Olde Barn.* • *(dated or humorous)* **Ye Gods** can be used to show surprise.

yea /jeɪ/ *adv* [not gradable] *old use* yes • *They have the power to hire and fire managers and say* **yea or nay** (=yes or no) *to big investment projects.*

yeah /jeə/ *adv* [not gradable] *infml* yes • *"Do you like your job?" "Yeah, it's all right I suppose."* • *Yeah, I understand what you're saying.* • *"Will you drive?" "Yeah, sure."* • *Yeah, that's really great.* • *"I can run faster than you any day!"* **"(Oh) yeah?** (=I don't believe you)**"** • *"Anyway, we're just good friends."* **"Yeah, yeah** (=I don't believe you)*!"*

year /£jɪəʳ, $jɪr/ *n* [C] a period of twelve months, esp. from January 1st to December 31st • *Annette worked in Italy for two years.* • *We'll have been together four years next April.* • *1988 was one of the worst years of my life.* • *Is it a three-year course?* • *She brought along her three-year-old daughter.* • *Have a wonderful Christmas and I hope to see you both in the* **new** *year* (=the year that is about to begin). • *It's been a good year for the roses* (=they have been very successful during this year). • *Trade is good all (the) year (round)* (=through the year) *but it is a little less busy in the winter.* • *We went to Egypt on holiday* **last** *year.* • *At this* **time of** *year the beaches are almost deserted.* • In an educational establishment a year refers to the part of the year during which courses are being taught: *September sees the start of the new* **school/academic** *year.* ○ *She's now* **in** *her second year at Manchester university.* ○ *He had a nervous breakdown* **(during/in)** *his* **final** *year at college.* • *(Br and Aus)* Year also refers to students in a particular year of school, college or university: *A couple of my fifth-year pupils are real trouble-makers.* ○ *I like teaching the younger kids – the first- and second-years.* • *He looks good/dances well* **for a** *man* **of** *his* **years** (=considering how old he is). • The expression **for years** means for a long time: *Roz and I have been going there for years.* • **For years** (also **in years**) also means since a long time ago: *How are you – I haven't seen you for/in years!* • *I've never once seen her angry* **in/through all the years** (=in all the time) *I've known her.* • A thing or person **of the year** is one that has been chosen as the best in a particular year, esp. in a competition: *Young Musician of the Year* • If something **puts years on** a person, it makes them appear much older: *Being tired and unhappy puts years on you.* • If something **takes years off** a person, it makes them appear or feel much younger: *"Have you seen James without his beard?" "I know – it takes years off him!"* • *(Br and Aus infml)* **The year dot** means an extremely long time ago: *Men and women must have had this argument* **from/since** *the year dot!* • If something happens **year in year out** it happens in the same way every year, often so that it is boring: *We go to Mike's parents every summer – it's the same thing year in year out.* • LP› **Dates, Holidays, Periods of time**

year·ly /£ˈjɪə·li, $ˈjɪr-/ *adv* [not gradable] • Yearly means every year or once every year: *Individual copies of the magazine sell for $2·95 and yearly subscriptions cost $21.* ○ *We get a yearly pay-increase.* ○ *Members receive a twice yearly newsletter.* ○ *Last month, the inflation rate was up 0·2% on a monthly basis and 3·1% on a yearly basis.*

year·book /£ˈjɪə·bʊk, $ˈjɪr-/ *n* [C] a book published every year by a school or other organization that gives various facts about the events and achievements of the previous or present year • *There was a photo of her in the school yearbook holding a trophy that she'd won for playing tennis.*

yearn /£jɜːn, $jɜːrn/ *v* to desire very strongly, esp. something that you cannot have or something that is very difficult to have • *The whole country seems to yearn* **for** *its lost empire.* [I] • *Is it not in the nature of all human beings to yearn* **for** *freedom?* [I] • *Despite his great commercial success he still yearns* **for** *critical approval.* [I] • *It's better to be happy with what you've got than to be always yearning* **towards** *something you can't have.* [I] • *Sometimes I just yearn* **to** *be alone.* [+ *to* infinitive]

yearn·ing /£'jɜː·nɪŋ, $'jɜːr-/ *n* • *All the great love stories are about* **frustrated** *yearning rather than contented fulfillment.* [U] • *I suppose it's because I live in a crowded city that I have this yearning* **for** *open spaces.* [C] • *His poems are full of unfulfilled yearnings and desires.* [C]

yeast /jiːst/ *n* [U] a type of FUNGUS (=simple organism) which is used in making alcoholic drinks such as beer and wine, and for making bread swell and become light • *dried/fresh yeast* • *yeast extract*

yeast·y /'jiː·sti/ *adj* **-ier**, **-iest** • *This bread has a wonderful yeasty taste.*

yell *(obj)* /jel/ *v* to shout (words) or make a loud noise, usually when you are angry, in pain or excited • *Our neighbours were yelling* **(obscenities) at** *each other this morning.* [T/I] • *My sister's baby started yelling in the middle of the night.* [I] • *I can't bear it when a bar is so noisy that you have to yell* **to** *make yourself heard.* [I] • *We could clearly hear them screaming and yelling.* [I] • *I could hear one of the kids yelling* **for** *me from the bedroom.* [I] • *When she gets excited she doesn't speak so much as yell.* [I] • *"Just get out of here – I can't stand you!" she yelled.* [+ clause] • (J)

yell /jel/ *n* [C] • *I thought I heard a yell from the bathroom so I came up to see what was the matter.* • *Suddenly she let out a* **loud/great** *yell.*

yel·low COLOUR /£'jel·əʊ, $-oʊ/ *adj, n* **-er**, **-est** (of) a colour like that of a lemon or gold or the sun • *She was wearing a bright yellow T-shirt.* • *You should wear more yellow – it suits you.* • *It was early autumn and the leaves were turning yellow.* • *(Am)* The yoke of an egg is sometimes called its yellow. • **Yellow fever** is an infectious tropical disease which causes the skin to become yellow and can result in death. • In Britain a **yellow line** is line of yellow paint which is put along the sides of particular roads to show that vehicles cannot be parked there at stated times. • *(trademark)* A **Yellow Pages** is a large yellow book which contains the addresses and telephone numbers of businesses and people offering services, listing them in groups according to what type of business they are. • *"Follow the yellow brick road"* (from the book and film of L.Frank Baum's *The Wizard of Oz*, 1900)

yel·low *(obj)* /£'jel·əʊ, $-oʊ/ *v* • *The newspaper had yellowed* (= become yellow) *over the years.* [T] • *A lot of white and cream paints yellow over time.* [I]

yel·low·ish /£'jel·əʊ·ɪʃ, $-oʊ-/, **yel·low·y** /£'jel·əʊ·i, $-oʊ-/ *adj* • If something is yellowish or yellowy it is slightly yellow: *The leaves vary from yellowish-green to dark green.*

yel·low·ness *n* [U]

yel·low PEOPLE /£'jel·əʊ, $-oʊ/ *adj* [not gradable] belonging to a race that has pale yellowish brown skin. This is generally considered offensive.

yel·low COWARDLY /£'jel·əʊ, $-oʊ/ *adj* **-er**, **-est** *infml* cowardly; not brave • *You're yellow – running away like that.*

yelp /jelp/ *v* [I] to make a sudden short high sound, usually when in pain • *I accidentally trod on the dog's foot and it yelped.*

yelp /jelp/ *n* [C] • *She let out a yelp of fear.*

yen /jen/ *n* [C usually sing] *infml* a strong feeling of wanting or desiring • *I have a yen* **for** *mountains and snow.*

yeo·man /£'jəʊ·mən, $'joʊ-/ *n* [C] *pl* **-men** (in the past) a man who was not a servant and owned and cultivated an area of land

yep /jep/ *adv infml* yes • *"You mean they just ran away to Mauritius together?" "Yep, that's right."*

yer /£jəʳ, $jɚ/ *determiner infml* your • *Give us yer coat, love.* • *Get yer hands off me!*

yes /jes/, *infml* **yeah** /jeə/, **yep** /jep/, **yah** /jɑː/ *adv* [not gradable] used to express acceptance, willingness or agreement • *"Did you say a kilo?" "Yes."* • *"Would you like a glass of wine?" "Yes please."* • *"Do you like Indian food?" "Yes, I love it."* • *"Would you post those for me?" "Yeah, sure."* • *"Was everything all right at the hotel?" "Yes, fine."* • *"She's happy enough, isn't she?" "Yes, I think so."* • *"He's a really nice guy." "Yes he is."* • *"He should have said so earlier." "Yes, you're right."* • *"Report to me at nine o'clock tomorrow morning." "Yes, sir."* • *"Now go and clean your bedroom." "Yes, dad, anything you say, dad."* • *"You do know what he's like, don't you?" "Oh yes, don't worry."* • *"Peter, are you listening to me?" "Yes, yes, yes, I heard what you said!"* • *"Have you got enough money with you?" "Yes, thank you, I do know how much I'll need!"* • *If you'd* **say** *yes* (= agree) *to the request you'd save a lot of trouble.* • Yes can be used to show that you are ready to listen to someone or to answer their request for information: *"Johnny" "Yes?" "Can I have a word?"* ○ *"Dad." "Yes, what do you want, honey?"* ○ *"You see, I think I, I..." "Yes?" "I think I love you."* ○ *Yes, can I help you?* • You can also use yes when you are disagreeing with a negative statement: *"I'm not a very good cook though." "Yes you are – you make wonderful food!"* ○ *"I don't have many clothes." "Yes you do – you've got loads!"* • You can also use yes when you have just remembered something that you were saying: *What was I talking about – Oh yes, I was telling you what happened at the shops.* • If you answer **yes and no** to a question, you are expressing that you cannot answer it in a certain way: *"It's better now that Sara works for you, isn't it?" "Well, yes and no – there are good points and bad."* • *(disapproving)* A **yes-man** is a person who agrees with everything their employer, leader, etc. says in order to please them: *Philip won't stand up to the boss – he's such a yes-man.*

yes /jes/ *n* [C] • A yes is a vote supporting a particular plan of action or an acceptance of an invitation: *The plan was passed by four yeses to three noes.* • *"Have you had any replies yet?" "Yeah, six yeses, two noes and a don't know."*

yes *obj* /jes/ *v* [T] *Am* • *I hate it when my students yes* (= say yes to) *me all the time.*

yes·ter·day /£'jes·tə·deɪ, $-tɚ-/ *adv* [not gradable], *n* (on) the day before today • *We only got home from France yesterday.* • *He rang yesterday while you were out.* • *I saw her yesterday afternoon.* • *"Is that today's paper?" "No, it's yesterday's."* [U] • Yesterday can also refer more generally to the recent past: *But this is a fickle world and nobody's interested in yesterday's pop-stars.* [U] • *Yes, I know they're having an affair – I* **wasn't born yesterday** (= I'm not stupid)*!* • *"Yesterday, all my troubles seemed so far away"* (from the song *Yesterday* by The Beatles, 1965) • LP **Calendar**

yes·ter·year /£'jes·tə·jɪəʳ, $-tɚ·jɪr/ *n* [U] *literary* the past, esp. the recent past • *In this TV series we look back with fondness and nostalgia at the Hollywood stars of yesteryear.*

yet UNTIL NOW /jet/ *adv* [in negatives and questions; not gradable] still; until the present time • *I haven't spoken to her yet!* • *Haven't you eaten your lunch yet?* • *He hasn't finished yet.* • *She hasn't told him yet.* • *I got the book a month ago and I haven't yet had a chance to read it.* • *"Are you ready?" "Not yet – wait a moment."* • *Of all the songs I've heard tonight that's the best yet.* • *"Is the cake cooked?" "Not (quite) yet – give it five more minutes."* • *(fml)* **As** *yet* (= Until now) *we haven't needed extra staff, but it's only a matter of time.* • *"Give me chastity and continence, but not yet"* (from the *Confessions* of St Augustine, 354-430)

yet IN THE FUTURE /jet/ *adv* [not gradable] in the future • *She won't be back for a long time yet.* • *The delights of motherhood are yet* **to come.** • If you **have yet to** do something you have not done it: *"What did your dad say about it?" "I've yet to tell him."* ○ *She seems so sad – I've yet to see her smile.* ○ *I came in from work two hours ago but I've been so busy I've yet to sit down!*

yet DESPITE THAT /jet/ *adv* [not gradable], *conjunction* despite that • *He's got a huge nose, he's overweight and he's bald* **(and)** *yet somehow he's incredibly attractive.* • *I say all these dreadful things about her* **(and)** *yet I like her.* • *She says she's a vegetarian* **(and)** *yet she eats chicken.* • *They're a most unlikely couple* **(and)** *yet they get on really well together.* • *She manages to be firm yet kind with the kids.*

yet EVEN /jet/ *adv* [not gradable] used to add emphasis, esp. to words such as 'another' and 'again' and *(fml)* to comparatives • *Rachel bought yet* **another** *pair of shoes to add to the thirty pairs she already owns.* • *Yet* **again** *we are seeing violence break out in our streets.* • *Yet more snow is forecast for the already hard-hit south-east region.* • *(fml) I met the older sister who is yet more beautiful.* • *(fml) Yet more food! Where will it all end?*

yet EVEN NOW /jet/ *adv* [not gradable] even at this stage or time • *We* **may** *yet succeed – you never know.* • *She* **may** *yet be proven to be right – we'll have to wait and see.* • *You might yet prove me wrong.* • *So you know someone who met the love *of her life on her fortieth birthday? Well, there's hope for me yet!*

yet·i /£ˈjet·i, $ˈjet̬-/, **a·bom·in·a·ble snow·man** (*pl* **-men**) *n* [C] a big hairy human-like creature believed by some people to live in the Himalayan mountains

yew /juː/ *n* an evergreen tree with flattened, needle-like leaves and small red CONES, or the wood from this tree • *In Britain you often see yews in churchyards.* [C] • *A large bowl made from yew stood on the table.* [U] • PIC› **Tree**

yid /jɪd/ *n* [C] *taboo* (a very offensive word for) a Jew

Yid·dish /ˈjɪd·ɪʃ/ *n* [U] a language spoken by some Jewish people which is related to German

yield *obj* PRODUCE /jiːld/ *v* [T] to supply or produce (something positive such as a profit, an amount of food or information) • *The talks with management failed to yield any results.* • *Police have been interviewing people in the area in the hope that it will yield further information about the crime.* • *Organic farmers in the United States yield only 5-15% less than mainstream farmers.* • *Some people prefer to put their money into higher-yielding financial assets instead of bank accounts.*

yield /jiːld/ *n* [C usually pl] • *Yields* (= Profits) *on gas and electricity shares are consistently high.* • *Over the past 50 years* **crop** *yields* (= the amount of crops produced) *have risen steadily in the US by 1-2% a year.*

yield *(obj)* GIVE UP /jiːld/ *v* to give up the control of or responsibility for (something), often because you have been forced to • *They were forced to yield* **(up)** *some of their lands during the war.* [T] • *Carl's failing as a boss is that he refuses to yield any responsibility.* [T] • *Despite renewed pressure to give up the occupied territory they will not yield.* [I] • If you yield **to** something, you accept that you have been defeated by it: *It's very easy to yield to the temptation to sign for a lot of money.* [I] ○ *"We will not yield to pressure," said the president.* [I] • *(Am)* To yield **to** traffic coming from another direction is to wait and allow it to go first. [I]

yield BEND/BREAK /jiːld/ *v* [I] *slightly fml* to bend or break under pressure • *His legs began to yield under the sheer weight of his body.* • *Eventually the bridge yielded because of the weight.*

yield·ing /ˈjiːl·dɪŋ/ *adj slightly fml* • A material that is yielding is soft and able to move or bend: *Baby toys are usually made out of yielding materials.* ○ *(fig.) Part of his success as a negotiator is that he can be yielding when necessary.*

yin /jɪn/ *n* [U] **yin and yang** the two basic principles of the universe in Chinese PHILOSOPHY • *Yin is the female principle, characterized as dark and negative, and Yang the male principle, being light and positive.*

yip·pee /£jɪˈpiː, $ˈjɪp·iː/ *exclamation infml* used to express happiness, excitement or great satisfaction • *No school for five weeks – yippee!*

yo /£jəʊ, $joʊ/ *exclamation slang* used as an informal greeting between people who know each other or as an expression of approval • *"Mickie!" "Yo brother!"* • *"Party at my place?" "Yo baby!"*

yob /£jɒb, $jɑːb/, **yob·bo** (*pl* **yobbos**) /£ˈjɒb·əʊ, $ˈjɑː·boʊ/ *n* [C] *Br and Aus infml* a young man who behaves in a very rude, offensive and sometimes violent way • *Gangs of loud-mouthed yobs with shaven heads and tattoos roam the streets at night.* • *Police officers arrested a few yobs who had started fighting at the football match.* • *What we are witnessing in this country is the spread of yob culture.*

yo·del /£ˈjəʊ·dəl, $ˈjoʊ-/ *v* [I] **-ll-** or *Am usually* **-l-** to sing by making a series of very fast changes between the natural voice and a much higher voice • *Yodelling is associated with folk songs of the Swiss Alps.*

yo·del /£ˈjəʊ·dəl, $ˈjoʊ-/ *n* [C] • A yodel is a song or a part of a song that is yodelled.

yo·ga /£ˈjəʊ·gə, $ˈjoʊ-/ *n* [U] a set of physical and mental exercises, Indian in origin, which is intended to give control over the body and mind • *Roz spent last summer doing yoga in India.* • *He teaches yoga at the local hospital.* • *I thought I might try out a new yoga class tonight.* • Yoga is a Hindu system of PHILOSOPHY which aims at the union of the self with god.

yo·gic /£ˈjəʊ·gɪk, $ˈjoʊ-/ *adj* [not gradable] • *yogic exercises*

yo·gi /£ˈjəʊ·gi, $ˈjoʊ-/ *n* [C] • A yogi is a person who has spent a lot of their life doing yoga and studying its PHILOSOPHY.

yog·urt, **yo·ghurt**, **yo·ghourt** /£ˈjɒg·ət, $ˈjoʊ·gɚt/ *n* a slightly sour thick liquid made from milk with bacteria added to it, sometimes sweetened and flavoured with fruit and sometimes eaten plain • *natural/plain yogurt* [U] • *strawberry yogurt* [U] • *Greek yogurt* [U] • *low-fat yogurt* [U] • *drinking yogurt* [U] • *I only had a yogurt* (= a container of this) *for lunch.* [C]

yoke WOODEN BAR /£jəʊk, $joʊk/ *n* [C] a wooden bar which is fastened over the necks of two animals, esp. cattle, and connected to the vehicle or load that they are pulling • *The oxen are led up to the sledges, and tricked into the yoke.* • *(literary)* Yoke can also be used to refer to something which unfairly limits freedom: *It was during those years that the British colonial yoke was lifted.* ○ *Both countries had recently thrown off the communist yoke.* ○ *She did not want the yoke of marriage.*

yoke *obj* /£jəʊk, $joʊk/ *v* [T] • *Two oxen yoked* **to** *a plough walked wearily up and down the field.* • *(fig.) All these different political elements have somehow been yoked* **together** (= combined) *to form a new alliance.*

yoke CLOTHES /£jəʊk, $joʊk/ *n* [C] a fitted part of an item of clothing, esp. a strip which goes around the shoulders or waist, to which is sewn a looser piece of material

yo·kel /£ˈjəʊ·kəl, $ˈjoʊ-/ *n* [C] a stupid or awkward person who lives in the countryside rather than a town, esp. one whose appearance is in some way strange or amusing • *He plays the* **country** *yokel in the butter ad.*

yolk /£jəʊk, $joʊk/ *n* the yellow middle part of an egg • *I like eggs lightly cooked so that the yolk is still runny.* [U] • *Separate the yolks from the whites.* [C] • *I used three egg yolks in this pastry.* [C]

Yom Kip·pur /£ˌjɒm·kɪˈpʊəʳ, $ˌjɑːm'kɪp·ɚ/, **Day of A·tone·ment** *n* [U] a Jewish holy day in September or October when nothing is eaten all day and people say prayers in the SYNAGOGUE asking for forgiveness for things they have done wrong

yon·der /£ˈjɒn·dəʳ, $ˈjɑːn·dɚ/, **yon** /£jɒn, $jɑːn/ *adj, adv* [not gradable] *old use or regional* in the place or direction shown; over there • *Do you see yonder cloud that's almost in the shape of a camel?* • *She lives in that village yonder.*

yonks /£jɒŋks, $jɑːŋks/ *n* [U] *Br and Aus infml dated* a very long time, usually a number of years • *How is Gareth? I haven't seen him for yonks!*

yoo–hoo /ˈjuː·huː/ *exclamation* used to attract a person's attention • *Yoo-hoo, we're over here!* • *"It's for yoo-hoo!"* (advertisement for the British Telecom telephone service, 1985-)

yore /£jɔːʳ, $jɔːr/ *n* [U] **of yore** *old use literary* of a long time ago • *This was once a Roman road* **in days** *of yore.* • *Nowadays, of course, people are better educated than in the backward village communities of yore.*

York·shire pud·ding /£ˈjɔːk·ʃəˌpʊd·ɪŋ, $ˈjɔːrk·ʃɚ-/ *n* [C/U] a savoury dish which consists of a baked mixture of flour, milk and eggs which is traditionally eaten in Britain with BEEF

you PERSON/PEOPLE ADDRESSED /juː, jʊ/ *pronoun* the person or people being addressed • *You look nice.* • *I love you.* • *I'll help you if you like.* • *You're coming tonight, aren't you?* • *You know it makes sense.* • *You made that especially for me? You are a sweetie!* • *Are you two ready?* • *You've made an old lady very happy.* • *You painted that yourself? You clever girl!* • *You, too, can have a body like mine.* • *You complete idiot! What did you do that for?* • *Hey, you with the hat – come here and say that!* • *(Am) "Would you get me a coffee?" "Sure,* **you got it** (= what you have asked will be done, esp. quickly)*!"*

your /£jɔːʳ, $jʊr, £jəʳ, $jɚ/ *determiner* • Your means of or belonging to the person or group of people being spoken or written to: *Is this your bag?* ○ *I love your dress – it's so pretty.* ○ *She's told both of you before – it's none of your business!* ○ *Go to the end of this street and you'll see the shop on your right.* ○ *Your mother is driving me crazy.* ○ *What's your problem?* • LP› **Determiners**

yours /£jɔːz, $jʊrz/ *pronoun* • Yours is used to show that something belongs to or is connected with the person or group of people being spoken or written to: *Mine's the smaller plate of food and that one there is yours.* ○ *Is this pen yours? I found it under my desk.* ○ *Unfortunately my legs aren't as long as yours.* ○ *I'll show you my answers if you'll show me yours.* ○ *Our tent is a bit too small so were wondering if we could borrow yours.* ○ *I've got something* **of** *yours* (= that belongs to you). ○ *That recipe* **of** *yours for cheesecake was wonderful!* ○ *You know, that dog* **of** *yours smells!* • You can write yours at the end of an informal letter: *Yours, Jack* ○ *Yours, as ever, Ellis.* • LP› **Letters**

your·self /£jɔːˈself, £jə-, $jʊr-, $jɚ-/ *pronoun pl* **yourselves** /£jɔːˈselvz, £jə-, $jʊr-, $jɚ-/ • Yourself is used when both the subject and object of the verb are you: *Be careful with that knife or you'll cut yourself!* ○ *You could have killed yourselves!* • Yourself is sometimes used to give special attention to the subject of the sentence: *And you actually made this yourself instead of buying it?* ○ *You yourself said that you sometimes find your mother a pain.* ○ *You could write to him yourself, you know.* ○ *You can do that yourself – you don't need me to help you.* • If you do something **(all) by** yourself you do it alone or without help from anyone else: *Did you tie your laces all by yourself Joe? You clever boy!* • *So have you got the whole house* **to** *yourself* (=for your own use only) *now that Neil and Sam are on holiday?* • *The best thing you can do is to go into the interview and* **(just) be yourself** (=do and say what seems right to you rather than behaving in a way that you think other people might like). • *(Br dated) How are you* **in yourself** (=How do you feel despite being physically ill of having other problems)? • LP› **Reflexive pronouns and verbs**

you PEOPLE GENERALLY /juː, jʊ/ *pronoun* people in general • *You learn from experience.* • *You can't get a driving licence till you're seventeen in this country.* • *They're saying now that margarine is bad for you.* • *You meet a lot of people through work.* • *You see, you can't be too careful.* • *How do you get this thing to start?*

your /£jɔːʳ, $jʊr, £jəʳ, $jɚ/ *determiner* • Your means of or belonging to people generally: *Garlic is good for your blood.* ○ *Of course you want the best for your children.* ○ *You do your best but it's never quite good enough.* ○ *Whatever your opinion of the man, you have to admit he's clever.* • *(infml)* Your is sometimes said before a typical example of something is given: *He's your standard middle-class liberal wimp!* ○ *This is not your usual science-fiction offering but then Brinkworth isn't exactly your typical author.*

yours /£jɔːz, $jʊrz/ *pronoun* • Yours is used to show that something belongs to or is connected with people generally: *Someone else's dirty handkerchief is revolting but it's okay if it's yours.*

your·self /£jɔːˈself, £jə-, $jʊr-, $jɚ-/ *pronoun* • Yourself is used when both the subject and object of the verb are you and you is also being used to refer to people generally: *You tell yourself everything's all right but you know it's not really.*

young /jʌŋ/ *adj* **-er, -est** (esp. of something living) at an early stage of development or existence; not old • *The trees in this part of the forest are still quite young.* • *A young couple have just moved in downstairs.* • *His girlfriend's very young.* • *He looks very young for his age.* • *Philippa is the youngest person in the family.* • *Angela is two years younger than Clare.* • *The younger generation don't know how lucky they are.* • *Relatively speaking, it's quite a young planet.* • *The course is specifically intended to help with the problems experienced by young adults.* • *At 28 he's exceptionally young* **to** *be manager of a major league club.* [+ *to* infinitive] • *You must remember – she's still young and impressionable.* • *Mind your language, young lady!* • *He's a member of the Young Conservatives.* • *She's got very young-***looking** *skin for someone of fifty.* • *I couldn't believe how young-***looking** *his parents were.* • *Be honest now – do you think this dress* **is** *a bit/too* **young for** *me* (=would be more suitable for someone younger)? • *(approving) My mother's* **young at heart** (=thinks and behaves as if she was younger than she really is). • *Isn't* **young love** (=love between young people) *sweet?* • **Young blood** means young and interesting people: *I felt that we needed a bit of young blood in the organization.* • *(dated or humorous)* Someone's **young lady** or **young man** is the woman/girl or man/boy with whom they have a loving and/or sexual relationship: *If you'd care to bring your young man along too we should be delighted.* • A **young offenders' institution** is a special place for people who have done bad things and are too young to be sent to prison. • **Young ones** are children: *a news programme specially for the young ones* • *"Young, gifted and black"* (title of a song written by Weldon J. Irvine and Nina Simone, 1970) • *"The Young Ones"* (title of a film and song by Cliff Richard, 1961, later used for a British television programme) • *"Bliss was it in that dawn to be alive, / But to be young was very heaven!"* (William Wordsworth in the poem *The Prelude*, 1850) • *"When We Were Very Young"* (title of a book of poems for children by A.A.Milne, 1924) • LP› **Age**

young /jʌŋ/ *pl n* • **The** young can be used to refer to young people as a group: *I have nothing against mini-skirts but I think they're strictly for the young.* • Young are the babies of an animal: *Meanwhile the mother flies back to the nest to feed her young.* ○ *In this type of animal* **the** *young are born with fur and open eyes.*

young·ster /£ˈjʌŋk·stəʳ, $-stɚ/ *n* [C] • A youngster is a young person, usually an older child: *We try to find college places for youngsters who haven't done as well as they'd hoped with their exams.* ○ *The government have set up a scheme to build hostels for homeless youngsters.* ○ *You youngsters – you don't know how lucky you are!*

youth /juːθ/ *n* the period of your life when you are young, the state of being young, or a young person or people • *It seems a shame to spend the whole of your youth shut away studying.* [U] • *With parents that strict I don't imagine she ever really had a youth.* [C] • *I was a fairly good football player* **in** *my youth.* [U] • *I left my sister counting her grey hairs and mourning her* **lost** *youth.* [U] • *The first volume is the author's account of his* **misspent** *youth in the bars of Dublin.* [U] • *We live in a society that worships youth* (=the state of being young). [U] • *He looks like a man who's found the secret to* **eternal** *youth* (=being young). [U] • *You may not have played tennis as often as him but at least you've got youth on your side* (=you are young). [U] • A youth is a boy or a young man: *She brought home another spotty youth last week.* [C] ○ *Gangs of youths were throwing stones and bottles at the police.* [C] ○ *For these offences he received a nine-month youth custody sentence.* ○ *(literary) In the film he is portrayed very much as a* **callow** *youth* (=a young person lacking experience). [C] • Youth can also mean can mean young people, both male and female, considered as a group: *Oh, the arrogance of youth!* [U] ○ *The youth of today – they've got no manners!* [U] ○ *They were the first rock band to really capture the imagination of the nation's disaffected youth.* [U] ○ *Like most capital cities in Europe it has a thriving youth culture.* ○ *This area has the second highest youth unemployment rate in England.* • A **youth club** is a place that older children can go to in order to meet other children, play sports and do other social activities: *Rosie is off to a disco at the local youth club tonight.* • A **youth hostel** is a place where people, esp. young people, can stay cheaply for short periods when they are travelling: *When we went on our cycling tour, we stayed mainly in youth hostels.* ○ *I used to go* **youth-hostelling** *when I was a student.* • *"Love like youth is wasted on the young"* (from the song *The Second Time Around* written by Sammy Cahn, 1960) • LP› **Age**

youth·ful /ˈjuːθ·fəl/ *adj approving* • Youthful means having the qualities that are typical of young people: *At the time I admired his youthful* **enthusiasm/vigour**. ○ *She has very youthful skin.* ○ *He's a very youthful-***looking** *60 – I thought he was more like 50.* • Youthful can also just mean young: *A youthful president can be good for a country's morale.*

youth·ful·ly /ˈjuːθ·fəl·i/ *adv* • *Slim and sprightly with youthfully cropped hair, you'd never believe he's fifty-six.*

youth·ful·ness /ˈjuːθ·fəl·nəs/ *n* [U] • *He has a youthfulness about him that nothing seems to affect.*

yowl /jaʊl/ *v* [I] to make a long, high-sounding cry, usually because of pain • *I was woken up by cats yowling outside my window.*

yowl /jaʊl/ *n* [C]

yo-yo /£ˈjəʊ·jəʊ, $ˈjoʊ·joʊ/ *n* [C] *pl* **yoyos** a toy which consists of a circular object that can be made to go up and down a long piece of string to which it is tied

yuc·ca /ˈjʌk·ə/ *n* [C] a plant with long stiff leaves on a thick woody stem and sometimes white bell-shaped flowers

yuck, yuk /jʌk/ *exclamation infml* an expression of disgust • *"There's a horrible smell outside." "Yuck, how revolting!"* • *What have you got in that sandwich – chocolate and cheese? Yuk!*

yuck·y (-ier, -iest), yuk·ky (-ier, -iest) /ˈjʌk·i/ *adj infml* • Yucky means disgusting or unpleasant: *I like the style of the jacket but I don't like the yucky green colour.* ○ *It got a bit yucky towards the end of the film with all those murders.* ○ *'Loving Peter' is the film's rather yukky title.*

Yule /juːl/ *n* [U] *dated or literary* Christmas • A **yule log** is a cylindrical chocolate cake eaten at Christmas which is decorated to look like a LOG (=a thick piece of tree branch or trunk).

Yule·tide /ˈjuːl·taɪd/ *n* [U] *dated or literary* the period around Christmas • *Yuletide greetings*

yum·my /ˈjʌm·i/ *adj* **-ier, -iest** *infml* (esp. of food) tasting extremely good • *I think I'll have some more of that yummy chocolate cake.* • *"What's the tart like?" "It's totally yummy."* • *There are some yummy-***looking** *desserts over there.* • *(fig.)*

Tell her to bring along that yummy (= attractive) *brother of hers.*

yup·pie, yup·py /ˈjʌp·i/ *n* [C] *disapproving* a young person who lives in a city, earns a lot of money and spends it doing fashionable things and buying expensive possessions • *The problem is that if you smarten up an area of the city you get a load of yuppies moving in.* • *They're just a couple of yuppies with more money than sense.*

yup·pi·fy *obj* /ˈjʌp·ɪ·faɪ/ *v* [T usually passive] *infml disapproving* • When a part of a town is yuppified, its appearance is changed to suit or attract people who earn and spend a lot of money: *Over the past ten years this traditionally working-class neighbourhood has been yuppified beyond recognition.*

Zz

Z (*pl* **Z's** or **Zs**), **z** (*pl* **z's** or **zs**) /£zed, $ziː/ *n* [C] the 26th and last letter of the English alphabet • *(Am infml)* If you **catch/get/make some/a few z's**, you sleep: *"Do you want to come back for a drink after the film?" "No thanks, I need to go home and catch some z's."*

za·ny /ˈzeɪ·ni/ *adj* **-ier, -iest** *infml* strange, surprising or uncontrolled in an amusing way • *a zany film* • *a zany cartoon* • *zany clothing* • *zany ideas* • *Daisy is a pretty zany character.*

zap *obj* [DESTROY] /zæp/ *v* [T] **-pp-** *infml* to destroy or kill, esp. intentionally • *We've got the kind of weapons that can zap the enemy from thousands of miles away.* • *We're really going to zap the competition with this new product, guys!* • *Don't you know that the sun zaps your skin cells?*

zap /zæp/ *exclamation* • *One day, zap! – it suddenly hit him that he was nearly 40 and he'd achieved nothing with his life.* • Zap! is often written in CARTOONS (= picture stories) to show that someone or something has been hit or destroyed.

zap *(obj)* [GO QUICKLY] /zæp/ *v* [always + adv/prep] **-pp-** *esp. Am infml* to go somewhere or do (something) quickly • *They're always zapping off somewhere or other.* [I] • *Have I got time to zap into town and do some shopping before we have to catch the train?* [I] • *George zapped through his homework and rushed out to play football.* [I] • *There are now over a million American fax machines zapping* (= sending quickly) *messages from coast to coast.* [T] • To zap is also to use a device to change channels quickly, sometimes to avoid watching advertisements: *It really annoys me when people zap* **between** *channels.* [I] ○ *Advertising agencies have become concerned that television advertising could lose its effectiveness because of zapping.* [I] • See also ZIP [SPEED].

zap /zæp/ *n* [U] *esp. Am infml* • Zap means energy and enthusiasm: *We need someone with a lot of zap for this job.* ○ *"OK," said the play's producer, "Let's do that scene again, and this time* **put** *some zap* **into it**.*"*

zap·py /ˈzæp·i/ *adj* **-ier, -iest** *esp. Am infml* • *a zappy advertising campaign* • *a zappy tune*

zap·per /£ˈzæp·əʳ, $-ɚ/ *n* [C] *Am infml* • A zapper is a device for controlling a machine from a distance: *Use the zapper to turn off the TV.*

zeal /ziːl/ *n* [U] great enthusiasm or eagerness • *reforming zeal* • *missionary zeal* • *revolutionary zeal* • *religious zeal* • *He thinks that with the new zeal* **for** *money-making, a certain quality of life has been lost.* • *They are pursuing their aims* **with a** *determined zeal*/**an** *evangelical zeal.* • **With (all)** *the zeal* **of a convert**, *she strongly disapproves of people who smoke now she's stopped herself.* • **In** *his zeal* **to** *get his work finished on time, he made a lot of mistakes.* [+ to infinitive]

zeal·ot /ˈzel·ət/ *n* [C] • A zealot is a person who has very strong opinions about something, and tries to make other people have them too: *a religious zealot* ○ *a feminist zealot* ○ *a right-wing zealot* ○ *zealots* **of** *the nationalist movement*

zeal·ous /ˈzel·əs/ *adj* • Zealous means enthusiastic and eager: *She has become a zealous convert to the environmentalist cause.* ○ *He has remained a zealous supporter of the government's policies.* ○ *It was thanks to a zealous member of the public that the bomb was discovered before it went off.* ○ *They have been extremely zealous in their attempts to get smoking banned in their office.*

zeal·ous·ly /ˈzel·ə·sli/ *adv* • *The actress Greta Garbo always zealously guarded her privacy.* • *He has been zealously carrying out the tasks he's been given.*

zeal·ous·ness /ˈzel·ə·snəs/ *n* [U]

zeb·ra /ˈzeb·rə, ˈziː·brə/ *n* [C] *pl* **zebras** or **zebra** an African wild animal which looks like a horse, and which has black or brown and white lines on its body • *(Br and Aus)* A **zebra crossing** (*Am* **crosswalk**) is a place on a road, esp. one where there is a lot of traffic, across which wide black and white lines are painted, and at which vehicles must stop to allow people to walk across the road: *She was taken to hospital after being knocked over on a zebra crossing.* Compare **pedestrian crossing** at PEDESTRIAN [WALKER]; **pelican crossing** at PELICAN. • [PIC] Road

zeit·geist /ˈtsaɪt·gaɪst/ *n* [U] the general set of ideas, beliefs, feelings etc. which is typical of a particular period in history • *The film's success may reflect the country's zeitgeist: anxiety, economic hardship, suspicion and fear.* • *He described the designer, Mary Quant, as part of the zeitgeist* **of** *the sixties.*

Zen /zen/ *n* [U] a form of Buddhism which developed in Japan and which emphasizes that religious knowledge is achieved through clearing the mind of thoughts and giving attention to only one thing, rather than by reading religious writings • *Zen is a mystic religion, which emphasizes the importance of meditation.* • *Zen Buddhism* • *a Zen master* • *"Zen and the art of motorcycle maintenance"* (title of a book by Robert Pirsig, 1974)

zen·ith /ˈzen·ɪθ/ *n* [C] the best or most successful point or time • *In the early 1900s, Tolstoy was* **at the zenith of** *his achievement.* • *His dancing career is now past its zenith.* • *The newspaper* **reached** *its zenith in the 1960s, but has since declined.* • Compare NADIR.

zeph·yr /£ˈzef·əʳ, $-ɚ/ *n* [C] *poetic or literary* a light wind

zep·pel·in /ˈzep·əl·ɪn/ *n* [C] a large AIRSHIP (= an aircraft without wings, containing gas to make it lighter than air, and with an engine)

ze·ro /£ˈzɪə·rəʊ, $ˈzɪr·oʊ/ *n pl* **zeros** or **zeroes** (the number) 0; nothing • *Five, four, three, two, one, zero.* [U] • *My car goes from zero (esp. Br also* **nought**) *to 60 mph in 4 seconds.* [U] • *The number one million is written with a one and six zeroes (esp. Br also* **noughts**). [C] • *Driving conditions are dangerous because heavy rain has reduced visibility almost to zero* (= its lowest point). [U] • Zero is also, on a set of numbers for comparing temperature in degrees CELSIUS, the level of temperature at which water freezes: *The temperature is expected to drop to ten degrees below zero tonight.* [U] ○ *Temperatures barely reached above zero all day.* [U] • **Zero hour** is the time at which something, esp. some type of military activity, is planned to begin: *Zero hour is 6 a.m.*

ZERO

The number 0 can be said as zero, and also as nought (/nɔːt/) in British English: *Registration number 905 RUK (nine zero five . . .)* • *(Br) 10.05g (ten point nought five grams)*

Zero is often read informally as 'o' /£əʊ/ or /$oʊ/ *Call me on 30885 (three o eight . . .)* • *room number 602 (six o two)*

In giving the results of sports games other words are used:

SOCCER	*Liverpool won 3-0* (three nil)
TENNIS	*Becker leads Edberg 30–0* (thirty love)
AMERICAN TEAM GAMES	*(Am) The Chicago Cubs beat the Cincinnati Reds 5–0* (five nothing; five to nothing; *(infml)* five zip)

ze·ro /£ˈzɪə·rəʊ, $ˈzɪr·oʊ/ *adj* [not gradable] • Zero means not any or no: *These measures will enable us to increase our market at zero extra cost.* ○ *The government is aiming to achieve zero inflation.* ○ *The economy showed zero* **growth** *in the first quarter of this year.* ○ *Fishermen support the decision to close the fishing area under a 'zero* **tolerance***' policy designed to prevent any oil-tainted fish from reaching market.* ○ *(infml) He said that his chances of getting the job were zero* (=he had no chance). ○ *(Br) I think books and newspapers should be zero-***rated** *for VAT* (=that no tax should be paid on them).

ze·ro in /£ˈzɪə·rəʊ, $ˈzɪr·oʊ/ *v adv* [I] he/she/it **zeros** or **zeroes**, **zeroing**, *past* **zeroed** to aim (esp. a weapon) directly (at something or someone) • *The pilot was told to wait until he could see the target, then zero in.* • *Modern military aircraft use computers to help them zero in* **on** (=aim weapons at) *their targets.* • *(fig.) We must decide on our target market, then zero in* **on** (=aim attention directly at) *it.* • *(fig.) His opponents in the election have zeroed in* **on** *his weaknesses.*

zest EXCITEMENT /zest/ *n* [U] enthusiasm, eagerness, energy and interest • *He approached every task* **with** *a boundless zest.* • *Whatever that family does, they do* **with** *more zest than anybody else.* • *After last week's defeat, the teams seem now to have recovered some of their zest.* • *The recording captures the zest* **of** *this live concert performance.* • *We invited Bill and Ed along to* **add** *some zest* **to** *the party.* • *It's wonderful to see the children's zest* **for life**.

zest·ful /ˈzest·fᵊl/ *adj* • *The reviewer complimented the cast's zestful performance.*

zest·ful·ly /ˈzest·fᵊl·i/ *adv* • *She sang zestfully in the shower.*

zest FRUIT SKIN /zest/ *n* [U] the skin of an orange, lemon or LIME, used for flavouring food • *Add two teaspoons of* **grated** *lemon zest to the cake mixture.*

zig·zag /ˈzɪg·zæg/ *n, v* **-gg-** (to move in) a line which looks like a row of W's joined together • *The sales graph was a series of zigzags.* [C] • *a zigzag path* • *a zigzag road* • *a zigzag coastline* • *a dress with a zigzag pattern/ a pattern of zigzags on it* • *(fig.) The country seems to have been following a zigzag course* (=keeps moving) *between democracy and dictatorship.* • *The children ran in a zigzag/***in zigzags** *around the playground.* • *He watched his daughter zigzag down the road as she was learning to ride her bike.* [I] • To zigzag is sometimes said as to zig and zag: *The footpath zigs and zags through the forest.* • PIC> **Patterns** (T)

zilch /zɪltʃ/ *pronoun, adj* [not gradable] *infml* nothing; none; no • *There's absolutely zilch to do around here.* • *He told me zilch about what's going on.* • *"How many points did you score?" "Zilch."* • *We've had zilch success so far.*

zil·li·on /ˈzɪl·jən, -i·ən/ *n* [C] *infml* an extremely large, but not a stated, number • *I've told you* **a** *zillion times/ zillions* **of** *times not to do that.*

Zim·mer frame *Br trademark* /£ˈzɪm·əʳ, $-ɚ/, *Br also and Aus* **walk·ing frame**, *Am* **walk·er** *n* [C] a rectangular metal frame with four legs which esp. old people who have difficulty in walking can put on the ground in front of them and hold on to in order to help them move forward • *At the age of 95, she can still get about by herself, though not without the aid of a Zimmer frame.* • People sometimes refer to Zimmer frames as a humorous way of talking about old people, or becoming old: *I may have passed 40, but I'm not ready for a Zimmer frame yet.* • PIC> **Frame, Medical equipment**

zinc /zɪŋk/ *n* [U] a bluish white metal that is used in making other metals or for covering other metals to protect them • *Brass is made from copper and zinc.* • *Zinc, which is found naturally in many foods, is important in the body for fighting disease, making wounds heal and for the development of unborn babies.*

zing /zɪŋ/ *n* [U] *infml* a quality that makes something interesting or exciting; enthusiasm or energy • *We want to* **put** *more zing* **into** *our advertising.* • *He wants the title of his book to have a bit of zing* **to** *it.* • *A bit of lemon juice will* **add** *zing* **to** *the sauce.*

zing·y /ˈzɪŋ·i/ *adj* **-ier, -iest** *infml* • *a zingy* (=interesting and exciting) *slogan*

Zi·on·i·sm /ˈzaɪə·nɪ·zᵊm/ *n* [U] a political movement which had as its original aim the creation of a country for Jewish people, and which now works to help the development of Israel

Zi·on·ist /ˈzaɪə·nɪst/ *adj* [C], *n* • *a Zionist leader* • *the Zionist cause* • *Zionist ideals* • *He became a Zionist while he was still a schoolboy.*

zip FASTENER /zɪp/, *Br also* **zip fas·ten·er**, *Am and Aus usually* **zip·per** *n* [C] a fastener consisting of two rows of metal or plastic teeth-like parts which are brought together by pulling a small sliding piece over them, and which is used for closing openings in esp. clothing or bags • *She tugged at the zip on her skirt.* • *I can't open my bag – the zip has* **stuck**. • *This zip has got some teeth missing, so it won't* **do up**. • **Do** *the zip* **up** *on your jacket – it's cold outside.* • LP> **Dressing and undressing**

zip *(obj)* /zɪp/ *v* **-pp-** • *I've got so much stuff in this bag, I don't think I'm going to be able to zip it shut* (=close it using the zip). [T] • *This dress zips* **(up)** (=fastens with a zip) *at the back, and I can't do it up by myself.* [I] • *Excuse me, but you've forgotten to zip your trousers* **up** (=close them using the zip). [M] • If you zip someone **up** you fasten their clothing using the zip: *Could you zip me up, please?* [T] • *(fig. slang) He told me to zip my mouth* (=not to say anything). [T]

zip SPEED /zɪp/ *n* [U] *infml* energy; speed • *The two new players have added some zip to the football team.* • *These new measures are intended to put a bit of zip back into the economy.* • *The new engine has given the car a lot of zip.* • In the US, a **zip code** is a series of numbers that forms part of an address, and which is used to help organize post so that it can be delivered more quickly.

zip *(obj)* /zɪp/ *v* [always + adv/prep] **-pp-** *infml* • *I'm just going to zip* (=go quickly) **along** *to the shops – I won't be long.* [I] • *He zipped through the traffic on his bike.* [I] • *We were about to cross the road when a car suddenly zipped past.* [I] • *If you want your book back today, I can zip it round to you later.* [T] • See also ZAP.

zip·py /ˈzɪp·i/ *adj* **-ier, -iest** *infml approving* • Zippy means energetic or fast: *a zippy car* ○ *a zippy performance* ○ *a zippy enterprise*

zip NOTHING /zɪp/ *pronoun Am infml* nothing • *I know zip about computers.* • *We reported the problem with our phone, but the phone company has done zip about it.* • LP> **Zero**

zip·per /£ˈzɪp·əʳ, $-ɚ/ *n* [C] *Am and Aus for* ZIP FASTENER

zit /zɪt/ *n* [C] *infml* a temporary small raised spot on the skin • *This lotion is really good for treating zits.*

zi·ther /£ˈzɪð·əʳ, $-ɚ/ *n* [C] a musical instrument shaped like a flat box which has many strings that you pull at with your fingers or with a small piece of plastic

zo·di·ac /£ˈzəʊ·di·æk, $ˈzoʊ-/ *n* (in the study of the planets and their influence on life) an area of the sky through which the sun, moon and most of the planets appear to move, or the representation of this area in the form of a usually circular drawing. The area of sky is divided into twelve equal parts, each of which has a name, is connected with a time of year, and is represented by a symbol. • *Astrologers use the position of the planets within* **the** *zodiac to predict the future.* [U] • *The astrologer used a zodiac to prepare my horoscope.* [C]

zo·di·a·cal /£zəʊˈdaɪ·ə·kᵊl, $zoʊ-/ *adj* [not gradable] • *a zodiacal sign* • *a zodiacal prediction*

zom·bie /£ˈzɒm·bi, $ˈzɑːm-/ *n* [C] *infml disapproving* a person who lacks energy, seems to act without thinking and is not aware of what is happening around them • *All these kids do is sit in front of the TV all day like zombies.* • *My job is so boring it's turning me into a zombie.* • In some Caribbean religions, a zombie is a dead person who has been brought back to life by magic.

zone /£zəʊn, $zoʊn/ *n* [C] an area, esp. one which is different from the areas around it because it has different characteristics or is used for different purposes • *San Francisco is in an earthquake zone.* • *He was charged with driving 75 mph in a 55 mph zone.* • *This stretch of coast has been* **designated** *a* **danger** *zone.* • *Medical teams have been flown into the* **war/combat** *zone to care for the wounded.* • *After the explosion at the Chernobyl power station, Ukraine* **declared** *itself a* **nuclear-free** *zone.* • *The UN Security Council has* **established/created** *a* **no-fly** *zone* (=one into which aircraft are not permitted to fly). • *Your lips are an* **erogenous** *zone* (=an area of your body from which you can get sexual pleasure). • *(specialized)* A zone is also one of the five parts into which the Earth is divided according to temperature, marked by imaginary lines going round it from east to west. They are the **torrid** zone, two **temperate** zones, and two **frigid** zones: *These trees only grow in temperate zones.*

zon·al /£ˈzəʊ·nᵊl, $ˈzoʊ-/ *adj* [not gradable] *esp. specialized* • Zonal means of or arranged in zones: *zonal boundaries* ○ *zonal divisions* ○ *These geraniums have zonal markings on the leaves.*

zon·al·ly /£ˈzəʊ·nᵊl·i, $ˈzoʊ-/ *adv* [not gradable] *esp. specialized*

zone *obj* /£zəʊn, $zoʊn/ *v* [T] *esp. specialized* • To zone is to give a special purpose to a particular area, such as an area in a town: *400 acres of commercially zoned land* ○ *The former dockyard has been zoned* **for** *tourist, leisure, residential and office use.* ○ *This area has been zoned* **as** *agricultural.*

zon·ing /£ˈzəʊ·nɪŋ, $ˈzoʊ-/ *n* [U] *esp. specialized* • Zoning is the act of deciding, or the decision that has been taken about, what particular use a particular area should have: *The council is responsible for zoning.* ○ *Zoning laws/regulations/restrictions/rules/ordinances do not allow buildings over a certain height to be built in the city.* ○ *Under current zoning* (= the decision that has been made about its use), *nothing can be built on this site.*

zonked /£zɒŋkt, $zɑːŋkt/ *adj slang* extremely tired • *We were really zonked after our long journey.* • *You look completely zonked* **out** *– why don't you go to bed?*

zoo /zuː/, *dated fml* **zo·o·log·i·cal gar·dens** *n* [C] *pl* **zoos** an area in which animals, esp. wild animals, are kept so that people can go and look at them, or study them • *I think zoos should let their animals roam around as freely as possible, not keep them in cages.* • *The zoo has so far had no success in breeding pandas.* • *Soon the only black rhinoceroses left may be those in zoos.* • *The prisoners said that they felt like animals in a zoo.* • *We watched the* **zoo-keeper** (= a person who works in a zoo, taking care of the animals) *feeding the lions.*

zo·ol·o·gy /£zuˈɒl·ə·dʒi, £zəʊ-, $zoʊˈɑː·lə-/ *n* [U] the scientific study of animals, esp. their structure • *marine zoology* • *vertebrate zoology*

zo·o·log·i·cal /£ˌzəʊ·əˈlɒdʒ·ɪ·kᵊl, £ˌzuː·ə-, $ˌzoʊ·əˈlɑː·dʒɪ-/ *adj* [not gradable] • *zoological research* • *zoological classification* • *zoological discoveries* • **Zoological gardens** is *dated fml for* ZOO.

zo·ol·o·gist /£zuˈɒl·ə·dʒɪst, £zəʊ-, $zoʊˈɑːlə-/ *n* [C] • *Charles Darwin was a famous zoologist* (= a person who scientifically studies animals).

zoom [MOVE QUICKLY] /zuːm/ *v* [I] *infml* to move very quickly • *They got into the car and zoomed off.* • *The way the traffic zooms along this road is very dangerous.* • *We went zooming down the ski slopes.* • *In the last few metres of the race, she suddenly zoomed ahead.* • *This last year has just zoomed past.* • If costs, sales etc. zoom, they increase suddenly and quickly: *House prices zoomed last year.* ○ *The company's sales zoomed from $11 million to $160 million.* • (I)

zoom [CAMERA] /zuːm/ *v* [I] (of a camera) to operate so that the person or thing being photographed appears to be nearer or further away • *Does this camera zoom, or not?* • *At the beginning of the film, the camera zooms* **in** *to show two people sitting by the side of a river.* • *Television cameras were zooming* **in on** *incidents of players swearing.* • *(fig.) Henry immediately zoomed* **in on** (= noticed and gave his attention to) *the weakest part of my argument.* • (I)

zoom (lens) /zuːm/ *n* [C] • *I want to get a camera with a zoom lens* (= a device that can make the thing being photographed appear nearer). • *These photographs were taken from some distance away, using a high-powered zoom.*

Zo·ro·as·tri·an·i·sm /£ˌzɒr·əʊˈæs·tri·ə·nɪ·zᵊm, $ˌzɔːr·oʊ-/ *n* [U] a religion which developed in ancient Iran, and is based on the idea that there is a continuous fight between a god who represents good and one who represents evil

zuc·chi·ni /£zʊˈkiː·ni, $zuː-/ *n pl* **zucchini** or **zucchinis** *Am and Aus for* COURGETTE • [PIC] **Vegetables**

Zu·lu /ˈzuː·luː/ *adj* [not gradable], *n* (of) the language of or a member of a race of people who live in South Africa • *a Zulu warrior* • *He speaks Zulu.* [U] • *They are Zulus.* [C]

zy·gote /£ˈzaɪ·gəʊt, $-goʊt/ *n* [C] *specialized* the cell which is formed when a female reproductive cell and a male reproductive cell join

zzz /z/ *exclamation* used in a picture or a piece of writing to represent the noise that people make when they are sleeping

Defining Vocabulary
(words used in definitions)

The definitions in this dictionary are written using a list of UNDER 2000 WORDS. Explanations in Language Portraits and Usage Notes are also written using these words. The words in this list have been carefully chosen, according to these principles:

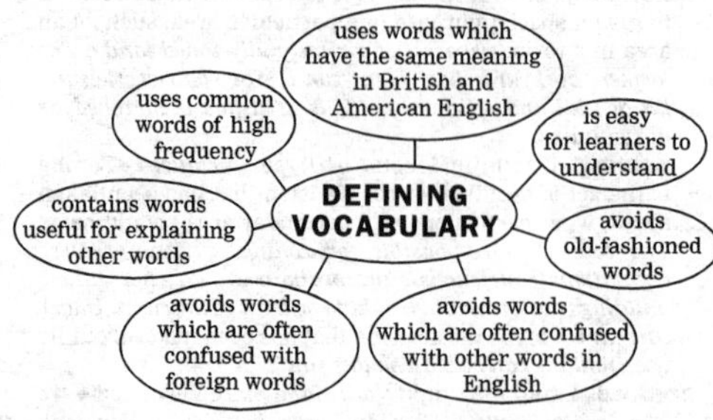
DEFINING VOCABULARY
uses words which have the same meaning in British and American English
uses common words of high frequency
is easy for learners to understand
contains words useful for explaining other words
avoids old-fashioned words
avoids words which are often confused with foreign words
avoids words which are often confused with other words in English

a
abbreviate
abbreviation
ability (POWER)
able (CAN DO)
about (CONNECTED WITH)
(APPROXIMATELY)
(IN THIS PLACE)
(INTENDING)
above
absence
absent
absorb
absorbent
absorbency
absorption
accept
acceptable
acceptably
acceptability
acceptance
accepted
access
accessible
accessibility
accident
accidental
accidentally
according to (FOLLOWING)
account (FINANCIAL SERVICE)
accountant
accountancy
accounts
accurate
accurately
accuracy
accuse
accusation
accused
accuser
achieve
achievable
achiever
achievement
acid (LIQUID SUBSTANCE)
acidic
acidify
acidity
across
act (DO SOMETHING)
(PERFORM)
acting
actor
action (SOMETHING DONE)
(MOVEMENT)
active
actively
activity
add
addition
additional
additionally
address (HOME DETAILS)
address (SPEAK TO)
adjective
adjectival
adjust
adjustable
adjuster
adjustment
admire
admirable
admirably
admiration
admirer
admiring
admiringly
admit (ACCEPT)
admission
admittedly
adult
adulthood
advance
advanced
advancement
advantage
advantageous
advantageously
adverb
adverbial
advertise
advertisement
advertiser
advertising
advice
advise
advisable
advisedly
adviser
affection
affectionate
affectionately
after
afternoon
again
against (IN OPPOSITION)
(TOUCHING)
age (TIME SPENT ALIVE)
ago
agree
agreement
aim (POINT)
(INTEND)
air (GAS)
(AREA)
aircraft
airport
alcohol
alcoholic
alcoholism
alive
all
allow (PERMIT)
allowable
almost
alone (WITHOUT PEOPLE)
along (BESIDE)
aloud
alphabet
alphabetical
alphabetically
already
also
although
always
among
amount
amuse
amusement
amusing
amusingly
an
ancient
and
anger
angry
angrily
angle (SPACE)
angled
animal (CREATURE)
announce
announcement
announcer
annoy
annoyance
annoyed
annoying
annoyingly
another
answer (REACTION)
anxiety
anxious
anxiously
any
anyone
anything
anywhere
apart (SEPARATE)
apartment
appear (BE PRESENT)
(SEEM)
appearance
apple
appreciate (VALUE)
appreciation
appreciative
appreciatively
approach (COME NEAR)
approve (GOOD OPINION)
approval
approving
approvingly
approximate
approximately
approximation
arch (CURVED STRUCTURE)
arched
area (PLACE)
(MEASURE)
argue (DISAGREE)
argument
argumentative
argumentatively
arm (BODY PART)
(PROVIDE WEAPONS)
armed
army
around (IN THIS DIRECTION)
arrange (PLAN)
(PUT IN POSITION)
arrangement
arrive
arrival
arrow
art
artist
artistic
artistically
arts
article (NEWSPAPER)
artificial
artificially
artificiality
as
ashamed
ashamedly
ask (QUESTION)
at
atom
atomic
atomically
attack
attacker
attempt
attention (NOTICE)
attend
attentive
attentively
attract
attraction
attractive
attractively
attractiveness
aunt
authority
authoritative
authoritatively
authorities
automatic (INDEPENDENT)
automatically
autumn
auxiliary
available
availability
average (AMOUNT)
(USUAL STANDARD)
averagely
avoid
avoidable
avoidance
awake
aware
awareness
away
awkward (GRACELESS)
awkwardly
baby
back (RETURN)
(FARTHER AWAY)
(FARTHEST PART)
(BODY PART)
background (THINGS BEHIND)
backwards
backward
bacteria
bacterial
bad (UNPLEASANT)
(LOW QUALITY)
badly
bag (CONTAINER)
bake
baker
baker's
bakery
balance (EQUALITY)
balanced
ball (ROUND OBJECT)
bank (ORGANIZATION)
banker
banking
(RAISED GROUND)
bar (POLE)
barred
(DRINKING PLACE)
bare
base (BOTTOM)
(MAIN PART)
-based
baseball
basic
bath
bathroom
be
beach
beak (BIRD'S MOUTH)
beam (LIGHT)
bean
bear (ANIMAL)
(ACCEPT)
bearable
beat (HIT)
(DEFEAT)
(MOVEMENT)
beauty
beautiful
beautifully
because
become
bed (FURNITURE)
bedroom
bee (INSECT)
beer
before
begin
beginner
beginning
behave
behaviour
behind (BACK)
being (PERSON)
belief
believe
believable
believer
bell
belong (PROPERTY)
below
belt (CLOTHING)
bend
bendable
bendy
benefit
beneficial
beside
between
beyond
bicycle
big (LARGE)
biology
biological
biologically
biologist
bird (CREATURE)
birth
biscuit (FLAT CAKE)
bit (AMOUNT)
bite
bitter (TASTE)
bitterness
black (DARK IN COLOUR)
blacken
(PEOPLE)
blade (PART OF KNIFE)
blame
bleed
blind (SIGHT)
blindness
block (LUMP)
(PREVENT)
blockage
blocked
blood (LIQUID)
bloody
-blooded
blow (SEND OUT AIR)
blue (COLOUR)
bluish
board (WOOD)
boat
boating
body (PHYSICAL STRUCTURE)
bodied
bodily
boil (HEAT)
boiled
boiling
bomb (WEAPON)
bombing
bomber
bone
-boned
bony
book (TEXT)
boot (SHOE)
border (DIVISION)
bordering
(EDGE)
bore (FAIL TO INTEREST)
bored
boring
boringly
boredom
born (BEGAN TO EXIST)
borrow
borrower
borrowing
both
bottle (CONTAINER)
bottom (LOWEST PART)
(BODY PART)
bounce (JUMP)
bouncy
bowels
bowl (DISH)
box (CONTAINER)
boxing
boxer
boy
brain
branch (TREE PART)
brave (FEARLESS)
bravely
bravery
bread
break (DAMAGE)
breakable
breakage
(NOT KEEP)
breast (OF A WOMAN)
breath
breathe
breathing
breathless
breed
breeder
breeding
brick (BUILDING BLOCK)
bridge (LARGE STRUCTURE)
brief (SHORT IN TIME)
briefly
bright (LIGHT)
brighten
brightly
brightness
(COLOUR)
bring (TAKE)
(CAUSE)
broadcast
broadcaster
broadcasting
broken (DAMAGED)
brother
brown
brownish
brush (TOOL)
bubble
bubbly
build
builder
built
building
bullet
burn (BE ON FIRE)
(DAMAGE)
burning
burnt
burst
bury
bus
bush (PLANT)
business (SELLING)
busy
busily
but (DIFFERENCE)
butter
button
buy (PAY FOR)
buyer
by
cage
cake (FOOD)
calculate
calculation
calculator
call (NAME)
(TELEPHONE)
caller
(SHOUT/CRY)
calm
calmly
calmness
camera
can (ABILITY)
(PERMISSION)
(REQUEST)
(POSSIBILITY)
candle
cannot
capital (CITY)
capital (letter)
capitalize
capitalization
car
carbon
card (STIFF PAPER)
(GAME)
cardboard
care (PROTECTION)
care for
carer
caring
(ATTENTION)
careful
carefully
careless
carelessly
carelessness
carriage (VEHICLE)
carry (TRANSPORT)
carrier
case (PROBLEM)
(CONTAINER)
castle
cat
catch (TAKE HOLD)
(TRAVEL)
(BECOME INFECTED)
cattle
cause (REASON)
cave
ceiling
celebrate (ENJOY AN OCCASION)
celebration
cell (ORGANISM)
-celled
cellular

centimetre
central (NEAR THE MIDDLE)
centrally
centre (MIDDLE)
(PLACE)
century
ceremony (FORMAL ACTS)
ceremonial
ceremonially
certain (IN NO DOUBT)
(EXTREMELY LIKELY)
certainly
certainty
chain (RINGS)
chair (FURNITURE)
chance (LUCK)
(LIKELIHOOD)
change (BECOME DIFFERENT)
changeable
changed
changing
channel (PASSAGE)
character (QUALITY)
characteristic
characteristically
(PERSON)
charge (ASK)
(SUPPLY ENERGY)
(CONTROL)
charm (ATTRACTION)
charmed
charming
charmingly
chase (FOLLOW)
cheap
cheaply
cheapness
cheat
cheese
chemical
chemically
chemistry
chemist
chest (BODY PART)
chew
chewy
chicken (BIRD)
child
childhood
childish
childishly
childishness
chocolate
choice (ACT)
(VARIETY)
choose
chosen
church (BUILDING)
cigarette
cinema
circle (SHAPE)
circular
city (LARGE PLACE)
claim (SAY)
(DEMAND)
clap (MAKE NOISE)
class (TEACHING GROUP)
(ECONOMIC GROUP)
classless
clause (GRAMMAR)
clay
clean (NOT DIRTY)
cleaner
cleaning
cleanliness
cleanness
clear (UNDERSTANDABLE)
(NOT CONFUSED)
clearly
clever
cleverly
cleverness
cliff
climb (RISE)
climber
clock (TIME)
close (NOT OPEN)
closed
close (NEAR)
(RELATED)
closeness
closely
cloth
clothes
clothing
cloud
cloudless
cloudy
coal
coast (LAND)
coastal
coat (CLOTHING)
coffee
coin (MONEY)
coinage
cold (LOW TEMPERATURE)
collar (NECK)
collect (GATHER)
(GET)
collection
collector
college (EDUCATION)
colour (APPEARANCE)
coloured
-coloured
colourful
colourfully
colouring
colourless
column (BUILDING)
combine
combination
come
comfort
comfortable
comfortably
comma
commit (CRIME)
common (USUAL)
commonly
communicate
communication
companion (PERSON)
company (BUSINESS)
comparative
compare (EXAMINE DIFFERENCES)
comparison
compass (DEVICE)
compete
competition
competitor
competitive
complain
complaint
complete (FINISH)
completion
(VERY GREAT)
completely
complicate
complicated
complication
computer
computing
computerize
computerization
concrete (HARD MATERIAL)
condition (STATE)
cone
confidence (CERTAINTY)
confident
confidently
confuse
confused
confusing
confusion
conjunction (CONNECTING WORD)
connect (JOIN)
(RELATE)
connected
connecting
connection
conscious (THINKING)
consciousness
consider (THINK)
(OPINION)
(GIVE ATTENTION)
consideration
consist of
consonant
contain (HOLD)
container
contents
continent (LAND)
continue
continual
continually
continuation
continued
continuity
continuous
continuously
control
controller
convenient
conveniently
convenience
conversation
conversational
cook
cooked
cooker
cookery
cooking
cool (COLD)
cooling
coolness
copy (PRODUCE)
cord (ROPE)
corner
correct
correctly
correctness
correction
cost (MONEY)
cotton
cough
could
count (NUMBER)
countable
country (POLITICAL UNIT)
countryside
course (CLASSES)
court (LAW)
cover (PLACE OVER)
-covered
covering
cow (ANIMAL)
coward
cowardly
cowardliness
crack (BREAK)
cream
creamy
creaminess
create (MAKE)
creation
creator
creature
cricket (GAME)
cricketer
cricketing
crime
criminal
criminally
criminalize
critic
critical
critically
criticism
criticize
crop (PLANT)
crop
cross (GO ACROSS)
crossing
cross (MARK)
crowd
crowded
cruel
cruelly
cruelty
crush (PRESS)
crushed
cry (PRODUCE TEARS)
crying
cultivate
cultivated
cultivation
cultivator
culture (WAY OF LIFE)
cultural
culturally
cup (DRINKING CONTAINER)
cupful
cupboard
cure (MAKE WELL)
curl
curly
curliness
current (MOVEMENT)
curtain
curve
curved
curvy
custom (TRADITION)
customer
cut (KNIFE)
cylinder (SHAPE)
cylindrical
damage
damaged
dance
dancer
danger
dangerous
dangerously
dark (WITHOUT LIGHT)
darken
darkly
darkness
date (AGE)
dated
daughter
day
dead (NOT LIVING)
deal with (TAKE ACTION)
death
debt
decay
deceive
decide
decision
decisive
decisively
decorate
decoration
decorative
decoratively
decorator
deep (DOWN)
deepen
(COMPLICATED)
deer
defeat
defend
defence
defenceless
defender
degree (AMOUNT)
(UNIT)
(COURSE)
delay
delicate (EASILY DAMAGED)
(SOFT)
delicacy
delicately
deliver (TAKE)
delivery
demand
dense (THICK)
densely
density
department
departmental
depend on/upon (SUPPORT)
dependant
dependence
dependency
dependent
depth (DISTANCE DOWN)
describe
description
descriptive
descriptively
desert (SANDY AREA)
deserve
deserved
deservedly
deserving
design (PLAN)
designer
desire (WANT)
desirable
desirably
desirability
despite
destroy
destruction
destructive
destructively
destructiveness
detail (INFORMATION)
detailed
determined
determinedly
determine
determination
determiner
develop (GROW)
developed
developer
developing
development
device (OBJECT)
diagonal
diagonally
dictionary
die (STOP LIVING)
differ
difference
different
differently
difficult
difficulty
dig (MOVE EARTH)
digest (EAT)
digestion
digestive
direct (STRAIGHT)
directly
directness
(AIM)
direction
dirt
disadvantage
disadvantaged
disadvantageous
disagree
disagreement
disappear
disappearance
disappoint
disappointed
disappointedly
disappointing
disappointingly
disappointment
disapprove
disapproval
disapproving
disapprovingly
disc
discourage (MAKE LESS CONFIDENT)
discouraging
discouragement
discover
discoverer
discovery
discuss
discussion
disease
diseased
disgust
disgusted
disgustedly
disgusting
disgustingly
dish (CONTAINER)
(FOOD)
dishonest
dishonestly
dishonesty
dislike
dismiss (SEND AWAY)
dismissal
disobey
dissatisfied
dissatisfaction
dissolve (BE ABSORBED)
distance
distant
distantly
divide (SEPARATE)
division
(CALCULATE)
divisible
do
doctor (MEDICINE)
document
documentary
documentation
dog (ANIMAL)
door
doubt
doubtful
doubtfully
down (LOWER POSITION)
(LOWER LEVEL)
draw (PICTURE)
drawing
drawer
dream (SLEEP)
dress (PIECE OF CLOTHING)
(PUT ON CLOTHES)
dressed
drink (LIQUID)
drinking
drinker
drive (USE VEHICLE)
driver
driving
drop (FALL)
(SMALL AMOUNT)
droplet
drug (MEDICINE)
(NOT MEDICINE)
drum (INSTRUMENT)
drunk (TOO MUCH ALCOHOL)
drunken
drunkenly
drunkenness
dry (NOT WET)
dried
dryer
dryness
during
dust
dusty
duty (RESPONSIBILITY)
dutiful
dutifully
E (EAST)
each
eager
eagerly
eagerness
ear (BODY PART)
-eared
early
earlier
earliest
earliness
earn
earnings
earner
earth (PLANET)
(SUBSTANCE)
east
eastern
eastward
eastwards
easy (NOT DIFFICULT)
easily
eat (HAVE FOOD)
eatable
eater
economy (SYSTEM)
economic
economically
economics
economist
edge (OUTER POINT)
(BLADE)
-edged
edible
educate
educated
education
educational
educationally
effect (RESULT)
effective
effectively
effectiveness
effort
effortless
effortlessly
effortlessness
egg (REPRODUCTION)
(FOOD)
eight
eighth
either
elastic
elasticated
elasticity
elect
election
electoral
electorally
electricity
electric
electrical
electrically
electrician
electrify
electrification
electronic
electronically
element (SIMPLE SUBSTANCE)
eleven
eleventh
else
embarrass
embarrassing
embarrassingly
embarrassment
emergency
emotion
emotional
emotionally
emotionless
emotionlessly
emphasize
emphasis
emphatic
emphatically
empire
employ
employee
employer
employment
empty
emptiness
enclose (SURROUND)
enclosure
encourage
encouraged
encouraging
encouragingly
encouragement
end (LAST POINT)
ending
endless
enemy
energy (STRENGTH)
energetic
energetically
(POWER)
engine
enjoy (PLEASURE)
enjoyable
enjoyment
enough
enter (GO IN)
entertain (AMUSE)
entertainer
entertainingly
entertaining
entertainment
enthusiasm
enthusiast
enthusiastic
enthusiastically
entrance (WAY IN)
entry (WAY IN)
envelope
environment (NATURE)
environmental
environmentally
equal (SAME)
equality
equally
equator
equatorial
equip (PROVIDE)
equipped
equipment
escape
especially
establish (START)
establishment
(BECOME ACCEPTED)
etc.
even (SURPRISE)
(EMPHASIS)
(FLAT)
evening
event
ever
evergreen
every
everyone
everything
everywhere
evil
exact (CORRECT)
exactly
exactness
exam
examine
examiner
examine
examination
example (TYPICAL CASE)
excellent
excellently
excellence
except
exception
exchange
exchangeable
excite (MAKE HAPPY)
excitable
excited
excitedly
exciting
excitingly
excitement
exclaim
exclamation
excrete
excretion
excrement
excuse (EXPLANATION)
exercise (HEALTHY ACTIVITY)
(PRACTISING)
exist
existence
expect (THINK)
expectancy
expectant
expectantly
expectation
expense
expensive
expensively
experience
experienced
experiment
experimental
experimentally
experimentation
expert
expertise
expertly
explain
explanation
explode (BURST)
explosion
explosive

explosively
explosiveness
express (SHOW)
expression
expressionless
expressionlessly
expressive
expressively
expressiveness
expression (WORDS)
extra (MORE)
extreme (GREAT)
extremely
eye
eye
face (HEAD)
facial
(TURN TOWARDS)
-facing
fact
factual
factually
factory
fail (NOT SUCCEED)
failure
fair (RIGHT)
fairly
fairness
fall (ACCIDENT)
(MOVE DOWN)
false (NOT CORRECT)
falsely
fame
familiar (WELL KNOWN)
familiarity
family (SOCIAL GROUP)
famous
far
farm
farmer
farming
fashion (CLOTHING)
fashionable
fashionably
fast (QUICK)
fasten
fastener
fastening
fat (BIG)
fatness
fatten
fattening
(SUBSTANCE)
fatty
father (PARENT)
fault (MISTAKE)
faultless
faultlessly
faulty
fear
fearful
fearfully
fearless
fearlessly
feather
feathered
feathery
feature (QUALITY)
feed (GIVE FOOD)
feel (EXPERIENCE)
feeling
(TOUCH)
female (SEX)
fence (STRUCTURE)
fencing
fever
few (SOME)
(NOT MANY)
fibre (MATERIAL)
fibrous
field (LAND)
(SPORT)
fierce
fiercely
fierceness
fifth
fight
fighter
fighting
figurative (LANGUAGE)
figuratively
fill
-filled
filling
film (MOVING PICTURES)
filming
final (LAST)
finalize
finalization
finally
finance
financial
financially
find (DISCOVER)
finger
finish
fire (FLAMES)
(SHOOT)
fireplace
firm (FIXED)
(SOLID)
firmly
firmness
first
firstly
fish (ANIMAL)
fishing
fit (CORRECT SIZE)
(SUIT)
five
fix (FASTEN)
fixed
fizz (PRODUCE GAS)
fizzy
fizziness
flag (SYMBOL)
flame
flash (SHINE)
flat (LEVEL)
flatness
flatten
flavour
-flavoured
flavouring
flavourless
flesh
fleshy
flight (FLYING)
float (NOT SINK)
flood (COVER WITH WATER)
flooded
flooding
floor (SURFACE)
floored
flooring
(LEVEL OF BUILDING)
flour
floury
flow
flowing
flower
flowered
flowering
flowery
fly (TRAVEL)
flier
flying
fog
foggy
fold (BEND)
folding
follow (GO AFTER)
following
(OBEY)
follower
food
fool (PERSON)
foolish
foolishly
foolishness
foot (BODY PART)
football (GAME)
footballer
for
forbid
forbidden
force (INFLUENCE)
forceful
forcefully
forcefulness
(PHYSICAL POWER)
(DO UNWILLINGLY)
(GROUP)
foreign
foreigner
forest
forever
forget
forgetful
forgetfully
forgetfulness
forgive
forgivable
forgiveness
forgiving
fork (TOOL)
form (SHAPE)
formation
(DOCUMENT)
(TYPE)
formal
formally
formality
forwards
forward
four
fourth
frame (BORDER)
framed
(STRUCTURE)
free (NOT LIMITED)
freely
(NO CHARGE)
(WITHOUT)
freedom
freeze
freezing
freezer
frequent (COMMON)
frequently
fresh (RECENT)
freshly
freshness
(NATURAL)
freshen
friend
friendly
friendliness
friendship
fright (FEAR)
frighten
frightened
frightening
frighteningly
from
front (PLACE)
fruit (PLANT PART)
fruity
fry (COOK)
fuel
fulfil (MAKE HAPPEN)
fulfilment
full (CONTAINING A LOT)
fullness
funeral
fur (HAIR)
furry
furniture
future
game (ENTERTAINMENT)
garden
gardener
gardening
gas (MATTER)
gaseous
gassy
gate
gather (COLLECT)
(COME TOGETHER)
general (COMMON)
generally
generous
generosity
generously
gentle
gently
gentleness
get (OBTAIN)
(BECOME)
(MOVE)
girl
give (OFFER)
(PRODUCE)
give up
glass
glasses
glue
go (TRAVEL)
(LEAVE)
(BECOME)
goal (GAME)
goat (ANIMAL)
god (SPIRIT)
going to
gold (METAL)
(COLOUR)
golden
golf
golfer
golfing
good (VERY SATISFACTORY)
(MORAL RIGHT)
goodness
goodbye
goods
govern (RULE)
governing
government
governmental
governor
grace (BEAUTY)
graceful
gracefully
gracefulness
graceless
gracelessly
gracelessness
gradual
gradually
grain (SEED)
(SMALL PIECE)
gram (MEASUREMENT)
grammar
grammatical
grammatically
granddaughter
grandfather
grandmother
grandparent
grandson
grass
grassy
grateful
gratefully
gratitude
great (BIG)
greatly
(FAMOUS)
greatness
green (COLOUR)
greenish
greenness
greet
greeting
grey
greying
greyish
greyness
ground (LAND)
group
grow (INCREASE)
grown
growth
guard
guess
guest
guilt (FEELING)
(RESPONSIBILITY)
guilty
guiltily
guitar
gun
habit (REPEATED ACTION)
habitual
habitually
hair
-haired
hairless
hairy
hairstyle
half
halve
hammer (TOOL)
hand (BODY PART)
handle (PART)
hang (FIX AT TOP)
happen (HAVE EXISTENCE)
happy (PLEASED)
happily
happiness
hard (SOLID)
harden
hardness
(USING EFFORT)
harm
harmful
harmfully
harmfulness
harmless
harmlessly
harmlessness
hat
hate
hated
-hater
have
he
head (BODY PART)
heal
healing
health
healthy
healthily
hear (RECEIVE SOUND)
hearing
heart (ORGAN)
(SHAPE)
heat (TEMPERATURE)
heated
heater
heating
heaven
heavenly
heavy (WEIGHING A LOT)
(FORCEFUL)
heavily
heaviness
heel (BODY PART)
height
hell (PLACE)
hello
help (MAKE EASIER)
helper
helpful
helpfully
helpfulness
helpless
helplessly
helplessness
her
herself
herb
herbal
herbalist
here
hide (OUT OF VIEW)
high (DISTANCE)
(SOUND)
(ABOVE AVERAGE)
highly
hill
hilly
him (MALE)
himself
hip (BODY PART)
his (MALE)
history (PAST EVENTS)
historian
historic
historical
historically
hit (TOUCH)
hitter
hobby
hold (SUPPORT)
holder
(CONTAIN)
hole (SPACE)
holiday
hollow (EMPTY)
hollowness
holy (GOOD)
holiness
home
(HOUSE/APARTMENT)
homeless
homelessness
homosexual
homosexuality
honest
honestly
honesty
honour (RESPECT)
honourable
honourably
(REWARD)
hook (DEVICE)
hope
hopeful
hopefully
hopeless
hopelessly
hopelessness
horizontal
horizontal
horizontally
horn (ANIMAL)
horned
horse (ANIMAL)
hospital
hot (VERY WARM)
(SPICY)
hotel
hour
hourly
house (HOME)
housing
how
human
human (being)
humour (AMUSEMENT)
humorous
humorously
humourless
hunger (FOOD)
hungry
hungrily
hunt (CHASE)
hunter
hunting
hurry
hurried
hurriedly
hurt
hurtful
hurtfully
husband (MAN)
I (PERSON SPEAKING)
ice (FROZEN WATER)
icy
idea (SUGGESTION)
if
ignore
ill (NOT WELL)
illness
illegal
illegality
illegally
image (PICTURE)
imagine
imaginable
imaginary
imagination
imaginative
imaginatively
immediate
immediately
immediacy
immoral
immorally
immorality
important
importantly
importance
impossible
impossibility
impossibly
improve
improvement
in
inability
include
included
including
inclusion
income
inconvenience
inconvenient
inconveniently
increase
increasingly
independent (NOT INFLUENCED)
independently
independent (NOT RULED)
independent (NOT HELPED)
independence
indirect (NOT OBVIOUS)
(NOT STRAIGHT)
indirectly
industry (PRODUCTION)
industrial
industrially
industrialize
industrialized
industrialization
(TYPE OF WORK)
infect
infection
infectious
infinitive
influence
influential
inform
information
informative
informed
informal
informally
informality
injure
injured
injury
ink
inner
insect
inside (INNER PART)
instead
instruct (ORDER)
instruction
instrument (MUSIC)
instrumental
insult
insulting
insultingly
intelligence
(CLEVERNESS)
intelligent
intelligently
intend
intention
intentional
intentionally
interest (INVOLVEMENT)
interested
interesting
interestingly
international
internationally
interrupt
interruption
into
introduce (MAKE KNOWN)
introduction
introductory
invent
invention
inventive
inventively
inventiveness
inventor
invest
investment
investor
invite (ASK TO AN EVENT)
invitation
involve
involvement
inward
iron (METAL)
irregular (SHAPE)
(TIME/SPACE)
(RULE)
irregularity
irregularly
island
it
its
itself
item
jacket
jazz (MUSIC)
jewel
jewelled
jewellery
job (EMPLOYMENT)
jobless
joblessness
(PIECE OF WORK)
join (CONNECT)
joint (CONNECTION)
joke (AMUSING)
jokey
jokingly
journey
judge (PERSON)
judgment
(DECIDE)
judgment
juice (LIQUID)
juicy
juiciness
jump (IN THE AIR)
jumper
just (NOW)
(ONLY)
(ALMOST)
justice (LAW)
keep (POSSESS)
(STAY)
key (METAL SHAPE)
(MOVABLE PART)
keyboard
kick (HIT)
kill
killer
killing
kilogram
kilometre
kind (GOOD)
kindly
kindness
king
kiss
kitchen
knee
knife
knock (MAKE NOISE)
knot (FASTENING)
know (HAVE INFORMATION)
(BE FAMILIAR WITH)
known
knowledge
knowledgeable
knowledgeably
lack
lacking
lake
land (DRY SURFACE)
(ARRIVE)
landing
language
large
largeness
last (FINAL)
lastly
(MOST RECENT)
(CONTINUE)
lasting
late (NEAR THE END)
lately
lateness
(AFTER)
laugh
laughter
law (RULE)
lawful
lawfully
(PRINCIPLE)

lawyer
layer
 layered
lead (CONTROL)
 leader
 leadership
 (SHOW WAY)
leaf (PLANT)
 leafy
 -leaved
lean (SLOPE)
 leaning
learn
 learner
 learning
least
leather
 leathery
leave (GO AWAY)
 (NOT TAKE)
left (DIRECTION)
leg (BODY PART)
 -legged
legal
 legality
 legalize
 legalization
 legally
lemon
lend
 lender
length (DISTANCE)
 lengthen
 -length
less (SMALLER AMOUNT)
 lessen
 lesser
let (ALLOW)
letter (MESSAGE)
 (SYMBOL)
 lettering
level (HORIZONTAL)
lid
lie (POSITION)
 (SPEAK FALSELY)
life
lift (RAISE)
light (BRIGHTNESS)
 lightness
 lighten
 lighting
 (NOT HEAVY)
 (NOT STRONG)
 lightly
lightning
like (ENJOY)
 likeable
 (WANT)
 (SIMILAR TO)
 -like
 likeness
likely
 likelihood
limit
 limitation
 limited
line (LONG MARK)
 lined
lion
lip (BODY PART)
liquid (SUBSTANCE)
 liquidize
list (RECORD)
listen
 listener
literary
literature (WRITING)
litre
little (SMALL)
 (NOT ENOUGH)
live (HAVE LIFE)
 living
 (HAVE A HOME)
load (AMOUNT CARRIED)
loaf (BREAD)
local (AREA)
 locally
lock (FASTEN)
 lockable
long (DISTANCE)
 (TIME)
 longish
look (SEE)
 (SEARCH)
 (SEEM)
 -looking
loose (NOT FIXED)
 loosely
 (NOT TIGHT)
 loosen
 looseness
lose (NOT HAVE)
 lost
 loss
 (BE DEFEATED)
 loser
lot (LARGE AMOUNT)
loud (NOISY)
 loudly
 loudness
love (LIKE SOMEONE)
 lovable
 lover
 loving
 lovingly
low (NOT HIGH)
 lower
 (SMALL IN AMOUNT)
loyal
 loyally
 loyalty
luck
 lucky
 luckily
lump (PIECE)
 lumpy
lung
luxury
 luxurious
 luxuriously
machine
 machinery
magazine (BOOK)
magic (IMAGINARY POWER)
 magical
 magically
 magician
magnet
 magnetic
 magnetism
 magnetize
main (MOST IMPORTANT)
mainly
maintain (CONTINUE TO HAVE)
 maintenance
make (PRODUCE)
 maker
 making
 (CAUSE)
make-up
male (SEX)
mammal
man (MALE)
manage (SUCCEED)
 manageable
 (CONTROL)
 management
 manager
 manageress
 managerial
manner (WAY)
 (BEHAVIOUR)
many
map
march (WALK)
 marcher
mark (DIFFERENT AREA)
 marking
 (JUDGMENT)
market (PLACE)
marriage
marry
 married
mass (LARGE AMOUNT)
 (MATTER)
match (EQUAL)
material (SUBSTANCE)
mathematics
 mathematical
 mathematically
 mathematician
matter (SITUATION)
 (SUBSTANCE)
me (PERSON)
meal (FOOD)
mean (EXPRESS)
 meaning
 meaningless
measure (SIZE)
 measurable
 measurement
meat (FOOD)
medical
 medically
medicine (TREATMENT)
 medicinally
medium (VALUE)
meet (BECOME FAMILIAR WITH)
meet (COME TOGETHER)
 meeting
melt
member (PERSON)
 membership
memory (ABILITY TO REMEMBER)
 (EVENT REMEMBERED)
mental
 mentally
mention
message (INFORMATION)
 messenger
metal
 metallic
method
metre (MEASUREMENT)
middle
might (POSSIBILITY)
mile
military
milk
 milky
mind (THOUGHTS)
mine (BELONGING TO ME)
minute (TIME)
mirror (GLASS)
misfortune
miss (NOT HIT)
 (NOT DO)
mistake (WRONG ACTION)
mix (COMBINE)
 mixer
 mixture
modal
model
 (REPRESENTATION)
 (COPY)
modern (MOST RECENT)
modest (QUIETLY SUCCESSFUL)
 modestly
 modesty
moment (SHORT TIME)
 (OCCASION)
money
monkey (ANIMAL)
month
 monthly
mood
moon (PLANET)
moral
 moralistic
 morality
 morally
 morals
more
morning
most
 mostly
mother (PARENT)
motor (DEVICE)
motorcycle
 motorcyclist
mountain
 mountainous
mouse (ANIMAL)
mouth (BODY PART)
move (POSITION)
 movable
 movement
 moving
much (AMOUNT)
multiply
 multiplication
murder
 murderer
muscle
 muscular
 muscly
music
 musical
 musicality
 musically
 musician
must (NECESSARY)
my (OF ME)
 myself
mystery
 mysterious
 mysteriously
N (NORTH)
nail (METAL)
 (BODY PART)
naked
 nakedness
name
 nameless
narrow
 narrowly
 narrowness
nation
 national
 nationality
 nationally
 nationalism
 nationalist
 nationalistic
nature (LIFE)
 natural
 naturally
navy
 naval
near
 nearness
nearly
necessary
 necessarily
neck (BODY PART)
 -necked
need (MUST HAVE)
needle (SEWING TOOL)
 (MEDICAL TOOL)
negative (NO)
 (WITHOUT HOPE)
 negatively
 (ELECTRICITY)
 (BELOW ZERO)
neither
nerve (FIBRES)
 nervous
nerves
 nervous
 nervously
 nervousness
nest (HOME)
net (MATERIAL)
 netting
never
new (RECENTLY CREATED)
 (DIFFERENT)
 (NOT USED)
 (RECENTLY DISCOVERED)
news
newspaper
next
night (DARK PERIOD)
 nightly
nine
 ninth
no (NOT ANY)
 (NEGATIVE ANSWER)
noise (SOUND)
 noisy
 noisily
 noisiness
none
nonsense
 nonsensical
nor
north
 northern
 northwards
nose (BODY PART)
 -nosed
not
note (SOUND)
 (MONEY)
 (WRITING)
nothing
notice (SEE)
 notice
 noticeable
 noticeably
 (INFORMATION)
noun
now (AT PRESENT)
nowhere
nuclear
number (SYMBOL)
 (AMOUNT)
nurse (PERSON)
 nursing
nut (FOOD)
 nutty
o'clock
obedient
 obediently
 obedience
obey
object (THING)
 (GRAMMAR)
obtain (GET)
 obtainable
obvious
 obviously
occasion (PARTICULAR TIME)
of
off (NOT OPERATING)
 (REMOVED)
offence (UPSET FEELINGS)
 offensive
 offensively
 offensiveness
offer (AGREE TO GIVE)
office (WORK ROOM)
 (RESPONSIBILITY)
 officer
 official
 officially
often
oil
 oily
old (EXISTED MANY YEARS)
 (OF AGE)
 (FROM THE PAST)
omit
 omission
on
once (ONE TIME)
one (NUMBER)
onion
only (SINGLE OR FEW)
 (LIMIT)
onto
open (NOT CLOSED)
 opener
 opening
 (READY)
opera
 operatic
operate (WORK)
 operation
 operational
 operationally
 operator
 (MEDICAL PROCESS)
 operation
opinion
opportunity
oppose
 opposed
 opposing
 opposition
opposite (DIFFERENT)
or (POSSIBILITIES)
 (IF NOT)
orange (FRUIT)
 (COLOUR)
order (INSTRUCTION)
 (ARRANGEMENT)
 (PURPOSE)
ordinary
 ordinarily
 ordinariness
organ (BODY PART)
 organic
organism
organization
organize (ARRANGE)
 (MAKE A SYSTEM)
 organization
 organizational
 organized
 organizer
origin
 original
 originally
 originate
 originator
other (PART OF A SET)
 (ADDITIONAL)
our
 ours
 ourselves
out
outer
outside (OUTER PART)
oval
over (HIGHER POSITION)
owe (HAVE DEBTS)
 owing
own (BELONGING)
 owner
 ownership
oxygen
 oxygenate
page (PAPER)
pain
 painful
 painfully
 painless
 painlessly
paint
 painter
 painting
pair
pale
 palish
pan (CONTAINER)
paper
 papery
parallel (POSITION)
parcel
parent
 parental
park (AREA OF LAND)
 (STOP)
 parked
 parking
parliament
 parliamentary
part (SOME)
 partly
 (SEPARATE PIECE)
participle
particular (SPECIAL)
 particularly
partner
 partnership
party (CELEBRATION)
 (POLITICAL GROUP)
 (VISITING GROUP)
pass (SUCCEED)
passage (CONNECTING WAY)
passenger (TRAVELLER)
passive (GRAMMAR)
past (TIME BEFORE)
 (GRAMMAR)
 (BEYOND)
pasta
pastry
path (DIRECTION)
patience
 patient
 patiently
pattern
 (ARRANGEMENT)
 patterned
pause
pay (BUY)
 payment
 (WORK)
peace (NO VIOLENCE)
 peaceful
 peacefully
 peacefulness
pen (WRITING DEVICE)
pencil
penis
people
per cent
 percentage
perfect (FAULTLESS)
 perfectly
 perfection
perform (DO)
 (ENTERTAIN)
 performance
 performer
period (TIME)
permanent
 permanently
 permanence
permit
 permission
person
 personal
 personally
 personality
persuade
 persuasion
 persuasive
 persuasively
 persuasiveness
pet (ANIMAL)
petal
 -petalled
photograph
 photographer
 photographic
 photographically
 photography
phrase (GRAMMAR)
 phrasal
 (EXPRESSION)
physical (BODY)
 physically
 (MATERIAL)
physics
 physical
piano
 pianist
pick (REMOVE)
picture
 (REPRESENTATION)
piece (PART)
 (ITEM)
pig (ANIMAL)
 piglet
pile (MASS)
pill (MEDICINE)
pin (METAL STICK)
pink (COLOUR)
 pinkish
pipe (TUBE)
 piping
place (AREA)
plain (NOT DECORATED)
 plainly
 plainness
plan (DECISION)
 planning
 (DRAWING)
planet
 planetary
plant (LIVING THING)
plastic (SUBSTANCE)
plate (DISH)
play (ENJOY)
 playful
 playfully
 playfulness
 (ACT)
 (PRODUCE SOUNDS/PICTURES)
 (GAME)
 player
pleasant
 pleasantly
please (POLITE REQUEST)
 (MAKE HAPPY)
 pleased
 pleasing
 pleasingly
pleasure
 pleasurable
plural (GRAMMAR)
 pluralize
pocket (BAG)
poem
 poet
 poetic
 poetical
 poetically
 poetry
point (TIME OR PLACE)
 (UNIT)
 (SHARP END)
 (SHOW)
 (MARK)
 pointer
poison
 poisonous
pole (STICK)
police
polite
 politely
 politeness
politics
 political
 politically
 politician
pollute
 pollutant
 polluter
 pollution
pool (LIQUID)
poor (NO MONEY)
 poorly
 poorness
popular (LIKED)
 popularity
port (TOWN)
position (PLACE)
 (RANK)
positive (HOPEFUL)
 positively
 positiveness
 (ABOVE ZERO)
 (ELECTRICITY)
possess (OWN)
 possession
 possessive
possible (ACHIEVABLE)
 (UNCERTAIN)
 possibly
 possibility
post (LETTERS)
 postage
 postal
 (POLE)
potato
pour (CAUSE TO FLOW)
powder
 powdered
 powdery
power (CONTROL)
 (STRENGTH)
 (ENERGY)
 powerful
 powerless
 powerlessly
 powerlessness
 powered
practical (EXPERIENCE)
 practically
 (SUITABLE)
practise (TRAIN)
praise
pray (SPEAK TO GOD)
 prayer
precious (VALUABLE)
predeterminer
prefer (CHOOSE)
 preferable
 preferably
 preference

pregnant (FEMALE)
pregnancy
prepare
preparation
preposition
prepositional
present (NOW)
(SOMETHING GIVEN)
(PLACE)
presence
preserve (KEEP)
preservative
preservation
press (PUSH)
pressure
pressurize
pressurization
pretend
pretence
prevent
preventable
preventative
prevention
previous
previously
price
pride (SATISFACTION)
priest
principle (BASIC IDEA)
(MORAL RULE)
print (TEXT)
printer
printing
prison
prisoner
private (PERSONAL)
privacy
privately
prize (REWARD)
probable
probably
probability
problem
process
processed
processor
produce (MAKE)
producer
product
production
profit
profitable
profitably
program
programmer
programme (BROADCAST)
promise
pronoun
pronominal
pronounce (MAKE SOUND)
pronunciation
proof (SHOWING TRUTH)
proven
property (THINGS OWNED)
protect
protected
protection
protective
protectively
protectiveness
proud (SATISFIED)
proudly
provide (SUPPLY)
public (PEOPLE)
publicly
publish
publisher
publishing
pull (MOVE TOWARDS YOU)
punish (CRIME)
punishment
pure (NOT MIXED)
purify
purification
purifier
purity
purple
purplish
purpose (REASON)
push (USE PRESSURE)
put (MOVE)
qualify (STANDARD)
qualification
qualified
quality (STANDARD)
(CHARACTERISTIC)
quarter (FOURTH PART)
queen (WOMAN)
question (ASKING)
quick (FAST)
quicken
quickly
quickness
quiet
quietly
quietness
quite (NOT VERY)
rabbit (ANIMAL)
race (COMPETITION)
racing
(PEOPLE)
racial
racially
radio
railway
rain
raise (LIFT)
(DEVELOP)
range (LIMIT)
(SET)
rank (POSITION)
ranking
rare (NOT COMMON)
rarely
rate (MEASURE)
rather (PREFERENCE)
raw (NOT PROCESSED)
reach (ARRIVE)
(STRETCH)
react
reaction
read (UNDERSTAND)
reader
reading
ready (PREPARED)
readily
readiness
real (NOT IMAGINARY)
realistic
realistically
reality
really
reason (EXPLANATION)
(JUDGMENT)
reasonable
reasonableness
reasonably
reasoned
reasoning
receive (GET)
receipt
recent
recently
recognize (KNOW)
recognition
recognizable
recognizably
record (STORE INFORMATION)
(STORE ELECTRONICALLY)
recording
recorded
rectangle
rectangular
red (COLOUR)
reddish
redden
redness
reduce
reduction
refer to (TALK ABOUT)
reflect (RETURN)
reflective
reflection
reflector
reflexive
reflexively
refuse (SAY NO)
refusal
region
regional
regionally
regret
regretful
regretfully
regrettable
regrettably
regular (EVEN)
(USUAL)
regularity
regularly
relate (CONNECT)
related
relation
relationship
relate to
relationship
relative (FAMILY MEMBER)
relax
relaxation
relaxed
relaxing
release (MAKE FREE)
religion
religious
religiously
remark
remember
remove
removable
removal
removed
remover
rent (PAYMENT)
rental
repair
repairable
repeat
repeated
repeatedly
repetition
repetitive
replace (PUT BACK)
report (TELL)
reported
reporter
represent (ACT FOR)
(DESCRIBE)
representation
representational
representative
reproduce (PRODUCE YOUNG)
reproduction
reproductive
reputation
request
respect (ADMIRATION)
respected
respectful
respectfully
respectfulness
(HONOUR)
responsible (BLAME)
(GOOD JUDGMENT)
(DUTY)
responsibly
responsibility
rest (STOP)
restaurant
result
return (GO BACK)
(PUT BACK)
reward
rewarding
rhythm
rhythmic
rhythmically
rice
rich
rid
ride
riding
ridicule
ridiculous
ridiculously
right (DIRECTION)
(CORRECT)
(ACCEPTABLE)
ring (CIRCLE)
(SOUND)
ripe
ripen
ripeness
rise (MOVE UP)
(INCREASE)
rising
risk
risky
river
road
rock (STONE)
rocky
rod
roll (MOVE)
(FOLD)
roller
romance (LOVE)
romantic
roof
-roofed
roofing
roofless
room (PLACE)
root (PLANT PART)
rooted
rootless
rope
rose (PLANT)
rough (UNEVEN)
roughen
roughly
round (CIRCULAR)
rounded
(AROUND)
route
row (LINE)
royal
royalty
rub
rubber (SUBSTANCE)
rubbery
rubbish
rude (NOT POLITE)
rudely
rudeness
rule (INSTRUCTION)
(CONTROL)
ruler
ruling
run (GO QUICKLY)
runner
running
S (SOUTH)
sad (NOT HAPPY)
sadly
sadness
sadden
safe (NOT IN DANGER)
safely
safety
safeness
sail (TRAVEL)
sailing
sailor
(MATERIAL)
salad
sale
salt
saltiness
salty
same (EXACTLY ALIKE)
(NOT ANOTHER)
sand (SMALL GRAINS)
sandy
satisfaction
satisfactory
satisfactorily
satisfy
satisfied
satisfying
sauce (THICK LIQUID)
save (MAKE SAFE)
(KEEP)
saver
savings
savoury
say (SPEAK)
saying
scatter
scattered
school (EDUCATION)
science
scientific
scientifically
scientist
score (WIN)
scorer
screen (PICTURE)
screening
screw (METAL OBJECT)
sea
search
season (PART OF YEAR)
seasonal
seasonally
seat (FURNITURE)
seated
seating
second (POSITION)
(TIME)
secret
secretive
secretiveness
secretly
secrecy
see (USE EYES)
seed (PLANT)
-seeded
seedless
seem
self (PERSONAL ADVANTAGE)
selfish
selfishly
sell (MONEY)
seller
send (POST)
sender
sentence (WORD GROUP)
separate
separable
separately
separation
series (SET OF EVENTS)
serious (BAD)
(NOT JOKING)
seriously
seriousness
servant
serve (DEAL WITH CUSTOMER)
service (PROVIDE SOMETHING NECESSARY)
set (GET READY)
(GROUP)
seven
seventh
several (SOME)
severe (VERY SERIOUS)
(NOT KIND)
severly
severity
sew
sewing
sex (MALE OR FEMALE)
(ACTIVITY)
sexual
sexuality
sexually
sexy
sexily
shake (MOVE)
shaky
shakily
shakiness
shape (FORM)
shaped
-shaped
shapeless
shapelessly
shapelessness
share (PART)
shared
sharp (ABLE TO CUT)
sharpen
sharpener
sharply
sharpness
she
sheep
sheet
sheeting
shelf
shelving
shell (COVERING)
shelter
sheltered
shine
shininess
shining
shiny
ship (BOAT)
shipping
shirt
shock (SURPRISE)
shocked
shocking
shockingly
shoe
shoot (WEAPON)
(SPORT)
shooting
shot
shop (PLACE TO BUY THINGS)
shopper
shopping
short (DISTANCE)
(TIME)
shortish
shortness
should (DUTY)
(PROBABLE)
shoulder (BODY PART)
shout
shouting
show (MAKE SEEN)
(DIRECT)
(EXPLAIN)
(PUBLIC EVENT)
(ENTERTAINMENT)
shy (NERVOUS)
shyly
shyness
side (SURFACE)
(EDGE)
-sided
(PART)
sideways
(OPPOSING GROUP)
sight (ABILITY TO SEE)
sign (MARK)
(NOTICE)
(BODY MOVEMENT)
signal (SHOWING)
(WAVE)
signature
silence (QUIET)
silent
silently
silk
silky
silkiness
silly (FOOLISH)
silliness
silver
silvery
similar
similarity
similarly
simple (PLAIN)
(EASY)
simplicity
simplify
simplification
simply
since (TIME)
sincere
sincerely
sincerity
sing (MAKE MUSIC)
singer
single (ONE)
singly
singular (GRAMMAR)
sink (GO DOWN BELOW)
sister
sit (BE SEATED)
situate
situated
situation
six
sixth
size (LARGENESS)
-sized
(MEASURE)
skill
skilful
skilfully
skilled
skin
skinless
-skinned
skirt (CLOTHING)
sky
slang (INFORMAL LANGUAGE)
sleep (RESTING STATE)
sleepy
sleepily
sleeve (ARM COVER)
-sleeved
sleeveless
slice (PIECE)
sliced
slide (MOVE SMOOTHLY)
slight (SMALL IN AMOUNT)
slightly
slope
sloping
slow
slow down
slowly
small (LIMITED)
smallness
smell (ABILITY)
(CHARACTERISTIC)
-smelling
smelly
smelliness
smile
smiling
smilingly
smoke (CLOUDY AIR)
smoked
smoky
smokiness
(BREATHE SMOKE)
smoker
smoking
smooth (REGULAR)
smoothness
snake (ANIMAL)
sneeze
snow (WEATHER)
snowy
so
soap
soapy
social
socially
sociable
socialize
society (PEOPLE)
social
socially
sock (CLOTHES)
soft (NOT HARD)
soften
softener
softness
(GENTLE)
softly
soldier
solid (HARD)
solidly
(NOT LIQUID/GAS)
solidify
solidification
solidity
solution
soluble
solubility
solve
solution
solvable
some (UNKNOWN AMOUNT)
someone
something
sometimes
somewhere (PLACE)
son
song
soon
sore (PAINFUL)
soreness
sorry (SAD)
(REGRET)
sound (NOISE)
soundless
soundlessly
soup
sour
sourly
sourness
south
southern
southward
southwards
space (EMPTY PLACE)
spacing
spacious
(BEYOND EARTH)
spacecraft
speak (SAY WORDS)
(KNOW A LANGUAGE)
speaker
-speaking
special (NOT USUAL)
speciality
specially
(PARTICULAR)
specialism
specialist
speciality
specialize
specialization
specialized
speech (SAY WORDS)
speed (RATE OF MOVEMENT)
spell (FORM WORDS)
spelling
spend (MONEY)
spending
(TIME)
sperm
sphere (ROUND OBJECT)
spherical
spice
spiced
spicy
spicily
spiciness
spin (TURN)
spirit (NOT MATTER)
spiritual
spiritually
splendid
splendidly
spoil (DESTROY)
spoon
sport (GAME)
sportsperson
sporty
spot (CIRCLE)
spotted
spotty
spring (SEASON)
(CURVED METAL)
springy
square (SHAPE)
squared
stage (PART)
(THEATRE)
stair
stamp (LETTER)
stand (VERTICAL)
standard (USUAL)
standardize
standardization
(QUALITY)
star (OBJECT IN SPACE)
start (BEGIN)
state (CONDITION)
(EXPRESS)
statement
station (BUILDING)
(BROADCASTING)
statue
stay (NOT LEAVE)
(CONTINUE)

(LIVE)
steal (TAKE AWAY)
steam
steel (METAL)
steep (NOT GRADUAL)
steeply
steepness
stem (CENTRAL PART)
-stemmed
step (FOOT MOVEMENT)
(SURFACE)
stick (THIN PIECE)
(FIX)
sticker
sticky
stickiness
stick out (GO BEYOND)
stiff (FIRM)
stiffen
stiffly
stiffness
still (CONTINUING)
(NOT MOVING)
sting (HURT)
stitch (THREAD)
stitching
stomach
stone (ROCK)
stony
stop (FINISH)
stoppage
(PREVENT)
store (KEEP)
storage
storm (VIOLENT WEATHER)
stormy
stormily
story (DESCRIPTION)
straight (NOT CURVING)
straighten
strange (UNUSUAL)
strangeness
strangely
strap
stream (SMALL RIVER)
strength (EFFORT)
strengthen
strengthener
stress (EMPHASIZE)
stretch(LENGTHEN)
stretchable
stretchy
stretchiness
string (CORD)
stringy
stringiness
(MUSIC)
stringed
strip (PIECE)
strong (NOT WEAK)
(DIFFICULT TO BREAK)
strongly
structure
(ARRANGEMENT)
(BUILDING)
structural
structurally
student
study (LEARN)
stupid
stupidity
stupidly
style (WAY)
style
(HIGH QUALITY)
stylish
stylishly
stylishness
(DESIGN)
stylist
subject (AREA OF STUDY)
(GRAMMAR)
substance (MATERIAL)
subtract
subtraction
succeed (ACHIEVE SOMETHING)
success
successful
successfully
such (SO GREAT)
(OF THAT TYPE)
suck (PULL IN)
sudden
suddenly
suddenness
suffer (FEEL PAIN)
sufferer
suffering
sugar
sugary
suggest (MENTION)
suggestion
suit (BE RIGHT)
suited
suitable
suitably
suitability
sum (AMOUNT OF MONEY)
summer
summery
sun (STAR)
sunny
superlative (GRAMMAR)
supply
supplier
support (ENCOURAGE)
supporter
supportive
(STOP FROM FALLING)

surface
surprise
surprised
surprising
surprisingly
surround
surrounding
surroundings
swallow (THROAT)
swear (USE RUDE WORDS)
sweet
sweeten
sweetener
sweetness
swell (INCREASE)
swelling
swollen
swim (MOVE IN WATER)
swimmer
swimming
swing (MOVE SIDEWAYS)
switch (DEVICE)
sword
syllable
syllabic
symbol
symbolic
symbolically
symbolize
sympathy (SADNESS)
sympathetic
sympathetically
sympathize
system (METHOD)
systematic
systematically
table (FURNITURE)
taboo
tail (ANIMAL)
-tailed
take (ACT)
(ACCEPT)
(HOLD)
(MOVE)
(NEED)
take off (LEAVE)
talk
tall
tallish
tallness
taste (FLAVOUR)
tasteless
-tasting
tasty
tax (MONEY)
taxable
taxation
tea
teach
teacher
teaching
team
tear (CRY)
tear (SEPARATE)
technical
technically
telephone
television
tell (SPEAK)
temperature
temporary
temporarily
ten
tenth
tend (BE LIKELY)
tendency
tennis
tense (VERB FORM)
tent
test
tester
text
textual
than
thank
thankful
thankfulness
that
the
theatre (BUILDING)
(PERFORMING ARTS)
theatrical
theatrically
their
them
themselves
then
theory
theoretical
theoretically
there
therefore
these
they
thick (NOT THIN)
(NOT FLOWING)
thickly
thickness
thicken
thief
thin (NOT THICK)
(FLOWING EASILY)
thinly
thing (OBJECT)
think (CONSIDER)
(REASON)
third
thirst
thirstily
thirsty
this

those
thought (THINKING)
thread (FIBRE)
threadlike
threat
threaten
threateningly
three
throat
through (PLACE)
(TIME)
throw (SEND THROUGH AIR)
throw away
thumb
thunder
ticket (PROOF OF PAYMENT)
tidy (ORDERED)
tidily
tidiness
tie (FASTEN)
tight
tightly
tightness
tighten
time (MINUTES/DAYS/YEARS)
(PARTICULAR POINT)
(OCCASION)
tire (LOSE ENERGY)
tired
tiredness
tissue (CELLS)
title (NAME)
(PERSON)
to
tobacco
today
toe (BODY PART)
-toed
together (WITH EACH OTHER)
(AT THE SAME TIME)
(COMBINED)
toilet (CONTAINER)
tongue (MOUTH PART)
too (MORE)
(ALSO)
tool (EQUIPMENT)
tooth (MOUTH)
top (HIGHEST PART)
total (AMOUNT)
touch (USE FINGERS)
(CLOSE TOGETHER)
towards (MOVEMENT)
tower
town
toy (GAME)
track (PATH)
trade (BUYING AND SELLING)
trader
trading
trademark
tradition
traditional
traditionally
traffic (VEHICLES)
train (VEHICLE)
(PREPARE)
trained
trainee
trainer
training
transparent
transparency
transport
transportation
travel
traveller
travelling
treat (DEAL WITH)
(GIVE MEDICAL CARE)
treatment
tree
trial (LEGAL PROCESS)
triangle
triangular
trick (ACT OF DECEIVING)
tropic
tropical
tropically
trouble (DIFFICULTIES)
troubled
trousers
truck (VEHICLE)
true (NOT FALSE)
truly
trunk (MAIN PART)
trust (BELIEVE)
trusted
trustworthy
trustworthiness
truth
truthful
truthfully
truthfulness
try (ATTEMPT)
(TEST)
tube (PIPE)
tubing
tune (MUSICAL NOTES)
tuneful
tuneless
turn (GO ROUND)
(OPPORTUNITY)
twelve
twelfth
twice
twist (TURN)

twisted
twisting
two
type (GROUP)
typical
typically
tyre
ugly (VERY UNATTRACTIVE)
ugliness
unable
unacceptable
unacceptably
unattractive
uncertain
uncertainly
uncertainty
uncle
unclear
unclearly
uncomfortable
uncomfortably
unconscious
unconscious
unconsciously
unconsciousness
uncontrollable
uncontrollably
uncontrolled
uncountable
under (LOWER POSITION)
(LESS THAN)
underground
underground
understand (KNOW)
understandable
understandably
understanding
underwear
unemployed
unemployment
uneven
unevenly
unevenness
unexpected
unexpectedly
unfair
unfairly
unfairness
unfasten
unfriendly
unfriendliness
unhappy
unhappily
unhappiness
unhealthy
unhealthily
uniform (CLOTHES)
unimportant
unintentional
unintentionally
unit (MEASUREMENT)
(SEPARATE PART)
unite
united
unity
union
universe
university
unkind
unkindly
unkindness
unknown
unlikely
unlimited
unload
unlucky
unluckily
unnatural
unnaturally
unnecessary
unnecessarily
unofficial
unofficially
unpleasant
unpleasantly
unpleasantness
unpopular
unreasonable
unreasonably
unskilled
unsuccessful
unsuccessfully
unsuitable
unsuitably
untidy
untidily
untidiness
until (TIME)
unusual
unusually
unwanted
unwilling
unwillingness
unwillingly
unwise
unwisely
up
upper (HIGHER)
upset (WORRY)
upsetting
upside down
urgent (IMPORTANT)
urgency
urgently
urine
urinate
urination
us (GROUP)
use (PURPOSE)
usable

usage
useful
usefully
usefulness
useless
uselessly
uselessness
user
usual
usually
utensil
vagina
vaginal
valley
value (IMPORTANCE)
(MONEY)
valuable
valueless
valuation
variety (DIFFERENCE)
various
vary
varied
variable
variance
variant
variation
vegetable
vehicle
verb
vertical
vertically
very (EXTREMELY)
victory
victorious
victoriously
view (SIGHT)
viewer
village
vinegar
vinegary
violence
violent
violently
virus (SMALL ORGANISM)
viral
visit
visitor
voice (SOUNDS)
voiced
voiceless
volume (AMOUNT)
vomit
vote
voter
vowel
W (WEST)
waist
wait
wake (STOP SLEEPING)
waken
walk
walking
wall
want (DESIRE)
war
warm (HIGH TEMPERATURE)
warmly
warmth
warn
warning
wash (CLEAN)
washable
washing
waste (BAD USE)
wastage
wasteful
wastefully
(UNWANTED MATTER)
watch (SMALL CLOCK)
(LOOK AT)
water
watery
waterproof
wave (HAND MOVEMENT)
(WATER)
(ENERGY)
wavy
wax (SUBSTANCE)
waxy
waxiness
way (ROUTE)
(DISTANCE)
(POSSIBILITY)
we (GROUP)
weak (NOT STRONG)
weaken
weakly
weakness
wealth (MONEY)
wealthy
weapon
weaponry
wear (ON BODY)
wearer
weather (AIR CONDITIONS)
weave (MAKE CLOTH)
weaving
week
weekly
weekend
weigh (HEAVINESS)
weight
welcome (MEET)
well (HEALTHY)
(IN A GOOD WAY)
west (DIRECTION)
western

westward
wet (NOT DRY)
wetness
what
whatever
wheat
wheel (ROUND OBJECT)
-wheeled
when
where
whether
which
while (DURING)
whip (DEVICE FOR HITTING)
whipping
white (COLOUR)
(PEOPLE)
whiten
whitish
who
whole
wholeness
wholly
whom
whose
why
wide
widely
widen
width
wife
wild (NATURAL)
(NOT CONTROLLED)
wildly
wildness
will (FUTURE)
(INTENTION)
(REQUEST)
willing
willingly
willingness
win
winner
winning
wind (CURRENT OF AIR)
windy
window (GLASS)
wine
wing (STRUCTURE FOR FLYING)
winged
winter
wintry
wire (METAL THREAD)
wiring
wise (CLEVER)
wisely
wisdom
wish (DESIRE)
(REGRET)
with
within
without
woman
womb
wood (MATERIAL)
wooden
woody
(GROUP OF TREES)
wooded
woods
wool
woollen
woolly
word (LANGUAGE UNIT)
worded
wording
work (JOB)
worker
working
(OPERATE)
(OBJECT)
world (THE EARTH)
worry
worried
worriedly
worrying
worryingly
worse (LESS PLEASANT)
worsening
worsh
worshipping
worshipper
worth (MONEY)
(IMPORTANCE)
worthless
worthlessly
worthlessness
would
wrap
wrapper
wrapping
wrist
write
wrong (NOT CORRECT)
wrongly
(IMMORAL)
year
yearly
yellow (COLOUR)
yellowish
yes
yet (UNTIL NOW)
you (PERSON/PEOPLE ADDRESSED)
your
yours
yourself
young
zero

The Phrase Index

The Phrase Index helps you to:

- find a group of words when you don't know which word to look up
- find compound verbs (phrasal verbs) and other verb combinations which might be confused with them

For example, if you want to find the phrase 'over my dead body', you look for *any* of the most important words in the phrase, and you will find a page and line number:

over my dead **body** 350R33
over my **dead** body 350R33
over my dead body 350R33

Sometimes a word, such as **go**, can take up a lot of space in the dictionary. In these cases the Phrase Index is particularly helpful.

A reference like 133L16 means page 133, left column, line 16.

Stress in phrases is shown using the symbol ˈ for the main stress and ˌ for any secondary stress, as in a ˌbed and ˈbreakfast'.

ˌtake *someone* aˈback 1R48
aˌbandon ˈship 1R65
as ˌeasy as ABˈC 438R39
aˈbet in 2R6
ˌaid and aˈbet 28R20
ˈlaw-aˌbiding 801L41
ˌmixed aˈbility 2R49 908L57
to the ˌbest of *one's* aˈbility 119L74
set the ˈworld/the ˈThames aˌblaze 1299L34
ˌable-ˈbodied 3L8/12
ˌno fixed aˈbode 528L55
aˌbominable ˈsnowman 3L83 1697L3
ˌanti-aˈbortion 49R60
ˌback-alley aˈbortion 89R16
ˌback-street aˈbortion 89R15
aˈbound with/in 3R56
a ˌcut aˈbove 339L15
above ˈall ˌthings 1512R10
above ˈstairs 1407R49
ˌhead and ˈshoulders above 653L72
keep *one's* ˌhead above ˈwater 653L79
ˌover and aˈbove 1005R67
put/stick *one's* ˌhead above the ˈparapet 653R29
ˈrear above 1181L83
ˌrise aˈbove 1226R30/32/75
ˌabseil ˈdown 5L10
ˌleave of ˈabsence 807R64
ˌabsent-ˈminded 5L32/35
ˌabsentee ˈballot 5L48 1100R73
ˌabsentee ˈlandlord 5L52
ˌabsentee ˈvote 5L48 1100R74
ˌabsolute maˈjority 5R14
ˌabsolute ˈzero 5R16
deˌcree ˈabsolute 356R10
in ˌabsolute ˈterms 5R12
abˈsolve from/of 5R21/22
abˈsorb by/in/into 5R34/43/35
ˈshock abˌsorber 1318R79
abˈstain from 5R65/66
ˌabstract ˈnoun 6L12
ˈchild aˌbuse 6R6 226L22
ˈdrug abˌuse 428R37
ˌsexual aˈbuse 1304L11
ˈsubstance aˌbuse 1452R84 1453L1
ˌterm of aˈbuse 6R14 1501R38
the ˌgroves of ˈacademe 627L47
Aˌcademy Aˈward 7L11
ˌmilitary aˈcademy 896R4/5
acˈcede to 7L24/26
ˈparticle acˌcelerator 1029R15
ˈaccess ˌcourse 7R61
ˈaccess ˌroad/ˌroute 7R65
ˈaccess ˌtime 7R66
disˈabled ˌaccess 388L61
acˌcessory after/before the ˈfact 8L17/18
ˈaccident-ˌprone 8L31
more by ˈaccident than deˌsign 8L28
ˌaccidental ˈdeath 8L42
acciˌdentally on ˈpurpose 8L47
ˌchapter of ˈaccidents 216R32
acˈclaim as/for 8L58/53
acˈcommodate in 8R3
acˈcommodate *oneself* to 8R20
acˈcommodate *someone* with 8R22
accommoˈdation adˌdress 8R9
ˌsheltered accommoˈdation 1315L23
ˌfait accomˈpli 496L26
acˈcord *something* to *someone* 9L48
acˈcord with 8R74
acˌcording to ˈplan 9L56
acˌcording to the ˈclock 246L67
acˈcordion ˌfile 9L65 281L84
acˈcount for 10L8/32
acˈcount to 10L12
ˈbank acˌcount 9L76 97R39
ˌbring/ˌcall to acˈcount 9R58
ˈcharge acˌcount 217R13/23 322L45
ˈchecking acˌcount 221R80 224L29 336R78
ˈcheque acˌcount 224L28
ˈcredit acˌcount 322L44
ˈcurrent acˌcount 336R78
deˈposit acˌcount 368R44
exˈpense acˌcount 481R70
NOˈW acˌcount 965R68
on ˌno acˈcount 9R68
ˌrender an acˈcount of 1203L19
ˈsavings acˌcount 368R45 1257R79
ˌsettle an acˈcount 1301R39
ˌtake into acˈcount 9R79
ˌturn/ˌuse to (ˌgood) acˈcount 10L3
ˌcertified ˌpublic acˈcountant 211R1
ˈturf acˌcountant 1568R56
creˌative acˈcounting 321R40
ˌfalse acˈcounting 499R67
by/from ˌall acˈcounts 9R56
ˌsquare the acˈcounts 1402L68
acˈcrue on 10L57
acˈcrue to 10L58
acˈcuse of 10R18/19/20
acˈcustom to 10R40
ˌace in the ˈhole 10R57
ˈace up *one's* ˈsleeve 10R56
be/ˌcome within an ˈace of 10R54
hold/have ˌall the ˈaces 10R60
aˌcetic acˈid 11L6
ˈache for 11L27
Aˌchilles ˈheel 11L62
Aˌchilles ˈtendon 11L66
aˌcetic acˈid 11L6
ˈacid ˌhead 11R17
ˌacid ˈrain 11L79
ˈacid ˌtest 11L82
aˌmino ˈacid 41R15
aˌscorbic ˈacid 67R15
carˌbolic ˈacid 194L56
ˌcitric ˈacid 234L61
ˌfatty ˈacid 506L63
ˌfolic ˈacid 542R65
ˌhydrochloric ˈacid 696R53
ˌlactic ˈacid 791R64
ˌnitric ˈacid 956R39
nuˌcleic ˈacid 966L75
ˌprussic ˈacid 1140L43
sulˌfuric ˈacid 1458R25
sulˌphuric ˈacid 1458R25
ˌtannic ˈacid 1490L62
tarˌtaric ˈacid 1492L28
acˈknowledge *someone* as 11R24
aˌcoustic ˈcoupler 11R67
aˌcoustic guiˈtar 631R39
acˈquaint with 12L1
ˌmake *someone's* acˈquaintance 12L31
ˌnodding acˈquaintance 958R3
on ˌfurther acˈquaintance 12L33
acquiˈesce to/in 12L41
acˈquit of 12L77/79
aˌcross ˈcountry 12R49 313R37
aˌcross the ˈboard 12R54/58
ˌcome aˈcross 264R56
ˌget the ˈmessage across 890L55
ˌput one aˈcross 12R59
ˈstumble across 1448R31
a ˌhard/ˌtough act to ˈfollow 13L52
ˈact as 12R82/83/84
ˈact ˌlike 13L2
ˌact of ˈGod 13L16
ˈact on 13L3
ˌact ˈout 13L26
ˌact the ˈfool/ˈgoat 544L81 608R1
ˌact ˈup 13L6/8
ˈbalancing ˌact 95L15
ˌclean up *one's* ˈact 241L52
get *one's* ˈact toˌgether 13L48
get/muscle ˈin on the ˌact 13L44
ˈjuggling ˌact 772L4/14
Oˌfficial ˈSecrets ˌAct 977R68
ˌput on an ˈact 13L55
read the ˈRiot ˌAct 1178R24
ˌsmarten up *one's* ˈact 1358R25
a ˌpiece/ˌslice of the ˈaction 13R13
ˈaction-ˌpacked 13R7
ˌaction ˈreplay 13R15
ˈaction ˌstations 13R34
afˌfirmative ˈaction 22R4
ˌcivil ˈaction 235L13
ˌdirect ˈaction 386R50
inˌdustrial ˈaction 723R77
ˈjob ˌaction 765R41
ˈpump-ˌaction 1145R83
ˈrearguard ˌaction 1181R5
ˌswing into ˈaction 1477L47
on ˌactive ˈservice 13R74 1298L29
a ˌhive of acˈtivity/ˈindustry 673R74
disˈplacement acˌtivity 396R46
ˌextracurricular acˈtivity 487L57/60
ˌleading ˈactor 803R75
ˌleading ˈactress 803R75
in ˌactual ˈfact 14L30
ˈad ˌagency 14R41
ˌad ˈhoc 16L32
ˌad infiˈnitum 16L40
ˌad ˈlib 17L44/48
ˌad ˈnauseam 18L24
ˌclassified ˈad 238R70
ˌpersonal ˈad 1052R72
ˈsmall ˌad 238R71
ˈwant ˌad 238R71 1636R33
ˌAdam's ˈapple 14R49
not ˌknow *someone* from ˈAdam 787R19
ˌsweet ˌfanny ˈadams 1475R51
add ˈflesh to *one's* ˌargument 533L63
add ˈfuel to the ˌfire/ˌflames 571L75
ˌadd ˈin 15L26
add ˌinsult to ˈinjury 15L42
ˌadd ˈon 15L27/28/29/44
ˌadd ˈup to 15L31/32/33/37/38 1598L67
it ˌdoesn't add ˈup 15L40
ˈpuff ˌadder 1143R58
ˌnon-adˈdictive 959L55
ˈfood ˌadditive 544L53
accommoˈdation adˌdress 8R9
adˈdress as 15R49
adˈdress ˌbook 15R35
ˈforwarding adˌdress 555R7
ˌhome adˈdress 679R71
ˌno fixed adˈdress 528L55
ˌpublic adˈdress (ˌPˈA) (ˌsystem) 1142L20
ˌstamped addressed ˈenvelope 1409R24
adˈhere to 16L11/20
adˈjudicate on/upon 16R81
ˌwell-adˈjusted 1652L14
ˈloss adˌjuster 17L30 842L57
adˈminister to 17L80/82/83
ˌfleet ˈadmiral 533L22
ˌrear ˈadmiral 1181L58
ˌred ˈadmiral 1188R65
adˈmire for 17R12
ˌsecret adˈmirer 17R26 1280L70
ˌopen adˈmissions 988R59
adˌmit deˈfeat 17R45 358L48
adˈmit of 18L1
adˈmit to 17R43/62/63
adˈmonish *someone* to 18L15
aˈdopt as 18R2
aˌdopt the ˈveil 1611L43
ˌopen aˈdoption 988L43
aˈdorn with 18R44/45
aˈdulterate with 19L29
adˌvance diˈrective 19L69
adˈvance on 19L54/64
adˌvanced ˈclass/ˈcourse 19L76
ˈAdvent ˌcalendar 19R29
ˌSeventh-Day ˈAdventist 1302L38
adˈventure ˌplayground 19R48
ˈadvertise for 20R31
adˈvice ˌcolumn 27L44/49
ˌCitizens Adˈvice ˌBureau 234L30
proˌfessional adˈvice 1128L13
be ˌill adˈvised to 21L9
be ˌwell adˈvised to 21L6
ˌill-adˈvised 703L70
ˌwell-adˈvised 1652L21
ˌdevil's ˈadvocate 378L63
ˌunder the ˈaegis of 21L36
ˌaerial reˈconnaissance 1186R20
ˈstep aeˌrobics 1420L29
ˈlove afˌfair 21R82 843R38
afˌfairs of ˈstate 21R78
ˌcurrent afˈfairs 336R75
ˌforeign afˈfairs 549R21
ˌsettle *one's* afˈfairs 1301L82/R6
ˌstate of afˈfairs 1414R16
afˈfiliate with 22L50
affiliˈation ˌorder 22L57
afˌfirmative ˈaction 22R4
ˈlife-afˌfirming 819L22
afˈflict with 22R25
afˈford to 22R40/42/44
afˈfront by 22R65
afˈfronted at 22R66
ˌAfghan ˈhound 22R67
ˌfar aˈfield 22R73
with ˌmalice aˈforethought 857R58
ˌblack ˈAfrica 132L31
ˌAfrican ˈviolet 23L46
acˌcessory after the ˈfact 8L17/18
ˈafter efˌfects 23R21
ˌafter ˈhours 688R76/78
ˌafter *one's* own ˈheart 656R53
ˌafter *one's* ˈscalp 1261L80
beˌfore ˈtax/ˌafter ˈtax 1493L78
ˌday after ˈday 23L77 349L61
ˌhour after ˈhour 689L1
ˌlife after ˈdeath 818R62
ˈlust after 848R76
ˌmorning-ˈafter ˌpill 918R48
ˌnight after ˈnight 955L26/50
ˌone after anˈother 47R83 983R69
ˌone thing after anˈother 1512L8
shut/close the stable/barn ˌdoor after the ˈhorse has bolted 411R52
ˈsought-after 1378L46
ˌstrain after efˈfect 1433R81/82
the ˌcalm after the ˈstorm 186R20
ˈthirst after 1513R44
throw ˌgood money after ˈbad 1517L10
ˌtime after ˈtime 1523R81
ˌweek after ˈweek 23L77 1649R7
ˌafternoon ˈtea 1493R83
good ˌafterˈnoon 612L43
ˈAga ˌcooker 24L34
aˌgainst all (the) ˈodds 974R80
aˌgainst *one's* better ˈjudgment 24R4
aˌgainst the ˈrules 1239R57
aˌgainst ˈtime/the ˈclock 24R18
ˌbeat/ˌbang/ˌknock *one's* ˌhead against a brick ˈwall 653L33
camˈpaign against 187R38/59
ˌcome ˈup aˌgainst 265L42
ˌcount/ˌgo/ˌwork aˈgainst 24R15
cruˈsade against 330R78 331L4
ˌcry ˈout against 331R69
ˌdead ˈset aˌgainst 351L17
ˈfight against 516R81 517L55
go/ˌmove aˌgainst the ˈflow 538L5
ˌgo/ˌswim against the ˈtide 1519L24/25
ˌhope against ˈhope 684R83
ˌkick against the ˈpricks 778R74
play both ˌends against the ˈmiddle 1078L42
ˈprejudice against 1113L66/R2/15
ˈrace against 1165L82
ˌraise *one's* ˈhand against 1170L39
ˌrun ˈup against 1243L70
ˌsail against the ˈwind 1249R28
ˈset against 1298R59 1299L31/R52
ˌstrike a ˈblow against 1441R1/4
the ˌodds/ˌcards are stacked aˈgainst *someone* 1405R61
up against a ˌbrick ˈwall 24R7
up aˈgainst it 24R11
ˌage of conˈsent 25L47
ˈage-ˌold 25L68
ˈage-reˌlated 24R80
ˈBronze ˌAge 168R21
ˌcome/ˌbe of ˈage 24R75
ˌcome of ˈage 24R78
ˌgolden ˈage 610L35
ˌgrand old ˈage 617R73
ˈIce ˌage 597R28 698R65
in ˌthis day and ˈage 349R3
ˈIron ˌAge 752R22
maˈture-age ˌstudent 875R58
ˌmental ˈage 887L51
ˌmiddle ˈage 894L10
ˌmiddle-age ˈspread 894L18
ˌNew ˈAge 952L27/33
ˌold ˈage 979R53
ˌold age ˈpension 979R/5660 1046L40 1292L42
ˌripe old ˈage 1226L69
school-ˈleaving age 1265R9
ˈspace-ˌage 1382L27
ˈStone ˌAge 1429R27
ˌunder ˈage 24R70/82
ˌmiddle-ˈaged 894L14
ˌanti-ˈageing 49R53
ˈad ˌagency 14R41
ˈdating ˌagency 348L43 868L11
ˈescort ˌagency 468L22
esˈtate ˌagency 469L47
ˈnews ˌagency 953L15
ˌagent provocaˈteur 26L6
ˌdouble ˈagent 413R62
esˈtate ˌagent 469L46
ˌfree ˈagent 560R47
ˈliterary ˌagent 830L78
ˈreal estate ˌagent 469L46 1180R34/35 1181L4
ˌsecret ˈagent 1280L72
ˈtravel ˌagent 1553L22
ˈDark ˌAges 346L64
ˌdown/ˌthrough the ˈages 439R83
the ˈMiddle ˌAges 894L20
ˌaggravated asˈsault 26L35
ˌaggravated ˈburglary 26L34
ˌnon-agˈgression 959L57
ˈagitate for/against 26R60/61

▪many ▫moons ago 916R59
▪agony ▫aunt/▫column/▫uncle 27L44/49/48
▫pile on the ▪agony 1066L76
a▪gree about/on/to 27R4/7/23
a▫gree to ▪differ 27R32
a▪gree with 27R5/8/28/29/63
▫couldn't agree ▪more/▪less 27R35
▫gentleman's a▪greement 589L29
post▫nuptial a▪greement 1102L15
▪sweetheart a▫greement 1476L41
▫run a▪ground 1241R1
a▫head of 1523L52
a▫head of ▪time 1522R5/69
▫full steam a▪head 573L29
go a▪head 606R18/28/34
▫one/a ▫jump a▪head 773L6
▪streets a▫head of 1437L19
▫aid and a▪bet 28R20
▫Aid to Families with Dependent ▪Children 28R12 226L25
▪aid *someone* with 28R20
▪Band-▫Aid 96R75 1076R21 1423L41
▫band-aid so▪lution 96R77
▪deaf ▫aid 351R10
▫first ▪aid 525R25
▫foreign ▪aid 549R22
▫grant-in-▪aid 618R82
▪hearing ▫aid 656L4
▫legal ▪aid 809L51
▫marital ▪aid 865L80
▪nursing ▫aid 968L21
▪sex ▫aid 1303R44
▫sexual ▪aid 1303R44
▪study ▫aid 1094L60
▫visual ▪aid 1627R18
▫aide-de-▪camp 28R28/29/31
▫grant-▪aided 618R82
▫first-▪aiders 525R30
▪aim at 28R71/72/73/77/78 29L4/5
▪aim for 28R70/78 29L3
a ▫breath of fresh ▪air 162R44/43
a ▪nip in the ▫air 956R1
▪air ▫brake 29L41
▪air-con▫ditioned 29L48
▪air con▫ditioner 29L44/46
▪air-▫cooled 29L50
▪air-▫cushioned 29L52
▪air ▫drop 29L78
▪air ▫force 29L80
▪air ▫freshener 29L55
▪air host▫ess 29L82
▪air ▫mattress 29L57/R70 823L54
▪air-▫pistol 29L61
▪air ▫pocket 29L58
▪air ▫power 29L84
▪air ▫raid 29R4
▪air re▫sistance 1209L82
▪air-▫rifle 29L61
▫air-sea ▪rescue 29R5
▪air ▫terminal 29R9
▫air-to-▪air 29R12
▫air to-▪ground 29R14
▫air traffic con▪trol 29R20/17
▫breath of ▪air 162R41
▪castles in the ▫air 202R48
▫clear the ▪air 242R72/70
com▫pressed ▪air 277R54
▫dead ▪air 351L21
disap▪pear/▫vanish into thin ▪air 1511R36
▫float on ▪air 535R2
(so much/just) ▫hot ▪air 687R26
hot-▪air bal▫loon 687R27
hot-▪air ▫gun 687R30
▫leave up in the ▪air 807R8
▫Marshal of the Royal ▪Air ▫Force 868R57
▫nose in the ▪air 962L38
out of ▫thin ▪air 1511R38
▫pluck out of the ▪air 1083L50
put/stick two ▪fingers in the ▫air 1576L17
▫surface-to-▪air 1468L12
the ▫open ▪air 988R18
▫up in the ▪air 29R23
▫walk/▫float on ▪air 29L41
▫walk on ▪air 1634R1
▫airbrush ▪out 30L10
▪aircraft ▫carrier 30L17
▫anti-▪aircraft 49R56
▫light ▪aircraft 821L55
▪airing ▫cupboard 29R50
▫airs and ▪graces 29R39
▫put on/▫give *oneself* ▫airs (and ▪graces) 29R36
▫airy-▪fairy 30R51
▫take down the ▪aisle 30R61
▫rolling in the ▪aisles 1231L28
▫drop *one's* ▪aitches 427R24
▫al ▪dente 32L41
▫et ▪al 469R32
a▪las and a▪lack 31R64
A▫laddin's ▪cave 31L51
▫alarm bells start to ▪ring/▪sound 115R38 1638R44
▪alarm ▫call 31R50
▪burglar a▫larm 176R70
▫false a▪larm 500L5
▪fire a▫larm 523L42
▫radio a▪larm (▫clock) 1167R63
a▪las and a▪lack 31R64
▫baked A▪laska 94R18
▪photo ▫album 1059L12
▫demon ▪alcohol 364R73
▫ethyl ▪alcohol 470L31/R32
▫rubbing ▪alcohol 1238R9 1468R21
▫non-alco▪holic 959L59
▫ginger ▪ale 595R18
▫pale ▪ale 1020L20
▫real ▪ale 1180L66
▪smart ▫alec 1358R33
▪smart ▫aleck 1358R33
a▪lert to 32L55/66
▫red a▪lert 1188R67
▫blue-green ▪algae 140L1
▫inter ▪alia 740R75
▪Alice ▫band 32R16 636R39
▪alienate from 32R47
a▪light from 32R63
a▪light on/upon 32R67/68/70
set the ▪world/the ▪Thames a▫light 1299L34
a▪lign with/behind 32R76/73
▫non-a▪ligned 959L60/63
▪look-alike 839R53
▫share and share a▪like 1311L83
▫alimentary ca▪nal 33L7
a▫live and ▪well/▪kicking 33L35/36
▫flay *someone* a▪live 532R33
▫look a▪live 839R47
▫skin *someone* a▪live 1346R57
▪Allen ▫key 34L20
▪Allen ▫wrench 34L20
▫back-alley a▪bortion 89R16
▫blind ▪alley 135L71
▪bowling ▫alley 154R66
▫Tin Pan ▪Alley 1524R84
▫up/▫down *someone's* ▪alley 34L45 1437L34
▫Allied ▪forces 34L51
▪allocate for/to 34L82/84/80/84
al▪lot to/for 34R10/6/9
al▪low for 35L4
allow *something* ▫full ▪play 1079L48/49
allow ▫nature to take its ▪course 943L6
allow the ▪dust to ▫settle 433L14
make al▪lowance(s) for 35L10/13
▪baggage al▫lowance 93R58
▫family al▪lowance 500R71
▫personal al▪lowance 1052R75
recom▫mended daily al▪lowance 1186L32
▪tax al▫lowance 34R72 1493L81
▪ally *oneself* to/with 35R40
▫alma ▪mater 35R66
▫Christ Al▪mighty 35R83
▫God al▪mighty 35R83 608R77
▫almond ▪paste 36L9 869R35
▫aloe ▪vera 36L37
▫go it a▪lone 36L55 605L61
▫leave ▫well a▪lone 807R10 1651R44
let a▪lone 812R51
▪stand-a▫lone 1410R50
▫all along the ▪line 826L23
a▫long for the ▪ride 36R7
a▫long the ▪way 36L74
▫go a▪long with 606R40
▫jog a▪long 766R58
▫push a▪long 1152L58
▫rub a▪long (together) 1238L69
▪somewhere along the ▫line 826L20
▫think a▪loud 1513L52
Inter▫national Pho▫netic ▪Alphabet 744L25
▫Latin ▪alphabet 1232L31
▫Roman ▪alphabet 1232L30
▪also-▫ran 37L5
▫alter ▪ego 37L33
▪mind-▫altering 899L6
▪alternate with 37L40/42
▫male ▪alto 313L81
an▫other matter/thing alto▪gether 48L12
▫always a/the ▪bridesmaid ▫never the ▪bride 164L24
a▪malgamate as/into/with 38L11/9
▫amateur dra▪matics 38L38
▫vaulting am▪bition 1609R73
▫amble a▪long/▪down/▪off 39L69/72/70
▪ambulance-▫chaser 39R13/9
make a▪mends 39R72
▫Middle A▪merica 894L24/27 895L20
A▫merican ▪dream 41L23
A▫merican ▪football 41L25
A▫merican ▪Indian 41L30
A▫merican ▪muffin 928L35
▫Anglo-A▪merican 45R16
as A▫merican as ▫apple ▪pie 41L20
▫Irish-A▪merican 752L78
▫Latin A▪merican 799R5
▫modified American ▪plan 637R27 911L55
▫Native A▪merican 939R20
▫ugly A▪merican 1577R69
un-A▪merican 1579R10
a▫mino ▪acid 41R15
▫not go/come a▪miss 41R26/28
▫take a▪miss 41R30
am▫monium ▪sulphate 41R41
▫Amnesty Inter▪national 41R63
a▫moebic ▪dysentery 41R81
▫run a▪mok 41R83
▫first among ▪equals 525R8
put/set the ▫cat among the ▪pigeons 203L64
a▪mount to 42L57
it all amounts to the ▫same ▪thing 1252R42
▪gene ampli▫fication 586R58
▫run a▪muck 41R83
a▪musement ar▫cade 43L15
a▪musement ▫park 43L16 574R79 1509L22
▫anabolic ▪steroid 43L33
▫sickle-cell a▪naemia 1333L70
▫general anaes▪thetic 43L75 587L25
▫anal re▪tentive 51R53
in the ▫last/▫final/▫ultimate a▪nalysis 43R42
▪systems ▫analyst 1482R59
▫weigh ▪anchor 44L32 1650L67
ane▫cdotal ▪evidence 44R58
▫sickle-cell a▪nemia 1333L70
▪sea a▫nemone 1276L2
▪angel ▫food ▫cake 44R82
▫guardian ▪angel 629R42
▫ministering ▪angel 901L78
▫Hell's ▪Angels 661L58
on the ▫side of the ▪angels 44R79
▫cor ▪anglais 305L52
a ▫new/▫fresh ▪angle on 45L72
▪angle at/for 45L76/74
▪right angle 1223R73
▫supplementary ▪angle 1464R18
▫wide-angle (▪lens) 1663R22
▫right-▪angled ▪triangle 1223R75
comple▫mentary ▪angles 275R14
▫Anglo-A▪merican 45R16
▫Anglo-▪Catholic 45R18
▫Anglo-▪Indian 45R20
▫Anglo-▪Saxon 45R23
▫animal ▪husbandry 46L9
▪animal ▫kingdom 46L11
do▫mestic ▪animal 45R77 410R16
like a ▫caged ▪animal 183L41
▪pack ▫animal 1016L8
▪party ▫animal 1030L67
▫stuffed ▪animal 1371R25
▫animated car▪toon 200R16
su▫spended ani▪mation 1471R72
▪ankle ▫boots 46L81
▪ankle ▫sock 46L83
Queen ▫Anne's ▪lace 317L52 1161L30
▫annual (general) ▪meeting 47L28
▫annual re▪ports 47L26
▫annual ▪ring 1554R68
per ▪annum 1047L28
▫annus mi▪rabilis 47L60
a▪noint as 47R2
▫ever and a▪non 473L20
and an▪other ▫thing 1512R13/27
an▫other bite of the ▪cherry 130R40
an▫other matter/thing alto▪gether 48L12
an▫other ▪story 48L19
another ▫string to *one's* ▪bow 1443R47
at/on an▫other ▪level 813R59
in an▫other ▪world 48L22
live to ▫fight another ▪day 831R64
▫one after an▪other 47R83 983R69
▫one/an▪other of ▫life's great ▪mysteries 818R72
▫one thing after an▪other 1512L8
▫one thing ▫leads to an▪other 1512L30
▫one way or an▪other 48L10
▫tell me an▪other 1498L40/41
what with ▫one thing and an▪other 1512L6
▫answer ▪back 48L66/67
▪answer for 48R3
▪answer to 48L33/41/R14
▫question-and-▪answer 1161R17
▪answering ma▫chine 48L69/R25
▪answering ▫service 48L70
know ▫all the ▪answers 786L60
▫white ▪ant 1503R64 1660R1
▫penny-▪ante 1045R73
▫national ▪anthem 938R81
▫anti-a▪bortion 49R60
▫anti-▪ageing 49R53
▫anti-▪aircraft 49R56
▫anti-▪choice 49R63
▫anti-▪clerical 49R67/72
▫anti-▪clockwise 49R73
▫anti-con▪sumerist 49R76
▫anti-de▪pressant 49R81
▫anti-▪federal(ist) 49R84
▪anti-▫hero 50L7
▫anti-in▪flammatory 50L13/15
▫anti-▪lock 50L16
▫anti-▪missile 50L18
▫anti-▪noise 50L20
▫anti-▪nuclear 50L23
▫anti-▪oxidant 50L27
▫anti-person▪nel 50L31
▫anti-▪perspirant 50L33
▫anti-▪racist 50L36
▫anti-▪Semite 50L40/45
▫anti-Se▪mitic 50L44
▫anti-▪social 50L45/51
▫anti-▪tank 50L52
▫anti-▪viral 50L54/56
▪ants in *one's* ▫pants 48R34
▫anyone who is ▪anyone 52L69
▫wouldn't wish *something* on ▪anyone 1671R75
▫anything ▪goes 605R84
▫anything's ▪possible 1099R56
▫anything that ▫turns *you* ▪on 1570L81
as ▫easy as ▪anything 438R39
not ▫anything ▪near 944R42
▫turn *one's* hand to ▪anything 1569R38
would ▫give ▪anything for 596R21
▫anywhere ▪near 52R54/56
▫miles from ▪anywhere 896L32
not ▫anywhere ▪near 944R44/56/58
▫not ▪anywhere to be ▪found 520R55
not ▫getting/▫going ▪anywhere 52R60
▫fall a▪part 498L82/R1
▫grow a▪part 627R69
▫joking a▪part 768R29
▪poles a▫part 1091L53
▫set a▪part 1298R65
▫take a▪part 1487L42
▫tell a▪part 1498L57
a▪partment ▫building 53L26 136R42
a▪partment ▫house 53L25 136R43 531R63
▪garden a▫partment 582R74
▪studio a▫partment 1447R29
▫go ▪ape-shit 53L42
a▪pologize for 54L18/20
a▪pologize to 54L18
ap▪palled at/by 54R51
▫heir ap▪parent 660R46
ap▪peal for/against 55L46/61/63/67/44/51/55
ap▪peal to 55L29/30/32/46/51/62/64/66
▪sex ap▫peal 55L34 1303R47
ap▪pear as 55R65
ap▪pear for 55R6
ap▪pear in 55R6
ap▪pear to 55R22/23/24/28
▫keep up ap▪pearances 55R54 777L33
to ▫all ap▪pearances 55R51
▫grumbling ap▪pendix 628R14
apper▪tain to 56L23
▫Adam's ▪apple 14R49
▫Apple ▪Macintosh 851L8
▫apple pie ▪order 56L67
as A▫merican as ▫apple ▪pie 41L20
▪cooking ▫apple 302R17
▪eating ▫apple 439L54
the ▫apple of *someone's* ▪eye 56L68
the ▫Big ▪Apple 124L70
▪toffee ▫apple 1531R23
up▫set the ▪apple cart 1600L53
do▫mestic ap▪pliance 410R18
ap▪ply for/to 56R10/11/12/25/34/11
▫well-ap▪pointed 1652L24
ap▪portion among/between 57L27
ap▫portion ▪*something* to 57L29
ap▪preciate it 57L78
ap▪prentice to 57R55/56
ap▪prise of 57R62
ap▪proach for/about 57R77
the ▫closest ap▪proach to 58L12
give *one's* ▫seal of ap▪proval 1276L84
ap▪prove of 58L78/79/80
ap▫proved ▪school 58R23
ap▪proximate to 58R77
▫après-▪ski 59L15
▫April ▪fool 59L31
▫April ▪Fools' ▫Day 59L33
▫apron ▪stage 59L57
▪apron ▫strings 59L45
▪aptitude ▫test 59R3
▪Aqua ▫Lung 59R10
▫arabic ▪numerals 59R69
▪arbitrate between 60L42
▫arc a▪cross 60L80
▪arc ▫lamp 60L75
▪arc ▫light 60L75
▫arc ▪welding 60L76
a▪musement ar▫cade 43L15
▪video ar▫cade 1622L51
▫arch ▪over 60R23
▫lever ▪arch ▫file 814L78
in▫dustrial archae▪ology 723R78
▫landscape ▪architect 795L37/40
the ▫Arctic ▪Circle 61L66
▪area ▫code 61R24 254L41 379R25
▪catchment ▫area 205L76
de▪velopment ▫area 377R55
▫grey ▪area 623R4
▫no-▪go ▫area 957R61
▪penalty ▫area 1044R19
re▪ception ▫area 1184L15
▪rest ▫area 803L58 1212R9
▪staging ▫area 1406R64
▪argue over/about 61R53
▫argue the ▪toss 61R54
▪argue with 61R52
▫well-▪argued 1652L29
add ▪flesh to *one's* ▫argument 533L63
put ▫flesh on *one's* ▪argument 533L64
the ▫cosmological ▪argument 309L79
▫argy-▪bargy 62L15
a▪rise from 62L46
arith▫metic pro▪gression 62L80
▫mental a▪rithmetic 62L75 887L54
go ▫out with the ▪ark 1000R37
▫Noah's ▪ark 62R1 958L17
the ▫Ark of the ▪Covenant 62R6
a ▫list as ▫long as *one's* ▪arm 829R10
an ▫arm and a ▪leg 62R28
▪arm *oneself* for 62R73
▫arm in ▪arm 62R29
▪arm-▫twisting 62R31
▪arm *oneself* with 62R71
▪arm ▫wrestling 62R34
as ▫long as *one's* ▪arm 838L7
at ▫arm's ▪length 62R24
▫chance *one's* ▪arm 214R40
give *one's* ▫right ▪arm 1223R69
long ▫arm of the ▪law 838L8
▫put the ▪arm on 1154L36
▫shot in the ▪arm 1320R82
▪strong-▫arm 1445R21
would ▫give *one's* right ▪arm for 596R21
▫armed ▪combat 261L56
▫armed ▪forces 62R80
▫one-armed ▪bandit 984L57 1355L46
▫armour-▪plated 63L75
▪body ▫armour 63L65
▫knight in shining ▪armour 783R73
▫armoured person▪nel ▫carrier 63L82
▫armpit of the ▪Universe 63R17
▪arms-con▫trol 63L9
▪arms ▫race 63L11
▫babe in ▪arms 88L65
▫coat of ▪arms 252L41
▪small ▫arms 1357R41
▫under ▪arms 63L6
▫up in ▪arms 63L7
with ▫open ▪arms 987R23
▫army dis▪posals ▫store 63R34
▫army-▪navy ▫store 63R33
▫army ▪surplus 63R29
▫Red ▪Army 1189L52
Sal▫vation ▪Army 1252L57
Swiss ▪army ▫knife 1477R75
the ▫Sally ▪Army 1251L67
the ▫Territorial ▪Army 1504R74
a▫round the ▪clock 246L62
a▫round the ▪corner 63R79
▫arse a▪round 65L36
▫ass a▪round 65L36 71L79
▫beat around the ▪bush 109L29
▫bum a▪round 175L6/4
▫can't get *one's* ▪head a▫round 653R69
▫cast a▪round 202R9
▫come a▪round 266R49/55
▫doss a▪round 413L16
▫faff a▪round 493R19
▫fart a▪round 504R28
▫float a▪round 535L81/84
▫fly a▪round 540L81
▫fool a▪round 544R33
▫frig a▪round 565R71
▫fuck a▪round 571L15
▫gad a▪round 579L20
get *one's* ▪tongue around 1534R50
▫go a▪round 607R40
▫goof a▪bout/a▪round 612R82
have a ▪noose around *one's* ▫neck 960R45
have ▫been around the ▪ridges 1222L79
▫horse a▪round/a▪bout 686L73
▫just a▫round the ▪corner 306L79
▫knock a▪round 785L55
▫know *one's* way a▪round 787R12
▫lark a▪round 796R51
▫lie a▪round 818L21

▫make the ▪world go a▫**round** 1683R60
▫mess **a▪round** 889R72
▫mill **a▪round** 897L50
▫muck a▪bout/**a▪round** 927R16
▫piss **a▪round** 1070L73
▫play **a▪round** 1077R67
▫ponce **a▪round** 1093R80 1094L1
▫prat **a▪round** 1108R17
▫put the ▪word **around** 1679L12
▫run **a▪round** with 1242L82
▫sleep **a▪round** 1351L68
▪something **a▫round** 1375L11
the ▫right way **a▪round** 1223L48
the ▫wrong way **a▪round** 1693L66
▫throw *one's* ▪weight **around** 1517L22
▫twist/▫wrap *someone* **around** *one's* little ▪finger 1573R84 1689L69
▫up and **a▪round** 1598L30
▫way **a▪round** 1236R40 1645L54
▫word gets **a▪round** 1679L16
ar▪raign on 64L41
ar▪range for 64L50/53/76
ar▪range with 64L52
ar▫ranged ▪marriage 64L57 868L1
▪flower **ar▫ranging** 538L30
ar▪rest *someone* for 64R36
▪house **ar▫rest** 689L38
ar▪rive at 64R53/65
ar▫rive ▪back to 64R54
ar▪rive in 64R53
▪**arrogate** to 65L5
a ▫pain in the ▪**arse** 1018R30
▫arse **a▪bout/a▪round** 65L36
▫**arse** about ▪face 65L29
▪**arse**-▫kisser 65L32
▪**arse**-▫licker 65L32
▫**arse** over ▪tit/▪tip 65L28
get *one's* ▪**arse** in ▫gear 65L27
▫get off *one's* ▪**arse** 65L26
▫kick up/in the ▪**arse** 779L34
▫kiss my ▪**arse** 781R65
▫move/▫shift *one's* ▪**arse** 65L24
▫not know *one's* ▫**arse** from *one's* elbow 65L22
▫sit on *one's* ▪**arse** 1343L44
▪smart ▫**arse** 1358R39
▫half-▪**arsed** 637R24
▪rat-▫**arsed** 1174R11
▫**art** ▪deco 65L84
▫**art** nou▪veau 65R2
▫down/▫off to a ▫fine ▪**art** 521L61
▫fine ▪**art** 521L57
▫graphic ▪**art** 619R7
▪op ▫**art** 987L82
per▪formanance ▫**art** 1048R40
▪pop ▫**art** 1095R13
▫state of the ▪**art** 1414R20/24
▫work of ▪**art** 1682L83
ar▫tesian ▪well 65R68
▫rheumatoid **arth▪ritis** 1220L5
▫globe ▪**artichoke** 600L66
Je▫rusalem ▪**artichoke** 762R8
▫**article** of ▪faith 66L29
▫definite ▪**article** 359R35
in▫definite ▪**article** 720L51
▫leading ▪**article** 442L49 803R73
the ▫genuine ▪**article** 589L71
▫doing/▫in ▪**articles** 66L31
ar▫ticulated ▪lorry 66L64 841R45
▫**artificial** insemi▪nation 66L79
▫**artificial** in▪telligence 66L83
▫**artificial** respi▪ration 66R3 1211L57
▪con ▫**artist** 65R12 279R41
es▪cape ▫**artist** 467R84
▪mime ▫**artist** 897R55
▪piss ▫**artist** 1070L68
▪sidewalk ▪**artist** 1037R63
tat▪too ▫**artist** 1493L13
▫**arts** and ▪crafts 65L82
▫liberal ▪**arts** 816L70
▫martial ▪**arts** 869L3
▫Master of ▪**Arts** 871R60
per▪forming ▫**arts** 1048R25
▫visual ▪**arts** 1627R22
▫**artsy**-▪craftsy 65R39
▫**arty**-▪crafty 65R39
▫**arty**-▪farty 65R42
as▫cend the ▪throne 67L65
a▫scorbic ▪acid 67R15
as▪cribe to 67R23
▫**ash** ▪blond(e) 67R43
▫**Ash** ▪Wednesday 67R46
▫sackcloth and ▪**ashes** 1247L41
▫run **a▪shore** 1241R1
▫joking **a▪side** 768R29
▫step **a▪side** 1420R50
▫**ask** a ▪favour of 70L1/3/54
▪**ask** about 70L3/4/5
▪**ask** after 70L31/33
▫**ask** a▪round 70L30
▪**ask** for 70L20/53
▪**ask** for it 70L37/39
▫**ask** ▪in 70L72
▫**ask** ▪out 70L69/70
need *one* ▪**ask** 946R74
▫well may *one* ▪**ask** 70L18
you may ▫well ▪**ask** 70L17
▫look **a▪skance** 70L74
▫no-▫questions-▪**asked** 957R83
▪**asking** ▫price 70L45
▫fast **a▪sleep** 505R59
▫cast **as▪persions** on 70R67 202L31
as▪phyxiate on 70R77
as▪pire to/after 71L15
a ▫pain in the ▪**ass** 1018R30
▫**ass** a▪bout/a▪round 65L36 71L79
▪**ass**-▫kisser 65L33
▪**ass**-▫licker 65L32
▫**ass** over ▪teakettle 65L29 1494R10
▫bet *one's* ▪**ass** 119R82
▫bore the ▪**ass** off *someone* 71L57
▪candy-▫**ass** 189L81
▫cover *one's* ▪**ass** 316L33
▪haul ▫**ass** 651L13
▫horse's ▪**ass** 686L50
▫kick (some) ▪**ass** 778R77
▪kiss ▫**ass** 781R63
▫kiss my ▪**ass** 781R65
make a *com▪plete* ▫**ass** of 71L46
not within an ▫**ass's** ▪roar of 71L42
▫piece of ▪**ass** 1064R56
▫shove/▫stick/▫ram *something* up *someone's* ▪**ass** 71L65
▫sit on *one's* ▪**ass** 1343L44
▪smart ▫**ass** 1358R38
▫talk *one's* ▪**ass** off 71L63/64
▫up my ▪**ass** 71L69/70
▫work *one's* ▪**ass** off 71L61
▫work the/*one's* ▪**ass** off 71L59
as▪sail with 71L83/R1/6
as▪sailed by 71R3/5/7
▪character **as▫sassin▫ation** 216R83
▫aggravated **as▪sault** 26L35
as▫sault and ▪battery 71R54
as▫sault ▫course 71R47/51
in▫decent **as▪sault** 719R59
▫half-▪**assed** 637R24
▪rat-▫**assed** 1174R11
the **as▫sembled** ▪company 71R78
as▪sembly ▫language 72L36
as▪sembly ▫line 72L28/32/33
▫General **As▪sembly** 587L28
▫legislative **as▪sembly** 809R71
▫Royal **As▪sent** 72L45 1238L2
as▪sertiveness ▫training 72L70
as▪sess at 72L77
as▫sessable ▪income 72L82
con▫tinuous **as▪sessment** 297L53
▪tax **as▫sessment** 1493L82
▪**asset**-▫stripping 72R19/22
▫capital ▪**asset** 191R43
in▫tangible ▪**asset** 739L62
▫fixed ▪**assets** 528L59
as▫sign a ▪day for 72R50/56
as▪sign to 72R41/43/44/46/48/53/72
as▪similate into 72R78
as▪sist in 73L7
as▪sist with 73L8
▫come to *someone's* **as▪sistance** 73L18
Di▫rectory **As▪sistance** 387R68
▪sales **as▫sistant** 73L24 1250R68
▪shop **as▫sistant** 1321L28
▫power(-assisted) ▪steering 1106R7
as▪sisting the po▫lice with/in their in▪quiries 73L9
as▫sociate's de▪gree 73L51
as▫sociate pro▪fessor 73L49
as▪sociate with 73L35/36/38/39/40
as▫sociation ▪football 73L70
▫free **associ▪ation** 560R53
▪housing **as▫sociation** 689L81
▫parent-▪teacher **associ▫ation** 1026L58
▫savings and ▪loan **as▫sociation** 173R12 1257R83
▪word **associ▫ation** 1678R25
▫ill-**as▪sorted** 703L72
as▪sure *someone* of 73R52/74 74L2
▫rest **as▪sured** 73R56 1212R47
▫**astral** ▪body 74R61
▫**astral** ▪plane 74R57
▫**astral** pro▪jection 74R60
▪lunatic **a▫sylum** 75L84 847R64
po▫litical **a▪sylum** 1092L48
▫**athlete's** ▪foot 76L28
ath▫letic sup▪port 76L35 766R13
AT▪M ▫card 201R31
▪**atom** ▫bomb 76R16
▫smash the ▪**atom** 1359L23
a▫tomic ▪bomb 76R25
a▪tone for 76R36/37
▫Day of **A▪tonement** 349R28 1697R29
at▪tach to 76R71/74/77/83 77L2
at▪taché ▫case 77L32
▪strings **at▫tached** 1443L78
▪heart **at▫tack** 656L76
▪panic **at▫tack** 1022L36
at▪tempt to 77R20/25/26
or ▫die in the **at▪tempt** 381R63
at▪tend to 77R52/53 78L32
▫dance **at▪tendance** on 345L40
▪flight **at▫tendant** 29L83 534L43
▫well-**at▪tended** 1652L34
at▪tention ▫span 78L23
▫centre of **at▪tention** 209L47
re▫pay *someone's* **at▪tention** 1204L16
▫steal **at▪tention** 1418L9
▪**attitude** ▫problem 78R1
▫strike ▪**attitudes** 1443L13
At▫torney ▪General 78R16/17
▫district **at▪torney** 400L58
▫power of ▪**attorney** 1105R81
at▪tribute to 78R71
▫**au** ▪fait 79R43
au ▪gratin 79R61
▫**au** ▪pair 80L12
▪vol-**au**-▫vent 1629R64
▫captive ▪**audience** 193L68
▫**audio**-▪visual 79R10
▫digital ▪**audio** ▫tape 383R75
au▪dition for 79R29/30/32
for ▫aught *anyone* ▪cares/▪knows 79R51 547L45
▫**augur** ▪ill/▪badly 79R68
▫**augur** ▪well 79R66
▪agony ▫**aunt** 27L44/49/48
▫maiden ▪**aunt** 853L73
au▫rora aus▪tralis 80L32/31
au▫rora bore▪alis 80L36/37
▫under the ▪**auspices** of 80L43
▫High ▫Court of **Au▪stralia** 668R18
au▫rora **aus▪tralis** 80L32/31
have it on the ▪highest **au▫thority** 668L76
▪health **au▫thority** 655L83
▫local **au▪thority** 834R8
▪**authorize** *someone* to 80R75
▫infantile ▪**autism** 80R81
▫**auto-im▪mune** 82L52
▪**auto**-▫pilot 82R55
▫**automated** ▪teller ma▫chine 82L69
▫**automatic** ▪pilot 82R55
▫**automatic** ▪teller 201R38
▫**automatic** trans▪mission 82L80
▫semi-**auto▪matic** 1290R34/36
▫**autumn** ▪years 83L12
aux▪iliary ▫nurse 83L22
▫modal **aux▪iliary** 909R80
a▫vail *oneself* of the oppor▪tunity 83L43/41/45
it **a▫vails** *one* ▪nothing 83L40
▫**avant**-▪garde 83L78
▫**average** ▪out 83R75
▫Dow Jones (Industrial) ▪**Average** 415R4
▪grade point ▫**average** 616L49
▫law of ▪**averages** 801L78
a▪version ▫therapy 85L27
a▪vert from 85L40/41
a▫void like the ▪plague 85R28
▫**aw**-▪shucks 87L63
a▪wake to 85R71/78
▫wide **a▪wake** 85R67 1663R42
a▪waken in 85R82
a▪waken *someone* to 86L3
A▫cademy **A▪ward** 7L11
▫blow *someone* **a▪way** 138R62/65
blow the ▪cobwebs **a▫way** 138R69
▫fall **a▪way** 498L38/39 497R32
get **a▪way** (with ▫you) 591R29
get **a▪way** with 593L8
▫get **away** with ▪murder 593L13
▪**give-away** 596R28/51/54 597L27/34
give the ▪game **away** 581L67
go **a▪way** 604R3
go **a▪way** with *one's* ▫tail between *one's* ▪legs 1485R29
▫grow **a▪way** 627R69
▪light years **a▫way** 820R42
make **a▪way** with 856L10
▪miles **away** 86L72 896L28
▫right **a▪way** 1224L72
▫run **away** to ▪sea 1275R82
▫run **a▪way** with 1242R8
▫shy **a▪way** from 1332R26
▫tail **a▪way** 1485R36/33
take *someone's* ▪breath **a▫way** 162R46
▫throw **a▪way** 1517L70
▫trail **a▪way** 1548L81
▫turn **a▪way** from 1569R3
▫walk **a▪way** from 1634L62/65/68
▫walk **a▪way** with 1634L70
▪well **a▫way** 1651R53
▫whittle **a▪way** 1661L84
▪**awe** ▫into 86R28
▪god-▫**awful** 609L1
have an ▪**axe** to ▫grind 87L70
▪**Axis** ▫Powers 87R8
▫vitamin **B▪2** 1220R74
▪**babble** about 88L43
▫**babe** in ▪arms 88L65
▪**baby** ▫boom 88R19/14
▫**baby's** ▪bottle 151R21
▪**baby** ▫carriage/▫buggy 88R21 1108L67
▪**baby** ▫fat 1148L25
▪**baby** ▫milk 88R23
▪**baby**-▫minder 88R22
▪**baby** ▫talk 88R24
▪**baby** ▫tooth 88R26
▪blue ▫**baby** 139R68
▪cry-▫**baby** 331R52
▪jelly ▫**baby** 761R62
▫leave *someone* holding the ▪**baby**/▪**bag** 807L77
▫test tube ▪**baby** 1505R31
throw out the ▫**baby** with the ▪bath-water 1516R77
▪**babysit** for 88R43
▪**bachelor's** de▫gree 88R62
▪**bachelor** ▫party 1406L34
at/in the ▫**back** of *one's* ▪mind 89L75
▫**back**-alley a▪bortion 89R16
▫**back** and ▪forth 89L32 554R29
▫**back** a▪way 89L40
▪**back** ▫copy 89L19
▫**back** ▪down 89L45
▫**back** ▪down from/on 89L48
▫**back** handed ▪compliment 808R40
▫**back** in ▪harness 648R59
▪**back** into 89L36
▫**back** is to the ▪wall 89R68
▫**back** ▪issue/▪number 89L20
▪**back** of 89L52/56/57/58/59/60/61/63/72
▫**back** ▪off 89L42/44
▫**back** ▪out 89L49
▫**back** ▪passage 89R12
▫**back** ▪road 89R13
▪**back** ▫saw 89L79
▫**back**-seat ▪driver 89R2
▪**back**-▫stabber 89R73
▫**back** ▪street 89R14
▫**back**-street a▪bortion 89R15
▪**back** ▫talk 89L22 90L47
▫**back** to ▪basics 102R21
▫**back** to ▪front 89L65/67
▫**back** to ▪nature 943L1
▫**back** to square ▪one 89L11
back to the ▪drawing ▫board 89L11
▫**back** ▪up 89L39/R34/36/37 90L1/6 1485R33
▪**back** with 89R19
be▫hind *someone's* ▪**back** 89R61
▫bite ▪**back** 130R5
▫bounce ▪**back** 152R62
▫break the ▪**back** of 159R59/61
▫bring **back** to ▪earth 437L69
▫cast *one's* ▪mind **back** 202L36
▫clap on the ▪**back** 236R82
come ▫**back** from the ▪dead 350R65
come **back** to ▪earth 437L70
▫come **back** to ▪roost 1233R40
▫eyes in the **back** of *one's* ▪head 488L58
▫fall ▪**back** on/upon 499L5
get ▪**back** at 593L17
▫get off *someone's* ▪**back** 89R70
get *one's* ▪own ▫**back** 1012R79
go **back** a ▫long ▪way 838L17
go ▪**back** on 606R44
go **back** to ▪sleep 1351L37
go to ▪hell and ▫**back** 661L29
have *one's* ▫**back** to the ▪wall 89R68
▫knock *something* ▪**back** 785L25
▫laid-▪**back** 792R83
like the ▫**back** of *one's* ▪hand 89L73
make a ▫rod for *one's* ▫own ▪**back** 1230R11
▫never look ▪**back** 839L30
on the ▫**back** ▪burner 89R8
on the ▫**back** of an ▪envelope 463L34
▫one step ▪forward ▫two steps ▪**back** 1420R9
▫out/▫round the ▪**back** 89L68
▫pat on the ▪**back** 1034R31/35
▪piggy **back** (▫ride) 1065R6
▫pin **back** *your* ▪ears 1067R54
▫pin *your* ▪ears ▫**back** 1067R54
▫pull ▪**back** 1144R83
put *one's* ▪**back** into it 89R71
▫put/▫get *someone's* ▪**back** up 89R72
▫put/▫turn the ▪clock ▫**back** 246L58
▫round the ▪**back** 89L70
▫short **back** and ▪sides 1321R70
▫slap on the ▪**back** 1349L61/73
▫small of *someone's* ▪**back** 1357R35
▫stab *someone* in the ▪**back** 1405L15
▫straw that breaks the camel's ▪**back** 1435R26
▫sweep ▪**back** 1476R1
▫tail ▪**back** 1485R36/33
take a/the ▫**back** ▪seat 89L84
▫take ▪**back** 1486R60
the ▫**back** of be▪yond 89L74
the ▫shirt off *someone's* ▪**back** 1317L76
▫throttle ▪**back** 1516L66
▫throw *something* ▫**back** in *someone's* ▪face 1516R79
▫thrown ▪**back** on *one's* ▫own resources 1517L32
▫turn *one's* ▪**back** on 1569R3/5
▫turn **back** the ▪clock 246L60
▫turn the ▪clock ▫**back** 1570R10
▫you scratch ▪my **back** and ▫I'll scratch ▪yours 1271R41
back▪date to 90L55
back▪fire on 90L68
back▪pedal on 91L2
▪**backroom** ▫boy 91L8
a ▫boot/▫kick up the **back▪side** 91L13
a ▫pain in the **back▪side** 1018R30
▫get off *one's* ▪**backside** 91L15
▫kick up/in the ▪**backside** 779L34
▫sit (a▫round) on *one's* **back▪side** 91L16
back▪slide over/on/from 91L34
▪**backtrack** from/on 91L69/68
a ▫**backward** ▪step 1420R8
▫**backward** in coming ▪forward 91R8
▪**backward**-▫looking 91R34
a ▫step ▪**backwards** 1420R8
▫**backwards** and ▪forwards 91R24
▫bend/▫lean over ▪**backwards** 91R26
▫know ▪**backwards** 787L69
▫lean ▫over ▪**backwards** 805R49
▫**bacon** and ▪eggs 91R72
▫bring home the ▪**bacon** 91R74/75
▫save *someone's* ▪**bacon** 1257R51
▫**bad** ▪blood 92L43
▫**bad** ▪breath 92L46 638L75
▫**bad** ▪debt 92L47 353L76
▫**bad** ▪faith 92R2
▫**bad** ▪feeling 92L44
▫**bad** ▪language 92R5
▫**bad** ▪luck on *someone* 846L8
▫**bad**-▪tempered 92L15
▫**bad** ▪turn 1570R35
give *something* ▫up as a **bad** ▪job 92L35
go from ▫**bad** to ▪worse 92L38
go through a ▫**bad** ▪patch 1034R56
▫got it ▪**bad** 92L41
in a ▫**bad** ▪light 820R20
in ▫**bad** re▪pair 1203R73
▫leave a **bad** ▪taste 807L69
make the ▫best of a **bad** ▪job 119L62
▫not too ▪**bad** 92L28
on ▫**bad** ▪terms 1504L11
take the ▫**bad** with the ▪good 92L53
the ▫best of a **bad** ▪bunch 175R36
throw ▫good money after ▪**bad** 1517L10
▫too ▪**bad** 92L30/32 1535L62
▫turn up like a ▫**bad** ▪penny 1571L51
▪**badger** *someone* into/with 92R56/52
a ▫**bag** of ▪bones 93L52
▪**bag** *something* for 93L73
▪**bag** ▫lady 93L61
▪**bag** ▫lunch 155L29
▫**bag** of ▪tricks 93L53
▪barf ▫**bag** 100L3
▪bin ▫**bag** 127L3
▪body ▫**bag** 142R57
▪brown-▫**bag** 169L52
▫brown-**bag** ▪lunch 169L56
▪clutch ▫**bag** 251L1
▪cold ▫**bag** 256R6 302R57
▪cool ▫**bag** 302R43
▪cooler ▫**bag** 256R7 302R56
diplo▪matic ▫**bag** 386R3
▪doggy ▫**bag** 409L77
▪duffel ▫**bag** 431L69
▪duffle ▫**bag** 431L69
▪dustbin ▫**bag** 433L50
▫fight *one's* ▫way out of a paper ▪**bag** 517L27
▪freezer ▫**bag** 256R7 563L54/56
▪garbage ▫**bag** 433L51 582R49
▪garment ▫**bag** 583R48 1458L11
▪grab ▫**bag** 615L44/47
▪Jiffy ▫**bag** 764L43
▪kit ▫**bag** 782L24
▫leave *someone* holding the ▪baby/▪**bag** 807L77
let the ▪cat out of the ▫**bag** 203L51
▫mixed ▪**bag** 908L59
▫plastic ▪**bag** 1093L14
▪poly ▫**bag** 1093L14
▫pull *something* out of the ▪**bag** 1144L44
▪saddle-▫**bag** 1247R82
▪sag ▫**bag** 107R44 1249L53
▪shopping ▫**bag** 199L14 1321L53/56
▪shoulder ▫**bag** 1325R72
▪sleeping ▫**bag** 1351R7
▪sponge ▫**bag** 1395R79
▫string ▪**bag** 1443L82
▪suit ▫**bag** 583R48 1458L11
▪tea ▫**bag** 1494L8
▪toilet ▫**bag** 1532R12

▪tote ▫**bag** 1540L28
▪trash ▫**bag** 433L52 1552R36
▪**baggage** al▫lowance 93R58
▪**baggage** ▫car 93R63
▪**baggage** ▫handler 93R61
▪**baggage** ▫room 93R64
▫excess ▪**baggage** 476R32
▪hand ▫**baggage** 641L13
▫**bags** under *someone's* ▪eyes 93L57
▫**bail** ▪out 94L41/43/50
re▫manded on ▪**bail** 1201L22
▫stand ▪**bail** 1410R35
▪**bait** *something* with 94L77
▫fish or cut ▪**bait** 526R19
▫rise to the ▪**bait** 1226R39
▫swallow the ▪**bait** 1473L35
▫batch-▪**bake** 104L12
▫**baked** A▪laska 94R18
▫**baked** ▪beans 94R21
▫**baked** ▪custard 338L38
▫half-▪**baked** 637R23
▪sun-▫**baked** 1459R63
▫**baker's** ▪dozen 94R41
▪**baking** ▫dish 94R27
▪**baking** ▫powder/▫soda 94R23/25 123L34 1105L52
▪**baking** ▫sheet 94R29
▪**baking** ▫tin 94R31
▪**baking** ▫tray 94R32
▪**balance** against 95L4
▫**balance** of ▪payments 94R79
▫**balance** of ▪trade 94R79
▪**balance** on 95L2/3
▫**balance** ▪out 95L7
▪**balance** ▫sheet 95L42
▫**balance** the ▪books 95L9
▫**balance** the ▪budget 95L12
▫**balance** the e▪conomy 95L13
▪bank ▫**balance** 95L42 97R41
hold the ▫**balance** of ▪power 94R73
re▫dress the ▪**balance** 94R60
▫strike a ▪**balance** 1442R26
▫swing the ▪**balance** 1477L50
the ▫**balance** of ▪power 94R71
▫throw off ▪**balance** 94R69
▫tilt the ▪**balance** 1520R33
▫tip the ▪**balance** 1526L70
▪trade ▫**balance** 1546L61
▫**balanced** ▪diet 95L23
▫well-▪**balanced** 1652L38
▫checks and ▪**balances** 221R37
▪**balancing** ▫act 95L15
as ▫**bald** as a ▪coot 95L52
▫**bald** ▪eagle 95L53
▪**bald** ▫patch 95L54
▪**bald** ▫spot 95L54
▫**bald** ▪tyre 95L55
▫**bale** ▪out 94L50 95R1
▪**balk** at 95R9
a ▫whole new/com▫pletely different ▪**ball** ▫game 95R36
▫**ball**-and-▪socket 95R40 1371L26
▫**ball** ▪bearing 95R29
▪**ball** ▫boy/▫girl 95R32
▪**ball** ▫game 95R35
▪beach ▫**ball** 107L21
▪cannon ▫**ball** 189R63
▫crystal ▪**ball** 332L84
▫curve ▪**ball** 337R72
▫foul ▪**ball** 556L4
▪golf ▫**ball** 610R9/11
▪ground ▫**ball** 626L45/82
▫masked ▪**ball** 870L35
▫play ▪**ball** 1078L39
▪punch ▫**ball** 1146L64/67
▪slime ▫**ball** 1353L45
start/set/get the ▪**ball** ▫rolling 95R24
▪tea ▫**ball** 1494L12
the **ball** is in ▪*someone's* ▫court 95R27
the ▫belle of the ▪**ball** 115R60
▫prima **balle**▪rina 1121R11
▪**ballet** ▫shoes 95R63
▫corps de ▪**ballet** 307R3
bal▫**listic** ▪missile 95R75
bal▪**loon** into 96L8
▪barrage **bal**▫**loon** 101L22
go down like a ▫lead **bal**▪**loon** 804R41
hot-▪air **bal**▫**loon** 687R27
▫prick the **bal**▪**loon** 1120R70
▫sink like a ▫lead **bal**▪**loon** 1341R42 1429R21
the **bal**▪**loon** goes ▫up 96L1
▫absentee ▪**ballot** 5L48 1100R73
▪**ballot**-▫rigging 96L14
▫put to the ▪**ballot** 96L12
▫secret ▪**ballot** 1280L77
▪**ballpark** ▫figure 96L23
▫**ballpoint** ▪pen 96L28
▫**ballroom** ▪dancing 96L34
▫**balls** ▪up 96L49/53
▫brass ▪**balls** 158R12
▪cotton ▫**balls** 310R45
▫freeze the ▫**balls** off a ▫brass ▪monkey 563L25
▪green ▫**ban** 622R10
▪test ▫**ban** 1505R16
ba▫**nana** re▪public 96R26
ba▪**nana** ▫skin 96R29
ba▫**nana** ▪split 96R33
▪Alice ▫**band** 32R16 636R39
▪**Band**-▫Aid 96R75 1076R21 1423L41
▫**band**-aid so▪lution 96R77
▫**band** to▪gether 96R65
▫big ▪**band** 124L73
▫brass ▪**band** 158L82
▪Citizens' **Band** (▫radio) 234L34
e▫lastic ▪**band** 445R27 1238R27
▫military ▪**band** 896R8
▫one-man ▪**band** 984L77
▫rubber ▪**band** 1238R26
▫steel ▪**band** 1418R31
▪sweat ▫**band** 1474R67
▪wave ▫**band** 1644R68
▪wedding ▫**band** 1648R75
▫one-armed ▪**bandit** 984L57 1355L46
▫jump/▫climb/▫get on the ▪**bandwagon** 97L21
▫**bandy** a▪bout 97L28/29
▫**bandy** ▪words 97L30
the ▫**bane** of *someone's* ▪life 97L34
▫**bang** a▪bout 97L40
▪**bang** at 97L39
▫**bang** a▪way 97L42/69
▪**bang** ▫goes *something* 97L60
▫**bang** *one's* ▫head against a brick ▪wall 653L33
▫**bang** *one's* ▪head against/on 97L65
▫**bang** the ▪drum 97L46 428R69
▫**bang** ▪up 97L77
▫big ▪**bang** ▫theory 124L76
▪gang-▫**bang** 581R71
go ▫over with a ▪**bang** 97L53
go with a ▪**bang** 97L52
▪**banish** from/to 97R12/10/11/15
▪**bank** ac▫count 9L76 97R39
▪**bank** ▫balance 95L42 97R41
▪**bank** ▫charges 97R42
▫**bank** ▪holiday 97R45
▪**bank** ▫manager 97R33
▪**bank** on 98L1/4
▪**bank** ▫rate 97R47
▪**bank** ▫statement 97R50
▫**bank** ▪up 97R78/79
▪**bank** with 97R52
▪blood ▫**bank** 137L55
▪bottle ▫**bank** 151R29
▫break the ▪**bank** 159R66
▪clearing ▫**bank** 243L22
▪cloud ▫**bank** 248R42
▪data ▫**bank** 347L71
▪fog ▫**bank** 542L24
▫laugh all the way to the ▪**bank** 800L1
▫merchant ▪**bank** 888L71
▪needle ▫**bank** 947L40
▪piggy ▫**bank** 1065R8
▪river ▫**bank** 1227R21
▪savings ▫**bank** 1257R84
▪snow ▫**bank** 1367L66
▪sperm ▫**bank** 1390L80
▫World ▪**Bank** 1683R81
▪**banker's** ▫card 97R64 224L40
▫**banker's** ▪order 97R66
▫**banner** ▪headline 98L39
▫Star-Spangled ▪**Banner** 1412R31
▫**baptism** of ▪fire 98L79
all ▫over **bar** the ▪shouting 99L29
▪**bar** ▫chart/▫graph 98R16
▪**bar** ▫code 98R19
▪**bar**-code ▫reader 820R37
▪**bar** from 99L17
▪**bar** ▫line 99L10
▫**bar** ▪mitzvah 100R20
▪cash ▫**bar** 201R27
▪coffee ▫**bar** 255L7
▪colour ▫**bar** 260L33
▪heel-▫**bar** 660L40
▪lounge ▫**bar** 843L31
▪milk ▫**bar** 896R71
▫public ▪**bar** 1142L23
▪roll ▫**bar** 1231L63
▪salad ▫**bar** 1250R1
sa▪loon ▫**bar** 1251R14
▪sandwich ▫**bar** 1254R12
▪singles ▫**bar** 1341L64
▪snack ▫**bar** 1363R19
▪space-▫**bar** 1381R64
▪tow ▫**bar** 1542R69
▪wine ▫**bar** 1668R83
▫**barbecue** ▪sauce 99R9
▫**barbed** ▪wire 99L53
▫**barber's** ▪pole 99R15
▫**bare** ▪bones 99R46
▫**bare** *one's* ▪heart/▪soul 99R59
▫**bare** in▪finitive 99R52
▫cupboard is ▪**bare** 335R41
▫lay ▪**bare** 99R43 802L81
with *one's* ▫**bare** ▪hands 99R45
▫**barely** hear *oneself* ▪think 655R77
barely put ▫one foot in front of the ▪other 545R46
▪**barf** ▫bag 100L3
▫**bargain** a▪way 100L18
▫**bargain** ▪basement 100L36
▪**bargain** for 100L21/23
▪**bargain** ▫hunter 100L40
▪**bargain** on 100L19
▪**bargain** with 100L16
▫drive a hard ▪**bargain** 425R44
▪**bargaining** ▫chip/▫counter 100L26
▪**bargaining** ▫power 100L31
co▫llective ▪**bargaining** 258L25
▫free collective ▪**bargaining** 560R60
▪plea ▫**bargaining** 1080L39
▫**barge** ▪in 100L49/50
▪**barge** into 100L47
▫**barge** ▪through 100L45
▫**barge** *one's* ▪way 100L46
▫touch *something* with a ▪**barge** pole 1540L72
▫argy-▪**bargy** 62L15
▫**barium** ▪meal 100L60
▫**barium** ▪sul▫phate 100L61
▪**bark** is ▫worse than *one's* ▪bite 100L71
▫**bark** up the wrong ▪tree 100L73
▪stringy-▫**bark** 1443R22
▪**barley** ▫sugar 100R12
▪**barley** ▫water 100R13
▪**barn** ▫dance 100R28
shut/close the **barn** ▫door after the ▪horse has bolted 411R52
▪press ▫**baron** 1118R68
▪**barrack** for 101L1
▪**barrage** bal▫loon 101L22
▫no holds ▪**barred** 675R57 957R68
a ▫**barrel** of ▪laughs/▪fun 101L40
▪**barrel** ▫organ 101L44
▪**barrel** ▫roll 101L48
▫lock stock and ▪**barrel** 835L17
▫over a ▪**barrel** 101L41
▪pork-▫**barrel** 1096R53
▪rain ▫**barrel** 1642L83
▫scrape (the bottom of) the ▪**barrel** 1271L41
▫double-▪**barrelled** ▪name 413R68/66/65
▪**barricade** *someone* into 101L70/72
▪**barrier** ▫cream 101R2
▪crash ▫**barrier** 320L68
▪crush ▫**barrier** 331L23
the ▪sound ▫**barrier** 1378R33
▪**barrow** ▫boy 101R11
be▫hind ▪**bars** 98R10
▫parallel ▪**bars** 1024R20
▫Stars and ▪**Bars** 1412R30
▪**barter** for 101R20/21
▫bas-re▪lief 103L76
▪**base** ▫camp 101R51
▪**base** ▫form 101R63
▪**base** ▫metal 101R78
▪**base** on 101R66/69
▪**base** ▫rate 101R36
▫first ▪**base** 525R31
▪power ▫**base** 1105R19
▪**baseball** ▫cap 102L22
▪**baseball** ▫jacket 102L25
▫bargain ▪**basement** 100L36
▪**bash** against 102L48
▫**bash** ▪on 102L54/74
▪Bible-▫**basher** 102L58/64 122R82 123L3
▪gay/▪queer ▫**basher** 102L56/62
▪queer ▫**bashing** 1161L50
▪union-▫**bashing** 102L63
▫**basic** ▪salary 102R12
▫back to ▪**basics** 102R21
▪pudding ▫**basin** 1143L53
▫pudding-**basin** ▪haircut 1143L54
on a ▪first-name ▫**basis** with 526L9
▪**bask** in 102R77/78
▪**basket** ▫case 103L44/46
▪bicycle ▫**basket** 123L66
▪bread ▫**basket** 159L80/81
▪clothes ▫**basket** 248R5
▫hanging ▪**basket** 643R82
▪laundry ▫**basket** 800R34
▪linen ▫**basket** 826R82
put all *one's* ▫eggs in ▫one ▪**basket** 444L83
waste▪paper ▫**basket** 1641L34
▫**bass** ▪drum 103R10
▫**bass** ▪saxophone 103R10
▫double ▪**bass** 413R70
as ▫blind as a ▪**bat** 135L66
▪fruit ▫**bat** 569R45
not ▫**bat** an ▪eyelid 104L2
▪vampire ▫**bat** 1606L29
▫**batch**-▪bake 104L12
▫**batch** ▪processing 104L14
with ▫**bated** ▪breath 104L16
▪swimming ▫**bath(s)** 1476R70
▪**bath** ▫mat 104L41 872L69
▪**bath** ▫rack 104L44
▪**bath** ▫towel 104L47
▪bed-▫**bath** 111L56
▪bubble ▫**bath** 171L45
throw out the ▫baby with the ▪**bath**-water 1516R77
▫Turkish ▪**bath** 1569L13
▪**bathe** in 104L61/82/84/R1
▪**bathe** *something* with 104L81
▪**bathing** ▫costume 104L74 1476R65
▪**bathing** ▫suit 1476R66
▪**bathing** ▫trunks 104L75 1476R75 1565L5
▪**bathroom** ▫suite 104R16
▪**bathroom** ▫tissue 1527L37
go to the ▪**bathroom** 104R14
▪**baton** ▫charge 104R45
have ▫**bats** in the ▪belfry 103R79
▫**batten** down the ▪hatches 104R62
▪**batten** on 104R66
▫**batter's** ▪box 103R73
▫**batter** ▪down 104R77
▫recharge *one's* ▪**batteries** 1184R5
▪**battering** ▫ram 105L36
as▫sault and ▪**battery** 71R54
▪storage ▫**battery** 10L76
▫cotton ▪**batting** 310R45
▪**battle** ▫cry 105L82 1637L33
▪**battle** for 105L77/78/R45
▫**battle** of ▪wits 105L80
▪**battle** with/against 105R47/L75/R45
▫**battle** with the ▪elements 105R47
▫fight a losing ▪**battle** 517L33
▫half the ▪**battle** 637L54
▫join ▪**battle** 767R43
▫pitched ▪**battle** 1071R12
▫running ▪**battle** 1241R33
▪**bawl** at 106L13
▫**bay** for ▪blood 106L31
▫**bay** ▪window 106L24
▫hold/▫keep at ▪**bay** 106L36
▪loading ▫**bay** 833R5
BB▫**C** Pronunci▪ation 106L73
be ▪dying to 381R66
▫**be** on the re▪ceiving end of 1183R23
▫**be**-all and ▪end-all 106R35/36
▪**beach** ▫ball 107L21
▪**beach** ▫buggy 107L22
▪**beach** ▫bum 107L24
▫**beach** re▪sort 107L26
Be▫lisha ▪**beacon** 115R19
▪**beam** at 107R20
▪**beam** with 107R19
▫broad in the ▪**beam** 167R18
on *one's* ▪**beam**-▫ends 107R16
▪**bean** ▫counter 107R31
▪**bean** ▫curd 107R30 1531R29
▪**bean** ▫feast 107R38
▫black-eyed ▪**bean** 131R27
▫broad ▪**bean** 167R20
▪butter ▫**bean** 180L44 823L78
▪coffee ▫**bean** 254R72
▫French ▪**bean** 563R1
▪jelly ▫**bean** 761R63
▪kidney ▫**bean** 779R37
▪lima ▫**bean** 823L78
▪mung ▫**bean** 930L4
▫not worth a ▪**bean** 1687L64
▫runner ▪**bean** 1243R24
▪soya ▫**bean** 1381R10
▫string ▪**bean** 1443R2
▪**beanbag** ▫chair 107R43
▫baked ▪**beans** 94R21
full of ▪**beans** 572L21
▫green ▪**beans** 622L71
▫spill the ▪**beans** 1391R15
▫**bear** a ▪grudge/any ill ▪feeling against/towards 108L37
▫**bear** ▪down 108R9
▫**bear** false ▪witness 108L56
▫**bear** ▫hug 107R59
▫**bear** *someone* ill-▪will 703R30
▪**bear** ▫market 108R1
▪**bear** ▫on 108R13/23
▫**bear** ▪out 108R21
▫**bear** ▪testimony/▪witness 108L51
▫**bear** ▪up 108R25
▪**bear** with 108R30
▫**bear** ▪witness 1674L77
▫grin and ▪**bear** it 624L66
like a ▫**bear** with a sore ▪head 107R57
▫not **bear** ▪thinking about 108L22
▫polar ▪**bear** 1091L48
▫**beard** the ▫lion in *his/her* ▪den 108R49
▪standard-▫**bearer** 1411R60
▪stretcher-▫**bearer** 1440L39
▫ball ▪**bearing** 95R29
▫Teddy **Bears'** ▪picnic 1495R75
▫**beast** of ▪burden 108R72
the ▪nature of the ▫**beast** 943R23
▫**beat** a ▫path to *someone's* ▪door 109L25
▫**beat** a (hasty) re▪treat 109L42
▫**beat** about/around the ▪bush 109L29
▪**beat** *someone* at 109L67
▫**beat** *someone* at *their* ▫own ▪game 109L84
▫**beat** ▪back 109L11
▫**beat** *someone's* ▪brains ▫out 109L33/35
▫**beat** *one's* ▪breast/▪chest 109L38
▪**beat** by 109L67
▫**beat** ▪down 109L11/7/8
▫**beat** ▪down on 109L6
▪**beat** gener▫ation 109R48
▫**beat** ▫hands ▪down 109L71 641L9
▫**beat** *one's* ▫head against a brick ▪wall 653L33
▫**beat** *someone* ▪hollow 109R5
▫**beat** ▪off 109L12
▫**beat** ▪out 109L14/73/R27
beat ▫swords into ▪ploughshares 1479R9
▫**beat** the ▪drum 97L46 428R69
▫**beat** the ▪pants off 109R4
▫**beat** the ▪rap 109R6 1173L63
▫**beat** the ▪stuffing out of 1448L47
▫**beat** the ▪tar out of 1491L65
▫**beat** *a* ▪*path* through 109L24
▫dead ▪**beat** 109R47 351L10
▫heart skips/misses a ▪**beat** 656L74
▪**beat-up** 109L16/R67
▫off the **beaten** ▪path/▪track 109L50
▪weather-▫**beaten** 1648L36
▪world-▫**beater** 1683R83 1684L72
▫take some ▪**beating** 109R18
▫that **beats** ▪everything 109R7
▫**beau** ▪monde 109R73
the ▫**beautiful** ▪people 110L48/50
▫think **beautiful** ▪thoughts 1513L58
▪**beauty** ▫contest/▫pageant 110L19
▪**beauty** ▫parlour/▫salon 110L22
▪**beauty** ▫queen 110L21
▪**beauty** ▫shop 110L23
▪**beauty** ▫sleep 110L25
▪**beauty** ▫spot 110L28/29
▫**beaver** a▪way 110L82/83
▪**Beaver** ▫Scout 110L78
▫eager ▪**beaver** 434R56
▫**beckon** *someone* ▪over 110R32
▪**beckon** to 110R31/33/34
be▪**come** of *someone* 110R57
a ▫**bed** of ▪nails 111L48
a ▫**bed** of ▪roses 111L80 1234R66
▫**bed** and ▪board 111L49 141R17
▫**bed** and ▪breakfast 111L50
▪**bed**-▫bath 111L56
▫**bed** ▪down 111L71/69
▪**bed** ▫linen 111L57 826R78
▫**bed** ▪out 111L82
▫**bed**-▪sitting room 111L59/R74
▪**bed**-▫wetting 111L60
▪bunk ▫**bed** 176L25
▪camp ▫**bed** 187L80
▫double ▪**bed** 413R72
get out of ▫**bed** (on) the ▫wrong ▪side 111L43
get up on the ▫wrong side of the ▪**bed** 111L43
go to ▪**bed** with 111L41
▫make the ▪**bed** 111L45
▪oyster ▫**bed** 1013R51
▫put to ▪**bed** 110R73 1152R44
▪river-▫**bed** 1227R24
▫single ▪**bed** 1341L10
▪sofa ▫**bed** 1371L84
▪tanning ▫**bed** 1460L29
▪trundle ▫**bed** 1564R26
▫twin ▪**bed** 1573L59
▪water ▫**bed** 1642L72
▫twin-**bedded** ▪room 1573L60
▪**bedding** ▫plant 111R1
be▪**deck** with 111R15
be▪**devil** by 111R19
between ▫you me and the ▪**bedpost** 111R38 121R7
▪**bedroom** com▫munity 111R61
▪master ▫**bedroom** 111R57 871R20
▫**bedside** ▪manner 111R68
▫**bedside** ▪table 111R71
a ▫busy ▪**bee** 112L52
as ▫busy as a ▪**bee** 112L52
▪**bee**-▫keeping 112L62/60
have a ▪**bee** in *one's* ▫bonnet 112L54
▪spelling ▫**bee** 1389R25
▪**beef** about 112R48/49
▫**beef** ▪up 112R41/45
▫corned ▪**beef** 306L58
▫ground ▪**beef** 626R36 898L40
make a ▪**beeline** for 112R68
▪**beep** at 112R79
▪**beer** ▫belly/▫gut 113L7
▪**beer** ▫garden 113L9
▪**beer** ▫mat 113L10
▫ginger ▪**beer** 595R18
▪guest ▫**beer** 630L64
▪root ▫**beer** 1233R54
▪small ▫**beer** 1358L19
the ▫**bees'** ▪knees 112L57
the ▫birds and the ▪**bees** 128L49
▪sugar ▫**beet** 1457L14
▫**beetle** a▪way 113L29
▫**beetle**-▪browed 113L30
▫Colorado po▫tato ▪**beetle** 259L67
▫deathwatch ▪**beetle** 352R68
po▪tato ▫**beetle** 1102R83
go/turn as ▫red as a ▪**beetroot** 113L37/38
go/turn ▪**beetroot** (▫red) 113L37

ac▫cessory **before** the ▪fact 8L17/18
as ▫never **be▪fore** 951R23
be▫fore ▪last 798L40
be▫fore (very/▫too) ▪long 838L71
be▫fore much ▪longer 838L72
be▫fore ▪tax/▫after ▪tax 1493L78
be▫fore the ▪Flood 536L46
before ▪then 1509L57
before ▪this 1514L13
be▫fore *one's* ▪time 113L54 1523L52 1524L23
be▫fore *one's* very ▪eyes 488L57
be▫fore you can/could say Jack ▪Robinson 757R80 1259L69
▫best **be▪fore** date 118R76
cast ▫pearls **before** ▪swine 202L41
▪come **before** 265R30
▫ever **be▫fore** 473L15
▫leg **before** ▪wicket 809L17
▫not **before** ▪time 1523L50
put the ▫cart **before** the ▪horse 200L36
the ▫calm **before** the ▪storm 186R20
the ▫lull **before** the ▪storm 847L16
▪**beg** for 113R13/14
▫**beg** ▪off 113R28/30
▪**beg** *something* off/from 113R17
▫**beg** *someone's* ▪pardon 1026L12/16/19/22
▫**beg** the ▪question 113R23/27
▪**beg** *someone* to 113R18
▫**beg** to ▪differ/disa▪gree 113R33
I ▫**beg** your ▪pardon 113R38
▫**beggar** be▪lief/de▪scription 113R64
▫**beggar**-my-▪neighbour 113R56
go ▪**begging** 113R31
be▪gin at 113R79
be▪gin on 113R81
be▪gin with 113R81/82
be▫ginner's ▪luck 114L16
be▪ginners' ▫slope 114L17
be▫ginning of the ▪end 114L28 455L30
the ▫fur **begins** to ▪fly 575R40
be▪guile into 114L54
▪well-**be▪haved** 1652L48
be▪haviour ▫therapy 114R1
on *one's* ▫best **be▪haviour** 114L81 118R61
be▫hind *someone's* ▪back 89R61
be▫hind ▪bars 98R10
be▫hind closed ▪doors 247L64
be▫hind the ▪scenes 1263R41
be▫hind the ▪times 1524L26
be▫hind the ▪wheel 114R41
▫power **behind** the ▪throne 1105R66
▫right **be▪hind** 1224L67
▫wet **behind** the ▪ears 1654R7
▫lo and **be▪hold** 114R62 833L53
▫all/▫other things **being** ▪equal 1512R6
ce▫lestial ▪**being** 208L16
every ▫fibre of *one's* ▪**being** 515L33
for the ▫time ▪**being** 547L23 1521R42
Su▫preme ▪**Being** 1466R48
▪well-▫**being** 1652L52
be▪labour with 115L15/16
have ▫bats in the ▪**belfry** 103R79
▫beggar **be▪lief** 113R64
▫pass (all) **be▪lief** 1031L6
to the ▫best of *one's* **be▪lief** 115L54 119L75
be▫lieve a ▪word 115L74
be▪lieve in 115L69/71
be▫lieve it or ▪not 115L75
be▫lieve *something* when *one* ▪sees it 115L84
could ▫hardly/▫could not **believe** *one's* ▪eyes/▪ears 115L77
make **be▪lieve** 115L81 856R77
not **be▫lieve** *one's* ▪luck 115L79
▫have to be ▫seen to be **be▪lieved** 1283L61
▫non-**be▪liever** 959L64
Be▫lisha ▪beacon 115R19
▪**bell**-▫bottoms 115R42
▪**bell** ▫jar 115R44
▪**bell** ▫pull/▫push 115R47/46
▪**bell**-▫ringer 115R49
▫clear/▫sound as a ▪**bell** 115R34
▪diving ▫**bell** 401L79
▫give *someone* a ▪**bell** 115R36
▫ring a ▪**bell** 1225R35
the ▫**belle** of the ▪ball 115R60
▫hear ▪warning **bells** 1638R43
▫hear ▪wedding **bells** 655R74
▫hell's ▪**bells** 661R25
▫warning/▫alarm **bells** start to ▪ring/▪sound 115R38 1638R44
▪beer ▫**belly** 113L7
▪**belly** ▫button 116L10 944L23
▪**belly**-▫dancer 116L11/10
▪**belly** ▫flop 116L12
▪**belly** ▫laugh 116L14
▫**belly** ▪out 116L27
eyes too ▫big for *one's* ▪**belly** 488R33
go/turn ▫**belly** ▪up 116L17
be▪long in 116L35/39/40
be▪long to 116L42
be▫low ▪decks 355L27
be▫low ▪par 1023R42/53
be▫low ▪stairs 1407R48
be▫low ▪strength 1437R83
be▫low the ▪belt 116L75
be▫low the ▪**belt** 116L75
▪**belt** along/down 116R15
▫**belt** and ▪braces 116R3
▫**belt** ▪out 116R20
▫**belt** ▪up 116R12/22
▪Bible ▫**Belt** 123L6
▫black ▪**belt** 131R16
▪chastity ▫**belt** 220L9
com▪muter ▫**belt** 116R1
▪cotton ▫**belt** 116R3
▪fan ▫**belt** 501L74
▪green ▫**belt** 622R29
▪life ▫**belt** 819L24/58
▪safety ▫**belt** 1248R47
▪seat ▫**belt** 1278L46
▪stockbroker ▫**belt** 116R1 1428L23
su▪spender ▫**belt** 1472L31
▫tighten *one's* ▪**belt** 1520L30
▫under *one's* ▪**belt** 116R7
▫**bend** ▪double 116R76
▫**bend** ▪down 116R61
▫**bend** ▪forward/▪over 116R62
▫**bend** over ▪backwards 91R26
▫**bend** the ▪rules 1239R61
▫drive/▫send ▪round the **bend** 117L1
▫hairpin ▪**bend** 636R83
▫round the ▪**bend** 116R80/81
▪S-▫**bend** 1245L51
▫tight ▪**bend** 1520L16
▪U-▫**bend** 1577L46
on ▫**bended** ▪knee 117L8
▪fender ▫**bender** 1108R1
▪gender-▫**bender** 586R48
▪mind-▫**bending** 899L3
▫marry **be▪neath** *oneself* 117L30 868L62
▫marry **beneath** *one's* ▪station 868L64
▫scratch **beneath** the ▪surface 1271R42
▪**benefit** ▫concert 117L70
▪**benefit** from 117L62
▫child ▪**benefit** 226L25
▪fringe ▫**benefit** 566R11
give *someone* the ▫**benefit** of the ▪doubt 117L65
▪sickness ▫**benefit** 1333L12
unem▪ployment ▫**benefit** 1587R5
be▪nevolent ▫fund 117L78
be▪nevolent so▫ciety 117L80
▪Gordon ▫**Bennett** 613L64
▫hell-▪**bent** on 661R22
be▪queath *something* to 117R35/37
be▪rate for 117R44
St ▪**Bernard** 1417L72
▫give *something* a wide ▪**berth** 1663R18
be▪seech *someone* to 118L36
be▫side the ▪point 118L48 1089R6
▪pale **beside** 1020L28
at the ▪**best** of ▫times 119L43
▫**best** be▪fore date 118R76
▫**best** ▪bet 118R78 120L13
▫**best** bib and ▪tucker 122R68
▫**best** ▪boy 118R81
▫**best** ▪card 195L32
▫**best** ▪man 118R84
▫**best** of ▪luck 119L46
▫**best** ▪seller/▪selling 119R53
▫**best** ▪wishes 119L2 1672L1/2
▫do as *you* think ▪**best** 119L14
▫do *one's* level ▪**best** 813R27
for ▫reasons **best** ▫known to *one▪self* 1181R42
▫give of *one's* ▪**best** 596R39/18
had ▪**best** 635L61
▫have the ▪**best** of 119R1/2
▫know ▪**best** 786R31/37/28
make the ▪**best** of ▫*something* 119L62
▫man's **best** ▪friend 859L49
may the ▫**best** man/person ▪win 118R64
on *one's* ▫**best** be▪haviour 114L81 118R61
put *one's* ▫**best** foot ▪forward 118R67
▫six of the ▪**best** 1344L44
▫Sunday ▪**best** 1460L80
the ▫**best** days of *someone's* ▪life 118R73
the ▫**best** of a bad ▪bunch 175R36
the ▫**best** of ▪both worlds 119L51
the ▫**best** of the ▪bunch 175R35 1062L37
the ▫**best** ▪part of 1028R55
the ▫**best** ▫thing since sliced ▪bread 118R69
to the ▫**best** of *one's* a▪bility 119L74
to the ▫**best** of *one's* ▪knowledge/be▪lief 115L54 119L75
to the ▫**best** of *my* recol▪lection 1186L12
▫turn out/be ▫all for the ▪**best** 119L70
with the ▫**best** will in the ▪world 118R74 1665R57
be▪stir *oneself* to 119R19
be▪stow on/upon 119R27/28/31
be▪strew with 119R40
▫best ▪**bet** 118R78 120L13
▫**bet** *one's* ▪boots/▫bottom ▪dollar/▪shirt/▪ass 119R82
▪**bet** on 119R61/62 120L3
▫don't ▪**bet** on it 119R78
▫I/▫I'll ▪**bet** 119R68
make a ▪**bet** with 120L5
(How ▫much) *do you* want to ▪**bet**? 119R74
▪Phi ▪**Beta** ▪Kappa 1057R34
▫**bête** ▪noire 120L30
▫woe **be▪tide** *someone* 1675L67
be▪tray *someone* to 120L46
be▫tray *someone's* ▪trust 120L52
be▪troth to 120L72
▫hedge *one's* ▪**bets** 659R58
a▫gainst *one's* **better** ▪judgment 24R4
▫**better** ▪half 120R34
▫**better** luck ▪next time 120R18
▫**better** ▪nature 120R36
▫**better** ▪still 120R67
▫**better** than ▪nothing 120R12
▫change for the ▪**better** 215L4
de▫serve ▪**better** 372L2
for ▫**better** or (for) ▪worse 121L10
▫get ▪**better** 120R22/24
▫get the ▪**better** of 121L18/19
go ▫one ▪**better** 120R26
had ▪**better** 635L61
have seen ▫**better** ▪days 1283L48
move on to ▫**better** ▪things 925R12
▫so much/▫all the ▪**better** 121L9
the ▫**better** ▪part of 1028R55
the ▫bigger the ▪**better** 124L67
▫think ▪**better** of it 1513L16
▪**betting** ▫shop 120L20
between a ▫rock and a ▪hard ▫place 1229R45
between the ▫devil and the deep blue ▪sea 378L57
be▪tween ▫times 121L63
between ▫you me and the ▪bedpost/▪gatepost 111R38 121R7
be▫twixt and **be▪tween** 121R29
▪come **between** 121R26
▫fall **between** two ▪stools 497R66
▫few and far **be▪tween** 514R57
▪go-**be▫tween** 604L21
go off/away with *one's* ▫tail **between** *one's* ▪legs 1485R29
have/get/take the ▫bit **between** *one's* ▪teeth 130L27
▫hit *someone* **between** the ▪eyes 673L7
▫little/not ▫much to ▪choose **between** 229L49
▫no/▫little ▪love ▫lost **between** 843R36
▫read **between** the ▪lines 1178L83
▪torn **be▫tween** 121L82 1538R14
▪wedge **between** 1648R84 1649L5
be▫twixt and **be▪tween** 121R29
be▪ware of 121R66/67/68
be▫yond a ▪joke 122L79
beyond a ▫shadow of a ▪doubt 122R5
be▫yond (all) dis▪pute 397L73
be▫yond ▪help 122L64
be▫yond *one's* ▪ken 777L78
be▫yond *one's* ▪means 122L65 832L71 879L42
beyond ▫reasonable ▪doubt 122R1/L84 1182L1
be▫yond the ▪grave 620R64
be▫yond the ▪pale 122L82
beyond *one's* ▫wildest ▪dreams 122R9 1664R25
▫cannot see **be▪yond** *something* 122L34
▫can't see **be▫yond** the ▫end of *one's* ▪nose 1283L59
from **be▫yond** the ▪grave 122L76
is/goes **be▫yond** all ▪reason 1181R55
the ▫back of **be▪yond** 89L74
▪**bias** against 122R33/45
▫best **bib** and ▪tucker 122R68
▪**Bible**-▫basher 102L58/64 122R82 123L3
▪**Bible** ▫Belt 123L6
▪**Bible**-▫thumper 122R82 123L4
▫Holy ▪**Bible** 122R70
in the ▫**biblical** ▪sense 123L14
bi▫carbonate of ▪soda 123L32
▫sodium **bi▪carbonate** 123L33 1371L71
▪**bicker** with 123L51
▫big ▪**bickies** 124R50
▪**bicycle** ▫basket 123L66
▪**bicycle** ▫pump 123L67
▪**bid** against 123L43
▪**bid** for 123L77/78/82/R5/12
make a ▪takeover ▫**bid** 1487R60
▫**bide** *one's* ▪time 123R48
▫spina ▪**bifida** 1392L69
a **big** ▫girl's ▪blouse 596L10
▫**big** ▪band 124L73
▫**big** ▪bang ▫theory 124L76
▫**big** ▪bickies 124R50
▪**Big** ▫Board 124L79
▫**big** ▪boys 125L27
▫**Big** ▪Brother 125L33
▫**big** ▪bucks 124R50
▫**big** ▪business 125L39/44
▫**big** ▪day 125L1 349L50
▫**big** ▪deal 125L8
▫**Big** ▪Dipper 124L82/R39 1231L76
▫**big** ▪end 124R40
▫**big** ▪fish/▪gun/▪noise/▪shot 125L47
▫**big** ▪game 124R43
▪**big**-▫head 125L52
▫**big**-▪headed 125L52
▫**big**-▪hearted 124R46
▪**big** ▫league 125L57
▫**Big** ▪Mo 125L65
▫**big** ▪money 124R49
▫**big** ▪mouth 124R54
▫**big** ▪name 125L68
▫**Big** ▪Smoke 124R58
▫**big** ▪toe 124R59
▫**big** ▪top 124R60
▫**big** ▪wheel 124R62
▫**big** ▪word 124R65
▪dirty ▫**big** 388L44
eyes too ▫**big** for *one's* ▪belly/▪stomach 488R33
have ▫**big** i▪deas 125L16
▫makes it ▪**big** 125L26
▫Mister ▪**Big** 907L66
▫no **big** ▪deal 125L12
▫really/▫very ▪**big** of *someone* 124L63
the ▫**Big** ▪Apple 124L70
the ▪**big** ▫time 125L70
▫think ▪**big** 1513L26
too ▫**big** for *one's* ▪boots 125L23
▫what's the ▫**big** i▪dea? 125L20
have ▫**bigger** fish to ▪fry 526L71
the ▫**bigger** the ▪better 124L67
▪**bike** ▫rack 340R76
▪**bike** ▫shed 125R44
▪exercise ▫**bike** 478R70
▪mountain ▫**bike** 922R82
▫on yer ▪**bike** 125R43
▪racing ▫**bike** 1165R25/13
▪**bilge** ▫water 126L13
▫**bill** and ▪coo 126R19
▪**bill** as 126R9/10
▫**bill** of ▪fare 126R4
▫**bill** of ▪rights 126L78
▪**bill** ▫poster 126R5/6
▪**bill** ▫sticker 126R5
▫clean **bill** of ▪health 241R45
▫double ▪**bill** 413R73
▫fill/▫fit the ▪**bill** 126R2 527L66
▫head/▫top the ▪**bill** 126R1
▫pick up the ▪**bill** 1062R4 1483L32
sell *someone* a ▫**bill** of ▪goods 1290L18
▪tax ▫**bill** 1493L82
▪water ▫**bill** 1642L73
▫duck-**billed** ▪platypus 430R59 1077R32
▫**billet**-▪doux 126R32
▪**billow** into 126R56
like ▪**billy**-o 126R66
▪**bin** ▫bag/▫liner 127L3
▪**bin** ▫man 127L4 433L65
▪bread ▫**bin** 159R1
▪loony ▫**bin** 840R5
▪sin-▫**bin** 1340L47
▪wheelie ▫**bin** 1656R19
▪**binary** ▫number 127L11
▫**bind** to▪gether 127L17/18
▫double ▪**bind** 413R75
▫reaper-▪**binder** 1181L33
▪ring ▫**binder** 1225L27
▪**binge**-▫eating 127L69/74
▪**binge** on 127L73
▫non-▪**bio** 959L66
bio▫logical ▪clock 127R49/54
bio▫logical con▪trol 127R56
bio▫logical ▪father/▪mother/▪parent 127R58
bio▫logical ▪warfare 127R61 590L31
bio▫logical ▪washing ▫liquid/▫powder 127R64
bio▫logical ▪weapon 127R62
▫non-**bio▪logical** 959L67
mo▫lecular **bi▪ology** 912L16
bi▫polar de▪pression 128L27
▫silver ▪**birch** 1338R79
a ▫**bird's** eye ▪view 128L55
a ▫little **bird** ▪told me (so) 831L35
▪**bird**-▫brain 128L54/55
▪**bird** ▫dog 128L58 632R4
▫**bird** of ▪paradise 128L59
▫**bird** of ▪passage 128L61/R5
▫**bird** of ▪prey 128L63
▪**bird**-▫scarer 128L65
▪**bird** ▫table 128L67
▪**bird**-▫watcher 128L69/71
▪dolly ▫**bird** 410L63
▪early ▫**bird** 436R57
▫rare ▪**bird** 1173R81
▪wading ▫**bird** 1632L58
▪water ▫**bird** 1642L75
▫watch the ▪**birdie** 128R26
▫**birds** of a ▪feather 128R9
kill ▫two **birds** with one ▪stone 779R75
the ▫**birds** and the ▪bees 128L49
▪**birth** cer▫tificate 128R65
▪**birth** con▫trol 128R67
▪**birth** control ▫pill 128R69
▪**birth** ▫defect 128R71
▪**birth** ▫mother/▫parent 128R73
▪**birth** ▫rate 128R75
▫give ▪**birth** 128R60
▫multiple ▪**birth** 929L56
▫strangle at ▪**birth** 1434R36
▪**Birthday** ▫honours 683L76
wearing/in *one's* ▪**birthday** ▫suit 128R83
▪dog ▫**biscuit** 408R65
▪ginger ▫**biscuit** 595R22
▫wafer ▪**biscuit** 1632R20
▪water ▫**biscuit** 1642L77
a ▫**bit** ▪much 927L51/53
a ▫**bit** of a ▪lad 791R80
a ▫**bit** of all ▪right 35L42 130L13
▫**bit** by ▪bit 130L4
▫**bit** of ▪fluff/▪stuff/▪skirt 130L14
▫**bit** on the ▪side 130L16
▪**bit** ▫part 130L22
▫brace and ▪**bit** 156L63
▫chafe/▫champ at the ▪**bit** 130L25
have/get/take the ▫**bit** between *one's* ▪teeth 130L27
not take a ▫blind **bit** of ▪notice 135L69
the ▫biter is ▪**bit** 130R47
the ▫whole ▪**bit** 1662L13
▪two-▫**bit** 1576L23
▪**bitch** about 130L45
▫payback's a ▪**bitch** 1039L6
▫son of a ▪**bitch** 1375R33/34
a/an▫other/a ▫double/a ▫second **bite** of the ▪cherry 130R40
▪bark is ▫worse than *one's* ▪**bite** 100L71
▫**bite** ▪back 130R5
▪**bite** into 130L81/82
▫**bite** ▪off 130L63
▫**bite** off ▫more than *one* can ▪chew/▪cope with/▪manage 130R7
▪**bite**-▫sized 130R44
▫**bite** the ▪bullet 130R15
▫**bite** the ▪dust 130R19
▫**bite** the hand that ▪feeds 130R13
▫**bite** *one's* ▪tongue 130R24
have a ▫**bite** to ▪eat 130R39
▫put the ▪**bite** on 1154L36
the ▫**biter** is ▪bit 130R47
▪nail-▫**biting** 935R84 936L64
▫**bits** and ▪bobs 130L21
▫**bits** and ▪pieces 130L20
▫thrilled to ▪**bits** 1515R59
▫itsy-▪**bitsy** 757L33
▫hard-▪**bitten** 647L10
▫**bitter** ▪chocolate 130R61 1074R22
▫**bitter** ▪end 131L11
▫**bitter** ▪fruit 130R65
▫**bitter** ▪lemon 130R63
▫**bitter** ▪medicine 130R68
▫**bitter** ▪pill (to ▫swallow) 130R67
to the ▫**bitter** ▪end 131L13
▫**bittersweet** ▪chocolate 130R61 131L34
as ▫**black** as ▪thunder 131R63
▫**black** ▪Africa 132L31
▫**black** and ▪blue 131L84
▫**black** and ▪white 131R4/14
▫**black** ▪belt 131R16
▫**black** ▪box 131R19
▫**black** ▪coffee 131R21 254R69
▫**black** ▪comedy 131R67
▪**Black** ▫Country 131R22
▫**Black** ▪Death 131R70
▫**black** e▪conomy 131R72
▫**black** ▪eye 131R24
▫**black**-eyed ▪bean 131R27
▫**black**-eyed ▪pea 131R27
▫**black** ▪hole 131R28
▫**black** ▪humour 131R74
▫**black** ▪ice 131R36
▫**black** ▪look 131R75
▫**black** ▪magic 131R76
▫**Black** Ma▪ria 131R39
▫**black** ▪mark 131R78
▫**black** ▪market 131R81
▫**black** market▪eer 131R84
▫**Black** ▪Mass 132L1
▫**black** ▪mood 132L2

▫black ▪out 132R29/38
▫black ▪pepper 131R40
▫black ▪pudding 131R41
▫black ▪sheep 132L5
▪black ▫spot 132L10
▫black ▪tie 131R44
▫black ▪treacle 1553R30
▫black ▪widow 132L14
▫blue-▪black 139R70
▫coal ▪black 251R15
▫jet-▪black 763L23
not as ▫black as ▪painted 131R66
▫paint a (very) ▫black ▪picture 131R64
▫pitch-▪black 1071L81
▫see things in black and ▪white 131R10
the ▫Black Hole of Cal▪cutta 131R33
▫blackboard ▪jungle 132L52
▪gall ▫bladder 580L81
▪shoulder ▫blade 1325R74
▪blame for 132R65/71
▪blame *something* on 132R67
▫carte ▪blanche 200L53
at ▫point-blank ▪range 1090L36
▫blank ▪cheque 133L82
▫blank ▪out 133R16
▫blank ▪verse 133L84
▫draw a ▪blank 420L76
▫point-▪blank 1090L33/38
▪blanket ▫bombing 133R37
▪fire ▫blanket 523L47
se▪curity ▫blanket 1281R74 1282L57
▫wet ▪blanket 1654R9
▪blare across 133R41
▫blare ▪out 133R42
▫blast a▪way 133R69
▫blast from the ▪past 133R83
▪blast ▫furnace 134L1
▫blast ▪off 133R74 134L3
▪blast with 133R65
▪ghetto ▫blaster 594L15
▫blather ▪on 134L31/32
▫blaze a ▪trail 134L59
▫blaze ▪down 134L38
▪blaze with 134L40/42
▪trail ▫blazer 1548L58
go to ▪blazes 134L70
with ▪guns ▫blazing 632L83
▫bleed *someone* ▪dry/▪white 134R19 1403R69
▫bleeding ▪heart 134R24
▫heart ▪bleeds for 656L70/73
▪blench at 134R64/66
▪blend into 134R72
▪blend with 134R70/71
▫bless *your* ▪heart 135L11
▫bless my ▪soul 135L10
▫God ▪bless 608R77
▫Blessed ▪Virgin 135L21
the ▫blessed e▪vent 645R27
▫well I'm ▪blessed 135L10
▫blessing in dis▪guise 135L33
▫mixed ▪blessing 908L63
▫count *one's* ▪blessings 312L4
▫cordon ▪bleu 305R18
▪planning ▫blight 1075L84
po▪tato ▫blight 135L41
▫Colonel ▪Blimp 258R72
as ▫blind as a ▪bat 135L66
▫blind ▪alley 135L71
▫blind ▪date 135L74
▫blind ▪drunk 135R40 429R1
▫blind man's ▪buff 135L79
▪blind ▫side 135L81
▪blind ▫spot 135L83
▪blind to 135L62/R10
▫blind with ▪science 135R12
▪colour ▫blind 259R45
▫double-▪blind 413R79
▫eff and ▪blind 443L30
not take a ▫blind bit of ▪notice 135L69
▪roller ▫blind 1231L73
▪snow-▫blind 1367L70
▫swear ▪blind 1474R26
the ▫blind leading the ▪blind 135R16
▫turn a blind ▪eye 1569R31
ve▫netian ▪blind 1613L18
▫vertical ▪blind 1615R54
▪night ▫blindness 955L30
▪snow ▫blindness 1367L67
a ▫blink of an ▪eye 135R64
▪blink at 135R60
▫blink *one's* ▪tears back 135R58
▫blithering ▪idiot 136L41
▪blitz on 136L48/56
en ▪bloc 453R17
a ▫chip off the old ▪block 227R16
▫block and ▪tackle 136R26
▫block ▪capitals 136R22
▫block ▪in 136R57/65
▫block ▪letters 136R22
▫block ▪off 136R54
▫block ▪out 136R60
▫block ▪vote 136R33
▪brake ▫block 157R36
▫chock-a-▪block 228L82
▪cinder ▫block 232L41
▪ice ▫block 700L3
▫mental ▪block 887L58
▪office ▫block 977R17
▪stumbling ▫block 1448R17
▪tower ▫block 1543L78
▫writer's ▪block 1692L9
▫Joe ▪Bloggs 766R42
▫ash ▪blond(e) 67R43
per▫oxide ▪blonde 1051L77
▫platinum ▪blonde 1077R9
▫strawberry ▪blonde 1435R51/54
▫bad ▪blood 92L43
▫bay for ▪blood 106L31
▫blood and ▪guts 137L49
▪blood ▫bank 137L55
▫blood ▪brother 137R38
▪blood ▫count 137L57
▪blood ▫donor 137L58
▪blood ▫group 137L60
▪blood ▫lust 137L63
▪blood ▫money 137L65/67
▪blood ▫plasma 1076L67
▪blood ▫poisoning 137L70
▪blood ▫pressure 137L74
▫blood-▪red 137L78
▪blood re▫lation 137R41
▪blood ▫sport 137L79
▪blood ▫test 137L82
▪blood ▫ties 137R42
▪blood trans▫fusion 137L84 1550R25
▪blood ▫type 137L61
▪blood *is* ▫up 137L52
▪blood ▫vessel 137R3
▫burst a ▪blood ▫vessel 137R6/8
▫curdle *one's* ▪blood 336L25
▫flesh and ▪blood 533L59/61
get ▫blood out of a ▪stone 137L54
in ▫cold ▪blood 256R57
▫make *someone's* ▪blood ▫boil 137L42
▫make *someone's* ▪blood ▫curdle 336L25
make *someone's* ▫blood run ▪cold 137L48 1242L6
▫new ▪blood 952L34
▫own flesh and ▪blood 1013L9
▫red ▪blood ▫cell 1188R69
▫running with ▪blood 1242L4
▫smell ▪blood 1360L60
▫spill ▪blood 1391R17
▫spit ▪blood 1393R44
▫stirs *someone's* ▪blood 1427L10
▫sweat ▪blood 1474R43
▫white ▪blood ▫cell 1660R1
▫young ▪blood 1698L64
▫blue-▪blooded 139R71
▫cold-▪blooded 256R10/61
▫full-▪blooded 572L80/81
▫hot-▪blooded 687R33 688L30
▫red-▪blooded 1188R71
▫warm-▪blooded 1638L28
▫bloody ▪hell 138L15
▫bloody ▪mary 137R12
▫bloody-▪minded 138L23/19
▫scream bloody ▪murder 930L42
▫come into ▪bloom 138L47
the ▫bloom of ▪youth 138L50
▫late ▪bloomer 799L12
▪blossom into 138R2/4
▫blot *one's* ▪copybook 138R15/13
▫blot *one's* ▪lips 138R26
▫blot on the ▪landscape 138R16
▫blot ▪out 138R19/21
▫blot ▪up 138R27
▪blotting ▫paper 138R28
a big/great ▫girl's ▪blouse 596L10
▫blow a ▪gasket 139L40
▫blow a ▪kiss 138R67 781R76
▫blow *someone* a▪way 138R62/65/53 139L79
▫blow-by-▪blow 139L75
▫blow *one's* ▪chance 139L51
▫blow *one's* ▪cool 139L37
▫blow *someone's* ▪cover 139L39
▫blow *something* ▪down 138R54
▪blow-▫dry 139L12
▫blow ▫hot and ▪cold 138R74/77
▪blow it 139L51
▪blow ▫job 139L14 511R32
▫blow *one's* ▪lid/▪top/▪stack 139L42
▫blow *someone's* ▪mind 139L54
▫blow ▪off 138R55/56 139L31
▫blow off ▪steam 138R80
▪blow on 138R55/73
▫blow ▪out 139L2/4/6
▫blow ▪over 139L7/71
▫blow *one's* own ▪trumpet/▪horn 138R81
▫blow ▪smoke 138R58 139L57
blow the ▪cobwebs a▫way 138R69
▫blow the ex▪pense 139L59
▫blow the ▪gaff 138R72
▫blow the ▪lid off 138R78 817R47
▫blow the ▪whistle 138R83
▫blow ▪up 139L8/9/11/31
▪body ▫blow 142R59
▫cushion the ▪blow 338L3
▫Joe ▪Blow 766R43
▫strike a ▪blow against/at/for 1441R1/4
I'm ▪blowed if I'm ▫going to 139L65
well ▫I'll be ▪blowed 139L63
▪glass-▫blower 598R10
▪whistle-▫blower 1660L50
▪mind-▫blowing 898R83
which way the ▪wind is ▫blowing 1645R26
▫full-▪blown 572L83
come ▫close to ▪blows 139L70 247R67
which way the ▪wind ▫blows 1645R26
▪Blu-▫Tack 141L18
a ▫bolt from/out of the ▪blue 145L52
between the ▫devil and the deep blue ▪sea 378L57
▫black and ▪blue 131L84
▪blue ▫baby 139R68
▫blue-▪black 139R70
▫blue-▪blooded 139R71
▫blue ▪cheese 139R73
▫blue ▪chip 139R75
▫blue ▪collar 139R79
▫blue-eyed ▪boy 139R81
▫blue-eyed ▪soul 139R84
▫blue-green ▪algae 140L1
▪blue ▫jeans 140L2 761L66
▪blue ▫law 140L4
▪blue ▫pencil 140L9
▫blue ▪riband 140L10
▫blue ▪ribbon 140L11/15
▪blue ▫tit 140L16
▫boys in ▪blue 155R70
▫ice-▪blue 698R66
in a ▫blue ▪funk 139R65
▫once in a blue ▪moon 139R62
▫peacock ▪blue 1040L64
▫royal ▪blue 1238L3
▫scream/▫shout blue ▪murder 139R62 930L42
▫sky-▪blue 1348L5
▫talk a ▫blue ▪streak 1488R2
▫true-▪blue 1563R56
until *someone is* ▫blue in the ▪face 139R56
▫rhythm and ▪blues 1220L84
▪bluff *one's* ▪way 140R2
▫call *someone's* ▪bluff 185R81
▫double ▪bluff 413R84
▫blunder a▪round 140R21
▪blunder into/towards 140R23
▫put ▪bluntly 1153R44
to ▫put it ▪bluntly 1153R43
▫blurt ▪out 140R74
▫spare *someone's* ▪blushes 1383L40
▪peep-▫bo 1042R9/53
▫feather ▪boa 508R82
▫wild ▪boar 1664L57
a▫cross the ▪board 12R54/58
back to the ▪drawing ▫board 89L11
▫bed and ▪board 111L49 141R17
▪Big ▫Board 124L79
▫board and ▪lodging 141R17 836L42
▪board ▫game 141L51
▫board of edu▪cation 141L80
▫board ▪out 141R13
▪board ▫shorts 141L61 1476R75
▪board with 141R7
▫bring on ▪board 141R47
▪bulletin ▫board 174R18/20 964R31
▪diving ▫board 401L82
▪draining ▫board 418R55
▪drawing ▫board 419R66
▫full ▪board 572L84
▫go by the ▪board 141L59
▫half ▪board 637R27
▪ironing ▫board 752R57
▪notice ▫board 964R30
▪ouija ▫board 999L59
▫room and ▪board 141R18 1233L71
▪sandwich ▫board 1254R14
▪skirting ▫board 1347L82
▪sounding ▫board 1378R82
▫sweep the ▪board 1475R6
▫take/▫bring on ▪board 141R48/49/50/51/45
▪boarding ▫card 141R53
▪boarding ▫fees 141R28
▪boarding ▫house 141R33
▪boarding ▫kennels 141R32
▪boarding ▫pass 141R54
▪boarding ▫school 141R27
▫tread the ▪boards 1553R59
▪boast of/about 141R72/71
▪boat ▫hook 142L12
▪boat ▫people 142L14
▪boat ▫train 142L16
ca▪nal ▫boat 188R29
▪flying ▫boat 540R4
▪gravy ▫boat 621L53
in the ▫same ▪boat 1253L36
▫miss the ▪boat 906L16
▪narrow ▫boat 188R29 938L60
▫push the ▪boat out 1151L67
▪river ▫boat 1227R25
▫rock the ▪boat 1230L5
▪rowing-▫boat 1237R60
▪sailing ▫boat 1249R51
▪U-▫boat 1577L60
▫straw ▪boater 1435R2
▫burn *one's* ▪boats 177L77
▫bob a ▪curtsy to 142L50
▫bob ▪up 142L46
▫bob's your ▪uncle 142L62
not ▫short of a ▪bob or two 1324L40
▪bobble ▫hat 142L72
▪bobby ▫pin 142L81 636R64
▫bits and ▪bobs 130L21
▪bodice-▫ripper 142R31
▫fitted ▪bodice 142R30
▫able-▪bodied 3L8/12
▫full-▪bodied 573L61
▫wide-▪bodied 1663R24
▫grievous bodily ▪harm 623R77
▫astral ▪body 74R61
▪body ▫armour 63L65
▪body ▫bag 142R57
▪body ▫blow 142R59
▪body ▫builder 142R64
▪body-building 142R63
▪body ▫clock 142R66
▪body ▫language 142R67
▪body ▫odour 142R72
▫body ▪politic 143L76
▪body ▫snatcher 142R74
▪body ▫stocking 142R77
▫governing ▪body 614R11
▫heavenly ▪body 658R51
keep ▫body and ▪soul to▫gether 142R54
over ▫*my* dead ▪body 350R33
▫bog ▪down 143R62/55
▫bog ▪Irish 143R47
▫bog ▪off 143R70
▫bog ▪standard 144L6
▪peat ▫bog 1041L8
▪bogey ▫man 143R76
▪boggle at 144L1/3
▪mind-▫boggling 899L2
▫boil a▪way 144L35
▫boil ▪down 144L36/37/40/44
▫boil ▪over 144L53/48/50
▫boil ▪up 144L57/54
▫can't boil an ▪egg 144L60
▫make *someone's* ▪blood ▫boil 137L42
▫boiled ▪sweet 144L72
▫hard-▪boiled 646L41 647L15
▪boiler ▫suit 144R9
▪boiling ▫point 144L79
reach ▪boiling ▫point 144L82
if I may be/▫make so ▪bold (as to) 144R38
▫bollix ▪up 144R66
▫bollocks ▪up 144R66
spa▫ghetti bolo▪gnese 1382R32
a ▫bolt from/out of the ▪blue 145L52
▪bolt-▫hole 145L61
▪bolt onto/to 145L47/48/56
▫bolt ▪upright 1599R70
▫dead ▪bolt 350R34 919R42
make a ▪bolt for 145L60
▫shoot *one's* ▪bolt 1319R35
shut/close the stable/barn ▫door after the ▪horse has bolted 411R52
▫nuts and ▪bolts 968R60
▪atom ▫bomb 76R16
a▫tomic ▪bomb 76R25
▪bomb dis▫posal ▫unit 145R1
▫bomb ▪out 145R11
▪bomb ▫scare 145R4
▪bomb ▫squad 145R1
▪car ▫bomb 193R18
▪carpet ▫bomb 198L66
▪cluster ▫bomb 250R74
▪dive-▫bomb 401L64/65/67
fragment▪ation ▫bomb 558L23
go a ▪bomb 145L83
go like a ▪bomb 145L82/83
▪H-▫bomb 653L4 696R67
▪hydrogen ▫bomb 696R67
▪letter ▫bomb 813L37
▪neutron ▫bomb 951L77
▪parcel ▫bomb 1025R50
▪petrol ▫bomb 1056L43/40
▪smart ▫bomb 1358R46
▪smoke ▫bomb 1361L75
▪stink ▫bomb 1426L67
▪time ▫bomb 1522R19/21
bom▪bard with 145R33/35
▪bomber ▫jacket 145R21
▪Stealth ▫bomber 1418L33
▪blanket ▫bombing 133R37
satur▪ation ▫bombing 1256R79
▫bon ▪mot 146R35
▫bon vi▪vant 146R60
▫bon vi▪veur 146R61
▫bon vo▪yage 146R64
▫bona ▪fide 145R67
▫bona ▪fides 145R70
▪bond to 146L9
▪premium ▫bond 1114L82
▪Treasury ▫bond 1554L51
one's ▫word is *one's* ▪bond 1679L41
▫male ▪bonding 857R1
▫skin and ▪bone(s) 1346R35
a ▪bone to ▫pick with 146L54
▫bone ▪china 146L59
▫bone ▪dry 146L61 429R47
▫bone ▪idle 146L64
▪bone ▫marrow 146L64 868L32/36
▪bone ▫meal 146L65
▫bone of con▪tention 146L51
▫bone ▪up 146L78/80
▫chill to the ▪bone 226R15
▫close to the ▪bone 247R68
▪collar ▫bone 257R12
▪funny ▫bone 575L57
▪jaw ▫bone 760R46
▪marrow ▫bone 868L38
▫pare (▫down) to the ▪bone 1026L43
rag and ▪bone ▫man 1168R1
▫T-bone (▪steak) 1483L7
▫work *one's* fingers to the ▪bone 1679R43
▫raw-▪boned 1176R71
a ▫bag of ▪bones 93L52
▫bare ▪bones 99R46
▫feel it in *one's* ▪bones 510L78
▫make no ▪bones about 146L57
▪bonfire ▫night 146R10
have a ▪bee in *one's* ▫bonnet 112L54
▫no-▪claims ▫bonus 957L49
▪boo-▫boo 147L5
▫boo ▪off 146R73
▫never say ▪boo 146R75
not say ▫boo (to a ▪goose) 1259R61
▫peek-a-▪boo 1042R8
▪booby ▫prize 147L9
▪booby ▫trap 147L11/13/17/19
▫turn-up for the ▪book(s) 1571L53
ad▪dress ▫book 15R35
▪book ▫club 147L47
▪book for 147L72/R15
▫book ▪in 147L81/83
▪book ▫token 147L50
▫book ▪up 147L80
▫bring to ▪book 166L39
▪check ▫book 224L31
▫check book ▪journalism 224L35
▪cheque ▫book 224L31
▫cheque book ▪journalism 224L34
▫closed ▪book 247L68
▪coffee-table ▫book 255L11
▪comic ▫book 267R21
▪cookery ▫book 302R9
▫double-▪book 414L5
every ▫trick in the ▪book 1557L31
▪guest ▫book 630L67
▪log ▫book 836R48
▫nose in a ▪book 962L40
▫on/▫reach the ▪statute ▫book 1416R48
▫open ▪book 988L47
▪order ▫book 993R82
▪phone ▫book 1058R2 1496R66
▪picture ▫book 1063R62
▪reference ▫book 1191L6
regis▪tration ▫book 836R48
▪rule ▫book 1239R70
take a ▫leaf from/out of *someone's* ▪book 805L47
▫talking ▪book 1488R30
the ▫good ▪book 612L5
▫throw the ▪book at 1516R82
▪visitors' ▫book 1627L68
▪booking ▫clerk 147R6
▪booking ▫office 147R8
▫balance the ▪books 95L9
▫cook the ▪books 302L61
▫square the ▪books 1402L68
▪baby ▫boom 88R19/14
▪boom ▫box 148L9 594L16
▫boom ▪in 147R80
▪boom ▫town 148L3
▫sonic ▪boom 1376L7
▪boomerang on 148L27
▪booster ▫seat 148L59
a ▫boot up the back▪side 91L13
▪boot up 148R8
▫car-▪boot ▫sale 193R19
▫get/*be* ▫given the ▪boot 148L78
▫hobnailed ▪boot 674R44
▫put the ▪boot in 148L82
the ▫boot is on the other ▪foot 148L71 545L54
▪phone ▫booth 1058R3/7
▪polling ▫booth 1092R38
▪telephone ▫booth 1058R4
▪ankle ▫boots 46L81
▫bet *one's* ▪boots 119R82
▪bossy ▫boots 150L83
▪bovver ▫boots 153R76
▪desert ▫boots 371R68
▫heart in *one's* ▪boots 656R63
▪hiking ▫boots 669R83
too ▫big for *one's* ▪boots 125L23
▫tough as old ▪boots 1541R5/L84

▫pull/▫haul *oneself* ▫up by *one's* ▪bootstraps 148R34
▪booze ▫bus 148R51
▪booze-up 148R48
▪border on 149L7
her▫baceous ▪border 663R25
▪bore into 149L68
▫bore the ▪ass off *someone* 71L57
▫bore ▪through 149L65
au▫rora bore▪alis 80L36/37
▫bored ▪rigid 149L49
▫bored ▪stiff 149L48
▫bored to ▪death 149L48
▫bored to ▪tears 149L48
as (▫if) to the ▫manner ▪born 861R56
▫born-again ▪Christian 149R25
▫born and ▪bred 149R17
▫born with a silver ▪spoon in *one's* ▫mouth 149R18
▫curse the ▫day *one* was ▪born 337L52
▫first-born (▪child) 525R36
▫not born ▪yesterday 149R20 1696R40
wish *someone* had ▫never been ▪born 149R22
▫borne ▪in on/upon 149R45
▪borrow from/off 149R56/61/56
live/exist on ▫borrowed ▪time 149R61
▫bosom ▪friend/▪buddy/▪pal 150L63
▫boss a▪round/a▪bout 150L79
▫boss-▪eyed 150R54
▪bossy ▫boots 150L83
bo▫tanic(al) ▪garden 150R61
▪botch it 150R72
▪bother about 151L76
▫bother ▪doing/to ▪do 151L45
▫cannot be ▪bothered 151L55
▫hot and ▪bothered 151R3 687R12
▫baby's ▪bottle 151R21
▪bottle ▫bank 151R29
▪bottle-▫feed 151R26/28
▫bottle ▪out 151R58
▪bottle ▫top 151R32
▫bottle ▪up 151R42
de▪posit ▫bottle 368R47
▫hit the ▪bottle 151R51 673L17
hot-▪water ▫bottle 687R67
▫non-returnable ▪bottle 959R23
▪squeeze ▫bottle 1403R84
▫take to the ▪bottle 151R53
▪water ▫bottle 1642L78
▫bottled ▪water 151R39
▫bet *one's* ▫bottom ▪dollar 119R82
▫bottom ▪drawer 152L67
▫bottom ▪line 152L70/73
▫bottom ▪out 152L83
▫bottom rung of the ▪ladder 1243R15
▫false ▪bottom 499R70
from the ▫bottom of *one's* ▪heart 152L63
from ▫top to ▪bottom 1536R76/77
get to the ▪bottom of 152L58
▫knock the ▪bottom out of 785L18
▫rock ▪bottom 1229R47/51
the ▫bottom of the ▪heap 655R45
▫copper-▪bottomed 304R14
▫bottomless ▪pit 152R10
▪bell-▫bottoms 115R42
▫bottoms ▪up 152L64
▪store-▫bought 1431L61
▪bouillon ▫cube 152R35 1428L37
▫bounce ▪back 152R62
▫bounce ▪in 152R59
▫bounce ▪off 152R54
▫bound and de▪termined 153L13
▪bound by 153L24
▫bound ▪up 153L66
▪desk-▫bound 373L17
▫duty ▪bound 433R13
▪muscle-▫bound 930R34
▫outward-▪bound 1004R75
▪pot-▫bound 1102R20
▪spiral-bound 1393L4
▫bounden ▪duty 153R1
by/in ▫leaps and ▪bounds 806L22
▫know no ▪bounds 153L42 787R8
▫lady ▪bountiful 792L72
▪bounty ▫hunter 153R12
▫petit ▪bourgeois 1055R55/61/63
▫petty ▪bourgeois 1055R61/55 1056L77
▪bovver ▫boots 153R76
▪bovver ▫boy 153R77
another ▫string/a ▫second string/▫two strings to *one's* ▪bow 1443R47
▫bow and ▪scrape 154L11
▫bow ▪down 154L3/5
▫bow-▪legged 154L59
▫bow ▪out 154L9
▫bow ▪tie 154L75
▪bow to 153R82/83 154L7
▫bow ▪window 154L61
▫bow-▪wow 155L4
▫cupid's ▪bow 335R52
▪bowel ▫movement 154R8
▪bowl down/along 154R44
▫bowl ▪over 154R74
▪finger ▫bowl 522L3
▪goldfish ▫bowl 610L74
▫life is just a ▫bowl of ▪cherries 154R29
▪punch ▫bowl 1146R24
▪Super ▫Bowl 1461R8
▫clean ▪bowled 241R39
▫bowler-▪hatted 155L1
▪pace ▫bowler 1014L59
▫spin ▪bowler 154R48 1391R56/59
▪bowling ▫alley 154R66
▪bowling ▫green 154R55
▫lawn ▪bowling 801R83
▫tenpin ▪bowling 154R61 1500R58
▫batter's ▪box 103R73
▫black ▪box 131R19
▪boom ▫box 148L9 594L16
▫box ▪in 155L49/50
▫box into a ▪corner 306R11
▪box ▫junction 155L25
▪box ▫lunch 155L28 1016L15
▪box ▫number 155L30
▪box ▫office 155L33
▪box ▫spanner 155L38
▪box ▫spring 155L41
▪box ▫wrench 155L38
▪bread ▫box 159R1
▪call ▫box 184R14
▪chocolate ▫box 228R18
▪Christmas ▫box 230L75
▪commentary ▫box 269R29
▪deed ▫box 357L26
dis▪patch ▫box 396L43
▪fuse ▫box 577L27
▪gift ▫box 594R49
give *someone* a ▫box on the ▪ears 155L79
▪glory ▫box 152L68 601L8
▪glove ▫box 601R2/6
▪goggle-▫box 609R4
▪ice-▫box 565L40 698R67
▪jack-in-the-▫box 757R70
▪junction ▫box 773L53
▪jury ▫box 774L24
▪musical ▫box 931L51/71
▪nesting ▫box 949R47
▪paint ▫box 1019L11
Pan▫dora's ▪box 1021R57
▪penalty ▫box 1044R20/28
▪pepper ▫box 1046R71
▪phone ▫box 1058R6
▪pillar-▫box 1066R61
P▪O ▫Box 1087R2
▪press ▫box 1118R70
▪safety de▫posit box 1248R53 1249L10/9
▪sentry ▫box 1294R28
▪shadow-▫box 1306R4/1
▪signal ▫box 1336R23
▪strong-▫box 1445R56
▪telephone ▫box 1058R7
▪tool ▫box 1535R36
▪voice ▫box 796R72 1629L71
▪window ▫box 1667R84
▪witness ▫box 1674R33
▪boxer ▫shorts 155L83
▪Boxing ▫Day 155R47
▪boxing ▫glove 155L72
▪boxing ▫ring 155L74
▪backroom ▫boy 91L8
▪ball ▫boy 95R32
▪barrow ▫boy 101R11
▫best ▪boy 118R81
▫blue-eyed ▪boy 139R81
▪bovver ▫boy 153R77
▫boy-meets-▪girl 155R79
▫boy ▪scout 155R80 1270L49
▫boy ▫toy 155R81
▫boy ▪wonder 155R83
▪bully ▫boy 174R66
▪bus ▫boy 178L45
▪cabin ▫boy 182L62
▪cover ▫boy 316L48
▪day ▫boy 349R34
▪errand ▫boy 467L22
▫fair-haired ▪boy 139R82 495L70
▪golden ▫boy 610L39
local ▫boy made ▪good 155R62
▪mama's ▫boy 858L78
▫man and ▪boy 858R55
▪mummy's ▫boy 929R61
▪new ▫boy 952L45
▫old ▪boy 979R64/69 980L47
▫old-▪boy ▫network 980L51/55
▫principal ▪boy 1122R19
▪rent ▫boy 1203R18
▪stable ▫boy 1405R10
▪teddy ▫boy 1495R80
▪there's a good ▫boy 1509R80
▪toy ▫boy 1544L44
▪whipping ▫boy 1659L29
▪wide ▫boy 1663R27
▫live-in ▪lover/▪boyfriend 832L34
▪big ▫boys 125L27
▫boys in ▪blue 155R70
▫jobs for the ▪boys 765R35
▪bric-a-▫brac 163R49
▫brace and ▪bit 156L63
▪brace *oneself* for 156L56
▪brace with 156L71
▪charm ▫bracelet 219L9
▫belt and ▪braces 116R3
▫bracket to▪gether 156R58
▪bracket with 156R59
▫square ▪bracket 1402L35
▫round ▪brackets 156R6 1236L70
▪brag about 156R70
▪bird-▫brain 128L54/55
▪brain ▫dead 157L30
▪brain ▫death 157L28
▪brain ▫drain 157L33
▪brain ▫power 157L37
▪brain ▫teaser 157L39
▪brain ▫trust 157L44
▪brain ▫wave 157L46
▪pea-▫brain 1039R6
▫beat *someone's* ▪brains ▫out 109L33/35
▫cudgel *one's* ▪brains 333R61
more ▫brains than ▪brawn 157L64
▫pick *someone's* ▪brains 157L62 1062L74
▫rack *one's* ▪brains 1166L53
▫shit for ▪brains 1317R66
▪braising ▫steak 1417R75
▪air ▫brake 29L41
▪brake ▫block 157R36
▪brake ▫cable 157R39
▪brake ▫light 157R34
▪brake ▫pedal 157R41 1041R34
▪disc ▫brake 389R79 390L2
e▪mergency ▫brake 450L76 642L3
▪foot ▫brake 545R58
▪parking ▫brake 642L4 1027L6
put a ▪brake on 157R32
▫ screech/▫squeal of ▪brakes 157R30
put the ▪brakes on 157R32
▪branch ▫line 157R68
▫branch ▪off 157R75
▫branch ▪out 158L4
▫branch ▪out from/into 158L7/9
▪olive ▫branch 980R60
▫root and ▪branch 1233R53
▪Special ▫Branch 1386L38
▪brand ▫loyalty 158L20
▪brand ▫name 158L19
▫brand ▪new 158L42 952R35
ge▫neric ▪brand/▪label 1013L11
▫own ▪brand 1013L10
▪store ▫brand 1013L11
▪branding ▫iron 158L31
▪brandish *something* at 158L41
▪brandy ▫butter 158L50
▪brandy ▫snap 158L52
▫brass ▪balls 158R12
▫brass ▪band 158L82
▫brass ▪hat 158L71
▫brass ▪knuckles 158L72 787R80
▫brass ▪monkey ▫weather 158L67
▪brass ▫neck 158R12
▪brass-▫rubbing 158L73
▫freeze the ▫balls off a ▫brass ▪monkey 563L25
get down to ▫brass ▪tacks 158L68
▫top ▪brass 1537L80
▫brave it ▪out 158R68
▪brave new 158R55
put a ▫brave ▪face on 158R51
put on a ▫brave ▪face 158R50
more ▫brains than ▪brawn 157L64
▫brazen ▪hussy 159L20
▪brazen it 159L28
▫brazen ▪out 159L24
Bra▪zil ▫nut 159L35
▫breach of the ▪peace 159L47
▫step into the ▪breach 1420L53
▫bread and ▪butter 159L71/72
▫bread and ▪circuses 159L75
▪bread ▫basket 159L80/81
▪bread ▫bin 159R1
▪bread ▫box 159R1
▪bread ▫knife 159R2 783L83
▫bread ▪roll 1231R77
▫break ▪bread 160R66/67
▫brown ▪bread 169L57
▪corn ▫bread 306L26
▫daily ▪bread 342R52
▫earn *one's* (daily) ▪bread 159L68
▪fairy ▫bread 495R68
▫French ▪bread 563R3
▫garlic ▪bread 583L84
▪granary ▫bread 617R57
know which side *one's* ▪bread is ▫buttered (on) 786R57
▪rye ▫bread 1245R39
the ▫best ▫thing since sliced ▪bread 118R69
▪breadth of ▪mind 159R38
▪hair's ▫breadth 636L71
the ▫length and ▪breadth 810R81
▫break a▪way 160L53/R51
▫break *one's* ▪back 159R57
▫break ▪bread 160R66/67
▫break ▪camp 161L65
▫break ▪cover 161R26
▪break-▫dancing 162L10
▫break ▪down 159R67/69 160L55/R52/54 1064R23
▫break ▪even 161L67
▫break ▪faith with 496L55
▫break fresh/new ▪ground 160R64
▪break from 160L53/R51 161L35
▫break ▪ground 160R62
▪break ▪in 160L61/73 161L12/R60/67 1242R49
▪break into 160L64/R55 161R73
▫break it/something ▪up 161L64
▫break ▪off 160R56
▫break ▪out 160L68 161R77
▪break over 161R25
▫break ▫point 161R56
▫break ▪ranks 160R73
▪break ▫serve 161R50
▫break the ▪back of 159R59/61
▫break the ▪bank 159R66
▫break the ▪ice 160R68
▫break the ▪mould 160R71
▫break ▪through 160L69
▫break ▪up 160L71/R58/59 161L8/60/9
▫break ▪wind 161R28
▪break with 161L59/70/R48 1673L49
▪coffee ▫break 254R74
▫give *someone* a ▪break 161L35
▪lunch ▫break 848L6
make a ▫clean ▪break (of it) 241L77/35
▫make a/the ▪break 161L78
▫make-or-▪break situation 159R70 855L20
▪station ▫break 1415R5
▪tea ▫break 1494L10
▪tie-▫break 1519R51/52
▪breakdown ▫truck 162L20
▫nervous ▪breakdown 949R10
▪breaker's ▫yard 160R76
▪circuit ▫breaker 232R60
▪ice-▫breaker 698R69/71
▪law-▫breaker 801L46
▫bed and ▪breakfast 111L50
▫breakfast ▪television 162L37
▫continental ▪breakfast 296R70
▫cooked ▪breakfast 302L82
▫dog's ▪breakfast 408R53
▫eat *someone* for ▪breakfast 439L34
▫English ▪breakfast 458L16
▪power ▫breakfast 1105R22
▫breaking and ▪entering 160L72
▪breaking ▫point 159R71
▪ground-▫breaking 626L46
▪record-▫breaking 1187R19
all ▪hell breaks ▫loose 661L24
▫straw that breaks the camel's ▪back 1435R26
▫sea ▪bream 162L70
▫beat *one's* ▪breast 109L38
▪breast-▫feed 162L81/79
▫breast ▪pocket 162R8
▪chimney ▫breast 226R74
make a ▫clean ▪breast (of it) 241L77/35
▫double ▪breasted 162R12 414L2
▫single ▪breasted 162R15 1341L11
a ▫breath of fresh ▪air 162R44/43
▫bad ▪breath 92L46 638L75
▪breath ▫freshener 162R53
▫breath of ▪air 162R41
▪breath ▫test 162R56
▫catch *one's* ▪breath 204L71
▫don't hold your ▪breath 676L66
▫draw ▪breath 162R29 420R54
in the ▫same/▫next ▪breath 162R48 1253L38
random ▪breath ▫test 1172L19
▫save *one's* ▪breath 1258L16
▫short of ▪breath 162R33 1324L37
take *someone's* ▪breath a▫way 162R46
▫under *one's* ▪breath 162R50 933R64
▫waste *one's* ▪breath 1640R3
with ▫bated ▪breath 104L16
with *one's* ▫last/▫dying ▪breath 162R52
▫breathe a ▪word 1678L71
▫breathe down *someone's* ▪neck 162R72
▫breathe *one's* ▪last 162R71
▫breathe ▪life into 162R69
▫live and ▪breathe 832R3
have/▫take a ▪breather 162R84
▫heavy ▪breather 659L57
▪breathing ▫space 162R81
▫born and ▪bred 149R17
▫ill-▪bred 703L77
▫well-▪bred 1652L58
▫breed like ▪rabbits 1164R43
▫breeze ▪in 163L70
▪breeze into 163L72
▫breeze ▪through 163L80
▫sea ▪breeze 163L63 1276L4
▫shoot the ▪breeze 1319R39
▫bright and ▪breezy 163L74 165L66
▫brew ▪coffee 163R14
▫witches' ▪brew 1672L77
▫organize a ▫piss-up in a ▪brewery 995R13
▪bric-a-▫brac 163R49
▫beat/▫bang/▫knock *one's* ▫head against a brick ▪wall 653L33
▫brick ▪in/▪up 163R64
▫brick ▪off 163R68
▫drop a ▪brick 427R19
▫shit a ▪brick 1318L12
up against a ▫brick ▪wall 24R7
▫bricks and ▪mortar 163R57
like a ▫ton of ▪bricks 1534L3
▫shit ▪bricks 1318L12
▫always a/the ▪bridesmaid ▫never the ▪bride 164L24
▫child ▪bride 164L9
▪war ▫bride 1637L23
▫always a/the ▪bridesmaid ▫never the ▪bride 164L24
▫cantilever ▪bridge 190R11
cross ▪that bridge when you ▪come/▪get to it 327R6
▫humpback ▪bridge 693R83
pon▪toon ▫bridge 1094L47
▫rope ▪bridge 1234L69
su▪spension ▫bridge 164L32 1472L21
▪swing ▫bridge 1477L54
▫water under the ▪bridge 1642L69
▫burn *one's* ▪bridges 177L77
▪bridging ▫loan 164L44
▪bridle at 164R2
▪bridle ▫path 164L79
▪brief about/on 164R33
▫put ▪briefly 1153R44
to ▫put it ▪briefly 1153R43
▪fire ▫brigade 523L52
▫brigadier-▪general 164R64/68
▫bright and ▪breezy 163L74 165L66
▫bright and ▪early 165L67
bright-▫eyed and bushy-▪tailed 165L69
▫bright ▪spark 165L60
look on the ▪bright ▫side 839L55
▫full to the ▪brim 572L26/46
▫fire-and-▪brimstone 523L20
bring a▪bout 166R17
▫bring a▪long 166L19
▫bring an ▫action for ▪libel against 166R10
▫bring and ▪buy ▫sale 166L41
▫bring a▪round 166R26/30
▫bring ▪back 166L51
▫bring back/down/back down to ▪earth 437L69
▫bring ▪down 166L54/55/57
▫bring *someone* ▪down a ▫peg (or two) 1043L72
▫bring ▪forward 166L58
▫bring home the ▪bacon 91R74/75
▫bring ▪home to 166L60 680L50
▫bring ▪in 166L20/62/63/65
▫bring into ▪play 1079L43
▫bring ▪off 166R20
▫bring ▪on 166L68/69
▫bring on ▪board 141R48/49/50/51/47/45
▫bring ▪out 166L26/70/72
▫bring *someone* out of *their* ▪shell 1314R40
▫bring ▪round 166R26/30
▫bring some ▫colour to *someone's* ▫cheeks 259R40
▫bring ▪through 166L28
▫bring ▪to 144L64 166L14/29/31/32/34/48/73/75/77 /R33/34/40
▫bring to a ▪head 653L42
▫bring to ac▪count 9R58
▫bring to ▪book 166L39
▫bring *someone* to *their* ▪knees 782R70
▫bring to ▪life 818R47
▫bring to ▪light 820R10
▫bring to ▪mind 184R80 899L47
▫bring to ▪terms 1503R72
▫bring ▪up 166L34/36/R36 1598L35
▫bring up ▪short 166R3
▫bring up the ▪rear 166L37 1181L57
▫teeter on the ▪brink of 166R49 1496L61
▪bristle at 166R83
▪bristle with 167L1
▫British ▪Summer ▫Time 167L12
▫peanut ▪brittle 1040R21
▫broad ▪bean 167R20
▫broad in the ▪beam 167R18
▪broad ▫jump 167R20 838L36
in ▫broad ▪daylight 167R16 349R75
▫outside ▪broadcast 1004L48
▫party political ▪broadcast 1030R21
▫broaden hor▪izons 685L55
▪broiler ▫pan 168L28 624L11
go for ▪broke 168L34
▫stone-▪broke 1429R73
▫stony ▪broke 1429R73
▫broken-▪down 168L44

▫broken-▪hearted 168L45
▫honest ▪broker 681R15
▪power ▫broker 1105R25
▪real estate ▫broker 469L46 1180R34/35 1181L4
▫Bronx ▪cheer 168R14
▪Bronze ▫Age 168R21
▪brood ▫mare 168R37
▪brood on/over 168R50
▫new ▪broom 952L38
▫Scotch ▪broth 1269R27
▫Big ▪Brother 125L33
▫blood ▪brother 137R38
▪brother-in-▫law 169L14/16
▫everyone and his ▪brother 1683R51
▪half-▫brother 638L9
▪lay ▫brother 802R14
like ▫something the ▪cat brought in 203L61
▫well-brought-▪up 1652L63
▫wrinkle *one's* ▪brow 1691L33
▪browbeat into 169L46
▫beetle-▪browed 113L30
▪brown-▫bag 169L52
▫brown-bag ▪lunch 169L56
▫brown ▪bread 169L57
▫brown ▪paper 169L60
▫brown ▪rice 169L59
▫brown ▪sugar 169L63
▪Brownie ▫Guide 169L75
get/score ▪brownie ▫points 169L80
▫hash ▪browns 649R7
▫knit *one's* ▪brows 784L66
▪browse on 169R19
▫browse ▪through 169R11/15
▫bruit a▪broad/a▪round 169R48
▪brush against 170L57
▫brush a▪side 170L46
▫brush a▪way 170L44
▫brush ▪down 170L39
▫brush ▪off 169R81/83 170L47/48
▫brush ▪past/▪by 170L59
▫brush ▪up on 170L80
▪clothes ▫brush 248R6
▫give *someone* the ▪brush-off 170L49
▪nail ▫brush 936L65
▪scrubbing ▫brush 1274L33/34
▫tar with the same ▪brush 1491L70
▪toilet ▫brush 1532L74
▫wire ▪brush 1670R58
▫brussels ▪sprout 170R58
▫bubble and ▪squeak 171L43
▪bubble ▫bath 171L45
▪bubble ▫gum 171L48
▪bubble-▫jet 171L50
▪bubble ▫wrap 171L52 1689R2
▫prick the ▪bubble 1120R70
▪speech ▫bubble 1388L70
bu▫bonic ▪plague 171L70
▫buck ▪naked 171R83
▪buck-▫passing 171R8
▫buck the ▪trend 171R19
▫buck ▪tooth 172L6
▫buck ▪up 171R30
▫pass the ▪buck 1031L60
▪bucket-▫loads 171R46
▪bucket ▫seat 171R47
▪bucket ▫shop 171R52
▫kick the ▪bucket 778R78
▫weep ▪buckets 171R45
▫buckle ▪down 171R80/81
▫big ▪bucks 124R50
▪bucks ▫party 171R4 1406L34
look/feel like a ▫million ▪bucks 897R5
▪cotton ▫bud 310R37
▫nip in the ▪bud 956L71
▫bosom ▪buddy 150L63
▪budge from/on 172L42
▫budge ▪up 172L43
not ▫budge an ▪inch 716L44
▫balance the ▪budget 95L12
▪budget for 172L61
▪taste ▫buds 1492L84
▫blind man's ▪buff 135L79
▪water ▫buffalo 1642L80
▪buffer ▫state 172R13
▫old ▪buffer 172R18/19 979R68
▪buffet ▫car 172R26
▪finger ▫buffet 522L5
▫bug-▪eyed 172R39
▪bug ▫eyes 172R39
▫bugger a▪bout 173L4/5
▫bugger ▪off 173L8/10
play ▪silly ▫buggers 1078R59 1338L61
▪baby ▫buggy 88R21 1108L67
▪beach ▫buggy 107L22
▪build around 173L46
▫build ▪in 173L49
▪build into 173L40/47
▪build on/onto 173L50/51/41
▫build ▪up 173L72/79/83/74
▪body ▫builder 142R64
▫spec ▪builder 1385R34
a▪partment ▫building 53L26 136R42
▪body-building 142R63
▪building ▫site 173R10
▪building so▫ciety 173R11
▫heritage-listed ▪building 665L1 829R19
▫landmarked ▪building 794R82 829R18
▫listed ▪building 829R18
▪office ▫building 977R17
▫built in obso▪lescence 972L81
▫built-▪up 173L70
▫custom-▪built 338R6
▪jerry-▫built 762L68
▫purpose-▪built 1150L12
▫well-▪built 1652L68
▪light ▫bulb 820R26
▫bulge at the ▪seams 174L2
▫bulge ▪out 173R83
▫bulge ▪over 173R84
▫bulk ▪large 174L30
▫bulk ▪out 174L29
a ▫bull in a ▪china ▫shop 174L46
▪bull's-▫eye 174L53/58
▫bull ▪terrier 174R57
▫cock-and-▪bull ▫story 252R29
▫John ▪Bull 767L19
like a ▫red rag to a ▪bull 1188R64
▫pit bull (▪terrier) 1070R59
take the ▫bull by the ▪horns 174L51
▪bulldog ▫clip 174L73
▫bite the ▪bullet 130R15
▫bullet-▪headed 174R10
▪bullet-▫proof 174R8
▫plastic ▪bullet 1076R43
▪bulletin ▫board 174R18/20 964R31
▫sweat ▪bullets 1474R46
▪bully ▫boy 174R66
▪bully into 174R62
▪beach ▫bum 107L24
▫bum a▪round/a▪bout 175L6/4
▪bum *something* off *someone* 175L4
▫bum ▪steer 175L11
▫sit on *one's* ▪bum 1343L44
▫bumble a▪long 175L17
▫bump a▪long 175L54
▪bump into 175L57/58
▫bump ▪off 175L72
▪bump ▫start 175L66 1151L83/R1
▫bump ▪up 175L74
▪speed ▫bump 1389L19
▫things that go bump in the ▪night 1512L47
▪bumper ▫car 175L82
▫bumper to ▪bumper 175L81
▫country ▪bumpkin 175R8
▪goose ▫bumps 613L15/39
▫bums on ▪seats 1278L39
a ▪bun in the ▫oven 175R19
▫hot-cross ▪bun 687R36
▪rock ▫bun 1229R56
▫bunch to▪gether/▪up 175R48/47
give *someone* a ▫bunch of ▪fives 175R39
the ▫best of a bad ▪bunch 175R36
the ▫best/▫pick of the ▪bunch 175R35 1062L37
a ▫bundle of ▪laughs/▪joy 175R59
a ▫bundle of ▪nerves 175R60 949L69
▪bundle into 175R66/68/70
▫bundle ▪off 175R71
▫bundle ▪up 175R72
go a ▪bundle (on) 175R62
make a ▪bundle 175R63
▪bung in/into 176L1
▫bung ▪up 175R80
▪bungee ▫jump 176L9
▪bungy ▫jump 176L9
▪bunk ▫bed 176L25
▫bunk ▪off 176L39
▪coal ▫bunker 251R16
▫bunsen ▪burner 176L52
▪life ▫buoy 819L24
▫burble a▪way 176R3
▫beast of ▪burden 108R72
▫burden of ▪proof 176R12
▪burden *someone* with 176R17
▫lighten *someone's* ▪burden 821L66
▫bureau de ▪change 176R51
▫Citizens Ad▪vice ▫Bureau 234L30
▪marriage ▫bureau 868L10
▪burglar a▫larm 176R70
▪cat ▫burglar 203L67
▫aggravated ▪burglary 26L34
▪burial ▫ground 177L3
▫hurly-▪burly 695L77
▫burn a ▪hole in *someone's* ▫pocket 177L71
▫burn at the ▪stake 177L75 1407R84
▫burn *one's* ▪boats/▪bridges 177L77
▫burn ▪down 177L81
▫burn *one's* ▪fingers 177R6
▫burn ▪off 177L27
▫burn the ▫candle at both ▪ends 177L37
▫burn the ▫midnight ▪oil 177L41
▫burn to the ▪ground 177L82
▫burn ▪up 177L31
▪burn with 177L34/36
▫first-degree ▪burn 525R54
▫money to ▪burn 913R27
▫slow ▪burn 1355R48
▫third-degree ▪burn 1513R24
▫bunsen ▪burner 176L52
on the ▫back ▪burner 89R8
▫ears are ▪burning 434R84
▪fiddle while ▫Rome ▪burns 515R41
▫burnt ▪offering 177R17
▫burnt si▪enna 1335L2
get/have *one's* ▪fingers ▫burnt 177R6
▪burst(ing) to 177R77/78
▫burst a ▪blood ▫vessel 137R6/8
▫burst at the ▪seams 177R81
▫burst ▪in 177R72
▫burst into ▪flames 178L1
▫burst into ▪song/▪tears/▪laughter 177R72/83 746R72 747L 1494R49
burst ▪out 178L6
▫burst out ▪laughing/▪crying 178L5
▪burst with 177R79
▪cloud-▫burst 248R42
▫fit to ▪burst 527L79/75/76
▫full to ▪bursting 572L22/47
▫go for a ▪burton 178L16/15
bury *one's* ▫head in the ▪sand 653L38
▫bury the ▪hatchet 178L32
▪booze ▫bus 148R51
▪bus ▫boy 178L45
▪bus con▫ductor 178L48
▪bus ▫lane 178L49
▪bus-▫shelter 178L52
▪bus ▫station 178L54
▪bus ▫stop 178L55
▫beat about/around the ▪bush 109L29
▪bush ▫fire 178L82
▫bush ▪telegraph 178R2
bright-▫eyed and bushy-▪tailed 165L69
▫big ▪business 125L39/44
▪business ▫class 178R52
▪business ▫end 178R55
▪business ▫park 178R57
▪business ▫people 178R58
▪funny ▫business 575R7/8
▫get down to ▪business 178R47
like ▪nobody's ▫business 179L6
▫mean ▪business 878R24
▫mind *one's* own ▪business 179L8 899R19
▪monkey ▫business 915L4
▪show ▫business 1328L33
▫busman's ▪holiday 179L29
go ▪bust 179L49
▪sanctions-▫busting 1253R69
▫bustle a▪bout 179L70
▫bustle ▪in 179L71
▫hustle and ▪bustle 696R6
a ▫busy ▪bee 112L52
as ▫busy as a ▪bee 112L52
▫ifs and/or ▪buts 702R51
no/not any ▫buts (a▪bout it) 179R39
a ▫pain in the ▪butt 1018R30
▫butt ▪in 180L18 227R47
▫butt ▪naked 180L11
cigar▪ette ▫butt 232L22
▪head-▫butt 653L57/59
▪water ▫butt 1642L83
▪brandy ▫butter 158L50
▫bread and ▪butter 159L71/72
▪butter ▫bean 180L44 823L78
▫butter ▪up 180L34
▫butter wouldn't ▫melt in *someone's* ▪mouth 180L29
▪cocoa ▫butter 253R71
▪coconut ▫butter 253R80
▫peanut ▪butter 1040R22
know which side *one's* ▪bread is ▫buttered (on) 786R57
▪butterflies in *one's* ▫stomach 180L55
▪butterfly ▫stroke 180L60
▫tortoiseshell ▪butterfly 1539L28
at the ▫push of a ▪button 180L84
▪belly ▫button 116L10 944L23
▪button ▫day 529L38
▫button-down ▪collar 180R9
▪button-▫fly 180R3
▪button it 180R7
▪hot-▫button 687R35
▪panic ▫button 1022L39
▪push-button 1151L79
▫right on the ▪button 180R1
▪snooze ▫button 1367L1
▪tummy ▫button 944L23 1567R15
▫flying ▪buttress 540R6
▫bring and ▪buy ▫sale 166L41
▪buy for 180R37
▪buy from 180R39
▫buy ▪in 180R40
▪buy into 180R42/75
▪buy it 180R77
▫buy ▪off 180R40
▫buy the ▪farm 180R57
▫buy ▪time 180R59
▫buy ▪up 180R53
▪buy-out 180R47
▫buyer's ▪market 180R69 867L18
▫first-time ▪buyer 526L43
▪home ▫buyer 679R73
▪panic ▫buying 180R60 1022L45
▫leveraged ▪buyout 814R66
▫buzz a▪round 181L1/2/4
▫buzz ▪off 181L24
▪buzz with 181L8
▪buzz ▫word 181L31
▫get a ▪buzz from 181L17
▫give *someone* a ▪buzz 181L18
▫cheery-▪bye 223L18
▫go ▪bye-bye 181R1
go to ▪bye-byes 181R3
go to ▪bye-byes 181R3
let ▫bygones be ▪bygones 181R15
▫highway and ▪byway 669R47
▪cab ▫stand 182L31
▪cabin ▫boy 182L62
▪cabin ▫crew/▫staff 182L63
▪cabin ▫cruiser 182L64
▫log ▪cabin 836R27
▪cabinet ▫maker 182L75
▫kitchen ▪cabinet 782L35
▪brake ▫cable 157R39
▪cable ▫car 182R10
▪cable ▫railway 182R13
▪cable ▫stitch 182R14
▪jumper cables 772R32
the ▫whole (kit and) ca▪boodle 1662L22
▫cack-▪handed 182R37
▫cut the ▪cackle 339R35
▪caddie for 182R66
▪tea ▫caddy 182R67 1494L14
▪cadge from/off 182R80
▪transport ▫café 1552L11
▪rib ▫cage 1220R28
like a ▫caged ▪animal 183L41
ca▪jole into 183L69
a ▫piece of ▪cake 183L83 1064R13
▪angel ▫food ▫cake 44R82
▫cake ▪in 183R17
▪cake with 183R16
▪cattle ▫cake 206L31
▪Christmas ▫cake 230L78
▪coffee ▫cake 254R76
▪devil's ▫food ▫cake 378L68
▪fairy ▫cake 495R70
have *one's* cake and ▪eat it 183R5
▪layer ▫cake 803L76
▪rock ▫cake 1229R56
▫slice of the ▪cake 1352L51
go/▫sell like ▫hot ▪cakes 687R24
▪calculate as/at 183R48
▪calculate on 183R49/63
▫calculated ▪risk 183R72
the ▫Black Hole of Cal▪cutta 131R33
▪Advent ▫calendar 19R29
▪calendar ▫month 184L14
▪calendar ▫year 184L16
Gre▫gorian ▪calendar 623L49/50
per ▪calendar ▫month 1047L31
▪calf-▫length 184L36
▫kill the fatted ▪calf 779R68
a/the ▫call of ▪nature 186L9
▪alarm ▫call 31R50
call a ▫spade a ▪spade 185L77
▫call ▪back 184L84/R32/78
▫call *someone's* ▪bluff 185R81
▪call ▫box 184R14 1058R7
▫call ▪by 184R33
▫call col▪lect 184R3 1218L17
▪call for 184R8/35 185R67/70 186L4/6/8
▫call ▪forth 186L22
▪call ▫girl 184R17
▪call-in 184R20/73/76/77 1058R9
▪call into 184R75
▫call into ▪question 184R83
▫call it a ▪day 185L76
▫call it ▪quits 185L74
▫call *someone* ▪names/a ▫name 936R84
▫call ▪off 186L25/31
▪call on 184R50 185R70/72/73
▫call ▪out 184R57
▫call ▪over 184R70
▫call *one's* ▪shot 185R83
▫call the ▪roll 1231R67
▫call the ▪tune/▪shots 186L1
▪call to 184R2/59/72
▫call to ac▪count 9R58
▫call to ▪mind 184R80 899L47
▫call ▪up 184R3 186L35/38/41
▪clarion ▫call 237R3
▫close ▪call 247R76 1512L14
▫cold ▪call 256R13
▪curtain ▫call 337R35
▪house ▫call 689L41
▫pay a ▪call 184R49 1038R79/80
▪phone ▫call 258L21
▪photo-▫call 1059L14
▫port of ▪call 1097L18
▪roll ▫call 1231R70
▫so-▪called 1370L23
▫crank ▪caller 319R84
▪name-▫calling 937L4
▫calm ▪down 186R9
the ▫calm before/after the ▪storm 186R20
▪traffic ▫calmed 1547R42
▪Calor ▫gas 186R28
plenty ▫more where ▪that ▫came from 1081R39
▪camel ▫hair 187L6
▫straw that breaks the camel's ▪back 1435R26
▪camera ▫operator 187L39
▪camera-▫shy 187L32
▪camera ▫work 187L35
▪video ▫camera 1622L53
▫aide-de-▪camp 28R28/29/31
▪base ▫camp 101R51
▫break ▪camp 161L65
▪camp ▫bed 187L80
▪camp ▫follower 187R32
▫camp it ▪up 187R23
▫camp ▪out 187R3
concen▪tration ▫camp 280R32
▪holiday ▫camp 677R60
▪labour ▫camp 789R55
▪prison ▫camp 187L80 1123R35
refu▪gee ▫camp 1192R63
▫strike ▪camp 1441R8
▪transit ▫camp 1550R68
cam▪paign against 187R38/59
▫campaign of ▪violence 187R40
cam▪paign ▫trail 187R43
e▪lection cam▫paign 187R42 446L42
▪whispering cam▫paign 1660L3
▪camper ▫van 187R5 412R52
▪camping ▫ground 187R11/75
▪camping ▫site 187R75
▪trailer ▫camping 193R70
a foot in ▪both ▫camps 545L52
▪can it 188L33
▫French Ca▪nadian 563R6
▫alimentary ca▪nal 33L7
ca▪nal ▫boat 188R29
▫cancel ▪out 189L6
▫Tropic of ▪Cancer 1560R32
▫candied ▪peel 189R5
▫burn the ▫candle at both ▪ends 177L37
▫can't hold a ▪candle 189L59
can't ▫hold a ▪candle to 675R38
▫Roman ▪candle 1232L33
the ▫game is worth the ▪candle 581L74
▪candy-▫ass 189L81
▪candy-▫striped 189L83
▫cotton ▪candy 189R8 310R39
▫hard ▪candy 144L72
▪rock ▫candy 1229R42/44
▪sugar ▫cane 1457L15
▫white ▪cane 1660R63
▫canister ▪vacuum ▫cleaner 189R34
▫canned ▪laughter 188L38
▫canned ▪music 188L43
▪cannon ▫ball 189R63
▪cannon ▫fodder 189R65
▪water ▫cannon 1642R1
▫paddle *one's* ▫own ca▪noe 1017R32
ca▪noodle with 190L33
▫cantilever ▪bridge 190R11
▫under ▪canvas 190R21
▫canvass sup▪port/▪votes 18L14 54L21 132R68 190R28 198L73 326L45 337L50 546R83 547L4/10 782R37/38 1038L49
▪baseball ▫cap 102L22
▫cap in ▪hand 190R60
▪cap with 190R83 191L3
▪dunce ▫cap 432L66/65
▫Dutch ▪cap 191L9 433L77
▪feather in *someone's* ▪cap 509L3
▪ice ▫cap 698R73
▪pen ▫cap 1044L45
put *one's* ▪thinking ▫cap on 1513L75
▪stocking ▫cap 142L72 1428L84
▪toe ▫cap 1531L71
▫capable ▪hands 191L22
di▫minished ca▪pacity 385L22
▫caper ▪through 191R5
per ▪capita 1047L35
▫capital ▪asset 191R43
▫capital ex▪penditure 191R51
▫capital ▪gain 191R45
▫capital in▪tensive 191R47
▫capital in▪vestment 191R51
▫capital ▪punishment 191R69
make ▪capital (out) of/from 191R54
▪venture ▫capital 1613R42
▪working ▫capital 1679R80
▫venture ▪capitalist 1613R47
▪capitalize on 192L72
▫under ▪capitalized 191R60

▫block ▪**capitals** 136R22
▪cloud-▫**capped** 248R43
▪snow-▫**capped** 1367L70
▫Tropic of ▪**Capricorn** 1560R33
▪time(d)-release ▫**capsule** 1522R30
▪time ▫**capsule** 1524L35
▫**captain** of ▪industry 193L39
▪group ▫**captain** 626R76
▪sea ▫**captain** 1276L5
▫**captive** ▪audience 193L68
▪data ▫**capture** 347L74
▪baggage ▫**car** 93R63
▪buffet ▫**car** 172R26
▪bumper ▫**car** 175L82
▪cable ▫**car** 182R10
▪**car** ▫bomb 193R18
▫**car**-▪boot ▫sale 193R19
▪**car** ▫dealer/▫showroom 582R37
▪**car** ▫ferry 193R22
▪**car** ▫park 193R23
▪**car** ▫phone 193R26
▪**car** ▫pool 193R32/28/30 1094R20
▪**car** ▫wash 193R34
▫classic ▪**car** 238L75
▫company ▪**car** 272R34
▪dining ▫**car** 385L69 1213L18
▪kiddy ▫**car** 779R14
▪motor ▫**car** 193R8 921R4
pa▪trol ▫**car** 1036R45 1401R43
▪racing ▫**car** 1165R25/28
▪restaurant ▫**car** 193R16 385L70 1213L17
▪sleeping ▫**car** 193R17 1351R8
▪sports ▫**car** 1396R64
▪squad ▫**car** 1401R43
▪**caravan** ▫park 193R65
▪**caravan** ▫site 193R64
▪motor ▫**caravan** 921R6
car▫**bolic** ▪acid 194L56
▫**carbon** ▪copy 194L69
▫**carbon** ▪dating 194L76
▫**carbon** di▫oxide 194L70
▫**carbon** mon▪oxide 194L72
AT▪M ▫**card** 201R31
▪banker's ▫**card** 97R64 224L40
▫best ▪**card** 195L32
▪boarding ▫**card** 141R53
▫**card**-carrying ▪member 195L63
▪**card** ▫index 195L10 721L23
▫**card** up *one's* ▪sleeve 195L23
▪**card** ▫vote 195L12
▪cash ▫**card** 201R30
▪charge ▫**card** 217R24
▪cheque ▫**card** 224L40
▪Christmas ▫**card** 230L80
▪credit ▫**card** 322L48
▪debit ▫**card** 353L44
▪discount ▫**card** 391R33
▪donor ▫**card** 411L65
▪flash ▫**card** 530R75
▫gold ▪**card** 609R60
▫green ▪**card** 622L73/75
▪greeting ▫**card** 623L37/36
▫I.▪D. **card** 700R19
i▪dentity ▫**card** 701R24
▪place ▫**card** 1073R55
▪playing ▫**card** 195L17 1078L62
re▪port ▫**card** 1205L29
▪smart ▫**card** 1358R48
▪store-▫**card** 1431L64
▪test ▫**card** 1505R18
▪time ▫**card** 1522L21
▪trump ▫**card** 1564L38
▪wild ▫**card** 1664R10/13/17
▫**cardinal** ▪point 196L5
have/hold ▫all the ▪**cards** 195L39
hold ▫all the ▪**cards** 676R60
▫house of ▪**cards** 689L48
keep/hold *one's* ▫**cards** close to *one's* ▪chest 195L28
on the ▪**cards** 195L41
▫play *one's* ▪**cards** ▫right 1078L37
▫put/▫lay *one's* ▫**cards** on the ▪table 195L36
▫stack the ▪**cards** 1405R57
the ▫**cards** are stacked a▪gainst *someone* 1405R61
▫**care** a ▪damn 344R21
▫**care** a ▪sod 1371L40
▫**care** a ▪toss 1539R36
▪**care** about 196R63
▪**care** for 196L70 197L1
▪child ▫**care** 226L28
▪day ▫**care** 349R24
▫devil-may-▪**care** 378L41
▪easy ▫**care** 438R53
in▫tensive ▪**care** 740R23
not ▫**care** a ▪fig 516R64
not ▫**care** a ▪hoot/two ▪hoots 684R16
▫not **care** ▪tuppence 1568L53
not/without a ▫**care** in the ▪world 196R55
▫pastoral ▪**care** 1034L60/63
▫take ▪**care** 196L59/R9/11/12
▫take ▪**care** of *oneself* 196L59/48/54
▫take/▫put into ▪**care** 196L62
ca▫**reen** ▪down 197L11
▪**career** down 197L40
▫**careful** how you ▪go 196R29
for ▫all/▫aught *anyone* ▪**cares** 79R51 547L45
the **cares** of the ▪world on *one's* ▫shoulders 196R54
▪**caring** pro▫fession 196L83
▫**carnal** ▪knowledge 197R56
▫chilli con ▪**carne** 226R46
▪**carol** ▫singer 198L9/5
▪**carp** at 198L40
▪**carpet** ▫bomb 198L66
▪**carpet** ▫slippers 198L65
▪**carpet** ▫sweeper 198L68
▫magic ▪**carpet** 852L51
▫Persian ▪**carpet** 1052L37
▫pull the ▪**carpet** from under 1144L48
▫red ▪**carpet** 1188R73
▫sweep under the ▪**carpet** 1475L21
▪baby ▫**carriage** 88R21 1108L67
▪**carriage** ▫clock 198R21
▫**carriage** ▪forward 198R17
▫**carriage** ▪free/▪paid 198R19
▪gun ▫**carriage** 632R2
▫dual ▪**carriageway** 430L54
▪aircraft ▫**carrier** 30L17
▫armoured person▪nel ▫**carrier** 63L82
▪**carrier** ▫pigeon 199L16
▪letter ▫**carrier** 813L39 1101R67
▪mail ▫**carrier** 853R11
person▪nel ▫**carrier** 1053R37
▪spear ▫**carrier** 1385L83
▪troop ▫**carrier** 1560R7
▪**carrion** ▫crow 198R36
▫**carrot**-and-▪stick 198R51/55
▪**carrot**-▫top 198R41
as ▫fast as *one's* legs would ▪**carry** *one* 505R40
▫**carry** a ▪torch for 198R82
▫**carry** a▪round 198R70
▫**carry** a▪way 198R72 199R25
▫**carry** ▪back 198R77/59/63/68/77 199R6/8 200L7
carry ▫coals to ▪Newcastle 251R11
▫**carry** ▪down 198R66
▫**carry** ▪forward 199R9
▫**carry** ▪off 198R74/76 199R36
▫**carry** ▪on 198R84 199R42/55/65
▫**carry** ▪on about 199R61
▫**carry** ▪on at 199R60
▫**carry** ▪on with 199R47/63
▫**carry** ▪out 199R79
▫**carry** ▪over 200L3
▫**carry** ▪over from/into 200L9/8
▫**carry** ▪through 200L11/15
▫cash and ▪**carry** 201R22/25
▫fetch and ▪**carry** 513R71
▫**card-carrying** ▪member 195L63
▪**carrying** ▫charge 199L50
▫**cart** a▪round 200L49
▫**cart** a▪way 200L47
▫**cart** ▪off 200L51
▪**cart** ▫track 200L39
put the ▫**cart** before the ▪horse 200L36
▪tea ▫**cart** 1494L36
up▫set the ▪apple **cart** 1600L53
à la ▪**carte** 31L40
▫**carte** ▪blanche 200L53
▫animated **car**▪**toon** 200R16
car▪**toon** ▫character 200R22
car▪**toon** ▫strip 200R11 267R24
▪strip ▫**cartoon** 267R24 1444R44
▪**cartridge** ▫paper 200R37
▪**cartridge** ▫pen 200R33
▪**carve** from 200R51
▪**carve** into/on 200R54/52
▫**carve** ▪out 200R58/60/62
▫**carve** ▪up 200R64 201L1
▪**carve** with 200R54
▫**carved** in (▫tablets of) ▪stone 200R71 1429R26
▪**carving** ▫knife 200R83 783L84
a ▫**case** in ▪point 201L29
as/what▫ever the ▫**case** might ▪be 201L30
at▪taché ▫**case** 77L32
▪basket ▫**case** 103L44/46
▫**case** ▪history 201L53
▪**case** ▫law 201L63
▪**case** ▫study 201L55
▫hard ▪**case** 646R80
I ▫rest my ▪**case** 1212R51
▫lower ▪**case** 845L6
▫make out a ▪**case** 856L48
my ▫**case** ▪rests 1212R52
▫not the ▪**case** 201L35
▫on *someone's* ▪**case** 982R80
▪packing ▫**case** 1016L29
▪test ▫**case** 1505R22
▫upper ▪**case** 1599R27
▫worst **case** sce▪nario 1263R19 1686R81
▫**cash** and ▪carry 201R22/25
▪**cash** ▫bar 201R27
▪**cash** ▫card 201R30
▪**cash** ▫crop 201R33
▪**cash** ▫desk 201R35
▪**cash** dis▫penser 201R32/36
▪**cash** ▫flow 201R40
▫**cash** ▪in 201R48
▫**cash** ▪in on 201R48
▪**cash** ma▫chine 201R37
▪**cash** ▫register 201R43
▫**cash** ▪up 201R52
▫hard ▪**cash** 646L44
▫petty ▪**cash** 1056L71
cas▪**sette** ▫player 202L7
▫video **cas**▪**sette** 1622L58
▫video **cas**▪**sette** re▫corder 1622L71
▫**cast** a ▪shadow over/on 202L18
▫**cast** a ▪spell on 202L44
▫**cast** an ▪eye/a ▪glance over 202L35
▫**cast** a▪round/a▪bout 202R9
▪**cast** as 202L52/58
▫**cast** a▪side/a▪way/▪off 202L27
▫**cast** as▪persions on 70R67 202L31
▫**cast** ▪down 202L46
▫**cast** in ce▪ment/▪concrete 208R9 282L78
▫**cast** in the same ▪mould 202L71
▫**cast** ▪iron 202L78
▫**cast** ▪light on 820R13
▫**cast** *one's* ▪mind back 202L36
▫**cast** *one's* net ▪wide 202L38
▫**cast** ▪off 202L26/R12/14
▫**cast**-off ▪clothes 202L29
▪**cast**-▫offs 202L30
▫**cast** ▪on 202R17
▪**cast** on/over 202L17
▫**cast** ▪out 202L29
cast ▫pearls before ▪swine 202L41
▪die-▫**cast** 382L4
▪plaster ▫**cast** 1076L81
sup▫porting ▪**cast** 202L66
the ▫die is ▪**cast** 382L7
▪worm ▫**cast** 1685L81
▪half-▫**caste** 637R32
▪**caster** ▫sugar 202R37
▪**casting** ▫couch 202L60
▫**casting** ▪vote 202R5
▪**castles** in the ▫air 202R48
▪**castor** ▪oil 202R61
a ▫**cat** in ▪hell's ▫chance 203L44
▫**cat** and ▪mouse 203L38
▪**cat** ▫burglar 203L67
▫**cat's** ▪cradle 203L72
▪**cat's** ▫eyes 203L76
▫**cat**-o'-▪nine-▫tails 203L69
▫**cat's** ▪whiskers 203L81
▪cool ▫**cat** 203L83
▫fat ▪**cat** 506L22
has the ▫**cat** got *your* ▪tongue 203L48
▪hep ▫**cat** 203L83
let the ▪**cat** out of the ▫bag 203L51
like a ▫**cat** on a hot tin ▪roof 203L55
like ▫**cat** and ▪dog 203L58
like ▫something the ▪**cat** brought/dragged in 203L61
▫Manx ▪**cat** 863L49
▫Persian ▪**cat** 1052L41
put/set the ▫**cat** among the ▪pigeons 203L64
▫Siamese ▪**cat** 1332R36
▫tortoiseshell ▪**cat** 1539L30
▫**catalytic** con▪verter 203R44
▪**catapult** into 203R63
▫**Catch**-▪22 205L41
▫**catch** a few/some ▪rays 204L82
▫**catch** *someone* ▪at *something* 204L56
▪**catch** between 204L58
▫**catch** *one's* ▪breath 204L71
▫**catch** *one's* ▫death (of ▪cold) 352R2
▫**catch** *someone's* ▪fancy 501R83
▫**catch** ▪fire 205L35
▫**catch** ▪hold of 204L58
▫**catch** in the ▪crossfire 328L69
▫**catch** ▪napping 204R68
▫**catch** off-▪guard 629L69 976L68
▫**catch** ▪on 204L52 205L49/52
▫**catch** on the ▪hop 684R46
▫**catch** on the wrong ▪foot 1692R78
▫**catch** ▪on to 205L54
▫**catch** ▪out 205L65/55/59/63
▫**catch** some/a few ▪z's 1699L16
▫**catch** the ▪sun 204L79
▫**catch** ▪up 205L68/72/74 1598L47
▫**catch** ▪up with/on 205L70
▫**catch** *someone* with *their* ▪trousers/▪pants ▫down 204R73/78
if you ▫**catch** my ▪drift 1486L83
▪safety ▫**catch** 1248R47
▪eye-▫**catching** 488R35
▪**catchment** ▫area 205L76
▪**cater** for 205R30/39
▪**cater** to 205R42
ex **ca**▪**thedra** 476L3
▪**catherine** ▫wheel 205R78
▫Anglo-▪**Catholic** 45R18
▫Roman ▪**Catholic** 1232L35
▫Roman **Catholic** ▪Church 1232L38
▫Roman **Ca**▪**tholicism** 1232L40
▪**cattle** ▫cake 206L31
▪**cattle** ▫grid 206L32
▫**caught** ▪short 1322R69
▫**caught** ▪up in 204L54
▫**cauliflower** ▪cheese 206L64
▫**cauliflower** ▪ear 206L66
▪**causative** ▫factor 206R16
▫**cause** a dis▪turbance 206R2
▫**cause** a ▪stink 1426L80
▫**cause** a ▪stir 1427L12
▫**cause** cé▫lèbre 206R28
▫good ▪**cause** 206R25 612L5
▫lost ▪**cause** 206R26 842L35
▫make common ▪**cause** with 270R79
▪**caution** against/about 206R69
▫err on the side of ▪**caution** 467L13
throw ▫**caution** to the ▪wind(s) 1517L2
▫**cautionary** ▪tale 206R78
▫**cautious** ▪optimism 206R52 992L41
A▫laddin's ▪**cave** 31L51
▫**cave** ▪in 207L26
▫**caveat** ▪emptor 207L36
▪**cavil** at 207L54
▫**cavity** ▪wall 207L62
▫**cayenne** ▪pepper 207L71
▫**CD**-▪**ROM** 207R4
▫**cease** ▪fire 207R16/18 523R34
▫glass ▪**ceiling** 598R13
▫hit the ▪**ceiling** 673L19
▫cause **cé**▪**lèbre** 206R28
ce▫**lestial** ▪being 208L16
ce▫**lestial** ▪music 208L17
▪**cell** ▫phone 208L43
con▫demned ▪**cell** 282R77
▪germ ▫**cell** 590L24
▪nerve ▫**cell** 949L27 950R68
▫padded ▪**cell** 1017L73
▫photoelectric ▪**cell** 1059L36/63
▫red ▪blood ▫**cell** 1188R69
se▪clusion ▫**cell** 1278R82
▫sickle-**cell** a▪naemia 1333L70
▫sickle-**cell** a▪nemia 1333L70
▫white ▪blood ▫**cell** 1660R1
▪root ▫**cellar** 1233R56
▪salt ▫**cellar** 1251R42
▫**cellular** ▪phone 208L42
ce▪**ment** ▫mixer 208R6
▫set/▫cast in **ce**▪**ment** 208R9 282L78
▪**censor** from 208R37
not give a ▫red ▪**cent** for 1188R78
per ▪**cent** 1047L59
cor▪rectional ▫**center** 307R72
de▪tention ▫**center** 1201L34
▪nerve ▫**center** 949L28
recre▪ation ▫**center** 1188L10
▪shopping ▫**center** 1321L61/62
▫**central** con▪trol 209L9
▫**central** ▪government 209L12
▫**central** ▪heating 209L14
▫**central** ▪nervous ▫system 209L17
▫**central** reser▪vation 209L20 881R22
▪**centre** around/round/on/upon 209L66
▫**centre** of at▪tention 209L47
▫**centre** of ▪gravity 209L50
▪**centre**-▫spread 209L52
▫**centre** ▪stage 209L57
▫city ▪**centre** 234L72
com▪munity ▫**centre** 272L31
de▪tention ▫**centre** 375L73
detoxifi▪cation ▫**centre** 376L74
▪garden ▫**centre** 582R77
▪health ▫**centre** 655R1
▪job ▫**centre** 765R44
▫left of ▪**centre** 808R51
▪leisure ▫**centre** 810L65
▪music ▫**centre** 931L52
▪nerve ▫**centre** 949L28
recre▪ation ▫**centre** 1188L10
re▪mand ▫**centre** 1201L33
▫right ▫left and ▪**centre** 1223R72
▪shopping ▫**centre** 1321L61/62
take ▫**centre** ▪stage 1406R14
▫town ▪**centre** 1543R34
two ▪**cents** ▫worth 1574R70
ce▫**ramic** ▪hob 209R63
▫**cerebral** ▪palsy 209R79
▫master of ▪**ceremonies** 871R23
initi▪ation ▫**ceremony** 731L66
▫stand on ▪**ceremony** 1410L49
make ▪**certain** 855R3
to a ▪**certain** ex▫tent 486L47
▪birth **cer**▫**tificate** 128R65
▪gift **cer**▫**tificate** 1532R60
Post▫graduate **Cer**▫**tificate** in Edu▪cation 1101R47
▫**certified** ▪mail 211L78
▫**certified** ▫public ac▪countant 211R1
▫**cervical** ▪smear 211R16
▫**chafe** at the ▪bit 130L25
the ▫wheat from the ▪**chaff** 1656L1
▪**chain** ▫letter 212L62
▪**chain** ▫mail 212L42
▫**chain** re▪action 212L67
▪**chain** ▫saw 212L45
▪**chain**-▫smoke 212L73/72
▪**chain** ▫stitch 212L48
▪**chain** ▫store 212L76
▫**chain** ▪up 212L55
▪food ▫**chain** 544L54
▪beanbag ▫**chair** 107R43
▪**chair** ▫lift 212R1
▪easy ▫**chair** 439L7
▫fall off *one's* ▪**chair** 497L32
▪high ▫**chair** 667L53
▪rocking ▫**chair** 1230L9
se▪dan ▫**chair** 1282R3
the e▫lectric ▪**chair** 446L79
▫wing ▪**chair** 1669L17
▫musical ▪**chairs** 931L73
▫**chaise** ▪longue 212R32
▫poisoned ▪**chalice** 1090R37
▫**chalk** and/from ▪cheese 212R54/49
▫**chalk** ▪up 212R75/68
not by a ▪long ▫**chalk** 838L20
▫rise to the ▪**challenge** 1226R40
▪**chamber** ▫music 213R48
▫**chamber** of ▪commerce 213R66
▫**chamber** of ▪horrors 213R69
▪**chamber** ▫orchestra 213R51
▪**chamber** ▫pot 213R53
▪cloud-▫**chamber** 248R45
com▪bustion ▫**chamber** 213R79 261R47
decom▪pression ▫**chamber** 356L11
▪gas ▫**chamber** 584L14
▫star ▪**chamber** 1412R26
the ▫upper ▪**chamber** 1599R40
▫**champ** at the ▪bit 130L25
cham▪**pagne** ▫flute 214L23
▫**champagne** ▪socialist 214L25
▫**champion** ▪hurdler 695L60
a ▫cat in ▪hell's ▫**chance** 203L44
a ▪dog's ▫**chance** 408R56
not a ▫snowball's **chance** in ▪hell 203L45 1367R20
not a/the ▪ghost of a ▫**chance** 594L38
▫blow *one's* ▪**chance** 139L51
▪**chance** *it* 214R40
▫**chance** *one's* ▪arm 214R40
▪**chance** ▫*something* on 214R38
▪**chance** on/upon 214L69/71
▫**chance** would be a ▪fine ▫thing 214R26
▫fighting ▪**chance** 517L75
given ▫half a ▪**chance** 214R28 637L58
▫given the ▪**chance** 596L74
have an ▫eye to/for the main ▪**chance** 488L67
▫sporting ▪**chance** 1396R58
▫stand a (good) ▪**chance** 1411L19
▫**Chancellor** of the Ex▪chequer 214R53
▫vice-▪**chancellor** 1621L38
▫bureau de ▪**change** 176R51
▫**change** a▪bout/a▪round/▪round 215L2
▫**change** ▪down 215R41
▪**change** *something* for/into 214R73 215R14/16
▫**change** for the ▪better 215L4
▪**change** from 214R78 215L1
▫**change** ▪hands 215L6
▫**change** ▫horses in mid▪stream 686L43
▪**change** into 215L77/R40
▫**change** *one's* ▪mind 215L8
▫**change** of di▪rection 215L45
▫**change** of ▪heart 215L47 656R42
▫**change** of ▪pace 215L49
▫**change** of ▪scene 215L44
▫**change** ▪places with 215L13
▫**change** ▪tack 215L14
▫**change** *one's* ▪tune 215L20
▫**change** ▪up 215R43
▫**change** *one's* ▪ways 215L23
▫**change** with the ▪times 1524L29
▫chop and ▪**change** 229R5
▫loose ▪**change** 840R62
▫sea ▪**change** 1276L7
▪sex ▫**change** (operation) 1303L75
▫short-▪**change** 1324L41
▫small ▪**change** 1357R44
▫ring the ▪**changes** 1225R37
▪**changing** ▫room 215R1
the ▫**changing** of the ▪guard 629L72
▪**channel**-▫hopping 215R55
▪**channel** into 216L14/15
▫**Channel** ▪Tunnel 215R72
the ▫English ▪**Channel** 215R68
Gre▫gorian ▪**chant** 623L54
▪**chaos** ▫theory 216L38
▫**chapter** and ▪verse 216R20
▫**chapter** of ▪accidents 216R32
▪**char** for 216R49
▫**char**-▪grilled 216R42
car▪toon ▫**character** 200R22
▪**character** as▫sassin▫ation 216R83

▪character ▫reference 217L2
▫optical ▫character recog▪nition 992L10
re▫formed ▪character 1192L75
▪baton ▫charge 104R45
▪carrying ▫charge 199L50
▫charge a▪bout/a▪round 217R64
▪charge ac▫count 217R13/23 322L45
▪charge ▫card 217R24
▪charge for 217R6/19
▪charge into 217R66
▪charge ▫nurse 218L5
▪charge ▫sheet 217R55
▫charge ▪up 217R67
▪charge with 217R34/35/36 218L12
▪cover ▫charge 316L58
▪depth ▫charge 369R64
pre▫scription ▫charge 1116L70
▪service ▫charge 1297L47
▪bank ▫charges 97R42
re▫verse the ▪charges 1218L16
▪charity ▫shop 218R12
▪charley ▫horse 218R35
▪charm ▫bracelet 219L9
▪charm into 218R57
▪charm of▫fensive 218R51
▫charm the ▪pants off 218R59
▫work like a ▪charm 1682L14
a ▫charmed ▪life 219L19
▪snake ▫charmer 1364L9
▫Prince ▪Charming 1122L76
▪bar ▫chart 98R16
▪flip ▫chart 535L8
▪pie ▫chart 1064L71
▫chase a▪bout/a▪round/▪round 219R18
▫chase a▪way 219R40/41
▫chase out 219R42
▫chase *one's* ▪tail 219R21
▫chase the ▪dragon 219R19
▫chase ▪up 219R54
▫give ▪chase 219R29
▫lead *someone* a (merry) ▪chase 804L32
wild-▪goose ▫chase 1664R21
▪ambulance-▫chaser 39R13/9
▪chastity ▫belt 220L9
▪chat about 220L31/47
▫chat a▪way 220L33
▪chat ▫show 220L49
▫chat ▪up 220L34/38/39
▪chat-up ▫line 220L52 826L63
▪chit-▫chat 228L24/28
▫goods and ▪chattels 612R50
▫chatter a▪way 220L77/80
▫chatter ▪on 220L78
▪chattering ▫classes 220L84
▫male ▪chauvinism 220R29 857R8
▫male ▪chauvinist 857R3
▫male chauvinist ▪pig 857R6
▫cheap and ▪cheerful 220R73
▫cheap and ▪nasty 220R75 938R39
▫cheap at ▪half the ▫price 220R76
▫cheap ▪labour 220R56
▫cheap ▪rate 221L1
▫dirt ▪cheap 220R47 388L3/4
▫not come ▪cheap 221L8
pile it ▫high (and) sell it ▪cheap 1066L69
▪cheat at 221L48
▪cheat on 221L61
▪cheat out of 221L55
▪check ▫book 224L31
▫check book ▪journalism 224L35
▪check for 221L79/81
▪check-in 222L3/10
▫check ▪in at 222L7
▪check into 222L9
▫check ▪off 222L17
▪check on 221L82/R21/22 222L33/34
▫check ▪out 221R7 222L26
▫check ▪out of/from 222L27
▫check ▪up 222L29
▪check with 221R7/14/65
▫double-▪check 414L8
▫hold/▫keep *something* in ▪check 221R34
▪sound ▫check 1378R38
▪spell-▫check 1389R3/4/3
▫spot ▪check 1398L82
take a ▪rain ▫check 1169R69
▪traveler's ▫check 1553L45
▪checking ac▫count 221R80 224L29 336R78
▫checks and ▪balances 221R37
▫cheek by ▪jowl 222R4
▫tongue in ▪cheek 1534R60
▫turn the other ▪cheek 1569R50
with *one's* ▪tongue in *one's* ▫cheek 1534R60
▫hollow-▪cheeked 679L18
▫put some ▪colour in/▫bring some ▪colour to *someone's* ▫cheeks 259R40
▫put the ▪roses (back) into *someone's* ▫cheeks 1234R63
▫be of good ▪cheer 222R61
▫Bronx ▪cheer 168R14
▪cheer for ▫*someone* 222R40
▫cheer ▪up 222R54/56
▫cheap and ▪cheerful 220R73
▫cheery-▪bye 223L18
▫blue ▪cheese 139R73
▫cauliflower ▪cheese 206L64
▫chalk and/from ▪cheese 212R54/49
▪cheese it 223L64
▪cheese ▫knife 223L47
▫cheese ▪off 223L67
▫cottage ▪cheese 310R18
▫cream ▪cheese 321L51
▫curd ▪cheese 336L15
▫hard/▫tough/▫stiff ▪cheese 223L52
▫lemon ▪cheese 810R14
maca▫roni ▪cheese 850L59
▫say ▪cheese 223L51
▫chef ▪d'oeuvre 223R34
▫chemical engin▪eering 223R53
▫chemical e▪quation 223R55
▫chemical ▪formula 223R57
▫chemical re▪action 223R59 1178L7
▫chemical ▪warfare 127R61 223R62 590L31
▫chemical ▪weapon 223R64
▫inorganic ▪chemistry 733L57
or▫ganic ▪chemistry 995L62
▫blank ▪cheque 133L82
▪cheque ac▫count 224L28
▪cheque ▫book 224L31
▫cheque book ▪journalism 224L34
▪cheque ▫card 224L40
▫traveller's ▪cheque 1553L44
▫chequered ▪flag 224L57
▫Chinese ▪chequers 227L36
▫life is just a ▫bowl of ▪cherries 154R29
▫maraschino ▪cherries 864L4
a/an▫other/a ▫double/a ▫second bite of the ▪cherry 130R40
▪chess ▫set 224R21
▫beat *one's* ▪chest 109L38
▫chest of ▪drawers 224R55
▪chest ▫pain 224R36
com▪munity ▫chest 272L33
get *something* ▫off *one's* ▪chest 224R38
▪hope ▫chest 152L67 684R71
keep/hold *one's* ▫cards close to *one's* ▪chest 195L28
▪tea ▫chest 1494L15
▫that'll put ▪hairs on your chest 636L37
▫flat-▪chested 224R45 531L43
▫pigeon-▪chested 1065R43
▫horse ▪chestnut 686R1
▫sweet ▪chestnut 1475R48
▫bite off ▫more than *one* can ▪chew 130R7
▪chew ▫on 225L6/31
▪chew ▫on/▫chew ▪over 225L17
▫chew the ▪cud 333L61
▫chew the ▪fat 225L20
▫chew ▪through 225L9/11
▫chew ▪up 225L16
▪chewing ▫gum 225L23
▫t'ai ▪chi 1485R7
▫chicken and ▪egg 225L71
▫chicken ▪out 225R7
▪chicken ▫wire 225L76
▫play ▪chicken 225L84
▫spring ▪chicken 1399R79/81
▫chief ▪constable 225R52
▫chief ex▪ecutive 225R54/56
▫chief ▪justice 225R58
▫chief of ▪staff 225R63
com▫mander-in-▪chief 269L26
▫Joint Chiefs of ▪Staff 767R69
▪child a▫buse 6R6 226L22
▫child ▪benefit 226L25
▫child ▪bride 164L9
▪child ▫care 226L28
▪child mo▫lester 226L35 912L32
▪child's ▫play 226L18
▫child ▪prodigy 1126R76
▪child-▫rearing 226L38
▪latchkey ▫child 798R33
▪love ▫child 843R42
▫only ▪child 985R76
▫natural ▪childbirth 943L39
▫Early ▪Childhood Education 436R43
▫second ▪childhood 1279L45
▫Aid to Families with Dependent ▪Children 28R12 226L25
▪children's ▫home 226L33
▪flower ▫children 538L32
▪hothouse ▫children 688R9
▫chill ▪out 226R40
▫chill the ▪marrow of 226R13
▫chill to the ▪bone 226R15
▫take the ▪chill off 226R23
the ▫chill ▪wind of 226R31
▪wind-▫chill 1667L1
▫chilli con ▪carne 226R46
▪chilli ▫powder 226R44
▪spine-chilling 1392R12
▫chime ▪in 226R57
▫chime ▫with 226R60/62
▪wind ▫chimes 1667L3
▪chimney ▫breast 226R74
▪chin ▫rest 227L19
▫chuck under the ▪chin 231L24/28
▫double ▪chin 414L11
▫keep *one's* ▪chin up 227L13
▫take it on the ▪chin 227L15
a ▫bull in a ▪china ▫shop 174L46
▫bone ▪china 146L59
for ▫all the tea in ▪China 1494L4
▫Chinese ▪chequers 227L36
▫Chinese ▪gooseberry 227L39 782R13
▫Chinese ▪lantern 227L40
▫Chinese ▪puzzle 227L42
▫chinless ▪wonder 227L64
a ▫chip off the old ▪block 227R16
a ▪chip on *one's* ▫shoulder 227R18
▪bargaining ▫chip 100L26
▫blue ▪chip 139R75
▫chip ▪in 227R15/43/47/50
▪chip ▫shop 227R3
po▪tato ▫chip 1102R84
▫silicon ▪chip 1337R36
▪corn ▫chips 306L27
▫fish and ▪chips 526R8
▪hickory ▫chips 666R7
tor▫tilla ▪chips 1539L17
when the ▫chips are ▪down 227R36
▪chit-▫chat 228L24/28
▫chivvy a▪long/▪up 228L51
▪chivvy *someone* into 228L52
▫sodium ▪chloride 1371L73
▪choc-▫ice 228L77 698R60
▫chock-a-▪block 228L82
▫bitter ▪chocolate 130R61 1074R22
▫bittersweet ▪chocolate 130R61 131L34
▪chocolate ▫box 228R18
▫dark ▪chocolate 346L69 1074R23
▫milk ▪chocolate 896R72
▫plain ▪chocolate 1074R22
▫anti-▪choice 49R63
▫given the ▪choice 596L74
▫Hobson's ▪choice 674R56
▫multiple-▪choice 929L59
▫pro-▪choice 1126L57
▫choke ▪back 228R73
▪choke on 228R64
▪choke with 228R72
▪chomp on 229L30
▪choo-▫choo 229L32
▪choose as 229L43
▪choose between 121L80 229L39
▪choose for 229L42
▪choose from 229L40
▪choose to 229L45/46
▫little/not ▫much to ▪choose between 229L49
▫chop and ▪change 229R5
▫chop-▪chop 229R10
▫chop ▪down 229L66
▫chop ▪off 229L68
▫chop ▪suey 229R42
▫chump ▪chop 231L68
▫strike a ▪chord 1442R34/54
▫vocal ▪chords 1628R41
▫dawn ▪chorus 348R81
a ▫few well-▫chosen ▪words 1652L75
▫well-▪chosen 1652L71
▫choux ▪pastry 230L19
▫Christ Al▪mighty 35R83
▫Christ ▪knows 786R2
for ▫Christ's ▪sake 1250L52
▫vicar of ▪Christ 1620R71
▪christen after 230L33
▫born-again ▪Christian 149R25
▪Christian ▫name 230L54
▫Christian ▪Science 230L57
▪Christmas ▫box 230L75
▪Christmas ▫cake 230L78
▪Christmas ▫card 230L80
▫Christmas ▪cracker 230L82 319L10
▫Christmas ▪Day 230R2
▫Christmas ▪Eve 230R3 471R84
▫Christmas ▪pudding 230R4
▫Christmas ▪stocking 230R8
▪Christmas-▫time 230R11
▪Christmas ▫tree 230R12
▫Father ▪Christmas 506R47 1255L25
▫Merry ▪Christmas 230L74 889L64
▫white ▪Christmas 1660R3
▫chrome ▪yellow 230R33
▪X-▫chromosome 1694L17
▪Y-▫chromosome 1694L63
▫chronic fa▪tigue ▫syndrome 877R18
▫chuck in at the ▪deep ▫end 357L58
▫chuck in the ▪towel 1543L51
▫chuck ▪out 231L17/15/17
▫chuck ▪overboard 1006R60
▫chuck under the ▪chin 231L24/28
▫chum ▪up 231L55
be/go ▫off *one's* ▪chump 231L66
▫chump ▪chop 231L68
▪chunter about 231R6
▫Church of ▪England 231R29
E▫piscopal ▪Church 464L52
es▪tablished ▪church 469L20
▫Free ▪Church 560R58
▫high ▪Church 667R31
▫low ▪church 844R1
▫Roman Catholic ▪Church 1232L38
▫churn a▪bout 231R57
▫churn ▪out 231R64
cigar▪ette ▫butt 232L22
cigar▪ette ▫end 232L22
cigar▪ette ▫holder 232L25
cigar▪ette ▫lighter 232L27
cigar▪ette ▫paper 232L28
▫filter-tipped cigar▪ette 519R48
▪cinder ▫block 232L41
▪dress ▫circle 422R63
▫family ▪circle 232R45 500R73
go ▫round in a ▪circle 232R20
▪semi-▫circle 1290R38
▫square the ▪circle 1402L50
the ▫Arctic ▪Circle 61L66
▫things have/the ▫wheel has come full ▪circle 572L68
▪traffic ▫circle 1237L25 1547R49
▪turning ▫circle 1569L50
▫vicious ▪circle 1621L76
go ▫round in ▪circles 232R20
▫run round in ▪circles 232R20 1241L6
▫smart ▪circles 1358R1
▪circuit ▫breaker 232R60
▪circuit ▫diagram 232R62
▪circuit ▫training 232R74
▫closed circuit ▪television 247L70
▫integrated ▪circuit 739R9
▪logic ▫circuit 837L24
▫printed ▪circuit (▫board) 1123L21
▫short-▪circuit 1321R72/76
▫semi-▪circular 1290R40
▫pomp and ▪circumstance 1093R53
re▫duced ▪circumstances 1190L7
▫under the ▪circumstances 233R18
▫bread and ▪circuses 159L75
▫op ▪cit 987R3
▪cite as 233R76/78 234L6
▪cite for 234L14
▫senior ▪citizen 1292L41
▫Citizens Ad▪vice ▫Bureau 234L30
▪Citizens' Band (▫radio) 234L34
▫parents and ▪Citizens 1026L60
▫citric ▪acid 234L61
▪citrus ▫fruit 234L59
▪citrus ▫tree 234L58
▫city ▪centre 234L72
▫city ▪council 234L75
▫city ▪councillor 234L76
▪City ▫Desk 234R17
▫city ▪fathers 234L77
▫city ▪hall 234L79/82
▫city ▪slicker 234R84
▫city-▪state 234R4
▫garden ▪city 582R79
▫inner ▪city (area) 732L81
▫civil ▪action 235L13
▫civil de▪fence 234R47
▫civil diso▪bedience 234R50
▫civil engin▪eer 234R56/59
▫civil ▪law 235L17
▫civil ▪liberty 234R59
▪civil ▫list 234R63
▫civil ▪rights 234R65
▫civil ▪servant 234R71
▫civil ▪service 234R68
▫civil ▪war 234R72
keep a civil ▪tongue in *one's* ▫head 234R81
▫not have a civil ▪word to ▫say for 234R83
▪civvy ▫street 235L69
▫iron-▪clad 752R26
▪claim for 235R43/61
▪claim ▫form 235R67
▪claim from 235R39
▪claim on 235R44/60
▫claim the moral ▪high ▫ground 235R52
▫claim to ▪fame 235R31
compen▪sation ▫claim 273R77
▫lay ▪claim to 802R55
▫make no ▪claim to 235R29
▪pay ▫claim 1038R54
▫stake a ▪claim 1408L7
▫no-▪claims ▫bonus 957L49
▫small ▪claims 1357R48
▫clam ▪up 236L9
shut ▫up like a ▪clam 236L5
▪clamber into/onto 236L20/21
▪clamber over/up 236L20
▪clamour against 236L33
▪clamour for 236L32/39
▪clamour to 236L34
▫clamp ▪down on 236L71
▫clamp ▪on 236L63
▫clamp to▪gether 236L58
▪wheel ▫clamp 1656L51/55
▫drop a ▪clanger 427R19
▫gathering of the ▪clans 236R2
▫clap a▪long 236R54
▫clap ▪eyes on 236R73 488L73
▪clap into/in 236R72
▪clap on 236R80 237L1
▫clap on the ▪back 236R82
▫clap ▪out 236R56
▫clap *something* ▪over 236R71
▫man/▫woman on the Clapham ▪omnibus 981L83
▪clarion ▫call 237R3
▪clash over 237R11
▪clash with 237R10/16/32/38
person▪ality ▫clash 1053L47
▪clasp ▫knife 237R57
ad▫vanced ▪class 19L76
▪business ▫class 178R52
▪class among/with 238L38
▪class as 238L37
▫class ▫conflict/▫struggle 238L9
▪class-▫conscious 238L5
e▫conomy ▫class 440L62
▪evening ▫class 472R22
▫first ▪class 525R40/48
▫first-class de▪gree 525L82
▫high-▪class 667R38
▫lower ▪class 845L11/9
▪master ▫class 871R64
▫middle ▪class 237R83 894L31
▫ruling ▪class 1240L16
▫second class de▪gree 1279R27
▫third ▪class 1513R19
▪tourist ▫class 1542L79
▫upper ▪class 237R81 1599R28
▫working ▪class 237R81 1679R83
▫world-▪class 1684L73
▪chattering ▫classes 220L84
▫ruling ▪classes 1240L16
▫classic ▪car 238L75
▫classic ▪cut 238L75
▫classified ▪ad 238R70
▪classify into 238R70
▪classify under/as 238R69
▫open ▪classroom 988R62
▪Santa ▫Claus 1255L24
con▫cessive ▫clause 281R41
▫relative ▪clause 1196R19
▪claw at 239L73
▫claw ▪back 239L81
▫claw *one's* ▪way 239L78/77
▫get *one's* ▪claws into 239L63
▫clay ▪pigeon 239R8
▫feet of ▪clay 545L64
▫clean bill of ▪health 241R45
▫clean ▪bowled 241R39
▫clean ▪cut 241L61/65/66
▫clean ▪down 239R31
▫clean ▪off 239R35/33/34/36
▫clean ▪out 239R37/38 241R53/56
▫clean-▪shaven 241L70
▫clean ▪slate/▪sheet 241R50
▫clean ▪up 239R39/42/47 241L40/43/50/R58/61
▫clean up *one's* ▪act 241L52
▫come ▪clean 239R83 266L10
▫dry-▪clean 429R57/54
keep *one's* ▪nose ▫clean 961R72
make a ▫clean ▪break/▪breast (of it) 241L77/35
make a ▫clean ▪sweep 241L81/82
▫slate wiped ▪clean 1350L31
▫spring-▪clean 1399R84/83
▫squeaky-▪clean 1403L59/61
▫wipe the ▪slate clean 1670L60
▫canister ▪vacuum ▫cleaner 189R34
▫cylinder ▪vacuum ▫cleaner 189R35
▪pipe ▫cleaner 1069R37
▫take to the ▪cleaner's 239R60/62
▪cleansing ▫cream 241R75
▪cleansing ▫lotion 241R75
▫ethnic ▪cleansing 470L72
▫clear as a ▪bell 115R34
▫clear a▪way/▪up 242R10/12
▫clear-▪cut 242L32
▪clear ▫*something* for 243L32
▫clear-▪headed 242L45
▪clear of 242L62/66/67/71/R84 243L2/5/6/49
▫clear ▪off 187R76
▪clear off/from 242R16
▫clear ▪out 242R18/19/42 243L47
▫clear-▪sighted 242L48
▫clear ▪snow from 242R15
▫clear the ▪air 242R72/70
▫clear the ▪decks 242R23
▫clear the ▪way 242R28
▫clear *one's* ▪throat 242R25
▫clear ▪up 242L36/38/R22 243L51
▪clear *it* with 243L34
▫crystal ▪clear 332L68/70
leave the ▫field ▪clear 516L27
▫loud and ▪clear 842R81
the ▪coast is ▫clear 251R62
▪clearance ▫sale 242R36
▪clearing ▫bank 243L22
▪clearing ▫house 243L24

▪cleave to 243L78
▪G ▫clef 1554R50
▫treble ▪clef 1554R50
▫cleft ▪lip 243R3
▫cleft ▪palate 243R3
▫anti-▪clerical 49R67/72
▫clerical ▪collar 243R40 257R5
▪booking ▫clerk 147R6
▪desk ▫clerk 373L25
▫parish ▪clerk 1026R47
▫town ▪clerk 1543R58
▪clever-▫clever 243R73
▪clever ▫dick 243R68
too ▫clever by ▪half 243R70
▫click *twice* on 244L34
▪click with 244L20/22
▫double-▪click 414L14
▫client ▪state 244L40
▫climb ▪down 244R18/36/54/59
▪climb into 244R52
▫climb on the ▪bandwagon 97L21
▫climb the ▪walls 244R28
▫climb ▪up/▪over 244R23/17/35
▫social ▪climber 1370R23
▪climbing ▫frame 244R47
▪clinch it 244R66
infer▪tility ▫clinic 726R60
▫clinical de▪pression 245L36 369L69
▫clinical ther▪mometer 245L42
▪bulldog ▫clip 174L73
▫clip-▪clop 245R48/51
▪clip ▫joint 245R54
▫clip ▪off 245R14
▪clip-▫on 245R3/L81/84/R2
▫clip *someone's* ▪wings 245R15
▪paper ▫clip 1023L41
▪cycle ▫clips 340R66
▫cloak-and-▪dagger 245R79/82
▪cloak in 246L7/8
a▫gainst ▪time/the ▪clock 24R18
bio▫logical ▪clock 127R49/54
▪body ▫clock 142R66
by/ac▫cording to the ▪clock 246L67
▪carriage ▫clock 198R21
▪clock at 246L82
▫clock ▪in/▪on 246L84/R4
▫clock ▪out/▪off 246R2/6
▫clock ▪radio 246L76 1167R64
▪clock ▫tower 246L78
▫clock ▪up 246R18/23
▪clock-▫watcher 246L73/74
▪cuckoo ▫clock 332R74
▪grandfather ▫clock 618L76
keep *one's* ▫eye(s) on the ▪clock 246L70
▫put/▫turn the ▪clock ▫back 246L58
▫round/a▫round the ▪clock 246L62
▪time ▫clock 1522R27
▫turn back the ▪clock 246L60
▫turn the ▪clock ▫back 1570R10
▫twenty-four-hour ▪clock 1572R45
▫up with the ▪clock 1598L59
▫watch the ▪clock 246L71 1641L82
▫anti-▪clockwise 49R73
▪clog with 246R63
▪clever ▫clogs 243R68
▫pop *one's* ▪clogs 1095L81
clip-▪clop 245R48/51
a ▫close ▪thing 1512L13
▪close at 247L81
▫close ▪call 1512L14
▫close-▪cropped 247R71
▫close ▪down 247L80
▫close-▪fitting 247R72
▫close-▪grained 247R73
▫close ▪in 248L22/39
▫close ▪in on 248L40
▫close on *someone's* ▪heels 660L31
▫close ▪ranks 247L58
▫close-▪set 247R75
▫close ▪shave/▪call 247R76
▫close the ▪door on 411R46
close the stable/barn ▫door after the ▪horse has bolted 411R52
▫close to the ▪bone 247R68
▪close-up 247R80/L53
▫close up ▪shop 1321L79
▪close with 247L77
come ▫close to ▪blows 139L70 247R67
keep/hold *one's* ▫cards close to *one's* ▪chest 195L28
▫sail close to the ▪wind 1249R30
too ▫close for ▪comfort 247R65
be▫hind closed ▪doors 247L64
▫closed ▪book 247L68
▫closed circuit ▪television 247L70
▪closed ▫season 247L84
▫closed ▪shop 247L73
the ▫closest ap▪proach to 58L12
▪closet with 248L58
▫early-▪closing ▫day 436R46
▪cloth-▫ears 248L74
▪floor ▫cloth 536R25
▪J-▫cloth 757L58
▪Jeye ▫cloth 757L58 763R50
▫man of the ▪cloth 858R72
▪tea ▫cloth 1494L32
▪terry ▫cloth 1505L35
▫cast-off ▪clothes 202L29
▪clothes ▫basket 248R5
▪clothes ▫brush 248R6
▪clothes-▫hanger 248R8 644R53
▪clothes ▫horse 248R8/10
▪clothes ▫line 248R12 824R57
▪clothes ▫peg 248R14
▪clothes ▫pin 248R14
▪clothes ▫rack 248R16
▫plain ▪clothes 1074R24
a ▫wolf in sheep's ▪clothing 1675R32
▫clotted ▪cream 248L66
▪cloud ▫bank 248R42
▪cloud-▫burst 248R42
▪cloud-▫capped 248R43
▪cloud-▫chamber 248R45
▫cloud-▪cuckoo-▫land 248R57
▪cloud hanging ▫over 248R48
▪cloud on the ho▫rizon 248R51
▫cloud ▪over 248R76/70
▫cloud the ▪issue 248R74
▪mushroom ▫cloud 931L22
on ▫cloud ▪nine 248R59
▪storm ▫cloud 1431R82
▫under a ▪cloud 248R54
▫head in the ▪clouds 653L62
▪war ▫clouds 1637L25
▫four-leaf/▫four-leaved ▪clover 556R50
▫live/be in ▪clover 249R78
▫clown a▪round 250L9
▪book ▫club 147L47
▪club-▫house 250L24
▫club ▪sandwich 250L26
▫club ▪soda 250L28 1371L59
▫club to▪gether 250R6
▪country ▫club 313R41
▪fan ▫club 501R52
▪golf ▫club 610R14/15
in the ▪pudding ▫club 1143L52
▫Indian ▪club 721L51
▫join the ▪club 767R25
▪strip ▫club 1444R10
▪youth ▫club 1698R35
▫clue ▪in 250R33/35/31
▫clue ▪up 250R31/36
not have a ▪clue 250R26
▫clump a▪round 250R45
▫clump to▪gether 250R41/42
▪cluster around 250R77
▪cluster ▫bomb 250R74
▫cluster to▪gether 250R78
▪clutch at 250R83
▫clutch at ▪straws 1435L80
▪clutch ▫bag 251L1
in/▫fall into the ▪clutches of 251L4 497R78
▫co-▪ed 254R4/7/14
▫co-edu▪cation 254R13/9
▫co-▪opt 303R61
▫co-pro▪duction 304R29
▫co-res▪pondent 305R56
▫co-▪star 310L26/30
▫co-▪worker 317R82
▫co-▪write 318L19/12
▪coach ▫station 251L67
▫drive a ▫coach and ▪horses through 424R75
▫coal ▪black 251R15
▪coal ▫bunker 251R16
▪coal ▫face 251R18
▪coal ▫field 251R21
▫coal-▪fired 251R22 523R10
▪coal ▫miner 251R25
▪coal ▫scuttle 251R26
▪coal ▫tar 251R28
▫hard ▪coal 49R14
carry/take ▫coals to ▪Newcastle 251R11
▫haul/▫drag *someone* over the ▪coals 251R8
▫coast to ▪coast 251R66/67
▫East ▪Coast 438L70
the ▪coast is ▫clear 251R62
▫West ▪Coast 1654L8
▪roller ▫coaster 124L83 1231L76
▪coat-▫hanger 252L11 644R54
▪coat-▫hook 252L12
▪coat in/with 252L25/26
▫coat of ▪arms 252L41
▪coat-▫peg 252L12
▪coat-▫tails 252L13
▪duffel ▫coat 431L72
▪duffle ▫coat 431L72
▪frock ▫coat 567L20
▪sugar-▫coat 1066R36
▪tail ▫coat 1485R16
▪trench ▫coat 1555R54
▫sugar-▪coated 252L39 1457L17/20
▫corn on the ▪cob 306L31
▫cobble to▪gether 252L65
blow the ▪cobwebs a▫way 138R69
▫Coca ▪Cola 252R6
▫cock-a-doodle-▪doo 252R35
▫cock-a-▪hoop 252R67
▫cock-a-▪leekie 252R36
▫cock a ▪snook at 252R62
▫cock-and-▪bull ▫story 252R29
▪cock ▫crow 252R26
▪cock ▫fight 252R38
▫cock-of-the-▪walk 252R33
▪cock-▫tease 252R42 1120R80/82
▫cock ▪up 252R70/75
▫sulphur-crested cocka▪too 1458R19
go ▫off half-▪cocked 637R36/37
▫cocker ▪spaniel 253L44
warm the ▫cockles of *someone's* ▪heart 1638L65
▫cockney ▪rhyming ▫slang 253L64
▪cocktail ▫dress 253R46
▪cocktail ▫lounge 253R48
▪cocktail ▫stick 253R50
▫Molotov ▪cocktail 912L58
▪cocoa ▫butter 253R71
▪coconut ▫butter 253R80
▪coconut ▫shy 253R81
co▪coon against/from 254L4
▫cod-liver ▪oil 254L10
▪area ▫code 61R24 254L41 379R25
▪bar ▫code 98R19
▪bar-code ▫reader 820R37
▪code ▫name 254L42/45
▫code of ▪practice 254L57 1107R21
▪dialling ▫code 379R24
▪dress ▫code 422L84
ge▫netic ▪code 588L45
▫Highway ▪Code 669R48
ma▪chine ▫code 850R44
▪penal ▫code 1044L65
▪sorting ▫code 1377R62
▪zip ▫code 254L39 1700R26
▫colour-▫coded 259R49
co▪erce into 254R29
▫cri de ▪coeur 323R67
▫black ▪coffee 131R21 254R69
▪coffee ▫bean 254R72
▪coffee ▫break 254R74
▪coffee ▫cake 254R76
▪coffee-▫coloured 254R70
▪coffee-▫grinder 254R79 624R1
▪coffee ▫house 254R81
▪coffee ▫klatch 254R83
▪coffee ▫mill 254R79
▪coffee-▫morning 255L1
▪coffee ▫pot 255L4
▪coffee ▫shop/▫bar 255L7
▪coffee ▫table 255L9
▪coffee-table ▫book 255L11
▪filter ▫coffee 519R44/45
▫Irish ▪coffee 752L80
drive a ▫nail into *someone's* ▪coffin 935R57
▪cog in a/the ma▫chine 255L33
▪cogitate about/on/upon 255L47
▫cognitive psy▪chology 255L62
▫cognitive ▪therapy 255L64
▫take ▪cognizance of 255L75
co▪habit with 255R8
▪coil around 255R69
▪coil into 255R71
shuffle ▫off this mortal ▪coil 1331L45
a ▫spin of the ▪coin 1391R81
▫coin ▪money 256L2
▫spin a ▪coin 1391R52
the ▫other side of the ▪coin 1333R7
to ▫coin a ▪phrase 256L10
▫toss a ▪coin 1539R22
coin▪cide with 256L19/20/22/26
▫post-▪coital 1101L39
▫coitus inter▪ruptus 256L44
▫Coca ▪Cola 252R6
as ▫cold as ▪ice 256L74
▫blow ▫hot and ▪cold 138R74
▪cold ▫bag 256R6 302R57
▫cold-▪blooded 256R10/61
▫cold ▪call 256R13
▫cold ▪comfort 256R17
▪cold ▫cream 256R19
▪cold ▫cuts 256R21
▫cold-▪eyed 256R62
▫cold ▪fish 256R64
▪cold ▫frame 246L30 256R22
▫cold ▪front 256R27
▫cold-▪hearted 256R66
▫cold-▪shoulder 256R53
▪cold ▫shower 256R30
▪cold ▫snap 256R32
▪cold ▫sore 256R84
▪cold ▫storage 256R34
▫cold ▪sweat 256R35
▫cold ▪truth 256R67
▫cold ▪turkey 256R39
▫cold ▪war 256R68
▫common ▪cold 270R56
▫get ▪cold 256L83
get/have ▫cold ▪feet 256L80
▪head ▫cold 653R32
▫ice-▪cold 698R76
in ▫cold ▪blood 256R57
▫leave *someone* ▪cold 807L73
leave ▫out in the ▪cold 807L75
make *someone's* ▫blood run ▪cold 137L48 1242L6
▫pour/▫throw cold ▪water on 256R2
▫stone-▪cold 1429R36
▫stone-cold ▪sober 1369R64 1429R39
▫throw cold ▪water on 1517L5
col▪laborate on 257L18
col▪laborate with 257L19/34
col▪lapse with 257L56
▫blue ▪collar 139R79
▫button-down ▪collar 180R9
▫clerical ▪collar 243R40 257R5
▪collar ▫bone 257R12
▪dog ▫collar 243R41 257R5 408R66
▫hot under the ▪collar 687R17
▫Peter Pan ▪collar 1055R53
▪pink-▫collar 1068R21
▫white-▪collar 1660R6
▫wing ▪collar 1669L18
▫call col▪lect 184R3 1218L17
col▪lect for 257R54
col▫lect *one's* ▪wits 1674R52
col▫lective ▪bargaining 258L25
col▫lective ▪farm 258L28
col▫lective ▪noun 258L31
▫free collective ▪bargaining 560R60
col▪lector's ▫item/▫piece 257R68
▪garbage col▫lector 582R52
▪refuse col▫lector 433L66 1193L15
e▫lectoral ▪college 446L62
▫junior ▪college 773R16
▪teacher's ▫college 1494L75/74
teacher-▪training ▫college 1494L74
col▫legiate uni▪versity 258L67
col▪lide into 258L77
col▪lide with 258L75/77
on a col▪lision ▫course 258R2
▪collocate with 258R17/20
col▪lude with 258R49
▫eau de co▪logne 258R59 439L83
▫Colonel ▪Blimp 258R72
co▫lonial men▪tality 259L40
▫crown ▪colony 329L72
▪penal ▫colony 1044L67
▪color ▫line 260L34
▫Colorado po▪tato ▫beetle 259L67
▪colour ▫bar 260L33
▪colour ▫blind 259R45
▪colour-▫coded 259R49
▪colour-▫fast 259R52
▫colour ▪in 259R70
▪colour ▫prejudice 260L36
▪colour ▫scheme 259R54
▪colour ▫supplement 259R56
▪colour with 259R72
▪earth ▫colour 437R23
have a ▫high ▪colour 259R38
▫local ▪colour 834R11
▪poster ▫colour 1101R9/32
▫primary ▪colour 1121R42
▫put some ▪colour in *someone's* ▫cheeks 259R40
▫riot of ▪colour 1226L9
see the ▫colour of *someone's* ▪money 1283L67
▫troop the ▪colour 1560L73
▪coffee-▫coloured 254R70
▪flesh-▫coloured 533L66
▫plain-▪coloured 1074R28
▫nail *one's* ▫colours to the ▪mast 935R77
see *someone* in *their* ▫true ▪colours 260L64
▫show *one's* true ▪colours 260L63
under ▫false ▪colours 499R58
with ▫flying ▪colours 541L10
▫pre-Co▪lumbian 1108R80
ad▪vice ▫column 27L44/49
▪agony ▫column 27L44/49/48
▪debit ▫column 353L47
▫fifth ▪column 528L39/41
▪gossip ▫column 614L12
▪personal ▫column 1052R77
▫spinal ▪column 260R60 1392R1/46
▪steering ▫column 1419L57
▪comb *somewhere* for 261L49
▫comb ▪out 261L47
with a ▫fine-▪tooth comb 521L84
▫armed ▪combat 261L56
▫single ▪combat 1341L14
▫unarmed ▪combat 261L57
▫non-▪combatant 959L68
com▪bine against 261L82
com▪bine ▪forces 548L28
▫combine ▪harvester 261R6
com▪bining ▫form 261R9
com▪bustion ▫chamber 213R79 261R47
internal com▪bustion ▫engine 743R52
spon▫taneous com▪bustion 1396L42
▫come a ▪cropper 327L58
▫come a▪bout 265R8 266L12
▫come a▪cross 264R56 266L25
▫come a▪cross/▪over as 264R62
▫come ▪after 265R21/22
▫come a▪long 261R66 265L23 266L29/78/R1
▫come and ▪go 265L46
▫come a▪way 261R70
▫come ▪back 88R81 261R71 265L24
come back/down/back down to ▪earth 437L70
come ▫back from the ▪dead 350R65
▫come back/home to ▪roost 1233R40
▪come before 265R30
▪come between 121R26 266L31
▪come ▫by 261R76/77 266L34
▫come ▪clean 239R83 266L10
come ▫close to ▪blows 139L70 247R67
▫come ▪down 261R79/80/81/83 264L49/52 265L59/R38 266R59/L39
come ▪down in the ▫world 1685L16
▫come down on one side of the fence or ▪other 1333R13
▫come ▪down to 266L44 416L32/35
▫come ▪down with 416L24
come ▫face-to-▪face with 490R22
▪come for 264L55/56/57 265L13 266L41
▫come ▪forward 264L58/R69
▪come from 264L51/59 265L59/66/67/68/69/70/71 266R57
come ▫hell or high ▪water 661L33
▫come ▪home to 680L50
▫come ▪in 264L62 265L25/26/28/30/32/39/76/77/78/79/R17/18 266L50
▫come in the ▫world 416L28
▫come ▪into 264L64/65/67
▫come into ▪bloom 138L47
▫come into ▪flower 538L26
▫come into ▪play 1079L42
▫come of ▪age 24R75/78
come ▪off 265R41/42/43/44/46/47/48 266L58/63/68/73 1032L21
▫come ▪on 265L35/R51/53 266L78/R1/5/6/11/63 267L7
▪come-on ▫line 220L52 825R83 826L64
▫come on ▪strong 1445R30
▫come ▪out 264L69/70/74 265L55/57/61/R57/58/60/62/64/67 266R16/21/29/23/26 1000L61
▫come ▪out a▫gainst 266R20
▫come ▪out in ▪sympathy with 1480R45
come ▫out of *one's* ▪shell 1314R39
▫come out of the ▪woodwork 1677R73
▫come ▪over 264R57 266R40/44
come ▫rain or ▪shine 1169R67
▫come ▪round 265R7
▫come ▪round/a▪round 266R49/55
▫come ▪round/▪over 264L78 265L14
▫come the raw ▪prawn 1176R52
▫come ▪through 264L80 265L39/40/R71
▪come to 264L52/80/81/83/84/R72/79 265L14/R76/78/80/81 266R8/51/58/79
▫come to a full ▪stop 572R67
▫come to a ▪head 653L42
▫come to a pretty ▪pass 1119R71
▫come to a sticky ▪end 1423R7
▫come to an ▪end 455L25
▫come to *someone's* as▪sistance 73L18
▫come to ▪grief 623R54
▫come to ▪grips with 624R58
▫come to ▪heel 660L29
▫come to ▪life 818R50
▫come to ▪light 820R10
▫come to ▪nothing 266R72
▫come to ▪pass 265R9
▫come to ▪pieces 1064R22
▫come to ▪rest 1212L83
▫come to ▪terms 266R73 1503R75/78
▫come to the ▪conclusion 282L12
▫come to the ▫end of the ▪road 1228L39
▪come towards 264R46
▫come ▪true 1563R13
▫come ▪under 265R24/26/82
▫come under the ▪hammer 639R26
▫come un▪glued 1588R68
▫come un▪stuck 266L5/8 1596L13
▫come ▪up 266R60/82 267L1 1598L36
▫come ▪up a▫gainst 265L42
▫come up ▫smelling of ▪roses 1360L29
▫come ▪up to 264R47 265L44
▫come up ▪trumps 1564L30
▫come ▪up with 267L4
come ▫up with the ▪goods 612R49
▪come upon 267L7
▫come-▪uppance 267L51
▪come with 264R48/69/73 265L80 266L22/66/R27
▫come with the ▪territory 1504R63
▫come within an ▪ace of 10R54

cross ▪that bridge when you ▪come to it 327R6
easy ▫come easy ▪go 438R80
first ▫come first ▪served 525R4
have come a ▫long ▪way 838L12
have ▫come to ▪stay 1417L9
▫hour has ▪come 689L4
▫not come a▪miss 41R26/28
▫not come ▪cheap 221L8
▫not come ▫up to expec▪tation(s) 480R81
the ▫shape of things to ▪come 1310R63 1512L62
▫things have/the ▫wheel has come full ▪circle 572L68
till/until ▫kingdom ▪come 781L53
till/until the ▪cows come ▫home 317L48
to ▫kingdom ▪come 781L55
▫how ▪come? 690R12/15
▫black ▪comedy 131R67
▫comedy of ▪manners 267L29
situ▫ation ▪comedy 1344L28
if the ▫worst comes to the ▪worst 1687L26
if/when it ▫comes to the ▪crunch 330R70
if/when it ▫comes to the ▪push 1151R20
if/when ▫push comes to ▪shove 1151L62
it all comes to the ▫same ▪thing 1252R42
▫cold ▪comfort 256R17
▪comfort ▫food 267L70
▪comfort ▫station 267L72
▪comfort ▫stop 267L73
▫eat for ▪comfort 439L36
▫take ▪comfort from 267L67
too ▫close for ▪comfort 247R65
▫comic ▫book 267R21
▫comic ▪opera 267R32
▪comic ▫strip 267R24
▫backward in coming ▪forward 91R8
▫coming up ▪roses 1234R65
▫saw/could ▫see it ▪coming 1283L52
the ▫Second ▪Coming 1279L50
▫up-and-▪coming 1597R76
▫comings and ▪goings 265L50
▫comity of ▪nations 267R38
in▫verted ▪comma 749R72 1164R12
▪command ▫module 267R73
com▪mand per▫formance 267R75
▫second-in-com▪mand 1279L79
com▫mander-in-▪chief 269L26
the ▫Ten Com▪mandments 269L34 1499R42
▫comme il ▪faut 269L42
com▪mend for/on 269L70
com▪mend to 269L72
▪comment on/about 269R6/13
▪commentary ▫box 269R29
▫running ▪commentary 269R28 1241R36
chamber of ▪commerce 213R66
high com▪mission 668R4/5/L83/R7
om▫missioned ▪officer 270L38
om▫mit ▪suicide 270L55
e▫lect com▪mittee 1286L58
steering com▫mittee 1419L60
y ▫common con▪sent 289R83
common ▪cold 270R56
common de▪nominator 270R83 271L2
common ▪ground 270R75 626R11
common ▪knowledge 270R43 787R54
common ▪law 270R57
common ▪man 270R45
Common ▪Market 271L7 443L8
common ▪noun 271L9
common-or-▪garden 270R47
common ▫room 271L13
common ▪sense 270R64
r the ▫common ▪good 270R53
lowest common de▪nominator 844R16
make common ▪cause with 270R79
e ▫common ▪touch 270R50
House of ▪Commons 689R30
om▪mune with 264R80
om▪municate by/through/in 271R24
om▪municate with 271R26/29/35
ommuni▪cation ▫cord 271R52
ommuni▪cations ▫satellite 271R73
om▫munion of ▪saints 271R13
Holy Com▪munion 679L81
bedroom com▫munity 111R61
om▪munity ▫centre 272L31
om▪munity ▫chest 272L33
om▪munity ▫service 272L36
om▪munity ▫spirit 272L39
uropean Com▪munity 471L49
commu▪tation ▫ticket 272L55 1277R60
com▪mute from 272L64
com▪mute into 272L60/62
com▪mute to 272L65
com▪muter ▫belt 116R1
com▪muter ▫train 272L50
▫compact ▪disc 272L75
▫company ▪car 272R34
▪company ▫man 272R35
▫company ▪policy 272R37
▪company ▫style 1449R46
▪company ▫town 272R39
▪holding ▫company 677L70
in ▫good ▪company 272R70
▫joint-stock ▪company 767R77
▫listed ▪company 829R22
▫parent ▪company 1026L57
▫part ▪company 1028R77
▫present ▫company ex▪cepted 272R54 476L75 1116R67
▫public ▪company 1142L25
▪repertory ▫company 1204R12
the as▫sembled ▪company 71R78
com▫pare ▪notes 273L20/18
com▪pare to/with 273L43/44/45/16/17/14/47/48/51
▪pale in com▫parison with 1020L28
▪freezer com▫partment 563L52
▪glove com▫partment 601R6
▪compass ▫point 273L81
▪compass ▫reading 273L83
com▪passion fa▫tigue 273R16 507L17
com▫passionate ▪leave 273R22
▪compensate for 273R72/81/83 274L60
compen▪sation ▫claim 273R77
com▪pete against/with 274L84/R61
com▪pete for 274L79/83
com▪pete in 274L82
com▪pete to 274L80
com▪plain about 275L56
com▪plain of 275L62
com▪plain to 275L61
comple▫mentary ▪angles 275R14
comple▫mentary ▪medicine 275R15
com▪plete and ▫utter 275R45
it's a com▫plete ▪mystery 934R58
a com▫pletely different ▪ball ▫game 95R36
▫complex ▪sentence 275R62
▫complex ▪word 275R66
▪guilt ▫complex 631L57
inferi▪ority ▫complex 726R29
▫military-in▪dustrial ▫complex 896R20
▪Oedipus ▫complex 975L51
perse▪cution ▫complex 1052L8
superi▪ority ▫complex 1462R56
▪compliment(s) ▫slip 276L69
▫left-handed/▫back-handed ▪compliment 808R40
▫fish for ▪compliments 276L57
▫compos ▪mentis 277L28
▫non compos ▪mentis 959R76
com▪pose for 276R41/42/43
com▪pose into 276R69
com▪posed of 276R71/72/73/74
▫composite ▪photograph 1059L66
▫composite ▪sketch 701R3
▫compound ▪fracture 277L63
▫compound ▪leaf 277L65
com▪pound with 277L72
compre▫hensive in▪surance 277R34
com▪press into 277R52/53
com▫pressed ▪air 277R54
com▪prised of 277R72
▪compromise at/on 279L3
▪compromise between 277R80
▪compromise with 279L1
com▫pulsory ▪purchase ▫order 279L48
com▪puter ▫dating 279L77
com▪puter ▫game 279L80
com▪puter ▫program 1129L55
com▪puter ▫science 279L82
▫laptop com▪puter 963R53
▫personal com▪puter 1052R82
▫chilli con ▪carne 226R46
▪con ▫artist 65R12 279R41
▪con into 279R36
▪con ▫man 279R42 286L37
▪con ▫rod 288R12
▫mod ▪con 910L4
con▪ceal from 279R64/65
con▪cede to 279R83 280L7
con▪ceive of 280L27/29/26/28/30/32/34
▫ill-con▪ceived 703L79
▪concentrate on 280L67/69/71/73
concen▪tration ▫camp 280R32
Im▫maculate Con▪ception 705L83
con▪cern *oneself* with 280R82
to ▫whom it may con▪cern 281L1
as far as ▪I'm con▫cerned 281L19
at ▪concert ▫pitch 281L63
▪benefit ▫concert 117L70
▪concert-▫goer 281L60
▫concert ▪grand 281L61 618L43
concer▪tina ▫file 281L83
concer▪tina into 281R7/9
con▪cessive ▫clause 281R41
con▪ciliate between 281R59
▫come to the ▪conclusion 282L12
▫forgone con▪clusion 549L63 551L53
▫jump to a con▪clusion 772R79
▫concrete ▪jungle 282L79
▪concrete ▫mixer 282L82
▫concrete ▪noun 282R10
▫concrete ▪over 282R2
▫reinforced ▪concrete 1195R19
▫set/▫cast in ▪concrete 208R9 282L78
con▪cur with *someone* on/in 282R24
con▪demn as 282R51/54
con▪demn for 282R52
con▪demn to 282R63/65/66
con▫demned ▪cell 282R77
con▫densed ▪milk 283L5
conde▪scend to 283L19
in ▫mint con▪dition 902L1
▪air-con▫ditioned 29L48
▪air con▫ditioner 29L44/46
▫under the con▪ditions of 283L62
▫safe-▪conduct 1248R7
▪bus con▫ductor 178L48
▪lightning con▫ductor 822L22
▫cone ▪off 285L60
▪ice cream ▫cone 306R44 698R80
▪nose ▫cone 962L66
▪pine ▫cone 1068L59
▪traffic ▫cone 1547R49
con▪fectioners' ▫sugar 285L79
con▪fer on/upon 285R20
con▪fer with 285R17
▪news ▫conference 953L17
▪press ▫conference 1118R72
▪confidence ▫man/▫trickster 286L36
▪confidence ▫trick 286L33
in the ▫strictest ▪confidence 1440R36
▫take *someone* into *one's* ▪confidence 286L11
▫vote of ▪confidence 1631L37
vote of ▫no ▪confidence 1631L45
con▪fine to 286L53/55/56/59/61/62
▫solitary con▪finement 1373R36
▪class ▫conflict 238L9
con▪flict with 286R52/61/63/67
con▪form to 286R81
con▪form with 286R81
con▪front by/with 287L33/28/24
▫conger ▪eel 287R10
▪congregate around 287R54
con▪jecture about 288L14
▫conjugal ▪rights 288L24
a ▫name to ▪conjure with 937L29
▫conjure ▪up 288L59/64/66/68
▪conjuring ▫trick 288L61
▫conk ▪out 288L77
con▫nect ▪up to 288R2/3/52
con▪nect with 288R32/33/51/61
▫well-con▪nected 1652L78
con▪necting ▫rod 288R12
con▪nective ▫tissue 288R66
con▪nive at 288R74
con▪nive with 288R71
▫Norman ▪Conquest 961L27
▪conscience-▫stricken 289L59
▫guilty ▪conscience 289L42 631L73
in ▫good ▪conscience 289L58
▫prick *someone's* ▪conscience 1120R71
▫prisoner of ▪conscience 1123R55
▫social ▪conscience 1370R25
consci▫entious ob▪jector 289L63
▪class-▫conscious 238L5
▪fashion-▫conscious 505L40
▪price-▫conscious 1120R31
▪consciousness ▫raising 289R28
▫stream of ▪consciousness 1436R12
con▪script into 289R33
▫consecrate *one's* ▪life to 289R50
▫age of con▪sent 25L47
by ▫common con▪sent 289R83
con▪sent to 289R75/77
▫suffer/▫take the ▪consequences 290L11
con▪sider *it* ▪done 290R76
con▪sider for 290R16/17
▫all things con▪sidered 1512L52/R4
con▫sidered o▪pinion 290R22
con▪sign to 291L5/16/18/20/21
con▪sist in 291L28
con▪sist of 291L23
conso▪lation ▫prize 291L73
con▪sole with 291L61
con▫solidate *one's* ▪hold on 291R6/7
the con▫solidated ▪fund 291R12
con▪sort together 291R32
con▪sort with 291R33
▫prince ▪consort 1122L78
con▪spiracy ▫theory 291R82
con▪spire against 291R61
con▪spire to 291R59/64/67
con▪spire together 291R59
con▪spire with 291R61
▫chief ▪constable 225R52
po▫lice ▪constable 1091R17
▫constitutional ▪monarchy 293L14
con▪struct of 293L81
con▪strue as 293R32
con▪sult on 293R52
con▪sult with 293R56
con▪sumed by/with 294L1
con▫sumer ▪durables 294L18
con▫sumer ▪price ▫index 294L21 1214R79
con▫sumer pro▪tection 294L22
con▪sumer so▫ciety 294L25
▫anti-con▪sumerist 49R76
▪time-con▫suming 1521R72
fit for ▫human con▪sumption 527L72 692L73
▪contact ▫lenses 294R22
▪contact ▫sports 294R19 1396R39
▪eye ▫contact 488R36
have ▪contact with 179L46 294L82 635L76
con▪taminated by 295L43
▫contemplate *one's* ▪navel 944L27
con▪tempt of ▪court 295R61
con▪tend against 295R80
con▪tend for 295R80
con▪tent with 296L15/21
to *one's* ▫heart's con▪tent 656R77
▫bone of con▪tention 146L51
▫in/▫out of con▪tention for 296L51
▪beauty ▫contest 110L19
▪talent ▫contest 1488L51
▫continental ▪breakfast 296R70
▫continental ▪drift 296R55
▫continental ▪quilt 296R73 433R34
▫continental ▪shelf 296R57
con▪tinue as 297L27
con▪tinue on 297L29/32
con▪tinue to 297L19/20
con▪tinue with 297L24
con▫tinuous as▪sessment 297L53
▫past con▪tinuous 1033R14
▫past perfect con▪tinuous 1033R26
▫present con▪tinuous 1116R42
con▪tort with 297R76
▪contour ▫lines 298L17
con▫tract ▪in 298L60
con▫tract ▪out 298L63
con▪tract to 298L49/58/62/65/75
con▪tract with 298L59
con▪tractile ▫tissue 298L79
▫contradiction in ▪terms 298R31
a ▫mass of contra▪dictions 870R36
▫contrary to popular o▪pinion 298R83
con▪trast with 299L19/27
con▪tribute to/towards 299L52/56/51/54
con▫tributory ▪negligence 299L79
con▫tributory ▪pension ▫scheme 299L74
▫non-con▪tributory 959L72
con▪trive to 299R13
▫air traffic con▪trol 29R20/17
▪arms-con▫trol 63L9
bio▫logical con▪trol 127R56
▪birth con▫trol 128R67
▪birth control ▫pill 128R69
▫central con▪trol 209L9
con▪trol ▫key 299R67
con▪trol ▫tower 299R70
mission con▪trol 906R18
▪quality con▫trol 1158L33
re▫mote con▪trol 1202R9/13
▪spin con▫trol 1392L30
▪stock con▫trol 1427R51
con▪venience ▫food 300R8
▫flag of con▪venience 529L42
▫marriage of con▪venience 868L13
▫public con▪venience 1142L27
▪convent ▫school 300R14
Ge▫neva Con▪vention 588L59
con▪verge on 300R60/61
conver▪sation ▫piece 301L13
con▪vert into 301L44/46
con▪vert to 301L46/48/52/53
▫preach to the con▪verted 1109L32
▫catalytic con▪verter 203R44
the ▫courage of *one's* con▪victions 314R19
con▪vince of 301R58
con▪vince to 301R60
con▪vulse with/in 302L28/27
▫bill and ▪coo 126R19
▪coo over 302L46
▪cook for 302L52
▫cook *someone's* ▪goose 302L64
▫cook the ▪books 302L61
▫cook ▪up 302L65
▫cooked ▪breakfast 302L82
▫cooked to a ▪turn 1570R52
▪Aga ▫cooker 24L34
▪pressure ▫cooker 1118L61
▪cookery ▫book 302R9
▪fortune ▫cookie 555L49
▪cooking ▫apple 302R17
▫blow *one's* ▪cool 139L37
▪cool ▫bag 302R43
▪cool ▫cat 203L83
▫cool ▪customer 303L44
▫cool ▪down/▪off 302R76/46
▪cool it 302R83
keep a ▫cool ▪head 302R69 653R80
▫play it ▪cool 1078R26
▪air-▫cooled 29L50
▪water-▫cooled 1642R6
▪cooler ▫bag 256R7 302R56
▫cooling-▪off ▫period 303L32 1049L34
▪cooling ▫tower 302R58
▫coop ▪up 303L81/77
co▪operate in 303R39/40/42
co▪operate with 303R40/41
as ▫bald as a ▪coot 95L52
▫cop a ▪plea 304L41
▪cop for 304L30
▪cop it 304L43/55
▫cop ▪out 304L79/R1
▪cop ▫shop 304L49
it's a ▫fair ▪cop 494R79
▪traffic ▫cop 1547R70
▫bite off ▫more than *one* can ▪cope with 130R7
▪cope with 304L59/61/62
▫copper-▪bottomed 304R14
▪back ▫copy 89L19
▫carbon ▪copy 194L69
▪copy *something* from 304R52
▪copy from/off 304R58
▫fair ▪copy 495R26
▫hard ▪copy 646L45
▫blot *one's* ▪copybook 138R13
▫cor ▪anglais 305L52
▫coral ▪reef 305L49
communi▪cation ▫cord 271R52
e▪mergency ▫cord 271R53
ex▪tension ▫cord 485R67/66
▪sash ▫cord 1255R56
▫spinal ▪cord 1392R48
um▪bilical ▫cord 1578R30
▫lime ▪cordial 823R25
▫cordon ▪bleu 305R18
▫cordon ▪off 305R15
▫vocal ▪cords 1628R41
▫core cur▪riculum 305R47
▪hard ▫core 646L47/R50/54
▫hard-core ▪music 646R56
▫cork ▪up 305R81/82
▪corn ▫bread 306L26
▪corn ▫chips 306L27
▪corn ▫oil 306L29
▫corn on the ▪cob 306L31
▫corn ▪syrup 306L33
▫Indian ▪corn 854L79
▪seed ▫corn 1284R4
▪corncob ▫pipe 306L49
▫corned ▪beef 306L58
a▫round the ▪corner 63R79
▫box/▫force into a ▪corner 306R11
▫corner a/the ▪market 306R31
▫corner on a ▪market 306R8
▪corner ▫shop 306R14
▫cut a ▪corner 339R61
▫distant/▫far corner of the ▪globe/▪world/▪earth 306R84
▪doll ▫corner 410L35
▫fight *one's* ▪corner 517L29
▫just a▫round the ▪corner 306L79
on/at ▫every ▪corner 473R3
out of/from the ▫corner of *one's* ▪eye 306R5
▫round the ▪corner 1236R73
▫tight ▪corner 1520L14
▫turn the ▪corner 1569R7
▫all the corners of the ▪world/▪earth 306R2
▫cut ▪corners 339R62
▫Cornish ▪pasty 306R69
▫coronary ▪heart ▫disease 307L25
▫coronary throm▪bosis 307L16
▫corporal ▪punishment 307L43
▫lance ▪corporal 793R65
▫corporate ▪image 307L64
corpo▪ration ▫tax 307L61
▫corps de ▪ballet 307R3
diplo▪matic ▫corps 386R8
es▫prit de ▪corps 468L83
Ma▫rine ▫Corps 865L58
the ▪Peace ▫Corps 1039R58
▫habeas ▪corpus 634L54
▫red ▪corpuscle 1188R70
▪white cor▫puscle 1660R1
cor▫rect me if I'm ▪wrong 307R37
▫make (all) the cor▫rect ▪noises 958R61
po▫litically cor▪rect 1092L65/69
▫stand cor▪rected 1410R36
▫house of cor▪rection 689L50

cor▪rectional ▫center/fa▫cility 307R72
po▫litical **cor▪rectness** 1092L52
corre▪spond to 307R84 308L2/3
corre▪spond with 308L4/6/18
corres▪pondence ▫course 308L29
▪court **corre▫spondent** 315L75
▪lobby **corre▫spondent** 834L51
▫**corridors** of ▪power 308L43
cos▫metic ▪surgery 308R80
the ▫**cosmological** ▪argument 309L79
at ▪all ▫**cost(s)** 310L13
▫count the ▪**cost(s)** 312L6/9
at ▪any ▫**cost** 310L13
▫**cost** *someone* ▪dear 309R69 310L19/20 352L37
▫**cost-ef▪fective** 309R36
▫**cost** of ▪living 309R41
▫**cost** of ▪living ▫index 309R45 1214R78
▪**cost** ▫price 309R47
▫hang the ▪**cost** 644L52
▫indirect ▪**cost** 722L39
▪running ▫**costs** 1241R66
▪bathing ▫**costume** 104L74 1476R65
▪**costume** ▫drama 310L50
▪**costume** ▫jewellery 310L53
▪swimming ▫**costume** 1476R64
▪tea ▫**cosy** 1494L18
▪**cot** ▫death 310L84
▫**cottage** ▪cheese 310R18
▫**cottage** ▪industry 310R20
▫**cottage** ▪loaf 310R21
▫**cottage** ▪pie 310R22 1315L46
▫tied ▪**cottage** 1519R22
▪**cotton** ▫balls 310R45
▫**cotton** ▪batting 310R45
▪**cotton** ▫belt 116R3
▪**cotton** ▫bud 310R37
▫**cotton** ▪candy 189R8 310R39
▪**cotton** ▫gin 310R40
▫**cotton** ▪on 310R57
▪**cotton** ▫pads 310R49
▪**cotton**-▫picking 310R42
▪**cotton** to 310R54
▫**cotton** ▪wool 310R44
▪casting ▫**couch** 202L60
▪**couch** in 310R68
▪**couch** po▫tato 310R61
▪**cough** ▫drop 311L13
▪**cough** ▫lollies 311L14
▪**cough** ▫medicine 311L11
▪**cough** ▫mixture 311L12
▪**cough** ▫sweet 311L13
▫**cough** ▪up 311L16
▫hacking ▪**cough** 635L37
▪whooping ▫**cough** 1662R47
▪**coughing** ▫fit 310R84
▫city ▪**council** 234L75
▪**council** ▫housing 311R10
▫**council** of ▪war 311R12
▫county ▪**council** 311R6 314L8
▫legislative ▪**council** 809R77
▫parish ▪**council** 1026R49
▫Privy ▪**Council** 1124R15
Se▪curity ▫**Council** 1281R80
▫city ▪**councillor** 234L76
▫Privy ▪**Councillor** 1124R18
▪**counsel** against 311R27
▫**counsel** for the de▪fence 311R35
▫**counsel** of de▪spair 311R40
▫**counsel** of per▪fection 311R42
▪**counsel** on 311R25
keep *one's* ▫own ▪**counsel** 311R38
▫marriage ▪**counselling** 868L22
▪guidance ▫**counsellor** 197L35
▪blood ▫**count** 137L57
▫**count** a▪gainst 24R15 312L50/51
▪**count** among 312L53/54
▪**count** as 312L56/58
▫**count** *one's* ▪blessings 312L4
▫**count** ▪down 311R75
▪**count** for 312L65
▫**count** ▪heads 312L10
▫**count** me ▪out 339L79
▪**count** ▫noun 312L32/38
▫**count** on the ▫fingers of one ▪hand 312L14
▫**count** ▪out 311R79
▫**count** *someone* ▪out/▪in 311R84
▫**count** the ▫cost(s) 312L6/9
▪**count** towards 312L59
▫keep ▪**count** of 312L29
▫lose ▪**count** of 312L30
▪pollen ▫**count** 1092R46
▪sperm ▫**count** 1390L82
▫stand (up) and be ▪**counted** 1410L70
▪bargaining ▫**counter** 100L26
▪bean ▫**counter** 107R31
▪**counter**-▫culture 312R54
▫**counter**-in▪tuitive 312R59
▪**counter** ▫lunch 312R25
▫**counter**-revo▪lution 312R62
▪**counter**-▫suit 312R64
▪**counter** with 312R42
▪Geiger ▫**counter** 586L73
▫over the ▪**counter** 312R26
▫under the ▪**counter** 312R28
the ▫Home ▪**Counties** 680L65
de▪veloping ▫**countries** 377R5
a▫cross ▪**country** 12R49 313R37
▪Black ▫**Country** 131R22
▫**country** ▪bumpkin 175R8
▪**country** ▫club 313R41
▫**country** ▪dance 313R45
▫**country** ▪house 313R47
▫**country** ▪seat 313R50
▫cross-▪**country** 327R13/15
▫flee the ▪**country** 532R84
▫free ▪**country** 560R64/67
go to the ▪**country** 313R22
▪mother ▫**country** 506R77 920L65
▪old ▫**country** 980L58
▫up-▪**country** 1598R60
▪West ▫**Country** 1654L10
▫**county** ▪council 311R6 314L8
▫**county** ▪court 314L10
▫**county** ▪seat 314L12
▫**county** ▪town 314L12
▫**coup de** ▪grâce 314L34
▫palace ▪**coup** 1019R53
a **couple** of ▫shakes (of a ▫duck's/lamb's ▪tail) 1307R14
be ▫with you in a ▫**couple** of ▪ticks 1518R5
▪**couple** onto 314L75
▫**couple** to▪gether 314L76
▪**couple** with 314L77
▫courting ▪**couple** 315R7
a▫coustic ▪**coupler** 11R67
▫Dutch ▪**courage** 433L78
▫liquid ▪**courage** 433L78 829L6
▫pluck up the/*one's* ▪**courage** 1083L59
▫screw up *one's* ▪**courage** 1273L34
the ▫**courage** of *one's* con▪victions 314R19
▪access ▫**course** 7R61
ad▫vanced ▪**course** 19L76
allow ▫nature to/let ▫nature take its ▪**course** 943L6
as a ▫matter of ▪**course** 492R17 874R26 1122R57
as▪sault ▫**course** 71R47/51
corres▪pondence ▫**course** 308L29
▫**course** ▪down 315L26
▫**course** ▪through 315L27/29
▪crash ▫**course** 320R5
▪damp ▫**course** 344R83
▪damp proof ▫**course** 344R83
foun▪dation ▫**course** 556L68
▪golf ▫**course** 610R17
in ▫due ▪**course** 431L31
in the ▫**course** of ▪time 314R70/71 1520R69
intro▪ductory ▫**course** 556L69
▫main ▪**course** 315L20 853R53
▪obstacle ▫**course** 71R47 972R13
on a col▪lision ▫**course** 258R2
▫par for the ▪**course** 1023R46
per▫vert the **course** of ▪justice 1054R67
re▪fresher ▫**course** 1192R33
▫run *its* ▪**course** 1240R76
▪sandwich ▫**course** 1254R20
▫stay the ▪**course** 1417L43
▪hare ▫**coursing** 647R79
con▫tempt of ▪**court** 295R61
▫county ▪**court** 314L10
▪**court** corre▫spondent 315L75
▫**court** ▪martial 315R54/57
▫**court** of in▪quiry 315L48
▫**court** ▪order 315L53 993R41
▪**court** ▫shoe 315L77
▪criminal ▫**court** 324L66
▫crown ▪**court** 329L69
▫high ▪**court** 668R11/17
▫High ▪**Court** of Au▫stralia 668R18
▫hold ▪**court** 676R63
▫Inns of ▪**Court** 732R75
▫kangaroo ▪**court** 775R39
▫laugh *someone* out of ▪**court** 800L25
▪motor ▫**court** 920L39
the ball is in ▪*someone's* ▫**court** 95R27
▫**courting** ▪couple 315R7
▫first ▪**cousin** 315R70 525R51
▫second ▪**cousin** 1279L52
▫haute **cou▪ture** 315R82 651L80
the ▫Ark of the ▪**Covenant** 62R6
▫send to ▪**Coventry** 1292L8
▫blow *someone's* ▪**cover** 139L39
▫break ▪**cover** 161R26
▪**cover** against/for 316R11
▫**cover** *one's* ▪ass 316L33
▪**cover** ▫charge 316L58
▪**cover** for 316R44/56
▪**cover** ▫girl/▫boy/▫model 316L48
▫**cover** ▪in 316L28
▪**cover** ▫note 316R13
▪**cover** ▫story 316L50
▫**cover** ▪up 316R52/58
▪**cover** with 316L24/25/27/30
▪**cover** with/in 316L27
▪duvet ▫**cover** 433R38
from ▫**cover** to ▪**cover** 316L52
▪ground ▫**cover** 626L48
▪quilt ▫**cover** 433R38
under ▫plain/▫separate ▪**cover** 316L62
▪**covered** by/with 316L31
▪**covering** ▫letter/▫note 316L35
▫loose ▪**covers** 840R64
▪**cow** ▫into 317L66/67
▪**cow** ▫parsley 317L51
▫mad ▪**cow** dis▫ease 851L49
▫sacred ▪**cow** 1247L62
till/until the ▪**cows** come ▫home 317L48
▪**cox** for 318L31
▪**crab** ▫lice 318L75
▫dressed ▪**crab** 318L65 422R41
a ▫hard/▫tough ▪nut to ▫**crack** 968L79
a ▫sledgehammer to **crack** a ▪nut 1351L2
▪**crack** against 318R41
▫**crack** ▪down 318R77
▫**crack** of ▪dawn 318R24
▪**crack** on 318R51/78/80
▫**crack** the ▪whip 318R46
▫**crack** ▪up 318R16/17/66
▫**crack** *it* ▪up to be 318R68
▪**crack** with 318R45
▫fair **crack** of the ▪whip 494R82
▫just a ▪**crack** 318R22
▫slip through the ▪**crack** 1354L6
▫Christmas ▪**cracker** 230L82 319L10
▫cream ▪**cracker** 321L52
▫get ▪**cracking** 318R50
▫paper over the ▪**cracks** 1023L65
▫cat's ▪**cradle** 203L72
▪**cradle** ▫snatcher 319L44
▪**craft** ▫fair 319L64
▪**craft** ▫shop 319L66
▪**craft** ▫union 319L67
▪landing ▫**craft** 794R21
▫arts and ▪**crafts** 65L82
▫artsy-▪**craftsy** 65R39
▫arty-▪**crafty** 65R39
▫**cram** ▪down 319R21
▪**cram** for 319R28
▪**cram** into 319R18/19/20
▫writer's ▪**cramp** 1692L11
▪**crane** ▫fly 319R75
▫**crane** ▪forward 319R71
▫**crane** ▪over 319R70
▪**crank** ▫caller 319R84
▫**crank** ▪out 320L16
▫**crank** ▪up 320L20
▫nook and ▪**cranny** 320L30 960R28
▫cut the ▪**crap** 339R37
▪**crash** ▫barrier 320L68
▪**crash** ▫course 320R5
▫**crash** ▪diet 320R8
▪**crash** ▫helmet 320L71
▪**crash** into 320L64
▫**crash**-▪landing 320L73
▪packing ▫**crate** 1016L30
▫stick in *one's* ▪**craw** 1423L37
▪**crawl** across 320R49
▫**crawl** into *one's* ▪shell 1314R43
▫**crawl** out of the ▪woodwork 1677R73
▪**crawl** with 320R63/64/66
make *someone's* ▪flesh ▫**crawl** 533L62
▪pub ▫**crawl** 1141R60
▫creepy-▪**crawlie** 322R66
▪kerb ▫**crawling** 777R13
▫creepy-▪**crawly** 322R64
▫**crazy** ▪paving 321L17
▫drive *someone* ▪**crazy** 425L80
like ▪**crazy** 822R50
▪stir-▫**crazy** 1427L47
▪barrier ▫**cream** 101R2
▪cleansing ▫**cream** 241R75
▫clotted ▪**cream** 248L66
▪cold ▫**cream** 256R19
▫**cream** ▪cheese 321L51
▫**cream** ▪cracker 321L52
▫**cream** of ▪tartar 321L53
▫**cream** ▪soda 321L55
▫**cream** ▪tea 321L56
▫double ▪**cream** 414L17
▪face ▫**cream** 490R35
▫heavy ▪**cream** 414L17
▪ice ▫**cream** 698R77
▪ice **cream** ▫cone 306R44 698R80
▫ice-**cream** ▪soda 698R81
▫light ▪**cream** 1341L13
▪salad ▫**cream** 1250R3
▪shower ▫**cream** 1328R84
▫single ▪**cream** 1341L13
▫sour ▪**cream** 1380L26/25
▫**crease** ▪up 321R01
▫**create** a ▪stink 1426L82
cre▫ate a ▪stir 1427L12
▪**create** *something* from 321R7
cre▫ative ac▪counting 321R40
▪street-▫**cred** 321R79 1437L38/45/37
credi▪bility ▫gap 322L17
▪**credit** ac▫count 322L44
▪**credit** ▫card 322L48
▪**credit** ▫crunch 322L58
▪**credit** ▫note 322L51
▪**credit** ▫rating 322L55
▪**credit** ▫squeeze 322L58 1403R83
▪**credit** ▫terms 322L60
▪**credit** with 322L78/R6
▫family ▪**credit** 500R73
▫letter of ▪**credit** 813L40
▪film ▫**credits** 1529L29
▫up the ▪**creek** 322R34
▫**creep** a▪long 322R41
▫**creep** ▪in 322R48
▪**creep** into 322R50
▫**creep** ▪over 322R47
▫**creep** ▪through 322R38
▫**creep** ▪up 322R43
make *someone's* ▪flesh ▫**creep** 533L62
vir▫ginia ▪**creeper** 1625R23
▪**creeping** ▫plant 322R54
▫give *someone* the ▪**creeps** 322R68
▫**creepy**-▪crawlie 322R66
▫**creepy**-▪crawly 322R64
▫**creme de** ▪menthe 322R83
▫**crepe** ▪paper 323L27
▫**crêpe su▪zette** 323L20
▫Red ▪**Crescent** 1188R80
▫sulphur-**crested** cocka▪too 1458R19
▪cabin ▫**crew** 182L63
▪**crew** ▫cut 323R10
▪**crew** ▫neck 323R11
▪ground ▫**crew** 626L52
▫**cri de** ▪coeur 323R67
▪**crib** from 323R32
▪**crib** ▫notes 323R34
▫**crime** of ▪passion 324L50
▪**crime** ▫wave 324L53
▪**crime** ▫writer 324L54
extra▫ditable ▪**crime** 487L68
▫organized ▪**crime** 995R51
▫petty ▪**crime** 323R81 1056L65
▪war ▫**crime** 1637L32/29
▪**criminal** ▫court 324L66
▫**criminal** ▪damage 324L68
▫**criminal** ▪justice ▫system 324L76
▫**criminal** ▪law 324L70
▫**criminal** ▪record 324L72 1187L30
▪**cringe** at 324R71
▪**cringe**-▫making 324R73
▫cultural ▪**cringe** 334R56
▪**crinkle**-▫cut 324R78
▫**crinkle** ▪up 324R77
i▪dentity ▫**crisis** 701R27
▫mid-life ▪**crisis** 893R48
po▫tato ▪**crisp** 1103L1
▪**criss**-▫**cross** 325R77/83
▪lit ▫**crit** 830L14
▫literary ▪**criticism** 326L38 830L79
▪**crochet**-▫hook 326R4
▪**crocodile** ▫tears 326R32
by ▫hook or by ▪**crook** 684L23
▪cash ▫**crop** 201R33
▪**crop** ▫dusting 327L33
▪**crop** ro▫tation 327L30 1235L78
▪**crop** ▫spraying 327L33
▫**crop** ▪up 327L57/54
▪root ▫**crop** 1233R57
▫close-▪**cropped** 247R71
▫come a ▪**cropper** 327L58
at ▫**cross**-▪purposes 328R4
▪**criss**-▫**cross** 325R77/83
▫**cross**-▪country 327R13/15
▫**cross**-▪dressing 328L38
▫**cross**-ex▪amine 328L51/43/55
▪**cross**-▫eyed 328L57
▫**cross**-fertiliz▪ation 328L59
▫**cross** ▪fingers 327R28
▪**cross**-▫hatch 328L75/71/77 650L52
▪**cross** into 327L79
▫**cross**-▪legged 327R36
▫**cross** *one's* ▪mind 327R3
▫**cross** ▪off 328L11
▫**cross** ▪out 328L16
▫**cross**-▪purposes 328R3
▫**cross**-▪question 328L43/R9
▫**cross**-re▪fer 328R11/14
▪**cross**-▫section 328R24/28
▪**cross**-▫stitch 327R47
▫**cross** ▪swords with 327R31
cross ▪that bridge when you ▪come/▪get to it 327R6
▪**cross** with 327R76 328L7
dot the ▫i's and **cross** the ▪t's 413R4
▫double-▪**cross** 414L18/22
▫Greek ▪**cross** 622L48
▫hot-**cross** ▪bun 687R36
▫make the sign of the ▪**cross** 327R53
▫Maltese ▪**cross** 858L64
▫paths ▪**cross** 1035R37
▫Red ▪**Cross** 1188R83
▫Southern ▪**Cross** 1380R53
the ▫Stations of the ▪**Cross** 1415R18
▫skull and ▪**crossbones** 1347R67/71
▫**cross▪check** with 328L37
▫**crossed** ▪line 327R39
get *one's* ▪wires ▫**crossed** 1670R54
keep *one's* ▪fingers ▫**crossed** 521R79
▪star-▫**crossed** 1412R64
▫noughts and ▪**crosses** 965L1
the ▫thought **crosses** *someone's* ▪mind 1514R42
▫catch in the ▪**crossfire** 328L69
▪grade ▫**crossing** 616L81 813R33
▫level ▪**crossing** 813R32
pe▫destrian ▪**crossing** 1042L23
▫pelican ▪**crossing** 1043R70
▫zebra ▪**crossing** 1699R15
▫cryptic ▪**crossword** 332L33
as the ▪**crow** ▫flies 328R84
▪carrion ▫**crow** 198R36
▪cock ▫**crow** 252R26
▪**crow** about/over 329L14
▪**crow's** ▫feet 329L4
▪**crow's** ▫nest 329L6
▫eat ▪**crow** 439L50
▫Jim ▪**Crow** 764R76
▪**crowd** into 329L41/42/43
▫**crowd** ▪out 329L47
▪**crowd**-▫puller 329L34
▪**crowd** round/about 329L38
go/move with the ▪**crowd** 604L17
▫**crown** ▪colony 329L72
▫**crown** ▪court 329L69
▫**crown** ▪jewels 329L76
▫**crown** ▪prince 329L79
▫**crown** prin▪cess 329L80
▫**crown** ▪prosecutor 329L83
▫jewel in the ▪**crown** 763R14
▫**crowned** ▪head 329R8
▫stone the ▪**crows** 1429R56
▫**crude** ▪oil 330L10
be ▫**cruel** to be ▪kind 330L40
▫**cruelty**-▪free 330L53
▫mental ▪**cruelty** 330L51 887L61
▪cabin ▫**cruiser** 182L64
the ▫thinking woman's/man's ▪**crumpet** 1513L83
▫**crumple** ▪up 330R43
▪**crumple** with 330R46
▪**crumple** ▫zone 330R49
▪credit ▫**crunch** 322L58
▪**crunch** on 330R57
▫**crunch** ▪up 330R59
if/when it ▫comes to the ▪**crunch** 330R70
▪number-▫**cruncher** 967L32/36
cru▪sade against 330R78 331L4
cru▪sade for 330R77 331L3
▪**crush** ▫barrier 331L23
▪**crush** into 331L13
▪pie ▫**crust** 1064L75
▫upper ▪**crust** 1599R29
a ▫far ▪**cry** from 504L12
▪battle ▫**cry** 105L82 1637L33
▪**cry** at 331R80
▪**cry**-▫baby 331R52
▫**cry** *one's* ▪eyes out 331R49
▫**cry** ▪foul 331R78
▫**cry** ▪off 332L16
▫**cry** ▪out 331R68
▫**cry** ▪out against 331R69
▫**cry** ▪wolf 331R82
▫hue and ▪**cry** 691R34
in ▫full ▪**cry** 332L11/14 573L34
not ▫know whether to ▫laugh or ▪**cry** 786R72
▫shoulder to ▪**cry** on 1325R61
▪war ▫**cry** 1637L33
▫burst out ▪**crying** 178L5
▫**crying** ▪shame 332L21
for ▫**crying** out ▪loud 331R76
▫no good/use **crying** over spilt ▪milk 331R55
▫**cryptic** ▪crossword 332L33
▫**crystal** ▪ball 332L84
▫**crystal** ▪clear 332L68/70
▪**crystal**-▫gaze 332R3
liquid-▪**crystal** dis▫play 829L7
▫**crystallized** ▪fruit 332L55
C▪S ▫gas 332R9
▪**cub** re▫porter 332R14
▪bouillon ▫**cube** 152R35 1428L37
▫**cube** ▪root 332R33 1234L50
▪ice ▫**cube** 698R83
▪stock ▫**cube** 1428L37
▫cloud-▪**cuckoo**-▫land 248R57
▪**cuckoo** ▫clock 332R74
▫chew the ▪**cud** 333L61
▫**cuddle** ▪up 333L69
▫**cuddly** ▪toy 333L77
▫**cudgel** *one's* ▪brains 333R61
▫take up (the) ▪**cudgels** 333L81
▫take *one's* ▪**cue** from 333R74/78
▪**cuff** ▫link 334L14
▫haute **cui▪sine** 651R1
▫nouvelle **cui▪sine** 965L42
▪**cul-de-▫sac** 334L34
▪**cull** from 334L53/54
▪**culminate** in 334L57
▪**cult** ▫figure 334R10
▪**cult** ▫following 334R9
person▪ality ▫**cult** 334R8 1053L52
▫**cultural** ▪cringe 334R56
▫**cultural** ▪desert 334R79
▫multi-▪**cultural** 928R67

▪counter-▫**culture** 312R54
▪**culture** ▫gap 334R42
▪**culture** ▫shock 334R44
▪**culture** ▫vulture 334R71
▪enterprise ▫**culture** 461L37
▫**cultured** ▪pearl 335L9
▫**cup** ▪final 335R11
▪**cup** ▫holder 335R14
▪**cup** ▫tie 335R17
▪egg ▫**cup** 444R2
▫FA ▪**Cup** 490L25
▪measuring ▫**cup** 879R12
not *someone's* **cup** of ▪tea 335L78
▪suction ▫**cup** 1455R66
▫World ▪**Cup** 335R9 1684L75
▪airing ▫**cupboard** 29R50
▫**cupboard** is ▪bare 335R41
▪**cupboard** ▫love 335R42
▫**cupid's** ▪bow 335R52
▫**curate's** ▪egg 335R76
▪bean ▫**curd** 107R30 1531R29
▫**curd** ▪cheese 336L15
▫lemon ▪**curd** 810R14
▪soya ▫**curd** 1381R20
▫**curdle** *one's* ▪blood 336L25
▫make *someone's* ▪blood ▫**curdle** 336L25
▪**cure** of 336L31/32/34/36
▫kill or ▪**cure** 779R63
▪rest ▫**cure** 1212R4
curi▪osity ▫value 336L77
▫**curl** *one's* ▪lip 336R32
▫**curl** ▪round 336R23/26
▫**curl** ▪through 336R23
▫**curl** ▪up 336R29/28/27/28
▫**curl** up and ▪die 336R31
▪kiss ▫**curl** 781R82
▫make *someone's* ▪hair ▫**curl** 636L40
▪spit ▫**curl** 781R83
▪toes ▫**curl** 1531L74
have (got) *someone* by the ▫short and ▪**curlies** 1321R68
▪toe-▫**curling** 1531L73
▫decimal ▪**currency** 354R74
▫hard ▪**currency** 646L49
▪**current** ac▫count 336R78
▫**current** af▪fairs 336R75
▫swim/▫drift/▫go with the ▪**current** 337L9
▫core **cur▪riculum** 305R47
cur▫riculum ▪vitae 337L25
▫national **cur▪riculum** 337L17 938R83
▫**curry** ▪paste 337L31
▪**curry** ▫powder 337L32 1105L53
▫**curse** the ▫day *one* was ▪born 337L52
▪**curtain** ▫call 337R35
▫**curtain** ▪off 337R51
▪**curtain** ▫rail 337R25
▪**curtain** ▫raiser 337R37
▪**curtain** ▫rod 337R27
▪**curtain** ▫time 337R33
▫Iron ▪**Curtain** 752R30
▪safety ▫**curtain** 1248R50
the ▫final ▪**curtain** 337R43/45
▪**curve** ▫ball 337R72
▫**cushion** the ▪blow 338L3
▪scatter ▫**cushion** 1263L50
▪air-▫**cushioned** 29L52
▫give a ▫tinker's (▪**cuss**) 1525R2
▫baked ▪**custard** 338L38
▫**custard** ▪pie 338L34
▪**custard** ▫powder 338L36
▫**custard** ▪tart 338L38
pro▫tective ▪**custody** 1137L82
re▫manded in ▪**custody** 338L61
▫**custom**-▪built 338R6
▫**custom**-▪made 338R8
▫cool ▪**customer** 303L44
▫**customer** ▪services 338R14
▫slippery ▪**customer** 1354L39
Customs and ▪Excise 338R35
customs ▫officer 338R37
a ▫**cut** a▪bove 339L15
classic ▪**cut** 238L75
clean ▪**cut** 241L61/65/66
clear-▪**cut** 242L32
crew ▫**cut** 323R10
crinkle-▫**cut** 324R78
cut a ▪corner 339R61
cut a fine ▪figure 339R77
cut a ▪swath through 338R75
cut a▪cross 340L3
cut and ▪dried 339L21/23
cut and ▪paste 339L80
cut and ▪run 339R64
▫**cut** a▪way/▪out 338R62
cut ▪back/▪down 338R63/65 339L51/R53/L46
cut ▪both/▪two ▫ways 338R74
cut ▪corners 339R62
cut down to ▪size 339L53
cut for ▪dealer 339L42/R70
cut ▪glass 339L26 598R13
cut ▪in 338R53 339L64/66/R27/29/55/71
cut in ▪front of 339R58
cut *something* in/into 338R60
▫**cut** ▪in on 338R47 339R28/55/71
▪**cut** into 338R66
▫**cut** into ▪ribbons 1220R66
▫**cut** it 339R83
▫**cut** it/that ▪out 339R33
▪**cut** it/things ▪fine 339L2
▫**cut** ▪loose 339R80
▫**cut** *one's* ▪losses 339L55
▫**cut** ▪lunch 339L27 1016L16
▫**cut** me ▪out 339L79
▫**cut** no/very little ▪ice with 338R81
▫**cut** ▪off 338R69 339L43 340L7/22/27/31/32
▫**cut** ▪off from 340L25/26
cut off *one's* ▫nose to spite *one's* ▪face 338R83
cut ▫off without a ▪penny 339L76
▫**cut** ▪out 338R71/72 339L75/R23/24/59
▫**cut** *someone* ▫out of *one's* ▪will 339L75
▫**cut**-▪price 339L59/61
▫**cut** quite a ▪figure/▪dash 339R77
▫**cut**-▪rate 339L62
▫**cut** *one's* ▪teeth on 339R45
▫**cut** the ▪cackle 339R35
▫**cut** the ▪crap 339R37
▫**cut** the ▪ground from under *someone's* ▪feet 339L83
▪**cut** through/across/over 338R61/77 339R51/50
▫**cut** to the ▪quick/▪heart 339R14
▫**cut** ▪up 338R48 339R16 340L31/36
▫**cut** ▪up about 339R16
▫**cut** up ▪rough 339R81
▪**cut** with 338R44/45/47
▫**cut** with a ▪knife 338R79
▫fish or **cut** ▪bait 526R19
▫half-▪**cut** 637R41
have *one's* ▪work **cut** ▫out (for *one*) 1679R3
▫low-▪**cut** 844L38/40
▫open-▪**cut** 988R22 989L18
▪power ▫**cut** 1106L69
▫short ▪**cut** 1321R78
the ▫**cut** and ▪thrust 339L16
to **cut** a ▫long story ▪short 339L57
▫**cutoff** ▪jeans 340R8
▪cold ▫**cuts** 256R21
▪glass-▫**cutter** 598R11
▫**cutthroat** ▪razor 340R28
▫**cutting** ▪edge 339L5
▪press ▫**cutting** 1118R75
▪**cycle** ▫clips 340R66
▪**cycle** ▫helmet 340R70
▪**cycle** ▫lane/▫path/▫way 340R74
▪**cycle** ▫rack 340R76
▪**cycle** ▫shed 125R44 340R78
▪**cycle** ▫shorts 340R72
▪life ▫**cycle** 819L27
▪menstrual ▫**cycle** 886R62
▪racing ▫**cycle** 1165R25/13
▪**cycling** ▫helmet 340R70
▪**cycling** ▫shorts 340R72
▪**cyclone** ▫fence 341L63
▫**cylinder** ▪vacuum ▫cleaner 189R35
hot ▪water ▫**cylinder** 687R69
▪measuring ▫**cylinder** 879R14
▫**cystic** fib▪rosis 341R79
▫la-di-▪**da** 792L34
▪**dab** at 342L54/56
▫**dab** ▪hand 342L53
▪**dab** on 342L31
▪**dabble** in 342L41/44/52
▪**dabble** with 342L42
▫**daddy** ▪longlegs 319R75 342L78/79/80/81 649L75
▪sugar ▫**daddy** 1457L23
▫cloak-and-▪**dagger** 245R79/82
at ▫**daggers** ▪drawn 342R28
▫look ▪**daggers** 839L43
▫lah-di-▪**dah** 792L34/R80
▫**daily** ▪bread 342R52
recom▫mended **daily** al▪lowance 1186L32
the/*someone's* ▫**daily** ▪round 1237L2
▪**dairy** ▫products 1127L24
▫push up (the) ▪**daisies** 1151L71
▪oops-a-▫**daisy** 987L31
▪ups-a-▫**daisy** 987L31
▫**Dalai** ▪Lama 344L12
over ▫hill and ▪**dale** 344L14
up ▫hill and down ▪**dale** 670L43
▪**dally** over 344L35
▪**dally** with 344L25/37
▫**dam** ▪up 344L51
▪dental ▫**dam** 366R12
▫criminal ▪**damage** 324L68
▪**damage** limi▫tation 344L68
the ▫**damage** is ▪done 344L66
▫road to **Da▪mascus** 1228L42
▪**damn** for 344R53
▫**damn** with faint ▪praise 344R53
▫give a ▫tinker's (▪**damn**) 1525R2
▫give/▫care a ▪**damn** 344R21
▫God ▪**damn** 609L45
damned if *you* ▫do and damned if *you* ▪don't 344R50
▫I'm ▪**damned** 344R32
▫sword of ▪**Damocles** 1479R5
▪**damp** ▫course 344R83
▫**damp** ▪down 345L15
▪**damp** ▫proof 345L2
▪**damp** proof ▫course 344R83
▫**damp** ▪squib 344R76
▫rising ▪**damp** 1226R44
▪barn ▫**dance** 100R28
▫country ▪**dance** 313R45
▫**dance** at▪tendance on 345L40
▪**dance** ▫floor 345L60
▪**dance** ▫hall 345L61
▪**dance** ▫studio 345L64
▪dinner ▫**dance** 385R44
▫lead *someone* a (merry) ▪**dance** 804L32
▫modern ▪**dance** 910R51
▪morris ▫**dance** 919L14/10/15
▫song and ▪**dance** 1375R65/69
▪square ▫**dance** 1402L38
▪war ▫**dance** 1637L37
▪belly-▫**dancer** 116L11/10
e▫xotic ▪**dancer** 480L63
▪go-go ▫**dancer** 606L74
▫ballroom ▪**dancing** 96L34
▪break-▫**dancing** 162L10
▫jim-▪**dandy** 345R10 765L3/7
▪**danger** ▫list 345R27
▪**danger** ▫money 345R30
on ▫**dangerous** ▪ground 626R12
▫**Danish** ▪pastry 345R52
▫**dare** I ▪say (it) 346L6
▫don't/▫just you ▪**dare** 346L10
a ▫shot in the ▪**dark** 1320L59
▪**Dark** ▫Ages 346L64
▫**dark** ▪chocolate 346L69 1074R23
▫**dark** ▪glasses 346L71 1460R38
▫**dark** ▪horse 346R25/28
▫leap in the ▪**dark** 806L25
▫pitch-▪**dark** 1071L82
never ▫**darken** these doors/*someone's* door a▪gain 346R5
▫pitch ▪**darkness** 1071L84
▫Prince of ▪**Darkness** 1122L80
the ▫powers of ▪**darkness** 1105R71
▪**darning** ▫needle 346R55
▫**dart** ▪out 346R76
▫shoot ▪**darts** at 1319R42
▫cut quite a ▪**dash** 339R77
▪**dash** against 347L20/21
▫**dash** a▪long 347L4
▫**dash** a▪round 347L5
▫**dash** ▪off 347L7
make a ▪**dash** for it 347L14
▪**data** ▫bank 347L71
▪**data** ▫capture 347L74
▪**data** ▫processing 347L76
▫best be▪fore **date** 118R76
▫blind ▪**date** 135L74
▪**date** at 347R76
▪**date** ▫rape 348L37
expi▪ration ▫**date** 347R63 482R37
Inter▫national ▪**Date** Line 744L15
▫make it a ▪**date** 348L36
▪pull ▫**date** 1144R51 1290L21
▪sell-by ▫**date** 1290L20
▪start ▫**date** 1413R67
▪starting ▫**date** 1413R66
▫up-to-▪**date** 1597R29/31
▫carbon ▪**dating** 194L76
com▪puter ▫**dating** 279L77
▪**dating** ▫agency 348L43 868L11
▪**dating** ▫service 348L44
▫wattle and ▪**daub** 1644L75
▪**daughter**-in-▫law 348R36
▫nothing ▪**daunted** 348R45 964L60
▫Star of ▪**David** 1412R28
▪**Davy** ▫lamp 1248R62
▫crack of ▪**dawn** 318R24
▫**dawn** ▪chorus 348R81
▪**dawn** on 348R74 349L18
▫**dawn** ▪raid 348R69/71 1169L9
▫false ▪**dawn** 500L11
a ▫rainy ▪**day** 1170L5
▫all in a **day's** ▪work 349L55
▫any **day** ▪now 349L58
▫April ▪Fools' ▫**Day** 59L33
at the ▫end of the ▪**day** 455L20
▫big ▪**day** 125L1 349L50
▪Boxing ▫**Day** 155R47
▪button ▫**day** 529L38
▫call it a ▪**day** 185L76
▫Christmas ▪**Day** 230R2
▫curse the ▫**day** *one* was ▪born 337L52
▪D-▫**Day** 350L64
▫**day** after ▪day 23L77 349L61
▫**day** and ▪night 349L62
▫**day** by ▪day 349L67
▪**day** ▫care 349R24
▪**day** ▫girl/▫boy 349R34
▪**Day**-▫Glo 349R66
day ▫in day ▪out 349L69
▪**day** ▫nursery 349R26
▫**Day** of A▪tonement 349R28 1697R29
▫**Day** of ▪Judgment 349R28 771L69
▪**day** ▫pupil 349R33
▪**day** re▫lease 349R36
▫**day** re▪turn 349R40
▪**day** ▫school 349R43
▪**day** ▫student 349R34
▫**day**-to-▪**day** 349L72/73
▪**day** ▫trip 349R45/49
▫early-▪closing ▫**day** 436R46
▪field ▫**day** 516L8
▪flag ▫**day** 529L38/40
from ▫one **day** to the ▪next 349L76
from ▫that **day** ▪forward 555R20
▫give *one something* ▪any **day** 596R35
good ▪**day** 612L45
have a ▪field ▫**day** 516L10
have a ▫good/▫nice ▪**day** 349L77
in ▫this **day** and ▪age 349R3
Inaugur▪ation ▫**Day** 715L27
Inde▪pendence ▫**Day** 720R58/60
▪Judgment ▫**Day** 771L69
▪labour ▫**day** 789R57
▫late in the ▪**day** 798R83
▪latter-**day** 799R39
live to ▫fight another ▪**day** 831R64
▫lose the ▪**day** 842L70
make a ▪**day** of it 855L13
▫Midsummer('s) ▪**Day** 895L2
▪Mother's ▫**Day** 920L80
▫name the ▪**day** 937L76
▫New Year's ▪**Day** 952R14
▫night and ▪**day** 955L28
not ▫give *someone* the ▫time of ▪**day** 1522R16
▪open ▫**day** 988R65
▪Pancake ▫**Day** 1021R19
▫pass the time of ▪**day** 1031R34
▪polling ▫**day** 1092R37
▫present-▪**day** 1116R40
red-▪letter ▫**day** 1189L20
Re▪membrance ▫**Day** 1201R46
▫rue the ▪**day** 1239L60
▪saint's ▫**day** 1250L20
▫save the ▪**day** 1257R52
▫see the light of ▪**day** 1284L22
▫Seventh-**Day** ▪Adventist 1302L38
▪sick ▫**day** 1332R68
▪speech ▫**day** 1388R17
▪tag ▫**day** 529L38
the ▫**day** of ▪reckoning 349R30
the ▫happy ▪**day** 645R25
the ▫heat of the ▪**day** 657R75
the ▫order of the ▪**day** 994L21/23
▪Veterans ▫**Day** 1619R81
▫win the ▪**day** 1666R9
▫working ▪**day** 1681L57
▫**daylight** ▪robbery 349R76
▫**daylight** ▪saving 349R80
▫**daylight** ▪saving ▫time 349R80
in ▫broad ▪**daylight** 167R16 349R75
something's ▫**days** are ▪numbered 349L63/65
▪dog ▫**days** 408R69
▫early ▪**days** 436R39
▪glory ▫**days** 600R70
▫halcyon ▪**days** 637L28
have seen ▫better ▪**days** 1283L48
in *one's* ▪salad ▫**days** 1250R7
▫nine **days'** ▪wonder 955R78
the ▫best **days** of *someone's* ▪life 118R73
▪razzle-▫**dazzle** 1177L37
▫**de** ▪facto 357R68/75
▫**de** ▪jure 361R17
▫**de** ▪luxe 363R12
▫**de** ri▪gueur 370R20
▫**de** ▪trop 376R83
▫eau **de** co▪logne 258R59 439L83
es▫prit **de** ▪corps 468L83
▫fin-**de**-▪siècle 521L23
▫fleur-**de**-▪lis 533R1
▫joie **de** ▪vivre 767L55
▫nom **de** ▪plume 959L12
▫pas-**de**-▪deux 1030R65
pi▫èce **de** rési▪stance 1064R65
▫tour **de** ▪force 1542L44
as ▫**dead** as a ▪doornail 350R26
as ▫**dead** as the/a ▪dodo 350R28
▪brain ▫**dead** 157L30
come ▫back from the ▪**dead** 350R65
▫**dead** ▪air 351L21
▫**dead** ▪beat 109R47 351L10
▫**dead** ▪bolt 350R34 919R42
▫**dead** ▪duck 350R35
▫**dead** ▪end 351L24
▫**dead** ▪heat 351L30
▫**dead** ▪language 350R39
▫**dead** ▪letter 350R41/44
▫**dead** ▪loss 351L35
▫**dead** of ▪night 350R67
▫**dead** of ▪winter 350R67
▫**dead** on *one's* ▪feet 350R29
▫**dead** on ▪target 351L14
▫**dead** on ▪time 1523L59
▫**dead** ▪reckoning 350R46
▫**dead** ▪ringer 351L35
▫**dead** ▪set a▫gainst 351L17
▫**dead** ▪set on 351L15
▫**dead** to ▪rights 351L38
▫**dead** to the ▪world 350R31
▫**dead** ▪weight 350R49
▫**dead** ▪wood 350R53
▫drop ▪**dead** 427R12/8
▫flog a **dead** ▪horse 536L6
▫half-▪**dead** 637R43
▫knock 'em ▪**dead** 785L22
over ▫*my* **dead** ▪body 350R33
▫stone-▪**dead** 1429R41
▫wouldn't be seen ▪**dead** 1283L79
▫**deadly** ▪nightshade 350R81
in ▫**deadly** ▪earnest 351L52
▫seven **deadly** ▪sins 1302L25
▪**deaf** ▫aid 351R10
▫**deaf** as a ▪post 351R9
▫**deaf**-▪mute 351R11
▫fall on ▫**deaf** ▪ears 497R82
▫stone-▪**deaf** 1429R45
▫tone-▪**deaf** 1534L82
▫turn a **deaf** ▪ear 1569R34
a ▫good ▪**deal** 351R46 611L63 612R1/2
a ▫raw ▪**deal** 1176R65
▫big ▪**deal** 125L8
▪**deal** in 351R35
▪**deal** to 351R25
▪**deal** with 351R34/72/78
▫**deal** with *someone* with kid ▪gloves 779L79
▫no big ▪**deal** 125L12
▪package ▫**deal** 1016R56
▫square ▪**deal** 1402L64
▪sweetheart ▫**deal** 1476L40
▫wheel and ▪**deal** 1656R22/29
▪car ▫**dealer** 582R37
▪hardware ▫**dealer** 647R53 752R71
▪news ▫**dealer** 953L33
▪scrap ▫**dealer** 1270R72
▫wheeler-▪**dealer** 1656R34
▫double-▪**dealing** 414L23
in▫sider ▪**dealing** 735L45
▫cost *someone* ▪**dear** 309R69 310L19/20 352L37
▫**Dear** ▪John (letter) 352L28
for ▫**dear** ▪life 352L26
▫oh ▪**dear** 352L45
▫nearest and ▪**dearest** 944R71
a ▫fate worse than ▪**death** 506R14
▫accidental ▪**death** 8L42
at ▫**death's** ▪door 352R3
▫Black ▪**Death** 131R70
▫bored to ▪**death** 149L48
▪brain ▫**death** 157L28
▫catch *one's* ▫**death** (of ▪cold) 352R2
▪cot ▫**death** 310L84
▪**death**-de▫fying 352R7
▪**death** ▫duty 352R9
▪**death's** ▫head 352R11
▪**death** ▫knell 352R13
▪**death** ▫mask 352R20
▪**death** ▫penalty 352R22
▫**death** ▪row 352R26
▪**death** ▫sentence 352R27 1294L21
▪**death** ▫squad 352R30
▪**death** ▫tax 352R9
▪**death** ▫throes 352R33
▪**death** ▫toll 352R34 1533L69
▪**death** ▫trap 352R36
▪**death** ▫warrant 352R40
▪**death** ▫wish 352R47
▫dice with ▪**death** 380R42
▫die a ▪**death** 381R46
▫flog to ▪**death** 536L10
hang/hold ▫on like grim ▪**death** 624L28
▫kiss of ▪**death** 781R79
▫life after ▪**death** 818R62
▫life and ▪**death** 818R64
▫living ▪**death** 831R84
▫look/▫feel like ▪**death** ▫warmed ▪up/▪over 352R4
▫matter of ▫life and/or ▪**death** 874R29
▫merchant of ▪**death** 888L74
▫near-▪**death** ex▫perience 945L6
▫sentence of ▪**death** 1294L21
▫sign *one's* own ▪**death** ▫warrant 1336L39
▫sound/▫toll the ▪**death** knell 352R16
▫stone to ▪**death** 1429R53
▫tickled to ▪**death** 1518R75
▫worried to ▪**death** 1686L22
▫**deathwatch** ▪beetle 352R68
▪**debit** ▫card 353L44
▪**debit** ▫column 353L47
▫direct ▪**debit** 386R53
▫bad ▪**debt** 92L47 353L76
▫national ▪**debt** 939L1
de▪ceive *someone* into 354L39
▫flatter to de▪ceive 532L2
▫half-▪**decent** 637R45
de▪cide on 354R20
de▪cide to 354R21
de▪ciding ▫factor 354R30
de▫ciding ▪vote 354R32
▫**decimal** ▪currency 354R74
▫**decimal** ▪fraction 354R64
▫**decimal** ▪point 354R69 1090L12

Dewey **decimal** system 379L12
recurring/repeating **decimal** 1188R19
deck in 355L44
deck out 355L42/44
deck with 355L42
flight **deck** 534L45/47
hit the **deck** 673L21
stack the **deck** 1405R58
tape **deck** 1491L19
move/rearrange the **deckchairs** on the Titanic 355L52
double-**decker** (sandwich) 355L33 414L26/27
single-**decker** 355L34 1341L16
below **decks** 355L27
clear the **decks** 242R23
declare for/against 355R7
declare war on 355L81/83
declining years 355R41
art **deco** 65L84
decompression chamber 356L11
decompression syndrome/sickness 356L6
interior **decorator** 742L76
decoy duck 356L75
decoy into 356L78
decree absolute 356R10
decree nisi 356R8
dedicate *oneself* to 356R35/36/44
deduce from 356R69
deduct from 357L2
tax-**deductible** 357L8 1493L84
deed box 357L26
deed poll 357L27
good **deed** 611R71
title **deed** 1529L21
deep(ly)-rooted 357L67
be in/get into **deep** water 357L53
between the devil and the **deep** blue sea 378L57
deep-down (inside) 357L62
deep freeze 357L63 563L48
deep-fry 357L64
deep-laid 357L65
deep-seated 357L67
deep-set 357L70
Deep South 357L71
dig (**deep**) into *one's* pocket(s)/resources/savings 383R8
go off the **deep** end 357L55
in too **deep** 1535L68
jump/plunge in at the **deep** end 357L57
knee-**deep** 782R73
run/go **deep** 357L61
skin-**deep** 1346R36
throw/chuck/pitch in at the **deep** end 357L58
at/on a **deeper** level 813R59
dig (**deeper**) into *one's* pocket(s)/resources/savings 383R8
fallow **deer** 499R37
red **deer** 1189L2
roe **deer** 1230R27
default on 358L10/12/13
default to 358L27
admit **defeat** 17R45 358L48
birth **defect** 128R71
defect from 358L82
defect to 358L81
mentally **defective** 887L77
civil **defence** 234R47
counsel for the **defence** 311R35
defend against 358R10
defer to *someone* on 359L19/24
deficiency disease 359L47
define as 359L78
well-**defined** 1652L81
defining moment 359R18
definite article 359R35
definite maybe 359R38 877L21
high **definition** television 667R40
deflect away 360L8
deflect from 360L8/14
deflect off 360L9
defraud of 360L62
defy to 360R26
death-**defying** 352R7
degenerate into 360R52/53
degrade into 361L9
associate's **degree** 73L51
bachelor's **degree** 88R62
degree with honours 683L73/71
first-class **degree** 525L82
first-**degree** burn 525R54
first-**degree** murder 525R55
honours **degree** 683L73/70
Master's **degree** 871R66
pass **degree** 1031R3/6
second class **degree** 1279R27
the third **degree** 1513R21
third-**degree** burn 1513R24
to a **degree** 361L25
to the nth **degree** 966L31
deign to 361L73
déjà vu 361R6
have/take a **dekko** 361R22
delegate to 361R62/64/71/73/74
delete from 361R80/81
deliberate on 362L26
delight in 362R23/25
in a transport of **delight** 1552L9
Turkish **delight** 1569L19
delirium tremens 362R76
deliver from 363L32
deliver of 363L24
deliver on 363L48
deliver the goods 612R49
deliver to 362R79 363L10/11
stand and **deliver** 1410L32
signed sealed and **delivered** 1336L34
delivery room/suite/unit 363L26
general **delivery** 587L30 1101R11/18
recorded **delivery** 1187L58
special **delivery** 1385R59
delude into 363L68
delusions of grandeur 363L78
delve for 363R16
delve in 363R16
delve into 363R19/21
Lib **Dem** 816L48
demand from 363R39
demand of 363R46/57
demand to 363R41
final **demand** 363R53 520L3
law of supply and **demand** 801L82 1464R67
demarcation dispute 363R83
senile **dementia** 1292L31
Social **Democrat** 1370R27
Democratic Party 364R8
Social **Democratic** Party 1370R28
Liberal **Democrats** 816R8
demolition derby 364R61
demon alcohol 364R73
the **demon** drink 364R72
demonstrate for 365L80
demonstrate to 365L20
demote to 365R20
demur at 365R32
beard the lion in *his/her* **den** 108R49
lion's **den** 828L55
common **denominator** 270R83 271L2
lowest common **denominator** 844R16
denounce as 366L39/49
relative **density** 1196R72
dental dam 366R12
dental floss 366R16
dental hygienist 366R18 697L17
dental practitioner 366R20
dental surgeon 366R20
al **dente** 32L41
denude of 366R37
deny to 366R47/59
depart from 367L12/34
depart this life 367L13
department store 367L58
fire **department** 523L52
State **Department** 1414R48
departure lounge 367L31
depend on/upon 367L81/83/70/79/R15
Aid to Families with **Dependent** Children 28R12 226L25
depict as 367R53
deplete of 367R77
deport from 368L52
deport to 368L50
deportation order 368L57
depose as 368L69
depose from 368L70
deposit account 368R44
deposit bottle/can 368R47
direct **deposit** 386R58
safety **deposit** box 1248R53 1249L10/9
anti-**depressant** 49R61
bipolar **depression** 128L27
clinical **depression** 245L36 369L69
manic **depression** 860R82
manic **depressive** 860R79
deprive of 369R32
sink to such **depth(s)** 1341R75
depth charge 369R64
plumb the **depths** 1084R23
demolition **derby** 364R61
local **derby** 370L65 834R14
roller **derby** 1231L81
deride as 370R13
deride for 370R12
derive from/out of 370R31/37/32
des res 374L30
descant recorder 371L1
descend from 371L22
descend into 371L7
descend on/upon 371L40
descend to 371L8
describe as 371L58
describe to 371L57
beggar **description** 113R64
job **description** 765R47
desensitize to 371R23
cultural **desert** 334R79
desert boots 371R68
desert island 371R71
get *one's* just **deserts** 774R34
deserve a medal 372L12
deserve better 372L2
deserve whatever/everything *one* gets 372L13
the **deserving** poor 372L30
design for 372L46/48/52/53/79
graphic **design** 619R11/8
interior **design** 742L79/81
more by accident than **design** 8L28
designer drug 372L69
designer socialism 372L72
designer socialist 372L71
designer stubble 372L75
heart's **desire** 372R53 656R62
leave a lot to be **desired** 807L71
desist from 373L9
cash **desk** 201R35
City **Desk** 234R17
desk-bound 373L17
desk clerk 373L25
desk job 373L19
reception **desk** 1184L15
roll-top **desk** 1231R36
writing **desk** 1692L36
desktop publishing 373L33
counsel of **despair** 311R40
despair at/over 373L77
despair of 373L66/78/80
throw up *one's* hands in **despair** at 1517L41
despise for 373R60
dessert wine 374L37
soul-**destroying** 1378L58
detach from 374R65
semi-**detached** (house) 1290R41
go into **detail** 375L33
detain at His/Her Majesty's pleasure 375L59
detective work 375R20
private **detective** 1124L32
store **detective** 1431L67
lie **detector** 818L73
metal **detector** 890R23
detention center 1201L34
detention centre 375L73
detention home 1201L33
deter from 375R34
laundry **detergent** 1639R41
bound and **determined** 153L13
detoxification centre 376L74
detract from 376L77
deus ex machina 377L11
pas-de-**deux** 1030R65
develop into 377L68/69/70/R38
less **developed** countries 377R5
well-**developed** 1652R3
late **developer** 377R1 799L12
property **developer** 1134R56
the **developing** world 377R5
development area 377R55
housing **development** 377R51 689L84
research and **development** 1208L28
ribbon **development** 1220R70
deviate from 377R80/81
explosive **device** 483L61
logic **device** 837L24
storage **device** 1431R9
timing **device** 1522R48
leave *someone* to *their* own **devices** 807R6
a/the **devil** of 378L38
between the **devil** and the deep blue sea 378L57
devil's advocate 378L63
devil's food cake 378L68
devil-may-care 378L41
give the **devil** his due 596R30
go to the **devil** 378L45
speak/talk of the **devil** 378L47
the **devil** to pay 378L54
devolve on/upon 378R29
devote to 378R35
Dewey decimal system 379L12
dewy-eyed 379L9
manual **dexterity** 862R80
la-di-**da** 792L34
lah-di-**dah** 792L34/R80
diagnose as 379L61/62
circuit **diagram** 232R62
flow **diagram** 538L17
Venn **diagram** 1613L46
dial tone 379R28 1534R21
dialling code 379R24
dialling tone 379R27
diamond in the rough 380L24 1235R54
diamond jubilee 380L25
diamond wedding (anniversary) 380L27
rough **diamond** 1235R53
verbal **diarrhoea** 1614L43
dice with death 380R42
clever **dick** 243R68
spotted **dick** 1397R66
Tom **Dick** and/or Harriet 1533R13
dicker with 380R72
dictate to 381L15/16/56
elective **dictatorship** 446L53
as straight as a **die** 1433L56
curl up and **die** 336R31
die a death 381R46
die away 381R55
die-cast 382L4
die down 381R58
die for 381R38/67
die hard 381R68
die of/from 381R48/36
die out 381R60
I'd rather **die** 1688R23/25
or **die** in the attempt 381R63
right-to-**die** 1223R32
the **die** is cast 382L7
balanced **diet** 95L23
crash **diet** 320R8
starvation **diet** 1414L77
dietary fibre 382L51 515L34
agree to **differ** 27R32
beg to **differ** 113R33
differ about/over/on 382L74
differ between 382L71
differ from 382L67/68
differ in 382L66
differ with 382L74
for all the **difference** *something makes* 382R13
make a (big) **difference** 382R3
make a world of **difference** 382R4
make all the **difference** (in the world) 382R3
make no **difference** 382R8
not make any/the slightest **difference** 382R8
same **difference** 1252R45
split the **difference** 1394R72
tell the **difference** 1498L59
sink *one's* **differences** 1341R80
a completely **different** ball game 95R36
set/go/start off on a **different** tack 1484L83
differentiate between 382R56/58
differentiate from 382R59
go through a **difficult** patch 1034R56
learning **difficulties** 383L5 806L81
dig *one's* heels in 383R28
dig in 383L61/63/64/67
dig *someone* in the ribs 1220R25
dig into 383R6/7/22/24
dig (deep/deeper) into *one's* pocket(s)/resources/savings 383R8
dig out/up 383L73/R16/18/L72/69/70/R14
dig *one's* own grave 383L74
dig *oneself* (into) a hole 383L57
infra **dig** 728R43
digestive system 383R48
gold **digger** 609R62/65
digital audio tape 383R75
stand on *one's* **dignity** 1410L52
digress from 384L48/50
dilate on/upon 384L77
on the horns of a **dilemma** 685R6
dilute with 384R42
dim witted 384R65 1674R81
a **dime** a dozen 384R79 1045R70
nickel-and-**dime** 954R46/48
fourth **dimension** 556R84
multi-**dimensional** 928R69
three-**dimensional** 1515L65
two-**dimensional** 1576L29/31
diminished capacity 385L22
diminished responsibility 385L21
diminishing returns 385L27
din into 385L56
dine at 385L63
dine on/upon 385L68
dine out 385L62
dine with 385L61
wine and **dine** 1669L3
ding-dong 385R1/4/6
rubber **dinghy** 1238R29
dining car 385L69 1213L18
dining hall 385L72
dining room 385L71
dining table 385L74
lay/set the **dining** table 1483L61
rinky-**dink** 1225R72
fair **dinkum** 495L18
dinner dance 385R44
dinner jacket 385R46
dinner service 385R48
dinner set 385R49
dinner table 385R52
done/dressed/got up like a dog's **dinner** 408R58
TV **dinner** 1572L43
carbon **dioxide** 194L70
sulphur **dioxide** 1458R13
dip in/into 386L11/12/14/19/34/47/48/13/21/25/36/16
dip-switch 386L49
double-**dip** 414L29/32
lucky **dip** 846L59
skinny-**dip** 1346R83/80
gunboat **diplomacy** 632R33
shuttle **diplomacy** 1332L62
diplomatic bag 386R3
diplomatic corps 386R8
diplomatic immunity 386R10
diplomatic pouch 386R3
diplomatic relations 386R1 1196R47
diplomatic service 386R14
Big **Dipper** 124L82/R39 1231L76
direct action 386R50
direct against/at 387L11/12
direct debit 386R53
direct deposit 386R58
direct discourse 386R69
direct hit 386R60 673L40/41
direct mail 386R61
direct object 386R73
direct speech 386R69
direct tax 386R65
direct towards 387L13
change of **direction** 215L45
stage **direction** 1406R15
advance **directive** 19L69
director general 387L36
Director of Public Prosecutions 387L37
funeral **director** 574R68
managing **director** 859R43
Directory Assistance 387R68
Directory Enquiries 387R67
ex-**directory** 478L70
telephone **directory** 387R66 1496R66
dirt cheap 220R47 388L3/4
dirt poor 388L5
dirt road 388L6 1227R81
dirt track 388L6
dish the **dirt** 394L14
pay **dirt** 1038R67
rub *someone's* nose in the **dirt** 1238R4
dirty great/big 388L44
dirty look 388L27
dirty old man 388L28
dirty weekend 388L30
dirty word 388L24
talk **dirty** 1488R4
wash *one's* **dirty** linen in public 1639L74
disabled access 388L61
disabuse of 388L82
beg to **disagree** 113R33
disagree on 388R44/45/56
disagree with 388R44/49/54/65
disappear behind 389L1
disappear from 389L3
disappear into 389L2
disappear into thin air 1511R36
disappear off the face of the earth 490R74
disapprove of 389L47/48
disbar for 389R54
compact **disc** 272L75
disc brake 389R79 390L2
disc jockey 389R82
gold **disc** 609R66
laser **disc** 797L16
Mini **Disc** 900R60
slipped **disc** 1353R34
tax **disc** 1493R1
video **disc** 1622L59
discharge from 390L42/53
discharge into 390L57
multi-**disciplinary** 928R71
disconcerted at/to 391L14/13
disconnect from 391L26
discount card 391R33
discount store 391R36
discount warehouse 391R37
discourage from 391R73
direct **discourse** 386R69
discourse on/upon 391R83 392L
indirect **discourse** 722L49
discriminate against 392R10
discriminate between 392R29
discriminate from 392R27
positive **discrimination** 1098R77 1218L31
reverse **discrimination** 1218L3
discuss with 392R50
disdain to 392R66
coronary heart **disease** 307L2
deficiency **disease** 359L47

Dutch elm disease 433L81
foot-and-mouth disease 545R55
industrial disease 723R80
legionnaire's disease 809R58
mad cow disease 851L49
occupational disease 973R27
sexually transmitted disease 1304L31
venereal disease 1613L13
disembark from 393L8
disengage from 393L47/49/51
disentangle oneself from 393L58/59
blessing in disguise 135L33
baking dish 94R27
can dish it out but you can't take it 394L24
dish liquid 393R81
dish out 394L18
dish rack 393R82 1077L6
dish the dirt 394L14
dish towel 393R84 1494L33
dish up 394L31
petri dish 1056L7
satellite dish 394L6 1256L32
dry the dishes 430L3
disintegrate into 394R51/52
disinvest from 394R74
disk drive 395L1
disk operating system 395L3
floppy disk 537L24
hard disk 646L51
dislodge from 395L33/35/36
dismayed by/at 395L67
dismiss as 395L79
dismiss from 395L81/R8
civil disobedience 234R50
personality disorder 1053L55
post-traumatic stress disorder 1101L51
disparage as 396L2
dispatch box 396L43
dispatch rider 396L46
mentioned in dispatches 396L41
dispense with 396R4
cash dispenser 201R32/36
dispensing optician 396L82 992L28
displace as 396R37
displaced person 396R40
displacement activity 396R46
display in 396R54
LED display 808L40
liquid-crystal display 829L7
disposable income 397L25
bomb disposal unit 145R1
army disposals store 63R34
dispose of/to/towards 396R83 397L6
disposed someone to 396R84
ill-disposed 703L82
well-disposed 1652R10
of a nervous disposition 949R7
dispossess of 397L40
beyond (all) dispute 397L73
demarcation dispute 363R83
dispute over 397L68/71/72
dispute with 397L70
open to dispute 397L77
disqualify from 397R21/22/24
dissent from 398L54
dissenting voice 398L60
dissociate from 398R7/8
dissolve in/into 398R23
dissuade from 398R44
at/from a distance 398R53
distance learning 398R62
go the distance 398R54
in/within spitting distance 1393R51
keep one's distance 398R61
long-distance 838L20
middle distance 894L41/43
within hailing distance of 636L4
within/in shouting distance 1326L84
within striking distance 1441R39/42
distant corner of the globe/world/earth 306R84
distant relative 399L1
not too distant future 398R83 578L27
distinguish between 399R1/4
distinguish from 399R3
distract from 399R44
distribute among 400L26
distribute between 400L27
distribute to 400L29
district attorney 400L58
district nurse 400L61
red-light district 1189L25
disturb the peace 400R4
cause a disturbance 206R2
last-ditch 797R41
dither over 400R81
dive after 401R8
dive-bomb 401L64/65/67
dive for 401L53/60/70/R4
dive in 401L53
dive into 401L54/R6/9/11/13
dive off 401L54
dive under 401L57/R5
swallow dive 1473L72
swan dive 1473L73/R24
pearl diver 1040R49
scuba diver 1274R50/53
skin-diver 1346R44/40
diverge from 401R27/28
divert from 401R69/71/75 402L2
divert into 401R75/76
divert to 401R72
divest from 402L25
divest of 402L16
divide and rule 402L60
divide between 402L48/50/68
divide down the middle 893R72/71
divide from 402L43
divide into 402L31/32/33/R38/39 747L15
divide up among/between 402L39
North-South divide 961L47/50
divided highway 402L74 430L55
divided on/over 402L55
peace dividend 1039R61
diving bell 401L79
diving board 401L82
division lobby 402R13
division of labour 402R15
long division 838L24
divorce for 403L37
divorce from 403L38/44
divvy up 403L73/70
Mason-Dixon Line 870L75
do about 404R48/52
do as 405L71/72
do by 406R76
do down 406R83
do for 404R54/56/69 406L4/5/17/49/65/66/73/75/R23/34 407L2/3
do in 407L12/47/48
do it 404R76
do out 407L18/21
do over 406L7 407L30
do to 404R61 405L74 406L68/70/71
do up 407L33/39/46 1700R11
do with 404R72/73/75/78 405R58 407L50/54
do without 407L69
dob in 407L77/83/77/R1
dob on 407L78
Doc Martens 407R6 417R59
dock at 407R32
dock money from 407R51
dock someone's pay/wages 407R49
dry dock 429R58
loading dock 833R6
doctor's orders 408L13
family doctor 500R75
flying doctor 540R8
just what the doctor ordered 408L11
spin doctor 1392L34
drama documentary 419L13
well-documented 1652R14
draft dodger 418L8
as dead as the/a dodo 350R28
Jane Doe 767L26
John Doe 767L26
a dog's chance 408R56
a dog's life 408R57
bird dog 128L58 632R4
dog biscuit 408R65
dog's breakfast 408R53
dog collar 243R41 257R5 408R66
dog days 408R69
dog-eared 408R70
dog-eat-dog 408R71
dog in the manger 408R51
dog paddle 409L80
dog tag 408R74
dog-tired 408R76
done/dressed/got up like a dog's dinner 408R58
guard dog 629L76
guide dog 630R44
gun dog 128L59 632R3
hot dog 342L60 687R40/42/45/46
like cat and dog 203L58
put on the dog 408R64
sausage dog 342L60 1257L77
sea dog 1276L10
see a man about a dog 1284L10
Seeing-Eye dog 1283L81
shaggy dog story 1307L23
sick as a dog 1333L18
sniffer dog 1366L9
the hair of the dog 636L51
the tail wagging the dog 1485R29
there's a good dog 1509R80
top dog 1537L82
tracker dog 1545L84
work like a dog 1679R41
lie doggo 409L69 818L23
doggy bag 409L77
doggy paddle 409L79
go to the dogs 408R60
Play-Doh 1076R70 1078L5
okey-doke 979R31
la dolce vita 792L47
dole out 410L24/22
doll corner 410L35
doll's house 410L31
doll up 410L41
rag doll 1168R5
bet one's bottom dollar 119R82
dollar sign 410L51
dollar signs in one's eyes 410L53
pay top dollar 1038R3
pink dollar 1068R27
sixty-four-thousand-dollar question 1344R2
look/feel like a million dollars 897R5
dolly bird 410L63
dolly mixture 410L64
in the public domain 410L83 1142L16
public domain 1142L29
domestic animal 45R77 410R16
domestic appliance 410R18
domestic science 410R21
domino effect 411L19
Don Juan 411L48
consider it done 290R76
done to a turn 1570R52
done (up) to the nines 955R74
done up like a dog's dinner 408R58
easier said than done 438R45
hard-done-by 646R27
no sooner said than done 1376L53
not the done thing 1512R43
over and done with 1006L53
the damage is done 344L66
the done thing 1512R40
well done 406R5 1651R19 1652R19
when all is said and done 1260L6
ding-dong 385R1/4/6
do (all) the donkey work 411L55
donkey jacket 411L56
donkey's years 411L52
talk the hind leg(s) off a donkey 1488R7
prima donna 1121R16/22
blood donor 137L58
donor card 411L65
don't come it 266L23
dos and don'ts 405L65
cock-a-doodle-doo 252R35
cock-a-doodle-doo 252R35
merchant of doom 888L75
prophet of doom 1135L11
a foot in the door 545L51
at death's door 352R3
beat a path to someone's door 109L25
door to door 411R41/43 689L60
door-to-door salesman 411R44 1251L23
fire door 523L54
front door 568L36
keep the wolf from the door 1675R34
leave the door open 807R2
never darken someone's door again 346R5
next door 411R40 953R52/56/59
open-door 987R29
open the door to 411R46
revolving door 1219L29
screen door 1272R58
show someone the door 1327L78
shut/close the stable/barn door after the horse has bolted 411R52
shut/slam the door in someone's face 411R49
shut/slam the door on 411R50
stage door 1406R19
storm door 1432L3
swing door 1477L57
the knock at/on the door 784R64
as dead as a doornail 350R26
behind closed doors 247L64
French doors 563R9/52
never darken these doors again 346R5
dope test 412L48
dopp kit 1532R13
Doppler effect 412L75
dormitory town 412R48
hunky dory 694R56
John Dory 767L33
dos and don'ts 405L65
MS-DOS 926R45
a dose of one's own medicine 882L43/54
lethal dose 412R73
like a dose of salts 412R80
in small doses 412R78
doss around/about 413L16
doss down 413L10
dot-matrix printer 413L46
dot the i's and cross the t's 413R4
in the year dot 413L45
polka dot 1092R9
the year dot 1695R67
dote on/upon 413R18
dotted line 413R9
sign on the dotted line 1336L37
double(-page) spread 414L80
a double bite of the cherry 130R40
at/on the double 413R57
bend double 116R76
double agent 413R62
double as 414R29
double back 414R32
double-barrelled name 413R68/66/65
double bass 413R70
double bed 413R72
double bill 413R73
double bind 413R75
double-blind 413R79
double bluff 413R84
double-book 414L5
double breasted 162R12 414L2
double-check 414L8
double chin 414L11
double-click 414L14
double cream 414L17
double-cross 414L18/22
double-dealing 414L23
double-decker (sandwich) 355L33 414L26/27
double-dip 414L29/32
double Dutch 414L35/37
double-edged 414L39
double-edged sword 414L46
double entendre 414L48
double fault 414L52
double feature 414L54
double figures 517R56
double-header 414L55
double helix 414L57 661L10
double jeopardy 414L59
double-jointed 414L61
double negative 414L64
double or quits 413R59
double over with 414R38
double-park 414L69
double play 414L72
double-quick 414L74
double room 414L73
double-space 414L80/77
double standards 414L83
double take 414R2
double-talk 414R5
double-team 414R9
double time 414R11
double trouble 414R14
double up/over 414R36/39/35
double up with laughter 414R38
double vision 414R16
double whammy 414R17
in double-quick time 414L75
mixed doubles 908L65
beyond a shadow of a doubt 122R5
beyond reasonable doubt 122R1/L84 1182L1
give someone the benefit of the doubt 117L65
doubting Thomas 415L8
douse in/with 415L61
billet-doux 126R32
dove-grey 415L72
dovetail with/into 415L79/82
Dow Jones (Industrial) Average 415R4
a shiver/shivers (up and) down one's spine 1318L52
batten down the hatches 104R62
bear down 108R9
beat hands down 109L71 641L9
bed down 111L69
bog down 143R62
boil down 144L44
break down 159R67/69 1064R23
breathe down someone's neck 162R72
bring down to earth 437L69
bring/take someone down a peg (or two) 1043L72
broken-down 168L44
burn down 177L81
button-down collar 180R9
cast down 202L46
catch someone with their trousers/pants down 204R73/78
clamp down on 236L71
climb down 244R18/36/54/59
come down 266L39
come down in the world 1685L16
come down on one side of the fence or other 1333R13
come down to 266L44 416L32/35
come down to earth 437L70
come/go down with 416L24
cut down to size 339L53
deep-down (inside) 357L62
divide/split down the middle 893R71
down someone's alley 34L45 1437L34
down-at-heel 416L47
down-at-the-heel 416L47
down in the mouth 924L10
down on one's luck 846L9
down payment 416R12
down river 1227R16
Down's syndrome 417L35
down the ages 439R83
down the drain/toilet/tube(s)/plughole/pan/gurgler 415R30 1021L69
down the gurgler 633L19
down the line 826L25
down the road/line/track 416L77
down to a fine art 521L61
down-to-earth 416L51
down to the last 797R32
down tools 416L2
down under 415R75
down vest 143R25 416R26
down your way 416L70
dressing-down 422R70
fall down 497L59/61
fall down on one's knees 497L72
force/thrust/ram down someone's throat 1516L2
get down to 593L28
get down to brass tacks 158L68
get down to business 178R47
get/put one's head down 653L48/51
go down/fall like ninepins 956L17
go down in the world 416L28
go down like a lead balloon 804R41
go down on 603R66 606R71
go down the tubes 1566R11
go down the wrong way 1692R75
go down with 603R64
hand-me-down 641R2
hands down 641L6/12
it's tipping (it) down 1526L54
jump down someone's throat 772R56
jump up and down 772R11
keep one's head down 653L82
kick/hit someone when they're down 415R77
lay down 802L42
lay down one's life 802L46 818R58
lay down the law 802R60
lead someone down the garden path 804L35
let one's hair down 812L49
let the side down 812R80 1334L26
lie down on the job 818L25
look down one's nose 839L34
look down on 839L34
low-down 844R52
move down in the world 1685L17
mow down 926L49
on the down grade 616L48
pop-down 1095L61
pull someone down 1144R47
put down 1058L76 1152R73/75/77/79/81 1153L83 1154R1/6/10/14
put down as 1153R10
put it down to 620L8 1153R11
put it/something down to experience 482L22 1153R13
put one's foot down 545L76/79
put the phone down on 1058L78
ram down someone's throat 1171L33
run-down 1241R74 1242R18/21/29/33/39/42 1243R3
scream the place down 1272L43
sell down the river 1290L8
send down 1291R61/64/55
shoot down 1319R44/47
simmer down 1339L63
splash-down 1394L36
split/divide down the middle 893R72
step down 1420R50
strip down 1444R30
struck down 1441R11 1442L69
suit right down to the ground 1457R51
take a stroll/trip/walk down memory lane 886L22
take down the aisle 30R61
take lying down 818L40 1486L57
talk down 1489L5
that's two down eight to go 416L41
throttle down 1516L66
throw down the gauntlet 585L55
thumbs down 1517R36
top-down 1537L8

ˌtouch ˈ**down** 1540R35
ˌtrickle-ˈ**down** 1557L43
ˌturn upside ˈ**down** 1569R69
ˌup and ˈ**down** 1597R17/50 1598L11/14/R26/27
up ˌhill and **down** ˈdale 670L43
ˌupside ˈ**down** 1600L69
ˌweigh ˈ**down** 1649R75
when the ˌchips are ˈ**down** 227R36
ˌwin hands ˈ**down** 641L8 1666R3
ˌ**downhill** ˈskiing 416R72
ˈ**Downing** ˌStreet 416R78
ˌups and ˈ**downs** 1598R35
ˌ**doze** ˈoff 417R31
a ˌdime a ˈ**dozen** 384R79 1045R70
ˌbaker's ˈ**dozen** 94R41
ˌnineteen/ˌten to the ˈ**dozen** 417R52
ˌround ˈ**dozen** 1236L77
six of ˌone and half a **dozen** of the ˈother 1344L43
ˌ**Dr** ˈMartens 417R58
ˌolive ˈ**drab** 980R65
in ˌdribs and ˈ**drabs** 423R67
ˈ**draft** ˌdodger 418L8
ˌ**draft** ˈin 418L26
ˈ**draft** into 418L13
ˌ**drag** aˈway 418L38
ˌ**drag** ˈdown 418L40
ˌ**drag** *one's* ˈheels/ˈfeet 418L54
ˈ**drag** into 418L41/44
ˈ**drag** ˌlift 418L60
ˌ**drag** ˈout 418L46/50
ˌ**drag** *someone* over the ˈcoals 251R8
ˈ**drag** ˌqueen 418R6
ˌmain ˈ**drag** 853R57
like ˌsomething the ˈcat **dragged** in 203L61
ˈfoot-ˌ**dragging** 545R60
ˌchase the ˈ**dragon** 219R19
draˈ**goon** into 418R33
ˈbrain ˌ**drain** 157L33
ˌdown the ˈ**drain** 415R30 1021L69
ˈ**drain** of 418R50
ˌlaugh like a ˈ**drain** 800L14
ˈ**draining** ˌboard 418R55
ˈcostume ˌ**drama** 310L50
ˌ**drama** docuˈmentary 419L13
ˌamateur **dra**ˈ**matics** 38L38
draˌ**matis** perˈsonae 419L64
ˌ**drape** all ˈover 419L75
ˈ**drape** around 419L70
ˈ**drape** in/with 419L71
ˈ**drape** over 419L72
ˌ**draw** a ˈblank 420L76
ˌ**draw** a ˈveil over 420L64
ˌ**draw** aˈway/ˈout 419R76
ˌ**draw** ˈback 419R80
ˌ**draw** ˈbreath 162R29 420R54
ˈ**draw** for 420L75
ˈ**draw** from/on/upon 420R50/70/61
ˌ**draw** ˈin 419R82 420R75
ˌ**draw** in *one's* ˈhorns 685R4
ˈ**draw** into 419R81 420L62
ˌ**draw** ˈoff 420R47
ˈ**draw** on 420L34/R63/64/78
ˌ**draw** ˈout 420R47/81 421L3
ˌ**draw** the ˈline at 419R55
ˌ**draw** the short ˈstraw 1321R64
ˈ**draw** towards 420L44
ˌ**draw** ˈup 419R82 420L59 421L7/11
ˌluck of the ˈ**draw** 846L18
ˌbottom ˈ**drawer** 152L67
ˌchest of ˈ**drawers** 224R55
back to the ˈ**drawing** ˌboard 89L11
ˈ**drawing** ˌboard 419R66
ˈ**drawing** ˌpin 419R63
ˈ**drawing** ˌroom 421L32
ˈline ˌ**drawing** 824R22
at ˌdaggers ˈ**drawn** 342R28
ˌhanged/ˌhung **drawn** and ˈquartered 644L20
ˌlong-**drawn**-ˈout 838R33
ˌ**dread** to ˈthink 421L59
ˌ**dreaded** ˈlurgy 421L66
Aˌmerican ˈ**dream** 41L23
ˈ**dream** about/of 421R3/15/16/61
ˌ**dream** ˈon 421R67
ˈ**dream** ˌticket 421R54
ˌ**dream** ˈup 421R76
ˈpipe ˌ**dream** 1069R39
ˌwet ˈ**dream** 1654R11
beyond *one's* ˌwildest ˈ**dreams** 122R9 1664R25
ˌmust have ˈ**dreamt** *it* 421R19
ˌ**dredge** for 422L10
ˌ**dredge** ˈup 422L11/12
ˈ**dredge** with 422L18
ˌ**drenched** to the ˈskin 1346R28
ˈsun-ˌ**drenched** 1459R67
ˈcocktail ˌ**dress** 253R46
ˈ**dress** ˌcircle 422R63
ˈ**dress** ˌcode 422L84
ˌ**dress** ˈdown 422L47
ˈ**dress** in 422L56
ˈ**dress** reˌhearsal 422R3
ˈ**dress** ˌsense 422R6
ˌ**dress** the ˈpart 1028R53
ˌ**dress** ˈup 422L50/54/57
ˈ**dress** with 422L61
ˌevening ˈ**dress** 472R27/30
ˌfancy ˈ**dress** 503L46
ˌlong ˈ**dress** 838L27
ˈmorning ˌ**dress** 918R51
ˈpinafore ˌ**dress** 1067R79
ˌ**dressed** ˈcrab 318L65 422R41
ˌ**dressed** to ˈkill 422R17
ˌ**dressed** (up) to the ˈnines 955R74
ˌ**dressed** up like a ˌdog's ˈdinner 408R58
ˌmutton **dressed** (up) as ˈlamb 933R82
ˌwell-ˈ**dressed** 1652R23
ˌcross-ˈ**dressing** 328L38
ˌ**dressing**-ˈdown 422R70
ˈ**dressing** ˌgown 422L62
ˈ**dressing** ˌroom 422L64
ˈ**dressing** ˌtable 422L66
ˌFrench ˈ**dressing** 563R10 1624L39
ˈpower ˌ**dressing** 1105R29
ˈsalad ˌ**dressing** 1250R5
ˈwindow ˌ**dressing** 1668L43/46
ˌ**dribble** ˈdown 422R84
in ˌ**dribs** and ˈdrabs 423R67
ˌcut and ˈ**dried** 339L21/23
ˌsun-ˈ**dried** 1459R69
ˈhair ˌ**drier** 636L54
ˈtumble ˌ**drier** 1567L68
ˌwasher-ˈ**drier** 1639R21
ˌcontinental ˈ**drift** 296R55
ˈ**drift** against 423R80
ˌ**drift** aˈway 423R81
ˌ**drift** ˈin 423R78
ˌ**drift** ˈup 423R79
ˌ**drift** with the ˈcurrent 337L9
ˌ**drift** with the ˈtide 424L3
if you ˌcatch my ˈ**drift** 1486L83
ˈ**drill** for 424L33
ˌ**drill** in 424L44
ˈ**drill** into 424L46
ˈfire ˌ**drill** 523L57
pneuˌmatic ˈ**drill** 1087L72
ˌcannot hold *one's* ˈ**drink** 675R81
ˌ**drink**-ˈdriving 424L80
ˌ**drink** *one's* ˈfill 518R75
ˌ**drink** ˈin 424L59
ˌ**drink** like a ˈfish 424R16
ˈ**drink** ˌproblem 424L83/82
ˈ**drink** to 424R11/14
ˌ**drink** *someone* under the ˈtable 424R18
ˌ**drink** ˈup 424L58
ˌdrive *someone* to ˈ**drink** 425L77
ˌhard ˈ**drink** 647L54
ˌlong ˈ**drink** 838L29
ˌmeat and ˈ**drink** 880L60
ˌmixed ˈ**drink** 908L67
ˌsoft ˈ**drink** 1372L8
ˌtake to ˈ**drink** 424L77
the ˌdemon ˈ**drink** 364R72
the ˌworse for ˈ**drink** 1686L65
ˌhard ˈ**drinker** 646R4
ˈ**drinking** ˌfountain 424L66
ˌ**drinking**-ˈup ˌtime 424R26
ˈ**drinking** ˌwater 424L65
ˈ**drinks** maˌchine 424L52
ˌ**drip**-ˈdry 424R38
ˌ**drip** (ˈdown) onto 424R35
ˌnon-ˈ**drip** 959L74
ˈdisk ˌ**drive** 395L1
ˌ**drive** a ˌcoach and ˈhorses through 424R73
ˌ**drive** a hard ˈbargain 425R44
drive a ˌnail into *someone's* ˈcoffin 935R57
ˌ**drive** a ˈwedge 425R49
ˈ**drive** at 424R72 427L15
ˈ**drive** between 425R53
ˌ**drive** ˈdown 425R60
ˌ**drive** ˈhome 680L54
ˈ**drive** into 424R70 563R68
ˌ**drive** *someone* ˈmad/ˈcrazy/inˈsane 425L80
ˌ**drive** *one's* ˈmessage/ˈpoint ˌhome 425R47
ˌ**drive** ˈoff 424R70
ˌ**drive** ˈon/ˈpast/aˈway 424R69
ˌ**drive** ˈround the bend 117L1
ˈ**drive** ˌshaft 425R61
ˌ**drive** *someone* to ˈdrink 425L77
ˌ**drive** to exˈtremes 487R23
ˌ**drive** under the ˈinfluence 425L56
ˌ**drive** while inˈtoxicated 425L57
ˌ**drive** *someone* ˈwild 425R40
eˈconomy ˌ**drive** 427L11 440L65
ˌfly-drive ˈholiday 540R2
ˌfly-drive vaˈcation 540R2
ˌfour-wheel ˈ**drive** 556R75
ˌfront-wheel ˈ**drive** 568L55
ˌleft-hand ˈ**drive** 808R31
ˌrear wheel ˈ**drive** 1181L62
ˌright-hand ˈ**drive** 1223R82
ˈsales ˌ**drive** 1250R70
ˈtest ˌ**drive** 1505R24
ˈwhist ˌ**drive** 1660L18
ˈmenu-ˌ**driven** 888L14
ˌback-seat ˈ**driver** 89R2
ˈ**driver's** ˌlicence 425L51
ˈ**driver's** ˌlicense 425L51
ˈengine ˌ**driver** 457R70
ˈL-ˌ**driver** 803R52
ˈpile-ˌ**driver** 1066R1
ˈracing ˌ**driver** 1165R27
ˈslave ˌ**driver** 1350R5
ˌSunday ˈ**driver** 1460L82
ˈtrain ˌ**driver** 457R70
ˌdrink-ˈ**driving** 424L80
ˈ**driving** ˌforce 427L4
ˈ**driving** ˌlicence 425L51
ˌdrunk-ˈ**driving** 424L81
in the ˈ**driving** ˌseat 425L55/54
ˈ**drool** over 427L59/60/61
a ˌ**drop** too ˌmuch (to ˈdrink) 427R78
ˈair ˌ**drop** 29L78
at the ˌ**drop** of a ˈhat 427R33
ˈcough ˌ**drop** 311L13
ˌ**drop** a ˈbrick/ˈclanger 427R19
ˌ**drop** *someone* a ˈline 427R14
ˌ**drop** *one's* ˈaitches/ˈh's 427R24
ˌ**drop** aˈway/ˈoff 427R45
ˌ**drop** beˈhind/ˈback/aˈway 427L80
ˌ**drop** ˈby 428L13
ˌ**drop** ˈdead 427R12/8
ˌ**drop** ˈeverything 427R68
ˈ**drop** from/off 427L77/79/R67
ˌ**drop** in the ˈocean 427R81
ˈ**drop** ˌkick 427R34
ˌ**drop**-leaf ˈtable 427R47
ˌ**drop** like a ˈstone 1429R20
ˌ**drop** like ˈflies 540R58
ˌ**drop** off (to ˈsleep) 427R10
ˌfit to ˈ**drop** 527L79/75/76
ˌlet ˈ**drop** 629L65 812L71/74
ˌlet it ˈ**drop** 812L72
ˈmail ˌ**drop** 8R10
ˈname-ˌ**drop** 937L53/54/50
ˈknockout ˌ**drops** 786L8
the ˌpenny ˈ**drops** 1045R55
ˌwork till/until *one* ˈ**drops** 1679R41
ˈ**drown** in 428L72
ˈ**drown** *something* in/with 428L70
ˌ**drown** *one's* ˈsorrows 428L58
ˌ**drowned** ˈrat 428L60
deˈsigner ˌ**drug** 372L69
ˈ**drug** abˌuse 428R37
preˈscription ˌ**drug** 1116L73
ˌsoft ˈ**drug** 1372L10
ˈwonder ˌ**drug** 1676R33
ˌsmart ˈ**drugs** 1358R55
ˌbang/ˌbeat the ˈ**drum** 97L46 428R69
ˌbass ˈ**drum** 103R10
ˈ**drum** into 429L61
ˈ**drum** ˌkit/ˌset 428R74
ˈ**drum** maˌchine 428R75
ˌ**drum** ˈmajor 428R77
ˌ**drum** majorˈette 428R78 854R55
ˈ**drum** on 428R82/84
ˌ**drum** ˈup 429L67
ˈside ˌ**drum** 1333R15 1365L5
ˌsnare ˈ**drum** 1365L5
ˌsteel ˈ**drum** 1418R28
ˌblind ˈ**drunk** 135R40 429R1
ˌ**drunk**-ˈdriving 424L81
ˈpunch-ˌ**drunk** 1146L69/73
ˌroaring ˈ**drunk** 1228R84
a dry ˌeye in the ˈhouse 429R48
ˌbleed *someone* ˈ**dry** 134R19 1403R69
ˈblow-ˌ**dry** 139L12
ˌbone ˈ**dry** 146L61 429R47
ˌdrip-ˈ**dry** 424R38
ˌ**dry**-ˈclean 429R57/54
ˌ**dry** ˈdock 429R58
ˌ**dry**-ˈeyed 429R61
ˌ**dry** ˈginger 595R19
ˈ**dry** ˌgoods 419R4 429R64 634L60
ˌ**dry** ˈice 429R65
ˌ**dry** ˈland 429R68
ˌ**dry** ˈout 429R82 430L26
ˌ**dry** ˈrot 429R69
ˌ**dry** ˈrun 1241R26
ˌ**dry** stone ˈwall 429R71
ˌ**dry** the ˈdishes 430L3
ˌ**dry** ˈup 429R82 430L1/3
ˈfreeze-ˌ**dry** 563L28
ˌhome and ˈ**dry** 680L24
ˌleave *someone* high and ˈ**dry** 667L47
ˌspin-ˈ**dry** 1391R59/63
ˌsqueeze ˈ**dry** 1403R68
watch ˈpaint ˌ**dry** 1641R40
ˈhair ˌ**dryer** 636L54
ˈtumble ˌ**dryer** 1567L68
ˌdo the ˈ**drying** ˈup 430L4
ˌ**dual** ˈcarriageway 430L54
ˌ**dual** ˈpurpose 430L47/58
ˈ**dub** into 430L78
ˌ**dub** ˈover 430L79
a couple of/two ˌshakes (of a **duck's** ˈtail) 1307R14
ˌdead ˈ**duck** 350R35
ˈdecoy ˌ**duck** 356L75
ˌ**duck**-billed ˈplatypus 430R59 1077R32
ˌlame ˈ**duck** 793L65/70
ˌsitting ˈ**duck** 1343L53
take to *something* like a ˌ**duck** to ˈwater 430R25
ˌugly ˈ**duckling** 1577R73
ˌ**ductless** ˈgland 430R72 455R68
ˈfuddy-ˌ**duddy** 571L43
ˈ**dude** ˌranch 430R84
in ˌhigh ˈ**dudgeon** 667R28
ˌgive *someone their* ˈ**due** 431L18 596R30
give the ˌdevil his ˈ**due** 596R30
in ˌ**due** ˈcourse 431R31
with ˌall **due** reˈspect 431L14 1210R43
ˌpay *one's* ˈ**dues** 1038L69
ˌ**duff** ˈup 431L65
ˈ**duffel** ˌbag 431L69
ˈ**duffel** ˌcoat 431L72
ˈ**duffle** ˌbag 431L69
ˈ**duffle** ˌcoat 431L72
ˈ**dum-dum** (ˌbullet) 431R78
ˈ**dumb** ˌshow 431R60
ˌ**dumb** ˈwaiter 431R61
ˌstrike ˈ**dumb** 431R57 1441R15
ˌ**dummy** ˈrun 1241R26
venˌtriloquist's ˈ**dummy** 1613R31
ˈ**dump** *something* on 432L21
ˈ**dump** ˌtruck 432L28/47 1526L56
have/ˌtake a ˈ**dump** 432L42
ˈrefuse ˌ**dump** 1193L16
ˈ**dumping** ˌground 432L31
ˈ**dunce** ˌcap 432L66/65
ˈsand ˌ**dune** 1254L11
ˈ**dunk** *something* in 432R4/5
ˈslam ˌ**dunk** 1348R64
ˈ**dupe** *someone* into 432R22
conˌsumer ˈ**durables** 294L18
ˌ**during** the ˈspace of 1381R62
allow the ˈ**dust** to ˌsettle 433L14
ˌbite the ˈ**dust** 130R19
ˈ**dust** ˌjacket 433L18
ˌ**dust** ˈoff 433L28
ˈ**dust**-up 433L20
ˈ**dust** with 433L25
ˌgather ˈ**dust** 584R64
ˈgold ˌ**dust** 609R69
let the ˈ**dust** ˌsettle 433L14
not ˌsee *someone* for ˈ**dust** 1283L54
ˌwait until the ˈ**dust** has settled 433L15
ˈ**dustbin** ˌbag/ˌliner 433L50
ˈ**dustbin** ˌlorry 433L54
ˌfeather ˈ**duster** 509L4
ˈknuckle-ˌ**duster** 787R80
ˈcrop ˌ**dusting** 327L33
ˌdouble ˈ**Dutch** 414L35/37
ˌ**Dutch** ˈcap 191L9 433L77
ˌ**Dutch** ˈcourage 433L78
Dutch ˈelm diˌsease 433L81
go ˈ**Dutch** 433L74
ˌbounden ˈ**duty** 153R1
ˈdeath ˌ**duty** 352R9
ˌ**duty** ˈbound 433R13
ˌ**duty**-ˈfree 433R28/25
ˌ**duty**-ˈfree ˌshop 433R26
ˈescort ˌ**duty** 468L18
hazardous-ˈ**duty** ˌpay 345R31
ˌheavy-ˈ**duty** 659L13
in the ˌline of ˈ**duty** 826R27
ˈ**duvet** ˌcover 433R38
ˈ**dwell** in 433R65
ˈ**dwell** on 433R67
ˈ**dwell** with 433R57
ˈ**dwindle** to 433R74
ˈtie-ˌ**dye** 1519R55
ˌ**dyed**-in-the-ˈwool 433R82
with *one's* ˌ**dying** ˈbreath 162R52
aˌmoebic ˈ**dysentery** 41R81
ˌmuscular ˈ**dystrophy** 930R49
ˌ**eager** ˈbeaver 434R56
ˌbald ˈ**eagle** 95L53
ˈ**eagle** ˌeye 434R65
ˌgolden ˈ**eagle** 610L20
spread-ˈ**eagled** 1399R39
a ˈflea in *one's* ˌ**ear** 532R38
a ˌword in *someone's* ˈ**ear** 1678R77
ˌcauliflower ˈ**ear** 206L66
ˈ**ear** ˌsplitting 436L69
ˌeasy on the ˈ**ear** 438R52
ˈglue ˌ**ear** 601R70
go ˌin ˈone **ear** and ˌout the ˈother 436L55
have/keep an/*one's* ˈ**ear** to the ˌground 434R82/81
ˌlend an ˈ**ear** 810R46
make a ˌpig's ˈ**ear** of 1065L75
ˌmiddle ˈ**ear** 894L47
ˌplay it by ˈ**ear** 1078R31
ˌturn a deaf ˈ**ear** 1569R34
ˈdog-ˌ**eared** 408R70
ˌbright and ˈ**early** 165L67
ˈ**early** ˌbird 436R57
ˌ**Early** ˈChildhood Education 436R43
ˌ**early**-ˈclosing ˌday 436R46
ˌ**early** ˈdays 436R39
ˌ**early** ˈmusic 436R48
early ˈwarning ˌsystem 436R51
to an ˌ**early** ˈgrave 436R41
ˈ**earmark** for 436R75
ˌ**earn** *one's* (daily) ˈbread 159L68
ˌhard-ˈ**earned** 646R11
ˌwell-ˈ**earned** 1652R25
ˌnice little ˈ**earner** 954L55
ˈwage ˌ**earner** 1632R70
in ˌdeadly ˈ**earnest** 351L52
imˌmoral ˈ**earnings** 706R12
ˈcloth-ˌ**ears** 248L74
could ˌhardly/ˌcould not believe *one's* ˈ**ears** 115L77
ˌ**ears** are ˈburning 434R84
ˌ**ears** are ˈflapping 436L52
ˌfall on ˌdeaf ˈ**ears** 497R82
give *someone* a ˌbox on the ˈ**ears** 155L79
ˌmusic to *someone's* ˈ**ears** 931L48
ˌpin back *your* ˈ**ears** 1067R54
ˌpin *your* ˈ**ears** ˌback 1067R54
ˌup to *one's* ˈ**ears** in 436L68
ˌup to the/*one's* ˈ**ears** 1597R35
ˌwet behind the ˈ**ears** 1654R7
ˌall the corners/the ˌfour corners/the ˌfar corners of the ˈ**earth** 306R2
ˌbring back/down/back down to ˈ**earth** 437L69
come back/down/back down to ˈ**earth** 437L70
Did the ˌ**earth** ˈmove for you? 437R2
disapˌpear off/be ˌwiped off the ˌface of the ˈ**earth** 490R74
ˌdistant/ˌfar corner of the ˈ**earth** 306R84
ˌdown-to-ˈ**earth** 416L51
ˈ**earth** ˌcolour 437R23
ˈ**earth** ˌmother 437R5
ˈ**earth** ˌscience 437R8
ˈ**earth**-ˌshaking 437R10
ˈ**earth**-ˌshattering 437R10
ˈ**earth** ˌtone 437R23
ˌFriends of the ˈ**Earth** 565R1
ˌfruit of the ˈ**earth** 569R47
go to ˈ**earth** 604L15
ˌhell on ˈ**earth** 661L20
move ˌheaven and ˈ**earth** 925L17
ˌpromise *someone* the ˈ**earth** 1131L30
ˌrun to ˈ**earth** 1241L8
scorched-ˈ**earth** policy 1268R10
the ˌ**earth** ˈmoved 437R2
the ˌsalt of the ˈ**earth** 1251R39
the ˌscum of the ˈ**earth** 1275L68
ˌwipe off the face of the ˈ**earth** 1670L59
ˈ**ease** *something* into 438L24
ˌ**ease** *oneself* ˈthrough 438L23
ˌill at ˈ**ease** 703L74
set/put *someone's* ˈmind at ˌ**ease** 898R72
ˌstand at ˈ**ease** 438L37
easier ˌsaid than ˈdone 438R45
the ˌ**easiest** thing in the ˈworld 438R47
ˌ**East** ˈCoast 438L70
ˌ**East** ˈEnd 438L72
ˌ**East** ˈEnder 438L73
ˌFar ˈ**East** 504L14
ˌMiddle ˈ**East** 894L49
ˈ**Easter** ˌegg 438R19
ˌ**Easter** ˈSunday 438R20
ˌMiddle ˈ**Eastern** 894L53
as ˌ**easy** as ABˈC/ˈanything/ˈpie/ˈwinking /ˌfalling off a ˈlog 438R39
ˈ**easy** ˌcare 438R53
ˈ**easy** ˌchair 439L7
easy ˌcome easy ˈgo 438R80
ˌ**easy** ˈgame 438R55
ˌ**easy**-ˈgoing 439L9
ˌ**easy** ˈlistening 438R58
ˌ**easy** ˈmark 438R56
ˌ**easy** ˈmeat 438R55
ˌ**easy** ˈmoney 438R50
ˌ**easy** on the ˈeye/ˈear 438R52
ˌ**easy** ˈoption 1371R82
ˌ**easy**-ˈpeasy 438R60
ˌ**easy** ˈtouch 438R62
ˌfree and ˈ**easy** 560R72
go ˈ**easy** 439L1
go ˈ**easy** on/with 438R83
on ˈ**easy** ˌstreet 439L12
on ˌ**easy** ˈterms 1504L5
ˌrest ˈ**easy** 1212R46
ˌtake it ˈ**easy** 439L6 589L11
ˌtake it/things ˈ**easy** 439L3/4
ˌtake things ˈ**easy** 1512L66
ˌdog-eat-ˈdog 408R71
ˌ**eat** aˈway 439L74
ˌ**eat** ˈcrow 439L50
ˌ**eat** *one's* ˈfill 518R75
ˌ**eat** *someone* for ˈbreakfast 439L34
ˌ**eat** for ˈcomfort 439L36
ˌ**eat** *one's* ˈhat 439L53
ˌ**eat** *one's* ˈheart out 439L45
eat ˌhumble ˈpie 439L49
ˌ**eat** ˈin 439L26

eat into 439L75/76
eat like a horse 439L31
eat out 439L26
eat out of *someone's* hand 439L42 1020R29
eat *someone* out of house and home 439L39
eat up 439L29/77
eat *one's* words 439L49
have a bite to **eat** 130R39
have *one's* cake and **eat** it 183R5
I am so hungry I could eat a horse 439L30
eaten up with/by 439L80
moth-**eaten** 920L46
worm-**eaten** 1685L84
fire-**eater** 523L62
lotus **eater** 842R68
man-**eater** 858R68 859L51/53
binge-**eating** 127L69/74
eating apple 439L54
man-**eating** 859L53
shit-**eating** grin 1317R79
eau de cologne 258R59 439L83
eavesdrop on 439R8
at a low **ebb** 439R18
ebb and flow 439R18
ebb tide 439R20
echo round 439R75
echo sounder 439R70
echo with 439R76
index of leading **economic** indicators 721L34
economical with the truth 440L82
home **economics** 679R74
balance the **economy** 95L13
black **economy** 131R72
economy class 440L62
economy drive 427L11 440L65
economy pack 440L68
economy-sized 440L68
false **economy** 500L16
mixed **economy** 908L70
ectopic pregnancy 440R62 1113L13
co-**ed** 254R4/7/14
op-**ed** 987R10
Garden of **Eden** 441L44 582R82
cutting **edge** 339L5
edge out 441L83
edge *someone* towards 441L81
edge trimmer 441L59 1443L62
edge up 441L80
leading **edge** 804R13/14
on a knife-**edge** 783R56/57/52
razor's **edge** 1177L20
set *someone's* teeth on **edge** 1535R70
take the **edge** off 441L72/73
teeter on the **edge** of 1496L61
double-**edged** 414L39
double-**edged** sword 414L46
gilt-**edged** securities 595L53
two-**edged** 1576L35/36
get a word in **edgeways** 1678L79
edit down 441R72
edit out 441R73
limited **edition** 442L70 824L31
educate *someone* in/on/about 442L80
educated guess 442R46
well-**educated** 1652R31
board of **education** 141L80
co-**education** 254R13/9
Early Childhood **Education** 436R43
further **education** 576R47
higher **education** 669L45 1505L53
physical **education** 1060R51
Postgraduate Certificate in **Education** 1101R47
special **education** 1385R74
conger **eel** 287R10
eff and blind 443L30
eff off 443L38
domino **effect** 411L19
Doppler **effect** 412L75
knock-on **effect** 785L43
ripple **effect** 1226R8
side **effect** 1333R56
snowball **effect** 1367R23
special **effect** 443R25 1385R61
strain after/for **effect** 1433R81/82
the greenhouse **effect** 623L10
cost-**effective** 309R36
after **effects** 23R21
personal **effects** 443R32 1053L1
sound **effects** 1378R42
team **effort** 1494R24
can't boil an **egg** 144L60
chicken and **egg** 225L71
curate's **egg** 335R76
Easter **egg** 438R19
egg-and-spoon race 444R5
egg cup 444R2
egg on 444R16
egg on *someone's* face 444L80
egg roll 444R4 1400L7
egg timer 444R6
egg white 444R8
egg yolk 444R10
kill the goose that lays the golden **egg** 779R70
nest **egg** 949R40
over-**egg** the pudding 1005R79
Scotch **egg** 1269R29
white of an **egg** 444R9
yolk of an **egg** 444R11
bacon and **eggs** 91R72
put all *one's* **eggs** in one basket 444L83
teach *one's* grandmother to suck **eggs** 1494L68
walk on **eggs** 1634R2
walk on **eggshells** 1634R2
alter **ego** 37L33
ego trip 444R37
figure **eight** 517R64
figure of **eight** 517R64
pieces of **eight** 1064R55
seventy-**eight** 1302L59
eighth note 445L7 1161L4
in **either** event 472R59
eject from 445L64
ejector seat 445L68
eke out 445L72
elaborate on 445R7/8
elastic band 445R27 1238R27
elbow grease 445R60
elbow room 445R63
give *someone* the **elbow** 445R57
more power to *your* **elbow** 1106L37
not know *one's* arse from *one's* **elbow** 65L22
tennis **elbow** 1500R36
rub **elbows** with 1238R3
elect *someone* as 446L21
election campaign 187R42 446L42
general **election** 587L31
elective dictatorship 446L53
electoral college 446L62
electoral register/roll 446L63
electric(al) storm 446R17
electric eye 1059L37
electric fence 446L81
electric fire 446L83
electric guitar 631R40
electric heater 446L83
electric razor 446R1 1177L18
electric shock 446R3
the **electric** chair 446L79
electrical engineer 446R14
electroconvulsive therapy 446R41
electron microscope 446R71
electronic mail 446R83
electronic mailbox 447L1
electroshock therapy 446R42
trace **element** 1544R46
elementary particle 447L62
elementary school 447L65
memory like an **elephant** 886L21
pink **elephant** 1068R24
white **elephant** 1660R9
elevate to 447R1
elevator music 447R26 1635R54
eleven-plus 447R35
the **eleventh** hour 447R45
elicit from 447R57
eliminate from 447R78
elimination tournament 448L2 786L12
Dutch **elm** disease 433L81
elope with 448L79
if all **else** fails 493R80
something **else** 1374R54 1375L1
the **Elysian** fields 448R52
emanate from 448R69
embark on/upon 449L28
embezzle from 449L80
embitter *someone* towards 449R5
emblazon across/on 449R10/8
emblazon with 449R9
embroil in 449R83/84 450L3
the **Emerald** Isle 450L37
emerge from 450L41/42/43/44
emergency brake 450L76 642L3
emergency cord 271R53
emergency room 203L25 450L78
state of **emergency** 1414R17
emigrate from/to 450R13
éminence grise 450R46
grey **eminence** 450R46 623R7
pre-**eminent** 1108R84 1109L4/2
tired and **emotional** 1526R69
employ *someone* as 452L69
employ in 452L81
empower *someone* to 452R33
pre-**empt** 1109L9/5
caveat **emptor** 207L36
empty-handed 452R60
empty-headed 452R66
empty into 452R77/81
empty of 452R51/55/75
empty threat 1515L50
on an **empty** stomach 452R59 1429L63
en bloc 453R17
en masse 459L32
en passant 459R44
en route 460L38
en suite 460R17
nail **enamel** 936L69
encapsulate in 453R37
encase in 453R42/44
the whole **enchilada** 1662L14
encourage *somebody* in 454R4
a means to an **end** 879L30
at a loose **end** 840R60
at the **end** of *one's* tether 1506L53
at the **end** of the day 455L20
at *one's* wits' **end** 1674R65
beginning of the **end** 114L28 455L30
big **end** 124R40
bitter **end** 131L11
business **end** 178R55
can't see further than/beyond the **end** of *one's* nose 1283L59
cigarette **end** 232L22
come to an **end** 455L25
come to/meet a sticky **end** 1423R7
come to the **end** of the road 1228L39
dead **end** 351L24
East **End** 438L72
end as 455L78
end in 455L71
end of story 455L15
end-of-terrace 1504L40
end on 455L73
end product 455L56
end result 455L60 1214L30
end up 455L74 1598R46
end user 455L61
end with 455L72
fag **end** of 493R27
for weeks on **end** 1649L82
get (hold of) the wrong **end** of the stick 1692R73
go off the deep **end** 357L55
hear the **end** of *something* 656L31 798L17
jump/plunge in at the deep **end** 357L57
keep/hold *one's* **end** up 455L50
light at the **end** of the tunnel 820R4
make *someone's* hair stand on **end** 636L48
on/at the receiving **end** 1183R23
put an **end** to 455L26
rear-**end** 1181L47
split **end** 1394R79
tail **end** of 1485R15
the **end** of the line 826L14
the **end** of the road 455L8
the **end** of the world 455L33/32
the sharp **end** 1312L26
the thin **end** of the wedge 1511R15
throw/chuck/pitch in at the deep **end** 357L58
to the bitter **end** 131L13
West **End** 1654L13
endear to 455R30
open-**ended** 988L26
East **Ender** 438L73
never-**ending** 951R42
endocrine gland 455R68
well-**endowed** 1652R37
endowment mortgage 456L47
endowment policy 456L51
burn the candle at both **ends** 177L37
loose **ends** 840R66
make **ends** meet 455L54
odds and **ends** 975L16
on *one's* beam-**ends** 107R16
play both **ends** against the middle 1078L42
sworn **enemies** 1479R27
one's own worst **enemy** 1686R76
public **enemy** number one/no. 1 1142L30
wouldn't wish *something* on *one's* worst **enemy** 1671R75
enfant terrible 456R48
engage in 457L65
engage with 457L37/44
engagement ring 457R41
speaking **engagement** 1385L27
engine driver 457R70
fire **engine** 523L66
internal combustion **engine** 743R52
jet **engine** 762R58
traction **engine** 1546L31
civil **engineer** 234R56/59
electrical **engineer** 446R14
chemical **engineering** 223R53
genetic **engineering** 588L47
mechanical **engineering** 880R77
social **engineering** 1370R29
Church of **England** 231R29
Middle **England** 894L24/27 895L20
English breakfast 458L16
English horn 305L53
English muffin 928L32
plain **English** 1074R45
the **English** Channel 215R68
flavour **enhancer** 532L65
enlarge on/upon 458R55
enlighten *somebody* about 458R76
enlightened self-interest 458R83
enlist in 459L20
enmesh in 459L39/40/41
be good **enough** to 611L75
enough and to spare 459R33
enough is enough 459R34
enough said 459R36
fair **enough** 495L1
funnily **enough** 575R1
give *someone* **enough** rope to hang *them*selves 459R38
near **enough** 944R55
strangely **enough** 1434R8
sure **enough** 1467L66
enquire about/after 459R51/56/58/59
enquire into 459R60/61
enquire of 459R55
enquire with 459R63
Directory **Enquiries** 387R67
enraged at 460L5
enrich *something* with 460L17
enrol at 460L26
enrol for/in/on 460L27
open **enrollment** 988R59
double **entendre** 414L48
enter *a place* 231R28
enter for/in 460R75
enter *something* in 460R82
enter into 460R81/84 461L7/10
enter into the spirit of 1393L30
enter on/upon 461L11
enter through/by 460R62
breaking and **entering** 160L72
enterprise culture 461L37
enterprise zone 461L42
free **enterprise** 560R76
private **enterprise** 461L28 1124L37
in-flight **entertainment** 534L56
enthrone in/on 461R20
entice *someone* into 461R54
entice *someone* to 461R56
entitle to 461R81/82/83
entomb in 462L18
entrance exam 462L47
entrance fee 462L49
tradesmen's **entrance** 1547L32
entre nous 462R21
entrust *something* to 462R43/45
entrust with 462R44/47
entwine in 463L6
envelop in 463L27
on the back of an **envelope** 463L34
pay **envelope** 1038R56
stamped addressed **envelope** 1409R24
Episcopal Church 464L52
epoch-making 464R24
Epsom salts 464R48
all/other things being **equal** 1512R6
equal opportunity 464R70
on **equal** terms 1504L8
first among **equals** 525R8
equate to 465L52/53
equate *something* with 465L51
chemical **equation** 223R55
quadratic **equation** 1157L26
vernal **equinox** 1615L51
equip *someone* for 465R53
equip with 465R31/33/51
ill-**equipped** 703R1
erase from 466R4
err on the side of caution 467L13
errand boy 467L22
errand of mercy 467L25
fool's **errand** 544R11
run **errands** 1240R78
knight-**errant** 783R81
error of judgment 467L61
margin of **error** 864R68
see the **error** of *one's* ways 467L59
trial and **error** 1556L68
erupt in 467R1
escape artist 467R84
escape from 467R38/57
escape hatch 467R65
escape key 467R61
escape velocity 467R68
fire **escape** 523L69
have a narrow **escape** 467R52
there's no **escaping** the fact that 467R44
escort agency/service 468L22
escort duty 468L18
industrial **espionage** 723R83
esprit de corps 468L83
essential oil 468R53
essential services 468R58
establish *oneself* as 469L16
establish in/at 469L18
established church/religion 469L20
long-**established** 469L7
old-**established** 469L7
well-**established** 1652R42
estate agency 469L47
estate agent 469L46
housing **estate** 689L83
industrial **estate** 724L1
real **estate** 1134R49 1180R32
real **estate** agent/broker 469L46 1180R34/35 1181L4
real **estate** office 469L48
the Fourth **Estate** 557L5
trading **estate** 1546R45
sink in *someone's* **estimation** 1341R78
et al 469R32
son **et** lumière 1375R48
eternal student 470L8
eternal triangle 470L11
send to **eternity** 470L29
Protestant work **ethic** 1137R84
work **ethic** 1679R9
ethnic cleansing 470L72
ethyl alcohol 470L31/R32
European Community 471L49
European Union 471L55
evacuate from 471L69
job **evaluation** 765R49
evaporated milk 471R73
Christmas **Eve** 230R3 471R84
New Year's **Eve** 952R16
break **even** 161L67
even better 120R67
even-handed 472L66
even now 472L21
even out 472R1/4
even so 472L24/26
even-tempered 472L52
even up 472L84
on an **even** keel 472L45
evening class 472R22
evening dress 472R27/30
evening gown 472R30
evening primrose 472R32/34
evening star 472R35
good **evening** 612L48
make a **evening** of it 855L13
field **event** 516L30
in either **event** 472R59
media **event** 881R12
non-**event** 959L76
the blessed **event** 645R27
the happy **event** 645R26
track **event** 1545R46
turn of **events** 1570L22
ever and anon 473L20
ever before 473L15
ever so 473L49 1368L68
ever such 473L49
hardly **ever** 473L8 647R16
rarely if **ever** 473L9
the same as **ever** 1253L3
worst-**ever** 1686R78
everyone and his brother 1683R51
on **everyone's** lips 828L83
deserve **everything** *one* gets 372L13
drop **everything** 427R68
everything but/except the kitchen sink 474L18
hold **everything** 676R8
that beats **everything** 109R7
how's **everything**? 690R29
evict from 474L35
anecdotal **evidence** 44R58
king's **evidence** 474L68
queen's **evidence** 474L67
state's **evidence** 1414R50
force of **evil** 548L61
necessary **evil** 945L80
the **evil** eye 474R9
the lesser of two **evils** 811R83
evolve from/into 474R51/50
deus **ex** machina 377L11
ex cathedra 476L3
ex-directory 478L70
ex gratia 479L34
ex officio 480L39
ex-serviceman 485L79
Tipp-**Ex** 1526R9 1661L29
exact a toll 1533L71
exact *something* from 475L37
exactly on time 1523L59
exactly so 1369L19
my point **exactly** 1089R8
entrance **exam** 462L47
external **examination** 486R21
cross-**examine** 328L51/43/55
examine *something* for 475R15/16
examine *somebody* on 475R2/23

external examiner 486R24
satisfy the examiners 1256R33
excel at/in 476L42
par excellence 1023R37 1026R29
everything except the kitchen sink 474L18
except from 476L74
present company excepted 272R54 476L75 1116R67
take exception (to) 476R2
excerpt from 476R18/22
excess luggage/baggage 476R32
exchange for 476R48
exchange rate 476R62
Exchange Rate Mechanism 476R65
exchange words 476R53
foreign exchange 549R25
part exchange 1028R13
rate of exchange 476R63 1174R64
stock exchange 1428L7
telephone exchange 1496R68
Chancellor of the Exchequer 214R53
Customs and Excise 338R35
excise *something* from 476R84
nothing to get excited about 477L17
exclaim in 477L43
exclamation mark/point 477L48
exclude from 477L52/54/55
excuse for 478L35/58/68
excuse from 478L41/42
make excuses 478L66/65
stay of execution 1417L69
chief executive 225R54/56
exempt from 478R53/55/57
exercise bike 478R70
the object of the exercise 970R17
heat exhaustion 657R80
exhibition match 479R7
make an exhibition of 479R4
exhort *someone* (not) to 479R33
tax exile 1493R5
exist on 479R68
exist on borrowed time 149R61
pre-exist 1109L17
hand-to-mouth existence 640L73
non-existent 959L80
exit poll 480L19
exit visa 480L23 1626L72
exonerate *someone* from 480L47
exotic dancer 480L63
expand horizons 685L55
expanded polystyrene 480L72
expanding file 281L84
mind-expanding 899L6
expatiate on/upon/about 480R35
expect *something* from 481L3
life expectancy 819L32
expectant mother 480R67
not come/live up to expectation(s) 480R81
expel from 481L52/53/54
capital expenditure 191R51
no expense(s) spared 481R65
blow the expense 139L59
expense account 481R70
hang the expense 644L52
all expenses paid 481R76/78/79
out-of-pocket expenses 1087R73
travel expenses 1553L25
near-death experience 945L6
put *it/something* down to experience 482L22 1153R13
work experience 1679R10
experiment on 482L55/65
experiment with 482L64
expert system 482R10
expert witness 72R7 1674R29
expiration date 347R63 482R37
explain away 482R60
explain to 482R46
explode into 483L29/33/34
explode with/in 483L26
explore for 483R53
Explorer Scout 1613R66
explosive device 483L61
high explosive 667R42
plastic explosive 1076R56
export to 484L12
invisible exports 750R56
expose a raw nerve/spot 1176R68 1540L76
expose *someone* as 484L53
expostulate on/about/against 484R10
expostulate with *someone* about 484R9
indecent exposure 719R61
expound on 484R18
express as 484R26
if you'll pardon the expression 1026L5
expunge from 485L48/49
extend for 485R19
extend into 485R18/40
extend to 485R22/28/77/78/83
extended family 485R52
extension cord/lead 485R67/66
to a great extent 486L43
to some extent 486L47
to such an extent 486L49
to the same extent as 486L46
external examination 486R21
external examiner 486R24
external student 486R24
fire extinguisher 523L71
extol as 486R70
extort money from 486R73/75/76
extra time 487L17
extract from 487L35/36/39/43
malt extract 858L57
extracurricular activity 487L57/60
extraditable crime 487L68
extradite *someone* from 487L65
extradite to 487L64
extradition treaty 487L72
extraordinary meeting 487R7
extrapolate from 487R15/16/15
extrasensory perception 487R21
go from one extreme to the other 487R71
drive to extremes 487R72
extricate from 488L6
exude from 488L32
exult in/at/over 488L36
keep *one's* eye(s) on the clock 246L70
a bird's eye view 128L55
a blink of an eye 135R64
a dry eye in the house 429R48
as far as the eye can/could see 488L56
black eye 131R24
bull's-eye 174L53/58
cast an eye over 202L35
eagle eye 434R65
easy on the eye 438R52
electric eye 1059L37
eye-catching 488R35
eye contact 488R36
eye-opener 488R41
eye-patch 488R44
eye shadow 488R47
eye socket 488R49
fish-eye lens 526L79
get/keep *one's* eye in 488L63
have a roving eye 1237R32
have an eye to/for the main chance 488L67
hook and eye 684L25
in the public eye 1142L18
in the twinkling of an eye 1573R35
keep an/*one's* eye on 488L71
keep an/*one's* eye out for 488R27
look *someone* in the eye 839L50
meet *someone's* eye 883L80/81
mind's eye 899L11
more to *something* than meets the eye 488L81
out of/from the corner of *one's* eye 306R5
red-eye 1189L5
run *one's* eye over 1241R5
see eye to eye with 1283R34
Seeing-Eye dog 1283L81
the apple of *someone's* eye 56L68
the evil eye 474R9
the glad eye 597R41
the naked eye 936R52
turn a blind eye 1569R31
watchful eye 1641R60/62
eyeball to eyeball 488R72
up to *one's* eyeballs 488R74
up to the/*one's* eyeballs 1597R35
raise (a few) eyebrows 1170L42
black-eyed bean 131R27
black-eyed pea 131R27
blue-eyed boy 139R81
blue-eyed soul 139R84
boss-eyed 150R54
bright-eyed and bushy-tailed 165L69
bug-eyed 172R39
cold-eyed 256R62
cross-eyed 328L57
dewy-eyed 379L9
dry-eyed 429R61
goggle-eyed 609R7
hawk-eyed 652L83
hollow-eyed 679L20
misty-eyed 907L17
open-eyed 987R32
pie-eyed 1064L78
pop-eyed 1095L57
round-eyed 1236L65
square-eyed 1402L40
starry-eyed 1412R13
wide-eyed 1663R30
get an eyeful 488R67
flutter *one's* eyelashes 540L36
not bat an eyelid 104L2
a sight for sore eyes 1335R28
bags under *someone's* eyes 93L57
before/under *one's* very eyes 488L57
bug eyes 172R39
cat's eyes 203L76
clap/lay/set eyes on 236R73 488L73
could hardly/could not believe *one's* eyes 115L77
cry *one's* eyes out 331R49
dollar signs in *one's* eyes 410L53
eyes in the back of *one's* head 488L58
eyes out on stalks 1408R65
eyes too big for *one's* belly/stomach 488R33
feast *one's* eyes (up)on 508R64
four-eyes 556R48
gimlet eyes 595L67
hit *someone* between the eyes 673L7
keep *one's* eyes open/peeled/skinned for 488R28
lift/raise *one's* eyes heavenward 658R61
make eyes at 488L75
pull the wool over *someone's* eyes 1678L17
rub/wipe the sleep out of *one's* eyes 1351R35
shut *one's* eyes to 1331R7
take *one's* eyes off 488L79
the scales fall from *someone's* eyes 1260R57
undress *someone* with *one's* eyes 1586R74
up to *one's* eyes in 488L84
up to the/*one's* eyes 1597R35
with *one's* eyes open 488R32 987R25
with *one's* eyes shut 488R23/25
give *one's* eyeteeth 489R77
would give *one's* eyeteeth for 596R21
FA Cup 490L25
a slap in the face 1349L59
arse about face 65L29
coal face 251R18
come face-to-face with 490R22
cut off *one's* nose to spite *one's* face 338R83
disappear off/be wiped off the face of the earth 490R74
egg on *someone's* face 444L80
face cream 490R35
face pack 490R36
face powder 490R39
face-saving 492L33
face the music 492L21
face-to-face 490R21
face up to 492L20 1402R6
face value 490R41/78
face washer 492L41
face with 492L13/16
fly in the face of 540L82
get out of my face 490R33
if your face fits 490R30
laugh on the other side of *one's* face 800L17
let's face it 812R35
long face 838L32
look *someone* in the face 839L50
pizza-face 1072R4
pull a face 1144L54
put a brave face on 158R51
put on a brave face 158R50
show *one's* face 1327L16
shut/slam the door in *someone's* face 411R49
shut your face 1331R11
stare in the face 1413L30
take at face value 490R81
the unacceptable face of 1579L28
throw *something* back in *someone's* face 1516R79
until *someone is* blue in the face 139R56
volte-face 1630L31
wipe off the face of the earth 1670L59
wipe the smile off *someone's* face 1670L65
written all over *someone's* face 1692L50
faced in/with 492L3
freckle-faced 560R31
fresh-faced 564L60
grim-faced 624L31
hatchet-faced 650L69
pasty-faced 1034R25
po-faced 1088R62
poker-faced 1090R74/73
straight-faced 1433L63
two-faced 1576L41
grind the faces of the poor 624L82
the same old faces 1253L44
multi-faceted 928R75
prima facie 1121R25
correctional facility 307R72
accessory after/before the fact 8L17/18
as a matter of fact 492R17 874R26 1122R57
fact-finding 492R25
fact of life 492R22
in actual fact 14L30
in point of fact 492R17
matter-of-fact 875L69/72/64
the fact remains 1200R61
there's no escaping the fact that 467R44
de facto 357R68/75
ipso facto 752L32
causative factor 206R16
deciding factor 354R30
Rh factor 1219R45 1220L9
rhesus factor 1219R45
sleaze factor 1350R63
factory farming 492R81 493L2
factory floor 493L2 536R41
factory gate 493L7
factory ship 493L9
facts and figures 492R27
facts of life 492R24
fade away/out 493L77
fade into 493L75
fading fast 493L82
faff about/around 493R19
fag end of 493R27
fag for 493R45
fag hag 493R51
fail in 493R75 494L21/43
fail-safe 494L58
fail to see 494L22
pass-fail 1031R8
words fail *someone* 1678R42
if all else fails 493R80
heart failure 656L82
damn with faint praise 344R53
faint from 494R29
faint-hearted 494R9
fainting fit 494R32
a fair hearing 495L9
by fair means or foul 494R78
craft fair 319L64
fair and square 495L15/17
fair copy 495R26
fair crack of the whip 494R82
fair dinkum 495L18
fair enough 495L1
fair's fair 495L6
fair game 495L21
fair go 495L23
fair-haired boy 139R82 495L70
Fair Isle 495R53
fair-minded 495L25
fair play 495L30
fair shake 494R82
fair to middling 495L76 894R12
fair-weather friend 495R19
it's a fair cop 494R79
it's fair to say 494R74
it is only fair 494R72
play fair 1078L45
the fair sex 495R24
trade fair 1546L63
with *one's* own fair hand 495R25
laissez-faire 793L14
savoir-faire 1258L40
fairly and squarely 495L48
airy-fairy 30R51
fairy bread 495R68
fairy cake 495R70
fairy floss 189R8
fairy godmother 495R71
fairy lights 495R79
fairy story/tale 495R81 496L8
tooth fairy 1535R75
au fait 79R43
fait accompli 496L26
article of faith 66L29
bad faith 92R2
break faith with 496L55
faith healer 496R38/43
in good faith 612L3
keep faith 496L50
keep the faith 496R34
party faithful 496L83 1030R24
peregrine falcon 1047R78
fall among 498R82
fall apart 498L82/R1
fall around 498R75
fall away/off 497R31/32/35 498L38/39
fall back 498L22 499L1
fall back on/upon 499L5
fall behind 499L15/32
fall between two stools 497R66
fall by 498L25
fall by the wayside 497L68 1646L80
fall down/over 497L59/61/22/55/49
fall flat 497L45
fall for 499L20/23
fall foul of 498R4/6
fall from 497L23
fall from grace 497L84 615R31
fall guy 497R7
fall in 497L24/25 498L45/46/48 499L2/4/30
fall in/into line 498R12
fall in love 498R8
fall into 497L26/27/28/R43/44/69 498R68
fall into place 497R75/76/72
fall into the clutches of 251L4
fall into the hands/clutches of 497R78
fall into the wrong hands 1693L61
fall like a stone 1429R20
fall off 497L31
fall off *one's* chair 497L32
fall off the wagon 1633L28
fall on 497L34/R28/37/40/46/47/49 498L68/R34/62 499L41
fall on deaf ears 497R82
fall on *one's* feet 545L59
fall on hard times 497R84
fall on stony ground 497R83
fall out 497L36/37/38/R50/52 499L46/53
fall out with 498R11/17/19 499L17/18/48
fall over 497L62 497R56 499L48
fall short 498R20
fall through 497L40 499L56
fall to 497L41/64/R29 498L27/R38/39/75 499L60/62/64
fall to *one's* knees 497L72
fall to pieces 1064R25/30
fall under 498L72/74/R70
fall upon 499L41
free fall 561R62
go down/fall like ninepins 956L17
let fall 629L65 812L71/74
riding for a fall 1222L27
stand or fall by 1410L69
take a/the fall for 497R5
the scales fall from *someone's* eyes 1260R57
fallen idol 497R16
fallen woman 497R19
as easy as falling off a log 438R39
falling star 498L3 891L41 1320L45
fallopian tube 499R9
fallout shelter 499R23
fallow deer 499R37
bear false witness 108L56
false accounting 499R67
false alarm 500L5
false bottom 499R70
false dawn 500L11
false economy 500L16
false friend 500L73
false imprisonment 500L21
false modesty 500L57
false move/step 500L26
false start 500L32/35
put on a false front 500L56
ring false 1225R42
under false colours 499R58
under false pretences 499R61
claim to fame 235R31
hall of fame 638R13
rise to fame 1226R37
on familiar terms 500R29
Aid to Families with Dependent Children 28R12 226L25
extended family 485R52
family allowance 500R71
family circle 232R45 500R73
family credit 500R73
family doctor 500R75
family man 500R75
family name 500R77 1468R71
family planning 500R78
family tree 500R80
in the family way 500R70
nuclear family 966L71
one-parent family 984R14
run in the family 1241R6
single-parent family 984R14
start a family 1414L31
famous last words 501L59
world-famous 1684L79
fan belt 501L74
fan club 501R52
fan heater 501L75
fan mail 501R54
fan the flames 501R47
fan *oneself* with 501L82
pigeon fancier 1065R45
catch/take/tickle *someone's* fancy 501R83
fancy *oneself* as 503L22
fancy dress 503L46
(footloose and) fancy-free 503L11
fancy man/woman 503L13
fancy that! 503L26
flight of fancy 503L31 534L38/41
tickle *someone's* fancy 1518R74

fannies in the seats 1278L39
fanny pack 175L12 503L66
sweet fanny adams 1475R51
a far cry from 504L12
as far as I could throw 503R49
as far as I'm concerned 281L19
as far as it goes 503R51
as far as the eye can/could see 488L56
as/so far as 503R45/46/48
far afield 22R73
far corner of the globe/world/earth 306R84
Far East 504L14
far-fetched 503R61
far-flung 503R63/64
far-gone 503R67
far-reaching 503R75
far-sighted 503R78/82
few and far between 514R57
from far and wide 503R56
not trust someone as far as one can/could throw 1565L39
so far so good 503R59
the far corners of the world/earth 306R2
thus far 1518L48
bill of fare 126R4
buy the farm 180R57
collective farm 258L28
farm out 504L78/80/81
fish farm 526L81
funny farm 575R23
health farm 655R3
sewage farm 1303L45
truck farm 1562R71/67
factory farming 492R81 493L2
intensive farming 740R27
mixed farming 908L72
fart about/around 504R28
pissed as a fart 1070R8
penny-farthing 1045R75
arty-farty 65R42
fashion-conscious 505L40
fashion victim 505L41
parrot-fashion 1028L14
full-fashioned 573L10
old-fashioned 980L62/65
as fast as one's legs would carry one 505R40
colour-fast 259R52
fading fast 493L82
fast and furious 505L68
fast asleep 505R59
fast food 505L69
fast-forward 505R42/46
fast lane 505L71 795L64
fast link 505L74
fast-talk 505R47
fast-talker 505R49
fast track 505L76
hard and fast 646L36/39
pull a fast one 1145L21
sinking fast 1341R73
snap fastener 1118L35 1364L43
zip fastener 1700R4
baby fat 1148L25
chew the fat 225L20
fat cat 506L22
fat-free 506L57
puppy fat 1148L25
he fat is in the fire 506L55
he fat of the land 506L53
femme fatale 512R7
fate worse than death 506R14
empt fate 1499R8
ill-fated 703R6
iological father/mother/parent 127R58
Father Christmas 506R47 1255L25
father figure 506R47
father-in-law 506R60
founding father 556L29
one father 837R38
city fathers 234L77
chronic fatigue syndrome 877R18
ompassion fatigue 273R16 507L17
metal fatigue 507L23 890R28
kill the fatted calf 779R68
fatty acid 506L63
mixer faucet 908R5
double fault 414L52
fault line 507R9/11
find fault with 507L71 520R53
foot fault 545R63
flora and fauna 507R21 537L30
comme il faut 269L42
faux pas 507R23
ithout fear or favour 508L82
Guy Fawkes Night 633R74
fawn on/upon 508L31/34
fawn over 508L33/36
fear for 508R7
n fear of one's life 508L73
never fear 508R14 951R25/28
put the fear of God into/in 508L79
strike fear 1441R18
without fear or favour 508L82
god-fearing 609L3
feasibility study 508R52
bean feast 107R38
feast one's eyes (up)on 508R64
feast on/off 508R62
midnight feast 894R49
movable feast 925L32
no mean feat 508R75
birds of a feather 128R9
feather boa 508R82
feather duster 509L4
feather in someone's cap 509L3
feather one's nest 509L8
feathered friend 509L14
ruffle someone's feathers 1239L78
double feature 414L54
feature-length 509L65
fed up 509R36
well-fed 1652R49
anti-federal(ist) 49R84
entrance fee 462L49
fee-paying 509R47
transfer fee 1550L44
feeble-minded 509R54
bottle-feed 151R26/28
breast-feed 162L81/79
feed someone a line 510L20
feed into 510L13/16
feed off/on 509R66/79
feed over 510L14
feed through 510L11
feed to the lions 509R81
feed up 509R75
feed with 509R68/78
mouth to feed 924L12
spoon-feed 1396L79/81
feeding time at the zoo 509R83
bite the hand that feeds 130R13
feel at home 679R54
feel for 510L73/R78 511L32
feel free 510L76 560R39
feel ill-will for 703R30
feel it in one's bones 510L78
feel like 511L37
feel like a million dollars/bucks 897R5
feel like death warmed up/over 352R4
feel like it 511L41
feel up 510R84
feel one's way 510R81
get the feel of 511L33
put out feelers 511L10
bad feeling 92L44
fellow feeling 511R67
gut feeling 633L84
have a nasty feeling 938R43
Monday morning feeling 913L46
sinking feeling 1341R69
hard feelings 646R44
mixed feelings 908L74
touchy-feely 1540R22
boarding fees 141R28
crow's feet 329L4
cut the ground from under someone's feet 339L83
dead on one's feet 350R29
drag one's feet 418L54
fall/land on one's feet 545L59
feet of clay 545L64
find one's feet 520R46
flat feet 531L46/44
get/have cold feet 256L80
have both feet on the ground 545L57
have one's feet on the ground 545L56
have the world at one's feet 1683R66
in one's stocking feet 1428L83
itchy feet 756R69
jump in with both feet 772R60
land on one's feet 794L81
rush/run someone off their feet 545R49
sit at the feet of 1343L38
six feet under 1344L47
stand on one's own (two) feet 1410L66
sweep someone off their feet 1475L48
take the weight off one's feet 1650L11
the patter(ing) of tiny feet 1037L21
think on one's feet 1513L54
under someone's feet 545R52
vote with one's feet 1631L21
Sinn Fein 1342L29
feint to 511L57
feline friend 511R18
at/with one fell swoop 511R29
fellow feeling 511R67
fellow man 511R70
fellow traveller 511R63
hail-fellow-well-met 636L8
felt-tip (pen) 512L16
make one's presence felt 1116R78
femme fatale 512R7
come down on one side of the fence or other 1333R13
cyclone fence 341L63
electric fence 446L81
fence in/off 512R25/29
picket fence 1063L49
shark fence 1311R52
sit on the fence 1343L42
mend fences 886L73
fend for 512R46
fend off 512R50
fender bender 1108R1
tree fern 1554R63
ferret around/about 513L28
ferret out 513L30
Ferris wheel 124R62 513L32
car ferry 193R22
cross-fertilization 328L59
in vitro fertilization 751L48
harvest festival 649L61
the festive season 513R44
festoon with 513R64
fetch and carry 513R71
fetch up 513R81
far-fetched 503R61
feud over 514L70/73
feud with 514L72
glandular fever 598L38
hay fever 652R29
rheumatic fever 1220L1
run a fever 1240R77
scarlet fever 1263L10
swine fever 1477L29
yellow fever 1696L39
hi-fi 667L25/28/R45
sci fi 1266R59 1267L57
glass fiber 515L45 598R17
dietary fibre 382L51 515L34
every fibre of one's being 515L33
fibre optics 515L22
fibre-tip (pen) 512L17
glass fibre 515L45 598R17
optical fibre 992L13
cystic fibrosis 341R79
non-fiction 959L84
science fiction 1266R59
fiddle about/around 515R32/34/36
fiddle while Rome burns 515R41
fiddle with 515R24
play second fiddle 1079L11
second fiddle 1279R12/73
bona fide 145R67
high fidelity 667R44
bona fides 145R70
fidget about 515R74
fidget with 515R73
coal field 251R21
field day 516L8
field event 516L30
field glasses 516L15
field hockey 516L33 674R78
field marshal 516L16 868R56
field trip 516L17
have a field day 516L10
lead the field 804L78
leave the field clear 516L27
left field 808R25
level playing field 813R31
magnetic field 852R54
out in left field 808R28
play the field 1078L51
playing field 1078L65
right field 1223R77
track and field 1545R45
the Elysian fields 448R52
something fierce 516R13
fifth column 528L39/41
fifty-fifty 516R46
fig leaf 516R66/68
not care/give a fig 516R64
not worth a fig 516R65
cock fight 252R38
fight a losing battle 517L33
fight about 517L2/50/57
fight against 516R81 517L55
fight one's corner 517L29
fight fire with fire 517L32
fight for 517L13
fight it out 517L26
fight off 517L16/18
fight on 516R83
fight over 516R84 517L4
fight shy of 517L36
fight one's way out of a paper bag 517L27
fight with 516R81 517L3/49
fist-fight 526R78
live to fight another day 831R64
spoiling for a fight 1395R27
freedom fighter 562L63
Stealth fighter 1418L33
fighting chance 517L75
fighting fit 517L78
fighting spirit 517L79
fighting talk/words 517L82
figment of the/someone's imagination 517R3
ballpark figure 96L23
cult figure 334R10
cut a fine figure 339R77
cut quite a figure 339R77
father figure 506R47
figure as 517R75
figure eight 517R64
figure in 517R75/76/78
figure of eight 517R64
figure of fun 517R41
figure of speech 517R43
figure on 517R82
figure out 518L5
figure skating 517R66
fine figure of a man/woman 517R39
hourglass figure 689L21
matchstick figure 873L33 1422R67
mother figure 920L69
public figure 1142L34
put a figure on it 517R62
stick figure 873L34 1422R66
facts and figures 492R27
round figures 1236L80
single/double figures 517R56
that/it figures 517R83
trade figures 1546L67
accordion file 9L65 281L84
concertina file 281L83
expanding file 281L84
file for 518L83
file through 518R12/22
file something under 518L81
folding file 281L84
lever arch file 814L78
nail file 936L66
single file 1341L17
the rank and file 1172R38
eat/drink one's fill 518R75
fill in/out 518R47/66/69/72 1411L67
fill someone's shoes 1319L55
fill the bill 126R2 527L66
fill up 518R53
fill with 518R44/52/57/61/64
smoke-filled room 1361L78
stocking-filler 1428R1
filling station 518R73 1056L44
film credits 1529L29
film over 519L59/60
film strip 519L52
horror film 686L10
silent film 1337R2
filter coffee 519R44/45
filter down 519R35
filter in 519R35/42
filter out 519R35
filter paper 519R46
filter through 519R35
filter tip 519R48
filter-tipped cigarette 519R48
water filter 1642R9
filthy rich 519R67
fin-de-siècle 521L23
cup final 335R11
final demand 363R53 520L3
final solution 520L11
final straw 1435R25
grand final 618L17
in the final analysis 43R42
semi-final 1290R44
the final curtain 337R43/45
the final Judgment 771L68
financial year 520L68
find against 520R84
find fault with 507L71 520R53
find one's feet 520R46
find for 520R9/81
find oneself in 520R31
find it in one's heart 520R50
find out 521L6/10/13
find out how the land lies 794L13
find one's own level 813R65
find one's tongue 520R52
range finder 1172L59
fact-finding 492R25
all very fine 1617L67
chance would be a fine thing 214R26
cut a fine figure 339R77
cut it/things fine 339L2
down/off to a fine art 521L61
fine art 521L57
fine figure of a man/woman 517R39
fine kettle of fish 777R51
fine print 521R5 1357R66
fine-tune 521R7
not to put too fine a point on it 521L82
spot fine 1398R57
with a fine-tooth comb 521L84
you're a fine one to talk 1488R25
fines herbes 521R41
a finger in every pie 521R71
finger bowl 522L3
finger buffet 522L5
finger food 522L10
finger on the pulse 1145R35
finger someone to 522L24
fish-finger 526L83
give someone the finger 521R66
have a finger in the pie 521R73
index finger 549L43 721L46
lady's finger 792L75 979R35
lay a finger on 802L62
lift/raise a finger 521R81
little finger 831L39
middle finger 894L55
point the finger at 1089L37
pull/get one's finger out 521R83
put one's finger on 522L2
ring finger 1225L29
twist/wrap someone around/round one's little finger 1573R84 1689L69
light-fingered 821L56
genetic fingerprinting 588L50
all fingers and thumbs 521R63
burn one's fingers 177R6
count on the fingers of one hand 312L14
cross fingers 327R28
fingers in the till 521R76
get/have one's fingers burnt 177R6
give someone two fingers 1576L18
green fingers 622R26/29
have sticky fingers 1423L79
keep one's fingers crossed 521R79
ladies' fingers 792L77
put/stick two fingers in the air/up 1576L17
slip through someone's fingers 1354L8
snap one's fingers 1364L57
to the tips of one's fingers 1525R80
two fingers 1603L60
work one's fingers to the bone 1679R43
finish off 522R4/5/6
finish up 522R11/13 1598R45
finish with 522L73/79/80
from start to finish 522R34 1413R41
photo finish 1059L19
finishing school 522R22
put the finishing touches on/to 522R27/28
fink on 522R78
fink out 522R81
add fuel to the fire 571L75
baptism of fire 98L79
bush fire 178L82
catch fire 205L35
cease fire 207R16/18 523R34
electric fire 446L83
fight fire with fire 517L32
fire alarm 523L42
fire-and-brimstone 523L20
fire at 523R13
fire away 523R20
fire blanket 523L47
fire brigade 523L52
fire department 523L52
fire door 523L54
fire drill 523L57
fire-eater 523L62
fire engine 523L66
fire escape 523L69
fire extinguisher 523L71
fire from 523R28/36
fire house 523L80
fire hydrant 523L73
fire into 523R14
fire-plug 523L74
fire-raiser 523L78/76
fire starter 524L68
fire station 523L80
fire up 523R54
fire someone with 523R51/52
friendly fire 565R34
gas fire 584L10
go through fire and water 523L32
hang fire 644L61
have/keep many/several irons in the fire 752R13
open fire 988R23
play with fire 1078L3
rapid fire 1173R18/19
set fire to 523L28
set on fire 523L27
set the world/the Thames on fire 1299L34
the fat is in the fire 506L55
coal-fired 251R22 523R10
oil-fired 523R8 979L24

▫open ▪**fireplace** 988R23
▪**firing** ▫squad 523R30
in/on the ▪**firing** ▫line 523R23/26/22/26
▫**firm** ▪up 525L34
▫terra ▪**firma** 1504L52
at ▫**first** ▪hand 525R71 640L66
▫**first** ▪aid 525R25
▫**first**-▪aiders 525R30
▫**first** among ▪equals 525R8
▫**first** and ▪foremost 525R15
▫**first** and ▪last 525R16
▫**first** ▪base 525R31
▫**first**-born (▪child) 525R36
▫**first** ▪class 525R40/48
▫**first**-class de▪gree 525L82
first ▫come first ▪served 525R4
▫**first** ▪cousin 315R70 525R51
▫**first**-degree ▪burn 525R54
▫**first**-degree ▪murder 525R55
▫**First** ▪Fleet 525R57
▫**first** ▪fleeter 525R58
▫**first** ▪floor 525R60 626L55
▪**first** ▫fruit 525R72
▫**first** ▪gear 525R62
▫**first**-▪hand 525R67
▫**first** ▪lady 525R76
▫**first** ▪language 525R78
▫**first** ▪light 525R81
▫**first** ▪mate 525R84
▪**first** ▫name 526L2
▫**first** ▪night 526L14
▫**first** of▪fender 526L17
▫**first** ▪officer 525R84
▫**first**-past-the-▪post 526L20
▫**first** ▪person 526L27
▫**first** ▪principles 526L32 1122R45
▫**first**-▪rate 526L36 1174R82
▫**first** ▪strike 526L41
▫**first** ▪thing 525R22 1512L3
▫**first** things ▪first 525R23
▫**first**-time ▪buyer 526L43
▪**first**-▫year 526L48
in the ▫**first** ▪flush of 525R12
in the ▪**first** ▫instance 525R20
in the ▪**first** ▫place 525R19 1073L65
make the ▫**first** ▪move 925R57
not know the ▫**first** ▪thing about 786R62
on a ▪**first**-name ▫basis with 526L9
on ▪**first**-name ▫terms with 526L9
▫safety-▪**first** 1248R54
the ▪**first** ▫thing 1512R46
▫twenty-▪**first** 1572R43
▪**fiscal** ▫year 526L59
▫big ▪**fish** 125L47
▫cold ▪**fish** 256R64
▫drink like a ▪**fish** 424R16
▫**fish** and ▪chips 526R8
▫**fish**-eye ▪lens 526L79
▪**fish** ▫farm 526L81
▫**fish**-▪finger 526L83
▪**fish** for 526R31/32
▫**fish** for ▪compliments 276L57
fish in ▫troubled ▪waters 526R21
▪**fish** ▫kettle 526R1
▪**fish**-▫knife 526R2
▫**fish** or cut ▪bait 526R19
▫**fish** ▪out 526R35/37
▪**fish**-▫slice 526R3
▪**fish** ▫stick 526L83
▪**fish** ▫tank 526R6 1490L31
▫flying ▪**fish** 540R10
have ▫bigger/▫other **fish** to ▪fry 526L71
▫kettle of ▪**fish** 777R49
▫little ▪**fish** 831R35
▪pretty/▪fine ▫kettle of ▫**fish** 777R51
there are (▫plenty) more/(▫plenty of) other **fish** in the ▪sea 526L75
▪fly-▫**fishing** 540R78
▫smell ▪**fishy** 1360L33
▪**fist**-▫fight 526R78
▫hand over ▪**fist** 640R45
with an ▫iron ▪**fist** 752R18
▫ham-▪**fisted** 639R6
▫tight-▪**fisted** 1520L8
a ▫tight ▪**fit** 1519R84
▪coughing ▫**fit** 310R84
▪fainting ▫**fit** 494R32
▫fighting ▪**fit** 517L78
fit for ▫human con▪sumption 527L72 692L73
▫**fit** ▪in 528L5/9
▫**fit** ▪in with 528L6
▫**fit** ▪out 528L12
▫**fit** the ▪bill 126R2 527L66
▫**fit** to ▪burst/▪drop 527L79/75/76
▫**fit** ▪up 528L16/19
▫**fit** ▪up as 528L18
▫keep-▪**fit** 777L11
▫see ▪**fit** 1283R74
if your ▪face ▫**fits** 490R30
in/by ▫**fits** and ▪starts 527R82
one-▫size-**fits**-▪all 984R34
▫**fitted** ▪bodice 142R30
▫**fitted** ▪kitchen 527R49 782L34
sur▫vival of the ▪**fittest** 1470R55
▫close-▪**fitting** 247R72
▫loose-▪**fitting** 841L16
▪sanitary ▫**fittings** 1254R73
▫**five** o'clock ▪shadow 528L30
▫**five**-▪star 528L33
▫gimme ▪**five** 528L28
▫give *someone* ▪**five** 528L26
▫high-▪**five** 667L55
▫nine to ▪**five** 955R84
▫not last **five** ▪minutes 798L76
put ▫two and two together and ▫make ▪**five** 1574R75/78
▫take/▫have ▪**five** 528L26
give *someone* a ▫bunch of ▪**fives** 175R39
▪**fix** at 528L65
▪**fix** *something* for 528R3
▪**fix** on 528L48/R22/34
▪**fix** *something* to 528L46
▪**fix** *someone* with 528L49/R35
▫quick ▪**fix** 1162L56
▫**fixed** ▪assets 528L59
▫**fixed** ▪star 528L56
▫no **fixed** a▪bode/ad▪dress 528L55
▫**fizzle** ▪out 528R80
▫chequered ▪**flag** 224L57
▪**flag** ▫day 529L38/40
▫**flag** ▪down 529L67
▫**flag** of con▪venience 529L42
▪**flag**-▫waving 529L45
keep the ▪**flag** ▫flying 529L35
▫red ▪**flag** 1189L7
the ▫Red ▪**Flag** 1189L10
▪Union ▫**Flag** 1590R27
▫wave/▫show/▫fly the ▪**flag** 529L30
▫white ▪**flag** 1660R12
▫put out the ▪**flags** 529L32
put the ▪**flags** out 529L32
▪**flak** ▫jacket 529R36
▫**flake** ▪out 529R56
▪soap ▫**flakes** 1369L81
▫**flaky** ▪pastry 529R46
▪flim ▫**flam** 534R1
▪**flame** re▫tardant 530L1
▪**flame**-▫thrower 529R83
▫old ▪**flame** 980L67
add ▪fuel to the ▫**flames** 571L75
▫burst into ▪**flames** 178L1
▫fan the ▪**flames** 501R47
go ▫up in ▪**flames** 529R80
▫non-▪**flammable** 959R2
▫**flap** a▪bout/a▪round 530R3
▫ears are ▪**flapping** 436L52
▪**flare**-up 530R15/23
▪**flash** at 530R38/72
▪**flash** ▫back 530R61
▫**flash** ▪by/▪past 530R59
▪**flash** ▫card 530R75
▪**flash** ▫flood 530R54
▪**flash**-▫fry 530R62
▪**flash** in the ▪pan 530R45
▫**flash** ▪money about/around 530R68
▪**flash** ▫point 530R48/52
▫hot ▪**flash** 687R48
▫quick as/like/in a ▪**flash** 530R42
▪hip ▫**flask** 531L30 671L70
▪thermos ▫**flask** 1604L67
▪vacuum ▫**flask** 531L30 1604L67
as ▫**flat** as a ▪pancake 531L42
▫fall ▪**flat** 497L45
▫**flat**-▪chested 224R45 531L43
▫**flat** ▪feet 531L46/44
▪**flat** ▫racing 531L48
▪garden ▫**flat** 582R83
▪granny ▫**flat** 618R65
▫lay ▪**flat** 802L50
▪studio ▫**flat** 1447R29
▫**flatter** to de▪ceive 532L2
▪**flavour** en▫hancer 532L65
▫**flavour** of the ▪month 532L63
▪**flavour** *something* with 532L70
▫**flay** *someone* a▪live 532R33
a ▪**flea** in *one's* ▫ear 532R38
▪**flea** ▫market 532R39
▪**fleck** *something* with 532R67
▫full-▪**fledged** 573L12/13
▫**flee** the ▪country 532R84
▫First ▪**Fleet** 525R57
▫**fleet** ▪admiral 533L22
▪**Fleet** ▫Street 533L38
▫first ▪**fleeter** 525R58
add ▪**flesh** to *one's* ▫argument 533L63
▫**flesh** and ▪blood 533L59/61
▪**flesh**-▫coloured 533L66
▫**flesh** ▪out 533L79/81
▪**flesh**-▫tone 533L66
▪**flesh** ▫wound 533L69 1688R47
make *someone's* ▪**flesh** ▫crawl/▫creep 533L62
mortifi▫cation of the ▪**flesh** 919R32
▫own **flesh** and ▪blood 1013L9
▫pound of ▪**flesh** 1104R8
put ▫**flesh** on *one's* ▪argument 533L64
▪thorn in the ▫**flesh** 1514L55
▫**fleur**-de-▪lis 533R1
▪muscle-▫**flexing** 930R24
▪**flick** ▫knife 533R64
▫**flick** *something* ▪off 533R60
▫**flick** ▪out 533R56
▪**flick** ▫through 533R62/71
▪skin ▫**flick** 1346R45
as the ▪crow ▫**flies** 328R84
▫drop like ▪**flies** 540R58
the ▫shit ▪**flies** 1317R69
▪**flight** at▫tendant 29L83 534L43
▪**flight** ▫deck 534L45/47
▫**flight** lieu▪tenant 534L48
▫**flight** of ▪fancy 503L31 534L38/41
▪**flight** ▫path 534L50
▪**flight** re▫corder 534L53
▪**flight** ▫sergeant 534L54
▫in-**flight** enter▪tainment 534L56
in the ▫top ▪**flight** 534L42
▫put to ▪**flight** 534L71
▫scheduled ▪**flight** 1264R6
▫take ▪**flight** 534L73
▫top-▪**flight** 1537L83
▫white ▪**flight** 1661L18
▪**flim** ▫flam 534R1
▪**flinch** from 534R16/18
▫**fling** ▪on/▪off 534R46/54
▫**fling** ▪out 534R48/53
▫**fling** up *one's* ▪hands 534R49
▫highland ▪**fling** 669L83
▪**flip** ▫chart 535L8
▪**flip**-▫flop 535L23
▫**flip** *one's* ▪lid 535L7/4
▫**flip** ▪over 534R78/79/81
▪**flip** ▫side 535L15/16
▪**flip** through 534R83
▪**flirt** with 535L49
▫do a ▫moonlight ▪**flit** 917L1
▫**flit** a▪round/a▪bout 535L69
▫**float** a▪round/a▪bout 535L81/84/R35
▫**float** ▪down/a▪long 535R18
▪**float** in/on 535L80
▪**float** into/through/across 535R29/28
▪**float** on 535L78/R21/52
▫**float** on ▪air 29L41 535R2
▪horse ▫**float** 686L83
▪milk ▫**float** 896R77
▫**floating** ▪voter 535R44
▫free-▪**floating** 561R70
▪**flock** to 535R80/81
▪ice ▫**floe** 700L1
▫**flog** a dead ▪horse 536L6
▫**flog** to ▪death 536L10
be▫fore the ▪**Flood** 536L46
▪flash ▫**flood** 530R54
▫**flood** ▪back 536L70
▫**flood** ▪in 536L63
▪**flood** into 536L58
▫**flood** ▪out 536L31/75
▪**flood** ▫plain 536L39
▪**flood** ▫tide 536L41/42
▪**flood** with 536L27/60/66
▫open the ▪**floodgates** 987R64
in ▫**floods** of ▪tears 536R3
▪dance ▫**floor** 345L60
▫factory ▪**floor** 493L2 536R41
▫first ▪**floor** 525R60 626L55
▪**floor** ▫cloth 536R25
▪**floor** ▫lamp 536R26 1411R65
▪**floor** ▫show 536R51
go through the ▪**floor** 536R23
▫ground ▪**floor** 626L54
▫put *one's* ▫foot to the ▪**floor** 545L79
▫second ▪**floor** 1279L70
▫shop ▪**floor** 1321L69
▫take the ▪**floor** 536R48/50
▫wipe the ▪**floor** with 1670L55
▪belly ▫**flop** 116L12
▪flip-▫**flop** 535L23
▪**flop** over/into 537L3/4
▫**floppy** ▪disk 537L24
▫**flora** and ▪fauna 507R21 537L30
▪dental ▫**floss** 366R16
▪fairy ▫**floss** 189R8
▫**flotsam** and ▪jetsam 537L74
▫**flounce** a▪bout 537R2
▫plain ▪**flour** 1074R29
▫self-▪raising **flour** 1289L15
▪soya ▫**flour** 1381R20
▪cash ▫**flow** 201R40
▫ebb and ▪**flow** 439R18
▪**flow** ▫diagram 538L17
▫**flow** ▪down 537R57
▪**flow** from 537R59
▫**flow** ▪in 537R75
▪**flow** into/to 537R61/60/73
▫**flow** ▪through 537R60/62
go/▫move a▫gainst the ▪**flow** 538L5
go/move with the ▪**flow** 538L3 604L17
in ▫full ▪**flow** 572L71
▫come into ▪**flower** 538L26
▪**flower** ar▫ranging 538L30
▪**flower** ▫children 538L32
▪**flower** ▫people 538L32
▪**flower** ▫power 538L33
▫land **flowing** with milk and ▪honey 794L45
▫high-▪**flown** 668R21
▪**fluctuate** between 538L72
▫bit of ▪**fluff** 130L14
▪**fluff** *it/something* 538R33
▫**fluff** ▪up/▪out 538R20
▫**fluid** ▪ounce 538R48
▫far-▪**flung** 503R63/64
▫**flunk** ▪out 538R80
▪**flush** down 539R66
▫**flush** ▪out 539R72/77
▪**flush** with 539L77/79/R53
▫hot ▪**flush** 687R48
in the ▫first ▪**flush** of 525R12
▫royal ▪**flush** 1238L4
cham▪pagne ▫**flute** 214L23
▫**flutter** a▪bout 540L24
▫**flutter** ▪down 540L23
▫**flutter** *one's* ▪eyelashes 540L36
▪button-▫**fly** 180R3
▪crane ▫**fly** 319R75
▫**fly** a ▪kite 541L5
▫**fly** a▪bout/a▪round 540L81/67
▫**fly** at 540L60/R32
▫**fly** a▪way/▪off 540L68/R30
▪**fly**-by-▫night 541L19
▫**fly** ▪by/▪past 540R27
▫**fly**-by-▪wire 540R1
▫**fly**-drive ▪holiday 540R2
▫**fly**-drive va▪cation 540R2
▪**fly**-▫fishing 540R78
▫**fly** ▪in/▪out 540L78/80/73/75/76/74
▫**fly** in the ▪face of 540L82
▫**fly** in the ▪ointment 540R61
▫**fly** into a ▪rage/▪temper/▪fury 540R35
fly ▫off at/on a ▪tangent 1489R70/69/68
▫**fly** off the ▪handle 540R35
▪**fly**-on-the-▫wall 540R69/65
▫**fly** the ▪flag 529L30
▪fruit ▫**fly** 569R49
go ▫**fly** a ▪kite 541L8
▫let ▪**fly** 812R24/28
make the ▫fur ▪**fly** 575R42
▫no-▪**fly** ▫zone 957R54 1700R76
▪pop ▫**fly** 1095L59
the ▫fur begins/starts to ▪**fly** 575R40
the ▫sparks ▪**fly** 1383R39
▪tsetse ▫**fly** 1566L61
▪tzetze ▫**fly** 1577R35
▫wouldn't harm/hurt a ▪**fly** 540R73
▫high-▪**flyer** 667R57/50
▪**flying** ▫boat 540R4
▫**flying** ▪buttress 540R6
▫**flying** ▪doctor 540R8
▫**flying** ▪fish 540R10
▫**flying** ▪fox 540R12 569R45
▫**flying** ▪jump/▪leap 540R13
▫**flying** ▪picket 540R40
▫**flying** ▪saucer 540R14
▪**flying** ▫squad 540R43
▫**flying** ▪start 540R45
▫**flying** ▪visit 540R47 1627L48
keep the ▪flag ▫**flying** 529L35
▪kite-▫**flying** 782L55
set the ▪fur ▫**flying** 575R43
with ▫**flying** ▪colours 541L10
▫Venus ▪**flytrap** 1614L12
▫**foam** at the ▪mouth 541L83
▫**fob** ▪off 541R16/17/10
▫**focal** ▪length 541R58
▫**focal** ▪point 541R34/35
▪**focus** on 541R27/28/62
▪cannon ▫**fodder** 189R65
▪**fog** ▫bank 542L24
▪**fog** ▫lamp 542L25
▪**fog** ▫light 542L25
▪**fog** ▫up 542L31
▪**fogged** ▫in 542L29
▫silver ▪**foil** 1339L1
▫tin ▪**foil** 1524R74
▪**foist** on/upon 542L80
▫**fold** a▪round 542R11
▫**fold** ▪back 542R7
▫**fold** ▪down 542R8
▫**fold** ▪in 542R11/48
▫**fold** ▫into 542R47
▪**fold** under 542R16
▫**fold** ▪up 542R6
▫**folding** ▪file 281L84
▫**folic** ▪acid 542R65
▪**folk** ▫hero 542R76
▪**folk** ▫medicine 543L12
▪**folk** ▫memory 543L14
▪**folk** ▫tale 543L17
▪**folk** ▫wisdom 543L19
▪little ▫**folk** 831L42
a ▫hard/▫tough act to ▪**follow** 13L52
▪**follow** from 543R71
▫**follow** my/the -▪leader 543R17
▫**follow** *one's* ▪nose 543L78/83
▫**follow** ▪suit 543R1
▫**follow** ▪through 543R3/4
▫**follow** ▪up on 543R11
▫**follow** ▪up with 543L65
▪**follow-up** 543R15/16
▪camp ▫**follower** 187R32
▪cult ▫**following** 334R9
▫**following** ▪wind 543R25
▪**fondue** ▫set 544L34
▪angel ▫**food** ▫cake 44R82
▪comfort ▫**food** 267L70
con▪venience ▫**food** 300R8
▪devil's ▫**food** ▫cake 378L68
▫fast ▪**food** 505L69
▪finger ▫**food** 522L10
▪**food** ▫additive 544L53
▪**food** ▫chain 544L54
▫**food** for ▪thought 544L63
▪**food** ▫poisoning 544L58
▪**food** ▫processor 544L59
▪**food** ▫stamp 544L61
▪health ▫**food** 655R5
▪junk ▫**food** 773R46
▫act/▫play the ▪**fool** 544L81 608R1
▫April ▪**fool** 59L31
▫**fool** a▪bout/a▪round 544R27/29/33/31/29/35
▫**fool's** ▪errand 544R11
▫**fool's** ▪gold 544R12
▪**fool** into 544R24
▫**fool's** ▪paradise 544R16
▫gooseberry ▪**fool** 544R61 613L35
make a ▪**fool** of *one▫self* 544R2/L84
▫no/▫no one's/▫nobody's ▪**fool** 544R9
penny-▫wise and pound-▪**foolish** 1045R66
▫April ▪**Fools'** ▫Day 59L33
not suffer ▫**fools** ▪gladly 1456L79
a **foot** in ▪both ▫camps 545L52
a ▪**foot** in the ▫door 545L51
▫athlete's ▪**foot** 76L28
▫catch on the wrong ▪**foot** 1692R78
foot-and-▪mouth dis▫ease 545R55
▪**foot** ▫brake 545R58
▪**foot**-▫dragging 545R60
▪**foot** ▫fault 545R63
▪**foot** ▫soldier 545R65 726L44
from ▫head to ▪**foot** 653L46
▫hand and ▪**foot** 640R80
hardly/barely put ▫one **foot** in front of the ▪other 545R46
have one ▫**foot** in the ▪grave 545L58
▫hot ▪**foot** 687R51
▫never put/set a **foot** ▪wrong 545L75
on the ▫right/▫wrong ▪**foot** 545L71
put *one's* ▫best **foot** ▪forward 118R67
put *one's* ▪**foot** ▫down 545L76/79
put *one's* ▪**foot** in it 545L82
▫put *one's* ▪**foot** in *one's* ▫mouth 545L83
▫put *one's* ▫**foot** to the ▪floor 545L79
▫set ▪**foot** 545R51
the ▫boot/▫shoe is on the other ▪**foot** 148L71 545L54
▫touch *something* with a ten-**foot** ▪pole 1540L72
▫wrong-▪**foot** 1692R79
A▫merican ▪**football** 41L25
as▫sociation ▪**football** 73L70
▪**football** ▫player 546L24
▪**football** ▫pools 546L22 1094R39
▫rugby ▪**football** 1239R6
▫touch ▪**football** 1540R4
▫web ▪**footed** 1648R47
▫play ▪**footsie** 1078L47
▫**footslog** a▪round 546R9
▪**forage** for 547R25/26/27
for▪**bear** from 547R48
▫God/▫heaven **for**▪**bid** 547R74
for▫**bidden** ▪fruit 547R83
a ▫**force** to be ▪reckoned with 548L57
▪air ▫**force** 29L80
▪driving ▫**force** 427L4
▫**force** ▪back 548R5
▫**force** down *someone*'s ▪throat 1516L2
▫**force** into a ▪corner 306R11
▫**force** of ▪evil 548L61
▫**force** of ▪habit 548L63
▪**force** *something* on 548R8
▫**force** ▪out 548R11
▫**force** *someone* to *their* ▪knees 782R70
in/into ▪**force** 548R34
▪labour ▫**force** 789R59
▫Marshal of the Royal ▪Air ▫**Force** 868R57
▪sales ▫**force** 1250R75
▪task ▫**force** 1492L48
▫tour de ▪**force** 1542L44
▫Allied ▪**forces** 34L51
▫armed ▪**forces** 62R80
com▫bine/▫join ▪**forces** 548L28
▫market ▪**forces** 867L32
▪weather ▫**forecast** 1648L42/45/39
fore▪**close** on 549L20
▫**foreign** af▪fairs 549R21
▫**foreign** ▪aid 549R22
▫**foreign** ex▪change 549R25
▫**Foreign** ▪Legion 563R15

Foreign ▫Office 549R29
foreign ▪soil 549R31
French Foreign ▪Legion 563R15
tug at/▫touch one's ▪forelock
549R45
first and ▪foremost 525R15
ore▫seeable ▪future 550L12
can't see the ▫forest for the
▪trees 1677L74
rain ▫forest 1169R71
ore▪warn about 550R11
forge a▪head 550R64
or▪get about 550R70/75
or▪get it 551L1
or▪give someone for 551L29
forgone con▪clusion 549L63
551L53
fork-lift (▪truck) 551L60
fork ▪out 551R45
fork something ▪out for/on
551R47
fork ▪over 551R45
fork ▪up 551R45/46
able ▫fork 1483L63
oasting ▫fork 1530R36
uning ▫fork 1567R62
forked ▪tongue 551R43
base ▫form 101R63
claim ▫form 235R67
om▪bining ▫form 261R9
form into 551R76
form of ▪words 553L66
form ▪up 551R79
ree-▫form 561L5
1 ▫any ▫shape or ▪form 1310L70
/on ▫top ▪form 1537L78
life ▫form 819L35
order ▫form 993R84
sixth ▫form 1344L60/62/63
rue to ▪form 1563R64
pro ▪forma 1128R66
pro forma ▪invoice 1128R72
shadow of one's former ▪self
1306L81
abit-▫forming 634R46
chemical ▪formula 223R57
nfant ▫formula 726L14
god-for▫saken 609L6
Fort ▪Knox 554R20
hold the ▪fort 676R69
nd ▪so forth 44R19
nd ▫so on and ▪so forth 44R19
back and ▪forth 89L32 554R29
roaring ▪forties 1229L6
fortified ▪wine 554R66
fortify oneself with 554R56/59/61
tes▫tinal ▪fortitude 746R3
small ▪fortune 1357R38
fortune ▫cookie 555L49
fortune ▫hunter 555L39
fortune ▪smiles on 555L45
fortune ▫teller 555L51
ostage to ▪fortune 687L53
soldier of ▪fortune 1372R28
ell someone's ▪fortune 1498L39
ell ▪fortunes 1498L39
forty ▪winks 555L62
▫step ▪forward 1420R4
backward in coming ▪forward
91R8
arriage ▪forward 198R17
ast-▪forward 505R42/46
forward-▫looking 555R27
om ▫that day/time ▪forward
555R20
ook ▪forward 840L39
ne step ▪forward ▫two steps
▪back 1420R9
ut one's ▫best foot ▪forward
118R67
stride ▪forward 1440R80 1441L25
orwarding ad▫dress 555R7
backwards and ▪forwards 91R24
ossil ▫fuel 555R37
ard-▪fought 647L19
▫fair means or ▪foul 494R78
ry ▪foul 331R78
all ▪foul of 498R4/6
oul ▪ball 556L4
oul ▪language 555R75
oul-▪mouthed 555R76
oul ▪play 555R79 556L5
oul ▪up 556L15/21
o▫fessional ▪foul 1128L15
ound upon 556L62
ost-and-▪found ▫office 842L40
owhere/▫not ▪anywhere to be
▪found 520R55
ried and found ▪wanting
1636R62
un▪dation ▫course 556L68
un▪dation ▫stone 556L74
vell-▪founded 1652R52
ounder ▪member 556L50
ounder on 556R15
ounding ▪father/▪mother
556L29
ounding ▪member 556L36
rinking ▫fountain 424L66
ountain ▫pen 556R34
▪water ▫fountain 424L66
▪four-▫eyes 556R48
▫four leaf ▪clover 556R50
▫four-letter ▪word 556R53
▫four-▫pack 556R58
▫four-poster (▪bed) 556R61
▫four-▪square 556R64/68
▫four-star (▪petrol) 556R72/70
▫four-wheel ▪drive 556R75
▫petit ▪four 1055R69
▫sixty-four-thousand-dollar
▪question 1344R2
▫ten-▪four 1499R45
the ▫four corners of the
▪world/▪earth 306R2
▫twenty-four-hour ▪clock 1572R45
▫two-by-▪four 1576L25
▫plus ▪fours 1085R63
▫fourth di▪mension 556R84
▫Fourth of Ju▪ly 557L8
the ▫Fourth Es▪tate 557L5
▪guinea ▫fowl 631R18
▫flying ▪fox 540R12 569R45
▪fox someone into 557L61
▫fox ▪terrier 557L42
▫decimal ▪fraction 354R64
im▫proper ▪fraction 711R65
▫proper ▪fraction 1134L73
▫compound ▪fracture 277L63
▫simple ▪fracture 1339R40
fragmen▪tation ▫bomb 558L23
▫fromage ▪frais 567R69
▪climbing ▫frame 244R47
▪cold ▫frame 246L30 256R22
▫frame of ▪mind 558L84 898R77
▫frame of ▪reference 558R49
▪freeze-▫frame 563L30
▪photo ▫frame 1059L22
▪picture ▫frame 1063R64
▪time ▫frame 1521R74
▪walking ▫frame 1634R62 1700L56
▪Zimmer ▫frame 1700L55
▫lingua ▪franca 827L69
▫Frankenstein's ▪monster 559L66
▪fraternize with 559R44/46
▪Fraud ▫Squad 559R66
▪tempers get ▫frayed 1498R39
▪freak ▫show 560L82
▪freckle-▫faced 560R31
▫carriage ▪free 198R19
▫cruelty-▪free 330L53
▫duty-▪free 433R28/25
▫duty-▪free ▫shop 433R26
(footloose and) ▫fancy-▪free 503L11
▫fat-▪free 506L57
▫feel ▪free 510L76 560R39
▫free ▪agent 560R47
▫free and ▪easy 560R72
▫free associ▪ation 560R53
▫Free ▪Church 560R58
▫free collective ▪bargaining
560R60
▫free ▪country 560R64/67
▫free ▪enterprise 560R76
▫free ▪fall 561R62
▫free-▪floating 561R70
▪free-▫form 561L5
▪free from 561R9 562L9/10/12
▫free ▪gift 561R19
▫free ▪hand 561L7
▫free ▪house 561L10
▫free ▪jazz 561L14
▫free ▪kick 561L17
▫free ▪love 561L20
▫free ▪market 561L24
▪free of 561R55 562L3/13
▫free ▪pardon 561L84
▫free ▪pass 561L30/R22
▫free ▪port 561R27
▫free ▪press 561L34
▫free-▪range 561R3
▫free ▪speech 561L38
▫free ▪spirit 561L41
▫free-▪standing 561R74
▫free ▪throw 561L44
▪free to 560R37/38/39
561L9/66/R43
▫free ▪trade 561L46
▫free ▪verse 561L52
▫free ▪will 561L53
▫free ▪world 561L58
give ▫free ▪rein 1195L52
▫home ▪free 680L28
make ▪free with 562L23
▫nuclear-▪free 966L63
of one's ▫own free ▪will 1665R54
▫post ▪free 1100L76
▫rent-▪free 1203R20/21
▫scot-▪free 1269R50
▫sugar-▪free 1457L26
▫toll-free ▪number 562R37
▪freedom ▫fighter 562L63
▫freedom of the ▪press 1118R61
▫give someone the ▪freedom of
562L60
▫deep ▪freeze 357L63 563L48
▪freeze-▫dry 563L28
▪freeze-▫frame 563L30
▫freeze ▪out 563L64/62
▫freeze the ▫balls off a ▫brass
▪monkey 563L25
▪wage ▫freeze 1632R71
▪freezer ▫bag 256R7 563L54/56
▪freezer com▫partment 563L52
▪freezer ▫pack 563L57
▫fridge ▪freezer 565L43
re▪frigerator-▫freezer 565L43
1192R52
▫hell freezes ▪over 661L49
▪freezing ▫point 563L36
▫French ▪bean 563R1
▫French ▪bread 563R3
▫French Ca▪nadian 563R6
▫French ▪doors 563R9/52
▫French ▪dressing 563R10 1624L39
▫French Foreign ▪Legion 563R15
▫French ▪fry 227L83 563R17
▫French ▪horn 563R20
▫French ▪kiss 563R24
▫French ▪leave 563R26
▫French ▪letter 563R30
▫French ▪loaf 94L17 563R32
▫French ▪manicure 563R36
▫French ▪polish 563R46/39/43
▫French ▪stick 94L17 563R48
▫French ▪toast 563R49
▫French ▪windows 563R52
a ▫breath of fresh ▪air 162R44/43
a ▫fresh ▪angle on 45L72
▫break fresh ▪ground 160R64
▫fresh-▪faced 564L60
▫freshen ▪up 564L43/R20
▪air ▫freshener 29L55
▪breath ▫freshener 162R53
▪fret about/over 564R62
▫Freudian ▪slip 565L4
▪friction ▫tape 738R9
▫Friday the thir▪teenth 1513R60
▫Girl ▪Friday 596L11
▫Good ▪Friday 612L9
▫man ▪Friday 858R70
▫fridge ▪freezer 565L43
▫bosom ▪friend 150L63
▫fair-weather ▪friend 495R19
▫false ▪friend 500L73
▫feathered ▪friend 509L14
▫feline ▪friend 511R18
▫man's best ▪friend 859L49
▫mutual ▪friend 934L14
my ▫honourable ▪friend 565L75
my ▫learned ▪friend 565L74
▪pen ▫friend 1044L39
▫plumber's ▪friend 1084L83
1085L45
▫friendly ▪fire 565R34
▪friendly so▫ciety 565R37
▫ozone-▪friendly 1013R69
▫user-▪friendly 565R48 1602L55/58
▫friends in high ▪places 565L82
▫Friends of the ▪Earth 565R1
▫frig a▪bout/a▪round 565R71
▪stage ▫fright 1406R23
▫take ▪fright 566L1
▫put the ▪frighteners on 566L35
▪Frigid ▫Zones 566L72
▪fringe ▫benefit 566R11
the ▫lunatic ▪fringe 847R61
▫fritter a▪way 566R72
▫to-ing and ▪fro-ing 1530R13/19
▪frock ▫coat 567L20
a ▪frog in one's ▫throat 567L29
▫frogmarch a▪way/▪off 567L47/48
▫fromage ▪frais 567R69
▫back to ▪front 89L65/67
▫cold ▪front 256R27
▫cut in ▪front of 339R58
▫front ▪door 568L36
▪front for 568R8/22
▫front ▪loader 568L39
▪front ▫man/▫woman 568L41/R14
▫front-of-▪house 568L29
▪front-▫page 568L44 1018L29
▫front ▪room 568L47
▫front-▪runner 568L50
▫front-wheel ▪drive 568L55
▪front with 568L63
hardly/barely put ▫one foot in
front of the ▪other 545R46
in the ▫front ▪line 568R46
▫National ▪Front 939L3
▫put on a false ▪front 500L56
▪shop ▫front 567R84 1321L30
the ▫home ▪front 679R76
▫up ▪front 568L28
▫frontal lo▪botomy 568L69
▪frontal ▫system 568R30
▫full-frontal ▪picture 572R45/44
▫Y-▪fronts 1694L67
▫frost ▪over 569L21
▫frost ▪up 569L21
▪frost with 569L22
▪ground ▫frost 626L56
▪hoar ▫frost 674L56
▫Jack ▪Frost 757R68
▫froth at the ▪mouth 569L61/64
▫froth ▪up 569L60
▪frou-▫frou 569L74
▪frown at/upon 569L81/82
▫bitter ▪fruit 130R65
▪citrus ▫fruit 234L59
▫crystallized ▪fruit 332L55
▪first ▫fruit 525R72
for▫bidden ▪fruit 547R83
▪fruit ▫bat 569R45
▪fruit ▫fly 569R49
▪fruit ma▫chine 569R51 1355L47
▫fruit of the ▪earth 569R47
▫fruit ▪salad 569R52
▫soft ▪fruit 1371R16
▪deep-▫fry 357L64
▪flash-▫fry 530R62
▫French ▪fry 227L83 563R17
▪fry-up 570R49
have ▫bigger/▫other fish to ▪fry
526L71
▪pan-▫fry 1021L32
▪shallow-▫fry 1308R19
▪small ▫fry 1358L23
▪stir-▫fry 1426R65/72
▪frying ▫pan 570R47
▫FTSE ▪100 (Index) 570R69
▫kung ▪fu 788R70
▫fuck a▪bout/a▪round 571L15
▫fuck ▪off 571L18/20
▫fuck ▪up 571L23/30
▪fuddy-▫duddy 571L43
add ▪fuel to the ▫fire/▫flames
571L75
▪fossil ▫fuel 555R37
▪fuel-in▫jected 571L76
▪fuel ▫rod 571L78
▫solid ▪fuel 1373L59
▪wish-ful▫fillment 1671R42
at ▫full ▪pelt 1044L24
at ▫full ▪strength 1438L2
at ▫full ▪stretch 1438R66
▫come to a full ▪stop 572R67
▫full-▪blooded 572L80/81
▫full-▪blown 572L83
▫full ▪board 572L84
▫full-▪bodied 573L61
▫full-▪fashioned 573L10
▫full-▪fledged 573L12/13
▫full-frontal ▪picture 572R45/44
▫full-▪grown 572R40/39
▫full ▪house 572L40/R41
▫full ▪length 572R47/48/50/51
▫full ▪marks 573L19/20 866L74
▫full ▪moon 572R53 916R54
full of ▪beans 572L21
▫full of one's own im▪portance
572L35
full of the ▫joys of ▪spring 572L39
▫full-▪page 572R55
▫full-▪scale 572R56/60 573L36
▫full-▪service 572R61
▫full steam a▪head 573L29
▫full ▪stop 572R62/65
▫full ▪time 572R68/74
▫full to ▪bursting 572L22/47
▫full to the ▪brim 572L26/46
▫full to to the ▪gunwales 633L6
▫full ▪well 572R79
give/allow something ▫full ▪play
1079L48/49
have one's ▪hands ▫full 640L78
in ▫full ▪cry 332L11/14 573L34
in ▫full ▪flow 572L71
in ▫full ▪sail 572L73/74
in ▫full ▪swing 572L76
in ▫full ▪view of 572L79
on a ▫full ▪stomach 572L48
1429L64
▫things have/the ▫wheel has come
full ▪circle 572L68
in the ▫fullness of ▪time 573L1
▪fulminate about 573L79
▫fumble a▪round/a▪bout 573R14
▪fumble for 573R11/21
▪fumble with 573R13
▪fume at 573R28
a ▫barrel of ▪fun 101L40
▫figure of ▪fun 517R41
for ▪fun/for the ▪fun of it/for the
▪fun of the ▫thing 573R58
▫fun and ▪games 573R74/76
▪fun ▫house 573R61
▪fun ▫run 573R64
make ▪fun of 573R59
▫poke ▪fun at 1090R59
▫sense of ▪fun 1293L29
▫sound ▪fun 1378R81
▪function as 573R83 574L5
▪function ▫key 574L30
▫functional il▪literacy 574L39
▫functional il▪literate 574L39
be▪nevolent ▫fund 117L78
▪fund-▫raiser 574L79/76
Inter▫national ▪Monetary ▫Fund
744L23
▪mutual ▫fund 934L17 1590L53
▪pension ▫fund 574L70 1046L28
▪sinking ▫fund 1342L26
▪slush ▫fund 1356R71
the con▫solidated ▪fund 291R12
▪trust ▫fund 574L75 1565L82
▫joint-▪funded 768L2
▪funeral di▫rector 574R68
▪funeral ▫home 574R70
▪funeral ▫parlour 574R70
in a ▫blue ▪funk 139R65
▪funnel-▫web 575L34
▫funnily e▪nough 575R1
▪funny ▫bone 575L57
▪funny ▫business 575R7/8
▪funny ▫farm 575R23
funny ha-▪ha 575L60
▫rib-ticklingly ▪funny 1220R30
▫screamingly ▪funny 1272L56
make the ▫fur ▪fly 575R42
set the ▪fur ▫flying 575R43
the ▫fur begins/starts to ▪fly
575R40
▫fast and ▪furious 505L68
▪blast ▫furnace 134L1
▪furnish with 576L25/39/41
▫soft ▪furnishings 1371R19
▫part of the ▪furniture 1028L84
repro▫duction ▫furniture 1206L78
▪street ▫furniture 1437L45
▫can't see ▫further than the ▫end
of one's ▪nose 1283L59
▫further edu▪cation 576R47
▫further from one's
▪mind/▪thoughts 576R21
on ▫further ac▪quaintance 12L33
▫fly into a ▪fury 540R35
▪fuse ▫box 577L27
▫short ▪fuse 1321R84
▪fuss at 577R18
▪fuss over 577R30
▪fuss with 577R31
▫kick up a ▪fuss 779L9
make a ▪fuss of 577R12
for ▫future ▪reference 578R1
fore▫seeable ▪future 550L12
▫future ▪perfect 578R6
▫not too distant ▪future 398R83
578L27
▫fuzzy ▪logic 578R54
▫gab ▪on 578R78
the ▫gift of the ▪gab 594R59/60
▫gabble a▪way 579L5/7
▫gad a▪bout/a▪round 579L20
▫blow the ▪gaff 138R72
▪gag on 579L75
▪gag ▫order 579L62
▪gag ▫rule 579L62
go ▪ga▫ga 579R4
▫capital ▪gain 191R45
▪gain from 579R24/26
▫gain ▪ground 579R46
▪gain on 579R60
▫gain one's ▪spurs 1401L28
▫gales of ▪laughter 580L48
▪gall ▫bladder 580L81
▫play to the ▪gallery 1078R62
▪press ▫gallery 1118R77
▫rogues' ▪gallery 1230R45
▪shooting ▫gallery 1320L41/R70
▫gallivant a▪round 580R26
▫gallows ▪humour 580R56
▫gamble a▪way 581L33
▪gamble on 581L20/24
a ▪mug's ▫game 928L71
a ▫whole new/▫com▫pletely
different ▪ball ▫game 95R36
▪ball ▫game 95R35
▫beat someone at their ▫own ▪game
109L84
▫big ▪game 124R43
▪board ▫game 141L51
com▪puter ▫game 279L80
▫easy ▪game 438R55
▫fair ▪game 495L21
▪game ▫plan 581L78
give the ▪game away 581L67
▪numbers ▫game 967L45
▪parlour ▫game 1027R12
▫play the ▪game 1078L58
▪team ▫game 1494R19
the ▪game is ▫up 581L69
the ▫game is worth the ▪candle
581L74
the ▫name of the ▪game 937L40
▫two can play at ▪that ▫game
1576L9
▪video ▫game 1622L62
▪waiting ▫game 1633R49
▪war ▫game 1637L40
▫poacher turned ▪gamekeeper
1087R31
▫fun and ▪games 573R74/76
▫Highland ▪Games 669L84
O▫lympic ▪Games 981L10
▫play ▪games 1078L59
▪gaming ▫table 581R32
▫gamma ▪globulin 581R37
▫gamma radi▪ation 581R41
have/▫take a ▪gander 581R59
▪gang-▫bang 581R71
▫gang ▪up 581R77/74
credi▪bility ▫gap 322L17
▪culture ▫gap 334R42
▪gap-▫toothed 582L72
gener▪ation ▫gap 587R73
▪gape at 582L76
▪garage ▫sale 193R20 582R38
▪parking ▫garage 193R25

▪garbage ▫bag 433L51 582R49
▪garbage col▫lector 582R52
▪garbage ▫truck 433L55 582R52
▫avant-▪garde 83L78
▪beer ▫garden 113L9
bo▫tanic(al) ▪garden 150R61
▫common-or-▪garden 270R47
▪garden a▫partment 582R74
▪garden ▫centre 582R77
▫garden ▪city 582R79
▫garden ▪flat 582R83
▫Garden of ▪Eden 441L44 582R82
▪garden ▫party 582R84
▫kitchen ▪garden 782L37
▫lead someone up/down the garden ▪path 804L35
▫market ▪garden 866R82/84 867L2
▪rock ▫garden 1229R58 1230L51
▪roof ▫garden 1233L19
▪tea ▫garden 1494L20
▫landscape ▪gardener 795L37/40
zoo▫logical ▪gardens 1701L24/39
▫garlic ▪bread 583L84
▪garlic ▫press 583R40
▪garment ▫bag 583R48 1458L11
▪Calor ▫gas 186R28
C▪S ▫gas 332R9
▪gas ▫chamber 584L14
▪gas ▫fire 584L10
▪gas ▫guzzler 584L34
▪gas ▫heater 584L10
▪gas ▫mark 584L11
▪gas ▫mask 584L17
▪gas ▫station 582R34 584L35 1056L45
▫gas ▪up 584L37
▫greenhouse ▪gas 623L14
▪laughing ▫gas 800L33
▪marsh ▫gas 868R22
▪mustard ▫gas 933L29
▫natural ▪gas 943L42
▪nerve ▫gas 949L32
▫poison ▪gas 1090R11
▪tear ▫gas 1494R55
▫blow a ▪gasket 139L40
▫last-▪gasp 797R41
▫factory ▪gate 493L7
▪gate ▫money 584R24
between ▫you me and the ▪gatepost 111R38 121R7
the ▫pearly ▪gates 1040R56
▫gather a▪bout/a▪round 584R62
▫gather ▪dust 584R64
▫gather ▪in 584R55
▫gather to▫gether 584R57
▫gather ▪up 584R53
▫gather one's ▪wits 1674R52
▫gathering of the ▪clans 236R2
▪narrow-▫gauge 938L61
▪rain ▫gauge 1169R74
▪wind ▫gauge 1667L7
▫pick up the ▪gauntlet 585L58
▫throw down the ▪gauntlet 585L55
▪gawk at 585L83/84
▪gay -▫basher 102L56/62
▫gay liber▪ation 585R10
▪crystal-▫gaze 332R3
▫gaze at one's ▪navel 944L27
▫first ▪gear 525R62
▪gear ▫lever/▫stick 586L14
▪gear to 586L21/26
▪gear toward/towards 586L22
▫gear ▪up 586L24
get one's ▪arse in ▫gear 65L27
▫high ▪gear 667R59
▪landing ▫gear 794R11
step/move ▪up a ▫gear 586L11
▪gee-▫gee 586L58
▫gee ▪up 586L54
▫gee-▪whiz 586L65
▪Geiger ▫counter 586L73
▪hair ▫gel 636L57
▪shower ▫gel 1328R84
▫gen ▪up 586R36/32
▪gender-▫bender 586R48
▪gene amplifi▫cation 586R58
▪gene ▫pool 586R60
▪gene ▫therapy 586R63
as a ▫general ▪rule 587L17
At▫torney ▪General 78R16/17
▫brigadier-▪general 164R64/68
di▫rector ▪general 387L36
▫general anaes▪thetic 43L75 587L25
▫General As▪sembly 587L28
▫general de▫livery 587L30 1101R11/18
▫general e▫lection 587L31
▫general ▪hospital 587L34
▫general ▪knowledge 587L35
▫general ▪practice 587L40
▫general ▪public 587L44 1142L71
▫general ▪staff 587L53
▫general ▪store 587L51
▫general ▪strike 587L55
▫governor-▪general 614R63
▫major-▪general 854R30
▫Secretary-▪General 1280R75
▫Surgeon ▪General 1468L78
the ▫general ▪interest 587L24
the ▫general ▪run of 1242L55
▪beat gener▫ation 109R48
gener▪ation ▫gap 587R73
ge▫neric ▪brand/▪label 1013L11
ge▫netic ▪code 588L45
ge▫netic engin▪eering 588L47
ge▫netic ▪fingerprinting 588L50
Ge▫neva Con▪vention 588L59
▫genito-▪urinary 588R6
▫human ▪genome ▫project 692L78
in gen▫teel ▪poverty 588R62
▫gentleman's a▪greement 589L29
▫take it ▪gently 589L10
the ▫genuine ▪article 589L71
▫physical ge▪ography 589R17 1060R84
geo▫metric(al) pro▪gression 589R50
▪germ ▫cell 590L24
▫germ of an i▪dea 590L29
▫germ ▪warfare 590L31
▪wheat ▫germ 1655R81
▫German ▪measles 590L48
▫German ▪shepherd 36R82 590L53
ge▫stalt psy▪chology 590R7
ge▫stalt psycho▪therapy 590R8
▫can't get one's ▪head a▫round 653R69
▫can't get ▪over 593R15
cross ▪that bridge when you ▪get to it 327R6
▫get a ▪buzz from 181L17
▫get a ▪grip on 624R61
get a ▪jump on 773L8
get a ▪load of 833L74
get a ▪move on 924R54
get a ▪rise ▫out of 1226R51
get a ▫word in ▪edgeways 1678L79
▫get a▫cross 591L70
get one's ▪act to▫gether 13L48
get a▪long 591R25 593L65/69
get an ▪eyeful 488R67
get one's ▪arse in ▫gear 65L27
▪get ▫at 592R53/80 593L1/5
get a▪way 591R26/28/29
get a▪way with 593L8
get away with ▪murder 593L13
▫get ▪back 88R79 162R31 590R82 592L75
get ▪back at 593L17
▫get someone's ▪back up 89R72
▫get/be ▪shot of 1324R77
▫get ▪better 120R22/24
get ▫blood out of a ▪stone 137L54
▫get ▪brownie ▫points 169L80
▫get ▪by 593L21
▫get one's ▪claws into 239L63
▫get ▪cold 256L83
▫get ▫cold ▪feet 256L80
▫get ▪cracking 318R50
▫get ▪down 591L73/76/77/R32
get ▪down to 593L28
get down to ▫brass ▪tacks 158L68
get down to ▪business 178R47
▫get one's ▪eye in 488L63
▫get one's ▪finger out 521R83
get one's ▪fingers ▫burnt 177R6
▫get (on) someone's ▪goat 608R2
▫get ▪going/▪moving 591L52
▫get someone's ▪hackles up 635L43
▫get one's ▪hands on 640L76
get one's ▪head ▫down 653L48/51
▫get ▪hitched 673R35
▫get ▪hold 675R54/56
▫get one's ▪hooks on/into 684L29
▫get ▪in 590R82/83 591L2/5/36/81/R34 592L78/79 593L33/38 714L7/14
▫get ▪in someone's ▪hair 636L42
get ▪in on the ▫act 13L44
▪get into 591L42/R35 1310R83
▫get into deep ▪water 357L53
get into ▫hot ▪water 687R21
get ▫into one's ▪stride 1441L6
▫get into the ▪spirit of 1393L30
get ▫into the ▪swing of it/things 1477L84
get into the ▫wrong ▪hands 1693L61
▫get someone into ▪trouble 1561R16
▫get it in the ▪neck 945R40
▫get it to▫gether 1531R75 1532L25
get one's ▫just de▪serts 774R34
get one's ▪knickers in a ▫twist 783L68
▫get one's ▪knife into/in 783R43
▫get ▪knotted 786L36
get one's ▪leg ▫over 809L9
▫get ▪lost 842L33
▫get ▪lucky 846L53
get one's ▪mind ▫round 898R47
get one's ▪money's worth 913R15
▫get ▪needles 947L39
get ▪off 591L6/84/R35/37/40/42 641R58/59 782L24
▫get off one's ▪arse 65L26
▫get off someone's ▪back 89R70
▫get off one's ▪backside 91L15
get something ▫off one's ▪chest 224R38
get ▪on 593L1/25/65/69/73/76 1217R42
▫get on one's ▪hands 640L81
▫get on one's ▪soapbox 1369R10
▫get on the ▪bandwagon 97L21
▫get on someone's ▪tits 1527L58
▫get ▪out 591R44/48
get out of ▫bed (on) the ▫wrong ▪side 111L43
get ▫out of my ▪face 490R33
get ▫out of one's ▪sight 1335R3
get ▫out of the/my ▪road 1227R82
get something ▫out of one's ▪system 1482R24
get ▪over 593R6 1006L64
▫get something ▪over with 1006L50
▫get one's ▪own ▫back 1012R79
▫get ▪real 591L30 1179R35
▫get-rich-▪quick 1221L8
get ▪rid of 1221R54/57/60
▫get one's ▪rocks ▫off 1229R71
▫get ▪round 591R49 593R21 1236R39
get ▪round to 593R25
get one's ▪skates ▫on 1344R75
▫get some/a few ▪z's 1699L16
▪get ▫somewhere 1375L73
▫get ▪started 1413R20
▫get ▪stuck into 1447L38
▫get ▪stuffed 1448L40
get one's ▪teeth into 1535R67
get the ▪ball ▫rolling 95R24
get the ▪better of 121L18/19
get the ▫bit between one's ▪teeth 130L27
▫get the ▪boot 148L78
get the ▪feel of 511L33
get the ▪hang of 644L56
▫get the ▫hell ▪out of 661L80
▫get the ▪measure of 879R32
▫get the ▪message 890L53
▫get the ▪message across 890L55
▫get the ▪picture 591R75 1064L18
▫get the short ▪straw 1321R64
get the/this ▪show on the ▫road 1328L62
▫get the ▪wind up 1666R77
get (hold of) the ▫wrong end of the ▪stick 1692R73
get ▪through 591R5 592R56/59 593R26 1516L83/R19/27/53
get to ▪grips with 624R60
get to ▪know 787R1
get to the ▪bottom of 152L58
▫get to ▪work 1679R1
▪get-to▫gether 591L45 593R64 1531R66
get one's ▪tongue round/around 1534R50
get ▫under someone's ▪skin 1346R30
▫get ▪up 591R50/51/53/54 593R41/44/46/49/56 1598L27
▫get-up-and-▪go 593R69
get ▫up someone's ▪nose 961R66
get up on the ▫wrong side of the ▪bed 111L43
▫get up ▪steam 1418L46
▫get ▪up to 591L48
▫get ▪weaving 1648R33
get ▪wind of 1666R74
get one's ▪wires ▫crossed 1670R54
▫get ▪with 591R10 593L25/52/68/71/74 1672R43
▫get someone ▪wrong 591R67/69 1693L14
have/get one's ▪shit to▫gether 1317R61
nice ▫work if you can ▪get it 954L50
▫nothing to get ex▫cited about 477L17
on your ▫marks/▫mark get ▫set ▪go! 866L40
play ▫hard to ▪get 1078R19
▪tempers get ▫frayed/▫short 1498R39
de▫serve what▫ever/▫everything one ▪gets 372L13
give as ▫good as one ▪gets 596R25 611L82
▫word gets a▪bout/a▪round/▪round 1679L16
▪go-▫getter 606L65/69
▪vote-▫getter 1631L49
not ▫getting ▪anywhere 52R60
▪ghetto ▫blaster 594L15
not a/the ▪ghost of a ▫chance 594L38
▪ghost ▫ship 594L41
▪ghost ▫story 594L42
▪ghost ▫town 594L43
▪ghost ▫train 594L46
▪ghost-▫writer 594L62
▫give up the ▪ghost 594L40
▫Holy ▪Ghost 679R16
▫lay the ▫ghost of something to ▪rest 802L71
▫giant ▪panda 594R14 1021R32
▫red ▪giant 1189L10
▫free ▪gift 561R19
▪gift ▫box 594R49
▪gift cer▫tificate 1532R60
▫gift from the ▪gods 594R47
▪gift ▫shop 594R49
▪gift ▫token 594R51
▪gift-▫wrapped 594R54
▫God's ▪gift 609L9
the ▫gift of the ▪gab 594R59/60
▫gild the ▪lily 595L32
▫green/▫pale about the ▪gills 595L43
▫gilt-edged se▪curities 595L53
take the ▫gilt off the ▪gingerbread 595L55
▫gimlet ▪eyes 595L67
▫gimme ▪five 528L28
▪cotton ▫gin 310R40
▪gin ▫palace 595R7
▫gin ▪rummy 595R9
▫sloe ▪gin 1354R19
▫dry ▪ginger 595R19
▫ginger ▪ale 595R18
▫ginger ▪beer 595R18
▪ginger ▫group 595R24
▪ginger ▫nut/▫biscuit/▫snap 595R22
▫ginger ▪up 595R30
▫ginger ▪wine 595R21
▪gingerbread ▫man 595R36
take the ▫gilt off the ▪gingerbread 595L55
▫gippy ▪tummy 595R58
▪gird oneself for 595R68
▫gird (up) one's ▪loins 595R71
a big/great ▫girl's ▪blouse 596L10
▪ball ▫girl 95R32
▫boy-meets-▪girl 155R79
▪call ▫girl 184R17
▪cover ▫girl 316L48
▪day ▫girl 349R34
▫Girl ▪Friday 596L11
▫Girl ▪Guide 596L13 631L3
▫Girl ▪Scout 596L14 1270L49
▪go-go ▫girl 606L75
▪golden ▫girl 610L40
▪new ▫girl 952L45
▫old ▪girl 979R64/69 980L47
▪stable ▫girl 1405R11
▪there's a good ▫girl 1509R80
▪working ▫girl 1681R49
▪trophy ▫girlfriend 1560R22
▫don't/▫couldn't give a ▪monkey's 914R79
▫give someone a ▪bell 115R36
give someone a ▫box on the ▪ears 155L79
▫give someone a ▪break 161L35
give someone a ▫bunch of ▪fives 175R39
▫give someone a ▪buzz 181L18
▫give a ▪damn 344R21
▫give something a ▪go 596R83
give someone a ▫hard ▪time 1523R77
give someone a helping ▪hand 662L38
give someone a ▫leg ▪up 809L10
▫give something a ▪miss 906L27
▫give someone a ▪rocket 1230L66
give someone a ▫rough ▪time/▪ride 1236L26
give someone a ▪run for their ▫money 1241L40
▫give a ▪sod 1371L40
▫give a ▪talk 1488R44
▫give a ▫tinker's (▪cuss/▪damn) 1525R2
▫give someone a ▪tinkle 1525R15
give someone a ▫torrid ▪time 1538R81
▫give a ▪toss 1539R36
▫give something a ▪whirl 1659R9
▫give something a wide ▪berth 1663R18
▫give oneself ▫airs (and ▪graces) 29R36
▫give-and-▪take 596R58/61
▫give one something ▪any day/every ▪time 596R35
give as ▫good as one ▪gets 596R25 611L82
▪give-away 596R51/54/R28 597L27/34
▫give ▪back 596R6/7
▫give ▪birth 128R60
▫give ▪chase 219R29
▫give someone their ▪due 431L18 596R30
▫give someone enough ▫rope to ▪hang themselves 459R38
▫give one's ▪eyeteeth 489R77
▫give someone ▪five 528L26
▫give ▪anything for 596L78/79
give ▫free ▪rein 1195L52
give something ▫full ▪play 1079L48/49
▫give someone (a lot of) ▪grief 623R57
▫give someone their ▪head 653L53/54
▫give someone ▪hell 661L40
▫give ▪in 596R8 597L37
▫give it a ▪rest 1212R2
▫give one's ▪life 596R37 818R58
▫give ▪lip service to 828L76
▫give of one's ▪best 596R18
▫give of one's ▪money/▪time/▪bes[t] 596R39
▫give ▪off 596R81
▪give onto 597L42
▫give or ▪take 596R48
▫give ▪out 597L45
▫give ▪over 597L51
▫give ▪over/▪up 597L56
▫give someone ▪pause 1037R33
give one's ▫right ▪hand/▪arm 1223R69
▫give ▪rise 1226R68
give one's ▫seal of ap▪proval 1276L84
give someone ▫something to ▪talk about 1488R28
▫give me ▪strength 1437R35
give someone the ▫benefit of the ▪doubt 117L65
▫give someone the ▪brush-off 170L49
▫give someone the ▪creeps 322R68
give the ▫devil his ▪due 596R30
▫give someone the ▪elbow 445R57
▫give someone the ▪finger 521R66
▫give someone the ▪freedom of 562L60
give the ▪game away 581L67
▫give the glad ▪hand 597R43
give the ▫green ▪light 622L67
give someone the (▫cold) ▫heave ▪h[o] 658R26
▫give someone the ▪jitters 765L65
▫give the ▪lie 818L70
give someone the ▪push 1151R19/15/19
▫give someone the ▫rough side of one's ▪tongue 1236L25
▫give someone the ▪runaround 1243L75
▫give someone the ▪shits 1318L28
▫give someone the ▪shivers 1318L59
▫give someone the ▪slip 1354L16
▫give someone the ▪works 1683R3
▫give something to someone on a ▪plate 1076R80
▫give someone to under▪stand 597L2
give someone ▫two ▪fingers 1576L18
▫give ▪up 596R44 597L61
give something ▫up as a bad ▪job 92L35
▫give ▪up on 597L67/69
▫give up the ▪ghost 594L40
▫give ▪vent 1613L82
▫give ▪voice 1629L66/R5
▫give ▪way 1645R10/51/47
▫give ▪way to 1645R54
not ▫give a ▪fig 516R64
not ▫give a ▪hoot/two ▪hoots 684R16
not ▫give a ▫red ▪cent for 1188R78
not ▫give a ▪shit 1317R59
not ▫give an ▪inch 716L44
not ▫give someone the ▫time of ▪day 1522R16
▫not give ▪tuppence 1568L53
would ▫give ▪anything/a ▪lot/the ▪world/one's ▪eyeteeth/one's right ▪arm for 596R21
▫wouldn't give ▪tuppence for 1568L58
at ▫any given ▪time 1522R11
given ▫half a ▪chance 214R28 637L58
▪given ▫name 526L3 597R8
be ▫given the ▪boot 148L78
▫given the ▪chance/▪choice 596L74
▪God-▫given 609L12/14
▪life-▫giving 819L37
▪glacial ▫period 597R28
▫give the ▪glad ▪hand 597R43
▪glad-▫handing 597R43
▪glad ▫rags 597R47
▫glad ▪tidings 597R49
the ▫glad ▪eye 597R41
not suffer ▫fools ▪gladly 1456L79
▫glam ▪up 597R74
▫cast a ▪glance over 202L35
▪glance off 598L27
▪glance on 598L25
▫shoot a ▪glance 1319R49
▫throw a ▪glance 1517L8
▫ductless ▪gland 430R72 455R68
▫endocrine ▫gland 455R68
▪lymph ▫gland 849R28
se▫baceous ▪gland 1278R42
▪mammary ▫glands 858R6
sa▪livary ▫glands 1251L52
▪sweat ▫glands 1474R70
▫glandular ▪fever 598L38

▫cut ▪glass 339L26 598R13
▪glass-▫blower 598R10
▫glass ▪ceiling 598R13
▪glass-▫cutter 598R11
▫glass ▪fibre/▪fiber 515L45 598R17
▫glass ▪in 598R22
▫glass ▪over 598R25
▪looking ▫glass 598R1 839L66
▪magnifying ▫glass 853L16
▫plate ▪glass 1077L22
▪safety ▫glass 1248R59/56
▫smoked ▪glass 1361R24
▫stained ▪glass 1407R10
▫dark ▪glasses 346L71 1460R38
▪field ▫glasses 516L15
▫half-moon ▪glasses 637R81
▪opera ▫glasses 989L28
▫glaze ▪over 598R68
▫triple ▪glazing 1558R61
▪gleam with/in 598R84
▪glean *something* from 599L10
▫glide ac▪ross/▪over 599L37
▪glide into 599L35/36
▪glide through 599L38/47
▪hang-▫glider 643R78/82
▪glimmer with 599L57
▪glint with 599R2
▪glisten with 599R10
▪glitter with 599R29/30
▪Day-▫Glo 349R66
▪gloat at 599R78
▪gloat over/about 599R76
▫global ▪search 600L20
▫global ▪warming 600L28
the ▫global ▪village 600L23
▫distant/▫far corner of the ▪globe 306R84
▫globe ▪artichoke 600L66
▪light ▫globe 820R30
▫gamma ▪globulin 581R37
▫merchant of ▪gloom 888L75
in ▫glorious ▪technicolour 1495R21
▪glory ▫box 152L68 601L8
▪glory ▫days 600R70
▪glory in 600R73
▫knickerbocker ▪glory 783L57
▫gloss ▪over 601L61
▪lip ▫gloss 601L29 828R37
▫glossy maga▪zine 601L43
▫glottal ▪stop 601L77
▪boxing ▫glove 155L72
▪glove ▫box 601R2/6
▪glove com▫partment 601R6
▪glove ▫puppet 601R8
▫hand and ▪glove 640L82
▫hand in ▪glove 640L82
▪oven ▫gloves 1005L44
▫treat/▫deal with *someone* with kid ▪gloves 779L79
▪glow-▫worm 601R31
▪glue ▫ear 601R70
▪glue-▫sniffer 601R75/80 1366L7
▫monosodium ▪glutamate 915R48
▫glutton for ▪punishment 602L43
▫gnash *one's* ▪teeth 602L78/80
▫gnashing of ▪teeth 602L82
▪gnaw at 602R12/20
▫gnomes of ▪Zurich 602R37
▫ leave ▪go of 807R33
a ▫long way to ▪go 838L9
▫careful how you ▪go 196R29
▫come and ▪go 265L46
easy ▫come easy ▪go 438R80
▫fair ▪go 495L23
from the ▫word ▪go 1679L55
▫get-up-and-▪go 593R69
▫give *something* a ▪go 596R83
go a ▪bomb 145L83
go a ▪bundle (on) 175R62
go a ▫long ▪way 838L16
go a ▫long way to▪wards 838L14
go a▪bout 606R4 607L79
go ▪after 603R24/25
▫go a▪gainst 24R15 605R21 606R11
go a▫gainst the ▪flow 538L5
▫go against/with the ▪tide 1519L24/25
go a▪head 606R18/28/34
go ▫all the ▪way 1646L2
go a▪long 603R26/29
▫go a▪long with 606R40
▫go ▪ape-shit 53L42
▫go a▪round/▪round/a▪bout 603R30/32/34/36/39 605R67 607R40
go (▫down in the ▪record books) as 606R56
go as ▫red as a ▪beetroot 113L37/38
▪go at *something* 606L44/54/58 607L80
▫go at it ▫hammer and ▪tongs 639R21
go a▪way 604L53/R3
go ▪back 602R79 603R41
go back a ▫long ▪way 838L17
go ▪back on 606R44
go back to ▪sleep 1351L37
go ▪beetroot (▫red) 113L37
go ▪begging 113R31
go ▫belly ▪up 116L17
▪go-be▫tween 604L21
go ▪bust 179L49
go ▪by 603L12/R43/44/45/47/49 604L6 606L13/25/R50
▫go by the ▪board 141L59
go by the ▪name of 937L5
▫go ▪bye-bye 181R1
▫go ▪deep 357L61
go ▪down 415R32 603L13/14/R49/51/53/55/56/58/60/63 604L60/R59/61/63 606R54/58/64/68
go ▫down/▫fall like ▪ninepins 956L17
▫go ▪down in the ▫world 416L28
go down like a ▫lead bal▪loon 804R41
go ▪down on 603R66 606R71
go down the ▪tubes 1566R11
go down the ▫wrong ▪way 1692R75
▫go ▪down with 416L24 603R64
go ▪Dutch 433L74
go ▪easy 439L1
go ▪easy on/with 438R83
go ▫fly a ▪kite 541L8
▪go for 603L17 605R38/40/45 606L21/R73/81 607L3/7
▫go for a ▪burton 178L16/15
go for ▪broke 168L34
go for ▪gold 609R77
go (▪over) from 603L53/55 604L60
go from ▫bad to ▪worse 92L38
go from ▫one extreme to the ▪other 487R71
go from ▫strength to ▪strength 1437R39
go ▪ga▫ga 579R4
▪go-▫getter 606L65/69
▪go-▫go 606L70
▪go-go ▫dancer 606L74
▪go-go ▫girl 606L75
▫go ▪gold 609R59
go ▪great ▫guns 621R33
go ▪halves 637L61
go ▪hang 644L47
go ▪in 603L20/21/23/25 604R64 605R22 606R56
go ▫in for the ▪kill 780L1
go ▫in ▪one ear and ▫out the ▪other 436L55
go in ▫terror of *one's* ▪life 1505L10
▪go into 231R28 603L26/27/28/30/32 604R66/68/69/71/72 605R14/15 607L17
go into a ▪huddle 691R18
go into ▪detail 375L33
go into ▪rhapsodies 1219R26
▫go into *one's* ▪shell 1314R43
▫go it a▪lone 36L55 605L61
go (and) ▫jump in the ▪lake 772R26
▪go-▫kart 609R39/44
▪go (something) ▫like 605R62
go like a ▪bomb 145L82/83
go like ▫hot ▪cakes 687R24
go ▪mad 605L27
go ▪native 939R43
go ▪off 603L34 604R74/76/78/80/82/84 605L2/4 607L32/41
go ▫off at/on a ▪tangent 1489R70/69/68
go off/away with *one's* ▫tail between *one's* ▪legs 1485R29
go ▫off *one's* ▪chump 231L66
go ▫off half-▪cocked 637R36/37
go off on a ▫different ▪tack 1484L83
go off the ▪deep ▫end 357L55
go ▫off the ▪rails 1169L42
go ▪on 603L35/37/R69 605L10/12 606L26/29 607L53/63/82/R4 608L2
▫go on ▪line 825R83
▫go on ▪record 1187L41
go on the ▪stage 1406R13
go ▫one ▪better 120R26
go ▪out 603L42/43 604L65/67/73/75/78/81/82 605L14/16/17/19
go ▫out like a ▪light 820R17
go ▪out of 604L80
go ▫out of *one's*/the ▪way 1645R13
go ▫out of *one's* ▪mind 898R49
go ▫out with the ▪ark 1000R37
go ▪over 603L53/54/R71 606R58 607R7/25/30/32
go ▫over *something* in *one's* ▪mind 898R51
go ▫over with a ▪bang 97L53
go ▪overboard 1006R54
go *one's* ▫own ▪way 1645R19
go ▪phut 1060L66
▪go ▫places 1072R59
▫go ▪round 607R40 1236R41
go ▫round in ▪circles/a ▪circle 232R20
go *one's* ▫separate ▪way 1294R47
▫go ▪shares 1311L43
▫go ▪slow 605L63/68
▫go ▪spare 1383R22
▫go ▪stag 1406L32
▫go ▪steady 1417R44
go the ▪distance 398R54
go the ▪rounds 1237L10
go the ▫same ▪way 1252R40
go the ▫whole ▪hog 1662L19
go ▪through 603R72/73 604R36 607R43/47/51/56
go through a ▫bad/▫difficult/▫rough/▫sticky ▪patch 1034R56
go through ▫fire and ▪water 523L32
go through the ▪floor 536R23
go through the ▪motions 920R75
go through the ▪roof 1233L16/14
go to ▪bed with 111L41
go to ▪blazes 134L70
go to ▪bye-byes 181R3
go to ▪earth 604L15
go to ▫great/▫any ▪lengths 811L23
go to ▫great ▪pains 1018R43
go to ▪ground 604L14 626L40
go to *someone's* ▪head 653R75/78
go to ▪hell 661L18/44
go to ▪hell and ▫back 661L29
go to ▪law 801L35
▫go to ▪pieces 1064R25/30
go to ▪pot 1102R65
go to ▪press 1119L9
▫go to ▪prove/▪show 606L33
▫go to ▪sea 1275R82
go to ▪sleep 1351L32
go to the ▪bathroom 104R14
go to the ▪country 313R22
go to the ▪devil 378L45
▫go to the ▪dogs 408R60
go to the ▪polls 1092R34
go to the ▪toilet 1532L72
go to the ▪wall 1635L44
▫go to ▪town 1543R47
go to ▪waste 1640L67
go to ▪work 1679R1
▫go to▪gether 603R36 605R29/30/79 607R71 1531R79
go ▪under 603R80/81/83 604L1 606L14/15
▫go under the ▪hammer 639R26
go ▫un▪heard 1589L22
go ▫up in ▪flames 529R80
go ▫up in ▪smoke 1361L58
go ▪up in the ▫world 1685L16
go ▪west 1654L6
▪go with 603L82/R1/38 604L84 605L53/R8/31/32/80/81 606R21/62 607L66/68/R33/79/83
go with a ▪bang 97L52
go with a ▪swing 1477L82
go with the ▪crowd/the ▪flow/the ▪stream/the ▪times 604L17
▫go with the ▪current 337L9
go with the ▪flow 538L3
go with the ▪territory 1504R63
▫go with▪out 608L4
▫go ▪wrong 1693L16/54/57/R49
▫good as *things* ▪go 611L71
▫happy-go-▪lucky 645R28
▫let *something* ▪go 812L40/R1/2
make a ▪go of 606L60
▫make the ▪world go a▫round/▫round 1683R60
▪merry-go-▫round 889L67
▫mind how you ▪go 899L81
▫no ▪go ▫area/▫zone 957R61
▫not go a▪miss 41R26/28
on your ▫marks/▫mark get ▫set ▪go! 866L40
▫ready steady ▪go 1179L67
▫stop-and-▪go 1430R39
▫stop-▪go 1430R42
that's ▫*two* down *eight* to ▪go 416L41
▫things that go bump in the ▪night 1512L47
▫touch-and-▪go 1540L74
watch the ▪world go ▫by 1641L84
▪goal ▫line 608L38
▫move the ▪goalposts 925L20
▫act/▫play the ▪goat 544L81 608R1
▫get (on) *someone's* ▪goat 608R2
separate/tell/sort (out) the ▫sheep from the ▪goats 1313R81
▫shut your ▪gob 1331R12
▫gobble ▪up 608R27
▫act of ▪God 13L16
by the ▫grace of ▪God 615R32
for ▫God's ▪sake 1250L52
▫God al▪mighty 35R83
▪god-▫awful 609L1
▫God ▪bless 608R77
▫God ▪damn 609L45
▪god-▫fearing 609L3
▫God for▪bid 547R74
▪god-for▫saken 609L6
▫God's ▪gift 609L9
▪God-▫given 609L12/14
▫God ▪help *someone* 662L43
▫God ▪knows 786R2
▫God's ▪truth 609L16
▫God ▪willing 608R80
▫house of ▪God 689L53
in ▫God's/▫heaven's ▪name 937L24
in the ▫name of ▪God/▪heaven 937L24
make a ▪god of 608R60
▫man of ▪God 858R72
▫My ▪God 608R77
▫please ▪God 1080R59
put the ▫fear of ▪God into/in 508L79
▪sun-▫god 1459R73
▫surely to ▪God 1467L82
▫thank ▪God 1506R66
▫tin ▪god 1524R79
▫fairy ▪godmother 495R71
▫gift from the ▪gods 594R47
in the ▫lap of the ▪gods 795R47
▫ye ▪Gods 1695R22
▪concert-▫goer 281L60
▫anything ▪goes 605R84
as ▫far as it ▪goes 503R51
▪bang ▫goes *something* 97L60
goes be▫yond all ▪reason 1181R55
it ▫goes without ▪saying 1259L83
the bal▪loon goes ▫up 96L1
what ▫*I* say ▪goes 1260L5
▫what *someone* ▫says ▪goes 1655R11
▪goggle at 609L84
▪goggle-▫box 609R4
▫goggle-▪eyed 609R7
▫easy-▪going 439L9
▫get ▪going 591L52
▫going-▪over 607R18/35 609R32
▫hard ▪going 604L34 646L79
▫have something ▪going with 1374R79
▫heavy ▪going 604L33 659L66
I'm ▪blowed if I'm ▫going to 139L65
not ▫going ▪anywhere 52R60
while the ▫going is ▪good 604L41
▫how's it ▪going? 690R29
▫comings and ▪goings 265L50
as ▫good as ▪gold 611R79
▫fool's ▪gold 544R12
go for ▪gold 609R77
▫go ▪gold 609R59
▫gold ▪card 609R60
▪gold ▫digger 609R62/65
▫gold ▪disc 609R66
▫gold ▪dust 609R69
▫gold ▪leaf 609R71
▫gold-▪plated 609R78 1231R27
▪gold re▫serve 609R80
▪gold ▫rush 609R82
▪gold ▫standard 609R84
▫heart of ▪gold 656R71
▫paved with ▪gold 1037R43
▫rolled ▪gold 1231R27
▫worth *one's* weight in ▪gold 1687L70
▫golden ▪age 610L35
▫golden ▪boy 610L39
▫golden ▪eagle 610L20
▪golden ▫girl 610L40
▫golden ▪goose 610L44
▫golden ▪handcuffs 610L48
▫golden ▪handshake 610L53
▫golden ▪jubi▫lee 610L6
▫golden oppor▪tunity 610L31
▫golden ▪parachute 610L59
▫golden re▪triever 610L22
▫golden ▪rule 610L64
▫golden ▪syrup 610L23
▫golden ▪wedding (anni▫versary) 610L9
kill the ▫goose that lays the golden ▪egg 779R70
the ▫golden ▪triangle 610L61
▪goldfish ▫bowl 610L74
▪golf ▫ball 610R9/11
▪golf ▫club 610R14/15
▪golf ▫course 610R17
▪golf ▫links 827R64
▫far-▪gone 503R67
a ▫good ▪deal 351R46 611L63 612R1/2
a ▫good ▪mind to 899L55
▫all in good ▪time 611L65
▫all very ▪good 1617L67
▫all well and ▪good 1651R62
as ▫good as ▪gold 611R79
▫be of good ▪cheer 222R61
be so ▪good as to 611L75
▫do a good ▪turn 611R82
▫do a ▪power of ▫good 1106L35
for ▫good ▪measure 611L79
for ▫good or ▪ill 703R34
for the ▫common ▪good 270R53
give as ▫good as *one* ▪gets 596R25 611L82
good ▫after▪noon 612L43
▫good and ▪proper 611R2
▫good as *things* ▪go 611L71
▫good ▪cause 206R25 612L5
good ▪day 612L45
▫good ▪deed 611R71
good ▪evening 612L48
▫good for ▪nothing 611R6/8
▫Good ▪Friday 612L9
▫good-▪hearted 612L11
▫good ▪humoured 611R45 693R58
▫good ▪looker 839R65
▫good ▪looks 611R48/50
good ▪morning 612L50
▫good-▪natured 612L12
good ▪night 612L51
▫good ▪offices 612L14
▫good ▪riddance 1221R63
▫good Sa▪maritan 612L17
▫good ▪show 611R13 1327R64
▪good ▫time 611L19/R51 1523L57/R70
▫good ▪times 612L74
▫good ▪turn 1570R35
▫good ▪word 611R54 1678R72 1679L11
have a ▫good ▪day 349L77
▫have a good ▪innings 612R10
have a ▫good ▪run for *one's* ▫money 1241L38
have ▫good ▪lungs 848L46
▫hold ▪good 676L30
in ▫good ▪company 272R70
in ▫good ▪conscience 289L58
in ▫good ▪faith 612L3
in ▫good re▪pair 1203R73
in ▫good ▪time 611R16
it's a ▫good ▪job/▪thing 611R17
▫jolly ▪good 769L47
▫jolly good ▪show 769L45
keep a ▫good ▪table 1483L59
local ▫boy made ▪good 155R62
▫make ▪good 611R19/22
▫make good ▪time 611R25
▫no ▪good 611R27
▫no good crying over spilt ▪milk 331R55
on ▫good ▪terms 1504L11
on to a ▫good ▪thing 1512L18
▫set a ▫good ▪table 1483L60
so ▫far so ▪good 503R59
▫stand in good ▪stead 1410R40 1417R3
take the ▫bad with the ▪good 92L53
the ▫good ▪book 612L5
the ▫great and the ▪good 621R59
▪there's a good ▫boy/▫girl/▫dog 1509R80
throw ▫good money after ▪bad 1517L10
too ▫good to be ▪true 611R31 1535L71
▫too good to ▪last 611R34 798L67
▫too good to ▪miss 906L4 1535L70
▫too much of a good ▪thing 611R37 1535L79
▫up to no ▪good 612L27
▪what ▫good is 611R41
while the ▫going is ▪good 604L41
▪your ▫guess is as ▫good as ▪mine 630L25
▫kiss *something* good▪bye 781R48
▫wave good▪bye to 1644R4
for ▫goodness ▪sake 1250L49
▫goodness ▪knows 786R2
▫honest-to-▪goodness 681R10
▫surely to ▪goodness 1467L82
▫thank ▪goodness 1506R66
come ▫up with/de▫liver the ▪goods 612R49
▪dry ▫goods 419R4 429R64 634L60
▫goods and ▪chattels 612R50
▫heavy ▪goods vehicle 659L16
▫household ▪goods 690L32
▪luxury ▫goods 849L66
▪package ▫goods 1016R57
sell *someone* a ▫bill of ▪goods 1290L18
▪soft ▫goods 1371R19
▪white ▫goods 1660R27
the ▫season of good▪will 1277R50
▪goody-▫goody 612R63
▫goody ▪gumdrops 612R60
▫goof a▪bout/a▪round 612R82
▫goof ▪off 613L1
▫cook *someone's* ▪goose 302L64
▫golden ▪goose 610L44
▪goose ▫bumps 613L15/39
▪goose-▫pimples 613L45/16/38
▫goose ▪up 613L26
kill the ▫goose that lays the golden ▪egg 779R70
wild-▪goose ▫chase 1664R21
▫Chinese ▪gooseberry 227L39 782R13
▫gooseberry ▪fool 544R61 613L35
▫play ▪gooseberry 1078R16
▫Gordian ▪knot 613L59
▪Gordon ▫Bennett 613L64
▪gorge *oneself* on/with 613R12
▫hot-▫gospeller 687R55
▪gossip ▫column 614L12
▪gossip-▫monger 614L14
▫got it ▪bad 92L41

got up like a dog's dinner 408R58
has the cat got *your* tongue 203L48
have (really) got something 1374R71
have got something there 1374R76
we've got a right one here 1224L79
you've got to be joking 768R37
you've got to laugh 800L31
a man's gotta do what a man's gotta do 614L48
ill-gotten 703R8
gouge out 614L62/64
governing body 614R11
central government 209L12
Her/His Majesty's Government 614R44
local government 834R16
governor-general 614R63
dressing gown 422L62
evening gown 472R30
grab at 615L28
grab bag 615L44/47
grab from 615L30
smash-and-grab raid 1359L24
up for grabs 615L43
by the grace of God 615R32
coup de grâce 314L34
fall from grace 497L84 615R31
grace with 615R2/3
saving grace 1257R59
airs and graces 29R39
grade crossing 616L81 813R33
grade into 616L62
grade point average 616L49
grade school 616L73
high-grade 616L35 667R61
make the grade 616L47 855R80
on the up/down grade 616L48
graduate from 616R68/74
graduate in/into 616R83/51/70/84
graduate school 616R62 1265R27
graft away 617L39
graft on/onto 617L28/30/26
skin-graft 617L22 1346R46
the Holy Grail 679R1
close-grained 247R73
grammar school 617R18
granary bread 617R57
granary loaf 617R57
concert grand 281L61 618L43
grand final 618L17
grand jury 618L19
grand old age 617R73
grand old man 618L15
grand opera 617R77
grand piano 617R78
grand prix 618R35
grand slam 618L22/23/25
grand sum 618L28
grand total 618L28
grand tour 617R80
delusions of grandeur 363L78
grandfather clock 618L76
teach *one's* grandmother to suck eggs 1494L68
granny flat 618R65
granny knot 618R68
grant-aided 618R82
grant-in-aid 618R82
grant-maintained school 619L1
take for granted 619L20/25
sour grapes 1380L20
hear *something* on/through the grapevine 619L63
bar graph 98R16
graphic art 619R7
graphic design 619R11/8
graphic novel 619R11
grapple for 619R40
grapple with 619R39/41
grappling iron/hook 619R32/42
Mardi Gras 864R24
grasp at 619R49
grasp at straws 1435L80
grasp the nettle 619R51
grass on *someone* 620L29/32
grass over 620L25
grass widow 620L15
lemon grass 810R17
pampas grass 1021L12
put out to grass 620L11
knee-high to a grasshopper 782R77
persona non grata 1053R7/8
grate on 620L59/63
grateful for small mercies 1357R31
ex gratia 479L34
au gratin 79R61
beyond the grave 620R64
dig *one's* own grave 383L74
from beyond the grave 122L76
have one foot in the grave 545L58
this side of the grave 1334L6
to an early grave 436R41
turn in *one's* grave 1569R46
watery grave 1643L53
gravel pit 621L2
graven image 621L12
graveyard shift 621L25
gravitate toward/to 621L32
centre of gravity 209L50
specific gravity 1386R50
gravy boat 621L53
the gravy train 621L54
graze in 621L66
grazing land 621L71
elbow grease 445R60
grease gun 621L76
grease monkey 621L79
like greased lightning 621R2
greaseproof paper 621R17
greasy spoon 621R13
a great girl's blouse 596L10
dirty great 388L44
go great guns 621R33
go to great lengths 811L23
go to great pains 1018R43
no great shakes 621R35
one/another of life's great mysteries 818R72
pearl of great price 1040R47
put/set great store 1431R33
the great and the good 621R59
think great thoughts 1513L58
to a great extent 486L43
with great respect 1210R43
with the greatest of respect 1210R43
greedy-guts 622L41
Greek cross 622L48
a green thumb 622R26
blue-green algae 140L1
bowling green 154R55
give the green light 622L67
green about the gills 595L43
green ban 622R10
green beans 622L71
green belt 622R29
green card 622L73/75
green fingers 622R26/29
green-light 622L68
green paper 622L78
green pepper 622R32
Green Revolution 622R37
green salad 622R37 1250L78
green tea 622R38
green-thumbed 622R29
lime-green 823R27
olive green 980R66
pea green 1039R7
putting green 1155R36
sage-green 1249L83
greenhouse gas 623L14
the greenhouse effect 623L10
spring greens 1400L3
Greenwich Mean Time 623L17
greet *someone* with 623L25/26
greeting card 623L37/36
Season's Greetings 1277R47
Gregorian calendar 623L49/50
Gregorian chant 623L54
hand grenade 641L17
dove-grey 415L72
grey area 623R4
grey eminence 450R46 623R7
grey matter 623R8
gunmetal grey 632R65
steel grey 1418R31
cattle grid 206L32
grid reference 623R31
national grid 939L6
come to grief 623R54
give *someone* (a lot of) grief 623R57
grief-stricken 623R59
grievous bodily harm 623R77
grill *someone* about 624L18
grill pan 624L11
mixed grill 908L76
char-grilled 216R42
grim-faced 624L31
grim reaper 624L33
hang/hold on like grim death 624L28
paint a grim picture 1019L30
grin and bear it 624L66
shit-eating grin 1317R79
grind down 624L74/R9/10
grind into 624L77/78
grind on 624R31 626L77
grind the faces of the poor 624L82
grind to a halt/standstill 624R35/37
have an axe to grind 87L70
coffee-grinder 254R79 624R1
meat grinder 624R2 898L45
organ grinder 995L47
keep/put *one's* nose to the grindstone 961R82
get/keep a grip on 624R61
loosen *one's* grip 840R77
gripe water 624R74
come to grips with 624R58
get to grips with 624R60
éminence grise 450R46
grist to the mill 624R56
grit *one's* teeth 625L24
nitty-gritty 956R48
grocery shop 625L67
grocery store 625L67
sly grog 1357L12
well-groomed 1652R57
gross out 625R69
Santa's grotto 1255L30
grouch about 626L16
air-to-ground 29R14
break fresh/new ground 160R64
break ground 160R62
burial ground 177L3
burn to the ground 177L82
camping ground 187R11/75
claim the moral high ground 235R52
common ground 270R75 626R11
cut the ground from under *someone's* feet 339L83
dumping ground 432L31
fall on stony ground 497R83
gain ground 579R46
go/run to ground 604L14 626L40
ground ball 626L45/82
ground beef 626R36 898L40
ground-breaking 626L46
ground cover 626L48
ground crew 626L52
ground floor 626L54
ground frost 626L56
ground level 626L58 813R56
ground plan 626L61
ground rent 626L65
ground rules 626L67
ground speed 626L70
ground staff 626L72
ground stroke 626L73
have both feet on the ground 545L57
have *one's* feet on the ground 545L56
have/keep an/*one's* ear to the ground 434R82/81
hold *one's* own/hold *one's* (own) ground 676L46
hunting ground 695L32
lose ground 842L72
middle ground 894L56
on safe/dangerous ground 626R12
parade ground 1024L24
proving ground 1138R36
recreation ground 1188L8
rough ground 1235R44
run to ground 1241L8
shift *one's* ground 1315R53
spawning ground 1384L74
stamping ground 1409R44
stand *one's* ground 1410L45
stone-ground 1429R47
suit right down to the ground 1457R51
the happy hunting ground 695L35
thick on the ground 1511L44
thin on the ground 1511R35
grounded in 626R30
well-grounded 1652R61
blood group 137L60
ginger group 595R24
group captain 626R76 Group of Seven 626R78
group practice 626R77
group therapy 626R82
interest group 741R69
minority group 901R49
peer group 1043L39
peer group pressure 1043L41
pressure group 1118R41
special interest group 1385R68
splinter group 1394R33
support group 1465L61
grouse about 627L25
the groves of academe 627L47
grow apart 627R69
grow away 627R69
grow into 627L69/R75
grow up 627R2/L80/83
not grow on trees 627R5
growing pains 627R26/29/31
growing up 627L82 1598R5
full-grown 572R40/39
grown-up 627R7/10
growth hormone 627R58
growth ring 1554R68
old growth 979R70
grub around/about 628L22
grub from 628L26
grub off 628L25
grub up/out 628L26
money-grubbing 913R31
grudge *something* to 628L49
grumble about 628R4/6
grumbling appendix 628R14
grunt with 628R52
catch off guard 629L69
guard against 629L68/R11/17
guard dog 629L76
guard of honour 629L77
guard post 629L80
guard rail 629L81
guard's van 629L84
mount guard 922R56
old guard 980L69
security guard 1282L2
splash guard 928L8 1394L46
stand/keep guard 629L55 1410L48
take/catch off guard 976L68
the changing of the guard 629L72
under guard 629L53
well-guarded 1652R66
guardian angel 629R42
educated guess 442R46
second-guess 1279L60/63
your guess is as good as mine 630L25
keep *someone* guessing 630L7
no marks for guessing 866L75
there are no prizes for guessing 1124R31
guest beer 630L64
guest book 630L67
guest of honor 630L70
guest of honour 630L69
guest worker 630L72
mystery guest 934R64
guidance counsellor 197L35
marriage guidance 868L21
Brownie Guide 169L75
Girl Guide 596L13 631L3
guide dog 630R44
guide round 630R29
guide through 630R33
guide word 630R55
Ranger Guide 1172R22
guided missile 630R46
guiding principle 630R49
guiding spirit/light 630R53
guilt complex 631L57
guilt trip 631L60/64
guilty conscience 289L42 631L73
guinea fowl 631R18
guinea pig 631R20/24
acoustic guitar 631R39
electric guitar 631R40
Gulf Stream 631R61
stick in *one's* gullet 631R78
gulp back 632L12
gulp down 632L8/9
bubble gum 171L48
chewing gum 225L23
gum shield 632L23
gum tree 470R59 632L40
gum up the works 632L52
scribbly gum 1273R24
spotted gum 1397R68
up a gum tree 632L42
goody gumdrops 612R60
gummed up 632L50
at gun point 1089L9
big gun 125L47
grease gun 621L76
gun carriage 632R2
gun dog 128L59 632R3
gun down 632R16
gun for 632R22
gun-runner 632R6/5
hot-air gun 687R30
jump the gun 772R69
machine gun 850R56/58
pull a gun on 1144R48
ray gun 1177L1
smoking gun 1361R15
son of a gun 1375R38
spray gun 1399L75
squirt gun 1404R61 1642R19
staple-gun 1412L68
Sten gun 1419R57
stun gun 1448R80
submachine gun 1451R30
tommy gun 1533R61
gunboat diplomacy 632R33
gung-ho 632R55
gunmetal grey 632R65
go great guns 621R33
spike *someone's* guns 1391L70
stick to *one's* guns 1423R36
with guns blazing 632L83
helicopter gunship 660R78
full to the gunwales 633L6
hurdy gurdy 695L65
gurgle with 633L13
down the gurgler 415R30 633L19 1021L69
beer gut 113L7
gut feeling/reaction 633L84
gut-wrenching 633R4
blood and guts 137L49
greedy-guts 622L41
sweat/work *one's* guts out 633R14 1474R44
gutter press 633R44
fall guy 497R7
Guy Fawkes Night 633R74
no more Mr Nice Guy 926R11
wise guy 1671L54
gas guzzler 584L34
jungle gym 773L83
funny ha ha 575L60
ha ha! 635R71
hoo-ha 684L9
habeas corpus 634L54
force of habit 548L63
habit-forming 634R46
kick a/the habit 778R80
riding habit 1222L65
hack about 635L1
hack at 634R82
hack down 635L6
hack into 635L18
hack off 634R83
hack *one's* way through 634R84
hacking cough 635L37
make *someone's* hackles rise 635L42
raise *someone's* hackles 635L43
fag hag 493R51
haggle *someone* down 635R56
haggle over/about 635R55
hum and hah 652L77 692L62
hail-fellow-well-met 636L8
hail from 636L18
Hail Mary 636L12
within hailing distance of 636L4
camel hair 187L6
get in *someone's* hair 636L42
hair's breadth 636L71
hair drier/dryer 636L54
hair gel 636L57
hair lacquer 791R52
hair mousse 636L58
hair-raising 636L62
hair salon 636L64
hair slide 636L66 1352R66
hair spray 636L68 791R52
hair-trigger 636L73
harm a hair of/on *someone's* head 648L62
head of hair 653L66
keep your hair on 636L46 777L8
let *one's* hair down 812L49
make *someone's* hair curl 636L40
make *someone's* hair stand on end 636L48
not see hide nor hair of 1284L15
not turn a hair 1569R36
tear *one's* hair out over 1495L17
thatch of hair 1507R52
the hair of the dog 636L51
pudding-basin haircut 1143L54
fair-haired boy 139R82 495L70
wire-haired 1670R59
receding hairline 636R71 1183L84
hairpin bend 636R83
have (got) *someone* by the short hairs 1321R68
split hairs 1394R65
that'll put hairs on your chest 636L37
halcyon days 637L28
hale and hearty 637L32 657R43
better half 120R34
cheap at half the price 220R76
don't know/haven't heard the half of it 637L51
given half a chance 214R28 637L58
go off half-cocked 637R36/37
half a mind to 899L54
half an hour 637R50
half and half 637R9
half-arsed 637R24
half-assed 637R24
half-baked 637R23
half board 637R27
half-brother 638L9
half-caste 637R32
half-cut 637R41
half-dead 637R43
half-decent 637R45
half-hearted 637R50/47
half-hour 637R50
half-hourly 637R57
half-joking 637R61/60
half-life 637R64
half-light 637R67
half-marathon 637R71
half-mast 637R73
half-measure 637R75
half-moon 637R78 916R53
half-moon glasses 637R81
half note 637R83 900R62
half-price 638L4
half-sister 638L8
half-size 638L11
half-staff 637R73
half step 638L13/54 1291L63
half term 638L14 1501R10
half the battle 637L54

▫half the *person one* ▪used to be 638L2
▫**half**-▪timbered 638L17
▫**half**-▪time 638L20
▪**half** ▫tone 1291L64 1534L82
▪**half**-▫truth 638L24
▫**half** ▪volley 638L27
▪**half**-▫wit 638L29/33
how the ▪other **half** ▫lives 637L65
six of ▫one and **half** a dozen of the ▪other 1344L43
▫time and a ▪**half** 1521R67
too ▫clever by ▪**half** 243R70
▫**halfway** ▪house 638L67
▫meet *someone* **half**▪**way** 883L38
▫city ▪**hall** 234L79/82
▪dance ▫**hall** 345L61
▪dining ▫**hall** 385L72
▫**hall** of ▪fame 638R13
▪mess ▫**hall** 890L27
▪music ▫**hall** 931L53 1607L25
▫town ▪**hall** 1543R59
▫**halogen** ▪hob 639L9
▫**halogen** ▪lamp 639L12
▫grind to a ▪**halt** 624R35/37
▫do things by ▪**halves** 637L72
go ▪**halves** 637L61
▫**ham**-▪fisted 639R6
▫**ham** *something* ▪up 639L70
▫come/▫go under the ▪**hammer** 639R26
▫go at it ▫**hammer** and ▪tongs 639R21
▫**hammer** and ▪sickle 639R27
▫**hammer** a▪way 639R44
▪**hammer** *someone* for 639R64
▫**hammer** *something* ▪home 639R48
▫**hammer** *something* ▪in 639R37/52
▪**hammer** *something* into 639R36/38/52
▪**hammer** on/at 639R65/42
▫**hammer** ▪out 639R40/72
▪**hammer**-▫throwing 639R31
▫John ▪**Hancock** 767L37
a ▫heavy ▪**hand** 659L60
at ▫first ▪**hand** 525R71 640L66
at ▫second ▪**hand** 640L68
▫bite the **hand** that ▪feeds 130R13
▫cap in ▪**hand** 190R60
▫count on the ▫fingers of one ▪**hand** 312L14
▫dab ▪**hand** 342L53
▫eat out of *someone's* ▪**hand** 439L42 1020R29
▫first-▪**hand** 525R67
▫free ▪**hand** 561L7
give/lend *someone* a helping ▪**hand** 662L38
give *one's* ▫right ▪**hand** 1223R69
▫give the glad ▪**hand** 597R43
▫**hand** and ▪foot 640R80
▫**hand** and ▪glove 640L82
▫**hand** ▪back 641L60
▪**hand** ▫baggage/▫luggage 641L13
▫**hand** ▪down 641L61/77
▪**hand** gre▫nade 641L17
▪**hand**-▫held 641L21
▫**hand** ▪in 641L63/64/R36/38
▪**hand** in ▪glove 640L82
▫**hand** in ▪hand 640R39/41
▪**hand**-me-▫down 641R2
▫**hand** ▪on 640L52 641L66
▫**hand** ▪out 641L67/69
▫**hand** ▪over 641L70/72/73/80
▫**hand** over ▪fist 640R45
▫**hand**-▪picked 641L38
▪**hand** ▫puppet 601R8
▫**hand** ▪round 641L75
▪**hand** (over) to 641L59/61/66/82
▫**hand**-to-▪hand 641L41
▫**hand**-to-mouth ex▪istence 640L73
▫**hand** *something* to *someone* on a ▪plate 1076R80
▪**hand** ▫truck 641L48
in the ▫palm of *one's* ▪**hand** 1020R28
▫job at ▪**hand** 766L10
▫job in ▪**hand** 640R54 766L10
keep *one's* ▪**hand** ▫in 641R40
▫lay a ▪**hand** on 802L63
▫leading ▪**hand** 803R74
▫left-**hand** ▪drive 808R31
like the ▫back of *one's* ▪**hand** 89L73
▫matter at ▪**hand** 874R24
▫matter in ▪**hand** 874R23
▪minute ▫**hand** 902L60
▫near at ▪**hand** 944R54
▫old ▪**hand** 979R74
over▫play *one's* ▪**hand** 1009R9
put *one's* ▫**hand** in *one's* ▪pocket 641L1
▫put in ▪**hand** 640R61
▫raise *one's* ▪**hand** to/against 1170L39
▫right-▪**hand** 1223R79
▫right-**hand** ▪drive 1223R82
▫right-**hand** ▪man 1224L6
▪second ▫**hand** 641R13 1279L67/R56
▫show *one's* ▪**hand** 1327L20
▫sleight of ▪**hand** 1352L4
the ▫upper ▪**hand** 1599R36
the ▫whip ▪**hand** 1658R83
▫tip *one's* ▪**hand** 1526L24
▫try *one's* ▪**hand** 1565R72
▫turn *one's* **hand** to ▪anything 1569R38
with an ▫iron ▪**hand** 752R18
with *one's* ▫own fair ▪**hand** 495R25
▫slow ▪**handclap** 1355R51
▫golden ▪**handcuffs** 610L48
▫cack-▪**handed** 182R37
▫empty-▪**handed** 452R60
▫even-▪**handed** 472L66
▫heavy-▪**handed** 659L65
▫high-▪**handed** 668R25/29
▫left-▪**handed** 808R30/34/38
▫left **handed** ▪compliment 808R40
▫open-▪**handed** 988R68
▫red-▪**handed** 1189L12
▫right-▪**handed** 1224L1
▫single-▪**handed** 1341L21/18
▫two-▪**handed** 1576L45
▫right-▪**hander** 1224L1/4
▫two-▪**hander** 1576L48
▫mental ▪**handicap** 642L66 887L65
▪glad-▫**handing** 597R43
▫pocket-▪**handkerchief** 1087R76/78
▫fly off the ▪**handle** 540R35
▫too hot to ▪**handle** 688L25
▫**handlebar** mous▪tache 643L36
▪baggage ▫**handler** 93R61
▪love ▫**handles** 843R44
▫shipping and ▪**handling** 1100R65
a ▫safe pair of ▪**hands** 641R63
▫beat ▫**hands** ▪down 109L71 641L9
▫capable ▪**hands** 191L22
▫change ▪**hands** 215L6
▫fling up *one's* ▪**hands** 534R49
get/fall into the ▫wrong ▪**hands** 1693L61
▫get/▫lay/▫put *one's* ▪**hands** on 640L76
▫get on *one's* ▪**hands** 640L81
▫**hands** ▪up/▪down 641L6/12
have *one's* ▪**hands** ▫full 640L78
▫hold ▪**hands** 675R29
in/▫fall into the ▪**hands** of 497R78
in ▫safe ▪**hands** 641R53 1248L84
▫join ▪**hands** 767L71
▫laying ▫on of ▪**hands** 802L72
▫show of ▪**hands** 1327R65
▫sit on *one's* ▪**hands** 1343L43
▫stand on *one's* ▪**hands** 1410L55
▫take *one's* ▫life in *one's* ▪**hands** 819L8
take matters into *one's* ▪own ▫**hands** 874R46
take the ▫law into *one's* own ▪**hands** 801L37
▫thieving ▪**hands** 1511L81
throw up *one's* ▫**hands** in ▪horror/de▪spair at 1517L41
▪time on *one's* ▪**hands** 1521R50
▫wash *one's* ▪**hands** of 1639L76
▫win **hands** ▪down 641L8 1666R3
with *one's* ▫bare ▪**hands** 99R45
▫wring *one's* ▪**hands** 1690R82
▫golden ▪**handshake** 610L53
▫**handwriting** is on the ▪wall 643R20 1692L30
▫can't **hang** ▪that on 190L59
get the ▪**hang** of 644L56
▫give *someone* enough ▫rope to ▪**hang** *them*selves 459R38
go ▪**hang** 644L47
hang a▪bout/a▪round 643R59 644L65/71/65/71
▪**hang** at 644L82
▫**hang** ▪back 644R1
▫**hang** by a ▪thread 643R70
▫**hang** ▪down 643R60
▫**hang** ▪fire 644L61
▪**hang** from 643R61
▪**hang**-▫glider 643R78/82
▫**hang** ▪in 643R62
▫**hang** ▪loose 840R61
▪**hang** on 644R7/12/16/20/45 982R73
hang ▫on like grim ▪death 624L28
▫**hang** ▪on to 644R14
hang ▪out 644R26
▫**hang** ▪over 644L38
hang ▪round 644L71
▫**hang** round *one's* ▪neck 644L80
▫**hang** the ▪cost/ex▪pense 644L52
▫**hang** to▪gether 644R33/38
hang ▪up 643R76 644R41/78 645L3 1225R13
▪**hang** upon 644R16/20
let it ▫all **hang** ▪out 812L58
▫**hanged** drawn and ▪quartered 644L20
▫I'll be/▫I'm ▪**hanged** 644L54
▪clothes-▫**hanger** 248R8 644R53
▪coat-▫**hanger** 252L11 644R54
▪cloud **hanging** ▫over 248R48
▫**hanging** ▪basket 643R82
▫thereby **hangs** a ▪tale 1510L63
▪**hanker** ▫after/▫for 645L10/15/10
▫**hanky**-▪panky 645L19
▫**happen** a▪long/▪by/▪past 645L83
▪**happen** on/upon 645L80
▪**happen** to 645L54/71/75/77
▫as things ▪**happened** 67L20
▫stranger things have ▪**happened** 1434R3
▫as it ▪**happens** 67L19/18
▫**happy**-go-▪lucky 645R28
▪**happy** ▫hour 645R31
▫**happy** ▪medium 645R33
▫many **happy** returns (of the ▪day) 863L82
the ▫**happy** ▪day 645R25
the ▫**happy** e▪vent 645R26
the ▫**happy** ▪hunting ground 695L35
▪trigger-▫**happy** 1557R24
▫**hara**-▪kiri 645R65
▪**harbour**-▫master 646L15
a ▫**hard** act to ▪follow 13L52
a ▫**hard** ▪nut to ▫crack 968L79
between a ▫rock and a ▪**hard** ▫place 1229R45
▫die ▪**hard** 381R68
▫drive a **hard** ▪bargain 425R44
▫fall on ▫**hard** ▪times 497R84
give *someone* a ▫**hard** ▪time 1523R77
▫**hard** and ▪fast 646L36/39
▫**hard**-▪bitten 647L10
▫**hard**-▪boiled 646L41 647L15
▫**hard** ▪candy 144L72
▫**hard** ▪case/▪nut 646R80
▫**hard** ▪cash 646L44
▫**hard** ▪cheese 223L52
▫**hard** ▪coal 49R14
▫**hard** ▪copy 646L45
▪**hard** ▫core 646L47/R50/54
▫**hard**-core ▪music 646R56
▫**hard** ▪currency 646L49
▫**hard** ▪disk 646L51
▫**hard**-▪done-by 646R27
▫**hard** ▪drink 647L54
▫**hard** ▪drinker 646R4
▫**hard**-▪earned 646R11
▫**hard** ▪feelings 646R44
▫**hard**-▪fought 647L19
▫**hard** ▪going 604L34 646L79
▫**hard** ▫hat 646L53
▫**hard**-▪headed 646R58
▫**hard**-▪hearted 646R61
▫**hard**-▪hitting 647L22
▫**hard** ▪knock 646R64
▫**hard** ▪labour 646R65
▫**hard**-▪line 646R68
▫**hard**-▪liner 646R70
▫**hard** ▫liquor 647L55
▫**hard** ▪luck 646R32/36
▫**hard**-▪luck ▫story 646R72
▫**hard** ▪margin 646L58
▫**hard**-▪nosed 646R76
▫**hard** of ▪hearing 646L80
▫**hard** on *someone's* ▪heels 660L31
▫**hard** ▪porn 646R82
▫**hard** ▪pressed 647L24
▫**hard** ▪rock 647L1
▫**hard** ▪science 647L72
▫**hard** ▪sell 647L3
▫**hard** ▪shoulder 646L57
▫**hard** ▫stuff 647L57
▫**hard** to ▪swallow 646L78
▫**hard** to ▪take 646R43
▫**hard** ▪up 647R40
▫**hard**-▪wearing 647L32
▪**hard**-▫won 646R14
▫**hard**-▪working 646R16
▫learn *one's* ▫lesson the ▪**hard** way 806L56
play ▫**hard** to ▪get 1078R19
▫rock ▪**hard** 1229R53
▫school of **hard** ▪knocks 1265R31
take a ▫long **hard** ▪look at 840L9
the ▪**hard** ▫way 646L75/R46
▫think ▫long and ▪**hard** 1513L45
▫too much like **hard** ▪work 1535L81
▫play ▪**hardball** 1078L60
▫**harden** *one's* ▪heart 647L39
can ▫**hardly** ▪wait 1633R7
could ▫**hardly** believe *one's* ▪eyes/▪ears 115L77
▫**hardly** ▪ever 473L8 647R16
▫**hardly** hear *oneself* ▪think 655R77
hardly put ▫one foot in front of the ▪other 545R46
need ▫**hardly** ▪say 946R74
▪**hardware** ▫dealer 647R53 752R71
▪**hardware** ▫store 647R54 752R73
▪**hare** ▫coursing 647R79
▫**Hare** ▪Krishna 648L7
▫**hare** ▪off 647R83
▫**hark** at ▪*someone* 648L23
▫**hark** ▪back 648L31/33/29
▪**Harley** ▫Street 648L38
▫grievous bodily ▪**harm** 623R77
harm a ▫hair of/on *someone's* ▪head 648L62
out of ▫**harm's** ▪way 648L54
▫wouldn't **harm** a ▪fly 540R73
▫back in ▪**harness** 648R59
▪**harness** into 648R65
▪**harp** about 648R75/77
▫**harp** ▪on 648R77
▫Jew's ▪**harp** 763L68
▫Tom Dick and/or ▪**Harriet** 1533R13
▫**harum**-▪scarum 649L47
▫**harvest** ▪festival 649L61
▫combine ▪**harvester** 261R6
▫**hash** ▪browns 649R7
▫**hash** ▪up 649R1
▫make ▪**haste** 649R36
at the ▫drop of a ▪**hat** 427R33
▪bobble ▫**hat** 142L72
▫brass ▪**hat** 158L71
▫eat *one's* ▪**hat** 439L53
▪hard ▫**hat** 646L53
▪**hat** ▫trick 650R76
▫hold out the ▪**hat** 675R32
▫old ▪**hat** 979R77
▫pass round the ▪**hat** 675R33
▫pass the ▪**hat** (round) 1031L64
▫pull *something* out of the ▪**hat** 1144L44
▪slouch ▫**hat** 1355R10
▪sun-▫**hat** 1459R74
▫take *one's* ▪**hat** off to 649R69
▫talk through *one's* ▪**hat** 1488R18
throw/toss *one's* ▪**hat** into the ▫ring 649R76
▫tin ▪**hat** 1524R81
▫top ▪**hat** 1537R55
▪cross-▫**hatch** 328L75/71/77 650L52
e▪scape ▫**hatch** 467R65
▫batten down the ▪**hatches** 104R62
▫bury the ▪**hatchet** 178L32
▪**hatchet**-▫faced 650L69
▪**hatchet** ▫job 650L70
▪**hatchet** ▫man 650L74
▪**hate** ▫mail 650L82
▫bowler-▪**hatted** 155L1
▪**haul** ▫ass 651L13
▫**haul** a▪way 651L8
▪**haul** on 651L9
▫**haul** *someone* over the ▪coals 251R8
▫**haul** ▪up 651L7
▫**haul** *oneself* ▫up by *one's* ▪bootstraps 148R34
▪road ▫**haulage** 651L19 1563L1
▫**haute** cou▪ture 315R82 651L80
▫**haute** cui▪sine 651R1
▫**have** *someone* ▪back 651R82/84
▫**have** *someone* ▪down 652L20
▫**have** *someone* (▪up) for 652L29 1143L51
▪**have** it 652L54/56
▫**have** *something* ▪off 652L19
▫**have** *someone* ▪on 651R38/40/43 652L48
▫**have** ▪out 652L22/23/53
▫**have** *something* ▪out with *someone* 651R55 652L56 1488R43
▫**have** *someone* ▪over/▪round 652L24
▪tax ▫**haven** 1493R6
▪hee-▫**haw** 660L11
▫hem and ▪**haw** 692L63
▫hum and ▪**haw** 652L77 692L62
▪**hawk**-▫eyed 652L83
▪**hay** ▫fever 652R29
▫hit the ▪**hay** 673L25
make ▫**hay** while the ▪sun shines 652R28
a ▫needle in a ▪**haystack** 947L30
▪**hazard** (▪warning) ▫light 652R48
occu▫pational ▪**hazard** 973R29
hazardous-▪duty ▫pay 345R31
▫**haze** ▪over 652R69
▪heat ▫**haze** 652R68 657R83
▪witch-▫**hazel** 1672R16
▪wych-▫**hazel** 1672R16 1694R3
a ▪roof over *one's* ▫**head** 1233L12
▪acid ▫**head** 11R17
an ▫old/a ▫wise **head** on ▫young ▪shoulders 653L29
▫beat/▫bang/▫knock *one's* ▫**head** against a brick ▪wall 653L33
▪big-▫**head** 125L52
▫bring to a ▪**head** 653L42
bury/have *one's* ▫**head** in the ▪sand 653L38
▫can't get *one's* ▪**head** a▫round 653R69
▫can't make ▫**head** (n)or ▪tail of 654L26
▫come to a ▪**head** 653L42
▫crowned ▪**head** 329R8
▪death's ▫**head** 352R11
▫don't worry your ▫pretty little ▪**head** 1685R79
▫eyes in the back of *one's* ▪**head** 488L58
from ▫**head** to ▪foot 653L46
from ▫**head** to ▪toe 653L46
get/put *one's* ▪**head** ▫down 653L48/51
▫give *someone their* ▪**head** 653L53/54
go to *someone's* ▪**head** 653R75/78
harm a ▫hair of/on *someone's* ▪**head** 648L62
▫**head** and ▪shoulders above 653L72
▪**head**-▫butt 653L57/59
▪**head** ▫cold 653R32
▪**head** for 654L77/78
▫**head** in the ▪clouds 653L62
▪**head** ▫louse 653R35
▫**head** ▪nurse 1292L69
▫**head** of ▪hair 653L66
▫**head** of ▪state 654L49
▫**head** ▪off 653L64 654R1
▫**head** ▪office 654L55
▫**head** over ▫heels (in ▪love) 653L68
▪**head** re▫straint 653R39
▪**head** screwed ▫on 653L69
▫**head** ▪start 653R41/45
▫**head** the ▪bill 126R1
▫**head**-to-▪head 653R33
▪**head** towards 654L76
▫**head** ▪up 654L62
hit the ▫nail on the ▪**head** 672R51
hold *one's* ▪**head** (up) ▫high 675R35
hold/put a ▪pistol to *someone's* ▫**head** 1070R31
▫hole in *one's* ▪**head** 677R2/1
▫in over *one's* ▪**head** 653L76
keep a civil ▪tongue in *one's* ▫**head** 234R81
keep a ▫cool ▪**head** 302R69 653R80
▫keep *one's* ▪**head** 653R80
keep *one's* ▫**head** above ▪water 653L79
keep *one's* ▪**head** ▫down 653L82
▫knock on the ▪**head** 785L32
▫laugh *one's* ▪**head** off 800L8
like a ▫bear with a sore ▪**head** 107R57
▫lose *one's* ▪**head** 841R75
magnetic ▪**head** 852R57
▫need *something* like (I need) a hole in the ▪**head** 946L76
not (quite) ▫right in the ▪**head** 1224L43
off the ▫top of *one's* ▪**head** 1536R82
▫out of *one's* ▪**head** 1001L11
▫over *one's* ▪**head** 653L84
▫pissed out of *one's* ▪**head** 1070R8
put an ▫idea into *someone's* ▪**head** 700R43
put/stick *one's* ▫**head** above the ▪parapet 653R29
▫run through *one's* ▪**head** 1243L43
▫running in *one's* ▪**head** 1241R7
▫scratch *one's* ▪**head** 1271R35
▫scream *one's* ▪**head** off 1272L43
▪smack ▫**head** 1357L73
▫stand *something* on *its* ▪**head** 1410L60/55
▫standing on *one's* ▪**head** 1410L58
▫swelled ▪**head** 1479L51
▫swollen ▪**head** 1479L55/50
▫take *something* into *one's* ▪**head** 654L7
▫talk *one's* ▪**head** off 1488R5
▫turn *something* on *its* ▪**head** 1569R43
▫use *one's* ▪**head** 1601R67
▫sick ▪**headache** 1332R70
▫thumping ▪**headache** 1517R78
▫big-▪**headed** 125L52
▫bullet-▪**headed** 174R10
▫clear-▪**headed** 242L45
▫empty-▪**headed** 452R66
▫hard-▪**headed** 646R58
▫**headed** ▪notepaper 654L42
▫level-▪**headed** 813R36
▫light-▪**headed** 821L57
▫muddle-▪**headed** 927R79
▫wrong-▪**headed** 1693L68/73
▫double-▪**header** 414L55
▫banner ▪**headline** 98L39
▫hit the ▪**headlines** 673L27
▫count ▪**heads** 312L10
▫**heads** or ▪tails? 654L23
▫**heads** will ▪roll 653L75
put *their* ▪**heads** to▫gether 654L4
▫make ▪**headway** 655L40
▪faith ▫**healer** 496R38/43
▫spiritual ▪**healer** 1393L78/74
▫clean bill of ▪**health** 241R45
▪**health** au▫thority 655L83
▪**health** ▫centre 655R1
▪**health** ▫farm 655R3
▪**health** ▫food 655R5
▪**health** in▫surance 655R8 738R83
▪**health** ▫maintenance organi▫zation 655R11
▪**health** ▫spa 655R3
▪**health** ▫visitor 655R16
▫National ▪**Health** (▫Service) 939L9

World **Health** Organization 1684L81
have a **healthy** pair of lungs 848L46
heap on 655R51/53
heap with 655R52
scrap **heap** 1270R73
the bottom of the **heap** 655R45
the top of the **heap** 655R46
hear about 656L13
hear from 656L15
hear hear 656L32
hear of 656L21/22/23
hear *something* on/through the grapevine 619L63
hear *someone* out 656L48
hear tell (of) 656L31
hear the end/last of *something* 656L31 798L17
hear things 1512L43
hear warning bells 1638R43
hear wedding bells 655R74
not/hardly/barely **hear** *oneself* think 655R77
will not **hear** of 656L37
don't know/haven't **heard** the half of it 637L51
a fair **hearing** 495L9
hard of **hearing** 646L80
hearing aid 656L4
must be **hearing** things 655R75
after *one's* own **heart** 656R53
bare *one's* **heart** 99R59
bleeding **heart** 134R24
bless *your* **heart** 135L11
change of **heart** 215L47 656R42
coronary **heart** disease 307L25
cut to the **heart** 339R14
eat *one's* **heart** out 439L45
find it in *one's* **heart** 520R50
from the bottom of *one's* **heart** 152L63
harden *one's* **heart** 647L39
have a heavy **heart** 658R70
heart and soul 656R69
heart attack 656L76
heart bleeds for 656L70/73
heart's desire 372R53 656R62
heart failure 656L82
heart in *one's* boots 656R63
heart in *one's* mouth 656R67
heart in the right place 656R70
heart murmur 656R29
heart of gold 656R71
heart of stone 656R73
someone's **heart** sank 656R52 1341R66
heart-searching 656R83
heart skips/misses a beat 656L74
heart-to-**heart** 656R80
hole in the **heart** 677R9
in *one's* **heart** of hearts 656R74
light **heart** 821L81
lose **heart** 657L19 841R66
lose *one's* **heart** to 841R67
open *one's* **heart** 987R70
open-**heart** surgery 987R36
Purple **Heart** 1149R50
put **heart** and soul into 657L24
set *one's* **heart** on 656R76
sick at **heart** 1333L39
sob *one's* **heart** out 1369R49
strike at the **heart** of 1441R21
take **heart** 657L20
tear at *someone's* **heart** 1495L20
to *one's* **heart's** content 656R77
warm the cockles of *someone's* **heart** 1638L65
warm the **heart** 1638L65
wear *one's* **heart** on *one's* sleeve 1647L79
young at **heart** 1698L61
big-**hearted** 124R46
broken-**hearted** 168L45
cold-**hearted** 256R66
faint-**hearted** 494R9
good-**hearted** 612L11
half-**hearted** 637R50/47
hard-**hearted** 646R61
heavy **hearted** 658R70
kind-**hearted** 780R2
light-**hearted** 821L78
lion-**hearted** 828L58
open-**hearted** 988L53
soft-**hearted** 1371R45
stout-**hearted** 1432R4
tender-**hearted** 1500L40
warm-**hearted** 1638L83
whole-**hearted** 1662L30/27
hearten to 657L76
hearth and home 657R9
in *one's* heart of **hearts** 656R74
lonely **hearts** 837R53
hale and **hearty** 637L32 657R43
dead **heat** 351L30
heat exhaustion 657R80
heat haze 652R68 657R83
heat prostration 657R81
heat rash 658L3 1174L49
heat-seeking 658L5
heat shield 658L9
heat stroke 658L11
heat-treated 658L13
heat treatment 658L15/17
heat wave 658L19
in the **heat** of the moment 658L41
on/in **heat** 658L55
prickly **heat** 658L3 1121L30
put the **heat** on 657R68 1154L33
take the **heat** off 657R71
the **heat** of the day 657R75
white **heat** 1660R16
electric **heater** 446L83
fan **heater** 501L75
gas **heater** 584L10
immersion **heater** 706L36
space **heater** 1381R67
storage **heater** 1431R11
Heath Robinson 658L74
central **heating** 209L14
give *someone* the (old) **heave** ho 658R26
heave a sigh 658R15/17
heave ho 658R23/26
heave to 658R29
heave *oneself* up/out 658R2
thank **heaven(s)** 1506R66
a marriage made in **heaven** 868L8
heaven forbid 547R74
heaven help *someone* 662L43
Heaven knows 786R2
heaven-sent 658R43
in God's/**heaven's** name 937L24
in seventh **heaven** 1302L38
in the name of God/**heaven** 937L24
manna from **heaven** 861R40
move **heaven** and earth 925L17
heavenly body 658R51
heavenly host 658R52
for **heavens** sake 1250L49
the **heavens** open 658R56
lift/raise *one's* eyes **heavenward** 658R61
a **heavy** hand 659L60
have a **heavy** heart 658R70
heavy breather 659L57
heavy cream 414L17
heavy-duty 659L13
heavy going 604L33 659L66
heavy goods vehicle 659L16
heavy-handed 659L65
heavy hearted 658R70
heavy industry 659L18
heavy metal 658R73/74
heavy petting 659L68
heavy sea 659L42
heavy-set 659L21
heavy water 658R76
make **heavy** weather of 659L53
top-**heavy** 1537L50
light **heavyweight** 821L60
hedge *one's* bets 659R58
hedge-trimmers 659R49
hee-haw 660L11
heebie-jeebies 659R75
Achilles **heel** 11L62
come to **heel** 660L29
down-at-**heel** 416L47
down-at-the-**heel** 416L47
heel-bar 660L40
under the **heel** of 660L39
high-**heeled** shoes 660L53 667L58
well-**heeled** 1652R68/71
close/hard/hot on *someone's* **heels** 660L31
dig *one's* **heels** in 383R28
drag *one's* **heels** 418L54
head over **heels** (in love) 653L68
high **heels** 660L52 667L58
hot on the **heels** of 687R82
kick *one's* **heels** 778R83
kick up *one's* **heels** 779L1
snap at *someone's* **heels** 1364L54/55
spike **heels** 1391L55
take to *one's* **heels** 660L36
heigh-ho 660L74
heir apparent 660R46
hand-**held** 641L21
helicopter gunship 660R78
double **helix** 414L57 661L10
a cat in **hell's** chance 203L44
not a hope in **hell** 684R68
not a snowball's chance in **hell** 203L45 1367R20
all **hell** breaks loose 661L24
bloody **hell** 138L15
come **hell** or high water 661L33
get the **hell** out of 661L80
give *someone* **hell** 661L40
go to **hell** 661L18/44
go to **hell** and back 661L29
Hell's Angels 661L58
hell's bells 661R25
hell-bent on 661R22
hell for leather 661L47
hell freezes over 661L49
hell on earth 661L20
hell's teeth 661R26
hell to pay 661L52
make *someone's* life **hell** 661L55
play (merry) **hell** with 1078R22
raise **hell** 1170L62
see in **hell** 1284L16
the **hell** *you* do/are 661R11
hello stranger 1434R26
crash **helmet** 320L71
cycle/cycling **helmet** 340R70
pith **helmet** 1071R53
beyond **help** 122L64
God/heaven **help** *someone* 662L43
help out 662L13
help screen 662L65
help with 662L5/6/55
home **help** 679R82
professional **help** 1128L18
so **help** me (God) 662L47
plumber's **helper** 1084L83 1085L46
give/lend *someone* a **helping** hand 662L38
helter-skelter 662R15/20/23
hem and haw 692L63
hem in 662R37
hen night/party 662R76
Hooray **Henry** 684R4
John **Henry** 767L38
hep cat 203L83
hepatitis B 663L32
herald as 663L81
herbaceous border 663R25
herbal tea 663R18 1527L26
fines **herbes** 521R41
herd instinct 663R51
hereditary peer 664R40
heritage-listed building 665L1 829R19
anti-**hero** 50L7
folk **hero** 542R76
hero worship 665L55/59
unsung **hero** 1596L25
red-**herring** 1189L13
hesitate to 665R35/36
het up 666L15
rough-**hewn** 1235R56/58
hey presto 666L39
hi-fi 667L25/28/R45
hi-tech 673R44
hickory chips 666R7
hide-and-seek 666R29
hide behind 666R21
hide from 666R29
not see **hide** nor hair of 1284L15
save *one's* own **hide** 1257R56
tan *someone's* **hide** 1489R42
tan the **hide** off 1489R43
hidey-hole 666R34
on a **hiding** to nothing 666R82
hidy-hole 666R34
higgledy-piggledy 667L32
as **high** as a kite 669L11
claim the moral **high** ground 235R52
come hell or **high** water 661L33
for the **high** jump 667L68
friends in **high** places 565L82
have a **high** colour 259R38
high and low 667R14
high and mighty 668L79
high-**heeled** shoes 660L53 667L58
high chair 667L53
high Church 667R31
high-class 667R38
high commission 668R4/5/L83/R7
high court 668R11/17
High Court of Australia 668R18
high definition television 667R40
high explosive 667R42
high fidelity 667R44
high-five 667L55
high-flown 668R21
high-flyer 667R57/50
high gear 667R59
high-grade 616L35 667R61
high-handed 668R25/29
high-heeled shoes 660L53 667L58
high heels 660L52 667L58
high jinks 669L12
high jump 667L67/61
high-level 668R37
high-level language 667R65
high-level waste 667R69
high life 667R73
high-minded 667R78
high noon 667L72/75
high-octane 667R82 974L53
high on/off the hog 668R82
high-pitched 667L78 669L27/28
high point 668L2
high-powered 668L7/R40/45
high-pressure 668L12/16/20
high priest 668R49
high priestess 668R50
high profile 668L23
high-ranking 668R78
high rise 667L81
high-risk 668L29
high roller 668L34
high school 669L36/38
high seas 668R53
high season 668L37
high society 1370R15
high-sounding 668R22
high-speed 668L43
high-spirited 669L18/22 1393L43
high spirits 669L16
high street 668R56/60
high table 668R63
high tea 668R65
high tech 673R44
high technology 673R44 1495R51
high tension 668L46
high tide 667L84/R2
high time 1522R83
high treason 668R67
high up 668R71
high water 667L84 1642L60
high water mark 667R4
hold *one's* head (up) **high** 675R35
in **high** dudgeon 667R28
in **high** places 668L75
junior **high** (school) 773R26
knee-**high** 782R75
knee-**high** to a grasshopper 782R77
leave *someone* **high** and dry 667L47
on *one's* **high** horse 668R32
passions run **high** 1032R45
pile it **high** (and) sell it cheap 1066L69
return a **high** rate of interest 1217L37
riding **high** 1222L29
running **high** 1242L22
sky-**high** 1348L7/8
higher education 669L45 1505L53
higher-up 668R74
move on to **higher** things 925R12
have it on the **highest** authority 668L76
highland fling 669L83
Highland Games 669L84
highly-strung 668L68
think **highly** of 1513L17
Royal **Highness** 1238L7
hightail out 669R34/35
divided **highway** 402L74 430L55
highway and byway 669R47
Highway Code 669R48
highway robbery 349R77
hike up 670L10
hitch-**hike** 673R37/42
take a **hike** 669R79
hiking boots 669R83
hill start 670L37
hill station 670L45
over **hill** and dale 344L14
over the **hill** 670L40
up **hill** and down dale 670L43
as old as the **hills** 979R51
talk the **hind** leg(s) off a donkey 1488R7
hinder *someone* from 670R58
hinder *someone* in 670R56
without let or **hindrance** 812R71
with the wisdom of **hindsight** 1671R2
hinge on/upon 671L12
hint at 671L34
hip flask 531L30 671L70
hip hip hooray/hurray 671R1
hip-hop 671R8
rose **hip** 671L75 1234R69
hippocratic oath 671R17
hire out 671R65
hire purchase 671R44 736R83
hire *someone* to 671R41
historic present 672L76
case **history** 201L53
life **history** 672L53 819L28/39
make legal **history** 809L49
natural **history** 943L43
oral **history** 992R73
the rest is **history** 1213L5
direct **hit** 386R60 673L40/41
hit a raw nerve/spot 1176R68 1540L76
hit-and-miss 672R48
hit-and-run 672R55/60/62
hit back 673L75
hit *someone* between the eyes 673L7
hit *someone* (up) for 673R11
hit home 673L31
hit it off with 673L74
hit list 673L48
hit man 673L54
hit on/upon 672R40/67 673L47/82/R1
hit-or-miss 672R48
hit out 673L80/R8/5
hit parade 673L67
hit *one's* stride 1441L7
hit the bottle 151R51 673L17
hit the ceiling/roof 673L19
hit the deck 673L21
hit the hay/sack 673L25
hit the headlines 673L27
hit the jackpot 672R44
hit the nail on the head 672R51
hit the road 673L33
hit the roof 1233L16
hit the spot 673L36
hit up 673R10
hit *someone* when *they're* down 415R77
hit *someone* where it hurts 673L2
make a **hit** with 673L64
not know what **hit** *one* 786R65
one-**hit** wonder 984L66
hitch-hike 673R37/42
hitch up 673R29
get **hitched** 673R35
hither and thither 673R53
hard-**hitting** 647L22
HIV-positive 673R66
a **hive** of activity/industry 673R74
hive off 673R78
give *someone* the (old) heave **ho** 658R26
gung-**ho** 632R55
heave **ho** 658R23/26
heigh-**ho** 660L74
ho-hum 675L45
tally-**ho** 1489L72
hoar frost 674L56
hoax into 674R3
ceramic **hob** 209R63
halogen **hob** 639L9
hobby-horse 674R33/37
hobnailed boot 674R44
hobnob with 674R50/51
Hobson's choice 674R56
ad **hoc** 16L32
field **hockey** 516L33 674R78
ice **hockey** 700L2
jolly **hockey** sticks 769L21
hocus-pocus 675L1
go the whole **hog** 1662L19
high on/off the **hog** 668R82
hog the road 675L30
road **hog** 1228L47
hoi polloi 675L51
hoist(ed) with/by *one's* own petard 675L69
hoity-toity 675L75
leave **hold** of 807R33
cannot **hold** *one's* drink/liquor 675R81
can't **hold** a candle 189L59
can't **hold** a candle to 675R38
don't **hold** your breath 676L66
get **hold** 675R54/56
hold a pistol to *someone's* head 1070R31
hold against 677L29
hold all the aces 10R60
hold all the cards 195L39 676R60
hold at bay 106L36
hold back 675R79 676L74/80/84/R2
hold *one's* cards close to *one's* chest 195L28
hold court 676R63
hold down 675R10 676L28/29/R59
hold *one's* end up 455L50
hold everything 676R8
hold forth about/on 677L36/34
hold good 676L30
hold hands 675R29
hold *one's* head (up) high 675R35
hold *one's* horses 676R31
hold in 675R7/8/25/78
hold *something* in check 221R34
hold it 676R10 677L31
hold off 676R12
hold on 675R26 676R19
hold on like grim death 624L28
hold on/tight 676L32
hold out 675R15/16 676L37/39 677L39
hold out the hat 675R32
hold over 676L42
hold *one's* own/**hold** *one's* (own) ground 676L46
hold prisoner 1123R48
hold still 676R22
hold sway 676R77/21/77
hold the balance of power 94R73
hold the fort 676R69
hold the key 676R74
hold the press 1119L10
hold the reins 676R75
hold the road 676L52
hold the stage 676R66
hold tight 676R23
hold to 676L56 677L22

hold together 675R27 676L19/25
hold *one's* tongue 676R24
hold up 675R18/19/28 676L58/R27/30 677L52/57/60/61
hold water 676R48
take hold 1486R25
cigarette holder 232L25
cup holder 335R14
stall holder 1409L14
holding company 677L70
leave *someone* holding the baby/bag 807L77
road-holding 676L55
no holds barred 675R57 957R68
ace in the hole 10R57
black hole 131R28
bolt-hole 145L61
burn a hole in *someone's* pocket 177L71
dig *oneself* (into) a hole 383L57
hidey-hole 666R34
hidy-hole 666R34
hole in *one's* head 677R2/1
hole in the heart 677R9
hole in the wall 677R11/27
hole punch(er) 677R14
hole up 677R41
make a hole in 677R5
need *something* like (I need) a hole in the head 946L76
nineteenth hole 956L30
the Black Hole of Calcutta 131R33
toad-in-the-hole 1530L74
watering hole 1642R68
pick holes in 1062L79
bank holiday 97R45
busman's holiday 179L29
fly-drive holiday 540R2
holiday camp 677R60
holiday package 1016R62
holiday season 513R44
package holiday 1016R61
public holiday 1142L37
holier-than-thou 679L79
holy of holies 679R8/9
His/Your Holiness 679R24
holistic medicine 679L3
beat *someone* hollow 109R5
hollow-cheeked 679L18
hollow-eyed 679L20
hollow out 679L26
hollow ring 679L35
ring hollow 1225R41
Holy Bible 122R70
Holy Communion 679L81
Holy Ghost 679R16
holy of holies 679R8/9
holy orders 679R11
Holy Spirit 679R15
holy war 679R17
Holy Week 679R20
the Holy Grail 679R1
the Holy See 679R14
be/feel at home 679R54
bring home the bacon 91R74/75
bring home to 166L60 680L50
children's home 226L33
come home to 680L50
come home to roost 1233R40
detention home 1201L33
drive home 680L54
drive *one's* message/point home 425R47
eat *someone* out of house and home 439L39
funeral home 574R70
hammer *something* home 639R48
hearth and home 657R9
hit home 673L31
home address 679R71
home and dry 680L24
home and hosed 680L25
home buyer 679R73
home economics 679R74
home free 680L28
home from home 679R80/79
home help 679R82
home in 680L78/77
home loan 679R84
home movie 680L2
home (phone) number 679R71
Home Office 680L66
home rule 680L70
home run 680L31
Home Secretary 680L68
home stretch 680L34 1440L8/9
home truth 680L37
make *oneself* at home 679R56
mobile home 909L61
motor home 921R6
nothing to write home about 1691R65
nursing home 968L23
old people's home 980L13
rest home 1212R6
scrape home 1271L69
show home 1327R82
spiritual home 1393L70
stately home 1415L29
stay at home 1417L8/14
strike home 1441R27
take-home pay 1486R64
the Home Counties 680L65
the home front 679R76
till/until the cows come home 317L48
justifiable homicide 775L10
Homo sapiens 681L56
Rt Hon 1238L52
honest broker 681R15
honest-to-goodness 681R10
make an honest living 681R14
make an honest woman of 681R12
in all honesty 713L38
honey trap 681R37
land flowing with/land of milk and honey 794L45
honeymoon in 681R76
second honeymoon 1279L72
honky-tonk 682L65/68
guest of honor 630L70
honor roll 1231R73
guard of honour 629L77
guest of honour 630L69
honour with 683L59
lap of honour 795R69
maid of honour 853L66
roll of honour 1231R72
Scout's honour 1270L56
honourable mention 683L61
my honourable friend 565L75
time-honoured 1521L3
degree with honours 683L73/71
honours degree 683L73/70
honours list 683L76
military honours 896R11
New Year's honours 683L76
hoo-ha 684L9
yoo-hoo 1697R41
hoodwink into 683R80
hoof it 684L7
boat hook 142L12
by hook or by crook 684L23
coat-hook 252L12
crochet-hook 326R4
grappling hook 619R32/42
hook and eye 684L25
hook line and sinker 684L22
hook-nosed 684L27
hook up 684L37/40
sling *one's* hook 1353L68
wriggle off the hook 1690R65
get *one's* hooks on/into 684L29
play hooky 684L62 1562R34
put through (the) hoop(s) 684L74
cock-a-hoop 252R67
hula hoop 692L18
hip hip hooray/hurray 671R1
Hooray Henry 684R4
hoot *one's* horn at 684R11
not care/give a hoot 684R16
not care/give two hoots 684R16
catch on the hop 684R46
hip-hop 671R8
hop *it* to 684R41/43
short hop 684R49
not a hope in hell 684R68
hope against hope 684R83
hope chest 152L67 684R71
hope for 684R75/77
pious hope 1069L51
white hope 1660R20
pin *one's* hopes on 1067L70
channel-hopping 215R55
cloud on the horizon 248R51
broaden/expand/widen horizons 685L55
growth hormone 627R58
hormone replacement therapy 685L75
blow *one's* own horn 138R81
English horn 305L53
French horn 563R20
horn in 685R24/27
horn-rimmed 685R8
hornet's nest 685R30
draw/pull in *one's* horns 685R4
lock horns 835R24
on the horns of a dilemma 685R6
take the bull by the horns 174L51
horror film 686L10
horror movie 686L11
horror of horrors 686L9
horror story 686L13
horror-stricken 686L18
horror-struck 686L18
shock horror 1318R53
throw up *one's* hands in horror at 1517L41
chamber of horrors 213R69
horror of horrors 686L9
hors d'oeuvre 686L29
charley horse 218R35
clothes horse 248R8/10
dark horse 346R25/28
eat like a horse 439L31
flog a dead horse 536L6
hobby-horse 674R33/37
horse around/about 686L73
horse's ass 686L50
horse chestnut 686R1
horse float 686L83
horse manure 686L52
horse sense 686L53
horse trailer 686L82
I am so hungry I could eat a horse 439L30
on *one's* high horse 668R32
one-horse race 984L68
one-horse town 984L72
pantomime horse 1022R48
put the cart before the horse 200L36
rocking horse 1230L11
shire horse 1317L48
shut/close the stable/barn door after the horse has bolted 411R52
stalking horse 1408R79
Trojan horse 1559R66
vaulting horse 686L69
change/swap horses in midstream 686L43
drive a coach and horses through 424R73
hold *one's* horses 676R31
white horses 1660R24
wild horses 1664L55
hose down 686R61/67
home and hosed 680L25
general hospital 587L34
mental hospital 887L66
psychiatric hospital 1140R35
heavenly host 658R52
hostage to fortune 687L53
youth hostel 1698R38/42
air hostess 29L82
blow hot and cold 138R74
get into hot water 687R21
go/sell like hot cakes 687R24
(so much/just) hot air 687R26
hot-air balloon 687R27
hot-air gun 687R30
hot and bothered 151R3 687R12
hot-blooded 687R33 688L30
hot-button 687R35
hot-cross bun 687R36
hot dog 342L60 687R40/42/45/46
hot flash 687R48
hot flush 687R48
hot foot 687R51
hot-gospeller 687R55
hot off the press 687R16
hot on *someone's* heels 660L31
hot on the trail/tracks/heels of 687R82
hot potato 687R58
hot shit 687R60
hot spot 687R62 688L48
hot stuff 688L12/32
hot to trot 688L33
hot tub 687R64
hot under the collar 687R17
hot up 688L52
hot-water bottle 687R67
hot water cylinder 687R69
hot-wire 688R32
in hot pursuit 687R83
in hot water 687R20
in the hot seat 687R14
like a cat on a hot tin roof 203L55
piping hot 687R11 1069R70
red-hot 1189L16
shit hot 687R60
strike while the iron is hot 1441R31
too hot to handle 688L25
white-hot 1660R26
hotfoot 688L76
hothouse children 688R9
Afghan hound 22R67
hound out 688R43
half an hour 637R50
half-hour 637R50
happy hour 645R31
hour after hour 689L1
hour has come 689L4
in *one's* hour of need 689L3
lunch hour 848L6
rush hour 1244R67
the eleventh hour 447R45
the witching hour 1672L79/R21
twenty-four-hour clock 1572R45
waking hour 1634L20
working hour 860R29
zero hour 1699R57
hourglass figure 689L21
half-hourly 637R57
after hours 688R76/78
office hours 977R19
opening hours 988L17
small hours 1357R52
till all hours 688R84
visiting hours 1627L38
a dry eye in the house 429R48
apartment house 53L25 136R43 531R63
boarding house 141R33
clearing house 243L24
club-house 250L24
coffee house 254R81
country house 313R47
doll's house 410L31
eat *someone* out of house and home 439L39
fire house 523L80
free house 561L10
front-of-house 568L29
full house 572L40/R41
fun house 573R61
halfway house 638L67
house arrest 689L38
house call 689L41
house-hunting 689L42
house husband 689L44
house journal 689R14
house lights 689R45
house martin 689L46
house of cards 689L48
House of Commons 689R30
house of correction 689L50
house of God 689L53
House of Lords 689R32
House of Representatives 689R37
house organ 689R14
house-room 689L54
house-sitter 689L56/57
house sparrow 689L58
house style 1449R46
house-to-house 689L60
house-trained 689L63
lodging house 836L45
lower house 689R31/36 845L15
meeting house 883L72
move house 925L69
open house 988R65/68/72
opera house 989L30
pizza house 1072R6
public house 1141R48 1142L40
publishing house 1143L26
ranch house 1171R75/78
ranch-style house 1171R78
rooming house 836L46 1233L80
row house 1237R42 1504L43
safe house 1248R11
set/put *one's* own house in order 689L35
show house 1327R82
software house 1372L25
station house 1415L81
steak house 1417R68
tea-house 1494L23
the upper house 1599R40
tied house 1519R22/24
town house 1543R62
tract house 1546L4
tree house 1554R65
upper house 689R32/37
Wendy house 1079R37 1653R59
White House 1660R29
household goods 690L32
household name 689R75
household word 689R77
housemaid's knee 690L8
all round the houses 689L34
as safe as houses 1248R2
Houses of Parliament 689R30
council housing 311R10
housing association 689L81
housing development 377R51 689L84
housing estate 689L83
housing project 689R4
public housing 311R10 689L79 1142R12
sheltered housing 1315L23
hove in(to) sight/view 690L55
hover between 690L72
the how(s) and the why(s) 690R73
go into a huddle 691R18
huddle round/together 691R12/13
hue and cry 691R34
huff and puff 691R38/41
bear hug 107R59
hula hoop 692L18
ho-hum 675L45
hum and hah/haw 652L77 692L62
fit for human consumption 527L72 692L73
human genome project 692L78
human interest 692L80
human nature 692L82
human relations 692R3
human rights 692R8
human shield 692R10
the human race 692R2
the human touch 692R15
the milk of human kindness 896R69
secular humanism 1281R22
eat humble pie 439L49
relative humidity 1196R74
sense of humor 1293L29
black humour 131R74
gallows humour 580R56
lavatorial humour 800R69
sense of humour 693R17/18/19 1293L32
good humoured 611R45 693R58
over the hump 693R65
speed hump 1389L19
humpback bridge 693R83
ninety-nine times out of a hundred 956L37
round hundred 1236L79
hung drawn and quartered 644L20
hung-over 694R38
hung up on 1058L78
hunger after 694R29
hunger for 694R25/26/28
hunger strike 694R12/14
hunger to 694R30
I am so hungry I could eat a horse 439L30
hunker down 694R51
hunky dory 694R56
hunt down 695L24
hunt for 694R65 695L22/23/32/38/40/41
hunt out 695L26
hunt saboteur 694R79
hunt up 695L29
treasure hunt 1554L25
witch-hunt 1672L80
bargain hunter 100L40
bounty hunter 153R12
fortune hunter 555L39
house-hunting 689L42
hunting ground 695L32
the happy hunting ground 695L35
champion hurdler 695L60
hurdy gurdy 695L65
hurl at 695L70/72/75
hurl *oneself* into 695L73
hurl mud 927R49
hurly-burly 695L77
hip hip hooray/hurray 671R1
hurricane lamp 695R5
hurry along 695R17
hurry back 695R19
hurry into 695R16
hurry on 695R20
hurry up 695R22
in a tearing hurry 1495L30
in no hurry 695R39
wouldn't hurt a fly 540R73
hit *someone* where it hurts 673L2
it never hurts 695R70
as husband and wife 696L15
house husband 689L44
animal husbandry 46L9
hush-hush 696L35
hush money 696L38
hush up 696L50
brazen hussy 159L20
hustle and bustle 696R6
Nissen hut 956R20
Quonset hut 1164L1
Jekyll and Hyde 761R27
fire hydrant 523L73
hydrochloric acid 696R53
hydrogen bomb 696R67
hydrogen peroxide 1051L72
dental hygienist 366R18 697L17
hype up 697L40/38
hypodermic needle 947L34
I.D. card 700R19
as cold as ice 256L74
black ice 131R36
break the ice 160R68
choc-ice 228L77 698R60
cut no/very little ice with 338R81
dry ice 429R65
Ice age 597R28 698R65
ice block 700L3
ice-blue 698R66
ice-box 565L40 698R67
ice-breaker 698R69/71
ice cap 698R73
ice-cold 698R76
ice cream 698R77
ice cream cone 306R44 698R80
ice-cream soda 698R81
ice cube 698R83
ice floe 700L1
ice hockey 700L2
ice lolly 700L3
ice over 700L25
ice pack 700L5
ice pick 700L7
ice rink 700L8
ice skate 700L10/11
ice up 700L25
ice water 700L13
pack ice 1016L61
put on ice 698R63

skate on thin ice 1344R82
water ice 1376R71 1642R11
tip of the iceberg 1525R77
icing sugar 700L44
germ of an idea 590L29
haven't the remotest idea 1202R8
put an idea into *someone's* head 700R43
rough idea 1235R78
what's the big idea? 125L20
have big ideas 125L16
identical twins 701L53
personal identification number 1053L5
identify with 701L70/74
identity card 701R24
identity crisis 701R27
identity parade 701R30
blithering idiot 136L41
bone idle 146L64
idle away 702L31
idling speed 702L29
fallen idol 497R16
matinée idol 874L25
ifs and/or buts 702R51
comme il faut 269L42
be ill advised to 21L9
bear *someone* ill-will 703R30
feel ill-will for 703R30
for good or ill 703R34
ill-advised 703L70
ill-assorted 703L72
ill at ease 703L74
ill-bred 703L77
ill-conceived 703L79
ill-disposed 703L82
ill-equipped 703R1
ill-fated 703R6
ill-gotten 703R8
ill-informed 703R10
ill-mannered 703R12
ill-omened 703R12
ill-starred 703R12
ill-tempered 703R14/15
ill-timed 703R17
ill-treat 703R21
functional illiteracy 574L39
functional illiterate 574L39
optical illusion 992L17
illustrate with 704L51/54
corporate image 307L64
graven image 621L12
mirror image 902R47
the spitting image of 1393R53
by no stretch/not by any stretch of the imagination 1438R69
figment of the/*someone's* imagination 517R3
imagine things 1512L43
magnetic resonance imaging 852R65
thermal imaging 1510L83
imbue with 705L45
pale imitation 1020L22
Immaculate Conception 705L83
from/since time immemorial 1524L28
immerse in 706L31
immersion heater 706L36
immoral earnings 706R12
auto-immune 82L52
immune response 706R49
immune system 706R54
diplomatic immunity 386R10
impact on 707L27
impart to 707L59
speech impediment 1388L73
impinge on/upon 709L9
implant in 709L26
silicone implant 1337R42
implicate in 709L56/57
full of *one's* own importance 572L35
impose on 299R53 710L27/30/32/33/41
impregnate with 710R72
impress on/upon 711L24
imprint on 711R18
imprison for 711R29
false imprisonment 500L21
life imprisonment 819L42
improper fraction 711R65
improve on/upon 712L4
room for improvement 1233R23
improvise on 712L33
impute to 712R14
hove in(to) sight/view 690L55
put in(to) perspective 1053R57
in/within spitting distance 1393R52
Inauguration Day 715L27
incarcerate in 715R33
inch by inch 716L39
not budge/give/move an inch 716L44
not trust *someone* an inch 1565L40
within an inch of 1674L22/24/22/23
incidental music 716L81
incite *someone* to 716R51
include in 717L12/14
assessable income 72L82
disposable income 397L25
income support 717L48
income tax 717L51 1493L83
private income 1124L40
unearned income 1587L25
incorporate into/in 718R20
increase to 718R65
inculcate in/into 719L83
inculcate with 719L84
indecent assault 719R59
indecent exposure 719R61
indefinite article 720L51
Independence Day 720R58/60
independent means 720R69
independent school 720R70
card index 195L10 721L23
consumer price index 294L21 1214R79
cost of living index 309R45 1214R78
index finger 549L43 721L46
index-linked 721L37
index of leading economic indicators 721L34
retail price index 1214R77
india rubber 721L63
American Indian 41L30
Anglo-Indian 45R20
Indian club 721L51
Indian corn 854L79
Indian ink 721L54
Indian mynah 934R16
Indian summer 721L56
Red Indian 1189L19
West Indian 1654L15
index of leading economic indicators 721L34
indict for/on 721R30/32/27/29
indirect cost 722L39
indirect discourse 722L49
indirect object 722L43
indirect speech 722L48
indirect tax(ation) 722L54
indoctrinate *someone* in 723L34
indulge in 723R36/37
indulge with 723R35
industrial action 723R77
industrial archaeology 723R78
industrial disease 723R80
industrial espionage 723R83
industrial estate 724L1
industrial medicine 723R82
industrial park 724L1
industrial relations 724L3
industrial revolution 724L4
industrial tribunal 724L12
military-industrial complex 896R20
post-industrial 1101L42
a hive of activity/industry 673R74
captain of industry 193L39
cottage industry 310R20
heavy industry 659L18
light industry 821L62
smokestack industry 1362L19
inertia reel 724R80
inertia selling 724R83
infant formula 726L14
infant prodigy 1126R76
infantile autism 80R81
infect with 726L60
opportunistic infection 990L58
infer from 726L84/R1/2/4
inferiority complex 726R29
infertility clinic 726R60
infest with 726R66
infiltrate into 727L20
in *someone's* infinite wisdom 727L38
bare infinitive 99R52
split infinitive 1394R82
ad infinitum 16L40
inflame with 727L80
non-inflammable 959R2
anti-inflammatory 50L13/15
inflation rate 1174R42
rate of inflation 1174R42
inflationary spiral 727R49
inflected language 727R61
inflict on 727R83/84 728L2
drive under the influence 425L56
under the influence 728L26
inform about 728L55
inform against 728L58
inform of 728L56
inform on 728L58
information retrieval 728L74
information technology 728L75
ill-informed 703R10
well-informed 728R7 1652R74
infra dig 728R43
infuse into 728R80
infuse with 728R79
to-ing and fro-ing 1530R13/19
ingratiate with 729L71
inherit from 729R39
inheritance tax 729R46
inhibit from 729R55
man's inhumanity to man 859L50
initiate into 731L60/61
initiation ceremony 731L66
inject against 731R28
inject into 731R30/32
inject with 731R26
fuel-injected 571L76
add insult to injury 15L42
injury time 731R70
Repetitive Strain Injury 1204L55
Indian ink 721L54
ink in 732L10
ink-jet 732L4
invisible ink 750R59
Inland Revenue 732L29
inner city (area) 732L81
inner man/woman 732R1
inner sole 736L22
inner tube 732R4
have a good innings 612R10
Inns of Court 732R75
inoculate against 733L13/15
inorganic chemistry 733L57
input into 733L62/71
assisting the police with/in their inquiries 73L9
court of inquiry 315L48
Spanish Inquisition 733R2
make inroads 733R28
ins and outs 713L8
drive *someone* insane 425L80
stick insect 1422R69
artificial insemination 66L79
insert in/into 734R3
inside job 734R82
inside lane 734R34/37/40
inside leg 734R64
the inside track 734R43
insider trading/dealing 735L45
pale into insignificance 1020L32
insist on 736L1/2
inspire in 736R24
inspire to 736R16
inspire with 736R15/24
install as 736R71
installment plan 671R44 736R83
in the first instance 525R20
instil in/into 737L62
herd instinct 663R51
killer instinct 780L20
Women's Institute 1675R67
young offenders' institution 1698L69
instruct in 737R72/74
musical instrument 738L13
precision instrument 1110R37
reed instrument 1190L47
string instrument 1443R55/41/56
wind instrument 1667L8
insulate from/against 738R7/26/28
insulating tape 738R8
add insult to injury 15L42
comprehensive insurance 277R34
health insurance 655R8 738R83
insurance policy 739L2
life insurance 738R83 819L46
national insurance 939L14
term insurance 1501R25
third-party insurance 1513R28
unemployment insurance 1587R10
insure against 738R68/74
insure for 738R70/72
intangible asset 739L62
integrate *oneself* into 739L83/R2
integrate *something* with 739R4
integrated circuit 739R9
vertical integration 1615R57
intellectual property 739R42
artificial intelligence 66L83
intend as 740L40/42
intend for 740L39
capital intensive 191R47
intensive care 740R23
intensive farming 740R27
labour-intensive 789R64
well-intentioned 740L67 1652R83
to/for all intents and purposes 740L53
inter alia 740R75
inter in 740R41
interact with 740R55
interbreed with 740R81/83
intercede with 741L4
enlightened self-interest 458R83
human interest 692L80
interest group 741R69
interest rate 810R58
place of interest 1072R60
repay *someone's* interest 1204L16
return a high/low rate of interest 1217L37
simple interest 1339R36
special interest group 1385R68
take interest in 1487L22
the general interest 587L24
vested interest 741R60 1617R81 1619L51/52/56/46
interested in 741R7/8/23
think interesting thoughts 1513L58
special interests 1385R65
interfere between 742L25/26
interfere in/with 742L25/27/29/34/27
interior decorator 742L76
interior design 742L79/81
interlace with 742R18/20
intermediate school 743L42
intermingle with 743L68
internal combustion engine 743R52
internal medicine 743R55
Internal Revenue Service 743R58
Amnesty International 41R63
International Date Line 744L15
international law 744L20
International Monetary Fund 744L23
International Phonetic Alphabet 744L25
interpolate into 744R30
interpret as 744R54/55
coitus interruptus 256L44
intersect with 745R11
intersperse among 745R30
intersperse between 745R32
intersperse with 745R28/29
intertwine with 745R56
at *15-second* intervals/at intervals of *15 seconds* 745R65
intervene between 746L29
intervene in 745R84 746L1/5
interweave with 746L72
intestinal fortitude 746R3
large intestine 796R15
small intestine 1357R56
intimidate into 746R53
drive while intoxicated 425L57
introductory course 556L69
intrude into 748R26/27
counter-intuitive 312R59
inundate with 749L2/3
inure to 749L15
invalid out 749L75/77
inveigh against 749R17
inveigle *someone* into 749R22/23
inverted comma 749R72 1164R12
inverted snob 749R81/78
invest in 750L21/22/23/25/26
invest with 750L42
investigative journalism 750L74/78 770L25
capital investment 191R51
invisible exports 750R56
invisible ink 750R59
invoice *someone* for 751L56
pro forma invoice 1128R72
involve in 751R24
involve with 751R22
iodized salt 751R68
ipso facto 752L32
bog Irish 143R47
Irish-American 752L78
Irish coffee 752L80
Irish stew 752L83
branding iron 158L31
cast iron 202L78
grappling iron 619R32/42
Iron Age 752R22
iron-clad 752R26
Iron Curtain 752R30
iron lung 752R33
iron man 752R36
iron out 752R64
iron rations 752R38
pig iron 1065R80
pump iron 1146L26
soldering iron 1372R22
steam iron 1418L52
strike while the iron is hot 1441R31
with an iron hand/fist 752R18
wrought iron 1693R68
ironing board 752R57
have/keep many/several irons in the fire 752R13
irradiate with 753L41
desert island 371R71
traffic island 1547R53/56
Fair Isle 495R53
the Emerald Isle 450L37
isolate from 755L54/55
isosceles triangle 755L78
back issue 89L20
cloud the issue 248R74
issue from 755R39
issue with 755R37
make an issue of 755R23
take issue with 755R28
Do you want to make something of it? 856L30
would you believe it? 115L75
itch for 756R59
seven-year itch 1302L29
itchy feet 756R69
itchy palm 756R73
collector's item 257R68
item by item 757L5
line item 826L43
luxury item 849L66
itsy-bitsy 757L33
stick-to-it-iveness 1423R56
tinkle/tickle the ivories 757R31
ivory tower 757R22
Ivy League 757R37
poison ivy 1090R14
jab at 757L66
jab in 757L65/75
before you can/could say Jack Robinson 757R80 1259L69
Jack Frost 757R68
jack in 759L40
jack-in-the-box 757R70
jack-knife 759L75
jack-o'-lantern 757R77
jack-of-all-trades 757R74
jack plug 759L79
Jack the Lad 757R84
jack up 757R59
Union Jack 1590R28
laughing jackass 788L64
baseball jacket 102L25
bomber jacket 145R21
dinner jacket 385R46
donkey jacket 411L56
dust jacket 433L18
flak jacket 529R36
jacket potato 759L68
life jacket 819L51/59
lumber jacket 847L47
safari jacket 1248L53
smoking jacket 1361R68
sports jacket 1396R66
hit the jackpot 672R44
jam into 760L9
jam on 760L10
jam-packed 760L11
jam roll 1477R77
jam sandwich 759R54
jam session 760L4
jam today 759R59
jam tomorrow 759R57
jam with 760L13
log jam 836R28
money for jam 913R24
traffic jam 1547R57
Jane Doe 767L26
bell jar 115R44
jar on 760L73
jar with 760L73
jaunt off 760R24
jaw bone 760R46
slack-jawed 1348L56
free jazz 561L14
jazz up 761L15/17/18
modern jazz 910R54
jazzed-up 761L6
je ne sais quoi 762L3
blue jeans 140L2 761L66
cutoff jeans 340R8
heebie-jeebies 659R75
jeer at 761L82
Jehovah's Witness 761R17
Jekyll and Hyde 761R27
Jell-O 761R37
jelly baby 761R62
jelly bean 761R63
jelly roll 761R65 1477R77
K-Y jelly 788R79
mint jelly 901R72
petroleum jelly 761R55 1056L50
double jeopardy 414L59
jerk off 762L45/50
knee-jerk 782R80
tear jerker 1494R57
physical jerks 1060R54
jerry-built 762L68
Jerusalem artichoke 762R8
jest about 762R25
jest with 762R25
bubble-jet 171L50
ink-jet 732L4
jet-black 763L23
jet engine 762R58
jet in 763L18
jet lag 762R84 763L8
jet off 763L18
jet propulsion 762R63
jet set 763L14/8/12
Jet Ski 762R68/73
jet stream 762R75
flotsam and jetsam 537L74
jettison for 763L47
Jew's harp 763L68
jewel in the crown 763R14
costume jewellery 310L53

▫crown ▪jewels 329L76
▪Jeye ▫cloth 757L58 763R50
▪jib at 763R64
▪jibe at 763R78
▪jibe with 763R80
▪Jiffy ▫bag 764L43
▪jig a▪bout 764L55
he ▪jig is ▫up 764L62
▪jiggery-▪pokery 764L81
▪jiggle a▪bout 764R42
▪jilt for 764R72
▪Jim ▪Crow 764R76
▪jim-▪dandy 345R10 765L3/7
▫sonny ▪Jim 1376L15
high ▪jinks 669L12
ju-▪jitsu 772L49
give someone the ▪jitters 765L65
blow ▫job 139L14 511R32
desk ▫job 373L19
lo/make a ▪job of 766L4
ive something ▫up as a bad ▪job 92L35
hatchet ▫job 650L70
inside ▫job 734R82
's a ▫good ▪job 611R17
job ▫action 765R41
job at ▪hand 766L10
job ▫centre 765R44
job de▫scription 765R47
job evalu▫ation 765R49
ob in ▪hand 640R54 766L10
ob satis▫faction 765R52 1256L82
ob se▫curity 765R58 1282L39
ust the ▪job 766L38
ust the man/woman for the ▪job 766L14
ie ▪down on the ▫job 818L25
ube ▫job 845R27
ake the ▫best of a bad ▪job 119L62
nore than someone's ▪job's ▫worth 765R40
ose ▫job 962L57
odd-▪job ▫man 974R40
ushed ▪job 1244R71
now-▫job 1367R11
e ▫patience of ▪Job 1036L33
odd-▪jobber 974R40
obs for the ▪boys 765R35
disc ▫jockey 389R82
ockey for po▪sition 1098R19
ockey into 766R6
Joe ▪Bloggs 766R42
Joe ▪Blow 766R43
Joe ▪Public 766R47
og a▪long 766R58 767L9
og down 767L7
og someone's ▪memory 766R81
og-▫trot 766R60
ogging ▫suit 766R74
oggle a▪bout 767L12
Dear ▪John (letter) 352L28
John ▪Bull 767L19
John ▪Doe 767L26
John ▪Dory 767L33
John ▪Hancock 767L37
John ▪Henry 767L38
John Q ▪Public 766R48
ong ▫johns 838L33
oie de ▪vivre 767L55
oin ▪battle 767R43
oin ▪forces 548L28
oin ▪hands 767L71
oin ▪in 767R4/6/9/41/42
oin in ▪marriage/▪matrimony 767L69
oin on/onto 767L67
oin the ▪club 767R25
oin the ▪ranks 767R24
oin to▪gether 767L65
oin ▪up 767L73/64/R29
oin with 767R8/42
lip ▫joint 245R54
oint Chiefs of ▪Staff 767R69
oint-▪funded 768L2
oint reso▪lution 767R72
oint-stock ▪company 767R77
ut out of ▪joint 768L13/17
trip ▫joint 1444R10
niversal ▪joint 1590R46
ouble-▪jointed 414L61
eyond a ▪joke 122L79
oke about 768R16
ake a ▪joke of 768R2
lay a ▪joke 1078R34
ractical ▪joke 1107L34/31
ee the ▪joke 1283R44
tanding ▪joke 1412L3
ake a ▪joke 1486L61
e ▪joker in the ▫pack 768R83
alf-▪joking 637R61/60
oking a▪part/a▪side 768R29
u ▫must be ▪joking 768R37
olly someone a▪long 769L64
olly ▪good 769L47
olly good ▪show 769L45
olly ▪hockey sticks 769L21
olly into 769L62
olly ▪up 769L67/65
olly well (▪do something) 769L53
the ▫Jolly ▪Roger 769L30
▫jolt a▪long 769L72
▫Dow Jones (Industrial) ▪Average 415R4
keep ▫up with the ▪Joneses 777L3
▫mah-▪jong 853L51
▪joss ▫stick 769R25
▪jostle for 769R35
▫jostle for po▪sition 1098R19
▫jot and ▪tittle 769R73
▫jot ▪down 769R55
▪jot something in 769R54
▪house ▫journal 689R14
▫learned ▪journal 806L68
▫check book ▪journalism 224L35
▫cheque book ▪journalism 224L34
in▫vestigative ▪journalism 750L74/78 770L25
▪joust for 770L64
▫cheek by ▪jowl 222R4
a ▫bundle of ▪joy 175R59
in a ▫transport of ▪joy 1552L9
▫jump for ▪joy 772R24
full of the ▫joys of ▪spring 572L39
▫ju-▪jitsu 772L49
▫Don ▪Juan 411L48
▫diamond ▪jubilee 380L25
▫golden ▪jubi▫lee 610L6
▫silver ▪jubilee 1338R81
▪judge by/on 771L28
▪judge something to 771L21
▫sober as a ▪judge 1369R65
to ▪judge by/from 771L33
▪judging by/from 771L33
a▫gainst one's better ▪judgment 24R4
▫Day of ▪Judgment 349R28 771L69
▫error of ▪judgment 467L61
▪Judgment ▫Day 771L69
more by ▫luck than ▪judgment 846L20
▫sit in ▪judgment on/over 1343L40
the ▫final/▫last ▪Judgment 771L68
▪value ▫judgment 1605R24
▫non-▪judg▪mental 959R4
▫sub ▪judice 1451L54
▫Punch and ▪Judy ▫show 1146R39
▪measuring ▫jug 879R12
▪toby ▫jug 1531L9
▪juggle with 771R83
▪juggling ▫act 772L4/14
▫stew (in one's own ▪juice) 1422L50
▪lime ▫juice 823R25
▫mint ▪julep 772L57 901R69
▫Fourth of Ju▪ly 557L8
▪jumble ▫sale 772L75 1240R13
▫mumbo ▪jumbo 929R52
▪broad ▫jump 167R20 838L36
▪bungee ▫jump 176L9
▪bungy ▫jump 176L9
▫flying ▪jump 540R13
for the ▪high ▫jump 667L68
get a ▪jump on 773L8
go (and) ▫jump in the ▪lake 772R26
▪high ▫jump 667L67/61
▪jump at 772R53
▫jump down someone's ▪throat 772R56
▫jump for ▪joy 772R24
▪jump in 772R58
jump in at the ▪deep ▫end 357L57
▪jump in/into 772R7/52
▫jump in with ▫both ▪feet 772R60
▪jump leads 772R33/32
▪jump on 772R63
▫jump on the ▪bandwagon 97L21
▫jump out of one's ▪skin 1346R32
▪jump ▫rope 772R35 1347L12/18
▪jump-start 772R37/38
▫jump the ▪gun 772R69
▪jump to 772R76/78 773L15
▫jump to a con▪clusion 772R79
▫jump ▪up 772R9/51
▫jump up and ▪down 772R11
▪long ▫jump 838L35
▫one/a ▫jump a▪head 773L6
▪scissor ▫jump 1267R56
▪show ▫jump 1329L30
▪ski ▫jump 1345R70
▫take a running ▪jump 1241L52
▫triple ▪jump 1558R70/66
▪water ▫jump 1642R12
▪jumped-up 773L2
▪jumper cables/leads 772R32
▪show ▫jumper 1329L30
jumping-▪off ▫point 772R30
▪queue-▫jumping 1162L21
▪box ▫junction 155L25
▪junction ▫box 773L53
Spa▫ghetti ▪Junction 1382R33
▫staggered ▪junction 1407L43
▪T-▫junction 1483L9
▫blackboard ▪jungle 132L52
▫concrete ▪jungle 282L79
▪jungle ▫gym 773L83
the ▫law of the ▪jungle 801L53
▫urban ▪jungle 1601L29
▫junior ▪college 773R16
▫junior ▪high (school) 773R26
▫office ▪junior 773R21 977R22
▪junk ▫food 773R46
▪junk ▫mail 773R49
▪junk ▫shop 773R51
▫de ▪jure 361R17
▫grand ▪jury 618L19
▪jury ▫box 774L24
get one's ▫just de▪serts 774R34
▫just a ▪crack 318R22
▫just a ▪minute/▪moment/▪second 774L34/35/37
▫just a▫round the ▪corner 306L79
▫just as ▪well 774L62/63 1651R73
just ▪kidding 779R8
▫just somebody's ▪luck 774L66
▫just ▪now 774L45 965R25
just ▪so 1369L19
▫just ▪talk 1488R52
▫just the ▪job 766L38
▫just the man/woman for the ▪job 766L14
▫just the ▪thing 1512R56
▫just the ▪ticket 1518R50
▫just this ▪once 983L56
▫just what the ▫doctor ▪ordered 408L11
▫just you ▪dare 346L10
▫just you ▪wait 1633R9
▫life is just a ▫bowl of ▪cherries 154R29
▫only ▪just 774R14/15/16 986L45/48
▫mot ▪juste 921L52
▫chief ▪justice 225R58
▫criminal ▪justice ▫system 324L76
▫Justice of the ▪Peace 774R76
mis▫carriage of ▪justice 774R65 903R1
per▫vert the course of ▪justice 1054R67
po▫etic ▪justice 1088R41
▫rough ▪justice 1236L23
justi▫fiable ▪homicide 775L10
juxta▪pose with 775R20
▫kangaroo ▪court 775R39
▪Phi ▪Beta ▪Kappa 1057R34
▪go-▫kart 609R39/44
▪shish ke▫bab 776L3 1317R43
▫keel ▪over 776L16
on an ▫even ▪keel 472L45
as ▫keen as ▪mustard 776L30
▫ ▫keep the ▪lid on 817R46
keep a civil ▪tongue in one's ▫head 234R81
keep a ▫cool ▪head 302R69 653R80
keep a ▫good ▪table 1483L59
▫keep a ▪grip on 624R61
▫keep a/the ▪tally 1489L66/65/64
keep a ▫tight ▪rein on 1195L55
keep a ▪watch out 1641R50
keep an/one's ▪ear to the ▫ground 434R82/81
▫keep an/one's ▪eye on 488L71
▫keep an/one's ▪eye out for 488R27
▫keep ▪at something 777L21
▫keep at ▪bay 106L36
▫keep a▪way/▪back 89L26 776R33/35
keep ▫body and ▪soul to▫gether 142R54
keep one's ▫cards close to one's ▪chest 195L28
▫keep one's ▪chin up 227L13
▫keep ▪count of 312L29
▫keep one's ▪distance 398R61
▫keep something ▪down 776R38/41/43
▫keep one's ▪end up 455L50
▫keep one's ▪eye in 488L63
keep one's ▫eye(s) on the ▪clock 246L70
keep one's ▪eyes ▫open/▫peeled/▫skinned for 488R28
▫keep ▪faith 496L50
keep one's ▪fingers ▫crossed 521R79
▫keep-▪fit 777L11
▪keep from 776R33/46/48 1280L69
▫keep ▪guard 629L55 1410L48
▫keep someone ▪guessing 630L7
keep one's ▪hand ▫in 641R40
▫keep one's ▪head 653R80
keep one's ▫head above ▪water 653L79
keep one's ▪head ▫down 653L82
▫keep ▪in 776R53/54
▫keep something in ▪check 221R34
▫keep someone in ▪stitches 1427R17
▫keep one in the ▪picture 1064L19
▪keep it 777L23/25/32
keep ▫many/▫several irons in the ▪fire 752R13
keep one's ▪mouth ▫shut 924L15
keep one's ▪nose ▫clean 961R72
keep one's ▪nose ▫out of 961R77
keep one's ▫nose to the ▪grindstone 961R82
▫keep ▪off 776R61/62
keep on a ▫tight ▪rein 1195L56
▫keep on ▪trucking 1562R79
▫Keep ▪Out 776R64 999R54
keep one's ▫own ▪counsel 311R38
▫keep one's ▪pecker up 1041L49
▫keep ▪prisoner 1123R48
▫keep one's ▪shirt on 636L47 777L8
▫keep ▪shut 608R15 1552R1
▫keep someone ▪sweet 1475R40
▫keep ▪tabs on 1483L36
▫keep the ▪faith 496R34
keep the ▪flag ▫flying 529L35
keep the ▪wolf from the ▫door 1675R34
keep things ▫ticking ▪over 1518R6
▪keep to 776R70/71
▫keep ▪track 1545L53
▫keep under re▪straint 1213R40
▫keep ▪up 776R78/80 777L31 912R82 1598L49
▫keep up ap▪pearances 55R54 777L33
keep ▫up with the ▪Joneses 777L3
keep ▫up with the ▪times 1524L29
▫keep (all) one's ▪wits about 1674R59
keep your ▪hair ▫on 636L46 777L8
▪lock ▫keeper 835R7
▪park ▫keeper 1026R69
▪wicket ▫keeper 1663L84
▪zoo-▫keeper 1701L31
▪bee-▫keeping 112L62/60
▪keg ▫party 777L70
▪powder ▫keg 1105L62
be▫yond one's ▪ken 777L78
▪boarding ▫kennels 141R32
▫kept ▪woman/▪man 777L55
▫well-▪kept 1653L5/8
▪kerb ▫crawling 777R13
▪pine ▫kernel 1068L62
to▫mato ▪ketchup 777R40 1533R28
▪fish ▫kettle 526R1
▫kettle of ▪fish 777R49
▪pretty/▪fine ▫kettle of ▫fish 777R51
▪Allen ▫key 34L20
con▪trol ▫key 299R67
es▪cape ▫key 467R61
▪function ▫key 574L30
▫hold the ▪key 676R74
▪key into 777R83
▪key ▫money 777R67
▪key ▫ring 777R70
▪key ▫signature 778L63
▪key to 778L58/59/60/71
▫key ▪up 778L74
▫low-▪key 844R6
▪master ▫key 871R22
▪shift ▫key 1315R58
▪skeleton ▫key 1345R7
under ▫lock and ▪key 835L83/R1
▫keyhole ▪surgery 778R13
▫put the ▪kibosh on 778R49
a ▫kick up the back▪side 91L13
▪drop ▫kick 427R34
▫free ▪kick 561L17
▫kick a/the ▪habit 778R80
▫kick a▪bout 778R59 779L49
▪kick against 778R61
▫kick against the ▪pricks 778R74
▫kick a▪round 778R64 779L49
▫kick (some) ▪ass 778R77
▫kick one's ▪heels 778R83
▫kick ▪in/▪down 778R55/66
▫kick in the ▪teeth 779L31
▫kick into ▪touch 779L5
▫kick ▪off 778R68/71/79/69
▫kick ▪out 778R73
▫kick over the ▪traces 779L6
▪kick-▫start 779L22
▫kick the ▪bucket 778R78
▫kick the ▪stuffing out of 1448L47
▫kick up a ▪fuss/▪row 779L9
▫kick up a ▪rumpus 1240R50
▫kick up a ▪stink 1426L82
▫kick up one's ▪heels 779L1
▫kick up/in the ▪arse/▪backside/▪pants 779L34
▫kick up▪stairs 779L13
▫kick someone when they're ▪down 415R77
▪penalty ▫kick 1044R17
▪scissor ▫kick 1267R56
a▫live and ▪kicking 33L35/36
▪kid ▫stuff 779L72
▫treat/▫deal with someone with kid ▪gloves 779L79
▪whizz ▫kid 1661R20
just/only ▪kidding 779R8
▪kiddy ▫car 779R14
▪kidney ▫bean 779R37
▪kidney ▫machine 779R33
▪kidney ▫stone 779R36
▫steak and kidney ▪pie/▪pudding 1417R69
▫dressed to ▪kill 422R17
▫kill ▪off 779R59
▫kill or ▪cure 779R63
▫kill the fatted ▪calf 779R68
kill the ▫goose that lays the golden ▪egg 779R70
▫kill ▪time 779R72
kill ▫two birds with one ▪stone 779R75
▫kill someone with ▪kindness 779R66
move/go ▫in for the ▪kill 780L1
▪killer ▫instinct 780L20
▪killer ▫whale 780L21
▪lady-▫killer 792L78
▪serial ▫killer 1296L43
make a ▪killing 780L27
▪mercy ▫killing 888R24
▫kith and ▪kin 782L65
▫next of ▪kin 780L78 953R60
be ▫cruel to be ▪kind 330L40
▫kind-▪hearted 780R2
▫nothing of the ▪kind 964L34
the ▪marrying ▫kind 868L67
▫two of a ▪kind 1576L4
▫look ▪kindly on 839L52
not ▫take ▪kindly to 780R13
▫kill someone with ▪kindness 779R66
the ▫milk of human ▪kindness 896R69
▫kindred ▪spirit 780R67
a ▫king's ▪ransom 781L32
at the ▫King's ▪pleasure 1081L28
▫king's ▪evidence 474L68
▫king of all ▫sur▪veys 1470L78
▪king-▫size 781L33
▫live like a ▪king 832R10
▫pearly ▪king 1040R58
▫uncrowned ▪king 1582R3
▪animal ▫kingdom 46L11
the U▫nited ▪Kingdom 1590R9
till/until ▫kingdom ▪come 781L53
to ▫kingdom ▪come 781L55
▫hara-▪kiri 645R65
▫blow a ▪kiss 138R67 781R76
▫French ▪kiss 563R24
▫kiss-and-▪tell 781R56
▪kiss ▫ass 781R63
▪kiss a▪way 781R52
▪kiss ▫curl 781R82
▫kiss something good▪bye 781R48
▫kiss my ▪arse/▪ass 781R65
▫kiss of ▪death 781R79
▫kiss of ▪life 781R81
▪kiss on 781R45/75
▪sun-▫kissed 1459R75
▪arse-▫kisser 65L32
▪ass-▫kisser 65L33
▪dopp ▫kit 1532R13
▪drum ▫kit 428R74
▪kit ▫bag 782L24
▫kit ▪out 782L29/27
sur▪vival ▫kit 1470R52
▪tool ▫kit 1535R39
▫everything but/except the kitchen ▪sink 474L18
▫fitted ▪kitchen 527R49 782L34
▫kitchen ▪cabinet 782L35
▫kitchen ▪garden 782L37
▫kitchen ▪paper 782L39/46 1494L33
▫kitchen-▪sink 782L44
▫lay/▫set the ▪kitchen ▫table 1483L61
▪soup ▫kitchen 1379R75
as ▫high as a ▪kite 669L11
▫fly a ▪kite 541L5
go ▫fly a ▪kite 541L6
▪kite-▫flying 782L55
▪Kite ▫mark 782L60
▫kith and ▪kin 782L65
▪sex ▫kitten 1303R48
▫Ku Klux ▪Klan 788R61/62
▪coffee ▫klatch 254R83
▫Ku Klux ▪Klan 788R61/62
▪knick-▫knack 783L75
▪knacker's ▫yard 782R46
at one's ▫mother's ▪knee 920L64
▫housemaid's ▪knee 690L8
▫knee-▪deep 782R73
▫knee-▪high 782R75
▫knee-high to a ▪grasshopper 782R77
▪knee-▫jerk 782R80
▪knee-▫length 782R84
on ▫bended ▪knee 117L8
▫knock-▪kneed 784R61
▫weak-▪kneed 1646R51
▫bring/▫force someone to their ▪knees 782R70
▫fall to/ fall ▫down on one's ▪knees 497L72
▪knees-up 783L40
the ▫bees' ▪knees 112L57
▫weak at the ▪knees 1646R48
▪death ▫knell 352R13
▫sound/▫toll the ▪death knell 352R16
▪knick-▫knack 783L75
▫knickerbocker ▪glory 783L57

get *one's* ▪**knickers** in a ▫twist 783L68
at ▪**knife** ▫point 1089L9
▪bread ▫**knife** 159R2 783L83
▪carving ▫**knife** 200R83 783L84
▪cheese ▫**knife** 223L47
▪clasp ▫**knife** 237R57
▫cut with a ▪**knife** 338R79
▪fish-▫**knife** 526R2
▪flick ▫**knife** 533R64
▫get/▫have *one's* ▪**knife** into/in 783R43
▪jack-▫**knife** 759L75
on a ▪**knife**-edge 783R56/57/52
▪palette ▫**knife** 1020L50
▪paper ▫**knife** 813L45 1023L43
▪paring ▫**knife** 1026L50
▫put/▫stick the ▪**knife** in/into 783R40/39
▪razor ▫**knife** 1177L21 1412L56
▪sheath ▫**knife** 1313R29
▪Stanley ▫**knife** 1177L21 1412L56
▪steak ▫**knife** 1417R71
Swiss ▪army ▫**knife** 1477R75
▪table ▫**knife** 1483L63
twist/turn the ▫**knife** (in the ▪wound) 783R49
▫under the ▪**knife** 783R59
▫**knight**-▪errant 783R81
▫**knight** in shining ▪armour 783R73
▫white ▪**knight** 1660R32
▫**knit** *one's* ▪brows 784L66
▫hard ▪**knock** 646R64
▫**knock** a▪bout/a▪round 785L55/13/60
▪**knock** against 784R48
▫**knock** *something* ▪back 785L25/68/72
▫**knock** ▪down/▪over 784R58 785L75/80/83/84/R1/3/4
▫**knock** 'em ▪dead 785L22
▫**knock** *somebody* for ▪six 785L25
▫**knock** *one's* ▫head against a brick ▪wall 653L33
▫**knock** ▪in 785L1
▪**knock** into 784R74
▫**knock** ▪into each ▫other/▪through 785L3
▫**knock** into ▪shape 1311L8
▫**knock**-▪kneed 784R61
▫**knock** ▪off 784R75/76 785R3/7/9/14/19/21/24/32/35
▫**knock** *someone* off *their* ▪pedestal 785L28
▪**knock** on 784R42 785L46
▪**knock** on/at 784R43
knock-▪on ef▫fect 785L43
▫**knock** on the ▪head 785L32
▫**knock** on ▪wood 784R60
▫**knock** ▪out 784R84 785L5/8/R39/51/56/L9
▫**knock** ▪over 784R82 785R61
▫**knock** ▪sense into 785L37
▫**knock** *somebody* ▪sideways 785L24
▫**knock** ▪spots off 785L40
▫**knock** the ▪bottom out of 785L18
▫**knock** the ▪stuffing out of 1448L48/47
▫**knock** the ▪tar out of 1491L65
▫**knock** to▪gether 785L61/R62
▫**knock** ▪up 785R66/70/72/76
▫**knock** ▪wood 784R60
the ▫**knock** at/on the ▪door 784R64
▪**knockout** ▫drops 786L8
▫school of hard ▪**knocks** 1265R31
▫Gordian ▪**knot** 613L59
▪granny ▫**knot** 618R68
▪reef ▫**knot** 1190L66
▪square ▫**knot** 1190L66 1402L43
▫tie the ▪**knot** 1519R20
at a ▫rate of ▪**knots** 1174R50
▫tie (up) in ▪**knots** 1519R20
▫get ▪**knotted** 786L36
▫don't know/▫haven't heard the ▪half of it 637L51
get to ▪**know** 787R1
▪**know** a thing or ▫two 786R25
▪**know** about 786L66/R27 787L31/38/68
know ▫all the ▪answers 786L60
know ▫all there ▪is to know 786R23
▫**know** ▪backwards 787L69
▫**know** ▪best 786R31/37/28
▫**know** by ▪name 787R5
▫**know** by ▪sight 787R6
▪**know** *something* from *something* 787L77
▫**know** no ▪bounds 153L42 787R8
▪**know** of 787L72
▫**know** *one's* ▪onions 787R10
▫**know** *one's* own ▪mind 786R41
▫**know** *one's* ▪place 786R42
▫**know** *one's* ▪stuff 787R10
▫**know** the ▪ropes 787R13
▫**know** the ▪score 786R45
▫**know** *someone* to ▪speak to 1384R64
▫**know** *one's* way a▪round 787R12
▫**know** what *one is* ▪talking about 786R52 787R15
know which side *one's* ▪bread is ▫buttered (on) 786R57
▫let *someone* ▪**know** 812R8
▫not **know** *one's* ▫arse from *one's* ▪elbow 65L22
not ▫**know** *someone* from ▪Adam 787R19
not **know** the ▫first ▪thing about 786R62
not **know** ▫what ▪hit *one* 786R65
▫not **know** when *one's* is ▫well ▪off 1653L42
not **know** ▫where to ▪put *oneself* 786R69
not ▫**know** whether to ▫laugh or ▪cry 786R72
not **know** ▫which way to ▪turn 786R75
you ▪**know** ▫something 787L5
you ▫**know** what I ▪mean 787L7/14
you ▫never ▪**know** 787L19
there's ▫no ▪**knowing** 956R78
▫carnal ▪**knowledge** 197R56
▫common ▪**knowledge** 270R43 787R54
▫general ▪**knowledge** 587L35
▪reading ▫**knowledge** 1179L11
to the ▫best of *one's* ▪**knowledge** 115L54 119L75
for ▫reasons best ▫**known** to *one's*self 1181R42
▫let *something* be ▪**known** 812R12
▫make ▪**known** 787R38/39/43
▫well-▪**known** 1653L11
as ▫every ▪schoolboy/▪schoolchild ▫**knows** 1265R67
for ▫all/▫aught *anyone* ▪**knows** 79R51 547L45
▫goodness/▫God/▫Heaven/▫Christ ▪**knows** 786R2
▫Fort ▪**Knox** 554R20
▫**knuckle** ▪down 788L36/39/45
▫**knuckle**-▫duster 787R80
▫**knuckle** ▪under 788L41
▫near the ▪**knuckle** 787R79
▪white-▫**knuckle** 1660R37
▫brass ▪**knuckles** 158L72 787R80
▫Kris ▪**Kringle** 788R53
▫**Kris** ▪Kringle 788R53
▫Hare ▪**Krishna** 648L7
▫**Ku** ▫Klux ▪Klan 788R61/62
▫**kung** ▪fu 788R70
à **la** ▪carte 31L40
à **la** ▪mode 31L56/59
▫c'est **la** ▪vie 211R33
▫**la**-di-▪da 792L34
la ▫dolce ▪vita 792L47
▫Shangri-▪**La** 1309R54
ge▫neric ▪brand/▪**label** 1013L11
▪luggage ▫**label** 846R27
▫own ▪**label** 1013L10
▪store ▫**label** 1013L11
▪**labor** ▫union 1546R74
▪language **la**▫**boratory** 795R1
▫cheap ▪**labour** 220R56
di▫vision of ▪**labour** 402R15
▫hard ▪**labour** 646R65
▪**labour** ▫camp 789R55
▪**labour** ▫day 789R57
▪**labour** ▫force 789R59
▫**labour**-in▪tensive 789R64
▪**labour** ▫market 789R67
▫**labour** of ▪love 789R70
▪**labour** re▫lations 789R74
▪**labour**-▫saving 789R76
▪**labour** to 791L2
▫slave ▪**labour** 1350R7/8
▫**lace** ▪up 791L75
▪**lace**-▫ups 791L79
▪**lace** with 791L84/R2
Queen ▫Anne's ▪**lace** 317L52 1161L30
▪hair ▫**lacquer** 791R52
▫**lactic** ▪acid 791R64
a ▫bit of a ▪**lad** 791R80
▫Jack the ▪**Lad** 757R84
▪stable ▫**lad** 1405R11
▫lowest/▫bottom rung of the ▪**ladder** 1243R15
▫rope ▪**ladder** 1234L66
▫snakes and ▪**ladders** 1364L12
▪**ladies'** ▫fingers 792L77
▪**ladies'** ▫man 792L82
▪**ladies'** ▫room 792R5 1532R2
▫**ladle** ▪out 792L44
▪bag ▫**lady** 93L61
▫first ▪**lady** 525R76
▫**lady** ▪bountiful 792L72
▪**lady's** ▫finger 792L75 979R35
▫**lady**-in-▪waiting 792R8
▪**lady**-▫killer 792L78
▫**Lady** ▪Muck 792R23
▫leading ▪**lady** 803R75
▪lollipop ▫**lady** 837R18
▫old ▪**lady** 979R82
▫young ▪**lady** 1698L66
▪jet ▫**lag** 762R84 763L8
▫**lag** be▪hind 792R39/41
▪time ▫**lag** 792R47 1521R78
▪**lager** ▫louts 792R73
▫**lah**-di-▪dah 792L34/R80
▫deep-▪**laid** 357L65
▫**laid**-▪back 792R83
▫**laid** ▪up 793L6
▫**laissez**-▪faire 793L14
go (and) ▫jump in the ▪**lake** 772R26
▫Dalai ▪**Lama** 344L12
a couple of/two ▫shakes (of a **lamb's** ▪tail) 1307R14
like a ▫**lamb** to the ▪slaughter 793L39
▫mutton dressed (up) as ▪**lamb** 933R82
▫sacrificial ▪**lamb** 1247L81
▪**lambing** ▫season 793L46
▫**lame** ▪duck 793L65/70
▪arc ▫**lamp** 60L75
▪Davy ▫**lamp** 1248R62
▪floor ▫**lamp** 536R26 1411R65
▪fog ▫**lamp** 542L25
▫halogen ▪**lamp** 639L12
▪hurricane ▫**lamp** 695R5
▪safety ▫**lamp** 1248R62
▪standard ▫**lamp** 1411R65
▪table ▫**lamp** 1483L64
▫**lance** ▪corporal 793R65
▫cloud-▪cuckoo-▫**land** 248R57
▫dry ▪**land** 429R68
find out/see how the ▪**land** ▫lies 794L13
▪grazing ▫**land** 621L71
▫**land** flowing with milk and ▪honey 794L45
▪**land** *someone* in/with 794L71
▫**Land** of the Midnight ▪Sun 794L49
▫**Land** of the Rising ▪Sun 794L54
▫**land** on *one's* ▪feet 545L59 794L81
▪**land** *someone* ▫one 983R68
▪**land**-▫poor 794L16
▪**Land** ▫Rover 794L17
▪**land** ▫tenure 794L20
▫**land** ▪up 794R1/4
▪**land**-▫use 794L23
▫lay of the ▪**land** 818L48
▫marginal ▪**land** 864R57
▫never-▪never ▫**land** 951R49
▪no-man's-▫**land** 957R75
▫spy out the ▪**land** 1401R11
the ▫fat of the ▪**land** 506L53
the ▫**land** of ▪nod 794L52
the ▫**land** of the ▪living 794L44
the ▫lie of the ▪**land** 818L47
the ▫Promised ▪**Land** 1131L34
▫crash-▪**landing** 320L73
▪**landing** ▫craft 794R21
▪**landing** ▫gear 794R11
▪**landing** ▫stage 794R24
▪**landing** ▫strip 30R14 794R14
▫pancake ▪**landing** 1021R22
▫soft ▪**landing** 1371R79
▫absentee ▪**landlord** 5L52
▫**landmarked** ▪building 794R82 829R18
▫blot on the ▪**landscape** 138R16
▫**landscape** ▪gardener/▪architect 795L37/40
▪bus ▫**lane** 178L49
▪cycle ▫**lane** 340R74
▪fast ▫**lane** 505L71 795L64
▫inside ▪**lane** 734R34/37/40
▫outside ▪**lane** 1004L7/11/13
over▪taking ▫**lane** 1011L73
▪passing ▫**lane** 1031L26
▪sea ▫**lane** 1276L12
take a ▫stroll/▫trip/▫walk down memory ▪**lane** 886L22
as▪sembly ▫**language** 72L36
▫bad ▪**language** 92R5
▪body ▫**language** 142R67
▫dead ▪**language** 350R39
▫first ▪**language** 525R78
▫foul ▪**language** 555R75
▫high-level ▪**language** 667R65
in▫flected ▪**language** 727R61
▫**language** la▫boratory 795R1
▫natural ▪**language** 943L46
▫second ▪**language** 1279L83
▪sign ▫**language** 1335R77
▪source ▫**language** 1380L68
▫speak/▫talk the same ▪**language** 795L82
▫strong ▪**language** 1445R24
▪target ▫**language** 1491R30
▪tone ▫**language** 1534L84
▫modern ▪**languages** 911L10
▫Chinese ▪**lantern** 227L40
▫jack-o'-▪**lantern** 757R77
▪storm ▫**lantern** 695R5
in the ▫**lap** of ▪luxury 795R43
in the ▫**lap** of the ▪gods 795R47
▪**lap** against 795R60
▫**lap** of ▪honour 795R69
▫**lap** ▪up 795R53/54/56
▪**lapse** into 796L34
▪time-▫**lapse** 1521R81
▫**laptop** com▪puter 963R53
▪**lard** with 796L62
▫bulk ▪**large** 174L30
in (a) ▫**large** ▪part 1028L77
▫**large** in▪testine 796R15
▫loom ▪**large** 840L81
on the ▪**large** ▫side 1334L7
the ▫world at ▪**large** 1683R69
to a ▪**large** ex▫tent 486L43
▫writ ▪**large** 1691L72/74
▫**larger** than ▪life 796R12
▫**lark** a▪bout/a▪round 796R51
▫up with the ▪**lark** 796R36
▪**laser** ▫disc 797L16
▪**laser** ▫printer 797L19/23
▪**lash** against 797L30/44
▫**lash** a▪round 797L31
▪**lash** into 797L34
▫**lash** ▪out 797L41/43/37/67
▫**lash** ▪out for/on 797L70/69
▪**lash** to 797L63
▫**lash** to▪gether 797L64
▪under the ▫**lash** 797L52
▪tongue-▫**lashing** 1534R66
as a ▫**last** re▪sort 798L26
at ▫long ▪**last** 797R27
be▫fore ▪**last** 798L40
▫breathe *one's* ▪**last** 162R71
▫down to the ▪**last** 797R32
▫famous **last** ▪words 501L59
▫first and ▪**last** 525R16
▫hear the ▪**last** of *something* 656L31 798L17
in the ▫**last** a▪nalysis 43R42
in the ▫**last** re▪sort 798L26
▫**last** but not ▪least 797R37
▫**last**-▪ditch 797R41
▫**last**-▪gasp 797R41
▫**last** ▪laugh 797R46
▫**last** ▪minute 797R49/55/56
▪**last** ▫name 797R58 1468R72
▫**last** ▪night 798L32 955L68
▫**last** ▪orders 797R62
▫**last** ▪out 798L70
▫**last** ▪post 797R64
▫**last** re▪sort 1210L28
▫**last** ▪rites 797R66 1227L55
▫**last** ▪straw 1435R25
▫**Last** ▪Supper 797R70
▫**last** ▪thing 797R72 798L52/53 1512L3
▫**last** will and ▪testament 797R75
▫**last** ▪word 797R77
▫next-to-▪**last** 953R81
▫not **last** five ▪minutes 798L76
on *one's* ▫**last** ▪legs 798L19/22
▫pay *one's* **last** re▪spects 1210R83
▫see the ▪**last** of 1283L72
the ▫**last** ▪Judgment 771L68
the ▫**last** ▪thing 1512R47
the ▫**last** ▪time 797R40
▫too good to ▪**last** 611R34 798L67
with *one's* ▫**last** ▪breath 162R52
▫long-▪**lasting** 838L82
▫**latch** ▪on/▪onto 798R25/23/27
▪**latchkey** ▫child 798R33
▫**late** ▪bloomer 799L12
▫**late** de▪veloper 377R1 799L12
▫**late** in the ▪day 798R83
too ▫little too ▪**late** 798R83 1535L73
▫see you ▪**later** 1284L8
▫sooner or ▪**later** 1376L56
▫**lateral** ▪thinking 799L42
▫**Latin** ▪alphabet 1232L31
▫**Latin** A▪merican 799R5
▫**Latin** ▪lover 799R3
▪**latter**-day 799R39
▫**lattice** ▪window 799R56
▪belly ▫**laugh** 116L14
▫don't make me ▪**laugh** 799R83
for a ▪**laugh** 800L55
▫last ▪**laugh** 797R46
▫**laugh** all the way to the ▪bank 800L1
▪**laugh** at 799R76/77/80/81
▫**laugh** *one's* ▪head off 800L8
▫**laugh** like a ▪drain 800L14
▫**laugh** *something* ▪off 800L15
▫**laugh** on the other side of *one's* ▪face 800L17
▫**laugh** *someone* out of ▪court 800L25
▫**laugh** out of the other side of *one's* ▪mouth 800L18
▫**laugh** *oneself* ▪silly 800L23
▫**laugh** up *one's* ▪sleeve 800L27
▫make *someone* ▪**laugh** 799R82
not ▫know whether to ▫**laugh** or ▪cry 786R72
you've ▫got to ▪**laugh** 800L31
▫burst out ▪**laughing** 178L5
▪**laughing** ▫gas 800L33
▪**laughing** ▫jackass 788L64
▪**laughing** ▫stock 800L36/39
no ▪**laughing** ▫matter 800L29 874R37
a ▫barrel of ▪**laughs** 101L40
a ▫bundle of ▪**laughs** 175R59
for ▪**laughs** 800L55
▫burst into ▪**laughter** 177R83 1494R49
▫canned ▪**laughter** 188L38
▫gales of ▪**laughter** 580L48
▪**launch** *oneself* at 800L83
▪**launch** into/on 800R13/14
▫**launch** ▪out 800R17
▪**launch** ▫pad 800L84
▪**launch** ▫party 800R19
▪**laundry** ▫basket 800R34
▫**laundry** de▪tergent 1639R41
▫Poet ▪**Laureate** 1088R25/29
▪**laurel** ▫wreath 800R51 1689R83
▫look to *one's* ▪**laurels** 839R81
▫rest on *one's* ▪**laurels** 1212R61
lava▫torial ▪humour 800R69
a ▫**law** unto *one*▪self 801L32
▪blue ▫**law** 140L4
▪brother-in-▫**law** 169L14/16
▪case ▫**law** 201L63
▫civil ▪**law** 235L17
▫common ▪**law** 270R57
▫criminal ▪**law** 324L70
▪daughter-in-▫**law** 348R36
▪father-in-▫**law** 506R60
go to ▪**law** 801L35
inter▫national ▪**law** 744L20
▪**law**-a▫biding 801L41
▫**law** and ▪order 801L42
▪**law**-▫breaker 801L46
▪**law**-▫maker 801L51
▫**law** of ▪averages 801L78
law of ▫supply and de▪mand 801L82 1464R67
▫lay ▫down the ▪**law** 802R60
▪leash ▫**law** 806R27
▪lemon ▫**law** 810R19
long ▫arm of the ▪**law** 838L8
▪lynch ▫**law** 849R40
▫martial ▪**law** 869L8
▪mother-in-▫**law** 920R21
▫Murphy's ▪**law** 930R9
on the ▫right/▫wrong ▫side of the ▪**law** 1333R83
▪Parkinson's ▫**law** 1027L25
▫Roman ▪**law** 1232L41
▫rule of ▪**law** 1240L9
▪sister-in-▫**law** 1342R80/81
▫Sod's ▪**law** 930R9 1371L45
▪son-in-▫**law** 1375R30/31
take the ▫**law** into *one's* own ▪hands 801L37
the ▫**law** of the ▪jungle 801L53
the ▫letter of the ▪**law** 813L54
▫**lawn** ▪bowling 801R83
▪**lawn** ▫party 583L40 801R84
▫**lawn** ▪tennis 802L2
▪licensing ▫**laws** 817L58
▫**lay** a ▪finger on 802L62
▫**lay** a ▪hand on 802L63
▫**lay** ▪against 802R54
▫**lay** a▪side 802L36/37/R76
▫**lay** ▪back 802L39
▫**lay** ▪bare 99R43 802L81
▫**lay** ▫brother 802R14
▫**lay** *one's* ▫cards on the ▪table 195L36
▫**lay** ▪claim to 802R55
▫**lay** ▪down 802L40/R56/82/L42
▫**lay** down *one's* ▪life 802L46 818R58
▫**lay** ▫down the ▪law 802R60
▫**lay** ▪eyes on 236R73 488L73
▫**lay** ▪flat 802L50
▫**lay** *one's* ▪hands on 640L76
▫**lay** ▪in 803L1
▫**lay** ▪into 803L4
▫**lay** *someone* ▪low 802L83/R1
▫**lay** of the ▪land 818L48
▫**lay** ▪off 803L8/15/18
▫**lay** ▪on 802L34/R41/43/44 803L24/28/44
▫**lay** on the ▪line 802R45/46 824R4
▫**lay** ▪out in/on 803L34/32/40/42/45
▫**lay** ▪over 802L35
▫**lay** ▪sister 802R15
▫**lay** the ▪dining/▪kitchen ▫table 1483L61
▫**lay** the ▫ghost of *something* to ▪rest 802L71
▫**lay** to ▪rest 802L68/70
▫**lay** to ▪waste 802R4
▫**lay** ▪up 803L48/51
▫**lay** up ▪trouble 803L51
▫**lay** (to) ▪waste 802R3
▪**layer** ▫cake 803L76
▪**layer** with 803L82
▪ozone ▫**layer** 1013R63
▫**laying** ▫on of ▪hands 802L72
kill the ▫goose that **lays** the gold ▪egg 779R70
▫**lazy** ▪Susan 803R25
ex▫tension ▫**lead** 485R67/66
go down like a ▫**lead** bal▪loon 804R41
have/put ▪**lead** in *someone's* ▫pencil 804R61
▫**lead** *someone* a (merry) ▪chase/▪dance 804L32
▫**lead** *someone* by the ▪nose 803R
▪**lead** into 804L60

▫lead ▪off 804L31
▫lead ▪on 804R26
▪lead onto 804L52
▪lead over/through 804L25
▫lead-▪poisoning 804R40
▫lead the ▪field/▪pack/▪world 804L78
▫lead the life of ▪Riley 818R84
▫lead the ▪way 840L26/28 1645L59
▪lead ▫time 804L66
▪lead to 804L49/50
▫lead someone up/down the garden ▪path 804L35
▪lead with 804L31
▫sink like a ▫lead bal▪loon 1341R42 1429R21
▪lead-in 804L28/38/81
▫leaded ▪lights 804R47
▫leaded ▪windows 804R48
▫follow- my/the ▪leader 543R17
▪loss ▫leader 842L60
▪Scout ▫leader 1270L59
▪squadron ▫leader 1401R51
▫index of ▫leading eco▪nomic ▫indicators 721L34
▫leading ▪article 442L49 803R73
▫leading ▪edge 804R13/14
▫leading ▪hand 803R74
▫leading ▪lady/▪actress 803R75
▫leading ▪light 803R78
▫leading ▪man/▪actor 803R75
▫leading ▪question 804R31
the ▫blind leading the ▪blind 135R16
▪jump leads 772R33/32
▪jumper leads 772R32
▫one thing ▫leads to an▪other 1512L30
▫compound ▪leaf 277L65
▫drop-leaf ▪table 427R47
▪fig ▫leaf 516R66/68
▫four leaf ▪clover 556R50
▫gold ▪leaf 609R71
▪leaf ▫mould 805L9
▫leaf ▪through 805L51
▫loose-▪leaf 840R68
take a ▫leaf from/out of someone's ▪book 805L47
turn over a ▫new ▪leaf 1569R52
▪big ▫league 125L57
in the ▫same ▪league 1253L41
▫Ivy ▪League 757R37
▫Rugby ▪League 1239R9
▫leak ▪out 805R15/18
▪leak to 805R18
▫take a ▪leak 805R27
▪lean against 805R39/40
▫lean ▪forward 805R41
▪lean on 805R43/44
▫lean ▪over 805R48
▫lean over ▪backwards 91R26 805R49
▪lean to 805R47/51/53/79
▫flying ▪leap 540R13
▫leap in the ▪dark 806L25
▫leap out of one's ▪skin 1346R32
▫leap to ▪mind 806L14
▪leap ▫year 806L28
▫quantum ▪leap 1158R57
by/in ▫leaps and ▪bounds 806L22
▪learn about/of 806L51
▫learn by ▪rote 1235L84
▫learn one's ▫lesson the ▪hard way 806L56
▫learn the ▪ropes 1234L80
▫learn to ▪live with 806L58
▫live and ▪learn 831R61
▫learned ▪journal 806L68
my ▫learned ▪friend 565L74
▪distance ▫learning 398R62
▪learning ▫difficulties 383L5 806L81
▪rote ▫learning 1235R1
▫seat of ▪learning 1278R30
new ▫lease of ▪life 952L51
new ▫lease on ▪life 952L51
▪leash ▫law 806R27
it is/was the ▫least one can/could ▪do 806R48
▫last but not ▪least 797R37
▫path/▫line of ▫least re▪sistance 1209R2
to ▫say the ▪least 806R57 1259L84
▫hell for ▪leather 661L47▫tough as ▪shoe leather 1541R5
▫ leave ▪go of 807R33
com▫passionate ▪leave 273R22
▫French ▪leave 563R26
▫leave a bad/a sour/an unpleasant ▪taste 807L69
▫leave a ▫lot to be de▪sired 807L71
▫leave a▪side 807R25
▫leave be▪hind 807L8/10
▫leave someone ▪cold 807L73
▪leave ▫some for 807L13/18/62
▫leave someone high and ▪dry 667L47
▫leave someone holding the ▪baby/▪bag 807L77
▫leave in the ▪lurch 807L80
▫leave in the ▪shade 1304R70
▫leave ▫something in one's ▪wake 1634L27
▫leave one's ▪mark 865R30
▫leave ▫no stone un▪turned 807L83
▫leave of ▪absence 807R64
▫leave ▪off 807L48/R29/31/32
▫leave ▪out 807L50
leave ▫out in the ▪cold 807L75
▫leave ▪over 807L19
▫leave someone standing/on the ▪sidelines 807R4
▪leave-▫taking 807R68
leave the ▪door ▫open 807R2
leave the ▫field ▪clear 516L27
▫leave ▪doing something till/to 807L65
▫leave someone to their own de▪vices 807R6
▫leave up in the ▪air 807R8
▫leave ▫well a▪lone 807R10 1651R44
▪leave with 807L23/R50/52
ma▪ternity ▫leave 873R84
▪sick ▫leave 1332R72
▫take it or ▪leave it 1486R10
▫take ▪leave 807R66
take ▫leave of one's ▪senses 807R70 1292R64
without so much as a ▫by your ▪leave 807R56 1674L46
▫four leaved ▪clover 556R50
▪school ▫leaver 1265R6
school-▪leaving age 1265R9
▪lech after 808L3
▪lecture in/on 808L18/21/24/26/23
▫LE▪D dis▫play 808L40
▪window-▫ledge 1668L51/77
▫cock-a-▪leekie 252R36
▪leer at 808L9
▫left ▪field 808R25
▫left-hand ▪drive 808R31
▫left-▪handed 808R30/34/38
▫left handed ▪compliment 808R40
▫left-▪luggage office 807R14
▫left ▪wing 808R51
▫left-▪winger 808R52
out in ▪left ▫field 808R28
▫right ▫left and ▪centre 1223R72
▫stage ▪left 1406R26
talk the ▫hind leg(s) off a ▪donkey 1488R7
a ▫leg to ▪stand on 809L7
an ▫arm and a ▪leg 62R28
get one's ▪leg ▫over 809L9
give someone a ▫leg ▪up 809L10
have a ▫leg ▪up on 809L12
▫inside ▪leg 734R64
▫leg before ▪wicket 809L17
▪leg it 809L28
▪leg-▫puller 809L16
▪peg-▫leg 1043L84
▫pull someone's ▪leg 809L13 1144L60
▫pull the ▪other leg (it's got ▪bells on) 1144L63
▫shake a ▪leg 1307R6
without a ▫leg to ▪stand on 809L6
▫legal ▪aid 809L51
▫legal ▪tender 809L54
▫make legal ▪history 809L49
▫bow-▪legged 154L59
▫cross-▪legged 327R36
▫three-legged ▪race 1515L68
▫Foreign ▪Legion 563R15
▫French Foreign ▪Legion 563R15
legion▪naire's dis▫ease 809R58
▪legislate against 809R63
▫legislative as▪sembly 809R71
▫legislative ▪council 809R77
as ▫fast as one's legs would ▪carry one 505R40
go off/away with one's ▫tail between one's ▪legs 1485R29
on one's ▫last ▪legs 798L19/22
▪sea ▫legs 1276L13
▫stretch one's ▪legs 1439L77
take the ▪weight off one's ▫legs 1650L11
▪leisure ▫centre 810L65
▫bitter ▪lemon 130R63
▫lemon ▪curd/▪cheese 810R14
▫lemon ▪grass 810R17
▪lemon ▫law 810R19
▫lemon ▪sole 810R21
▫lemon ▪squash 810R22
lend someone a helping ▪hand 662L38
▫lend an ▪ear 810R46
▫lend one's ▪name to 810R52
▪lending ▫library 810R54
▪lending ▫rate 810R57
at ▫arm's ▪length 62R24
▪calf-▫length 184L36
▪feature-▫length 509L65
▫focal ▪length 541R58
▫full ▪length 572R47/48/50/51
▪knee-▫length 782R84
▫stretch the ▪length of 1439R72
the ▫length and ▪breadth 810R81
three-▪quarter ▫length 1515R2
go to ▫great/▫any ▪lengths 811L23
▫Marxist-▪Leninist 869R34/33/21
▫fish-eye ▪lens 526L79
▫telephoto ▪lens 1496R73
▪contact ▫lenses 294R22
the ▫lesser of two ▪evils 811R83
▫learn one's ▫lesson the ▪hard way 806L56
▪object ▫lesson 970R28
re▪medial ▫lesson 1201L78
▫teach a ▪lesson 812L18 1494L57
let a▫lone 812R51
▫let something be ▪known 812R12
let ▫bygones be ▪bygones 181R15
▫let ▪down 812L81/83/R75
▫let's ▪face it 812R35
▫let ▪go 812R1/2
▫let something ▪go/▪pass 812L40
let one's ▪hair ▫down 812L49
▫let someone ▪in 812L52
▫let into 812L54/56/R6
let it ▫all hang ▪out 812L58
▫let it ▪slip/▪drop 812L72
▫let it/▫things ▪lie 812L61
▫let someone ▪know 812R8
▫let ▪loose 840R52
▫let me ▪see 1283R72
let ▫nature take its ▪course 943L6
▫let ▪off 812L63/66/R14 1269R52
▫let off ▪steam 812R16
▫let ▪on 812R64 813L4/11
▫let ▪on about 813L6
▫let ▪out 251L15 812L68/70/R21/22
▫let something ▪ride 1222L25
▫let ▪rip/▪fly 812R24/28
▫let's ▪see 812R36
▫let ▪slip/▪drop/▪fall 629L65 812L71/74
let the ▪cat out of the ▫bag 203L51
let the ▪dust ▫settle 433L14
let the ▪side ▫down 812R80 1334L26
▪let something to 144L64 812R60
▫let ▪up 813L9
▫live and ▪let live 832R5
without ▫let or ▪hindrance 812R71
▫lethal ▪dose 412R73
▪chain ▫letter 212L62
▪covering ▫letter 316L35
▫dead ▪letter 350R41/44
▫four-letter ▪word 556R53
▫French ▪letter 563R30
▪letter ▫bomb 813L37
▪letter ▫carrier 813L39 1101R67
▫letter of ▪credit 813L40
▪letter ▫opener 813L45 1023L43
▫letter-▪perfect 813L62 1678R31
▪love ▫letter 843R45
▫open ▪letter 988L54
▫poison-▪pen ▫letter 1090R17
red-▪letter ▫day 1189L20
▫silent ▪letter 1337R4
the ▫letter of the ▪law 813L54
▫block ▪letters 136R22
▫man of ▪letters 858R73
▪A/▪S ▫level 70R14
at/on an▫other/a ▫deeper ▪level 813R59
▫do one's level ▪best 813R27
find one's ▫own ▪level 813R65
▪ground ▫level 626L58 813R56
▫high-▪level 668R37
▫high-level ▪language 667R65
▫high-level ▪waste 667R69
▪level against/at 814L59
▪level something at 814L59
▫level ▪crossing 813R32
▫level-▪headed 813R36
▫level ▪off/▪out 813R78/74
▫level ▪playing ▫field 813R31
▪level with 813R13/14/17/39 814L61
▪O ▫level 969L61
on a more ▫serious ▪level 813R60
▪Ordinary ▫level 994R75
▪sea ▫level 1276L16
▫sink to such a ▪level 1341R75
▪spirit-level 1393R26
▫split-▪level 1395L3
▫top-▪level 1537L84
▪gear ▫lever 586L14
▫lever ▪arch ▫file 814L78
▫lever ▪up 814L84
▫leveraged ▪buyout 814R66
▪ley ▫line 815R74
li▪aise with 816L23
▫ad ▪lib 17L44/48
▫Lib ▪Dem 816L48
▫women's ▪lib 816L42/44 1675R72 1675R76
▫liberal ▪arts 816L70
▫Liberal ▪Democrats 816R8
▪Liberal ▫Party 816R12
▪liberate someone from 816R30
▫gay liber▪ation 585R10
liber▫ation the▪ology 816R42
▫women's liber▪ation 1675R72
▫take ▪liberties with 816R77/79
▫civil ▪liberty 234R59
▫take the ▪liberty of 816R74
▪lending ▫library 810R54
▫mobile ▪library 909L64
▪reference ▫library 1191L8
▪crab ▫lice 318L75
▪driver's ▫licence 425L51
▪driving ▫licence 425L51
▫licence to ▫print ▪money 817L47
po▫etic ▪licence 1088R46
pro▫visional ▪licence 1139L82
▫under ▪licence 817L51
▪driver's ▫license 425L51
▫license plate ▪number 817L52 1193R82
▫licensed ▫practical ▪nurse 817L61
▪licensing ▫laws 817L58
a ▫lick and a ▪promise 817R16
▫lick into ▪shape 1311L8
▫lick one's ▪lips 817R4
▫lick one's ▪wounds 817R12
▪salt-▫lick 1251R44
▪arse-▫licker 65L32
▪ass-▫licker 65L32
▫lickety-▪split 817R39
▫ put/▫keep the ▪lid on 817R46
▫blow one's ▪lid 139L42
▫blow the ▪lid off 138R78
▫flip one's ▪lid 535L7/4
▪pen ▫lid 1044L45
▫put a ▪lid on 817R52
▫put the ▪lid on 817R50
▫take/▫blow the ▪lid off 817R47
▫give the ▪lie 818L70
▫let it/▫things ▪lie 812L61
▪lie about 818L56/57
▫lie a▪bout/a▪round 818L16/21
▫lie ▪back 89L27 817R63
▫lie be▪hind 818L2
▪lie de▫tector 818L73
▫lie ▪doggo 409L69 818L23
▫lie ▪down 817R66/67 818L43
▫lie ▪down on the ▫job 818L25
▪lie in 818L5/27/45
▫lie in ▪state 818L29
▫lie in ▪wait 1633R63
▫lie ▪low 818L31
▫lie through one's ▪teeth 818L61
▫lie ▪up 818L37
▪lie with 803L50 818L11
▫live a ▪lie 832L84
▫nail a ▪lie 935R79
▫tell a ▪lie 818L72 1498L27
the ▫lie of the ▪land 818L47
▫white ▪lie 1660R40
a ▫pack/▫tissue of ▪lies 818L68
find out/see how the ▪land ▫lies 794L13
▫tell lies 818L72 1498L27
▫flight lieu▪tenant 534L48
a ▫charmed ▪life 219L19
a ▪dog's ▫life 408R57
a ▫slice of ▪life 1352L49
be/go/live in ▫terror of one's ▪life 1505L10
▫breathe ▪life into 162R69
▫bring to ▪life 818R47
▫come to ▪life 818R50
de▫part this ▪life 367L13
▫fact of ▪life 492R22
▫facts of ▪life 492R24
for ▫dear ▪life 352L26
▫give/▫lay down one's ▪life 818R58
▫give one's ▪life 596R37
▪half-▫life 637R64
▪high ▫life 667R73
▫how's life treating ▪you? 818R61
in ▫fear of one's ▪life 508L73
it's the ▫story of my ▪life 1432L59
▫kiss of ▪life 781R81
▫larger than ▪life 796R12
▫lay down one's ▪life 802L46
▫lead/▫live the life of ▪Riley 818R84
▪life-af▫firming 819L22
▫life after ▪death 818R62
▫life and ▪death 818R64
life and ▫soul of the ▪party 818R68
▪life ▫belt 819L24/58
▪life ▫buoy 819L24
▪life ▫cycle 819L27
▪life ex▫pectancy 819L32
▪life ▫form 819L35
▪life-▫giving 819L37
▫life ▪history 672L53 819L28/39
▫life im▪prisonment 819L42
▪life in▫surance 738R83 819L46
▫life is just a ▫bowl of ▪cherries 154R29
▪life ▫jacket 819L51/59
▫life ▪peer 819L54
▪life ▫peerage 819L58
▪life pre▫server 819L58
▪life ▫raft 819L59
▫life's rich ▪tapestry 818R75
▪life-▫saver 819L64/66/62
▪life ▫science 819L69
▫life ▪sentence 819L74
▪life-▫size(d) 819L72
▪life ▫story 819L39
▫life-sup▪port system 819L80/83
▪life-▫threatening 819R4
▫life's ▪work 819R6
▫live one's own ▪life 832R11
▫long-▪life 838L84
▪lotus ▫life 842R70
▪love ▫life 843R9
▪low ▫life 844R49
▫make someone's life ▪hell 661L55
▫make/▫start a new ▪life 818R77
▫matter of ▫life and/or ▪death 874R29
▫mid-life ▪crisis 893R48
new ▫lease of ▪life 952L51
new ▫lease on ▪life 952L51
▫not to ▫save my ▪life 1257R58
▫one/an▫other of ▫life's great ▪mysteries 818R72
▫pro-▪life 1130R11
▫public ▪life 818R17 1142L34
▫quality of ▪life 1158L36
▫real ▪life 1179R41
▫right-to-▪life 1223R36
▫school of ▪life 1265R29
▫see ▪life 1284L20
▪sex ▫life 818R18 1303R52
▪shelf ▫life 1314R14
▪social ▫life 1370L40
▫still ▪life 1425L67
▫such is ▪life 1455L39
▫take one's (own) ▪life 819L7
▫take one's ▫life in one's ▪hands 819L8
the ▫bane of someone's ▪life 97L34
the ▫best days of someone's ▪life 118R73
the ▫light of someone's ▪life 820R9
the ▫man/▫woman in someone's ▪life 818R78
the ▫miracle of ▪life 902R22
the ▫staff of ▪life 1406L20
the ▫time of one's ▪life 1524L1
▫true-life ▪story 1563R21
▫true-to-▪life 1563R24
▫walk(s) of ▪life 1634R46
▫way of ▪life 1646L18
▫working ▪life 1681R50 1682L35
▫how's ▪life? 690R29
▫once in a ▪lifetime 819R79 983L58/59
▪chair ▫lift 212R1
▪drag ▫lift 418L60
▫fork-lift (▪truck) 551L60
▫lift a ▪finger 521R81
▫lift ▪down 820L31
▫lift one's ▫eyes ▪heavenward 658R61
▫lift ▪off 820L26/32
▫lift ▪up 820L3
▪ski ▫lift 1345R73
▪arc ▫light 60L75
▪brake ▫light 157R34
▫bring to ▪light 820R10
▫cast/▫shed/▫throw ▪light on 820R13
▫come to ▪light 820R10
▫first ▪light 525R81
▪fog ▫light 542L25
give the ▫green ▪light 622L67
go ▫out like a ▪light 820R17
▫green-▪light 622L68
▫guiding ▪light 630R53
▪half-▫light 637R67
▪hazard (▪warning) ▫light 652R48
in a ▫bad ▪light 820R20
in the ▫light of 820R23
▫leading ▪light 803R78
▫light ▪aircraft 821L55
▫light at the ▫end of the ▪tunnel 820R4
▪light ▫bulb 820R26
▫light ▪cream 1341L13
▫light-▪fingered 821L56
▪light ▫globe 820R30
▫light-▪headed 821L57
▫light ▪heart 821L81
▫light-▪hearted 821L78
▫light ▪heavyweight 821L60
▫light ▪industry 821L62
▪light ▫meter 820R31
▪light on/upon 822L7
▪light-▫open 820R37
▫light ▪railway 821L64
▫light ▪up 820R77
▪light ▫year 820R40
▪light years a▫way 820R42
▫make ▪light of 821L82
▪parking ▫light 1027L7 1334L64
▫red ▪light 1189L23
red-▪light ▫district 1189L25
▫see the ▪light 1283R38
▫see the light of ▪day 1284L22
▪strobe ▫light 1445L6
▫sweetness and ▪light 1476L26
the ▫light of someone's ▪life 820R9
▪traffic ▫light 1547R61/64
▫trick of the ▪light 1556R83

lighten *someone's* burden/load 821L66
lighten up 821R45
cigarette lighter 232L27
lighting-up time 820R54
strip lighting 1444R44
lightning conductor 822L22
lightning rod 822L23/27
lightning strike 822L31
like a streak of lightning 1436L14
like greased lightning 621R2
sheet lightning 1314L59
fairy lights 495R79
house lights 689R45
leaded lights 804R47
tail lights 1485R20
the Northern lights 961L79
like to 822L56/58/R6/7/9/12/14/19/20
well-liked 1653L17
a likely story 823L26
gild the lily 595L32
lily-livered 823L67
lily of the valley 823L67
lily pad 823L69
lily-white 823L71/73/75
water lily 1642R14
lima bean 823L78
limber up 823R8
lime cordial 823R25
lime-green 823R27
steal the limelight 1418L9
speed limit 1389L23
the sky's the limit 1348L3
time limit 1522L1
damage limitation 344L68
limited edition 442L70 824L31
stretch limo 1438R27/28
limp wrist 824L65/68/69
all along the line 826L23
assembly line 72L28/32/33
bar line 99L10
bottom line 152L70/73
branch line 157R68
chat-up line 220L52 826L63
clothes line 248R12 824R57
color line 260L34
come-on line 220L52 826L64
crossed line 327R39
dotted line 413R9
down the line 416L77 826L25
draw the line at 419R55
drop *someone* a line 427R14
fall in/into line 498R12
fault line 507R9/11
feed *someone* a line 510L20
go/come on line 825R83
goal line 608L38
hard-line 646R68
hook line and sinker 684L22
in-line skate 713R37 1231R82
in/on the firing line 523R23/26/22/26
in the front line 568R46
in the line of duty 826R27
International Date Line 744L15
lay on the line 802R45/46 824R45
ley line 815R74
line drawing 824R22
line item 826L43
line manager 826R37
line of least resistance 1209R2
line *one's* pocket(s) 825R46
line up 825L82/63 1162L25
line up against 825L81/83
line up behind 825L78
line up for 825L74
line up to 825L77
main line 826L10 853R59
Mason-Dixon Line 870L75
parallel line 1024R29
party line 1030R29/52
picket line 1063L33
Plimsoll line 1082L21
plot line 1082R33
plumb line 1084R16
poverty line 1105L21
production line 1127L38
punch line 1146R11
put on the line 824R43
sign on the dotted line 1336L37
somewhere along the line 826L20
starting line 824R39 1413R64
step out of line 1420L59
story line 1432L65
the end of the line 826L14
three-line whip 1515L71 1659L49
throwaway line 1517L81
toe the line 1531L82
yellow line 1696L41
tree-lined 1554R67
bed linen 111L57 826R78
linen basket 826R82
table linen 826R80 1483L65
wash *one's* dirty linen in public 1639L74
bin liner 127L3
dustbin liner 433L50
hard-liner 646R70
liner note 825R53
panty liner 1022R68
trash can liner 433L51 1552R37
contour lines 298L17
read between the lines 1178L83
ting-a-ling 1525L35
linger on 827L39/41
linger over 827L42
lingua franca 827L69
linguistic science 827R8
cuff link 334L14
fast link 505L74
link together 827R33/34
link up 827R49/60
link with 827R24/57
missing link 906L55/59
weak link 1646R54
index-linked 721L37
sex-linked 1303L79
linking verb 827R36
golf links 827R64
linseed oil 827R76
beard the lion in *his/her* den 108R49
lion's den 828L55
lion-hearted 828L58
lion's share 828L59
mountain lion 310R74 923L35
sea lion 1276L19
feed to the lions 509R81
cleft lip 243R3
curl *one's* lip 336R32
give/pay lip service to 828L76
lip gloss 601L29 828R37
lip-read 828R39/42
lip salve 828R43
lip-smacking 828R45
lip-sync(h) 828R47
stiff upper lip 1424L60
tight-lipped 1520L10
lick *one's* lips 817R4
lips *are* sealed 828L80
on everyone's lips 828L83
smack *one's* lips 1357L55
biological washing liquid 127R64
dish liquid 393R81
liquid courage 433L78 829L6
liquid-crystal display 829L7
Liquid Paper 829L13 1526R10 1661L29
washing liquid 1639R40
washing-up liquid 1639R38
cannot hold *one's* liquor 675R81
hard liquor 647L55
fleur-de-lis 533R1
a list as long as *one's* arm 829R10
civil list 234R63
danger list 345R27
hit list 673L48
honours list 683L76
list price 829R12
mailing list 853R21
on the sick-list 1332R65
reading list 1179L13
shit list 1317R82
short list 1322L55/60
transfer list 1550L48/50
waiting list 1633R52
heritage-listed building 665L1 829R19
listed building 829R18
listed company 829R22
listen to reason 1181R57
easy listening 438R58
lit crit 830L14
wagon-lit 1633L29
literary agent 830L78
literary criticism 326L38 830L79
litmus test 830R72
litter lout 831L8
litter with 831L12/16/18
a little bird told me (so) 831L35
cut very little ice with 338R81
don't worry your pretty little head 1685R79
little by little 831L63
little finger 831L39
little fish 831R35
little folk 831L42
little love lost between 843R36
little one 831L74
little people 831L41
little something 831L44/R36
little to choose between 229L49
little toe 831L47
little wonder (that) 1676R29
make little of 831R34
nice little earner 954L55
put/set little store 1431R33
something a little stronger 1375L14
there's little to be said for 1259R83
too little too late 798R83 1535L73
twist/wrap *someone* around/round *one's* little finger 1573R84 1689L69
learn to live with 806L58
live a lie 832L84
live and breathe 832R3
live and learn 831R61
live and let live 832R5
live by/on *one's* wits 832R14
live down 832R63
live for 831R57 832L72
live in 832L17/18/19/20/25/36
live in clover 249R78
live-in lover/boyfriend 832L34
live in sin 832L30
live in terror of *one's* life 1505L10
live (on) in the memory 832R36
live it up 832R59
live like a king/lord 832R10
live off/on 832L46/48/49/21/50/51/R35
live on borrowed time 149R61
live out 832L22/74/76 999R55
live *one's* own life 832R11
live the life of Riley 818R84
live to fight another day 831R64
live to tell the tale 831R66
live together 832L29
live up to 832R68
live wire 832R47
live with 832L23/30/80
live with/through 832L77
live without 832L82
long live *someone* 838R35
not live up to expectation(s) 480R81
short-lived 1322R79
look lively 839R47
liven up 833L8
cod-liver oil 254L10
liver sausage 833L16
lily-livered 823L67
how the other half lives 637L65
cost of living 309R41
cost of living index 309R45 1214R78
living death 831R84
living memory 832L8
living room 832L38
living room suite 832L41 1515L77
living standard 1411R54
living wage 832L60 1632R67
living will 832L1
make an honest living 681R14
owe *someone* a living 1012R10
scrape a living 1271L72
standard of living 1411R53
the land of the living 794L44
lo and behold 114R62 833L53
a load of (old) rubbish 1238R56
a load off *one's* mind 898R61
get a load of 833L74
lighten *someone's* load 821L66
load onto 833R2
shoot *one's* load 1319R55
front loader 568L39
loading bay 833R5
loading dock 833R6
bucket-loads 171R46
cottage loaf 310R21
French loaf 94L17 563R32
granary loaf 617R57
meat loaf 880L65
use *one's* loaf 1601R68
bridging loan 164L44
home loan 679R84
loan shark 833R75
savings and loan association 173R12 1257R83
student loan 1447R12
lob *something* into 834L28
lob *something* over 834L27
division lobby 402R13
lobby correspondent 834L51
lobby for/against 834L40
frontal lobotomy 568L69
lobster pot 834L77
local authority 834R8
local boy made good 155R62
local colour 834R11
local derby 370L65 834R14
local government 834R16
local time 834R19
locate at 834R67
locate in 834R68/71
locate on 834R69
anti-lock 50L16
lock away/up 835L66/68/70
lock horns 835R24
lock in 835L65/74/R15/16
lock keeper 835R7
lock out 835L76/R60
lock stock and barrel 835L17
lock up 835L79/80
mortise lock 350R34 919R41
under lock and key 835L83/R1
locker room 835R42/45
in loco parentis 732L50
lodge in 836L35/59/60/61
lodge with 836L37/68/72/73
motor lodge 920L39 921R10
board and lodging 141R17 836L42
lodging house 836L45
pigeon loft 1065R38
as easy as falling off a log 438R39
log book 836R48
log cabin 836R27
log in/on 836R64
log in/out 836R60/61
log in to 836R62
log jam 836R28
log off/out 836R66
log up 836R56/59
sleep like a log 1351L51
yule log 1698R75
fuzzy logic 578R54
logic circuit 837L24
logic device 837L24
gird (up) *one's* loins 595R71
loiter about 837L82/84
loll about/around 837R14
loll out 837R16
cough lollies 311L14
lollipop man/lady 837R18
ice lolly 700L3
lone parent/mother/father 837R38
lone wolf 837R39
lonely hearts 837R53
by/on *one's* lonesome 837R73
a list as long as *one's* arm 829R10
a long way to go 838L9
as long as *one's* arm 838L7
as/so long as 838R62
at long last 797R27
before (very/too) long 838L71
go a long way 838L16
go a long way towards 838L14
go back a long way 838L17
have come a long way 838L12
in the long run 1241R23/26
in the long term 1501R21
long arm of the law 838L8
long-distance 838L20
long division 838L24
long-drawn-out 838R33
long dress 838L27
long drink 838L29
long-established 469L7
long face 838L32
long for 838R53
long in the tooth 838L79
long johns 838L33
long jump 838L35
long-lasting 838L82
long-life 838L84
long live *someone* 838R35
long-lost 838R40
long memory 838L38
long-range 838L40
long-running 838R43
long shot 838L42
long-sighted 838L45
long-standing 838R45 1412L21
long-suffering 838R47
long suit 838L49
long-time 838R3
long vacation 838R4
long wave 1644R61
long weekend 838R6
long-winded 838L51
not by a long chalk/shot 838L20
not last long 798L76
not long for this world 838R39
so long 838L70
take a long hard look at 840L9
take long 1486R80
the long and the short of 838L77
think long and hard 1513L45
to cut a long story short 339L57
before much longer 838L72
no longer 838L73
daddy longlegs 319R75 342L78/79/80/81 649L75
chaise longue 212R32
black look 131R75
by the look of things/it 839R62
dirty look 388L27
look after 840L27
look ahead 840L17
look-alike 839R53
look alive/lively/sharp 839R47
look askance 70L74
look at 839L20/21/49/80 840L5/6/7
look at/over/through 839R76
look back 839L27
look daggers 839L43
look down *one's* nose 839L34
look down on 839L34
look for 839R11/12/24 840L21/52
look for trouble 839R13 1561L76
look forward 840L39
look in 839L44 840L69
look in on 839L47/48
look *someone* in the eye/face 839L50
look into 839R16
look kindly on 839L52
look like 822R38 839R38/39/42/44
look like a million dollars/bucks 897R5
look like death warmed up/over 352R4
look on *someone* as 840L47/48
look on the bright side 839L55
look on/upon 840L45
look onto 840L14
look out 839R17 840L50
look out for number one 840L52
look over 839L29/R79
look-see 839L82
look small 839R50 1358L13
look the part 1028R53
look to 839R80 840L20/21/22/23
look to *one's* laurels 839R81
look towards 840L19
look up 381L75 839L40/R21 840L66
look up to 839L41
look who's talking 1488R24
never look back 839L30
take a long hard look at 840L9
throw a look 1517L8
wet-look 1654R9
good/nice looker 839R65
backward-looking 91R34
forward-looking 555R27
looking glass 598R1 839L66
good looks 611R48/50
loom large 840L81
loony bin 840R5
loop the loop 840R24
all hell breaks loose 661L24
at a loose end 840R60
cut loose 339R80
hang/stay loose 840R61
have a screw loose 1272R84
let loose 840R52
loose change 840R62
loose covers 840R64
loose ends 840R66
loose-fitting 841L16
loose-leaf 840R68
loosen *one's* grip 840R77
loosen up 841L2/6
lop off 841L54
lop *something* off/from 841L56
live like a lord 832R10
lord it over *someone* 841R1
lord of all one surveys 1470L78
Lord's Prayer 841R24
Lord's Supper 841R26
House of Lords 689R32
articulated lorry 66L64 841R45
dustbin lorry 433L54
tipper lorry 1526L55
lose count of 312L30
lose ground 842L72
lose *one's* head 841R75
lose heart 657L19 841R66
lose *one's* heart to 841R67
lose *one's* marbles 841R78
lose *one's* mind 841R80
lose out 842L68
lose *one's* rag 842L1 841R83
lose *one's* shirt 842L3/2
lose sight of 842L4 1335R22
lose sleep over/about 842L6
lose the day 842L70/72 1492L79
lose the toss 1539R34
lose to 842L67
lose track 842L8
no time to lose 1521R55
fight a losing battle 517L33
dead loss 351L35
loss adjuster 17L30 842L57
loss leader 842L60
cut *one's* losses 339L55
get lost 842L33
long-lost 838R40
lost-and-found office 842L40
lost cause 206R26 842L35
lost property 842L37
lost property office 842L39
make up for lost time 856R61
no/little love lost between 843R36
cleansing lotion 241R75
lotus eater 842R68
lotus life 842R70
lotus position 842R71
for crying out loud 331R76
loud and clear 842R81
cocktail lounge 253R48
departure lounge 367L31
lounge around/about 843L41
lounge bar 843L31
lounge room 832L39 843L35
lounge suit 843L36
head louse 653R35
louse up 843L54/55
litter lout 831L8
lager louts 792R73
lovable rogue 843R54
cupboard love 335R42
fall in love 498R8

free love 561L20
labour of love 789R70
love affair 21R82 843R38
love child 843R42
love for 843R83
love handles 843R44
love letter 843R45
love life 843R9
love-making 843R32
love to 843R80/81/83
love triangle 470L11
make love 843R33/31
no/little love lost between 843R36
puppy love 1148L27
tug-of-love 1567L28
young love 1698L63
loved one 843L76
Latin lover 799R3
live-in lover/boyfriend 832L34
peace-loving 1039R63
at a low ebb 439R18
high and low 667R14
lay someone low 802L83/R1
lie low 818L31
low church 844R1
low-cut 844L38/40
low-down 844R52
low-key 844R6
low life 844R49
low-lying 844L40
low-pitched 844R63
low-rise 844L42
low season 844R8
low spirited 844R68 1393L43
low-tech 844R13
low tide 844L44
low water 844L44 1642L59
low water mark 844L46
return a low rate of interest 1217L37
sink so low 1341R76
lower case 845L6
lower class 845L11/9
lower house 689R31/36 845L15
lower one's sights 1335R51
lower oneself to 844R58
lowest common denominator 844R16
lowest rung of the ladder 1243R15
brand loyalty 158L20
lube job 845R27
as proud as Lucifer 845R58
bad luck on someone 846L8
beginner's luck 114L16
best of luck 119L46
better luck next time 120R18
down on one's luck 846L9
hard luck 646R32/36
hard-luck story 646R72
in luck 846L14
just somebody's luck 774L66
luck into 846L29
luck of the draw 846L18
luck out 846L32
more by luck than judgment 846L20
no such luck 846L23/25
not believe one's luck 115L79
pot luck 1103R35
rough luck 1236L23
try one's luck 1566L18
worse luck 1686L72
get lucky 846L53
happy-go-lucky 645R28
lucky dip 846L59
should be so lucky 846L64
strike it lucky 1442R8
thank one's lucky stars 1507L5
lug around/about/round 846R9
excess luggage 476R32
hand luggage 641L13
left-luggage office 807R14
luggage label 846R27
luggage rack 846R30
luggage tag 846R27
luggage van 846R32
lull into 847L10
the lull before the storm 847L16
lumber jacket 847L47
son et lumière 1375R48
a lump in one's throat 847R7
lump it 847R35
lump of sugar 847L84
lump sum 847R14
lump together 847R20/23
lump with 847R22
take one's lumps 847R12
lunar month 847R71
lunatic asylum 75L84 847R64
the lunatic fringe 847R61
bag lunch 155L29
box lunch 155L28 1016L15
brown-bag lunch 169L56
counter lunch 312R25
cut lunch 339L27 1016L16
lunch hour 848L6
lunch meat 848L19
lunch on 848L12
lunch room 848L8
lunch with 848L11
packed lunch 1016L15
power lunch 1105R22
luncheon meat 848L19
luncheon voucher 848L23
Aqua Lung 59R10
iron lung 752R33
lunge at/toward(s) 848L50/52/55
have good lungs 848L46
leave in the lurch 807L80
lurch forward 848L66
lurch from 848L67/69/72
lurch to 848L68/70/72/77
lure into 848R4/7
dreaded lurgy 421L66
lurk about 848R33
lurk behind 848R34
lurk in 848R33/37
blood lust 137L63
lust after/for 848R76
de luxe 363R12
luxuriate in 849L55
in the lap of luxury 795R43
luxury goods/item 849L66
low-lying 844L40
take lying down 818L40 1486L57
lymph gland 849R28
lymph node 849R28
lynch law 849R40
lynch mob 849R38
macaroni cheese 850L59
papier-mâché 1023R8
deus ex machina 377L11
answering machine 48L69/R25
automated teller machine 82L69
cash machine 201R37
cog in a/the machine 255L33
drinks machine 424L52
drum machine 428R75
fruit machine 569R51 1355L47
kidney machine 779R33
machine code 850R44
machine gun 850R56/58
machine-readable 850R42
machine tool 850R63
machine translation 850R46
milking machine 897L18
pinball machine 1068L2
poker machine 1090R77 1355L47
sanding machine 1254L32
sausage machine 1257L79
sewing machine 1303L26
slot machine 1355L46/50 1612L65
time machine 1521L7
vending machine 1612L64
voting machine 1631L26
washing machine 1639R30
Apple Macintosh 851L8
drive someone mad 425L80
go mad 605L27
like mad 822R50
mad cow disease 851L49
a marriage made in heaven 868L8
custom-made 338R8
local boy made good 155R62
made of money 855L26 913R22
made of sterner stuff 1421R76
made-to-measure 851R40
made-up 851R42/44
man-made 859L58
mind is made up 899L58
ready-made 1179L72
tailor-made 1485R64/68/73
method to/in one's madness 891R74/75
glossy magazine 601L43
black magic 131R76
magic carpet 852L51
magic wand 852L52
magic word 852L56
white magic 1660R42
work like magic 1682L14
milk of magnesia 896R79
magnetic field 852R54
magnetic head 852R57
magnetic north/south 852R58
magnetic poles 852R60
magnetic resonance imaging 852R65
magnetic tape 852R69
magnifying glass 853L16
order of magnitude 994R35
magnum opus 853L35
mah-jong 853L51
maid of honour 853L66
old maid 979R84
maiden aunt 853L73
maiden name 853L70
maiden speech 853L78
by return mail 1217L19
certified mail 211L78
chain mail 212L42
direct mail 386R61
e-mail 446R83 448R65
electronic mail 446R83
fan mail 501R54
hate mail 650L82
junk mail 773R49
mail carrier 853R11
mail drop 8R10
mail order 853R12
mail slot 813L67
registered mail 1193R76
voice mail 1629L71
electronic mailbox 447L1
mailing list 853R21
mass mailing 853R40 870R55
have an eye to/for the main chance 488L67
main course 315L20 853R53
main drag 853R57
main line 826L10 853R59
main road 853R62
main street 853R65
main verb 853R66
water main 853R73 1642R16
grant-maintained school 619L1
health maintenance organization 655R11
maintenance order 854L63
maitre d' 854L76
detain at His/Her Majesty's pleasure 375L59
Her/His Majesty's Government 614R44
drum major 428R77
major-general 854R30
major in 854R40
sergeant major 1296L18
drum majorette 428R78 854R55
absolute majority 5R14
majority rule 854R68
moral majority 917R27
silent majority 1337L84
can't make head (n)or tail of 654L26
Do you want to make something of it? 856L30
don't make me laugh 799R83
have or make a stab at something 1405L27
if I may make so bold (as to) 144R38
make a complete ass of 71L46
make a beeline for 112R68
make a bet with 120L5
make a bolt for 145L60
make a bundle 175R63
make a clean break/breast (of it) 241L77/35
make a clean sweep 241L81/82
make a dash for it 347L14
make a day/night/evening/weekend of it 855L13
make a (big) difference 382R3
make a fool of oneself 544R2/L84
make a fuss of 577R12
make a go of 606L60
make a god of 608R60
make a hit with 673L64
make a hole in 677R5
make a job of 766L4
make a joke of 768R2
make a killing 780L27
make a man (out) of 858R51
make a meal (out) of 877R50
make a mess of 889R55
make a mockery 909R39
make a monkey out of 914R83
make a mountain out of a molehill 922R80
make a move 924R55 925R54
make a new life 818R77
make a noise about 958R53
make a nuisance of oneself 966R59
make a pig's ear of 1065L75
make a (real) pig of oneself 1065R25
make a play for 1078L80
make a point of 1089R18
make a practice of 1107R23
make a representation to 1205R36
make a rod for one's own back 1230R11
make a spectacle of oneself 1387L79
make a splash 1394L43
make a takeover bid 1487R60
make a/the break 161L78
make a (big) thing (out) of 1512L26
make a virtue (out) of 1626L9
make a world of difference 382R4
make someone's acquaintance 12L31
make all the difference (in the world) 382R3
make allowance(s) for 35L10/13
make amends 39R72
make an exhibition of 479R4
make an honest living 681R14
make an honest woman of 681R12
make an issue of 755R23
make oneself at home 679R56
make away with 856L10
make believe 115L81 856R77
make someone's blood boil 137L42
make someone's blood curdle 336L25
make someone's blood run cold 137L48 1242L6
make capital (out) of/from 191R54
make certain/sure 855R3
make common cause with 270R79
make do 855L17
make ends meet 455L54
make excuses 478L66/65
make eyes at 488L75
make someone's flesh crawl/creep 533L62
make for 854R81 856L12/15/51/62
make free with 562L23
make fun of 573R59
make good 611R19/22
make good time 611R25
make someone's hackles rise 635L42
make someone's hair curl 636L40
make someone's hair stand on end 636L48
make haste 649R36
make hay while the sun shines 652R28
make headway 655L40
make heavy weather of 659L53
make inroads 733R28
make something into 855L5/7 856L73
make it a date 348L36
make it a rule 1239R70
make it snappy 1364R1
make it up 856R65/36
make known 787R38/39/43
make someone laugh 799R82
make legal history 809L49
make someone's life hell 661L55
make light of 821L82
make little of 831R34
make love 843R33/31
make one's mark 865R32
make matters worse 874R42 1686L59
make mincemeat of 898L67
make one's mind up 899L57
make mischief 903R44
make someone's mouth water 924L16
make much of 856L27
make no bones about 146L57
make no claim to 235R29
make no difference 382R8
make no mistake about it 907L58
make noises 958R56/59
make (a) nonsense of 960L72
make off 856L33
make-or-break situation 159R70 855L20
make out 856L38/53/60/63
make out a case 856L48
make something out of/from 855L1
make over 856L67/71/76
make one's presence felt 1116R78
make someone (want to) puke 1144L19
make short shrift of 1324L2
make short work 1322R73
make some/a few z's 1699L16
make the bed 111L45
make the best of something 119L62
make the first move 925R57
make the fur fly 575R42
make the grade 616L47 855R80
make (all) the right/proper/correct noises 958R61
make the rounds 1237L8
make the running 1241R67
make the sign of the cross 327R53
make the ultimate/supreme sacrifice 1247R20
make the world go around/round 1683R60
make time 855L21/R26 856R26
make to 854R82 855R41 856L62/70/R30/52
make towards 856L80
make tracks 1545L58
make up 856L83/R7/18/22/33/39/43/49 857L3/7
make up for 856R55
make up for lost time 856R61
make up one's mind 856R49 899L56
make up to 856R65/70
make oneself useful 1602L31
make waves 1644R49
make way for 1645R54
make someone welcome 1650R82
make whoopee 1662R44
make with 27R57 856L65/R37/74
make it worth someone's while 1687L61
not make any/the slightest difference 382R8
put the make on 856L8
put two and two together and make five 1574R75/78
cabinet maker 182L75
law-maker 801L51
meet one's maker 883L41
money-maker 913R34
makes it big 125L26
that makes two of us 1576L6
what makes someone tick 1518R8
non-profit(-making) 959R10
cringe-making 324R73
epoch-making 464R24
love-making 843R32
merry-making 889L83
mischief-making 903R48
music-making 931L47
male alto 313L81
male bonding 857R1
male chauvinism 220R29 857R8
male chauvinist 857R3
male chauvinist pig 857R6
male menopause 857R9
male organ 857R13
male prostitute 1136R77
with malice aforethought 857R58
pedestrian mall 1042L28
shopping mall 858L14 1321L61
malt extract 858L57
malt whisky 858L58
malted milk 858L60
Maltese cross 858L64
mama's boy 858L78
mammary glands 858R6
a man's gotta do what a man's gotta do 614L48
a man's man 858R61
best man 118R84
bin man 127L4 433L65
blind man's buff 135L79
bogey man 143R76
common man 270R45
company man 272R35
con man 279R42 286L37
confidence man 286L36
dirty old man 388L28
family man 500R75
fancy man 503L13
fellow man 511R70
fine figure of a man 517R39
front man 568L41/R14
G-man 602L65
gingerbread man 595R36
grand old man 618L15
hatchet man 650L74
hit man 673L54
inner man 732R1
iron man 752R36
just the man for the job 766L14
kept man 777L55
ladies' man 792L82
leading man 803R75
lollipop man 837R18
make a man (out) of 858R51
man about-town 1543R55
man and boy 858R55
man and wife 858R56
man's best friend 859L49
man-eater 858R68 859L51/53
man-eating 859L53
man Friday 858R70
man in the moon 858R58
man in the street 1437L61
man's inhumanity to man 859L50
man-made 859L58
man of God 858R72
man of his word 1679L44
man of letters 858R73
man of straw 859L54/56 1435R7/10
man of the match 872R9
man of the people 1046R39
man of the world 1683R79
man on the Clapham omnibus 981L83
man-sized 858R74
man-to-man 858R65
marked man 866R64
may the best man win 118R64
medallion man 881L64
Neanderthal man 944R31
New Man 952L56
no-man's-land 957R75

▫odd-▪job ▫man 974R40
▫odd man ▪out 974R26
▫old ▪man 980L3
▫one-man ▪band 984L77
▪pace ▫man 1014L59
rag and ▪bone ▫man 1168R1
Re▫naissance ▪man 1202R77
▫right-hand ▪man 1224L6
see a ▫man about a ▪dog 1284L10
▪straight ▫man 1433L66
▫straw ▪man 859L57 1435R6/10
▫stunt ▫man 1449L14
the ▫man in *someone's* ▪life 818R78
the ▫thinking man's ▪crumpet 1513L83
▫twelfth ▪man 1572R35
▫well ▪man 1651L69
▪yes-▫man 1696R23
▫young ▪man 1698L66
▫bite off ▫more than *one* can ▪manage 130R7
▪manage on 859R25
▪manage to 859R13/14/17
▫middle ▪management 894L59
▪stress ▫management 1438L46
▪bank ▫manager 97R33
▪line ▫manager 826R37
▫middle ▪manager 894L63
▪stage ▫manager 1406R29
▫managing di▪rector 859R43
▫dog in the ▪manger 408R51
▫sex ▪maniac 1303R53
▫manic de▪pression 860R82
▫manic de▪pressive 860R79
▫French ▪manicure 563R36
▪manicure ▫set 861L5
▪manifest *itself* in/as 861L25/23/24/26
▫manna from ▪heaven 861R40
as (▫if) to the ▫manner ▪born 861R56
▫bedside ▪manner 111R68
in a ▫manner of ▪speaking 861R59
not by ▪any manner of ▫means 861R63
▫ill-▪mannered 703R12
▫mild-▪mannered 896L11
▫well ▪mannered 862L25 1653L19
▫comedy of ▪manners 267L29
▪table ▫manners 1483L70
man▪oeuvre into 862L66
▫room/▫scope for man▪oeuvre 862L58
▫praying ▪mantis 862R35 1108R56
▫manual dex▪terity 862R80
▫manual trans▪mission 862R83
▪horse ma▫nure 686L52
▫Manx ▪cat 863L49
▫map ▪out 863R56
▫put *something* on the ▪map 863R43
re▪lief ▫map 1200L35
▪sketch ▫map 1345R20
▫wipe off the ▪map 1670L59
▫maple ▪syrup 863R68
▫maraschino ▪cherries 864L4
▫half-▪marathon 637R71
▫lose *one's* ▪marbles 841R78
▫march ▪off 864R4
▪march-▫past 864L82
▫quick ▪march 864L65
▪route ▫march 1237R4
▫steal a ▪march on 1418L12
▪marching ▫orders 864L70
▫Mardi ▪Gras 864R24
▪brood ▫mare 168R37
▫shank's ▪mare 1309R65
▫hard ▪margin 646L58
▫margin of ▪error 864R68
▪profit ▫margin 1128R23
▫marginal ▪land 864R57
▫Black Ma▪ria 131R39
Ma▪rine ▫Corps 865L58
▫marital ▪aid 865L80
▫marital ▫status 865L84
▫black ▪mark 131R78
▫easy ▪mark 438R56
excla▪mation ▫mark 477L48
▪gas ▫mark 584L11
▫high ▪water ▫mark 667R4
▪Kite ▫mark 782L60
▫leave *one's* ▪mark 865R30
▫low ▪water ▫mark 844L46
▫make *one's* ▪mark 865R32
▫mark ▪down 866L80/R27/40
mark ▪down as 866R42/43
▫mark *something* ▪down/▪up 866R30
▫mark ▪off 866L12
▫mark ▪time 866R18
▫mark ▪up 866R46
▫mark *my* ▪words 866R23
▫miss the ▪mark 906L19
on your ▫mark get ▫set ▪go! 866L40
over▫step the ▪mark 1011L27
▪pass ▫mark 1031R11
▪Plimsoll ▫mark 1082L21
punctu▪ation ▫mark 1146R75
▪question ▫mark 1161R13
▪strawberry ▫mark 1435R55
▪stress ▫mark 1438R5
▫wide of the ▪mark 1663R21
▫marked ▪man/▪woman 866R64
▪bear ▫market 108R1
▫black ▪market 131R81
▫buyer's ▪market 180R69 867L18
▫Common ▪Market 271L7 443L8
▫corner a/the ▪market 306R31
▫corner on a ▪market 306R8
▪flea ▫market 532R39
▫free ▪market 561L24
▪labour ▫market 789R67
▫market ▪forces 867L32
▫market ▪garden 866R82/84 867L2
▫market ▪price 867L37
▫market re▪search 867L42/39
▪market ▫town 867L3
▫mass ▪market 870R56/62
▪money ▫market 913R32
▪niche ▫market 954R8
▫open ▪market 867L31 988R74
▫price *oneself* out of the ▪market 1120R50
▫rig the ▪market 1222R60
▪stock ▫market 1428L7
▫up-▪market 1598R69
▫black market▪eer 131R84
▫full ▪marks 573L19/20 866L74
▫no marks for ▪guessing 866L75
on your ▫marks get ▫set ▪go! 866L40
quo▫tation ▫marks 1164R11
▪quote ▫marks 1164R12
▪skid ▫marks 1346L18
a ▫marriage made in ▪heaven 868L8
ar▫ranged ▪marriage 64L57 868L1
▫join in ▪marriage 767L69
▪marriage ▫bureau 868L10
▫marriage ▪counselling 868L22
▫marriage ▪guidance 868L21
▫marriage of con▪venience 868L13
▫open ▪marriage 988R77
▫shotgun ▪marriage 1325L10
▪married ▫name 868R2
▪bone ▫marrow 146L64 868L32/36
▫chill the ▪marrow of 226R13
▪marrow ▫bone 868L38
▫vegetable ▪marrow 868L42
▫marry be▪neath *oneself* 117L30 868L62
▫marry beneath *one's* ▪station 868L64
▪marry into 868L57
▫marry ▪money 868L66 913R23
▫marry *someone* ▪off 868L58
the ▪marrying ▫kind 868L67
▪marsh ▫gas 868R22
▪field ▫marshal 516L16 868R56
▫Marshal of the Royal ▪Air ▫Force 868R57
▫Doc ▪Martens 407R6 417R59
▫Dr ▪Martens 417R58
▫court ▪martial 315R54/57
▫martial ▪arts 869L3
▫martial ▪law 869L8
▪house ▫martin 689L46
▫Marxist-▪Leninist 869R34/33/21
▫bloody ▪mary 137R12
▫Hail ▪Mary 636L12
▫mash ▪up 870L8/10
▫mashed-▪up 870L14
▪death ▫mask 352R20
▪gas ▫mask 584L17
▪mask with 870L41
▪oxygen ▫mask 1013R34
▪stocking ▫mask 1428R4
▫masked ▪ball 870L35
▪masking ▫tape 870L43
▫Mason-▪Dixon Line 870L75
masque▪rade as 870R21
a ▫mass of contra▪dictions 870R36
▫Black ▪Mass 132L1
▫mass ▪mailing 853R40 870R55
▫mass ▪market 870R56/62
▫mass ▪media 870R63 881R10
▫mass ▪murder 930L39
▫mass-pro▪duce 870R70
▫mass ▪production 870R75
▪massage ▫parlour 871L46/48
en ▪masse 459L32
▫half-▪mast 637R73
▫nail *one's* ▫colours to the ▪mast 935R77
▪harbour-▫master 646L15
▪master ▫bedroom 111R57 871R20
▪master ▫class 871R64
▪Master's ▫degree 871R66
▪master ▫key 871R22
▫master of all *one* sur▪veys 1470L78
▫Master of ▪Arts 871R60
▫master of ▪ceremonies 871R23
▫Master of ▪Philosophy 871R68
▫Master of ▪Science 871R73
▪master ▫plan 871R26
▪master ▫race 871R30
▪master ▫switch 871R32
▫old ▪master 980L6
▫past ▪master 1033R7
▪bath ▫mat 104L41 872L69
▪beer ▫mat 113L10
▪place ▫mat 872L73 1073R59
▪prayer ▫mat 1108R70
▫put the ▪welcome mat ▫out 1650R65
▫sweep under the under the ▪mat 1475L21
▪table ▫mat 1483L67
▪welcome ▫mat 1650R59
exhi▪bition ▫match 479R7
▫man/▫woman of the ▪match 872R9
▪match against 872R17
▫match ▪point 872R11
▫match ▪up 872R56/59/62
▪match with 872R6/58/61
▫meet *one's* ▪match 872R77 883L42
▫put a ▪match to 872R26
re▪turn ▫match 1217L45
▪safety ▫match 1248R65
▪shouting ▫match 1326R4
▪slanging ▫match 1349L25
▫strike a ▪match 872R25 1441R36
▪tennis ▫match 1500R34
▫well-▪matched 1653L23
▪matchstick ▫figure 873L33 1422R67
▫first ▪mate 525R84
▪mate with 873L60
▪running ▫mate 1242L38
▪soul ▫mate 1378L71
▪team-▫mate 1494R20
▫alma ▪mater 35R66
ma▪ternity ▫leave 873R84
ma▪ternity ▫ward 363L27 874L2
▪matinée ▫idol 874L25
▫join in ▪matrimony 767L69
▫dot-matrix ▪printer 413L46
a ▫matter of o▪pinion 989R82
an▫other matter alto▪gether 48L12
as a ▫matter of ▪course/▪fact/▪principle 492R17 874R26 1122R57
▪grey ▫matter 623R8
▫matter at ▪hand 874R24
▫matter in ▪hand 874R23
▫matter-of-▪fact 875L69/72/64
▫matter of ▫life and/or ▪death 874R29
▫matter of o▪pinion 874R32
▫matter of ▪record 874R35
▫matter of ▪time 1520R78
▫mind over ▪matter 899L16
no ▪laughing ▫matter 800L29 874R37
no ▫matter ▫how you ▪slice it 1352L64
▫not matter ▪tuppence 1568L56
▪printed ▫matter 1123L23
▫make matters ▪worse 874R42 1686L59
take matters into *one's* ▪own ▫hands 874R46
▪air ▫mattress 29L57/R70 823L54
ma▪ture-age ▫student 875R58
ma▪ture ▫student 875R57
▫definite ▪maybe 359R38 877L21
the ▫real Mc▪Coy 877R2 1180L77
▪water ▫meadow 1642R17
▫barium ▪meal 100L60
▪bone ▫meal 146L65
make a ▪meal (out) of 877R50
▪meal ▫ticket 848L23 877R54/55
▫square ▪meal 1402L43
▫meals on ▪wheels 877R59
▫Greenwich ▪Mean ▫Time 623L17
▫mean ▪business 878R24
▪mean by 878L4/5/24
▪mean for 878L61/R13/18
▫mean ▪mischief 878R27
▫mean (all) the ▪world 1685L29
▪mean to 878L62/63/64/R8/9/11/12/13/14/16/53
▫mean ▪well 878R29
▫no mean ▪feat 508R75
you ▫know what I ▪mean 787L7/14
if you ▫take my ▪meaning 878L44 1486L83
▫well-▪meaning 1653L28
a ▫means to an ▪end 879L30
be▫yond *one's* ▪means 122L65 832L71 879L42
by ▫fair means or ▪foul 494R78
▫independent ▪means 720R69
▪means ▫test 879L46
not by ▪any manner of ▫means 861R63
▫private ▪means 879L41 1124L40
▫ways and ▪means 1646L44
within *one's* ▪means 879L44
▫well-▪meant 1653L31
in the ▪meantime/▪meanwhile 879L50
in the ▪meantime/▪meanwhile 879L50
▫German ▪measles 590L48
for ▫good ▪measure 611L79
▫get/▫take the ▪measure of 879R32
▫half-▪measure 637R75
▫made-to-▪measure 851R40
▪measure against 879L82
▪measure as 879L84
▪measure in 879R2
▫measure ▪up to 879R7
▪tape ▫measure 1490R82
▪measuring ▫cup 879R12
▪measuring ▫cylinder 879R14
▪measuring ▫jug 879R12
▫easy ▪meat 438R55
▪lunch ▫meat 848L19
▪luncheon ▫meat 848L19
▫meat and ▪drink 880L60
▫meat-and-po▪tatoes 880L62
▫meat and two ▪veg 880L58
▪meat ▫grinder 624R2 898L45
▫meat ▪loaf 880L65
▫red ▪meat 1189L26
▪sausage ▫meat 1257L81/83
var▪iety ▫meat 976R57
▪white ▫meat 1660R43
me▫chanical engin▪eering 880R77
me▫chanical ▪pencil 1134L44
▫quantum me▪chanics 1158R60
Ex▪change Rate ▫Mechanism 476R65
de▫serve a ▪medal 372L12
me▪dallion ▫man 881L64
▪meddle in 881L74/75
▪meddle with 881L72
▫mass ▪media 870R63 881R10
▪media e▫vent 881R12
▪median ▫strip 209L20 881R22
▪mediate between 881R29
▪mediate through 881R34
a ▫dose/▫taste of *one's* own ▪medicine 882L43/54
▫bitter ▪medicine 130R68
comple▫mentary ▪medicine 275R15
▪cough ▫medicine 311L11
▪folk ▫medicine 543L12
ho▫listic ▪medicine 679L3
in▫dustrial ▪medicine 723R82
in▫ternal ▪medicine 743R55
▫orthodox ▪medicine 997L53
▫patent ▪medicine 1035L49
pre▪scription ▫medicine 1116L73
▫socialized ▪medicine 1370R1
▪meditate on/upon 882L79
▫transcendental medit▪ation 1549R65
▫happy ▪medium 645R33
in the ▪medium ▫term 1501R21
▫make ends ▪meet 455L54
▫meet a sticky ▪end 1423R7
▫meet *someone's* ▪eye 883L80/81
▫meet *someone* half▪way 883L38
▫meet *one's* ▪maker 883L41
▫meet *one's* ▪match 872R77 883L42/45
▫meet ▪up 883L28
▫meet *one's* Water▪loo 883L46
▪meet with 883R18
▫pleased to ▪meet you 1080R78
▪swap ▫meet 1391R20 1474L3
▪track ▫meet 1545R50
▫annual (general) ▪meeting 47L28
extra▫ordinary ▪meeting 487R7
▪meeting ▫house 883L72
▫meeting of ▪minds 883L70
▪meeting ▫point 883L49
▪race ▫meeting 1165R1
▫town ▪meeting 1543R65
▫boy-meets-▪girl 155R79
▫more to *something* than ▫meets the ▪eye 488L81
▫peach ▪Melba 1040L45
▫pell-▪mell 1044L3
▫mellow ▪out 884R78
▫butter wouldn't ▫melt in *someone's* ▪mouth 180L29
▫melt a▪way 885L36
▪melt into 885L37
▪melting ▫point 885L53
▪melting ▫pot 885L54/59
▫card-carrying ▪member 195L63
▫founder ▪member 556L50
▫founding ▪member 556L36
▫Member of ▪Parliament 885L82
▫sitting ▪member 1343R9
▫mucous ▪membrane 927R34
▪war me▫morial 1637L42
▪folk ▫memory 543L14
▫jog *someone's* ▪memory 766R81
live (▫on) in the ▪memory 832R36
▫living ▪memory 832L8
▫long ▪memory 838L33
▫memory like a ▪sieve 1335L19
▫memory like an ▪elephant 886L21
▪memory ▫span 886L28
▫photographic ▪memory 1059R18
re▫fresh *someone's* ▪memory 1192R24
▫short ▪memory 1322R81
▫slip *someone's* ▪memory 1354L10
take a ▫stroll/▫trip/▫walk down memory ▪lane 886L22
within *one's* ▪memory 886L25
all ▫things to all ▪men 1512R8
▪men's ▫room 792R5 858R75 1532R2
▫ménage à ▪trois 886L60
▫mend ▪fences 886L73
▫mend *one's* ▪ways 886L79
▫male ▪menopause 857R9
▪menstrual ▫cycle 886R62
▫menstrual ▪period 886R62 1049L49
▫mental ▪age 887L51
▫mental a▪rithmetic 62L75 887L54
▫mental ▪block 887L58
▫mental ▪cruelty 330L51 887L61
▫mental ▪handicap 642L66 887L65
▪mental ▫hospital 887L66
▫mental ▪note 887L68 963L59
co▪lonial men▪tality 259L40
▪siege men▫tality 887R51 1334R83
▫mentally de▪fective 887L77
▫creme de ▪menthe 322R83
▫honourable ▪mention 683L61
▫rate a ▪mention 1174R78
▫mentioned in dis▪patches 396L41
▫compos ▪mentis 277L28
▫non compos ▪mentis 959R76
▪menu-▫driven 888L14
▫merchant ▪bank 888L71
▫merchant ▪navy 888L79
▫merchant of ▪death 888L74
▫merchant of ▪doom/▪gloom 888L75
▫merchant ▪seaman 888L81
▫merchant ▪shipping 888L79
▪scrap ▫merchant 1270R72
▫grateful/▫thankful for small ▪mercies 1357R31
▫errand of ▪mercy 467L25
▪mercy ▫killing 888R24
▪merge with 888R83
▫post me▪ridiem 1101R84
▫Merry ▪Christmas 223L74 889L64
▪merry-go-▫round 889L67
▪merry-▫making 889L83
▪mesh with 889R24
make a ▪mess of 889R55
▫mess a▪bout/a▪round 889R72/64/69/76
▪mess ▫hall 890L27
▪mess-up 889R58/63/78/82/84
▪mess with 889R68/71 890L1/4/6
▫drive *one's* ▪message ▫home 425R47
▫get the ▪message 890L53
▫get the ▪message across 890L55
▪voice ▫messaging 1629L71
▫messed-▪up 890L14
▫hail-fellow-well-▪met 636L8
▫base ▪metal 101R78
▫heavy ▪metal 658R73/74
▪metal de▫tector 890R23
▪metal fa▫tigue 507L23 890R28
▫precious ▪metal 1109R79
meta▪morphose into 890R68
▫mixed ▪metaphor 908L79
▫mix *one's* ▪metaphors 908L35
▫mete ▪out 891L37
Meteoro▪logical ▫Office 891L62
▪light ▫meter 820R31
▪parking ▫meter 891L73 1027L9
▫read the ▪meter 891L74 1178R13
▪method to/in *one's* ▫madness 891R74/75
▪rhythm ▫method 1220R3
as ▫old as Me▪thuselah 892L27
▫methylated ▪spirits 892L29
▫metric ▪ton 892L69 1535L34
▫Tex-▪Mex 1506L65
▫Mexican ▪stand off 892R20
▫Mexican ▪wave 892R23
e▫lectron ▪microscope 446R71
▫mid-life ▪crisis 893R48
di▫vide/▫split down the ▪middle 893R71
▫middle ▪age 894L10
▫middle-age ▪spread 894L18
▫middle-▪aged 894L14
▫Middle A▪merica/▪England 894L24/27 895L20
▫middle ▪C 894L30
▫middle ▪class 237R83 894L31
▫middle ▪distance 894L41/43
▫middle ▪ear 894L47
▫Middle ▪East 894L49
▫Middle ▪Eastern 894L53
▫middle ▪finger 894L55
▫middle ▪ground 894L56
▫middle ▪management 894L59
▫middle ▪manager 894L63
▫middle ▪name 894L63
▫middle-of-the-▪road 894L69
▪middle ▫school 894L75
▫Middle ▪West 894L77 895L20
▫piggy/▫pig in the ▪middle 1065L82
play both ▫ends against the ▪middle 1078L42
▫split/di▫vide down the ▪middle 893R72

the Middle Ages 894L20
fair to middling 495L76 894R12
midi system 894R32
burn the midnight oil 177L41
Land of the Midnight Sun 794L49
midnight feast 894R49
midnight sun 894R50
change/swap horses in midstream 686L43
Midsummer('s) Day 895L2
high and mighty 668L79
migrate from 895R49/51
migrate into 895R50/61
migrate to 895R51/55
mild-mannered 896L11
put mildly 1153R44
to put it mildly 1153R43
can see/tell a mile off 896L35
nautical mile 944L16
run a mile 1240R82
sea mile 944L16
stand/stick out a mile 896L38
the Square Mile 1402L29
miles away 86L72 896L28
miles from anywhere/nowhere 896L32
miles too 896L35
military academy 896R4/5
military band 896R8
military honours 896R11
military-industrial complex 896R20
Military Police 896R15
military policeman 896R17
military service 896R19 1298L28
militate against 896R47
baby milk 88R23
condensed milk 283L5
evaporated milk 471R73
land flowing with/land of milk and honey 794L45
malted milk 858L60
milk bar 896R71
milk chocolate 896R72
milk float 896R77
milk of 897L18
milk of magnesia 896R79
milk round 896R81
milk run 896R84
milk shake 897L3
milk tooth 88R27 897L6
milk truck 897L7
no good/use crying over spilt milk 331R55
skimmed milk 1346R1
soya milk 1381R21
the milk of human kindness 896R69
milking machine 897L18
Milky Way 897L23
coffee mill 254R79
grist to the mill 624R56
mill about/around 897L50
pepper mill 1046R68
put through the mill 897L38
rolling mill 1231R47
run-of-the-mill 1242L56
steel mill 1418R32
look/feel like a million dollars/bucks 897R5
mime artist 897R55
mime to 897R60
mince pie 898L71
mince words 898L53
make mincemeat of 898L67
a good mind to 899L55
a load/weight off *one's* mind 898R61
a piece of *one's* mind 1064R16
at/in the back of *one's* mind 89L75
blow *someone's* mind 139L54
breadth of mind 159R38
call/bring to mind 184R80 899L47
cast *one's* mind back 202L36
change *one's* mind 215L8
cross *one's* mind 327R3
frame of mind 558L84
from/since time out of mind 1524L28
further from *one's* mind 576R21
get *one's* mind round 898R47
go out of *one's* mind 898R49
go over *something* in *one's* mind 898R51
half a mind to 899L54
know *one's* own mind 786R41
leap to mind 806L14
lose *one's* mind 841R80
make *one's* mind up 899L57
make up *one's* mind 856R49 899L56
mind-altering 899L6
mind-bending 899L3
mind-blowing 898R83
mind-boggling 899L2
mind-expanding 899L6
mind's eye 899L11
mind how you go 899L81
mind is made up 899L58
mind like a sieve 1335L19
mind-numbing 899L14
mind out for 899L80
mind over matter 899L16
mind *one's* own business 179L8 899R19
mind *one's* p's and q's 899R3
mind reader 899L20
mind-set 899L24
mind *one's* step 1420L5
never mind 951R30/32/34
never mind that 951R36
not in *one's* right mind 1224L40
of sound/unsound mind 898R75
of the same/of one mind 899L61
one-track mind 984R55
open mind 988L29
out of *one's* mind 1001L11
pissed out of *one's* mind 1070R8
presence of mind 1117L7
put *someone* in mind of 899L48
put *something* out of *one's* mind 1154R77
run through *one's* mind 1243L43
set/put *someone's* mind at rest/ease 898R72
set/put *one's* mind to 898R70
slip *someone's* mind 1354L10
speak *one's* mind 1384R52
spring to mind 1400L45
state/frame of mind 898R77
take *someone's* mind off 898R78
the thought crosses *someone's* mind 1514R42
turn of mind 1570L14
turn over in *one's* mind 898R51
absent-minded 5L32/35
bloody-minded 138L23/19
fair-minded 495L25
feeble-minded 509R54
high-minded 667R78
money-minded 913R37
narrow-minded 938L70/64
open-minded 988L33/31
petty-minded 1056L69
right minded 1223L76
simple-minded 1339R68/71
single-minded 1341L21/24
small-minded 1357R59/64
strong-minded 1445R69
weak-minded 1646R59
baby-minder 88R22
in two minds 1574R83
meeting of minds 883L70
of two minds 1574R84
mine for 899R80/81
coal miner 251R25
mineral oil 900L26
mineral water 900L27
mingle together 900L55
mingle with 900L48/53
Mini Disc 900R60
mini-series 900L65
mini-system 900L67
minimum wage 900R80 1632R66
strip mining 1444R47
minister to 901L73
prime minister 1121R73
ministering angel 901L78
moaning minnie 909L25
minor planet 74L66
minority group 901R49
minstrel show 901R60
in mint condition 902L1
mint jelly 901R72
mint julep 772L57 901R69
mint sauce 901R72
B minus 88L21
C minus 182L16
minus sign 902L12
just a minute 774L34/35/37
last minute 797R49/55/56
minute hand 902L60
minute steak 902L62
up-to-the-minute 902L53 1597R33
wait a minute 1633R13
not last five minutes 798L76
annus mirabilis 47L60
the miracle of life 902R22
work miracles 1682L17
mirror image 902R47
rear view mirror 1181L59
two-way mirror 1576L70
smoke and mirrors 1361L71
miscarriage of justice 774R65 903R1
miscast as 903R11
make mischief 903R44
mean mischief 878R27
mischief-making 903R48
misconstrue as 904L8
misdirect to 904L40
put *an animal* out of *its* misery 904L77
misinform about 904R74
mislead about 905L30
mislead into 905L32/34
mispronounce as 905R6
misrepresent as 905R36
give *something* a miss 906L27
hit-and-miss 672R48
hit-or-miss 672R48
miss a trick 906L22
miss out 906L74/67/72
miss the boat 906L16
miss the mark 906L19
near miss 944R72/76
too good to miss 906L4 1535L70
heart misses a beat 656L74
anti-missile 50L18
ballistic missile 95R75
guided missile 630R46
missing link 906L55/59
missing person 906L63
mission control 906R18
missionary position 906R42
mist over 907L3
mist up 907L3
Scotch mist 1269R31
make no mistake about *it* 907L58
mistake for 907L26
Mister Big 907L66
mistress of all *one* surveys 1470L78
misty-eyed 907L17
oven mitts 1005L45
bar mitzvah 100R20
mix in 908L29
mix *something* in with/into 908L30
mix it up 908R49
mix *one's* metaphors 908L35
mix up/together 908R41/46/52/L30
mix with 908L26/R22/28
pick 'n' mix 1061R82
mixed ability 2R49 908L57
mixed bag 908L59
mixed blessing 908L63
mixed doubles 908L65
mixed drink 908L67
mixed economy 908L70
mixed farming 908L72
mixed feelings 908L74
mixed grill 908L76
mixed metaphor 908L79
mixed up 908R57/63
cement mixer 208R6
concrete mixer 282L82
mixer tap/faucet 908R5
cough mixture 311L12
dolly mixture 410L64
Big Mo 125L65
moan about 909L19
moan of 909L14
moan with 909L10
moaning minnie 909L25
lynch mob 849R38
mobile home 909L61
mobile library 909L64
mobile phone/telephone 909L67
upwardly mobile 1601L12
upward mobility 909L80 1600R80
Möbius strip 909R12
mock turtleneck 1571R65
mock up 909R63/70
make a mockery 909R39
mod con 910L4
modal auxiliary 909R80
modal verb 909R80
à la mode 31L56/59
cover model 316L48
model on 910L56/57
role model 1230R65
modern dance 910R51
modern jazz 910R54
modern languages 911L10
post-modernism 1101L45/49/50
false modesty 500L57
modified American plan 637R27 911L55
command module 267R73
modus operandi 911R23
modus vivendi 911R27
molecular biology 912L16
make a mountain out of a molehill 922R80
child molester 226L35 912L32
Molotov cocktail 912L58
at/for the moment 912R51
defining moment 359R18
from one moment to the next 912L81 953R33
in the heat of the moment 658L41
just a moment 774L34/35/37
moment of truth 912R59
not a moment too soon 912L82
psychological moment 1141L35
spur of the moment 1401L33
wait a moment 1633R13
constitutional monarchy 293L14
Monday morning feeling 913L46
Monday-morning quarterback 913L48
beau monde 109R73
International Monetary Fund 744L23
big money 124R49
blood money 137L65/67
coin money 256L2
danger money 345R30
easy money 438R50
gate money 584R24
get/have *one's* money's worth 913R15
give *someone* a run for *their* money 1241L40
give of *one's* money 596R39
have a good run for *one's* money 1241L38
hush money 696L38
key money 777R67
licence to print money 817L47
made of money 855L26 913R22
marry money 868L66 913R23
money for jam/old rope 913R24
money-grubbing 913R31
money-maker 913R34
money market 913R32
money-minded 913R37
money order 913R42
money-spinner 913R35
money supply 913R45
money to burn 913R27
monopoly money 915R29
old money 980L7/72
paper money 1023L44
pocket money 1087R80/84 1088L2
pots of money 1102R19
pump money into 1146L28
put *one's* money where *one's* mouth is 913R28
ready money 1179L77
rolling in money 1231L25
see the colour of *someone's* money 1283L67
seed money 1284R8
smart money 1358R57
spending money 1087R80 1390L20
throw good money after bad 1517L10
throw money at 1517L13
gossip-monger 614L14
rumour-monger 1240R28
video monitor 1622L66
brass monkey weather 158L67
don't/couldn't give a monkey's 914R79
freeze the balls off a brass monkey 563L25
grease monkey 621L79
I'll be a monkey's uncle 914R82
make a monkey out of 914R83
monkey about/around 915L13/9
monkey business 915L4
monkey-puzzle (tree) 915L16
monkey suit 915L19
monkey wrench 915L21
rhesus monkey 1219R42
spider monkey 1391L14
serial monogamy 1296L48
monopoly money 915R29
monosodium glutamate 915R48
carbon monoxide 194L72
Frankenstein's monster 559L66
a month of Sundays 916L55
calendar month 184L14
flavour of the month 532L63
lunar month 847R71
per calendar month 1047L31
mooch off 916R21/23
black mood 132L2
full moon 572R53 916R54
half-moon 637R78 916R53
half-moon glasses 637R81
man in the moon 858R58
moon about/around 916R68
moon over 916R69
new moon 916R53 952L61
once in a blue moon 139R62
over the moon 916R60
promise *someone* the moon 1131L30
all moonlight and roses 916R83
do a moonlight flit 917L1
many moons ago 916R59
mop up 917L67/72
squeegee mop 1403R36
mope about/around 917L79
claim the moral high ground 235R52
moral majority 917R27
moral support 917R32
need I say more? 946R77
coffee-morning 255L1
good morning 612L50
Monday morning feeling 913L46
Monday-morning quarterback 913L48
morning-after pill 918R48
morning dress 918R51
morning noon and night 918R48
morning sickness 918R56
morning star 918R58
morning suit 918R52
morris dance 919L14/10/15
mortal sin 919L43
shuffle off this mortal coil 1331L45
bricks and mortar 163R57
endowment mortgage 456L47
mortification of the flesh 919R32
rigor mortis 1224R38
mortise lock 350R34 919R41
mosquito net 919R70
bon mot 146R35
mot juste 921L52
moth-eaten 920L46
at *one's* mother's knee 920L64
biological father/mother/parent 127R58
birth mother/parent 128R73
earth mother 437R5
expectant mother 480R67
founding mother 556L29
lone mother 837R38
mother country 506R77 920L65
Mother's Day 920L80
mother figure 920L69
mother-in-law 920R21
mother Nature 920L72
mother-of-pearl 920L76
mother tongue 920R3
Queen Mother 1161L29
working mother 1681R52
motion picture 920R84
motion sickness 921L1 1553L31
motion to 921L9/11/15
put/set in motion 920R79
set the wheels in motion 1656L45
slow motion 1355R54
time-and-motion study 1521R69
go through the motions 920R75
motor along 921R25
motor car 193R8 921R4
motor caravan 921R6
motor court 920L39
motor home 921R6
motor lodge 920L39 921R10
motor mower 921L75
motor racing 921R11
motor scooter 921R14
motor vehicle 921R18 1610R62
break the mould 160R71
cast in the same mould 202L71
leaf mould 805L9
mould into 922L55/60
mould out of/from/in 922L56
mould to/round 922L62
moulder away 922L77
mount guard 922R56
mount in 922R49
mount on 922R47/49
mount to 922R31
mount up 922R32
make a mountain out of a molehill 922R80
mountain bike 922R82
mountain lion 310R74 923L35
move mountains 925L17
mounted police 922R17
mourn for/over 923L64/61
cat and mouse 203L38
hair mousse 636L58
handlebar moustache 643L36
walrus moustache 1635R77
all mouth 33R41
big mouth 124R54
born with a silver spoon in *one's* mouth 149R18
butter wouldn't melt in *someone's* mouth 180L29
by word of mouth 1678L76
down in the mouth 924L10
foam at the mouth 541L83
foot-and-mouth disease 545R55
froth at the mouth 569L61/64
hand-to-mouth existence 640L73
heart in *one's* mouth 656R67
keep *one's* mouth shut 924L15
laugh out of the other side of *one's* mouth 800L18
make *someone's* mouth water 924L16
mouth off 924R8/11/5
mouth organ 648L79 924L19
mouth to feed 924L12
mouth-to-mouth (resuscitation) 924L19
mouth-watering 924L21
open *one's* mouth 987R72
put *one's* foot in *one's* mouth 545L83

put *one's* money where *one's* **mouth** is 913R28
put words in/into *someone's* **mouth** 1678R9
shoot *one's* **mouth** off 1319R57
shut your **mouth** 1331R11
smart **mouth** 1358R63
take the words out of *someone's* **mouth** 1678R13
wash *someone's* **mouth** out (with soapy water) 1639L81
foul-**mouthed** 555R76
open-**mouthed** 924L71 987R38
movable feast 925L32
Did the earth **move** for you? 437R2
false **move** 500L26
get a **move** on 924R54
make a **move** 924R55 925R54
make the first **move** 925R57
move a muscle 924R48
move about/around 924R34 925L73/75
move against the flow 538L5
move ahead 924R42
move along/on 924R37/74
move along/over/up 924R34
move among/with 924R44
move *one's* arse 65L24
move aside/over 925L77
move away 925L79
move back 925L81
move down 924R79/80
move for 926L1
move from 925L8/71/R6
move heaven and earth 925L17
move house 925L69
move in 925L11/73 926L13
move in/among 924R46
move in for the kill 780L1
move into 925L59/73/R3/7
move it 924R47
move off 925R11
move off/away 925L3
move on 924R41 925L52/R9/45
move on to better things 925R12
move out 925R2
move the deckchairs on the Titanic 355L52
move the goalposts 925L20
move towards 925L54/56/R51
move up a gear 586L11
move up/down in the world 1685L17
move with the crowd/the flow/the stream/the times 604L17
move with the flow 538L3
move with the times 1524L29
not **move** an inch 716L44
the earth **moved** 437R2
bowel **movement** 154R8
pincer **movement** 1068L11
women's **movement** 1675R77
mover and shaker 925R70/71
prime **mover** 1121R76
as/when the spirit **moves** 1393L57
B-**movie** 88L7
home **movie** 680L2
horror **movie** 686L11
movie star 926L29
movie theater 232L52 926L29
movie theatre 232L53
snuff **movie** 1368L32
get **moving** 591L52
mow down 926L49
motor **mower** 921L75
Mr Punch 1146R36
no more **Mr** Nice Guy 926R11
MS-DOS 926R45
Lady **Muck** 792R23
muck about/around 927R16/18
muck in 927R21
muck out 927R12
muck-raker 927R2/L79
muck up 927R24/30
stuck in the **muck** 1423L35
mucous membrane 927R34
hurl/throw/sling **mud** 927R49
mud pie 927R56
mud-slinging 927R53
mud sticks 927R55
mud wrestling 927R57
someone's name is **mud** 937L36/39
stick-in-the-**mud** 1423L51
muddle about 928L1
muddle along 928L2
muddle-headed 927R79
muddle through 928L4
muff it 928L30
American **muffin** 928L35
English **muffin** 928L32
stud-**muffin** 1447L56
muffle *oneself* (up) against 928L51
muffle in 928L54
muffle up 928L52/53
a **mug's** game 928L71
mug shot 928L76
mug up 928R10/5
mull over 928R51
multi-cultural 928R67
multi-dimensional 928R69
multi-disciplinary 928R71
multi-faceted 928R75
multi-racial 928R77
multi-storey 928R80/82
multi-tasking 928R83
multiple birth 929L56
multiple-choice 929L59
multiple sclerosis 929L62
multiplication table 929R7
multiply by 929R2
a **multitude** of sins 929R18
mumbo jumbo 929R52
mummy's boy 929R61
mung bean 930L4
first-degree **murder** 525R55
get away with **murder** 593L13
mass **murder** 930L39
scream bloody **murder** 930L42
scream/shout blue **murder** 930L42 139R62
serial **murderer** 1296L43/47
heart **murmur** 656R29
Murphy's law 930R9
move a **muscle** 924R48
muscle-bound 930R34
muscle-flexing 930R24
muscle in 930R40/37
muscle in on the act 13L44
muscular dystrophy 930R49
muse about/on 930R66
museum piece 930R82
mushroom cloud 931L22
mushy peas 931L11
canned **music** 188L43
celestial **music** 208L17
chamber **music** 213R48
early **music** 436R48
elevator **music** 447R26 1635R54
face the **music** 492L21
hard-core **music** 646R56
incidental **music** 716L81
music centre 931L52
music hall 931L53 1607L25
music-making 931L47
music system 931L57
music theatre 931L59
music to *someone's* ears 931L48
music video 1622L47
piped **music** 1069L75
popular **music** 1095R17 1096L10
sheet **music** 1314L61
wallpaper **music** 1635R54
world **music** 1684L84
musical box 931L51/71
musical chairs 931L73
musical instrument 738L13
must be hearing things 655R75
must have dreamt *it* 421R19
must needs 947L21
must say 1259L82
needs **must** 947L19/20
you **must** be joking 768R37
as keen as **mustard** 776L30
cut the **mustard** 339R83
mustard gas 933L29
muster point 933L50
muster station 933L50
pass **muster** 1031L77
deaf-**mute** 351R11
mute swan 933R9
mutton dressed (up) as lamb 933R82
muttonchop whiskers 934L4
mutual friend 934L14
mutual fund 934L17 1590L53
Indian **mynah** 934R16
one/another of life's great **mysteries** 818R72
it's a complete **mystery** 934R58
mystery guest 934R64
mystery tour 934R67
mystery voice 934R64
nick-nack 783L75 954R54
naff off 935L80
drive a **nail** into *someone's* coffin 935R57
hit the **nail** on the head 672R51
nail a lie 935R79
nail-biting 935R84 936L64
nail brush 936L65
nail *one's* colours to the mast 935R77
nail down 935R66/70/68/71
nail enamel 936L69
nail file 936L66
nail polish 936L69
nail scissors 936L71
nail up 935R67
nail varnish 936L69
tooth and **nail** 1535R72
a bed of **nails** 111L48
spit **nails** 1393R44
tough as **nails** 1541L84
buck **naked** 171R83
butt **naked** 180L11
the **naked** eye 936R52
namby-pamby 936R60
a **name** to conjure with 937L29
big **name** 125L68
brand **name** 158L19
call *someone* names/a **name** 936R84
Christian **name** 230L54
code **name** 254L42/45
double-barrelled **name** 413R68/66/65
family **name** 500R77 1468R71
first **name** 526L2
given **name** 526L3 597R8
go by the **name** of 937L5
household **name** 689R75
in God's/heaven's **name** 937L24
in **name** only 937L8
in the **name** of God/heaven 937L24
know by **name** 787R5
last **name** 797R58 1468R72
lend *one's* **name** to 810R52
maiden **name** 853L70
married **name** 868R2
middle **name** 894L63
name after/for 937L61
name-calling 937L4
name-drop 937L53/54/50
someone's **name** is mud 937L36/39
name names 937L68
name the day 937L76
name your poison 1090R9
not have a penny to *one's* **name** 1045R64
on a first-**name** basis with 526L9
on first-**name** terms with 526L9
pen **name** 1044L41
pet **name** 1055R19
place **name** 1072R65
rejoice in the **name** of 1196L21
second **name** 1279R4 1468R72
stage **name** 1406R31
the **name** of the game 937L40
trade **name** 1546L71
under the **name** of 937L48
call *someone* **names**/a name 936R84
name **names** 937L68
napkin ring 937R58
sanitary **napkin** 1254R78
catch **napping** 204R68
nappy rash 937R67
narked with 938L14
have a **narrow** escape 467R52
narrow boat 188R29 938L60
narrow down 938L81/84/83
narrow-gauge 938L61
narrow-minded 938L70/64
narrow squeak 938L71
a **nasty** piece of work 938R48
cheap and **nasty** 220R75 938R39
have a **nasty** feeling 938R43
video **nasty** 1622L69
nation state 938R66
national anthem 938R81
national curriculum 337L17 938R83
national debt 939L1
National Front 939L3
national grid 939L6
National Health (Service) 939L9
national insurance 939L14
national park 939L20
national service 939L24/29
national socialism 939L32
National Trust 939L33
comity of **nations** 267R38
developing **nations** 377R5
the United **Nations** 1590R6
go **native** 939R43
Native American 939R20
native speaker 939R26
nativity play 939R49
natter away 939R62
natural childbirth 943L39
natural gas 943L42
natural history 943L43
natural language 943L46
natural resources 943L49
natural science 943L52
natural selection 943L54
natural wastage 943L58
a/the call of **nature** 186L9
allow **nature** to take its course 943L6
back to **nature** 943L1
better **nature** 120R36
human **nature** 692L82
in the **nature** of things 943R22
mother **Nature** 920L72
nature reserve 943L7
nature strip 943L10
nature trail 943L13
second **nature** 1279R9
the **nature** of the beast 943R23
good-**natured** 612L12
ad **nauseam** 18L24
nautical mile 944L16
contemplate/gaze at/stare at *one's* **navel** 944L27
army-**navy** store 63R33
merchant **navy** 888L79
Royal **Navy** 1238L9
yea or **nay** 1695R25
NC-17 944R7
je ne sais quoi 762L3
Neanderthal man 944R31
a **near** thing 1512L13
anywhere **near** 52R54/56
near at hand 944R54
near-death experience 945L6
near enough 944R55
near miss 944R72/76
near-sighted 944R84 1322L63/66
near the knuckle 787R79
near thing 944R66/73/79
nothing/not anything **near** 944R42
nowhere/not anywhere **near** 944R44/56/58
nearest and dearest 944R71
necessary evil 945L80
a pain in the **neck** 1018R27
brass **neck** 158R12
breathe down *someone's* **neck** 162R72
by the scruff of the/*one's* **neck** 1274L50
crew **neck** 323R11
get it in the **neck** 945R40
hang round *one's* **neck** 644L80
have a noose around *one's* **neck** 960R45
neck and neck 945R44
neck of the woods 945R51
polo **neck** 1092R81
roll **neck** 1092R81 1231R35
save *someone's* **neck** 1257R51
scoop-**neck** 1268L25
stick *one's* **neck** out 1423R76
talk through *one's* **neck** 1488R18
up to *one's* **neck** in 945R48
up to the/*one's* **neck** 1597R35
V-**neck** 1603L50/53
open-**necked** 987R41
in *one's* hour of **need** 689L3
need *one* ask 946R74
need hardly say 946R74
need I say more? 946R77
need *something* like (I need) a hole in the head 946L76
need *one* say 946R75
need to 946L63/R6/16/18/20/42/43/44/45/60
need (all) *one's* wits about 1674R59
that/this is all *we* **need** 33L74
a **needle** in a haystack 947L30
darning **needle** 346R65
hypodermic **needle** 947L34
needle bank 947L40
pine **needle** 1068L61
get **needles** 947L39
pins and **needles** 1067L61/64
needless to say 947L10
must **needs** 947L21
needs must 947L19/20
special (educational) **needs** 1385R70/73
ne'er-do-well 947L76
double **negative** 414L64
negative pole 947R29
contributory **negligence** 299L79
non-**negotiable** 959R6
negotiate for 948L3
negotiate with 948L2/5
negro spiritual 1393R30
beggar-my-**neighbour** 113R56
neighbourhood watch 948L60
neither here nor there 948R20
neither one thing nor the other 948R16
nerve cell 949L27 950R68
nerve center 949L28
nerve centre 949L28
nerve gas 949L32
strain every **nerve** 1433R79
touch/strike/hit/expose a raw **nerve** 1176R68 1540L76
a bundle of **nerves** 175R60 949L69
strong **nerves** 1445R54
central **nervous** system 209L17
nervous breakdown 949R10
nervous system 949L38
of a **nervous** disposition 949R7
crow's **nest** 329L6
feather *one's* **nest** 509L8
hornet's **nest** 685R30
nest egg 949R40
nesting box 949R47
nestle among 949R59
nestle between 949R60
nestle down 949R58
cast *one's* **net** wide 202L38
mosquito **net** 919R70
net for 950L54
safety **net** 1248R67
tighten the **net** 1520L26
trawl **net** 1553R1
wire **netting** 1670R61
grasp the **nettle** 619R51
nettle rash 950L84
stinging **nettle** 1426L15
neural **network** 950R42
old-boy **network** 980L51/55
support **network** 1465L64
neural network 950R42
neutron bomb 951L77
always a/the bridesmaid **never** the bride 164L24
as **never** before 951R23
it **never** hurts 695R70
never darken these doors/*someone's* door again 346R5
never-ending 951R42
never fear 508R14 951R25/28
never look back 839R65
never mind 951R30/32/34
never mind that 951R36
never-never land 951R49
never put/set a foot wrong 545L75
never say boo 146R75
never the same again 1252R57
on the **never**-never 951R44
that will **never** do 406L54
well I **never** 951R38
will **never** do 951R40
wish *someone* had **never** been born 149R22
would **never** *do something* for the world 1685L25
you **never** can tell 1498L62
you **never** know 787L19
a **new** angle on 45L72
a whole **new** ball game 95R36
brand **new** 158L42 952R35
brave **new** 158R55
break **new** ground 160R64
make/start a **new** life 818R77
New Age 952L27/33
new blood 952L34
new boy 952L45
new broom 952L38
new girl 952L45
new lease of life 952L51
new lease on life 952L51
New Man 952L56
new moon 916R53 952L61
new pastures 1034R13
new potatoes 951R77
new town 952L71
new wave 952L74/79
New Year 952R7 1695R38
New Year's Day 952R14
New Year's Eve 952R16
New Year's honours 683L76
New Year's Resolution 952R19
pastures **new** 1034R12
see in the **New** Year 1284L32
the **New** Right 952L62
the **New** Testament 952L65
the **New** World 952L82
the **new** world order 952L84
turn over a **new** leaf 1569R52
carry/take coals to **Newcastle** 251R11
have **news** for *someone* 953L13
news agency 953L15
news conference 953L17
news dealer 953L33
news roundup 1237L53
pissed as a **newt** 1070R8
better luck **next** time 120R18
from one day to the **next** 349L76
from one moment to the **next** 912L81 953R33
in **next** to no time 1521R51
in the **next** breath 162R48 1253L38
next door 411R40 953R52/56/59
next of kin 780L78 953R60
next-to-last 953R81
the **next** thing 1512R46
pince-**nez** 1068L3
nibble away 954L21/23/21
have a **nice** day 349L77
nice little earner 954L55
nice looker 839R65
nice work if you can get it 954L50
no more Mr **Nice** Guy 926R11
niche market 954R8
in the **nick** of time 954R18
nick for 954R26
nick-nack 783L75 954R54
old **Nick** 980L12
nickel-and-dime 954R46/48
nickel-plated 954R41
nicotine patch 954R66
well-**nigh** 1653L35
bonfire **night** 146R10
day and **night** 349L62

▫dead of ▪night 350R67
▫first ▪night 526L14
▪fly-by-▫night 541L19
good ▪night 612L51
▫Guy ▪Fawkes Night 633R74
▪hen ▫night 662R76
▫last ▪night 798L32 955L68
make a ▪night of it 855L13
▫morning noon and ▪night 918R48
▫night after ▪night 955L26/50
▫night and ▪day 955L28
▪night ▫blindness 955L30
▫night-▪night 955L52
▫night on the ▪town 955L54
▪night ▫owl 955L61
▪night ▫school 955L63
▪night ▫shift 955L31 1315R76/77
▪night ▫stand/▫table 111R71 955L34/35
▪night-▫time 955L36
▫night ▪watchman 955L37
▫one-night ▪stand 984L81/R1
▫opening ▪night 526L14 988R1
▫Saturday night ▪special 1257L14
▫sleepless ▪night 1351R20
▫spend the ▪night to▫gether/▫with 955L24 1390L48
▪stag ▫night 1406L34
▫stay the ▪night 1417L57
▫things that go bump in the ▪night 1512L47
▫Twelfth ▪Night 1572R36
▫deadly ▪nightshade 350R81
▫willy-▪nilly 1666L35
▫cat-o'-▪nine-▫tails 203L69
▫nine days' ▪wonder 955R78
▫nine times out of ▪ten 955R80
▫nine to ▪five 955R84
▫ninety-nine times out of a ▪hundred 956L37
on ▫cloud ▪nine 248R59
go ▫down/▫fall like ▪ninepins 956L17
▫done/▫dressed (up) to the ▪nines 955R74
▫nineteen to the ▪dozen 417R52
▫nineteenth ▪hole 956L30
▫ninety-nine times out of a ▪hundred 956L37
a ▫nip ▪here and a ▫tuck ▪there 956L81
a ▪nip in the ▫air 956R1
▫nip a▪cross 956L59
▫nip a▪long 956L62
▫nip and ▪tuck 956L76/77
▪nip at 956L70
▫nip ▪in 956L60
▫nip in the ▪bud 956L71
▫nip ▪out/▪round 956L58
de▫cree ▪nisi 356R8
▪Nissen ▫hut 956R20
▫nitric ▪acid 956R39
▫nitty-▪gritty 956R48
▫public ▫enemy no. ▪1 1142L30
▫Noah's ▪ark 62R1 958L17
No▫bel ▪prize 958L30
no▫blesse ob▪lige 958L58
like ▪nobody's ▫business 179L6
▫nobody's ▪fool 544R9
▫nod in a▪greement 958L80
▫nod ▪off 958R13
the ▫land of ▪nod 794L52
▫nodding ac▪quaintance 958R3
▪lymph ▫node 849R28
▫bête ▪noire 120L30
▫anti-▪noise 50L20
▫big ▪noise 125L47
make a ▪noise about 958R53
▪noise pol▫lution 958R65
▫white ▪noise 1660R45
▫make ▪noises 958R56/59
▫make (all) the ▫right/▫proper/cor▫rect ▪noises 958R61
▫nom de ▪plume 959L12
▪nominate as 959L44
▪nominate *someone* for/as 959L32
▫non-ad▪dictive 959L55
▫non-ag▪gression 959L57
▫non-alco▪holic 959L59
▫non-a▪ligned 959L60/63
▫non-be▪liever 959L64
▫non-▪bio 959L66
▫non-bio▪logical 959L67
▫non-▪combatant 959L68
▫non compos ▪mentis 959R76
▫non-con▪tributory 959L72
▫non-▪drip 959L74
▫non-e▪vent 959L76
▫non-ex▪istent 959L80
▫non-▪fiction 959L84
▫non-▪flammable 959R2
▫non-in▪flammable 959R2
▫non-judg▪mental 959R4
▫non-ne▪gotiable 959R6
▫non-▪payment 959R8
▫non-▪profit(-▫making) 959R10
▫non-prolifer▪ation 959R13
▫non-▪racist 959R16
▫non-▪resident 959R19
▫non-re▪turnable 959R22
▫non-returnable ▪bottle 959R23
▫non ▪sequitur 960R7
▫non-▪slip 959R35
▫non-▪smoker 959R26/25
▫non-▪standard 959R29/32
▫non-▪starter 959R38
▫non-▪stick 959R41
▫non-▪stop 959R43
▫non-▪U 959R47
▫non-▪verbal 959R49
▫non-▪violence 959R54/50
▫non-▪white 959R54
per▫sona non ▪grata 1053R7/8
▫sine qua ▪non 1340R34
▪nonce ▫word 959R61
make (a) ▪nonsense of 960L72
▪nonsense ▫verse/▫rhyme/▫poem 960L80
▪nonsense ▫word/▫syllable 960L84
▫stand no ▪nonsense 960L78
▫stuff and ▪nonsense 1448L19
▫talk ▪nonsense 1488R8
won't ▫stand any ▪nonsense 960L78
▫nook and ▪cranny 320L30 960R28
▫high ▪noon 667L72/75
▫morning noon and ▪night 918R48
have a ▪noose around *one's* ▫neck 960R45
neither ▫here nor ▪there 948R20
neither ▫one thing nor the ▪other 948R16
▫not see ▫hide nor ▪hair of 1284L15
▫Norman ▪Conquest 961L27
mag▫netic ▪north 852R58
▫North ▪Pole 961L61
▫North-South di▪vide 961L47/50
▫North ▪Star 961L62
▫north ▪wind 961L60
▫true ▪north 1563R25
the ▫Northern ▪lights 961L79
▫can't see ▫further than/be▫yond the ▫end of *one's* ▪nose 1283L59
cut off *one's* ▫nose to spite *one's* ▪face 338R83
▫follow *one's* ▪nose 543L78/83
get ▫up *someone's* ▪nose 961R66
keep *one's* ▪nose ▫clean 961R72
keep *one's* ▪nose ▫out of 961R77
keep/put *one's* ▫nose to the ▪grindstone 961R82
▫lead *someone* by the ▪nose 803R72
▫look down *one's* ▪nose 839L34
no ▫skin off ▪*someone's* ▫nose 1346R33
▫nose a▫bout/▪round 962L80
▪nose ▫cone 962L66
▫nose in a ▪book 962L40
▫nose in the ▪air 962L38
▪nose into 962L73/81
▪nose ▫job 962L57
▫nose ▪out 962L71/83
▫nose to ▪tail 962L65
▪nose ▫wheel 962L68
▫pay through the ▪nose 1038L83
▫poke/▫stick *one's* ▪nose into 962L41
▫powder *one's* ▪nose 1105L76
▫right out from under *someone's* ▪nose 962L49
▫Roman ▪nose 1232L43
rub *someone's* ▪nose in it/the ▫dirt 1238R4
▫thumb *one's* ▪nose at 1517R49
▫turn *one's* ▪nose up 1571L61
▫wrinkle (up) *one's* ▪nose 1691L36
▫hard-▪nosed 646R76
▫hook-▪nosed 684L27
▫sharp-▪nosed 1312R28
▪snub-▫nosed 1368L12/13
▫toffee-▪nosed 1531R26
▫count ▪noses 312L10
▪nosh-up 962R23
▫nosy ▪parker 962R49
▪notch ▪up 963L50/51
▫top-▪notch 1537R3
▪C-▫note 182L7
▪cover ▫note 316R13
▪covering ▫note 316L35
▪credit ▫note 322L51
▪eighth ▫note 445L7 1161L4
▪half ▫note 637R83 900R62
▪liner ▫note 825R53
▫mental ▪note 887L68 963L59
▪promissory ▫note 1131L63
▪quarter ▫note 328R55 1160L59
six▪teenth ▫note 1291L54 1344L81
▫strike a ▪note 1442R56
▫take ▪note of 963R37
▪whole ▫note 1290R68 1662L30
▫headed ▪notepaper 654L42
com▫pare ▪notes 273L18
▪crib ▫notes 323R34
▪sleeve ▫notes 1351R79
▫better than ▪nothing 120R12
▫come to ▪nothing 266R72
▫double or ▪nothing 413R59
▫good for ▪nothing 611R6/8
have/be ▫nothing to ▪do with 964L41/44
▫have ▪nothing on 651R52 982L30
have ▫nothing to ▪say for *oneself* 1259L74
it a▫vails *one* ▪nothing 83L40
it's ▪nothing 964L14
▫nothing ▪daunted 348R45 964L60
▫nothing ▪near 944R42
▫nothing of the ▪sort/▪kind 964L34
▫nothing ▪short of 964L61
▫nothing ▪special 964L40
▫nothing to get ex▪cited about 477L17
▫nothing to ▫write ▪home about 1691R65
on a ▫hiding to ▪nothing 666R82
▫something for ▪nothing 1375L4
▫stop at ▪nothing 1430R32
▫think ▪nothing of 1513L25/22
to ▫say ▪nothing of 1260L4
▫sweet ▪nothings 1475R53
▪D-▫notice 403R42
not take a ▫blind bit of ▪notice 135L69
▪notice ▫board 964R30
sit ▫up and take ▪notice 1343R62
▫take ▪notice 964R1 1487L23
▪notify of 964R41
▫noughts and ▪crosses 965L1
▫abstract ▪noun 6L12
col▫lective ▪noun 258L31
▫common ▪noun 271L9
▫concrete ▪noun 282R10
▪count ▫noun 312L32/38
▪noun ▫phrase 965L10
▪proper ▫noun 1134L75
▪nourish *oneself* on/with 965L19
▫entre ▪nous 462R21
▫art nou▪veau 65R2
▫nouveau ▪riche 965L35/40
▫nouvelle cui▪sine 965L42
▫graphic ▪novel 619R11
▫any day ▪now 349L58
▫even ▪now 472L21
▫every now and a▪gain/▪then 473R31
▫just ▪now 774L45 965R25
NO▪W ac▫count 965R68
▫now ▪now 965R62
▫right ▪now 1224L70
▪there ▫now 1510L43
▫miles from ▪nowhere 896L32
▫nowhere ▪near 944R44/56/58
▪nowhere to be ▪found 520R55
to the ▫nth de▪gree 966L31
▫anti-▪nuclear 50L23
▫nuclear ▪family 966L71
▫nuclear-▪free 966L63
▫nuclear re▪actor 1178L38
▫nuclear ▪winter 966L66
nu▫cleic ▪acid 966L75
nudge ▫nudge (wink ▪wink) 966R35
make a ▪nuisance of *oneself* 966R59
▫null and ▪void 966R69
▫back ▪number 89L20
▪binary ▫number 127L11
▪box ▫number 155L30
▪E ▫number 434L46
▫home (▪phone) ▫number 679R71
▫license plate ▪number 817L52 1193R82
look ▫out for number ▪one 840L52
▪number among 967L83/R1
▪number-▫cruncher 967L32/36
▪number ▫plate 967L43
▫Number ▪Ten 967L49
someone's ▫number *is* ▪up 967L30
▫opposite ▪number 990R42
▫personal identifi▪cation ▫number 1053L5
▫prime ▪number 1121R78
▫public ▫enemy number ▪one 1142L30
re▫curring ▪number 1188R18
▫round ▪number 1236L75
▪serial ▫number 1296L51
▫toll-free ▪number 562R37
▫whole ▪number 1662L31
something's ▫days are ▪numbered 349L63/65
▪numbers ▫game 967L45
▪mind-▫numbing 899L14
▫arabic ▪numerals 59R69
▫Roman ▪numerals 1232L44
aux▪iliary ▫nurse 83L22
▪charge ▫nurse 218L5
▫district ▪nurse 400L61
▫head ▪nurse 1292L69
▫licensed ▫practical ▪nurse 817L61
▫nursery ▫nurse 968L42
▪staff ▫nurse 1406L3
▪wet ▫nurse 1654R13/15
▪day ▫nursery 349R26
▪nursery ▫nurse 968L42
▪nursery ▫rhyme 968L45
▪nursery ▫school 968L43
▪nursery ▫slopes 968L48
▪nursing ▫aid 968L21
▪nursing aux▫iliary 83L22
▪nursing ▫home 968L23
▫senior ▪nursing officer 1292L68
a ▫hard/▫tough ▪nut to ▫crack 968L79
a ▫sledgehammer to crack a ▪nut 1351L2
Bra▪zil ▫nut 159L35
▪ginger ▫nut 595R22
▫hard ▪nut 646R80
▪pine ▫nut 1068L62
▪wing ▫nut 1669L21
▫nuts and ▪bolts 968R60
▫O.▪D. on 974L84
▫put/▫stick *one's* ▪oar in 969R77
▫hippocratic ▪oath 671R17
▫rolled ▪oats 1231R45
▫sow *one's* wild ▪oats 1381R2
▫direct ▪object 386R73
▫indirect ▪object 722L43
▪object ▫lesson 970R28
▪object-▫oriented 970R4
ob▪ject to 970R42
▪sex ▫object 1303R55
the ▫object of the ▪exercise 970R17
consci▫entious ob▪jector 289L63
▫objet ▪d'art 970R80
no▫blesse ob▪lige 958L58
o▪blige *someone* with 971L31
obser▪vation ▫post 971R82
▫built-in/▫planned obso▪lescence 972L81
▪obstacle ▫course 71R47 972R13
ob▪tain from 972R82
ob▪trude upon 973L13
▫screamingly ▪obvious 1272L57
▫rise to the oc▪casion 1226R40
▫sense of oc▪casion 1293L37
▫state oc▪casion 1414R55
occu▫pational dis▪ease 973R27
occu▫pational ▪hazard 973R29
occu▫pational ▪therapy 973R33
▫Occupied ▪Territories 1504R55
▫owner-▪occupied 1013L36
▫owner-▪occupier 1013L35
▪occupy with 973R40
▫drop in the ▪ocean 427R81
▫high-▪octane 667R82 974L53
▫odd-▪job ▫man 974R40
▫odd-▪jobber 974R40
▫odd man ▪out 974R26
a▫gainst all (the) ▪odds 974R80
▫odds and ▪ends 975L16
▫odds and ▪sods 975L16
▫over the ▪odds 975L12
the ▫odds are stacked a▪gainst *someone* 1405R61
▪body ▫odour 142R72
▪Oedipus ▫complex 975L51
▫first of▪fender 526L17
of▫fender ▪profile 976R75
▪sex of▫fender 1303R57
▫young of▪fenders' insti▫tution 1698L69
▪charm of▫fensive 218R51
▫under ▪offer 977L57
▫burnt ▪offering 177R17
▪peace ▫offering 1039R66
▪booking ▫office 147R8
▪box ▫office 155L33
▪Foreign ▫Office 549R29
▫head ▪office 654L55
▪Home ▫Office 680L66
▫left-▪luggage office 807R14
▫lost-and-▪found ▫office 842L40
▫lost ▪property ▫office 842L39
Meteoro▪logical ▫Office 891L62
▪office ▫block 977R17
▪office ▫building 977R17
▪office ▪hours 977R19
▫office ▪junior 773R21 977R22
▪office ▫tower 977R17 1543L75
▪Oval ▫Office 1005L21
▪post ▫office 1100L72/74
▪real estate ▫office 469L48
▪register ▫office 1193R72 1194L6
▪registry ▫office 1194L6
▪sorting ▫office 1377R66
▫take (up) ▪office 1486R37
com▫missioned ▪officer 270L38
▪customs ▫officer 338R37
▫first ▪officer 525R84
pa▪trol ▫officer 1036R46
▪petty ▫officer 1056L79
po▪lice ▫officer 1091R16
pro▪bation ▫officer 1125L33/40
▫senior ▪nursing officer 1292L68
▪staff ▫officer 1406L7
▪truant ▫officer 1562R31
▪warrant ▫officer 1639L8
▫good ▪offices 612L14
of▫ficial ▪receiver 977R61 1183R63
of▫ficial ▪secret 977R65
Of▫ficial ▪Secrets ▫Act 977R68
ex of▪ficio 480L39
off▪load onto 978L52
▪cast-▫offs 202L30
▪offset against 978L59
off▪set by 978L57
▫every so ▪often 473R35
▫oh ▪dear 352L45
▫Oh ▪God 608R77
▫right ▪oh 1224L53
▫burn the ▫midnight ▪oil 177L41
▫castor ▪oil 202R61
▫cod-liver ▪oil 254L10
▪corn ▫oil 306L29
▫crude ▪oil 330L10
es▫sential ▪oil 468R53
like ▫oil and ▪water 979L22
▫linseed ▪oil 827R76
▪mineral ▫oil 900L26
▫no ▪oil ▫painting 979L29
▪oil-▫fired 523R8 979L24
▪oil ▫painting 979L26/27
▪oil ▫slick 979L30
▪oil ▫tanker 979L33 1490L53
▫oil the ▪wheels 979L40
▪oil ▫well 979L34
▫olive ▪oil 980R67
▪palm ▫oil 1020R52
pour ▫oil on troubled ▪waters 1104R60
▪soya ▫oil 1381R20
▫vegetable ▪oil 1610L82
▫well-▪oiled 1653L53/54
▫oilseed ▪rape 1173R8
▫fly in the ▪ointment 540R61
▫rule O▪K 1239R84
▫okey-▪doke 979R31
a ▫chip off the old ▪block 227R16
▪age-▫old 25L68
an ▫old head on ▫young ▪shoulders 653L29
as ▫old as Me▪thuselah 892L27
as ▫old as the ▪hills 979R51
▫dirty ▫old ▪man 388L28
for old ▪times' ▫sake 980R4
▫grand old ▪age 617R73
▫grand old ▪man 618L15
have a ▪rare old ▫time 1173R83
▫money for old ▪rope 913R24
▫old ▪age 979R53
▫old age ▪pension 979R56/60 1046L40 1292L42
▫old ▪boy/▪girl 979R64/69 980L47
▫old-▪boy ▫network 980L51/55
▫old ▪buffer 172R18/19 979R68
▪old ▫country 980L58
▫old-es▪tablished 469L7
▫old-▪fashioned 980L62/65
▫old ▪flame 980L67
▫old ▪growth 979R70
▪old ▫guard 980L69
▫old ▪hand 979R74
▫old ▪hat 979R77
▫old ▪lady 979R82
▫old ▪maid 979R84
▫old ▪man 980L3
▫old ▪master 980L6
▪old ▫money 980L7/72
▫old ▪Nick 980L12
▫old ▪people's ▫home 980L13
▪old ▫school 980L76
▫old school ▪tie 980L77
▪old-▫time 980L84
▫old-▪timer 980L16
▫old ▪wives' ▫tale 980L18
▫old ▪woman 980L21
▫Old ▪World 980R7/11
▫ripe old ▪age 1226L69
the ▫Old ▪Testament 980L81
the ▫same old ▪faces 1253L44
the ▫same old ▪story 1253L45
▫tough as old ▪boots 1541R5/L84
▫olde ▪worlde 980R27
▫older ▪student 875R58
▫oldest pro▫fession (in the ▪world) 979R52
▪olive ▫branch 980R60
▫olive ▪drab 980R65
▫olive ▪green 980R66
▫olive ▪oil 980R67
O▫lympic ▪Games 981L10
▫Special O▪lympics 1385R82
▫ill-▪omened 703R12
o▪mit from 981L61
o▪mit to 981L64
▫man/▫woman on the Clapham ▪omnibus 981L83
every ▫once in a ▪while 473R32
▫just this ▪once 983L56
▫once in a blue ▪moon 139R62
▫once in a ▪lifetime 819R79 983L58/59
▫once or ▪twice 983L74
▪once-▫over 983R3/8
▫once upon a ▪time 983L76/80
in ▫ones and ▪twos 983R76
▪young ▫ones 1698L72
▫spring ▪onion 1400L5
▫know *one's* ▪onions 787R10
by ▫ticket ▪only 1518R49
in ▫name ▪only 937L8
it is ▫only ▪fair 494R72
▫only ▪child 985R76
▫only ▪just 774R14/15/16 986L45/48

only kidding 779R8
only resort 1210L28
only too 1535L56
standing room only 1410R3
slip-ons 1353R37
onward and upward 986R75
oops-a-daisy 987L31
ooze from 987L35/37/41
ooze out 987L38
op art 987L82
op cit 987R3
op-ed 987R10
op-shop 991R74
photo op 1059L14
keep *one's* eyes open for 488R28
leave the door open 807R2
open admissions 988R59
open adoption 988L43
open-and-shut 987R27
open book 988L47
open classroom 988R62
open-cut 988R22 989L18
open day 988R65
open-door 987R29
open-ended 988L26
open-eyed 987R32
open fire 988R23
open-handed 988R68
open *one's* heart 987R70
open-heart surgery 987R36
open-hearted 988L53
open house 988R68/72
open letter 988L54
open market 867L31 988R74
open marriage 988R77
open mind 988L29
open-minded 988L33/31
open *one's* mouth 987R72
open-mouthed 924L71 987R38
open-necked 987R41
open out/up 988R39
open-pit 988R27 989L18
open-plan 988R28
open prison 988R30
open sandwich 988R33
open season 988R80
open secret 988L57
open sesame 987R73
open the door to 411R46
open the floodgates 987R64
open to dispute 397L77
Open University 988R55
open up 987R54/59 988L61 989L8
open up about 988L62
open verdict 988L34 1614R8
the heavens open 658R56
the open air 988R18
wide open 987R20 1663R40/42
with *one's* eyes open 488R32 987R25
with open arms 987R23
eye-opener 488R41
letter opener 813L45 1023L43
tin opener 188L27 1524R82
opening hours 988L17
opening night 526L14 988R1
opening time 988L19
comic opera 267R32
grand opera 617R77
opera glasses 989L28
opera house 989L30
soap opera 1369R14
modus operandi 911R23
operate in 989L49
operate on 989R36
disk operating system 395L3
operating room 989R39
operating system 989L52
operating table 989R37
operating theatre 989R38
standard operating procedure 1411R23
operational research 989L81
operations research 989L81
operative word 989R6
camera operator 187L39
switchboard operator 1479L28
ophthalmic optician 989R63 992L25
opine about/on 989R67
a matter of opinion 989R82
considered opinion 290R22
contrary to popular opinion 298R83
matter of opinion 874R32
opinion poll 990L15 1092R20
opportunistic infection 990L58
equal opportunity 464R70
golden opportunity 610L31
opportunity shop 990R3
photo opportunity 1059L14
opposite number 990R42
the opposite sex 990R46
co-opt 303R61
opt for 991R78
opt out 991R82 992L1
opt to 991R79
optical character recognition 992L10
optical fibre 992L13
optical illusion 992L17
dispensing optician 396L82 992L28
ophthalmic optician 989R63 992L25
fibre optics 515L22
cautious optimism 206R52 992L41
easy option 1371R82
soft option 1371R81
magnum opus 853L35
oral history 992R73
oral sex 992R84
oral tradition 992R75
orang-utan 993L24
orange soda 993L20
orange squash 993L16 1402R73
orbital road 993L61
chamber orchestra 213R51
orchestra pit 993L72 1070R52
affiliation order 22L57
apple pie order 56L67
banker's order 97R66
compulsory purchase order 279L48
court order 315L53 993R41
deportation order 368L57
gag order 579L62
law and order 801L42
mail order 853R12
maintenance order 854L63
money order 913R42
of the order of 994R32
order about/around 993R60
order book 993R82
order form 993R84
order of magnitude 994R35
order out 993R59
order paper 994L31
Order! Order! 994L81
pecking order 1041L39
point of order 1089R20
postal order 1100R75
preservation order 1117R24
restraining order 1213R12
set/put *one's* own house in order 689L35
standing order 1411R84
tall order 1489L49
the new world order 952L84
the order of the day 994L21/23
just what the doctor ordered 408L11
doctor's orders 408L13
holy orders 679R11
last orders 797R62
marching orders 864L70
orders are orders 993R50
sealed orders 1276R38
under starter's orders 1413R50
in the ordinary way 994R74
Ordinary level 994R75
the Ordnance Survey 995L3
barrel organ 101L44
house organ 689R14
male organ 857R13
mouth organ 648L79 924L19
organ grinder 995L47
sense organ 1293L18
vital organ 1627R73
organic chemistry 995L62
health maintenance organization 655R11
parent-teacher organization 1026L59
World Health Organization 1684L81
organize a piss-up in a brewery 995R13
organized crime 995R51
personal organizer 519L74 1053L6
object-oriented 970R4
original sin 996R18
orthodox medicine 997L53
oscillate between 997R17/20
osmotic pressure 997R46
ouija board 999L59
fluid ounce 538R48
oust as 999R16
oust from 999R17/20
power outage 1106L69
outer space 1002L1
outlay on 1002R49
outline in 1002R75
outlive *one's* usefulness 1002R81 1602L37
outraged at/by 1003L76
ins and outs 713L8
outside broadcast 1004L48
outside lane 1004L7/11/13
outstay *one's* welcome 1004R31
outward-bound 1004R75
Oval Office 1005L21
standing ovation 1005L34 1410L80
a bun in the oven 175R19
oven gloves 1005L44
oven mitts 1005L45
oven-ready 1005L47
a roof over *one's* head 1233L12
all over bar the shouting 99L29
all over the place 33R33 1072R57
arse over tit/tip 65L28
ass over teakettle 65L29 1494R10
bend/lean over backwards 91R26
boil over 144L53
can't get over 593R15
cast an eye/a glance over 202L35
climb over 244R17/35
cloud hanging over 248R48
cloud over 248R76
come over 264R57
dispute over 397L68/71/72
drape all over 419L75
draw a veil over 420L64
fall over 497L59/61/62
get *one's* leg over 809L9
get over 593R6 1006L64
get *something* over with 1006L50
give over 597L56
go over *something* in *one's* mind 898R51
go over with a bang 97L53
going-over 607R18/35 609R32
hand over fist 640R45
hang over 644L38
haul/drag *someone* over the coals 251R8
head over heels (in love) 653L68
hell freezes over 661L49
hold over 676L42
hung-over 694R38
in over *one's* head 653L76
keep *things* ticking over 1518R6
kick over the traces 779L6
lean over backwards 805R49
look/feel like death warmed over 352R4
lord it over *someone* 841R1
lose sleep over 842L6
mind over matter 899L16
no good/use crying over spilt milk 331R55
once-over 983R3/8
over a barrel 101L41
over and above 1005R67
over and done with 1006L53
over and over (again) 1006L57
over *my* dead body 350R33
over-egg the pudding 1005R79
over *one's* head 653L84
over hill and dale 344L14
over the counter 312R26
over the hill 670L40
over the hump 693R65
over the moon 916R60
over the odds 975L12
over the top 1536R84
paper over the cracks 1023L65
pull the wool over *someone's* eyes 1678L17
put over on 1154L71
ramble over 1171L62/R3
rear over 1181L83
ride roughshod over 1222L39
run *one's* eye over 1241R5
score (points) over 1268R64
sit in judgment over 1343L40
something over 1375L21
swap over 1473R76
tear *one's* hair out over 1495L17
throw over for 1517L44
tick over 1518R2
turn over a new leaf 1569R52
turn over in *one's* mind 898R51
up-and-over 1597R41
voice-over 1629L73
walk all over 1634L59
warm over 1638L56
written all over *someone's* face 1692L50
chuck/throw/toss overboard 1006R60
go overboard 1006R54
overburden with 1006R73
overcharge *someone* by 1006R84
overcome with/by 1007L24/28/26
overcompensate by 1007L34
overcompensate for 1007L37
overcompensate with 1007L37
overdose on 1007L77/78
overflow into/onto 1007R72
overflow pipe 1008L5
overflow with 1007R79/82/83
overhang with 1008L28
overindulge in 1008R20
overlap with 1008R52
overlay with 1008R75/76
overload with 1009L4/6/9
stay overnight 1417L57
overplay *one's* hand 1009R9
overreact to 1009R81/82
overrun by 1010L67/69
overrun on 1010L70/74
overrun with 1010L58/59
overspend on 1010R76
overstep the mark 1011L27
overstock with 1011L32/34
overtaking lane 1011L73
overwhelmed with/by 1012L29
owe *someone* a living 1012R10
owe *someone* for 1012R2
night owl 955L61
own to 1013L48/49/52
own up 1013L50
as if/like *someone* owned the place 1013L26
owner-occupied 1013L36
owner-occupier 1013L35
anti-oxidant 50L27
oxygen mask 1013R34
oxygen tent 1013R38
oyster bed 1013R51
ozone-friendly 1013R69
ozone layer 1013R63
at a snail's pace 1363R81
change of pace 215L49
pace bowler 1014L59
pace man 1014L59
put *someone* through *their* paces 1014L73
a pack of lies 818L68
economy pack 440L68
face pack 490R36
fanny pack 175L12 503L66
four-pack 556R58
freezer pack 563L57
ice pack 700L5
lead the pack 804L78
pack a punch 1016R23/25
pack animal 1016L8
pack away 1014R70
pack down 1016L60
pack ice 1016L61
pack in 1016L36/R27
pack in/into 1014R67/76/77 1016L35
pack it in 1016R29
pack off 1016R35
pack off to 1016R37
pack *something* round 1014R79
pack up 1014R71 1016R39
pack with 1014R62 1016L39/41
six-pack 1344L50
the joker in the pack 768R83
waist pack 175L12 1633L51
holiday package 1016R62
package as 1016R71
package deal 1016R56
package goods 1016R57
package holiday 1016R61
package in 1016R70
package store 1016R59
package tour 1016R61
software package 1372L26
action-packed 13R7
jam-packed 760L11
packed like sardines 1255R5
packed lunch 1016L15
vacuum-packed 1604L70
pay packet 1038R56/58
wage packet 1632R74
packing case 1016L29
packing crate 1016L30
postage and packing 1100R64
send packing 1291R68
suicide pact 1457R28
launch pad 800L84
lily pad 823L69
pad with 1017L69
sanitary pad 1254R79
scouring pad 1269R83
padded cell 1017L73
dog paddle 409L80
doggy paddle 409L79
paddle *one's* own canoe 1017R32
paddle steamer 1017R20
paddle wheel 1017R19/23
paddling pool 1017R38
paddy wagon 1017R59 1036R48
rice paddy 1220R83
cotton pads 310R49
shoulder pads 1017L23 1325R78
paedophile ring 1018L5
double(-page) spread 414L80
front-page 568L44 1018L29
full-page 572R55
page three 1018L36
page-turner 1018L38
title page 1527R49
beauty pageant 110L19
White Pages 1660R47
Yellow Pages 1696L44
all expenses paid 481R76/78/79
carriage paid 198R19
paid-up 1018R7/10
post paid 1100L76
put paid to 1038R81
reply-paid 1204R79
a pain in the back side/arse/butt/ass 1018R30
a pain in the neck 1018R27
chest pain 224R36
on/under pain of 1018R33
go to great pains 1018R43
growing pains 627R26/29/31
shooting pains 1320R42
take pains 1018R42
paint a (very) black picture 131R64
paint a picture 1019L28 1064L10
paint a rosy/grim picture 1019L30
paint box 1019L11
paint over 1019L20
paint stripper 1019L12 1444L68
paint the town (red) 1019L33
poster paint 1101R32
war paint 1637L44/46
watch paint dry 1641R40
not as black as painted 131R66
no oil painting 979L29
oil painting 979L26/27
a safe pair of hands 641R63
au pair 80L12
have a good pair of lungs 848L46
pair off 1019L76
pair up 1019L80
pair with 1019L80
bosom pal 150L63
pal around 1019R38
pal up 1019R40
pal up with 1019R41
pen pal 1044L38
gin palace 595R7
palace coup 1019R53
palace revolution 1019R53
cleft palate 243R3
beyond the pale 122L82
pale about the gills 595L43
pale ale 1020L20
pale beside 1020L28
pale imitation 1020L22
pale in comparison with 1020L28
pale into insignificance 1020L32
palette knife 1020L50
in the palm of *one's* hand 1020R28
itchy palm 756R73
palm off 1020R40/42/38/41
palm oil 1020R52
Palm Sunday 1020R54
palpitate with 1020R81
cerebral palsy 209R79
namby-pamby 936R60
pampas grass 1021L12
broiler pan 168L28 624L11
down the pan 415R30 1021L69
flash in the pan 530R45
frying pan 570R47
grill pan 624L11
pan across 1021L74
pan-fry 1021L32
pan out 1021L82
pan scourer 1021L34 1269R82
Peter Pan 1055R49
Peter Pan collar 1055R53
Tin Pan Alley 1524R84
as flat as a pancake 531L42
Pancake Day 1021R19
pancake landing 1021R22
pancake roll 1400L7
giant panda 594R14 1021R32
pander to 1021R51
Pandora's box 1021R57
panel in 1022L6
panic attack 1022L36
panic button 1022L39
panic buying 180R60 1022L45
panic into 1022L64
panic over/about 1022L63
panic selling 1022L50
panic stations 1022L56
panic-stricken 1022L58
hanky-panky 645L19
puff and pant 1143R3
pantomime horse 1022R48
ants in *one's* pants 48R34
beat the pants off 109R4
by the seat of *one's* pants 1278R7
catch *someone* with *their* pants down 204R73/78
charm the pants off 218R59
kick up/in the pants 779L34
piss/shit *one's* pants 1022R58
seat-of-the-pants 1278R11
ski pants 1345R76
smarty-pants 1358R67
wear the pants 1647L83
wet *one's* pants 1022R57
panty liner 1022R68
Pap smear 1023R23 1359R13
blotting paper 138R28
brown paper 169L60
cartridge paper 200R37
cigarette paper 232L28
crepe paper 323L27
fight *one's* way out of a paper bag 517L27
filter paper 519R46
greaseproof paper 621R17
green paper 622L78

▫kitchen ▪**paper** 782L39/46 1494L33
▫Liquid ▪**Paper** 829L13 1526R10 1661L29
▫not worth the ▫**paper** *it* is ▪printed on 1687L66
▪order ▫**paper** 994L31
▪**paper** ▫clip 1023L41
▪**paper** ▫knife 813L45 1023L43
▫**paper** ▪money 1023L44
▫**paper** ▪over 1023L64
▫**paper** over the ▪cracks 1023L65
▫**paper** ▪profit 1023L45
▪**paper** ▫round 1023L50
▪**paper** ▫route 1023L50
▪**paper** ▫shop 1023L51
▫**paper** ▪thin 1023L54
▫**paper** ▪tiger 1023L55
▫**paper** ▪towel 782L40
▪**paper** ▫trail 1023L59
put/set ▫pen(cil) to ▪**paper** 1044L36/R77
▪rice ▫**paper** 1220R84
▫rough ▪**paper** 1235R84
▫scrap ▪**paper** 1271L6
▪scratch ▫**paper** 1271L6/R56
▫silver ▪**paper** 1339L1
▪term-▫**paper** 1501R12
▪tissue ▫**paper** 1527L34
▪toilet ▫**paper** 1532L76
▪tracing ▫**paper** 1544R35
▫waxed ▪**paper** 1645L24
▫white ▪**paper** 1660R51
▪wrapping ▫**paper** 1689R30
▪writing ▫**paper** 1023L15 1692L37
▪walking ▫**papers** 864L71 1634R28
▪working ▫**papers** 1681R59
▫**papier-**▪**mâché** 1023R8
be▫low/▫under ▪**par** 1023R42/53
▫not up to ▪**par** 1023R44
▫**par** ▪excellence 1023R37 1026R29
▫**par** for the ▪course 1023R46
▫golden ▪**parachute** 610L59
▪hit **pa**▫**rade** 673L67
i▪dentity **pa**▫**rade** 701R30
pa▪**rade** ▫ground 1024L24
▪ticker-tape **pa**▫**rade** 1518R38
▫bird of ▪**paradise** 128L59
▫fool's ▪**paradise** 544R16
▫**parallel** ▪bars 1024R20
▫**parallel** ▪line 1024R29
▫**parallel** ▪processing 1024R26
put/stick *one's* ▫head above the ▪**parapet** 653R29
▪**parcel** ▫bomb 1025R50
▫**parcel** ▪out 1025R59
▪**parcel** ▫post 1025R51
▫**parcel** ▪up 1025R56
▫part and ▪**parcel** of 1028L80
▫beg *someone's* ▪**pardon** 1026L12/16/19/22
▫free ▪**pardon** 561L84
I ▫beg your ▪**pardon** 113R38
if you'll ▫**pardon** the ex▪pression 1026L5
▪**pardon** for 1025R84
▫royal ▪**pardon** 1238L11
▫**pare** (▫down) to the ▪bone 1026L43
bio▫logical ▪father/▪mother/▪**parent** 127R58
▪birth ▫mother/▫**parent** 128R73
▫lone ▪**parent** 837R38
▫one-**parent** ▪family 984R14
▫**parent** ▪company 1026L57
▫**parent**-▪teacher associ▫ation 1026L58
▫**parent**-▪teacher organiz▫ation 1026L59
▫single-**parent** ▪family 984R14
▫planned ▪**parenthood** 1075L54
in ▫loco **pa**▪**rentis** 732L50
▫**parents** and ▪Citizens 1026L60
▪**paring** ▫knife 1026L50
▫plaster of ▪**Paris** 1076L79/82
▫**parish** ▪clerk 1026R47
▫**parish** ▪council 1026R49
a▪musement ▫**park** 43L16 574R79 1509L22
▪business ▫**park** 178R57
▪car ▫**park** 193R23
▪caravan ▫**park** 193R65
▫double-▪**park** 414L69
in▫dustrial ▪**park** 724L1
▫national ▪**park** 939L20
▪**park** ▫keeper 1026R69
sa▪fari ▫**park** 1248L56
▪science ▫**park** 1266R63
▪theme ▫**park** 1509L22
▪trailer ▫**park** 193R64
▫nosy ▪**parker** 962R49
▪**parking** ▫brake 642L4 1027L6
▪**parking** ▫garage 193R25
▪**parking** ▫light 1027L7 1334L64
▪**parking** ▫meter 891L73 1027L9
▪**parking** po▫liceman 1547R74
▪**parking** ▫ticket 1027L12
▪valet ▫**parking** 1605L25
▪**Parkinson's** ▫law 1027L25
▪**parlay** into 1027L48/50
▪**parley** with 1027L56
▫Houses of ▪**Parliament** 689R30
▫Member of ▪**Parliament** 885L82
▪beauty ▫**parlour** 110L22
▪funeral ▫**parlour** 574R70
▪massage ▫**parlour** 871L46/48
▪**parlour** ▫game 1027R12
pa▪**rochial** ▫school 1027R27
▪**parrot**-▫fashion 1028L14
▫sick as a ▪**parrot** 1333L37
▪cow ▫**parsley** 317L51
▪bit ▫**part** 130L22
▫dress/▫look the ▪**part** 1028R53
in (a) ▫large ▪**part** 1028L77
▫**part** and ▪parcel of 1028L80
▫**part** ▪company 1028R77
▫**part** ex▪change 1028R13
▪**part** from 1028R71
▫**part** of ▪speech 1028R59
▫**part** of the ▪furniture 1028L84
▫**part**-▪time 1028R1/2/5
▪**part** with 1028R80 1673L47
▫play a ▪**part** 1078R55
▫spare-**part** ▪surgery 1383L75
the ▫best/▫better ▪**part** of 1028R55
par▪**take** in 1029L41
par▪**take** of 1029L36
▫**partially** ▪sighted 1029L54
par▪**ticipate** in 1029L72/73
▫past ▪**participle** 1033R18
▫perfect ▪**participle** 1048L51
▫present ▪**participle** 1116R47
ele▫mentary ▪**particle** 447L62
▪**particle** ac▫celerator 1029R15
▫**parting** of the ▪ways 1029L9
▫**parting** ▪shot 1029L18
par▪**tition** *something* into 1030L10
▫**partition** ▪off 1030L11
▫silent ▪**partner** 1337R5 1351R10
▫sleeping ▪**partner** 1337R6 1351R10
▪sparring ▫**partner** 1383L23
▫private ▪**parts** 1124L10
▫spare ▪**parts** 1383L72
▪bachelor ▫**party** 1406L34
▪bucks ▫**party** 171R4 1406L34
Demo▪cratic ▫**Party** 364R8
▪garden ▫**party** 582R84
▪hen ▫**party** 662R76
▪keg ▫**party** 777L70
▪launch ▫**party** 800R19
▪lawn ▫**party** 583L40 801R84
▪Liberal ▫**Party** 816R12
life and ▫soul of the ▪**party** 818R68
▪**party** ▫animal 1030L67
▫**party** ▪faithful 496L83 1030R24
▪**party** ▫line 1030R29/52
▪**party** ▫piece 1030L70
▫**party** political ▪broadcast 1030R21
▫**party** ▪politics 1030R31
▪**party** ▫pooper 1030L74
▪**party** ▫popper 1030L76
▫**party** ▪wall 1030R55
Re▪publican ▫**Party** 1206R23
▪search ▫**party** 1277L50
▫Social Demo▪cratic **Party** 1370R28
▫spoil the ▪**party** for 1395L82
▪stag ▫**party** 1406L34
▪tea ▫**party** 1494L24
▫third ▪**party** 1513R25
▫third-**party** in▪surance 1513R28
▫throw a ▪**party** 1517L54
▪working ▫**party** 1681R54
▫faux ▪**pas** 507R23
▫**pas-de**-▪**deux** 1030R65
▫be at/▫reach/▫come to a pretty ▪**pass** 1119R71
▪boarding ▫**pass** 141R54
▫come to ▪**pass** 265R9
▫free ▪**pass** 561L30/R22
▫let *something* ▪**pass** 812L40
▫**pass** a▪cross 1030R74
▪**pass** among 1030R75
▪**pass** as 1031R49 1032L8/27/28/29
▫**pass** a▪way 1032L14
▫**pass** (all) be▪lief 1031L6
▫**pass** ▪by 1030R78
pass ▫by on the other ▪side 1030R81
▪**pass** de▫gree 1031R3/6
▫**pass**-▪fail 1031R8
▪**pass** for 1032L8/45
▪**pass** from 1031L44/R72 1032L38
▪**pass** into 1030R83
▫**pass** ▫mark 1031R11
▫**pass** ▪muster 1031L77
▫**pass** ▪off 1032L21/24
▫**pass** ▪on 1030R84 1031L47/49/R55/68/69 1032L14
▫**pass** ▪out 1032L31/36
▫**pass** ▪over 1031L1 1032L41
▪**pass** ▫rate 1031R14
▫**pass** ▪round/a▪round/▪out 1031L50
▫**pass** round the ▪hat 675R33
▫**pass** the ▪buck 1031L60
▫**pass** the ▪hat (round) 1031L64
▫**pass** the time of ▪day 1031R34/36
▫**pass** ▪up 1032L47
▫**pass** ▪water 1031R63
▫back ▪**passage** 89R12
▫bird of ▪**passage** 128L61/R5
▫rite of ▪**passage** 1227L56
en ▪**passant** 459R44
▪buck-▫**passing** 171R8
▪**passing** ▫lane 1031L26
▪**passing** ▫shot 1031L31
▫crime of ▪**passion** 324L50
▪**passion** ▫play 1032R65
▫ruling ▪**passion** 1240L17
▫**passions** run ▪high 1032R45
▫**passive** re▪sistance 1032R79
▫**passive** ▪smoking 1032R83
a ▫thing of the ▪**past** 1512R32
▫blast from the ▪**past** 133R83
▫first-**past**-the-▪post 526L20
▫march-▫**past** 864L82
▫**past** con▪tinuous 1033R14
▫**past** ▪master 1033R7
▫**past** ▪participle 1033R18
▫**past** ▪perfect 1033R22
▫**past** perfect con▪tinuous 1033R26
▫**past** pro▪gressive 1033R14 1129R60
▫**past** ▪simple 1033R27
▫**past** ▪tense 1033R31
▫simple ▪**past** 1033R27
▫wouldn't put it ▪**past** *someone* 1033R52
▫almond ▪**paste** 36L9 869R35
▫curry ▪**paste** 337L31
▫cut and ▪**paste** 339L80
▪**paste**-up 1033R74
▫scissors and ▪**paste** 1267R52
▫**pastoral** ▪care 1034L60/63
▫choux ▪**pastry** 230L19
▫Danish ▪**pastry** 345R52
▫flaky ▪**pastry** 529R46
▫puff ▪**pastry** 1143R59
▫new ▪**pastures** 1034R13
▫**pastures** ▪new 1034R12
▫Cornish ▪**pasty** 306R69
▪**pasty**-▫faced 1034R25
▫**pat** on the ▪back 1034R31/35
▪bald ▫**patch** 95L54
▪eye-▫**patch** 488R44
go through a ▫bad/▫difficult/▫rough/▫sticky ▪**patch** 1034R56
▪nicotine ▫**patch** 954R66
▪**patch** into 1035L17
▫**patch** ▪through 1035L16
▫**patch** to▪gether 1035L7/9
▫**patch** ▪up 1035L11/13
▫**patent** ▪medicine 1035L49
▫beat a ▫**path** to *someone's* ▪door 109L25
▪bridle ▫**path** 164L79
▪cycle ▫**path** 340R74
▪flight ▫**path** 534L50
▫lead *someone* up/down the garden ▪**path** 804L35
▫off the beaten ▪**path** 109L50
▫**path** of ▫least re▪sistance 1209R2
▫**paths** ▪cross 1035R37
the ▫**patience** of ▪Job 1036L33
try the ▫**patience** of a ▪saint 1036L35 1566L41
pa▪**trol** ▫car 1036R45 1401R43
pa▪**trol** ▫officer 1036R46
pa▪**trol** ▫wagon 1036R48
▫**patron** ▪saint 1036R61
the ▫**patter(ing)** of tiny ▪feet 1037L21
▫**patter** a▪bout/a▪round 1037L19
▪**patter** against/on 1037L18
▪pitter-▫**patter** 1072L8/13
▪**pattern** after 1037R3
▪**pattern** *oneself* on 1037R2
▪test ▫**pattern** 1505R18
▪willow ▫**pattern** 1666L20
▫give *someone* ▪**pause** 1037R33
▫**pave** the ▪way for/to 1037R46
▪**pave** with 1037R42
▫**paved** with ▪gold 1037R43
▫crazy ▪**paving** 321L17
▪**paving** ▫stone 1037R53
▪**pawn** ▫shop 1038L15
hazardous-▪duty ▫**pay** 345R31
▪hell to ▫**pay** 661L52
▫**pay** a ▪call 184R49 1038R79/80/79
▫**pay** a ▪price 1120R24
▫**pay** ▪back 1038L43/44/51
▪**pay** ▫claim 1038R54
▪**pay** ▫dirt 1038R67
▫**pay** *one's* ▪dues 1038L69
▪**pay** ▫envelope 1038R56
▪**pay** for 1038L39/52/R44
▫**pay** ▪in 1038L40
▪**pay** into 1038L41
▫**pay** *one's* last re▪spects 1210R83
▫**pay** ▪lip service to 828L76
▫**pay** ▪off 1038L54/55/57/59
▫**pay** ▪out 1039L1
▫**pay** ▪over 1038L62
▪**pay** ▫packet 1038R56/58
▫**pay**-per-▪view 1038R8
▪**pay** ▫phone 1038R10 1058R4
▫**pay** the ▪price 1038L77
▫**pay** the ▫ultimate ▪price 1038L80
▫**pay** through the ▪nose 1038L83
pay ▫top ▪dollar 1038R3
▫**pay** ▪up 1038L65 1598R48
▫**pay** *one's* ▪way 1038R6
▪**pay** with/by 1038L46
▪sick ▫**pay** 1332R74
▪strike ▫**pay** 1442L42
▪take-home ▫**pay** 1486R64
the ▪devil to ▫**pay** 378L54
▫**payback's** a ▪bitch 1039L6
▪**payback** ▫period 1039L11
▪fee-▫**paying** 509R47
▫down ▪**payment** 416R12
▫non-▪**payment** 959R8
re▪dundancy ▫**payment** 1190L33
▫balance of ▪**payments** 94R79
pol▫luter ▪**pays** 1092R65
▫black-eyed ▪**pea** 131R27
▪**pea**-▫brain 1039R6
▫**pea** ▪green 1039R7
▫**pea** ▪soup 1039R8
▫**pea**-▪souper 1039R8
▪snap ▫**pea** 1364L44 1457L29
▪snow ▫**pea** 860L65 1367L71 1457L29
▫split ▪**pea** 1395L6
▪sugar ▫**pea** 860L66
▫sweet ▪**pea** 1475R55
at ▫**peace** with the ▪world 1040L18
▫breach of the ▪**peace** 159L47
▫disturb the ▪**peace** 400R4
▫Justice of the ▪**Peace** 774R76
▪**peace** ▫dividend 1039R61
▪**peace**-▫loving 1039R63
▪**peace** ▫offering 1039R66
▪**peace** ▫pipe 1039R68
▪**peace** ▫sign 1039R70
▫rest in ▪**peace** 1212L59
the ▪**Peace** ▫Corps 1039R58
▫**peach** ▪Melba 1040L45
▫**peacock** ▪blue 1040L64
▫**peal** ▪out 1040R10
▫**peanut** ▪brittle 1040R21
▫**peanut** ▪butter 1040R22
▪**pear**-▫shaped 1040R32
▫prickly ▪**pear** 1121L30
▫cultured ▪**pearl** 335L9
▫mother-of-▪**pearl** 920L76
▪**pearl** ▫diver 1040R49
▫**pearl** of great ▪price 1040R47
cast ▫**pearls** before ▪swine 202L41
▫**pearly** ▪king 1040R58
▫**pearly** ▪queen 1040R58
the ▫**pearly** ▪gates 1040R56
as like as/like ▫two **peas** in a ▪pod 822R53
▫mushy ▪**peas** 931L11
▫easy-▪**peasy** 438R60
▪**peat** ▫bog 1041L8
▪**peck** at 1041L32/34/36
▪**peck** on 1041L39
▫keep *one's* ▪**pecker** up 1041L49
▪**pecking** ▫order 1041L39
funny **pe**▪**culiar** 575L60
▪brake ▫**pedal** 157R41 1041R34
▫soft-▪**pedal** 1371R47
▫knock *someone* off *their* ▪**pedestal** 785L28
▫put on a ▪**pedestal** 1042L11
pe▫**destrian** ▪crossing 1042L23
pe▫**destrian** ▪mall 1042L28
pe▫**destrian** ▪precinct 1042L27
▫**peek-a-**▪**boo** 1042R8
▫**peek** ▪in 1042R2
▫**peek** ▪out from 1042R7
▫candied ▪**peel** 189R5
▫**peel** a▪way/▪off 1042R37/35/44/18/39
keep *one's* ▪eyes ▫**peeled** for 488R28
▪**peep** at/into 1042R51/52
▪**peep**-▫bo 1042R9/53
▫**peep** ▪out 1042R63/64
▫**peeping** ▪Tom 1042R54
he▫reditary ▪**peer** 664R40
▫life ▪**peer** 819L54
▪**peer** ▫group 1043L39
▪**peer** group ▫pressure 1043L41
▫**peer** of the ▪realm 1043L17
▪**peer** ▫pressure 1043L40
▪life ▫**peerage** 819L58
▫bring/▫take *someone* ▪down a ▫**peg** (or two) 1043L72
▪clothes ▫**peg** 248R14
▪coat-▫**peg** 252L12
▪**peg**-▫leg 1043L84
▫**peg** ▪out 1043R38/40
square ▫**peg** (in a round ▪hole) 1402L31
▪tuning ▫**peg** 1567R66
▫**pelican** ▪crossing 1043R70
▫**pell**-▪**mell** 1044L3
▪slug ▫**pellet** 1356L32
at ▫full ▪**pelt** 1044L24
put/set ▫**pen(cil)** to ▪paper 1044L36/R77
▫ballpoint ▪**pen** 96L28
▪cartridge ▫**pen** 200R33
▪fountain ▫**pen** 556R34
▪light-▫**pen** 820R37
▪**pen** ▫cap 1044L45
▪**pen** ▫friend 1044L39
▪**pen** ▫lid 1044L45
▪**pen** ▫name 1044L41
▪**pen** ▫pal 1044L38
▪**pen** ▫pusher 1044L43
▫poison-▪**pen** ▫letter 1090R17
the ▫stroke of a ▪**pen** 1445L25
▪**penal** ▫code 1044L65
▪**penal** ▫colony 1044L67
▫**penal** re▪form 1044L68
▪**penal** ▫settlement 1044L67
▪death ▫**penalty** 352R22
▪**penalty** ▫area 1044R19
▪**penalty** ▫box 1044R20/28
▪**penalty** ▫kick 1044R17
▫**penalty** ▪shoot-out 1044R22
▪**penalty** ▫spot 1044R26
▫blue ▪**pencil** 140L9
have/put ▪lead in *someone's* ▫**pencil** 804R61
me▫chanical ▪**pencil** 1134L44
▫**pencil** ▪in 1045L1
▪**pencil** ▫pusher 1044L44/R80
▫**pencil**-▪thin 1044R80
pro▫pelling ▪**pencil** 1134L44
▫not have two ▫**pennies** to rub to▪gether 1045R64
▫pinch ▪**pennies** 1068L29
a ▫**penny** for your ▪thoughts 1045R61
a ▫pretty ▪**penny** 1119R74
cut ▫off without a ▪**penny** 339L76
▫not have a ▫**penny** to *one's* ▪name 1045R64
▫**penny**-▪ante 1045R73
▫**penny**-▪farthing 1045R75
▪**penny**-▫pinching 1045R77
▫**penny** ▪whistle 1045R80
penny-▫wise and pound-▪foolish 1045R66
▫spend a ▪**penny** 1390L15
the ▫**penny** ▪drops 1045R55
▫turn up like a ▫bad ▪**penny** 1571L51
▫two/▫ten a ▪**penny** 384R79 1045R70
con▫tributory ▪**pension** ▫scheme 299L74
▫old age ▪**pension** 979R56/60 1046L40 1292L42
▪**pension** ▫fund 574L70 1046L28
▫**pension** ▪off 1046L32
▪**pension** ▫plan 1046L25
▪**pension** ▫scheme 1046L25
re▪tirement ▫**pension** 979R57 1216L14
▫state ▪**pension** 979R57
▫**pent**-▪**up** 1046R5
all ▫things to all ▪**people** 1512R8
▪boat ▫**people** 142L14
▪business ▫**people** 178R58
▪flower ▫**people** 538L32
▪little ▫**people** 831L41
▫man/▫woman of the ▪**people** 1046R39
of ▫all ▪**people** 975R56
▫old ▪**people's** ▫home 980L13
▪street ▫**people** 1437L48
the ▫beautiful ▪**people** 110L48/50
▪**pep** ▫pill 1046R55
▪**pep** ▫talk 1046R56
▫**pep** ▪up 1046R60
▫black ▪**pepper** 131R40
▫cayenne ▪**pepper** 207L71
▫green ▪**pepper** 622R32
▫**pepper-and-**▪**salt** 1046R74
▪**pepper** ▫box/▫shaker 1046R71
▪**pepper** ▫mill 1046R68
▪**pepper** ▫pot 1046R71
▪**pepper** with 1047L5/6
▫red ▪**pepper** 1189L28/29
▫salt and ▪**pepper** 1046R68/74 1251R41
▫sweet ▪**pepper** 1475R56
▫**peppercorn** ▪rent 1047L9
▫as **per** ▪usual 1047L27
▫pay-**per**-▪view 1038R8
per ▪annum 1047L28
per ▪calendar ▫month 1047L31
per ▪capita 1047L35
per ▪cent 1047L59
▫**per** ▪se 1051R73
▫extrasensory **per**▪**ception** 487R21
▫**peregrine** ▪falcon 1047R78
▫future ▪**perfect** 578R6
▫letter-▪**perfect** 813L62 1678R31
▫past ▪**perfect** 1033R22
▫past **perfect** con▪tinuous 1033R26
▫**perfect** ▪participle 1048L51
▫present ▪**perfect** 1116R53
▫word-▪**perfect** 1678R31
▫counsel of **per**▪**fection** 311R42
per▪**formance** ▫art 1048R40
com▪mand **per**▫**formance** 267R75
per▪**forming** ▫arts 1048R25
▫cooling-▪off ▫**period** 303L32 1049L34

▪glacial ▫period 597R28
▫menstrual ▪period 886R62 1049L49
▪payback ▫period 1039L11
▪period ▫piece 1049L44
▪safe ▫period 1248R14
peri▫odic ▪table 1049L70
▫perish the ▪thought 1050L21
▫perk ▪up 1050L75/R10/L79
▫permanent ▪secretary 1050R38
▫permanent ▪wave 1050R11/43
▪permeate into 1050R62
▪planning per▫mission 1051L32 1075R3
per▫missive so▪ciety 1051L41
per▪mit of 1051L8
per▪mit to 1051L2/4/19
▪work ▫permit 1679R17
▫weather per▪mitting 1051L11 1648L30
▫hydrogen per▪oxide 1051L72
per▫oxide ▪blonde 1051L77
▪perpetrate against 1051R19
▪persecute for 1052L2
perse▪cution ▫complex 1052L8
perse▪vere in 1052L21
perse▪vere with 1052L23
▫Persian ▪carpet/▪rug 1052L37
▫Persian ▪cat 1052L41
per▪sist in 1052L54
per▪sist with 1052L56
▫displaced ▪person 396R40
▫first ▪person 526L27
may the ▫best person ▪win 118R64
▫missing ▪person 906L63
▫on/a▫bout *one's* ▪person 1052R18
▫person-to-▪person 1052R31/34
per▫sona non ▪grata 1053R7/8
dra▫matis per▪sonae 419L64
▫personal ▪ad 1052R72
▫personal al▪lowance 1052R75
▪personal ▫column 1052R77
▫personal com▪puter 1052R82
▫personal ef▪fects 443R32 1053L1
▫personal identifi▪cation ▫number 1053L5
▫personal ▪organizer 519L74 1053L6
▫personal ▪pronoun 1053L10
▫personal ▪property 1053L12 1134R47
▫personal ▪stereo 1053L14 1634R79
▪personal ▫touch 1053L18
person▪ality ▫clash 1053L47
person▪ality ▫cult 334R8 1053L52
person▪ality dis▫order 1053L55
▫split person▪ality 1395L11
▫anti-person▪nel 50L31
▫armoured person▪nel ▫carrier 63L82
person▪nel ▫carrier 1053R37
▫put in(to) per▪spective 1053R57
▫anti-▪perspirant 50L33
per▪suade of 1054L27
per▪suade to 1054L25
per▪tain to 1054L62
per▫vert the course of ▪justice 1054R67
▪pester for 1055L58
▪pester to 1055L59
▫pet ▪name 1055R19
▫teacher's ▪pet 1055R9 1494L76
▫hoist(ed) with/by *one's* own pe▪tard 675L69
for ▫Pete's ▪sake 1250L49
▫peter a▪way 1055R44
▫peter ▪out 1055R44
▫Peter ▪Pan 1055R49
▫Peter Pan ▪collar 1055R53
▫petit ▪bourgeois 1055R55/61/63
▫petit ▪four 1055R69
▫petit ▪pois 1056L4
pe▪tition for/about 1055R78/84/80
pe▪tition *someone* to 1055R82
▪petri ▫dish 1056L7
▪petrol ▫bomb 1056L43/40
▪petrol ▫station 1056L44
pe▫troleum ▪jelly 761R55 1056L50
▫heavy ▪petting 659L68
▪petting ▫zoo 1055R30
▫petty ▪bourgeois 1055R61/55 1056L77
▫petty ▪cash 1056L71
▫petty ▪crime 323R81 1056L65
▫petty-▪minded 1056L69
▫petty ▪officer 1056L79
▫take a ▪pew 1056R11
PG-▪13 1056R24
▫phantom ▪pregnancy 1056R84
▫in/▫out of ▪phase 1057L49
▫phase ▪in 1057L41/55
▫phase ▪out 1057L58
▪Phi ▪Beta ▪Kappa 1057R34
▫D ▪Phil 1057L61
▫Master of ▪Philosophy 871R68
▪car ▫phone 193R26
▪cell ▫phone 208L43
▫cellular ▪phone 208L42
▫mobile ▪phone 909L67
▪pay ▫phone 1038R10 1058R4
▪phone ▫book 1058R2 1496R66
▪phone ▫booth 1058R3/7
▪phone ▫box 1058R6
▪phone ▫call 258L21
▪phone-in 1058R9/21/22
▪phone-▫tapping 1058R13 1490R62
▫put the ▪phone down on 1058L78
▪Touch-Tone ▫phone 1540R6
Inter▫national Pho▫netic ▪Alphabet 744L25
▫phoney ▪war 1058R58
▪photo ▫album 1059L12
▪photo-▫call 1059L14
▫photo ▪finish 1059L19
▪photo ▫frame 1059L22
▪photo ▫op 1059L14
▪photo oppor▫tunity 1059L14
▪photo ▫session 1059L25 1298R14
▫photochemical ▪smog 1059L44
▫photoelectric ▪cell 1059L36/63
▫composite ▪photograph 1059L66
▫photographic ▪memory 1059R18
▫phrasal ▪verb 1059R64
▪noun ▫phrase 965L10
to ▫coin a ▪phrase 256L10
▫turn a ▪phrase 1569L43
▫turn of ▪phrase 1569L60
go ▪phut 1060L66
a ▫physical ▪wreck 1060L84
▫physical edu▪cation 1060R51
▫physical ge▪ography 589R17 1060R84
▫physical ▪jerks 1060R54
▫physical ▪sciences 1061L13
▫grand pi▪ano 617R78
pi▪ano ▫stool 1061L79
pi▪ano ▫tuner 1061L81 1567R79
▪stride ▫piano 1440R81
▫upright pi▪ano 1599R72
a ▪bone to ▫pick with 146L54
▪ice ▫pick 700L7
▪pick at 1061R49
▫pick *someone's* ▪brains 157L62 1062L74
▫pick ▪clean 1062L68
▪pick *someone* for 1061R26 1063L14
▫pick ▪holes in 1062L79
▪pick-me-up 1062R19
▫pick 'n' ▪mix 1061R82
▪pick of 1062L35/R14/16/18
▫pick ▪off 1061R53 1062L52/53/54/55
▪pick on 1061R62 1062R39 1063L13
▫pick on someone *your* ▪own size 1061R67
▫pick ▪out 1061R82/72/76 1062L82
▫pick ▪over 1061R59
▫pick *someone's* ▪pocket 1062L84
▫pick to ▪pieces 1064R32
▫pick ▪up 1062L56/57/58/62/R35/50/53/66/81 1063L5/7/11
▫pick ▪up on 1063L15
▫pick up ▪steam 1418L46
▫pick up the ▪bill/▪tab 1062R4 1483L32
▫pick up the ▪gauntlet 585L58
▫pick up the ▪pieces 1062R9
▫pick up the ▪slack 1348L65
▫pick up the ▪threads 1062R14
▪pick-up ▫truck 1062R76/74
▫take your ▪pick 1062L30
the ▫pick of the ▪bunch 175R35 1062L37
▫hand-▪picked 641L38
▫flying ▪picket 540R40
▪picket ▫fence 1063L49
▪picket ▫line 1063L33
▪cotton-▫picking 310R42
▫slim ▪pickings 1063L57 1353L16
▫seem like a ▪picnic 1063R10
▫Teddy Bears' ▪picnic 1495R75
▫full-frontal ▪picture 572R45/44
▫get the ▪picture 591R75 1064L18
▫keep *one* in the ▪picture 1064L19
▪motion ▫picture 920R84
▫paint a (very) ▫black ▪picture 131R64
▫paint a ▪picture 1019L28 1064L10
▫paint a ▫rosy/▫grim ▪picture 1019L30
▪picture as 1064L3
▪picture ▫book 1063R62
▪picture ▫frame 1063R64
▫picture ▪postcard 1063R66/69
▪picture ▫window 1063R70
▫put *someone* in the ▪picture 1064L22
a ▫finger in every ▪pie 521R71
▫apple pie ▪order 56L67
as A▫merican as ▫apple ▪pie 41L20
as ▫easy as ▪pie 438R39
▫cottage ▪pie 310R22 1315L46
▫custard ▪pie 338L34
eat ▫humble ▪pie 439L49
have a ▫finger in the ▪pie 521R73
▫mince ▪pie 898L71
▫mud ▪pie 927R56
▪pie ▫chart 1064L71
▪pie ▫crust 1064L75
▫pie-▪eyed 1064L78
▫pie in the ▪sky 1064L68
▫pizza ▪pie 1072L80
▫pork ▪pie 1096R42/44/60
▫shepherd's ▪pie 310R23 1315L46
▫steak and kidney ▪pie 1417R69
a ▪nasty piece of ▫work 938R48
a ▫piece of ▪cake 183L83 1064R13
a ▫piece of *one's* ▪mind 1064R16
a ▫piece of the ▪action 13R13
col▪lector's ▫piece 257R68
conver▪sation ▫piece 301L13
mu▪seum ▫piece 930R82
▫one-piece ▪swimsuit 984R24
▪party ▫piece 1030L70
▪period ▫piece 1049L44
pièce de rési▪stance 1064R65
▫piece of ▪skirt/▪tail/▪ass 1064R56
▫piece to▪gether 1064R37
▪puff ▫piece 1143R69
▫say *one's* ▪piece 1259R67
▫set ▪piece 1299R60
▫three-piece ▪suit 1515L75
▫three-piece ▪suite 832L41 1515L76
▫two-▪piece 1576L49
▪villain of the ▫piece 1624L24
▫bits and ▪pieces 130L20
▫come to ▪pieces 1064R22
▫go/▫fall to ▪pieces 1064R25/30
▫pick/▫pull to ▪pieces 1064R32
▫pick up the ▪pieces 1062R9
▫pieces of ▪eight 1064R55
▫pied à ▪terre 1065L3
Pied ▫Piper (of ▪Hamelin) 1064R83
▪ear ▫piercing 436L69
a ▫pig in a ▪poke 1065L70
▪guinea ▫pig 631R20/24
make a ▫pig's ▪ear of 1065L75
▫make a (▫real) ▪pig of *oneself* 1065R25
▫male chauvinist ▪pig 857R76
▫pig in the ▪middle 1065L82
▫pig ▫iron 1065R80
▪pig-out 1065R28/30
▫pig ▪out on 1065R28
▪carrier ▫pigeon 199L16
▫clay ▪pigeon 239R8
▫not ▪your ▫pigeon 1065R40
▫pigeon-▪chested 1065R43
▪pigeon ▫fancier 1065R45
▪pigeon ▫loft 1065R38
▫pigeon-▪toed 1065R46
▪stool ▫pigeon 1430L68
▫put *something* in a ▪pigeonhole 1065R55
▫put *something* in ▪pigeonholes 1065R56
put/set the ▫cat among the ▪pigeons 203L64
▪racing ▫pigeons 1165R28
▫higgledy-▪piggledy 667L32
▪piggy back (▫ride) 1065R6
▪piggy ▫bank 1065R8
▫piggy in the ▪middle 1065L82
▪pile-▫driver 1066R1
▫pile ▪in 1066R5
pile it ▫high (and) sell it ▪cheap 1066L69
▫pile on the ▪agony 1066L76
▫pile ▪out of/▪pile ▫into 1066R6
▫pile ▪up 1066L66/68/79
▪birth control ▫pill 128R69
▫bitter ▪pill (to ▫swallow) 130R67
▫morning-▪after ▫pill 918R48
▪pep ▫pill 1046R55
▪pill-▫popping 1066R39
▪sleeping ▫pill 1351R13
▫sweeten/▫sugar the ▪pill 1066R36
from ▫pillar to ▪post 1066R58
▪pillar-▫box 1066R61
▪pillow ▫talk 1067L5
▪pop ▫pills 1095L83
▪auto-▫pilot 82R55
▫automatic ▪pilot 82R55
▫pilot ▪through 1067L30
▪test ▫pilot 1505R27
▪goose-▫pimples 613L45/16/38
▪bobby ▫pin 142L81 636R64
▫can't pin ▪that on 190L59
▪clothes ▫pin 248R14
▪drawing ▫pin 419R63
▫pin back *your* ▪ears 1067R54
▫pin ▪down 1067R49/56/58
▫pin *your* ▪ears ▫back 1067R54
▫pin *one's* ▪hopes on 1067L70
▫pin ▪on 1067L69/R52
▪pin to 1067R48
▫pin ▪up 1067L70/74
▪rolling ▫pin 1231R48
▪safety ▫pin 1248R73
▫split ▪pin 1395L8
▫straight as a ▪pin 1432R78
▪tuning ▫pin 1567R66
▪pinafore ▫dress 1067R79
▪pinball ma▫chine 1068L2
▫pince-▪nez 1068L3
▪pincer ▫movement 1068L11
▪pinch *oneself* 1068L24
▫pinch and ▪scrape 1068L29
▫pinch ▪pennies 1068L29
▫take with a ▫pinch of ▪salt 1068L45
▪penny-▫pinching 1045R77
▪pine ▫cone 1068L59
▪pine for 1068L71
▪pine ▫kernel 1068L62
▪pine ▫needle 1068L61
▪pine ▫nut 1068L62
▪ping-▫pong 1068L83
▪pinion to 1068R10
▪pink-▫collar 1068R21
▫pink ▪dollar 1068R27
▫pink ▪elephant 1068R24
▫pink ▪pound 1068R26
▫pink ▪slip 1068R33/30
▫salmon-▪pink 1251L78
▫shocking ▪pink 1318R38
▫tickled ▪pink 1518R75
▪pinking ▫shears 1068R53
▫pins and ▪needles 1067L61/64
▪pint-▫size(d) 1069L17
▫pious ▪hope 1069L51
▫pip *someone* at the ▪post 1069L62
▪corncob ▫pipe 306L49
▪overflow ▫pipe 1008L5
▪peace ▫pipe 1039R68
▪pipe ▫cleaner 1069R37
▫pipe ▪down 1069R48
▪pipe ▫dream 1069R39
▫pipe ▪up 1069R47
▫put/▫stick in your ▫pipe and ▪smoke it 1069R34
Pied ▫Piper (of ▪Hamelin) 1064R83
▫piped ▪music 1069L75
▫piping ▪hot 687R11 1069R70
▫squeeze *someone* until the ▪pips squeak 1403R68
▫organize a ▫piss-up in a ▪brewery 995R13
▫piss a▪bout/a▪round 1070L73
▪piss ▫artist 1070L68
▫piss a▪way 1070L77
▫piss ▪off 1070L80/R1
▫piss *one's* ▪pants 1022R58
▫piss-▪poor 1070L60/61
▪piss-▫take 1070L63/65
▪piss-up 1070R21
▫take the ▪piss (out of) 1070L57
▫pissed as a ▪newt/▪fart 1070R8
▫pissed out of *one's* ▪head/▪mind/▪skull 1070R8
▪air-▫pistol 29L61
hold/put a ▪pistol to *someone's* ▫head 1070R31
▪pistol-▫whip 1070R34
▪water ▫pistol 1642R19
▫bottomless ▪pit 152R10
▪gravel ▫pit 621L2
▫open-▪pit 988R27 989L18
▪orchestra ▫pit 993L72 1070R52
▪pit against 1070R71 1674R50
▫pit bull (▪terrier) 1070R59
▫pit of *the/one's* ▪stomach 1070R56
▪pit ▫pony 1070R50
▪pit with 1070R65
at ▪concert ▫pitch 281L63
▪pitch at 1071L44/46/45/46/59
▫pitch-▪black 1071L81
▫pitch-▪dark 1071L82
▫pitch ▪darkness 1071L84
▫pitch ▪forward 1071L8
▫pitch ▪in 1071R1/4/6
▫pitch in at the ▪deep ▫end 357L58
▪pitch into 1071L5/13/R7
▪pitch onto 1071L5
▫pitch ▪up 1071R10
▪sales ▫pitch 1250R71
▫high-▪pitched 667L78 669L27/28
▫low-▪pitched 844R63
▫pitched ▪battle 1071R12
▪pitchfork into 1071R25
▪pith ▫helmet 1071R53
▪pitter-▫patter 1072L8/13
for ▫pity's ▪sake 1250L49
▪pivot on 1072L70/72
▪pizza-▫face 1072R4
▪pizza ▫house 1072R6
▫pizza ▪pie 1072L80
▪pizza ▫place 1072R6
all ▪over the ▫place 33R33 1072R57
as ▫if/like *someone* ▪owned the ▫place 1013L26
between a ▫rock and a ▪hard ▫place 1229R45
▫fall into ▪place 497R75/76/72
▫heart in the ▫right ▪place 656R70
in the ▪first ▫place 525R19 1073L65
in the right ▫place at the right ▪time 1223L54
▫know *one's* ▪place 786R42
▪pizza ▫place 1072R6
▪place ▫card 1073R55
▫place in the ▪sun 1073R52
▪place ▫mat 872L73 1073R59
▪place ▫name 1072R65
▫place of ▪interest 1072R60
▫place of ▪work 1072R62
▫place of ▪worship 1072R63
▪place ▫setting 1299L84
▫place under re▪straint 1213R40
▫pride of ▪place 1121L43
▫put *someone* in *their* ▪place 1074L21
▪resting-▫place 1212L65
same ▫time same ▪place 1253L47
▫scream the ▪place down 1272L43
▫take ▪place 1073R53
▫take the ▪place of 1073L82
▫change ▪places with 215L13
▫friends in high ▪places 565L82
▪go ▫places 1072R59
in ▫high ▪places 668L75
of ▫all ▪places 975R56
a▫void like the ▪plague 85R28
bu▫bonic ▪plague 171L70
▪plague for 1074L71
▪plague with 1074L69
▪flood ▫plain 536L39
▫plain ▪chocolate 1074R22
▫plain ▪clothes 1074R24
▫plain-▪coloured 1074R28
▫plain ▪English 1074R45
▫plain ▪flour 1074R29
▫plain ▪sailing 1074R47
▫plain ▪speaking 1074R50
▫plain-▪spoken 1074R53
under ▫plain ▪cover 316L62
ac▫cording to ▪plan 9L56
▪game ▫plan 581L78
▪ground ▫plan 626L61
in▪stallment ▫plan 671R44 736R83
▪master ▫plan 871R26
▫modified American ▪plan 637R27 911L55
▫open-▪plan 988R28
▪pension ▫plan 1046L25
▪plan for 1075L29/30/53
▪plan on 1075L50/51
▫plan ▪out 1075L47
▫astral ▪plane 74R57
▪transport ▫plane 1552L6
▫minor ▪planet 74L66
as ▫thick as two short ▪planks 1511L58
▫planned obso▪lescence 972L81
▫planned ▪parenthood 1075L54
▫town ▪planner 1543R67/70
▫family ▪planning 500R78
▫planning ▫blight 1075L84
▪planning per▫mission 1051L32 1075R3
▪bedding ▫plant 111R1
▪creeping ▫plant 322R54
▪plant in 1075R79/80 1076L21
▫plant ▪out 1076L2
▪plant ▫pot 1075R74
▪plant with 1075R84
▪pot ▫plant 690L25 1102R21
▪power ▫plant 1106L77/R12
re▪processing ▫plant 1206L40
▪rubber ▫plant 1238R30
▪sewage (▫treatment) ▫plant 1303L44
▪spider ▫plant 1391L17
▪blood ▫plasma 1076L67
▪plaster ▫cast 1076L81
▫plaster of ▪Paris 1076L79/82
▪plaster to 1076R8
▪plaster with 1076R10/11
▪sticking ▫plaster 1076R21 1423L41
▫plastic ▪bag 1093L14
▫plastic ▪bullet 1076R43
▫plastic ex▪plosive 1076R56
▫plastic ▪surgery 1076R61
▫plastic ▪wrap 245L14 1076R49
▫give/▫hand *something* to *someone* on a ▪plate 1076R80
▪L-▫plate 845L67
▫license plate ▪number 817L52 1193R82
▪number ▫plate 967L43
▫plate ▪glass 1077L22
▪plate ▫rack 393R82 1077L6
▪plate with 1077L30
▫silver ▪plate 1339L3
▪vanity ▫plate 1604R77
▫armour-▪plated 63L75
▫gold-▪plated 609R78 1231R27
▫nickel-▪plated 954R41
▫silver-▪plated 1339L5
▪platform ▫shoes 1077L84
▪space ▫platform 1382L30
▫platinum ▪blonde 1077R9
▫duck-billed ▪platypus 430R59 1077R32
▫bring into ▪play 1079L43
▪child's ▫play 226L18
▫come into ▪play 1079L42
▫double ▪play 414L72
▫fair ▪play 495L30
▫foul ▪play 555R79 556L5
give/allow *something* ▫full ▪play 1079L48/49
make a ▪play for 1078L80
na▪tivity ▫play 939R49
▪passion ▫play 1032R65
▫play a ▪joke/▪trick 1078R34
▫play a ▪part 1078R55
▪play across/over/on 1079L26

▫play a▪long 1077R62
▫play a▪round 1077R67
▪play at 1077R54/55/57 1078R12
▫play ▪back 1079L7
▫play ▪ball 1078L39
play both ▫ends against the ▪middle 1078L42
▫play *one's* ▪cards ▫right 1078L37
▫play ▪chicken 225L84
▪Play-▫Doh 1076R70 1078L5
▫play ▪down 1079L57
▫play ▪fair 1078L45
▫play ▪footsie 1078L47
▪play for 1078L26
▫play for ▪time 1078L50
▪play for/to 1078R84
▫play ▪games 1078L59
▫play ▪gooseberry 1078R16
play ▫hard to ▪get 1078R19
▫play ▪hardball 1078L60
▫play (merry) ▪hell with 1078R22
▫play ▪hooky 684L62 1562R34
▫play it by ▪ear 1078R31
▫play it ▪cool 1078R26
▫play ▪off 1078L33/67 1079L62
▫play ▪off against 1079L65
▪play on/upon 1078R42
▫play on ▪words 1078L11
▫play ▪out 1078R47
▫play ▪politics 1077R75
▫play ▪possum 1078R57
▫play second ▪fiddle 1079L11
play ▪silly ▫buggers 1078R59 1338L61
▫play the ▪field 1078L51
▫play the ▪fool/▪goat 544L81 608R1
▫play the ▪game 1078L58
▫play to the ▪gallery 1078R62
▫play ▪truant 1562R34
▫play ▪up 1079L68
▫play ▪up to 1078R64
▪play with 1077R51/53/62/68/76 1078L1/24/47
▫play with ▪fire 1078L3
▪role ▫play 1230R59/79
▫two can play at ▪that ▫game 1576L9
cas▪sette ▫player 202L7
▪football ▫player 546L24
▪record ▫player 1187L77
▪sax ▫player 1258R13/26
ad▪venture ▫playground 19R48
▫level ▪playing ▫field 813R31
▪playing ▫card 195L17 1078L62
▪playing ▫field 1078L65
▫cop a ▪plea 304L41
▪plea ▫bargaining 1080L39
▪plead for 1080L46
▪plead with 1080L49/47/49
▫special ▪pleading 1385R84
▫please ▪God 1080R59
as ▫pleased as ▪Punch 1080R78
▫pleased to ▪meet you 1080R78
at the ▫King's/▫Queen's ▪pleasure 1081L28
de▪tain at His/Her ▫Majesty's ▪pleasure 375L59
it's a/my ▪pleasure 1081L24
▪pledge to 1081L61/77/78
▫take/▫sign the ▪pledge 1081L68
plenty ▫more where ▪that ▫came from 1081R39
▫solar ▪plexus 1372R15
▫plight *one's* ▪troth 1082L10
▪Plimsoll ▫line/▫mark 1082L21
▫plod a▪long 1082L36/42
▫plod a▪way 1082L40/41
▫plod ▪on 1082L37/44
▫plonk a▪way 1082L59
▫plonk ▪down 1082L69
▪plonk in 1082L69
▪plonk on 1082L57/59/64/66
▫plonked ▪out 1082L61
▫plop ▪down 1082R3/4
▪plop into 1082L79/82
▪plop onto 1082R2
▪plot against 1082R19
▪plot ▫line 1082R33
▪plot to 1082R10/20/24
▪plot with 1082R24
▫plough ▪in/▪back 1082R62 1083L11
▪plough into 1082R61 1083L3/10/11
▫plough ▪on 1082R82/84 1083L1
▫plough ▪through 1082R72/73/75/76/77/79/80
▫plough ▪up 1082R65
▫under the ▪plough 1082R56
beat/turn ▫swords into ▪ploughshares 1479R9
▪pluck from 1083L36/38/39/47/49
▪pluck off 1083L37
▫pluck ▪out 1083L39
▫pluck out of the ▪air 1083L50
▫pluck ▪up 1083L59
▫pluck up the/*one's* ▪courage 1083L59
▪fire-▫plug 523L74
▪jack ▫plug 759L79
▫plug a▪way 1084L22/19
▫plug ▪in 1083R58/61/66/69
▪plug into 1083R60/62/67/70/71/74/76
▫plug-▪ugly 1084L28/30
▪plug with 1084L7
▫pull the ▪plug 1144L67
▪spark ▫plug 1383R40/42
▪travel ▫plug 1553L27
▫down the ▪plughole 415R30 1021L69
▫plum ▪pudding 1084L36
sat▪suma ▫plum 1256R49
▫plumb ▪in 1084L79
▪plumb into 1084L78
▪plumb ▫line 1084R16
▫plumb the ▪depths 1084R23/24
▫plumber's ▪friend 1084L83 1085L45
▫plumber's ▪helper 1084L83 1085L46
▫nom de ▪plume 959L12
▫plummet ▪down 1084R35
▪plummet to/towards 1084R36
▫plump ▪down 1084R56/60
▪plump ▫for 1084R63
▪plump ▫on 1084R59
▫plump ▪up 1084R52
▪plunder from 1084R74
▫plunge ▪in 1085L7/28/34/35/37
plunge in at the ▪deep ▫end 357L57
▪plunge into 1085L3/8/10/11/16/19/22/23/26
▫plunge ▪over 1085L6
▫take the ▪plunge 1085L37
▫B ▪plus 88L20
▫C ▪plus 182L15
e▫leven-▪plus 447R35
▫plus ▪fours 1085R63
▪plus ▫sign 1085R37
▪ply between 1087L34
▪ply with 1087L37
▪three-▫ply 1515L82/83
▫two-▪ply 1576L52
pneu▫matic ▪drill 1087L72
P▪O ▫Box 1087R2
▫po-▪faced 1088R62
▪poach from 1087R26
▪poach on 1087R21
▫poacher turned ▪gamekeeper 1087R31
▫line *one's* ▪pocket(s) 825R46
dig (▫deep/▫deeper) into *one's* ▪pocket(s)/▪resources/▪savings 383R8
▪air ▫pocket 29L58
▫breast ▪pocket 162R8
▫burn a ▪hole in *someone's* ▫pocket 177L71
▫out-of-pocket ex▪penses 1087R73
▫pick *someone's* ▪pocket 1062L84
▫pocket-▪handkerchief 1087R76/78
▪pocket ▫money 1087R80/84 1088L2
▪pocket-▫sized 1088L5/7
▫pocket ▪veto 1088L8
put *one's* ▫hand in *one's* ▪pocket 641L1
▫hocus-▪pocus 675L1
as like as/like ▫two peas in a ▪pod 822R53
▪nonsense ▫poem 960L80
▫Poet ▪Laureate 1088R25/29
po▫etic ▪justice 1088R41
po▫etic ▪licence 1088R46
▪pogo ▫stick 1088R69
a ▫case in ▪point 201L29
at ▪gun/▪knife ▫point 1089L9
at ▫point-blank ▪range 1090L36
be▫side the ▪point 118L48 1089R6
▪boiling ▫point 144L79
▪break ▫point 161R56
▪breaking ▫point 159R71
▫cardinal ▪point 196L5
▪compass ▫point 273L81
▫decimal ▪point 354R69 1090L12
▫drive *one's* ▪point ▫home 425R47
excla▪mation ▫point 477L48
▪flash ▫point 530R48/52
▫focal ▪point 541R34/35
▪freezing ▫point 563L36
▪grade point ▫average 616L49
▪high ▫point 668L2
in ▫point of ▪fact 492R17
jumping-▪off ▫point 772R30
make a ▪point of 1089R18
▫match ▪point 872R11
▪meeting ▫point 883L49
▪melting ▫point 885L53
▪muster ▫point 933L50
▫my point ex▪actly 1089R8
not to put ▫too fine a ▪point on it 521L82
▪point at 1089L24/27
▫point-▪blank 1090L33/38
▫point of no re▪turn 1089R59
▫point of ▪order 1089R20
▫point of ▪view 1089R63
▫point ▪out 1089L45
▫point ▪taken 1089R2 1486L64
▫point the ▪finger at 1089L37
▫point the ▪way 1089L42
▪point to 1089L31/44/48
▫point ▪up 1089L54
▪power ▫point 1106L72
▪pressure ▫point 1118L63
reach ▪boiling ▫point 144L82
satur▪ation ▫point 1089R43 1256R74
▫see the ▪point of 1283R42
▪selling ▫point 1290L22
▫set ▪point 1300L46
▪shaver ▫point 1313L50
▫sore ▪point 1377L14
▪start ▫point 1413R67
▪starting ▫point 1089R47/49 1413R67
▪sticking ▫point 1423L47
▫stretch a ▪point 1438R59
▪strong ▫point 1445R26
▪talking ▫point 1488R32
▫three-point ▪turn 1515L78
▪turning ▫point 1569R73
▫up to a ▪point 1089R55/57
▪vantage ▫point 1606R29
▫white ▪pointer 1660R56
get/score ▪brownie ▫points 169L80
▫petit ▪pois 1056L4
▫name your ▪poison 1090R9
▫poison ▪gas 1090R11
▫poison ▪ivy 1090R14
▫poison *someone's* ▪mind 1090R37
▫poison-▪pen ▫letter 1090R17
▫poisoned ▪chalice 1090R37
▪blood ▫poisoning 137L70
▪food ▫poisoning 544L58
▫lead-▪poisoning 804R40
a ▫pig in a ▪poke 1065L70
▫poke a▪round/a▪bout 1090R56
▫poke ▪fun at 1090R59
▫poke ▪in 1090R53/55/59/62
▫poke *someone* in the ▪ribs 1220R25
▪poke into 1090R54
▫poke/▫stick *one's* ▪nose into 962L41
▫poke ▪through 1090R67
▪poker-▫faced 1090R74/73
▫strip ▪poker 1444R14
▫jiggery-▪pokery 764L81
▫polar ▪bear 1091L48
▫barber's ▪pole 99R15
▫negative ▪pole 947R29
▫North ▪Pole 961L61
▪pole po▫sition 1091R4
▪pole ▫vault 1091L32/35
▫South ▪Pole 1380R38
▪telegraph ▫pole 1496R36
▪telephone ▫pole 1496R37
the ▪Pole ▫Star 1091L42
▪totem ▫pole 1540L34
▫touch *something* with a ▪barge pole 1540L72
▫touch *something* with a ten-foot ▪pole 1540L72
mag▫netic ▪poles 852R60
▪poles a▫part 1091L53
▪ski ▫poles 1345R79
as▪sisting the po▫lice with/in their in▪quiries 73L9
▫Military Po▪lice 896R15
▫mounted po▪lice 922R17
po▫lice ▪constable 1091R17
po▪lice ▫officer 1091R16
po▪lice ▫state 1091R21
po▪lice ▫station 1091R19
▪riot po▫lice 1226L6
▫secret po▪lice 1280L81
▪traffic po▫lice 1547R70
▫military po▪liceman 896R17
▪parking po▫liceman 1547R74
▫sleeping po▪liceman 1351R14 1389L20
▫company ▪policy 272R37
en▫dowment ▪policy 456L51
in▪surance ▫policy 739L2
scorched-▪earth policy 1268R10
▫French ▪polish 563R46/39/43
▪nail ▫polish 936L69
▫polish ▪off 1091R80
▫polish ▪up 1091R63/65
▫spit and ▪polish 1393R64
▫body ▪politic 143L76
▫party political ▪broadcast 1030R21
po▫litical a▪sylum 1092L48
po▫litical cor▪rectness 1092L52
po▫litical ▪prisoner 1092L55
po▫litical ▪science 1092L59
po▫litically cor▪rect 1092L65/69
▫party ▪politics 1030R31
▫play ▪politics 1077R75
▪power ▫politics 1105R31
▪polka ▫dot 1092R9
▪deed ▫poll 357L27
▪exit ▫poll 480L19
o▫pinion ▪poll 990L15 1092R20
▫straw ▪poll 1435R18
▪pollen ▫count 1092R46
▪polling ▫booth 1092R38
▪polling ▫day 1092R37
▪polling ▫station 1092R40
▫hoi pol▪loi 675L51
go to the ▪polls 1092R34
pol▫luter ▪pays 1092R65
▪noise pol▫lution 958R65
▪polo ▫neck 1092R81
▪polo ▫shirt 1093L1
▪water ▫polo 1642R21
▪poly ▫bag 1093L14
▫roly-▪poly 1232L12/15
ex▫panded poly▪styrene 480L72
▪pom-▫pom 142L70 1093R58
▫pomp and ▪circumstance 1093R53
▫ponce a▪bout/a▪round 1093R80 1094L1
▪ponder on 1094L17
▪ping-▫pong 1068L83
pon▪tificate on/about 1094L42
pon▪toon ▫bridge 1094L47
▪pit ▫pony 1070R50
▪pony-▫tail 1094L52
▪pony ▫trekking 1094L56
▫shanks's ▪pony 1309R65
▫Shetland ▪pony 1315L80
▪show ▫pony 1328L49
▫pooh ▪pooh 1094R4
▪car ▫pool 193R32/28/30 1094R20
▪gene ▫pool 586R60
▪paddling ▫pool 1017R38
▪rock ▫pool 1229R58
▫scoop the ▪pool 1268L39
▪swimming ▫pool 1094R14 1476R69
▪toddlers ▫pool 1017R39
▪wading ▫pool 1017R39 1632L55
▪football ▫pools 546L22 1094R39
▪poop ▫scoop 1094R45
▪poop ▫sheet 1094R52
▪party ▫pooper 1030L74
▪pooper ▫scooper 1094R46
▫dirt ▪poor 388L5
▫grind the ▫faces of the ▪poor 624L82
▪land-▫poor 794L16
▫piss-▪poor 1070L60/61
▫poor re▪lation 1094R70
the de▫serving ▪poor 372L30
▪pop ▫art 1095R13
▫pop *one's* ▪clogs 1095L81
▪pop-▫down 1095L61
▫pop-▪eyed 1095L57
▪pop ▫fly 1095L59
▫pop ▪in 1095L77
▫pop ▪in/▪over 1095L71
▪pop into 1095L68/78
▫pop ▪off 1095L73/80
▫pop ▪on 1095L79
▫pop ▪out 1095L49/70
▪pop ▫pills 1095L83
▫pop ▪round 1095L78
▫pop the ▪question 1095R1
▫pop ▪up 1095L52/59/61/63
▪pop with 1095L59
▪soda ▫pop 1371L62
▫vox ▪pop 1631R18
▪party ▫popper 1030L76
▪pill-▫popping 1066R39
▫contrary to popular o▪pinion 298R83
▫popular ▪music 1095R17 1096L10
▪pore over 1096R37
▪pork-▫barrel 1096R53
▫pork ▪pie 1096R42/44/60
▫pork ▪scratchings 1096R45
▫hard ▪porn 646R82
▫soft ▪porn 1372L12
▫free ▪port 561R27
▫port of ▪call 1097L18
▫portion ▪out among/between 1097R45/43
▪pose as 1098L38
▪pose for 1098L20/22
▪posing ▫pouch 1098L22
▫jockey/▫jostle for po▪sition 1098R19
▪lotus po▫sition 842R71
▪missionary po▫sition 906R42
▪pole po▫sition 1091R4
▫HIV-▪positive 673R66
▫positive discrimi▪nation 1098R77 1218L31
▫positive ▪vetting 1098R80
▫proof ▪positive 1132R14
▫vacant pos▪session 1603R67
theo▫retical possi▪bility 1509R30
within the ▫realms of possi▪bility 1180R76
▫anything's ▪possible 1099R56
as ▫soon as ▪possible 1099R35 1376L46
▫play ▪possum 1078R57
▫deaf as a ▪post 351R9
▫first-past-the-▪post 526L20
from ▫pillar to ▪post 1066R58
▪guard ▫post 629L80
▫last ▪post 797R64
obser▪vation ▫post 971R82
▪parcel ▫post 1025R51
▫pip *someone* at the ▪post 1069L62
▫post-▪coital 1101L39
▫post ▪free 1100L76
▫post-in▪dustrial 1101L42
▫post me▪ridiem 1101R84
▫post-▪modernism 1101L45/49/50
▪post ▫office 1100L72/74
▫post ▪on 1101L14
▪post to 1100L84 1101L25/26
▫post-traumatic ▪stress dis▫order 1101L51
▫registered ▪post 1193R75
▪staging ▫post 1406R66
▪trading ▫post 1546R47
▪winning ▫post 1666R49
▪postage and ▪packing 1100R64
▪postage ▫stamp 1100R68 1409R10
▪postal ▫order 1100R75
▫picture ▪postcard 1063R66/69
▫poste ▪restante 1101R10/17
▪bill ▫poster 126R5/6
▫four-poster (▪bed) 556R61
▪poster ▫colour 1101R9/32
▪poster ▫paint 1101R32
Post▫graduate Cer▫tificate in Edu▪cation 1101R47
post▫nuptial a▪greement 1102L15
▪chamber ▫pot 213R53
▪coffee ▫pot 255L4
go to ▪pot 1102R65
▪lobster ▫pot 834L77
▪melting ▫pot 885L54/59
▪pepper ▫pot 1046R71
▪plant ▫pot 1075R74
▪pot-▫bound 1102R20
▫pot ▪luck 1103R35
▪pot ▫plant 690L25 1102R21
▪pot ▫roast 1102R22
▪tin-▫pot 1525L3
▫Colorado po▪tato ▫beetle 259L67
▪couch po▫tato 310R61
▫hot po▪tato 687R58
▫jacket po▪tato 759L68
po▪tato ▫beetle 1102R83
po▪tato ▫blight 135L41
po▪tato ▫chip 1102R84
po▫tato ▪crisp 1103L1
po▫tato ▪salad 1103L1
▫sweet po▪tato 1475R57
▫meat-and-po▪tatoes 880L62
▫new po▪tatoes 951R77
▪seed po▫tatoes 1284R9
▪shoestring po▫tatoes 1319L78
▫small po▪tatoes 1358L20
▫pots of ▪money 1102R19
▫potter a▪bout 1103R69
▫potter a▪long 1103R71/75
▫potter a▪round 1103R67/72/73
▫potter's ▪wheel 1102R43
▪potting ▫shed 1102R29
▪potty-▫trained 1104L11
▪potty-▫trainer 1104L14
diplo▪matic ▫pouch 386R3
▪posing ▫pouch 1098L22
▪pounce on 1104L51/53/55
penny-▫wise and pound-▪foolish 1045R66
▫pink ▪pound 1068R26
▫pound a▪way 1104R32
▫pound for ▪pound 1104L78
▪pound into 1104R27
▫pound of ▪flesh 1104R8
▪pound on 1104R29
▪pound ▫sign 1104L75
▫pound ▪sterling 1104L76
▫pour cold ▪water on 256R2
▪pour ▫down 1104R77/78/81
▪pour from 1104R74/75
▪pour into 1104R48/69/76
pour ▫oil on troubled ▪waters 1104R60
▫pour ▪out 1104R55/68
in gen▫teel ▪poverty 588R62
▪poverty ▫line 1105L21
▪poverty-▫stricken 1105L25
▪poverty ▫trap 1105L30
▪baking ▫powder 94R23/25 123L34 1105L52
bio▫logical ▪washing ▫powder 127R64
▪chilli ▫powder 226R44
▪curry ▫powder 337L32 1105L53
▪custard ▫powder 338L36
▪face ▫powder 490R39
▪powder ▫keg 1105L62
▪powder *one's* ▪nose 1105L76
▪powder ▫puff 1105L66
▪powder ▫room 1105L68
▪talcum ▫powder 1105L51 1488L27
▪washing ▫powder 1639R40
▫power(-assisted) ▪steering 1106R7
▪air ▫power 29L84
▪bargaining ▫power 100L31
▪brain ▫power 157L37
▫corridors of ▪power 308L43
▫do a ▪power of ▫good 1106L35
▪flower ▫power 538L33
hold the ▫balance of ▪power 94R73
more ▫power to *your* ▪elbow 1106L37
▫power a▪way 1106L45

power base 1105R19
power behind the throne 1105R66
power breakfast 1105R22
power broker 1105R25
power cut 1106L69
power dressing 1105R29
power lunch 1105R22
power of attorney 1105R81
power outage 1106L69
power plant 1106L77/R12
power point 1106L72
power politics 1105R31
power station 1106L76
power structure 1105R34
power struggle 1105R38 1446R28
power tool 1106L81
power up 1106R19
power vacuum 1105R40
pulling power 1144R62
purchasing power 1148L40
staying power 1417L47
the balance of power 94R71
world power 1105R63 1684R71
high-powered 668L7/R40/45
Axis Powers 87R64
the powers of darkness 1105R71
for all practical purposes 1107L29
licensed practical nurse 817L61
practical joke 1107L34/31
code of practice 254L57 1107R21
general practice 587L40
group practice 626R77
make a practice of 1107R23
restrictive practice 1213R83
restrictive trade practice 1214L2
sharp practice 1312L31
practise as 1107R72
practise what one preaches 1107R30
dental practitioner 366R20
damn with faint praise 344R53
praise for 1108L40/48/49
sing the praises of 1340R61
prance about/around 1108L77/74/76
prat about/around 1108R17
prattle on 1108R28
come the raw prawn 1176R52
pray for 1108R45/47
pray to 1108R49/50/54
Lord's Prayer 841R24
prayer mat/rug 1108R70
praying mantis 862R35 1108R56
pre-Columbian 1108R80
pre-eminent 1108R84 1109L4/2
pre-empt 1109L9/5
pre-exist 1109L17
Pre-Raphaelite 1115R64
preach about 1109L38/40
preach at/to 1109L40/22
preach to the converted 1109L32
practise what one preaches 1107R30
precede with 1109R19
pedestrian precinct 1042L27
precious metal 1109R79
precious stone 1109R81
semi-precious 1290R49
precipitate into 1110L47
precipitate onto 1110L69
precision instrument/tool 1110R37
preclude from 1110R57/60
predatory pricing 1111L60
predispose to/towards 1112L16/18
ectopic pregnancy 440R62 1113L13
phantom pregnancy 1056R84
pregnancy test 1113L14
colour prejudice 260L36
prejudice against 1113L66/R2/15
state premier 1414R58
premium bond 1114L82
prep school 1115L80
prep-time 1114R59
preparatory school 1115L28/80
prepositional verb 1115L62
royal prerogative 1238L16
prescription charge 1116L70
prescription drug/medicine 1116L73
make one's presence felt 1116R78
presence of mind 1117L7
historic present 672L76
present company excepted 272R54 476L75 1116R67
present continuous 1116R42
present-day 1116R40
present participle 1116R47
present perfect 1116R53
present simple 1116R58
present you to 1117L17/20/41/43
present with 1117L12/13/16
preservation order 1117R24
preserve in 1117L82
well-preserved 1653L56
life preserver 819L58
preside at 1117R62
preside over 1117R63/64/65/67
Vice President 1621L39
free press 561L34
freedom of the press 1118R61
garlic press 583R40
go to press 1119L9
gutter press 633R44
hold the press 1119L10
hot off the press 687R16
press ahead/on 1118R14
press baron 1118R68
press box 1118R70
press conference 1118R72
press cutting 1118R75
press down 1118L18/20
press for 1118L30/R12
press gallery 1118R77
press into service 1118R17
press on 1118R15/L83/84 1119L15
press release 1118R80 1197R17
press secretary 1118R83
press-stud 1118L35
press someone to 1118L79/81
press-up 1118L38
printing press 1123L36
stop press 1430R46
trouser press 1562L82
vanity press 1604R75
hard pressed 647L24
blood pressure 137L74
high-pressure 668L12/16/20
osmotic pressure 997R46
peer group pressure 1043L41
peer pressure 1043L40
pressure cooker 1118L61
pressure group 1118R41
pressure of work 1118R28
pressure point 1118L63
tyre pressure 1577R29
hey presto 666L39
presume on 1119L61/63
presume to 1119L44/65
under false pretences 499R61
pretend to 1119R12/17
a pretty penny 1119R74
be at/reach/come to a pretty pass 1119R71
don't worry your pretty little head 1685R79
not a pretty sight 1119R70 1335L77
pretty kettle of fish 777R51
sit pretty 1343L55
prevail over 1120L10
prevaricate over 1120L29
prevent from 1120L36
sneak preview 1365L79
bird of prey 128L63
prey on 1120R3
asking price 70L45
at/for a price 1120R19
cheap at half the price 220R76
consumer price index 294L21 1214R79
cost price 309R47
cut-price 339L59/61
half-price 638L4
list price 829R12
market price 867L37
pay a price 1120R24
pay the price 1038L77
pay the ultimate price 1038L80
pearl of great price 1040R47
price at 1120R44
price-conscious 1120R31
price oneself out of the market 1120R50
price-sensitive 1120R33
price sticker 1120R35
price tag/ticket 1120R37 1485L62
retail price index 1214R77
starting price 1413R73
sticker price 1423L70
trade price 1546L73
predatory pricing 1111L60
prick someone's conscience 1120R71
prick-tease 1120R82/79
prick the balloon/bubble 1120R70
prick up 1121L4
prickly heat 658L3 1121L30
prickly pear 1121L30
kick against the pricks 778R74
pride of place 1121L43
pride oneself on 1121L53
puff oneself with pride 1143R49
swallow one's pride 1473L53
high priest 668R49
high priestess 668R50
prima ballerina 1121R11
prima donna 1121R16/22
prima facie 1121R25
primary colour 1121R42
prime minister 1121R73
prime mover 1121R76
prime number 1121R78
prime time 1121R81
prime to 1122L18
evening primrose 472R32/34
crown prince 329L79
Prince Charming 1122L76
prince consort 1122L78
Prince of Darkness 1122L80
Prince of Wales 1122L73
crown princess 329L80
principal boy 1122R19
as a matter of principle 492R17 874R26 1122R57
guiding principle 630R49
first principles 526L32 1122R45
fine print 521R5 1357R66
in print 1122R79
licence to print money 817L47
print from 1123L48
print on 1123L4
print out 1122R82 1123L6
print run 1123L1
small print 1357R65
not worth the paper it is printed on 1687L66
printed circuit (board) 1123L21
printed matter 1123L23
the printed word 1123L17
dot-matrix printer 413L46
laser printer 797L19/23
printing press 1123L36
screen printing 1272R13
top priority 1537R4
open prison 988R30
prison camp 187L80 1123R35
hold/keep prisoner 1123R48
political prisoner 1092L55
prisoner of conscience 1123R55
prisoner of war 1123R57
take prisoner 1123R45
private detective 1124L32
private enterprise 461L28 1124L37
private income 1124L40
private means 879L41 1124L40
private parts 1124L10
private school 1124L43
Privy Council 1124R15
Privy Councillor 1124R18
grand prix 618R35
booby prize 147L9
consolation prize 291L73
Nobel prize 958L30
prize off 1124R48
take the prize for 1124R30
there are no prizes for guessing 1124R31
pro-choice 1126L57
pro forma 1128R66
pro forma invoice 1128R72
pro-life 1130R11
pro rata 1136L24
pro tem 1137R37
quid pro quo 1162R21
probation officer 1125L33/40
probe for 1125L56/64
probe in/into 1125L57/67/62
probe with 1125L60
space probe 1382L32
attitude problem 78R1
drink problem 424L83/82
no problem 956R77
teething problems 1496L76
standard operating procedure 1411R23
proceed against 1125R70
proceed to 1125R60
proceed with 1125R59/63
batch processing 104L14
data processing 347L76
parallel processing 1024R26
word processing 1678R39/35
food processor 544L59
proclaim from the rooftops 1233L41
prodigal son 1126R55
child/infant prodigy 1126R76
mass-produce 870R70
end product 455L56
waste product 1640R53
co-production 304R29
mass production 870R75
production line 1127L38
dairy products 1127L24
profess to 1127R47/48
caring profession 196L83
oldest profession (in the world) 979R52
professional advice 1128L13
professional foul 1128L15
professional help 1128L18
semi-professional 1290R52
associate professor 73L49
high profile 668L23
offender profile 976R75
psychological profile 1141L41/36
non-profit(-making) 959R10
paper profit 1023L45
profit by/from 1128R30/33
profit margin 1128R23
profit sharing 1128R26
computer program 1129L55
progress report 1129R31
progress to 1129R38
arithmetic progression 62L80
geometric(al) progression 589R50
past progressive 1033R14 1129R60
prohibit from 1129R71
housing project 689R4
human genome project 692L78
project onto 1130L50/52
astral projection 74R60
non-proliferation 959R13
a click and a promise 817R16
promise someone the earth/moon 1131L30
the Promised Land 1131L34
promises promises 1131L44
promissory note 1131L63
promote to 1131R30/31/36
prompt to 1131R46
accident-prone 8L31
personal pronoun 1053L10
reflexive pronoun 1191R65
relative pronoun 1196R23
pronounce on/upon 1132L71
pronounce sentence 1294L19
BBC Pronunciation 106L73
Received Pronunciation 1183R59
bullet-proof 174R8
burden of proof 176R12
damp proof 345L2
damp proof course 344R83
proof positive 1132R14
prop against 1132R67
prop up 1132R68/70/74
propelling pencil 1134L44
good and proper 611R2
make (all) the proper noises 958R61
proper fraction 1134L73
proper noun 1134L75
properly speaking 1134R8
intellectual property 739R42
lost property 842L37
lost property office 842L39
personal property 1053L12 1134R47
property developer 1134R56
real property 1180R32
prophet of doom 1135L11
proportional representation 1135R11
propose a toast 1135R79 1530R56
propose to 1135R38/70/73/83
jet propulsion 762R63
prosecute for 1136L61
Director of Public Prosecutions 387L37
crown prosecutor 329L83
public prosecutor 1142R13
prospect for 1136R42
tremble at the prospect of 1555L55
male prostitute 1136R77
heat prostration 657R81
protect against 1137L39/50
protect from 1137L43
consumer protection 294L22
protection racket 1137L74 1166R14
protective custody 1137L82
protest about 1137R45/55
protest against 1137R43/56
protest song 1137R50
protest to 1137R57
protest too much 1137R65
under protest 1137R46
Protestant work ethic 1137R84
protrude from 1138L55
as proud as Lucifer 845R58
go to prove 606L33
prove to 1138R34
provide against 1138R75
provide for 1138R77/80/82
provide with 1138R71
tempt providence 1499R8
proving ground 1138R36
provisional licence 1139L82
agent provocateur 26L6
pruning shears 1140L29 1278R53
prussic acid 1140L43
pry into 1140L47/48
pry out 1140L57
pseudo-science 1140L76
psych out 1140R9
psych up 1140R14
psychiatric hospital 1140R35
psychological moment 1141L35
psychological profile 1141L41/36
psychological warfare 1141L42
cognitive psychology 255L62
gestalt psychology 590R7
gestalt psychotherapy 590R8
pub crawl 1141R60
certified public accountant 211R1
Director of Public Prosecutions 387L37
general public 587L44 1142L71
in the public domain 410L83 1142L16
in the public eye 1142L18
John Public 766R47
John Q Public 766R48
public address (PA) (system) 1142L20
public bar 1142L23
public company 1142L25
public convenience 1142L27
public domain 1142L29
public enemy number one/no. 1 1142L30
public figure 1142L34
public holiday 1142L37
public house 1141R48 1142L40
public housing 311R10 689L79 1142R12
public life 818R17 1142L34
public phone 1058R4
public prosecutor 1142R13
public relations 1142L40
public school 1142L44/R20
public servant 1142R22 1297R13
public-spirited 1142L50 1393L44
public transport 1142L53 1551R83
the public purse 1142R16
wash one's dirty linen in public 1639L74
desktop publishing 373L33
publishing house 1143L26
black pudding 131R41
Christmas pudding 230R4
in the pudding club 1143L52
over-egg the pudding 1005R79
plum pudding 1084L36
pudding basin 1143L53
pudding-basin haircut 1143L54
rice pudding 1221L1
steak and kidney pudding 1417R69
summer pudding 1459L63
Yorkshire pudding 1697R49
huff and puff 691R38/41
powder puff 1105L66
puff adder 1143R58
puff and pant 1143R3
puff (away) on/at 1143R18
puff out 1143R36/44/46
puff pastry 1143R59
puff piece 1143R69
puff sleeves 1143R61
puff up 1143R47/48
puff oneself with pride 1143R49
puffed up 1143R50
puffer train 1143R41
make someone (want to) puke 1144L19
puke up 1144L18
bell- pull 115R47/46
pull a face 1144L54
pull a fast one 1145L21
pull a gun on 1144R48
pull ahead 1144R76
pull at 1144L42/58
pull away 1144R77
pull back 1144R83/78
pull date 1144R51 1290L21
pull down 1144L40/R43/47 1145L24
pull one's finger out 521R83
pull in 1144R82 1145L8/27
pull in one's horns 685R4
pull into 1144R79
pull someone's leg 809L13 1144L60
pull off 1144R36 1145L30
pull on 1144L71/79 1145L21/22
pull out 1144L41/51/R26/39/40/52/81 1145L36/41
pull out all the stops 1144R1
pull out of 1145L38
pull something out of the bag/hat 1144L44
pull over 1144R82
pull one's punches 1144L73
pull rank 1144L78
pull one's socks up 1144L81
pull strings 1144R3
pull-tab 1144R28 1225L33
pull the carpet/rug from under 1144L48
pull the other leg (it's got bells on) 1144L63
pull the plug 1144L67
pull the strings 1144R7
pull the wool over someone's eyes 1678L17
pull through 1145L45
pull to pieces 1064R32
pull together 1144R9

pull up 1144R41/42 1145L4/56
pull oneself up by one's bootstraps 148R34
pull someone up for/over 1145L57
pull up short 1145L4
pull up stakes 1422R64
pull one's weight 1144R16
ring-pull 1225L32
crowd-puller 329L34
leg-puller 809L16
pulling power 1144R62
wood pulp 1677L48
finger on the pulse 1145R35
pulse through 1145R45
quicken someone's pulse 1145R32
bicycle pump 123L67
pump-action 1145R83
pump for 1146L21
pump into 1146L4
pump iron 1146L26
pump money into 1146L28
pump out 1146L7/9
pump round 1146L6
pump through 1146L5
pump up 1146L17
stomach pump 1429L72
vacuum pump 1604L72
pumping station 1146L31
turn into a pumpkin 1146L42 1570L48
pun on 1146L54
hole punch(er) 677R14
as pleased as Punch 1080R78
Mr Punch 1146R36
one-two punch 984R60
pack a punch 1016R23/25
Punch and Judy show 1146R39
punch ball 1146L64/67
punch bowl 1146R24
punch-drunk 1146L69/73
punch line 1146R11
punch out 1146L83
punch-up 1146R5
punch with 1146R6
pull one's punches 1144L73
roll with the punches 1231L36
punctuated by/with 1146R67/66
punctuation mark 1146R75
capital punishment 191R69
corporal punishment 307L43
glutton for punishment 602L43
sell a pup 1290L18
day pupil 349R33
glove puppet 601R8
hand puppet 601R8
puppy fat 1148L25
puppy love 1148L27
compulsory purchase order 279L48
hire purchase 671R44 736R83
purchase for 1148L37
purchase of 1148L43/44/54
purchase with 1148L39
purchasing power 1148L40
pure and simple 1149L9
purely and simply 1149L18
purge from 1149L56
purge something of 1149L53/55/59/62/68
purge one's soul from/of 1149L66
Purple Heart 1149R50
purport to 1149R61/62/64
accidentally on purpose 8L47
dual purpose 430L47/58
purpose-built 1150L12
at cross-purposes 328R4
cross-purposes 328R3
for all practical purposes 1107L29
to/for all intents and purposes 740L53
purr of 1150L65
the public purse 1142R16
the purse strings 1150L69
in hot pursuit 687R83
at the push of a button 180L84
bell- push 115R47/46
give someone the push 1151R19/15/19
if/when it comes to the push 1151R20
if/when push comes to shove 1151L62
push ahead/along/forward/on 1151R33/75/39/32
push along/off 1152L58
push around/about 1151L64
push aside 1151R41/43
push-button 1151L79
push down 1151R53
push for 1151L49/R54/59 1152L13
push forward 1151R44 1152L36/38
push in 251L14 1151R76
push into 1152L9
push one's luck/push it 1151L75
push off 1151L47/R79 1152L61
push on with 1151R36
push out 1151R48
push over 1151L42
push start 1151L83/R1
push the boat out 1151L69/70/67
push through 1151R49/51 1152L2/11
push up 1151R2/52/82
pushing up (the) daisies 1151L71
push up/down 1151R54
pen pusher 1044L43
pencil pusher 1044L44/R80
pussy willow 1152R12
pussyfoot around/about 1152R24
put the lid on 817R46
hardly/barely put one foot in front of the other 545R46
never put a foot wrong 545L75
not know where to put oneself 786R69
not to put too fine a point on it 521L82
put a brake/the brakes on 157R32
put a brave face on 158R51
put a figure on it 517R62
put a lid on 817R52
put a match to 872R26
put a pistol to someone's head 1070R31
put a sock in it 1371L10
put a spanner in the works 1383L15
put a spoke in someone's wheel 1395R48
put a stop to 1430R58
put about/around 1153R31 1154L67
put across 1154L71
put across/over 1153R36
put all one's eggs in one basket 444L83
put an end to 455L26
put an idea into someone's head 700R43
put one's arm round 1152R42
put away 1152R56 1153L60/63 1154L77
put back 1152R58/64/65 1153L64 1154L81
put one's back into it 89R71
put someone's back up 89R72
put behind one 1153L66
put one's best foot forward 118R67
put bluntly/simply/briefly/mildly 1153R44
put by 1152R71
put one's cards on the table 195L36
put down 1058L76 1152R73/75/77/79/81 1153L83 1154R1/6/10/14
put down as 1153R10
put it down to 620L8 1153R11
put it/something down to experience 482L22 1153R13
put one's finger on 522L2
put flesh on one's argument 533L64
put one's foot down 545L76/79
put one's foot in it 545L82
put one's foot in one's mouth 545L83
put one's foot to the floor 545L79
put forth 1154R20/21
put forward 1152R68 1153L3 1154R20
put great/little store 1431R33
put one's hand in one's pocket 641L1
put one's hands on 640L76
put one's head above the parapet 653R29
put one's head down 653L48/51
put their heads together 654L4
put heart and soul into 657L24
put in 1152R30/31/32 1153L6/80/R16/51/54 1154L52/R33/41/47/84
put something in a pigeonhole 1065R55
put in for 1154L38/39/R38/40/56/57 1155L39/48/49/61
put in hand 640R61
put someone in mind of 899L48
put in motion 920R79
put in(to) perspective 1053R57
put something in pigeonholes 1065R56
put someone in their place 1074L21
put someone in the picture 1064L22
put in the shade 1304R70
put in train 1548R79
put in your pipe and smoke it 1069R34
put into 13L79 90L39 1152R34/36/64 1153R55 1154L18/20/21/23 1700L75
put into care 196L62
put lead in someone's pencil 804R61
put someone's mind at rest/ease 898R72
put one's mind to 898R70
put one's money where one's mouth is 913R28
put one's nose to the grindstone 961R82
put one's oar in 969R77
put off 1154R53/65/77
put someone off their stride/stroke 1154R73 1441L11
put someone off the scent 1264L16
put someone off the scent/track/trail 1153R74
put on a brave face 158R50
put on a false front 500L56
put on a pedestal 1042L11
put on airs (and graces) 29R36
put on an act 13L55
put on ice 698R63
put on/out 1153R57
put on the dog 408R64
put on the line 824R43
put something on the map 863R43
put on the spot 1398L78
put one across 12R59
put out 89R59 898R67 1153L6/7/8/10/13/73/R39/41/61/62/67/70 1155L31/37/R62
put out feelers 511L10
put out for tender 1500L78
put out of joint 768L13/17
put something out of one's mind 1154R77
put an animal out of its misery 904L77
put out the flags 529L32
put out to grass 620L11
put over 1152R42
put over on 1154L71
put one's own house in order 689L35
put paid to 1038R81
put pen(cil) to paper 1044L36/R77
put right 1153R64 1154R69/83 1223L181224L45
put one's shirt on 1317L73
put one's skates on 1344R75
put some colour in someone's cheeks 259R40
put stock in 1427R44
put the arm/bite on 1154L36
put the boot in 148L82
put the cart before the horse 200L36
put the cat among the pigeons 203L64
put the clock back 246L58
put the fear of God into/in 508L79
put the finishing touches on/to 522R27/28
put the flags out 529L32
put the frighteners on 566L35
put the heat on 657R68
put the heat/screws on 1154L33
put the kibosh on 778R49
put the knife in/into 783R40/39
put the lid on 817R50
put the make on 856L8
put the phone down on 1058L78
put the record straight 1187L48
put the roses (back) into someone's cheeks 1234R63
put the screws on 1273L3
put the seal on 1276R2/3
put the shot 1154L62
put the skids under 1346L32
put the squeeze on 1154L36
put the welcome mat out 1650R65
put the wind up 1666R77
put the word about/around/out/round 1679L12
put one's thinking cap on 1513L75
put through 1152R43 1153L17/20 1154L30
put through (the) hoop(s) 684L74
put someone through their paces 1014L73
put through the mill 897L38
put through the wringer 1691L10
put to bed 110R73 1152R44
put to flight 534L71
put (out) to sea 1275R81
put to sleep 1351L36
put to the/a vote 1631L32
put to the ballot 96L12
put to the sword 1479R4
put to the test 1505R13
put together 1152R63 1153L25/26/29/30/32/33 1532L12
put towards 1153L76
put two and two together and make five 1574R75/78
put two fingers in the air/up 1576L17
put someone under 337L62 1153R73
put up 545L49 1153L38/41/51 1155L41/46/50/55/62 1250R53
put up as 1155L60
put up to 1155L66
put up with 1155L70
put upon 1155L77/80
put words in/into someone's mouth 1678R9
put years on 1695R62
shot put 1324R61/63
that'll put hairs on your chest 636L37
to put it bluntly/simply/briefly/mildly 1153R43
wouldn't put it past someone 1033R52
putting green 1155R36
Chinese puzzle 227L42
monkey-puzzle (tree) 915L16
puzzle about 1155R65
puzzle out 1155R68
puzzle over 1155R66
pyramid scheme 1156R9
pyramid selling 1156R13
pyrrhic victory 1156R46
sine qua non 1340R34
quadratic equation 1157L26
well-qualified 1653L62
qualify as 1157R38/47
qualify for 1157R40/45/82/84
qualify someone to 1157R49 1158L2
quality control 1158L33
quality of life 1158L36
quality time 1158L49
quantity surveyor 1158R43
unknown quantity 1591L81
quantum leap 1158R57
quantum mechanics 1158R60
quarrel about/over 1160L24
quarter note 328R55 1160L59
three-quarter length 1515R2
Monday-morning quarterback 913L48
hanged/hung drawn and quartered 644L20
three quarters 1515L84
string quartet 1443R42
at the Queen's pleasure 1081L28
beauty queen 110L21
drag queen 418R6
pearly queen 1040R58
Queen Anne's lace 317L52 1161L30
queen's evidence 474L67
Queen Mother 1161L29
queen of all one surveys 1470L78
uncrowned queen 1582R3
queer -basher 102L56/62
queer bashing 1161L50
beg the question 113R23
call into question 184R83
cross-question 328L43/R9
leading question 804R31
pop the question 1095R1
question-and-answer 1161R17
question mark 1161R13
question of time 1520R78
question time 1161R17
rhetorical question 1219R65
sixty-four-thousand-dollar question 1344R2
trick question 1556R84
no-questions-asked 957R83
queue-jumping 1162L21
quibble about 1162L34
quibble over 1162L35
cut to the quick 339R14
double-quick 414L74
get-rich-quick 1221L8
in double-quick time 414L75
quick as a flash 530R42
quick fix 1162L56
quick march 864L65
quick on the uptake 1600R43
quick-temper 1162L62/63
quick-witted 1162L64 1674R77
quicken someone's pulse 1145R32
quid pro quo 1162R21
quiet down 1162R64/43
continental quilt 296R73 433R34
quilt cover 433R38
call it quits 185L74
double or quits 413R59
quid pro quo 1162R21
the status quo 1416L74
je ne sais quoi 762L3
Quonset hut 1164L1
quotation marks 1164R11
quote from 1164L29
quote marks 1164R12
quote someone on 1164L31
quote unquote 749R74 1164L35
rabbit warren 1164L79 1639L21
Welsh rabbit 1653R42
breed like rabbits 1164R43
rabble-rouser 1164R61/56
arms race 63L11
egg-and-spoon race 444R5
master race 871R30
one-horse race 984L68
race across 1165R76
race against 1165L82
race by 1165R80
race for 1165L77/R78
race meeting 1165R1
race on/off/away 1165R77
race relations 1165R54
race to 1165L76/81/84/R79
rat race 1174R9
sack race 1247L8
space race 1382L35
the human race 692R2
three-legged race 1515L68
multi-racial 928R77
flat racing 531L48
motor racing 921R11
racing bike/cycle 1165R25/13
racing car 1165R25/28
racing driver 1165R27
racing pigeons 1165R28
racing start 1165R31
anti-racist 50L36
non-racist 959R16
bath rack 104L44
bike rack 340R76
clothes rack 248R16
cycle rack 340R76
dish rack 393R82 1077L6
luggage rack 846R30
plate rack 393R82 1077L6
rack and ruin 1166L72
rack one's brains 1166L53
rack up 1166L77
roof-rack 1233L20
toast rack 1530R28
wine rack 1668R84
racked by/with 1166L46/47/52/50
protection racket 1137L74 1166R14
squash rackets 1402R54
squash racquets 1402R55
radar trap 1166R45
radiate from 1166R68/79/83/84
gamma radiation 581R41
radiation sickness 1167L51
clock radio 246L76 1167R64
radio alarm (clock) 1167R63
radio telescope 1167R65
riff-raff 1222R32
Rafferty's rules 1168L42
life raft 819L59
like a red rag to a bull 1188R64
lose one's rag 841R83
rag someone about 1168R12
rag and bone man 1168R1
rag doll 1168R5
rag trade 1168R10
fly into a rage 540R35
rage at 1168R42
rage on 1168R46
run ragged 1241L2
glad rags 597R47
rags-to riches 1168R6
air raid 29R4
dawn raid 348R69/71 1169L9
ram-raid 1171L37/39/43
smash-and-grab raid 1359L24
curtain rail 337R25
guard rail 629L81
rail against/at 1169R15
rail off 1169R13
railroad into 1169R30
railroad something through 1169R29
go off the rails 1169L42
cable railway 182R13
light railway 821L64
railway station 1169R43 1415L68/69
acid rain 11L79
as right as rain 1224L37
come rain or shine 1169R67
rain barrel 1642L83
rain forest 1169R71
rain gauge 1169R74
rain water 1169R75
take a rain check 1169R69
a rainy day 1170L5
raise a finger 521R81
raise a rumpus 1240R50

raise a stink 1426L82
raise (a few) eyebrows 1170L42
raise *one's* eyes heavenward 658R61
raise *someone's* hackles 635L43
raise *one's* hand to/against 1170L39
raise the roof 1170L62/64/70 1233L18
raise the stakes 1408L37
curtain raiser 337R37
fire-raiser 523L78/76
fund-raiser 574L79/76
consciousness raising 289R28
hair-raising 636L62
self-raising flour 1289L15
raison d'être 1170R14
rake about/around 1170R29
rake in 1170R35/31/33
rake out 1170R36
rake over 1170R38
rake through 1170R30
rake up 1170R41/42/44
muck-raker 927R2/L79
rally against 1170R74 1171L20
rally around/round 1171L5/4
rally *one's* forces 1170R78/84 1171L1
rally *people* in favour of/against 1170R82
rally to/behind 1171L3
battering ram 105L36
ram down 1171L31/32
ram down *someone*'s throat 1516L2
ram down *someone's* throat 1171L33
ram into 1171L25
ram-raid 1171L37/39/43
ram *something* up *someone's* ass 71L65
ramble on 1171L71
ramble over 1171L62/R3
ramble through 1171L58/62/R4
rampage through 1171R35
as stiff/straight as a ramrod 1171R63
also-ran 37L5
dude ranch 430R84
ranch house 1171R75/78
ranch-style house 1171R78
random breath test 1172L19
at point-blank range 1090L36
free-range 561R3
long-range 838L40
range about/over 1172R7/4
range against 1172L82
range between 1172L63
range finder 1172L59
range through/over 1172R5
range *oneself* with 1172R1
rifle-range 1222R38
short-range 1322L60
Ranger Guide 1172R22
wide ranging 1172R8 1663R43
pull rank 1144L78
rank as 1172R55/56
rank *something* in 1172R58
the rank and file 1172R38
high-ranking 668R78
rankle with 1173L7
break ranks 160R73
close ranks 247L58
join the ranks 767R24
rise through the ranks 1226R35
ransack *something* for 1173L12
a king's ransom 781L32
ransom for 1173L15/25
rant about 1173L31/35
beat the rap 109R6 1173L63
rap on 1173L50/57
date rape 348L37
oilseed rape 1173R8
Pre-Raphaelite 1115R64
rapid fire 1173R18/19
rapid transit 1173R20 1550R67
have a rare old time 1173R83
rare bird 1173R81
Welsh rarebit 1653R42
rarely if ever 473L9
heat rash 658L3 1174L49
nappy rash 937R67
nettle rash 950L84
drowned rat 428L60
rat-arsed 1174R11
rat-assed 1174R11
rat on 1174R16
rat race 1174R9
smell a rat 1360L68
pro rata 1136L24
at a rate of knots 1174R50
bank rate 97R47
base rate 101R36
birth rate 128R75
cheap rate 221L1
cut-rate 339L62
exchange rate 476R62
Exchange Rate Mechanism 476R65
first-rate 526L36 1174R82
inflation rate 1174R42
interest rate 810R58
lending rate 810R57
pass rate 1031R14
rate a mention 1174R78
rate as 1174R68/73/74
rate of exchange 476R63 1174R64
rate of inflation 1174R42
return a high/low rate of interest 1217L37
second-rate 1279R12
third rate 1513R19
rateable value 1175L17
I'd rather die 1688R23/25
would rather/sooner 1688R17
credit rating 322L55
ration out 1175R2/L84
iron rations 752R38
rattle along/down/over 1175R76/75
rattle off 1175R77
rattle on/away 1175R79
rattle through 1175R82
sabre-rattling 1246L84
rave about/at 1176L49/47/49/50/62/64
rave against 1176L47
ravel up 1176L76
a raw deal 1176R65
come the raw prawn 1176R52
raw-boned 1176R71
raw sienna 1335L2
touch on the raw 1176R69
touch/strike/hit/expose a raw nerve/spot 1176R68 1540L76
ray gun 1177L1
ray of sunshine 1176R81
X-ray 1694R36/49
catch a few/some rays 204L82
cutthroat razor 340R28
electric razor 446R1 1177L18
razor's edge 1177L20
razor knife 1177L21 1412L56
razor-sharp 1177L22/23
razor-thin 1177L24
razor wire 1177L25
safety razor 1248R76
straight razor 340R28
razzle-dazzle 1177L37
reach a pretty pass 1119R71
reach boiling point 144L82
reach *somewhere* by 1177R24
reach down/out 1177R10
reach for 1177R7/8/17/52
reach for the stars 1177R28
reach out 1177R11
reach over/across 1177R9
reach the statute book 1416R48
reach up 1177R14
far-reaching 503R75
react against 1177R67
react on 1177R71
react to 1177R66/69
react with 1177R72
chain reaction 212L67
chemical reaction 223R59 1178L7
gut reaction 633L84
nuclear reactor 1178L38
lip-read 828R39/42
read about 1178L46
read between the lines 1178L83
read *something* into 1178R2
read over/through 1178L77
read the meter 891L74 1178R13
read the Riot Act 1178R24
read the runes 1178R28
read to 1178L51/62/63/R27
read *someone* to sleep 1178L64
sight-read 1335L57/58/53
take as read 1178R39
well-read 1653L67/71
machine-readable 850R42
bar-code reader 820R37
mind reader 899L20
compass reading 273L83
reading knowledge 1179L11
reading list 1179L13
reading room 1179L15
oven-ready 1005L47
ready and waiting 1179L63
ready-made 1179L72
ready money 1179L77
ready steady go 1179L67
ready-to-wear 1179L69
rough and ready 1235R50/82
get real 591L30 1179R35
in real terms 1179R38
real ale 1180L66
real estate 1134R49 1180R32
real estate agent/broker 469L46 1180R34/35 1181L4
real estate office 469L48
real life 1179R41
real property 1180R32
real-time 1179R45
the real McCoy 877R2 1180L77
the real thing 1180L69 1512R53
the real world 1179R50
virtual reality 1625R59
really big of *someone* 124L63
peer of the realm 1043L17
within the realms of possibility 1180R76
ream out 1181L10
reap what *one* has sown 1181L25
grim reaper 624L33
reaper-binder 1181L33
bring up the rear 166L37 1181L57
rear above/over 1181L83
rear admiral 1181L58
rear-end 1181L47
rear view mirror 1181L59
rear wheel drive 1181L62
rearguard action 1181R5
child-rearing 226L38
rearrange the deckchairs on the Titanic 355L52
is/goes beyond all reason 1181R55
it stands to reason 1410R43
listen to/see reason 1181R57
reason out 1181R67
reason with 1181R72/74
rhyme or reason 1220L66
see reason 1283R36
beyond reasonable doubt 122L84/R1 1182L1
for reasons best known to *oneself* 1181R42
rebel against 1182L60/61
rebel at 1182L65/68
rebound off 1182R21
rebound on 1182R25
rebuke for 1182R62/67/68
total recall 1183L24
recapture from 1183L66
recast as 1183L75
recede into 1183L82
receding hairline 636R71 1183L84
receive as 1183R50
receive into 1183R53
Received Pronunciation 1183R59
official receiver 977R61 1183R63
on/at the receiving end 1183R23
reception area/desk 1184L15
reception room 1184L26
recharge *one's* batteries 1184R5
reckon from 1185L42
reckon in 1185L45
reckon to/on 1185L34/48
reckon up 1185L53
reckon with 1185L54
a force to be reckoned with 548L57
dead reckoning 350R46
the day of reckoning 349R30
reclaim from 1185L78/80
recline against/on 1185R12/11
optical character recognition 992L10
recoil at 1185R75/76
to the best of *my* recollection 1186L12
recommend for 1186L20
recommend *something* to 1186L21
recommended daily allowance 1186L32
recompense for 1186L56/57/59/64
reconciled with/to 1186L75/76
aerial reconnaissance 1186R20
reconstitute as 1186R48
criminal record 324L72 1187L30
go on record 1187L41
matter of record 874R35
record-breaking 1187R19
record *something* on 1187L68
record player 1187L77
set/put the record straight 1187L48
track record 1545R53
world record 1187R18 1683R46
recorded delivery 1187L58
descant recorder 371L1
flight recorder 534L53
tape recorder 1491L22
video cassette recorder 1622L71
video recorder 1622L71
videotape recorder 1622L72
recover from/after 1187R61/63/71
recreation center/centre 1188L10
recreation ground 1188L8
recreational vehicle 1188L14
recuperate from 1188R7
recurring decimal 1188R19
recurring number 1188R18
blood-red 137L78
go/turn as red as a beetroot 113L37/38
like a red rag to a bull 1188R64
not give a red cent for 1188R78
red admiral 1188R65
red alert 1188R67
Red Army 1189L52
red blood cell 1188R69
red-blooded 1188R71
red carpet 1188R73
red corpuscle 1188R70
Red Crescent 1188R80
Red Cross 1188R83
red deer 1189L2
red-eye 1189L5
red flag 1189L7
red giant 1189L10
red-handed 1189L12
red-herring 1189L13
red-hot 1189L16
Red Indian 1189L19
red-letter day 1189L20
red light 1189L23
red-light district 1189L25
red meat 1189L26
red pepper 1189L28/29
red tape 1189L31
the Red Flag 1189L10
robin redbreast 1229L67
redeem from 1189L82
redress the balance 94R60
reduce to 1189R83/84 1494R52
reduced circumstances 1190L7
reduced time 1190L9 1324L5
redundancy payment 1190L33
reed instrument 1190L47
coral reef 305L49
reef knot 1190L66
reek of/with 1190L69/70/71
inertia reel 724R80
reel back 1190L82
reel from/with 1190R33
reel in/out 1190R33/37
cross-refer 328R11/14
refer back 1190R69
refer to 1190R51/64/82/54
character reference 217L2
for future reference 578R1
frame of reference 558R49
grid reference 623R31
reference book 1191L6
reference library 1191L8
terms of reference 1504L13/17
reflect in 1191R7/26
reflect off 1191R8
reflect on 1191R39
reflexive pronoun 1191R65
reflexive verb 1191R64
penal reform 1044L68
reformed character 1192L75
refresh *someone's* memory 1192R24
refresher course 1192R33
refrigerator-freezer 565L43 1192R52
women's refuge 1192R59 1675R82
refugee camp 1192R63
refuse collector 433L66 1193L15
refuse dump 1193L16
in this/that regard 1193L62
regard *someone* as 1193L50
regard with 1193L50/52
cash register 201R43
electoral register 446L63
register as 1193R62
register at 1193R63
register for 1193R60
register office 1193R72 1194L6
register on 1194L13
register with 1193R59/64
registered mail 1193R76
registered post 1193R75
registration book 836R48
registry office 1194L6
regret at/for 1194L60
regret to 1194L56
send *one's* regrets 1194L64
dress rehearsal 422R3
Third Reich 1195L27
reign of terror 1195L34
reign over 1195L32
reimburse for 1195L42/44
give free rein 1195L52
keep a tight rein on 1195L55
keep on a tight rein 1195L56
rein in/back 1195L59/60
reinforce with 1195R6/19
reinforced concrete 1195R19
hold the reins 676R75
reinstate in 1195R39
reject *someone* for 1195R70
reject shop 1196L4
rejoice at 1196L17
rejoice in 1196L18
rejoice in the name of 1196L21
have/suffer a relapse 1196L55
relapse into 1196L52
relate to 1196R35/37
age-related 24R80
blood relation 137R41
in/with relation to 1196R4
poor relation 1094R70
diplomatic relations 386R1 1196R47
have sexual relations with 1196R48
human relations 692R3
industrial relations 724L3
labour relations 789R74
public relations 1142L40
race relations 1165R54
distant relative 399L1
relative clause 1196R19
relative density 1196R72
relative humidity 1196R74
relative pronoun 1196R23
relatively speaking 1197L1
relax by 1197L16
relax with 1197L18
day release 349R36
press release 1118R80 1197R17
release from 1197L62/63/64/79
release into 1197L74
release to 1197R8
time(d)-release capsule 1522R30
relegate from/to 1197R33/26/28/30/33
bas-relief 103L76
relief map 1200L35
relief road 1199L81
tax relief 1493R7
established religion 469L20
relinquish responsibility 1200L55
relocate to 1200R1
rely on/upon 1200R16/18/19
remain to 1200R51
it remains to be seen 1200R62
the fact remains 1200R61
remake as 1201L13
remand centre 1201L33
remand *someone* to 1201L20
remanded in custody 338L61
remanded on bail 1201L22
remark on 1201L41/44
throwaway remark 1517L81
remedial teaching/lesson 1201L78
remember *someone* as 1201R11
remember for 1201R22
remember *someone* in 1201R30
remember to 1201R13/14/32
Remembrance Day 1201R46
Remembrance Sunday 1201R47
remind *somebody* about 1201R52
remind *somebody* of 1201R53/54
remind *somebody* to 1201R54/56
reminisce about 1201R75
remit to 1202L19/29/30/31
remonstrate against 1202L57
remote control 1202R9/13
haven't the remotest idea 1202R8
remove *something* from 1202R22
several/many removes (away) from 1202R34
remunerate for 1202R61
Renaissance man 1202R77
rend *something* in/into 1203L1/2
render an account of 1203L19
render down 1203L13
render *something* into/to 1203L10/20
rendezvous with 1203L37
renege on 1203L47
renounce *something* for 1203L77
ground rent 626L65
peppercorn rent 1047L9
rent-a- 1203R32
rent boy 1203R18
rent *something* for 1203R30
rent-free 1203R20/21
rent from/to 1203R30/28
rent strike 1203R22
sales rep 1250R73
in a *terrible* state of repair 1203R74
in good/bad repair 1203R73
repair to 1203R69/78
repay by 1204L14
repay *someone* for 1204L13
repay *someone's* interest/attention/time 1204L16
repay to 1204L12
repay with 1204L14
repeat *something* to 1204L29/30
repeating decimal 1188R19
water-repellant 1642R23
repent of 1204L76
repertory company 1204R12
Repetitive Strain Injury 1204L55
replace with 1204R30
hormone replacement therapy 685L75
action replay 13R15
reply-paid 1204R79
reply to 1204R73/74/75

progress report 1129R31
report back 1205L18
report card 1205L29
report for 1205L14/50
report on 1205L5/6/8/23/25
report to/at 1205L5/10/13/15/52 1208L33
reported speech 722L48 1205L38
cub reporter 332R14
annual reports 47L26
repose in 1205L62
represent *oneself* as 1205R33
represent *something* to 1205R30
make a representation to 1205R36
proportional representation 1135R11
make representations to 1205R36
sales representative 1250R72
House of Representatives 689R37
reprieve from 1205R73
reprimand for 1205R78/81
reproach *someone* for 1206L20/21
reproach *someone* with 1206L19
reprocessing plant 1206L40
reproduction furniture 1206L78
reprove *someone* for 1206L81
banana republic 96R26
Republican Party 1206R23
request stop 1207L64
request to 1207L56/70
require *something* of 1207L81
require to 1207L83/R34
des res 374L30
air-sea rescue 29R5
rescue from 1208L10/12
market research 867L42/39
operational research 989L81
operations research 989L81
research and development 1208L28
research in/into 1208L32
central reservation 209L20 881R22
gold reserve 609R80
nature reserve 943L7
reserve for 1208L79/80/R4
resettle in 1208R55/56
non-resident 959R19
resign as 1209L33
resign from 1209L31
resigned to 1209L42
air/wind resistance 1209L82
passive resistance 1032R79
path/line of least resistance 1209R2
pièce de résistance 1064R65
sales resistance 1250R76
joint resolution 767R72
New Year's Resolution 952R19
resolve into 1209R63
resolve on/against 1209R43
resolve to 1209R44
magnetic resonance imaging 852R65
resonate through 1209R75
resonate with 1209R76/79/82 1210L1
as a last resort 798L26
beach resort 107L26
in the last resort 798L26
only/last resort 1210L28
resort to 1210L21/27
resound with 1210L34
resource with 1210L55
natural resources 943L49
thrown back on *one's* own resources 1517L32
respect for 1210L80/R7/26/27
with all due respect 431L14
with great/with the greatest of/with all due respect 1210R43
pay *one's* last respects 1210R83
artificial respiration 66R3 1211L57
respiratory system 1211L70
respond by/with 1211R24/17/23
respond to 1211R19/20/21/22/24/25/27
co-respondent 305R56
immune response 706R49
diminished responsibility 385L21
chin rest 227L19
come to rest 1212L83
give it a rest 1212R2
I rest my case 1212R51
lay the ghost of *something* to rest 802L71
lay to rest 802L68/70
rest against 1212R57
rest area 803L58 1212R9
rest assured 73R56 1212R47
rest cure 1212R4
rest easy 1212R46
rest home 1212R6
rest in peace 1212L59
rest on 1212R42/43/56/58/59
rest on *one's* laurels 1212R61
rest room 1212R8
rest stop 803L58 1212R9
rest up 1212L50
rest with 1212R40/60
set/put *someone's* mind at rest 898R72
the rest is history 1213L5
poste restante 1101R10/17
restaurant car 193R16 385L70 1213L17
resting-place 1212L65
restore to 1213L43/45/46/56
restrain from 1213R9
restraining order 1213R12
head restraint 653R39
keep/place under restraint 1213R40
restrict to 1213R50/51
restrictive practice 1213R83
restrictive trade practice 1214L2
my case rests 1212R52
end result 455L60 1214L30
result from 1214L53/55
result in 1214L56/57/58
resurface as 1214R20
resurrect from 1214R38
retail at/for 1215L2
retail price index 1214R77
retaliate against 1215L64
retaliate by 1215L62/63
flame retardant 530L1
anal retentive 51R53
retire as 1215R73
retire from 1215R72/76/79
retire into *one's* shell 1314R43
retire to 1216L23
retirement pension 979R57 1216L14
retrace *one's* steps 1216L42
beat a (hasty) retreat 109L42
retreat from 1216L61/67/71
retreat into *one's* shell 1314R43
retreat to 1216L63
sound the retreat 1378R59
information retrieval 728L74
golden retriever 610L22
retro-rocket 1216R21
by return mail 1217L19
day return 349R40
point of no return 1089R59
return a high/low rate of interest 1217L37
return a verdict of 1217L49
return from 1216R69/78
return match 1217L45
return ticket 1217L2
return to 1216R67/69/71/72/74/75/80/83 1217L12
sale or return 1250R58
tax return 1493R9
non-returnable 959R22
non-returnable bottle 959R23
diminishing returns 385L27
many happy returns (of the day) 863L82
reunite with 1217L58
revel in 1217R19
revenge *oneself* on 1217R47
Inland Revenue 732L29
Internal Revenue Service 743R58
reverberate through/around 1217R62
reverberate with/to 1217R60
revere *someone* for 1217R68
role reversal 1230R67
reverse discrimination 1218L30
reverse the charges 1218L16
revert to 1218L47
review section 1218L82
revile *someone* for 1218R10
revise for 1218R26
revolt against 1218R68
revolted by 1218R76
counter-revolution 312R62
Green Revolution 622R37
industrial revolution 724L4
palace revolution 1019R53
sexual revolution 1304L15
revolve around 1219L26/28
revolving door 1219L29
reward for 1219L55/61/62
reward *something* with 1219L63/66
Rh factor 1219R45 1220L9
go into rhapsodies 1219R26
rhesus factor 1219R45
rhesus monkey 1219R42
rhetorical question 1219R65
rheumatic fever 1220L1
rheumatoid arthritis 1220L5
nonsense rhyme 960L80
nursery rhyme 968L45
rhyme or reason 1220L66
rhyme with 1220L49
skipping rhyme 1347L19
cockney rhyming slang 253L64
rhyming slang 1220L49
rhythm and blues 1220L84
rhythm method 1220R3
rhythm section 1220R7
rib *someone* about 1220R33
rib cage 1220R28
rib-tickling 1220R30
rib-ticklingly funny 1220R30
blue riband 140L10
blue ribbon 140L11/15
ribbon development 1220R70
cut/torn into ribbons 1220R66
poke/dig *someone* in the ribs 1220R25
stick to *someone's* ribs 1423L39
brown rice 169L59
rice paddy 1220R83
rice paper 1220R84
rice pudding 1221L1
filthy rich 519R67
get-rich-quick 1221L8
life's rich tapestry 818R75
mine a rich seam 899R83
stinking rich 1426R14
strike it rich 1442R10
nouveau riche 965L35/40
rags-to riches 1168R6
Richter scale 1221R14
ricochet off 1221R41
get rid of 1221R54/57/60
rid of 1221R52/54
good riddance 1221R63
riddle with 1222L5
talk/speak in riddles 1222L1
along for the ride 36R7
give *someone* a rough ride 1236L26
let *something* ride 1222L25
ride (on) a wave of 1222L22
ride *somewhere* by 1222L16
ride by/past 1222L20
ride on 1222L15/17/47/48/49
ride out 1222L35
ride roughshod over 1222L39
ride up 1222L41
take for a ride 1222L54
dispatch rider 396L46
have been around the ridges 1222L79
ridicule for 1222R7
from the sublime to the ridiculous 1451R12
riding for a fall 1222L27
riding habit 1222L65
riding high 1222L29
riding school 1222L67
riff-raff 1222R32
air-rifle 29L61
rifle-range 1222R38
rifle through 1222R46
rift valley 1222R54
rig-out 1222R82 1223L1 1224R63
rig the market 1222R60
ballot-rigging 96L14
a bit of all right 35L42 130L13
as right as rain 1224L37
give *one's* right hand/arm 1223R69
heart in the right place 656R70
in the right place at the right time 1223L54
make (all) the right noises 958R61
not in *one's* right mind 1224L40
not (quite) right in the head 1224L43
on the right foot 545L71
on the right road/track 1228L37
on the right side of 1333R81/79 1334L1
on the right side of the law 1333R83
play *one's* cards right 1078L37
put/set right 1224L45
right angle 1223R73
right-angled triangle 1223R75
right away 1224L72
right behind 1224L67
right field 1223R77
right-hand 1223R79
right-hand drive 1223R82
right-hand man 1224L6
right-handed 1224L1
right-hander 1224L1/4
right left and centre 1223R72
right minded 1223L76
right now 1224L70
right of way 1223R29
right on the button 180R1
right on time 1523L59
right out from under *someone's* nose 962L49
right-to-die 1223R32
right-to-life 1223R36
right way round 1236R43
right wing 1224L16/17/20
right-winger 1224L21
right you are 1224L53
see *someone* right 1284L49
serve *someone* right 1297R8
sit right 1343L46
stage right 1406R26
suit right down to the ground 1457R51
the New Right 952L62
the right way round/around 1223L48
too right 1224L54
we've got a right one here 1224L79
would give *one's* right arm for 596R21
bill of rights 126L78
civil rights 234R65
conjugal rights 288L24
dead to rights 351L38
human rights 692R8
the rights and wrongs of 1223L84
within *one's* rights 1223R23
bored rigid 149L49
rigor mortis 1224R38
de rigueur 370R20
lead/live the life of Riley 818R84
horn-rimmed 685R8
annual ring 1554R68
boxing ring 155L74
engagement ring 457R41
growth ring 1554R68
hollow ring 679L35
key ring 777R70
napkin ring 937R58
paedophile ring 1018L5
ring a bell 1225R35
ring back 1225R6
ring binder 1225L27
ring finger 1225L29
ring for 1225R5
ring hollow 1225R41
ring in 1225L83/R29
ring *something* on 1225R37
ring out 1225R31/32/33
ring-pull 1225L32
ring road 1225L35
ring round 1225R9
ring the changes 1225R37
ring toss 684L77
ring true/false 1225R42
ring up 1225R12/43
ring with 1225R34
signet ring 1336R58
throw/toss *one's* hat into the ring 649R76
tree ring 1554R68
vice ring 1621L18
warning/alarm bells start to ring 115R38 1638R44
wedding ring 1648R74
ringed by/with 1225L79
bell-ringer 115R49
dead ringer 351L35
run rings round 1225L24
ice rink 700L8
skating rink 1345L33
rinky-dink 1225R72
read the Riot Act 1178R24
riot of colour 1226L9
riot police 1226L6
let rip 812R24/28
rip off 1226L39/44/49/51
rip out 1226L38
rip-roaring 1226R14
rip through 1226L40
rip up 1226L33/35/41
ripe old age 1226L69
the time is ripe 1226L66 1523L64
bodice-ripper 142R31
ripple effect 1226R8
get/take a rise out of 1226R51
give rise 1226R68
high rise 667L81
low-rise 844L42
make *someone's* hackles rise 635L42
rise above 1226R30/32/75
rise and shine 1226R42
rise from 1226R19/20
rise in/at 1226R63/65/75/24
rise through the ranks 1226R35
rise to fame 1226R37
rise to the bait 1226R39
rise to the occasion/challenge 1226R40
Land of the Rising Sun 794L54
rising damp 1226R44
rising star 1226R45
calculated risk 183R72
high-risk 668L29
risk *it* 1227L35
risk *everything* on 1227L36
run the risk of 1227L31
security risk 1282L7
rite of passage 1227L56
last rites 797R66 1227L55
rival for/in 1227L84
sibling rivalry 1332R45
down river 1227R16
river bank 1227R21
river-bed 1227R24
river boat 1227R25
sell down the river 1290L8
up river 1227R15
rivet *something* on 1227R37/39
rivet together 1227R35
access road 7R65
back road 89R13
come to the end of the road 1228L39
dirt road 388L6 1227R81
down the road 416L77
get out of *the/my* road 1227R82
get the/this show on the road 1328L62
hit the road 673L33
hog the road 675L30
hold the road 676L52
main road 853R62
middle-of-the-road 894L69
no through road 1516R43
on the right road 1228L37
orbital road 993L61
relief road 1199L81
ring road 1225L35
road haulage 651L19 1563L1
road hog 1228L47
road-holding 676L55
road safety 1228L48
road sense 1228L52
road tax 1228L55
road test 1228L57/58
road to Damascus 1228L42
road toll 1228L60
road trip 1228L62
service road 1297R78
slip road 1354L13
take to the road 1228L46
the end of the road 455L8
trunk road 1564R36
roam around 1228R61
not within an ass's roar of 71L42
roar with 1228R73
a roaring trade 1229L4
rip-roaring 1226R14
roaring drunk 1228R84
roaring forties 1229L6
roaring success 1229L2
roaring twenties 1229L9
pot roast 1102R22
rob *someone* of 1229L41/43
daylight robbery 349R76
highway robbery 349R77
robbery with violence 1229L55
robin redbreast 1229L67
round robin 1236L81/82
before you can/could say Jack Robinson 757R80 1259L69
Heath Robinson 658L74
between a rock and a hard place 1229R45
hard rock 647L1
like a shag on a rock 1307L14
rock and roll 1230L35
rock back 1229R81
rock bottom 1229R47/51
rock bun 1229R56
rock cake 1229R56
rock candy 1229R42/44
rock garden 1229R58 1230L51
rock hard 1229R53
rock 'n' roll 1230L35
rock pool 1229R58
rock salt 1229R60
rock solid 1229R54
rock the boat 1230L5
solid as a rock 1229R55
steady as a rock 1417R37
give *someone* a rocket 1230L66
retro-rocket 1216R21
rocket ship 1230L69
rocket to 1230L74/75
rocket up 1230L74
rocking chair 1230L9
rocking horse 1230L11
get *one's* rocks off 1229R71
run onto the rocks 1241R1
con rod 288R12
connecting rod 288R12
curtain rod 337R27
fuel rod 571L78
lightning rod 822L23/27
make a rod for *one's* own back 1230R11
roe deer 1230R27
the Jolly Roger 769L30
lovable rogue 843R54
rogues' gallery 1230R45
role model 1230R65
role play 1230R59/79
role reversal 1230R67
title role 1527R51
barrel roll 101L48
bread roll 1231R77
egg roll 444R4 1400L7
electoral roll 446L63
heads will roll 653L75
honor roll 1231R73
jam roll 1477R77

▪jelly ▫roll 761R65 1477R77
▫kitchen ▪roll 782L39/46 1494L33
▫pancake ▪roll 1400L7
▫rock and ▪roll 1230L35
▫rock 'n' ▪roll 1230L35
▫roll ▪back 1231R17/19
▪roll ▫bar 1231L63
▪roll ▫call 1231R70
▪roll into 1231R12
▫roll ▪neck 1092R81 1231R35
▫roll of ▪honour 1231R72
▪roll on 1231L29/38
▫roll-▪on ▫roll-▪off 1231L42
▫roll ▪out 1231R44
▫roll-top ▪desk 1231R36
▫roll ▪up 1231L30/R13/20/38 1351R67
▫roll up one's ▪sleeves 1231R21
▫roll ▪up! ▫roll ▪up! 1231L33
▫roll with the ▪punches 1231L36
▫sausage ▪roll 1257L82
▫spring ▪roll 1400L6
▫Swiss ▪roll 1477R77
▫take/▫call the ▪roll 1231R67
▪till ▫roll 1520R11
▪toilet ▫roll 1532L80
▫rolled ▪gold 1231R27
▫rolled ▪oats 1231R45
▫high ▪roller 668L34
▪roller ▫blind 1231L73
▪roller ▫coaster 124L83 1231L76
▪roller ▫derby 1231L81
▪roller ▫skate 1231R4/L84/R5
▪roller ▫towel 1231R5
▫rolling in ▪money 1231L25
▫rolling in the ▪aisles 1231L28
▪rolling ▫mill 1231R47
▪rolling ▫pin 1231R48
▪rolling ▫stock 1231L43
start/set/get the ▪ball ▫rolling 95R24
▫roly-▪poly 1232L12/15
▫CD-▪ROM 207R4
▫Roman ▪alphabet 1232L30
▫Roman ▪candle 1232L33
▫Roman ▪Catholic 1232L35
▫Roman Catholic ▪Church 1232L38
▫Roman Ca▪tholicism 1232L40
▫Roman ▪law 1232L41
▫Roman ▪nose 1232L43
▫Roman ▪numerals 1232L44
▪fiddle while ▫Rome ▪burns 515R41
▫romp a▪round/a▪bout 1232R63
▪romp ▫home/▫in 1232R65
▪romp through 1232R66/71
▪romper ▫suit 1232R73
▪rood ▫screen 1232R83
a ▪roof over one's ▫head 1233L12
go through the ▪roof 1233L16/14
▫hit the ▪roof 673L19
like a ▫cat on a hot tin ▪roof 203L55
▫raise the ▪roof 1170L62/64 1233L18
▪roof ▫garden 1233L19
▪roof-▫rack 1233L20
▪roof with 1233L23
under the ▫same ▪roof 1233L13
▫shout/pro▫claim from the ▪rooftops 1233L41
▪baggage ▫room 93R64
▫bed-▪sitting room 111L59/R74
▪changing ▫room 215R1
▪common ▫room 271L13
de▪livery ▫room 363L26
▪dining ▫room 385L71
▫double ▪room 414L73
▪drawing ▫room 421L32
▪dressing ▫room 422L64
▪elbow ▫room 445R63
e▪mergency ▫room 203L25 450L78
▫front ▪room 568L47
▪house-▫room 689L54
▪ladies'/▪men's ▫room 792R5 1532R2
▪living ▫room 832L38
▪living room ▫suite 832L41 1515L77
▪locker ▫room 835R42/45
▪lounge ▫room 832L39 843L35
▪lunch room 848L8
▪men's ▫room 858R75
▪operating ▫room 989R39
▪powder ▫room 1105L68
▪reading ▫room 1179L15
re▪ception ▫room 1184L26
▪rest ▫room 1212R8
▫room and ▪board 141R18 1233L71
▫room for im▪provement 1233R23
▫room for man▪oeuvre 862L58
▪room ▫service 1233L72
▪room with 1233L78/79
▪rumpus ▫room 1240R52
se▪clusion ▫room 1278R82
▫single ▪room 1341L26
▪sitting ▫room 832L38 1343L62
▫smallest ▪room 1357R72
▫smoke-filled ▪room 1361L78
▪standing ▫room 1410L83
▫standing room ▪only 1410R3
▪tack ▫room 1484R64
▪tally-▫room 1489L67
▪tea ▫room 1494L26
▫twin-bedded ▪room 1573L60
u▪tility ▫room 1603L21
▪waiting ▫room 1633R58
▪rooming ▫house 836L46 1233L80
▫come back/home to ▪roost 1233R40
▫rule the ▪roost 1240L2
▫cube ▪root 332R33 1234L50
▫root and ▪branch 1233R53
▪root ▫beer 1233R54
▪root ▫cellar 1233R56
▪root ▫crop 1233R57
▪root ▫for 1234L54/56
▪root through/among 1234L53
▫root ▪up/▪out 1233R77/75
▫take ▪root 1233R50/52
▫deep(ly)-▪rooted 357L67
▫rooted to the ▪spot 1234L33
▫send out ▪roots 1233R50
▫give someone enough ▫rope to ▪hang themselves 459R38
▪jump ▫rope 772R35 1347L12/18
▫money for old ▪rope 913R24
▫rope ▪bridge 1234L69
▫rope ▪in 1234R34
▫rope ▪into 1234R37
▫rope ▪ladder 1234L66
▫rope ▪off 1234R32
▫rope to▪gether 1234L84
▪skipping ▫rope 1347L17/12
▫know the ▪ropes 787R13
▫learn the ▪ropes 1234L80
▫show/▫teach someone the ▪ropes 1234L78
▪rose ▫hip 671L75 1234R69
▪rose-▫water 1234R71
▫rose ▪window 1234R72
a ▫bed of ▪roses 111L80
▫all/a ▫bed of ▪roses 1234R66
all ▫moonlight and ▪roses 916R83
▫come up ▫smelling of ▪roses 1360L29
▫coming up ▪roses 1234R65
▫put the ▪roses (back) into someone's ▫cheeks 1234R63
▫paint a ▫rosy ▪picture 1019L30
▫dry ▪rot 429R69
▫rot set ▪in 1235L54
▫stop the ▪rot 1235L56
ro▪tate around 1235L68
▪crop ro▫tation 327L30 1235L78
▫learn by ▪rote 1235L84
▪rote ▫learning 1235R1
▫cut up ▪rough 339R81
▫diamond in the ▪rough 380L24 1235R54
give someone a ▫rough ▪time/▪ride 1236L26
▫give someone the ▫rough side of one's ▪tongue 1236L25
go through a ▫rough ▪patch 1034R56
▫rough and ▪ready 1235R50/82
▫rough and ▪tumble 1236L37/38
▫rough ▪diamond 1235R53
▫rough ▪ground 1235R44
▫rough-▪hewn 1235R56/58
▫rough ▪idea 1235R78
▫rough ▪justice/▪luck 1236L23
▫rough ▪out/▪in 1236L7/6
▫rough ▪paper 1235R84
▫rough ▪trade 1236L28
▫rough someone ▪up 1236L42
▫sleep ▪rough 1236L33
take the ▫rough with the ▪smooth 1235R68
▫ride ▪roughshod over 1222L39
▫Russian rou▪lette 1244R83
▫all round the ▪houses 689L34
▫come ▪round 266R49/55
▫drive/▫send ▪round the bend 117L1
get one's ▪mind ▫round 898R47
▫get ▪round 591R49 593R21 1236R39
get ▪round to 593R25
get one's ▪tongue round 1534R50
▫go ▪round 607R40
go ▫round in ▪circles/a ▪circle 232R20
▫hang round one's ▪neck 644L80
▫make the ▪world go ▫round 1683R60
▪merry-go-▫round 889L67
▪milk ▫round 896R81
▪paper ▫round 1023L50
▫pass round the ▪hat 675R33
▫put the ▪word round 1679L12
▫right/▫wrong way ▪round 1236R43
▫round ▪brackets 156R6 1236L70
▫round ▪dozen 1236L77
▫round-▪eyed 1236L65
▫round ▪figures 1236L80
▫round ▪hundred 1236L79
▫round ▪number 1236L75
▫round ▪off/▪out 1236R48/50
▪round on 1236R51
▫round ▪robin 1236L81/82
▫round-▪shouldered 1236R1
▫Round-▪table 1236R3
▫round the ▪back 89L70/68
▫round the ▪bend 116R80/81
▫round the ▪clock 246L62
▫round the ▪corner 1236R73
▫round the ▪twist 1574L16
▫round ▪trip 1236R5
▫round ▪up/▪down 1236R8/11/54 1598R49
▫run ▪rings round 1225L24
▫run round in ▪circles 232R20 1241L6
▫send round the ▪twist 1574L16
▫swap ▪round 1473R76
the/someone's ▫daily ▪round 1237L2
the ▫right way ▪round 1223L48
the ▫wrong way ▪round 1693L66
▫theatre in the ▪round 1508R15
▫twist/▫wrap someone round one's little ▪finger 1573R84 1689L69
▫way ▪round 1236R40 1645L54
▪whip-▫round 1659L75
▫word gets ▪round 1679L16
▫well-▪rounded 1653L75
go the ▪rounds 1237L10
▫make/▫do the ▪rounds 1237L8
▫roundtrip ▪ticket 1216R84
▪news ▫roundup 1237L53
▪rouse from 1237L63
▪rabble-▫rouser 1164R61/56
▫rout ▪out 1237L77/75
▪access ▫route 7R65
en ▪route 460L38
▪paper ▫route 1023L50
▪route ▫march 1237R4
▪stock ▫route 1428L41
▪trade ▫route 1546L76
▪Land ▫Rover 794L17
have a ▫roving ▪eye 1237R32
▫death ▪row 352R26
▫kick up a ▪row 779L9
▪row about/over 1237R52
▪row ▫house 1237R42 1504L43
▫skid ▪row 1346L24
▪rowing-▫boat 1237R60
▫Marshal of the Royal ▪Air ▫Force 868R57
▫Royal As▪sent 72L45 1238L2
▫royal ▪blue 1238L3
▫royal ▪flush 1238L4
▫Royal ▪Highness 1238L7
▫Royal ▪Navy 1238L9
▫royal ▪pardon 1238L11
▫royal pre▪rogative 1238L16
▫Royal ▪Society 1238L9
the ▫three ▪Rs 1515R3
▫Rt ▪Hon 1238L52
▫not have two ▫pennies to rub to▪gether 1045R64
▪rub against/on 1238L66/68
▫rub a▪long (together) 1238L69
▫rub ▪clean 1238L63
▫rub ▪down 1238L71/72/74/75/R11
▫rub ▪elbows with 1238R3
▫rub ▪in 1238L77
▪rub into 1238L61
rub someone's ▪nose in it/the ▫dirt 1238R4
▫rub ▪off 1238L79/80
▫rub ▪out 466R10 1238L84
▫rub ▪shoulders with 1238R3
rub the ▪sleep out of one's ▫eyes 1351R35
▫rub up the wrong ▪way 1238R7/8
▪rub with 1238L62
▫india ▪rubber 721L63
▫rubber ▪band 1238R26
▫rubber ▪dinghy 1238R29
▪rubber ▫plant 1238R30
▫rubber-▪stamp 1238R32/36
▪rubber ▫tree 1238R38
▫sponge ▪rubber 1395R82
▪brass-▫rubbing 158L73
▫rubbing ▪alcohol 1238R9 1468R21
a ▫load of (old) ▪rubbish 1238R56
▫talk ▪rubbish 1488R8
▫ruck ▪up 1239L1
▫rue the ▪day 1239L60
▫ruffle someone's ▪feathers 1239L78
▫Persian ▪rug 1052L37
▪prayer ▫rug 1108R70
▫pull the ▪rug from under 1144L48
▪scatter ▫rug 1263L50
▫sweep under the under the ▪rug 1475L21
▫rugby ▪football 1239R6
▫Rugby ▪League 1239R9
▫Rugby ▪Union 1239R10
▫rack and ▪ruin 1166L72
as a ▫general ▪rule 587L17
di▫vide and ▪rule 402L60
▪gag ▫rule 579L62
▫golden ▪rule 610L64
▫home ▪rule 680L70
ma▪jority ▫rule 854R68
▫make it a ▪rule 1239R70
▪rule ▫book 1239R70
▪rule for/in ▫favour of/against 1240L20
▫rule of ▪law 1240L9
▫rule of ▪thumb 1239R65
▫rule ▪off 1240L34
▫rule O▪K 1239R84
▪rule on 1240L20
▫rule ▪out 1240L25
▫rule the ▪roost 1240L2
▪slide ▫rule 1352R32
▫work to ▪rule 1679R46/49
a▫gainst the ▪rules 1239R57
▫bend/▫stretch the ▪rules 1239R61
▪ground ▫rules 626L67
▫Rafferty's ▪rules 1168L42
▫ruling ▪class 1240L16
▫ruling ▪passion 1240L17
▪rumble ▫strip 1240L59 1389L19
▪rummage in/through 1240R9
▪rummage ▫sale 772L75 1240R13
▫gin ▪rummy 595R9
▪rumour-▫monger 1240R28
▫rump ▪steak 1240R36
▫kick up a ▪rumpus 1240R50
▫raise a ▪rumpus 1240R50
▪rumpus ▫room 1240R52
▫cut and ▪run 339R64
▫dummy/▫dry ▪run 1241R26
▪fun ▫run 573R64
give someone a ▪run for their ▫money 1241L40
have a good ▪run for one's ▫money 1241L38
▫hit-and-▪run 672R55/60/62
▫home ▪run 680L31
in the ▪long ▫run 1241R23/26
in the ▪short ▫run 1241R25
make someone's ▫blood run ▪cold 137L48 1242L6
▪milk ▫run 896R84
▫passions run ▪high 1032R45
▪print ▫run 1123L1
▫run a ▪fever 1240R77
▫run a ▪mile 1240R82
▫run a ▪temperature 1499L23
▫run a▪cross 1241L63 1242L44/68
▫run ▪after 1242L72
▪run against 1240R64 1241L77 1242L32
▫run a▫ground/a▪shore/onto the ▪rocks 1241R1
▫run a▪long 1241L65 1242L78
▫run along/down 1241L79
▫run a▪mok/a▪muck 41R83
▫run and ▪run 1241R10
▫run a▪round 1240R70 1241L65
▫run a▪round/▪round 1241L66
▫run a▪round with 1242L82
▫run a▪way/▪off 1240R60 1242R1
▫run away to ▪sea 1275R82
▫run a▪way to▫gether 1242R4
▫run a▪way with 1242R8
▫run something ▪back 1241L80
▫run ▪by 1242R14
▫run its ▪course 1240R76
▫run ▪deep 357L61
▫run-▪down 1241R74 1242R18/21/29/33/39/42 1243R3
▫run ▪down in/to 1242R43
▫run ▪errands 1240R78
▫run one's ▪eye over 1241R5
▪run for 1240R61/79 1241L17/67/68/70/R29 1242L33/R70 1243L20/66
▪run from 1242R2/6
▫run someone ▪home 1241L82
▫run ▪in 1240R66 1242R45/48
▫run in the ▪family 1241R6
▪run into 1241L63/R79/84 1242L3/45/R57/60
▫run-of-the-▪mill 1242L56
▪run-off 1241L14/72 1242R64/67
▫run someone off their ▪feet 545R49
▫run ▪on 1241L73/R45/80 1242L48/50/51/R74
▫run on the ▪spot 1240R83
▫run ▪out 1242R78 1243L4
▫run ▪out for/on 1243L8
▫run out of ▪steam 1243L2
▫run ▫out of ▪town 1241R9
▫run ▪over 1243L14/18/24/28
▫run ▪ragged 1241L2
▫run ▪rings round 1225L24
▫run round in ▪circles 232R20 1241L6
▫run the ▪risk of 1227L31
▪run the ▫show 1241R62
▫run ▪through 1241L63/74/75/76/83 1243L31/34/36/41/46/49
▫run through one's ▪mind/▪head 1243L43
▪run to 1241L22 1242R2 1243L52
run to ▪ground 604L14 626L40
▫run to ▫ground/▪earth 1241L8
▪run-up 1241L18 1243L58/61/63/68
▫run ▪up against 1243L70
▫run ▪wild 1242L23 1664R47
▪run with 1241R77 1242R5/66 1243L22/39
the ▫general/▫usual ▪run of 1242L55
▫trial ▪run 1556L72
▫give someone the ▪runaround 1243L75
▫read the ▪runes 1178R28
▫lowest/▫bottom rung of the ▪ladder 1243R15
▫front-▪runner 568L50
▪gun-▫runner 632R6/5
▫runner ▪bean 1243R24
▫runner-▪up 1243R27
▫scarlet ▪runner 1243R24
▫long-▪running 838R43
▫make/▫take the ▪running 1241R67
▫running ▪battle 1241R33
▫running ▪commentary 269R28 1241R36
▪running ▫costs 1241R66
▫running ▪high 1242L22
▫running in one's ▪head 1241R7
▪running ▫mate 1242L38
▪running ▫shoe 1549L1
▫running ▪sore 1242L13
▫running ▫stitch 1241R37
▫running with ▪blood 1242L4
▫take a running ▪jump 1241L52
the sands of ▫time are running ▪out 1254L20
▫up and ▪running 1241R46 1598L79
▫year ▪running 547L25
▪gold ▫rush 609R82
▪rush ▫hour 1244R67
▪rush into 1244L64
▫rush someone off their ▪feet 545R49
▫rush ▪through 1243R71
▫rushed ▪job 1244R71
▫Russian rou▪lette 1244R83
▫rust a▪way/▪through 1245L11
▫rustle ▪up 1245L40
▪rye ▫bread 1245R39
▪hunt sabo▫teur 694R79
▪sabre-▫rattling 1246L84
▫sabre-toothed ▪tiger 1246R67
▪cul-de-▫sac 334L34
▫hit the ▪sack 673L25
▫sack ▪out 1247L20
▪sack ▫race 1247L8
▫sackcloth and ▪ashes 1247L41
▫sacred ▪cow 1247L62
make the ▫ultimate/su▫preme ▪sacrifice 1247R20
▫sacrificial ▪lamb 1247L81
▫sad to ▪say 1247R67
▫sadder but ▪wiser 1247R48
▪saddle-bag 1247R82
▪saddle-▫sore 1248L1
▫saddle ▪up 1248L5
▪saddle with 1248L16
sa▪fari ▫jacket 1248L53
sa▪fari ▫park 1248L56
sa▪fari ▫suit 1248L55
a ▫safe pair of ▪hands 641R63
as ▫safe as ▪houses 1248R2
▪fail-▫safe 494L58
in ▫safe ▪hands 641R53 1248L84
on ▫safe ▪ground 626R12
on the ▪safe ▫side 1248R4
▫safe and ▪sound 1248R6
▫safe-▪conduct 1248R7
▪safe ▫house 1248R11
▪safe ▫period 1248R14
▫safe ▪seat 1248L83
▫safe ▪sex 1248R16
▪road ▫safety 1228L48
▪safety ▫belt 1248R47
▪safety ▫catch 1248R47
▪safety ▫curtain 1248R50
▪safety de▫posit box 1248R53 1249L10/9
▫safety-▪first 1248R54
▪safety ▫glass 1248R59/56
▪safety ▫lamp 1248R62
▪safety ▫match 1248R65
▪safety ▫net 1248R67
▪safety ▫pin 1248R73
▪safety ▫razor 1248R76
▪safety ▫valve 1248R78
▪sag ▫bag 107R44 1249L53
▪sag under 1249L47
▫sage-▪green 1249L83
easier ▫said than ▪done 438R45
e▫nough ▪said 459R36
no sooner ▫said than ▪done 1376L53
there's ▫little to be ▪said for 1259R83
there's ▫something/a ▫lot to be ▪said for 1259R81
when ▫all is said and ▪done 1260L6

in ▫full **▪sail** 572L73/74
▫sail against the ▪wind 1249R28
▫sail a▪long 1249R74
▫sail close to the ▪wind 1249R30
▪sail for 1249R24/67
▫sail ▪into 1249R75/77
▫sail ▪on 1249R81
▪sail over 1249R80
▪sail ▫through 1249R82 1345L47
▫set **▪sail** 1249R66
▫under **▪sail** 1249R68
▫plain **▪sailing** 1074R47
▪sailing ▫boat 1249R51
▫smooth **▪sailing** 1074R48
▪sailor ▫suit 1249R59
take the ▪wind out of *someone's* ▫**sails** 1666R79
▫patron **▪saint** 1036R61
▪saint's ▫day 1250L20
try the ▫patience of a **▪saint** 1036L35 1566L41
com▫munion of **▪saints** 271R13
je ne **sais** ▪quoi 762L3
for ▫God's/▫Christ's **▪sake** 1250L52
for ▫goodness/▫Pete's/▫heavens/▫pity's **▪sake** 1250L49
for old ▪times' ▫**sake** 980R4
sa▪laam to 1250L62
▫fruit **▪salad** 569R52
▫green **▪salad** 622R37 1250L78
in *one's* **▪salad** ▫days 1250R7
po▫tato **▪salad** 1103L1
▪salad ▫bar 1250R1
▪salad ▫cream 1250R3
▪salad ▫dressing 1250R5
▫basic **▪salary** 102R12
▪starting ▫**salary** 1413R76
▫bring and ▪buy ▫**sale** 166L41
▫car-▪boot ▫**sale** 193R19
▪clearance ▫**sale** 242R36
▪garage ▫**sale** 193R20 582R38
▪jumble ▫**sale** 772L75 1240R13
▪rummage ▫**sale** 772L75 1240R13
▫**sale** or ▪return 1250R58
▪sales as▫sistant 73L24 1250R68
▪sales ▫drive 1250R70
▪sales ▫force 1250R75
▪sales ▫pitch 1250R71
▪sales ▫rep 1250R73
▪sales repre▫sentative 1250R72
▪sales re▫sistance 1250R76
▪sales ▫slip 1250R79
▪sales ▫talk 1250R80
▪sales ▫tax 1250R82
▫door-to-door **▪salesman** 411R44 1251L23
▫travelling **▪salesman** 1553L55
sa▪livary ▫glands 1251L52
▫**sally** ▪forth 1251L65
the ▫**Sally** ▪Army 1251L67
▫**salmon**-▪pink 1251L78
▫**salmon** ▪trout 1251L76
▫smoked **▪salmon** 845L29 1251L74
▪beauty ▫**salon** 110L22
▪hair ▫**salon** 636L64
sa▪loon ▫bar 1251R14
▫iodized **▪salt** 751R68
▫pepper-and-**▪salt** 1046R74
▪rock ▫**salt** 1229R60
▫**salt** and ▪pepper 1046R68/74 1251R41
▫**salt** a▪way 1251R68
▪salt ▫cellar 1251R42
▪salt-▫lick 1251R44
▫take with a ▫pinch of **▪salt** 1068L45
the ▫**salt** of the ▪earth 1251R39
▫worth *one's* **▪salt** 1687L68
▫Epsom **▪salts** 464R48
like a ▫dose of **▪salts** 412R80
▪smelling ▫**salts** 1360L72
sa▪lute as 1252L25
sa▪lute *someone* for 1252L24
▫take the **sa▪lute** 1252L18
Sal▫vation ▪Army 1252L57
▪lip ▫**salve** 828R43
▫Uncle **▪Sam** 1581L71
▫good **Sa▪maritan** 612L17
at the ▫**same** ▪time 1253L31/32 1522L72
by the ▫**same** ▪token 1252R35
▫cast in the **same** ▪mould 202L71
go the ▫**same** ▪way 1252R40
in the ▫**same** ▪boat 1253L36
in the ▫**same** ▪breath 162R48 1253L38
in the ▫**same** ▪league 1253L41
in the ▫**same** ▪street 1253L42
it all amounts/comes to the ▫**same** ▪thing 1252R42
▫never the **same** a▪gain 1252R57
not on the ▫**same** ▪wavelength 1644R75
of the ▫**same** ▪mind 899L61
on the ▫**same** ▪terms 1504L8
▫**same** ▪difference 1252R45
same ▫time same ▪place 1253L47
▫speak/▫talk the **same** ▪language 795L82
▫tar with the **same** ▪brush 1491L70
the ▫**same** as ▪ever 1253L3
the ▫**same** old ▪faces 1253L44
the ▫**same** old ▪story 1253L45
the ▫**same** ▪thing 1512R52
to the ▫**same** ex▪tent as 486L46
under the ▫**same** ▪roof 1233L13
▪sanctify by 1253R38
▪sanctions-▫busting 1253R69
bury/have *one's* ▫head in the **▪sand** 653L38
▪sand ▫dune 1254L11
▪sand ▫trap 176L47 1254L15
▪sanding ma▫chine 1254L32
the **sands** of ▫time are running ▪out 1254L20
▫club **▪sandwich** 250L26
▫jam **▪sandwich** 759R54
▫open **▪sandwich** 988R33
▪sandwich ▫bar 1254R12
▪sandwich ▫board 1254R14
▪sandwich ▫course 1254R20
▪submarine ▫**sandwich** 665L77
▪sanitary ▫fittings 1254R73
▪sanitary ▫napkin 1254R78
▪sanitary ▫pad 1254R79
▪sanitary ▫towel 1254R78
sani▪tation ▫worker 1255L2
someone's ▫heart **▪sank** 656R52 1341R66
▪Santa ▫Claus 1255L24
▫**Santa's** ▪grotto 1255L30
▫Homo **▪sapiens** 681L56
▫packed/▫squashed like **sar▪dines** 1255R5
▪sash ▫cord 1255R56
▫**sash** ▪window 1255R54
communi▪cations ▫**satellite** 271R73
▪satellite ▫dish 394L6 1256L32
▪satellite ▫state 1256L36
▪satellite te▪levision 1256L34
▪job **satis▫faction** 765R52 1256L82
▫**satisfy** the ▪examiners 1256R33
sat▪suma ▫plum 1256R49
▪saturate with/in 1256R55
▫**saturated** so▪lution 1256R70
satur▪ation ▫bombing 1256R79
satur▪ation ▫point 1089R43 1256R74
▫**Saturday** night ▪special 1257L14
▫barbecue **▪sauce** 99R9
▫mint **▪sauce** 901R72
▫soy(a) **▪sauce** 1381R18
▪tartar ▫**sauce** 1492L34
▪tartare ▫**sauce** 1492L34
▫white **▪sauce** 1660R58
▫Worcester **▪sauce** 1678L53
▫Worcestershire **▪sauce** 1678L53
▫flying **▪saucer** 540R14
▫**saunter** ▪by 1257L64
▪liver ▫**sausage** 833L16
▪sausage ▫dog 342L60 1257L77
▪sausage ma▫chine 1257L79
▪sausage ▫meat 1257L81/83
▪sausage ▪roll 1257L82
▫not to ▫**save** *my* ▪life 1257R58
▫**save** *someone's* ▪bacon/▪neck 1257R51
▫**save** *one's* ▪breath 1258L16
▪save for 1258L6/7/12/35
▪save *someone* from 1257R40 1258L10
▪save it 1258L15
▪save on 1258L11
▫**save** *one's* ▫own ▪skin/▪hide 1257R56
▫**save** the ▪day/situ▪ation 1257R52
▫scrimp and **▪save** 1273R35
▪life-▫**saver** 819L64/66/62
▫screen ▫**saver** 1272R16
▫daylight **▪saving** 349R80
▫daylight **▪saving** ▫time 349R80
▪face-▫**saving** 492L33
▪labour-▫**saving** 789R76
▫**saving** ▪grace 1257R59
▪space-▫**saving** 1381R69
▪savings ac▫count 368R45 1257R79
▫**savings** and ▪loan as▫sociation 173R12 1257R83
▪savings ▫bank 1257R84
▫**savoir-▪faire** 1258L40
▫**savour** of 1258L53
▪back ▫**saw** 89L79
▪chain ▫**saw** 212L45
▫**saw** a▪way 1258L83
▫**saw** *something* ▪down 1258L80
▫**saw** it ▫coming 1283L52
▫**saw** ▪off 1258L78
▫**saw** ▪up 1258L79
▪tenon ▫**saw** 1500R43
▫**sawn**-off ▪shotgun 1258R2
▪sax ▫player 1258R13/26
▫Anglo-**▪Saxon** 45R23
▫bass **▪saxophone** 103R10
be▫fore you can/could **say** Jack ▪Robinson 757R80 1259L69
▫dare I **▪say** (it) 346L6
have ▫nothing to **▪say** for *one*self 1259L74
it's ▫fair to **▪say** 494R74
▪must ▫**say** 1259L82
need ▫hardly **▪say** 946R74
▫need I **say** ▪more? 946R77
need *one* **▪say** 946R75
▫needless to **▪say** 947L10
▫never **say** ▪boo 146R75
▫not have a civil ▪word to ▫**say** for 234R83
not **say** ▫boo (to a ▪goose) 1259R61
▫sad to **▪say** 1247R67
▫**say** a ▪word 1678L71
▫**say** *something* a▪gainst 1258R78
▫**say** ▪cheese 223L51
▫**say** *one's* ▪piece 1259R67
▪say-so 1259L59 1260L43/46
▪say ▫something/a ▫lot about 1259R68
▫**say** the ▪word 1259R75 1679L49
▫**say** ▪uncle 1259R70
▫sorry to **▪say** 1377L80
to ▫**say** ▪nothing of 1260L4
to ▫**say** the ▪least 806R57 1259L84
what ▫*I* **say** ▪goes 1260L5
it ▫goes without **▪saying** 1259L83
there's ▫no **▪saying** 956R78
▫what *someone* ▫**says** ▪goes 1655R11
▫full-**▪scale** 572R56/60 573L36
▪Richter ▫**scale** 1221R14
▫**scale** ▪up/▪down 1260R46
▫sliding **▪scale** 1352R27
▪time ▫**scale** 1522L10
the **▪scales** fall from *someone's* ▫eyes 1260R57
▫tilt the **▪scales** 1520R33
▫tip the **▪scales** 1526L70/77
▫out for/▫after *one's* **▪scalp** 1261L80
▫**scamper** ▪down 1261R26
▫**scamper** ▪off 1261R25
▪scan *something* for 1261R35
▫**scan** ▪through 1261R40
▪bomb ▫**scare** 145R4
▫**scare** a▪way/▪off 1262R18/21
▫**scare** *someone* ▪shitless 1262R33/54
▫**scare** ▪up 1262R69/66
▪bird-▫**scarer** 128L65
▫**scarlet** ▪fever 1263L10
▫**scarlet** ▪runner 1243R24
▫**scarlet** ▪woman 1263L13
▫harum-**▪scarum** 649L47
▪scatter ▫cushion 1263L50
▪scatter ▫rug 1263L50
▫**scatter** to the (four) ▪winds 1263L45
▫worst case **sce▪nario** 1263R19 1686R81
▫change of **▪scene** 215L44
▫set the **▪scene** 1263R48 1299L57
▫steal the **▪scene** 1418L16
the ▫**scene** *is* ▪set 1299L56
be▫hind the **▪scenes** 1263R41
▫put/▫throw *someone* off the **▪scent** 1153R74
▫throw/▫put *someone* off the **▪scent** 1264L16
▪schedule for/to 1264L82/83/81
▫**scheduled** ▪flight 1264R6
▪colour ▫**scheme** 259R54
con▫tributory ▪pension ▫**scheme** 299L74
▪pension ▫**scheme** 1046L25
▪pyramid ▫**scheme** 1156R9
▪scheme against 1264R39
▪scheme for 1264R22/27/38/39
▪scheme of ▫things 1264R29
▪scheme to 1264R23/40
▫**schlep** a▪round 1265L1
▫**schlep** ▪down 1265L3
ap▫proved **▪school** 58R23
▪boarding ▫**school** 141R27
▪convent ▫**school** 300R14
▪day ▫**school** 349R43
ele▪mentary ▫**school** 447L65
▪finishing ▫**school** 522R22
▪grade ▫**school** 616L73
▪graduate ▫**school** 616R62 1265R27
▪grammar ▫**school** 617R18
▫grant-maintained **▪school** 619L1
▪high ▫**school** 669L36/38
▫independent **▪school** 720R70
inter▪mediate ▫**school** 743L42
▪middle ▫**school** 894L75
▪night ▫**school** 955L63
▪nursery ▫**school** 968L43
▪old ▫**school** 980L76
▫old **school** ▪tie 980L77
pa▪rochial ▫**school** 1027R27
▪prep ▫**school** 1115L80
pre▪paratory ▫**school** 1115L28/80
▫private **▪school** 1124L43
▫public **▪school** 1142L44/R20
▪riding ▫**school** 1222L67
▪school *someone* in 1265R39/41
▪school ▫leaver 1265R6
school-▪leaving age 1265R9
▫**school** of hard ▪knocks 1265R31
▫**school** of ▪life 1265R29
▫**school** of ▪thought 1265R53
▪school *oneself* to 1265R40
▫special **▪school** 1386L42
▪summer ▫**school** 1459L56/59
▪Sunday ▫**school** 1460L83
▫teach **▪school** 1494L56
▪trade ▫**school** 1546R65
as ▫every **▪schoolboy** ▫knows 1265R67
as ▫every **▪schoolchild** ▫knows 1265R67
▪sci ▫fi 1266R59 1267L57
▫blind with **▪science** 135R12
▫Christian **▪Science** 230L57
com▪puter ▫**science** 279L82
do▫mestic **▪science** 410R21
▪earth ▫**science** 437R8
▫hard **▪science** 647L72
▪life ▫**science** 819L69
lin▫guistic **▪science** 827R8
▫Master of **▪Science** 871R73
▫natural **▪science** 943L52
po▫litical **▪science** 1092L59
▪pseudo-▫**science** 1140L76
▫**science** ▪fiction 1266R59
▪science ▫park 1266R63
▫social **▪science** 1370R31
▪soil ▫**science** 1372L59
▫physical **▪sciences** 1061L13
the ▫social **▪sciences** 1370R34
▪scissor ▫jump/▫kick 1267R56
▪nail ▫**scissors** 936L71
▫**scissors** and ▪paste 1267R52
▫multiple **scle▪rosis** 929L62
▪scoff at 1267R72/74
▪poop ▫**scoop** 1094R45
▪scoop-▫neck 1268L25
▫**scoop** ▪out 1268L35
▫**scoop** the ▪pool 1268L39
▫**scoop** ▪up 1268L34/38
▪pooper ▫**scooper** 1094R46
▪motor ▫**scooter** 921R14
▫**scope** for man▪oeuvre 862L58
▪scorch down 1268R26
▫**scorch** ▪past 1268R27
scorched-▪earth policy 1268R10
▫know the **▪score** 786R45
on ▪that/▪this ▫**score** 1269L36
▪score against/for 1268R35 1269L14/15
score ▪brownie ▫points 169L80
▫**score** (▪points) off/over 1268R64
▫**score** ▪out/▪through 1269L20
▪score over 1268R47
▪score with 1268R63
▫settle a **▪score** 1301R8
▫settle (old) **▪scores** 1301R8
▫**scot**-▪free 1269R50
▫**Scotch** ▪broth 1269R27
▫**Scotch** ▪egg 1269R29
▫**Scotch** ▪mist 1269R31
▫**Scotch** ▪tape 1269R32 1290L56/63
▫**Scotch** ▪terrier 1269R33
▫**Scotland** ▪Yard 1269R55
▫**scour** a▪way 1269R76
▪scour for 1270L6/7
▪pan ▫**scourer** 1021L34 1269R82
▪scouring ▫pad 1269R83
▪Beaver ▫**Scout** 110L78
▫boy **▪scout** 155R80 1270L49
Ex▪plorer ▫**Scout** 1613R66
▫Girl **▪Scout** 596L14 1270L49
▫**scout** a▪round/▪round 1270L33
▫**Scout's** ▪honour 1270L56
▪Scout ▫leader 1270L59
▫**scout** ▪out 1270L36
▪talent ▫**scout** 1488L53
▪Venture ▫**Scout** 1613R66/73
▪scowl at 1270L65
▫**scrabble** a▪bout 1270L72
▫**scrabble** a▪round 1270L71
▪scrabble for 1270L79
▫**scrabble** ▪through 1270L73
▪scrabble with 1270L75
▪scramble for 1270R24/34
▪scramble into 1270R21
▫**scramble** ▪over 1270R18
▫**scramble** ▪through 1270R19
▫**scramble** ▪up/▪down 1270R17
▪scrap ▫dealer 1270R72
▪scrap ▫heap 1270R73
▪scrap ▫merchant 1270R72
▪scrap over 1271L13
▫**scrap** ▪paper 1271L6
▪scrap ▫yard 1270R80
▫bow and **▪scrape** 154L11
▫pinch and **▪scrape** 1068L29
▫**scrape** a ▪living 1271L72
▪scrape against 1271L30/38
▫**scrape** a▪way 1271L32
▫**scrape** ▪by/a▪long 1271L64/34
▫**scrape** ▪home 1271L69
▪scrape into 1271L62
▫**scrape** ▪off 1271L31
▫**scrape** (the bottom of) the ▪barrel 1271L41
▫**scrape** the ▪surface 1468L3
▫**scrape** ▪through 1271L63
▫**scrape** to▪gether 1271L77/78
▫**scrape** ▪up 1271L79
▫**scratch** a▪bout/a▪round 1271R21/20
▫**scratch-and-▪sniff** 1271R45
▪scratch at 1271R30
▫**scratch** beneath the ▪surface 1271R42
▪scratch from 1271R82/84
▫**scratch** *one's* ▪head 1271R35
▫**scratch** *something* ▪off 1271R27
▪scratch *oneself* on 1271R15/26
▪scratch ▫paper 1271L6/R56
▫**scratch** the ▪surface 1468L3
▫up to **▪scratch** 1271R66
▫you **scratch** ▪my back and ▫I'll scratch ▪yours 1271R41
▫pork **▪scratchings** 1096R45
▪scream at 1272L31/33
▫**scream** bloody ▪murder 930L42
▫**scream** blue ▪murder 139R62 930L42
▪scream for 1272L23/31
▫**scream** ▪out 1272L30
▫**scream** ▪past 1272L39
▫**scream** *one*self ▪hoarse 1272L43
▫**screamingly** ▪funny 1272L56
▫**screamingly** ▪obvious 1272L57
▫ **screech** of ▪brakes 157R30
▪screech with 1272L69/70
▪help ▫**screen** 662L65
▪rood ▫**screen** 1232R83
▪screen ▫door 1272R58
▪screen for 1272R34/57
▪screen *something* from 1272R63
▫**screen** ▪off 1272R63
▫**screen** ▪out 1272R38
▪screen ▫printing 1272R13
▪screen ▫saver 1272R16
▪silk ▫**screen** 1337R54/57
▪small ▫**screen** 1357R73
have a **▪screw** ▫loose 1272R84
▫**screw** a▪round 1273L45
▪screw *someone* for 1273L40
▫**screw** ▪in/to▪gether 1273L23
▪screw it/you/them 1273L48
▫**screw** *something* ▪round 1273L28
▫**screw** *things* to▪gether 1273L14
▪screw ▫top 1273L8
▫**screw** ▪up 1273L74/66
▫**screw** up *one's* ▪courage 1273L34
▫**screw** *something* ▪up/▪on 1273L20
▫turn of the **▪screw** 1569L57
▪head **screwed** ▫on 653L69
▫put the **▪screws** on 1154L33
▫put/▫tighten the **▪screws** on 1273L3
▫**scribble** all ▪over/▪scribble ▫on 1273R9
▪scribbly ▫gum 1273R24
▫**scrimp** and ▪save 1273R35
▪scrimp on 1273R32/35
▫**scroll** ▪through 1273R80
▫**scrounge** a▪round 1274L13/11
▫**scrounge** *something* off/from 1274L10/11
▫**scrounge** ▪up 1274L14
▫**scrub** ▪round 1274L43
▫**scrub** ▪up 1274L31
▪scrubbing ▫brush 1274L33/34
by the ▫**scruff** of the/*one's* ▪neck 1274L50
▪scuba ▫diver 1274R50/53
▪sculpture into 1275L41
▪sculpture out of/from 1275L39
the ▫**scum** of the ▪earth 1275L68
▪scurry across 1275R10
▫**scurry** ▪back 1275R14
▪scurry for 1275R12
▪coal ▫**scuttle** 251R26
▫**scuttle** a▪way/▪off 1275R25/24
▫per **▪se** 1051R73
▫air-sea ▪rescue 29R5
between the ▫devil and the deep blue **▪sea** 378L57
▫heavy **▪sea** 659L42
▫put (out) to **▪sea** 1275R81
▫run away to **▪sea** 1275R82
▪sea a▫nemone 1276L2
▫**sea** ▪bream 162L70
▫**sea** ▪breeze 163L63 1276L4
▪sea ▫captain 1276L5
▫**sea** ▪change 1276L7
▫**sea** ▪dog 1276L10
▪sea ▫lane 1276L12
▪sea ▫legs 1276L13
▪sea ▫level 1276L16
▪sea ▫lion 1276L19
▫**sea** ▪mile 944L16
▪sea ▫urchin 1276L22
▫**sea** ▪wall 1276L24
there are (▫plenty) more/(▫plenty of) other fish in the **▪sea** 526L75
give *one's* ▫**seal** of ap▪proval 1276L84
▪seal by 1276R28
▫**seal** ▪in 1276R22
▫**seal** ▪off 1276R24

▪seal with 1276R28
▫set/▫put the ▪seal on 1276R2/3
▫lips *are* ▪sealed 828L80
▫sealed ▪orders 1276R38
▫signed and ▪sealed 1336L34
▫signed sealed and de▪livered 1336L34
▪sealing ▫wax 1276R5
▫mine a rich ▪seam 899R83
▫merchant ▪seaman 888L81
▫bulge at the ▪seams 174L2
▫burst at the ▪seams 177R81
▫global ▪search 600L20
▪search after 1277L40
▪search for 1277L20/22/23/24/30/45
▫search ▪out 1277L31
▪search ▫party 1277L50
▪strip-▫search 1444L82/R5
▪heart-▫searching 656R83
▪soul-▫searching 1378L62
▪seared into 1277L7
▫high ▪seas 668R53
▪closed ▫season 247L84
▫high ▪season 668L37
▪holiday ▫season 513R44
▪lambing ▫season 793L46
▪low ▫season 844R8
▫open ▪season 988R80
▫Season's ▪Greetings 1277R47
▪season ▫ticket 1277R55
▪season with 1278L2
▪silly ▫season 1338L63
the ▪festive ▫season 513R44
the ▫season of good▪will 1277R50
▫back-seat ▪driver 89R2
▪booster ▫seat 148L59
▪bucket ▫seat 171R47
by the ▫seat of *one's* ▪pants 1278R7
▫country ▪seat 313R50
▫county ▪seat 314L12
e▪jector ▫seat 445L68
have/▫take a ▪seat 1278L40
in the ▪driving ▫seat 425L55/54
in the ▪hot ▫seat 687R14
▫safe ▪seat 1248L83
▪seat ▫belt 1278L46
▫seat of ▪learning 1278R30
▫seat-of-the-▪pants 1278R11
take a/the ▫back ▪seat 89L84
▫take *one's* ▪seat 1278L44
▪window ▫seat 1668L52/55
▫deep-▪seated 357L67
▫two-▪seater 1576L54
▫bums on ▪seats 1278L39
▫fannies in the ▪seats 1278L39
se▫baceous ▪gland 1278R42
se▪cede from 1278R61
se▪clusion ▫cell/▫room 1278R82
a ▫second bite of the ▪cherry 130R40
a ▫second string to *one's* ▪bow 1443R47
at ▫second ▪hand 640L68
▫just a ▪second 774L34/35/37
on ▫second ▪thought 1279L35
▫play second ▪fiddle 1079L11
▫second ▪childhood 1279L45
▫second class de▪gree 1279R27
▫second ▪cousin 1279L52
▫second ▪fiddle 1279R12/73
▫second ▪floor 1279L70
se▪cond from 1279R73/74
▫second-▪guess 1279L60/63
▪second ▫hand 641R13 1279L67/R56
▫second ▪honeymoon 1279L72
▫second-in-com▪mand 1279L79
▫second ▪language 1279L83
▫second ▪name 1279R4 1468R72
▫second ▪nature 1279R9
▫second-▪rate 1279R12
▫second ▪sight 1279R14
▫second ▪thoughts 1279L32
▫second ▪wind 1279R18
▫split ▪second 1395L13
the ▫Second ▪Coming 1279L50
▫wait a ▪second 1633R13
without a ▫second ▪thought 1279L36
o▫fficial ▪secret 977R65
▫open ▪secret 988L57
▫secret ad▪mirer 17R26 1280L70
▫secret ▪agent 1280L72
▫secret ▪ballot 1280L77
▫secret po▪lice 1280L81
▫secret ▪service 1280R1
▫secret so▪ciety 1280R8
▫secret ▪weapon 1280R10
▫top ▪secret 1280L67 1537R7
▫trade ▪secret 1546R68
▫Home ▪Secretary 680L68
▫permanent ▪secretary 1050R38
▪press ▫secretary 1118R83
▫Secretary-▪General 1280R75
▫Secretary of ▪State 1280R57/66
▫under-▪secretary 1583L5
O▫fficial ▪Secrets ▫Act 977R68
▪cross-▫section 328R24/28
re▪view ▫section 1218L82
▪rhythm ▫section 1220R7
▫secular ▪humanism 1281R22
se▪cure against 1281R41/46 1282L67
se▪cure from 1281R42/47
se▪cure *something* to 1282L28
▫gilt-edged se▪curities 595L53
▪job se▫curity 765R58 1282L39
se▪curity ▫blanket 1281R74 1282L57
Se▪curity ▫Council 1281R80
se▪curity ▫guard 1282L2
se▪curity ▫risk 1282L7
▫social se▪curity 979R57 1370R34
▫top se▪curity 1537R7/11
se▪dan ▫chair 1282R3
se▪duce into 1282R59
as far as the ▫eye can/could ▪see 488L56
can ▫see a ▪mile off 896L35
▫cannot see be▪yond *something* 122L34
▫can't see ▫further than/be▫yond the ▫end of *one's* ▪nose 1283L59
▫can't see the ▫wood/▫forest for the ▪trees 1677L74
could ▫see it ▪coming 1283L52
▫fail to ▪see 494L22
▫let me ▪see 1283R72
▫let's ▪see 812R36
▪look-▫see 839L82
not ▫see *someone* for ▪dust 1283L54
▫not see ▫hide nor ▪hair of 1284L15
see a ▫man about a ▪dog 1284L10
▪see about 1284L53
▫see *someone* a▪round 1284L2
▪see *somebody* as 1283R59/60/61
see ▫eye to ▪eye with 1283R34
▫see ▪fit 1283R74
▫see how the ▪land ▫lies 794L13
▫see in ▪hell 1284L16
see ▫in the New ▪Year 1284L32
see *someone* in *their* ▫true ▪colours 260L64
▫see ▪life 1284L20
▫see ▪off 1284L30/35
▫see ▪out 1284L56
▫see ▪over 1283L42
▫see ▪reason 1181R57
▫see *someone* ▪right 1284L49
▫see ▪round/▪through/▪over 1284L7
▫see ▪sense/▪reason 1283R36
▫see ▪stars 1283L66
see the ▫colour of *someone's* ▪money 1283L67
see the ▫error of *one's* ▪ways 467L59
▫see the ▪joke 1283R44
▫see the ▪last of 1283L72
▫see the ▪light 1283R38
▫see the light of ▪day 1284L22
▫see the ▪point of 1283R42
▪see ▫things 1512L43
▫see things in black and ▪white 131R10
▪see to it 1284L63
▫see *one's* way (▪clear) to 1283R78
▫see you ▪later 1284L8
the ▫Holy ▪See 679R14
▫wait and ▪see 44R31 1633R19
▪seed ▫corn 1284R4
▪seed ▫money 1284R8
▪seed po▫tatoes 1284R9
▪seed with 1284R19
▫sow the ▪seeds of 1381L84
Seeing-▪Eye ▫dog 1283L81
▪seeing ▫things 1283L77
▫hide-and-▪seek 666R29
▫seek ▪out 1284R78
▪seek to 1285L8/11
▪heat-▫seeking 658L5
▪seem as if/as though/like 1285L22
▫seem like a ▪picnic 1063R10
▪seem to 1285L29/31/32/33/37/38/39/41
have seen ▫better ▪days 1283L48
▫have to be ▫seen to be be▪lieved 1283L61
it re▫mains to be ▪seen 1200R62
▫wouldn't be seen ▪dead 1283L79
▪seep into 1285L65/67
▫seep ▪out 1285L69
▫seep ▪through 1285L66
be▫lieve *something* when *one* ▪sees it 115L84
▪segregate from 1285R49
▪segregate into 1285R46
▪seize on/upon 1286L14
▫seize ▪up 1286L19
▪seize with 1286L29
se▫lect com▪mittee 1286L58
se▪lect for/to 1286L53/54
se▪lect from 1286L48/52
se▫lect ▪out 1286L56
▫natural se▪lection 943L54
▫hard ▪sell 647L3
pile it ▫high (and) sell it ▪cheap 1066L69
sell *someone* a ▫bill of ▪goods 1290L18
▫sell a ▪pup 1290L18
▪sell at/for 1289R61
▪sell-by ▫date 1290L20
▫sell down the ▪river 1290L8
▪sell for 1289R60
▫sell like ▫hot ▪cakes 687R24
▫sell ▪on 1290L4/52
▪sell-out 1289R73/74/82 1290L6
sell ▪short 1290L11
sell *one's* ▫soul (to the ▪devil) 1290L15
▪sell to 1289R75 1290L2
▫sell ▪up 1289R75/79
▫soft ▪sell 1371R50
▫best- ▪seller 119R53
▫best- ▪selling 119R53
in▪ertia ▫selling 724R83
▪panic ▫selling 1022L50
▫pyramid ▪selling 1156R13
▪selling ▫point 1290L22
▫semi-auto▪matic 1290R34/36
▪semi-▫circle 1290R38
▫semi-▪circular 1290R40
▫semi-detached (▪house) 1290R41
▫semi-▪final 1290R44
▫semi-▪precious 1290R49
▫semi-pro▪fessional 1290R52
▫anti-▪Semite 50L40/45
▫anti-Se▪mitic 50L44
▫send a ▪signal to 1292L6
▫send ▪down 1291R61/64/55/83
▪send for 1291R25
▪send-off 1291R71
▫send ▪on 1291R34
▫send ▪out 1292L13
▫send out ▪roots 1233R50
▫send ▪packing 1291R68
▫send *one's* re▪grets 1194L64
▫send ▪round the bend 117L1
▫send round the ▪twist 1574L16
▪send to 1291R21/23/49/50
▫send to ▪Coventry 1292L8
▫send to e▪ternity 470L29
▫send ▪up 1291R59/64 1292L3/18/23
▫send ▪word 1291R37
▫senile de▪mentia 1292L31
▫senior ▪citizen 1292L41
▫senior ▪nursing officer 1292L68
▫senior ▪statesman/▪stateswoman 1292L53
▫common ▪sense 270R64
▪dress ▫sense 422R6
▪horse ▫sense 686L53
in a ▪sense 1293L65
in the ▫biblical ▪sense 123L14
▫knock ▪sense into 785L37
▪road ▫sense 1228L52
▫see ▪sense 1283R36
▫sense of ▪fun 1293L29
▫sense of ▪humor 1293L29
▫sense of ▪humour 693R17/18/19 1293L32
▫sense of oc▪casion 1293L37
▪sense ▫organ 1293L18
▫sixth ▪sense 1344L64
▫talk ▪sense 1488R15
take ▫leave of *one's* ▪senses 807R70 1292R64
▪price-▫sensitive 1120R33
▫heaven-▪sent 658R43
▫complex ▪sentence 275R62
▪death ▫sentence 352R27 1294L21
▫life ▪sentence 819L74
pro▫nounce ▪sentence 1294L19
▫sentence of ▪death 1294L21
▪sentence to 1294L24/25
▫simple ▪sentence 1339R29
▪sentry ▫box 1294R28
go *one's* ▫separate ▪way 1294R47
▪separate from 1294R42/53/62/65
▪separate into 1294R55
separate the ▫sheep from the ▪goats 1313R81
under ▫separate ▪cover 316L62
▫septic ▪tank 1295L52
▫non ▪sequitur 960R7
▪flight ▫sergeant 534L54
▫sergeant ▪major 1296L18
▪serial ▫killer/▫murderer 1296L43
▫serial mo▪nogamy 1296L48
▪serial ▫murderer 1296L47
▪serial ▫number 1296L51
▪mini-▫series 900L65
▫World ▪Series 1684R73
on a more ▫serious ▪level 813R60
in ▫all ▪seriousness 713L38
▫civil ▪servant 234R71
▫public ▪servant 1142R22 1297R13
▪break ▫serve 161R50
▪serve as 1297R50/51/53/56
▪serve in/on 1297L84/R1/L83
▫serve ▪out 1297L69
▫serve *someone* ▪right 1297R8
▫serve ▪time 1297R41 1521R35
▪serve to 1297L64/R56
▪serve under 1297R2
▫serve ▪up 1297L69
▪serve with 1297L63 1298L20
first ▫come first ▪served 525R4
▪answering ▫service 48L70
▫civil ▪service 234R68
com▪munity ▫service 272L36
▪dating ▫service 348L44
▪dinner ▫service 385R48
diplo▪matic ▫service 386R14
▪escort ▫service 468L22
▫full-▪service 572R61
▫give/▫pay ▪lip service to 828L76
In▫ternal ▪Revenue ▫Service 743R58
▫military ▪service 896R19 1298L28
▫national ▪service 939L24/29
on ▫active ▪service 13R74 1298L29
▫press into ▪service 1118R17
▪room ▫service 1233L72
▫secret ▪service 1280R1
▪service ▫charge 1297L47
▪service ▫road 1297R78
▪service ▫station 1297R80
▪skeleton ▫service 1345R6
▪tea ▫service 1494L28
▪valet ▫service 1605L26
▪wire ▫service 1671L7
▫ex-▪serviceman 485L79
▫customer ▪services 338R14
es▫sential ▪services 468R58
▫social ▪services 1370R40
▫open ▪sesame 987R73
▪jam ▫session 760L4
▪photo ▫session 1059L25 1298R14
▪chess ▫set 224R21
▫close-▪set 247R75
▫dead ▪set a▫gainst 351L17
▫dead ▪set on 351L15
▫deep-▪set 357L70
▪dinner ▫set 385R49
▪drum ▫set 428R74
▪fondue ▫set 544L34
▫heavy-▪set 659L21
▪jet ▫set 763L14/8/12
▪manicure ▫set 861L5
▪mind-▫set 899L24
▫never set a foot ▪wrong 545L75
on your ▫marks/▫mark get ▫set ▪go! 866L40
▫rot set ▪in 1235L54
▫set a ▫good ▪table 1483L60
▫set a▪bout 1300L51/57/53/55
▪set against 1298R59 1299L31/R52
▫set a▪part 1298R65/69/65
▫set a▪side 1298R49/51 1299L4
▫set at 1299R21
▫set ▪back 1298R71/74 1300L59
▪set by 1299L48
▫set ▪down 1298R53/55/58
▫set ▪eyes on 236R73 488L73
▫set ▪fire to 523L28
▫set ▪foot 545R51
▪set for 1299L49/55/60/61/64/R13/15 1300L69/77
▫set ▪forth 1300L64/R27
▫set great/little ▪store 1431R33
▫set *one's* ▪heart on 656R76
▫set ▪in 1298R31/35 1300L66/R53
▫set in ce▪ment/▪concrete 208R9 282L78
▪set in/into 1299R23
▫set in ▪motion 920R79
▫set in (▫tablets of) ▪stone 1429R26
▫set in ▪train 1548R79
▫set in *one's* ▪ways 1299R59
set *someone's* ▪mind at ▫rest/▫ease 898R72
▫set *one's* ▪mind to 898R70
set off on a ▫different ▪tack 1484L83
▫set ▪off/▪out 1298R78 1300R20/27/L79/R7/L75
▪set ▫on 1298R28 1299R17 1300L78/R12/16
▫set on ▪fire 523L27
set *one's* ▪own ▫house in ▫order 689L35
set ▫pen(cil) to ▪paper 1044L36/R77
▫set ▪piece 1299R60
▫set ▪point 1300L46
▫set ▪right 1224L45
▫set ▪sail 1249R66
▫set *one's* ▪sights on 1335R49
▫set *someone* ▪talking 1488R29
▫set *someone's* ▪teeth on ▫edge 1535R70
set the ▪ball ▫rolling 95R24
set the ▫cat among the ▪pigeons 203L64
▫set the ▪dining/▪kitchen ▫table 1483L61
set the ▪fur ▫flying 575R43
set the ▪record ▫straight 1187L48
▫set the ▪scene/▪stage 1263R48 1299L57
▫set the ▪seal on 1276R2/3
▫set the ▪tone 1534L43/50
set the ▪wheels in ▫motion 1656L45
set the ▪world/the ▪Thames on ▫fire/a▫light/a▫blaze 1299L34
▫set ▪to 1299L45/66/69/70/R12 1300R23/25/34/37/40
▫set to ▪work 1298R82 1679R1
set ▪tongues ▫wagging 1534R55
▫set ▪up 1299L1/46/R9/10 1300R45/58/63/70/78 1598L40
▫set ▪up as 1300R54
▫set up ▪shop 1321L76
▪set upon 1300R16
▪set with 1299R24 1300L58/R21/66
▪smart ▫set 1300L34
▪socket ▫set 1371L26
▪tea ▫set 1494L28
▪television ▫set 1300L37
the ▫scene/▫stage *is* ▪set 1299L56
▪train ▫set 1548R19
▪twin ▫set 1573L62
▪place ▫setting 1299L84
allow the ▪dust to ▫settle 433L14
let the ▪dust ▫settle 433L14
▫settle a ▪score 1301R8
▫settle *one's* af▪fairs 1301L82/R6
▫settle an ac▪count 1301R39
▫settle ▪back 1301L26
▫settle ▪down 1301L27/28/29/55/56/R61
▪settle for 1301L74/78
▫settle ▪in 1301L33/37/R54
▪settle into 1301L29
▪settle on/upon 1301L73/R37/84 1302L3/13/14
▫settle ▪up 1301R34
▪settle with 1301R36/39
▫wait until the ▪dust has settled 433L15
▪penal ▫settlement 1044L67
▫Group of ▪Seven 626R78
▫seven deadly ▪sins 1302L25
▫seven-year ▪itch 1302L29
at ▫sixes and ▪sevens 1344L40
in ▫seventh ▪heaven 1302L38
▫Seventh-Day ▪Adventist 1302L38
▫seventy-▪eight 1302L59
▪sever from 1302L80
have/keep ▫several irons in the ▪fire 752R13
▫several removes (a▪way) from 1202R34
▫sew ▪on 1303L7/9
▫sew to▪gether 1303L5
▫sew ▪up 1303L11/13/14
▪sewage ▫farm 1303L45
▪sewage (▫treatment) ▫plant 1303L44
▪sewage ▫works 1303L45
▪sewing ma▫chine 1303L26
▫oral ▪sex 992R84
▫safe ▪sex 1248R16
▪sex ▫aid 1303R44
▪sex ap▫peal 55L34 1303R47
▪sex ▫change (operation) 1303L75
▪sex ▫kitten 1303R48
▪sex ▫life 818R18 1303R52
▪sex-▫linked 1303L79
▫sex ▪maniac 1303R53
▪sex ▫object 1303R55
▪sex of▫fender 1303R57
▪sex ▫shop 1303R60
▪sex-▫starved 1303R62
▪sex ▫symbol 1303R65
▫sex ▪therapy 1303R67/68
▫single-▪sex 1341L24
the ▪fair ▫sex 495R24
the ▫opposite ▪sex 990R46
the ▪weaker ▫sex 1646R68
have ▫sexual re▪lations with 1196R48
▫sexual a▪buse 1304L11
▪sexual ▫aid 1303R44
▫sexual revo▪lution 1304L15
▫sexually transmitted dis▪ease 1304L31
▫shack ▪up 1304R34/38/36
▫put/▫leave in the ▪shade 1304R70
▪shade from 1306L33
▪shade into 1306L33/35/37
▪shade ▫tree 1304R75
▪window ▫shade 1666L58
beyond a ▫shadow of a ▪doubt 122R5
▪eye ▫shadow 488R47
▫five o'clock ▪shadow 528L30
in/▫under the ▪shadow of 1306L75/76
▪shadow-▫box 1306R4/1
▫shadow of *one's* former ▪self 1306L81
▪drive ▫shaft 425R61
like a ▫shag on a ▪rock 1307L14
shaggy ▪dog ▫story 1307L23
▫fair ▪shake 494R82
▪milk ▫shake 897L3
▫more than you can shake a ▪stick at 1307R5
▫shake a ▪leg 1307R6
▫shake ▪down 1308L1/9/16
▫shake ▪off 1307L41/R80/81/83
▫shake ▪out 1307L43/44
▪shake-up 1307L47 1308L20/31
▪shake with 1307L53/55
▫mover and ▪shaker 925R70/71
▪pepper ▫shaker 1046R71

a couple of/two shakes (of a duck's/lamb's tail) 1307R14
no great shakes 621R35
earth-shaking 437R10
world shaking 1684R76
shallow-fry 1308R19
shilly shally 1316L23
thou shalt 1308R51
crying shame 332L21
shame into 1309L54
Shangri-La 1309R54
shank's mare 1309R65
shanks's pony 1309R65
shanty town 1309R76
in any shape or form 1310L70
knock/lick/whip into shape 1311L8
shape *something* into 1310L75
shape up 1311L18/15/19
shape up or ship out 1311L22
the shape of things to come 1310R63 1512L62
pear-shaped 1040R32
V-shaped 1603L54
all shapes and sizes 1310L66
lion's share 828L59
share among 1311L74
share and share alike 1311L83
share between 1311L60/75
share in/of 1311L33/35/36/37/38/41/43/44/R2/3/L39/40/R17
share out 1311L84
share with 1311L55/57/73/80/81
time share 1522L14
go shares 1311L43
profit sharing 1128R26
time-sharing 1522L17/19
loan shark 833R75
shark fence 1311R52
look sharp 839R47
razor-sharp 1177L22/23
sharp-nosed 1312R28
sharp practice 1312L31
short sharp shock 1322R75
the sharp end 1312L26
sharpen up 1312R76
earth-shattering 437R10
world shattering 1684R76
close shave 247R76
shave off/from 1313L34/38/40
clean-shaven 241L70
shaver point 1313L50
pinking shears 1068R53
pruning shears 1140L29 1278R53
sheath knife 1313R29
the whole shebang 1313R41 1662L25
bike shed 125R44
cycle shed 125R44 340R78
potting shed 1102R29
shed light on 820R13
shed tears 1494R53
tool shed 1535R40
a wolf in sheep's clothing 1675R32
black sheep 132L5
separate/tell/sort (out) the sheep from the goats 1313R81
sheep station 1314L1
sheer off/away 1314L40
baking sheet 94R29
balance sheet 95L42
charge sheet 217R55
clean sheet 241R50
ice sheet 698R73
poop sheet 1094R52
sheet against 1314L66
sheet lightning 1314L59
sheet music 1314L61
time sheet 1522L21
continental shelf 296R57
shelf life 1314R14
shelf space 1314R16
bring *someone* out of *their* shell 1314R40
come out of *one's* shell 1314R39
crawl/go/retreat/retire into *one's* shell 1314R43
shell out 1314R75/73
shell-shock 1314R60/62/57
shell suit 1314R48
bus-shelter 178L52
fallout shelter 499R23
shelter from 1315L8/11/13
tax shelter 1493R11
women's shelter 1675R82
sheltered accommodation 1315L23
sheltered workshop 1315L28
German shepherd 36R82 590L53
shepherd's pie 310R23 1315L46
Shetland pony 1315L80
gum shield 632L23
heat shield 658L9
human shield 692R10
shield from 1315R35/37/39
graveyard shift 621L25
night shift 955L31 1315R76/77
shift *one's* arse 65L24
shift from 1315R42
shift *one's* ground 1315R53
shift key 1315R58
shift onto/to 1315R42/45/46/47
stick shift 586L15 1422R72
shilly shally 1316L23
shin splints 1316L49
shin up 1316L56
come rain or shine 1169R67
rise and shine 1226R42
shine at/in 1316L66/76
shine out 1316L71
shine with 1316L68/69
take a shine to 1316L82
make hay while the sun shines 652R28
knight in shining armour 783R73
abandon ship 1R65
factory ship 493L9
ghost ship 594L41
rocket ship 1230L69
shape up or ship out 1311L22
ship off 1316R40
ship over 1316R39
transport ship 1552L6
merchant shipping 888L79
shipping and handling 1100R65
shire horse 1317L48
bet *one's* shirt 119R82
keep *one's* shirt on 636L47 777L8
lose *one's* shirt 842L2
polo shirt 1093L1
put *one's* shirt on 1317L73
shirt-sleeve 1317L71
stuffed shirt 1448L61
T-shirt 1483L12
tee shirt 1483L12 1496L56
the shirt off *someone's* back 1317L76
shish kebab 776L3 1317R43
go ape-shit 53L42
have/get *one's* shit together 1317R61
hot shit 687R60
not give a shit 1317R59
shit a brick 1318L12
shit bricks 1318L12
shit-eating grin 1317R79
shit for brains 1317R66
shit hot 687R60
shit list 1317R82
shit *one's* pants 1022R58
shit stirrer 1318L1
the shit flies 1317R69
tough shit 1541R76
scare *someone* shitless 1262R33/54
give *someone* the shits 1318L28
a shiver (up and) down *one's* spine 1318L52
give *someone* the shivers 1318L59
shivers (up and) down *one's* spine 1318L52
a shock to the system 1318R7
culture shock 334R44
electric shock 446R3
shell-shock 1314R60/62/57
shock absorber 1318R79
shock horror 1318R53
shock *someone* into 1318R27
shock tactics 1318R17
shock therapy/treatment 1318R19
shock to 1318R48
shock troops 1318R21
shock wave 1318R82
short sharp shock 1322R75
shocking pink 1318R38
court shoe 315L77
running shoe 1549L1
tennis shoe 1500R38
the shoe is on the other foot 148L71 545L54
tough as shoe leather 1541R5
track shoe 1545R57
training shoe 1549L1
ballet shoes 95R63
high-heeled shoes 660L53 667L58
platform shoes 1077L84
step into/fill *someone's* shoes 1319L55
shoestring potatoes 1319L78
shoo *someone* away 1319R9
penalty shoot-out 1044R22
shoot a glance 1319R49
shoot at/for 1319R31/15/29
shoot *one's* bolt 1319R35
shoot darts at 1319R42
shoot down 1319R44/47
shoot *one's* load 1319R55
shoot *one's* mouth off 1319R57/60
shoot over 1320L82
shoot the breeze 1319R39
shoot the works 1319R66
shoot through 1320R40
shoot up 1320L84/R38/69
shoot *one's* wad 1319R56
six-shooter 1344L52
shooting gallery 1320L41/R70
shooting pains 1320R42
shooting star 891L41 1320L45
shooting stick 1320L48
a bull in a china shop 174L46
all over the shop 33R33
beauty shop 110L23
betting shop 120L20
bucket shop 171R52
charity shop 218R12
chip shop 227R3
close up shop 1321L79
closed shop 247L73
coffee shop 255L7
cop shop 304L49
corner shop 306R14
craft shop 319L66
duty-free shop 433R26
gift shop 594R49
grocery shop 625L67
junk shop 773R51
op-shop 991R74
opportunity shop 990R3
paper shop 1023L51
pawn shop 1038L15
reject shop 1196L4
set up shop 1321L76
sex shop 1303R60
shop around 1321L34
shop assistant 1321L28
shop floor 1321L69
shop front 567R84 1321L30
shop steward 1321L72
shut up shop 1321L78 1331R83
sweet shop 1475R82
talking shop 1488R15
tea shop 1494L26
thrift shop 1515R33
window-shop 1668L59/60
shopping bag 199L14 1321L53/56
shopping center/centre 1321L61/62
shopping mall 858L14 1321L61
shore up 1321R47
shorn of 1313R10/11
as thick as two short planks 1511L58
bring up short 166R3
caught/taken short 1322R69
draw/get the short straw 1321R64
fall short 498R20
have (got) *someone* by the short and curlies 1321R68
in the short run 1241R25
in the short term 1501R21
in/within a short space of time 1381R61
make short shrift of 1324L2
make short work 1322R73
not short of a bob or two 1324L40
nothing short of 964L61
pull up short 1145L4
sell short 1290L11
short and sweet 1322R77
short back and sides 1321R70
short-change 1324L41
short-circuit 1321R72/76
short cut 1321R78
short fuse 1321R84
short hop 684R49
short list 1322L55/60
short-lived 1322R79
short memory 1322R81
short of breath 162R33 1324L37
short-range 1322L60
short sharp shock 1322R75
short shrift 1322R82
short-sighted 934R19/22 1322L63/66/69
short-staffed 1324L47/R36
short story 1322L73
short-tempered 1324L67
short time 1190L10 1324L5
short wave 1644R66
stop short of 1430R36
tempers get short 1498R39
the long and the short of 838L77
to cut a long story short 339L57
shorthand typist 1324R32
board shorts 141L61 1476R75
boxer shorts 155L83
cycle/cycling shorts 340R72
a shot in the dark 1320L59
big shot 125L47
call *one's* shot 185R83
get/be shot of 1324R77
long shot 838L42
mug shot 928L76
not by a long shot 838L20
parting shot 1029L18
passing shot 1031L31
put the shot 1154L62
shot in the arm 1320R82
shot put 1324R61/63
sawn-off shotgun 1258R2
shotgun marriage 1325L10
shotgun wedding 1325L9
call the shots 186L1
a chip on *one's* shoulder 227R18
cold-shoulder 256R53
hard shoulder 646L57
shoulder aside 1326L9
shoulder bag 1325R72
shoulder blade 1325R74
shoulder pads 1017L23 1325R78
shoulder strap 1325R80
shoulder to cry on 1325R61
shoulder to shoulder 1325R65
round-shouldered 1236R1
an old/a wise head on young shoulders 653L9
head and shoulders above 653L72
rub shoulders with 1238R3
the cares of the world on *one's* shoulders 196R54
shout at 1326L53/60
shout blue murder 139R62 930L42
shout down 1326L69
shout from the rooftops 1233L41
shout out 1326L59
all over bar the shouting 99L29
shouting match 1326R4
within/in shouting distance 1326L84
if/when push comes to shove 1151L62
shove around 1326R25
shove aside 1326R42
shove down 1326R41/45
shove in 1326R39
shove it 1326R30
shove off 1326R51/55
shove on 1326R40
shove over/along 1326R48
shove up 1326R50
shove *something* up *someone's* ass 71L65
steam shovel 476L26 1418L54
chat show 220L49
dumb show 431R60
floor show 536R51
freak show 560L82
get the/this show on the road 1328L62
go to show 606L33
good show 611R13 1327R64
jolly good show 769L45
minstrel show 901R60
Punch and Judy show 1146R39
run the show 1241R62
show-and-tell 1327L37
show business 1328L33
show every sign/all the signs that 1336L12
show *one's* face 1327L16
show *one's* hand 1327L20
show home 1327R82
show house 1327R82
show in 1326R84
show jump 1329L27
show jumper 1329L30
show of hands 1327R65
show off 1327L23 1328L64/69
show out 1327L76
show over 1327R2
show pony 1328L49
show round/around 1327L81
show *someone* the door 1327L78
show the flag 529L30
show *someone* the ropes 1234L78
show the way 1327R25
show the way forward 1327R26
show through 1327L49
show trial 1328L50
show *one's* true colours 260L63
show up 1327L50/52/62/63/64 1328L72/78
steal the show 1418L16
talk show 1488R55/60
that will show 1327L28
trade show 1546L64
cold shower 256R30
shower cream/gel 1328R84
shower on 1328R66
shower tea 1329L9
shower with 1328R63/64/65
car showroom 582R37
make short shrift of 1324L2
short shrift 1322R82
shrink at 1330L23
shrink by 1330L6
shrink from 1330L24/25
shrink-wrap 1330L12/6
shrinking violet 1330L29
shroud in 1330L49
Shrove Tuesday 1330L64
shrug off/aside 1330R16/17/10
shuck off 1330R42
aw-shucks 87L63
shudder to think 1330R63
shuffle off 1331L44/39
shuffle off this mortal coil 1331L45
shunt aside 1331L71
shunt between 1331L68
shunt off 1331L70
keep *one's* mouth shut 924L15
keep shut 608R15 1552R1
open-and-shut 987R27
shut away 1331R44/45/48
shut down 1331R70
shut *one's* eyes to 1331R7
shut in 1331R28/29/30/32
shut it 1331R12
shut off 1331R55/56/52/53/72/74/76/78/81
shut out 1331R34/36/38/39 1332L7 1661L63
shut the door in *someone's* face 411R49
shut the door on 411R50
shut the stable/barn door after the horse has bolted 411R52
shut up 1331R57/58
shut up like a clam 236L5
shut up shop 1321L78 1331R83
shut your face 1331R11
shut your gob 1331R12
shut your mouth 1331R11
snap shut 1364L70
with *one's* eyes shut 488R23/25
shuttle diplomacy 1332L62
shuttle from/to 1332L69/71/69/71
space shuttle 1382L37
camera-shy 187L32
coconut shy 253R81
fight shy of 517L36
shy at 1332R18/20/21
shy away from 1332R26
Siamese cat 1332R36
Siamese twins 1332R38
sibling rivalry 1332R45
on the sick-list 1332R65
sick as a dog 1333L18
sick as a parrot 1333L37
sick at heart 1333L39
sick day 1332R68
sick headache 1332R70
sick leave 1332R72
sick pay 1332R74
sick to *one's* stomach 1333L19/51
sick up 1333L31
worried sick 1333L45 1686L20
hammer and sickle 639R27
sickle-cell anaemia 1333L70
sickle-cell anemia 1333L70
decompression sickness 356L6
morning sickness 918R56
motion sickness 921L1 1553L31
radiation sickness 1167L51
sickness benefit 1333L12
sleeping sickness 1351R16
travel sickness 1553L30
B side 88L10 535L15
bit on the side 130L16
blind side 135L81
come down on one side of the fence or other 1333R13
err on the side of caution 467L13
flip side 535L15/16
from side to side 1333R69
get out of bed (on) the wrong side 111L43
get up on the wrong side of the bed 111L43
give *someone* the rough side of *one's* tongue 1236L25
have time on *one's* side 1520R82
know which side *one's* bread is buttered (on) 786R57
laugh on the other side of *one's* face 800L17
laugh out of the other side of *one's* mouth 800L18
let the side down 812R80 1334L26
look on the bright side 839L55
on the large/small side 1334L7
on the right/wrong side of 1333R81/79 1334L1
on the right/wrong side of the law 1333R83
on the safe side 1248R4
on the side of the angels 44R79
pass by on the other side 1030R81
side by side 1333R47
side drum 1333R15 1365L5
side effect 1333R56
side-wheeler 1333R17
side with/against 1334L32
the other side of the coin 1333R7
this side of the grave 1334L6
thorn in the side 1514L55
time is on *someone's* side 1520R81
leave *someone* on the sidelines 807R4
stay on the sidelines 1417L41
sidereal time 1334R11
short back and sides 1321R70
split *one's* sides 1394R69
take sides 1334L22
sidewalk artist 1037R63
knock *somebody* sideways 785L24
sidle past 1334R72
fin-de-siècle 521L23
siege mentality 887R51 1334R83
under siege 1334R78/80

ˌburnt siˈenna 1335L2
ˌraw siˈenna 1335L2
ˌmemory/ˌmind like a ˈ**sieve** 1335L19
ˌ**sieve** ˈout 1335L17
ˌ**sift** ˈthrough 1335L35
ˌheave a ˈ**sigh** 658R15
ˈ**sigh** with 1335L41
a ˌ**sight** for sore ˈeyes 1335R28
get ˌout of one's ˈ**sight** 1335R3
ˌhove in(to) ˈ**sight** 690L55
ˌknow by ˈ**sight** 787R6
ˌlose ˈ**sight** of 842L4 1335R22
ˌnot a pretty ˈ**sight** 1119R70 1335L77
ˌsecond ˈ**sight** 1279R14
ˈ**sight**-ˌread 1335L57/58/53
ˌ**sight** unˈseen 1335R30
ˌstand the ˈ**sight** of 1410R78
ˌclear-ˈ**sighted** 242L48
ˌfar-ˈ**sighted** 503R78/82
ˌlong-ˈ**sighted** 838L45
ˌnear-ˈ**sighted** 944R84 1322L63/66
ˌpartially ˈ**sighted** 1029L54
ˌshort-ˈ**sighted** 934R19/22 1322L63/66/69
ˌlower *one's* ˈ**sights** 1335R51
ˌset *one's* ˈ**sights** on 1335R49
a ˌ**sign** of the ˈtimes 1336L20
ˈdollar ˌ**sign** 410L51
ˌmake the **sign** of the ˈcross 327R53
ˈminus ˌ**sign** 902L12
ˈpeace ˌ**sign** 1039R70
ˈplus ˌ**sign** 1085R37
ˈpound ˌ**sign** 1104L75
ˌshow every ˈ**sign** 1336L12
ˌ**sign** *something* aˈway 1336L41
ˈ**sign** for/with/to 1336L32/2/44
ˌ**sign** ˈin 1336L46
ˈ**sign** ˌlanguage 1335R77
ˌ**sign** ˈoff 1336L49/51/52
ˌ**sign** on the dotted ˈline 1336L37
ˌ**sign** ˈon/ˈup 1336L58/55/56
ˌ**sign** ˈout 1336L48/62
ˌ**sign** ˈover 1336L64
ˌ**sign** *one's* own ˈdeath ˌwarrant 1336L39
ˌ**sign** the ˈpledge 1081L68
ˈstar ˌ**sign** 1412R65
ˈstop ˌ**sign** 1430R50
ˈV-ˌ**sign** 1603L54
ˈvee ˌ**sign** 1603L54
ˈwarning ˌ**sign** 1638R50/52/48
ˌsend a ˈ**signal** to 1292L6
ˈ**signal** ˌbox 1336R23
ˈ**signal** to/for 1336R4/L75/R3/4/5/L77/84
ˈ**signal** ˌtower 1336R23
ˈsmoke ˌ**signal** 1361L81
ˈtime ˌ**signal** 1522R32
ˈturn ˌ**signal** 721R13 1569R81
ˈkey ˌ**signature** 778L63
ˈ**signature** ˌtune 1336R53
ˈtime ˌ**signature** 1524L57
ˌ**signed** and ˈsealed 1336L34
ˌ**signed** sealed and deˈlivered 1336L34
ˈ**signet** ˌring 1336R58
ˈdollar ˌ**signs** in *one's* ˌeyes 410L53
ˌshow all the ˈ**signs** that 1336L12
ˌvital ˈ**signs** 1627R75
ˌ**silent** ˈfilm 1337R2
ˌ**silent** ˈletter 1337R4
ˌ**silent** maˈjority 1337L84
ˌ**silent** ˈpartner 1337R5 1351R10
silhouˈette against/on 1337R23
ˌ**silicon** ˈchip 1337R36
ˈ**silicone** ˌimplant 1337R42
ˈ**silk** ˌscreen 1337R54/57
ˌtake ˈ**silk** 1337R54
ˌlaugh *oneself* ˈ**silly** 800L23
play ˈ**silly** ˌbuggers 1078R59 1338L61
ˈ**silly** ˌseason 1338L63
ˌ**silt** ˈup 1338L83
ˌborn with a **silver** ˈspoon in *one's* ˌmouth 149R18
ˌ**silver** ˈbirch 1338R79
ˌ**silver** ˈfoil 1339L1
ˌ**silver** ˈjubilee 1338R81
ˌ**silver** ˈpaper 1339L1
ˌ**silver** ˈplate 1339L3
ˌ**silver**-ˈplated 1339L5
ˌ**silver** ˈtongued 1339L7 1535L5
ˌ**silver** ˈwedding (anniversary) 1339L9
ˌ**simmer** ˈdown 1339L63
ˈ**simmer** with 1339L58
ˈ**simper** at 1339L68
ˌpast ˈ**simple** 1033R27
ˌpresent ˈ**simple** 1116R58
ˌpure and ˈ**simple** 1149L9
ˌ**simple** ˈfracture 1339R40
ˌ**simple** ˈinterest 1339R36
ˌ**simple**-ˈminded 1339R68/71
ˌ**simple** ˈpast 1033R27
ˌ**simple** ˈsentence 1339R29
ˌpurely and ˈ**simply** 1149L18
ˌput ˈ**simply** 1153R44
to ˌput it ˈ**simply** 1153R43
as ˌugly as ˈ**sin** 1577R72
ˌlive in ˈ**sin** 832L30
ˌmortal ˈ**sin** 919L43
ˌoriginal ˈ**sin** 996R18
ˈ**sin**-ˌbin 1340L47
ˈ**sin** ˌtax 1340L51
ˌ**sine** qua ˈnon 1340R34
ˌ**sinews** of ˈwar 1340R43
ˈ**sing** for/to 1340R56/55
ˌ**sing** ˈout 1340R60
ˌ**sing** the ˈpraises of 1340R61
ˌ**sing** ˈup 1340R60
ˈcarol ˌ**singer** 198L9/5
ˌ**single** ˈbed 1341L10
ˌ**single** ˈbreasted 162R15 1341L11
ˌ**single** ˈcombat 1341L14
ˌ**single** ˈcream 1341L13
ˌ**single**-ˈdecker 355L34 1341L16
ˌ**single** ˈfigures 517R56
ˌ**single** ˈfile 1341L17
ˌ**single**-ˈhanded 1341L21/18
ˌ**single**-ˈminded 1341L21/24
ˌ**single** ˈout 1341L70/66/68
ˌ**single**-parent ˈfamily 984R14
ˌ**single** ˈroom 1341L26
ˌ**single**-ˈsex 1341L24
ˈ**singles** ˌbar 1341L64
ˌeverything but/except the kitchen ˈ**sink** 474L18
ˌkitchen-ˈ**sink** 782L44
ˌ**sink** *one's* ˈdifferences 1341R80
ˌ**sink** ˈin 1342L13/15
ˌ**sink** in *someone's* estimˈation 1341R78
ˈ**sink** into 1341R35/36/37/38/59/60/61 1342L3/14/17
ˌ**sink** like a ˈstone/a ˌlead balˈloon 1341R42 1429R21
ˌ**sink** or ˈswim 1341R40
ˌ**sink** so ˈlow 1341R76
ˈ**sink** to 1341R57
ˌ**sink** to a ˈwhisper 1341R63
ˌ**sink** to such a ˈlevel 1341R75
ˌ**sink** to such ˈdepth(s) 1341R75
ˈ**sink** ˌunit 1342L23
ˌ**sink** *one's* voice to a ˈwhisper 1341R65
ˌspirits ˈ**sink** 1341R66
ˌhook line and ˈ**sinker** 684L22
ˌ**sinking** ˈfast 1341R73
ˈ**sinking** ˌfeeling 1341R69
ˈ**sinking** ˌfund 1342L26
ˌ**sinking** ˈstandards 1341R72
ˌ**Sinn** ˈFein 1342L29
a ˈmultitude of ˌ**sins** 929R18
ˌseven deadly ˈ**sins** 1302L25
ˌ**siphon** ˈout 1342L63
ˈsoda ˌ**siphon** 1342L58
ˈhalf-ˌ**sister** 638L8
ˌlay ˈ**sister** 802R15
ˈ**sister**-in-ˌlaw 1342R80/81
ˌ**sister** under the ˈskin 1342R64
ˌ**sit** aˈbout/aˈround 1343R15
ˈ**sit** at/in 1343L19/7/15
ˌ**sit** at the ˈfeet of 1343L38
ˌ**sit** ˈback 1343R20
ˌ**sit** ˈby 1343R26
ˈ**sit** for 1343L22/37/R7/14/66
ˌ**sit** ˈin 1343L8/R29/34/36
ˌ**sit** ˈin for 1343R41
ˌ**sit** in ˈjudgment on/over 1343L40
ˈ**sit** ˌon 1343L8/12/18/20/33/R5/38/43/48/51
ˌ**sit** on *one's* ˈarse/ˈass/ˈbum 1343L44
ˌ**sit** (aˌround) on *one's* backˈside 91L16
ˌ**sit** on *one's* ˈhands 1343L43
ˌ**sit** on the ˈfence 1343L42
ˌ**sit** ˈout 1343L23/R54
ˌ**sit** ˈpretty 1343L55
ˌ**sit** ˈright/ˈwell 1343L46
ˌ**sit** ˈthrough 1343L24
ˌ**sit** ˈtight 1343L49/47
ˌ**sit** ˈup 1343L26/27/69/R60/64
sit ˌup and take ˈnotice 1343R62
ˈ**sit**-down 1343L11/57/58/61
ˈbuilding ˌ**site** 173R10
ˈcamping ˌ**site** 187R75
ˈcaravan ˌ**site** 193R64
ˈhouse-ˌ**sitter** 689L56/57
ˌbed-ˈ**sitting** room 111L59/R74
ˌ**sitting** ˈduck 1343L53
ˌ**sitting** ˈmember 1343R9
ˈ**sitting** ˌroom 832L38 1343L62
ˌ**sitting** ˈtarget 1343L65
ˌ**sitting** ˈtenant 1343L67
ˌmake-or-ˈbreak **situation** 159R70 855L20
make the ˌbest of a bad **situˈation** 119L62
ˌsave the **situˈation** 1257R52
situˈation ˌcomedy 1344L28
ˌtight **situˈation** 1520L14
ˌ**Situations** ˈVacant 1344L23
ˌknock *somebody* for ˈ**six** 785L25
ˌ**six** feet ˈunder 1344L47
six of ˌone and half a dozen of the ˈother 1344L43
ˌ**six** of the ˈbest 1344L44
ˈ**six**-ˌpack 1344L50
ˌ**six**-ˈshooter 1344L52
at ˌ**sixes** and ˈsevens 1344L40
sixˈteenth ˌnote 1291L54 1344L81
ˈ**sixth** ˌform 1344L60/62/63
ˌ**sixth** ˈsense 1344L64
ˌ**sixty-four-thousand-dollar** ˈquestion 1344R2
ˈlife-ˌ**size(d)** 819L72
ˈpint-ˌ**size(d)** 1069L17
ˌcut down to ˈ**size** 339L53
ˈhalf-ˌ**size** 638L11
ˈking-ˌ**size** 781L33
one-ˌ**size-fits**-ˈall 984R34
ˌpick on someone *your* ˈown **size** 1061R67
ˌ**size** ˈup 1344R60
ˌtry for ˈ**size** 1566L5/7
ˈbite-ˌ**sized** 130R44
eˈconomy-ˌ**sized** 440L68
ˈman-ˌ**sized** 858R74
ˈpocket-ˌ**sized** 1088L5/7
ˌall shapes and ˈ**sizes** 1310L66
ˈice ˌ**skate** 700L10/11
ˌin-line ˈ**skate** 713R37 1231R82
ˈroller ˌ**skate** 1231R4/L84/R5
ˌ**skate** aˈround/ˈround 1345L40
ˌ**skate** ˈon/across/over 1344R79
ˌ**skate** on thin ˈice 1344R82
ˌ**skate** ˈover 1345L40
ˌ**skate** ˈthrough 1345L47
get/put *one's* ˈ**skates** ˌon 1344R75
ˈfigure ˌ**skating** 517R66
ˈ**skating** ˌrink 1345L33
ˈspeed ˌ**skating** 1389L29
ˈ**skeleton** ˌkey 1345R7
ˈ**skeleton** ˌservice 1345R6
ˈ**skeleton** ˌstaff 1345R3
ˌhelter-ˈ**skelter** 662R15/20/23
ˌcomposite ˈ**sketch** 701R3
ˌ**sketch** ˈin 1345R27/32
ˈ**sketch** ˌmap 1345R20
ˌ**sketch** ˈout 1345R25/29
ˌthumbnail ˈ**sketch** 1517R59
ˌ**skew**-ˈwhiff 1345R53
ˌaprès-ˈ**ski** 59L15
ˈJet ˌ**Ski** 762R68/73
ˌ**ski** ˈdown 1346L1
ˈ**ski** ˌjump 1345R70
ˈ**ski** ˌlift 1345R73
ˈ**ski** ˌpants 1345R76
ˌ**ski** ˈpast 1346L1
ˈ**ski** ˌpoles 1345R79
ˈ**ski** ˌsticks 1345R80
ˈ**skid** ˌmarks 1346L18
ˌ**skid** on 1346L12
ˌ**skid** ˈrow 1346L24
ˌput the ˈ**skids** under 1346L32
ˌdownhill ˈ**skiing** 416R72
ˈwater ˌ**skiing** 1642R24/31
ˌ**skim** aˈlong 1346L67
ˈ**skim** from 1346L81
ˌ**skim** ˈoff 1346L82
ˌ**skimmed** ˈmilk 1346R1
baˈnana ˌ**skin** 96R29
by the ˌ**skin** of *one's* ˈteeth 1346R27
ˌdrenched/ˌsoaked/ˌwet to the ˈ**skin** 1346R28
get ˌunder *someone's* ˈ**skin** 1346R30
ˌjump/ˌleap out of *one's* ˈ**skin** 1346R32
no ˌ**skin** off ˈ*someone's* ˌnose 1346R33
ˌsave *one's* ˌown ˈ**skin** 1257R56
ˌsister under the ˈ**skin** 1342R64
ˌ**skin** *someone* aˈlive 1346R57
ˌ**skin** and ˈbone(s) 1346R35
ˌ**skin**-ˈdeep 1346R36
ˈ**skin**-ˌdiver 1346R44/40
ˈ**skin** ˌflick 1346R45
ˈ**skin**-ˌgraft 617L22 1346R46
ˌ**skin**-ˈtight 1346R49
keep *one's* ˈeyes ˌ**skinned** for 488R28
ˌthick-ˈ**skinned** 1511L32
ˌthin-ˈ**skinned** 1511R19
ˈ**skinny**-ˌdip 1346R83/80
ˌ**skip** aˈbout 1347L6
ˌ**skip** ˈdown 1347L7
ˌ**skip** ˈoff/ˈout 1347L29
ˌ**skip** over/across/off 1347L26
ˈ**skipping** ˌrhyme 1347L19
ˈ**skipping** ˌrope 1347L17/12
ˌheart **skips** a ˈbeat 656L74
ˈ**skirmish** with 1347L63
ˌbit of ˈ**skirt** 130L14
ˌpiece of ˈ**skirt** 1064R56
ˈ**skirting** ˌboard 1347L82
ˌ**skitter** aˈbout/aˈround 1347R7
ˌ**skive** ˈoff 1347R31
ˈ**skivvy** for 1347R42
ˈ**skulk** in 1347R58
ˌpissed out of *one's* ˈ**skull** 1070R8
ˌ**skull** and ˈcrossbones 1347R67/71
ˌpie in the ˈ**sky** 1064L68
ˌ**sky**-ˈblue 1348L5
ˌ**sky**-ˈhigh 1348L7/8
the ˌ**sky's** the ˈlimit 1348L3
ˌpick up/ˌtake up the ˈ**slack** 1348L65
ˌ**slack**-ˈjawed 1348L56
ˌ**slack** ˈoff/ˈup 1348L83/81/82
ˌgrand ˈ**slam** 618L22/23/25
ˈ**slam** ˌdunk 1348R64
ˈ**slam** into 1348R62
ˌ**slam** ˈon 1348R58
ˌ**slam** the ˌdoor in *someone's* ˈface 411R49
ˌ**slam** the ˈdoor on 411R50
teˌquila ˈ**slammer** 1501L75
ˌcockney ˈrhyming ˌ**slang** 253L64
ˌrhyming ˈ**slang** 1220L49
ˈ**slanging** ˌmatch 1349L25
a ˌ**slap** in the ˈface 1349L59
ˌ**slap** and ˈtickle 1349L65
ˌ**slap** aˈround 1349L71
ˌ**slap** ˈdown 1349R3
ˌ**slap** ˈon 1349L79
ˈ**slap** on/onto 1349R7
ˌ**slap** on the ˈback 1349L61/73
ˌ**slap** on the ˈwrist 1349L63
ˈ**slap**-up 1349R24
ˈ**slash** at 1349R33/35/75
ˌ**slash** ˈthrough 1349R32
ˌclean ˈ**slate** 241R50
ˈ**slate** for 1350L36/37
ˈ**slate** to 1350L34
ˌ**slate** wiped ˈclean 1350L31
ˌwipe the ˈ**slate** clean 1670L60
ˌ**slather** aˈround 1350L50
ˈ**slather** with 1350L49
like a ˌlamb to the ˈ**slaughter** 793L39
ˈ**slave** at 1350R14
ˈ**slave** ˌdriver 1350R5
ˌ**slave** ˈlabour 1350R7/8
ˈ**slave** over 1350R16
ˈ**slave** ˌtrade 1350R10
ˈ**slaver** over 1350R37
ˈ**sleaze** ˌfactor 1350R63
a ˌ**sledgehammer** to crack a ˈnut 1351L2
ˌ**sleek** ˈback/ˈdown 1351L15
a ˌwink of ˈ**sleep** 1669R26
ˈbeauty ˌ**sleep** 110L25
go back to ˈ**sleep** 1351L37
go to ˈ**sleep** 1351L32
ˌlose ˈ**sleep** over/about 842L6
ˌput to ˈ**sleep** 1351L36
ˌread *someone* to ˈ**sleep** 1178L64
rub/wipe the ˈ**sleep** out of *one's* ˌeyes 1351R35
ˌ**sleep** a ˈwink 1669R26
ˌ**sleep** aˈround 1351L68
ˌ**sleep** ˈin 1351L50
ˌ**sleep** like a ˈlog 1351L51
ˌ**sleep** ˈoff 1351L57
ˈ**sleep** on 1351L53
ˌ**sleep** ˈover 1351L58/75
ˌ**sleep** ˈrough 1236L33
ˌ**sleep** ˈthrough 1351L64
ˈ**sleep** together 1351L70
ˈ**sleep** with 1351L72
ˈ**sleeping** ˌbag 1351R7
ˈ**sleeping** ˌcar 193R17 1351R8
ˈ**sleeping** ˌpartner 1337R6 1351R10
ˈ**sleeping** ˌpill/ˌtablet 1351R13
ˌ**sleeping** poˈliceman 1351R14 1389L20
ˈ**sleeping** ˌsickness 1351R16
ˌ**sleepless** ˈnight 1351R20
ˌace up *one's* ˈ**sleeve** 10R56
ˌcard up *one's* ˈ**sleeve** 195L23
have *something* up *one's* ˈ**sleeve** 1351R68
ˌlaugh up *one's* ˈ**sleeve** 800L27
ˌshirt-ˈ**sleeve** 1317L71
ˈ**sleeve** ˌnotes 1351R79
ˌwear *one's* ˌheart on *one's* ˈ**sleeve** 1647L79
ˌpuff ˈ**sleeves** 1143R61
ˌroll up *one's* ˈ**sleeves** 1231R21
ˌ**sleight** of ˈhand 1352L4
ˌ**slew** aˈround 1352L37
a ˌ**slice** of ˈlife 1352L49
a ˌ**slice** of the ˈaction 13R13
ˌany way you ˈ**slice** it 1352L64
ˈfish-ˌ**slice** 526R3
ˌ**slice** of the ˈcake 1352L51
ˌ**slice** *me* ˈoff 1352L57/58/62
the ˌbest ˌthing since **sliced** ˈbread 118R69
ˈoil ˌ**slick** 979L30
ˌ**slick** ˈback 1352R15
ˌ**slick** ˈdown 1352R16
ˌcity ˈ**slicker** 234R84
ˈhair ˌ**slide** 636L66 1352R66
ˌ**slide** ˈback 1352R48
ˈ**slide** ˌrule 1352R32
ˌ**sliding** ˈscale 1352R27
not make the ˌ**slightest** ˈdifference 382R8
ˌ**slim** ˈdown 1353L24
ˌ**slim** ˈpickings 1063L57 1353L16
ˈ**slime** ˌball 1353L45
ˌ**sling** *one's* ˈhook 1353L68
ˌ**sling** ˈmud 927R49
ˌ**sling** ˈover 1353L72/73/75
ˌ**sling** toˈgether 1353L63
ˈmud-ˌ**slinging** 927R53
ˈcompliment(s) ˌ**slip** 276L69
ˌFreudian ˈ**slip** 565L4
ˌgive *someone* the ˈ**slip** 1354L16
ˌlet it ˈ**slip** 812L72
ˌlet ˈ**slip** 629L65 812L71/74
ˌnon-ˈ**slip** 959R35
ˌpink ˈ**slip** 1068R33/30
ˈsales ˌ**slip** 1250R79
ˈ**slip** into 1353R49/50/51/52
ˌ**slip** *someone's* ˈmemory/ˈmind 1354L10
ˌ**slip** of the ˈtongue 1353R78
ˌ**slip** *something* ˈon 1353R54
ˈ**slip**-ons 1353R37
ˈ**slip** ˌroad 1354L13
ˌ**slip** through *someone's* ˈfingers 1354L8
ˌ**slip** through the ˈcrack 1354L6
ˌ**slip** ˈup 1353R80/83
ˌ**slipped** ˈdisc 1353R34
ˈcarpet ˌ**slippers** 198L65
ˌ**slippery** ˈcustomer 1354L39
ˌ**slippery** ˈslope 1354L40
ˌ**slob** aˈbout 1354R1
ˌ**slob** aˈround 1354R1
ˈ**slobber** over 1354R10
ˌ**sloe** ˈgin 1354R19
ˌ**slog** aˈway 1354R24
ˌ**slog** ˈon 1354R25/27
ˌ**slop** aˈbout 1354R58
ˌ**slop** aˈround 1354R58
ˌ**slop** ˈout 1354R61
beˈginners' ˌ**slope** 114L17
ˌslippery ˈ**slope** 1354L40
ˌ**slope** ˈoff 1354R82
ˌ**slope** ˈup/ˈdown 1354R74
ˈnursery ˌ**slopes** 968L48
ˌ**slosh** aˈbout 1355L37
ˈmail ˌ**slot** 813L67
ˌ**slot** ˈin 1355L66
ˈ**slot** into 1355L53
ˈ**slot** maˌchine 1355L46/50 1612L65
ˈ**slouch** ˌhat 1355R10
ˌ**slough** ˈoff 1355R16
ˌgo ˈ**slow** 605L63/68
ˌ**slow** ˈburn 1355R48
ˌ**slow** ˈdown/ˈup 1355R83/76/77/79/80/82
ˌ**slow** ˈhandclap 1355R51
ˌ**slow** ˈmotion 1355R54
ˌ**slow** on the ˈuptake 1600R43
ˌ**slow**-ˈwitted 1355R58 1674R78
ˌ**slowly** but ˈsurely 1356L2 1467L77
ˈ**slug** ˌpellet 1356L32
ˌ**sluice** ˈdown/ˈout 1356L63
ˌ**slurp** ˈdown 1356R44
ˈ**slush** ˌfund 1356R71
ˈ**sly** ˌgrog 1357L12
ˌ**smack** ˈdown 1357L54
ˈ**smack** ˌhead 1357L73
ˌ**smack** *one's* ˈlips 1357L55
ˈ**smack** of 1357L75
ˈlip-ˌ**smacking** 828R45
a ˌ**small** ˈfortune 1357R38
ˌgrateful/ˌthankful for **small** ˈmercies 1357R31
in ˌ**small** ˈdoses 412R78
ˌlook ˈ**small** 839R50 1358L13
on the ˈ**small** ˌside 1334L7
ˈ**small** ˌad 238R71
ˈ**small** ˌarms 1357R41
ˌ**small** ˈbeer 1358L19
ˌ**small** ˈchange 1357R44
ˌ**small** ˈclaims 1357R48
ˈ**small** ˌfry 1358L23
ˌ**small** ˈhours 1357R52
ˌ**small** inˈtestine 1357R56
ˌ**small**-ˈminded 1357R59/64
ˌ**small** of *someone's* ˈback 1357R35
ˌ**small** poˈtatoes 1358L20
ˈ**small** ˌprint 1357R65
ˈ**small** ˌscreen 1357R73
ˈ**small** ˌtalk 1358L26
ˌ**small**-ˈtimer 1358L33
ˈ**small**-ˌtown 1357R76
ˌ**small** ˈwonder (that) 1676R29
ˌ**smallest** ˈroom 1357R72
ˈ**smart** ˌalec/ˌaleck 1358R33
ˈ**smart** ˌarse 1358R39
ˈ**smart** ˌass 1358R38
ˈ**smart** at 1359L5
ˈ**smart** ˌbomb 1358R46
ˈ**smart** ˌcard 1358R48
ˈ**smart** ˈcircles 1358R1
ˈ**smart** ˈdrugs 1358R55
ˈ**smart** from 1358R83 1359L1
ˈ**smart** ˈmoney 1358R57
ˈ**smart** ˌmouth 1358R63
ˈ**smart** ˌset 1300L34
ˌ**smart** soˈciety 1358R1
ˌ**smarten** ˈup 1358R17
ˌ**smarten** up *one's* ˈact 1358R25
ˈstreet ˌ**smarts** 1437L51
ˈ**smarty**-ˌpants 1358R67
ˌ**smash**-and-ˈgrab ˌraid 1359L24
ˌ**smash** ˈdown 1359L34

▪smash into 1359L37
▫smash the ▪atom 1359L23
▫smash ▪through 1359L35
▫smash ▪up 1359L16/18/47
▫cervical ▪smear 211R16
▪Pap ▫smear 1023R23 1359R13
▫smear ▪on 1359R6
▫smear ▪over 1359R8
▪smear with 1359R7/9
▫smell a ▪rat 1360L68
▫smell ▪blood 1360L60
▫smell ▪fishy 1360L33/36
▪smell like/of 1360L24/3/21/22/76
▫smell ▪out 1360L63/64
▫smell ▪up 1360L37
▫come up ▫smelling of ▪roses 1360L29
▪smelling ▫salts 1360L72
▪smile at/on/to 1360R17/49/53/42
▫wipe the ▪smile off *someone's* face 1670L65
▫fortune ▪smiles on 555L45
▫wreathed in ▪smiles 1360R34 1690L11
▪smirk at 1360R81
▫photochemical ▪smog 1059L44
▫Big ▪Smoke 124R58
▫blow ▪smoke 139L57
▪chain-▫smoke 212L73/72
go ▫up in ▪smoke 1361L58
▫put/▫stick in your ▫pipe and ▪smoke it 1069R34
▫smoke and ▪mirrors 1361L71
▪smoke ▫bomb 1361L75
▫smoke-filled ▪room 1361L78
▫smoke ▪out 1361R19
▪smoke ▫signal 1361L81
▫smoked ▪glass 1361R24
▫smoked ▪salmon 845L29 1251L74
▫non-▪smoker 959R26/25
▪smokestack ▫industry 1362L19
▫passive ▪smoking 1032R83
▪smoking ▫gun 1361R15
▪smoking ▫jacket 1361R68
▪smooch to 1362L33
▪smooch with 1362L30
▫smooth a▪way 1362L57
▫smooth ▪out 1362L62/63
▫smooth ▪over 1362L54/R1/2
▫smooth ▪sailing 1074R48
take the ▫rough with the ▪smooth 1235R68
▪smother in 1362R61/62
▪smother with 1362R59
▫smoulder ▪on 1363L7
▪smoulder with 1363L11
▪smuggle into 1363L64
▪snack ▫bar 1363R19
▪snack on 1363R25
▫snaffle ▪up 1363R31/33
▪snag from 1363R68
▪snag on 1363R54/61
at a ▪snail's ▫pace 1363R81
▪snake ▫charmer 1364L9
▫snake *one's* ▪way 1364L24
▫snakes and ▪ladders 1364L12
▪brandy ▫snap 158L52
▪cold ▫snap 256R32
▪ginger ▫snap 595R22
▪snap at 1364R9
▫snap at *someone's* ▪heels 1364L54/55
▫snap a▪way 1364R35
▫snap ▪back 1364L50/52/R14
▪snap ▫fastener 1118L35 1364L43
▫snap *one's* ▪fingers 1364L57
▫snap it ▪up 1364L75
▫snap ▪off 1364L35
▫snap ▪out 1364R11
▫snap ▪out of it 1364L69
▪snap ▫pea 1364L44 1457L29
▫snap ▪shut 1364L70
▫snap ▪up 1364L77/78
make it ▪snappy 1364R1
▪snare ▫drum 1365L5
▪snarl at 1365L12/14
▪snarl-up 1365L24
▪snatch at 1365L41
snatch ▫victory (from the jaws of de▪feat) 1365L46
▪body ▫snatcher 142R74
▪cradle ▫snatcher 319L44
▫sneak ▪in 1365L70/72
▪sneak into 1365L73
▪sneak on 1365R7
▫sneak ▪preview 1365L79
▪sneer at 1365R29/30
▫scratch-and-▪sniff 1271R45
▪sniff at 1365R76/77
▫sniff ▪out 1360L64 1365R81/83
▪glue-▫sniffer 601R75/80 1366L7
▪sniffer ▫dog 1366L9
▪snigger at/about 1366L34/33
▫snip ▪off 1366L43
▪snipe at 1366L56/58
▪snitch on 1366L81
in▫verted ▪snob 749R81/78
▫cock a ▪snook at 252R62
▫snoop a▪bout/a▪round 1366R58/60
▪snoop on 1366R56/63
▪snooze ▫button 1367L1
▪snow ▫bank 1367L66
▪snow-▫blind 1367L70
▪snow ▫blindness 1367L67
▪snow-▫capped 1367L70
▫snow ▪in/▪up 1367L82
▪snow-▫job 1367R11
▪snow ▫pea 860L65 1367L71 1457L29
▪snow ▫tire 1367L72
▪snow ▫tyre 1367L72
▫snow-▪white 1367L75
not a ▫snowball's chance in ▪hell 203L45 1367R20
▫snowball ef▪fect 1367R23
▪snowed ▪under 1367R1
a▫bominable ▪snowman 3L83 1697L3
▪snub-▫nosed 1368L12/13
▪snuff ▫it 1368L32
▪snuff ▫movie 1368L32
▫snuff ▪out 1368L24/25
▫snuggle ▪down 1368L60
▫snuggle ▪up 1368L59
and ▪so forth 44R19
and ▫so on and ▪so forth 44R19
as/so ▪long as 838R62
be so ▪good as to 611L75
▫even ▪so 472L24/26
▪ever ▫so 473L49 1368L68
▫every so ▪often 473R35
I am ▫so hungry I could ▫eat a ▪horse 439L30
if I may be/▫make so ▪bold (as to) 144R38
in ▫so many ▪words 863L77
just/ex▫actly ▪so 1369L19
▪say-so 1259L59 1260L43/46
▫should be so ▪lucky 846L64
▫sink so ▪low 1341R76
▪so-and-▫so 1369L59/66
▫so-▪called 1370L23
so ▪far as 503R45/46/48
so ▫far so ▪good 503R59
so ▫help me (▪God) 662L47
so ▫*something* it's not ▪true 1563R20
▫so ▪long 838L70
▫so much the ▪better 121L9
▫so-▪so 1378L27
▫so to ▪speak 1384R60
▪tell *someone* ▫so 1498L31
without so much as a ▫by your ▪leave 807R56 1674L46
▫how ▪so? 690R12/15
▪soak in 1369L33
▪soak into 1369L26
▫soak ▪out 1369L31
▫soak ▪through 1369L27
▫soak ▪up 1369L34
▫soaked to the ▪skin 1346R28
▪soap ▫flakes 1369L81
▪soap ▫opera 1369R14
▫soft-▪soap 1371R22
▪toilet ▫soap 1532R14
▫get on *one's* ▪soapbox 1369R10
▫sob *one's* ▪heart out 1369R49
▪sob ▫story 1369R52
▪sob-▫stuff 1369R57
▫sober as a ▪judge 1369R65
▫sober ▪up 1369R68/69
▫stone-cold ▪sober 1369R64 1429R39
▫anti-▪social 50L45/51
▫social ▪climber 1370R23
▫social ▪conscience 1370R25
▫Social ▪Democrat 1370R27
▫Social Demo▪cratic Party 1370R28
▫social engin▪eering 1370R29
▪social ▫life 1370L40
▫social ▪science 1370R31
▫social se▪curity 979R57 1370R34
▫social ▪services 1370R40
▪social ▫work 1370R44/43
the ▫social ▪sciences 1370R34
de▫signer ▪socialism 372L72
▫national ▪socialism 939L32
▫champagne ▪socialist 214L25
de▫signer ▪socialist 372L71
▫socialized ▪medicine 1370R1
be▪nevolent so▫ciety 117L80
▪building so▫ciety 173R11
con▪sumer so▫ciety 294L25
▪friendly so▫ciety 565R37
▫high so▪ciety 1370R15
per▫missive so▪ciety 1051L41
▫Royal ▪Society 1238L9
▫secret so▪ciety 1280R8
▫smart so▪ciety 1358R1
▪ankle ▫sock 46L83
▫put a ▪sock in it 1371L10
▪sock *someone* ▫one 983R68
▫ball-and-▪socket 95R40 1371L26
▪eye ▫socket 488R49
▪socket ▫set 1371L26
▫pull *one's* ▪socks up 1144L81
▫care/▫give a ▪sod 1371L40
▪sod it 1371L48
▫Sod's ▪law 930R9 1371L45
▫sod ▪off 1371L48
▪baking ▫soda 94R23/25 123L34 1105L52
bi▫carbonate of ▪soda 123L32
▫club ▪soda 250L28 1371L59
▫cream ▪soda 321L55
▫ice-cream ▪soda 698R81
▫orange ▪soda 993L20
▪soda ▫pop 1371L62
▪soda ▫siphon 1342L58
▫sodium bi▪carbonate 123L33 1371L71
▫sodium ▪chloride 1371L73
▫odds and ▪sods 975L16
▪sofa ▫bed 1371L84
▫soft ▪drink 1372L8
▫soft ▪drug 1372L10
▫soft ▪fruit 1371R16
▫soft ▪furnishings 1371R19
▪soft ▫goods 1371R19
▫soft-▪hearted 1371R45
▫soft ▪landing 1371R79
▫soft ▪option 1371R81
▫soft-▪pedal 1371R47
▫soft ▪porn 1372L12
▫soft ▪sell 1371R50
▫soft-▪soap 1371R22
▫soft-▪spoken 1371R53
▪soft ▫spot 1371R57
▫soft ▪target 1371R84
▫soft ▪top 301L72 1371R24
▫soft ▪touch 1372L3
▫soft ▪toy 1371R25
▫soft ▪water 1372L14
▫soften ▪up 1371R63
▪water ▫softener 1642R27
▫softly-▪softly 1371R71
▪software ▫house 1372L25
▪software ▫package 1372L26
▫foreign ▪soil 549R31
▪soil ▫science 1372L59
▫solar ▪plexus 1372R15
▪solar ▫system 1372R6
▫solar ▪year 1372R7
▪soldering ▫iron 1372R22
▪foot ▫soldier 545R65 726L44
▫soldier of ▪fortune 1372R28
▫soldier ▪on 1372R32
▫inner ▪sole 736L22
▫lemon ▪sole 810R21
▫rock ▪solid 1229R54
▫solid as a ▪rock 1229R55
▫solid ▪fuel 1373L59
▫solid-▪state 1373L39
▫solitary con▪finement 1373R36
▪water-▫soluble 1642R29
▫band-aid so▪lution 96R77
▫final so▪lution 520L11
▫saturated so▪lution 1256R70
▫pick on someone *your* ▪own size 1061R67
▫break something ▪up 161L64
Do you ▫want to make something ▪of it? 856L30
give *someone* ▫something to ▪talk about 1488R28
have (really) ▪got ▫something 1374R71
have ▫got something ▪there 1374R76
▫have something ▪going with 1374R79
like ▫something the ▪cat brought/dragged in 203L61
▫little ▪something 831L44/R36
▫put *something* down to ex▪perience 482L22 1153R13
▪say ▫something about 1259R68
▫something a little ▪stronger 1375L14
▫something ▪else 1374R54 1375L1
▫something ▪fierce 516R13
▫something for ▪nothing 1375L4
▪something ▫like/a▫round 1375L11
▪something ▫over/▫under 1375L21
▪start ▫something 1414L33
there's ▫something to be ▪said for 1259R81
you ▪know ▫something 787L5
▪get ▫somewhere 1375L73
▪somewhere along the ▫line 826L20
▫prodigal ▪son 1126R55
▫son et lum▪ière 1375R48
▪son-in-▫law 1375R30/31
▫son of a ▪bitch 1375R33/34
▫son of a ▪gun 1375R38
▫burst into ▪song 177R83 1494R49
▪protest ▫song 1137R50
▫song and ▪dance 1375R65/69
▪song ▫thrush 1375R73 1517R1
▫sonic ▪boom 1376L7
▫sonny ▪Jim 1376L15
as ▫soon as ▪possible 1099R35 1376L46
not a ▫moment too ▪soon 912L82
▫speak too ▪soon 1384R69
would (▫just) as ▪soon 1376L59
no sooner ▫said than ▪done 1376L53
▫sooner or ▪later 1376L56
would ▪rather/▪sooner 1688R17
would ▪sooner 1376L59
▫soothe ▪down 1376L74
▫sop ▪up 1376R9
a ▫sight for sore ▪eyes 1335R28
▪cold ▫sore 256R84
like a ▫bear with a sore ▪head 107R57
▫running ▪sore 1242L13
▪saddle-▫sore 1248L1
▫sore ▪point 1377L14
stand/stick ▫out like a sore ▪thumb 1377L17
▪sorrow over/for 1377L60
▫drown *one's* ▪sorrows 428L58
▫sorry to ▪say 1377L80
▫nothing of the ▪sort 964L34
▪sort into 1377R59
▫sort ▪out 1377R61/64 1378L1/7
sort (out) the ▫sheep from the ▪goats 1313R81
▪sorting ▫code 1377R62
▪sorting ▫office 1377R66
▫sotto ▪voce 1378L32
▪sought-after 1378L46
▫bare *one's* ▪soul 99R59
▫bless my ▪soul 135L10
▫blue-eyed ▪soul 139R84
▫heart and ▪soul 656R69
keep ▫body and ▪soul to▫gether 142R54
life and ▫soul of the ▪party 818R68
put ▫heart and ▪soul into 657L24
sell *one's* ▫soul (to the ▪devil) 1290L15
▪soul-des▫troying 1378L58
▪soul ▫mate 1378L71
▪soul-▫searching 1378L62
of ▫sound ▪mind 898R75
▫safe and ▪sound 1248R6
▫sound as a ▪bell 115R34
▪sound ▫board for 1378R82
▪sound ▫check 1378R38
▪sound ef▫fects 1378R42
▫sound ▪fun 1378R81
▪sound like 1378R74/79
▫sound ▪off a▫bout 1379L82/83/R35
▫sound ▪out 1379R32
▪sound ▫system 1378R44
▫sound the ▪death knell 352R16
▫sound the re▪treat 1378R59
▪sound ▫wave 1378R47
the ▪sound ▫barrier 1378R33
▫warning/▫alarm bells start to ▪sound 115R38 1638R44
▪echo ▫sounder 439R70
▫high-▪sounding 668R22
▪sounding ▫board 1378R82
▫pea ▪soup 1039R8
▪soup ▫kitchen 1379R75
▪soup ▫spoon 1379R77
▫soup ▪up 1379R81
▪souped-up 1380L3
▫pea-▪souper 1039R8
▫leave a sour ▪taste 807L69
▫sour ▪cream 1380L26/25
▫sour ▪grapes 1380L20
▫sweet-and-▪sour 1475R45
▪source ▫language 1380L68
▫Deep ▪South 357L71
mag▫netic ▪south 852R58
▫North-South di▪vide 961L47/50
▫South ▪Pole 1380R38
▫Southern ▪Cross 1380R53
▪sow in/on 1381L79/80
▫sow the ▪seeds of 1381L84
▫sow *one's* wild ▪oats 1381R2
▪sow with 1381L81
▫reap what *one* has ▪sown 1181L25
▫soy(a) ▪sauce 1381R18
▪soya ▫bean 1381R10
▪soya ▫curd 1381R20
▪soya ▫flour 1381R20
▪soya ▫milk 1381R21
▪soya ▫oil 1381R20
▪health ▫spa 655R3
▪breathing ▫space 162R81
▫double-▪space 414L80/77
in/within a ▫short space of ▪time 1381R61
in/within/▫during the ▪space of 1381R62
▫outer ▪space 1002L1
▪shelf ▫space 1314R16
▪space-▫age 1382L27
▪space-▫bar 1381R64
▪space ▫heater 1381R67
▫space ▪out 1382L1
▪space *things* over 1382L1
▪space ▫platform 1382L30
▪space ▫probe 1382L32
▪space ▫race 1382L35
▪space-▫saving 1381R69
▪space ▫shuttle 1382L37
▪space ▫station 1382L40
▫space-▪time 1381R71
▫waste of ▪space 1640L68
▫watch this ▪space 1641R30
call a ▫spade a ▪spade 185L77
spa▫ghetti bolo▪gnese 1382R32
Spa▫ghetti ▪Junction 1382R33
spa▫ghetti ▪western 1382R37
at▪tention ▫span 78L23
▪memory ▫span 886L28
▫spick and ▪span 1391L5
▫Star-Spangled ▪Banner 1412R31
▫cocker ▪spaniel 253L44
▫Spanish Inquis▪ition 733R2
▪box ▫spanner 155L38
put/throw a ▫spanner in the ▪works 1383L15
▪spar with 1383L22
e▫nough and to ▪spare 459R33
▫go ▪spare 1383R22
▫spare a ▪thought for 1383R13 1514R39
▫spare *someone's* ▪blushes 1383L40
▫spare ▪*something* for 1383R10/11/13
▫spare-part ▪surgery 1383L75
▫spare ▪parts 1383L72
▫spare ▪tyre 1383L70 1577R29
▫no expense(s) ▪spared 481R65
▫bright ▪spark 165L60
▪spark into 1383R47
▫spark ▪off 1383R52
▪spark ▫plug 1383R40/42
the ▫sparks ▪fly 1383R39
▪sparring ▫partner 1383L23
▪house ▫sparrow 689L58
▪spat with 1384L34/35
▪spatter in/with 1384L35/53
▪spatter on 1384L54
▪spatter over 1384L52
▪spawning ▫ground 1384L74
▫couldn't/▫didn't speak a ▪word of 1385L6
▫know *someone* to ▪speak to 1384R64
▫none to ▪speak of 1384R56
▫so to ▪speak 1384R60
▪speak against 1385L22
▪speak as 1384R30
▪speak for 1384R19/22/23 1385L21/50
▫speak in ▪riddles 1222L1
▫speak *one's* ▪mind 1384R52
▪speak of 1384R14/16/26 1385L47
▫speak of the ▪devil 378L47
▪speak on/about 1385L20/50
▫speak ▪out 1384R32
▫speak out of ▪turn 1570R26
▫speak the same ▪language 795L82
▪speak to 1384R5/7/9/10 1385L18/20
▫speak too ▪soon 1384R69
▫speak ▪up 1384R74/34 1598L20
▫speak ▪volumes 1385L50
▫speak ▪well for 1385L52
▫speak when you're ▪spoken to 1384R79
▫native ▪speaker 939R26
in a ▫manner of ▪speaking 861R59
on ▪speaking ▫terms 1384R65/63
▫plain ▪speaking 1074R50
▫properly ▪speaking 1134R8
▫relatively ▪speaking 1197L1
▪speaking en▫gagement 1385L27
▫strictly ▪speaking 1384R45 1440R57
▪spear ▫carrier 1385L83
▪spec ▪builder 1385R34
▫nothing ▪special 964L40
▫Saturday night ▪special 1257L14
▪Special ▫Branch 1386L38
▫special de▪livery 1385R59
▫special edu▪cation 1385R74
▫special ef▪fect 443R25 1385R61
special ▪interest ▫group 1385R68
▫special ▪interests 1385R65
▫special (educational) ▪needs 1385R70/73
▫Special O▪lympics 1385R82
▫special ▪pleading 1385R84
▪special ▫school 1386L42
spe▫cific ▪gravity 1386R50
make a ▪spectacle of *oneself* 1387L79
spec▪tator ▫sport 1387R45
▪speculate about 1388L9
▪speculate in 1388L40/41
▪speculate on 1388L7/8/38
▫direct ▪speech 386R69
▫figure of ▪speech 517R43
▫free ▪speech 561L38
▫indirect ▪speech 722L48
▫maiden ▪speech 853L79
▫part of ▪speech 1028R59
re▫ported ▪speech 722L48 1205L38
▪speech ▫bubble 1388L70
▪speech ▫day 1388R17
▪speech im▫pediment 1388L73
▫speech ▪therapy 1388L77/75
▪speech ▫writer 1388R20
at ▫top ▪speed 1537L77
▪ground ▫speed 626L70
▫high-▪speed 668L43
▪idling ▫speed 702L29
▫speed a▪long 1388R67
▫speed a▪way/▪off 1388R68
▪speed ▫bump 1389L19

▫**speed** ▪by/▪past 1388R70
▫**speed** ▪down 1388R69
▪**speed** ▫hump 1389L19
▫**speed** ▪in 1388R84
▪**speed** ▫limit 1389L23
▫**speed** *someone* on *their* ▪way 1388R81
▪**speed** ▫skating 1389L29
▪**speed** ▫trap 1389L26
▫**speed** ▪up 1388R75/77/78/79/80/83
▫up to ▪**speed** 1388R54/57
▫cast a ▪**spell** on 202L44
▪**spell**-▫check 1389R3/4/3
▫**spell** ▪out 1389L83
▪**spelling** ▫bee 1389R25
▫**spend** a ▪penny 1390L15
▪**spend** on 1390L11/12/13/22
▫**spend** spend ▪spend 1390L18
▫**spend** the ▪night to▫gether/▫with 955L24 1390L48/50/51
▪**spending** ▫money 1087R80 1390L20
▪**sperm** ▫bank 1390L80
▪**sperm** ▫count 1390L82
▪**sperm** ▫whale 1390R10
▫**spew** ▪out 1390R16/17
▫**spice** ▪up 1390R76
▪**spice** with 1390R75/79
▫sugar and ▪**spice** 1457L12
▫**spick** and ▪span 1391L5
▪**spider** ▫monkey 1391L14
▪**spider** ▫plant 1391L17
▪**spider's** ▫web 252R3
▫**spiff** ▪up 1391L36
▫**spike** *someone's* ▪guns 1391L70
▫**spike** ▪heels 1391L55
▪**spike** with 1391L75/76
▫**spill** ▪blood 1391R17
▫**spill** down 1391L83
▪**spill** into 1391R5/6/8
▪**spill** on 1391L83
▪**spill** onto 1391R9
▫**spill** ▪out 1391R12/14
▫**spill** ▪over 1391R2/6/8
▫**spill** the ▪beans 1391R15
▫no good/use crying over **spilt** ▪milk 331R55
a ▫**spin** of the ▪coin 1391R81
▫**spin** a ▪coin 1391R52
▫**spin** a▪long 1392L41
▫**spin** a▪round/▪round 1391R40/42
▫**spin** ▪bowler 154R48 1391R56/59
▪**spin** con▫trol 1392L30
▪**spin** ▫doctor 1392L34
▫**spin**-▪dry 1391R59/63
▪**spin** into 1392L8
▫**spin** ▪off 1392L46/54
▫**spin** ▪out 1392L62
▫**spina** ▪bifida 1392L69
▫**spinal** ▪column 260R60 1392R1/46
▫**spinal** ▪cord 1392R48
a ▪shiver/▪shivers (up and) ▫down *one's* ▫**spine** 1318L52
▪**spine**-chilling 1392R12
▪**spine**-tingling 1392R16
▪money-▫**spinner** 913R35
▪**spinning** ▫top 1391R65
▪**spinning** ▫wheel 1392L18
in▫flationary ▪**spiral** 727R49
▪**spiral**-bound 1393L4
as/when the ▫**spirit** ▪moves 1393L57
com▪munity ▫**spirit** 272L39
▫enter/▫get into the ▪**spirit** of 1393L30
▫fighting ▪**spirit** 517L79
▫free ▪**spirit** 561L41
▫guiding ▪**spirit** 630R53
▫Holy ▪**Spirit** 679R15
▫kindred ▪**spirit** 780R67
▪**spirit**-level 1393R26
▫surgical ▪**spirit** 1468R20
▫white ▪**spirit** 1660R60
▫high-▪**spirited** 669L18/22 1393L43
▫low ▪**spirited** 844R68 1393L43
▫public-▪**spirited** 1142L50 1393L44
▫high ▪**spirits** 669L16
▫methylated ▪**spirits** 892L29
▫**spirits** ▪sink 1341R66
▫negro ▪**spiritual** 1393R30
▫**spiritual** ▪healer 1393L78/74
▫**spiritual** ▪home 1393L70
▫**spit** and ▪polish 1393R64
▫**spit** ▪blood/▪venom/▪nails/▪tacks 1393R44
▪**spit** ▫curl 781R83
▫**spit** ▪out 1393R39/40
cut off *one's* ▫nose to **spite** *one's* ▪face 338R83
in/within ▪**spitting** ▫distance 1393R51
the ▫**spitting** ▪image of 1393R53
make a ▪**splash** 1394L43
▪**splash**-▫down 1394L36
▪**splash** ▫guard 928L8 1394L46
▪**splash** into 1394L26
▫**splash** ▪out 1394L49
▫**splash** ▪out ▫on 1394L51/53
▪**splatter** with 1394L64
▫**splay** ▪out 1394L70
▫**splice** to▪gether 1394R18
▪**splinter** ▫group 1394R33
▪**splinter** into 1394R41
▪shin ▫**splints** 1316L49
ba▫nana ▪**split** 96R33
▫lickety-▪**split** 817R39
▪**split** between 1394R44/47 1395L22
▫**split** down the ▪middle 893R72/71
▫**split** ▪end 1394R79
▪**split** from 1394R62
▫**split** ▪hairs 1394R65
▫**split** in▪finitive 1394R82
▫**split**-▪level 1395L3
▪**split** on 1395L39
▫**split** ▪pea 1395L6
▫**split** person▪ality 1395L11
▫**split** ▪pin 1395L8
▫**split** ▪second 1395L13
▫**split** *one's* ▪sides 1394R69
▫**split** the ▪difference 1394R72
▫**split** ▪up 1394R46/49/77/78/79 1395L17
▪ear ▫**splitting** 436L69
▫**splosh** a▪bout 1395L45
▪**splurge** on 1395L50/51/53
▪**spoil** for 1395R27
▫**spoil** the ▪party for 1395L82
▪**spoiling** for a ▪fight 1395R27
put a ▪**spoke** in *someone's* ▫wheel 1395R48
▫plain-▪**spoken** 1074R53
▫soft-▪**spoken** 1371R53
▫speak when you're ▪**spoken** to 1384R79
▫well-▪**spoken** 1653L81
▪**sponge** ▫bag 1395R79
▪**sponge** ▫off 1396L9/10
▫**sponge** ▪rubber 1395R82
▫throw in the ▪**sponge** 1517L7
spon▫taneous com▪bustion 1396L42
▫born with a silver ▪**spoon** in *one's* ▫mouth 149R18
egg-and-▪**spoon** ▫race 444R5
▫greasy ▪**spoon** 621R13
▪soup ▫**spoon** 1379R77
▪**spoon**-▫feed 1396L79/81
▪**spoon** into 1396R4
▪**spoon** ▫over 1396R4
▫wooden ▪**spoon** 1677L61/62
▪blood ▫**sport** 137L79
spec▪tator ▫**sport** 1387R45
▪water ▫**sport** 1642R30
▫**sporting** ▪chance 1396R58
▪contact ▫**sports** 294R19 1396R39
▪**sports** ▫car 1396R64
▪**sports** ▫jacket 1396R66
▫winter ▪**sports** 1396R42 1669R66
▪bald ▫**spot** 95L54
▪beauty ▫**spot** 110L28/29
▪black ▫**spot** 132L10
▪blind ▫**spot** 135L83
▪G-▫**spot** 578L71
▫hit the ▪**spot** 673L36
▪hot ▫**spot** 687R62 688L48
▪penalty ▫**spot** 1044R26
▫put on the ▪**spot** 1398L78
▫rooted to the ▪**spot** 1234L33
▫run on the ▪**spot** 1240R83
▪soft ▫**spot** 1371R57
▫**spot** ▪check 1398L82
▪**spot** ▫fine 1398R57
▪**spot**-▫welding 1397R58
▫tight ▪**spot** 1520L14
▫touch/▫strike/▫hit/ex▫pose a raw ▪**spot** 1176R68 1540L76
▪trouble ▫**spot** 1561R19/22
▪weak ▫**spot** 1646R60
▫turn the ▪**spotlight** on 1569R54
▫knock ▪**spots** off 785L40
▫**spotted** ▪dick 1397R66
▫**spotted** ▪gum 1397R68
▫well ▪**spotted** 1398L61
▪talent ▫**spotter** 1488L53
▪train ▫**spotter** 1548R21
▫up the ▪**spout** 1399L17/18
▪hair ▫**spray** 636L68 791R52
▪**spray** ▫gun 1399L75
▫**spray** ▪on 1399L80
▪**spray** over 1399L81
▪**spray** with 1399L78/79
▪crop ▫**spraying** 327L33
▪centre-▫**spread** 209L52
▫double(-page) ▪**spread** 414L80
▫middle-age ▪**spread** 894L18
spread-▪eagled 1399R39
▫**spread** like ▪wildfire 1399R28 1664R75
▫**spread** ▪on 1399R16
▫**spread** ▪out 1399R11/14/28
▫**spread** ▪over 1399R24
▫**spread** the ▪word 1399R34
▫**spread** *one's* ▪wings 1399R31
a ▪**spring** in *one's* ▫step 1400L21
▪box ▫**spring** 155L41
full of the ▫joys of ▪**spring** 572L39
▫**spring** ▪chicken 1399R79/81
▫**spring**-▪clean 1399R84/83
▪**spring** from 1400L52/57
▫**spring** ▪greens 1400L3
▫**spring** ▪onion 1400L5
▫**spring** ▪roll 1400L6
▫**spring** to ▪mind 1400L45
▫**spring** ▪up 1400L50
▫**sprinkle** ▪on 1400L83
▫brussels ▪**sprout** 170R58
▪**sprout** from 1400R62
▫**sprout** ▪up 1400R64
▫**spruce** ▪up 1400R74
▫**spur** of the ▪moment 1401L33
▫**spur** ▪on 1401L38
▫win/▫gain *one's* ▪**spurs** 1401L28
▪**spy** on 1401R6/7
▫**spy** ▪out 1401R9
▫**spy** out the ▪land 1401R11
▪bomb ▫**squad** 145R1
▪death ▫**squad** 352R30
▪firing ▫**squad** 523R30
▪flying ▫**squad** 540R43
▪Fraud ▫**Squad** 559R66
▪**squad** ▫car 1401R43
▪vice ▫**squad** 1621L15
▪**squadron** ▫leader 1401R51
▫back to **square** ▪one 89L11
▫fair and ▪**square** 495L15/17
▫four-▪**square** 556R64/68
▫**square** ▪bracket 1402L35
▪**square** ▫dance 1402L38
▫**square** ▪deal 1402L64
▪**square**-▫eyed 1402L40
▪**square** ▫knot 1190L66 1402L43
▫**square** ▪meal 1402L43
▫**square** ▪off 1402R1
square ▫peg (in a round ▪hole) 1402L31
▫**square** the ac▪counts/▪books 1402L68
▫**square** the ▪circle 1402L50
▫**square** ▪up 1402L67/R1
▫**square** ▪up to 1402R6
▪**square** with 1379L32
▪T-▫**square** 1483L18
the ▫**Square** ▪Mile 1402L29
▫fairly and ▪**squarely** 495L48
▫lemon ▪**squash** 810R22
▫orange ▪**squash** 993L16 1402R73
▫**squash** ▪in 1402R43/44
▪**squash** ▫rackets 1402R54
▪**squash** ▫racquets 1402R55
▫**squash** ▪up 1402R45/46
▫**squashed** like sar▪dines 1255R5
▫**squat** ▪down 1402R80
▪**squat** in 1403L8
▪**squat** on 1403L11
▪**squat**-▫thrust 1402R84
▪**squawk** about 1403L36
▫bubble and ▪**squeak** 171L43
▫narrow ▪**squeak** 938L71
▫**squeak** ▪by 1403L73
▫**squeak** ▪through 1403L72
▫**squeeze** *someone* until the ▪pips **squeak** 1403R68
▫**squeaky**-▪clean 1403L59/61
▫ ▫**squeal** of ▪brakes 157R30
▪**squeal** on 1403R12
▪**squeal** with 1403R4
▪**squeegee** ▫mop 1403R36
▪credit ▫**squeeze** 322L58 1403R83
▫put the ▪**squeeze** on 1154L36
▪**squeeze** ▫bottle 1403R84
▫**squeeze** ▪dry 1403R68
▫**squeeze** ▪in 1404L14/15/16/20
▫**squeeze** ▪out 1403R53
▫**squeeze** ▪through 1404L22
▫**squeeze** ▪under 1404L23
▫**squeeze** *someone* until the ▪pips squeak 1403R68
▫damp ▪**squib** 344R76
▫**squinch** ▪up 1404L83
have *or* ▫take a ▪**squint** at *something* 1404R6
▫**squirrel** a▪way 1404R40
▪**squirt** ▫gun 1404R61 1642R19
▫**squirt** *something* ▪on 1404R47
▫**squirt** ▪out 1404R50
▪**squirt** *someone* with 1404R51
St ▪Bernard 1417L72
have *or* ▫make a ▪**stab** at *something* 1405L27
▪**stab** at 1405L11
▫**stab** *someone* in the ▪back 1405L15
▪**stab** *something* with 1405L10
▪back-▫**stabber** 89R73
shut/close the **stable** ▫door after the ▪horse has bolted 411R52
▪**stable** ▫boy 1405R10
▪**stable** ▫girl 1405R11
▪**stable** ▫lad 1405R11
▫blow *one's* ▪**stack** 139L42
▪**stack** against 1405R57/60
▪**stack** ▫system 1405R42
▫**stack** the ▪cards 1405R57
▫**stack** the ▪deck 1405R58
▫**stack** ▪up 1405R55/67
the ▫odds/▫cards are **stacked** a▪gainst *someone* 1405R61
▪cabin ▫**staff** 182L63
▫chief of ▪**staff** 225R63
▫general ▪**staff** 587L53
▪ground ▫**staff** 626L72
▫half-▪**staff** 637R73
▫Joint Chiefs of ▪**Staff** 767R69
▪skeleton ▫**staff** 1345R3
▪**staff** ▫nurse 1406L3
▪**staff** ▫officer 1406L7
▪**staff** with 1406L10
the ▫**staff** of ▪life 1406L20
▫short-▪**staffed** 1324L47/R36
▫go ▪**stag** 1406L32
▪**stag** ▫party 1406L34
▫apron ▪**stage** 59L57
▫centre ▪**stage** 209L57
go on the ▪**stage** 1406R13
▫hold the ▪**stage** 676R66
▪landing ▫**stage** 794R24
▫set the ▪**stage** 1263R48 1299L57
▪**stage** di▫rection 1406R15
▫**stage** ▪door 1406R19
▪**stage** ▫fright 1406R23
▫**stage** ▪left 1406R26
▪**stage** ▫manager 1406R29
▪**stage** ▫name 1406R31
▪**stage**-▫struck 1406R34
▪**stage** ▫whisper 1406R38/42
take ▫centre ▪**stage** 1406R14
▫take the ▪**stage** 1406R10
the ▫**stage** *is* ▪set 1299L56
▫**staggered** ▪junction 1407L43
▪**staging** ▫area 1406R64
▪**staging** ▫post 1406R66
▫**stained** ▪glass 1407R10
▫**stainless** ▪steel 1407R28
above ▪**stairs** 1407R49
be▫low ▪**stairs** 1407R48
▫burn at the ▪**stake** 177L75 1407R84
▫**stake** a ▪claim 1408L7
▫**stake** ▪out 1408L77
▪**stake** *someone* to *something* 1408L67
▫pull up ▪**stakes** 1422R64
▫raise/▫up the ▪**stakes** 1408L37
▪**stalking** ▫horse 1408R79
▫eyes out on ▪**stalks** 1408R65
▪**stall** ▫holder 1409L14
▫**stall** ▪off 1409L41
▪food ▫**stamp** 544L61
▪postage ▫**stamp** 1100R68 1409R10
▫rubber-▪**stamp** 1238R32/36
▪**stamp** *someone* as 1409R70/72
▪**stamp** on 1409R38/39/58/59/66/73
▫**stamp** ▪out 1409R37
▪**stamp** with 1409R56/75
▫**stamped** addressed ▪envelope 1409R24
stam▪pede into 1410L2
▪**stamping** ▫ground 1409R44
a ▫leg to ▪**stand** on 809L7
▫as things ▪**stand** 67L19/20 1512L58
▪cab ▫**stand** 182L31
▫make *someone's* ▪hair **stand** on ▫end 636L48
▫Mexican ▪**stand** off 892R20
▪night ▫**stand** 111R71 955L34/35
▫one-night ▪**stand** 984L81/R1
▫**stand** a (good) ▪chance 1411L21/19
▪**stand** against 1410L20 1411L40/44
▪**stand**-a▫lone 1410R50
▫**stand** (up) and be ▪counted 1410L70
▫**stand** and de▪liver 1410L32
▫**stand** a▪round 1410L21
▫**stand** a▪side 69R60 1410L25
▫**stand** at ▪ease 438L37
▫**stand** ▪back 1410L27
▫**stand** ▪bail 1410R35
▫**stand** ▪by 1410L34/42
▫**stand** cor▪rected 1410R36
▫**stand** ▪down 1411L56
▪**stand** for 547R4 1410L40/R42/48 1411L18/50/59/63/68
▫**stand** *one's* ▪ground 1410L45
▫**stand** ▪guard 629L55 1410L48
▫**stand** ▪in 1410L25/R23/64 1411L67/70
▫**stand** in good ▪stead 1410R40 1417R3
▫**stand** no ▪nonsense 960L78
▪**stand** on 1410L24 1411L7/9/42
▫**stand** on ▪ceremony 1410L49
▫**stand** on *one's* ▪dignity 1410L52
▫**stand** on *one's* ▪hands/▪head 1410L55
▫**stand** *something* on *its* ▪head 1410L60
▫**stand** on *one's* own (two) ▪feet 1410L66
▫**stand** or ▪fall by 1410L69
▫**stand** ▪out 1411L75
▫**stand** out a ▪mile 896L38
▫**stand** ▪out from 1411L77
stand ▫out like a sore ▪thumb 1377L17
▫**stand** ▪over 1410R28
▫**stand** ▪tall 1489L47
▫**stand** the ▪sight of 1410R78
▫**stand** the test of ▪time 1410R77
▫**stand** ▪to 1410R12/14
▫**stand** to▪gether 1410R30
▫**stand** ▪trial 1410R47
▫**stand** ▪up 1410L75 1411L80
▫**stand** ▪up for 1411R1
▫**stand** ▪up to 1411R4
without a ▫leg to ▪**stand** on 809L6
won't ▫**stand** any ▪nonsense 960L78
▫bog ▪**standard** 144L6
▪gold ▫**standard** 609R84
▪living ▫**standard** 1411R54
▫non-▪**standard** 959R29/32
▪**standard**-▫bearer 1411R60
▪**standard** ▫lamp 1411R65
▫**standard** of ▪living 1411R53
▫**standard** ▪operating procedure 1411R23
▫**standard** ▪time 1411R26
▫double ▪**standards** 414L83
▫sinking ▪**standards** 1341R72
▫free-▪**standing** 561R74
▫leave *someone* **standing** 807R4
▫long-▪**standing** 838R45 1412L21
▫**standing** ▪joke 1412L3
▫**standing** on *one's* ▪head 1410L58
▫**standing** ▪order 1411R84
▫**standing** o▪vation 1005L34 1410L80
▪**standing** ▫room 1410L83
▫**standing** room ▪only 1410R3
▫**standing** ▪start 1410L82
▫as it ▪**stands** 67L19/18
it ▫**stands** to ▪reason 1410R43
▫grind to a ▪**standstill** 624R35/37
▪**Stanley** ▫knife 1177L21 1412L56
▪**staple**-▫gun 1412L68
▫**staple** to▪gether 1412L71
▫co-▪**star** 310L26/30
▫evening ▪**star** 472R35
▫falling ▪**star** 498L3 891L41 1320L45
▫five-▪**star** 528L33
▫fixed ▪**star** 528L56
▫four-**star** (▪petrol) 556R72/70
▫morning ▪**star** 918R58
▪movie ▫**star** 926L29
▫North ▪**Star** 961L62
▫rising ▪**star** 1226R45
▫shooting ▪**star** 891L41 1320L45
▫**star** ▪chamber 1412R26
▪**star**-▫crossed 1412R64
▪**star** in 1412R51
▫**Star** of ▪David 1412R28
▪**star** ▫sign 1412R65
▫**Star**-Spangled ▪Banner 1412R31
▪**star**-studded 1412R41
▫**star** ▪turn 1412R47
▪**star** ▫wars 1275R46 1412R9
the ▪Pole ▫**Star** 1091L42
▪three-▫**star** 1515R4
▪**stare** at 1413L22/23/26
▫**stare** at *one's* ▪navel 944L27
▫**stare** ▪down 1413L28
▫**stare** in the ▪face 1413L30
▫ill-▪**starred** 703R12
▫**starry**-▪eyed 1412R13
▫reach for the ▪**stars** 1177R28
▫see ▪**stars** 1283L66
▫**Stars** and ▪Bars 1412R30
▫**Stars** and ▪Stripes 1412R30
▫thank *one's* lucky ▪**stars** 1507L5
▫written in the ▪**stars** 1692L52
▪bump ▫**start** 175L66 1151L83/R1
▫false ▪**start** 500L32/35
▫flying ▪**start** 540R45
from ▫**start** to ▪finish 522R34 1413R41
▫head ▪**start** 653R41/45
▪hill ▫**start** 670L37
▪jump-**start** 772R37/38
▪kick-▫**start** 779L22
▪push ▫**start** 1151L83/R1
▫racing ▪**start** 1165R31
▫standing ▪**start** 1410L82
▫**start** a ▪family 1414L31
▫**start** a new ▪life 818R77
▪**start** at/from 1413R82 1414L38/4
▪**start** by 1414L7
▪**start** ▫date 1413R67
▪**start** from 1413R82
▫**start** ▪off as 1414L12
start off on a ▫different ▪tack 1484L83
▫**start** ▪on about 1413R13
▪**start** ▫point 1413R67
▪**start** ▫something 1414L33
start the ▪ball ▫rolling 95R24
▪**start** ▫time 1413R68
start ▪tongues ▫wagging 1534R55
▫**start** ▪work 1413R20
▫warning/▫alarm bells **start** to ▪ring/▪sound 115R38 1638R44
▫get ▪**started** 1413R20
▪fire ▫**starter** 524L68
▫non-▪**starter** 959R38
under ▫**starter's** ▪orders 1413R50
▪**starting** ▫date 1413R66
▪**starting** ▫line 824R39 1413R64
▪**starting** ▫point 1089R47/49 1413R67
▪**starting** ▫price 1413R73
▪**starting** ▫salary 1413R76
▪**starting** ▫time 1413R68

in/by ▫fits and ▪**starts** 527R82
the ▫fur **starts** to ▪fly 575R40
star▪vation ▫diet 1414L77
▪**starve** of 1414L68
▪sex-▫**starved** 1303R62
▫**stash** a▪way 1414L83
af▫fairs of ▪**state** 21R78
▪buffer ▫**state** 172R13
▫city-▪**state** 234R4
▫client ▪**state** 244L40
▫head of ▪**state** 654L49
in a ▫*terrible* **state** of re▪pair 1203R74
▫lie in ▪**state** 818L29
▫nation ▪**state** 938R66
po▪lice ▫**state** 1091R21
▪satellite ▫**state** 1256L36
▫Secretary of ▪**State** 1280R57/66
▫solid-▪**state** 1373L39
▪**State** De▫partment 1414R48
▫**state's** ▪evidence 1414R50
▫**state** oc▪casion 1414R55
▫**state** of af▪fairs 1414R16
▫**state** of e▪mergency 1414R17
▫**state** of ▪mind 898R77
▫**state** of the ▪art 1414R20/24
▫**state** ▪pension 979R57
▫**state** ▪premier 1414R58
▫**state** ▪visit 1414R59
suc▪cessor ▫**state** 1454R44
▫welfare ▪**state** 1651L59
▫**stately** ▪home 1415L29
▪bank ▫**statement** 97R50
▫senior ▪**statesman** 1292L53
▫senior ▪**stateswoman** 1292L53
▪bus ▫**station** 178L54
▪coach ▫**station** 251L67
▪comfort ▫**station** 267L72
▪filling ▫**station** 518R73 1056L44
▪fire ▫**station** 523L80
▪gas ▫**station** 582R34 584L35 1056L45
▪hill ▫**station** 670L45
▫marry beneath *one's* ▪**station** 868L64
▫muster ▪**station** 933L50
▪petrol ▫**station** 1056L44
po▪lice ▫**station** 1091R19
▪polling ▫**station** 1092R40
▪power ▫**station** 1106L76
▪pumping ▫**station** 1146L31
▪railway ▫**station** 1169R43 1415L68/69
▪service ▫**station** 1297R80
▪sheep ▫**station** 1314L1
▪space ▫**station** 1382L40
▪**station** ▫break 1415R5
▪**station** ▫house 1415L81
▪**station** in 1415R11
▪**station** ▫wagon 469L59 1415L82
▪tracking ▫**station** 1545L75
▪train ▫**station** 1415L69
▪way ▫**station** 1645R30
▪weather ▫**station** 1648L48
▪action ▫**stations** 13R34
▪panic ▫**stations** 1022L56
the ▫**Stations** of the ▪Cross 1415R18
▫vital **sta▪tistics** 1627R79/83
▪marital ▫**status** 865L84
▪**status** ▫symbol 1416L83
the ▫**status** ▪quo 1416L74
▫on/▫reach the ▪**statute** ▫book 1416R48
▫**stave** ▪in 1416R73
▫**stave** ▪off 1416R78
have ▫come to ▪**stay** 1417L9
▪**stay** at 1417L55/61
▫**stay** at ▪home 1417L8/14
▪**stay** for 1417L2
▫**stay** ▪in 1417L22/54/63
▫**stay** ▪loose 840R61
▫**stay** of exe▪cution 1417L69
▫**stay** on the ▪sidelines 1417L41
▫**stay** ▪out 1417L29
▫**stay** over▪night 1417L57
▫**stay** the ▪course 1417L43
▫**stay** ▪up 1417L31
▪**stay** with 1417L56/63
▪**staying** ▫power 1417L47
▫stand in good ▪**stead** 1410R40 1417R3
▫go ▪**steady** 1417R44
▫ready **steady** ▪go 1179L67
▫**steady** as a ▪rock 1417R37
▪minute ▫**steak** 902L62
▫rump ▪**steak** 1240R36
▫**steak** and kidney ▪pie/▪pudding 1417R69
▪**steak** ▫house 1417R68
▪**steak** ▫knife 1417R71
▫**steak** tar▪tare 1417R72
▫stewing/▪braising ▫**steak** 1417R75
▫**steal** a ▪march on 1418L12
▫**steal** at▪tention 1418L9
▫**steal** ▪out 1418L8
▫**steal** the ▪show/▪scene 1418L16
▪**Stealth** ▫bomber/▫fighter 1418L33
▫blow off ▪**steam** 138R80
▫full **steam** a▪head 573L29
▫get/▫pick up ▪**steam** 1418L46
▫let off ▪**steam** 812R16
▫run out of ▪**steam** 1243L2
▪**steam** ▫iron 1418L52
▫**steam** ▪off 1418L61
▪**steam** ▫shovel 476L26 1418L54
▫**steam** *it* ▪up 1418L63/62
under *one's* ▫own ▪**steam** 1418L49
▫**steamed** ▪up 1418L67
▪paddle ▫**steamer** 1017R20
▫stainless ▪**steel** 1407R28
▫**steel** ▪band 1418R31
▫**steel** ▪drum 1418R28
▫**steel** ▪grey 1418R31
▪**steel** ▫mill 1418R32
▪**steel** *oneself* to 1418R44
▫**steel** ▪wool 1418R33
▫bum ▪**steer** 175L11
▪**steer** towards 1419L56
▫power(-assisted) ▪**steering** 1106R7
▪**steering** ▫column 1419L57
▪**steering** com▫mittee 1419L60
▪**steering** ▫wheel 1419L65
from ▫**stem** to ▪stern 1419R15
▪**stem** from 1419R24/25/27
▪**Sten** ▫gun 1419R57
a ▪spring in *one's* ▫**step** 1400L21
a ▫**step** at a ▪time 1420R13
a ▫**step** ▪backwards 1420R8
a ▫**step** ▪forward 1420R4
▫false ▪**step** 500L26
▪half ▫**step** 638L13/54 1291L63
▫mind/▫watch *one's* ▪**step** 1420L5
▫one **step** ▪forward ▫two steps ▪back 1420R9
▪**step** ae▫robics 1420L29
▫**step** ▪back 1420L40/41/42/R43/48/53
▫**step** by ▪step 1420R14/16
▫**step** ▪down as 1420R53
▫**step** ▪down/a▪side 1420L39/R50/55
▫**step** ▪forward 1420L44
▫**step** ▪in 1420R60
▫**step** into *someone's* ▪shoes 1319L55
▫**step** into the ▪breach 1420L53
▫**step** on 1420L48/R31/32
▫**step** on *someone's* ▪toes 1531L68
▫**step** ▪out 1420L49/51
▫**step** out of ▪line 1420L59
▫**step** ▪up 1420L53/80/R68
step ▪up a ▫gear 586L11
▫watch *one's* ▪**step** 1642L8
▪**stepping** ▫stone 1420L65
▫one step ▪forward ▫two **steps** ▪back 1420R9
re▫trace *one's* ▪**steps** 1216L42
▫personal ▪**stereo** 1053L14 1634R79
▫pound ▪**sterling** 1104L76
from ▫stem to ▪**stern** 1419R15
made of ▫**sterner** ▪stuff 1421R76
▫anabolic ▪**steroid** 43L33
▫Irish ▪**stew** 752L83
▫**stew** (in *one's* own ▪juice) 1422L50
▫shop ▪**steward** 1321L72
▪**stewing** ▫steak 1417R75
▫carrot-and-▪**stick** 198R51/55
▪cocktail ▫**stick** 253R50
▪fish ▫**stick** 526L83
▫French ▪**stick** 94L17 563R48
▪gear ▫**stick** 586L14
get (hold of) the ▫wrong end of the ▪**stick** 1692R73
▪joss ▫**stick** 769R25
▫more than you can shake a ▪**stick** at 1307R5
▫non-▪**stick** 959R41
▪pogo ▫**stick** 1088R69
▫poke/▫**stick** *one's* ▪nose into 962L41
▪shooting ▫**stick** 1320L48
▫**stick** a▪round 1423R20/21
▪**stick** at 1423R23
▫**stick** ▪by 1423R24
▫**stick** ▪down 1423L18
▪**stick** ▫figure 873L34 1422R66
stick *one's* ▫head above the ▪parapet 653R29
▫**stick** in *one's* ▪gullet 631R78
▪**stick**-in-the-▫mud 1423L51
▫**stick** in *one's* ▪throat/▪craw 1423L37
▫**stick** in your ▫pipe and ▪smoke it 1069R34
▪**stick** ▫insect 1422R69
▪**stick** into 1423L7/8/9/12
▪**stick** it 1424L14
▫**stick** *one's* ▪neck out 1423R76
▫**stick** *one's* ▪oar in 969R77
▫**stick** ▪out 1423R68 1424L3/10
▫**stick** out a ▪mile 896L38
stick ▫out like a sore ▪thumb 1377L17
▪**stick** ▫shift 586L15 1422R72
▫**stick** the ▪knife in/into 783R40/39
▪**stick** through 1423L13
▪**stick** to 1423L24/26/27/R29
▫**stick** to *one's* ▪guns 1423R36
▫**stick**-▪to-it-iveness 1423R56
▫**stick** to *someone's* ▪ribs 1423L39
▫**stick** to▪gether 1423L29/30/R40
stick two ▪fingers in the ▫air/▫up 1576L17
▫**stick** ▪up 1423L19 1424L17/23/26
▫**stick** *something* up *someone's* ▪ass 71L65
▫**stick** ▪up for 1424L29
▪**stick** with 1423L19/R43
▪swizzle ▫**stick** 1479L43
▫take a ▪**stick** to 1422R62
▫white ▪**stick** 1660R63
▪bill ▫**sticker** 126R5
▪price ▫**sticker** 1120R35
▪**sticker** ▫price 1423L70
▪**sticking** ▫plaster 1076R21 1423L41
▪**sticking** ▫point 1423L47
that's ▫my ▫story and I'm ▪**sticking** to it 1432L64
▫jolly ▪hockey **sticks** 769L21
▫mud ▪**sticks** 927R55
▪ski ▫**sticks** 1345R80
▫up ▪**sticks** 1422R64
▫come to/▫meet a **sticky** ▪end 1423R7
go through a ▫**sticky** ▪patch 1034R56
have ▫**sticky** ▪fingers 1423L79
▪**sticky** ▫tape 1290L56 1423R10
▫**sticky** ▪wicket 1423R11
as ▫**stiff** as a ▪ramrod 1171R63
▫bored ▪**stiff** 149L48
▫**stiff** ▪cheese 223L52
▫**stiff** upper ▪lip 1424L60
▫better ▪**still** 120R67
▫hold ▪**still** 676R22
▫**still** ▪life 1425L67
▫stock-▪**still** 1428R27
▫worse ▪**still** 1425L53
▪**stimulate** into 1425R45
▪**stimulate** to 1425R42
have a ▫**sting** in the/one's ▪tail 1426L24
▪**sting** for 1426L35
▪**sting** into 1426L14
▫take the ▪**sting** out of 1426L29
▪**stinging** ▫nettle 1426L15
▫cause a ▪**stink** 1426L80
▫create/▫kick up/▫raise a ▪**stink** 1426L82
▪**stink** ▫bomb 1426L67
▪**stink** of 1426L60/66
▫**stink** ▪out 1426L62
▪**stink** up 1426L63
▪**stinking** ▪rich 1426R14
▪**stint** on 1426R25
▫cause/cre▫ate a ▪**stir** 1427L12
▪**stir**-▫crazy 1427L47
▪**stir**-▫fry 1426R65/72
▪**stir** into 1426R63
▪**stir** to 1427L5
▫**stir** ▪up 1427L36/7
▪shit ▫**stirrer** 1318L1
▫**stirs** *someone's* ▪blood 1427L10
▪cable ▫**stitch** 182R14
▪chain ▫**stitch** 212L48
▪cross-▫**stitch** 327R47
▪running ▫**stitch** 1241R37
▪**stitch** *back* onto 1427R1
▫**stitch** to▪gether 1427R3
▫**stitch** ▪up 1427R5/7/20/23
have/▫keep *someone* in ▪**stitches** 1427R17
▫joint-**stock** ▪company 767R77
▪laughing ▫**stock** 800L36
▫lock **stock** and ▪barrel 835L17
▫put ▪**stock** in 1427R44
▪rolling ▫**stock** 1231L43
▪**stock** con▫trol 1427R51
▪**stock** ▫cube 1428L37
▪**stock** ex▫change 1428L7
▫**stock**-in-▪trade 1428L61
▪**stock** ▫market 1428L7
▪**stock** ▫route 1428L41
▫**stock**-▪still 1428R27
▫**stock** ▪up on/▪up with 1427R64
▫take ▪**stock** (of) 1427R47
▪**stockbroker** ▫belt 116R1 1428L23
▪body ▫**stocking** 142R77
▫Christmas ▪**stocking** 230R8
in *one's* ▫**stocking** ▪feet 1428L83
▪**stocking** ▫cap 142L72 1428L84
▪**stocking**-▫filler 1428R1
▪**stocking** ▫mask 1428R4
▪**stocking**-▫stuffer 1428R2
▫**stoke** ▪up 1429L8
▫**stoke** ▪up on/▪up with 1429L13
a ▫strong ▪**stomach** 1445R54
▪butterflies in *one's* ▫**stomach** 180L55
eyes too ▫big for *one's* ▪**stomach** 488R33
have ▫no ▪**stomach** for 1429L65/68
on a ▫full ▪**stomach** 572L48
on an ▫empty ▪**stomach** 452R59 1429L63
▫pit of *the/one's* ▪**stomach** 1070R56
▫sick to *one's* ▪**stomach** 1333L19/51
▪**stomach** ▫pump 1429L72
a ▪**stone's** ▫throw 1429R23
▫carved in ▪**stone** 200R71
▫dry **stone** ▪wall 429R71
▫fall/▫drop like a ▪**stone** 1429R20
foun▪dation ▫**stone** 556L74
get ▫blood out of a ▪**stone** 137L54
▫heart of ▪**stone** 656R73
▪kidney ▫**stone** 779R36
kill ▫two birds with one ▪**stone** 779R75
▫leave ▫no **stone** un▪turned 807L83
▪paving ▫**stone** 1037R53
▫precious ▪**stone** 1109R81
▫set/▫carved in (▫tablets of) ▪**stone** 1429R26
▫sink like a ▪**stone** 1341R42 1429R21
▪stepping ▫**stone** 1420L65
▪**Stone** ▫Age 1429R27
▫**stone**-▪broke 1429R73
▫**stone**-▪cold 1429R36
▫**stone**-cold ▪sober 1369R64 1429R39
▫**stone**-▪dead 1429R41
▫**stone**-▪deaf 1429R45
▪**stone**-▫ground 1429R47
▫**stone** the ▪crows 1429R56
▫**stone** to ▪death 1429R53
▫fall on ▫**stony** ▪ground 497R83
▫**stony** ▪broke 1429R73
pi▪ano ▫**stool** 1061L79
▪**stool** ▫pigeon 1430L68
▫fall between two ▪**stools** 497R66
▫**stoop** ▪down 1430L74
▪bus ▫**stop** 178L55
▫come to a full ▪**stop** 572R67
▪comfort ▫**stop** 267L73
▫full ▪**stop** 572R62/65
▫glottal ▪**stop** 601L77
▫non-▪**stop** 959R43
▫put a ▪**stop** to 1430R58
re▪quest ▫**stop** 1207L64
▪rest ▫**stop** 803L58 1212R9
▫**stop**-and-▪go 1430R39
▫**stop** a▪round/▪round 1431L24
▪**stop** at 1430R20 1431L16
▫**stop** at ▪nothing 1430R32
▫**stop** ▪by 1431L12
▫**stop**-▪go 1430R42
▫**stop** ▪in 1431L10/18
▫**stop** ▪off 1431L15
▫**stop** ▪over 1431L19
▫**stop** ▪press 1430R46
▫**stop** ▪short of 1430R36
▪**stop** ▫sign 1430R50
▫**stop** the ▪rot 1235L56
▫**stop** ▪up 1431L11
▪truck ▫**stop** 1552L11 1562R71
▫whistle-**stop** ▪tour 1660L52
▪**stoppage** ▫time 1430R75
▫pull out all the ▪**stops** 1144R1
▫cold ▪**storage** 256R34
▪**storage** ▫battery 10L76
▪**storage** de▫vice 1431R9
▪**storage** ▫heater 1431R11
▫army dis▪posals ▫**store** 63R34
▫army-▪navy ▫**store** 63R33
▪chain ▫**store** 212L76
de▪partment ▫**store** 367L58
▪discount ▫**store** 391R36
▫general ▪**store** 587L51
▪grocery ▫**store** 625L67
▪hardware ▫**store** 647R54 752R73
▪package ▫**store** 1016R59
▫put/▫set great/little ▪**store** 1431R33
▫**store** a▪way 1431L80
▪**store**-▫bought 1431L61
▪**store** ▫brand/▫label 1013L11
▪**store**-▫card 1431L64
▪**store** de▫tective 1431L67
var▪iety ▫**store** 1607L14
▫multi-▪**storey** 928R80/82
a ▫**storm** in a ▪teacup 1431R79
e▫lectric(al) ▪**storm** 446R17
▪**storm** ▫cloud 1431R82
▪**storm** ▫door/▫window 1432L3
▪**storm** into 1432L12
▪**storm** ▫lantern 695R5
▪**storm** ▫trooper 1432L35
▫take by ▪**storm** 1432L31
the ▫calm before/after the ▪**storm** 186R20
the ▫lull before the ▪**storm** 847L16
▫weather the ▪**storm** 1648L68
a ▪likely ▫**story** 823L26
an▫other ▪**story** 48L19
▫cock-and-▪bull ▫**story** 252R29
▪cover ▫**story** 316L50
▫end of ▪**story** 455L15
▪fairy ▫**story** 495R81 496L8
▪ghost ▫**story** 594L42
▫hard-▪luck ▫**story** 646R72
▪horror ▫**story** 686L13
it's the ▫**story** of *my* ▪life 1432L59
▪life ▫**story** 819L39
shaggy ▪dog ▫**story** 1307L23
▫short ▪**story** 1322L73
▪sob ▫**story** 1369R52
▪**story** ▫line 1432L65
suc▪cess ▫**story** 1454L72
▫tall ▪**story** 1489L51
that's ▫my ▫**story** and I'm ▪sticking to it 1432L64
the ▫same old ▪**story** 1253L45
to cut a ▫long **story** ▪short 339L57
▫true-life ▪**story** 1563R21
▫**stout**-▪hearted 1432R4
▫**stow** a▪way 1432R25/26
as ▫**straight** as a ▪die 1433L56
as ▫**straight** as a ▪ramrod 1171R63
set/put the ▪record ▫**straight** 1187L48
▫**straight** as a ▪pin 1432R78
▫**straight**-▪faced 1433L63
▪**straight** ▫man 1433L66
▫**straight** ▪razor 340R28
▫**straight** ▪up 1433L54/55
▫think ▪**straight** 1513L56
Repetitive ▪**Strain** ▫Injury 1204L55
▫**strain** after/for ef▪fect 1433R81/82
▫**strain** every ▪nerve 1433R79
▫**strain** ▪off 1434L11
▫**strain** the ▪truth 1433R84
▪tea ▫**strainer** 1494L31
▫**strangely** e▪nough 1434R8
hel▫lo ▪**stranger** 1434R26
▫**stranger** things have ▪happened 1434R3
▫**strangle** at ▪birth 1434R36
▪shoulder ▫**strap** 1325R80
strap ▪in 1434R71
strap ▪up 1434R73
▫draw/▫get the short ▪**straw** 1321R64
▫final ▪**straw** 1435R25
▫last ▪**straw** 1435R25
▫man of ▪**straw** 859L54/56 1435R7/10
▫**straw** ▪boater 1435R2
▫**straw** in the ▪wind 1435R32
▫**straw** ▪man 859L57 1435R6/10
▫**straw** ▪poll 1435R18
▫**straw** that breaks the camel's ▪back 1435R26
▫**strawberry** ▪blonde 1435R51/54
▪**strawberry** ▫mark 1435R55
▫clutch/▫grasp at ▪**straws** 1435L80
▫waifs and ▪**strays** 1633L35
like a ▫**streak** of ▪lightning 1436L14
▫**streak** a▪head 1436L54
▫**streak** ▪down 1436L50
▫**streak** ▪past 1436L51
▫**streak** ▪through 1436L48
▪**streak** with 1436L18/20/21
▫talk a ▫blue ▪**streak** 1488R2
go/move with the ▪**stream** 604L17
▪Gulf ▫**Stream** 631R61
▪jet ▫**stream** 762R75
▫**stream** ▪down 1436R21
▪**stream** from/into 1436R25/23
▫**stream** of ▪consciousness 1436R12
▫**stream** ▪out 1436R27
▫**stream** ▪through 1436R27
▫back ▪**street** 89R14
▫back-**street** a▪bortion 89R15
▪civvy ▫**street** 235L69
▪Downing ▫**Street** 416R78
▪Fleet ▫**Street** 533L38
▪Harley ▫**Street** 648L38
▪high ▫**street** 668R56/60
in the ▫same ▪**street** 1253L42
▫main ▪**street** 853R65
▫man/▫woman in the ▪**street** 1437L61
on ▪easy ▫**street** 439L12
▪**street**-▫cred 321R79 1437L38/45/37
▪**street** ▫furniture 1437L45
▪**street** ▫people 1437L48
▪**street** ▫smarts 1437L51
▪**street** ▫theatre 1437L54
▪**street** ▫value 1437L58
▫two-way ▪**street** 1576L69
▫up *someone's* ▪**street** 1437L33
▪Wall ▫**Street** 1635L58
▪**streets** a▫head of 1437L19
▫take to the ▪**streets** 1437L30
▫walk the ▪**streets** 1437L23/27
at ▫full ▪**strength** 1438L2
be▫low ▪**strength** 1437R83
▫give *me* ▪**strength** 1438L4
go from ▫**strength** to ▪strength 1437R39
▪tensile ▫**strength** 1500R77
▫tower of ▪**strength** 1543L81
▫**strep** ▪throat 1438L25
▫post-traumatic ▪**stress** dis▫order 1101L51
▪**stress** ▫management 1438L46
▪**stress** ▫mark 1438R5
▫**stress** ▪out 1438L62

at ▫full ▪stretch 1438R66
by ▫no stretch of the imagin▪ation 1438R69
▪home ▫stretch 680L34 1440L8/9
▫stretch a ▪point 1438R59
▫stretch a▪cross 1439L84
▫stretch a▪long 1439R65
▫stretch ▪back 1440L15/17
▪stretch for 1439R66
▪stretch from 1439R68 1440L18
▪stretch into 1440L20
▫stretch *one's* ▪legs 1439L77
▫stretch ▪limo 1438R27/28
▫stretch ▪out 1438R79/81/82/84 1439L76 1440L22
▫stretch the ▪length of 1439R72
▫stretch the ▪rules 1239R61
▪stretch to 1438R23/58 1439R68/70
▪stretcher-▫bearer 1440L39
▪strew with 1440L68/70/71
▪conscience-▫stricken 289L59
▪grief-▫stricken 623R59
▪horror-▫stricken 686L18
▪panic-▫stricken 1022L58
▪poverty-▫stricken 1105L25
▪terror-▫stricken 1505L15
in the ▫strictest ▪confidence 1440R36
▫strictly ▪speaking 1384R45 1440R57
get ▫into *one's* ▪stride 1441L6
▫hit *one's* ▪stride 1441L7
put *someone* ▫off *their* ▪stride 1154R73 1441L11
▫stride a▪cross 1440R78
▫stride ▪forward 1440R80 1441L25
▪stride ▫piano 1440R81
▫take in *one's* ▪stride 1441L14/15
▫first ▪strike 526L41
▫general ▪strike 587L55
▪hunger ▫strike 694R12/14
▪lightning ▫strike 822L31
▪rent ▫strike 1203R22
▫strike a ▪balance 1442R26
▫strike a ▪blow against/at/for 1441R1/4
▫strike a ▪chord 1442R34/54
▫strike a ▪match 872R25 1441R36
▫strike a ▪note 1441R44/46 1442R60/56
▫strike a raw ▪nerve/▪spot 1176R68 1540L76
▪strike about *something* 1441L69
▪strike *something* among 1442R37
▪strike as 1442R43
▪strike at 1441L73
▫strike at the ▪heart of 1441R21
▫strike ▪attitudes 1443L13
▪strike between 1442R30/33
▫strike ▪camp 1441R8
▫strike ▪dumb 431R57 1441R15
▫strike ▪fear/▪terror 1441R18
▪strike for 1442L18
▪strike from 1442L65
▫strike ▪home 1441R27
▫strike it ▪lucky 1442R8
▫strike it ▪rich 1442R10
▪strike ▪off 1442L67/69
▫strike ▪out 1441L74 1443L16/19/37
▪strike ▫pay 1442L42
▫strike ▪up 1443L50/55
strike while the ▪iron is ▫hot 1441R31
▪strike with 1442R36
▫wildcat ▪strike 822L31 1664R49
within ▪striking ▫distance 1441R39/42
another ▫string to *one's* ▪bow 1443R47
▪G-▫string 578L73
▫string a▪long 1444L13
▫string ▪bag 1443L82
▫string ▪bean 1443R2
▪string ▫instrument 1443R55/41/56
▫string ▪out 1443R77
▫string quar▪tet 1443R42
▪string ▫theory 1443R3
▫string to▪gether 1443R75
▫string ▪up 1443R7
▪apron ▫strings 59L45
▫pull ▪strings 1144R3
▫pull the ▪strings 1144R7
▪strings at▫tached 1443L78
the ▪purse ▫strings 1150L69
▫two strings to *one's* ▪bow 1443R47
▪stringy-▫bark 1443R22
car▪toon ▫strip 200R11 267R24
▪comic ▫strip 267R24
▪film ▫strip 519L52
▪landing ▫strip 30R14 794R14
▪median ▫strip 209L20 881R22
▫Möbius ▪strip 909R12
▪nature ▫strip 943L10
▪rumble ▫strip 1240L59 1389L19
▫strip a▪way 1444L59
▪strip ▫cartoon 267R24 1444R44
▪strip ▫club 1444R10
▫strip ▪down 1444R29/30
▪strip ▫joint 1444R10
▪strip ▫lighting 1444R44
▪strip ▫mining 1444R47
▪strip of 1444L53/60/62/R39
▫strip ▪off 1444L54/55/73/75
▫strip ▪poker 1444R14
▪strip-▫search 1444L82/R5
▫tear a ▪strip off 1495L8
▫tear *someone* ▪off a ▫strip 1495L8
▪candy-▫striped 189L83
▫Stars and ▪Stripes 1412R30
▪paint ▫stripper 1019L12 1444L68
▪asset-▫stripping 72R19/22
▪strive for/to 1444R84 1445L2/3/4
▪strobe ▫light 1445L6
▪butterfly ▫stroke 180L60
▪ground ▫stroke 626L73
▪heat ▫stroke 658L11
put *someone* ▫off *their* ▪stroke 1154R73 1441L11
the ▫stroke of a ▪pen 1445L25
take a ▫stroll down memory ▪lane 886L22
▫come on ▪strong 1445R30
▪strong-▫arm 1445R21
▪strong-▫box 1445R56
▫strong ▪language 1445R24
▫strong-▪minded 1445R69
▫strong ▪nerves 1445R54
▪strong ▫point 1445R26
▫strong ▪suit 1445R26
▫strong-▪willed 1445R72
▫something a little ▪stronger 1375L14
▫strongest ▪card 195L32
▪horror-▫struck 686L18
▪stage-▫struck 1406R34
▪struck by 1442R45
▫struck ▪down 1441R11 1442L69
▪terror-▫struck 1505L15
▪power ▫structure 1105R34
▪class ▫struggle 238L9
▪power ▫struggle 1105R38 1446R28
▪struggle for 1446R1/9/11
▫struggle ▪on 1446R4
▪struggle to 1446L81/82/83/R12/14
▪struggle with/against 1446R24/21/23/26
▫highly-▪strung 668L68
▫strung ▪up 1446R46
▫strut *one's* ▪stuff 1446R55/52
▫stub ▪out 1446R73
de▫signer ▪stubble 372L75
▫get ▪stuck into 1447L38
▫stuck in the ▪muck 1423L35
▫stuck-▪up 1447L45
▪press-▫stud 1118L35
▪stud-▫muffin 1447L56
▪star-▫studded 1412R41
▪day ▫student 349R34
e▫ternal ▪student 470L8
ex▪ternal ▫student 486R24
ma▪ture-age ▫student 875R58
ma▪ture ▫student 875R57
▫older ▪student 875R58
▫student ▪loan 1447R12
▫student ▪union 1447R16
▪women's ▫studies 1676L1
▪dance ▫studio 345L64
▪studio a▫partment 1447R29
▪studio ▫flat 1447R29
▪case ▫study 201L55
▫feasi▪bility ▫study 508R52
▪study ▫aid 1094L60
▪study for 1447R50
▪study under 1447R53
time-and-▪motion ▫study 1521R69
▫bit of ▪stuff 130L14
▪hard ▫stuff 647L57
▫hot ▪stuff 688L12/32
▪kid ▫stuff 779L72
▫know *one's* ▪stuff 787R10
made of ▫sterner ▪stuff 1421R76
▪sob-▫stuff 1369R57
▫strut *one's* ▪stuff 1446R55/52
▫stuff and ▪nonsense 1448L19
▫stuff ▪down 1448L29
▫get ▪stuffed 1448L40
▫stuffed ▪animal 1371R25
▫stuffed ▪shirt 1448L61
▫stuffed-▪up 1448L63
▪stocking-▫stuffer 1428R2
▫beat/▫kick/▫knock the ▪stuffing out of 1448L47
▫knock/▫take the ▪stuffing out of 1448L48
▫stumble a▪bout/a▪round 1448R23
▪stumble across/on/upon/onto 1448R31
▪stumble on 1448R15
▪stumble over 1448R29
▪stumble to 1448R20
▪stumbling ▫block 1448R17
▫stump ▪out 1448R50
▫stump ▪up 1448R60
▪stun ▫gun 1448R80
▪stunt ▫man/▫woman 1449L14
▪company/▪house ▫style 1449R46
▪ranch-style ▫house 1171R78
▪style *oneself* as 1450L19
▪sub for 1450L46
▫sub ▪judice 1451L54
▫subcon▪tract to 1450R23/25
subdi▪vide among 1450R40
▫subdi▪vide into 1450R38/40
▪subject to 1451L16/23/35
▪subjugate *oneself* to 1451L68/69
▪sublimate into 1451R2
from the sub▫lime to the ri▪diculous 1451R12
subma▪chine ▫gun 1451R30
▪submarine ▫sandwich 665L77
sub▪merge in 1451R45
sub▪mit to 1451R64/82/84
sub▪ordinate to 1452L16/26
sub▪poena *somebody* as/to 1452L41/40
sub▪scribe for/to 1452L49/51/52/54/67/56
sub▪sist by/on 1452R59/58
▪substance a▫buse 1452R84 1453L1
▪substitute for 1453L56/57/60/62/68
sub▪sume into 1453R8/9
sub▪sume under 1453R11
sub▪tract *something* from 1453R66/67
suc▪ceed *someone* as 1454R15
suc▪ceed in 1454L45/49/51
suc▪ceed to 1454R17
▫roaring suc▪cess 1229L2
suc▪cess ▫story 1454L72
suc▪cessor ▫state 1454R44
suc▪cumb to 1454R80/82/83 1455L1
▪ever ▫such 473L49
▫no such ▪luck 846L23/25
▫sink to such a ▪level 1341R75
▫sink to such ▪depth(s) 1341R75
▪such and ▫such 1455L52
▫such is ▪life 1455L39
there's ▫no such ▪thing as 1455L31
to ▫such an ex▪tent 486L49
▪suck at 1455L69/71
▫suck ▪dry of 1455L77
▫suck ▪in 1455R7
▪suck into 1455R5
▫suck ▪off 1455L78
▪suck on 1455L69/71
▫suck ▪up to 1455L80
teach *one's* ▫grandmother to ▫suck ▪eggs 1494L68
▪sucker into 1455R22
▪suction ▫cup 1455R66
▪sue for 1456L24/26/27
▫chop ▪suey 229R42
▫suffer a ▪relapse 1196L55
not suffer ▫fools ▪gladly 1456L79
▪suffer from 1456L45/46/47/77
▫suffer the ▪consequences 290L11
▫long-▪suffering 838R47
suf▪fuse with 1456R67/68/69
▪barley ▫sugar 100R12
▫brown ▪sugar 169L63
▪caster ▫sugar 202R37
con▪fectioners' ▫sugar 285L79
▪icing ▫sugar 700L44
▫lump of ▪sugar 847L84
▫sugar and ▪spice 1457L12
▪sugar ▫beet 1457L14
▪sugar ▫cane 1457L15
▪sugar-▫coat 1066R36
▫sugar-▪coated 252L39 1457L17/20
▪sugar ▫daddy 1457L23
▫sugar-▪free 1457L26
▪sugar ▫pea 860L66
▫sugar the ▪pill 1066R36
com▫mit ▪suicide 270L55
▪suicide ▫pact 1457R28
▪bathing ▫suit 104L74 1476R66
▪boiler ▫suit 144R9
▪counter-▫suit 312R64
▫follow ▪suit 543R1
▪jogging ▫suit 766R74
▫long ▪suit 838L49
▪lounge ▫suit 843L36
▪monkey ▫suit 915L19
▪morning ▫suit 918R52
▪romper ▫suit 1232R73
sa▪fari ▫suit 1248L55
▪sailor ▫suit 1249R59
▪shell ▫suit 1314R48
▫strong ▪suit 1445R26
▪suit ▫bag 583R48 1458L11
suit ▫right down to the ▪ground 1457R51
▪sweat ▫suit 1474R71
▫three-piece ▪suit 1515L75
▪trouser ▫suit 1562L84
wearing/in *one's* ▪birthday ▫suit 128R83
▪wet ▫suit 1654R17
▪bathroom ▫suite 104R16
de▪livery ▫suite 363L26
en ▪suite 460R17
▪living room ▫suite 832L41 1515L77
▫three-piece ▪suite 832L41 1515L76
sul▫furic ▪acid 1458R25
am▫monium ▪sulphate 41R41
▫barium ▪sul▫phate 100L61
▫sulphur-crested cocka▪too 1458R19
▫sulphur di▪oxide 1458R13
sul▫phuric ▪acid 1458R25
▫grand ▪sum 618L28
▫lump ▪sum 847R14
▫sum ▪total 1458R71
▫sum ▪up 1458R78 1459L11
▫British ▪Summer ▫Time 167L12
▫Indian ▪summer 721L56
▫summer ▪pudding 1459L63
▪summer ▫school 1459L56/59
▪summon to 1459R20
▪sumo ▫wrestler 1459R33/39
have *one's* ▪sums ▫wrong 1458R61
▫catch the ▪sun 204L79
▫Land of the Midnight ▪Sun 794L49
▫Land of the Rising ▪Sun 794L54
make ▫hay while the ▪sun shines 652R28
▫midnight ▪sun 894R50
▫place in the ▪sun 1073R52
▪sun-▫baked 1459R63
▪sun-▫drenched 1459R67
▫sun-▪dried 1459R69
▪sun-▫god 1459R73
▪sun-▫hat 1459R74
▪sun-▫kissed 1459R75
▪sun-up 1459R80 1461L3
▪sun ▫visor 1459R81
▫under the ▪sun 1459R61
▫Easter ▪Sunday 438R20
▫Palm ▪Sunday 1020R54
Re▫membrance ▪Sunday 1201R47
▫Sunday ▪best 1460L80
▫Sunday ▪driver 1460L82
▪Sunday ▫school 1460L83
a ▫month of ▪Sundays 916L55
▫sunk in ▪thought 1341R78
▫ray of ▪sunshine 1176R81
▪sup on/off 1461L83
▫sup ▪up 1461L78
▪Super ▫Bowl 1461R8
▫superim▪pose on 1462R6
▫superim▪pose over 1462R7
superi▪ority ▫complex 1462R56
▫supermarket ▪tabloid 1463L24
▫super▪sede as 1463R28
▫Last ▪Supper 797R70
▫Lord's ▪Supper 841R26
▪colour ▫supplement 259R56
▪supplement with 1464R5
▫supplementary ▪angle 1464R18
▪supplicate for 1464R24
▪supplicate from 1464R23
law of ▫supply and de▪mand 801L82 1464R67
▪money ▫supply 913R45
sup▪ply ▫teacher 1464R70
sup▪ply to 1464R44
sup▪ply with 1464R47/48
▪water sup▫ply 1642R34
ath▫letic sup▪port 76L35 766R13
▫canvass sup▪port 18L14 54L21 132R68 198L73 326L45 337L50 546R83 547L4/10 782R37/38 1038L49
▫income sup▪port 717L48
▫life-sup▪port system 819L80/83
▫moral sup▪port 917R32
sup▪port ▫group 1465L61
sup▪port *someone* in 1465L53/54
sup▪port ▫system/▫network 1465L64
sup▫porting ▪cast 202L66
▫white ▪supremacy 1661L20/22
make the su▫preme ▪sacrifice 1247R20
Su▫preme ▪Being 1466R48
▪surcharge on 1467L2/4
make ▪sure 855R3
▫sure e▪nough 1467L66
▫sure ▪thing 1467L48
▫slowly but ▪surely 1356L2 1467L77
▫surely to ▪God/▪goodness 1467L82
▫air-to ▪surface 29R14
▫scratch beneath the ▪surface 1271R42
▫scratch/▫scrape the ▪surface 1468L3
▫surface ▪tension 1468L8
▫surface-to-▪air 1468L12
▫surface-to-▪surface 1468L15
▪work ▫surface 1679R19 1683R27
▪dental ▫surgeon 366R20
▫Surgeon ▪General 1468L78
▫veterinary ▪surgeon 1619R51 1620L5
cos▫metic ▪surgery 308R80
▫keyhole ▪surgery 778R13
▫open-▫heart ▪surgery 987R36
▫plastic ▪surgery 1076R61
▫spare-part ▪surgery 1383L75
▫surgical ▪spirit 1468R20
▫army ▪surplus 63R29
sur▫prise sur▪prise 1469L47
▫take by sur▪prise 1486R62
sur▪render to 1469R24/26
the ▫Ordnance ▪Survey 995L3
▪quantity sur▫veyor 1158R43
▫lord/▫master/▫mistress/▫king/▫queen of all *one* sur▪veys 1470L78
sur▪vival ▫kit 1470R52
sur▫vival of the ▪fittest 1470R55
sur▪vive on 1470R23
▫lazy ▪Susan 803R25
su▪spect of 1471L57
su▪spend between 1472L11
su▪spend from 1471R70/71 1472L8/10
su▪spend in 1472L17/18
su▫spended ani▪mation 1471R72
su▪spender ▫belt 1472L31
su▪spension ▫bridge 164L32 1472L21
▫suss ▪out 1472L65/67
▫crêpe su▪zette 323L20
▫swab ▪out 1472R71
▪swaddle in 1472R78
▫swagger a▪bout 1473L5
▫hard to ▪swallow 646L78
▪swallow ▫dive 1473L72
▫swallow *one's* ▪pride 1473L53
▫swallow the ▪bait 1473L35
▫swallow *one's* ▪words 1473L61
▪swamp with 1473R12/14
▫mute ▪swan 933R9
▫swan a▪round 1473R31
▪swan ▫dive 1473L73/R24
▫swan ▪off 1473R32
▪swank about 1473R38
▪swap for 1473R67/68/70/72
▫swap ▫horses in mid▪stream 686L43
▪swap ▫meet 193R20 1474L3
▫swap ▪over/▪round 1473R76
▪swap with 1473R65
▪wife ▫swapping 1664L26
▪swarm with 1474L16/17
▫cut a ▪swath through 338R75
▪swathe in 1474L57/58
▫hold ▪sway 676R77
▪sway into 1474L71
▪swear at 1474R2
▫swear ▪blind 1474R26
▫swear ▪in 1474R16
▫swear ▪off 1474R30
▪swear on 1474R14
▪swear ▫word 1474R2
▫cold ▪sweat 256R35
no ▪sweat 956R77
▪sweat ▫band 1474R67
▫sweat ▪blood 1474R43
▫sweat ▪bullets 1474R46
▪sweat ▫glands 1474R70
▫sweat *one's* ▪guts out 633R14 1474R44
▪sweat ▫suit 1474R71
▪sweat with 1474R37/43
make a ▫clean ▪sweep 241L81/82
▫sweep a▪long 1475L53
▫sweep a▪side 1475L42/44
▫sweep a▪way/a▪long 1475L37/46
▫sweep ▪back 1475L37 1476R1
▪sweep into 1475L18/38/39/56
▫sweep *someone* off *their* ▪feet 1475L48
▫sweep ▪out 1475L18
▫sweep ▪over 1475L54
▫sweep the ▪board 1475R6
▫sweep ▪through 1475L57/59
▫sweep under the ▪carpet/under the ▪rug/under the ▪mat 1475L21
▫sweep ▪up 1475L20/39
▪carpet ▫sweeper 198L68
▫boiled ▪sweet 144L72
▪cough ▫sweet 311L13
▫keep *someone* ▪sweet 1475R40
▫short and ▪sweet 1322R77
▫sweet-and-▪sour 1475R45
▫sweet ▪chestnut 1475R48
▫sweet f ▪a 1475R51
▫sweet ▫fanny ▪adams 1475R51
▫sweet ▪nothings 1475R53
▫sweet ▪pea 1475R55
▫sweet ▪pepper 1475R56
▫sweet po▪tato 1475R57
▪sweet ▫shop 1475R82
▪sweet-▫talk 1475R59/64
▫sweet ▪tooth 1475R65
▫sweeten the ▪pill 1066R36
▪sweetheart a▫greement 1476L41
▪sweetheart ▫deal 1476L40
▫sweetness and ▪light 1476L26
▫swelled ▪head 1479L51
▪swerve from 1476R9
▪swerve into 1476R7
▫swill ▪out 1476R37
▫sink or ▪swim 1341R40
▫swim against/with the ▪tide 1519L24/25
▫swim with the ▪current 337L9
▪swimming ▫bath(s) 1476R70
▪swimming ▫costume 1476R64
▪swimming ▫pool 1094R14 1476R69
▪swimming ▫trunks 1476R75 1565L4
▫synchronized ▪swimming 1481L78
▫one-piece ▪swimsuit 984R24

▪**swindle** from 1477L14
cast ▫pearls before ▪**swine** 202L41
▪**swine** ▫fever 1477L29
get ▫into the ▪**swing** of it/things 1477L84
go with a ▪**swing** 1477L82
in ▫full ▪**swing** 572L76
▪**swing** at 1477L43/63
▪**swing** between 1477L44
▪**swing** ▫bridge 1477L54
▫**swing** ▪door 1477L57
▪**swing** for 1477R23/28
▫**swing** into ▪action 1477L47
▪**swing** it 1477R23
▫**swing** ▪round 1477L40/42
▫**swing** the ▪balance 1477L50
▫**swing** *one* ▪up 1477L37
▪**swipe** at 1477R37/41/42
▪**swipe** *someone* round 1477R38
▫**swirl** a▪cross 1477R53
▫**swirl** a▪round 1477R52/53
Swiss ▪army ▫knife 1477R75
▫**Swiss** ▪roll 1477R77
▪dip-▫**switch** 386L49
▪master ▫**switch** 871R32
▪**switch** *something* for 1479L8
▪**switch** from/to 1478L74/R79/81/83 1479L1/2
▫**switch** ▪off/▪on 1478L75/76
▫**switch** ▪over 1478L76 1479L1
▪**switch** with 1479L6
▪time ▫**switch** 1522R35/52
▪trip ▫**switch** 1558R25
▪**switchboard** ▫operator 1479L28
▫**swivel** ▪round 1479L34/35
▪**swizzle** ▫stick 1479L43
▫**swollen** ▪head 1479L55/50
▪**swoon** over 1479L62
▪**swoon** with 1479L61
at/with ▫one fell ▪**swoop** 511R29
▫**swoop** ▪down 1479L74/78
▪**swoop** on 1479L75
▫double-edged ▪**sword** 414L46
▫put to the ▪**sword** 1479R4
▫**sword** of ▪Damocles 1479R5
beat/turn ▫**swords** into ▪ploughshares 1479R9
▫cross ▪**swords** with 327R31
▫**sworn** ▪enemies 1479R27
▪**swot** for 1479R33
▫**swot** ▪up 1479R34
in words of ▫one ▪**syllable** 1678R5
▪nonsense ▫**syllable** 960L84
▪sex ▫**symbol** 1303R65
▪status ▫**symbol** 1416L83
▫come out in ▪**sympathy** with 1480R45
▪**sympathy** ▫vote 1480R9
▫tea and ▪**sympathy** 1494L6
with▪drawal ▫**symptoms** 1673R19
▪lip-▫**sync(h)** 828R47
▪**synchronize** with 1481L72
▫**synchronized** ▪swimming 1481L78
▫chronic fa▪tigue ▫**syndrome** 877R18
decom▪pression ▫**syndrome** 356L6
▪Down's ▫**syndrome** 417L35
Tour▪ette's ▫**syndrome** 1542L51
▫corn ▪**syrup** 306L33
▫golden ▪**syrup** 610L23
▫maple ▪**syrup** 863R68
a ▫shock to the ▪**system** 1318R7
▫central ▪nervous ▫**system** 209L17
▫criminal ▪justice ▫**system** 324L76
▫Dewey ▪decimal ▫**system** 379L12
di▪gestive ▫**system** 383R48
▪disk ▫operating ▫**system** 395L3
early ▪warning ▫**system** 436R51
▪expert ▫**system** 482R10
▪frontal ▫**system** 568R30
get *something* ▫out of *one's* ▪**system** 1482R24
im▪mune ▫**system** 706R54
▫life-sup▪port **system** 819L80/83
▪midi ▫**system** 894R32
▪mini-▫**system** 900L67
▪music ▫**system** 931L57
▪nervous ▫**system** 949L38
▪operating ▫**system** 989L52
re▪spiratory ▫**system** 1211L70
▪solar ▫**system** 1372R6
▪sound ▫**system** 1378R44
▪stack ▫**system** 1405R42
sup▪port ▫**system** 1465L64
▪**systems** ▫analyst 1482R59
▫**ta**-▪**ta** 1492R75
▫pick up the ▪**tab** 1062R4 1483L32
▪pull-▫**tab** 1144R28 1225L33
▫wait (at/on) ▪**table(s)** 1633R41/42
▫bedside ▪**table** 111R71
▪bird ▫**table** 128L67
▪coffee ▫**table** 255L9
▪coffee-**table** ▫book 255L11
▪dining ▫**table** 385L74
▪dinner ▫**table** 385R52
▪dressing ▫**table** 422L66
▫drink *someone* under the ▪**table** 424R18
▫drop-leaf ▪**table** 427R47
▪gaming ▫**table** 581R32
▫high ▪**table** 668R63
keep a ▫good ▪**table** 1483L59
▫lay/▫set the ▪dining/▪kitchen ▫**table** 1483L61
multipli▪cation ▫**table** 929R7
▪night ▫**table** 111R71 955L34/35
▪operating ▫**table** 989R37
peri▫odic ▪**table** 1049L70
▫put/▫lay *one's* ▫cards on the ▪**table** 195L36
▫round-▪**table** 1236R3
▫set a ▫good ▪**table** 1483L60
▫**table** ▪d'hôte 1483R53
▪**table** ▫fork 1483L63
▪**table** ▫knife 1483L63
▪**table** ▫lamp 1483L64
▪**table** ▫linen 826R80 1483L65
▪**table** ▫manners 1483L70
▪**table** ▫mat 1483L67
▪**table** ▫tennis 1483L71
▪**table** ▫wine 1483L73
▪tide-▫**table** 1519L26
▪trestle ▫**table** 1556L41
▫under the ▪**table** 1483L57
▪water ▫**table** 1642R37
▫turn the ▪**tables** 1569R58
▪sleeping ▫**tablet** 1351R13
▫supermarket ▪**tabloid** 1463L24
▫keep ▪**tabs** on 1483L36
▪Blu-▫**Tack** 141L18
▫change ▪**tack** 215L14
set/go/start off on a ▫different ▪**tack** 1484L83
▫**tack** ▪down 1484L77
▪**tack** ▫room 1484R64
▪**tack** to 1484L76/R58
▫tick-**tack**-▪toe 965L2 1518R83
▫block and ▪**tackle** 136R26
▪**tackle** about 1484R75
get down to ▫brass ▪**tacks** 158L68
▫spit ▪**tacks** 1393R44
▪shock ▫**tactics** 1318R17
▪dog ▫**tag** 408R74
▪luggage ▫**tag** 846R27
▪price ▫**tag** 1120R37 1485L62
▫**tag** a▪long with/after/behind 1485L83/81
▪**tag** ▫day 529L38
▪**tag** for 1485L69
▫**tag** ▪on 1485R1/2/4
a couple of/two ▫shakes (of a duck's/lamb's ▪**tail**) 1307R14
▫chase *one's* ▪**tail** 219R21
go off/away with *one's* ▫**tail** between *one's* ▪legs 1485R29
have a ▫sting in the/one's ▪**tail** 1426L24
▫nose to ▪**tail** 962L65
▫piece of ▪**tail** 1064R56
▪pony-▫**tail** 1094L52
▫**tail** a▪way/▪back 1485R36/33
▪**tail** ▫coat 1485R16
▫**tail** ▪end of 1485R15
▪**tail** ▫lights 1485R20
▪**tail** ▫wind 1485R21
the ▫**tail** wagging the ▪dog 1485R29
▫turn ▪**tail** 1569R63
bright-▫eyed and bushy-▪**tailed** 165L69
▪**tailor** *something* for 1485R71
▫**tailor**-▪made 1485R64/68/73
▫cat-o'-▪nine-▫**tails** 203L69
▪coat-▫**tails** 252L13
▫heads or ▪**tails**? 654L23
allow ▫nature to/let ▫nature **take** its ▪course 943L6
can ▫dish it ▪out but *you* ▫can't ▪**take** it 394L24
▫double ▪**take** 414R2
▫give-and-▪**take** 596R58/61
▫give or ▪**take** 596R48
▫hard to ▪**take** 646R43
have/▫**take** a ▪dekko 361R22
have/▫**take** a ▪gander 581R59
have *or* ▫**take** a ▪squint at *something* 1404R6
if you ▫**take** my ▪meaning 878L44 1486L83
not **take** a ▫blind bit of ▪notice 135L69
not ▫**take** ▪kindly to 780R13
▪piss-▫**take** 1070L63/65
sit ▫up and **take** ▪notice 1343R62
▫**take** a ▪breather 162R84
▫**take** a ▪dump 432L42
▫**take** a ▪hike 669R79
▫**take** a ▪joke 1486L61
take a ▫leaf from/out of *someone's* ▪book 805L47
▫**take** a ▪leak 805R27
take a ▫long hard ▪look at 840L9
▫**take** a ▪pew 1056R11
take a ▪rain ▫check 1169R69
take a ▪rise ▫out of 1226R51
▫**take** a running ▪jump 1241L52
▫**take** a ▪seat 1278L40
▫**take** a ▪shine to 1316L82
▫**take** a ▪stick to 1422R62
take a ▫stroll/▫trip/▫walk down memory ▪lane 886L22
take a/the ▫back ▪seat 89L84
take a/the ▪fall for 497R5
▫**take** a ▪toll 1533L70
take a ▫turn for the ▪worse 1570L66
▫**take** *someone* a▪back 1R48
▪**take** ▫after 1487L70
▫**take** a▪gainst 1487L73
▫**take** a▪miss 41R30
▫**take** a▪part 1487L42
▫**take** as ▪read 1178R39
take at ▫face ▪value 490R81
▫**take** *someone* at *their* ▪word 1679L37
▫**take** a▪way 1486L13/14
▫**take** *it* ▪back 1486L79/80/81/R47/60
take *someone's* ▪breath a▫way 162R46
▫**take** by ▪storm 1432L31
▫**take** ▪care 196L59/R9/11/12
▫**take** ▪care of *oneself* 196L59/48/54
take ▫centre ▪stage 1406R14
take ▫coals to ▪Newcastle 251R11
▫**take** ▪cognizance of 255L75
▫**take** ▪comfort from 267L67
▫**take** *one's* ▪cue from 333R74/78
▫**take** *someone* ▪down a ▫peg (or two) 1043L72
▫**take** down the ▪aisle 30R61
▫**take** ▪down/▪up 1485R48/50 1487L47
▫**take** ex▪ception (to) 476R2
▫**take** *one's* ▪eyes off 488L79
▫**take** *someone's* ▪fancy 501R83
▫**take** ▪five 528L26
▫**take** ▪flight 534L73
▪**take** *somebody* ▫for 1173L64 1486L69/R59 1487L11
▫**take** for a ▪ride 1222L54
▫**take** for ▪granted 619L20/25
▫**take** ▪fright 566L1
▪**take** from 1317R56 1486L17/18 1487R55
▫**take** *one's* ▪hat off to 649R69
▫**take** ▪heart 657L20
▫**take** ▪hold 1486R25
▪**take**-home ▫pay 1486R64
▪**take** ▪in 641R47 1486R3/63 1487L76/83/R1/4
▫**take** in *one's* ▪stride 1441L14/15
▫**take** ▪interest in 1487L22
▫**take** into ac▪count 9R79
▫**take** into ▪care 196L62
▫**take** *someone* into *one's* ▪confidence 286L11
▫**take** *something* into *one's* ▪head 654L7
▫**take** ▪issue ▫with 755R28
▪**take** it 1486L58/R5
▫**take** it ▪easy 439L6 589L11
▫**take** it from ▪me 1486R8
▫**take** it ▪gently 589L10
▫**take** it in ▪turns 1570R22
▫**take** it on the ▪chin 227L15
▫**take** it or ▪leave it 1486R10
▫**take** it ▪out of 1486L26
▫**take** it/things ▪easy 439L3/4
▫**take** ▪leave 807R66
take ▫leave of *one's* ▪senses 807R70 1292R64
▫**take** ▪liberties with 816R77/79
▫**take** *one's* (own) ▪life 819L7
▫**take** *one's* ▫life in *one's* ▪hands 819L8
▫**take** ▪long 1486R80
▫**take** *one's* ▪lumps 847R12
▫**take** lying ▪down 818L40 1486L57
take matters into *one's* ▪own ▫hands 874R46
▫**take** *someone's* ▪mind off 898R78
▫**take** ▪note of 963R37
▫**take** ▪notice 964R1 1487L23
▫**take** ▪off 248R4 1486L18/20/21/22/23/24 1487R8/15/18/23
▫**take** off-▪guard 976L68
▫**take** (up) ▪office 1486R37
▫**take** ▪on 1487R26/34/38 1488L4
▫**take** on ▪board 141R48/49/50/51/45
▫**take** on ▪trust 1565L54
take ▫one (thing) at a ▪time 1487L17
▫**take** ▪out 424R80 1486L24/R57 1487R40
▫**take** ▪over 1487R49
▫**take** ▪pains 1018R42
▫**take** ▪place 1073R53
▫**take** ▪prisoner 1123R45
▫**take** ▪root 1233R50/52
▫**take** *one's* ▪seat 1278L44
▫**take** ▪sides 1334L22
▫**take** ▪silk 1337R54
▫**take** some ▪beating 109R18
▫**take** ▪stock (of) 1427R47
▫**take** *someone's* ▪temperature 1499L25
take the ▫bad with the ▪good 92L53
take the ▫bit between *one's* ▪teeth 130L27
take the ▫bull by the ▪horns 174L51
▫**take** the ▪chill off 226R23
▫**take** the ▪consequences 290L11
▫**take** the ▪edge off 441L72/73
▫**take** the ▪floor 536R48/50
take the ▫gilt off the ▪gingerbread 595L55
▫**take** the ▪heat off 657R71
take the ▫law into *one's* own ▪hands 801L37
▫**take** the ▪liberty of 816R74
▫**take** the ▪lid off 817R47
▫**take** the ▪measure of 879R32
▫**take** the ▪piss (out of) 1070L57
▫**take** the ▪place of 1073L82
▫**take** the ▪pledge 1081L68
▫**take** the ▪plunge 1085L37
▫**take** the ▪prize for 1124R30
▫**take** the ▪roll 1231R67
take the ▫rough with the ▪smooth 1235R68
▫**take** the ▪running 1241R67
▫**take** the sa▪lute 1252L18
▫**take** the ▪stage 1406R10
▫**take** the ▪sting out of 1426L29
▫**take** the ▪stuffing out of 1448L48
▫**take** the ▪time to 1486R83
▫**take** the ▪veil 1611L39/43
▫**take** the ▪view that 1487L26
take the ▪weight off *one's* ▫feet/▫legs 1650L11
take the ▪wind out of *someone's* ▫sails 1666R79
take the ▫words out of *someone's* ▪mouth 1678R13
▫**take** the ▪wraps off 1689R6
▫**take** things ▪easy 1512L66
▫**take** ▪time 1486R82/84 1487L3 1521R21/58
▫**take** to ▪drink 424L77
▫**take** to *one's* ▪heels 660L36
take to *something* like a ▫duck to ▪water 430R25
▫**take** to ▪task 1492L58
▫**take** to the ▪bottle 151R53
▫**take** to the ▪cleaner's 239R60/62
▫**take** to the ▪road 1228L46
▫**take** to the ▪streets 1437L30
▫**take** ▪turns 1570R21
▫**take** ▪umbrage 1578R35
▫**take** una▪wares/by sur▪prise 1486R62
▫**take** under *one's* ▪wing 1669L14
▫**take** ▪up 1486R51 1487R76 1488L1/5
▫**take** up (the) ▪cudgels 333L81
▫**take** *someone* ▪up on 977L51 1488L9
▫**take** up the ▪slack 1348L65
▫**take** ▪up ▫with 36R5 196R7 1486R45 1488L3/7/8/12
▫**take** with a ▫pinch of ▪salt 1068L45
▫**take** ▪years ▫off 1695R64
▫**take** your ▪pick 1062L30
▫vertical ▪**take**-off 1615R62
▫point ▪**taken** 1089R2 1486L64
▫**taken** ▪short 1322R69
▪**taken** with/by 1488L22
make a ▪**takeover** ▫bid 1487R60
▫winner-**takes**-▪all 1666R39
▪leave-▫**taking** 807R68
▪**talcum** ▫powder 1105L51 1488L27
▫cautionary ▪**tale** 206R78
▪fairy ▫**tale** 495R81 496L8
▪folk ▫**tale** 543L17
▫live to tell the ▪**tale** 831R66
▫old ▪wives' ▫**tale** 980L18
▫**tale** of ▪woe 1488L35 1675L66
▪tattle-▫**tale** 1493L1
▪tell-▫**tale** 1493L2 1498L47
▫thereby hangs a ▪**tale** 1510L63
▪**talent** ▫contest 1488L51
▪**talent** ▫scout 1488L53
▪**talent** ▫spotter 1488L53
▫tell ▪**tales** 1498L34
▫all ▪**talk** 33R41
▪baby ▫**talk** 88R24
▪back ▫**talk** 89L22 90L47
▪double-▫**talk** 414R5
▫fast-▪**talk** 505R47
▫fighting ▪**talk** 517L82
▫give a ▪**talk** 1488R44
give *someone* ▫something to ▪**talk** about 1488R28
▫just ▪**talk** 1488R52
▪pep ▫**talk** 1046R56
▪pillow ▫**talk** 1067L5
▪sales ▫**talk** 1250R80
▪small ▫**talk** 1358L26
▪sweet-▫**talk** 1475R59/64
▫**talk** a ▫blue ▪streak 1488R2
▪**talk** a▫bout 1488L73/74/76/R44
▫**talk** a▪round 1489L31
▫**talk** *one's* ▪ass off 71L63/64
▪**talk** at 1488R75
▫**talk** ▪back 48L67 1488R78
▫**talk** ▪dirty 1488R4
▫**talk** ▪down 1488R81 1489L1/5
▫**talk** *one's* ▪head off 1488R5
▫**talk** in ▪riddles 1222L1
▪**talk** in ▫terms of 1504L2
▫**talk** ▫into 1489L9
▫**talk** ▪nonsense/▪rubbish 1488R8
▫**talk** of the ▪devil 378L47
▫**talk** ▪out 1489L13
▫**talk** out of ▪turn 1570R26
▫**talk** ▪over 1488L79 1489L23
▫**talk** ▪round 1489L27/31
▫**talk** ▪sense 1488R15
▪**talk** ▫show 1488R55/60
talk the ▫hind leg(s) off a ▪donkey 1488R7
▫**talk** the same ▪language 795L82
▫**talk** through *one's* ▪hat/▪neck 1488R18
▪**talk** to/with 1488L67/69/70/R42 1489L25/29
▫**talk** ▪turkey 1488R23
▫**talk** ▪up 1489L80
the ▫**talk** of the ▪town 1488R50
▪you're a ▫fine one to ▫**talk** 1488R25
▫fast-▪**talker** 505R49
▫walkie-▪**talkie** 1634R75
▫know what *one is* ▪**talking** about 786R52 787R15
▫look who's ▪**talking** 1488R24
▫set *someone* ▪**talking** 1488R29
▫**talking** ▪book 1488R30
▪**talking** ▫point 1488R32
▪**talking** ▫shop 1488R15
▫stand/▫walk ▪**tall** 1489L47
▫**tall** ▪order 1489L49
▫**tall** ▪story 1489L51
▫keep a/the ▪**tally** 1489L66/65/64
▫**tally**-▪ho 1489L72
▪**tally**-▫room 1489L67
▫**tally** ▪up 1489L71
▪**tally** ▫with 1489L60
▪**tamper** ▫with 1489R23
▫**tan** *someone's* ▪hide 1489R42
▫**tan** the ▪hide ▫off 1489R43
fly/go ▫off at/on a ▪**tangent** 1489R70/69/68
▪**tangle** with 1490L16
▫anti-▪**tank** 50L52
▪fish ▫**tank** 526R6 1490L31
▫septic ▪**tank** 1295L52
▪**tank** ▫top 1490L57
▪think ▫**tank** 1513L66
▪water ▫**tank** 1642L84
▫**tanked** ▪up 1490L47
▪oil ▫**tanker** 979L33 1490L53
▫**tannic** ▪acid 1490L62
▪**tanning** ▫bed 1460L29
▪mixer ▫**tap** 908R5
▪**tap** against 1490R37
▫**tap** a▪way 1490R42
▪**tap** for 1490R54
▪**tap** ▫water 1490R30
▫digital ▪audio ▫**tape** 383R75
▪friction ▫**tape** 738R9
▪insulating ▫**tape** 738R8
mag▫netic ▪**tape** 852R69
▪masking ▫**tape** 870L43
▫red ▪**tape** 1189L31
▫Scotch ▪**tape** 1269R32 1290L56/63
▪sticky ▫**tape** 1290L56 1423R10
▪**tape** ▫deck 1491L19
▪**tape** ▫measure 1490R82
▪**tape** re▫corder 1491L22
▪**tape** to/on/onto 1491L5
▪ticker-**tape** pa▫rade 1518R38
▫have *someone* ▪**taped** 1491L30
▫**taper** ▪off 1491L37/39
▫life's rich ▪**tapestry** 818R75
▪phone-▫**tapping** 1058R13 1490R62
▪wire-▫**tapping** 1670R62
▫beat/▫knock/▫whale the ▪**tar** out of 1491L65
▪coal ▫**tar** 251R28
▫**tar** with the same ▪brush 1491L70
▫dead on ▪**target** 351L14
▫sitting ▪**target** 1343L65
▫soft ▪**target** 1371R84
▪**target** at/on 1491R15/17/20
▪**target** ▫language 1491R30
▫custard ▪**tart** 338L38
▫**tart** ▪up 1492L10
▫cream of ▪**tartar** 321L53
▪**tartar** ▫sauce 1492L34
▫steak **tar**▪**tare** 1417R72
▪**tartare** ▫sauce 1492L34
tar▫**taric** ▪acid 1492L28
▫take to ▪**task** 1492L58
▪**task** ▫force 1492L48
▫multi-▪**tasking** 928R83
a ▫**taste** of *one's* own ▪medicine 882L43/54
▫leave a bad/a sour/an unpleasant ▪**taste** 807L69
▪**taste** ▫buds 1492L84
▪**taste** of 1492L71/72/R11
▫tit for ▪**tat** 1527R7/15
▪**tattle**-▫tale 1493L1
▪tittle-▫**tattle** 1529L38
tat▪**too** ▫artist 1493L13
tat▪**too** on 1493L10
▫indirect **tax**▪**(ation)** 722L54
be▫fore ▪**tax**/▫after ▪**tax** 1493L78

corporation tax 307L61
death tax 352R9
direct tax 386R65
income tax 717L51 1493L83
inheritance tax 729R46
road tax 1228L55
sales tax 1250R82
sin tax 1340L51
tax allowance 34R72 1493L81
tax assessment/bill 1493L82
tax-deductible 357L8 1493L84
tax disc 1493R1
tax exile 1493R5
tax haven 1493R6
tax relief 1493R7
tax return 1493R9
tax shelter 1493R11
tax year 1493L84
withhold tax 1673R75
water taxi 1642R38
afternoon tea 1493R83
cream tea 321L56
for all the tea in China 1494L4
green tea 622R38
herbal tea 663R18 1527L26
high tea 668R65
not *someone's* cup of tea 335L78
shower tea 1329L9
tea and sympathy 1494L6
tea bag 1494L8
tea ball 1494L12
tea break 1494L10
tea caddy 182R67 1494L14
tea chest 1494L15
tea cloth 1494L32
tea cosy 1494L18
tea garden 1494L20
tea-house 1494L23
tea party 1494L24
tea room/shop 1494L26
tea service/set 1494L28
tea strainer 1494L31
tea towel 1494L32
tea tray 1494L34
tea trolley 1494L36 1560L7
tea wagon 1494L36
teach a lesson 812L18 1494L57
teach *one's* grandmother to suck eggs 1494L68
teach school 1494L56
teach *someone* the ropes 1234L78
parent-teacher association 1026L58
parent-teacher organization 1026L59
supply teacher 1464R70
teacher's college 1494L75/74
teacher's pet 1055R9 1494L76
teacher-training college 1494L74
remedial teaching 1201L78
a storm in a teacup 1431R79
pass over teakettle 65L29 1494R10
double-team 414R9
team effort 1494R24
team game 1494R19
team-mate 1494R20
team up 1494R33/35/30
team work 1494R27
a tempest in a teapot 1431R80
tear a strip off 1495L8
tear at *someone's* heart 1495L20
tear down 1495L14
tear gas 1494R55
tear *one's* hair out over 1495L17
tear into 1064R6 1495L22
tear jerker 1494R57
tear off 1495L6
tear *someone* off a strip 1495L8
tear out 1494R77
tear up 1494R77/79
wear and tear 1647R39
in a tearing hurry 1495L30
bored to tears 149L48
burst into tears 177R83 1494R49
crocodile tears 326R32
in floods of tears 536R3
shed tears 1494R53
this vale of tears 1605L2
cock-tease 252R42 1120R80/82
prick-tease 1120R82/79
tease about 1495L41
tease out 1495L53
brain teaser 157L39
hi-tech 673R44
high tech 673R44
low-tech 844R13
in glorious technicolour 1495R21
high technology 673R44 1495R51
information technology 728L75
Teddy Bears' picnic 1495R75
teddy boy 1495R80
tee off 1496L19/24
tee shirt 1483L12 1496L56
tee up 1496L22
teem down 1496L28
teem with 1496L28/30
teeter on the brink/edge of 1496L61
teeter on the brink of 166R49
teeter-totter 1285L83 1496L64
by the skin of *one's* teeth 1346R27
cut *one's* teeth on 339R45
get *one's* teeth into 1535R67
gnash *one's* teeth 602L78
gnashing of teeth 602L82
grit *one's* teeth 625L24
have/get/take the bit between *one's* teeth 130L27
hell's teeth 661R26
kick in the teeth 779L31
lie through *one's* teeth 818L61
set *someone's* teeth on edge 1535R70
teething troubles/problems 1496L76
bush telegraph 178R2
telegraph pole 1496R36
mobile telephone 909L67
telephone booth 1058R4
telephone box 1058R7
telephone directory 387R66 1496R66
telephone exchange 1496R68
telephone pole 1496R37
telephoto lens 1496R73
radio telescope 1167R65
breakfast television 162L37
closed circuit television 247L70
high definition television 667R40
satellite television 1256L34
television set 1300L37
can tell a mile off 896L35
hear tell (of) 656L34
kiss-and-tell 781R56
live to tell the tale 831R66
show-and-tell 1327L37
tell a lie/lies 818L72 1498L27
tell *someone* about 1498L18/83
tell against 1498L69
tell apart 1498L57
tell *something* by/from 1498L56
tell *someone's* fortune 1498L39
tell me another 1498L40/41
tell of 1498L18/19
tell off 1498L81/83
tell on 1498L35/71
tell *someone* so 1498L31
tell-tale 1493L2 1498L47
tell tales 1498L34
tell the difference 1498L59
tell the sheep from the goats 1313R81
tell the time 1498L33 1522L56
tell the truth 1498L29
tell to 1498L16/24/26
to tell the truth 1498L29
truth to tell 1565R29
you never can tell 1498L62
automated teller machine 82L69
automatic teller 201R38
fortune teller 555L51
there's no telling 956R78
pro tem 1137R37
fly into a temper 540R35
quick-temper 1162L62/63
temper with 1498R51
run/have a temperature 1499L23
take *someone's* temperature 1499L25
bad-tempered 92L15
even-tempered 472L52
ill-tempered 703R14/15
short-tempered 1324L67
tempers get frayed/short 1498R39
a tempest in a teapot 1431R80
up-tempo 1598R73
tempt fate/providence 1499R8
tempt into 1499R7
nine times out of ten 955R80
Number Ten 967L49
ten a penny 384R79 1045R70
ten-four 1499R45
ten to the dozen 417R52
the Ten Commandments 269L34 1499R42
top ten 1537R13
touch *something* with a ten-foot pole 1540L72
sitting tenant 1343L67
tend to/towards 1500L5/3/4/25
legal tender 809L54
put out for tender 1500L78
tender for 1500L73/84
tender-hearted 1500L40
Achilles tendon 11L66
lawn tennis 802L2
table tennis 1483L71
tennis elbow 1500R36
tennis match 1500R34
tennis shoe 1500R38
tenon saw 1500R43
tenpin bowling 154R61 1500R58
past tense 1033R31
tense up 1501L6
tensile strength 1500R77
high tension 668L46
surface tension 1468L8
oxygen tent 1013R38
land tenure 794L20
tequila slammer 1501L75
half term 638L14 1501R10
in the long/medium/short term 1501R21
term insurance 1501R25
term of abuse 6R14 1501R38
term-paper 1501R12
air terminal 29R9
bring to terms 1503R72
come to terms 266R73 1503R75/78
contradiction in terms 298R31
credit terms 322L60
in absolute terms 5R12
in no uncertain terms 1501R45
in real terms 1179R38
on easy terms 1504L5
on equal/on the same terms 1504L8
on familiar terms 500R29
on first-name terms with 526L9
on good/bad terms 1504L11
on speaking terms 1384R65/63
terms of reference 1504L13/17
think/talk in terms of 1504L2
terra firma 1504L52
end-of-terrace 1504L40
pied à terre 1065L3
enfant terrible 456R48
terrible twins 1504R2
bull terrier 174R57
fox terrier 557L42
Scotch terrier 1269R33
territorial waters 1504R72
the Territorial Army 1504R74
Occupied Territories 1504R55
go/come with the territory 1504R63
be/go/live in terror of *one's* life 1505L10
reign of terror 1195L34
strike terror 1441R18
terror-stricken 1505L15
terror-struck 1505L15
terry cloth 1505L35
terry towelling 1505L35
acid test 11L82
aptitude test 59R3
blood test 137L82
breath test 162R56
dope test 412L48
litmus test 830R79
means test 879R46
pregnancy test 1113L14
put to the test 1505R13
random breath test 1172L19
road test 1228L57/58
stand the test of time 1410R77
test ban 1505R16
test card 1505R18
test case 1505R22
test drive 1505R24
test for 1505R39/43
test on 1505R35
test pattern 1505R18
test pilot 1505R27
test the water(s) 1505R52
test tube 1505R29
test tube baby 1505R31
last will and testament 797R75
the New Testament 952L65
the Old Testament 980L81
time-tested 1521L9
testify against 1505R79
testify for 1505R78
testify to 1505R79/83
bear testimony 108L51
testing times 1505R63
tête-à-tête 1506L43/46
at the end of *one's* tether 1506L53
tether to 1506L56/57
Tex-Mex 1506L65
set the Thames on fire/alight/ablaze 1299L34
thank for 1506R58/60/63/73
thank God/goodness/heaven(s) 1506R66
thank *one's* lucky stars 1507L5
thankful for small mercies 1357R31
vote of thanks 1631L52
fancy that! 503L26
thatch of hair 1507R52
thaw out 1507R67
the benefit of 117L52
the run of 1241R15 1242R79
movie theater 232L52 926L29
vaudeville theater 931L53
movie theatre 232L53
music theatre 931L59
operating theatre 989R38
street theatre 1437L54
theatre in the round 1508R15
theme park 1509L22
liberation theology 816R42
theoretical possibility 1509R30
big bang theory 124L76
chaos theory 216L38
conspiracy theory 291R82
string theory 1443R3
aversion therapy 85L27
behaviour therapy 114R1
cognitive therapy 255L64
electroconvulsive therapy 446R41
electroshock therapy 446R42
gene therapy 586R63
group therapy 626R82
hormone replacement therapy 685L75
occupational therapy 973R33
sex therapy 1303R67/68
shock therapy 1318R19
speech therapy 1388L77/75
thereby hangs a tale 1510L63
thermal imaging 1510L83
thermal underwear 1510R34
clinical thermometer 245L42
thermos flask 1604L67
as thick as thieves 1511L42
as thick as two short planks 1511L58
thick on the ground 1511L44
thick-skinned 1511L32
as thick as thieves 1511L42
thieving hands 1511L81
a thin time (of it) 1511R55
disappear/vanish into thin air 1511R36
out of thin air 1511R38
paper thin 1023L54
pencil-thin 1044R80
razor-thin 1177L24
skate on thin ice 1344R82
the thin end of the wedge 1511R15
thin down 1511R26
thin on the ground 1511R35
thin on top 1511R35
thin-skinned 1511R19
wafer-thin 1632R18
wear thin 1647R29
a close/near thing 1512L13
a thing of the past 1512R23
a thing or two 1512R17/18/21
and another thing 1512R13/27
another thing altogether 48L12
chance would be a fine thing 214R26
first thing 525R22 1512L3
for fun/for the fun of it/for the fun of the thing 573R58
have not a thing to wear 1512L84
it's a good thing 611R17
it all amounts/comes to the same thing 1252R42
know a thing or two 786R25
last thing 797R72 798L52/53 1512L3
make a (big) thing (out) of 1512L26
near thing 944R66/73/79
neither one thing nor the other 948R16
not know the first thing about 786R62
not the done thing 1512R43
on to a good thing 1512L18
one thing after another 1512L8
one thing leads to another 1512L30
sure thing 1467L48
the best thing since sliced bread 118R69
the done thing 1512R40
the easiest thing in the world 438R47
the first/next thing 1512R46
the last thing 1512R47
the real thing 1180L69 1512R53
the same thing 1512R52
the very thing 1512R56
the whole thing 1512R57/58
there's no such thing as 1455L31
too much of a good thing 611R37 1535L79
what with one thing and another 1512L6
above all things 1512R10
all/other things being equal 1512R6
all things considered 1512L52/R4
all things to all men/people 1512R8
as things are/stand 67L19
as things are/stand/turned out/happened 67L20
by the look of things 839R62
cut things fine 339L2
do things by halves 637L72
first things first 525R23
get into the swing of things 1477L84
hear/imagine/see things 1512L43
in the nature of things 943R22
let things lie 812L61
move on to better things 925R12
must be hearing things 655R75
of all things 975R56
scheme of things 1264R29
see things in black and white 131R10
seeing things 1283L77
stranger things have happened 1434R3
take things easy 439L3/4 1512L66
the shape of things to come 1310R63 1512L62
the way things are 1512L58
things have come full circle 572L68
things that go bump in the night 1512L47
how are things? 690R29
do as *you* think best 119L14
dread to think 421L59
let me think 812R36
not/hardly/barely hear *oneself* think 655R77
shudder to think 1330R63
think about/of 1512R83 1513R7/9/12/13/L14/65
think aloud 1513L52
think better of it 1513L16
think big 1513L26
think great/beautiful/interesting thoughts 1513L58
think highly of/a lot of/well of/the world of 1513L17
think in terms of 1504L2
think long and hard 1513L45
think nothing of 1513L25/22
think of 1513L1/R11/L1
think of/think up 1513L44
think on *one's* feet 1513L54
think *something* over/through 1513L49
think straight 1513L56
think tank 1513L66
think twice 1513L45
tremble to think 1555L55
lateral thinking 799L42
not bear thinking about 108L22
put *one's* thinking cap on 1513L75
right thinking 1223L76
the thinking woman's/man's crumpet 1513L83
to my way of thinking 1513L33
wishful thinking 1672L9
the third degree 1513R21
the Third World 1513R30
third class/rate 1513R19
third-degree burn 1513R24
third party 1513R25
third-party insurance 1513R28
Third Reich 1195L27
thirst after/for 1513R44
thirsty work 1513R50
Friday the thirteenth 1513R60
hither and thither 673R53
doubting Thomas 415L8
thorn in the flesh/side 1514L55
no thoroughfare 1516R44
holier-than-thou 679L79
thou shalt 1308R51
food for thought 544L63
on second thought 1279L35
perish the thought 1050L21
school of thought 1265R53
spare a thought for 1383R13 1514R39
sunk in thought 1341R78
the thought crosses *someone's* mind 1514R42
well-thought-of 1653R5
well-thought-out 1653R9
without a second thought 1279L36
a penny for your thoughts 1045R61
further from *one's* thoughts 576R21
second thoughts 1279L32
think great/beautiful/interesting thoughts 1513L58
sixty-four-thousand-dollar question 1344R2
thrash out 1515L9
hang by a thread 643R70
pick up the threads 1062R14
empty threat 1515L50
under threat of 1515L48
life-threatening 819R4
page three 1018L36
the three Rs 1515R3
three-D 1515L64
three-dimensional 1515L65
three-legged race 1515L68
three-line whip 1515L71 1659L49
three-piece suit 1515L75
three-piece suite 832L41 1515L76
three-ply 1515L82/83

three-point turn 1515L78
three-quarter length 1515R2
three quarters 1515L84
three-star 1515R4
three-wheeler 1515R5
thrift shop 1515R33
thrilled to bits 1515R59
thrive on 1515R74
a frog in *one's* throat 567L29
a lump in *one's* throat 847R7
clear *one's* throat 242R25
jump down *someone's* throat 772R56
ram down *someone's* throat 1171L33
stick in *one's* throat 1423L37
strep throat 1438L25
death throes 352R33
coronary thrombosis 307L16
ascend the throne 67L65
power behind the throne 1105R66
throng to 1516L54
throttle back/down 1516L66
a stone's throw 1429R23
as far as I could throw 503R49
free throw 561L44
not trust *someone* as far as *one* can/could throw 1565L39
throw a glance/look 1517L8
throw a party 1517L54
throw a spanner in the works 1383L15
throw about/around 1516R84/73
throw away/out 1517L70
throw back 1517L27/28
throw *something* back in *someone's* face 1516R79
throw caution to the wind(s) 1517L2
throw cold water on 256R2 1517L5
throw down the gauntlet 585L55
throw good money after bad 1517L10
throw *one's* hat into the ring 649R76
throw in at the deep end 357L58
throw in the sponge 1517L7
throw in the towel 1543L51
throw light on 820R13
throw money at 1517L13
throw mud 927R49
throw off 1517L37
throw off balance 94R69
throw *someone* off the scent 1264L16
throw *someone* off the scent/track/trail 1153R74
throw out the baby with the bath-water 1516R77
throw over for 1517L44
throw overboard 1006R60
throw the book at 1516R82
throw together 1517L38/39
throw up 1517L74/43
throw up *one's* hands in horror/despair at 1517L41
throw *one's* voice 1517L19
throw *one's* weight around/about 1517L22
throwaway line/remark 1517L81
flame-thrower 529R83
hammer-throwing 639R31
thrown back on *one's* own resources 1517L32
song thrush 1375R73 1517R1
squat-thrust 1402R84
the cut and thrust 339L16
thrust at 1517R12/13/14
thrust down *someone's* throat 1516L2
a green thumb 622R26
rule of thumb 1239R65
stand/stick out like a sore thumb 1377L17
thumb a lift 1517R48
thumb *one's* nose at 1517R49
thumb through 1517R51
green-thumbed 622R29
well-thumbed 1517R54
thumbnail sketch 1517R59
all fingers and thumbs 521R63
thumbs down 1517R36
thumbs up 1517R37
twiddle *one's* thumbs 1572R81
Bible-thumper 122R82 123L4
thumping headache 1517R78
tub-thumping 1566R45
as black as thunder 131R63
thunder at 1518L11
thus far 1518L48
tick away/by 1518L83
tick off 1518R29/34
tick over 1518R2
tick round 1518L81
tick-tack-toe 965L2 1518R83
what makes *someone* tick 1518R8
ticker-tape parade 1518R38
by ticket only 1518R49
commutation ticket 272L55 1277R60
dream ticket 421R54
just the ticket 1518R50
meal ticket 848L23 877R54/55
parking ticket 1027L12
price ticket 1120R37 1485L62
return ticket 1217L2
roundtrip ticket 1216R84
season ticket 1277R55
timed ticket 1522R45
keep *things* ticking over 1518R6
slap and tickle 1349L65
tickle *someone's* fancy 501R83 1518R74
tickle the ivories 757R31
tickle to death 1518R76
tickled pink 1518R75
rib-tickling 1220R30
rib-ticklingly funny 1220R30
be with you in a couple of ticks 1518R5
tidal wave 1519L34
drift with the tide 424L3
ebb tide 439R20
flood tide 536L41/42
go/swim against/with the tide 1519L24/25
high tide 667L84/R2
low tide 844L44
tide over 1519L41
tide-table 1519L26
glad tidings 597R49
tidy away 1519L58/59
tidy out 1519L60/61
tidy-up 1519L57/67
black tie 131R44
bow tie 154L75
cup tie 335R17
old school tie 980L77
tie back 1519L78
tie-break 1519R51/52
tie down 1519L79/81/82
tie down on 1519L83
tie-dye 1519R55
tie for 1519R46/49
tie in 786L27 1519L77/84/R1/2/10
tie (up) in knots 1519R20
tie into 1519L77
tie the knot 1519R20
tie up 1519R8/10/12/14 1598L72
tie with 1519L84/R2/14/47
twist-tie 1574L4
white-tie 1660R66
have *one's* tubes tied 1566R7
tied cottage 1519R22
tied house 1519R22/24
tongue-tied 1534R69
blood ties 137R42
paper tiger 1023L55
sabre-toothed tiger 1246R67
a tight fit 1519R84
hold tight 676R23
keep a tight rein on 1195L55
keep on a tight rein 1195L56
sit tight 1343L49/47
skin-tight 1346R49
tight bend 1520L16
tight-fisted 1520L8
tight-lipped 1520L10
tight situation/corner/spot 1520L14
tight turn 1520L16
tighten *one's* belt 1520L30
tighten the net 1520L26
tighten the screws on 1273L3
walk/tread a tightrope 1520L42
fingers in the till 521R76
till all hours 688R84
till kingdom come 781L53
till roll 1520R11
till the cows come home 317L48
up till 1520L84 1597R27
work till *one* drops 1679R41
tilt at windmills 1520R41
tilt away from/towards 1520R29/26
tilt the balance/scales 1520R33
half-timbered 638L17
time(d)-release capsule 1522R30
a step/one step at a time 1420R13
a thin time (of it) 1511R55
a whale of a time 1654R74
about time (too) 1522R83 1523L50
access time 7R66
against time/the clock 24R18
ahead of time 1522R5/69
all in good time 611L65
all the time in the world 1521R34
at (any) one time 1522R11
at the due time 431L31
at the same time 1253L31/32 1522L72
before *one's* time 113L54 1523L52 1524L23
better luck next time 120R18
bide *one's* time 123R48
British Summer Time 167L12
buy time 180R59
by this time 1514L13
Christmas-time 230R11
curtain time 337R33
daylight saving time 349R80
do/serve time 1521R35
double time 414R11
drinking-up time 424R26
exactly/dead/right on time 1523L59
extra time 487L17
feeding time at the zoo 509R83
first-time buyer 526L43
for the time being 547L23 1521R42
from/since time immemorial 1524L28
from that time forward 555R20
from time to time 1523R76
full time 572R68/74
give *someone* a hard time 1523R77
give *someone* a rough time 1236L26
give *one something* every time 596R35
give of *one's* time 596R39
good time 611L19/R51 1523L57/R70
Greenwich Mean Time 623L17
half-time 638L20
have a rare old time 1173R83
have/give *someone* a torrid time 1538R81
have time on *one's* side 1520R82
in double-quick time 414L75
in good time 611R16
in no time (at all) 1521R51
in the course of time 314R70/71 1520R69
in the fullness of time 573L1
in the nick of time 954R18
in the right place at the right time 1223L54
in/within a short space of time 1381R61
injury time 731R70
kill time 779R72
lead time 804L66
lighting-up time 820R54
live/exist on borrowed time 149R61
local time 834R19
long-time 838R3
make good time 611R25
make time 855L21/R26 856R26
make up for lost time 856R61
mark time 866R18
matter/question of time 1520R78
night-time 955L36
no time to lose 1521R55
not give *someone* the time of day 1522R16
old-time 980L84
once upon a time 983L76/80
opening time 988L19
part-time 1028R1/2/5
pass the time of day 1031R34
play for time 1078L50
prep-time 1114R59
prime time 1121R81
quality time 1158L49
question time 1161R17
real-time 1179R45
reduced time 1190L9 1324L5
repay *someone's* time 1204L16
same time same place 1253L47
serve time 1297R41
short time 1190L10 1324L5
sidereal time 1334R11
space-time 1381R71
stand the test of time 1410R77
standard time 1411R26
start time 1413R68
starting time 1413R68
stoppage time 1430R75
take one (thing) at a time 1487L17
take the time to 1486R83
take time 1486R82/84 1487L3 1521R21/58
tell the time 1498L33 1522L56
the big time 125L70
the last time 797R40
the sands of time are running out 1254L20
the time is ripe 1226L66 1523L64
the time of *one's* life 1524L1
time after time 1523R81
time and a half 1521R67
time-and-motion study 1521R69
time bomb 1522R19/21
time capsule 1524L35
time card 1522L21
time clock 1522R27
time-consuming 1521R72
time frame 1521R74
time-honoured 1521L3
time is on *someone's* side 1520R81
time lag 792R47 1521R78
time-lapse 1521R81
time limit 1522L1
time machine 1521L7
time on *one's* hands 1521R50
time scale 1522L10
time share 1522L14
time-sharing 1522L17/19
time sheet 1522L21
time signal 1522R32
time signature 1524L57
time switch 1522R35/52
time-tested 1521L9
time travel 1521L13
time's up 1521R62
time warp 1521L14
time zone 1522R36
two-time 1576L55/59
ill-timed 703R17
timed ticket 1522R45
well-timed 1653R12
egg timer 444R6
old-timer 980L16
small-timer 1358L33
a sign of the times 1336L20
at the best of times 119L43
behind the times 1524L26
between times 121L63
fall on hard times 497R84
for old times' sake 980R4
go/move with the times 604L17
good times 612L74
keep up/move/change with the times 1524L29
nine times out of ten 955R80
ninety-nine times out of a hundred 956L37
testing times 1505R63
timing device 1522R48
baking tin 94R31
like a cat on a hot tin roof 203L55
tin foil 1524R74
tin god 1524R79
tin hat 1524R81
tin opener 188L27 1524R82
Tin Pan Alley 1524R84
tin-pot 1525L3
tin whistle 1525L5
ting-a-ling 1525L35
tinge with 1525L44/46
tingle with 1525L53/55
spine-tingling 1392R16
give a tinker's (cuss/damn) 1525R2
tinker about 1525L78
tinker with 1525L73/74/76/79/81
give *someone* a tinkle 1525R15
tinkle the ivories 757R31
the patter(ing) of tiny feet 1037L21
arse over tip 65L28
felt-tip (pen) 512L16
fibre-tip (pen) 512L17
filter tip 519R48
on the tip of *someone's* tongue 1525R74
Q-tip 310R37 1156R63
tip as 1526L15
tip for 1526L7/9/16/82
tip *one's* hand 1526L24
tip of the iceberg 1525R77
tip off 1526L21/30/29/33
tip out 1526L52/63
tip over 1526L64/65/66
tip the scales 1526L77/76
tip the scales/balance 1526L70
tip *someone* the wink 1526L18
tip the wink to 1526L19
tip-top 1526R43
tip truck 432L48 1526L56
tip up 1526L62
Tipp-Ex 1526R9 1661L29
filter-tipped cigarette 519R48
tipper truck/lorry 1526L55
it's tipping (it) down 1526L54
to the tips of *one's* fingers 1525R80
snow tire 1367L72
tire of 1526R62/63
tire *someone* out 1526R60
dog-tired 408R76
tired and emotional 1526R69
a tissue of lies 818L68
bathroom/toilet tissue 1527L37
connective tissue 288R66
contractile tissue 298L79
tissue paper 1527L34
arse over tit 65L28
blue tit 140L16
tit for tat 1527R7/15
move/rearrange the deckchairs on the Titanic 355L52
title deed 1529L21
title page 1527R49
title role 1527R51
get on *someone's* tits 1527L58
jot and tittle 769R73
tittle-tattle 1529L38
toad-in-the-hole 1530L74
toady to 1530R5
French toast 563R49
propose a toast 1135R79 1530R56
toast rack 1530R28
toast with 1530R67
toasting fork 1530R36
toby jug 1531L9
jam today 759R59
today *something* tomorrow the world 1531L30
toddle off 1531L39
toddlers pool 1017R39
big toe 124R59
from head to toe 653L46
from top to toe 1536R76/77
little toe 831L47
tick-tack-toe 965L2 1518R83
toe cap 1531L71
toe-curling 1531L73
toe the line 1531L82
pigeon-toed 1065R46
web toed 1648R47
toes curl 1531L74
tread/step on *someone's* toes 1531L68
toffee apple 1531R23
toffee-nosed 1531R26
tog up/out 1531R43/38
get *one's* act together 13L48
get it together 1531R75 1532L25
get-together 591L45 593R64 1531R66
have/get *one's* shit together 1317R61
keep body and soul together 142R54
mix together 908R41/46/52
not have two pennies to rub together 1045R64
put *their* heads together 654L4
put together 1152R63 1153L25/26/29/30/32/33 1532L12
put two and two together and make five 1574R75/78
spend the night together 955L24 1390L48
throw together 1517L38/39
toggle between 1532L37
toil away 1532L54
down the toilet 415R30 1021L69
go to the toilet 1532L72
toilet bag 1532R12
toilet brush 1532L74
toilet paper 1532L76
toilet roll 1532L80
toilet soap 1532R14
toilet tissue 1527L37
toilet-trained 1104L11 1532L82
toilet water 1532R16
hoity-toity 675L75
book token 147L50
by the same token 1252R35
gift token 594R51
a little bird told me (so) 831L35
death toll 352R34 1533L69
exact a toll 1533L71
road toll 1228L60
take a toll 1533L70
toll-free number 562R37
toll the death knell 352R16
peeping Tom 1042R54
Tom Dick and/or Harriet 1533R13
tom-tom 1533R79
Uncle Tom 1581L76
tomato ketchup 777R40 1533R28
tommy gun 1533R61
jam tomorrow 759R57
like there was/as if there were/as if there was no tomorrow 1533R73
today *something* tomorrow the world 1531L30
like a ton of bricks 1534L3
metric ton 892L69 1535L34
dial tone 379R28 1534R21
dialling tone 379R27
earth tone 437R23
flesh-tone 533L66
half tone 1291L64 1534L82
set the tone 1534L43/50
tone-deaf 1534L82
tone down 1534R24
tone in 1534L62
tone language 1534L84
Touch-Tone phone 1540R6
two-tone 1576L62
go at it hammer and tongs 639R21
bite *one's* tongue 130R24
find *one's* tongue 520R52
forked tongue 551R43
get *one's* tongue round/around 1534R50
give *someone* the rough side of *one's* tongue 1236L25
has the cat got *your* tongue 203L48
hold *one's* tongue 676R24

keep a civil ▪**tongue** in *one's* ▫head 234R81
▫mother ▪**tongue** 920R3
on the ▫tip of *someone's* ▪**tongue** 1525R74
▫slip of the ▪**tongue** 1353R78
▫**tongue** in ▪cheek 1534R60
▪**tongue**-▫lashing 1534R66
▪**tongue**-▫tied 1534R69
▪**tongue** ▫twister 1534R73
▫trip off the ▪**tongue** 1558R17
with *one's* ▪**tongue** in *one's* ▫cheek 1534R60
▫silver ▪**tongued** 1339L7 1535L5
set/start ▪**tongues** ▫wagging 1534R55
▪honky-▫**tonk** 682L65/68
a ▫drop **too** ▫much (to ▪drink) 427R78
▪all/▪only ▫**too** 1535L56
be▫fore (▫**too**) ▪long 838L71
eyes **too** ▫big for *one's* ▪belly/▪stomach 488R33
▫in **too** ▪deep 1535L68
▪miles **too** 896L35
not a ▫moment **too** ▪soon 912L82
not to put ▫**too** fine a ▪point on it 521L82
▫not **too** ▪bad 92L28
▫not **too** distant ▪future 398R83 578L27
pro▫test **too** ▪much 1137R65
▫speak **too** ▪soon 1384R69
▫**too** ▪bad 92L30/32 1535L62
too ▫big for *one's* ▪boots 125L23
too ▫clever by ▪half 243R70
too ▫close for ▪comfort 247R65
too ▫good to be ▪true 611R31 1535L71
▫**too** good to ▪last 611R34 798L67
▫**too** good to ▪miss 906L4 1535L70
▫**too** hot to ▪handle 688L25
too ▫little too ▪late 798R83 1535L73
▫**too** ▪much 927L51/53
▫**too** much like hard ▪work 1535L81
▫**too** much of a good ▪thing 611R37 1535L79
▫**too** ▪right 1224L54
ma▫chine ▫**tool** 850R63
▪power ▫**tool** 1106L81
pre▪cision ▫**tool** 1110R37
▪**tool** ▫box 1535R36
▪**tool** ▫kit 1535R39
▪**tool** ▫shed 1535R40
▫**tooled** ▪up 1535R52
▫down ▪**tools** 416L2
▫**tools** of the ▪trade 1535R32
▪baby ▫**tooth** 88R26
▫buck ▪**tooth** 172L6
▫long in the ▪**tooth** 838L79
▪milk ▫**tooth** 88R27 897L6
▫sweet ▪**tooth** 1475R65
▫**tooth** and ▪nail 1535R72
▪**tooth** ▫fairy 1535R75
▪wisdom ▫**tooth** 1671R4
with a ▫fine-▪**tooth** comb 521L84
▪gap-▫**toothed** 582L72
▫sabre-**toothed** ▪tiger 1246R67
at the ▫**top** of *one's* ▪voice 1537L7
at ▫**top** ▪speed 1537L77
▫big ▪**top** 124R60
▫blow *one's* ▪**top** 139L42
▪bottle ▫**top** 151R32
▪carrot-▫**top** 198R41
from ▫**top** to ▪bottom/▪toe 1536R76/77
in/on ▫**top** ▪form 1537L78
in the ▫**top** ▪flight 534L42
off the ▫**top** of *one's* ▪head 1536R82
on ▫**top** of the ▪world 1536R78
▫over the ▪**top** 1536R84
pay ▫**top** ▪dollar 1038R3
▫roll-**top** ▪desk 1231R36
▪screw ▫**top** 1273L8
▫soft ▪**top** 301L72 1371R24
▪spinning ▫**top** 1391R65
▪tank ▫**top** 1490L57
the ▫**top** of the ▪heap 655R46
▫thin on ▪**top** 1511R35
▫tip-▪**top** 1526R43
▫**top** ▪brass 1537L80
▫**top** ▪dog 1537L82
▫**top**-▪down 1537L8
▫**top**-▪flight 1537L83
▫**top** ▪hat 1537R55
▫**top**-▪heavy 1537L50
▫**top**-▪level 1537L84
▫**top**-▪notch 1537R3
▫**top** ▪off with 1537L22/25/R27/L24
▫**top** pri▪ority 1537R4
▫**top** ▪secret 1280L67 1537R7
▫**top** se▪curity 1537R7/11
▫**top** ▪ten 1537R13
▫**top** the ▪bill 126R1
▫**top** ▪up 1537L27/34/35
▫**top** ▪whack 1537R18
▫**topsy**-▪**turvy** 1538L24
▫carry a ▪**torch** for 198R82
▪**torn** be▫tween 121L82 1538R14
▫**torn** into ▪ribbons 1220R66
have/give *someone* a ▫**torrid** ▪time 1538R81
tor▫**tilla** ▪chips 1539L17
▫**tortoiseshell** ▪butterfly 1539L28
▫**tortoiseshell** ▪cat 1539L30
▪**torture** *oneself* 462R46 847L40/41
▫argue the ▪**toss** 61R54
▫give/▫care a ▪**toss** 1539R36
▪ring ▫**toss** 684L77
▫**toss** a ▪coin 1539R22
▫**toss** and ▪turn 1539R19
▫**toss** a▪round 1539R7
▫**toss** a▪side 1539R4
▫**toss** a▪way 1539R6
▪**toss** between 1539R30
▪**toss** for 1539R24/26
toss *one's* ▪hat into the ▫ring 649R76
▪**toss** in 1539R16
▫**toss** ▪off 1539R40
▫**toss** ▪overboard 1006R60
▫**toss** ▪up 1539R27
▪**toss** with 1539R14
▫win/▫lose the ▪**toss** 1539R34
▫**tot** ▪up 1539R56/53
▫grand ▪**total** 618L28
▫sum ▪**total** 1458R71
▫**total** ▪recall 1183L24
▫**tote** a▪long 1540L24
▫**tote** a▪round 1540L25
▪**tote** ▫bag 1540L28
▪**totem** ▫pole 1540L34
▪teeter-▫**totter** 1285L83 1496L64
▫easy ▪**touch** 438R62
▫in ▪**touch** 1540R43
▫kick into ▪**touch** 779L5
▪personal ▫**touch** 1053L18
▫soft ▪**touch** 1372L3
the ▫common ▪**touch** 270R50
the ▫human ▪**touch** 692R15
▫**touch** a raw ▪nerve/▪spot 1176R68 1540L76
▫**touch**-and-▪go 1540L74
▫**touch** ▪down 1540R35
▫**touch** ▪football 1540R4
▪**touch** for 1541L1
▫**touch** *one's* ▪forelock 549R45
▫**touch** ▪in 1541L4
▫**touch** ▪off 1541L6
▫**touch** on the ▪raw 1176R69
▪**touch** on/upon 1540L81
▪**Touch**-Tone ▫phone 1540R6
▪**touch**-▫type 1540R12
▫**touch** ▪up 1540L83 1541L11
▪**touch** with 1540L63/65/R40/43/45/47
▫**touch** *something* with a ▪barge pole 1540L72
▫**touch** *something* with a ten-foot ▪pole 1540L72
▫**touch** ▪wood 1540R2
put the ▫finishing ▪**touches** on/to 522R27/28
▫**touchy**-▪**feely** 1540R22
a ▫**tough** act to ▪follow 13L52
a ▫**tough** ▪nut to ▫crack 968L79
▫**tough** as old ▪boots 1541R5/L84
▫**tough** as ▪shoe leather 1541R5
▪**tough** ▪cheese 223L52
▪**tough** it 1541R30
▫**tough** ▪out 1541R27
▫**tough** ▪shit 1541R76
▫grand ▪**tour** 617R80
▪mystery ▫**tour** 934R67
▪package ▫**tour** 1016R61
▫**tour** de ▪force 1542L44
▪**tour** with 1542L31
▫whistle-stop ▪**tour** 1660L52
Tour▪**ette's** ▫syndrome 1542L51
▪**tourist** ▫class 1542L79
▪**tourist** ▫trap 1542R2
elimi▪nation ▫**tournament** 448L2 786L12
▪**tout** as 1542R36/37
▪**tout** for 1542R38/41/47
▫**tow** a▪way/▪off 1542R61/63/60
▪**tow** ▫bar 1542R69
▪**tow** ▫truck 1062R77 1542R70
▪gravitate **to**▫**ward**/to 621L32
go a ▫long way **to**▪**wards** 838L14
▪move **towards** 925L54/56/R51
▪bath ▫**towel** 104L47
▪dish ▫**towel** 393R84 1494L33
▫kitchen ▪**towel** 782L39/46 1494L33
▫paper ▪**towel** 782L40
▪roller ▫**towel** 1231R5
▪sanitary ▫**towel** 1254R78
▪tea ▫**towel** 1494L32
▫throw/▫chuck in the ▪**towel** 1543L51
▫**towel** *oneself* ▪down 1543L59
▫terry ▪**towelling** 1505L35
▪clock ▫**tower** 246L78
con▪trol ▫**tower** 299R70
▪cooling ▫**tower** 302R58
▫ivory ▪**tower** 757R22
▪office ▫**tower** 977R17 1543L75
▪signal ▫**tower** 1336R23
▪**tower** ▫block 1543L78
▫**tower** of ▪strength 1543L81
▪water ▫**tower** 1642R41
▪boom ▫**town** 148L3
▪company ▫**town** 272R39
▫county ▪**town** 314L12
▪dormitory ▫**town** 412R48
▪ghost ▫**town** 594L43
▫go to ▪**town** 1543R47
▫man-about ▪**town** 1543R55
▪market ▫**town** 867L3
▪new ▫**town** 952L71
▫night on the ▪**town** 955L54
▫one-horse ▪**town** 984L72
▫paint the ▫**town** (▪red) 1019L33
▫run ▫out of ▪**town** 1241R9
▪shanty ▫**town** 1309R76
▪small-▫**town** 1357R76
the ▫talk of the ▪**town** 1488R50
▫**town** ▪centre 1543R34
▫**town** ▪clerk 1543R58
▫**town** ▪hall 1543R59
▪**town** ▫house 1543R62
▫**town** ▪meeting 1543R65
▫**town** ▪planner 1543R67/70
▫twin ▪**town** 1573L66
▪boy ▫**toy** 155R81
▫cuddly ▪**toy** 333L77
▫soft ▪**toy** 1371R25
▪**toy** ▫boy 1544L44
▪**toy** ▫with 700R47 1544L49/54
▪**trace** ▫element 1544R46
▫**trace** ▪out 1544R28
▪**trace** to 1544L67/71/73/77
▫kick over the ▪**traces** 779L6
▪**tracing** ▫paper 1544R35
▪cart ▫**track** 200L39
▪dirt ▫**track** 388L6
▫down the ▪**track** 416L77
▪fast ▫**track** 505L76
▫keep ▪**track** 1545L53
▫lose ▪**track** 842L8
▫off the beaten ▪**track** 109L50
on the ▫right ▪**track** 1228L37
▫one-**track** ▪mind 984R55
▫put/▫throw *someone* off the ▪**track** 1153R74
the ▫inside ▪**track** 734R43
▫**track** and ▪field 1545R45
▫**track** ▪down 1545L69/70
▪**track** e▫vent 1545R46
▪**track** ▫meet 1545R50
▪**track** ▫record 1545R53
▪**track** ▫shoe 1545R57
▪**tracker** ▫dog 1545L84
▪**tracking** ▫station 1545L75
▫hot on the ▪**tracks** of 687R82
▫make ▪**tracks** 1545L58
▪**tract** ▫house 1546L4
▪**traction** ▫engine 1546L31
▪**tractor**-▫trailer 771R76 1546L36
a ▪roaring ▫**trade** 1229L4
▫balance of ▪**trade** 94R79
▫free ▪**trade** 561L46
▪rag ▫**trade** 1168R10
restrictive ▪**trade** ▫practice 1214L2
▫rough ▪**trade** 1236L28
▪slave ▫**trade** 1350R10
▫stock-in-▪**trade** 1428L61
▫tools of the ▪**trade** 1535R32
▪**trade** ▫balance 1546L61
▫**trade** ▪down to/for 1546R25/28
▪**trade** ▫fair 1546L63
▪**trade** ▫figures 1546L67
▪**trade** for 1546R9/10/11/14/22
▫**trade** ▪in 1546L46/48/60/83/R20/23
▪**trade** ▫name 1546L71
▪**trade** ▫on 1547L3
▪**trade** ▫price 1546L73
▪**trade** ▫route 1546L76
▪**trade** ▫school 1546R65
▫**trade** ▪secret 1546R68
▪**trade** ▫show 1546L64
▫**trade** ▪union 1546R79/73/78/73
▫**trade** ▪up 1546R23
▪**trade** upon 1547L3
▪**trade** with 1546L49/82
▫trick of the ▪**trade** 1557L34
▫jack-of-▪all-▫**trades** 757R74
▪**tradesmen's** ▫entrance 1547L32
in▫sider ▪**trading** 735L45
▪**trading** es▫tate 1546R45
▪**trading** ▫post 1546R47
▫oral **tra**▪**dition** 992R75
▫air **traffic** con▪trol 29R20/17
▫no through ▪**traffic** 1516R44
▪**traffic** ▫calmed 1547R42
▪**traffic** ▫circle 1237L25 1547R49
▪**traffic** ▫cone 1547R49
▪**traffic** ▫cop 1547R70
▪**traffic** in 1547R84 1548L2
▪**traffic** ▫island 1547R53/56
▪**traffic** ▫jam 1547R57
▪**traffic** ▫light 1547R61/64
▪**traffic** po▫lice 1547R70
▪**traffic** ▫warden 1547R73
▫blaze a ▪**trail** 134L59
cam▪paign ▫**trail** 187R43
▫hot on the ▪**trail** of 687R82
▪nature ▫**trail** 943L13
▪paper ▫**trail** 1023L59
▫put/▫throw *someone* off the ▪**trail** 1153R74
▫**trail** a▪way/▪off 1548L81
▫**trail** be▪hind 1548L75
▪**trail** ▫blazer 1548L58
▪vapour ▫**trail** 1606R53
▪horse ▫**trailer** 686L82
▪tractor-▫**trailer** 771R76 1546L36
▪**trailer** ▫camping 193R70
▪**trailer** ▫park 193R64
▪boat ▫**train** 142L16
com▪muter ▫**train** 272L50
▪ghost ▫**train** 594L46
▪puffer ▫**train** 1143R41
▫put/▫set in ▪**train** 1548R79
the ▪gravy ▫**train** 621L54
▪**train** ▫driver 457R70
▪**train** ▫set 1548R19
▪**train** ▫spotter 1548R21
▪**train** ▫station 1415L69
▪house-▫**trained** 689L63
▪potty-▫**trained** 1104L11
▪toilet-▫**trained** 1104L11 1532L82
▪potty-▫**trainer** 1104L14
as▪sertiveness ▫**training** 72L70
▪circuit ▫**training** 232R74
teacher-▪**training** ▫college 1494L74
▪**training** ▫shoe 1549L1
▪**training** ▫wheels 1405L70
▪weight ▫**training** 1650L14
▫**traipse** ▪round 1549L6
▫**traipse** ▪through 1549L8
▪**trample** ▫on 1549L64
▫**transcendental** medit▪ation 1549R65
▪**transfer** ▫fee 1550L44
▪**transfer** ▫list 1550L48/50
▪blood **trans**▫**fusion** 137L84 1550R25
▫rapid ▪**transit** 1173R20 1550R67
▪**transit** ▫camp 1550R68
ma▫chine **trans**▪**lation** 850R46
▫automatic **trans**▪**mission** 82L80
▫manual **trans**▪**mission** 862R83
▫sexually **transmitted** dis▪ease 1304L31
in a ▫**transport** of de▪light/▪joy 1552L9
▫public ▪**transport** 1142L53 1551R83
▪**transport** ▫café 1552L11
▪**transport** ▫plane 1552L6
▪**transport** ▫ship 1552L6
▪booby ▫**trap** 147L11/13/17/19
▪death ▫**trap** 352R36
▪honey ▫**trap** 681R37
▪poverty ▫**trap** 1105L30
▪radar ▫**trap** 1166R45
▪sand ▫**trap** 176L47 1254L15
▪speed ▫**trap** 1389L26
▪tourist ▫**trap** 1542R2
▪**trash** ▫bag 433L52 1552R36
▪**trash** can ▫liner 433L51 1552R37
▫white ▪**trash** 1661L23
▫post-**traumatic** ▪stress dis▫order 1101L51
▫have *something* ▫will ▪**travel** 1553L11
▪time ▫**travel** 1521L13
▪**travel** ▫agent 1553L22
▪**travel** ex▫penses 1553L25
▪**travel** ▫plug 1553L27
▪**travel** ▫sickness 1553L30
▪**traveler's** ▫check 1553L45
▫fellow ▪**traveller** 511R63
▫**traveller's** ▪cheque 1553L44
▫**travelling** ▪salesman 1553L55
▪**trawl** ▫net 1553R1
▪baking ▫**tray** 94R32
▪tea ▫**tray** 1494L34
▫black ▪**treacle** 1553R30
▫**tread** a ▪tightrope 1520L42
▫**tread** ▪down 1553R48
▪**tread** in 1553R49
▪**tread** into 1553R50
▪**tread** on 1553R42/58
▫**tread** on *someone's* ▪toes 1531L68
▫**tread** the ▪boards 1553R59
▫**tread** ▪water 1553R62
▫high ▪**treason** 668R67
▫**treasure** ▫hunt 1554L25
▫**treasure** ▪trove 1554L27
▪**Treasury** ▫bond 1554L51
▫ill-▪**treat** 703R21
▪**treat** as 1554L60
▪**treat** for 1554L76
▪**treat** to 1554R11/12
▪**treat** with 295R58 1554L64/78/R19
▫**treat** with *someone* with kid ▪gloves 779L79
▫trick or ▪**treat** 1557L2
▪heat-▫**treated** 658L13
▫how's life **treating** ▪you? 818R61
▪heat ▫**treatment** 658L15/17
▪shock ▫**treatment** 1318R19
extra▪dition ▫**treaty** 487L72
▫**treble** ▪clef 1554R50
▫bark up the wrong ▪**tree** 100L73
▪Christmas ▫**tree** 230R12
▪citrus ▫**tree** 234L58
▫family ▪**tree** 500R80
▪gum ▫**tree** 470R59 632L40
▪rubber ▫**tree** 1238R38
▪shade ▫**tree** 1304R75
▪**tree** ▫fern 1554R63
▪**tree** ▫house 1554R65
▪**tree**-▫lined 1554R67
▪**tree** ▫ring 1554R68
up a ▪gum ▫**tree** 632L42
▫can't see the ▫wood/▫forest for the ▪**trees** 1677L74
▫not grow on ▪**trees** 627R5
▪pony ▫**trekking** 1094L56
▫**tremble** at the ▪prospect of 1555L55
▫**tremble** to ▪think 1555L55
de▫lirium ▪**tremens** 362R76
▪**trench** ▫coat 1555R54
▫buck the ▪**trend** 171R19
▪**trespass** on/upon 1556L22
▪**trestle** ▫table 1556L41
▪show ▫**trial** 1328L50
▫stand ▪**trial** 1410R47
▫**trial** and ▪error 1556L68
▫**trial** ▪run 1556L72
▫**trials** and tribul▪ations 1556L84
e▫ternal ▪**triangle** 470L11
i▫sosceles ▪**triangle** 755L78
▪love ▫**triangle** 470L11
▫right-angled ▪**triangle** 1223R75
the ▫golden ▪**triangle** 610L61
▫trials and **tribul**▪**ations** 1556L84
in▫dustrial **tri**▪**bunal** 724L12
▪confidence ▫**trick** 286L33
▪conjuring ▫**trick** 288L61
every ▫**trick** in the ▪book 1557L31
▪hat ▫**trick** 650R76
▫miss a ▪**trick** 906L22
▫play a ▪**trick** 1078R34
▪**trick** into 1557L12/14
▫**trick** of the ▪light 1556R83
▫**trick** of the ▪trade 1557L34
▫**trick** or ▪treat 1557L2
▪**trick** ▫question 1556R84
▫**trickle**-▪down 1557L43
▫bag of ▪**tricks** 93L53
▪confidence ▫**trickster** 286L36
▫**tried** and found ▪wanting 1636R62
▫well-▪**tried** 1653R18
▪**trifle** ▫with 1557R13
▫hair-▪**trigger** 636L73
▪**trigger**-▫happy 1557R24
▫**trigger** ▪off 1557R33
▫**trim** ▪off 1557R69
▪edge ▫**trimmer** 441L59 1443L62
▪hedge-▫**trimmers** 659R49
▪day ▫**trip** 349R45/49
▪ego ▫**trip** 444R37
▪field ▫**trip** 516L17
▪guilt ▫**trip** 631L60/64
▪road ▫**trip** 1228L62
▫round ▪**trip** 1236R5
take a ▫**trip** down memory ▪lane 886L22
▫**trip** ▪down 1558R16
▫**trip** off the ▪tongue 1558R17
▪**trip** on 1558L65/73
▫**trip** ▪over 1558L62/64
▪**trip** ▫switch 1558R25
▫**trip** ▪up 1558L66/69/70
▫**triple** ▪glazing 1558R61
▫**triple** ▪jump 1558R70/66
▫well-▪**trodden** 1653R20
▫ménage à ▪**trois** 886L60
▫**Trojan** ▪horse 1559R66
▫work like a ▪**Trojan** 1679R40
▪tea ▫**trolley** 1494L36 1560L7
▫**trompe** ▪l'oeil 1560L39
▫**troop** ▪after 1560L67
▪**troop** ▫carrier 1560R7
▫**troop** ▪down 1560L72
▪**troop** into 1560L71
▫**troop** ▪off 1560L69
▫**troop** the ▪colour 1560L73
▪storm ▫**trooper** 1432L35
▪shock ▫**troops** 1318R21
▫de ▪**trop** 376R83
▪**trophy** ▫wife/▫girlfriend 1560R22
▫**Tropic** of ▪Cancer 1560R32
▫**Tropic** of ▪Capricorn 1560R33
▫hot to ▪**trot** 688L33
▪jog-▫**trot** 766R60
▫**trot** ▪along 1560R74/79
▪**trot** down 1560R76/81
▫**trot** ▪off 1560R81
trot ▪out 1561L9
▪**trot** through 1560R77 1561L3
▫plight *one's* ▪**troth** 1082L10
▫double ▪**trouble** 414R14
▫get *someone* into ▪**trouble** 1561R16
it's more ▫**trouble** than it's ▪worth 1561R63
▫lay up ▪**trouble** 803L51
▪look for ▫**trouble** 839R13 1561L76
▪**trouble** ▫spot 1561R19/22
fish in ▫**troubled** ▪waters 526R21
pour ▫oil on **troubled** ▪waters 1104R60
▪teething ▫**troubles** 1496L76
▪**trouser** ▫press 1562L82
▪**trouser** ▫suit 1562L84

ˌcatch *someone* with *their* ˈ**trousers** ˌdown 204R73/78
ˌwear the ˈ**trousers** 1647L82
ˌsalmon ˈ**trout** 1251L76
ˌtreasure ˈ**trove** 1554L27
ˌplay ˈ**truant** 1562R34
ˈ**truant** ˌofficer 1562R31
ˈbreakdown ˌ**truck** 162L20
ˈdump ˌ**truck** 432L28/47 1526L56
ˈgarbage ˌ**truck** 433L55 582R52
ˈhand ˌ**truck** 641L48
ˈmilk ˌ**truck** 897L7
ˈpick-up ˌ**truck** 1062R76/74
ˈtip ˌ**truck** 432L48 1526L56
ˈtipper ˌ**truck** 1526L55
ˈtow ˌ**truck** 1062R77 1542R70
ˈ**truck** ˌfarm 1562R71/67
ˈ**truck** ˌstop 1552L11 1562R71
ˌkeep on ˈ**trucking** 1562R79
ˌcome ˈ**true** 1563R13
ˌring ˈ**true** 1225R42
see *someone* in *their* ˌ**true** ˈcolours 260L64
ˌshow *one's* **true** ˈcolours 260L63
so ˌ*something* it's not ˈ**true** 1563R20
too ˌgood to be ˈ**true** 611R31 1535L71
ˌ**true**-ˈblue 1563R56
ˌ**true**-life ˈstory 1563R21
ˌ**true** ˈnorth 1563R25
ˌ**true** to ˈform/ˈtype 1563R64
ˌ**true**-to-ˈlife 1563R24
ˌwell and ˈ**truly** 1651R31
ˈ**trump** ˌcard 195L32 1564L38
ˌ**trump** ˈup 1564L50
ˌblow *one's* own ˈ**trumpet** 138R81
ˌturn up/ˌcome up ˈ**trumps** 1564L30
ˈ**trundle** ˌbed 1564R26
ˌ**trundle** ˈout 1564R24
ˈ**trunk** ˌroad 1564R36
ˈbathing ˌ**trunks** 104L75 1476R75 1565L5
ˈswimming ˌ**trunks** 1476R75 1565L4
ˌ**truss** ˈup 1565L10
beˌtray *someone's* ˈ**trust** 120L52
ˈbrain ˌ**trust** 157L44
ˌNational ˈ**Trust** 939L33
not ˌ**trust** *someone* an ˈinch 1565L40
not ˌ**trust** *someone* as ˌfar as *one* can/could ˈthrow 1565L39
ˌtake on ˈ**trust** 1565L54
ˈ**trust** ˌfund 574L75 1565L82
ˈ**trust** in 1565L34/51
ˈ**trust** with 1565L32
ˌunit ˈ**trust** 1590L53
ˌcold ˈ**truth** 256R67
econˌomical with the ˈ**truth** 440L82
ˌGod's ˈ**truth** 609L16
ˈhalf-ˌ**truth** 638L24
ˌhome ˈ**truth** 680L37
ˌmoment of ˈ**truth** 912R59
ˌstrain the ˈ**truth** 1433R84
ˌtell the ˈ**truth** 1498L29
to ˌtell the ˈ**truth** 1498L29
ˌ**truth** to ˈtell 1565R29
in ˌall ˈ**truthfulness** 713L38
ˈ**try** for 1565R65/66 1566L25/35
ˌ**try** for ˈsize 1566L5/7
ˌ**try** *one's* ˈhand 1565R72
ˌ**try** *one's* ˈluck 1566L18
ˌ**try** ˈon 1566L3/5/15
ˌ**try** ˈout 1566L2/22
try the ˌpatience of a ˈsaint 1036L35 1566L41
ˌ**try** *one's* ˈutmost 1603R5
ˈ**tsetse** ˌfly 1566L61
tu-ˌwhit tu-ˈwhoo 1572L35
ˌhot ˈ**tub** 687R64
ˈ**tub**-ˌthumping 1566R45
ˌdown the ˈ**tube(s)** 415R30 1021L69
falˌlopian ˈ**tube** 499R9
ˈinner ˌ**tube** 732R4
ˈtest ˌ**tube** 1505R29
ˌtest **tube** ˈbaby 1505R31
go down the ˈ**tubes** 1566R11
have *one's* ˈ**tubes** ˌtied 1566R7
a ˌnip ˈhere and a ˌ**tuck** ˈthere 956L81
ˌnip and ˈ**tuck** 956L76/77
ˌ**tuck** aˈway 1566R64/71
ˌ**tuck** ˈin/ˈinto 1566R54/55/56/60/66/81/83 1567L4
ˌ**tuck** ˈunder 1566R57/61/62/73/74
ˈ**tucked** along/down 1566R69
ˌbest bib and ˈ**tucker** 122R68
ˌShrove ˈ**Tuesday** 1330L64
ˌ**tug** at *one's* ˈforelock 549R45
ˌ**tug**-of-ˈlove 1567L28
ˌ**tug**-of-ˈwar 1567L34
ˌrough and ˈ**tumble** 1236L37/38
ˈ**tumble** ˌdrier 1567L68
ˈ**tumble** ˌdryer 1567L68
ˌgippy ˈ**tummy** 595R58
ˈ**tummy** ˌbutton 944L23 1567R15
ˌcall the ˈ**tune** 186L1
ˌchange *one's* ˈ**tune** 215L20
ˌfine-ˈ**tune** 521R7
ˈsignature ˌ**tune** 1336R53
ˌ**tune** ˈin 1568L2/3/9/3/6
ˌ**tune** ˈup 1567R76 1568L22
piˈano ˌ**tuner** 1061L81 1567R79
ˈ**tuning** ˌfork 1567R62
ˈ**tuning** ˌpeg 1567R66
ˈ**tuning** ˌpin 1567R66
ˌChannel ˈ**Tunnel** 215R72
ˌlight at the ˌend of the ˈ**tunnel** 820R4
ˈ**tunnel** under 1568L44
ˌ**tunnel** ˈvision 1568L38/40
ˈwind ˌ**tunnel** 1667L10
ˌnot care/give ˈ**tuppence** 1568L53
ˌnot matter ˈ**tuppence** 1568L56
ˌwouldn't give ˈ**tuppence** for 1568L58
ˈwind ˌ**turbine** 1667L14
ˈ**turf** acˌcountant 1568R56
ˌ**turf** ˈout 1568R66/69
ˌcold ˈ**turkey** 256R39
ˌtalk ˈ**turkey** 1488R23
ˌ**Turkish** ˈbath 1569L13
ˌ**Turkish** deˈlight 1569L19
ˌcooked/ˌdone to a ˈ**turn** 1570R52
ˌdo a good ˈ**turn** 611R82
ˌgood/ˌbad ˈ**turn** 1570R35
in ˈ**turn** 1570R25
not know ˌwhich way to ˈ**turn** 786R75
ˌnot **turn** a ˈhair 1569R36
ˌspeak/ˌtalk out of ˈ**turn** 1570R26
ˌstar ˈ**turn** 1412R47
take a ˌ**turn** for the ˈworse 1570L66
ˌthree-point ˈ**turn** 1515L78
ˌtight ˈ**turn** 1520L16
ˌtoss and ˈ**turn** 1539R19
ˌ**turn** a blind ˈeye 1569R31
ˌ**turn** a deaf ˈear 1569R34
ˌ**turn** a ˈphrase 1569L43
ˌ**turn** aˈround 1570R55
turn as ˌred as a ˈbeetroot 113L37/38
ˌ**turn** aˈway/ˈback 1569L79
ˌ**turn** aˈway from 1569R3
ˌ**turn** ˈback 1569L79
ˌ**turn** *one's* ˈback on 1569R3/5
ˌ**turn** back the ˈclock 246L60
turn ˈbeetroot (ˌred) 113L37
turn ˌbelly ˈup 116L17
ˌ**turn** ˈdown 1570L72/R66
ˈ**turn** for 1569R65/80
ˌ**turn** *one's* hand to ˈanything 1569R38
ˌ**turn** ˈin 1570R72/80
ˌ**turn** in *one's* ˈgrave 1569R46
ˈ**turn** into 1570L41/47
ˌ**turn** into a ˈpumpkin 1146L42 1570L48
ˈ**turn** into/to 1570L40
ˌ**turn** *one's* ˈnose up 1571L61/63
ˌ**turn** of eˈvents 1570L22
ˌ**turn** of ˈmind 1570L14
ˌ**turn** of ˈphrase 1569L60
ˌ**turn** of the ˈscrew 1569L57
ˌ**turn** ˈoff/ˈout 1569L69/R78 1570L76/83/71
ˌ**turn** *something* on *its* ˈhead 1569R43
ˈ**turn** *something* on/to 1569R19
ˈ**turn** onto 1569R20
ˌ**turn** ˈout 1570R82 1571L3/6/16
ˌ**turn** out for the ˈbest 119L70
ˌ**turn** ˈout of 1571L4
ˌ**turn** ˈover 1569R9 1570L75 1571L20/23/37
turn over a ˌnew ˈleaf 1569R52
ˌ**turn** over in *one's* ˈmind 898R51
ˌ**turn** ˈround 1569L73/82 1570R55
ˈ**turn** ˌsignal 721R13 1569R81
turn ˌswords into ˈploughshares 1479R9
ˌ**turn** ˈtail 1569R63
ˌ**turn** the ˈclock ˌback 246L58 1570R10
ˌ**turn** the ˈcorner 1569R7
turn the ˌknife (in the ˈwound) 783R49
ˌ**turn** the other ˈcheek 1569R50
ˌ**turn** the ˈspotlight on 1569R54
ˌ**turn** the ˈtables 1569R58
ˈ**turn** to 78L19 1569L77/R16/23/25/34/36/63 1570L62/64/R9/17/19/23/78 1571L21
ˌ**turn** ˈup 1570L73 1571L44/53/57/66
ˌ**turn**-up for the ˈbook(s) 1571L53
ˌ**turn** up like a ˌbad ˈpenny 1571L51
ˌ**turn** up ˈtrumps 1564L30
ˌ**turn** upside ˈdown 1569R69
ˌ**turn**/ˌuse to (ˌgood) acˈcount 10L3
ˈU-ˌ**turn** 1577L63
ˌwait *one's* ˈ**turn** 1633R45
ˈ**turn**-ˌon 89R57 1569L35/36/R17/22/61 1570L72/R6
ˌas things **turned** ˈout 67L20
ˌpoacher **turned** ˈgamekeeper 1087R31
ˌwell-ˈ**turned** 1569L45 1653R25
ˈpage-ˌ**turner** 1018L38
ˈ**turning** ˌcircle 1569L50
ˈ**turning** ˌpoint 1569R73
ˌanything that/whatˌever ˌ**turns** *you* ˈon 1570L81
ˌas it **turns** ˈout 67L19/18
by ˈ**turns** 1570R25
ˌtake it in ˈ**turns** 1570R22
ˌtake ˈ**turns** 1570R21
the ˌworm ˈ**turns** 1685L76
ˌmock ˈ**turtleneck** 1571R65
ˌtopsy-ˈ**turvy** 1538L24
ˈ**tussle** over 1571R77
ˈ**tussle** with 1571R79/81
ˌTV ˈdinner 1572L43
ˌ**tweak** ˈout 1572L70
ˌ**twelfth** ˈman 1572R35
ˌ**Twelfth** ˈNight 1572R36
ˌroaring ˈ**twenties** 1229L9
ˌ**twenty**-ˈfirst 1572R43
ˌ**twenty**-four-hour ˈclock 1572R45
ˌ**twenty**-twenty ˈvision 1572R49
ˌonce or ˈ**twice** 983L74
ˌthink ˈ**twice** 1513L45
ˌ**twiddle** *one's* ˈthumbs 1572R81
ˈ**twig** to 1573L23
ˈ**twilight** ˌyears 1573L38
ˈ**twilight** ˌzone 1573L38
ˌ**twin** ˈbed 1573L59
ˌ**twin**-bedded ˈroom 1573L60
ˈ**twin** ˌset 1573L62
ˌ**twin** ˈtown 1573L66
ˈ**twin** ˌwith 1573L71/74
ˈ**twine** round/up 1573L78
ˌ**twine** toˈgether 1573L79
in the ˌ**twinkling** of an ˈeye 1573R35
iˌdentical ˈ**twins** 701L53
ˌSiamese ˈ**twins** 1332R38
ˌterrible ˈ**twins** 1504R2
get *one's* ˈknickers in a ˌ**twist** 783L68
ˌround the ˈ**twist** 1574L16
ˌsend round the ˈ**twist** 1574L16
ˌ**twist** *someone* around/round *one's* little ˈfinger 1573R84 1689L69
ˌ**twist** ˈoff 1573R70
twist the ˌknife (in the ˈwound) 783R49
ˈ**twist**-ˌtie 1574L4
ˈ**twist** with 1573R73
ˈtongue ˌ**twister** 1534R73
ˈarm-ˌ**twisting** 62R31
a ˈthing or ˌ**two** 1512R17/18/21
as like as/like ˌ**two** peas in a ˈpod 822R53
as ˌthick as **two** short ˈplanks 1511L58
be ˌwith you in ˌ**two** ˈticks 1518R5
ˌcut ˈ**two** ˌways 338R74
ˌfall between **two** ˈstools 497R66
give *someone* ˌ**two** ˈfingers 1576L18
in ˌ**two** ˈminds 1574R83
kill ˌ**two** birds with one ˈstone 779R75
ˈknow a thing or ˌ**two** 786R25
ˌmeat and **two** ˈveg 880L58
ˌno **two** ˌways aˈbout it 1574R66
not ˌcare/ˌgive **two** ˈhoots 684R16
ˌnot have **two** ˌpennies to rub toˈgether 1045R64
not ˌshort of a ˈbob or **two** 1324L40
of ˌ**two** ˈminds 1574R84
ˌone step ˈforward ˌ**two** steps ˈback 1420R9
ˌone-ˈ**two** ˌpunch 984R60
put/stick **two** ˈfingers in the ˌair/ˌup 1576L17
put ˌ**two** and two together and ˌmake ˈfive 1574R75/78
ˌthat makes ˈ**two** of us 1576L6
the ˌlesser of **two** ˈevils 811R83
ˌ**two** a ˈpenny 384R79 1045R70
ˈ**two**-ˌbit 1576L23
ˌ**two**-by-ˈfour 1576L25
ˌ**two** can play at ˈthat ˌgame 1576L9
two ˈcents ˌworth 1574R70
ˌ**two**-diˈmensional 1576L29/31
ˌ**two**-ˈedged 1576L35/36
ˌ**two**-ˈfaced 1576L41
ˌ**two** ˈfingers 1603L60
ˌ**two**-ˈhanded 1576L45
ˌ**two**-ˈhander 1576L48
ˌ**two** of a ˈkind 1576L4
ˌ**two**-ˈpiece 1576L49
ˌ**two**-ˈply 1576L52
ˌ**two**-ˈseater 1576L54
two ˌshakes (of a duck's/lamb's ˈtail) 1307R14
ˌ**two** strings to *one's* ˈbow 1443R47
ˈ**two**-ˌtime 1576L55/59
ˈ**two**-ˌtone 1576L62
ˌ**two**-ˈway 1576L63/64/65
ˌ**two**-way ˈmirror 1576L70
ˌ**two**-way ˈstreet 1576L69
in ˌones and ˈ**twos** 983R76
ˌblood ˈ**type** 137L61
ˈtouch-ˌ**type** 1540R12
ˌtrue to ˈ**type** 1563R64
ˌ**type** ˈB 1576R26
ˌ**type** ˈup 1576R64/66
ˌshorthand ˈ**typist** 1324R32
ˌbald ˈ**tyre** 95L55
ˈsnow ˌ**tyre** 1367L72
ˌspare ˈ**tyre** 1383L70 1577R29
ˈ**tyre** ˌpressure 1577R29
ˈ**tzetze** ˌfly 1577R35
as ˌ**ugly** as ˈsin 1577R72
ˌplug-ˈ**ugly** 1084L28/30
ˌ**ugly** Aˈmerican 1577R69
ˌ**ugly** ˈduckling 1577R73
in the ˌ**ultimate** aˈnalysis 43R42
make the ˌ**ultimate** ˈsacrifice 1247R20
ˌpay the ˌ**ultimate** ˈprice 1038L80
umˈ**bilical** ˌcord 1578R30
ˌtake ˈ**umbrage** 1578R35
un-Aˈmerican 1579R10
the ˌ**unacceptable** ˈface of 1579L28
ˌ**unarmed** ˈcombat 261L57
ˌtake **una**ˈ**wares** 1486R62
in ˌno **uncertain** ˈterms 1501R45
ˈagony ˌ**uncle** 27L44/49/48
ˌbob's your ˈ**uncle** 142L62
ˌI'll be a monkey's ˈ**uncle** 914R82
ˌsay ˈ**uncle** 1259R70
ˌ**Uncle** ˈSam 1581L71
ˌ**Uncle** ˈTom 1581L76
ˌ**uncrowned** ˈking 1582R3
ˌ**uncrowned** ˈqueen 1582R3
ˌbags **under** *someone's* ˈeyes 93L57
ˌchuck **under** the ˈchin 231L24/28
ˌcome/ˌgo **under** the ˈhammer 639R26
ˌcut the ˈground from **under** *someone's* ˈfeet 339L83
ˌdown ˈ**under** 415R75
ˌdrink *someone* **under** the ˈtable 424R18
ˌdrive **under** the ˈinfluence 425L56
get ˌ**under** *someone's* ˈskin 1346R30
ˌhot **under** the ˈcollar 687R17
ˌkeep/ˌplace **under** reˈstraint 1213R40
ˌpull the ˈcarpet/ˈrug from **under** 1144L48
ˌput the ˈskids **under** 1346L32
ˈput *someone* **under** 337L62 1153R73
ˌright out from **under** *someone's* ˈnose 962L49
ˌsister **under** the ˈskin 1342R64
ˌsix feet ˈ**under** 1344L47
ˌsnowed ˈ**under** 1367R1
ˈsomething ˌ**under** 1375L21
ˌsweep **under** the ˈcarpet/under the ˈrug/under the ˈmat 1475L21
ˌsweep under the **under** the ˈrug 1475L21
ˌtake **under** *one's* ˈwing 1669L14
ˌ**under** a ˈcloud 248R54
ˌ**under** ˈage 24R70/82
ˌ**under** ˈarms 63L6
ˌ**under** *one's* ˈbelt 116R7
ˌ**under** *one's* ˈbreath 162R50 933R64
ˌ**under** ˈcanvas 190R21
ˌ**under** ˈcapitalized 191R60
under ˌfalse ˈcolours 499R58
under ˌfalse preˈtences 499R61
ˌ**under** *someone's* ˈfeet 545R52
ˌ**under** ˈguard 629L53
ˌ**under** ˈlicence 817L51
under ˌlock and ˈkey 835L83/R1
ˌ**under** ˈoffer 977L57
under *one's* ˌown ˈsteam 1418L49
ˌ**under** ˈpain of 1018R33
ˌ**under** ˈpar 1023R42/53
under ˌplain/ˌseparate ˈcover 316L62
ˌ**under** ˈprotest 1137R46
ˌ**under** ˈsail 1249R68
ˌ**under**-ˈsecretary 1583L5
ˌ**under** ˈsiege 1334R78/80
under ˌstarter's ˈorders 1413R50
ˌ**under** the ˈaegis of 21L36
ˌ**under** the ˈauspices of 80L43
ˌ**under** the ˈcircumstances 233R18
ˌ**under** the conˈditions of 283L62
ˌ**under** the ˈcounter 312R28
ˌ**under** the ˈheel of 660L39
ˌ**under** the ˈinfluence 728L26
ˌ**under** the ˈknife 783R59
ˈ**under** the ˌlash 797L52
ˌ**under** the ˈname of 937L48
ˌ**under** the ˈplough 1082R56
under the ˌsame ˈroof 1233L13
ˌ**under** the ˈshadow of 1306L75/76
ˌ**under** the ˈsun 1459R61
ˌ**under** the ˈtable 1483L57
ˌ**under** the ˈweather 1648L34
ˌ**under** ˈthreat of 1515L48
ˌ**under** *one's* very ˈeyes 488L57
ˌ**under** ˈway 1583L53 1645L62
ˌ**under** ˈwraps 1689R4
ˌwater **under** the ˈbridge 1642L69
ˌgive *someone* to **under**ˈ**stand** 597L2
ˌthermal ˈ**underwear** 1510R34
unˌ**dress** *someone* with *one's* ˈeyes 1586R74
ˌ**unearned** ˈincome 1587L25
unemˈ**ployment** ˌbenefit 1587R5
unemˈ**ployment** inˌsurance 1587R10
ˌcome **un**ˈ**glued** 1588R68
go ˌ**un**ˈ**heard** 1589L22
ˈcraft ˌ**union** 319L67
Euroˌpean ˈ**Union** 471L55
ˈlabor ˌ**union** 1546R74
ˌRugby ˈ**Union** 1239R10
ˌstudent ˈ**union** 1447R16
ˌtrade ˈ**union** 1546R79/73/78/73
ˈ**union**-ˌbashing 102L63
ˈ**Union** ˌFlag 1590R27
ˌ**Union** ˈJack 1590R28
ˈbomb disˌposal ˌ**unit** 145R1
deˈlivery ˌ**unit** 363L26
ˈsink ˌ**unit** 1342L23
ˌ**unit** ˈtrust 1590L53
ˈvanitory ˌ**unit** 1606R18
ˈvanity ˌ**unit** 1604R80 1606R18
the Uˌ**nited** ˈKingdom 1590R9
the Uˌ**nited** ˈNations 1590R6
ˌ**universal** ˈjoint 1590R46
ˌarmpit of the ˈ**Universe** 63R17
colˌlegiate **uni**ˈ**versity** 258L67
ˌOpen **Uni**ˈ**versity** 988R55
ˌ**unknown** ˈquantity 1591L81
ˌleave an **unpleasant** ˈtaste 807L69
ˌquote ˈ**unquote** 749R74 1164L35
ˌsight **un**ˈ**seen** 1335R30
of ˌ**unsound** ˈmind 898R75
ˌcome **un**ˈ**stuck** 266L5/8 1596L13
ˌ**unsung** ˈhero 1596L25
ˌsqueeze *someone* **until** the ˈpips squeak 1403R68
until *someone is* ˌblue in the ˈface 139R56
until ˌkingdom ˈcome 781L53
until the ˈcows come ˌhome 317L48
unˌ**til** ˈthen 1509L57
ˌup **un**ˈ**til** 1597R27
ˌwait **until** the ˈdust has settled 433L15
ˌwork **until** *one* ˈdrops 1679R41
a ˌlaw **unto** *one*ˈself 801L32
ˌleave ˌno stone **un**ˈ**turned** 807L83
a ˌboot/ˌkick **up** the backˈside 91L13
ˈace **up** *one's* ˈsleeve 10R56
ˌact ˈ**up** 13L6/8
ˌadd ˈ**up** to 15L33/37/38
ˌback ˈ**up** 90L6 1485R33
ˌbark **up** the wrong ˈtree 100L73
ˈblood *is* ˌ**up** 137L52
ˌboil ˈ**up** 144L57
ˌbollix ˈ**up** 144R66
ˈbooze-ˌ**up** 148R48
ˌbottle ˈ**up** 151R42
ˌbottoms ˈ**up** 152L64
ˌbound ˈ**up** 153L66
ˌbreak it/something ˈ**up** 161L64
ˌbreak ˈ**up** 160R59 161L8
ˌbring **up** ˈshort 166R3
ˌbring **up** the ˈrear 166L37 1181L57
ˌbrush ˈ**up** on 170L80
ˌbuild ˈ**up** 173L72/79/83
ˌbuilt-ˈ**up** 173L70
ˌcamp it ˈ**up** 187R23
ˌcard **up** *one's* ˈsleeve 195L23
ˌcatch ˈ**up** 1598L47
ˌcaught ˈ**up** in 204L54
ˈchat-**up** ˌline 220L52 826L63
ˌclean **up** *one's* ˈact 241L52
ˌclimb ˈ**up** 244R17/35
ˈclose-**up** 247R80
ˌclose **up** ˈshop 1321L79
ˌclue ˈ**up** 250R36
ˌcock ˈ**up** 252R70/75
ˌcome ˈ**up** aˌgainst 265L42
ˌcome **up** ˌsmelling of ˈroses 1360L29
ˌcome ˈ**up** to 264R47 265L44
ˌcome ˈ**up** with 267L4
come ˌ**up** with the ˈgoods 612R49
ˌcoming **up** ˈroses 1234R65
ˌcoop ˈ**up** 303L81
ˌcork ˈ**up** 305R81/82
ˌcover ˈ**up** 316R52/58
ˌcrack ˈ**up** 318R16/17
ˌcrack *it* ˈ**up** to be 318R68
ˌcurl ˈ**up** 336R29
ˌcurl **up** and ˈdie 336R31
ˌcut **up** ˈrough 339R81

▫do the ▫drying ▪up 430L4
▫done/▫dressed/▫got up like a ▫dog's ▪dinner 408R58
▫drinking-▪up ▫time 424R26
▫dry up (the ▪dishes) 430L3
▪dust-up 433L20
▫eaten ▪up with/by 439L80
▫face ▪up to 492L20 1402R6
▫fed ▪up 509R36
▪flare-up 530R15/23
▫fling up *one's* ▪hands 534R49
▫follow ▪up on 543R11
▪fry-up 570R49
▫gen ▪up 586R36
▫get/▫pick up ▪steam 1418L46
▫get ▪up 591R50/51/53/54 593R41/44/46/49/56 1598L27
▫get-up-and-▪go 593R69
get ▫up *someone's* ▪nose 961R66
get up on the ▫wrong side of the ▪bed 111L43
get ▪up to 591L48
give *someone* a ▫leg ▪up 809L10
▫give ▪up 596R44 597L56
give *something* ▫up as a bad ▪job 92L35
▫give ▪up on 597L67/69
▫give up the ▪ghost 594L40
go/turn ▫belly ▪up 116L17
go ▫up in ▪flames 529R80
go ▫up in ▪smoke 1361L58
go ▪up in the ▫world 1685L16
▫grow ▪up 627R2
▫growing ▪up 627L82 1598R5
▫grown-▪up 627R7/10
▫gum up the ▪works 632L52
▫gummed ▪up 632L50
▫ham *something* ▪up 639L70
▫hands ▪up 641L6/12
hang ▪up 645L3
▫hard ▪up 647R40
have a ▫leg ▪up on 809L12
have *something* up *one's* ▪sleeve 1351R68
het ▪up 666L15
▫high ▪up 668R71
▫higher-▪up 668R74
▫hold ▪up 676R27
▫hung ▪up on 1058L78
▫hype ▪up 697L40
it ▫doesn't add ▪up 15L40
▫jazzed-▪up 761L6
▫join ▪up 767L73
▫jump up and ▪down 772R11
▪jumped-up 773L2
▫keep *one's* ▪chin up 227L13
▫keep/▫hold *one's* ▪end up 455L50
▫keep *one's* ▪pecker up 1041L49
▫keep up ap▪pearances 55R54 777L33
keep ▫up with the ▪Joneses 777L3
keep ▫up with the ▪times 1524L29
▫kick up a ▪fuss/▪row 779L9
▫kick up a ▪rumpus 1240R50
▫kick up a ▪stink 1426L82
▫kick up *one's* ▪heels 779L1
▫kick up the ▪arse/▪backside/▪pants 779L34
▪knees-up 783L40
▫laid ▪up 793L6
▫laugh up *one's* ▪sleeve 800L27
▫lay up ▪trouble 803L51
▫lead *someone* up the garden ▪path 804L35
▫leave up in the ▪air 807R8
▫lighten ▪up 821R45
▫lighting-▪up ▫time 820R54
▫line ▪up 825L82
▫link ▪up 827R49/60
▫live it ▪up 832R59
live ▪up to 832R68
▫look/▫feel like ▪death ▫warmed ▪up 352R4
look ▪up to 839L41
▫loosen ▪up 841L2/6
▫louse ▪up 843L54/55
▫made-▪up 851R42/44
▫make it ▪up 856R65/36
▫make *one's* ▪mind up 899L57
▫make ▪up 856L83/R7/18/22/33/39/43/49 857L73/7
make ▪up for 856R55
make up for ▫lost ▪time 856R61
▫make up *one's* ▪mind 856R49 899L56
make ▪up to 856R65/70
▫mashed-▪up 870L14
▫measure ▪up to 879R7
▪mess-up 889R58/63/78/82/84
▫messed-▪up 890L14
▫mind is made ▪up 899L58
▫mix it ▪up 908R29
▫mix ▪up 908R41/46/52
▫mixed ▪up 908R57/63
move ▪up in the ▫world 1685L17
▪nosh-up 962R23
▫not come/live ▫up to expec▪tation(s) 480R81
▫not up to ▪par 1023R44
someone's ▫number *is* ▪up 967L30
on the ▫up and ▪up 1597R64
on the ▪up ▫grade 616L48
▫open ▪up 988R39
▫organize a ▫piss-up in a ▪brewery 995R13
▫paid-▪up 1018R7/10
▪paste-up 1033R74
▫pent-▪up 1046R5
▪pick-me-up 1062R19
▫pick ▪up on 1063L15
▫pick up the ▪bill/▪tab 1062R4 1483L32
▫pick up the ▪gauntlet 585L58
▫pick up the ▪pieces 1062R9
▫pick up the ▪slack 1348L65
▫pick up the ▪threads 1062R14
▪pick-up ▫truck 1062R76/74
▫pile ▪up 1066L66/68/79
▪piss-up 1070R21
▫play ▪up to 1078R64
▫pluck up the/*one's* ▪courage 1083L59
▫pop ▪up 1095L52/59/61/63
▫power ▪up 1106R19
▪press-up 1118L38
▫puffed ▪up 1143R50
▫pull/▫haul *oneself* ▫up by *one's* ▪bootstraps 148R34
▫pull *one's* ▪socks up 1144L81
▫pull ▪up 1145L4
▫pull up ▪short 1145L4
▫pull up ▪stakes 1422R64
▪punch-up 1146R5
▫push up (the) ▪daisies 1151L71
▫put/▫get *someone's* ▪back up 89R72
▫put/▫get the ▪wind up 1666R77
put/stick two ▪fingers ▫up 1576L17
put ▪up to 1155L66
put ▪up with 1155L70
▫ride ▪up 1222L41
▫ring ▪up 1225R43
▫roll up *one's* ▪sleeves 1231R21
▫roll ▪up! ▫roll ▪up! 1231L33
▫rough *someone* ▪up 1236L42
▪run-up 1241L18 1243L58/61/63/68
▫run ▪up against 1243L70
▫runner-▪up 1243R27
▫screw ▪up 1273L74
▫screw up *one's* ▪courage 1273L34
▫send ▪up 1291R59/64 1292L3/18/23
▫set up ▪shop 1321L76
▫shack ▪up 1304R38
▪shake-up 1307L47 1308L20/31
▫shape ▪up or ▫ship ▪out 1311L22
▫shove/▫stick/▫ram *something* up *someone's* ▪ass 71L65
shut ▫up like a ▪clam 236L5
▫shut up ▪shop 1321L78 1331R83
sit ▫up and take ▪notice 1343R62
▪slap-up 1349R24
▫smarten up *one's* ▪act 1358R25
▫smell ▪up 1360L37
▫snap it ▪up 1364L75
▪snarl-up 1365L24
▫soften ▪up 1371R63
▪souped-up 1380L3
▫speak ▪up 1384R74
▫square ▪up to 1402R6
▫stand ▪up 1410L75 1411L80
▫stand ▪up for 1411R1
▫stand ▪up to 1411R4
▫steam ▪up 1418L62
▫steamed ▪up 1418L67
step/move ▪up a ▫gear 586L11
▫stick ▪up for 1424L29
▫stir ▪up 1427L36
▫stock ▪up on 1427R64
▫stoke ▪up on 1429L13
▫straight ▪up 1433L54/55
▫strung ▪up 1446R46
▫stuck-▪up 1447L45
▫stuffed-▪up 1448L63
▫suck ▪up to 1455L80
▫sum ▪up 1459L11
▪sun-up 1459R80 1461L3
▫take up (the) ▪cudgels 333L81
▫take *someone* ▪up on 977L51 1488L9
▫take ▪up ▫with 1488L12
▫tanked ▪up 1490L47
▫tense ▪up 1501L6
the bal▪loon goes ▫up 96L1
the ▪game is ▫up 581L69
the ▪jig is ▫up 764L62
▫throw ▪up 1517L43
throw up *one's* ▫hands in ▪horror/de▪spair at 1517L41
▫thumbs ▪up 1517R37
▫time's ▪up 1521R62
▫tog ▪up 1531R38
▫tooled ▪up 1535R52
▫toss ▪up 1539R27
▫turn *one's* ▪nose up 1571L61
▫turn-up for the ▪book(s) 1571L53
▫turn up like a ▫bad ▪penny 1571L51
▫turn up ▪trumps 1564L30
up a ▪gum ▫tree 632L42
up against a ▫brick ▪wall 24R7
up a▪gainst it 24R11
▫up *someone's* ▪alley 34L45 1437L34
▫up and a▪bout/a▪round 1598L30
▫up-and-▪coming 1597R76
▫up and ▪down 1597R17/50 1598L11/14/R26/27
▫up-and-▪over 1597R41
▫up and ▪running 1241R46 1598L79
▫up-▪country 1598R60
▫up for ▪grabs 615L43
▫up ▪front 568L28
up ▫hill and down ▪dale 670L43
▫up in ▪arms 63L7
▫up in the ▪air 29R23
▫up-▪market 1598R69
▫up my ▪ass 71L69/70
▫up ▪river 1227R15
▫up ▪sticks 1422R64
▫up *someone's* ▪street 1437L33
▪up-▫tempo 1598R73
▫up the ▪creek 322R34
▫up the ▪spout 1399L17/18
▫up the ▪stakes 1408L37
▫up the ▪wall 1635L48
▪up ▫till 1520L84 1597R27
▫up to a ▪point 1089R55/57
▫up-to-▪date 1597R29/31
▫up to *one's* ▪ears in 436L68
▫up to *one's* ▪eyeballs 488R74
▫up to *one's* ▪eyes in 488L84
▫up to *one's* ▪neck in 945R48
▫up to no ▪good 612L27
▫up to ▪scratch 1271R66
▫up to ▪speed 1388R54/57
▫up to the/*one's* ▪ears/▪eyeballs/▪eyes/▪neck 1597R35
▫up-to-the-▪minute 902L53 1597R33
▫up un▪til 1597R27
▫up with the ▪clock 1598L59
▫up with the ▪lark 796R36
▪walk-up 1634R31
▫warm ▪up 1638L32/41/44/45/47/48/51
▫washed-▪up 1639R69
▫washing-▪up 1639R33
▫washing-▪up ▫liquid 1639R38
▫weigh ▪up 1650L59
▫well-brought-▪up 1652L63
▫whoop it ▪up 1662R36
▫wire ▪up 1670R73 1671L11
▫worked ▪up 1598L23 1682R71
up▪date *someone* on 1599L18/19
up▪grade to 1599L38
▫come-▪uppance 267L51
▫stiff upper ▪lip 1424L60
the ▫upper ▪chamber 1599R40
the ▫upper ▪hand 1599R36
the ▫upper ▪house 1599R40
▫upper ▪case 1599R27
▫upper ▪class 237R81 1599R28
▫upper ▪crust 1599R29
▫upper ▪house 689R32/37
▫bolt ▪upright 1599R70
▫upright pi▪ano 1599R72
▪lace-▫ups 791L79
▪ups-a-▫daisy 987L31
▫ups and ▪downs 1598R35
up▫set the ▪apple cart 1600L53
▫turn upside ▪down 1569R69
▫upside ▪down 1600L69
▫kick up▪stairs 779L13
▫quick/▫slow on the ▪uptake 1600R43
▫onward and ▪upward 986R75
▫upward mo▪bility 909L80 1600R80
▫upwardly ▪mobile 1601L12
▫urban ▪jungle 1601L29
▪sea ▫urchin 1276L22
▫genito-▪urinary 588R6
▫that makes ▪two of us 1576L6
▪land-▫use 794L23
▫no use crying over spilt ▪milk 331R55
▫turn/▫use to (▫good) ac▪count 10L3
▫use *one's* ▪head 1601R67
▫use *one's* ▪loaf 1601R68
▫use ▪up 1602L67
▫what's the ▪use of 1602L14
▫half the *person one* ▪used to be 638L2
▫make *oneself* ▪useful 1602L31
out▫live *one's* ▪usefulness 1002R81 1602L37
▪end ▫user 455L61
▫user-▪friendly 565R48 1602L55/58
▫usher ▪in 1602R43
▪usher ▫into 1602R41
▫as per ▪usual 1047L27
the ▫usual ▪run of 1242L55
▫orang-u▪tan 993L24
u▪tility ▫room 1603L21
▫do/▫try *one's* ▪utmost 1603R5
com▪plete and ▫utter 275R45
▫Situations ▪Vacant 1344L23
▫vacant pos▪session 1603R67
▫fly-drive va▪cation 540R2
▫long va▪cation 838R4
▫canister ▪vacuum ▫cleaner 189R34
▫cylinder ▪vacuum ▫cleaner 189R35
▪power ▫vacuum 1105R40
▪vacuum ▫flask 531L30 1604L67
▫vacuum-▪packed 1604L70
▪vacuum ▫pump 1604L72
this ▫vale of ▪tears 1605L2
▪valet ▫parking 1605L25
▪valet ▫service 1605L26
▫lily of the ▪valley 823L67
▪rift ▫valley 1222R54
curi▪osity ▫value 336L77
▫face ▪value 490R41/78
▫rateable ▪value 1175L17
▪street ▫value 1437L58
take at ▫face ▪value 490R81
▪value ▫judgment 1605R24
▪safety ▫valve 1248R78
▫vamp ▪up 1606L23
▪vampire ▫bat 1606L29
▪camper ▫van 187R5 412R52
▪guard's ▫van 629L84
▪luggage ▫van 846R32
▪weather ▫vane 1648L50
▫vanish into thin ▪air 1511R36
▪vanitory ▫unit 1606R18
▪vanity ▫plate 1604R77
▪vanity ▫press 1604R75
▪vanity ▫unit 1604R80 1606R18
▪vantage ▫point 1606R29
▪vapour ▫trail 1606R53
▪water ▫vapour 1642R43
▫varicose ▪vein 1606R74
var▪iety ▫meat 976R57
var▪iety ▫store 1607L14
▪nail ▫varnish 936L69
▪vary between 1607L75
▪vary in 1607L77
▪vaudeville ▫theater 931L53
▪pole ▫vault 1091L32/35
▪vault over 1609R64
▫vaulting am▪bition 1609R73
▪vaulting ▫horse 686L69
▪vee ▫sign 1603L54
▫veer ▪off 1610L33
▪veer onto 1610L40
▪veer to 1610L35/41
▫meat and two ▪veg 880L58
▫veg ▪out 1610L47/R19
▫vegetable ▪marrow 868L42
▫vegetable ▪oil 1610L82
▫heavy ▪goods vehicle 659L16
▪motor ▫vehicle 921R18 1610R62
recre▫ational ▪vehicle 1188L14
▫draw a ▪veil over 420L64
▫take/a▫dopt the ▪veil 1611L43
▫take the ▪veil 1611L39
▫varicose ▪vein 1606R74
es▪cape ve▫locity 467R68
▪vending ma▫chine 1612L64
ve▫nereal dis▪ease 1613L13
ve▫netian ▪blind 1613L18
▪Venn ▫diagram 1613L46
▫spit ▪venom 1393R44
▫give ▪vent 1613L82
▪vol-au-▫vent 1629R64
ven▫triloquist's ▪dummy 1613R31
▪venture ▫capital 1613R42
▫venture ▪capitalist 1613R47
▪venture on 1613R63/65
▪Venture ▫Scout 1613R66/73
▪venture to 1613R53
▫Venus ▪flytrap 1614L12
▫aloe ▪vera 36L37
▪linking ▫verb 827R36
▫main ▪verb 853R66
▫modal ▪verb 909R80
▫phrasal ▪verb 1059R64
▫prepositional ▪verb 1115L62
re▫flexive ▪verb 1191R64
▫non-▪verbal 959R49
▫verbal diar▪rhoea 1614L43
▫open ▪verdict 988L34 1614R8
re▫turn a ▪verdict of 1217L49
▪verge on 1614R37
▫vernal ▪equinox 1615L51
▫vice ▪versa 1621L49
▫blank ▪verse 133L84
▫chapter and ▪verse 216R20
▫free ▪verse 561L52
▪nonsense ▫verse 960L80
▫well-▪versed 1615R3 1653R27
▫vertical ▪blind 1615R54
▫vertical inte▪gration 1615R57
▫vertical ▪take-off 1615R62
▪blood ▫vessel 137R3
▫burst a ▪blood ▫vessel 137R6/8
▫down ▪vest 143R25 416R26
▪vest in/with 1617R79/80/84/77
▫vested ▪interest 741R60 1617R81 1619L51/52/56/46
▪Veterans ▫Day 1619R81
▫veterinary ▪surgeon 1619R51 1620L5
▫pocket ▪veto 1088L8
▫positive ▪vetting 1098R80
▪vex with 1620L31
vi▪brate with 1620R49/50
▫vicar of ▪Christ 1620R71
▫vice-▪chancellor 1621L38
▫Vice ▪President 1621L39
▪vice ▫ring 1621L18
▪vice ▫squad 1621L15
▫vice ▪versa 1621L49
▫vicious ▪circle 1621L76
▪fashion ▫victim 505L41
▫pyrrhic ▪victory 1156R46
snatch ▫victory (from the jaws of de▪feat) 1365L46
▪music ▫video 1622L47
▪video ar▫cade 1622L51
▪video ▫camera 1622L53
▫video cas▪sette 1622L58
▫video cas▪sette re▫corder 1622L71
▪video ▫disc 1622L59
▪video ▫game 1622L62
▪video ▫monitor 1622L66
▫video ▪nasty 1622L69
▪video re▫corder 1622L71
▪videotape re▫corder 1622L72
▫c'est la ▪vie 211R33
▪vie for 1622R15/16/18
a ▫bird's eye ▪view 128L55
▫hove in(to) ▪view 690L55
in ▫full ▪view of 572L79
▫pay-per-▪view 1038R8
▫point of ▪view 1089R63
▫rear ▫view ▪mirror 1181L59
▫take the ▪view that 1487L26
the ▫global ▪village 600L23
▪villain of the ▫piece 1624L24
▫wither on the ▪vine 1673R41
▫campaign of ▪violence 187R40
▫non-▪violence 959R54/50
▫robbery with ▪violence 1229L55
▫African ▪violet 23L46
▫shrinking ▪violet 1330L29
▫anti-▪viral 50L54/56
▫Blessed ▪Virgin 135L21
vir▫ginia ▪creeper 1625R23
▫virtual re▪ality 1625R59
make a ▪virtue (out) of 1626L9
▫vis-a-▪vis 1626L81
▪exit ▫visa 480L23 1626L72
▫double ▪vision 414R16
▫tunnel ▪vision 1568L38/40
▫twenty-twenty ▪vision 1572R49
▫flying ▪visit 540R47 1627L48
▫state ▪visit 1414R59
▪visiting ▫hours 1627L38
▪health ▫visitor 655R16
▪visitors' ▫book 1627L68
▪sun ▫visor 1459R81
▫audio-▪visual 79R10
▫visual ▪aid 1627R18
▫visual ▪arts 1627R22
la ▫dolce ▪vita 792L47
cur▫riculum ▪vitae 337L25
▫vital ▪organ 1627R73
▫vital ▪signs 1627R75
▫vital sta▪tistics 1627R79/83
▫vitamin B▪2 1220R74
in ▫vitro fertili▪zation 751L48
▫viva ▪voce 1628L44
▫bon vi▪vant 146R60
▫modus vi▪vendi 911R27
▫bon vi▪veur 146R61
▫joie de ▪vivre 767L55
▫vocal ▪cords 1628R41
▫sotto ▪voce 1378L32
▫viva ▪voce 1628L44
at the ▫top of *one's* ▪voice 1537L7
dis▫senting ▪voice 398L60
▫give ▪voice 1629L66/R5
▫mystery ▪voice 934R64
▫sink *one's voice* to a ▪whisper 1341R65
▫throw *one's* ▪voice 1517L19
▪voice ▫box 796R72 1629L71
▪voice ▫mail 1629L71
▪voice-▫over 1629L73
▫null and ▪void 966R69
▪vol-au-▫vent 1629R64
▫half ▪volley 638L27
▫volte-▪face 1630L31
▫speak ▪volumes 1385L50
▫absentee ▪vote 5L48 1100R74
▫block ▪vote 136R33
▪card ▫vote 195L12
▫casting ▪vote 202R5
de▫ciding ▪vote 354R32
▫put to the/a ▪vote 1631L32
▪sympathy ▫vote 1480R9
▫vote ▪down 1631L15
▪vote-▫getter 1631L49
▫vote of ▪confidence 1631L37
vote of ▫no ▪confidence 1631L45
▫vote of ▪thanks 1631L52
▫vote ▪through 1631L18
▫vote with *one's* ▪feet 1631L21
▫floating ▪voter 535R44
▫canvass ▪votes 18L14 54L21 132R68 198L73 326L45 337L50 546R83 547L4/10 782R37/38 1038L49
▪voting ma▫chine 1631L26
▪vouch for 1631L66/69
▪luncheon ▫voucher 848L23
▫vox ▪pop 1631R18
▫bon vo▪yage 146R64
▫déjà ▪vu 361R6
▪culture ▫vulture 334R71

▫shoot *one's* ▪**wad** 1319R56
▫**wade** ▪in 1632L64
▪**wade** into 1632L71
▫**wade** ▪through 1632L54/74
▪**wading** ▫bird 1632L58
▪**wading** ▫pool 1017R39 1632L55
▫**wafer** ▪biscuit 1632R20
▫**wafer**-▪thin 1632R18
▫**waffle** ▪on 1632R27
▫living ▪**wage** 832L60 1632R67
▫minimum ▪**wage** 900R80 1632R66
▪**wage** ▫earner 1632R70
▪**wage** ▫freeze 1632R72
▪**wage** ▫packet 1632R74
▫**wage** ▪war on/against 1632R84
set/start ▪tongues ▫**wagging** 1534R55
the ▫tail **wagging** the ▪dog 1485R29
▫fall off the ▪**wagon** 1633L28
▪paddy ▫**wagon** 1017R59 1036R48
pa▫trol ▫**wagon** 1036R48
▪station ▫**wagon** 469L59 1415L82
▪tea ▫**wagon** 1494L36
▫**wagon**-▪lit 1633L29
▪Welcome ▫**Wagon** 1650R66
▫**waifs** and ▪strays 1633L35
▪**waist** ▫pack 175L12 1633L51
▫wasp-▪**waisted** 1640L29
can ▫hardly ▪**wait** 1633R7
▫just you ▪**wait** 1633R9
▫lie in ▪**wait** 1633R63
▫**wait** a ▪minute/▪moment/▪second 1633R13
▫**wait** and ▪see 44R31 1633R19
▫**wait** a▪round 1633L79
▫**wait** a▪round/a▪bout 1633L79
▫**wait** be▪hind 1633R20
▪**wait** for 1633L72/74/75/81/84/R4/62
▫**wait** in the ▪wings 1633R30
▫**wait** (at/on) ▪table(s) 1633R41/42
▫**wait** *one's* ▪turn 1633R45
▫**wait** until the ▪dust has settled 433L15
▫**wait** ▪up 1633R46
▫dumb ▪**waiter** 431R61
▫lady-in-▪**waiting** 792R8
▫ready and ▪**waiting** 1179L63
▪**waiting** ▫game 1633R49
▪**waiting** ▫list 1633R52
▪**waiting** ▫room 1633R58
▫leave ▫*something* in *one's* ▪**wake** 1634L27
▪**wake** out of/from 1634L6
▫**wake** ▪up 1634L3/4/6
▫**wakey** ▪wakey 1634L16
▫**waking** ▪hour 1634L20
▫Prince of ▪**Wales** 1122L73
▫**walk(s)** of ▪life 1634R46
▫cock-of-the-▪**walk** 252R33
take a ▫**walk** down memory ▪lane 886L22
▫**walk** a ▪tightrope 1520L42
▫**walk** all ▪over 1634L59
▫**walk** a▪way from 1634L62/65/68
▫**walk** a▪way/▪off with 1634L70
▪**walk** into 1634L78
▪**walk** it 1634L43
▫**walk** ▪off 1634L81
▫**walk** on ▪air 29L41 1634R1
▫**walk** on ▪eggs/▪eggshells 1634R2
▫**walk** ▪out 1634R10
▫**walk** ▪tall 1489L47
▫**walk** the ▪streets 1437L23/27
▪**walk**-up 1634R31
▫**walkie**-▪talkie 1634R75
▪**walking** ▫frame 1634R62 1700L56
▪**walking** ▫papers 864L71 1634R28
▫back is to the ▪**wall** 89R68
▫beat/▫bang/▫knock *one's* ▫head against a brick ▪**wall** 653L33
▫cavity ▪**wall** 207L62
▫dry stone ▪**wall** 429R71
▪fly-on-the-▫**wall** 540R69/65
go to the ▪**wall** 1635L44
▫handwriting is on the ▪**wall** 643R20
have *one's* ▫back to the ▪**wall** 89R68
▫hole in the ▪**wall** 677R11/27
▫party ▪**wall** 1030R55
▫sea ▪**wall** 1276L24
up against a ▫brick ▪**wall** 24R7
▫up the ▪**wall** 1635L48
▫**wall** ▪off 1635L65
▪**Wall** ▫Street 1635L58
▫**wall**-to-▪wall 1635L53
▫**wall** ▪up 1635L66
▫writing/▫handwriting is on the ▪**wall** 1692L30
▪**wallow** in 1635R35/36/40
▪**wallpaper** ▫music 1635R54
▫climb the ▪**walls** 284R28
▫**walrus** mous▪tache 1635R77
▫**waltz** ▪round 1636L4
▪**waltz** through 1636L13
▫magic ▪**wand** 852L52
▫**wander** a▪round 1636L29
▫**wander** ▪off 1636L32
▫wax and ▪**wane** 1645L36
▫**wangle** *one's* ▪way into 1636L68
Do you ▫**want** to make something ▪of it? 856L30
▪**want** ▫ad 238R71 1636R33
▪**want** ▫for 1636R52
▫**want** ▪out of/▪in 1636R31
(How ▫much) *do you* **want** to ▪bet? 119R74
▫tried and found ▪**wanting** 1636R62
▫civil ▪**war** 234R72
▫cold ▪**war** 256R68
▫council of ▪**war** 311R12
▫holy ▪**war** 679R17
▫phoney ▪**war** 1058R58
▫prisoner of ▪**war** 1123R57
▫sinews of ▪**war** 1340R43
▫tug-of-▪**war** 1567L34
▪**war** ▫bride 1637L23
▪**war** ▫clouds 1637L25
▪**war** ▫crime 1637L32/29
▪**war** ▫cry 1637L33
▪**war** ▫dance 1637L37
▪**war** ▫game 1637L40
▪**war** me▫morial 1637L42
▪**war** ▫paint 1637L44/46
▫world ▪**war** 1684R80/81/79
ma▫ternity ▫**ward** 363L27 874L2
▫**ward** ▪off 1637R17
▪traffic ▫**warden** 1547R73
▪discount ▫**warehouse** 391R37
bio▫logical/▫chemical ▪**warfare** 127R61 590L31
▫chemical ▪**warfare** 223R62
▫germ ▪**warfare** 590L31
psycho▫logical ▪**warfare** 1141L42
▫**warm**-▪blooded 1638L28
▫**warm**-▪hearted 1638L83
▫**warm** ▪over 1638L56
warm the ▫cockles of *someone's* ▪heart 1638L65
▫**warm** the ▪heart 1638L65
▫**warm** ▪through 1638L39
▪**warm** to/towards 1638L58
▫**warm** ▪up 1638L32/41/44/45/47/48/51/49
▫look/▫feel like ▪death ▫**warmed** ▪up/▪over 352R4
▫global ▪**warming** 600L28
▪**warn** against/▫warn ▪off 1638R23
▪**warn** of 1638R24
early ▪**warning** ▫system 436R51
▫hear ▪**warning** bells 1638R43
▫**warning** bells start to ▪ring/▪sound 115R38 1638R44
▪**warning** ▫sign 1638R50/52/48
▪time ▫**warp** 1521L14
▪death ▫**warrant** 352R40
▫sign *one's* own ▪death ▫**warrant** 1336L39
▪**warrant** ▫officer 1639L8
▪rabbit ▫**warren** 1164L79 1639L21
▪star ▫**wars** 1275R46 1412R9
▪car ▫**wash** 193R34
▪**wash** against 1639R49
▫**wash** a▪way 1639R50
wash *one's* dirty ▫linen in ▪public 1639L74
▫**wash** *one's* ▪hands of 1639L76
wash *someone's* ▫mouth out (with soapy ▪water) 1639L81
▫**wash** ▪out 1639L65/66/R64
▪**wash** over 1639R49
▫**wash** ▪up 1639L70
▫**washed**-▪up 1639R69
▪face ▫**washer** 492L41
▫**washer**-▪drier 1639R21
bio▫logical ▪**washing** ▫liquid/▫powder 127R64
▪**washing** ma▫chine 1639R30
▪**washing** ▫powder/▫liquid 1639R40
▫**washing**-▪up 1639R33
▫**washing**-▪up ▫liquid 1639R38
▪wishy-▫**washy** 1672L15
▫**wasp**-▪waisted 1640L29
▫natural ▪**wastage** 943L58
go to ▪**waste** 1640L67
▫high-level ▪**waste** 667R69
▫lay to ▪**waste** 802R4
▫lay (to) ▪**waste** 802R3
▫**waste** a▪way 1640R61
▫**waste** *one's* ▪breath 1640R3
▫**waste** of ▪space 1640L68
▪**waste** ▫product 1640R53
▫**waste** ▪words 1640R7
▫**waste**▪**paper** ▫basket 1641L34
keep a ▪**watch** out 1641R50
▫neighbourhood ▪**watch** 948L60
▫**watch** *one's* ▪back 1642L4
▪**watch** it 1642L1/3
▫**watch** ▪out 1642L10
▫**watch** ▪over 1641R36
watch ▪paint ▫dry 1641R40
▫**watch** *one's* ▪step 1420L5 1642L8
▫**watch** the ▪birdie 128R26
▫**watch** the ▪clock 246L71 1641L82
watch the ▪world go ▫by 1641L84
▫**watch** this ▪space 1641R30
▪bird-▫**watcher** 128L69/71
▪clock-▫**watcher** 246L73/74
▪**watchful** ▪eye 1641R60/62
▫night ▪**watchman** 955L37
▫test the ▪**water(s)** 1505R52
▪barley ▫**water** 100R13
be in/▫get into deep ▪**water** 357L53
▪bilge ▫**water** 126L13
▫bottled ▪**water** 151R39
come ▫hell or high ▪**water** 661L33
▪drinking ▫**water** 424L65
get into ▫hot ▪**water** 687R21
go through ▫fire and ▪**water** 523L32
▪gripe ▫**water** 624R74
▫heavy ▪**water** 658R76
▫high ▪**water** 667L84 1642L60
▫high ▪**water** ▫mark 667R4
▫hold ▪**water** 676R48
hot-▪**water** ▫bottle 687R67
hot ▪**water** ▫cylinder 687R69
▪ice ▫**water** 700L13
in ▫hot ▪**water** 687R20
keep *one's* ▫head above ▪**water** 653L79
like ▫oil and ▪**water** 979L22
▫low ▪**water** 844L44 1642L59
▫low ▪**water** ▫mark 844L46
make *someone's* ▪mouth ▫**water** 924L16
▪mineral ▫**water** 900L27
▫pass ▪**water** 1031R63
▫pour/▫throw cold ▪**water** on 256R2
▪rain ▫**water** 1169R75
▪rose-▫**water** 1234R71
▫soft ▪**water** 1372L14
take to *something* like a ▫duck to ▪**water** 430R25
▪tap ▫**water** 1490R30
▫throw cold ▪**water** on 1517L5
throw out the ▫baby with the ▪bath-**water** 1516R77
▪toilet ▫**water** 1532R16
▫tread ▪**water** 1553R62
▪**water** ▫bed 1642L72
▪**water** ▫bill 1642L73
▪**water** ▫bird 1642L75
▪**water** ▫biscuit 1642L77
▪**water** ▫bottle 1642L78
▪**water** ▫buffalo 1642L80
▪**water** ▫butt 1642L83
▪**water** ▫cannon 1642R1
▪**water**-▫cooled 1642R6
▫**water** ▪down 1642R59
▪**water** ▫filter 1642R9
▪**water** ▫fountain 424L66
▪**water** ▫ice 1376R71 1642R11
▪**water** ▫jump 1642R12
▪**water** ▫lily 1642R14
▪**water** ▫main 853R73 1642R16
▪**water** ▫meadow 1642R17
▪**water** ▫pistol 1642R19
▪**water** ▫polo 1642R21
▪**water**-re▫pellant 1642R23
▪**water** ▫skiing 1642R24/31
▪**water** ▫softener 1642R27
▪**water**-▫soluble 1642R29
▪**water** ▫sport 1642R30
▪**water** sup▫ply 1642R34
▪**water** ▫table 1642R37
▪**water** ▫tank 1642L84
▪**water** ▫taxi 1642R38
▪**water** ▫tower 1642R41
▫**water** under the ▪bridge 1642L69
▪**water** ▫vapour 1642R43
▫white ▪**water** 1660R69
▪mouth-▫**watering** 924L21
▪**watering** ▫hole 1642R68
▫meet *one's* **Water**▪loo 883L46
fish in ▫troubled ▪**waters** 526R21
pour ▫oil on troubled ▪**waters** 1104R60
▫territorial ▪**waters** 1504R72
▫**watery** ▪grave 1643L53
▫**wattle** and ▪daub 1644L75
▪brain ▫**wave** 157L46
▪crime ▫**wave** 324L53
▪heat ▫**wave** 658L19
▪long ▫**wave** 1644R61
▫Mexican ▪**wave** 892R23
▫new ▪**wave** 952L74/79
▫permanent ▪**wave** 1050R11/43
▫ride (on) a ▪**wave** of 1222L22
▪shock ▫**wave** 1318R82
▪short ▫**wave** 1644R66
▫sound ▪**wave** 1378R47
▪tidal ▫**wave** 1519L34
▫**wave** a▪way 1644R10
▪**wave** ▫band 1644R68
▫**wave** good▪bye to 1644R4
▫**wave** ▪off 1644R8
▫**wave** the ▪flag 529L30
▪**wave** to/at 1644L81
not on the ▫same ▪**wavelength** 1644R75
▪**waver** between 1644R84 1645L3/4
▪**waver** in 1644R81
▫make ▪**waves** 1644R49
▪flag-▫**waving** 529L45
▪sealing ▫**wax** 1276R5
▫**wax** and ▪wane 1645L36
▫**waxed** ▪paper 1645L24
a ▫long way to ▪go 838L9
a▫long the ▪**way** 36L74
▫any way you ▪slice it 1352L64
▫clear the ▪**way** 242R28
▪cycle ▫**way** 340R74
▫down ▪*our* ▫**way** 416L70
▫fight *one's* ▫**way** out of a paper ▪bag 517L27
▫give ▪**way** 1645R10/51/47
▫give ▪**way** to 1645R54
go a ▫long ▪**way** 838L16
go a ▫long **way** to▪wards 838L14
go ▫all the ▪**way** 1646L2
go back a ▫long ▪**way** 838L17
go down the ▫wrong ▪**way** 1692R75
go ▫out of *one's*/the ▪**way** 1645R13
go *one's* ▫own ▪**way** 1645R19
go *one's* ▫separate ▪**way** 1294R47
go the ▫same ▪**way** 1252R40
have come a ▫long ▪**way** 838L12
in the ▪family ▫**way** 500R70
in the ▫ordinary ▪**way** 994R74
▫know *one's* **way** a▪round 787R12
▫laugh all the way to the ▪bank 800L1
▫lead the ▪**way** 840L26/28 1645L59
▫learn *one's* ▫lesson the ▪hard **way** 806L56
▫Milky ▪**Way** 897L23
▫no through ▪**way** 1516R43
not know ▫which way to ▪turn 786R75
▫one way or an▫other 48L10
out of ▫harm's ▪**way** 648L54
▫pave the ▪**way** for/to 1037R46
▫pay *one's* ▪**way** 1038R6
▫point the ▪**way** 1089L42
▫right of ▪**way** 1223R29
▫right/▫wrong way ▪round 1236R43
▫rub *up* the wrong ▪**way** 1238R7/8
▫see *one's* way (▪clear) to 1283R78
▫show the ▪**way** 1327R25
▫snake *one's* ▪**way** 1364L24
▫speed *someone* on *their* ▪**way** 1388R81
the ▪hard ▫**way** 646L75/R46
the ▫right way ▪round/a▪round 1223L48
the ▫way things ▪are 1512L58
the ▫wrong way ▪round/a▪round 1693L66
to ▪my way of ▫thinking 1513L33
▫two-▪**way** 1576L63/64/65
▫two-**way** ▪mirror 1576L70
▫two-**way** ▪street 1576L69
▫under ▪**way** 1583L53 1645L62
▫**way** a▪round/▪round 1236R40 1645L54
▫**way** of ▪life 1646L18
▪**way** ▫station 1645R30
▫wend *one's* ▪**way** 1653R56
which way the ▪wind ▫blows/is ▫blowing 1645R26
▫change *one's* ▪**ways** 215L23
▫cut ▪both/▪two ▫**ways** 338R74
▫mend *one's* ▪**ways** 886L79
▫no two ▫**ways** a▪bout it 1574R66
▫parting of the ▪**ways** 1029L9
see the ▫error of *one's* ▪**ways** 467L59
▫set in *one's* ▪**ways** 1299R59
▫**ways** and ▪means 1646L44
▫fall by the ▪**wayside** 497L68 1646L80
▫**weak** at the ▪knees 1646R48
▫**weak**-▪kneed 1646R51
▫**weak** ▪link 1646R54
▫**weak**-▪minded 1646R59
▪**weak** ▫spot 1646R60
▫**weak**-▪willed 1646R63
the ▪**weaker** ▫sex 1646R68
▪**wean** *someone* off/from 1647L51
▪**wean** on 1647L49
bio▫logical ▪**weapon** 127R62
▫chemical ▪**weapon** 223R64
▫secret ▪**weapon** 1280R10
have not a ▫thing to ▪**wear** 1512L84
▫ready-to-▪**wear** 1179L69
the ▫worse for ▪**wear** 1686L68
▫**wear** and ▪tear 1647R39
▫**wear** a▪way 1647R23/50
▫**wear** ▪down 1647R51/55/56
▫**wear** *one's* ▪hair up 1647L77
▫**wear** *one's* ▫heart on *one's* ▪sleeve 1647L79
▫**wear** ▪off 1647R25
▫**wear** ▪on 1647R66
▫**wear** ▪out 1647R27/53/59
▫**wear** the ▪pants 1647L83
▫**wear** the ▪trousers 1647L82
▫**wear** ▪thin 1647R29
▫hard-▪**wearing** 647L32
wearing *one's* ▪birthday ▫suit 128R83
▪**weary** of 1647R78 1648L1
▫world-▪**weary** 1684R82 1685L2
▪**weasel** ▫words 1648L14
▫brass ▪monkey ▫**weather** 158L67
▫fair-**weather** ▪friend 495R19
▫make heavy ▪**weather** of 659L53
▫under the ▪**weather** 1648L34
▪**weather**-▫beaten 1648L36
▪**weather** ▫forecast 1648L42/45/39
▫**weather** per▪mitting 1051L11 1648L30
▪**weather** ▫station 1648L48
▫**weather** the ▪storm 1648L68
▪**weather** ▫vane 1648L50
▪**weave** from 1648R21
▪**weave** into 1648R4
▪**weave** through/between 1648R29
▫**weave** to▪gether 1648R19
▫get ▪**weaving** 1648R33
▪funnel-▫**web** 575L34
▪spider's ▫**web** 252R3
▫**web** -▪footed/-▪toed 1648R47
▫diamond ▪**wedding** (anni▫versary) 380L27
▫golden ▪**wedding** (anni▫versary) 610L9
▫hear ▪**wedding** bells 655R74
▫shotgun ▪**wedding** 1325L9
▫silver ▪**wedding** (anniversary) 1339L9
▪**wedding** ▫band 1648R75
▪**wedding** ▫ring 1648R74
▫white ▪**wedding** 1660R71
▫drive a ▪**wedge** 425R49
the ▫thin end of the ▪**wedge** 1511R15
▪**wedge** between 1648R84 1649L5
▫Ash ▪**Wednesday** 67R46
▫**weed** ▪out 1649L49
▪**weed** ▫whacker 1443L63 1649L40
from ▫week to ▪week 1649R1
▪Holy ▫**Week** 679R20
▫**week** after ▪week 23L77 1649R7
▫**week** by ▪week 1649R1
week ▫in week ▪out 1649R7
▫working ▪**week** 1649L65 1679R75
▫dirty **week**▪end 388L30
▫long **week**▪**end** 838R6
make a **week**▪**end** of it 855L13
▫wet **week**▪**end** 1654R6
for ▫weeks on ▪end 1649L82
▫**weep** ▪buckets 171R45
▪**weep** over 1649R43
▪**weep** with 1649R42
▫**weeping** ▪willow 1649R57
▪**weigh** against 1650L54
▫**weigh** ▪anchor 44L32 1650L67
▫**weigh** ▪down 1649R75/81
▫**weigh** ▪in 1649R82 1650L30
▫**weigh** ▪in with 1649R77/79 1650L29/34
▪**weigh** on 1650L70
▫**weigh** ▪out 1649R74/75
▫**weigh** ▪up 1650L62/59
▫**weigh** *one's* ▪words 1650L55
a ▪**weight** off *one's* ▫mind 898R61
▫dead ▪**weight** 350R49
▫pull *one's* ▪**weight** 1144R16
take the ▪**weight** off *one's* ▫feet/▫legs 1650L11
▫throw *one's* ▪**weight** around/about 1517L22
▪**weight** ▫training 1650L14
▫worth *one's* **weight** in ▪gold 1687L70
▪**welch** ▫on 1650R35/37
▫make *someone* ▪**welcome** 1650R82
out▫stay *one's* ▪**welcome** 1004R31
▫put the ▪**welcome** mat ▫out 1650R65
▪**welcome** ▫mat 1650R59
▪**Welcome** ▫Wagon 1650R66
▪**weld** into/to 1651L22/34/35
▫arc ▪**welding** 60L76
▪spot-▫**welding** 1397R58
▫**welfare** ▪state 1651L59
a ▫few **well**-chosen ▪words 1652L75
a▫live and ▪**well** 33L35/36
▫all very ▪**well** 1617L67
▫all **well** and ▪good 1651R62
ar▫tesian ▪**well** 65R68
▫augur ▪**well** 79R66
be ▫**well** ad▪vised to 21L6
▫full ▪**well** 572R79
▫hail-fellow-**well**-▪met 636L8
▫jolly **well** (▪do something) 769L53
▫just as ▪**well** 774L62/63 1651R73
▫leave ▫**well** a▪lone 807R10 1651R44
▫mean ▪**well** 878R29
▪ne'er-do-▫**well** 947L76
▫not know when *one's* is ▫**well** ▪off 1653L42
▪oil ▫**well** 979L34
▫sit ▪**well** 1343L46
▫speak ▪**well** for 1385L52
▫think ▪**well** of 1513L17
▫**well**-ad▪justed 1652L14
▫**well**-ad▪vised 1652L21
▫**well** and ▪truly 1651R31
▫**well**-ap▪pointed 1652L24
▫**well**-▪argued 1652L29
▫**well**-at▪tended 1652L34
▪**well** a▫way 1651R53
▫**well**-▪balanced 1652L38

▪well-be▪haved 1652L48
▫well-▫being 1652L52
▫well-▪bred 1652L58
▫well-brought-▪up 1652L63
▫well-▪built 1652L68
▫well-▪chosen 1652L71
▫well-con▪nected 1652L78
▫well-de▪fined 1652L81
▫well-de▪veloped 1652R3
▫well-dis▪posed 1652R10
▫well-▪documented 1652R14
▫well ▪done 406R5 1651R19 1652R19
▫well-▪dressed 1652R23
▫well-▪earned 1652R25
▫well-▪educated 1652R31
▫well-en▪dowed 1652R37
▫well-es▪tablished 1652R42
▫well-▪fed 1652R49
▫well-▪founded 1652R52
▫well-▪groomed 1652R57
▫well-▪grounded 1652R61
▫well-▪guarded 1652R66
▫well-▪heeled 1652R68/71
▫well I ▪never 951R38
well ▫I'll be ▪blowed 139L63
▫well I'm ▪blessed 135L10
▫well-in▪formed 728R7 1652R74
▫well-in▪tentioned 740L67 1652R83
▫well-▪kept 1653L5/8
▫well-▪known 1653L11
▫well-▪liked 1653L17
▫well ▪mannered 862L25 1653L19
▫well-▪matched 1653L25
▫well may *one* ▪ask 70L18
▫well-▪meaning 1653L28
▫well-▪meant 1653L31
▪well-▫nigh 1653L35
▫well-▪oiled 1653L53/54
▫well-pre▪served 1653L56
▫well-▪qualified 1653L62
▫well-▪read 1653L67/71
▫well-▪rounded 1653L75
▫well-▪spoken 1653L81
▫well ▪spotted 1398L61
▫well-▪thought-of 1653R5
▫well-thought-▪out 1653R9
▫well-▪thumbed 1517R54
▫well-▪timed 1653R12
▫well-▪tried 1653R18
▫well-▪trodden 1653R20
▫well-▪turned 1569L45 1653R25
▫well ▪up 1652L13
▫well-▪versed 1615R3 1653R27
▪well-▫wisher 1653R29
▫well ▪woman/▪man 1651L69
▫well-▪worn 1653R34
▫wish *someone* ▪well 1671R84
you may ▫well ▪ask 70L17
▫Welsh ▪rabbit 1653R42
▫Welsh ▪rarebit 1653R42
▫wend *one's* ▪way 1653R56
▪Wendy ▫house 1079R37 1653R59
go ▪west 1654L6
▫Middle ▪West 894L77 895L20
▫West ▪Coast 1654L8
▪West ▫Country 1654L10
▫West ▪End 1654L13
▫West ▪Indian 1654L15
▫Wild ▪West 1664R29
spa▫ghetti ▪western 1382R37
▫wet behind the ▪ears 1654R7
▫wet ▪blanket 1654R9
▫wet ▪dream 1654R11
▪wet-▫look 1654R9
▪wet ▫nurse 1654R13/15
▫wet *one's* ▪pants 1022R57
▪wet ▫suit 1654R17
▫wet to the ▪skin 1346R28
▫wet week▪end 1654R6
▫wet *one's* ▪whistle 1654R30
▪bed-▫wetting 111L60
▫top ▪whack 1537R18
▪weed ▫whacker 1443L63 1649L40
a ▪whale of a ▫time 1654R74
▪killer ▫whale 780L21
▪sperm ▫whale 1390R10
▫whale the ▪tar out of 1491L65
▫double ▪whammy 414R17
de▫serve what▫ever *one* ▪gets 372L13
what▫ever the ▫case might ▪be 201L30
what▪ever the ▫cost 310L13
what▪ever ▫turns *you* ▪on 1570L81
the ▫wheat from the ▪chaff 1656L1
▪wheat ▫germ 1655R81
be▫hind the ▪wheel 114R41
▫big ▪wheel 124R62
▪catherine ▫wheel 205R78
▪Ferris ▫wheel 124R62 513L32
▫four-wheel ▪drive 556R75
▫front-wheel ▪drive 568L55
▪nose ▫wheel 962L68
▪paddle ▫wheel 1017R19/23
▫potter's ▪wheel 1102R43
put a ▪spoke in *someone's* ▫wheel 1395R48
▫rear **wheel** ▪drive 1181L62
▪spinning ▫wheel 1392L18
▪steering ▫wheel 1419L65
the ▫wheel has come full ▪circle 572L68
▫wheel and ▪deal 1656R22/29
▪wheel ▫clamp 1656L51/55
▫wheel ▪out 1656L64/65
▫wheel ▪round 1656L83
▪side-▫wheeler 1333R17
▫three-▪wheeler 1515R5
▫wheeler-▪dealer 1656R34
▪wheelie ▫bin 1656R19
▫meals on ▪wheels 877R59
▫oil the ▪wheels 979L40
set the ▪wheels in ▫motion 1656L45
▪training ▫wheels 1405L70
▫wheels within ▪wheels 1656L48
▫whys and ▪wherefores 1663L36
▫whet *someone's* ▪appetite for 1657R35
▫skew-▪whiff 1345R53
▫drive **while** in▪toxicated 425L57
every ▫once in a ▪while 473R32
▪fiddle **while** ▫Rome ▪burns 515R41
make ▫hay **while** the ▪sun shines 652R28
make *it* ▫worth *someone's* ▪while 1687L61
strike **while** the ▪iron is ▫hot 1441R31
▪while away 1658R3
while the ▫going is ▪good 604L41
▫worth *one's* ▪while 1687R30
▫crack the ▪whip 318R46
▫fair crack of the ▪whip 494R82
▪pistol-▫whip 1070R34
the ▫whip ▪hand 1658R83
▫three-line ▪whip 1515L71 1659L49
▫whip a▪way 1659L38
▫whip into ▪shape 1311L8
▫whip ▪out 1659L34
▪whip-▫round 1659L75
▫whip ▪up 1659L15/56
▪whipping ▫boy 1659L29
▫give *something* a ▪whirl 1659R9
▫whisk a▪way 1659R40
within a ▪whisker 1659R63
▫cat's ▪whiskers 203L81
▫muttonchop ▪whiskers 934L4
▫malt ▪whisky 858L58
▫sink to a ▪whisper 1341R63
▫sink *one's* voice to a ▪whisper 1341R65
▪stage ▫whisper 1406R38/42
▪whispering cam▫paign 1660L3
▪whist ▫drive 1660L18
▫blow the ▪whistle 138R83
▫penny ▪whistle 1045R80
▫tin ▪whistle 1525L5
▫wet *one's* ▪whistle 1654R30
▪whistle-▫blower 1660L50
▫whistle-stop ▪tour 1660L52
▪wolf-▫whistle 1675R37
tu-▫whit tu-▪whoo 1572L35
▫black and ▪white 131R4/14
▫bleed *someone* ▪white 134R19 1403R69
▪egg ▫white 444R8
▫lily-▪white 823L71/73/75
▫non-▪white 959R54
▫see things in black and ▪white 131R10
▫snow-▪white 1367L75
▫white ▪ant 1503R64 1660R1
▫white ▪blood ▫cell 1660R1
▫white ▪cane 1660R63
▫white ▪Christmas 1660R3
▫white-▪collar 1660R6
▫white ▪elephant 1660R9
▫white ▪flag 1660R12
▫white ▪flight 1661L18
▫white ▫goods 1660R27
▫white ▪heat 1660R16
▫white ▪hope 1660R20
▫white ▪horses 1660R24
▫white-▪hot 1660R26
▪White ▫House 1660R29
▫white ▪knight 1660R32
▪white-▫knuckle 1660R37
▫white ▪lie 1660R40
▫white ▪magic 1660R42
▫white ▪meat 1660R43
▫white ▪noise 1660R45
▫white of an ▪egg 444R9
▫white ▪out 1661L25
▪White ▫Pages 1660R47
▫white ▪paper 1660R51
▫white ▪pointer 1660R56
▫white ▪sauce 1660R58
▫white ▪spirit 1660R60
▫white ▪stick 1660R63
▫white ▪supremacy 1661L20/22
▫white-▪tie 1660R66
▫white ▪trash 1661L23
▫white ▪water 1660R69
▫white ▪wedding 1660R71
▫whiter than ▪white 1660L82
▫whiter than ▪white 1660L82
▫whittle a▪way 1661L84/R1
▫whittle ▪down 1661R7
▫gee-▪whiz 586L65
▫whizz ▪by/▪past 1661R12/15
▪whizz ▫kid 1661R20
▫whizz ▪through 1661R13
a ▫whole new ▪ball ▫game 95R36
go the ▫whole ▪hog 1662L19
the ▫whole ▪bit 1662L13
the ▫whole (kit and) ca▪boodle 1662L22
the ▫whole enchi▪lada 1662L14
the ▫whole she▪bang 1313R41 1662L25
the ▫whole ▪thing 1512R57/58
▫whole-▪hearted 1662L30/27
▪whole ▫note 1290R68 1662L30
▫whole ▪number 1662L31
to ▫whom it may con▪cern 281L1
tu-▫whit tu-▪whoo 1572L35
▫whoop it ▪up 1662R36
▫make ▪whoopee 1662R44
▪whooping ▫cough 1662R47
the ▫how(s) and the ▪why(s) 690R73
▫whys and ▪wherefores 1663L36
▫leg before ▪wicket 809L17
▫sticky ▪wicket 1423R11
▪wicket ▫keeper 1663L84
▫cast *one's* net ▪wide 202L38
from ▫far and ▪wide 503R56
▫give *something* a **wide** ▪berth 1663R18
▫wide-angle (▪lens) 1663R22
▫wide a▪wake 85R67 1663R42
▫wide-▪bodied 1663R24
▪wide ▫boy 1663R27
▫wide-▪eyed 1663R30
▫wide of the ▪mark 1663R21
▫wide ▪open 987R20 1663R40/42
▫wide ▪ranging 1172R8 1663R43
▫widen hor▪izons 685L55
▫black ▪widow 132L14
▫grass ▪widow 620L15
as ▫husband and ▪wife 696L15
▫man and ▪wife 858R56
▪trophy ▫wife 1560R22
▪wife ▫swapping 1664L26
▫drive *someone* ▪wild 425R40
▫run ▪wild 1242L23 1664R47
▫sow *one's* **wild** ▪oats 1381R2
▫wild ▪boar 1664L57
▪wild ▫card 1664R10/13/17
wild-▪goose ▫chase 1664R21
▫wild ▪horses 1664L55
▫Wild ▪West 1664R29
▫wildcat ▪strike 822L31 1664R49
beyond *one's* ▫wildest ▪dreams 122R9 1664R25
▫spread like ▪wildfire 1399R28 1664R75
▫bear *someone* ill-▪will 703R30
▫cut *someone* ▫out of *one's* ▪will 339L75
▫feel ill-▪will for 703R30
▫free ▪will 561L53
▫have *something* ▫will ▪travel 1553L11
▫heads **will** ▪roll 653L75
▫last **will** and ▪testament 797R75
▫living ▪will 832L1
of *one's* ▫own free ▪will 1665R54
that **will** ▪never ▫do 406L54
▪that will ▫show 1327L28
will ▪never ▫do 951R40
will not ▪hear of 656L37
▫will-o'-the-▪wisp 1666L15
with the ▫best **will** in the ▪world 118R74 1665R57
▫strong-▪willed 1445R72
▫weak-▪willed 1646R63
▫God ▪willing 608R80
▫pussy ▪willow 1152R12
▫weeping ▪willow 1649R57
▪willow ▫pattern 1666L20
▫willy-▪nilly 1666L35
▫wimp ▪out 1666L60
may the ▫best man/person ▪win 118R64
▫win hands ▪down 641L8 1666R3
▫win ▪over/▪round 1666R4
▫win *one's* ▪spurs 1401L28
▫win the ▪day 1666R9
▫win the ▪toss 1539R34
▫win ▪through 1666R12
throw ▫caution to the ▪wind(s) 1517L2
▫break ▪wind 161R28
▫following ▪wind 543R25
get ▪wind of 1666R74
▫north ▪wind 961L60
▫put/▫get the ▪wind up 1666R77
▫sail against the ▪wind 1249R28
▫sail close to the ▪wind 1249R30
▫second ▪wind 1279R18
▫straw in the ▪wind 1435R32
▪tail ▫wind 1485R21
take the ▪wind out of *someone's* ▫sails 1666R79
the ▫chill ▪wind of 226R31
which way the ▪wind ▫blows/is ▫blowing 1645R26
▫wind a▪round/▪round 1667L65/66
▫wind ▪back 1667L53
▫wind ▪back/▪forward 1667L50
▪wind-▫chill 1667L1
▪wind ▫chimes 1667L3
▫wind ▪down/▪up 1597L65 1667L49/75/82R5/9/15/20/22
▪wind ▫gauge 1667L7
▪wind ▫instrument 1667L8
▫wind ▪on 1667L51
▪wind re▫sistance 1209L82
▪wind ▫tunnel 1667L10
▪wind ▫turbine 1667L14
▫long-▪winded 838L51
▫tilt at ▪windmills 1520R41
▫bay ▪window 106L24
▫bow ▪window 154L61
▫lattice ▪window 799R56
▪picture ▫window 1063R70
▫rose ▪window 1234R72
▫sash ▪window 1255R54
▪storm ▫window 1432L3
▪window ▫box 1667R84
▪window ▫dressing 1668L43/46
▪window-▫ledge 1668L51/77
▪window ▫seat 1668L52/55
▪window ▫shade 1668L58
▪window-▫shop 1668L59/60
▫French ▪windows 563R52
▫leaded ▪windows 804R48
▫scatter to the (four) ▪winds 1263L45
▪windscreen ▫wiper 1668R45
▪windshield ▫wiper 1668R45
des▪sert ▫wine 374L37
▫fortified ▪wine 554R66
▫ginger ▪wine 595R21
▪table ▫wine 1483L73
▫wine and ▪dine 1669L3
▪wine ▫bar 1668R83
▪wine ▫rack 1668R84
▫left ▪wing 808R51
▫right ▪wing 1224L16/17/20
▫take under *one's* ▪wing 1669L14
▫wing ▪chair 1669L17
▫wing ▪collar 1669L18
▪wing ▫nut 1669L21
▫left-▪winger 808R52
▫right-▪winger 1224L21
▫clip *someone's* ▪wings 245R15
▫spread *one's* ▪wings 1399R31
▫wait in the ▪wings 1633R30
a ▫wink of ▪sleep 1669R26
▫sleep a ▪wink 1669R26
▫tip *someone* the ▪wink 1526L18
▫tip the ▪wink to 1526L19
▪wink at 1669R14/16/17/19/20
as ▫easy as ▪winking 438R39
▫winkle ▪out 1669R33
▫forty ▪winks 555L62
▫winner-takes-▪all 1666R39
▪winning ▫post 1666R49
▫dead of ▪winter 350R67
▫nuclear ▪winter 966L66
▫winter ▪sports 1396R42 1669R66
▫wipe ▪off 1670L52
▫wipe off the ▪map 1670L59
▫wipe ▪out 1670L72/76
▫wipe the ▪floor with 1670L55
▫wipe the ▪slate clean 1670L60
wipe the ▪sleep out of *one's* ▫eyes 1351R35
▫wipe the ▪smile off *someone's* face 1670L65
▫wipe ▪up 1670L48/51
be ▫wiped off the ▫face of the ▪earth 490R74
▫slate **wiped** ▪clean 1350L31
▪windscreen ▫wiper 1668R45
▪windshield ▫wiper 1668R45
▫barbed ▪wire 99L53
▪chicken ▫wire 225L76
▫fly-by-▪wire 540R1
▪hot-▫wire 688R32
▪live ▫wire 832R47
▪razor ▫wire 1177L25
▫wire ▪brush 1670R58
▫wire-▪haired 1670R59
▫wire ▪netting 1670R61
▪wire ▫service 1671L7
▪wire-▫tapping 1670R62
▫wire ▪up 1670R71/73 1671L11
▫wire ▪wool 1418R33 1670R65
get *one's* ▪wires ▫crossed 1670R54
▪folk ▫wisdom 543L19
in *someone's* ▫infinite ▪wisdom 727L38
▪wisdom ▫tooth 1671R4
with the ▫wisdom of ▪hindsight 1671R2
a ▫wise head on ▫young ▪shoulders 653L29
penny-▫wise and pound-▪foolish 1045R66
▪wise ▫guy 1671L54
▫wise ▪up 1671L64
▫worldly-▪wise 1685L54
▫sadder but ▪wiser 1247R48
▪death ▫wish 352R47
▪wish-ful▫fillment 1671R42
wish *someone* had ▫never been ▪born 149R22
▫wish *someone* ▪well 1671R84
▫wouldn't **wish** *something* on ▪anyone/on *one's* worst ▪enemy 1671R75
▪well-▫wisher 1653R29
▫best ▪wishes 119L2 1672L1/2
▫wishful ▪thinking 1672L9
▪wishy-▫washy 1672L15
▫will-o'-the-▪wisp 1666L15
▪half-▫wit 638L29/33
▪witch-▫hazel 1672R16
▪witch-▫hunt 1672L80
▫witches' ▪brew 1672L77
the ▪witching ▫hour 1672L79/R21
with▪drawal ▫symptoms 1673R19
▫wither on the ▪vine 1673R41
with▫hold ▪tax 1673R75
be/▫come **within** an ▪ace of 10R54
en▫quire **with▪in** 459R63
not **within** an ▫ass's ▪roar of 71L42
▫wheels **within** ▪wheels 1656L48
within a ▫short space of ▪time 1381R61
within a ▪whisker 1659R63
within an ▪inch of 1674L22/24/22/23
within ▪hailing ▫distance of 636L4
within *one's* ▪means 879L44
within *one's* ▪memory 886L25
within *one's* ▪rights 1223R23
within ▪shouting ▫distance 1326L84
within ▪spitting ▫distance 1393R51
within ▪striking ▫distance 1441R39/42
within the ▫realms of possi▪bility 1180R76
within the ▪space of 1381R62
▫bear false ▪witness 108L56
▫bear ▪witness 108L51 1674L77
▫expert ▪witness 72R7 1674R29
Je▫hovah's ▪Witness 761R17
▪witness ▫box 1674R33
at *one's* ▫wits' ▪end 1674R65
▫battle of ▪wits 105L80
col▫lect/▫gather *one's* ▪wits 1674R52
have/▫keep/▫need (all) *one's* ▪wits about 1674R59
▫live by/on *one's* ▪wits 832R14
▫dim ▪witted 384R65 1674R81
▫quick-▪witted 1162L64 1674R77
▫slow-▪witted 1355R58 1674R78
▫witter ▪on 1675L2/1/2
▫old ▪wives' ▫tale 980L18
▫tale of ▪woe 1488L35 1675L66
▫woe be▪tide *someone* 1675L67
a ▫wolf in sheep's ▪clothing 1675R32
▫cry ▪wolf 331R82
keep the ▪wolf from the ▫door 1675R34
▫lone ▪wolf 837R39
▪wolf-▫whistle 1675R37
▫fallen ▪woman 497R19
▪fancy ▫woman 503L13
▪fine figure of a ▫woman 517R39
▪front ▫woman 568L41/R14
▫inner ▪woman 732R1
▫just the **woman** for the ▪job 766L14
▫kept ▪woman 777L55
make an ▫honest ▪woman of 681R12
▫marked ▪woman 866R64
▫old ▪woman 980L21
▫scarlet ▪woman 1263L13
▪stunt ▫woman 1449L14
the ▫thinking **woman's** ▪crumpet 1513L83
the ▫woman in *someone's* ▪life 818R78
▫well ▪woman 1651L69
▫woman about-▪town 1543R55
▫woman in the ▪street 1437L61
▫woman of her ▪word 1679L44
▫woman of the ▪match 872R9
▫woman of the ▪people 1046R39
▫woman of the ▪world 1683R79
▫woman on the Clapham ▪omnibus 981L83
▫Women's ▪Institute 1675R67
▫women's ▪lib 816L42/44 1675R72/76
▫women's liber▪ation 1675R72
▪women's ▫movement 1675R77
▫women's ▪refuge 1192R59 1675R82
▪women's ▫shelter 1675R82
▪women's ▫studies 1676L1
▪hard-▫won 646R14
▫boy ▪wonder 155R83
▫chinless ▪wonder 227L64
▫little/▫small ▪wonder (that) 1676R29
▫nine days' ▪wonder 955R78
▫one-hit ▪wonder 984L66
▪wonder ▫drug 1676R33
▫do/▫work ▪wonders 1676R36
▫work ▪wonders 1682L17
▫woo a▪way 1677L23/25/23/25
▪woo with 1677L21/29

▫can't see the ▫**wood** for the ▪trees 1677L74
▫dead ▪**wood** 350R53
▫knock on ▪**wood** 784R60
▫knock ▪**wood** 784R60
▫touch ▪**wood** 1540R2
▪**wood** ▫pulp 1677L48
▫**wooden** ▪spoon 1677L61/62
▫neck of the ▪**woods** 945R51
▫come/▫crawl out of the ▪**woodwork** 1677R73
▪**woof** at 1678L11
▫cotton ▪**wool** 310R44
▫dyed-in-the-▪**wool** 433R82
▫pull the ▪**wool** over *someone's* ▫eyes 1678L17
▫steel ▪**wool** 1418R33
▫wire ▪**wool** 1418R33 1670R65
▪**Woop** ▫Woop 1678L44
▫**Worcester** ▪sauce 1678L53
▫**Worcestershire** ▪sauce 1678L53
a ▫**word** in *someone's* ▪ear 1678R77
be▫lieve a ▪**word** 115L74
▫big ▪**word** 124R65
▫breathe/▫say a ▪**word** 1678L71
▪buzz ▫**word** 181L31
by ▫word of ▪mouth 1678L76
▫complex ▪**word** 275R66
▫couldn't/▫didn't speak a ▪**word** of 1385L6
▫dirty ▪**word** 388L24
▪f-▫**word** 490L16
▫four-letter ▪**word** 556R53
from the ▫**word** ▪go 1679L55
get a ▫**word** in ▪edgeways 1678L79
▫good ▪**word** 611R54 1678R72 1679L11
▪guide ▫**word** 630R55
▫household ▪**word** 689R77
▫last ▪**word** 797R77
▫magic ▪**word** 852L56
▫man of his ▪**word** 1679L44
▪nonce ▫**word** 959R61
▪nonsense ▫**word** 960L84
▫not have a civil ▪**word** to ▫say for 234R83
▫operative ▪**word** 989R6
▫put the ▪**word** about/around/out/round 1679L12
▫say the ▪**word** 1259R75 1679L49
▫send ▪**word** 1291R37
▫spread the ▪**word** 1399R34
▪swear ▫**word** 1474R2
▫take *someone* at *their* ▪**word** 1679L37
▫take my ▪**word** for it 1486R8
the ▫printed ▪**word** 1123L17
▫weigh each ▪**word** 1650L55
▪**word** associ▫ation 1678R25
▫**word** for ▪word 1678R17/20
▫**word** gets a▪bout/a▪round/▪round 1679L16
one's ▫**word** is *one's* ▪bond 1679L41
▫**word**-▪perfect 1678R31
▪**word** ▫processing 1678R39/35
▫written ▪**word** 1692L55
a ▫few well-chosen ▪**words** 1652L75
▫bandy ▪**words** 97L30
▫eat *one's* ▪**words** 439L49
ex▫change ▪**words** 476R53
▫famous last ▪**words** 501L59
▫fighting ▪**words** 517L82
▫form of ▪**words** 553L66
in ▫so many ▪**words** 863L77
in **words** of ▫one ▪syllable 1678R5
▫mark *my* ▪**words** 866R23
▫mince ▪**words** 898L53
▫play on ▪**words** 1078L11
put ▫**words** in/into *someone's* ▪mouth 1678R9
▫swallow *one's* ▪**words** 1473L61
take the ▫**words** out of *someone's* ▪mouth 1678R13
▫waste ▪**words** 1640R7
▪weasel ▫**words** 1648L14
▫weigh *one's* ▪**words** 1650L55
▫**words** ▪fail *someone* 1678R42
a ▪nasty piece of ▫**work** 938R48
▫all in a day's ▪**work** 349L55
▪camera ▫**work** 187L35
de▪tective ▫**work** 375R20
▫do (all) the ▪donkey ▫**work** 411L55
▫get/▫go/▫set to ▪**work** 1679R1
have *one's* ▪**work** cut ▫out (for *one*) 1679R3
▫life's ▪**work** 819R6
▫make short ▪**work** 1322R73
nice ▫**work** if you can ▪get it 954L50
▫place of ▪**work** 1072R62
▫pressure of ▪**work** 1118R28
▫Protestant ▪**work** ▫ethic 1137R84
▫set to ▪**work** 1298R82
▪social ▫**work** 1370R44/43
▫start ▪**work** 1413R20
▪team ▫**work** 1494R27
▫thirsty ▪**work** 1513R50
▫too much like hard ▪**work** 1535L81
▫**work** a▪gainst 24R15 1682R13
▪**work** as 1679R26
▫**work** *one's* ▪ass off 71L61
▪**work** at 1679R35 1682R52
▪**work** ▫ethic 1679R9
▪**work** ex▫perience 1679R10
▫**work** *one's* fingers to the ▪bone 1679R43
▪**work** for 1679R28 1682L20/R14
▫**work** *one's* ▪guts out 633R14 1474R44
▫**work** ▪in 1679L84 1682R7/22
▪**work** it 1682R19
▫**work** like a ▪charm 1682L14
▫**work** like a ▪dog 1679R41
▫**work** like a ▪Trojan 1679R40
▫**work** ▪miracles/▪wonders 1682L17
▫**work** of ▪art 1682L83
work ▪off 1682L74
work ▪on 1679R2/33 1682R23
▫**work** ▪out 1682R28/40/49/55
▫**work** ▪over 1682R61
▪**work** ▫permit 1679R17
▪**work** ▫surface 1679R19 1683R27
▫**work** the/*one's* ▪ass off 71L59
▫**work** till/until *one* ▪drops 1679R41
▫**work** to ▪rule 1679R46/49
▫**work** ▪up 1682L68/70/R65/75
work *oneself* ▪up into 1682R5/68/77
▫**work** ▪wonders 1676R36
▫**worked** ▪up 1598L23 1682R71
▫co-▪**worker** 317R82
▪guest ▫**worker** 630L72
sanit▪ation ▫**worker** 1255L2
▫hard-▪**working** 646R16
▪**working** ▫capital 1679R80
▫**working** ▪class 237R81 1679R83
▫**working** ▪day 1681L57
▪**working** ▫girl 1681R49
▫**working** ▪hour 860R29
▫**working** ▪life 1681R50 1682L35
▫**working** ▪mother 1681R52
▪**working** ▫papers 1681R59
▪**working** ▫party 1681R54
▫**working** ▪week 1649L65 1679R75
▫give *someone* the ▪**works** 1683R3
▫gum up the ▪**works** 632L52
put/throw a ▫spanner in the ▪**works** 1383L15
▪sewage ▫**works** 1303L45
▫shoot the ▪**works** 1319R66
▫sheltered ▪**workshop** 1315L28
▫all the corners/the ▫four corners/the ▫far corners of the ▪**world** 306R2
all the ▫time in the ▪**world** 1521R34
at ▫peace with the ▪**world** 1040L18
▫come/▫go ▪down in the ▫**world** 416L28
▫dead to the ▪**world** 350R31
▫distant/▫far corner of the ▪**world** 306R84
▫free ▪**world** 561L58
go ▪up/come ▪down in the ▫**world** 1685L16
have the ▫**world** at *one's* ▪feet 1683R66
in an▫other ▪**world** 48L22
▫lead the ▪**world** 804L78
make a ▪**world** of ▫difference 382R4
▫make the ▪**world** go a▫round/▫round 1683R60
▫man/▫woman of the ▪**world** 1683R79
▫mean (all) the ▪**world** 1685L29
move ▪up/▪down in the ▫**world** 1685L17
not ▫long for this ▪**world** 838R39
not/without a ▫care in the ▪**world** 196R55
▫Old ▪**World** 980R7/11
on ▫top of the ▪**world** 1536R78
set the ▪**world** on ▫fire/a▫light/a▫blaze 1299L34
the cares of the ▪**world** on *one's* ▫shoulders 196R54
the de▫veloping ▪**world** 377R5
the ▫easiest thing in the ▪**world** 438R47
the ▫end of the ▪**world** 455L33/32
the ▫New ▪**World** 952L82
the ▫new **world** ▪order 952L84
the ▫real ▪**world** 1179R50
the ▫Third ▪**World** 1513R30
the ▫**world** at ▪large 1683R69
▫think the ▪**world** of 1513L17
today ▫*something* tomorrow the ▪**world** 1531L30
watch the ▪**world** go ▫by 1641L84
with the ▫best will/▫all the will in the ▪**world** 1665R57
with the ▫best will in the ▪**world** 118R74
▫**World** ▪Bank 1683R81
▪**world**-▫beater 1683R83 1684L72
▫**world**-▪class 1684L73
▫**World** ▪Cup 335R9 1684L75
▫**world**-▪famous 1684L79
▫**World** ▪Health Organization 1684L81
▫**world** ▪music 1684L84
▫**world** ▪power 1105R63 1684R71
▫**world** ▪record 1187R18 1683R46
▫**World** ▪Series 1684R73
▪**world** ▫shattering 1684R76
▫**world** ▪war 1684R80/81/79
▫**world**-▪weary 1684R82 1685L2
would ▫give the ▪**world** for 596R21
would ▫never/would not *do something* for the ▪**world** 1685L25
▫olde ▪**worlde** 980R27
▫**worldly**-▪wise 1685L54
the ▫best of ▪both **worlds** 119L51
▪glow-▫**worm** 601R31
the ▫**worm** ▪turns 1685L76
▪**worm** ▫cast 1685L81
▪**worm**-▫eaten 1685L84
▪**worm** *oneself* into 1685R35
▫**worm** ▪out 1685R38
▫well-▪**worn** 1653R34
▫**worried** ▪sick 1333L45 1686L20
▫**worried** to ▪death 1686L22
▫don't **worry** your ▫pretty little ▪head 1685R79
▪**worry** about 1685R66/82 1686L9
▪**worry** at 1685R76
a ▫fate **worse** than ▪death 506R14
▪bark is ▫**worse** than *one's* ▪bite 100L71
for ▫better or (for) ▪**worse** 121L10
go from ▫bad to ▪**worse** 92L38
▫make matters ▪**worse** 874R42 1686L59
take a ▫turn for the ▪**worse** 1570L66
the ▫**worse** for ▪drink 1686L65
the ▫**worse** for ▪wear 1686L68
▫**worse** ▪luck 1686L72
▫**worse** ▪still 1425L53
▪hero ▫**worship** 665L55/59
▫place of ▪**worship** 1072R63
if the ▫**worst** comes to the ▪worst 1687L26
one's ▫own **worst** ▪enemy 1686R76
▫**worst** case sce▪nario 1263R19 1686R81
▫**worst**-▪ever 1686R78
▫wouldn't wish *something* on *one's* **worst** ▪enemy 1671R75
▫get/▫have *one's* ▪money's **worth** 913R15
it's more ▫trouble than it's ▪**worth** 1561R63
make *it* ▫**worth** *someone's* ▪while 1687L61
▫more than *someone's* ▪job's ▫**worth** 765R40
▫not **worth** a ▪bean 1687L64
▫not **worth** a ▪fig 516R65
▫not **worth** the ▫paper *it* is ▪printed on 1687L66
the ▫game is **worth** the ▪candle 581L74
two ▪cents ▫**worth** 1574R70
▫**worth** *one's* ▪salt 1687L68
▫**worth** *one's* weight in ▪gold 1687L70
▫**worth** *one's* ▪while 1687R30
▪flesh ▫**wound** 533L69 1688R47
▫lick *one's* ▪**wounds** 817R12
▫bow-▪**wow** 155L4
▪bubble ▫**wrap** 171L52 1689R2
▫plastic ▪**wrap** 245L14 1076R49
▪shrink-▫**wrap** 1330L12/6
▫**wrap** *someone* around/round *one's* little ▪finger 1573R84 1689L69
▫**wrap** ▪up 1598L73 1689R32/36/33
▪gift-▫**wrapped** 594R54
▪**wrapping** ▫paper 1689R30
▫take the ▪**wraps** off 1689R6
▫under ▪**wraps** 1689R4
▪laurel ▫**wreath** 800R51 1689R83
▫**wreathed** in ▪smiles 1360R34 1690L11
a ▫physical ▪**wreck** 1060L84
▪Allen ▫**wrench** 34L20
▪box ▫**wrench** 155L38
▪monkey ▫**wrench** 915L21
▪gut-▫**wrenching** 633R4
▫**wrest** a ▪living from 1690L83/R1/2
▪**wrestle** with 1690R14
▪sumo ▫**wrestler** 1459R33/39
▪arm ▫**wrestling** 62R34
▪mud ▫**wrestling** 927R57
▫**wriggle** off the ▪hook 1690R65
▫**wring** *one's* ▪hands 1690R82/83
▫put through the ▪**wringer** 1691L10
▫**wrinkle** *one's* ▪brow 1691L33
▫**wrinkle** (up) *one's* ▪nose 1691L36
▫limp ▪**wrist** 824L65/68/69
▫slap on the ▪**wrist** 1349L63
▫**writ** ▪large 1691L72/74
▫co-▪**write** 318L19/12
▫nothing to ▫**write** ▪home about 1691R65
▪**write** about/on 1691R69
write ▪back 1691R60
▪**write** for 1691R49/51/62/70
▪**write** into 1691R74
▫**write**-▫off 1692L65/69/75/78
▪**write** to 1691R40/41/52/55/58/78
write ▪up 1692L80/R9
▪crime ▫**writer** 324L54
▪ghost-▫**writer** 594L62
▪speech ▫**writer** 1388R20
▫**writer's** ▪block 1692L9
▫**writer's** ▪cramp 1692L11
▫**writhe** a▪round 1692R16
▪**writing** ▫desk 1692L36
▫**writing** is on the ▪wall 1692L30
▪**writing** ▫paper 1023L15 1692L37
▫**written** all over *someone's* ▪face 1692L50
▫**written** in the ▪stars 1692L52
▫**written** ▪word 1692L55
▫bark up the **wrong** ▪tree 100L73
▫catch on the **wrong** ▪foot 1692R78
cor▫rect me if I'm ▪**wrong** 307R37
get/fall into the ▫**wrong** ▪hands 1693L61
get out of ▫bed (on) the ▫**wrong** ▪side 111L43
get (hold of) the ▫**wrong** end of the ▪stick 1692R73
get up on the ▫**wrong** side of the ▪bed 111L43
▫get *someone* ▪**wrong** 591R67/69 1693L14
go down the ▫**wrong** ▪way 1692R75
▫go ▪**wrong** 1693L16/54/57/R49
have *one's* ▪sums ▫**wrong** 1458R61
▫never put/set a foot ▪**wrong** 545L75
on the ▫**wrong** ▪foot 545L71
on the ▫**wrong** ▪side of 1333R81/79 1334L1
on the ▫**wrong** ▫side of the ▪law 1333R83
▫rub *up* the **wrong** ▪way 1238R7/8
the ▫**wrong** way ▪round/a▪round 1693L66
▫**wrong**-▪foot 1692R79
▫**wrong**-▪headed 1693L68/73
▫**wrong** way ▪round 1236R43
the ▫rights and ▪**wrongs** of 1223L84
▫**wrought** ▪iron 1693R68
▪**wych**-▫hazel 1672R16 1694R3
▫yin and ▪**yang** 1697L46
▫**yank** ▪out 1695L20/21
▪breaker's ▫**yard** 160R76
▪knacker's ▫**yard** 782R46
▫Scotland ▪**Yard** 1269R55
▪scrap ▫**yard** 1270R80
▫**yards** and ▪yards 1695L45
▫**yawning** ▪gap 1695R10
▫**ye** ▪Gods 1695R22
▫**yea** or ▪nay 1695R25
▪calendar ▫**year** 184L16
fi▫nancial ▪**year** 520L68
▪first-▫**year** 526L48
▪fiscal ▫**year** 526L59
in the ▫**year** ▪dot 413L45
▪leap ▫**year** 806L28
▪light ▫**year** 820R40
▫New ▪**Year** 952R7 1695R38
▫New **Year's** ▪Day 952R14
▫New **Year's** ▪Eve 952R16
▫New **Year's** ▪honours 683L76
▫New **Year's** Reso▪lution 952R19
see ▫in the New ▪**Year** 1284L32
▫seven-**year** ▪itch 1302L29
▫solar ▪**year** 1372R7
▪tax ▫**year** 1493L84
the ▫**year** ▪dot 1695R67
year ▫in year ▪out 1695R69
▫**year** ▪running 547L25
▫autumn ▪**years** 83L12
de▫clining ▪**years** 355R41
▪donkey's ▫**years** 411L52
in/through ▫all the ▪**years** 1695R58
▪light **years** a▫way 820R42
put ▪**years** on 1695R62
▫take ▪**years** ▫off 1695R64
▪twilight ▫**years** 1573L38
▫chrome ▪**yellow** 230R33
▪**yellow** ▫fever 1696L39
▫**yellow** ▪line 1696L41
▫**Yellow** ▪Pages 1696L44
▫on yer ▪bike 125R43
▪**yes**-▫man 1696R23
▫not born ▪**yesterday** 149R20 1696R40
▫yin and ▪**yang** 1697L46
▪**yoke** to 1697R14
▫**yoke** to▪gether 1697R16
▪egg ▫**yolk** 444R10
▫**yolk** of an ▪egg 444R11
▪**yoo**-▫hoo 1697R41
▫**Yorkshire** ▪pudding 1697R49
Did the ▫earth ▪move for **you**? 437R2
▫how's life treating ▪**you**? 818R61
an ▫old/a ▫wise head on ▫**young** ▪shoulders 653L29
▫**young** at ▪heart 1698L61
▫**young** ▪blood 1698L64
▫**young** ▪lady 1698L66
▫**young** ▪love 1698L63
▫**young** ▪man 1698L66
▫**young** of▪fenders' insti▫tution 1698L69
▪**young** ▫ones 1698L72
the ▫bloom of ▪**youth** 138L50
▪**youth** ▫club 1698R35
▪**youth** ▫hostel 1698R38/42
▪**yule** ▫log 1698R75
▪**zap** between 1699L44
▫**zebra** ▪crossing 1699R15
▫absolute ▪**zero** 5R16
▪**zero** ▫hour 1699R57
▫**zero** ▪in 1700L12/16/18/19
▪**Zimmer** ▫frame 1700L55
▫**zip** a▪long 1700R30
▪**zip** ▫code 254L39 1700R26
▫**zip** ▪fastener 1700R4
▫**zip** ▪up 1700R17/18
▪crumple ▫**zone** 330R49
▪enterprise ▫**zone** 461L42
▫no-▪fly ▫**zone** 957R54 1700R76
▫no-▪go ▫**zone** 957R61
▪time ▫**zone** 1522R36
▪twilight ▫**zone** 1573L38
▪Frigid ▫**Zones** 566L72
▫feeding time at the ▪**zoo** 509R83
▪petting ▫**zoo** 1055R30
▪**zoo**-▫keeper 1701L31
zoo▫**logical** ▪gardens 1701L24/39
▫**zoom** ▪in 1701R16/18/19/18/19
▫gnomes of ▪**Zurich** 602R37

Pictures, Language Portraits and lists of False Friends

*Language Portraits are marked **

Accommodation 9
Adjectives* 16
Adverbs* 20
Age* 25
Aircraft 31
American spelling* 40
Apes and monkeys 53
Apostrophe* 54
Approximate numbers* 58
Arm 62
Articles* 68
Asterisk* 74
Australian English* 81
Auxiliary verbs* 84
Axe 87

Bags 93
Bar 98
Basket 103
Bathroom 105
Bed 111
Beds and bedroom 112
Berries 118
Bicycles 124
Bill 126
Birds 129
Blade 133
Body 143
Bolt 145
Borrow* 150
Bottles and flasks 152
Bow 154
Box 155
Brackets* 156
Bread and cakes 160
Bridge 165
Britain* 167
Brush 170
Building and construction 173

Calendar* 185
Canal 188
Capital letters* 192
Car 194
Cards* 195
Cats 204
Cereals 210
'ch' pronunciation* 211
Chair 213
Clauses* 240
Cleaning 241
Clocks and watches 247
Clothes 249
Club 250
Coats and jackets 253
Colon* 259
Column 260
Columns 260
Comb 261
Combining forms* 262
Comma* 268
Comparing and grading* 274
Compound verbs* 278
Conditionals* 284
Cone 285
Consonant doubling* 292
Containers 295
Continuous form* 297
Cooking 303
Cosmetics 309
Coverings 317
Crimes and criminals* 324
Crop 327
Crustaceans 331
(CS) Czech false friends 333
Cutlery 341

(D) German false friends 343
Dash* 347
Dates* 348
Determiners* 376
Diamond 380
Directions* 387
(DK) Danish false friends 404
Do: verbs meaning 'perform'* 405
Dogs 409
Doors 412
Dots* 413
Drawing and painting 420
Dressing and undressing* 423
Driving* 425
Drum 429
Dutch false friends (NL) 957

(E) Spanish false friends 435
Each other* 436
-ed and -ing adjectives* 441
Edge 442
Emergency services 451
Energy 457
'-et' words* 469
Exclamation mark* 477
Expensive* 481
Eye 488
Eye and seeing* 489

(F) French false friends 491
False friends* 502
Family tree 501
Farming 505
Feelings and pains* 510
File 518
Filter 519
Fires and space heaters 524
Fish 527
Flowers and plants 539
Food preparation 545
Fork 551
Forms of words (spelling)* 552
Frame 558
Fruit 570
Full stop* 572

Games 582
Garden 583
German false friends (D) 343
Get: verbs meaning 'cause'* 592
(GR) Greek false friends 616

Hair 636
Hand 640
Handicraft 642
Hats 650
Head 653
Heart 656
Herbs and spices 664
Holidays* 678
Homophones and homographs* 682
Hundred* 694
Hyphen* 697

(I) Italian false friends 699
'ie' or 'ei' spelling* 702
Imaginary creatures 705
-ing form of verbs* 730
Insects 735
It* 756
Italics* 756

(J) Japanese false friends 758
Jack 759
Jewellery 764
Jug 771

Key 778
King 781
Kitchen 783
Knife 784
(KOR) Korean false friends 788

Labels* 790
Laboratory 789
Law* 801
Leaf 805
Letters* 814
Lights 821
Line 825
Linking verbs* 828
Locks and home security 835
Luggage 846

Mark 865
Match 872
Mathematics* 875
Measurements* 880
Medical equipment 882
Meeting someone* 884
Memory* 887
Meters and gauges 891
Mill 898
Mini 900
Molluscs 912
Money 914
Motorway 923
Mouth 924
Music 931
Musical instruments 932
Muzzle 934

(N) Norwegian false friends 936
Nail 936
Nations and nationalities* 940
Neck 945
Net 950
(NL) Dutch false friends 957
Nose 962

Note 963
Nut 968

Office 978
One* 984
Opposites* 991
'-ough' pronunciation* 999
Outdoor games for children 1001

(P) Portuguese false friends 1015
Pad 1017
Pair* 1019
Pan 1021
Patterns 1037
Peas and beans 1039
Peg 1043
Periods of time* 1049
Phrases and customs* 1060
Pick 1062
Pins and needles 1067
Pipe 1069
(PL) Polish false friends 1073
Playground 1080
Plugs 1083
Plurals* 1086
Possessive form* 1100
Prepositions of movement 1115
Pronunciation* 1133

Quantity words* 1159
Question mark* 1161
Quotation marks* 1163

'r' pronunciation* 1165
Rack 1167
Rail 1169
Reel 1190
Reflexive pronouns and verbs* 1192
Relationships* 1198
Reptiles and amphibians 1207
Ring 1225
Road 1228
Room 1234
(RUS) Russian false friends 1244

(S) Swedish false friends 1246
Say* 1259
Scales 1261
Schools and colleges* 1266
Sculpture 1275
Semicolon* 1291
Sexist language* 1305
Shapes 1310
Sharp 1312
Ships and boats 1317
Shoes 1320
Shopping goods* 1322
Short forms* 1323
Silent letters* 1338
Skate 1345
Slash* 1349
Smells* 1359
Sound* 1379
Spade 1382
Spanish false friends (E) 435
Spine 1392
Sports* 1397
Stationery 1416
Stick 1422
Stress in pronunciation* 1439
Supermarket 1463
Switching on and off* 1478
Symbols* 1481

(T) Thai false friends 1484
Table 1483
Telephone* 1497
Tenses* 1502
There* 1510
Time* 1523
Titles and forms of address* 1528
Tools 1536
Top 1536
Toy 1545
Tree 1555
Trunk 1564
Two* 1574
Two objects* 1575

Units* 1591

Varieties of English* 1608
Vegetables 1611
Vehicles 1612
Verbs* 1616
Very, completely* 1618

Wasps and bees 1641
Water sports 1643
Wild animals in Britain 1665
Window 1668
Wing 1669
Winter sports 1670
Words used together* 1680
Work* 1681
World regions* 1684
Worm 1685
Writing 1691
Writing instruments 1692

Zero* 1699

Phonetic symbols

£ rock /£rɒk/	British pronunciation
$ rock /$rɑːk/	American pronunciation

LONG VOWELS

iː	ɑː	ɔː	uː	ɜː
sheep	farm	horse	shoe	bird
/ʃiːp/	/£fɑːm/ /$fɑːrm/	/£hɔːs/ /$hɔːrs/	/ʃuː/	/£bɜːd/ /$bɜːrd/

SHORT VOWELS

ɪ	e	æ	ʌ	(Br) ɒ	ʊ	ə	(Am) ɚ
ship	head	hat	cup	sock	foot	above	mother
/ʃɪp/	/hed/	/hæt/	/kʌp/	/£sɒk/	/fʊt/	/ə'bʌv/	/$'mʌð·ɚ/

DIPHTHONGS (Two vowel sounds together)

eɪ	aɪ	ɔɪ	aʊ	(Br) əʊ	(Am) oʊ	(Br) ɪə	(Br) eə	(Br) ʊə
day	eye	boy	mouth	nose	nose	ear	hair	pure
/deɪ/	/aɪ/	/bɔɪ/	/maʊθ/	/£nəʊz/	/$noʊz/	/£ɪəʳ/	/£heəʳ/	/£pjʊəʳ/

CONSONANTS

voiceless	p pen /pen/	t town /taʊn/	k cat /kæt/	f fish /fɪʃ/	θ think /θɪŋk/	s say /seɪ/	ʃ she /ʃiː/	tʃ cheese /tʃiːz/
voiced	b book /bʊk/	d day /deɪ/	g give /gɪv/	v very /'ver·ɪ/	ð the /ðə/	z zoo /zuː/	ʒ vision /vɪʒn/	dʒ jump /dʒʌmp/
	l look /lʊk/	r run /rʌn/	j yes /jes/	w we /wiː/	m moon /muːn/	n name /neɪm/	ŋ sing /sɪŋ/	h hand /hænd/

OTHER SYMBOLS

ˈ main stress ˌ secondary stress
expectation /ˌek·spek'teɪ·ʃᵊn/

· syllable division
system /'sɪs·təm/

ʳ linking r is pronounced only before a vowel in British English:
four /£fɔːʳ/ → four apples /fɔː'ræp·l̩z/

italic letters can be omitted:
lunch /lʌn*t*ʃ/

l̩
little
/'lɪt·l̩/

ᵊl ᵊm ᵊn pronounced either /əl/ or /l̩/ etc.
label /'leɪ·bᵊl → /'leɪ·bəl/ or /'leɪ·bl̩/

i
happy
/'hæp·i/

(Am) t̬
butter
/$'bʌt̬·ɚ/

ɔ̃ː
restaurant
/£'res·tᵊr·ɔ̃ː/

▶ see Language Portraits on **Pronunciation** at PRONOUNCE, **Stress**, **Pronunciation of 'r'** at R, and **Varieties of English** at VARIETY.